Off Broadway Musicals,
1910–2007

Off Broadway Musicals, 1910–2007

Casts, Credits, Songs, Critical Reception and Performance Data of More Than 1,800 Shows

DAN DIETZ

McFarland & Company, Inc., Publishers
Jefferson, North Carolina, and London

ISBN 978-0-7864-3399-5

(library binding : 50# alkaline paper) ∞

Library of Congress control number 2008043968

Library of Congress cataloguing data are available

British Library cataloguing data are available

Manufactured in the United States of America

McFarland & Company, Inc., Publishers
Box 611, Jefferson, North Carolina 28640
www.mcfarlandpub.com

To my mother, Celia,
and to the memory of my father, Frank

Table of Contents

Preface 1

OFF BROADWAY MUSICALS 5

Appendices:
A: Chronology 507
B: Discography 513
C: Published Scripts 515
D: Filmography 516
E: Black Musicals and Revues 516
F: Children's Musicals and Revues 517
G: Gay Musicals and Revues 517
H: Jewish Musicals and Revues 517
I: Women's Musicals and Revues 517
J: Burlesque Musicals and Revues 518
K: Musicals Based on Writings of Lewis B. Carroll 518
L: Musicals and Revues Based on Writings of William Shakespeare 518
M: Composer and Lyricist Tribute Revues 518
N: Al Carmines Musicals and Revues 519
O: Kurt Weill Musicals and Revues 519
P: Ben Bagley Revues 519
Q: Julius Monk Revues 520
R: Rod Warren Revues 520
S: Forbidden Broadway 520
T: Second City Revues 520
U: Theatre "Curses" 520

Bibliography 521

Song Index 523

Name Index 591

Theatre Index 646

Preface

The Off Broadway musical was born during the second week of March 1954. On two consecutive nights, New York saw the openings of two musicals which forever changed the public's perception of Off Broadway: on March 10, Marc Blitzstein's adaptation of Bertolt Brecht and Kurt Weill's *The Threepenny Opera* opened at the Theatre de Lys, and the next evening John LaTouche and Jerome Moross' *The Golden Apple* premiered at the Phoenix Theatre.

There had been Off Broadway musicals before *The Threepenny Opera* and *The Golden Apple*. In the 1920s, a few editions of the *Greenwich Village Follies* and the *Grand Street Follies* had opened there, and, in the 1930s, Richard Lewine, Ted Fetter, and John Van Antwerp's spoofs of old-time musical melodramas were popular. And there were other occasional revues and musicals as well. But none of these made an impact on the Off Broadway theatre scene, which continued to be more distinguished for its dramatic rather than its musical offerings. Everything changed with the openings of *The Threepenny Opera* and *The Golden Apple*. The two musicals were emphatically different from anything previously seen Off Broadway, and contrasted sharply with the Broadway offerings of the 1953-1954 season.

In fact, within a month of the premieres of *The Threepenny Opera* and *The Golden Apple*, Broadway saw the opening of *By the Beautiful Sea*, one of the season's most lavish productions. A nostalgic turn-of-the-century piece, the musical was by all accounts a pleasant if conventional effort which featured a star turn by Shirley Booth. Brooks Atkinson in the *New York Times* noted it offered "good picnic song numbers" (indeed, the charming score by Arthur Schwartz and Dorothy Fields is sadly underrated), but the work itself was little more than an old-fashioned star vehicle.

The Threepenny Opera and *The Golden Apple* were light years away from the plots, characters, and song structures of *By the Beautiful Sea*, *Carnival in Flanders*, *Kismet*, *The Girl in Pink Tights*, and other musicals which opened on Broadway that season. *The Threepenny Opera* offered a dissonant, jagged score by Kurt Weill (a score which had fallen into obscurity in the United States following the failure of its Broadway production two decades earlier). Marc Blitzstein's new adaptation about lowlifes in the seedy underside of London couldn't have been more different from the romantic beggars of *Kismet* and the barbershop quartets, acrobats, and other sunny Coney Island types inhabiting *By the Beautiful Sea*. As for *The Golden Apple*, not only was it sung through (and written in rhymed couplets, no less), it was an adaptation of Homer's *Iliad* and *Odyssey* transported to the world and music of early twentieth-century America. Beginning in the 1970s and 1980s, sung-through musicals (such as *Jesus Christ Superstar*, *Evita*, *Cats*, and *Les Misérables*) became familiar fare to Broadway audiences, but this unconventional method of telling a musical story was virtually unheard of in the world of 1950s musical theatre (the exceptions being the occasional opera produced on Broadway and *The Most Happy Fella*, which premiered in 1956).

So it's no wonder everyone took notice when *The Threepenny Opera* and *The Golden Apple* opened. Broadway was where you went to see the latest musicals, and now suddenly the most talked-about musicals in New York were playing in a place called Off Broadway, a place which was as much a concept as a location. Until March 1954, Off Broadway was the last place you'd expect to see the two most discussed musicals in town.

The Threepenny Opera was an immediate hit, and ran out the season. Because of a prior booking commitment at the Theatre de Lys, the musical went on a long hiatus, but returned the following year for a marathon run of 2,611 record-breaking performances. *The Golden Apple* received rapturous reviews and quickly transferred to Broadway. It won the New York Critics Award for Best Musical, its script was published by Random House, and, like *The Threepenny Opera*, it enjoyed a cast recording; the musical even made the cover of *Life*.

Suddenly the Off Broadway musical was on the map, and musicals and revues flourished, many productions enjoying long runs Off Broadway and others transferring to Broadway. In fact, seven musicals running on Broadway during summer 2007 had first been seen Off Broadway (*Avenue Q*, *Grey Gardens*, *Rent*, *Spring Awakening*, *The 25th Annual Putnam County Spelling Bee*, and the revivals of *A Chorus Line* and *Grease* [see below for more information regarding the contractual status of the original 1972 production of the latter]).

During the 1953-1954 season, six musicals opened Off Broadway; in the 1954-1955 and 1955-1956 seasons, five apiece; and in 1956-1957, ten. But as Off Broadway became institutionalized as a way of New York theatrical life, the numbers jumped: in 1957-1958, nineteen Off Broadway musicals opened; in 1958-1959, twenty; in 1959-1960, twenty-two; in 1960-1961, twenty-seven; and in 1961-1962, thirty-six.

This book covers 1,804 musicals and revues (including the occasional performance piece, magic show, and mime show as well as plays with incidental songs) which opened in New York from 1910 to 2007, and includes not only Off Broadway musicals (including those which closed in previews and even one which closed during rehearsals) but also numerous Off Off Broadway musicals, showcases, workshops, and cabaret revues. The book also includes American operas which premiered in New York from 1910 through 2007 (including one foreign opera, which used an American short story as its source) because operas are generally ignored in traditional reference books about musical theatre. Purists may question why traditional operas are included in a book about Off Broadway musicals, but most operas in New York have indeed opened "Off Broadway" (that is, not in Broadway theatres) and since they are lyric works, this book provides a unique opportunity to get them on the record in a survey of New York musical theatre. And there's actually a precedent for including operas as part of New York's Off Broadway history. In the early 1960s, the *Best Plays* volumes included new operas presented by the New York City Opera and other companies in the Off Broadway section of its seasonal surveys.

Over the years, it's become increasingly difficult to define the terms "Off Broadway" and "Off Off Broadway." It used to be so easy: if a show wasn't on Broadway and in a traditional Broadway theatre, then it had to be an Off Broadway show. But as the years passed, the definitions of and the distinctions between Broadway and Off Broadway blurred and constantly shifted. Even such venerable reference books as *Best Plays* and *Theatre World* sometimes disagreed, and a musical would be categorized as "Broadway" in one and "Off Broadway" in the other. Of course, the definition often comes down to the matter of contracts. A basic standard to determine if a production was Off (or Off Off) Broadway was based not on location (although for the general public, location is probably the key factor which defines and identifies Off and Off Off Broadway shows) but on such factors as whether the performers are under Actors' Equity Association contracts, the size of the theatre, the number of weekly performances, whether the production is open-ended, and whether the production offers an official opening date to which critics are invited for the purpose of writing reviews.

To arrive at a definition of Off Broadway, let's examine *The Best Plays of 1979-1980*, which indicated for its purposes an Off Broadway production was one which had an Equity cast; gave eight performances a week; was in an Off Broadway theatre; and invited critics for public comment. Further, *Best Plays* reported that Paul Libin, the president of the League of Off-Broadway Theatres, defined an Off Broadway theatre as a venue which had 499 or fewer seats and was located outside the area bounded by Fifth and Ninth avenues between 34th and 56th streets, and by Fifth Avenue and the Hudson River between 56th and 72nd streets. But *Best Plays* was quick to note there were exceptions to these rules and that "no dimension of off Broadway can be applied exactly." The reference book also noted that Off Broadway "isn't an exact location." Off Off Broadway plays and musicals are usually offered for limited runs, don't necessarily invite critics, and don't always set a specific opening night. *The Best Plays of 1977-1978* offers a then-current definition for such productions, mentioning "special contractual arrangements like the Equity showcase code" which allowed concessions for employing Equity members for productions limited to a total run of twelve performances (often over a period of two or three weekends). Further, special "mini-contracts" allowed for longer runs (and higher ticket prices).

Although most productions covered in this book were under one variation or another of specific Off Broadway and Off Off Broadway contracts, it seems likely that many revues produced in nightclub venues during the mid to late 1950s and early 1960s weren't under traditional contracts at all. Further, for a period beginning in the early 1970s, some productions were under so-called Limited or Middle Broadway contracts (some reference books define productions under these contracts as Broadway shows, others classify them as Off Broadway productions).

The Best Plays of 1970-1971 noted that the Limited Gross Broadway Theatre Agreement (which had been known previously as Middle Theatre or Limited Broadway) applied to theatres with 600 seats or more (*Best Plays* noted that during this period traditional Off Broadway theatres could sell tickets for no more than 299 seats). For Limited or Middle Broadway contracts, a producer could sell tickets for no more than 600 seats, even if there were more seats in the theatre. Further, the weekly gross ticket sales couldn't exceed $25,000 and the top ticket price couldn't exceed five dollars. If the producer met these conditions, then his show could open under the Limited Broadway contract and he would receive special concessions from the various theatre unions. *Best Plays* reported that if a Limited Broadway production became a hit, the producer could move to "full Broadway status (and cost levels)" only *after* four weeks of performances under the Limited Broadway contract (with the caveat that a production under a Broadway contract could never change to Limited Broadway). To be as inclusive as possible, I've included musicals under Limited and Middle contracts in this book.

I've also included musicals which were produced in Brooklyn, such as those productions offered by the Brooklyn Academy of Music. Further, the 1968 musical *Frère Jacques* opened at a theatre in Brooklyn, but the production appears to have been under the era's standard Off Broadway contract for shows which played in Manhattan, and so I've included the production in this book. The book also includes a few musicals which were produced at Jones Beach and one which was produced at the Paper Mill Playhouse. Because the line between Broadway and Off Broadway, and between Off Broadway and Off Off Broadway, often blurred, my goal for this book was to be as inclusive as possible. For example, when the original New York production of *Grease* opened in February 1972 at the Eden Theatre (a traditional Off Broadway house), the audiences who saw the musical there undoubtedly assumed they were seeing an Off Broadway musical. The production played at the Eden until June, when it transferred to Broadway at the Broadhurst Theatre. But it turns out that *Grease* was under a Broadway contract during its entire run at the Eden. The general perception at the time was that *Grease* was an Off Broadway musical when it played the Eden, and that it "became" a Broadway musical when it transferred to the Broadhurst. So rightly or wrongly, I've included *Grease* and its Eden Theatre run in this book.

Further, *Smith*, a musical which played at the Eden the following year, had a somewhat more ambiguous contractual background. *Variety* reported the production had been capitalized for Broadway, but when complete funding wasn't forthcoming, the musical opted for Off Broadway (and Off Broadway contracts [with the exception of the performers, who were paid under Broadway contracts]). So *Smith* is included in this book as an Off Broadway production, even though its performers were under Broadway contracts.

Every production covered in this book follows a basic template of information, which is explained below. Incidentally, for the musicals discussed in this book, a mélange of terms exist, both as nouns and adjectives: Off Broadway, Off-Broadway, off Broadway, off-Broadway; and Off Off Broadway, Off-Off-Broadway, off off Broadway, off-off- Broadway; for consistency's sake, this book uses the terms Off Broadway and Off Off Broadway throughout, both as adjectives and nouns.

The following information is included for the productions in this book:

The musical's identification "tag" (when applicable). For example, *The Better 'Ole* (1918) called itself "A Fragment From France in Two Explosions, Seven Splinters and a Short Gas Attack," and *Get Thee to Canterbury* (1969) called itself "A Medieval Happenynge";

The name of the theatre in which the musical originally opened (if a musical transferred to another theatre, I've added the transfer date and the name of the new theatre, when known);

The opening date. Opening dates for Off (and Off Off) Broadway musicals are sometimes difficult to pinpoint; but to be consistent, I've opted to use the opening dates provided by *Best Plays*. However, some musicals aren't covered in either *Best Plays* or in *Theatre World*. Sometimes I've been able to identify the month and year a musical opened, but not the specific date. And occasionally the precise year is unknown, and so I've provided a best guess. In both the Chronology (Appendix A) and in the specific entries, I've noted when the precise opening dates are unknown;

The number of performances. Again, for consistency, I've used the performance numbers given in *Best Plays*; in some instances, if the performance numbers are unknown, the entry indicates such; in other cases, I've been able to make a best guess, and these performance numbers are identified as estimated performances;

The names of the librettist, sketch writer, lyricist, and composer (when applicable);

The name of the director;

The name of the choreographer. Sometimes choreography credits are identified in programs as "dances by" or "musical staging by"; for consistency, I've used the word "choreography" to denote the staging of dances and musical numbers;

The name of the scenic designer;

The name of the costume designer;

The name of the lighting designer. If the name of the lighting designer, costume designer, and so on is unknown, the entry omits the complete notation (that is, a typical notation would be "Lighting: Johnny Broadway," but if the lighting designer is unknown, I haven't included a notation such as "Lighting: Unknown");

The name of the musical director (generally the musical director is the conductor and so the term "musical direction" is used in this book);

The name of the producer;

The names of the cast members. In parenthesis, following each cast member's name, is, when applicable, the name of the character portrayed by the performer (most revues and cabaret musicals didn't assign names to the characters); whenever possible, the cast members' names are listed in the order of appearance, and, when known, the names of starring and major featured players are given in capital letters;

The musical's source (if applicable);

The location where the musical takes place and the time when the action occurs are given (when known);

The number of acts (when known);

A list of the titles of songs (and, when applicable, the titles of sketches). Each song or sketch is followed by the name of the performer (not the character) who introduced the song or sketch. When specific singing or sketch assignments are unknown, that fact is noted in each entry. The song titles are listed in performance order, but if such information isn't known, the titles are listed alphabetically.

Most entries are followed by a note section in which a variety of topics are discussed, including the plot, critical comments, and cast album/published script/film version/London production and other information. The book also includes appendices, including one with a seasonal chronology as well as ones for scripts, recordings, and films. There are also appendices which list entries by composer (Kurt Weill, Al Carmines), producer (Julius Monk, Ben Bagley, Rod Warren, Second City), or subject matter (musicals based on writings by Shakespeare and by Lewis B. Carroll).

In his invaluable series of books which analyze Broadway musicals decade by decade, Ethan Mordden wrote there was nothing more obscure than an Off Broadway flop. But over the decades some Off Broadway hits and almost-hits have fallen into theatrical limbo. This book will hopefully remedy that situation by providing an overview of each musical which includes esoteric and even seemingly trivial information. I believe such details help to personalize so many of these forgotten musicals. Here are some brief examples of the kind of trivia offered throughout the book:

There was no Off Broadway cast album of the long-forgotten 1959 musical *She Shall Have Music*; but the score was recorded four years later when it was mounted for a college production (the college-student cast members included John Davidson and John Kuhner).

A number of songs from the 1961 revue *Another Evening with Harry Stoones* resurfaced in the 1965 revue *That Thing at the Cherry Lane*.

The 1962 revue *This Was Burlesque* included a song from the flop musical *The Amazing Adele*, which closed during its pre–Broadway tryout during the 1955-1956 theatre season.

The three revues *Street Jesus* (1974), *Fire of Flowers* (1976), and *New York City Street Show* (1977) are for all purposes one and the same, as all three share about a dozen songs apiece.

The 1976 musical *Two of Everything* was a revised version of *Innocent as Hell*, a 1961 London flop.

There are also a number of songs which traveled from musical to musical, and this book summarizes their theatrical journeys. For example, the 1976 revue *2 by 5*, which was a tribute to John Kander and Fred Ebb, included the song "Military Man"; in 1999, the song was performed by Dorothy Loudon and Mario Cantone in a regional production of Kander and Ebb's *Over & Over*, their musical adaptation of Thornton Wilder's play *The Skin of Our Teeth*; and the song was heard again in *All About Us*, a revised version of *Over & Over* which played in regional theatre in 2007.

Incidentally, the 1962 revue *Les Poupées de Paris* proves there's nothing really new under the theatrical sun. It was for the most part a "naughty" puppet show (sound familiar?), and in fact its souvenir program warned that it was "FOR ADULTS ONLY!" And the revue even included a sketch about Florence Foster Jenkins.

This book also takes occasional detours into general musical theatre trivia, such as the convoluted history of Howard Dietz and Arthur Schwartz' song "Triplets," which at one point was sung *solo* by Beatrice Lillie during the tryout of a Broadway musical (see entry for *That's Entertainment*) and unlucky shows which shared the same performer or producer or locale or subject matter (see Appendix U for theatre curses).

Whenever possible, the information in this book comes from original source material, such as playbills, programs, souvenir programs, flyers, window cards, scripts, recordings, and advertisements (I estimate that I used original source material for about seventy percent of the musicals covered in the book). Moreover, a number of reference books and databases have been extremely helpful, and these are credited in the bibliography. In this preface, I particularly want to salute Off Broadway performers, Off Broadway Babies all (and some who were Broadway Babies as well): Ceil Cabot, Jane Connell, Cherry Davis, Bob Fitch, June Gable, Annie Golden, Ronny Graham, Dorothy Greener, Patti Karr, Alix Korey, Dick Latessa, Sue Lawless, Tom Mixon, Ted Pugh (whose program bio for *In the Nick of Time* noted his "dark, statuesque good looks will tell you immediately that he hails from Anadarko, Oklahoma"), Mary Testa, Elmarie Wendel, and so many others who contributed to the world of Off Broadway musicals and revues. Finally, I want to thank my mother Celia for her help and support in the writing of this book, and I also want to thank my friends Mike Baskin and Don Cushing for their suggestions and insights.

Off Broadway Musicals

1 A ... My Name Is Alice. "A New Musical Revue." THEATRE: American Place Theatre; transferred to Upstairs/The Village Gate on April 8, 1984; OPENING DATE: February 24, 1984; PERFORMANCES: 353; SKETCHES: David Crane, Marta Kauffman, Richard LaGravanese, Anne Meara, Cassandra Medley, and Art Murray; LYRICS: Calvin Alexander, Maggie Benson, Susan Birkenhead, David Crane, Carol Hall, Georgia Holof, Winnie Holzman, Marta Kauffman, Amanda McBroom, Susan Rice, Mark Saltzman, James Shorter, June Siegal, Steve Tesich, Don Tucker, and David Zippel; MUSIC: Calvin Alexander, David Evans, Carol Hall, Cheryl Hardwick, Doug Katsaros, Stephen Lawrence, Amanda McBroom, David Mettee, Susan Rice, Glen Roven, James Shorter, Lucy Simon, Michael Skloff, and Don Tucker; DIRECTION: Joan Micklin Silver and Julianne Boyd; CHOREOGRAPHY: Edward Love; SCENERY: Adrianne Lobel; COSTUMES: Mimi Maxmen; LIGHTING: Ann Wrightson; MUSICAL DIRECTION: Michael Skloff; PRODUCERS: Anne Wilder, Douglas F. Goodman, and Rosita Sarnoff, by special arrangement with The Women's Project.

CAST—Roo Brown, Randy Graff, Mary Gordon Murray, Alaina Reed, Charlaine Woodard

The revue was presented in two acts (the song and sketch list below is compiled from information in both the program and the published script).

ACT ONE—"All Girl Band" (lyric by David Zippel, music by Doug Katsaros) (Company), "A ... My Name Is Alice Poems" (by Marta Kauffman and David Crane) (Company), "At My Age" (lyric by June Siegel, music by Glen Roven) (Roo Brown, Randy Graff), "Trash" (lyric by Marta Kauffman and David Crane, music by Michael Skloff) (Company), "For-Women-Only Poems" (by Marta Kauffman and David Crane) (Roo Brown), "Good Thing I Learned to Dance" (lyric by Mark Saltzman, music by Stephen Lawrence) (Charlaine Woodard), "Welcome to Kindergarten, Mrs. Johnson" (lyric by Marta Kauffman and David Crane, music by Michael Skloff) (Mary Gordon Murray, Roo Brown), "I Sure Like the Boys" (lyric by Steve Teisch, music by Lucy Simon) (Randy Graff), "Ms. Mae" (sketch by Cassandra Medley) (Alaina Reed), "Good Sports: Detroit Persons" (lyric and music by Susan Rice) and "Educated Feet" (lyric and music by Carol Hall) (Company), "Harbour Lady" (lyric by Steve Tesich, music by Lucy Simon) (Mary Gordon Murray), "The Portrait" (lyric and music by Amanda McBroom) (performer unknown), "I'm Bluer Than You" (lyric by Winnie Holzman, music by David Evans) (Randy Graff, Alaina Reed, Charlaine Woodard)

ACT TWO—"Watching All the Pretty Young Men" (lyric by Susan Birkenhead, music by Lucy Simon) (Mary Gordon Murray, Alaina Reed, Roo Brown), "Demigod" (sketch by Richard LaGravanese) (Charlaine Woodard), "The French Monologue" (sketch by Art Murray), "The French Song" (lyric and music by Don Tucker, monologue by Art Murray) (Mary Gordon Murray), "Hot Lunch" (sketch by Anne Meara) (Mary Gordon Murray, Charlaine Woodard), "Pay Them No Mind" (lyric and music by Calvin Alexander and James Shorter) (performer unknown), "Emily, The M.B.A." (lyric by Mark Saltzman, music by Stephen Lawrence) (Randy Graff, Alaina Reed, Charlaine Woodard, Mary Gordon Murray), "Sisters" (lyric by Maggie Benson, music by Cheryl Hardwick) (Roo Brown), "Honeypot" (lyric by Mark Saltzman, music by Stephen Lawrence) (Randy Graff, Alaina Reed), "Friends" (lyric by Georgia Holof, music by David Mettee) (Mary Gordon Murray, Randy Graff), "All Girl Band" (reprise) (lyric by David Zippel, music by Doug Katsaros) (Company)

NOTES—The feminist revue *A...My Name Is Alice* was followed by two sequels, *A...My Name Is Still Alice* (which opened Off Broadway at the Second Stage Theatre on November 22, 1992, for ninety-seven performances; see entry) and *A...My Name Will Always Be Alice* (originally titled *Alice Revisited*, the revue had its world premiere with the Barrington Stage Company in Great Barrington, Massachusetts, on August 2, 1995; as of this writing, the third revue hasn't been seen in New York). Before its February 1984 opening at the American Place Theatre, the musical had been presented there earlier in the season on November 2, 1983, for twelve performances, and Lynnie Godfrey, Randy Graff, Polly Pen, Alaina Reed, and Grace Roberts were in the production. Frank Rich in the *New York Times* said that "feminism is worn lightly" in the "delightful" revue, and singled out a number of sketches and songs, including the evening's "dizziest solo bit," a Piaf-like torch song ("The French Song") written in "intricately rhymed Franglais" by Don Tucker and performed by Mary Gordon Murray. Rich also liked the evening's running gag (written by future *Friends* writers and creators Marta Kauffman and David Crane) in which Roo Brown continuously recites a cycle of "self-martyring verses" (all accompanied by the "accusatory" refrain, "*He* did it/*he* did it"). Rich also liked Kauffman and Crane's lyrics for the song "Trash," which depicted a hapless receptionist who wonders why her life can't be as interesting as those lives depicted in romance novels. In 1996, Original Cast Records released *A...My Name Will Always Be Alice* (CD # OC-9543); it included thirteen songs from *A...My Name Is Alice* ("All Girl Band," "A...My Name Is Alice Poems," "At My Age," "Trash," "I Sure Like the Boys," "Welcome to Kindergarten, Mrs. Johnson," "Watching All the Pretty Young Men," "The Portrait," "I'm Bluer Than You," "The French Monologue," "The French Song," "Honeypot," and "Friends") and six numbers from *A...My Name Is Still Alice* ("Sensitive New Age Guys," "Wheels," "Once and Only Thing," "Lifelines," and both the sketch and song of "Painted Ladies").

In 1985 and 1993, respectively, Samuel French, Inc., published the scripts of *A...My Name Is Alice* and *A...My Name Is Still Alice.*

2 A ... My Name Is Still Alice. "A Musical Revue." THEATRE: Second Stage Theatre; OPENING DATE: November 22, 1992; PERFORMANCES: 92; SKETCHES: Dan Berkowitz, Douglas Bernstein, John Gorka, Georgia Bogardus Holof, Christine Lavin, Lisa Loomer, Denis Markell, David Mettee, Lynn Nottage, Mark Saltzman, Kate Shein, and Steve Tesich; LYRICS: Marion Adler, Douglas Bernstein, Francesca Blumenthal, Craig Carnelia, John Gorka, Carol Hall, Georgia Bogardus Holof, Michael John LaChiusa, Christine Lavin, Denis Markell, Amanda McBroom, David Mettee, Mary Bracken Phillips, Stephen Schwartz, June Siegel, Carolyn Sloan, and Mark St. Germain; MUSIC: Douglas Bernstein, Craig Carnelia, Randy Courts, John Gorka, Carol Hall, Georgia Bogardus Holof, Doug Katsaros, Michael John LaChiusa, Christine Lavin, Denis Markell, Amanda McBroom, David Mettee, Mary Bracken Phillips, and Jimmy Roberts; DIRECTION: Joan Micklin Silver and Julianne Boyd; CHOREOGRAPHY: Hope Clarke; SCENERY: Andrew Jackness; COSTUMES: David C. Woolard; LIGHTING: David F. Segal; MUSICAL DIRECTION: Ian Herman; PRODUCER: Second Stage Theatre (Carole Rothman, Artistic Director; Suzanne Schwartz Davidson, Producing Director).

CAST—Roo Brown, Laura Dean, Cleo King, KT Sullivan, Nancy Ticotin

The revue was presented in two acts.

ACT ONE—*Opening:* "Two Steps Forward" (lyric and music by Stephen Schwartz and Mary Bracken Phillips) (Company), "It Ain't Over" (lyric and music by Carol Hall) (Roo Brown, Cleo King), "Non-Bridaled Passion" (sketch by Kate Shein) (Laura Dean), "Once and Only Thing" (lyric and music by Michael John LaChiusa) (Nancy Ticotin), "Cover-Up #1" (sketch by Dan Berkowitz) (Roo Brown), "Why Doesn't She Call on Me?" (lyric by Mark St. Germain, music by Randy Courts) (Company), "Juanita Craiga (for Juanita Craiga Weight Loss Centers)" (sketch by Lisa Loomer) (Nancy Ticotin), "So Much Rain" (lyric and music by Craig Carnelia) (KT Sullivan), "The Group" (sketch's concept, lyric, and music by Georgia Bogardus Holof and David Metee, additional material by Dan Berkowitz) (Company), "Ida Mae Cole Takes a Stance" (sketch by Lynn Nottage) (Cleo King), "Cover-Up #2" (sketch by Dan Berkowitz) (Roo Brown), "Wheels" (lyric and music by Amanda McBroom) (Laura Dean), "The Sorghum Sisters" (lyric by Mark St. Germain, music by Randy Courts) (Roo Brown, KT Sullivan, Cleo King, Laura Dean)

ACT TWO—"Painted Ladies" (sketch, lyric, and music by Douglas Bernstein and Denis Markell) (Company), "Sensitive New-Age Guys" (sketch, lyric and music by Christine Lavin and John Gorka) (Nancy Ticotin, Band), "A Lovely Little Life" (sketch by Steve Tesich) (KT Sullivan), "Play Nice" (sketch, lyric, and music by Douglas Bernstein and Denis Markell) (Laura Dean, Cleo King, Nancy Ticotin), "Gross Anatomy Lecture" (sketch by Douglas Bernstein) (Roo Brown), "Hard-Hat Woman" (lyric by Francesca Blumenthal, music by Doug Katsaros) (Nancy Ticotin, Laura Dean, Cleo King), "Cover-Up #3" (sketch by Douglas Bernstein) (Roo Brown), "Baby" (lyric and music by Amanda McBroom)

(Company), "Women Behind Desks" (sketch by Mark Saltzman) (Company), "What Did I Do Right?" (lyric by June Siegel, music by Jimmy Roberts) (Roo Brown), "Lifelines" (lyric by Marion Adler, music by Carolyn Sloan) (Company), *Finale:* "Two Steps Forward" (reprise) (Company)

NOTES—*A...My Name Is Still Alice* was a belated sequel to the 1984 feminist revue *A...My Name Is Alice* (see entry, which also includes information about a third revue [*A...My Name Will Always Be Alice*] which was produced in regional theatre).

Mel Gussow in the *New York Times* generally liked the revue, although he noted it had its "obvious" moments. He singled out a number of songs and sketches, including "Sensitive New-Age Guys" and "Hard-Hat Woman," and he mentioned that the evening's most "assertive" numbers (such as "Painted Ladies") were written by men. The script for *A...My Name Is Still Alice* was published by Samuel French in 1993.

Six numbers from *A...My Name Is Still Alice* ("Sensitive New Age Guys," "Wheels," "Once and Only Thing," "Lifelines," and both the sketch and song of "Painted Ladies") were heard on the recording *A...My Name Will Always Be Alice*, which was released by Original Cast Records (CD # OC-9543).

3 Abby's Song. THEATRE: City Center; OPENING DATE: November 14, 1999; PERFORMANCES: 19; BOOK: Mary Pat Kelly; LYRICS: Mary Pat Kelly; MUSIC: Elliot Willensky; DIRECTION: Randy Skinner; CHOREOGRAPHY: Randy Skinner; SCENERY: Bill Clarke; COSTUMES: David C. Woolard; LIGHTING: Nancy Schertler; MUSICAL DIRECTION: Stephen Bates; PRODUCERS: Spirit Lake Productions, Mickey Kelly, Susan Kelly Panian, and Michael Kelly

CAST—Paul Sorvino (Mentor), David A. Tay (Danny), Judy Malloy (Judith), Jacquiline Rohrbacker (Bertha), Monica L. Patton (Leah), Sebastian Sozzi (Ethan), Maggie Panian (Becky), Courtney Leigh (Susannah), Ally Hilfiger (Lilly), John Wilkerson (John), Daniel Elborne (Josh), Michael-Leon Wooley (Bennie), Jackie Angelescu (Abby), John Paul Almon (Ruben)

The action occurs in Whispering Pines, Montana.

The musical was presented in two acts (division of acts and song assignments unknown; songs are listed in performance order).

MUSICAL NUMBERS—"An Ordinary Town," "Woman's Work," "Fly a Rainbow," "More Than Ever," "Wolf Song," "I Am Home," "Another Girl Who's Just Like Me," "There's a Price," "You Just Gotta Be You," "She Left Without a Word," "A Little Girl in the Night," "Beyond," "I Did It," "An Angel Has a Message," "A Mother's Heart," "Pass the Wine," "The Revelation," "How Do You Follow a Star," "Who Is This Child," "Abby's Song," "One Small Voice"

NOTES—A self-described "holiday fable," *Abby's Song* played at City Center for a limited engagement of two weeks. Possibly produced under an Off Off Broadway contract, the musical's cast included Paul Sorvino as a special guest star. The musical's flyer indicated the plot was about "a delightful, lovable girl who wants to 'fly a rainbow,' while everybody else is telling her to keep her feet on the ground." Specifically, the musical was a variation on the Christmas story, and in this case dealt with a young girl in modern-day Montana who wants to be a shepherd and who encounters an angel as well as a couple who take shelter in a barn when there's no room at a nearby inn.

4 Abelard and Heloise. "A Music Drama." THEATRE: City Center Theatre; OPENING DATE: May 31, 1984; PERFORMANCES: 2; LIBRETTO: Jan Hartman; MUSIC: Robert Ward; DIRECTION: Gayle Swymer Olsen; MUSICAL DIRECTION: Leigh Gibbs Gore; PRODUCERS: The New York Opera Repertory Theatre in association with the 55th Street Dance Theatre Foundation, Inc.

CAST—Ron De Fesi (Peter the Venerable, Zophas), Phyllis Hunter (Heloise), Stephen Len White (Thibault), Alexandra Hughes (Job's Wife, Berthe), Nicholas Solomon (Job, Alberic), Charles Walker (Eliphaz, Lotulf), Cindy C. Oxberry (Bildad, Sister Simone), Tony Dillon (First Tradesman, A Court Clerk), Ronald Forsmo (Second Tradesman), Mark Jackson (Abelard), Glenn Martin (Bernard), Douglas Perry (Fulbert), Lawrence Cooper (Denys); The New York Opera Repertory Theatre Orchestra and Chorus

The action occurs throughout France during the period 1116–1140.

The opera was presented in three acts.

NOTES—The opera told the familiar story of the love affair between Abelard, a cleric and theologian, and Heloise, one of his students. When she becomes pregnant, her uncle has had Abelard castrated, who then devotes his life to God (as does Heloise, who joins a convent). Ultimately, Abelard is tried and found guilty of heresy for his belief in the power of reason to resolve religious matters and other related questions.

The New York Opera Repertory Theatre's concert version marked the New York premiere of the opera, which had originally been produced in 1981. Will Crutchfield in the *New York Times* found fault with the libretto ("'reason' is tossed about as though it were a campaign slogan" and Heloise "is made to spout simplistic distillations of 20th-century feminism"). Further, he had reservations about Robert Ward's score ("always promising a great tune and never delivering it") and only occasional praise ("a nice duet" here, a passage of "dramatic tension" there).

Another work about the ill-fated lovers was Ronald Millar's play *Abelard and Heloise*, which premiered in London during the 1969-1970 season with Keith Michell and Diana Rigg in the title roles. They also appeared in the 1971 Broadway production of the drama.

5 Abi Gezunt. THEATRE: Town Hall; OPENING DATE: April 6, 1980; PERFORMANCES: 6; PRODUCER: Shalom Yiddish Musical Comedy Theatre

CAST—MOLLY PICON, HENRY GERRO, ROSITA LONDNER

The revue was presented in two acts.

NOTES—The flyer for the Off Off Broadway revue *Abi Gezunt* said the evening was a "musical entertainment rich in Yiddish-English humor and nostalgia." For the first act, the married team of Henry Gerro and Rosita Londner provided comedy and songs, and for the second Molly Picon appeared alone in a series of songs, patter, and even a little dancing.

Richard F. Shepard in the *New York Times* noted that with "vivacity and vigor" Picon made "a lively present of her long past." Perhaps the highlight of her presentation was a sequence titled "Lesson in Yiddish," in which she showed the audience how Yiddish can do what no other spoken or written language can accomplish. Shepard also praised Gerro and Londner, and indicated if there were any doubt Gerro was a "true comedian in the most orthodox (lower case) tradition," such doubts would be put to rest in a number in which he played a violin in the grand tradition of such comics as Jack Benny and Henny Youngman.

6 Absolutely Fascinating. THEATRE: Acorn Theatre; OPENING DATE: September 26, 2004; PERFORMANCES: 57; DIRECTION: Simon Green; SCENERY: Chris Lee; LIGHTING: Chris Lee; MUSICAL DIRECTION: Russell Churney; PRODUCER: Edward Snape

CAST—Fascinating Aida (Adele Anderson, Dillie Keane, Liza Pulman)

The revue was presented in two acts.

NOTES—In the revue *Absolutely Fascinating*, the three-woman group Fascinating Aida offered up political and topical comments accompanied by music. After the Off Broadway engagement, the trio played Off Off Broadway at the Kirk Theatre on April 11, 2005, for forty performances. The trio had first appeared in New York at the Firebird Café in March 1998, and had presented an earlier version of *Absolutely Fascinating* Off Off Broadway at the 59E59 Theatre on May 18, 2004, for thirty-two performances.

7 Absolutely Freeee. "A Musical Entertainment." THEATRE: Garrick Theatre; OPENING DATE: May 24, 1967; PERFORMANCES: 208; LYRICS: Frank Zappa; MUSIC: Frank Zappa; LIGHTING: Buddy from L.A.; PRODUCER: Herb Cohen

CAST—The Mothers of Invention (Frank Zappa, Don Preston, Ray Collins, Jimmy Clark Black, Bunk Gardner, Roy Estrada, Billy Mundi)

NOTES—Originally titled *Pigs and Repugnant*, the revue *Absolutely Freee* was a program of songs and instrumental pieces by cult musician Frank Zappa and his band Mothers of Invention.

Dan Sullivan in the *New York Times* suggested that while the Flower Generation might like the revue, the Pepsi Generation probably would not. He noted a ticket for *Absolutely Freee* would cost you "threee" dollars, and whether or not the money was well spent would depend "how old you are, or wish you were."

Sullivan complained that the music was pitched at a "headachey" volume, making the lyrics largely unintelligible; further, he felt the jabs at mainstream targets seemed mild. He remarked that the music was at its best in parodies of 1950's rock-and-roll.

8 Abyssinia. THEATRE: CSC Repertory Theatre; OPENING DATE: April 4, 1987; PERFORMANCES: 14; BOOK: James Racheff and Ted Kociolek; LYRICS: James Racheff; MUSIC: Ted Kociolek; DIRECTION: Tazewell Thompson; CHOREOGRAPHY CONSULTANT: Julie Arenal; SCENERY: Evelyn Sakash; COSTUME CONSULTANT: Amanda Klein; LIGHTING: Clarke W. Thornton; MUSICAL DIRECTION: Daryl Waters (?); PRODUCER: Musical Theatre Works (Anthony J. Stimac, Artistic Director; Mark Herko, Associate Artistic Director)

CAST—Jennifer Leigh Warren (Abyssinia Jackson [Abby]), Tina Fabrique (Mother Vera), Cheryl Freeman (Patience Jackson), Lehman Beneby (Minister), Karen Jackson (Trembling Sally), Zelda Pulliam (Lily Noreen, Mother Samuels), LaDonna Mabry (Selma), Connie Fredericks (Mavis), Bambi Jones (Corine), Jaison Walker (Marcus), Clyde Jones (Leon), Roderick Cloud (Jesse), Stanley Earl Harrison (Brother Samuels)

SOURCE—The 1982 novel *Marked by Fire* (*One Land Saga*) by Joyce Carol Thomas.

The action occurs some in the past in rural Oklahoma.

The musical was presented in two acts.

ACT ONE—"Rise and Fly" (Company), "Song of the Field" (Tina Fabrique, Cheryl Freeman, LaDonna Mabry, Bambi Jones, Connie Fredericks), "Abyssinia" (Company), "Lift Up Your Voice!" (Jennifer Leigh Warren, Company), "Song of Mother Samuels" (Jennifer Lee Warren, Zelda Pulliam, Company), "Recipe" (Tina Fabrique, Cheryl Freeman, Jennifer Lee Warren), "There Has to Be a Reason" (Jennifer Lee Warren), "The Sound of a Ragtime Band" (Tina Fabrique, Company), "I Have Seen the Wind" (Jennifer Lee Warren, Karen Jackson); "Blackberry Wine" (Jaison Walker, Clyde Jones, Roderick Cloud), "Cry" (Performer[s] unknown), "Lightnin' Bug" (Cheryl Freeman), "Abby's Lament" (Jennifer Lee Warren, Company)

ACT TWO—"Pickin' Up the Pieces" (Lehman Beneby, Company), "Get Thee Behind Me, Satan!" (LaDonna Mabry, Bambi Jones, Connie Fredericks), "Sisters of Healing" (Cheryl Freeman, LaDonna Mabry, Bambi Jones, Connie Fredericks), "Honey and Lemon" (Tina Fabrique), Finale (Company)

NOTES—*Abyssinia* told the story of the title character, a young girl who was born after a catastrophic tornado was miraculously dispatched by her community's spiritual leader. Abyssinia grows up blessed with healing powers, but tragedy follows her when an evil woman, who lost four children in the tornado, conspires to destroy her.

Stephen Holden in the *New York Times* praised the book's "strong narrative drive" and the "simple, appealing score." He felt the musical, "part folk tale, part gospel service," was ideal for community and church productions.

After its Off Off Broadway production, *Abyssinia* was produced at the Goodspeed Opera House's Norma Terris Theatre on August 11, 1987, and then again on June 8, 1988. Numbers in the Goodspeed productions which weren't heard in the Off Off Broadway version were "Lift Up Your Voice!," "Abby's Song (Sweet, Sweet Music)," "Ten Little Children," "If I Were You," and "Ragtime Promenade" (the latter may have been a revised version of "The Sound of a Ragtime Band").

A promotional CD of five songs from the score was issued in anticipation of a March 1999 Broadway opening (which never materialized). The songs on the CD are "Lift Up Your Voice!," "There Has to Be a Reason," "Recipe," "Pickin' Up the Pieces," and "Honey and Lemon."

9 Adam. "A New Musical Drama." THEATRE: Harry DeJur Henry Street Settlement Playhouse; OPENING DATE: January 20, 1983; PERFORMANCES: 12; BOOK: June Tansey; LYRICS: Richard Ahlert; MUSIC: Richard Ahlert; DIRECTION: Don Evans; CHOREOGRAPHY: Dianne McIntyre; SCENERY: Llewellyn Harrison; COSTUMES: Judy Dearing; LIGHTING: Shirley Prendergast; MUSICAL DIRECTION: Neal Tate; PRODUCER: New Federal Theatre (Woodie King, Jr., Producer)

CAST—Jeff Bates (Charley, Reporter, Maitre D'), Frederic Beals (Congressman Mudd), Bill Boss (Congressman Gilgo, Television Voice), Richard Chiffy (Reporter), Dawn Davis (Sally, Louise, Southern Belle), Randy Flood (Doug Marshall), Rueben Green (Adam Clayton Powell, Jr.), Suzanne Hall (New York Socialite), Hugh Harrell III (Adam Clayton Powell, Sr.), Jackee' Harry (Rachel Watts), Rosetta Jefferson (Serena Crawford), Jim Keels (Congressman Shanklin), S. Epatha Merkerson (Addie Carmicheal), Kevin Ramsey (M.C., Bellboy, Young Jim), Deborah Smith (Annie, Barmaid), Raymond Stough (Sam Bradbury), Robin Wilson (Madame Rochais, Miss Lee), Kevin Wynn (Photographer, Young Brad, Old Joe)

The musical was presented in two acts.

ACT ONE—Overture (Orchestra), "Walk Just a Few Feet" (Rueben Green, Ensemble). "The Strike" (Rueben Green, Randy Flood, S. Epatha Merkerson, Rosetta Jefferson, Ensemble), "Operator" (Rueben Green, S. Epatha Merkerson, Randy Flood, Kevin Ramsey, Kevin Wynn, Jeff Bates, Hugh Harrell III, Ensemble), "Prettiest Politician" (Robin Wilson, Rosetta Jefferson, Jeff Bates, Kevin Ramsey, S. Epatha Merkerson), "Give Me the Power" (Rueben Green, Ensemble), "A Hundred and Twenty-Fifth Street" (Ensemble), "L'Amour Dangereux" (Jackee' Harry), "The Best Is None Too Good for Me" (Jackee' Harry, Deborah Smith, Rueben Green), "When I'm Your Woman" (Jackee' Harry), "I'd Like to Propose a Bill" (Rueben Green, Bill Boss, Jim Keels, Frederick Beals, Raymond Stough), "He Should Have Been Mine" (S. Epatha Merkerson), "He's Gotta Go" (Bill Boss, Jim Keels, Frederick Beals)

ACT TWO—"Mr. Harlem" (Rueben Green, Bill Boss, Jim Keels, Frederick Beals, Jeff Bates, Richard Chiffy, Others [Two Girls]), "Giglo, Shanklin and Mudd" (Raymond Stough, Randy Flood), "We Got Grounds, Good Ole Boys" (Bill Boss, Jim Keels, Frederick Beals), "Lament and Argument" ('Old Timer,' 'Young Militants'), "I Never Thought I'd See the Day" (Jackee' Harry), "Let's Do It for Adam" (Performers Unknown), "(Oh Lord) Did I Get Too Far Away from You" (Rueben Green), "In Bimini" (Rueben Green), "We Kept the Faith" (Performers Unknown), "Look Who's Coming to Harlem" (Rosetta Jefferson, Jeff Bates, Kevin Ramsey, Ensemble)

NOTES—Unlike another musical about a New York City congressman (*Fiorello!*, 1959), *Adam*, an Off Off Broadway musical which dealt with Congressman Adam Clayton Powell, Jr., went nowhere.

Mel Gussow in the *New York Times* noted that Powell was a "flamboyant" and "contradictory political figure," and his story had the potential to be "an urban America *Evita*" or even one which challenged *Fiorello!* But the writers avoided giving the musical a "hard edge," and so Powell's life got a "simplistic storybook treatment" in an evening that was a "catalogue of missed opportunities." Gussow complained that some of the dialogue sounded like soap opera, that the characterizations were "as deep as press releases," and that Powell himself sounded like a "sermon."

10 Adrift in Macao. "The New Musical." Theatre: 59E59 Theatres; OPENING DATE: February 13, 2007; PERFORMANCES: 24; BOOK: Christopher Durang; LYRICS: Christopher Durang; MUSIC: Peter Melnick; DIRECTION: Sheryl Kaller; CHOREOGRAPHY: Christopher Gattelli; SCENERY: Thomas Lynch; COSTUMES: Willa Kim; LIGHTING: Jeff Croiter; MUSICAL DIRECTION: Fred Lassen; PRODUCERS: Primary Stages (Casey Childs, Founder and Executive Producer; Andrew Leynse, Artistic Director; Elliot Fox, Managing Director; Michelle Bossy, Associate Artistic Director) in association with Ina Meibach, Susan Dietz, Jennifer Manocherian, and Barbara Manocherian

CAST—Will Swenson (Rick Shaw), Orville Mendoza (Tempura), Michele Ragusa (Corinna), Jonathan Rayson (Trenchcoat Chorus [Joe]), Elisa Van Duyne (Trenchcoat Chorus [Daisy]), Alan Campbell (Mitch), Rachel de Benedet (Lureena)

The action occurs in 1952 in Macao, China.

The musical was performed in one act.

MUSICAL NUMBERS—"In a Foreign City" (Rachel de Benedet), "Grumpy Mood" (Alan Campbell), "Tempura's Song" (Orville Mendoza, Alan Campbell), "Mister McGuffin" (Orville Mendoza, Michele Ragusa, Joanthan Rayson, Elisa Van Duyne), "Mambo Malaysian" (Michelle Ragusa), "Sparks" (Rachel de Benedet, Alan Campbell), "Mitch's Story" (Alan Campbell, Michele Ragusa, Rachel de Benedet), "Adrift in Macao" (Rachel de Benedet, Michele Ragusa, Alan Campbell, Orville Mendoza), "So Long" (Rachel de Benedet), ["Rick's Song"; performed by Will Swenson], "The Chase" (Alan Campbell, Ensemble), "Revelation (I'm Actually Irish)" (Orville Mendoza), "Ticky Ticky Tock" (Rachel de Benedet, Michele Ragusa, Jonathan Rayson, Elisa Van Duyne)

NOTES—Peter Melnick and Christopher Durang's *Adrift in Macao* played a limited run of three weeks, but its daffy and deranged (if not duranged) send-up of film noir should ensure it a long life in regional and community theatre. Even those critics who found fault with the musical nonetheless admitted it was a guilty pleasure. Charles Isherwood in the *New York Times* noted that while the jokes were less than inspired and the plot "could be scrawled on a cocktail napkin," he nonetheless had a "pretty good time." Isherwood also noted that Melnick's score ran the gamut from Kurt Weill to big-band pastiche. Further, the score embraced occasional film-noir background-music moodiness; offered a mambo; and included an amusing comedy song for Tempura (originally titled "Revelation" and later "I'm Actually Irish") in which he reveals that at will he can morph into any nationality or sex, depending on the needs of the moment. Melnick, incidentally, is the grandson of Richard Rodgers, and his score is further proof that musical theatre DNA is in the family's bloodlines. For almost a full century, the American musical has been enriched by the contributions of Richard Rodgers, Mary Rodgers, Adam Guettel, and Peter Melnick.

Marilyn Stasio in *Variety* praised the sets, costumes, and props, and found the music "bright" and the lyrics "drolly inane." Perhaps the score's best song was the utterly irresistible "Ticky Ticky Tock," a deliriously entertaining show-stopper and the kind of old-fashioned musical-comedy song they don't seem to write anymore. But be forewarned! Once heard, the ingratiating and insinuating melody will hard wire into your brain and will never, ever leave it.

The musical took place in Rick Shaw's club, where a group of mysterious film-noir types hang out, including Lureena, a glamorous platinum doll; Corinna, a hard-boiled dame; Tempura, an inscrutable Oriental (who has been battered by life); and Mitch, an American dick who is on the trail of an elusive Mr. McGuffin.

Besides film noir, *Adrift in Macao* also kidded musicals themselves. Isherwood mentioned a scene in which one character says to another, "See you around, I hope," to which another character responds, "Well, it's a small cast." And Stasio noted that Rick Shaw, annoyed because he didn't get a solo number in the show, had to hire "outside songwriters" in order to get a number of his own (adding insult to injury, Rick's song isn't listed in the program, and even the cast album dismissively calls it "Rick's Song"). A first reading of the musical took place as part of The York Theatre Developmental Series, and later was seen at Vassar's Powerhouse Theatre on July 10, 2002; it was also produced by the Philadelphia Theatre Company on October 19, 2005 (for the latter production, Michael Rupert performed the role of Rick Shaw).

As of this writing, the cast recording is scheduled for release in early 2008 via LML Music (the CD is unnumbered); the recording omits one song ("Mitch's Story") and adds one ("Pretty Moon Over Macao"); "Rick's Song" is also heard on the recording (and in performance sequence, no less; so Rick can be happy his song wasn't included as a bonus track, or, worse, a hidden track). The recording also includes an instrumental prologue. The script was published by Samuel French, Inc., in 2009.

As mentioned, the CD represents a slightly revised version of the musical as seen in New York, and on the album "Ticky Ticky Tock" now includes Tempura as one of the singers (here, Tempura is in drag as "Billie Holliday Wong"); the audience is also asked to join in the song, and "everyone" sings it "one hundred more times."

11 Aesop's Fables. "A Rock Musical." THEATRE: Mercer Arts Center, OPENING DATE: August 17, 1972; PERFORMANCES: 58; TEXT: Jon Swan; MUSIC: William Russo; DIRECTION: William Russo; staged by Dan Sanders; SCENERY: Vanessa James; COSTUMES: Vanessa James; MUSICAL DIRECTION: Joseph Reiser, Choral Director; Frank Shaney, Associate Music Director; PRODUCER: William Russo

CAST—The Performing Ensemble of the Chicago Free Theatre (Mike Shacochis, Trisha Long, John Davenport, Denise Walther, Bill Williams, Frank Shaney, Richard Kravets, Ken Hayden, Kat Buddeke)

SOURCES—Stories from *Aesop's Fables*. The revue was presented in one act.

MUSICAL NUMBERS—"The Lion and the Mouse" (Mike Shacochis, Trisha Long). "The Fox and the Stork" (John Davenport, Denise Walther), "The Mice in Council" (Bill Williams, Frank Shaney, Kat Buddeke, Trish Long), "The Lion and the Boar" (Bill Williams, Frank Shaney), "The Wolves and the Jackal" (John Davenport, Richard Kravets, Ken Hayden), "The Donkey and the Grasshopper" (Bill Williams), "The Frog and the Ox" (Kat Buddeke, Trish Long), "The Trees and the Ax" (Denise Walther, Mike Shacochis, Bill Williams), "The Cat and the Rooster" (Mike Shacochis, Denise Walther), "The Ants and the Cocoon" (Frank Shaney), "The Crow and the Fox" (Trish Long)

NOTES—*Aesop's Fables* had originally been produced in Chicago, and appears similar in style to *Story Theatre* and *Metamorphoses*, two other Chicago-based offerings which appeared on Broadway during the 1970-1971 season.

The revue was set to a rock score by William Russo, and Howard Thompson in the *New York Times* found the music "imaginative ... thoughtful, melodic, often striking," and he singled out "The Mice in Council," "The Trees and the Ax," and "The Lion and the Boar." But he noted the drumming "was the loudest thumping I have heard since one voodoo night in the hills above Port-au-Prince, Haiti."

12 Africanis Instructus. THEATRE: St. Clement's Theatre; OPENING DATE: January 14, 1986; PERFORMANCES: 34; TEXT: Richard Foreman; MUSIC: Stanley Silverman; DIRECTION: Richard Foreman; SCENERY: Richard Foreman and Nancy Winters; COSTUMES: Jim Buff; LIGHTING: William Armstrong; MUSICAL DIRECTION: David Oei; PRODUCERS: Music-Theatre Group/Lenox Arts Center (Lyn Austin, Producer and Director; Diane Wondisford and Mark Jones, Associate Producing Directors); produced in association with the Ontological-Hysterical Theatre

CAST—Alan Scarfe (Otto), Eve Bennett-Gordon (Rhoda), David Sabin (Max), Kate Dezina (Eleanor), Keith David (Ben), Tommy Hollis (Black Max), Susan Browning (Nurse), Clark Brown (Attendant), Gerald Gilmore (Attendant), Charles Richardson (Lion, Headless Man), Peter Davis (Lion, Headless Man)

NOTES—Mel Gussow in the *New York Times* reported that the Off Off Broadway musical *Africanis Instructus* dealt with the themes of colonial expansionism and African exploration, and centered around Rhoda (Eve Bennett-Gordon), a Victorian woman who voyages to Africa. But Gussow felt the musical never quite focused on its subject matter, and as a result the evening was "a series of stops and starts ... like a ship that keeps waiting for its passengers to arrive." Gussow was nonetheless impressed with the music, design, and performance, and noted that Stanley Silverman's score included over forty songs and recitatives, "all linked by the composer's talent for transcending pastiche." Gussow wrote that the songs were "filled with verve" and ran a gamut of styles, from Cy Coleman to Puccini.

13 After the Ball. THEATRE: Irish Repertory Theatre; OPENING DATE: December 6, 2004; PERFORMANCES: 54 (estimated); BOOK: Noel Coward; book edited by and additional material by Barry Day; this production was also adapted by Tony Walton; LYRICS: Noel Coward; MUSIC: Noel Coward; DIRECTION: Tony Walton; Kelly Hanson, Assistant Director; CHOREOGRAPHY: Lisa Shriver; SCENERY: Tony Walton; Kelly Hanson, Assistant Designer; COSTUMES: Tony Walton; LIGHTING: Brian Nason; MUSICAL DIRECTION: Mark Hartman; PRODUCER: The Irish Repertory Theatre (Charlotte Moore, Artistic Director; Ciaran O'Reilly, Producing Director)

CAST—Kathleen Widdoes (Duchess of Berwick), Mary Illes (Mrs. Erlynne), Kristin Huxhold (Lady Windermere), Paul Carlin (Lord Windemere), David Staller (Lord Darlington), Collette Simmons (Lady Agatha), Greg Mills (Mr. Hopper), Josh Grisetti (Mr. Dumby), Drew Eshelman (Lord Augustus), Elizabeth Inghram (Lady Plymdale)

SOURCE—The 1892 play *Lady Windermere's Fan* by Oscar Wilde.

The action occurs in London in 1892.

The musical was presented in two acts.

ACT ONE—"Why Is It the Woman Who Pays?" (Ladies), "I Knew That You Would Be My Love" (Paul Carlin, Kristin Huxhold), "Mr. Hooper's Chanty" (Greg Mills, Josh Grisetti, Kathleen Widdoes), "Sweet Day" (Kristin Huxhold), "Stay on the Side of the Angels" (David Staller), "Oh, What a Century It's Been" (Drew Eshelman, Greg Mills, Paul Carlin, Josh Grisetti), "May I Have the Pleasure" (Greg Mills, Kathleen Widdoes), "Good Evening, Lady Windermere" (Mary Illes, Drew Eshelman, Ensemble), "Let's Say Goodbye" (Mary Illes), "I Offer You My Heart" (David Staller, Kristin Huxhold)

ACT TWO—"I Feel So Terribly Alone" (Lady Windermere's Aria) (Kristin Huxhold), "London at Night" (Gentlemen), "Letter Song"/"Never Again" (David Staller), "Why Is It the Woman Who Pays?" (reprise) (Ladies), "Clear, Bright Morning" (Kristin Huxhold), "Remember Me" (Mary Illes), "Something on a Tray" (Kathleen Widdoes), "Faraway Land" (Greg Mills), "Let's Say Goodbye" (reprise) (Mary Illes, Drew Eshelman), "Light Is the Heart" (Mary Illes, Ensemble), Finale (Company)

NOTES—A musical adaptation by Noel Coward of a play by Oscar Wilde would seem to have been an inspired combination. But despite its witty book, lyrics, and score, Coward's *After the Ball*, based on Wilde's *Lady Windermere's Fan*, was a disappointment, running only 188 performances in its original London production which opened at the Globe Theatre on March 1, 1954. The Irish Rep's Off Off Broadway production was based in part on a newly adapted concert version of the musical by Barry Day which had first been seen on May 27, 1999, at the Peacock Theatre in London as part of the Covent Garden Festival. The adaptation's American premiere occurred in Chicago on November 13, 1999, at the Auditorium Theatre as part of the Chicago Humanities Festival, and its New York premiere was on April 21, 2001, by the New York Library for the Performing Arts at Lincoln Center at the U.S. Custom House.

Besides using Day's concert adaptation, director Tony Walton repositioned some of the material; deleted five songs; and interpolated two from other musicals by Coward.

Deleted were "Crème de la Crème," "What Can It Mean?," "Go, I Beg You Go," "All My Life Ago," and "Farewell Song." Added to the production were "Let's Say Goodbye" and "Never Again." "Let's Say Goodbye" had been introduced in the 1932 London revue *Words and Music* (when the revised revue opened in New York in 1938 it was titled *Set to Music*; the song wasn't included in the New York production); "Never Again" was introduced in *Set to Music*, and was later interpolated into the 1945 London revue *Sigh No More* (further, early versions of the song, written in the 1920s, were known as "You've Gone Away" and "The Dream Is Over"). The cast album of the Irish Rep's production was released by Kritzerland Records (CD # KR-20010-1). The original 1954 production was recorded by Philips Records (LP # BBL-7005) and has been issued on CD by Sepia Records (CD # 1043); this recording includes "Crème de la Crème" and "All My Life Ago."

The script of Barry Day's concert version of *After the Ball* was published by Samuel French, Inc., in 2002.

For another musical version of *Lady Windermere's Fan*, see entry for the 1960 production *A Delightful Season*. For other musical adaptations of works by Wilde, see entries for *Dorian* (which also references *Dorian Gray*, another musical adaptation of the material [both musicals opened within a month of one another in 1990]); *Dorian Gray*, another musical adaptation (which opened in 1996); and *Ernest in Love* (which also references other musical versions of *The Importance of Being Earnest*).

For musicals based on Wilde's life, see entries for *Dear Oscar* and *It's Wilde!* as well as *Utterly Wilde!!!*, a one-man musical biography.

14 After the Fair. "A New Romantic Musical." THEATRE: The Theatre at Saint Peter's Church; OPENING DATE: July 15, 1999; PERFORMANCES: 30; BOOK: Stephen Cole; LYRICS: Stephen Cole; MUSIC: Matthew Ward; DIRECTION: Travis L. Stockley; SCENERY: James Morgan; COSTUMES: Michael Bottari and Ronald Case; LIGHTING: Michael Lincoln; MUSICAL DIRECTION: Georgia Stitt; PRODUCER: The York Theatre Company (James Morgan, Artistic Director; Robert A. Buckley, Managing Director

CAST—Michele Pawk (Edith Harnham), Jennifer Piech (Anna), James Ludwig (Charles Bradford), David Staller (Arthur Harnham)

SOURCE—The short story "On the Western Circuit," which appeared in Thomas Hardy's short story collection *Life's Little Ironies* (1894).

The action occurs in Melchester, England, and in London during 1897.

The musical was presented in two acts.

ACT ONE—Prologue (Company), "The World at My Window" (Company), "After the Fair" (Jennifer Piech, Michele Pawk), "Just in Case" (Michele Pawk), "Just Then" (Jennifer Piech, Michele Pawk), "Beloved" (Michele Pawk), "Summer Fancy" (James Ludwig), "Another Letter" (Company), "Nothing Stays" (David Staller, Michele Pawk), "This Is Not the End" (Michele Pawk, Jennifer Piech), "Nothing Will Ever Be the Same" (Michele Pawk, Company)

ACT TWO—Opening (Michele Pawk, Jennifer Piech, James Ludwig), "A Spot of Tea" (David Staller, Michele Pawk), "Between the Lines" (James Ludwig, Michele Pawk), "There's a Woman"/"What Is Real" (Michele Pawk, Jennifer Piech), "Men and Wives" (James Ludwig, David Staller), "Your Words Were Music" (James Ludwig, Michele Pawk, Jennifer Piech), Finale (Company)

NOTES—*After the Fair* told the story of a vaguely unhappy married couple (Edith and Arthur) and their illiterate maid (Anna), who meets and falls in love with a barrister (Charles) at the annual county fair. Edith conspires with Anna by writing letters on Anna's behalf to Charles, and soon discovers she's falling in love with him. In the meantime, Charles has fallen in love with the woman who writes him the letters (believing, of course, that Anna is the letter-writer). When Anna becomes pregnant, she and Charles marry. But when the letter-writing deception is revealed, matters become tenuous but nonetheless go on somewhat routinely with the two married couples. After the passage of a year, Edith receives a letter from Charles and when she read it, she smiles enigmatically. As the curtain falls, the three other characters, and the audience, don't know what in the letter has made Edith smile. The pleasant score was recorded by Varese Sarabande Records (CD # 302-066-075-2).

The musical was first produced at Lyric Stage in Irving, Texas.

The Day After the Fair, a dramatic adaptation of Hardy's story by Frank Harvey, premiered in London in 1972 with Deborah Kerr (as Edith), who also toured with the play in the United States during the

1973-1974 season. In 1987, a made-for-television film (as *The Day After the Fair*) was also produced.

15 The Agony of Paul. THEATRE: Judson Poets' Theatre; OPENING DATE: October 3, 1980; PERFORMANCES: 16; BOOK: Al Carmines; LYRICS: Al Carmines; MUSIC: Al Carmines; DIRECTION: Bob Herget; CHOREOGRAPHY: Bob Herget; SCENERY: Steve Priest; COSTUMES: Jim Correy; LIGHTING: Andrew Taines; MUSICAL DIRECTION: Al Carmines; PRODUCER: The Judson Poets' Theatre

CAST—Tony Calabro, Michael Lynch, Jackie Beech, Essie Borden, Carmelo Bruno, Molly Stark, Lee Hayden, Maggie Wise, Paul Rounsaville, Bill Altham, Marvin Foster, David Summers, Richard Battaglia, Robert Atwood, Georgia Creighton, Fiddle Viracola, Peter Oliver-Norman, Patricia Woodard, Peter Alfano, Dwight Arno, Amanda Marx, Susan Chasin, David McCracken, Ronn Smith, Robert McNamara, Lynne Miller, Alice Bosveld, Matthew Lipton, Nathaniel Bucknell, Judith Elaine, Kathleen Cardy, Helena Andreyko, Brugh Pettrey, Rosemary Loar, Carol Estey, Christopher Foster, Nancy Giles, Heather Godwin, Marianna Allen, Robert Herrig, Juliana Hamel, Terence Burk, Jim King, Linda Blackwood

NOTES—Al Carmines' Off Off Broadway musical *The Agony of Paul* examined St. Paul's attitude towards women and sex. Mel Gussow in the *New York Times* felt the work was one of Carmines' least successful, noting the book and lyrics wavered between "the didactic and the simplistic." He felt the evening's strongest asset was Carmines' music, which included a "low-down" "Get Your Man" and a song of "sapphic love" sung to "an old-fashioned 'Moonlight Bay' beat." Tony Calabro performed the title role, and Gussow reported his character sang a "sheaf of self-accusing soliloquies."

16 Ah, Men. "An Entertainment on the Male Experience (With Music)." THEATRE: South Street Theatre; OPENING DATE: May 11, 1981; PERFORMANCES: 14; SKETCHES: Paul Shyre; LYRICS: Will Holt; MUSIC: Will Holt; DIRECTION: Paul Shyre; SCENERY: Eldon Elder; COSTUMES: Eldon Elder; LIGHTING: John Gisondi; MUSICAL DIRECTION: Christopher Denny; PRODUCER: Jay Garon

CAST—Jane White (Narrator), Curt Dawson (Player A), Jack Betts (Player B), Stephen Lang (Player C)

The revue was presented in one act.

MUSICAL NUMBERS—"Ah, Men" (Company)/ *Sons*: "Man Is for the Woman Made" (Curt Dawson)/*Lovers*: "When After You Pass My Door" (Jane White), "My First" (Stephen Lang), "The Last Minute Waltz" (Jack Betts), "Truck Stop" (Jane White)/ "It's Time" (Company)/*Husbands*: "Illusions" (Jane White)/*Fathers*: "Daddy Blues" (Curt Dawson, Jack Betts, Stephen Lang)/"Ah, Men" (reprise) (Company)

NOTES—*Ah, Men* was another loosely connected evening of songs and dialogue sequences (and with nameless characters, no less). But at least it was another (albeit brief) opportunity to see the always fascinating Jane White, who was the revue's narrator. Mel Gussow in the *New York Times* remarked that someone should come up with a musical to "take advantage of her considerable musical talents," including her "dramatic ability to convey the emotion within the lines of a lyric."

Ah, Men was a look at "the male experience," as told through four sequences (*Sons, Lovers, Husbands,* and *Fathers*). Each sequence contained at least one song and also included readings from writings by, and interviews with, such disparate personalities as Mickey Rooney, Rudolph Valentino, Ayatollah Khomeni, and Lenny Bruce. Gussow found the revue a "mildly engaging collage ... an amiable but unadventurous interlude." He also noted the revue wasted time by offering "detailed information on ... distasteful subjects," such as male-related diseases and the "chemical components" of the male anatomy.

During previews, the revue was presented in two acts, with the intermission taking place after the *Lovers* sequence and the song "It's Time." Once the intermission was omitted, "We're Back," the opening number of the second act, was dropped. The song "The Life We Lead" was also dropped during previews.

17 Ain't Doin' Nothin' But Singin' My Song. THEATRE: Theatre Off Park; OPENING DATE: October 11, 1978; PERFORMANCES: 12; LYRICS: Johnny Brandon; MUSIC: Johnny Brandon; DIRECTION: Lucia Victor; CHOREOGRAPHY: Mabel Robinson; SCENERY: Don Jensen; COSTUMES: Don Jensen; LIGHTING: Jeff Davis; MUSICAL DIRECTION: Carl Maultsby; PRODUCER: Theatre Off Park (Patricia Flynn Peate, Executive Director; Jeffrey Solis, General Manager)

CAST—Pi Douglass, Pat Lundy, Ken Prescott, Judy Stevens, Marian Taylor

NOTES—The apostrophe-loving *Ain't Doin' Nothin' but Singin' My Song* was the first of three musicals by Johnny Brandon which were produced Off Off Broadway during the 1978-1979 season (see entries for *Helen* and *Suddenly the Music Starts*).

18 Ain't Misbehavin'. "A Musical Tribute to Fats Waller." THEATRE: Cabaret/Manhattan Theatre Club; OPENING DATE: February 8, 1978; PERFORMANCES: 28; DIRECTION: Richard Maltby, Jr.; CHOREOGRAPHY: Arthur Faria; COSTUMES: Pegi Goodman; MUSICAL DIRECTION: Thom Birdwell; PRODUCER: Manhattan Theatre Club (Lynne Meadow, Artistic Director; Barry Grove, Managing Director)

CAST—Irene Cara, Nell Carter, Andre De Shields, Armelia McQueen, Ken Page

The revue was presented in two acts.

ACT ONE—"Ain't Misbehavin'" (from *Hot Chocolates* [a/k/a *Connie's Hot Chocolates*], 1929; lyric by Andy Razaf, music by Thomas [Fats] Waller and Harry Brooks) (Company), "Lookin' Good but Feelin' Bad" (lyric by Lester A. Santly, music by Fats Waller) (Company), "'T Ain't Nobody's Biz-ness If I Do" (lyric and music by Porter Grainger and Everett Robbins; additional lyric by Richard Maltby, Jr., and Murray Horwitz) (Andre De Shields, Company), "Honeysuckle Rose" (lyric by Andy Razaf, music by Fats Waller) (Ken Page, Nell Carter), "Squeeze Me" (lyric by Clarence Williams, music by Fats Waller) (Armelia McQueen), "Handful of Keys" (lyric by Richard Maltby, Jr., and Murray Horwitz, based on an idea by Marty Grosz, music by Fats Waller) (Company), "I've Got a Feeling I'm Falling" (lyric by Billy Rose, music by Fats Waller and Harry Link) (Nell Carter, Company), "The Ladies Who Sing with a Band" (*Early to Bed*, 1943; lyric by George Marion, Jr., music by Fats Waller) (Andre De Shields, Ken Page), "Yacht Club Swing" (lyric by J.C. Johnson, music by Fats Waller and Herman Autry) (Irene Cara), "When the Nylons Bloom Again" (*Early to Bed*, 1943; lyric by George Marion, Jr., music by Fats Waller) (Armelia McQueen, Irene Cara, Nell Carter), "Cash for Your Trash" (lyric by Ed Kirkeby, music by Fats Waller) (Nell Carter), "Off-Time" (lyric by Andy Razaf, music by Fats Waller and Harry Brooks) (Company), "The Joint Is Jumpin'" (lyric by Andy Razaf and J.C. Johnson, music by Fats Waller) (Company)

ACT TWO—"Lounging at the Waldorf" (lyric by Richard Maltby, Jr., music by Fats Waller) (Armelia McQueen, Irene Cara, Ken Page, Nell Carter). "The Viper's Drag" (music by Fats Waller)/"The Reefer Song" (traditional) (Andre De Shields, Company). "Mean to Me" (lyric by Roy Turk, music by Fred E. Ahlert) (Nell Carter), "Your Feet's Too Big" (lyric and music by Ada Benson and Fred Fisher) (Ken Page), "That Ain't Right" (lyric by Irving Mills, additional lyric by Richard Maltby, Jr., and Murray Horwitz, music by Nat "King" Cole) (Andre De Sheilds, Armelia McQueen, Company), "Keepin' Out of Mischief Now" (lyric by Andy Razaf, music by Fats Waller) (Irene Cara), "Find Out What They Like" (lyric by Andy Razaf, music by Fats Waller) (Armelia McQueen, Nell Carter), "Fat and Greasy" (lyric and music by Porter Grainger and J.C. Johnson) (Andre De Shields, Ken Page), "Black and Blue" (*Hot Chocolates*, 1929; lyric by Andy Razaf, music by Fats Waller and Harry Brooks) (Company). *Finale:* "I'm Gonna Sit Right Down and Write Myself a Letter" (lyric by Fred E. Ahlert, music by Joe Young) (Ken Page), "Two Sleepy People" (1938 film *Thanks for the Memory*; lyric by Frank Loesser, music by Hoagy Carmichael) (Armelia McQueen, Ken Page), "I've Got My Fingers Crossed" (1936 film *King of Burlesque*; lyric by Ted Koehler, music by Jimmy McHugh) (Armelia McQueen, Irene Cara, Nell Carter), "I Can't Give You Anything But Love" (*Blackbirds of 1928*; lyric by Dorothy Fields, music by Jimmy McHugh) (Andre De Shields, Irene Cara), "It's a Sin to Tell a Lie" (lyric and music by Billy Mayhew) (Nell Carter, Company), "Honeysuckle Rose" (reprise) (Company)

NOTES—The Manhattan Theater Club was committed to producing limited-run revues of various lyricists and composers, and they hit pay dirt with their Off Off Broadway tribute to Fats Waller (1904–1943). *Ain't Misbehavin'* immediately transferred to Broadway, where it played for 1,604 performances. For the Broadway transfer, Irene Cara was replaced by Charlaine Woodard, and the scenery was by John Lee Beatty, the costumes by Randy Barcelo, and the lighting by Pat Collins.

The following numbers were added for the Broadway production: "How Ya Baby" (lyric by J.C. Johnson, music by Fats Waller), "The Jitterbug Waltz" (lyric by Richard Maltby, Jr., music by Fats Waller), and "Spreadin' Rhythm Around" (lyric by Ted Koehler, additional lyric by Richard Maltby, Jr., music by Jimmy McHugh; the song was originally introduced in the 1936 film *King of Burlesque*).

The first five songs heard in the finale weren't written by Fats Waller, but were popularized by him. The Broadway cast recording of *Ain't Misbehavin'* was released by RCA Victor on a 2-LP set (# CBL2-2965); the revue was later televised by NBC on June 21, 1982 (the cast included Nell Carter and Charlaine Woodard); and was revived with the original Broadway cast on August 15, 1988, at the Ambassador Theatre for 176 performances.

The revue included two numbers ("The Ladies Who Sing with a Band" and "When the Nylons Bloom Again") from Waller's 1943 hit musical *Early to Bed*, which appears to be the first Broadway musical about Whites composed by a Black. The musical ran for a year, and the half-dozen or so songs which have surfaced (including "Slightly Less Than Wonderful" and "There's a Man in My Life") are an ingratiating mixture of haunting ballads and amusing comedy songs; a studio cast album of the score would be a valuable addition to the legacy of recorded American theatre music.

19 Airtime. "A Light Musical Revue on Flying and Breathing." THEATRE: Main Theatre/New York Stage Works; OPENING DATE: April 25, 1980; PERFORMANCES: 20; LYRICS: Tom Michael; MUSIC: Tom Michael; DIRECTION: Kevin E. Thompson; LIGHTING: Terry Alan Smith; PRODUCER: New York Stage Works (Cecily and Craig LaPlount, Nick Roberts, and Terry Alan Smith, Founders)

CAST—Victoria Gilmore, Stephanie Nighbert, Craig Wells

The revue was presented in two acts.

ACT ONE—"Airtime" (Company), "Delivery Boy" (Victoria Gilmore), "Tuned-Out" (Stephanie Nighbert), "Winded" (Company), "My Song"/"Ding Ding" (Craig Wells, Victoria Gilmore, Stephanie Nighbert), "Long Distance" (Stephanie Nighbert), "Extramarital Relationships" (Victoria Gilmore), "Undesirable" (Craig Wells), "I Could Never Be Your Lover Again" (Company), "Alone at Last" (Craig Wells), "Echoes" (Company), "Meditation" (Stephanie Nighbert), "Some Minor Turbulence" (Victoria Gilmore), "Disco Nights" (Company)

ACT TWO—"Tell Me What to Do" (Company), "Duet" (Victoria Gilmore, Stephanie Nighbert), "Right from the Start" (Craig Wells), "I Will Love You" (Stephanie Nighbert), "Jim" (Victoria Gilmore), "Revival on Broadway" (Company), "Breathless" (Company)

NOTES—A program note for the Off Off Broadway revue *Airtime* indicated the evening was inspired by the lyricist-composer's childhood, when he watched planes circling Linden Airport in New Jersey. "Majestically inspired" by the sight of planes, "he dreamed of writing an Off-Broadway musical about Cerebral Aviation" (which the program explained was the "flight of the imagination"). The production of *Airtime* thus "allowed a little boy's dream to come true."

20 Akhnaten. THEATRE: The New York State Theatre; OPENING DATE: November 4, 1984; PERFORMANCES: Unknown; LIBRETTO: Philip Glass, Shalom Goldman, Robert Israel, and Richard Riddell; MUSIC: Philip Glass; MUSICAL DIRECTION: Christopher Keene; PRODUCERS: The New York City Opera and the Houston Grand Opera

CAST—Cast included Christopher Robson (Akhnaten)

The action occurs around 1370 B.C. in Thebes and Akhetaten.

The opera was performed in three acts (singing assignments unknown).

ACT ONE—"Prelude: Refrain, Verse 1, Verse 2," "Funeral of Amenhotep III," "The Coronation of Akhnaten," "The Window of Appearances," "The Temple," "Akhnaten and Nefertiti"

ACT TWO—"The City"/"Dance (Beginning)," "The City," "The City"/"Dance (Conclusion)," "Hymn" (a/k/a "Hymn to Aten")

ACT THREE—"The Family," "Attack and Fall," "The Ruins," Epilogue

NOTES—*Akhnaten* was one of Philip Glass' three "portrait" operas (see entries for *Einstein on the Beach* [1976] and *Satyagraha* [1980]). The opera was first seen on March 24, 1984, when it was produced by the Stuttgart State Opera; the New York City Opera's production marked the work's American premiere.

The opera was sung in three languages (Egyptian, Hebrew, and Arcadian), and only one sequence in the opera ("Hymn to Aten") was sung in the language of the audience.

The libretto dealt with Akhnaten, the Egyptian pharaoh who murdered his father, had an affair with his mother, and married Nerferti (the latter had her own musical, *Nefertiti*, which closed in Chicago during its pre–Broadway tryout in 1977 [Andrea Marcovicci was Nefertiti and Robert LuPone was Akhnaten]). Donal Henahan in the *New York Times* felt the evening was boring and monotonous, and he complained that Glass' score was "going-nowhere music, music that flutters its wings but does not try to fly."

The opera was recorded by the Stuttgart State Opera, Orchestra, and Chorus on a 2-CD set released by Sony Classical Records (# SM2K-91141); the musical sequences listed above are taken from this recording.

21 Akokawe. THEATRE: St. Marks Playhouse; OPENING DATE: May 19, 1970; PERFORMANCES: 44; DIRECTION: Afolabi Ajayi; CHOREOGRAPHY: Percival Borde; SCENERY: Chuck Vincent; LIGHTING: Ernest Baxter; PRODUCER: The Negro Ensemble Company

CAST—Mbari-Mbayo Players (Afolabi Ajayi, from Nigeria; Amandina Lihamba, Tanzania; Paul Makgoba, South Africa; Ifatumbo Oyebola, New York; Babfemi Akinlana, New York; Louis Espinosa, New York); Negro Ensemble Company Players (Norman Bush, Frances Foster, Esther Rolle, Clarice Taylor, Allie Woods); Guest Performer, Andre Womble

The revue was presented in two acts.

ACT ONE—*Traditional Times*—"Opening Call of Drums" (Babafemi Akinlana, Ifatumbo Oyebola), "Poem of Greetings" (Company), "Song of Ojo" (Afolabi Ajayi, Norman Bush, Paul Makgoba, Andre Womble), "Song of Wisdom" (Amandina Lihamba, Clarice Taylor), "The Storyteller" (Afolabi Ajayi, Company)/*The First Contact*—"The European" (Frances Foster, Amandina Lihamba, Esther Rolle), "The Prayer That Got Away" (Afolabi Ajayi, Norman Bush), "Song of War" (Paul Makgoba, Company)

ACT TWO—*Poets in Exile*—"Invocation" (by Wole Soyinka) (Esther Rolle), "New York" (Clarice Taylor, Andre Womble), "First Impressions" (by Laffiaji) (Amandina Lihamba), "Vending Machine" (by J.P. Clark) (Norman Bush), "American Impressions" (by Ifeanyi Menkiti), "Harlem Blonde Bombshell" (Amandina Lihamba), "Manhattan" (Paul Makgoba), "Selma" (Frances Foster, Esther Rolle, Clarice Taylor), "Integration" (Paul Makgoba), "New York Skyscrapers" (by J. Mbiti) (Clarice Taylor), "Telephone Conversation" (Afolabi Ajayi), "Paris in the Snow" (by Senghor) (Frances Foster)/*Negritude Poets*—"Prayer to Masks" (by Senghor) (Paul Makgoba, Company), "Africa" (by Birago Diop) (Esther Rolle), "Nights of Sine" (by Senghor) (Paul Makgoba, Company), "Dawn in the Heart of Africa" (Afolabi Ajayi), "Defiance Against Force" (Afolabi Ajayi, Norman Bush, Company)/*New Songs*—"Merinda Love Song" (Norman Bush, Frances Foster), "Popular Love Song" (Amandina Lihamba, Paul Makgoba), "Song of Proverbs" (Company), "Drum Finale" (Ifatumbo Oyebola, Babfrmi Akinlana)

NOTES—*Akowawe* (*Initiation*) was an evening of traditional and modern African poems, songs, music, and dances performed by members of the Negro Ensemble Company as well as by members of the Mbari-Mbayo Players.

Mel Gussow in the *New York Times* praised a number of sequences (one about a Black renting an apartment via the telephone, another about an exchange student who discovers how little Americans know about Africa), but felt some of the material was lacking (such as an "interminable" tale about why the tortoise has an uneven shell). He also noted the evening could do with more songs and dances.

22 Alarums and Excursions. THEATRE: Square East; OPENING DATE: May 29, 1962; PERFORMANCES: 619; SCENES AND DIALOGUE: Created by the Company; MUSIC: William Mathieu; later in run, the program credited music to Fred Kaz DIRECTION: Alan Myerson; SCENERY: Larry Klein; LIGHTING: Ronald Colby; PRODUCERS: Bernard Sahlins, Howard Alk, and Paul Sills

CAST—Howard Alk, Alan Arkin, John Brent, Andrew Duncan, Patricia Englund, Anthony Holland, Lynda Segal, Eugene Troobnick

The revue was performed in two acts (sketch and song assignments unknown).

ACT ONE—"Everybody's in the Know but Me," "Technical Assistants in Vietnam," "The Commercial," "The Drawing Room," "The Pretzel Peddler," "Do It Yourself Playwriting," "Die Konzert," "The Adventures of Businessman"

ACT TWO—"A Group Improvisation," "BBC-TV Presents," "'Dink' Smith's Teen Age Band Party," "A Grecian Urn," "Wigs," "Springtime at Vassar," "Kennedy-Khrushchev Interview," "Joey's Song"

NOTES—*Alarums and Excursions* was the third Second City revue, and the second to play Off Broadway. It was the longest entry in the series, playing for 619 performances. (See entry for *Seacoast of Bohemia* for a complete list of the Second City revues which were presented in New York; also see Appendix T.)

The "Kennedy-Khrushchev Interview" was a holdover from *Seacoast of Bohemia*. Notice how prescient the group was in their subject matter: "Technical Assistants in Vietnam" appeared in the revue more than two years before the general public became aware of the United States' widespread political and military involvement in that country. In 1962, Vietnam was decidedly a non-issue for most Americans. Arthur Gelb in the *New York Times* singled out the Vietnam sketch as well as two others, one about the stock market and another about nuclear weapons (President Kennedy soothingly states that each time we denotate a nuclear bomb we are slowly but surely depleting our supply). Later in the run, direction was credited to Larry Arrick, and music to Fred Kaz. Lynda Segal, an original Stewed Prune (see entry for *Stewed Prunes*) joined the Second City for this excursion.

23 Alec Wilder/Clues to a Life. THEATRE: Vineyard Theatre; OPENING DATE: February 3, 1982; PERFORMANCES: 20; LYRICS: See song list for credits; MUSIC: See song list for credits; DIRECTION: Norman Rene; CHOREOGRAPHY: Louise Quick; SCENERY: Jane Thurn; COSTUMES: Oleksa; LIGHTING: Debra J. Kletter; MUSICAL DIRECTION: Elliot Weiss; PRODUCERS: The Production Company (Norman Rene, Producing Director) in association with Vineyard Theatre (Barbara Zinn, Artistic Director)

CAST—Christine Andreas, D'Jamin Bartlett, Keith David, Craig Lucas

The revue was presented in two acts.

ACT ONE—"A Child Is Born" (lyric by Alec Wilder, music by Thad Jones) (Christine Andreas), "The Echoes of My Mind (Life)" (lyric by Rogers Bracket, music by Alec Wilder) (Christine Andreas, Company), "Photographs" (lyric by Fran Landesman, music by Alec Wilder) (D'Jamin Bartlett), "That's My Girl" (lyric by William Engvick, music by Alec Wilder) (Keith David, Craig Lucas), "Ellen" (lyric by William Engvick, music by Alec Wilder) (Keith David), "Unbelievable" (lyric by William Engvick, music by Alec Wilder) (Craig Lucas), "Give Me Time" (lyric and music by Alec Wilder) (Christine Andreas), "Where Is the One?" (lyric by Alec Wilder, music by Edwin Finckel) (D'Jamin Bartlett, Christine Andreas), "Don't Deny" (lyric by William Engvick, music by Alec Wilder) (Craig Lucas), "Moon and Sand" (lyric by William Engvick, music by Alec Wilder) (D'Jamin Bartlett), "Where Is the One" (medley) (Company), "I'd Do It All Again" (lyric and music by Alec Wilder) (Keith David), "Lovers and Losers" (lyric by William Engvick, music by Alec Wilder) (Company), "I'll Be Around" (lyric and music by Alec Wilder) (Company), "While We're Young" (lyric by William Engvick, music by Alec Wilder and Morty Palitz), "I'd Do It All Again" (reprise) (Company)

ACT TWO—"Night Talk" (lyric and music by Alec Wilder) (Keith David), "The Wrong Blues" (lyric by William Engvick, music by Alec Wilder) (Craig Lucas), "I've Been There" (lyric by Loonis McGlohon, music by Alec Wilder) (D'Jamin Bartlett), "Rain, Rain (Don't Go 'Way)" (lyric by Marshall Barer, music by Alec Wilder) (Company), "Blackberry Winter" (lyric and music by Alec Wilder and Looonis McGlohon) (Keith David), "I'll Be Around" (reprise) (D'jamin Bartlett), "Trouble Is a

Man" (lyric and music by Alec Wilder) (Christine Andreas), "You Wrong Me" (lyric and music by Alec Wilder) (Christine Andreas, Craig Lucas, D'Jamin Bartlett), "The Worm Has Turned" (lyric by Loonis McGlohon, music by Alec Wilder) (Christine Andreas, Craig Lucas, D'Jamin Bartlett), "It's So Peaceful in the Country" (lyric and music by Alec Wilder) (Keith David), "Do (Did) You Ever Cross Over to Sneden's?" (lyric and music by Alec Wilder) (Craig Lucas), "Mimosa and Me" (lyric by William Engvick, music by Alec Wilder) (Christine Andreas), "I See It Now" (lyric by William Engvick, music by Alec Wilder) (Keith David, Christine Andreas), "While We're Young" (reprise) (D'Jamin Bartlett)

NOTES—This welcome Off Off Broadway revue of Alec Wilder's songs included such expected pieces as "I'll Be Around," "Blackberry Winter," "It's So Peaceful in the Country," "Trouble Is a Man," and "While We're Young," but nothing from *Kittiwake Island* (see entry) and *Nobody's Earnest*, the latter Wilder's 1974 musical adaptation of *The Importance of Being Earnest* which was performed in regional theatre. The revue was conceived by Barbara Zinn and Elliot Weiss, and included excerpts from Wilder's book *Letters I Never Mailed* (1975). Some songs had additional lyrics by Mike Champagne and Elliot Weiss.

Alec Wilder (1908–1981) wrote *American Popular Song: The Great Innovators* (1972), perhaps the most important analysis of popular American music ever written. He wrote a few musicals (including *Kittiwake Island*, an overlooked gem with a richly melodic score) as well as a major body of songs written independent of any musicals. Wilder lived at the Algonquin Hotel, and legend has it that his possessions never filled more than three suitcases. He died on Christmas Eve 1981.

The cast album of *Clues to a Life* was released on Original Cast Records (LP # OC-8237). It omitted a handful of songs from the production, but included at least one ("A Long Night") which wasn't listed in the program (but which may have been added to the revue during its run).

24 Ali Baba and the 40 Thieves. THEATRE: Bil Baird Theatre; OPENING DATE: December 26, 1970; PERFORMANCES: 91; BOOK: Alan Stern; LYRICS AND MUSIC: George Kleinsinger, Bil Baird, and Joe Darion; DIRECTION: Gordon Hunt; MUSICAL DIRECTION: Alvy West; DESIGNS: Bil Baird; PRODUCERS: American Puppet Arts Council (Arthur Cantor, Executive Director) and a Bil Baird Marionettes Production

CAST—Cary Antebi (Danhasch), Bil Baird (alternating in the roles of Danhasch and Cassim), Peter Baird (Robber), Pady Blackwood (Zsa-Zsa), David Canaan (Selim), Olga Felgemacher (Morgiana, Mrs. Ali), Frank Sullivan (Ali Baba), Byron Whiting (Mahmoud, Cassim)

NOTES—Set in the "Land of Persia," *Ali Baba and the 40 Thieves* was a new puppet musical in the second of three programs offered by Bil Baird during the 1970-1971 theatre season. It was accompanied by *Holiday on Strings*, a story of Christmas and other winter holidays, and it also included demonstrations of puppet techniques (similar to *A Pageant of Puppet Variety*, which wasn't included on this bill).

Mel Gussow in the *New York Times* noted that *Ali Baba* was perhaps a bit too complicated for younger children, and he felt the story was "a little long on love and a little short on humor." But he nonetheless found it an "ornate, colorful spectacle" on the order of the Christmas show at Radio City Music Hall or a production of *Kismet*.

25 Alias Jimmy Valentine. THEATRE: Musical Theatre Works; OPENING DATE: March 4, 1988; PERFORMANCES: 8; BOOK: Jack Wrangler; LYRICS: Hal Hackady; MUSIC: Bob Haber; DIRECTION: Charles Repole; CHOREOGRAPHY: Sam Viverito; SCENERY: Michael Keith; COSTUMES: Stephen L. Bornstein; LIGHTING: Clarke W. Thornton; MUSICAL DIRECTION: Arnold Gross; PRODUCER: Musical Theatre Works (Anthony J. Stimac, Artistic Director; Mark S. Herko, Associate Artistic Director)

CAST—Faith Prince (Lillian Deluxe), Shelly Burch (Beatrice, Carla Fox), Keith Savage (Rufus, John Chase), Lillian Graff (Valerie, Viola), Robert McCormick (Detective Benjamin Price), Denise Lor (Hattie), Billy Hipkins (Murk, Gambler), Bill Buell (Bowery Boy, Mr. Thompson), Katharine Buffaloe (Ellen Longstreth), Thomas Ruisinger (Thaddeaus Longstreth), Kurt Peterson (Jimmy Valentine), Dick Decareau (Dink), Boo-Boo Prince (Scruffy)

SOURCE—The short story "A Retrieved Reformation" by O. Henry (William Sydney Porter), which appeared in the short story collection *Con Men and Hoboes*.

The action occurs in Spring 1912 in the Bowery of New York and in Willow Run, Idaho.

The musical was presented in two acts.

ACT ONE—"Winner Take All" (Faith Prince, Shelly Burch, Lillian Graff), "Jimmy's Comin' Back" (Faith Prince, Company), "What's Your Hurry, Mister?" ("Canaries," Denise Lor, Faith Prince), "I'm Free" (Kurt Peterson, Dick Decareau), "I'm Free" (reprise) (Robert McCormick, Kurt Peterson, Dick Decareau), "Flim-Flam" (Kurt Peterson, Denise Lor, Dick Decareau), "You're So Good, John" (Katharine Buffaloe), "Flim-Flam" (reprise) (Kurt Peterson, Dick Decareau), "She'll Get You Yet" (Kurt Peterson, Keith Savage), "That Girl" (Kurt Peterson), "Dink's Lament" (Dick Decareau), "Leave It to Me" (Faith Prince, Robert McCormick, Kurt Peterson, Dick Decareau, Denise Lor, Katharine Buffaloe, Keith Savage)

ACT TWO—"Today Is on Me" (Kurt Peterson, Company), "Love Is a Four-Letter Word" (Faith Prince, Katharine Buffalo, Denise Lor), "Small Town" (Kurt Peterson), "You're So Good, John" (reprise) (Katharine Buffaloe, Keith Savage), "I'm Gettin' Off Here" (Denise Lor), "I'm Free" (reprise) (Kurt Peterson), "I Love You, Jimmy Valentine" (Company)

NOTES—The Off Off Broadway musical *Alias Jimmy Valentine* was based on O. Henry's short story "A Retrieved Reformation." The plot dealt with a con man who is released from prison, only to slide back into a life of flim flam. He's tracked down by a detective, but when Jimmy performs a good deed, the detective pretends not to know him and sends him on his way.

26 Alice. THEATRE: Brooklyn Academy of Music; OPENING DATE: October 6, 1995; PERFORMANCES: Unknown; TEXT: Adaptation by Robert Wilson; Book by Paul Schmidt; LYRICS: Tom Waits and Kathleen Brennan; MUSIC: Tom Waits and Kathleen Brennan; DIRECTION: Robert Wilson; PRODUCER: The Next Wave Festival

CAST—Annette Paulmann, Stefan Kurt, Jorg Holm, Drik Ossig, Sven-Eric Bechtolf

SOURCES—The novels *Alice's Adventures in Wonderland* (1865) and *Through the Looking Glass* (1872) by Lewis B. Carroll.

NOTES—*Alice* had originally been produced in Hamburg in 1992; it was performed in both English and German.

Stephen Holden in the *New York Times* indicated the evening was a "breathtakingly elegant realization" of Lewis Carroll's novels. Mel Gussow in *The Best Plays of 1995-1996* reported that the production began with "a chorus of Carrolls" which ultimately concentrated on Carroll as photographer, not author, as he zeroed in on Alice with a "snake-like camera." Gussow noted that Alice's fall into Wonderland was presented by a "perspective-distorting magic trick" in which the scenery around Alice grew larger and larger as she seemed to grow smaller and smaller. He also mentioned that the score was "Weill-tinged." The songs were performed in English, and the dialogue was spoken in both English and German.

27 Alice in Concert. THEATRE: Anspacher Theatre/The Public Theatre; OPENING DATE: November 29, 1980; PERFORMANCES: 32; BOOK: Elizabeth Swados; LYRICS: Elizabeth Swados; MUSIC: Elizabeth Swados; DIRECTION: Joseph Papp; CHOREOGRAPHY: Graciela Daniele; SCENERY: Michael H. Yeargan; COSTUMES: Theoni V. Aldredge; LIGHTING: Arden Fingerhut; MUSICAL DIRECTION: Elizabeth Swados; PRODUCER: The New York Shakespeare Festival (Joseph Papp, Producer)

CAST—Betty Aberlin, Stuart Baker-Bergen, Richard Cox, Sheila Dabney, Rodney Hudson, Michael Jeter, Charles Lanyer, Mark Linn-Baker, Kathryn Morath, Amanda Plummer, Deborah Rush, Meryl Streep

SOURCES—The novels *Alice's Adventures in Wonderland* (1865) and *Through the Looking Glass* (1872) by Lewis B. Carroll.

The musical was presented in two acts.

ACT ONE—"What There Is" (lyric based on a poem by Kenneth Patchen) (Meryl Streep), "The Rabbit's Excuse" (Mark Linn-Baker, Company), "Down Down Down" (Meryl Streep, Betty Aberlin, Company), "Drink Me" (Deborah Rush, Rodney Hudson, Michael Jeter, Stuart Baker-Bergen, Company), "Good-By Feet" (Meryl Streep, Company), "The Rabbit's House" (Michael Jeter, Amanda Plummer, Mark Linn-Baker, Company), "Bill's Lament" (Michael Jeter, Men), "Caterpillar's Advice" (Richard Cox, Company), "Beautiful Soup" (Meryl Streep), "Wow Wow Wow" (Sheila Dabney, Company), "Pretty Piggy" (Meryl Streep, Company), "Cheshire Puss" (Rodney Hudson, Meryl Streep), "If You Knew Time" (Betty Aberlin, Company), "No Room No Room" (Richard Cox, Mark Linn-Baker, Michael Jeter, Meryl Streep, Company), "Starting Out Again" (Meryl Streep, Company), "White Roses Red" (Stuart Baker-Bergen, Michael Jeter, Rodney Hudson, Deborah Rush), "Alphabet" (Company), "Red Queen" (Deborah Rush, Company), "Never Play Croquet" (Meryl Streep, Company), "Mock Turtle Lament" (Mark Linn-Baker, Deborah Rush, Meryl Streep), "The Lobster Quadrille" (Richard Cox, Betty Aberlin, Company), "Eating Mushrooms" (Meryl Streep, Company)

ACT TWO—"Child of Pure Unclouded Brow" (Deborah Rush, Stuart Baker-Bergen), "Jabberwocky" (Richard Cox, Company), "The Bird Song" (Deborah Rush, Mark Linn-Baker, Michael Jeter), "Humpty Dumpty" (Meryl Streep, Company), "Tweedledum and Tweedledee" (Michael Jeter, Stuart Baker-Bergen), "The Walrus and the Carpenter" (Charles Lanyer, Amanda Plummer, Company), "The White Queen" (Meryl Streep), "The White Knight" (Mark Linn-Baker, Meryl Streep), "An Aged, Aged Man" (Meryl Streep, Mark Linn-Baker), "The Examination" (Kathryn Morath, Betty Aberlin, Deborah Rush, Sheila Dabney), "What There Is" (reprise) (Sheila Dabney), "Queen Alice" (Company), "What Is a Letter" (Meryl Streep, Betty Aberlin, Company)

NOTES—According to the program notes, Elizabeth Swados worked on *Alice in Concert* for seven years (in fact, an earlier version of the piece, a workshop which also starred Meryl Streep, had been produced at the Public as *Wonderland in Concert* for three performances beginning on December 27, 1978), and this led some critics to question why the long-aborning musical was such a cheerless, vague, and disjointed affair, lacking a coherent point of view. Writing in *Time*, T.E. Kalem said that both Swados and Joseph Papp (the director) didn't have "the foggiest notion of Carroll's substance or sensibility."

As for the score, Frank Rich in the *New York Times* conceded Swados' "right to compose tuneless music," but wondered why she didn't even bother to match the score to the material. Kalem felt her best numbers sounded like what the writers of *Hair* "threw in the wastebasket."

As for Streep, the critics were generally enthusiastic, but one or two mentioned the mature actress wasn't convincing as a delicate young girl; Kalem noted that she "is so far from being petite that she might have intimidated" Carroll himself. Indeed, Streep's likeness on the musical's poster confirms why some critics questioned her physical suitability for the role.

The script was published by Samuel French, Inc. (apparently in 1987; the title page of the script isn't clear about the publication date). On January 16, 1982, the musical was televised on NBC as *Alice at the Palace* (with Streep reprising her stage role). For a list of other *Alice* adaptations both on Broadway and off, see entry for *Alice with Kisses*; also see Appendix K.

28 Alice in Wonderland (March 1975; Joe Raposo). THEATRE: Bil Baird Theatre; OPENING DATE: March 1, 1975; PERFORMANCES: 51; PRODUCER: The American Puppet Arts Council (Arthur Cantor, Executive Producer)

NOTES—*Alice in Wonderland* was of course based on Lewis B. Carroll's 1865 novel *Alice's Adventures in Wonderland*. Its book was by A.J. Russell, lyrics by Sheldon Harnick, and music by Joe Raposo. It was directed by Paul Leaf, and the musical director was Alvy West. The scenery was by Howard Mandel, and the lighting was designed by Peggy Clark. The production incorporated the original Tenniel drawings into the marionettes' designs; Alice was portrayed by both a puppet and a live actress.

The cast was as follows: Peter Baird (White Rabbit, Tweedledee, Frog Footman, First Creature, Lobster, Violet), Rebecca Bondor (Alice, Turtle, Cheshire Cat, Dormouse, Second Creature, Whiting), Olga Felgemacher (Alice Queen, Tiger Lily, Turtle, Third Creature, Caterpillar), Steven Hansen (Duchess, Walrus, Knave of Hearts, Humpty Dumpty, March Hare, Five of Spades, Mock Turtle), William Tost (Fish Footman, Tweedledum, Mad Hatter, King, Lobster, Violet), Steven Widerman (Three of Spades, Executioner, Cook, Carpenter, Violet).

The singing voices were: George S. Irving (Duchess), Sheldon Harnick (White Rabbit, March Hare, Tweedleee), Rose Mary Jun, Ivy Austin, and Margery Gray (Violet Trio), William Tost (Mad Hatter, Tweedledum, Whiting), Margery Gray (Dormouse), Bil Baird (Mock Turtle, Walrus, Caterpillar)

NOTES—Mel Gussow in the *New York Times* felt the "lively" evening was "funniest at its wildest" in the Mad Tea Party sequence. He also noted that Sheldon Harnick and Joe Raposo's score sounded as if "it had been written between lunch and dinner."

The musical was accompanied by the perennial *Bil Baird's Variety*.

The production returned later in the year for its only revival (see entry).

29 Alice in Wonderland (November 1975; Joe Raposo). THEATRE: Bil Baird Theatre; OPENING DATE: November 2, 1975; PERFORMANCES: 87; PRODUCERS: The American Puppet Arts Council (Arthur Cantor, Executive Producer)

NOTES—Based on the Lewis B. Carroll's 1865 novel *Alice's Adventures in Wonderland*, the puppet musical had been previously presented by Bil Baird earlier in 1975 for fifty-one performances (see entry).

The two-act musical had a book by A.J. Russell, lyrics by Sheldon Harnick, and music by Joseph (Joe) G. Raposo; it was directed by Paul Leaf; the scenery was by Howard Mandel; the lighting was by Peggy Clark; the musical direction was by Alvy West; and the puppet were designed and produced by Bil Baird and Susanna Baird. Olga Felgemacher appeared as the "live" Alice; the puppet Alice was performed by Puppeteer Rebecca Bondor. The puppeteer cast also included: Peter Baird (White Rabbit, Tweedledee, Frog Footman, First Creature, Lobster, Violet); Rebecca Bondor (besides Alice, she also was the puppeteer for Turtle, Cheshire Cat, Dormouse, Second Creature, Snail); Olga Felgemacher (besides the "live" Alice, she was also the puppeteer for Queen, Tiger Lily, Caterpillar, Turtle, Third Creature); Brian Stashick (Duchess, Walrus, Knave of Hearts, Humpty Dumpty, March Hare, Five of Spades, Mock Turtle); William Tost (Fish Footman, Tweedledum, Mad Hatter, King, Lobster, Violet); Steven Widerman (Three of Spades, Executioner, Cook, Carpenter, Violet).

The singing voices were by: Mary Case (Alice); George S. Irving (Duchess); Sheldon Harnick (White Rabbit, March Hare, Tweedledee); Rose Mary Jun, Ivy Austin, and Margery Gray (Violet Trio); William Tost (Mad Hatter, Tweedledum); Margery Gray (Dormouse); Bil Baird (Mock Turtle, Walrus, Caterpillar).

Alice in Wonderland was also presented on a bill with the returning *Bil Baird's Variety*, which, as usual, presented many styles of puppetry. The program included such sequences as: Bill Tost and Purseface; Introducing Slugger Ryan; Froggy Piano; The Rain Forest; the Bughouse Band; and Finale.

30 Alice in Wonderland. (2007; TayWah). "An Adult Musical Comedy." THEATRE: The Kirk Theatre at Theatre Row; OPENING DATE: circa 2007; PERFORMANCES: Unknown; BOOK: Bill Osco; LYRICS: TayWah; MUSIC: TayWah; DIRECTION: Bill Osco; CHOREOGRAPHY: Tania L. Pearson; SCENERY: Josh Iacovelli; COSTUMES: Laura Frecon; LIGHTING: Chris Hudacs; PRODUCERS: Bill Osco in association with Gary Abena, Edmund Gaynes and Louis S. Salamone and TOY for After School Productions

CAST—Unknown

SOURCE—The 1865 novel *Alice's Adventures in Wonderland* by Lewis B. Carroll.

The action occurs in a trailer park in Weehawken, New Jersey.

NOTES—The flyer for this Off Off Broadway version of Lewis B. Carroll's *Alice's Adventures in Wonderland* noted the production was for "Mature Audiences ONLY!!" Set in a trailer park in Weehawken, New Jersey, the musical took Alice to an "erotic Wonderland" where she learns to "let go, grab on, and drink the zest of life."

31 Alice with Kisses. "The Exciting New Musical." THEATRE: 41st Street Theatre; SCHEDULED OPENINGS: May 7, 1964; then May 14, 1964; PERFORMANCES: No official performances (closed in previews); BOOK: Joseph L. Blankenship; LYRICS: Joseph L. Blankenship; MUSIC: Sammy Fields, Joseph L. Blankenship, and Nevett Bartow; DIRECTION: Joseph L. Blankenship; CHOREOGRAPHY: Joseph L. Blankenship; PRODUCERS: Richard J. Martin and Joseph L. Blankenship

CAST—Alice Rawlings, Keith Baker, and (according to the musical's window card) a "Big Singing & Dancing Company"

SOURCE—The 1865 novel *Alice's Adventures in Wonderland* by Lewis B. Carroll.

NOTES—*Alice with Kisses* is one of the most obscure of all Off Broadway musicals, and for good reason: It never officially opened. A "mod" version of *Alice's Adventures in Wonderland*, the "Exciting New Musical" (according to the show's window card) was scheduled to open at the 41st Street Theatre on May 7, 1964, after a series of eight previews beginning on May 1; the opening night was changed to May 14, and the musical continued in previews until a day or two before the official opening. At that point, the opening night was cancelled and the musical permanently closed. Sam Zolotow in the *New York Times* reported that Joseph L. Blankenship, the musical's book writer, lyricist, co-composer, director, choreographer, and co-producer, announced the work would re-open in the fall at the 41st Street Theatre after undergoing "polishing and recasting." Zolotow also reported that Blankenship and the musical's other producer, Richard J. Martin, had taken a five-year lease on the 41st Street Theatre. But *Alice with Kisses* never resurfaced the following fall, or at any other time.

But *Alice with Kisses* has a special distinction. Its window card is featured in the original 1967 film version of *The Producers*. The card can be seen in the film's early scenes, on the wall of Max Bialystock's office, which is covered with window cards of (mostly) flop musicals and plays. Among the other window cards on Max's wall are *The Astrakhan Coat* (1967; 19 performances), *Baby Want a Kiss* (1964; 145 performances), *Beekman Place* (1964; 29 performances), *Café Crown* (the 1964 musical version; 3 performances), *Diamond Orchid* (1965; 5 performances), *Entertaining Mr. Sloane* (1965; 13 performances), *First One Asleep, Whistle* (1966; one performance), *Foxy* (1964; 72 performances [see entry for the *Musicals Tonight!* revival]), *The Great Indoors* (1966; 7 performances), *La Grosse Valise* (1965; 7 performances), *Nature's Way* (1957; 61 performances), *Night Life* (1962; 63 performances), *Nobody Loves an Albatross* (1963; 212 performances), *The Perfect Setup* (1962; 5 performances), *Photo Finish* (1963; 159 performances; this is not the 1968 Off Broadway revue of the same name [see entry]), *The Playroom* (1965; 33 performances), *Poor Bitos* (1964; 17 performances), *Something More!* (1964; 15 performances), *That Summer—That Fall* (1967; 12 performances), and *We Have Always Lived in the Castle* (1966; 9 performances).

Alice with Kisses was one of some dozen musical versions (Broadway [and Broadway-bound], Off and Off Off Broadway, film, and television) which were based on *Alice's Adventures in Wonderland* (1865) and/or *Through the Looking Glass* (1872); many of the adaptations were failures. The Off Broadway *Alice with Kisses* (1964) closed during previews; the Off Off Broadway *For the Snark Was a Boojum, You See* (1977; see entry) quickly disappeared; Micki Grant's stunningly produced *Alice* closed early during the run of its pre–Broadway tryout in Philadelphia in 1978; *But Never Jam Today* (1979) closed on Broadway after seven performances (see entry for its earlier Off Off Broadway production); *The Passion of Alice* was an obscure Off Off Broadway adaptation in the late 1970s (see entry); and *Alice in Concert* (1980) played Off Broadway for thirty-two performances (see entry). In 1995, the Brooklyn Academy of Music presented Robert Wilson's *Alice* (see entry) with lyrics and music by Tom Waits and Kathleen Brennan. There was even an "adult" musical version which opened Off Off Broadway in 2007 (see entry for TayWah's *Alice in Wonderland*).

The Eva Le Gallienne-Florida Friebus adaptation, which did well during its initial 1932 Broadway production as well as in its first Broadway revival in 1946, floundered after twenty-one performances when it returned to Broadway in 1982. Further, *Once on a Summer's Day* (which included both real-life and Wonderland characters) had a brief Off Off Broadway run in 1984, and its announced Off Broadway opening in 1985 was cancelled due to financing problems (see entry).

Bil Baird's puppet version of the material was popular and enjoyed two Off Broadway engagements (see entries for both the original and the revival, both of which were produced in 1975), and perhaps the most critically successful and certainly the longest running of all the different *Alice* adaptations during the period was the Manhattan Project's Off Broadway non-musical version, which originally opened in 1970 and returned for two engagements in 1972 and 1975, for a total of 192 performances.

The Walt Disney cartoon film musical adaptation was released in 1951 (with lyrics by Bob Hilliard and music by Sammy Fain); and there were two television versions, in 1966 (lyrics by Lee Adams and music by Charles Strouse) and in 1972 (lyrics by Don Black and music by John Barry).

32 All by Myself. THEATRE: 41st Street Theatre; OPENING DATE: June 15, 1964; PERFORMANCES: 40; SKETCHES: Anna Russell; LYRICS: Anna Russell; MUSIC: Anna Russell; DIRECTION: Kurt Cerf; SCENERY: Robert E. Darling; COSTUMES: Stephanya; MUSICAL DIRECTION: "Miss Russell Assisted at the Piano by Frank Bartholomew"

CAST—ANNA RUSSELL

The revue was presented in two acts.

ACT ONE—A Summer Festival: "Festival President," "Prima Donna," "Madrigal Group," "Lieder Singer," "Ballad Singer," "Contemporary Music," "Les Cigarettes," "South American, Polite and Rude"/Status: "I Am a Splendid American Man," "Oh, Levittown!," "'Oh Sponsor,' Said She, "Jolly Old Sigmund Freud," "Who He? Don't Know!" "Cossack," "Community Sing"

ACT TWO—The Same Festival, Later: Backwards with the Popular Song: "The Latest," "Schizophrenic," "Chlorophyl Solly," "Santa Claus," "That Man," "Red Hot Mamma," "Hamletto"

NOTES—Anna Russell (1911–2006) was a British singer-comedienne who satirized musical styles and singers, everything from grand opera and operetta to music hall, nightclub and folk music. In her 1953 Broadway revue *Anna Russell's Little* Show, she interpreted Cole Porter's "Night and Day" if it had been composed by Handel and performed by a choir boy. In "Les Cigarettes" (which also appeared in *All by Myself*) she spoofed the Edith Piaf-styled chanteuse. Another Broadway number carried over for *All by Myself* was "Chlorophyl Solly."

Russell was extremely popular in her time, recording numerous albums for Columbia Records and performing her revues and concerts worldwide. Her brand of musical satire has all but vanished; of course, her humor was predicated on the sophistication of her audience, and it's questionable if there's now enough of a public to support, appreciate, and even understand her style of sophisticated and knowing musical humor.

33 All in Love. "A New Musical Comedy." THEATRE: Martinique Theatre; OPENING DATE: November 10, 1961; PERFORMANCES: 141; BOOK: Bruce Geller; LYRICS: Bruce Geller; MUSIC: Jacques Urbont; DIRECTION: Tom Brennan; CHOREOGRAPHY: Jack Beaber; SCENERY: Charles Lisanby; COSTUMES: Charles Lisanby; LIGHTING: Jules Fisher; MUSICAL DIRECTION: Jacques Urbont; PRODUCERS: Jacques Urbont, J. Terry Brown, and Stella Holt, in association with George Peters and Herbert Steinmann

CAST—Sean Gillespie (Page), Bonita Belle (Page), CHRISTINA GILLESPIE (Lucy), MIMI RANDOLPH (Mrs. Malaprop), LEE CASS (Sir Anthony Absolute), GAYLEA BYRNE (Lydia Languish), DAVID ATKINSON (Jack Absolute), Charles Kimbrough (Bag), DOM DE LUISE (Bob Acres), MICHAEL DAVIS (Sir Lucius O'Trigger), Fidel Romann (Sir Percival Crumble), Robert Quint (Sir William Holdfast), Roy Hausen (Sir Roger Stepback), John Dennison (Sir Thomas Standpat), Lorraine Bergstrom (Lady Garter), Elizabeth Burgess (Lady Climber), Wanda Cooke (Lady Barter), Mary Jane Wilson (Lady Slattern-Lounger)

SOURCE—The 1775 play *The Rivals* by Richard Brinsley Sheridan.

The musical was presented in two acts.

ACT ONE—"To Bath Derry-O" (Charles Kimbrough, Gentry), "Poor" (Gaylea Byrne, David Atkinson), "What Can It Be" (Christina Gillespie, Gentry), "Odds" (Dom de Luise, David Atkinson), "I Love a Fool" (David Atkinson), "A More Than Ordinary Glorious Vocabulary" (Mimi Randolph), "Women Simple" (Lee Cass), "The Lady Was Made to Be Loved" (Lee Cass, David Atkinson), "The Good Old Ways" (Grenadiers), "Honour" (Michael Davis), "The Good Old Ways" (reprise) (Lee Cass, Grenadiers)

ACT TWO—"I Found Him"/"Day Dreams" (Christina Gillespie), "Don't Ask Me" (David Atkinson, Gaylea Byrne), "Why Wives" (Michael Davis, Charles Kimbrough, Grenadiers), "I Love a Fool" (reprise) (Gaylea Byrne), "Quickly" (Mimi Randolph, Gaylea Byrne, Christina Gillespie, Charles Kimbrough), "All in Love" (David Atkinson, Company), Finale (Company)

NOTES—Bruce Geller and Jacques Urbont, here returning to musical theatre after the disappointing reception of *Livin' the Life* (1957; see entry), provided a sparkling set of songs for *All in Love*, a lyric adaptation of Sheridan's classic *The Rivals*. Their delightful score was thankfully preserved on a lavish cast album released by Mercury Records (LP # OCS-6204 and # OCM-2204). But despite a rave review from Milton Esterow in the *New York Times*, the musical closed within a few months and for all purposes vanished. Esterow found the evening a "grand show," and noted that Geller and Urbont had "dug into a classic and have struck it rich." He found the book and lyrics full of "wit and ingenuity" and the music "tuneful and original." The lilting "What Can It Be" is one of the score's most memorable numbers (and can also be heard on Jerry Orbach's collection of Off Broadway songs; see discography [Appendix B]), but Mrs. Malaprop's "A More Than Ordinary Glorious Vocabulary" is not only the show's best song, it's also one of the best show songs of the era. With an irresistible melody and an amusingly malapropic lyric, the song is sung by Mrs. Malaprop, who is "answered" by Sir Anthony Absolute in his number "Women Simple," and finally the two songs merge into a thrilling contrapuntal duet. The song "I Found Him" has two distinctions: it was heard in two concurrently-running Off Broadway musicals and was recorded on both their cast albums (a month before the opening of *All in Love*, the song was introduced in *Seven Come Eleven* [see entry]).

Photographs from *All in Love* reveal a stylishly designed musical, one which in fact looks like no other musical of the era, on Broadway or off: the costumes look slightly off-kilter, and have a certain surreal elegance. Esterow found the costumes and scenery "especially imaginative ... opulent ... colorful." He noted that the three-sided stage was white, as were the stage furnishings and the backdrop, and he found this effect "striking." The designer of the scenery and costumes was Charles Lisanby, who also created the musical's poster artwork. It's a mystery why he never had a major career in theatre design. The musical was briefly seen in London in 1964, quickly folding after a disappointing run of twenty-two (or thirty-two, depending on the source) performances; the cast included Annie Ross, Mary Miller, and Ronnie Barker.

34 All Kinds of Giants. "A Musical." THEATRE: Cricket Theatre; OPENING DATE: December 18, 1961; PERFORMANCES: 16; BOOK: Tom Whedon; LYRICS: Tom Whedon; MUSIC: Sam Pottle; DIRECTION: Peter Conlow; SCENERY: Merrill Sindler; COSTUMES: Merrill Sindler; LIGHTING: Pat Simmons; MUSICAL DIRECTION: Milton Setzer; PRODUCER: Noel Weiss

CAST—Ralph Purdum (A King), Claiborne Cary (A Princess), Richard Morse (A Tailor), Tom Rummler (A Prince), Bill Hinnant (A Giant)

The action occurs in the Royal Courtyard, the Throne Room, the Tailor's Shop, and the Great Forest.

The musical was presented in three acts.

ACT ONE—"State of the Kingdom" (Ralph Purdum, Claiborne Cary, Richard Morse), "My Prince" (Claiborne Cary), "Paint Me a Rainbow" (Claiborne Cary, Richard Morse), "Logic!" (Ralph Purdum, Claiborne Cary, Richard Morse), "If I Were Only Someone" (Richard Morse)

ACT TWO—"To Be King" (Ralph Purdum), "Suddenly Stop and Think" (Richard Morse, Claiborne Cary), "My Star" (Claiborne Cary), "All Kinds of Giants" (Bill Hinnant), "Friends" (Bill Hinnant, Richard Morse)

ACT THREE—"Here Are We" (Claiborne Cary, Ralph Purdum), "Be Yourself" (Bill Hinnant), "Be Myself" (Richard Morse), "Duel" (Richard Morse, Tim Rummler), Finale (Company)

NOTES—*All Kinds of Giants* played for just sixteen performances, but cast member Bill Hinnant received good reviews (Lewis Funke in the *New York Times* compared his clowning to that of Nancy Walker's) and he later enjoyed a long-running success when he created the role of Snoopy in *You're a Good Man, Charlie Brown*, one of the biggest hits in the history of the Off Broadway musical (see entry). Funke reported that the tongue-in-cheek musical dealt with a kingdom threatened by a giant. Because a giant isn't good for the tourist trade, the king offers his daughter in marriage to whoever can dispatch him (it later turns out the giant is the diminutive Hinnant). Naturally, the king assumes only high-born heroes will apply, and doesn't bargain for a lowly commoner (a tailor, no less) to enter the picture (as the chorus sang in *Love Me Tonight*, Richard Rodgers and Lorenz Hart's brilliant 1932 fairy-tale-like film musical, "The Son of a Gun Is Nothing but a Tailor"). Funke praised Tom Whedon and Sam Pottle's score, singling out no less than seven songs ("My Prince," "Paint Me a Rainbow," "My Star," "Friends," "Logic!," "Here We Are," and "To Be a King"). But he was less than pleased with the ordinary book (which threatened "to get lost in its own forest"), and concluded that another Off Broadway fairy-tale musical (*Once Upon a Mattress*; see entry) was better.

35 The All Night Strut! THEATRE: Theatre Four; OPENING DATE: October 4, 1979; PERFORMANCES: 6; DIRECTION: Fran Charnas; CHOREOGRAPHY: Fran Charnas; COSTUMES: Celia Eller; LIGHTING: Glenn Heinmiller; MUSICAL DIRECTION: Michael Dansicker; PRODUCERS: Karen Kantor, Philip Swaebe, Stanley A. Glickman, and Ashton Springer

CAST—Andrea Danford, Tony Rich, Jess Richards, Jana Robbins

The revue was presented in two acts (song assignments weren't identified in the program).

ACT ONE—"Chattanooga Choo-Choo" (from 1941 film *Sun Valley Serenade*; lyric by Mack Gordon, music by Harry Warren), "Minnie the Moocher" (*Cotton Club Revue*, 1931; lyric by Clarence Gaskill, Cab Calloway, Irving Mills, music by Cab Calloway), "Brother, Can You Spare a Dime?" (*Americana*, 1932; lyric by E.Y. Harburg, music by Jay Gorney), "In the Mood" (lyric and music by Joe Garland, additional lyric by Bette Midler and Barry Manilow), "Gimme a Pigfoot (and a Bottle of Beer)" (lyric and music by Wesley "Socks" Wilson and Coot Grant; some sources credit only Wilson as the lyricist and composer of the song), "A Nightingale Sang in Berkeley Square" (1940 British musical *New Faces*; lyric by Eric Maschwitz, music by Manny Sherwin), "Fascinating Rhythm" (*Lady, Be Good!*, 1924; lyric by

Ira Gershwin, music by George Gershwin), "Java Jive" (by Milton Drake and Ben Oakland)

World War II Medley (songs unidentified in program, but the following lyricists and composers were credited: Johnny Mercer; Moore; Burton-Kent; Brown-Tobias-Stept; Evans-Loeb; Freed and Skinner; Irving Berlin; Harold Adamson and Jimmy McHugh; and Irving Kahal and Sammy Fain)

ACT TWO—"I Get Ideas" (by Dorcas Cochran and Sanders), "Ain't Misbehavin'" ([*Connie's*] *Hot Chocolates*, 1929; lyric by Andy Razaf, music by Thomas [Fats] Waller and Harry Brooks), "Operator" (lyric and music by William Spivery), "Dream" (not written for a musical, but interpolated into the score of the 1955 film *Daddy Long Legs*; lyric and music by Johnny Mercer), "Beat Me, Daddy, Eight to the Bar" (lyric and music by Don Raye, Hughie Prince, and Eleanore Sheehy), "A Fine Romance" (1936 film *Swing Time*; lyric by Dorothy Fields, music by Jerome Kern), "Tuxedo Junction" (lyric and music by Erskine Hawkins, Buddy Feyne, William Johnson, and Julian Dash), "Juke Box Saturday Night" (*Stars on Ice*, 1942; lyric by Al Stillman, music by Paul McGrane), "As Time Goes By" (*Everybody's Welcome*, 1931; lyric and music by Herman Hupfield), "Hit That Jive, Jack" (lyric and music by Tolbert and Alston), "Billie's Bounce" (lyric and music by Charlie Parker), "It Don't Mean a Thing (If It Ain't Got That Swing)" (lyric and music by Duke Ellington), "Lullaby of Broadway" (film *Gold Diggers of 1935*; lyric by Al Dubin, music by Harry Warren)

NOTES—*The All Night Strut!*, an anemic revue of nostalgic songs of the 1920s, 1930s, and 1940s, would have been better served as a television special. There was no particular rhyme or reason to the order in which the songs were performed, and the aimlessness gave the four-member revue no shape or substance. A Broadway song from 1932 would be followed by a big-band song, a Broadway song from 1924 would be followed by a 1940s jive tune. Walter Kerr in the *New York Times* noted that the evening's highlight was "Fascinating Rhythm." First sung in a straightforward manner, it was then performed as a cha-cha-cha, a waltz, and finally in a "burst" of boogie-woogie.

Prior to its New York production, the revue had been presented with a cast of sixteen in such cities as Cleveland, Boston, and Washington, D.C. (William Roy had been the musical director), and during the tour the material was presented in distinct segments (Big Band; Harlem; El Morocco; Broadway; Stage Door Canteen; New Orleans; and Hollywood). The Cleveland production was recorded live and was released on Playhouse Square Records, Inc. (LP # PHS-CLE-1S-1001).

36 All of the Above. "A Musical Entertainment." THEATRE: Perry Street Theatre; OPENING DATE: July 14, 1982; PERFORMANCES: 7; SKETCHES: Michael Eisenberg; LYRICS: Michael Eisenberg; MUSIC: Michael Eisenberg; DIRECTION: Tony Berk; SCENERY: Lou Anne Gilleland; COSTUMES: Carla Kramer; LIGHTING: Victor En Yu Tan; MUSICAL DIRECTION: Ed Ellner; PRODUCERS: Victoria Lang and Peter Golden in association with Eugene Albert

CAST—Ann Morrison, Linda Gelman, Michelan Sisti, Ed Ellner

The revue was presented in one act (the program didn't provide song assignments for musical numbers, all of which were listed alphabetically).

MUSICAL NUMBERS—"A Cry from the Coast," "Be My Bland Romantic Lead," "Born Again," "California Love," "Child of a Sweater," "Dancin' Shoes," "For Alice," "Game Show Hosts," "It Just Ain't a Party Without You," "Las Vegas Post-Blitz," "Little Rubik's Room," "Memories of Kong," "Mom Kills Child Comma Self," "My Heart's Intact," "New Year's Eve at the Computer Center," "Pianist's Fingers," "School on Saturday Night," "Talk to My Machine," "The Dictator Who Ran Away," "Willy's Prize," "Your Show"

NOTES—The Off Off Broadway revue *All of the Above* was gone within a week. John S. Wilson in the *New York Times* noted the program listed the songs alphabetically, and suggested that perhaps the revue's creators weren't sure of the final running order of the songs and "were just winging it." He then added, "Unfortunately, they don't have much to wing it with." Wilson also noted that much of the revue's material indicated the writer had been overexposed to television. Further, he felt the lyrics struggled "to find something to say" and the melodies "simply tread water." But Wilson praised the "cheerful energy" of the cast, and said their confidence almost gave the impression that something was happening on stage. "Pianist's Fingers" was a musical sequence based on traditional blues, with piano improvisations by Ed Ellner. "Memories of Kong" and "Talk to the Machine" were composed by Bruce Lieberman, and "Dancin' Shoes" had music by Bruce Molloy and Mike Eisenberg. Ann Morrison had made her Broadway debut the previous fall, creating the role of Mary Flynn in Stephen Sondheim's *Merrily We Roll Along* (1981). With her powerful, brassy voice, she seemed destined for a great career in musical theatre, and while she appeared in Off Broadway, regional, and London productions, but didn't create another role on Broadway until *LoveMusik* in 2007.

37 Almost Heaven: Songs of John Denver. THEATRE: Promenade Theatre; OPENING DATE: November 9, 2005; PERFORMANCES: 61; ORIGINAL CONCEPT: Harold Thau; DIRECTION: Randal Myler; SCENERY: Kelly Tighe; Jan Hartley, Projection Technical Advisor; COSTUMES: Tobin Ost; LIGHTING: Don Darnutzer; MUSICAL DIRECTION: Charlie Alterman; PRODUCERS: Harold Thau in association with Lexie Potamkin, R.H. and Ann Crossland, Lawrence J. Winnerman, and Robert Courson; Ken Denison, Associate Producer

CAST—Jennifer Allen, Terry Burrell, Valisia Lekae Little, Lee Morgan, Jim Newman, Nicholas Rodriguez

The revue was presented in two acts.

ACT ONE—"All of My Memories" (Jim Newman, Lee Morgan, Company), "For Bobbie" (Nicholas Rodriguez, Lee Morgan, Jim Newman), "Rhymes and Reasons" (Valisia Lekae Little), "Draft Dodger Rag" (Lee Morgan), "I Wish I Could've Been There (Woodstock)" (Jim Newman, Company), "Take Me Home, Country Roads" (Jennifer Allen, Company), "Fly Away" (Terry Burrell), "I Guess He'd Rather Be in Colorado" (Terry Burrell, Jennifer Allen, Valisia Lekae Little), "Rocky Mountain High" (Lee Morgan, Company), "Matthew" (Jim Newman), "Let Us Begin (What Are We Making Weapons For?)" (Nicholas Rodriguez, Terry Burrell), "Calypso" (Nicholas Rodriguez, Company)

ACT TWO—"This Old Guitar" (Lee Morgan, Jim Newman), "Thank God I'm a Country Boy" (Jim Newman), "Grandma's Feather Bed" (Company), "Annie's Song" (Jennifer Allen), "Goodbye Again" (Jim Newman, Jennifer Allen), "How Can I Leave You Again" (Lee Morgan, Terry Burrell), "Back Home Again" (Nicholas Rodriguez, Valisia Lekae Little), "Leaving on a Jet Plane" (Terry Burrell, Company), "For You" (Nicholas Rodriguez), "I'm Sorry" (Jennifer Allen), "Sunshine on My Shoulders" (Valisia Lakae Little), "Looking for Space" (Jim Newman), "Wild Montana Skies" (Jennifer Allen, Terry Burrell, Valisia Lekae Little, "Songs Of" (Lee Morgan, Company), "Poems, Prayers and Promises" (Terry Burrell, Jim Newman, Company), "Yellowstone" (Company)

NOTES—*Almost Heaven: Songs of John Denver* was a short-lived revue which featured songs by and stories about singer and songwriter John Denver (1943–1997). Neil Genzlinger in the *New York Times* found the evening a "pale imitation of a biographical musical." He reported that Denver's songs were often undercut by a lack of subtlety, and so "Take Me Home, Country Roads" "morphed into a braying torch song"; "Rocky Mountain High" came across like a "beer-drinking song on a pirate ship"; and "Leaving on a Jet Plane" used clichéd and obvious projections (of an airport, of a plane flying into the clouds) to accompany the lyric. Randal Myler, the director of *Almost Heaven*, was associated with three other Off Broadway musicals which looked at the lives and careers of pop singers (see entries for *Dream a Little Dream* [The Mamas and The Papas], *Hank Williams: Lost Highway*, and *Love, Janis* [Joplin]).

38 Altar Boyz. THEATRE: Dodger Stages; OPENING DATE: March 1, 2005; PERFORMANCES: Still playing as of December 31, 2007; BOOK: Kevin Del Aguila; LYRICS AND MUSIC: Gary Adler and Michael Patrick Walker (see song list for specific credits); DIRECTION: Stafford Arima; CHOREOGRAPHY: Christopher Gattelli; SCENERY: Anna Louizos; COSTUMES: Gail Brassard; LIGHTING: Natasha Katz; MUSICAL DIRECTION: Lynne Shankel; PRODUCERS: Ken Davenport and Robyn Goodman in association with Walt Grossman, Ruth Hendel, Sharon Karmazin, Matt Murphy, and Mark Shacket; Stephen Kocis, Associate Producer

CAST—Scott Porter (Matthew), Tyler Maynard (Mark), Andy Karl (Luke), Ryan Duncan (Juan), David Josefsberg (Abraham); also, Shadoe Stevens (The Voice of G.O.D.)

The action occurs in New York City at the present time.

The musical was presented in one act.

MUSICAL NUMBERS—"We Are the Altar Boys" (lyric and music by Gary Adler) (Company), "Rhythm in Me" (lyric and music by Michael Patrick Walker) (Company), "Church Rulez" (lyric and music by Gary Adler) (Company), "The Calling" (lyric and music by Gary Adler) (Company), "The Miracle Song" (lyric and music by Michael Patrick Walker) (Company), "Everybody Fits (lyric and music by Gary Adler) (Company; Lead Vocal, David Josefsberg), "Something About You" (lyric and music by Gary Adler) (Company; Lead Vocal, Scott Porter), "Body, Mind and Soul" (lyric and music by Michael Patrick Walker) (Company; Lead Vocal, Andy Karl), "La Vida Eternal" (lyric and music by Gary Adler) (Company; Lead Vocal, Ryan Duncan), "Epiphany" (lyric and music by Michael Patrick Walker) (Company; Lead Vocal, Tyler Maynard), "Number 918" (lyric and music by Michael Patrick Walker) (Company), Finale "I Believe" (lyric and music by Michael Patrick Walker) (Company)

NOTES—*Altar Boyz*, a good-natured revue-like musical about a five-boy Christian band (four are named Matthew, Mark, Luke, and Juan; the fifth member, Abraham, is Jewish), was presented as a concert in which the band is making its New York debut.

Christopher Isherwood in the *New York Times* said the musical "makes a nice sound, looks pretty (if you like pretty boys) and sends you home with a smile"; he further noted that the cast members had "terrific voices and nimble limbs" and said the choreography paid "energetic homage to the athletic gyrations of boy-band music videos." With its likeable cast and its non-stop energy, the musical quickly caught on, and its ebullient score was recorded by Sh-K-Boom Records (CD # 79155860050-2). As of this writing, the musical has been playing for almost three years.

Altar Boyz was first produced Off Off Broadway at the 47th Street Theatre on September 16, 2004, as part of the New York Musical Theatre Festival.

The musical will probably never be confused with Stephen Magowan's Off Broadway play *Altar Boys*, which played for one performance at Theatre Four on November 18, 1979.

39 Always ... Patsy Cline. THEATRE: Variety Arts Theatre; OPENING DATE: June 24, 1997; PERFORMANCES: 192; BOOK: Ted Swindley; LYRICS: See song list for credits; MUSIC: See song list for credits; DIRECTION: Ted Swindley; SCENERY: Christopher Pickart; COSTUMES: Thom Heyer; LIGHTING: Stephen Quandt; MUSICAL DIRECTION: Vicki Masters; PRODUCERS: Opryland Theatricals in association with the Randy Johnson Company

CAST—Tori Lynn Palazola (Patsy Cline), Margo Martindale (Louise)

The revue was presented in two acts.

ACT ONE—"Honky Tonk Merry Go Round" (lyric and music by Stan Gardner and Frank Simon), "Back in Baby's Arms" (lyric and music by Bob Montgomery), "Anytime" (lyric and music by Herbert Happy Lawson), "Walkin' After Midnight" (lyric and music by Don Hecht and Allen W. Block), "I Fall to Pieces" (lyric and music by Hank Cochran and Harlan Howard), "It Wasn't God Who Made Honky Tonk Angels" (lyric and music by J.D. Miller), "Come On In (and Sit Right Down)" (lyric and music by Michael B. Clark), "Your Cheatin' Heart" (lyric and music by Hank Williams, Sr.), "She's Got You" (lyric and music by Hank Cochran), "San Antonio Rose" (lyric and music by Bob Willis), "Lovesick Blues" (lyric and music by Irving Mills and C. Friend)

ACT TWO—"Sweet Dreams" (lyric and music by Don Gibson), "Three Cigarettes in an Ashtray" (lyric and music by Eddie Miller and W.S. Stevenson), "Crazy" (lyric and music by Willie Nelson), "Seven Lonely Days" (lyric and music by Earl Shuman, Alden Shuman, and Marshall Brown), "If I Could See the World (Through the Eyes of a Child)" (lyric and music by Sammy Masters, Richard Pope, and Tex Satterwhite), "Just a Closer Walk with Thee" (traditional), "Blue Moon of Kentucky" (lyric and music by Bill Monroe), "Gotta Lot of Rhythm in My Soul" (lyric and music by Barbara Ann Vaughan and W.S. Stevenson), "Faded Love" (lyric and music by John Wills and Bob Wills), "True Love" (from 1956 film *High Society*; lyric and music by Cole Porter)

NOTES—*Always...Patsy Cline*, a tribute-revue to country-western singer Patsy Cline (who died in an airplane crash in 1963), was one of many such revues which opened during the era and paid homage to country-western and other popular singers. Off Broadway saw *Our Sinatra* (Frank; 1999), *Love, Janis* (Joplin; 2001), *Hank Williams: Lost Highway* (2003), *The Jackie Wilson Story* (2003), and *Dream a Little Dream* (The Mamas and the Papas; 2003); see entries. Broadway (via London) got *Buddy: The Buddy Holly Story* (1990).

Sweet Dreams, a film version of Patsy Cline's life, was released in 1985 (Jessica Lange portrayed Cline).

The Off Broadway production of *Always...Patsy Cline* wasn't recorded, but an earlier version seen in Nashville in 1995 was recorded live at Ryman Auditorium (the Grand Ole Opry) by MCA Records (CD # MCAD-11205). Mandy Barnett portrayed Patsy Cline, and the recording included two numbers not heard in the Off Broadway production, "Come On In (and Make Yourself at Home)" (lyric and music by V.F. [Pappy] Stewart) and "Always" (lyric and music by Irving Berlin).

40 Amelia Goes to the Ball. THEATRE: Metropolitan Opera House; OPENING DATE: March 3, 1938; PERFORMANCES: 4; LIBRETTO: Gian-Carlo Menotti; MUSIC: Gian-Carlo Menotti; DIRECTION: Leopold Sachse; SCENERY: Donald Oenslager; MUSICAL DIRECTION: Leopold Sachse; PRODUCER: The Metropolitan Opera

CAST—Muriel Dickson (Amelia), John Brownlee (Husband), Mario Chamlee (Lover), Helen Olheim (Friend), Norman Cordon (Chief of Police), Lucielle Browning (Cook), Charlotte Symons (Maid)

The action occurs in Milan.

The opera was produced in one act.

NOTES—*Amelia al Ballo* was originally written in Italian by Gian-Carlo Menotti, and its first production (which was in English in a translation by George Mead) took place on April 1, 1937, at the Curtis Institute of Music in Philadelphia. One week later, on April 7, 1937, the opera was apparently presented for one performance at the New Amsterdam Theatre. If so, the opera was the last lyric work to be performed at the legendary theatre for almost sixty years, when Alan Menken's *King David* was seen there for five performances beginning on May 18, 1997. The opera was first seen at the Met on March 3, 1938, eleven months after the special performance at the New Amsterdam Theatre. The work's Italian premiere occurred in San Remo on April 4, 1938, and on March 24, 1954 the opera was performed at La Scala (see below). The comic opera's title said it all: Amelia goes to the ball. Throughout the opera, she's determined to get there, come hell or high water. Her husband demands to know who her lover is, and she promises to tell him ... after the ball. The lover wants her to run away with him ... and she agrees to, but only after the ball. When the husband and lover meet, a contretemps occurs, and Amelia knocks out the husband with a convenient vase. The police are called, and they arrest her lover for assaulting the husband. And Amelia goes to the ball ... with the chief of police himself.

Writing in the *New York Times*, Olin Downes praised Menotti's libretto, a "jest" of "capital fooling ... deliberately foolish, planned excellently for effect in the theatre." Further, he noted Menotti's "instinctive talent" for music, including solos, duos and trios, and mentioned that his recitative didn't make the English language sound "stupid or futile."

The La Scala production was recorded in Italian by Columbia Records (LP # FCX-335). An Australian production of the opera was televised on ABC on May 11, 1966 (earlier television adaptations of the opera had been seen on Italian television on January 9, 1957, and on German television on September 12, 1965). For the Met production, the opera was seen on a double bill with Richard Strauss' *Elektra* (1909).

41 America Kicks Up Its Heels. "A Musical Comedy." THEATRE: Playwrights Horizons; OPENING: The production gave preview performances from March 3 through March 27, 1983, and then cancelled its official opening.; PERFORMANCES: 28 preview performances; LYRICS: William Finn; MUSIC: William Finn; DIRECTION: Mary Kyte and Ben Levit; CHOREOGRAPHY: Mary Kyte; SCENERY: Santo Loquasto; COSTUMES: Santo Loquasto; LIGHTING: Frances Aronson; MUSICAL DIRECTION: Michael Starobin; PRODUCER: Playwrights Horizons (Andre Bishop, Artistic Director; Paul Daniels, Managing Director)

CAST—Dick Latessa (Boris), Patti LuPone (Cleo), I.M. Hobson (Polly), Robin Boudreau (Thyra), Lenora Nemetz (Hennie), Alexandra [Alix] Korey (Zoe), Robert Dorfman (Julie), Rodney Hudson (Harlan), Peggy Hewett (Mrs. Roosevelt)

The action occurs in New York City in the present and in a 1930's soup kitchen.

The musical was presented in two acts.

ACT ONE—"All of Us Are Niggers" (Company), "Put It Together" (Dick Latessa, Patti LuPone), "Eleanor Roosevelt (A Discussion of Soup)" (Peggy Hewett, Rodney Hudson, Company), "A Better World" (Lenora Nemetz, Dick Latessa, Patti LuPone, Robin Boudreau), "Cutting Hair (A Recitative)" (Company), "Red Faces at the Kremlin" (I.M. Hobson, Company), "Lullaby" (Alexandra Korey), "America, Kick Up Your Heels" (Patti LuPone), "Papa, You Won" (Patti LuPone, Dick Latessa, Company), "Daddy and Me" (Robin Boudreau, Patti LuPone), "Push and Pull (A Recitative)" (Dick Latessa, Rodney Hudson), "All Fall Down" (Alexandra Korey), "The Depression Is Over" (Dick Latessa, Company)

ACT TWO—"I Don't Want to Be Fired Again" (Patti LuPone, Company), "Happiest Moment of My Life" (Dick Latessa, Company), "Ask Me No Question" (Rodney Hudson), "Pull It Together (A Response)" (Peggy Hewett, Patti LuPone, Company), "Nobody's Ever Gonna Step on Me" (Lenora Nemetz), "Why" (Peggy Hewett, I.M. Hobson, Lenora Nemetz, Robert Dorfman, Company), "It Was Fun" (Robin Boudreau, Dick Latessa, Patti LuPone), "America, Kick Up Your Heels (A Choral Arrangement)" (reprise) (Robert Dorfman, Lenora Nemetz, Rodney Hudson, Peggy Hewett, I.M. Hobson, Alexandra Korey, Robin Boudreau, Dick Latessa), "My Day Has Come" (Patti LuPone), "Papa Says" (Dick Latessa, Patti LuPone, Robin Boudreau), "All of Us Are Brothers" (Company)

NOTES—The ill-fated musical *America Kicks Up Its Heels*, which juxtaposed life during the Depression with life in the 1980s, never officially opened. After four weeks of preview performances, the opening night was cancelled. However, during previews the musical was constantly worked on, and at one point a program was issued which indicated the action took place only in the present. For this "revised" version, the following numbers were dropped: "Lullaby," "Papa, You Won," "Daddy and Me," and "All of Us Are Brothers." Added to the production was "Sex Stories in Hard Times."

In November 1989, a radically revised version of the musical was presented by the Public Theatre as *Romance in Hard Times* (see entry). This time around, most of the characters were Black; there were two holdovers from the 1983 production (Peggy Hewett and Alexandra [now Alix] Korey); among the other cast members were Lillias White and Cleavant Derricks. The revised version was set in a Depression-era soup kitchen in New York City, and no action took place in the present. When the original production opened at Playwrights Horizons, there were twenty-four individual numbers; there were thirty-one in the Public Theatre version. Only three numbers from the original production were carried over ("Red Faces in the Kremlin," "Eleanor Roosevelt: A Discussion of Soup," and "All Fall Down"). *Romance in Hard Times* played for only six performances at the Public, and at that point Finn seems to have completely given up on the project.

42 The American Dance Machine. "A Living Archive of Broadway Theatre Dance." THEATRE: Century Theatre; OPENING DATE: June 14, 1978; PERFORMANCES: 198; Entire production supervised and directed by Lee (Becker) Theodore; COSTUMES: John David Ridge; LIGHTING: Jeremy Johnson; MUSICAL DIRECTION: David Krane; PRODUCERS: Lee Theodore and Gloria Sher

CAST (The Alpha Company)—Guests Artists (Harold Cromer, Patti Mariano, and Don Swanson); Soloists (Nancy Chismar, Louise Hickey, and Don Johanson); Ensemble (Helena Andreyko, Amy Lester, Greg Minahan, Christine Oren, Candice Prior, Kevin Ryan, Alexandra Visitor, Derek Wolshonak, and Donald Young). Other performers who appeared in the production during its New York run were Zan Charisse, Grover Dale, Janet Eilber, Steven Gelfer, Liza Gennaro, John Jones, Brian Kelly, Kristina Koebel, David Kottke, Anita Morris, Barry Preston, Debbi Bier Prouty, Joseph Pugliese, Morgan Richardson, Denny Shearer, and Swen Swenson.

The dance revue was presented in two acts.

ACT ONE—"Mamie Is Mimi" (from *Gentlemen Prefer Blondes*, 1949; lyric by Leo Robin, music by Jule Styne; choreography by Agnes de Mille, reconstructed by Evelyn Taylor) "Popularity" (*George M!*, 1968; music by George M. Cohan; choreography by Joe Layton, reconstructed by Karin Baker and Patti Mariano), "June Is Bustin' Out All Over" (*Carousel*, 1945; lyric by Oscar Hammerstein II, music by Richard Rodgers; choreography by Agnes de Mille, reconstructed by Gemze de Lappe), "Whip Dance" (*Destry Rides Again*, 1959; music by Harold Rome; choreography by Michael Kidd, reconstructed by Swen Swenson), "All Aboard for Broadway" (*George M!*, 1968; lyric and music by George M. Cohan; choreography by Joe Layton, reconstructed by Karin Baker and Patti Mariano), "Won't You Charleston with Me?" (*The Boy Friend*, 1954; lyric and music by Sandy Wilson; choreography by Buddy Schwab, reconstructed by Eleanor Treiber), "The Telephone Dance" (*Cabaret*, 1966; lyric by Fred Ebb, music by John Kander; choreography by Ron Field, reconstructed by Marianne Selbert), "Next to Lovin,' I Like Fightin'" (*Shenandoah*, 1975; lyric by Peter Udell, music by Gary Gelb; choreography by Bob Tucker, reconstructed by Bob Tucker), "Rich Kids' Rag" (*Little Me*, 1962; music by Cy Coleman; choreography by Bob Fosse, reconstructed by Gene Galvin).

Intermission dances performed by Harold Cromer, including "Mr. Bojangles" by Jerry Jeff Walker.

ACT TWO—"If the Rain's Gotta Fall" (*Half a Sixpence*, 1965; lyric and music by David Heneker; choreography by Onna White, reconstructed by Tom Panko and Ron Bostick), "Satin Doll" (from a television special; music by Duke Ellington; choreography by Carol Haney, reconstructed by Buzz Miller), "Monte Carlo Crossover"/"Up Where the People Are" (*The Unsinkable Molly Brown*, 1960; music by Meredith Willson; choreography by Peter Gennaro, reconstructed by Vito Durante), "Come to Me, Bend to Me"/"Funeral Dance" (*Brigadoon*, 1947; lyric by Alan Jay Lerner, music by Frederick Loewe; choreography by Agnes de Mille, reconstructed by Gemze de Lappe and Jamie Jamieson), "Quadrille" (*Can-Can*, 1953; music by Cole Porter; choreography by Michael Kidd, reconstructed by Eleanor Treiber and Ken Urmstrum), "You Can Dance with Any Girl at All" (*No, No, Nanette*, 1971 revival; lyric by Irving Caesar, music by Vincent Youmans; choreography by Donald Saddler, reconstructed by Helen Gallagher, Donald Saddler, and Swen Swenson), "Clog Dance" (*Walking Happy*, 1966; music by Jimmy Van Heusen; choreography by Danny Daniels, reconstructed by Dick Korthaze)

NOTES—The American Dance Machine was an important dance company and *The American Dance Machine* was an important dance revue; here for the first time original choreography from Broadway musicals was authentically reproduced. Many dances were thought lost forever, but thanks to Lee Theodore, the company's visionary founder, a number of such dances were reclaimed for posterity in a "living archive." Lee (Becker) Theodore had been a Broadway dancer (she created the role of Anybodys in the original 1957 production of *West Side Story*) and a Broadway choreographer (*Baker Street*, 1965; *Flora, the Red Menace*, 1965; *The Apple Tree*, 1966).

Thanks to Theodore's tenacity, the American Dance Machine thrived on and off for about ten years. Alas, with her untimely death the dance company disbanded and has never re-surfaced under another director. If someone had taken over Theodore's role, and if funding had been made available, who knows what lost Broadway dances might have been reconstructed: "The Sale" from *Make a Wish* (1951)? "The Assembly Dance" from *First Impressions* (1959)? "The Juke-Box Hop" from *Do Re Mi* (1960)? "Be a Santa," "Subway Rush," and "Subway Incident" from *Subways Are for Sleeping* (1961)? The possibilities are endless, and it's a pity that the preservation of Broadway dances seems to have ended with the death of Lee Theodore and the demise of the American Dance Machine. Theodore worked with original choreographers and with dancers who had performed in the original productions, and with perseverance and detective-like work she built up an impressive repertoire of lost Broadway dances. And it couldn't have always been easy to obtain the legal rights to the dances, or the cooperation of choreographers and/or their estates. Swen Swenson, one of the company's guest artists, told me that at first Bob Fosse refused to allow "I've Got Your Number" (Swenson's show-stopping number from *Little Me* [1962]) to be part of the Dance Machine's repertoire, even though Swenson himself would be performing it. Only after many discussions between Fosse and Swenson (and much cajoling on Swenson's part) did Fosse give permission for the number to be included in the revue. Other dance numbers seen during the show's pre–Broadway engagement or numbers added during the Broadway run were "That Terrific Rainbow" (from the 1952 revival of *Pal Joey*), "Harlem Makes You Feel" (*Bubbling Brown Sugar*, 1976), and "Cane Dance" (*The Magic Show*, 1974).

In 1981, *The American Dance Machine* was released on videocassette by MGM/CBS Home Video (# CV-400056); it included many of the dances seen in the New York production as well as Michael Kidd's "Dance o' the Golden Crock" from *Finian's Rainbow* (1947).

In 1982, *Steps in Time*, a sequel of sorts to *The American Dance Machine*, was mounted for a brief tour, which never played New York. It included such dances as "Moon-Faced, Starry-Eyed" (*Street Scene*, 1947), "Another Autumn" (*Paint Your Wagon*, 1951), and "Express Yourself" (*Flora, the Red Menace*, 1965) as well as "I Guess I'll Have to Change My Plan" (as choreographed by Michael Kidd for the 1953 film *The Band Wagon*).

43 American Enterprise.

THEATRE: Playhouse 46/St. Clement's Church; OPENING DATE: April 13, 1994; PERFORMANCES: 15; BOOK: Jeffrey Sweet; LYRICS: Jeffrey Sweet; MUSIC: Jeffrey Sweet; additional music by Michael Vitali; DIRECTION: Patricia Birch; SCENERY: Richard Finkelstein; COSTUMES: Brent Griffin; LIGHTING: John McLain; MUSICAL DIRECTION: Betsy Riley; PRODUCER: The New York State Theatre Institute (Patricia Di Benedetto Snyder, Producing Director)

CAST—John Romeo (George M. Pullman), Erol K.C. Landis (J. Patrick Hopkins), David Bunce (George Jr., Paymaster), Gerard Curran (Eugene V. Debs, Beman, Buisnessman McCormick, Priest), Bernard J. Tarver (John P. Altgeld, Jackson, Clayton, Porter), Paul Villani (Stephens, Harahan, Agent), Marshall Factora (Thomas Wickes, Commissioner, Wright, Porter), Joel Aroeste (Heathcote, Railroad Owner, Commissioner Worthington), Erika Newell (Jennie Curtis, Florence Pullman), Betsy Riley (Soloist), Kelley Sweeney (Soloist), John T. McGuire III (the Rev. E.C. Oggel, Businessman Field), Michael Steese (Mayor Harrison, Businessman Swift, Delegate Cosgrove, Federal Marshal), Jack Seabury (Railroad Assistant, Porter, Servant), Jason W. Bowman (Club Attendant), Tracey E. Madison (Secretary), Ensemble (Laura Roth, Allison Sharpley); Aaron Hagan (Keyboards, Synthesizer)

The action occurs in Chicago during the latter half of the nineteenth century.

The play with music was presented in two acts.

NOTES—*American Enterprise* was a play with music dealt with George M. Pullman, the railroad car manufacturer, and it took on the larger theme of the differing goals of capitalist and laborer.

David Richards in the *New York Times* felt the evening didn't really prove its assertion that Pullman was a "real-life American King Lear," and while he felt the production provided a "helpful overview" of the era's management-and-labor problems, it all too often was the "theatrical equivalent of a W.P.A. mural."

The following songs were included in the production (all lyrics and music by Jeffrey Sweet unless otherwise noted): "Shall We Plant a Tree?" (Soloists, Ensemble); "Porters on a Pullman Train" (lyric by Charles D. Crandall, music by Michael Vitali) (Porters); "Leave a Light" (Soloist); "It's a Trust" (Pullman, Hopkins, McCormick, Railroad Owner, Oggel, Harrison, Club Attendant); "The Columbian Exposition" (Ensemble); "Maggie Murphy" (lyric and music by Ned Harrington and Dave Braham) (Soloist); "Step by Step" (traditional Irish song) (Ensemble); and "The Pullman Strike" (lyric by William M. Delaney, music by Lewis Hall) (Soloist). All songs not by Sweet were authentic songs of the period. For information on other musicals with a railroad theme, see entry for *Frimbo*.

44 The American Hamburger League.

THEATRE: New Theatre; OPENING DATE: September 16, 1969; PERFORMANCES: 1; SKETCHES: Norman Kline. INCIDENTAL MUSIC: Arthur Siegel; DIRECTION: George Luscombe; SCENERY: Nancy Jowsey; COSTUMES: Nancy Jowsey; Joseph Aulisi, Costume Consultant; LIGHTING: Paul Sullivan; PRODUCERS: Leonard Sillman and Orin Lehman; presented by special arrangement with Toronto Workshop Productions

CAST—Jack Fletcher, Bill Hinnant, Jane Hoffman, Dorothy Lyman, Liz Sheridan, Richard B. Shull

The revue was presented in two acts (sketch and song assignments unknown).

ACT ONE—Prologue, "They're Here," "They've Put Up a New Lampost," "I Know What You're Thinking," "Are You Charles Waltz?," "I Have Always Had a Plain Face," "Where's Seth?," "Once a Week I Put My Television Set on the Windowsill," "Nice Shot," "Do You Clean Birthday Suits?," "Yoo-Hoo, Raymond, Breakfast Is Ready," "Mary, I'm a Fool," "I'm a Member in Good Standing of a Reform Congregation," "Charles, This Isn't Easy for Me to Have to Say," "All Those Who Want Their Hamburgers Rare, Raise Their Hand"

ACT TWO—"Are You Waiting for Vito?," "I Have These Pains in My Back," "Who Would Write Something Like That?," "Are You Coming Bowling with Me Tonight, or Not?," "Candlelight Graces a Woman's Face," "Who Is It? The Grocery Boy," "I Have Come to the Conclusion That I Am Unable to Compete in the Normal Labor Market," "Where Did You Come From?," "Closeup of Jack Entering Room," "No-Cal, Norma?"

NOTES—The one-performance flop *The American Hamburger League* was a revue of twenty-five comic "playlets" (with incidental music by Arthur Siegel), and had been first produced in Toronto. Over the next few years there would be a mini-invasion of musicals from north of the border, all of them failures (such as *A Bistro Car on the CNR* and *Love Me, Love My Children* [see entries] Off Broadway and *Rockabye Hamlet* on Broadway).

Writing in the *New York Times*, Clive Barnes noted that the revue dealt with "sweet, sentimental failures." He remarked that the "feyness of the piece is indescribable," and noted the first word to describe the evening was "cute," the second word was "cute," and the third word was "quite unprintable." He said *The American Hamburger League* was " underdone with onions" and had the "wrong kind of ketchup."

45 American Passion.

THEATRE: Joyce Theatre; OPENING DATE: July 10, 1983; PERFORMANCES: 1; BOOK: Fred Burch; LYRICS: Willie Fong Young and

Fred Burch; MUSIC: Willie Fong Young; DIRECTION: Patricia Birch; CHOREOGRAPHY: Patricia Birch; COSTUMES: William Ivey Long; LIGHTING: Richard Winkler; MUSICAL DIRECTION: Timothy Graphenreed; PRODUCER: Stuart Ostrow

CAST—Rosko (Sam), Taryn Grimes (Mary O'Ryan), Margie Perez (Gracie Darcel), Laura Dean (Patty Chance), Christal Wood (Joy Spitz), Don Kehr (Nick), William Morrison (Stanley Blau), Sam Slovick (Joel), Todd Graff (Johnny), Liza Lauber (Debbie), Keri Leff (Clarise), Tia Riebling (Kathy), Robert Downey, Jr. (Jackson)

The action occurs in New York City at the present time.

The musical was presented in one act.

MUSICAL NUMBERS—"American Passion" (Company), "I Think I Like His Eyes" (Taryn Grimes, Company), "There Ain't No Virgins in Queens" (Margie Perez, with Laura Dean, Christal Wood, and Taryn Grimes), "Limo to the Plaza" (Robert Downey, Jr.), "The Gospel According to Rock" (Laura Dean, Company), "Trashin' and Tourin'" (Liza Lauber, Keri Leff, Tia Riebling), "Loud Enough" (Todd Graff), "Concert Tonight" (Company)/"Air Guitar" (Don Kehr, Company), "Balcony of the Faithful" (Christal Wood), "Shirts" (Company), "In the Hallway" (Company), "We'll Sleep with the Radio On" (Margie Perez), "Hi" (Taryn Grimes), "I Light a Light" (Company)

NOTES—*American Passion* dealt with a group of aspiring show business wannabes competing in a talent contest (a kind of early version of *American Idol*, perhaps). Frank Rich in the *New York Times* found the evening the "latest and perhaps the least—but probably not the last" in a long line of *A Chorus Line* clones, and remarked that while the one-act musical was a few minutes shorter than *A Chorus Line*, it seemed four times longer. In *A Chorus Line*, the performers stood on an empty stage while they were interviewed by an unseen director. Rich noted that in a "daring" move, *American Passion* broke with precedent by having the performers questioned by a disk jockey. The one-performance flop underwent a tumultuous preview period. It had originally been presented in two acts, but by opening night the intermission had been dropped, as well as seven songs ("One of Us Lucky Listeners Out There," "Tickets," "Baseball Cards," "Backstage Girls," "Anticipation," "I Like His Ass," and "Romance Is the Way"). Further, Jane Krakowski was replaced by Taryn Grimes, Erica Gimpel by Margie Perez, Anne Marie Bobby by Laura Dean, Martha Plimpton by Christal Wood, and Lisa Ann Graff by Keri Leff.

During previews, Heidi Landesman was credited with the scenery, but by opening night she was listed as "scenic consultant." Rosko, in the tradition of Yuriko and Bhaskhar, seems to have disappeared; but Robert Downey, Jr., went on to an erratic film career and a *Page Six*-styled personal life. The musical had originally been presented by The Musical Theatre Lab in Cambridge, Massachusetts.

46 American Rhapsody.

"A New Musical Revue." THEATRE: Triad Theatre; OPENING DATE: November 10, 2000; PERFORMANCES: 231; TEXT: Ruth Leon, KT Sullivan, and Mark Nadler; LYRICS: Unless otherwise noted, all lyrics by Ira Gershwin; MUSIC: George Gershwin; DIRECTION: Ruth Leon; CHOREOGRAPHY: Donald Saddler; SCENERY: William Barclay; COSTUMES: Roz Goldberg; LIGHTING: Phil Monat and John Tees III; PRODUCERS: Louise Westergaard, Stephen Downey, Jay Harris, and Peter Martin in association with Linda Wassong

CAST—Mark Nadler, KT Sullivan

The revue was presented in two acts (division of acts and song assignments unknown; songs are listed in performance order).

MUSICAL NUMBERS—"Fascinating Rhythm" (from *Lady, Be Good!*, 1924)/"Sweet and Low-Down" (*Tip-Toes*, 1925)/"The Real American Folk Song Is a Rag" (*Ladies First*, 1918) "Love Is Here to Stay" (1938 film *The Goldwyn Follies*), "By Strauss" (*The Show Is On*, 1936)/"Little Jazz Bird" (*Lady, Be Good!*, 1924), "Isn't It a Pity" (*Pardon My English*, 1933), "But Not for Me" (*Girl Crazy*, 1930), "Blah, Blah, Blah" (1931 film *Delicious*), "Vodka" (*Song of the Flame*, 1925; lyric by Otto Harbach and Oscar Hammerstein II, music by George Gershwin and Herbert Stothart), "An American in Paris" (1928)/"Mademoiselle in New Rochelle" (*Strike Up the Band*, 1930)/"Embraceable You" (*Girl Crazy*, 1930), "The Man I Love" (dropped during the tryout of *Lady, Be Good!* [1924]; later used in 1927 version of *Strike Up the Band* [which closed during its pre–Broadway tryout]; later considered for, but not used in, *Rosalie* [1928])

Medley from *Porgy and Bess* (1935): "Summertime" (lyric by DuBose Heyward), "Bess, You Is My Woman Now" (lyric by DuBose Heyward and Ira Gershwin), "It Ain't Necessarily So," "The Lorelei" (*Pardon My English*, 1933) "Slap That Bass" (1937 film *A Damsel in Distress*), "(I've Got) Beginner's Luck" (1937 film *Shall We Dance*), "They All Laughed" (1937 film *Shall We Dance*), "They Can't Take That Away from Me" (1937 film *Shall We Dance*), "Shall We Dance" (1937 film *Shall We Dance*), S'Wonderful (*Funny Face*, 1927)/"Rhapsody in Blue" (1924), "Swanee" (*Demi-Tasse/Capitol Revue*, 1919; later interpolated into tour of *Sinbad* [also 1919]; lyric by Irving Caesar), "Who Cares?" (*Of Thee I Sing*, 1931)

NOTES—For another Off Broadway evening of Gershwin, see entry for *Do It Again!*

47 An American Tragedy.

THEATRE: Metropolitan Opera House; OPENING DATE: December 2, 2005; PERFORMANCES: 8; LIBRETTO: Gene Scheer; MUSIC: Tobias Picker; DIRECTION: Francesca Zambello; CHOREOGRAPHY: Doug Varone; SCENERY: Adrianne Lobel; COSTUMES: Dunya Ramicova; LIGHTING: James F. Ingalls; MUSICAL DIRECTION: James Conlon; PRODUCER: The Metropolitan Opera

CAST—Graham Phillips (Young Clyde Griffiths), Dolora Zajick (Elvira Griffiths), Anna Christy (Hortense), Nathan Gunn (Clyde Griffiths), Kim Begley (Samuel Griffiths), William Burden (Gilbert Griffiths), Patricia Racette (Roberta Alden), Clare Gormley (Grace Marr), Jennifer Larmore (Elizabeth Griffiths), Jennifer Alymer (Bella Griffiths), Susan Graham (Sondra Finchley), Mark Schowalter (the verend McMillan)

SOURCE—The 1925 novel *An American Tragedy* by Theodore Dreiser.

The action occurs in the United States during the late nineteenth and early twentieth centuries.

The opera was presented in two acts.

NOTES—The operatic world premiere of the classic novel *An American Tragedy* told the familiar story of the socially ambitious middle-class Clyde Griffiths (Nathan Gunn), who murders his poor and pregnant girlfriend Roberta Alden (Patricia Racette) when he realizes she'll ruin his chance to marry the wealthy Sondra Finchley (Susan Graham). The novel had been dramatized on Broadway in 1926 by Patrick Kearney, and in 1951 it had been filmed by George Stevens as *A Place in the Sun* with Montgomery Clift, Elizabeth Taylor, and Shelley Winters.

Anthony Tommasini in the *New York Times* noted that Tobias Picker's opera was "conventional," but felt the score "would not be out of place in a Broadway theatre." He remarked that the opera was "accomplished, dramatically effective and thoroughly professional." Greg Sandow in the *Washington Post* felt the story was set to "music in a somewhat lurid operatic style" and complained that the libretto "unfolds at a ponderous, slow pace, with every plot twist telegraphed." However, the various reviews singled out a few set pieces for praise: a duet separately sung by Roberta and Sondra of their love for Clyde; a hymn (the *Times* noted its harmonies were "gritty, astringent and wonderfully strange, with weirdly high chords in the orchestra"); an amusing routine for some businessmen; and a vaudeville-styled sequence.

Adrianne Lobel's three-tiered set allowed for swift scene changes, and Tommasini noted that while the set was "elaborate" it was also "magically simple" in its use of the tiers as a metaphor for the three social classes represented in the opera. And *Variety*'s Eric Myers reported the tiers were also used for one particularly dramatic and stunning effect: on the top tier, Clyde and Roberta are in a boat; Roberta falls off the boat, and then on the tier below she is suddenly seen fighting for her life before she drowns.

Nathan Gunn came close to becoming a matinee idol; the good-looking, muscular baritone appeared shirtless in one scene and wore a bathing suit in another. Myers reported that "few male opera singers would look as good in a 1906 swimsuit."

48 The Amorous Flea.

THEATRE: East 78th Street Playhouse; transferred to the York Theatre on March 20, 1964; OPENING DATE: February 17, 1964; PERFORMANCES: 93; BOOK: Jerry Devine; LYRICS: Bruce Montgomery; MUSIC: Bruce Montgomery; DIRECTION: Jack Sydow; SCENERY: Bill Hargate; COSTUMES: Donald Brooks; LIGHTING: Jane Reisman; MUSICAL DIRECTION: Ted Simmons; PRODUCERS: Charles Hollerith, Jr., and Jerry Devine

Cast—LEW PARKER (Arnolphe), David C. Jones (Chrysalde), JACK FLETCHER (Alain), ANN MITCHELL (Georgette), IMELDA DE MARTIN (Agnes), PHILIP PROCTOR (Horace), Ted Tiller (Oronte), Bryce Holman (Enrique)

SOURCE—The 1662 play *The School for Wives* by Jean-Baptiste Poquelin (Moliere). The action occurs on a street and in a secluded garden in seventeenth-century Paris.

The musical was presented in three acts.

ACT ONE—"All About Me" (Lew Parker), "All About Me" (reprise) (Lew Parker), "All About He" (Imelda de Martin), "All About Him" (Jack Fletcher, Ann Mitchell), "Learning Love" (Philip Proctor), "There Goes a Mad Old Man" (Jack Fletcher, Ann Mitchell), "Dialogue on Dalliance" (Imelda de Martin, Lew Parker)

ACT TWO—"March of the Vigilant Vassals" (Jack Fletcher, Ann Mitchell), "Lessons on Life" (Imelda de Martin, Lew Parker), "Man Is a Man's Best Friend" (Philip Proctor, Lew Parker), "The Other Side of the Wall" (Imelda de Martin), "Closeness Begets Closeness" (Philip Proctor, Imelda de Martin)

ACT THREE—"It's a Stretchy Day" (Lew Parker, Imelda de Martin, Jack Fletcher, Ann Mitchell), "When Time Takes Your Hand" (David C. Jones), "Learning Love" (reprise) (Philip Proctor, Imelda de Martin), "The Amorous Flea" (Lew Parker), Finale (Company)

NOTES—*The Amorous Flea* was another Off Broadway musical adaptation of a classic comedy (in this case, Moliere's *The School for Wives*), and despite a delightful score and a well-received performance by Broadway veteran Lew Parker (Moliere's "best friend," according to Lewis Funke in the *New York Times*), the show ran for only three months. However, the musical continued to have an afterlife, with occasional regional and college theatre productions.

Despite his praise of Parker's performance and the score (there were "several winning songs"), Funke wasn't completely happy with the musical and noted that while it "meant to be a frolic," there were "arid patches that wear you down." Book-writer Jerry Devine had earlier written *The Cuckold's Nest*, a non-musical adaptation of Moliere's comedy; it doesn't appear to have been produced.

The script for *The Amorous Flea* was published by Dramatists Play Service, Inc., in 1964. For other musicals based on Moliere's comedies, see entries for *The Misanthrope*, *Monsieur de Pourceaugnac*, *Show Me Where the Good Times Are*, and *'Toinette*.

49 Amphigorey. "A Musicale." THEATRE: Perry Street Theatre; OPENING DATE: April 7, 1994; PERFORMANCES: 50; TEXT: Edward Gorey; MUSIC: Peter Golub; DIRECTION: Daniel Levans; CHOREOGRAPHY: Daniel Levans; SCENERY: More Than Just Scenery; COSTUMES: James P. Hammer, Jr.; LIGHTING: Brian Nelson; MUSICAL DIRECTION: Frederick Willard; PRODUCER: The Q.R.V. Company

CAST—Mark Baker, Allison DeSalvo, Ken Jennings, Kathleen Mahoney-Bennett, Kevin McDermott, Jennifer Naimo, Richard Parent, Dale Sandish, Joyce Sozen, Clare Stollak

SOURCE—Various writings by Edward Gorey.

The revue was presented in two acts (song assignments weren't credited in the program).

ACT ONE—"Q.R.V.," "The Frozen Man," "The Weeping Chandelier," "The Doubtful Guest," "The Deranged Cousins," "Q.R.V. Too," "The Forty-Seven Questions," "The Blue Aspic"

ACT TWO—"The Nursery Frieze," "The Object Lesson," "The Enraged Telephone," "The Osbick Bird," "The Inanimate Tragedy," "The Admonitory Hippopotamus," Finale "Q.R.V. Also"

NOTES—A program note for *Amphigorey* indicated the revue's sequences were comprised of mostly unpublished material by Edward Gorey, and that in the case of previously published material (such as "The Blue Aspic" and "The Deranged Cousins"), the adaptations were by Gorey. The scenery and costumes were based on designs by Gorey.

Amphigorey had been previously seen as *Tinned Lettuce* in a student production by NYU Undergraduate Drama and was later developed in a series of workshops at Bennington College and at Musical Theatre Works. Its first public performances were at the American Music Theatre Festival in Philadelphia; later, a revised version was presented at the American Repertory Theatre. *Amphigorey* was again revised (as *The Gorey Details*), with music by Peter Matz; this production was seen Off Broadway in 2000 (see entry).

On October 30, 1978, Broadway offered the revue *Gorey Stories* (which played for one performance at the Booth Theatre and had originally been produced Off Off Broadway on December 8, 1977, at the WPA Theatre for twelve performances). Gorey's greatest theatrical success was the Broadway revival of *Dracula*, which opened on October 20, 1977, at the Martin Beck (now Hirschfeld) Theatre and played for 925 performances; Gorey designed the clever scenery and costumes, and won the Tony Award for Best Costume Design.

50 ...And in This Corner. THEATRE: Upstairs at the Downstairs OPENING DATE: February 12, 1964; PERFORMANCES: 410; SKETCHES: Treva Silverman; LYRICS: Allison Roulston, Michael McWhinney, and Rod Warren; MUSIC: Jay Foote, Jerry Powell, and Rod Warren; DIRECTION: Jonathan Lucas; COSTUMES: Gowns by Baba; MUSICAL DIRECTION: Daniel Strickland; PRODUCERS: Michael McWhinney and Rod Warren

CAST—Bill Brown, Marian Mercer, Virgil Curry, Carol Morley

The revue was presented in two acts (sketch and song assignments unknown).

ACT ONE—"...And in This Corner" (lyric and music by Rod Warren) "Happiness Is" (lyric and music by Rod Warren) "Prince Edward Skool" (lyric by Michael McWhinney, music by Jerry Powell) "Service for Two" (sketch by Treva Silverman) "Tristan and Isolated" (lyric and music by Rod Warren) "The Judy Garland National Anthem" (lyric by Michael McWhinney, music by Jerry Powell) "Out of Session" (sketch by Treva Silverman) "The Dying Schwann" (lyric and music by Rod Warren), "Smoke Signals" (sketch by Treva Silverman) "Where the Bulls Are" (lyric by Allison Roulston, music by Jay Foote)

ACT TWO—"Tokyo, Mon Amour" (lyric and music by Rod Warren), "Ads Infinitum" (lyric by Michael McWhinney, music by Rod Warren), "Subways Are for Skiing" (lyric by Michael McWhinney, music by Rod Warren) "When I Was Learning to Read" (lyric and music by Rod Warren) "The Tree" (sketch by Treva Silverman) "Elephant Joke" (lyric by Michael McWhinney, music by Rod Warren) "Our New Best Friends" (lyric by Michael McWhinney, music by Jerry Powell), "Dear Abbey" (lyric by Allison Roulston, music by Jay Foote) "The Envelope, Please" (sketch by Treva Silverman) "Mr. Wanamaker's Home" (lyric by Michael McWhinney and Rod Warren, music by Rod Warren)

NOTES—With the opening of ... *And in This Corner*, Rod Warren began a series of satiric revues at the Upstairs at the Downstairs. Unlike Julius Monk and Ben Bagley, Warren was a composer and lyricist, and wrote much of his own material. Bagley used the word "shoestring" in the titles of some of his revues, and, of course, Monk used numerical references. Warren, in order to tie his revues together and to give them an overall identity via their titles, worked in sporting references. Besides ... *And in This Corner*, there were eleven other Warren revues (see entries; also see Appendix R): *The Game Is Up* (three editions, one in 1964 and two in 1965), *Just for Openers* (1965), *Below the Belt* (1966), *Mixed Doubles* (1966), *The Playoffs of Mixed Doubles* (1967), *Dark Horses* (1967), *Photo Finish* (1968), *Instant Replay* (1968), and *Free Fall* (1969), the latter in collaboration with Ronny Graham. Brian O'Doherty in the *New York Times* said the "bright, smooth, fast and witty" revue "deserves all the success it's going to get." He singled out a number of songs and sketches, including "The Judy Garland National Anthem" ("Our lives would be hell/If she ever got well") and a spoof of the Academy Awards in which an Oscar is given to the writer of "the most outstanding single line" of dialogue.

Note that the finale of ...*And in This Corner* was "Mr. Wanamaker's Home," a tribute to the owner of the townhouse where the Upstairs at the Downstairs was located. The song was later heard in *The Playoffs of Mixed Doubles*., "Tokyo, Mon Amour" also appeared in the first edition of *The Game Is Up*. "Happiness Is," "When I Was Learning to Read," "The Envelope, Please," and "The Tree" were later heard in the retrospective revue *Below the Belt* (1966), and "The Envelope, Please" was also heard in *The Playoffs of Mixed Doubles*. During its run, ...*And in This Corner* was filmed intact for pay television. It appears to have never surfaced on home video; if it did, it would be an invaluable theatrical time capsule, the only complete visual record available of the revues which played at the Upstairs at the Downstairs.

51 And Still I Rise. THEATRE: AMAS Repertory Theatre; OPENING DATE: October 18, 1979; PERFORMANCES: 14; TEXT: Maya Angelou; MUSIC: Lalo Schifrin; DIRECTION: Maya Angelou; CHOREOGRAPHY: Joseph J. Cohen; SCENERY: Patrick Mann; COSTUMES: Leslie V. Day; LIGHTING: Paul Sullivan; MUSICAL DIRECTION: Don Sturrock; PRODUCER: AMAS Repertory Theatre (Rosetta LeNoire, Founder and Artistic Director)

CAST—Cast included J.J. Cole, Brenda Pressley, David Dawud

NOTES—The Off Off Broadway musical *And Still I Rise* was written and directed by Maya Angelou.

52 And the World Goes 'Round. "The Songs of Kander & Ebb." THEATRE: Westside Theatre; OPENING DATE: March 18, 1991; PERFORMANCES: 408; LYRICS: Fred Ebb; MUSIC: John Kander; DIRECTION: Scott Ellis; CHOREOGRAPHY: Susan Stroman; SCENERY: Bill Hoffman; COSTUMES: Lindsay W. Davis; LIGHTING: Phil Monat; MUSICAL DIRECTION: David Loud; PRODUCERS: R. Tyler Gatchell, Jr., Peter Neufeld, Patrick J. Patek, and Gene R. Korf in association with the McCarter Theatre

CAST—Bob (Robert) Cuccioli, Karen Mason, Brenda Pressley, Jim Walton, Karen Ziemba

The revue was presented in two acts.

ACT ONE—"And the World Goes 'Round" (from 1977 film *New York, New York*) (Brenda Pressley), "Yes" (*70, Girls, 70*, 1971) (Company), "Coffee in a Cardboard Cup" (*70, Girls, 70*, 1971) (Company), "The Happy Time" (*The Happy Time*, 1968) (Bob Cuccioli), "Colored Lights" (*The Rink*, 1984) (Karen Mason), "Sara Lee" (independent song) (Jim Walton, with Karen Mason, Brenda Pressley, and Karen Ziemba), "Arthur in the Afternoon" (*The Act*, 1977) (Karen Ziemba, Bob Cuccioli), "My Coloring Book" (independent song) (Brenda Pressley), "I Don't Remember You" (*The Happy Time*, 1968) (Bob Cuccioli), "Sometimes a Day Goes By" (*Woman of the Year*, 1981) (Jim Walton), "All That Jazz" (*Chicago*, 1975) (Karen Ziemba, Jim Walton), "Class" (*Chicago*, 1975) (Brenda Pressley, Karen Mason), "Mr. Cellophane" (*Chicago*, 1975) (Jim Walton), "Me and My Baby" (*Chicago*, 1975) (Company), "There Goes the Ball Game" (1977 film *New York, New York*) (Brenda Pressley, Karen Mason, Karen Ziemba), "How Lucky Can You Get" (1975 film *Funny Lady*) (Karen Mason, with Bob Cuccioli and Jim Walton), "The Rink" (*The Rink*, 1984) (Company)

ACT TWO—"Ring Them Bells" (independent song; used in 1972 television special *Liza with a 'Z'*) (Karen Mason, Company), "Kiss of the Spider Woman" (*Kiss of the Spider Woman*, 1993) (Bob Cuccioli), "Only Love" (*Zorba*, 1968) (Brenda Pressley), "Marry Me" (*The Rink*, 1984) (Jim Walton), "A Quiet Thing" (*Flora, the Red Menace*, 1965) (Karen Ziemba), "When It All Comes True" (independent song) (Jim Walton, Karen Ziemba), "Pain" (independent song) (Company), "The Grass Is Always Greener" (*Woman of the Year*, 1981) (Brenda Pressley, Karen Mason), "We Can Make It" (*The Rink*, 1984) (Bob Cuccioli), "Maybe This Time" (1972 film *Cabaret*) (Brenda Pressley), "Isn't This Better?" (1975 film *Funny Lady*) (Karen Mason), "Money, Money, Money" (1972 film *Cabaret*) (Company), "Cabaret" (*Cabaret*, 1966) (Company)

NOTES—*And the World Goes 'Round*, a tribute revue to John Kander and Fred Ebb, introduced the title song from *Kiss of the Spider Woman* to New York audiences two years before the show itself premiered on Broadway.

The revue's cast recording was released by RCA Victor Records (CD # 09026-60904-2).

For another Kander and Ebb tribute, see entry for *2 by 5* (1976). Also, on February 4, 1976, the Manhattan Theater Club presented another Kander and Ebb tribute, *A Kander & Ebb Cabaret*, which played for twelve performances; the cast included Kay Cummings and Tommy Breslin, the former of whom appeared in *2 by 5* later in the year.

53 Angel Levine. THEATRE: 92nd Street Y; OPENING DATE: October 5, 1985; PERFORMANCES: Unknown; LIBRETTO: Edward Mabley; MUSIC: Elie Siegmeister; SCENERY: Tony Castrigno; LIGHTING: Victor En Yu Tan; MUSICAL DIRECTION: Amy Kaiser; PRODUCER: Jewish Opera at the Y

CAST—Richard Frisch (Nathan Manischevitz), John Freeman-McDaniels (Alexander Levine), Molly Stark (Mrs. Manischevitz), Teresa Bowers (Blues Singer); also, Raymond Murcell

SOURCE—Bernard Malamud's 1955 short story "The Angel Levine."

The action occurs in New York City.

The opera was presented in one act.

NOTES—The world premiere of Elie Siegmeister's one-act opera *Angel Levine* was presented on a double bill with *The Lady of the Lake* (see entry), another world premiere by Siegmeister; the libretti for both operas were written by Edward Mabley, and both operas were based on short stories by Bernard Malamud.

Malamud's comic yet touching short story "The Angel Levine" was first published in 1955, and in 1970 was filmed with Zero Mostel and Harry Belafonte. After its 1985 premiere, the opera seems to have disappeared, but in 1999 it was revived on a double bill with the world premiere of Jack Beeson's opera *Sorry, Wrong Number* (see entry).

Angel Levine dealt with Nathan Manischevitz, a long-suffering Jewish man who is visited by a Black man claiming to be a Jewish angel named Alexander Levine. Nathan dismisses Levine, but his wife insists he take the subway to Harlem in order to find the angel.

In reviewing the opera's premiere for the *New York Times*, Will Crutchfield felt that Siegmeister's music was most successful in the "jazzy" sequences associated with the title character as well as a scene in a Harlem nightclub. Otherwise, he felt the music for Nathan and his wife consisted of a "drab, highly dissonant sort of recitative."

54 Angry Housewives. THEATRE: Minetta Lane Theatre; OPENING DATE: September 7, 1986; PERFORMANCES: 137; BOOK: A.M. Collins; LYRICS: Chad Henry; MUSIC: Chad Henry; DIRECTION: Mitchell Maxwell; CHOREOGRAPHY: Wayne Cilento; Lisa Mordente, Assistant Choreographer; SCENERY: David Jenkins; COSTUMES: Martha Hally; LIGHTING: Allen Lee Hughes; MUSICAL DIRECTION: Jonny Bowden; PRODUCERS: M Square Entertainment, Inc., Mitchell Maxwell, Alan J. Schuster, Marvin R. Meit, and Alice Field; Robert and Trinity Lind, Associate Producers

CAST—Michael Manasseri (Tim), Carolyn Casanave (Bev), Lorna Patterson (Wendy), Vicki Lewis (Jetta), Camille Saviola (Carol), Nicholas Wyman (Larry), Michael Lemback (Wallace), Lee Wilkof (Lewd)

The musical was presented in two acts.

ACT ONE—"Think Positive" (Carolyn Casanave), "It's Gonna Be Fun" (Lorna Patterson, with Carolyn Casanave, Camille Saviola, Vicki Lewis), "Generic Women" (Camille Saviola, with Carolyn Casanave, Lorna Patterson, Vicki Lewis), "Not at Home" (Vicki Lewis), "Betsy Moberly" (Lee Wilkof, Michael Lemback), "Cold Cruel Dark" (Company)

ACT TWO—"First Kid on the Block" (Michael Manasseri, with Carolyn Casanave, Camille Saviola, Vicki Lewis, Lorna Patterson), "Love-O-Meter" (Michael Lemback, Lorna Patterson), "Trouble with Me" (Lorna Patterson, Nicholas Wyman), "Stalling for Time" (Lee Wilkof, Nicholas Wyman, Michael Lemback, Michael Manasseri), "Eat Your @*!#@*!@#! Cornflakes" (The Angry Housewives [Carolyn Casanave, Lorna Patterson, Vicki Lewis, Camille Saviola), Finale (Company)

NOTES—According to Jeffrey Sweet in *The Best Plays of 1986–1987*, the title characters of the musical rebel against their middle class lives by forming a punk rock band. Sweet felt the material might have worked as a brief revue sketch, but noted the two-act musical was too long and repetitive and its characters were both caricatures and stereotypes. Oh, yes, when as a rock group the ladies perform their big number (called "Eat Your @*!#@*!@#! Cornflakes" in the program), the song was heard as "Eat Your Fucking Cornflakes."

The musical had been previously produced in Seattle in 1983, and then later in Chicago.

The script, published by Samuel French, Inc., in 1988, included three numbers not listed in the program of the Off Broadway production ("Hell School," "Saturday Night," and "Man from Glad"). Two songs heard in the Off Broadway production ("Cold Cruel Dark" and "Trouble with Me") weren't included in the script.

55 Ann Reinking ... Music Moves Me. THEATRE: Joyce Theatre; OPENING DATE: December 23, 1984; PERFORMANCES: 16; SPECIAL LYRICS: Ellen Fitzhugh; ORIGINAL MUSICAL MATERIAL: Larry Grossman; DIRECTION: Alan Johnson; CHOREOGRAPHY: Alan Johnson; Stephen Jay, Assistant Choreography; SCENERY: Thomas Lynch; COSTUMES: Albert Wolsky; LIGHTING: Ken Billington; MUSICAL DIRECTION: Ronald Melrose; PRODUCER: Lee Gross Associates, Inc.

CAST—ANN REINKING, Reed Jones, Michael Kubala, Rob Marshall, Sara Miles, Christina Saffran, Gary Chryst

The dance revue was presented in one act.

MUSICAL NUMBERS—"Another Mr. Right" (from the unproduced musical *Going Hollywood* [see entry]; lyric by David Zippel, music by Jonathan Sheffer), "Anything Goes" (*Anything Goes*, 1934; lyric and music by Cole Porter), "Ballin' the Jack" (lyric by Jim Burris, music by Chris Smith), "Higher and Higher" (lyric and music by Gary Jackson, Carl Smith, and Raymond Miner), "Hit Me with a Hot Note" (lyric and music by Duke Ellington and Don George), "I Can't Turn You Loose" (lyric and music by Otis Redding), "If Love Were All" (*Bitter Sweet*, 1929 [London], also New York [1929]; lyric and music by Noel Coward), "Isn't It Romantic" (1932 film *Love Me Tonight*; lyric by Lorenz Hart, music by Richard Rodgers), "Just Once" (lyric and music by Barry Mann and Cynthia Weil), "Moonlight Sonata" (Piano Sonata, Opus 27, No. 2) (music by Ludwig V. Beethoven), "Music Moves Me" (lyric by Ellen Fitzhugh, music by Larry Grossman), "Nowhere to Run" (lyric and music by Eddie Holland, Lamont Dozier, and Brian Holland), "Oh Baby, Won't You Please Come Home" (lyric and music by Clarence Williams and Charles Warffield), "Rescue Me" (lyric and music by Carl Smith and Raynard Miner), "Satin Doll" (lyric by Johnny Mercer, music by Billy Strayhorn and Duke Ellington), "Sing, Sing, Sing" (lyric and music by Louis Prima), "Stompin' at the Savoy" (lyric by Andy Razaf, music by Benny Goodman, Chick Webb, and Edgar Sampson), "Tea for Two" (*No, No, Nanette*, 1925; lyric by Irving Caesar, music by Vincent Youmans), "Unchained Melody" (lyric by Hy Zaret, music by Alex North), "Why Not? (Manhattan Carnival)" (lyric and music by Michael Camilo, Hilary Koski, and Julie Eigenberg), "Wild Women" (lyric and music by Ida Cox), "You and Me" (lyric and music by Carole Bayer Sager and Peter Allen)

NOTES—*Ann Reinking...Music Moves Me* was the second of two dance revues which played at the Joyce Theatre starring Ann Reinking (see entry for *One More Song/One More Dance*). "Another Mr. Right" was written for the unproduced musical *Going Hollywood* (which was based on the 1930 play *Once in a Lifetime* by George S. Kaufman and Moss Hart); it was also heard in the revue *It's Better with a Band* (see entries).

The trumpet solo sequence in "Sing, Sing, Sing" was choreographed by Bob Fosse and had originally been seen in the 1978 Broadway dance revue *Dancin'* (the cast of which included Ann Reinking).

Ann Reinking and Rob Marshall would later share a *Chicago* (1975) connection. Reinking had appeared as Roxie Hart in the original stage production of the musical as a replacement for Gwen Vernon. In 1996, she appeared as Roxie Hart in the musical's revival (which as of this writing is now in its second decade on Broadway) and also created the production's choreography ("in the style of" Bob Fosse). In 2002, Marshall directed the film version of *Chicago* (which won the Academy Award as Best Picture).

56 Anne of Green Gables (1971). "A Musical." THEATRE: New York City Center; OPENING DATE: December 21, 1971; PERFORMANCES: 16; BOOK: Donald Harron; LYRICS: Donald Harron and Norman Campbell; additional lyrics by Mavor Moore and Elaine Campbell; MUSIC: Norman Campbell; DIRECTION: Alan Lund; CHOREOGRAPHY: Alan Lund; SCENERY: Murray Laufer; COSTUMES: Marie Day; LIGHTING: Ronald Montgomery; MUSICAL DIRECTION: John Fenwick; PRODUCERS: City Center of Music and Drama, Inc. (Norman Singer, Executive Director) in association with The Charlottestown Festival (Prince Edward Island, Canada); a Canadian National Musical Theatre Production

CAST—Maud Whitmore (Mrs. Rachel Lynde), Cleone Duncan (Mrs. MacPherson, Lucilla), Nancy Kerr (Mrs. Barry), Flora MacKenzie (Mrs. Sloane, Mrs. Spencer), Kathryn Watt (Mrs. Pye), Lloyd Malenfant (Minister), Bill Hosie (Earl, Stationmaster), George Merner (Cecil), ELIZABETH MAWSON (Marilla Cuthbert), PETER MEWS (Matthew Cuthbert), GRACIE FINLEY (Anne Shirley), Roma Hearn (Mrs. Blewett, Miss Stacy), Glenda Landry (Diana Barry), Sharlene McLean (Prissy Andrews), Barbara Barsky (Josie Pye), Patti Toms (Ruby Gillis), Lynn Marsh (Tillie Boulter), Deborah Miller (Gertie Pye), JEFF HYSLOP (Gilbert Blythe), George Juriga (Charlie Sloane), Dan Costain (Moody MacPherson), Andre Denis (Gerry Buote), John Powell (Tommy Sloane), Calvin McRae (Malcolm Andrews), Jack Northmore (Mr. Phillips)

SOURCE—The 1908 novel *Anne of Green Gables* by Lucy Maud Montgomery.

The action occurs in Avonlea, a tiny village in Prince Edward Island, around 1900.

The musical was presented in two acts.

ACT ONE—"Great Workers for the Cause" (Maud Whitmore, with Cleone Duncan, Nancy Kerr, Flora MacKenzie, Kathryn Watt), "Where Is Matthew Going?" (Townspeople), "Gee, I'm Glad I'm No One Else but Me" (Gracie Finley). Trio: "We Clearly Requested a Boy" (Elizabeth Mawson, Gracie Finley, Peter Mews), "The Facts" (Gracie Finley, Flora MacKenzie, Roma Hearn, Elizabeth Mawson), "Where'd Marilla Come From?" (Bill Hosie, George Merner, Maud Whitmore, Cleone Duncan, Nancy Kerr, Flora MacKenzie, Kathryn Watt), "Humble Pie" (Peter Mews, Gracie Finley), "Oh Mrs. Lynde!" (a/k/a "Apology") (Gracie Finley), "Back to School Ballet" (Pupils), "Avonlea We Love Thee" (Jack Northmore, Pupils), "Wondrin'" (Jeff Hyslop), "Did You Hear?" (Barbara Barsky, Kathryn Watt, Cleone Duncan, Nancy Kerr, Bill Hosie, George Merner, Maud Whitmore), "Ice Cream" (Glenda Landry, Company), "The Picnic" (Company)

ACT TWO—"Where Did the Summer Go To?" (Pupils), "Kindred Spirits" (Gracie Finley, Glenda Landry), "Open the Window!" (a/k/a "Learn Everything!") (Roma Hearn, Pupils), "The Words" (Peter Mews), "Open the Window!" (reprise) (Roma Hearn, Pupils), "Nature Hunt Ballet" (Pupils), "I'll Show Him" (Gracie Finley, Jeff Hyslop), "General Store" (Cleone Duncan, Peter Mews, Townspeople), "Pageant Song" (Pupils), "If It Hadn't Been for Me" (Company), "Where Did the Summer Go To?" (reprise) (Gracie Finley, Jeff Hyslop), "Anne of Green Gables" (Peter Mews), "The Words" (reprise) (Elizabeth Mawson), "Wondrin'" (reprise) (Gracie Finley, Jeff Hyslop)

NOTES—*Anne of Green Gables* was based on the popular novel about an orphaned girl who finds her place in the world when she's adopted by a brother and sister in the Canadian town of Avonlea. The musical was first produced for Canadian television in 1955 (and again in 1958), and was later expanded for the stage and premiered at the Charlottestown Festival in Canada during Summer 1965 (and for many consecutive summers thereafter); it was recorded by Ready Records (LP # LR-045). The musical opened in London at the New Theatre on April 16, 1969, where it ran for 300 performances; Anne was played by Polly James, who had played opposite Tommy Steele in both the original London and New York productions of *Half a Sixpence*. The London cast recording was released by CBS Records (LP # 70053). For the London production, a new song ("When I Say My Say") was added to the score.

The script was published by Samuel French, Inc., in 1972.

The musical's book writer and co-lyricist was Donald Harron, a Canadian who performed in Broadway plays in the 1950s and early 1960s. He created the title role in Paddy Chayevsky's hit drama *The Tenth Man* (1959), and when Jean Kerr's hit comedy *Mary, Mary* (1961) was produced in London in 1963, Maggie Smith assumed the role originated by Barbara Bel Geddes, and Harron played the role created by Barry Nelson. For another musical version of *Anne of Green Gables*, see entry for the 2007 production.

57 Anne of Green Gables (2007). THEATRE: Lucille Lortel Theatre; OPENING DATE: March 29, 2007; PERFORMANCES: 41; BOOK: Gretchen Cryer; LYRICS: Gretchen Cryer; MUSIC: Nancy Ford; DIRECTION: Tyler Merchant; SCENERY: Beowulf Borrit; COSTUMES: David C. Woolard; LIGHTING: Clifton Taylor; MUSICAL DIRECTION: W. Brent Sawyer; PRODUCERS: TheatreworksUSA (Barbara Pasternack, Artistic Director; Ken Arthur, Managing Director) by special arrangement with the Lucille Lortel Theatre Foundation

CAST—Erick Devine (Matthew Cuthbert), Bethe B. Austin (Marilla Cuthbert), Piper Goodeve (Anne Shirley), Heath MacRae (Rachel Lynde), Michael Mendiola (Man), Alison Faircloth (Woman), Andrew Gehling (Gilbert Blythe), Jessica Grove (Diana Barry)

SOURCE—The 1908 novel *Anne of Green Gables* by Lucy Maud Montgomery.

The action occurs in Avonlea, a tiny village in Prince Edward Island, around 1900.

The musical was presented in one act.

MUSICAL NUMBERS—Overture (Orchestra), "Around the Bend" (Piper Goodeve), "A Pretty Kettle of Fish" (Bethe B. Austin, Erick Devine, Piper Goodeve), "I Can Stay" (Piper Goodeve), "It's the Strangest Thing" (Heather MacRae, Alison Faircloth, "Postmaster"), "Kindred Spirits" (Piper Goodeve, Erick Devine), "Making Up for Lost Time" (Piper Goodeve, Jessica Grove), "The Use of the Colon" ("Mr. Philips," Piper Goodeve, Josie, Andrew Gehling, Jessica Grove), "Two Weeks" (Andrew Gehling, Piper Goodeve), "It Was Not Because of Gilbert Blythe" (Piper Goodeve, Jessica Grove), "Drunk!" (Heather MacRae, "Mrs. Barry," Piper Goodeve, Bethe B. Austin, Erick Devine), "The Clock Keeps Ticking" (Piper Goodeve, Jessica Grove, "Mary Jo"), "It's the Strangest Thing" (reprise) (Heather MacRae, Alison Faircloth, "Postmaster"), "First Day at the Academy" (Piper Goodeve), "It's Nice to Know" (Piper Goodeve, Andrew Gehling), "Around the Bend" (reprise) (Piper Goodeve), "Making Up for Lost Time" (reprise) (Piper Goodeve, Andrew Gehling), Finale (Company)

NOTES—Mark Blankenship in *Variety* was less than impressed with Gretchen Cryer and Nancy Ford's musical version of *Anne of Green Gables*, the classic children's book about Anne Shirley, the orphan who finds a new life on Green Gables Farm when a sister and a brother adopt her. He found the book more "like Cliff Notes with songs ... events that take chapters to unfold now occur in minutes," and he noted the score relied on "clichés," with "standard-issue" ballads and lyrics which "bulge[d] with stock phrases."

The program didn't identify the performers who played the roles of the Postmaster, Mr. Philips, Mrs. Barry, and Mary Jo; the roles were probably assumed by Michael Mendiola and Alison Faircloth, who were credited in the program as the "Man" and the "Woman."

The cast recording was released by Jay Records (CD# CDJAY-1404).

For another musical version of *Anne of Green Gables*, see entry for 1971 production.

58 Annie Warbucks. "A New Musical Comedy." THEATRE: Variety Arts Theatre; OPENING DATE: August 9, 1993; PERFORMANCES: 200; BOOK: Thomas Meehan; LYRICS: Martin Charnin; MUSIC: Charles Strouse; DIRECTION: Martin Charnin; CHOREOGRAPHY: Peter Gennaro; SCENERY: Ming Cho Lee; COSTUMES: Theoni V. Aldredge LIGHTING: Ken Billington; MUSICAL DIRECTION: Keith Levenson; PRODUCERS: Ben Sprecher, William P. Miller, Dennis Grimaldi by special arrangement with Karen Walter Goodwin; Amy Miller, Matthew Garffield, David Young, Bulldog Theatrical Prods., Inc., and Eve-Lynn Miller, Associate Producers

CAST—KATHRYN ZAREMBA (Annie Warbucks), Cindy Lou (Sandy), HARVE PRESNELL (Oliver Warbucks), Marguerite MacIntyre (Grace Farrell), Kip Niven (Drake), Brooks Almy (Mrs. Pugh, Dr. Margaret Whittleby, White House Aide), J.B. Adams (Warbucks' Staff Member, Trainman, White House Aide, Man in a Stetson Hat, Wedding Guest), Colleen Fitzpatrick (Warbucks' Staff Member, Miss Clark, Gladys, Wedding Guest), Michael E. Gold (Warbucks' Staff Member, Warbucks' Accountant, Fletcher, Mr. Stanley, David Lillianthal), Jennifer L. Neuland (Warbucks' Staff Member, Hobo, White House Aide, Wedding Guest), Steve Steiner (Warbucks' Staff Member, Warbucks' Accountant, Harry, Hobo, Senator Arthur I. Vandenberg, Wedding Guest), Joel Hatch (Simon Whitehead), ALENE ROBERTSON (Commissioner Harriet Doyle), Ashley Pettet (Molly), Missy Goldberg (Pepper), Elisabeth Zaremba (Tessie), Rosie Harper (Kate), Natalia Harris (Peaches), DONNA MCKECHNIE (Mrs. Sheila Kelly), Harvey Evans (Alvin T. Paterson), Jackie Angelescu (C.G. Paterson), Molly Scott (Ella Paterson), RAYMOND THORNE (President Franklin Delano Roosevelt)

SOURCES—Harold Gray's comic strip *Little Orphan Annie* and the 1977 Broadway musical *Annie* (book by Thomas Meehan, lyrics by Martin Charnin, music by Charles Strouse).

The action occurs in 1933 and 1934.

The musical was presented in two acts.

ACT ONE—"A New Deal for Christmas" (Company), "Annie Ain't Just Annie Anymore" (Kathryn Zaremba, Harve Presnell, Marguerite MacIntyre, Kip Niven, J.B. Adams, Colleen Fitzpatrick, Michael E. Gold, Jennifer L. Neuland, Steve Steiner), "Above the Law" (Alene Robertson), "Changes" (Harve Presnell, Kathryn Zaremba), "The Other Woman" (Ashley Pettet, Missy Goldberg, Elizabeth Zaremba, Rosie Harper, Natalia Harris), "The Other Woman" (reprise) (Ashley Pettet, Missy Goldberg, Elizabeth Zaremba, Rosie Harper, Natalia Harris), "That's the Kind of Woman" (Kip Niven, Kathryn Zaremba, Harve Presnell, Servants), "A Younger Man" (Harve Presnell), "But You Go On" (Donna McKechnie), "Above the Law" (reprise) (Alene Robertson, Donna McKechnie), "When You Smile" (Harve Presnell, Kathryn Zaremba, Ashley Pettet, Missy Goldberg, Elizabeth Zaremba, Rosie Harper, Natalia Harris), "I Got Me" (Kathryn Zaremba, Ashley Pettet, Missy Goldberg, Elizabeth Zaremba, Rosie Harper, Natalia Harris), "I Got Me" (reprise) (Kathryn Zaremba)

ACT TWO—"Love" (Molly Scott), "Love" (reprise) (Kathryn Zaremba, Jackie Angelescu), "Somebody's Gotta Do Somethin'" (Kathryn Zaremba, Harvey Evans, Jackie Angelescu, Molly Scott, Raymond Thorne, Marguerite MacIntyre, J.B. Adams, Brooks Almy, Jennifer Neuland), "Leave It to the Girls" (Alene Robertson, Donna McKechnie), "All Dolled Up" (Ashley Pettet, Missy Goldberg, Elizabeth Zaremba, Rosie Harper, Natalia Harris, Kathryn Zaremba, Harve Presnell, Marguerite MacIntyre, Raymond Thorne, Kip Niven, J.B. Adams, Colleen Fitzpatrick, Michael E. Gold, Jennifer L. Neuland, Steve Steiner), "The Tenement Lullaby" (Donna McKechnie) "It Would Have Been Wonderful" (Marguerite MacIntyre), "Changes" (reprise) (Harve Presnell, Kathryn Zaremba), "Wedding, Wedding" (Company), "I Always Knew" (Kathryn Zaremba)

NOTES—The original Broadway production of *Annie* played for 2,377 performances, and was a perfect example of an entertaining old-fashioned musical comedy. When its sequel *Annie 2: Miss Hannigan's Revenge* was announced, hopes were high that another family-friendly hit was on its way to Broadway. But the musical's very first preview performance at the Kennedy Center's Opera House on December 22, 1989, immediately dashed those hopes. The sequel was a cheerless, confusing affair which lacked the charm and theatrical know-how of the original. It had lively performances by Dorothy Loudon (reprising her role of Miss Hannigan) and Ronny Graham, one or two pleasant songs, and a couple of amusing politically incorrect jokes, and that was just about all. Once the negative reviews appeared, the musical quickly folded. But its creators didn't give up, and so the following summer another production (as *Annie 2*) was mounted in a Goodspeed Opera House production at the Norma Terris Theatre, and then in 1992 the musical resurfaced as *Annie Warbucks*, and played at various venues throughout the country.

Annie Warbucks was expected to reach Broadway in a production which was capitalized at five-million dollars. Instead, it opened Off Broadway with a capitalization of about one-fifth that amount. The sequel began where the original left off, on Christmas Day of 1933, with the cast singing "A New Deal for Christmas" from the 1977 production. The new plot involved the shenanigans of Commissioner Harriet Doyle, who informs Daddy Warbucks that as a single man he can't adopt Annie; he must marry within sixty days or the adoption will become invalid. Meanwhile, Doyle is in cahoots with a husband-killer who's an all-too- willing candidate for Warbucks' hand in marriage. (The character of Miss Hannigan no longer figured in the plot.)

The Off Broadway production enjoyed some good if not particularly enthusiastic reviews (John Simon in *New York* wrote "you could do a lot worse; you could, for example, see *Tommy*" [which had opened on Broadway a few months earlier]). Recalling the sequel's long journey to New York, Jeremy Gerard in *Variety* hoped the Off Broadway production would allow the musical's creatois to "finally... get on with their lives, for which we can all be grateful." Jan Stuart in *New York Newsday* mentioned that Peter Gennaro's choreography forced the orphan-girl chorus "to shake their fannies kooch-dancer-style one time too many," and noted if a similar chorus of boys had done bumps and grinds "like aspiring Chippendales waiters," the musical would have been forced to close in previews on indecency charges.

The critics felt *Annie Warbucks* looked cramped on the small stage of the Variety Arts Theatre, and several were disappointed with its scaled-down scenery. Because the musical didn't enjoy must-see notices, and perhaps because it wasn't playing at a Broadway theatre, the production never quite caught on and lasted for just six months. Despite its entertaining if not particularly memorable score, the musical was released on a lavish 2-CD set by Broadway Angel Records (# CDQ-7243-5-55040-29).

The Off Broadway production retained four songs from the disastrous 1989 tryout: "A Younger Man," "When You Smile," "Tenement Lullaby," and "Changes." Another song from the 1989 tryout, Annie's "All I've Got Is Me," may have been recycled for *Annie Warbucks* as "I Got Me."

59 Anonymous. THEATRE: AMAS Repertory Theatre; OPENING DATE: October 25, 1984; PERFORMANCES: 16; BOOK: Vincenzo Stornaiuolo; LYRICS: Vincenzo Stornaiuolo; additional English lyrics by Jack Everly; MUSIC: Vincenzo Stornaiuolo; additional music by Giancarlo De Matteis; DIRECTION: Vincenzo Stornaiuolo; CHOREOGRAPHY: Gui Andrisano; SCENERY: Janice Davis; COSTUMES: Robert Locke; LIGHTING: William H. Grant III; MUSICAL DIRECTION: Jack Everly; PRODUCER: AMAS Repertory Theatre (Rosetta LeNoire, Founder and Artistic Director)

CAST—Ed Battle (Motivator), Steven Cates (Black Pope, Ensemble), Sarah C. Clark (Ensemble), Michael Duran (Secretary of State, Father Cardinal, Ensemble), Ivy Fox (Ensemble), Lisa LaCorte (Holy Ghost, Ensemble), Paul Loper (Cardinal, Son, Ensemble), Janice Lorraine (Ensemble), Dick Lombard (Pope Anonymous), Jayne Ackley Lynch (Ensemble), Maura Miller (Motivator), Mark Pennington (Cardinal, Ensemble), Phillip Perry (Cardinal, Ensemble), Kevin Ramsey (Ensemble), Tug Wilson (Cardinal, Ensemble).

The action occurs sometime in the future in Rome and New York City.

The musical was presented in two acts (division of acts and song assignments unknown; songs are listed in performance order).

MUSICAL NUMBERS—Overture, "Anonymous," "Conclave," "What Can It Be?," "Church of the World," "Smoke, Smoke," "Praised Be to the Lord Our Savior," "Brothers," "Figli," "God, I Beg Your Forgiveness," "Come with Us," "Fire," "They're Killing the Pope," "New York," "Monotheism," "How Much Love," "Mon Marte," "Trinity," "Vatican," "Our Decision," "We Want the Pope," "I Shall Condemn," "I Bless You," "We Have the Pope," Finale

NOTES—John S. Wilson in the *New York Times* reported that the Off Off Broadway musical *Anonymous* dealt with the Catholic Church in the twenty-first century when the Vatican moves to New York City and the Empire State Building becomes Vatican City; further, the Church is about to elect Pope Anonymous, whose selection sets off riots, and so Anonymous steps down, leading the way for the first Black Pope. Wilson noted that despite the "potentially provocative material," the musical's creators did "virtually nothing" with it except to "leave it hanging in the air" without conflict or resolution. As for the score, it offered both recitative and a "steady disco throb."

60 Another Evening with Harry Stoones. THEATRE: Gramercy Arts Theatre; OPENING DATE: October 21, 1961; PERFORMANCES: 1; SKETCHES: Jeff Harris; LYRICS: Jeff Harris; MUSIC: Jeff Harris; DIRECTION: G. Adam Jordan; CHOREOGRAPHY: Joe Milan; SCENERY: Robert E. Darling; COSTUMES: Ruth Wagner; LIGHTING: Robert E. Darling; MUSICAL DIRECTION: Abba Bogin; PRODUCER: Stenod Productions

CAST—Diana Sands, Ben Keller, Dom De Luise, Susan Belink, Sheila Copelan, Kenny Adams, Virgil Curry, Barbra Streisand

The revue was presented in two acts (sketch and song assignments unknown).

ACT ONE—(*The Civil War*), "Carnival in Capri," "To Belong," "Communication," "Ballad to the International," "You Won't Believe Me," "The Wrong Plan," "Ballet," "Bang!," "Don't Laugh at Me," "Museum Piece," "Tableau," "Indian Nuts," "Uh-Oh," "Ragtime," "Minnesota," "Ballad of the Tree," "Value," "Session," "My Doggie," "Jersey," "Dancin' Free and Easy," "Dr. Rosalyn Green," "Invitation to the Basketball," "Party of the First Part"

ACT TWO—(*The Roaring Twenties*), "Big Barry," "Miss Greenwich Village," "Stephanie," "Betty Simpson," "The Rage," "Upstairs at the Downstairs," "Hail to Thee!," "Serena," "Butterfingers," "Human Side of the News," "Miss Heinschlinger," "Strangers on a Train," "Water on the Brain," "Dream House"

NOTES—*Another Evening with Harry Stoones* closed after just one performance. Of the revue's eight cast members (Diana Sands, Ben Keller, Dom De Luise, Susan Belink, Sheila Copelan, Kenny Adams, Virgil Curry, and Barbra Streisand), one went on to superstardom.

Lewis Funke in the *New York Times* noted that while the revue was stuffed with material, quantity didn't mean quality; overall, he found *Harry Stoones* "not exactly unbearable" and with occasional flashes of wit (such as a tourist agency's "rhythmic hymn" to "Minnesota").

In the 1965 revue *That Thing at the Cherry Lane* (see entry), Jeff Harris (now billed as Jeff Steve Harris) recycled five numbers from *Harry Stoones* ("To Belong," "Communication," "You Won't Believe Me," "Jersey," and the aforementioned "Minnesota"). Another *Harry Stoones*' number, "Museum Piece," was briefly heard in *That Thing* during previews, and "Ragtime" may have been performed in *That Thing* as "Ragtime Max."

On her 1968 album "Barbra Streisand/A Happening in Central Park" (reissued by Columbia Records on CD # CK-9710), Streisand sang "Value," a song she first introduced in *Another Evening with Harry Stoones*.

And in an interesting twist of show-business fate, a few years later two of the revue's cast members, Streisand and Diana Sands, crossed paths when they shared the same role. In 1964, Sands created the role Doris in Bill Manhoff's hit Broadway play *The Owl and the Pussycat*, and for the 1970 film version, Streisand played the character.

For another twist of show-business fate, here's a story completely unrelated to *Harry Stoones*. In 1950, the film musical *My Blue Heaven* included the song "The Friendly Islands" (lyric by Ralph Blane and music by Harold Arlen), a parody of Richard Rodgers and Oscar Hammerstein II's *South Pacific*, which had opened on Broadway the previous year. The number even managed to work into its lyric some of the song titles from *South Pacific*, and Dan Dailey offered a mean vocal impression of Enzo Pinza (although he may have been dubbed). "The Friendly Islands" was part of a television-show-within-the-movie, and, in her film debut, Mitzi Gaynor, as a television hostess, introduced the song to the film's television audience. And eight years later when *South Pacific* was filmed, Gaynor played the role of Nellie Forbush (her delightful and touching performance is one of the most underrated in the history of the film musical).

61 Antiques. "A Revue." THEATRE: Mercer-O'Casey Theatre; OPENING DATE: June 19, 1973; PERFORMANCES: 8; SPECIAL MATERIAL: Dore Schary; LYRICS AND MUSIC: Alan Greene and Laura Manning; DIRECTION: Marco Martone; CHOREOGRAPHY: Jeffrey K. Neill; SCENERY: Bruno C. Scordino; COSTUMES: William Christians; LIGHTING: R.H. Rizzio; MUSICAL DIRECTION: Alan Greene; PRODUCERS: Video Techniques, Inc., in association with Dore Schary Productions, Inc.

CAST—Charles Hudson, Laura Manning, Richard Marr, Betty Oakes, Eugene Smith, Ward Smith, Molly Stark

The revue was presented in two acts (division of acts and song assignments unknown; songs are listed in performance order).

MUSICAL NUMBERS—"Antiques," "The Pill," "They Don't Write Songs Like That Anymore," "Rent-a-Grandma," "To Love Again," "Papa Bird," "Don't Grow Old Gracefully," "Bridges," "Grandma's Diary," "The 'Hey, Ma, You Were Right' Cantata," "The Red Kimono," "Oh, What a Time We Had," "We Got Married," "Look Underneath," "Love Is Everything," "Conversations," "Victims of the Past," "Solutions," Finale

NOTES—According to Clive Barnes in the *New York Times*, *Antiques* dealt with the "joys and tribulations of being old," but he felt mediocre material defeated the evening's message. The program indicated the revue would be performed without an intermission; but "after a period of some pain," Barnes noted an intermission was announced and so "bang went another 15 minutes of my existence." *Antiques* had originally been seen on cable television.

62 Antony and Cleopatra. THEATRE: Metropolitan Opera House; OPENING DATE: September 16, 1966; PERFORMANCES: 8; LIBRETTO: William Shakespeare and Franco Zeffirelli; MUSIC: Samuel Barber; DIRECTION: Franco Zeffirelli; CHOREOGRAPHY: Alvin Ailey; SCENERY: Franco Zeffirelli; COSTUMES: Franco Zeffirelli; MUSICAL DIRECTION: Thomas Schippers

CAST—Justino Diaz (Mark Antony), Leontyne Price (Cleopatra), Jess Thomas (Octavius Caesar), Ezio Flagello (Enobarbus), Rosalind Elias (Charmian), Belen Amparan (Iras), Andrea Velis (Mardian), Paul Franke (Messenger), Raymond Michalski (Alexas), Lorenzo Alvary (Soothsayer), Clifford Harvuot (Rustic), Mary Ellen Pracht (Octavia), Russell Christopher (Maecenas), John Macurdy (Agrippa), Robert Nagy (Lepidus), Robert Goodloe (Thidias), Gabor Carelli (Soldier of Caesar), Bruce Scott (Eros), Gene Boucher (Dolabella), Lloyd Strang (Canidius), Norman Giffin (Demetrius), Ron Bottcher (Scarus), Louis Sgarro (Decretas), Dan Marek (Captain), Robert Schmorr (Guard), Norman Scott (Guard), John Trehy (Solider of Mark Antony), Paul De Paola (Watchman), Luis Forero (Watchman), Peter Sliker (Sentinel) Dancers (Sally Brayley, Nira Paaz, Rhodie Jorgenson, Hope Clarke, Jan Mickens, Lance Westergard)

SOURCE—The play *Antony and Cleopatra* (circa 1603–1607) by William Shakespeare. The opera was performed in three acts.

ACT ONE—Prologue; Scene 1, "I Am Sick and Sullen"; Orchestra Interlude; Scene 2; Scene 3, "Slaves' Dance"; Scene 4, "When First She Met Mark Antony" (Aria), "Vision of Cleopatra's Barge"

ACT TWO—Scene 1; Scene 2, "Hush, Here Come the Queen and Anthony"; Scene 3; Scene 4, "Oh Take, Oh Take Those Lips Away"; Scene 5, "Hark! The Land Bids Me Tread No More Upon It"; Scene 6; Scene 7, "O Sov'reign Mistress" (Aria); Orchestral Interlude; Scene 8, "Where's Antony?"

ACT THREE—Scene 1, "My Lord, My Lord! Noblest of Men" (Trio), "The Breaking of So Great a Thing"; Prelude; Scene 2, "Here Is a Rural Fellow," "Give Me My Robe" (Aria), "Death of Cleopatra"

NOTES—*Antony and Cleopatra* was commissioned by the Metropolitan to celebrate the opening of its new theatre at Lincoln Center. However, the opera was poorly received, and never became part of the standard repertory. But Barber later revised the opera, and it has since been performed by various companies. In 1992, a Spoleto Festival production was recorded by New World Records on a 2-CD set (# 80322-2); the song sequences above are taken from this recording.

In reviewing the "grand, grand" opening of the Metropolitan's new home (and the new opera, which he felt got "somewhat lost in the shuffle"), Harold C. Schonberg in the *New York Times* facetiously noted the evening was "situated on the cosmic scale" somewhat above the Big Bang and below the creation of the Milky Way. He wrote that huge amounts of scenery for the new production ensured that "things" were screwed, locked, and bolted, and got pushed, pulled, and revolved. Pieces of scenery "ponderously" moved across the stage "like a Sherman tank passing over a wheat ffield." Further, the image of the Sphinx was turned "this way and that," Cleopatra's barge floated across the stage, and, oh, yes, there were also live camels, goats, and horses. Schonberg reported the "exhibitionist" evening was "artiffice masquerading ... as art." As for Barber's music, it was a "hybrid," not quite traditional, not quite modern. Further, the words were difficult to understand because the cast "tended to enunciate ... like an untalented myna bird" and the chorus sounded like "gabble in Babel." As for Leontyne Price, Schonberg criticized her elaborate if "unbecoming" costumes, and noted the way in which she was directed emanated from "queer ideas" in "certain circles" of the Met's then-current hierarchy. The world premiere performance was broadcast live on radio.

63 Anything Goes. THEATRE: Orpheum Theatre; OPENING DATE: May 15, 1962; PERFORMANCES: 239; BOOK: Guy Bolton, P.G. Wodehouse, Howard Lindsay, and Russel Crouse (book of 1962 production revised by Guy Bolton); LYRICS: Cole Porter; MUSIC: Cole Porter; DIRECTION: Lawrence Kasha; CHOREOGRAPHY: Ronald (Ron) Field; SCENERY: Don Jensen; COSTUMES: Bill Hargate; LIGHTING: Don Jensen; MUSICAL DIRECTION: Julian Stein; Ted Simons ("musical conductor"); PRODUCERS: Jane Friedlander, Michael Parver, Gene Andewski, in association with Mrs. Judson Todd

CAST—WARREN WADE (Elisha J. Whitney), Robert (Bob) Fitch (Steward), BARBARA LANG (Hope Harcourt), KENNETH MARS (Sir Evelyn Oakleigh), MILDRED CHANDLER (Mrs. Wadsworth T. Harcourt), Jim Franklin (Reporter), Jim Jarrett (Photographer), Bonnie Walker (Girl Passenger), Kay Norman (Girl Passenger), Rawley Bates (Girl Passenger), Neal Patrick (Bishop), Jeff Siggins (Ching), Martin J. Cassidy (Ling), EILEEN RODGERS (Reno Sweeney), The Angels (Diane McAfee [Purity], Sally Anne Carlson [Chastity], Tobie Lynn [Charity], Chee Davis [Virtue]), HAL LINDEN (Billy Crocker), D. Bruce Rabbino (Purser), MARGERY GRAY (Bonnie), MICKEY DEEMS (Moon), Neal Patrick (Captain)

The action occurs aboard the S.S. *American*.

The musical was presented in two acts.

ACT ONE—Opening (Company), "You're the Top" (Eileen Rodgers, Hal Linden), "Bon Voyage" (Passengers, Crew), "It's Delovely" (Hal Linden, Barbara Lang, Passengers), "Heaven Hop" (Margery Gray, Diane McAfee, Sally Ann Carlson, Tobie Lynn, Chee Davis), "Friendship" (Eileen Rodgers, Hal Linden, Mickey Deems), "I Get a Kick Out of You" (Eileen Rodgers), "Anything Goes" (Eileen Rodgers, Passengers, Crew)

ACT TWO—"Public Enemy Number One" (Passengers, Crew), "Let's Step Out" (Margery Gray, Robert Fitch, Passengers), "Let's Misbehave" (Eileen Rodgers, Kenneth Mars), "Blow, Gabriel, Blow" (Eileen Rodgers, Passengers), "All Through the Night" (Hal Linden, Barbara Lang), "Be Like the Bluebird" (Mickey Deems), "Take Me Back to Manhattan" (Eileen Rodgers, Diane McAfee, Sally Ann Carlson, Tobie Lynn, Chee Davis), Finale (Company)

NOTES—The 1960 Off Broadway revival of Cole Porter's *Gay Divorce* (see entry) was a quick failure, but the 1962 revival of his 1934 hit *Anything Goes* was well received by critics and audiences. Like *Gay Divorce*, this revival omitted some songs from the original production and added others from various Porter musicals, but the interpolated songs and the revised book (by Guy Bolton, one of the librettists of the 1934 production) were in the spirit of the original. In fact, for many years the Off Broadway version became the standard acting edition of the musical (at least until the 1987 long-running Broadway revival came along, with a revised book by Jerome Weidman and another re-tooled song listing).

Anything Goes had an interesting cast. Eileen Rodgers shined in the role originally created by Ethel Merman; she had earlier been seen Off Broadway, and had appeared in the original Broadway productions of *Fiorello!* (1959) and *Tenderloin* (1960), introducing "Gentleman Jimmy" in the former and "My Gentle Young Johnny" in the latter. She also sang the role of Bobo (played by Abbe Lane on the stage) for the cast recording of *Oh Captain!* (1958). Sadly, after *Anything Goes* she appeared in just one more Broadway musical, the notorious flop *Kelly* (1965). On the brighter side, the revival proved to be a major stepping stone in Hal Linden's career; he would go on to win the Tony Award for Best Actor in a Musical for *The Rothschilds* (1970), and, of course, found his greatest success in television.

Margery Gray, one of Eileen Rodgers' cohorts from *Tenderloin*, also proved to be a delight (she later became Mrs. Sheldon Harnick, *Tenderloin*'s lyricist); and Off Broadway stalwart Robert (Bob) Fitch had the smash *Annie* (1977) in his future. Unfortunately, Diane McAfee's claim to Broadway fame was that she created the role of Eve in the tryout of *Applause* (1970), but was replaced by Penny Fuller before the show reached New York. Ronald (Ron) Field later choreographed two major Broadway hits, *Cabaret* (1966) and *Applause* (1970).

Four numbers from the 1934 production of *Anything Goes* weren't used in the revival: "Sailors' Chanty (There'll Always Be a Lady Fair)," "Where Are the Men," "The Gypsy in Me," and "Buddie Beware" (the latter, one of the gems in the Cole Porter songbook, was also dropped during the Broadway run of the original production).

The following Cole Porter songs were added to the revival: "It's Delovely" (from *Red Hot and Blue!*, 1936), "Heaven Hop" (*Paris*, 1928), "Friendship" (*DuBarry Was a Lady*, 1939), "Let's Step Out" (added to *Fifty Million Frenchmen* [1929] during its New York run), "Let's Misbehave" (written for, but not used in, *Paris* [1928]), and "Take Me Back to Manhattan" (*The New Yorkers*, 1930).

The Off Broadway cast album was released by Epic Records (LP # FLM-13100).

A script of the 1935 London production was published by Samuel French, Limited (London) in 1936.

64 Ape Over Broadway. "A New Gorilla Musical." THEATRE: Bert Wheeler Theatre; OPENING DATE: March 12, 1975; PERFORMANCES: 11; BOOK: Mary McCartney and Bart Andrews; LYRICS: Bill Vitale; MUSIC: Stephen Ross; DIRECTION: Jeffrey K. Neill; CHOREOGRAPHY: Jeffrey K. Neill; SCENERY: Dan Leigh and Gail Van Voorhis; COSTUMES: Brent J. Porter; LIGHTING: Dan Leigh and Gail Van Voorhis; MUSICAL DIRECTION: Frederick S. Roffman; PRODUCERS: Allan Brown, Renee Semes Herz, and Bill Vitale in association with Octagon: The American Musical Theatre Company

CAST—Jacqueline Reilly (Rose), Robert Calvert (Lanford Gotham), Phylis Ward (Ramona, Smitty, Jungle Jill, Shirley, Flamingo Fusser, Betty, Mrs. O'Hara), Freyda-Ann Thomas (Renee, Miss Frump, Jungle Jill, Shirley, Flamingo Fusser, Pinky Chiffon), Jim Cyrus (Delivery Boy, Pilot, Native Guide, Higgins, Flamingo Fusser, Johnson, Cop), Robert Lydiard (Ernest Boles), Norb Joerder (Sam Stud, Martini, Stevens, King, Delivery Man, TV Announcer), Barbara Coggin (Jane Peskowitz), Curt Ralston (Max)

The action occurs in New York City and in "Deepest Darkest Africa."

The musical was presented in two acts (division of acts and song assignments unknown; songs are listed in performance order).

MUSICAL NUMBERS—"Nude-Lewd," "The Star Number," "Broadway," "I've Had Everything but a Man," "The Man-Eating Ape Waltz," "Saga of Men and Marriage," "An Ape Can Save the World," "Mixed-Up Media," "I'm in Like with You," "Flamingo Fuss," "Triangle Song," "Just Whistle," "My Friend," "Ape Over Broadway," Finale

NOTES—*Theatre World 1974-1975 Season* reported that *Ape Over Broadway* was presented for a limited engagement of eleven performances (the musical was apparently produced under an Off Off Broadway contract). With such intriguing song titles as "I've Had Everything but a Man" and "The Man-Eating Ape Waltz," perhaps this musical deserves another hearing.

The musical was later revived Off Off Broadway at The Fantasy Factory on November 21, 1980, for sixteen performances; this time around, the book was credited to Andrew Herz.

65 Apple Pie. "A New Musical Work." THEATRE: Anspacher Theatre/The Public Theatre; OPENING DATE: January 27, 1976; PERFORMANCES: 64; LIBRETTO: Myrna Lamb; MUSIC: Nicholas Meyers; DIRECTION: Joseph Papp; CHOREOGRAPHY: Lynne Weber; SCENERY: Design by David Mitchell; Visuals by Thom Lafferty and David Mitchell; COSTUMES: Timothy Miller; LIGHTING: Pat Collins; MUSICAL DIRECTION: Liza Redfield; PRODUCER: The New York Shakespeare Festival (Joseph Papp, Producer; Bernard Gersten, Associate Producer)

CAST—Stephanie Cotsirilos (Lise), Ilsebet Anna Tebesli (The Mirror), Lucille Paton (Mother Marlene), Spain Logue (Streicher), Robert Polenz (American), Joseph Neal (Doctor), John Watson (Boss), Robert Guillaume (Marshall), Lee Allen (Harry, Father)

The musical was presented in one act.

MUSICAL NUMBERS—Overture/"Yesterday Is Over" "I'm Lise" (Stephanie Cotsirilos, Company), "Waltz of Lise's Childhood" (Stephanie Cotsirilos, Ilsebet Anna Tebesli, Company), "Father's Waltz" (Lee Allen), "Men Come with Guns" (Stephanie Cotsirilos, Company), "Hundsvieh" (Stephanie Cotsirilos, Company), "Mother's March" (Lucille Patton, Company), "The Trial" (Lucille Patton, Ilsebet Anna Tebesli, Company), "Marshall's Blues" (Robert Guillaume), "The Counterman" (Lee Allen), "America — We're in New York (Company), "The Victim Dream" (Stephanie Cotsirilos, Lee Allen), "The Stockboy Blues" (Robert Guillaume, Stephanie Cotsirilos), "The Too Much Motet" (Lucille Patton, Company), "The Mating Dance" (Lee Allen, Stephanie Cotsirilos), "Love Scene" (Robert Guillaume, Stephanie Cotsirilos), "The Doctor" (Joseph Neal, Stephanie Cotsirilos, Ilsebet Anna Tebesli), "Lise Dear" (Lucille Patton, Stephanie Cotsirilos, Company), "The Wedding" (Stephanie Cotsirilos, Robert Polenz, Lucille Patton, Company), "Gun Scene" (Robert Guillaume, Stephanie Cotsirilos), "Harry's Rag" (Lee Allen, Company), "Freedom Anthem" (Robert Guillaume, Stephanie Cotsirilos, Company), "Reiffied Expression" (Robert Guillaume, Lee Allen), "Yesterday Is Over" (reprise) (Lucille Patton, Company), "Break-up Rag" (Lee Allen, Stephanie Cotsirilos, Robert Guillaume), "Marshall's Reply" (Robert Guillaume), "Survival Song" (Stephanie Cotsirilos), "Survival Song" (reprise) (Stephanie Cotsirilos, Company), "Final Judgment" (Company), "Yesterday Is Over" (reprise) (Company), "I'm Lise" (reprise) (Stephanie Cotsirilos)

NOTES—*Apple Pie* told the story of a Jewish woman who flees Hitler's Germany for the United

States, but apparently finds life in America just as evil and oppressive. (Is this the message the authors really intended to convey?) The production had been in workshop for a number of years, but all the nurturing by the Public Theatre was to no avail. The critics found the piece chaotic and confusing.

The musical diatribe was a collection of feminist grievances told in such overwrought terms it was all but indecipherable. Martin Gottfried in the *New York Post* said the musical's "incomprehensible" story was "impossible to follow"; Clive Barnes in the *New York Times* noted the music sounded as if it "came out of Kurt Weill's wastepaper basket"; Christopher Sharp in *Women's Wear Daily* commented that he sometimes felt he was watching "the worst show ever written, *Springtime for Hitler*"; and Leonard Propst on NBC said he felt he was in "a bizarre cabaret with Marlene Dietrich ... somehow ending up in New Jersey."

Further, the critics had a field day with the title: *Apple Pie* was "fairly flakey" (the headline of Gottfried's review in the *New York Post*); "difficult to digest" (the headline of Douglas Watt's review in the *New York Daily News)*; "no matter how you slice it, [*Apple Pie*] is indigestible" (Probst on NBC); and "Did the pastry have to be so dry?" (Clive Barnes in the *Times*). The musical was privately recorded on an unlabeled LP (# 4743) which was distributed as a souvenir to those associated with the show. It included approximately seventy-five percent of the musical numbers as well as a two-page synopsis of the confusing plot.

The script was published in the Winter 1984 volume of *Women & Performance/A Journal of Feminist Theory*.

For another musical by Myrna Lamb, see entry for *Mod Donna*, which was also produced at the Public.

66 Arabian Nights. "A New Musical Extravaganza." THEATRE: Jones Beach Marine Theatre; OPENING DATE: June 24, 1954; PERFORMANCES: Unknown; BOOK: George Marion, Jr.; LYRICS: Carmen Lombardo and John Jacob Loeb; MUSIC: Carmen Lombardo and John Jacob Loeb; ballet music "developed" by Alan Moran; DIRECTION: Robert H. Gordon; Allan Zee, Production Director; water sequences by Lottie Mayer; CHOREOGRAPHY: Yurek Lazowski; "Disappearing Water Ballet" dances devised by the Ballet Theatre; SCENERY: Richard Rychtarik; COSTUMES: Richard Rychtarik; LIGHTING: Paul Morrison; MUSICAL DIRECTION: Pembroke Davenport; PRODUCER: Guy Lombardo

CAST—JACK DABDOUB (Genie), HOPE HOLIDAY (Na-eel-ah, Teeny-Weeny-Genie), MIA SLAVENSKA (Prima Ballerina), ADRIANO VITALE (Premier Danseur), Ralph Herbert (Grand Vizier), Ralph Lowe (Trumpeter), HELENA SCOTT (Scheherazade, Chinese Princess), WILLIAM CHAPMAN (Prince Ahmed, Aladdin), Harding Dorn (Ali), Winifred Ainslee (A Slave Girl), LAURITZ MELCHIOR (Sultan, Chinese Emperor), THE MOROCCANS (Acrobats), JANICK AND ARNAUT (Snake and Charmer), Herbert Estrow (Major Domo); Dancing Ensemble — Girls: Margot Campbell, Jean Barrozo, Jeanette Maroulis, Sally Mortimer, Moira Paul, Mary Haywood, Ruth Hanna, Nina Popova, Eda Wyatt, Janice Cioffi, Jan Miller, Paula Tennyson, Marilyn Pendell, Naomi Boneck, Nanette Blair, Mariann Bollin, Karolyn Bruder, Pat Diamond, Joan Ann Einwick, June Evans, Janise Gardner, Helen Gorst, Ellen Kampman, Natasha Kelepovska; Dancing Ensemble — Boys: Victor Duntiere, Hubert Farrington, Albert Fiorella, Bruce Hoy, John Kelly, Arthur Mitchel, Tom Reed, George Tomal, Martin Fredriks, Harding Dorn, Angelo Nicelli, Edward Stinnett; Singing Ensemble — Contraltos: Jane Copeland, Ethel Madsen, Gerrianne Raphael, Ruth Schumacher; Sopranos: Winifred Ainslee, Rosanne Jun, Beth Hawkins, Sybil Lamb, Jane Carlyle, Lucille Lewis, Gloria Van Dorpe, Lois Van Pelt, Astrid Neilson, Betty Zollinger, Toby Dale, Rosalind Phillips, Marie Saucier, Iona Nobel, Doras Smith; Baritones: Carlos Sherman, Mike Roberts, Larry Anderson, Max Hart, George Geyer, Thomas Rieder, Herbert Estrow, Howard Shaw, James Fox, Steve Roland, Charles Rule, Marvin Zeller, Frank Bouley, Charles Aschmann, Robert Price; Tenors: Herbert Mazzini, Ralph Lowe, Keith Kaldenberg, Feodore Tedick, Don Phillips, Thomas Edwards, Arthur Ulisse, John Schickling, Gene Varrone; Water Ballet Girls — Inge Bredehorst, Gaar Marvin, Merlyn Gensler, Eileen Grady, Eileen Hiferty, Charlene Hornor, Lesley Ann Knoll, Phoebe Kruge, Kathy McLaughlin, Marjorie Paveglio, Sanita Pelkey, Irene Roberts, Marlaine Sharak, Pat Sikes, Sandra Smith, Helen Vukotich, Barbara Wallace

Most of the action occurs in Baghdad and Peking.

The musical was presented in two acts.

ACT ONE—"What a Pity" (Ralph Herbert, Soldiers), "It's Great to Be Alive" (Hope Holiday, Singing Girls; danced by Mia Slavenska, Adriano Vitale, and Girl and Boy Dancers), "A Thousand and One Nights" (William Chapman, Helena Scott), "Grand Vizier's Lament" (Ralph Herbert, Singing Boys and Girls), "Hail to the Sultan" (Lauritz Melchior, Ralph Herbert, Singing Boys and Girls, Dancing Boys and Girls), "Hero of My Dreams" (Helena Scott), "A Whale of a Story" (William Chapman, 'The 'Bo'sun' [Performer Unknown], Singing Boys, Sea Sirens), "Valley of Jewels" (Janick and Arnaut, Dancing Boys and Girls)

ACT TWO—"Bath Parade" (Gloria Van Dorpe, Singing and Dancing Girls, Sea Sirens), "Disappearing Water Ballet" (Water Ballet Girls), "How Long Has It Been" (William Chapman, Helena Scott), "Teeny-Weeny Genie" (Hope Holiday, Singing Boys), "Genie Ballet" (Hope Holiday, Dancing Boys), "A Long Ago Love" (Lauritz Melchior), "Marry the One You Love" (Lauritz Melchior), "Teeny-Weeny Genie" (reprise) (Jack Dabdoub), "How Long Has It Been" (reprise) (Lauritz Melchior), "Marry the One You Love" (reprise) (Lauritz Melchior, Singing Boys and Girls), "Grand Vizier's Lament" (reprise) (Ralph Herbert, Singing Boys and Girls), "Bridal Fete" (Mia Slavenska, Adriano Vitale, Dancing Boys and Girls), Finale (Company)

NOTES—Six months before the opening of *Arabian Nights* at the Jones Beach Marine Theatre (formerly Marine Stadium), *Kismet* ("A Musical Arabian Night") had opened on Broadway, and so during the summer of 1954 New Yorkers had dueling Arabian Night musicals to choose from.

L.F. (Lewis Funke) in the *New York Times* reported that the new musical at Jones Beach was "entirely successful" in its lavish re-telling of some of Scheherazade's stories, and, in order to make use of the theatre's lagoon, the extravaganza managed to work in the story of Sinbad and the whale (Funke reported it was a "first-class monster" with a beach umbrella on its snout and eyes which constantly changed color).

As for the music, Funke said it was a "pleasant" mix of Eastern rhythms and "sprightly" tunes worthy of any "respectable juke box." He also noted that the lyrics refused to take the story too seriously, and thus made anachronistic allusions to the Brooklyn Dodgers, refrigerators, and the Long Island railroad.

One of the musical's cast members was Hope Holiday, who made memorable comic impressions in two films during the early 1960s. She played Margie MacDougall, Jack Lemmon's pick-up in Billy Wilder's classic 1960 comedy-drama *The Apartment*, and the following year she appeared in Jerry Lewis' surreal *The Ladies' Man*.

Among the chorus members in *Arabian Nights* were Gene Varrone, Gerrianne Raphael, and Steve Roland. *Arabian Nights* was revived at Jones Beach the following summer, opening on June 23, 1955; the production included most of the principals from the original cast. The musical returned to Jones Beach on July 2, 1967, for a run of sixty-three performances (David Hurst and Linda Bennett were the leads). The cast album was released on Decca Records (LP # DL-9013).

67 The Ark. THEATRE: 37 Arts Theatre; OPENING DATE: November 14, 2005; PERFORMANCES: 8; BOOK: Michael McLean and Kevin Kelly; LYRICS: Michael McLean and Kevin Kelly; MUSIC: Michael McLean; DIRECTION: Ray Roderick; CHOREOGRAPHY: Ray Roderick; SCENERY: Beowulf Boritt; COSTUMES: Lisa L. Zinni; LIGHTING: Eric T. Haugen; PRODUCERS: Erik Orton and Karen Walter Goodwin in association with D. Keith and Suzanne Ross, Jr.

CAST—Marie-France Arcilla (Martha), D.B. Bonds (Ham), Justin Brill (Shem), Janeece Aisha Freeman (Egyptus), Annie Golden (Eliza), Jacquelyn Piro (Sariah), Rob Sutton (Japheth), Adrian Zmed (Noah)

The musical was presented in two acts.

ACT ONE—"What a Sight" (Annie Golden, Jacquelyn Piro, Rob Sutton, Justin Brill, Marie-France Arcilla), "Ship Without an Ocean" (Adrian Zmed, Annie Golden, Jacquelyn Piro, Rob Sutton, Justin Brill, Marie-France Arcilla), "More Than I Asked For" (D.B. Bonds, Janeece Aisha Freeman), "Noah's Prayer" (Adrian Zmed, Annie Golden, Janeece Aisha Freeman, Jacquelyn Piro, Rob Sutton, Justin Brill, Marie-France Arcilla), "Whenever He Needs a Miracle" (D.B. Bonds), "It Takes Two" (Adrian Zmed, Annie Golden), "Lift Me Up" (Company), "Rain Song #1" (Annie Golden), "You Cannot Be a Beauty Queen Forever" (Jacquelyn Piro), "Rain Song #2" (Janeece Aisha Freeman), "Rain Song #3" (Jacquelyn Piro), "I Got a Man Who Loves Me" (Marie-France Arcilla), "I Got a Man Who Loves Me" (reprise) (Marie-France Arcilla, Jacquelyn Piro), "Oh, Yeah" (Rob Sutton, Justin Brill, D.B. Bonds), "Rain Song #4" (Company), "Song of Praise" (Company), "Why Can't We?" (Janeece Aisha Freeman, Company)

ACT TWO—"Couple of Questions" (Company), "Couple of Questions" (reprise) (Janeece Aisha Freeman), "In a Perfect World" (Janeece Aisha Freeman, Adrian Zmed, D.B. Bonds), "Eliza's Breakdown"/"Hold On" (Annie Golden, Adrian Zmed), "Dinner" (D.B. Bonds, Annie Golden, Jacquelyn Piro, Marie-France Arcilla, Justin Brill, Janeece Aisha Freeman, Rob Sutton), "You Must Believe in Miracles #1" (Janeece Aisha Freeman), "You Must Believe in Miracles #2" (Janeece Aisha Freeman, Justin Brill, Marie-France Arcilla), "You Must Believe in Miracles #3" (Janeece Aisha Freeman, Rob Sutton, Jacquelyn Piro), "You Must Believe in Miracles #4" (Janeece Aisha Freeman, Company), "(So Much) More Than I Asked For" (reprise) (D.B. Bonds, Janeece Aisha Freeman), "Lift Me Up"/"Hold On" (reprises) (Adrian Zmed, D.B. Bonds, Company), "I Thought I Was Alone" (D.B. Bonds), "Lift Me Up" (Company), "Song of Praise" (Company)

NOTES—*The Ark*, a musical which dealt with the Biblical story of Noah and the Flood, lasted one week, four weeks shy of the length of the apocalyptic flood. Miriam Horn in the *New York Times* noted the musical's characters were like refugees in a "kind of extended sitcom" as the plot dealt with a "meddling" mother-in-law and "neglected" wives. Further, Noah's son Ham (played by B.D. Bonds in black leather) complains his father is too busy to address his own emotional needs; as for Noah, Adian Zmed gave his character a "slouchy, lounge-lizard style." Horn indicated the musical's anachronisms and pop-culture references were so dated that they themselves were anachronistic. But Horn found one performer who transcended the production: Annie Golden's performance as Eliza was "tender and funny ... with a lovely voice."

Another musical about the subject, Richard Rodgers' *Two by Two*, opened at the Imperial Theatre on November 10, 1970, and managed to run out the season for a total of 343 performances, apparently even turning a small proffit. Based on Clifford Odets' 1954 play *The Flowering Peach*, *Two by Two* looked as though its scenery and costumes cost at least $14.93, and it suffered from an indifferent performance by Danny Kaye (who played the role of Noah). At one performance, Kaye seemed more animated during the curtain calls, when he waved to children in the audience. But the musical left one treasure behind, "I Do Not Know a Day I Did Not Love You," one of the loveliest songs in the Rodgers songbook; it was hauntingly sung by Walter Willison.

68 Around the World in 80 Days. "A New Musical Spectacle on Stage!." THEATRE: Jones Beach Marine Theatre; OPENING DATE: June 22, 1963; PERFORMANCES: 73; BOOK: Sig Herzig; LYRICS: Harold Adamson; MUSIC: Sammy Fain; DIRECTION: Production under the "supervision" of Arnold Spector; staged by June Taylor; CHOREOGRAPHY: June Taylor; SCENERY: George Jenkins; COSTUMES: Winn Morton; LIGHTING: Peggy Clark; MUSICAL DIRECTION: Mitchell Ayres; PRODUCER: Guy Lombardo was credited as presenting "Michael Todd's *Around the World in 80 Days*."

CAST—Lloyd Harris (Hinshaw, Captain of the *Henrietta*), Jane Laughlin (Cora, Mary Lou), Mary Jane Moncrieff (Millie), Leigh Wharton (Stuart, Paku), KEITH HERRINGTON (Sir Ralph, Sir Francis), FRITZ WEAVER (Phileas Fogg), ROBERT CLARY (Passepartout), DOM DE LUISE (Mr. Fix), EDMUND LYNDECK (M. Gasse, Maharajah of Panjipur, Silk Hat Harry), LAURIE FRANKS (Gaby, Kitty), Michael J. Gentry (Ahmed), ELAINE MALBIN (Princess Aouda), Joey Fitter (Clerk at Lloyd's), Marvin Goodis (Conductor [India]), Peter Gladke (One Draw Dillon), Harry Goz (Bartender, Warden), Ralph Vucci (Conductor [U.S.A.]), GUY LOMBARDO AND HIS ROYAL CANADIANS; Singers — Girls: Katherine Barnes, Jane Carlyle, Terri Deshane, Doris Galiber, Eleanor R. Geffert, Maria Graziano, Frances Koll, Leonore Lanzillotti, Marilyne Mason, Janet Moody Morris, Mary Ann Rydzeski, Elise Warner; Boys — Darrell J. Askey, Irving D. Barnes, John (Peter) Clark, Eugene Edwards, Kenneth Emmery, Norman Fredericks, Nino Galanti, Marvin Goodis, Theodore Lambrinos, Herbert J. Pordum, Ralph Vucci, Edmund Walenta; Dancers — Girls: Trudy Carson, Kathryn Doby, Shelley Frankel, Mimi Funes, Judy Kay Gillespie, Gloria Jones, Patti Kelton, Donna Lee Leonard, Joan Leonard, Jari Lynn, Deedee Lyons, Diana Lee Nielsen, Carol Perry, Toni Reither, Renee Louise Rose, Rani Sanford, Geri Seignious, Patti Ann Watson; Boys — Jose Ahumada, Bob Bernard, Kim Bray, Robert Ellis, Robert Fitch, Raphael Gilbert, Joseph M. Gentry, Roy D. Harsh, Joe Helms, Nat Horne, James Maher, Charles Moore, Harold Pierson, Rec Russel, Andre R. Saint-Jean, Richard Prescott, Henry Kip Watson

SOURCE—The 1873 novel *Around the World in 80 Days* by Jules Verne.

The action occurs around the world during an eighty-day period.

The musical was presented in two acts.

ACT ONE—"Grand Opening" (Guy Lombardo and His Royal Canadians), Overture (Orchestra), "March of the Grenadiers" (Ensemble), "Long Live the English Scene" (Ensemble), "Have You Heard About Phileas Fogg?" (Ensemble), "Hide Your Sister" (Robert Clary, Ensemble), "Long Live the English Scene" (reprise) (Fritz Weaver), "I'm a Sleuth" (Dom De Luise), "Sidewalks of Paris" (Robert Clary, Ensemble), "I Hate to Travel" (Fritz Weaver, Edmund Lyndeck), "Sky Symphony" (Singers), "Fiesta in Spain" (Dancers), "Are We Talking About the Same Thing?" (Elaine Malbin, Fritz Weaver), "Lloyd's of London" (Singers), "His Little World" (Elaine Malbin), "One-Woman Man" (Robert Clary, Girls), "Once I Wondered" (Elaine Malbin), "Dance of Sacriffice" (Ensemble), Finale Act I: "Around the World" (Ensemble)

ACT TWO—Entr'acte (Orchestra), "Hong Kong" (Singers), "Barbary Coast" (Jane Laughlin, Peter Gladke), "Carry On" (Fritz Weaver, Robert Clary), "Way Out West" (Fritz Weaver, Singers), "I Hate to Travel" (reprise) (Fritz Weaver), "I Love to Travel" (reprise version of "I Hate to Travel") (Robert Clary), "His Little World" (reprise) (Elaine Malbin), "Around the World" (reprise) (Fritz Weaver), "Burning the *Henrietta*" (Fritz Weaver, Robert Clary, Dancers), "Lloyd's of London" (reprise) (Ensemble), "I'm a Sleuth" (reprise) (Dom De Luise), "Once I Wondered" (reprise) (Elaine Malbin, Fritz Weaver), "Lloyds of London" (reprise) (Ensemble), Finale (Company)

NOTES—Based on Jules Verne's popular novel (and clearly inspired by the recent success of the 1956 film version, which had won the Academy Award for Best Picture), *Around the World in 80 Days* was a musical extravaganza typical of the summer offerings at Jones Beach; it even boasted a hot-air balloon (for the hot-air balloon curse and the problems *Around the World* had with its own hot-air balloon, see entry for *Nellie*).

Lewis Funke in the *New York Times* noted the book, lyrics, and music were "serviceable," and he praised the "sumptuous" production values (besides the hot-air balloon, the musical also employed a yacht as well as huge barges which floated on the theatre's lagoon and represented various locales [and let's not forget the camel and the elephant, either]). Funke noted that dramatic actor Fritz Weaver, who had recently played Hamlet at the American Shakespeare Festival in Stratford, Connecticut, was now "relaxing" in the role of Phileas Fogg, who wagers he can circle the world in eighty days. *Around the World* was Weaver's second excursion into the world of musical comedy: in 1962, he appeared in the Broadway musical *All American*, and two years after the lavish *Around the World* he played the role of Sherlock Holmes in another spectacular, Alexander Cohen's 1965 Broadway musical *Baker Street*, in which he introduced the song "A Married Man" (the number enjoyed a brief vogue thanks to a popular recording by Richard Burton). Weaver had earlier won the 1956 Tony Award for Best Featured Actor in a Play for *The Chalk Garden*, and in 1970 would win the Tony for Best Actor in a Play for his performance in the thriller *Child's Play*.

The 1956 film version of Verne's story (released as *Around the World in Eighty Days*; David Niven played Fogg; Cantinflas, Passepartout; Robert Newton, Mr. Fix; and Shirley MacLaine, Princess Aouda) boasted a hit title theme song (lyric by Harold Adamson and music by Victor Young). While the program for *Around the World* listed Harold Adamson and Sammy Fain for the respective lyrics and music of the stage musical, a special note in the program credited Young with the "original motion picture music," and so it seems that some of Young's music was heard in the stage production; indeed, later programs credited both Fain and Young with the score.

Although there was no cast recording of the musical, a few years prior to its production there was a studio cast album of a "lyrical adaptation" of the film, with lyrics by Adamson which were based on music from Young's film background music. The album (released on Everest Records [LP # SDBR-1020]) included Court Benson (as Fogg) and Leon Janney (as Passepartout), and among the songs were "Long Live the English Scene," "Sky Symphony," "Lloyds of London," and "Hong Kong," all of which are listed in the program of *Around the World*. As for Adamson and Young's popular title song, it was included in the stage version, as the first-act finale (sung by the ensemble) and then in a second-act reprise by Weaver.

Around the World in 80 Days returned to Jones Beach the following summer, opening on June 27, 1964, and playing for seventy performances. Many of the cast members returned (such as Robert Clary, Edmund Lyndeck, and Dom De Luise), but for this production the role of Phileas Fogg was performed by David Atkinson and the role of Princess Aouda was played by Jan McArt. All the songs were retained for the 1964 production, and "Indian Raid," which followed the "Way Out West" sequence, was added.

The musical eventually found its way to summer stock; one tour starred Jose Ferrer (Phileas Fogg) and Don Potter (Passepartout), and another, at the St. Louis Municipal Opera, with Cyril Ritchard (Fogg) and Pierre Olaf (Passepartout). For the tour which starred Ferrer, the following numbers were added (or were perhaps revised titles for older ones): "Spanish Villa" (which may have been a new title for "Fiesta in Spain"), "Processional"/"Ritual Ceremony" ("Dance of Sacriffice"), "Silver Dollars" ("Barbary Coast"), and "London" (which seems to have been added to the "Hong Kong" sequence). Prior to the production of *Around the World in 80 Days* at Jones Beach, the musical had first been seen at the Municipal Opera in St. Louis, Missouri, beginning on June 11, 1962.

Broadway had seen an earlier musical version of Verne's novel. On May 31, 1946, *Around the World in Eighty Days* opened at the Adelphi Theatre; the adaptation was by Orson Welles (who also directed the production and starred as Dick Fix [Arthur Margetson was Phileas Fogg, Larry Laurence, later Enzo Stuarti, was Passepartout, and Mary Healy was Princess Aouda) and the lyrics and music were by Cole Porter. The musical played for seventy-five performances, making it the shortest-running of all Porter's Broadway musicals, but it included some pleasant if minor songs, including "Look What I Found," "Should I Tell You I Love You?," "Pipe Dreaming," and "If You Smile at Me."

69 As Thousands Cheer. THEATRE: Greenwich House Theatre; OPENING DATE: June 14, 1998; PERFORMANCES: 44; SKETCHES: Moss Hart; LYRICS: Irving Berlin; MUSIC: Irving Berlin; DIRECTION: Christopher Ashley; CHOREOGRAPHY: Kathleen Marshall; SCENERY: Allen Moyer; Wendall K. Harrington, Projections; COSTUMES: Jonathan Bixby and Gregory A. Gale; LIGHTING: Kirk Bookman; MUSICAL DIRECTION: David Evans; PRODUCER: Drama Dept. (Douglas Carter Beane, Artistic Director; Michael S. Rosenberg, Managing Director)

CAST—Kevin Chamberlin, Judy Kuhn, Howard McGillin, Paula Newsome, Mary Beth Peil, B.D. Wong, Thursday Farrar, Thom Sesma

The revue was presented in two acts.

ACT ONE—"Man Bites Dog" (Company), "How's Chances?" (Judy Kuhn, Kevin Chamberlin, Howard McGillin, B.D. Wong), "Heat Wave" (Mary Beth Peil, Kevin Chamberlin, Howard McGillin, B.D. Wong), "Debts" (Company), "Lonely Heart" (Judy Kuhn), "The Funnies" (B.D. Wong), "Let's Have Another Cup of Coffee" (Company)

ACT TWO—"Metropolitan Opening" (Company), "Metropolitan Opens in Old-Time Splendor" (Company), "Supper Time" (Paula Newsome), "Our Wedding Day" (a/k/a "Society Wedding") (Company), "(I've Got) Harlem on My Mind" (Paula Newsome), "Through a Keyhole" (Howard McGillin, Company), Finale "Not for All the Rice in China" (Company)

NOTES—The original production of *As Thou-*

sands Cheer opened on Broadway at the Music Box Theatre on September 30, 1933, and played for 400 performances. With witty sketches by Moss Hart and one of Irving Berlin's most brilliant scores, the star-studded musical (its cast included Marilyn Miller, Ethel Waters, Clifton Webb, and Helen Broderick) remains one of the definitive examples of the era's sophisticated revues.

The musical took its cue from newspaper headlines, and so the song "Heat Wave" served as the weather report; the comics section was represented by "The Funnies"; the rotogravure section by "Easter Parade" (which for some reason was listed in the program as "Her Easter Bonnet" for the entire run of the revue); and the lonely hearts column by the ballad "Lonely Heart." The celebrity gossip section of the newspaper was covered by "Through a Keyhole"; news about Noel Coward's return to England by a sketch in which his servants have taken on the airs of some of the playwright's most sophisticated characters; and the news of Josephine Baker being the rage of Paris was covered by her admission that she still has "Harlem on My Mind." In the musical's final scene, the newspaper reports a landmark decision by the Supreme Court: a musical does not have to end with a reprise. And so for the finale there was a completely new song ("Not for All the Rice in China") which hadn't been heard earlier in the evening. The revue's most serious moment occurred in a news report of an "Unknown Negro Lynched by Frenzied Mob"; for this, Ethel Waters memorably sang "Supper Time," her realization that her husband would never again return to her and their children.

The Drama Dept.'s revival of the revue was recorded by Varese Sarabande Records (CD # VSD-5999); the liner notes indicated that at the time of the production, the rights for "Easter Parade" weren't available, and so Irving Berlin's family offered the production a "replacement" song, "Let's Have Another Cup of Coffee" from Hart and Berlin's 1932 musical *Face the Music*. The number was a perfect choice, because *As Thousands Cheer* didn't address the Depression, and the song as staged in *Face the Music* dealt with unemployed New Yorkers enjoying a cup of coffee (and a piece of pie) at the automat. By the time the revival was to be recorded, "Easter Parade" had become available, and so the song was included on the CD (and "Let's Have Another Cup of Coffee" was added as a bonus track).

Since "Easter Parade" was ultimately added to the revival's recording, it appears the only song from the original 1933 production of *As Thousands Cheer* which wasn't heard in the revival or on the recording is "To Be or Not to Be."

The Complete Lyrics of Irving Berlin (edited by Robert Kimball and Linda Emmet, and published by Alfred A. Knopf in 2001) indicates that among the songs written for, but not used in, the revue were: "Mr. and Mrs. Hoover," about the Hoovers' last day in the White House before Roosevelt's inauguration; a song about the repeal of the Eighteenth Amendment; a song about Al Capone; and one about the Chicago World's Fair.

70 Assassins. THEATRE: Playwrights Horizons; OPENING DATE: January 27, 1991; PERFORMANCES: 25; BOOK: John Weidman; LYRICS: Stephen Sondheim; MUSIC: Stephen Sondheim; DIRECTION: Jerry Zaks; CHOREOGRAPHY: D.J. Giagni; SCENERY: Loren Sherman; COSTUMES: William Ivey Long; LIGHTING: Paul Gallo; MUSICAL DIRECTION: Paul Gemignani; PRODUCER: Playwrights Horizons (Andre Bishop, Artistic Director; Paul S. Daniels, Executive Director)

CAST—William Parry (Proprietor, Bystander, Fairgoer, James Garffield, Gerald Ford), Terrence Mann (Leon Czolgosz), Greg Germann (John Hinckley), Jonathan Hadary (Charles Guiteau), Eddie Korbich (Giuseppe Zangara), Lee Wilkof (Samuel Byck), Annie Golden (Lynette "Squeaky" Fromme), Debra Monk (Sara Jane Moore), Victor Garber (John Wilkes Booth), Patrick Cassidy (Balladeer), Marcus Olson (David Herold, Bystander, Fairgoer, Hangman), John Jellison (Bartender, Bystander, Fairgoer, James Blaine, Warden), Joy Franz (Bystander, Benjamin's Mother), Lyn Greene (Bystander, Emma Goldman, Fairgoer), Michael Shulman (Benjamin, Billy), Jace Alexander (Lee Harvey Oswald)

The musical was performed in one act.

MUSICAL NUMBERS—"Everybody's Got the Right" (William Parry, Terrence Mann, Greg Germann, Jonathan Hadary, Eddie Korbich, Lee Wilkof, Annie Golden, Debra Monk, Victor Garber), "The Ballad of Booth" (Patrick Cassidy, Victor Garber), "How I Saved Roosevelt" (Joy Franz, Lyn Greene, John Jellison, Marcus Olson, William Parry, Eddie Korbich), "Gun Song" (Terrence Mann, Victor Garber, Jonathan Hadary, Debra Monk), "The Ballad of Czolgosz" (Patrick Cassidy, Lyn Greene, John Jellison, Marcus Olson, William Parry), "Unworthy of Your Love" (Greg Germann, Annie Golden), "The Ballad of Guiteau" (Jonathan Hadary, Patrick Cassidy), "Another National Anthem" (Terrence Mann, Victor Garber, Greg Germann, Annie Golden, Eddie Korbich, Jonathan Hadary, Debra Monk, Lee Wilkof, Patrick Cassidy), "Everybody's Got the Right" (reprise) (Victor Garber, Terrence Mann, Debra Monk, Jonathan Hadary, Eddie Korbich, Lee Wilkof, Greg Germann, Annie Golden, Jace Alexander)

NOTES—*Assassins* is perhaps the most controversial of Stephen Sondheim's musicals because assassins (and would-be assassins) of U.S. Presidents are its subject matter; the work may well be the most misunderstood musical ever written. It runs the risk of alienating its audience by analyzing the assassins to such a degree that it almost seems to excuse their acts. While this interpretation is clearly off the mark, it may be the reason the musical hasn't quite found its place in the canon of frequently-produced Sondheim works in college, regional, and other venues (*Assassins* was not part of the Kennedy Center's 2002 Sondheim Celebration).

Assassins takes place in the here and now as well as in the past, and the time warp allows the assassins of the nineteenth and twentieth centuries to move through time and space in order to mingle with and encourage one another. Considering the disparate tales it had to tell, the plot could have easily been disjointed and confusing. But Weidman's terse and underrated book used the first presidential assassin, John Wilkes Booth, as a unifying device by anointing him the spiritual mentor for all assassins to come. Further, Sondheim's score employed traditional story ballads (three for the musical) and a panoply of American-styled music to tell its story. Besides the folk-like ballads, the music evoked Copeland, Sousa, and Carpenters-like Seventies songs.

Critics and lovers of Sondheim's musicals have pondered over the musical's message. Are these assassins, losers all, the dark underside of the American Dream? Well, yes, of course. But it may be going too far to say that since America has produced them, the nation is therefore responsible for their actions and is just as guilty as the assassins. The converse of that theory could celebrate the countless dedicated citizens in, say, the teaching and medical professions ... these people too are part of the American Dream, its best side, and if America is responsible for its killers it must also be credited for its teachers and nurses and doctors, and all the ordinary, average citizens who go about their business in a law-abiding manner. If society has produced good people as well as assassins, murderers, terrorists, and rapists, then perhaps this melting pot of the good and the evil is the natural result of any nation which is home to over three-hundred million people. When *Assassins* premiered Off Broadway in 1991, the critics were divided on its merits, and the lack of strongly positive reviews scotched any chance of a Broadway transfer. As a result, the musical was gone after three weeks. But the RCA Victor cast recording (CD # 60737-2-RC) insured that Sondheim's richly melodic and hypnotic score would lead to other productions. In fact, a London production soon followed in 1993 (and included a new song, "Something Just Broke"), and occasional U.S. regional mountings were seen. Finally, in 2004, a Broadway production opened; although it won the Tony Award for Best Revival of a Musical (despite the fact the musical had never been seen on Broadway before and so wasn't a Broadway revival), the musical lasted a disappointing 101 performances (but happily left behind a cast album released by PS Classics [CD # PS-421] which included "Something Just Broke"). *Assassins* will probably never enjoy mainstream, Broadway-styled popularity, but it will surely continue to be produced by adventurous regional and college theatres.

The script of the original production was published by Theatre Communications Group in 1991. At one point, a cable television version of *Assassins* was in discussion stages, but unfortunately the production never materialized.

71 Asylum: The Strange Case of Mary Lincoln. "A Musical." THEATRE: St. Peter's Theatre; OPENING DATE: September 14, 2006; PERFORMANCES: 21; BOOK: Carmen Owen; LYRICS: Carmen Owen; MUSIC: June Bingham; DIRECTION: Fabrizio Melano; "additional" musical staging by Brian Blythe; SCENERY: James Morgan; COSTUMES: Terese Wadden; LIGHTING: Chris Robinson; MUSICAL DIRECTION: Bob Goldstone; PRODUCER: The York Theatre Company (James Morgan, Artistic Director; W. David McCoy, Chairman of the Board)

CAST—Carolann Page (Mary Lincoln), Edwin Cahill (Robert Lincoln, Ensemble), John Jellison (Dr. Patterson, Lincoln, Ensemble), Bertilla Baker (Myra Bradwell, Ensemble), Daniel Spiotta (Franc Wilkie, Ensemble), Joy Lynn Matthews (Delia, Ensemble)

The action occurs in 1875 and in the memory of Mary Lincoln.

The musical was presented in two acts.

ACT ONE—"Mother, I Need You" (Edwin Cahill), "A National Disgrace" (Ensemble), "Dear Mr. Lincoln" (Carolann Page), "Mother, I Need You" (reprise) (Edwin Cahill), "This Is the Solution" (Edwin Cahill, Carolann Page), "Doctor" (Carolann Page, John Jellison), "Crystal Wisdom" (Carolann Page), "I Remember Him" (Edwin Cahill), "The Run" (Joy Lynn Matthews), "The Lincoln Waltz" (Carolann Page, John Jellison), "Warm Mist" (Carolann Page), "Oregon" (Carolann Page, John Jellison), "The Letter" (Carolann Page)

ACT TWO—"What a Story" (Bertilla Baker, Daniel Spiotta), "Looking at You" (Carolann Page, Bertilla Baker), "It Won't Be Long Now" (Carolann Page), "Here's the Story" (reprise of "What a Story") (Daniel Spiotta, Bertilla Baker, Ensemble), "Easy for You" (Edwin Cahill), "Rockabye Child Jesus" (Joy Lynn Matthews), "Why Robert, Why" (Carolann Page, Edwin Cahill), "Why Robert, Why" (Coda) (Carolann Page), "It Won't Be Long Now" (reprise) (Carolann Page)

NOTES—Mary Todd Lincoln had been a leading character in three plays which opened during the 1972-1973 theatre season (see below). *Asylum: The Strange Case of Mary Lincoln* told her story as a musical, and it not only dealt with her being judged insane and committed to an asylum but also in flashbacks told the story of her courtship and marriage to Abraham Lincoln. By the musical's end, the verdict of insanity is reversed and she regains her freedom.

Neil Genzlinger in the *New York Times* felt the musical deserved a fuller and more compelling book. Nonetheless, he found it a "respectable pocket musical" which might find future life in college and regional theatre. He singled out three songs for praise ("The Run," "The Lincoln Waltz," and "Oregon").

The musical was recorded by Original Cast Records (CD # 6221); for the recording, Ken Krugman sang the roles originally created on the stage by John Jellison.

As mentioned, three plays during the 1972-1973 season featured Mary Todd Lincoln as a leading character: *The Lincoln Mask* by V.J. Longhi (Eva Marie Saint was Mary Lincoln); *The Last of Mrs. Lincoln* by James Prideaux (Julie Harris won the Tony Award for Best Actress in a Play for her performance); and *Look Away* by Jerome Kilty (a two-character drama with Geraldine Page as Mary Lincoln and Maya Angelou as her companion).

72 **At Least It's Pink.** THEATRE: Ars Nova Theatre; OPENING DATE: January 25, 2007; PERFORMANCES: 24 (estimated) BOOK: Bridget Everett, Michael Patrick King, and Kenny Mellman; LYRICS AND MUSIC: Kenny Mellman and Bridget Everett; DIRECTION: Michael Patrick King; SCENERY: Lauren Helpern; COSTUMES: Angela Wendt; LIGHTING: Tyler Micoleau; PRODUCERS: Ars Nova (Jon Steinhart, Jenny Wiener, and Jason Eagan); Kimberly Rosenstock, Associate Producer

CAST—Bridget Everett (as Herself), Kenny Mellman (as Himself), Rosa Curry (Woman), Sean Jenness (Straight Man), Peter Kim (Gay Man), Michael-Leon Woolsey (Simon)

The revue was presented in one act.

NOTES—*At Least It's Pink* was a bawdy revue-like evening (Zachary Pincus-Roth reported in *Playbill* that the production's press release described the evening as a "trashy little show") which starred newcomer Bridget Everett, formerly of Manhattan, Kansas. According to Christopher Isherwood in the *New York Times*, the show was a "woozy combination" of cabaret and stand-up comedy, not to mention a "particularly volatile episode of *The Jerry Springer Show*," and he felt one's enjoyment of the evening depended on one's tolerance for "loudmouthed, dirty-talking girls with attitudes stretching from here to Kansas." As for Everett, he found her "bold and brash — O.K., frightening." Frank Scheck in the *New York Post* found her a "lascivious dynamo ... entertainingly and unapologetically licentious ... a sort of profane Mae West." Everett's outré antics delighted the crowds, and the limited engagement was extended into the spring.

73 **At Wit's End.** THEATRE: Michael's Pub; OPENING DATE: October 8, 1991; PERFORMANCES: 27; PLAY: Joel Kimmel; DIRECTION: Barbara Karp; SCENERY: Alan Kimmel, Scenic Consultant; LIGHTING: Andrew Taines; PRODUCERS: Lawrence Kasha and Ronald A. Lachman in association with Warner/Chappell Music Group; Richard T. Hart, Associate Producer

CAST—Stan Freeman (Oscar Levant)

SOURCES—Oscar Levant's three autobiographies (*A Smattering of Ignorance* [1940], *Memoirs of an Amnesiac* [1965], and *The Unimportance of Being Oscar* [1968]).

The revue was presented in two acts (division of acts unknown; musical numbers are listed in performance order).

MUSICAL NUMBERS—"Rhapsody in Blue" (music by George Gershwin; 1924), "Second Rhapsody" (a/k/a "Rhapsody in Rivets"; music by George Gershwin; 1931), "Preludes I, II, and III" (music by George Gershwin; 1926), "An American in Paris" (music by George Gershwin; 1928), "Concerto in F" (music by George Gershwin; 1925), "Swanee" (from *Demi Tasse/Capitol Revue*, 1919; lyric by Irving Caesar, music by George Gershwin; later used in *Sinbad* [also 1919]), "Somebody Loves Me" (*George White's Scandals* [Sixth Edition], 1924; lyric by B.G. [Buddy] DeSylva and Ballard MacDonald, music by George Gershwin), "Lady Play Your Mandolin" (lyric by Irving Caesar, music by Oscar Levant), "True Blue Lou" (1929 film *Dance of Life*; lyric by Sam Coslow and Leo Robin, music by Richard A. Whiting), "That Old Feeling" (lyric by Lew Brown, music by Sammy Fain), "Wacky Dust" (lyric by Stanley Adams, music by Oscar Levant), "Blame It on My Youth" (lyric by Edward Heyman, music by Oscar Levant), "That's Entertainment" (1953 film *The Band Wagon*; lyric by Howard Dietz, music by Arthur Schwartz)

NOTES—*At Wit's End*, a one-man show in which Stan Freeman portrayed Oscar Levant (1906–1972), had toured prior to its New York production.

The evening was supposedly a recreation of a typical concert performance by Levant in the 1950s. Stephen Holden in the *New York Times* reported the "highly entertaining" portrait of the self-described "deeply superficial" Levant included numerous musical interludes as well as anecdotes about his career and his addiction to pain-killers (Levant states that when he and Judy Garland first met, it may well have been "the greatest moment in pharmaceutical history"). Holden noted that Levant's reminiscences about George Gershwin formed the show's "tenderest moments."

74 **The Athenian Touch.** "A New Musical Comedy." THEATRE: Jan Hus Playhouse; OPENING DATE: January 14, 1964; PERFORMANCES: 1; BOOK: Arthur Goodman and J. Albert Fracht; LYRICS: David Eddy; MUSIC: Willard Straight; DIRECTION: Alex Palermo; CHOREOGRAPHY: Alex Palermo; SCENERY: Robert T. Williams; COSTUMES: Don Foote; LIGHTING: Robert T. Williams; MUSICAL DIRECTION: Glen Clugston; PRODUCERS: David Brown in association with Ronald Toyser

CAST—John Baylis (Flictus), Betsy Durkin (Lamia), Annette Brandler (Kita), Marty Clarke (Thea), BUTTERFLY MCQUEEN (Ora), Lois Rooks (Rhodia), MARION MARLOWE (Attalea), James Harder (Polycharides), William Martel (Cleon), John Kordel (Colonis), ROBERT COSDEN (Aristophanes), Will Richter (Socrates), Bill Caskey (Nicias), Ronn Hansen (Citizen-Soldier), Mark Holliday (Citizen-Soldier), Richard Ianni (Citizen-Soldier)

The action occurs in Athens during the third year of the 88th Olympiad ("A Long Time Ago").

The musical was presented in two acts.

ACT ONE—"There Goes Time" (Marion Marlowe), "Today's the Day" (Butterfly McQueen, John Baylis, Betsy Durkin, Annette Brandler, Marty Clarke, Boys), "No Garlic Tonight" (Marion Marlowe, Butterfly McQueen, Chorus), "Have a Little Sooth on Me" (James Harder), "Harmony, Sweet Harmoni" (Marion Marlowe, William Martel, John Baylis, Betsy Durkin), "The Singer and the Song" (John Kordel, Betsy Durkin), "When You Write Greek Comedy" (Robert Cosden), "What Is a Woman" (Marion Marlowe), "Eleleu!" (Robert Cosden, Company), "Look Away" (Butterfly McQueen), "There Goes Time" (reprise) (Robert Cosden), "Love, You Are So Difficult" (Marion Marlowe)

ACT TWO—"A Lady of Leisure" (Marion Marlowe, Butterfly McQueen), Dance (Chorus), "An Awkward Little Boy" (John Kordel), "An Agent's Blood" (John Baylis), "Lysistrata" (James Harder, Ronn Hansen, Mark Holliday, Richard Ianni), "What Is a Woman" (reprise) (Robert Cosden), "All We Need To Know" (Marion Marlowe, Robert Cosden, Company)

NOTES—*The Athenian Touch* dealt with the romantic goings-on of Attalea (Marion Marlowe), a courtesan about to become the mistress of the wealthy Cleon. She's also involved with Aristophanes, on trial for treason because his latest play *Lysistrata* advocates that women withhold their sexual favors from men until such time as men stop fighting wars. Attalea succeeds in getting Aristophanes' trial thrown out of court, and, with his help, manages to restore Cleon to his wife. Moreover, she and Aristophanes enter into their own romantic arrangement.

Because Lewis Funke in the *New York Times* didn't know who was speciffically responsible for *The Athenian Touch*, he said blame would be "distributed equally" among the writers of the show's book, lyrics, and music. He concluded his review with a lament for "poor" Aristophanes and the penalty he paid for having originally written *Lysistratra*. But Aristophanes had his revenge: *The Athenian Touch* lasted for only one performance.

A recording of the show's rather bland score was released by Broadway East Records (LP # OCS-101; later issued on CD by AEI Records [# AEI-CD-010]), which included most of the songs (with one additional number, "The Contract"). For the recording, Peter Sands and Alice Cannon sang the numbers performed in the production by John Kordel and Betsy Durkin.

For information about other musicals based on Aristophanes' comedies, see entries for *Wings* (1975) and *Lyz!*

75 **Austentatious.** NOTES—See entry for *The New York Musical Theatre Festival.*

76 **Autumn's Here!** THEATRE: Bert Wheeler Theatre; OPENING DATE: October 25, 1966; PERFORMANCES: 80; BOOK: Norman Dean; LYRICS: Norman Dean; MUSIC: Norman Dean; DIRECTION: Hal Le Roy; CHOREOGRAPHY: Hal Le Roy; SCENERY: Robert Conley; COSTUMES: Eve Henriksen; LIGHTING: Arthur Terjeson; MUSICAL DIRECTION: Gordon Munford; PRODUCER: Bob Hadley

CAST—Leslie Wilkinson (Diedrich Knickerbocker), Fred Gockel (Brom Bones), Karin Wolfe (Katrina), Bob Riehl (Ichabod Crane), Allan Lokos (Mr. Van Tassel), Joyce Lynn (Mrs. Van Tassel), Joyce Devlin (Jo), Les Freed (Ben), John Johann (Douglas), Zona Kennedy (Etta), Dan Leach (Will), Regina Lynn (Dora), Pamela Privette (Della), Gordon Ramsey (Lew)

SOURCE—The 1820 story *The Legend of Sleepy Hollow* by Washington Irving.

The musical was presented in two acts.

ACT ONE—"Sleepy Hollow" (Company), "Boy, Do I Hate Horse Races" (The Boys and The Girls), "Me and My Horse" (Fred Gockel), "Autumn's Here" (Karin Wolfe), "Song of the 13 Colonies" (The Boys and The Girls), "Patience" (Bob Riehl), "For the Harvest Safely Gathered" (Company), "Who Walks Like a Scarecrow" (Fred Gockel, Company), "This Is the Girl for Me" (Bob Riehl), "Do You Think I'm Pretty?" (Karin Wolfe, Bob Riehl, Allan Lokos, Joyce Lynn), "Fine Words and Fancy Phrases" (Allan Lokos, Joyce Lynn, Karin Wolfe), "Private Hunting Ground" (Les Freed, Gordon Ramsey, Dan Leach), "It's a Long Road Home" (Les Freed, Zona Kennedy), "Brom and Katrina" (Pamela Privette, Zona Kennedy, Joyce Devlin, Fred Gockel), "Dark New England Night" (Company; danced by Pamela Privette, John Johann, Joyce Devlin)

ACT TWO—"Dutch Country Table" (Company), "You Never Miss the Water" (Fred Gockel, Les Freed, Gordon Ramsey, Dan Leach), "Any Day Now" (Karin Wolfe), "You May Be the Someone" (Karen Wolfe, Bob Riehl), "Beware as You Ride Through the Hollow" (Company), "The Chase" (Company), "Sleepy Hollow" (reprise) (Company)

NOTES—With its irresistible story, colorful characters, and rich atmosphere, a musical version of *The Legend of Sleepy Hollow* seems a natural. But *Autumn's Here*, the inaugural production at the Bert Wheeler Theatre (former stage and film comic Bert

Wheeler was in attendance for the opening), barely made it through the autumn. Writing in the *New York Times*, Dan Sullivan found the evening clumsy, but liked the new theatre, which had formerly been the Plantation Room of the Dixie (now Carter) Hotel. He described the space as "1947 Moderne, with studded leatherette ceiling and mirrored pillars," and a "fun" décor which was a welcome change from the "customary austerity" of typical Off Broadway venues. It's unclear who performed the role of Diedrich Knickerbocker on opening night (either Leslie Wilkinson or James L. O'Neill).

Sleepy Hollow, another musical version of Irving's story, had opened on Broadway in 1948 and was the first musical to play the St. James Theatre after the marathon run of *Oklahoma!* (1943); it lasted only twelve performances. In 1977, Tommy Tune appeared at Town Hall in *Ichabod* (see entry) a one-man musical version of the material, but it too quickly disappeared. On June 27, 2006, *The Legend of Sleepy Hollow* was presented at the York Theatre, apparently for a limited engagement of just one performance (the book was by Robert Stempin, and the lyrics and music were by James Crowley). The score was recorded on an unnumbered 2-CD set released by CE (Crowley Entertainment) Records.

77 **Avenue Q.** THEATRE: Vineyard Theatre; OPENING DATE: March 19, 2003; PERFORMANCES: 47; BOOK: Jeff Whitty; LYRICS: Robert Lopez and Jeff Marx; MUSIC: Robert Lopez and Jeff Marx; DIRECTION: Jason Moore; CHOREOGRAPHY: Ken Roberson; SCENERY: Anna Louizos; Puppets conceived and designed by Rick Lyon; COSTUMES: Mirena Rada; LIGHTING: Frances Aronson; MUSICAL DIRECTION: Gary Adler; PRODUCERS: Vineyard Theatre (Douglas Aibel, Artistic Director; Bardo S. Ramirez, Managing Director; Jennifer Garvey-Blackwell, Executive Director, External Affairs) and The New Group (Scott Elliottt, Artistic Director; Geoffrey Rich, Executive Director)

CAST—John Tartaglia (Princeton, Rod), Alexander Gemignani (Brian), Stephanie D'Abruzzo (Kate Monster, Lucy, Others), Rick Lyon (Nicky, Trekkie Monster, Bear, Others), Ann Harada (Christmas Eve), Natalie Venetia Belcon (Gary Coleman), Jennifer Barnhart (Mrs. T. Bear, Others)

The action occurs in an outer borough of New York City in the present.

The revue was presented in two acts.

ACT ONE—"Avenue Q Theme" (Company) Opening (Company), "If You Were Gay" (Rick Lyon, John Tartaglia), "Purpose" (John Tartaglia), "Everyone's a Little Bit Racist" (John Tartaglia, Stephanie D'Abruzzo, Natalie Venetia Belcon, Alexander Gemignani, Ann Harada), "The Internet Is for Porn" (Stephanie D'Abruzzo, Rick Lyon, John Tartaglia, Alexander Gemignani), "A Mix Tape" (Stephanie D'Abruzzo, John Tartaglia), "I'm Not Wearing Underwear Today" (Alexander Gemignani), "Special" (Stephanie D'Abruzzo), "You Can Be as Loud as the Hell You Want (When You're Making Love)" (Natalie Venetia Belcon, Bad Idea Bears, Company), "Fantasies Come True" (John Tartaglia, Stephanie D'Abruzzo), "My Girlfriend, Who Lives in Canada" (John Tartaglia), "There's a Fine, Fine Line" (Stephanie D'Abruzzo)

ACT TWO—"There Is Life Outside Your Apartment" (Alexander Gemignani, Company), "The More You Ruv Someone" (Ann Harada, Stephanie D'Abruzzo), "Schadenfreude" (Natalie Venetia Belcon, Rick Lyon), "I Wish I Could Go Back to College" (Stephanie D'Abruzzo, Rick Lyon, John Tartaglia), "The Money Song" (Rick Lyon, John Tartaglia, Natalie Venetia Belcon, Ann Harada, Alexander Gemignani), "For Now" (Company)

NOTES—*Avenue Q*, an Off Off Broadway puppet revue for adults, seemed to go out of its way to wear its left-leaning heart on its sleeve and to embrace crudeness; but for all that, its lyrical ideas were obvious and rather bland. Nonetheless, the musical quickly transferred to Broadway, where it opened at the John Golden Theatre on July 31, 2003, for 2,534 performances (and then transferred back to Off Broadway). It won Tony Awards for Best Book, Best Score, and Best Musical.

The Broadway cast recording was released by RCA Victor Records (CD # 82876-55923-2) and came with a parental advisory for explicit content (strong language and sexual content) just in case clueless parents thought the musical was a Broadway riff of television's *Sesame Street.* A separate recording of "Tear It Up and Throw It Away (The Jury Duty Song)," a song cut from the musical during rehearsals, was released on a single CD (unidentified label # 04021013).

The script was published in a lavish edition by Hyperion Books in 2006 with a warning that it was "for children over 18 only!" and a notation that no puppets were harmed during the making of the book.

The 2007 documentary film *ShowBusiness: The Road to Broadway* chronicled *Avenue Q* and three other musicals (*Wicked*, *Taboo*, and *Caroline*, or *Change* [see entry for the latter production]) which opened on Broadway during the 2003-2004 season; the film was released on DVD by Genius Products and Liberation Entertainment (# 80543).

78 **Avenue X.** "The A Capella Musical." THEATRE: Playwrights Horizons; OPENING DATE: February 21, 1994; PERFORMANCES: 48; BOOK: John Jiler; LYRICS: John Jiler; MUSIC: Ray Leslee; DIRECTION: Mark Brokaw; CHOREOGRAPHY: Ken Roberson; SCENERY: Loy Arcenas; COSTUMES: Ellen McCartney; LIGHTING: Donald Holder; MUSICAL DIRECTION: Chapman Roberts; PRODUCER: Playwrights Horizons (Don Scardino, Artistic Director; Leslie Marcus, Managing Director)

CAST—Ted Brunetti (Pasquale), Roger Mazzeo (Ubazz), John Leone (Chuck), Colette Hawley (Barbara), Harold Perrineau (Milton), Chuck Cooper (Roscoe), Alvaleta Guess (Julia), Keith Johnston (Winston); Note: When performers weren't singing a "lead" in a speciffic number, they sometimes performed as back-up or chorus members.

The action occurs in Gravesend, Brooklyn, in Summer 1963.

The musical was presented in two acts.

ACT ONE—"Where Is Love?" (Performer[s] unknown), "A Thousand Summer Nights" (John Leone, Ted Brunetti, Roger Mazzeo), "Scat" (Ted Brunetti, Harold Perrineau), "Serves You Right" (Ted Brunetti, Harold Perrineau), "Waitin'" (Chuck Cooper, Alvaleta Guess), "Io Sono Cosi Stanco" (Roger Mazzeo, Colette Hawley), "Woman of the World" (Colette Hawley, Ted Brunetti, Harold Perrineau, Roger Mazzeo), "She's Fifteen" (Ted Brunetti, John Leone, Roger Mazzeo), "Stay with Me Baby" (Chuck Cooper, Harold Perrineau, Keith Johnston, Ted Brunetti, Roger Mazzeo), "Where Are You Tonight?" (John Leone, Men), "Big Lucy" (Chuck Cooper, Harold Perrineau, Keith Johnston, Ted Brunetti, Roger Mazzeo), "Why?" (Harold Perrineau, Men), "Follow Me" (Harold Perrineau, Ted Brunetti, Chorus), "Follow Me" (reprise) (Harold Perrineau, Chorus)

ACT TWO—"Palermo" (John Leone), "Command Me" (Chuck Cooper, Alvaleta Guess, Keith Johnston, Harold Perrineau, Roger Mazzeo), "Rap" (a/k/a "Roscoe's Rap") (Chuck Cooper), "Moonlight in Old Sicily" (Ted Brunetti, Colette Hawley, Chorus), "Gloria" (Entire Company [except Ted Brunetti]), "Africa" (Keith Johnston, Harold Perrineau, Chorus), "Go There" (Alvaleta Guess, Chorus [except Harold Perrineau]), "'Til the End of Time" (Chuck Cooper, John Leone, Keith Johnston, Roger Mazzeo), Epilogue/"Where Is Love?" (reprise) (Chorus)

NOTES—*Avenue X* was unusual in that its score was sung a capella; as for the plot, it told the overly familiar story of racial tensions in New York (in this case, racial divisions between Italian-American and Black families in Brooklyn in 1963). According to the musical, different ethnic groups can get along if they just sing together (it's too bad the Jets and the Sharks didn't follow this philosophy). In 1995, the script was published by Samuel French, Inc., as a one-act musical, and included some changes in the song sequences. While the New York production opened with the song "Where Is Love?," the script opens with "A Thousand Summer Nights"; the script also includes the number "Santa Cecilia," which apparently was not heard in New York.

In 1997, RCA Victor released a recording (CD # 09026-63208-2) of songs from the musical which included four of the original cast members (Colette Hawley, Ted Brunetti, John Leone, and Chuck Cooper). The recording also included a new song ("Darling Can't You See"), and the album indicated additional lyrics were by Ray Leslee.

The musical had been previously been produced by Playwrights Horizons on June 3, 1993, for fourteen performances, and was later revived Off Off Broadway for two weeks beginning on March 1, 2007, at the 45th Street Theatre. For the latter production, Marilyn Stasio in *Variety* noted that the musical's recipe for racial harmony was a "fairy-tale concept," and she regretted the characters weren't developed "beyond their initial attitudes." But she praised Ray Leslee's score, "a multi-faceted musical language of blues, jazz, pop, do-wop, gospel, liturgical church music, Italian folk songs and African chants."

79 **Babalooney.** "An Improvisational Comedy Revue with Music!"; THEATRE: Provincetown Playhouse; OPENING DATE: February 15, 1984; PERFORMANCES: 24; MUSIC: Larry Schanker and the Practical Theatre Co.; DIRECTION: Brad "Thing" Hall; SCENERY: Louis "El Rukn" DiCrescenzo; COSTUMES: Iwo "Buddy" Jima and Jen "J5" Crawford; LIGHTING: Tom "Yogi Bubba" Larson; MUSICAL DIRECTION: Uncredited (Probably Larry Schanker); PRODUCERS: Arthur "Skippy" Cantor, Brad "Skippy" Hall, Bruce "Skippy" Ostler, Paul "Skippy" Barrosse, and Bonnie Nelson "Skippy" Schwartz present a Practical Theatre Co. Production

CAST—Rush Pearson ("Chip" and "The Skipper too"), Jamie Baron ("Rob" and "The Millionaire and His Wife"), Bekka Eaton ("Ernie" and "The Rest"), Uncle Charlie (as "Himself" and "Gilligan"), Jane Muller ("Steve" and "The Movie Star"), Paul Barrosse ("Doug, our smelly little cousin"); and the Ba Ba Ba Babalooney Band with Larry Schanker (Piano, Synthesizers) and Rockin' Ronny Crawford (Drums, Toys, Stuff)

The revue was presented in two acts (the program didn't include a list of songs and sketches).

NOTES—The *Babalooney* Company was based in Evanston, Illinois, where the Practical Theatre Company developed its material through improvisation "and actual combat missions." Frank Rich in the *New York Times* found the revue a "mostly innocuous" attempt at a "low-budget *Hellzapoppin*"; further, the evening's main point of reference was television (*To Tell the Truth*, *The Twilight Zone*, *Family Affair*, *Gilligan's Island*) as well as topics which were hopelessly passé (such as a parody of Peter, Paul and Mary's popular early-1960s song "Puff the Magic Dragon"). However, Rich singled out "McBroadway," a sketch which dealt with offering Broadway theatre fare as if it were fast food (Rich reported customers could "order" highlights from *Macbeth* and *The Music Man*, with a side order of "fries" [that is, highlights from plays by Christopher Fry]).

80 Babes in the Wood. "A New Musical"; THEATRE: Orpheum Theatre; OPENING DATE: December 28, 1964; PERFORMANCES: 45; BOOK: Rick Besoyan; LYRICS: Rick Besoyan; MUSIC: Rick Besoyan; DIRECTION: Rick Besoyan; CHOREOGRAPHY: Ralph Beaumont; SCENERY: Paul Morrison; COSTUMES: Howard Barker; LIGHTING: Paul Morrison; MUSICAL DIRECTION: Natalie Charlson; PRODUCERS: Sandy Farber and Aaron Schroeder

CAST—Richard Charles Hoh (Oberon), Elmarie Wendel (Robin Goodfellow), Carol Glade (Titania), Ruth Buzzi (Helena), Danny Carroll (Demetrius), Kenneth McMillan (Bottom), Don Stewart (Lysander), Joleen Fodor (Hermia), Edward Miller (An Addition)

SOURCE—William Shakespeare's play *A Midsummer Night's Dream* (written circa 1595-1596).

The action occurs in 300 B.C. in a wood near Athens on a midsummer's night.

The musical was presented in two acts.

ACT ONE—"This State of Affairs" (Richard Charles Hoh, Elmarie Wendel), "Titania's Philosophy" (Carol Glade), "A Lover Waits" (Richard Charles Hoh), "The Gossip Song" (Ruth Buzzi), "I'm Not for You" (Danny Carroll), "I'm Not for You" (reprise) (Ruth Buzzi, Danny Carroll), "Mother" (Kenneth McMillan), "Old Fashioned Girl" (Kenneth McMillan, with Elmarie Wendel), "Love Is Lovely" (Don Stewart, Joleen Fodor), "Babes in the Wood" (Elmarie Wendel), "Love Is Lovely" (reprise) (Don Stewart, with Ruth Buzzi), Finale (Company)

ACT TWO—Opening (Company), "Anyone Can Make a Mistake" (Elmarie Wendel), "Cavorting" (Carol Glade, Kenneth McMillan), "There's a Girl" (Richard Charles Hoh, Danny Carroll), "There's a Girl" (reprise) (Danny Carroll), "I'm Not for You" (reprise) (Don Stewart), "Little Tear" (Joleen Fodor), "Babes in the Wood" (reprise) (Elmarie Wendel), "Helena's Solution" (Ruth Buzzi, with Don Stewart and Danny Carroll), "Helena" (Danny Carroll, Don Stewart), "Midsummer Night" (Richard Charles Hoh, Carol Glade), "Moon Madness" (Carol Glade, Kenneth McMillan), "A Lover Waits" (reprise) (Richard Charles Hoh), "The Alphabet Song" (Carol Glade, Joleen Fodor, Ruth Buzzi), Finale (Company)

NOTES—The disappointing six-week run of *Babes in the Wood* brought Rick Besoyan's short career to an end. The show reads well (a slightly revised script was published by Broadway Play Publishing, Inc., in 1983), and with such inspired comics as Ruth Buzzi, Elmarie Wendel, Danny Carroll, and Kenneth McMillan among the company, it appears to have been superbly cast.

But Howard Taubman in the *New York Times* felt Besoyan stretched himself thin with his book, lyrics, music, and direction, and noted that only in his music did Besoyan shine (a score with "flowing, singable melodies"); otherwise, Taubman felt "a tough-minded librettist" is what Besoyan needed. "Old Fashioned Girl" is probably the same "Old Fashioned Girl" which Kenneth McMillan introduced in the "Gems from *Little Mary Sunshine*" sequence from *In Your Hat* (1957; see entry). The number wasn't used in *Little Mary Sunshine* when the musical was expanded for its Off Broadway production in 1959 (see entry). If it's the same song, then McMillan finally got his song back, albeit after an eight-year delay.

For another adaptation of the material, see entry for *The Donkey Show*. Other musical versions of Shakespeare's comedy include the Off Off Broadway production *Puck and the Magic Flower*, which opened at Theatre Off Park on October 27, 1979, for twelve performances (book by Ken Berman and Leon Odenz, lyrics by Nick De Noia [with additional lyrics by Anthony Calabrese], and music by Leon Odenz), and at least two regional theatre versions, *A Midsummer Night's Dream*, which opened in Dallas at the Dallas Theatre Center on November 20, 1973, with adaptation, lyrics, and music by Randolph Tallman and Steven Mackenroth, and *Another Midsummer Night*, which opened at the Goodman Theatre in Chicago on June 26, 1995 (book and lyrics by Arthur Perlman, music by Jeffrey Lunden).

81 The Babes in Toyland. "A Musical Extravaganza"; THEATRE: Felt Forum/Madison Square Garden; OPENING DATE: December 21, 1979; PERFORMANCES: 16; BOOK: Ellis Weiner (based on an idea by Barry Weissler); the book of the original production was by Glenn McDonough; LYRICS: New lyrics by Shelly Markham and Annette Leisten; the lyrics of the original production were by Glenn McDonough; MUSIC: New music by Shelly Markham and Annette Leisten; the music of the original production was by Victor Herbert; DIRECTION: Munson Hicks; CHOREOGRAPHY: Tony Stevens; SCENERY: Michael J. Hotopp and Paul de Pass; COSTUMES: Michael J. Hotopp and Paul de Pass; LIGHTING: Associated Theatrical Designers; MUSICAL DIRECTION: Bob Christianson; PRODUCERS: American Entertainment Enterprises; Barry Weissler and Fran Weissler

CAST—Tom Holleran (Tom, Vendor #2), Roger Lawson (Sugarbear, Vendor #1), Michael Calkins (Horace, Vendor #3), Mona Finston (Puppette, One of the Children in the Shoe [Mary], Toy Soldier, Puppeteer), Edward T. Jacobs (Puppette, Haystack, A Lady of the Grand Ballet), Robert Hancock (Puppette, The Wall, Toy Soldier, Puppeteer, Computer Bob), Lynn Hippen (Puppette, The Old Woman in the Shoe [Lucy], Toy Soldier, Puppeteer), Steve Mathews (Puppette, One of the Children in the Shoe [Little Boy Blue], Toy Soldier, Puppeteer), Alan F. Seiffert (Puppette, Jack Be Nimble, Drummer Boy, Humpty Dumpty, A Shroud, Toy Soldier, Puppeteer), Dan Kruger (Promoter, Old King Cole, Toy Soldier), Edward T. Jacobs (Haystack), Ken Bonafons (Grandfather, Humpty Dumpty), Debbie McLeod (Mary), S. Barkley Murray (Mother Goose, A Lady of the Grand Ballet, A Shroud, Toy Soldier), C.A. Hutton (Barnaby), Shari Watson (Little Bo Peep, A Lady of the Grand Ballet); (NOTE—The souvenir program identified the roles of Tom [Mark Holleran], Sugarbear [Roger Lawson], Horace [Michael Calkins], and Mary [Debbie McLeod]) as "The Babes.")

The musical was presented in two acts.

ACT ONE—"Big Baby" (Mark Holleran, Roger Lawson, Michael Calkins, Debbie McLeod, Mona Finston, Edward T. Jacobs, Robert Hancock, Lynn Hippen, Steve Mathews, Dan Kruger), "It's a Sweet Life" (Mark Holleran, Roger Lawson, Michael Calkins, Debbie McLeod), "Something Must Be Done" (Mark Holleran, Roger Lawson, Michael Calkins, Debbie McLeod, Dan Kruger, Ken Bonafons, Alan F. Seiffert, Robert Hancock, S. Barkley Murray, Lynn Hippen, Mona Finston, Steve Mathews), "Don't Cry, Bo Peep" (Mark Holleran, Roger Lawson, Michael Calkins, Debbie McLeod), "Bare Facts" (see NOTES below), "Step Out in Front" (Mark Holleran, Roger Lawson, Michael Calkins, Debbie McLeod), "Dream Toyland" (Ken Bonafons, S. Barkley Murray, Edward T. Jacobs, Shari Watson, Roger Lawson, Mark Holleran, Michael Calkins, Nursery Rhyme Characters, Toyland Visitors)

ACT TWO—"The Two of Us" (Mark Holleran, Debbie McLeod), "March of the Wooden Soldiers" (Mona Finston, Robert Hancock, Lynn Hippen, Dan Kruger, Steve Mathews, S. Barkley Murray, Alan F. Seiffert), "Disco Toyland" (Company)

NOTES—*The Babes in Toyland* was an updated version of Victor Herbert's venerable operetta *Babes in Toyland*, which had originally opened at the Majestic Theatre on October 13, 1903, and played for 192 performances.

It's unclear if *The Babes in Toyland* was under a Broadway or an Off Broadway contract. *Theatre World 1979-1980 Season* includes the production in its Off Broadway survey, and while *The Best Plays of 1979-1980* mentioned the musical in passing (identifying it as "a special holiday attraction for children"), it didn't classify it as either a Broadway or an Off Broadway production.

In the musical, The Babes, a trio performing on a cross-country tour, hope to find success in show business. During the tour, they meet Mary, and soon the trio becomes a quartet. (This being the late 1970s, one number was called "Disco Toyland.")

The cast album and the souvenir program were subtitled "A Musical Fantasy for the 80's"; the album (released by the Dream Music Company and produced by Barry and Fran Weissler [LP # BIT-91550]) had limited distribution, and was apparently sold only in theatres where the musical played. The musical premiered on November 2, 1979, at the American Shakespeare Theatre in Stratford, Connecticut. According to the souvenir program, after the run in New York, the musical was scheduled to play in a number of cities, including Boston, Atlanta, and Philadelphia. "Where will it all end?" asked the souvenir program (and its answer was, "Not until there's a Babe in every borough").

Although the song "Bare Facts" wasn't mentioned along with the other numbers in the souvenir program, it was included on the cast album between "Don't Cry, Bo Peep" and "Step Out in Front" (the album didn't identify performers or names of the musical's characters); according to Richard C. Norton's *A Chronology of American Musical Theatre*, the song was performed by "The Babes" (that is, Mark Holleran, Roger Lawson, Michael Calkins, and Debbie McLeod).

For two weeks during December 1979, New York audiences had the chance to see dueling *Babes*. While *The Babes in Toyland* was playing at Felt Forum for its limited two-week engagement, a traditional version of the Herbert classic was produced by the Light Opera of Manhattan on November 28, 1979, for a limited run of thirty-five performances; this version didn't use Glenn McDonough's book and lyrics; instead, the revised book was by William Mount-Burke and Alice Hammerstein Mathias (the latter also wrote the new lyrics).

82 Back in the Big Time. "A New Musical"; THEATRE: South Street Theatre; OPENING DATE: October 2, 1986; PERFORMANCES: 12; BOOK: Abe Kroll; LYRICS: Johnny Brandon; MUSIC: Johnny Brandon; DIRECTION: Bernard Johnson; CHOREOGRAPHY: Henry LeTang; musical staging by Henry LeTang and Bernard Johnson; SCENERY: Don Jensen; COSTUMES: Bernard Johnson; LIGHTING: Kenneth Tabachnik; MUSICAL DIRECTION: Barry Levitt; PRODUCER: Robert E. Richardson

CAST—Jimmy W. Tate (Bongo), Marc Heller (Zoot), Shaun Baker-Jones (Little B), Bernard Pollock (Vincent Tedesco), Adam Bryant (Tom Booth), Nancy Salo (Melanie Tedesco), Ruth Adams (Linda Jones), HAROLD NICHOLAS (Ruddy Mack), Deborah Mitchell (Vi), Germaine Goodson (Bunny), Rashamella Cumbo (Sally), Michael Mitorotondo (Alex Heckler), Patrons of Kelly's Bar, etc. (Jeffrey Adams, Louis Baldonieri, Deonne Martin), MABLE LEE (Dawn Kingsley)

The musical was presented in two acts.

ACT ONE—"Street Rap" (Jimmy W. Tate, Marc Heller, Shaun Baker-Jones), "At Kelly's (You're a Star)" (Harold Nicholas, Company), "We've Got Quite a Future" (Harold Nicholas, Mable Lee), "We Did It" (Harold Nicholas, Shaun Baker-Jones), "Torching My Way Through Life" (Mable Lee), "Feel the Heat" (Deborah Mitchell, Germaine Goodson, Rashamella Cumbo), "Higher and Higher" (Ruth Adams, Adam Bryant), "If That's What Everyone Wants" (Ruth Adams), "Song and Dance Man" (Harold Nicholas)

ACT TWO—"Song and Dance Man" (reprise) (Harold Nicholas), "Street Rap" (reprise) (Jimmy W. Tate, Marc Heller, Shaun Baker-Jones), "Age Is Nothin'" (Harold Nicholas, Jimmy W. Tate, Marc Heller, Shaun Baker-Jones), "I've Tried Before" (Mable Lee), "The Hustling Executive" (Adam Bryant), "I Wasn't Prepared" (Adam Bryant, Ruth Adams), "Lady Lingerie" (Deborah Mitchell, Germaine Goodson, Rashamella Cumbo), "I Wasn't Prepared" (reprise) (Adam Bryant, Ruth Adams), "You'll Fit Right In" (Harold Nicholas, Adam Bryant), "Back in the Big Time" (Harold Nicholas, Mable Lee, Company)

NOTES—*Back in the Big Time* was one of two show business-themed musicals by Johnny Brandon produced Off Off Broadway during the 1986-1987 season (see entry for *Prime Time*).

The final scene and song in *Back in the Big Time* took place at the Walnut Street Theatre in Philadelphia.

83 Back to Bacharach and David. "A New Musical Revue"; THEATRE: Club 53; OPENING DATE: March 25, 1993; PERFORMANCES: 69; LYRICS: Hal David; MUSIC: Burt Bacharach; DIRECTION: Kathy Najimy; CHOREOGRAPHY: Javier Velasco; SCENERY: Peter Rogness; COSTUMES: David Loveless; LIGHTING: Maura Sheridan; MUSICAL DIRECTION: John Boswell; PRODUCERS: Daryl Roth, Hal Luftig, Alan D. Perry, Jim David, and Kathy Najimy

CAST—Melinda Gibb, Steve Gunderson, Sue Mosher, Lillias White

The revue was apparently presented in one act (the program listed songs in alphabetical order and didn't credit song assignments).

MUSICAL NUMBERS—"A House Is Not a Home," "Alfie" (from 1966 film *Alfie*), "Always Something There to Remind Me," "Another Night," "Any Old Time of Day," "Anyone Who Had a Heart," "Are You There with Another Girl," "Close to You," "Do You Know the Way to San Jose," "Don't Make Me Over," "I Just Have to Breathe," "I Say a Little Prayer for You," "I'll Never Fall in Love Again" (*Promises, Promises*, 1968), "Just Don't Know What to Do with Myself," "Knowing When to Leave" (*Promises, Promzises*, 1968), "Let Me Be Lonely," "Let Me Go to Him," "Message to Michael," "My Little Red Book," "Nikki," "One Less Bell to Answer," "Promises, Promises" (*Promises, Promises*, 1968), "Reach Out for Me," "The April Fools" (1969 film *The April Fools*), "The Look of Love" (1967 film *Casino Royale*), "This Empty Place," "This Guy's in Love with You," "Trains and Boats and Planes," "24 Hours from Tulsa," "Walk On By," "What the World Needs Now," "Whoever You Are, I Love You" (*Promises, Promises*, 1968), "You'll Never Get to Heaven"

NOTES—The short-running revue included many of Burt Bacharach and Hal David's pop songs, film songs, and even songs from *Promises, Promises*, their only Broadway musical ... but, alas, not a single number from their 1973 flop film musical *Lost Horizon*.

The revue had begun performances two weeks earlier at Club 53, when it opened under an Off Off Broadway contract beginning on March 11, 1993. It transferred to Off Broadway status on March 25. At one point or another during its run, "Another Night" and "The Windows of the World" were included in the score.

Another Bacharach-David tribute revue, *The Look of Love*, was seen on Broadway in 2003, playing for just forty-nine performances (it too ignored the *Lost Horizon* score).

On April 2, 1998, the Old Globe Theatre in San Diego offered *What the World Needs Now ... A Musical Fable* with a cast which included Sutton Foster. For this Bacharach-David tribute, one song from *Lost Horizon* was included ("The World Is a Circle"). Yet another recycling of Bacharach-David songs occurred when *Love Sweet Love* premiered in regional theatre at the Mesa Arts Center in Mesa, Arizona, on November 20, 2007; according to the musical's press release, thirty-one of the team's songs were used to tell the story of "four contemporary Los Angeles women looking for love during the week leading up to Valentine's Day." No word on whether any songs from *Lost Horizon* were used.

84 A Backers' Audition (1983). THEATRE: UpStage/Manhattan Theatre Club; OPENING DATE: December 13, 1983; PERFORMANCES: 48; BOOK: Douglas Bernstein and Denis Markell; LYRICS: Douglas Bernstein and Denis Markell; MUSIC: Douglas Bernstein and Denis Markell; DIRECTION: Martin Charnin; CHOREOGRAPHY: Janie Sell; SCENERY: Ray Recht; COSTUMES: Linda Fisher; LIGHTING: Marc B. Weiss; MUSICAL DIRECTION: William Roy; PRODUCER: Manhattan Theatre Club (Lynne Meadow, Artistic Director; Barry Grove, Managing Director)

CAST—Dana Vance (Nora, Maxine Abbott), Douglas Bernstein (Leonard, Haji Rahaji, Jed Rubin), Barbara Barrie (Esther Kanner), William Roy (Andrew Marks), Scott Robertson (Arthur Jay Kalodner), Mary D'Arcy (Kim Terry), Bill Fagerbakke (Don Costello), Nicholas Woodeson (Peter Pouncey)

The action occurs in Esther Kanner's living room at 850 Park Avenue at the present time.

The musical was presented in two acts.

ACT ONE—"Another Backer's Audition" (Ensemble), "Kalodner and Marks Revisited" (Scott Robertson, William Roy), "Herman" (Barbara Barrie), "Better" (Nicholas Woodeson)

ACT TWO—"Ick" (Mary D'Arcy), "Collaboration" (Scott Robertson, William Roy), "Over the Top" (Ensemble), "Herman" (reprise) (Barbara Barrie), "Over the Top" (reprise) (Ensemble)

Musical Selections from *Raggedy Romeo* performed during *A Backers' Audition*: (performers unknown [probably Mary D'Arcy, Bill Fagerbakke, William Roy, and Scott Robertson]):

ACT ONE—"Another New York Day," "A Regular Guy," "The Story of Lou," "What Do They Want," "Noah and Jeff," Finale

ACT TWO—"Blue Manhattan Nights," "Love Duet," "Over the Top"

NOTES—Backstage "let's-put-on-a-show" musicals have always been popular on stage and in film, and beginning in the mid-1970s the Broadway and Off Broadway musical saw a mini-trend in which fictitious new plays and musicals were viewed from the perspective of cast members, directors, writers, critics, and other insiders. *A Chorus Line* (1975; see entry) dealt with an upcoming new musical which was seen from the perspective of aspiring chorus dancers trying to land roles in the show (all we ever really know about the musical is that it will star a well-known actress who is perhaps singing-and-dancing challenged, and that the score will include a bouncy song called "One"); *A Broadway Musical* (1978; see entry) focused on the troubled rehearsal and tryout periods of a new musical called *Sneakers*; *Musical Chairs* (1980; see entry) was seen from the perspective of an opening-night audience attending a new play (*Forest of Shadows*); and *42nd Street* (1980) dealt with the trials and tribulations surrounding the rehearsals and tryout of a new Broadway musical called *Pretty Lady*.

The Off Off Broadway production of *A Backers' Audition* told the story of a backers' audition for *Raggedy Romeo*, a new musical for which a wealthy Park Avenue woman (Barbara Barrie) is the "angel."

Perhaps Richard Rodgers and Oscar Hammerstein II's *Me and Juliet* (1953) remains the ultimate look at a musical from almost every conceivable angle (the performers, the creators, the musicians, the stage hands, and audience).

Included in the cast of *A Backers' Audition* was William Roy, who played the composer of *Raggedy Romeo* (he was also the musical director for *A Backers' Audition*). Roy was an occasional contributor to Off Broadway revues as well as the composer and lyricist of the Broadway musical *Maggie* (1953) and the Off Broadway musical *The Penny Friend* (1966; see entry).

A Backers' Audition was revived by the American Jewish Theatre on December 7, 1992, for thirty-one performances; the cast included Sheila Smith and Tom Ligon.

85 Bad Habits of 1926. THEATRE: Greenwich Village Theatre; OPENING DATE: April 30, 1926; PERFORMANCES: 19; LYRICS: Arthur Herzog, Jr.; MUSIC: Manning Sherwin; PRODUCER: Irving Strouse

CAST—Elsie Bonwit, Flora Borden, Molly Burnside, Hume Derr, Kathleen Edwards, Harriet Hamil, Kathryn Hamil, Ann Schmidt, Florence Selwyn, John Mahin, Robert Montgomery, Billy Murray, Larry Starbuck, Willard Tobias, Day Tuttle, Marvin Vogel, Martin Wolfson

The revue was produced in two acts.

MUSICAL NUMBERS (division of acts and song and sketch assignments unknown; songs and sketches are listed in performance order)—"Are We Downhearted?" "When," "Gone Away Blues," "Station L-O-V-E," "Would-ja?" "Cinderella of Our Block," "Funeral of Charleston," "Manhattan Transfer," "Chorus Girl Blues," "Geisha Girl," "Let Me Be Myself," "The Student Robin Hood of Pilsen" (lyric by Perry Ivins, music by Randall Thompson), "Keep Your Shirt On," "The Lifeguards"

NOTES—In his review of *Bad Habits of 1926* in the *New York Times*, (J.) Brooks Atkinson noted one of the *worst* habits of the theatrical year was the proliferation of amateur revues on the New York stage. In the current instance, he found the cast members in a "transitional" period between amateur and professional standing, and suggested their performances gave more delight to themselves and their friends than to "hardened" theatergoers. He noted the chorus had a "frantic" quality about it, the dancers wore "forced smiles," the solo dancer offered "clumsy insinuations," and the lead comedian gave forth with "naughty innuendo." However, Atkinson singled out a couple of "limber tunes" with "serviceable" lyrics as well as a "dry lecture on the telephone that almost makes it point." "The Student Robin Hood of Pilsen" was a spoof of male musical-comedy chorus numbers.

Two of the revue's cast members went on to lengthy careers in show business; Robert Montgomery made his mark in film and television, and Martin Wolfson's stage appearances included the 1954 revival of *The Threepenny Opera* (see entry); early during the revival's run, he succeeded Leon Lishner in the role of Mr. Peachum, and it is Wolfson who is heard on the musical's cast album.

86 Bags. THEATRE: Three Muses Theatre; OPENING DATE: April 6, 1982; PERFORMANCES: 18; BOOK: Elizabeth Perry; LYRICS: Elizabeth Perry; MUSIC: Robert Mitchell; DIRECTION: Wally Strauss; Maggy Gorrill and Carole D'Andrea, Assistants; CHOREOGRAPHY: Wally Strauss; SCENERY: John Falabella; COSTUMES: David Murin; LIGHTING: David Segal; MUSICAL DIRECTION: Robert Mitchell; PRODUCERS: Jo Anne Vallier and Joseph Feury

CAST—Peggy Atkinson (Mrs. Rodriguez), Michael Blevins (Dangerous, Dealer), Juanita Fleming (Ms. Head), Don Gantry (Gus Rinalto), Maggy Gorrill (Lucky), Tiger Haynes (Bobby), Audre Johnston (Magda), Susan Kaslow (Badmouth, Sabrett's Woman), Stephani Low (Kiria), Thom McCleister (Buyer, Sonny, Demolition Man), Brian Sutherland

(Cop, Mambo), Fiddle Viracola (Meg), Michael Zaslow (Dr. Sheinberg)

The action occurs at the present time in New York City.

The musical was presented in two acts (division of acts and song assignments unknown; songs are listed in performance order).

MUSICAL NUMBERS—"It's Mine," "I Was Beautiful," "Bobby's Songs," "The Clean Ones," "Lady Wake Up," "This Is Where We Met," "So Much for Marriage," "Honky Jewish Boy," "Out on the Streets," "Street People's Anthem," "Lucky Me," "Song to Endangered Species," "Street Corner Song," "Schwesters," "The Freedom Song"

NOTES—The heroine of the 1965 Broadway musical *Skyscraper* found herself in battle with a construction company which wants to build on the site of her Manhattan brownstone. The bag-lady heroines of *Bags* faced a similar dilemma when they fight to save a block of brownstones from demolition in order to make way for a high-rise apartment building.

John S. Wilson in the *New York Times* complained that *Bags* was too often padded with the stories of the homeless women, and noted the "erratic" plot wavered between "the plausible and the inept." But he felt the score had a certain Kurt Weill-like flavor, and indicated the music was "most effective in the background that it establishes." Wilson remarked that the title of "Song to Endangered Species" brought to mind Weill and Bertolt Brecht, but the song was actually similar in subject matter to Richard Rodgers and Oscar Hammerstein II's "My Favorite Things" from *The Sound of Music* (1959).

The musical, which may have been produced under an Off Off Broadway contract, opened at the Three Muses Theatre, which was located in the Ansonia Hotel.

87 Baker's Dozen. "A New Post-Prandial Prank ... A Farinaceous Farrago"; THEATRE: PLaza 9-Room; OPENING DATE: January 9, 1964; PERFORMANCES: 469; SKETCHES: William F. Brown, Dee Caruso, Robert Elliott, Bill Levine, and Treva Silverman; LYRICS: Louis Botto, Michael Brown, Lesley Davison, Clark Gesner, Bud McCreery, Don Parks, George Ploner, June Reizner, William Roy, Fred Tobias, Rod Warren, and G. Wood; Compere Continuity written by William F. Brown; MUSIC: Michael Brown, Lesley Davison, William Dyer, Clark Gesner, Stan (Stanley) Lebowsky, Bud McCreery, Margaret Perrin, June Reizner, William Roy, John Simon, Rod Warren, and G. Wood; DIRECTION: Frank Wagner and Julius Monk; CHOREOGRAPHY: Julius Monk; COSTUMES: Bill Belew; LIGHTING: Don Lamb; MUSICAL DIRECTION: William Roy and Robert Colston at the plural pianos, and Paul Trueblood at the singular piano; PRODUCER: Julius Monk

CAST—Gerry Matthews, Jamie Ross, Nagle Jackson, Ruth Buzzi, Barbara Cason, Delphi Harrington, Richard Blair, Jan Templeton

The revue was presented in two acts.

ACT ONE—Overture (William Roy and Robert Colston), "Baker's Dozen" (lyric and music by William Roy) (Company) "Avis" (sketch by Dee Caruso and Bill Levine) (Gerry Matthews, Barbara Cason) "Megalopolis" (lyric and music by Lesley Davison) (Richard Blair, Ruth Buzzi, Jan Templeton) "White House Comics" (sketch by Robert Elliott and William F. Brown) (Gerry Matthews, Barbara Cason, Nagle Jackson, Delphi Harrington), "Water Pollution" (lyric by Rod Warren, music by William Roy) (Ruth Buzzi, Jan Templeton, Jamie Ross, Richard Blair) "Never Say Die" (sketch by William F. Brown) (Jamie Ross, Delphi Harrington, Gerry Matthews, Nagle Jackson) "Avon Garde" (lyric and music by Rod Warren) (Richard Blair) "Mescaline Hat Dance" (lyric by Louis Botto, music by John Simon, introduction by William F. Brown) (Gerry Matthews, Jamie Ross, Nigel Jackson, Richard Blair) "The Gripe of the Group" (lyric by Don Parks, music by William Dyer) (Delphi Harrington), "The Bag with Which You Shop" (lyric and music by Lesley Davison, introduction by William F. Brown) (Ruth Buzzi, Barbara Cason, Delphi Harrington, Jan Templeton, [and some of the male members of the cast, specific ones not identified]) "The Old Eight-Ten" (lyric and music by G. Wood) (Jamie Ross) "Who's Afraid of I. J. Fox" (sketch by William F. Brown) (Gerry Matthews, Barbara Cason, Jan Templeton, Nagle Jackson) "A New Italian Folk Song" (lyric by Fred Tobias, music by Stan [Stanley] Lebowsky) (Gerry Matthews) "(Cries in the) Common Marketplace" (lyric and music by Lesley Davison) (Company) ACT TWO, "Double-O Or Nothing" (sketch by William F. Brown) (Gerry Matthews, Jamie Ross, Ruth Buzzi, Nagle Jackson) "National Service Corps" (lyric and music by Bud McCreery) (Ruth Buzzi) "Fourteen Hours and Thirty-Seven Minutes" (lyric and music by Clark Gesner) (Nagle Jackson) "Wherefore Are Thou, Romeo" (lyric by George Ploner, music by Margaret Perrin) (Jan Templeton), "Hang Down Your Head, Jane Dooley" (sketch by William F. Brown) (Gerry Matthews, Barbara Cason), "Merry-Go-Round" (lyric and music by G. Wood) (Barbara Cason), "Barry's Boys" (lyric and music by June Reizner) (Gerry Matthews, Jamie Ross, Nagle Jackson), "East Side, West Side" (sketch by Treva Silverman) (Gerry Matthews, Barbara Cason, Delphi Harrington, Jamie Ross, Nagle Jackson) "The Wonderful World-Wide Fair" (lyric and music by Michael Brown) (Company)

NOTES—The "Farinaceous Farrago" *Baker's Dozen* was another successful long-running revue by Monk and many of his stock company of writers, composers, and performers.

Michael Brown contributed another one of his songs dedicated to specific New York sites (this time, the World's Fair). "Who's Afraid of I.J. Fox" was a parody of Edward Albee, and other spoofs included swipes at astronauts, Ian Fleming, Mary McCarthy, the Common Market, Charles de Gaulle, and folk songs. "Barry's Boys" had been previously heard in *Dime a Dozen* (1962; see entry), and can be heard on that show's cast album; it was later used in *Bits and Pieces XIV*. "Merry-Go-Round" had been used in *Four Below Strikes Back* (1959; see entry) as "Merry-Go, Merry-Go-Round," and it was recorded on that revue's cast album. Milton Esterow in the *New York Times* noted that *Webster's Dictionary* defined "farinaceous" as "consisting of meal or flour" and "farrago" as a "medley." He concluded that *Baker's Dozen* was "delicious" and a "delight," an "entertaining platter" which was "well-baked" but needed "more dough" and "more seasoning." He praised a number of sketches and songs, but felt some were not particularly witty or imaginative.

In 1964, Random House published the complete script of the revue (all sketches and lyrics), and thus *Baker's Dozen* has the distinction of being the only classic revue of the period which was published in its entirety. Monk cites two performers in particular for the book's dedication, Ceil Cabot and Jenny Lou Law.

For a complete list of Julius Monk's revues, see entry for *Four Below*; also see Appendix Q.

88 The Baker's Wife. "A Musical Love Story"; THEATRE: Church of the Heavenly Rest; OPENING DATE: March 24, 1985; PERFORMANCES: 20; BOOK: Joseph Stein; LYRICS: Stephen Schwartz; MUSIC: Stephen Schwartz; DIRECTION: Stephen Schwartz; CHOREOGRAPHY: Lynne Taylor-Corbett; SCENERY: James Morgan; COSTUMES: Holly Hynes; LIGHTING: Mary Jo Dondlinger; MUSICAL DIRECTION: Tim Weil; PRODUCER: The York Theatre Company (Janet Hayes Walker, Producing Director; Molly Pickering Grose, Managing Director)

CAST—JACK WESTON (Aimable Castagner), Joyce Leigh Bowden (Genevieve), Kevin Gray (Dominique), Charles Goff (M. Le Marquis), Hal Robinson (Claude), Judith Lander (Denise), Gabriel Barre (Priest), Florence Anglin (Therese), Bert Fraser (Antoine), Paul O'Keefe (Phillipe), Pamela Clifford (Simone), Mayla McKeehan (Inez), Gail Pennington (Nicole)

SOURCE—The 1938 French film *La Femme du Boulanger* (screenplay by Marcel Pagnol and Jean Giono).

The action occurs in a small village in the South of France.

The musical was presented in two acts.

ACT ONE—"Chanson" (Judith Lander), "Voila" (Jack Weston, Joyce Leigh Bowden), "Bread" (Villagers), "Proud Lady" (Kevin Gray), "Gifts of Love" (Jack Weston, Joyce Leigh Bowden), "Chanson" (reprise) (Judith Lander), "Serenade" (Kevin Gray, Paul O'Keefe, Jack Weston, Joyce Leigh Bowden), "Meadowlark" (Joyce Leigh Bowden)

ACT TWO—"Any-Day-Now-Day" (Jack Weston, Villagers), "Chanson" (reprise) (Judith Lander), "I Could Never Get Enough of You" (Joyce Leigh Bowden, Kevin Gray), "Feminine Companionship" (Charles Goff, Pamela Clifford, Mayla McKeehan, Gail Pennington, Jack Weston), "If I Have to Live Alone" (Jack Weston), "New Musketeers" (Charles Goff, Villagers), "Where Is the Warmth?" (Joyce Leigh Bowden, Jack Weston, Judith Lander)

NOTES—Stephen Schwartz has enjoyed many successes (*Godspell* [see entry], *Pippin, The Magic Show, Wicked*) but perhaps his best score is *The Baker's Wife*. The musical closed during its pre-Broadway tryout in 1976, and its later (1989) London production was a failure, running a disappointing fifty-six performances; but the musical has surfaced in many regional theatres, and the Off Off Broadway production by the York Theatre Company marked its first New York engagement. The book is somewhat slow and lacks true dramatic action, but it's nonetheless a charming, atmospheric mood piece. The plot, a love triangle concerning a young woman, a young man, and an older man, is somewhat similar to two other musicals set in France, *Fanny* (which was based on a play by Marcel Pagnol, who had also co-written the screenplay of the 1938 film *La Femme du Boulanger*, the source of *The Baker's Wife*) and *The Umbrellas of Cherbourg* (see entry), as well as one set in the Napa Valley, *The Most Happy Fella*. What made *The Baker's Wife* memorable was Schwartz' richly romantic and melodic score, which included "Meadowlark," one of the finest songs ever written for the musical theatre. In the original 1976 production, "Meadowlark" was thrillingly sung by Patti LuPone, and Paul Sorvino was a warm and touching Aimable who sang with brio; he replaced Topol, whose performance lacked the heart-breaking intensity which Sorvino brought to the role. Included in the original cast were Portia Nelson, Kurt Peterson, Teri Ralston, and David Rounds. The York production didn't include all the songs which were heard during the original production's five-month tryout (for example, "Merci, Madame," a delightful duet for Aimable and Genevieve was omitted), but offered four songs not heard in the 1976 production ("New Musketeers," "Voila," "I Could Never Get Enough of You," and "Feminine Companionship"). "Voila" had been heard in a 1983 Chicago version of the musical, and "Feminine Companionship" was later included in the 1989 London production.

There are two recordings of the score: the original (Sorvino-LuPone) cast on Original Cast Records (LP # THT-772; CD # THT-CD-891) and the 2-LP London cast recording on That's Entertainment Records (# TER2-1175; CD # CDTER-1175).

89 Balancing Act. "A New Musical Comedy"; THEATRE: Westside Theatre; OPENING DATE: June

15, 1992; PERFORMANCES: 56; BOOK: Dan Goggin; LYRICS: Dan Goggin; MUSIC: Dan Goggin; DIRECTION: "Directed and Staged by" Tony Parise and Dan Goggin; SCENERY: Barry Axtell; COSTUMES: Mary Peterson; LIGHTING: Paul Miller; MUSICAL DIRECTION: Michael Rice; PRODUCER: The N.N.N. Company

CAST—The Main Character: Craig Wells (The Ambitious Side), Diane Fratantoni (The Sensitive Side), Christine Toy (The Optimistic Side), J.B. Adams (The Skeptical Side), Suzanne Hevner (The Humorous Side); Everybody Else—Anyone, Harriet Stottlemeier, Maisie, Mr. Revere, Jane Pickford-Bellingham, Dr. Sybil (Nancy E. Carroll)

The action occurs in Hometown, U.S.A., New York, and Hollywood at the present time.

The musical was presented in two acts.

ACT ONE—"Life Is a Balancing Act" (Company), "Next Stop: New York City" (Craig Wells, Diane Fratantoni, Christine Toy, J.B. Adams, Suzanne Hevner), "Home Sweet Home" (Craig Wells, Diane Fratantoni, Christine Toy, J.B. Adams, Suzanne Hevner), "Play Away the Blues" (Nancy E. Carroll), "My Bio Is a Blank" (Nancy E. Carroll, Craig Wells, Diane Fratantoni, Christine Toy, J.B. Adams, Suzanne Hevner), "A Tough Town" (Craig Wells, Diane Fratantoni, Christine Toy, J.B. Adams, Suzanne Hevner), "I Left You There" (Diane Fratantoni), "A Tough Town" (reprise) (Craig Wells, Diane Fratantoni, Christine Toy, J.B. Adams, Suzanne Hevner), "A Twist of Fate" (Craig Wells, Diane Fratantoni, Christine Toy, J.B. Adams, Suzanne Hevner), "A Casting Call" (Nancy E. Carroll, Craig Wells, Diane Fratantoni, Christine Toy, J.B. Adams, Suzanne Hevner), "The Fifth from the Right" (Suzanne Hevner), "You Heard It Here First" (J.B. Adams), "A Long, Long Way" (Christine Toy), "The Woman of the Century" (Nancy E. Carroll, Craig Wells, Diane Fratantoni, Christine Toy, J.B. Adams, Suzanne Hevner)

ACT TWO—"Welcome, Bienvenue" (Nancy E. Carroll), "Where Is the Rainbow" (Craig Wells), "I Am Yours" (Craig Wells, Diane Fratantoni, Christine Toy, J.B. Adams, Suzanne Hevner), "That Kid's Gonna Make It" (Nancy E. Carroll), "Chew Chewy Chow" (Nancy E. Carroll, Craig Wells, Diane Fratantoni, Christine Toy, J.B. Adams, Suzanne Hevner), "Hollywood 'n' Vinyl" (Christine Toy, Diane Fratantoni, Suzanne Hevner), "California Suite" (Craig Wells, Diane Fratantoni, Christine Toy, J.B. Adams, Suzanne Hevner, Nancy E. Carroll), "I Am Yours" (reprise) (Craig Wells, Diane Fratantoni, Christine Toy, J.B. Adams, Suzanne Hevner), "I Knew the Music" (Craig Wells, Diane Fratantoni, Christine Toy, J.B. Adams, Suzanne Hevner), "Life Is a Balancing Act" (reprise) (Company)

NOTES—*Balancing Act* was Dan Goggin's first musical after his enormously successful (and then still-running) *Nunsense* (see entry); but instead of presenting a deliberately silly and amusing free-for-all in the style of *Nunsense*, he opted for a pretentious story of an aspiring show business wannabe (who is played by five performers) told from the perspective of the character's five sides (ambitious, sensitive, optimistic, skeptical, and humorous). The result was a dreary and tiresome evening which told its revue-like story without wit and freshness.

The musical struggled on for seven weeks, but eventually joined *Nunsense* in repertory, playing at the Douglas Fairbanks Theatre for a brief period on Sunday nights when *Nunsense* was dark. The musical had first been presented by the Seven Angels Theatre in Waterbury, Connecticut. The cast album was released by DRG Records (CD # 19004). A much earlier version of the musical was produced in the early 1980s as *One-Way Ticket to Broadway* (see entry), which included five songs later used in *Balancing Act*.

90 Ballad for a Firing Squad. "A Musical"; THEATRE: Theatre de Lys; OPENING DATE: December 13, 1968; PERFORMANCES: 7; BOOK: Jerome Coopersmith; LYRICS: Martin Charnin; MUSIC: Edward Thomas; DIRECTION: Martin Charnin; CHOREOGRAPHY: Alan Johnson; SCENERY: James Tilton; COSTUMES: Theoni V. Aldredge; LIGHTING: James Tilton; MUSICAL DIRECTION: Joyce Brown; PRODUCERS: Edward Thomas; presented by special arrangement with Lucille Lortel Productions, Inc.

CAST—BRUCE SCOTT (The Young Solider), STANLEY CHURCH (Major Bonnard), JAMES HURST (LaFarge), Liz Sheridan (Countess, Claudine), RENATA VASELLE (Mata Hari), ADELLE RASEY (Paulette), Elliott Savage (General Delacorte), George Marcy (Duvalier, Philipe), Vi Velasco (Pistolette), Neva Small (Michele), Irma Rogers (Mme. Dupre), Dominic Chianese (Maurice, Old French Soldier), Peter Shawn (First American Soldier), Joseph Corby (Second American Soldier)

The action occurs during World War I (specifically, 1917) on the battlefields, in the salons, and in the offices of the French Intelligence Service in Paris.

The musical was presented in two acts.

ACT ONE—"Ballad for a Firing Squad" (Bruce Scott), "Is This Fact?" (James Hurst, Stanley Church), "Dance at the Salon" (Renata Vaselle), "There Is Only One Thing to Be Sure Of" (Renata Vaselle, Company), "How Young You Were Tonight" (James Hurst, Adelle Rasey), "I'm Saving Myself for a Soldier" (George Marcy, Vi Velasco, Company), "Everyone Has Something to Hide" (Renata Vaselle), "Fritzie" (Bruce Scott), "The Choice Is Yours" (Renata Vaselle, James Hurst), "Sextet" (Adelle Rasey, Liz Sheridan, Irma Rogers, George Marcy, Neva Small, Dominic Chianese), Maman (Bruce Scott), "Not Now, Not Here" (Renata Vaselle), "Is This Fact?" (reprise) (James Hurst), "Maman" (reprise) (Bruce Scott)

ACT TWO—"I Did Not Sleep Last Night" (Renata Vaselle), "Hello Yank" (Bruce Scott, Dominic Chianese, Peter Shawn, Joseph Corby), "I Don't See Him Very Much Any More" (Adelle Rasey), "Sextet" (reprise) (Adelle Rasey, Liz Sheridan, Irma Rogers, George Marcy, Neva Small, Dominic Chianese), "What Then?" (James Hurst), "What Might Have Been" (Renata Vaselle), "Ballad for a Firing Squad" (reprise) (Bruce Scott)

NOTES—This small-scale revival of *Mata Hari*, now titled *Ballad for a Firing Squad*, opened almost a year to the day of the original's closing, which had collapsed during its tryout at the National Theatre in Washington, D.C., at a loss of $500,000.

Originally titled *Façade*, *Mata Hari* quickly joined *Kelly* (1965) and *Holly Golightly/Breakfast at Tiffany's* (1966) as one of the most infamous flops in the history of the American musical. The first chaotic preview performance of *Mata Hari* became the stuff of legend, and the hopelessly inept musical closed a week early in Washington; it cancelled its second tryout engagement (in Philadelphia) and its January 13 opening at the Alvin (now Neil Simon) Theatre.

Despite a fine score and a fascinating if flawed book, *Mata Hari* was clearly not ready to face an audience. The book was too scattershot, awkwardly leaping back and forth between a French intelligence officer's affair with Mata Hari and his love of wife and family. (He wants Exciting Mistress ... but also wants Dependable Little Wife, and thus experiences the eternal musical-comedy dilemma of not being able to make up his mind.)

Perhaps having the same actress play the roles of both Mata Hari and the wife would have added a layer of ironic subtext to the plot. As it was, the musical shambled back and forth between the two stories, occasionally interrupted by scenes on the war front with a symbolic Young Soldier who sang the anti-war song "Maman." He was apparently a distant cousin to the M.C. in *Cabaret* (1966) and a forerunner to the Courier in *1776* (1969), the latter of whom sang the anti-war song "Mamma, Look Sharp." Further, *Mata Hari* had almost non-existent direction (literally, since director Vincente Minnelli decamped half-way through the Washington run), frequent-but-trite choreography (which came to life only once, in "I'm Saving Myself for a Soldier"), and bland performances (Pernell Roberts seemed stiff and uncomfortable, and Marisa Mell, in the words of that song about Bella Darvi in *The Billy Barnes Revue* [see entry], was mighty cute but awfully hard to understand). But *Mata Hari* was *big* ... it had lavish, spare-no-expense scenery, boutiques-full of costumes, and a large cast of actors, singers, and dancers.

When the tiny *Ballad for a Firing Squad* opened, it apparently had solved none of *Mata Hari*'s problems, and was just a miniature version of the original, thus coming across as *Mata Hari*-lite. The new version, which lost its entire investment of $60,000, emphasized the original's anti-war viewpoint but still could not create a compelling story about the two leading protagonists. (Incidentally, it appears that *Ballad for a Firing Squad* was originally considered for Lincoln Center's Mitzi E. Newhouse Theatre.)

New numbers used in *Ballad for a Firing Squad* were "There Is Only One Thing to Be Sure Of," "Fritzie," "I Did Not Sleep Last Night," "What Then?" and "What Might Have Been" and a title song. Numbers heard in Washington but which were not used in the revival were "This Is Not a Very Nice War," "Curiosity," "No More Than a Moment," "In Madrid," "Dance at the Café del Torro," "You Have No Idea," "There Is No You," "There Will Be Love Again," "Waltz at the Salon," and "Interrogation and Ballet" (a/k/a "The Arrest Ballet"). (By the second week of the Washington run, "This Is Not a Very Nice War," "Curiosity," and "No More Than a Moment" had been dropped from the show.)

The revival's "Dance at the Salon" was called "Mata Hari's Dance at the Salon" in Washington.

In 1996, the York Theatre revived the piece (as *Mata Hari*; see entry) in a limited engagement, but, like the original Washington, D.C., production, the York version closed a week early. However, the production led to the first and only recording of the score (by Original Cast Records; CD # OC-8600), incorporating numbers from the 1967 and 1968 versions as well as new songs specifically written for the York production. The CD included artwork of the posters for both *Mata Hari* and *Ballad for a Firing Squad*.

91 Ballad for Bimshire. "A New Musical of Barbados"; THEATRE: Mayfair Theatre; OPENING DATE: October 15, 1963; PERFORMANCES: 74; BOOK: Irving (Lord Burgess) Burgie and Loften Mitchell; LYRICS: Irving (Lord Burgess) Burgie; MUSIC: Irving (Lord Burgess) Burgie; DIRECTION: Ed Cambridge; CHOREOGRAPHY: Talley Beatty; SCENERY: Donald Ryder; COSTUMES: Mozelle Forte; LIGHTING: Verdon Enoch; MUSICAL DIRECTION: Sammy Benskin; PRODUCERS: Ossie Davis, Bernard Waltzer, and Page Productions

CAST—Alyce Webb (Vendor), Miriam Burton (Iris Boyce), CHRISTINE SPENCER (Daphne Byfield), FREDERICK O'NEAL ("Captain" Neddie Boyce), Ural Wilson (Grafton), Jim Trotman (Spence), Bobby Dean (Robert) Hooks (Dennis Thornton), Clebert Ford (Howie), Sylvia Moon (Millie), JIMMY RANDOLPH (Johnny Williams), OSSIE DAVIS (Sir Radio), Fran Bennett (Matron), Joe A. Callaway (Arthur Roundville), Lauren (Gloria) Jones (Maude), Hilda Harris (Hilda), Charles Moore (Watchman, Rooster), Eugene Edwards (Lead Man); Various Singers and Dancers: Barbara Alston, Lew Camacho, Ray Gilbert, Gloria Higdon, Lauren (Gloria) Jones, Hilary Kelley, Joan Peters, Geri Seignious, Ella Thompson

The action occurs in the recent past on the Windward Island of Barbados.

The musical was presented in two acts.

ACT ONE—Prologue: "Ballad for Bimshire" (Alyce Webb, Eugene Edwards, Clebert Ford), "Street Cries" (Alyce Webb), "Lately I've Been Feeling So Strange" (Christine Spencer, Alyce Webb), "'Fore Day Noon in the Mornin'" (Chorus, Frederick O'Neal), "Deep in My Heart" (Christine Spencer), "Have You Got Charm?" (Christine Spencer, Frederick O'Neal), "Hail Britannia" (Ossie Davis, Chorus), "Welcome Song" (Chorus), "Belle Plain" (Chorus), "I'm a Dandy" (Chorus), "Silver Earring" (Jimmy Randolph), "My Love Will Come By" (Christine Spencer, Jimmy Randolph), "Chicken's a Popular Bird" (Joe A. Callaway, with Charles Moore)

ACT TWO—"Deep in My Heart" (reprise) (Christine Spencer), "Pardon Me, Sir" (Clebert Ford), "Yesterday Was Such a Lovely Day" (Jimmy Randolph, Christine Spencer), "My Master Plan" (Christine Spencer), "Chant" (Alyce Webb), "Have You Got Charm?" (reprise) (Performer[s] Unknown), "Vendor's Song" (Alyce Webb), "We Gon' Jump Up" (Ensemble)

NOTES—*Ballad for Bimshire*, a short-lived musical concerning the romance of a Barbados Island girl and a New York playboy, has many delightful songs which were preserved on the cast album released by London Records (LP # AMS-78002).

Howard Taubman in the *New York Times* suggested the weak book be ignored and the lively score emphasized. He singled out no less than eight songs, including "Chicken's a Popular Bird," a production number which strutted and shuffled with "irresistible abandon" and "gleaming humor." Taubman felt the musical brought its own heat wave from the Caribbean, and noted that with such numbers as the "sizzling" "Chant," the Mayfair Theatre need not worry about heating bills upon the arrival of fall weather.

As Mozelle, the musical's costume designer Mozelle Forte designed memorable poster artwork for such Broadway musicals as *The Gay Life* (1961) and *Purlie* (1970). *Ballad for Bimshire* was briefly revived Off Off Broadway by the Negro Ensemble Company on November 19, 1994.

92 The Ballad of Baby Doe. "An Opera"; THEATRE: New York City Center; OPENING DATE: April 3, 1958; PERFORMANCES: Unknown; BOOK: John LaTouche; MUSIC: Douglas Moore; DIRECTION: Vladimir Rosing; SCENERY: Donald Oenslager; COSTUMES: Donald Oenslager; MUSICAL DIRECTION: Emerson Buckley; PRODUCER: New York City Opera Company

CAST—Howard Fried (An Old Silver Miner), Chester Ludgin (A Saloon Bartender, A Denver Politician), Walter Cassel (Horace Tabor), Keith Kaldenberg (Sam. Clerk), Jack De Lon (Bushy, President Chester Alan Arthur), George Del Monte (Barney), Arthur Newman (Jacob, Footman), Frances Bible (Augusta), Beverly Sills (Mrs. Elizabeth [Baby] Doe), Greta Wolff (Kate), Helen Baisley (Mag, Silver Dollar [Elizabeth as an adult]), Lynda Jordan (Samantha), Robert Atherton (Albert), Mary Lesawyer (Sarah), Jennie Andrea (Mary), Lou Rodgers (Emily), Dorothy White (Effie), Beatrice Krebs (Mama McCourt), Four Washington Dandies (Edson Hoel, Dan Marek, Peter Sliker, John Dennison), McCourt Family (Greta Wolff, Helen Baisley, Donald Arthur, William Saxon), Grant Williams (Father Chappelle), Lynn Taussig (Elizabeth as a child), William Saxon (Mayor of Leadville), Joshua Hecht (Stage Doorman of the Tabor Grand Theatre), Chorus (Jennie Andrea, Donald Arthur, Robert Atherton, Anthony Balestrieri, George Del Monte, John Dennison, Frank Ehrhardt, William Golden, Edson Hoel, Lynda Jordan, Mary Lesawyer, Dan Marek, Rita Metzger, Margaret Rae, Lou Rodgers, William Saxon, Peter Sliker, Lynn Starling, Marshall Stone, Dorothy White, Greta Wolff, Maria Yavne)

The action occurs in Leadville, Denver, and Washington, D.C.

The opera was presented in two acts.

ACT ONE—Opening (Orchestra), "It's a Bang-Up Job" (Walter Cassel, Jack De Lon, Keith Kaldenberg, George Del Monte, Arthur Newman), "Horace, What Is This?" (Frances Bible), "I Beg Your Pardon" (Beverly Sills), "What a Lovely Evening" (Leadville Ladies and Men), "Willow, Where We Met Together (Willow Song)" (Beverly Sills), "Oh, Mr. Tabor" (Beverly Sills), "Warm as the Autumn Light" (Walter Cassel), "Now, Where Do You Suppose?" (Frances Bible), "Have You Seen Her?" (Frances Bible), "What Are You Looking For, Horace?" (Frances Bible), "Why, Mrs. Doe!" (Keith Kaldenberg), "Dearest Mama (Letter Song)" (Beverly Sills), "Excuse Me" (Frances Bible), "I Knew It Was Wrong" (Beverly Sills), "No! No! No!" (Beverly Sills, Walter Cassel), "What Do You Intend to Do?" (Mary Lesawyer, Jennie Andrea, Lou Rodgers, Dorothy White, Frances Bible), "Everything Looks Beautiful" (Beatrice Krebs), "Gold Is a Fine Thing (Silver Aria)" (Beverly Sills), "And I'll Show You Something Else" (Walter Cassel)

ACT TWO—Opening (Orchestra), "The Fine Ladies" (Beverly Sills), "Mama, Go Inside!" (Beverly Sills), "Augusta, What Are You Doing Here?" (Walter Cassel), "I'll Raise You" (Jack De Lon, Keith Kaldenberg, George Del Monte, Arthur Newman), "Turn Tail and Run!" (Walter Cassel), "La, La, La, La" (Leadville Ladies), "Good People of Leadville" (Joshua Hecht), "Extra! Extra!" (Newsboys), "Augusta! Augusta!" (Frances Bible), "Hey, Mister!" (Grant Williams), "The Cattle Are Asleep" (Walter Cassel), "Tabor Owns the Big Hotel" (Chorus), "Horace!" (Beverly Sills), "Always Through the Changing" (Beverly Sills)

NOTES—One of the greatest of American operas, *The Ballad of Baby Doe* told the true story of the young and beautiful Baby Doe, who left her poor husband for the rich, powerful, and already-married Horace Tabor. Horace divorced his wife Augusta and married Baby Doe at the Willard Hotel in Washington, D.C., with President Chester Alan Arthur in attendance. But when the United States adopted the gold standard, Horace's fortune was lost, and he died penniless in 1899. Baby Doe, true to his memory, lived on at the Matchless Mine just outside Leadville, and there froze to death in 1935.

The colorful characters and dramatic action, along with atmospheric settings in Colorado and Washington, D.C., had the makings of a fine fictional opera, and so the opera was all the more touching because it told a true story. Its premiere took place on July 7, 1956, in Central City, Colorado, at the Central City Opera House (Baby Doe had actually attended productions at the theatre in the late nineteenth century). Baby Doe was played by Dolores Wilson, Walter Cassel was Tabor, and Martha Lipton was Augusta (the alternating cast members were respectively Lenya Gabriele, Clifford Harvuot, and Frances Bible).

On April 3, 1958, Cassel and Bible reprised their roles for the first New York performance, and Beverly Sills made her triumphant debut as Baby Doe, forever assuring her place in the history of American opera. Because of opera's tradition of alternating cast members, at the third New York performance the role of Augusta was played by Ruth Kobart.

Douglas Moore's rich, melodic score and John LaTouche's poetic text (the New York program identified his contributions as the "book" of the opera; the words "libretto" and "text" weren't used, although the original Central City production identified his contribution as the "libretto") have all but guaranteed the opera its permanent place in the repertory of modern opera. The musical sequences for Baby Doe's character are particularly memorable, and include the "Willow" and "Letter" songs as well as the moving finale ("Always Through the Changing") which she sings as the snow begins to fall around her. Perhaps the highlight of the work is "Gold Is a Fine Thing," which, ironically, is actually known as the Silver Aria. In this magnificent wedding of words and music, Baby Doe sings of the glory of gold, but finds silver more precious because it is hidden in the "core" of dreams.

The opera has been revived numerous times by the New York City Opera, and in 1976 it was shown on public television (Ruth Welting was Baby Doe, Richard Fredricks was Tabor, and Frances Bible reprised her role of Augusta).

The opera was recorded by MGM Records on a 3-LP set (# 3GC-1) which was reissued first by Heliodor Records (# H/HS-25035-3) and then by Deutsche Grammophon (# 2709-061; later released on CD by Deutsche Grammophon in 1999 [# 289-465-148-2-GH-2]). The above cast list and song list is taken from this CD. A recording of a 1996 revival by the Central City Opera was released by Newport Classic Records (# NPD-85593/2); Jan Grissom was Baby Doe, Brian Steele was Tabor, and Dana Kreuger was Augusta.

One edition of the libretto was issued by the Program Publishing Company in 1966; another edition was published in the mid-1990s as a Washington Opera Publication (with permission of Warner Brothers Publications, Inc.).

There was *almost* a film version of the opera. In the early 1970s, *Variety* reported that filming by Winter-Atlas Productions/Oceana Films was to begin during Summer 1971, with a budget of four million dollars. The opera was to be filmed on location in Leadville, Central City, Denver, and Washington, D.C., and Beverly Sills was to recreate her role. Alas, the project never came to fruition.

Another lyric work based on the Baby Doe saga is *Silver Dollar*, which was briefly produced by Goodspeed Musicals at the Norma Terris Theatre in Chester, Connecticut, beginning on November 2, 1995. The book and lyrics were by Mary Bracken Phillips, and the music by Jack Murphy. Elizabeth Richmond was Baby Doe, George Ball was Horace Tabor, and Phillips was Augusta. *Silver Dollar*, a film version of the story, was released in 1932, three years before Baby Doe's death (the characters' names were changed), and the cast included Bebe Daniels, Edward G. Robinson, and Aline MacMahon.

93 The Ballad of Johnny Pot. THEATRE: Theatre Four; OPENING DATE: April 26, 1971; PERFORMANCES: 16; BOOK: Carolyn Richter; LYRICS: Carolyn Richter; MUSIC: Clinton Ballard; DIRECTION: Joshua Shelley; CHOREOGRAPHY: Jay Norman; SCENERY: Lloyd Burlingame; COSTUMES: Alvin Colt; LIGHTING: Lloyd Burlingame; MUSICAL DIRECTION: Harrison Fisher; PRODUCERS: Wyler Productions and Bob McDevitt

CAST—Leroy Lessane (Leroy, White Cloud), BETTY BUCKLEY (Sarah), JOHN BENNETT PERRY (Johnny Pot), Sandra Thornton (Sandra), Colin Garrey (Watson), Nancy Dalton (Nancy), Tony Stevens (Tony, The Fugitive, The Hayseed), Sharron Miller (Sharron), Robert Berdeen (Bob, Preacher), David Eric (David, Happy Man), Ben Bryant (Garwood Heever), Peter Jason (Marshal), Barbara Brownell (Desiree), Jim Weston (H.L.), The Boys (Robert Berdeen, David Eric, Tony Stevens), Kids (Sharron Miller, Nancy Dalton, Sandra Thornton)

The action occurs in the early 1970s, in the United States of America "as it was then."

The musical was presented in two acts.

ACT ONE—"The Ballad of Johnny Pot" (Leroy Lessane, Company), "Johnny's Creed" (John Bennett Perry, Friends), "The Ballad of Johnny Pot" (reprise) (Company), "Hard Hat Stetsons" (Ben Bryant, Peter Jason), "The Letter" (Betty Buckley,

Ben Bryant, Peter Jason, John Bennett Perry), "Discarded Blues" (Barbara Brownell, Robert Berdeen, David Eric, Tony Stevens), "Whaddaya Say Kid" (Jim Weston, Company), "Crazy" (John Bennett Perry, Betty Buckley), "Head Down the Road" (John Bennett Perry), "A Carol" (Jim Weston, Company), "Lonely Is the Life" (John Bennett Perry, Barbara Brownell, Colin Garrey), "What About Me" (Betty Buckley), "Have Some Pot" (Company)

ACT TWO—"The Ballad of Johnny Pot" (reprise) (Company), "Scared" (John Bennett Perry, Colin Garrey), "How Wonderful It Is" (Betty Buckley), "I Like It" (John Bennett Perry), "Dance of Distraction" (Barbara Brownell, Robert Berdeen, David Eric, Tony Stevens), "Johnny's Creed" (reprise) (John Bennett Perry), "The Ballad of Johnny Pot" (reprise) (Sandra Thornton, Sharron Miller, Nancy Dalton), "Saskatchewan" (Colin Garrey), "Little Sparrows" (Ben Bryant, Jim Weston, Peter Jason), "Find My Way Alone" (John Bennett Perry, Betty Buckley), "The Ballad of Johnny Pot" (reprise) (Company)

NOTES—The burning question for audiences attending the next rock musical was always, What will be the name of the musical's band? For *The Ballad of Johnny Pot*, the band was called Bandana.

The title role of Johnny Pot was performed in previews by John Carradine, who left the production two days before the opening because of "artistic differences." He was replaced by his understudy, John Bennett Perry, who had earlier been seen in *Now Is the Time for All Good Men* (1967), *Month of Sundays* (1968), and *Show Me Where the Good Times Are* (1970); see entries. (Perry later appeared in the New York premiere of Leonard Bernstein's *Mass* [see entry]). Mel Gussow in the *New York Times* noted the opening-night "cliff-hanger" was whether or not Perry would remember his lines (Yes) and if a new star was born (No). Gussow didn't think much of the musical, and noted the choreography was of the "crowded discotheque" variety. He also mentioned the scenery consisted of "enough lumber to build six barns and 10 corrals," and said if the show ran long enough, the producers would "be faced with dry rot." The producers never had to deal with that problem, because the musical closed after two weeks of performances.

The musical dealt with a Johnny Appleseed-type, a hippie who unfortunately plants marijuana instead of apple trees. (Only in the 1970s.)

94 Ballet Ballads.

THEATRE: East 74th Street Theatre; OPENING DATE: January 3, 1961; PERFORMANCES: 40; WORDS: John LaTouche; MUSIC: Jerome Moross; CHOREOGRAPHY: Mavis Ray, John Butler, and Glen Tetley; SCENERY: Gary Smith; COSTUMES: Hal George; LIGHTING: Jules Fisher; MUSICAL DIRECTION: Don Smith; PRODUCER: Ethel Watt

The evening of three ballet ballads, *Riding Hood Revisited*, *Willie the Weeper*, and *The Eccentricities of Davy Crockett (as told by himself)*, was presented in three acts.

ACT ONE—*Riding Hood Revisited* (choreography by Mavis Ray)

CAST—Lisa Brummett (Mrs. Nature), Alice Scott (Cloud), Lorraine Roberts (Cloud), Sallie Bramlette (Cloud), Dounia Rathbone (Dragon Fly), Veronika Mlakar (Riding Hood), Gregg Nickerson (Good Humor Man), Buck Heller (Viennese Wolf), Dianne Nicholson (Granny); The Dancers (portraying Trees, Flowers, Animals, and Skyscrapers): Pauline de Groot, Betty de Jong, Ellen Graff, Phyllis Lamhut, Fred Herko, Steve Paxton, Bob Powell, Jon Rager, Dounia Rathbone, Robert Helloway; The Singers (portraying Trees, Flowers, Animals, and Skyscrapers): Sallie Bramlette, Dianne Nichols, Lorraine Roberts, Alice Scott, Ted Bloecher, Derek de Cambra, Ted Lambrinos, Gregg Nickerson, Ed Zimmerman, Abbe Todd

MUSICAL NUMBERS—Overture, "Rhumba," "Pastorale," "Waltz and Variations," "Coda"

ACT TWO—*Willie the Weeper* (choreography by John Butler)

CAST—Glen Tetley (Dancing Willie), Carmen de Lavallade (Cocaine Lil), Arne Markussen (Singing Willie); Pauline de Groot, Betty de Jong, Ellen Graff, Phyllis Lamhut, Fred Herko, Steve Paxton, Bob Powell, Jon Rager, Robert Helloway (Dancers); Sallie Bramlette, Dianne Nichols, Lorraine Roberts, Alice Scott, Ted Bloecher, Derek de Cambra, Ted Lambrinos, Gregg Nickerson, Ed Zimmerman, Abbe Todd (Singers)

The action takes place in Willie's "untidy mind."

MUSICAL NUMBERS—Introduction, "Did You Ever Hear About Willie the Weeper?" Episode I—Rich Willie, "Has a Million Cattle," Episode II—Lonely Willie, "I'm Mister Nobody," Episode III—Famous Willie, "He's Wonderful," Episode IV—Baffled Willie, "No Thoroughfare," Episode V—Super Willie, "They Can't Scare Me," Episode VI—Self-Sufficient Willie, "I've Got Me," Episode VII—Lover Willie, "Introducin' Yuh to Cocaine Lil," "Oh Baby and Gee Baby," Finale, "Poor Dreamy Willie"

ACT THREE—*The Eccentricities of Davy Crockett (as told by himself)* (choreography by Glen Tetley)

CAST—Jack Mette (Davy Crockett), Betty de Jong (First Girl, Dancing Grace Sherwood), Pauline de Groot (Second Girl), Ellen Graff (Third Girl, Dancing Ann Hutchinson), Sallie Bramlette (Sally Ann), Ed Zimmerman (Indian Chief, Singing John Oldman, President Andrew Jackson), Fred Herko (Indian, Hunter, Dancing Nathaniel Bacon, Congressman), Steve Paxton (Indian, Brown Bear, Dancing John Oldman, Congressman), Bob Powell (Indian, Hunter, Congressman), Jon Rager (Indian, Hunter, Congressman), Ted Bloecher (Soldier, Singing Nathaniel Bacon), Derek de Cambra (Soldier), Ted Lambrinos (Soldier, Ghost Bear), Gregg Nickerson (Soldier), Alice Scott (Mermaid), Carmen de Lavallade (The Comet), Dianne Nichols (Singing Ann Hutchinson), Lorraine Roberts (Singing Grace Sherwood); Dancers and Singing Ensemble portrayed Voters, Gallery Spectators, Friends, and Neighbors

MUSICAL NUMBERS—Introduction/The People Gather to Celebrate the Memory of Davy Crockett, "Oh, the Western Star Is Riding Low," Young Davy in the Backwoods, "Funny Kind of Lad Is Davy," The Courtship of Davy, "Young Women," Davy Marries Sally Ann, "Sally Ann," They Journey to the Frontier, They Build a House in the Wilderness, "Peace Be on This House of Logs," The Indian War, "Cherokee, Choctaw, Shawanoe," On the Banks of the Tennessee River, "You're My Yaller Flower," Davy Catches a Mermaid in the River, "I Swam Upstream This Morning," Davy Saves the World from Halley's Comet, "There's a Comet A-Comin'," Davy Goes on a Bear Hunt, "Oh, Davy Would a-Huntin' Ride," Davy in the Haunted Cave, "Brave Hunter," Davy Goes to Congress, "Maybe I Should Cut Some Public Capers," "Ridin' on the Breeze," Finale, "Davy Journeyed to the Alamo"

NOTES—Although *Ballet Ballads* was a critical success when it originally opened on Broadway in 1948, it ran for a disappointing two months (sixty-nine performances). Reviewing the original production in the *New York Post*, Richard Watts found the evening a "happy" blend of the "gayest features of ballet, music, and folk drama." The sung-through all danced musical consisted of three folk-dance-plays, with words by John LaTouche and music by Jerome Moross, both of whom collaborated on another critical (and limited audience) success, *The Golden Apple* (see entry), which is one of the greatest of American musicals.

In his review of the 1961 Off Broadway revival of *Ballet Ballads* for the *New York Times*, Howard Taubman hoped the "curiosity of venturesome theatergoers" would allow the production "a new lease on life," but, unfortunately, the production folded in five weeks.

The 1948 production consisted of three ballet ballads: *Susanna and the Elders*, choreographed by Katherine Litz; *Willie the Weeper*, choreographed by Paul Godkin; and *The Eccentricities of Davy Crockett (as told by himself)*, choreographed by Hanya Holm. *Susanna* told the Biblical story as a sermon presented at a revival meeting. *Willie* took place in Willy's "untidy mind"; as a result of his marijuana smoking, Willie's dreams take him through a number of unrelated hallucinatory episodes which include his attendance at his own funeral as well as meeting Cocaine Lil (Sono Osato in the original Broadway production) who lives on Cocaine Hill with her cocaine dog and her cocaine cat (not to mention the cocaine rats). *Davy Crockett* depicted a series of Davy's tall tales, including his encounter with a mermaid; his adventures on a bear hunt; in a haunted cave; in the Indian War; and the time he stopped Halley's Comet in its track.

When *Ballet Ballads* was revived Off Broadway in 1961, *Susanna and the Elders* was replaced by *Riding Hood Revisited*, which as *Red Riding Hood* had been intended for the original 1948 production but had never been fully completed. It may be that *Susanna* wasn't retained for the current program because of the popularity in the intervening years of Carlisle Floyd's operatic version of the piece (as *Susannah*; see entry). As for the two ballet ballads from the original production, the original choreography for *Willie* and *Davy* by Paul Godkin and Hanya Holm wasn't retained, and John Butler and Glen Tetley created new choreography for the pieces.

Ballet Ballads was a fascinating experiment, and it's a shame it hasn't become part of the American ballet repertoire. Maybe one day a ballet company will see fit to revive it.

The scintillating boogie-woogie, blues-inflected score of *Willie the Weeper* was recorded by Naxos Records (CD # 8-559086) in a collection of Jerome Moross' music called *Moross: Frankie and Johnny*; identifying *Willie* as a "dance cantata," the CD offered *Willie* in a thirty-five-minute sequence performed by the Hot Springs Music Festival Symphony Orchestra and Chamber Chorus and the tenor John DeHaan. The CD identified the musical's numbers as "Introduction," "Rich Willie," "Lonely Willie," "Famous Willy," "Baffled Willie," "Big Willie," "Contented Willie," and "Sexy Willie."

Windflowers, a collection of Jerome Moross' music recorded by PS Classics (CD # 0307-01022), included "My Yellow Flower" ("You're My Yeller Flower") and "Ridin' on the Breeze" from *The Eccentricities of Davy Crockett*; "I've Got Me" from the "Contented Willie" (a/k/a "Self-Sufficient Willie") sequence of *Willie the Weeper*; and "Oh Baby, Gee Baby" (a/k/a "Oh, Oh, Baby" and "Oh Baby and Gee Baby") from the "Sexy Willie" (a/k/a "Lover Willie") sequence of *Willie the Weeper*. The recording also included "Come Live with Me," which it attributed to *Willie the Weeper*; however, the song doesn't appear in either the Naxos recording of the complete score or in the published script, and the lyric itself doesn't seem to match Willie's character (unless it was intended for a proposed sequence in which Willie dreams he's a straight-laced suburbanite, which, for Willie, would be a true nightmare indeed).

The 2000 John LaTouche tribute-revue *Taking a Chance on Love* (see entry) included four songs from *The Eccentricities of Davy Crockett* ("Opening," "My Yellow Flower," "Ridin' on the Breeze," and "Finale") and two numbers from *Willie the Weeper*, "Oh, Oh, Baby" (a/k/a "Oh Baby, Gee Baby" "Oh Baby and Gee Baby") from the "Sexy Willie" (a/k/a "Lover Willie") sequence and "Mr. Nobody" from the "Lonely Willie" sequence. All the songs are included on the revue's cast recording which was released by Original Cast Records (CD # OC-4444).

The script of the original Broadway production was published by Chappell & Co. in 1949; each of the three ballet ballads was published separately as well as together in one volume. The script includes all lyrics and stage directions as well as the piano score.

95 Ballet Russes. THEATRE: American Theatre of Actors; OPENING DATE: January 6, 1994; PERFORMANCES: 6; BOOK: Bernard Myers; LYRICS: David Reiser; MUSIC: David Reiser; DIRECTION: Karen Berman; CHOREOGRAPHY: Oleg Briansky; SCENERY: Michael Stepowany; COSTUMES: Rodney Munoz; LIGHTING: Kevin Lawson; MUSICAL DIRECTION: C. Colby Sachs; PRODUCER: American Theatre of Actors

CAST—Carmen DeMichael (Serge Diaghilev), Gary Martin (Gregoriev), Peter Jacobsson (Vaslav Nijinksy), Robert Maiorano (Fokine), Jenni Hjalmarson (Tata), Rachel Hennelly (Mattilda), Stephen DeLorenzo (Baron DeGunzburg), Christie Cox (Romola), Brad Menendez (Stravinsky)

The action occurs during the period 1909-1923.

The musical was presented in two acts (division of acts and song/dance assignments unknown; musical numbers are listed in performance order).

MUSICAL NUMBERS—"Le Dieu Bleu," "Golden Slave," "Something Wonderful," "When You're Intimate with the Czar," "When You're in Love," "Les Sylphides," "Afternoon of a Faun," "I'm Through with You," "Waltz," "We Need Money," "Petrouchka," "Le Spectre de la Rose," "He's So Near," "Rite of Spring," "Les Sirens," "Prayer," "A Revelation," "Final Dance"

NOTES—The Off Off Broadway musical *Ballet Russes* dealt with the love affair of Nijinksy and Diaghilev, two legends of the ballet world. Other figures of the era, such as Fokine and Stravinsky, were also depicted in the musical, which included sequences from various ballets associated with the main characters.

96 Band-Wagon. Theatre: Bil Baird's Theatre; OPENING DATE: March 16, 1973; PERFORMANCES: 75; PRODUCERS: The American Puppet Arts Council (Arthur Cantor, Executive Producer)

NOTES—*Band-Wagon* (a/k/a *Bandwagon*), directed by Lee Theodore and with musical direction by Alvy West, was performed by the Bil Baird's Marionette Company. The sequences in the two-act musical are as follows:

ACT ONE—"Lift Off!" "It's Happening!" "Tables," "Punch and Judy," "The Dance," "Toy Bird," "The Tale of the Caliph Stork," "You're My Everything," "Spring, Sun and Flowers"

ACT TWO—"About Puppets," "Bill Bailey," "The Dying Swan," "Whaddya Read?" "The Stars," "Rope Dancers," "Old MacDonald Had a Farm," "Cecilia"; Finale

The evening was in effect an expanded version of *Bil Baird's Variety* (a/k/a *A Pageant of Puppetry*), the sequence which usually followed all of Bil Baird's puppet musicals and which explained the background and techniques of puppetry to the children in the audience. For *Band-Wagon*, Mel Gussow in the *New York Times* reported that the evening of variety offered background about puppetry as well as a number of comic and musical sequences (including guest appearances by Winnie the Pooh, Davy Jones, and the Wolf, all stars from other Baird musicals).

97 Banjo Dancing, or The 48th Annual Squitters Mountain Song Dance Folklore Convention and Banjo Contest ... and How I Lost. THEATRE: Century Theatre; OPENING DATE: October 21, 1980; PERFORMANCES: 38. Devised by Stephen Wade (with Milton Kramer); DIRECTION: Milton Kramer; SCENERY: David Emmons; LIGHTING: Dennis Parichy; PRODUCERS: Stuart Oken, Jason Brett, and The Klezmer Corporation; An Apollo Group Production in association with Jeffrey Wachtel

CAST—STEPHEN WADE

The revue was presented in two acts (spoken sequences and songs not listed in program).

NOTES—Stephen Wade's one-man revue was an amiable evening of music, stories, jokes, and a bit of clog dancing, and while it didn't last long in New York, it had a long and healthy life in regional theatre. *Banjo Dancing* was first performed in Chicago in May 1979, and with its brief New York run as well as its regional theatre engagements (including a marathon run at Washington D.C.'s Arena Stage), the revue played continuously until May 1989; at that time, it was followed by *On the Way Home*, a new Stephen Wade revue which opened at the Arena Stage during Summer 1989. In 1990, Flying Fish Records released *Dancing Home* (CD # FF-70543), which included numbers from both *Banjo Dancing* and *On the Way Home*.

98 The Banker's Daughter. "A New Musical"; THEATRE: Jan Hus House; OPENING DATE: January 21, 1962; PERFORMANCES: 68; BOOK: Edward Eliscu; LYRICS: Edward Eliscu; MUSIC: Sol Kaplan; DIRECTION: David Brooks; CHOREOGRAPHY: Lee Sherman; SCENERY: Kim Swados; COSTUMES: Peter Joseph; LIGHTING: Jules Fisher; MUSICAL DIRECTION: Arthur Lief; PRODUCERS: Claire Nichtern, Paul Libin

CAST—TONY KRABER (Captain Fairweather), KAREN MORLEY (Mrs. Charlotte Fairweather), Karen Duke (Nursemaid), TOM NOEL (Jonas Puffy), LLOYD GOUGH (Gideon Bloodgood), PHIL LEEDS (Oliver Badger), Kermit Herd (Financial Investor, Florist), Cliff Wayne (Financial Investor, Valet), Frank Groseclose (Financial Investor, Edwards), Fred Patrick (Financial Investor, Police Officer, Rowe Schuyler), Kathryn Humphreys (Financial Investor, Lady's Maid, Sophie), Evelyn Kingsley (Financial Investor, Lily, Parlor Maid), JOELLE JONS (Lucy Fairweather), Cliff Wayne (John Taylor), HELENA SCOTT (Alida Bloodgood), DAVID DANIELS (Mark Livingstone)

SOURCE—Dion Boucicault's early nineteenth-century play *Streets of New York*.

The action occurs in New York City in 1837 and 1857.

The musical was presented in two acts.

ACT ONE—"Gentlemen's Understanding" (Lloyd Gough, Tony Kraber, Phil Leeds), "Such a Beautiful World" (Lloyd Gough, Kermit Herd, Cliff Wayne, Frank Groseclose, Fred Patrick, Kathryn Humphreys, Evelyn Kingsley), "Genteel" (Helena Scott), "In a Brownstone Mansion" (David Daniels, Joelle Jons), "Such a Beautiful World" (reprise) (David Daniels), "Both Ends Against the Middle" (Phil Leeds, Tom Noel), "The Sun Rises" (Helena Scott), "Father's Daughter" (Lloyd Gough, Helena Scott), "Say No More" (Joelle Jons, David Daniels), "Father's Daughter" (reprise) (Lloyd Gough, Helena Scott)

ACT TWO—"One More Chance" (Tom Noel, Kermit Herd, Cliff Wayne, Frank Groseclose, Fred Patrick, Kathyrn Humphreys, Evelyn Kingsley), "Unexpectedly" (Joelle Jons), "In Time" (Helena Scott, David Daniels), "In Time" (reprise) (Helena Scott), "Nero, Caesar, Napoleon" (Lloyd Gough), "Head in the Stars" (Evelyn Kingsley, Kathryn Humphreys), "Sleep, O Sleep" (Karen Morley, Phil Leeds), "A Carriage for Alida" (Helena Scott), "It's So Heartwarming" (Frank Groseclose, Cliff Wayne, Kathryn Humphreys, Evelyn Kingsley), Finale (Company)

NOTES—*The Banker's Daughter* was the first of two musical adaptations of Boucicault's play *Streets of New York* which opened Off Broadway within two seasons (see entry for *The Streets of New York* [1963]).

Howard Taubman in the *New York Times* was ecstatic over the score for *The Banker's Daughter*, finding it "one of the most ambitious and flowingly melodic" of the season; he noted that Sol Kaplan's songs were "spacious and long-breathed" and occasionally reminded him of the "great romantic composers." He pronounced the songs as "the real thing ... generous, lilting and sentimental," and singled out five in particular ("In a Brownstone Mansion," "In Time," "Nero, Caesar, Napoleon," "Sleep, O Sleep," and "It's So Heartwarming"). Unfortunately, the musical was never recorded.

The song list is taken from a January 1962 program, which is either a preview program or one issued soon after the opening, and it's at variance with the musical numbers listed in *Theatre World Season 1961-1962*. For the record, the reference book lists a first-act opening number ("One More Day") and a second-act opening number ("More Than One More Day"), both of which are not in the program; moreover, the songs "One More Chance" and "In Time" are listed in the program, but not in *Theatre World*; and a comparison of the program with *Theatre World* reveals a considerable re-ordering of the songs in the second act.

Incidentally, *The Banker's Daughter* was a reunion of sorts for Kaplan and David Brooks. Brooks, who starred in the original Broadway productions of *Bloomer Girl* (1944) and *Brigadoon* (1947), played the leading role of Billy the Kid in Kaplan's *Shootin' Star*, which closed during its pre-Broadway tryout in 1946.

99 Banned in France. THEATRE: O'Neals' 43rd Street Cabaret; OPENING DATE: July 21, 1983; PERFORMANCES: Unknown; MATERIAL: Terry Sweeney, Carey Cromelin, Ginger Donelson, Lanier Laney, and Walter Thomas; DIRECTION: Arthur Collis; PRODUCER: Arthur Collis

CAST—Terry Sweeney, Carey Cromelin, Ginger Donelson, Lanier Laney, Walter Thomas

NOTES—The five writers-performers in *Banned in France* called themselves The Bess Truman Players. In his review for the *New York Times*, Stephen Holden found the material (with one important exception) all too one-note in its comic targets (the snooty French; a television program which each week presents "a different Christian dilemma"). But Holden had glowing words for Terry Sweeney and his vicious impersonation of a certain female television talk-show hostess who like a "famished piranha" zeroes in on her celebrity targets. Sweeney played Connie Chutzpah with "fiendish zeal" as she "navigates through the limousine-infested currents" of celebrity in her quest to interview Linda Evans, Brooke Shields' mother, and "Princess Caroline of Morocco." Holden noted that having Connie played by a man only added to the sketch's amusement.

100 Bar Mitzvah Boy. THEATRE: American Jewish Theatre; OPENING DATE: June 10, 1987; PERFORMANCES: 16 (estimated); BOOK: Jack Rosenthal; American adaptation by Martin Gottfried; LYRICS: Don Black; MUSIC: Jule Styne; DIRECTION: Robert Kalfin; Andrew Glant-Linden, Assistant Director; CHOREOGRAPHY: Larry Hayden; SCENERY: Eugene Gurlitz; COSTUMES: Gail Cooper-Hecht; LIGHTING: Brian MacDevitt; MUSICAL DIRECTION: Buster Davis; PRODUCER: American Jewish Theatre (Stanley Brechner, Artistic Director)

CAST—Peter Smith (Eliot Green), Harold Shepard (Rabbi Kaplan), Mary Gutzi (Rita), Mary Stout (Lucille), John Barone (Solly), Michael Callan (Herbert), Eleanor Reissa (Lesley), Daniel Marcus (Harold), Kimberly Stern (Denise), Reuben Schafer (Grandfather)

SOURCE—The 1976 BBC-teleplay *Bar Mitzvah Boy* by Jack Rosenthal.

The action occurs in Brooklyn in 1946.

The musical was presented in two acts.

ACT ONE—Overture, "Taxis at Midnight" (Company), "Why" (Harold Shepard), "If Only a Little Bit Sticks" (Peter Smith), "The Cohens Are Coming" (Company), "I'm Grown Up" (Peter Smith), "This Time Tomorrow" (Mary Gutzi, Eleanor Reissa, Michael Callan, Reuben Schafer, Daniel Marcus), "The Harolds of This World" (Daniel Marcus, Eleanor Reissa), "We've Done All Right" (Michael Callan, Mary Gutzi), "Simcha" (Mary Gutzi, Company), "You Wouldn't Be You" (Eleanor Reissa), "Sabbath Services" (Harold Shepard)

ACT TWO—"Kill Me" (Mary Gutzi), "Why Did I Do It" (Peter Smith), "Why Can't He Be Like Me" (Michael Callan, Daniel Marcus, Harold Shepard, Reuben Schafer), "That's Grown Up" (Eleanor Reissa, Peter Smith), "Hamakom" (Harold Shepard), "I've Just Begun" (Peter Smith), "I've Just Begun" (reprise) (Peter Smith)

NOTES—British-born Jule Styne wrote just one musical for the London stage, *Bar Mitzvah Boy*, which opened at Her Majesty's Theatre on October 31, 1978, for a disappointing run of seventy-seven performances (the London production was directed by Martin Charnin and choreographed by Peter Gennaro). The musical told the story of Eliot Green, who on the eve of his bar mitzvah is overwhelmed by the brouhaha of the social aspects of the ceremony. On his big day, he runs away, leaving his family and friends in the lurch at the synagogue. When his sister sees him on a playground, she accuses him of running away because he didn't know his prayers, but in fact he's able to recite all of them. When his rabbi discovers Eliot said his prayers, the rabbi concludes God is everywhere, and that prayers spoken on a playground are just as valid as those spoken in a synagogue. The rabbi then pronounces Eliot bar mitzvahed, and Eliot reconciles with his family and goes to the ceremony, now a little older and wiser and ready to journey into adulthood.

The slight story wasn't helped by Styne's pleasant if generally unmemorable score. Indeed, the best song was recycled from another of Styne's shows: the music of "The Harolds of This World" was taken from "Not Mine," a lovely ballad from *Hallelujah, Baby!* (1967).

The American Jewish Theatre's production represented the American premiere of the musical. During previews, the show was called *Song for a Saturday*, but by opening night the musical had reverted to its original title. During the preview period, Larry Keith played the role of Rabbi Kaplan, and Michael Cone was Solly.

Songs from the London production which weren't used in the American version were "The Bar Mitzvah of Eliot Green," "Thou Shalt Not," "The Bar Mitzvah," "Where Is the Music Coming From?" and "The Sun Shines Out of Your Eyes." Numbers heard in New York but not in London were "The Cohens Are Coming," "I'm Grown Up," "Sabbath Services," "Why Did I Do It," "Why Can't He Be Like Me," "That's Grown Up," and "Hamakom." Apparently Rita's London song "Rita's Request" was heard as "Kill Me" in New York.

The original London cast album was released on LP by CBS Records (# 70162), and was later issued on CD by Sony West End Records (# SMK-53498).

In a January 25, 2007, *Playbill* article, Zachary Pincus-Roth reported that a special reading of *Bar Mitzvah Boy* was scheduled for January 26 at the Chelsea Studios; among the cast members for the reading were Faith Prince, Daniel Reichard, Peter Friedman, and Larry Keith (the latter had played the role of Rabbi Kaplan during the preview period of the production's Off Off Broadway run in 1987). Pincus-Roth noted the reading would include "never-before-heard Styne tunes that were not necessarily intended for *Bar Mitzvah Boy*," and that Don Black was writing lyrics for these songs as well as revising lyrics for some of the old ones.

101 The Bar That Never Closes. "A New Musical"; THEATRE: Astor Place Theatre; OPENING DATE: December 3, 1972; PERFORMANCES: 33; BOOK: Louisa Rose; SKETCHES: Marco Vassi; LYRICS: Louisa Rose, John Braswell, and Tom Mandel; MUSIC: Tom Mandel; DIRECTION: John Braswell; SCENERY: Bar drop painting (and logo) by Susan Haskins; MUSICAL DIRECTION: Cathy MacDonald; PRODUCERS: Albert Poland and Bruce Mailman; Ina Lea Meibach, Associate Producer

CAST—Jennie Mortimer (Anybody, Little Woman), Susan Haviland (Mistaken Man, Mrs. Schneider), Nancy Schwartz (Old Woman), Richard Westlein (Michael, Table and Spigot), Mary Jo Kaplan (Mrs. Dear, Anybody's Friend's Friend), Kyle Andersen (Mr. Dear), Lane Binkley (Girl), Bill Eddy (God), Ralph Smith and Kyle Anderson (Lovers), Sara Parker (Anybody's Friend), Barbara Greca (Homosexual, Elevator Girl, Debutante), Jean Andalman (Singing Bar), Raina Hefner (Nurse, Harry), Christopher Lamal (Doctor), Barbara Greca and Bill Eddy (The Libidoes), Kyle Andersen (Riddle's Woman), Camille Tibaldeo (Butch Medusa), Mad People (Ensemble)

The revue was presented in two acts.

ACT ONE—"Walking with You, Two by Two" (lyric by Louisa Rose) (Ensemble), "Do It" (lyric by John Braswell) (Jennie Mortimer, Ensemble), "Recipe for Love" (lyric by John Braswell) (Nancy Schwartz, Ensemble), "Kaleidoscope" (lyric by Louisa Rose) (Sara Parker)

ACT TWO—"I Don't Think I'll Ever Love You" (lyric by John Braswell) (Ensemble), "Dear, Dear" (lyric by Tom Mandel) (Raina Hefner), "Tears of Ice" (lyric by Louisa Rose) (Jean Andalman), "Circus of Jade" (lyric by John Braswell) (Camille Tibaldeo), "Precious Little Darkness" (lyric by Louisa Rose) (Jennie Mortimer)

NOTES—*The Bar That Never Closes* was a loosely constructed book musical which dealt with the general topic of sexual loneliness.

Clive Barnes in the *New York Times* felt the subject matter was more suited to revue or cabaret format, but noted that while the evening was "not perfect" he "liked it a lot." It was a show with "a style, a manner and an attitude," but he warned it was also sometimes "rude and raw" (although not necessarily "tasteless"). The musical had previously been produced Off Off Broadway at La Mama Experimental Theatre Club (ETC) on September 9, 1972, as *Everything for Anybody*. In reviewing that production for the *New York Times*, Mel Gussow found the self-described "amatorio in 12 scenes" a kind of "sexual Story Theatre," and noted that while the evening offered very "specialized" delectations, it was "much funnier than several highly commercial erotic shows" that he could name.

102 Das Barbecu. "A New Musical Comedy"; THEATRE: Minetta Lane Theatre; OPENING DATE: November 10, 1994; PERFORMANCES: 30; BOOK: Jim Luigs; LYRICS: Jim Luigs; MUSIC: Scott Warrender; DIRECTION: Christopher Ashley; CHOREOGRAPHY: Stephen Terrell; SCENERY: Eduardo Sicangco; COSTUMES: Eduardo Sicangco; LIGHTING: Frances Aronson; MUSICAL DIRECTION: Jeff Halpern; PRODUCERS: Thomas Viertel, Steven Baruch, Richard Frankel, Jack Viertel, Dasha Epstein, Margery Klain, Leavitt/Fox/Mages, and Daryl Roth; Mitchell Maxwell and Alan Schuster, Co-Producers

CAST—Julie Johnson (Narrator, Fricka, Erda, Needa Troutt, Back-Up Singer, Katsy Snapp, Rivermaiden, Valkyrie), J.K. Simmons (Wotan, Gunther, Hagen, Texas Ranger, Dwarf, Giant), Jerry McGarity (Siegfried, Norn Triplet, Milam Lamar, Alberich, Giant), Carolee Carmello (Gutrune, Norn Triplet, Texas Ranger, Dwarf, Freia, Y-Vonne Duvall, Rivermaiden, Valkyrie, Tambourine Girl), Sally Mayes (Brunnhilde, Norn Triplet, Texas Ranger, Dwarf, Rivermaiden, Valkyrie)

SOURCE—Richard Wagner's four-part opera cycle *Der Ring des Nibelungen* (*Das Rheingold* [1854], *Die Walkure* [1856], *Siegfried* [1871], and *Gotterdammerung* [1874]).

The action occurs in a variety of locations throughout present-day Texas.

The musical was presented in two acts.

ACT ONE—"A Ring of Gold in Texas" (Company), "What I Had in Mind" (Sally Mayes, Jerry McGarity, Carolee Carmello, J.K. Simmons), "Hog-Tie Your Man" (Carolee Carmello, Sally Mayes, Jerry McGarity), "Makin' Guacamole" (Julie Johnson, Jerry McGarity, Carolee Carmello), "Rodeo Romeo" (Jerry McGarity, Julie Johnson, Carolee Carmello), "County Fair" (Sally Mayes), "Public Enemy Number .1" (Carolee Carmello, Sally Mayes, J.K. Simmons)

ACT TWO—"A Little House for Me" (Carolee Carmello), "River of Fire" (J.K. Simmons), "If Not Fer You" (J.K. Simmons, Jerry McGarity), "Slide a Little Closer" (Jerry McGarity, Sally Mayes), "Barbecue for Two" (Sally Mayes, Carolee Carmello), "After the Gold Is Gone" (Carolee Carmello, Julie Johnson, Sally Mayes), "Wanderin' Man" (Jerry McGarity, Julie Johnson), "Turn the Tide" (Sally Mayes, Julie Johnson, J.K. Simmons), Closing (Company)

NOTES—*Das Barbecu* was an amiable spoof of Wagner's *Ring* cycle, here transplanted to modern-day Texas. Although essentially a one-joke show (which might have worked better as a short one-act musical), the book and score were amusing, and so it's surprising the musical ran no more than a month.

Ben Brantley in the *New York Times* generally liked the show; he found it "slightly risque" and "mildly arch," and noted it was "middle camp, something you could happily take the kids to." The score was "mostly forgettable ... but tuneful," and Christopher Ashley's direction was "as smooth as chiffon pie."

The cast recording was released by Varese-Sarabande Records (CD # VSD-5593), and the script was published by Samuel French, Inc., in 1995. The musical had premiered at the Seattle Opera in 1991, and was later seen at the Goodspeed Opera House in Chester, Connecticut, and Center Stage in Baltimore, Maryland.

For another spoof of the *Ring*, see entry for *Der Ring Gott Farblonjet*.

103 Bare. "A Pop Opera"; THEATRE: Chernuchin Theatre/American Theatre of Actors; OPENING DATE: April 19, 2004; PERFORMANCES: 43; BOOK: John Hartmere, Jr., and Damon Intrabartolo; LYRICS: John Hartmere, Jr.; MUSIC: Damon Intrabartolo; DIRECTION: Kristin Hanggi; CHOREOGRAPHY: Sergio Trujillo; SCENERY: David Gallo; COSTUMES: David C. Woolard; LIGHTING: Mike Baldassari; MUSICAL DIRECTION: Damon Intrabartolo; PRODUCERS: Dodger Stage Holding and Jack Grossbart/Marc Schwartz; William M. Apfelbaum and Amanda DuBois, Associate Producers

CAST—Sasha Allen (Tanya), Michael Arden (Peter), Romelda T. Benjamin (Sister Chantelle), Isaac Calpito (Alan), Mike Cannon (Zach), Adam Fleming (Lucas), Kearran Giovanni (Kyra), Jenna Leigh Green (Ivy), John Hill (Jason), Kaitlin Hopkins (Claire), Natalie Joy Johnson (Nadia), Aaron Lohr (Matt), Jim Price (Priest), Lindsay Scott (Rory), Kay Trinidad (Diane) The action occurs in a Catholic boarding school.

The musical was presented in two acts.

ACT ONE—"Epiphany" (Company), "You and I" (John Hill, Michael Arden, Students), "Role of a Lifetime" (Michael Arden), "Auditions" (Students,

Romelda T. Benjamin, Kaitlin Hopkins), "Love, Dad" (Natalie Joy Johnson, John Hill), "Wonderland" (Adam Fleming, Sasha Allen, Aaron Lohr, Natalie Joy Johnson, Jenna Leigh Green, John Hill, Michael Arden), "A Quiet Night at Home" (Natalie Joy Johnson), "Rolling" (Students), "Best Kept Secret" (Michael Arden, John Hill), "Confession" (Students, Jim Price), "Portrait of a Girl" (Jenna Leigh Green, Aaron Lohr), "Birthday, Bitch!" (Students), "One Kiss" (Jenna Leigh Green, John Hill), "Are You There?" (Aaron Lohr, Michael Arden) "911! Emergency!" (Romelda T. Benjamin, Kearran Giovanni, Sasha Allen, Michael Arden), "Reputation Stain'd" (Students), "Ever After" (Michael Arden, John Hill), "Spring" (Natalie Joy Johnson), "One" (Jenna Leigh Green, John Hill, Aaron Lohr, Natalie Joy Johnson, Michael Arden)

ACT TWO—"Wedding Bells" (Company), "In the Hallway" (Students, Jim Price), "Touch My Soul" (Jenna Leigh Green, John Hill), "See Me" (Michael Arden, Kaitlin Hopkins), "Warning" (Kaitlin Hopkins), "Pilgrim's Hands" (Students), "God Don't Make No Trash" (Romelda T. Benjamin, Michael Arden), "All Grown Up" (Jenna Leigh Green), "Promise" (John Hill, Jenna Leigh Green, Aaron Lohr, Michael Arden, Natalie Joy Johnson), "Once Upon a Time" (John Hill), "Cross" (Jim Price, John Hill), "Two Households" (Students, Romelda T. Benjamin), "Queen Mab" (Michael Arden, John Hill), "Bare" (Michael Arden, John Hill), "A Glooming Peace" (Students), "Absolution" (Jim Price, Michael Arden), "No Voice" (Company)

NOTES—During its limited Off Off Broadway engagement, *Bare* created the kind of theatrical buzz which seemed to assure it an eventual Off Broadway run or even a Broadway production. But nothing happened, and two years later another musical about the same subject (sexual coming-of-age among teenagers) opened Off Broadway to new theatrical buzz and an eventual Broadway production, and so *Spring Awakening* (see entry) eclipsed whatever momentum *Bare* had once enjoyed. *Bare* was originally produced in Los Angeles at the Hudson Theatre on October 14, 2000.

Sh-K-Boom Records released an unnumbered "promotional use"–only cast album which included eleven songs from the production.

Incidentally, the musical eventually underwent a title change, from *Bare* to *bare*.

In 2007, a "deluxe edition" 2-CD studio cast album (among the singers were Kaitlin Hopkins and Jim Price, two original cast members) was released in a package which included a one-hour documentary DVD about the musical and the recording's history (the set was unlabeled and unnumbered). With the new recording, *bare* is likely to find its niche in regional, college, and community theatre. This recording represents the official licensed version of the musical, and includes the following songs (the names of the characters follow the song titles):

ACT ONE—"Epiphany" (Company), "You & I" (Jason, Peter, Students), "Role of a Lifetime" (Peter), "Auditions" (Sister Chantelle, Students), "Plain Jane Fat Ass" (Nadia, Jason), "Wonderland" (Lucas, Nadia, Ivy, Jason, Peter, Matt, Tanya), "A Quiet Night at Home" (Nadia), "Rolling," "Best Kept Secret" (Peter, Jason), "Confession" (Students, Priest), "Portrait of a Girl" (Ivy, Matt), "Birthday, Bitch!" (Students), "One Kiss" (Ivy, Jason), "Are You There" (Peter, Matt), "911! Emergency!" (Virgin Mary, Cherubs), "Reputation Stain'd" (Matt, Jason, Ivy, Nadia, Peter), "Ever After" (Peter, Jason), "Spring" (Nadia), "One" (Ivy, Jason, Nadia, Matt, Peter)

ACT TWO—"Wedding Bells" (Company), "In the Hallway" (spoken sequence; Jason, Peter, Matt, Ivy, Nadia, Lucas, Tanya), "Touch My Soul" (Ivy, Jason), "See Me" (Peter, Claire), "Warning" (Claire), "Pilgrim's Hands" (Jason, Peter), "God Don't Make No Trash" (Sister Chantelle), "All Grown Up" (Ivy), "Promise" (Jason, Ivy, Matt, Peter, Nadia), "Once Upon a Time" (Jason), "Cross" (Priest, Jason), "Two Households" (Sister Chantelle, Students), "Bare" (Jason, Peter), "Queen Mab" (Jason, Peter), "A Glooming Peace" (Students), "Absolution" (Peter, Priest), "No Voice" (Company)

104 Bartleby. THEATRE: York Playhouse; OPENING DATE: January 24, 1961; PERFORMANCES: 15; LIBRETTO: James Hinton, Jr., and Edward Albee; MUSIC: William Flanagan; DIRECTION: Bill Penn; SCENERY: William Ritman; COSTUMES: William Ritman; LIGHTING: William Ritman; MUSICAL DIRECTOR: James Leon; PRODUCERS: A Theatre 1961 Production (Richard Barr and Clinton Wilder)

CAST—Bruce MacKay (Mr. Allen), Allen Gildersleeve (Turkey), Emory Bass (Nippers), Edmund Gaynes (Ginger Nut), Robert Blossom (Bartleby)

SOURCE—The 1853 short story "Bartleby, the Scrivner" by Herman Melville.

NOTES—*Bartleby*, for which Edward Albee was the co-librettist, was a one-act opera which opened on a double bill with Albee's now-classic one-act play *The American Dream*. Due to poor reviews, *Bartleby* was dropped on February 5, after giving fifteen performances. On February 7, it was replaced with performances by the Valerie Bettis Dance Theatre (twenty-four performances through February 26); and in turn the dance company was replaced by Albee's one-act play *The Death of Bessie Smith* on February 28 (the play had been performed in Europe, and this production marked its New York premiere).

Howard Taubman in the *New York Times* praised William Flanagan's score, which he found graceful and not afraid to be "old-fashioned and melodic." But he felt *Bartleby*'s score did little to enhance to the overall mood of the work. *Bartleby* remains the most obscure work in the Albee canon. Even his libretto of *Breakfast at Tiffany's* (which closed during Broadway previews in 1966) is better known. In the early 2000s, the announcement that Albee's works would be collected in a series of volumes raised the (faint) hope that the scripts of *Bartleby* and *Breakfast at Tiffany's* would be included. Alas, they were not (but pirated scripts of *Breakfast at Tiffany's* have surfaced, which doesn't seem to be the case with *Bartleby*). Herman Melville has been frequently adapted for the musical stage. Besides *Bartleby*, there was a 1969 Broadway adaptation of *Billy Budd*, titled *Billy*. Despite a breath-taking set, exciting choreography by Grover Dale, and a few first-rate songs, the show closed on opening night. However, Benjamin Britten's 1951 operatic adaptation of *Billy Budd* has become one of the few modern operas to be performed with regularity on the world's opera stages. Not so with George and Gene Rochberg's 1982 operatic adaptation of *The Confidence Man*, which seems to have disappeared after its world premiere by the Santa Fe Opera (for a musical comedy adaptation of the novel, see entry for Jim Steinman and Ray Erol Fox's *The Confidence Man*). Also see entries for the Off Off Broadway musical *Moby Dick*, which vanished after its scheduled two-week run by the York Theatre Company, and the Off Broadway play with music *Pequod/The Next Voyage*, with closed after one performance.

105 Basin Street. "The Storyville Musical"; THEATRE: New Federal Theatre; OPENING DATE: September 8, 1983; PERFORMANCES: 15; BOOK: Michael Hulett and G. William Oakley; LYRICS: Michael Hulett; MUSIC: Turk Murphy; DIRECTION: G. William Oakley; CHOREOGRAPHY: Michael Gorman; SCENERY: Robert Edmonds; COSTUMES: Judy Dearing; LIGHTING: Jeremy Johnson; MUSICAL DIRECTION: Thom Birdwell; PRODUCER: Henry Street Settlement's New Federal Theatre (Woodie King, Jr., Producer; Barbara Tate, Executive Assistant of Arts and Administration; and Michael Frey, Executive Vice President)

CAST—Jeff Bates (Umbrella Man), Gloria Jones, Keith Williams, and Kevin DeVoe (Spasm Kids), J. Lee Flynn (Tom Anderson), Charles H. Patterson (Chauncey), Danny Rounds (Billy Struve), Erik Geier (Reporter), Shaun Jones (Aberdeen), Clebert Ford (Joe Oliver), Tamara Tunie (Yvette), Michael Potter (Creese), James Young (Leander), Lawrence Vincent (the Reverend Hapgood, Councilman Pelligrew), Sandra Reaves-Phillips (Harmony), Alexana Ryer (Adele), Pat Yankee (Lulu White), Jeffrey Bryan (Man #1), George Bernhard (Man #2); Female Ensemble (Patrice Hollrah, Mary Ann Lamb, Stephanie M. Pope, Diana Blue, Lise Simms, Alexana Ryer); Male Ensemble (George Bernhard, Jeffrey Bryan, Danny Rounds, James Young, Erik Geier)

The action occurs in the Storyville District of New Orleans in September 1917.

The musical was presented in two acts.

ACT ONE—"Chauncey's Tune" (Orchestra), "Call the Children Home" (Chorus), "All That It Takes" (J. Lee Flynn), "Penny Whistle Sweet" (Clebert Ford, J. Lee Flynn), "After" (Tamara Tunie), "The Sporting House Professor Blues" (Charles H. Patterson), "The Blue Book" (J. Lee Flynn, Chorus), "Soldiers of the Lord" (Lawrence Vincent, Chorus), "Song of My Fathers" (Sandra Reaves-Phillips, Charles H. Patterson), "Lady Gets Me There" (Charles H. Patterson), "Miss Lulu White" (Pat Yankee, Chorus), "After" (reprise) (Tamara Tunie)

ACT TWO—"Razzy Dazzy" (Spasm Band), "Ragtime Man" (Alexana Ryer, Tamara Tunie), "Chicago Drag" (Charles H. Patterson, Tamara Tunie), "Ragtime Man" (reprise) (Sandra Reaves-Phillips, Tamara Tunie, Alexana Ryer), "The Ham Kick" (Orchestra), "Don't Much Matter Any More" (J. Lee Flynn, Pat Yankee), "The Naked Dance" (Orchestra), "Elegy" (Sandra Reaves-Phillips), "Call the Children Home" (reprise) (Chorus)

NOTES—The Off Off Broadway *Basin Street* was yet another in the seemingly endless flow of failed Broadway and Off (and Off Off) Broadway musicals set in New Orleans, many of which took place in the early years of the twentieth century in the Storyville section of that city. But the success of *One Mo' Time!* (see entry) ensured that producers would try to duplicate its long run with other similar offerings. A point in *Basin Street*'s favor was that it offered a new score, rather than rehashing a slew of old standards.

While there have been a few successful musicals which took place either fully or partly in New Orleans (or Louisiana in general), such as *Naughty Marietta* (1910, 136 performances), *Louisiana Purchase* (1940, 444 performances), and the aforementioned *One Mo' Time!* (1979, 1,372 performances), most musicals set in that area of the country have been failures, including *Deep River* (1926, 32 performances); *The Lace Petticoat* (1927, 15 performances); *Great Day* (1929, 36 performances); *A Noble Rouge* (1929, 9 performances); *Great Day in New Orleans* (1929; closed prior to Broadway); *Sunny River* (1941, 36 performances); *In Gay New Orleans* (1947; closed prior to Broadway; the musical's scenery and costumes, as well as its poster artwork, were then used in *Louisiana Lady*, which opened later in the 1946-1947 season and played for just 3 performances); *Saratoga* (1959, 80 performances); *Pousse-Café* (1966, 3 performances); *House of Leather* (1970, one performance; see entry); *Prettybelle* (1971; closed prior to Broadway); *Doctor Jazz* (1975, 5 performances); *Fat Tuesday* (1976, number of performances unknown; see entry); *Saga* (1979, 12 performances; see entry); *Storyville* (1979; closed prior to Broadway); *Daddy Goodness* (1979; closed prior to Broadway); *Jam* (1980, 14 performances; see entry); *Louisiana Summer* (1982, 16 performances; see entry); *1,000 Years of Jazz* (1982; closed prior to Broadway); *Basin*

Street (1983, 15 performances); *Staggerlee* (1987, 118 performances; see entry); *A Walk on the Wild Side* (1988, 20 performances; see entry); *The Middle of Nowhere* (1988, 20 performances; see entry); *Further Mo'* (1990, 174 performances; see entry); *The High Rollers Social and Pleasure Club* (1992, 14 performances); *Whistle Down the Wind* (1996; closed prior to Broadway); *Marie Christine* (1999, 44 performances); *Call the Children Home* (2000; performances unknown [probably a two-week run]; see entry); *Thou Shalt Not* (2001, 85 performances); *Caroline, or Change* (2003, 106 performances; see entry); and *Lestat* (2006, 39 performances).

Dramas set in New Orleans (such as *A Streetcar Named Desire* ([1947, 855 performances] and *Toys in the Attic* [1960, 556 performances]) have done far better than musicals.

Besides New Orleans, another geographical "curse" for musicals is Italy (see entry for *Fortuna*).

106 Bat Boy. "The Musical"; THEATRE: Union Square Theatre; OPENING DATE: March 21, 2001; PERFORMANCES: 260

Book (and Story): Keythe Farley and Brian Flemming; LYRICS: Laurence O'Keefe; MUSIC: Laurence O'Keefe; DIRECTION: Scott Schwartz; CHOREOGRAPHY: Christopher Gattelli; SCENERY: Richard Hoover and Bryan Johnson; COSTUMES: Fabio Toblini; LIGHTING: Howell Binkley; MUSICAL DIRECTION: Alex Lacamoire; PRODUCERS: Nancy Nagel Gibbs, Riot Entertainment, Robyn Goodman, Michael Alden, Jean Doumanian and The Producing Office; Pam Pariseau, Greg Schaffert, and Mike Skipper, Associate Producers

CAST—Deven May (Bat Boy), Daria Hardeman (Ruthie Taylor, Ned), Doug Storm (Rick Taylor, Mr. Dillon, Lorraine), Kathy Brier (Ron Taylor, Clem, Maggie), Richard Pruitt (Sheriff Reynolds), Jim Price (Bud, Daisy, King of the Forest), Kerry Butler (Shelley Parker), Kaitlin Hopkins (Meredith Parker), Trent Armand Kendall (Roy, Mrs. Taylor, the Reverend Hightower, Institute Man); Storytellers, Townspeople, and Animals were portrayed by the full company

SOURCE—The story "Bat Child Found in Cave" in the *Weekly World News* (June 23, 1992, issue).

The action occurs in the present in Hope Falls, West Virginia.

The musical was presented in two acts.

ACT ONE—"Hold Me, Bat Boy" (Company), "Christian Charity" (Richard Pruitt, Kaitlin Hopkins, Kerry Butler), "Ugly Boy" (Kerry Butler), "Watcha Wanna Do?" (Doug Storm, Kerry Butler), "A Home for You" (Kaitlin Hopkins, Deven May), "Another Dead Cow" (Townsfolk), "Dance with Me, Darling" (Sean McCourt), "Ruthie's Lullaby" (Trent Armand Kendall), "Show You a Thing or Two" (Company), "Christian Charity" (reprise) (Richard Pruitt, Sean McCourt, Townsfolk), "A Home for You" (reprise) (Deven May), "Comfort and Joy" (Company)

ACT TWO—"A Joyful Noise" (Trent Armand Kendell, Congregation), "Let Me Walk Among You" (Deven May), "Three-Bedroom House" (Kaitlin Hopkins, Kerry Butler), "Children, Children" (Jim Price, Company), "More Blood" (Sean McCourt), "Inside Your Heart" (Kerry Butler, Deven May), "Apology to a Cow" (Deven May), "Revelations" (Kaitlin Hopkins, Sean McCourt, Company), Finale: "I Imagine You're Upset" (Company), "Hold Me, Bat Boy" (reprise) (Company)

NOTES—This science fiction musical (which Jeffrey Eric Jenkins in *The Best Plays of 2000-2001* noted was "like a backwoods version" of *Little Shop of Horrors*) told the amusing but sometimes touching tale of Bat Boy, a half-bat/half-boy who just wants to wear blazers and bow ties and live a normal life in Hope Falls, West Virginia. But such hopes are dashed when the insular, prejudiced community turns on him. (Indeed, as scores of science fiction films have taught us, these things never turn out well.)

The musical's relatively short run was surprising because the script and score were entertaining and had genuinely quirky touches (when Bat Boy kills a cow, he sings a song of apology to the unfortunate animal, noting "I shouldn't work my problems out with food").

RCA Victor released the cast album (CD # 09026-63800-2), and the script was published by Dramatists Play Service, Inc., in 2002.

The musical was first produced at the Actors' Gang Theatre in Los Angeles on Halloween Night 1997.

107 Bayou Legend. THEATRE: Church of St. Paul and St. Andrew; OPENING DATE: January 10, 1975; PERFORMANCES: 12; BOOK: Owen Dodson; LYRICS: Jack Landron; MUSIC: Jack Landron; DIRECTION: Shauneille Perry; CHOREOGRAPHY: Deborah (Debbie) Allen; Clinton Turner Davis, Assistant Choreographer; SCENERY: C. Richard Mills; COSTUMES: Sherri Brewer; LIGHTING: Paul Sullivan; MUSICAL DIRECTION: Neal Tate; PRODUCER: AMAS Repertory Theatre, Inc. (Rosetta LeNoire, Founder and Artistic Director)

CAST—Carolyn Byrd (Naomi, Bijou's Mother), Zaida Coles (Maud), Lori Chinn (Teaka, Bettesue, Tulip), Billy Davis (Willie Silver, Second Counselor), Clinton T. Davis (Yancey, Third Counselor), Erni Adano (Bijou's Father, Ballon, Ted Goodridge (Grave, Zempoaltepec), Karen Grannum (Sophie-Louise), Yvette Johnson (Bijou, Oleander), Jack Landron (Reve), Edward Love (Troy, First Counselor), Emett "Babe" Wallace (Apocalypse, Old Priest), Tom White (King Loup, Man), Dorian Williams (Charlotte, Clove), Sundra Williams (Mrs. Candymayme), Binky Wood (Hethabella, Woman)

The action occurs in the 1800s.

The musical was presented in two acts (division of acts and song assignments unknown; songs are listed in performance order).

MUSICAL NUMBERS—"Alligator Dance," "Rice Hulling Song," "I Wasn't Born to Die No Common Way," "You Only Fool Me 'Cause I Want You To," "Le Carabine," "Sophie-Louise," "I'm Bad," "King of the Rock," "I Belong Right Here," "My Only Son," "I Cut Their Throats," "Teaka's Dance," "Hello, Out There," "Reason Died Last Night," "Something in the Wind," "Graveyard Chant," "Another Day"

NOTES—*Bayou Legend*, an Off Off Broadway production which played for a limited engagement of twelve performances, was a fantasy about a young Black boy who is a combination of devil and hero.

108 Be. THEATRE: Union Square Theatre; OPENING DATE: March 15, 2007; PERFORMANCES: 121; Created and Directed by Eylon Nuphar and Boaz Berman; and by Mayumana; SCENERY: Nizan Refaeli; COSTUMES: Neta Haker; LIGHTING: Eyal Tavori and Roy Milo; PRODUCERS: Marc Routh, Tom Viertel, Steven Baruch, Roy Ofer, Mayumana Ltd., Annette Niemtzow, and Pamela Cooper

CAST—Sharon Ben Naim, Alba Bonal Garcia, Eva Boucherite Martin, Vicente De Andres, Silvia Garcias De Ves, Michael Feigenbaum, Ido Kagan, Yael Mahler, Taly Minkov, Reut Rotem, Ido Stadler, Aka Jean Claude Thiemele, Hila Yaffe

The revue was presented in one act (the program didn't identify specific dance and musical sequences).

NOTES—Mayumana was an Israeli performance troupe, and their production of *Be* (meaning "skill" in Hebrew) was, according to Frank Scheck in the *New York Post*, somewhat difficult to classify. He noted that while the revue included dance, music, movement, and mime, it wasn't quite like the percussion-driven piece *Stomp* (1994; see entry), and it included humorous sequences, formalized choreography, and rock music. He also mentioned the troupe showed the influences of Blue Man Group (see entry), Cirque de Soleil, and Mummenchanz. While he enjoyed parts of the "ultimately bland" evening, Scheck felt the revue had an overall "undeniable air of familiarity."

At the time of *Be*'s Off Broadway closing, *Broadway.com* reported that the revue had been performed more than 5,000 times in over thirty countries.

109 Be Kind to People Week. "The Smiling Musical"; THEATRE: Belmont Theatre; OPENING DATE: March 23, 1975; PERFORMANCES: 100; BOOK: Jack Bussins and Ellsworth Olin; LYRICS: Jack Bussins and Ellsworth Olin; MUSIC: Jack Bussins and Ellsworth Olin; DIRECTION: Quinton Ranes; CHOREOGRAPHY: Bobby Lee; SCENERY: Bruce Monroe; LIGHTING: Centaur Productions; PRODUCERS: J. Arthur Elliot; a Quinton Raines Production

CAST—Naura Hayden (Hope Healy), Kenneth Cory (Norman), Alan Kass (Alan), Daniel Brown (Dan), Nell N. Carter (Nell), Judy Congress (Judy), Grenoldo Frazier (Grenoldo), Bobby Lee (Bobby), Dana Lorge (Dana), Randy Martin (Randy), Maureen Moore (Maureen)

The musical was presented in two acts.

ACT ONE—"Whatever Happened to the Good Old Days" (Daniel Brown, Bobby Lee, Randy Martin, Grenoldo Frazier), "I Will Give Him Love" (Kenneth Cory, Naura Hayden), "Mad About You, Manhattan" (Daniel Brown, Judy Congress), "I Have a Friend at the Chase Manhattan Bank" (Dana Lorge), "All I Got Is You" (Kenneth Cory, Naura Hayden), "I'm in Like with You" (Kenneth Cory), "When We See a Pretty Girl We Whistle" (Kenneth Cory, Daniel Brown, Grenoldo Frazier, Bobby Lee, Randy Martin, Naura Haydon, Nell N. Carter, Judy Congress, Dana Lorge, Maureen Moore), "Ecology" (Kenneth Cory), "I Will Give Him Love" (reprise) (Naura Hayden)

ACT TWO—"All I Got Is You" (reprise) (Bobby Lee, Grenoldo Frazier), "I Need You" (Kenneth Cory), "I'm in Like with You" (reprise)/"To Love Is to Live" (Randy Martin, Maureen Moore), "Freud Is a Fraud" (Alan Kass), "Black Is Beautiful" (Kenneth Cory, Daniel Brown, Grenoldo Frazier, Bobby Lee, Randy Martin, Naura Hayden, Nell N. Carter, Judy Congress, Dana Lorge, Maureen Moore), "A Smile Is Up" (Grenoldo Frazier), "To Love Is to Live" (reprise) (Nell N. Carter), "You're Divine" (Naura Hayden), Finale: "Be Kind to People Week"; "I'm in Like with You" (reprise); "A Smile Is Up" (reprise); "Be Kind to People Week" (reprise) (Company)

NOTES—*Be Kind to People Week* was the first attraction at the new Belmont Theatre, which was located on the second floor of the Belmont Hotel. The musical dealt with a young woman (Naura Hayden) who tries to bring together all sorts of disparate groups (Blacks, Whites, feminists, peace activists, blue collar workers) by asking New Yorkers to sign a petition declaring they will all be kind to one another.

Clive Barnes in the *New York Times* noted Hayden was a television actress and author of a high-protein cookbook, and he felt the musical itself could have used some protein. But he praised one song ("To Love Is to Live"), and applauded Nell N. Carter, whose "strong singing may shatter a chandelier."

Shortly after the run of the musical, the song "Mad About About You Manhattan! ... & Nutty for You New York" was released on an unnumbered 45 RPM record by Nutty for You New York Records which was sponsored by The Citizens Committee for New York City, Inc. The song was performed by "The Million Dollar Chorus" and included, among others, Barbara Barrie, Polly Bergen, Arlene Dahl, Ossie Davis, Ruby Dee, Rocky Graziano, Tammy

Grimes, Henny Youngman, Celeste Holm, Linda Hopkins, Guy Lombardo, Jake La Motta, Dina Merrill, Bess Myerson, Otto Preminger, Cliff Robertson, and Naura Hayden, the heroine of *Be Kind to People Week*.

Intended as a promotional song "to mobilize the vast resources of New York in New York's cause," perhaps there was hope that "Mad About You Manhattan" would become the city's unofficial anthem. But the matter was officially settled two years later with the release of a new Martin Scorsese film which starred Liza Minnelli and Robert DeNiro and included songs by John Kander and Fred Ebb.

110 Bea's Place. "A New Musical Play"; THEATRE: Westbeth Theatre Center; OPENING DATE: May 26, 1979; PERFORMANCES: 16; BOOK: Daniel O'Connor and John Goodwin; LYRICS: John Goodwin; MUSIC: John Goodwin; DIRECTION: Daniel O'Connor; SCENERY: Jack McGroder; COSTUMES: Jack McGroder; LIGHTING: Gail Dahl; MUSICAL DIRECTION: Michael Holmes; PRODUCER: Public Players, Inc.

CAST—Janey Kelly (Bea), Al Franz (Willy), Shyrl Ryanharrt (Dot), Scott Stevensen (Mitch), Jonathan Bricklin (Tommy), Barbara Trunz (Martha Ann), Howard Hagan (Floyd), Gail Titunik (Evie), Corrine Coutlangus (Voice of the Juke)

The action occurs in Bea's Place, a bar just outside Las Vegas.

The musical was presented in one act.

MUSICAL NUMBERS—"Slow Town Small Time Step" (Company), "Bea's Place" (Scott Stevensen, Shyrl Ryanharrt, Jonathan Bricklin, Janey Kelly, Al Franz), "Mannequine Lady" (Scott Stevensen, Jonathan Bricklin), "Mornin's Lovely Rose" (Gail Titunik), "Easy Love" (Barbara Trunz, Corrine Coutlangus), "Lovin' Tree" (Scott Stevensen), "Love a Stranger" (Company), "You Could've Told Me" (Janey Kelly), "Funky Piano Man" (Janey Kelly), "You Could've Told Me" (reprise) (Shyrl Ryanharrt), "Midnight Love Song" (Jonathan Bricklin), "Mama's (Daddy's) Little Girl" (Barbara Trunz, Howard Hagan), "Holy Hanna" (Janey Kelly), "This Lullabye Is for You" (Janey Kelly)

NOTES—This showcase didn't go anywhere; like *Piano Bar* (see entry), which opened earlier in the 1978-1979 season, *Bea's Place* was also set in a bar (on the outskirts of Las Vegas). There have been many successful "barroom" plays (*The Time of Your Life* [1939], *The Iceman Cometh* [1946], and *Happy Birthday* [1946]), but the Great American Barroom Musical has yet to be written.

111 The Beast: A Meditation on Beauty. THEATRE: Judson Poets' Theatre; OPENING DATE: November 5, 1976; PERFORMANCES: Unknown; BOOK: Al Carmines; LYRICS: Al Carmines; MUSIC: Al Carmines; DIRECTION: Dan Wagoner; CHOREOGRAPHY: Dan Wagoner; SCENERY: Lee Guilliatt; COSTUMES: Dean H. Reiter; LIGHTING: Earl Eidman; MUSICAL DIRECTION: Al Carmines; PRODUCER: The Judson Poets' Theatre

CAST—Trisha Long (Narrator), Wendell Cordtz (Father), Gretchen Van Aken (Big Sister), Margaret Wright (Goodness), Essie Borden (Beauty), Lee Guilliatt (Nurse), Eric Ellenburg (Rose)

SOURCE—The eighteenth-century fairy tale "Beauty and the Beast."

The musical was presented in two acts.

ACT ONE—"Daughters, Daughters" (Wendell Cordtz, with Gretchen Van Aken, Margaret Wright, and Essie Borden), "I'm Ugly" (Essie Borden), "Big Sister Blues" (Gretchen Van Aken), "Surrounded by Women" (Wendell Cordtz), "Journeys" (Trisha Long), "Dreams" (Lee Guilliatt), "The Land of Desolation" (Lee Guilliatt, Eric Ellenburg), "Lullabye" (Eric Ellenburg, Wendell Cordtz), "The Bloom Is Gone" (Gretchen Van Aken, Margaret Wright), "Good-Bye" (Wendell Cordtz, Margaret Wright, Gretchen Van Aken, Eric Ellenburg), Dance (Lee Guilliatt, Essie Borden)

ACT TWO—"Born Again" (Margaret Wright, Wendell Cordtz, Gretchen Van Aken), "God Bless All" (Margaret Wright), "Pas De Deux" (Essie Borden, Eric Ellenburg), "Art Is the Imitation of an Action (Beauty Is an Action)" (Company)

NOTES—With Al Carmines at the helm, this Off Off Broadway musical version of the classic fairy tale "Beauty and the Beast" was nothing like the Disney version presented on Broadway in 1994. According to Mel Gussow in the *New York Times*, Carmines' Beauty (Essie Borden) has a "speckled face, blackened teeth, gunny-sack costumes and droopy socks," and is in love with a male beauty named Rose (Eric Ellenburg). But all ends well when Beauty decides to "toss off her ugly looks and evil ways and become Beautiful."

The Beast: A Meditation on Beauty was a departure from the usual Carmines' musical; instead of a large cast and chorus, its company numbered seven, and indeed Gussow noted that instead of an opera the work was a chamber opera. Gussow felt the book wasn't up to par, but he praised the score, a "squadron of rafter-shaking tunes," including a "lowdown" "Big Sister Blues" for Gretchen Van Aken. He also noted that the finale, "Art Is the Imitation of an Action," was the show's key song, and because it set the tone for the musical, the "pulsating" sequence would have been better placed as the evening's opening number.

112 Beautiful Dreamer. "A Musical Play"; THEATRE: Madison Avenue Playhouse; OPENING DATE: December 27, 1960; PERFORMANCES: 24; BOOK: William Engvick; LYRICS: Stephen Foster; MUSIC: Stephen Foster; DIRECTION: Ernestine Perrie; CHOREOGRAPHY: Tom Ribbink; COSTUMES: Joe Crosby; LIGHTING: Maralyn S. Miller; PRODUCERS: Joseph F. Moon, Catherine Connor, and the Wickland Company in association with Robert Bruce Holley

CAST—Don Liberto (George Cooper, Tambo), Don Gunderson (Morrison Foster), Howard Kahl (Herr Von Kleber), Carolyn Maye (Jane McDowell Foster), James Morris (Stephen Foster), Ted Lawrie (E.P. Christy), Stephen Lloyd (Bones, Charley, Hospital Clerk), Jud Bartlett (Banjo, Bob, Turk), Jeanne Schlegel (Mrs. MacDowell), Kate Hurney (Miss Tilton,), Lillian Fields (Henrietta Hoctor, Lottie), Reese Burns (Andy, Mr. Rice), Clinton Dolan (Harvey, Algy); Kate Hurney and Stephen Lloyd (New York Couple)

The division of acts is unknown, as are song assignments (the songs are listed in performance order).

MUSICAL NUMBERS—"Minstrel Parade," "Temperance Trio," "Oleo," "Dolcey Jones," "Linger in Blissful Repose," "The Shanghai Rooster," "Comrades, Fill No Cup for Me," "I Dream of Jeannie," "Some Folks Do," "Nellie Bly," "Ah, May the Red Rose," "Our Bright Summer Days Are Gone," "If You've Only Got a Moustache," "My Old Kentucky Home," "Beautiful Dreamer"

NOTES—*Beautiful Dreamer* was Off Broadway's answer to Hollywood and Broadway's Great Composer genre, a lode successfully mined in the 1944 Broadway musical *Song of Norway* (Edvard Grieg) and the 1945 film *A Song to Remember* (Frederic Chopin). But Off Broadway's life of Stephen Collins Foster (1826-1864) didn't result in a long-running *Song of Kentucky*; *Beautiful Dreamer* was gone in three weeks.

The musical began at a memorial for Foster, ten years after his death. Participants at the service remember him, and flashbacks told the story of his life and music. Howard Taubman in the *New York Times* found the book "respectful, truthful and well-intentioned," but as drama it was "elementary" and verged on being a "tear-jerker." But when the musical sang, Taubman had nothing but praise, singling out both famous songs (such as "My Old Kentucky Home") and lesser-known ones (Taubman was particularly taken with "Some Folks Do," which he mentioned twice). He noted that Foster's songs are "tender and gay" and continue "to touch and move you."

Hollywood made no less than three films about Stephen Foster: *Harmony Lane* (1935), *Swanee River* (1939), and *I Dream of Jeanie* (1952). Don Ameche portrayed Foster in *Swanee River*, and, cinematically speaking, 1939 was a busy year for him, what with composing the likes of "Beautiful Dreamer" and "Swanee River" as well as inventing the ameche, that is, the telephone.

In 1934, the Broadway-bound musical *America Sings* told the story of Foster and his songs, but the show never made it to New York, closing in Boston during its pre-Broadway tryout (Allan Jones performed the role of Foster).

In 1980, another stage version of Stephen Foster's life and songs, also called *Beautiful Dreamer*, opened in Britain; the "musical melodrama" was written by Roy Hudd and wasn't presented in the usual earnest and straightforward approach of the typical composer biography; instead, the musical was fashioned in the style of a nineteenth-century melodrama (scenes were individually named, such as "CUPID—fires his bewitching darts!"; "The DEMON DRINK!—begins to take its FATAL hold"; and "A dastardly VILLAIN—attempts an UNHOLY alliance"); the score included "I Dream of Jeannie," "Camptown Races," "The Old Folks at Home," and "Oh, Susanna."

113 Becoming. "A New Style Musical"; THEATRE: Circle in the Square (Downtown); OPENING DATE: June 15, 1976; PERFORMANCES: 2; SKETCHES, LYRICS, AND MUSIC: Gail Edwards and Sam Harris; DIRECTION: John Mineo; CHOREOGRAPHY: John Mineo; SCENERY: Dan Leigh; COSTUMES: Dee Dee Fote; additional costumes by Nolan Drummond; LIGHTING: Martin Tudor; MUSICAL DIRECTION: Robert Stecko; PRODUCERS: Heartsong Productions in association with Drew Murphy (Dennis I. Gould, Associate Producer)

CAST—Norman Meister (Norman), Anne Sward (Anne), Gail Edwards (Gail)

The revue was presented in two acts (division of acts and song assignments unknown; songs are listed in performance order).

MUSICAL NUMBERS—"It Feels So Good to Be Alive Today," "Believe in You," "It's Not Easy to Change Your Life," "Goin' Back to That Feelin'," "Mama," "Valentine Song," "Lonely Times," "Lordy," "Choices," "Birthday Song," "From Now On," "Let It Be Today," "Love Me Lightly," "Freer Love," "Look Inside," "Let's Get Started"

NOTES—The revue *Becoming* had first been seen at the University of Miami. Richard Eder in the *New York Times* found the evening generally bland, and noted its only attitude seemed to be that "everything's O.K." He said the revue offered itself as a "bit of fresh air" but soon induced "hyperventilation."

114 Bed and Sofa. "A Silent Movie Opera"; THEATRE: Vineyard Theatre; OPENING DATE: February 1, 1996; PERFORMANCES: 52; LIBRETTO: Laurence Klavan; MUSIC: Polly Pen; DIRECTION: Andre Ernotte; SCENERY: G.W. Mercier; COSTUMES: G.W. Mercier; LIGHTING: Phil Monat; MUSICAL DIRECTION: Alan Johnson; PRODUCER: The Vineyard Theatre (Douglas Aibel, Artistic Director; Barbara Zinn Krieger, Executive Director; Jon Nakagawa, Managing Director)

CAST—Terri Klausner (Ludmilla), Michael X. Martin (Nikolai [Kolya]), Jason Workman (Volodya)

SOURCE—The 1926 silent film *Bed and Sofa* (*Tretya Meschanskaya*) (screenplay by Victor Shklovsky, direction by Abram Room).

The action occurs in Moscow in 1926.

The musical was presented in one act.

MUSICAL NUMBERS—"Anthem" (instrumental), "The Train" (Company), "My Name" (Company), "Lunch"/"Without My Work" (Company), "The Night" (Company), "The War" (Michael X. Martin, Jason Workman), "Bed and Sofa #1 (Volodya Moves In)" (Company), "13 Meschanskaia Lane" (Company), "News"/"Over the Moon" (Terri Klausner, Michael X. Martin, Jason Workman, Radio Singers), "Bed and Sofa #2 (Ludmilla and Volodya Are Alone)" (Terri Klausner, Jason Workman), "Silent Movie" (Terri Klausner, Jason Workman), "Bed and Sofa #3 (Ludmilla and Volodya Go To Bed)" (Terri Klausner, Jason Workman), "Kolya's Return"/ "Beans" (Company), "Big and Complicated" (Michael X. Martin, Jason Workman), "Do You Mean to Stay Here?"/"Without My Wife" (Michael X. Martin, Jason Workman), "The Night"/"Over the Moon" (reprise) (Company), "Back and Forth" (Company), "Bed and Sofa #4 (Kolya Takes the Sofa)" (Company), "Checkers" (Company), "I Am Hungry" (Company), "The Dressing Screen" (Company), "A Walk" (Company), "I Am Hungry" (reprise) (Company), "U.S.S.R." (Terri Klausner), "Bed and Sofa #5 (Volodya Takes the Sofa)" (Terri Klausner, Jason Workman), "Back and Forth" (reprise) (Michael X. Martin), "To Have a Child" (Company), "Abortion" (Terri Klausner), "Her Husband" (Michael X. Martin, Jason Workman), "The Letter" (Company), "The Ending" (Company), "Anthem" (reprise) (instrumental)

NOTES—The Off Off Broadway musical *Bed and Sofa* was sung-through, and the song list is derived from information on the cast recording (released by Varese Sarabande Records [CD # VSD-5729]).

The fascinating three-character musical was based on a 1926 silent Russian film about a poor young married couple (Ludmilla and Kolya) who live in a cramped apartment in Moscow, which is in the midst of a housing crisis. They are soon joined by a young man named Volodya, who sleeps on their sofa, but when he and Ludmilla become lovers, Kolya is forced to sleep on the sofa. When both of the boorish men become obsessed with playing checkers, Ludmilla claims the bed for herself and relegates Volodya to the sofa, too. When she realizes she's pregnant, the two men wonder who the father is and insist Ludmilla abort the child. But she decides the two aren't worthy of being fathers, and leaves them. At the end of the musical, Kolya and Volodya are left alone, the former claiming the bed and the latter the sofa.

As befits a musical based on a silent film, the scenery and costumes were in black and white; further, some sequences of the musical weren't sung or spoken, but were instead performed in the style of a silent film.

The script was published by Dramatists Play Service, Inc., in 1997.

115 Beehive. THEATRE: Top of the Gate/The Village Gate Upstairs; OPENING DATE: March 30, 1986; PERFORMANCES: 600; LYRICS: See song list for credits; MUSIC: See song list for credits; DIRECTION: Larry Gallagher; CHOREOGRAPHY: Leslie Dockery; SCENERY: John Hickey; COSTUMES: David Dille; LIGHTING: John Hickey; MUSICAL DIRECTION: Skip Brevis; PRODUCERS: BETMAR and Charles Allen

CAST—Pattie Darcy, Alison Fraser, Jasmine Guy, Adriane Lenox, Gina Taylor, Laura Theodore

The revue was presented in two acts.

ACT ONE—"The Name Game" (lyric and music by Elliston and Chase) (Ensemble), "My Boyfriend's Back" (lyric and music by Feldman, Goldstein, and Gottehrer) (Alison Fraser), "Sweet Talkin' Guy" (lyric and music by D. Morris and E. Greenberg) (Adriane Lenox), "One Fine Day" (lyric and music by G. Goffen and C. King) (Jasmine Guy), "I Sold My Heart to the Junkman" (lyric and music by L. Rene and O. Rene) (Gina Taylor), "Academy Award" (lyric and music by C. Bolling) (Gina Taylor), "Will You Still Love Me Tomorrow" (lyric and music by Carole King) (Laura Theodore), "Give Him a Great Big Kiss" (lyric and music by G. Morton) (Pattie Darcy), "Remember (Walking in the Sand)" (lyric and music by G. Morton) (Pattie Darcy), "I Can Never Go Home Again" (lyric and music by G. Morton) (Pattie Darcy), "Where Did Our Love Go?" (lyric and music by Brian Holland, Lamont Dozier, and Edward J. Holland) (Jasmine Guy), "Come See About Me" (lyric and music by Brian Holland, Lamont Dozier, and Edward J. Holland) (Jasmine Guy), "I Hear a Symphony" (lyric and music by Brian Holland, Lamont Dozier, and Edward J. Holland) (Jasmine Guy), "It's My Party" (lyric and music by Gold, Gluck, and Wiener) (Pattie Darcy), "I'm Sorry" (lyric and music by Self and Britten) (Alison Fraser), "Rockin' Around the Christmas Tree" (lyric and music by M. Marks) (Alison Fraser), "I Dream About Frankie" (lyric and music by Hemric and Steiner) (Jasmine Guy), "She's a Fool" (lyric and music by B. Raleigh and M. Barkan) (Adriane Lenox), "You Don't Own Me" (lyric and music by J. Madara and D. White) (Pattie Darcy), "Judy's Turn to Cry" (lyric and music by B. Ross and E. Lewis) (Pattie Darcy), "Where the Boys Are" (from 1960 film *Where the Boys Are*; lyric and music by Neil Sedaka and Howard Greenfield) (Alison Fraser), "The Beehive Dance" (lyric and music by Claudia Brevis) (Ensemble), "The Beat Goes On" (lyric and music by Sonny Bono) (Adriane Lenox), "Downtown" (lyric and music by Anthony Peter Hatch) (Alison Fraser), "To Sir, with Love" (1967 film *To Sir, with Love*; lyric by Mark London, music by Donald [Don] Black) (Laura Theodore), "Wishin' and Hopin'" (lyric by Hal David, music by Burt Bacharach) (Pattie Darcy), "Don't Sleep in the Subway" (lyric and music by Anthony Peter Hatch) (Alison Fraser), "You Don't Have to Say You Love Me" (lyric and music by P. Donaggio, Vito Pallavicini, Vicky Wickham, S.N. Bell, and Napier) (Pattie Darcy)

ACT TWO—"A Fool in Love" (lyric and music by Ike Turner) (Gina Taylor), "River Deep, Mountain High" (lyric and music by Phil Spector, Jeff Barry, and Ellie Greenwich) (Jasmine Guy), "Proud Mary" (lyric and music by J.C. Fogerty) (Gina Taylor), "Society's Child" (lyric and music by Janis Ian) (Alison Fraser), "Respect" (lyric and music by Otis Redding) (Gina Taylor), "A Natural Woman" (lyric and music by Goffen, King, and Wexler) (Pattie Darcy), "Do Right Woman" (lyric and music by D. Penn and C. Moman) (Gina Taylor), "Piece of My Heart" (lyric and music by Jerry Ragovoy and Berns) (Laura Theodore), "Try (Just a Little Bit Harder)" (lyric and music by Jerry Ragovoy and Chip Taylor) (Laura Theodore), "Me and Bobby McGee" (lyric and music by Kris Kristofferson and F. Foster) (Laura Theodore), "Ball and Chain" (lyric and music by W. Thornton) (Laura Theodore), "Make Your Own Kind of Music" (lyric by Cynthia Weil, music by Barry Mann) (Ensemble)

NOTES—*Beehive*, a tribute to individual "girl" singers of the 1960s as well as "girl" groups of the period (see entries for *Suds* and *The Taffetas*, two other "girl group" musicals, as well as the entry for *Shout!* a tribute to British "girl" singers of the 1960s), was the first of an onslaught of mostly dreary, unimaginative evenings which strung together popular songs from the 1950s and 1960s into pop-song and composer-tribute revues. The practice is still with us, but now it's mostly in the form of jukebox musicals, a bastard form of modern musical theatre which takes independently written popular songs (written of course without regard to character, plot, and atmosphere) and then grafts them into book musicals (for which the songs are suddenly supposed to reflect character, plot, and atmosphere). (If a *Dreamgirls*-styled musical was planned for Broadway today, the producer would undoubtedly try to buy up the rights to the Motown catalogue rather than hire a lyricist and composer to create a new score.)

Beehive was recorded on a 2-LP set released by Rock Dream Records (# RDR-003) with the original cast members (with the exception of Gina Taylor, who was replaced by Cookie Watkins).

116 Before the Flood. THEATRE: AMAS Repertory Theatre; OPENING DATE: November 29, 1979; PERFORMANCES: 12; BOOK: Rudy Gray; LYRICS: David Blake; MUSIC: Paul Piteo; DIRECTION: Billie Allen; CHOREOGRAPHY: Mabel Robinson; SCENERY: Patrick Mann; COSTUMES: Leslie Day; LIGHTING: Fred Jason Hancock; PRODUCER: AMAS Repertory Theatre (Rosetta LeNoire, Founder and Artistic Director)

CAST—John McCurry, C.J. Benson, Joella Breedlove, Christofer de Oni, Ann Duquesnay, Clebert Ford, Edna Goode, Jeannie Kauffman, Pat Lundy, Charles "C.B." Murray, Damon Pearce, Steiv Semien, Dan Seymour

NOTES—The musical *Before the Flood* was an Off Off Broadway production.

117 The Beggar's Opera. THEATRE: McAlpin Rooftop Theatre; OPENING DATE: May 30, 1972; PERFORMANCES: 224; BOOK: John Gay; LYRICS: John Gay; MUSIC: Johann Christoph Pepusch; musical score "newly realized" by Ryan Edwards; DIRECTION: Gene Lesser; CHOREOGRAPHY: Elizabeth Keen; SCENERY: Robert U. Taylor; COSTUMES: Carrie F. Robbins; LIGHTING: William Mintzer; MUSICAL DIRECTION: Roland Gagnon; PRODUCER: The Chelsea Theatre Center of Brooklyn (Robert Kalfin, Artistic Director; Michael David, Executive Director)

CAST—Joseph Palmieri (The Beggar [Jemmy Twicher]), Gordon Connell (Mr. Peachum), John Long (Filch), Jeanne Arnold (Mrs. Peachum), Kathleen Widdoes (Polly Peachum), Timothy Jerome (Macheath), Roy Brocksmith (Ben Budge), William Newman (Mart of the Mint), Jill Eikenberry (Dolly Trull), Lynn Ann Leveridge (Mrs. Coaxer), Tanny McDonald (Jenny Diver), Irene Frances Kling (Suky Tawdry), Ralston Hill (Lockit), Marilyn Sokol (Lucy Lockit)

The action occurs in London early in the eighteenth century.

The musical was presented in two acts.

NOTES—*The Beggar's Opera* premiered in 1728, and was of course the inspiration for *The Threepenny Opera* (see entries for 1954, 1955, and other productions). The first American production of *The Beggar's Opera* appears to have taken place during the 1855-1856 theatre season, and the work has been revived periodically.

The Off Broadway production was originally mounted by the Chelsea Theatre Center of Brooklyn at the Brooklyn Academy of Music on March 21, 1972, for twenty-nine performances. When it transferred to Manhattan, Timothy Jerome assumed the role of Macheath, which Stephen D. Newman had played in Brooklyn; Ralston Hall replaced Reid Shelton; and Jill Eikenberry replaced Joan Nelson. For the Off Broadway production, the roles of Crook-Fingered Jack and Diane Mapes were omitted (these roles had been performed by Neil Hunt and Connie Van Ess in Brooklyn).

Polly, Gay's sequel to *The Beggar's Opera*, was published in 1729, and appears to have been produced in London shortly thereafter. The first American production was seen Off Broadway at the Cherry Lane Theatre (then called the Cherry Lane Playhouse) on October 10, 1925 (see entry). On April

29, 1975, the Chelsea Theatre Center presented *Polly*, with Betsy Beard in the title role, Stephen D. Newman as Macheath, and Patricia Elliott as Jenny Diver. The production played for thirty-two performances, and didn't transfer to a Manhattan theatre. See entry for this revival.

There is no song listing available for the numbers performed in the 1972 revival of *The Beggar's Opera*; the list below is taken from a 1957 revival of the opera which was produced at the New York City Center, and which starred Jack Cassidy as Macheath and Shirley Jones as Polly. Cassidy and Jones had married the previous summer while performing in another production of *The Beggar's Opera* at Cambridge. The City Center production also included another married couple: George S. Irving played the role of Mr. Peachum and Maria Karnilova the role of Dolly Trull.

Among the recordings of *The Beggar's Opera* is a 2-LP set released by London Records (# LDR-72008) in 1981; the cast includes Kiri Te Kanawa, James Morris, Joan Sutherland, Angela Lansbury, Alfred Marks, Regina Resnik, and Michael Hordern.

Another musical inspired by *The Beggar's Opera* was *The Beggar's Soap Opera* (see entry). The 1961 musical *Big Deal* was also based on Gay's work; it was produced in Chicago on August 16 by the Playwrights' Theatre (book by Paul Sills, lyrics by David Shepherd, and music by William Mathieu).

ACT ONE—"Let Us Take the Road" (Macheath, Gang), "My Heart Was So Free" (Macheath), Duet: "Were I Laid on Greenland Coast" (Macheath, Polly), "Virgins Are Like the Fair Flower" (Polly), Trio: "Our Polly Is a Sad Slut" (Peachum, Mrs. Peachum, Polly), "The Turtle Thus with Plaintive Crying" (Polly), "'Tis Woman That Seduces All Mankind" (Lockit), Duet: "Through All the Employments of Life" (Peachum, Lockit), "Hanging Is My Only Sport" (Peachum), Reprise Duet: "Were I Laid on Greenland Coast" (Polly, Macheath), "O, What a Pain It Is to Part" (Polly, Macheath), "No Power on Earth Can E'er Divide" (Polly), "Man May Escape from Rope and Gun" (Prisoners), Trio: "Why How Now Madam Flirt" (Lucy, Polly, Macheath), Quartet: "Is Then His Fate Decreed, Sir?" (Polly, Lucy, Peachum, Lockit)

ACT TWO—"Fill Every Glass" (Matt, Gang, Ladies of the Town), "The Ways of the World" (Dolly Trull, Bob Booty), Reprise: "Let Us Take the Road" (Gang, Ladies of the Town), "If the Heart of a Man" (Mrs. Coaxer), "Youth's a Season Made for Joys" (Ladies of the Town), "When Young at the Bar" (Jenny Diver), Trio: "In the Days of My Youth" (Mrs. Coaxer, Peachum, Lockit), "At the Tree I Shall Suffer with Pleasure" (Macheath), Reprise: "When Young at the Bar" (Jenny Diver), "I'm Like a Skiff on the Ocean Toss'd" (Lucy), Duet: "Come Sweet Lass" (Lucy, Polly), "The Charge Was Prepar'd" (Macheath, Chorus), "Would I Might Be Hanged" (Lucy, Polly, Macheath), "Since Laws Were Made for Every Degree" (Company), Finale: "See the Conquering Hero" (Company)

118 The Beggar's Soap Opera.

"A Musical Satire"; THEATRE: INTAR Theatre; OPENING DATE: July 5, 1979; PERFORMANCES: Unknown; BOOK: Dolores Prida; LYRICS: Dolores Prida; MUSIC: Paul Radelat; DIRECTION: Manuel Martin, Jr.; CHOREOGRAPHY: Rosemary Rios and Daria Atandian; SCENERY: Diego Vallejo; COSTUMES: Bud Santora; LIGHTING: Jenny Ball; PRODUCER: The Duo Theatre Spanish-English Ensemble Theatre

CAST—Brenda Feliciano (Jenny Dive), Dionis Enrique (Maki Navaja), Juan Manuel Aguero (Juan Ramon Pichon, the Reverend Eualio Perez), Brunilda Colon (Receptionist, Mimi, Western Union Messengrer), Armando Rivas (Felipe Filcho, Tigre Bravo), Henry Ravelo (Mr. Bemba, Papo), Miguel Sierra (Mr. Pluma, Pipo, Prison Guard), Richard Adan (Mr. Buche, Pepe), Cynthia Lopez (Maria Josefa Pichon), Sandra Nieves (Poli Pichon), Jeannie Kauffman (Fifi, Lucy), Paula Denise Martinez (Chichi, Western Union Messenger)

SOURCE—The 1728 opera *The Beggar's Opera* by John Gay.

The musical was presented in two acts.

The action occurs in the South Bronx during the present time.

NOTES—A satire of *The Beggar's Opera* and *The Threepenny Opera* (see entries) as well as Spanish television soap operas, the flyer for the Off Off Broadway production boasted that the musical contained twenty songs and "a million laughs."

The plot included such familiar characters as Maki Navaja, Poli Pichon, and Jenny Dive, and took place in the South Bronx. The less-than-honest Mr. Peachum (that is, Mr. Pichon) runs an agency to help the poor (its acronym is SCAM), and his daughter Poli becomes involved with the thief Maki Navaja, who is best known for his graffiti "artwork." Maki eventually hangs himself, but John Corry in the *New York Times* nonetheless felt the work was "still a cheerful musical." Corry also singled out Paul Radelat's score, a mixture of Latino and American pop, but he noted the music demanded "great" or "maybe only exuberant" choreography. He singled out "Macho Mirror Dance," a gym workout sequence for Maki and his cronies, but was disappointed when the number morphed into a kind of marital-arts ballet. As for a salsa number at Maki and Poli's wedding, Corry mentioned it was too short to be really effective.

119 Bei Mir Bistu Schoen.

THEATRE: Yiddish Anderson Playhouse (Phyllis Anderson Theatre); OPENING DATE: October 21, 1961; PERFORMANCES: 88; BOOK: Louis Freiman; LYRICS: Jacob Jacobs; MUSIC: Sholom Secunda; DIRECTION: Leo Fuchs; SCENERY: Arthur Aronson; LIGHTING: Arthur Aronson; MUSICAL DIRECTION: Probably Sholom Secunda; PRODUCER: Jacob Jacobs

CAST—Leon Liebgold (Rabbi Itchele Edelman), Jacob Jacobs (Leizer Elie), Seymour Rexsite (Bennie), Leo Fuchs (Shlome Edelman), Rose Greenfield (Sarah Gitel), Miriam Kressyn (Shoshanah), Mordecal Yachsen (Mr. Greenstein), Rebecca Richman (Rivkaleh), Thelma Mintz (Geraldine), Charlotte Cooper

MUSICAL NUMBERS—Overture (Orchestra), "Nachas Fun Kinder (Joys from Children)" (Leon Liebgold), "Social Security" (Jacob Javits, Charlotte Cooper), "Folgen A Tatten (Obeying Father)" (Jacob Javits, Leon Liebgold, Seymour Rexite), "Hob Mich Lieb (Love Me)"/"Bei Mir Bistu Schoen" (Leo Fuchs, Miriam Kressyn), "Machest Mich Feelen Yinger (You Make Me Feel Younger)" (Leon Fuchs, Rebecca Richman), "Hora" (Leo Fuchs, Ensemble), "B'rochos L'Havdoloh (Blessings of the Havdoloh)" (Leon Liebgold, Ensemble), Itsche (Jacob Javits), "Mein Hartz Flegt Zogen Mir (My Heart Told Me)" (Miriam Kressyn, Rebecca Richman), "T'Ain't Kosher" (Leo Fuchs, Ensemble), Finale: "Hob Mich Lieb"/"Machst Mich Feelen Yinger"/"T'Ain't Kosher"/"Hora" (Company)

NOTES—The song list for *Bei Mir Bistu Schoen* is based on information from the cast album, which was released by Decca Records (LP # DL-79115). Interpolated into Sholom Secunda's score was his hit song "Bei Mir Bistu Schoen."

The musical dealt with a twice-widowed rabbi, his two sons (one a Talmudic scholar), a matchmaker, and the matchmaker's daughter, the latter of whom is pursued by both the rabbi and his son the scholar. Milton Esterow in the *New York Times* noted that a marriage eventually occurs, but "not before everyone experiences a lot of difficulties."

Esterow also reported that Secunda had written the music for "Bei Mir Bistu Schoen" in the 1930s (the lyric was by Jacob Jacobs), but in 1937 had sold his rights to a music publisher for thirty dollars. At that point, the song became one of the biggest hit songs in the country, and had Secunda owned the rights, he could have earned $350,000. Esterow reported that in February 1961, the copyright for the song reverted to Secunda. Songs from the musical were also released on a Tikva Records album (LP # T-72) which included numbers from another Jewish-themed musical, *Go Fight City Hall* (see entry).

120 The Believers.

"The Black Experience in Song"; THEATRE: Garrick Theatre; OPENING DATE: May 9, 1968; PERFORMANCES: 310; TEXT: Josephine Jackson and Joseph A. Walker; LYRICS: Benjamin Carter, Dorothy Dinroe, Josephine Jackson, Anje Ray, Ron Steward, and Joseph A. Walker; MUSIC: Benjamin Carter, Dorothy Dinroe, Josephine Jackson, Anje Ray, and Ron Steward; DIRECTION: Barbara Ann Teer; SCENERY: Joseph A. Walker; COSTUMES: Robert Pusilo; LIGHTING: R. Robert Lussier and J.P. Regan; MUSICAL DIRECTION: Brooks Alexander; PRODUCERS: Jesse DeVore and Harold L. Oram, in association with Gustav Heninburg

CAST—Voices, Inc. (Dorothy Dinroe, Josephine Jackson, Sylvia Jackson, Shirley McKie, Veronica Redd, Anje Ray, Jesse Devore, Barry Hemphill, Don Oliver, Ron Steward, James Wright, Benjamin Carter, Joseph A. Walker)

The revue was presented in two acts.

ACT ONE—(*The Gone Years*), "African Sequence" (Voices), "Believers' Chants" (Barry Hemphill, Shirley McKie), "Believers' Lament" (Voices), Drum Solo: "Abio, Oalla, Bondoyika"; "Hey Twa Nah"; "Ya, Ya" (Ladji Camara), "This Old Ship"/"Where Shall I Go?"/"What Shall I Believe in Now?" (Voices), Field Hollers and Work Songs: "Ho, Hee"; "Had to Get Up This Morning, Soon"; "Look a Yonder"; "Pick Dis Cotton, Lord"; "Do I Wonder" (Voices), Church Sequence: "What Shall I Believe in Now?" (reprise) (Voices), "He's Got the Whole World in His Hands" (Jo [Josephine] Jackson, Voices) "Jesus, Light Up the World" (Don Oliver, Voices), Sermon: "The Life of Peter" (Jesse DeVore), "I Turn to Jesus" (Anje Ray, Voices), "I'm So Glad" (Voices)

ACT TWO—(*The Then and Now Years*), "I Just Got in the City" (Barry Hemphill), "City Blues" (Ron Steward), "You Never Really Know" (Voices), "Naked Foot" (Voices), "Early One Morning Blues" (Anje Ray, Voices), "Daily Buzz" (Joseph A. Walker), "Children's Games" (Voices), "School Don't Mean a Damn Thing" (Voices), "I'm Gonna Do My Thing" (Ron Steward, Voices), "Where Do I Go from Here?" (Veronica Redd, Voices), "Burn This Town" (Ron Steward), "Learn to Love" (Anje Ray, Voices), Finale (Voices)

NOTES—Through songs, dances, and dramatic readings, the revue *The Believers* told the story of the Black experience from the pre-slavery period through 1967.

Dan Sullivan in the *New York Times* cited a number of recent shows which had dealt with the same theme (*In White America*, *Jerico-Jim Crow* [see entry], *A Hand Is on the Gate*, and *Hallelujah, Baby!*), and seemed to feel *The Believers* took a somewhat tougher and more aggressive stance than its predecessors. He praised the singing ("I don't care: Negroes do sing better than anybody"), but felt the evening could have been tightened and could have explored its subject matter in more depth.

Individual songs weren't listed in the program; the song list reflects the numbers on the RCA Victor cast recording (LP # LOC-1151-RE and # LOC-LSO-1151-RE).

The "Field Hollers," "Work Songs," and "Naked Foot" sequences are in the public domain.

The musical had first been seen in April 1967 at

the Voices Musical Theatre/St. Paul's Chapel, Columbia University.

121 Bella. "A Very Musical Comedy"; THEATRE: Gramercy Arts Theatre; OPENING DATE: November 16, 1961; PERFORMANCES: 6; BOOK: Tom O'Malley and Lance Barklie; LYRICS: Tom O'Malley; MUSIC: Jane Douglass; DIRECTION: Richard C. Shank; CHOREOGRAPHY: Don Sky; SCENERY: Richard B. Hughes; COSTUMES: Dorine Ackerman; LIGHTING: Richard B. Hughes; MUSICAL DIRECTION: Jane Douglass; PRODUCERS: Lance Barklie and Ned Hendrickson

CAST—Marc McCrary (Dr. Xanadu Chu), "?????" (Performer's name not given in program for the character of "Silhouette"), Gloria LeRoy (Blondine), Glenn Dunno (Bob Lamont), F.J. O'Neil (Count Alex D'Nasti), Jaycee Collins (Dorie), Will B. Able (Lord Evelyn Mason-Mason, Rosetta Stone Mason-Mason, Juan Mason-Mason, Stone Mason, Tex Mason-Dixon), Dodo Denney (Lady Bella Mason), Roger Allan Raby (Bell Hop, Member of Quartette, Ensemble), Otto Lohmann (Gong Boy), D. Bruce Rabbino (Captain Jinks, Member of Quartet, Ensemble), J. David Kirby (Night Club M.C., Porter, Ensemble), Hazel Steck (Kewpie Doll, Madame from Paree), Millie Hruska (Kewpie Doll), Essie Mistarka (Kewpie Doll), Ruth Jaroslow (Kewpie Doll), Rebecca Margolis (Kewpie Doll), Marilyn Sonner (Kewpie Doll), Don Hull (Henchman), Keith Carsey (Henchman), Bill Chase (Henchman), Diane McAfee (Mexican Singer, Train Passenger, Ensemble), Mary Margaret (Script Girl, Ensemble), Charles Sarell (Dresser), Gene Foote (Guide, Member of Quartet, Ensemble), Mervin Crook (Stage Hand, Member of Quartette, Train Passenger, Ensemble), Jami Landi (Train Passenger, Ensemble), Betsy Speller (Train Passenger, Ensemble), Ann Hodges (Ensemble) The action occurs in the 1930s.

The musical was presented in two acts (song assignments unknown).

ACT ONE—"On the Seashore by the Sea," "It Isn't the Same," "All About Evelyn," "Could Be," "Time," "The Seven Seas," "Hand in Hand," "Love Doesn't Grow on Trees," "I'm Happy," "My Card," "Kiss Me"

ACT TWO—"Madame from Paree," "Big, Big," "Could Be" (reprise), "Take a Chance," "Way Down in Lil' Old Texas," "For Love or Money"

NOTES—*Bella* was a musical whodunit; in 1976, Broadway had no luck with a similar murder mystery musical, *Something's Afoot*; but compared to 1991's *Nick & Nora*, the delightful and unappreciated *Something's Afoot* was a masterpiece of musical mystery malarkey. Another mystery musical, Rupert Holmes' *The Mystery of Edwin Drood* (1985; see entry), was successful, and as of this writing John Kander, Fred Ebb, and Holmes' *Curtains* is still playing on Broadway after its Spring 2007 premiere.

Arthur Gelb in the *New York Times* noted that *Bella* "opened noisily" and should "close quietly." He found the book, lyrics, and music "uninspired," "vapid," and "tasteless." He also noted the musical offered "more accents and dialects than the Delegates' Lounge at the United Nations": the characters included an Oriental ("menacing"), a Hungarian ("oily"), a French soubrette, a British Lord ("leering"), and "assorted Mexicans, Texas cowboys and sailors."

Bella's brand of humor might be sampled from the names of the five characters played by Will B. Able: Lord Evelyn Mason-Mason, Rosetta Stone Mason-Mason, Juan Mason-Mason, Stone Mason, and Tex Mason-Dixon.

122 Belle Epoque. THEATRE: The Mitzi E. Newhouse Theatre/Lincoln Center Theatre; OPENING DATE: November 21, 2004; PERFORMANCES: 49; TEXT: Martha Clarke and Charles L. Mee, Jr.; lyric translations by Michael Feingold; DIRECTION: Martha Clarke; CHOREOGRAPHY: Martha Clarke; SCENERY: Robert Israel; COSTUMES: Jane Greenwood; LIGHTING: Christopher Akerlind; MUSICAL DIRECTION: Jill Jaffe; PRODUCER: Lincoln Center Theatre (Andre Bishop, Artistic Director; Bernard Gersten, Executive Producer)

CAST—Mark Povinelli (Henri de Toulouse-Lautrec), Honora Fergusson (Comtesse de Toulouse-Lautrec), Vivienne Benesch (Suzanne), Michael Stuhlbarg (Francois), Joyce Castle (Yvette), Ruth Maleczech (La Goulue), Robert Besserer (Valentin the Boneless), Tome Cousin (Chocolat), Paola Styron, Gabrielle Malone, Robert Wersinger, Nina Goldman, Rebecca Wender, Jill Jaffe, Will De Vos, Hector "Tito" Castro, Sam Davis

The action occurs in Paris around 1900.

The music-dance piece was presented in one act

NOTES—Like Martha Clarke and Charles L. Mee's theatre-music-dance piece *Vienna: Lusthaus* (see entry), *Belle Epoque* was set in a turn-of-the-century European city, in this case Paris "waltzing toward the edge of the abyss" (according to Charles Isherwood in the *New York Times*). In fact, Isherwood noted that despite the milieu of Parisian nightclubs with colorful characters (such as Henri de Toulouse-Lautrec), Clarke and Mee were more interested in "gloom" than "gaiety." Further, he felt one of the central female characters was more like a modern-day feminist than a "good-time girl" of the late nineteenth century. But Isherwood praised the "seductive" look of the production, particularly Robert Israel's "smoky, tilted mirrors," and Clarke's choreography, which offered "expected variations" of the can-can and quadrille. Isherwood also commented on the "bouncy" song translations provided by Michael Feingold.

For a list of theatre works by Martha Clarke which are discussed in this book, see entry for *The Garden of Earthly Delights*.

For more musicals about Toulouse-Lautrec, see entry for *Times and Appetites of Toulouse-Lautrec* (incidentally, Michael Feingold provided lyric translations for this musical as well).

123 La Belle et la Bete. "An Opera for Ensemble and Film"; THEATRE: Brooklyn Academy of Music; OPENING DATE: December 7, 1994; PERFORMANCES: 4; LIBRETTO: Philip Glass; MUSIC: Philip Glass; DIRECTION: Charles Otte; SCENERY: John Michael Deegan; COSTUMES: Mary Myers; LIGHTING: John Michael Deegan; MUSICAL DIRECTION: Michael Reisman

CAST—Alexandra Montano (La Belle), Hailie Neill (Felice, Adelaide), Gregory Purnhagen (La Bete, The Prince, Avenant), Zheng Zhou (Le Pere, Ludovic, Usurier), and The Philip Glass Ensemble; PRODUCER: The Next Wave Festival

MUSICAL NUMBERS—Overture, "Les Soeurs" ("The Sisters"), "La Demande en Mariage d'Avenant" ("Avenant Proposes"), "Le Voyage du Pere" ("The Father's Journey"), "La Domaine de la Bete" ("The Beast's Domain"), "La Retour de Pere" ("The Father Returns"), "La Belle va au Chateau" ("Beauty Goes to the Chateau"), "Le Diner" ("Dinner with the Beast"), "Les Tourments de la Bete" ("The Beast's Anguish"), "Promenade dans le Jardin" ("Promenade in the Garden"), "La Saisie des Meubles" ("The Furniture Is Seized"), "La Confiance de la Bete en la Belle" ("The Beast's Pledge of Faith"), "Belle Retourne Chez Son Pere" ("Beauty's Return Home"), "Belle Raconte Son Histoire" ("Beauty Tells Her Story"), "Le Plan" ("The Plan"), "La Passion d'Avenant" ("Avenant's Passion"), "La Magnifique Apparait" ("Magnificence Appears"), "Le Miroir" ("The Mirror"), "Le Pavillon" ("The Pavilion"), "La Metamorphose" ("The Transformation"

NOTES—*La Belle et la Bete* was originally produced in Gibellina, Sicily, on June 21, 1994, and received its American premiere six months later at the Brooklyn Academy of Music as part of the Next Wave Festival.

Philip Glass stripped Jean Cocteau's classic 1946 film of it spoken dialogue and its background music by Georges Auric and in their place he set the film's dialogue to music and also composed new background music. In the theatre, the film was shown on a screen above the stage while a live orchestra and ensemble sang and played in time to the action on the screen (the opera was sung in French).

Edward Rothstein in the *New York Times* felt that despite its occasional flaws, *La Belle et la Bete* "should not be missed." He noted that Glass and Cocteau's sensibilities were different, and that Glass emphasized musical "effects" over Cocteau's "mystery." For all that, Rothstein praised the minimalist music used for Beauty's sisters and the "bluesy flavor" of the Beast's yearning for Beauty. Moreover, he noted that Glass' music offered "wonderful effects" which matched Cocteau's filmic imagery, and concluded that he hoped to hear the opera again. The opera was recorded by Nonesuch Records on a 2-CD set (# 79347-2); the song titles above are taken from the recording.

La Belle et la Bete was the second in Glass' trilogy inspired by films by Cocteau. The first, *Orphee* (1993), was based on the 1949 film, and unlike *La Belle et la Bete*, it was fully staged without a screening of the film. The final work in the trilogy was *Les Enfant Terribles* (1996), which was based on a Cocteau film released in 1949.

124 La Belle Helene. THEATRE: The AMAS Repertory Theatre; OPENING DATE: February 13, 1986; PERFORMANCES: 16; BOOK: John Fearnley; from A.P. Herbert's *Helene* Lyrics: David Baker; from A.P. Herbert's *Helene*; MUSIC: Jacques Offenbach; DIRECTION: John Fearnley; CHOREOGRAPHY: J. Randall Hugill; SCENERY: Donald L. Brooks; COSTUMES: Howard Behar; LIGHTING: Deborah Matlack; MUSICAL DIRECTION: Patrick Holland; PRODUCER: The AMAS Repertory Theatre, Inc. (Rosetta LeNoire, Founder and Artistic Director) by special arrangement with Dorothy Dickson

CAST—Philip Anderson (Philicomus, Ajax II), Alexander Barton (Agamemnon), Marcia Brushingham (Minerva), Beverly Burchett (Eleni), Larry Campbell (Menelaus), Cliff Hicklen (Mercury), Jozie Hill (Parthenis), Jay Aubrey Jones (Calchas), Francesca MacAaron (Anais, Juno), Saundra McClain (Bacchis), Susan McDonnell (Leora), Kenneth McMullen (Hector), Steve Riedel (Pylades), Alex Santoriello (Paris), Brad Scott (Oresties), Vanessa Shaw (Helen), Ted Simmons, Jr. (Ajax I), Sunder (Venus), Marzetta Tate (Juno), Ivan Thomas (Achilles)

SOURCE—The 1865 operetta *La Belle Helene*, music by Jacques Offenbach, and A.P. Herbert's adaptation, *Helene*.

The action occurs in Sparta, Greece, some 3,000 years ago.

The musical was presented in three acts.

ACT ONE—Opening (Worshippers, Jay Aubrey Jones, Philip Anderson), "Oh, Gods of Love" (Vanessa Shaw, Maidens), "Oom Pah Pah" (Brad Scott, Jay Aubrey Jones), "Oom Pah Pah" (reprise) (Vanessa Shaw, Brad Scott), "Paris' Song" (Alex Santoriello), "Judgement" (Alex Santoriello, Marzetta Tate, Marcia Brushingham, Sunder), "Entrance of Kings" (Company), "Conference"/Finale (Company)

ACT TWO—"Bacchis' Song" (Vanessa Shaw, Saundra McClain, Maidens), "Struggle in Vain" (Vanessa Shaw, Brad Scott), "Bolero" (Company), "Love Duet" (Vanessa Shaw, Brad Scott), Finale (Company)

ACT THREE—"The Warrior's Song" (The Men), "The Face That Launched a Thousand Ships" (The Men, Vanessa Shaw), Finale (Company)

NOTES—The Off Off Broadway production of *La Belle Helene* was based on a translation by A.P. Herbert of Jacques Offenbach's 1865 operetta. A program note indicated that Rosetta LeNoire, the founder and artistic director of AMAS, had appeared as Bacchis in a 1941 production of Herbert's adaptation; for the 1941 production, John Fearnley directed (he also directed the current production and adapted the book for the revival). For other musical versions of the legendary tale of Helen, Paris, et al., see entries for *The Golden Apple*, *Sing Muse!* and *Helen*; for a list of musicals which utilized music by Jacques Offenbach, see entry for *Bon Voyage*.

125 Le Bellybutton. "A Sexy Musical"; THEATRE: Diplomat Cabaret Theatre; OPENING DATE: April 2, 1976; PERFORMANCES: 28; SKETCHES: Scott Mansfield; additional sketch material by Johnathan Copley and Joel Scott; LYRICS: Scott Mansfield; MUSIC: Scott Mansfield; DIRECTION: Scott Mansfield; CHOREOGRAPHY: Katherine Hill and Louise Quick; SCENERY: David Chapman; COSTUMES: David Chapman; associate costume designer, Ben Gutierrez-Soto; LIGHTING: Richard Winkler, Associate Lighting Designer; MUSICAL DIRECTION: Ken Werner; PRODUCERS: Jolandrea Music Inc. in association with Gail Davis, Parker Willson, and Edmund Gaynes.

CAST—MARILYN CHAMBERS, Thommie Bush, Jessie Hill, Adrienne Frimet, Larry Kingery, Debbie Kinney, Alan Lee Kootsher, Billy Padgett, Paulette Sanders, Jim Sbano, Alan Scott, Suzanne Walker

The revue was presented in two acts (program didn't indicate division of acts).

MUSICAL NUMBERS—"Disco Baby"/"Dance for Me" (Jim Sbano, Marilyn Chambers, Company), "BiSexual Blues" (Alan Lee Kootsher), "The S & M Polka" (Company), "Gotta Get Back to You" (Marilyn Chambers, Thommie Bush, Larry Kingery), "Night Lady" (Jim Sbano, Larry Kingery, Marilyn Chambers), "Love Child" (Thommie Bush, Company), "I Never Let Anyone Beat Me but You" (Debbie Kinney), "Jenny" (Jessie Hill), "A Sucker's Soliloquy" (Billy Padgett, Paulette Sanders, Company), "Marilyn's Theme" (Marilyn Chambers), "She" (Jim Sbano), "Disco"/"Apache" (Company), "Morning Light" (Alan Scott, Suzanne Walker, Marilyn Chambers), "Come Back Home Baby" (Paulette Sanders, Jim Sbano), "Let Me Make Love to You" (Marilyn Chambers)

NOTES—*Le Bellybutton* was another *Oh! Calcutta!* (1969; see entry) wannabe, and despite the presence of an authentic porn-film star (Marilyn Chambers), the revue didn't last a full month. Perhaps the era of the porn/nudie musical was finally over. But another era was now upon us: The Age of Disco. And because it appears to be the first musical to incorporate a disco number into its score (two, in fact: "Disco Baby" and "Disco"), *Le Bellybutton* may be one of the most important works in the history of the American musical.

126 Below the Belt. "A Retrospective ReView"; THEATRE: Downstairs at the Upstairs; OPENING DATE: June 21, 1966; PERFORMANCES: 186; SKETCHES: Dee Caruso, Bill Kaufman, Paul Koreto, Bill Levine, Gayle Parent, Treva Silverman, Kenny Solms, and Rod Warren; LYRICS: Lesley Davison, David Finkle, Howard Liebling, Michael McWhinney, James Rusk, and Rod Warren; MUSIC: Lesley Davison, Marvin Hamlisch, Jerry Powell, James Rusk, Rod Warren, and Bill Weeden; DIRECTION: Sandra Devlin; supervised by Rod Warren; CHOREOGRAPHY: Sandra Devlin; MUSICAL DIRECTION: Michael Cohen CAST—Richard Blair, Genna Carter, Madeline Kahn, Robert Rovin, Lily Tomlin; PRODUCER: Rod Warren

The revue was presented in two acts.

ACT ONE—"Below the Belt" (lyric and music by Rod Warren) (Company) "Happiness Is" (lyric and music by Rod Warren) (Genna Carter, Lily Tomlin, Richard Blair) (*), "Gentlemen's Resale Shop" (sketch by Rod Warren) (Richard Blair, Robert Rovin) (*****), "Camp" (lyric and music by Rod Warren) (Genna Carter, Madeline Kahn, Lily Tomlin) (****), "Lady Bird" (lyric and music by Lesley Davison) (Madeline Kahn, Robert Rovin) (****), "If the Crown Fits" (sketch by Kenny Solms and Gayle Parent) (Richard Blair, Genna Carter, Madeline Kahn, Lily Tomlin) (*****), "When I Was Learning to Read" (lyric and music by Rod Warren) (Robert Rovin) (*), "The Telephone Hang-Up" (sketch by Bill Kaufman and Paul Koreto) (Madeline Kahn, Lily Tomlin) (*****), "Anyone Who's Anyone" (lyric by David Finkle, music by Bill Weeden) (Genna Carter, Madeline Kahn, Richard Blair, Robert Rovin) (*****), "The Envelope, Please" (sketch by Treva Silverman) (Company) (*), "Suburbia Square Dance" (lyric by Michael McWhinney, music by Rod Warren) (Company) (****)

ACT TWO—"The Great Society Waltz" (lyric and music by Rod Warren) (Company) (***), "Love's Labour Lost" (lyric by Michael McWhinney, music by Jerry Powell) (Genna Carter) (**), "Eye on New York" (sketch by Dee Caruso and Bill Levine) (Lily Tomlin, Robert Rovin) (***), "The Doll Song" (lyric and music by James Rusk) (Madeline Kahn) (**), "The Tree" (sketch by Treva Silverman) (Genna Carter, Richard Blair) (*), "Introductions" (sketch by John Meyer and David Neuburge) (Lily Tomlin) "Doris" (lyric by Howard Liebling, music by Marvin Hamlisch) (Richard Blair, Company) (***), "International Monopoly" (lyric and music by Rod Warren) (Company) (****), Finale: "Below the Belt" (lyric and music by Rod Warren) (Company)

NOTES—*Below the Belt* was a collection of songs and sketches (some of which were updated for this revue) which had appeared in Rod Warren's previous "sporting title" revues (*...And in This Corner* [1964], *The Game Is Up* [one edition in 1964 and two in 1965], and *Just for Openers* [1965]); see entries for these revues. *Below the Belt* and the next Warren revue (*Mixed Doubles*; 1966; see entry) were released together in a 2-LP set by Upstairs at the Downstairs Records (# UD-37W56) (the album's number reflected the address of Upstairs at the Downstairs, 37 West 56th Street).

* = from ... *And in This Corner* (1964); ** = from *The Game Is Up* (First Edition; 1964); *** = from *The Game Is Up* (Second Edition; 1965). **** = from *The Game Is Up* (Third Edition; 1965); ***** = from *Just for Openers* (1965); it is unclear from which revue the number "Introductions" was first presented. "The Great Society Waltz," "Camp," and "The Envelope, Please" were also heard in *The Playoffs of Mixed Doubles* (see entry). "Suburbia Square Dance" had first been introduced in the third edition of *The Game Is Up* (see entry); after being heard in *Below the Belt* (and recorded on that revue's cast album), the song appeared for a third time in the 1972 revue *Hark!* (see entry) and was recorded for the *Hark!* cast album. "Lady Bird" had first been heard in *That Thing at the Cherry Lane* and then later in *The Game Is Up* (Third Edition); see entries.

For a complete list of Rod Warren's revue, see entry for *...And in This Corner*; also see Appendix R.

127 Beowulf. THEATRE: AMAS Repertory Theatre; OPENING DATE: December 1, 1977; PERFORMANCES: 12; BOOK: Betty Jane Wylie; LYRICS: Betty Jane Wylie; MUSIC: Victor Davies; DIRECTION: Voight Kempson; CHOREOGRAPHY: Voigt Kempson; SCENERY: Michael Meadows; COSTUMES: Lindsay Davis; LIGHTING: Paul Sullivan; MUSICAL DIRECTION: Clyde Williams; PRODUCER: The AMAS Repertory Theater (Rosetta LeNoire, Artistic Director)

CAST—Robert Anderson, Nora M. Cole, Joey Ginza, Susanne Montgomery, Michelle Stubbs

NOTES—*Beowulf*, which was based on the ancient epic, was produced Off Off Broadway. On October 16, 2005, another musical version of the story, also titled *Beowulf*, was produced Off Off Broadway by the Irish Repertory Theatre; the adaptation was by Lenny Pickett and Lindsey Turner.

For an operatic look at the Beowulf legend, see entry for *Grendel*.

128 Berlin to Broadway with Kurt Weill (1972). "A Musical Voyage"; THEATRE: Theatre de Lys; OPENING DATE: October 1, 1972; PERFORMANCES: 152; TEXT (AND FORMAT): Gene Lerner; LYRICS: See song list for credits; MUSIC: Kurt Weill; DIRECTION: Donald Saddler; SCENERY: Herbert Senn and Helen Pond; COSTUMES: Frank Thompson; LIGHTING: Thomas Skelton; MUSICAL DIRECTION: Newton Wayland; PRODUCERS: Hank Kaufman and Gene Lerner in association with Michael Arthur Film Productions

CAST—Margery Cohen, Ken Kercheval (who played the part of the revue's "guide" through the "musical voyage"), Judy Lander, Jerry Lanning, Hal Watters The revue was presented in two acts.

ACT ONE—*The Threepenny Opera* (1928; original German lyrics by Bertolt Brecht; English lyrics by Marc Blitzstein): "Morning Anthem" (Margery Cohen, Judy Lander, Jerry Lanning, Hal Watters), "Mack the Knife" (Jerry Lanning), "Jealousy Duet" (Margery Cohen, Judy Lander), "Tango Ballad" (Jerry Lanning, Judy Lander), "Love Duet" (Jerry Lanning, Margery Cohen), "Barbara Song" (Judy Lander), "Useless Song" (Hal Watters), "How to Survive" (Jerry Lanning, Hal Watters, Margery Cohen, Judy Lander); *Happy End* (1929; original German lyrics by Bertolt Brecht): "Bilbao Song" (English lyric by Michael Feingold) (Jerry Lanning, Hal Watters), "Surabaya Johnny" (English lyric by George Tabori) (Judy Lander); *The Rise and Fall of the City of Mahagonny* (1930; original German lyrics by Bertolt Brecht; English lyrics by Arnold Weinstein): "Alabama Song" (English lyric by Bertolt Brecht) (Margery Cohen, with Jerry Lanning, Hal Watters, Judy Lander), "Deep in Alaska" (Hal Watters, with Jerry Lanning), "Oh, Heavenly Salvation" (Hal Watters, Jerry Lanning, Margery Cohen, Judy Lander), "As You Make Your Bed" (Company); *The Threepenny Opera* (1928; original German lyric by Bertolt Brecht; English lyric by Marc Blitzstein): "Pirate Jenny" (Judy Lander); *Marie Galante* (1934; original French lyric by Jacques Deval; English lyric by Gene Lerner and Alice Baker): "I Wait for a Ship" (Margery Cohen); *Happy End* (1929; original German lyric by Bertolt Brecht; English lyric by Michael Feingold): "Sailor Tango" (Jerry Lanning, Hal Watters, Margery Cohen, Judy Lander)

ACT TWO—*Johnny Johnson* (1936; lyrics by Paul Green): "Songs of Peace and War" (Jerry Lanning, with Margery Cohen and Judy Lander), "Song of the Guns" (Jerry Lanning, Margery Cohen, Judy Lander), "Hymn to Peace" (Hal Watters), "Johnny's Song (Listen to My Song)" (Hal Watters); *Knickerbocker Holiday* (1938; lyrics by Maxwell Anderson): "How Can You Tell an American?" (Jerry Lanning, Hal Watters, Margery Cohen, Judy Lander), "September Song" (Jerry Lanning); *Lady in the Dark* (1941; lyrics by Ira Gershwin): "My Ship" (Margery Cohen), "Girl of the Moment" (Jerry Lanning, Hal Watters), "The Saga of Jenny" (Judy Lander, with Jerry Lanning, Hal Watters); *One Touch of Venus* (1943; lyrics by Ogden Nash): "That's Him" (Margery Cohen), "Speak Low" (Jerry Lanning, Hal Watters, Margery Cohen, Judy Lander); *Love Life* (1948; lyric by Alan Jay Lerner): "Progress" (Jerry Lanning, Hal Watters); staged by Richard Landon); *Street Scene* (1947; lyrics by Langston Hughes): "Moon-Faced, Starry-Eyed" (Hal Watters), "Ain't It Awful, the Heat" (Jerry Lanning, Hal Watters, Margery Cohen, Judy Lander), "Lonely House" (Hal

Watters), "Lullaby" (Margery Cohen, Judy Lander); *Lost in the Stars* (1949; lyrics by Maxwell Anderson): "Train to Johannesburg" (Hal Watters, with Jerry Lanning, Margery Cohen, Judy Lander), "Trouble Man" (Judy Lander), "Cry the Beloved Country" (Margery Cohen, with Jerry Lanning, Hal Watters, Judy Lander), "Lost in the Stars" (Jerry Lanning); *Love Life* (1948; lyric by Alan Jay Lerner): "Love Song" (Jerry Lanning, Hal Watters, Margery Cohen, Judy Lander); *The Threepenny Opera* (1928; original German lyric by Bertolt Brecht; English lyric by Marc Blitzstein): "Happy Ending" (Ken Kercheval)

NOTES—Every season seemed to offer either a revival of a Weill musical or a revue of his songs; this season it was *Berlin to Broadway with Kurt Weill* (which returned in 2000; see entry).

The revue offered the not particularly inspired concept of a voyage to depict the two worlds of Weill's German and American music; it was released on a two-LP set by Paramount Records (# PAS-4000). The cast album also included material (from *Happy End* and *Johnny Johnson*) not heard on opening night, and so perhaps the revue underwent changes shortly after it opened.

If the album is any indication of the performance style, some numbers were performed in the upbeat and perky manner of the era's television variety shows; the dissonance and world weariness inherent in most of the material was often missing.

129 Berlin to Broadway with Kurt Weill (2000). THEATRE: Triad Theatre; OPENING DATE: August 19, 2000; PERFORMANCES: 121; TEXT (AND FORMAT): Gene Lerner; LYRICS: See entry for 1972 production; MUSIC: Kurt Weill; DIRECTION: Hal Simons; CHOREOGRAPHY: Hal Simons; SCENERY: William Barclay; COSTUMES: Suzy Benzinger; LIGHTING: Phil Monat; MUSICAL DIRECTION: Eric Stern; PRODUCERS: Laura Heller, Carol Ostrow, and Edwin W. Schloss

CAST—Lorinda Lisitza (Mezzo), Veronica Mittenzwei (Soprano), Bjorn Olsson (Baritone), Michael Winther (Tenor), Eric Stern (Pianist)

The revue was presented in two acts.

NOTES—The revival of the 1972 Kurt Weill tribute offered essentially the same songs as the original (but in a somewhat reordered presentation). For a list of songs, see entry for the original production.

130 Bernarda Alba. THEATRE: The Mitzi E. Newhouse Theatre/Lincoln Center Theatre; OPENING DATE: March 6, 2006; PERFORMANCES: 40 Words: Michael John LaChiusa; MUSIC: Michael John LaChiusa; DIRECTION: Graciela Daniele; CHOREOGRAPHY: Graciela Daniele; SCENERY: Christopher Barreca; COSTUMES: Toni-Leslie James; LIGHTING: Stephen Strawbridge; MUSICAL DIRECTION: Deborah Abramson; PRODUCER: Lincoln Center Theatre (Andre Bishop, Artistic Director; Bernard Gersten, Executive Producer)

CAST—Phylicia Rashad (Bernarda Alba), Saundra Santiago (Augustias), Judith Blazer (Magdalena), Sally Murphy (Amelia), Daphne Rubin-Vega (Martirio), Nikki M. James (Adela), Yolande Bavan (Maria Josepha), Candy Buckley (Poncia), Laura Shoop (Young Maid), Nancy Ticotin (Servant, Prudencia)

SOURCE—The play *The House of Bernarda Alba* by Federico Garcia Lorca (the play was written in 1936, and first produced in 1945).

The action occurs in a small village in rural Spain in the 1930s.

The musical was presented in three acts (with no intermissions).

ACT ONE—Prologue (Candy Buckley, Women), "The Funeral" (Phylicia Rashad, Women), "On the Day That I Marry"/"Bernarda's Prayer" (Laura Shoop, Phylicia Rashad, Candy Buckley, Nancy Ticotin), "Love, Let Me Sing You" (Sally Murphy, Daphne Rubin-Vega, Judith Blazer, Nikki M. James, Nancy Ticotin), "Let Me Go to the Sea" (Yolande Bavan, Women)

ACT TWO—"Magdalena" (Judith Blazer), Augustias (Saundra Santiago), "Amelia" (Sally Murphy), "Martirio" (Daphne Rubin-Vega), "Adela" (Nikki M. James), "I Will Dream of What I Saw" (Women), "Thirty Odd Years" (a/k/a "Poncia") (Candy Buckley), "Limbrada's Daughters" (Phylicia Rashad, Women)

ACT THREE—"One Moorish Girl" (Laura Shoop, Nancy Ticotin, Candy Buckley), "The Smallest Stream" (Phylicia Rashad), "The Stallion" (Saundra Santiago, Judith Blazer, Sally Murphy, Daphne Rubin-Vega, Nikki M. James), "Lullaby" (Yolande Bavan), "Open the Door" (Nikki M. James, Women), Finale (Women)

NOTES—Michael John LaChiusa's impressive score told the tragic story of Bernarda Alba, a fierce, dominating woman who won't give her five daughters the freedom to leave home and find love and fulfillment in the outside world.

Ben Brantley in the *New York Times* found the production lacking. Some of the roles were miscast (he noted Phylicia Rashad in the title role was more in keeping with "a generally jolly suburban matron in a bad mood") and Graciela Daniele's "flamenco-ish" choreography was sometimes "unintentionally comic." And he found a "nagging repetitiveness" in LaChiusa's score, which often erupted into "antimelodic harshness" more in keeping with chamber opera than conventional Broadway music. Brantley concluded it was all too easy to identify with Magdalena, Bernarda Alba's narcoleptic daughter who tended to fall asleep during much of the stage action.

The score was recorded by Ghostlight Records (CD # 1915584412-4).

131 Bernice Bobs Her Mullet.

NOTES—See entry for *The New York Musical Theatre Festival.*

132 Best Foot Forward. "The Bright Musical Comedy"; THEATRE: Stage 73; OPENING DATE: April 2, 1963; PERFORMANCES: 224; BOOK: John Cecil Holm; LYRICS: Hugh Martin and Ralph Blane; MUSIC: Hugh Martin and Ralph Blane; DIRECTION: Danny Daniels; CHOREOGRAPHY: Danny Daniels; SCENERY: Robert Fletcher; COSTUMES: Robert Fletcher; LIGHTING: Jules Fisher; MUSICAL DIRECTION: Buster Davis; PRODUCERS: Arthur Whitelaw, Buster Davis, Joan D'Incecco, and Lawrence Baker, Jr.

CAST—Ronald (Christopher) Walken (Clayton "Dutch" Miller), Paul Charles (Fred Jones), Edmund Gaynes (Monroe "Hunk" Hoyt), Gene Castle (LeRoy "Goofy" Clarke), Don Slaton (Harrison "Satchel" Moyer), Edwin Cooper (Doctor Reeber), Kay Cole (Minerva Brooks), Susie Martin (Lois Street), Karen Smith (Debbie Baxter), Renee Winters (Linda Ferguson), Liza Minnelli (Ethel Hofflinger), Jill Choder (Winnie McKaye), Jack Irwin (Old Grad), Glenn Walken (Bud Hooper), Patricia Stewart (Waitress, Nurse), Grant Walden (Jack Haggerty), Paula Wayne (Gale Joy), Truman Smith (Chester Billings), Tony Manzi (Professor Lloyd), Karin Wolfe (Helen Schlessinger), Paul Kastl (Chet Evans)

The action occurs in a small town in Pennsylvania in Spring 1940.

The musical was presented in two acts.

ACT ONE—"Wish I May" (Ensemble), "Three Men on a Date" (Glenn Walken, Ronald [Christopher] Walken, Edmund Gaynes), "The Old Hollywood Story" (Paula Wayne, Grant Walden), "Three B's" (Liza Minnelli, Kay Cole, Renee Winters) (NOTE—Although not listed in program, "That's How I Love the Blues" was incorporated into this sequence.), "Everytime" (Karin Wolfe), "Alive and Kicking" (Paula Wayne), "The Guy Who Brought Me" (Paula Wayne, Grant Walden, Edmund Gaynes, Ronald [Christopher] Walken, Glenn Walken), "Shady Lady Bird" (Karin Wolfe, Paul Kastl, Gene Castle, Don Slaton, Paul Charles)

ACT TWO—"Buckle Down, Winsocki" (Jack Irwin, Edmund Gaynes, Paul Charles, Ensemble), "You're Lucky" (Paula Wayne), "What Do You Think I Am?" (Edmund Gaynes, Liza Minnelli, Kay Cole, Ronald [Christopher] Walken, Ensemble), "Raving Beauty" (Ronald [Christopher] Walken, Kay Cole), "Just a Little Joint with a Juke-Box" (Liza Minnelli, Gene Castle, Don Slaton, Paul Charles), "You Are for Loving" (Liza Minnelli), "Buckle Down, Winsocki" (reprise) (Company)

NOTES—*Best Foot Forward* was a Broadway hit in 1941, and this well-received revival was a welcome addition to the Off Broadway season, affording theatre-goers the chance to see an old favorite. And a new favorite, too, as the musical marked Liza Minnelli's New York theatrical debut.

Earlier in the season, *O Say Can You See!* (1962; see entry) had offered a character (Veronica Van Whitney) modeled on 1940s film star Veronica Lake. But *Best Foot Forward* offered the real McCoy. A happy surprise of the revival was that at one point during its run, the character of Hollywood Actress Gale Joy was performed by the legendary Veronica Lake herself.

The following numbers were added for the revival: "Wish I May," "Alive and Kicking," and "You're Lucky," all of which had been written for the 1943 MGM film version; "Raving Beauty" and "You Are for Loving," which had been written for a 1960 summer stock production of Hugh Martin and Ralph Blane's 1944 film musical *Meet Me in St. Louis*; and, according to Miles Kreuger's liner notes for the CD release of the cast album, "The Old Hollywood Story" had originally been intended for Judy Garland in the 1954 film *A Star Is Born*. The following numbers from the original production weren't used in the revival: "Don't Sell the Night Short," "I Know You by Heart," "My First Promise," "Where Do You Travel?" and "I'd Gladly Trade."

Incidentally, although the songs are attributed to both Martin and Blane, they almost always wrote their songs separately, and so some numbers were written solely by Blane, others only by Martin. And although it's not officially attributed to Richard Rodgers, "The Guy Who Brought Me" was composed by him, and Rodgers and Martin co-wrote the lyric (the original production was anonymously produced by Rodgers; Kreuger noted that Rodgers did so in order not to offend Lorenz Hart, who was ill at the time; and so George Abbott, the musical's director, was credited as producer).

The revival was recorded by Cadence Records (LP # CLP-4012 and # CLP-24012), and was later reissued on Picc-A-Dilly Records; the CD was issued by Varese Sarabande Records (# 302-666-221-2).

Note that performer Ronald Walken later changed his name to Christopher Walken. His brother (Glenn Walken) was also in the production.

A self-described "straight play version" of the script (by John Cecil Holm) was published by the Dramatic Publishing Company in 1943; the copyright page indicates the work had originally been copyrighted in 1939 as an unpublished work titled *And One for the Lady.*

133 The Best Little Whorehouse in Texas. "A New Musical Comedy"; THEATRE: Entermedia Theatre; OPENING DATE: April 17, 1978; PERFORMANCES: 64; BOOK: Larry L. King and Peter Masterson; LYRICS: Carol Hall; MUSIC: Carol Hall; DIRECTION: Peter Masterson and Tommy Tune; CHOREOGRAPHY: Tommy Tune; Thommie Walsh, Associate Choreographer; SCENERY: Marjorie Kellogg; COSTUMES: Ann Roth; LIGHTING: Dennis

Parichy; MUSICAL DIRECTION: Robert Billig; PRODUCER: Universal Pictures

CAST—Rio Grande Band (Craig Chambers, Leader; Pete Blue, Ben Brogdon, Lynn Frazier, Chris Laird, Ernie Reed), Girls (Lisa Brown, Carol Chambers, Donna King, Susan Mansur, Louise Quick-Bowen, Debra Zalkind), Cowboys (Jay Bursky, Bradley Clayton King, Michael Scott, Paul Ukena, Jr.), Clint Allmon (Farmer, Melvin P. Thorpe), Gerry Burkhardt (Shy Kid), Edna Milton (Miss Wulla Jean), Jay Garner (Traveling Salesman, Scruggs, T.V. Colorman, Governor), Cameron Burke (Slick Dude, Soundman), Choir (Jay Bursky, Becky Gelke, Delores Hall, Jan Merchant, James Rich, Marta Sanders), Pamela Blair (Amber), Joan Ellis (Shy), Delores Hall (Jewel), Don Crabtree (Cokeman, Edsel Mackey), Carlin Glynn (Masterson) (Mona Stangley), The Girls at Miss Mona's (Donna King, Linda Lou; Lisa Brown, Dawn; Louise Quick-Bowen, Ginger; Jan Merchant, Beatrice; Carol Chambers, Taddy Jo; Becky Gelke, Ruby Rae; Marta Sanders, Eloise; Debra Zalkind, Duria), Bradley Clayton King (Leroy Sliney), The Dogettes (Gerry Burkhardt, Jay Bursky, Michael Scott, Paul Ukena, Jr.), Tom Cashin (Stage Manager, Cameraman), Melvin Thorpe Singers (Becky Gelke, Bradley Clayton King, Susan Mansur, Jan Merchant, James Rich, Marta Sanders), Henderson Forsythe (Sheriff Ed Earl Dodd), J. Frank Lucas (Mayor Rufus Poindexter, Senator Wingwoah), Susan Mansur (Doatsey Mae), Townspeople (Carol Chambers, Bradley Clayton King, Edna Milton, James Rich, Marta Sanders), T.V. Announcer (Voice of Larry L. King), Lisa Brown (Angelette Imogene Charlene), Angelettes (Carol Chambers, Becky Gelke, Donna King, Debra Zalkind, Jan Merchant), Paul Ukena, Jr. (Aggie #21), Michael Scott (Aggie #71), Jay Bursky (Aggie #11), Cameron Burke (Ukranian Placekicker—Aggie #1), James Rich (Aggie #17), Gerry Burkhardt (Aggie #7), Tom Cashin (Aggie #12—Specialty Dance), Bradley Clayton King (Aggie #77), Photographers (Michael Scott, Paul Ukena, Jr., James Rich, Jay Bursky), Susan Mansur (Reporter #1), Paul Ukena, Jr. (Reporter #2), Jay Bursky (Governor's Aide), Michael Scott (Reporter #3)

The action occurs in the State of Texas at the present time.

The musical was presented in two acts.

ACT ONE—Prologue (Craig Chambers and The Rio Grande Band), "20 Fans" (Carlin Glynn, Lisa Brown, Carol Chambers, Donna King, Susan Mansur, Louise Quick-Bowen, Debra Zalkind, Jay Bursky, Bradley Clayton-King, Michael Scott, Paul Ukena, Jr., Clint Allmon, Gerry Burkhardt, Edna Milton, Jay Garner, Cameron Burke, Becky Gelke, Delores Hall, Jan Merchant, James Rich, Marta Sanders), "A Li'l Ole Bitty Pissant Country Place" (Carlyn Glynn, Donna King, Lisa Brown, Louise Quick-Bowen, Jan Merchant, Carol Chambers, Becky Gelke, Marta Sanders, Debra Zalkind), "Girl You're a Woman" (Carlin Glynn, Joan Ellis, Delores Hall, Donna King, Lisa Brown, Louise Quick-Bowen, Jan Mechant, Carol Chambers, Becky Gelke, Marta Sanders, Debra Zalkind), "Watch Dog Theme" (Clint Allmon, Gerry Burkhardt, Jay Bursky, Michael Scott, Paul Ukena, Jr.), "Texas Has a Whorehouse in It" (Clint Allmon, Becky Gelke, Bradley Clayton King, Susan Mansur, Jan Merchant, James Rich, Marta Sanders, Gerry Burkhardt, Jay Burksy, Michael Scott, Paul Ukena, Jr.), "Twenty-Four Hours of Lovin'" (Delores Hall, Donna King, Lisa Brown, Louise Quick-Bowen, Jan Merchant, Carol Chambers, Becky Gelke, Marta Sanders, Debra Zalkind), "Watch Dog Theme" (reprise) (Gerry Burkhardt, Jay Bursky, Michael Scott, Paul Ukena, Jr.), "Texas Has a Whorehouse in It" (reprise) (Clint Allmon, Gerry Burkhardt, Jay Bursky, Michael Scott, Paul Ukena, Jr., J. Frank Lucas, Jay Garner, Don Crabtree, Susan Mansur, Townspeople and Others), "Doatsey Mae" (Susan Mansur), "Angelette March" (Lisa Brown, Carol Chambes, Becky Gelke, Donna King, Debra Zalkind, Jan Merchant), "The Aggie Song" (Paul Ukena, Jr., Michael Scott, Jay Bursky, Cameron Burke, James Rich, Gerry Burkhardt, Tom Cashin, Bradley Clayton King), "Bus from Amarillo" (Carlin Glynn)

ACT TWO—"The Sidestep" (Jay Garner, Jay Bursky, J. Frank Lucas, Clint Allmon, Gerry Burkhardt, Jay Bursky, Michael Scott, Paul Ukena, Jr., Becky Gelke, Bradley Clayton King, Susan Mansur, Jan Merchant, James Rich, Marta Sanders), "No Lies" (Carlin Glynn, Delores Hall, Donna King, Lisa Brown, Louise Quick-Bowen, Jan Merchant, Carol Chambers, Becky Gelke, Marta Sanders, Debra Zalkind), "Good Old Girl" (Henderson Forsythe, Paul Ukena, Jr., Michael Scott, Jay Bursky, Cameron Burke, James Rich, Gerry Burkhardt, Tom Cashin, Bradley Clayton King), "Hard Candy Christmas" (Pamela Blair, Donna King, Louise Quick-Bowen, Lisa Brown, Becky Gelke, Jan Merchant), "Hard Candy Christmas" (reprise) (Pamela Blair, Donna King, Louise Quick-Bowen, Lisa Brown, Becky Gelke, Jan Merchant), Finale (Company)

NOTES—The blockbuster *The Best Little Whorehouse in Texas* first played a brief workshop engagement at the Actors Studio in November 1977, and then transferred to Off Broadway at the Entermedia Theatre (formerly the Phoenix and Eden, respectively) in April 1978. By June, it was on Broadway, for a run of 1,584 performances. The Actors Studio version included four songs which were dropped before the Off-Broadway run ("A Little Bit of Fixin'," "Memory Song," "Two Blocks from the Capitol Building," and "Goddam Everything"). Another song ("Have a Memory on Me") was written for, but apparently never performed in, the workshop; it can be heard in the collection *Lost in Boston IV* (Varese Saraband Records CD # VSD-5768).

Tommy Tune joined the production as co-director and co-choreographer for the regular Off Broadway engagement; it was his inventive musical staging which put him on the map as one of the leading musical theatre directors/choreographers of the era.

Carol Hall's score hit just the right note. "Hard Candy Christmas" was one of the finest theatre songs of the 1970s. The score's weakest number was the lugubrious "Doatsey Mae," a song written for a minor character.

Despite its long Broadway run, the musical's 1982 Broadway revival lasted just sixty-three performances; the London production, which opened on February 26, 1981, at the Drury Lane (with Henderson Forsythe and Carlin Glynn repeating their original roles), was short-lived; and the 1982 film version, which starred Dolly Parton and Burt Reynolds and was released by Universal-RKO, will never make anyone's list of best movie musicals (to be sure, Charles Durning's "The Sidestep" was a memorable delight). (The film retained little more than a half-dozen songs from the Broadway production, and included two songs written by Dolly Parton, "Sneakin' Around" and "I Will Always Love You.") *The Best Little Whorehouse Goes Public*, a misguided and out-of-control sequel which opened on Broadway in 1994, checked out after two weeks. Its strongest asset was Carol Hall's catchy score (which was recorded by Varese Sarabande Records [CD # VSD-5542]).

The original Broadway cast album of *The Best Little Whorehouse in Texas* was released on MCA Records (LP # MCA-3049 and CD # MCAD-11683) as was the film's soundtrack (CD # MCAD-31007). In 2001, a national tour was mounted with Ann-Margret as Miss Mona, and it too was recorded (by Fynsworth Alley Records [CD # 302-062-1172]); the revival included a new song, "A Friend to Me."

134 The Best of Burlesque. THEATRE: Carnegie Playhouse; OPENING DATE: September 27, 1957; PERFORMANCES: Unknown; MATERIAL: Narrative, musical, and dramatic continuity written by Jack Vaughan; traditional sketches revised and edited by Jack Vaughan and Vini Faye; DIRECTION: Jack Vaughan; CHOREOGRAPHY: Nelle Fisher; SCENERY: Howard Bay; LIGHTING: Howard Bay; MUSICAL DIRECTION: Herbert Harris; PRODUCER: Banner Productions (Howard Da Sylva, Sanford Friedman, Arnold Perl, and Myron Weinberg)

CAST—Sherry Britton, Tom Poston, Vini Faye, Nelle Fisher, Joan Pierce, Lilly White, Emmett Rose, Nelle's Belles, Sugar Glaze, Nancee Ward

The revue was presented in two acts.

ACT ONE—Prologue (Emmett Rose), Overture (The Band); OPENING: "Hello, Everybody" and "Autumn Salutation" (Nelle's Belles), "Higher Education" (Tom Poston, Vini Faye, Nancee Ward, Sugar Glaze, Lilly White, Emmett Rose), "Pagan Love Song" and "Dagger Dance" (Vini Faye, Nelle's Belles), "I'm Forever Blowing Bubbles" (Nelle's Belles) (During Intermission, Candy Butcher sequence [performed by Emmett Rose])

ACT TWO—Prelude (The Band), "Pagan Love Song (Ballet)" (Nelle's Belles), "Fleugel Street" (Tom Poston, Emmett Rose, Nancee Ward, Sugar Glaze, Lilly White, Vini Faye), "Strip Tease" (Sherry Britton), Finale: "Sophisticated Lady" (Nelle's Belles, Vini Faye)

NOTES—Information regarding musical numbers was taken from the cast album, which was released by MGM Records (LP # E-3644). *Best of Burlesque* was the first of many successful and not-so-successful burlesque revues which appeared Off Broadway for the better part of four decades (see Appendix K for a list of burlesque revues). "A. G." in the *New York Times* praised newcomer Tom Poston and noted that in the grand tradition of slapstick "he can hang out his tongue and roll his eyes ... like a pair of unattached marbles."

The revue was first performed during weekends, but appears to have eventually settled into a regular eight-performance-week schedule.

135 Betjemania. "A Musical Entertainment"; THEATRE: St. Bart's Playhouse; OPENING DATE: September 23, 1980; PERFORMANCES: 12

Words: Sir John Betjeman; MUSIC: John Gould Direction: Peter Delaney; LIGHTING: Pauline Tonkin; PRODUCERS: St. Bartholomew's Church (the Reverend Thomas Dix Bowers, Rector; the Rev. Andrew J. Mullins, Assistant Rector), St. Bartholomew Community House; produced for St. Bartholomew's by Joe Sutherin

CAST—Richard Bartlett, David Firth, John Gould, Gay Soper

The revue was presented in two acts.

ACT ONE—*Childhood*: "Cornish Cliffs" (David Firth, Gay Soper, Richard Bartlett) (**), "Trebetherick" (Gay Soper) (**), "Indoor Games Near Newbury" (Company) (*), "Trebetherick" (Richard Bartlett) (**), "Pot Pourri from a Surrey Garden" (David Firth) (*), "North Coast Recollections" (Richard Bartlett, Gay Soper) (*), "Trebetherick" (John Gould) (**), "Huntrer Trials" (Gay Soper) (**), "Winthrop Mackworth Redivivus" (John Gould) (**), "Trebetherick" (Company) (**); *Church*: "Summoned by Bells" (Gay Soper, Richard Bartlett) (*), "Our Padre" (Company) (**), "Hymn" (Company) (**), "Diary of a Church Mouse" (Richard Bartlett) (*), "Lenten Thoughts of a High Angelican" (David Firth) (**), "Christmas" (Company) (**), "Wantage Bells" (David Firth) (*); *England*: "Dorset" (David Firth) (**), "The Town Clerk's Views" (John Gould) (*) "Inexpensive Progress"/"Executive" (John Gould, Company) (**), "Slough" (Richard Bartlett) (**), "The Village Inn" (Company) (*), "Harvest Hymn" (Richard Bartlett, John Gould, David Firth) (**); *Wartime*: "In Westminster Abbey" (Gay Soper) (**), "Station Syren" (Company) (**), "Before Invasion

1940" (Richard Bartlett) (*), "Invasion Exercise on the Poultry Farm" (Gay Soper) (*)

ACT TWO—*Love*: "A Russell Flint" (Richard Bartlett) (**), "The Licorice Fields at Pontefract" (David Firth) (*), "In a Bath Tea Shop" (Gay Soper, David Firth) (**); *Alma Mater*: "Caprice"/"Summoned by Bells" (Company) (*), "Cricket Master" (Richard Bartlett, Company) (**), "The Varsity Students Rag" (Company) (**); *People*: "County" (David Firth) (*), "Mortality" (Gay Soper, John Gould) (*), "Eunice" (David Firth) (**) "Middlesex" (Gay Soper) (**), "The Wykehamist" (Richard Bartlett) (*), "Monody on the Death of a Platonist Bank Clerk" (John Gould) (**), "Shattered Image" (Richard Bartlett, David Firth, John Gould) (*), "Narcissus" (David Firth, Gay Soper) (*), "The Arrest of Oscar Wilde at the Cadogan Hotel" (Gay Soper, Richard Bartlett, David Firth) (**), "On Seeing an Old Poet in the Café Royal" (John Gould, David Firth) (*); *Mortality*: "Sun and Fun" (Gay Soper) (**), "A Child Ill" (Richard Bartlett) (*), "In Memoriam Walter Ramsden" (Company) (**), "Goodbye" (David Firth) (*), "Besides the Seaside" (Company) (**); *Golf*: "Seaside Gold" (Company) (**)

NOTES—*Betjemania*, a limited-run revue from Great Britain, was based on the works of Sir John Betjeman (1906-1984), the Poet Laureate of England. Devised by David Benedictus and John Gould, the revue was a collection of readings of Betjeman's writings as well as songs based on his poetry. It was an esoteric piece; probably 99.9 percent of Americans couldn't identify America's, let alone Britain's, Poet Laureate.

John Gould and Gay Soper reprised their roles for the engagement at St. Bart's, which appears to have been under an Off Off Broadway contract. The British cast album was released by That's Entertainment Records in a limited edition of 1,000 copies (LP # TER-1002).

SPECIAL NOTE—(*) denotes spoken piece, (**) denotes song.

136 The Better 'Ole, or The Romance of Old Bill. "A Fragment from France in Two Explosions, Seven Splinters and a Short Gas Attack"; THEATRE: Greenwich Village Theatre; transferred to Broadway at the Cort Theatre on November 18, 1918, and then later to the Booth Theatre; OPENING DATE: October 19, 1918; PERFORMANCES: 32 (estimated); see NOTES below; SCRIPT: Captain Bruce Bairnsfather and Captain Arthur Eliot; MUSIC: Herman Darewski and Percival Knight; DIRECTION: Percival Knight; CHOREOGRAPHY: Lily Leonora; SCENERY: Ernest Albert; COSTUMES: Madame Broich and Chrisdie & Company; MUSICAL DIRECTION: Elliott Schenck

CAST—Edwin Taylor (Sergeant-Major), Gwen Lewis (Angele), Charles McNaughton (Bert), Colin Campbell (Alf) Charles Coburn (Old Bill), Eugenie Young (Rachel), Henry Warwick (Colonel), Lark Taylor (A Spy, Captain Milne), Mona Desmond (Suzette), Albert Kenway (A Tommy), Mrs. Charles Coburn (Victoire), Lillian Spencer (Captain of the Women War Workers), Marguerite Torrey (Mollie from Ireland), Hazel O'Brien (Suzette from France), Athalie Jenkins (Maggie from Scotland), Mollie Carroll (Helene from Belgium), Eugenie Young (Nancy from England), Ruth Urban (Mary Brown from America), Therese Josephs (Rosa from Italy), Theodora Keene (Peg from Canada), Helen Tilden (Berthe), Howard Taylor (French Officer), Eugene Borden (French Porter), Kenyon Bishop (Maggie [Mrs. Bill Busby]), Ruth Vivian (Kate), George Logan (Vicar), Nevin Clark (Old Villager), Tommies (Albert Kenway, Rene Wren, J.M. Deeter, Charles Engels, William Swayne, Henry Ward, Vincenze Ioucelli, William Fish, Nevin Clark, George Logan)

The action occurs in the present in both France and in England.

The play with music was presented in two "explosions" (acts); the program didn't denote division of acts (songs are listed in performance order).

MUSICAL NUMBERS—"Tommy" (Mona Desmond, Tommies), "That Trip Across the Rhine" (Lillian Spencer, Women War Workers), "Carrying On" (Charles McNaughton, Colin Campbell, Charles Coburn), "We Wish We Was in Blighty" (Charles McNaughton, Colin Campbell, Charles Coburn), "The Garden of Roses" (Lark Taylor), "Venus de Milo" (Charles Coburn), "Je Sais Que Vous Etes Gentil" (Helen Tilden, Charles McNaughton), "Regiment of Our Own" (Charles McNaughton, French Girls), "Regiment of Our Own" (dance) (Charles McNaughton, Marguerite Torrey)

NOTES—*The Better 'Ole* had been previously seen in Britain; when it arrived in New York, it was an immediate hit and within a month of its opening transferred to Broadway, where it played for the better part of a year (the play with music is credited with 353 performances; it's unclear if this figure includes the approximately 32 Off Broadway performances).

The play dealt with Old Bill (Charles Coburn) and his misadventures during World War One. He's mistakenly arrested as a spy, but is exonerated by the final curtain. The Better 'Ole was the name of a small English village.

A silent film version of *The Better 'Ole* was released in 1926.

137 Between Whisky and Vodka. THEATRE: Barbizon-Plaza Theatre; OPENING DATE: October 3, 1961; PERFORMANCES: 8; SKETCHES: Kay and Lore Lorentz, and Eckard Hachfeld; MUSIC: Werner Krause (Kruse), Emile Schuchardt, and Rolf Liebermann; PRODUCERS: Felix Gerstman and Gert von Gontard in association with the Deutsches Theatre of New York

CAST—Das Kom(m)odchen (a German cabaret troupe), which included Kay and Lore Lorentz

NOTES—*Between Whisky and Vodka*, a German-language revue which played for a limited engagement of just one week, was performed by Das Kom(m)odchen, an eight-member political cabaret troupe which was based in Dusseldorf. The troupe had played throughout Germany and Europe, and here was making its New York debut.

Milton Esterow in the *New York Times* explained the troupe's name derived from, and was a pun based upon, the words "little comedy." Esterow found the company "talented ... with a sharp sense of timing." He singled out one sketch which depicted two couples, one from West Germany and the other from East Germany, and how the former couple use American words like "cocktail party" and "darling" in their conversation while the latter talk about "work quotas." He also mentioned a song about a little girl named Berlina, who is imprisoned by her bad Uncle Khrushchev and hopes to be saved by her good uncle from Texas (Vice-President Lyndon Johnson). Esterow wondered if Berlina lived happily ever after, and noted the revue didn't provide an answer. In 1966, the company returned to the Barbizon-Plaza Theatre with the revue *Why Do I Deserve This?* (see entry); over the years, the theatre would occasionally offer other foreign entertainments, such as evenings of German (non-musical) plays and at least one Indian dance company.

138 Beware the Jubjub Bird. THEATRE: Theatre Four; OPENING DATE: June 14, 1976; PERFORMANCES: 2; PLAY: Sandra Jennings; LYRICS: Sandra Jennings; MUSIC: Sandra Jennings and Richard Cameron; DIRECTION: Harold Guskin; SCENERY: Lee Goldman; LIGHTING: Lee Goldman; PRODUCER: Pegasus III

CAST—Lisa (Jenny Sanford), Kevin Kline (Daniel), Peter G. Skinner (Jason), Cheryl Scammon (Jean), Jared Sakren (Owen)

The action occurs in the present in New York City.

The play was presented in two acts.

NOTES—*Beware the Jubjub Bird* dealt with a group of actors rehearsing a revival of Anton Chekhov's *The Seagull* (1896), and how their personal lives become confused with the characters they portray in the revival. The play included five incidental songs (titles unknown).

Richard Eder in the *New York Times* found the play wordy, and noted it "confuses self-explication with dialogue"; but he mentioned it was often "intelligent" and "wry." The songs themselves amounted to "lyrical hectoring," and of the performers, Eder singled out Kevin Kline as the "most interesting."

See entry for *Birds of Paradise*, a 1987 musical which dealt with two theatre companies collaborating on a revival of *The Seagull*. Also see entry for *The Seagull*, Thomas Pasatieri's operatic version of Chekhov's play. As of this writing, Pasadena's The Theatre @ Boston Court is scheduled to present *Gulls*, a musical version of *The Seagull*, on July 26, 2008. Set in Greenwich Village and Hollywood in 1959, the book and lyrics are by Nick Salamone and the music is by Maury McIntyre.

An interesting parallel to *Beware the Jubjub Bird* and *Birds of Paradise* is the 1994 (non-musical) film *Vanya on 42nd Street* (directed by Louis Malle) which dealt with actors rehearsing a production of Chekhov's *Uncle Vanya* (1900); during the course of the rehearsal, the actors' personal lives intersect with the roles they are playing. Incidentally, the film was photographed in a dark, crumbling, and haunted New Amsterdam Theatre years before its glorious restoration by the Disney Company.

139 Bewilderness. THEATRE: 47th Street Theatre; OPENING DATE: November 7, 2002; PERFORMANCES: 61; LIGHTING: Josh Monroe; PRODUCERS: WestBeth Entertainment, Islington Entertainment, Jam Theatricals, and BBC America Comedy Live

CAST—Bill Bailey

The revue was presented in two acts.

NOTES—Bill Bailey, a British comic, performed songs and stories in a potpourri of "religion, politics and physics," according to *The Best Plays of 2002-2003*.

The revue had been previously produced Off Off Broadway at the Westbeth Theatre Center on March 7, 2002. In reviewing the earlier production for the *New York Times*, Lawrence Van Gelder reported that Bailey was a "treat for the funny bone, the brain and the ear" and singled out many comic and musical bits, including Bailey's interpretation of a Tom Clancy thriller as written by Jane Austen.

140 Beyond Desire. "A Play with Music"; THEATRE: Theatre Four; OPENING DATE: October 10, 1967; PERFORMANCES: 8; PLAY: Constance Loux; DIRECTION: Jean Dalrymple; SCENERY: Feder; COSTUMES: Pat Stuart; LIGHTING: Feder; PRODUCER: Jean Dalrymple

CAST—FRANCHOT TONE (Karl Klingman [Narrator]), Mary Bell (Leah Mendelssohn), Jay Velie (Abraham Mendelssohn), Ethel Smith (Anna Bach), Norman Budd (Herr Weinlick, Herman Schmidt), John Scanlan (Herr Grumler, Pastor Hagen, Gustave), RICHARD STERNE (Felix Mendelssohn), Andre Plamondon (Frederic Chopin), Ben Yaffee (Amschel Rothschild, Herr Howlitz), BETSY VON FURSTENBERG (Cecile Jeanrenaud), Jane Marla Robbins (Nina), Jay Barney (Mayor Muller), Richard Kuss (Herr Kruger), Samuel Behar (Otto Reinbach), Deidre Sullivan (Kristine Reinbach), Michael Pedersen (Tanzen), Jo Flores Chase (Magdalena Klupp)

SOURCE—The novel *Beyond Desire* by Pierre La Mure.

The action occurs between the years 1750 and 1847 in various European countries.

The play was presented in two acts.

NOTES—*Beyond Desire* was based on the life of Felix Mendelssohn (1809-1847); the play included selections of Mendelssohn's music (arranged by Max Marlin), apparently as background and "interlude" sequences. The music wasn't utilized to tell the story in the form of a book musical.

Dan Sullivan in the *New York Times* criticized the evening as "pure romantic slush" and "tripe," and noted it played so fast and loose with the facts surrounding Mendelssohn's life it could have been titled *Beyond Recognition*. He also quoted some of the dialogue ("lines you thought they'd never dare use again"), such as "It's almost as if we were ... meant for each other" and "Felix, someday you'll be ... world-famous."

The cast included Franchot Tone, who sat on the sidelines and acted as narrator for the proceedings.

141 The Bible Salesman.

NOTES—See entry for *Double Entry* (1961), an evening which was comprised of two one-act musicals, *The Bible Salesman* and *The Oldest Trick in the World*.

142 Big Bad Burlesque! THEATRE: Orpheum Theatre; OPENING DATE: August 14, 1979; PERFORMANCES: 112; DIRECTION: Celeste Hall; CHOREOGRAPHY: Don Brockett; SCENERY: Charles Vanderpool; LIGHTING: Charles Vanderpool; MUSICAL DIRECTION: Jim Walton; PRODUCERS: David Richmond in association with Alan Schuster

CAST—Tamara Brandy (Tamara, Chorus), Michael Danek (Juvenile, Chorus), Nina David (Nina, Dancer), Danny Herman (Danny, Dancer), Tina Kay (Tina, Ecdysiast), Steve Liebman (Top Banana), Susan Orem (Soubrette), Eva Parmelee (Eva, Chorus), Deborah Pollack (Debbie, Showgirl), Donna Sontag (Donna, Chorus), Mitchell Steven Tebo (Mitch, Second Banana), Jim Walton (Jim the Piano Man)

The revue was presented in two acts (division of acts and sketch and song assignments unknown).

MUSICAL NUMBERS—"Big Bad Burlesque," "Glamour Girls," "Patriotic Finale," "School Daze," "Bug," "Wonderful Burlesque Days"; SKETCHES: "Meet Me Round the Corner (The Shed House Four)," "The Westfall Murder," "The Bullfight (Positions)," "Schoolroom," "Crazy House (The Nervous Wreck)," "Man on the Street"

NOTES—Off Broadway burlesque revues still kept coming along, although there were fewer and fewer of them; and not one of them matched the success of Ann Corio's *This Was Burlesque* (1962; see entry). John Corry in the *New York Times* noted that while the material in *Big Bad Burlesque!* was "surpassingly bad," it was nonetheless a "tiny triumph" because the evening never pretended to be anything more than it was, a salute to old-time burlesque. Corry found that the direction, choreography, and performers aimed for "exuberance and fun," and he singled out a number of cast members, including Donna Sontag (who played "Glowworm" on a flute, sang "Poor Butterfly," and enjoyed herself "enormously") and Nina David (who tap danced and enjoyed herself, too). Two months after the opening of *Big Bad Burlesque!* perhaps the ultimate burlesque musical opened on Broadway, the lavish and supremely entertaining *Sugar Babies*. With former MGM stars Mickey Rooney and Ann Miller at the helm, the smash hit was a mixture of classic burlesque sketches and song standards by Jimmy McHugh. It played for 1,208 performances.

143 The Big Bang. THEATRE: Douglas Fairbanks Theatre; OPENING DATE: March 1, 2000; PERFORMANCES: 55; BOOK: Boyd Graham; LYRICS: Boyd Graham; MUSIC: Jed Feuer; DIRECTION: Boyd Graham; Christopher Scott, Assistant Director; SCENERY: Edward T. Gianfrancesco; COSTUMES: Basil du Maurier; LIGHTING: James Vermeulen; MUSICAL DIRECTION: Albert Ahronheim; PRODUCERS: Eric Krebs and Nancy Nagel Gibbs in association with Pam Klappas-Pariseau

CAST—Jed Feuer, Boyd Graham

The action occurs in an apartment on Park Avenue.

The musical was presented in one act (all songs performed by Jed Feuer and Boyd Graham, including songs sung by the fictional characters in the musical-within-a-musical).

MUSICAL NUMBERS—"The Big Bang" (Jed Feuer, Boyd Graham), "Free Food and Frontal Nudity" ('Adam and Eve'), "Pyramid" ('Slaves'), "Viva La Diva" ('Nefertiti'), "Pyramid" (reprise) ('Slaves'), "Wake Up, Caesar" ('Caesar and Soothsayer'), "Hell of a Job" ('The Blessed Virgin Mary,' 'Mrs. Gandhi'), "Coliseum" ('Leo'), "Emperor Man" ('Constantine the Great'), "Number One" ('Attila the Hun'), "Cantata" ('Sisters of the Sacre Bleu'), "A New World" ('Columbus and Queen Isabella'), "Cooking for Henry" ('Chefs'), "The True Tale of Pocahontas" ('Pocahontas and Minihaha'), "Today's Just Yesterday's Tomorrow" ('Napoleon and Josephine'), "Freedom" ('Inertia and Phlegm'), "Potato" ('Paddy O'-Gratin'), "Two Asian Ladies" ('Shanghai Lil and Tokyo Rose'), "We're Gonna Fly" ('The Wright Brothers'), "Loving Him" ('Eva Braun'), "The Twentieth Century" (Jay Feuer, Boyd Graham), "The Big Bang" (finale) (Jay Feuer, Boyd Graham)

NOTES—In *The Big Bang*, two authors/stars of a new musical about the history of civilization put on a backers' audition for prospective angels. Bruce Weber in the *New York Times* found the evening "tedious" and the anachronistic humor tiresome.

The script was published by Samuel French in 2001, and the cast album was recorded by Original Cast Records.

For a similar musical, see entry for *A Backers' Audition*.

144 Big Noise of '92. "Diversions from the New Depression"; THEATRE: Cherry Lane Theatre; OPENING DATE: December 16, 1991; PERFORMANCES: 1; CHOREOGRAPHY: Tony Musco; SCENERY: Ann Davis; COSTUMES: Gregg Barnes; LIGHTING: Douglas O'Flaherty; PRODUCERS: Neilan Tyree; Gregg Wilcynski, Assistant Producer

CAST—Neilan Tyree, Mink Stole, Kit McClure and Her All-Girl Orchestra, Joel Forrester (Piano), Timi Michael (Marie-France), Tom Kosis (Hector)

The revue was presented in two acts.

NOTES—*The Applause/Best Plays Theatre Yearbook of 1991-1992* described *Big Noise of '92* as a variety show of "satirical vignettes and characterizations." More to the point, Stephen Holden in the *New York Times* noted the evening was a "vanity showcase" for Neilan Tyree, who performed in a "seasick monotone that occasionally" echoed Tallulah Bankhead. Further, Holden indicated *Big Noise of '92* "aspires to be the tackiest variety show ever produced" with "heavily sequined" production numbers staged with "hyperkinetic klutziness." The one-performance *'92* closed in '91, two weeks before '92 arrived.

145 The Big Show of 1936. THEATRE: The Felt Forum/Madison Square Garden Center; OPENING DATE: May 30, 1972; PERFORMANCES: 8 (estimated); PRODUCERS: Madison Square Garden Productions in association with Stan Seiden and Darren M. Seiden

CAST—Vince Barnett, Jackie Coogan, Cass Daley, The Ink Spots, Beatrice Kay, Virginia O'Brien, Sally Rand, Arthur Tracy, Allan Jones; with Shari Sue Robinson, Carl Stevens, Gene Bell

The revue was presented in two acts.

ACT ONE—Overture (The Panama Francis Orchestra), Allan Jones, Master of Ceremonies, The Ink Spots, Shari Sue Robinson, Arthur "The Street Singer" Tracy, Cass Daley, Carl "Harmonica" Stevens, Virginia "Dead Pan" O'Brien

ACT TWO—Panama Francis Orchestra, Vince Barnett, Beatrice (Gay 90's) Kay, Gene Bell (The World's Fastest Dancer), Sally Rand, Jackie "The Kid" Coogan, Allan Jones, Finale (Company)

NOTES—*The Big Show of 1936* offered a number of many forgotten performers who sang, danced, told stories, and did whatever they were famous for, all without benefit of lavish sets, costumes, and backup choruses of dancers and singers.

Some of them had been second-stringers even in their modest hey-day, and by the time of the revue's production they had long been out of the limelight. The revue afforded them another chance to strut their stuff, to give older audiences a chance to reminisce, and to provide younger audiences a once-in-a-lifetime opportunity to see in person a cultural icon like Sally Rand (who did indeed perform her fan dance) or a half-remembered MGM supporting player such as cut-up Virginia O'Brien, who, come to think of it, was actually famous for not cutting up.

A few months earlier the revue had toured as *The Big Show of 1928 (...And Ensuing Years)*, and among the cast members of this production (who weren't in the later *1936* version) were Rudy Vallee, George Givot, Louis Jordan and His Orchestra, and Diosa Costello. The latter had appeared in Richard Rodgers and Lorenz Hart's 1939 Broadway musical *Too Many* Girls, introducing "(All Dressed Up) Spic and Spanish" and, with Desi Arnaz, "She Could Shake the Maracas."

146 The Big Voice: God or Merman? "A Musical Comedy in Two Lives"; THEATRE: Actors Temple Theatre; OPENING DATE: November 30, 2006; PERFORMANCES: 125; TEXT, LYRICS, AND MUSIC: Jim Brochu and Steve Schalchlin; additional lyrics by Marie Cain; DIRECTION: Anthony Barnao; SCENERY: Clifton Taylor; COSTUMES: Elizabeth Flores; LIGHTING: Clifton Taylor; PRODUCERS: Murphy Cross, Paul Kreppel, Edmund Gaynes, and BarBar Productions, Ltd.; Nancy Bianconi, Pamela Hall, and Louis S. Salamone, Associate Producers

CAST—Steve Schalchlin (Steve), Jim Brochu (Jim)

The musical was presented in two acts (songs were not listed in the program).

NOTES—In *The Big Voice: God or Merman?* Steve Schalchlin and Jim Brochu (who had written the impressive *The Last Session* [see entry]) examined both their personal relationship and their love of musical theatre. Steve Suskin in *Variety* found the revue-like musical "funny, touching and warmly endearing," and singled out two songs, "I Want to Make Music" and "You Are a Stranger."

The musical's title derived from Brochu's dilemma concerning his calling. As a teenager, he had once met Merman and asked her whether he should become a priest or an actor. With deep philosophical wisdom and insight she responded, "How the hell should I know?"

The script was published by Samuel French, Inc., in 2007, and a cast recording of the Los Angeles production was released, which included the following songs: "Why?," "I Want to Make Music," "Us Catholics," "James Robertson," "The Closet," "Where Is God?," "Beyond the Light," "Near You," "Christmastime," "Where Is God? II," "You Are a Stranger," "One New Hell," "A Simple Faith," "Scarecrows," and "Why" (reprise).

147 The Big Winner. THEATRE: Eden Theatre; OPENING DATE: October 20, 1974; PERFORMANCES: 119; BOOK: David Opatoshu; LYRICS: Wolf Younin; MUSIC: Sol Kaplan; DIRECTION: David Opatoshu; Bryna Wasserman, Assistant to the Director; CHOREOGRAPHY: Sophie Maslow; SCENERY: Jeffrey B. Moss; COSTUMES: Jeffrey B. Moss; LIGHTING: Tom Meleck; MUSICAL DIRECTION: Jack Easton; PRODUCERS: Harry Rothpearl and Jewish Nostalgic Productions, Inc.

CAST—Bruce Adler (Old Man, Kopel), Stan Porter (Motel), Diane Cypkin (Bailke), Miriam Kressyn (Ety-Meny), David Opatoshu (Shimele Soroker), David Carey (Solomon Fine), Herschel Rosen (Osher Fine), Shifra Lerer (Perel), Jack Rechtzeit (Solovaitchik), William Gary (Goldentaller), Elia Patron (Mendel), Shmulik Goldstein (Rubinchik), Jaime Lewin (Vigdorchik, Sexton), Reizl Bozyk (Madame Fine), Shifra Lerer (Madame Flaum); Townspeople, Guests (Richard Ammon, Winifred Berg, Susan Fox, Joseph Goode, Cheryl Hartley, Marcus Williamson

SOURCE—An unidentified play by Sholem Aleichem.

The action occurs in 1910 in a Jewish town in Russia.

The musical was presented in two acts.

ACT ONE—"How Can I Tell Him She Loves Me?" (Stan Porter, Bruce Adler), "We're the People" (David Opatoshu, Miriam Kressyn, Stan Porter, Bruce Adler, Diane Cypkin), "Lottery Celebration" (Company), "Money, Wealth, Gold" (Stan Porter, Bruce Adler), "It's Delicious" (David Opatoshu, Miriam Kressyn), "Movie Montage" (David Opatoshu, Miriam Kressyn, Shmulik Goldstein, Jaime Lewin), "I Am a Tailor's Daughter" (Diane Cypkin), "Tango Rehearsal" (David Opatoshu, Miriam Kressyn)

ACT TWO—"The Tango" (Company), "In-Laws" (Miriam Kressyn, Reizl Bozyk), "Love Song" (Stan Porter, Diane Cypkin), "Winners, Losers" (Bruce Adler), "Wedding Dance" (David Opatoshu, Miriam Kressyn, Stan Porter, Diane Cypkin, Bruce Adler, Company)

NOTES—*The Big Winner* was performed in Yiddish, with narration in English.

Based on an unidentified play by Sholem Aleichem, *The Big Winner* was the story of a poor tailor (David Opatoshu) who wins the lottery and forsakes old friends for newer ones as he enjoys a life of untold wealth. But he's soon robbed of his fortune by two con artists, and he ultimately returns to his old life and friends, poorer but wiser for the experience.

Richard F. Shepard in the *New York Times* hailed *The Big Winner* as the "most polished production staged here in many years." Further, Sol Kaplan and Wolf Younin's score was "lively, creative and contemporary," and Shepard singled out a "funny" number, "The Tango."

A 1989 production of *The Big Winner* was taped live and released on videocassette by Jewish Video Library (# 1333). The revival was seen at the Folksbiene Playhouse, and was directed by Rina Elisha; the cast included Zypora Spaisman, David Rogow, and Mina Bern.

Sol Kaplan hadn't been heard from since 1962, when he was one of the two composers of *The Banker's Daughter* (see entry). He was also the composer of *Shootin' Star*, a 1946 musical about Billy the Kid which closed during its pre-Broadway tryout.

148 Billion Dollar Baby. THEATRE: York Theatre Company; OPENING DATE: September 11 (?), 1998; PERFORMANCES: Unknown; BOOK: Betty Comden and Adolph Green; LYRICS: Betty Comden and Adolph Green; MUSIC: Morton Gould; DIRECTION: BT McNicholl; Joe Marchese, Assistant Director; CHOREOGRAPHY: Mark Esposito; SCENERY: James Morgan; COSTUMES: Robin L. McGee; LIGHTING: Alexandra J. Pontone; MUSICAL DIRECTION: Michael Lavine; PRODUCER: The York Theatre Company (James Morgan, Artistic Director; Joseph V. De Michele, Managing Director)

NOTES—*Billion Dollar Baby* was presented by the York Theatre Company in 1998 as part of its *Musicals in Mufti* series (see entry for information on this series). The revival eventually led to the first recording of the score, which was "based" on the *Mufti* presentation. Released by Original Cast Records (CD # OC-4304) in 2000, the recording's cast included Kristin Chenoweth as Maribelle Jones (the billion dollar baby of the title), Debbie Shapiro Gravitte, Marc Kudisch, and Richard B. Schull.

The original Broadway production opened at the Alvin (now Neil Simon) Theatre on December 21, 1945, and was in a sense a follow-up to the successful *On the Town*, which had opened on Broadway one year earlier. The two musicals shared the same lyricists and book writers (Betty Comden and Adolph Green), director (George Abbott), choreographer (Jerome Robbins), set designer (Oliver Smith), musical director (Max Goberman), and producers (Oliver Smith and Paul Feigay). And, like *On the Town*, the cast included a number of fresh faces (Joan McCracken [as Maribelle Jones], Mitzi Green, Danny Daniels, and James Mitchell) as well as such seasoned performers as David Burns and Robert Chisholm. The cast also included Helen Gallagher (as a "chorine") and Jeri Archer (as a "cigarette girl"). Unfortunately, while *On the Town* enjoyed Leonard Bernstein's melodic score, *Billion Dollar Baby* offered pleasant if formulaic music by Morton Gould.

The musical, which was advertised as "A Musical Play of the Terrific Twenties," was a satire of the era, and the plot dealt with Prohibition, speakeasies, gangsters, Atlantic City beauty contests, and dance marathons.

The critics were divided over the merits of the original production. Howard Barnes in the *New York Herald Tribune* found the book "slyly refreshing and curiously nostalgic" and the score "rich and varied"; he noted the musical was "sung and danced brilliantly" and said the evening was "great good fun." But Lewis Nichols in the *New York Times* said the show was "far from even" and "doesn't completely come off." The original production of *Billion Dollar Baby* managed to run out the season, for a total of 220 performances; it apparently returned its investment and even showed a small profit, and so technically the musical was a hit.

But for almost forty-five years after its closing, *Billion Dollar Baby* wasn't much more than a memory. It didn't leave behind a cast album or even a hit song to establish itself in the public's mind, there wasn't a national tour or a London production, and it doesn't seem to have found its way into the rich summer stock circuit of the 1940s, 1950s, and early 1960s.

But in 1989, the Jerome Robbins' retrospective revue *Jerome Robbins' Broadway*, which opened at the Imperial Theatre on February 26 and played for 634 performances, included in its dance sequences the "Charleston" number from *Billion Dollar Baby* (the number was recorded for the 2-CD cast album released by RCA Victor Records [# 60150-2RC]). In his review for the *Wall Street Journal*, Edwin Wilson noted that for the "Charleston," Robbins had "cleverly exploited" the clichés of the 1920s and said the dance wasn't "just another Charleston number but a pastiche of character types and physical attitudes that is continually amusing."

The following is a list of musical numbers from the original 1945 production (followed by the names of the original performers who introduced them):

ACT ONE—"Million Dollar Smile (Billion Dollar Baby)" (Alan Gilbert), "Who's Gonna Be the Winner?" (Joan McCracken, Jacqueline Dodge, Beverly Hosier, Betty Saunders, Doris Hollingsworth, Bathing Beauties), "Dreams Come True" (Joan McCracken, James Mitchell, Fed Hearn, Bill Skipper), "Charleston" (Dancers), "Broadway Blossom" (Mitzi Green), "Speaking of Pals" (David Burns, Dave Thomas, Tony Gardell, William Tabbert, Ensemble), "There I'd Be" (Mitzi Green, Robert Chisholm), "One Track Mind" (Shirley Van, Danny Daniels), "Bad Timing" (William Tabbert, Joan McCracken), "The Marathoners" (Dance Ensemble), "A Lovely Girl" (Mitzi Green, Joan McCracken, Jollities Beauties)

ACT TWO—"Funeral Procession" (The Mob), "Havin' a Time" (Mitzi Green), "The Marathon Dance" (Danny Daniels), "Faithless" (Robert Chisholm, Joan McCracken), "I'm Sure of Your Love" (William Tabbert), "A Life with Rocky" (Joan McCracken, James Mitchell, Dancers), "The Wedding" (Company)

149 The Billy Barnes Revue (June 1959). THEATRE: York Playhouse; OPENING DATE: June 9, 1959; PERFORMANCES: 64; SKETCHES (AND DIALOGUE): Bob Rodgers; LYRICS: Billy Barnes; MUSIC: Billy Barnes; DIRECTION: Bob Rodgers Scenery: Glenn Holse; COSTUMES: "Supervision" by Berman Costume Co.; LIGHTING: Peggy Clark; MUSICAL DIRECTION: Billy Barnes; PRODUCERS: George Eckstein in association with Bob Reese

CAST—Joyce Jameson, Bert Convy, Patti Regan, Ken Berry, Ann Guilbert, Bob Rodgers, Jackie Joseph, Len Weinrib

The revue was presented in two acts.

ACT ONE—"Do a Revue" (Company), "Where Are Your Children?" (Ken Berry, Bert Convy, Jackie Joseph, Ann Guilbert, Patti Regan, Len Weinrib) "Medic" (Len Weinrib, Ann Guilbert, Patti Regan) "Foolin' Ourselves" (Bert Convy, Ken Berry) "Safari a la Marilyn" (Len Weinrib [as Papa Hemingway], Bob Rodgers [Arthur Miller], Joyce Jameson [Marilyn Monroe]) "The Pembroke Story" (Ken Berry, Ann Guilbert, Jackie Joseph, Bert Convy, Len Weinrib) "Where Is the Place, Kid?" (Joyce Jameson, Ann Guilbert, Jackie Joseph) "Listen to the Beat!" (Company) "Home in Mississippi" (Patti Regan [Maggie], Len Weinrib [Big Daddy], Ann Guilbert [Big Mama], Bob Rodgers [Brick], and "Themselves" [uncredited] as the No-Neck Monsters), "Las Vegas" (Joyce Jameson, Bert Convy, Ken Berry), "Blocks" (Bob Rodgers, Jackie Joseph) "The Thirties" (Company)

ACT TWO—"A Dissertation on Transportation, or It All Started with the Wheel" (Company) "The Fights" (Joyce Jameson, Bob Rodgers), "The Vamp and the Friends" (Ann Guilbert, Ken Berry, Patti Regan, Len Weinrib) "Tyler My Boy" (Bert Convy), "Hellahahana" (Bert Convy, Ken Berry, Joyce Jameson, Len Weinrib, Jackie Joseph, Ann Guilbert) "World at Large" (Bert Convy) "World at Large #1" (Joyce Jameson, Len Weinrib, Ann Guilbert) "Station Break" (Patti Regan), "World at Large #2" (Bob Rodgers, Choral Group [uncredited]) "World at Large Preview" (Ken Berry, Patti Regan) "(Have I Stayed) Too Long at the Fair?" (Joyce Jameson) "One of Those Days" (Company) NOTES—The liner notes of the cast album for *The Billy Barnes Revue* (Decca Records LP # DL-9076) indicated the revue had been intended for Rex Harrison and Julie Andrews and was to have taken place in River City, Iowa. The plot was to have dealt with a variety of characters, including the mother of a Chinese strip-tease artist (from the west side of River City), a redheaded man, and a tights-wearing Frenchman from the Jamaican section of the city ... "but the entire project was junked as 'uncommercial.'"

Billy Barnes was the Ben Bagley and Julius Monk of West Coast revues, albeit he wrote the lyrics and music for his revues and left the producing to others. But the name "Billy Barnes" evoked the same response as the names of Bagley and Monk, because his revues guaranteed an evening of topical and irreverent sketches and songs.

Over the course of his career, Barnes wrote a number of such revues (*In League with Ivy* [date unknown], *Fooling Ourselves* [1957], *Something Cool* [1957], *Billy Barnes Summer Revue* [1958, 1962], *Billy Barnes Revue* [1960], *Billy Barnes Party* [1961], *The Billy Barnes People* [1961], *Billy Barnes' L.A.*. [1962], *Billy Barnes' Hollywood* [1964], *Best Friends* [1980], and *Movie Star* [1982]), most if not all of which were performed in Los Angeles. Two of the revues, *The Billy Barnes Revue* and *The Billy Barnes People*, went on to New York. Usually the same performers would crop up in his revues (Joyce Jameson, Ken Berry, Patti Regan, Jackie Joseph), providing him a stock company of sorts. In 1989, Barnes returned to New York with the Off Broadway revue *Blame It on the Movies!* (see entry).

Lewis Funke in the *New York Times* found *The Billy Barnes Revue* "crisply played" and "highly polished," but said the humor was funny only "in a collegiate sort of way." He noted the revue's topics included beatniks, television, Marilyn Monroe, and Tennessee Williams, "all subjects of standing in the revue world."

The Billy Barnes Revue played a number of New York theaters, traveling almost as much as *Once Upon a Mattress* (1959; see entry). The revue opened at the York Playhouse on June 9, 1959, for sixty-four performances, and then transferred to Broadway on August 4 of that year (as *Billy Barnes Revue*) where it opened at the John Golden Theatre; on September 28, it transferred to another Broadway theater, the Lyceum, for a total of eighty-seven Broadway performances. Three days after it closed at the Lyceum, it re-opened Off Broadway as *Billy Barnes Revue* on October 20 at the Carnegie Hall Playhouse, where it ran for forty-eight performances (for more information on run at the Carnegie Hall Playhouse, see entry). The revue's total number of New York performances (at all four theatres) was 199.

The songs and sketches for the Broadway run were presented in a slightly different running order from the York Playhouse production, and included some new material: a trio of related songs for Patti Regan ("Whatever," "Whatever Happened," and, "Whatever Happened To") and "City of the Angels," a song for Joyce Jameson, Ann Guilbert, and Jackie Joseph. The "Whatever" songs and "City of the Angels" were also heard in the Carnegie Hall Playhouse production.

The revue was also performed in London, opening at the Lyric Opera House, Hammersmith, on April 4, 1960, for a run of twenty-four performances. The British cast included four members of the original Off Broadway and Broadway cast (Joyce Jameson, Ann Guilbert, Patti Regan, and Jackie Joseph, as "Four American Girls"). The males in the cast were "Four English Boys" (Ronnie Stevens, Ted Rogers, Terence Cooper, and Richard Owens).

The Billy Barnes Revue was a major stepping stone for some of its performers. Bert Convy later created roles in the original Broadway productions of *Fiddler on the Roof* (1964) and *Cabaret* (1966), and Ken Berry and Ann Guilbert found a certain amount of fame on television. The latter, as Ann Morgan Guilbert, created the role of Millie Helper, Dick Van Dyke and Mary Tyler Moore's next-door neighbor in the long-running series *The Dick Van Dyke Show*.

In the first act of *The Billy Barnes Revue*, Joyce Jameson portrayed Marilyn Monroe in a comic sketch which depicted her and Arthur Miller on safari with Ernest Hemingway. In the second act, she sang "(Have I Stayed) Too Long at the Fair?" a torch song generally acknowledged as a melancholy tribute to Monroe (who was alive at the time). The number became a standard, one of the few Off Broadway songs to achieve wide popularity.

In fact, Joyce Jameson made something of a career playing Marilyn Monroe types. In Henry Denker's Broadway comedy *Venus at Large* (1962), she portrayed a famous blonde Hollywood actress who seeks fame on the New York stage. She can also be seen giving a Marilyn Monroe impersonation of sorts in Billy Wilder's 1960 film *The Apartment*. Jameson plays "The Blonde," a pick-up whom the Ray Walston character takes to Jack Lemmon's apartment (Walston asks Lemmon to clear out of his apartment so he can have a tryst with a girl "who looks like Marilyn Monroe").

Besides "(Have I Stayed) Too Long at the Fair?" the revue offered a number of memorable songs: a lovely, underrated ballad, "Foolin' Ourselves"; a catchy upbeat number, "One of Those Days"; and "Listen to the Beat," an amusing song satirizing the beatnik movement (we're told that a fellow was inspired to write beat poetry after encountering Jack Kerouac in the men's room of a Greyhound bus terminal).

One of the "Whatever" songs asked what became of actress Bella Darvi. For those not steeped in 1950s move lore, Bella Darvi was a Polish actress who was taken under the wings of Hollywood producer Darryl F. Zanuck and his wife Virginia (Darvi's last name was a combination of their first names). Due to her extremely limited acting skills and her very thick European accent, Darvi probably didn't get even a full fifteen minutes of fame under the Hollywood sun. "Whatever" asked us to salute this "wonderful gal" who was mighty cute but "awfully hard to understand."

Incidentally, Billy Barnes' second (and last) revue to open on Broadway, *The Billy Barnes People*, premiered at the Royale Theatre on June 13, 1961, for seven performances. The cast included four holdovers from *The Billy Barnes Revue* (Joyce Jameson, Patti Regan, Ken Berry, and Jackie Joseph). Another cast member, Jo Anne Worley, later found fame in television's *Laugh-In*. Verve Records was set to record the cast album, but due to the show's brief New York run, the recording was cancelled.

At least one theatre reference book indicates the number called "Callas Tonight" appeared in *The Billy Barnes Revue*. It may well have, but various programs from the York, Royale, Lyceum, and Carnegie Hall Playhouse runs don't include the number.

Five numbers in *The Billy Barnes Revue* ("Hellahahana," "The Thirties," "Too Long at the Fair," "Tyler My Boy," and "Where Are Your Children?") appeared in an earlier Billy Barnes revue, *Fooling Ourselves* (a/k/a *Foolin' Ourselves*); it seems likely that the ballad "Foolin' Ourselves" originated with this this production.

In 1999, the CD *Billy Barnes Revued* was released by Ducy Lee Recordings (# DLR-900107), a revue which presented material from throughout Barnes' career, including the song "Dance, Dance, Dance," which had been added during the run of *Billy Barnes Revue* when it played the Carnegie Hall Playhouse (see entry). For the CD, the "Whatever Happened To" songs were updated, and one referenced Molly Ringwald. Other numbers on the CD were "Do a Revue," "Where Are Your Children?" "Foolin' Ourselves," "City of the Angels," and "(Have I Stayed) Too Long at the Fair?"

Incidentally, the Los Angeles cast recording of *Billy Barnes' L.A.* (which opened on October 10, 1962, at the Coronet Theatre) was recorded by BB Records (LP # 1001); the cast included Joyce Jameson, Ken Berry, Marilyn Mason, and Steve Franken, and the score contained another melancholy number which brought to mind Marilyn Monroe ("Does Anybody Here Love Me?") as well as a comic number about "Sister Aimee" (see entry for *Sister Aimee* [1981]).

In 1962, *The Billy Barnes Summer Revue* played in summer stock, and the cast included Joyce Jameson, Patty (formerly Patti) Regan, Ken Barry, Marlyn (Marilyn?) Mason, Jack Grinnage, and Bob Rodgers (with Barnes and Al Morley at the pianos). New numbers included "Something to Do," "Something to Do Blackouts," "Rich People of Texas," "The Interview," "A Tennessee Williams Note," "Fairly Fresh," "What Am I?" "The Doctors," "Classic Ingredients," "Little Italy," and "I'm a Butterfly." Other numbers in the revue which were retained from earlier editions of *The Billy Barnes Revue* were: "(Have I Stayed) Too Long at the Fair," "Blocks," "The Thirties," "The Fights," "A Dissertation on Transportation, or It All Started with the Wheel," "Hellahahana," "City of the Angels," and new versions of the "Whatever" sequences. Further, five numbers were used which had been heard in *The Billy Barnes People*: "I Like You," "Dolls," "The End?" "Where Is the Clown?" and "Liberated Woman."

150 Billy Barnes Revue (October 1959).

THEATRE: Carnegie Hall Playhouse; OPENING DATE: October 20, 1959; PERFORMANCES: 48; SKETCHES AND DIALOGUE: Bob Rodgers; LYRICS: Billy Barnes; MUSIC: Billy Barnes; DIRECTION: Bob Rodgers; CHOREOGRAPHY: Ken Berry; SCENERY: Glenn Holse; COSTUMES: "Supervision" by Berman Costume Co.; "New York Costume Supervision" by Peggy Morrison; PRODUCERS: George Brandt and Samuel J. Friedman, presenting a George Eckstein production

CAST—See NOTES below for the names of the two sets of casts in the production; the song and sketch credits below are from a later program, and reflect the second cast.

The revue was presented in two acts.

ACT ONE—"Do a Revue" (Company) "Where Are Your Children?" (Company) "Las Vegas" (Charles Nelson Reilly, Arlene Fontana, Virginia de Luce, Larry Hovis, James Inman) "Medic" (Charles Nelson Reilly, Ronnie Cunningham, Jane A. Johnston) "Foolin' Ourselves" (Larry Hovis, James Inman), "Whatever" (Ronnie Cunningham) "The Pembroke Story" (James Inman, Jane A. Johnston, Arlene Fontana, Tom Williams, Larry Hovis) "City of the Angels" (Virginia de Luce, Ronnie Cunningham, Arlene Fontana), "Listen to the Beat!" (Larry Hovis, James Inman, Arlene Fontana, Tom Williams, Virginia de Luce) "Dance, Dance, Dance" (Virginia de Luce) "Home in Mississippi" (Ronnie Cunningham, Charles Nelson Reilly [Big Daddy], Jane A. Johnston, Larry Hovis, and "Themselves" [uncredited] as the No-Neck Monsters) "Tyler My Boy" (Tom Williams) "Whatever Happened" (Ronnie Cunningham) "The Thirties" (Company)

ACT TWO—"A Dissertation on Transportation, or It All Started with the Wheel" (The Company) "(The) Fights" (Jane A. Johnston, Charles Nelson Reilly), "The Vamp and Friends" (Virginia de Luce, Larry Hovis, Ronnie Cunningham, Charles Nelson Reilly), "Hellahahana" (Charles Nelson Reilly, Larry Hovis, Arlene Fontana, James Inman, Jane A. Johnston, Virginia de Luce) "Whatever Happened To" (Ronnie Cunningham) "World at Large" (Larry Hovis) "World at Large No. 1" (Virginia de Luce, Tom Williams, Arlene Fontana), "Station Break" (Ronnie Cunningham), "World at Large No. 2" (Charles Nelson Reilly, Choral Group [uncredited]) "World at Large Preview" (James Inman, Ronnie Cunningham), "(Have I Stayed) Too Long at the Fair?" (Jane A. Johnston), "One of Those Days" (Charles Nelson Reilly, Tom Williams, Arlene Fontana, James Inman) Finale (Company)

NOTES—When *The Billy Barnes Revue* re-opened Off Broadway (as *Billy Barnes Revue*) after first being seen Off Broadway and then on Broadway, there was a new cast as well as some minor production changes (the earlier versions didn't credit the choreography, but the second Off Broadway production listed Ken Berry as choreographer). This production also reflects various song and sketch changes which occurred during the York Playhouse-Royale Theatre-Lyceum Theatre-Carnegie Hall Playhouse versions. "Safari a la Marilyn," "Blocks," and "Where Is the Place, Kid?" were omitted from the Carnegie Hall Playhouse production (the latter was also omitted from the Broadway production). Those songs added to the Broadway production (the "Whatever" trio of songs and "City of the Angels") were retained for the Carnegie Hall Playhouse version, and a song which hadn't appeared elsewhere ("Dance, Dance, Dance") was added for the final New York version of the revue. As mentioned in the entry for *The Billy Barnes Revue*, "Dance, Dance, Dance" was recorded for *Billy Barnes Revued* (1999).

It seems odd that the sure-fire sketch "Safari a la Marilyn" would have been omitted from this production, but perhaps Joyce Jameson was essential for its success.

The *New York Times* reported a contretemps which occurred soon after the production opened. Seven of the revue's cast members flew to Chicago to tape a television performance of material from the production, and they missed their return flight to New York. As a result, a performance had to be cancelled (the *Times* reported that 198 ticket-holders were refunded a total of $800) and the producers of the revue took up the matter with Actors' Equity, saying they would also file charges against Billy Barnes and the company's stage manager.

Two weeks later, the *Times* noted that the revue underwent a "drastic" casting change, and except for Virginia de Luce all the revue's cast (Ann Guilbert, Jackie Joseph, Patti Regan, George Eckstein, Ken Berry, Bob Rodgers, and Len Weinrib) were replaced (by Ronnie Cunningham, Arlene Fontana, Jane Johnston, Larry Hovis, James Inman, Charles Nelson Reilly, and Tom Williams). Further, Barnes and Andy Lesko, who played pianos for the production, were replaced by Eddie Johnson and Eddie Cooke. Both the revue's producers and Actors' Equity denied that the casting changes were in retaliation against those cast members who missed the performance in question. One wonders if the tapes which had been made in Chicago (according to the *Times* "under the auspices of *Playboy* magazine" for ABC) still exist.

(For more information about the first Off Broadway production as well as a list of other Billy Barnes' revues, see entry for *The Billy Barnes Revue*.)

151 Billy Bishop Goes to War. THEATRE: Theatre de Lys; OPENING DATE: June 17, 1980; PERFORMANCES: 78; BOOK: John Gray; Eric Peterson, Script Collaborator; LYRICS: John Gray; MUSIC: John Gray; DIRECTION: John Gray; SCENERY: David Gropman; LIGHTING: Jennifer Tipton; MUSICAL DIRECTION: John Gray; PRODUCERS: Mike Nichols and Lewis Allen; co-produced by Vancouver East Cultural Center (Christopher Wootten, Executive Director); Stephen Graham and Ventures West Capital, Inc., Associate Producers; presented by special arrangement with Lucille Lortel Productions, Inc.

CAST—Eric Peterson (Billy Bishop, Upperclassman, Adjutant Perrault, Officer, Sir Hugh Cecil, Lady St. Helier, Cedric, Doctor, General John Higgins, Tommy, Lovely Helene, Albert Ball, Walter Bourne, Officer, Hugh M. Trenchard, Servant, King George V), John Gray (Narrator, Pianist)

SOURCE—The life and times of Billy Bishop (1894-1956).

The musical was presented in two acts (individual numbers weren't listed in the program; the list below is derived from information on the cast album; the numbers were sung by Erik Peterson, and John Gray was the narrator and pianist).

ACT ONE—"Off to Fight the Hun," "Canada at War," "The Good Ship Caledonia," "Buried Alive in the Mud," "December Nights," "The RE-7," "Nobody Shoots No-One in Canada," "Lady St. Helier," "My First Solo Flight," "In the Sky"

ACT TWO—"As Calm as the Ocean," "Friends Ain't Supposed to Die," "General Sir Hugh M. Trenchard," "The Empire Soiree," "In the Sky" (reprise)

NOTES—Billy Bishop was a World War One Canadian flying ace, a legendary pilot who in slightly more than one year shot down seventy-two enemy aircraft (twenty-five of them in one ten-day period). The musical *Billy Bishop Goes to War* was a pleasant if ephemeral evening, not particularly memorable but nonetheless entertaining in its modest way.

The musical premiered in Canada in 1979 (with Eric Peterson and John Gray), and the cast album was recorded by Tapestry Records (LP # GD-7372); the script was published by Talonbooks in 1991, and by 2002 the book was in its ninth printing. The American premiere took place at the Arena Stage in Washington, D.C., followed by the Broadway opening at the Morosco Theatre on May 29, 1980, where it played for only twelve performances. Many Off Broadway musicals (and plays) have transferred to Broadway, but in the case of *Billy Bishop Goes to War*, the sequence was reversed. Just ten days after the Broadway closing, the musical opened at the Theatre de Lys, where it remained for almost two months. *Billy Bishop* was the second Broadway musical to transfer Off Broadway (after *Cambridge Circus* [see entry]. Moreover, four musicals (*Simply Heavenly*, *The Billy Barnes Revue*, *Young Abe Lincoln*, and *Avenue Q* [see entries]) opened Off Broadway, transferred to Broadway, and then after their Broadway runs returned to Off Broadway. Incidentally, John Howard Lawson's expressionist drama *Roger Bloomer* opened on Broadway at the 48th Street Theatre on March 1, 1923, and within the month transferred Off Broadway to the Greenwich Village Theatre). *Billy Bishop* was televised in 1982, and was later revived by the York Theatre Company on February 19, 1987, for twelve performances.

152 Billy Noname. "A New Musical"; THEATRE: Truck and Warehouse Theatre; OPENING DATE: March 2, 1970; PERFORMANCES: 48; BOOK: William Wellington Mackey; LYRICS: Johnny Brandon; MUSIC: Johnny Brandon; DIRECTION: Lucia Victor; CHOREOGRAPHY: Talley Beatty; SCENERY: Jack Brown; COSTUMES: Pearl Somner; LIGHTING: David F. Segal; MUSICAL DIRECTION: Sammy Benskin; PRODUCERS: Robert E. Richardson and Joe Davis

CAST—DONNY BURKS (Billy Noname), Andrea Saunders (Louisa), Andy Torres (Li'l Nick), Charles Moore (Big Nick, G.I., Dean), Roger Lawson (Young Billy), Thommie Bush (Young Tiny), Eugene Edwards (the Reverend Fisher, Mr. Milton), Hattie Winston (Dolores), Alan Weeks (Tiny Shannon), Glory Van Scott (Barbara, Woman in Labor), Urylee Leonardos (Harriet Van witherspoon, Neighbor); People of Bay Alley, U.S.A.: Thommie Bush, Doris DeMendez, Eugene Edwards, J.L. Harris, Marilyn Johnson, Roger Lawson, Urylee Leonardos, Charles Moore, Joni Palmer, Andrea Saunders, Andy Torres, Glory Van Scott, Alan Weeks, Hattie Winston

The action occurs in Bay Alley, U.S.A., from 1937 to the present.

The musical was presented in two acts.

ACT ONE—"King Joe" (People of Bay Alley), "Seduction" (Andrea Saunders, Andy Torres, Charles Moore, Glory Van Scott), "Billy Noname" (Donny Burks), "Boychild" (Donny Burks, Roger Lawson, People of Bay Alley), "A Different Drummer" (People of Bay Alley, Charles Moore), "Look Through the Window" (Hattie Winston), "It's Our Time Now" (Donny Burks, Alan Weeks, Roger Lawson, Andy Torres, Thommie Bush), "Hello World" (Donny Burks, Hattie Winston), "At the End of the Day" (Urylee Leonardos), "I Want to Live" (Donny Burks)

ACT TWO—"Manchild" (Hattie Winston, Alan Weeks), "Color Me White" (Donny Burks, Alan Weeks, Hattie Winston, Charles Moore, Roger Lawson, Tommie Bush, Andy Torres, Doris DeMendez, Andrea Saunders, Joni Palmer), "We're Gonna Turn On Freedom" (Alan Weeks, Company), "Mother Earth" (Glory Van Scott, Donny Burks), "Sit In—Wade In" (Alan Weeks, Company), "Movin'" (Donny Burks, Company), "The Dream" (Marilyn Johnson, Company), "Black Boy" (Donny Burks), "Burn, Baby, Burn" (Alan Weeks, Glory Van Scott, Militants), "We Make a Promise" (Eugene Edwards, Integrationists), "Get Your Slice of Cake" (Urylee Leonardos), "I Want to Live" (reprise) (Donny Burks)

NOTES—*Billy Noname*, which was the first production to play at the Truck and Warehouse Theatre, was another Johnny Brandon musical, and unlike his earlier light-hearted musicals (*Cindy* [1964] and *Who's Who, Baby?* [1968]; see entries), it was a serious one which dealt with civil rights in the United States. But perhaps due to the meandering plot, inconclusive ending, and sometimes indifferent songs, audiences weren't interested in hearing the story of the title character who must choose how to live out his life: by embracing Black separatism; by choosing Martin Luther King's vision of peaceful nonviolence and coexistence; or by pursuing capitalism. The plot points seemed a little too pat (and rigid), and the message that racism is unacceptable was an obvious one, even for 1970. The show disappeared in six weeks, but left behind a cast album on Roulette Records (LP # SROC-11).

Clive Barnes in the *New York Times* praised the "powerhouse" performances as well as the "brilliant" choreography, which was the "best" he had seen "for some time." But he found the book unclear and "simplistic," and noted the score offered "gutsiness at second hand."

153 Bingo! (1985). "A New Musical"; THEATRE: The AMAS Repertory Theatre; OPENING DATE: October 24, 1985; PERFORMANCES: 16; BOOK: Ossie Davis and Hy Gilbert; LYRICS: Hy Gilbert; MUSIC: George Fischoff; DIRECTION: Ossie Davis; CHOREOGRAPHY: Henry LeTang; Ellie Letang, Associate Choreographer; Christian Holder, Assistant Choreographer; SCENERY: Tom Barnes; COSTUMES: Christina Giannini; other costumes by Howard Behar; LIGHTING: Jeffrey Schissler; MUSICAL DIRECTION: Neal Kenyon and George Fischoff; PRODUCER: The AMAS Repertory Theatre, Inc. (Rosetta LeNoire, Founder and Artistic Director)

CAST—Louis Baldonieri (Team Member, Ensemble), David Winston Barge (Country Joe Calloway), Ethel S. Beatty (Lonnette), Ron Bobb-Semple (Sallee Boggs), Brian Evaret Chandler (Team Member, Cecil, Isaac), Joyce Dara (Chessie Girl, Choppette), Melissa Haizlip (Harlot, Choppette, Nurse), Christian Holder (Team Member, Ensemble), Andy Hostettler (Team Member, Ensemble), Donna Ingram-Young (Church Lady, Choppette), David L. King (Owner, Ensemble), Norman Matlock (Bingo Long), John R. McCurry "Pops" Foster), Monica Parks (Church Lady, Choppette), Barbara Passolt (Church Lady, Choppette), Jackie Patterson (Louis Keystone), James Randolph (Leon Price), Sharon E. Scott (Church Lady, Choppette), Keith Tyrone (Team Member, Raymond, Chessie), Ronald Wyche (Team Member, Methuselah, Owner)

SOURCE—The 1973 novel *The Bingo Long Travelling All-Stars and Motor Kings* by William Brashler.

The action occurs in 1939.

The musical was presented in two acts.

ACT ONE—"The Wheels Keep Turnin'" (Norman Matlock, James Randolph, Ron Bobb-Semple, The Team), "Gentleman Caller" (Ethel S. Beatty, Ensemble), "It's All in the Timin'" (Norman Matlock, John R. McCurry, Company), "Get While the Getting's Good" (James Randolph, Norman Matlock), "Country Boy/City Girl" (Ethel S. Beatty, Brian Evaret Chandler, David Winston Barge), "You Gotta Give 'Em a Show" (Norman Matlock, John R. McCurry, The Team)

ACT TWO—"Saturday Night in Kansas City" (Company), "We're a Team" (Norman Matlock, Ethel S. Beatty, The Team), "The Bingo Long Travelling All-Stars and Motor Kings" (Company), "We're a Team" (reprise) (Norman Matlock, Ethel S. Beatty), "The Wheels Keep Turnin'" (reprise) (Company)

NOTES—Based on the novel *The Bingo Long Travelling All-Stars and Motor Kings* (which was filmed in 1976), the Off Off Broadway musical *Bingo!* told the story of a baseball player who starts his own team (independent of the Negro National League).

Considering the inherent drama in its story about racism in baseball as well as the conflict between Black baseball owners and Black players, Mel Gussow in the *New York Times* was surprised the musical sidestepped these issues and instead concentrated on the romance between one of the baseball players and a nightclub singer; in fact, Gussow noted that for much of the evening the players seemed to mostly visit nightspots.

Gussow further noted that the lyrics, the book, and George Fischoff's "modestly tuneful" score never capitalized on the "ballpark background" or on the "rambunctious flavor of the game itself."

Apparently the success of *Damn Yankees* (1955) was a happy fluke, because *Bingo!* continued the tradition of baseball-themed plays and musicals which went nowhere (see entry for *Diamonds*).

George Fischoff composed the music for *The Prince and the Pauper* (see entry); the delightful score for the short-running 1971 Broadway musical *Georgy*; and the musical adaptation of *Sayonara*, which premiered in regional theatre in 1987 (see entry). Also see entry for his *Gauguin/Savage Light*.

154 Bingo (2005). "A Winning New Musical"; THEATRE: St. Luke's Theatre; OPENING DATE: November 7, 2005; PERFORMANCES: 92; BOOK: Michael Heitzman and Ilene Reid; LYRICS: Michael Heitzman, Ilene Reid, and David Holcenberg; MUSIC: Michael Heitzman, Ilene Reid, and David Holcenberg; DIRECTION: Thomas Caruso; CHOREOGRAPHY: Lisa Stevens; SCENERY: Eric Renschler; COSTUMES: Carol Brys; LIGHTING: John Viesta; MUSICAL DIRECTION: Steven Bishop; PRODUCERS: Aruba Productions and Buddy and Sally Productions

CAST—Liz McCartney (Vern), Janet Metz (Patsy), Liz Larsen (Honey), Chevi Colton (Minnie), Patrick Ryan Sullivan (Sam, Frank), Klea Blackhurst (Bernice, Marilyn), Beth Malone (Alison)

The musical was presented in one act.

MUSICAL NUMBERS—Overture (Orchestra), "Girls' Night Out" (Liz McCartney), "Anyone Can Play Bingo" (Chevi Colton), "I Still Believe in You" (Janet Metz), "I've Made Up My Mind" (Beth Malone), "Under My Wing" (Liz McCartney), "Gentleman Caller" (Liz Larsen), "The Birth of Bingo" (Patrick Ryan Sullivan), "Ratched's Lament" (Beth Malone), "Anyone Can Play Bingo" (reprise) (Liz McCartney), "Swell" (Liz McCartney), "Gentleman Caller" (reprise) (Patrick Ryan Sullivan), "I Still Believe in You" (reprise) (Janet Metz, Company), "B4" (Beth Malone), "I've Made Up My Mind" (reprise) (Beth Malone), "Girls' Night Out" (reprise) (Company)

NOTES—*The Best Plays Theatre Yearbook 2005-2006* described *Bingo* as an interactive musical which dealt with the "pleasures and pitfalls" of playing bingo (each audience member got to play two games of bingo and even received a free bag of popcorn). But "pitfalls"? Who knew?!

Jason Zinoman in the *New York Times* noted the cast members were in a show "clearly beneath their talents"; further, he reported their characters' traits were essentially from the same cookie-cutter which created the four women in the television sitcom *The Golden Girls* (one was "acerbic," one "promiscuous," one "batty," and one a "wisecracking older woman"). But Zinoman felt the songs were "peppy," and he praised "Girls' Night Out," the "quite catchy" opening number. With such an "accomplished" cast, he felt *Bingo* might find its audience, and, if so, he wondered if a musical about canasta was around the corner.

The cast album was recorded by Bingo Records (the CD was unnumbered).

The musical was first produced at the Hermosa Beach Playhouse in California on April 23, 2001.

155 Birdbath. THEATRE: Quaigh Theatre; OPENING DATE: August 1, 1982; PERFORMANCES: 7; LIBRETTO: Kenneth Lieberson; MUSIC: Kenneth Lieberson; DIRECTION: John Margulis; MUSICAL DIRECTION: Patrick Mullins

CAST—Martha Ihde (Velma Sparrow), Michael Kutner (Frankie Basta)

SOURCE—The 1965 play *Birdbath* by Leonard Melfi.

The action occurs one night in February in a midtown cafeteria, on the streets outside, and in a basement apartment in New York City.

The opera was presented in one act.

NOTES—Kenneth Lieberson's opera *Birdbath* was based on the play of the same name by Leonard Melfi. The plot dealt with a young poet who works as a cashier in a cafeteria and the neurotic (and murderous) waitress whom he takes to his apartment one night.

The play had originally opened at St. Mark's Church-in-the-Bowery in 1965 (with Kevin O'Connor as the young man), and in 1966 was produced at the Martinique Theatre as one of six short plays under the umbrella title of *Six from LaMama* (the 1966 production was directed by Tom O'Horgan and O'Connor reprised his original role).

In reviewing the opera for the *New York Times*, Bernard Holland felt the music was most successful in the opera's final sequence when Lieberson's abandoned his "half-spoken, half-parlando vocal writing" and instead concentrated on "long lyric lines." In this scene, the poet writes a valentine poem for the sleeping waitress, and here the "eloquent" music had "real grace and attraction."

156 Birdland. THEATRE: New Federal Theatre; OPENING DATE: February 1978; PERFORMANCES: Unknown; BOOK: Barry Amyer Kaleem; LYRICS: Some lyrics possibly by Barry Amyer Kaleem; see song list for other credits; MUSIC: All original music composed by Elliot Weiss; see song list for other credits; DIRECTION: Anderson Johnson; CHOREOGRAPHY: Frank Ashley; SCENERY: Alvin Perry; COSTUMES: Karen Perry; LIGHTING: Jeff Miller; PRODUCER: Henry Street Settlement's New Federal Theatre (Woodie King, Jr., Producer)

CAST—Cary L. Barnes (Musa), Michelle Beteta (Dancer), Starletta DuPois (Dot), Wayne Elbert (D. of A.J. & D. [Dave the Rave]), Grenoldo Frazier (Chocolate), Jamil Garland (Dancer, Mr. Wonderful), Marion Knox (Pat), Crystal Lilly (Zainub), Juanita Mahone (Louise), Jeannine Otis (A. of A.J. & D. [Annie the Rose]), Jim Patricia (Sid), Reyno (J. of A.J. & D. [Jon the Dove]), Bernard Riddick (Dancer), Carole Simpson (Dancer), Steve Simpson (Red, Historian), Reginald Vel Johnson (M.C.), Samm-Art Williams (Pittsburgh)

The musical was presented in two acts.

ACT ONE—"OP" (music by Oscar Peterson) (Orchestra), "Blue Train" (lyric by Barry Amyer Kaleem and Anderson Johnson) (Jeannine Otis, Reyno, Wayne Elbert), "Black Coffee" (lyric by Paul Francis Webster and Sonny Burke, music by Paul Francis Webster and Sonny Burke) (Orchestra), "Give the Bad Cat Some" (lyric by Barry Amyer Kaleem and Anderson Johnson) (Jeannine Otis, Reyno, Wayne Elbert), "So What" (music by Miles Davis) (Orchestra), "Milestones" (music by Miles Davis) (Orchestral), "Lover Man" (lyric and music by J. Davis, R. Ramirez, and J. Sherman) (Juanita Mahone), "Give the Bad Cat Some" (reprise) (lyric by Barry Amyer Kaleem and Anderson Johnson) (Jeannine Otis, Reyno, Wayne Elbert), "Straight, No Chaser" (music by Thelonious Monk) (Orchestra), "What a Difference a Day Made" (a/k/a "What a Diff'rence a Day Makes") (lyric and music by M. Grever and S. Adams) (Juanita Mahone) "Round Midnite" (music by Thelonious Monk) (Orchestra), "Fine Clothes" (lyric by Barry Amyer Kaleem and Anderson Johnson) (Jeannine Otis, Reyno, Wayne Elbert), "Save Your Love for Me" (Starletta DuPois), "OP" (reprise) (music by Oscar Peterson) (Orchestra), "(In My) Solitude" (lyric by Eddie DeLange and Irving Mills, music by Duke Ellington) (intermission solo by Bross Towsend)

ACT TWO—"Blue Monk" (music by Thelonious Monk) (Orchestra), "Bounce Back" (lyric by Anderson Johnson) (Jeannine Otis, Reyno, Wayne Elbert), "Yardbird Suite" (music by Charlie Parker) (Orchestra), "Hi-Fly" (music by R. Weston) (Orchestra), "Ode to a Junkie Player" (lyric by Barry Amyer Kaleem and Anderson Johnson) (Jeannine Otis), "Hi-Fly" (reprise) (music by R. Weston) (Orchestra), "Lady One & One" (lyric by Barry Amyer Kaleem and Anderson Johnson) (Juanita Mahone), "Just Before Daylight" (lyric by Barry Amyer Kaleem and Anderson Johnson) (Starletta DuPois, Cary L. Barnes), "Birdland" (music by Reyno) (Orchestra)

NOTES—Samm-Art Williams, who played Pittsburgh in the Off Off Broadway *Birdland*, was an actor and playwright. As a writer, his greatest success was the long-running *Home* (1979), which played Off Broadway for eighty-two performances and then transferred to Broadway for a run of 288 performances.

157 Birds of Paradise. "A New Musical"; THEATRE: Promenade Theatre; OPENING DATE: October 26, 1987; PERFORMANCES: 24; BOOK: Winnie Holzman and David Evans; LYRICS: Winnie Holzman; MUSIC: David Evans; DIRECTION: Arthur Laurents; CHOREOGRAPHY: Linda Haberman; SCENERY: Philipp Jung; COSTUMES: David Murin; LIGHTING: Paul Gallo; MUSICAL DIRECTION: Frederick Weldy; PRODUCER: John A. McQuiggan; Douglas M. Lawson, Executive Producer

CAST—Barbara Walsh (Stella), Mary Beth Peil (Marjorie), Andrew Hill Newman (Dave), J.K. Simmons (Andy), Donna Murphy (Hope), Todd Graff (Homer), John Cunningham (Lawrence Wood), Crista Moore (Julia)

SOURCE—The 1896 play *The Seagull* by Anton Chekhov. The action occurs in the present time in the meeting hall of the oldest church on Harbor Island, a small fictional island somewhere on the eastern seaboard.

The musical was presented in two acts.

ACT ONE—"So Many Nights" (Todd Graff, Mary Beth Peil, Barbara Walsh, J.K. Simmons, Donna Murphy, Andrew Hill Newman), "Diva" (Donna Murphy, Arthur Hill Newman, J.K. Simmons), "Every Day Is Night" (Crista Moore), "Somebody" (John Cunningham, Company), "Coming True" (Todd Graff, Crista Moore), "It's Only a Play" (Todd Graff, Company), "She's Out There" (J.K. Simmons), "Birds of Paradise" (Mary Beth Peil, Barbara Walsh, Donna Murphy), "Imagining You" (Company)

ACT TWO—"Penguins Must Sing" (Andrew Hill Newman, Donna Murphy, J.K. Simmons), "You're Mine" (Mary Beth Peil), "Things I Can't Forget" (Todd Graff, Mary Beth Peil), "After Opening

Night" (Todd Graff, Mary Beth Peil), "Chekhov" (Company), "Something New" (Company)

NOTES—Despite its short run, *Birds of Paradise* offered a delightful score and a book which was an interesting variation on Anton Chekhov's play *The Seagull* (1896). The musical dealt with an amateur group putting on *Seagull*, a musical version of Chekhov's play set in Antarctica and featuring singing-and-dancing penguins (this musical-within-the-musical pre-dates the 2006 film *Happy Feet* by nineteen years), and what happens to them when a formerly famous actor agrees to direct and star in their production.

The cast recording was released by That's Entertainment Records (CD # CDTER-1196), and the script was published by Samuel French, Inc., in 1988.

See entries for *Beware the Jubjub Bird*, which dealt with a group of actors rehearsing a revival of *The Seagull*, and for *The Seagull*, Thomas Pasatieri's operatic adaptation of Chekhov's play. (The entry for *Beware the Jubjub Bird* also references *Gulls*, another musical based on *The Seagull*.)

158 The Birth of the Poet. "An Opera"; THEATRE: Opera House/Brooklyn Academy of Music; OPENING DATE: December 3, 1985; PERFORMANCES: 8; LIBRETTO: Kathy Acker; MUSIC: Peter Gordon; DIRECTION: Richard Foreman; SCENERY: David Salle; COSTUMES: David Salle; LIGHTING: Pat Collins; PRODUCER: The Next Wave Festival

CAST—Frank Dahill (Stabbed Arab Lover), Zach Grenier (Ali, Hinkley), Jan Leslie Harding (Cynthia), Stuart Hodes (Maccenas), Anne Iobst (Shadow from San Francisco), Max Jacobs (Propertius), Warren Keith (Hassidic, Book Delivery Man), Anne Lange (Barbarella), Brooke Myers (Stabbed Arab Wife), Danielle Ingrid Reffert (Street of Dogs Town Crier, Harsh Nayyar), Valda Setterfeld (Lady with the Whip)

NOTES—*The Birth of the Poet*, which had originally premiered in Rotterdam in April 1984, was presented at the Brooklyn Academy of Music as part of the Next Wave Festival.

John Rockwell in the *New York Times* described the evening as a "rather lurid, cartoon-eroticized vision" of three periods in world history: the first period, set in a futuristic New York, dealt with the explosion of a nuclear power plant; the second took place during the late Roman Empire; and the third in contemporary Iran. Rockwell found the work "a well-intentioned, neatly crafted mess" with "often interesting" contributions from the collaborators and performers.

Much of the music was pre-recorded, and a Brechtian touch was added to the evening when the stagehands changed scenery in view of the audience.

159 A Bistro Car on the CNR. "A Musical Journey on the C.N.R."; THEATRE: Playhouse Theatre; OPENING DATE: March 23, 1978; PERFORMANCES: 61; BOOK: D.R. Andersen; LYRICS: Merv Campone and Richard Ouzounian; MUSIC: Patrick Rose; DIRECTION: Richard Ouzounian; CHOREOGRAPHY: Lynne Gannaway ("Associate Choreographer"); SCENERY: John Falabella; COSTUMES: John Falabella; LIGHTING: Ned Hallick; MUSICAL DIRECTION: John Clifton; PRODUCERS: Jeff Britton and Bob Bisaccia

CAST—Marcia McLain (Kathy), Patrick Rose (Ted), Henrietta Valor (Jessica), Tom Wopat (Dan)

The action occurs during the final performance of the entertainers on the Bistro Car of the Canadian National Rapido train traveling from Toronto to Montreal.

The revue was presented in two acts.

ACT ONE—Overture, "CNR" (Company), "Twenty-five Miles" (Marcia McClain), "Guitarist" (Patrick Rose), "Passing By" (Tom Wopat, Marcia McClain), "Madame La Chanson" (Henrietta Valor), "Oh God, I'm Thirty" (Patrick Rose), "Ready or Not" (Marcia McClain, Henrietta Valor), "Sudden Death Overtime" (Patrick Rose), "Bring Back Swing" (Company), "Yesterday's Lover" (Henrietta Valor), "Four Part Invention" (Company), "Nocturne" (Company)

ACT TWO—"La Belle Province" (Company), "Ensemble" (Henrietta Valor, Patrick Rose), "Dewey and Sal" (Tom Wopat, Marcia McClain), "Here I Am Again" (Patrick Rose), "Street Music" (Company), "Other People's Houses" (Marcia McClain), "Genuine Grade A Canadian Superstar" (Tom Wopat, Company), "I Don't Live Anywhere Anymore" (Tom Wopat), "The Lady Who Loved to Sing" (Company), "Somebody Write Me a Love Song" (Henrietta Valor), Finale (Company)

NOTES—During the five-hour train trip between Toronto and Montreal, passengers on the bistro car of the Canadian National Rapido were entertained by a group of singers and musicians. The musical *A Bistro Car on the CNR* depicted one such journey and the entertainment offered to the passengers.

The musical had been first produced in Canada as *Jubalay*, where it opened on May 8, 1974, at the Manitoba Theatre Center; it then transferred to the Arts Club Theatre on June 27. *Jubalay* had music by Patrick Rose and lyrics by Merv Campone, and the cast members were Brent Carver, Ruth Nichol, Patrick Rose, and Diane Stapley. The show was recorded by Jubalay Productions Records (LP # JP-9001), and included five numbers later heard in the New York production ("Bring Back Swing," "Yesterday's Lover," "CNR," "Dewey and Sal," and "La Belle Province"); the other numbers on the album which weren't heard in New York were "Jubalay," "Craftsman," "Wailing Wall," "Sailor," "Find Me," "His Name Is Love," and "Lullabye." Songs heard in *Jubalay* which weren't on the cast album and which weren't heard in New York were "The Craftsman," "The Child," "Indian Trilogy," "Peace," "The City," "Harry," "La Piece Bien Faite," "Old Jocks," "What Am I Bid?" "I Am the Light," "On My Pillow," and "20th Century." "The Anarchist," which was heard during New York previews, was also in *Jubalay* (but not on the cast album). The New York program credited the lyrics for "Yesterday's Lover" and "Guitarrero" to D. Berwick.

Jubalay had its American premiere at the Ceres Theatre/Theatre by the Sea on November 10, 1977, for forty-five performances. The songs heard in this production were, in performance order: "Share with You," "Jubalay," "The Last Man," "Eighty-Seven Cents," "Bring Back Swing," "Yesterday's Lover," "Oh, God, I'm Thirty," "The Sailor," "What Am I Bid?" "Street Music," "Senator Bach," "Ready or Not," "C.N.R.," "Wailing Wall," "Peace Will Come Again," "Opiate for the Masses," "The Guitarist," "La Piece Bien Faite," "Dewey and Sal," "Remember Me," "Old Jocks," "La Belle Province," "The Anarchist," "Lullaby," and "20th Century"; the lyrics for "Bring Back Swing" and "La Piece Bien Faite" were credited to E. Henderson and the lyric for "Yesterday's Lover" was credited to D. Berwick.

The New York production of *A Bistro Car on the CNR* was a revised version of *Jubalay*, and included lyrics by Richard Ouzounian as well as by Merv Campone; later, as *A Bistro Car*, the musical was produced in Calgary at the Lunchbox Theatre on January 16, 1979, and then in Edmonton, Vancouver, and Toronto. This version was recorded (as *A Bistro Car*) by Berandol Records (LP # BER-9069), and included nine songs (and one reprise), all of which had been heard in the New York version: "Ensemble," "Oh God, I'm Thirty," "Other People's Houses," "I Don't Live Anywhere Anymore," "(Genuine Grade A) Canadian Superstar," "Four Part Invention," "Here I Am Again," "The Lady Who Loved to Sing," and "Somebody Write Me a Love Song." During New York previews, the following songs were dropped: "Share with You," "At the Movies," "Lady, Lady," "The Anarchist," "Whodunit," "Through Glass," and "Eleven O'Clock Number."

In reviewing the Off Broadway production, Richard Eder in the *New York Times* wrote that while the train in the musical ran between Toronto and Montreal, the show itself "might just get by on the BMT in a blizzard." Further, he noted the score "is to music as typewriting is to writing," and said the "dismal" evening should be "towed away" because "the whole thing" could not "possibly move under its own power." But he praised Tom Wopat and Marcia McClain, and noted they shared a "bright" number ("Dewey and Sal") about "leather freaks timorously in love."

For information on musicals centering around trains, see entry for *Frimbo*.

160 Bits and Pieces XIV. THEATRE: PLaza 9- Room; OPENING DATE: October 6, 1964; PERFORMANCES: 426; SKETCHES: Ronald Axe, William F. Brown, Dee Caruso, Richard Craven, Bill Dana, Rory Harrity, Bill Levine, and Sol Weinstein Lyrics: David Axelrod, Michael Brown, William F. Brown, Ernest A. Chambers, Lesley Davison, Clark Gesner, Howard Liebling, June Reizner, Fred Tobias, and Tom Whedon Music: Michael Brown, Lesley Davison, Clark Gesner, Marvin Hamlisch, Stan (Stanley) Lebowsky, George W. Linsenmann, Sam Pottle, June Reizner, and William Roy; DIRECTION: Julius Monk; staged by Frank Wagner; CHOREOGRAPHY: Frank Wagner; COSTUMES: Bill Belew; LIGHTING: Don Lamb; MUSICAL DIRECTION: William Roy; PRODUCER: An Orion Production presented by Thomas Hammond

CAST—Gerry Matthews, Jamie Ross, Barbara Cason, Nagle Jackson, Barbara Minkus, Nancy Myers

The revue was presented in two acts (sketch and song assignments unknown).

ACT ONE—"Bits & Pieces XIV" (lyric and dialogue by William F. Brown, music by William Roy), "Feathered Friends" (lyric by Howard Liebling, music by Marvin Hamlisch) "You're Something More Than I Bargained For" (lyric by David Axelrod and Tom Whedon, music by Sam Pottle) "An Ode to Those Anchor Men" (sketch by Dee Caruso and Bill Levine) "New York on Five Dollars a Day" (lyric by David Axelrod and Tom Whedon, music by Sam Pottle) "Take the Bus" (sketch by William F. Brown) "Won't You Come Home, Judge Crater" (lyric and music by Michael Brown) "Stand Up and Flex" (lyric and music by Lesley Davision) "Wonderful, Wonderful, Wonderful" (lyric and music by Lesley Davison) "The Controversial Play's the Thing" (sketch by Ronald Axe and Sol Weinstein) "From the Unisphere with Love" (sketch by William F. Brown) "Don't Let Them Take the Paramount" (lyric and music by Michael Brown)

ACT TWO—"Alexander's Discount Rag" (lyric by Fred Tobias, music by Stan [Stanley] Lebowsky) "The Late Show" (sketch by William F. Brown) "The Gathering of the Clan" (lyric by Ernest A. Chambers, music by George W. Linsenmann) "H.M.S. Brownstone" (sketch by Rory Harrity and Richard Craven) "The Peanut Butter Affair" (lyric and music by Clark Gesner) "Ballad for a Park" (lyric and music by Clark Gesner) "Barry's Boys" (lyric and music by June Reizner) "The Game Is Over!" (lyric by Fred Tobias, music by Stan [Stanley] Lebowsky) "Conference Call" (sketch by Bill Dana) "Love Letters Written to My Mother" (lyric and music by Michael Brown), Finale (lyric and music by Michael Brown)

NOTES—The long-running *Bits and Pieces XIV* included another of Michael Brown's songs about vanishing New York ("Don't Let Them Take the Paramount"); and the revue marked another early appearance by Marvin Hamlisch ("Feathered

Friends"). Brown also offered another song about New York, specifically one which centered around a New York mystery; "Won't You Come Home, Judge Crater" dealt with Judge Joseph Force Crater, who disappeared on August 6, 1930 (the last time he had ever been seen was when he was getting into a taxi on his way to see a Broadway show). "Conference Call" had been first been performed in *Demi-Dozen* (1958; see entry), and "H.M.S. Brownstone" had earlier been used in *Fourth Avenue North* (1961) and *Dime a Dozen* (1962) (see entries). "Barry's Boys" had first been heard in *Dime a Dozen* and then later in *Baker's Dozen* (1964; see entry); it can be heard on the former's cast album.

Clark Gesner's "The Peanut Butter Affair" was later used in *The Jello Is Always Red* (see entry), and can be heard on that revue's cast album.

Among the revue's topics were sketches about Chet Huntley and David Brinkley ("An Ode to Those Anchor Men"), James Bond in a caper set at the New York World's Fair ("From the Unisphere with Love"), and school busing ("Take the Bus"). Milton Esterow in the *New York Times* found the evening "uproarious, fresh, breezy joyfully poisonous or poisonously joyful or as funny as anything in town."

For a complete list of Julius Monk's revues, see entry for *Take Five*; also see Appendix Q.

161 Bittersuite (1984). "A New Musical"; THEATRE: Quaigh Theatre; OPENING DATE: January 20, 1984; PERFORMANCES: 23; LYRICS: Michael Champagne; MUSIC: Elliot Weiss; DIRECTION: Bert Michaels; COSTUMES: Eric Newland; LIGHTING: Eric Cornwell; PRODUCER: Quaigh Theatre (Will Lieberson, Artistic Director; Peggy Ward, Managing Director)

CAST—Claudine Casson, Del Green, Anthony Mucci, Theresa Rakov, Richard Roemer

The revue was presented in two acts.

ACT ONE—"Let's Do It Right" (Company), "The Life That Jack Built" (Anthony Mucci, Company), "Ice Cream" (Claudine Casson, Anthony Mucci), "Our Favorite Restaurant" (Richard Roemer, Theresa Rakov, Claudine Casson, Anthony Mucci), "You're Not Getting Older" (Theresa Rakov, Claudine Casson), "Meg and Joe" (Del Green), "The Influence of Scotch" (Anthony Mucci), "The Recipe" (Theresa Rakov, Richard Roemer), "I'll Be There" (Anthony Mucci, Company), "Twentieth Reunion" (Richard Roemer, Company), "Mama Don't Cry" (Claudine Casson, Company), "Narcissism Rag" (Richard Roemer, Company)

ACT TWO—"Snap Back" (Company), "John's Song" (Anthony Mucci, Company), "Soap Opera" (Theresa Rakov), "The Apology" (Richard Roemer), "Pretty Lady" (Anthony Mucci), "Pay the Piper" (Del Green, Company), "Cliché" (Claudine Casson, Company), "Win and Lose" (Richard Roemer), "Fathers and Sons" (Anthony Mucci), "How Little We've Learned" (Theresa Rakov), "Dream Like a Child" (Richard Roemer, Company)

NOTES—*Bittersuite* was an Off Off Broadway song cycle dealing with modern living and urban angst; in other words, it was another in a long string of similarly plotted revues and book musicals which opened in New York during the period. But John S. Wilson in the *New York Times* felt the revue built a "sustained flow of excellence," and he praised Michael Champagne's lyrics and Elliot Weiss' music (the latter was sometimes reminiscent of Kurt Weill and Stephen Sondheim, but also had its own "fresh qualities"). Wilson singled out "Twentieth Reunion," "Narcissism Rag," "How Little We've Learned," and "The Recipe."

The revue was revived Off Off Broadway at the Duplex Theatre on April 12, 1987, and then later Off Broadway for 211 performances at Palsson's Supper Club on October 5, 1987. A new edition of the latter opened in an Off Broadway production on May 16, 1988, at Palsson's; titled *Bittersuite—One More Time*, the musical played for eighteen more performances. (See separate entries for these productions.)

The script, which was published by Samuel French, Inc., in an undated edition, included a considerable re-ordering of the songs, adding some and dropping others. The script also indicates a later production eliminated one of the women's roles.

162 Bittersuite (April 1987). "Songs of Experience"; THEATRE: The Duplex; OPENING DATE: April 12, 1987; PERFORMANCES: Unknown; LYRICS: Michael Champagne; MUSIC: Elliot Weiss; DIRECTION: Michael Champagne; COSTUMES: Judy Dearing; LIGHTING: Clay Coury, Matt Burman, and Linda Wallen; MUSICAL DIRECTION: Steve Flaherty; PRODUCERS: Next Wave Management (David Musselman and Mary T. Nealon) in association with Laric Entertainment CAST—Claudine Cassan-Jellison, Joy Franz, John Jellison, Joseph Neal

The revue was presented in two acts (song assignments unknown).

ACT ONE—"The Bittersuite," "The Life That Jack Built," "You're Not Getting Older," "Our Favorite Restaurant," "John's Song," "Soap Opera," "The Recipe," "Ice Cream," "Win and Lose," "Fathers and Sons," "Mama Don't Cry"

ACT TWO—"Snap Back," "The Cliché Waltz," "The Apology," "Narcissism Rag," "Dungeons and Dragons," "Twentieth Reunion," "I'll Be There," "How Little We've Learned," "World Without End," "Flight of the Phoenix"

NOTES—This Off Off Broadway production was the second of four editions of *Bittersuite* which played both Off Broadway and Off Off Broadway from 1984 to 1988 (for more information, see entry for the original Off Off Broadway 1984 production; also see entries for the Off Broadway productions in October 1987 and in 1988).

Note that Steve(n) Flaherty was the revue's musical director.

163 Bittersuite (October 1987). "Songs of Experience"; THEATRE: Palsson's Supper Club; OPENING DATE: October 5, 1987; PERFORMANCES: 211; LYRICS: Michael Champagne; MUSIC: Elliot Weiss; DIRECTION: Michael Champagne; LIGHTING: Eric Cornwell; MUSICAL DIRECTION: Elliot Weiss; PRODUCERS: Palsson's Supper Club; M & P Enterprises, Executive Producer

CAST—Susanne Blakeslee, David Edwards, Barbara Marineau, Byron Nease

The revue was presented in two acts.

ACT ONE—"The Bittersuite" (Company), "The Life That Jack Built" (David Edwards, Company), "You're Not Getting Older" (Barbara Marineau, Susanne Blakeslee), "Our Favorite Restaurant" (Company), "John's Song" (Byron Nease, Company), "Soap Opera" (Barbara Marineau), "The Recipe" (Byron Nease, Barbara Marineau), "Ice Cream" (Susanne Blakeslee, David Edwards), "Win and Lose" (Byron Nease), "Fathers and Sons" (David Edwards), "Mama Don't Cry" (Susanne Blakeslee, Company)

ACT TWO—"Snap Back" (Company), "The Cliché Waltz" (Susanne Blakeslee, Company), "The Apology" (David Edwards), "Narcissism Rag" (Byron Nease, Barbara Marineau, Susanne Blakeslee), "Dungeons and Dragons" (Barbara Marineau), "Twentieth Reunion" (Byron Nease, Company), "I'll Be There" (Byron Nease, David Edwards), "How Little We've Learned" (Company), "Flight of the Phoenix" (Company)

NOTES—This Off Broadway edition was the third of four editions of *Bittersuite* which played both Off Broadway and Off Off Broadway from 1984 to 1988 (for more information, see entry for the original 1984 Off Off Broadway production; also see entries for the Off Off Broadway production in April 1987 as well as the 1988 Off Broadway version).

164 Bittersuite—One More Time (1988). THEATRE: Palsson's Supper Club; OPENING DATE: May 16, 1988; PERFORMANCES: 16; LYRICS: Michael Champagne; MUSIC: Elliot Weiss; DIRECTION: Michael Champagne; PRODUCER: The Bittersuite Company

CAST—David Edwards, Suellen Estey, Roger Neil, Barbara Scanlon

The revue was presented in two acts (song assignments unknown).

ACT ONE—"The Bittersuite," "The Life That Jack Built," "Try a Little Harder," "Lonely Man, Lonely Woman," "Rank and File," "The Recipe," "Ice Cream," "Soap Opera," "I'll Make a Place," "Win and Lose," "Fathers and Sons," "Mama Don't Cry"

ACT TWO—"Snap Back," "The Cliché Waltz," "I've Got to Be Famous," "Money Is Honey," "Narcissism Rag," "Dungeons and Dragons," "Twentieth Reunion," "I'll Be There," "I'm Going to Live Forever," "One More Time"

NOTES—This Off Broadway edition was the fourth and final version of *Bittersuite* which played both Off Broadway and Off Off Broadway from 1984 to 1988 (for more information, see entry for the original 1984 Off Off Broadway production; also see entries for the Off Off Broadway production in April 1987 as well as the Off Broadway edition in October 1987).

165 Black Broadway. THEATRE: Town Hall; OPENING DATE: May 4, 1980; PERFORMANCES: 24; Production Designer: Leo Gambacorta; MUSICAL DIRECTION: Frank Owens; PRODUCERS: George Wein in associated with Honi Coles, Robert Kimball, and Bobby Short; John P. Fleming, Associate Producer

CAST—JOHN W. BUBBLES, NELL CARTER, HONI COLES, ADELAIDE HALL, GREGORY HINES, BOBBY SHORT, ELISABETH WELCH, EDITH WILSON, Charles "Cookie" Cook, Leslie "Bubba" Gaines, Mercedes Ellington, Carla Earle, Terri Griffin, Wyetta Turner

The revue was presented in two acts.

ACT ONE—Overture: Medley from *Runnin' Wild* (1923; music by James P. Johnson): "Ginger Brown," "Old-Fashioned Love," and "Charleston") (Frank Owens and Orchestra), "The Story of Black Broadway" (by George Wein, Dick Hyman, Honi Coles, and Robert Kimball) (Bobby Short or Honi Coles), "Liza" (Entrance of Copasetics) (Gregory Hines or Honi Coles, Cookie Cook, Bubba Gaines), "Blue Turning Grey Over You" (Cookie Cook), "I Can't Believe That You're in Love with Me" (lyric by Clarence Gaskill, music by Jimmy McHugh)/"Perdido" (lyric by Ervin Drake and Hans Lengsfelder, music by Juan Tizol)/"Who?" (*Sunny*, 1925; lyric by Oscar Hammerstein II and Otto Harbach, music by Jerome Kern) (Bubba Gaines), "Christopher Columbus" (Gregory Hines or Honi Coles, Cookie Cook, Bubba Gaines), "Under the Bamboo Tree" (lyric and music by Bob Cole, Jr., J. Rosamond Johnson, and James Weldon Johnson); "Wouldn't It Be a Dream" (lyric and music by Earl Jones and Joe Jordan); "Broadway in Dahomey" (from *In Dahomey*, 1902; lyric and music by Alex Rogers, Bert Williams, and George Walker) (Bobby Short), "Black and Blue" (*Hot Chocolates*, 1929; lyric by Andy Razaf, music by Thomas [Fats] Waller and Harry Brooks) (Edith Wilson), "He May Be Your Man but He Comes to See Me Sometimes" (*The Plantation Revue*, 1922; lyric and music by Lemuel Fowler) (Edith Wilson), "The Unbeliever" (lyric and music by Chris Smith, Frederick Bryan, and Bert Williams) (Bobby Short), "The Mayor of Harlem" (patter by Honi Coles)/ "Doin' the New Low Down" (*Blackbirds of 1928*;

lyric by Dorothy Fields, music by Jimmy McHugh) (Gregory Hines or Honi Coles, Cookie Cook, Bubba Gaines, Girls), "Creole Love Call" (lyric and music by Duke Ellington) (Adelaide Hall), "I Must Have That Man" (*Blackbirds of 1928*; lyric by Dorothy Fields, music by Jimmy McHugh) (Adelaide Hall), "Diga, Diga, Do"/"I Can't Give You Anything but Love, Baby" (*Blackbirds of 1928*; lyrics by Dorothy Fields, music by Jimmy McHugh) (Adelaide Hall); Harlem Medley: "She's Tall, She's Tan, She's Terrific"/"Posin'"/"Truckin'"/Breakfast in Harlem"/"Gimme a Pigfoot (and a Bottle of Beer)" (lyric and music by Wesley Wilson) (Bobby Short), "Ill Wind" (*Cotton Club Revue*, 1934; lyric by Ted Koehler, music by Harold Arlen), (Adelaide Hall), "Between the Devil and the Deep Blue Sea" (*Rhythmania*, 1931; lyric by Ted Koehler, music by Harold Arlen) (Adelaide Hall, Bobby Short), "As Long as I Live" (*Cotton Club Revue*, 1934; lyric by Ted Koehler, music by Harold Arlen) (Bobby Short), "The Brown-Skin Gal in the Calico Gown" (*Jump for Joy*, 1941 [revue never played New York]; lyric by Paul Francis Webster, music by Duke Ellington) (Bobby Short), "Jump for Joy" (*Jump for Joy*, 1941 [revue never played New York]; lyric by Paul Francis Webster, music by Duke Ellington) (Bobby Short, Company)

ACT TWO—"Cotton Club Stomp" (lyric and music by Duke Ellington, Johnny Hodges, and Harry Carney) (Frank Owens and Orchestra), "Tan Manhattan" (*Tan Manhattan*, 1940; lyric by Andy Razaf, music by Eubie Blake) (Gregory Hines), "Charleston Rag" (music by Eubie Blake) (Gregory Hines); Entrance of Elisabeth Welch to "When Lights Are Low" (lyric and music by Spencer Williams and Benny Carter); "Love for Sale" (*The New Yorkers*, 1930; lyric and music by Cole Porter); "Solomon" (British musical *Nymph Errant*, 1933; lyric and music by Cole Porter) (Elisabeth Welch), "Charleston" (*Runnin' Wild*, 1923; lyric by Cecil Mack, music by James P. Johnson) (Elisabeth Welch), "Ain't Misbehavin'" (*Hot Chocolates*, 1929; lyric by Andy Razaf, music by Thomas [Fats] Waller and Harry Brooks) (Nell Carter), "I've Got a Feeling I'm Falling" (lyric by Billy Rose, music by Thomas [Fats] Waller and Harry Link) (Nell Carter), "Legalize My Name" (*St. Louis Woman*, 1946; lyric by Johnny Mercer; music by Harold Arlen) (Nell Carter), "I'm a Little Blackbird Looking for a Bluebird" (*Dixie to Broadway*, 1924; lyric and music by George W. Meyer, Arthur Johnston, Grant Clarke, and Roy Turk) (Edith Wilson) (NOTE—This number was a tribute to Florence Mills.), "Silver Rose" (*Blackbirds of 1926*; lyric and music by George W. Meyer) (Elisabeth Welch), "Heat Wave" (*As Thousands Cheer*, 1933; lyric and music by Irving Berlin) (Nell Carter) (NOTE—This number was a tribute to Ethel Waters.), "You're Lucky to Me" (*Blackbirds of 1930*; lyric by Andy Razaf, music by Eubie Blake) (Edith Wilson), "Suppertime" (*As Thousands Cheer*, 1933; lyric and music by Irving Berlin) (Adelaide Hall), "Honey in the Honeycomb" (*Cabin in the Sky*, 1940; lyric by John LaTouche, music by Vernon Duke) (Nell Carter), "Stormy Weather" (*Cotton Club Parade*, 1933; lyric by Ted Koehler, music by Harold Arlen) (Elisabeth Welch), "Takin' a Chance on Love" (*Cabin in the Sky*, 1940; lyric by John LaTouche and Ted Fetter, music by Vernon Duke) (Adelaide Hall, Edith Wilson, Elisabeth Welch, Nell Carter, Gregory Hines or Honi Coles), "Dinah" (*The Plantation Revue*, 1925; lyric and music by Sam Lewis, Joe Young, and Harry Akst) (Gregory Hines or Bobby Short), "Sweet Georgia Brown" (lyric and music by Ben Bernie, Maceo Pinkard, and Kenneth Casey) (Gregory Hines, Ensemble), "It Ain't Necessarily So"/"There's a Boat That's Leavin' Soon for New York" (*Porgy and Bess*, 1935; lyrics by Ira Gershwin, music by George Gershwin) (John W. Bubbles), "Memories of You" (*Blackbirds of 1930*; lyric by Andy Razaf, music by Eubie Blake) (John W. Bubbles, Company), "Jump for Joy" (reprise) (Company)

NOTES—The performances of *Black Broadway* were historic. Here was an evening of legendary Black entertainers, many of them singing famous songs they had introduced decades earlier. Imagine: the song "Charleston" is so iconic it seems to have been around forever. But Elisabeth Welch introduced it on Broadway in 1923, and fifty-seven years later she was back on a New York stage, singing it again. Similarly, she had introduced the saga of "Solomon" in the London production of Cole Porter's *Nymph Errant* forty-seven years earlier. And so it went: here was Adelaide Hall singing one of the hottest torch songs ever written, "I Must Have That Man," which she had introduced in *Blackbirds of 1928*, fifty-two years ago to the month, and there was John W. Bubbles, the original Sportin' Life in *Porgy and Bess*, singing his two big numbers from that opera forty-five years after its world premiere. And there was "new" Broadway, too: Nell Carter and Gregory Hines. Alas, their early deaths deprived audiences from seeing them in a future *Black Broadway*-styled evening. There was no taping for cable or public television, there wasn't even a recording. At least one reference book lists the production as a "Broadway" revue, but it seems likely the evening was under an Off Broadway contract.

166 Black Nativity (1961).

THEATRE: 41st Street Theatre; transferred to the York Theatre on January 9, 1962; OPENING DATE: December 11, 1961; PERFORMANCES: 57; BOOK: Langston Hughes; DIRECTION: Vinnette Carroll; CHOREOGRAPHY: Louis Johnson; SCENERY: Joe Eula; COSTUMES: Bill Hargate; LIGHTING: Martin Aronstein; PRODUCERS: Michael R. Santoangelo and Barbara Griner in association with Eric Franck

CAST—Howard Sanders (Narrator), Clive Thompson (Joseph), Cleo Quitman (Mary), Henrietta Waddy (Woman), Carl Ford (Shepard), Princess Stewart (Angel), Alex Bradford (Balthazar, Preacher), Calvin White (Melchior), Kenneth Washington (Caspar); Townsfolk (Madeline Bell, Alex Bradford, Bernie Durant, Jr., Willie James McPhatter, Kitty Parham, Frances Steadman, Henrietta Waddy, Kenneth Washington, Calvin White, Marion Williams, Mattie Williams)

The musical was presented in two acts (song assignments unknown).

ACT ONE—(*The Child Is Born*), "Joy to the World" "My Way Is Cloudy," "No Room at the Inn," "Most Done Traveling," "Oh, Jerusalem in the Morning," "Poor Little Jesus," "What You Gonna Name Your Baby?" "Wasn't That a Mighty Day!" "Christ Was Born," "Go Tell It on the Mountain," "Rise Up, Shepherd, and Follow," "What Month Was Jesus Borned In?" "Sweet Little Jesus Boy," "Oh, Come All You Faithful," "If Anybody Asked You Who I Am?" "Children, Go Where I Send Thee"

ACT TWO—(*The Word Is Spread*), "Meetin' Here Tonight," "Holy Ghost, Don't Leave Me," "We Shall Be Changed," "The Blood Saved Me," "Leak in the Building," "Nobody Like the Lord," "His Will Be Done," "Said I Wasn't Gonna Tell Nobody," "Get Away Jordan," "Packin' Up," "God Be with You"

NOTES—*Black Nativity*, a Christmas story song-cycle by Langston Hughes, used gospel and traditional music to tell its story. The musical has continued to be produced, especially during the Christmas season.

In reviewing the original production for the *New York Times*, Howard Taubman noted the first act (*The Child Is Born*) told the traditional Christmas story and the second act (*The Word Is Spread*) took place in the present at a "jubilant revival meeting." Taubman felt the evening's "slim" text served as an excuse for a series of musical numbers performed with "uninhibited spirits and unlimited lung power." Taubman also mentioned that for "cultivated musical ears a little gospel singing may go a long way."

The production's original title seems to have been either *Wasn't That a Mighty Day!* or *Wasn't It a Mighty Day?*

The musical was seen in London at the Phoenix Theatre in 1962, and the cast included Alex Bradford and other members of the New York production.

VeeJay Records released an LP of thirteen of the cycle's songs (# VJL-5022). The musical was revived Off Broadway at The Duke on 42nd Street Theatre on November 30, 2007, for a one-month engagement; this time around, the musical took place on 42nd Street in 1973 (see entry). As of this writing, Fox Searchlight plans to release a film version of the musical in 2010.

167 Black Nativity (2007).

"A Gospel Celebration"; THEATRE: The Duke on 42nd Street; OPENING DATE: November 30, 2007; PERFORMANCES: 36; BOOK: Langston Hughes; DIRECTION: Alfred Preisser; Tracy Jack, Assistant Director; CHOREOGRAPHY: Tracy Jack; SCENERY: Troy Hourie; COSTUMES: Kimberly Glennon; LIGHTING: Aaron Black; MUSICAL DIRECTION: Kelvyn Bell; PRODUCER: A New 42nd Street and a Classical Theatre of Harlem Presentation (Alfred Preisser, Founder and Artistic Director); Jaime Robert Carrillo, Producer

CAST—Andre De Shields (Narrator, Pastor), Enrique Cruz DeJesus (Joseph), Tracy Jack (Mary); Lead Singers/Chorus: Melvin Bell III, Ebony Blake, Alexander Elisa, Phyre Hawkins, Laiona Michelle, Nikki Stephenson, Tryphena Wade, Rejinald Woods; Chorus of Angels: Shangilia Youth Choir of Kenya (Kennedy Malumbe Anyanzwa, Brian Kamau Gitonga, Francis Kimani Irungu, Mary Wambui Kamau, Muchiri Kariuki, Gladys Wanjiku Mbugua, Dennis Mutwiri Micheni, Phresia Wangare)

The musical was presented in one act.

NOTES—The revival of *Black Nativity* was set in the Times Square area during the Christmas season of 1973 and its cast of characters included pimps and prostitutes. Sam Thielman in *Variety* liked the "rich and unique" 1970s time setting for the musical, but Caryn James in *New York Times* said "the '70s transplant just doesn't work." She felt the evening was "flat" and "disappointing," while Thielman felt the revival was "a really great show" of "boundless enthusiasm."

The production apparently included new music composed by Kelvyn Bell, who was also the revival's musical director.

For more information, see entry for the original 1961 production.

168 The Black Rider.

THEATRE: Brooklyn Academy of Music/Opera House; OPENING DATE: November 20, 1993; PERFORMANCES: 10; BOOK: William S. Burroughs; LYRICS: Tom Waits; MUSIC: Tom Waits; DIRECTION: Robert Wilson; SCENERY: Robert Wilson; COSTUMES: Frida Parmeggiani; LIGHTING: Heinrich Brunke and Robert Wilson; MUSICAL DIRECTION: Greg Cohen; PRODUCER: The Brooklyn Academy of Music/The Next Wave Festival and The Thalia Theatre of Hamburg

CAST—Heinz Vossbrink (Kuno, Old Forrester), Dominque Horwitz (Pegleg), Annette Paulmann (Katchen), Stefan Kurt (Wilhelm, Clerk), Gerd Kunath, Jorg Holm

NOTES—A horrific old German folk tale was the basis for *The Black Rider*. The tale had been previously adapted into the 1821 opera *Der Freischutz* by Carl Maria von Weber, who softened the story considerably. But the new adaptation, about a young man who makes a pact with the devil for magic bullets to help him succeed both as marksman and lover, was, according to Edward Rothstein in the

New York Times, a "post-modern nihilistic carnival" which finds "the stench of blood" in middleclass mores.

Rothstein found *The Black Rider* "brilliant and disturbing," and praised Tom Waits' new but purposely familiar-sounding score, songs which seemed to be "walking around in drag" (thus "gospel turns demonic; vaudeville turns acidic; 1930's ballads turn morbid"). Rothstein summed up the evening as one of the "most persistently insinuating and affecting" musicals of recent seasons.

The musical had first been presented in Hamburg in 1990.

169 Black Roses.
NOTES—See entry for *Murder in 3 Keys*.

170 Black Sea Follies. THEATRE: Playwrights Horizons; OPENING DATE: December 16, 1986; PERFORMANCES: 31; PLAY: Paul Schmidt; play conceived and additional material by Stanley Silverman Lyrics: Russian lyrics translated by Paul Schmidt; MUSIC: Dmitri Shostakovich and other composers; all music adapted by Stanley Silverman; DIRECTION: Stanley Silverman; CHOREOGRAPHY: Liz Lerman; SCENERY: James Noone; COSTUMES: Jim Buff; LIGHTING: Ken Tabacknick; PRODUCERS: Playwrights Horizons and Music-Theatre Group

CAST—David Chandler (Shostakovich), Alan Scarfe (Stalin), Henry Stram (Misha), Deborah Milson (Katerina Lvovna), David Dosing (Seryozha), Robert Osborne (Stepanych), Martha Caplin (Violin), Carol Zeavin (Violin), Sarah Clarke (Viola), Matthias Naegele (Cello), Elena Ivanina (Piano)

The action occurs in Moscow in the early 1970s.

The play with music was presented in two acts.

ACT ONE—Rehearsal, "Leningrad—What War Was It?" (from Quartet # 8, Opus 110)/Song: "United Nations on the March" (lyric by Harold Roma), "By the Beautiful Black Sea," "The State Film Industry at Work" /Song: "I'm Single" (Opus 121, No. 2), "A Night at the Movies"/Song: "The King Goes Out to War" (Opus 62, No. 6), "War and Peace (Dialectic Inaction!)"/Song: "Comin' Through the Rye" (Opus 62, No. 4) (text by R. Burns), Rehearsal Break/"Skipping Dance," "The Composing of 'Tahiti Trot'"

ACT TWO—"March vs. Waltz (Dialectic Inaction!)" (Quartet # 3, Opus 73)/"Prison Camp Scene" and "Katerina's Aria" from 1934 opera *Lady Macbeth of Mtsensk* (Opus 29), "The Mad Tea Party" (Quartet # 13, Opus 138)/Song: "Tchaikovsky" (*Lady in the Dark*, 1941; lyric by Ira Gershwin, music by Kurt Weill)/Duet from "Moscow Cheryomushki" (Opus 105; from Quartet # 1, Opus 49), "Truth and Lies (Dialectic Inaction!)" (Quartet # 7, Opus 108), "Dancing to the Tick of Terror" (Coda [First Movement, 5th Symphony]), Rehearsal: "Cantabile" (Piano Quintet, Opus 57), "Ant and Grasshopper (More Dialectic Inaction!)"/"We Were Together" (Opus 127, No. 3)

NOTES—In *Black Sea Follies*, Dmitri Shostakovich coaches an ensemble of young musicians in his chamber music. As he works with them, his thoughts go back to the years of Stalin's regime and his meetings with the Soviet dictator. It seems the evening took a turn which the authors didn't expect, because Mel Gussow in the *New York Times* noted that Shostakovich, the would-be hero of the play with music, was "pallid" and far less interesting than the exuberant Stalin, who all but stole the show. Gussow singled out two highlights (both of which weren't listed in the program). One was a series of variations on the "Star-Spangled Banner," which was performed in a number of styles (including a minuet and a Russian-harvest song), and the other was a "Sovietized" version of "Tea for Two" (from *No, No, Nanette*, 1925; lyric by Otto Harbach, music by Vincent Youmans). Gussow also mentioned that the evening offered a "rewriting" of Ira Gershwin and Kurt Weill's "Tchaikovsky" (from *Lady in the Dark*, 1941), which this time around included the names of artists banned under Stalin's regime. The *Times* later made a correction about the number, stating that Gershwin's lyric was used in the production; it's unclear whether his original lyric from 1941 was used or whether he had indeed at one time revised the original lyric to include the names of banned Soviet composers. A program note by Alex DeJonge noted that under Stalin no film could be released without his approval; Stalin also considered himself the arbiter of "good" music, and ordered Shostakovich to write hummable music; further, Stalin condemned Shostakovich's 1934 opera *Lady Macbeth of Mtsensk*.

171 Blackberries. "A Minstrel-Vaudeville Spectacular"; THEATRE: The AMAS Repertory Theatre; OPENING DATE: April 19, 1984; PERFORMANCES: 16; BOOK: Joseph George Caruso; SKETCHES: Billy K. Wells; ADDITIONAL MATERIAL AND DIALOGUE: Andre De Shields; DIRECTION: Andre De Shields; CHOREOGRAPHY: Andre De Shields; Gui Andrisano, Co-Choreographer; SCENERY: Edward Goetz; COSTUMES: Mardi Philips; LIGHTING: Deborah Tulchin; MUSICAL DIRECTION: John McMahon; PRODUCER: The AMAS Repertory Theatre (Rosetta LeNoire, Founder and Artistic Director) by special arrangement with William De Sylva and Betsy Rosenfield

CAST—Steven Bland (Georgia Berry), Anthony Bova (Virginia Berry), Clent Bowers (Mr. Interlocutor Berry), Christina Britton (North Carolina Berry), Marion Caffey (Florida Berry), Ellia English (South Carolina Berry), Janice Holt (Tambo Berry), Allynne Johnson (Arkansas Berry), Lynda Joy (Mississippi Berry), Cynthia Pearson (Maryland Berry), Mardi Philips (Tennessee Berry), Gary Sullivan (Kentucky Berry), Steve Tapp (Alabama Berry), Tug Wilson (Texas Berry), Andrea Wright (Bones Berry); On-Stage Musicians (John McMahon, Piano; Babafumi Ohene Kwado Larbi, Drums and Percussion)

The musical was presented in two acts.

ACT ONE—*Minstrels on Parade!*

Prologue: "The Parade" (Steven Bland), "The International Rag" (lyric and music by Irving Berlin) (Steven Bland, The Berries), "Down in Dixie" (Clent Bowers), "Are You from Dixie?" (lyric by Jack Yellen, music by George L. Cobb) (Steven Bland, Anthony Bova, Marion Caffey, Janice Holt, Gary Sullivan, Andrea Wright), "My Sunny Tennessee" (possibly from *The Midnight Rounders of 1921*; lyric and music by Bert Kalmar, Harry Ruby, and Herman Ruby) (Clent Bowers), "Walkin' the Dog" (lyric and music by Shelton Brooks) (Janice Holt, Andrea Wright), "When the Midnight Choo-Choo Leaves for Alabam'" (lyric and music by Irving Berlin) (Clent Bowers, The Berries), "Alice Blue Gown" (*Irene*, 1919; lyric by Joe McCarthy, music by Harry Tierney) (Christina Britton, Mardi Philips, Tug Wilson), "St. Louis Blues" (lyric and music by W.C. Handy) (Allynne Johnson), "Poor Papa" (lyric by Billy Rose, music by Harry Woods) (Ellia English), "The Singer" (sketch by Billy K. Wells) (Christina Britton, Steve Tapp), "The Birth of the Blues" Operetta (The song "Birth of the Blues" was introduced in *George White's Scandals* [Eighth Edition], 1926; lyric by B.G. [Buddy] DeSylva and Lew Brown, music by Ray Henderson) (Clent Bowers; danced by Janice Holt; oboe solo by Allynne Johnson; The Berries), "The Perfect Night" (sketch by Billy K. Wells) (Steven Bland, Tug Wilson, Andrea Wright), "Swanee" (interpolated into the score of *Sinbad*, 1918; lyric by Irving Caesar and B.G. [Buddy] DeSylva, music by George Gershwin) (Marion Caffey), "April Showers" (added for the tour of *Bombo*, 1921; lyric by B.G. [Buddy] DeSylva, music by Louis Silvers) (Linda Joy), "Toot, Toot, Tootsie! (Goodbye)" (added to the tour of *Bombo*, 1921; lyric by Ted Fio Rito, Gus Kahn, Robert King, and Dan Russo, music by Ernie Erdman) (Anthony Bova), "Waiting for the Robert E. Lee" (lyric by Sam Lewis and Joe Young, music by Walter Donaldson) (Tug Wilson), "My Mammy" (*Sinbad*, 1918; lyric by Sam Lewis and Joe Young, music by Walter Donaldson) (Anthony Bova, Marion Caffey, Lynda Joy, Tug Wilson), "Friendly Reunion" (sketch by Billy K. Wells) (Clent Bowers, Allynne Johnson), "Old Fashioned Garden" (*Hitchy-Koo of 1919*; lyric and music by Cole Porter) (Steve Tapp, The Sunflowers [Ellia English, Janice Holt, Lynda Joy, Andrea Wright), "Whispering" (lyric and music by John Schonberger, Richard Coburn, and Vincent Rose) (Christina Britton), "Carolina's Calling Me" (lyric and music by Bob Charles) (The Sunflowers and The Rose [Mardi Philips]), "Lazy Moon" (lyric by Bob Cole, music by Rosamond Johnson) (Clent Bowers, Steve Tapp, Christina Britton, The Sunflowers, The Rose), "Stump Speech by Speakin' Sam" (Marion Caffey), "Sit Down, Sister" (traditional) (Ellia English, The Congregation), "The International Rag" (reprise) (The Berries), "We'll Say So Long, but Not Goodbye" (lyric and music by Jack Mahoney) (Steven Bland)

ACT TWO—*And Now... Vaudeville!* "Under the Bamboo Tree" (lyric and music by Bob Cole, Jr., J. Rosamund Johnson, and James Weldon Johnson) (Clent Bowers, Ellia English), "Chloe" (lyric by Gus Khan, music by Neil Moret) (Marion Caffey, The Berries), "Ja-Da" (lyric and music by Bob Carleton) (Janice Holt), "That's A Plenty" (lyric by Ray Gilbert, music by Lew Pollack) (dance; performed by Janice Holt, Steven Bland, Gary Sullivan), "Pagan Love Song" (1929 film *The Pagan*; lyric by Arthur Freed, music by Nacio Herb Brown) (Steve Tapp, Andrea Wright, The Berries), "Limehouse Blues" (*A to Z*, 1922 [London], *Charlot's Revue of 1924* [New York]; lyric by Douglas Furber and Ronald Jeans, music by Philip Braham) (John McMahon), "Gimme a Pigfoot (and a Bottle of Beer)" (lyric and music by Wesley "Socks" Wilson and Coot Grant; some sources credit only Wilson as the lyricist and composer of the song) (Janice Holt), "Georgia on My Mind" (lyric and music by Hoagy Carmichael) (Andrea Wright), "Strange Fruit" (lyric and music by Lewis Allan) (Ellia English), "Do You Know What It Means to Miss New Orleans?" (1947 film *New Orleans*; lyric by Eddie De Lange, music by Louis Alter) (Ellia English, Janice Holt, Andrea Wright), "The Apartment" (sketch by Billy K. Wells) (Steven Bland, Steve Tapp), "I Wanna Be Loved by You" (*Good Boy*, 1928; lyric by Bert Kalmar, music by Harry Ruby) (Lynda Joy, after Helen Kane), "Transplant" (sketch by Billy K. Wells) (Anthony Bova, Christina Britton, Marion Caffey, Lynda Joy, Mardi Philips, Tug Wilson), "Si J'Etais Blanche" (lyric and music by L. Falk, H. Varna, and R. Lelievre) (Janice Holt, after Josephine Baker), "Paradise" (lyric by Nacio Herb Brown and Gordon Clifford, music by Nacio Herb Brown) (Christina Britton, after Pola Negri), "You're the Cream in My Coffee" (*Hold Everything!* 1928; lyric by B.G. [Buddy] DeSylva and Lew Brown, music by Ray Henderson) (Marion Caffey and Lynda Joy, after Bill "Bojangles" Robinson and Shirley Temple), "The Flying Linguinis (Pasta Medley)" (Anthony Bova, Christina Britton, Allynne Johnson, Mardi Philips, Gary Sullivan, Steve Tapps), "Bill Bailey (Won't You Please Come Home?)" (lyric and music by Hughie Cannon) (Ellia English, after Bessie Smith), "Fascinating Rhythm" (*Lady, Be Good!* 1924; lyric by Ira Gershwin, music by George Gershwin) (Gary Sullivan and Andrea Wright, after Fred and Adele Astaire), "Some of These Days" (lyric and music by Shelton Brooks) (Lynda Joy, after Sophie Tucker), "I'll See You in My Dreams" (lyric by Gus Kahn, music by Isham Jones) (Steven Bland, after Dick Powell; featuring The Dreamgirls [Christina

Britton, Janice Holt, Lynda Joy, Mardi Philips, Andrea Wright), "The International Rag" (reprise) (The Berries)

NOTES—This Off Off Broadway evening of musical nostalgia was a self-described "Minstrel-Vaudeville Spectacular ... not an obituary to a by-gone era — it is a notice of a permanent life in America's musical history."

172 Blame It on the Movies! "The Reel Music of Hollywood"; THEATRE: Criterion Center Stage Left; OPENING DATE: May 16, 1989; PERFORMANCES: 3; MATERIAL: Ron Abel, Billy Barnes, and David Galligan; LYRICS: Billy Barnes; MUSIC: Billy Barnes; DIRECTION: David Galligan; CHOREOGRAPHY: Larry Hyman; SCENERY: Fred Duer; COSTUMES: Bonnie Stauch; LIGHTING: Michael Gilliam; MUSICAL DIRECTION: Ron Abel; PRODUCERS: Roger Berlind, Franklin R. Levy, and Gregory Harrison

CAST—Sandy Edgerton, Kathy Garrick, Bill Hutton, Christine Kellogg, Peter Marc, Dan O'-Grady, Barbara Sharma, Patty Tiffany

The revue was presented in two acts (sketch and song assignments not listed in program).

ACT ONE—"Blame It on the Movies," The Forties, The War Years, Foreign Film Tribute, Fox in Love

ACT TWO—Entr'acte, Saturday Matinee, Oscar Losers, A Tribute to the Hollywood Film Score: *A Place in the Sun* Ballet, Finale

NOTES—This short-lived affectionate tribute to the movies used a combination of standard film songs and new ones by Billy Barnes, a welcome name from the early years of the Off Broadway revue who hadn't been represented in New York since the early 1960s (see entries for *The Billy Barnes Revue* and *Billy Barnes Revue*).

Jeffrey Sweet in *The Best Plays of 1988-1989* praised the revue's ballet *A Place in the Sun* (which used Franz Waxman's background music from the 1951 film) and also chose Christine Kellogg as Best Actress in a Secondary Role for her performance in the revue (along with Faith Prince for her roles in the Broadway production of *Jerome Robbins' Broadway*).

Stephen Holden in the *New York Times* also liked the aforementioned ballet, saying it represented the revue's "one moment of genuine movie magic." He also praised an "inventive" sequence in which an "unglamorous" movie-going couple (who are viewing the 1966 French film *A Man and a Woman*) are magically transformed into "sexy icons of 60's Continental sophistication." Holden also mentioned the "Fox in Love" segment, which paid tribute to the overripe title songs from 20th Century-Fox movies of the 1950s (Holden referred to the title songs from *Love Is a Many Splendored Thing* [1955] and *April Love* [1957], and one hopes there was room in the revue for the title numbers from *Woman's World* [1954], *A Certain Smile* [1958], and *The Best of Everything* [1959]).

Blame It on the Movies! had been previously produced in Los Angeles.

173 Blitzstein! THEATRE: Provincetown Playhouse; OPENING DATE: November 30, 1966; PERFORMANCES: 7; LYRICS: Marc Blitzstein; MUSIC: Marc Blitzstein; DIRECTION: Ellen Pahl; SCENERY: Cynthia Bernardi; LIGHTING: Thomas Kelly; PRODUCERS: Herbert Dorfman and Stage Associates

CAST—Mira Gilbert, Norman Frieden, Peter Basquin (piano)

NOTES—No information available concerning which songs were in the program.

If composer-tribute revues must exist, then one devoted to Marc Blitzstein's songs at least makes sense, given that his exquisite theatre music is often unfamiliar to even the most ardent lovers of musical theatre. His work includes *The Cradle Will Rock* (1937), *No for an Answer* (1941), *Regina* (1949), *Reuben Reuben* (1955), and *Juno* (1959), and his songs ("Monday Morning Blues," "Bird Upon the Tree," "One Kind Word," and "We're Alive") are among the finest ever written for the musical theatre. See entries for *The Cradle Will Rock, No for an Answer, Juno*, and *The Blitzstein Project.*

Possibly the finest (and certainly one of the most thoroughly researched) of all theatre biographies is Eric A. Gordon's *Mark the Music/The Life and Work of Marc Blitzstein* (published by St. Martin's Press in 1989), a fascinating study of one of the least-known figures in American musical theatre.

174 The Blitzstein Project: The Harpies and I've Got the Tune. THEATRE: St. Bart's Playhouse/Soho Rep; OPENING DATE: September 14, 1988; PERFORMANCES: 24; BOOKS: Marc Blitzstein; LYRICS: Marc Blitzstein; MUSIC: Marc Blitzstein; DIRECTION AND ADDITIONAL TEXTS: Carol Corwen; CHOREOGRAPHY: Barry R. Gallo; SCENERY: Jeffrey D. McDonald; COSTUMES: G.A. Howard; LIGHTING: Donald Holder; MUSICAL DIRECTION: Donald Sosin; PRODUCER: Soho Rep (Marlene Swartz and Jerry Englebach, Artistic Directors)

The Harpies:

CAST—Paul Binotto (Phineus), Joanna Seaton (Aello), Loretta Giles (Ocypete), Helen Zelon (Calaeno), Daniel Blum (Zetes), Don Mayo (Jason), Peter Schmitz (Calais), Jennifer Lee Andrews (Iris), Mary Eileen O'Donnell (Chorus), Andre Montgomery (Chorus)

NOTES—*The Blitzstein Project: The Harpies and I've Got the Tune* was an Off Off Broadway production.

The Harpies was a one-act opera, a spoof of the myth of Jason and the Argonauts. It was written in 1931, and it was first performed by the Manhattan School of Music on May 25, 1953. The complete opera was recorded by Premier Recordings (CD # PRCD-1009) for the collection *3 American One-Act Operas* (the recording also included William Schuman's *The Mighty Casey* [1953] and Samuel Barber's *A Hand of Bridge* [1959], both in abridged versions).

I've Got the Tune:

CAST—Andre Montgomery (Mr. Musiker), Joanna Seaton (Beetzie), Mary Eileen O'Donnell (Madame Arbutus), Peter Schmitz (Captain Bristlepunkt), Daniel Baum (Private Schnook), Mimi Higgins (The Mongrel), Helen Zelon (The Suicide), Don Mayo (Choral Director), Others (Paul Binotto, Loretta Giles, Jennifer Lee Andrews)

NOTES—*I've Got the Tune* had been commissioned by CBS radio, and the agit-prop musical, somewhat in the style of Blitzstein's *The Cradle Will Rock* and *No for an Answer* (see entries for the Off Broadway productions), was first aired on October 14, 1937. Prior to the Soho Rep production, the work had been occasionally staged over the years.

175 Blood. THEATRE: Martinson Hall/The Public Theatre; OPENING DATE: March 7, 1971; PERFORMANCES: 14 (or 39, depending on source); CONCEIVED BY: Doug Dyer; BOOK: Doug Dyer in collaboration with the *Blood* Company; LYRICS: Alex Ander, Mary Boylan, Christopher Cox, Doug Dyer, Patrick Fox, Horald Griffiths, and Avra Petrides; MUSIC: Alex Ander, David Cohen, Christopher Cox, Margaret Dorn, Doug Dyer, Patrick Fox, Horald Griffiths, Elizabeth Howard, Maggie Hyatt, Linda Swenson, Jim Turner, and Tom Willis Direction: Doug Dyer; CHOREOGRAPHY: Cora Cahan; SCENERY: Doug Dyer; COSTUMES: Theoni V. Aldredge; LIGHTING: Keith Nelson; MUSICAL DIRECTION: Patrick Fox; PRODUCER: New York Shakespeare Festival Public Theatre (Joseph Papp, Producer; Bernard Gersten, Associate Producer)

CAST—Alex Ander, Roberta Baum, Alexandra Borrie, Mary Boylan, Christopher Cox, Margaret Dorn, Doug Dyer, William Ellington, Patrick Fox, Horald Griffiths, Elizabeth Howard, Maggie Hyatt, Madge Sinclair, Joyce Stanton, Jack Starkey, Linda Swenson, Jim Turner

SOURCE—Aeschylus' 458 B.C. trilogy *The Oresteia* (*Agamemnon, The Libation Bearers*, and *The Eumenides*).

MUSICAL NUMBERS (division of acts and song assignments unknown; songs are listed in performance order)—"Baby Rue," "High Lonesome," "Hard Time War Time," "Hear the Guns," "Lullaby," "Snake," "Cold Steel," "Every Father," "I Had a Son," "There You Go Again," "Father, Father," "Gas Can," "Dance of Murder," "Nobody's Fault," "I Dreamt About My Home," "Madness Murder," "Whistles," "I Woke Up Today," "Prophesy," "4,000 Years," "Walk on Home," "Heebie-Jeebie Furies," "Don't Call Us," "Before You Knew I Love You," "Destruction," "Rhythms," "Monkey in a Tree," "Minute by Minute," "Love Came to Me," "New Snow," "Just a Little Bit," "Hail to the Blood"

NOTES—Doug Dyer, who had been responsible for *Stomp* (see entry) during the 1969-1970 season, returned to the Public Theatre with this anti-war piece about a Vietnam veteran's homecoming. An updated version of the Greek trilogy *The Oresteia* by Aeschylus, the piece ran for just a few weeks. Apparently the musical's message was that blood-letting (war and murder) in the present day reaches back to ancient times (or maybe it was the other way around, blood-letting in ancient times continues to the present day). Either way, these sophomoric revelations were hardly awe-inspiring, leading Leonard Probst of NBC to call the production a "myth-take" and for Jerry Tallmer in the *New York Post* to complain that *Blood* was "the 47,000th spin-off" of *Hair* (see entry). The scenes were performed on elongated, movable platforms, and much of the audience was seated on stools or on the floor; at times, audience members had to get out of the way of the moving platforms, taking their stools with them (Tallmer mentioned that the typical "built-in" Public audience of "True Believers" would no doubt not mind the inconvenience).

Dyer was back at the Public later in the year for yet another musical re-telling of a Greek tragedy; like *Blood, The Wedding of Iphigenia/Iphigenia in Concert* (see entry) was quickly forgotten and classical Greek tragedy was safe from musical adaptation ... at least until the next such arrival, the disappointing *Marie Christine* (1999). Based on Euripides' *Medea* (431 B.C.), Michael John LaChiusa's strong score had to battle a ponderous book, unsympathetic characters, and a sometimes pretentious production; the musical opened (and quickly closed) at Lincoln Center, but happily left behind a cast album.

176 Bloolips in "Lust in Space." "A Musical Space Epidemic"; THEATRE: Orpheum Theatre; OPENING DATE: March 19, 1981; PERFORMANCES: 124

Conceived by Jon Taylor, Rex Lay, and The Bloolips; "Androgeny" lyric by Jimmy Camicia; DIRECTION: Bette Bourne; SCENERY: The Bloolips; COSTUMES: The Bloolips; LIGHTING: David K. H. Elliott; PRODUCERS: Bloolips, Ltd., Mitchell Maxwell, and Alan Schuster in association with The Eastside Theatre Corporation CAST—The Bloolips (Bossy Bette, Gretel Feather, Lavina Co-Op, Naughty Nickers, Diva Dan, Precious Pearl [Paul Shaw])

The revue was presented in two acts.

NOTES—Songs titles for *Bloolips in "Lust in Space"* weren't listed in the program. The evening, a spoof of science-fiction films which centered around a trip to the Moon, was performed by the Bloolips, a sextet of British men in drag. Mel Gussow in the *New York Times* found the Bloolips "bizarrely funny," and noted their outré costumes were "an unfashion show of unparalleled tackiness."

The program bio for the Bloolips' founder, Bette Bourne, indicated he had played King Lear, Tamburlaine, Othello, Macbeth, Mephistopheles, Noah, and Wotan, but "now feels his public demands more than mere pertness."

The Bloolips occasionally returned to Off Off Broadway in limited engagements such as *Belle Reprieve* (which opened at La Mama on February 14, 1991, and was inspired by *A Streetcar Named Desire*); *Bloolips/Get Hur* (which opened at the Dance Theatre Workshop's Bessie Schonberg Theatre on January 26, 1993); and *Bloo Review: A Bloolips Retrospectacle* (which opened at the Theatre for the New City on April 30, 1998, and included sketches and lyrics by Neil Bartlett, Jimmy Camicia, Ray Dobbins, Paul Shaw, "and Oscar Wilde").

177 The Blue Magi. THEATRE: St. Peter's Gate Theatre; OPENING DATE: December 11, 1972; PERFORMANCES: 20; BOOK: Sally Dixon Wiener; LYRICS: Sally Dixon Wiener; MUSIC: Sally Dixon Wiener; DIRECTION: Miriam Fond; SCENERY: Billy Puzo; COSTUMES: Danny Morgan; LIGHTING: Richard Delahanty; MUSICAL DIRECTION: William Foster McDaniel; PRODUCER: Theatre at Noon (Miriam Fond, Artistic Director)

CAST—Sy Travers (Jessie), Ruth Brisbane (Mme. Sophronie), Ross Gilford (Gaspard), Roger Woodson (Jim), Leilani Johnson (Della), Bill LaVallee (Clarinetist)

SOURCE—O. Henry (William Sydney Porter)'s short story "The Gift of the Magi," which first appeared in the short story collection *The Big City*.

NOTES—*The Blue Magi* was an Off Off Broadway musical adaptation of O. Henry's short story "The Gift of the Magi." For other musical versions of the material, see entries for Ronnie Britton's *Gift of the Magi* (1975) and Mark St. Germain and Randy Courts' *The Gifts of the Magi* (1984); these two entries also include information about television and regional musical adaptations of the famous short story.

178 Blue Man Group.
NOTES—See entry for *Tubes*.

179 Blue Plate Special. "A Musical Country Soap Opera"; THEATRE: UpStage/Manhattan Theatre Club; OPENING DATE: October 18, 1983; PERFORMANCES: 48; BOOK: Tom Edwards; LYRICS: Mary L. Fisher; MUSIC: Harris Wheeler; DIRECTION: Art Wolff; CHOREOGRAPHY: Douglas Norwick; SCENERY: David Jenkins; COSTUMES: David Murin; LIGHTING: Arden Fingerhut; PRODUCER: Manhattan Theatre Club (Lynne Meadow, Artistic Director; Barry Grove, Managing Director; Connie L. Alexis, General Manager)

CAST—Steven Adler (Floor Manager), Gretchen Cryer (Della Juracko), Gordon Paddison (Ronnie Frank Flaugher), David Strathairn (Ricky Jim Robinson), Ron Holgate (Preacher Larry Finney), Mary Gordon Murray (Connie Sue Day), Tina Johnson (Ramona Juracko)

The musical is Episode 41 of the continuing daytime drama of a soap opera broadcast from Morning Glory Mountain in Tennessee at the present time.

The musical was presented in two acts.

ACT ONE—"Morning Glory Mountain" (Gretchen Cryer, Company), "At the Bottom Lookin' Up" (Mary Gordon Murray), "Ramona's Lament" (Tina Johnson), "Never Say Never" (Tina Johnson, Gordon Paddison), "Halfway to Heaven" (Mary Gordon Murray, Tina Johnson, Gretchen Cryer), "Satisfaction Guaranteed" (Ron Holgate, Gretchen Cryer, Company)

ACT TWO—"Blue Plate Special" (Gretchen Cryer, Company), "Twice as Nice" (Gretchen Cryer, Ron Holgate), "All American Male" (Gordon Paddison), "Side of Fries" (Gretchen Cryer, Mary Gordon Murray, Tina Johnson), "Honky Tonk Queens" (Mary Gordon Murray, Tina Johnson), "I Ain't Looking Back" (Mary Gordon Murray, Company), "I'm Gonna Miss Those Tennessee Nights" (Gretchen Cryer)

NOTES—*Blue Plate Special* was a musical spoof of soap operas, in this case Episode 41 of a soap set in a diner in the mountains of Tennessee. In this episode, a nuclear waste dump is discovered under the vegetable patch of the diner. Sounds amusing, but, unfortunately, *Blue Plate Special* disappeared after its limited engagement at the Manhattan Theatre Club. Moreover, Frank Rich in the *New York Times* wasn't impressed with the offering, noting "it's not easy to parody what is already ridiculous." But he had nothing but praise for David Jenkins' depiction of an old-time diner, a mélange of "curdled oranges and blues suggesting vintage color postcards."

The musical had previously been produced at Upstairs at Gene & Gabe's (produced by Gene Dale and Gabe Bencivenga).

180 Blues in the Night (1980). THEATRE: Playhouse 46; OPENING DATE: March 26, 1980; PERFORMANCES: 51; LYRICS: See song list for credits; MUSIC: See song list for credits; DIRECTION: Sheldon Epps; CHOREOGRAPHY: Gregory Hines; SCENERY: June De Camp; COSTUMES: Jeanette Oleksa; LIGHTING: Debra J. Kletter; PRODUCER: The Production Company (Norman Rene, Artistic Director; Sheldon Epps, Associate Artistic Director)

CAST—David Brunetti, Suzanne M. Henry, Rise Collins, Gwen Shepherd

The action occurs in a cheap hotel in Chicago during the late 1930s.

The revue was presented in two acts.

ACT ONE—"Blue Blues" (lyric and music by Bessie Smith) (Company), "Four Walls Blues" (lyric and music by Willard Robison) (David Brunetti), "Stompin' at the Savoy" (lyric and music by Andy Razaf, Benny Goodman, Chick Webb, and Edgar Sampson) (Rise Collins), "New Orleans Hot Scop Blues" (lyric and music by George W. Thomas) (Gwen Shepherd), "It Makes My Love Come Down" (lyric and music by Bessie Smith) (Suzanne M. Henry, Rise Collins, Gwen Shepherd), "Copenhagen" (lyric by Walter Melrose, music by Charlie Davis) (Suzanne M. Henry), "Lush Life" (lyric and music by Billy Strayhorn)/"Sophisticated Lady" (lyric by Mitchell Parish and Irving Mills, music by Duke Ellington) (Rise Collins, David Brunetti), "Take Me for a Buggy Ride" (lyric and music by Leola and Wesley Wilson) (Gwen Shepherd), "Willow Weep for Me" (lyric and music by Ann Ronell) (Suzanne M. Henry), "Kitchen Man" (lyric and music by Andy Razaf and Alex Bellenda) (Gwen Shepherd), "Take It Right Back" (lyric and music by H. Grey) (Suzanne M. Henry, Rise Collins, Gwen Shepherd)

ACT TWO—"Blues in the Night" (from the 1941 film *Blues in the Night*; lyric by Johnny Mercer, music by Harold Arlen) (Rise Collins and Suzanne M. Henry), "When a Woman Loves a Man" (lyric by Johnny Mercer, music by Bernard Hanighen and Gordon Jenkins)/"Am I Blue" (1929 film *On with the Show*; lyric by Grant Clarke, music by Harry Akst) (Rise Collins), "Something to Live For" (lyric and music by Duke Ellington and Billy Strayhorn) (Rise Collins), "Reckless Blues" (lyric and music by Bessie Smith) (Suzanne M. Henry), "Wasted Life Blues" (lyric and music by Bessie Smith) (Gwen Collins), "Baby Doll" (lyric and music by Bessie Smith) (David Brunetti), "Nobody Knows You When You're Down and Out" (lyric and music by Jimmy Cox) (Suzanne M. Henry, Rise Collins, Gwen Shepherd), "I Gotta Right to Sing the Blues" (*Earl Carroll Vanities* [Tenth Edition], 1932); lyric by Ted Koehler, music by Harold Arlen) (Company), "Blue Blues"/"Blues in the Night" (reprises) (Company)

NOTES—Beginning in the 1970s, Broadway and Off Broadway musicals seemed to feed upon one another with an almost unending parade of revues and loosely-structured book musicals, each one drawing upon the same well of nostalgic songs from the Twenties, Thirties, and Forties. Some were entertaining enough, but their lack of imagination and the familiarity of their songs and points of view made them tiresome. Such offerings included *Bubbling Brown Sugar* (1976; see entry), *Ain't Misbehavin'* (1978; see entry), *Eubie!* (1978), *One Mo 'Time!* (1979; see entry), *Sophisticated Ladies* (1980), and *Blues in the Night* (1980), and the genre continued well into the 1980s and 1990s with such later revues as *Uptown...It's Hot!* (1986), *Black and Blue* (1989), *Rollin' on the T.O.B.A.* (1999; see entry), and *It Ain't Nothin' but the Blues* (1999; see entry). Another revue, *Evolution of the Blues*, seemed poised for a New York production in the early 1980s, but the closest it got to New York was its Kennedy Center engagement in Washington, D.C. Another such revue seen during the era, and which was also produced in Washington, D.C. (at Ford's Theatre in 1982) was *1,000 Years of Jazz* (subtitled "A New Orleans Revue").

Perhaps the most ambitious of all these musicals was *The Last Minstrel Show* (1978). A tough but entertaining look at Black minstrel shows of the 1920s, it was memorably sung by Della Reese and thrillingly danced by Gregory Hines. But a *Black* minstrel show which had something important to say about racial issues in the United States was probably too far ahead of its time in the politically correct climate of the late 1970s. Sadly, the musical closed during its Philadelphia tryout.

A revised *Blues in the Night* opened at the Rialto Theatre on June 2, 1982, for fifty-three performances with a cast which included Leslie Uggams and Debbie Shapiro (see entry). Another revised version toured in the mid-1980s; Della Reese and Neva Small were in the cast. Moreover, a revival was mounted at the Minetta Lane Theatre on September 14, 1988, for forty-five performances (see entry); it was based on a 1987 London production which had included Carol Woods and Maria Friedman in its cast (the London production was recorded by First Night Records [LP # SCENE-9]).

181 Blues in the Night (1982). THEATRE: Rialto Theatre; OPENING DATE: June 2, 1982; PERFORMANCES: 53; DIRECTION: Sheldon Epps; SCENERY: John Falabella; COSTUMES: David Murin; LIGHTING: Ken Billington; MUSICAL DIRECTION: Chapman Roberts; Sy Johnson (Co-Musical Director), Charles Coleman (Conductor) Producers: Mitchell Maxwell, Alan J. Schuster, Fred H. Krones, M2 Entertainment, Inc.; Joshua Silver, Associate Producer

CAST—LESLIE UGGAMS (Woman #1), DEBBIE SHAPIRO (GRAVITT) (Woman #2), JEAN DU SHON (Woman #3), Charles Coleman (Saloon Singer)

The action occurs in a hotel in Chicago in 1938.

The revue was presented in two acts.

ACT ONE—"Blue Blues" (lyric and music by Bessie Smith) (Company), "Four Walls (and One Dirty Window) Blues" (lyric and music by Willard Robison) (Charles Coleman), "I've Got a Date with a Dream" (lyric by Mack Gordon, music by Harry Revel) (Leslie Uggams, Debbie Shapiro), "These Foolish Things (Remind Me of You)" (from 1936 London musical *Spread It Around*; lyric by Eric Maschwitz [a/k/a Holt Marvell], music by James Strachey and Harry Link) (Leslie Uggams), "New Orleans Hot Scop Blues" (lyric and music by George W. Thomas) (Jean Du Shon), "It Makes My Love Come Down" (lyric and music by Bessie Smith) (Leslie Uggams, Debbie Shapiro, Jean Du Shon),

"Copenhagen" (lyric by Walter Melrose, music by Charlie Davis) (Debbie Shapiro), "Wild Women Don't Have the Blues" (lyric and music by Ida Cox) (Charles Coleman), "Lover Man" (lyric and music by Jimmy Davis, Roger "Ram" Ramirez, and Jimmy Sherman) (Leslie Uggams), "Take Me for a Buggy Ride" (lyric and music by Leola and Wesley Wilson) (Jean Du Shon), "Willow Weep for Me" (lyric and music by Ann Ronell) (Debbie Shapiro), "Kitchen Man" (lyric and music by Andy Razaf and Alex Bellenda) (Jean Du Shon), "Low" (lyric and music by Vernon Duke, Milton Drake, and Ben Oakland) (Leslie Uggams), "Take It Right Back" (lyric and music by H. Grey) (Leslie Uggams, Debbie Shapiro, Jean Du Shon)

ACT TWO—"Wild Women Don't Have the Blues" (reprise) (lyric and music by Ida Cox) (Band), "Blues in the Night" (from the 1941 film *Blues in the Night*; lyric by Johnny Mercer, music by Harold Arlen) (Leslie Uggams, Debbie Shapiro), "Dirty No-Gooder Blues" (lyric and music by Bessie Smith) (Jean Du Shon), "When a Woman Loves a Man" (lyric by Johnny Mercer, music by Bernard Hanighen and Gordon Jenkins) (Charles Coleman), "Am I Blue" (1929 film *On with the Show*; lyric by Grant Clarke, music by Harry Akst) (Leslie Uggams, Debbie Shapiro, Jean Du Shon), "Rough and Ready Man" (lyric and music by Alberta Hunter) (Leslie Uggams), "Reckless Blues" (lyric and music by Bessie Smith) (Debbie Shapiro), "Wasted Life Blues" (lyric and music by Bessie Smith) (Jean Du Shon), "Baby Doll" (lyric and music by Bessie Smith) (Charles Coleman), "Nobody Knows You When You're Down and Out" (lyric and music by Jimmy Cox) (Leslie Uggams, Debbie Shapiro, Jean Du Shon), "I Gotta Right to Sing the Blues" (*Earl Carroll Vanities* [Tenth Edition, 1932]; lyric by Ted Koehler, music by Harold Arlen) (Leslie Uggams, Debbie Shapiro, Jean Du Shon), "Blue Blues"/"Blues in the Night" (reprises) (Leslie Uggams, Debbie Shapiro, Jean Du Shon)

NOTES—See entries for the original 1980 production as well as the 1988 revival.

The 1982 revival may have been presented under a Limited or Middle Broadway contract. The musical numbers differed somewhat from the original 1980 production (for example, "Stompin' at the Savoy," "Lush Life," and "Something to Live For" were deleted, and "I've Got a Date with a Dream" and "These Foolish Things [Remind Me of You]" were added).

During previews, Ruth Brown performed the role of Woman # 3; by opening night, Jean Du Shon had assumed the role.

182 Blues in the Night (1988).

THEATRE: Minetta Lane Theatre; OPENING DATE: September 14, 1988; PERFORMANCES: 45; DIRECTION: Sheldon Epps; Patricia Wilcox, Assistant Director; SCENERY: Michael Pavelka; COSTUMES: Michael Pavelka; LIGHTING: Susan A. White; MUSICAL DIRECTION: David Brunetti; PRODUCERS: M Square Entertainment, Inc., and TV Asahi; Joshua Silver and Victoria Maxwell, Co-Producers; Colin Hooper, Betsy Lifton, and Showpeople, Ltd., Associate Producers

CAST—Carol Woods (Lady from the Road), Brenda Pressley (Woman of the World), Leilani Jones (Girl with a Date), Lawrence Hamilton (Man in the Saloon)

The action occurs in the late 1930s in a cheap hotel.

The revue was presented in two acts.

ACT ONE—"Blue Blues" (lyric and music by Bessie Smith) (Company), "Four Walls (and One Dirty Window) Blues" (lyric and music by Willard Robison) (Lawrence Hamilton, Carol Woods), "I've Got a Date with a Dream" (lyric by Mack Gordon, music by Harry Revel) (Brenda Pressley, Leilani Jones), "New Orleans Hot Scop Blues" (lyric and music by George W. Thomas) (Carol Woods), "Stompin' at the Savoy" (lyric and music by Benny Goodman, Andy Razaf, Edgar Sampson, and Chick Webb) (Brenda Pressley), "Taking a Chance on Love" (from *Cabin in the Sky*, 1940; lyric by John LaTouche and Ted Fetter, music by Vernon Duke) (Leilani Jones), "It Makes My Love Come Down" (lyric and music by Bessie Smith) (Carol Woods, Brenda Pressley, Leilani Jones), "Lush Life" (lyric and music by Billy Strayhorn) (Brenda Pressley), "I'm Just a Lucky So-and-So" (lyric by Mack David, music by Duke Ellington) (Lawrence Hamilton), "Take Me for a Buggy Ride" (lyric and music by Leola and Wesley Wilson) (Carol Woods), "Wild Women Don't Have the Blues" (lyric and music by Ida Cox) (Lawrence Hamilton), "Lover Man" (lyric and music by Jimmy Davis, Roger "Ram" Ramirez, and Jimmy Sherman) (Carol Woods), "Willow Weep for Me" (lyric and music by Ann Ronell) (Leilani Jones), "Kitchen Man" (lyric and music by Andy Razaf and Wesley Wilson) (Carol Woods), "When Your Lover Has Gone" (lyric and music by A.E. Swan) (Brenda Pressley, Leilani Jones), "Take It Right Back" (lyric and music by H. Grey) (Carol Woods, Brenda Pressley, Leilani Jones)

ACT TWO—Jam Session ("Wild Women Don't Have the Blues" [reprise]) (Band), "Blues in the Night" (1941 film *Blues in the Night*; lyric by Johnny Mercer, music by Harold Arlen) (Company) "Dirty No-Gooder [Gooder's] Blues" (lyric and music by Bessie Smith) (Carol Woods), "When a Woman Loves a Man" (lyric by Johnny Mercer, music by Bernard Hanighen and Gordon Jenkins)/"Am I Blue" (1929 film *On with the Show*; lyric by Grant Clarke, music by Harry Akst) (Company), "Rough and Ready Man" (lyric and music by Alberta Hunter) (Carol Woods, Brenda Pressley, Leilani Jones), "Reckless Blues" (lyric and music by Bessie Smith) (Leilani Jones), "Wasted Life Blues" (lyric and music by Bessie Smith) (Carol Woods), "Baby Doll" (lyric and music by Bessie Smith) (Lawrence Hamilton), "Nobody Knows You When You're Down and Out" (lyric and music by Jimmy Cox) (Company), "I Gotta Right to Sing the Blues" (*Earl Carroll Vanities* [Tenth Edition, 1932]; lyric by Ted Koehler, music by Harold Arlen) (Carol Woods, Brenda Pressley, Leilani Jones), "Four Walls (and One Dirty Window) Blues" (reprise) (Company)

NOTES—See entries for the original 1980 production as well as the 1982 revival.

The 1988 revival was based on a 1987 London production, and it differed slightly from the other New York versions (numbers such as "Taking a Chance on Love" and "I'm Just a Lucky So-and-So" were added for this production and songs such as "Low," "Copenhagen" and "Something to Live For," which had been heard in earlier versions, were not used).

This was the third and presumably final New York visit of *Blues in the Night*; each production played roughly six weeks.

183 Boccaccio.

"A Musical"; THEATRE: Edison Theatre; OPENING DATE: November 24, 1975; PERFORMANCES: 7; BOOK: Kenneth Cavander; LYRICS: Kenneth Cavander; MUSIC: Richard Peaslee; DIRECTION: Gene Lesser; CHOREOGRAPHY: Elizabeth Keen; SCENERY: Robert U. Taylor; COSTUMES: Linda Fisher; LIGHTING: William Mintzer; MUSICAL DIRECTION: Ken Bichel; PRODUCERS: Rita Fredricks, Theatre Now, Inc., and Norman Kean

CAST—Michael Zaslow (Beltramo, Egano), Virginia Vestoff (Giletta, Abbess), Armand Assante (Masetto, Ferondo), Caroline McWilliams (Beatrice, Sister Teresa, Ferondo's Wife), D'Jamin Bartlett (Isabella, Sister Angelica), Jill Choder (Alibech, Sister Makaria), Munson Hicks (Rustico, Leonetto, Brother Perdurabo), Richard Bauer (Anichino, Nuto, Abbot)

SOURCE—Giovanni Boccaccio's stories from *The Decameron* (approximately one-hundred stories, written circa 1348-1353). The musical adapted six of the stories: *Devil in Hell*, Day II, Story 10; *Masetto*, Day III, Story 1; *Ferondo*, Day III, Story 8; *The Doctor's Daughter*, Day III, Story 9; *Madonna Isabella*, Day VII, Story 6; and *Anichino*, Day VII, Story 7.

The action occurs in a villa outside Florence in 1348.

The musical was presented in two acts.

ACT ONE—Introduction: "Time to Go" (Company)

Masetto: "Masetto's Song" (Armand Assante, Richard Bauer), "Nun's Song" (Virginia Vestoff, Caroline McWilliams, D'Jamin Bartlett, Jill Choder), "God Is Good" (Armand Assante, Virginia Vestoff, Caroline McWilliams, D'Jamin Bartlett, Jill Choder), "Now My Season's Here" (Company); Anichino: "Only in My Song" (Richard Bauer), "Egano D'Galluzzi" (Richard Bauer, Michael Zaslow), "The Men Who Have Loved Me" (Caroline McWilliams), "In the Garden" (Richard Bauer, Michael Zaslow), "Lucky Anichino" (Company), "Pretend You're Living" (D'Jamin Bartlett), "Devil in Hell" (Jill Choder, Munson Hicks, Company)

ACT TWO—The She Doctor: "She Doctor" (Virginia Vestoff, Michael Zaslow), "Lover Like a Blind Man" (Virginia Vestoff), "If You Had Seen" (Virginia Vestoff), "Love Was Just a Game" (Michael Zaslow), "Madonna Isabella" (D'Jamin Bartlett, Company); Ferondo: "My Holy Prayer" (Richard Bauer, Monks), "Hold Me Gently" (Caroline McWilliams), Finale (Company)

NOTES—This was the second Off Broadway flop based on Boccaccio's *The Decameron* (the work is comprised of approximately one-hundred separate tales). The first, *The Decameron*, opened in 1961, and played for thirty-nine performances (see entry). *Boccaccio* was apparently produced under a Limited (Middle) Broadway contract.

The musical dealt with a group of refugees fleeing the Black Death, the plague which killed an estimated one-third to one-half of the population of Europe. The group, seeking safe haven in a villa outside Florence, pass the time by entertaining one another with earthy tales of love.

Martin Gottfried in the *New York Post* felt the evening was little more than a "patchwork job" which told Boccaccio's tales in the manner of *Story Theatre*; the score ("art music with a rock beat") reminded him of *Godspell* (see entry). Douglas Watt in the *New York Daily News* felt the evening was too mild, offering only "tasteful bawdiness." He said the lyrics were "properly improper" and "nice," the music was "refined" rock (and "nice"), the characters were "nicely promiscuous," and the direction was "naughty but nice." He concluded that the proceedings induced little more than a "polite yawn."

Boccaccio opened at Arena Stage in Washington, D.C., on November 15, 1974 (following two earlier productions, one in showcase at the Williamstown Playhouse in 1972 and another in 1973 by the Manhattan Theatre Club). Of the Arena cast members, only Jill Chodor appeared in the New York production. Also in the Arena version was Robert LuPone (as Masetto), a few months away from his most famous role, that of Zach in the original production of *A Chorus Line* (1975; see entry). (His program bio noted he had a sister in show business, one Patti Ann.) Incidentally, the musical director for the Arena production was Steve Ross, one of the finest cabaret performers of the era.

Songs dropped during the New York preview period were "The Best of Times" and "Let Your Body Have Its Way." Some song titles were altered: "Apples in the Garden" became "In the Garden" and "A Game I've Lost" became "Love Was Just a Game."

184 Bodo. "The New Musical Hero!"

NOTES—Because it never opened, *Bodo* may be the most obscure musical in this book. Other musicals in these pages (such as *Alice with Kisses*, 1964; *The Way It Is!!!* 1969; and *America Kicks Up Its Heels*, 1983) never officially opened, but they gave preview performances. But poor *Bodo* shut down before its first preview.

Bodo takes place in the year 1125, and its titular hero is a lowly goatherd who falls in love with a girl above his station; but he ends up as an advisor to a baron, and so all ends well. In an interview with the *New York Times*, Hugh Wheeler, the librettist, explained that the title character becomes involved in elaborate and farcical schemes and situations and ultimately lands at the top of the heap, inadvertently becoming "the first modern man."

The musical had been seen in workshop for Goodspeed Foundation members for twelve performances between August 4 and 14, 1983, in a barn on the grounds of Johnsonville, a restored Victorian village near Moodus, Connecticut. From there, a full-scale production at the Goodspeed Opera House was planned for the 1983-1984 theatre season.

Instead, Producer Jerry Schlossberg optioned *Bodo* for an immediate Off Broadway production at the Promenade Theatre. Previews were to begin on December 16, 1983, with an opening night of December 29. Later, an advertisement in the *New York Times* announced the first preview would begin on December 20, with an opening night of January 4 (the ad further stated that all pre-holiday previews would be at "medieval prices," that is, each seat in the theatre would sell for $11.25 [1125 was the year in which the show took place]). Later, the first preview was announced for January 8, and so apparently the "pre-holiday" special was cancelled.

The Off Broadway production went into rehearsal on November 26, the sets and lights were hung in the Promenade Theatre, and the programs were printed. However, on January 3, Schlossberg abandoned the production after he was unable to complete its full capitalization, which was estimated at $350,000 (the musical was apparently $100,000 short in funding).

The programs, which were printed but never handed out to would-be *Bodo* audiences, are probably among the rarest of musical theatre memorabilia.

The following are the credits and song listing for *Bodo*; had it opened, it would have been the first Off Broadway visit in twenty-three years for the team of Anne Croswell and Lee Pockriss, who had collaborated on the delightful score for *Ernest in Love* in 1960 (see entry); the team was later represented Off Off Broadway with *Conrack* in 1987 (see entry): BOOK: Hugh Wheeler; LYRICS: Anne Croswell; MUSIC: Lee Pockriss; DIRECTION: Dan Held; CHOREOGRAPHY: Jerry Yoder; SCENERY: Tony Castrigno; COSTUMES: Franne Lee; LIGHTING: Marcia Madeira; MUSICAL DIRECTION: Albin Konopka; PRODUCER: Jerry Schlossberg; Isabel Brenner and William T. Rich III, Associate Producers

CAST—Hal Cline (Second Male Goat, Canon), Gabriel Barre (First Male Goat, The Bishop), Marianna Allen (Female Goat, Canon), Steven Jacob (Bodo), Arthur Howard (Peter the Leper), Joel Kramer (Baron Arnulf), James Judy (Squire, Jailer), Stephen Fenning (Page), John Tillotson (John of Piquet), Judy Dewey (Alison), Ruth Williamson (Lady Gutrun), Elizabeth King (Lady Marianne), Christopher Coucill (Sir Gawain) The action occurs in the village of Dulac, France, in 1125 A.D.

The musical was presented in two acts.

ACT ONE—"Goat Prologue" (Hal Cline, Gabriel Barre, Marianna Allen), "Hey!" (Steven Jacob, Serfs), "I Love My Serfs" (Joel Kramer, James Judy, Steven Jacobs, Arthur Howard, Serfs), "Picture Yerself" (Steven Jacob, Judy Dewey), "I Can Change!" (Steven Jacob, Hal Cline, Gabriel Barre, Marianna Allen), "My Moppets, My Poppets and Me" (John Tillotson, Steven Jacob, Arthur Howard), "One Last Embrace" (Christopher Coucill, Elizabeth King), "The Song of Milady Gutrun" (Ruth Williamson, Steven Jacob, Arthur Howard, James Judy, Stephen Fenning, Servants), "So Short the Day" (Joel Kramer, Stephen Fenning), "What an Honor!" (Judy Dewey, Serfs, Steven Jacob, James Judy)

ACT TWO—"It Could Be Worse" (Arthur Howard, Steven Jacob), "The Deflowering" (Joel Kramer, Judy Dewey, Steven Jacob, Gabriel Barre, Marianna Allen, Hal Cline), "It's Me She Loves" (Stephen Jacob, Hal Cline, Gabriel Barre, Marianna Allen), "Pay a Forfeit!" (Stephen Jacob, Gabriel Barre, Joel Kramer, Gentry, Serfs), "What an Honor!" (reprise/finale) (Company)

185 Body Shop. "The Stripsational New Musical"; THEATRE: Westbeth Theatre Center; OPENING DATE: December 5, 1994; PERFORMANCES: 56; BOOK: Walter Marks; LYRICS: Walter Marks; MUSIC: Walter Marks; DIRECTION: Sue Lawless; CHOREOGRAPHY: Tony Stevens; SCENERY: Tim Goodmanson; COSTUMES: Franne Lee; LIGHTING: Don Coleman; MUSICAL DIRECTION: Deborah Hurwitz; PRODUCERS: Bank Street Productions in association with Westbeth Theatre Center (Arnold Engelman, Producing Director)

CAST—Tiffany Cooper (Keisha), Justine DiConstanzo (Esmeralda), Donna Drake (Leanne), Susan Flynn (Tiffany Silver), Beth Glover (Samantha), Christopher Scott (Franklin Francesa, Others), Jodi Stevens (Doris), Marine Jahan (Angeline)

The action occurs in a small-town strip club.

The musical was presented in two acts.

ACT ONE—"Desire" (Tiffany Cooper, Donna Drake, Marine Jahan, Jodi Stevens, Beth Glover), "Maybe It's Not Too Late" (Susan Flynn), "You're a Natural" (Susan Flynn, Donna Drake), "Desire" (reprise) (Ensemble), "Suffer" (Tiffany Cooper), "Esmeralda" (performed by Justine DiConstanzo [?]), "You Like Me" (Beth Glover), "My Turn" (Jodi Stevens), "Class Act" (Susan Flynn), "My Turn" (reprise) (Jodi Stevens), "Doris' Nightmare" (Jodi Stevens, Ensemble)

ACT TWO—"A Matter of Time" (Susan Flynn), "Mr. Maybe" (Tiffany Cooper, Ensemble), "The Woman in Me" (Marine Jahan), "Find a Way" (Donna Drake), "Virtual Sexuality" (Beth Glover), "Desire" (reprise) (Ensemble), "Class Act" (reprise) (Susan Flynn), Finale (Susan Flynn, Ensemble)

NOTES—The Off Off Broadway musical *Body Shop* played two slightly separated engagements at the Westbeth Theatre Center for a total of fifty-six performances. The plot dealt with strippers who work at a club in a small town and a Hollywood director hoping to cast an authentic stripper for his new movie. Ben Brantley in the *New York Times* indicated the book and score were of an "utterly conventional blandness" which in some respects updated stage and film clichés involving chorus girls (here with the addition of an "aspiring transsexual"). He felt the "irony-free" evening about "doing your best and respecting yourself" was aimed at tired businessmen who want an "eyeful without feeling depraved." But Brantley reported that a rape sequence was "truly offensive." During the second engagement, the song "Esmeralda" was replaced by "Angeline" (performed by Marine Jahan).

Body Shop marked Walter Marks' return to the musical stage in twenty-six years. His first Broadway musical *Bajour* (1964) was a failure, but ran over six months; its score wasn't particularly memorable, but included a few clever numbers. His second (and final) Broadway musical was *Golden Rainbow* (1968), a weak vehicle for Steve Lawrence and Eydie Gorme which ran for a year but nevertheless lost money; its generally undistinguished score was pleasantly old-fashioned (and included "I Gotta Be Me" [a/k/a "I've Got to Be Me"], a certifiable pop hit in an era when Broadway songs were becoming increasingly irrelevant to the record-buying public).

186 La Boheme. THEATRE: Anspacher Theatre/The Public Theatre; OPENING DATE: November 29, 1984; PERFORMANCES: 38; ADAPTATION AND LYRICS: David Spencer; MUSIC: Giacomo Puccini; DIRECTION: Wilford Leach; SCENERY: Bob Shaw; COSTUMES: Jane Greenwood; LIGHTING: Paul Gallo; MUSICAL DIRECTION: William Elliott

CAST—Howard McGillin (Marcel), David (-James) Carroll (Rodolfo), Keith David (Colline), Neal Klein (Schaunard), Joe Pichette (Benoit, Student, Hall Porter), Linda Ronstadt (Mimi), Cass Morgan (Musette), Merwin Goldsmith (Alcindoro), John Herrera (The Maitre D', Sweeper), Bill Carmichael (Waiter, Sweeper), Daniel Marcus (Waiter, Night Clerk), James Judy (Trumpet Vendor, Head Sweeper), Marcie Shaw (Bonnet Vendor, Dairymaid), Nancy Heikin (Lady with Pearls, Dairymaid), Margaret Benczak (Student, Dairymaid), Carol Dennis (Student, Dairymaid), Caroline Peyton (Student, Dairymaid), Michael Willson (Parpignol, Hall Porter) SOURCE—The 1896 opera *La Boheme* (music by Giacomo Puccini, original libretto by Giuseppe Giacosa and Luigi Illica), which was based on the novel *Scenes de la Vie de Boheme* by Henri Murger (the scenes in the novel were first published in the journal *Le Corsair* between 1847 and 1849).

The action occurs in Paris from Christmas Eve through the early fall.

The opera was presented in four acts.

NOTES—The Public Theatre's revival of *La Boheme* didn't duplicate its popular revival of *The Pirates of Penzance* (see entry); in fact, *La Boheme* went the way of the Public's now virtually forgotten *Non Pasquale* (see entry). The production's big attraction was Linda Ronstadt, who received poor notices for her portrayal of Mimi (although the critics gave her credit for trying): Thor Eckert, Jr. (*The Christian Science Monitor*) found her singing "tenuous" and noted she seemed "desperately ill-at-ease"; Clive Barnes (*The New York Post*) said she was "robustly mediocre"; Howard Kissel (*Women's Wear Daily*) wrote that she was listless and unemotional; and John Skow (*Time*) said her voice was "small and uncertain." Writing in the *New York Times*, Frank Rich said Ronstadt's performance was "lackluster and anxiety-inducing," and noted the revival itself was a "benign collegiate mishmash." Rich also made an interesting observation: he felt the revival's creators seemed uncertain whether the opera should remain in its original timeframe or moved "to contemporary TriBeCa (a not unpromising fancy)." In 1996, *Rent*, Jonathan Larson's updated version of *La Boheme* (with all-new music, of course) took place in the East Village (see entry).

As for the other performers in *La Boheme*, David (-James) Carroll received excellent notices for his Rodolfo, as did Howard McGillin for his Marcel. The critics were divided on Cass Morgan's approach to Musette: Rich said she was "excessively vulgar" while Douglas Watt found her "splendid."

The revival offered two alternates for Mimi (Patti Cohenour and Caroline Peyton) as well as one alternate for Rodolfo (Gary Morris). Howard Kissel noted that Cohenour's Mimi offered "a much richer voice and an astonishing ability to shape words, lines and musical emotions." (On November 18, a few days before the musical's official opening, Leslie Bennetts in the *New York Times* reported that on the advice of her throat doctor Ronstadt would perform three rather than four performances a week; since Cohenour was already scheduled to sing four times a week, Caroline Peyton was signed to perform for one performance each week.)

187 Bohikee Creek. THEATRE: Stage 73; OPENING DATE: April 28, 1966; PERFORMANCES: 30; PLAY: Robert Unger; LYRICS: Robert Unger; MUSIC: Donald Moreland; DIRECTION: Donald Moreland; SCENERY: Tad Gesek; PRODUCERS: Patrick Baldauff, Frank Boone, and Gillian Crowe

CAST—Richard Havens (Folk Singer), James Earl Jones (Arnie, Bo), Georgia Burke (Aunty Mom), Moses Gunn (Able, Coke), Wayne Grice (Tinch), Dennis Tate (Halfbeak), Billie Allen (Reba), Julius Harris (Harold)

NOTES—Robert Unger's *Bohikee Creek* was an evening of four numbered but unnamed short one-act plays about Blacks living in the South Carolina Islands (there was apparently an intermission between the second and third plays).

The evening included incidental songs performed by a ballad singer (the lyrics were by Unger, and the music was by the director, Donald Moreland). Stanley Kauffman in the *New York Times* found the evening somewhat insubstantial but felt the four plays offered good roles for the performers, which included James Earl Jones and Moses Gunn.

188 Bomarzo. THEATRE: The New York State Theatre; OPENING DATE: March 14, 1968; PERFORMANCES: Unknown; LIBRETTO: Manuel Mujica Lainez; MUSIC: Alberto Ginastera; DIRECTION: Tito Capobianco; CHOREOGRAPHY: Jack Cole; SCENERY: Ming Cho Lee; COSTUMES: Jose Varona; MUSICAL DIRECTION: Julius Rudel; PRODUCER: The New York City Opera

CAST—Robert Harwood (Shepherd Boy), Salvador Novoa (Pier Francesco Orsini [The Duke of Bomarzo]), Richard Torigi (Silvio de Narni), Joaquin Romaguera (Nicolas Orsini), Claramae Turner (Diana Orsini), Patriccio Pooras (Pier Francesco [as a child]), Emillio Crespo (Girolamo [as a child]), Michael Devlin (Gian Corrado Orsini), Buzz Miller (Skeleton), Nico Castel (Messenger), Joanna Simon (Pantasilea), Charles Moore (Abul), Robert Gregori (Girolamo), Isabel Penagos (Julia Farnese), Raymond Gibbs (Maerbale)

The opera was presented in two acts.

NOTES—Alberto Ginastera's opera *Bomarzo* told the story of the hunchback Pier Francesco Orsini, The Duke of Bomarzo, who is poisoned by his nephew. As he dies, he recalls major events in his life, which are depicted in flashbacks.

The opera's world premiere took place at the Lisner Auditorium in Washington, D.C., on May 19, 1967, by the Opera Society of Washington, and had been scheduled for production on August 4 of that year in Buenos Aires, where Ginastera lived. But the opera was banned there because of its violence and alleged sexual frankness. Reviewing the New York premiere, Harold C. Schonberg in the *New York Times* wondered what all the fuss was about. He noted that except for an erotic ballet (which was "mild stuff"), there was little sex in the opera, and compared to *Lulu* and *Il Trovatore*, the sex and violence were "small-time." Schonberg found Ginastera's music more "old-hat" than modern, and noted the "melodic lines never really sing." He indicated Ginastera's use of "ultra-modern and traditional techniques" might point the way for the future operas, but noted that other composers would have to use "more originality, more imagination, and especially more lyricism."

The opera had been recorded by the Washington, D.C., cast, and was released on a 3-LP set by CBS Records (# 548113) prior to the New York premiere. The libretto was published by Boosey & Hawkes, Inc., in 1967.

Broadway choreographer Jack Cole created the dances for the opera, and the cast itself included Claramae Turner and Buzz Miller. Turner had performed the role of Nettie Fowler in the 1956 film version of *Carousel*, singing "June Is Bustin' Out All Over" and "You'll Never Walk Alone." Miller was a memorable Broadway dancer, creating roles in a number of musicals, including *The Pajama Game* (1954) and *Redhead* (1959). In the former, he introduced (along with Carol Haney and Peter Gennaro) "Steam Heat," and in the latter he and Gwen Vernon danced "The Pick-Pocket Tango." He also danced in the original productions of *Magdalena* (1948), *Two's Company* (1952), *Me and Juliet* (1953), *Bravo Giovanni* (1962), *Hot Spot* (1963), and *Funny Girl* (1964) as well as in the long-running 1952 revival of *Pal Joey*.

189 The Bomb-itty of Errors. THEATRE: 45 Bleecker; OPENING DATE: December 12, 1999; PERFORMANCES: 216; TEXT: Jordan Allen-Dutton, Jason Catalano, G.Q., and Erik Weiner; MUSIC: J.A.Q.; DIRECTION (AND DEVELOPMENT): Andy Goldberg; SCENERY: Scott Pask; COSTUMES: David C. Woolard; LIGHTING: James Vermeulen; PRODUCERS: Daryl Roth, Michael Lynne, Q Brothers, and Hal Luftig; Andrew Kato, Associate Producer

CAST—Jordan Allen-Dutton a/k/a Rodan (Antipholus of Ephesus, Adriana, Bike Messenger, Others), Jason Catalano a/k/a Gruff (Dromio of Syracuse, Desi, Dr. Pinch, Others), Gregory J. Qaiyum a/k/a G.Q. (Antipholus of Syracuse, Hendelberg, Abbess, Others), Erik Weiner a/k/a Red Dragon (Dromio of Ephesus, Luciana, Policeman, Stranger, Others), Jeffrey Qaiyum a/k/a J.A.Q. (D.J.)

SOURCE—The play *The Comedy of Errors* by William Shakespeare (written between 1589 and 1594).

NOTES—*The Bomb-itty of Errors*, a self-described "add-rap-tation" of "Willy" Shakespeare's *The Comedy of Errors*, was performed to rap music and hip-hop lyrics by a group of former New York University drama students.

Bruce Weber in the *New York Times* noted the evening was "cheerfully executed" with "admirable zest," but he couldn't quite cotton to the amiable if self-indulgent performance style of the piece. But he reported the college students around him enjoyed themselves immensely and left the theatre "as jazzed as any group of theatergoers I've seen in a long time." So he concluded there was "a generation gap at work here." For a more traditional lyric adaptation of Shakespeare's comedy, see entry for *The Boys from Syracuse*.

190 Bon Voyage. "A New Musical Play"; THEATRE: Church of the Heavenly Rest Opening Date: November 18, 1977; PERFORMANCES: 12; BOOK: Edward Mabley; LYRICS: Edward Mabley; MUSIC: Jacques Offenbach; music freely adapted by Vera Brodsky Lawrence; DIRECTION: Edward Mabley; CHOREOGRAPHY: Kay DeMetz; SCENERY: James Morgan; COSTUMES: Judy Gillespie; LIGHTING: Charles F. Morgan and Jesse Ira Berger; MUSICAL DIRECTION: Mark Hastings and Justin Blasdale (Duo-Pianists); PRODUCER: The York Players

CAST—John Newton (Gaspard Perrichon), Janet Hayes (Therse Perrichon), Kathleen McKearney (Henriette Perrichon), Harry Danner (Armand Desroches), Michael D. Wickenheiser (Daniel Savary), Neal Schwantes (Commandant Mathieu), Mel Black (Porter, Traveler), Dale DeGroff (Ticket Clerk, Traveler), Peter J. Saputo (Customer Officer), Jennifer Pritchett (English Lady, Jeanne), Alison H. Campbell (Bookseller, Proprietress)

SOURCE—The 1860 play *Le Voyage de Monsieur Perrichon* by Eugene Marin Labiche.

The action occurs in Paris, the Swiss Border, and an Alpine Inn during 1860.

The musical was presented in two acts.

ACT ONE—Overture (Mark Hastings, Justin Blasdale), "Bon Voyage!" (John Newton, Janet Hayes, Kathleen McKearney, Mel Black, Dale DeGroff), "We'll Still Be Friends" (Harry Danner, Michael D. Wickenheiser), "Love! Love! Love!" (Neal Schwantes), "Lucky Star" (Harry Danner, Michael D. Wickenheiser, Kathleen McKearney), "Know Your Man" (Michael D. Wickenheiser), "I'll Always Remember This Day" (Harry Danner, Kathleen McKearney), "Man Is Small" (John Newton), "I Love Her So" (Harry Danner), "What a Fine Young Man!" (John Newton, Janet Hayes)

ACT TWO—Entr'acte (Mark Hastings, Justin Blasdale), "Home" (John Newton, Janet Hayes), "You Know Your Love Is True" (Kathleen McKearney), "Me and the Mountain" (John Newton), "Monsieur Le Prefet" (Michael D. Wickenheiser, Janet Hayes, John Newton), "I'll Always Remember This Day" (reprise) (Harry Danner, Kathleen McKearney), "Know Your Man" (reprise) (Michael D. Wickenheiser), Finale (Company)

NOTES—The Off Off Broadway musical was based on the play *Le Voyage de Monsieur Perrichon* by Eugene Marin Labiche, who with Marc-Michel wrote *The Italian Straw Hat* (the basis for two Off Broadway musicals; see entries for *The Italian Straw Hat* [1957] and *That Hat!* [1964]).

Bon Voyage is one of many unsuccessful musicals which utilized themes composed by Jacques Offenbach. On Broadway, *Helen Goes to Troy* (1944) and *The Happiest Girl in the World* (1961) bombed after ninety-seven and ninety-six respective performances, and the New York-bound *La Belle* (1962) didn't get beyond its Philadelphia tryout. And in 1986, *La Belle Helene* (see entry) disappeared after its scheduled two-week engagement at the AMAS Repertory Theatre. (Incidentally, 1976 saw the premiere of a "new" opera about Christopher Columbus; based on music of Offenbach, the score for *Christophe Columbus* was adapted by Patric Schmid and the libretto was by Don White; the New York premiere occurred in 1987.)

Perhaps the most tantalizing musical based on Offenbach's music is *Anatol*, which was based on Arthur Schnitzler's *The Affairs of Anatol*. The musical opened at the Boston Arts Center on July 31, 1961, for twenty-four performances; the book and lyrics were by Tom Jones, and the cast included Jean-Pierre Aumont and Marisa Pavan. After the Boston run, the musical seems to have surfaced just one more time, in a production by the Playhouse in the Park in Cincinnati; it opened on August 31, 1967, for twenty-nine performances. (A few months after *Anatol*'s 1961 premiere, *The Gay Life*, another musical based on *The Affairs of Anatol*, opened on Broadway on November 18 with Walter Chiari and Barbara Cook; the work offered a lushly melodic score by Arthur Schwartz and witty lyrics by Howard Dietz.) (For other musicals based on works by Schnitzler, see entry for *Rondelay*.)

191 The Bone Room. THEATRE: Portfolio Theatre; OPENING DATE: February 28, 1975; PERFORMANCES: 12 or 29 (depending on source); BOOK: Tom Jones; LYRICS: Tom Jones; MUSIC: Harvey Schmidt; DIRECTION: John Schak; CHOREOGRAPHY: Janet Kerr; COSTUMES: Charles Blackburn; MUSICAL DIRECTION: Ken Collins; PRODUCERS: Drew Katzman and John Schak

CAST—John Cunningham (Male Lecturer), Ray Stewart (Smith), Susan Watson (Female Lecturer)

The action occurs in the Museum of Natural History.

The musical was presented in one act.

NOTES—The program didn't list individual musical numbers for *The Bone Room*, a showcase production which was billed as a work in progress. Tom Jones and Harvey Schmidt's musical about male menopause dealt with Jones (Ray Stewart), who is sometimes called Smith and is a gluer of bones in the bone room of the Museum of Natural History. As he works, he muses over the opportunities missed in his life, and is suddenly visited by an array of figures, including Aphrodite and Death (these and other roles were performed by Susan Watson and John Cunningham).

Mel Gussow in the *New York Times* found the musical "felicitous" and "lively and diverting," and despite its offbeat subject matter he noted Jones and Schmidt made all the right choices in telling their eighty-minute story. Gussow singled out the "bouncy" title song and the "wistful" "September Song"-like "The Middle of the Road." But he said he could have done without "Blessed Relief," an "arch ditty" about constipation.

While the Portfolio production of *Philemon* (see entry) was recorded and later shown on television, and another (*Celebration*) had been produced on Broadway in 1969 and recorded by Capitol Records, *The Bone Room* quickly disappeared and remains one of those tantalizing lost musicals. One of the songs from *The Bone Room*, "Isn't That a Wonderful Way to Die?" was first heard in *Portfolio Revue* (1974; see entry) and then later in *The Show Goes On* (1997; see entry); it was recorded for the latter's cast album. Another song from *The Bone Room*, the aforementioned "The Middle of the Road," was recorded by *Bone Room* cast member Susan Watson in her priceless collection of songs by Jones and Schmidt (*Earthly Paradise* [Nassau Records CD # 96598]).

192 The Bonus Army. THEATRE: Judson Poets' Theatre; OPENING DATE: February 20, 1976; PERFORMANCES: Unknown; BOOK: David Epstein; LYRICS: Al Carmines; MUSIC: Al Carmines; DIRECTION: Jacques Levy

CAST—Reathel Bean, Gordon Hammett, Daniel Keyes, William Knight, Anne Korzen, Peter Lombard, Richard Miller, Leslie Ann Ray, Rick Warner, Ronald Willoughby, Alex Wipf

NOTES—Two songs ("It's a Man's World" and "My Old Man") from this obscure Off Off Broadway musical surfaced in *The Gospel According to Al* (see entry).

193 Boobs! The Musical (The World According to Ruth Wallis). THEATRE: Triad Theatre; OPENING DATE: May 19, 2003; PERFORMANCES: 304; BOOK: Steve Mackes and Michael Whaley; LYRICS: Ruth Wallis; MUSIC: Ruth Wallis; DIRECTION: Donna Drake; CHOREOGRAPHY: Lawrence Leritz; COSTUMES: Robert Pease and J. Kevin Draves; PRODUCERS: SRU Productions LLC, Lawrence Leritz, and Michael Whaley

CAST—Kristy Cates, Robert Hunt, Max Perlman, J. Brandon Savage, Jenny-Lynn Suckling, Rebecca Young

NOTES—The revue was based on naughty party songs written by Ruth Wallis during the 1950s.

Anita Gates in the *New York Times* found the evening "a saucy bit of silliness," and reported that among the show's songs were "Queer Things Are Happening," "Johnny's Got a Yo-Yo," "I Need a Man of My Own," and "Mama Was a Star." Apparently other numbers included in the revue were "Drill 'Em All," "Marriage Jewish Style," "The Pop-Up Song," "De Gay Young Lad," and "Hawaiian Lei Song."

The cast album was recorded by MOL Records (as of this writing, the recording has not yet been released).

194 The Boogie-Woogie Rumble of a Dream Deferred. THEATRE: Urban Arts Theatre; OPENING DATE: December 1982 (possibly December 5); PERFORMANCES: Unknown; BOOK: Vinnette Carroll; LYRICS: Micki Grant; MUSIC: Vinnette Carroll; DIRECTION: Vinnette Carroll; CHOREOGRAPHY: Talley Beatty; Ralf Paul Haze, Co-Choreographer; COSTUMES: Hope Hanafin; LIGHTING: Richard Winkler; MUSICAL DIRECTION: Charles A. Johnson III; PRODUCER: Urban Arts Theatre (Vinnette Carroll, Artistic Director; Anita MacShane, Managing Director)

CAST—Charles Abruzzo, Ed Battle, Elizabeth Bruzzese, Harry L. Burney III, Alan Campbell, Lynne Clifton-Allen, Nora Cole, Joseph Warren Davis, John De Luca, Douglas Easley, Ellia English, William Gabriner, Martron Gales, Jamil K. Garland, Kent B. Gash, Ruthanna Graves, Stanley E. Harrison, Rufus Jackson, Tommi Johnson, Rob Marshall, Stephanie Murphy, Dwayne Phelps, Steiv Semien, Phillip Trice, Reginald Veljohnson, Marilynn Winbush; NOTE—The program didn't identify the names of the characters.

SOURCE—The 1936 play *Bury the Dead* by Irwin Shaw.

The musical was presented in two acts.

ACT ONE—"That's What the Bible Say" (Alan Campbell, Company), "Correspondent's Correspondence" (Stephanie Murphy), "Battle Ballet" (Ed Battle, William Gabriner, Martron Gales, Stanley E. Harrison, Phillip Trice, Steiv Semien), "It Takes a Soldier" (Alan Campbell, Jamil K. Garland, Joseph Warren Davis, John De Luca, Kent B. Gash, Reginald Veljohnson), "Poor General" (Rob Marshall), "I Ain't Had My Fill" (Charles Abruzzo), "War Is Made for Generals" (Douglas Easley), "Body Count" (Rob Marshall, Stephanie Murphy, Company), "Step Lively, Boy" (Alan Campbell, Jamil K. Garland, Joseph Warren Davis, John De Luca, Kent B. Gash, Reginald Veljohnson), "Hey General" (Lynne Clifton-Allen), "Walking the Dog" (Alan Campbell, John De Luca, Jamil K. Garland, Joseph Warren Davis, Kent B. Gash, Reginald Veljohnson), "Walking the Dog" (reprise) (John De Luca, Company), "I Love the Army" (Alan Campbell, Kent B. Gash, Jamil K. Garland), "Our Cause Is Righteous" (Charles Abruzzo, Harry L. Burney III), "When Every Man Is Everyman" (Harry L. Burney III, Company)

ACT TWO—"Sound Off" (Reginald Veljohnson, Company), "Love Is Like a Water Faucet" (Ellia English, Jamil K. Garland), "Have a Drink" (Rob Marshall, John De Luca), "Step Lively Boy" (reprise) (Alan Campbell), "Boogie-Woogie Rumble" (Rob Marshall, Ed Battle, William Gabriner, Martron Gales, Stanley E. Harrison, Steiv Semien, Phillip Trice), "My Dear" (Elizabeth Bruzzese), "Call Me Ursula" (Lynne Clifton-Allen), "The Women" (Douglas Easley, Rob Marshall, Women), "Widow's Lament" (Nora Cole), "I Ain't Had My Fill" (reprise) (Charles Abruzzo, John De Luca, Company), "That's What the Bible Say" (reprise) (Company), Finale (Company)

NOTES—The Off Off Broadway musical *The Boogie-Woogie Rumble of a Dream Deferred* (the title was taken from the writings of Langston Hughes) was based on Irwin Shaw's surreal 1936 Broadway play *Bury the Dead*, in which soldiers killed in battle refuse to stay buried, much to the consternation of their commanders, fellow soldiers, and even their loved ones.

The two-act musical was an expanded and retitled version of the Urban Arts Theatre's 1973 one-act musical *Step Lively, Boy!* (see entry). *The Boogie Woogie Rumble* included most of the songs from *Step Lively, Boy!* and added about ten others.

In his review of *The Boogie-Woogie Rumble* in the *New York Times*, Stephen Holden wrote that despite its "many inadequacies," the antiwar musical had "heart, vitality and tunefulness," and he praised Micki Grant's "passionately melodic score" which embraced "a Richard Rodgers-style melodiousness." He singled out many numbers, including "I Ain't Had My Fill" (the musical's "most chilling" song, a "cantorially flavored lament" which recalled Rodgers's "Soliloquy" from *Carousel* [1945]); "When Every Man Is Everyman" ("an inspirational polemic that hits home through the sheer sweep of its melody"); "Love Is Like a Water Faucet" ("an amusing Bessie Smith-styled blues song"); "Sound Off" (a rap-like number); and "That's What the Bible Say" ("a rousing pop spiritual"). Holden also praised the "lusty" ensemble singing of the cast which "rocks the theatre to its rafters." Holden's comments make one want to rush out and buy the cast album, but, unfortunately, an album was never recorded. But Holden's perceptive and intriguing review leads one to add *The Boogie Woogie Rumble* to a wish list of musicals which should one day be revived and recorded.

Harry Kleiner's 1945 drama *Skydrift* also dealt with soldiers who return from the dead. In this case, seven paratroopers who are killed in action return to life and visit their relatives; before the soldiers leave their families forever, they assure their kinfolk they are resigned to their deaths and can adjust to their new existence. The play lasted for seven performances at the flop-prone Belasco Theatre.

195 Book of the Dead (Second Avenue). THEATRE: Martinson Hall/The Joseph Papp Public Theatre; OPENING DATE: November 20, 2000; PERFORMANCES: 32; CONCEIVED BY John Moran; DIRECTION: John Moran; Cabell Tomlinson, Assistant Director; SCENERY AND PROJECTIONS: John Moran; Cabell Tomlinson, Mask and Puppet Designs; COSTUMES: James Schuette; LIGHTING: Jonathan Spencer; PRODUCER: The Joseph Papp Public Theatre/New York Shakespeare Festival (George C. Wolfe, Producer; Rosemarie Tichler, Artistic Producer; Mark Litvin, Managing Director)

CAST—Theo Bleckmann, Patricia R. Floyd, Darryl Gibson, Anthony Henderson, Michael Huston, John Moran, Laine Satterfield, Cabell Tomlinson, David West, M. Drue Williams; Uma Thurman (Recorded Narration)

The musical performance piece was presented in one act.

NOTES—*Theatre World Season 2000-2001* described John Moran's *Book of the Dead (Second Avenue)* as a "theme park ride" through comparative religion, from ancient Egypt through the present day, and Margo Jefferson in the *New York Times* wrote that the evening was "as full of aural and visual stimuli as a Disneyland attraction" (she also noted that Moran himself referred to the work as an "attraction").

The one-hour "attraction" first covered the period of ancient Egypt (including the ritual of preparing the dead for afterlife), then modern times (much of the action took place in a Lower East Side bar and, according to Moran's program notes, dealt with death and the difficulty of "letting go" of one's life), and finally concluded with a condensed version of *The Tibetan Book of the Dead*. Jefferson noted that in performance the work wasn't always clear to the audience, and felt that one shouldn't have to read Moran's program notes for an understanding of the action on stage (she wondered if a "sympathetic collaborator" might help clarify Moran's "private associations" for the audience). She also mentioned that when the performance was over, the audience wasn't really sure it had concluded, and she felt that the work was "still explaining itself to itself." Jefferson nonetheless admired the "true sweetness" of Moran's visual and aural images. Incidentally, the entire production was pre-recorded, including the voices of the performers, who lip-synched.

196 Born to Sing! THEATRE: Union Square Theatre; OPENING DATE: August 6, 1996; PERFORMANCES: 134; BOOK: Vy Higginsen and Ken Wydro; LYRICS: Vy Higginsen and Ken Wydro; MUSIC: Wesley Naylor; DIRECTION: Ken Wydro; Charles Stewart, Stage Movement; SCENERY: Mike Fish; COSTUMES: Carlos Falchi and Malissa Drayton, Costume Supervision; LIGHTING: Marshall Williams; MUSICAL DIRECTION: W. Naylor; PRODUCERS: Vy Higginsen and Ken Wydro, Mitchell Maxwell and Alan J. Shuster; in association with SuperVision Productions and Workin' Man Theatricals; Kery Davis and Victoria Maxwell, Co-Producers; Lesley Mazzotta, Associate Producer

CAST—Lisa Fischer (Doris Winter), Kellie D. Evans (Mama Winter), Tanya Blount (Dottie Winter), Stacy Francis (Samantha Summers), Charles Stewart (Minister of Music), Charles Perry (Auditioner), Jessica Care Moore, Debora Rath, Shari Headley, and Samantha Davis (Alternating Narrators), Anita Wells, Anissia Bunton, and Kim Summerson (Harris Sisters), Pierre Cook, Tyrone Flower, Richard Hartley, Damon Horton (Four Guys), Choir Members (Anissia Bunton, Dawn Green, Sheila Slappy, Kim Summerson [Sopranos]; Robin Cunningham, Lorraine Moore, Anita Wells [Altos]; Pierre Cook, Tyrone Flower, Richard Hartley, Damon Horton, Ronnie McLeod, Charles Perry [Tenors])

The action occurs in the United States, Tokyo, Istanbul, Venice, Cairo, Berlin, Paris, and London.

The musical was presented in two acts.

ACT ONE—"Lead Us On" (Kellie D. Evans), "Interpretations" (Charles Perry), "Lord Keep Us Day by Day" (Anita Wells, Anissia Bunton, Kim Summerson), "Sweeping Through the City" (Kellie D. Evans, Girls), "Blessed Assurance" (Stacy Francis), "Is My Living in Vain" (Pierre Cook, Tyrone Flower, Richard Hartley, Damon Horton), "Blessed Assurance" (reprise) (Tanya Blount), "Narration"/"Poem" (Jessica Care Moore [?]), "Give the Child a Break" (Kellie D. Evans, Lisa Fischer), "And the Winner Is" (Lisa Fischer, Ensemble), "Your Time Will Come" (Lisa Fischer, Tanya Blount), "Born to Sing" (Stacy Francis, Ensemble)

ACT TWO—"Harmony" (Lisa Fischer, Ensemble), "Who Needs Who?" (Stacy Francis, Lisa Fischer, Kellie D. Evans, Ensemble), "Lord Keep Us Day by Day" (reprise) (Anita Wells, Anissia Bunton, Kim Summerson), "Take a Stand" (Kellie D. Evans, Tanya Blount, Lisa Fischer), "The Sky's the Limit" (Stacy Francis, Ensemble), "Who You Gonna Blame?" (Stacy Francis, Tanya Blount), "Center Peace" (Kellie D. Evans), "Attention Must Be Paid" (Lisa Fischer, Tanya Blount), "Poem" (Jessica Care Moore [?]), "Face to Face" (Kellie D. Evans, Lisa Fischer, Tanya Blount, Stacy Francis), "Take the High Way" (Tanya Blount, Ensemble), "Lead Us On" (reprise) (Kellie D. Evans, Ensemble)

NOTES—*Born to Sing!* continued the saga of Doris Winter (that is, Vy Higginsen), whose story had been told in two previous musicals, *Mama, I Want to Sing* and *Mama, I Want to Sing—Part II: The Story Continues*, both of which had been previously seen Off Off Broadway (see entries). The third musical in the trilogy opened Off Broadway, and found Doris Winter a gospel star recruiting singers for a worldwide gospel tour. The musical had been previously produced Off Off Broadway at the Paramount Theatre in March 1996 as *Born to Sing! (Mama 3)*.

197 Boston Boston. "A New Musical"; THEATRE: The AMAS Repertory Theatre; OPENING DATE: April 27, 1978; PERFORMANCES: 12; BOOK: William Michael Maher; LYRICS: Bill Brohn and William Michael Maher; MUSIC: Bill Brohn; DIRECTION: William Michael Maher; CHOREOGRAPHY: William Michael Maher; SCENERY: Michael Meadows; COSTUMES: Sydney Brooks; LIGHTING: Paul Sullivan; MUSICAL DIRECTION: John Lenehan; PRODUCER: The AMAS Repertory Theatre, Inc. (Rosetta LeNoire, Artistic Director)

CAST—Charles Serrano (Enoch Pitt), Robert Bays (Police Officer, Patrick Murray), Allen W. Lane (Captain Charles Philip Reade), Charles Grimes (the Reverend Nathaniel Thorndike), David Lile (George Adam Hood), Susan J. Baum (Anne Reade), Rodney Wooding (Frederick J. Deane), Diane Tarleton (Margaret Reade), Corliss Taylor-Dunn (Abigail Hood), Chuck Newcome (John, Man in Revere House Inn, Officer O'Brian), James Rainbow (Robert, Man in Revere House Inn), Granville Burgess (Rufus Cruger), Philip Shaw (Major Titus T. Flagstaff), Lina Manning (Flora), Mary Graebler (Harriet Quigley), Barbb Louis (Molly Boone), Sheryl Martin (Mary Peachum)

SOURCE—The play *The Merry Wives of Windsor* (circa 1597) by William Shakespeare.

The action occurs in Boston on July 4, 1905.

The musical was presented in two acts.

ACT ONE—"In Boston" (People of Boston), "Lost and Won" (Philip Shaw), "I Remember Rosey" (Granville Burgess, Robert Bays, Men), "It Makes January Feel Like July" (Allen W. Lane, David Lile, Charles Grimes, Charles Serrano), "The Piper Must Be Paid" (Mary Gaebler, Barbb Louis), "Imperfections" (Susan J. Baum, Rodney Wooding, People of Boston), "Quigley's Message" (Mary Gaebler, Philip Shaw), "Bully Song" (Philip Shaw, Lina Manning, Men), "Should We?" (David Lile, Susan J. Baum)

ACT TWO—"The Game Is Mate" (People of Boston), "Let's Do Something New Tonight" (Susan J. Baum, Rodney Wooding), "Where Do All the Old Soldiers Go?" (Philip Shaw), "Ladies of Louisburg Square" (Allen W. Lane, Diane Tarleton, David Lile, Corliss Taylor-Dunn), "Fourth of July" (Robert Bayes, People of Boston), Finale (People of Boston)

NOTES—The Off Off Broadway musical *Boston Boston* was based on Shakespeare's *The Merry Wives of Windsor*; a program note stated the musical was about "the amorous jousts of a funny, portly, old soldier in the land of the F.F.B.'s ... First Families of Boston."

Giuseppe Verdi's 1893 opera *Falstaff* remains the definitive lyric adaptation of Shakespeare's comedy; but the 2004 Off Off Broadway musical *Lone Star Love*, or *The Merry Wives of Windsor, Texas*, makes a good case for an irreverent musical version of the play, now set in Texas during the period just following the Civil War (see entry).

Another musical version of Shakespeare's play was produced on November 29, 1985, at the American Stage Theatre in St. Petersburg, Florida; titled *I Love Alice*, this time around the merry wives live in Windsor, an American suburb of the 1950s.

198 Box Office of the Damned, Part 2. THEATRE: West Bank Café; OPENING DATE: September 12, 1989; PERFORMANCES: 5; BOOK: Michael James Ogborn; LYRICS: Michael James Ogborn; MUSIC: Michael James Ogborn; DIRECTION: James Ireland; CHOREOGRAPHY: James V. Flynn; SCENERY: Will Klein; MUSICAL DIRECTION: James Lopardo; PRODUCER: Act Four

CAST—Matthew Cloran, Bethanne Collins, Jim Flynn, Susan Kurowski, Robert MacCallum, Tracie Normoyle, John O'Hara, Anne Robinson

The action occurs in and around a theatre box office.

The musical was presented in two acts (song assignments unknown).

ACT ONE—"A Season You'll Never Forget," "Festival Fever"/"Gala Galore," "Please Hold," "Go Away, Mrs. Levittown," "Just Say NO," "Viva La Matinee," "Metropolitan Midge," "I'm in the Show," "We See It All," "Our Exchange Policy," "Remember Me," "The New Non-Union Usher Polka"

ACT TWO—"One Ticket," "Stranger," "8:00 Auto-Pilot," "Incantation to the T.M.I.," "This Job Is for the Birds," "Clerk," "Curtain Speech," "Subscribe!" "LATE," Finale

NOTES—There had been musicals seen from the perspective of backers' auditions (*A Backers' Audition*), casting calls (*A Chorus Line*), out-of-town tryouts (*A Broadway Musical*), and even one about an opening-night audience (*Musical Chairs*) (see entries); so why not one from the perspective of the poor beleaguered souls who man the box office? *Box Office of the Damned, Part 2* sounds amusing, but unfortunately the Off Off Broadway revue didn't last even one full week.

As *Box Office of the Damned*, the musical was revived Off Off Broadway at the CSC Theatre on June 3, 1994, apparently for just one performance. Among the revival's cast members was one Kristy Chenoweth. New songs for the revival included "Mrs. Levittown's Complaint" (this was not the song "Go Away, Mrs. Levittown"), "Ladies, Please!" "Daddy Long Legs," "Clerk 2 Clerk" (possibly a different title for "Clerk"), and "General Public Burn-Out."

199 The Boy Friend. THEATRE: Downtown Theatre; OPENING: January 25, 1958; transferred to the Cherry Lane Theatre on April 28, 1958; PERFORMANCES: 763; BOOK: Sandy Wilson; LYRICS: Sandy Wilson; MUSIC: Sandy Wilson; DIRECTION: Gus Schirmer, Jr.; CHOREOGRAPHY: Buddy Schwab; SCENERY: Charles Brandon; COSTUMES: Joe Crosby; LIGHTING: Charles Brandon; MUSICAL DIRECTION: Natalie Charlson; PRODUCER: The New Princess Company

CAST—Margaret Hall (Hortense), Christina Gillespie (Nancy), Gerrianne Raphael (Maisie), Michele Burke (Fay, Lolita), June Squibb (Dulcie), Ellen McGown (Polly), Thom Molinaro (Marcel, Pepe), Neal Kenyon (Pierre), Jeanne Beauvais (Mme. DuBonnet), Peter Conlow (Bobby Van Husen)*, Leon Shaw (Percival Brown), Bill Mullikin (Tony), David Vaughn (Lord Brockhurst), Phoebe Mackay (Lady Brockhurst)

(*Indicates that for Friday night performances the role of Bobby Van Husen was played by Eddie Weston.)

The action occurs in 1925 (1926, according to the published scripts).

The musical was presented in three acts.

ACT ONE—"Perfect Young Ladies" (Margaret Hall, Girls), "The Boy Friend" (Ellen McGown, Girls), "Won't You Charleston with Me?" (Gerrianne Raphael, Peter Conlow), "Fancy Forgetting" (Jeanne Beauvais, Leon Shaw), "I Could Be Happy with You" (Ellen McGown, Bill Mullikin)

ACT TWO—"Sur le Plage" (Boys, Girls), "Room in Bloomsbury" (Ellen McGown, Bill Mullikin), "Nicer in Nice" (Margaret Hall, Boys, Girls), "I've Got the 'You-Don't-Want-To-Play-With-Me' Blues" (Jeanne Beauvais, Leon Shaw, Girls), "Safety in Numbers" (Gerrianne Raphael, Boys), "I Could Be Happy with You" (reprise) (Ellen McGown, Bill Mullikin)

ACT THREE—"The Riviera" (Boys and Girls), "Room in Bloomsbury" (reprise) (Bill Mullikin), "It's Never Too Late to Fall in Love" (June Squibb, David Vaughan), "The Tango" (Thom Molinaro, Michele Burke), "Poor Little Pierette" (Jeanne Beauvais, Ellen McGown), Finale (Company)

NOTES—*The Boy Friend* was an affectionate British spoof of 1920s musicals which targeted such Broadway (and London) hits as Richard Rodgers and Lorenz Hart's *The Girl Friend* (1926) and Vincent Youmans' *No, No, Nanette* (1925). The musical was first seen on April 14, 1953, at the Players' Theatre and returned there in October of that year; in December, it opened at the Embassy Theatre; and finally it premiered in the West End on January 14, 1954, at Wyndham's Theatre. It was a resounding success, playing for 2,084 performances (Anne Rogers originated the role of Polly). The musical's Broadway premiere occurred at the Royale (now the Bernard B. Jacobs) Theatre on September 30 of that year, with Julie Andrews in her Broadway debut as Polly. The show was a hit all over again, and ran for 485 performances. The Off Broadway revival opened just twenty-five months after the successful Broadway run, and it might have seemed premature to bring back the show so soon. But the revival actually doubled the run of the Broadway production, running for a total of 763 performances (albeit at two Off Broadway theatres which were considerably smaller than the Royale).

The musical was revived on Broadway in 1970, with *Laugh-In*'s Judy Carne in the role of Polly; it was a failure, running only 119 performances. A belated film version directed by Ken Russell was released by MGM in 1972 (Twiggy played Polly), and it may well be the most misguided stage musical adaptation in the history of film musicals. Russell took a surefire audience-pleasing spoof and turned it into a charmless anti-musical. Indeed, Russell's skewed directorial vision led the way for a slew of well-known film directors to helm the adaptations of various Broadway musical hits. These directors seemed clueless to the intrinsic merits of their source material, and managed to miss almost every opportunity to capture the essence of what made the original a hit on Broadway (watch, if you must, *The Wiz* [Sidney Lumet, director], *Annie* [John Huston], and *A Chorus Line* [Richard Attenborough]). Prior to the release of the 1972 film version, there were two earlier attempts to bring the musical to the screen. In the February 1958 issue of *Screen Stories*, Columnist Mike Connolly reported that he asked Debbie Reynolds what her "next" film would be "after *The Boy Friend*." Further, Hugh Fordin in *The Movies' Greatest Musicals* noted that by March 23, 1967, George Kirgo had completed a first, second, and final draft screenplay for a film version of the musical (the screenplay for the version which was eventually filmed was by Ken Russell). The 1972 film interpolated into its score two classic songs from earlier MGM films, "All I Do Is Dream of You" (1934 film *Sadie McKee*) and "You Are My Lucky Star" (1935 film *Broadway Melody of 1936*), both with lyrics by Arthur Freed and music by Nacio Herb Brown. Incidentally, Debbie Reynolds had performed both songs in the 1952 film *Singin' in the Rain*, the former with chorus and the latter as a solo (the latter was deleted from the final print, but can be seen as bonus material on the DVD release of *Singin' in the Rain*). Incidentally, Sandy Wilson wrote a sequel to *The Boy Friend*; *Divorce Me, Darling!* dealt with the characters from *The Boy Friend* ten years later. It opened in London at the Globe Theatre on February 1, 1965, and played for only ninety-one performances (Polly was Patricia Michael). The musical was recorded by Decca Records (LP # LK-4675 and # SLK-4675; later reissued by DRG Records [LP # DS-15009]; the CD was released by Must Close Saturday Records # MCSR-3013]). Sandy Wilson later revised the musical, and a 1997 British production was recorded by That's Entertainment Records (CD # CDTER-1245). The musical has been seldom seen in the United States; probably its most important U.S. production was a 1984 mounting by Houston's Theatre Under the Stars which paired both *The Boy Friend* and *Divorce Me, Darling!*

While the Off Broadway revival wasn't recorded, there have been a number of recordings of *The Boy Friend*, including the original London (HMV Records LP # DLP-1078; Sepia Records CD # 1042) and New York (RCA Victor LP # LOC-1018 and CD # 60056-2-RG) casts; the 1970 Broadway revival (Decca LP # DL-79177; Broadway Decca CD # B0004736-02); and the 1972 film soundtrack (MGM Records LP # 1SE-32ST). Other recordings are a 1967 London cast revival (Parlophone Records LP # PMC-7044 and # PCS-7044, later reissued by That's Entertainment Records LP # TER-1054); a 1984 London revival (That's Entertainment Records LP # TER-1095); and a 1996 German cast album recorded by Prasentiert Records (CD # S11-1997). The script was published in hardback by Andre Deutsch (London) in 1955 and by E.P. Dutton & Company, Inc. (New York) in 1955, and a paperback edition was published by Samuel French (London) in 1960.

200 Boy Meets Boy. "A New Musical Comedy"; THEATRE: Actors' Playhouse; OPENING DATE: September 17, 1975; PERFORMANCES: 463; BOOK: Bill Solly and Donald Ward; LYRICS: Bill Solly; MUSIC: Bill Solly; DIRECTION: Ron Troutman; CHOREOGRAPHY: Robin Reseen; SCENERY: David Sackeroff; COSTUMES: Sherry Buchs; LIGHTING: David Sackeroff; MUSICAL DIRECTION: David Friedman; PRODUCERS: Edith O'Hara in association with Lee Barton and Christopher Larkin

CAST—Joe Barrett (Casey O'Brien), Paul Ratkevich (Andrew), David Gallegly (Guy Rose), Bobby Bowen (Bellboy, Alphonse), Raymond Wood (Clarence Cutler), Rita Gordon (Lady Rose, Josephine, La Rosa), Bobby Reed (Bruce, Reporter), Gene Borio (Head Waiter), Richard King (Assistant Hotel Manager, Porter, Reporter), Kathy Willinger (Rosita), Mary-Ellen Hanlon (Lolita), Jam Crean (Pepita, Photographer), Monica Grignon (Jan, Photographer), Dan Rounds (Reporter), Bobby Bowen and Kathy Willinger (The Van Wagners)

The action occurs in December 1936 in both London and Paris.

The musical was presented in two acts.

ACT ONE—OPENING: "Boy Meets Boy"/"Party in Room 203" (Boys and Girls), "Giving It Up for Love" (Joe Barrett, Paul Ratkevich), "Me" (Raymond Wood, Chorus), "The English Rose" (Richard King, Bobby Reed, Dan Rounds, Jan Crean, Monica Grignon), "Marry an American" (Girls and Boys), "It's a Boy's Life" (Joe Barrett, David Gallegly), "Does Anybody Love You?" (David Gallegly), "You're Beautiful" (David Gallegly), "Let's" (Joe Barrett, Chorus), "Let's" (Dance) (Joe Barrett, David Gallegly), "Giving It Up for Love" (reprise) (Joe Barrett), Finaletto (Raymond Wood, Chorus)

ACT TWO—"Just My Luck" (Joe Barrett, Raymond Wood, Girls), "It's a Dolly" (Rita Gordon, Boys, Girls), "What Do I Care?" (David Gallegly), "Clarence's Turn" (Raymond Wood), "Does Anybody Love You?" (reprise) (Joe Barrett, David Gallegly), Finale (Company)

NOTES—*Boy Meets Boy* was the first openly gay Off Broadway book musical; it broke the jinx which had befallen most gay-oriented revues, and ran over a year. Because it didn't preach and instead emphasized old-fashioned entertainment values (albeit with a gender-bending twist), the musical was a success and turned a profit.

The story utilized the framework of the Fred Astaire and Ginger Rogers film musicals of the 1930s and patterned its pastiche score after Cole Porter and Noel Coward.

The cast album was released by Records & Publishing Records (LP # JO-13), and a second cast album (with expanded musical sequences) was recorded in 1979 from a Minneapolis, Minnesota, production (released by Front Row Center Productions Records [LP # FRC-PES-1]).

The straight Broadway musical *The Gay Life* (1961) underwent a title change when its script was published some twenty years after the original production had closed. At the time of publication, the word "gay" had taken on a different meaning, and so the script was published as *The High Life*. *Boy Meets Boy* also underwent a title change. When the musical was produced regionally, at least one production gave the show a neutral-sounding name, calling it *Boy Oh Boy* (presumably with the authors' blessings).

201 The Boys from Syracuse. THEATRE: Theatre Four; OPENING DATE: April 15, 1963; PERFORMANCES: 500; BOOK: George Abbott; LYRICS: Lorenz Hart; MUSIC: Richard Rodgers; ballet music by Peter Matz; DIRECTION: Christopher Hewett; CHOREOGRAPHY: Bob Herget; SCENERY: Herbert Senn and Helen Pond; COSTUMES: Guy Kent; PRODUCER: Richard York

CAST—Gary Oakes (Sergeant), Fred Kimbrough (Duke), MATTHEW TOBIN (Aegeon), CLIFFORD DAVID (Antipholus of Ephesus), RUDY TRONTO (Dromio of Ephesus), Jim Pompeii (Tailor, Merchant of Ephesus), STUART DAMON (Antipholus of Syracuse), DANNY CARROLL (Dromio of Syracuse), Richard Colacino (Merchant of Syracuse), Jeane Deeks (Apprentice, Maid, Amazon), Richard Nieves (Angelo, Pygmalian), Dom Salinaro (Corporal), KAREN MORROW (Luce), ELLEN HANLEY (Adriana), JULIENNE MARIE (Luciana), Betsy Hepburn (Maid), Svetlana McLee (Maid, Amazon), Matthew Tobin (Sorcerer), CATHRYN DAMON (Courtesan), Zebra Nevins (Fatima), Violetta Landek (Courtesan, Galatea), Charlene Carter (Courtesan, Amazon) SOURCE—The play *The Comedy of Errors* (written between 1589 and 1594) by William Shakespeare.

The action occurs in Ephesus, Greece.

The musical was presented in two acts.

ACT ONE—"I Had Twins" (Matthew Tobin, Gary Oakes, Fred Kimbrough, Richard Nieves, Ensemble), "Dear Old Syracuse" (Stuart Damon, Danny Carroll), "What Can You Do with a Man?" (Karen Morrow, Rudy Tronto), "Falling in Love with Love" (Ellen Hanley), "Falling in Love with Love" (reprise) (dance) (Julienne Marie, Jean Deeks), "The Shortest Day of the Year" (Clifford David), "The Shortest Day of the Year" (reprise) (Ellen Hanley), "This Can't Be Love" (Stuart Damon, Julienne Marie), "This Can't Be Love" (reprise) (Julienne Marie), "Ladies' Choice Ballet" (Clifford David, Cathryn Damon, Ellen Hanley, Zebra Nevins, Richard Colacino, Jim Pompeii, Dom Salinaro, Violetta Landek, Richard Nieves, Svetlana McLee. Charlene Carter, Jeane Deeks)

ACT TWO—"Ladies of the Evening" (Gary Oakes, Company), "He and She" (Karen Morrow, Danny Carroll), "You Have Cast Your Shadow on the Sea" (Stuart Damon, Julienne Marie), "Come with Me" (Clifford David, Gary Oakes, Dom Salinaro, Jim Pompeii, Richard Nieves, Richard Colacino, Fred Kimbrough), "Big Brother" (Rudy Tronto), "Big Brother" (dance) (Danny Carroll, Rudy Tronto), "Sing for Your Supper" (Ellen Hanley, Julienne Marie, Karen Morrow), "Oh, Diogenes!" (Cathryn Damon, Company), Finale (Company)

NOTES—Two weeks after New Yorkers got the chance to see *Best Foot Forward* (see entry) for the first time in twenty-two years, Off Broadway gave them their first glimpse of *The Boys from Syracuse* (1938) in a quarter-century (the original production opened at the Alvin [now Neil Simon] Theatre on November 23, 1938, and played for 235 performances). The book had lost none of its charm, and the Rodgers and Hart songs were as fresh as ever. As a result, happy audiences flocked to the revival for an even 500 performances.

One number, "Ladies Choice Ballet," was added for the production, replacing "Let Antipholus In." Otherwise, all the original songs were retained for the revival.

The production gave Karen Morrow her best opportunity yet, and from then on she was in constant demand for a string of Broadway musicals (alas, all of them failures). Clifford David would create major roles in the original Broadway productions of *On a Clear Day You Can See Forever* (1965) and *1776* (1969). He introduced "She Wasn't You" in the former, and "Molasses to Rum" in the latter.

In *The Boys from Syracuse*, Stuart Damon and Julienne Marie sang classic Richard Rodgers standards; in 1965, they had the opportunity to introduce new Rodgers' songs in *Do I Hear a Waltz?* (lyrics by Stephen Sondheim). Stuart Damon perhaps became best known for his continuing (some thirty years as of this writing) role of Alan Quartermaine in the daytime television soap opera *General Hospital*.

The Boys from Syracuse revival was recorded by Capitol Records (LP # STAO-1933 and # TAO-1933), and was later released on CD (Broadway Angel # ZMD-0777-7-64695-2-2). When the Off Broadway revival was produced in London at the Drury Lane Theatre on November 7, 1963, it was the first time the musical had been seen in the West End (it played for a disappointing 100 performances); it was recorded by Decca Records (LP # LK-4564 and # SLK-4564); was later reissued by Stet Records (LP # DS-15016); and a Decca CD release (# 422-882-281-2) included bonus tracks of Rudy Vallee and Frances Langford singing six songs from the score. Other recordings of the score include a 1953 studio cast album (which included Portia Nelson and Jack Cassidy) on Columbia Records (LP # ML-4837; later released on CD by Sony Broadway Records [# SK-53329]) and a cast recording from the 1997 *Encores!* Production (Davis Gaines, Rebecca Luker, Debbie Shapiro Gravitt, and Malcolm Gets) which was released by DRG Records (CD # 94767).

The script was published by Chappell & Co., Inc., in 1965. In 1940, a film version of the musical was released by Universal; it included two songs by Rodgers and Hart which had been written specifically for the film ("The Greeks Have No Word for It" and "Who Are You?"). The musical was also shown on Canadian television on December 28, 1986, in a production which had been taped live from a revival at the Stratford Festival. The success of *Syracuse* no doubt inspired another Off Broadway revival of a Rodgers and Hart musical set in ancient Greece: *By Jupiter* (1942) opened in 1967 (see entry). And for a very different musical adaptation of *The Comedy of Errors*, see entry for *The Bomb-itty of Errors*.

With a revised book by Nicky Silvers, *The Boys from Syracuse* was revived on Broadway by the Roundabout Theatre Company on August 28, 2002, for seventy-three performances.

202 The Brain from Planet X.
NOTES—See entry for *The New York Musical Theatre Festival.*

203 El Bravo! "A Merry Musical Myth"; THEATRE: Entermedia Theatre; OPENING DATE: June 16, 1981; PERFORMANCES: 48; BOOK: Jose Fernandez and Thom Schiera; LYRICS: John Clifton; MUSIC: John Clifton; DIRECTION: Patricia Birch; CHOREOGRAPHY: Patricia Birch; SCENERY: Tom Lynch; COSTUMES: Carrie Robbins; LIGHTING: Neil Peter Jampolis; MUSICAL DIRECTION: Herbert Kaplan; PRODUCERS: Kenneth Waissman with Edward Mezvinsky and Sidney Shlenker

CAST—Aurelio Padron (Pepe DeMarco [El Bravo]), Chamaco Garcia (Beggar), Dennis Daniels (Alan), Charlie Serrano (Juanito), Ray De Mattis (Honest John), Keith Jochim (Sergeant Noble), Michael Jeter (Cruikshank), Michele Mais (Lola), Vanessa Bell (Kitty), Starr Danias (Annabelle), Frank Kopyc (Father Tucker), Lenka Peterson (Mrs. Krekelberg), Yamil Borges (Mariana [Chiquita Bonita]), Olga Merediz (Aunt Rosa), Kevin Rogers (Willy), Duane Bodin (Mr. Louie Woodknot, Narrator), Jesse Corti (Mr. Jose Ensalada), S.J. Davis (Mrs. Betty Ensalada), Julia Lema (Julia Farichide), Alaina Warren Zachary (Duchess Hilda Pinchik), Jenifer Lewis (Officer Walker), Stephen Jay (Officer Chase), Quitman Fludd III (Officer Cruz)

The action occurs "once upon a time" in El Barrio, somewhere in New York City.

The musical was presented in two acts.

ACT ONE—Prologue (Duane Bodin, Aurelio Padron, Chamaco Garcia, Dennis Daniels, Charlie Serrano, Ray DeMattis, Company), "El Bravo" (Aurelio Padron, Dennis Daniels, Charlie Serrano, Company), "Cuchifrito Restaurant" (Aurelio Padron, Friends), "Que Pasa, My Love?" (Aurelio Padron, Yamil Borges), "Honest John's Game" (Ray De Mattis, Henchman), "Chiquita Bonita" (Yamil Borges, Olga Merediz, Company), "Shoes" (Michele Mais, Vanessa Bell, Starr Danias), "Hey Chico" (Aurelio Padron, Dennis Daniels, Charlie Serrano), "Criminal" (Olga Merediz, Yamil Borges, Company)

ACT TWO—"He Says" (Aurelio Padron, Yamil Borges), "The Talent Contest" (Jenifer Lewis, S.J. Davis, Alaina Warren Zachary, Starr Danias), "Gotta Get Out" (Kevin Rogers, The Creampuffs), "Honest John's Game" (reprise) (Ray De Mattis, Henchmen), "Adios Barrio" (Yamil Borges, Olga Merediz, Company), "Fairy Tales" (Aurelio Padron), "Torture" (Yamil Borges, Olga Merediz, Ray De Mattis, Keith Jochim), "That Latin Lure" (Ray De Mattis), "Congratulations!" (Aurelio Padron and His Band, Ray De Mattis), "Bailar!" (Olga Merediz), "And Furthermore" (Chamaco Garcia), Finale (Company)

NOTES—*El Bravo!* was an updated re-telling of the Robin Hood story set in a barrio in New York City. It was John Clifton's first Off Broadway book musical since *Man with a Load of Mischief* (1966; see entry); unfortunately, it disappeared after six weeks. Clifton had also written a musical version of *I Remember Mama*, which premiered at Buffalo's Studio Arena and starred Celeste Holm and Jill O'Hara. His adaptation was produced three years before Richard Rodgers' version opened on Broadway in 1979.

Clive Barnes in the *New York Post* found *El Bravo!* a "terrific show," a "charming winner, full of guts and humor." He thought Clifton's score was better than the one he wrote for *Man with a Load of Mischief*, and he noted that Patricia Birch's choreography gave "speed and flow" to the production. During the preview period of *El Bravo*, the role of Willy was played by Ray Stephens, who was replaced by Kevin Rogers, and the songs "Mariana" and "At the Door" were dropped.

El Bravo! appears to be the first Off Broadway musical to enjoy a program cover in full color. During the nineteenth century and the early decades of the twentieth century, most Broadway programs had color covers which were generic in nature and which had nothing to do with the shows at hand. It seems the first color cover (of sorts) for a non-musical was for the 1935 Broadway revival of *Rain* with Tallulah Bankhead ("of sorts" because the photograph of Bankhead seems to be a black-and-white one which was tinted). The first full-fledged color cover for a non-musical was the 1958 three-week flop *Edwin Booth* (in his opening night review for the *New York Herald Tribune*, Walter Kerr noted the "two gloriously technicolored portraits of star Jose Ferrer" on the cover). Although *This Is the Army* (1942) had red, white, and blue colors for the lettering on its cover, *Baker Street* (1965) is generally credited as the first Broadway musical to boast a color cover. But *Jotham Valley* (1951) got there first, with a colorful artwork logo on its program cover.

204 Brecht on Brecht. THEATRE: Theatre de Lys; OPENING DATE: January 3, 1962; PERFORMANCES: 424; TEXT ARRANGED AND TRANSLATED BY George Tabori; DIRECTION: Gene Frankel; Frances Frankel, Assistant Director; SCENERY: Wolfgang Roth; MUSICAL DIRECTION: Lys Bert Symonette; PRODUCERS: The Greater New York Chapter of ANTA and Cheryl Crawford

CAST—Dane Clark, Anne Jackson, Lotte Lenya, Viveca Lindfors, George Voskovec, Michael Wager

The revue was presented in two acts.

NOTES—*Brecht on Brecht* was a staged reading of Bertolt Brecht's writings; however, the evening included the following songs: "The Solomon Song" (from *The Threepenny Opera*, 1928; original German lyric by Brecht, English lyric by Marc Blitzstein, music by Kurt Weill); "Song of a German Mother" (lyric by Hanns Eisler, music by Eric Bentley); "Pirate Jenny" (*The Threepenny Opera*, 1928; original German lyric by Bertolt Brecht, English lyric by Marc Blitzstein, music by Kurt Weill); and an unidentified song from *Mother Courage* (music by Paul Dessau). All songs were performed by Lotte Lenya.

The work had been previously seen as *Brecht on Brecht: His Life and Art* for two performances at the Theatre de Lys on November 14 and 20, 1961; the cast members were: George Gaynes, Dolly Haas, Anne Jackson, Lotte Lenya, Viveca Lindfors, George Voskovec, Michael Wager, and Eli Wallach. *Brecht on Brecht* was recorded on a 2-LP set by Columbia Records (# 02L-278 and # 02S-203).

For an evening of similar material, see entry for *An Evening with Ekkehard Schall.*

205 A Brief History of White Music. THEATRE: Village Gate; OPENING DATE: November 19, 1996; PERFORMANCES: 308; LYRICS: See song list for credits; MUSIC: See song list for credits; DIRECTION: Ken Roberson; CHOREOGRAPHY: Ken Roberson; SCENERY: Felix E. Cochren; COSTUMES: Debra Stein; LIGHTING: Alan Keen; Matt Berman, Associate Lighting Designer; MUSICAL DIRECTION: Alva Nelson; PRODUCERS: Gene Wolsk, RAD Productions Inc., and Art D'Lugoff

CAST—James Alexander, Wendy Edmead, Deborah Keeling

The revue was presented in one act.

MUSICAL NUMBERS—Overture (Orchestra), "Who Put the Bomp" (lyric and music by Barry Mann and Gerry Coffin) (Company), "Bei Mir Bistu Schoen" (lyric and music by Jacob Jacobs and Shalom Secunda, English lyric by Sammy Cahn and Saul Chaplan) (Deborah Keeling, Company), "I Got a Gal in Kalamazoo" (from 1942 film *Orchestra Wives*; lyric by Mack Gordon, music by Harry Warren) (James Alexander, Company), "That'll Be the Day" (lyric and music by Buddy Holly) (Company), "Teenager in Love" (lyric and music by Doc Pomus and Mort Shuman) (Company), "Where the Boys Are" (1960 film *Where the Boys Are*; lyric and music by Neil Sedaka and Howard Greenfield) (Wendy Edmead), "Leader of the Pack" (lyric and music by Jeff Barry, Ellie Greenwich, and George "Shadow" Morton) (Wendy Edmead, Company), "Walk Like a Man" (lyric and music by Bob Crewe and Bob Gaudio) (James Alexander, Company), "Love Potion No. 9" (lyric and music by Jerry Leiber and Mike Stoller) (Company), "Blue Suede Shoes" (lyric and music by Carl Lee Perkins) (Deborah Keeling), *Love Me Tender* Medley (1956 film; lyrics and music by Elvis Presley and P. Matson) (Company) "Jailhouse Rock" (1957 film *Jailhouse Rock*; lyric and music by Jerry Leiber and Mike Stoller) (Company), "California Dreaming" (lyric and music by John Phillips and M. Gilliam) (Company), "Monday, Monday" (lyric and music by John Phillips) (Company), "Surfin' USA" (lyric and music by Brian Wilson and Chuck Berry) (James Alexander, Company), "I Got You Babe" (lyric and music by Sonny Bono) (James Alexander, Deborah Keeling), "Itsy Bitsy Teeny Weeny Yellow Polka Dot Bikini" (lyric by Paul J. Vance, music by Lee Pockriss) (Wendy Edmead), "These Boots Are Made for Walking" (lyric and music by Lee Hazelwood) (Company), "Do Wah Diddy Diddy" (lyric and music by Jeff Barry and Ellie Greenwich) (James Alexander), "Son of a Preacher Man" (lyric and music by J. Hurley and R. Wilkins) (Deborah Keeling), "To Sir, with Love" (1967 film *To Sir, with Love*; lyric by Mark London, music by Donald [Don] Black) (Wendy Edmead), "Downtown" (lyric and music by Anthony Peter Hatch) (Deborah Keeling), "She Loves You" (lyric and music by John Lennon and Paul McCartney) (Company), "I Wanna Hold Your Hand" (lyric and music by John Lennon and Paul McCartney) (James Alexander), "With a Little Help from My Friends" (lyric and music by John Lennon and Paul McCartney) (Company), "Sgt. Pepper's Lonely Hearts Club Band" (lyric and music by John Lennon and Paul McCartney) (Company), "Imagine" (lyric and music by John Lennon) (Company), "We Can Work It Out" (lyric and music by John Lennon and Paul McCartney)

NOTES—With so many revues celebrating Black music, why not an evening devoted to White music? And so *A Brief History of White Music* offered up four decades' worth of "White" music. But the joke was that all the songs in the evening were performed by Black singers.

206 Bright Lights, Big City. THEATRE: New York Theatre Workshop; OPENING DATE: February 24, 1999; PERFORMANCES: 31; BOOK: Paul Scott Goodman; LYRICS: Paul Scott Goodman; MUSIC: Paul Scott Goodman; DIRECTION: Michael Greif; CHOREOGRAPHY: Michael Greif; Lisa Shriver, Associate Choreographer; SCENERY: Paul Clay; COSTUMES: Angela Wendt; LIGHTING: Blake Burba; MUSICAL DIRECTION: Richard Barone; PRODUCER: The New York Theatre Workshop (James C. Nicola, Artistic Director; Linda S. Chapman, Associate Artistic Director)

CAST—Paul Scott Goodman (Writer), Patrick Wilson (Jamie), Carla Bianco (Tuff Babe #1, Mary O'Brien McCann, Sally), Natascia Diaz (Tuff Babe #2, Theresa, Vicky), Liza Lapira (Drug Girl, Coma Baby, Elise), Jerry Dixon (Tad), Kerry O'Malley (Pinkie, Megan), Napiera Daniele Groves (Amanda), Jacqueline Arnold (Statue of Liberty, Clara), John Link Graney (Yasu, Michael, Drug Dealer #1), Ken Marks (Alex, Drug Dealer #2, Mad Person), Annmarie Milazzo (Elaine, Mom)

SOURCE—The 1984 novel *Bright Lights, Big City* by Jay McInerney.

The action occurs in New York City during one week in 1984.

The musical was presented in two acts.

ACT ONE—Prologue (Paul Scott Goodman), "Bright Lights, Big City" (Patrick Wilson, Company), "I Love Drugs" (Patrick Wilson, Liza Lapira), "1984"/"Heartbreak" (Jerry Dixon, Patrick Wilson, Company), "Missing" (Carla Bianco), "Beautiful Sunday" (Patrick Wilson, Napiera Daniele Groves, Paul Scott Goodman), "Bright Lights, Big City" (reprise) (Jacqueline Arnold, Company), "Coma Baby"/"Gotham Magazine" (James Paul Goodman, Patrick Wilson, Company), "Can I Come Over, Please" (Carla Bianco, Kerry O'Malley, John Link Graney), "Fact and Fiction" (Jacqueline Arnold, Ken Marks, Carla Bianco, Kerry O'Malley, John Link Graney, Patrick Wilson), "You Don't Show Me Your Stories Anymore" (Ken Marks, Patrick Wilson), "I Hate the French" (Patrick Wilson, Co-Workers), "Brother" (John Link Graney), "Monstrous Events" (Jerry Dixon, Patrick Wilson, Carla Bianco, Kerry O'Malley, John Link Graney, Jacqueline Arnold, Ken Marks), "Odeon"/"Club Crawl" (Annmarie Milazzo, Natascia Diaz, Company), "I Wanna Have Sex Tonight" (Jerry Dixon, Patrick Wilson, Company), "Forest Hills 9 A.M." (Liza Lapira, Patrick Wilson), "Happy Birthday, Darling" (Annmarie Milazzo), "Come Baby"/"Missing" (Patrick Wilson, Carla Bianco, Company), "Fact and Fiction" (reprise) (Ken Marks, Kerry O'Malley, John Link Graney, Carla Bianco, Patrick Wilson), "New Literature" (Patrick Wilson), "Walk" (Patrick Wilson, Paul Scott Goodman, John Link Graney), "To Model" (Napiera Daniele Groves, Patrick Wilson), "So Many Little Things" (Patrick Wilson, Company)

ACT TWO—"It's Great to Be Back in the City" (Jerry Dixon, Company), "Monstrous Events" (reprise) (Patrick Wilson, Jerry Dixon), "Thinkers and Drinkers"/"Kindness" (Natascia Diaz), "Perfect Feeling" (Patrick Wilson, Natascia Diaz, Company), "Tonight I Am Happy" (Patrick Wilson), "We Couldn't Handle It, Jamie" (Jacqueline Arnold), "Come On" (Paul Scott Goodman, Patrick Wilson), "Wednesday" (Paul Scott Goodman, Patrick Wilson, Company), "Heart and Soul" (John Link Graney, Natascia Diaz, Company), "The Letter" (Patrick Wilson), "Bad Blow" (Patrick Wilson, Jerry Dixon), "Camera Wall" (Napiera Daniele Groves, Models, Patrick Wilson), "Fact and Fiction?" (reprise) (Co-Workers), "How About Dinner at My Place?" (Kerry O'Malley, Patrick Wilson), "My Son" (Kerry O'Malley, Patrick Wilson), "Missing" (Carla Bianco), "Brother 2" (John Link Graney, Patrick Wilson), "Mummies at the Met" (Patrick Wilson, Company), "Are You Still Holding My Hand?" (Annmarie Milazzo), "Monstrous Events" (reprise) (Jerry Dixon), "Stay in My Life" (Patrick Wilson, Natascia Diaz, Company), "Bright Lights, Big City" (reprise) (Patrick Wilson), "Wordfall" (Paul Scott Goodman, Patrick Wilson, Company)

NOTES—Based on Jay McInerney's novel *Bright Lights, Big City* (which was also the basis for a 1988 film), this ambitious musical depicted a young man caught up in the drug culture and nightlife of Manhattan in the 1980s. Perhaps because its theme was too off-putting, and its main character unsympathetic, the musical disappeared after its limited run at the New York Theatre Workshop. David Lefkowitz in *The Best Plays of 1998-1999* noted that while some critics saw the work as "a soulless *Rent* wannabe" (Michael Greif, the director of *Bright Lights*, had directed *Rent*), others were impressed with the musical's depiction of "1980s self-indulgence and mindlessness ...finding it more cohesive than" *Rent*.

In 2005, Sh-K-Boom Records released a recording of the score (CD # 1984-2); Patrick Wilson reprised his leading role, and Sherie Rene Scott, Gavin Creel, Christine Ebersole, and Richard Kind were among the studio cast members.

On the evening of March 5, 2007, two performances of a revised world premiere version of the musical were given at Harvard University's Adams House Pool Theatre.

207 Bring in 'da Noise, Bring in 'da Funk. THEATRE: Newman Theatre/The Joseph Papp Public Theatre; OPENING DATE: November 15, 1995; PERFORMANCES: 85; BOOK: Reg E. Gaines; LYRICS: Reg E. Gaines; additional lyrics by George C. Wolfe and Ann Duquesnay; MUSIC: Ann Duquesnay, Zane Mark, and Daryl Waters; DIRECTION: George C. Wolfe; CHOREOGRAPHY: Savion Glover; SCENERY: Riccardo Hernandez; Batwin + Robin, Projection Design; COSTUMES: Karen Perry; LIGHTING: Jules Fisher; MUSICAL DIRECTION: Zane Mark; PRODUCER: The New York Shakespeare Festival (George C. Wolfe, Producer; Rosemarie Tichler, Artistic Producer; Joey Parnes, Executive Producer; Laurie Beckelman, Executive Director; Wiley Hausam, Associate Producer; Kevin Kline, Artistic Associate)

CAST—Vincent Bingham, Jared Crawford, Ann Duquesnay, Reg E. Gaines, Savion Glover, Dule Hill, Raymond King, Jimmy Tate, Baakari Wilder

The dance revue was presented in two acts.

ACT ONE—*In 'Da Beginning*: "Bring in 'Da Noise, Bring in 'Da Funk" (Company), "The Door to Isle Goree" (Reg E. Gaines), "Slave Ships" (Ann Duquesnay, Savion Glover); *Som'Thin' from Nuthin'*: "Som'thin' from Nuthin'"/"The Circle Stomp" (Baakari Wilder, Dule Hill, Jimmy Tate, Vincent Bingham), "The Pan Handlers" (Jared Crawford, Raymond King); *Urbanization*: "The Lynching Blues" (Baakari Wilder, Ann Duquesnay, Company), "Chicago Bound" (Savion Glover, Ann Duquesnay, Company), "Shifting Sounds" (Reg E. Gaines), "Industrialization" (Savion Glover, Baakari Wilder, Jimmy Tate, Vincent Bingham, Raymond King), "The Chicago Riot Rag" (Savion Glover, Baakari Wilder, Jimmy Tate, Vincent Bingham), "I Got the Beat"/"Dark Tower" (Ann Duquesnay, Reg E. Gaines, Company), "The Whirligig Stomp" (Company)

ACT TWO—*Where's the Beat?*: "Now That's Tap" (Jimmy Tate, Vincent Bingham), "The Uncle Huck-a-Buck Song" (Baakari Wilder, Savion Glover, Company), "Kid Go!" (Dule Hill, Company), "The Lost Beat Swing" (Ann Duquesnay, Company), "Green, Chaney, Buster, Slyde" (Savion Glover); *Street Corner Symphony*: 1956—"Them Conkheads" (Company); 1967—"Hot Fun" (Company); 1977—"Blackout" (Savion Glover, Baakari Wilder, Jimmy Tate, Vincent Bingham); 1987—"Gospel"/"Hip Hop Rant" (Reg E. Gaines, Savion Glover, Ann Duquesnay); *Noise/Funk*: "Drummin'" (Jared Crawford, Raymond King), "Taxi" (Savion Glover, Jimmy Tate, Baakari Wilder, Vincent Bingham), "Conversations" (Jared Crawford, Raymond King, Savion Glover, Jimmy Tate, Baakari Wilder, Vince Bingham), "Hittin'" (Savion Glover, Baakari Wilder, Vincent Bingham), "Bring in 'da Noise Bring in 'da Funk" (reprise) (Company)

NOTES—After its Off Broadway run at the Public, the dance revue *Bring in 'Da Noise, Bring in 'Da Funk* transferred to the Ambassador Theatre on April 25, 1996, where it played for 1,130 performances. "Conversations" may not have been performed during the Off Broadway engagement.

The revue attempted to create the history of the Black experience in America through tap, hip hop, and other forms of dance. Writing in *Time*, Martha Duffy noted the episodic evening offered little or no connection in its vignettes ("the book is weak ... the feet have it"). Donald Lyons in the *Wall Street Journal* said that while the revue dealt with slave ships, plantations, lynchings, riots, and "endless prejudice ... the larger historical narrative is an uninflected litany of victimized innocence." Further, he found the revue condescending and smug in its "superiority" to Black entertainers of the past. Clive Barnes in the *New York Post* also noted that Savion Glover seemed to frown on "the old buck and wing of historical showbiz tap," and felt he was "a little too satirically tough" on such legendary Black dancers as Bill "Bojangles" Robinson and the Nicholas Brothers.

The cast recording was released by RCA Victor Records (CD # 09026-68565-2). The night after *'Da Noise* opened Off Broadway, another similarly styled hip-hop dance revue premiered (see entry for *Jam on the Groove*).

208 Bring in the Morning. "A New Musical"; THEATRE: Variety Arts Theatre; OPENING DATE: April 23, 1994; PERFORMANCES: 51; ADAPTATION AND LYRICS: Herb Schapiro; MUSIC: Gary William Friedman; DIRECTION: Bertin Rowser; CHOREOGRAPHY: Michele Assaf; SCENERY AND PROJECTIONS: Ken Foy; COSTUMES: Robert MacKintosh; LIGHTING: Ken Billington; MUSICAL DIRECTION: Louis St. Louis; PRODUCERS: Jeff Britton in association with Edgar M. Bronfman

CAST—Yassmin Alers (Sonya), Roy Chicas (Roberto), Nicole Leach (Alicia), Shannon Reyshard Peters (Jamal), Imelda de los Reyes (Judy), Sean Grant (Cougar), Inaya Fafa'n (Lakesha), Yvette Lawrence (Inez), Raquel Polite (Mavis), Steven X. Ward (Hector), Kevin R. Wright (Nelson)

SOURCE—The writings of young people participating in the program "Poets in Public Service, Inc."

The action occurs at the present time in the inner city.

The revue was presented in two acts.

ACT ONE—"Come Into My Jungle" (Sean Grant, Company), "Bring in the Morning (Nicole Leach, Company), "Let It Rain" (Imelda de los Reyes, Kevin R. Wright, Yassmin Alers, Roy Chicas, Yvette Lawrence, Company), "You (Tu)" (Yvette Lawrence,

Roy Chicas), "Not Your Cup of Tea" (Imelda de los Reyes), "Ghetto of My Mind" (Sean Grant), "Funky Eyes" (Steven X. Ward), "Another Cry" (Yvette Lawrence), "I'm on My Way" (Inaya Jafa'n, Company), "Never Stop Believing" (Company)

ACT TWO—"Never Stop Believing" (reprise) (Company), "Something Is Wrong with Everyone Today" (Yassmin Alers), "Missing Person" (Kevin R. Wright), "The Light of Your Love (La Luz de Tu Amor)" (Roy Chicas), "Ghetto of My Mind" (reprise) (Sean Grant), "Hector's Dream" (Steven X. Ward, Company), "Trip" (Shannon Reyshard Peters), "The Glory of Each Morning" (Company), "Deliver My Soul" (Raquel Polite, Inaya Jafa'n, Company), "I Want to Walk in a Garden" (Company)

NOTES—Gary William Friedman and Herb Schapiro's revue *Bring in the Morning* was a less successful sequel to their (and Will Holt's) 1970 revue *The Me Nobody Knows* (see entry); in both cases, the revues set to music the writings of young people (in the case of *Bring in the Morning*, their ages ranged from 16 to the early 20s, and the music included contemporary pop and gospel).

Stephen Holden in the *New York Times* noted the cast members brought "vitality and grittiness" to their material, but said the "mushy vagueness" of the lyrics worked against the revue's success. Further, except for two rap songs (see below), he felt the music didn't speak to the contemporary characters and was instead reflective of a time warp which suggested a "sophisticated hybrid" of Burt Bacharach and the score for the 1980 film *Fame* ("with a dash of Kurt Weill"). The two rap numbers ("Best Kept Secret" and "Awake and a Dream") were by Bertin Rowser, and the program noted they were inspired by students of Boys Harbor Performing Arts in East Harlem, New York.

Friedman and Holt also collaborated on a revue based on the writings of older people (see entries for *Turns* [1980] and *Taking My Turn* [1983]).

209 A Broadcast Baby. THEATRE: American Jewish Theatre; OPENING DATE: June 18, 1985; PERFORMANCES: 16 (estimated); PLAY: Isaiah Sheffer; DIRECTION: Dan Held; PRODUCER: American Jewish Theatre

CAST—MARILYN SOKOL, HENDERSON FORSYTHE, Stan Free, Mark Hulswit

The action occurs in 1936.

NOTES—The flyer for the Off Off Broadway play *A Broadcast Baby* indicated that the plot, set in 1936, dealt with a live cost-to-coast radio show. During the broadcast, a popular Jewish comedienne confronts her ethnic identity and "pandemonium breaks loose." The evening included popular songs of the 1930s as well as songs from Yiddish theatre. It appears that during rehearsals or during preview performances Lanny Meyers performed the role ultimately assumed by Stan Free.

210 Broadway Babylon—The Musical That Never Was! THEATRE: Paper Moon Cabaret; OPENING DATE: May 18, 1984; PERFORMANCES: 20, "Created" by Christopher Adams and David Agress; DIRECTION: Susan Stroman; CHOREOGRAPHY: Susan Stroman; SCENERY: Salvatore Taliarino; COSTUMES: Carol Wenz; MUSICAL DIRECTION: Eric Diamond; PRODUCERS: Chris Adams and David Agress; Roni Gallion, Associate Producer

CAST—Scott Bakula, Jossie De Guzman, Melinda Gilb

MUSICAL NUMBERS (division of acts and song assignments unknown; songs are listed in performance order)—"A Broadway Musical" (from *A Broadway Musical*, 1978; lyric by Lee Adams, music by Charles Strouse), "You Mustn't Be Discouraged" (*Fade Out-Fade In*, 1964; lyric by Betty Comden and Adolph Green, music by Jule Styne), "Where Was I When They Passed Out the Luck?" (*Minnie's Boys*, 1970; lyric by Hal Hackady, music by Larry Grossman), "Everybody Needs Something" (possibly "Everything Needs Something" from *La Strada*, 1969; lyric by Martin Charnin, music by Elliot Lawrence) "A Quiet Thing" (*Flora, the Red Menace*, 1965; lyric by Fred Ebb, music by John Kander), "Go Visit Your Grandmother" (*70, Girls, 70*, 1971; lyric by Fred Ebb, music by John Kander), "Yenta Power" (*A Broadway Musical*, 1978; lyric by Lee Adams, music by Charles Strouse), "You I Like" (*The Grand Tour*, 1979; lyric and music by Jerry Herman), "He Touched Me" (*Drat! The Cat!* 1964; lyric by Ira Levin, music by Milton Schafer), "Once Upon a Time" (*All American*, 1962; lyric by Lee Adams, music by Charles Strouse), "What's New at the Zoo?" (*Do Re Mi*, 1960; lyric by Betty Comden and Adolph Green, music by Jule Styne), "Lawyers" (*A Broadway Musical*, 1978; lyric by Lee Adams, music by Charles Strouse), "Ten Percent" (dropped during the pre-Broadway tryout of *Chicago*, 1975; lyric by Fred Ebb, music by John Kander) "I Like What I Do" (*Bring Back Birdie*, 1981; lyric by Lee Adams, music by Charles Strouse), "It's an Art" (*Working*, 1978; lyric and music by Stephen Schwartz), "Be Happy" (*Minnie's Boys*, 1970; lyric by Hal Hackady, music by Larry Grossman), "Go to Sleep Early" (source unknown; lyricist and composer unknown), "Dance a Little Closer" (*Dance a Little Closer*, 1983; lyric by Alan Jay Lerner, music by Charles Strouse), "This Is a Great Country" (*Mr. President*, 1962; lyric and music by Irving Berlin)

NOTES—This revue is an early entry from Susan Stroman. The Off Off Broadway production featured mostly unfamiliar songs from shows which, for the most part, had short Broadway runs.

211 Broadway by the Year.

NOTES—*Broadway by the Year* is an invaluable series which offers evenings of songs from Broadway shows by specific years (not specific Broadway seasons). The series was created by its producer, Scott Siegel, who also serves as host, and the performances are given at Town Hall.

The following years have been thus far celebrated (asterisks denote which have been recorded and released [as of this writing]): 1925 (*), 1926 (*), 1928, 1929, 1930, 1933 (*), 1935 (*), 1938, 1939 (*), 1940 (*), 1943 (*), 1945, 1949 (*), 1951 (*), 1953 (*), 1955 (*), 1956, 1959, 1960 (*), 1962, 1963 (*), 1964 (*), 1968, and 1978. For the 2008 series, the years 1947, 1954, 1965, and 1979 are scheduled to be saluted.

The recordings have been released by Bayview Recording Company. A typical recording in the series is the one which celebrates the Broadway musicals of 1939 (CD # RNBW025). It features such performers as Amanda McBroom, Annie Golden, and Steve Ross, and includes familiar songs from the musicals of that year, such as "Friendship" (*DuBarry Was a Lady*) and "All the Things You Are" (*Very Warm for May*), but also offers an obscure number, the premiere recording of "Papa's Got a Job" (*Sing for Your Supper*).

212 Broadway Dandies. "A Musical Romp Through New York"; THEATRE: International Cabaret Theatre; OPENING DATE: December 17, 1974; PERFORMANCES: 8; DIRECTION: Robert Johnnene Choreography: Henry Le Tang; SCENERY: Wilfred Surita; COSTUMES: Cheena Lee; MUSICAL DIRECTION: Don Whisted; PRODUCER: Robert Johnnene

CAST—Robert (Bob) Fitch (Tour Guide), Hal James Pederson (Cabaret Host, Opera Star, Club #4), Diane Nicole (Cabaret Performer), Suzi Swanson (Dance Hall Hostess), Michael Radigan (Recording Artist), Teddy Williams (Club #1), Marilyn Anderson (Club #2), Janet Saunders (Club #3), Don Swanson and Suzi Swanson (Dance Team), Sharon Bruce ("Send in the Clowns")

The revue was presented in two acts (division of acts and song assignments unknown; songs are listed in performance order).

MUSICAL NUMBERS—"On Broadway" (lyric and music by Cynthia Weill, Jerry Leiber, and Mike Stoller), "Lullaby of Broadway" (from 1935 film *Gold Diggers of 1935*; lyric by Al Dubin, music by Harry Warren), "Give Our (My) Regards to Broadway" (*Little Johnny Jones*, 1905; lyric and music by George M. Cohan) "Wilkommen" (*Cabaret*, 1966; lyric by Fred Ebb, music by John Kander), "Cabaret" (*Cabaret*, 1966; lyric by Fred Ebb, music by John Kander), "Carousel" (probably "Carousel Waltz" from *Carousel*, 1945; music by Richard Rodgers), "Standing on the Corner" (*The Most Happy Fella*, 1956; lyric and music by Frank Loesser), "Big Spender" (*Sweet Charity*, 1966; lyric by Dorothy Fields, music by Cy Coleman), "Ten Cents a Dance" (*Simple Simon*, 1930; lyric by Lorenz Hart, music by Richard Rodgers), "I'm All Smiles" (*The Yearling*, 1965; lyric by Herbert Martin, music by Michael Leonard), "Questa Quela," "Let's Dance" (possibly Benny Goodman's theme song; if so, lyric and music by Fanny Baldridge, Gregory Stone, and Joseph Bonine), "Ain't Misbehavin'" (*Hot Chocolates*, 1929; lyric by Andy Razaf, music by Thomas [Fats] Waller), "Honeysuckle Rose" (lyric by Andy Razaf, music by Fats Waller), "Adelaide's Lament" (*Guys and Dolls*, 1950; lyric and music by Frank Loesser), "Summertime" (*Porgy and Bess*, 1935; lyric by DuBose Heyward, music by George Gershwin), "I Never Has Seen Snow" (*House of Flowers*, 1954; lyric by Truman Capote and Harold Arlen, music by Harold Arlen), "Night and Day" (*Gay Divorce*, 1932; lyric and music by Cole Porter), "Too Darn Hot" (*Kiss Me, Kate*, 1948; lyric and music by Cole Porter), "Sisters" (1954 film *White Christmas*; lyric and music by Irving Berlin), "Aquarius" (*Hair*, 1967 [see entry]; lyric by James Rado and Gerome Ragni, music by Galt MacDermot), "Send in the Clowns" (*A Little Night Music*, 1973; lyric and music by Stephen Sondheim), "That's Entertainment" (1953 film *The Band Wagon*; lyric by Howard Dietz, music by Arthur Schwartz), "Another Op'nin', Another Show" (*Kiss Me, Kate*, 1948; lyric and music by Cole Porter)

NOTES—*Broadway Dandies*, a self-described "musical romp through New York," had just one week to do its romping.

The revue included mostly well-known standards from theatre and films (such as "Summertime") and offered only one relatively obscure number ("I'm All Smiles").

213 Broadway Jukebox. THEATRE: John Houseman Theatre; OPENING DATE: July 19, 1990; PERFORMANCES: 50; DIRECTION: Bill Guske; production conceived and supervised by Ed Linderman; CHOREOGRAPHY: Bill Guske; SCENERY: James Morgan; COSTUMES: Barbara Forbes; LIGHTING: Stuart Duke; PRODUCERS: Eric Krebs in association with Joanne Macan and Carol Wernli; also produced in association with Theodore Rawlings, James R. Singer, Sanford Levitt, Joseph Scalzo, Jana Robbins, and Joyous Music Productions

CAST—Robert Michael Baker, Susan Flynn, Beth Leavel, Gerry McIntyre, Amelia Prentice, Sal Vivano; Ed Linderman and Ken Lundie (Pianos)

The revue was presented in two acts.

NOTES—*Broadway Jukebox* was an evening devoted to obscure Broadway (and Off Broadway) show tunes, some of them selected by the audience from a list of eighty-two relatively unknown songs. Included in the list were forty-three "Up Tempo and Comedy Songs," such as "Unrequited Love" (*Promenade*, 1969; lyric by Maria Irene Fornes, music by Al Carmines; see entry), "A Girl Can Go Wacky" (*Swing*, 1980; lyric by Alfred Uhry, music by Robert Waldman; see entry for *Dream Time*), "Feather in My Shoe" (*Come Summer*, 1969; lyric by Will Holt, music by David Baker), and "Sur Les Quais" (*Lolita, My Love*, 1970; lyric by Alan Jay Lerner, music by John Barry). Thirty-nine "Ballads and Love Songs" were listed, including "All at Once You Love Her" (*Pipe Dream*, 1955; lyric by Oscar Hammerstein II, music by Richard Rodgers), "I Never Know When (to Say When)" (*Goldilocks*, 1958; lyric by Walter Kerr, Jean Kerr, Joan Ford, music by Leroy Anderson), "His Own Little Island" (*Let It Ride!* 1961; lyric and music by Jay Livingston and Ray Evans), and "Nothing More to Look Forward To" (*Kwamina*, 1961; lyric and music by Richard Adler).

At each performance, about 30 numbers were performed. The revue included one new song, "We Love a Broadway Song," lyric and music by Ed Linderman.

214 A Broadway Musical. "A Musical About a Broadway Musical"; THEATRE: Theatre of the Riverside Church; OPENING DATE: October 10, 1978; PERFORMANCES: 26; BOOK: William F. Brown; LYRICS: Lee Adams; MUSIC: Charles Strouse; DIRECTION: George Faison; CHOREOGRAPHY: George Faison; SCENERY: Peter Wexler; COSTUMES: Randy Barcelo; LIGHTING: John DeSantis and Peter Wexler; PRODUCER: Norman Kean in association with Garth H. Drabinsky

CAST—Ron Ferrell (James Lincoln), Julius La Rosa (Eddie Bell), Larry Riley (Paul Johnson), Dan Strayhorn (Lonnie Wright), Calvin McRae (Scott Bernard), Alan Weeks (Stan Howard, African Figment), Dom Guastaferro (Sid Froman, University Figment), Helen Gallagher (Maggie Simpson), Gwyda Donhowe (Kean), Larry Marshall (Sylvester Lee, Richie Taylor), Julia Lema (Jamala King, Pleasure Figment), Sidney Anderson (Lawyer), Michael Gallagher (Lawyer), Maggie Gorrill and Loretta Devine (Stan's Ladies), Anne Francine (Shirley Wolfe), Maris Clement and Sydney Anderson and Jackee Harry (Shirley's Associates); Ensemble (Sydney Anderson, Gwen Arment, Adrian Bailey, Nate Barnett, Shirley Black-Brown, Maris Clement, Don Detrick, Loretta Devine, Michael Gallagher, Maggie Gorrill, Jackee Harry, Leon Jackson, Christina Kumi Kimball, Michael Kubala, Calvin McRae, Joni Palmer, Karen Peskow, Dan Strayhorn)

The action occurs in the present in both New York City and Washington, D.C.

The musical was presented in two acts.

ACT ONE—"Here in the Playbill" (Ron Ferrell), "A Broadway Musical" (Julius La Rosa, Ron Ferrell, Larry Riley, Dan Strayhorn, Calvin McRae, Alan Weeks, Dom Guastaferro, Helen Gallagher, Gwyda Donhowe, Ensemble), "I Hurry Home to You" (Julius La Rosa, Gwyda Donhowe), "The 1934 Hot Chocolate Jazz Babies Revue" (Larry Marshall, Ron Ferrell, Ensemble), "You Only Get One Chance" (Julia Lema, Dancers), "Lawyers" (Julius La Rosa, Dom Guastaferro, Sydney Anderson, Michael Gallagher), "A Wrong Song" (Ron Ferrell, Alan Weeks, Maggie Gorrill, Loretta Devine), "Who Says You Always Have to Be Happy?" (Helen Gallagher, Ron Ferrell), "Who Am I" (Ron Ferrell, Alan Weeks, Dom Guastaferro, Julia Lema), "Yenta Power" (Anne Francine, Maris Clement, Sydney Anderson, Jackee Harry, Ensemble), "Let Me Sing My Song" (Larry Marshall)

ACT TWO—"Out-A-Town" (Ron Ferrell, Company), "Jokes" (Ron Ferrell, Alan Weeks, Dom Guastaferro, Julia Lema, Larry Riley, Helen Gallagher, Julius La Rosa, Gwyda Donhowe, Larry Marshall), "Out-A-Town" (reprise) (Helen Gallagher, Larry Riley, Ron Ferrell, Julius La Rosa, Gwyda Donhowe, Alan Weeks, Dom Guastaferro, Larry Marshall, Julia Lema, Ensemble), "Goin' to Broadway" (Larry Marshall, Julia Lema, Ensemble), "What We Go Through" (Julius La Rosa, Gwyda Donhowe), "I've Been in Those Shoes" (Helen Gallagher, Ensemble), "Don't Tell Me" (Julius La Rosa), "Be Like a Basketball and Bounce Right Back" (Ron Ferrell, Julius La Rosa, Helen Gallagher, Gwyda Donhowe, Alan Weeks, Dom Guastaferro, Larry Riley, Ensemble), "A Broadway Musical" (reprise) (Company)

NOTES—The Broadway musical *A Broadway Musical* had its pre-Broadway tryout Off Broadway at the Theatre of the Riverside Church from October 10 through November 19, 1978, giving twenty-six performances there before opening on Broadway at the Lunt-Fontanne Theatre on December 21, where it closed after its first performance.

The musical dealt with the making of a Broadway musical, one with Black subject matter (the musical-within-the-musical was called *Sneakers*, and seemed patterned after *Runaways* [see entry]; the artwork logo of the prop playbill for *Sneakers* was similar to the logo of *Runaways*). The musical was a lighthearted look at the iffy subject matter of White writers and directors who create Black-themed Broadway musicals. The creators of *A Broadway Musical* were Charles Strouse, Lee Adams, and William F. Brown, all of whom were White. Strouse and Adams had previously written the score for *Golden Boy* (1964); while not a specifically Black musical, its star was Black and the plot dealt with racism. Brown had written the book for *The Wiz* [1975], which of course was a Black version of *The Wizard of Oz*. The director and choreographer of *A Broadway Musical* was George Faison, a Black.

Ironically, during the course of *A Broadway Musical*'s trek to Broadway, Faison was replaced by a White director and choreographer (Gower Champion, who received a "production supervised by" credit; George Bunt was credited as co-choreographer). Among the cast members, Ron Ferrell was replaced by Irving Allen Lee; Julius La Rosa by Warren Berlinger; and Helen Gallagher by Patti Karr.

Between Off Broadway and Broadway, the following songs were deleted: "Here in the Playbill," "I Hurry Home to You," "You Only Get One Chance," "A Wrong Song," "Who Says You Always Have to Be Happy?" "Who Am I," "Out-a-Town," "Goin' to Broadway," "I've Been in Those Shoes," and "Be Like a Basketball and Bounce Right Back." Added for Broadway were: "Broadway, Broadway," "Smoke and Fire," "It's Time for a Cheer-Up Song," "You Gotta Have Dancing," and "Together."

With the success of *A Chorus Line* (see entry), there was a brief vogue for musicals which dealt with putting together Broadway productions. Three, *A Broadway Musical*, *Musical Chairs* (1982; see entry), and *A Backers' Audition* (1982; see entry), were failures; however, the 1980 stage version of the 1933 film musical *42nd Street* was a long-running hit.

With *A Broadway Musical*, Charles Strouse returned to Broadway after his smash success *Annie* (1977); but the new musical seemed to jinx him, and beginning with the one-performance *A Broadway Musical*, Strouse had six consecutive Broadway failures: *Charlie and Algernon* (1979, 17 performances), *Bring Back Birdie* (1981, 4 performances), *Dance a Little Closer* (1983, 1 performance), *Rags* (1986, 4 performances; see entry for the Off Off Broadway revival), and *Nick & Nora* (1991, 9 performances). Moreover, some of his musicals (such as *Bojangles*) were never produced, others (*Annie 2: Miss Hannigan's Revenge* [1989] and *Marty* [2002]) never got beyond their tryouts. At best, Strouse had just two modest runs, both Off Broadway (*Mayor* [1985, 268 performances] and *Annie Warbucks* [1993, 200 performances]; see entries for both productions). As of this writing, *A Broadway Musical* is Lee Adams' most recent Broadway show.

The two producers of *A Broadway Musical* had even worse luck than the writers. Norman Kean was reportedly depressed over his inability to break into the Broadway-producer winner's circle (his major credit was the long-running 1976 revival of *Oh! Calcutta!* [see entry] at the Edison, a theatre which he managed), and after murdering his wife, Gwyda Donhowe (who played a producer's wife in *A Broadway Musical*), he committed suicide. As for Garth Drabinsky, he became an active producer in his native Canada and later on Broadway (among his credits are *Kiss of the Spider Woman* [1993] and *Ragtime* [1998]). However, after allegations regarding questionable accounting practices, he returned to Canada.

215 Broadway Scandals of 1928. "A New Musical Revue"; THEATRE: O'Neals' Times Square/Club Broadway (O'Neals' 43rd Street Cabaret); OPENING DATE: July 7, 1982; PERFORMANCES: 39; SCENARIO: Walter Willison; LYRICS: Walter Willison; MUSIC: Jefrey Silverman; DIRECTION: Walter Willison; CHOREOGRAPHY: Jo Anna Lehmann and Gwen Hillier Lowe; additional choreography by Douglas Norwick; SCENERY: Ron Placzek; COSTUMES: Robert Turturice; LIGHTING: Malcolm Sturchio; MUSICAL DIRECTION: Jefrey Silverman; PRODUCERS: Walter Willison and Jefrey Silverman in association with Ted Van Antwerp and David Plattner Productions/Theacom Entertainment

CAST—Jefrey Silverman (Tony), Kenny D'Aquila (Joey Staccato), Jo Anna Lehmann (Rusty Parker), Gwen Hillier Lowe (Trixie Dugan), Rose Scudder (Roberta Kelley), JESSICA JAMES (Texas Guinan), Shelley Bruce (Sandy McGuire), Steve Jerro (Big Phil Castanza), Bill Johnson (Rosie), Walter Willison (Kid Kotten); The Broadway Boys (Steve Singer, Percussion; David Reinheimer, Bass; John Reinheimer, Banjo, Guitar)

The revue was presented in two acts.

ACT ONE—Scandals Opening: "Scandals!" (Tex's Girls), "Let's Go Boating" (Jessica James, Girls), "Picture Me with You" (Shelley Bruce, Jessica James, Girls), "Scandals!" (reprise) (Jessica James, Shelley Bruce, Girls), "Nobody Needs a Man as Bad as That!" (Jessica James), "Charleston Under the Moon" (Gwen Hillier Lowe, Girls), "When You Come to the End of Your Rainbow" (Shelley Bruce), "Happy Jest Bein' with Me" (Kenny D'Aquila, Jessica James), "Blowing Bubbles in the Bathtub" (Jo Anna Lehmann, Girls), "I Gotta Hear a Song" (Shelley Bruce), "A Good Ol' Mammy Song" (Walter Willison), "Things Have Never Been Better" (Company)

ACT TWO—"The Man at the Piano" (Rose Scudder), "Sodomangamor" (Jessica James, Walter Willison, Girls), "I Couldn't Say" (Kenny D'Aquila), "Tango" (Jo Anna Lehmann, Kenny D'Aquila), "Give a Girl a Break!" (Shelley Bruce, Girls), "Broadway Wedding" (Company), "Better Bein' Loved" (Jessica James), "Scandals' Finale"/"Maxie" (Company)

NOTES—The "scenario," lyrics, and direction for the Off Off Broadway revue *Broadway Scandals of 1928* were by Walter Willison, who was also one of the co-producers as well as a member of the cast.

The revue had originally been conceived as a book musical about the relationship of Ruby Keeler and Al Jolson.

Three songs from *Broadway Scandals of 1928* were later heard in Willison and Jefrey Silverman's 1985 Off Broadway musical *Options* (see entry): "Blowing Bubbles in the Bathtub," "A Good Ol' Mammy Song," and "The Man at the Piano."

In 1980, Willison and Jefrey Silverman's revue *Front Street Gaieties* opened in Santa Monica, California; it never played New York, but was recorded by AEI Records (LP # AEI-1133). Three songs from that revue were later heard in *Options* ("Life Don't Always Work Out," "Mostly Love," and "I Went and Found Myself a Cowboy").

216 Broken Toys! THEATRE: Actors' Playhouse; OPENING DATE: July 16, 1982; PERFOR-

MANCES: 29; BOOK: Keith Berger; LYRICS: Keith Berger; MUSIC: Keith Berger; DIRECTION: Carl Haber; SCENERY: Lisa Beck; COSTUMES: Mara Lonner and Karen Dusenbury; LIGHTING: Kevin Jones; PRODUCERS: Dani Ruska and Marina Spinola

CAST—Debra Greenfield (Melissa), Keith Berger (Rooty Kazooty), Nerida Normal (Kanga), Oona Lind (Big Dolly), Cheryl Lee Stockton (Kandy), Lonnie Lichtenberg (Randy), Daud Svitzer (Golly), Lucille (Pretty Polly), Jhonny Zeitz (3-D Jesus)

The action occurs in the bedroom and attic of a suburban house.

The musical was presented in two acts (the program didn't identify song assignments).

ACT ONE—"This Life's the Right One for Me," "We're on a Shelf in Your Attic," "Play with Me," "Broken & Bent," "Let's Play Let's Stay," "I Don't Play with Humans," "Prayer Song," "Johnny Space," "Choo Choo Rap," "Lady Ride with Me," "Not of Her World," "Kangaroo Court," "I Don't Think I Like This Game"

ACT TWO—"The Temperance Song," "So Ya Wanna Be a Toy," "I Got That Other Lady's with My Baby Feeling," "Ain't Worth a Dime," "Rag Doll Rag," "Funny Wind-Up Toy," "Left Alone to Be," "Weird Fun," "Wind-Up in New York City"

NOTES—*Broken Toys!* appears to have been a fey piece trying for ironic effect; it dealt with a young girl who finds a toy soldier, which comes to life.

217 The Brooklyn Bridge. THEATRE: Quaigh Theatre; OPENING DATE: August 17, 1983; PERFORMANCES: 28; BOOK: Dorothy Chansky; LYRICS: Dorothy Chansky; MUSIC: Scott Maclarty; DIRECTION: Marjorie Melnick; CHOREOGRAPHY: Missy Whitchurch; SCENERY: Terry Bennett; COSTUMES: Karen Gerson; LIGHTING: Leslie Spohn; MUSICAL DIRECTION: Harrison Fisher; PRODUCERS: Dorothy Chansky and The Bridge Theatre Production Company

CAST—David Higlen (The Man in the Street), Anne Gartlan (Mrs. O'Malley, Lady Reporter, Landlady), Nick Jolley (William Kingsley, Eddie), Bijou Clinger (Emily Warren Roebling), Paul Merrill (Henry Murphy, General G. K. Warren), Jack Sevier (John Roebling, Dr. Smith, E.F. Farrington, Mayor Low), John Leslie Wolfe (Washington Roebling)

The action occurs in Brooklyn and New York City from 1865 to 1883, and in 1983.

The musical was presented in two acts.

ACT ONE—"Brooklyn" (Company), "Love Means" (Bijou Clinger), "Can I Do It All" (John Leslie Wolfe), "Bridge to the Future" (Jack Sevier), "Cash Politics" (Nick Jolley, Paul Merrill), "The Roebling Plan" (Company), "Love Means" (reprise) (Bijou Clinger), "Can I Do It All" (reprise) (John Leslie Wolfe), "Keep Me Out of the Cassion" (David Higlen), "When You're the Only One" (Bijou Clinger, Anne Gartlan)

ACT TWO—"Ain't No Women There" (Nick Jolley, Paul Merrill, Jack Sevier, David Higlen), "Every Day for Four Years" (Company), "The Man in the Window" (John Leslie Wolfe), "All That I Know" (Bijou Clinger), Finale (Company)

NOTES—The musical premiered on the occasion of the centennial of the Brooklyn Bridge, and dealt with the building of the bridge as well as with the professional and personal life of the bridge's architect, Washington Roebling (1837–1926). Richard F. Shepard in the *New York Times* found the modest musical "refreshingly old-fashioned in format, pleasing in its execution and easy on the ears."

218 Brownstone (1984). "A Musical"; THEATRE: Hudson Guild Theatre; OPENING DATE: May 23, 1984; PERFORMANCES: 28; BOOK: Josh Rubins, Peter Larson, and Andrew Cadiff; LYRICS: Josh Rubins; MUSIC: Peter Larson and Josh Rubins; DIRECTION: Andrew Cadiff; CHOREOGRAPHY: Cheryl Carty; SCENERY: Paul Wonsek; COSTUMES: Tom McKinley; LIGHTING: Paul Wonsek; MUSICAL DIRECTION: Yolanda Segovia; PRODUCER: Hudson Guild Theatre (David Kerry Heefner, Producing Director; Daniel Swee, Associate Director)

CAST—Loni Ackerman (Claudia), Ralph Bruneau (Stuart), Kimberly Farr (Joan), Maureen McGovern (Mary), Lenny Wolpe (Howard). The action occurs in and around a Manhattan brownstone at the present time over the course of one year (autumn to autumn). The musical was presented in two acts (individual songs weren't listed in the program).

ACT ONE—Prelude, First Movement—*Someone's Moving In,* Second Movement—*Night Thoughts*

ACT TWO—Third Movement—*Spring Cleaning,* Fourth Movement—*Someone's Moving Out,* Epilogue

NOTES—The Off Off Broadway *Brownstone* was yet another look at lives and loves in modern Manhattan, in the mode of *Company* (1970), *Sextet* (1974; see entry), *Weekend* (which had played earlier during the 1983-1984 season; see entry), and many others in this seemingly endless vogue of similarly-themed musicals.

The musical briefly resurfaced in a revised version on October 8, 1986, when it was produced by the Roundabout Theatre Company for sixty-nine performances (see entry, which includes list of musical numbers). For the 1986 revival, Kimberly Farr reprised her role of Joan, and the other cast members were Rex Smith (Stuart), Liz Callaway (Claudia), Ben Harney (Howard), and Ernestine Jackson (Mary); the book was credited to Josh Rubins and Andrew Cadiff. In 2003, Original Cast Records released a combined studio and cast album (CD # OC-6052) of a revised production which had been seen in regional theatre in 2002; the album included three new songs ("Pretty City," "If It's Time to Go," and "The Cellphone Song"); and the album's cast included Liz Callaway from the original production as well as Brian D'Arcy James, Debbie Shapiro Gravitte, and Rebecca Luker.

219 Brownstone (1986). "A New Musical"; THEATRE: The Christian C. Yegen Theatre/Roundabout Theatre Company; OPENING DATE: October 8, 1986; PERFORMANCES: 69; BOOK: Josh Rubins and Andrew Cadiff; LYRICS: Josh Rubins; MUSIC: Peter Larson and Josh Rubins; DIRECTION: Andrew Cadiff; Don Bondi, Additional Musical Staging; SCENERY: Loren Sherman; COSTUMES: Ann Emonts; LIGHTING: Richard Nelson; MUSICAL DIRECTION: Don Jones; PRODUCER: Roundabout Theatre Company (Gene Feist, Artistic Director; Todd Haimes, Executive Director)

CAST—Liz Callaway (Claudia), Rex Smith (Stuart), Ben Harney (Howard), Ernestine Jackson (Mary), Kimberly Farr (Joan)

The action occurs in and around a Manhattan brownstone at the present time over the course of one year (autumn to autumn).

The musical was presented in two acts.

ACT ONE—"Someone's Moving In" (Company), "Fiction Writer" (Ben Harney), "I Just Want to Know" (Liz Callaway), "There She Goes" (Kimberly Farr, Liz Callaway), "We Should Talk" (Ernestine Jackson, Ben Harney), "Camouflage" (Company), "Thanks a Lot" (Kimberly Farr, Rex Smith, Liz Callaway), "Neighbors Above, Neighbors Below" (Company), "I Wasn't Home for Christmas" (Rex Smith), "What Do People Do?" (Liz Callaway), "Not Today" (Kimberly Farr, Company), "The Water Through the Trees" (Kimberly Farr, Rex Smith), "You Still Don't Know" (Ernestine Jackson), "Babies on the Brain" (Ben Harney, Company), "Almost There" (Company)

ACT TWO—"Don't Tell Me Everything" (Ernestine Jackson, Ben Harney, Liz Callaway, Rex Smith), "One of Them" (Kimberly Farr, Rex Smith), "Spring Cleaning" (Liz Callaway, Rex Smith), "Fiction Writer Duet" (Ben Harney, Ernestine Jackson), "He Didn't Leave It Here" (Kimberly Farr, Liz Callaway), "It Isn't the End of the World" (Ernestine Jackson, Ben Harney), "See That Lady There" (Rex Smith, Kimberly Farr), "Since You Stayed Here" (Liz Callaway), "We Came Along Too Late" (Kimberly Farr, Rex Smith, Liz Callaway), "Hi There, Joan" (Company), "It's a Funny Thing" (Kimberly Farr, Rex Smith), "It Isn't the End of the World" (reprise) (Ben Harney), "There She Goes" (reprise) (Kimberly Farr, Liz Callaway), "Nevertheless" (Ernestine Jackson, Ben Harney), "Almost There" (reprise) (Rex Smith, Liz Callaway), "Someone's Moving Out" (Company)

NOTES—*Brownstone* was a revised version of the musical which had played Off Off Broadway in 1984 (see entry for more information about that production and about the musical's 2003 cast/studio recording). For the 1986 production, Kimberly Farr reprised her role of Joan.

For her collection *The Story Goes On/Liz Callaway On & Off Broadway* (Varese Sarabande Records CD # VSD-5585), Callaway included a song from *Brownstone* ("Since You Stayed Here").

220 Bubbe Meises Bubbe Stories. THEATRE: Cherry Lane Theatre; OPENING DATE: October 29, 1992; PERFORMANCES: 186; TEXT: Ellen Gould; LYRICS AND MUSIC: Holly Gewandter and Ellen Gould; DIRECTION: Gloria Muzio; SCENERY: David Jenkins; COSTUMES: Elsa Ward; LIGHTING: Peter Kaczorowski; MUSICAL DIRECTION: Bob Goldstone; PRODUCERS: Richard Frankel, Paragon Park Productions, and Renee Blau

CAST—Ellen Gould

The revue was presented in one act (all songs performed by Ellen Gould).

MUSICAL NUMBERS—"Bubbe Meises Bubbe Stories," "You're Dancing Inside Me," "The Road I'm Taking," "Take More Out of Life" (lyric and music by Ellen Gould), "Fifty-Fifty" (original Yiddish lyric by Louis Gilrod, English lyric by Jacques Levy, Zalman Mlotok, Moishe Rosenfeld, and Bruce Adler, music by Joseph Romshinsky), "Oy, How I Hate That Fellow Nathan" (lyric by Lew Brown, music by Albert Von Tilzer), "Oy, I Like Him" (based on "Oy, I Like She," lyric and music by Aaron Lebedeff and Alexander Olshanetsky, English lyric by Jacques Levy), "It's a Bubbe Meise" (lyric and music by Holly Gewandter and Ellen Gould), "The Bridge Song" (The Bubbe Rag) (lyric by Holly Gewandter and Ellen Gould, music by Scott Joplin), "Goldstein, Swank & Gordon," "Chocolate Covered Cherries" (lyric and music by Holly Gewandter)

NOTES—*Bubbe Meises Bubbe Stories,* a one-woman show starring Ellen Gould, covered familiar territory, that of Jewish immigrants in New York City at the turn of the twentieth century. In this case, the revue was a tribute to Gould's grandmothers ("bubbes") and their lives as young immigrants.

A cast recording was released on audiocassette only (by BMR Chrome Records). The musical was later telecast in 1994 (with Gould recreating her stage role), and in 1995 the television version was released on videocassette by SISU Home Entertainment, Inc. (# 176). In 2008, the telecast was released on DVD (by SISU).

221 Bubbling Brown Sugar. "A Musical Journey Through Harlem"; THEATRE: The Church of St. Paul and St. Andrew; OPENING DATE: February 14, 1975; PERFORMANCES: 12; BOOK: Loften Mitchell and Rosetta LeNoire; LYRICS: See song list for credits; MUSIC: See song list for credits; DIRECTION: Robert M. Cooper; CHOREOGRAPHY: Fred Benjamin; Karen Burke, Assistant Choreographer; SCENERY: Gene Fabricatore; COSTUMES: "Coordinated" by Carol Luiken; LIGHTING: Ian Johnson; PRODUCER: The AMAS Repertory Theatre, Inc. (Rosetta LeNoire, Founder and Artistic Director)

CAST—Spence Adams (Sophie, Mrs. Roberts),

Joseph (C.) Attles (Checkers, Rusty), Ethel Beatty (Ella, Club Singer), Thommie Bush (Bud, M.C.), Sandi Hewitt (Neighbor, Club Singer), Yvette Johnson (Neighbor, Stroller, Club Singer), Alton Lathrop (Neighbor, Stroller, Club Singer), Avon Long (John Sage, Bert Williams, Dusty), Mary Louise (Irene Paige), Julienne Marshall (Judy, Club Singer), Dale McIntosh (Joe, Count), Howard Porter (Jim, Lunky, Singer), Vivian Reed (Joyce, Georgia Brown, Club Singer), Anthony Whitehouse (Mr. Roberts, Dutch, Waiter)

The action occurs in Harlem between 1910-1940.

The musical was presented in two acts.

ACT ONE—"Bubbling Brown Sugar" (lyric by Lillian Lopez and Emme Kemp, music by Danny Holgate), "Harlem Sweet Harlem" (lyric by Loften Mitchell, music by Danny Holgate), "(I Ain't Never Done Nothing to) Nobody" (from *Ziegfeld Follies of 1910*; lyric and music by Axel Rogers and Bert Williams), "Some of These Days" (lyric and music by Shelton Brooks), "Through the Years" "Strolling" (music by Danny Holgate), "Honeysuckle Rose" (lyric by Andy Razaf, music by Thomas ["Fats"] Waller), "I'm Going to Tell God All My Troubles" (traditional), "His Eye Is on the Sparrow" (traditional), "Swing Low Sweet Chariot" (traditional), "Sweet Georgia Brown" (lyric and music by Maceo Pinkard, Ben Bernie, and Kenneth Casey), "Stormy Monday Blues" (lyric and music by Earl "Fatha" Hines, Billy Eckstine, and Bob Crowder), "Rosetta" (lyric and music by Earl "Fatha" Hines and Henri Woode), "S'posin'" "(In My) Solitude" (lyric by Eddie DeLange and Irving Mills, music by Duke Ellington), "Stompin' at the Savoy" (lyric by Andy Razaf, music by Benny Goodman, Edgar Sampson, and Chick Webb), "Take the 'A' Train" (lyric by Billy Strayhorn, music by Duke Ellington)

ACT TWO—"Love Will Find a Way" (*Shuffle Along*, 1922; lyric by Noble Sissle, music by Eubie Blake), "Crying My Heart Out," "Dutch's Song" (lyric and music by Emme Kemp), "Pray for the Lights to Go Out" (lyric and music by Renton Tunnah and Will Skidmore), "Brown Gal" (lyric and music by Avon Long and Lil Armstrong), "Memories of You" (*Blackbirds of 1930*; lyric by Andy Razaf, music by Eubie Blake), "Moonlight Cocktail" (lyric by Kim Gannon, music by Lucky Roberts), "I Got It Bad (and That Ain't Good)" (*Jump for Joy*, which closed in 1941 during its pre-Broadway tryout; lyric by Paul Francis Webster, music by Duke Ellington), "Harlem Tour," "Jim, Jam, Jumpin' Jive" (lyric and music by Cab Calloway), "It's All Your Fault," "God Bless the Child" (lyric and music by Arthur Herzog, Jr., and Billie Holiday), "It Don't Mean a Thing (If It Ain't Got That Swing)" (lyric by Irving Mills, music by Duke Ellington)

NOTES—Before *Ain't Misbehavin'* (1978; see entry), *Eubie!* (1978), and *Sophisticated Ladies* (1981), there was *Bubbling Brown Sugar*, which was probably the best of all the Black musicals seen in New York during the period. A few months after its Off Off Broadway production, the musical began a national tour in Summer 1975, and on March 2, 1976, it opened on Broadway at the ANTA (now August Wilson) Theatre for a run of almost two years (766 performances). The Broadway cast album was released by H & L Records (LP # 69011-698), and the script (dialogue only, no lyrics) was published by Broadway Play Publishing, Inc., in 1985. The London production opened at the Royalty Theatre on September 28, 1977, and a 2-LP cast album was released by Pye Records (# NSPD-504).

When the musical played Off Off Broadway, the action took place during the period 1910–1940; by the time the musical began its national tour, the lighter-than-air revue-like book took place in 1970 and dealt with a group of old-time performers who take the younger generation on a time-travel tour of Harlem during the hey-day of Bert Williams, Florence Mills, and other legendary Black performers.

With the endearing and devilish Avon Long and Joseph C. Attles as the main tour guides, the musical offered a number of show-stopping routines. Among the highlights were "Sweet Georgia Brown," one of the most sizzling dance sequences of the entire theatrical era, thrillingly sung and danced by Vivian Reed; "Jim, Jam, Jumpin' Jive," in which Vernon Washington, Lonnie McNeil, and Newton Winters seemed to literally dance on air; Reed's explosive rendition of "God Bless the Child"; Attles' comic and naughty "Pray for the Lights to Go Out"; Long's sweetly sad "Nobody"; and the razz-ma-tazz finale "It Don't Mean a Thing."

During most of the pre-Broadway tour, the role of Irene Paige (which was played by Mary Louise in the Off Off Broadway production) was performed by Thelma Carpenter (who had co-starred with Avon Long in the 1952 Broadway revisal of *Shuffle Along*). At the end of the tour, and for Broadway, the role was assumed by Josephine Premice. Such songs as "Through the Years," "S'posin'," and "It's All Your Fault" were heard in the Off Off Broadway production, but were dropped for the national tour and Broadway. Numbers added for the pre-Broadway national tour and for Broadway included "Harlem Makes Me Feel Alive" (lyric and music by Emme Kemp"), "Harlem '70" (lyric by Loften Mitchell, music by Danny Holgate), "There'll Be Some Changes Made" (lyric and music by Benton Overstreet and Billy Higgins), and "That's What Harlem Is to Me" (lyric by Andy Razaf, music by Russell Wooding and Paul Denniker).

222 The Bubbly Black Girl Sheds Her Chameleon Skin. THEATRE: Playwrights Horizons; OPENING DATE: June 20, 2000; PERFORMANCES: 32; BOOK: Kirsten Childs; LYRICS: Kirsten Childs; MUSIC: Kirsten Childs; DIRECTION: Wilfredo Medina; CHOREOGRAPHY: A.C. Ciulla; SCENERY: David Gallo; COSTUMES: David C. Woolard; LIGHTING: Michael Lincoln; MUSICAL DIRECTION: Fred Carl; PRODUCERS: Playwrights Horizons (Tim Sanford, Artistic Director; Leslie Marcus, Managing Director; William Russo, General Manager) in association with Wind Dance Theatre; Ira Weitzman, Associate Producer

CAST—LaChanze (Viveca), Cheryl Alexander (Miss Pain, Harriet Tubman, Secretary, Tallulah, Granny), Natalie Venetia Belcon (Emily, Nilda, Sandra), Duane Boutte (Larry, Keith), Darius de Haas (Gregory), Angel Desai (Chitty Chatty Pal #1, Secretary, Ballet Teacher, Sophia), Jerry Dixon (Jazz Teacher, Dance Captain, Lucas), Jonathan Dokuchitz (Prince, Cosmic, Policeman, Director Bob), Felicia Finley (Chitty Chatty Pal #2, Secretary, Modern Teacher, Scarlett), Robert Jason Jackson (Daddy, Policeman), Debra M. Walton (Mommy, Yolanda, Delilah)

The action occurs from the early 1960s in Los Angeles to the mid-1990s in New York City.

The musical was presented in one act.

MUSICAL NUMBERS—"Welcome to My L.A." (LaChanze, Company), "Sweet Chitty Chatty" (LaChanze, Angel Desai, Felicia Finley), "Smile, Smile" (Robert Jason Jackson, Fathes), "I Am in Dance Class" (LaChanze, Natalie Venetia Belcon, Darius de Haas, Debra M. Walton, Cheryl Alexander), "The Skate" (LaChanze, Girls in the Gym), "Sticks and Stones" (Company), "Walk on the Water" (LaChanze, Cheryl Alexander, Nightriders, Runaways), "Pass the Flame" (Ancestors #1 and #2, Debra M. Walton, LaChanze), "War Is Not Good" (Flower Children, LaChanze), "Brave New World" (Debra M. Walton, LaChanze, Company), "Give It Up" (LaChanze, Natalie Venetia Belcon, Boys & Girls), "Belle of the Ball" (LaChanze, Robert Jason Jackson, Company), "Beautiful Bright Blue Sky" (Darius de Haas, Company), "Legacy" (Jonathan Dokuchitz, Robert Jason Jackson, LaChanze, Darius de Haas), "The Argument" (LaChanze, Darius de Haas), "Wonderland" (Company), "Who's That Bubbly Black Girl?" (Company, LaChanze), "Secretarial Pool" (LaChanze, Cheryl Alexander, Angel Desai, Felicia Finley), "Pretty" (LaChanze, Back-Up Boys), "Three Dance Classes" (Three Dance Teachers, LaChanze, Duane Boutte), "Director Bob" (LaChanze, Chorines), "Come with Me" (Jerry Dixon, Company), "Come with Me" (reprise) (LaChanze), "Granny's Advice" (Cheryl Alexander, Jerry Dixon, LaChanze, Debra M. Walton, Robert Jason Jackson, Company), "Smile, Smile" (reprise) (Robert Jason Jackson), "Who's That Bubbly Black Girl?" (reprise) (Company), "Listen!" (LaChanze, Company), "The Skate" (reprise) (Company), "There Was a Girl" (LaChanze)

NOTES—*The Bubbly Black Girl Sheds Her Chameleon Skin* dealt with a young Black woman's encounters with racism and sexism in her quest to be a Broadway dancer. Jeffrey Eric Jenkins in *The Best Plays of 2000-2001* noted that despite its favorable buzz during its limited engagement at Playwrights Horizons, the musical never enjoyed a future life, perhaps because its message "makes better fodder for children's theatre or afterschool television programming." But the belated release of the cast album in 2007 by Ghostlight Records (CD # 8-4419) might give the show an eventual afterlife in regional and community theatre.

The script was published by Dramatists Play Service, Inc., in 2003.

223 The Buck Stops Here! THEATRE: The AMAS Repertory Theatre; OPENING DATE: October 27, 1983; PERFORMANCES: 16; BOOK: Norman J. Fedder; LYRICS: Richard A. Lippman; additional lyrics by Norman J. Fedder; MUSIC: Richard A. Lippman; additional music by Lea Richardson; DIRECTION: Regge Life; CHOREOGRAPHY: Tim Millett; SCENERY: Kalina Ivanov; COSTUMES: Eiko Yamaguchi; LIGHTING: Gregg Marriner; MUSICAL DIRECTION: Lea Richardson; PRODUCER: The AMAS Repertory Theatre, Inc. (Rosetta LeNoire, Founder and Artistic Director)

CAST—Scott Banfield (John Snyder, General McArthur, Ensemble), Mary Dunn (Martha Truman), Andrew Gorman (Charlie Ross, Eddie Jacobson), Janet Hayes (Tilly Brown, Reporter, Ensemble), Paul Hewitt (Paul Pendergast, Reporter, Ensemble), Janice L. Holt (Reporter, Ensemble), Laurel Lockhart (Madge Wallace), Fredric Marco (Bon Hannigan, Reporter, Ensemble), Jim McNickle (Eddie McKim, Grand Wizard, Ensemble), Kimberly Mucci (Young Bess Wallace, Young Margaret Truman), Ilona Papp (Reporter, Ensemble), Brian Pew (Young Harry Truman), Peter Piekarski (Reporter, Ensemble), Stephanie M. Pope (Reporter, Ensemble), Alexana Ryer (Bess Wallace Truman), Harris Shore (Harry S. Truman), Paul Tardi (Lloyd Stark, Reporter, Ensemble), Jacqueline Trudeau (Margaret Truman)

The action occurs between 1894 and 1953, primarily in and around Independence, Missouri, and Washington, D.C.

The musical was presented in two acts.

ACT ONE—"The Thirty-Third President" (Janet Hayes, Paul Hewitt, Janice L. Holt, Fredric Marco, Ilona Papp, Peter Piekarski, Stephanie M. Pope, Paul Tardi), "If You Try" (Mary Dunn, Brian Pew), "My Best Friend" (Kimberly Mucci, Brian Pew), "That Boy's Not Good Enough for You" (Laurel Lockhart), "Haberdashery Blues" (Harris Shore, Alexana Ryer, Customers), "That Boy's Not Good Enough for You" (reprise) (Laurel Lockhart), "When Will You Learn" (Harris Shore), "I Believe in the Man" (Alexana Ryer), "The Buck Stops Here" (Harris Shore), "My One Day" (Harris Shore), "I Believe in the Man" (reprise) (Alexana Ryer), "If You Try" (reprise) (Harris Shore), "Dear Dad" (Harris Shore, Kimberly Mucci)

ACT TWO—"Simple But Not an Ordinary Man" (Alexana Ryer, Jacqueline Trudeau, Mary Dunn), "Never Look Back" (Harris Shore), "Never Look Back" (reprise) (Harris Shore), "Harry, This Time We're Clapping for You" (Janet Hayes, Paul Hewitt, Janice L. Holt, Fredric Marco, Ilona Papp, Peter Piekarski, Stephanie M. Pope, Paul Tardi, Harris Shore), "The Buck Stops Here" (reprise) (Harris Shore), "My Best Friend" (reprise) (Harris Shore, Alexana Ryer)

NOTES—*The Buck Stops Here!* was a trite, strictly by-the-numbers musical biography of Harry S. Truman. The Off Off Broadway musical was later performed at the Baird Auditorium in the Smithsonian Institution's National Museum of Natural History for five performances. Harris Shore recreated his role of Truman, and the production included one new number ("It's Over"). The character of Bess Truman also appeared in Michael John LaChiusa's *Olio*, one of four musicals in his *First Lady Suite* (1993; see entry).

224 Bugles at Dawn. "A Musical Play"; THEATRE: The Chernuchin Theatre; OPENING DATE: October 10, 1982; PERFORMANCES: 12; BOOK: David Vando; LYRICS: David Vando; MUSIC: Mark Barkan; DIRECTION: Robert Pesola; CHOREOGRAPHY: Jerri Garner; SCENERY: David C. Woolard; COSTUMES: Johnetta Lever; LIGHTING: David N. Weiss; MUSICAL DIRECTION: Stan Free; PRODUCER: Courage Productions

CAST—Joseph Breen (Johnny Fleming), Marcus Neville (The Rebel Flagbearer), Jay Devlin (Spirit of Johnny's Father [who assumes guises of The Veteran, Sergeant Asford, and The Photographer), Brent Rogers (Recruiter, Chaplin), Edward Crotty (Oscar Redgrave), Nancy Ringham (Alma, Scarlet), Peggy Atkinson (Johnny's Mother, Battlefield Annie), Luke Lynch (A Sergeant), David Nighbert (Bill Burnside), W. Michael Crouch (J.C.), Chuck Stanley (A Lieutenant), Philip Shultz (Private Smith, Gaylord), Mimi Bessette (Cherry, Roseanna), Margaret Benczak (Ruby, Pearl)

SOURCE—The 1895 novel *The Red Badge of Courage* by Stephen Crane.

The action occurs on the battlefields of the American Civil War and in the mind of Johnny Fleming.

The musical was presented in two acts.

ACT ONE—"Marching to Victory" (Ensemble), "Blow, Bugles, Blow" (Nancy Ringham, Joseph Breen), "Take by Giving" (Peggy Atkinson), "More Is Less" (W. Michael Crouch, David Nighbert, Joseph Breen), "The Interlude" (Joseph Breen, Marcus Neville), "Alma's Poem" (Nancy Ringham, Joseph Breen), "Covered in the Rear" (Soldierettes, Philip Schultz), "Sermon" (Brent Rogers, Joseph Breen, Marcus Neville, Philip Schultz, Ensemble), "What Is Wrong with Alma" (Nancy Ringham), "Run" (Marcus Neville, Joseph Breen, Ensemble), "Give Me Love" (W. Michael Crouch), "Marching to Victory" (reprise) (Ensemble)

ACT TWO—"Picture Perfect" (Jay Devlin, Philip Shultz), "Annie's Song" (Peggy Atkinson), "Dream" (Ensemble), "Life's Odyssey" (Joseph Breen, Jay Devlin), "Battle Montage" (Nancy Ringham, Stephen Breen), "The Flag of Death" (Marcus Neville), "Marching to Victory" (reprise) (Ensemble), Finale (Ensemble)

NOTES—*Bugles at Dawn* was based on Stephen Crane's classic novel of the Civil War, *The Red Badge of Courage*. The musical was presented in showcase; including previews, it played from October 7 through October 24, 1982.

Herbert Mitgang in the *New York Times* felt the evening was a "valiant effort that has its moments," but noted that too often the musical tried for vaudeville effect and used anachronisms in a "U.S.O. style."

225 A Bundle of Nerves. "A New Musical Revue"; THEATRE: Top of the Gate; OPENING DATE: March 13, 1983; PERFORMANCES: 33; LYRICS: Geoff Leon and Edward Dunn; MUSIC: Brian Lasser; DIRECTION: Arthur Faria; SCENERY: Barry Arnold; COSTUMES: David Toser; LIGHTING: Barry Arnold; MUSICAL DIRECTION: Clay Fullum; PRODUCERS: Leonard Finger, Howard J. Burnett, and Terry Spiegel

CAST—Gary Beach, Carolyn Casanave, Ray Gill, Vicki Lewis, Karen Mason

The revue was presented in two acts.

ACT ONE—"A Bundle of Nerves" (Company), "The News" (Company), "I Eat" (Karen Mason), "She Smiled at Me" (Ray Gill), "Boogey Man" (Carolyn Casanave, Karen Mason, Vicki Lewis), "Flying" (Gary Beach), "Old Enough to Know Better" (Carolyn Casanave, Vicki Lewis), "Studs" (Gary Beach, Ray Gill), "That's What'll Happen to Me" (Carolyn Casanave), "I Don't Know How to Have Sex" (Karen Mason, Vicki Lewis, Gary Beach, Ray Gill)

ACT TWO—"The Fatality Hop" (Company), "Waiting" (Company), "After Dinner Drinks" (Carolyn Casanave, Gary Beach), "Slice of Life" (Vicki Lewis, Ray Gill), "What Do You Do" (Karen Mason), "Connie" (Ray Gill, Carolyn Casanave, Karen Mason, Vicki Lewis), "I'm Afraid" (Company), "That Sound" (Company), "A Bundle of Nerves" (reprise) (Company)

NOTES—The short-lived revue *A Bundle of Nerves* spoofed the foibles of modern neuroses. It sounds amusing, especially with cut-ups Gary Beach and Vicki Lewis in the cast. But Mel Gussow in the *New York Times* felt the revue dealt with too many phobias (eating, drinking, flying, having sex, aging, dying, even one involving a childless couple who feel disdain for their friends' children), and so he noted that while watching the revue he too developed a phobia ("fear of boredom").

Gussow singled out Karen Mason's "I Eat" as the revue's most "amusing" spoof, one in which a woman describes herself as a "calorie nymphomaniac" who is having an unrequited love affair with her refrigerator; he also enjoyed Mason's "What Do You Do," which he felt was the evening's best ballad; and he praised Gary Beach's fear of "Flying." Gussow noted the revue's funniest sight gag was a neon sign hanging over the stage which spelled out the title of the revue: the letters in the word "nerves" quivered.

226 Burlesque on Parade. THEATRE: Village Theatre; OPENING DATE: December 10, 1963; PERFORMANCES: 33; LYRICS: Eric Blau; MUSIC: David Fleischman; DIRECTION: Charlie Robinson; CHOREOGRAPHY: Elna Laun; COSTUMES: Peter Joseph; LIGHTING: Walter S. Russell; MUSICAL DIRECTION: David Fleischman; PRODUCERS: WBW Productions (Joseph Burstin, Bernard Waltzer, and Milt Warner)

CAST—Blaze Starr, Charlie Robinson, Dick Dana, Billy Reed, Ken Martin, Charley Schultz, June Knight, Jean Carroll, Paul Brown, Thelma Pelish; The New Village Corps de Burlesque (Erin Adair, Patti Boxall, Juanita Boyle, Pamela Burrell, Judy Cassmore, Altovise Gore, Billie Mahoney, Nomi Mitty, Linda Shoop, Renee Slade, John Cashman, Robert St. Clair); La Troupe Classique (Lorraine DeLong, Joan Lynn, Deeda Hymes)

The revue was presented in two acts (sketch and song assignments unknown).

ACT ONE—Prologue, "Talking Man," "Parade," "Flirtation Scene," "Lollitapop," "Arabella," "Bright Footed," "Moanin' Low," "Easy Does It," "Stage Door," "Circus"

ACT TWO—"Calendar Girls," "Pantomime Wine," "Kiss Off," "Jazz Games," "I Love Paris," "Dishes," "Funny Bunny," "Court Room Scene," "Passing Parade," "Passion Street," Finale

NOTES—Blaze Starr was the star of *Burlesque on Parade*; the supporting cast included Charley Robinson, who had appeared with Ann Corio in *This Was Burlesque* (1962, see entry), and Broadway veteran Thelma Pelish, of the original casts of *The Pajama Game* (1954) and *Milk and Honey* (1961).

Burlesque on Parade was gone in a month. *This Was Burlesque* had cornered the market on burlesque revues, and there wasn't much demand for more of the same. But that didn't keep optimistic producers from trying to hit the jackpot with other *This Was Burlesque*-styled revues, including *International Playgirls '64* (1964), *The Wonderful World of Burlesque* (1965), and *Follies Burlesque '67* (1967); see entries; also see Appendix J.

227 Bush Is Bad. "The Musical Cure for the Blue-State Blues"; THEATRE: Triad Theatre; OPENING DATE: September 29, 2005; PERFORMANCES: 200 (estimated); LYRICS: Joshua Rosenblum; MUSIC: Joshua Rosenblum; DIRECTION: Gary Slavin; Janet Bushor, Assistant Director; CHOREOGRAPHY: Gary Slavin; Janet Bushor, Assistant Choreographer; COSTUMES: Anne Auberjonois; LIGHTING: Tonya Pierre; PRODUCERS: Tim Peierls and Shrubbery Productions

CAST—Kate Baldwin, Neal Mayer, Michael McCoy, Joshua Rosenblum (Piano)

The revue was presented in one act.

MUSICAL NUMBERS—"How Can 59 Million People Be So Dumb?" (Company), "Bush Is Bad Intro" (Company), "Bush Is Bad" (Company), "New Hope for the Fabulously Wealthy" (Company), "Das Busch Ist Schlecht" (Michael McCoy), "Good Conservative Values I" (Company), "The Gay Agenda" (Neal Mayer), "I May Be Gay (But I'm No Lesbian)" (Company), "I'm Losing You, Karl" (Company), "Love Song of W. Mark Felt" (Neal Mayer, Kate Baldwin), "John Bolton Has Feelings, Too" (Michael McCoy), "Crazy Ann Coulter" (Kate Baldwin), "Lying Liars" (Company), "Survivor: Beltway Scumbag Edition" (Company), "The 'I' Word" (Company), "Get Real" (Kate Baldwin), "The Inauguration Was Marvelous" (Neal Mayer), "Good Conservative Values II" (Company), "Culture of Life" (Company), "Beaten by a Dead Man" (Michael McCoy), "Sure, You Betcha, Georgie" (Kate Baldwin), "In His Own Words" (Company), "On Our Way" (Company), "Good Conservative Values III" (Encore) (Company)

NOTES—*Bush Is Bad* was an Off Off Broadway revue which bashed President George W. Bush, Republicans, and conservatives. The partisan revue didn't seem to tolerate any beliefs and views but its own; as Neil Genzlinger in the *New York Times* noted, works of this nature preach to the converted and "lead them in comfortably laughing or booing at familiar targets."

The revue was first presented by the York Theatre Company as part of its developmental reading series, and then opened at the Triad Theatre in September 2005, where it played until August 2006. The revue reopened a few weeks later in a revised edition titled *Bush Is Bad/Impeachment Edition*, which closed on December 30, 2006. For much of its run, the revue was presented on an abbreviated schedule of three performances a week.

The revised edition contained about seventy-five percent new material, including thirteen new numbers: "Wake Me When It's 2009," "Anyone Can Grow Up to Be President," "The Man from Diebolt," "Torture Has Been Very Good to Me," "You Can Never Have Enough Bush," "Down in Crawford," "The Social Security Song," "Won't You Please," "Our Job," "Poor Jack Abramoff," "Mr. Whittington Regrets," "Heck of a Job," and "Can't Help Lovin' That Bush."

After the revue's closing, Joshua Rosenblum, its creator, announced the next edition might be titled *Bush Is Bad/Lame Duck Edition*, or, if the Democrats didn't do well in the House and the Senate, other editions might be titled *Pelosi Is Pathetic* or *Reid Is Ridiculous*.

The information in the credits section as well as in the song list is taken from the cast album, which was released on OC/Original Cast Records (CD # OC-6160).

A similar preaching-to-the-converted Bush-bashing revue during the same period was *Bush Wars* (subtitled "Musical Revenge") which opened at the Rattlesnake Theatre in March 2006 with song parodies and sketches conceived by Jim Russek and written by Nancy Holson; first scheduled as a limited run through April 16, the revue transferred to the Actors' Playhouse and played there for the better part of the year. George Hunka in the *New York Times* wrote that if the thought of President Bush, Osama bin Laden, and their mothers "engaging in a salad-fork duel at an Olive Garden restaurant to the tune of 'America,' from *West Side Story*, sound appealing, this show is for you."

228 Bush Wars.
NOTES—See entry for *Bush Is Bad*.

229 Buskers. "The New Musical"; THEATRE: Stage Arts Center/Actors Outlet Theatre Center; OPENING DATE: April 27, 1986; PERFORMANCES: Unknown; BOOK: Howard Goldberg; LYRICS: Howard Goldberg; MUSIC: Howard Goldberg; DIRECTION: Howard Goldberg; CHOREOGRAPHY: Lillo Way; SCENERY: Chris J. Shriver; COSTUMES: Muriel Stockdale; LIGHTING: Betsy M. Pool; MUSICAL DIRECTION: Hillel Dolgenas; PRODUCERS: Howard Goldberg and Aumont Productions

CAST—Tony Azito, Timothy Bennett, Sasha Charnin, Bob Flannigan, Kimberly Hall, JoAnn Hunter, Phil LaDuca, Anthony Marciona, Krista Tesreau, Lyn Vaux, Jim Wagg, Kelly Woodruff

The musical was presented in two acts (the program didn't credit song assignments).

ACT ONE—"Power in the Air," "I Walk Alone," "Movie Stars"/"Monday Mornings," "Down to the Foodstore," "All of My Love," "Myrna P.," "Pain in My Heart," "Selena," "Born to Love"

ACT TWO—"Love at First Sight," "Hinton Went Down," "My Parents' House," "Alien Love," "Soap Is Good for You," "I Know What Love Can Bring," "Etude," "Maybe I'm Lonely," "Ice Cream"

NOTES—*Buskers* was an Off Off Broadway presentation.

230 But Never Jam Today. THEATRE: Urban Arts Corps Theatre; OPENING DATE: August 1978; PERFORMANCES: 12; BOOK: Vinnette Carroll; DIRECTION: Vinnette Carroll; CHOREOGRAPHY: Talley Beatty; SCENERY: Marty Kappell; LIGHTING: Jeffrey Schissler; PRODUCER: Urban Arts Corps (Vinnette Carroll, Artistic Director; Anita MacShane, Managing Director)

CAST—Clinton Derricks-Carroll, Cleavant Derricks, Marilynn Winbush, Reginald Vel Johnson

SOURCE—Various works by Lewis B. Carroll.

NOTES—In May and June of 1978, Vinnette Carroll's fascinating *Alice* opened and quickly closed during its Philadelphia tryout. With a terrific cast which included Debbie Allen in the title role, a good, solid score by Micki Grant, galvanic choreography, and striking décor, the musical's short tryout run was heartbreaking. It was a musical which deserved a second chance. Vinnette Carroll then revisited the basic source material by Lewis B. Carroll with a version titled *But Never Jam Today*, which she had first developed with Anita MacShane at the Actors Studio in 1962 and which was later presented at New York City Center for one performance on April 23, 1969. For this version, the "Afro-American Adaptation" was by Carroll, and the music by Gershon Kingsley; it was directed by Carroll, the choreography was by Talley Beatty, and the cast included Marie Thomas (as Alice) and Sherman Hemsley (as the Mad Hatter and the Seven of Spades). In August 1978, just a few weeks after *Alice*'s closing, *But Never Jam Today* was seen in a workshop production for a limited Off Off Broadway run of twelve performances.

A year later, on July 31, 1979, *But Never Jam Today* opened on Broadway at the Longacre Theatre; the adaptation was credited to Vinnette Carroll and Bob Larimer, the lyrics were by Larimer, and the music was composed by Larimer and Bert Keyes (Larimer had earlier provided the score for *King of the Whole Damn World* [see entry]).

Unfortunately, the new version played just eight performances. Mel Gussow in the *New York Times* found the "contemporary, urbanized" musical "a rabbit's hole away from the spirit and the humor of the original" source material by Carroll. The critics noted the score was an eclectic mixture of blues, gospel, ballads, calypso, rock, boogie woogie, reggae, disco, and Kurt Weill-styled music, and Joel Siegel on WABC-TV said "as a concert it's a hit. Unfortunately, it's not a concert." He regretted that the book got "curiouser and curiouser" and never really pulled itself together to tell a coherent story.

The Broadway version was presented in two acts, with the following songs:

ACT ONE—"Curiouser and Curiouser," "Twinkle, Twinkle Little Star," "Long Live the Queen," "A Real Life Lullabye," "The More I See People," "My Little Room," "But Never Jam Today," "Riding for a Fall," "All the Same to Me," "I've Got My Orders"

ACT TWO—"God Could Give Me Anything," "But Never Jam Today" (reprise), "I Like to Win," "And They All Call the Hatter Mad," "Jumping from Rock to Rock," "They," "Long Live the Queen" (reprise), "I've Got My Orders" (reprise)

For a list of musicals adapted from the works of Lewis B. Carroll, see entry for *Alice with Kisses*; also see Appendix K.

231 Butterfly McQueen and Friends. THEATRE: Bert Wheeler Theatre; OPENING DATE: August 4, 1969; PERFORMANCES: 7; PIANIST: Joe Burns; COSTUMES: African Market, Inc.; PRODUCER: "The United States of America"

CAST—BUTTERFLY MCQUEEN, Wanetta Hope, Jonathan Nicoll, Paul Searcy, Delilah Jackson, Jill Jackson, William Hoffler, Mitchell Marco

The revue was presented in two acts.

NOTES—Beloved character actress Butterfly McQueen, who had recently joined the cast of *Curley McDimple* (1967; see entry), offered this self-described "happening" on a succession of Monday nights when *Curley McDimple* was dark. The evening included songs, dances, and reminiscences.

232 Buy Bonds, Buster! "A New 40s Musical"; THEATRE: Theatre de Lys; OPENING DATE: June 4, 1972; PERFORMANCES: 1; BOOK: Jack Holmes; LYRICS: Jack Holmes; MUSIC: Bill Conklin and Bob Miller; DIRECTION: John Bishop; CHOREOGRAPHY: Bick Goss; SCENERY: William Pitkin; LIGHTING: William Strom; MUSICAL DIRECTION: Shelly Markham; PRODUCER: Wits' End

CAST—William Dalton (Jamie, Joey), Phil Erickson (J.P., FDR, Sgt. Cracker), Suellen Estey (Bea, Betty), Jay Gregory (Nicholas, Tony), Winston DeWitt Hemsley (Tommy, Harrington, Redcap, Washburn, Syracuse), Pamela Hunt (Debbie, Trixie), Virginia Martin (Veronica, Eunice), Rick Podell (Elmer, Flatbush), Jane Robertson (Fannie, Martha), Rowena Rollins (Lollie, Eleanor Roosevelt, Sgt. Crisp), Frank Root (Clay, Student)

The action occurs in the present as well as in the early 1940s.

The musical was presented in two acts (division of acts and song assignments unknown; songs are listed in performance order).

MUSICAL NUMBERS—"Pearl," "So Long for Now," "The Freedom Choo-Choo (Is Leavin' Today)," "Tan 'n' Hot," "Dreamboat from Dreamland," "These Are Worth Fighting For," "The Woogie Boogie," "Canteen Serenade," "Donuts for Defense," "Now and Then," "The Master Race Polka," "Us Two," "Flim Flam Flooie," "When the Bluebirds Fly All Over the World," "Hat Crossover," "Buy Bonds, Buster," "Chico Chico," "My G.I. Joey," "O Say Can You See"

NOTES—The busy 1972-1973 Off Broadway season began with a one-performance flop, *Buy Bonds, Buster!* a revised version of *O Say Can You See!* (see entry), which had played for one month in 1962 and had left behind an ingratiating cast album (unlabeled LP # 76-34; AEI Records CD # AEI-CD-034).

The earlier musical had taken place in the War Forties, but the revised version, which premiered in Atlanta, alternated between the 1940s and the present time. The new version, which in Atlanta was titled *O Say Did You See!* (the liner notes of *O Say Can You See!* indicate the new title was inspired by a comment made by Ben Bagley regarding the brief run of the original production), played for a year in Atlanta, and was eventually brought to New York under the title of *Buy Bonds, Buster!* In reviewing *Buy Bonds, Buster!* for the *New York Times*, Clive Barnes noted the production originated in Atlanta and "will doubtless soon be gone with the wind." He also felt the musical was a formulaic evening of nostalgic references on the order of *Dames at Sea* (see entry), but, to be fair, *O Say Can You See!* had opened six years before the premiere of *Dames at Sea*.

Numbers written for the new version were: "Pearl," "So Long for Now," "Tan 'n' Hot," "The Woogie Boogie," "Now and Then," "Hat Crossover," and the intriguingly titled "The Master Race Polka." Numbers from the original 1962 production not used in *Buy Bonds, Buster!* were "Take Me Back to Texas," "Someone a Lot Like You," "Veronica Takes Over," and "Just the Way You Are." "Us Two" had been dropped during the run of *O Say Can You See!* and wasn't included on its cast recording; it wasn't used in *Buy Bonds, Buster!* either, but when *O Say Can You See!* was issued on CD, "Us Two" was recorded and included on the reissue as a bonus track.

233 Buzzsaw Berkeley. "The Musical with a Touch of Slash!"; THEATRE: WPA Theatre; OPENING DATE: August 1, 1989; PERFORMANCES: 28; BOOK: Doug Wright; LYRICS: Michael John LaChiusa; MUSIC: Michael John LaChiusa; DIRECTION: Christopher Ashley; CHOREOGRAPHY: Joe Lanteri; SCENERY: Edward T. Gianfrancesco; COSTUMES: Don Newcomb; LIGHTING: Craig Evans; PRODUCER: WPA Theatre (Kyle Renick, Artistic Director; Donna Lieberman, Managing Director)

CAST—Peter Bartlett (Mr. Krupps, James Looney, Zack Fleece, Ace), Shauna Hicks (Judy Gorgon), Keith Reddin (Mickey Looney), John Hickok (Edgore Soames, Howie Stubbs), Ethyl Eichelberger (Old Miss Soames, Mary Looney, Buzzsaw Berkeley), Becky Gelke (Mona Starch), Vicki Lewis (Prudy Doody)

NOTES—The Off Off Broadway musical *Buzzsaw Berkeley* (subtitled "The Musical with a Touch of Slash!") is an early work by Michael John LaChiusa. The flyer for the production indicated the plot dealt with kids "full of pluck and moxie" who live in a world without music because a serial killer is murdering all the singers and dancers in their hometown of Grave Hollow. When a show-biz producer comes to town, it looks as if the kids can put on a show in the barn, but little do they know that they'll be "singing and dancing for their lives" because the producer is actually Buzzsaw Berkeley, the deranged killer. In fact, Mel Gussow in the *New York Times* noted that one of the evening's most amusing lines occurred when on the opening night of the kids' musical Mickey Looney tells the cast, "We're all going out on the stage tonight, but we're not all coming back."

Gussow mentioned that although the evening was a crossbreed of *Babes in Arms*, *Summer Stock*, and *The Texas Chain Saw Massacre*, the work was "paltry as a musical satire." But he singled out "I'm Taking This Show to Hell," in which a Stephen Sondheim-like number morphed into Cole Porter. The musical's second act included a mini-musical called *The History of Civilization*, and for the patriotic finale Ethyl Eichelberger portrayed the Statue of Liberty. Certainly any musical in which Ethyl Eichelberger impersonated the Statue of Liberty had to have been worth seeing.

234 By Bernstein. THEATRE: The Westside Theatre; OPENING DATE: November 23, 1975; PERFORMANCES: 17; CONTINUITY DIALOGUE: Betty Comden and Adolph Green; LYRICS: See song list for credits; MUSIC: Leonard Bernstein; DIRECTION: Michael Bawtree; SCENERY: Lawrence King and Michael H. Yeargan; COSTUMES: Lawrence King and Michael H. Yeargan; LIGHTING: Marc B. Weiss; MUSICAL DIRECTION: Clay Fullum; PRODUCERS: The Chelsea Theatre Center of Brooklyn (Robert Kalfin, Artistic Director; Michael David, Executive Director; and Burl Hash (Production Director)

CAST—Jack Bittner, Margery Cohen, Jim Corti, Ed Dixon, Patricia Elliott, Kurt Peterson, Janie Sell

The revue was presented in one act.

MUSICAL NUMBERS—"Welcome" (lyric by Betty Comden and Adolph Green; song was probably especially written for *By Bernstein*) (Company), "Gabey's Comin'" (written for, but not used in, *On the Town*, 1944; lyric by Betty Comden and Adolph Green) (Kurt Peterson, Janie Sell, Margery Cohen), "Lonely Me" (written for, but not used in, *On the Town*, 1944; lyric by Leonard Bernstein) (Kurt Peterson), "Say When" (written for, but not used in, *On the Town*, 1944; lyric by Betty Comden and Adolph Green) (Patricia Elliott), "I'm Afraid It's Love" (written for, but not used in, *On the Town*, 1944); lyric by Betty Comden and Adolph Green) (Kurt Peterson), "Like Everybody Else" (written for, but not used in, *West Side Story*, 1957; lyric by Stephen Sondheim) (Janie Sell, Ed Dixon, Jim Corti), "I'm Afraid It's Love" (reprise) (Kurt Peterson), "(And So I've Had) Another Love" (source unknown; lyric by Betty Comden, Adolph Green, and Leonard Bernstein) (Patricia Elliott), "I Know a Fellow" (source unknown; lyric by Leonard Bernstein) (Jim Corti), "It's Got to Be Bad to Be Good" (written for, but not used in, *On the Town*, 1944; lyric by Leonard Bernstein) (Janie Sell, Jim Corti), "Dream with Me" (apparently written for *Peter Pan*, 1950; lyric by Betty Comden, Adolph Green, and Leonard Bernstein) (Margery Cohen, Ed Dixon, Company), "(And So I've Had) Another Love" (reprise) (Company), "Ringaroundarosy" (written for, but not used in, *Candide*, 1956; lyric by John LaTouche), (Ed Dixon, Jim Corti, Company), "Captain Hook's Soliloquy" (a/k/a "The Captain Hook Aria — Soliloquy") (written for, but not used in, *Peter Pan*, 1950; lyric by Leonard Bernstein) (Jack Bittner), "The Riobamba" (music adapted from Bernstein's 1944 ballet *Fancy Free*; lyric by Leonard Bernstein) (Patricia Elliott, Janie Sell, Margery Cohen, Company), "The Intermission's Great" (written for, but not used in, *On the Town*, 1944; lyric by Betty Comden and Adolph Green) (Company), "The Story of My Life" (written for, but not used in, *Wonderful Town*, 1953; lyric by Betty Comden and Adolph Green) (Janie Sell), "Ain't Got No Tears Left" (music adapted from Bernstein's 1949 symphony *Age of Anxiety*; lyric by Leonard Bernstein) (Patricia Elliott), "The Coolie's Dilemma" (appears to have been written for unproduced musical *The Exception and the Rule*, or *A Pray by Bletch*; lyric by Jerry Leiber) (Jim Corti, Company), "In There" (appears to have been written for unproduced musical *The Exception and the Rule*, or *A Pray by Bletch*; lyric by Stephen Sondheim) (Jack Bittner, Jim Corti, Company), "Here Comes the Sun" (written for unproduced musical version of *The Skin of Our Teeth*; lyric by Betty Comden and Adolph Green) (Company), "Spring Will Come Again" (written for unproduced musical version of *The Skin of Our Teeth*; lyric by Betty Comden and Adolph Green) (Margery Cohen, Company), "Here Comes the Sun" (reprise) (Company)

NOTES—In 1965, *Leonard Bernstein's Theatre Songs*, which included only familiar Bernstein material, ran for eighty-eight performances (see entry). On the other hand, the more imaginative *By Bernstein* offered unfamiliar Bernstein songs, and played for just two weeks. Go figure. But those venturesome theatergoers who sought out *By Bernstein* were treated to an evening of extremely obscure theatre songs by one of the masters of musical theatre. In fact, one of the advertisements for the revue proclaimed the evening was "a celebration of the newly liberated theatre music of Leonard Bernstein heretofore existing only in exile."

The revue was performed in one act. During previews, there were two acts, with an intermission between "The Riobamba" and "The Intermission's Great." The program for *By Bernstein* is one of the most curious of all Off Broadway (and Broadway) programs: It was a large-magazine-sized program designed in the format of a book of matches, and, when opened, the performers' bios were part of the "matches" themselves.

The musical was originally titled *The Bernstein Show*, and an early script not only includes "Like Everybody Else," which was deleted from *West Side Story*, but also two other numbers which were cut from that iconic musical ("Rocket to the Moon" and "Mix").

The revue included two songs ("Here Comes the Sun" and "Spring Will Come Again") from Comden, Green, and Bernstein's unproduced musical version of *The Skin of Our Teeth* (Phyllis Newman's *The Madwoman of Central Park West* [see entry] also included a song from the adaptation ["Up, Up, Up"] which was recorded on that show's cast album). For information about another musical version of *The Skin of Our Teeth*, see entry for the John Kander and Fred Ebb tribute revue *2 by 5*.

235 By Hex. "A Musical Play"; THEATRE: Tempo Playhouse; OPENING DATE: June 18, 1956; PERFORMANCES: 40; BOOK: John Rengier; LYRICS: Howard Blankman; additional lyrics by Richard Gehman and John Rengier; MUSIC: Howard Blankman; DIRECTION: Bill Penn; CHOREOGRAPHY: Ed Balin; SCENERY: Ed Flesh; COSTUMES: Rennie Procopio; LIGHTING: Jules Moffitt; MUSICAL DIRECTION: George Seaman; PRODUCERS: Lester Hackett, George Ortman, and Julie Bovasso

CAST—Robert Caesar (Bishop), Wynne Miller (Nancy), Rita Shay (Lydia), Ken Cantril (Jonas), Diane Griffith (Annie), Tom Mixon (Eli), Bob David (David), Lewis Kraus (Tractor Salesman), Jerry Wallace (Luther), Anita Huffington (Rebecca), Tom Pocorobba (Henner), Lucie Gillam (Alma), Arnold Soboloff (Jailer) (NOTE—For the published script, the character of Luther was re-named Levi.)

SOURCE—Based on an idea suggested by Richard Gehman.

The action occurs at the present time in Lancaster County, Pennsylvania.

The musical was presented in two acts.

ACT ONE—"Market Day" (Robert Caesar, Company), "Shunned" (Robert Caesar), "Ferhuddled and Ferhexed" (Wynne Miller), "Wonderful Good" (Rita Shay, Tom Mixon, Company), "Wonderful Bad" (Rita Shay, Tom Mixon), "Antiques" (performer unknown) (Note: This number is not in the published script.) "What Is Love?" (Diane Griffith), "I Can Learn" (Ken Cantril, Wynne Miller), "What Is Love?" (reprise) (Wynne Miller), "Shunned" (reprise) (Robert Caesar, Company), "Only a Man" (Robert Caesar) ACT TWO, "An Amishman" (Tom Mixon, Rita Shay, Jerry Wallace, Anita Huffington, Tom Pocorobba, Lucie Gillam), "I Have Lived" (Diane Griffith), "I Know My Love" (Wynne Miller), "The Trouble with Me" (Ken Cantril), "Something New" (Ken Cantril, Wynne Miller), "It Takes Time" (Robert Caesar), "An Amishman" (reprise) (Company)

NOTES—*By Hex* would appear to be a *Plain and Fancy* (1955) wannabe, but, in fact, this musical about Amish life premiered in Lancaster, Pennsylvania, on August 20, 1953, a full seventeen months before *Plain and Fancy* opened on Broadway. But it also appears that *By Hex* (which opened in New York three months after *Plain and Fancy* closed) wouldn't have been produced Off Broadway but for the success of *Plain and Fancy* and the producers' hope that New York was ready for another Amish musical. (It wasn't.) But the show found some success in regional theatre, and the script, published by Dramatists Play Service, Inc., in 1956, is still in print. The cast album was recorded on LP by a private label and had extremely limited distribution.

Although the musical dealt with a rebellious Amish farmer (who is shunned when he buys a tractor) and his romance with the headstrong daughter of one of the sect's elders, all ends well when the independent twosome realize they belong with their community.

Arthur Gelb in the *New York Times* found a lot to like: the "fresh and winsome" cast, "bright and airy" scenery, and a "pleasant and literate" score (he singled out "I Can Learn" and "Something New" as two "charming" ballads). He also praised a "gay and wonderful" bucolic dance which opened the second act. Gelb also noted that the entire orchestra consisted of one organ, which he found "eminently suitable" for the musical.

Eight musical numbers which appeared in the original Pennsylvania production weren't used in the Off Broadway version: "Don't Be Afraid," "The Senoritas" (*"The Senoritas"*—?? !!), "Marriage Is Fer Me (But Not to You)," "Getting Ready for a Wedding," "Hexed," "The Hex Ballet," "Hand in Hand," and "Bachelor Song." Incidentally, Wynne Miller was the niece of legendary band leader Glenn Miller. She later appeared in *A Thurber Carnival* and *Tenderloin* (both 1960), and her lovely voice and presence should have established her along with Anita Gillette and Susan Watson as one of the leading ingénues of the 1960s. But after *Tenderloin* she seems to have disappeared.

236 By Jupiter. THEATRE: Theatre Four; OPENING DATE: January 19, 1967; PERFORMANCES: 118; BOOK: Richard Rodgers and Lorenz Hart; additional material by Fred Ebb; LYRICS: Lorenz Hart; MUSIC: Richard Rodgers; DIRECTION: Christopher Hewett; CHOREOGRAPHY: Ellen Ray; SCENERY: Herbert Senn and Helen Pond; COSTUMES: Winn Morton; LIGHTING: Robert L. Steele; MUSICAL DIRECTION: Milton Setzer; PRODUCERS: Robert Cherin in association with Christopher Hewett

CAST—Robert R. Kaye (Theseus), Emory Bass (Homer), Charles Rydell (Hercules), Richard Marshall (Herald), Ben Gerard (Achilles), Rosemarie Heyer (Buria), Renata Vaselle (Sergeant, Penelope), Fayn Le Veille (First Sentry), Alice Glenn (Second

Sentry, Messenger, Hunter), Joyce Maret (Third Sentry, Trumpeter), Ronnie Cunningham (Caustica), Norma Doggett (Heroica), Irene Byatt (Pomposia), Debra Lyman (Trumpeter, A Runner), Jackie Alloway (Hippolyta), BOB DISHY (Sapiens), Sheila Sullivan (Antiope); Amazon and Greek Women: Violetta Landek, Fayn Le Veille, Alice Glenn, Renata Vaselle, Joyce Maret, Debra Lyman; Greek Warriors and Men: Hamp Dickens, Fred Kimbrough, Richard Natkowski, Ben Gerard

SOURCE—The 1932 play *The Warrior's Husband* by Julian F. Thompson.

The action occurs in ancient Greece.

The musical was presented in two acts.

ACT ONE—"For Jupiter and Greece" (Robert R. Kaye, Emory Bass, Charles Rydell, Richard Marshall, Greek Men), "Ride, Amazon, Ride" (Rosemarie Heyer, Amazons), "Jupiter Forbid" (Jackie Alloway, Irene Byatt, Ronnie Cunningham, Norma Doggett, Amazon Warriors and Men), "Life with Father" (Bob Dishy, Amazon Men), "Nobody's Heart" (Susan Sullivan), "In the Gateway of the Temple of Minerva" (Robert R. Kaye), Ballet (Renata Vaselle, Ronnie Cunningham, Norma Doggett, Fayn Le Veille, Violetta Landek, Alice Glenn, Debra Lyman, Joyce Maret, Hamp Dickens, Richard Natkowski, Ben Gerard, Fred Kimbrough), "Life with Father" (reprise) (Bob Dishy, Irene Byatt), "Here's a Hand" (Robert R. Kaye, Sheila Sullivan), Finale Act One ("No, Mother, No") (Jackie Alloway, Irene Byatt, Bob Dishy, Ronnie Cunningham, Norma Doggett, Amazon Warriors and Men)

ACT TWO—"Wait Till You See Her" (Robert R. Kaye, Emory Bass, Richard Marshall, Charles Rydell, Greek Men), "The Boy I Left Behind Me" (Rosemarie Heyer, Amazons), "Nobody's Heart" (reprise) (Bob Dishy), "Ev'rything I've Got" (Jackie Alloway, Bob Dishy), "Bottoms Up" (Jackie Alloway, Sheila Sullivan, Richard Marshall, Emory Bass, Ben Gerard, Ronnie Cunningham, Norma Doggett, Amazon Warriors, Greek Warriors), "Careless Rhapsody" (Sheila Sullivan, Robert R. Kaye), Finaletto (Jackie Alloway, Bob Dishy, Irene Byatt, Ronnie Cunningham, Norma Doggett, Amazon Warriors), "Ev'rything I've Got" (reprise) (Jackie Alloway), "Now That I've Got My Strength" (Bob Dishy, Camp Followers, Greek Men), Finale (Company)

NOTES—After the tremendous success of the Off Broadway revival of *The Boys from Syracuse* (1963; see entry), Rodgers and Hart's other "Greek" musical, *By Jupiter,* seemed an obvious candidate for revival. With its built-in humor (war-mongering women, effeminate men) and its wonderful score, *By Jupiter* seemed a natural. Moreover, it hadn't been seen in New York since its original production, which opened at the Shubert Theatre on June 3, 1942.

Based on *The Warrior's Husband* (which had featured Katharine Hepburn in the role of Antiope), *By Jupiter* had starred Ray Bolger, and its run of 427 performances was the longest of all the original Rodgers and Hart productions (in fact, it ran almost twice as long as the 1938 production of *The Boys from Syracuse*). But the Off Broadway production faltered after three months. Happily, the lively score was recorded by RCA Victor (LP # LOC-1137 and LSO-1137; later issued on CD by DRG Records [# DRG-CD-19105]), and the sparkling cast album remains the only complete recording of one of Rodgers and Hart's most attractive scores.

The revival reinstated one of Rodgers' most beguiling waltzes, "Wait Till You See Her," which had been heard during the musical's tryout but dropped from the Broadway production at the last minute (literally, because the Broadway playbills had already been printed for the show's first week, and the number was in the song listing). What's especially surprising is that the song continued to appear in the playbills for most if not all of the New York run. Some sources indicate the song was performed on opening night and throughout the run; however, the song may have been dropped before the opening, but reinstated at some point during the show's run. Although there's no evidence to support the latter scenario, it's certainly possible. With three ballads in the show ("Nobody's Heart," "Careless Rhapsody," and "Wait Till You See Her"), perhaps George Abbott thought one was expendable, and so "Wait Till You See Her" was dropped. Further, "Wait Till You See Her" was sung very late in the second act (the Off Broadway revival placed the song at the beginning of the second act), and so perhaps Abbott felt the song slowed up the musical at the moment when it was time to start wrapping up the action.

The evidence for assuming the song wasn't heard on the Broadway opening night comes indirectly from the eight New York newspaper critics who reviewed the musical. In those days, critics devoted a good portion of their reviews to discussions of a show's songs, and they particularly liked to predict which numbers would soon be heard in the better boites or on the nation's jukeboxes. The eight critics singled out the following songs: "Nobody's Heart" (five of eight critics), "In the Gateway of the Temple of Minerva" (four), "Life with Father" (four), "Jupiter Forbid" (three), "Here's a Hand" (three), "Ev'rything I've Got" (two),"Careless Rhapsody" (one), "No, Mother, No" (one), and "Bottoms Up" (one). Not one of the eight critics referred to "Wait Till You See Her," and surely this exquisite waltz, one of the finest in the Rodgers' songbook, would have been mentioned by at least one or more of the critics if the song had been heard on opening night.

But the score of *By Jupiter* doesn't just rest on "Wait Till You See Her." "Nobody's Heart" is one of the loveliest of ballads, "Ev'rything I've Got" is the supreme song of comic insults, and the jubilant almost-title song "Jupiter Forbid" is one of the most pulsating and rhythmic in the Rodgers and Hart catalogue. And one can't forget "In the Gateway of the Temple of Minerva," in which the hero tells us he was given the gate.

The revival included every song from the original production, including "No, Mother, No," which was incorporated into the first act finale and was not specifically listed in the revival's program or on the cast album.

237 By Strouse. "An Evening of Music by Charles Strouse, The Broadway Composer"; THEATRE: The Ballroom; OPENING DATE: February 1, 1978; PERFORMANCES: 156; LYRICS: Lee Adams and Martin Charnin; additional lyrics by David Rogers and Fred Tobias; MUSIC: Charles Strouse; DIRECTION: Charles Strouse; CHOREOGRAPHY: Mary Kyte; SCENERY: Connie and Peter Wexler; MUSICAL DIRECTION: Randy Barnett; PRODUCER: Norman Kean

CAST—Gary Beach, Donna Marshall, Maureen Moore, Gail Nelson

The revue was presented in one act (song assignments were not credited in the program).

MUSICAL NUMBERS—"Stick Around" (from *Golden Boy*, 1964; lyric by Lee Adams), "A Lot of Livin' to Do" (*Bye Bye Birdie*, 1960; lyric by Lee Adams), "The Immigration and Naturalization Rag" (early version of "Melt Us," from *All American* [1962]; lyric by Lee Adams), 'This Is the Life" (*Golden Boy*, 1964; lyric by Lee Adams), "Colorful" (*Golden Boy*, 1964; lyric by Lee Adams), "What a Country" (*All American*, 1962; lyric by Lee Adams), "N.Y.C." (*Annie*, 1977; lyric by Martin Charnin), "Don't Forget 127th Street" (*Golden Boy*, 1964; lyric by Lee Adams), "I'm Not in Philadelphia" (written for, but not used in, *All American* [1962]; lyric by Lee Adams), "Half of Life" (unproduced musical *The Borrowers*; lyric by Lee Adams) "One Boy" (*Bye Bye Birdie*, 1960; lyric by Lee Adams), "One Last Kiss" (*Bye Bye Birdie*, 1960; lyric by Lee Adams), "We Love You Conrad" (*Bye Bye Birdie*, 1960; lyric by Lee Adams), "Born Too Late" (independent song; lyric by Fred Tobias), "Bye Bye Birdie" (1963 film *Bye Bye Birdie*; lyric by Lee Adams), "How Lovely to Be a Woman" (*Bye Bye Biridie*, 1960; lyric by Lee Adams), "Livin' Alone" (source unknown; lyric by Charles Strouse), "Some Bright Morning" (*Charlie and Algernon*, 1980; lyric by David Rogers) "Marjorie Morningstar" (unproduced musical *Marjorie Morningstar*; lyric by Lee Adams), "Welcome to the Theatre" (*Applause*, 1970; lyric by Lee Adams), "But Alive" (*Applause*, 1970; lyric by Lee Adams), "In a Silly Mood" (source and lyricist unknown), "One of a Kind" (*Applause*, 1970; lyric by Lee Adams), "Good Friends" (*Applause*, 1970; lyric by Lee Adams), "Everything's Great" (*Golden Boy*, 1964; lyric by Lee Adams), "Hunky Dory" (unproduced musical *Hunky Dory*; lyric by Charles Strouse), "You're Never Fully Dressed without a Smile" (*Annie*, 1977; lyric by Martin Charnin), "Put on a Happy Face" (*Bye Bye Birdie*, 1960; lyric by Lee Adams), "Tomorrow" (*Annie*, 1977; lyric by Martin Charnin), "Once Upon a Time" (*All American*, 1962; lyric by Lee Adams), "Lorna's Here" (*Golden Boy*, 1964; lyric by Lee Adams), "Night Song" (*Golden Boy*, 1964; lyric by Lee Adams), "Those Were the Days" (theme song from CBS television series *All in the Family*; lyric by Lee Adams), "Applause" (*Applause*, 1970; lyric by Lee Adams), "A Broadway Musical" (from [then] forthcoming musical *A Broadway Musical* [which opened later in 1978; see entry]; lyric by Lee Adams)

NOTES—*By Strouse* was first produced Off Off Broadway at the Manhattan Theatre Club's Cabaret November 9, 1977, for a limited engagement of twenty-eight performances (with the exception of Kim Fedena, who was replaced by Donna Marshall, all the principals remained when the revue transferred to the Off Broadway Ballroom).

The onslaught of lyricist-composer tributes wasn't going away. In fact, with the previous Broadway season's hit *Side by Side by Sondheim* (1977) and the successful Broadway transfer of the Manhattan Theatre Club's *Ain't Misbehavin'* (1978; see entry), the heretofore almost exclusively Off Broadway genre was quickly becoming institutionalized on Broadway.

An insert in the *By Strouse* program indicated the evening would offer songs from five forthcoming Charles Strouse musicals (*Hunky Dory, Palm Beach, The Borrowers, Marjorie Morningstar*, and *A Broadway Musical*). As of this writing, some three decades after *By Strouse* opened, only *A Broadway Musical* has been produced (see entry).

238 Cabin in the Sky. "A Musical Fantasy"; THEATRE: Greenwich Mews Theatre; OPENING DATE: January 21, 1964; PERFORMANCES: 47; BOOK: Lynn Root; LYRICS: John LaTouche; MUSIC: Vernon Duke; DIRECTION: Brian Shaw; CHOREOGRAPHY: Pepe Dechazza; SCENERY: Alan Kimmel; COSTUMES: Alan Kimmel; LIGHTING: Daniel Forer; MUSICAL DIRECTION: Eric W. Knight; PRODUCERS: Arthur Whitelaw, Leo Friedman

CAST—Helen Ferguson (Lily), Joseph (C.) Attles (Brother Green, John Henry), KETTY LESTER (Georgia Brown), Albert Popwell (Dr. James, Domino Jackson), ROSETTA LE NOIRE (Petunia Jackson), BERNARD JOHNSON (Headman), Harold Pierson (First Henchman, Messenger), Morton Winston (Second Henchman, Messenger), TONY MIDDLETON ("Little Joe" Jackson), SAM LAWS (The Lord's General), D'urville Martin (Fleetfoot), Cleo Quitman (Angel), Jeannet Rollins de Ramos (Angel), Vernon Washington (Dude) The action occurs "then and now."

The musical was presented in two acts.

ACT ONE—Overture (Orchestra), "Wade in the Water" (Ensemble), "We'll Live All Over Again" (Rosetta Le Noire), "The Man Upstairs" (Sam Laws,

Tony Middleton, D'urville Martin, Cleo Quitman, Jeannet Rollins de Ramos), "Taking a Chance on Love" (Rosetta Le Noire), "Cabin in the Sky" (Rosetta Le Noire, Tony Middleton), "Gospel: Great Day" (Ensemble), "Do What You Want to Do" (Bernard Johnson, Harold Pierson, Morton Winston) "Taking a Chance on Love" (reprise) (Rosetta Le Noire, Tony Middleton)

ACT TWO—"Fugue" (Ensemble), "Not a Care in the World" (Rosetta Le Noire, Tony Middleton), "Do What You Want to Do" (reprise) (Ketty Lester, Harold Pierson, Morton Winston), "Not So Bad to Be Good" (Sam Laws), "Love Me Tomorrow (but Leave Me Alone Today)" (Ketty Lester, Tony Middleton), "Love Turned the Light Out" (Rosetta Le Noire), "Cross Over—Off to John Henry's" (Ensemble), "Living It Up" (Ketty Lester, Tony Middleton), "Honey in the Honeycomb" (Ketty Lester), "Savannah" (Rosetta Le Noire, Ensemble), "Cabin in the Sky" (reprise) (Rosetta Le Noire, Tony Middleton, Company)

NOTES—Off Broadway continued to revive musicals which had otherwise gone unseen in New York for decades. Previous seasons had offered *On the Town, Gay Divorce, Oh, Kay! Anything Goes, Best Foot Forward*, and *The Boys from Syracuse* (see entries), and now the legendary *Cabin in the Sky* joined the steady stream of revivals. *Cabin in the Sky*, a fable about the struggle between the lord and the devil for Little Joe's soul, had lost money during its original production, which opened at the Martin Beck (now Al Hirschfeld) Theatre on October 25, 1940, and played for only 156 performances. But the musical was fondly remembered for its score (which included the hit song "Taking a Chance on Love") and Ethel Waters' performance as Little Joe's wife Petunia. In 1943, *Cabin in the Sky* was filmed by MGM, with Waters reprising her stage role (the film also included new songs by E.Y. Harburg and Harold Arlen). Unfortunately, the 1964 revival was gone in eight weeks (but thankfully was recorded by Capitol Records [LP # W-2073], and was reissued on CD by Broadway Angel Records [# ZDM-0777-7-64892-2-3] and later by DRG Records [# 19088]). To this day *Cabin in the Sky* has never enjoyed another major revival (and, with political correctness running amok, probably never will). The Off Broadway cast album is a delight, and Rosetta LeNoire gives an especially memorable performance as Petunia; vocally, she is a worthy successor to Ethel Waters. Five songs from the 1940 production were recorded by Ethel Waters and the original Broadway orchestra (conducted by Max Meth), and these were included on an LP released by AEI Records (# AEI-1107; later issued on CD by AEI [# AEI-CD-017]). In 1980, Hollywood Soundstage Records released an LP of the film's soundtrack (# 5003), and in 1996 Rhino Records released the soundtrack (# R-272245), complete with outtakes as well as extended versions of songs, including Harburg and Arlen's "Ain't It the Truth," which was sung by Lena Horne and deleted from the final print (fourteen years later, Horne starred in Harburg and Arlen's 1957 Broadway musical *Jamaica*, and performed the song in that production [and recorded it for the Broadway cast album]). For the film, Harburg and Arlen also contributed "Happiness Is a Thing Called Joe," which became a minor standard.

Further, the 2000 tribute-revue to John La-Touche, *Taking a Chance on Love* (see entry), included several songs from *Cabin in the Sky*, and these can be heard on the revue's cast album (Original Cast Records CD # OC-4444).

"We'll Live All Over Again" was dropped from the original production, but reinstated for the revival. Similarly, "It's Not So Good to Be Bad," which had been added to the production after the Broadway opening, was used in the revival (as "Not So Bad to Be Good"). For the revival, Vernon Duke wrote the lyric and music for a new song, "Living It Up"; and "Not a Care in the World" (from Duke and LaTouche's 1941 musical *Banjo Eyes*) was interpolated into the revival.

"Gospel: Great Day" and "Cross Over" don't seem to have been used in the original production, and so Duke may have written these especially for the revival. It's also possible that "Gospel: Great Day" was heard in the original as "Holy Unto the Lord." "The General's Song" is also known as "General's Entrance" and "Make Way"; "Wade in the Water" is also known as "God's A'Going to Trouble the Water"; and "The Man Upstairs" is sometimes titled "Pay Heed"; Incidentally, "Taking a Chance on Love" had been originally written by Duke and Ted Fetter (the latter a cousin to Cole Porter) as "Fooling Around with Love" for a different (and unproduced) musical. When an extra number was needed for Ethel Waters to sing in the original production, Duke remembered "Fooling Around with Love," and three days before the opening LaTouche re-wrote the original lyric (with an assist from Fetter, who is also credited as co-lyricist of "Savannah").

The following songs from the 1941 production weren't used in the revival: "Dem Bones," "In My Old Virginia Home (on the River Nile)," "Egyptian Ballet," "Lazy Steps," and "Boogy Woogy."

239 Call Me Ethel! (1988); THEATRE: Don't Tell Mama; OPENING DATE: January 1988; PERFORMANCES: Unknown; WRITTEN BY Rita McKenzie and Christopher Powich; DIRECTION: Christopher Powich

CAST—Rita McKenzie

NOTES—*Call Me Ethel!* was a one-woman show in which Rita McKenzie impersonated Ethel Merman (1909-1984) and sang numbers associated with her. It was a dandy evening of cabaret, and McKenzie had the patter and songs down perfectly. For the Off Off Broadway production, McKenzie was accompanied by Christopher Powich on the piano (for other cities, Fred Barton was the pianist). The revue returned to Off Off Broadway at the American Jewish Theatre on June 9, 1989, for sixty-seven performances. In a program note for that production, McKenzie indicated she was grateful to Sister Viterbia "for convincing her that she was not Julie Andrews."

In 1992, Rita McKenzie portrayed Merman once again, this time in *Ethel Merman's Broadway* (see entry).

240 Call the Children Home. THEATRE: Primary Stages; OPENING DATE: September 23, 2002; PERFORMANCES: Unknown; BOOK: Thomas Babe; additional book material by JD Myers; LYRICS: Mildred Kayden; MUSIC: Mildred Kayden; DIRECTION: Kent Gash; CHOREOGRAPHY: Tanya Gibson-Clark; SCENERY: Emily Beck; COSTUMES: Austin K. Sanderson; LIGHTING: William H. Grant III; MUSICAL DIRECTION: William Foster McDaniel; PRODUCERS: Primary Stages (Casey Childs, Executive Director; Andrew Leynse, Artistic Director) in association with RACK Enterprises

CAST—Tamara Tunie (Mary), Eugene Fleming (Professor), Angela Robinson (Pia), Sophia Salguero (Blondie), Julian Gamble (Anderson), Caesar Samayoa (Papa), Christiane Noll (Kathleen), Sean McDermott (Henry)

The action occurs in St. Louis and New Orleans during 1912.

The musical was presented in two acts.

ACT ONE—Overture (Orchestra), "Welcome to My World" (Tamara Tunie), "Welcome to My World" (reprise) (Tamara Tunie), "Hometown Blues of New Orleans" (Eugene Fleming), "No Holdin' Back" (Eugene Fleming, Tamara Tunie, Angela Robinson, Sophia Salguero), "Forever Mine" (Caesar Samayoa, Christiane Noll), "Catering" (Angela Robinson, Sophia Salguero, Christiane Noll), "Blue Book" (Tamara Tunie, Angela Robinson, Sophia Salguero, Caesar Samayoa), "Harlots" (Sean McDermott), "Never Gonna Run Again" (Tamara Tunie, Eugene Fleming), "Crystal Glass" (Sean McDermott, Tamara Tunie), "Buddy Bolden's Horn"/"Call the Children Home" (Eugene Fleming, Angela Robinson, Sophia Salguero)

ACT TWO—Entr'acte (Orchestra), "Cuttin' Out and Crossin' Over" (Caesar Samayoa, Eugene Fleming), "Do I Need a Man?" (Tamara Tunie), "Chilling Stream, Drink" (Sean McDermott), "Funeral March" (Orchestra), "The Last to Know" (Angela Robinson, Sophia Salguero), "Le Bal de L'Amour" (Company), "Your Home Within My Life" (Christiane Noll, Tamara Tunie), "The Game" (Tamara Tunie, Sean McDermott, Eugene Fleming), Finale (Company)

NOTES—The Off Off Broadway musical *Call the Children Home* dealt with life in a New Orleans house of prostitution, and among its characters were the madam, one of her "girls" (a teenager who is pursued by a photographer), two brothers into whips, and the brothel's Black piano player (what he really wants to do is compose opera).

The plot was reminiscent of Louis Malle's 1978 film *Pretty Baby*, which was set in a New Orleans' brothel during World War I and dealt with a twelve-year-old prostitute who marries a photographer.

Bruce Weber in the *New York Times* found the late Thomas Babe's book "wildly overwrought" with "pompous baloney," and Mildred Kayden's score "varied but undistinguished" and "disappointingly unadventurous." But he singled out two of Kayden's contributions, the "rollicking" "Buddy Bolden's Horn" and the "unusual" duet "Forever Mine." At the end of the musical, the piano player notes he has plenty of material for his opera; but Weber predicted that what he had wouldn't add up to "grand" opera, only "soap."

Babe, who had co-written the book for another musical, William Bolcom's *Casino Paradise* (see entry), was a prolific playwright whose works include *Kid Champion* (1975), *Rebel Women* (1976), *A Prayer for My Daughter* (1977), *Taken in Marriage* (1979), *Salt Lake City Skyline* (1980), and *Buried Inside Extra* (1983). He died in 2000.

241 Cambridge Circus. THEATRE: Square East; OPENING DATE: October 28, 1964; PERFORMANCES: 90; WRITTEN BY: Tim Brooke-Taylor, Graham Chapman, John Cleese, David Hatch, Jo Kendall, Jonathan Lynn, and Bill Oddie; MUSIC: Bill Oddie, Hugh McDonald, and David Palmer; DIRECTION: Humphrey Barclay; SCENERY: Stephen Mullin; COSTUMES: Unknown (possibly Stephen Mullin); LIGHTING: Pedar Ness; PRODUCERS: David Black in association with Jay Julien and Andre Goulston

CAST—Tim Brooke-Taylor, Graham Chapman, John Cleese, David Hatch, Jo Kendall, Jonathan Lynn, Bill Oddie

NOTES—*Cambridge Circus* was first seen as *A Clump of Plinths* when it was produced as an undergraduate revue at Cambridge University in Spring 1963; as *Cambridge Circus*, it opened in London at the Lyric Theatre on August 14, 1963, and then on October 6, 1964, it premiered on Broadway. Despite generally enthusiastic reviews, the piece floundered after less than three weeks. However, four days after its Broadway closing, the revue re-opened with the Broadway cast at Square East for a run of almost three months; it was followed by a second edition (*New Cambridge Circus*; 1965; see entry) which played for over two months.

The list of sketches and songs which appear below were in the Broadway production (presumably most if not all appeared Off Broadway as well). The Broadway production credited the cast with most of the material, with additional contributions by Anthony Buffery, John Cameron, John Cassels, Richard

Eyre, Tony Hendra, Terry Jones, David Lewis, David Lipscomb, and Chris Stuart-Clark. Sketches and songs weren't differentiated, but most if not all the contributions by Bill Oddie are songs.

One of the revue's highlights was "I Wanna Hold Your Handel," which presented a Beatles' song as if it had been written by Handel. The revue's sense of the ridiculous is perhaps best sampled in a sketch in which a man phones for two cups of coffee, only to call back and cancel the order because he wants to place a new order (for two cups of coffee). Of the cast members, Bill Oddie was singled out by most critics as the revue's outstanding performer. And John Cleese and Graham Chapman would of course find immortality as members of the satiric group Monty Python.

In his review of the Broadway production, Walter Kerr in the *New York Herald Tribune* noted that Cardinal Richelieu was credited for some of the revue's numbers, and said he felt Richelieu showed great promise as a revue writer. Kerr noted that the "small" revue offered a "vast sense of humor" and said he hoped he made it clear that the revue was "royally welcome."

ACT ONE—"Bring Out the Beast" (by Cardinal Richelieu) (Company), "Cloak and Dagger" (by John Cleese and David Hatch) (John Cleese, David Hatch, Jonathan Lynn), "London Bus" (by Bill Oddie and Tim Brooke-Taylor) (Jonathan Lynn, Tim Brooke-Taylor, David Hatch, Bill Oddie), "Stage Coach" (by Graham Chapman and David Lipscomb) (Graham Chapman), "Final Episode" (by John Cleese and Graham Chapman) (Company), "Traffic Island" (by Bill Oddie) (Bill Oddie, Jo Kendall), "Patients, for the Use Of" (by Bill Oddie, Tim Brooke-Taylor, and Chris Stuart-Clark) (Tim Brooke-Taylor, Bill Oddie, Jo Kendall, Jonathan Lynn), "Scatty" (by Bill Oddie and Hugh MacDonald) (Jo Kendall), "How Black Was My Valley" (by David Lewis, John Cassels, and Jonathan Lynn) (Jonathan Lynn), "Sing Sing" (by Bill Oddie) (Bill Oddie, Tim Brooke-Taylor, Jo Kendall, John Cleese, Graham Chapman), "BBCBC" (by Bill Oddie, John Cleese, et al.) (David Hatch, John Cleese), "Boring Straight Song" (by Bill Oddie) (Bill Oddie), "Humor Without Tears" (by Terry Jones) (David Hatch, Tim Brooke-Taylor, Bill Oddie, Jonathan Lynn, Jo Kendall)

ACT TWO—"I Wanna Hold Your Handel" (by John Cameron) (Bill Oddie, Tim Brooke-Taylor, David Hatch, Jo Kendall), "Prophet" (by Graham Chapman) (Graham Chapman), "West End Saga" (by Cardinal Richelieu) (Company), "Music-Hall 1600" (by Bill Oddie, Tim Brooke-Taylor, Chris Stuart-Clark) (Jonathan Lynn, Tim Brooke-Taylor), "Those Were the Days" (by Bill Oddie) (Bill Oddie), "Pride and Joy" (by Bill Oddie) (David Hatch, Jo Kendall), "To Bury Caesar" (by Tony Hendra) (Graham Chapman, David Hatch), "On Her Majesty's Service" (by Bill Oddie) (Bill Oddie, Tim Brooke-Taylor, David Hatch, Jonathan Lynn), "Banana" (by Anthony Buffery and Richard Eyre) (Jonathan Lynn, Graham Chapman), "Bigger Than Both of Us" (by John Cleese and Bill Oddie) (Jo Kendall, John Cleese), "Judge Not" (by John Cleese) (John Cleese, Bill Oddie, David Hatch, Jonathan Lynn, Tim Brooke-Taylor, Graham Chapman), "Foot Note" (by Cardinal Richelieu) (Company)

The London production was recorded by Odeon/E.M.I. Records Limited (LP # PCS-3046), and included "Patients, for the Use of," "Pride and Joy," "BBCBC," "Sing Sing," "Boring Straight Song," "Those Were the Days," and "Judge Not"; among the other numbers on the album was "Green Line Bus," which was probably performed in New York as "London Bus."

242 Camp Meeting (1977).

THEATRE: Greenwich Mews Theatre; OPENING DATE: August 5, 1977; PERFORMANCES: Unknown; BOOK: Al Carmines; LYRICS: Al Carmines; MUSIC: Al Carmines; DIRECTION: Bob Herget; SCENERY: John Pitt; PRODUCER: The Judson Poets' Theatre

NOTES—The Off Off Broadway *Camp Meeting* was a revised version of *Camp Meeting: 1840*, which had opened at the Judson Poets' Theatre on May 20, 1976. The new version opened at the Greenwich Mews Theatre because the Judson Memorial Church was undergoing extensive renovations.

For more information about this production, see entry for the earlier version.

243 Camp Meeting: 1840 (1976).

THEATRE: Judson Poets' Theatre; OPENING DATE: May 20, 1976; PERFORMANCES: Unknown; BOOK: Al Carmines; LYRICS: Al Carmines; MUSIC: Al Carmines

NOTES—The Off Off Broadway musical *Camp Meeting: 1840* was revised the following season, opening on August 5, 1977, at the Greenwich Mews Theatre as *Camp Meeting* (see entry); the following information is from a program of the revised version which noted that "the Camp Meeting was a religious phenomenon of American frontier life ... several communities would gather periodically for a large, open-air religious revival service [which included] politicking, weddings, baptisms, memorial service, and (on the edges) gambling, drinking, and trading ... In 1846 Abraham Lincoln ran for public office against one of the most famous of camp meeting revivalists, Peter Cartwright. This is the kernel of fact upon which *Camp Meeting* is based."

The credits and song titles for the 1977 version are as follows: DIRECTION: Bob Herget; SCENERY: John Pitts; COSTUMES: Michele Edwards and Blae Hannahan; LIGHTING: Edward I. Byers; MUSICAL DIRECTION: Al Carmines and John R. Williams, Pianists

CAST—Joel Higgins (the Rev. Carton Wheelwright), Essie Borden (Evelyn Wheelwright). Gretchen Van Aken (Shouting Alice), Vickie Patik (Daughter Binnie), Lisa Essary (Daughter Ellie), Tony Clark (Abraham Lincoln), Lou Bullock (Brother Thomas), Lee Guilliatt (Sister Maggie James), Barbara Sandek (Sister Mexico), Peter Gordon (Brother Amoriah), Stu Silver (Mean Jim), Karl Heist (Brother Peter Dumpston), William Beckham (Brother Willard Dumpston), Margaret Wright (Sister Geraldine), David Summers (Son Joe), Trisha Long (Sister Callie)

The action occurs in late Summer 1846 in a campground in Southeastern Illinois.

The musical was presented in one act.

MUSICAL NUMBERS—"Doxology" (lyric and music based on "Old Hundredth" by L.M. Genevan Psalter [1551]) (Congregation) "Open Your Heart" (Joel Higgins, Congregation), "He Comes Home in the Evening" (Essie Borden, Women), "I Will Never Let You Go" (David Summers), "The Day of the People Is Coming" (Trisha Long, Congregation), "Does God Ever Make Mistakes?" (Lou Bullock), "Everything That God Does Is Perfect" (Joe Higgins, Congregation), "Joy in the Earth" (Congregation), "Testimony" (Lee Guilliatt), "Atheism" (Stu Silver), "Threnody" (Vickie Patik), "Children Break Your Heart" (Margaret Wright, with Gretchen Van Aken), "Forgiveness" (Tony Clark), "I Want to Go Home to God" (Congregation), "God Be with You" (lyric and music by Jeremiah Rankin and William Tomer [1832]) (Congregation)

244 Candide.

THEATRE: Brooklyn Academy of Music; OPENING DATE: December 11, 1973; PERFORMANCES: 48; BOOK: Hugh Wheeler; LYRICS: Richard Wilbur; additional lyrics by Stephen Sondheim and John LaTouche; MUSIC: Leonard Bernstein; DIRECTION: Harold Prince; Ruth Mitchell, Assistant Director; CHOREOGRAPHY: Patricia Birch; SCENERY: Eugene and Franne Lee; COSTUMES: Eugene and Franne Lee; LIGHTING: Eugene and Franne Lee; MUSICAL DIRECTION: John Mauceri; PRODUCER: The Chelsea Theatre Center of Brooklyn (Robert Kalfin, Artistic Director; Michael David, Executive Director; Burl Hash, Productions Director)

CAST—Lewis J. Stadlen (Dr. Voltaire, Dr. Pangloss, Governor, Host, Sage), Jim Corti (Chinese Coolie, Westphalian Soldier, Priest, Spanish Don, Rosary Vendor, Sailor, Lion, Guest), Mark Baker (Candide), David Horwitz (Huntsman, First Recruiter, Agent, Executioner, Spanish Don, Cartagenian, Priest, Third Sailor, Eunuch), Deborah St. Darr (Paquette), Joe Palmieri (Baron, Grand Inquisitor, Slave Driver, First Sailor), Mary-Pat Green (Baroness, Harpsichordist, Penitente, Steel Drummer, Houri, Cow), Maureen Brennan (Cunegonde), Sam Freed (Maximillian), Robert Hendersen (Servant, Bulgarian Sergeant, Agent of the Inquisition, Executioner, Spanish Don, Cartagenian, Sailor), Jeff Keller (Second Recruiter, Rich Jew, Judge, Man in Black, Cartagenian, Pirate, German Botanist, Guest), Gail Boggs (Penitente, Whore, Houri), Lynne Gannaway (Penitente, Cartagenian, Houri), Marti Morris (Aristocrat, Cartagenian, Second Sheep), Chip Garnett (Westphalian Soldier, Agent, Guard, Governor's Aide, Pirate, Guest), Carlos Gorbea (Bulgarian Soldier, Aristocrat, Fruit Vendor, Second Sailor, Pygmy, Cow), Renee Semes (Lady with Knitting, Cartagenian, First Sheep), Kathryn Ritter (Aristocrat, Whore, Houri), June Gable (Old Lady)

SOURCE—The 1759 novel *Candide*, or *Optimism* by Voltaire (Francois-Marie Arouet).

The musical was presented in one act.

MUSICAL NUMBERS—"Life Is Happiness Indeed" (lyric by Stephen Sondheim) (Mark Baker, Maureen Brennan, Sam Freed, Deborah St. Darr), "The Best of All Possible Worlds" (lyric by Stephen Sondheim) (Lewis J. Stadlen, Mark Baker, Maureen Brennan, Sam Freed, Deborah St. Darr), "Oh Happy We" (lyric by Richard Wilbur) (Mark Baker, Maureen Brennan), "O Miserere" (Lynne Gannaway, Gail Boggs, Marti Morris), "Oh Happy We" (reprise) (Mark Baker, Maureen Brennan), "Glitter and Be Gay" (lyric by Richard Wilbur) (Maureen Brennan), "Auto Da Fe (What a Day)" (lyric by John LaTouche and Stephen Sondheim) (Company), "This World" (a/k/a "Candide's Lament") (lyric by Stephen Sondheim) (Mark Baker), "You Were Dead, You Know" (lyric by John LaTouche) (Mark Baker, Maureen Brennan), "I Am Easily Assimilated" (lyric by Leonard Bernstein) (June Gable, Jim Corti, Robert Hendersen, David Horwitz), "I Am Easily Assimilated" (reprise) (June Gable, Mark Baker, Maureen Brennan), "My Love" (lyric by John LaTouche and Richard Wilbur) (Lewis J. Stadlen), "Fons Pietatis" (Company), "Sheep's Song" (lyric by Stephen Sondheim) (Marti Morris, Renee Semes, Jim Corti, Deborah St. Darr, Mark Baker), "Bon Voyage" (lyric by Richard Wilbur) (Lewis J. Stadlen, Company), "The Best of All Possible Worlds" (reprise) (June Gable, Mark Baker, Deborah St. Darr, Renee Semes, Marti Morris), "You Were Dead, You Know" (reprise) (Mark Baker, Maureen Brennan), "Make Our Garden Grow" (lyric by Richard Wilbur) (Company)

NOTES—Once upon a time there was a great musical called *Candide*, which opened at the Martin Beck (now Al Hirschfeld) Theatre on December 1, 1956. Based on Voltaire's picaresque satire of religion, philosophy, and society in general, the musical offered an uncommonly witty and incisive book by Lillian Hellman; clever lyrics by Richard Wilbur, John LaTouche, Lillian Hellman, Dorothy Parker, and Leonard Bernstein (LaTouche had died a few months before the production went into rehearsal, and at the time of his death had completed only a few lyrics); and a richly melodic score by Leonard Bernstein, a score which is one of the greatest ever written for the musical theatre.

Candide premiered on Broadway soon after the openings of *Li'l Abner* and *Bells Are Ringing*, and just before *Happy Hunting*, and while these three light-hearted musicals ran for a year or more, *Candide* could manage only nine weeks (seventy-three performances). One of the myths surrounding the original production is that the New York critics didn't appreciate the show. But of the seven New York newspaper critics, only one (Walter Kerr of the *New York Herald Tribune*) dismissed it. The other six critics were in agreement that *Candide* was a memorable and important musical: John Chapman in the *New York Daily News* wrote that *Candide* "was a truly notable event ... an artistic triumph — the best light opera since Richard Strauss wrote *Der Rosenkavalier* in 1911." Tom Donnelly in the *New York World-Telegram* noted that when the score "isn't as voluptuous as velvet, it is as frostily pretty as a diamond bell ... one of the most attractive scores anyone has written for the musical theatre." Richard Watts in the *New York Post* found "so much that is brilliant about it, so much in the way of musical excellence." Further, John McClain in the *Journal American* wrote that the musical is "ambitious and brilliant"; Robert Coleman in the *Daily Mirror* noted the "colorful and cynical" musical offered a score "of operatic calibre"; and Brooks Atkinson in the *New York Times* felt "the performance is a triumph of stage arts ... a wonderful score ... the most stunning production of the season."

These reviews clearly show that the majority of the critics appreciated the musical and recognized its value. (As for Walter Kerr, he found the musical "a really spectacular disaster ... a great ghostly wreck ... [a] singularly ill-conceived venture.")

Further, Gerald Weales' fascinating *American Drama Since World War II* (published by Harcourt, Brace & World, Inc., in 1962) noted that *Candide* "is not only the most sophisticated product of the American musical stage," it is "probably the most imaginative American play to reach Broadway since the war."

Candide was recorded by Columbia Records (LP # OS-2350; the CD was most recently released by Sony Classical/Columbia/Legacy Records [# SK-86859]), and in 1957 the script was published by Random House. It was the cast recording that kept the show alive, and it soon took on cult status among lovers of theatre music.

A second myth about the musical is that except for its cast album it was virtually ignored after its original production and that it didn't surface until the 1973 revival. But this theatrical legend is far from the truth. In 1958, Lester Osterman (one of the musical's original producers) and Hillard Elkins presented a touring concert version with two leads from the original cast (Robert Rounseville [Candide] and Irra Pettina [The Old Lady]); the cast also included Martyn Green (Pangloss) and Mary Costa (Cunegonde). The adaptation was by Michael (Mike) Stewart, and Samuel Krachmalnick, who conducted the original Broadway production, did the same for the tour.

On April 30, 1959, the musical premiered in London at the Saville Theatre (playing a disappointing sixty performances). Costa was again Cunegonde; Denis Quilley, Candide; Laurence Naismith, Pangloss; Edith Coates, The Old Lady; Ron Moody, The Governor; and Victor Spinetti, The Marquis. The book was credited to Lillian Hellman ("assisted" by Michael Stewart).

In 1967, another concert version was produced, this time in an adaptation by Sheldon Patinkin.

Moreover, on November 10, 1968, a special one-performance-only production was presented at Philharmonic Hall with William Lewis (Candide) and Madeline Kahn (Cunegonde) heading the cast. The revival was a combination of Hellman, Stewart, and Patinkin's adaptations.

Further, in 1971 a lavish national touring production was mounted, which played for four months. Frank Porretta was Candide and Costa (in her third *Candide* production) was Cunegonde. The adaptation was by Patinkin, and Oliver Smith, who had designed the scenery for the original production, contributed the décor for the revival.

The *Candide* overture became a staple of American light music, and the cast album continued to sell well over the decades (in fact, since its release on December 31, 1956, the cast album has never been out of print).

So by the time of the 1973 revival at the Brooklyn Academy of Music, *Candide* was hardly an overlooked and forgotten musical.

But what happened to *Candide* in 1973 is a mixed blessing. For the revival, the acerbic wit of Hellman's original libretto was ignored; instead, Harold Prince's direction and Hugh Wheeler's script offered up a cutesy production which emphasized silly *Laugh-In*-styled comedy and staging. The glorious, epic sweep of Bernstein's score seemed an afterthought in this production, and it was subjugated to the silly goings-on and juvenile humor of the new adaptation.

The production soon transferred to the Broadway Theatre on March 5, 1974; the venue had been gutted in 1971 for the so-called "environmental" staging of Galt McDermot's flop musical *Dude*, or *The Highway Life*, and so when *Candide* moved into the Broadway it too was presented in an "environmental" production. The auditorium was turned into a series of nooks and crannies where the audience sat on bleachers and watched a kindergarten-styled *Candide* performed (the published script [see below] noted there were ten performance areas throughout the theatre as well as four separate orchestra sections, all of these connected by ramps, drawbridges, trap doors, and "hidden passageways").

The revival unaccountably won the Tony Award for Best Book of a Musical (it tied with the stage adaptation of *Gigi*); it also won for Best Director, Best Scenic Design, and Best Costumes; moreover, it received a special Tony Award for "outstanding contribution to the artistic development of the musical theatre." It was also named Best Musical by the New York Drama Critics Circle.

The production, which played for 740 performances, was recorded on a 2-LP set by Columbia Records (LP # S2X-32923; the CD was released by Sony/Masterworks Broadway Records # 82876-88391-2), and Schirmer Books/MacMillan Performing Arts Series released a lavish edition of the script in 1976. The upside of Prince and Wheeler's free-for-all version is that even though it lost money after almost two years on Broadway, it nonetheless allowed the work to enjoy a more solid foothold in the musical theatre and operatic repertory, and thus it is now frequently produced (albeit in often "cute" *Hellzapoppin*-styled stagings reminiscent of the 1973 production).

As a result, the work has been produced five times by the New York City Opera (1982, 1983, 1984, 1986, and 1989; as of this writing, a sixth revival by the company is scheduled to open on April 8, 2008, for fourteen performances), and on April 29, 1997, it was revived on Broadway at the Gershwin Theatre for 103 performances (again in Wheeler's adaptation, and with direction by Prince and choreography by Patricia Birch). Jason Danieley was Candide; Harolyn Blackwell, Cunegonde; Jim Dale, Pangloss; and Andrea Martin, The Old Lady. The production was recorded by RCA Victor Records (CD # 09026-68835-2).

Other recordings of the score include a 2-LP set by New Worlds Records of the 1982 New York City Opera production (LP # NW-340/341); David Eisler was Candide; Erie Mills, Cunegonde; John Lankston, Pangloss; and Joyce Castle, The Old Lady. A 1988 production by the Scottish Opera was released by That's Entertainment Records (LP # TER-1156; CD # TER-1156 [the CD includes six extra tracks]). A "final revised version, 1989" released by Deutsche Grammophon Records was conducted by Bernstein, and the singers include Jerry Hadley (Candide), June Anderson (Cunegonde), Adolph Green (Pangloss/Martin), and Crista Ludwig (The Old Lady); the recording was released on a 2-LP set (# 429-734-1) and a 2-CD set (# 429-734-2). A 1999 Royal National Theatre production was released by First Night Records (CD # CD-75).

All these recordings offer variations of the score, including songs written for, but not used in, the original production. Among the "other" *Candide* songs heard in these recordings are "Universal Good," "We Are Women," "Nothing More Than This," "Ring Around a Rosy," and "The Kings' Barcarolle." Probably a *complete* recording of *Candide*, with all the songs from the 1956, 1974, and 1997 Broadway productions as well as songs which were not used in the original production (including songs deleted during the tryout), would require three or four CDs.

Two versions of *Candide* were filmed. A concert version which preceded the Deutsche Grammophon recording was taped at London's Barbican Centre on December 13, 1989, and was released on DVD by Deutsche Grammophon (# B0006905-09). Later, a four-performance concert staging at Lincoln Center's Avery Fisher Hall was taped live from the May 5, 2005, performance and was shown on public television's *Great Performances* series; it was later released on DVD by Image Entertainment (# ID2762EM DVD); Paul Groves was Candide; Kristin Chenoweth, Cunegonde; Patti LuPone, The Old Lady; Sir Thomas Allen, Pangloss; Jeff Blumenkrantz, Maximillian; and Janine LaManna, Paquette; unfortunately, this production is marred by unsubtle, overly precious staging.

As of this writing, Hellman's will precludes the use of her libretto in any productions. Until such time as her libretto may be released for a future staging, perhaps some forthcoming revival will offer a libretto in the Hellman style, bereft of the dumbed-down touches which have become standard with so many recent productions. Maybe one day we'll actually see a *Candide* for adults, just like those lucky audiences did for those seventy-three performances during the 1956-1957 Broadway theatre season.

245 The Canterbury Pilgrims. THEATRE: Metropolitan Opera House; OPENING DATE: March 8, 1917; PERFORMANCES: 7; LIBRETTO: Percy MacKaye; MUSIC: Reginald De Koven; DIRECTION: Richard Ordynski; SCENERY: James Fox (designs for Act One) and Homer F. Emens (designs for Acts Two and Three); COSTUMES: Hildreth Meiere; MUSICAL DIRECTION: Artur Bodanzky; PRODUCER: The Metropolitan Opera

CAST—Johannes Sembach (Chaucer), Robert Leonhardt (Knight, Man of Law), Paul Althouse (Squire), Max Bloch (Friar), Basil Ruysdael (Miller), Pompilio Malatesta (Cook), Mario Laurenti (Shipman), Carl Schlegel (Summoner), Julius Bayer (Pardoner), Giulio Rossi (Host), Pietro Audisio (Joannes), Albert Reiss (King Richard II), Riccardo Tegani (Herald), Margaret Ober (Alisoun [The Wife of Bath]), Edith Mason (Prioress), Marie Sundelius (Johanna), Minnie Egener (Girl), Marie Tiffany (Girl)

SOURCE—Geoffrey Chaucer's collection of short stories *The Canterbury Tales* (written between 1387 and 1400).

The opera was presented in three acts.

NOTES—The world premiere of the operatic version of Chaucer's *The Canterbury Tales* had an interesting pedigree. Its composer Reginald De Koven had written the music for *Robin Hood* (1891), one of the most popular of American operettas (its score included "Brown October Ale," and, during the run, "Oh, Promise Me" was added to the production), and its librettist Percy MacKaye had written one of the finest of American plays, *The Scarecrow* (1911), which enjoyed a magnificent revival at the Kennedy Center in Washington, D.C., in 1975 (William Atherton, Leonard Frey, and Barbara Baxley headed the cast).

An unsigned reviewer in the *New York Times* noted the Met had given the new opera a "really sumptuous" production." The piece was described as "light and gay in spirit, without a serious moment." The "unceasingly melodious" score was filled with marches, waltzes, and other dance music, and the libretto was full "of situation and action, full of life and humor ... an ingenious and elaborate plot" (the *Times* noted MacKaye had fashioned the libretto from his 1903 play *The Canterbury Pilgrims* [which apparently has never been produced in New York]).

Despite the acclaim for the new work, it has disappeared from the operatic repertory. For two other musicals based on Chaucer's tales, see entries for *Get Thee to Canterbury* and *The Canterbury Tales.*

246 The Canterbury Tales. "The Bawdy Musical Comedy"; THEATRE: Rialto Theatre; OPENING DATE: February 12, 1980; PERFORMANCES: 16; BOOK: Martin Starkie and Nevill Coghill; LYRICS: Nevill Coghill; MUSIC: Richard Hill and John Hawkins; DIRECTION: Robert Johanson; CHOREOGRAPHY: Randy Hugill; SCENERY: Michael Anania; COSTUMES: Sigrid Insull; LIGHTING: Gregg Marriner; MUSICAL DIRECTION: John Kroner; PRODUCERS: Burry Fredrik and Bruce Schwartz

CAST—Earl McCarroll (Chaucer, January), Robert Stoeckle (Knight), Robert Tetirick (Squire, Nicholas, Damian, Horse), Andy Ferrell (Yeoman, John, King Arthur), Mimi Sherwin (Prioress), K.K. Preece (Nun, Proserpina), Kaylyn Dillehay (Molly, Guenevere), Tricia Witham (May), Krista Neumann (Alison, Sweetheart), Andrew Traines (Friar, Justinus), Vance Mizelle (Merchant, Gervase), Richard Stillman (Clerk, Robin, Page, Horse), Polly Pen (Cook, Miller's Wife, Duenna), Win Atkins (Miller), Ted Houck, Jr. (Stewart, Carpenter, Placebo), Maureen Sadusk (Wife of Bath, Old Woman), Kelly Walters (Summoner, Absolon, Alan), Martin Walsh (Pardoner, Executioner), George Maguire (Host, Pluto)

SOURCE—Geoffrey Chaucer's collection of stories *The Canterbury Tales* (written between 1387 and 1400); the production was based on a translation by Nevil Coghill.

The action occurs during a four-day pilgrimage to Canterbury Cathedral in the late 1300s.

The musical was presented in two acts.

ACT ONE—Prologue (Earl McCarroll, Company), "Welcome Song" (George Maguire, Company), "Goodnight Hymn" (Company), "Canterbury Day" (Company), "Horse Rise" (Company), "I Have a Noble Cock" (Robert Tetirick), "There's the Moon" (Robert Tetirick, Krista Neumann), "Darling, Let Me Teach You How to Kiss" (Kelly Walters), "It Depends on What You're At" (Maureen Sadusk, K.K. Preece), "Beer Is Best" (Win Atkins, Polly Pen, Kaylyn Dillehay, Kelly Walters, Andy Ferrell), "Love Will Conquer All" (Mimi Sherwin, K.K. Preece, Company), "Canterbury Day" (reprise) (Company)

ACT TWO—"Come On and Marry Me, Honey" (Maureen Sadusk, Company), "Where Are the Girls of Yesterday" (George Maguire; danced by Krista Neumann, Tricia Witham, Kaylyn Dillehay), "April Song" (Company), "If She Has Never Loved Before" (Earl McCarroll, Tricia Witham), "I'll Give My Love a Ring" (Robert Tetirick, Tricia Witham), "Pear Tree Sextet" (Earl McCarroll, Tricia Witham, Robert Tetirick, George Maguire, K.K. Preece, Vance Mizelle), "What Do Women Most Desire" (Robert Stoeckle, Ladies), "I Am All Ablaze" (Robert Stoeckle; danced by Andy Ferrell and Kaylyn Dillehay), "Love Will Conquer All" (reprise) (Mimi Sherwin, K.K. Preece, Company)

NOTES—*The Canterbury Tales* was a hit in London, opening on March 21, 1968, at the Phoenix Theatre and playing for 2,082 performances. The following year the musical premiered on Broadway at the Eugene O'Neill Theatre on February 3, where it had a disappointing run of only 121 performances. Both productions were recorded, the British cast by Decca (LP # LK-4956 and # SKL-4956; later reissued by That's Entertainment Records [LP # TER-1076]) and the Broadway cast by Capitol Records (LP # SW-229; later released on CD by Broadway Angel Records [# ZDM-5-65171-2]). In 1969 there was also an Off-Broadway musical version of the material, *Get Thee to Canterbury* (see entry), which lasted just one week. Also see entry for *The Canterbury Pilgrims*, an operatic version of the material which premiered at the Met in 1917.

The current revival opened at the Equity Library Theatre on November 29, 1979, where it played for thirty performances. But when the musical transferred to the Rialto on February 12 of the following year, it lasted only two weeks. Perhaps the material is too "literary" and too British for American audiences. A 2006 (non-musical) adaptation of the material (which played at the Kennedy Center in Washington, D.C.) was victim to the protests of a few audience members, who unwittingly or not, were members of the Politically Correct Police when they objected to the content of the material. (It's odd: politically correct censorship is never called censorship, it's called "sensitivity.") But Chaucer has survived for some eight centuries, and will continue to do so, in spite of the PC Police who continuously try to disembowel works of the past and not-so-recent past.

247 Capitol Steps. "Musical Political Satire"; THEATRE: John Houseman Theatre; OPENING DATE: February 13, 1997; PERFORMANCES: 152; MATERIAL: Bill Strauss and Elaina Newport, with contributions from the cast "and Congress"; DIRECTION: Bill Strauss and Elaina Newport; SCENERY: R.J. Matson; COSTUMES: Robyn Scott; LIGHTING: Robert Bessoir; PRODUCERS: Eric Krebs and Anne Strickland Squadron in association with the Capitol Steps

CAST—Mike Carruthers, Janet Davidson Gordon, Ann Johnson, Mike Loomis, Tyjuana Morris, Elaina Newport, Bill Strauss, Mike Tilford, Brad Van Grack, Amy Felices Young, Jamie Zemarel; Bo Ayars, Howard Breitbart, and Lenny Williams, Pianists

The revue was presented in two acts.

NOTES—The Capitol Steps is a Washington, D.C.-based political comedy group which formed in December 1981; many of the cast members were former Congressional staff members, and thus the group particularly enjoyed satirizing Congress. The program noted the revue's material was based on "the trials and tribulations, scandals, and screw-ups of our elected officials ... typically the Republicans goof up and the Democrats party. Or the Democrats goof up and the Republicans party. That's what we call the two party system."

The March 1997 program noted the Capitol Steps had performed for four presidents, "five if you count Hillary."

Five members of the company and one pianist appeared at each performance, and the material changed nightly, "according to the political scandals of the day."

The production had been previously seen in Washington, D.C., which of course was the home base for the company. Nonetheless, the group occasionally returned to New York for a bit of merry-making: *It Ain't Over 'Til the First Lady Sings!* opened at the Douglas Fairbanks Theatre on June 6, 2000, for ninety-two performances; *When Bush Comes to Shove*, played for 124 performances at the John Houseman Theatre beginning on May 16, 2002; and on July 19, 2003, *Between Iraq and a Hard Place* opened at the same theatre for fifty performances.

248 Captain Louie. "A New Family Musical"; THEATRE: Little Shubert Theatre; OPENING DATE: October 31, 2005; PERFORMANCES: 16; BOOK: Anthony Stein; LYRICS: Stephen Schwartz; MUSIC: Stephen Schwartz; DIRECTION: Meridee Stein; CHOREOGRAPHY: Joshua Bergasse; SCENERY: Jeff Subik; based on the illustrations of Erza Jack Keats; GRAPHIC DESIGN: Frank Dain; based on the illustrations of Erza Jack Keats; COSTUMES: Elizabeth Flauto; based on the illustrations of Erza Jack Keats; LIGHTING: Jason Lyons; MUSICAL DIRECTION: Ray Fellman; PRODUCERS: Meridee Stein, Kurt Peterson, and Bob Reich in association with Lynne Halliday, Susan Hoffman, Kevin Lyle, and Gary Sitomer

CAST—Douglas Fabian (Louie), Sara Kapner (Amy, Broom), Katelyn Pippy (Roberta, Mouse), Paul Pontrelli (Ziggy), Ricky Smith (Archy), Ronny Mercedes (Julio), Ryan Appleby (New Kid, Ensemble), Rachel Cantor (New Kid, Ensemble), Noemi Del Rio (New Kid, Ensemble), Remy Zaken (New Kid, Ensemble)

SOURCE—The 1978 book *The Trip* by Erza Jack Keats.

The action occurs in New York City on Halloween.

The musical was presented in one act.

MUSICAL NUMBERS—"New Kid in the Neighborhood" (Douglas Fabian, Company), "Big Red Plane" (Douglas Fabian, Company), "A Welcome for Louie" (Katelyn Pippy, Sara Kapner, Paul Pontrelli, Ricky Smith), "Shadows" (Company), "Trick or Treat" (Company), "Looza on the Block" (Company), "Spiffin' Up Ziggy's" (Company), "Captain Louie" (Douglas Fabian, Company), "Home Again" (Douglas Fabian, Company), Finale: "New Kid in the Neighborhood" (reprise) (Company)

NOTES—*Captain Louie* was a children's musical about a lonely little boy named Louie whose family has moved to a new neighborhood. On Halloween, Louie's toy plane Red suggests he and Louie fly off to their old haunts. Louie agrees, and in his imagination he's soon back with his old friends as well as Julio, a lonely boy who's just moved into the neighborhood; in fact, Julio and his family are now living in Louie's former home. Louie and his gang befriend Julio, who quickly fits into the group. When Louie and Red return home, Louie finds that although he's the new kid on the block, he now has the courage to make new friends in his new neighborhood.

With its sweet story (and its gentle lessons about growing up), its colorful setting (the New York production's décor was based on illustrations from the original novel upon which the musical was based), and Stephen Schwartz' attractive score, *Captain Louie* should find its place in the permanent repertoire of children's musicals. A recording of the score was released by PS Classics (CD # PS-530).

An early version of *Captain Louie* had first been presented by New York's First All Children's Theatre on December 2, 1983. In October 2004, the musical was produced at the New York Music Theatre Festival, and then on May 8, 2005, it was produced by James Morgan and the York Theatre Company in association with Meridee Stein, Pam Koslow, and Kurt Peterson at the Theatre at St. Peter's Church for forty-six performances.

Meridee Stein was the founder and artistic director of The First All Children's Theatre, and it's probably not a stretch to say that she is the driving force for a vibrant children's theatre in this country. Thanks to her tenacity and foresight, she has over the years presented family-friendly musicals, and these have provided opportunities for young people to develop their acting and singing skills.

249 Captains Courageous, the Musical. THEATRE: City Center Stage I/Manhattan Theatre Club; OPENING DATE: February 16, 1999; PERFORMANCES: 56; BOOK: Patrick Cook; LYRICS: Patrick Cook; MUSIC: Frederick Freyer; DIRECTION: Lynne Meadow; CHOREOGRAPHY: Jerry Mitchell; SCENERY: Derek McLane; COSTUMES: Catherine Zuber; LIGHTING: Brian MacDevitt; MUSICAL DIRECTION: Robert Gustafson; PRODUCER: Manhattan Theatre Club (Lynne Meadow, Artistic Director; Barry Grove, Executive Producer)

CAST—Erick Buckley (Harris), Dick Decareau (Evans, Eliot), Michael DeVries (Mr. Cheyne, Peters), Brandon Espinoza (Harvey E. Cheyne), J. Lee Flynn (Ollie), Pete Herber (Hemans, Parent), George Kmeck (Walters), Norm Lewis (Doc), Michael X. Martin (Long Jack), Michael Mulheren (Captain Troop), Gary Schwartz (Murphy, Attendant #2), Dan Sharkey (Simon, Teacher), Daniel Siford (Tom Platt, Attendant #1), Jim Stanek (Dan), Erik Stein (Stephens, Principal), Treat Williams (Manuel)

SOURCES—The 1897 novel *Captains Courageous* by Rudyard Kipling and the 1937 MGM film adaptation (screenplay by John Lee Mahin, Marc Connelly, and Dale Van Every).

The action occurs in 1928 over the course of three months on various spots on the North Atlantic and in the port of Gloucester, Massachusetts.

The musical was presented in two acts.

ACT ONE—"Out on the Sea" (Michael Mulheren, Crew), "Little Fish" (Treat Williams), "I'm Harvey Ellesworth Cheyne" (Brandon Espinoza, Michael Mulheren), "Not So Bad" (Treat Williams), "I Married a Woman" (Dan Sharkey), "I Make Up This Song" (Treat Williams, Brandon Espinoza), "A Hundred Years Ago" (Crew), "Goodnight, Sweet Molly" (Dick Decareau), "She Waits for Me" (Daniel Siford, Michael Mulheren), "That's Where I'm Bound" (Michael Mulheren, Crew), "Jonah" (Michael X. Martin, Crew), "You Never Saw" (Brandon Espinoza)

ACT TWO—"Song of the Sea" (Jim Stanek, Treat Williams, Crew), "Grand Banks Sequence"/"Not This Year" (Michael Mulheren, Brandon Espinoza, Crew), "Regular Fellas" (Treat Williams, Brandon Espinoza), "I'm Home" (Treat Williams, Brandon Espinoza), "I Make Up This Song" (reprise) (Brandon Espinoza), "Song of the Sea" (reprise) (Crew)

NOTES—This musical version of Rudyard Kipling's 1897 novel (and its 1937 film version) *Captains Courageous* told the familiar story of the spoiled rich boy who is lost at sea, is rescued by a Portuguese fisherman, and finds maturity when he learn the values of work, friendship, and character as he lives with the fisherman, the captain, and the crew of a small fishing vessel. For his role of the fisherman in the film adaptation, Spencer Tracy won the Academy Award for Best Actor.

The musical moved the action forward by about thirty years (the novel was set in the late 1800s). Further, the relationship between the fisherman and the boy wasn't part of the novel; it was created for the film version (hence the film version was credited in the program).

Peter Marks in the *New York Times* noted that one didn't have to wait for Fleet Week to find the hardest-working crew in or out of New York Harbor: the "lusty, vocally trained sailors" in the musical's cast more than filled the bill. But he felt for all its busyness in giving the "illusion of something happening," the "rather static and pale" evening was the equivalent of a "torpid cruise in shallow water." Marks singled out a couple of songs ("Regular Fellas" and "I'm Home"), but said the overall score, while "full of verve," never achieved much in the way of individuality.

Sony Classical Records was scheduled to record the musical, but the recording was later cancelled.

Captains Courageous had previously been seen at Ford's Theatre in Washington, D.C., in a 1992 production directed and choreographed by Graciela Daniele. John Dossett played the fisherman, Don Chastain was the Captain, and the boy was played by Kel O'Neill. The cast also included John Mineo and Joseph Kolinski. Numbers heard in the production which were dropped prior to New York were "Nothin' to Do," "Ten Seconds," "Anybody Else," "Right Here," and "Lord, She Could Go." "One More Year" may have been later heard in New York as "Not This Year."

250 Carmilla. "A Vampire Tale"; THEATRE: La Mama Experimental Theatre Club (ETC); OPENING DATE: February 2, 1973; PERFORMANCES: Unknown; TEXT: Wilford Leach; MUSIC: Ben Johnston; DIRECTION: Wilford Leach and John Braswell; MUSICAL DIRECTION: Zizi Mueller; PRODUCER: The ETC Company of La Mama

CAST—Margaret Benczak (Laura), Donald Harrington (Father), Camille Tibaldeo (Mlle. De la Fontaine), Sandra Johnson (Carmilla), Murrel Gehman (Woman, Nurse), John Braswell (Mountebank)

SOURCE—A novella by J.S. LeFanu.

The musical appears to have been presented in one act.

MUSICAL SEQUENCES—Our household. A dream; By Moonlight. On the odyllic influence of the moon; An invitation. Carmilla stays; We compare notes; A saunter. Twilight; A funeral passed by; A mountebank. The amulet; A strange Agony; Passing days; Descending.; About the Ompire; Mesmerized; Conclusion.

NOTES—*Carmilla* had been widely produced throughout the United States and Europe prior to its production in New York by La Mama, and it appears the original cast album, released by Vanguard Records (LP # VSD-79322), was recorded prior to the New York run (the recording omitted two sequences, the interlude "By Moonlight. On the odyllic influence of the moon" and "About the Ompire," the latter mostly spoken text). Cast information and the song list are taken from information on the cast album.

Carmilla received good reviews, but didn't make much of an impact and didn't transfer to a regular Off Broadway theatre once it played Off Off Broadway at La Mama (the musical was twice revived at La Mama, on March 27, 1978, and on October 1, 1986).

Plays about vampires tend to do well, but musicals don't. The granddaddy of such plays was of course *Dracula*. Based on Bram Stoker's novel, the stage adaptation by Hamilton Deane and John L. Balderston opened on Broadway in 1927 with Bela Lugosi in the title role; it ran throughout the season, for a total of 261 performances. It toured widely, and in 1931 was filmed with Lugosi repeating his classic and best-known role. The play was revived on Broadway in 1977, and was the surprise smash of the season, running over two years, for a total of 925 performances. Frank Langella performed the title role, and his toothsome goings-on were accented by Edward Gorey's clever and striking costumes and scenery, all in black and white (with occasional splashes of red).

Another 1977 play about Dracula (which was also based on Stoker's novel) was the Off Broadway *The Passion of Dracula* by Bob Hall and David Richmond. It was a long-running hit, playing for a total of 714 performances (Christopher Bernau was Dracula).

But vampire musicals have been spectacularly less successful. During the early 2000s, no less than three flop vampire musicals opened and quickly closed on Broadway, with a total estimated loss of thirty million dollars. The first, *Dance of the Vampires*, opened in 2002 with Michael Crawford as the leading vampire, and played for only fifty-six performances. The next, *Dracula, the Musical* opened in 2004 with Tom Hewitt as Dracula. It managed to hang on for 157 performances, losing millions in the process. The third and final flop in the vampire "trilogy" was *Lestat*, which opened in 2006 and played for just thirty-nine performances (Hugh Panero played the title role).

Further, Stanley Silverman's *Hotel for Criminals* (see entry) didn't have an afterlife, and *Dracula Sabbat*, which was based on Stoker's novel and which premiered at the Judson Poets' Theatre during the 1970-1971 season, seems to have disappeared after its initial run there (the book and lyrics were by Leon Katz and the music was by John Herbert McDowell).

In 1828, Heinrich Marschner's opera *Der Vampyr* premiered in Germany, and fell into general neglect, not receiving its New York premiere until 1980, when it opened at the Encompass Theatre on September 24 for twenty-four performances. The original libretto was by Wilhelm August Wohlbruck, and the new version enjoyed an English translation by Michael Feingold. Peter G. Davis in the *New York Times* hailed the "splendid production," and noted it offered a "melodiously pleasant" score.

In the 1990s, the Wings Theatre Company presented the Off Off Broadway musical *Fangs* ("The Vampire Musical") with book and lyrics by Clint Jefferies and music by Michael Calderwood.

There have also been two (apparently unproduced) vampire musicals, both of which have received studio cast recordings. *Possessed/The Dracula Musical* was released by Wild Twin Tunes Records (CD # WT-1004) in 1989; the book was by Robert Marasco and Jason Darrow, the lyrics by Darrow, and the music by Carter Cathcart. And a 1995 British musical, *Nosferatu the Vampire*, was released on a 2-CD set by Dress Circle Records (# NVDC/20; the lyrics were by Bernard J. Taylor and Eric Vickers, and the music was by Taylor.

251 Carmines Sings Whitman Sings Carmines. THEATRE: Playwrights Horizons; OPENING DATE: February 18, 1985; PERFORMANCES: 14; DIRECTION: Al Carmines; LIGHTING: David N. Weiss; PRODUCER: Playwrights Horizons (Andre Bishop, Artistic Director; Paul Daniels, Managing Director)

CAST—Al Carmines

The revue was presented in two acts. NOTES: *Carmines Sings Whitman Sings Carmines* was an evening of Al Carmines performing both his and other composers' songs. He also introduced songs set to the poems of Walt Whitman; in addition, *Theatre World 1984-1984 Season* reported that Carmines read passages from Peter Parnell's *Romance Language* (see entry), which had been produced by Playwrights Horizons earlier in the season and in which Carmines had played the role of Walt Whitman. Besides his own songs, Carmines sang numbers by such writers, lyricists and composers as Abel Baer, Irving Berlin, Anne Caldwell, David Epstein, Maria Irene Fornes, L. Wolfe Gilbert, Jerome Kern, Gertrude Stein, Mao Tse Tung, and P.G. Wodehouse.

See Appendix N for a list of revues and musicals by Carmines.

252 Caroline, *or* Change. THEATRE: Newman Theatre/The Public Theatre; OPENING DATE: November 30, 2003; PERFORMANCES: 106; BOOK: Tony Kushner; LYRICS: Tony Kushner; MUSIC: Jeanine Tesori; DIRECTION: George C. Wolfe; CHOREOGRAPHY: Hope Clarke Scenery: Riccardo Hernandez; COSTUMES: Paul Tazewell; LIGHTING: Jules Fisher and Peggy Eisenhauer; MUSICAL DIRECTION:

Linda Twine; PRODUCERS: The Public Theatre (George C. Wolfe, Producer; Mara Manus, Executive Director); Peter DuBois and Steven Tabakin, Associate Producers

CAST—Tonya Pinkins (Caroline Thibodeaux), Capathia Jenkins (The Washing Machine), Tracy Nicole Chapman/Marva Hicks/Ramona Keller (The Radio), Harrison Chad (Noah Gellman), Chuck Cooper (The Dryer, The Bus), Alice Playten (Grandma Gellman), Reathel Bean (Grandpa Gellman), Veanne Cox (Rose Stopnick Gellman), David Costabile (Stuart Gellman), Chandra Wilson (Dotty Moffett), Adriane Lenox (The Moon), Anika Noni Rose (Emmie Thibodeaux), Kevin Ricardo Tate (Jackie Thibodeaux), Marcus Carl Franklin (Joe Thibodeaux), Larry Keith (Mr. Stopnick)

The action occurs in Lake Charles, Louisiana, in November and December 1963.

The musical was presented in two acts (songs were not listed in the program; the list below is taken from the cast album).

ACT ONE—*Washer/Dryer*: "16 Feet Beneath the Sea" (Tonya Pinkins, Capathia Jenkins), "The Radio" (Tracy Nicole Chapman, Marva Hicks, Ramona Keller), "Laundry Quintet" (Tracy Nicole Chapman, Marva Hicks, Ramona Keller, Tonya Pinkins, Capathia Jenkins), "Noah Down the Stairs" (Harrison Chad), "The Cigarette" (Tonya Pinkins, Harrison Chad, Capathia Jenkins), "Laundry Finish" (Tracy Nicole Chapman, Marva Hicks, Ramona Keller), "The Dryer" (Chuck Cooper, Tracy Nicole Chapman, Marva Hicks, Ramona Keller), "I Got Four Kids" (Tonya Pinkins, Chuck Cooper, Capathia Jenkins); *Cabbage*: "Caroline, There's Extra Food" (Veanne Cox, Tonya Pinkins, Alice Playten, Reathel Bean, Harrison Chad); "There Is No God, Noah" (David Costabile); "Rose Stopnick Can Cook" (Alice Playten, Reathel Bean, David Costabile, Veanne Cox, Tonya Pinkins, Harrison Chad); *Long Distance*: "Long Distance" (Veanne Cox); *Moon Change*: "Dotty and Caroline" (Chandra Wilson, Tonya Pinkins, Adriane Lenox); "Moon Change" (Adriane Lenox); "Moon Trio" (Adriane Lenox, Chandra Wilson, Tonya Pinkins); "The Bus" (Chuck Cooper); "That Can't Be" (Chandra Wilson, Tonya Pinkins, Adriane Lenox); "Noah and Rose" (Harrison Chad, Veanne Cox); "Inside/Outside" (Adriane Lenox, Harrison Chad, Veanne Cox); "JFK" (Alice Playten, Reathel Bean, Chandra Wilson, Adriane Lenox, Harrison Chad); *Duets*: "No One's Waitin'" (Tracy Nicole Chapman, Marva Hicks, Ramona Keller, Noni Rose, Tonya Pinkins); "'Night Mamma" (Anika Noni Rose); "Gonna Pass Me a Law" (Tonya Pinkins, Harrison Chad); "Noah Go to Sleep" (Tonya Pinkins, Harrison Chad); *The Bleach Cup*: "Noah Has a Problem" (Tonya Pinkins, Veanne Cox); "Stuart and Noah" (David Costabile, Harrison Chad, Tonya Pinkins); "Quarter in the Bleach Cup" (Harrison Chad, Tonya Pinkins, Capathia Jenkins); "Caroline Takes My Money Home" (Harrison Chad, Tonya Pinkins, Anika Noni Rose, Kevin Ricardo Tate, Marcus Carl Franklin); "Roosevelt Petrucius Coleslaw" (Harrison Chad, Anika Noni Rose, Kevin Ricardo Tate, Marcus Carl Franklin, Tonya Pinkins)

ACT TWO—*Ironing*: "Santa Comin' Caroline" (Tracy Nicole Chapman, Marva Hicks, Ramona Keller, Capathia Jenkins); "Little Reward" (Capathia Jenkins, Tonya Pinkins, Tracy Nicole Chapman, Marva Hicks, Ramona Keller); "1943" (Tonya Pinkins, Tracy Nicole Chapman, Marva Hicks, Ramona Keller, Capathia Jenkins); "Mr. Gellman's Shirts" (Veanne Cox, Tonya Pinkins); "Ooh Child" (Capathia Jenkins, Tracy Nicole Chapman, Marva Hicks, Ramona Keller); "Rose Recovers" (Veanne Cox, Tonya Pinkins, Chuck Cooper); "I Saw Three Ships" (Kevin Ricardo Tate, Marcus Carl Franklin, Anika Noni Rose, Tonya Pinkins); *The Chanukah Party*: "The Chanukah Party" (David Costabile, Harrison Chad, Veanne Cox, Alice Playten, Reathel Bean, Larry Keith); "Dotty and Emmie" (Chandra Wilson, Anika Noni Rose, Tonya Pinkins); "I Don't Want My Child to Hear That" (Tonya Pinkins, Larry Keith, Alice Playten, Reathel Bean, Veanne Cox); "Mr. Stopnick and Emmie" (Anika Noni Rose, Larry Keith, Tonya Pinkins, Veanne Cox); "Kitchen Fight" (Chandra Wilson, Anika Noni Rose, Tonya Pinkins); "A Twenty Dollar Bill and Why" (Larry Keith, Veanne Cox, Harrison Chad, Alice Playten, Chandra Wilson); "I Hate the Bus" (Anika Noni Rose); "Moon, Emmie and Stuart Trio" (Adriane Lenox, Anika Noni Rose, David Costabile, Veanne Cox); *The Twenty Dollar Bill*: "The Twenty Dollar Bill" (Harrison Chad, Veanne Cox, Larry Keith, Reathel Bean, Alice Playten, Capathia Jenkins, Tonya Pinkins); "Caroline and Noah Fight" (Harrison Chad, Tonya Pinkins, Chuck Cooper); *Aftermath*: "Aftermath" (Veanne Cox, Harrison Chad, David Costabile, Larry Keith); *Lot's Wife*: "Sunday Morning" (Tonya Pinkins, Chandra Wilson); "Lot's Wife" (Tonya Pinkins); *How Long Has This Been Going On?*: "Salty Teardrops" (Tracy Nicole Chapman, Marva Hicks, Ramona Keller); "Why Does Our House Have a Basement?" (Harrison Chad, Veanne Cox, Capathia Jenkins); "Underwater" (Tonya Pinkins, Harrison Chad); *Epilogue*: Epilogue (Adriane Lenox, Anika Noni Rose, Kevin Ricardo Tate, Marcus Carl Franklin)

NOTES—*Caroline, or Change* transferred to Broadway after its Off Broadway run, opening at the Eugene O'Neill Theatre on May 2, 2004, for a disappointing run of 136 performances. The script was published by Theatre Communications Group in 2004, and a 2-CD cast album of the Broadway production was released by Hollywood Records (# 2061-62436-2).

A later production in Los Angeles did well, and perhaps the musical will eventually find its place in regional and community theatre.

Caroline, or Change was clearly a labor of love on the part of its creators, but perhaps the overly familiar plot (which dealt with race relations in the American South of 1963) and its somewhat unattractive score worked against it. Caroline is a Black maid who works for a Southern Jewish family whose members include a lonely and neglected eight-year-old boy whose widowed father has remarried, and so not only did the story go over familiar (and preachy) ground, it also brought to mind other plays about Southern families with Black servants, such as Carson McCullers' *The Member of the Wedding* (1950) and Alfred Uhry's *Driving Miss Daisy* (1987). McCullers' play dealt in part with a Black maid in a family with two children (a twelve-year-old girl and a six-year-old boy) who are neglected by their widowed father; and Uhry's masterful play, about a wealthy Southern Jewish widow who has a Black chauffeur in her employ, examined the immense racial and social changes occurring in the United States in a wry and affecting manner which was all the more powerful for its understatement. Further, audiences in 2003 were surely aware of racial problems in the United States of 1963, and certainly everyone knew the era was a turning point in American history with its array of momentous historical events (the civil rights march on Washington, D.C., political assassinations, and the Vietnam War). In 1963, tremendous social, cultural, and political changes were just around the corner, and it seemed smug, or perhaps just jejune, on the part of *Caroline*'s creators to offer the obvious as if it were ground-breaking news. Another problem with the musical was its coy use of inanimate household objects (such as a washing machine and a radio) as objective correlatives for Caroline's unhappiness; these appliances (as well as the Moon and a city bus) came to life, portrayed by actors; this device seemed desperate, and far too cute for the would-be serious story. Another problem with the libretto was that the characters seemed overly aware of themselves and their plight (particularly Noah, the eight-year-old boy). *Caroline, or Change* laid claim to be taken seriously; but too many factors in its libretto, lyrics, and music worked against it. Perhaps it wasn't entirely fair to label *Caroline, or Change* as "the sulky maid musical" (so termed by the *New York Post*'s Michael Reidel, whose twice-weekly columns are must-reads for the latest in Broadway news and gossip); and perhaps the unnamed source who told him the show was "*Beulah* without the laughs" wasn't quite accurate (*Beulah*, about a Black maid who works for a White family, was an ABC situation comedy series which ran from 1950 to 1953). But much of the material in *Caroline, or Change* seemed to ask for these kinds of flip comments (the musical seemed the perfect target for the *Forbidden Broadway* crew).

The 2007 documentary film *ShowBusiness: The Road to Broadway* chronicled *Caroline, or Change* and three other musicals (*Wicked*, *Taboo*, and *Avenue Q* [see entry for the latter production]) which opened on Broadway during the 2003-2004 season; the film was released on DVD by Genius Products and Liberation Entertainment (# 80543).

253 Carricknabauna. THEATRE: Greenwich Mews Theatre; OPENING DATE: March 30, 1967; PERFORMANCES: 21; WORDS: Padraic Colum; "dramatized" by Padraic Colum and Basil Burwell; MUSIC: Harriet Bailin; DIRECTION: Larry Arrick; SCENERY: Jock Stockwell; COSTUMES: Jock Stockwell; LIGHTING: Jock Stockwell; PRODUCERS: Greenwich Players, Inc. (a Stella Holt Production)

CAST—Martyn Green, Neil Fitzgerald, Hal Norman, Anne Draper, Tanny McDonald, Denise Huot, Rosemary McNamara, Mark Jenkins, Olive Murphy, Brid Lynch, Christopher Strater

The revue was presented in two acts.

ACT ONE—"The Old Poet" (Neil Fitzgerald), "When You Were a Lad" (Hal Norman, Christopher Strater, Mark Jenkins), "I Went Out in the Evening" (Martyn Green), "Fern's Castle" (Mark Jenkins), "The Crows" (Mark Jenkins), "Queen Gormlai" (Brid Lynch), "Carricknabauna" (Neil Fitzgerald, Hal Norman, Mark Jenkins, Christopher Strater), "For a Bride You Have Come" (Rosemary McNamara, Denise Huot), "The Well" (Mark Jenkins), "The Charm" (Christopher Strater), "Dirge of the Lone Woman" (by Mary Colum) (Tanny McDonald), "Dermott Donn MacMorna" (Denise Huot), "Tonight You See My Face" (Tanny McDonald), "No Bird That Sits" (Rosemary McNamara), "Sean O'Dwyer" (Martyn Green), "Old Scholar" (Neil Fitzgerald), "Sojourner" (Hal Norman), "Old Woman of the Roads" (Brid Lynch), "Cheap Jack" (Martyn Green), "The Lannan Shoe" (Brid Lynch, Denise Huot, Rosemary McNamara, Tanny McDonald), "The Fiddles Were Playing" (Anne Draper)

ACT TWO—"Stations of the Cross" (Martyn Green, Christopher Strater, Mark Jenkins, Tanny McDonald, Rosemary McNamara, Denise Huot, Brid Lynch), "One Came Before Her" (Rosemary McNamara, Christopher Strater), "Toymaker" (Martyn Green), "County Mayo" (Neil Fitzgerald), "Raftery" (Martyn Green), "Raftery's Repentence" (Neil Fitzgerald), "An Drinaun Donn" (Denise Huot), "The Terrible Robber Men" (Hal Norman, Christopher Strater, Rosemary McNamara), "The Cradle Song" (Tanny McDonald), "Spanish Lady" (Martyn Green), "White Faced Throng" (Brid Lynch), "Seumas-a-Ree" (Denise Huot), "The Rebel" (Martyn Green), "The Birds That Left the Cage" (Hal Norman, Christopher Strater, Neil Fitzgerald, Mark Jenkins, Denise Huot, Tanny McDonald, Rosemary McNamara), "O'Connell Bridge" (Mark Jenkins), "Meditation" (Anne Draper), "Age of Bronze" (Anne Draper, Mark Jenkins), "Over the Hills and Far Away" (Martyn Green, Company)

NOTES—*Carricknabauna* was an evening of Irish writer Padraic Colum's poetry and ballads set to music by Harriet Bailin. Walter Kerr in the *New York Times* felt the work would have been more successful as a succession of songs in a revue-styled format, and he regretted that Basil Burwell, the adaptor, tried to force the material into "one-eighth" of a story line. Kerr noted that amount was "too little for a story line, and too much for the verse." An earlier version of *Carricknabauna* had been previously produced in Dublin as *The Road Round Ireland*.

254 Carry Nation. "An Opera"; THEATRE: New York State Theatre; OPENING DATE: March 28, 1968; PERFORMANCES: 3; LIBRETTO: William North Jayme; MUSIC: Douglas Moore; DIRECTION: Frank Corsaro; SCENERY: Will Steven Armstrong; COSTUMES: Patton Campbell; MUSICAL DIRECTION: Samuel Krachmalnick; PRODUCER: The New York City Opera

CAST—Beverly Wolff (Carry Nation), Arnold Voketaitis (Carry Nation's Father), Ellen Faull (Carry Nation's Mother), Julian Patrick (Charles), Dan Kingman (First Man in Saloon), Don Carlo (Second Man in Saloon), Don Yule (City Marshal), Kellis Miller (Ben), Edward Pierson (Preacher), Young Men at Hoedown (Ronald Bentley, John Stewart), Arlene Adler (Young Woman at Hoedown), Jack Bittner (Toaster at Hoedown, Caretaker), Michael Ahearn (A Boy), Colette Martin (A Girl), Joan August (First Lady of Auxiliary), Maria West (Second Lady of Auxiliary), Lila Herbert (Third Lady of Auxiliary), Donna Owen (Fourth Lady of Auxiliary)

The action occurs in 1901 as well as during the period 1865-1867.

The opera was presented in two acts.

NOTES—Like Lizzie Borden, another real-life figure who was a leading character in a 1960s opera (see entry for *Lizzie Borden*), Carry Nation (1846-1911) was also identified with a hatchet. In her case, the hatchet was a symbol of her crusade against alcohol (and tobacco). However, the opera dealt with her back story, that is, her early years with her parents, her first husband, and the events which led to her becoming the nation's most well-known prohibitionist.

Harold C. Schonberg in the *New York Times* covered the New York premiere (the opera's world premiere had occurred two years earlier at the University of Kansas), and he noted that often the score was "more operetta than opera." Overall, the music "lacked point and variety," and the libretto dealt with "too much psychology and not enough action."

Douglas Moore's score is well-preserved on a 3-LP set by released by Desto Records (# DC-6463/65), and his music is intensely dramatic and well-suited to its story. But the opera has never found a foothold in the operatic repertory. Perhaps the image of Carry Nation is too much of the self-righteous scold, and her story lacks general appeal. She seems to share the fate of Dr. Andrew Brock, the leading character of the 1960 Broadway musical *Tenderloin*, who was another crusader against vice and corruption; the trouble was that, theatrically speaking, the Dr. Brock who sings of "Good Clean Fun" was not as much fun as the underworld denizens of the Tenderloin who celebrated the good times which naughty "Little Old New York" had to offer.

255 Cartoons for a Lunch Hour. THEATRE: Perry Street Theatre; OPENING DATE: November 11, 1978; PERFORMANCES: 12; BOOK: Loften Mitchell; LYRICS: Loften Mitchell; additional lyrics by Rudy Stevenson; MUSIC: Rudy Stevenson; DIRECTION: Percival Borde Choreography: Frank Hatchett; Rick Odums, Assistant Choreography; SCENERY: Phillip Graneto; COSTUMES: Bernard Johnson; LIGHTING: Terry Chandler; MUSICAL DIRECTION: Rudy Stevenson; PRODUCER: Seven Ages Performances, Ltd.

CAST—Johnny Barracuda (Labor Leader), Rosita Broadous (Noire), Don Butler (Vice President), Nora M. Cole (Mayda), Denise DeMirjian (Blanche), Clinton Derricks-Carroll (Jay), Charlene Harris (Carmella), Amy E. Hennessy (Dancer), Stephanie Madden (Ann), Brenda Mitchell (Heavenly Choir), Linda Morton (Heavenly Choir), Rick Odums (Gabriel), Geisha Otero (Satan), Claudia Peluso (Dina), Roy Rogers (Heavenly Choir), Arlena Rolant (Peter's Angel), Stephen J. Smith (Dancer, Herald), Grant Stewart (Business Executive), Nancy-Suzanne (Dancer), Anthony Whitehouse (Peter), Christopher Wynkoop (President), Linda E. Young (Heavenly Choir)

MUSICAL NUMBERS (number of acts and song assignments unknown; songs are listed in performance order): "Come On in This House," "This Angel's Arrivin'," "I Thought, Why Me?" "Wanna Go to Heaven," "Hail to Peter," "Ain't You Ashamed?" "Heaven Come and Help Us Out," "I Am the President," "Stay Ahead of the People," "I'll Demonstrate," "I'm Here," "Heaven in Your Eyes," "Stories," "Just a Little Italian Girl," "Smile Little Irish Girl," "There's a New Place," "Latin Girl," "A Place Somewhere," "A Party at Peter's Place," Finale

NOTES—*The Best Plays of 1978-1979* indicated that *Cartoons for a Lunch Hour* opened on November 11, 1978, and that the direction was by Percival Borde. On the other hand, *Theatre World 1978-1979 Season* gave the opening as November 28, and credited Akin Babatunde with direction (and cast member Arlena Rolant as assistant to the director). However, both reference books agreed that the Off Off Broadway musical played for twelve performances.

256 Casanova. THEATRE: The New York State Theatre; OPENING DATE: November 1, 1985; PERFORMANCES: Unknown; LIBRETTO: Dominick Argento; MUSIC: Dominick Argento; DIRECTION: Arthur Masella; CHOREOGRAPHY: Jessica Redel; SCENERY: Franco Colavecchia; COSTUMES: Lewis Brown; LIGHTING: Duane Schuler; MUSICAL DIRECTION: Scott Bergeson; PRODUCER: The New York City Opera.

CAST—Robert Brubaker (Montebank, Inquisitor, Tarraglia), Carol Sparrow (Vendor, Girl), Timothy Nolen (Casanova), David Hamilton (Lorenzo), Carolyn Sielski (Lady), Melissa Fogarty (Marcantonio), John Lankston (Marquis de Lisle), Ralph Bassett (Businello), Michele McBride (Barbara), Carol Gutknecht (Giuletta), Mark Thomsen (Gabrielle, Gondolier), Jane Bunnell (Timante, Young Woman), Dianne Iauco (Gianpaolo), Ruth Golden (Dircea), Susanne Marsee (Bellino), George Wyman (Demofoonte), Deborah Saverance (Cherinto), Susan Schafer (Matusio), Joyce Castle (Madame d'Urfe), Lee Bellaver (Servant to Madame d'Urfe), William Ledbetter (Chief of Police), Louis Perry (Officer), Jerold Siena (Charlatan, Inquisitor, Pulcinello), Joseph McKee (Inquisitor, Spanish Captain), Bernard Waters (Guard)

The action occurs in Venice during the first week of the Carnival Season in 1774.

The opera was presented in three acts.

NOTES—As *Casanova's Homecoming*, the opera premiered at the Minnesota Opera, St. Paul, Minnesota, on April 12, 1985, for four performances (Julian Patrick was Casanova).

In the opera, Casanova returns to Venice after having been exiled for eighteen years. The plot was filled with schemes and intrigues, including one in which an enemy hopes to discredit Casanova by having a castrato impersonate a woman and flirt with the legendary lover. But it turns out the castrato is really a woman who has been impersonating a castrato. Donal Henahan in the *New York Times* found the opera a "thorough going delight ... a witty theatre piece" that would charm audiences for many years to come. He further noted that as far as he could tell, the opera's New York premiere was an "historic event": the first time an opera in English used English supertitles.

In April 1985, a week after *Casanova* premiered at the Minnesota Opera, another lyric adaptation of the work opened in Geneva when Girolamo Arrigo's opera *Il Ritorno di Casanova* premiered. And Maury Yeston's 1982 Broadway musical *Nine* had earlier offered a Casanova sequence as a projected-film-musical-within-a-stage-musical. Yeston's music for this sequence ranks with the most memorable theatre music of the era.

257 Casino Paradise. THEATRE: The Ballroom; OPENING DATE: June 7, 1992; PERFORMANCES: 18; BOOK: Arnold Weinstein and Thomas Babe; LYRICS: Arnold Weinstein; MUSIC: William Bolcom; MUSICAL DIRECTION: Roger Trefousse

CAST—Joan Morris, Andre De Shields, Steven Goldstein

The musical was presented in two acts.

ACT ONE (song assignments unknown)—Little Overture, "Seaside Peace," "I Am the Landlord," "Gambling"/"Roll Up Your Sleeves," "A Great Man's Child," "My Father the Gangster," "Peculiar," "It Will Be Our Little Secret," "Casino Paradise," "Drive Me, Driver," "I'm His," "Nobody Takes My Paradise from Me," "Put Him In," Finale: "Power!"

ACT TWO—"This Is Not the Promised Land," "Boardwalkin' Blues," "Nurse's Song," "Here I Stand," "Night, Make My Day," "Ten Cent Piece of the Pie," "The Establishment Route," "The Road to You," "The Curse," Finale: "Boatman"/"Casino Paradise" (reprise)

NOTES—*Casino Paradise* told the saga of Ferguson, a ruthless and greedy mogul who buys up a small town in order to build a garish gambling center (The Casino Paradise).

The premiere of the fascinating "musical? theatre opera? cabaret opera? music theatre?" piece (so described by the composer, William Bolcom) took place at the American Music Theatre Festival in Philadelphia in April 1990; the following year, Koch International Classics Records released a cast recording (CD # 3-7047-2-H1) of the Philadelphia production with Timothy Nolen (as Ferguson). Joan Morris (Mrs. William Bolcom) and Eddie Korbich were also in the cast. (The above song list is taken from the recording.)

Two songs from the production ("Night, Make My Day" and "My Father the Gangster") were included in the collection *William Bolcom Songs* (Naxos CD # 8.559249) with Carole Farley (Soprano) and Bolcom on piano. The Off Off Broadway production at the Ballroom was an intimate, truly "cabaret" version of the work, with just three performers, including Joan Morris (thirteen cast members were in original Philadelphia production); the production at the Ballroom may not have included the entire score.

Bernard Holland in the *New York Times* found the nightclub venue just right for Arnold Weinstein's "wickedly funny" lyrics, Bolcom's "all-American synthesis of black and white pop and Latin styles," and the "clarity and force" of the three performers. Holland reported that Bolcom was said to be happier with the nightclub version of the work rather than the fully staged 1990 production in Philadelphia.

For other adventurous works by Bolcom, see entries for *Dynamite Tonight* (and *Dynamite Tonite!*) and *A View from the Bridge*.

258 The Cast Aways (1975).THEATRE: Marymount Manhattan College; OPENING DATE: September 19, 1975; PERFORMANCES: 12; BOOK: Anthony J. Stimac; LYRICS: Steve Brown; MUSIC: Don Pippin; DIRECTION: Anthony J. Stimac; CHOREOGRAPHY: Gene Kelton; SCENERY: Clarke W. Thornton; COSTUMES: Dean Reiter; LIGHTING: Clarke W. Thornton; MUSICAL DIRECTION: D. Bishop; PRO-

DUCERS: Marymount Manhattan College in association with BPS

CAST—Reid Shelton (Mr. Warren, Jasper, Indian), Marie Santell (Mrs. Warren, Christine), Peter Boyden (Mr. Cooke, Jerry, Pendragon, General), Patti Perkins (Mrs. Cooke, LaRole), Dennis Howard (Mr. Lewis, Captain Lenox), Sydney Blake (Mrs. Lewis, Adela), Gibby Brand (The Mate), Hank Berrings (Pirate Captain)

SOURCE—The 1819 play *She Would Be a Soldier* by Mordecai Noah.

The action occurs in 1819 in the hold of a Barbary pirate ship somewhere in the Mediterranean. The musical was presented in two acts (division of acts and song assignments unknown; songs are listed in performance order).

MUSICAL NUMBERS—"All the World's a Hold," "I Won't Love a Soldier Boy," "The Chase," "Let's Mop Up These Yankees and Go Back Home," "Bring Out Old Glory," "My Love," "She Would Be a Soldier," "Whipperwill," "Call Back the Times," "If I Had Wings," "Isn't She," "This Dawn"

NOTES—The team of Anthony Stimac, Steve Brown, and Don Pippin returned in a limited Off Off Broadway engagement of their newest musical, *The Castaways*. As *Castaways*, the piece was presented in 1977 at a regular Off Broadway house (see entry).

259 Castaways (1977). "A Musical"; THEATRE: Promenade Theatre; OPENING DATE: February 7, 1977; PERFORMANCES: 1; BOOK: Anthony Stimac, Dennis Andersen, and Ron Whyte; LYRICS: Steve Brown; MUSIC: Don Pippin; DIRECTION: Tony Tanner; SCENERY: Scott Johnson; COSTUMES: Patricia McGourty; LIGHTING: Richard Winkler; MUSICAL DIRECTION: Dorothy Opalach; PRODUCERS: Jeff Britton in association with Jimmy Merrill and Michael Shepley

CAST—Gibby Brand (Mate), Joel Kramer (Mr. Cooke), Maureen Maloney (Adele), Stephen James (Mr. Lewis), June Squibb (Mrs. Cooke), Wayne Sherwood (Mr. Noah), Kathleen Widdoes (Mrs. Kendall), Daniel Ziskie (Second Mate), Rick Ladson (Captain)

SOURCE—The 1819 play *She Would Be a Soldier* by Mordecai Noah.

The action occurs in 1819 in the hold of a Barbary pirate ship somewhere in the Mediterranean. The musical was presented in one act.

MUSICAL NUMBERS—"Exits and Entrances" (Company), "Isn't She" (Maureen Maloney, Company), "She Can't Resist Me" (Wayne Sherwood, Joel Kramer, Stephen James), "Exits and Entrances" (reprise) (Company), "I Won't Love a Soldier-Boy" (Kathleen Widdoes, Stephen James), "The Chase" (Kathleen Widdoes, Joel Kramer, Company), "Kind Sir" (Maureen Maloney, Wayne Sherwood), "Could Such a Face Be False" (Kathleen Widdoes), "Old Glory"/"She Would Be a Soldier" (Kathleen Widdoes, Company), "My Love" (Stephen James, Maureen Maloney), "Whipperwill" (Joel Kramer, June Squibb), "Dumplings" (Maureen Maloney, Gentlemen), "Call Back the Times" (Wayne Sherwood), "This Dawn" (Kathleen Widdoes, Company), Finale (Company)

NOTES—As *The Cast Aways* (see entry), Anthony Stimac, Steve Brown, and Don Pippin's musical had been seen Off Off Broadway in 1975; as *Castaways*, it returned in a regular Off-Broadway production, running for only one performance. It was the team's third and final musical adaptation of an early American play (see entries for *The Contrast* [1974] and *Fashion* [1975]). The musical dealt with a theatrical troupe from Philadelphia which is captured by pirates; in order to save their lives, the actors must amuse their captors with a production of Mordecai Noah's melodrama *She Would Be a Soldier*. Clive Barnes in the *New York Times* liked the notion of performers playing under peril and felt that "someone should write a musical about it," with a "proper" book and "more permanent music." He found the lyrics and music of *Castaways* "unnoticeable," and the book a "bore."

Songs from the 1975 production not used were "Let's Mop Up These Yankees and Go Back Home" and "If I Had Wings." One of the new songs for the 1977 production was "Kind Sir," with music by Gary William Friedman.

A 1994 studio cast recording of *Fashion* (Original Cast Records CD # OCR-9492) included bonus tracks of three songs from *Castaways* ("If [Could] Such a Face Be False," "I Won't Love a Soldier-Boy," and "Exits and Entrances").

260 Catch Me If I Fall. "A New Musical"; THEATRE: Promenade Theatre; OPENING DATE: November 12, 1990; PERFORMANCES: 16; BOOK: Barbara Schottenfeld; LYRICS: Barbara Schottenfeld; MUSIC: Barbara Schottenfeld; DIRECTION: Susan Einhorn; additional staging by Stuart Ross; SCENERY: G.W. Mercier; COSTUMES: G.W. Mercier; LIGHTING: Richard Nelson; MUSICAL DIRECTION: Joseph Church; PRODUCERS: The Never or Now Company; Frederick Schultz and Terry A. Johnson, Associate Producers

CAST—James Judy (Lonny Simon), David Burdick (Brian Simon), Jeanine Morick (Laurie Simon), Sal Vivano (Peter Bennington), Ronnie Farer (Godiva Harris), Laura Dean (Domnica Gruia), A.D. Cover (Andrei Gruia)

The action occurs in New York City during the late fall of 1989.

The musical was presented in two acts.

ACT ONE—Opening Number/"Catch Me If I Fall" (James Judy, Company), "Business Is an Art" (James Judy, Laura Dean), "Veterinarian" (James Judy, Ronnie Farer), "The Love That Came Before" (James Judy, Jeanine Morick), "Sometimes at Night" (Laura Dean), "The Beach House" (Laura Dean, James Judy, Sal Vivano), "I Want You to Be ..." (Sal Vivano), "It's Not a Real Wedding" (James Judy, Sal Vivano, Laura Dean, Ronnie Farer, David Burdick), "I Know the Feeling"/"Home Never Leaves You" (James Judy, Laura Dean)

ACT TWO—"When You Live in New York" (Laura Dean, Company), "Liberate" (A.D. Cover), "Isn't It Strange That We Can Love Again?" (Laura Dean), "Timing and Lighting" (Laura Dean, James Judy), "Chaperone" (Laura Dean, Janine Morick, Ronnie Farer), "Never or Now" (James Judy), "Isn't It Strange That We Can Love Again?" (reprise) (James Judy, Laura Dean)

NOTES—Despite an occasionally interesting score (*The Applause/Best Plays Theatre Yearbook of 1990-1991* singled out "The Beach House" as a worthy edition to a future [*Off*] *Broadway Jukebox* [see entry]), *Catch Me If I Fall* managed only a two-week run.

The overly busy plot dealt with Lonny Simon, a former sculptor undergoing an identity crisis on his fortieth birthday (shades of Bobby in *Company*). He's still involved with his ex-wife; has a new girlfriend; and is on the verge of a green-card marriage to a Romanian whose visa will soon expire. Moreover, his son, his boss, and the bride's uncle enter into the plot. Although Lonny first enters into the green-card marriage as a favor, he soon realizes he's come to love his wife, and by the finale he and his bride are taking off for Romania in order to help his wife's father, who is a political prisoner there. Mel Gussow in the *New York Times* felt that the "thicker" the plot became, the "thinner" the show became, and noted that almost every plot point became fodder for jokey humor or sentimentality. He felt the lyrics were bland and that the music had a "pseudo-Sondheim sameness" (but he singled out two songs, "Chaperone" ["amusing"] and "Never or Now" ["tuneful"]). The cast recording was released by Painted Smiles Records (CD # PSCD-133), and includes three numbers not listed in the program ("Peter's Dilemma," "I'm Changing," and "True").

The musical had been seen in workshop at the Ensemble Studio Theatre, and its pre-Off Broadway tryout was presented at the Nickerson Theatre in Norwell, Massachusetts.

261 The Cats' Pajamas. "A New Revue"; THEATRE: Sheridan Square Playhouse; OPENING DATE: May 31, 1962; PERFORMANCES: 34; SKETCHES: Unless otherwise noted, all material by The Stewed Prunes (Richard Libertini and MacIntyre Dixon); DIRECTION: Herb Suffrin; SCENERY: James A. Taylor; LIGHTING: Gigi Cascio; MUSICAL DIRECTION: Arthur Siegel, Monte Aubrey; PRODUCERS: P.G. J. Productions

CAST—The Stewed Prunes (Richard Libertini and MacIntyre Dixon), with "guest star" Sylvia Lord

The revue was presented in two acts.

ACT ONE—Overture, "Cyril Suitcase," "Monsier Toad," "Mr. Fisby," "Dual Pianists," "Presentation," "Parade," "The Cats' Pajamas," "Blues," "Ties," "The Tenor," "Puppets & People"

ACT TWO (all songs performed by Sylvia Lord)—Calypso Medley (lyricists and composers unknown); "John B. Sails"; "Tick-Tock"; "Cold Box of Chicken"; Standards: "Do It Again!" (from *The French Doll*, 1922; lyric by B.G. [Buddy] DeSylva, music by George Gershwin); "Makin' Whoopee" (*Whoopee*, 1928; lyric by Gus Kahn, music by Walter Donaldson); "Home on the Range" (traditional); "Love Is a Good Thing for You" (*New Faces of 1962*; lyric by June Carroll, music by Arthur Siegel); "It Depends on How You Look at Things" (*New Faces of 1962*; lyric by June Carroll, music by Arthur Siegel); "Over the River and Into the Woods" (*New Faces of 1962*; lyric and music by Jack Holmes); "In the Morning" (*New Faces of 1962*; lyric and music by Ronny Graham)

NOTES—Louis Calta in the *New York Times* wrote "there's lots of fun" in *The Cats' Pajamas*, and he found Richard Libertini and MacIntyre Dixon "clever" comedians with "a wonderful flair for amusing nonsense." The evening was "zany, irreverent and untamed," and the two leads were "expert ... in their art of lunacy." Calta singled out one sequence in which Libertini and Dixon portrayed two leering and drunk patrons at a nightclub who ask Sylvia Lord to sing "Home on the Range." Calta reported that her rendition of the venerable song was "one of the sizzlingest" and "most comic" versions ever heard.

The first *Stewed Prunes*' revue opened in 1960 as *Stewed Prunes* (see entry), and played for 295 performances (Libertini, Dixon, and Lynda Segal were the Stewed Prunes). The second edition (sans Segal) lasted only one month.

Sylvia Lord was a "new face" earlier in the year, when she appeared in the short-lived sixth Broadway edition of Leonard Sillman's occasional series of *New Faces* revues which began in 1934 (there would be one more edition in 1968). In *The Cats' Pajamas*, she sang four songs from *New Faces of 1962*, "It Depends on How You Look at Things" as well as three ("In the Morning," "Over the River and Into the Woods," and "Love Is Good for You") which she introduced in the revue. Another song from *New Faces of 1962* ("I Want You to Be the First to Know") turned up in another Off Broadway revue the following year as "We Want You to Be the First Ones to Know" (see entry for the second edition of *Seven Come Eleven*).

262 Celia. "The Life and Music of Celia Cruz"; THEATRE: New World Stages; OPENING DATE: September 26, 2007; PERFORMANCES: 269; BOOK: Carmen Rivera and Candido Tirado; DIRECTION: Jaime Azpilicueta; CHOREOGRAPHY: Rafi Maldonado-Lopez; SCENERY: Narelle Sissons; Jan Hartley, Projection Design; COSTUMES: Haydee Morales; LIGHTING: Sarah Sidman; MUSICAL DIRECTION: Isidro Infante; PRODUCERS: Henry Cardenas and David Maldonado; Gerry Fojo, Associate Producer; Daddy Yankee, Executive Producer

CAST—XIOMARA LAUGART SANCHEZ (Celia Cruz), MODESTO LACEN (Pedro Knight), PEDRO CAPO (Nurse), Joselin Reyes (Woman), Anissa Gathers (Ollita, Assistant), Sunilda Caraballo (Tia Ana, Stylist, Others), Lai-Si Fernandez (Ensemble), Elvis Nolasco (Simon, Rogelio Martinez, Ralph Mercado), Wilson Mendieta (Announcer, Theatre/Club Manager, Friend-Amigo, Tito Puente, Johnny Pacheco, Others), Rogelio Douglas, Jr. (Ensemble)

The musical was presented in two acts.

ACT ONE—*My Lady* (*Mi Mujer*), "Toro Mata" (lyric and music by De la Colinz Hadem) (Xiomara Laugart Sanchez, Ensemble), "Drume Negrita" (lyric and music by Ernesto Grenet)/"Canto Lucumi" (lyric and music by Isidro Infante) (Anissa Gathers), "El Cumbachero" (lyric and music by Rafael Hernandez) (Joselin Reyes, Xiomara Laugart Sanchez), "Caramelos" (lyric and music by Roberto Puentes Martinez) (Xiomara Laugart Sanchez), "Burundanga" (lyric and music by Buffartique)/"El Yerbero Moderno" (lyric and music by Nester Mili-Bustillo)/ "Que Bueno Baila Usted" (lyric and music by Benny Moor) (Xiomara Laugart Sanchez), "Mexico Lindo" (lyric and music by Isidro Infante) (Xiomara Laugart Sanchez), "Cao, Cao, Mani Picao" (lyric and music by [Jose Carbo?] Menendez) (Xiomara Laugart Sanchez), "Tu Voz" (lyric and music by Ramon Cabrera Argotes) (Xiomara Laugart Sanchez), "Drume Negrita" (reprise) (Joselin Reyes, Anissa Gathers), "La Guarachera" (lyric and music by Tito Puente) (Xiomara Laugart Sanchez), "Bamba Colora" (lyric and music by Jose Claro Fumero) (Xiomara Laugart Sanchez, Ensemble)

ACT TWO—*A Singer Becomes a Legend*: "Usted Abuso" (lyric and music by Pepe Avila, Jose Carlos Figueiredo, and Carlos Marques Pinto) (Joselin Reyes, Modesto Lacen, Pedro Capo); "Isadora Duncan" (lyric and music by Tite Curet Alonso)/"Encantigo" (lyric and music by Roy Brown)/"Guantanamera" (lyric and music by Jose Diaz Fernandez and Jose Marti) (Xiomara Laugart Sanchez); "Las Caras Lindas de Mi Gente Negra" (lyric and music by Tite Curet Alonso) (Anissa Gathers); "Quimbara" (lyric and music by Junior Cepeda) (Xiomara Laugart Sanchez); "Cucala" (lyric and music by Wilfredo Figueroa) (Pedro Capo, Xiomara Laugart Sanchez); "Canto a la Habana" (lyric and music by Jose Carbo Menendez) (Xiomara Laugart Sanchez); "Dos Jueyes" (lyric and music by Willie Colon) (Xiomara Laugart Sanchez); "Cuba" (lyricist and composer unknown) (Anissa Gathers); "Soy Antillana" (lyric and music by Marilyn Pupo)/"La Dicha Mia" (lyric and music by Johnny Pacheco)/"Cuando Volveras" (lyric and music by Oscar Gomez) (Xiomara Laugart Sanchez); "Celia's Oye Como Va" (lyric and music by Tito Puente) (Xiomara Laugart Sanchez); "El Guaba" (lyric and music by Johnny Pacheco) (Xiomara Laugart Sanchez); "Gracias" (a/k/a "Cancion del Enfermero") (lyric and music by Oscar Gomez) (Pedro Capo); "La Negra Tiene Tumbao" (lyric and music by Sergio George and Fernando Osorio) (Xiomara Laugart Sanchez); "Yo Vivire" (lyric and music by Dino Fekaris and Frederick J. Perren; Spanish lyric by Oscar Gomez) (Xiomara Laugart Sanchez); "La Vida es un Carnaval" (lyric and music by Victor Roberto Daniel) (Xiomara Laugart Sanchez, Ensemble)

NOTES—*Celia* was a tribute to Celia Cruz (1924-2003), the legendary "Queen of Salsa" who left her homeland of Cuba in 1960 after the 1959 revolution and settled in the United States. With over seventy recordings and over twelve Grammy nominations (winning two awards in 2002 and 2003), Cruz, with her strong voice and flashy style, was probably the ultimate singer of salsa.

The production was performed in Spanish six times each week, and in English twice.

263 Censored Scenes from King Kong.

"A Comic Extravaganza"; THEATRE: Princess Theatre; OPENING DATE: March 6, 1980; PERFORMANCES: 5; PLAY: Howard Schuman; LYRICS: Howard Schuman; MUSIC: Andy Roberts; DIRECTION: Colin Bucksey; CHOREOGRAPHY: David Toguri; SCENERY: Mike Porter; COSTUMES: Jennifer Von Mayrhauser; LIGHTING: Richard Nelson; PRODUCERS: Michael White and Eddie Kulukundis; Robert S. Fishko, Associate Producer

CAST—Stephen Collins (Stephen), Nicky Mieholes (The Voice of the Producer), Pete Flasher (The Voice of the Author), Peter Riegert (Vogels, Sagar, Chiaruggi), Carrie Fisher (Iris), Alma Cuervo (Deborah), Chris Sarandon (Benchgelter), Edward Love (Walter Wilma)

The action occurs in London at the present time.

The play with music was presented in two acts.

ACT ONE—"Ha-Cha" (Carrie Fisher, Alma Cuervo, Edward Love); "Banana Oil" (Carrie Fisher, Alma Cuervo, Edward Love); "He Ain't Scared of Nothing" (Stephen Collins)

ACT TWO—"Number One" (Carrie Fisher, Alma Cuervo, Edward Love); "Soft Shoe Freak" (Peter Reigert); "The Other Side of the Wall" (Edward Love)

NOTES—Previously produced in London, the campy *Censored Scenes from King Kong* was damned by the critics and lasted less than a week (it may have been presented under a Middle or Limited Broadway contract). The play with music dealt with the notion that the original 1933 film version of *King Kong* included information for secret agents; these scenes were supposedly cut from the film, thus forcing spies to wait for the sequel, *Son of Kong*. An investigative journalist (Stephen Collins) is on the trail of the mystery, and it all takes place in a tacky London nightclub.

The Princess Theatre had been previously known as the 22 Steps Theatre. In its glory days, the venue had been the home of the fabled Latin Quarter nightclub. Reviewing the debacle of *Censored Scenes from King Kong*, Clive Barnes suggested the theatre's recent names were too good for the "more to be pitied than censored" play. In order to amend for the "horror" perpetuated upon the Princess' stage, he suggested the name of the theatre be changed to either the 21 Steps Theatre or the Duchess Theatre because "no theatre is quite the same after an experience like" *Censored Scenes from King Kong*.

264 Central Park.

THEATRE: New York State Theatre; OPENING DATE: November 12, 1999; PERFORMANCES: 4; DIRECTION: Mark Lamos; SCENERY: Michael Yeargan; COSTUMES: Candice Donnelly; LIGHTING: Robert Wierzel; MUSICAL DIRECTION: Stewart Robertson; PRODUCERS: The New York City Opera and Glimmerglass Opera

NOTES—The New York premiere of *Central Park* offered three one-act operas, all taking place in New York's "big back yard."

The Festival of Regrets (libretto, Wendy Wasserstein, music, Deborah Drattell) centered around the Jewish ritual Tashlich (The Festival of Regrets) and included Lauren Flanigan in the cast. In his review for *New York*, John Leonard described the score as a pastiche of "synagogue melodies and klezmer blues."

Strawberry Fields (libretto, A.R. Gurney, music, Michael Torke) dealt with a woman with Alzheimer's who sits on a park bench and believes she's about to see an operatic performance of the story of her life; the cast included Joyce Castle and Jeffrey Lenz. Leonard felt the work veered towards the "lugubrious" and noted the music offered "pop, tending to the schmaltzy."

The Food of Love (libretto, Terrence McNally, music, Robert Beaser) told of a young unwed mother who comes across various people in the park, including a policeman and two self-absorbed yuppies. Lauren Flanigan played the mother, and Leonard found the opera "the darkest and most anguished" of the evening's presentations.

Central Park had first been produced earlier in the year by the Glimmerglass Opera in Cooperstown, New York. In his review of that production in the *New Yorker*, Alex Ross said the evening was an often "cruelly accurate snapshot" of modern life, and noted that the characters in the opera (including a screaming cell-phone user) can be seen "on the streets after the opera" and "even ... at intermission."

The opera was shown on public television on January 19, 2000.

265 Chad Mitchell's Counterpoint.

"Songs from the New Renaissance"; THEATRE: The Bitter End; OPENING DATE: November 25, 1968; PERFORMANCES: 12; DIRECTION: Moni Yakim; SCENERY: Chuck Eisler; PRODUCER: Bert Wainer

CAST—CHAD MITCHELL (Singer); Monte Dunn, Ron Eisenberg, Hal Gaylor, and Joe Hunt (Musicians)

The revue was presented in two acts.

ACT ONE—"Blowin' in the Wind" (lyric and music by Bob Dylan), "The Times They Are A-Changing" (lyric and music by Bob Dylan), "At the Zoo" (lyric and music by Paul Simon), "The Weight" (lyric and music by Jaime Robbie Robertson), "Sad Eyed Lady in the Lowlands" (lyric and music by Bob Dylan), "Genuine Limitation of Life" (lyric and music by Jake Holmes), "She Belonged to Me" (lyric and music by Jake Holmes), "Late Sleeping Day" (lyric and music by Jake Holmes), "The Dangling Conversation" (lyric and music by Paul Simon), "Big Bright Green Pleasure Machine" (lyric and music by Paul Simon), "Like a Rolling Stone" (lyric and music by Bob Dylan)

ACT TWO—"Sing This All Together" (lyric and music by Mick Jagger and Keith Richard), "White Rabbit" (lyric and music by Grace Slick), "Mr. Tambourine Man" (lyric and music by Bob Dylan), "Just Like a Woman" (lyric and music by Bob Dylan), "The 59th Street Bridge Song (Feelin' Groovy)" (lyric and music by Paul Simon), "Wish I Was Anywhere Else" (lyric and music by Jake Holmes), "The White Ship" (lyric and music by George Edwards, Dave Michaels and Tony Cavallari), "Light My Fire" (lyric and music by Jim Morrison, Ray Manzarek, Robert Krieger and John Densmore), "Rainy Day Woman #12 and 35" (lyric and music by Bob Dylan), "Goodbye and Hello" (lyric and music by Tim Buckley and Larry Beckett)

NOTES—This short-running revue consisted of singer Chad Mitchell (accompanied by four musicians) performing popular songs of the 1960s. The pretentious and inadvertently hilarious program notes stated that song-writers in the 1960s had done more for the quality of American song than any lyricists and composers of the last two generations. (Apparently the contributions of such luminaries as George Gershwin, Jerome Kern, Harold Arlen, Richard Rodgers, Cole Porter, Frank Loesser, Leonard Bernstein, and Hoagy Carmichael were minor.)

The program went on to hail Bob Dylan as the "Picasso of melody" and to expound that Paul Simon is great because he speaks the "new language" of "today's collegians." Apparently the height of song-writing achievement in the 1960s was the ability to speak the language of the era's collegians.

266 Champeeen!

"The Two-Fisted Musical"; THEATRE: Harry DeJur Henry Street Settlement Playhouse/New Federal Theatre; OPENING DATE: March 18, 1983; PERFORMANCES: 24; BOOK: Melvin Van Peebles; LYRICS: Melvin Van Peebles; MUSIC:

Melvin Van Peebles; DIRECTION: Melvin Van Peebles; CHOREOGRAPHY: Louis Johnson; SCENERY: Chris Thomas and Bob Edmonds; COSTUMES: Quay Truitt; LIGHTING: Shirley Prendergast; MUSICAL DIRECTION: Bob Carten; PRODUCER: New Federal Theatre (Woodie King, Jr.)

CAST—Sandra Reaves-Phillips (Bessie Smith), Ruth Brown (Lilly), David Connell (Old Man), Lawrence Vincent (Referee), Ted Ross (Jack Gee); Ensemble (Louis Albert, Gary Easterling, Denise Elliott, Johne Forges, Herbert Kerr, Marcia James, Meachie Jones, Manette LaChance, John D. McNally, DeNessa Tobin, Mario Van Peebles, Carolyn Webb, Charles LaVont Williams)

The action occurs during the period 1908 through 1937 (but also includes a "Disco" scene); the locales include Chattanooga, Philadelphia, New York City, Chicago, Cuba, and Sidney, Australia.

The musical was presented in two acts (the program didn't credit song assignments).

ACT ONE—"You Had Me Anyhow," "Like a Dream" (medley), "Home Ballet," "Come to Mama," "Opportunity," "Like a Dream" (reprise), "Knockout," "The World's a Stage"

ACT TWO—"Gimme a Pigfoot (and a Bottle of Beer)" (lyric and music by Wesley "Socks" Wilson; some sources credit song to both Wilson and Coot Grant), "Home," "'T Ain't Nobody's Biz-ness If I Do" (lyric and music by Porter Grainger and Everett Robbins), "Greasy Lightnin'" (medley), "Greasy Lightnin'" (reprise), "Knockout" (March)

NOTES—*Champeeen!* an Off Off Broadway musical about Bessie Smith, ran out its limited engagement as part of the New Federal Theatre's season, and was never heard from again. The musical used boxing as a metaphor to depict the life and career of Bessie Smith. But Mel Gussow in the *New York Times* noted the metaphor was "underdeveloped both musically and dramatically," and while he liked the cast and the "brisk" choreography, he felt the "one-fisted" *Champeeen!* wasn't a "contender" and needed more seasoning "before entering the ring."

Better known for his films, Melvin Van Peebles was active in stage musicals for a little over a decade (see entries for *Waltz of the Stork* and *Waltz of the Stork Boogie*; he was also represented on Broadway twice during the 1971-1972 season with *Aint Supposed to Die a Natural Death* and *Dont Play Us Cheap*). *Becky*, his proposed musical version of William Makepeace Thackeray's novel *Vanity Fair* (first published in serial form during 1847 and 1848), had been scheduled to open in London in Summer 1980, but was never produced. (Julian Slade's version of the material had opened in London in 1962 and was a major flop, lasting only seventy performances.) It would have been interesting to see Van Peebles' take on the classic novel. The *New York Times* reported that Glenda Jackson was committed to the project for a year, that Van Peebles had written the book, that the lyrics were co-written by him and Mildred Kayden, and that Kayden had composed the music.

267 A Change in the Heir.

"A New Musical Comedy"; THEATRE: Edison Theatre; OPENING DATE: April 29, 1990; PERFORMANCES: 17; BOOK: George H. Gorham and Dan Sticco; LYRICS: George H. Gorham; MUSIC: Dan Sticco; DIRECTION: David H. Bell; CHOREOGRAPHY: David H. Bell; SCENERY: Michael Anania; COSTUMES: David Murin; LIGHTING: Jeff Davis; MUSICAL DIRECTION: Rob Bowman; PRODUCER: Stewart F. Lane

CAST—BROOKS ALMY (Aunt Julia), Brian Sutherland (Giles), J.K. Simmons (Edwin), David Gunderman (Nicholas), Connie Day (Countess), Mary Stout (Lady Enid), JUDY BLAZER (Prince Conrad), JEFFREY HERBST (Princess Agnes), Jan Neuberger (Martha), Jennifer Smith (Lady Elizabeth)

The actions occurs "once upon a time, long, long ago, in a castle far, far away" and then "twenty years later" on a Friday, Saturday, and Sunday.

The musical was presented in two acts.

ACT ONE—Prologue (Company), "The Weekend" (Brooks Almy, Connie Day, Jan Neuberger, Mary Stout, J.K. Simmons, Brian Sutherland), "Here I Am" (Judy Blazer), "Exactly the Same as It Was" (Mary Stout, J.K. Simmons, Brian Sutherland, Brooks Almy, Connie Day, Jan Neuberger), "Look at Me" (Jeffrey Herbst, Judy Blazer), "Take a Look at That" (Jeffrey Herbst, Jennifer Smith), "I Tried and I Tried and I Tried" (J.K. Simmons, Mary Stout, Jeffrey Herbst, Connie Day, Judy Blazer), "Can't I?" (Judy Blazer), "When" (Brooks Almy, Jan Neuberger), "A Fairy Tale" (Jeffrey Herbst, Judy Blazer), "An Ordinary Family" (Company)

ACT TWO—"Happily Ever After, After All" (Jeffrey Herbst), "Shut Up and Dance" (David Gunderman, Jennifer Smith), "Can't I?" (reprise) (Judy Blazer), "Duet" (Jeffrey Herbst, Judy Blazer), "Hold That Crown" (Brooks Almy), "By Myself" (Judy Blazer, Company), Finale (Company)

NOTES—Set in medieval times (which for some reason always seems to bring out the twee and the cutesy in the creators of musicals [see entries for *Ride the Winds*, *Tricks*, and *Bodo*; even Bob Fosse's *Pippin* was guilty of occasional overarching coyness]), the pun-filled *A Change in the Heir* was about a boy and girl from two rival royal families, both raised as members of the opposite sex in order to help their chances of inheriting the throne when they grow up (hence, Jeffrey Herbst played Princess Agnes and Judy Blazer played Prince Conrad). Or something like that. Even the critics couldn't quite explain the musical's back story. Edwin Wilson in the *Wall Street Journal* found the story "sophomoric," and quickly added he meant "high school sophomoric, not college"; Clive Barnes in the *New York Post* said the musical "starts ridiculous and gets sillier"; and Stephen Holden in the *New York Times* noted the musical took place "in a low-rent district of fairyland where the royal garb resembles patterned bed sheets."

Howard Kissel in the *Daily News* reported that during the first act a fire alarm in the theatre went off (thus forcing the musical to take an unexpected intermission) and then midway in the second act the ventilators in the theatre started making noise. He noted that these events were the "two most interesting things" to happen during the performance.

During previews, "I Tried and I Tried and I Tried" was titled "Quintet."

The musical had first been produced by New Tuners Theatre in Chicago.

It appears the musical was presented in New York under a Middle Broadway contract.

268 Changes.

"A New Musical"; THEATRE: Theatre de Lys; OPENING DATE: February 19, 1980; PERFORMANCES: 7; LYRICS: Danny Apolinar; MUSIC: Addy Fieger; original dance music by Larry Fallon; DIRECTION: Dorothy Love; CHOREOGRAPHY: Ronn Forella; SCENERY: Don Jensen; COSTUMES: Miles White; LIGHTING: Richard Nelson; MUSICAL DIRECTION: Hal Serra; PRODUCERS: Dorothy Love and John Britton, by special arrangement with Lucille Lortel Productions, Inc.

CAST—Irving Allen Lee (Randy), Larry Kert (Mark), Trina Parks (Sanamu), Kelly Bishop (Anna); The Quintet (Hal Serra, Piano; Jeff Fuller, Bass; Ron Davis, Drums; Frank Perowksy, Reeds; David Samuels, Vibes and Percussion; Frank Cruz, Voice with the Quintet)

The action occurs in a city during the present time; the action spans the course of one year, beginning and ending on New Year's Eve.

The musical was presented in one act.

MUSICAL NUMBERS—Overture (Quintet); "Changes" (Company), *Winter:* "Have I Got a Girl for You" (Irving Allen Lee, Larry Kert), "Have I Got a Guy for You" (Trina Parks, Kelly Bishop), "So Much for Me" (Company), "Happy New Year" (Trina Parks), "Isn't This Fun" (Kelly Bishop, Larry Kert), "Three Beats Too Late" (Larry Kert), "Sunday" (Trina Parks, Irving Allen Lee), "Is This the Way" (Segue) (Larry Kert), "Keep Love Away" (Kelly Bishop); *Spring:* "All of a Sudden It's Spring" (Company), "The Man About Town" (Irving Allen Lee), "All Because of You" (Larry Kert), "Changes" (reprise) (Kelly Bishop, Trina Parks), "Do You Want to Go" (Company); *Summer:* "Summer Ain't So Hot" (Company); "Is This the Way" (reprise) (Company); *Fall:* "Sunday" (reprise) (Trina Parks, Irving Allen Lee), "Running Out of Time" (Trina Parks), "Love Is a Whole Other Scene" (Larry Kert), "The Ideal Deal" (Larry Kert, Irving Allen Lee), "Love Like Ours" (Kelly Bishop), "Changes" (reprise) (Company); *Winter:* "Merry Christmas to Me" (Irving Allen Lee); "Happy New Year" (reprise) (Kelly Bishop, Larry Kert)

NOTES—*Changes* sounds like a *Company* (1970) wannabe; in truth, almost every musical set in a large city which dealt with married and/or single couples begged comparison with the landmark Stephen Sondheim musical. *Company* centered around a birthday party, *Changes* around New Year's Eve. The latter's song titles ("Have I Got a Girl [Guy] for You," "Isn't This Fun," "Do You Want to Go") brought to mind Sondheim's lyrics and/or song titles for *Company* ("Have I Got a Girl for You," "Side by Side by Side," "Sorry-Grateful"), and Larry Kert's presence only reinforced the *Company* connection. Also in the cast was Kelly Bishop, who had earlier appeared in another big city/singles musical, Off Broadway's *Piano Bar* [1977; see entry).

John S. Wilson in the *New York Times* felt the creators of the sung-through musical came up "relatively empty-handed" with "paper-thin" characters and "predictable" situations. He singled out "The Ideal Deal," the score's "liveliest tune," for which Larry Kert built up "a joyous head of steam."

During previews, the musical was presented in two acts, with an intermission after the spring sequence.

Changes marked Addy Fieger's second failure in a row (after *Dear Oscar*, 1972; see entry).

269 Chanticleer.

NOTES—See entry for *Three by One.*

270 The Charles Pierce Show.

THEATRE: Top of the Gate; OPENING DATE: December 25, 1974; PERFORMANCES: 169; MATERIAL BY Charles Pierce; DIRECTION: Phil Oesterman; LIGHTING: Gary Weathersbee; PRODUCERS: Phil Oesterman and Jim Sink

CAST—Charles Pierce

The revue was presented in two acts.

NOTES—On Christmas Night, Charles Pierce made his New York debut in a one-man show of female impersonations. The revue ran out the season.

Clive Barnes in the *New York Times* found Pierce "the living equivalent of an Al Hirschfeld cartoon" who might give transvestism a "good name" by sending "perfectly normal sailors riffling through their mother's closets."

271 Charlotte Sweet.

"An All-Music Musical"; THEATRE: Cheryl Crawford Theatre/Westside Arts Center; OPENING DATE: August 12, 1982; PERFORMANCES: 102; LIBRETTO: Michael Colby; MUSIC: Gerald Jay Markoe; DIRECTION: Edward Stone; CHOREOGRAPHY: Dennis Dennehy; SCENERY: Homles Easley; COSTUMES: Michele Reisch; LIGHTING: Jason Kantrowitz; MUSICAL DIRECTION: Jan Rosenberg; PRODUCERS: Power Productions and Stan Raiff

CAST—Michael McCormick (Harry Host), Mara Beckerman (Charlotte Sweet), Christopher Seppe (Ludlow Ladd Grimble, "Queen Victoria"), Nicholas

Wyman (Bob Sweet, "Patrick O'Toole"), Alan Brasington (Barnaby Bugaboo), Sandra Wheeler (Katinka Bugaboo), Merle Louise (Cecily MacIntosh), Polly Pen (Skitzy Scofield)

The action occurs in turn-of-the-century England.

The musical was presented in two acts.

ACT ONE—"At the Music Hall" (Michael McCormick, Ensemble), "Charlotte Sweet" (Nicholas Wyman, Mara Beckerman, Ensemble), "A Daughter for Valentine's Day" (Mara Beckerman, Ensemble), "Forever" (Christopher Seppe, Mara Beckerman), "Liverpool Sunset" (Ensemble), "Layers of Underwear" (Nicholas Wyman, Sandra Wheeler, Alan Brasington, Mara Beckerman), "Quartet Agonistes" (Sandra Wheeler, Alan Brasington, Mara Beckerman, Nicholas Wyman), "The Circus of Voices" (Alan Brasington, Sandra Wheeler, Polly Pen, Merle Louise, Michael McCormick, Mara Beckerman), "Keep It Low" (Sandra Wheeler, Men's Chorus), "Bubbles in My Bonnet" (Merle Louise), "Vegetable Reggie" (Michael McCormick), "My Baby and Me" (Polly Pen), "A-Weaving" (Mara Beckerman, Women's Chorus), "Your High Note!" (Mara Beckerman, Alan Brasington, Sandra Wheeler), "Katinka"/"The Darkness" (Alan Brasington)

ACT TWO—"On It Goes" (Ensemble), "You See in Me a Bobby" (Nicholas Wyman, Alan Brasington, Sandra Wheeler), "A Christmas Buche" (Mara Beckerman, Merle Louise, Polly Pen, Michael McCormick), "The Letter (Me Charlotte Dear)" (Christopher Seppe), Dover (Polly Pen), "Good Things Come" (Merle Louise), "It Could Only Happen in the Theatre" (Michael McCormick, Nicholas Wyman, Polly Pen, Merle Louise), "Lonely Canary" (Mara Beckerman), "Queenly Comments" (Christopher Seppe, Alan Brasington, Sandra Wheeler, Nicholas Wyman, Mara Beckerman), "Surprise! Surprise!" (Ensemble), "The Reckoning" (Ensemble), "Farewell to Auld Lang Syne" (Ensemble)

NOTES—This sung-through musical drew upon the tradition of British music hall in its telling of the story of Charlotte Sweet, a music hall performer who can reach impossibly high notes. By performing so much, she loses her upper register; but the evil impresario of the music hall cunningly ensures Charlotte's addiction to the helium in balloons, an addiction which brings back her voice. But all ends well, as good triumphs and bad is punished.

John Corry in the *New York Times* wrote that the "delectable" musical mixed "the adorable and the strange." He praised the "glory" of Michael Colby's lyrics, the "wacky" costumes designed by Michele Reisch, the "moody lighting" by Jason Kantrowitz, and the "crisp and imaginative" direction by Edward Stone. The cast of *Charlotte Sweet* included Polly Pen, who soon became associated with a number of Off Broadway musicals which took place during the Victorian era. The ambitious score was recorded on a 2-LP set released by John Hammond Records (LP # W2X-38680), and the script was published by Samuel French, Inc., in 1983.

A sequel to the exploits of Charlotte Sweet and her beau Ludlow Ladd Grimble was later announced. Called *Happy Haunting*, it doesn't seem to have been produced.

272 Chase a Rainbow. THEATRE: Theatre Four; OPENING DATE: June 12, 1980; PERFORMANCES: 6; BOOK: Harry Stone; LYRICS: Harry Stone; MUSIC: Harry Stone; DIRECTION: Sue Lawless; CHOREOGRAPHY: Bick Goss; SCENERY: Michael Rizzo; COSTUMES: Rita Watson; LIGHTING: Jeff Davis; "Lighting Design" by Patricia Brown; MUSICAL DIRECTION: John Franceschina; PRODUCERS: Joan Dunham and Segue Productions

CAST—TED PUGH (Richard), VIRGINIA SANDIFUR (Jennifer, Cheerleader, Phyllis, Millie, Receptionist), Suzanne Dawson (Mrs. Keller, Cheerleader, TV Commercial Actress, Sandy, Shopper, Tessie, Secretary, Evie), Chuck Karel (Coach Brown, General, Steve, Kelly [The Cop], Office Boy, Mr. Foster, George F. Gaines, Mr. Mogul), Stephen McNaughton (Student, Madison Avenue Executive, Postman, Husband, Store Manager, Bobby Joe, Young Executive, Choreographer, Tony), Jan Neuberger (Trudi Christian, Cheerleader, Telephone Operator, Wife, Shopper, Mary, Secretary, Levy)

The musical was presented in two acts.

ACT ONE—"Let's Hear It for Me" (Ted Pugh, Company), "The People You Know" (Ted Pugh), "You've Gotta Have a Passion" (Suzanne Dawson, Ted Pugh), "We're # 1" (Chuck Karel, Team), "Masquerade" (Ted Pugh, Company), "Segue" (Suzanne Dawson, Ted Pugh, Company), "Everything Happens for the Best" (Stephen McNaughton, Jan Neuberger, Virginia Sandifur, Chuck Karel, Suzanne Dawson), "Out of Love" (Ted Pugh, Company), "Whenever You Want Me" (Virginia Sandifur, Ted Pugh), "The Big City" (Stephen McNaughton), "The Happiest People" (Virginia Sandifur, Jan Neuberger, Suzanne Dawson, Chuck Karel, Stephen McNaughton, Ted Pugh), "Segue" (reprise) (Company)

ACT TWO—"Have a Good Day" (Ted Pugh, Company), "Listen Little Boy" (Chuck Karel), "Gotta Have a Passion" (reprise) (Suzanne Dawson, Ted Pugh), "I'm in Showbiz" (Jan Neuberger, Stephen McNaughton), "I Just Want to Know That You're All Right" (Virginia Sandifur), "Life on the Rocks" (Stephen McNaughton), "To Be or Not to Be" (Chuck Karel), "I've Been Around the Horn" (Suzanne Dawson), "My Meadow" (Ted Pugh), "Mack Sennett, Where Are You Now?" (Ted Pugh, Virginia Sandifur), "All the Years" (Virginia Sandifur), "Listen, World!" (Ted Pugh), Finale (Company)

NOTES—*Chase a Rainbow* dealt with a writer torn between commerce and art. His dilemma lasted for just six performances.

Frank Rich in the *New York Times* noted that while the musical was sometimes reminiscent of Stephen Sondheim's *Company* (1970), the evening was "tedious" and offered a "tuneless" score. But he singled out the performance of Virginia Sandifur (who had created the role of Young Phyllis in Sondheim's *Follies* [1971]), finding her an "open-hearted, self-assured musical-comedy" performer, the kind "they don't write shows for anymore." Ted Pugh and Sue Lawless were familiar visitors to Off Broadway, and they seem to have been talented and amusing; but for one reason or another most of their ventures failed. They just never seemed to be associated with the right show at the right time.

273 Chef's Theatre. "A Musical Feast"; THEATRE: The Supper Club; OPENING DATE: April 14, 2004; PERFORMANCES: 50; LYRICS: See song list for credits; MUSIC: See song list for credits; DIRECTION: Stafford Arima; Jeffrey M. Markowitz, Production Supervisor; CHOREOGRAPHY: Casey Nicholaw; SCENERY: Beowulf Boritt; COSTUMES: Debbie Cheretun; LIGHTING: Ben Stanton; MUSICAL DIRECTION: Shawn Gough; PRODUCERS: West Egg Entertainment (Marty Bell, Greg Smith, and Stephen Fass) and Clear Channel Entertainment; Joe Allegro, Executive Producer

CAST—Paige Price, Jim Walton, Shannon Lewis, and The Shawn Gough Orchestra; each week of the show's run also offered a guest chef and musical guests as well. The chefs who appeared during the run were Todd English; Tom Valenti; Tyler Florence; Mary Sue Milliken and Susan Feniger; Michael Lomonaco; Michael Romano; and Rick Moonen; guest artists were Mylinda Hull; Janine Lamanna; Andrew Lippa; and Alice Ripley. At the Dessert Shows, guest artists were Jason Robert Brown; Daphne Rubin Vega; Andrew Lippa; and Alice Ripley. Sommeliers who appeared were Danielle Nally, Josh Wesson, Andrea Immer, and Steve Olsen.

The revue was presented in two acts, with dinner served during the intermission.

ACT ONE—"A Meal to Remember" (lyric by Lynn Ahrens, music by Stephen Flaherty) (Paige Price, Jim Walton, Shannon Lewis), Chef Interview (Guest Chef of the Week), "I'm Gonna Teach You How to Cook" (lyric by Marcy Heisler, music by Zina Goldrich) (Shannon Lewis), "This Is the Song That We Sing" (lyric by Marty Bell, music by Sam Davis and Casey Nicholaw)

ACT TWO—"Second Date" (lyric and music by Andrew Lippa) (Paige Price, Jim Walton) (NOTE: This song was performed during the week Andrew Lippa was the guest artist.), Chef's Trick of the Trade (Guest Chef of the Week); Dessert Preparation (Guest Chef of the Week); Guest Artist Performance; Goodnight and Bows

NOTES—In 1995, *Pomp Duck and Circumstance* provided both musical entertainment as well as dinner (see entry), and *Chef's Theatre* offered a similar evening. In this case, each week of the run offered a different guest chef (or chefs) as well as a different guest entertainer (plus a core group of performers who appeared throughout the run).

Besides dinners, weekend brunches as well as dessert programs were offered (among the performers who appeared at dessert shows were Jason Robert Brown, Daphne Rubin Vega, Andrew Lippa, and Alice Ripley).

Chef's Theatre was scheduled to run through June 27, but its final performance was on May 18. Among the performers who had been scheduled to appear after May 18 were Adam Pascal, LaChanze, Billy Porter, and Lauren Kennedy (some for more than one week); chefs who were scheduled to appear were David Burke, David Rosengarten, Marcus Samuelsson, Jacques Pepin, Alain Sailhac, Andre Soltner, Ed Brown, and Douglas Rodriguez.

As a sample of the menus, during the week when Michael Romano (of Union Square Café) was guest chef, the dinner consisted of baked ricotta and spinach tart; roasted lamb loin with red wine, shallot confit, and mushroom sauce; roasted asparagus and lentil-bulgur pilaf; and ginger-walnut tart with pineapple moscato zabaglione.

274 Cherry. THEATRE: Auditorium/Library and Museum of the Performing Arts, The New York Public Library at Lincoln Center; OPENING DATE: May 8, 1972; PERFORMANCES: 3; LYRICS: Ron Miller; MUSIC: Tom Baird; introductory narration composed and sung by Ilona Simon; DIRECTION: Tom Panko; CHOREOGRAPHY: Tom Panko; Ron Schwinn and Pi Douglas, Assistant Choreographers; PRODUCER: Stage Directors and Choreographers Workshop Foundation, Inc.

CAST—PAULA WAYNE (Cherry), DAVID CRYER (Beau), Seymour Penzner (Virge), Marilyn Cooper (Candy, Grace), Diane Blair, Greta Aldene; Dancers (Richard Benville, Don Bonnell, Bob (Robert) Fitch, Danny Joel, Dallas Johann, Gene Maysoner)

SOURCE—The 1955 play *Bus Stop* by William Inge.

The workshop was presented in one act.

MUSICAL NUMBERS—"Co-operatin' Nature" (David Cryer, Seymour Penzner, Ranch Hands), "Something to Believe In" (David Cryer), "Cherry's Soliloquy" (Paula Wayne), "I Feel Love" (Paula Wayne, Marilyn Cooper, Greta Aldene,, Patrons), "Montana" (David Cryer, Paula Wayne), "Take a Look at Life" (Paula Wayne, Marilyn Cooper, David Cryer, Seymour Penzner), "Men" (Paula Wayne, Marilyn Cooper), Dance Sequence (Beau and Cherry's characters danced by Gene Maysoner and Diane Blair), "Yesterday I Was You" (Seymour Penzner), "I've Never Been a Woman Before" (Paula Wayne)

NOTES—The workshop was open free to the public for three performances. *Cherry* was one of those musicals which always seemed to be announced for a Broadway production "next" season. But the next season never happened for this show. There was also talk of a London production, and it too never materialized (at one point, Joey Heatherson was mentioned for the title role).

The workshop didn't credit a book writer, but an unpublished (and undated) script for the proposed London production credits George Axelrod with the book, Joshua Logan with direction (Logan had directed the 1956 film version of *Bus Stop*, which starred Marilyn Monroe as Cherry and Don Murray as Beau), and Franklin Gollings and Peter Cranwell as Producer and Executive Producer, respectively.

Songs in the London script which weren't heard in the workshop were: "Would I Lie to You?" (Virge, Beau, Chorus); "Half Way Home" (Cherry; "Half Way Home" was possibly another title for "Cherry's Soliloquy"); "City Girls" (Carl, Virge, Chorus); "Green Grow the Lilacs" (Beau, Cherry); "If I Was a Man" (Cherry, Beau); "That Big Rodeo in the Sky" (Virge, Cherry, Grace); "Big Bar-B-Q-Below" (Carl); "Bar-B-Q-Dance"; and "What Is a Man?" (Beau).

The song "I've Never Been a Woman Before" was later recorded by Barbra Streisand and was included on her album *The Way We Were*.

Lyricist Ron Miller also wrote the lyrics and co-wrote the book for the 1979 musical *Daddy Goodness*, which closed permanently at the National Theatre in Washington, D.C., during its pre-Broadway tryout.

Jefry Silverman also wrote a musical adaptation of *Bus Stop* called *Perfect Strangers*, which apparently has never been produced (see entry for *Options*).

The first three of William Inge's seven Broadway plays were adapted into musicals. Besides *Bus Stop*, *Come Back, Little Sheba* (1950) was adapted as *Sheba*, which opened on July 24, 1974, at the First Chicago Center with Kaye Ballard as Lola and George D. Wallace as Doc (Kimberly Farr was Marie, and Gary Sandy played Turk). The book and lyrics were by Lee Goldsmith, and the music by Clint Ballard, Jr. The production was revived at least twice in regional theatre. As a work-in-progress, *Doc and Lola* opened at the Lenox Arts Center in Stockbridge, Massachusetts, on August 10, 1978, for approximately six performances; Edward Penn and Joanne Beretta performed the title roles, and this time around the book was credited to Rocco Bufano, and the lyrics to Goldsmith, Bufano, and Ballard. On August 31, 2001, the musical resurfaced as *Sheba* at the White Barn Theatre in Westport, Connecticut, for four performances. Donna McKechnie was Lola and Mark Peters was Doc; the book and lyrics were credited to Goldsmith; this production was recorded by Original Cast Records as *Come Back, Little Sheba* (CD # OC-6025). Inge's Pulitzer Prize-winning *Picnic* (1953) was adapted into the 1965 musical *Hot September*, which closed during its Boston tryout. One of its songs ("Show Me Where the Good Times Are") was later heard in a 1970 Off Broadway musical which also appropriated the song's title for the musical's title (see entry for *Show Me Where the Good Times Are*). A live recording of a Boston tryout performance of *Hot September* was released on Blue Pear Records (LP # BP-1012); the song "Show Me Where the Good Times Are" can be heard on Neva Small's *My Place in the World*, an enchanting collection which includes many obscure theatre songs (see Discography [Appendix B]).

As of this writing, there haven't been any announcements for upcoming musical versions of Inge's four other Broadway plays (*The Dark at the Top of the Stairs* [1957], *A Loss of Roses* [1959], *Natural Affection* [1963], and *Where's Daddy?* [1966]).

275 Chess. THEATRE: Master Theatre; OPENING DATE: February 1, 1992; PERFORMANCES: 83; BOOK: Tim Rice; LYRICS: Tim Rice; MUSIC: Benny Andersson and Bjorn Ulvaeus; DIRECTION: David Taylor; Madeline Paul, Assistant Director; CHOREOGRAPHY: Madeline Paul; SCENERY: Tony Castrigno; COSTUMES: Deborah Rooney; LIGHTING: John Hastings; MUSICAL DIRECTION: Phil Reno; PRODUCERS: The Artist's Perspective in association with Chess Players Ltd.

CAST—Kathleen Rowe McAllen (Florence Vassy), J. Mark McVey (Anatoly Sergievsky), Ray Walker (Frederick Trumper), Patrick Jude (Arbiter), Jan Horvath (Svetlana Sergievsky), Bob Frisch (Alexander Molokov); Ensemble (Mark Ankeny, Michael Gerhart, Mary Illes, David Koch, Nita Moore, Ric Ryder, Carol Schuberg, Rebecca Timms)

The action occurs in Merano, Italy, in 1972, and in Bangkok, Thailand, in 1973.

The musical was presented in two acts.

ACT ONE—Prologue (Patrick Jude), "Merano" (Patrick Jude, Ray Walker, Ensemble), "Where I Want to Be" (Bob Frisch, Jan Horvath, J. Mark McVey, Ensemble), "How Many Women" (Kathleen Rowe McAllen, Ray Walker), "US vs. USSR" (Ensemble), "The Arbiter's Song" (Patrick Jude, Ensemble), "Chess Game #1" (Orchestra), "A Model of Decorum and Tranquility" (Bob Frisch, Kathleen Rowe McAllen, Patrick Jude, J. Mark McVey), "Chess Hymn" (Ensemble), "Someone Else's Story" (Jan Horvath), "Nobody's on Nobody's Side" (Kathleen Rowe McAllen, Ensemble), "The Merchandisers' Song" (Ray Walker, Ensemble), "Mountain Top Duet" (Kathleen Rowe McAllen, J. Mark McVey), "Who'd Ever Guessed It?" (Ray Walker), "Chess Game #2" (Orchestra), "Florence Quits" (Ray Walker, Kathleen Rowe McAllen), "Pity the Child" (Ray Walker), "Where I Want to Be" (reprise) (J. Mark McVey, Kathleen Rowe McAllen), "Anthem" (J. Mark McVey)

ACT TWO—Prologue (Patrick Jude), "One Night in Bangkok" (Patrick Jude, Ensemble), "Heaven Help My Heart" (Kathleen Rowe McAllen), "Argument" (Kathleen Rowe McAllen, J. Mark McVey), "The Confrontation" (J. Mark McVey, Bob Frisch, Jan Horvath), "No Contest" (J. Mark McVey, Ray Walker), "I Know Him So Well" (Kathleen Rowe McAllen, Jan Horvath), "The Deal" (Company), "Endgame" (Company), "You and I"/Epilogue (Kathleen Rowe McAllen, J. Mark McVey)

NOTES—Despite its being the best of the "British Invasion" musicals of the 1980s, *Chess* had the shortest Broadway run (a heartbreaking sixty-eight performances in 1988). The musical began as a concept album, and was later produced in London in 1986 (reportedly, its almost three-year run barely turned a profit). The revised Broadway version (with a book by Richard Nelson) was followed by a number of U.S. and worldwide productions, either in staged or concert formats, and all of them "revisals" of both the British and New York productions. They all went nowhere. A "complete" *Chess*, with all its plot lines and the inclusion of all the songs written for it over the years, would probably take five hours to perform. In his program notes for the Off Broadway production, Tim Rice said the history of *Chess* "has become far more complicated than any of the storylines in its many different productions," and said of all his musicals *Chess* caused him the "most professional, personal and financial anguish." Rice and many critics blamed the failure of the Broadway production on the collapse of the Soviet empire and the end of the Cold War, political events which suddenly made the musical's plot seem out of date and old-fashioned. But films about World War II aren't criticized for being outdated, and since some two decades have passed since the fall of Communism, perhaps *Chess* will someday rise again, free of the baggage of "outdatedness"; the work may one day be seen for what it is, a story of innocent people trapped in the zeitgeist of their times and used as pawns between opposing political philosophies, and all of it told with a gloriously melodic score and alternately clever and touching lyrics. And, indeed, *Chess* may rise again. In early 2008, Michael Riedel in the *New York Post* reported that Tim Rice had revised the work by concentrating on its songs and whittling down its text. As a result, the new *Chess* was more opera than musical play. Rice announced that he was personally financing (to the tune of $250,000) a concert version of the revised *Chess* to be performed at London's Royal Albert Hall in May 2008, with Josh Grobin and Idina Menzel in leading roles, and with a full orchestra and a one-hundred-person chorus. The Broadway cast recording of *Chess* was released by RCA Victor Records (LP # 7700-1-RC and CD # 7700-2-RC), and the 1984 original concept album was also issued by RCA Victor (2-LP set # CPL2-5340 and 2-CD set # PCD2-5340). Other noteworthy recordings include *Chess in Concert*, a 1994 concert recorded live and released on a 2-CD set by Mono Music Production Records (# MMCD-010-2); a 2-CD set of the 2001-2002 Danish tour (Columbus Records # 81815); and a 2-CD 2002 Stockholm cast recording released by Mono Music Production Records (# MMCD-019-1).

The script was published by Samuel French, Inc., in 1989. An earlier book about the British production, *Chess/The Making of the Musical* by William Hartston, was published by Pavilion Books Limited in 1986, and included the lyrics from the musical as well as articles about the production.

276 Chez Garbo. "The New Musical"; THEATRE: Duo Theatre; OPENING DATE: May 26, 1995; PERFORMANCES: 10 (estimated); BOOK: Michelangelo Alasa'; LYRICS: Michelangelo Alasa'; MUSIC: Michelangelo Alasa' and David Welch; DIRECTION: Michelangelo Alasa'; PRODUCER: Duo Theatre

CAST—Lynne Charnay (Greta Garbo), Tony Louden (Joe Herrera), Michelle Powers (Young Garbo), Reet Roos Varnik (Linda Weinstar)

The action occurs in Greta Garbo's East Side living room (division of acts and song assignments unknown; songs are listed in performance order).

MUSICAL NUMBERS—"Never," "I See Myself," "I Have Always Collected," "Just Let Me Love You," "Where Does One Turn To," "An Artist Til the End," "As I Do," "Roses," "In a Perfect World," "How You've Changed," "Dreamers," "It's Not Like We Have Forever"

NOTES—The Off Off Broadway musical *Chez Garbo* (also known as Chez GARBO) dealt with the screen legend who looks back on her life and career when she befriends a young man during the latter years of her self-imposed retirement from the screen.

A studio cast album of the score was recorded by Duo Archival Records (CD # DAR-1000), and included one member from the Off Broadway production, Reet Roos Varnik (who played the character of Linda Weinstar in the stage version and the role of Garbo on the recording). The recording indicates the production played for 200 performances during the 1996-1997 season.

The CD credited Michelangelo Alasa' with the lyrics and music, and included just three songs from the production ("I See Myself," "Just Let Me Love You," and "In a Perfect World"). The following numbers are heard on the recording (song titles are followed by the characters who sang the numbers):

"Come to Me" (Young Garbo), "Only in a Film" (Joe, Fan #1, Fan #2), "I See Myself" (Garbo, Young Garbo), "Stiller Taught Me" (Garbo, Mauritz Stiller), "Born to Be an Artist" (Maurtiz Stiller), "I'm Free at Last" (Young Garbo), "Still Down There" (Young Garbo, Garbo, Joe), "Just Let Me Love You" (Joe), "Just Let Me Love You" (reprise) (Mercedes de Acosta), "In the Quiet Hours" (Young Garbo, Joe, Mauritz Stiller, Mercedes de Acosta), "Stars" (Joe), "Marry Me" (Cecil Beaton), "Pay the Price" (Marta), "Garbo on the Run" (Garbo, Joe), "Reach Out for

Love" (John Gilbert, Joe, Marta), "In a Perfect World" (Young Garbo, Joe), "Come to Me" (reprise) (Young Garbo, Garbo, John Gilbert)

277 Chic. "A New Musical Revue"; THEATRE: Orpheum Theatre; OPENING DATE: May 19, 1959; PERFORMANCES: 6; SKETCHES: Lester Judson; LYRICS: Lester Judson; MUSIC: Mostly by Julian Stein and Murray Grand; DIRECTION: Richard Altman; CHOREOGRAPHY: Jim Russell; SCENERY: Robert Soule; COSTUMES: Theoni Vachlioti Aldredge; LIGHTING: F. J. McAliece; MUSICAL DIRECTION: Dorothea Freitag; PRODUCER: Peter Pell

CAST—Beatrice Arthur, Emory Bass, Kelly Brown, Bob Dishy, John Myhers, Patty Ann Jackson, Dale Monroe, Eileen Rodgers, Evelyn Russell, Virginia de Luce

The revue was presented in two acts.

ACT ONE—"Chic" (music by Julian Stein) (Company), "Flattery" (music by Edward C. Redding) (Virginia de Luce, Kelly Brown, Bob Dishy, Dale Monroe), "The Truth About Camille" (sketch by Lester Judson and Murray Grand) (Evelyn Russell, Beatrice Arthur [as *Camille!*], Emory Bass, John Myhers), "The Mouse" (lyric by Lester Judson and Edward C. Redding, music by Edward C. Redding) (Kelly Brown, Patty Ann Jackson), "Charity" (lyric by Lester Judson and Robin Miller), music by Murray Grand) (Virginia de Luce, Eileen Rodgers, Evelyn Russell), "Gunfight" (sketch by Lester Judson, Bernie Kahn) (Kelly Brown, Bob Dishy, John Myhers), "Julie Is Mine" (music by Raymond Taylor) (Dale Monroe), "Mediocrity" (music by Murray Grand) (Eileen Rodgers, Kelly Brown, Patty Ann Jackson), "This Will Be Our Life" (sketch by Lester Judson, Robin Miller) (Dale Monroe, Beatrice Arthur, John Myhers, Evelyn Russell, Emory Bass, Virginia de Luce, Patty Ann Jackson), "The Thief" (music by Perry M. Lopez) (choreographed and danced by Kelly Brown), "Talk to Me" (music by Julian Stein) (Virginia de Luce), "The Angry Young Men" (music by Julian Stein) (Kelly Brown, Bob Dishy, Dale Monroe, John Myhers), "A Man Up My Sleeve" (lyric and music not credited) (Eileen Rodgers, Kelly Brown), "The East Side Story" (music by Julian Stein; additional music by Dorothea Freitag) (Company, five of whom played "The Whites" and five of whom played "The Off Whites")

ACT TWO—"In and Out" (song; not credited) (Company), "Later" (music by Dorothea Freitag) (Kelly Brown, Patty Ann Jackson), "A Summer Romance" (music by Raymond Taylor) (Eileen Rodgers), "To Soothe the Savage Beast," "Tallahassie Lassie" (lyric and music by Frank C. Slay, Bob Crewe, Frederick A. Picariello) (Bob Dishy, Virginia de Luce), "The Gull in My Life" (A Musical Version of *Make Mine Masha*) (translated by Lester Judson and Robin Miller; lyrics by Lester Judson and Robin Miller, music by Murray Grand) (Evelyn Russell, Eileen Rodgers, Beatrice Arthur, John Myhers, Emory Bass, Kelly Brown, Dale Monroe, Patty Ann Jackson), "The Three Eiffels" ("conceived and interpreted by Bob Dishy"), "There's No Room for People Anymore" (music by Julian Stein) (Dale Monroe, Virginia de Luce, John Myhers, Eileen Rodgers), "The Oath" (song or sketch; not credited) (Emory Bass), "The Man and the Mannequin" ("music arranged by Dorothea Freitag"; unclear if Freitag or Grand was the composer [probably Freitag]) (Kelly Brown, Patty Ann Jackson), "Tea" (uncredited) (Beatrice Arthur, John Myhers), "The Happy Years" (music by Raymond Taylor) (Beatrice Arthur), Finale (Company)

NOTES—This obscure revue lasted less than a week. Louis Calta in the *New York Times* found *Chic* amateurish and tiresome in its satire of East Side society types, angry young men, and television commercials. *Chic* included another Off Broadway appearance by Beatrice Arthur, whom Calta praised as a "vigorous clown" whose talents were wasted (her presence alone, including her parody of Camille, should have insured a longer run). Another cast member was Virginia de Luce, fondly remembered as the girl who lamented that "he takes me off his income tax" in *New Faces of 1952*.

Calta mentioned that a song in praise of "Mediocrity" ("you too can be saved by mediocrity") was belted out by Eileen Rodgers, whose rendition disproved the "song's point of view by demonstrating" her own " vivacious talent."

It appears that "Basic," "The Moscow Blues," "Teenage Love," and "We're Dying to Die" were dropped during rehearsals or previews; and that "A Man Up My Sleeve" may have been heard only during previews.

For the record, "Tallahassie Lassie" was a popular rock and roll song of the era, and it was interpolated into *Chic* as part of the sketch "To Soothe the Savage Beast."

278 Child of the Sun. THEATRE: Henry Street Settlement's New Federal Theatre; OPENING DATE: December 1, 1981; PERFORMANCES: 16; BOOK: Damien Leake; LYRICS: Damien Leake; MUSIC: Damien Leake; DIRECTION: Harold Scott; CHOREOGRAPHY: Otis Sallid; SCENERY: John Scheffler; COSTUMES: Judy Dearing; LIGHTING: Shirley Prendergast; MUSICAL DIRECTION: Lea Richardson; PRODUCER: Henry Street Settlement's New Federal Theatre (Woodie King, Jr., and Steven Tennen, Producers); Executive Producer, Dr. Niathan Allen

CAST—Kevin Harris (Joe), Nat Morris (James, Rainbow), Jackee Harry (Cassie), Pauletta Pearson (Marilyn), Count Stovall (Trinity, Preacher), Gordon Heath (Jake), Raymond Patterson (Jesse), Yolanda Lee (Maggie); Members of the Community (Alistair Butler, David Cameron, Bar Dell Conner, Leslie Dockery, Jacquelyn Gilliard, Diane Hayes, Dyane Harvey, Sonya Hensley, Perry Moore)

The musical was presented in two acts.

ACT ONE—Prologue (Company), "Whirling in Circles" (Company), "Rhythm & Rhyme" (Nat Morris, Community), "Basketball Game" (Nat Morris, Team), "Praises, Praises" (Jackee Harry, Friends), "Creation" (Pauletta Pearson), "Trinity's Theme" (Count Stovall), "Temptation" (Nat Morris, Community), "Wings to Fly" (Kevin Harris), "Weddings Bands" (Company), "Rhythm & Rhyme" (reprise) (Nat Morris), "When the Whistle Blows" (Kevin Harris, Pauletta Pearson), "Dance of the Unemployed" (Company), "Hush My Sweet Children" (Kevin Harris, Pauletta Pearson, Jackee Harry), "Honest Woman" (Pauletta Pearson), "Child of the Sun" (Jackee Harry, Nat Morris)

ACT TWO—"I Am a Windsong" (Company), "Games" (Raymond Patterson, Yolanda Lee), "Don't Buy the Lie" (Raymond Patterson, Friends), "Wedding Bands" (reprise) (Community Members), "Hello, It's Me Again" (Jackee Harry), "Honest Women" (reprise of "Honest Woman") (Pauletta Pearson, Friends), "Jake's Blues" (Raymond Patterson), "Wings to Fly" (reprise) (Raymond Patterson, Kevin Harris), "Sweet Refrain" (Gordon Heath, Kevin Harris, Prisoners), "Walking with Jesus" (Count Stovall, Company), "Amen" (Raymond Patterson, Company), "Rockin' My Soul" (Count Stovall, Raymond Patterson), "This New Identity" (Raymond Patterson, Community)

NOTES—*Child of the Sun* was an Off Off Broadway musical which had won the Richard Rodgers Award, but after its limited run at the New Federal Theatre it seems to have disappeared.

The plot dealt with Black urban life over a quarter-century, and Mel Gussow in the *New York Times* found the "fragmented" musical "sprawling and episodic," as if it were a "compilation" of plays by various Black writers. But Gussow noted there were some "lovely" songs, and singled out "I Am a Windsong."

279 Children of Adam. "The All-Music Musical"; THEATRE: Chelsea Westside Cabaret Theatre; OPENING DATE: August 17, 1977; PERFORMANCES: 69; LYRICS: Stan Satlin; MUSIC: Stan Satlin; DIRECTION: John Driver; CHOREOGRAPHY: Ruella Frank; SCENERY: Ernest Allen Smith; COSTUMES: Polly P. Smith; LIGHTING: Robert F. Strohmeier; MUSICAL DIRECTION: Jimmy Wisner

CAST—Gene Bua, Elizabeth Lathram, Karen Philipp, Robert Polenz, Roger Rathburn, Carole Schweid

The action occurs "during the span of a lifetime."

The revue was presented in one act.

MUSICAL NUMBERS—"Dreams" (Company), "Mr. and Mrs. Myth" (Company), "What's Your Name?" (Company), "Move Along" (Band), "Sex Is Animal" (Company), "It's Really You" (Robert Polenz), "Walkin'" (Company), "You've Got to Die to Be Born Again" (Gene Bua), "Rise in Love" (Company), "The Wedding" (Company), "The Flowers and the Rainbow" (Company), "Life" (Company), "It Ain't Easy"/"Equilib" (Company), "Sleep My Child" (Elizabeth Lathram), "I Must Go Now" (Karen Philipp), "Like a Park on Sunday" (Roger Rathburn), "Part of the Plan" (Gene Bua, Karen Philipp, Roger Rathburn, Carole Schweid), "I Can Feel" (Carole Schweid), "Sleepin' Around" (Company), "The Wooden People" (Company), "Cacophony" (Company), "Maybe You Can See Yourself" (Elizabeth Lathram), "Just a Feeling (My Spirit Awakening)" (Company), "The Flowers and the Rainbow" (reprise) (Elizabeth Lathram, Robert Polenz), "No More Games" (Carole Schweid, Roger Rathburn), "I Can Make It"/"Song Song" (Karen Philipp, Gene Bua), "The Sweetest Songs Remain To Be Sung" (Company), "Children of Adam" (Company)

NOTES—*Children of Adam* was another revue-cum-song-cycle, and it lasted for only two months. The program notes stated Stan Satlin's songs were inspired by Walt Whitman, Albert Camus, Herman Hesse, and "the master of them all, Life." Mel Gussow in the *New York Times* noted the bland and innocuous revue included more than two-dozen songs, most of which appear to "have been run through a blender"; moreover, the evening stressed "sunshine, flowers and rainbows," and the score ranged from "bouncy bubble-gum music to white gospel." Gussow also mentioned the lyrics tended to repeat the same words, and he decided the evening reached its heights ("or depths") with "You've Got to Die to Be Born Again," in which most of the lyric consisted of the "interminable repetition" of the song's title.

280 Children's Letters to God. "A New Musical"; THEATRE: Lamb's Theatre; OPENING DATE: June 30, 2004; PERFORMANCES: 146; BOOK: Stuart Hample; LYRICS: Douglas J. Cohen; MUSIC: David Evans; DIRECTION: Stafford Arima; CHOREOGRAPHY: Patty Wilcox; SCENERY: Anna Louizos; COSTUMES: Gail Brassard; LIGHTING: Kirk Bookman; MUSICAL DIRECTION: Larry Pressgrove; PRODUCERS: Carolyn Rossi Copeland and Marie B. Corporation/Broadway Overseas Management in association with the Lamb's Theatre Company

CAST—Gerard Canonico (Brett), Jimmy Dieffenbach (Theo), Libbie Jacobson (Iris), Sara Kapner (Joanna), Andrew Zutty (Kicker)

SOURCE—The 1966 collection *Children's Letters to God* by Stuart Hample and Eric Marshall.

The musical was presented in two acts.

ACT ONE—Prologue (Company), "Questions, Questions" (Company), "Thirteen" (Gerard Canonico), "Arnold" (Libbie Jacobson, Company), "Like Everybody Else" (Jimmy Dieffenbach, Company), "Questions for the Rain" (Libbie Jacobson, Company), "Ants" (Andrew Zutty), "A Simple Holiday Song" (Company), "Six Hours as a Princess" (Sara Kapner), "An Only Child" (Andrew Zutty, Sara Kapner), "When I Am in Charge" (Company)

ACT TWO—"Daydreams" (Company), "Kicker Brown" (Jimmy Dieffenbach), "Silly Old Hat" (Gerard Canonico), "How Come?" (Company), "Star Letters" (Libbie Jacobson, Sara Kapner, Jimmy Dieffenbach), "I Know" (Company), "I Know" (reprise) (Company)

NOTES—The title said it all for *Children's Letters to God,* a revue-like musical which was recorded by Jay Records (CD # CDJAY-1385). The cast album included a bonus track of "Joanna's Lament," which was dropped prior to the musical's opening. The script was published by Samuel French, Inc., in 2005.

Lawrence Van Gelder in the *New York Times* felt the evening lacked "character development and dramatic momentum," but noted the lyrics and music were "appealing." However, despite the musical's "sweet, warm heart," the show was a "mixed blessing" which fell "short of answering a theatregoer's prayer."

The musical had first been produced as a series of staged readings by the York Theatre Company in May 2001.

281 The Chinese Magic Revue of Taiwan. THEATRE: Promenade Theatre; OPENING DATE: September 4, 1984; PERFORMANCES: 16; DIRECTION: Production supervised by Ben Sprecher; LIGHTING: Alvin Ho; PRODUCERS: Bill Miller and I.A.I. Productions

CAST—The Chinese Magic Revue

The revue was presented in two acts.

ACT ONE—Opening Ceremony, Dragon Dance, Comedy Contortion, Juggling Cycle, Balancing Fantasy, Chinese Magic, Feet Balancing, Chinese Kung-Fu

ACT TWO—Precision Balancing, Flaming Circle, Chinese Comedy, High Act, Tower of Chairs, Human Pyramid, Bicycle Act, Finale

NOTES—The players in this Chinese magic revue were a Taiwanese troupe which included magicians, jugglers, acrobats, contortionists, and Kung-Fu artists.

282 Chinoiserie. THEATRE: Majestic Theatre/Brooklyn Academy of Music; OPENING DATE: November 11, 1995; PERFORMANCES: 5; TEXT AND LYRICS: Michael Matthews, Ping Chong, Regina Anna Seckinger, Ric Oquita; MUSIC: Guy Klucevsek; DIRECTION: Ping Chong; CHOREOGRAPHY: Shi-Zheng Chen; SCENERY AND PROJECTIONS: Jan Hartley; COSTUMES: Byron Lars; period costumes by Carol Ann Pelletier and Chan Kwok Yuen; LIGHTING: Thomas Hase; PRODUCER: The Next Wave Festival

CAST—Ping Chong, Shi-Zheng Chen, Aleta Hayes, Michael Edo Keane, Ric Oquita

NOTES—*Chinoiserie* was one of two works by Ping Chong which dealt with East-West relations (the other was *Deshima*). Mel Gussow in *The Best Plays of 1995-1996* praised the "outstanding" production, which used songs, stories, and slides to explore relationship between the two cultures, including racism. Stephen Holden in the *New York Times* felt the "stinging critique" of racism was often "informative" and "crisp," with "strikingly beautiful moments." But overall he said the work was not "especially compelling" and sometimes came across as an "illustrated lecture."

The evening included a mini-play (*Chinese Must Go*) and even found time to work in the song "Take Me Out to the Ball Game" (sung in Chinese) (as "Escorte-Moi," the 1984 revue *Diamonds* [see entry] had offered a French rendition of the song).

283 A Chorus Line. THEATRE: Newman Theatre/The Public Theatre; OPENING DATE: April 15, 1975; PERFORMANCES: 101; BOOK: James Kirkwood and Nicholas Dante; LYRICS: Edward Kleban; MUSIC: Marvin Hamlisch; DIRECTION: Michael Bennett; Bob Avian, Co-Choreographer; CHOREOGRAPHY: Michael Bennett; SCENERY: Robin Wagner; COSTUMES: Theoni V. Aldredge; LIGHTING: Tharon Musser; MUSICAL DIRECTION: Don Pippin; PRODUCER: The New York Shakespeare Festival Public Theatre (Joseph Papp, Director; Bernard Gersten, Associate Producer)

CAST—Scott Allen (Roy), Renee Baughman (Kristine), Carole (Kelly) Bishop (Sheila), Pamela Blair (Val), Wayne Cilento (Mike), Chuck Cissel (Butch), Clive Clerk (Butch), Kay Cole (Maggie), Ronald Dennis (Richie), Donna Drake (Tricia), Brandt Edwards (Tom), Patricia Garland (Judy), Carolyn Kirsch (Lois), Ron Kuhlman (Don), Nancy Lane (Bebe), Baayork Lee (Connie), Robert LuPone (Zach), Cameron Mason (Mark), Donna McKechnie (Cassie), Don Percassi (Al), Michael Serrecchia (Frank), Michel Stuart (Greg), Thomas (Thommie) J. Walsh (Bobby), Sammy Williams (Paul), Crissy Wilzak (Vicki)

The action occurs during an audition "here" (in the theatre in which *A Chorus Line* is playing) during the present time.

The musical was presented in one act.

MUSICAL NUMBERS—"I Hope I Get It" (Company), "Joanne" (Wayne Cilento), "And ..." (Thomas J. Walsh, Ronald Dennis, Pamela Blair, Patricia Garland), "At the Ballet" (Carole Bishop, Nancy Lane, Kay Cole), "Sing!" (Renee Baughman, Don Percassi), "Hello Twelve, Hello Thirteen, Hello Love" (Company), "Nothing" (Priscilla Lopez), "Dance: Ten, Looks: Three" (Pamela Blair), "The Music and the Mirror" (Donna McKechnie), "One" (Company), "The Tap Combination" (Company), "What I Did for Love" (Priscilla Lopez, Company), "One" (reprise) (Company)

NOTES—Much has been written about *A Chorus Line*, and so I'll try not to go over familiar territory.

When the first advertisement for the Newman Theatre engagement appeared in the *New York Times* (with ticket prices ranging from $3.50 to $8.00), Carole Schweid was listed among the cast members; by the time the show opened, she was no longer with the production. Although her bio remained in the first week's program (as the character "Barbara"), both her name and her character's name were omitted from the program's cast listing. All the opening night cast members transferred with the production when it opened on Broadway at the Shubert Theatre the following July 25, where it played for a then-record 6,137 performances.

One number was dropped during the Newman Theatre engagement: Mike's song "Joanne" was replaced with "I Can Do That."

Marvin Hamlisch's program bio is a bit odd. It states that with *A Chorus Line* he was making his "theatrical debut" (the program ignored his Off Broadway and Broadway contributions which stretched back eleven years to 1964).

The finest element of *A Chorus Line* was its magnificent choreography. Michael Bennett's dances were electric, among the best the musical theatre had ever seen (although he actually topped himself with *Ballroom* [1978], which may boast the most exciting choreography ever created for a musical). Unfortunately, Bennett's final musical, the vastly overpraised *Dreamgirls* (1981), had little dancing, and Bennett's main interest seemed to be in "choreographing" those pretentious, eternally-moving pylons which dominated the staging.

The weakest elements of *A Chorus Line* were its book and lyrics. The book was an endless round of belly-aching by the principals. The show was indeed a product of the 1970s, with characters incessantly talking about themselves. All the self-analysis became tiresome, and you sometimes wondered if these people really belonged in their profession. Maybe they would have been happier as clerks, waitresses, bus drivers, accountants, or florists.

Ed Kleban's lyrics didn't help, either. They were ordinary, bordering on the clichéd. Kleban was no Hammerstein, no Porter, no Sondheim. *A Class Act* (2000; see entry) was virtually a composer-lyricist tribute to him, although it was attached to a sketch-like book. Although Kleban was dead when *A Class Act* opened, the enterprise came across as a vanity production trying to sell Kleban as an unappreciated genius. In truth, *A Class Act* was a collection of mostly boring, derivative songs, and was without question one of the worst musicals this theatergoer ever encountered. Mercifully, the excrescence disappeared after 105 Broadway performances (105 too many).

Marvin Hamlisch's score for *A Chorus Line* deserved better lyrics; his sinewy music wrapped itself around the demands of the choreography, and yet at the same time managed to be incisive when it needed to complement a character or a plot point. And with "One," Hamlisch perhaps created the ultimate and eternal Broadway show tune. Dominated by an extenuated and irresistible vamp, the song defines the sound of brassy Broadway music. Columbia Records released the Broadway cast album (LP # PS-33581), and in 1995 the script was belatedly published (by Applause Books). The disastrous 1985 film adaptation by Polygram Pictures almost made the film versions of *Annie* and *The Wiz* look good. *A Chorus Line* would have been better served if a theatre performance had been taped for public television. The musical opened in London at the Drury Lane Theatre on July 22, 1976, and played there for approximately 1,200 performances. A reissue of the Broadway cast album on CD (Sony Classical/Columbia/Legacy Records # SK-65282) included an expanded version of "Hello Twelve, Hello Thirteen, Hello Love." The film's soundtrack was released by Casablanca Record and Filmworks Records (LP # 826-306-1M-1) and included two songs written especially for the screen version ("Surprise, Surprise" and "Let Me Dance for You"). Other recordings include the 1983 Oslo cast (NorDisc Records LP # NORLP-422); the 1988 German cast (LP # 835-485-1 and CD # 835-485-2); and the 1990 Italian cast (Carisch Records CD # CL-36); Incidentally, an unproduced, non-musical play by George Furth had first used the title *A Chorus Line* (Furth had written the book for *Company* [1970], which of course had been choreographed by Michael Bennett). Furth's play was announced for production in 1970 and had been optioned by David Merrick.

A Chorus Line was revived on Broadway in 2006, and this time around the critics seemed slightly cooler to the work; the production was still playing as of December 31, 2007. The revival's cast album, which was released by Sony Masterworks Broadway Records (CD # 82876-89785-2), is a testament to the enduring theatricality of Hamlisch's melodic score. *Every Little Step*, a documentary film about the casting of the revival, is scheduled for theatrical release in May 2008.

284 The Chosen. "A New Musical"; THEATRE: Second Avenue Theatre; OPENING DATE: January 6, 1988; PERFORMANCES: 6; BOOK: Chaim Potok; LYRICS: Mitchell Bernard; MUSIC: Philip Springer; DIRECTION: Mitchell Maxwell; CHOREOGRAPHY: Richard Levi; Patricia Wilcox, Assistant Choreographer; SCENERY: Ben Edwards; COSTUMES: Ruth Morley; LIGHTING: Thomas R. Skelton; MUSICAL DIRECTION: Eric Stern; PRODUCERS: M Square Entertainment, Inc. (Mitchell Maxwell, Alan J. Schuster, Marvin R. Meit, and Robert de Rothschild) in association with Edie and Ely Landau

CAST—Richard Cray (Danny Saunders), GEORGE HEARN (Reb Saunders), GERALD HIKEN (David Malter), Michael Ingram (Coach Galanter), Caryn Kaplan (Miriam), Daniel Marcus (Davey Cantor), Rob Morrow (Reuven Malter), Lynnette Perry (Hindie Saunders), Patricia Ben Peterson (Esther), Tia Riebling (Rachel), Joey Rigol (Levi Saunders), Mimi Turque (Mrs. Saunders), Ensemble (Patricia Alexander, Lawrence Asher, Zelie Daniels, Anny DeGange, Paul Dobie, Jack Drummond, Michael Erwin, Jeff Gardner, Jonathan Gold, Matthew Grant, Michael Greenwood, Joe Gustern, Eileen Hawkins, Linda Hess, Tracy Katz, Kevin Ligon, Gary Schwartz, Christopher Scott, Elaine Wright)

SOURCE—The 1967 novel *The Chosen* by Chaim Potok.

The action occurs in Williamsburg, Brooklyn, during 1944-1948.

The musical was presented in two acts (song assignments not listed in program).

ACT ONE—"Play to Win," "Words," "Holy Little World," "Processional," "Ladder to the Lord," "The Prince and Me," "Greetings to You, Sabbath Angels," "My World," "Wake Us with Your Song," "Our New Jerusalem," "The Chosen"

ACT TWO—"Tune in My Heart," "Tear Down the Wall," "Danny's Plea," "Words" (reprise), "Silence," "Tear Down the Wall" (reprise)

NOTES—*The Chosen* was based on Chaim Potok's novel (which was filmed in 1981) about the friendship of two Jewish boys, one Hassidic and one "Americanized" (that is, non-orthodox). It was the second musical of the season about teenage Jewish boys (see entry for *Bar Mitzvah Boy*). Mel Gussow in the *New York Times* found *The Chosen* "wordy," "ponderous," "bland," "unmusical," and "episodic"; further, he noted the way in which the relationship between the two boys was depicted brought to mind the love that dares not speak its name, surely something the authors never intended. Gussow also described a "dance for jumping Hasidim," which seemed to confuse the Hasidic and the Hellenic; so when "hirsute" actors started dancing and raising their arms and their chairs high above their heads, Gussow fully expected to see "Zorba the Hasid" appear on the stage.

During previews, Ron Holgate appeared in the role of David Malter (his role was assumed by Gerald Hiken), and Eugene Troobnik performed the role of Professor Reuven Malter (which was later played by Rob Morrow).

At least thirteen songs were dropped during previews: "The Gift You Left Behind," "Lazy Lou," "Soon You'll Be Here in My Arms," "Strangers Can Be Friends," "A Woman of Valor" (after *Proverbs*), "Coming Home/Street Boogie," "Remember the Children," "The Time Is Now," "Nostalgia Waltz," "Beautiful and Far," "Lana," and "In the Name of God."

Composer Philip Springer wrote two standards in the 1950s, the jaunty "(How Little It Matters) How Little We Know" (popularized by Frank Sinatra) and the saucy "Santa Baby," which is one of Eartha Kitt's signature songs. See entry for *A Song Floating*, a retrospective revue of the Springer songbook.

Lyricist Mitchell Bernard had also written the lyrics for the 1980 Off Broadway musical *Snapshots* (see entry).

285 Christina Alberta's Father. THEATRE: Vineyard Theatre; OPENING DATE: May 4, 1994; PERFORMANCES: 41; BOOK: Polly Pen; LYRICS: Polly Pen; MUSIC: Polly Pen; DIRECTION: Andre Ernotte; CHOREOGRAPHY: Lynne Taylor-Corbett; SCENERY: William Barclay; COSTUMES: Gail Brassard; LIGHTING: Michael Lincoln; MUSICAL DIRECTION: Paulette Haupt; PRODUCER: Vineyard Theatre (Douglas Aibel, Artistic Director; Barbara Zinn Krieger, Executive Director; Jon Nakagawa, Managing Director)

CAST—Henry Stram (Albert Edward Preemby), Alma Cuervo (Chris Hossett), Marla Schaffel (Christina Alberta Preemby), John Lathan (Teddy), Tina Johnson (Fay), Marceline Hugot (Miss Rewster), Don Mayo (Major Bone), Jan Neuberger (Mrs. Bone), Richard Holmes (Master Bone), Andy Taylor (Bobby)

SOURCE—The 1925 novel *Christina Alberta's Father* by H.G. Wells.

The action occurs in England during the period 1899-1920s.

The musical was presented in two acts (division of acts and song assignments unknown; songs are listed in performance order).

MUSICAL NUMBERS—"Greetings from the Paddlers on the Sheringham Front," "Sleep Little Red Object," "The Laundry," "Court of Conscience," "Alone in the World," "Boarding Houses," "Tunbridge Wells," "A Rock and a Body," "Waiting," "Dance in the Studio," "Early Amphibians," "I Am Reeling," "My World," "Running About," "Where Is the Lost and Found of London?" "Uneasy Armchairs," "Slow't Dow (Down?)," "Fricassee of Chicken," "Later Amphibians," "Christina Alberta and I," "Tra-La-La," "Daybreak," "Here in Love," "First Night of Summer"

NOTES—The Off Off Broadway musical *Christina Alberta's Father* was another offbeat excursion into the world of Victoriana by Polly Pen, who is often associated with musicals of that era, either as a writer and composer (*Goblin Market*) or as a performer (*Charlotte Sweet*) (see entries).

Based on the feminist novel by H.G. Wells, the musical is similar in subject matter to *Ann Veronica*, another feminist novel by Wells which was written in 1909 and which was also adapted into a musical. *Ann Veronica* opened in London at the Cambridge Theatre on April 17, 1969, and played for forty-four performances; the music was by Cyril Ornadel, the lyrics by David Croft, and the book by Ronald Gow. The title role was performed by Mary Millar, and the production was recorded by CBS Records (LP # 70052).

In reviewing *Christina Alberta's Father* for the *New York Times*, Ben Brantley said the "ambitious" musical had a "refreshingly original charm." However, he noted the evening was at its strongest in the "multifaceted jewel" of a first act, which dealt with the relationship between father and daughter. But when the second act turned dark, he felt the work lost its "conviction and confidence." But for all that, he praised Polly Pen's score of "winning tunefulness," and singled out a number of songs, including "Uneasy Armchairs," which he described as a "sinister street ballad."

286 Christmas Rappings. THEATRE: Judson Poets' Theatre; OPENING DATE: December 1969; PERFORMANCES: Unknown; TEXT: Adapted by Al Carmines from both the King James and the Revised Standard Versions of the Gospels of Luke, Matthew, and John; MUSIC: Al Carmines; CHOREOGRAPHY: John Jones, David Vaughan, and Dan Wagoner

NOTES—Al Carmines' *Christmas Rappings* was first presented at the Judson Poets' Theatre during the 1969 Christmas season. The Off Off Broadway oratorio-cum-cantata was presented at the theatre through Christmas 1980, for a total of twelve engagements. The 1976 edition was featured on the CBS television series *Camera Three*, and the 1979 edition was recorded on a 2-LP set (Judson Records # JU-1002). The song "No Room at the Inn" was included in *Songs from W.C. and Other Theatre Songs of Al Carmines* (CD # OC-9483). After many decades, the work returned to the Judson for a series of performances given in December 2007, and Robert Windeler in *Backstage.com* reported the singers included forty-four women and thirty-four men; with a large cast of singers and musicians which were typical of Carmines' productions, the revival must have evoked the memory and spirit of those long-ago evenings when Carmines and Company held forth on the Judson stage for *Christmas Rappings* and other musicals by the Off Broadway master. The following information is taken from a 1976 program and the 1979 cast album; DIRECTION: Dan Wagoner; CHOREOGRAPHY: Dan Wagoner; special choreography by David Vaughan; SCENERY: Earl Eidman; COSTUMES: Theo Barnes; LIGHTING: Earl Eidman

The self-described oratorio was presented in one act.

MUSICAL NUMBERS—Prologue, "In the Beginning Was the Word": Duet (Theo Barnes, Ira Siff), "Genealogy (With Homage)": Solo (Al Carmines),"Alleluia": Chorus, John the Baptist, "I Am the Angel Gabriel": Solo (Bill Conway, with Male Chorus), "For You Child Will Be Called the Prophet": (Chorus; dancer, Alexandra Galanopoulos), The Annunciation, "Hail Mary!"/Duet (Theo Barnes, Martin Meredith), "Dance of the Annunciation" (Dan Wagoner; choreographed by David Vaughan), "How Can These Things Be": Solo (Trisha Long, with Chorus and Instruments), "Blessed Art Thou Among Women": Solo (Zoelle Montgomery, with Chorus), "My Soul Magnifies the Lord": Solo (Julie Kurnitz, with Chorus), "Holy Mary, Mother of God": Chorus, Joseph, "Joseph, Son of David, Do Not Fear to Take Mary for Your Wife": Quartette (Semina De Laurentis, Julie Kurnitz, John Hinds, Craig Kuehl), "In Those Days a Decree Went Out": Solo (Jerry Fargo), The Birth and the Shepherds, "She Wrapped Him in Swaddling Clothes": Duet (Margaret Wright and David Vaughan) with Chorus; choreographed by David Vaughan, "No Room in the Inn": Solo (Lee Guilliatt) with Quartette (Eileen McNuit, Lou Bullock, Linda Larson, Paul Roundsaville), "And in That Region There Were Shepherds": Chorus, "And They Came with Haste": Octette (Essie Borden, Ellie Hondorp, Maggie Wise, Michele A. Katz, John Hinds, Fred Mills, Stephen Holt, Ronald Willoughby), "But Mary Kept All These Things in Her Heart": Solo (Margaret Wright) with Chorus, The Wise Men and Herod, "The Wise Men": Trio (Sandy Padilla, Barbara Sandek, Mary Meyer), "Go and Search Diligently for the Child": Solo (David Vaughan) with Tambourine (Alice Bosveld), "Nova": Solo (George Montgomery, with Instruments), "When They Saw the Star": Solo (Ira Siff) with Chorus); "Go and Search Diligently for the Child" (reprise): Solo (David Vaughan) with Tambourine (Alice Bosveld), "A Voice Was Heard Wailing": Solo (Maggie Wise) with Women's Chorus, Afterwards, "Prayer": Solo (Theo Barnes) with Chorus,"Lord, Now Let Thy Servant Depart in Peace": Chorus, "Waiting": Solo (Essie Borden)

CAST—NARRATORS: Brendan Elliott, Joan Cunningham, Melissa Sutphen, Judith Carroll, Susan Chasin, Julie Gregg, John Hinds, Fred Mills, Matthew Lipton, Peter Alfano, Bill Altham, Theo Barnes First Sopranos: Marilyn Bagner, Essie Borden, Alice Bosveld, Bonnie Carlson-Hiatt, Betty Collins, Joan Cunningham, Semina De Laurentis, Julie Gregg, Ellie Hondorp, Linda Larson, Barbara Mignone, Evelyn Schneider; SECOND SOPRANOS: Eve Edmond, Lynne Griffiths, Marti Lewis, Mia Mather, Eileen McNutt, Pamela Selensky, Melissa Sutphen; FIRST ALTOS: Susan Chasin, Karen Jare, Joan Kilpatrick, Julie Kurnitz, Trisha Long, Sandy Padilla, Barbara Sandek, Greta White, Maggie Wise; SECOND ALTOS: Judith Carroll, Brenda Lee Christman, Lee Guilliatt, Michele A. Katz, Mary Meyer, Zoelle Montgomery, Susan Owens, Margaret Wright, Marie E. Zwanziger; TENORS: Bill Conway, Martin Meredith, Ira Siff, John Tarrant; BARITONES: Peter Alfano, Bill Altham, Theo Barnes, John Barrett, Charles Behling, Lou Bullock, Brendan Elliott, Jerry Fargo, Eddie Harper, John Hinds, Stephen Holt, David Johnson, Tom Kilpatrick, Fred Mills, Tom Roderick, Paul Rounsaville, David Vaughan, John Witek; BASSES: Craig Kuehl, Matthew Lipton, Ronald Willoughby, Larry Wolf; DANCERS: Alexandra Galanopoulos, George Montgomery, Dan Wagoner; INSTRUMENTALISTS: Peter Alfano, Essie Borden, Alice Bosveld, Brenda Lee Christman, Betty Collins, Suzanne Dickinson, Eve Edmond, Eddie Harper, Karen Jare, Michele A. Katz, Marti Lewis, Matthew Lipton, Evelyn Schneider, Melissa Sutphen

287 Christopher's Wonders. THEATRE: Maidman Playhouse; OPENING DATE: September 26, 1960; PERFORMANCES: Unknown; PRODUCER: Brantz M. Bryan, Jr.

CAST—MILBOURNE CHRISTOPHER and His Company of Mystery Workers (Nancy Haskins, Bob Fischer, Ira Sanders, Diana Paoli, Frank Joglar)

The revue was presented in two acts.

ACT ONE—"A Whirlwind of Wizardry," "Knotty Problems," "Wonders from the Himalayas," "Cardology," "Poltergeist Phemomena," "Liquid Legerdemain," "Shanghai Sorcery," "Memories of LaFollette," "Christopher on the Air," "Behind the Scenes," "Miracle in Las Vegas," "An Explanation," "The Sidi Bou Said Mystery"

ACT TWO—"Dove Deceptions," "With Borrowed Money," "Contrasts," "Duck Dispatch," "Shooting Through a Girl," "The Wizard's Birthday," "Experiments in E.S.P.," "Séance Fantastique," "Cutting a Girl in 3 Pieces," "Metamorphosis Plus"

NOTES—A program note indicated that at an illusionist's performance, "program changes are not only possible but probable." *Christopher's Wonders* was apparently the first illusionist revue seen in New York in some twenty years. Arthur Gelb in the *New York Times* felt that while the show was perfect for children, adults might find themselves yawning.

Christopher's Wonders was also seen in London.

288 Christy. "The Darlin' Musical About a Daring Deed"; THEATRE: Bert Wheeler Theatre; OPENING DATE: October 14, 1975; PERFORMANCES: 40; BOOK: Bernie Spiro; LYRICS: Bernie Spiro; MUSIC: Lawrence J. Blank; incidental music by Robert Billig; DIRECTION: Peter David Heth; CHOREOGRAPHY: Jack Estes; SCENERY: Peter David Heth; COSTUMES: Peter David Heth Lighting: Marc Surver; MUSICAL DIRECTION: Robert Billig; PRODUCERS: Joseph Lillis in association with Joan Spiro

CAST—Jimi Elmer (Christopher [Christy] Mahon), Betty Forsyth (Pegeen Flaherty), Bea Swanson (Widow Quin), John Canary (Shawn Keogh), Alexander Sokoloff (Michael James Flaherty), Bruce Levitt (Old Mahon), Bill Hedge (Jimmy Farrell), Brian Pizer (Philly Cullen), Martha T. Kearns (Sara Malone), Lynn Kearney (Susan Brady), Marie Ginnetti (Maggie Tansey), Bebe Sacks Landis (Honor Blake)

SOURCE—The 1907 play *The Playboy of the Western World* by John Millington Synge.

The action occurs in Ireland.

The musical was presented in two acts.

ACT ONE—"Christy" (Jimi Elmer), "To Please the Woman in Me" (Betty Forsyth, Martha T. Kearns, Lynn Kearney, Marie Ginnetti, Bebe Sacks Landis), "To Please the Woman in Me" (reprise) (Betty Forsyth), "Grain of the Salt of the Earth" (Alexander Sokoloff, Bill Hedge, Brian Pizer, Betty Forsyth, Jimi Elmer), "Until the Likes of You" (Jimi Elmer, Betty Forsyth), "Picture Me" (Jimi Elmer), "The Morning After" (Betty Forsyth), "Rumors" (Martha T. Kearns, Lynn Kearney, Marie Ginnetti, Bebe Sacks Landis, Bea Swanson), "One Fell Swoop" (Jimi Elmer, Martha T. Kearns, Lynn Kearney, Marie Ginnetti, Bebe Sacks Landis, Bea Swanson), "All's Fair" (Bea Swanson, John Canary), "Picture Me" (reprise) (Martha T. Kearns, Lynn Kearney, Marie Ginnetti, Bebe Sacks Landis, Betty Forsyth, Jimi Elmer)

ACT TWO—"The Heart's a Wonder" (Betty Forsyth, Jimi Elmer), "Down the Hatch" (Alexander Sokoloff, Bill Hedge, Brian Pizer, Bea Swanson), Gallant Little Swearers (Alexander Sokoloff, Betty Forsyth, Jimi Elmer, Ensemble), "Christy" (reprise) (Jimi Elmer), "Until the Likes of You" (reprise) (Betty Forsyth)

NOTES—Although some of its songs seemed like filler in order to stretch out the evening, *Christy* nonetheless contained a melodic and lively score by Bernie Spiro and Lawrence J. Blank, and deserved a longer run than five weeks (incidentally, the music for "The Morning After" was by Robert Billig). The score was recorded by Original Cast Records (LP # OR-7913).

But Mel Gussow in the *New York Times* wasn't impressed with the musical, feeling it was an "abbreviated" version of Synge's play. He noted that the performers' Irish accents wavered between "Erin to Brooklyn," with "yer" often competing with "youse." He further noted that the women of the company smiled so broadly ("as if they were competing ... in a dimple contest") that the musical could well be titled *Christy McDimple* (in honor of *Curley McDimple*, which had originally premiered at the theatre in 1967 [see entry]). Gussow also noted that producer Joseph Lillis' program bio indicated his next productions would be *Hanky Panky*, a musical comedy adaptation of *Othello*, and a revue titled *Turkey Salad*.

Efforts to set *The Playboy of the Western World* to music have always failed. Besides the short-running *Christy*, a 1978 adaptation called *Back Country* (which switched the action from Ireland to Kansas) closed in Boston prior to its Broadway opening. (There was also a British musical produced in 1958; titled *The Heart's a Wonder*, it didn't make much of an impression, either.)

289 Chu Chem. "The First Chinese-Jewish Musical!"; THEATRE: Jewish Repertory Theatre; OPENING DATE: December 27, 1988; PERFORMANCES: 20; BOOK: Ted Allan; LYRICS: Jim Haines and Jack Wohl; MUSIC: Mitch Leigh; DIRECTION: Albert Marre; CHOREOGRAPHY: Rosalind Newman; SCENERY: Bob Mitchell; COSTUMES: Ken Yount; LIGHTING: Jason Sturm; MUSICAL DIRECTION: Don Jones; PRODUCER: Jewish Repertory Theatre (Ran Avni, Artistic Director; Edward M. Cohen, Associate Director)

CAST—Irving Burton (Yakob), Timm Fujii (The Prompter), Simone Gee (Na-Mi, Black Cloud, Concubine). Zoie Lam (Daf-ah-Dil, Villager, Concubine), Alvin Lum (The Elder), Kenji Nakao (Itsu-Hoke, Propman, Henchman), Marc C. Oka (Izu-Lo-Yeh, Propman, Henchman), Chev Rodgers (Hong Ho), Keelee Seetoo (Lei-An, Pink Cloud, Concubine), Thom Sesma (The Prince), Hechter Ubarry (The Prince's Brother), Emily Zacharias (Lotte), Mark Zeller (Chu Chem)

The action occurs six hundred years ago in the Village of Kai Feng, China.

The musical was presented in two acts.

ACT ONE—"Orient Yourself" (The Chinese Company), "Rain" (Chev Rodgers, Kenji Nakao, Marc C. Oka, Keelee Seetoo, Simone Gee), "What Happened, What?" (Mark Zeller, Villagers), "Welcome" (Villagers), "You'll Have to Change" (Emily Zacharias), "Love Is" (Thom Sesma), "I'll Talk to Her" (Mark Zeller, Thom Sesma, Hechter Ubarry), "Shame on You" (Mark Zeller, Simone Gee, Zoie Lam, Keelee Seetoo), "It Must Be Good for Me" (Emily Zacharias), "The Wise" (Mark Zeller), "You'll Have to Change" (reprise) (Thom Sesma), "The River" (Emily Zacharias, Thom Sesma), "We Dwell in Our Hearts" (Mark Zeller, Emily Zacharias, Thom Sesma)

ACT TWO—"Re-Orient Yourself" (Thom Sesma, Company), "What Happened, What?" (reprise) (Irving Burton), "I Once Believed" (Emily Zacharias), "It's Possible" (Mark Zeller), "Our Kind of War" (The Chinese Company), "Boom!" (Chev Rodgers), Finale (Company)

NOTES—*Chu Chem* (the name of the musical's main character, meaning "wise man") told the story of a group of fourteenth-century Jews searching for a lost tribe of Jews who settled in China during the eleventh century.

The original 1966 production of *Chu Chem* was Mitch Leigh's first musical after his 1965 hit *Man of La Mancha*; besides Leigh, other *La Mancha* veterans signed up for *Chu Chem*, including director Albert Marre, choreographer Jack Cole, and scenic and lighting designer Howard Bay. *Chu Chem*'s cast included Menasha Skulnik, Molly Picon, James Shigeta, Jack Cole, Marcia Rodd, and Buzz Miller.

But lightning didn't strike twice, and the original production of *Chu Chem* never got out of Philadelphia; in fact, the musical didn't even make it through the entire Philadelphia engagement, closing after just five days. Ernest Schier in the Philadelphia *Evening Standard* famously referred to the debacle as "The King and Oy."

But encouraged by the American Jewish Theatre's Off Off Broadway revival, Mitch Leigh brought the musical to Broadway, where it opened at the Ritz Theatre on March 17, 1989, twenty-three years after the musical had been scheduled to open at the George Abbott Theatre. With the exception of Thom Sesma (who was replaced by Kevin Gray), most of the American Jewish Theatre's cast transferred to Broadway. Despite an often ingratiating score (such as the haunting ballad "Love Is" and the rhythmic anti-war song "Our Kind of War"), the musical closed on Broadway after forty-five performances. "The Wise," a number heard in the Jewish Repertory production, wasn't retained for the Broadway version. Numbers on a 1966 demo recording which weren't used in the 1988-1989 revivals were "A Lovely Place," "Empty Yourself" (possibly an early version of "Orient Yourself"?), "One at a Time," "My Only Love," "It's Not the Truth," and the title song.

The 1966 demo recording reveals a melodic score, and no doubt the engaging music encouraged the later Off Broadway and Broadway revivals. But after the short Broadway run, *Chu Chem* disappeared. Even though the 1989 Broadway production was recorded, it's never been issued; for a while, there were rumors Leigh intended to issue on CD the recordings of three of his musicals (a transfer from LP to CD of his wonderful score of *Cry for Us All* [1970]; a transfer from audiocassette to CD of *Ain't Broadway Grand* [1993; the audiocassette had been sold in the theatre lobby during the musical's brief Broadway run]; and the 1989 production of *Chu Chem*), but unfortunately the releases never occurred.

290 Cinderella. THEATRE: Playhouse 91; OPENING DATE: December 19, 1991; PERFORMANCES: 70; BOOK: Norman Robbins; LYRICS: Amy Powers and Dan Levy; MUSIC: Dan Levy; DIRECTION: Laura Fine; SCENERY: Harry Feiner; COSTUMES: Gail Baldoni; LIGHTING: Stephen Petrilli; PRODUCER: Riverside Shakespeare Company (Gus Kaikkonen, Artistic Director; Stephen Vetrano, Managing Director)

CAST—Mark Honan (Buttons), Fredi Walker (Dandini), Melanie Wingert (Cinders), Pat Flick (Baron Hardupp), Diane Ciesla (Baroness Hardupp), Robert Mooney (Asphyxia), John Keene Bolton (Euthanasia), Jim Fitzpatrick (Ammer), Jay Brian Winnick (Tongs), Anthony Stanton (Prince Charming), Lora Lee Cliff (Old Lady, Fairy Godmother)

SOURCE—The 1697 fairy tale *Cinderella* by Charles Perrault.

The musical was presented in two acts.

ACT ONE—"Bright Spring Morn" (Company), "It's What You Do (That Makes Your Wishes Come True)" (Melanie Wingert), "His Highness" (Company), "I Am a Prince" (Anthony Stanton, Fredi Walker), "Your Sticks, Your Hat, Your Hand" (Anthony Stanton, Melanie Wingert), "Getting Ready for the Ball" (Melanie Wingert, Robert Mooney, John Keene Bolton, Pat Flick, Diane Ciesla), "It's What You Do" (reprise) (Melanie Wingert), "Dance at the Ball Tonight" (Lora Lee Cliff, Melanie Wingert, Mark Honan)

ACT TWO—"Waitin' on the Women" (Anthony Stanton, Fredi Walker, Pat Flick, Jim Fitzpatrick, Jay Brian Winnick, Mark Honan), "Keep the Castle Warm" (Mark Honan, Company), "La Petite Oiseau" (John Keene Bolton, Company), "Delighted You Invited Me" (Company), "It's What You Do" (reprise) (Melanie Wingert), "Happy Ending" (Company)

NOTES—*The Applause/Best Plays Theatre Yearbook of 1991-1992* described *Cinderella* as a "free-wheeling British 'panto'-like" adaptation of the classic Charles Perrault story.

D.J.R. Bruckner in the *New York Times* noted the evening offered "genial rowdiness" and a "very cheerful spirit," and he singled out one song, "Waitin' on the Women" (an "inspired ... nifty vocal sextet"). For another musical inspired by the fairy tale, see entry for *Cindy*.

291 Cindy. THEATRE: Gate Theatre Opening Date: March 19, 1964; transferred to the Orpheum Theatre on September 24, 1964; and to the Cricket Theatre on January 19, 1965; PERFORMANCES: 318; BOOK: Joe Sauter and Mike Sawyer; LYRICS: Johnny Brandon; MUSIC: Johnny Brandon; DIRECTION: Marvin Gordon; CHOREOGRAPHY: Marvin Gordon; SCENERY: Robert T. Williams; COSTUMES: Patricia Quinn Stuart; LIGHTING: Martin Aronstein; MUSICAL DIRECTION: Sammy Benskin; PRODUCER: Stuart Weiner

CAST—Thelma Oliver (Storyteller), Tommy Karaty (Storyteller), Mark Stone (Storyteller), Jacqueline Mayro (Cindy Kreller), Johnny Harmon (Lucky), Dena Dietrich (Della Kreller), Amelia Varney (Golsa Kreller), Frank Nastasi (Papa Kreller), Mike Sawyer (David Rosenfeld), Sylvia Mann (Mama Kreller), Lizabeth Pritchett (Ruth Rosenfeld), Joe Masiell (Chuck Rosenfeld)

SOURCE—The 1697 fairy tale *Cinderella* by Charles Perrault.

The action occurs in New York City at the Kreller delicatessen and home, the Rosenfeld penthouse, and the Plaza Hotel.

The musical was presented in two acts.

ACT ONE—Overture (Orchestra), "Once Upon a Time" (Thelma Oliver, Tommy Karaty, Mark Stone), "Let's Pretend" (Jacqueline Mayro, Johnny Harmon), "Is There Something to What He Said?" (Jacqueline Mayro), "Papa, Let's Do It Again" (Sylvia Mann, Frank Nastasi, Thelma Oliver, Tommy Karaty, Mark Stone), "A Genuine Feminine Girl" (Jacqueline Mayro), "Cindy" (Johnny Harmon), "Think Mink" (Amelia Varney, Dena Dietrich), "A Genuine Feminine Girl" (reprise) (Jacqueline Mayro), "Tonight's the Night" (Thelma Oliver, Tommy Karaty, Mark Stone), "Who Am I?" (Jacqueline Mayro, Joe Masiell), "Ballroom Sequence" (Company)

ACT TWO—Entr'acte (Orchestra), Opening (Thelma Oliver, Tommy Karaty, Mark Stone), "If You've Got It, You've Got It" (Amelia Varney, Dena Dietrich, Sylvia Mann, Frank Nastasi), "The Life That I Planned for Him" (Lizabeth Pritchett), "If It's Love" (Joe Masiell, Jacqueline Mayro), "Got the World in the Palm of My Hand" (Joe Masiell) "Call Me Lucky" (Johnny Harmon) "Got the World in the Palm of My Hand" (reprise) (Thelma Oliver, Tommy Karaty, Mark Stone), "Laugh It Up" (Jacqueline Mayro, Sylvia Mann, Frank Nastasi, Boys), "Is There Something to What He Said?" (reprise) (Performer[s] Unknown), "Let's Pretend" (reprise) (Jacqueline Mayro, Johnny Harmon), "Cindy" (reprise)/"Who Am I?" (Duet) (Jacqueline Mayro, Johnny Harmon), "What a Wedding" (Sylvia Mann, Frank Nastasi, Amelia Varney, Dena Dietrich, Mike Sawyer, Lizabeth Pritchett, Joe Masiell), Finale (Company)

NOTES—Johnny Brandon's *Cindy* was an updated version of the Cinderella story, here transplanted to modern-day New York City, where Cindy Kreller and her family live, operating a delicatessen adjoined to their home. The musical's familiar story and its pleasant if mild score enabled it to run for almost a year. But it seems to have completely disappeared from community and high school theatre, and lives on only in its cast recording released by ABC-Paramount Records (LP # ABCS-OC-2).

During the run, the second act reprise of "Is There Something to What He Said?" was dropped in favor of a reprise of "Once Upon a Time" (sung by the three Storytellers).

It appears that sometime during the run the credits for producer expanded from Stuart Weiner to Chandler Warren and Philip Temple, by arrangement with Stuart Weiner and Jerry Grace.

Jacquelyn Mayro, who played the title role of Cindy, had appeared in the original 1959 Broadway production of *Gypsy*, creating the role of Baby June. In early 1968, she appeared in another Off Broadway musical by Johnny Brandon, the short-lived *Who's Who, Baby?* and later that same year was in another Off Broadway failure, *Just for Love* (see entries). In 1971, she was in the dreadful Broadway musical *Ari*, and, with John Savage, sang "I See What I Choose to See," one of the dreariest songs of 1970s musicals. In case you were wondering ... Lane Bradbury, who created the role of the older June in the original Broadway production of *Gypsy*, doesn't seem to have appeared in any Broadway and Off Broadway musicals after *Gypsy*. However, she was in at least five dramas. Prior to *Gypsy*, she was in the original 1958 Broadway production of Archibald MacLeish's Pulitzer Prize-winning play *J.B.*, and after *Gypsy* she was in the original 1961 Broadway production of Tennessee Williams' *The Night of the Iguana*. She crossed theatrical paths with June Havoc again when she appeared in Havoc's 1963 play *Marathon '33*. She also created the role of Honey during the first few Broadway previews of the original production of Edward Albee's 1962 play *Who's Afraid of Virginia Woolf?* but by opening night Melinda Dillon had assumed the role. It seems Bradbury's final New York appearance was in an Off Broadway play titled *Graduation*, which opened (and closed) on January 5, 1965.

During *Cindy*'s run, screen legend Nancy Carroll succeeded Sylvia Mann in the role of Mama Kreller. The musical's run represented three slightly separated engagements, for a total of 318 performances. *Cindy* opened in London at the Fortune Theatre on May 29, 1968, for twenty-nine performances; Geraldine Morrow played the title role, and the cast included Hy Hazell, Rose Hill, Avril Angers, and Johnny Tudor.

292 City Scene (A double bill which included *Paradise Gardens East*). THEATRE: Fortune Theatre; OPENING DATE: March 10, 1969; PERFORMANCES: 16; SCRIPTS: Frank Gagliano; DIRECTION: Neil Israel; SCENERY: David F. Segal; COSTUMES: John David Ridge; LIGHTING: David F. Segal; PRODUCERS: Doris Kuller and Simon L. Saltzman

NOTES—*City Scene* (a/k/a *Frank Gagliano's City Scene*) consisted of two one-acts, the drama *City Scene I: Conerico Was Here to Stay* and the musical *City Scene II: Paradise Gardens East*. The above credits are for both plays.

The first play, *Conerico Was Here to Stay* included all the performers who appeared in the evening's second offering, *Paradise Gardens East*, which included songs with lyrics by Frank Gagliano and music by Mildred Kayden. *City Scene II: Paradise Gardens East*

The action occurs in a newly-painted efficiency on New York's Upper East Side.

CAST—Dominic Chianese (Workman), Terry Kiser (Workman), Raul Julia (Workman), Lynn Milgrim (Sis), Fran Stevens (Mrs. Super), Lenny Baker (Brother), M.K. Douglas/David Congden (William Saroyan O'Neill), Phillip Giambri (Narrator)

MUSICAL NUMBERS—(The following songs are listed as they appeared in the program, but may not have been performed in the order in which they were listed.) "Harmony" (Dominic Chianese, Terry Kiser, Raul Julia); "The Beat of the City" (Dominic Chianese, Terry Kiser, Raul Julia); "I'll Bet You're a Cat Girl" (Fran Stevens); "Gussy and the Beautiful People" (Fran Stevens); "Look at My Sister" (Lenny Baker); "Black and Blue Plumps" (Lenny Baker); "That's Right, Mr. Syph" (Lenny Baker); "Bodoni County" (Lynn Milgrim); "The Incinerator Hour" (David Congden)

MORE NOTES—It appears that the running order of the plays was reversed at some point during the two-week run.

Clive Barnes in the *New York Times* noted that *Paradise Gardens East* reminded him of Jules Feiffer's black comedy *Little Murders* (1967). Both works dealt with New Yorkers trying to survive in a violent city, and in the case of the musical the plot centered on Sis, a young woman who has just moved to the city. Barnes felt the work was flawed but "fun in its too quietly murderous way," and he mentioned that Mildred Kayden's "pastiche" score was "Weill-like" and a "modest but distinct plus" to the evening.

Conerico Was Here to Stay, which took place on a subway platform, had previously been produced at the Cherry Lane Theatre for twenty-one performances on March 3, 1965, as part of the Theatre 1965 New Playwrights Series.

The two scripts were published as *The City Scene* by Samuel French, Inc., in 1965, four years before the Off Broadway run at the Fortune Theatre; in the published version, *Paradise Gardens East* is a straight dramatic play, not a musical. Further, the running order of the script references *Paradise Gardens East* as Part One and *Conerico Was Here to Stay* as Part Two.

Paradise Gardens East was seen in London for eleven performances during the 1973-1974 theatre season.

293 The City Suite. THEATRE: Park Royal Theatre; OPENING DATE: March 15, 1979; PERFORMANCES: Unknown; BOOK: Carin Marie Zakes and Keith Levenson; "additional material" by Todd Graff and David Margolis; LYRICS: Keith Levenson; MUSIC: Keith Levenson; DIRECTION: Carin Marie Zakes; CHOREOGRAPHY: Carin Marie Zakes; SCENERY: Seth Levenson and Edwin Dixon; COSTUMES: Seth Levenson and Edwin Dixon; LIGHTING: Seth Levenson and Edwin Dixon (?); MUSICAL DIRECTION: Ronald Botting; PRODUCERS: TOMI in conjunction with Elaine Maran

CAST—Ronald Bottoms (Robbie), Lisa Essary (Susan), David Margolis (Jeffrey), Robin Curtis (Rachael), Nancy Wade (Jill), Peter Green (Kenneth), Jenny Rebecca Goldman (Lisa), Todd Graff (David), Dena Olstad (Lesley), Keith Levenson (Max)

The action occurs in Manhattan at the present time.

The musical was presented in two acts.

ACT ONE—*Past Fun:* "Tell Me Why I Love Him" Company), "My New York" (Company), "Party"

(Company), "Half a Couple" (David Margolis, Lisa Essary, Peter Green, Dena Olstad, Robin Curtis, Todd Graff), "Lullabye" (David Margolis, Company), "Where Do I Go" (Robin Curtis, Todd Graff, Nancy Wade), "Alone with Me" (Jenny Rebecca Goldman), "Fairytale" (David Margolis, Ronald Botting), "Lie with Me" (Ronald Botting, Peter Green, Dena Olstad, Lisa Essary), "Everybody Wants To Be in Love" (Company)

ACT TWO—*Present Games:* "I Am This Place" (Company), "What Ever Happened" (Robin Curtis), "A Love Scene for Who?" (Ronald Botting, Todd Graff, David Margolis), "Your Move" (Robin Curtis), "Game" (Company), "Take a Look" (Company), "Suite" (David Margolis, Lisa Essary, Company), "Was It Something That I Said" (Lisa Essary), "Just Friends" (David Margolis, Company)

NOTES—The program for the Off Off Broadway production of *The City Suite* stated the plot dealt with the lives and loves of "nine Manhattan-bred young adults ... The pace of New York exerts a certain frenzy in our lives; its influence in our relationships is what this new musical illustrates." (It appears the musical had a lot of *Company.*) Indeed, John S. Wilson in the *New York Times* acknowledged Keith Levinson's debt to Sondheim (particularly in the opening sequence of the musical), but he noted that for most of the score Levinson (a "warmly melodic and rhythmic" composer) found his own voice (particularly in "Lullabye [The Best Time to Be In Love in New York Is at Sunset]").

294 The CIVIL WarS: A Tree Is Best Measured When It Is Down. THEATRE: Brooklyn Academy of Music; OPENING DATE: December 14, 1986; PERFORMANCES: 10; TEXT: Maita di Nascemi and Robert Wilson; MUSIC: Philip Glass; Hans Peter Kuhn, Audio Score; DIRECTION: Robert Wilson; CHOREOGRAPHY: Ulysses Dove; SCENERY: Tom Kamm and Robert Wilson; COSTUMES: Christophe de Menil; LIGHTING: Beverly Emmons and Robert Wilson; MUSICAL DIRECTION: Bruce Ferden; PRODUCER: The Next Wave Festival

CAST—Claudia Cummings (Snow Owl, Alcmene), Ruby Hinds (Earth Mother, Mrs. Lincoln), Paul Spencer Adkins (Garibaldi), Harlan Foss (Abraham Lincoln), Bruce Kramer (Hercules), Paul Collins (Robert E. Lee), Jennifer Rohn (Young Mrs. Lincoln), Vernon Landix Scott (Eagle), Cristina Perera (Rain Priestess), Deadra Kaehler (Sun), Nancy Sakamoto (Serpent), Stacey Denham (Corn Maiden), Christine Clark (Corn Maiden), Mark Ruhala (Kachina Clown), Joel Kirby (Kachina Clown), Steve Bromer (Kachina Clown)

NOTES—The complete version of *The CIVIL WarS: A Tree Is Best Measured When It Is Down* was an epic twelve-hour opera by Robert Wilson and Philip Glass; for the Next Wave Festival, only the so-called "Rome Section" of the opera was produced. It consisted of a prologue and the opera's fourth act, and was sung and spoken in Latin, Italian, and English.

The plot itself was vague, and while the characters included Abraham Lincoln, Robert E. Lee, Hercules, and Garibaldi, most of the action took place in outer space where an occasional cartoon-like goose or swan flew by. Donal Henehan in the *New York Times* noted that the "metapoetical, obscurantist" libretto emphasized movement and tableau vivants, and thus the evening was closer to a dance work than to traditional musical theatre. As for Glass' score, Henehan noted it was "numbingly primitive" and "largely incidental and trivial." The complete opera also consisted of thirteen short "knee plays" which were to be presented between the various sections of the opera. *The Knee Plays* (see entry) had texts by Robert Wilson and music by David Byrne, and two weeks before *the CIVIL warS* sequences were given at the Brooklyn Academy of Music, they were produced at the Alice Tully Hall at Lincoln Center for four performances. On February 27, 1985, part of the opera (Act III/Scene E [credited to Robert Wilson], Act IV/Scene A [Wilson and Heiner Muller], and the Epilogue [Wilson and Muller]) was performed at the American Repertory Theatre in Cambridge, Massachusetts. Glass doesn't seem to have been credited for the music in this production, but Hans Peter Kuhn was credited for "compositions and sound."

295 The Class. "The New Ballet Musical"; THEATRE: Downstairs/New York City Center; OPENING DATE: April 28, 1978; PERFORMANCES: 4; BALLET CONCEIVED BY Jack Johnson; DIRECTION: Jack Johnson; CHOREOGRAPHY: Jack Johnson; Gloria Szymkowicz, Assistant; MUSIC: Original music by Andrew Asch; SCENERY AND MULTI-MEDIA EFFECTS by John Hawkins; photo sequences by David Bruce Cratsley; COSTUMES: Gloria Szymkowicz; LIGHTING: John Hawkins; MUSICAL DIRECTION: Andrew Asch (?); PRODUCER: Jerry B. Livengood

CAST—Rico Costa (Mark), Gisele Ferrari (Bobbie), Debra Lynn Jones (Heather), Donna McEntee (Sally), Robert Raimondo (Bob), Charles C. Sheek (Joe), Gloria Szymkowicz (Leslie), Whitney Wiemer (Ann)

The ballet-musical was presented in two acts.

ACT ONE—"Warm-Up Ballet" (Company), "Leslie's Fantasy of Warm-Up Ballet" (from "Jazz Ballet, Third Movement," music by George Riedel) (Gloria Szymkowicz), "Ann's Fantasy" (from "Sensation," music by David Shire) (Whitney Wiemer), "Joe's Fantasy" (from "Symphony No. 3, Final Movement," music by Roger Sessions) (Charles C. Sheek, Whitney Wiemer, Donna McEntee), "Heather's Fantasy Ballet" (from "Etude in D Minor," music by Franz Liszt) (Debra Lynn Jones, Rico Costa), "Leslie's Fantasy of Men's Combination" (from *Le Cid* ballet, music by Jules Massenet) (Gloria Szymkowicz, Rico Costa, Charles C. Sheek, Robert Raimondo), "Supported Adagio" (music by Andrew Asch) (Company)

ACT TWO—"Leslie's Fantasy of Women's Combination" (from "Symphony No. 4 in G," music by Gustav Mahler) (Gloria Szymkowicz, Gisele Ferrari, Debra Lynn Jones, Donna McEntee, Whitney Wiemer), "Love Duet" (from "Legend from Lake Malacen," music by Ture Rangstrom) (Rico Costa, Charles C. Sheek, Debra Lynn Jones), "Bob's Fantasy" (from "Concerto in F, Allegro," music by George Gershwin) (Robert Raimondo, Whitney Wiemer, Donna McEntee), "Bobbie's Fantasy" (from *Le Cid*'s "Madriene," music by Jules Massenet) (Gisele Ferrari, Robert Raimondo), "Mark's Fantasy" (from *Hamlet* Overture [1891], music by Peter Ilyich Tchaikovsky) (Rico Costa, Whitney Wiemer, Donna McEntee), "Leslie's Dance" (music by Andrew Asch) (Gloria Szymkowicz) Finale (from "Night on Disco Mountain" [from 1977 film *Saturday Night Fever*; adapted by David Shire from Modest Petrovich Mussorgsky's "Night on Bald Mountain"]) (Company)

NOTES—*The Class*, an obscure Off Off Broadway musical about ballet dancers, may have been inspired by *A Chorus Line* (1975; see entry).

296 A Class Act. THEATRE: City Center Stage II/Manhattan Theatre Club; OPENING DATE: November 9, 2000; PERFORMANCES: 29; BOOK: Linda Kline and Lonny Price; LYRICS: Edward Kleban; MUSIC: Edward Kleban; DIRECTION: Lonny Price; CHOREOGRAPHY: Scott Wise; Marguerite Derricks, Additional Choreography; SCENERY: James Noone; COSTUMES: Carrie Robbins; LIGHTING: Kevin Adams; MUSICAL DIRECTION: Todd Ellison; PRODUCERS: The Manhattan Theatre Club (Lynne Meadow, Artistic Director; Barry Grove, Executive Producer) in association with Musical Theatre Works

CAST—Nancy Anderson (Mona), Carolee Carmello (Lucy), Jonathan Freeman (Lehman), Randy Graff (Sophie), David Hibbard (Bobby), Julia Murney (Felicia), Lonny Price (Ed), Ray Wills (Charley)

The action occurs in February 1988 on the stage of the Shubert Theatre and in flashbacks from Ed Kleban's life from 1958 to 1987.

The musical was presented in two acts.

ACT ONE—"Light on My Feet" (additional lyric by Brian Stein) (Lonny Price, Company), "The Fountain in the Garden" (Company), "One More Beautiful Song" (Lonny Price, Randy Graff), "Fridays at Four" (Company), "Bobby's Song" (David Hibbard), "Charm Song" (Jonathan Freeman, Company), "Paris Through the Window" (additional lyric by Glenn Slater) (Lonny Price, David Hibbard, Ray Wills), "Mona" (Nancy Anderson), "Making Up Ways" (Performer[s] unknown), "Under Separate Cover" (Carolee Carmello, Lonny Price, Randy Graff), "Gauguin's Shoes" (Lonny Price, Company), "Follow Your Star" (Randy Graff, Lonny Price)

ACT TWO—"Better" (Lonny Price, Company), "Scintillating Sophie" (Lonny Price), "The Next Best Thing to Love" (Randy Graff), "Broadway Boogie Woogie" (Carolee Carmello). Excerpts from *A Chorus Line* (1975; music by Marvin Hamlisch; see separate entry) (Company): "Better" (reprise) (Lonny Price, Company); "I Choose You" (Lonny Price, Carolee Carmello); "Say Something Funny" (Company); "I Won't Be There (When the Dawn Breaks)" (Lonny Price); "Self Portrait" (Lonny Price); "Self Portrait" (reprise) (Lonny Price)

NOTES—Originally developed in workshop at Musical Theatre Works as *The Kleban Project* and then produced by the Manhattan Theatre Club as *A Class Act*, the revue-like musical celebrated the life and career of Edward Kleban (1939-1987), who had written the lyrics for *A Chorus Line* (see entry). After its Off Broadway run, *A Class Act* transferred to Broadway, opening at the Ambassador Theatre on March 11, 2001, for 105 performances.

Clearly a labor of love by its creators, the musical was nonetheless an extremely misguided effort on their behalf to expand what should have been a brief, intimate revue of Kleban's songs into a full-blown two-act musical. Kleban's life, and indeed his songs, weren't really enough to sustain a full-length evening, and the tiresome musical almost immediately wore out its welcome. The musical's awkward framework (in which Kleban's songs were sometimes used as "book" songs rather than as "performance" sequences) revolved around his memorial service, where his ghostly presence disagrees with comments made about him. In the script published by Stage & Screen Book Club in 2002, Lonny Price (the musical's director, star, and co-writer) outlined the four "multiple realities" in which the show takes place, and, in truth, perhaps all the layers of stories (Kleban's presence at the memorial service and his attempt to clarify and justify his life and career; the flashbacks of his life; the sequences in which one character interrupts Ed's stories in order to keep him focused; and finally the sequences in which Ed's ghost tries to deal with comments he hears about himself) were too much for the slender book to comfortably shoulder. For the Broadway run, "Don't Do It Again" and "The Nightmare" were added to the score.

"Better" had earlier been heard in *My Mother Was a Fortune-Teller* and *The Madwoman of Central Park West* (see entries), and was recorded for the latter's cast album. "Self Portrait" had been heard in the revue *Urban Blight* (see entry).

RCA Victor/BMG released the cast recording of the Broadway production of *A Class Act* (CD # 09026-63757-2).

297 Cleavage. "A New Musical ... Close to Where the Heart Is"; THEATRE: Playhouse Theatre; OPENING DATE: June 23, 1982; PERFORMANCES: 1; BOOK: Buddy and David Sheffield; LYRICS: Buddy Sheffield; MUSIC: Buddy Sheffield; DIRECTION: Rita Baker; CHOREOGRAPHY: Alton Geno; SCENERY: Morris Taylor; COSTUMES: James M. Miller; LIGHTING: Michael Hotopp and Paul De Pass (the latter also "supervised" scenery and costumes); MUSICAL DIRECTION: Keith Thompson; PRODUCER: Up Front Productions

CAST—Daniel David, Tom Elias, Mark Fite, Terese Gargiulo, Marsha Trigg Miller, Jay Rogers, Sharon Scruggs, Dick Sheffield, Pattie Tierce

The revue was presented in two acts.

ACT ONE—"Cleavage" (Ensemble), "Puberty" (Mark Fite, Ensemble), "Only Love" (Sharon Scruggs, Daniel David), "Surprise Me" (Terese Gargiulo), "Reprise Me" (Terese Gargiulo, Mark Fite), "Boys Will Be Girls" (Jay Rogers, Dancers), "Give Me an And" (Marsha Trigg Miller, Dancers), "Just Another Song" (Mark Fite), "Believe in Me, or I'll Be Leavin' You" (Pattie Tierce, Dick Sheffield)

ACT TWO—"The Thrill of the Chase" (Tom Elias, Mark Fite, Daniel David), "Lead 'Em Around by the Nose" (Marsha Trigg Miller, Pattie Tierce, Terese Gargiulo), "Sawing a Couple in Half" (Jay Rogers), "Only Love" (reprise) (Terese Gargiulo), "Bringing Up Badger" (Daniel David, Ensemble), "Voices of the Children" (Ensemble), "All the Lovely Ladies" (Tom Elias), "Living in Sin" (Tom Elias, Pattie Tierce, Ensemble), Finale (Ensemble)

NOTES—This one-performance flop dealt in revue-like fashion with a variety of couples and their romantic problems. The cast album was recorded on LP by BI Records and was coyly numbered (as # 36-24-36).

298 Cleopatra's Night. THEATRE: Metropolitan Opera House; OPENING DATE: January 31, 1920; PERFORMANCES: 6; LIBRETTO: Alice Leal Pollock; MUSIC: Henry Hadley; DIRECTION: Richard Ordynski; CHOREOGRAPHY: Rosina Galli; SCENERY: Norman Bel Geddes; COSTUMES: Norman Bel Geddes; MUSICAL DIRECTION: Gennaro Papi; PRODUCER: The Metropolitan Opera

CAST—Frances Alda (Cleopatra), Orville Harrold (Meiamoun), Marie Tiffany (Iras), Jeanne Gordon (Mardion), Millo Picco (Eunuch), Louis D'Angelo (Roman Officer), Vincenzo Reschiglian (Mark Antony), Dancers (Rosina Galli, Florence Rudolph, Giuseppe Bonfiglio)

SOURCE—The short story "Une Nuit de Cleopatre" by Theophile Gauthier.

The opera was presented in two acts.

NOTES—*Cleopatra's Night* was a world premiere, and it returned to the Met during the following season when it was presented for an additional three performances. The premiere was on a double bill with a revival of Ruggero Leoncavallo's *Pagliacci* (1892) with Enrico Caruso.

Richard Aldrich in the *New York Times* noted *Cleopatra's Night* was the tenth American opera to premiere at the Met under its present management, and he proclaimed it to be the "best," the most "competent," the "most skillfully made," and the most "viable." He praised the "excellent" performances," but found the libretto only serviceable. While he had some reservations with Henry Hadley's score, he nonetheless wrote of its "variety, depth, color, and significant detail of instrumental effect," and concluded it was "a pleasure to hear." The libretto told of a chaste Egyptian lion hunter named Meiamoun who falls in love with Cleopatra. She grants him one night of love under the condition that he must die with the dawn. He agrees, and the two spend the night together. By morning, Cleopatra is willing to hold back the dawn for a full month, but Meiamoun is resigned to his fate. He starts to drink a goblet of poison, but hesitates when Cleopatra implores him to not to. When a messenger tells Cleopatra that Antony will soon be arriving, she tells the messenger she eagerly awaits him. So Meiamoun drinks the poison, Cleopatra embraces his body, and then goes to meet Antony.

299 Close Enough for Jazz. "A Musical Comedy Revue"; THEATRE: Wonderhorse Theatre; OPENING DATE: June 18, 1981; PERFORMANCES: 12; BOOK: Joseph Keenan; LYRICS: Joseph Keenan; MUSIC: Scott Steidl; DIRECTION: David Rothkopf; CHOREOGRAPHY: Mary Duncan; SCENERY: Bill Motyka; COSTUMES: Amanda Klein; LIGHTING: Bill Motyka; MUSICAL DIRECTION: Douglas Bernstein; PRODUCER: David J. Rothkopf

CAST—Susan J. Baum, Stephen Berenson, Mary Duncan, Debra Jacobs, Joe Joyce, Nina Hennessey, Dietrich Snelling

The revue was presented in two acts.

ACT ONE—"Close Enough for Jazz" (Ensemble), "Required Reading" (Ensemble), "Somebody Else"/"First Interlude" (Ensemble), "A Playwright Remembered" (Ensemble), "Dressing Room" (Mary Duncan, Dietrich Snelling), "The Post" (Ensemble), "Paperback Writer" (Debra Jacobs, Joe Joyce), "This Is It"/"Second Interlude" (Ensemble)

ACT TWO—"Corporate Choreography" (Ensemble), "Anyone Else"/"Third Interlude" (Ensemble), "Don't Quote Me" (Ensemble), "Ballad"/"Fourth Interlude" (Nina Hennessey), "What I'm Looking For"/"Fifth Interlude" (Mary Duncan, Nina Hennessey), "Nobody Else"/"Final Interlude" (Ensemble), "Close Enough for Jazz" (reprise) (Ensemble)

NOTES—The Off Off Broadway revue *Close Enough for Jazz* played out its twelve-performance engagement and then disappeared. John S. Wilson in the *New York Times* noted the revue's title was misleading because the songs never got close to jazz; in fact, the "best" musical sequences ("Somebody Else," "Anyone Else," and "Nobody Else") were a "very capable parallel" to Stephen Sondheim's score for *Company* (1970). As for the sketches, Wilson felt they started promisingly but went on too long.

300 Closer Than Ever. THEATRE: Cherry Lane Theatre; OPENING DATE: November 6, 1989; PERFORMANCES: 288; LYRICS: Richard Maltby, Jr.; MUSIC: David Shire; DIRECTION: Richard Maltby, Jr.; CHOREOGRAPHY: Marcia Milgrom Dodge; SCENERY: Philipp Jung; COSTUMES: Jess Goldstein; LIGHTING: Natasha Katz; MUSICAL DIRECTION: Patrick Scott Brady; PRODUCERS: Janet Brenner, Michael Gill, and Daryl Roth

CAST—Brent Barrett, Patrick Scott Brady, Sally Mayes, Richard Muenz, Lynne Wintersteller

The revue was presented in two acts.

ACT ONE—"Doors" (Company), "She Loves Me Not" (Brent Barrett, Lynne Wintersteller, Richard Muenz), "You Wanna Be My Friend" (Sally Mayes, Brent Barrett), "Fandango" (Lynne Wintersteller, Richard Muenz), "What Am I Doing?" (Brent Barrett), "The Bear, the Tiger, the Hamster and the Mole" (Lynne Wintersteller), "If I Sing" (lyric by Richard Maltby, Jr., and David Shire) (Richard Muenz), "Miss Byrd" (Sally Mayes), "The Sound of Muzak" (Company), "One of the Good Guys" (Brent Barrett), "There's Nothing Like It" (Company), "Life Story" (Lynne Wintersteller), "Next Time" (Richard Muenz, Company), "I Wouldn't Go Back" (Company)

ACT TWO—"The March of Time" (Company), "There" (Sally Mayes, Patrick Scott Brady), "Cause I'm Happy" (lyric by David Shire) (Richard Muenz), "Three Friends" (Sally Mayes, Lynne Wintersteller, Brent Barrett), "Back on Base" (lyric by David Shire) (Sally Mayes), "Patterns" (Lynne Wintersteller), "Wedding Song" (Brent Barrett, Company), "Another Wedding Song" (lyric by David Shire) (Richard Muenz, Sally Mayes), "Father of Fathers" (Brent Barrett, Patrick Scott Brady, Sally Mayes), "It's Never That Easy"/"I've Been There Before" (Lynne Wintersteller, Sally Mayes), "Closer Than Ever" (Richard Muenz, Company)

NOTES—*Closer Than Ever* was another revue about life in the Big City, but was distinguished by Richard Maltby, Jr., and David Shire's score, which included new songs as well as numbers which had been either heard in or intended for other musicals. The revue was recorded on a 2-CD set released by RCA Victor (# 60399-2-RG).

"She Loves Me Not" was from the 1961 Off Broadway musical *The Sap of Life* (see entry); "The Sound of Muzak" had been in the 1963 revue *Graham Crackers* (see entry); "Next Time" was from *Love Match*, which closed prior to Broadway in 1968; "Patterns, "Like a Baby," "I Wouldn't Go Back," and "Father of Fathers" had been written for, but not used in, *Baby* (1983), although "Patterns" was included on *Baby*'s cast album; for *Closer Than Ever*, a new lyric was written for "Father of Fathers"; "The Bear, the Tiger, the Hamster, and the Mole" had been cut from *Baby* when the character who sang the number was written out of the script; and at least three numbers ("Life Story," "Miss Byrd," and "There") had been heard in *Urban Blight* (see entry); two songs, "What Am I Doing?" and "I've Been Here (There) Before," were written for an unfinished musical; further, while "You Want to Be My Friend?" and "There's Nothing Like It" don't appear in *Urban Blight*'s program, they were apparently heard in that production at one point or another; "Three Friends" was written for, but not used in, *Urban Blight*; and "One of the Good Guys" was written for *Urban Blight* but apparently not used. Also, "She Loves Me Not" and "It's Never That Easy" were early collaborations by Maltby and Shire.

Soon after the opening, the revue underwent various changes. Patrick Scott Brady, the revue's musical director, was no longer listed as a cast member, and a number of songs ("Wedding Song," "The March of Time," and "Cause I'm Happy") were either dropped, added ("Like a Baby"), or underwent minor title changes ("You Wanna Be My Friend" became "You Want to Be My Friend?" and "What Am I Doin'" became "What Am I Doing?"). "If I Sing" was later heard in Tovah Feldshuh's 1996 revue *Tovah: Out of Her Mind!* (see entry).

An earlier version of the revue appeared Off Off Broadway as *Next Time Now!* (it apparently opened during the 1988-1989 season); its three-member cast included Brent Barrett and Lynne Wintersteller, both of whom later appeared in *Closer Than Ever*, and the revue was directed by Steven Scott Smith and choreographed by Arthur Faria. *Next Time Now!* included songs which weren't heard in *Closer Than Ever*, including "Role Reversal" (which had been cut from *Baby*), "Please Don't Make Me Say Goodbye" (which had been written for *Urban Blight* and may have been heard in that revue sometime during its run), and one early collaboration by Maltby and Shire ("Mind Over Matter"). When the revue was revised as *Closer Than Ever*, it was seen at the Williamstown Theatre Festival prior to its Off Broadway production.

For another revue of Maltby and Shire's songs, see entry for *Starting Here, Starting Now*.

301 The Club. "A Musical Diversion"; THEATRE: Circle in the Square (Downtown); OPENING DATE: October 14, 1976; PERFORMANCES: 674; BOOK: Eve Merriam; LYRICS AND MUSIC: All songs performed in the production were from the period 1894-1905; see credits below; DIRECTION: T. (Tommy) Tune; SCENERY: Kate Carmel; COSTUMES: Kate Carmel; LIGHTING: Cheryl Thacker; MUSICAL DIRECTION: Alexandra Ivanoff; PRODUCERS: Circle in the Square (Theodore Mann, Artistic Director; Paul Libin, Managing Director)

CAST—M. (Marlene) Dell (Johnny), G. (Gloria) Hodes (Bertie), J. (Joanne) Beretta (Algy), C. (Carole) Monferdini (Freddie), J. (Julie) J. Hafner (Bobby), M. (Memrie) Innerarity (Maestro), T. (Terri) White (Henry)

The action occurs in a men's club in 1905.

The play with music was presented in one act.

MUSICAL NUMBERS—"Come to the Club Tonight" (by W. Loraine and G. Ade) (Members in Good Standing), "The Juice of the Grape" (by Th. Morse and E. Madden) (Imbibers), "To the Ladies" (Gentleman Songbirds and Steppers), "String of Pearls" (by J.W. Bratton and P. West) (Carole Monferdini, Friends), "Coquin de Printemps" (by I. Caryll) (Joanne Beretta), "Ticker Tape" (Marlene Dell, Company), "A Good Cigar (A Woman Is Only A Woman, but a Good Cigar Is a Smoke)" (from *Miss Dolly Dollars*, 1905; lyric by Harry B. Smith, music by Victor Herbert) (Gloria Hodes, Puffers), "Pinky Panky Poo" (Sporting Players), "If Money Talks (It Ain't On Speakin' Terms with Me)" (by J. Fred Helf) (Terri White), "New Shoes" (Ragtime Tappers), "A Little Valise" (Memrie Innerarity), "He Reminds Her of His Father" (by Charles Graham) (Julie J. Hafner), "Following in Father's Footsteps" (Dad and the Sonnyboys), "Dreams of a Rarebit Fiend" (Cane Dancers), "Bertie's Annual Aria" (Gloria Hodes), "Spring Frolic: Rose Garden" (Company), "Juice of the Grape" (Company), "Come to the Club Tonight" (Company)

NOTES—*The Club* was the longest-running musical of the 1976-1977 season, and, in retrospect, the piece seems less a feminist statement than a theatrical stunt in which seven actresses (whose first names are coyly identified in the program by their initials) portrayed men who belong to an all-male club in 1905 when (according to comments in the published script by Samuel French, Inc., in 1977) "male chauvinist behavior and banter were in full flower." By examining male chauvinism in 1905, the musical presumably intended to indirectly comment upon male chauvinism in 1976 (was the musical's message that nothing had changed in three-quarters of a century?). But, like so many plays and musicals with an axe to grind, *The Club* seems to have disappeared. Perhaps its lengthy run had less to do with its message and more to do with Tommy Tune's clever staging and the novelty of watching actresses acting butch in male drag.

Strangely enough, there was no original cast album. The only cast album of the musical appears to be a 1979 German production (*De Club*) released on Philips Records (LP # 6423-137); the recording includes twenty-nine musical sequences, many of which were not heard in the New York production.

302 Clue: The Musical. "The Musical"; THEATRE: Players Theatre; OPENING DATE: December 3, 1997; PERFORMANCES: 29; BOOK: Peter DePietro; LYRICS: Tom Chiodo; MUSIC: Galen Blum, Wayne Barker, and Vinnie Martucci; DIRECTION: Peter DePietro; CHOREOGRAPHY: Peter DePietro; COSTUMES: David R. Zyla; LIGHTING: Annmarie Duggan; MUSICAL DIRECTION: James Followell; PRODUCERS: Explorer Productions in association with DLR Entertainment and Manhattan Repertory Company

CAST—Robert Bartley (Mr. Boddy), Wysandria Woolsey (Mrs. Peacock), Ian Knauer (Professor Plum), Tiffany Taylor (Miss Scarlet), Michael Kostroff (Colonel Mustard), Daniel Leroy McDonald (Mrs. White), Marc Rubman (Mr. Green), Denny Dillon (Detective)

SOURCE—The Parker Brothers' Board Game "Clue."

The action occurs at the Boddy Manor in the present time.

The musical was presented in one act.

MUSICAL NUMBERS—"The Game" (Robert Bartley, Company), "Life Is a Bowl of Pits" (Daniel Leroy McDonald), "Everyday Devices" (Tiffany Taylor, Marc Rubman, Company), "Once a Widow" (Wysandria Woolsey), "Corridors and Halls" (Robert Bartley, Tiffany Taylor, Marc Rubman, Michael Kostroff, Ian Knauer, Daniel Leroy McDonald, Wysandria Woolsey), "The Murder" (Company), "The Game" (reprise) (Robert Bartley, Company), "She Hasn't Got a Clue" (Tiffany Taylor, Marc Rubman, Michael Kostroff, Ian Knauer, Daniel Leroy McDonald, Wysandria Woolsey), "Everyday Devices" (reprise) (Tiffany Taylor, Marc Rubman, Company), "Seduction Deduction" (Ian Knauer, Denny Dillon), "Foul Weather Friend" (Tiffany Taylor, Marc Rubman, Michael Kostroff, Ian Knauer, Daniel Leroy McDonald, Wysandria Woolsey), "Don't Blame Me" (Company), "The Final Clue" (Robert Bartley, Tiffany Taylor, Marc Rubman, Michael Kostroff, Ian Knauer, Daniel Leroy McDonald, Wysandria Woolsey), "The Game" (reprise) (Robert Bartley, Company)

NOTES—The highly successful board game "Clue" made for a less-than-successful musical; it was gone within a month. Anita Gates in the *New York Times* wasn't impressed with the evening, but she praised David R. Zyla's "fabulous" costumes, noting that characters hadn't looked this good since Warren Beatty's film version of *Dick Tracy* (1990). In fact, Gates mentioned that one of the characters in *Clue* notes that the wardrobe is "by Crayola."

The audience for *Clue* (as did the audience for *The Mystery of Edwin Drood*; see entry) determined who was the murderer. As they were seated, they received a special playing form on which to notate special clues which were given throughout the performance. The script was published by Samuel French, Inc., in 1998, and it provided different solutions, depending on how the audience "solved" the mystery.

The production had originally been produced in Chicago.

303 El Coca-Cola Grande (1973). "A Refreshment"; THEATRE: Mercer Arts Center; OPENING DATE: February 13, 1973; transferred to Plaza 9 Theatre on August 10, 1973; PERFORMANCES: 1,114; MATERIAL WRITTEN BY THE CAST (based on an idea by Ron House and Diz White); DIRECTION: Apparently by the cast; CHOREOGRAPHY: Anna Nygh; SCENERY: Mischa Petrow; COSTUMES: Possibly by Mischa Petrow; PRODUCERS: Jack Temchin, Gil Adler, and John A. Vaccaro (A Low Moan Spectacular Production)

CAST—Ron House (Sr. Don Pepe Hernandez), Alan Shearman (Miguel Hernandez), John Neville-Andrews (Juan Rodriquez), Diz White (Consuela Hernandez), Sally Willis (Maria Hernandez)

The action occurs in 1953 in a nightclub in a run-down section of Trujillo, Honduras.

The musical was presented in one act.

NOTES—Individual musical numbers weren't listed in the program.

El Coca-Cola Grande was the biggest hit of the Off Broadway season, running more than 1,000 performances. Perhaps not quite politically correct today, the farce was an inspired bit of silliness spoken in a mixture of English and pidgin Spanish. Clive Barnes in the *New York Times* said he found himself "roaring with laughter" during an evening of "bravura comedy ... outrageously silly and beautifully done."

A program note explained the plot: "Pepe Hernandez, a third-rate impresario, has boasted in the local press that he is bringing a group of famous international cabaret stars to Trujillo and has persuaded his uncle, manager of the local Coca-Cola bottling plant, to advance him enough money to rent the nightclub for one month. It is showtime for Pepe Hernandez's production of *Parasa de Esrellas* (Parade of Stars)." Of course, Pepe doesn't have a single star lined up for the floor show, and so he and his cohorts con their customers by impersonating well-known stars and singing such songs as "Da Mis Regards a Broadway" (helpfully translated as "Bestow My Sentiments of Affection to Broadway").

A slightly revised version of the musical opened on January 22, 1986, at the Village Gate Downstairs for eighty-six performances, and this production clarified the writing and the direction of the piece. The writers were identified as Ron House, Diz White, Alan Shearman, and John Neville-Andrews; and the direction was credited to Ron House, Diz White, and Alan Shearman. (For more information about the 1986 production, see entry.)

The musical had previously played in Britain at the Hampstead Theatre Club in 1971.

Bottle Cap Records released a 7" LP "original cast mini album" (# BC-1001) which was recorded live by the original New York cast on September 1, 1973, when the company performed the musical at the Montgomery Playhouse in San Francisco. The rather lavish gatefold cover includes photos and a wealth of amusing material. The script was published by Samuel French, Inc., in 1973.

When the musical opened in New York, the Coca-Cola company had reservations about its name being used in the title; and so on February 21, a week after the opening, the show's title was officially changed from *El Coca-Cola Grande* to *El Grande de Coca-Cola*. Apparently the original title was perceived as an indication that Coca-Cola sponsored the show, while the altered title presumably didn't suggest corporate sponsorship.

304 The Cockeyed Tiger (or The Last, Final, Farewell Performance Tour of Lilly Marlena Littleflea). THEATRE: Astor Place Theatre; OPENING DATE: January 13, 1977; PERFORMANCES: 5; BOOK: Eric Blau; LYRICS: Original lyrics by Eric Blau (see song list for other credits) Music: Original music by Nicholas Meyers (see song list for other credits); DIRECTION: Eric Blau; CHOREOGRAPHY: Gemze de Lappe and Buzz Miller; SCENERY: Donald Jensen; COSTUMES: Donald Jensen; LIGHTING: James Nisbet Clark (or possibly Crimmins & Smith); PRODUCER: James J. Wisner

CAST—James Nisbit Clark (Kishka Control), Robert Matthews (Larry Seasoner), Chris Campbell (Walda Barbras), Wendy Wolfe (Rhoda Boston), Janet McCall (Rosetta Bensonhurst), Leon Morenzie (Richard Bucharest), Joseph Neal (Rani Bengali), Jack Scalici (The Tiger, a/k/a Tigris, Tigris), ELLY STONE (Lilly Marlena Littleflea)

The action occurs in the newly refurbished facsimile of the old and celebrated Klub Kishka at Broome and Huston Streets, New York City.

The musical was presented in two acts.

ACT ONE—Overture (Orchestra), "My Dream of the South of France" (lyric by Bert Kalmar, music by Harry Ruby) (Wendy Wolfe, Janet McCall, Leon Morenzie, Joseph Neal), "Tyger, Tyger" (lyric adapted by Eric Blau from the poem by Richard Blake) (Wendy Wolfe, Janet McCall, Leon Morenzie, Joseph Neal), "The Littleflea Hop" (Wendy Wolfe, Janet McCall, Leon Morenzie, Joseph Neal), Miss Littleflea's Night Club Act: "God Is Good to Me"; "Whoopie"; and "Hold Me Thusly" (lyrics by Bert Kalmar, music by Harry Ruby) (Elly Stone), "We're Four of the Three Musketeers" (from *Animal Crackers*, 1928; lyric by Bert Kalmar, music by Harry Ruby) (Wendy Wolfe, Janet McCall, Leon Morenzie, Joseph Neal) "It's a Long, Long March to Kansas City" (Elly Stone, Wendy Wolfe, Janet McCall, Leon Morenzie, Joseph Neal), "They Were My Pals" (Elly Stone, Chris Campbell, Wendy Wolfe, Janet McCall, Leon Morenzie, Joseph Neal), "A Day in the Life of a Tiger" (lyric by Bert Kalmar, music by

Harry Ruby) (Jack Scalici), "America I Like You" (lyric by Bert Kalmar, music by Harry Ruby) (Elly Stone, Wendy Wolfe, Janet McCall, Leon Morenzie, Joseph Neal)

ACT TWO—"You've Got to Be a Tiger, Tiger" (Elly Stone), "Good Morning" (1939 film *Babes in Arms*; lyric by Arthur Freed, music by Nacio Herb Brown) (Elly Stone), "Confessions—1,2,3" (Wendy Wolfe, Janet McCall, Leon Morenzie, Joseph Neal), Miss Littleflea's Night Club Act: "Love Is Like a Rose"; "Tulip Told a Tale"; and "Show Me a Rose" (lyrics by Bert Kalmar, music by Harry Ruby) (Elly Stone), "Daddy Oh!" (Wendy Wolfe, Janet McCall, Leon Morenzie, Joseph Neal, Elly Stone), "You've Got to Be a Tiger, Tiger" (reprise) (Ensemble), "You Were a Hell of a Crowd Tonight" (Elly Stone, Ensemble)

NOTES—*The Cockeyed Tiger* was a whimsical, short-lived musical which dealt with a nightclub singer who is obsessed with the notion of the tiger becoming an extinct species. Clive Barnes in the *New York Times* found the evening a "paper tiger" of incomprehensibility, and noted it was "strange beyond the point of puzzlement." He reported that the book, lyrics, and music were "lost in a miasma of intent, and the intent was lost on a Sargasso Sea of uncertainty." The song list is based on a preview program. It appears that by opening night, the order of the songs changed considerably, and that at least two ("Good Times" and "We're Together at Kishka") were added, and five ("They Were My Pals," "A Day in the Life of a Tiger," "Good Morning," "Confessions—1,2,3" and "Love Is Like a Rose") were dropped.

A 7" LP cast album (on an unnamed but numbered [# 3121] label) was released, and included five numbers ("God Is Good to Me," "Good Times," "We're Four of the Three Musketeers," "You've Got to Be a Tiger, Tiger" and "You Were a Hell of a Crowd Tonight").

305 The Cocoanuts. THEATRE: American Place Theatre; OPENING DATE: August 15, 1996; PERFORMANCES: 165; BOOK: George S. Kaufman; adapted by Richard Sabellico; LYRICS: Irving Berlin; MUSIC: Irving Berlin; DIRECTION: Richard Sabellico; CHOREOGRAPHY: Richard Sabellico; SCENERY: Jeff Modereger; COSTUMES: Jonathan Bixby; LIGHTING: Herrick Goldman; MUSICAL DIRECTION: C. Lynne Shankel; PRODUCERS: Raymond J. Greenwald, Ltd.; an American Jewish Theatre Production (Stanley Brechner, Artistic Director); Stanley Brechner, Executive Producer

CAST—Michael Waldron (Jamison), Brad Bradley (Eddie), Alec Timerman (Robert Adams), Celia Tackaberry (Mrs. Potter), Laurie Gamache (Penelope Martyn), Becky Watson (Polly Potter), Michael Berresse (Harvey Yates), Michael McGrath (Henry W. Schlemmer [Groucho]), Peter Slutsker (Willie the Shill [Chico]), Robert Sapoff (Silent Sam [Harpo]), Richard Ziman (Hennessey)

The action occurs in 1925 in and around the Cocoanut Hotel in Cocoanut Beach, Florida.

The musical was presented in two acts.

ACT ONE—"Florida by the Sea" (Company), "A Little Bungalow" (Alec Timerman, Becky Watson), "Pack Up Your Sins and Go to the Devil" (Laurie Gamache, Michael Berresse), "We Should Care" (Alec Timerman, Becky Watson), "Florida by the Sea" (reprise) (Company), "Always" (Alec Timerman, Becky Watson)

ACT TWO—"Five O'Clock Tea" (Celia Tackaberry, Brad Bradley), "Tango Melody" (Michael McGrath, Celia Tackaberry), "When My Dreams Come True" (Alec Timerman, Becky Watson), "Shaking the Blues Away" (Laurie Gamache, Michael Berresse), "The Tale of a Shirt" (Company), "Always" (reprise) (Company)

NOTES—*The Cocoanuts* was a long-running success for the Marx Brothers when it opened on Broadway at the Lyric Theatre on December 8, 1925, for a run of 377 performances; they later recreated their roles in the film version, which was released in 1929. Perhaps because *The Cocoanuts* wasn't one of Irving Berlin's most memorable scores, the revival interpolated four songs (see below). Retained from the original score were just six numbers ("Florida by the Sea," "A Little Bungalow," "We Should Care," "Five O'Clock Tea," "Tango Melody," and "The Tale of a Shirt"). Songs not used in the revival were "Opening" (a sequence which included "The Guests" and "The Bellhops" [the latter also known as "The Bell Hop" and "Bellboy Opening"]), "With a Family Reputation," "Lucky Boy," "Why Am I a Hit with the Ladies?" "The Monkey-Doodle-Doo," "Opening Tea Dance" (the second act opening), "They're Blaming the Charleston," "Musical Days," and "Piano Specialty." During the original 1925 run, the production underwent various changes, including the omission of some songs and the addition of others; the revival didn't use any of the new songs ("Why Do You Want to Know Why?" "Gentlemen Prefer Blondes," "Ting-a-Ling, the Bells Will Ring," and "Everyone in the World Is Doing the Charleston").

Of the four songs interpolated into the revival, one ("When My Dreams Come True") had been introduced in the 1929 film version. Another ("Always") had been written by Berlin in 1925, independent of any stage production. "Pack Up Your Sins and Go to the Devil" had been introduced in *Music Box Revue 1922*, and "Shaking the Blues Away" in *Ziegfeld Follies of 1927*.

"The Tale of a Shirt" was an adaptation of "Habanera" ("The Toreador Song") from Georges Bizet's 1875 opera *Carmen*; incidentally, for the revival of *The Cocoanuts* the actors who performed the roles originally created by the Marx Brothers performed those roles in the style of the Marx Brothers.

The revival had first been produced Off Off Broadway at the American Jewish Theatre on May 12, 1996.

306 Colette (May 1970). THEATRE: Ellen Stewart Theatre; OPENING DATE: May 6, 1970; PERFORMANCES: 101; PLAY: Elinor Jones; LYRICS: Tom Jones; MUSIC: Harvey Schmidt; DIRECTION: Gerald Freedman; SCENERY: David Mitchell; COSTUMES: Theoni V. Aldredge; LIGHTING: Roger Morgan; MUSICAL DIRECTION: Harvey Schmidt; PRODUCERS: Cheryl Crawford in association with Mary W. John

CAST—ZOE CALDWELL (Colette), MILDRED DUNNOCK (Sido), Charles Siebert (Willy), Keene Curtis (The Captain, Max, George Wague, A Reporter), Holland Taylor (Daniele, Polaire, Ida, Amalia, Marguerite, A Reporter), Barry Bostwick (Leo, Jacques, Pierre, Jean, Henri de Jouvenel, Maurice Goudeket), Harvey Schmidt (Pianist)

SOURCE—*Earthly Paradise*, Robert Phelps' collection of Sidonie Gabrielle Colette's autobiographical writings.

The action occurs in France between 1873 and 1954.

The play was presented in two acts.

NOTES—*Colette* was the first of four plays and musicals which Tom Jones and Harvey Schmidt wrote about Colette. The first production was a play by Elinor Jones (who was married to Tom Jones) which included three songs by the team ("The Bouilloux Girls," "Femme Du Monde," and "Earthly Paradise") as well as background music composed by Schmidt (the three songs were later heard in *Portfolio Revue*; see entry). Mio International Records released the cast album (LP # MCS-3001), which included the three songs, background music, and dialogue sequences. (The play was revived the following season; see entry.) For her wonderful collection of songs by Jones and Schmidt, Susan Watson recorded "Earthly Paradise" (which was also the name of the CD collection [released by Nassau Records # 96568]).

For the record, the three other "Colette" works of Schmidt and Jones are *Colette* (1982), *Colette Collage* (1983; see entry), and a revised *Colette Collage* (1991; see entry).

The 1982 *Colette* was a lavish full-scale musical which closed prior to its Broadway opening; Diana Riggs portrayed Colette.

The first *Colette Collage* was produced Off Off Broadway by the York Theatre Company in 1983 for 17 performances, with Jana Robbins as Colette. The musical included new numbers as well as songs from the 1982 production which closed prior to Broadway; it also included "Earthly Paradise" from the 1970 play.

The second *Colette Collage*, a revised version of the former which opened Off Off Broadway at the Theatre at St. Peter's Church in 1991, was subtitled "Two Musicals About Colette"; the first act was titled *Willy*, the second *Maurice*. Betsy Joslyn portrayed Colette, and the musical played for twenty-eight performances. This production inspired a recording (with Judy Blazer as the Younger Colette and Judy Kaye as the Older Colette) which was released by Varese Sarabande Records (CD # VSD-5473); incidentally, in 1979 yet another Colette musical was produced, starring Cleo Laine. Titled *Colette*, the musical opened in London, with music by John Dankworth, Cleo Laine's husband. The delightful score was recorded by Sepia Records (LP # RSR-1006).

For another musical about Colette (which was based on her novel *L'Envers du Music-Hall*), see entry for *Music-Hall Sidelights*.

Of course, Colette's most enduring work is *Gigi*. The 1945 novella was filmed in France in 1948, with Daniele Delorme in the title role. On November 24, 1951, Anita Loos' stage adaptation opened on Broadway for a run of 219 performances (Audrey Hepburn was Gigi), and the London production, with Leslie Caron in the title role, opened on May 23, 1956, for 317 performances. Caron was of course cast in the 1958 musical film version, with screenplay and lyrics by Alan Jay Lerner and music by Frederick Loewe; also in the cast were Maurice Chevalier as Honore Lachaille and Louis Jourdan as Gaston Lachaille. The musical won nine Academy Awards, including Best Picture. The film was later adapted for the stage, opening at the Uris (now Gershwin) Theater on November 13, 1973, for 103 performances (Karin Wolfe, who replaced Terese Stevens during the tryout, was Gigi). In 1984, a national tour of the musical found Louis Jourdan playing Maurice Chevalier's role of Honore (Lisa Howard was Gigi); this production never played on Broadway.

307 Colette (October 1970). THEATRE: Ellen Stewart Theatre; OPENING DATE: October 14, 1970; PERFORMANCES: 7; PLAY: Elinor Jones; LYRICS: Tom Jones; MUSIC: Harvey Schmidt; DIRECTION: Gerald Freedman; SCENERY: David Mitchell; COSTUMES: Theoni V. Aldredge; LIGHTING: Roger Morgan; MUSICAL DIRECTION: Elman Anderson; PRODUCERS: Cheryl Crawford in association with Mary W. John

CAST—FENELLA FIELDING (Colette), Ruth Nelson (Sido), Albert Stratton (Willy), Erik Rhodes (The Captain, Max, George, A Reporter), Janet Dowd (Daniele, Polaire, Ida, Amalia, Marguerite, A Reporter), Michael Goodwin (Leo, Jacques, Pierre, Jean, Henri de Jouvenel, Maurce Goudeket), Elman Anderson (Pianist)

NOTES—The return engagement of *Colette*, with Fenella Fielding playing the role of Colette, lasted less than a week. In 1971, Fielding briefly toured in a British production of the play with music (which never played London).

For more information on Tom Jones and Harvey

Schmidt's *Colette* musicals, see entries for *Colette* (May 1970) and for two different *Colette Collage* musicals (1983 and 1991) which played Off Off Broadway. Jones and Schmidt also wrote another version of the material in 1982; titled *Colette*, the musical closed during its pre-Broadway tryout. Erik Rhodes, incidentally, was the famous character actor who specialized in playing conceited, continental types. He's perhaps best remembered for his performances in two Fred Astaire and Ginger Rogers' film musicals, *The Gay Divorcee* (1934) and *Top Hat* (1935). Playing the role of a dress designer in the latter, he announced to Fred Astaire that "I am no man, I am Bedini!" and further exclaimed that never again would he allow women to wear his dresses. In 1953, he appeared on Broadway in Cole Porter's *Can-Can*, and with Hans Conried introduced the saucy "Come Along with Me."

308 Colette Collage (1983). Theatre: The Church of the Heavenly Rest/The York Theatre Company; Opening Date: March 31, 1983; Performances: 17; Book: Tom Jones; Lyrics: Tom Jones; Music: Harvey Schmidt; Direction: Fran Soeder; Choreography: Janet Watson; Scenery: James Morgan; Costumes: Sigrid Insull; Lighting: Mary Jo Dondlinger; Musical Direction: Eric Stern; Producer: The York Theatre Company (Janet Hayes Walker, Producing Director)

Cast—Steven F. Hall (Maurice), George Hall (Jacques), Joanne Beretta (Sido), Timothy Jerome (Willy), Jana Robbins (Colette); Ensemble: Howard Pinhasik (Captain), Susan J. Baum (Nita, Fluff), Mayla McKeehan (Aimee), Dan Shaheen (Dr. Dutrate, Stage Manager), Suzanne Bedford (Claudine), Terry Baughan (Ida), Tim Ewing (Cheri); the Ensemble also appeared as Villagers, Writers, Music Hall Performers, Reporters, Photographers, Officials, and Luminaries.

The musical was presented in two acts.

Act One—Opening (Company), "Somewhere" (Jana Robbins), "Come to Life" (Timothy Jerome, Ensemble), "A Simple Country Wedding" (Jana Robbins, Timothy Jerome, Howard Pinhasik, Joanne Beretta, All), "Do It for Willy" (Timothy Jerome, Ensemble), "Woman of the World" (Jana Robbins, George Hall, Timothy Jerome), "There's Another World" (Jana Robbins, Timothy Jerome, Ensemble), "Why Can't I Walk Through That Door?" (Jana Robbins), "The Music Hall" (George Hall, Ensemble), "Dream of Egypt" (George Hall, Jana Robbins), "Love Is Not a Sentiment Worthy of Respect" (Joanne Beretta), Act One Finale (Jana Robbins, Ensemble)

Act Two—"Autumn Love" (Ensemble), "Riviera Nights" (George Hall, Jana Robbins, Stephen F. Hall), "Oo-La-La" (Stephen F. Hall, Jana Robbins), "Something for the Summer" (Stephen F. Hall, Jana Robbins), "Madame Colette" (Ensemble), "You Could Hurt Me" (Jana Robbins), "Be My Lady" (George Hall), "Earthly Paradise" (Joanne Beretta, Ensemble), "Growing Older" (Jana Robbins), "Joy" (Jana Robbins, Company)

Notes—For more information on Tom Jones and Harvey Schmidt's *Colette* musicals (all of which opened over a twenty-one year period), see entries for the Off Broadway play-with-music *Colette* (May 1970 as well as the October 1970 return engagement) and the 1991 Off Off Broadway production of the second *Colette Collage*. The entry for the original Off Broadway production of *Colette* (May 1970) includes information about the 1982 production of *Colette* which closed during its pre-Broadway tryout.

The following songs in the 1983 Off Off Broadway production of *Colette Collage* were also heard in the 1982 pre-Broadway tryout of *Colette*: "There's Another World," "Come to Life," "Do It for Willy," "Why Can't I Walk Through That Door?" "The Music Hall," "Dreams of Egypt," "Riviera Nights," "Oo-La-La," "Something for the Summer," "Madame Colette," "Be My Lady," "Growing Older," and "Joy." Thirteen numbers from the 1982 production weren't used in *Colette Collage*.

"Earthly Paradise," which was heard in the two 1970 productions of *Colette* but not in the 1982 version, was reinstated for the 1983 production.

For her priceless collection of songs by Jones and Schmidt (*Earthly Paradise*, released by Nassau Records [CD # 96568]), Susan Watson recorded five numbers from the various *Colette*/*Colette Collage* musicals ("Earthly Paradise," "Joy," "Growing Older," "The Room Is Filled with You," and "Decorate the Human Face").

309 Colette Collage (1991). "Two Musicals About Colette"; Theatre: The Theatre at St. Peter's Church; Opening Date: April 24, 1991; Performances: 26; Book: Tom Jones; Lyrics: Tom Jones; Music: Harvey Schmidt; Direction: Tom Jones and Harvey Schmidt; Choreography: Janet Watson and Scott Harris; Scenery: Ed Wittstein; Costumes: Ed Wittstein; Lighting: Mary Jo Dondlinger; Musical Direction: Norman Weiss; Producer: Musical Theatre Works (Anthony J. Stimac, Artistic Director)

Cast—Betsy Joslyn (Colette), Joanne Beretta, Paul Blankenship, John Bransdorf, Jamie Zee Eisner, Ralston Hill, Hilary James, Kenneth Kantor, James J. Mellon, Mary Setrakian, Craig Wells

Notes—The 1991 Off Off Broadway production of *Colette Collage* was a revised version of the 1983 musical and consisted of two separate one-act musicals, *Willy* and *Maurice*. In his liner notes for a studio cast recording released by Varese Sarabande Records (CD # VSD-5473), Tom Jones indicated the new *Colette Collage* represented the musical in its "final form."

The recording included Judy Kaye as the Older Colette and Judy Blazer as the Younger Colette. The following numbers from *Willy* and *Maurice* are heard on the CD:

Part I: Willy: Prelude (Orchestra), "Joy" (Younger Colette, Ensemble), "Come to Life" (Willy, Ensemble), "A Simple Country Wedding" (Younger Colette, Willy, Sido, Ensemble), "Do It for Willy" (Willy, Ensemble), The Claudine Craze:, "Claudine" (Younger Colette), "Two Claudines" (Younger Colette, Women), "The Father of Claudine" (Willy, Younger Colette, Ensemble), "Why Can't I Walk Through That Door?" (Younger Colette), "The Music Hall" (Jacques, Younger Colette, Ensemble), "The Dog and Cat Duet" (Younger Colette, Jacques), "I Miss You" (Sido, Unnamed Character), "La Vagabonde" (Younger Colette, Women), "Love Is Not a Sentiment Worthy of Respect" (Sido), "Now I Must Walk Through That Door" (Younger Colette, Ensemble)

Part II: Maurice: Prelude (Orchestra), "Autumn Afternoon" (Older Colette, Ensemble), "Decorate the Human Face" (Older Colette), "Riviera Nights" (Jacques, Older Colette, Maurice, Ensemble), "Ooh-La-La" (Maurice, Older Colette), "Something for the Summer" (Older Colette, Maurice, Ensemble), "Be My Lady" (Maurice), "The Room Is Filled with You" (Older Colette); Finale: "Victory" (Maurice, Older Colette); "Growing Older" (Older Colette); "Joy" (reprise) (Older Colette, Younger Colette, Ensemble)

The following songs in *Willy* and *Maurice* appear to be new and not heard in previous *Colette* productions: the "Claudine" sequence, "The Dog and Cat Duet," "I Miss You," "La Vagabonde," "Now I Must Walk Through That Door," "Decorate the Human Face," and "Victory."

For more information on Tom Jones and Harvey Schmidt's *Colette* musicals (all of which opened over a twenty-one-year period), see entries for the Off Broadway play-with-music *Colette* (May 1970 as well as the October 1970 return engagement) and the 1983 Off Off Broadway production of the first *Colette Collage*. The entry for the original Off Broadway production of *Colette* (May 1970) includes information about the 1982 production of *Colette* which closed during its pre-Broadway tryout.

For her must-have collection of songs by Jones and Schmidt (*Earthly Paradise*, released by Nassau Records [CD # 96568]), Susan Watson recorded five songs from the various *Colette*/*Colette Collage* musicals ("Earthly Paradise," "Joy," "Growing Older," "The Room Is Filled with You," and "Decorate the Human Face").

310 Columbus. Theatre: Direct Theatre; Opening Date: December 4, 1975; Performances: Unknown; Book: Allen R. Belknap; Lyrics: Beth Bowden; Music: Gary Levinson; Direction: Allen R. Belknap; Producer: Direct Theatre (Allen R. Belknap, Artistic Director)

Cast—Susan J. Baum, Jeff Brooks, Bob DelPazzo, Debra Dickinson, Gene Lindsey, George Maguire, Lilene Mansell, Milledge Mosley, Diana Schuster, Ted Wass

Source—The 1927 play *Christophe Colomb* by Michel de Ghelderode.

Notes—Besides the Off Off Broadway musical *Columbus*, there have been at least four other lyric works about Christopher Columbus: the 1930 opera *Christophe Colomb* (music by Darius Milhaud, libretto by Paul Claudel); Meredith Willson's *1491*, which closed during its pre-Broadway tryout in 1969 (John Cullum was Columbus and Jean Finn was Queen Isabella); *Christopher Columbus*, a 1976 European opera which used music by Jacques Offenbach (the score was adapted by Patric Schmid and the libretto was by Don White; the work was first heard in New York in 1987); and Philip Glass' opera *The Voyage*, which premiered at the Met on October 12, 1992 (see entry).

Further, the innovative 1945 film *Where Do We Go from Here?* (lyrics by Ira Gershwin, music by Kurt Weill) included an extended mini-musical sequence ("The Nina, the Pinta, the Santa Maria") about Columbus.

311 Coming Attractions. Theatre: Playwrights Horizons; Opening Date: December 3, 1980; Performances: 145; Play: Ted Tally; Lyrics: Bruce Sussman and Jack Feldman; Music: Jack Feldman; Direction: Andre Ernotte; Choreography: Theodore Pappas; Scenery: Andrew Jackness; Costumes: Ann Emonts; Lighting: Paul Gallo; Producers: Michael Frazier and Susan Madden Samson; a Playwrights Horizons Production

Cast—Larry Block (Manny Alter), Christine Baranski (Hostage, First TV Reporter, Secretary, Miss America, Backup Girl, Gofer), June Gable (Hostage, Newswoman, Bystander, Teri Sterling, Lab Coat #2, Backup Girl, Sunflower, Stenographer, Script Girl), Griffin Dunn (Lonnie Wayne Burke), Dan Strickler (Hostage, Second TV Reporter, Cop, Publisher, TV Interviewer, M.C., Lab Coat #3, Announcer, Interpreter, Private Eye #2, Prosecutor, Chaplain), Jonathan Hadary (Hostage, Second Newsman, Detective, Cameraman, Mister X, Lab Coat #1, Sammy Dazzle, Private Eye #1, Defense Attorney, Director), Allan Wasserman (Cop's Voice, First Newsman, Biff Braddock, Witness, Victim's Father, Tweed Jacket, Khaled El Hashish, Judge, Warden)

The play was presented in one act.

Notes—*Coming Attractions*, Ted Talley's cynical comedy in the mode of the 1926 play *Chicago* by Maurine Watkins (which was adapted into a musical in 1975), was about a killer who achieves media fame before eventually being executed in the electric chair on prime time television. The play included five incidental songs ("Miss America," "Sammy Dazzle's Song," "The Disco Death," "Look at Me Now," and "You Got to Go Out with a Bang").

Frank Rich in the *New York Times* noted the satirical thrusts couldn't match the grotesque events of real-life headlines; as a result, the play was one "we've already seen." He noted that while Tally tried to keep the proceedings "fast-paced," there was nonetheless a "static nature" about the evening. Rich singled out "The Magic of Me" (a/k/a "Sammy Dazzle's Song"); performed by Jonathan Hadary, the "hilarious" song was the "ultimate expression of the Sammy Davis-Mike Douglas school of Hollywood narcissism."

312 The Confidence Man. THEATRE: Cabaret/Manhattan Theatre Club; OPENING DATE: April 6, 1977; PERFORMANCES: 32 (estimated); LIBRETTO: Ray Errol Fox; MUSIC: Jim Steinman; DIRECTION: Gui Andrisano; MUSICAL DIRECTION: Bobby Blume

CAST—David Eric, Walter Niehenke, Joyce Nolen, Norman Snow; PRODUCER: The Manhattan Theatre Club (Lynne Meadow, Artistic Director)

SOURCE—The 1857 novel *The Confidence-Man* by Herman Melville.

NOTES—Perhaps the darkest and most cynical novel in American literature, Herman Melville's *The Confidence-Man* is not only his greatest work; it may be the greatest of all American novels. The story takes place on April Fool's Day, when a satanic master of disguises passes the day on a Mississippi River steamboat where he cons everyone he meets, first stripping his victims of their money, then later of their faith. Jim Steinman's musical version (also known as *Songs from "The Confidence Man"*) briefly appeared Off Off Broadway on April 6, 1976, and was later produced at New York's Queen College in 1986. In 2003, a studio cast recording was released by Original Cast Records (CD # OC-6058) with a cast which included Norbert Leo Butz, Chuck Cooper, LaChanze, Julia Murney, Andre De Shields, Andrea Marcovicci, and KT Sullivan. The CD included the following songs: "New Orleans Is Comin' to Me," "Pitch Penny," "Such Heaps of Fine Friends," "Edging Into Darkness," "Methinks," She Feels," "Give Us This Day Our Daily Flesh," "Sanctimonious Sambo," "Milady," "A Soft-Handed Gentleman (It's Your Life)," and "Something of This Masquerade May Follow."

An operatic adaptation, also called *The Confidence Man*, premiered at the Santa Fe Opera on July 31, 1982; the music was by George Rochberg and the libretto was by Gene Rochberg.

For more information about lyric adaptations of Melville's writings, see entry for *Bartleby*.

313 Conrack. THEATRE: The AMAS Repertory Theatre; OPENING DATE: October 15, 1987; PERFORMANCES: 16; BOOK: Granville Burgess, with Anne Croswell and Lee Pockriss; LYRICS: Anne Croswell; MUSIC: Lee Pockriss; DIRECTION: Stuart Ross; CHOREOGRAPHY: Sheila D. Barker; SCENERY: Dick Block; COSTUMES: Debra Stein; LIGHTING: Donald Holder; MUSICAL DIRECTION: James Followell; PRODUCER: The AMAS Repertory Theatre, Inc. (Rosetta LeNoire, Founder and Artistic Director)

CAST—Donald Acree (Top Cat), Peggy Alston (Mrs. Brown), Lisa Boggs (Cindy Lou), Harold Cromer (Quik Fella), J.P. Dougherty (Dr. Henry Piedmont), Ellia English (Edna Brown), Birdie M. Hale (Kate), Steven F. Hall (Pat Conroy [Conrack]), Pamela Isaacs (Dr. Jackie Brooks), Herb Lovelle (Sam), Jamila Perry (Anna), Victoria Platt (Mary), Kobie Powell (Prophet), Tarik Winston (Richard)

SOURCE—The 1972 novel *The Water Is Wide* by Pat Conroy.

The action occurs on the island of Yamacraw and in Beaufort, South Carolina, in 1969.

The musical was presented in two acts.

ACT ONE—"Find Me a Body" (J.P. Dougherty), "Yamacraw" (Stephen F. Hall), "He Gon' Stay" (Ellia English, Harold Cromer, Jamila Perry, Birdie M. Hale), "Bye, Bye, Conrack" (Kids), "The Water Is Wide" (Ellia English, Stephen F. Hall), "Hey, I'm Talkin' to You, Beethoven!" (Kids), "Southern Charm" (J.P. Dougherty, Steven F. Hall), "White Liberal to the Rescue" (Pamela Isaacs), "Tune in Tomorrow" (Stephen F. Hall, Pamela Isaacs), "Our Night to Howl" (Stephen F. Hall, Pamela Isaacs, Kids, Old Folks)

ACT TWO—"The 1920 Agricultural Exposition an' Fair" (Ellia English, Herb Lovelle, Harold Cromer, Birdie M. Hale), "A Regular Family" (Kids, Stephen F. Hall, Pamela Isaacs), "A Regular Family" (reprise) (Pamela Isaacs, Steven F. Hall), "Hopes an' Dreams" (Peggy Alston), "City Lights" (Victoria Platt, Stephen F. Hall), "He Gon' Stay" (reprise) (Old Folks, Kids), "I'm a Teacher" (Stephen F. Hall), "Bye, Bye, Conrack"/"The Water Is Wide" (reprises) (Kids, Old Folks)

NOTES—The Off Off Broadway musical *Conrack*, based on Pat Conroy's novel *The Water Is Wide* (which was filmed as *Conrack* in 1974 with Jon Voight in the title role), was an account of Conroy's teaching experiences with impoverished Black children on a remote island off the coast of South Carolina. Stephen Holden in the *New York Times* found the musical "a well-made family show that has something to say." He praised Anne Croswell and Lee Pockriss' score, including "The Water Is Wide," "The 1920 Agricultural Exposition an' Fair," "White Liberal to the Rescue," and "Hopes an' Dreams," the latter two boasting "excoriating" lyrics.

The musical was a rare visit from Croswell and Pockriss, who had contributed the delightful songs for *Ernest in Love* in 1960 (see entry); also see entry for their musical *Bodo* (which *almost* opened during the 1983-1984 season).

In 1992, the musical was briefly resurrected in regional theatre with Patrick Cassidy in the title role. Songs added for the production were "Pushing Thirty," "Lullaby for Anna," "Total Misfits," "Lookin' Good!" and "Letting Go." Pamela Isaacs recreated her role of Dr. Jackie Brooks, and Lonny Price directed.

314 Constance and the Musician. THEATRE: The American Place Theatre; OPENING DATE: June 10, 1981; PERFORMANCES: 12; BOOK: Caroline Kava; LYRICS: Caroline Kava; MUSIC: Mel Marvin; DIRECTION: Joan Micklin Silver; CHOREOGRAPHY: Wesley Fata; SCENERY: William Barclay; COSTUMES: Whitney Blausen; LIGHTING: Judy Rasmuson; PRODUCER: The American Place Theatre (Wynn Handman, Director; Julia Miles, Associate Director)

CAST—Jeff Brooks (John, Mr. Nisky), Marilyn Caskey (Young Woman, Marguerite, Rhonda), Philip Casnoff (Pauley), M'el Dowd (Alethea), Caroline Kava (Constance), Mel Marvin (The Musician), Stan Wilson (Gabriel, Young Man, Doctor, Northern Reporter)

The action occurs from the 1920s to the 1950s in the South and in New York City.

The Off Off Broadway musical was presented in one act.

MUSICAL NUMBERS—Prelude: "Aren't We Lucky" (M'el Dowd, Stan Wilson), "Constance and the Musician" (Caroline Kava, Mel Marvin), "Juliana Falconieri" (Caroline Kava, M'el Dowd), "Cotillion Song" (Caroline Kava, Marilyn Caskey, Stan Wilson), "My Mother's Hands" (Jeff Brooks, M'el Dowd), "Juliana Falconieri" (reprise) (Mel Marvin, Caroline Kava), "Constance and the Musician" (reprise) (Mel Marvin), "When I Was Ten" (M'el Dowd), "An Occasional Visit" (Caroline Kava, M'el Dowd, Company), "Aren't We Lucky" (reprise) (M'el Dowd, Caroline Kava), "Pauley's Song" (Philip Casnoff), "Juliana Falconieri" (reprise) (Mel Marvin, Caroline Kava), "If I Could Let It Slip My Mind" (Caroline Kava, Mel Marvin, M'el Dowd), "Dear Miss McMalley" (Marilyn Caskey), "Cotillion Song" (reprise) (Caroline Kava), "Juliana Falconieri" (reprise) (Mel Marvin, Company)

315 Contact. "A Dance Play"; THEATRE: The Mitzi E. Newhouse Theatre/Lincoln Center Theatre; OPENING DATE: October 7, 1999; PERFORMANCES: 101; BOOK: John Weidman; LYRICS: See song list for credits; MUSIC: See song list for credits; DIRECTION: Susan Stroman; CHOREOGRAPHY: Susan Stroman; SCENERY: Thomas Lynch; COSTUMES: William Ivey Long; LIGHTING: Peter Kaczorowski; PRODUCER: The Lincoln Center Theatre (Andre Bishop and Bernard Gersten, Directors)

Contact was presented in two acts, and was comprised of three dance-musicals (*Swinging*, *Did You Move?* and *Contact*); there was an intermission between *Did You Move?* and *Contact: Part I: Swinging*

The action occurs in a forest glade in 1767.

CAST—Sean Martin Hingston (Aristocrat), Stephanie Michels (Girl on a Swing), Scott Taylor (Servant)

MUSICAL SEQUENCE—"My Heart Stood Still" (from *A Connecticut Yankee*, 1928; lyric by Lorenz Hart, music by Richard Rodgers)

Part II: Did You Move?

The action occurs in an Italian restaurant in Queens in 1954.

CAST—Karen Ziemba (Wife), Jason Antoon (Husband), David MacGillivray (Headwaiter), Rocker Verastique (Busboy), Robert Wersinger (Waiter), Tome Cousin (Restaurant Patron), Peter Gregus (Restaurant Patron), Nina Goldman (Restaurant Patron), Dana Stackpole (Restaurant Patron), Scott Taylor (Waiter), Sean Martin Hingston (Uncle Vinnie), Pascale Faye (Photographer), Shannon Hammons (Cigarette Girl), Stacey Todd Holt (Busboy)

MUSICAL SEQUENCES—"Anitra's Dance" (*Peer Gynt Suite No. 1* by Edvard Grieg); "Waltz Eugene" (*Eugene Onegin*, Opus 24; the opera by Peter Ilyich Tchaikovsky premiered in 1879); "La Farandole" (*L'Arlesienne Suite No. 2* by Georges Bizet)

Part III: Contact

The action occurs in New York City in 1999.

CAST—Boyd Gaines (Michael Wiley), Deborah Yates (Girl in the Yellow Dress), Jason Antoon (Bartender, Voice-Mail Messages), Jack Hayes (Jakc), Robert Wersinger (Joe), Nina Goldman (Clubgoer), Scott Taylor (Clubgoer), Shannon Hammons (Clubgoer), Stephanie Michels (Clubgoer), Sean Martin Hingston (Johnny), Rocker Verastique (Clubgoer), Pascale Faye (Clubgoer), Mayumi Miguel (Clubgoer), Tome Cousin (Clubgoer), Dana Stackpole (Clubgoer), Peter Gregus (Clubgoer), Stacey Todd Holt (Clubgoer)

MUSICAL SEQUENCES—"You're Nobody Till Somebody Loves You" (lyric and music by Russ Morgan, Larry Stock, and James Cavanaugh); "Put a Lid On It" (lyric and music by Tom Maxwell); "Sweet Lorraine" (lyric by Mitchell Parish, music by Cliff Burwell); "Runaround Sue" (lyric and music by Ernest Maresca and Dion DiMucci); "Beyond the Sea" (lyric and music by Charles Trenet and Jack Lawrence); "See What I Mean?" (lyric and music by J. Chapman); "Simply Irresistible" (lyric and music by Robert Palmer); "Do You Wanna Dance?" (lyric and music by Bobby Freeman); "Topsy" (lyric and music by William Edgar Battle and Eddie Durham); "Sing Sing Sing (With a Swing)" (Parts 1 & 2) (lyric by Andy Razaf and Leon Berry, music by Louis Prima)

NOTES—There was much debate concerning whether Susan Stroman's *Contact* was "really" a musical because 1) it didn't have an original score and 2) it didn't employ an orchestra (the music was pre-recorded and used existing material by such artists as the New York Philharmonic, Dean Martin, and the Beach Boys). The debate became even more intense when *Contact* won the 2000 Tony Award for Best Musical. *Contact* called itself a "dance play," but most audience members didn't worry if was a "musical" or not; they were just happy to watch some of the most exciting choreography of the era which was danced by a splendid company (which included Karen Ziemba, Deborah Yates, David MacGillivray, and Rocker Verastique).

In truth, the real excitement of the piece was the third offering from which the overall dance-play took its name. The first sequence, *Swinging*, was a short, slight Fragonardesque fantasy set in the eighteenth century about a servant and his master vying for the romantic attentions of a young woman on a swing. The second, *Did You Move?* about a timid woman and her incredibly crude and boorish husband who are dining at an Italian restaurant in Queens in 1954, had some comic moments as well as the indelible presence of Karen Ziemba, but one felt the piece tried a little too hard to make politically correct points about sexual politics of the 1950s.

With *Contact* (the work's third sequence, which comprised the entirety of the second act), Stroman created the world of a downtown Manhattan dance hall in which club goers are obsessed with dancing, including a young man on the verge of suicide who finds solace and mystery on the dance floor when he encounters a haunting, elusive girl in a yellow dress who literally "owns" the floor when she takes on the male dancer of her choice. The dances in this segment gave the evening its electricity and were undoubtedly the greatest choreographic achievement seen in New York since Michael Bennett's *Ballroom* in 1978.

The three dance plays were connected by the word "contact": the men in *Swinging* are trying to seduce the girl in the swing; the lonely wife in *Did You Move?* finds release from her dull existence and loveless marriage through her dance fantasies with the waiters in the restaurant; and the would-be suicide in *Contact* hopes to dispatch his angst by dancing with the girl in the yellow dress. But the three dance pieces also shared surprise endings (spoiler alert). In *Swinging*, we watch master and servant flirt with the girl on the swing, only to discover at the end of the sequence that the two men had exchanged identities: the man we thought was the servant is actually the master, and vice versa. In *Did You Move?* the wife fantasizes about the waiters throughout dinner, but when she shoots her husband, the action seems to be real; but the "murder" turns out to be a fantasy, too, and so the hapless wife is doomed to go on living with a man she doesn't love. The ending of the *Contact* sequence reveals that the young man has never been to the dance club. During the moments in which he planned to hang himself, he had fantasized about a dance club somewhere downtown which he had once heard about, and which included a mysterious woman in a yellow dress. But all ends well: a neighbor who knocks on his door to complain about his noise turns out to be the image of the girl in his fantasy. (Shades of *One Touch of Venus*: in Kurt Weill's 1943 musical fantasy, the hero loses the elusive goddess but meets "Venus Jones," a girl who looks just like her.)

Contact transferred to the Vivian Beaumont Theatre, and with Broadway status it became Tony-eligible. Besides Best Musical, the show won Best Choreography for Susan Stroman and Best Performance for a Featured Actor and Actress in a Musical for Boyd Gaines and Karen Ziemba. *Contact* played for 1,010 performances, and was later shown on public television in September 2001.

RCA Victor/BMG Records released a CD of all the recorded music (# 09026-63764-2), but included one "original cast" track of sorts. In the production, Dean Martin's recording of "You're Nobody Till Somebody Loves You" was used; for the album, Boyd Gaines (who played the young man in the *Contact* sequence) sang the number.

A year or so after *Contact* closed, there was talk that Stroman planned to direct and choreograph a film version (which apparently would focus on the third sequence of the musical); as of this writing, the project hasn't materialized.

316 The Contrast. "A Musical"; THEATRE: Eastside Playhouse; OPENING DATE: November 28, 1972; PERFORMANCES: 24; BOOK: Anthony Stimac; LYRICS: Steve Brown; MUSIC: Don Pippin; DIRECTION: Anthony Stimac; CHOREOGRAPHY: Bill Guske; SCENERY: David Chapman; COSTUMES: Robert Pusilo; LIGHTING: C. Murawski; MUSICAL DIRECTION: Dorothea Freitag; PRODUCER: Peter Cookson

CAST—Connie Danese (Charlotte), Elaine Kerr (Letitia), Gene Kelton (Frank, Van Rough), Patti Perkins (Maria), Pamela Adams (Jenny), Ty McConnell (Dimple), Robert G. Denison (Colonel Manly), Grady Clarkson (Jessamy), Philip MacKenzie (Jonathan)

SOURCE—The 1787 play *The Contrast* by Royall Tyler.

The musical was presented in two acts.

ACT ONE—Prologue (Company), "A Woman Rarely Ever" (Connie Danese, Elaine Kerr), "A House Full of People" (Patti Perkins), "Keep Your Little Eye Upon the Main Chance, Mary" (Gene Kelton), "So They Call It New York" (Philip MacKenzie, Grady Clarkson), "Dear Lord Chesterfield" (Ty McConnell), "Dear Lord Chesterfield" (reprise) (Grady Clarkson), "A Sort of Courting Song" (Pamela Adams, Philip MacKenzie), "So Far" (Company)

ACT TWO—"She Can't Really Be" (Ty McConnell, Robert G. Denison), "That Little Monosyllable" (Connie Danese, Patti Perkins), "It's Too Much" (Ty McConnell, Connie Danese, Patti Perkins, Robert G. Denison, Elaine Kerr), "Keep Your Little Eye Upon the Main Chance, Mary" (reprise) (Gene Kelton), "Wouldn't I" (a/k/a "Were You Saying Something") (Patti Perkins, Robert G. Denison), "A Hundred Thousand Ways" (Grady Clarkson, Philip MacKenzie), "I Was in the Closet" (Company), "So Far" (reprise) (Company)

NOTES—Based upon the first successful comedy written by an American, *The Contrast* looked at plain American manners and European affectations.

Clive Barnes in the *New York Times* felt the musical tried too hard in its "epicene" and pun-filled humor (he noted that one song ["I Was in the Closet"] "strains credibility"), but he nonetheless found a number of laughs during the evening, and only regretted the "giggles" were too often "high-pitched."

Earlier in the season, the musical had been seen in an Off Off Broadway production at the Greenwich Mews Theatre.

The team of Anthony Stimac, Steve Brown, and Don Pippin wrote two more Off Broadway musicals based on or inspired by early American plays (*Fashion*, 1974, and *The Cast Aways*, 1975/*Castaways*, 1977; see entries). A later recording of *Fashion* (Original Cast Records CD # OCR-9492) included songs from *The Contrast* and *Castaways*; the two numbers from *The Contrast* were "Keep Your Little Eye on the Main Chance, Mary" and "Were You Saying Something." The script was published by Samuel French, Inc., in 1984.

317 Conversation Piece. "Musical Play"; THEATRE: Barbizon-Plaza Theatre; OPENING DATE: November 18, 1957; PERFORMANCES: 8; BOOK: Noel Coward; LYRICS: Noel Coward; MUSIC: Noel Coward; DIRECTION: Philip Wiseman; CHOREOGRAPHY: John Heawood; SCENERY: Tony Walton; COSTUMES: Audre; MUSICAL DIRECTION: John Kander; PRODUCERS: David Shaber, Philip Wiseman, William Synder, by special arrangement with Lance Hamilton and Charles Russell

CAST—LOUISE TROY (Sophie Oxford), SASHA VON SCHERLER (Martha James), Mildred Cook (Mrs. Dragon), RENE PAUL (Paul, Duc de Chaucigny-Varennes), JOAN KIBRIG (Rose), JOAN COPELAND (Melanie), GERALD GARRIGAN (Edward, Marquis of Sheere), William Woodson (The Earl of Harringford), WYMAN KANE (The Duke of Beneden), Jonathan Morris (Lord. St. Marys), CHERRY HARDY (The Duchess of Beneden), Mabel Cochran (The Countess of Harringford), Elwyn Harvey (Lady Braceworth), SARAH BURTON (Lady Julia Charteris), Corinna Manetto (Hannah), James Valentine (Butler), Leamond Dean (Sailor), Gloria Kaye (Girl), Sue Ann Gilfillan (Lady Kenyon) (NOTE: The performer who played Lord Doyning was not credited in the program.)

The action occurs in Brighton, England, 1811.

The musical was presented in three acts.

ACT ONE—Prologue (Louise Troy, Sasha von Scherler, Mildred Cook), "Brighton Parade" (Company), "I'll Follow My Secret Heart" (Joan Copeland), "Regency Rakes" (Wyman Kane, William Woodson, Jonathan Morris, [Lord Doyning]), "Charming! Charming! Charming!" (Joan Copeland, Joan Kibrig, Louise Troy, Sasha von Scherler, Mildred Cook), "March, Little Soldiers" (Joan Copeland, Joan Kibrig, Louise Troy, Sasha von Scherler)

ACT TWO—Prologue (Louise Troy, Sasha von Scherler, Mildred Cook), "The English Lesson" (Joan Copeland), "There Was Once a Little Village" (Louise Troy, Sasha von Scherler, Mildred Cook), Finale (Joan Copeland, Guests)

ACT THREE—"There's Always Something Fishy About the French" (Louise Troy, Sasha von Scherler, Mildred Cook), "Mothers and Wives" (Cherry Hardy, Mabel Cochran, Elwyn Harvey), "Nevermore" (Joan Copeland), Finale (Joan Copeland, Rene Paul)

NOTES—The original production of *Conversation Piece* opened in London at His Majesty's Theatre on February 16, 1934, for 177 performances, with Yvonne Printemps creating the role of Melanie. The musical premiered on Broadway later that year, opening at the 44th Street Theatre on October 23, with Printemps in the leading role. The American production was not a success, and closed after fifty-five performances.

Unfortunately, the Off Broadway revival was an even bigger failure, playing just one week. Joan Copeland (Arthur Miller's sister) played Melanie, and the few New Yorkers who saw the revival got the chance to hear one of Coward's loveliest songs, "I'll Follow My Secret Heart," a musical "scena" (as it might have been termed in a Jerome Kern musical) which is one of the theatre's great art songs. *Conversation Piece* also included two of Coward's wittiest comic numbers ("There's Always Something Fishy About the French" and "Regency Rakes").

Songs from the London production recorded by Yvonne Printemps and the original cast were released in various editions (including HMV Records LP # C-2654); a later studio cast recording was released on a 2-LP set by Columbia Records (# SL-163; reissued by Columbia Special Products Records # ASL-163; and later issued on CD by Must Close Saturday Night Records # MCSR-3039).

The script was published by Doubleday, Doran & Company, Inc., in 1934, and was later included in *The Collected Plays of Noel Coward* (*Play Parade, Volume Two*), published by William Heinemann, Ltd., in 1939 (new and enlarged edition published in 1950).

In reviewing the revival for the *New York Times*, Brooks Atkinson praised the "taste and splendor" of the musical, including Tony Walton's "excellent" scenic design, Andre's "gorgeous" costumes, and the "pleasantly conducted" orchestra by John Kander. And he found Joan Copeland a spirited and pleasing performer. But he couldn't help but miss Yvonne Printemps, for whom Coward had originally written the musical. Because the work had been specifically tailored for her "luminous, delicate" quality and her "daintiness and exquisite charm," he felt the revival fell short of perfection. Still, Atkinson's review was essentially favorable, and it's puzzling the revival lasted only a week.

318 Cooler Near the Lake. THEATRE: PLaza 9- Music Hall; OPENING DATE: February 7, 1971; PERFORMANCES: 26; SKETCHES: By the performers; MUSIC: Fred Kaz; DIRECTION: Bernard Sahlins; CHOREOGRAPHY: Mel Spinney; PRODUCERS: Bernard Sahlins and the PLaza 9- Music Hall

CAST—David Blum, Brian Doyle-Murray, Jim Fisher, Roberta Maguire, Judy Morgan, Joseph O'Flaherty, Dan Ziskie; Piano Interludes by Baldwin Bergersen

The revue was presented in two acts.

NOTES—Sadly, *Cooler Near the Lake*, the penultimate Second City revue and the tenth to play Off Broadway since 1962, couldn't manage a full month of performances and was the shortest run of any Second City production. Mel Gussow in the *New York Times* felt the evening wasn't on a par with the earlier offerings in the series, but he singled out one or two amusing sketches (such as a supermarket encounter between a food faddist and a meat-eater). Another sequence, about Moses getting his instructions from God, was played out like an episode of *Mission: Impossible* (Gussow noted that too frequently the evening referenced television, a complaint voiced by many critics about revues of the era). Gussow also focused on two serious sequences which didn't work. In one, a man visiting a mental institution acts "crazier" than the inmates, and is then revealed to be a member of the National Guard at Kent State University. In another, a flirtatious Southern soldier turns out to have been involved in the My-Lai massacre. Gussow felt there was no reason the Second City shouldn't take on important political matters, but he believed the last-minute revelations in the two sketches short-circuited their humorous moments and also deflated any inherent political statements the troupe was trying to make.

See entry for *Seacoast of Bohemia* for a list of all Second City revues which played in New York; also see Appendix T.

319 The Coolest Cat in Town. "A New Musical Comedy"; THEATRE: City Center Little Theatre; OPENING DATE: June 22, 1978; PERFORMANCES: 37; BOOK: William Gleason; LYRICS: William Gleason; MUSIC: Diane Leslie; DIRECTION: Frank Carucci; CHOREOGRAPHY: Mary Lou Crivello; SCENERY: Bil Mikulewicz; COSTUMES: Bennett; additional costumes by Faded Glory; LIGHTING: F. Fanelli; MUSICAL DIRECTION: Bob Goldstone; PRODUCERS: A. Arthur Altman, Joseph H. Lillis, Jr., and Jean Altman; a Pendragon Production

CAST—MICHAEL HAYWARD-JONES (Leon Bumpers), CHRISTOPHER CALLAN (Martha Bumpers), Lennie Del Duca, Jr. (Junior Bumpers), WILLIAM PARRY (Billy Dee Bumpers), Maura Silverman (Melinda Scheckeer), ROWENA ROLLINS (Ida Slagg), JOEY FAYE (Marvin Zeller), BILL BRITTEN (Dr. Albert Heinrich), JERRY SROKA (Igor), J. Gordon Matthews (Electrician), Mary Lou Crivello (Sue), Joni Masella (Gail), Pamela Ann Wilson (Terri), Adrienne Del Monte (Jane), Mark Morales (Leonard), Steven Hack (Joe), Danny Rounds (Bob), Bradley Jones (Ed)

The action occurs at the Midville High School Gymnasium on Senior Dance Night, and on the following day.

The musical was presented in two acts.

ACT ONE—"Disco Rag" (Lennie Del Duca, Jr., Students), "Born to Rock and Roll" (Lennie Del Duca, Jr., Students), "Don't Say Shoo-Be-Dobop" (Christopher Callan, Michael Hayward-Jones), "Melinda Schecker" (Boys, Girls), "Superstar" (Lennie Del Duca, Jr., Maura Silverman), "One Kiss" (Rowena Rollins, Joey Faye), "Suspended Animation" (Bill Britten, Boys), "Lost My Cool" (William Parry, Girls), "Rock Back the Clock" (Lennie Del Duca, Jr., Students)

ACT TWO—"The Bop Will Never Die" (Students), "The Bop Will Never Die" (reprise) (Christopher Callan, Michael Hayward-Jones), "Let's Live It Over Again" (Michael Hayward-Jones, Christopher Callan), "You're My Last Chance" (Rowena Rollins, Jerry Sroka, Joey Faye), "Hula Hoop" (William Parry), "The Coolest Cat in Town" (Girls), "Mr. Know It All" (Maura Silverman), "So What?" (Lennie Del Duca, Jr., Company), "Superstar" (reprise) (Lennie Del Duca, Jr., William Parry), Finale (Company)

NOTES—Previously showcased at La Mama Experimental Theatre Club (ETC) on February 23, 1978, *The Coolest Cat in Town* dealt with a 1950s rock-and-roll star who emerges from suspended animation (don't ask) and finds himself right smack in the middle of the disco era. The musical managed to hang on for almost five weeks.

Thomas Lask in the *New York Times* reported that the musical had first been presented at a high school in Brooklyn, and noted that what "look[ed] good in Flatbush" didn't have the "same luster on 55th Street." He found the book "awkward," the humor "low" and "sophomoric," the production values "skimpy," and the choreography "routine." As for the score, he mentioned the lyrics were "bright" and "crisp," and the music "memorable to the serviceable." He singled out one "embarrassing" number ("One Kiss"), a duet for Rowena Rollins and Joey Faye.

"Bite the Hand That Feed You" wasn't used in the production, but had been previously heard during the engagement at La Mama.

Top-billed Joey Faye always seemed to find himself in flop musicals. For more information about the The Joey Faye Curse, see entry for *Lyle*.

320 Corkscrews! "A Slightly Twisted Revue"/ "The Musical Comedy Revue That Unpeels the Big Apple!"

NOTE—*Corkscrews!* seems to have played in at least eight different cabarets and Off Broadway and Off Off Broadway theatres, four of them (Riverwest Theatre, T.O.M.I., Palsson's, and Jerry Kravat's Club 53) during the 1982-1983 season alone. *Theatre World 1982-1983 Season* indicates the revue played at the Theatre Opera Music Institute (T.O.M.I./Terrace Theatre) beginning on October 6, 1982, for fifteen performances, and *The Burns Mantle Yearbook/The Best Plays of 1982-1983* states the revue played at Palsson's in April 1983. In the meantime, an undated program shows the revue played at the Riverwest Theatre (at the Westbeth Arts Complex) sometime prior to Fall 1982 in a showcase production; and another undated program is from Club 53, which was located in the New York Hilton Hotel.

During the following years, the revue played at other nightclubs and theatres (Horn of Plenty, Michael's Pub, Steve McGraw's, and Theatre East). The information directly below is from the Riverwest program, and the NOTES section below reflects information from the T.O.M.I., Palsson's, and Club 53 productions; THEATRE: Riverwest Theatre; SKETCHES: Tony Lang; LYRICS: Tony Lang; MUSIC: Arthur Siegel; additional music by Paul Trueblood; DIRECTION: Miriam Fond; CHOREOGRAPHY: Miriam Fond; SCENERY: Vittorio Capecce; COSTUMES: Van Broughton Ramsey; LIGHTING: Victor En Yu Tan; MUSICAL DIRECTION: Albert Evans; PRODUCER: CHS Productions

CAST—Tony Aylward, Barbara Barsky, James Gleason, James Hosbein, Barbara Niles, Marilyn Wassell

The revue was presented in two acts.

ACT ONE—Opening (Company): "Brief Encounter" (Tony Aylward), "Pretty Babies" (Barbara Barsky, Barbara Niles), "I'm Into Music" (James Gleaso, James Hosbein), "Street Scene" (Tony Aylward, James Hosbein), "Maidens' Prayer" (Barbara Barsky, Barbara Niles, Marilyn Wassell), "The Daily Grind" (Tony Aylward), "Let It All Hang Out" (James Gleason, Barbara Niles), "The Family That Plays Together" (James Hosbein, Barbara Niles), "The New Varsity Drag" (Company), "What I Need the Most" (Marilyn Wassell, Tony Aylward), "You Have a Friend At" (James Gleason, Barbara Barsky, Marilyn Wassell), "The Betamax Blues" (Company), "Non-Matriculation" (Marilyn Wassell, Barbara Barsky), *Psychotic Overtures*: "The Ballad of Norman" (Company), "Send Out for Food" (Tony Aylward), "She Is Making Norman Antsy" (Company), "Not Getting Murdered Today" (Barbara Niles), "Up the Hill There" (Tony Aylward, Barbara Barsky), "I'm Not Queer" (Tony Aylward, Company), "Died and Died and Died" (Company)

ACT TWO—"I Like Me" (Company), "The David Somekind Show" (Tony Aylward, James Hosbein, James Gleason, Marilyn Wassell, Barbara Barsky), "Confession" (Barbara Niles), "Silent Treatment" (James Hosbein), "The Last Minority" (Marilyn Wassell, Barbara Niles, Tony Aylward, James Hosbein, James Gleason), "Creative Block" (Barbara Barsky), "Looking for Love" (Company), Finale (Company)

NOTES—The Riverwest production was a showcase in anticipation of the fall production (at T.O.M.I., where the revue appears to have been performed under an Off Broadway contract); numbers deleted during this production were "Aggressiveness Training," "Make It Another," "Street Scene II," and "The Golden Age." Paul Trueblood wrote the music for "Brief Encounter," "Let It All Hang Out," and "Silent Treatment." *Psychotic Overtures* was a spoof of the film *Psycho* (1960) and how it might have been adapted into a musical by Stephen Sondheim. Another extended Sondheim parody (*A Little Complex*) later appeared in *The Musical of Musicals* (see entry).

In 1993, the revue was recorded by Original Cast Records (CD # OC-9333), with material from various productions, including the song "Forever Fantastic" and the *Psychotic Overtures* sequence. When the revue played at T.O.M.I., the cast members were Tony Aylward, Barbara Barsky, James Hosbein, and Gail Oscar. There were various changes in the sketches and songs from Riverwest production:

ACT ONE—"I'm Into Music," "Maiden's Prayer," "The Daily Grind," "Let It All Hang Out," "The Betamax Blues," "You Have a Friend," "Make It Another," "The Family That Plays Together," "People," "Greetings," *Psychotic Overtures*: "The Ballad of Norman," "Send Out for Food," "She Is Making Norman Antsy," "Not Getting Murdered Today," "Up the Hill There," "I'm Not Queer," "Died and Died and Died"

ACT TWO—"I Like Me," "The David Somekind Show," "What I Need the Most," "The Golden Age," "Tina and Nina," "The Last Minority," "Confession," "Non-Matriculation," "Free Advice," "Creative Block," "Looking for Love," Finale

In April 1983, the revue reopened at Palsson's and then later at Club 53, and was subtitled "The Musical Comedy Revue That Unpeels the Big Apple!" (Both productions were apparently under Off Off Broadway contracts.) At Club 53, the revue was produced by Arthur Cantor and Edwin W.

Schloss; the scenery was by Leo B. Meyer; the lighting was designed by Randy Becker; and the cast members were Tony Lang, Arthur Siegel, and Miriam Fond. There was a considerable difference in the numbers in this production and the earlier one at Riverwest. For Club 53, the sketches and songs were presented in one act, as follows: Opening (Company), "Subway" (Miriam Fond), "I'm Into Music" (Tony Lang, Miriam Fond), "You Have a Friend" (Company), "People" (Arthur Siegel), "The Other Woman" (Tony Lang, Miriam Fond), "Rabid Transit" (Company), "Person to Person I" (Tony Lang, Miriam Fond), "Healthy Relationship" (Tony Lang, Miriam Fond), "Person to Person II" (Tony Lang, Miriam Fond), "Blues" (Arthur Siegel), "Adult Education" (Tony Lang, Miriam Fond), "Page Turners" (Company), "Person to Person III" (Tony Lang, Miriam Fond), "The Child Within" (Arthur Siegel), "Person to Person IV" (Tony Lang, Miriam Fond), "More Trouble" (Tony Lang), "Person to Person V" (Company), "Secret Love" (Miriam Fond), "Plan Ahead" (Tony Lang, Miriam Fond), "Backlash" (Arthur Siegel, Tony Lang), "The Odd Couplet" (Tony Lang, Miriam Fond), "Family Affair" (Arthur Siegel), "Brief Encounter" (Tony Lang, Miriam Fond), "Forever Fantastic" (Company), "Bleep" (Tony Lang, Miriam Fond), "Creative Block" (Miriam Fond), "Office Politics" (Tony Lang, Miriam Fond), "Take Out" (Tony Lang), "The Last Minority" (Company), "Looking for Love" (Company), "I Like Me" (Company), Finale (Company)

321 Cotton Patch Gospel. THEATRE: Lamb's Theatre; OPENING DATE: October 21, 1981; PERFORMANCES: 193; BOOK: Tom Key and Russell Treyz; LYRICS: Harry Chapin; MUSIC: Harry Chapin; DIRECTION: Russell Treyz; SCENERY: John Falabella; COSTUMES: John Falabella; LIGHTING: Roger Morgan; MUSICAL DIRECTION: Tom Chapin; PRODUCERS: Philip M. Getter; Louis F. Burke, Associate Producer

CAST—TOM KEY (Matthew and thirty-two other Biblical characters); The Cotton Pickers (Scott Ainslie, Pete Corum, Michael Mark, Jim Lauderdale)

SOURCE—The 1970 book *The Cotton Patch Version of Matthew and John* by Clarence Jordan.

The action occurs "here and now."

The revue was presented in two acts.

ACT ONE—"Somethin's Brewin' in Gainesville," "I Did It," "Mama Is Here," "It Isn't Easy," "Sho 'Nuff," "Turn It Around," "When I Look Up," "There Ain't No Busy Signals (on the Hot Line to God)"/"Spitball (Me Lord)," "(We're) Goin' to Atlanta," "What Does Atlanta Mean to Me"

ACT TWO—"Are We Ready?" "You Are Still My Boy," "We Got to Get Organized," "We're Gonna Love It (While It Lasts)," "Jubilation," "Agony Round," "(Well) I Wonder"

NOTES—Harry Chapin died in automobile accident three months before his last completed work, *Cotton Patch Gospel*, opened Off Broadway (his only other musical, *The Night That Made America Famous*, opened on Broadway in 1975 and played for seventy-five performances). *Cotton Patch Gospel* had premiered in Boston a month before Chapin's death as *Somethin's Brewin' in Gainesville* (the title of one of the musical's songs).

Songs dropped during the tryout were "I Wonder" and "Blind Date." The cast album was released by Chapin Productions Records (LP # CP-101), and included three numbers not listed in the program ("The Last Supper," "Jud," and "Thank God for Governor Pilate").

Like many revue-like musicals of the era, the show used the term "book" in its credits. But in truth *Cotton Patch Gospel* and other such musicals were in essence revues or song cycles. A concept or theme may have held the evening together, and the songs may have supported the framework of the evening's point of view, but no one confused these revues with traditional book musicals. *Cotton Patch Gospel* was revived Off Off Broadway on November 14, 1997, by the Melting Pot Theatre Company for twenty-six performances. The musical was also produced in London at the Westminster Theatre with Tom Key.

In 1985, the tribute-revue *Lies & Legends/The Musical Stories of Harry Chapin* opened Off Broadway (see entry). (Another revue, *Chapin*, was produced in Chicago in 1977.)

322 Cowboy. "The Legendary Charlie Russell and the Vanishing West"; THEATRE: Stage Arts Theatre; OPENING DATE: April 29, 1987; PERFORMANCES: 20; BOOK: Jess Gregg; LYRICS: Richard Riddle; MUSIC: Richard Riddle; DIRECTION: Robert Bridges; CHOREOGRAPHY: Dennis Dennehy; Musical Staging by Robert Bridges and Dennis Dennehy Scenery: Tom Hennes; COSTUMES: Barbara A. Bell; LIGHTING: Tom Hennes; MUSICAL DIRECTION: Wendell Kindberg; PRODUCER: Stage Arts Theatre Company (Nell Robinson and Ruth Ann Norris, Artistic Directors)

CAST—Ken Lundie (Bullnose, Janitor), Steven Riddle (Con Price), George Ball (Kid Russell), Lee Chew (Teddy Blue Abbott), Barry Finkel (Smitty, Buffaloe Moe), Craig Oldfather (Slim, Desk Clerk), Michael Mann (Territory, Sleeping Thunder), Dennis Edenfield (Sheriff), Carolyn DeLany (Mamie Nancy Cooper). Judith Tillman (Dan's Mrs., St. Louis Woman), Ilene Kristen (Dynamite), Madelyn Griffith-Haynie (Trixie La Tour), Mary Kilpatrick (Flo Le Fleur, Sleeping Bird), Joyce Fleming (Ruby La Rue), Mary Wing-Porter (Lou La Mulligan), Richard Bowne (Pretty Freddy, Brother Van, Carl Bledsoe), Audrey Lavine (Widow Jackson, Mrs. Bledsoe) The action occurs in Montana and "Points East" around 1900.

ACT ONE—Overture (Orchestra), "Hunker Down Cowboy" (George Ball, Cowboys), "Loud and Tacky" (Carolyn DeLany), "Loud and Tacky" (reprise) (George Ball, Steven Riddle, Lee Chew), "It Seems to Me" (George Ball), "The Dutchman's Pants" (Audrey Lavine, Steven Riddle), "I'll Dream Your Dream" (Carolyn DeLany), "Oh, Oh, Cowboy" (George Ball, Cowboys), "I'll Dream Your Dream" (reprise) (Carolyn DeLany), "The Horse" (Steven Riddle, Lee Chew, Cowboys), "You Look Like My Valley" (George Ball, Carolyn DeLany), "Hey, Kid" (Ilene Kristen, Madelyn Griffith-Haynie, Mary Kilpatrick, Joyce Fleming, Mary Wing-Porter), Finale (George Ball, Carolyn DeLany, Cowboys)

ACT TWO—"Light Doesn't Last That Long" (George Ball, Steven Riddle, Lew Chew, Ilene Kristen, Judith Tillman, Townswomen), "Pass the Bread and Butter, Brother Van" (Company), "The Blue Hen's Chick" (Audrey Lavine), "The Card Game" (Company), "Goin' East—St. Louis" (Carolyn DeLany, Company), "Singin' to 'Em" (George Ball), "Goin' East—Chicago" (Carolyn DeLany, Company), "Goin' East—New York" (Carolyn DeLany, Company), "Charles" (Carolyn DeLany), "Montana" (George Ball, Company), "She's a Shame, Shame, Shame" (Ilene Kristen), Finale (Company)

NOTES—The Off Off Broadway musical *Cowboy* was based on an idea by Ronnie Claire Edwards, and it told of the life and times of Charles M. Russell (1864-1926), the artist who painted scenes of the American West. Stephen Holden in the *New York Times* said the libretto had the "shallowness of a cartoon biography," and he noted the musical unaccountably painted Russell's wife Mamie as a "priggish pain in the neck" (perhaps she was cousin to Chairy, P.T. Barnum's scold of a wife in the musical *Barnum* [1980]). But Holden praised Richard Riddle's "eclectically folksy score," which was often a happy blend of "turn-of-the-century high-plains rusticity" and "Broadway-style razzle-dazzle."

323 Cowgirls. "The Musical"; THEATRE: Minetta Lane Theatre; OPENING DATE: April 1, 1996; PERFORMANCES: 319; BOOK: Betsy Howie; LYRICS: Mary Murfitt; MUSIC: Mary Murfitt; DIRECTION: Eleanor Reissa; CHOREOGRAPHY: Eleanor Reissa; SCENERY: James Noone; COSTUMES: Catherine Zuber; LIGHTING: Kenneth Posner; MUSICAL DIRECTION: Pam Drews Phillips; PRODUCERS: Denise Cooper, Susan Gallin, Rodger Hess, and Suki Sandler; Carollyne Ascher and Chanes/Shapiro, Associate Producers

CAST—Rhonda Coullet (Jo Carlson), Mary Ehrlinger (Rita), Lori Fischer (Lee), Mary Murfitt (Mary Lou), Betsy Howie (Mo), Jackie Sanders (Mickey)

The action occurs in the present at Hiram Hall, a country music hall in Rexford, Kansas.

The musical was presented in two acts.

ACT ONE—Overture (Ludwig van Beethoven's "Sonata Pathetique, Opus 13") (Mary Ehrlinger, Lori Fischer, Mary Murfitt), "Three Little Maids" (from *The Mikado*, 1885; lyric by W.S. Gilbert, music by Arthur Sullivan) (Mary Ehrlinger, Lori Fischer, Mary Murfitt), "Jesse's Lullaby" (music by Johannes Brahms) (Mary Ehrlinger, Lori Fischer, Mary Murfitt), "Ode to Connie Carlson" (Jackie Sanders, Betsy Howie), "Sigma, Alpha, Iota" (Mary Ehrlinger, Lori Fischer, Mary Murfitt), "Ode to Jo" (Jackie Sanders, Betsy Howie), "From Chopin to Country" (music by Frederick Chopin) (Mary Ehrlinge, Lori Fischer, Mary Murfitt), "Kingdom of Country" (music by C. Converse and Mary Murfitt) (Rhonda Coullet, Mary Ehrlinger, Lori Fischer, Mary Murfitt), "Songs My Mama Sang" (traditional hymns; additional music by Mary Murfitt) (Rhonda Coullet, Mary Murfitt), "Heads or Tails" (Lori Fischer, Mary Ehrlinger), "Love's Sorrow" (music by Kreisler) (Rhonda Coullet, Mary Ehrlinger, Lori Fischer), "Looking for a Miracle" (additional music by Wolfgang Amadeus Mozart) (Mary Murfitt, Rhonda Coullet, Company)

ACT TWO—"Don't Call Me Trailer Trash" (Jackie Sanders, Betsy Howie), "Honky Tonk Girl" (Mary Ehrlinger), "Every Saturday Night" (Rhonda Coullet, Mary Ehrlinger, Lori Fischer, Mary Murfitt), "Don't Look Down" (Lori Fischer, Mary Ehrlinger), "They're All Cowgirls to Me" (Rhonda Coullet, Mary Ehrlinger, Lori Fischer, Mary Murfitt), "Saddle Tramp Blues" (Mary Murfitt, Mary Ehrlinger, Lori Fischer), "It's Time to Come Home" (Rhonda Coullet), "We're a Travelin' Trio" (Mary Ehrlinger, Lori Fischer, Mary Murfitt), "Sunflower" (Mary Ehrlinger, Lori Fischer, Mary Murfitt), Concert Medley (Company), "House Rules" (Rhonda Coullet, Company), "Cowgirls" (Mary Ehrlinger, Lori Fischer, Mary Murfitt)

NOTES—The amusing one-joke premise of *Cowgirls* is that the female classical music trio (the *Coghill* Trio) is mistaken for the *Cowgirl* Trio. A saloon owner inadvertently books the Coghill Trio into her bar as a means of drawing in the crowds to save her honky-tonk from foreclosure. The predictable but enjoyable humor came from the "classical versus country" comparisons; but ultimately the characters find common ground, and the Coghill Trio girls are soon trading their violins for fiddles (actually, when the Coghill violinist is asked if there's a difference between a violin and a fiddle, she replies, "Of course there's a difference ... there must be").

The cast album was released by Varese Sarabande Records (CD # VSD-5740), and the script was published by Dramatists Play Service, Inc., in 1999.

The musical was first produced in 1994 by the Caldwell Theatre Company in Boca Raton, Florida. It then played in various regional theatres, including the Old Globe Theatre in San Diego, where it opened on January 13, 1996.

324 The Cradle Will Rock (1964). THEATRE: Theatre Four; OPENING DATE: November 8, 1964; PERFORMANCES: 82; BOOK: Marc Blitzstein; LYRICS: Marc Blitzstein; MUSIC: Marc Blitzstein; DIRECTION: Howard da Silva; CHOREOGRAPHY: Rhoda Levine; MUSICAL DIRECTION: Gershon Kingsley; PRODUCERS: Robert S. Fishko, John A. Prescott, and David Rubinson, in association with George Avakian

CAST—Lauri Peters (Moll), Ted Scott (Gent, Gus Polock), Wayne Tucker (Dick), Ben Bryant (Cop, Scott), Chris Warfield (the Reverend Salvation), Dean Dittman (Editor Daily), Hal Buckley (Yasha, President Prexy), Clifford David (Dauber, Professor Trixie), Nichols Grimes (Professor Mamie, Steve), Peter Meersman (Druggist), Nancy Andrews (Mrs. Mister), Joseph Bova (Junior Mister), Rita Gardner (Sister Mister), Gordon B. Clarke (Mr. Mister), Karen Cleary (Sadie Polock), Jerry Orbach (Larry Foreman), Micki Grant (Ella Hammer), Gershon Kingsley (Clerk)

The action occurs in Steeltown, U.S.A., during a union drive, in the 1930s.

The musical was presented in two acts.

ACT ONE—"Moll's Song"/"Moll and Gent"/"Moll and Dick" (Lauri Peters, Ted Scott, Wayne Tucker), "Moll and Drugist" (Lauri Peters, Peter Meersman), "Oh, What a Filthy Night Court!" (Ensemble), "Mrs. Mister and Reverend Salvation" (Nancy Andrews, Chris Warfield), "Croon-Spoon" (Joseph Bova, Rita Gardner), "The Freedom of the Press" (Dean Dittman, Gordon B. Clarke), "Let's Do Something" (Joseph Bova, Rita Gardner), "Honolulu" (Dean Dittman, Joseph Bova, Gordon B. Clarke, Rita Gardner), "Drugstore Scene" (Peter Meersman, Nichols Grimes, Wayne Tucker), "Gus and Sadie Love Song" (Ted Scott, Karen Cleary), "The Rich" (Hal Buckley, Clifford David), "Ask Us Again" (Nancy Andrews, Hal Buckley, Clifford David), "Art for Art's Sake" (Hal Buckley, Clifford David)

ACT TWO—"Nickel Under the Foot" (Lauri Peters), "Leaflets" (Performer[s] unknown), "The Cradle Will Rock" (Jerry Orbach), "Doctor and Ella" (Ben Bryant, Micki Grant), "Joe Worker" (Micki Grant), Finale/"The Cradle Will Rock" (reprise) (Jerry Orbach, Gordon B. Clarke, Lauri Peters, Peter Meersman, Company)

NOTES—Marc Blitzstein's "labor opera," originally scheduled to open at the Maxine Elliott Theatre, opened on Broadway at the Venice Theatre on June 16, 1937. The story of its controversial opening night is one of the legends of the Broadway musical, and has been told many times. (For a full re-telling, see Eric A. Gordon's masterful *Mark the Music/The Life and Work of Marc Blitzstein*, published by St. Martin's Press in 1989.) One of the enduring lessons from the episode is that government funding of the arts will almost always lead to heated controversy when artistic subject matter is deemed offensive to those who are paying for it. After its premiere at the Venice Theatre, the musical was produced at the Mercury Theatre on December 5, 1937, for a series of Sunday night performances, and was finally given a full production at the Windsor Theatre on January 3, 1938, for 108 performances. The piece was revived as a "complete concert performance" at the City Center for two performances on November 24 and 25, 1947. Leonard Bernstein conducted the New York City Symphony; Howard Da Silva created his original role of Larry Foreman, and Estelle Loring was Moll; the cast also included Shirley Booth, Jack Albertson, Will Geer, Robert Chisholm, Muriel Smith, and Jo Hurt. A month later the production was mounted on Broadway at the Mansfield (now Brooks Atkinson) Theatre; it opened on December 26 for a run of thirty-four performances. Alfred Drake was Larry Foreman, and Estelle Loring reprised her role as Moll. The production included some of the performers who had appeared in the City Center concert; for Broadway, Vivian Vance played Mrs. Mister, which had been performed by Shirley Booth in the concert version.

The musical was again revived at the City Center on February 11, 1960, with David Atkinson (Larry Foreman) and Tammy Grimes (Moll). On April 19, 1964, it was presented in an abridged version as part of the Marc Blitzstein Memorial Concert, with a cast which included Howard da Silva and Barbara Harris, and with Leonard Bernstein at the piano.

On September 12, 1978, the musical was revived Off Off Broadway at the Eighteenth Street Playhouse for four performances; and in 1983 the musical was revived Off Broadway (see entry) and was later shown on public television.

Jerry Orbach, who played the role of Larry Foreman in the revival, is now best remembered for his television work, and his important place in musical theatre is sometimes overlooked. He originated leading roles in no less than five hit musicals: *The Fantasticks* (1960; see entry), *Carnival!* (1961), *Promises, Promises* (1968), *Chicago* (1975), and *42nd Street* (1980). Not only were his performances in these shows recorded, but his "other," lesser known, appearances were recorded as well: *The Cradle Will Rock* and the Lincoln Center revivals of *Carousel* (1965) and *Annie Get Your Gun* (1966). The program for the 1964 revival of *The Cradle Will Rock* included a full-page ad by Columbia Records touting its upcoming cast recording; a cast recording was released, but not by Columbia; it was MGM Records which ultimately recorded and released the score. The musical has been frequently recorded: besides the 2-LP cast recording of the 1964 revival (MGM LP # SE-4289-2-OC), there's also a recording of the 1985 Off Broadway revival (with Patti LuPone as Moll) (Polydor LP # 827-937-1-Y-1; a complete version of this revival was issued on a 2-CD set by That's Entertainment Records [# CDTEM2-1105]). A 1994 Los Angeles production was recorded by Lockett Palmer Records (CD # LPR-940411).

And the most important recording of all is that of the original 1937 Broadway cast, which was recorded in April 1938 by Musicraft Records and is the first American musical to receive a full-length cast recording (it was later released on a limited-edition LP of 1,000 copies by American Legacy Records # T-1001).

A few songs from the musical can also be heard on the soundtrack of *Cradle Will Rock,* a 1999 film version which dealt with the mounting of the original 1937 production. The soundtrack was released by RCA Victor/BMG Records (CD # 09026-63577-2) and *Cradle Will Rock*, a lavish book about the film (which included the screenplay by Tim Robbins as well as lyrics by Blitzstein) was published by Newmarket Press in 2000.

Besides inspiring this film, the background surrounding the musical's opening in 1937 also led to the production of the play *It's All True* by Jason Sherman, which opened in Toronto on January 6, 1999, at the Terragon Theatre.

The script of *The Cradle Will Rock* was published by Random House in 1938, and was one of the first musicals to appear in hardback book format. See entry for Blitzstein's *No for an Answer*, which is in effect a companion piece to *The Cradle Will Rock* in its depiction of the conflict between labor and management.

325 The Cradle Will Rock (1983). THEATRE: American Place Theatre; later reopened at the Douglas Fairbanks Theatre on July 12, 1983; OPENING DATE: May 9, 1983; PERFORMANCES: 64; BOOK: Marc Blitzstein; LYRICS: Marc Blitzstein; MUSIC: Marc Blitzstein; DIRECTION: John Houseman; SCENERY: Mark Fitzgibbons; COSTUMES: Judith Dolan; LIGHTING: Dennis Parichy; MUSICAL DIRECTION: Michael Barrett; PRODUCER: Margot Harley

CAST—Patti LuPone (Moll, Sister Mister), Tom Robbins (Gent, Editor Dailey), Henry Stram (Dick, Junior Mister), Casey Biggs (Cop, Gus Polock), James Harper (the Reverend Salvation, Professor Trixie), Gerald Gutierrez (Yasha), Randle Mell (Dauber), Paul Walker (President Prexy), Brian Reddy (Professor Mamie, Harry Druggist), Charles Shaw-Robinson (Dr. Specialist, Bugs), Michael Barrett (Clerk), Mary Lou Rosato (Mrs. Mister), David Schramm (Mr. Mister), Daniel Corcoran (Steve, Professor Scoot, Reporter #1), Laura Hicks (Sadie Polock, Reporter #3), Randle Mell (Larry Foreman), Michele-Denise Woods (Ella Hammer), Susan Rosenstock (Reporter #2)

The action occurs in Steeltown, U.S.A., on the night of a union drive.

The musical was presented in two acts (no songs were listed in the program).

NOTES—This was the second Off Broadway revival of *The Cradle Will Rock,* Marc Blitzstein's 1937 left wing labor opera. It was also Patti LuPone's second Off Broadway musical of the season to take place during the Depression (see entry for *America Kicks Up Its Heels*). In 1987, she starred in yet another musical set during the Depression, Lincoln Center's hit revival of Cole Porter's *Anything Goes* (1934), which in style and tone was of course light years away from the two other serious musicals.

For more information about the labor opera, and for a list of songs, see entry for the 1964 production.

The revival closed on May 29 after twenty-four performances, but reopened on July 12 at the Douglas Fairbanks Theatre for an additional forty performances (sixty-four total performances); for the second production, Lisa Banes played Moll. On August 13, 1985, the musical opened in London at the Old Vic, with Patti LuPone (Moll) and Randle Mell (Larry Foreman). The production was recorded by Polydor Records (LP # 827-937-1-Y-1) and a complete recording was later issued on a 2-CD set by That's Entertainment Records (# CDTEM2-1105).

The New York production was shown on public television.

326 Crazy Now. "A Wild New Musical"; THEATRE: Eden Theatre; OPENING DATE: September 10, 1972; PERFORMANCES: 1; BOOK: Richard Smithies and Maura Cavanagh; LYRICS: Richard Smithies and Maura Cavanagh; MUSIC: Norman Sachs; DIRECTION: Voight Kempson; Richard Smithies, "Consulting Director"; CHOREOGRAPHY: Voight Kempson; COSTUMES: Margaret Tobin; LIGHTING: Wilson King; MUSICAL DIRECTION: Jim Litt; PRODUCER: B.F. Concerts

CAST—Carla Benjamin, William Buell, Glenn Mure, Rosalie, John Scoullar

The revue was presented in one act (sketch and song assignments unknown)

MUSICAL NUMBERS—"Crazy Now," "Shaftway Danger," "Marginal People," "Toll Basket," "Tears," "Great Connection," "Algae," "Beautiful," "Hard Times," "Get Naked," "Dirty Mind," "Regulation Purple," "Sherman's Mom," "Something to Do with My Hands," "Highway Narrows"

NOTES—*Crazy Now* was the first of two one-performance flops which opened during the 1972-1973 season. Although Richard Smithies and Maura Cavanagh were credited with the book, the evening was a revue which offered a loosely-connected series of songs and sketches dealing with modern-day life.

Clive Barnes in the *New York Times* found the evening "witless, tasteless and lacking in imagination," and noted the revue offered a "clever impersonation of being interminable." However, he singled out two songs, "Hard Times" and "Tears," the latter in the style of Kurt Weill. Barnes also mentioned that the opening night curtain was delayed while policemen and firemen searched the theatre because of a bomb scare ("with masterful restraint—no comment," remarked Barnes).

327 Croesus and the Witch. THEATRE: Urban Arts Theatre; OPENING DATE: March 14, 1973; PERFORMANCES: Unknown; BOOK: Vinnette Carroll; LYRICS: Micki Grant; MUSIC: Micki Grant; DIRECTION: Vinnette Carroll

The musical was presented in one act.

NOTES—A few weeks after Vinnette Carroll and Micki Grant's *Croesus and the Witch* closed Off Off Broadway, it was produced at the New Locust Theatre in Philadelphia (on a double bill with Carroll and Grant's *Step Lively, Boy!* [see entry for the latter as well as entry for its revised version, which was titled *The Boogie-Woogie Rumble of a Dream Deferred*]). The cast for the Philadelphia version of *Croesus and the Witch* included Sherman Hemsley, and the following songs were heard in the production: "Story Telling Time," "You Can Do What You Wanna Do," "Out There in the Forest," "Horrible Hecuba," "If I Had," "They Were Warned," "So Long," "You Can Do What You Wanna Do" (reprise), "Aha," "The Evil That You Do Will Turn on You," "You Can Do What You Wanna Do" (reprise)

328 Crossing Brooklyn. "A New Musical: A Woman, a Man, & 9/11"; THEATRE: Connelly Theatre; OPENING DATE: October 27, 2007; PERFORMANCES: 22; BOOK: Laura Harrington; Adam Perlman, Dramaturg; LYRICS: Laura Harrington; MUSIC: Jenny Giering; DIRECTION: Jack Cummings III; Christine O'Grady, Associate Director; CHOREOGRAPHY: Scott Rink; SCENERY: Sandra Goldmark; COSTUMES: Shana Albery; LIGHTING: R. Lee Kennedy; Cody Schindeldecker, Assistant Lighting Designer; MUSICAL DIRECTION: Brian J. Nash; PRODUCER: The Transport Group (Jack Cummings III, Artistic Director; Lori Fineman, Executive Director)

CAST—Jenny Fellner (Des), Bryce Ryness (AJ), Blythe Gruda (Madeline), Clayton Dean Smith (Travis), J. Bradley Bowers (Kevin), Susan Lehman (Olive), Kate Weiman (Beryl), Ken Triwush (Jimmy), Jason F. Williams (Bobby)

The action occurs in Brooklyn and Manhattan in late Spring 2002.

The musical was presented in one act.

MUSICAL NUMBERS—Opening (Bryce Ryness, Jenny Fellner, Chorus), "Every Day a New Day" (Bryce Ryness, Jenny Fellner), "Everything's Gonna Be All Right" (Bryce Ryness, Chorus), "Over the Edge"/"Can't Breathe" (Chorus), "I Think About It All the Time" (Jenny Fellner), "Off the Map"/"The Wrong Guy" (Chorus, Blythe Gruda), "Turn to Me" (Bryce Ryness, Blythe Gruda), "If I Could Escape" (Bryce Ryness), "Weed, Weed, Weed" (Chorus), "Imagine That" (Jenny Fellner), "Over the Edge" (reprise)/"Scraps of Paper" (Chorus), "Everybody Says" (Chorus), "Turn to Me" (reprise) (Bryce Ryness), "Common Little Catechism" (Jenny Fellner), "Don't Let Me Go" (Bryce Ryness, Jenny Fellner), "AJ on the Subway" (Bryce Ryness, Chorus), "What If?" (Bryce Ryness, Blythe Gruda), "Scraps of Paper" (reprise) (Chorus), "Everybody Says" (reprise) (Chorus), "First Grade" (Jenny Fellner), "If I'm Honest with You" (J. Bradley Bowers), "Four Square Blocks"/"Find Me" (Bryce Ryness, Chorus), "Talk to Me" (Jenny Fellner, Bryce Ryness), "Brooklyn Bridge"/"First Step" (Jenny Fellner, Bryce Ryness, Chorus)

NOTES—*Crossing Brooklyn* looked at the aftermath of 9/11 and how different people reacted to the terrorist attack. Frank Scheck in the *New York Post* noted the musical was well-intentioned but too generic and predictable, and lacked an edge. He remarked that the two-dozen songs were all "quietly introspective" and seemed to "blend together." Anne Midgette in the *New York Times* reported the musical was too often formulaic, and the characters and story lacked "credible development." But she found Jenny Giering's score "successful" in its creation of the "jagged, nervous energy" which captured the mood of post-9/11 Manhattan. A revised version of the musical is scheduled for a regional production in 2010.

329 Crossroads Café. THEATRE: 18th Street Playhouse; OPENING DATE: November 3, 1983; PERFORMANCES: 12; BOOK: Uncredited; LYRICS: John C. Introcaso; MUSIC: John C. Introcaso; DIRECTION: Carole Start; CHOREOGRAPHY: Dick Shell; SCENERY: Tony Damiano; COSTUMES: Jennie Weidmann; LIGHTING: Richard Clausen; PRODUCER: Autumn Productions

CAST—Diane Disque (McKinley), Tommy Re (Tommy), Annie Joe Edwards (Pearl), Lynne McCall (Alyson), Gale Gallione (Lacy), Susan Berkson (Mama), Frank M. Rosner (Sal), John C. Introcaso (Jarrett), Ken-Michael Stafford (Johnson)

The musical was presented in two acts (division of acts and song assignments unknown; songs are listed in performance order).

MUSICAL NUMBERS—"Ain't Doin' Nothin' Wrong," "Searching for That Sunset," "Rainy Day Blues," "Lovely Ladies," "Fool Inside of Me," "Give Before You Die," "Three O'Clock in the Mornin'," "You Wanna Go to Broadway," "Tell My Troubles To," "Woman's Work Ain't Never Done," "When I Dream," "Good Mornin' Mr. Sunshine," "Crossroads Café"

330 Crowns. "A Play with Gospel Music"; THEATRE: 2econd (Second) Stage Theatre; OPENING DATE: December 3, 2002; PERFORMANCES: 40; TEXT: Regina Taylor; DIRECTION: Regina Taylor; CHOREOGRAPHY: Ronald K. Brown; SCENERY: Riccardo Hernandez; COSTUMES: Emilio Sosa; LIGHTING: Robert Perry; MUSICAL DIRECTION: Linda Twine; PRODUCERS: 2econd Stage Theatre (Carole Rothman, Artistic Director; Carol Fisheman, Managing Director) in association with the McCarter Theatre Center

CAST—Lawrence Clayton (Man), Carmen Ruby Floyd (Yolonda), Harriett D. Foy (Jeanette), Lynda Gravatt (Mabel), Janet Hubert (Wanda), Ebony Jo-Ann (Mother Shaw), Lillias White (Velma)

SOURCE—The 2000 book *Crowns: Portraits of Black Women in Church Hats* by Michael Cunningham and Craig Marberry.

The musical was presented in one act (song assignments unknown).

MUSICAL NUMBERS—*Prologue*: "Where I Belong" (lyric by Regina Taylor); "In the Morning" (traditional); *Morning*: "Ain't That Good News" (traditional); *Procession*: "Oh, When the Saints Go Marching In" (traditional); "Marching to Zion" (traditional); *Morning Service*: "Oh Lord I'm Waiting on You" (traditional), "I'm on the Battlefield" (traditional), "That's All Right" (traditional), "Traditional Gullah/Geechee Shouts," "It's OK" (lyric and music by Mega Banton), "Touch the Hem of His Garment" (lyric and music by Sam Cooke), "His Eye Is on the Sparrow" (traditional), "None But the Righteous" (traditional); *Funeral*: "When I've Done the Best I Can" (traditional), "I'm Gonna Roll On a Few Days Longer" (traditional), "Mary Don't You Weep" (lyric and music by Inez Andrews); *Baptism*: "Wade in the Water" (traditional), "Ain't Gonna Let Nobody Turn Me Around" (traditional), "Take Me to the Water" (traditional), "Yonder Come Day" (traditional), "I've Got Peace Like a River" (traditional), "This Joy That I Have" (traditional); *Recessional*: "I Got a Crown" (traditional)

NOTES—*Crowns* was a revue-like musical in which a somewhat standoffish Black woman from Brooklyn comes to grips with her personal tragedies and finds her roots by learning the etiquette of "crowns" (hats) when she attends a Southern church while visiting an aunt. Through older Southern Black women, she learns there are crowns for every occasion, and these crowns are the conduits for stories about fashion and etiquette as well as about religion, slavery, and the history of African rituals.

The revue lasted only a few weeks in New York, but seems to have found its place in regional and community theatre where it promises to have a long and healthy life.

The script was published by Dramatists Play Service, Inc., in 2005.

331 The Crucible. New York City Center; OPENING DATE: October 26, 1961; PERFORMANCES: 3; LIBRETTO: Bernard Stambler; MUSIC: Robert Ward; DIRECTION: Allen Fletcher; SCENERY: Paul Sylbert; COSTUMES: Ruth Morley; MUSICAL DIRECTION: Emerson Buckley; PRODUCER: The New York City Opera Company

CAST—Joyce Ebert (Betty Parris), Norman Kelley (the Rev. Samuel Parris), Debria Brown (Tituba), Patricia Brooks (Abigail Williams), Mary Lesawyer (Ann Putnam), Paul Ukena (Thomas Putnam), Eunice Alberts (Rebecca Nurse), Spiro Malas (Francis Nurse), Maurice Stern (Giles Corey), Chester Ludgin (John Proctor), Norman Treigle (the Rev. John Hale), Frances Bible (Elizabeth Proctor), Joy Clements (Mary Warren), Harry Theyard (Ezekiel Cheever), Ken Neate (Judge Danforth), Joan Kelm (Sarah Good), Lorna Ceniceros (Ruth Putnam), Helen Guile (Susanna Walcott), Nancy Roy (Mercy Lewis), Elizabeth Schwering (Martha Sheldon), Beverly Evans (Bridget Smith)

SOURCE—The 1953 play *The Crucible* by Arthur Miller.

The action occurs in Salem, Massachusetts, in 1692.

The opera was presented in four acts.

ACT ONE—Beginning: "Gently, Sirs, Gently," "Jesus, My Consolation," "For Much in the World," "Oh, How Many Times, Mr. Parris," "Jesus, My Consolation"

ACT TWO—Beginning: "I've Forgotten Abigail," "But, Oh, the Dreams," "For Sarah Good Confessed," "You Will Go to That Court"

ACT THREE—Beginning: "In the Courtroom," "Open Thou, My Lips, O Lord," "These Girls Never Saw a Spirit," "No, No, It Is a Natural Lie to Tell"

ACT FOUR—Beginning: "But Sir, You Stir Rebellion," "What Word of the Children?" "God Does Not Need My Name"

NOTES—Harold G. Schonberg in the *New York Times* was disappointed with *The Crucible*, Robert Ward's operatic version of Arthur Miller's play about the Salem witch trials. Schonberg felt Ward's "musical platitudes" had "little distinction," and that overall the score was too "noncommittal" in telling its dark and powerful story. But Schonberg reported the audience's reaction indicated the opera was a "grand success." Further, he noted that midway through the first act, one audience member with an "enormous" voice yelled, "Sing out!" Schonberg suggested the New York City Opera find the man and offer him a contract, because his was a "baritone of a size and projection" which dwarfed the singers on the stage. The song list for *The Crucible* is taken from the 2-CD recording of the opera's original cast album which was released by Albany Records (# TROY025-26-2).

An earlier version of the opera was titled *Those Familiar Spirits. The Crucible* won the 1962 Pulitzer Prize for music and also received a New York Critics Circle Award citation.

There have been other musical adaptations of Arthur Miller's plays. *A View from the Bridge* (1955) has been twice adapted as an opera. The first adaptation, *Uno Squardo del Ponte*, premiered in Rome on January 17, 1961, at the Teatro dell'Opera (and was recorded at the time); the music was composed by Renzo Rossellini. The American premiere took place on October 17, 1967, at the Academy of Music in Philadelphia.

See entry for the second operatic adaptation, *A View from the Bridge*, which premiered on October 9, 1999, at the Lyric Opera of Chicago; the libretto was by Arnold Weinstein and Arthur Miller, and the music was composed by William Bolcom; the opera was later performed in New York at the Metropolitan Opera House. The work was recorded on a 2-CD set by New World Records.

Also see entry for *Up from Paradise*, which was a musical adaptation of Miller's 1972 play *The Creation of the World and Other Business.*

332 The Crystal Heart. "A New Musical"; THEATRE: East 74th Street Theatre; OPENING DATE: February 15, 1960; PERFORMANCES: 9; BOOK: William Archibald; LYRICS: William Archibald; MUSIC: Baldwin Bergersen; DIRECTION: William Archibald; CHOREOGRAPHY: William Archibald; SCENERY: Richard Casler; COSTUMES: Ted Van Griethuysen; LIGHTING: Richard Casler; MUSICAL DIRECTION: Baldwin Bergersen; PRODUCER: Charles Kasher

CAST—JOHN BAYLIS (Ted), JOHN STEWART (Jeremy John), JOE ROSS (Wellington Marchmount), Bob (Robert) Fitch (Herbert), Byron Mitchell (Percy), Vincent Warren (Donald), JEAN SHEA (Prudence), KATHERINE LITZ (Virtue), Barbara Janezic (Hope), Margot Harley (Charity), MILDRED DUNNOCK (Mistress Phoebe Ricketts), Virginia Vestoff (Alexandra Crowley), Robert Penn (The Captain)

The action occurs sometime between 1830 and 1840.

The musical was presented in two acts.

ACT ONE—"A Year Is a Day" (John Baylis), "A Monkey When He Loves" (John Baylis, Bob Fitch, Vincent Warren, Byron Mitchell), "Handsome Husbands" (Mildred Dunnock, Jeanne Shea, Katherine Litz, Barbara Janezic, Margot Harley), "Yes, Aunt" (Virginia Vestoff), "A Girl with a Ribbon" (John Baylis; danced by Maids and Sailors), "I Must Paint" (Virginia Vestoff), "I Wanted to See the World" (John Stewart; danced by Katherine Litz), "Fireflies" (dance; danced by Margot Harley, Barbara Jenezic, Byron Mitchell, Vincent Warren), "How Strange the Silence" (Jeanne Shea), "When I Drink with My Love" (Mildred Dunnock), "Desperate" (Joe Ross, John Stewart), "Lovely Island" (Katherine Litz, Barbara Janezic, Margot Harley, John Stewart, Virginia Vestoff), "Bluebirds" (Mildred Dunnock)

ACT TWO—"Agnes and Me" (Bob Fitch), "Madam, I Beg You" (Mildred Dunnock, Joe Ross), "My Heart Won't Learn" (Jeanne Shea), "Tea Party" (Mildred Dunnock, John Stewart, John Baylis, Sailors), "Lovely Bridesmaids" (Katherine Litz, Barbara Janezic, Margot Harley), "It Took Them" (Katherine Litz, Barbara Janezic, Margot Harley, Bob Fitch, Vincent Warren, Byron Mitchell), "D-O-G" (John Stewart), "A Year Is a Day" (reprise) (John Baylis)

NOTES—*The Crystal Heart* originally opened in London at the Saville Theatre on February 19, 1957, running just seven performances; the New York production did slightly better, with nine. In London, Gladys Cooper played the role of Mistress Phoebe Ricketts, and, like her New York counterpart, Mildred Dunnock, she made her musical debut in the production.

The musical dealt with a widow and her circle of female relations, friends, and servants, all living on an island bereft of the male sex. When a group of sailors lands on the island, the women's existence is forever changed because they're finally able to experience the male sex. Despite its somewhat earthy outlook on the nature of human existence, the work was nonetheless a delicate piece, perhaps a bit too brittle in its story-telling and perhaps with too much of the art song in its score. Its rarified air was not the stuff of popular entertainment: audiences didn't show up, and the critics, for the most part, weren't impressed. While he praised the score (the "well-bred music has a dainty humor"), Brooks Atkinson in the *New York Times* felt the musical's book lacked the final "fillip of imagination and daring" which could take the plot's "good idea" into the realm of "inspired madness"; and he suggested that Robert Louis Stevenson, Jean Giraudoux, and Lewis Carroll were "needed at the typewriter."

The elegant artificiality of the piece is perhaps best sampled by Mrs. Ricketts' final spoken sequence (preserved on the cast album) in which she recalls her youth, a time spent in a garden of tangerine and lavender butterflies which took to the sky while woodpeckers "pecked the moments away, like little clocks"; and she looked into her heart ("fashioned of crystal"), seeking the spark of love.

Happily, the New York production was recorded, not as a commercial venture but as a souvenir for those associated with the show (the LP was issued on an unnamed label which was numbered [#CK-1]). For years the album was the Holy Grail for cast album collectors; but in the 1980s it had a limited commercial release on a small label (Blue Pear Records LP # BP-1001).

The recording reveals *The Crystal Heart* a jewel of a musical. Its melodies and lyrics abound in wit and grace, and, along with *Kittiwake Island* (1960; see entry), it is clear that much of the best theatre music of the era was being heard Off Broadway. The London production was presented in three acts, and the running order of the musical numbers was somewhat different. The following songs were heard in London, but not in New York: "The Anchor's Down," "Hilltop Dance" (which might have been the "Fireflies" dance in New York), "Handsome Husbands," and "It's So British." Also, the London numbers "Pretty Little Bluebird" and "When I Dance with My Love" became "Bluebird" and "When I Drink with My Love" for New York. In both productions, the "Bluebird" number was sung by Mrs. Ricketts. However, while the London "When I Dance with My Love" was sung by Ted, in New York it was sung by Mrs. Ricketts. The songs "I Must Paint" and "D-O-G" were heard in New York, but weren't in the London production.

333 The Crystal Tree. THEATRE: AMAS Repertory Theatre; OPENING DATE: April 19, 1981; PERFORMANCES: 15; BOOK: Doris Julian; LYRICS: Doris Julian; MUSIC: Luther Henderson; DIRECTION: Billie Allen; CHOREOGRAPHY: Walter Raines; SCENERY: William R. Waithe; COSTUMES: Bernard Johnson; LIGHTING: Mark Diquinzio; MUSICAL DIRECTION: J. Leonard Oxley; PRODUCER: The AMAS Repertory Theatre, Inc. (Rosetta LeNoire, Founder and Artistic Director)

CAST—Marvin Foster (Jess), Christine Spencer (Hetty Johnson), Norman Matlock (Adam Johnson), Val Eley (Mary), Ira Hawkins (JoJo Johnson), Jean Du Shon (Della), Andre Morgan (Lasson Johnson), Grenoldo Frazier (Maxie), Albert S. Bennett (Doctor), Marta Vidal (Millie), Vanessa Thornton (Carole), T. Renee Crutcher (Edna Mae), Dolores Garcia (Rosie), Children (Teshina Haynes, Lisa Iglesias, Jamaal Richardson, Kim C. Stewart)

The musical was presented in two acts.

ACT ONE—"Bazaar—For the Lord" (Ensemble), "Home Is the Entire World" (Ira Hawkins, Ensemble), "The Tree Song" (Teshina Haynes, Lisa Iglesias, Jamaal Richardson, Kim C. Stewart), "Magical Man" (Grenoldo Frazier), "Just Got Me" (Andre Morgan, Val Eley), "Nothin' Funny" (Ensemble), "Nothin' Funny" (reprise) (Ensemble), "Small Aria" (Norman Matlock, Christine Spencer), "There's a Look to Him" (Jean Du Shon), "Dream Smoke" (Jean Du Shon), "River Song" (Ira Hawkins), "The Lord's Work" (Ira Hawkins), "Sorrow" (Ira Hawkins, Ensemble)

ACT TWO—"Satin-Skinned Doll" (Jean Du Shon), "Not Your Heart" (T. Renee Crutcher, Grenoldo Frazier), "Young Man" (Norman Matlock, Men), "Satin-Skinned Doll" (reprise) (Jean Du Shon), "What a Day" (Ensemble), "My Kind of Love" (Jean Du Shon), "Oh God" (Val Eley), "Lullabye" (Christine Spencer), "Magical Man" (reprise) (Grenoldo Frazier), "Magical Man" (reprise) (Val Eley), "Sweet Mary" (Ira Hawkins), "Love Stays" (Val Eley), "Magical Man" (reprise) (Grenoldo Frazier, Ensemble), "What a Day" (reprise) (Ensemble)

NOTES—Although *The Crystal Tree* had been written twenty years earlier, the Off Off Broadway production by AMAS marked the musical's premiere. John S. Wilson in the *New York Times* dismissed the "leaden" book with its "stereotyped" characters and "elementary" situations, all of which centered around the legend of a crystal tree possessed by the spirit of a vengeful woman. But Wilson praised Luther Henderson's "melodic" score, filled with "lively" rhythms and the occasional "sensuous, smoky" tune. He singled out "Small Aria," "Dream Smoke," "Satin-Skinned Doll," and "My Kind of Love." *The Crystal Tree* was a rare instance in which Luther Henderson, the noted Broadway arranger, orchestrator, and musical director, composed the score for a musical. His only Broadway score was the 1975 disaster *Doctor Jazz* (it appears his songs were the highlights of an otherwise forgettable evening).

It isn't clear if Marvin Foster played any performances; he was replaced by Leon Summers in the role of Jess either shortly before the opening or early during the musical's limited two-week engagement.

334 Cummings and Goings. THEATRE: Top of the Village Gate; OPENING DATE: February 26, 1984; PERFORMANCES: 5; WORDS: e.e. cummings; MUSIC: Ada Janik; additional songs by Steven Margoshes; DIRECTION: Nina Janik

CAST—Sharon Brown, Elisa Fiorillo, Nina Hennessey, Bruce Hubbard, Theodore Kilmer

The revue was presented in two acts.

NOTES—The Off Off Broadway revue *Cummings and Goings* was a tribute to the poet e.e. cummings (1894-1962). (And shouldn't that title have been *cummings and goings*—??)

The revue had earlier been seen Off Off Broadway at La Mama Experimental Theatre Club (ETC) on November 2, 1978; that production was directed by Annie Szamosi.

335 A Curious Evening with Gypsy Rose Lee. THEATRE: Mayfair Theatre; OPENING DATE: May 9, 1961; PERFORMANCES: 25

CAST—Gypsy Rose Lee (with pianist Sam Pottle)

NOTES—This was indeed a curious evening, one in which Gypsy Rose Lee sat on a stool and with the help of slides and home movies talked about her life and career. Milton Esterow in the *New York Times* felt the show could have been titled *The Gypsy Rose Lee Newsreel Theatre*, and while he noted that the legendary strip-tease artist was "never dull," he felt that two hours of home movies were "not always exciting."

There were no individual songs or sequences listed in the program (which also omitted the usual credits for direction, lighting, etc.); the evening appears to have been presented in one act. In the program, Miss Lee listed the names of about 100 people she wanted to thank, names ranging from Sarah Bernhardt to Stephen Sondheim, from John Gielgud to Lucille Ball.

The "curious evening" had been briefly presented at the Cherry Lane Theatre the previous winter.

336 Curley McDimple (1967). THEATRE: Bert Wheeler Theatre; OPENING DATE: November 22, 1967; PERFORMANCES: 931; BOOK: Mary Boylan and Robert Dahdah; LYRICS: Robert Dahdah; MUSIC: Robert Dahdah; DIRECTION: Robert Dahdah; CHOREOGRAPHY: Larry Stevens; SCENERY: Richard Jackson; COSTUMES: John Hirsch; LIGHTING: Barry Arnold; MUSICAL DIRECTION: Bob Atwood; PRODUCER: The Curley Company

CAST—Paul Cahill (Jimmy), Helon Blount (Sarah), Bernadette Peters (Bernadette Peters), Bayn Johnson (Curley McDimple), George Hillman (Bill), Norma Bigtree (Miss Hamilton), Gene Galvin (Mr. Gillingwater)

The action occurs in Sarah's Boarding House, a shabby brownstone in the West 40's in Manhattan; the time is the early to middle 1930s.

The musical was presented in two acts.

ACT ONE—Overture (Orchestra), "A Cup of Coffee" (Paul Cahill), "I Try" (Paul Cahill, Bernadette Peters), "Curley McDimple" (Bayn Johnson, Paul Cahill, Helon Blount, Bernadette Peters, George Hillman), "Love Is the Loveliest Love Song" (Bernadette Peters), "Are There Any More Rosie O'-Gradys?" (Helon Blount, Paul Cahill, Bernadette Peters, Bayn Johnson, George Hillman), "Dancing in the Rain" (Bayn Johnson, George Hillman, Company), "At the Playland Jamboree" (Bayn Johnson, Company), "I've Got a Little Secret" (George Hillman, Bayn Johnson)

ACT TWO—"Stars and Lovers" (Bernadette Peters, Paul Cahill, Company), "The Meanest Man in Town" (Bernadette Peters, Paul Cahill, Company), "I Try" (reprise) (Paul Cahill, Bernadette Peters), "Something Nice Is Going to Happen" (Bayn Johnson), "Swing-a-Ding-a-Ling" (Bayn Johnson), "Hi de hi de hi, Hi de hi de ho" (Helon Blount, Bernadette Peters, Paul Cahill, George Hillman, Gene Galvin, Norma Bigtree), "Dwarfs' Song" (Helon Blount, Bernadette Peters, Paul Cahill, George Hillman, Gene Galvin, Norma Bigtree), "Swing-a-Ding-a-Ling" (reprise) (Bayn Johnson, Company), "Something Nice Is Going to Happen" (reprise) (Norma Bigtree), "Love Is the Loveliest Love Song" (reprise) (Paul Cahill, Company), Finale (Company)

NOTES—In just one memorable show-stopping number ("You Mustn't Be Discouraged"), *Fade Out-Fade In* (1964) demolished every cliché of the Shirley Temple film musicals of the 1930s, and so a full evening's spoof of the genre might have seemed like overkill. But *Curley McDimple* was a cute self-described valentine to film musicals of the 1930s, and it ran for over two years, making it one of the longest-running Off Broadway musicals. Actually, Dan Sullivan in the *New York Times* felt the musical was less a spoof of Shirley Temple films than an actual replica of one, and he felt the show was too much in love with the "tyke that it's supposed to be kidding." But Sullivan noted the second act offered a "flurry" of songs and dances which were "easy to take," and because the musical offered so much tap dancing, he found he was typing his review in 6/8 time. But despite its run of over two years, *Curley McDimple* seems to have had a short shelf life; it's rarely if ever produced anymore, and is generally forgotten by musical theatre buffs. It didn't help that there wasn't a cast recording; in fact, only two songs (the title number and "I've Got a Little Secret") were recorded (by Capitol Records 45 RPM # 2116), both performed by two members of the original cast (Bayn Johnson and Paul Cahill). The script was published by Samuel French, Inc.; the copyright page indicates the pressing was in 1967, but the script was no doubt published sometime in 1968 or 1969.

Bernadette Peters seems to have left the musical sometime in December, a few weeks after the opening; meanwhile, Jill O'Hara had left *Hair* (see entry) after its engagement at the Public Theatre, and didn't transfer with the production when it re-opened at the Cheetah in late December. So presumably both had signed for *George M!* which was going into rehearsal soon after the first of the year.

Six months after its opening, Butterfly McQueen joined *Curley McDimple*; the character of "Hattie" was written for her, along with a new song ("Be Grateful for What You've Got"); the character of Hattie and the song don't appear in the published script.

Two other songs, "Curley's the Girlie for Me" and "You Little Monkey, You," were apparently heard in the show on opening night, but were immediately dropped (the former may have been heard only in previews).

The musical was briefly revived in New York in 1972 (see entry).

337 Curley McDimple (1972).

THEATRE: Plaza 9 Music Theatre; OPENING DATE: June 26, 1972; PERFORMANCES: 96; BOOK: Mary Boylan and Robert Dahdah; LYRICS: Robert Dahdah; MUSIC: Robert Dahdah; DIRECTION: Robert Dahdah; CHOREOGRAPHY: Don Emmons, George Hillman, and Dotty Morgan; COSTUMES: Gene D. Galvin; LIGHTING: April Adams; MUSICAL DIRECTION: Horace Diaz; PRODUCER: The Plaza 9 Music Hall

CAST—Don Emmons (Jimmy), Mary Boylan (Sarah), Lynn Brossman (Alice), Robbi Morgan (Curley McDimple), George Hillman (Bill), Jane Stuart (Miss Hamilton), Richard Durham (Mr. Gillingwater)

NOTES—See entry for the original 1967 production for information regarding musical numbers.

The revival of *Dames at Sea* (1970; see entry) had played the Plaza 9 Music Hall shortly after the original production had closed, and so did *Curley McDimple*. Again, it seemed rather too soon for a revival, but the musical played out the summer, chalking up almost 100 performances. Despite the jovial nature of the piece, it's all but disappeared and hasn't enjoyed a major revival since this production.

The revival included "Be Grateful for What You've Got," which had been added to the original production when Butterfly McQueen joined the cast.

338 Cut the Ribbons.

"A New Musical"; THEATRE: Westside Theater/Downstairs; OPENING DATE: September 20, 1992; PERFORMANCES: 25; LYRICS: Mae Richard; MUSIC: Cheryl Hardwick and Mildred Kayden; additional music by Nancy Ford; DIRECTION: Sue Lawless; CHOREOGRAPHY: Sam Viverito; SCENERY: Michael Hotopp; COSTUMES: Terence O'Neill Lighting: Michael Hotopp; MUSICAL DIRECTION: Sande Campbell; PRODUCERS: George Elmer and Phase Three Productions

CAST—GEORGIA ENGEL, BARBARA FELDON, DONNA MCKECHNIE

The musical was presented in two acts.

ACT ONE—Overture (The Band), "She Loves You" (music by Mildred Kayden) (Company), "Kick Me Again" (music by Nancy Ford) (Donna McKechnie), "Kick Me Again" (reprise) (music by Nancy Ford) (Georgia Engel), "Mommy Number Four" (music by Mildred Kayden) (Barbara Feldon), "Let Her Go" (music by Nancy Ford) (Georgia Engel), "The Door Is Closed" (music by Nancy Ford) (Georgia Engel), "A Period Piece" (music by Mildred Kayden) (Company), "Let Her Go" (reprise) (music by Nancy Ford) (Georgia Engel), "Lookin' Good" (music by Cheryl Hardwick) (Georgia Engel, Donna McKechnie), "It's a Party" (music by Cheryl Hardwick) (Georgia Engel, Donna McKechnie), "She Loves You" (reprise) (music by Mildred Kayden) (Donna McKechnie), "Four-Two-Two" (music by Mildred Kayden) (Barbara Feldon), "Two-Four-Four" (music by Mildred Kayden) (Donna McKechnie), "Because of Her" (music by Mildred Kayden) (Barbara Feldon, Donna McKechnie), "Try Not to Need Her" (music by Mildred Kayden) (Barbara Feldon), "Let Her Go" (reprise) (music by Nancy Ford) (Georgia Engel), "Balancing" (music by Cheryl Hardwick) (Company), "Mom Will Be There" (music by Mildred Kayden) (Company), "Balancing" (reprise) (music by Cheryl Hardwick) (Company)

ACT TWO—Entr'acte (The Band), "Am I Ready for This?" (music by Cheryl Hardwick) (Donna McKechnie), "Instinct" (music by Cheryl Hardwick) (Barbara Feldon), "She Loves You" (reprise) (music by Mildred Kayden) (Georgia Engel), "T'ai Chi" (music by Cheryl Hardwick) (Company), "Bed" (music by Cheryl Hardwick) (Barbara Feldon), "The Door Is Closed" (reprise) (music by Nancy Ford) (Donna McKechnie, Georgia Engel), "Isabel" (music by Cheryl Hardwick) (Barbara Feldon), "That Woman in the Mirror" (music by Cheryl Hardwick) (Georgia Engel), "Where's My Picture?" (music by Mildred Kayden) (Company), "I Dare You Not to Dance" (music by Cheryl Hardwick):, Take One (Barbara Feldon), Take Two (Donna McKechnie), Take Three (Georgia Engel), "Her Career" (music by Nancy Ford) (Barbara Feldon), "I Just Can't Move in Her Shadow" (music by Nancy Ford) (Donna McKechnie), "Cut the Ribbons" (music by Nancy Ford) (Barbara Feldon, Donna McKechnie), "That Woman in the Mirror" (reprise) (music by Cheryl Hardwick) (Company), "Cut the Ribbons" (reprise) (music by Nancy Ford) (Company)

NOTES—Mel Gussow in the *New York Times* felt that *Cut the Ribbons*, a revue about mother-and-daughter relationships, was far from the "cutting edge." As a result, the work was mostly bland, "mild-mannered" and predicable, and while it raised "issues," it didn't raise its "voice." The revue was occasionally satiric, but Gussow indicated Mae Richards, the lyricist, "prefers a soft brush to a stiff bristle." But the second act picked up speed when the three actresses (Donna McKenknie, Barbara Feldon, and Georgia Engel) performed a challenge dance in a sequence titled "I Dare You Not to Dance"; Gussow found this and "several" subsequent numbers invigorating because they allowed the three performers to "break loose from the restraints of cabaret-style staging." The script was published by Samuel French, Inc.

Gussow praised the cast, and noted that Georgia Engel must have "sprung full blown from the head of Carol Channing."

339 Cut to the Chase.

"The New Family Vaudeville Revue!"; THEATRE: 59E59 Theatres; OPENING DATE: December 12, 2007; PERFORMANCES: 30

NOTES—The Off Broadway children's revue *Cut to the Chase* was created by Joel Jeske, directed by Mark Lonergan, and produced by Parallel Exit. The cast included Laura Dillman (Dilly), Mike Dobson (Dobson), Joel Jeske (The Great Jeske), Ryan Kasprzak (Kasper), Andrea Kehler (Little Angela), and Roland Derek (Derek Roland).

Laurel Graeber in the *New York Times* said the one-hour show was "largely wordless," but included a few songs. She also noted the self-described vaudeville was "actually about vaudeville," and that much of the evening was inspired by the films of Buster Keaton and Charlie Chaplin. Graeber singled out a number of sequences, including a rendition of "Shine On, Harvest Moon" (which was performed as a duel by two romantic rivals); some "bravura" tap-dancing; and "nifty" magic tricks.

340 Cyrano.

THEATRE: Metropolitan Opera House; OPENING DATE: February 27, 1913; PERFORMANCES: 6; LIBRETTO: William J. Henderson; MUSIC: Walter Damrosch; DIRECTION: Jules Speck; SCENERY: Antonio Rovescalli; COSTUMES: Maison Muelle; MUSICAL DIRECTION: Alfred Hertz; PRODUCER: The Metropolitan Opera

CAST—Pasquale Amato (Cyrano de Bergerac), Frances Alda (Roxanne), Marie Mattfeld (Duenna), Vera Curtis (Lise), Louise Cox (Flower Girl), Florence Mulford (Mother Superior), Riccardo Martin (Christian), Albert Reiss (Ragueneau), Putnam Griswold (De Guiche), William Hinshaw (Le Bret), Basil Ruysdael (First Musketeer), Marcel Reiner (Second Musketeer), Lambert Murphy (Montfleury, Cadet), Antonio Pini-Corsi (Monk), Austin Hughes (Cavalier), Paolo Ananian (Cavalier), Louis Kreidler (Cavalier), Maurice Sapio (Cavalier)

SOURCE—The 1897 play *Cyrano de Bergerac* by Edmund Rostand.

The opera was presented in four acts.

NOTES—The world premiere of *Cyrano* was one of the earliest of some fourteen lyric adaptations of Rostand's play (see below). The *New York Times*' critic Richard Aldrich felt William J. Henderson's libretto showed "an unmistakable flair for the operatic stage" and had an "accomplished literary skill." Aldrich noted that Walter Damrosch's score included "more or less melodious arioso," and mentioned the evening was filled with ensembles, trios, quartets, and choruses. But for all that, he felt the score wasn't particularly inspired.

In 2005, the Met offered another opera based on Rostand's play when it presented its first production of Franco Alfano's 1936 opera *Cyrano de Bergerac*; Placido Domingo sang the title role. *Cyrano de Bergerac* is one of the most enduring plays in Western literature, and it appears to hold the record for the most musical adaptations. The original play opened in Paris on December 28, 1897, at the Theatre de la Porte Saint-Martin; Benoit Constant performed the title role. The New York premiere was on October 3, 1898, at the Garden Theatre, with Richard Mansfield in the lead. One of the play's most famous revivals occurred on October 8, 1946, at the Alvin (now Neil Simon) Theatre, when Jose Ferrer essayed the role for 195 performances (he later won the Academy Award for Best Actor for his role in the 1950 film version). The play's most recent New York visit occurred in 2007 when it was revived with Kevin Kline at the Richard Rodgers (formerly 46th Street) Theatre.

There have been at least fourteen musical adaptations of the work (counting two productions in 1932 and 1939 which shared a total of four titles between them; counting as one the 1967 and 1973 versions by Robert Wright and George Forrest; and counting the 1992 and 1994 Australian versions as two separate adaptations [the second version had a new lyricist]).

The first musical adaptation was *Cyrano de Bergerac*, which opened at the Knickerbocker Theatre on September 18, 1899, for twenty-eight performances; the music was by Victor Herbert, the lyrics by Harry B. Smith, and the book by Stuart Reed.

Two decades after *Cyrano*'s premiere at the Met, a Broadway-bound version of the story (titled *Cyrano de Bergerac*) began its tryout on November 4, 1932, with book and lyrics by Charles O. Locke and music by Samuel Pockriss. During the tryout, the title was changed to *Roxanne*. The production never reached New York, but seven years later the musical was revised (with additional songs by Vernon Duke) and given a new title. As *The White Plume*, the musical began its tryout on December 26, 1939, but during the run the musical was given its fourth title, *A Vagabond Hero*. Like the 1932 version, the 1939 adaptation closed during its pre-Broadway tryout.

Between the productions of *Cyrano de Bergerac/Roxanne* and *The White Plume/A Vagabond Hero*, Franco Alfano's operatic version premiered in 1936. In 1958, Richard Maltby, Jr., and David L. Shire, who were undergraduates at Yale, wrote the book, lyrics, and music for *Cyrano*, which was produced by the Yale Dramatic Association. The college cast members included John Cunningham, Richard Cavett, Carrie Nye McGeoy, Bill Hinnant, Austin Pendleton, and Roscoe Browne. The production was recorded on LP by the Association (# J8OP-4263/64) and was later issued on CD by Original Cast Records (# OC-9987); the CD also included highlights from another Maltby and Shire college show, *The Grand Tour* (1959).

In 1965, *Cyrano*, a children's version of the play (with music and lyrics by Judith Dvorkin) premiered in Winston-Salem, North Carolina; a recording of the score was released by Peter Pan Records (LP # S-8041). In 1967 and in 1973, *A Song for Cyrano* (with Jose Ferrer) was performed in summer stock, but the version was never produced on Broadway. The book was by J. Vincent Smith, and the lyrics and music were by Robert Wright and George Forrest.

On May 13, 1974, another musical version, *Cyrano*, opened at the Palace Theatre for forty-nine performances. Christopher Plummer played the title role and won the Tony Award for Best Actor in a Musical for his performance. The book and lyrics were by Anthony Burgess, and the music by Michael J. Lewis. The production was recorded on a 2-LP set by A & M Records, Inc. (# A&M-SP-3702; issued on CD by Decca Broadway Records # B-0004083-02).

On November 21, 1993, a 1992 version from the Netherlands opened at the Neil Simon (formerly Alvin) Theatre for 137 performances. Titled *Cyrano: The Musical*, the piece had book and lyrics by Koen Van Dijk (English lyrics by Peter Reeves, with additional lyrics by Sheldon Harnick) and music by Ad Van Dijk. There are at least two recordings of the musical: the Netherlands cast album (Indisc Records CD # DICD-3797) and a symphonic suite of the score recorded in 1993 by JE Music Records (CD # 51193).

A 1992 Australian adaptation called *Cyrano* had lyrics and music by David Reeves (with one song's lyric credited to Reeves and Terry Stapleton); this version doesn't seem to have been produced, but it left behind a "highlight album" which was recorded by EMI Records (CD # HA-0135). In 1994, a new version of the work was produced in Australia (the book and lyrics were by Hal Shaper, and this time around Reeves contributed only the music); this adaptation was recorded by Castle Communications (Australasia) Records (CD # CDSGP-9800)

Besides Damrosch and Alfano's operas, there have been at least three other operatic adaptations of the play, one by Eino Tamberg, the other by Marius Constant, and the third by David DiChiera. The latter version premiered in October 2007 at the Michigan Opera Theatre in Detroit and was presented by the Opera Company of Philadelphia in February 2008. The Alfano, Tamberg, and Constant operas have been recorded.

There have been at least six (non-musical) film versions of the play. Besides the 1950 version which starred Jose Ferrer, the other adaptations were released in 1900, 1925, 1945, 1987, and 1990. The 1987 version starred Steve Martin and was titled *Roxanne*.

341 Dames at Sea (1968).

"The New-30s Musical"; THEATRE: Bouwerie Lane Theatre; transferred to the Theatre de Lys on April 22, 1969; OPENING DATE: December 20, 1968; PERFORMANCES: 575; BOOK: George Haimsohn and Robin Miller; LYRICS: George Haimsohn and Robin Miller; MUSIC: Jim Wise; DIRECTION: Neal Kenyon; CHOREOGRAPHY: Neal Kenyon; Bonnie Ano, Assistant Choreographer; SCENERY: Peter Harvey; COSTUMES: Peter Harvey; LIGHTING: Martin Aronstein; MUSICAL DIRECTION: Richard J. Leonard; PRODUCERS: Jordan Hott and Jack Millstein

CAST—Tamara Long (Mona Kent), Sally Stark (Joan), Steve Elmore (Hennessey, The Captain), Bernadette Peters (Ruby), David Christmas (Dick), Joseph R. Sicari (Lucky)

The action occurs in any 42nd Street theatre (and later on a battleship) in the early Thirties.

The musical was presented in two acts.

ACT ONE—"Wall Street" (Tamara Long), "It's You" (David Christmas, Bernadette Peters), "Broadway Baby" (David Christmas), "That Mister Man of Mine" (Tamara Long, Chorus), "Choo-Choo Honeymoon" (Sally Stark, Joseph R. Sicari), "The Sailor of My Dreams" (Bernadette Peters), "Singapore Sue" (Joseph R. Sicari, Company), "Good Times Are Here to Stay" (Sally Stark, Company)

ACT TWO—"Dames at Sea" (Company), "The Beguine" (Tamara Long, Steve Elmore), "Raining in My Heart" (Bernadette Peters, Chorus), There's Something About You (David Christmas, Bernadette Peters), "Raining in My Heart" (reprise) (Bernadette Peters), "The Echo Waltz" (Tamara Long, Sally Stark, Bernadette Peters, Company), "Star Tar" (Bernadette Peters, Chorus), "Let's Have a Simple Wedding" (Company)

NOTES—In *Curley McDimple* (1967; see entry). Bernadette Peters played an Alice Faye-type character, and in the Broadway musical *Mack & Mabel* (1974), she played silent screen legend Mabel Normand; in *Dames at Sea*, she played Ruby (Keeler), who announces that she just got off the bus and wants to be in a Broadway show.

The musical affectionately spoofed the entire genre of the Warner Brothers 1930s musical, and the six-member cast in the postage-stamp-sized Bouwerie Lane Theatre seemed to fill the stage with a cast of thousands.

Dames at Sea had been around since May 1966 when a shorter, one-act version played for thirteen weeks at the Off Off Broadway Caffe Cino; during the run at Caffe Cino, the musical's title was *Dames at Sea*, or *Golddiggers Afloat*. In his fascinating history of the Caffe Cino, Wendell C. Stone reports that of the eleven performers who played the musical's seven roles during the Off Off Broadway run, only Bernadette Peters and David Christmas reprised their roles for the Off Broadway production.

The musical played over a year, opened in London at the Duchess Theatre on August 27, 1969, for 117 performances, and was revived Off Broadway in 1970 for 170 performances and then again in 1985 for 278 performances (see entries), All told, the three Off Broadway productions have tallied up over 1,000 performances. *Dames at Sea* was also revived Off Off Broadway at the Harold Clurman Theatre on December 2, 1994, for thirteen performances (Kristin Chenoweth performed the role of Ruby), and on September 3, 2004, it was briefly revived Off Off Broadway by the Jean Cocteau Repertory (formerly the Bouwerie Lane Theatre, where the original 1968 Off Broadway production had opened thirty-six years earlier), The musical was also shown in a one-hour television version scripted by George Haimsohn and Robin Miller; it starred Ann-Margret, Ann Miller, Anne Meara, Fred Gwynne, Dick Shawn, and Harvey Evans, and it was seen on NBC on November 15, 1971.

There have been at least four recordings of the score (Off Broadway [Columbia Records LP # OS-3330], television [a privately produced and unnumbered LP by the Bell System Family Theatre], the 1969 London Production [CBS Records LP # 70063], and a later 1989 British production [That's Entertainment Records LP # TER-1169 and CD # CDTER-1169]). The script was published by Samuel French, Inc., in 1969.

Most of the lyrics were jointly written by George Haimsohn and Robin Miller, with the exception of "The Sailor of My Dreams," "Singapore Sue," "Good Times Are Here to Stay," and "The Echo Waltz," which were written only by Haimsohn.

342 Dames at Sea (1970).

THEATRE: PLaza 9- Music Hall; OPENING DATE: September 23, 1970; PERFORMANCES: 170; BOOK: George Haimsohn and Robin Miller; LYRICS: George Haimsohn and Robin Miller; MUSIC: Jim Wise; DIRECTION: Neal Kenyon;

CHOREOGRAPHY: Neal Kenyon; assistant choreographer, Bonnie Ano; SCENERY: Peter Harvey; COSTUMES: Peter Harvey; LIGHTING: Chenault Spence; MUSICAL DIRECTION: Richard Demone; PRODUCERS: Jordan Hott and Jack Millstein

CAST—Janie Sell (Mona Kent), Carol Morley (Joan), Raymond Thorne (Hennessey, The Captain), Leland Palmer (Ruby), Kurt Peterson (Dick), Voight Kempson (Lucky)

NOTES—The original production of *Dames at Sea* (1968; see entry) had closed just four months before the 1970 revival opened, and so the revival seemed somewhat superfluous; nevertheless, it played for almost five months. For song list and other information, see entry for the 1968 production. The musical was also revived Off Broadway in 1985 for 278 performances (see entry), and Off Off Broadway at the Harold Clurman Theatre on December 2, 1994, for thirteen performances (Kristin Chenoweth performed the role of Ruby).

343 Dames at Sea (1985).

THEATRE: Lamb's Theatre; OPENING DATE: June 12, 1985; PERFORMANCES: 278; BOOK: George Haimsohn and Robin Miller; LYRICS: George Haimsohn and Robin Miller; MUSIC: Jim Wise; DIRECTION: Neal Kenyon; CHOREOGRAPHY: Neal Kenyon: Tap Sequences by Associate Choreographer Dirk Lumbard; SCENERY: Peter Harvey; COSTUMES: Peter Harvey; LIGHTING: Roger Morgan; MUSICAL DIRECTION: Janet Aycock; PRODUCERS: Jordan Hott and Jack Millstein in association with The Asolo State Theatre of Florida and Lee Star, Jack Tamen, Beverly Rich, and Victoria Pierce

CAST—Susan Elizabeth Scott (Mona Kent), Richard Sabellico (Hennesey, The Captain), Dorothy Stanley (Joan), Donna Kane (Ruby), George Dvorsky (Dick), Dirk Lumbard (Lucky)

The action occurs during the early 1930s in any 42nd Street theatre and on a battleship.

The musical was presented in two acts.

NOTES—This was the second New York revival of *Dames at Sea*, and it played for almost three-hundred performances. For song list and other information, see entry for the original 1968 production. The musical was also revived Off Broadway in 1970 for 170 performances (see entry), and Off Off Broadway at the Harold Clurman Theatre on December 2, 1994, for thirteen performances (Kristin Chenoweth performed the role of Ruby).

344 The Dance in Place Congo.

THEATRE: Metropolitan Opera House; OPENING DATE: March 23, 1918; PERFORMANCES: 5; STORY: Henry F. Gilbert; MUSIC: Henry F. Gilbert; DIRECTION: Ottokar Bartik; SCENERY: Livingston Platt; COSTUMES: Livingston Platt; MUSICAL DIRECTION: Pierre Monteux; PRODUCER: The Metropolitan Opera Company

CAST—Rosina Galli (Aurore), Giuseppe Bonfiglio (Remon), Ottokar Bartik (Numa)

SOURCE—A story of George W. Cable.

The action occurs in the bayous around New Orleans.

The "ballet pantomime" was presented in one act.

NOTES—*The Dance in Place Congo* had its world premiere at the Met on a triple bill which included another world premiere (*The Robin Woman: Shanewis*; see entry) and a revival (Franco Leoni's *L'Oracolo* [1905]). Charles Wakefield Cadman's music for *Shanewis* was based on Indian songs, and Henry F. Gilbert's music for *Congo* was similarly derived from other sources, including songs of the West Indies and the American South (the unsigned review in the *New York Times* found the adaptation "as genial a piece of symphonic writing as has come to local hearing in some time"), The plot of *Congo* was based on a story by George W. Cable.

The *Times* praised the choreography (it will "keep dancing feet busy") and singled out Rosina Galli's "kinky-haired, black-faced vixen" who danced a "tarantella of terpsichorean virtuosity, the last word in dancing on the Metropolitan stage or anywhere else" since Pavlowa danced in *Carmen*.

Although *Congo* wasn't an opera, it blended well into the triple bill because all the offerings were set in the United States (*Congo* in the bayous surrounding New Orleans, *Shanewis* in California and Oklahoma, and *L'Oraculo* in San Francisco), The ballet is also evidence of the Met's commitment to present American music on its stage; in the period between 1912 and 1920, the Met offered the world premieres of eight American operas and one American ballet.

345 Dance on a Country Grave.

"A Magical Folk Musical"; THEATRE: Hudson Guild Theatre; OPENING DATE: April 21, 1977; PERFORMANCES: 21 (estimated); BOOK: Kelly Hamilton; LYRICS: Kelly Hamilton; MUSIC: Kelly Hamilton; DIRECTION: Robert Brewer; CHOREOGRAPHY: Dennis Grimaldi; SCENERY: Tom Warren; COSTUMES: Donna Meyer; LIGHTING: Curt Ostermann; MUSICAL DIRECTION: Bill Grossman; PRODUCER: Hudson Guild Theatre (Craig Anderson, Producing Director)

CAST—Ghost Children (Bella Sirugo, Carol Sirugo, Gena Feist), Sam Freed (Diggory Venn), Donna Theodore (Eustacia Vye), Mike Dantuono (Damon Wildeve), Fiddle Viracola (Susan Nunsuch), Gail Kellstrom (Tess), Susan Berger (Olly Dowden), Paul Rosson (Grandfer Cantle), Timothy Wallace (Timothy Fairway), John B. Giletto (Humphrey), Kate Kelly (Thomasin Yeobright), Elizabeth Owens (Mrs. Yeobright), Trip Plymale (Christian Cantle), Deborah McHale (Jane Orchard), Carmen Peterson (Bathsheba), Jim Frank (Sam), Kevin Kline (Clym Yeobright)

SOURCE—The 1878 novel *The Return of the Native* by Thomas Hardy.

The action occurs in Egdon Heath, Wessex, England ("a face on which Time makes but little impression") in the middle of the nineteenth century.

The musical was presented in two acts.

ACT ONE—Prelude (Sam Freed), "Dance on a Country Grave" (Ensemble), "The Lonely Sparrows of Wessex" (Donna Theodore, Ensemble), "Sunday Morning Social Call" (Gail Kellstrom, Susan Berger, Deborah McHale), "Cities of Light" (Kevin Kline, Donna Theodore), "Can Ye Fancy That?" (Ensemble), "Unexpected Love" (Donna Theodore), "Unexpected Love" (reprise) (Donna Theodore, Trip Plymale), "Unexpected Love" (reprise) (Donna Theodore, Kevin Kline), "Self-Sacrificing Woman" (Elizabeth Owens, Ensemble), "The Dark Side of My Love" (Sam Freed), "Old Mister Fate" (Donna Theodore)

ACT TWO—"Tout le Monde" (Kevin Kline), "The East Egdon Band" (Ensemble), "Green Gravel" (Kate Kelly), "The Gamblin' Hand" (Mike Dantuono, Trip Plymale), "The Gamblin' Hand" (reprise) (Sam Freed, Mike Dantuono), "Who Would Have Thought?" (Donna Theodore, Kate Kelly, Mike Dantuono), "Country Spell" (Fiddle Viracola, Ensemble), "The Lonely Sparrows of Wessex" (reprise) (Ensemble), "The Dark Side of My Love" (reprise) (Sam Freed), "Dance on a Country Grave" (reprise) (Ensemble)

NOTES—Based on Thomas Hardy's *The Return of the Native*, the Off Off Broadway musical *Dance on a Country Grave* had originally been produced at Brigham Young University, and in 1974 a revised version played at Arlington Park Theatre in Chicago. Original Cast Records released a recording of a 1998 production which played in Philadelphia (CD # OC-8804), In reviewing the Off Broadway production, Thomas Lask in the *New York Times* thought the best aspect of the evening was Kelly Hamilton's score, which had "the fragrance and cadence of English folk songs." Lask singled out "Green Gravel," "The Lonely Sparrows of Wessex," "The Dark Side of My Love," and the title song.

Kevin Kline was a year away from his breakthrough role in the delightful art deco operetta *On the Twentieth Century* (1978).

346 Dance wi' Me, or The Fatal Twitch (1971).

THEATRE: Anspacher Theatre/The Public Theatre; OPENING DATE: June 10, 1971; PERFORMANCES: 53; PLAY: Greg Antonacci; LYRICS: Greg Antonacci; MUSIC: Greg Antonacci; DIRECTION: Joel Zwick; LIGHTING: Laura Rambaldi; PRODUCER: The New York Shakespeare Festival (Joseph Papp, Producer; Bernard Gersten, Associate Producer)

CAST—Greg Antonacci (Honey Boy), Johnny (John) Bottoms (Jimmy Dick), Judy Allen (Judy Jeanine), Alan Wynroth (Professor Alan), Joel Zwick (Venerable Zwish), Sarah Venable (Pepper Pot), Peter Alzado (Sailor Avocado), Tommy St. Cyr (Dr. Sincere), Jane Margaret Whitehill (Jane Trinculo), Peter Frumkin (The Band)

The action occurs in a subway station at the present time and, in the mind of Honey Boy, during the 1950s.

The play was performed in one act.

NOTES—Originally produced at La Mama Experimental Theatre Club, *Dance Wi' Me*, or *The Fatal Twitch* was a comedy with incidental songs. It dealt with Honey Boy, a perpetual loser who, while waiting for a subway, fantasizes he's a rock 'n' roll singer of the 1950s. In 1975, the comedy (now called *Dance with Me*) was revived Off Broadway and played for nearly a year (see entry).

347 Dance with Me (1975).

"A New Comedy with Music"; THEATRE: Mayfair Theatre; OPENING DATE: January 23, 1975; PERFORMANCES: 396; PLAY: Greg Antonacci; LYRICS: Greg Antonacci; MUSIC: Greg Antonacci; DIRECTION: Joel Zwick; CHOREOGRAPHY: Joel Zwick; SCENERY: Scott Johnson; COSTUMES: Susan Hum Buck; LIGHTING: Scott Johnson; PRODUCERS: Ted Ravinett and Steve Rubenstein

CAST—Annie Abbott (Tommie Sincere), Greg Antonacci (Honey Boy), John Bottoms (Jimmy Dick II), Peter Frumkin (Thumbs Bumpin), Patricia Gaul (Judy Jeanine), Scott Robert Redman (Wendell Crunchall), Deborah Rush (Goldie Pot), Stuart Silver (Smitner Tuskey), Skip Zipf (Don Tomm), Joel Zwick (Bulldog Allen)

The action occurs in a subway station at the present time and in the mind of Honey Boy during the 1950s.

The play was presented in two acts.

NOTES—*Dance with Me* was a revival of *Dance Wi' Me*, or *The Fatal Twitch*, which had played at the Public Theatre in 1971 for two months (see entry), The comedy with incidental songs had a slightly altered title this time around, and the play was revised as well as expanded into two acts (the revision also included different names for some of the characters).

The play dealt with a lovable loser who imagines he's a rock 'n' roll singer of the 1950s; the revival ran for almost a year.

Clive Barnes in the *New York Times* had found the original production a "merry romp," but the revised version seemed "overblown," He mentioned the original had offered a "minimum of scenery and a maximum of imagination," but the revival instead offered realistic scenery which was "out of all recognition" to what was seen in the original production.

348 Dancing in the Dark.

THEATRE: Cabaret/Manhattan Theatre Club; OPENING DATE: January 3, 1979; PERFORMANCES: 28; LYRICS: Except where noted, all lyrics by Howard Dietz; MUSIC:

Arthur Schwartz; DIRECTION: Christopher Chadman; CHOREOGRAPHY: Christopher Chadman; MUSICAL DIRECTION: Paul Trueblood; PRODUCER: Manhattan Theatre Club (Lynne Meadow, Artistic Director; Barry Grove, Managing Director; Stephen Pascal, Associate Artistic Director)

CAST—John Cunningham, Allyn Ann McLerie, Merilee Magnuson, Donn Simione

The revue was presented in two acts.

ACT ONE—"That's Entertainment" (from 1953 film *The Band Wagon*) (Company), "New Sun in the Sky" (*Flying Colors*, 1932) (Allyn Ann McLerie), "If There Is Someone Lovelier Than You" (*Revenge with Music*, 1934) (John Cunningham), "High and Low" (the stage production of *The Band Wagon*, 1931) (Merilee Magnuson), "This Is It" (*Stars in Your Eyes*, 1939; lyric by Dorothy Fields) (Donn Simione), "Love Isn't Born, It's Made" (1943 film *Thank Your Lucky Stars*; lyric by Frank Loesser) (Company), "Something to Remember You By" (*Three's a Crowd*, 1930) (Company), "They're Either Too Young or Too Old" (1943 film *Thank Your Lucky Stars*; lyric by Frank Loesser) (Allyn Ann McLerie, Merilee Magnuson), "I Can Never Get Anywhere on Time" (source unknown) (Allyn Ann McLerie), "Alone Together" (*Flying Colors*, 1932) (John Cunningham, Allyn Ann McLerie), "Triplets" (for background information concerning this song, see NOTES in entry for *That's Entertainment*, 1972) (John Cunningham, Allyn Ann McLerie), "My Son-in-Law" (*Park Avenue*, 1946; lyric by Ira Gershwin) (John Cunningham, Allyn Ann McLerie), "Rhode Island Is Famous for You" (*Inside U.S.A.*, 1948) (Donn Simione, Merilee Magnuson), "Louisiana Hayride" (*The Band Wagon*, 1931) (Company), "A Gal in Calico" (1946 film *The Time, the Place, and the Girl*; lyric by Leo Robin) (Company), "Why Go Anywhere at All?" (*The Gay Life*, 1961) (Allyn Ann McLerie), "When You're Far Away from New York Town" (*Jennie*, 1963) (Company).

ACT TWO—"I Guess I'll Have to Change My Plan" (*The Little Show*, 1929) (Donn Simione), "The Jog" (source unknown; lyric by Arthur Schwartz) (Company), "Confession" (*The Band Wagon*, 1931) (John Cunningham, Merilee Magnuson), "The Bloom Is Off the Rose" (*The Gay Life*, 1961) (John Cunningham), "Smokin' Reefers" (*Flying Colors*, 1932) (Allyn Ann McLerie, Donn Simione), "On the Other Hand" (source unknown) (Merilee Magnuson), "A Shine on Your Shoes" (*The Band Wagon*, 1931) (Donn Simione), "Before I Kiss the World Goodbye" (*Jennie*, 1963) (Allyn Ann McLerie), "Loadin' Time" (*At Home Abroad*, 1935) (Donn Simione, Merilee Magnuson, Allyn Ann McLerie), "Never Marry a Dancer" (*Revenge with Music*, 1934) (Donn Simione, Merilee Magnuson), "You and the Night and the Music" (*Revenge with Music*, 1934) (John Cunningham), "Get Yourself a Geisha" (*At Home Abroad*, 1935) (Allyn Ann McLerie, Merilee Magnuson), "A Rainy Night in Rio" (1946 film *The Time, the Place, and the Girl*; lyric by Leo Robin) (Allyn Ann McLerie, Donn Simione), "Tanya" (source unknown) (John Cunningham, Merilee Magnuson), "Love Should Be Free" (source unknown; lyric by Arthur Schwartz) (John Cunningham, Allyn Ann McLerie), "By Myself" (*Between the Devil*, 1937 (John Cunningham, Allyn Ann McLerie), "Dancing in the Dark" (*The Band Wagon*, 1931) (Company)

NOTES—The Off Off Broadway revue *Dancing in the Dark* was the second tribute to Arthur Schwartz in seven years (see entry for *That's Entertainment* [1972], which saluted Schwartz and his most frequent collaborator, Howard Dietz), In 1987, the Off Off Broadway revue *The Little Show and Friends* (see entry) was another tribute to Schwartz and Dietz.

Among the cast members of *Dancing in the Dark* was Allyn Ann McLerie, a virtually unknown legend of American musical theatre. She appeared in the original Broadway production of *One Touch of Venus* (1943), and later created the role of Amy (as in "once in love with") in *Where's Charley?* (1948), later reprising her role for the charming and very faithful 1952 film version. She was also the girl who posed for the Statue of Liberty in *Miss Liberty* (1949), and was prominently featured in the 1953 musical film *Calamity Jane* opposite Doris Day.

349 The Dangerous Christmas of Red Riding Hood. THEATRE: Actors' Outlet Theatre Center; OPENING DATE: December 19, 1986; PERFORMANCES: 17; BOOK: Robert Emmet; LYRICS: Bob Merrill; MUSIC: Jule Styne; DIRECTION: Lee Costello; CHOREOGRAPHY: Raymond Kurshals; SCENERY: James Finguerra; COSTUMES: Ann R. Emo; LIGHTING: Clay Shirky; MUSICAL DIRECTION: Jeanine T. Levenson; PRODUCER: Theatre and Dance Alliance (TADA) (Janine Nina Trevens and James Learned, Artistic Directors)

CAST—Rick Anthony (Chipmunk), Katisha Baldwin (Skunk), Erin Branch (Seal, Beaver), Kaila Colbin (Deer, Martha Hood), Andrea Davila (Bird), Simone Harrison (Bear), Saadiya Jackson (Monkey, Mouse), Conrad de Marez Oyens (Turtle), Astrid Prieto (Raccoon), Dawn Turnage (Kangaroo, Rabbit), Kwami Reynolds (Lone T. Wolf), Kyla Maull and Meredith Wechter (alternating the role of Red Riding Hood), Wolf Pack (Gerri Boone, Mark Felder, Evelyn Padilla, Randy Slaughter), Michael Halpner (Woodman)

The musical was presented in one act.

MUSICAL NUMBERS—Overture (Band), "We Wish the World a Happy Yule" (Animals, Kwami Reynolds), "My Red Riding Hood" (Kyla Maull or Meredith Wechter), "Sylvan Ballet" (Company), "Snubbed" (Gerri Boone, Mark Felder, Evelyn Padilla, Randy Slaughter, Kwami Reynolds), "Along the Way" (Michael Halpner), "I'm Naïve" (Kyla Maull or Meredith Wechter), "I'm Naïve" (reprise) (Kwami Reynolds), "We're Gonna Howl Tonight" (Gerri Boone, Mark Felder, Evelyn Padilla, Randy Slaughter), "Ding-A-Ling, Ding-A-Ling" (Kyla Maull or Meredith Wechter, Kwami Reynolds), "Poor Mouse" (Company), "Granny's Song" (Kyla Maull or Meredith Wechter, Kwami Reynolds), Finale (Company)

NOTES—The Off Off Broadway production of *The Dangerous Christmas of Red Riding Hood* marked the stage premiere of the television musical of the same name, which had first been seen on ABC on November 28, 1965 (Liza Minnelli was Red Riding Hood, Cyril Ritchard was the Wolf, Vic Damone was the Woodsman, and a 1960s pop group, the Animals, portrayed the wolf pack); the choreography was by Lee Theodore. The original television soundtrack album was released by ABC-Paramount Records (LP # 536), (The musical was re-telecast a year later.)

"Woodsman's Serenade (When I Chop, Chop, Chop)" was heard in the television production, but wasn't retained for the stage version.

"I'm Naïve" was later used in the 1992 musical *Some Like It Hot*, the British version of Jule Styne and Bob Merrill's 1972 Broadway musical *Sugar*, and can be heard on the British cast album released by First Night Records. The script of *The Dangerous Christmas of Red Riding Hood* was published by Samuel French, Inc., in 1992.

The original 1965 telecast of the musical was released on DVD in 2007 by Substance Video (# 12250).

350 Dark Horses. THEATRE: Upstairs at the Downstairs; OPENING DATE: December 30, 1967; PERFORMANCES: 280 (estimated); SKETCHES: Sidney Davis, Bob Lerner, Gayle Parent, Drey Shepard, Kenny Solms, and Rod Warren; LYRICS AND MUSIC: Gene Bissell, Suzanne Buhrer, David Finkle, Alan Foster Friedman, Kenny Jerome, Ed Kresley, Michael McWhinney, Lance Mulcahy, Tom Pasle, Drey Shepard, Ted Simons, Don Tucker, Rod Warren, and Bill Weeden; DIRECTION: Rod Warren; CHOREOGRAPHY: Ed Kresley; LIGHTING: Derek Whittlesey; MUSICAL DIRECTION: Edward Morris; PRODUCER: Upstairs at the Downstairs (Rod Warren)

CAST—Richard Blair, Gary Crabbe, Diane Deckard, Larry Moss, Carol Richards, Janie Sell

The revue was presented in two acts (sketch and song assignments unknown).

ACT ONE—"Dark Horses," "Dig We Must," "Singles on the Slopes," "Piggyback Partners," "Bloodshed and Brotherhood," "Little Brother," "Wednesday Matinee," "The Interview," "The Turn-On Song," "The Princess Lays a Golden Egg," "Charles," "Bedtime Story," "Nancy," "Whatever Happened To?"

ACT TWO—"The Tribute," "Token Gesture," "Won't Someone Give John Lindsay?," "Mr. Smith, Please Go Back to Washington," "I've Seen Shakespeare," "Ethel," "Requiem for the Queen," "High Finance," "Dark Horses"

NOTES—This was the ninth in Rod Warren's series of satiric revues; for a complete list of his revues, see entry for ... *And in This Corner*; also see Appendix R.

351 Dark Sonnet.
NOTES—See entry for *Murder in 3 Keys*.

352 Darwin's Theories. "A Revue"; THEATRE: Madison Avenue Playhouse; OPENING DATE: October 19, 1960; PERFORMANCES: 2; SKETCHES: Alan Alda; LYRICS: Darwin Venneri; MUSIC: Darwin Venneri; DIRECTION: Stanley Phillips; CHOREOGRAPHY: Louis Johnson; SCENERY: Robert Paine Grose; COSTUMES: Robert Paine Grose; LIGHTING: Warren Crane; MUSICAL DIRECTION: Nino Silva; PRODUCERS: Arthur Grasso, in association with Win Productions Ltd.

CAST—Alan Alda, James Coco, Austin Colyer, Patricia Fay, Albie Gaye, Bette Guy, Darwin Venneri

The revue was presented in two acts (sketch and song assignments unknown).

ACT ONE—Opening, "11th Hour Report," "Party Time," "I Know How You Wonder," "The Fledgling," "Love Is a Stranger," "Arrivederci," "Love Me a Little," "The Bard in the Park," "What's in a Name?," "The Stars Seem So Low Tonight," "Tennessee Williams' Heroine," "Mashoogie Boogie"

ACT TWO—"Darwin's Calypso," "The Bookworm," "Carried Away" "Strange Weather" "Marty's Room Is at the Top," "We'll Always Stay in Love" "A Day in the Park," "The Return of Tennessee Williams' Heroine," "I'm Living the Past," Finale

NOTES—This little-known revue was a fast flop. The headline for the *New York Times'* review by Howard Taubman proclaimed *Darwin's Theories* was "Not the Fittest," and Taubman warned his readers that the line of dialogue to heed was spoken in the middle of the first act when a cast member stated "I don't know about you, but I'm going home."

One of the sketches, "Marty's Room Is at the Top," was a spoof of the films *Marty* (1955) and *Room at the Top* (1959), and there was yet another Off Broadway sketch kidding Tennessee Williams (two sketches in fact), Of the show's two performer-writers, one (Alan Alda) went on to stage and later television fame, but the titular lead of the show, Darwin Venneri, drifted into show- business obscurity. Performer Jimmy Coco later enjoyed success on the stage, and he must have been an amusing Marty in the sketch "Marty's Room Is at the Top."

A few years after the show's closing, Darwin Venneri's solo LP, *To You from Darwin*, was released by Town Hall Records (# THM-1002), Darwin (as he now called himself) sang his own material as well as songs by other composers, including Billy Barnes' "(Have I Stayed) Too Long at the Fair?"; see entry for *The Billy Barnes Revue*.

The LP included five songs from *Darwin's Theories*: "Love Me a Little," "Strange Weather," "We'll Always Stay in Love," "I Know How You Wonder," and "Carried Away."

353 Davy Jones' Locker (1967). THEATRE: Bil Baird Theatre; OPENING DATE: April 19, 1967; PERFORMANCES: 18; BOOK: Arthur Birnkrant and Waldo Salt; LYRICS: Mary Rodgers; MUSIC: Mary Rodgers; DIRECTION: Burt Shevelove; COSTUMES: Fania Sullivan, Marianne Harms; MUSICAL DIRECTION: Unknown (possibly Alvy West); PRODUCERS: The American Puppet Arts Council, Inc. (Arthur Cantor, Executive Producer)

CAST (Puppeteers)—Franz Fazakas (Nick, Peddlefoot), Bil Baird (Billy [a goat], Captain Fletcher Scorn, The Sea Monster), Frank Sullivan (Mr. Merriweather, Davy Jones), Cora Baird (Miranda): Assorted Fishes, Ghosts, Pirates, "and Things": Jerry Nelson, Phyllis Nierendorf, Byron Whiting, Robin Kendall

SOURCE—A story by Bil Baird.

The action occurs on a deserted island in the Bahamas, aboard the ship of Captain Fletcher Scorn, and in Davy Jones' Locker.

The musical was presented in two acts.

NOTES—The program didn't list individual musical numbers. The musical premiered on March 28, 1959, at the Morosco Theatre, where it played for approximately sixteen performances. In the early 1960s, it was revived at the Hudson Theatre, and then in December 1966 it was again revived (for twenty performances; theatre unknown), Early programs of the musical credited the book to Arthur Burns and M.L. Davenport.

When *Davy Jones' Locker* opened at the Bil Baird Theatre on April 19, 1967, it played eighteen matinees in repertory with *People Is the Thing That the World Is Fullest Of* (see entry), which played evening performances. *Davy Jones' Locker* was presented on a bill with *A Pageant of Puppetry*, which was a series of variety acts. A program note indicated *Pageant* "will include various characters from Asia, Africa, Europe and both Americas, to be accompanied by classical, folk, and popular music and during which the puppeteers will disclose some of the secrets of the world of marionettes," *Pageant* was apparently first introduced on April 19, 1957, when it was included in one of Baird's puppet productions, and soon became a part of all his programs over the years (it was sometimes called *A Pageant of Puppet Variety* and *Bil Baird's Variety*).

Davy Jones' Locker was revived a number of times (see entries for 1972, 1976, and 1987 productions), The musical was also presented for five performances during the run of *Winnie the Pooh* in 1967 (see entry).

354 Davy Jones' Locker (1972). THEATRE: Bil Baird's Theatre; OPENING DATE: December 24, 1972; PERFORMANCES: 79; PRODUCERS: The American Puppet Council (Arthur Cantor, Executive Producer); a Bil Baird's Marionettes Production

NOTES—*Davy Jones' Locker* returned for another engagement (see entries for 1967, 1976, and 1987 productions), The musical was also presented for five performances during the run of *Winnie the Pooh* in 1967 (see entry).

The musical's book was by Arthur Birnkrant and Waldo Salt, and the lyrics and music were by Mary Rodgers; the production was directed by Lee Theodore, and the musical direction was by Alvy West. The cast were as follows: Peter Baird (Billy, Bosun), Pady Blackwood (Paddlefoot, Sea Monster), Olga Felgemacher (Miranda), John O'Malley (Nick), Frank Sullivan (Mr. Merriweather), William Tost (Capt. Fletcher Scorn), Byron Whiting (Davy Jones), The perennial *Bil Baird's Variety* accompanied the two-act musical.

355 Davy Jones' Locker (1976). THEATRE: Bil Baird's Theatre; OPENING DATE: October 15, 1976; PERFORMANCES: 97; THEATRE: The American Puppet Arts Council (Arthur Cantor, Executive Producer); A Bil Baird's Marionettes Production

NOTES—This revival of *Davy Jones' Locker* (accompanied by the perennial *Bil Baird's Variety*) was, sadly, the last production in the many seasons of puppet musicals offered by Bil Baird. With more and more television shows and films aimed at children, and with the era on the cusp of widespread cable television, videocassettes, and video games, perhaps children's puppet musicals were becoming too quaint and old-fashioned and couldn't compete with the newer entertainments. At any rate, after this engagement, children's puppet musicals no longer had a well-known and permanent New York venue. Besides the hundreds of performances of puppet musicals offered by Bil Baird, his puppets "starred" in the Broadway musical *Flahooley* (1951) and they performed in "The Lonely Goatherd" sequence in the film version of *The Sound of Music* (1965).

This production of *Davy Jones' Locker* was directed by Bill Dreyer; the musical direction was by Alvy West; the lighting was by Peggy Clark; and the puppets were produced and designed by Bil and Susanna Baird. The puppeteers were: Olga Felgemacher (Nick), Rebecca Bondor (Billy, Miranda), Peter B. Baird (Mr. Merriwether, Davy Jones), Neil Bleifeld (First Goon), William Tost (Captain Scorn, Sea Monster), and Ronnie Burkett (Paddlefoot), The puppeteers also played an assortment of "Fishes, Ghosts, Pirates & Things."

See entry for the original 1967 production; also, see entries for the 1972 and 1987 revivals (the latter was directed by Peter S. Baird), The musical had also been presented for five performances during the run of *Winnie the Pooh* in 1967 (see entry),

356 Davy Jones' Locker (1987). THEATRE: Orpheum Theatre; OPENING DATE: December 20, 1987; PERFORMANCES: 28; BOOK: Arthur Birnkrant and Waldo Salt; LYRICS: Mary Rodgers; MUSIC: Mary Rodgers; DIRECTION: Peter S. Baird; PRODUCER: Arthur Cantor

CAST—Sean O'Malley (Nick), Randy Carfagno (Billy, Goon), William Tost (Captain Fletcher Scorn), Peter S. Baird (Mr. Merriweather, Davy Jones), Pady Blackwood (Paddlefoot, Sea Monster, Goon), Sharon Lerner (Miranda)

NOTES—*Davy Jones' Locker* was revived over the holiday period in a series of matinee performances. See entries for the 1967, 1972, and 1976 productions; the musical had also been presented for five performances during the run of *Winnie the Pooh* in 1967 (see entry).

357 A Day in the Life of Just About Everyone. "New Musical"; THEATRE: Bijou Theatre; OPENING DATE: March 9, 1971; PERFORMANCES: 8; BOOK: Earl Wilson, Jr.; Michael Sawyer, Additional Dialogue; LYRICS: Earl Wilson, Jr.; MUSIC: Earl Wilson, Jr.; DIRECTION: Tom Panko; SCENERY: Andrew Greenhut; COSTUMES: Miles White; LIGHTING: Andrew Greenhut; MUSICAL DIRECTION: Elman R. Anderson; PRODUCER: Robert Shelley in association with Lawrence Simon

CAST—EARL WILSON, JR. (Smitty), JUNE GABLE (Penny), Friends and Acquaintances (Daniel Fortus, Dickie Evans, DeMarest Grey, Bennett Kinsey)

The action occurs "any place" at "any time."

The musical was presented in one act.

MUSICAL NUMBERS—Overture (Company), "If I Could Live My Life Again" (Earl Wilson, Jr.), "The View from My Window" (Earl Wilson, Jr.), "A Brief Dissertation on the Relevancy of a Liberal Education in a Contemporary Society" (Earl Wilson, Jr., Friends), "Fare Thee Well" (Earl Wilson, Jr., Friends), "A Waltz for Two Balloons" (June Gable), "Safe" (Earl Wilson, Jr., [Performer Unknown]), "When I Was a Child" (Earl Wilson, Jr.), "Give Us This Day" (Friends and Acquaintances), "Goin' Home" (Earl Wilson, Jr., [Performers Unknown]), "Out of Town" (Earl Wilson, Jr.), "Merrill, Lynch, Pierce, Fenner and Clyde" (Earl Wilson, Jr., [Performers Unknown]), "Everybody Loves a Single Girl" (June Gable, Earl Wilson, Jr.), "Two Grown-Up People at Play" (Company), "What Do I Do Now" (Company), "Got to Be a Woman Now" (Company), Reprise (reprise of which song is unknown) (Company), "He's Beginning to Look a Lot Like Me" (Earl Wilson, Jr.), "A Woman Is Just a Female" (June Gable, Friends), "Faces Without Names" (Earl Wilson, Jr., Acquaintances), "Paper Tiger" (Earl Wilson, Jr.), "The People in the Street" (performer unknown), "Visiting Hours" (June Gable), "The Man I Could Have Been" (Earl Wilson, Jr.), "The Man I Could Have Been" (reprise) (June Gable), "Isn't That What Makes Life Worthwhile" (Company), "If I Could Live My Life Again" (reprise) (Earl Wilson, Jr.)

NOTES—Like the hero of *Look Where I'm At!* (see entry), the hero of *A Day in the Life of Just About Everyone* was trying to find himself. He had only eight performances to do so.

Clive Barnes in the *New York Times* found the musical predictable and its point of view elusive, vacuous, and lacking in surprise. Ultimately, this was an evening in which "emptiness seems to be chasing blankness into an eternity of wilderness."

The program bio for Earl Wilson, Jr., was apparently serious when it stated he had first fallen in love with show business in childhood, when he appeared in a Christmas pageant at his private school. Further, giving "something of himself to his audience" was his "justification" for being a performer. He indeed gave a lot to the audiences who attended *A Day in the Life of Just About Everyone*; he appeared in twenty-two of the musical's twenty-six numbers.

Wilson returned to Off Broadway in 1974 as the lyricist and composer of the hit sex musical *Let My People Come*, which was just about the last of the *Oh! Calcutta!* wannabe sex-and-nudie musicals (see entries).

Wilson was the son of the famous entertainment columnist Earl Wilson (once referred to as the "Earl of Wilson" by Lucy McGillicuddy Ricardo when she attempted to impress a British acquaintance during her vacation in London).

358 The Day, the Night. "A Musical Journey"; THEATRE: Lenox Arts Center/St. Clement's Episcopal Church; OPENING DATE: May 18, 1983; PERFORMANCES: Unknown; TEXT: Welcome Msomi; MUSIC: Welcome Msomi; DIRECTION: Welcome Msomi; CHOREOGRAPHY: Thuli Dumakude; SCENERY: Rosaria Sinisi; COSTUMES: Karen Matthews; LIGHTING: Jackie Manassee; PRODUCER: Music-Theatre Group (Lyn Austin, Producing Director)

CAST—Robert Jason, Deborah Malone, Terrance T. Ellis, Stephanie R. Berry, Vanessa Shaw, Ghanniyya Green

The action occurs during one night and day in South Africa.

The musical appears to have been performed in one act.

NOTES—The Off Off Broadway production *The Day, the Night* was a self-described "musical journey through one day and one night in South Africa," and touched upon the oppression felt by the people of Johannesburg who are "flattened" but will nonetheless survive because "courage and strength conquer."

The program didn't list individual musical numbers, but a program synopsis singled out two song sequences ("We Are Going" and "We Ask") and three dance numbers ("Boot Dance," "Can Dance," and "Celebration Dance").

359 Dazy. THEATRE: The AMAS Repertory Theatre; OPENING DATE: February 12, 1987; PERFORMANCES: 16; BOOK: Allan Knee; LYRICS: Norman Simon; MUSIC: Lowell E. Mark; DIRECTION: Philip Rose; CHOREOGRAPHY: Clarence Teeters; SCENERY: Clarke Dunham; COSTUMES: Gail Cooper-Hecht; LIGHTING: Ken Billington; MUSICAL DIRECTION: Jeffrey Roy; PRODUCER: The AMAS Repertory Theatre (Rosetta LeNoire, Founder and Artistic Director)

CAST—Leah Hocking (Dazy), Jack Landron (Charlie), Tom Flagg (Eddie), Peter Gunther (Frank), Joie Gallo (Dorothy), Ensemble (Leslie Bates, Philip Carrubba, Norman Golden, Peter Lind Harris, Denise LeDonne, Richie McCall, Ken McMullen, Sel Vitella, LaTonya Welch, Teresa Wolf, Wendy Worth)

The action occurs in New York City in 1987 and then in 1967.

The musical was presented in two acts (division of acts and song assignments unknown; songs are listed in performance order).

MUSICAL NUMBERS—"Streets," "You Can Own the Whole World," "Two for a Quarter, Three for a Dime," "It Takes Time," "Rockaway Beach," "Better Get a Grip," "Telephones," "Where Did the World Go?," "In the Rainbow of My Mind," "Love Got in the Way," "Who Am I?," "Layin' in the Sand," "Some of It's Good," "The Other Side of Time," "A Mother's Love Song"

NOTES—The Off Off Broadway musical *Dazy* was reportedly based on the true story of a former child-star singer who in adulthood becomes homeless and destitute.

360 Dear Oscar. "A Musical"; THEATRE: Playhouse Theatre; OPENING DATE: November 16, 1972; PERFORMANCES: 5; BOOK: Caryl Gabrielle Young; LYRICS: Caryl Gabrielle Young; MUSIC: Addy O. Fieger; DIRECTION: Production "supervised" by John Allen; CHOREOGRAPHY: Margery Beddow; SCENERY: William Pitkin; COSTUMES: Mary McKinley; LIGHTING: David F. Segal; MUSICAL DIRECTION: Arnold Gross; PRODUCER: Mary W. John

CAST—RICHARD KNEELAND (Oscar Wilde), Nancy Cushman (Speranza, Lady Wilde), Jane Hoffman (Lady Mount-Temple), Len Gochman (Frank Harris), Garnett Smith (Charles Brookfield), Edward Penn (Charles Hawtry, Alfred Wood), Tinker Gillespie (Bootles), Sylvia O'Brien (Comtesse), Roger Leonard (Comtesse's Son, Sidney Mayor, Scotland Yard Detective), Jack Hoffman (Frederick), Kimberly Vaughn (Constance Lloyd), Grant Walden (Lord de Grey, Sir Edward Carson), Gary Krawford (Robert [Robbie] Ross), Richard Marr (Vicar), Jack Bittner (The Marquess of Queensbury), Edward McPhillips (Arthur, Theatre Attendant), Lynn Brinker (Nellie), Tommy Breslin (Clibburn), Bruce Heighley (Atkins), James Hosbein (Edward Shelly), Russ Thacker (Bosie, Lord Alfred Douglas), Richard Marr (Sir Edward Clark)

SOURCE—The life of Oscar Wilde (1854-1900).

The action occurs in London during the years 1883-1894.

The musical was presented in two acts.

ACT ONE—"We Like Things the Way They Are" (Richard Kneeland, Company), "Tite Street" (Richard Kneeland, Jane Hoffman, Kimberly Vaughn), "Oscar Wilde Has Said It" (Company), "Wot's 'Is Name" (Lynn Brinker, The Boys), "Poor Bosie" (Russ Thacker), "The Perfect Understanding" (Richard Kneeland, Russ Thacker), "Swan and Edgar's" (Kimberly Vaughn, Nancy Cushman), "We're Only Lovers" (Gary Krawford), "If I Could" (Richard Kneeland)

ACT TWO—"How Dare He" (Company), "We'll Have a Party" (Russ Thacker, Lynn Brinker, The Boys), "The Actor" (Richard Kneeland), "When Did You Leave Me?" (Kimberly Vaughn), "Good, Good Times" (Lynn Brinker), "There Where the Young Men Go" (Richard Kneeland)

NOTES—The critics found *Dear Oscar* dull and inept, and Leonard Harris on WCBS-TV suggested that after the words of the title "a letter of apology" should be written to Oscar Wilde. Kevin Sanders of WABC-TV felt if Wilde could have known he would be the subject of such a "mawkish and sentimental" musical, he would have raced off "in a desperate search for heterosexual obscurity."

Another Off Broadway musical about Wilde's life was also a flop: *It's Wilde* ran for seven performances in 1980 (see entry), Also see entry for *Utterly Wilde!!!*, a one-man musical biography

During previews two songs were dropped from *Dear Oscar* ("If I 'Ad 'Alf" and "For Woman") and one underwent a title change, from "We Dare You" to "How Dare He," The musical was briefly revived Off Off Broadway in 1980 at the Perry Street Theatre; "If I 'Ad 'Alf" was reinstated, three new songs were added ("You Ought to Meet My Mother," "Drinkin' Nights and Sleepin' Days," and "My Dear Oscar"), and four were omitted ("We Like Things the Way They Are," "Wot's 'Is Name," "Poor Bosie," and "How Dare He"), For the revival, Patrick Farrelly was Oscar Wilde, and Rex Thompson was Bosie. As a boy, the latter had played Anna Leonowens' son Louis in the 1956 film version of *The King and I* and the twelve-year-old Peter Duchin in *The Eddy Duchin Story*, also released in 1956.

Besides the three musicals, New York has seen at least seven plays about Wilde. Four were produced on Broadway: *Oscar Wilde* (1938, 247 performances; by Leslie and Sewell Stokes; Wilde was portrayed by Robert Morley); *The Importance of Being Oscar* (1961, 31 performances; by Michael MacLiammoir [who also portrayed Wilde]); *Diversions and Delights* (1978, 13 performances; by John Gay; Vincent Price); and *The Judas Kiss* (1998, 110 performances; by David Hare; Liam Neeson); and two Off Broadway: *Oscar Remembered* (1981, 23 performances; by Maxim Mazumdar, whose play told the story of Wilde through the eyes of Lord Alfred Douglas, [who was played by Mazumdar]) and *Gross Indecency: The Three Trials of Oscar Wilde* (1997, 534 performances; by Moises Kaufman; Michael Emerson), Further, an Off Off Broadway entry, *Lord Alfred's Lover* by Eric Bentley, opened in 1982 (15 performances; Maxim Mazumdar again portrayed Wilde, and Matthew Conlon was Lord Alfred).

The Importance of Being Oscar, *Diversions and Delights*, and *Oscar Remembered* were one-man shows.

For musical adaptations based on Wilde's work, see entries for *After the Ball* and *A Delightful Season*, both based on *Lady Windermere's Fan*; *Dorian* (which also references *Dorian Gray*, another musical adaptation of the material [both musicals opened within a month of one another in 1990]); *Dorian Gray*, another musical adaptation (which opened in 1996); and *Ernest in Love* (which also references other musical adaptations of *The Importance of Being Earnest*).

361 Dear Piaf. THEATRE: The Theatre at Mama Gail's; OPENING DATE: December 29, 1975; PERFORMANCES: 74; LYRICS: See song list for credits; all lyrics translated and adapted by Lucia Victor; MUSIC: See song list for credits; all music adapted by Ken Guilmartin; DIRECTION: Dorothy Chernuck; SCENERY: T. Winberry; COSTUMES: Adri; LIGHTING: T. Winberry; MUSICAL DIRECTION: Ken Guilmartin; PRODUCER: Ira Rubin

CAST—Michael Calkins, Irene Datcher, Linda Fields, Lou Rodgers, Michael Tartel, Norman Carey (pianist)

The revue was presented in one act.

MUSICAL NUMBERS—Overture, "Life Cry" ("Cri du Couer"; lyric and music by Prevert and Crolla) (Ensemble), "Words, Words, Words" ("Let Mots d'Amour"; lyric and music by Michel Rivgauche and Charles Dumont) (Linda Fields, Michael Tartel), "Music of Love" ("La Belle Histoire d'Amour"; lyric by Edith Piaf, music by Charles Dumont) (Lou Rodgers, Michael Tartel), "Lucien" ("Mon Vieux Lucien"; lyric and music by Charles Dumont and Michel Rivgauche) (Michael Calkins), "Grenadiers" ("Les Grognards"; lyric and music by De la Noe and Giraud) (Ensemble), "Hurdy-Gurdies" ("Les Orgues de Barbarie"; lyric and music by G. Moustaki) (Linda Fields), "You're Beautiful" ("T'Es Beau, Tu Sais"; lyric and music by Henri Contet and G. Moutstaki) (Irene Datcher), "Non, Je Ne Regrette Rien" (lyric and music by Charles Dumont and Michel Vaucaire) (Ensemble), "Snow from Finland" ("Les Neiges de Finlande"; lyric by Henri Contet, music by Marguerite Monnot) (Lou Rodgers), "I'm Yours Alone" ("Je Suis a Toi"; lyric and music by Boquet and Chauvigny) (Irene Datcher, Michael Calkins), "Running" ("Dans la Ville Inconnue"; lyric and music by Charles Dumont and Michel Vaucaire) (Michael Calkins), "Every Day That Passes" ("Tant Qu'il y Aura des Jours"; lyric by Michel Rivgauche, music by Marguerite Monnot) (Ensemble), "Lovers of Teruel" ("Les Amants de Teruel"; lyric and music by Plante and Theodorakis) (Michael Tartel, Lou Rodgers), "Mon Dieu" (lyric and music by Charles Dumont and Michel Vaucaire) (Irene Datcher), "Carnival" ("La Foule"; lyric and music by Charles Dumont, Michel Rivgauche, and possibly A. Cabral) (Linda Fields), "Bravo for the Clown" ("Bravo Pour le Clown"; lyric and music by Henri Contet and Louiguy) (Michael Tartel), "The Ones in White" ("Les Blouses Blanches"; lyric by Michel Rivgauche, music by Marguerite Monnot) (Lou Rodgers), "C'Est l'Amour Qui Fait Qu'on S'Aime" (lyric by Edith Piaf, music by Marguerite Monnot) (Ensemble), "Life Cry" (reprise) (Ensemble)

NOTES—Edith Piaf (1915-1963), a/k/a "The Little Sparrow," was an acquired taste; those who saw her perform thought she was the ultimate interpreter of intimate, melancholy song; for those who know her only through recordings, she sometimes comes across as an overly tremulous and whining singer.

Many of the songs in Piaf's repertoire were by Marguerite Monnot, who composed the music for the Paris, London, and New York hit musical *Irma La Douce* (which opened on Broadway in 1960). Her hurdy-gurdy songs for *Irma* are a delight; the score is one of the most melodic of the era.

There have been numerous productions about Piaf. Besides *Dear Piaf*, which opened Off Off Broadway, there were two Off Broadway tributes, *Piaf* (1977) and *Piaf...Remembered* (1993 (see entries) as well as a 1981 Broadway offering, the London import *Piaf* which played almost five months; written by Pam Gems, the play with music (which was published by Samuel French, Inc., in 1983) earned Jane Lapotaire a Tony Award for Best Actress in a Play. The latter production gave audiences the dubious opportunity of seeing the Piaf character urinate on stage. To paraphrase the title of an Off Broadway musical, *Fly, Sparrow*. But, alas, the sparrow hasn't yet flown. In 2007, *La Vie en Rose*, a French film biography of Piaf, was released, and for her performance as Piaf, Marion Cotillard won the Academy Award for Best Actress. Further, on December 8, 2007, the Off Broadway "musical drama" *Piaf: Love Conquers All* by Roger Peace opened for a six-week limited-engagement run at the SoHo Playhouse (Naomi Emmerson was Piaf, and the production included thirteen songs which were associated with the chanteuse).

362 A Death in the Family. THEATRE: Manhattan School of Music Opera Theatre; OPENING DATE: December 8, 1999; PERFORMANCES: 3 (estimated); LIBRETTO: William Mayer; MUSIC: William Mayer; DIRECTION: Rhoda Levine; SCENERY: Peter Harrison; COSTUMES: Tracy Dorman; LIGHTING: Dennis Parichy; MUSICAL DIRECTION: David Gilbert; PRODUCER: Manhattan School of Music

CAST—Bert K. Johnson (Jay Follet), Jennifer Goode (Mary Follet), Ian Samplin (Rufus Follet), Ted Schmitz (Andrew Lynch), Julie Cross (Hannah Lynch), Deborah Lifton (Catherine Lynch), John Bischoff (Joel Lynch), Darrell Babidge (Father Jackson), Christianne Rushton (Victoria), Ethan Watermeier (Ralph Follet), Deborah Domanski (Sally Follet), Daniel Gross (John Henry Follet), Jennifer Powell (Jesse Follet), Carissa Kett (Sadie Follet), Carl Kranz (Boy's Voice, Bully 2), Jay Glazer (Bully 1), Gabriel Levi (Bully 3), Robert Wickstrom (Sentimental Drunk), Stanford Felix (Bartender), Oshin Gregorian (Bar Patron 1), Marcos Vigil (Bar Patron 2, Fantasy Angel), Yanni Amouris (Banjo Player), Amanda Nisenson (Loud Speaker), Eric Cantania (Mr. Nashly), Rob Gildon (Salesman), Ted Huffman (Sales Helper), Henry Stenta (Gruff Clerk), Kyle Barisich (Clerk Assistant), Stanford Felix (Stranger), Offstage Chorus (Yanni Amouris, Stephan Bradley, Amanda Crider, Coralee Gallet, Suzanne Kantorski, Lisa Komara, Reverie Mott, Debra Pruitt, James Schaffner, Erin Smith, Kelly Smith, Giuseppe Spoletini, Marcos Vigil)

SOURCES—The 1957 novel *A Death in the Family* by James Agee and the 1960 play *All the Way Home* by Tad Mosel.

The action occurs in Knoxville, Tennessee, in 1915.

The opera was presented in three acts.

ACT ONE—Prologue ("Every Time the Sun Goes Down"), "Hey, Little Boy," "One Mother," "Gone, the Mountains, the Shady Hills" (Aria), "Damn!" "What a Lovely Night," "They're Here!" "By Golly, That's It!" "Lord, How My Baby Has Grown," "Hi, Mama!"

ACT TWO—"Ah! Child," "Daddy!" "Who Is It?" "Now Who the Hell at This Hour?" "Nashly, Calling Nashly"

ACT THREE—"Why Doesn't He Come?" "Mary, Mother of God," "Who Shall Tell the Sorrow?" "My Daddy's Dead," "Priggish, Mealy-Mouthed," "Look at the Basin"

NOTES—James Agee's unfinished autobiographical novel *A Death in the Family* was published posthumously in 1957 and won the Pulitzer Prize for fiction. In 1960, Tad Mosel dramatized the novel as *All the Way Home*, which won the Pulitzer Prize for drama. In 1963, the play was filmed, and in 1983 William Mayer's operatic version (which used both the novel and the play as its source) premiered at the Minnesota Opera. In 1999, the opera enjoyed its first New York performances in a production by the Manhattan School of Music.

The story told of a closely-knit family living in Knoxville, Tennessee, in 1915; when the father is killed in an automobile accident, his death has a profound impact on those left behind, particularly his little boy and his pregnant wife.

Reviewing the opera in the *New York Times*, Allan Kozinn praised Meyer's strong score: he wrote that Meyer's music had "tuneful accessibility" with orchestrations which were "rich, warm and picturesque," Further, he noted that the libretto and the music offered an "undercurrent of humor" which kept the work from becoming maudlin. Kozinn also noted that while Meyer used a "folk style," he also employed electronic music when appropriate.

Meyer's opera deserves a wider hearing, and hopefully American opera companies will discover its rich, intriguing score. The opera was recorded on a 2-CD set by Albany Records (# TROY-395); the titles of the song sequences are taken from the recording.

363 The Death of Klinghoffer. THEATRE: Brooklyn Academy of Music; OPENING DATE: September 5, 1991; PERFORMANCES: 5; LIBRETTO: Alice Goodman Music: John Adams; DIRECTION: Peter Sellars; CHOREOGRAPHY: Mark Morris; SCENERY: George Tsypin; COSTUMES: Dunya Ramicova; LIGHTING: James F. Ingalls; MUSICAL DIRECTION: Kent Nagano; PRODUCERS: The Brooklyn Academy of Musis, La Monnaie/De Munt, Opera de Lyon, Glyndebourne Productions Ltd., the Los Angeles Festival, and the San Francisco Opera

CAST—James Maddalena (The Captain), Thomas Hammons (The First Officer, Rambo), Janice Felty (Swiss Grandmother, Austrian Woman, British Dancing Girl), Thomas Young (Molqi, Jonathan Rumor), Eugene Perry (Mamoud), Sanford Sylvan (Leon Klinghoffer, Harry Rumor), Stephanie Friedman (Omar), Shelia Nadler (Marilyn Klinghoffer); Dancers: Alyce Bochette, Joe Bowie, Ruth Davidson, Tina Fehlandt, Dan Joyce, Oliva Maridjan-Koop, Clarice Marshall, Rachel Murray, Mark Nimkoff, Kraig Patterson, June Omura, Mireille Radawan-Dana, Guillermo Resto, Keith Sabado, William Wagner, Jean-Guilliaum Weis, Megan Williams The opera was presented in two acts.

ACT ONE—Prologue: "Chorus of Exiled Palestinains" and "Chorus of Exiled Jews," "It Was Just After One-Fifteen" (James Maddalena), "My Grandson Did, Who Was Two" (Janice Felty), "Give These Orders" (Thomas Young), "So I Said to My Grandson" (Janice Felty), "We Are Sorry for You" (Eugene Perry), "Ocean Chorus," "Now It Is Night" (Eugene Perry), "I Think If You Could Talk Like This" (James Maddalena), "I Have Often Reflected That This Is No Ship" (James Maddalena), "I Kept My Distance" (Janice Felty), "Those Birds Flying Above Us" (Eugene Perry), "Night Chorus"

ACT TWO—"Hagar Chorus," "Come Here. Look" (Thomas Young), "I've Never Been a Violent Man" (Sanford Sylvan), "You Are Always Complaining of Your Suffering" (Thomas Hammons), "I Must Have Been Hysterical" (Janice Felty), "It Is as if Our Earthly Life Were Spent Miserably" (Stephanie Friedman), "Desert Chorus," "My One Consolation" (Sheila Nadler), "Klinghoffer's Death," "Every Fifteen Minutes, One More Will Be Shot" (Eugene Perry), "Aria of the Falling Body (Gymnopedie)," "Day Chorus," "Mrs. Klinghoffer, Please Sit Down" (James Maddalena), "You Embraced Them!" (Sheila Nadler)

NOTES—The world premiere of *The Death of Klinghoffer* took place in Brussels on March 19, 1991, when it was presented by the Theatre Royal de la Monnaie for seven performances. The New York premiere took place at the Brooklyn Academy of Music on September 5 of that year.

Like John Adams' and Alice Goodman's previous opera *Nixon in China* (see entry), the work was based on recent news events, in this case the hijacking of the Italian cruise ship *Achille Lauro* in October 1985; during the course of the hijacking, the Palestinian terrorists threw overboard a Jewish-American passenger, the wheelchair-bound Leon Klinghoffer.

The opera ruminated over the events of the three-day period of the hijacking, and in his liner notes for the Elektra Nonesuch Records 2-CD release (# 9-79281-2; the above list of song sequences is taken from the recording), Michael Steinberg wrote that the action of the opera occurs in the present tense for the Klinghoffers and the Palestinian terrorists; in the past tense for the ship's captain and the survivors; and that the chorus stood "outside 'real' time altogether." To add to the layers of the libretto's complexity, the opera didn't take political sides and was in some ways perhaps too neutral about the action which occurred on the stage. Reviewing the New York premiere, Edward Rothstein in the *New York Times* found the music "either atmospheric or emotionally elementary" and the libretto written "in so unmusical a fashion" that surtitles were necessary to understand it. Further, he noted that traditional narrative techniques were instead replaced by "poetic monologues, meditations, and musings," all of which served to provide a certain sense of detachment to the work. Rothstein's comments are certainly valid, but repeated hearings of the opera also reveal a haunting and hypnotic score and a tightly written libretto (which, as Steinberg noted, carefully presents the opera in three levels of time [that is, present, past, and no time]); further, the libretto presents most of the chorus sequences from two points of view (the opening choruses for both Palestinians and Jews; the ocean and desert choruses; and the night and day choruses).

The opera was filmed in 2003, and was later released on DVD by Decca Music Group Limited (# B0001515-09).

364 The Death of Von Richthofen as Witnessed from Earth. "A Play with Flying and Songs"; THEATRE: Newman Theatre/The Public Theatre; OPENING DATE: July 29, 1982; PERFORMANCES: 45; BOOK: Des McAnuff; LYRICS: Des McAnuff; MUSIC: Des McAnuff; DIRECTION: Des McAnuff; CHOREOGRAPHY: Jennifer Muller; SCENERY: Douglas W. Schmidt; COSTUMES: Patricia McGourty; LIGHTING: Richard Nelson; MUSICAL DIRECTION: Michael S. Roth; PRODUCER: The New York Shakespeare Festival (Joseph Papp, Director)

CAST—Robert Westenberg (R. Raymond Barker), Marek Norman (N.C.O. Secull), Robert Joy (Robert Buie), Mark Linn-Baker (William Evans), Brent Barrett (Wolfram Von Richthofen), John Vickery (Manfred Von Richthofen), Jeffrey Jones (Karl Bodenschatz), Sigrid Wurschmidt (Violinst), Susan Berman (Lutanist), Peggy Harmon (Flautist), Mark Petrakis (A German Lance Corporal), Bob Gunton (Hermann Goering); The Flying Circus (Michael Brian, Eric Elice, Davis Gaines, Karl Heist, Tad Ingram, Ken Land, Martha Wingate)

The action occurs in France on the afternoon and evening of April 20 and the morning of April 21, 1918.

The musical was presented in two acts.

ACT ONE—"All I Wanted Was a Cup of Tea" (Robert Westenberg), "Our Red Knight" (Brent Barrett, Michael Brian, Eric Elice, Davis Gaines, Karl Heist, Tad Ingram, Ken Land, Martha Wingate), "Good Luck" (Michael Brian, Eric Elice, Davis Gaines, Karl Heist, Tad Ingram, Ken Land, Martha Wingate), "Speed" (John Vickery), "Sweet Eternity" (Robert Westenberg, Marek Norman), "Take What You Can" (Sigrid Wurschmidt, Susan Berman, Peggy Harmon), "If I Have the Will" (Mark Petrakis), "I've Got a Girl" (Robert Joy, Mark Linn-Baker, Marek Norman, Sigrid Wurschmidt, Susan Berman, Peggy Harmon), "England — The U.K," (Robert Westenberg, Marek Norman, Michael Brian, Eric Elice, Davis Gaines, Karl Heist, Tad Ingram, Ken Land, Martha Wingate), "Save the Last Dance" (Sigrid Wurschmidt, Susan Berman, Peggy Harmon, Bob Gunton, Jeffrey Jones), "If I Have the Will" (reprise) (Mark Petrakis, Sigrid Wurschmidt, Susan Berman, Peggy Harmon), "Here We Are" (John Vickery, Robert Joy, Mark Linn-Baker, Marek Norman, Michael Brian, Eric Elice, Davis Gaines, Karl Heist, Tad Ingram, Ken Land, Martha Wingate), "Congratulations" (Jeffrey Jones, Bob Gunton, Sigrid Wurschmidt, Susan Berman, Peggy Harmon), "Stand Up the Fatherland" (Jeffrey Jones, Bob Gunton, Brent Barrett, Robert Joy, Mark-Linn Baker, Marek Norman, Sigrid Wurschmidt, Susan Berman, Peggy Harmon, Michael Brian, Eric Elice, Davis

Gaines, Kart Heist, Tad Ingram, Ken Land, Martha Wingate)

ACT TWO—"Sitting in the Garden" (Marek Norman, Robert Westenberg, Robert Joy, Mark Linn-Baker, Michael Brian, Eric Elice, Davis Gaines, Karl Heist, Tad Ingram, Ken Land, Martha Wingate), "It's All Right God"/"Four White Horses" (Robert Joy, Mark Linn-Baker, Robert Westenberg, Marek Norman, John Vickery, Michael Brian, Eric Elice, Davis Gaines, Karl Heist, Tad Ingram, Ken Land, Martha Wingate), "1918" (Robert Westenberg, Marek Norman, Robert Joy, Mark Linn-Baker), "Dear Icarus" (Sigrid Wurschmidt, Susan Berman, Peggy Harmon), Sarah (John Vickery), "I Don't Ask About Tomorrow" (Mark Petrakis), "April Twenty One" (Robert Joy, Mark Linn-Baker, Robert Westenberg, Marek Norman, Michael Brian, Eric Elice, Davis Gaines, Karl Heist, Tad Ingram, Ken Land, Martha Wingate), "The Skies Have Gone Dry" (Jeffrey Jones, Bob Gunton, Brent Barrett), "Sarah" (reprise) (Sigrid Wurschmidt, Susan Berman, Peggy Harmon)

NOTES—Like *Billy Bishop Goes to War* (1980; see entry), *The Death of Von Richthofen as Witnessed from Earth* was about a World War I flying ace. But, unlike Billy Bishop, Von Richthofen (here called the Red Dragon, but popularly known as the Red Baron, who had downed eighty Allied planes) is killed in the war.

The lavish musical, apparently the most expensive in the Public's history, had been written by Des McAnuff over a period of six years; perhaps the musical gestated too long, because McAnuff's original conception seems to have been overwhelmed by the details of an overreaching if nonetheless ambitious and epic production. By all accounts the musical was thrillingly staged, with sweeping, cinematic direction and epic theatre effects (pouring rain, exploding bombs, mobile prop airplanes, even flying pianos). But the critics felt the evening lacked dramatic momentum, and they found the story disjointed, confusing, and heavy-handed in its posing the question of what might have happened to Germany if Von Richthofen had decided not to fly on his last mission and had instead assumed a leadership role in Germany's government. And skulking about on the periphery of the plot was a mysterious lance corporal (who turns out to be Hitler).

The critics found much to praise in the musical: a strange, surreal opening in which a pilot falls to his death from the sky while singing "All I Wanted Was a Cup of Tea"; a charming song in which von Richthofen recalls seeing a performance by Sarah Bernhardt when he was a boy; the vaudevillian antics of two American soldiers. But it was all for naught, because McAnuff's ambitious concept was more than his book, lyrics and music could handle. However, he deserves credit for an unusual evening, one that didn't fall into the typical Public Theatre trap of trendy left-wing diatribes and which eschewed the familiar themes of so many Off Broadway (and Broadway) musicals, such as clichéd plots dealing with show-business types. McAnuff was clearly a writer who had something to say, and his lofty vision could comfortably incorporate theatre of the absurd and epic theatre techniques into a viable musical theatre framework. It's a shame he never revisited the work; a revised version might have enjoyed a healthy afterlife in regional and college theatre.

The production boasted an impressive array of talented actors and singers (Brent Barrett, Robert Westenberg, Davis Gaines, Bob Gunton, Jeffrey Jones, and Mark Linn-Baker).

365 Debbie Does Dallas. THEATRE: Jane Street Theatre; OPENING DATE: October 29, 2002; PERFORMANCES: 127; BOOK: Erica Schmidt; MUSICAL CONCEIVED BY Susan L. Schwartz; MUSIC: Andrew Sherman; ADDITIONAL LYRICS AND MUSIC BY Tom Hitt and Jonathan Callicutt; DIRECTION: Erica Schmidt; CHOREOGRAPHY: Jennifer Cody; SCENERY: Christine Jones; COSTUMES: Juman Malouf; LIGHTING: Shelly Sabel; MUSICAL DIRECTION: Tom Hitt; PRODUCERS: The Araca Group, Jam Theatricals, and Waxman William Entertainment; Susan L. Schwartz, Clint Bond, Jr., and Aaron Harnich, Associate Producers

CAST—Paul Fitzgerald (Hardwick, Bradley, Nick, Tim, Ashley, Johnny), Mary Catherine Garrison (Lisa), Caitlin Miller (Tammy), Tricia Paoluccio (Donna), Del Pentecost (Greenfelt, Biddle, Kevin), Sherie Rene Scott (Debbie), Jon Patrick Walker (Rick, Hamilton, Bigtime), Jama Williamson (Roberta)

SOURCE—The 1978 film *Debbie Does Dallas*.

The action occurs somewhere in America in a small suburban town during the present.

The musical was presented in one act.

MUSICAL NUMBERS—"Debbie Benton" (Sherie Rene Scott), "Small Town Girl" (Sherie Rene Scott), "Ten Dollars Closer" (Parts I, II, and III) (Sherie Rene Scott), "The Dildo Rag" (Paul Fitzgerald, Girls), "I Wanna Do Debbie" (Jon Patrick Walker), "Bang, Bang" (Girls), "God Must Love a Fool" (Mary Catherine Garrison), "We Broke Up!" (Sherie Rene Scott), "Dallas ... I'm Coming!" (Sherie Rene Scott)

NOTES—This spoof of the 1970s pornographic film *Debbie Does Dallas* must have seemed like an Off Broadway natural; but it was gone in less than four months. Perhaps many potential audience members thought they were in for an X-rated evening, and thus avoided the musical.

The plot dealt with Debbie, the captain of her small-town high-school cheer-leading team whose dream is to become a Texas Cowgirl Cheerleader. She lacks money for the bus fare to Dallas, but she and her teammates come upon a novel way to earn all sorts of extra cash. And thus Debbie raises enough money to realize her dream.

With its tongue planted firmly in its cheek, the musical laughed at itself, even down to the blurbs on the script (which was published by Dramatists Play Service, Inc., in 2004): "The most important theatrical event of the twenty-first century ... a modern morality tale told as a comic musical of tragic proportions in the language of the rodeo-porno-football circus," The cast album was released by Sh-K-Boom Records (CD # 4002-2). The musical had first been produced at the New York International Fringe Festival in August 2001.

366 The Decameron. "A Musical"; THEATRE: East 74th Street Theatre; OPENING DATE: April 12, 1961; PERFORMANCES: 39; BOOK: Yvonne Tarr; LYRICS: Yvonne Tarr; MUSIC: Edward Earle; DIRECTION: Burry Fredrik; CHOREOGRAPHY: Edward Earle; SCENERY: John Conklin; COSTUMES: Frank Thompson; LIGHTING: Ian Cadenhead; PRODUCERS: Selma Tamber and William Tarr

CAST—Jan Miner (Pampinea), Louis Edmonds (Filostrato), Bob Roman (Dioneo), DeAnn Mears (Filomena), Alice Scott (Neifile), Betty McNamara (Lauretta), Ralph Hoffman (Folco), Sally Sewall (Maddelena), Robert Simpson (Pamfilo), Renee Byrns (Ninetta), Athan Karras (Alberto), Lois Grandi (Dianora), Frank Piper (Antonio), George Mamales (Torello)

SOURCE—Giovanni Boccaccio's stories from *The Decameron* (approximately one-hundred stories, written circa 1348-1353).

The action occurs in 1348 on Pampinea's country estate outside the city of Florence, Italy.

MUSICAL NUMBERS (division of acts and song assignments unknown; songs are listed in performance order)—Prologue, "1348," "Talk," "Deceive Me," "Ballad of Tancred," "Golden Goblet," "What's Wrong with Me?," "Women!," "Love Is Paradise," "I Know, I Know," "Cuckold's Delight," "Barnabo," "The Pirate's Song," "Nightingale," "Come Sweet Love," Finale

NOTES—This was the first of two musical failures based on *The Decameron* (see entry for *Boccaccio* [1975]). The musical dealt with a group of people fleeing the Black Death, the plague which killed an estimated one-third to one-half of the population of Europe during the fourteenth century. They seek safe haven in a villa outside Florence, and in order to pass the time they entertain one another with earthy tales of love.

Howard Taubman in the *New York Times* felt the evening offered more diversion "than some of the higher-priced musicals in town," and he praised the "agreeable melodic vein" of Edward Earle's score, which created an "agreeable lyrical atmosphere." He also liked the "ingratiating" choreography, the "colorful" sets, and the "handsome" costumes. Of the songs, he singled out the "smooth melody" of "Come Sweet Love." Two of *The Decameron*'s cast members frequently worked on the stage, but found their greatest success on television.

Louis Edmonds had created the role of Maximilian in the original Broadway production of *Candide* in 1956, and he stayed active on and Off Broadway, including a leading role in *Ernest in Love* (1960; see entry). But he's best known as the haughtier-than-thou Roger Collins in ABC's long-running daytime Gothic soap opera *Dark Shadows* (1966-1971).

Jan Miner became famous for her recurring character in a long-running television commercial. She played the manicurist Madge ("Your hands are soaking in it!"), The Palmolive Liquid Soap Girl.

367 The Decline and Fall of the Entire World as Seen Through the Eyes of Cole Porter Revisited (March 1965). THEATRE: Square East; OPENING DATE: March 30, 1965; PERFORMANCES: 273; CONTINUITY, SPECIAL VOCAL ARRANGEMENTS, AND GRAND FINALE WRITTEN BY: Bud McCreery; LYRICS: Cole Porter; MUSIC: Cole Porter; DIRECTION: Ben Bagley; CHOREOGRAPHY: Vernon Lusby; SCENERY: Collage paintings by Shirley Kaplan; projections photographed by Wallace Litwin; COSTUMES: Charles Fatone; LIGHTING: Jules Fisher; MUSICAL DIRECTION: Skip Redwine

CAST—KAYE BALLARD, HAROLD LANG, Carmen Alvarez, William Hickey, Elmarie Wendel

The revue was presented in two acts.

ACT ONE—"I Introduced" (from *Hitchy-Koo of 1919*) (Harold Lang, with Kaye Ballard, Carmen Alvarez, Elmarie Wendel), "Let's Do It, Let's Fall in Love"/"Don't Look at Me That Way" (both from *Paris*, 1928), "Wake Up and Dream"/"I'm a Gigolo" (both from *Wake Up and Dream*, London, March 1929; New York, December 1929) ("Gigolo" performed by William Hickey), "How's Your Romance?"/"I've Got You on My Mind" (both from *Gay Divorce*, 1932), "The Leader of a Big-Time Band" (*Something for the Boys*, 1943) (Kaye Ballard, Carmen Alvarez, Elmarie Wendel), "Red Hot and Blue!"/"Ridin' High"/"Down in the Depths (on the 90th Floor)" (all from *Red Hot and Blue!*, 1936) ("Depths" performed by Kaye Ballard), "Give Him the Oo-La-La" (*DuBarry Was a Lady*, 1939) (Elmarie Wendel), "Find Me a Primitive Man"/"I Worship You"/"The Tale of the Oyster" (all from *Fifty Million Frenchmen*, 1929

NOTE—"I Worship You" was deleted from *Frenchmen* during its pre-Broadway tryout; "The Tale of the Oyster" was deleted from the New York production soon after its opening.), "Let's Fly Away"/"I Happen to Like New York" (both from *The New Yorkers*, 1930) ("New York" performed by Harold Lang), "What Shall I Do?" (*You Never Know*, 1938) (Carmen Alvarez, with Harold Lang and William Hickey), "Most Gentlemen Don't Like

Love"/"Tomorrow" (both from *Leave It to Me!*, 1939) ("Gentlemen" performed by Kaye Ballard, Carmen Alvarez, and Elmarie Wendel; "Tomorrow" performed by entire company)

ACT TWO—"Come On In"/"But in the Morning, No" (both from *DuBarry Was a Lady*, 1939), "Make It Another Old-Fashioned, Please"/"I'm Throwing a Ball Tonight"/"I've Still Got My Health" (all from *Panama Hattie*, 1940) ("Old-Fashioned" performed by Carmen Alvarez), "Farming" (*Let's Face It!*, 1941) (Company), "I Loved Him, but He Didn't Love Me" (*Wake Up and Dream*, London, 1929; the song wasn't used in the New York production, which opened in December 1929) (Kaye Ballard) "Something for the Boys"/"I'm in Love with a Soldier Boy"/"By the Mississinewah" (all from *Something for the Boys*, 1943), "Girls" (*Mexican Hayride*, 1944), "When I Was a Little Cuckoo" (*Seven Lively Arts*, 1944), Finale (medley from various Cole Porter musicals) (Company): "My Mother Would Love You" (*Panama Hattie*, 1940), "Easy to Love" (1936 film *Born to Dance*), "I've Got You Under My Skin" (1936 film *Born To Dance*), "My Heart Belongs to Daddy" (*Leave It to Me!*, 1938), "Friendship" (*DuBarry Was a Lady*, 1939), "Well, Did You Evah!" (*DuBarry Was a Lady*, 1939), "It's All Right with Me" (*Can-Can*, 1953), "Get Out of Town" (*Leave It to Me!*, 1938), "It's De-Lovely" (*Red Hot and Blue!*, 1936), "Ev'rything I Love" (*Let's Face It!*, 1941), "Ev'ry Time We Say Goodbye" (*Seven Lively Arts*, 1944), "Another Op'nin', Another Show" (*Kiss Me Kate*, 1948), "Always True to You in My Fashion" (*Kiss Me Kate*, 1948), "C'est Magnifique" (*Can-Can*, 1953), "The Physician" (*Nymph Errant*, 1933 [London musical]), "Just One of Those Things" (*Jubilee*, 1935), "What Is This Thing Called Love?" (*Wake Up and Dream*, London, March 1929; New York, December 1929), "Love for Sale" (*The New Yorkers*, 1930), "You're the Top" (*Anything Goes*, 1934), "Begin the Beguine" (*Jubilee*, 1935), "The Laziest Gal in Town" (non-show song written in 1927; it may have later been heard in the nightclub revue presented at Edmond Sayag's Ambassadeurs Cafe; in 1950, the song was performed by Marlene Dietrich in the Alfred Hitchcock film *Stage Fright*)

NOTES—This early composer-tribute revue at least had the virtue of utilizing mostly unknown Cole Porter gems. Except for the finale, the songs were truly offbeat. Bagley ignored Porter standards (such as "Night and Day" and "Begin the Beguine") for such esoterica as "The Tale of the Oyster" and "Give Him the Oo-La-La," and for this reason alone the revue was worth seeing. Unfortunately, many composer-tribute revues (such as *Leonard Bernstein's Theatre Songs*; see entry) usually offered only the most obvious material, and rarely strayed from the well-worn path of familiar standards. Because *Decline* was so popular, another edition was offered the following season (see entry), Columbia Records recorded the highlights of the first edition (as well as the multi-song finale) on a one-LP cast album (# 549); a CD version included about a dozen bonus tracks by other performers, some of whom had later appeared in the revue during its two New York editions.

Sadly, the revue was Elmarie Wendel's last New York appearance, but the sparkling performer later enjoyed a busy career in television with a continuing role in the series *3rd Rock from the Sun* as well as appearances in such series as *Empty Nest*, *Murder, She Wrote*, *Murphy Brown*, and *Seinfeld*. Song assignments for some of the numbers are unclear, and the above list reflects the credits as they appear on the cast album.

368 The Decline and Fall of the Entire World as Seen Through the Eyes of Cole Porter Revisited (a/k/a New Cole Porter Revue) (December 1965). THEATRE: Square East; OPENING DATE: December 22, 1965; PERFORMANCES: 76; CONTINUITY: Bud McCreery Lyrics: Cole Porter; MUSIC: Cole Porter; DIRECTION: Ben Bagley; "new edition staged" by Buddy Schwab; CHOREOGRAPHY: New edition choreographed by Buddy Schwab; SCENERY: Collage paintings by Shirley Kaplan; projections photographed by Wallace Litwin; COSTUMES: Charles Fatone; LIGHTING: Jules Fisher; MUSICAL DIRECTION: Everett Gordon; PRODUCER: Square East

CAST—BOBBY SHORT, DODY GOODMAN, DANNY MEEHAN, Carol Arthur, Jane Manning, Virginia Vestoff

NOTES—The second edition of Ben Bagley's salute to Cole Porter was the last of the Bagley revues. No songs were listed in the program, but the song offerings were probably similar to the numbers heard in the first edition (see entry).

Note that cabaret legend Bobby Short was in the cast. His theatre appearances were few and far between. He made his theatrical debut in a 1956 New York City Center revival of *Kiss Me, Kate* (1948) which starred Kitty Carlisle, David Atkinson, and Barbara Ruick; he sang "Too Darn Hot" in the production. He also appeared in Sidney Kingsley's 1962 Broadway play *Night Life*, which took place in an exclusive New York key club (Short played the club's pianist). His last stage appearance was in the legendary *Black Broadway* (1980; see entry), which celebrated Black performers from Broadway's past and present. Short had also been seen in the 1951 film version of Harold Rome's revue *Call Me Mister* (he was featured in the "Going Home Train" sequence).

369 A Delightful Season. THEATRE: Gramercy Arts Theatre; OPENING DATE: September 28, 1960; PERFORMANCES: Unknown; BOOK: Don Allan Clayton; LYRICS: Don Allan Clayton; MUSIC: Don Allan Clayton; DIRECTION: Bill Butler; SCENERY: Robin Wagner; COSTUMES: Domingo A. Rodriguez; LIGHTING: Robin Wagner; MUSICAL DIRECTION: Jay Brower; PRODUCERS: New Enterprises (Allan Stern and Gerard A. Burke) in association with Nicholas Pavlik and Jerri Kenneally

CAST—Karen Thorsell (Lady Windermere), Edward Zimmerman (Parker), Nick Todd (Lord Darlington), Jane Lambert (Duchess of Berwick), Kay Brower (Lady Agatha Carlisle), Donald Symington (Lord Windermere), The Four Mrs. Plymdales (Frances Peter, Ruth Livingston, Barbary Newborn, Estelle Ritchie), Jonathan Taylor (Mr. Dumby), William Eddy (Mr. Rutherford), Nik Belong (Count Hall), James Baker (Sir JamesRoyston), Frederic Mueller (Mr. James Hopper), Charles Frasch (Lord Augustus Lorton), Brian Desmond (Mr. Cecil Graham), Joan Copeland (Mrs. Erlynne)

SOURCE—The 1892 play *Lady Windermere's Fan* by Oscar Wilde.

NOTES—The previous May had seen a modest reception for *Ernest in Love* (see entry), which had been adapted from Oscar Wilde's *The Importance of Being Earnest*. The musical played only a few months, but its witty lyrics and melodic score were recorded by Columbia Records and it occasionally appeared in summer stock and community theatre productions. But Don Allan Clayton's *A Delightful Season*, an adaptation of Wilde's *Lady Windermere's Fan*, was a quick failure. Howard Taubman in the *New York Times* found the musical "tepid Wilde and colorless Clayton," and warned that "those who venture on a style as gleaming and fragile as Wilde's do so at their own peril." There's no information available on the number of acts or the titles of the musical numbers, but Taubman singled out two songs for praise, "Yes, Mamma" and "Who's the Girl."

Even Noel Coward found disappointment with his own musical adaptation of the play. *After the Ball* opened at the Globe Theatre in London on June 10, 1954, and, despite a sparkling cast, a sumptuous production, and a memorable score (with perhaps "Something on a Tray" the highlight), the musical managed only 188 performances. Fifty years later, the musical was produced Off Off Broadway in a limited engagement by the Irish Repertory Theatre (see entry).

Besides entries for *Ernest in Love* (which also references other musical versions of *The Importance of Being Earnest*) and *After the Ball*, see entries for *Dorian* (which also references *Dorian Gray*, another musical adaptation of the material [both musicals opened within a month of one another in 1990]) and *Dorian Gray*, another musical adaptation (which opened in 1996).

For musicals about Wilde's life, see entries for *Dear Oscar* and *It's Wilde!* as well as *Utterly Wilde!!!*, a one-man musical biography.

370 Dementos. THEATRE: Theatre Guinevere; OPENING DATE: October 13, 1983; PERFORMANCES: 42; BOOK: Sebastian Stuart and Robert I.; LYRICS: Robert I.; MUSIC: Marc Shaiman; DIRECTION: Theodore Pappas; CHOREOGRAPHY: Theodore Pappas; SCENERY: Loy Arcenas; COSTUMES: Steven L. Birnbaum; LIGHTING: Debra J. Kletter; PRODUCER: The Production Company (Norman Rene, Artistic Director)

CAST—Joanne Beretta (Irene), Pi Douglass (Maria), Jane Galloway (Marcie), Annie Golden (Spike), Patrick Jude (Ruby), Jimmy Justice (Leon), Roger Lawson (Charles), Charlaine Woodard (Precious)

The action occurs in the Hotel Del Rio, a welfare hotel in New York City.

The musical was presented in two acts (song assignments unknown).

ACT ONE—"Crazy Crazy," "Hotel Del Rio," "I Saw God," "Hustlers Hookers Whores," "It's a Job," "Lowlife," "Dreams," "I'd Like to Spray the World," "High Class Bums," "Just Like You"

ACT TWO—"Woolworth's," "Never Had a Home," "Let Me Out," "What If," "New York Is a Party," "Shopping Bag Man," "God Save the City"

NOTES—The Off Off Broadway musical *Dementos* was an early work by Marc Shaiman.

The plot dealt with a group of misfits (two prostitutes, a pimp, a hustler, a bag lady, a drifter, and a transvestite) who live in a rundown welfare hotel in New York. Stephen Holden in the *New York Times* noted the "lively" evening was a series of "confessional monologues" which are spoken or sung by the motley group to a suburban liberal who has come into their lives.

Holden asked whether it was possible to create a musical based on "abject human misery" without sentimentalizing the subject, and his answer was a "very qualified yes." He praised Shaiman's "stylistically diverse" score, and singled out three songs ("New York Is a Party" [Charlaine Woodard], "Dreams" [Patrick Jude], and "Let Me Out" [Annie Golden]). (The musical didn't have a live orchestra, and so the performers sang their numbers to pre-recorded music.) "New York Is a Party" was later heard in the 1984 revue *Harlem Nocturne* (see entry).

371 Demi-Dozen. "A New Inconoclastic Intimacy in Two Acts"; THEATRE: Upstairs at the Downstairs; OPENING DATE: October 11, 1958; PERFORMANCES: 500; SKETCHES: Bill Dana; other writers unknown; LYRICS: Michael Brown, Tom Jones, Carolyn Leigh, Bud McCreery, Portia Nelson, Harvey Schmidt, Jay Thompson, and Joan Wile; MUSIC: Michael Brown, Cy Coleman, Michael Hughes, Bud McCreery, Portia Nelson, Harvey Schmidt, and Jay Thompson; DIRECTION: John Heawood; PRODUCER: Julius Monk; MUSICAL DIRECTION: Stan Keen and Gordon Connell "at the Plural Pianos"

CAST—Jean Arnold, Ceil Cabot, Jane Connell, Jack Fletcher, George Hall, Gerry Matthews

The revue was presented in two acts.

ACT ONE—"Grand Opening" (lyric by Tom Jones, music by Harvey Schmidt) (Company), "Yes, Siree" (lyric by Joan Wile, music by Michael Hughes) (Ceil Cabot), "Mr. (Mister) Off-Broadway" (lyric by Tom Jones, music by Harvey Schmidt) (Jack Fletcher) "You Fascinate Me So" (lyric by Carolyn Leigh, music by Cy Coleman) (Jean Arnold) "Conference Call, or Gray Flannel & How It Grew" (sketch by Bill Dana) (Jean Arnold, Gerry Matthews, George Hall, Jack Fletcher) "The Holy Man and the New Yorker" (lyric by Tom Jones, music by Harvey Schmidt) (Gerry Matthews) "The Race of the Lexington Avenue Express" (lyric by Tom Jones, music by Harvey Schmidt) (Jane Connell) "Sunday in New York" (lyric and music by Portia Nelson) (Ceil Cabot, Gerry Matthews), "The Intellectuals' Rag" (lyric and music by Jay Thompson) (Company)

ACT TWO—"A Seasonal Sonata" (lyric by Tom Jones, music by Harvey Schmidt) (Company) "One and All" (lyric and music by Harvey Schmidt) (George Hall) "Portofino" (lyric and music by Michael Brown) (Ceil Cabot, Jane Connell, Jean Arnold, Gerry Matthews, George Hall) "Guess Who Was There" (lyric and music by Bud McCreery) (Jack Arnold), "Third Avenue El" (lyric and music by Michael Brown) (Ceil Cabot, Jane Connell, Gerry Matthews, Jack Fletcher) "Statehood Hula" (lyric by Tom Jones, music by Harvey Schmidt) (Ceil Cabot) Grand Finale ("Monk's Merrie Minstrel Show!") (lyric and music by Bud McCreery) (Company)

NOTES—The opening number was indeed a "Grand Opening" because *Demi-Dozen* marked the first of Julius Monk's cabaret revues to be performed in the new West 56th Street location for Upstairs at the Downstairs (37 West 56th Street, to be precise), This revue was chock full of memorable goodies, including no less than six songs by Tom Jones and Harvey Schmidt, and one number with both lyric and music by Jones.

Among their contributions was the fascinating "A Seasonal Sonata," which presented a skewed look at the four seasons through the eyes of mostly jaded New Yorkers. Throughout their careers, Jones and Schmidt would return to the concept of the seasons, and how they affect us psychologically as well as physically. The seasons are important in both *The Fantasticks* (1960; see entry) and *Celebration* (1969). And, of course, hot, dry summer weather was the catalyst for the plot of their first Broadway musical *110 in the Shade* (1963), which took place from sunrise to midnight of "another hot day." Even their Broadway hit *I Do! I Do!* (1966; see entry for Off Broadway revival) found an aging Agnes looking back on youth when "young girls are April."

"Mr. Off-Broadway" was their affectionate salute to Off Broadway performers, theatres (among those mentioned in the lyric are the Cherry Lane and the Theatre de Lys), musicals (*Sandhog* was singled out), and dramas. The song was later heard in Jones and Schmidt's 1997 tribute-revue *The Show Goes On* (see entry) and was recorded on that show's cast album.

The highlight of the revue was the funniest comedy song ever written by the team and possibly the most amusing comedy song in the entire canon of musical theatre. The madcap "Statehood Hula" was sung in slightly pidgin-English by a seemingly naïve Hawaiian girl who wants her homeland to become the fiftieth state. However, for a "simple" native girl she's uncannily aware of Upper East Side culture, what with her knowing references to the likes of Lester Lanin. She also informs us that she makes a "marvelous lei," and could take us to a beach "where people naked go/Like Joshua Logan show." The song was devastatingly performed by Ceil Cabot, who was one of the welcome fixtures in Monk's revues.

Two ballads in the revue were also standouts: Portia Nelson's "Sunday in New York" and Carolyn Leigh and Cy Coleman's "You Fascinate Me So," The latter became a minor standard.

One sketch stood out in particular: Bill Dana's "Conference Call, or Gray Flannel & How It Grew" was a send-up of corporate-culture-speak, and it serves as a humorous time capsule of the business world of the 1950s, a world which was endlessly dramatized in the era's books, television dramas, and films (e.g., *The Man in the Gray Flannel Suit, Executive Suite, Patterns, The Best of Everything, The Power and the Prize, Woman's World, The Apartment*). "Conference Call" was also used in *Bits and Pieces XIV* (1964; see entry).

The revue also included a "Trinity of Requested Reprises" from earlier Monk revues: "Third Avenue El," from *Four Below* (1956; see entry), and which had also been heard in *The Littlest Revue* (1956; see entry); "Guess Who Was There," from *Son of Four Below* (1956; see entry); and "Portofino," from *Take Five* (1957; see entry). The latter can also be heard on Jerry Orbach's collection of Off Broadway songs (where it is erroneously attributed to *Dressed to the Nines*).

"Guess Who Was There" was later performed in the Chicago revue *Medium Rare* (1960), and "The Holy Man and the New Yorker" was reprised in the next Monk revue, *Pieces- of-Eight* (1959; see entry), "The Race of the Lexington Express" was later used in Rod Warren's revue *Below the Belt* (1966; see entry).

Demi-Dozen was recorded by Offbeat Records (LP # 0-4015), and the song and sketch list above is taken from information on the cast album.

"Mr. Off-Broadway," "The Holy Man and the New Yorker," and "A Seasonal Sonata" were later heard in Schmidt and Jones' Off Broadway *Portfolio Revue*; see entry. For a complete list of Julius Monk's revues, see entry for *Four Below*; also see Appendix Q.

372 The Derby (1980; John Braden). THEATRE: Theatre for the New City; OPENING DATE: January 31, 1980; PERFORMANCES: 12; BOOK: Barry Arnold; LYRICS: John Braden; MUSIC: John Braden; DIRECTION: John Vaccaro; CHOREOGRAPHY: Arthur Faria; SCENERY: Donald Eastman; COSTUMES: Max Hager; LIGHTING: Pat Collins; MUSICAL DIRECTION: Michael Dansicker; PRODUCER: Theatre for the New City (Bartenieff/Field)

CAST—Christine Anderson (Marge Brandt), Dick Bonelle (Lucky McCormick), Lou Criscuolo (Jim Streeter), Tyra Ferrell (Charlese Johnson), Ben Harney (Millard "The Rooster" Cox), Lloyd David Hart (Ernie Parker), Bonnie Hellman (Priscilla "Tiny" Wilson), Mark Kapitan (Cliff Gibbons), Elizabeth Lindsay (Dixie Dalton), Marcia McClain (Joy Costa), William Parry (Ron Wallinski)

The musical was presented in two acts.

ACT ONE—"Any Town" (Company), "That's the Way They Like It" (Lou Criscuolo, William Parry, Ben Harney, Mark Kapitan, Lloyd David Hart), "Flying" (Company), "Skate Away" (Tyra Ferrell, Elizabeth Lindsay, Marcia McClain, Bonnie Hellman), "Since When?" (Christine Anderson), "Show Me the Man" (Elizabeth Lindsay, Tyra Ferrell, Christine Anderson, Bonnie Hellman, Marcia McClain), "It Wouldn't Be So Bad" (Marcia McClain, William Parry, Christine Anderson, Dick Bonelle), "This Is Where I Belong" (Dick Bonelle, Company)

ACT TWO—"Helluva Night" (Company), "I'm Gonna Get Out Alive" (William Parry), "On the Inside" (Bonnie Hellman), "Dirty" (Company), "He's Not There" (Dick Bonelle, Christine Anderson), "Any Town" (reprise) (Company)

NOTES—The Off Off Broadway musical *The Derby*, which was about the roller derby, played for a limited engagement of three weekends at the Theatre for a New City.

Ben Harney and William Parry were among the cast members; Harney later won the Tony Award for Best Actor in a Musical for *Dreamgirls* (1981), and Parry created roles in two Stephen Sondheim musicals (*Sunday in the Park with George* [1984] and *Assassins* [1991]; see entries).

A revised version of *The Derby* resurfaced twenty-seven years later, when *Roller Derby* was presented for six performances at the 2007 New York Musical Theatre Festival beginning on September 20, 2007, at the Ailey Citigroup Theatre. The book was by Barry Arnold, and the music by John Braden; this time around, the lyrics were credited to both Braden and Arnold, and legendary Broadway orchestrator Harold Wheeler contributed additional music. (The production was dedicated to the memory of Braden, who had died in 1987.) *BroadwayWorld.com* reported that the press notes for the production indicated the plot, which took place in 1972, revolved around a derby rookie who hopes to take the title of Roller Derby Queen from the sport's "beloved but aging star."

373 The Derby (1981; Robert MacDougall). THEATRE: New York Stageworks; OPENING DATE: September 17, 1981; PERFORMANCES: Unknown; PLAY: Michael McClure; MUSIC: Robert MacDougall; DIRECTION: Angela Paton; CHOREOGRAPHY: John Medeiros; SCENERY: Ariel; COSTUMES: Ariel; LIGHTING: Terry Alan Smith; PRODUCERS: New York Stage Works in association with Berkeley Stage Company

CAST—Susan Hunter (Thought Two), Zita-Ann Geoffroy (Thought One), Kevin Reilley (King Lear), Maggie Schmidt (Mata Hari), Janice Kay Young (W), Laurence Roth (Patrick), Jill Merzon (Alpha Mouse), Paul Fegan (Beta Mouse)

NOTES—Michael McClure's most well-known play is his controversial *The Beard* (1967); the Off Off Broadway play *The Derby* appears to have been a whimsical piece (its characters included King Lear, Mata Hari, and two mice) with incidental music and dance.

The script had been privately published in 1974 in an (extremely!) limited edition of twenty copies.

The Derby was McClure's third play in three years to deal with mice in one way or another (his *Josephine the Mouse Singer* opened at the WPA Theatre on November 30, 1978, for twelve performances, and in 1978 his operetta *Minnie Mouse and the Tap-Dancing Buddha* premiered in San Francisco).

374 Desire Under the Elms. "An American Folk Opera"; THEATRE: City Center Theatre; OPENING DATE: January 11, 1989; PERFORMANCES: 3; LIBRETTO: Joe Masteroff; MUSIC: Edward Thomas; DIRECTION: David Gately; SCENERY: Michael Anania; COSTUMES: Gregg Barnes; LIGHTING: Kirk Bookman; MUSICAL DIRECTION: Leigh Gibbs Gore; PRODUCER: The New York Opera Repertory Theatre

CAST—Robert Paul Heimann (Simeon), William Livingston (Peter), James Schwisow (Eben Cabot), Nicholas Solomon (Ephraim Cabot), Judy Kaye (Abbie Putnam Cabot), Burton Fitzpatrick (Sheriff), Ensemble (Colette Black, Jim Curtin, Joe Fitzpatrick, Debbi Fuhrman, John Lynch, Heidi Mollenhauer, Stephanie Paul, Jacob Terry)

SOURCE—The 1924 play *Desire Under the Elms* by Eugene O'Neill.

The action occurs on Eben Cabot's farm in New England.

The opera was performed in three acts.

NOTES—Edward Thomas, the composer of *Desire Under the Elms*, had also written the score for the ambitious 1967 musical *Mata Hari*, which closed prior to New York but was later produced Off Broadway as *Ballad for a Firing Squad* (1968; see entry) and then Off Off Broadway as *Mata Hari* (1996; see entry), Joe Masteroff had written the books for the Broadway musicals *She Loves Me* (1963) and *Cabaret* (1966) as well as the light but ingratiating 1959 Broadway comedy *The Warm Peninsula*.

The opera had been developed during the 1978 National Music Theatre Conference at the Eugene O'Neill Theatre Center in Waterford, Connecticut. The City Center production marked the New York premiere of the work. The opera was recorded in 2002 on a 2-CD set released by Naxos Records (# 8.669001-02); for the recording, Jerry Hadley sang the role of Eben Cabot.

In reviewing the New York production, Allan Kozinn in the *New York Times* found Masteroff's libretto faithful to the original drama, but noted Thomas' score was perhaps too cautious and lacked variety. But he praised some "lovely" set pieces for the character of Abbie, and singled out in particular a "simple but sweetly melodic lullabye" in the second act.

375 Dessa Rose. THEATRE: The Mitzi E. Newhouse Theatre/Lincoln Center Theatre; OPENING DATE: March 21, 2005; PERFORMANCES: 80; BOOK: Lynn Ahrens; LYRICS: Lynn Ahrens; MUSIC: Stephen Flaherty; DIRECTION: Graciela Daniele; CHOREOGRAPHY: Graciela Daniele; SCENERY: Loy Arcenas; COSTUMES: Toni-Leslie James; LIGHTING: Jules Fisher and Peggy Eisenhauer; MUSICAL DIRECTION: David Holcenberg; PRODUCER: Lincoln Center Theatre (Andre Bishop and Bernard Gersten, Directors)

CAST—LaChanze (Dessa Rose), Rachel York (Ruth), Tina Fabrique (Rose, House Slave, Ada, Auntie Chole), Rebecca Eichenberger (Ruth's Mother, Mrs. Steele, Susannah), Kecia Lewis (Dorcas, Field Hand, Gemina, Janet), Eric Jordan Young (Kaine, Field Hand, Philip), David Hess (Sheriff Hughes, Trader Wilson, Bertie Sutton, Parishioner, Auctioneer), Michael Hayden (Adam Nehemiah), William Parry (Robert Steele, Parishioner, Auctioneer, Mr. Oscar, Sheriff Pine), Norm Lewis (Nathan), James Stovall (Harker, Joseph), Soara-Joye Ross (Field Hand, Parishioner, House Slave, Annabel, Joy)

SOURCE—The 1986 novel *Dessa Rose* by Sherley Anne Williams.

The action occurs in various locales in and around Charleston, South Carolina, and Linden, Alabama, during the summer of 1847.

The musical was presented in two acts.

ACT ONE—Prologue: "We Are Descended" (LaChanze, Rachel York, Company), "Comin' Down the Quarters" (Eric Jordan Young, Charleston Field Hands), "Old Banjar" (Eric Jordan Young, LaChanze), "Something of My Own" (LaChanze), "Ink" (Michael Hayden), "The Gold Band"/"Little Star" (Charleston Field Hands, Tina Fabrique, James Stovall, William Parry, Rebecca Eichenberger, David Hess, Michael Hayden, Norm Lewis, LaChanze), "Ladies" (Rebecca Eichenberger, Kecia Lewis), "Bertie's Waltz" (David Hess, Rachel York), "At the Glen" (Rachel York), "Capture the Girl" (Michael Hayden), "Fly Away" (David Hess, William Parry, Soara-Joye Ross, Rebecca Eichenbeger, LaChanze, Michael Hayden, Norm Lewis, Linden Field Hands), "Terrible" (Tina Fabrique, Soara-Joye Ross, Field Hands, Michael Hayden, Norm Lewis, James Stovall, Rachel York), "Twelve Children" (LaChanze)

ACT TWO—"Noah's Dove" (Norm Lewis, Rachel York, James Stovall, Eric Jordan Young, Kecia Lewis, Soara-Joye Ross, Tina Fabrique), "Fly Away" (reprise) (Kecia Lewis, Soara-Joye Ross, James Stovall, Eric Jordan Young, Tina Fabrique, Norm Lewis), "The Scheme" (Norm Lewis, James Stovall), "In the Bend of My Arm" (Eric Jordan Young, LaChanze, Rachel York, Norm Lewis, Michael Hayden), "Better If I Died" (Rachel York, LaChanze, Company), "Ten Petticoats" (Rebecca Eichenberger, Kecia Lewis, Rachel York), "Just Over the Line" (LaChanze, Rachel York, Norm Lewis, David Hess, Kecia Lewis, Tina Fabrique, Soara-Joye Ross, James Stovall, Eric Jordan Young, Michael Hayden), "A Pleasure" (Rachel York, William Parry, LaChanze), "White Milk and Red Blood" (Kecia Lewis), Epilogue: "We Are Descended" (reprise) (LaChanze, Rachel York, Michael Hayden, Company)

NOTES—*Dessa Rose* was the fourth in a series of recent musicals produced at Lincoln Center which in one way or another dealt with civil rights (Black, Jewish, gay, feminist); all were failures (the others were: *Parade* [1998, Vivian Beaumont Theatre]; *Marie Christine* [1999, Vivian Beaumont]; *A Man of No Importance* [see entry; 2002, Newhouse Theatre]). *Parade* offered a distinguished score by Jason Robert Brown, and Michael John LaChiusa's *Marie Christine* had many powerful moments; but *Dessa Rose* and *A Man of No Importance*, both with lyrics by Lynn Ahrens and music by Stephen Flaherty, lacked the musical muscle to make much of an impression.

(Similarly, *Ragtime*, another Ahrens and Flaherty musical which dealt in part with civil rights, was a major disappointment; opening on Broadway in 1998, the overproduced spectacle, filled with bombastic and often Euro-Pop-flavored power ballads, seemed to be an unending litany of politically correct affectations; it was the kind of evening in which the audience was apparently expected to sympathize with a character who attempts to murder her baby and another who becomes a terrorist and threatens to blow up a New York City building.) *Dessa Rose* dealt with the friendship of a Black woman (the title character) who leads a slave uprising and a White woman who gives refuge to the slaves.

Jacques Le Sourd in the *Journal News* found *Dessa Rose* "painfully turgid ... like a work from the age of Soviet Socialist Realism"; he further noted the musical was "so politically correct that it could make your teeth hurt." Frank Scheck in the *New York Post* wrote that the "plodding" *Dessa Rose* offered a "pedestrian score ... melodically unmemorable ... lyrically awkward," and felt the evening was like "an onerous high school assignment." Charles Isherwood in the *New York Times* described the musical as "inert ... a long, dreary sermon in song," and noted that the "constant lecturing" reinforced the musical's "faintly medicinal flavor." On the other hand, Michael Kuchwara of *Yahoo! News* and the *Associated Press* praised the score and its "robust collection of ... recitative, spirituals, ragtime and anthems." The cast recording of *Dessa Rose* was released on a 2-CD set by Jay Records (# CDJAY2-1392).

376 Diamond Studs. "The Life of Jesse James/An Outlaw Musical"; THEATRE: Westside Theatre; OPENING DATE: January 14, 1975; PERFORMANCES: 232; BOOK: Jim Wann; LYRICS: Bland Simpson and Jim Wann; MUSIC: Bland Simpson and Jim Wann; DIRECTION: John L. Haber; CHOREOGRAPHY: Patricia Birch; SCENERY: Larry King ("Design Adviser"); COSTUMES: Possibly Larry King ("Design Adviser"); LIGHTING: Possibly Burl Hash; PRODUCERS: The Chelsea Theatre Center of Brooklyn (Robert Kalfin, Artistic Director; Michael David, Executive Director; Burl Hash, Productions Director)

CAST—Jim Wann (Jesse James), Bland Simpson (C.C. Porkbarrel), John Foley (Bob Ford), Mike Sheehan (Allen Pinkerton), Jan Davidson (Major Edwards), Tommy Thompson (Zerelda James, Cole Younger), Jim Watson (Jim Younger), Bill Hicks (Bob Younger), Mike Craver (Berny Greencheese), Scott Bradley (William Clark Quantrill), Joyce Cohen (Zee James), Rick Simpson (Frank James), Madelyn Smoak (Belle Starr), Frances Tamburro (Tourist's Wife), Saloon People (Edith Davis, Anne Gilland, Abigail Lewis, Connie O'Connell, Penny Peyser, Bill Smith), The following cast members comprised the Southern States Fidelity Choir: Jim Wann (guitar), Bland Simpson (piano), John Foley (12-string guitar), Mike Sheehan (percussion), and Jan Davidson (bass), The following in the cast comprised the Red Clay Ramblers: Tommy Thompson (banjo), Jim Watson (mandolin), Bill Hicks (fiddle), Mike Craver (piano), Many of the performers also played a variety of minor roles (Engineer, Reporter, Newshawk, Huckster, Pappy Samuels, Pancho Villa, Tourist, etc.) (This cast list is assembled from information in the script as well as from programs.)

The action occurs in the American mid-west during the years 1863 through 1882.

The musical was presented in two acts.

ACT ONE—"Jesse James Robbed This Train" (Jim Wann, Engineer, Reporter), "These Southern States That I Love" (Tommy Thompson, Pappy, Rick Simpson, Jim Wann), "The Year of Jubilo" (traditional; by Henry C. Work, 1872) (Tommy Thompson, Bill Hicks, Jim Watson), "The Unreconstructed Rebel" (lyric and music by Jan Davidson) (Jan Davidson), "Mama Fantastic" (Jim Wann, Rick Simpson, Jim Watson, Tommy Thompson, Gang), "Saloon Piano" (Performer[s] unknown), "I Don't Need a Man to Know I'm Good" (Madelyn Smoak), "Northfield, Minnesota" (Jim Wann, Rick Simpson, Tommy Thompson, Bill Hicks, Jim Watson), "King Cole" (based on the traditional song "Duncan and Brady") (Tommy Thompson, Reporter, Doctor, Chorus), "New Prisoner's Song" (traditional) (Jim Watson, Tommy Thompson), "K.C. Line" (based on the traditional song "Mobile-Texas Line") (Jim Wann, Tommy Thompson, Chorus), "Cakewalk Into Kansas City" (Jim Wann, Chorus)

ACT TWO—"When I Was a Cowboy" (traditional) (Jim Watson), "Pancho Villa" (Jim Wann, Pancho Villa), "Put It Where the Moon Don't Shine" (Jim Wann, John Foley), "Sleepy Time Down South" (Jim Wann), "Jesse James Robbed This Train" (reprise) (Jim Wann, Chorus), "Bright Morning Stars" (traditional) (Congregation), "When I Get the Call" (Jim Wann, Chorus), "Cakewalk Into Kansas City" (reprise) (Cast)

NOTES—Like *Wanted* (1972; see entry), *Diamond Studs* dealt with famous American criminals, in this case, Jesse James, Frank James, and the Younger Brothers. The musical was more successful than *Wanted*, and played for over six months. The songs were both new and traditional, and they blended well into a seamless whole. Perhaps the most outstanding song was the brisk and lively "Cakewalk Into Kansas City."

The script was published by Samuel French, Inc., in 1976, and included the song "Steal Away" (which replaced "Saloon Piano"), A note in the script referred to the number "The Ballad of Jesse James," but the song isn't in the script or in various programs. A 7" LP was released by Pasquotank Records (# PS-33-7-003) which included four songs ("Jesse James Robbed This Train," "Cakewalk Into Kansas City," "Sleepy Time Down South," and "Abiding with You" [the latter was apparently written for the show after the New York production and its immediate tour]), The three singers on the LP are Jim Wann, Bland Simpson, and Cass (Cassandra) Morgan (the latter appeared in the show's tour, as Zerelda James).

The musical had been originally produced in Chapel Hill, North Carolina.

377 Diamonds. THEATRE: Circle in the Square (Downtown); OPENING DATE: December 16, 1984; PERFORMANCES: 122; SKETCHES: Bud Abbott, Ralph G. Allen, Roy Blount, Jr., Richard Camp, Lou Costello, Lee Eisenberg, Sean Kelly, Jim Wann, John Lahr, Arthur Masella, Harry Stein, John Weidman, and Alan Zweibel; LYRICS: Gerard Alessandrini, Howard Ashman, Craig Carnelia, Betty Comden, Fred Ebb, Ellen Fitzhugh, Adolph Green, Karl Kennett, Jack Norworth, Jim Wann, and David Zippel; MUSIC: Gerard Alessandrini, Craig Carnelia, Cy

Coleman, Pam Drews, Larry Grossman, John Kander, Doug Katsaros, Alan Menken, Jonathan Sheffer, Lynn Udall, Albert Von Tilzer, and Jim Wann; DIRECTION: Harold Prince; CHOREOGRAPHY: Theodore Pappas; SCENERY: Tony Straiges; COSTUMES: Judith Dolan; LIGHTING: Ken Billington; MUSICAL DIRECTION: Paul Gemignani; PRODUCERS: Stephen G. Martin, Harold DeFelice, Louis W. Scheeder, and Kenneth John Productions Inc. in association with Frank Basile

CAST—Loni Ackerman, Susan Bigelow, Jackee Harry, Scott Holmes, Dick Latessa, Larry Riley, Nestor Serrano, Chip Zien; Louis Padilla (Usher) and Bill McComb (Stadium Announcer); Alternating Performers, Dwayne Markee and Wade Raley

The revue was presented in two acts.

ACT ONE—"Winter in New York" (lyric by Fred Ebb, music by John Kander) (Company), "Batting Order" (sketch by Sean Kelly and Arthur Masella) (Company), "In the Cards" (lyric by David Zippel, music by Alan Menken) (Dwayne Markee/Wade Raley, Loni Ackerman), "Favorite Sons" (lyric by Ellen Fitzhugh, music by Larry Grossman) (Jackee Harry, Larry Riley, Nestor Serrano, Loni Ackerman, Chip Zien), "Warner Wolf #1" (sketch by Richard Camp) (Chip Zien), "Song for a Pinch Hitter" (lyric by Ellen Fitzhugh, music by Larry Grossman) (Susan Bigelow), "Vendors" (lyric by Betty Comden and Adolph Green, music by Cy Coleman) (Jackee Harry, Loni Ackerman, Dick Latessa, Nestor Serrano, Susan Bigelow, Dwayne Markee/Wade Raley), "Fanatics #1" (sketch by Harry Stein and Lee Eisenberg) (Larry Riley, Chip Zien, Scott Holmes), "What You'd Call a Dream" (lyric and music by Craig Carnelia) (Scott Holmes), "Kasi Atta Bat" (sketch by Sean Kelly) (Loni Ackerman, Susan Bigelow, Dick Latessa, Chip Zien, Nestor Serrano, Dwayne Markee/Wade Riley), "Ballparks of the Gods" (sketch by John Weidman; media design by Lisa Podgur) (Scott Holmes), "Escorte-Moi" ("Take Me Out to the Ballgame") (lyric by Jack Norworth, music by Albert Von Tilzer) (Chip Zien), "The Dodger Game" (sketch by Ralph G. Allen) (Nestor Serrano, Larry Riley, Susan Bigelow, Scott Johnson), "He Threw Out the Ball" (lyric by Ellen Fitzhugh, music by Larry Grossman) (Jackee Henry, with Loni Ackerman, Susan Bigelow, Scott Holmes, Larry Riley, Chip Zien, Nestor Serrano), "Hundreds of Hats" (lyric by Howard Ashman, music by Jonathan Sheffer) (Dick Latessa, Loni Ackerman, Scott Holmes, Susan Bigelow, Nestor Serrano, Jackee Harry, Larry Riley, Dwayne Markee/Wade Riley), "Warner Wolf #2" (sketch by Richard Camp) (Chip Zien), "1919" (lyric and music by Jim Wann) (Larry Riley, Dwayne Markee/Wade Riley, Scott Holmes, Company)

ACT TWO—"P.A. Announcement" (sketch by John Weidman) (Bill McComb), "Let's Play Ball" (lyric and music by Gerard Alessandrini) (Company), "Warner Wolf #3" (sketch by Richard Camp) (Chip Zien), "Psyched Out" (sketch by John Lahr) (Dick Latessa, Chip Zien), "Vendors" (reprise) (Nestor Serrano, Dick Latessa, Loni Ackerman, Susan Bigelow, Jackee Harry, Scott Holmes, Dwayne Markee/Wade Riley), "Fanatics #2" (sketch by Harry Stein and Lee Eisenberg) (Chip Zien, Larry Riley), Five Ives (sketch by Roy Blount, Jr.) (Scott Holmes), "The Boys of Summer" (lyric by Ellen Fitzhugh, music by Larry Grossman) (Susan Bigelow), "Fanatics #3" (sketch by Harry Stein and Lee Eisenberg) (Chip Zien, Larry Riley), "Song for a Hunter College Graduate" (lyric by Howard Ashman, music by Jonathan Sheffer) (Loni Ackerman), "Warner Wolf #4" (sketch by Richard Camp) (Chip Zien), "Who's on First" (sketch by Bud Abbott and Lou Costello) (Chip Zien, Dwayne Markee/Wade Riley), "Stay in Your Own Back Yard" (sketch by John Weidman, lyric by Karl Kennett, music by Lyn Udall, additional music by Pam Drews, media design by Lisa Podgur) (Jackee Harry), "Chief Surgeon" (sketch by Alan Zweibel) (Larry Riley, Loni Ackerman, Susan Bigelow, Dick Latessa, Nestor Serrano, Company), "Ka-razy" (lyric by David Zippel, music by Doug Katsaros) (Company), "Famous People Quotes" (sketch by John Weidman) (Company), "Batting Order" (sketch by Sean Kelly and Arthur Masella) (Company), "Diamonds Are Forever" (lyric by Fred Ebb, music by John Kander) (Company)

NOTES—Despite its dazzling pedigree of first-class theatre talents, the baseball revue *Diamonds* ran just a little more than three months; apparently the blue-vinyl baseball-stadium-seat-styled cushions (embellished with the revue's title) which were given to audience members as souvenirs weren't enough to compensate for sitting through the revue.

Howard Kissel, writing in *Women's Wear Daily*, found the production "dreary," "collegiate," "strained beyond belief," and "wretched." In the *New York Post*, Clive Barnes wondered whether anyone in the production got worried when they realized the revue's highpoint was a Gallic version of "Take Me Out to the Ball Game" ("Escorte-Moi"), and in the *New York Times* Frank Rich called the evening a "minor league affair" with "frail material."

During previews the following were deleted: the sketches "Box Score Family" by Jerry L. Crawford, "Man of the Year" by Richard Camp, and "Play at the Plate" by John Lahr, and the song "Cleaning Crew," lyric by Betty Comden and Adolph Green and music by Cy Coleman.

The sketch "Kasi Atta Bat" was titled "Yanquis Atta Bat" during previews; and the song "He Threw Out the Ball" was titled "God Threw Out the Ball" during previews. Also, during previews there were three "Vendors" sequences (two were in the final version) and two "P.A. Announcement" sequences (one in the final version).

The song "Hundreds of Hats" became the title of a revue which featured the lyrics of Howard Ashman (see entry). The number can be heard on *Unsung Musicals III* (Varese Sarabande Records CD # VSD-5769).

The script was published by Samuel French, Inc., in 1986. "What You'd Call a Dream" was recorded for the collection *Pictures in the Hall/Songs of Craig Carnelia* (released by Original Cast Records [CD # OC-914]).

Harold Prince was one of the co-producers of the original 1955 Broadway production of *Damn Yankees*, the hit musical which seemed to break the jinx of shows about baseball. But the very next year, the play *The Hot Corner* managed only five performances; *The First*, a 1981 Broadway musical about Jackie Robinson, managed only thirty-seven performances (although Bob Brush's score offered some fine numbers, including the gem "The Opera Ain't Over"); and *Bingo!* (see entry) disappeared after its limited two-week Off Off Broadway engagement. *The Dream Team* was another musical about baseball, and centered on two brothers (both play in the Negro Leagues, but only one is selected for the majors). With a book by Richard Wesley (who had written the powerful and underrated 1978 Broadway drama *The Mighty Gents* [which included a gripping and memorable performance by Morgan Freeman]), lyrics by Thomas Tierney, and music by John Forster, the musical was briefly seen at Goodspeed Opera House's Norma Terris Theatre in 1985. Further, three Off Broadway plays about baseball figures, *The Babe* (1984; Babe Ruth), *Cobb* (2000; Ty Cobb), and *Nobody Don't Like Yogi* (Yogi Berra; 2003), all ran for less than 100 performances. As for *Diamonds*, it opened six weeks after the 1984 World Series and was gone three weeks before the start of the 1985 season. But baseball-as-theatre made a home run during the 2002-2003 season with Richard Greenberg's *Take Me Out*, which played for 355 performances and won both the Tony Award and the New York Drama Critics' Circle Award for Best Play.

378 Dick Deterred. THEATRE: West Bank Café; OPENING DATE: September 24, 1983; PERFORMANCES: 19; BOOK: David Edgar; LYRICS: David Edgar; MUSIC: William Schimmel; DIRECTION: George Wolf Reily; CHOREOGRAPHY: Mary Pat Henry; SCENERY: Ted Reinert; COSTUMES: Marla R. Kaye; LIGHTING: Leslie Ann Kilian (?); PRODUCER: Lily Turner

CAST—Mary Kay Dean (Anne, Martha, Singer), Elf Fairservis (Plantagenet, York, Singer), Malcolm Gray (McClarence, Citizen, Tyrell, Forrest, Stanley), Richard Litt (Hastings), Steve Pudenz (Richard), Sylvester Rich (Buckingham), Rhonda Rose (Elizabeth, Lady Jackie, Singer), Carl Williams (Murderer, Dighton, Ely, Richmond)

SOURCE—The play *Richard III* by William Shakespeare (written circa 1592).

The action occurs in Washington, D.C., in the early 1970s.

The musical was presented in two acts.

ACT ONE—"Welcome Washington" (Performer[s] Unknown), "Gonna Win" (Steve Pudenz, Mary Kay Dean), "Don't Let Them Take Checkers Away" (Steve Pudenz), "You Are Bugging Me" (Malcolm Gray, Carl Williams) ACT TWO—"Hostess with the Mostess of Them All" (Mary Kay Dean), "The Buck Stops Here" (Steve Pudenz, Sylvester Rich, Richard Litt, Carl Williams), "Expletive Deleted" (Performer[s] Unknown), "I'm Leaving" (Richard Pudenz, Mary Kay Dean), "It's the End" (Performer[s] Unknown)

NOTES—Using William Shakespeare's *Richard III* (circa 1592) as its inspiration, the Off Off Broadway musical *Dick Deterred* was a spoof of Watergate. The musical had first been seen in London almost a decade earlier, when it opened on February 25, 1974, at the Bush Theatre (it then transferred to the ICA Terrace Theatre on March 4). Prior to the September 1983 New York production, the musical had been presented earlier in the year at the William Redfield Theatre (a/k/a No Smoking Playhouse) on January 13, where it played for nineteen performances, the same number as its run at the West Bank Café.

For New York, the music was by William Schimmel; Kurt Ganzl's *The British Musical Theatre Volume II 1915-1984* credits the music for the British production to Graham Field.

The musical was seen in New York almost eleven years after Watergate, and so perhaps it was a little late in the day for a satire on the subject. At least Barbara Garson's satire *MacBird!* (1967), which was patterned after Shakespeare's *Macbeth* and was a non-musical spoof of Lyndon Johnson and the Kennedys, had been produced during Johnson's presidency. The following songs were deleted prior to the run at the West Bank Café: "Gotta Know the Score," "Murderer, Murderer, Murderer," "How Many KKK's," "Everlasting Peace," "Ghost Song," and "It's All Over Now." During the January run, both Ted Reinert and Beate Kessler were credited with the set design.

379 The Difficult Woman. "A Musical"; THEATRE: Barbizon-Plaza Theatre

Opening Night: April 25, 1962; PERFORMANCES: 3; BOOK: Malcolm Stuart Boylan and Maurice Alevy; LYRICS: Morty Neff and George Mysels; MUSIC: Richard Freitas; DIRECTION: Maurice Alvey; production "supervised by" David Bines; CHOREOGRAPHY: Maurice Alvey; SCENERY: Louis Kennel; COSTUMES: Louis Kennel; LIGHTING: Louis Kennel; MUSICAL DIRECTION: Richard Freitas; PRODUCERS: Nikardi Productions and Donald C. Fetzko

CAST—Gerard Russak (Watchman, Magistrate, Leader of Banditos, Alphonso), Lilian Armijo (Rita), Devi Tina (Nieves), Odette McEwen (Isabel), Luis Hernandez (Pedrito), Jerry Cunliffe (Don Cosme, Hangman), Jack Russell (Victor), Charles Burks (Padre Lucindo), Warren Robertson (Ricardo), Ken "Slim" Martin (Don Jose, Inn Keeper), Jan Kirby

(Senor Mendoza), Paul Marlowe (Don Miguel), Joyce Orlando (Tina, Guest, One of Townspeople, Dancer), Robert Lorca (First Bandito, Guest, One of Townspeople, Dancer), Steven Rayow (Second Banditos, Guest, One of Townspeople, Dancer), Dena Dante (Guest, One of Townspeople), Joan Evans (Guest, One of Townspeople, Dancer), Maria Thome (Guest, One of Townspeople, Dancer), Yago Blass (One of Townspeople), Osvaldo Maurin (One of Townspeople, Dancer), Marta Viana (One of Townspeople)

SOURCE—A play by Conrado Nale Roxlo (translated by Ruth C. Gillespie).

The action occurs in Buenos Aires at the turn of the nineteenth century.

The musical was presented in two acts (song assignments unknown).

ACT ONE—"Grandioso," "Ulterior Motive," "Siesta," "One in My Position," "Malumbo," "The Hangman's Plea," "Ungrateful," "El Cuando Minuet," "Poor Isabel," "Milonga," "What a Life," "Bull Blood and Brandy," "Patience and Gentleness," "Dream Ballet"

ACT TWO—"Tormented," "Taking Inventory," "I Won't Take No for an Answer," "This Is the Day," "Throw the House Out the Window," "Ulterior Motive" (reprise), "Patience and Gentleness" (reprise)

NOTES—Spring 1962 was not the best of seasons for "bandito" musicals. Besides the short-running *The Difficult Woman*, the Broadway-bound *We Take the Town*, which starred Robert Preston as Pancho Villa (reportedly Preston's favorite role), collapsed during its tryout engagement in Philadelphia. Those songs which have surfaced from *We Take the Town*, such as "How Does the Wine Taste?" and "Silverware," are quite wonderful (the latter number has been identified by Stephen Sondheim as one he wishes he had written). And, who knows, maybe *The Difficult Woman*'s "Throw the House Out the Window" is a lost treasure; it sure has a great title, and was one of the few numbers praised by Milton Esterow in his review for the *New York Times*. Incidentally, Esterow felt one of the musical's most fascinating moments occurred when Warren Robertson sang of his wife's indifference while he shaved (the song was probably "Ungrateful"). With his face covered in foam, he shaved with a "gleaming" razor and without a mirror. And yet by the number's conclusion he wasn't even nicked. Otherwise, Esterow felt that another song ("Tormented") more appropriately summed up the feelings of the audience. *The Difficult Woman* and *We Take the Town* weren't the only "bandito" musicals to have a hard time of it. Almost thirty years to the day of the opening of *The Difficult Woman*, the 1932 Broadway musical *There You Are!* premiered where it lasted for just eight performances. In his review for the *New York Times*, Brooks Atkinson noted the "down in Mech-hi-co" musical was an evening of "hackneyed dullness" with "stock" songs and a "muddled" book. Incidentally, a open-to-the-public one-performance-only "run-through" of another musical about Pancho Villa was offered on March 29, 1978 (*Pancho Villa and Major Young* with book, lyrics, and music by Marcel Achille); after the performance, the musical seems to have disappeared.

380 Digging for Apples. THEATRE: Washington Square Theatre; OPENING DATE: September 27, 1962; PERFORMANCES: 28; SKETCHES: James E. Butler and Robert Bowers; LYRICS: James E. Butler; MUSIC: Robert Bowers; DIRECTION: James E. Butler and Robert Bowers; CHOREOGRAPHY: Gretchen VanAken, Robert Cotton; SCENERY: Gerald E. Proctor; LIGHTING: Robert Cotton; PRODUCERS: Ned Hendrickson and Frank Thomas

CAST—Robert (Bob) Cotton, Jeff Furst, Paula Shaw, Vinnie Van, Gretchen Van Aken

NOTES—Paul Gardner in the *New York Times* found the topical revue *Digging for Apples* generally bland and often on the level of a high school talent show. He felt that even the more promising sketches (such as one in which President Kennedy is obsessed by the television ratings of his press conferences) couldn't sustain a comic momentum. Gardner further noted the evening was a self-described "revue that asks a question," and then he had one of his own: Why did a straightforward anti-war song end with an armless and legless dummy on the stage? Gardner complained that the revue was "ammunition for uptown philosophers" who believe that virtually anything can get produced in Off Broadway's "lofts, basements and decorated caves."

381 Dime a Dozen. "The New Post-Prandial Prank"; THEATRE: PLaza 9- Theatre; OPENING DATE: October 18, 1962; PERFORMANCES: 728; DIRECTION: Frank Wagner and Julius Monk; CHOREOGRAPHY: Frank Wagner; SCENERY: Ed Wittstein and Robert (Bob) Miller; COSTUMES: Donald Brooks; LIGHTING: Don Lamb; MUSICAL DIRECTION: William Roy and Robert Colston at the Plural Pianos; Carl Norman, the Singular Pianist; PRODUCER: Orion Production Company (Julius Monk, Thomas Hammond, and Glen Boles)

CAST—Ceil Cabot, Gerry Matthews, Jack Fletcher, Mary Louise Wilson, Rex Robbins, Susan Browning

The revue was presented in two acts.

ACT ONE—"Dime a Dozen" (lyric by William F. Brown, music by William Roy) (Company), "Ode to an Eminent Daily" (lyric by Bruce Williamson, music by William Roy) (Mary Louise Wilson, Ceil Cabot, Jack Fletcher, Rex Robbins) "Philatelic" (sketch by Bruce Williamson) (Rex Robbins, Mary Louise Wilson) "Someone Like You" (lyric by Tom Whedon, music by Sam Pottle) (Ceil Cabot) "Barry's Boys" (lyric and music by June Reizner) (Jack Fletcher, Rex Robbins, Gerry Matthews), "Schmaltzy Waltz" (lyric and music by Bart Howard) (Performer[s] Unknown) "Collecting of the Plaid" (lyric and music by Lesley Davison) (Company) "From the Top" (sketch by William F. Brown) (Rex Robbins, Jack Fletcher) "Requiem for Everyone" (lyric and music by Bud McCreery) (Gerry Matthews, Rex Robbins) "P.T. Boat" (sketch by Dee Caruso and Bill Levine) (Rex Robbins, Gerry Matthews, Jack Fletcher) "The Making of a Man" (lyric by William Engvick, music by Alec Wilder) (Gerry Matthews), "Ten Per Cent Orlon" (lyric and music by Lesley Davison) (Ceil Cabot, Jack Fletcher) "Battle Hymn of the Rialto" (lyric by Allison Roulston, music by Jay Foote) (Rex Robbins) "Slow Down Moses" (lyric and music by Michael F. Brown) (Company)

ACT TWO—"Marching for Peace" (lyric and music by Lesley Davison) (Company) "Bless This School" (lyric by Maxwell E. Siegel, music by Jay Foote) (Ceil Cabot, Gerry Matthews) "The Minnows and the Sharks" (lyric by Allison Roulston, music by Jay Foote) (Ceil Cabot), "H.M.S. Brownstone" (sketch by Rory Harrity and Richard Craven) (Susan Browning, Gerry Matthews), "Johnny Come Lately" (lyric by Seymour Zogott, music by Claibe Richardson) (Susan Browning), "Barry's Boys" (reprise) (Jack Fletcher, Rex Robbins, Gerry Matthews) "Thor" (lyric and music by Jack Holmes) (Rex Robbins, Jack Fletcher) "The Habit" (sketch by Robert Elliott) (Performer[s] Unknown), "Alumnae Report" (lyric by Allison Roulston, music by Jay Foote) (Mary Louise Wilson) "Le Spot Hot" (lyric by Allison Roulston, music by Jay Foote) (Performer[s] Unknown) "Don't Be Absurd" (sketch by William F. Brown) (Rex Robbins, Ceil Cabot, Jack Fletcher, Mary Louise Wilson) "The Plaza Waltz-Waltz" (lyric and music by Michael Brown) (Company)

NOTES—*Dime a Dozen* was Julius Monk's first revue at his new location in the Plaza Hotel. His departure from Upstairs at the Downstairs/Downstairs at the Upstairs was not a happy one. The *New York Times* reported that on September 6, 1962, Monk filed a $2,500,000 lawsuit against his old venue, claiming his name was still being used at the nightclub and that material from *Seven Come Eleven* (see separate entries for both editions of the revue) had been copied in Ben Bagley's new revue. Since Bagley's *No Shoestrings* (see entry) was still some five weeks away from opening night, Monk's reported concerns are unclear. Monk's suit also demanded that the names of the Upstairs/Downstairs club be changed.

In the meantime, the owners of Upstairs/Downstairs filed a $210,000 lawsuit against Monk, claiming he had broken his contract with them by leaving prior to its termination and by not preparing a revue for their fall season. There seems to be no record of the results of these actions; however, the names of the Upstairs/Downstairs venues continued to be used for almost another full decade. Regarding Monk's allegations that material from *Seven Come Eleven* was used by Bagley, the titles of the sketches and songs heard in the opening night of *No Shoestrings* indicate the material had not been previously used in a Monk revue.

The cast album of *Dime a Dozen* was released by Cadence Records on a 2-LP set, thus making it the most complete recording of Monk's revues. It was also his longest-running work, playing for 728 performances.

Sometime between the revue's premiere (October 18, 1962) and the live performance when the album was recorded (January 13, 1964), the wonderful Ceil Cabot left the show (and seems to have completely vanished since then). She was replaced by Fredricka Weber, who is on the cast album.

There were various changes throughout the run of the revue. The following numbers were dropped, and aren't on the cast album: "Schmaltzy Waltz," "The Habit," and "Le Spot Hot." Added to the revue, and which are on the cast album, are "Cholesterol Love Song" (performed by Susan Browning), "Season's Greetings" (Fredricka Weber), and "Lincoln Center" (Gerry Matthews)

"Ten Per Cent Orlon" seems to have undergone a title change, to "Ten Percent Rayon," and it appears "Someone Like You" was revised as "Something Good Like You."

"Lincoln Center" had previously been heard in *Dressed to the Nines* (see entry); and "H.M.S. Brownstone" had been earlier heard in *Fourth Avenue North* (1961) and then later in *Bits and Pieces XIV* (1964) (see entries).

Dime a Dozen was another amusing entry in Monk's canon of sophisticated, intimate revues. The highlight of the show was "Barry's Boys," which mocked Goldwater's political philosophy; it was even performed on national television at the time (possibly on Jack Paar's late night television talk show); the song was reprised in Monk's *Baker's Dozen* (1964; see entry). "Thor" had also been heard *Ten-ish, Anyone?* (see entry).

For a complete list of Julius Monk's revues, see entry for *Four Below*; also see Appendix Q.

382 Dinah! "Queen of the Blues." THEATRE: Cheryl Crawford Theatre/Westside Arts Center; OPENING DATE: January 11, 1984; PERFORMANCES: 7; SCRIPT: Sasha Dalton and Ernest McCarty; DIRECTION: Woodie King, Jr.; SCENERY: Llewellyn Harrison; COSTUMES: Judy Dearing; LIGHTING: Llewellyn Harrison; MUSICAL DIRECTION: Bross Townsend; PRODUCERS: Woodie King, Jr., Raymond L. Gaspard, Martin Martinson, and Mary Card; Ashton Springer, Executive Producer

CAST—SASHA DALTON (Dinah Washington)

The action occurs one evening in 1963 at the jazz club Birdland.

The musical was presented in two acts.

ACT ONE—Overture, "I Wanna Be Loved by You" (from *Good Boy*, 1928; lyric and music by Herbert Stothart, Bert Kalmar, and Harry Ruby), "Dinah Washington," "Blow, Blow Soft Winds," "Dream" (lyric and music by Johnny Mercer; although not written for the 1955 film *Daddy Long Legs*, the song was interpolated into its score) "Lover Come Back to Me" (*The New Moon*, 1928; lyric by Oscar Hammerstein II, music by Sigmund Romberg) "Salty Papa Blues," "Evil Gal Blues," "I Don't Hurt Anymore," "The Blues Ain't Nothing," "They Didn't Believe Me" (*The Girl from Utah*, 1914; lyric by Herbert Reynolds, music by Jerome Kern) "Destination Moon," "Move on Up a Little Higher (Jesus Is All)," "There'll Be Some Changes Made"

ACT TWO—Overture, "This Can't Be Love" (*The Boys from Syracuse*, 1938; lyric by Lorenz Hart, music by Richard Rodgers) "Blow Top Blues #1," "Mixed Emotions (If It's the Last Thing I Do)," "I Could Write a Book" (*Pal Joey*, 1940; lyric by Lorenz Hart, music by Richard Rodgers) "Teach Me Tonight" (lyric by Sammy Cahn, music by Gene DePaul), "This Bitter Earth" (lyric and music by Clyde [?] Otis), "Love for Sale" (*The New Yorkers*, 1930; lyric and music by Cole Porter) "Am I Asking Too Much," Medley: "Harbor Lights," "Stairway to the Stars" (lyric by Mitchell Parish, music by Matt Malneck), "September in the Rain" (1935 film *Stars Over Broadway*; lyric by Al Dubin, music by Harry Warren) "Perdido" (lyric by Ervin Drake and Hans Lengsfelder, music by Juan Tizol), "Manhattan" (*The Garrick Gaities*, 1925; lyric by Lorenz Hart, music by Richard Rodgers), "Make Someone Happy" (*Do Re Mi*, 1960; lyric by Betty Comden and Adolph Green, music by Jule Styne) "What a Difference a Day Made" (a/k/a "What a Diff'rence a Day Makes") (lyric and music by Maria Grever and S. Adams), "Unforgettable" (lyric and music by Irving Gordon)

NOTES—This musical tribute to Dinah Washington (1924-1963) lasted just seven performances. The piece had originally been presented in a night club, and perhaps the musical worked better in that venue than in a formal theatre setting.

In 1998, another Off Broadway tribute to Dinah Washington was more successful. *Dinah Was* (see entry) ran for almost 250 performances.

In 2008, Theatre Alliance, a Washington D.C. theatre company, presented the cabaret revue *A Nite at the Dew Drop Inn*, which included a tribute to Dinah Washington.

383 Dinah Was. THEATRE: Gramercy Theatre; OPENING DATE: May 28, 1998; PERFORMANCES: 242; BOOK: Oliver Goldstick; LYRICS AND MUSIC: See song list for credits of some songs; DIRECTION: David Petrarca; CHOREOGRAPHY: George Faison; SCENERY: Michael Yeargan; COSTUMES: Paul Tazewell; LIGHTING: Stephen Strawbridge; MUSICAL DIRECTION: Lanny Hartley; PRODUCERS: Jean Doumnian in a WPA Theatre Production (Kyle Renick, Artistic Director)

CAST—Adriane Lenox (Maye, Waitress, Violet), Bud Leslie (Frick, Rollie), Yvette Freeman (Dinah Washington), Vince Viverito (Joe Spinelli, Sam Greenblatt), Darryl Alan Reed (Mama Jones, Boss, Chase Adams)

The action occurs in 1959 ("and stops along the way") in the lobby of the Sahara Hotel in Las Vegas.

The musical was presented in two acts.

ACT ONE—"Bad Luck" (Yvette Freeman), "Showtime" (Yvette Freeman), "Baby, You Got What It Takes" (Darryl Allen Reed, Yvette Freeman), "Slick Chick (On the Mellow Side)" (Yvette Freeman, Ensemble), "What a Difference a Day Made" (a/k/a "What a Diff'rence a Day Makes") (lyric and music by Maria Grever and S. Adams) (Yvette Freeman), "I Wanna Be Loved by You" (from *Good Boy*, 1928; lyric and music by Herbert Stothart, Bert Kalmar, and Harry Ruby) (Yvette Freeman)

ACT TWO—"Long John Blues" (Yvette Freeman), "I Won't Cry Anymore" (Yvette Freeman), "Come Rain or Come Shine" (*St. Louis Woman*, 1946; lyric by Johnny Mercer, music by Harold Arlen) (Yvette Freeman), "This Bitter Earth" (lyric and music by Clyde [?] Otis) (Yvette Freeman), "Sometimes I'm Happy" (*Hit the Deck*, 1927; lyric by Irving Caesar, music by Vincent Youmans) (Yvette Freeman), "A Rockin' Good Way" (Yvette Freeman, Adriane Lenox), "I Don't Hurt Anymore" (Yvette Freeman)

NOTES—This was the second Off Broadway musical about Dinah Washington (1924-1963); see entry for *Dinah! "Queen of the Blues"* (1984), The earlier musical took place at Birdland in 1963; the current one at the Sahara Hotel in 1959. *Dinah Was* had first been produced Off Off Broadway at the WPA Theatre on March 12, 1998, for forty-two performances.

In 2008, Theatre Alliance, a Washington, D.C., theatre company, presented the cabaret revue *A Nite at the Dew Drop Inn*, which included a tribute to Dinah Washington.

384 Dinny and the Witches. "A Frolic on Grave Matters"; THEATRE: Cherry Lane Theatre; OPENING DATE: December 9, 1959; PERFORMANCES: 29; PLAY: William Gibson; LYRICS: William Gibson; MUSIC: Bobby Scott; DIRECTION: Jess Kimmel; CHOREOGRAPHY: Dance Movement by Ted Cappy; SCENERY: John Robert Lloyd; COSTUMES: John Robert Lloyd; LIGHTING: Jason Robert Lloyd; MUSICAL DIRECTION: Bobby Scott; PRODUCERS: Jess Kimmel and Alfred Stern

CAST—Ellen Bogan Engel (Dawn), Sylvia Shay (Chloe), Renee Taylor (Bubbles), Harry Fritzius (Ben), Wil Albert (Jake), Dean Lyman Almquist (Stonehenge), Robert Leland (Tom), Jessie Jacobs (Dick), E. Francis Simon (Harry), Kay Doubleday (Amy), Bill Heyer (Dinny), Julie Bovasso (Luella), Bernard Reed (Ulga), Avril Gentles (Zenobia)

The action occurs in Central Park, and the time is "now, and again."

The musical was presented in three acts.

ACT ONE—"This Is How the World Was Made" (chant) (Avril Gentles, Julie Bovasso, Bernard Reed), "Don't Know Why I Came Here" (a/k/a "Don't Know What I'm Here For") (song) (Bill Heyer), "All Hail, King Dinny!" (chant) (Avril Gentles, Julie Bovasso, Bernard Reed), "All Hail, King Dinny!" (chant) (reprise) (Avril Gentes, Julie Bovasso, Bernard Reed), "Oh, Three Fun-Lovers Are We" (song) (Ellen Bogan Engel, Sylvia Shay, Renee Taylor), "Didn't Know What I Wanted" (song) (Bill Heyer, Kay Doubleday), "Didn't Know What I Wanted" (song) (reprise) Bill Heyer)

ACT TWO—"Why, Hail! It's Dinny!" (chant) (Avril Gentles, Julie Bovasso, Bernard Reed)

ACT THREE—"I Turned My Back" (song) (Bill Heyer), "Last Chance for Dinny" (chant) (Avril Gentles, Julie Bovasso, Bernard Reed), "Don't Know Why I Came Here" (a/k/a "Don't Know What I'm Here For") (song) (reprise) (Ensemble), "I'm a Girl that Likes to Go Along" (song) (Ellen Bogan Engel, Sylvia Shay, Renee Taylor), "Didn't Know What You Looked Like" (song) (Bill Heyer, Kay Doubleday), "This Is How the World Will End" (chant) (Avril Gentles, Julie Bovasso, Bernard Reed), "All Hail, to Dinny!" (chant) (Avril Gentles, Julie Bovasso, Bernard Reed)

NOTES—The song titles for *Dinny and the Witches* weren't listed in either the British or Off Broadway programs or in the published script; the above list represents "best guess" titles.

This curious, whimsical, and rather preachy little play with music was produced Off Broadway, following William Gibson's two Broadway hits *Two for the Seesaw* (1958) and *The Miracle Worker* (1959). The plot dealt with Dinny, a young man who is given the entire world by three witches; but he soon learns the old lesson that power doesn't necessarily buy happiness, and he ultimately realizes that the love of his wife and child is the most important thing in the world. The witches wryly note that he and his family live happily ever after.

Brooks Atkinson in the *New York Times* said that the fantasy never quite got off the ground, but he praised Jess Kimmel's "resourceful direction," John Robert Lloyd's "bizarre and ingeniously lighted scenery," Bobby Scott's "high-spirited" score, and Bill Heyer's "ideally cast" Dinny.

Dinny and the Witches had a brief run and was seldom heard from again. It originated as a one-act play (produced in Topeka, Kansas, in 1945), and was expanded into three acts for New York. It was published by Atheneum in 1960, under the title of *Two Plays and a Preface/The Miracle Worker and Dinny and the Witches.*

The Burns Mantle Yearbook/The Best Plays of 1959-1960 singled out "Don't Know What I'm Here For" ("Don't Know Why I Came Here") as the show's best song.

385 Disappearing Act. THEATRE: 47th Street Theatre; OPENING DATE: September 4, 1996; PERFORMANCES: 39; LYRICS: Mike Oster; MUSIC: Mike Oster; DIRECTION: Mark Frawley; CHOREOGRAPHY: Mark Frawley; SCENERY: Bill Clarke; COSTUMES: Gregg Barnes; LIGHTING: Tim Hunter; MUSICAL DIRECTION: Ron Roy; PRODUCERS: Jeff Bannon and Phyllis Miriam in association with Bosco, Ltd., Shawn Churchman, Norman Kurtz, Steven M. Levy and Adam Weinstock CAST—Jamie MacKenzie, Michael McElroy, Branch Woodman

The revue was presented in two acts.

ACT ONE—"Fear and Self-Loathing" (Company), "They Say" (Company), "Men Who Like Their Men" (additional lyric by Jeff Bannon, Mark Frawley, and Jamie MacKenzie) (Branch Woodman, with Michael McElroy and Jamie MacKenzie), "Gentrification" (Michael McElroy, Jamie McKenzie), "Just Go Shopping" (Branch Woodman, with Michael McElroy and Jamie MacKenzie), "I Had to Laugh" (Jamie MacKenzie), "A Secret" (Company), "Children Are a Blessing" (Branch Woodman, Michael McElroy), "A Friendly Vacation" (Company), "Let Me In" (Branch Woodman), "Something's Wrong with This Picture" (Company), "Rants and Raves" (Branch Woodman, Jamie MacKenzie), "I Slept with a Zombie" (Michael McElroy, with Branch Woodman and Jamie MacKenzie), "The Ride Home" (Jamie MacKenzie), "Looks Like It Might Rain" (Branch Woodman), "The Dance Floor" (Company)

ACT TWO—"All Tied Up on the Line" (Company), "In Here" (Jamie MacKenzie), "Dear Diary" (Company), "What Do Ya Know" (Michael McElroy), "Fruits of Domestic Bliss" (Branch Woodman, Jamie MacKenzie), "Old Flame" (Company), "In Our Community" (Company), "Ounce of Prevention" (Michael McElroy, with Branch Woodman), "An Ordinary Day" (Jamie MacKenzie), "Trio for Three Buddies" (Company), "Faded Levi Jacket" (Jason Woodman), "They Say" (reprise) (Company), "Disappearing Act" (additional lyrics by Jeff Bannon, Mark Frawley, and Jamie MacKenzie) (Company)

NOTES—Two weeks after the opening of *When Pigs Fly* (see entry), another gay revue, *Disappearing Act*, opened. But *Disappearing Act* took its title to heart and was gone in five weeks, while *When Pigs Fly* ran over two years.

D.R.J. Bruckner in the *New York Times* felt the evening was most successful in its light-hearted mockery of modern life (such as gentrification and compulsive shopping); but when the revue turned serious and dealt with such topics as AIDS, Bruckner felt the otherwise "sharp, fast and funny" evening became sentimental, repetitive, and self-indulgent.

386 Dispatches. "A Rock War Musical"; THEATRE: Martinson Hall/The Public Theatre; OPENING DATE: April 18, 1979; PERFORMANCES: 63; ADAPTATION: Elizabeth Swados; LYRICS: Elizabeth Swados; MUSIC: Elizabeth Swados; DIRECTION: Elizabeth Swados; SCENERY: Patricia Woodbridge; COSTUMES: Hilary Rosenfeld; LIGHTING: Jennifer Tipton; PRODUCER: The New York Shakespeare Festival (Joseph Papp, Director)

CAST—Penelope Bodry, Ray Contreras, Karen Evans, Tony Franklin, Rodney Hudson, Roger Lawson, Joan Macintosh, Paul McCrane, William Parry, David Schechter, Gedde Watanabe

SOURCE—The 1977 book *Dispatches* by Michael Herr.

The action occurs in Vietnam during the late 1960s and early 1970s.

The musical was presented in one act.

MUSICAL NUMBERS—"Crazy" (Joan Macintosh, Company), "Thou Shalt Not Be Afraid" (Roger Lawson, Company), "Breathing In" (Rodney Hudson, Company), "These Were the Faces" (Company), "The Ground Was Always in Play" (Ray Contreras, Company), "Song of the LURP (Long Range Reconnaissance Patrol)" (William Parry, Company), "Helicopter, Helicopter" (Paul McCrane, Company), "Stoned in Saigon" (Ray Contreras, Paul McCrane, William Parry, Company), "Beautiful for Once" (Gedde Watanabe, Rodney Hudson), "Tiger Lady" (Karen Evans, Company), "Prayers in the Delta" (Ray Contreras, Roger Lawson, Company), "Flip Religion" (David Schechter, Company), "Quakin' and Shakin'" (Penelope, Company), "Six Fucking Shades of Green" (Rodney Hudson, Paul McCrane, Ray Contreras, Company), "Bougainvillea" (Gedde Watanabe), "The Mix" (William Parry, Company), "I See a Road" (Penelope Bodry, Paul McCrane), "Take the Glamor Out of War" (Roger Lawson, Company), "This War Gets Old" (Rodney Hudson, Company), "Back in the World Now" (Company), "Freezing and Burning" (Joan Macintosh)

NOTES—Michael Herr's *Dispatches* was a highly regarded collection of the wartime correspondent's reminiscences of the Vietnam War and the American soldiers who fought it. Some of the critics felt Elizabeth Swados completely misunderstood Herr, and believed the misguided adaptation trivialized the subject matter, diminished the book, and portrayed American soldiers in a smug and patronizing manner.

Edwin Wilson, writing in the *Wall Street Journal*, stated Swados lacked even the slightest notion of the realities of war, that she seriously misrepresented American soldiers who took their jobs seriously, and that the musical was "dilettantism masquerading as political comment." In his review for *Women's Wear Daily*, Howard Kissel wrote that Swados reduced Herr's book to "an incoherent, meaningless shambles" and noted that her work would appeal mostly to "trendies and leftover Thirties Marxists." For another Off Broadway view of American soldiers in Vietnam, see entry for *Tracers*.

387 The Diva Is Dismissed. THEATRE: Susan Stein Shiva Theatre/The Public Theatre; OPENING DATE: October 30, 1994; PERFORMANCES: 34; MATERIAL: Jenifer Lewis and Charles Randolph-Wright; ADDITIONAL MATERIAL BY Mark Alton Brown; DIRECTION: Charles Randolph-Wright; LIGHTING: David Castaneda; MUSICAL DIRECTION: Michael Skloff; PRODUCER: The New York Shakespeare Festival (George C. Wolfe, Producer; Jason Steven Cohen, Managing Director; Rosemarie Tichler and Kevin Kline, Associate Producers)

CAST—Jenifer Lewis The revue was presented in one act.

MUSICAL NUMBERS—"Climb" (lyric and music by Jenifer Lewis), "Grandma Small" (lyric and music by Jenifer Lewis), "Killer Cheer" (lyric and music by Jenifer Lewis; additional lyric by Charles Randolph-Wright), "And I Was Fired" (lyric by Mark Brown, Jenifer Lewis, and Charles Randolph-Wright, music by Jenifer Lewis and Michael Skloff), Broadway Medley (songs in this sequence are unknown), "I Wanna Come Home" (lyric and music by Jenifer Lewis, Michael Skloff, and Charles Randolph-Wright), "Staring at the Moon" (lyric and music by Jenifer Lewis)

NOTES—Jenifer Lewis' *The Diva Is Dismissed* was a semi-autobiographical one-woman musical which told the story of an aspiring singer from the Midwest who tries her luck in Hollywood and on Broadway.

And Lewis knew about being dismissed. In early 1981, she created the role of Effie Melody White in Michael Bennett's workshop of *Dreamgirls* (then called *Big Dreams*). But by the time the musical opened on Broadway at the end of that year, she had been dismissed and replaced by another diva, Jennifer Holiday (when the belated 2006 film version of *Dreamgirls* was released, a third Jennifer [Jennifer Hudson] performed the role).

Stephen Holden in the *New York Times* praised the "snappy and amusing" evening in which Jenifer Lewis told the audience she wanted to be a "rich, famous and disgusting" diva (which she defined as "someone who pretends to know who she is and looks fabulous doing it"). Holden found Lewis "imperious and sharply funny," with a "brassy" voice and "hard-edged" good looks, and he concluded she fit the definition of "diva" "to a T." During the course of the evening, Lewis announced that among her accomplishments as a diva was to co-found Divas Anonymous; and at one point she sent "diva aid" to Russia (boxes of long-lashed mascara were dropped over Red Square). Perhaps the highlight of the evening was "Broadway Medley"; Holden reported Lewis sang fragments of two-dozen songs in a sequence which allowed her to compress "9 years of my life into 4 minutes and 22 seconds," and which, he noted, also allowed her to "parody every stock diva pose" in the book.

The Diva Is Dismissed played an irregular scheduled at the Public, alternating in repertory with Danny Hoch's one-man show *Some People*.

388 Diversions. "A Revue"; THEATRE: Downtown Theatre. OPENING NIGHT: November 7, 1958; PERFORMANCES: 58; SKETCHES: Steven Vinaver; LYRICS: Steven Vinaver; MUSIC: Carl Davis; DIRECTION: Steven Vinaver; SCENERY: A. William Strom; COSTUMES: Charles Hanford; LIGHTING: A. William Strom; MUSICAL DIRECTION: Carl Davis; PRODUCER: The New Princess Company

CAST—Aline Brown, Thom Molinaro, Nancy Dussault, Cy Young, Peter Feldman, Gubi Mann

The revue was presented in two acts (sketch and song assignments unknown).

ACT ONE—"Hello," "Five Plus One," "Detective Story," "Musicians," "You're Nothing," "Fill the Cup," "Touch and Go," "Subway Rag," "Boots," "Here Comes the Ballad," "Listening," "One Big Family"

ACT TWO—"Production Number," "He Wouldn't Care," "White Is the Dove," "Prayer," "Roll Call," "You're Wonderful," "Three Cans of Film," "He Follows Me Around," "Bolero," "Goodnight"

NOTES—Lewis Funke in the *New York Times* felt the revue *Diversions* was on the mild side, but he singled out two songs, "Here Comes the Ballad" and "You're Wonderful," and also praised the "Bolero" sequence, a "mad interlude" in which the performers worked themselves into a "wild crescendo of idiocy" as they exchanged a series of hats while scat-singing to Ravel's music.

"Here Comes the Ballad" surfaced on the compilation album *18 Interesting Songs from Unfortunate Shows* which was released by Take Home Tunes! Records (LP # THT-777). "Production Number" (lyric by Vinaver and music by Dan Silverstein and Anthony Tuttle) had been previously heard in Vinaver's college musical *Well I Never!*, which played at the Barbizon-Plaza Theatre in 1957 (see entry). During the brief run, Peg Murray was a cast replacement; she later won a Tony Award for Best Performance by a Featured Actress in a Musical when she originated the role of Fraulien Kost in the 1966 Broadway production of *Cabaret*.

389 D.M.Z. Revue. THEATRE: Forlini's Restaurant; OPENING DATE: 1967-1968 Season; PERFORMANCES: Unknown; SKETCHES AND LYRICS: Eric Bentley, Albert Bermel, Wolf Biermann, Jules Feiffer, Anthony Harrison, Robert Lowell, and Adrian Mitchell; MUSIC: Arnold Black, Bruce Kirle, Wolf Biermann, Irma Jurist, and Richard Peaslee; DIRECTION: Isaiah Sheffer; MUSICAL DIRECTION: Bruce Kirle; PRODUCER: D.M.Z. Cabaret (Isaiah Sheffer and Eric Bentley, Founders and Co-Producers)

CAST—James Antonio, Tony Harrison, Josephine Lemmo

NOTES—The D.M.Z. Cabaret ("yes, the demilitarized zone," noted R.J. Schroder in *The Best Plays of 1967-1968*) offered evenings of political cabaret at Forlini's Restaurant, which was located near Columbia University. The *D.M.Z. Revue* was a typical offering from the company.

390 Do It Again! "A Gershwin Musicade"; THEATRE: Promenade Theatre; OPENING DATE: February 8, 1971; PERFORMANCES: 14; LYRICS: Unless otherwise noted, all lyrics by Ira Gershwin Music: George Gershwin; DIRECTION: Bert Convy; SCENERY: Barry Arnold; LIGHTING: Roger Morgan; MUSICAL DIRECTION: William Cox; PRODUCERS: Jay H. Fuchs, with Stuart Duncan

CAST—MARGARET WHITING, CLIFTON DAVIS, Robin Benson, Susan Long, Marion Ramsey

The revue was presented in two acts.

NOTES—The revue *Do It Again!*, a tribute to the Gershwins, lasted just fourteen performances. Another such evening, *The Gershwins' Fascinating Rhythm*, opened on Broadway in 1999 and played for only seventeen performances. However, *American Rhapsody* (see entry), a 2000 Off Broadway Gershwin tribute, ran for 231 performances, and Hershey Felder's one-man *George Gershwin Alone* opened in 2001 for ninety-six performances. And two new Broadway book musicals which featured Gershwin songs were long-running hits (*My One and Only* [1983] and *Crazy for You* [1992]).

With so many songs listed in the *Do It Again!* program, some were undoubtedly shortened by omitting verses and extra choruses while others were probably sung in medley format (song assignments unknown): "The Babbitt and the Bromide" (from *Funny Face*, 1927), "Bess, You Is My Woman Now" (*Porgy and Bess*, 1935; lyric by DuBose Heyward and Ira Gershwin) "Bidin' My Time" (*Girl Crazy*, 1930) "By Strauss" (*The Show Is On*, 1936) "Clap Yo' Hands" (*Oh, Kay!*, 1926), "Do, Do, Do" (*Oh, Kay!*, 1926) "Do It Again" (*The French Doll*, 1922; lyric by B.G. [Buddy] DeSylva) "Don't Be a Woman If You Can" (*Park Avenue*, 1946) "Embraceable You" (*Girl Crazy*, 1930) "Fascinating Rhythm" (*Lady, Be Good!*, 1924) "A Foggy Day (in London Town)" (1937 film *A Damsel in Distress*), "For You, For Me, For Evermore" (1947 film *The Shocking Miss Pilgrim*), "Funny Face" (*Funny Face*, 1927) "How Long Has This Been Going On?" (dropped during the tryout of *Funny Face* [1927]; later used in *Rosalie* [1928]), "I Don't Think I'll Fall in Love Today" (*Treasure Girl*, 1928),

"If I Became the President" (*Strike Up the Band*, 1930 version) "I Got Plenty o' Nuthin'" (*Porgy and Bess*, 1935; lyric by Ira Gershwin and DuBose Heyward), "I Got Rhythm" (*Girl Crazy*, 1930) "I'm On My Way" (*Porgy and Bess*, 1935; lyric by DuBose Heyward) "It Ain't Necessarily So" (*Porgy and Bess*, 1935), "I've Got a Crush on You" (*Treasure Girl* [1928]; later used in the 1930 version of *Strike Up the Band*), "Let's Call the Whole Thing Off" (1937 film *Shall We Dance*), "Little Jazz Bird" (*Lady, Be Good!*, 1924) "Liza" (*Show Girl*, 1929) "Looking for a Boy" (*Tip-Toes*, 1925) "Love Is Here to Stay" (1938 film *The Goldwyn Follies*), "Love Is Sweeping the Country" (*Of Thee I Sing*, 1931), "Love Walked In" (1938 film *The Goldwyn Follies*), "The Man I Love" (dropped during the tryout of *Lady, Be Good!* [1924]; later used in 1927 version of *Strike Up the Band* [which closed during its pre-Broadway tryout]; later considered for, but not used in, *Rosalie* [1928]), "Maybe" (*Oh, Kay!*, 1926), "Mine" (*Let 'Em Eat Cake*, 1933) "My Man's Gone Now" (*Porgy and Bess*, 1935; lyric by DuBose Heyward) "Naughty Baby" (1924 London musical *Primrose*; lyric by Desmond Carter) "Nice Work If You Can Get It" (1937 film *A Damsel in Distress*), "Of Thee I Sing" (*Of Thee I Sing*, 1931), "Oh, Lady, Be Good!" (*Lady, Be Good!*, 1924), "Oh What She Hangs Out (She Hangs Out in Our Alley)" (*Spice of 1922*; lyric by B.G. [Buddy] DeSylva and E. Ray Goetz), "Prelude No. 2" (1926), "The Real American Folk Song Is a Rag" (*Ladies First*, 1918) "Rhapsody in Blue" (1924), "Slap That Bass" (1937 film *A Damsel in Distress*), "Somebody Loves Me" (*George White's Scandals* [Sixth Edition], 1924; lyric by B.G. [Buddy] DeSylva and Ballard MacDonald), "Someone to Watch Over Me" (*Oh, Kay!*, 1926), "Soon" (*Strike Up the Band*, 1930; part of the song was also heard in the 1927 version of *Strike Up the Band*, which closed during its tryout) "(I'll Build a) Stairway to Paradise" (*For Goodness Sake*, 1922; lyric by B.G. [Buddy] DeSylva and Arthur Francis [Ira Gershwin]), "Strike Up the Band" (*Strike Up the Band*, 1927 and 1930 versions), "Summertime" (*Porgy and Bess*, 1935; lyric by DuBose Heyward), "Swanee" (*Demi Tasse/Capitol Revue*, 1919; lyric by Irving Caesar; later used in *Sinbad* [also 1919]), "S'Wonderful" (*Funny Face*, 1927) "That Certain Feeling" (*Tip-Toes*, 1925), "There's a Boat Dat's Leavin' Soon for New York" (*Porgy and Bess*, 1935) "They All Laughed" (1937 film *Shall We Dance*), "They Can't Take That Away from Me" (1937 film *Shall We Dance*), "Who Cares?" (*Of Thee I Sing*, 1931) "Wintergreen for President" (*Of Thee I Sing*, 1931)

391 Doctor! Doctor! THEATRE: Players Theatre; OPENING DATE: March 26, 1997; PERFORMANCES: 31; LYRICS: Peter Ekstrom; MUSIC: Peter Ekstrom; ADDITIONAL MATERIAL AND LYRICS: David DeBoy; DIRECTION: Richard Rose; SCENERY: Crystal Tiala; COSTUMES: Amanda Aldridge; LIGHTING: David G. Silver-Friedl; MUSICAL DIRECTION: Albert Ahronheim; PRODUCER: The Barter Theatre (Richard Rose, Artistic Director)

CAST—Buddy Crutchfield (Jay), Jill Geddes (Audrey), Nancy Johnston (Gloria), James Weatherstone (William), Albert Ahronheim (Receptionist)

The revue was presented in two acts.

ACT ONE—"The Human Body" (Company), "Oh, Boy! How I Love My Cigarettes!" (Buddy Crutchfield, Jill Geddes), "The Consummate Picture" (Nancy Johnston), "I'm a Well-Known, Respected Practitioner" (James Weatherstone), "Tomorrow" (Jill Geddes), "A World of My Own" (Nancy Johnston), "And Yet I Lived On" (Company), "Willie" (Nancy Johnston), "The Right Hand Song" (Albert Ahronheim), "Please, Dr. Fletcher?" (Jill Geddes), "Take It Off, Tammy!" (James Weatherstone), "It's My Fat!" (Buddy Crutchfield), "Nine Long Months Ago" (Company)

ACT TWO—"Hymn" (Company), "Medicine Man Blues" (Nancy Johnston), "Private Practice" (James Weatherstone), "Nurse's Care" (Jill Geddes), "I'm Sure of It" (Jill Geddes, James Weatherstone), "I Loved My Father" (Buddy Crutchfield), "Jesus Is My Doctor" (Nancy Johnston, Company), "Bing, Bang, Boom!" (Jill Geddes, Buddy Crutchfield), "Eighty Thousand Orgasms" (Nancy Johnston, James Weatherstone), "Good Ole Days (of Sex)" (James Weatherstone, Jill Geddes), "Do I Still Have You" (James Weatherstone), "I Hope I Never Get It" (Buddy Crutchfield), "The Human Body" (reprise) (Company)

NOTES—Anita Gates began her review of *Doctor! Doctor!* in the *New York Times* with this memorable put-down: "Let's put it this way: the sing-along about hemorrhoids could have been much worse."

Gates found the revue "thoroughly unoriginal" and lacking a point of view; further, the music was "uninspired" and the lyrics "lead nowhere." But she liked the costumes, such as those worn by American tourists at Chartres or by WASPs on a golf course, and noted these made "the sight of hospital gowns a relief."

The script was published by Samuel French, Inc.

The short-lived revue about doctors and medicine had been originally performed as *Doctors and Diseases* at the Actors Theatre of Louisville in 1979 and at Barter Stage II in Abingdon, Virginia, in 1996.

392 Dr. Faustus Lights the Lights. "An Opera"; THEATRE: Judson Poets' Theatre; OPENING DATE: October 26, 1979; PERFORMANCES: 16; LIBRETTO: Gertrude Stein; adapted by Al Carmines; MUSIC: Al Carmines; DIRECTION: Lawrence Kornfeld; SCENERY: Ed Lazansky; COSTUMES: Theo Barnes; LIGHTING: Victor En Tu Yan; MUSICAL DIRECTION: Michael Kelly; PRODUCER: Judson Poets' Theatre

CAST—Jeff Weiss (Dr. Faustus), Al Carmines (Mephisto), Stephen English (A Dog), Aramis Estevez (A Little Boy), Zoelle Montgomery (Marguerite Ida Helena Annabel), Florence Tarlow (A Country Woman), Nathaniel Bucknell (A Man from Over the Seas), Sarah Kornfeld (A Little Girl); Chorus (Jackie Beech, Essie Borden, Lou Bullock, Esteban Chalbaud, Wendell Cordtz, Craig Kuehl, Barbara Sandek, Maggie Wise)

The opera was performed in two acts.

NOTES—The Off Off Broadway *Dr. Faustus Lights the Lights* was the sixth and final adaptation by Al Carmines of Gertrude Stein's works. See entries for *What Happened* (1963), *In Circles* (1967), *The Making of Americans* (1972), *Listen to Me* (1974), and *A Manoir* (1977).

Dr. Faustus Lights the Lights was Gertrude Stein's version of the Faust theme; in her telling, Faustus sells his soul to the devil for the power of light. In 1938, Stein wrote the piece as an opera libretto, which was to have been set to music by Lord Berners; but he was reportedly unable to compose due to his depression over Europe's political situation in the late 1930s. The libretto thus became the basis for non-musical productions of the work, and it took forty-one years for the libretto to finally be set to music. Another lyric adaptation of the work was presented at Lincoln Center's *Serious Fun!* festival in July 1992; this version was composed by Hans Peter Kuhn, and was directed by Robert Wilson.

393 Doctor Selavy's Magic Theatre (1972). THEATRE: Mercer-O'Casey Theatre; OPENING DATE: November 23, 1972; PERFORMANCES: 144; BOOK MATERIAL WRITTEN BY Richard Forman; LYRICS: Tom Hendry; MUSIC: Stanley Silverman; DIRECTION: Richard Foreman; PRODUCERS: Lyn Austin and Oliver Smith; A Lenox Arts Center Production

CAST—Denise Delapenha (Fortune Teller), Mary Delson (Female Pirate), Ron Faber (Patient), Jessica Harper (Rock Singer), George McGrath (Dr. Selavy), Steve Menken (Doctor with Most Hair), Jackie Paris (Little Girl), Robert Schlee (Shortest Male Doctor), Amy Taubin (Shortest Female Doctor)

The action occurs in a hospital.

The musical was presented in one act.

MUSICAL NUMBERS—*Introduction*: "I Live by My Wits" (Ron Faber), *First Day's Treatment*—"Facing the Pirates" (Female Doctors, George McGrath) "Three Menu Songs" (Mary Delson, Robert Schlee), "Bankrupt Blues" (Steve Menken), "Future for Sale" (Denise Delapenha), "Life on the Inside" (Amy Taubin), *Second Day's Treatment*—"Living the Good Life" (George McGrath), "Strawberry-Blueberry" (Jessica Harper, Steve Menken), "The More You Get" (Ron Faber), "Money in the Bank" (Jessica Harper, Ron Faber), "Life on the Inside" (reprise), "Long Live Free Enterprise" "Doesn't It Bug You," "Dusky Shadows," *Third Day's Treatment*—"Dreaming of Love" (George McGrath), "Poor Boy" (Ron Faber, with Denise Delapenha and Robert Schlee), "Dearest Man" (Mary Delson, with Amy Taubin), *Fourth Day's Treatment*—"The Symbolic Death and Rebirth" (George McGrath), "Where You Been Hiding Till Now" (Denise Delapenha, Doctors), "Fireman's Song" (Ron Faber), "What Are You Proposing," "Party's Gonna End," "Requiem" (Jessica Harper, Denise Delapenha, Company), *Fifth Day's Treatment*—"The Ecstasy and the Cure" (George McGrath), "Let's Hear It for Daddy Moola" (Denise Delapenha, Company), "Life on the Inside" (reprise) (Amy Taubin, Denise Delapenha, Jessica Harper)

NOTES—A sung-through musical, *Doctor Selavy's Magic Theatre* (read: c'est la vie) was a satiric look at therapy for mental illness and had first been produced at the Lenox Arts Festival in Lenox, Massachusetts, during Summer 1972.

Clearly a very specialized piece, the musical nonetheless played four months, thanks in part to its score and its unusual subject matter. Clive Barnes in the *New York Times* liked the "engaging madness" of the evening, and twice mentioned the "rare zaniness" of how the actors stared menacingly and coldly at the audience as they went about their songs and shtick, "generally behaving like the Marx Brothers at a Marxist rally." Barnes also praised the "original and yet sophisticatedly paraodistic" lyrics and music.

The cast recording was released by United Artists Records (LP # UA-LA196-G), with Barry Primus replacing Ron Faber, who had left the musical after its first week. The album, subtitled *Swinging at the Stock Exchange*, included two numbers not heard on opening night ("Swinging at the Stock Exchange" and "Every New Beginning").

The album also credited the lyric for "Poor Boy" to Stanley Silverman, and the lyric for "Requiem" to Richard Foreman and John Hirsch.

The piece was revived as *Dr. Selavy's Magic Theatre (C'est La Vie)* in 1984, for twenty performances (see entry); Jessica Harper, who was in the original production, also appeared in the revival.

394 Dr. Selavy's Magic Theatre (C'est La Vie) (1984). THEATRE: St. Clement's Theatre; OPENING DATE: January 27, 1984; PERFORMANCES: 20; BOOK MATERIAL WRITTEN BY Richard Foreman; LYRICS: Tom Hendry; MUSIC: Stanley Silverman; DIRECTION: Richard Foreman; SCENERY: Richard Foreman and Nancy Winters; COSTUMES: Lindsay W. Davis; LIGHTING: Pat Collins; MUSICAL DIRECTION: Michael Ward; PRODUCERS: Music-Theatre Group/Lenox Arts Center and Ontological-Hysteric Theatre

CAST—Roy Brocksmith, David Patrick Kelly, Dara Norman, Annie Golden, George McGrath, Charlie O'Connell, Jessica Harper, Kathi Moss, John Vining (program didn't identify names of characters; see entry for 1972 production for information regarding names of characters)

The action occurs in a hospital.

The musical was presented in one act.

MUSICAL NUMBERS—*Patient's Progress* (*Phases of the Cure*): *Prologue*—Doctors size up their patient (and vice versa?), "I Live by My Wits" (David Patrick Kelly), *First Day's Treatment*—Introducing him to aggressive forces (Pirates inside and out.), "Three Menu Songs" (Dara Norman, John Vining, Company), "Bankrupt Blues" (Roy Brocksmith, Company), "Future for Sale" (Jessica Harper), "Life on the Inside" (Annie Golden), *Second Day's Treatment*—Offering him sweets (and riches and the life of leisure), "Strawberry-Blueberry" (Roy Brocksmith, Kathi Moss), "The More You Get" (David Patrick Kelly), "Money in the Bank" (Jessica Harper, David Patrick Kelly, Company), "Life on the Inside" (reprise) (Annie Golden, John Vining), "If You're Proposing" (George McGrath), "Long Live Free Enterprise" (Company), "Doesn't It Bug You" (Annie Golden, Dara Norman, Kathi Moss, Jessica Harper), "Dusky Shadows" (Roy Brocksmith, Annie Golden, Jessica Harper, Kathi Moss, Dara Norman), *Third Day's Treatment*—Letting him dream of love, but warning that it probably won't last. "Poor Boy" (David Patrick Kelly, Annie Golden, John Vining), "Dearest Man" (Dara Norman, Jessica Harper), *Fourth Day's Treatment*—Tracking him down for the final confrontation. Death, rebirth, rage, momentary triumph—and that too passes. "Where You Been Hiding Til Now" (Kathi Moss, Company), "He Lived By His Wits" (John Vining, Roy Brocksmith, George McGrath), "Fireman's Song" (David Patrick Kelly, Annie Golden, Jessica Harper, Kathi Moss, Dara Norman), "What Are You Proposing" (George McGrath, John Vining), "Doctors in The Chase Scene" (Jessica Harper, John Vining), "Requiem" (Jessica Harper, Kathi Moss, Company), *Fifth Day's Treatment*—Treatment concluded, patient ready to re-enter the word; day 1, the courage to fight windmills, and the greater courage to know the battle ... has no resolution. "Let's Hear It for Daddy Moolah" (Kathi Moss, Company), "Life on the Inside" (reprise) (Annie Golden, Jessica Harper)

NOTES—This satiric Off Off Broadway musical had previously been produced Off Broadway in 1972 as *Doctor Selavy's Magic Theatre* (see entry for more information about the musical). Jessica Harper was in both the original production and the revival.

395 Dr. Sex. THEATRE: Peter Norton Space; OPENING DATE: September 21, 2005; PERFORMANCES: 23; BOOK: Larry Bortniker and Sally Deeting; LYRICS: Larry Bortniker; MUSIC: Larry Bortniker; DIRECTION: "Production Supervised" by Greg Hirsch; CHOREOGRAPHY: Mark Esposito; SCENERY: Rob Bissinger; COSTUMES: John Carver Sullivan; LIGHTING: Richard Winkler; MUSICAL DIRECTION: Alan Bukowiecki; PRODUCERS: Richard Ericson and Greg Young; Jann Cobler and Tom Wilson, Associate Producers

CAST—BRIAN NOONAN (Alfred C. Kinsey), Jared Bradshaw (Kinsey Player, Student, George, Bar Patron, Messenger, American), Linda Cameron (Kinsey Player, Miss Baxter, Mrs. Cavendish, Bar Patron, Miss Loretta Rockefeller, Telephone Operator, American), David Edwards (Kinsey Player, Student, Dean Howell, Mr. Cavendish, Dr. Wilhelm Hoffstedter, America), Christy Faber (Kinsey Player, Student, Daphne, Brenda, American), Colleen Hawks (Kinsey Player, Student, Phoebe, American), Benjie Randall (Kinsey Player, Student, Jack, Edgar Stevens, American), JENNIFER SIMARD (Clara Kinsey), CHRISTOPHER CORTS (Wally)

The musical was presented in two acts.

ACT ONE—"1, 2, 3, 4, 5, 6" (Brian Noonan, Company), "Rah, Rah, Rah, Rah" (Jared Bradshaw, Linda Cameron, David Edwards, Christy Faber, Colleen Hawks, Benjie Randall), "I'm in Love with My Zoology Professor" (Jennifer Simard), "Here in a Bog" (Brian Noonan, Jennifer Simard), "Gall Wasp Wedding"/"Honeymoon Dance" (Company), "The Call of the Wild" (Brian Noonan, Christopher Corts, Benjie Randall, Jared Bradshaw), "Angelface" (Brian Noonan, Christopher Corts, Jennifer Simard), "Dr. Sex" (Brian Noonan, Jared Bradshaw, Linda Cameron, David Edwards, Christy Faber, Colleen Hawks, Benjie Randall), "What People Really Do When the Lights Are Low" (Brian Noonan, Jennifer Simard, Christopher Corts), "Pharoah's Tomb" (Company)

ACT TWO—"Swingin' for Science" (Brian Noonan, Jennifer Simard, Christopher Corts, Company), "John D. Rockefeller" (Company), "They'll Tell You Everything" (Brian Noonan, Christopher Corts, Company), "The Doctor's Wife" (Jennifer Simard), "A Simple Rotational System" (Company), "I'm Still in Love with My Zoology Professor" (Jennifer Simard), "That Dirty Book" (Company), "Kinsey in the Eleventh Hour" (Company)

NOTES—Jason Zinoman in the *New York Times* found *Dr. Sex* a "small, silly musical in the guise of a big, silly one." The musical about Alfred Kinsey was "a harmless and derivative piece of fluff" in which the title character "likes to party at gay clubs and crack wise like a Catskills comic." Zinoman noted that Jennifer Simard's performance was the "highlight" of the evening (she "hits the right musical and parodic notes") and that she stopped the show with her torch song "The Doctor's Wife."

During early ads for the musical, Pamela Hunt was credited as director.

The musical was first produced at the Bailiwick Repertory Theatre in Chicago on September 5, 2003.

In 2004, *Kinsey*, a film version about the sex researcher's life, was released (Liam Neeson played the title role). On September 10, 2007, the Off Broadway play *Alfred Kinsey: A Love Story* by Mike Folie opened at the Michael Weller Theatre.

396 Dogs. "A New All-American Musical"; THEATRE: Perry Street Theatre; OPENING DATE: August 10, 1983; PERFORMANCES: 6; BOOK: James Stewart Bennett and Charles G. Horne; LYRICS: James Stewart Bennett; MUSIC: James Stewart Bennett; DIRECTION: Charles G. Horne; SCENERY: Jack Kelly; COSTUMES: Jack Kelly and Peyton Smith; LIGHTING: Edward RF Matthews; PRODUCER: Provincetown Theatre Ensemble in "Exile"

CAST—Lanny Green (Human), Linda Marie Larson (Duney), Caroline Cox (Judi), Kathryn Hunter (Poco), Terry Blaine (Sally), Valerie Santuccio (Dawn), Nicholas Searcy (Boomie), Mark Enis (Butchy), Neil Lyons (Rex), D. Jonathan Vaughn (Sammy)

The action occurs in New York City at the present time.

The musical was presented in two acts.

ACT ONE—"Welcome to Goodies" (Valerie Santuccio, Lanny Green [?], Female Dogs), "Tricks" (Lanny Green [?], Valerie Santuccio, Female Dogs), "Humpin' Hips" (Caroline Cox, Dog Company), "Dawn's Unemployment History" (Valerie Santuccio, Caroline Cox, Female Dogs), "Keep It Cool" (Female Dogs), "Tough Dogs"/"Chic Dogs" (Dog Company), "Jail Song" (Dog Company), "Somehow I Must Find a Way Out" (Nicholas Searcy), "I Hate Dogs" (Lanny Green), "Masters Song" (Dog Company), "I'm the Master of the City" (Lanny Green, Company), "Tricks" (reprise) (Lanny Green, Valerie Santuccio), "Somehow I Must Find a Way Out" (reprise) (Nicholas Searcy, Neil Lyons, Terry Blaine, Linda Marie Larson, Mark Enis, Kathryn Hunter), First Act Finale (Valerie Santuccio, Nicholas Searcy, Caroline Cox, Dog Company)

ACT TWO—"Dance at the Ritz" (Orchestra), "Awkward Waltz" (Valerie Santuccio, Nicholas Searcy, Lanny Green), "I Got a Plan" (Valerie Santuccio), "Bureau of Mutual Affairs" (Dog Company), "Don't Take Away All My Friends" (Valerie Santuccio, Company), Finale (Company)

NOTES—After the success of *Cats* (1982), *Dogs* was probably inevitable (and there was *Rats*, too [not to mention *Pets!*]; see entries).

Mel Gussow in the *New York Times* noted that the "dog-eared" musical opened during the "dog days" of August and would soon be "yapping its way into theatrical limbo." Further, the score was "composed of musical table scraps," and when the first act offered a reprise of "Somehow I Must Find My Way Out," Gussow felt the title perfectly matched his sentiments.

There was also a 1983 regional musical called *Dawgs!* with old and new songs by Richard M. Sherman and Robert B. Sherman and additional songs by John Henry; it was recorded by Glendale Records (LP # GLS-6032).

397 The $ Value of Man. THEATRE: Lepercq Space/Brooklyn Academy of Music; OPENING DATE: May 9, 1975; PERFORMANCES: 8; TEXT: Christopher Knowles and Robert Wilson; Carol Mullins, Vaudeville Script Coordinator; James Neu, Casino Script Coordinator Music: Michael Galasso; DIRECTION: Christopher Knowles and Robert Wilson; Ralph Hilton, Assistant Director; CHOREOGRAPHY: Andrew De Groat; Steven Crawford, Additional Movement; SCENERY: Gregory Payne, Terrence Chambers, and Charles Dennis; Mayra Levy, Props; COSTUMES: Richard Roth; LIGHTING: Carol Mullins; PRODUCER: The Brooklyn Academy of Music (A Byrd Hoffman Foundation Production)

CAST—Catherine Allport, Eric Appel, George Ashley, Ellen Benson, Robyn Brentano, Ritty Burchfield, Jacob Burckhardt, Julia Busto, Kevin Byrnes, Kathryn Cation, Steven Crawford, Roger Curtis, Frank DeGregorie, Andrew De Groat, Dale De Groff, Sandra Delaney, Charles Dennis, Laura Epstein, Nasar Farhangfar, Fahimeh Farhangfar, James Finguerra, Meredith Gang, Karin Greenblatt, Andy Gurian, Ester Grite, Edward Hadas, Julia Hanlon, Ralph Hilton, Melissa Homan, Arnold Horton, Julia Hymen, Maria Karrell, Christopher Knowles, Jan Kroeze, Robert Levithan, Mayra Levy, Robert Liebowitz, Cynthia Lubar, Elaine Luthy, Paul Mann, Richard Morrison, Carol Mullins, James Neu, Gregory Payne, Liz Pasquale, Ewa Pietkiewcz, Alfred Godot Pinhiero, Kathryn Ray, Marin Riley, Michael Rivlin, Richard Roth, Valda Setterfield, Shirley Soffer, Chris Stevens, Rosetta Stone, Ruth Tepper, Paul Thek, Ann Wooster, Sally Wormer, Shelley Valfer, Scotty Snyder

The work was presented in one act.

NOTES—*The Best Plays of 1974-1975* described *The $ Value of Man* as "another round of [Robert] Wilson's highly imaginative comments on the world around us." Clive Barnes in the *New York Times* reported the work's title and theme were derived from a Op-Ed piece which had appeared in the *New York Times* a year earlier, an article which speculated on the actual cash value of a human life (throughout the two-and-a-half-hour evening, the article was read to the audience). Further, Barnes indicated the action dealt with such topics as gambling, holdups, and cash registers, all of which were accompanied by incidental music ("a kind of baroque-cum-country-and-Western continuo") and some dancing (including a "mild dervish"). Barnes also reported that Wilson experimented with pre-recorded dialogue which was played in tandem with the "live" lines the performers were speaking ("a kind of uncoordinated instant replay" which was more interesting in theory than in action). Ultimately, Barnes felt Wilson never really had much to say about the subject of money, and noted that the evening was an arcane exercise more suited to the "theatrical laboratory than the theatre itself."

398 A Doll's Life. THEATRE: Saint Peter's Church/The York Theatre Company; OPENING DATE: December 21, 1994; PERFORMANCES: 34; BOOK: Betty Comden and Adolph Green; LYRICS: Betty Comden and Adolph Green; MUSIC: Larry Grossman; DIRECTION: Robert Brink; SCENERY: James Morgan; COSTUMES: Patricia Adshead; LIGHTING: Mary Jo Dondlinger; MUSICAL DIRECTION: David Kirshenbaum; PRODUCERS: The York Theatre Company (Janet Hayes Walker, Producing Director; Joseph V. De Michele, Managing Director) and One World Arts Foundation, Inc. (W. Scott McLucas, Executive Director; George Rondo, Artistic Director)

CAST—Seth Jones (Torvald), Jill Geddes (Nora), Howard Pinhasik (Conductor, Berg, Peterson, Butler, Muller, Hugo Zetterling), Jeff Herbst (Otto), Tamra Hayden (Lady of the Evening, Audition Singer, Jailed Woman, Johan's Secretary, Power Patron, Camilla Forrester), Jennifer Laura Thompson (Lady of the Evening, Audition Singer, Cannery Girl, Helga, Power Patron, Birgit), Michael Klashman (Pimp, Gustafson, Call Boy, Audition Singer, Kloster, Power Patron), Paul Schoeffler (Eric Didrickson), Robin Syke (Astrid Klemnacht, Dowager), Catherine Anne Gale (Respectable Woman, Guest, Cannery Girl, Jailed Woman, Jacqueline LeBeau), Eileen McNamara (Respectable Woman, Waitress, Guest, Selma, Cannery Girl, Jailed Woman, Power Patron, Berta), Paul Blankenship (Hamsun, Karl [The Stage Manager], Guest, Ambassador, Power Patron), Tom Galantich (Johan Blecker)

The action occurs in Norway during the late nineteenth century (1879-1883).

The musical was presented in two acts.

ACT ONE—"What Now?" (Jill Geddes), "A Woman Alone" (Part I) (Jill Geddes, Howard Pinhasik), "Letter to the Children" (Jill Geddes), "A Woman Alone" (Part II) (Jill Geddes, Howard Pinhasik, Jeff Herbst), "Arrival in Christiania" (Jill Geddes, Crowd), "New Year's Eve" (Tom Galantich, Paul Schoeffler, Howard Pinhasik, Michael Klashman), "Stay with Me, Nora" (Jeff Herbst, Jill Geddes), "The Arrival" (Robin Syke, Paul Blankenship, Catherine Ann Gale, Eileen McNamara), "Loki and Baldur" (Jeff Herbst, Male and Female Singer), "You Interest Me" (Tom Galantich), "The Departure" (Robin Syke, Paul Blankenship, Catherine Anne Gale, Eileen McNamara), "Letter from Klemnacht" (Robin Syke), "Learn to Be Lonely" (Jill Geddes), "Rats and Mice and Fish" (Jill Geddes, Eileen McNamara, Catherine Anne Gale, Eileen McNamara, Jennifer Laura Thompson), "Jailer, Jailer" (Catherine Anne Gale, Tamra Hayden, Eileen McNamara), "Rare Wines" (Paul Schoeffler, Jill Geddes)

ACT TWO—"You Puzzle Me" (Tom Galantich), "No More Mornings" (Jill Geddes) "There She Is" (Tom Galantich, Paul Schoeffler, Jeff Herbst), "Power" (Jill Geddes), "Letter to the Children" (reprise) (Jill Geddes), "At Last" (Tom Galantich), "Can't You Hear I'm Making Love to You" (Tom Galantich, Jill Geddes)

NOTES—It was miserable sitting through *A Doll's Life* in its gargantuan Broadway production, and it was equally miserable sitting through its tiny Off Off Broadway revival. Perhaps the most overproduced musical of its era, *A Doll's Life* opened on Broadway at the Mark Hellinger Theatre on September 23, 1982, and played for just five performances (its quick closing even made the front page of the *New York Times*). The musical was bloated and plot-heavy, and boasted ones of the most unlikable and unsympathetic characters in the history of musical theatre. As a sequel to Henrik Ibsen's *A Doll's House* (1879), the musical showed us what supposedly happened to the newly liberated Nora when she slammed the door on her hapless, clueless, but hardly evil husband (and her innocent children). The musical's message seemed to say the ultimate goal for a liberated woman is to become as much like a man as possible, a premise which would certainly have surprised Ibsen, not to mention modern-day feminists. The best which could be said for the York version was that it mercifully dropped some of the excesses of the original production, such as the opening sequence (which presented a group of actors in the present time who are rehearsing a production of *A Doll's House*) and the joyless dancing couples (who periodically twirled about the stage in portentous, if meaningless, fashion). But the York production still offered up a dull if not ludicrous book and a cold and unfeeling central character.

The laughably pretentious musical wore its angst and anger like a badge of honor, and it was hard to believe Broadway veterans Betty Comden and Adolph Green had written such a grim book and lyrics. Surely *A Doll's Life* was just the kind of pompous musical they had spoofed in the screenplay of their classic 1953 film *The Band Wagon*.

Only Larry Grossman, the musical's composer, emerged from the wreckage with honor. This vastly underrated composer left behind an often sweeping and melodic score which might have worked better sans lyrics as an independent *Suite from A Doll's Life*.

Most of the songs from the original production were retained for the revival, with the exception of "The Grand Café," one of best sequences in the score; added to the revival was "Can't You Hear I'm Making Love to You."

The original Broadway cast recording was released by Original Cast Records (LP # OC-8241, which was later reissued by CBS Special Products Records LP # P-18846; the CD was issued by Bay Cities Records # BCD-3031), and the script was published by Samuel French, Inc., in 1983.

399 The Donkey Show: A Midsummer Night's Disco. THEATRE: Club El Flamingo; OPENING DATE: August 18, 1999; PERFORMANCES: 1,488; CREATED BY Diane Paulus and Randy Weiner; DIRECTION: Diane Paulus and Randy Weiner; CHOREOGRAPHY: Maria Torres; SCENERY: Scott Park; COSTUMES: David C. Woolard; LIGHTING: Kevin Adams; PRODUCER: Jordan Roth

CAST—Rachel Benbow Murdy (Oberon, Mia), Anna Wilson (Tytania), Roman Pietrs (Rollerena), Jordin Ruderman (Helen, Vinnie 1), Emily Hellstrom (Dimitri, Vinnie 2), Anna Wilson (Sander), Oscar Estevez (Mustard Seed), Luke Miller (Cobweb), Dan Cryer (Moth), Quinn (Peasebottom), Orlando Santana (Rico Suave), Barbara Resstab (Disco Lady), Kevin Shand (DJ Hernando Pacheski)

SOURCE—William Shakespeare's play *A Midsummer Night's Dream* (written circa 1595-1596).

The action occurs in a disco in New York City in the 1970s.

The musical was presented in one act.

MUSICAL NUMBERS—"A Fifth of Beethoven," "Also Spach Zarathrustra," "Car Wash," "Dance with Me," "Disco Circus," "Don't Leave Me This Way," "I Love the Nightlife," "Never Knew Love Like This Before," "I'm Your Boogie Man," "Knock on Wood," "Ring My Bell," "Salsation," "That's the Way of the World," "You Sexy Thing," "We Are Family"

NOTES—*The Donkey Show*, a very loose adaptation of Shakespeare's *A Midsummer Night's Dream*, was set in a New York City disco during the height of the so-called disco era of the late 1970s and early 1980s, and it actually was performed in a club (Club El Flamenco, located in the Chelsea neighborhood). The musical's score was a collection of disco-era songs, all of them lip-synched by the performers.

Peter Marks in the *New York Times* found the musical a "rollicking hour of sex, drugs and sweaty gyrations ... a lark, an exuberant and witty splicing of" disco music and Shakespeare. He noted the show could easily have been titled *A Donna Summer Night's Dream*.

The musical became a long-running hit, chalking up approximately 1,800 performances. It first opened Off Off Broadway, and seems to have eventually transferred to Off Broadway status. In 2001, *The Donkey Show* was seen in London at the Hanover Grand Theatre.

For another Off Broadway adaptation of the material, see entry for *Babes in the Wood*. There was also a "swing" version of Shakespeare's comedy: *Swingin' the Dream* opened on Broadway at the Center Theatre on November 29, 1939, and played for thirteen performances. Its cast included Benny Goodman, Louis Armstrong, Dorothy McGuire, Maxine Sullivan, Butterfly McQueen, and the Dandridge Sisters (including Dorothy), and the lovely "Darn That Dream" was the highlight of the score by Eddie de Lange and Jimmy Van Heusen.

400 Dont Bother Me, I Cant Cope. "A New Musical Entertainment"; THEATRE: Playhouse Theatre; transferred to the Edison Theatre on June 13, 1972; OPENING DATE: April 19, 1972; PERFORMANCES: 1,065; LYRICS: Micki Grant; MUSIC: Micki Grant; DIRECTION: Vinnette Carroll; CHOREOGRAPHY: George Faison; SCENERY: Richard A. Miller; supervised by Neil Peter Jampolis; COSTUMES: Edna Watson; supervised by Sara Brook; LIGHTING: B.J. Sammler; supervised by Ken Billington; MUSICAL DIRECTION: Danny Holgate; PRODUCERS: Edward Padula and Arch Lustberg presenting Vinnette Carroll's Urban Arts Corps production, in association with Ford's Theatre Society

CAST—Alex Bradford, Micki Grant, Bobby Hill, Hope Clarke, Arnold Wilkerson; Singers (Alberta Bradford, Charles Campbell, Marie Thomas); Dancers (Thommie Bush, Gerald G. Francis, Ben Harney, Leona Johnson) The revue was presented in two acts.

ACT ONE—"I Gotta Keep Movin'" (Alex Bradford, Alberta Bradford, Charles Campbell, Bobby Hill; danced by Ben Harney), "Harlem Streets" (danced by Thommie Bush, Gerald G. Francis, Ben Harney, Leona Johnson), "Lookin' Over from Your Side" (Bobby Hill), "Don't Bother Me, I Can't Cope" (Company), "When I Feel Like Moving" (Hope Clarke; danced by Thommie Bush, Gerald G. Francis, Ben Harney, Leona Johnson), "Help" (Hope Clarke; danced by Thommie Bush, Gerald G. Francis, Ben Harney, Leona Johnson), "Fighting for Pharoah" (Alex Bradford, Bobby Hill, Alberta Bradford, Charles Campbell), "Good Vibrations" (Alex Bradford, Company), "Love Power" (Bobby Hill, Hope Clarke, Company), "You Think I Got Rhythm?" (danced by Thommie Bush, Gerald G. Francis, Ben Harney, Leona Johnson), "They Keep Coming" (Company), "My Name Is Man" (Arnold Wilkerson)

ACT TWO—"Questions" (Micki Grant), "It Takes a Whole Lot of Human Feeling" (Micki Grant), "You Think I Got Rhythm?" (reprise) (Arnold Wilkerson, Micki Grant), "Time Brings About a Change" (Micki Grant, Alex Bradford, Alberta Bradford, Charles Campbell, Marie Thomas, Arnold Wilkerson), "So Little Time" (Micki Grant), "Thank Heaven for You" (Bobby Hill, Micki Grant), "So Long Sammy" (Bobby Hill, danced by Hope Clarke, Thommie Bush, Gerald C. Francis, Ben Harney, Leona Johnson), "All I Need" (Alex Bradford, Company), "I Gotta Keep Movin'" (reprise) (Micki Grant, Alex Bradford, Company)

NOTES—The apostrophe (but not comma) challenged *Dont Bother Me, I Cant Cope* was first seen Off Off Broadway during the 1970-1971 season in a production by the Urban Arts Corps. The musical was later seen at Ford's Theatre in Washington,

D.C., in September 1971. A program note indicated that "'coping' is a basic commitment of a mature, purposeful, involved human being, that we sometimes laugh to keep from crying, that life is not necessarily fair, that happiness is a by-product not an end product, and that the ways we are similar are far greater than the ways we are different."

Like so many Off Broadway entertainments, the revue might have worked better in an intimate nightclub or cabaret venue; but the easy-going company (and the especially classy presence of Micki Grant) and the rather smooth, easy-listening songs overcame the confines of a larger-than-necessary theatre, and the revue ran for over 1,000 performances.

During the run, one song ("Show Me That Special Gene" [for Leona Johnson, Marie Thomas, and Micki Grant]) was added.

During the tryout, the musical numbers were divided into four sequences (*Resurrection City* [which included a section titled *Poetry Sequences by Langston Hughes & Micki Grant*], *Harlem Streets*, *Micki Sings Micki*, and *Elegy for Bessie, Billie & Jim*); this framework was dropped for the New York production. Numbers deleted during the Washington run were "Resurrection City," "Universe in Mourning," "My Love's So Good," "Liberated Woman," "So Now You Come," "Miss Bessie," and "Jimi." During the tryout, the song "My Name Is Man" seemed to be credited to both Langston Hughes and Grant; for New York, the number is credited only to Grant..

During subsequent productions, some numbers were omitted while others ("Lock Up the Doors," "Children's Rhymes," "Billy Holiday Song," "Billy Holliday Ballet," "Ghetto Life," "My Love's No Good," "Men's Dance," "Love Mississippi," "Prayer," "Sermon," and "Universe in Mourning"[the latter had originally been heard during the tryout]) were added. "Fighting for Pharoah" was retitled "Do a Little Living for Peace (Fighting for Pharoah)."

The cast album was recorded on Polydor Records (LP # PD-6013), and the script was published by Samuel French, Inc., in 1975.

Incidentally, Ben Harney won the Tony Award for Best Actor in a Musical for his performance in *Dreamgirls* (1981).

In 1978, Micki Grant wrote a fascinating, underrated score for a new version of *Alice's Adventures in Wonderland*. Titled *Alice*, the musical closed early during the run of its pre-Broadway tryout in Philadelphia. It was one of those shows which had all the necessary ingredients for success (the score, exciting choreography, wondrous scenery, and a galvanic performance by Debbie Allen in the title role); maybe it could have come together if the confused book had been more focused.

401 Don't Step on My Olive Branch. "A New Musical"; THEATRE: Playhouse Theatre; OPENING DATE: November 1, 1976; PERFORMANCES: 16; BOOK: Harvey Jacobs; LYRICS: Ron Eliran; MUSIC: Ron Eliran; DIRECTION: Jonathan Karmon; CHOREOGRAPHY: Jonathan Karmon; SCENERY: James Tilton; COSTUMES: Pierre D'Alby; LIGHTING: William H. Batchelder; MUSICAL DIRECTION: David Krivoshei; PRODUCERS: The Yael Company and Norman Kean

CAST—RIVKA RAZ, RON ELIRAN, RUTHI NAVON, RIKI GAL, HANAN GOLDBLATT, Gail Benedict, Darleen Boudreaux, Donald Ronci, Karen DiBianco, Carla Farnsworth, David Kottke, Joel Robertson, Lisa Gould Rubin, Daniel Stewart, John Windsor

The action occurs at the present time in a border settlement in Israel.

The musical was presented in one act (the program didn't identify individual singers and dancers for the musical numbers).

MUSICAL NUMBERS—"Moonlight," "The World's Greatest Magical Act," "I Believe," "Only Love," "My Land," "We Love a Conference," "Come with Me," "Tired Heroes," "Have a Little Fun," "I Hear a Song," "I Live My Life in Color," "Young Day," "Somebody's Stepping on My Olive Branch," "It Was Worth It," "Jerusalem"

NOTES—*Don't Step on My Olive Branch* was Jonathan Karmon's sixth and final offering of Jewish-related revues and musicals (for a complete list of his productions, see entry for *The Grand Music Hall of Israel*). For almost a fifteen-year period, the Paris-based director and choreographer offered a steady stream of good-natured, sometimes preachy, musical offerings about the precarious state of being a Jew in the Middle East.

During previews, *Don't Step on My Olive Branch* was presented in two acts, with an intermission between "Jerusalem" and "Tired Heroes." Once the revue was condensed into one act, "Jerusalem" became the show's finale. Further, "Nothing Like Home" was deleted, and "I Live My Life in Color" was added. Some songs heard in the production were later used in Ron Eliran's 1977 revue *Nightsong* (see entry).

402 Dori. THEATRE: The Cathedral Church of St. John the Divine; OPENING DATE: October 29, 1986; PERFORMANCES: 1; BOOK: Eric Blau; LYRICS: Eric Blau; MUSIC: Elliot Weiss; MUSICAL DIRECTION: Andrew Wilder; PRODUCER: Reuben Hoppenstein

CAST—Douglas Fairbanks, Jr. (Narrator), Joseph Neal (Dori), Valerie Anderson (Julie), Gary Krawford (Newlinksi), Gerard Edery (Degan), Rebecca Weiss (Pauline), Sarah Weiss (Trudi); Combined Choirs of the Cathedral Church of St. John the Divine Choir, Temple Emanu-El Choir, and Park Avenue Synogogue Choir; Selected Voices from St. Benedict's Youth Choir, Throgs Neck, New York; Cathedral Orchestra

The musical was presented in one act.

MUSICAL NUMBERS—Prologue (Company), "O Vienna Waltz" (Company), "On the Way Home to the Old Land" (Joseph Neal, Chorus), "Intrigue" (Gary Krawford; Violin Soloist, Elena Dumitrescu), "In the Wildest Dream" (Joseph Neal), "I Won't Be Home for a Long, Long Time" (Joseph Neal, Chorus), "Appearances" (Valerie Anderson), "Papa Is a Traveller" (Rebecca Weiss, Sarah Weiss), "Let's Play the Game" (Gary Krawford), "Diaspora" (Joseph Neal), "A World Without Us" (Gerard Edery), "Kishinev" (Gerard Edery, Chorus), "The Promise" (Joseph Neal, Chorus), "Do You Know What the Children Were Doing Today?" (Joseph Neal, Valerie Anderson), "Dancing in the Temple" (Company)

NOTES—*Dori* was performed in a concert production at the Cathedral Church of St. John the Divine for one performance on October 29, 1986. The evening included highlights from the score; Douglas Fairbanks, Jr., was the narrator, and Joseph Neal played the title role.

Theodore Herzl (a/k/a Dori) (1860-1904), considered the father of modern Zionism, was convinced that without a state of their own the Jewish people could not survive. The program noted that Reuben Hoppenstein, the producer, hoped to see *Dori* mounted on Broadway in 1987. The musical never materialized on Broadway, but in 1992 a revised version of *Dori* was produced Off Off Broadway as *A Rag on a Stick and a Star* (see entry).

Broadway had earlier seen a dramatic version of Herzl's life; titled *Herzl*, the play by Dore Schary and Amos Elon opened at the Palace Theatre on November 30, 1976, and played for eight performances (Paul Hecht performed the title role). *Herzl* was Schary's final play.

403 Dorian. THEATRE: Saval Theatre; OPENING DATE: March 10, 1990; PERFORMANCES: Unknown; BOOK: Nan Barcan; LYRICS: Michael Rubell and Nan Barcan; MUSIC: Michael Rubell; DIRECTION: Robert Petito; CHOREOGRAPHY: Irene Rubell; SCENERY: Joseph A. Varga; COSTUMES: Judy Kahn; LIGHTING: Jonathan Terry; MUSICAL DIRECTION: Marc Abel; PRODUCER: The American Ensemble Company (Robert Petito, Artistic Director)

CAST—Joel Briel (Basil Hallward), Hank Schob (Lord Wotten), William Broderick (Dorian Gray), Robert Schwarz (Lord Peck), Paula Newman (Lady Wotten), Elaine Terriss (Lady Peck), Gemma DeBiase (Lady Olivia), Jamie Stern (Adrian), Sarah Downs (Gladys), May Ellis (Mrs. Erskine), Ian Fleet (Peters, Mr. Erskine, Lord Charles), Kyle Waters (Sibyl Vane), Kurt Elftman (Victor, Lord Burton), Lorraine Serabian (Kate)

SOURCE—The 1890 (revised, 1891) novel *The Picture of Dorian Gray* by Oscar Wilde.

The action occurs in London during the period 1882-1900.

The musical was presented in two acts (division of acts and song assignments unknown; songs are listed in performance order).

MUSICAL NUMBERS—"Art Is Forever," "Creation," "Temptation," "Men on My Mind," "American Girls," "You Are the Magic," "I Love Him," "You Must Remember," "Night at the Theatre," "My Perfection," "The Lady Can't Act," "Till I Met You," "A Perfect Tragedy," "The Picture of Dorian Gray," "Dissipation," "Marriage," "For Old Time's Sake," "Jim's Song," "Prince Charming," "We Knew How to Live," "Chatter," "Confession," Finale

NOTES—*Dorian* was based on Oscar Wilde's *The Picture of Dorian Gray*, and was the second Off Off Broadway musical within a month to be based on the novel (on April 5, 1990, *Dorian Gray* opened at the Cubiculo Theatre; the book and lyrics were by Joseph Bravaco and the music by Robert Cioffi). Further, in 1996 another lyric adaptation of the novel (also titled *Dorian Gray*) opened Off Off Broadway (see entry).

For other musical adaptations of Wilde's work, see entries for *Ernest in Love* (which also references other musical versions of *The Importance of Being Earnest*), *A Delightful Season*, and *After the Ball* (the latter two were lyric adaptations of *Lady Windermere's Fan*), For musicals about Wilde's life, see entries for *Dear Oscar* and *It's Wilde!* Also see entry for *Utterly Wilde!!!*, a one-man musical biography of the subject.

404 Dorian Gray. THEATRE: Judith Anderson Theatre; OPENING DATE: September 17, 1996; PERFORMANCES: 16; BOOK: Allan Rieser and Don Price; LYRICS: Allan Rieser; MUSIC: Gary David Levinson; DIRECTION: Don Price; SCENERY: Sal Perrotta; COSTUMES: Mary Nemecek Peterson; LIGHTING: Kimo James; MUSICAL DIRECTION: James Mironchik; PRODUCER: Dorian Gray Productions

CAST—Tom Rocco (Basil Hallward), Chris Weikel (Lord Henry Wotton), Brian Duguay (Dorian Gray), Laura Stanczyk (Sibyl Vane), Gerrianne Raphael (Mrs. Vane), Ronald K. Morehead (James Vane), Ari Zohar Klingman (Victor), Mary Setrakian (Gladys), Amy D. Forbes (Polly), Jim Straz (Allan Campbell), John Greenbaum (Host), Whitney Allen (Hetty)

SOURCE—The 1890 (revised, 1891) novel *The Picture of Dorian Gray* by Oscar Wilde.

The action occurs in London during the late 1880s.

The musical was presented in two acts (division of acts and song assignments unknown; songs are listed in performance order).

MUSICAL NUMBERS—"Beauty Past All Dreaming," "Discover the Man You Are," "I Would Give My Soul for That," "Counterfeit Love," "Marriage," "Love That Lives Forever," "Don't Throw Your Love Away," "What Will Happen to Me Now?," "Dorian Gray," "Take Care of Your Heart," "What Dark November Thoughts"/"Let Me Believe in You," "The Prayer," "Blue Gate Fields Hotel," "As Long as There

Are Men," "Stay," "We Are But Patters of Paint," "I'll Call My Soul My Own"

NOTES—Based on Oscar Wilde's novel *The Picture of Dorian Gray*, the Off Off Broadway musical *Dorian Gray* was the third lyric adaptation of the musical within a six-year period. See entry for *Dorian* (which references an earlier musical also titled *Dorian Gray* [both *Dorian* and *Dorian Gray* opened within a month of one another in 1990; the latter was a completely different musical adaptation from the *Dorian Gray* which opened in 1996]).

For the 1996 *Dorian Gray*, Gerrianne Raphael created the role of Mrs. Vane; in 1960, she had originated the role of Cecily Cardew in the 1960 musical *Ernest in Love* (see entry), an adaptation of Wilde's *The Importance of Being Earnest*, and in 1994 she appeared in an Off Off Broadway production of *Ernest in Love*, this time around playing the role of Lady Bracknell.

For other musical adaptations of Wilde's work, also see entries for *After the Ball* and *A Delightful Season*, both based on *Lady Windermere's Fan*. For musicals about Wilde's life, see entries for *Dear Oscar* and *It's Wilde!* as well as *Utterly Wilde!!!*, the latter a one-man musical biography of the subject.

405 Double Entry. "Two New Musicals" Theatre: Martinique Theatre; OPENING DATE: February 20, 1961; PERFORMANCES: 56; BOOK: Jay Thompson; LYRICS: Jay Thompson; MUSIC: Jay Thompson; DIRECTION: Bill Penn; SCENERY: Howard Becknell; COSTUMES: Uncredited; possibly by Howard Becknell; Rossetta LeNoire's costumes by Olma Cunningham; LIGHTING: Howard Becknell; MUSICAL DIRECTION: Jay Thompson; PRODUCERS: Albert C. Lasher, Paul Lehman, and the Happy Medium Theatre

NOTE—*Double Entry* was a program of two one-act musicals, *The Bible Salesman* and *The Oldest Trick in the World. The Bible Salesman:*

CAST—Rosetta LeNoire (The Grandmother), Garrett Morris (LeRoy), Ted Lamrinos (The Man)

The action occurs at the present time a few miles outside a large city in East Texas.

MUSICAL NUMBERS—"Same Old Summer" (Rosetta LeNoire), "Miss Lucy Long" (Rosetta LeNoire, Garrett Morris), "I Twenty-One Years Old" (Garrett Morris), "Duet" (Garrett Morris, Rosetta LeNoire), "You Ain't One of Those Simpletons" (Ted Lambrinos), "The Question Is" (Ted Lambrinos), "It's a Hard Thing to Tell You" (Ted Lambrinos, Garrett Morris), "Sure Gets Lonesome" (Rosetta LeNoire), "I Wish You Could" (Aria) (Rosetta LeNoire), Duet and Finaletto (Garrett Morris, Rosetta LeNoire)

NOTES—*The Bible Salesman* was based on a short story of the same name by Alma Stone, which had been dramatized on television in the spring of 1960 by Albert McCleery. It appears that the non-musical television version and Jay Thompson's musical adaptation were produced almost concurrently, since the musical had first been produced on February 21, 1960, by the Broadway Chapel Players at the Broadway Congregational Church in New York (for a total of eleven performances given on a succession of eleven Sunday afternoons). The cast included Rosetta LeNoire and Garrett Morris, who later recreated their roles for the 1961 production, and Ted Thurston, who played the role of The Man.

The scripts of both musicals were published in the July 1961 issue of *Theatre Arts* magazine, which interviewed Jay Thompson about the two musicals (*The Oldest Trick in the World* was also published by Samuel French, Inc., in 1961). *The Bible Salesman* was sung-through; Thompson confusedly described it as "not an opera or a musical comedy ... not a musical setting of the short story or of a one-act play based on the story ... not a play with music ...*Salesman* is ... a musical work for the theatre ... *Trick* ... is a musical comedy."

The Oldest Trick in the World:; BOOK: Jay Thompson; LYRICS: Jay Thompson; MUSIC: Jay Thompson; DIRECTION: Bill Penn; SCENERY: Howard Becknell; COSTUMES: Uncredited; possibly by Howad Becknell; Rosetta LeNoire's costumes by Olma Cunningham; LIGHTING: Howard Becknell; MUSICAL DIRECTION: Jay Thompson; PRODUCERS: Albert C. Lasher, Paul Lehman, and the Happy Medium Theatre

CAST—Rosetta LeNoire (Madame Scarlatina), Doreese DuQuan (Enid), Jane Connell (Miss Spencer)

The action occurs at the present time on the best part of Eighth Avenue, New York City.

MUSICAL NUMBERS—"Sweep" (Rosetta LeNoire), "Kinda Sorta Doin' Nothing" (Doreese DuQuan), "Real Rich Ladies" (Rosetta LeNoire, Doreese DuQuan), "The Oldest Trick in the World" (Rosetta LeNoire, Doreese DuQuan), "Dear Madame Scarlatina" (Jane Connell), "The Fortune" (Rosetta LeNoire), "The White Slavery Fandango" (Rosetta LeNoire, Jane Connell), "All the Young Men" (Jane Connell), "The Oldest Trick in the World" (reprise) (Rosetta LeNoire, Doreese DuQuan)

NOTES—Jay Thompson was the co-librettist of *Once Upon a Mattress* (1959; see entry), and even though *Double Entry* was a commercial failure, *The Bible Salesman* was an ambitious piece of theatre writing and *The Oldest Trick in the World* was a genuinely amusing show which was enhanced by Thompson's clever lyrics. With *Mattress* and *Double Entry* behind him, one assumed that Thompson had a great future in musical theatre. Alas, after the failure of his next musical, *Royal Flush* (1965), he was never heard from again. *Royal Flush* was a big ambitious Broadway-bound musical laced with amusing and quirky touches, a pleasant score, and a cast which included such welcome clowns as Kaye Ballard and Jane Connell. But *Royal Flush* closed in Philadelphia, and didn't even get a second chance in the form of a small, revised Off Broadway version, which is occasionally what happened to big out-of-town bombs of that era (*Mata Hari* [1967] became *Ballad for a Firing Squad* [1968] and *Comedy* [1972] became *Smile, Smile, Smile* [1973]; see entries).

Royal Flush was based on Nino Savo's translation of Count Carlo Gozzi's play *L'Augellin Belvede* (*The Beautiful Green Bird*). In 2000, thirty-five years after *Royal Flush* went down the drain, Julie Taymor, flush from her success as director and co-designer of *The Lion King* (1997), directed and co-designed a new version of Gozzi's play, but her adaptation, *The Green Bird*, was a disaster, running only two months and losing every penny of its large investment (it had previously played Off Broadway in 1996 for fifteen performances; see entry).

406 Double Feature. THEATRE: The Common/The Theatre at St. Peter's Church; OPENING DATE: October 8, 1981; PERFORMANCES: 7; BOOK: Jeffrey Moss; LYRICS: Jeffrey Moss; MUSIC: Jeffrey Moss; DIRECTION: Sheldon Larry; CHOREOGRAPHY: Adam Grammis; Tina Paul, Assistant Choreographer; SCENERY: Stuart Wurtzel; COSTUMES: Rizia Von Brandenstein; LIGHTING: Marilyn Rennagel; MUSICAL DIRECTION: Michael Lee Stockler; PRODUCERS: Allen Grossman, Karl Allison, and Nan Pearlman in association with The Common at Saint Peter's Church

CAST—PAMELA BLAIR (Christine), CAROLE SHELLEY (Margaret), STEPHEN VINOVICH (Alan), DON SCARDINO (John), Michael Kubala ("He"), Tina Paul ("She")

The action occurs in the present time in New York City.

The musical was presented in two acts.

ACT ONE—"Just As It Should Be" (Company), "Morning" (Company), "Double Feature" (Stephen Vinovich, Carole Shelley), "When I Met Her" (Company), "What If I Asked Her for a Dance?" (Don Scardino, Pamela Blair), "We Saw a Movie Together" (Pamela Blair)

ACT TWO—"How's It Gonna End?" (Company), "One Step at a Time" (Don Scardino, Pamela Blair), "The First Touch of Autumn" (Carole Shelley), "Wallpaper" (Don Scardino), "Out Last Dance Together" (Stephen Vinovich), "A Little Bit of This" (Company)

NOTES—What's fascinating about this fast flop is its back story: some of the choreography used in its tryout later ended up as the show-stopper in a completely different musical.

Almost two years before it opened Off Broadway, *Double Feature* opened at the Long Wharf Theatre on November 15, 1979, with a stellar production team: Mike Nichols was the director and Tommy Tune the choreographer (Thommie Walsh was associate choreographer); the scenery was designed by Tony Walton; costumes were by Dona Granata and Michel Stuart; and Wally Harper was the musical director. The six cast members were Pamela Blair (two years later she reprised her role of Christine for the Off Broadway production), John Doolittle, Leland Palmer, Charles Kimbrough, Niki Harris, and Albert Stephenson (the latter two performed a dance number called "One Step at a Time").

When *Double Feature* finally reached Off Broadway two years later, Nichols, Tune, Walsh, Walton, Stuart, and Harper, not to mention Harris and Stephenson, were all long gone. But in the interim the hit Broadway musical *A Day in Hollywood, A Night in the Ukraine* had opened on May 1, 1980. A self-described "musical double feature," the show was a reunion of sorts for the Long Wharf *Double Feature* refugees: the choreography was by Tommy Tune (the co-choreographer was Thommie Walsh); the scenic designer was Tony Walton; the costume designer was Michel Stuart; the musical director was Wally Harper; and Niki Harris and Albert Stephenson were in the cast.

The show-stopping highlight of *Hollywood/Ukraine* was "Fancy Feet" (lyric by Dick Vosburgh, music by Frank Lazarus), and for this number Tommy Tune borrowed the choreographic conceit he had devised for "One Step at a Time" (which of course had been performed in *Double Feature* by Niki Harris and Albert Stephenson). For "Fancy Feet," Harris and Stephenson once again performed Tune's ingenious dance, which utilized a special mirrored scenic device which showed the audience only the legs and feet of Harris and Stephenson as they paid dancing homage to the "famous feet" of Hollywood legends. With only dancing styles and trademark shoes to identify such stars as Judy Garland, Marlene Dietrich, Charlie Chaplin, Ginger Rogers and Fred Astaire (and even Mickey and Minnie Mouse), "Famous Feet" stopped the show. Writing in the *New York Post*, Clive Barnes said Tune's ingenious staging took him to "the top of the class," joining legendary Broadway choreographers Michael Bennett, Bob Fosse, Joe Layton, and Jerome Robbins.

407 Down in the Valley and **Look at Us.** THEATRE: Actors' Playhouse; OPENING DATE: June 5, 1962; PERFORMANCES: 16

The two-act production consisted of a revival of *Down in the Valley* as well as a new revue, *Look at Us. Down in the Valley*; LIBRETTO: Arnold Sundgaard; MUSIC: Kurt Weill (based upon traditional American folk songs); DIRECTION: Jeff Warren; MUSICAL DIRECTION: Philip Ames-Fein; PRODUCERS: Fred Martin and Leo Brody

CAST—G. Brad Smith, Bill Mount, Charles

Baird, Cathi Romano, Mary Jane Vanhecke, Ed McDonald, Glenn Maggio, Jimmy Dove, Norman Lind, "and others"

NOTES—*Down in the Valley* premiered at the University of Indiana on July 15, 1948. The cast was comprised of university students, with the exception of guest performer Marion Bell, who had created the role of Fiona in the original Broadway production of *Brigadoon* the previous year. The opera was televised on NBC on January 14, 1950, with a cast which included Marion Bell; the television cast recording was released by RCA Victor (LP # LPV-503).

The one-act opera told the tragic story of two lovers, Jennie Parsons and Brack Weaver; the latter is in prison, awaiting execution for the murder of Thomas Bouche, a villain who threatened him and Jennie. In flashback sequences, the opera told of the lovers' first meeting and how events led Brack to kill Bouche.

Down in the Valley used a thematic device which Weill had employed in at least seven other operas and musicals, that of a leading character (who may or may not be guilty of a crime, be it murder or simply the fact of not being able to make up one's mind) who faces imprisonment, or, worse, execution (*The Threepenny Opera* [1928], *The Rise and Fall of the City of Mahagonny* [1930], *Knickerbocker Holiday* [1938], *Lady in the Dark* [1941], *The Firebrand of Florence* [1945], *Street Scene* [1947], and *Lost in the Stars* [1949]); see separate entries for *The Threepenny Opera* and *The Rise and Fall of the City of Mahagonny*.

Down in the Valley was revived Off Off Broadway in 1980 by the Union Square Theatre Company (on a double bill with Dylan Thomas' *A Child's Christmas in Wales*, as adapted by Joan White and Evadne Giannini).

Look at Us; LYRICS AND MUSIC: Lorenzo Fuller, Terry Morin, Constance Conrad, Frank Wille, Sano Marco, Carley Mills, Raoul Gonzalez, Benny Wagman, Alan Greene, Ray Passman, Johnny Meyers, and Jimmy Glitter; DIRECTION: Michael Wright; MUSICAL DIRECTION: Lorenzo Fuller; PRODUCERS: Fred Martin and Leo Brody

CAST—Bettye Voorhees, Cathi Romano, Didi DuBois, Rich Samuelson, Bonnie Snyder, Ray Ramirez, Sara Clark, Bill Mount, Jimmy Dove, Norman Lind

MUSICAL NUMBERS (song assignments unknown; songs are listed in performance order)—"Each Night Is a New Day" (music by Lorenzo Fuller), "Slow Rockin' Blues" (music by Terry Morin), "Rich Enough to Be Rude" (lyric by Carley Mills, music by Lorenzo Fuller), "Bored" (music by Constance Conrad), "Make Believe World" (music by Frank Wille), "It's Great to Hate Yourself" (music by Lorenzo Fuller), "Black Silence" (music by Sano Marco), "Odalie" (music by Raoul Gonzalez), "Whatever Happened to Spring" (music by Benny Wagman), "It's the Hat That Makes the Lady" (music by Constance Conrad), "Most People" (music by Frank Wille), "Caryl Ann" (music by Frank Wille), "A Helping Hand and a Willing Heart" (lyric and music by Alan Greene and Ray Passman), "One Woman Man" (music by Johnny Meyers), "The Sound of Laughter" (music by Jimmy Glitter)

NOTES—"Rich Enough to Be Rude" was first heard in *The World's My Oyster* (1956; see entry), which was the first Off Broadway Black musical. According to Ken Bloom's *American Song*, the lyricists weren't identified in the program.

408 Downriver. THEATRE: Musical Theatre Works; OPENING DATE: January 9, 1985; PERFORMANCES: 12; BOOK: Jeff Tambornino; LYRICS: John Braden; MUSIC: John Braden; DIRECTION: Michael Maurer; CHOREOGRAPHY: Mary Jane Houdina; SCENERY: Karl Eigsti; COSTUMES: Karen Roston; LIGHTING: Neil Peter Jampolis; MUSICAL DIRECTION: Michael Ward; PRODUCER: Michael Maurer

CAST—John Scherer (Huckleberry Finn), Todd Heughens (Tom Sawyer), Joe Lynn (Jim), Jack Fletcher (King of France), Don Harrington (Duke of Bridgewater), Frank Vohs (Tim Collins), Suzanne Bedford (Mary Jane), Clara Lunden (Susan), Andi Henig (Joanna), Timothy Jecko (Dr. Robinson), Ted Forlow (Silas Phelps), Helon Blount (Aunt Sally Phelps), Ensemble (Jack Brenton, Jayne Cacciatore, Tom Kosis, Kathy Lynn, Mark Manley, and Teressa Wylie)

SOURCE—The 1884 novel *The Adventures of Huckleberry Finn* by Mark Twain.

The action occurs along the Mississippi River before the Civil War.

The musical was presented in two acts (song assignments unknown).

ACT ONE—"Bound Away," "'Til Our Good Luck Comes Along," "It's a Hard Life," The Musicale: "Introduction," "Waltz of the Cameleopard," "Fare-Thee-Well," "You've Brightened Up My Day," "Come Home, Runaway," "Hallelujah, He's on His Way"

ACT TWO—"River Rats," "Just Like Love," "What a Fine Day for an Auction Sell," "Downriver," "Every Other Saturday Night," "Tom and Huck's Argument," "Shine Down, Lord"

NOTES—Six years before *Downriver* was performed Off Off Broadway, Take Home Tunes Records released an LP of the score (# THT-7811; Richard Dunne sang Huckleberry Finn, and Michael Corbett was Tom Sawyer).

The musical had first been produced Off Off Broadway on December 19, 1975, by the St. C. American Repertory at St. Clement's Church.

For more information about musicals based on *The Adventures of Tom Sawyer* (1876) and *The Adventures of Huckleberry Finn* (1884), see entry for *Livin' the Life*.

Also see entry for the Off Off Broadway musical *Lightin' Out*, which was based on both the life of Mark Twain and the fictional lives of his characters; the musical was later revised as *Mark Twain's Blues* and was seen Off Off Broadway in 2008.

409 Drat! THEATRE: McAlpin Rooftop Theatre; OPENING DATE: October 18, 1971; PERFORMANCES: 1; BOOK: Fred Bluth; LYRICS: Fred Bluth; MUSIC: Steven Metcalf; DIRECTION: Fred Bluth; SCENERY: Christian Thee ("design supervision"); COSTUMES: Tomianne Wiley ("costume supervision"); LIGHTING: Richard Nelson; MUSICAL DIRECTION: Steven Metcalf; PRODUCERS: Theatre 1972 (Richard Barr and Charles Woodward) in association with Michael Kasdan

CAST—BONNIE FRANKLIN (Sally Merryweather), JANE CONNELL (Widow Merryweather, General Arden Clobber), Gary Gage (Professor Souse), Walter Bobbie (Eddy Applebee), James "Red" Wilcher (Elmer Applebee), Carol Swarbrick (Lotta Lovejoy), Donna Sands (Poppy Applebee)

The action occurs in and around Plasterville, Ohio, and in New York City.

The musical was presented in two acts.

ACT ONE—Overture (Orchestra), "Little Fairies" (Bonnie Franklin), "Early Bird Eddie" (Walter Bobbie), "Walkin' in the Rain" (Walter Bobbie, Bonnie Franklin, Jane Connell, Company), "Friday, Friday" (Carol Swarbrick), "My Geranium" (James "Red" Wilcher), "Kick It Around" (Carol Swarbrick), "You and I" (Bonnie Franklin, Walter Bobbie), "Where Is the Man for Me?" (James "Red" Wilcher), "Frightened of the Dark" (Walter Bobbie, Company).

ACT TWO—Entr'acte (Orchestra), "Desperation Quintet" (Bonnie Franklin, Company), "Drat!" (Gary Gage), "Has Anyone Here Seen My Daddy?" (Donna Sands), "Lean on Me" (Carol Swarbrick), "Sally" (Walter Bobbie), "Bye and Bye" (Jane Connell), "You and I" (reprise) (Bonnie Franklin), "Bye and Bye" (reprise) (Jane Connell, Carol Swarbrick, James "Red" Wilcher, Donna Sands), "The Chase" (Company), "You and I" (reprise) (Company)

NOTES—*Drat!* was a spoof of Victorian melodrama, and had originally been produced at the Goodspeed Opera House in East Haddam, Connecticut. The campy and tasteless piece was passé; perhaps Off Broadway was indulging a bit too much in spoofs of earlier entertainment genres. Clive Barnes in the *New York Times* reported that the musical's title was "presumably spelled D-R-E-C-K," and said what he disliked most about the evening ("apart from its book, lyrics, music, scenery, costumes, lighting, staging, and acting") was its "extraordinarily fetid air of innuendo." He noted that *Drat!* was "the nastiest, the most unclean, the most prurient show in town."

Bonnie Franklin, fresh from *Applause* (1970), later found success in television, and then seems to have disappeared. On the other hand, Walter Bobbie was a stalwart Off Broadway and Broadway Baby (he appeared as Nicely-Nicely Johnson in the smash 1992 Broadway revival of *Guys and Dolls*). And then he really hit the jackpot with his sleek and stylish direction of the 1996 revival of *Chicago*, which, at this writing, is now in its second decade on Broadway.

As for Jane Connell, this was her second *Drat!* musical. In 1965, she had appeared on Broadway in *Drat! The Cat!* (despite an amusing book, witty lyrics, and a melodic score, the musical closed after eight performances). The song "Where Is the Man for Me?" may have been dropped from *Drat!* during previews, and thus might not have been heard on opening night.

410 The Dream. "A New American Musical"; THEATRE: The Westbeth Theatre; OPENING DATE: November 16, 1979; PERFORMANCES: 16 (estimated); BOOK: David Rexroad; LYRICS: David Rexroad; MUSIC: Walker Steady; DIRECTION: Ian McColl; CHOREOGRAPHY: Terry Rieser; COSTUMES: Deborah Benson; LIGHTING: Martin Tudor; MUSICAL DIRECTION: Elmer Gordon; PRODUCER: The Westbeth Theatre Center in association with Arnold Engelman and G. Richardson Cook

CAST—Joey Debenedetto (Nicky), Billy Hoffman (Bobby), Jay Larkin (Michael), Lane Ruoff (Denny)

The musical was presented in one act (specific song assignments weren't listed in the program).

MUSICAL NUMBERS—"A Voice," "Livin to the Beat," "One Long Party," "Street Talk," "Walk On," "Stars," "Photographer," "The Hook," "Just Like in the Movies: Rehearsal," "Quiet by Myself," "Just Like in the Movies: Production," "The Lovin," "A Voice: Refrain," "Dancin' with the One I Love"

NOTES—*The Dream* was probably presented under an Off Off Broadway contract. It played from November 16 through December 1, 1979, for approximately sixteen performances.

Additional book material and lyrics were by Edison Fast, Ian McColl, Billy Hoffman, and Arnold Engelman.

411 Dream a Little Dream. "The Mamas and The Papas Musical"; THEATRE: Village Theatre; OPENING DATE: April 23, 2003; PERFORMANCES: 119 (estimated); BOOK: Denny Doherty and Paul Ledoux; LYRICS: See song list for credits; MUSIC: See song list for credits; DIRECTION: Randal Myler; SCENERY: Walt Spangler; Jan Hartley, Video Projection Design; COSTUMES: David C. Woolard; LIGHTING: Brian Nason; MUSICAL DIRECTION: Ed Alstrom; PRODUCER: Eric Nederlander Productions

CAST—"PAPA" DENNY DOHERTY, Richard Burke, Angela Gaylor, Doris Mason

The revue was presented in two acts (song assignments not credited in program).

ACT ONE—"Dedicated to the One I Love" (lyric and music by Pauling and Bass), "The Man Who Wouldn't Sing Along with Mitch" (lyric and music by F. Hertz and C. Grean), "Wild Women" (lyric and music by Cass Elliott and Tim Rose), "500 Miles" (lyric and music by Hedy West), "Everybody's Been Talkin'" (lyric and music by Cass Elliott and Jim Hendricks), "Twist and Shout" (lyric and music by B. Russell and P. Medley), "Chanson, Chanson, Chanson" (lyric and music by Denny Doherty), "12:30" (lyric and music by John Phillips and Michelle Gilliam), "Go Where You Want to Go" (lyric and music by John Phillips), "California Dreamin'" (lyric and music by John Phillips and Michelle Gilliam)

ACT TWO—"Got a Feelin'" (lyric and music by Denny Doherty and John Phillips), "Theme from *Peyton Place*" (lyric by Paul Francis Webster, music by Franz Waxman), "I Saw Her Again" (lyric and music by Denny Doherty and John Phillips), "In Crowd" (lyric and music by Billy Page), "San Francisco (Be Sure to Wear Some Flowers in Your Hair)" (lyric and music by John Phillips), "Monday Monday" (lyric and music by John Phillips), "It Can Only Happen in America" (lyric and music by Denny Doherty and Henry "Bud" Fanton), "Dream a Little Dream of Me" (lyric and music by Wilber Schwant, Fabian Andre, and Gus Kahn), "Creeque Alley" (lyric and music by John Phillips and Michelle Gilliam)

NOTES—The revue *Dream a Little Dream* was a collection of songs made popular by the 1960s singing group The Mamas and the Papas (Denny Doherty, "Mama" Cass Elliott, John Phillips, and Michele Phillips), and its cast members included Denny Doherty, one of the two surviving members of the legendary quartet (Cass Elliott had died in 1974, John Phillips in 2001).

The revue premiered on November 29, 1996, at the White Point Theatre in White Point, Nova Scotia (Doherty's home), and toured throughout Canada for the rest of the decade. In 2001, the revue opened in Toronto.

Bruce Weber in the *New York Times* noted the evening was more of a "self-centered memoir" about Doherty (who at times came "dangerously close to lounge lizard territory") than it was about the famous quartet. But for all that, Weber noted the theatre was "packed" with an audience which seemed "ecstatic" in re-living 1960s nostalgia.

See entry for *Man on the Moon*, an original musical with lyrics and music by John Phillips.

Randal Myler, the director of *Dream a Little Dream*, was associated with three other Off Broadway musicals which looked at the lives and careers of pop singers (see entries for *Almost Heaven: Songs of John Denver, Hank Williams: Lost Highway*, and *Love, Janis* [Joplin]).

412 Dream Time. "A Musical Fable of the Swing Era"; THEATRE: The Harold Clurman Theatre; OPENING DATE: December 17, 1980; PERFORMANCES: Unknown; BOOK: Alfred Uhry; LYRICS: Alfred Uhry; MUSIC: Robert Waldman; DIRECTION: Robert LuPone and Myra Turley; CHOREOGRAPHY: Robert LuPone and Myra Turley; SCENERY: E.A. Smith; COSTUMES: E.A. Smith; LIGHTING: Tony Giovannetti; MUSICAL DIRECTION: Steven A. Freeman; PRODUCERS: Nina Lightstone and James F. Lightstone

CAST—Ann Morrison (Bebe Knight), Bruce Miller (Dave Tatum), Lon Mulvaney (Richard McGonagle)

SOURCE—The 1980 musical *Swing* (book by Conn Fleming, lyrics by Alfred Uhry, and music by Robert Waldman).

NOTES—*Dream Time* was a radically revised version of *Swing*, which had closed during its pre-Broadway tryout earlier in the year. *Dream Time* (which seems to have been produced under an Off Off Broadway contract) disappeared even more quickly than *Swing*, and so after this second attempt the musical disappeared for good. *Swing* is quite possibly the most ambitious concept musical ever produced. Yes, Conn Fleming's book overreached, and never quite made the leap from high-concept to basic theatre story-telling, and because the book couldn't live up to its ambitions, it never connected to most of its audience, and certainly to none of the critics.

Swing was an attempt to create a portrait of United States during the swing era (1937-1945), perhaps the last time the nation was unified in everything from its opinion of war to the kind of music it enjoyed. The end of the World War II (which coincided with the end of the Big Band Era) saw a more divided country, one which perhaps never again would experience the kind of national unity it knew during the swing era.

The basic plot dealt with the orchestra and singers of a big band who are playing a dance date, and the attendees at the dance. The hallucinatory, surreal concept was that of a single dance which begins in 1937 and ends in 1945. The characters experience the entire era in one night, and thus a young man in a zoot suit suddenly reappears in a military uniform. On the musical stage, only *Follies* (1971) used time and space in such a fluid manner.

Further, at stage left was a lighted sign which showed the audience where the dance was taking place (along the lines of "Stardust Ballroom, Boston"); but every few minutes the sign would change, showing the audience different locations. The dance essentially occurred all over the United States during the course of the one evening.

More than a dozen specific characters were bound together in the show's plot, and, at the beginning of the dance, life is nothing but sweet music and smooth dancing, reflected in the lush and creamy "Dream Time," the delicate "In the Shelter of Your Arms," the lazy and languid "A Piece of Cake," and the jaunty, blasé, and yet paradoxically heartfelt "Good from Any Angle." Moreover, two songs centered around the idea of home. One (a musical cousin to "Chattanooga Choo-Choo") is "Michigan Bound," which was belted out in pure show business splendor by Debbie Shapiro (Gravitte) as the big-band girl singer who sings of returning home to Michigan. The other "home" number, appropriately called "Home," was the show's own version of "The House I Live In," in which an Italian boy (Paul Binotto; read: Frank Sinatra) introduces the song on a nation-wide radio broadcast.Uhry and Waldman provided a cornucopia of Forties musical styles, even finding time for a typical Betty Hutton number ("A Girl Can Go Wacky") in which a scatterbrained character looks for a "permanent poppa" (a tinker, a tailor, a soldier, a sailor, any will do).

As the evening progressed, relationships which were warm and innocent took on an edge, and, by show's end, one of the leads (Janet Eilber) kisses off her boyfriend with "If You Can't Trot, Don't Get Hot," which, musically, was less Big Band and more in keeping with sleek late Forties' jazz-club music. Again, the literal (and metaphorical) dance was coming to a close.

At the very end of the musical, Shapiro and the band reprised "Dream Time," and then the dance and the era (and the show) were over.

Swing may have overreached. But its concept was brilliant, and it was thrilling to see a musical journey so far into such uncharted musical theatre territory.

Kenneth Rinker (in his only [almost] Broadway credit) created exciting and memorable choreography, and his work was on a par with the best theatre dances of the era (which included Michael Bennett's *A Chorus Line* [1975; see entry] and *Ballroom* [1978] and Susan Stroman's *Contact* [1999; see entry]). The authors clearly knew that audiences weren't "getting" the show, and so about midway through the musical's one-month tryout at the Kennedy Center, the one-dance-taking-place-over-eight-years-and-in-different-dance-venues was essentially scraped in favor of a more literal dance (that is, one dance during one evening and in one place), But since the show's theme was so big, the paring down of the concept only made the musical more confusing to the audience.

413 Dream True/My Life with Vernon Dexter. THEATRE: Vineyard Theatre; OPENING DATE: April 17, 1999; PERFORMANCES: 43; BOOK: Tina Landau; LYRICS: Tina Landau; additional lyrics by Ricky Ian Gordon; MUSIC: Ricky Ian Gordon; DIRECTION: Tina Landau; SCENERY: G.W. Mercier; COSTUMES: G.W. Mercier; LIGHTING: Scott Zielinski; MUSICAL DIRECTION: Joshua Rosenblum; PRODUCER: The Vineyard Theatre (Douglas Aibel, Artistic Director; Barbara Zinn Krieger, Executive Director and Founder; Jeffrey Solis, Managing Director)

CAST—Jeff McCarthy (Peter Emmons), Judy Kuhn (Madge), Alex Bowen (Peppy Cody [Young Peter]), Jase Blankfort (Verne Dexter [Young Vernon]), Jessica Molaskey (Sarah Cody), Amy Hohn (Dray Dexter), Steven Skybell (Dr. Howard Emmons), Francis Jue (Hal), Bryan T. Donovan (Bernard), Michael Cole (Jim), Daniel Jenkins (Vernon Dexter)

SOURCE—The 1891 novel *Peter Ibbetson* by George du Maurier.

The action occurs over a period of four decades (the 1940s through the 1980s) in various locations throughout the United States.

The musical was presented in two acts.

ACT ONE—"Wyoming Intro" (Company), "The Kingdom of Addo" (Alex Bowen, Jase Blankfort), "Finding Home" (Jessica Molaskey), "We Will Always Walk Together" (Part One) (Jase Blankfort, Alex Bowen), "The Way West" (Steven Skybell, Alex Bowen, Amy Hohn, Jase Blankford, Jessica Molaskey), "The Best Years of Our Lives" (Trio, Steven Skybell), "Ka Da Bing, Ka Da Bang" (Jeff McCarthy, Bryan T. Donovan, Francis Jue, Judy Kuhn), "God Is There" (Judy Kuhn), "Space" (Jeff McCarthy, Architects), "Peter's Dream" (Company), "Dream True" (Jeff McCarthy, Daniel Jenkins)

ACT TWO—"Have a Nice Day" (Jeff McCarthy, Daniel Jenkins, Judy Kuhn), "The Best for You" (Judy Kuhn, Jeff McCarthy), "Crick Crack" (Company), "Pride" (Daniel Jenkins, Men), "This Is How It Goes" (Steven Skybell, Jeff McCarthy), "Wyoming" (lyric by Ricky Ian Gordon) (Company), "Hold On" (Alex Bowen, Jeff McCarthy), "We Will Always Walk Together" (Part Two) (lyric by Ricky Ian Gordon) (Daniel Jenkins), Finale (Company)

NOTES—*Dream True* was the second lyric adaptation of George du Maurier's 1891 novel *Peter Ibbetson* (see entry for the Metropolitan Opera's 1931 production *Peter Ibbetson*). The new version was updated to the mid-twentieth-century; the musical began in the 1980s when the dying architect Peter Emmons recalls his life, including his childhood in Wyoming with his friend Vernon Dexter. When the two were boys in the 1940s, they conjured up the notion of "dreaming true," so that they might always be able to meet in their dreams. In the 1960s, they meet in both dream and reality, and become lovers. As an architect, Peter is obsessed with the notion of creating architectural space which feels "open," much like the openness of Wyoming (architectural space is also the objective correlative for Peter and Vernon being able to meet in the timeless and open space of dreams). At one point in the late 1960s, Peter "meets" Vernon in his dreams, and soon thereafter literally meets him at a gathering for gay rights; they become lovers, but eventually separate, although they continue to "meet" by "dreaming true." Vernon later becomes ill (and apparently dies [of AIDS?]); and Peter, on his deathbed, is transported to the open space of

Wyoming in the 1940s where he and Vernon are now together as boys. Ricky Ian Gordon's rich score was recorded by PS Classics Inc. Records in 2006 (CD # PS-9641). For the recording, Peter was sung by Brian d'Arcy James and Vernon by Jason Danieley. Jeff McCarthy (who created the role of Peter in the original production but who performed a different role for the album) and Jessica Molaskey (recreating her stage role on the album) were among the recording's cast members (which also included Victoria Clark).

The recording included the song "He's Gone," which had been dropped between the musical's workshop and the Vineyard production (other songs heard in the workshop were "Built to Last," "No Space," and "Crown of Stars"). One number from the production ("Ka Da Bing, Ka Da Bang") was revised and is heard on the recording as "A Beautiful Life" (the recording omitted two songs from the Vineyard production ["Crick Crack" and "This Is How It Goes"]). The song "We Can Fly" is heard on the recording, but isn't listed in the program.

414 Dreamstuff. THEATRE: WPA Theatre; OPENING DATE: April 2, 1976; PERFORMANCES: Unknown; BOOK: Howard Ashman; "additional material by William Shakespeare"; LYRICS: Dennis Green; MUSIC: Marsha Malamet; DIRECTION: James Nicola; CHOREOGRAPHY: Lynne Gannaway; SCENERY: Dan Leigh; COSTUMES: Marianne Powell-Parker; LIGHTING: Martin Tudor; MUSICAL DIRECTION: H. Ross Levy; PRODUCER: The WPA Theatre

CAST—Pat Lavelle (Lolly), Thomas Callaway (Stephen), Dick Latessa (Prospero), Betty Maul (Spirit of the Island), Barbara Niles (Spirit of the Island), Kitty Rea (Spirit of the Island), Alan Spitz (Ferdinand), David Lipman (Arthur), Deborah Weems (Miranda), David Patrick Kelly (Ariel), Albert Insinnia (Caliban)

SOURCE—The 1611 play *The Tempest* by William Shakespeare.

NOTES—The Off Off Broadway musical *Dreamstuff* was a modern-day adaptation of Shakespeare's *The Tempest*, and while it included in its cast of characters Ariel, Miranda, Caliban, and Prospero (the latter portrayed by Dick Latessa), it also offered a few new characters, including Arthur, a mogul of the garment industry who comes to be shipwrecked on Shakespeare's enchanted island. Clive Barnes in the *New York Times* generally found the juxtaposition of Shakespeare's "magic" and the garment industry's "wit" an "appealing" notion. However, he noted the music was "modestly attractive" but "forgettable," the lyrics were "commonplace," and while Howard Ashman's book was often "smart," it never quite came together.

According to Ken Bloom's *American Song*, the following songs were heard in the production: "Curse," "Full Fathom Five," "Get Down," "Goodbye Magic," "It's Beautiful," "My Own Way," "No More Enchantment," "One More Lullabye," "Tempest, "Where the Bee Sucks," and "You Love a Child."

For an operatic adaptation of Shakespeare's play, see entry for *The Tempest*.

On February 17, 1997, another musical titled *Dreamstuff* opened Off Off Broadway at the Samuel Beckett Theatre. Lawrence Van Gelder in the *New York Times* reported the "only intermittently magical" evening was a sometimes uneasy mix of the classic tale of Aladdin (from *The Arabian Nights*) and "20th-century urban smarts." But he noted Sal Lombarde's score was "easy on the ears." Aileen Quinn, who played the title role in the misbegotten 1982 film version of *Annie*, played the Princess.

415 Dressed to the Nines. "A Postprandial Prank"; THEATRE: Upstairs at the Downstairs; OPENING DATE: September 29, 1960; PERFORMANCES: 400 (estimated); SKETCHES: Linda Ashton, Ernest Chambers, Marian Grudeff, Ray Jessel, and Michael McWhinney; LYRICS: Louis Botto, Michael Brown, Lesley Davison, Jack Holmes, Bart Howard, Ray Jessel, Dion McGregor, Michael McWhinney, William Roy, Jack Urbont, Rod Warren, and G. Wood; MUSIC: Michael Brown, Michael Barr, Lesley Davison, Jack Holmes, Bart Howard, Ray Jessel, William Roy, Jack Urbont, Rod Warren, and G. Wood; DIRECTION: Julius Monk; staged by Frank Wagner; CHOREOGRAPHY: Frank Wagner; COSTUMES: Nilo; LIGHTING: George Curley; MUSICAL DIRECTION: William Roy and Carl Norman "at the Plural Pianos"; PRODUCER: Julius Monk

CAST—Ceil Cabot, Gordon Connell, Bill Hinnant, Gerry Matthews, Pat Ruhl, Mary Louise Wilson

The revue was presented in two acts.

ACT ONE—Overture, Gala Opening: "The Theatre's in the Dining Room" (lyric by Michael McWhinney, music by William Roy) and "Dressed to the Nines" (lyric and music by William Roy) (Company) "Tiny Town" (lyric and music by Jack Holmes) (Ceil Cabot, Gerry Matthews) "And That Was He and She" (sketch by Linda Ashton) (Mary Louise Wilson, Gordon Connell) "Sociable Amoeba" (lyric and music by Jack Urbant) (Bill Hinnant) "Con Edison" (sketch by Michael McWhinney) (Ceil Cabot, Bill Hinnant, Gerry Matthews) "Thanks to You" (lyric and music by Bart Howard) (Pat Ruhl) "Cook's Tour" (lyric and music by Lesley Davison) (Company) "Lincoln Center" (lyric and music by Rod Warren) (Gerry Matthews) "Hate Song" (lyric by Don McGregor, music by Michael Barr) (Ceil Cabot, Bill Hinnant) "Come In and Browse" (lyric and music by G. Wood) (Gordon Connell) "A Word from Our Sponsor" (sketch by Ernest Chambers) (Company) "Bring Back the Roxy to Me" (lyric and music by Michael Brown) (Gordon Connell, Bill Hinnant, Gerry Matthews), "Four Seasons" (lyric by Louis Botto, music by William Roy) (Company)

ACT TWO—"Keishi Attu Za Battu, or The Three Challenges" (sketch by Ernest Chambers) (Company), "Nanny" (lyric and music by Ray Jessel) (Ceil Cabot) "Smoke" (sketch by Michael McWhinney) (Mary Louise Wilson, Gerry Matthews) "Names" (lyric and music by Jack Holmes) (Mary Louise Wilson) "Billy's Blues" (lyric and music by William Roy) (Pat Ruhl) "Ft. Lauderdale" (lyric by Michael McWhinney, music by William Roy) (Gerry Matthews) "Unexpurgated Version" (sketch by Ray Jessel and Marian Grudeff) (Gerry Matthews, Pat Ruhl, Gordon Connell) "The New Yorker" (sketch by Michael McWhinney) (Ceil Cabot, Mary Louis Wilson, Bill Hinnant, Gerry Matthews) "Dressed to the Nines" (reprise) (Company)

NOTES—*Dressed to the Nines* was another of Julius Monk's satiric, intimate revues, and included most of his stock company along for the merry ride. Again, current aspects of New York City life were held up for loopy inspection (Con Edison, Lincoln Center), and Michael Brown contributed another of his tributes to old New York ("Bring Back the Roxy to Me"). "Smoke" was an amusing sketch about cigarettes, in the vein of Noel Coward. And "Names" even managed to work in a reference to a recent Broadway flop (*Christine*).

"Four Seasons" had previously been heard in *Four Below Strikes Back* (1959; see entry), and "Lincoln Center" was later used in *Dime a Dozen* (1962; see entry).

The length of the revue's run is a best guess; the cast album liner notes of *Dime a Dozen* indicate that *Dressed to the Nines* played for a year.

The cast album was recorded by MGM Records (LP # E-3914-OC and # SE-3914-OC), For a complete list of Julius Monk's revues, see entry for *Four Below*; also see Appendix Q.

416 A Drifter, the Grifter & Heather McBride. "A New Musical Comedy"; THEATRE: 47th Street Theatre; OPENING DATE: June 20, 1982; PERFORMANCES: 9; BOOK: John Gallagher; LYRICS: John Gallagher; MUSIC: Bruce Petsche; DIRECTION: Dick Sasso; CHOREOGRAPHY: George Bunt; SCENERY: Michael Sharp; COSTUMES: Michael Sharp; LIGHTING: Richard Winkler; MUSICAL DIRECTION: Jeremy Harris; PRODUCER: Popcorn Productions

CAST—Ronald Young (Sky Malinowski), Elizabeth Austin (Heather McBride), William Francis (G.W. Mosely), Dennis Bailey (Bernie Bernardo), Chuck Karel (Luigi O'Hara), Mary Ellen Ashley (Goodun Plenty)

The action occurs in Greenville, Indiana, a mythical Hoosier village caught in a time warp between the invention of indoor plumbing and the Rolling Stones.

The musical was presented in two acts.

ACT ONE—"Getaway" (Ronald Young, Elizabeth Austin, Dennis Bailey), "Remember the Dream" (Dennis Bailey, Elizabeth Austin, Ronald Young, William Francis), "Love Song" (Dennis Bailey, Elizabeth Austin), "Fat Luigi" (Dennis Bailey, Chuck Karel, Elizabeth Austin, Ronald Young), "Love Song" (reprise) (Ronald Young), "Holding the Bag" (Mary Ellen Ashley), "Just Our Way of Doing Business" (Chuck Karel, Dennis Bailey), "Find a Way" (Dennis Bailey)

ACT TWO—"Tippity Top" (Elizabeth Austin, Ronald Young, Dennis Bailey), "Tiny International Empire" (Dennis Bailey, Mary Ellen Ashley), "Honesty" (Dennis Bailey, Mary Ellen Ashley), "I Dream" (Elizabeth Austin), "Skidaddle" (William Francis), "Fly with Me" (Ronald Young, Elizabeth Austin), "Little Little" (Mary Ellen Ashley, Elizabeth Austin), "Hair Pulling Ballet" (Mary Ellen Ashley, Elizabeth Austin), "Hey Kiddo, You're Through" (Chuck Karel, Dennis Bailey), "Again" (Dennis Bailey, Chuck Karel, Mary Ellen Ashley)

NOTES—Stephen Holden in the *New York Times* suggested that his readers not bother to remember the musical's "difficult" title because "it probably won't be around very long." Indeed, *A Drifter, the Grifter & Heather McBride*, the first Off Broadway musical of the 1982-1983 season, was gone in nine performances.

The program noted the evening took place in a "mythical Hoosier village caught in a time warp between the invention of indoor plumbing and the Rolling Stones," and the whimsical plot dealt with a businessman of questionable ethics (the grifter), his secretary-girlfriend who longs for a wedding ring (Heather McBride), and a drifter who has commitment issues. Holden said the plot of the "wantonly inane" evening automatically assumed all Italians were members of the Mafia, and that the dialogue included the immortal line "Don't look a gift meatball sandwich in the buns"; he wasn't impressed with the score, either. During previews, Diane Findlay was replaced by Mary Ellen Ashley in the role of Goodun Plenty (the program couldn't decide on the spelling of the character's name, and thus referred to her as both Goodun and Goodie).

417 The Drunkard. "A New Musical Rendition"; THEATRE: The 13th Street Theatre; OPENING DATE: April 13, 1970; PERFORMANCES: 48; BOOK: Bro Herrod; LYRICS: Barry Manilow; MUSIC: Barry Manilow; DIRECTION: Bro Herrod; CHOREOGRAPHY: Carveth Wells; COSTUMES: Carol Luiken and Diana Hall; LIGHTING: Bill Hall; MUSICAL DIRECTION: Barry Manilow; PRODUCERS: Bro Herrod in association with Peter Perry

CAST—Susan Rush and Lou Vitacco (Jovial Leaders of the Songs), Marie Santell (Mary), Donna Sanders (Mrs. Wilson, Barmaid, A Salvation Worker), Christopher Cable (Lawyer Cribbs), Clay Johns (Edward Middleton), Drew Murphy (William

Dowton), Joy Garrett (Agnes, Mrs. Carry Nation, The Old Man's Darling), Lou Vitacco (The Preacher, The Barkeep), Susan Rush (Barmaid, Julia)

SOURCE—The 1844 play *The Drunkard, or The Fallen Saved* by W.H.S. Smith.

The action occurs in a humble cottage, a sylvan glade, a wooded grove, a rose-covered arbour, and a miserable garrett.

The musical was presented in three acts (division of acts unknown; songs are listed in performance order).

MUSICAL NUMBERS—"Something Good Will Happen Soon" (Marie Santell, Donna Sanders), "Whispering Hope" (Marie Santell, Donna Sanders), "Don't Swat Your Mother, Boys" (Christopher Cable), "Strolling Through the Park" (Marie Santell, Clay Johns), "Good Is Good" (Drew Murphy, Christopher Cable, Joy Garrett), "Mrs. Mary Middleton" (Lou Vitacco, Drew Murphy, Clay Johns, Donna Sanders, Marie Santell, Christopher Cable), "Have Another Drink" (Lou Vitacco, Clay Johns, Joy Garrett, Christopher Cable, Susan Rush, Donna Sanders), "The Curse of an Aching Heart" (Clay Johns), "For When You're Dead" (Christopher Cable), "A Cup of Coffee" (Clay Johns, Christopher Cable), "Something Good Will Happen Soon" (reprise) (Susan Rush, Drew Murphy, Marie Santell, Clay Johns, Donna Sanders), "Garbage Can Blues" (Clay Johns), "Shall I Be an Old Man's Darling" (Joy Garrett), "Julia's Song" (Susan Rush), "I'm Ready to Go" (Clay Johns), "Do You Wanna Be Saved" (Donna Sanders, Clay Johns, Marie Santell, Susan Rush, Joy Garrett, Drew Murphy, Christopher Cable, Lou Vitacco)

NOTES—This musical spoof of old-time melodramas lasted just six weeks. It included several new songs with lyrics and music by Barry Manilow (who noted in his program bio that the score didn't include any rock music) as well as old songs in the public domain (for which Manilow provided new arrangements).

The numbers in the public domain were "Whispering Hope," "Don't Swat Your Mother, Boys," "Strolling Through the Park," and "The Curse of an Aching Heart." The song "Shall I Be an Old Man's Darling" was by Will E. Haines and Jimmy Harper, and "I'm Ready to Go" was by Manilow (music) and Marty Panzer (lyric).

Clive Barnes in the *New York Times* felt the performance teetered between "the honest and the camp." But noting the musical was the only one in New York which offered free beer (and root beer), Barnes suggested that guzzling "as much of the free beer as you can get" would aid immeasurably in one's tolerance of, and goodwill toward, the "hiss-and-cheer" musical. Incidentally, the program indicated the action of the musical occurred in a humble cottage, a sylvan glade, a wooded grove, a rose-covered arbour, and a miserable garrett.

418 Dudu Fisher: Something Old, Something New. THEATRE: Mazer Theatre; OPENING DATE: October 15, 2002; PERFORMANCES: 63; TEXT: Richard Jay-Alexander; DIRECTION: Richard Jay-Alexander; SCENERY: Michael Brown; PRODUCERS: Elie Landau, Yeeshas Gross, Donny Epstein, in association with Ergo Entertainment

CAST—Dudu Fisher, Jason DeBord (Piano), Michael Blanco (Bass)

The revue was presented in one act.

NOTES—Dudu Fisher, a popular Israeli entertainer, reminisced about his career via songs and stories. Lawrence Van Gelder in the *New York Times* noted that Fisher "sets out to entertain, and that he surely does," Gelder reported that Fisher had at one time or another performed the role of Jean Valjean in the New York, London, and Tel Aviv productions of *Les Miserables*, and so for part of the evening Fisher performed Broadway songs (selections by George Gershwin, numbers popularized by Al Jolson, songs from *Oklahoma!*) as well as songs associated with Elvis Presley and the Red Hot Chili Peppers. He even performed a song set to a Kaddish prayer.

419 Duel. "A Romantic Opera"; THEATRE: Lion Theatre Opening Date: April 4, 1979; PERFORMANCES: 24; LIBRETTO: Randal Wilson; MUSIC: Randal Wilson; DIRECTION: Larry Carpenter; SCENERY: Ray Recht; COSTUMES: Kenneth M. Yount; LIGHTING: John Gisondi; MUSICAL DIRECTION: Jeffrey Olmsted; PRODUCER: The Lion Theatre Company (Gene Nye, Producing Director; Garland Wright, Company Director; Larry Carpenter, Managing Director)

CAST—Thomas Young (Fate), Randal Wilson (Lord Byron), Tom Westerman (Percy Shelley), Bertilla Baker (Teresa La Guiccioli); Holly Lipton and Barbara Niles were also in the cast (as Mary Shelley and Claire Clairmont [it's unclear which specific role each actress played])

The musical was presented in two acts.

ACT ONE—"Lovers" (Thomas Young, Company), "To Augusta"/"Spirit of Beauty" (Randal Wilson, Tom Westerman), "Two Men" ('Claire,' Randal Wilson, Tom Westerman), "'Tis Time"/"Frankenstein" ('Claire'/'Mary,' Thomas Young), "On and On" (Bertilla Baker, Thomas Young," "Ariel" (Randal Wilson), "Road Song"/"Willmouse" (Company/Tom Westerman), "I Am Not Listening" (Bertilla Baker, Randal Wilson, Thomas Young), First Act Finale (Thomas Young, Company)

ACT TWO—"Pageant in Exile": a) "Pisa" (Thomas Young), b) "There Are Moments" ('Claire'), c) "Come Again" (Bertilla Baker), d) "Murmurings" (Thomas Young), e) "When the Lamp" (Tom Westerman), f) "He Once Was Beautiful" ('Mary'), g) "Pageant of the Bleeding Heart" (Randal Wilson), "Feast or Famine" (Bertilla Baker), "Sarabande" (Company), "Milord" ('Claire'), "Fleshly Chain" (Tom Westerman, Randal Wilson), "I Must Stay with Him" ('Mary'), "Don't Tell Mary" (Tom Westerman), "Love" (Randal Wilson, Thomas Young)

NOTES—*Duel*, which dealt with the lives and deaths of the poets George Gordon Byron (Lord Byron) (1788-1824) and Percy Bysshe Shelley (1792-1822), was produced Off Off Broadway by the Lion Theatre Company, which had earlier presented the work as *Pageant in Exile* in March 1977.

Duel was recorded by Original Cast Records (LP # OC-7919) with members from the casts of both *Pageant in Exile* and *Duel* (the song titles are taken from the recording).

Duel was the second musical of the Off Off Broadway season about Shelley (see entry for *Shelley*).

420 Dunbar. THEATRE: AMAS Repertory Theatre; OPENING DATE: February 14, 1980; PERFORMANCES: 12; BOOK: Concept and original adaptation by Ayanna; adaptation for AMAS production by Ron Stacker Thompson in consultation with Ayanna; LYRICS: Paul Laurence Dunbar; additional lyrics by Quitman Fludd III; MUSIC: Quitman Fludd III, Lonnie Hewitt, and Paul E. Smith; DIRECTION: Ron Stacker Thompson; CHOREOGRAPHY: Joseph J. Cohen; SCENERY: Giles Hogya; COSTUMES: Jeffrey N. Mazor; LIGHTING: William H. Grant III; MUSICAL DIRECTION: Quitman Fludd III; PRODUCER: AMAS Repertory Theatre (Rosetta LeNoire, Founder and Artistic Director)

CAST—Dyane Harvey (Angelina), L. Edmond Wesley ("Saved" Deacon), Cle Thompson (Mrs. Conover), Steven Lang (Mr. Conover), Brenda D. Pressley (Eugenie), Larry J. Stewart (Preacher), Christine Campbell (Alice), T. Baomi Butts (Cleaning Lady), Gerald L.C. Mimd (Dely's Love), Mel Edmondson (Buddy), Jim Cyrus (Dunbar), Carl Lee (Father), Ruth Brisbane (Mother), Eleanor Cherry (Lucy)

NOTES—*Dunbar*, an Off Off Broadway musical about the life of Black poet Paul Laurence Dunbar (1872-1906), incorporated many of Dunbar's poems into the song's lyrics.

Michiko Kakutani in the *New York Times* found the episodic evening less a book musical than a "dramatic collage" of Dunbar's poems. But he felt the evening captured both the "sweetness" and "strength" of Dunbar's vision, and said the show had the potential to be a "fine" musical once the material was shaped into a "defined" point of view.

Kakutani noted the music was "appropriately lyrical," and singled out such songs as "A Hymn" and "A Death Song."

421 Dynamite Tonight (1964). "A Comic Opera for Actors"; THEATRE: York Playhouse; OPENING DATE: March 15, 1964; PERFORMANCES: 1; LIBRETTO: Arnold Weinstein; MUSIC: William Bolcom; DIRECTION: Paul Sills and Arnold Weinstein; CHOREOGRAPHY: Syvilla Fort; SCENERY: Willa Kim; special art curtain designed by Tom Keogh, Marisol, Ernest Trova, and Andy Warhol; COSTUMES: Willa Kim; LIGHTING: Peter Hunt; MUSICAL DIRECTION: Charles Turner; PRODUCER: The Actors Studio, Inc.

CAST—David Hurst (Captain), Anthony Holland (Sergeant), Gene Wilder (Smiley), George Gaynes (Prisoner), Lou Gilbert (Soldier), James Noble (Soldier), John Harkins (Soldier), Barbara Harris (Tlimpattia)

The action occurs in a bunker under an unspecified battlefield in a more unspecified war in a less specified time.

The opera was presented in one act.

NOTES—The satiric anti-war *Dynamite Tonight* sounds fascinating ... and what a cast. But apparently once the musical came out against war, it had nothing more to say; Howard Taubman in the *New York Times* felt the "alleged satire" was about effective as "birdshot fired off by an inattentive marksman." One critic singled out an amusing sequence in which a military officer discovers a forgotten military regulation which requires all prisoners about to be executed to smoke a cigarette as they say their last words.

As *Dynamite Tonite!*, the work was revived in 1967 for seven performances (see entry).

The CD collection *William Bolcom Songs* (Naxos Records # 8.559249) includes one number from the score ("When We Built the Church").

Bolcom's operas include *McTeague* (1992) and *A View from the Bridge* (1999; see entry).

422 Dynamite Tonite! (1967). THEATRE: Martinique Theatre; OPENING DATE: March 15, 1967; PERFORMANCES: 7; LIBRETTO: Arnold Weinstein; MUSIC: William Bolcom; DIRECTION: Paul Sills; SCENERY: Paul Shortt; COSTUMES: Thom Peterson; LIGHTING: F. Mitchell Dana; MUSICAL DIRECTION: John Strauss; PRODUCER: Paul Libin

CAST—Gene Troobnick (Captain), Alvin Epstein (Sergeant), George Gaynes (Prisoner), Bill Alton (Smiley), Ben Hayeem (Sad Soldier), Lou Gilbert (Shell-Shocked Soldier), Mark Epstein (Wounded Solider), Allyn Ann McLerie (Tlimpattia)

The action occurs at the home of the captain and the sergeant, which is a supply bunker beneath a battlefield after twenty years of fighting. The program did not list song titles.

NOTES—With a slightly revised title, *Dynamite Tonite!* was a revival of *Dynamite Tonight*, the 1964 anti-war opera which had played for just one performance. The revival opened three years to the date of the original production, and George Gaynes reprised his role of the Prisoner. In his *Opening Nights/Theatre Criticism of the Sixties* (G.P. Putnam's Sons, 1972), Martin Gottfried reviewed the revival when it was performed at the Yale School of Drama in December 1966 (four months before it opened Off Broadway). For the Yale production, Linda Lavin played the role of Tlimpattia, which had originally been performed by Barbara Harris in 1964 and which was played by Allyn Ann McLerie (Mrs. George Gaynes) when the revival reached New York in March 1967.

Gottfried praised Bolcom's score, a pastiche of vaudeville, tango, soft-shoe, and jazz, and noted occasional musical references to Stravinsky, Milhaud, and Weill. Gottfried found Weinstein's libretto perfect for an operatic setting, "a giddy horseplay about cartooned soldiers before a background of a terribly real war."

On November 24, 1975, the musical was again revived at Yale, for twenty-three performances; this time around, the cast included Linda Lavin, Eugene Troobnick, and Alvin Epstein; the revival was co-directed by Epstein and Walt Jones.

423 Earthlight. "A Play with Music." THEATRE: Garrick Theatre; OPENING DATE: January 17, 1971; PERFORMANCES: 56; SCRIPT: Allan Mann and the Earthlight Ensemble; LYRICS: Pure Love and Pleasure (?); MUSIC: Pure Love and Pleasure; DIRECTION: Allan Mann; CHOREOGRAPHY: Allan Mann (?); "additional" choreography by Peggy Chierseka; SCENERY: Ron Tannis; PRODUCER: Garrick Productions

CAST—Earthlight Ensemble (Wendy Blakely, Sheila Rachel Cohen, Ellyn Diskin, Doug Fowley, Tylar Gustavson, Barbara Pieters, Rick Pieters, Jane Richardson, Greg Stone, Richard Williams); Pure Love and Pleasure (musicians: John Allair, Bob Bohanna, Jacques Forman, Rob Moitaza; vocalists, Dave McAnally, Pegge May)

The revue was presented in one act.

NOTES—*Earthlight* had originally been seen Off Off Broadway. The rock revue consisted of approximately two-dozen topical sketches and songs concerning the Vietnam War, alienation, and other fashionable topics of the era; it appears the Earthlight Ensemble didn't sing, and that the vocals were handled by the two singers in the Pure Love and Pleasure band. (The band was later succeeded by another group, called Shaker.) *Earthlight* was part of a brief trend in rock musicals in which actors spoke dialogue and sang few if any of the songs, leaving a band and its vocalists to perform all (or most) of the score (see entries for the *The Last Sweet Days of Isaac* and *The Survival of St. Joan*). Reviewing the musical in the *New York Times*, Howard Taubman noted the Off Broadway production dropped the nude scene (which had been seen in the Off Off Broadway version) but retained a sprinkling of four-letter words. Taubman also noted (in a sequence typical of the era) that the cast members and some of the audience "locked together" (in this case, while eating slices of fresh oranges).

424 Eating Raoul. "The Musical." THEATRE: Union Square Theatre; OPENING DATE: May 13, 1992; PERFORMANCES: 47; BOOK: Paul Bartel; LYRICS: Boyd Graham; MUSIC: Jed Feuer; DIRECTION: Toni Kotite; CHOREOGRAPHY: Lynne Taylor-Corbett; SCENERY: Loren Sherman; COSTUMES: Franne Lee; LIGHTING: Peggy Eisenhauer; MUSICAL DIRECTION: Albert Ahronheim; PRODUCERS: Max Weitzenhoffer, Stewart F. Lane, Joan Cullman, and Richard Norton

CAST—Courtenay Collins (Mary Bland), Eddie Korbich (Paul Bland), M.W. Reid (Dr. Doberman, Ginger), Jonathan Brody (Mr. Kray, James, Junior), David Masenheimer (Mr. Leech, Howard, Bobby), Lovette George (Cop, Inez [Raoulette]), Cindy Benson (Donna the Dominatrix, Tyrone, Yolanda), ADRIAN ZMED (Raoul), Susan Wood (Gladys [Raoulette]); Tourists, Swingers, etc. (Cindy Benson, Jonathan Brody, Lovette George, Allen Hidalgo, David Masenheimer, M.W. Reid, Susan Wood)

SOURCE—The 1982 film *Eating Raoul* (screenplay by Paul Bartel).

The action occurs in Los Angeles in the mid-1960s.

The musical was presented in two acts.

ACT ONE—"Meet the Blands" (Company), "A Small Restaurant" (Eddie Korbich, Courtenay Collins), "La La Land" (Ensemble), "Swing, Swing, Swing" (Ensemble), "A Small Restaurant" (reprise) (Eddie Korbich, Courtenay Collins), "Happy Birthday, Harry" (M.W. Reid, Jonathan Brody), "You Gotta Takes Pains" (Cindy Benson, M.W. Reid, Jonathan Brody), "A Thought Occurs" (Eddie Korbich, Courtenay Collins), "Victim Update #1" (Ensemble), "Sexperts" (Girls), "Empty Bed" (Jonathan Brody, Courtenay Collins), "Basketball" (Cindy Benson), "Victim Update #2" (Ensemble), "Tool for You" (Adrian Zmed, Lovette George, Susan Wood), "A Thought Occurs" (reprise) (Adrian Zmed, Eddie Korbich, Courtenay Collins), "Think About Tomorrow" (Adrian Zmed, Eddie Korbich, Courtenay Collins)

ACT TWO—Opening/"Victim Update #3"/"Yolanda's" (Ensemble), "Hot Monkey Love" (Adrian Zmed, Lovette George, Susan Wood), "A Small Restaurant" (reprise) (Eddie Korbich, Courtenay Collins), "Momma Said" (M.W. Reid, Eddie Korbich, Courtenay Collins, Adrian Zmed), "Lovers in Love" (Adrian Zmed, Courtenay Collins), "Mary" (Eddie Korbich), "Victim Update #4" (Ensemble), "Eating Raoul" (Adrian Zmed, Lovette George, Susan Wood, Ensemble), "Mucho Macho Trio" (Adrian Zmed, Eddie Korbich, Courtenay Collins), "Eating Raoul" (reprise) (Adrian Zmed), "One Last Bop" (Courtenay Collins, Ensemble), Finale (Company)

NOTES—Based on the popular 1982 film of the same name, *Eating Raoul* told the satiric tale of Paul and Mary, a penniless couple whose only desire is to leave Los Angeles and open a small restaurant in the country. In order to achieve this goal, they lure unwitting victims to their apartment under the guise of its being a sex club; once the "clients" arrive, they're quickly dispatched, their money taken from their wallets, and, in *Sweeney Todd*-like fashion, their bodies sold to a dog food company. Raoul, a sexy Latino and wannabe rock singer, joins them in their venture, and pretty soon the money is rolling in ... and Mary and Raoul become lovers. When Paul discovers Raoul plans to kill him and run away with Mary ... well, take your pick of endings. The script, published by Samuel French, Inc., in 1993, indicates that as the curtain falls, frying-pan-wielding Mary has to decide whether to kill Raoul or Paul ("One Last Bop"). But according to the liner notes of the musical's cast album (released by Bay Cities Records [CD # BCD-3030]), Raoul is the one Mary bops, and, at musical's end, Paul and Mary invite their real estate agent for a home-cooked dinner in order to celebrate their purchase of a restaurant in the country. When the realtor asks Mary if the meat in the stew is French, she replies that it's "actually Mexican."

With its edgy black humor and pleasant score, it's surprising *Eating Raoul* didn't enjoy a long run. But audiences didn't come, and so the musical was gone in six weeks.

425 The Egg and I. THEATRE: Jan Hus Auditorium; OPENING DATE: September 10, 1958; PERFORMANCES: Unknown; BOOK: Hal Pockriss; LYRICS: Wilferd Sales; MUSIC: Frank Brent; DIRECTION: Ed Cambridge; CHOREOGRAPHY: Charles Martin; SCENERY: James Marshall; COSTUMES: Bob Tadlock; MUSICAL DIRECTION: Alonzo Hendricks; PRODUCERS: William Gyimes; Frank Brents, Associate Producer

CAST—Isabel Sanford (Ma Kettle), Jim Trotman (Pa Kettle), Clarice Taylor (Birdie Hicks), Carol Joy (Susie Hicks), Diana Sands (Betty), Clark Morgan (Bob), Allegro Kane (Mr. Hicks), Harold Scott (Albert), Clarence Williams 3rd (Elwin)

SOURCE—The 1945 novel *The Egg and I* by Betty MacDonald.

NOTES—This short-lived musical was adapted from Betty MacDonald's 1945 autobiographical novel *The Egg and I*, which dealt with her life as a city woman suddenly uprooted by marriage to a small chicken farm in Washington State. The book is now akin to Broadway's forgotten hits: Jean Kerr's wonderful comedy *Mary, Mary* (which opened in 1961 and played for over four years) is barely remembered today, and, similarly, Betty MacDonald's runaway best-seller is now unread and all-but-forgotten. But at the time, the book was a publishing phenomenon. Within the first eleven months of its publication, it had sold one million copies, and was eventually translated into thirty languages. In 1947, a film version was released (with Claudette Colbert in the "Betty MacDonald" role). Two minor characters in the film version, Ma and Pa Kettle (played by Marjorie Main and Percy Kilbride), were scene-stealers, and soon these supporting characters were promoted to the leads in a series of highly successful films dealing with the adventures of the Kettles. From 1949 through 1957, there was one Ma and Pa Kettle film released each year, a total of nine such films, all in which Main and Kilbride reprised their roles from the original 1947 film.

The musical version was surprising in that the White characters in the original were now Black. Diana Sands, who later found meaty roles in Broadway dramas and comedies, played Betty, and Isabel Sanford, who later found fame on the long-running CBS television series *The Jeffersons*, played Ma Kettle.

Brooks Atkinson in the *New York Times* had both positive and negative comments about the production. He praised the book ("witty ... with a sardonic point of view"), lyrics ("literate"), and music ("several romantic numbers" in the "melodic" style of Rudolf Friml ... "beguiling music ... serenades and ballads and square-dance tunes that have not been debauched by juke-box noises"). In particular, Atkinson praised "Spring Is on My Side," "Mountain Speaks to Me," and "The Equal of Kings."

On the other hand, Atkinson was appalled by the performances, which he found "shrill" and more in keeping with the standards of a minstrel show. He complained that the performers "whoop and holler as if nothing had happened since the days of blackface follies."

426 Egyptology (My Head Was a Sledgehammer). THEATRE: The Other Stage/The Public Theatre; OPENING DATE: May 17, 1983; PERFORMANCES: 48; TEXT: Richard Foreman; MUSIC: Richard Foreman; SCENERY: Richard Foreman and Nancy Winters; COSTUMES: Patricia McGourty; LIGHTING: Spencer Mosse; PRODUCER: The New York Shakespeare Theatre Festival (Joseph Papp, Producer; Jason Steven Cohen, Associate Producer)

CAST—Seth Allen, Raymond Barry, Gretel Cummings, William Duff-Griffin, Cynthia Gillette, Kate Manheim, Frank Maraden, George McGrath, Christine Morris, Lola Pashalinski

The revue was presented in one act.

NOTES—Produced at the Public Theatre, *Egyptology (My Head Was a Sledgehammer)* was a revue from the Foreman Ontological-Hysteric Theatre which offered sardonic commentary on various issues, many of which were accompanied by dance and musical interludes. Frank Rich in the *New York Times* indicated the evening's "fragmented, nonlinear" approach to cultural clashes, the randomness of existence, and the general "inability" of the characters to find their own and others' identities, was entertaining enough as long as one didn't dwell too long over the content; but he was disappointed that the evening's "transitions between segments" were more "willed and mechanical" than "genuinely associative." On January 16, 1994, the work (or at least a version of it) was produced Off Off Broadway at the Ontological-Hysteric Theatre as *My Head Was a Sledgehammer*, and was published under that title by Overlook Press.

427 Einstein on the Beach. THEATRE: Metropolitan Opera House; OPENING DATE: November 21, 1976; PERFORMANCES: 2; LIBRETTO: Philip Glass; MUSIC: Philip Glass; DIRECTION: Robert Wilson; CHOREOGRAPHY: Andrew deGroat; SCENERY: Design by Robert Wilson; Christina Gianniel, Scenic Supervision; COSTUMES: D'Arcangelo-Mayer; LIGHTING: Beverly Emmons; PRODUCER: Byrd Hoffman Foundation (in cooperation with the Metropolitan Opera)

CAST—George Andoniadis, Connie Beckley, Betty Ann Burchfield, Lucinda Childs, Frank Conversano, Andrew deGroat, Charles Dennis, Grethe Holby, Jeannie Hutchins, Mark Jacoby, Samuel M. Johnson, Paul Mann, Richard Morrison, Dana Reitz, Marie Rice, Ronald Resbury, Sheryl L. Sutton, Robert Wilson, David P. Woodberry

The opera was presented in five acts.

ACT ONE—"Knee Play 1" (text by Christopher Knowles) (Chorus, Electric Organ), "Train 1" (text by Christopher Knowles) (Ensemble with Solo Voice and Chorus), "Trial 1" (Chorus, Violin, Electric Organ, Flutes) (three sequences were included in this section: "Entrance," "Mr. Bojangles," and "All Men Are Equal"; in 1976, the latter sequence was different and was titled "Paris"; for "All Men Are Equal" and "Paris" had texts by Samuel M. Johnson)

ACT TWO—"Knee Play 2" (text by Christopher Knowles) (Violin Solo), "Dance 1" (Ensemble with Solo Voice and Dancers), "Night Train" (Two Voices, Chorus, Small Ensemble)

ACT THREE—"Knee Play 3" (Chorus a Capella), "Trial 2/Prison" (Chorus, Electric Organ; Ensemble at the End) (text by Christopher Knowles; this sequence included three sections: "Prematurely Air-Conditioned Supermarket," text by Lucinda Childs; an Ensemble sequence; and "I Feel the Earth Move"; the overall text for this sequence was by Christopher Knowles), "Dance 2" (Six Voices, Violin, Electric Organ)

ACT FOUR—"Knee Play 4" (Chorus, Violin), "Building/Train" (Chorus, Ensemble), "Bed" (Solo Electric Organ, Voice) (this sequence included three sections: "Cadenza," "Prelude," and "Aria"), "Spaceship" (Chorus, Ensemble)

ACT FIVE—"Knee Play 5" (Women's Chorus, Violin, Electric Organ) (two sequences included in this section were "Bus Driver (Lovers on a Park Bench)" and "Two Lovers" [text of latter by Samuel M. Johnson)

NOTES—*Einstein on the Beach* premiered in France on July 25, 1976, and was then performed in other European countries. The first performance in the United States took place on November 21 of that year when the opera was performed for two sold-out performances at the Met on nights when the Metropolitan Opera House wasn't offering performances from its regular season.

Both Mel Gussow and Clive Barnes of the *New York Times* reviewed the American premiere. Gussow found the opera a "mystical, monumental theatre piece," and while the opera was not really about Einstein (or a beach), Gussow noted that the work was "a dream of Einstein, an evolving exercise in time and space relations." The mesmerizing, hypnotic music of the five-act, five-hour opera (with no formal intermissions: the audience was at liberty to come and go during the performance) was connected by five so-called "knee plays" which were short choreographed sequences.

Clive Barnes found the work "bizarre" and "occasionally boring," but he nonetheless felt it offered a kind of "dramatic tension" rarely seen in the theatre. He praised Glass' "sensational" music and noted that the work's "visual beauty ... cannot be too highly stressed." He concluded by saying "you will never forget it, even if you hate it."

An abridged version of the opera was first recorded in 1978 on a 4-LP set released by Tomato Records (later on CD by CBS Masterworks Records [and then later by Sony Records]). In 1993, the complete opera was recorded on a 3-CD set released by Elektra Nonesuch Records (the list of musical sequences is taken from this recording).

Einstein on the Beach, *Satyagraha* (1980), and *Akhnaten* (1984) are known as Glass' three "portrait" operas (see entries for the latter two operas). As of this writing, *Satyagraha* is scheduled for its Met premiere on April 11, 2008.

Einstein on the Beach was later revived at the Brooklyn Academy of Music on December 11, 1984, for twelve performances, and then again on December 8, 1992.

428 Elaine Stritch at Liberty. THEATRE: Newman Theatre/The Joseph Papp Public Theatre; OPENING DATE: November 6, 2001; PERFORMANCES: 50; TEXT: Elaine Stritch and John Lahr; LYRICS: See song list for credits; MUSIC: See song list for credits; DIRECTION: George C. Wolfe; SCENERY: Riccardo Hernandez; COSTUMES: Paul Tazewell; LIGHTING: Jules Fisher and Peggy Eisenhauer; MUSICAL DIRECTION: Rob Bowman; PRODUCER: The New York Shakespeare Festival (George C. Wolfe, Producer; Fran Reiter, Executive Director)

CAST—Elaine Stritch

The revue was performed in one act.

MUSICAL NUMBERS (in alphabetical order; "the following songs may or may not be performed")—"All in Fun" (from *Very Warm for May*, 1939; lyric by Oscar Hammerstein II, music by Jerome Kern), "Broadway Baby" (*Follies*, 1971; lyric and music by Stephen Sondheim), "But Not for Me" (*Girl Crazy*, 1930; lyric by Ira Gershwin, music by George Gershwin), "If Love Were All" (*Bitter-Sweet*, 1929 [London]; also, New York [1929]; lyric and music by Noel Coward), "Can You Use Any Money Today?" (*Call Me Madam*, 1950; lyric and music by Irving Berlin), "Civilization" (a/k/a "Bongo, Bongo, Bongo") (*Angel in the Wings*, 1947; lyric by Bob Hilliard, music by Carl Sigman), "Hooray for Hollywood" (1938 film *Hollywood Hotel*; lyric by Johnny Mercer, music by Richard A. Whiting), "I'm Still Here" (*Follies*, 1971; lyric and music by Stephen Sondheim), "I've Been to a Marvelous Party" (a/k/a "I Went to a Marvelous Party") (*Set to Music*, 1938; lyric and music by Noel Coward), "I Want a Long Time Daddy" (lyric and music by Porter Grainger), "The Little Things You Do Together" (*Company*, 1970; lyric and music by Stephen Sondheim), "Something Good" (1965 film *The Sound of Music*; lyric and music by Richard Rodgers), "The Ladies Who Lunch" (*Company*, 1970; lyric and music by Stephen Sondheim), "The Party's Over" (*Bells Are Ringing*, 1956; lyric by Betty Comden and Adolph Green, music by Jule Styne), "There Never Was a Baby Like My Baby" (*Two on the Aisle*, 1951; lyric by Betty Comden and Adolph Green, music by Jule Styne), "There's No Business Like Show Business" (*Annie Get Your Gun*, 1946; lyric and music by Irving Berlin), "This Is All Very New to Me" (*Plain and Fancy*, 1954; lyric by Arnold B. Horwitt, music by Albert Hague), "Why Do the Wrong People Travel?" (*Sail Away*, 1961; lyric and music by Noel Coward), "Zip" (*Pal Joey*, 1940; lyric by Lorenz Hart, music by Richard Rodgers)

NOTES—The autobiographical evening of Broadway legend Elaine Stritch's life and theatre career soon transferred to Broadway at the Neil Simon (formerly Alvin) Theatre on February 21, 2002, for sixty-nine performances. The cast album was released by DRG Records (CD # 12994).

The revue was later shown on Home Box Office, and a DVD was released by Image Entertainment (# 1DO7231PDVD). The production was revived at the Café Carlyle beginning on January 1, 2008, for three weeks.

429 Eleanor Sleeps Here.

NOTES—See entry for *First Lady Suite*.

430 Elegies. "A Song Cycle." THEATRE: The Mitzi E. Newhouse Theatre/Lincoln Center Theatre; OPENING DATE: March 24, 2003; PERFORMANCES: 9; LYRICS: William Finn; MUSIC: William Finn; DIRECTION: Graciela Daniele; COSTUMES: Toni-Leslie James, Costume Consultant; LIGHTING: Donald Holder, Lighting Consultant; MUSICAL DIRECTION: Vadim Feichtner; PRODUCERS: Lincoln Center Theatre (Andre Bishop and Bernard Gersten, Directors; Ira Weitzman, Musical Theatre Associate Producer)

CAST—Christian Borle, Betty Buckley, Carolee Carmello, Keith Byron Kirk, Michael Rupert

The song cycle was presented in one act.

MUSICAL NUMBERS—"Looking Up Quintet" (Company), "Mister Choi & Madame G" (Keith Bryon Kirk, with Carolee Carmello and Christian Borle), "Mark's All-Male Thanksgiving" (Michael Rupert), "Only One" (Betty Buckley), "Joe Papp" (Keith Byron Kirk, with Christian Borle and Michael Rupert), "Peggy Hewitt & Misty del Giorno" (Christian Borle and Carolee Carmello, with Keith Byron Kirk and Michael Rupert), "Passover" (Carolee Carmello), "Infinite Joy" (Betty Buckley), "The Ballad of Jack Eric Williams (and Other 3-Named Composers)" (Michael Rupert), "Fred" (Christian Borle), "Dear Reader" (Betty Buckley, Carolee Carmello), "Monica & Mark" (Christian Borle, Keith Byron Kirk, Michael Rupert), "Anytime (I Am There)" (Carolee Carmello), "My Dogs" (Christian Borle), "Venice" (Michael Rupert), "14 Dwight Ave., Natick, Massachusetts" (Christian Borle, Betty Buckley), "When the Earth Stopped Turning" (Christian Borle), "Goodbye" (Keith Byron Kirk), "Boom Boom" (Carolee Carmello, with Christian Borle, Keith Byron Kirk, Michael Rupert), "Looking Up" (Betty Buckley), "Goodbye" (finale) (Company)

NOTES—*Elegies* was an affecting song cycle by William Finn in which the memories of the dead are evoked, and we are asked to remember that their "living was the prize" and their "ending's not the story." Among those remembered by Finn were his mother, Barbara Finn, Joe Papp, Peggy Hewitt, and Jack Eric Williams.

Peggy Hewett (1946-2002) had appeared in the original productions of Finn's *America Kicks Up Its Heels* and *Romance in Hard Times* (see entries), and had also been seen in the original Off Broadway productions of *Show Me Where the Good Times Are* and *Olympus on My Mind* (see entries). She's perhaps best remembered for her "Margaret Dumont" role in the 1980 Broadway musical *A Day in Hollywood, A Night in the Ukraine*.

Jack Eric Williams had written the lyrics and music for *Romance Language* (see entry), and as a performer created the role of Beadle Bamford in the original 1979 production of *Sweeney Todd/ The Demon Barber of Fleet Street*, introducing "Ladies in Their Sensitivities" and the numbers in the "Parlor Songs" sequence.

Among the memorable songs were "Mark's All-Male Thanksgiving," 'Anytime (I Am There)," "The Ballad of Jack Eric Williams (and Other 3-Named Composers)," and "Dogs."

The cycle (originally titled *Looking Up*) was presented as a limited engagement performed over a series of Sunday and Monday evenings at the Newhouse Theatre when Frank McGuinness' play *Observe the Sons of Ulster Marching Towards the Somme* was dark. *Elegies* was performed on the set used for *Ulster* (designed by Alexander Dodge).

The cast album was released by Fynsworth Alley Records (CD # 302-062-189-2); two numbers, "Fred" and "Dear Reader," weren't included on the recording.

431 Elephant Steps.

"A Multi-Media Pop-Opera Extravaganza"/"A Fearful Radio Show." THEATRE: Unknown; OPENING DATE: 1970; PERFORMANCES: Unknown; LIBRETTO: Richard Foreman; MUSIC: Stanley Silverman

The opera was presented in two acts.

ACT ONE—"Elephant Drone"/"Elephants," "Elephant Heartbeats," "Don't You Believe"/"My Ears," "All Shook Up," "Read My Palm[s]"/"Inside the Wall"/"Gavotte," "Gypsy Tango"/"Shoot Them," "You're on the Radio"/"Radio Waves," "Read My Palm[s]" (reprise)/"Watch Me Move"/"I'm No Closer"/"Look at My Hands," "Stop Seeing Reinhardt"

ACT TWO—Entr'acte/"Watch Me Put My Right Foot," "I Am No Longer Beautiful"/"Beautiful As Is"/"We Sit in the Window," "One and Two!," "Dreaming of Reinhardt," "Midnight Sun," "Photograph Song," "Madrigals," "Vaudeville Chase"/"Stirring Soup"/"A Strange Thing," Finale

NOTES—*Elephant Steps* was first produced at Tanglewood in Lenox, Massachusetts, on August 7, 1968, and in New York (in an apparently Off Off Broadway production) in 1970. It was recorded on a 2-LP set by Columbia Records in 1974 (# M2X-33044), and the album's performers included Larry Marshall, Marilyn Sokol, Patti Austin, and Michael Tilson Thomas (who also conducted).

The opera employed mixed-media effects (language, music, film, graphics, even incense) to tell the story of a man named Hartman who seeks enlightenment and thus searches for a mysterious guru named Reinhardt.

432 The Elevator.

NOTES—See entry for *The Last Sweet Days of Isaac.*

433 Elisabeth Welch: Time to Start Living.

"A Musical Entertainment." THEATRE: Lucille Lortel Theatre; OPENING DATE: March 20, 1986; PERFORMANCES: 22; SCENERY: Leo Meyer; MUSICAL DIRECTION: Peter Howard; PRODUCERS: Arthur Cantor and Edwin W. Schloss by arrangement with Lucille Lortel

CAST—ELISABETH WELCH

The revue was presented in one act.

NOTES—Elisabeth Welch's one-woman show (she was backed by a three-man combo) was a welcome opportunity for New Yorkers to hear the legendary performer in a program of songs covering her career from 1928 to the present.

A program note indicated a recording and a videocassette of the production were in preparation, but it appears they never materialized.

434 Elizabeth and Essex (1980).

"A Musical." THEATRE: Encompass, The Music Theatre; OPENING DATE: January 31, 1980; PERFORMANCES: 25; BOOK: Michael Stewart and Mark Bramble; LYRICS: Richard Engquist; MUSIC: Doug Katsaros; DIRECTION: Nancy Rhodes; CHOREOGRAPHY: Sharon Halley; SCENERY: Michael C. Smith; COSTUMES: A. Christina Giannini; LIGHTING: Carol B. Sealey; MUSICAL DIRECTION: Jack Gaughan; PRODUCER: The Encompass Theatre Company, Inc. (Roger Cunningham, Producer; Nancy Rhodes, Artistic Director)

CAST—ESTELLE PARSONS (Elizabeth), RICHARD WHITE (Essex), Florence Lacey (Penelope Gray), Brian Wolfe (The Fool), Lisa Ann Cunningham (Tressa, Old Woman), Paul Farin (Marvel), Fran Ferrone (Martha), Randy Hansen (Guard, Soldier, Courier), Wade L. Hardy III (Lord Herbert), Ted Kowal (Captain Armin, Man-at-Arms, Courier), Patricia Ludd (Lady Ann), Court Miller (Bacon), William Ryall (Walter Raleigh), Gordon Stanley (Cecil), Molly Stark (Lady Charlotte, Irish Woman)

SOURCE—The 1930 play *Elizabeth the Queen* by Maxwell Anderson.

The action occurs in the second half of the sixteenth century, at Whitehall Palace, Ireland; Essex' house on the Strand; and the Queen's apartment in the tower.

The musical was presented in two acts.

ACT ONE—"Fa La" (Company), "As You Are" (Estelle Parsons), "Cheers" (Richard White), "I'll Be Different" (Estelle Parsons, Richard White), "Gloriana" (Richard White, Company), "Gossip" (Randy Hansen, Ted Kowal), "The First to Know" (Estelle Parsons, Richard White), "Ireland" (Company), "Cheers" (reprise) (Richard White, Soldiers), "Love Knots" (Florence Lacey, Brian Wolfe, Patricia Ludd, Molly Stark), "Not Now" (Estelle Parsons)

ACT TWO—"She's a Woman" (Court Miller, William Ryall, Gordon Stanley), "Gossip" (reprise) (Florence Lacey, Patricia Ludd, Molly Stark), "It Takes a Man" (Richard White, Men), "The Lady Lies" (Estelle Parsons), "All I Remember Is You" (Wade L. Hardy III, Patricia Ludd, Estelle Parsons, Company), "The First to Know" (reprise) (Estelle Parsons, Richard White), "Ireland" (reprise) (Company), "Not Now" (reprise) (Estelle Parsons), Finale (Estelle Parsons, Richard White, Company)

NOTES—*Elizabeth and Essex* was based on Maxwell Anderson's successful play which starred Lynn Fontanne and Alfred Lunt. The 1939 film version (titled *The Private Lives of Elizabeth and Essex*) starred Bette Davis and Errol Flynn.

The Off Off Broadway musical generally impressed the critics, without actually overwhelming them. Doug Katsaros' score was compared favorably with Alan Jay Lerner and Frederick Loewe ... *and* with Kurt Weill (!). The musical was later produced Off Off Broadway (in 1984; see entry) with Evelyn Lear, and then disappeared for good.

435 Elizabeth and Essex (1984).

THEATRE: Church of the Heavenly Rest/The York Theatre Company; OPENING DATE: May 17, 1984; PERFORMANCES: 16; BOOK: Michael Stewart and Mark Bramble; LYRICS: Richard Engquist; MUSIC: Douglas Katsaros; DIRECTION: Sondra Lee; CHOREOGRAPHY: Onna White; SCENERY: James Morgan; COSTUMES: Willa Kim (Costume Consultant); LIGHTING: Mary Jo Dondlinger; MUSICAL DIRECTION: Douglas Katsaros; PRODUCER: The York Theatre Company (Janet Hayes Walker, Producing Director)

CAST—David Bryant (Fool), Nora Colpman (Lady Charlotte), Jennifer Naimo (Lady Ann), Willy Falk (Lord Herbert), Paul David Richards (Raleigh), Gordon Stanley (Cecil), D. Peter Samuel (Bacon), George Dvorsky (Armin), David Hart (Marvel), Jan Pessano (Penelope), Evelyn Lear (Elizabeth), Dennis Parlato (Essex), Sally Yorke (Ireland Lady), Paul Blankenship (Courier), Lisa Vroman (Lady Wicket), Barbara Scanlon (Martha)

SOURCE—The 1930 play *Elizabeth the Queen* by Maxwell Anderson.

The action occurs in late in the sixteenth century, in the palace and its grounds as well as in Ireland.

The musical was presented in two acts.

ACT ONE—Opening (David Bryant, Company), "As You Are" (Evelyn Lear), "Cheers" (Dennis Parlato), "I'll Be Different" (Evelyn Lear, Dennis Parlato), "Gloriana" (Dennis Parlato, Company), "Gossip" (David Bryant, Couriers), "The First to Know" (Evelyn Lear, Dennis Parlato), "Ireland" (Company), "Cheers" (reprise) (Dennis Parlato, English Soldiers), "Love Knots" (Jan Pessano, David Bryant, Nora Colpman, Jennifer Naimo, Lisa Vroman), "Not Now" (Evelyn Lear)

ACT TWO—"It Takes a Man" (Dennis Parlato, Soldiers), "She's a Woman" (D. Peter Samuel, Paul David Richards, Gordon Stanley), "Gossip" (reprise) (David Bryant, Nora Colpman, Jennifer Naimo, Lisa Vroman), "The Lady Lies" (Evelyn Lear), "All I Remember Is You" (Willy Falk, Jennifer Naimo, Company), "The First to Know" (reprise) (Evelyn Lear, Dennis Parlato), "Fool's Song" (David Bryant), "Not Now" (reprise) (Evelyn Lear), "The Last Encounter" (Evelyn Lear, Dennis Parlato), "Conclusion" (Evelyn Lear), Finale (Evelyn Lear, Company)

NOTES—This was the second Off Off Broadway production of *Elizabeth and Essex* (see entry for 1980 version). Estelle Parsons had taken critical brickbats for her vocals in the original production, and so the 1984 version boasted a genuine opera star in Evelyn Lear, who had made her debut in 1955 in Marc Blitzstein's *Reuben Reuben*, which never got out of Boston (it nonetheless boasts one of the great scores of musical theatre). Lear has recorded Sondheim (her recording of *Evelyn Lear Sings Sondheim and Bernstein* [Mercury Golden Imports Records LP # SRI-75136] is one of the earliest recorded collections of Sondheim material, and includes "Could I Leave You?" and "Losing My Mind" [from *Follies*, 1971] and "Green Finch and Linnet Bird" [*Sweeney Todd/The Demon Barber of Fleet Street*, 1979]).

436 Elsa Lanchester—Herself.

THEATRE: 41st Street Theatre; OPENING DATE: February 4, 1961; PERFORMANCES: 75; DIRECTION: "Censored by Charles Laughton"; SCENERY: Robert Soule; COSTUMES: Miss Lanchester's modern wardrobe by Stella of Magnin's "herself"; LIGHTING: Robert Soule; MUSICAL DIRECTION: Ray Henderson; PRODUCERS: Noel Behn and Robert Costello in association with Joe (Joseph) Beruh

CAST—Elsa Lanchester, with Ray Henderson and Don Dollarhide at the two pianos

The revue was presented in two acts.

ACT ONE—Overture, "Won't You Buy My Sweet Blooming Lavender?," "Charity," "He Didn't Oughter," "Cockney London," "Bits and Pieces," "St. Paul's Steeple," "When the Summer Comes Again," "Our Threepenny Hop," Don Dollarhide at the Piano, "Night Club Days," "It May Be Life," "The Ballad of Sister Anne," "I May Be Fast," "Cat's Meat," "Lola"

ACT TWO—Overture (After Offenbach), "I'm Glad to See You're Back," "Dancing Days and Stinkbombs," "Freedom and All That," "Un Bon Mouvement," Ray Henderson at the Piano, "Riverside Nights," "The Boatmen's Dance," "He's Nice, He's Clean...," "H.R.H. and N.Y.C.," "Catalogue Woman," "That-a-Way," "The Stork," "When a Lady Has a Piazza," Finale

NOTES—Elsa Lanchester's one-woman revue of obscure British music hall songs (although some of the numbers may have been written especially for the production, such as "H.R.H. and N.Y.C.") was directed ("censored," according to the program) by her husband, Charles Laughton. Milton Esterow in the *New York Times* reported that 17.4 inches of snow had just fallen on New York City, and so he encouraged his readers to use dog sleds, skis, or bulldozers to see the "wonderfully entertaining package" of songs by Lanchester, who could "purr and roar and get more out of a lifted eyebrow than a lot of Hollywood queens." To add to the atmosphere of the occasion, Esterow also reported that hot tea and British ginger beer were served at intermission (but, in a nod to Anglo-American relations, Pepsi-Cola was also offered).

Incidental music for "The Ballad of Sister Anne" and "Cat's Meat" sequences was composed by Ray Henderson, who was also the musical director for the production (he was not the Ray Henderson who composed *Good News* [1927] and other Broadway and Hollywood film musicals).

Material in the revue was credited to Harold Monro, Sir Osbert Sitwell, Sir Allan Herbert, Forman Brown, Herbert Farjeon, Thomas Wolfe, Euripides, "and others."

The revue was recorded by Verve Records (LP # V-15024).

437 Elvis Mania. THEATRE: Off On Broadway Theatre; OPENING DATE: September 4, 1984; PERFORMANCES: 18; PLAY: Johnny Seaton; DIRECTION: Leslie Irons; SCENERY: Paul Malec; COSTUMES: Jeffrey Wallach; PRODUCER: Off On Broadway Theatre

CAST—Johnny Seaton

The revue was presented in three acts.

NOTES—*Elvis Mania* was a concert-styled revue which covered the gamut of Elvis Presley's career (his early years with Sun Records, his emergence as a superstar during the mid and late 1950s [including his career with RCA Victor], his Army duty, his film and television years, and his Las Vegas period of the 1970s).

The revue had been previously produced Off Off Broadway for a brief run beginning on August 16, 1984.

There have been many Elvis Presley-related musicals, some in concert-style revue format, some based on his life, and others jukebox musicals which utilized songs associated with him to flesh out new books or books based on his films. In 1978, the concert *Elvis The Legend Lives* played on Broadway for 101 performances; the 1989 Off Off Broadway book-musical-cum revue *Elvis: A Rockin' Remembrance* offered three Elvis personas ("Young Elvis," "Heyday Elvis," and "Older Elvis") for thirty-one performances; and the 2005 jukebox musical *All Shook Up* lasted for 213 performances on Broadway. London saw *Elvis* (1977), *Are You Lonesome Tonight?* (1985), and *Jailhouse Rock* (2004). Canada has seen *The Elvis Story* (1997), and in 1984 Germany offered two competing musicals, both titled *Elvis*. In 1987, another German musical about Presley opened; titled *Elvis & John*, the evening consisted of two one-act musicals, one about Presley, the other about John Lennon (for more information regarding John Lennon and Beatles-related musicals, see entries for both *Sgt. Pepper's Lonely Hearts Club Band on the Road* and *Lennon*).

438 Emma.

NOTES—See entry for *The New York Musical Theatre Festival.*

439 Emmeline. THEATRE: New York State Opera; OPENING DATE: April 1, 1998; PERFORMANCES: 4; LIBRETTO: J.D. McClatchy; MUSIC: Tobias Picker; DIRECTION: Francesca Zambello; SCENERY: Robert Israel; COSTUMES: Dunya Ramicova; LIGHTING: Amy Appleyard; MUSICAL DIRECTION: George Manahan; PRODUCER: The New York City Opera

CAST—Patricia Racette (Emmeline Mosher), Curt Peterson (Matthew Gurney), Victor Ledbetter (Mr. Maguire), Anne-Marie Owens (Aunt Hannah Watkins), Kevin Langan (Henry Mosher), Kimm Julian (Hooker), Jennifer Dudley (Ella Burling), Melanie Sarakatsannis (Sophie), Josepha Gayer (Mrs. Bass), David Hutchinson (Mr. Summers), Joyce E. Greene (Mrs. Maguire), Marc Embree (Simon Fenton), Herbert Perry (Pastor Avery), Deanne Meek (Harriet Mosher), Kristen Garver (Sarah Mosher)

SOURCE—The novel *Emmeline* by Judith Rossner.

The action takes place in Maine and Massachusetts in the nineteenth century.

The opera was presented in two acts.

ACT ONE—"The Lord Has Spared This Child" (Anne-Marie Owens), "Give Her to Me" (Anne-Marie Owens), "Next! Next! Next!" (Kimm Julian), "There Now. That's Better" (Victor Ledbetter), "Patience ... Charity ... Prudence ... Lucy" (Josepha Gayer), "I've Never Seen My Face Before" (Patricia Racette), "So You Found the Library" (Victor Ledbetter), "Dearest Mother and Father (Letter Aria)" (Patricia Racette), "Like a Wood in Ireland This Is" (Victor Ledbetter), "Strange. From Inside the House" (Patricia Racette), "To Cheerfulness Inclining (Work Song)" (Girls), "Sing, Damn You, Sing" (Kimm Julian), "Have They Arrived? (Birth Scene)" (Patricia Racette)

ACT TWO—"I Know Nothing" (Patricia Racette), "The Railroad's Pushing North" (Kevin Langan), "I Forgot My Bible" (Patricia Racette), "No. No. No Secrets" (Patricia Racette), "I Need to Speak to Matthew" (Kevin Langan), "Matthew! If You Love Me (Love Duet)" (Patricia Racette, Curt Peterson), Wedding, "I Remember the Cold" (Curt Peterson), "I'm Relieved to See You" (Patricia Racette), "The Lord Is My Shepherd (The Wake)" (Herbert Perry), "Matthew Gurney?" (Anne-Marie Owens), "The Child Was a Girl" (Patricia Racette), "Emmeline! Is It True? (Revelation)" (Patricia Racette), "Funeral Procession," "Sinner! Abomination! Whore!" (Women), "Matthew! Everything I Want Is Gone" (Patricia Racette), "Everything I Want Is Gone" (Patricia Racette)

NOTES—The New York premiere of Tobias Picker's *Emmeline* was well received by the *New York Times*; Bernard Holland urged the City Opera to put the work into its permanent repertory and said the opera was a "model of its kind ... our hearts are touched."

The work was a re-telling of the Oedipus legend. The young and naïve Emmeline is seduced by her employer's son, and becomes pregnant. Against her will, her baby boy (whom she believes is a girl) is adopted by an unknown couple. Emmeline lives quietly for twenty years, until such time as she meets Matthew, a young man whom she marries. When it's revealed that Matthew is her son, he accuses her of not telling him the truth about his background. Emmeline tells him she never knew he was her son, and begs him to stay with her, as she can't bear the thought of having first lost her child and now her husband. But Matthew leaves, and Emmeline slowly goes mad.

The opera was seen on public television on April 2, 1997, and was recorded on a 2-CD set by Albany Records (# TROY-284-85) from a live performance by the Santa Fe Opera (the song list above is taken from the titles on the recording).

440 The Emperor Jones. THEATRE: Metropolitan Opera House; OPENING DATE: January 7, 1933; PERFORMANCES: 10; LIBRETTO: De Jaffa and Eugene O'Neill; MUSIC: Louis Gruenberg; DIRECTION: Alexander Sanine; SCENERY: Jo Mielziner Musical Direction: Tullio Serafin; PRODUCER: The Metropolitan Opera

CAST—Lawrence Tibbett (Brutus Jones), Marek Windheim (Henry Smithers), Pearl Besuner (Native Woman), Hemsley Winfield (Congo Witch Doctor)

SOURCE—The 1920 play *The Emperor Jones* by Eugene O'Neill.

The opera was presented in one act.

NOTES—The world premiere of *The Emperor Jones* was based on the play by Eugene O'Neill; it told the story of Brutus Jones, a crap-shooting Pullman porter who escapes from prison and flees to an island in the Caribbean where he becomes a brutal dictator. The juicy role of Jones was perhaps the highpoint in Lawrence Tibbett's illustrious career. Writing in the *New York Times*, Olin Downes said Tibbett's performance was a "great masterpiece of dramatic interpretation ... his supreme achievement," and noted that Tibbett might never again sing "with more ... excitement [and] electrical thrill."

As for the opera itself, Downes said it was the finest American opera ever written. Brooks Atkinson also reviewed the opera, but his was a much cooler assessment. He felt the play wasn't enhanced by music.

Some of the opera included non-singing dialogue, and so presumably that is why O'Neill is credited as one of the co-librettists. In 1967, the Met offered another world premiere of an opera based on an O'Neill play, *Mourning Becomes Electra* (1967; see entry). Other musical adaptations of O'Neill are *Dark Sonnet*, a one-act musical which appeared in *Murder in 3 Keys* (1956?), an evening of three one-act musicals; *Dark Sonnet* was based on O'Neill's 1916 play *Before Breakfast* (see entry for *Murder in 3 Keys*); *New Girl in Town* (1957), based on *Anna Christie* (1921); *Take Me Along* (1959), based on *Ah, Wilderness!* (1933; see entry for the Off Off Broadway version of *Take Me Along*, which includes information about another musical adaptation of *Ah, Wilderness!*, the 1948 film *Summer Holiday*); and the opera *Desire Under the Elms*, based on the 1924 play (1989; see entry). *The Emperor Jones* was again musicalized in 1984 when a "theatre dance work built around" O'Neill's play received its world premiere at the American Music Theatre Festival. The music was by Coleridge-Taylor Perkinson; Cleavon Little was Brutus; and the work was directed and choreographed by Donald McKayle.

441 Enchanting Melody. THEATRE: Folksbiene Playhouse; OPENING DATE: November 24, 1964; PERFORMANCES: 84; BOOK: Itzik Manger; LYRICS: Possibly by Itzik Manger; MUSIC: Henoch Kon; DIRECTION: David Licht; CHOREOGRAPHY: Yehudith and Felix Fibich; SCENERY: Marvin Gingold; COSTUMES: Dina Harris; LIGHTING: Marvin Gingold; MUSICAL DIRECTION: Tamara Bliss; PRODUCER: Folksbiene Company

CAST—Marilyn Gold (Chaneele, Young Girl, First Beggar Girl), Rochelle Gold (Mirele, Second Beggar Girl), Ada Singer (First Witches' Helper), Pauly Rosenblum (Second Witches' Helper, Middle Daughter), Felice Gold (Third Witches' Helper, Youngest Daughter), Sarah Stabin (Bobe Yachnes), Ely Aurnou (Avramche, Lyeh), Harry Freifeld (Eliyokum), Joshua Zeldis (First Hotzmah), Ziporah Spaisman (Oldest Daughter, Bayle), Rochelle Horowitz (Mirele), Mina Kern (Basya), George Davidsohn (First Salesman, Blind Organ Grinder), Jacob Belogorsky (Second Salesman, Coachman), Ben Feivelowitz (Second Hotzmah), Max Neiditch (Third Hotzmah), Joseph Silberberg (A Peddler); song "Enchanting Melody" sung by Rochelle Relis

NOTES—*Enchanting Melody* was performed in Yiddish and was a self-described Yiddish folk musical. It was presented for a series of weekend performances from November 24, 1964, through March 14, 1965. Richard F. Shepard in the *New York Times* found the evening "nostalgically traditional and impressionistically modern." He reported that the plot dealt with individuals who, by learning a magical melody ("Enchanted Melody"), hope to find happiness and a resolution of their problems. He noted that "some do, some don't—that's life."

Shepard also noted the Folksbeine Playhouse was celebrating its fifth birthday with the production of *Enchanted Melody*, and, "in Yiddish style," he hoped the theatre "should live until 120."

442 Encore. THEATRE: St. Malachy's Theatre; OPENING DATE: May 3, 1979; PERFORMANCES: 16; BOOK: Ronald Rogers and Bob Sonderskov; LYRICS AND MUSIC: Unknown; DIRECTION: Denny Shearer;

Ann Crowley, Assistant to the Director; CHOREOGRAPHY: Denny Shearer; SCENERY: Alan Kimmel; COSTUMES: Mariann Verheyen; LIGHTING: Michael Newton-Brown; MUSICAL DIRECTION: Stan Free; PRODUCER: National Musical Theatre (Paulette Attie, Executive Director)

CAST—Joe Silver (Host), Malita Barron (Leading Lady), Michael Hayward (Leading Man), Bob Morrisey (Juvenile), Sally Ann Swarm (Ingenue), Stan Free (Piano), Frank G. Martenez (Bass)

The musical was presented in one act.

NOTES—*Theatre World 1978-1979 Season* credited the Off Off Broadway musical *Encore* with two book writers, but no lyricist and composer (the songs in the musical may have been standards rather than new ones written specifically for the production).

Ann Crowley was the production's assistant to the director, and she seems to be the same Ann Crowley who appeared on Broadway as the flirtatious Lola Pratt in the 1951 musical *Seventeen*. Crowley had an interesting if brief Broadway career. She was a chorus replacement during the original Broadway runs of *Oklahoma!* (1943) and *Carousel* (1945), and then after creating the role of Lola Pratt in *Seventeen*, she replaced Olga San Juan in the original 1951 production of *Paint Your Wagon*. After that, her only other Broadway appearance was in the chorus of Richard Adler's charming and underrated *Music Is* [1976]).

443 Encores! The New York City Center *Encores!* series (Arlene Shuler, President and CEO; Mark Litvin, Sr., Vice President and Marketing Manager; Jack Viertel, Artistic Director; Paul Gemignani, Music Director) is devoted to presenting semi-staged concert productions of musicals. Beginning in 1994, three musicals have been presented for usually four performances apiece during each winter and spring over a two or three month period. Over the years, such performers as Len Cariou, Kristin Chenoweth, Christine Ebersole, Penny Fuller, Joel Grey, Celeste Holm, Marc Kudisch, Nathan Lane, Dorothy Loudon, Patti LuPone, Donna McKechnie, Bebe Neuwirth, Tony Randall, and Lynn Redgrave have appeared in *Encores!* productions.

While some selections in the series (*Wonderful Town*, *The Pajama Game*, *Bye Bye Birdie*, and *Follies*) are overly familiar and seem out of place within the context of what appears to have been the series' original mission (the restoration, preservation, and production of neglected musicals), *Encores!* has nonetheless done a terrific job of offering many esoteric and seldom-seen works (such as *Allegro*, *Sweet Adeline*, *Li'l Abner*, *St. Louis Woman*, and *Face the Music*), most of which will probably never enjoy fully staged revivals.

Thus far, only one *Encores!* production has been original. In 2007, *Stairway to Paradise* offered an evening of songs and sketches from various Broadway revues of the 1920s and 1930s.

The *Encores!* production of *Chicago* in 1996 led to its Broadway revival later that year, and as of this writing eleven years later, the musical is still playing on Broadway. And *Encores!* can probably be credited for the inspiration for the respective 2002, 2003, 2006, and 2006 Broadway revivals of *The Boys from Syracuse*, *Wonderful Town*, *The Pajama Game*, and *The Apple Tree* (the Broadway revival casts of *Chicago*, *Wonderful Town*, and *The Pajama Game* were recorded).

Eleven *Encores!* productions have been recorded: *Babes in Arms* (DRG Records CD # 94769), *The Boys from Syracuse* (DRG Records CD # 94767), *Call Me Madam* (DRG Records CD # 94761), *Do Re Mi* (DRG Records CD # 94768), *Face the Music* (DRG Records CD # 94781), *The New Moon* (Ghostlight Records CD # 4403-2), *Out of This World* (DRG Records CD # 94764), *Pal Joey* (DRG Records CD # 94763), *St. Louis Woman* (Mercury Records CD # 314-538-148-2), *Tenderloin* (DRG Records CD # 94770), and *Ziegfeld Follies of 1936* (Decca Broadway Records CD # 440-016-056-2).

The following is a chronological list of all *Encores!* productions through 2007 as well as the proposed *Encores!* offerings for 2008 (following the date of each *Encores!* production are the names of lyricists and composers; the year in which the original Broadway production opened; and the number of performances for the original Broadway run): *Fiorello!* (February 9, 1994; lyrics by Sheldon Harnick, music by Jerry Bock; 1959, 795 performances), *Allegro* (March 2, 1994; lyrics by Oscar Hammerstein II, music by Richard Rodgers; 1947, 315 performances), *Lady in the Dark* (May 4, 1994; lyrics by Ira Gershwin, music by Kurt Weill; 1941, 467 performances), *Call Me Madam* (February 16, 1995; lyrics and music by Irving Berlin; 1950, 644 performances), *Out of This World* (March 30, 1995; lyrics and music by Cole Porter; 1950, 157 performances), *Pal Joey* (June 4, 1995; lyrics by Lorenz Hart, music by Richard Rodgers; 1940, 374 performances; 1952 Broadway revival, 542 performances), *DuBarry Was a Lady* (February 15, 1996; lyrics and music by Cole Porter; 1939, 408 performances), *One Touch of Venus* (March 28, 1996; lyrics by Ogden Nash, music by Kurt Weill; 1943, 567 performances), *Chicago* (May 2, 1996; lyrics by Fred Ebb, music by John Kander; 1975, 898 performances; 1996 Broadway revival still playing as of this writing), *Sweet Adeline* (February 13, 1997; lyrics by Oscar Hammerstein II, music by Jerome Kern; 1929, 234 performances), *Promises, Promises* (March 20, 1997; lyrics by Hal David, music by Burt Bacharach; 1968, 1,281 performances), *The Boys from Syracuse* (May 1, 1997; lyrics by Lorenz Hart, music by Richard Rodgers; 1938, 235 performances; see entry for Off Broadway production), *Strike Up the Band* (February 12, 1998; lyrics by Ira Gershwin, music by George Gershwin; 1930, 191 performances), *Li'l Abner* (March 26, 1998; lyrics by Johnny Mercer, music by Gene de Paul; 1956, 693 performances), *St. Louis Woman* (April 30, 1998; lyrics by Johnny Mercer, music by Harold Arlen; 1946, 113 performances), *Babes in Arms* (February 11, 1999; lyrics by Lorenz Hart, music by Richard Rodgers; 1937, 289 performances), *Ziegfeld Follies of 1936* (March 25, 1999; lyrics by Ira Gershwin, music by Vernon Duke; 1936, 227 performances), *Do Re Mi* (May 7, 1999; lyrics by Betty Comden and Adolph Green, music by Jule Styne; 1960, 400 performances), *On a Clear Day You Can See Forever* (February 10, 2000; lyrics by Alan Jay Lerner, music by Burton Lane; 1965, 280 performances), *Tenderloin* (March 24, 2000; lyrics by Sheldon Harnick, music by Jerry Bock; 1960, 216 performances), *Wonderful Town* (May 4, 2000; lyrics by Betty Comden and Adolph Green, music by Leonard Bernstein; 1953, 559 performances), *A Connecticut Yankee* (February 8, 2001; lyrics by Lorenz Hart, music by Richard Rodgers; 1927, 418 performances; 1943 Broadway revival, 135 performances), *Bloomer Girl* (March 22, 2001; lyrics by E.Y. Harburg, music by Harold Arlen; 1944, 654 performances), *Hair* (May 3, 2001; lyrics by Gerome Ragni and James Rado, music by Galt McDermot; 1968, 1,742 performances; see entry for Off Broadway production), *Carnival!* (February 7, 2002; lyrics and music by Bob Merrill; 1961, 719 performances), *Golden Boy* (March 21, 2002; lyrics by Lee Adams, music by Charles Strouse; 1964, 569 performances; see entry for Off Off Broadway production), *The Pajama Game* (May 2, 2002; lyrics and music by Richard Adler and Jerry Ross; 1954, 1,063 performances), *House of Flowers* (February 13, 2003; lyrics by Harold Arlen and Truman Capote, music by Harold Arlen; 1954, 165 performances; see entry for Off Broadway production), *The New Moon* (March 27, 2003; lyrics by Oscar Hammerstein II, music by Sigmund Romberg; 1928, 509 performances), *No Strings* (May 8, 2003; lyrics and music by Richard Rodgers; 1962, 580 performances), *Can-Can* (February 12, 2004; lyrics and music by Cole Porter; 1953, 892 performances), *Pardon My English* (March 25, 2004; lyrics by Ira Gershwin, music by George Gershwin; 1933, 46 performances), *Bye Bye Birdie* (May 6, 2004; lyrics by Lee Adams, music by Charles Strouse; 1960, 607 performances), *A Tree Grows in Brooklyn* (February 10, 2005; lyrics by Dorothy Fields, music by Arthur Schwartz; 1951, 270 performances), *Purlie* (March 31, 2005; lyrics by Gary Geld, music by Peter Udell; 1970, 688 performances), *The Apple Tree* (May 12, 2005; lyrics by Sheldon Harnick, music by Jerry Bock; 1966, 463 performances), *Kismet* (2006; lyrics by Robert Wright and George Forrest, music by Alexander Borodin; 1953, 583 performances), *70, Girls, 70* (2006; lyrics by Fred Ebb, music by John Kander; 1971, 36 performances), *Of Thee I Sing* (2006; lyrics by Ira Gershwin, music by George Gershwin; 1931, 441 performances; see entries for Off Broadway productions), *Follies* (February 8, 2007; lyrics and music by Stephen Sondheim; 1971, 522 performances), *Face the Music* (March 29, 2007; lyrics and music by Irving Berlin; 1932, 165 performances), *Stairway to Paradise* (May 10, 2007; not based on any particular production, this revue used lyrics, music, and sketches of various Broadway revues), The following musicals are scheduled for the 2008 *Encores!* season:, *Applause* (February 7, 2008; lyrics by Lee Adams, music by Charles Strouse; 1970, 896 performances) *Juno* (March 27, 2008; lyrics and music by Marc Blitzstein; 1959, 16 performances; see entry for Off Broadway production), *No, No, Nanette* (May 8, 2008; lyrics by Otto Harbach and Irving Caesar, music by Vincent Youmans; 1925, 321 performances; 1971 Broadway revival, 861 performances)

444 Enter the Guardsman. THEATRE: Vineyard/Dimson Theatre; OPENING DATE: May 21, 2000; PERFORMANCES: 15; BOOK: Scott Wentworth; LYRICS: Marion Adler; MUSIC: Craig Bohmler; DIRECTION: Scott Wentworth; Jason King Jones, Associate Director; SCENERY: Molly Reynolds; COSTUMES: Molly Reynolds; LIGHTING: Jeff Croiter; MUSICAL DIRECTION: Nicholas Archer; PRODUCER: Weissberger Theatre Group and Jay Harris

CAST—Robert Cuccioli (The Actor), Marla Schaffel (The Actress), Mark Jacoby (The Playwright), Derin Altay (The Dresser), Kate Dawson (The Wardrobe Mistress), Rusty Ferracane (The Wigs Master), Buddy Crutchfield (The Stage Manager)

SOURCE—The 1910 play *The Guardsman* by Ferenc Molnar.

The action occurs in and around a theatre.

The musical was presented in two acts (song assignments unknown).

ACT ONE—"Tonight Was Like the First Night," "Chopin," "My One Great Love," "Language of Flowers," "Drama," "The Actor's Fantasy," "You Have the Ring," "Enter the Guardsman," "True to Me"

ACT TWO—"She's a Little Off," "I Can't Go On," "Waiting in the Wings," "My One Great Love" (reprise), "They Die," "The Long Run," "Tonight Was Like the First Night" (reprise), "Art Imitating Life"

NOTES—In 1924, Ferenc Molnar's 1910 play *The Guardsman* became the first major starring vehicle for the husband-and-wife team of Lynn Fontanne and Alfred Lunt; the play was a hit, and was later filmed with the Lunts in 1931 (and was in fact the only film in which they starred).

The plot dealt with a quarreling acting couple, and the husband's efforts to test his wife's fidelity by disguising himself as a guardsman. To the musical's disadvantage, more than one critic compared it to *Kiss Me, Kate*, another lyric work about a quarreling (and formerly married) acting couple (*Kate* had in fact been successfully revived on Broadway earlier in the season).

Lawrence Van Gelder in the *New York Times* said *Enter the Guardsman* was "a first-rate musical ... struggling to get out," and he felt "another coat of polish" might be what the musical needed to achieve major success. Mark Woods in *Variety* noted there were "some lovely retro songs" which wouldn't have been out of place in classic American musicals of the 1950s. He singled out "Tonight Was Like the First Night," "My One Great Love," and "Waiting in the Wings." Van Gelder also praised the latter song as well as the tango "Drama."

The musical had first been produced at London's Donmar Warehouse in 1997, and the American premiere occurred at the New Jersey Shakespeare Festival on September 7, 1999. An earlier musical version of *The Guardsman* was the 1941 MGM film *The Chocolate Soldier* (with Nelson Eddy and Rise Stevens) which appropriated the title and a few songs from the 1909 Oscar Straus operetta *The Chocolate Soldier* (which in turn had been based on George Bernard Shaw's 1894 play *Arms and the Man*).

445 The Entertainer. THEATRE: Stage One/ Roundabout Theatre Company; OPENING DATE: December 21, 1982; PERFORMANCES: 96; PLAY: John Osborne; MUSIC: John Addison; DIRECTION: William Gaskill; CHOREOGRAPHY: David Vaughn; SCENERY: Michael Sharp; COSTUMES: A. Christina Giannini; LIGHTING: Barry Arnold; MUSICAL DIRECTION: David Brunetti; PRODUCER: Roundabout Theatre Company, Inc. (Gene Feist, Producing Director)

CAST—Humphrey Davis (Billy Rice), Ellen Tobie (Jean Rice), NICOL WILLIAMSON (Archie Rice), Frances Cuka (Phoebe Rice), Keith Reddin (Frank Rice), Richard M. Davidson (William [Brother Bill] Rice), John Curless (Graham Dodd), David Brunetti (Conductor), Elizabeth Owens (Gorgeous Gladys)

The action occurs in 1956.

NOTES—*The Entertainer* was a play with incidental songs which dealt with Archie Rice, a shallow, immoral, and untalented music-hall performer. It premiered in London at the Palace Theatre on September 10, 1957, for fifty-four performances, with Lawrence Olivier in the title role; Olivier reprised his role for the Broadway premiere, which opened on February 12, 1958, at the Royale (now Schoenfeld)Theatre and ran for ninety-seven performances (the music for the London and New York productions was by John Addison). Olivier was also seen in the 1960 film version (a 1975 television version, with music by Marvin Hamlisch, starred Jack Lemmon).

The script was published by Faber & Faber in 1957.

The Entertainer was revived Off Off Broadway by the Joseph Jefferson Theatre Company on October 18, 1978, for twelve performances, and was again revived Off Off Broadway by the Classic Stage Company on November 13, 1996, for thirty-four performances.

446 Entre-Nous. THEATRE: Cherry Lane Theatre; OPENING DATE: December 30, 1935; PERFORMANCES: 47; LYRICS: Will B. Johnstone, Richard Lewine, Ted Fetter, and Norman Zeno; MUSIC: Harry Archer, Phillip Broughton, and Richard Lewine.

MUSICAL NUMBERS—"Entre-Nous" (lyric by Will B. Johnstone, music by Richard Lewine), "Let's Go High Hat" (lyric by Will B. Johnstone, music by Richard Lewine), "I'll See You Home" (lyric by Will B. Johnstone, music by Harry Archer), "Let's Get Married or Something" (lyric by Ted Fetter, music by Richard Lewine), "With You, with Me" (lyric and music by Richard Lewine), "Kick in the Pants" (lyric by Will B. Johnstone, music by Harry Archer), "Sunday Morning Churchman" (lyric by Norman Zeno, music by Richard Lewine, "Under My Skin" (lyric by Will B. Johnstone, music by Harry Archer), "What Can I Give You?" (lyric by Will B. Johnstone, music by Phillip Broughton), "A.J." (lyric by Will B. Johnstone, music by Harry Archer), "Am I?" (lyric by Will B. Johnstone, music by Harry Archer), "When Opportunity Knocks" (lyric by Ted Fetter, music by Richard Lewine)

447 Equity Library Theatre. *The Best Plays of 1944-45* indicates that the Equity Library Theatre (ELT), an organization "inspired, directed and sustained largely by the enthusiasm of the actors themselves," came into its own as a serious theatre enterprise during the 1943-1944 Broadway season. Admission was free, and all the actors and directors volunteered their services (ELT allowed twenty percent of the performers in any given production to be non-Equity [that is, amateur] casts). (The word "library" in the company's name derived from the fact that productions were given at libraries throughout the New York City area.) For over four decades, Equity's revivals served as showcases for its members and offered to audiences a rich and diverse selection of plays and musicals.

For the first two seasons, the ELT produced a total of forty-three productions over a sixty-six week period. As the seasons went by, musicals were added to the ELT's offerings, and by the 1960s each season offered about fifteen productions, almost always a mixture of plays and musicals. During the 1966-1965 season, the company officially changed its name to Equity Theatre, but old habits die hard and so the old name was still occasionally referenced by some sources, including programs of Equity productions. ELT's offerings were incredibly diverse. For non-musicals, Broadway failures (such as *Look After Lulu* [1965]), hits (*Come Back, Little Sheba* [1965]), and Shakespeare (*The Taming of the Shrew* [1978]) were seen.

As for musicals, ELT offered a mixture of hits and failures from the past (*A Tree Grows in Brooklyn* [1966], *Follies* [1975], *Panama Hattie* [1975], *Tenderloin* [1975], *Silk Stockings* [1977], and *Allegro* [1978]). One unusual aspect of Equity's musicals was that sometimes songs which had been deleted during a musical's tryout were reinstated. The Equity production of *Tenderloin* included two songs heard during the musical's tryout ("I Wonder What It's Like" and "Lovely Laurie") and one which was apparently dropped during rehearsals ("Nobody Cares"). For *Silk Stockings*, "Ode to a Tractor" was added.

The final Equity Theatre production was *Wonderful Town*, which opened on September 28, 1989. Sadly, *Theatre World 1989-1990 Season* reported that a lack of funds forced Broadway's longest-running showcase to close after its forty-seventh season.

See entries for *Mary* and *Nymph Errant*, perhaps two of the most unusual (and most welcome) revivals in Equity's history.

448 Ernest in Love. "A New Musical." THEATRE: Gramercy Arts Theatre; transferred to the Cherry Lane Theatre on June 14, 1960; OPENING DATE: May 4, 1960; PERFORMANCES: 111; BOOK: Anne Croswell; LYRICS: Anne Croswell; MUSIC: Lee Pockriss; DIRECTION: Harold Stone; CHOREOGRAPHY: Frank Derbas; SCENERY: Peter Dohanos; COSTUMES: Ann Roth; LIGHTING: Peter Dohanos; MUSICAL DIRECTION: Sam Pottle Producers: Noel Behn and Robert Kamlot

CAST—ALAN SHAYNE (Lane), GEORGE HALL (Perkins, Dr. Chasuble), John Hays (Greengrocer), Frank Simpson (Bootmaker), Hal Buckley (Piano Teacher), Sam Stoneburner (Tobacconist), D.P. Smith (Dancing Master), JOHN IRVING (John/Jack Worthing), MARGOT HARLEY (Alice), LEILA MARTIN (Gwendolen Fairfax), LOUIS EDMONDS (Algernon Moncrieff), SARA SEEGAR (Lady Bracknell), GERRIANNE RAPHAEL (Cecily Cardew), LUCY LANDAU (Miss Prism), CHRISTINA GILLESPIE (Effie)

SOURCE—The 1895 play *The Importance of Being Earnest* by Oscar Wilde.

The action occurs in London and Hertfordshire around 1900.

The musical was presented in two acts.

ACT ONE—"Come Raise Your Cup" (Alan Shayne, George Hall, John Hays, Frank Simpson, Hal Buckley, Sam Stoneburner, D.P. Smith), "How Do You Find the Words?" (John Irving), "The Hat" (Leila Martin, Margot Harley), "Mr. Bunbury" (Louis Edmonds, John Irving), "Perfection" (John Irving, Leila Martin), "A Handbag Is Not a Proper Mother" (Sara Seegar, John Irving), "A Wicked Man" (Gerrianne Raphael), "Metaphorically Speaking" (Lucy Landau, George Hall)

ACT TWO—"You Can't Make Love" (Christina Gillespie, Alan Shayne), "Lost" (Louis Edmonds, Gerrianne Raphael), "My Very First Impression" (Leila Martin, Gerrianne Raphael), "The Muffin Song" (John Irving, Louis Edmonds), "My Eternal Devotion" (Leila Martin, Gerrianne Raphael, Louis Edmonds, John Irving), "The Muffin Song" (reprise) (John Irving, Louis Edmonds, Leila Martin, Gerrianne Raphael), "Ernest in Love" (Company)

NOTES—*Ernest in Love* is one of the best of all Off Broadway scores; every number is a delight, and "The Muffin Song" is one of the best theatre songs ever written. Another standout number is "A Handbag Is Not a Proper Mother"; sung by the veddy proper Lady Bracknell, the melody is a whirligig pastiche of British music hall, slyly suggesting that perhaps the Lady isn't all she claims to be.

Brooks Atkinson in the *New York Times* felt that if the musical adaptation didn't "improve" upon Oscar Wilde's original play, it didn't "debase" it, either. Atkinson noted the "dry elegance" of the performances met the "highest standards" of Off Broadway; that Peter Dohanos' "exquisitely lighted settings look like a jewel-box"; and that Ann Roth's costumes were "elaborate and imposing," and even "ironically" commented on the social status of the characters. Atkinson found Lee Pockriss' music "deft and droll" and "excellent," and noted the score was humorous and yet still had the "decorous formality" of the period; further, Anne Croswell's book and lyrics were "clever." He even praised the "beautifully played" overture, which sounded like "well-bred chamber music."

The musical first saw life on television as *Who's Earnest?* Telecast by CBS as a *U.S. Steel Hour* presentation on October 9, 1957, it starred Edward Mulhare, Dorothy Collins, and Martyn Green. The musical numbers heard were: "Mr. Bunbury," "Metaphorically Speaking," "Perfection," "Lost," "My Eternal Devotion," "My Very First Impression," and "A Wicked Man," all of which were eventually used for the stage version.

Expanded for Off Broadway in 1960, the musical opened the night after the premiere of *The Fantasticks*, and while it didn't achieve a long run (it was gone in three months), the musical quickly became a favorite among small theatre companies.

The cast album was recorded by Columbia Records (LP # OL-5530), and was later released on CD by DRG Records (# 19045).

Anne Croswell and Lee Pockriss were heard from occasionally, collaborating together or with others. But they never found success on Broadway, and it's the theatre's misfortune, because they clearly had the talent, as proven by their memorable score for *Ernest in Love*. Probably their most obscure work is *Bodo* (see entry), which never got beyond rehearsals at the Promenade Theatre. Also see entry for their 1987 musical *Conrack*.

In 1958, Pockriss enjoyed a hit record with his

ballad "Catch a Falling Star," which was recorded by Perry Como (the lyric was by Paul Vance). And four months after the opening of *Ernest in Love*, Pockriss' song "Itsy Bitsy Teenie Weenie Yellow Polka Dot Bikini" (again with a lyric by Vance) was the number-one best-selling record in the country.

Counting *Who's Earnest?* (1957) and *Ernest in Love* (1960) separately, there have been at least twelve musical adaptations of Oscar Wilde's play: *Oh, Ernest!*, a fifty-six performance Broadway flop in 1927; *Half in Earnest* by Vivian Ellis, the composer and lyricist of *Salad Days* (see entry), a 1957 musical which had its premiere in U.S. regional theatre before being produced in Britain; numerous British versions (including *Found in a Handbag* [1957], *Earnest in Tune, or My Dark Gentleman* [1958], *Ernest* [1959], and *The Importance* [1984], of which apparently only the later played London); *Nobody's Earnest* (1974) by Alec Wilder which played in U.S. regional theatre; and *Dear Ernest* (1972), which appears to have been produced only in Britain. In 2000, Off Off Broadway offered another musical version of the play (titled *Ernest*), which opened on June 30 and played for seven performances (book and lyrics by Gayden Wren and music by Vance Lehmkuhl). A German musical adaptation, *Mein Freund Bunbury*, opened on October 2, 1964; the score was recorded by Nova Records (LP # 8-85-031).

The Importance of Being Earnest, along with *Cyrano De Bergerac*, *The Adventures of Tom Sawyer/The Adventures of Huckleberry Finn*, *Alice's Adventures in Wonderland/Through the Looking Glass*, and *Little Women*, have probably been adapted as musicals more often than any other works in Western literature. Besides the twelve *Earnest* adaptations, there are some fourteen of *Cyrano* (which appears to hold the record for the most musical adaptations), fourteen combined for *Tom Sawyer* and *Huckleberry Finn* (see entries for *Livin' the Life* and *Downriver*), twelve for *Alice* (for more information, see entry for *Alice with Kisses*), and ten of *Little Women* (see entries for the Off Broadway *Jo* and the opera *Little Women*). *Ernest in Love* later enjoyed a number of Off Off Broadway revivals. On May 14, 1980, it was produced for a limited engagement of sixteen performances by Theatre Off Park; on January 27, 1994, it played for ten performances at the All Soul's Theatre (with Gerrianne Raphael, who had originated the role of Cecily Cardew in the 1960 production, now playing the role of Lady Bracknell); and on March 20, 2007, it was revived in concert form for a limited run of two weeks at the McGinn/Cazale Theatre as part of the *Musicals Tonight!* series (with George S. Irving playing Lady Bracknell; see entry for the series).

For other musicals based on works by Oscar Wilde, see entries for *After the Ball* and *A Delightful Season*, both of which were based on *Lady Windermere's Fan*, and three adaptations of *The Picture of Dorian Gray*. See entries for *Dorian* (which also references *Dorian Gray* [both musicals opened within a month of each other in 1990]) and a 1996 adaptation, also called *Dorian Gray*. An operatic adaptation of Wilde's play *Salome* (written in French by Wilde in 1891, and translated by him into English in 1893 [the play wasn't produced in London until 1930]) with libretto and music by Richard Strauss premiered in 1905; Strauss' libretto was based on a German translation of Wilde's French text by Hedwig Lachmann.

For musicals based on Oscar Wilde's life, see entries for *Dear Oscar* and *It's Wilde!* as well as *Utterly Wilde!!!*, the latter a one-man musical biography.

449 The Establishment (1963 Edition). THEATRE: Strollers Theatre-Club; OPENING DATE: January 19, 1963; PERFORMANCES: 118; SKETCHES: Written by the cast (John Bird, Eleanor Bron, John Fortune, Jeremy Geidt, and Carole Simpson) and by Peter Cook; LYRICS: Christopher Logue, Stanley Myers, John Bird, Patrick Gowers, and Tony Kinsey; MUSIC: Christopher Logue, Stanley Myers, John Bird, Patrick Gowers, and Tony Kinsey; DIRECTION: Nicholas Garland; LIGHTING: Jules Fisher; PRODUCERS: Peter Cook and John Krimsky, with Nicholas Luard

CAST—John Bird, Eleanor Bron, John Fortune, Jeremy Geidt, Carole Simpson, and the Teddy Wilson Trio

The revue was presented in two "shows" (acts).

ACT ONE—"The English Class System," "Pregnancy," "Go to the Wall" "The Lambeth Walk" (film) "The Establishment's Window on the World (I)," "The Couple" "The Water and the Flame" "Cancer Operation (film)," "English version of *Advise and Consent*," "Sitting Around"

ACT TWO—"The Queen" "Interview on Soccer with Jomo Kenyatta" "Johny" "Abortion" "The Establishment's Window on the World (II)," "Potatoes, Potatoes" "Strangler Martin" "The Asses Song" "Advertising for the Labor Party," "Sitting Around"

NOTES—The program didn't list individual songs or sketches; the above listing is taken from *The Burns Mantle Yearbook/The Best Plays of 1962-1963*. *The Establishment* opened in London on October 5, 1961, and its American premiere took place in Chicago on October 2, 1962, for 117 performances (in something of the nature of a foreign-exchange program, *The Establishment* played at the Second City venue in Chicago while the Second City troupe took their revue to London where it played at the theatre where *The Establishment* had opened). The New York program explained that *The Establishment* differed from its American counterparts because the revue was written rather than improvised, and also used music, slides, and film.

The *New York Times* reported that the New York City License Commissioner received complaints concerning a sketch in the revue which dealt with the Crucifixion. In "The English Class System," three performers assumed the position of the cross and a spotlight produced a "halo effect" around one of them. Speaking in Cockney accents, the other two performers wondered why the third has an upper-class accent. John Krimsky, a co-producer of the revue, met with the Commissioner on a Friday to discuss the matter, and by that evening's performance the offensive sketch had been eliminated. The *Times* reported a spokesman for the revue said the sketch was a spoof of the tendency of the British to equate accents with social classes, and that the material hadn't been intended to offend Christians. A new edition of *The Establishment* opened later in the year (see entry), and in 1964 another edition was presented (see entry for *The Muffled Report*).

450 The Establishment (1963-1964 Edition). THEATRE: Strollers Theatre-Club; OPENING DATE: October 31, 1963; PERFORMANCES: 260; SKETCHES: Peter Cook; LYRICS: Steven Vinaver; MUSIC: Carl Davis (Special material by Peter Lewis, Peter Shaffer, John Braine, and Charles Lewsen); DIRECTION: William Francisco; PRODUCERS: Peter Cook and John Krimsky

CAST—Peter Bellwood, Alexandra Berlin, Francis Bethencourt, Roddy Maude-Roxby, Carole Simpson, the Teddy Wilson Trio (which during the run was replaced by the Marian McPartland Trio)

The revue was presented in two acts.

ACT ONE—"Stand Up" "MacMillan-Butler" "Galbraith" "Trouble," "Adam & Eve" "Philip & Elizabeth" "London Hilton" "Screen Test" "Mme. Nhu" "Heterosexual" "Great" "Religions"

ACT TWO—"News," "No" "Security," "Sick Man"

NOTES—The program for the second edition of *The Establishment* didn't list individual songs and sketches; however, *The Burns Mantle Yearbook/The Best Plays of 1963-1964* listed the above numbers (which included the Songs "Trouble," "Great," "No," and "Sick Man"). The yearbook also noted that "Cultural Warfare," a sketch by Kenneth Tynan, was written for, but not used in, the revue.

Richard F. Shepard in the *New York Times* was a bit disappointed with the edition, saying the humor this time around was less sophisticated and more collegiate. But he found much to like, especially the "good stuff" in "News," an extended spoof of television newscasts (Richard Nixon believes the introduction of stainless steel shaving blades will enhance his chances of winning the next election; Mrs. Ngo Dinh Nhu excoriates the Pope and the Kennedys for being "professional Catholics"; a toothpaste scandal reveals that families who were tested had twenty-one fewer teeth to begin with). Shepard also singled "Heterosexual," a "sad tale" of how a man's heterosexuality brought about his downfall.

The new edition ran more than twice as long as its predecessor (see entry for the earlier edition of *The Establishment*). There was also a third Establishment revue in 1964 (see entry for *The Muffled Report*).

Note that this edition included sketch material by playwright Peter Shaffer, who had made his New York debut in 1959 with the drama *Five Finger Exercise*. He continued to write many successful plays, including *Equus* and *Amadeus* (which had their respective Broadway premieres in 1974 and 1980).

451 Esther. THEATRE: New York State Theatre; OPENING DATE: October 10, 1993; PERFORMANCES: 2; LIBRETTO: Charles Kondek; MUSIC: Hugo Weisgall; DIRECTION: Christopher Mattaliano; SCENERY: Jerome Sirlin; COSTUMES: Joseph A. Citarella; LIGHTING: Jeff Davis; MUSICAL DIRECTION: Joseph Colaneri; PRODUCER: The New York City Opera

CAST—Lauren Flanigan (Esther), Joyce Castle (Zeresh), Robynne Redmon (Vashti), Allan Glassman (Haman), Eugene Perry (Xerxes), Joseph Corteggiano (Mordecai), Thomas Mark Fallon (Hegai)

SOURCE—The Biblical Book of Esther.

The opera was presented in three acts.

NOTES—Originally commissioned by the San Francisco Opera, Hugo Weisgall's *Esther* enjoyed its world premiere at the New York City Opera as part of the company's World Premiere Festival.

In his review for the *New York Times*, Edward Rothstein noted that Weisgall's music was difficult but "its power is unmistakable ... the score has rhythmic verve, sharp contrasts in texture and a youthful energy." (Weisgall [1912-1997] was eighty-one when *Esther* premiered.)

The opera had a limited engagement of just two performances, but Rothstein hoped it would be revived and recorded. In 1999, Naxos American Classics Records released *Scenes from Jewish Operas, Volume 2* (CD # 8-559450), which included approximately fifteen minutes' worth of music from the opera (excerpts from Act One, Scene Eight; Act Three, Scene Two; and Act Three, Scene Ten). The recording also included music from Elie Siegmeister's opera *Lady of the Lake* (see entry).

452 Ethel Merman's Broadway. "A Musical Tribute." THEATRE: John Houseman Theatre; OPENING DATE: June 17, 1992; PERFORMANCES: 64; DIRECTION: Christopher Powich; COSTUMES: Gail Cooper-Hecht; LIGHTING: Peter L. Smith; MUSICAL DIRECTION: Robert Bendorff; PRODUCERS: Eric Krebs and David Buntzman in association with Go Gi Go Productions and Scott Stander

CAST—RITA MCKENZIE (Ethel Merman)

NOTES—The always-welcome Rita McKenzie followed up her successful *Call Me Ethel!* with *Ethel Merman's Broadway*, a tribute in concert format. The songs included the familiar (such as "I Got Rhythm" [from *Girl Crazy*, 1930; lyric by Ira Gershwin, music by George Gershwin] and "Some People" [*Gypsy*, 1959; lyric by Stephen Sondheim, music by Jule

Styne]) and the slightly esoteric (such as "It's the Animal in Me" [filmed for, but not used in, the 1934 film *We're Not Dressing*; the sequence was later used in the 1935 film *The Big Broadcast of 1936*; lyric by Mack Gordon, music by Harry Revel] and "World, Take Me Back" [added to *Hello, Dolly!* when Merman joined the Broadway production in 1970]).

The production was recorded by Varese Sarabande Records (CD # VSD-5665).

453 The Evangelist. THEATRE: Wonderhorse Theatre; OPENING DATE: March 31, 1982; PERFORMANCES: 16; BOOK: Al Carmines; LYRICS: Al Carmines; MUSIC: Al Carmines; DIRECTION: William Hopkins; CHOREOGRAPHY: Ellen Krueger; Patricia Steigauf, Assistant Choreographer; SCENERY: Peter Harrison; COSTUMES: Paula Iasella; LIGHTING: Craig Kennedy; MUSICAL DIRECTION: Ernest Lehrer; PRODUCER: TRG Repertory Company (Marvin Kahan, Artistic Director)

CAST—Paul Farin (Ben Graham), Keith Baker (Garland Beauregard), Carlo Thomas (Bishop Brady), Kate Ingram (Florrie Thurlow), Judith Moore (Mathilda Beauregard), Donna Bullock (Raven); Chorus in St. Joe: Miles Herter (John McKeechen), Kevin Jones (Ernest), Judy Soto (Selina), Barbara Swift (Sister Elizabeth), Lee Teplitzky (Ragged Bumpus), Megan Lynn Thomas (Betsy)

The action occurs in St. Joseph, Missouri, Omaha, Nebraska, and Des Moines, Iowa, during the summer of 1924.

The musical was presented in two acts.

ACT ONE—"Hymns from the Darkness" (Lee Teplitzky, Barbara Swift), "Everything God Does Is Perfect" (Keith Baker, Congregation), "Holy Ghost Ride" (Keith Baker), "I Was a Black Sheep" (Carlo Thomas, Keith Baker, Congregation), "Home" (Congregation), "I Am a Preacher of the Lord" (Keith Baker, Judith Moore, Kate Ingram, Paul Farin), "Remember Joplin" (Carlo Thomas, Keith Baker), "Omaha I'm Here" (Keith Baker, Wranglers), "Cardboard Madonna" (Keith Baker), "Blame It on the Moon" (Donna Bullock, Keith Baker), "Little Children on the Grass" (Donna Bullock, Congregation), "Clinging to the Rock" (Congregation), "Good-bye" (Kate Ingram), "The Brother Blues" (Judith Moore, Congregation)

ACT TWO—"Serenade" (Paul Farin), "I Love You" (Keith Baker, Donna Bullock), "Do I Do It Through God?" (Donna Bullock), "The Buds of May" (Kate Ingram, Jaybirds), "Men Are Men" (Kate Ingram, Judith Moore), "We're Going to De Moines" (Congregation), "Who Is She?" (Paul Farin), "Garland Is My Man" (Donna Bullock), "I Am an Evangelist" (Keith Baker), "The Light" (Donna Bullock), "Navajo Woman" (Congregation), "Raven the Magnet" (Paul Farin, Keith Baker), "Home" (Judith Moore, Keith Baker, Congregation)

NOTES—From 1961 to 1981, Al Carmines had been an associate minister of the Judson Memorial Church and director of its art program. The Off Off Broadway musical *The Evangelist* was the first he wrote with the TRG Repertory Company.

The musical dealt with two rival evangelists, a Pentecostal minister (Keith Baker) and a Navajo Indian mystic (Donna Bullock). Complications arise when the two fall in love. Mel Gussow in the *New York Times* felt that Carmines' score was one of his strongest, but noted the book wavered between self-mockery and unintentional self-parody. Gussow singled out "Blame It on the Moon," which, he felt, should be "the last moon song" ever written because Carmines worked into its lyric "delirious" variations on every lunar theme imaginable. Gussow further noted that while he missed some of Carmines' stock company from the Judson Memorial Church, he also found it "refreshing" to hear Carmines interpreted by an entirely new company. "Everything That God Does Is Perfect" had been previously heard in *Camp Meeting* (see entry).

Reportedly, *The Evangelist* was intended to be a lyric adaptation of Sinclair Lewis' 1927 novel *Elmer Gantry*; when the rights weren't available, Carmines fashioned his story around another flashy preacher.

454 An Evening of Adult Fairy Tales. THEATRE: Wonderhorse Theatre; OPENING DATE: November 9, 1983; PERFORMANCES: 17

This Off Off Broadway evening presented two musicals (in three acts), *Miss Chicken Little* (libretto by William Engvick and music by Alec Wilder) and *The Journey of Snow White* (revival) (libretto and music by Al Carmines). The credits for both productions are as follows: DIRECTION: William Hopkins; CHOREOGRAPHY: Jerry Yoder; SCENERY: Peter Harrison; COSTUMES: Christopher Cole; LIGHTING: Carol Graebner; MUSICAL DIRECTION: Ernest Lehrer; PRODUCER: TRG Repertory (Marvin Kahan, Artistic Director)

CAST—Bob Arnold, Frank D'Ambrosio, Karen Merchant, Zoelle Montgomery, R.G. Moore, Donna Robinson, Hank Schob, Scott Sigler, Lee Teplitzky, Megan Lynn Thomas, Beth Williams

NOTES—*The Journey of Snow White* had originally been presented at the Judson Poets' Theatre on February 26, 1971 (see entry for information about the production, including musical numbers), and was revived there in May 1975.

455 An Evening with Ekkehard Schall. THEATRE: Harold Clurman Theatre; OPENING DATE: February 25, 1985; PERFORMANCES: 11; TEXT: from the writings of Bertolt Brecht; PRODUCERS: The Harold Clurman Theatre (Jack Garfein, Artistic Director) and Lucille Lortel; Naomi Konicus, Associate Producer

CAST—Ekkehard Schall, Karl-Heinz Nehring (Piano)

NOTES—Ekkehard Schall performed two evenings of material by Bertolt Brecht (Schall was Brecht's son-in-law). Both programs were performed in German; the first, *From Laughing at the World to Living in the World*, opened on February 25; the second, *Questions, Laments, Answers*, opened on February 27.

Both evenings included both spoken and sung excerpts from Brecht's writings and lyrics (Ekkehard was accompanied by pianist-composer Karl-Heinz Nehring). Included in the two programs were songs from *The Threepenny Opera* (1928), *Happy End* (1929), and *The Rise and Fall of the City of Mahagonny* (1930). For a similar evening, see entry for *Brecht on Brecht*.

456 An Evening with Joan Crawford. "A New Musical." THEATRE: Orpheum Theatre; OPENING DATE: January 28, 1981; PERFORMANCES: 15; BOOK: See NOTES below; LYRICS: See song list for credits; MUSIC: See song list for credits; DIRECTION: Julian Neil; CHOREOGRAPHY: Sydney Smith; SCENERY: J. Patrick Mann; COSTUMES: Barbara Gerard; LIGHTING: Paul Everett; MUSICAL DIRECTION: Joseph Church; PRODUCERS: Joe Bianco in association with Monroe Arnold; Philip S. Kaufman, Associate Producer

CAST—Kristine Zbornik (Lucifer), Frances Robertson (God), LEE SPARKS (Joan Crawford), Joyce Fullerton (Christina Crawford), Michael J. Hume (Christopher Crawford), Fracaswell Hyman (Jacques), Michael Kemmerling (Jules Beemus, Alfred Steele)

The musical was presented in two acts (song assignments weren't credited in the program).

ACT ONE—"The Devil's Song" (lyric and music by Nick Branch), "Hollywood Lullaby" (lyric and music by Joseph Church), "Give 'Em Hell" (lyric by Joseph Church and Kristine Zbornik, music by Joseph Church), "Blame It All on Me" (lyric by Joseph Church and Richard Schiff, music by Joseph Church)

ACT TWO—"Too Much Money Blues" (lyric and music by Julian Neil and Lee Sparks), "You Are One of a Kind" (lyric and music by Joseph Church), "Ain't No Place Like Home" (lyric and music by Nick Branch), "Take a Vacation" (lyric and music by Nick Branch), "What It's Like to Be a Legend" (lyric and music by Nick Branch)

NOTES—Joan Crawford (1904-1977) had two careers, first her classic period with MGM and other studios, in which she starred in such films as *Grand Hotel* (1932) and *Mildred Pierce* (1944; her Oscar-winning role), and then her camp period in the 1950s, when she starred in a string of juicy, over-the-top melodramas (*Harriet Craig*, 1950; *Sudden Fear*, 1952; *Torch Song*, 1953; *Johnny Guitar*, 1954 [itself the basis for an Off Broadway musical; see entry]; *Female on the Beach*, 1955; *Queen Bee*, 1955; *Autumn Leaves*, 1956; and *The Best of Everything*, 1959). Her last memorable role was in the black horror comedy *Whatever Happened to Baby Jane?* (1962) with her archrival Bette Davis.

But Crawford could never have anticipated her third career, which occurred after her death. When her adopted daughter Christina Crawford wrote a tell-all book about growing up with *Mommie Dearest*, the memoir took on instant camp status. And the 1979 film version (with Faye Dunaway as Joan Crawford) solidified Crawford's personal life as a subject for satire.

An Evening with Joan Crawford was perhaps too late in the cycle, because *Mommie Dearest* (book and film) had already attained cult status. And so the musical was gone in two weeks.

The work was conceived by Julian Neil, and was based upon Lee Sparks' female impersonation of Joan Crawford (some might say the terms "female impersonation" and "Joan Crawford" are synonymous). The basic outline of the musical was written by Neil and Sparks, and the dialogue was created through improvisational techniques by the original company of the production (which had played in a showcase version in February 1980).

During previews, the song "Except Of Course Men" (lyric by Joyce Fullerton, music by Nick Branch) was deleted.

457 An Evening with Max Morath at the Turn of the Century. THEATRE: Jan Hus Playhouse; OPENING DATE: February 17, 1969; PERFORMANCES: 140; SCENERY: Dennis Dougherty; LIGHTING: Dennis Dougherty; PRODUCER: Norman Kean

CAST—Max Morath

The revue was presented in two acts (division of acts unknown; all musical numbers performed by Max Morath).

MUSICAL NUMBERS—"Everybody's Doin' It" (lyric and music by Irving Berlin), "Don't Go in the Lion's Cage Tonight" (lyric and music by Goetz and Gilroy), "Maple Leaf Rag" (music by Scott Joplin), "Tiger Rag" (first recorded in 1917, the authorship is in dispute; at least twelve individuals have been credited with writing the song), "Come After Breakfast (Bring 'Long Your Lunch and Leave 'Fore Supper Time)" (lyric and music by Brymn, Smith, and Burris), Medley: "How Are You Goin' to Wet Your Whistle" (lyric and music by Byrne, Wenrich, and McIntyre), "Oh, You Don't Need Wine to Have a Wonderful Time (While They Make Those Beautiful Girls)" (lyric by Alex Rogers, music by Bert Williams), "The Pump Song" (lyric and music by Lerner, Fields, and Whiting), "Let It Alone" (lyric by Alex Rogers, music by Bert Williams), "Easy Winners" (music by Scott Joplin), "Alexander's Ragtime Band" (lyric and music by Irving Berlin), "How Do You Do It Mabel (on Twenty Dollars a Week)" (lyric and music by Irving Berlin), "Piano Rollin' Rag" (music by Scott Joplin)

NOTES—Pianist and singer Max Morath's one-man show was an evening of music and patter centering around ragtime and early twentieth-century American music (one of Morath's later "evenings" was titled *The Ragtime Years*, a one-man revue which he performed throughout the country); the revue consisted of material by Irving Berlin, Scott Joplin, Noble Sissle, Jelly Roll Morton, and other composers, lyricists, and performers.

The song listing is based on numbers from the original cast album, which was released by RCA Victor (as *Max Morath at the Turn of the Century*; LP # LSO-1159).

Morath also appeared in the 2004 Off Broadway one-man revue *Max Morath: Ragtime and Again*, another evening devoted to ragtime music; it opened at the Theatre at Saint Peter's Church on March 14, 2004, and played for forty-one performances.

458 An Evening with the Times Square Two. "A Musical Entertainment." THEATRE: Gramercy Arts Theatre; OPENING DATE: May 19, 1967; PERFORMANCES: 10; DIRECTION: Saul Gottlieb; "special staging" by Paul McDowell; SCENERY: Stuart Chapman; LIGHTING: Mark Solomon; PRODUCER: Roger Euster

CAST—Mycroft Partner, Andrew i (with Sara Hart and Marrin Sklar, musicians)

The revue was presented in two acts.

NOTES—The evening was a collection of satiric songs, skits, jokes, and juggling. It was gone in less than two weeks.

Edwin Bolwell in the *New York Times* described the "Times Square Two" as two men who affected Edwardian dress; one, Britisher Mycroft Partner, resembled Alistair Sim and Benjamin Disraeli, and the other, American-born Mr. i, looked like the child of "Mr. and Mrs. American Gothic" and sounded like the lead in the singing Chipmunks. And Bolwell's descriptions weren't meant as critical. He enjoyed their songs (such as "She Is More to Be Pitied Than Censured" and "I've Got a Feeling for Ophelia"), and felt the twosome would be delightful in a smaller venue, such as a coffeehouse. He also noted the "sophomoric" skits added little to the revue and made the ninety-minute evening "too long for too little."

459 An Evening with Wolfgang Roth (a/k/a Voices from the Past). "Berlin Theatre and Kabarett Songs from the Golden Twenties." THEATRE: Chelsea Theatre Center; OPENING DATE: December 8, 1977; PERFORMANCES: 8; WORDS AND MUSIC: Julian Arendt, Bertolt Brecht, Hanns Eisler, Werner Finck, Robert Gilbert, Friedrich Hollaender, Kurt Tucholsky, Kurt Weill, Frank Wedekind, Carl Zuckmayer, Walter Mehring, Wolfgang Roth, and "unknowns"; PRODUCER: Podium Management Associates

CAST—Wolfgang Roth, Alexandra Ivanoff (Piano), William Schimmel (Accordion), Michael Zuckerman (Drums); Michael S. Roth (Musical Arranger)

The revue was presented in one act.

NOTES—Wolfgang Roth began his theatre career in Berlin in 1930, when he performed in various political cabarets and worked with such artists as Bertolt Brecht. He later was the scenic designer for various operas as well as Off Broadway and Broadway musicals (including the lengendary 1958 flop *Portofino*).

The program notes indicated the revue would present a "cross-section of things as they were done then" (in the political cabarets of Berlin), and the evening would include ballads, songs, small talk, and drawings.

The program identified the revue as *An Evening with Wolfgang Roth*. However, *Theatre World 1977-1978 Season* identified the production as *Voices from the Past*.

460 An Evening with W.S. Gilbert. "A Musical Biography." THEATRE: Cherry Lane Theatre; OPENING DATE: February 28, 1980; PERFORMANCES: 33; PLAY: John Wolfson (based on writings of W.S. Gilbert); MUSIC: Arthur Sullivan, Osmond Carr, and Edward German; DIRECTION: Richard Smithies; SCENERY: Douglas McKeown; COSTUMES: Linda Sampson; LIGHTING: Joanna Schielke; MUSICAL DIRECTION: Alfred Heller; PRODUCER: Garrick Productions Inc.

CAST—LLOYD HARRIS

SOURCE—The writings of W.S. Gilbert (1836-1911).

The action occurs from 1877 to 1907 in the drawing room of W.S. Gilbert's country estate, Grim's Dyke, in Harrow, Great Britain.

The musical was presented in two acts (all musical sequences performed by Lloyd Harris).

ACT ONE—"Selene's Speech" (from *The Wicked World*, 1873), "The Distant Shore" (music by Arthur Sullivan), "At a Pantomime" (*The Bab Ballads*, written throughout the 1860s), "The Marquis of Mince Pie" (*The Miller and His Man*; by F.C. Burnand and Arthur Sullivan), "When I Was a Lad" (*H.M.S. Pinafore*, 1878; music by Arthur Sullivan), "Hymn to the Nobility" (deleted song from *The Pirates of Penzance*, 1879; music by Arthur Sullivan), "I Am a Pirate King" (*The Pirates of Penzance*, 1879; music by Arthur Sullivan; this sequence included both the first and second versions of the song), "Sleep On" (*Iolanthe*, 1882; music by Arthur Sullivan), "The Sentry Song" (*Iolanthe*, 1882; music by Arthur Sullivan), "If You Give Me Your Attention" (*Princess Ida*, 1884; music by Arthur Sullivan), "The Mikado's Song" (*The Mikado*, 1885; music by Arthur Sullivan)

ACT TWO—"When You Find You're a Broken-Down Critter" (*The Grand Duke*, 1896; music by Arthur Sullivan), "The Played-Out Humorist" (*His Excellency*, 1894; music by Arthur Sullivan and Osmond Carr), "In Yonder World (Luten's Song)" (*Fallen Fairies*, 1909; music by Arthur Sullivan and Edward German), "The Pantomime 'Super' to His Mask" (*The Bab Ballads*, written throughout the 1860s)

NOTES—This one-man musical biography of W.S. Gilbert included many of his writings (lyrics, speeches, letters, testimony, and interviews); besides the above-listed songs, the evening also included incidental music from various operettas by Gilbert and Sullivan.

The cast album was recorded by Original Cast Records (LP # OC-8026), and included most of the material listed above as well as some incidental music heard in the production (such as "Queen Victoria March," which had been deleted from *The Pirates of Penzance*).

461 Everybody's Gettin' Into the Act. "A Contemporary Vaudeville." THEATRE: Actors' Playhouse; OPENING DATE: September 27, 1981; PERFORMANCES: 33; SKETCHES: Bob Ost; LYRICS: Bob Ost; MUSIC: Bob Ost; DIRECTION: Darwin Knight; SCENERY: Frank J. Boros; COSTUMES: Dianne Finn Chapman; LIGHTING: Ric Barrett; MUSICAL DIRECTION: Bill McCauley (and Curtis Blaine?); PRODUCERS: Karen B. Gromis and Bunny Adir Ltd.; presented in association with Goz Enterprises, Inc.

CAST—Ann Hodapp (The Loser, Outtatown Broad, Female Friend, Louise Black, Mary Smith, Evie, The Swinger), Bill McCauley (The Piano Man), Leilani Mickey (The Looker, Rich Bitch, Female Stranger, Doris Gray, Gloria Vandenberg, Lonely Lady, Victim), Tuck Milligan (The Loner, GQ Man, Male Friend, Herbert Gray, Egon Vandenberg, Lonely Guy, Complainer), Ross Petty (The Lover, Macho Man, Male Friend, Fred Black, Charles Smith, Stu, The Romantic)

The revue was presented in two acts.

ACT ONE—"Everybody's Gettin' Into the Act" (Company), "That First Hello" (Bill McCauley), "The Pickup" (Tuck Milligan, Ann Hodapp) "Perfection" (Ross Petty), "Too Good" (Leilani Mickey) "Attitude #1" (Ann Hodapp), "So Close" (Company), "Attitude #2" (Leilani Mickey), "Attitude #3"/"Step Back" (Tuck Milligan), "Attitude #4" (Ross Petty), "I'm Available" (Ann Hodapp), "Love Me Just a Little Bit" (Company) "Strange Bedfellows"/"Love Duet" (Performer[s] unknown]), "Nothing's Changed"/"Looks Like Love" (Performer[s] Unknown]), "Life Is Perfect"/"You Never Take Me Anywhere" (Leilani Mickey, Tuck Milligan), "Success Stories" (Ann Hoddap, Ross Petty), "Social Intercourse"/First Act Finale (Company)

ACT TWO—"Appearance" (Ann Hoddap, Ross Petty) "Yes, I See a Woman" (Ross Petty) "Playing Hostess" (Ann Hoddap) "Party Games"/"To Wit" (Ann Hoddap, Ross Petty, Leilani Mickey, Tuck Milligan), "A Party in Southampton" (Ann Hodapp) "Sincere" (Ann Hodapp, Ross Petty) "It Always Seems to Rain" (Leilani Mickey) "Never, Never" (Tuck Milligan) "Keepin' It Together" (Bill McCauley), "Ballad of the Victim" (Leilani Mickey) "Alive and ... Well" (Tuck Milligan) "Valse Triste" (Ross Petty) "And I'm There!" (Ann Hoddap) "Don't I Know You?" (Company), "Everybody's Gettin' Into the Act" (reprise) (Company)

NOTES—Bob Ost's *Everybody's Getting' Into the Act,* another revue about life and love in contemporary Manhattan, told its story through a collection of vignettes and songs. It lasted a month.

Mel Gussow in the *New York Times* noted that despite the revue's timely treatment of romantic relationships ("including a drift toward bisexuality"), the evening was "old hat" and left him with a "bland aftertaste." Further, he felt the score was less a theatre piece than "a sheaf of songs for a piano bar," and noted some were reminiscent of other writers ("And I'm There!" was a "spinoff" of Stephen Sondheim's "I'm Still Here" [*Follies*, 1971], and another song was a parody of Bertolt Brecht and Kurt Weill's "Pirate Jenny" [*The Threepenny Opera*, 1928]). Gussow concluded he wasn't sure if these songs were meant to be "salutes or spoofs or simply imitations." He also mentioned the song "Keepin' It Together," and remarked that Mr. Ost had an annoying habit of "droppin' the final consonant." Twenty-two years after the Off Broadway production closed, Fynsworth Alley Records released a studio cast recording of some of the revue's songs (CD # 302-062-178-2). The singers on the recording included Robert Cuccioli, Marc Kudisch, Rebecca Luker, Karen Mason, Christiane Noll, Nancy Opel, Stephanie Pope, Evan Pappas, Jana Robbins, David Sabella, Emily Skinner, and Mary Testa. The following songs from the original production were heard on the album: "Everybody's Gettin' Into the Act," "That First Hello," "Perfection," "Too Good," "I'm Available," "Looks Like Love," "A Helluva State," "Yes, I See a (the) Woman," "To Wit," "A Party in Southhampton," "It Always Seems to Rain," "Never, Never," "Keepin' It Together," "Ballad of the Victim," "Valse Triste," "And I'm There!," and "Don't I Know You?" The recording also included two new songs ("I Gotta Sing!" and "Look at Me"), and omitted the following: "The Pickup," "So Close," "Love Me Just a Little Bit," "Strange Bedfellows," "Love Duet," "Nothing's Changed," "Life Is Perfect," "You Never Take Me Anywhere," "Success Stories," "Social Intercourse," "Appearance," "Playing Hostess," "Party Games," "Sincere," "Alive and ... Well," and the "Attitude" sequences.

462 Evil Dead: The Musical. THEATRE: Stage I/New World Stages; OPENING DATE: November 1, 2006; PERFORMANCES: 126; BOOK: George Reinblatt; LYRICS: George Reinblatt; additional lyrics by Christopher Bond; MUSIC: Frank Cipolla, Christopher Bond, Melissa Morris, and George Reinblatt; additional music by Rob Daleman; CO-DIRECTION: Hinton Battle and Christopher Bond;

CHOREOGRAPHY: Hinton Battle; SCENERY: David Gallo; COSTUMES: Cynthia Nordstrom; LIGHTING: Jason Lyons; MUSICAL DIRECTION: Daniel Feyer; PRODUCERS: Jenkay LLC, Jeffrey Latimer Entertainment, and Just for Laughs Live; Jay H. Harris, Bruce Hills, Jeffrey Latimer, Evi Regev, and Gilbert Rozon, Producers; William Franzblau, Executive Producer; by special arrangement with Renaissance Pictures, Ltd. & Studio Canal Image, S.A.

CAST—Jennifer Byrne (Linda), Jenna Coker (Cheryl), Renee Klapmeyer (Shelly, Annie), Ryan Ward (Ash), Brandon Wardell (Scott, Spirit of Knowby), Tom Walker (Ed, Moose), Darryl Winslow (Jake), Ryan Williams (Fake Shemp)

SOURCE—The 1983 film *The Evil Dead* (which was followed by two sequels, *Evil Dead II* [1987] and *Army of Darkness* [1993])

The musical was presented in two acts.

ACT ONE—"Cabin in the Woods" (Ryan Ward, Jennifer Byrne, Brandon Wardell, Renee Klapmeyer, Jenna Coker), "Housewares Employee" (Ryan Ward, Jennifer Byrne), "It Won't Let Us Leave" (Jenna Coker), "Look Who's Evil Now" (Jenna Coker, Renee Klapmeyer), "What the...?" (Ryan Ward, Brandon Wardell), "Join Us" (Jenna Coker, Tom Walker, House Spirits), "Good Old Reliable Jake" (Darryl Winslow, Renee Klapmeyer, Tom Walker), "Housewares Employee" (reprise) (Ryan Ward, Jennifer Byrne), "I'm Not a Killer" (Ryan Ward)

ACT TWO—"I'm Not a Killer" (reprise) (Ryan Ward), "Bit-Part Demon" (Tom Walker), "All the Men in My Life (Keep Getting Killed by Candarian Demons)" (Renee Klapmeyer, Ryan Ward, Darryl Winslow), "Ode to an Accidental Stabbing" (Darryl Winslow, Renee Klapmeyer, Jenna Coker), "Do the Necronomicon" (Candarian Demons), "It's Time" (Company), "We Will Never Die" (Candarian Demons), "You Blew That B**** Away" (Company)

NOTES—Based on the films in the *Evil Dead* franchise, the musical sounded like a sure thing. But, like other edgy Off Broadway science-fiction-themed, sure-fire-sounding musical spoofs (such as *Return to the Forbidden Planet* and *Bat Boy: The Musical* [see entries]), *Evil Dead: The Musical* lasted just four months. With the release of its cast album on Time Life Records (CD # M-19407), perhaps the musical will find a longer life in college, regional, and community theatre. The script was published by Samuel French, Inc., in 2007.

The plot dealt with a group of teenagers stranded in a lonely cabin in the woods. When evil spirits are unleashed, things go wrong ... terribly wrong.

Anita Gates in the *New York Times* enjoyed the "idiotic, but that's the point" musical. She liked the "deadpan" lyrics, "lively" music, and "playful" choreography, and she singled out "Do the Necromonicon" (the latest dance sensation) and "All the Men in My Life (Keep Getting Killed by Candarian Demons)" as the evening's best songs. She noted that seats in the first three rows of the theater ("the splatter zone") were covered in plastic, and audience members in those seats were thoughtfully provided white T-shirts by the management. Gates said that "apparently half the fun ... [is] being sprayed with geysers of stage blood." Frank Scheck in the *New York Post* said the musical is "for those who think the Greenwich Village Halloween parade isn't quite outrageous enough."

463 Exactly Like You.

"A Romantic Musical Comedy." THEATRE: Theatre at Saint Peter's Church/The York Theatre Company; OPENING DATE: April 19, 1999; PERFORMANCES: 31; BOOK: A.E. Hotchner; LYRICS: Cy Coleman and A.E. Hotchner; MUSIC: Cy Coleman; DIRECTION: Patricia Birch; Jonathan Cerullo, Assistant Director; CHOREOGRAPHY: Patricia Birch; Jonathan Cerullo, Assistant Choreographer; SCENERY: James Morgan; COSTUMES: Richard Schurkamp; LIGHTING: Kirk Bookman; MUSICAL DIRECTION: Doug Katsaros; PRODUCERS: The York Theatre Company (James Morgan, Artistic Director; Joseph V. De Michele, Managing Director) in association with Stuart Zimberg, Judith Ann Abrams, and David Day

CAST—Tony Hasting (TV Commentator), Doug Katsaros (Judge Maxmillian Meltzer), Edward Staudenmayer (Kevin Bursteter), Susan Mansur (Priscilla Vanderhosen), Kate Levering (Eve Bursteter), Lauren Ward (Arlene Murphy), Michael McGrath (Martin Murphy), Blair Ross (Winona Shook), Robert Bartley (Aaron Bates), Donya Lane (Stenographer), Frank Gravis (Lamarr), Donna Kelly (Juror)

The action occurs in and around a courtroom.

The musical was presented in two acts.

ACT ONE—Overture (Band), "Courtroom Cantata" (Ensemble), "Southern Comfort" (Blair Ross, Robert Bartley, Ensemble), "Thanks to Mom" (Kate Levering, Ensemble), "Why Did You Have to Be a Lawyer?" (Lauren Ward, Michael McGrath), "I Get Tired" (Frank Gravis, Blair Ross), "That's a Woman" (Robert Bartley), "Cottage by the Sea" (Edward Staudenmayer), "In the Name of Love" (Lauren Ward, Michael McGrath), "I Want the Best for Him" (Susan Mansur), "Don't Mess Around with Your Mother-in-Law" (Ensemble)

ACT TWO—"Good Day" (Tony Hastings), "She Makes Me Laugh" (Robert Bartley), "Rio" (Edward Staudenmayer, Michael McGrath, Ensemble), "At My Side" (Edward Staudemayer, Kate Levering), "No Further Questions, Please" (Lauren Ward), "Guilty" (Doug Katsaros, Susan Mansur), "Ain't He Cute?" (Lauren Ward), "Ain't She Cute?" (Michael McGrath), "Exactly Like You" (Ensemble)

NOTES—Here's the background on *Let 'Em Rot!/Welcome to the Club/Exactly Like You/Lawyers, Lovers & Lunatics* (perhaps only a master's thesis could do justice to this convoluted saga):

Exactly Like You was the third of four versions of Cy Coleman and A.E. Hotchner's musical about divorce; it was first produced as *Let 'Em Rot!* on February 16, 1988, at the Coconut Grove Playhouse in Coconut Grove, Florida, with a cast which included Ron Orbach William Parry, Martin Vidnovic, Cady Huffman, and Marilyn Sokol. As *Welcome to the Club*, the musical opened on Broadway at the Music Box Theatre on April 13, 1989, for twelve performances (it was the shortest-running of Coleman's Broadway musicals and the only one which wasn't recorded). The antithesis of Coleman's 1977 Broadway hit *I Love My Wife*, *Welcome to the Club* was a mean-spirited, misogynistic diatribe in which women were depicted as castrating harpies and gold-diggers, and husbands were pictured as being better off in alimony jail than in the clutches of their scheming and avaricious wives and ex-wives. Howard Kissel in the *Daily News* found the musical an "evening of spitefulness and recriminations ... unimaginably gross," and David Patrick Stearns in *USA Today* noted it "could be the ugliest, meanest Broadway show ever written."

For Broadway, only Marilyn Sokol remained from the Florida cast (the Broadway company also included Scott Waara, Jodi Benson, and Avery Schreiber). Between Florida and New York, the musical lost at least ten songs ("Alimony Rap," "Let 'Em Rot!," "Piece of Mind," "King of the Mound," "That's a Woman," "I Get Tired," "Aiken's Lament," "Bachelors," "The Honeymoon Is Over," and "To Live Again") and added five others ("Meyer Chickerman," "The Trouble with You," "Guilty," "Miami Beach," and "Love Behind Bars"). Another song, "Rio," may have been a new title for the tryout number "Boom Chicka Boom."

Despite the *Let 'Em Rot/Welcome to the Club* fiascos, Coleman and Hotchner revised the musical nine years later, and, as *Exactly Like You*, it opened at Goodspeed Opera House's Norma Terris Theatre on May 7, 1998. This version is the one which was later produced by the York Theatre Company in 1999, and the York production included many members from the Goodspeed cast. Numbers written for the Goodspeed production but which weren't heard in the York Theatre version were "A Man of the People," "The Trouble with You," "Thanks to Mum," "That's a Woman," and "I Forgive Him." *Exactly Like You* disappeared for a few years after its York Theatre revival, but Coleman and Hotchner still weren't through with it. Five years after the York production, the musical reappeared in its fourth (and presumably final) version in an Off Off Broadway production titled *Lawyers, Lovers & Lunatics*. The cast included four members from the York production (Donna Kelly, Donya Lane, Susan Mansur, and Michael McGrath) as well as Barbara Walsh, who had appeared in the Goodspeed production of *Exactly Like You*. New songs heard in *Lawyers, Lovers & Lunatics* were "Wake Up and Smell the Coffee," "Don't Let It Getcha," and "Pound of Flesh."

Two songs from *Exactly Like You* ("In the Name of Love" and "At My Side") can be heard on *Unsung Musicals* (I) (Varese Sarabande Records CD # VSD-5462).

464 Exchange.

THEATRE: Mercer-O'Casey Theatre; OPENING DATE: February 8, 1970; PERFORMANCES: 1; SPOKEN MATERIAL: Eric Levy; LYRICS: Mike Brandt, Michael Knight, and Robert J. Lowery; MUSIC: Mike Brandt, Michael Knight, and Robert J. Lowery; DIRECTION: Sondra Lee; SCENERY: Peter Harvey; COSTUMES: Stanley Simmons; LIGHTING: William Mintzer; MUSICAL DIRECTION: Tom Janusz; PRODUCERS: Stephanie Sills and Parallel Productions

CAST—Penelope (Anne) Bodry, Mike Brandt, Igors Gavon, Megan Kay, Michael Knight, Pamela Talus

The revue was presented in two acts (song assignments unknown).

ACT ONE—"All Over My Mind," "If You Listen to My Song," "Anthem," "If I Had the Answers," "Why Don't You Believe Me?," "Wondering," "A Madrigal," "Never Ever Land," "Dancing Through Lifetimes," "The Flower Song," "Carrion Train," "Come on Train," "Train," "L.A. Incident"

ACT TWO—"Santa Barbara" "Puddles," "Flying Somehow," "Mumble Nothing," "Understand It," "King," "Pied Piper," "Coonskin Cap," "Maybe Tomorrow," "I Can Make It"

NOTES—Clive Barnes in the *New York Times* felt that the revue *Exchange* was more in keeping with cabaret theatre. He also reported the musical contained two incredibly tasteless sequences, one in which there was a discussion about throwing bags of excrement at police and the other (a "quite repulsive suggestion") about performing taxidermy on dead United States Marines and then sending their remains to their parents. Despite his reservations about these two disgusting sequences, Barnes was still able to find the rest of the show "sweet" and "happy," and he indicated it would probably do well (like two other cabaret-styled revues, *Jacques Brel Is Alive and Well and Living in Paris* and *Joy*; see entries). But the public would have none of it, and the show's first performance was its last. Director Sondra Lee and cast member Igors Gavon had appeared together in the original production of *Hello, Dolly!* (1964), and they were (very) briefly reunited for the protest revue *Exchange*, which was one of four musicals to play just one performance during the 1969-1970 Off Broadway season. The revue is totally forgotten today, but it actually produced a cast album of sorts. Two months after the Off Broadway production opened and closed, Atlantic Records recorded *Tamalpais Exchange* (LP # SD-8263), which was the production's original title before being shortened to *Exchange* two weeks before the Off Broadway opening. The album cover doesn't resemble a traditional cast recording, and in fact the sparse album credits don't even indicate the material had ever been associated with a stage production. Of the six singers on the album, four (Penelope Anne Bodry, Mike Brandt, Michael Knight, and Pamela Talus) were in the stage production (a fifth singer, Susan Kay, might have been Megan Kay from the stage version). Of the fourteen numbers on the album, ten were sung in the show (the album credits Michael Knight with the lyrics and music for "Anthem," "King," "Flying Somehow," "L.A. Incident," "Pied Piper," and "Why Don't You Believe Me?"; Mike Brandt for "Never Ever Land" and "Maybe Tomorrow"; Mike Brandt and Michael Knight for "If I Had the Answers"; and Mike Brandt and Buckets Lowery for "Understand It").

Sondra Lee was associated with two "Neverland" musicals. *Peter Pan* (1954), in which she played Tiger Lily, introduced the classic song "Neverland," and *Exchange* introduced "Never Ever Land."

465 Exhalations. "A New Musical." THEATRE: Theatre Space/Madison Avenue Baptist Church; OPENING DATE: May 1984; PERFORMANCES: Unknown; BOOK: Al Carmines; LYRICS: Al Carmines; MUSIC: Al Carmines; DIRECTION: William Hopkins; CHOREOGRAPHY: Scott Sigler; PRODUCER: Rauschenbusch Memorial United Church of Christ

CAST—Roger Brown, Al Carmines, Nanci Grant, Miles Herter, Ernest Lehrer, Beverly Robinson, Kathrin King Segal

The musical was presented in one act.

MUSICAL NUMBERS—"Arizona" (Miles Herter, Nanci Grant), "The Navel" (Company), "Gerbils" (Kathrin King Segal), "Lullabye—Baby Men" (Al Carmines, Company), "Vis-à-vis" (Miles Herter, Beverly Robinson, Ernest Lehrer, Company), "Feelings" (Roger Brown, Nanci Grant, Kathrin King Segal, Al Carmines, Company), "I Can Bend My Arms" (Nanci Grant, Miles Herter, Women), "I Touch Myself Right Here" (Beverly Robinson), "Two Lonely Guys" (Roger Brown, Miles Herter), "Pretty Woman" (Nanci Grant, Male Trio), "Languishing" (Kathrin King Segal, Company), "Here We Go" (song adapted from John Thompson's *First Book of Piano*), (Al Carmines)

NOTES—This Off Off Broadway musical appears to be Al Carmines' last produced work. Carmines wrote in a program note that *Exhalations* "is a work of self-exploration ... Every exhalation of breath is a decision to give ... our life ... one more chance."

466 F. Jasmine Addams. "A New Musical." THEATRE: Circle in the Square (Downtown); OPENING DATE: October 27, 1971; PERFORMANCES: 6; BOOK: Carson McCullers, G. Wood, and Theodore Mann; LYRICS: G. Wood; MUSIC: G. Wood; DIRECTION: Theodore Mann; CHOREOGRAPHY: Patricia Birch; SCENERY: Marsha Louis Eck; COSTUMES: Joseph G. Aulisi; LIGHTING: Roger Morgan; MUSICAL DIRECTION: Liza Redfield; PRODUCERS: Circle in the Square (Theodore Mann and Paul Libin) and David J. Seltzer

CAST—THERESA MERRITT (Berenice Sadie Brown), NEVA SMALL (Frankie Addams), JOHNNY DORAN (John Henry West), NORTHERN J. CALLOWAY (Honey Camden), Robert Kya-Hill (T.T. Williams), William LeMassena (Mr. Addams), Alicia Marcelo (Sis Laura), Bill Biskup (Jarvis), Erika Petersen (Janice), Edmund Gaynes (Barney MacKean), Carol Anne Ziske (Mary Littlejohn), Page Miller (Helen Fletcher), Merry Flershem (Doris Mackey)

SOURCE—The novel and the 1950 play *The Member of the Wedding* by Carson McCullers.

The action occurs in the kitchen and backyard of the Addams' household in a small Southern town, from August to November 1945.

The musical was presented in one act.

MUSICAL NUMBERS—"How About You and Me" (Carol Anne Ziske, Page Miller, Merry Flershem), "If I Had A" (Johnny Doran, Theresa Merritt, Neva Small, Alicia Marcelo), "Miss Pinhead" (Johnny Doran, with Neva Small), "Baby, That's Love" (Theresa Merritt), "Did I Make a Good Impression?" (Neva Small), "Good as Anybody" (Northern J. Calloway, with Theresa Merritt and Robert Kya-Hill), "The We of Me" (Neva Small), "Travellin' On" (Neva Small, with Theresa Merritt and Johnny Doran), "Sunshine Tomorrow" (Theresa Merritt, Northern J. Calloway, with Neva Small, Johnny Doran, Robert Kya-Hill), "Baby, That's Love" (reprise) (Theresa Merritt), "F. Jasmine Addams" (Neva Small), "How Sweet Is Peach Ice Cream" (Theresa Merritt, with Johnny Doran and Neva Small), "Do Me a Favor" (Northern J. Calloway), "If I Had A" (reprise) (Johnny Doran, Theresa Merritt), "Another Day" (Theresa Merritt), "Quite Suddenly" (Neva Small, with Carol Anne Ziske), "How Sweet Is Peach Ice Cream" (reprise) (Theresa Merritt)

NOTES—*F. Jasmine Addams*, a musical version of Carson McCullers' beloved play *The Member of the Wedding*, was gone in less than a week. Clive Barnes in the *New York Times* felt the original play didn't need musical embellishment, and noted the often "slightly pallid evening" came across as a play with music rather than a full-fledged musical. He also indicated the play was still too new, and not enough time had passed to give the work the patina of a period piece. But he acknowledged the musical adaptation was done with "taste and discrimination."

In 2004, Neva Small (who had appeared in the musical's title role thirty-three years earlier) recorded "How Sweet Is Peach Ice Cream" in a wonderful collection which includes many generally obscure theatre songs; the CD was released by Theatre Voices Records (# NS-2211). If the song is any indication of the score's quality, then *F. Jasmine Addams* may be an undiscovered treasure. Perhaps some day an innovative regional theatre will revive it.

With *F. Jasmine Addams*, G. Wood wrote his only book musical. He was a welcome contributor to early Off Broadway revues, and can be found frequently in these pages.

During previews, *F. Jasmine Addams* was presented in two acts, and one number, "Gray Eyes," was deleted.

The musical had been scheduled to premiere at Ford's Theatre in Washington, D.C., on April 13, 1971, but the production was cancelled. According to a flyer, the tryout was to have been titled *Member of the Wedding*. Four years earlier, in March 1967, the *New York Times* reported that Theodore Mann was to produce a musical version of McCullers' novel and play on Broadway in early 1968. The lyrics were by Marshall Barer, the music by Mary Rodgers, and the libretto by McCullers. Although the Barer-Rodgers-McCullers version never materialized, Mann was clearly committed to producing a musical version of the play, and over four years later the Off Broadway adaptation with a score by G. Wood finally opened.

One song from Mary Rodgers and Marshall Barer's version ("Something Known") was heard in the 1993 revue *Hey, Love* (see entry) and was recorded for that show's cast album.

467 The Faggot. THEATRE: Truck and Warehouse Theatre; OPENING DATE: June 18, 1973; PERFORMANCES: 182; WORDS: Al Carmines; MUSIC: Al Carmines; DIRECTION: Al Carmines; CHOREOGRAPHY: David Vaughan; SCENERY: T.E. Mason; COSTUMES: T.E. Mason; LIGHTING: Gary Weathersbee; MUSICAL DIRECTION: John R. Williams; PRODUCERS: Bruce Mailman and Richard Lipton, and presented by special arrangement with Arthur D. Zinberg

CAST—Peggy Atkinson, Essie Borden, Lou Bullock, Marilyn Child, Tony Clark, Frank Coppola, Lee Guilliatt, Bruce Hopkins, Julie Kurnitz, Philip Owens, David Pursley, Bill Reynolds, Ira Siff, David Summers

The revue was presented in two acts.

ACT ONE—"Movie House" (Frank Coppola, Lou Bullock, Company), Overture (Company), "Women with Women—Men with Men" (Company), "The Hustler: A Five-Minute Opera" (David Pursley, Bill Reynolds), "I'll Take My Fantasy" (Tony Clark, David Summers, Company), "Mothers-in-Law" (Julie Kurnitz, Marilyn Child), "Hari Krishna" (Ira Siff, Philip Owens), "Desperation" (Bruce Hopkins, Essie Borden, Company), "A Gay Bar Cantata" (Marilyn Child, Lou Bullock, Tony Clark, Frank Coppola, Philip Owens, David Pursley, David Summers)

ACT TWO—"Nookie Time" (Lee Guilliatt, Company), "Your Way of Loving" (David Pursley, Ira Siff), "Fag Hag" (Essie Borden), "Puddin 'N' Tame" (Lou Bullock, Frank Coppola), "Ordinary Things" (Lee Guilliatt, Peggy Atkinson), "Art Song" (Julie Kurnitz, Essie Borden, Marilyn Child), "What Is a Queen" (Philip Owen, Company), "Women with Women—Men with Men" (reprise) (Company), Finale (Lee Guilliatt, David Pursley, Peggy Atkinson, Julie Kurnitz, Ira Siff, Company)

NOTES—Al Carmimes' *The Faggot* has the distinction of being the first openly gay musical. There had been other musicals which dealt with gay themes and characters (such as *Dear Oscar* [see entry], which had premiered the previous year), but *The Faggot* was the first to deal openly with gay subject matter, in-your-face and with no apologies; and, for its era, even the musical's title was startling. As such, *The Faggot* is a seminal work in the history of gay musical theatre. Originally produced by the Judson Poets' Theatre in April and May 1973 for sixteen performances, the revue played for five months. During the Judson Poets' run, and early in the Off Broadway run, Al Carmines appeared as Oscar Wilde in the "Your Way of Loving" and "Finale" sequences (later, David Pursley assumed the role).

The revue was recorded, but its release was put on hold, and it wasn't until the 1980s that the album was commercially released when it was issued by Blue Pear Records (LP # BP-1008); the recording includes Al Carmines in his original role of Oscar Wilde.

Carmines had previously adapted various writings of Gertrude Stein into six musicals (the entry for *What Happened* lists all the adaptations), and for *The Faggot* he wrote "Ordinary Things," a song for her and Alice B. Toklas (the number was also heard in the 1982 revue *The Gospel According to Al* [see entry]). *The Gospel According to Al* also included two songs ("New Boy in Town" and "Disposable Woman") credited to *The Faggot* (but the songs don't appear in the latter's program or cast album).

468 Fair Play for Eve. "A New Musical." THEATRE: The 3 Muses Opening Date: January 17, 1980; PERFORMANCES: 28 (estimated); BOOK: Paul Rawlings; LYRICS: Paul Rawlings; MUSIC: Jerry Markoe; DIRECTION: Robert Engstrom; CHOREOGRAPHY: Milena Melone; SCENERY: Robet Engstrom; COSTUMES: Karen Potter; LIGHTING: Sam Buccio; MUISCAL DIRECTION: Jerry Markoe; PRODUCER: Guild Media

CAST—Robert Anderson (Narrator), B.J. Wells (God), Stephen Schmidt (Adam), Mary Lou Belli (Eve)

The musical was presented in two acts.

ACT ONE—"We're Gonna Look Back" (Robert Anderson), "In the Beginning" (B.J. Wells, Robert Anderson, Angels), "It Was Good" (B.J. Wells, Robert Anderson), "An Help Meet I" (Mary Lou Belli), "Paradise Quartet" (Robert Anderson, B.J. Wells, Stephen Schmidt, Mary Lou Belli), "Temptation" (Robert Anderson, Mary Lou Belli), "Remember to Call Me Master" (Stephen Schmidt), "God of Wrath" (B.J. Wells, Robert Anderson), "Don't Dump on Eve" (Mary Lou Belli, Company)

ACT TWO—"We're Gonna Look Back" (reprise) (Robert Anderson), "Between an Ape and an Angel" (B.J. Wells, Robert Anderson), "Eve Sweet Eve" (Mary Lou Belli), "Wiser Than You Realize" (Mary Lou Belli), "Let Me Be Something to You" (Stephen Schmidt), "If He Has a Girl" (Mary Lou Belli), "Grand Design" (B.J. Wells), "We Go On" (Stephen Schmidt, Mary Lou Belli), "Wiser Than You Realize" (reprise) (Stephen Schmidt, Mary Lou Belli), "Going Back to Eden" (Company)

NOTES—The Off Off Broadway musical *Fair Play for Eve* was, like Sheldon Harnick and Jerry Bock's one-act musical *The Diary of Adam and Eve* (one of three musicals in the Broadway production of *The Apple Tree* [1966]), a light-hearted look at the story of Adam and Eve. For another musical which dealt with Adam and Eve, see entry for *Up from Paradise*.

John Corry in the *New York Times* found the "pleasantly unpretentious" musical a "winner" in its depiction of what *really* happened in the Garden of Eden. He praised Stephen Schmidt's Adam (a "primeval rube") and Mary Lou Belli's Eve (her "wholesome appeal" reminded him of June Allyson, only Belli "sings better"). Corry noted the evening was "helped immeasurably" by Jerry Markoe's score ("rock and jazz, with little suggestions of Scott Joplin") and Paul Rawlings' lyrics ("which sometimes reach inspired fancy"). The musical was presented on a double bill with the *My Cup Ranneth Over*, a one-act comedy by Robert Patrick (the author of *Kennedy's Children*) which opened the evening and which starred Harriet Z. Winkleman and Mary Joan Birmingham.

The 3 Muses was a theatre located in the Ansonia Hotel.

469 Fairy Tales. THEATRE: WPA Theatre; OPENING DATE: June 3, 1997; PERFORMANCES: 40; LYRICS: Eric Lane Barnes; MUSIC: Eric Lane Barnes; DIRECTION: Mark Cannistraro; CHOREOGRAPHY: Jackson McDorman; SCENERY: Hugh Walton; COSTUMES: Jennifer Kenyon; LIGHTING: Jack Mehler; MUSICAL DIRECTION: Daniel Harris; PRODUCER: WPA Theatre (Kyle Renick, Artistic Director; Lori Sherman, Prduction Manager)

CAST—Keith Anderson, Valerie Hill, Stephen Hope, Rob Maitner, Stephanie McClaine

The revue was presented in two acts (division of acts and song assignments unknown; songs are listed in performance order).

MUSICAL NUMBERS—"Flying Dreams," "Stonewall Serenade," "Gay Guys," "Illinois Fred," "You're the Bottom," "God Hates Fags," "Grace," "Heaven to Me," "Love, Don't Be a Stranger," "When You Meet an Angel," "Garbage," "Muses," "Parade," "My Ambition," "Letter Song," "Ballad of Tammy Brown," "Thanksgiving," "Anniversary Five," "Dear Dad," "American Beauty," "A Hummingbird," "A Few Words About Matthew," "Keepers of the Light"

NOTES—Lawrence Van Gelder in the *New York Times* found the Off Off Broadway gay revue *Fairy Tales* a "mixed blessing" of "sprightly and witty" as well as "obvious and sentimental" numbers.

Another version of the revue had been previously produced in cabaret format at the Duplex earlier in the season.

470 Faith Journey. THEATRE: Lamb's Theatre; OPENING DATE: July 21, 1994; PERFORMANCES: 193; BOOK: Clarence Cuthbertson; LYRICS: George Broderick and Clarence Cuthbertson; MUSIC: George Broderick; DIRECTION: Chuck Patterson; CHOREOGRAPHY: Barry Carrington; SCENERY: Visuals by Leon Oliver and Nelsena Burt Spano; COSTUMES: Nancy Brous; MUSICAL DIRECTION: George Broderick; PRODUCERS: Elohim Unlimited in association with Jesse L. DeVore, Jr.

CAST—Craig Anthony Grant (Paul), Loreal Steiner (Lucille), Claude Jay (Amos), Janet Weeden (Ruby), Henry C. Rawls (JP), Clarencia Shade (Sister Bell), Robert L. Evans (Brother), Claudette Evans (Traci), Jeff Benish (Policeman, Jason)

The action occurs during the period 1955-1964.

The musical was presented in two acts.

ACT ONE—Musical Prelude (Company), "Somebody's Knocking" (traditional) (Claude Jay, Company), "I Made a Vow" (Craig Anthony Grant), "Justice Is Knocking" (Claude Jay, Henry C. Rawls, Robert L. Evans), "Over My Head" (Clarencia Shade, Henry C. Rawls, Janet Weeden), "The Best of Both Worlds" (Janet Weeden), "Should I Wait" (Loreal Steiner), "Decide" (Craig Anthony Grant, Loreal Steiner, Robert L. Evans, Henry C. Rawls), "Don't Take Your Love" (Craig Anthony Grant), "One Day" (Craig Anthony Grant, Claude Jay), "We Got a Movement" (Craig Anthony Grant, Company), "By Any Means Necessary" (Claudette Evans), "We Got a Movement" (reprise) (Robert L. Evans, Company), "To Be Loved for Who I Am" (Loreal Steiner), "Help Me Find a Way" (Craig Anthony Grant, Claudette Evans), "I Wanna Be Ready" (Craig Anthony Evans, Company), "I Got to Go"/"I Just Wanna Be Loved" (Loreal Steiner, Claudette Evans), "Ain't Gonna Let Nobody Turn Me 'Round" (Company)

ACT TWO—"Woke Up This Morning" (traditional) (Claude Jay, Jeff Benish, Company), "There's a War in Mississippi" (Claude Jay, Jeff Benish, Company), "We Shall Overcome" (traditional) (Company), "My Country 'Tis of Thee" (traditional) (Clarencia Shade), "One Day" (reprise) (Janet Weeden, Company), "Freedom"/"Walk Together" (Company), "I Find a Friend in You" (Claudette Evans, Loreal Steiner), "I Miss You" (Claudette Evans, Craig Anthony Grant), "By Any Means Necessary" (reprise) (Henry C. Rawls, Company), "Ain't Gonna Let Nobody Turn Me 'Round" (reprise) (Company)

NOTES—Like many other Off Broadway musicals before it (such as *Fly Blackbird*, *Jerico-Jim Crow*, and *Selma*; see entries), *Faith Journey* told the story of the civil rights movement in America.

Ben Brantley in the *New York Times* noted that despite the musical's "ambitious" subject, it was "dispiritingly listless and confused" in its storytelling. As for the score, he felt it was "strangely" reminiscent of the "fizzy" sound of Burt Bacharach, and said that only when the musical offered traditional gospel numbers did it find its true sound.

471 Fallen Angel. THEATRE: Circle in the Square Downtown; OPENING DATE: April 14, 1994; PERFORMANCES: 32; BOOK: Billy Boesky; LYRICS: See song list for credits; MUSIC: See song list for credits; DIRECTION: Rob Greenberg; SCENERY: David Birn; COSTUMES: Wendy A. Rolfe; LIGHTING: Christopher Akerlind; MUSICAL DIRECTION: Steve Postell; PRODUCERS: Peter Holmes a Court and Roger Hess in association with Back Row Productions; Divonne Jarecki, Associate Producer

CAST—Jonathan Goldstein (Will), Corey Glover (Luke), Shannon Conley (Gretta), George Coe (Father, Stu Rosen), Susan Gibney (Dr. Bamberger, Alexandra)

The musical was presented in one act.

MUSICAL NUMBERS—"Coming and Going" (lyric by Billy Boesky, music by Billy Boesky and Steve Postell) (Corey Glover, Shannon Conley), "More Than You Know" (lyric by Billy Boesky and Deanna Kirk, music by Billy Boesky, Deanna Kirk, and Keven Bents) (Shannon Conley), "Falling in Line" (lyric and music by Billy Boesky) (Corey Glover), "Till I'm Gone" (lyric by Billy Boesky, music by Billy Boesky and Steve Postell) (Corey Glover, Shannon Conley), "Southbound Train" (lyric by Billy Boesky, music by Billy Boesky and Steve Postell) (Shannon Conley), "Hey Lady" (lyric by Billy Boeksy, music by Billy Boesky and Michael McCoy) (Corey Glover), "Silo" (lyric and music by Billy Boesky and Josh Klausner) (Shannon Conley, Corey Glover), "Fallen Angel" (lyric by Billy Boesky, music by Billy Boesky and Steve Postell) (Corey Glover), "Unveil My Eyes" (lyric and music by Billy Boesky) (Jonathan Goldstein), "All Right" (lyric and music by Billy Boesky) (Company)

NOTES—The short-lived musical *Fallen Angel* dealt with Will (Jonathan Goldstein), the leader and songwriter of a rock-and-roll band who tries to keep his group together when he loses his two leading singers. Will develops a skin rash which is partly due to the stress of the situation, and Stephen Holden in the *New York Times* noted that "no musical, Off Broadway or on, has devoted so much time to pondering the cause and treatment of a skin rash." Holden also commented that the score was "modestly catchy" but had little to do with the plot at hand.

Perhaps *Fallen Angel* should have borrowed the song "Miliaria Rubra" from *Swing* (which closed in Washington, D.C., during its pre-Broadway tryout in 1980); "Miliaria Rubra," which was dropped about midway during the tryout, may well be the only song in the history of the American musical devoted entirely to the pain caused by a skin condition (the character who had miliaria rubra sang that it "sounds like a dance ... and it burns").

Fallen Angel had been previously produced Off Off Broadway by La Mama Experimental Theatre Company (ETC).

472 Fallout. "A New Musical Revue." THEATRE: Renata Theatre; OPENING DATE: May 20, 1959; PERFORMANCES: 31; SKETCHES AND BLACKOUTS: Abe Goldsmith and Jerry Goldman, David Panich, and Martin Charnin; LYRICS: Martin Charnin, Robert (Bob) Kessler, and Paul Nassau; MUSIC: Martin Charnin, Robert (Bob) Kessler, and Paul Nassau; DIRECTION: Harvey Stuart; CHOREOGRAPHY: Buddy Schwab; SCENERY: Fred Voelpel; COSTUMES: Fred Voelpel; MUSICAL DIRECTION: Saul Schechtman; PRODUCERS: Harvey Stuart and David Taynton

CAST—Grover Dale, Paul Dooley, Judy Guyll, Margaret Hall, Jack Kauflin, Charles Nelson Reilly, Joe Ross, Joy Lynne Sica, Virginia Vestoff

The revue was presented in two acts.

ACT ONE—"We're Betting on You" (lyric by Martin Charnin, music by Robert Kessler) (Company), "Like the Beat, Beat, Beat" (sketch by David Panich) (Paul Dooley) "String Quartet" (lyric and music by Paul Nassau) (Charles Nelson Reilly, Jack Kauflin, Joe Ross, Margaret Hall) "Bwee Dah" (music by David Hollister, based on a theme by Robert Kessler; choreography by Grover Dale) (Grover Dale, Judy Guyll, Virginia Vestoff), "A Shipboard Romance" (sketch by David Panich) (Joe Ross, Margaret Hall) "Sixteenth Summer" (lyric by Martin Charnin, music by Robert Kessler) (Jack Kauflin, Joy Lynne Sica) "Initiation" (sketch by Martin Charnin) (Joe Ross, Grover Dale, Charles Nelson Reilly) "Someone Waiting" (lyric by Martin Charnin, music by Robert Kessler) (Margaret Hall) "The Victoria Trio" (lyric and music by Paul Nassau) (Jack Kauflin, Grover Dale, Virginia Vestoff, Joy Lynne Sica) "Rebeat" (sketch by David Panich) (Paul Dooley), "Something Forgotten in Denmark" (sketch by Martin Charnin) (Grover Dale), "Golden-Bull" (sketch by Abe Goldsmith and Jerry Goldman) (Joe Ross, Charles Nelson Reilly, Jack Kauflin, Joy Lynne Sica) "I Think I'd Like to Fall in Love" (lyric and music by Martin Charnin) (Virginia Vestoff) "That's When" (sketch by Martin Charnin) (Joy Lynne Sica, Grover Dale), "Clandestine" (lyric by Martin Charnin, music by Robert Kessler) (Charles Nelson Reilly, Margaret Hall, Jack

Kauflin, Judy Guyll, Joe Ross, Joy Lynne Sica) "The Kurds Had a Way" (sketch by David Panich) (Paul Dooley), "Oriental" (lyric by Martin Charnin, music by Robert Kessler) (Company)

ACT TWO—"Look!" (lyric by Martin Charnin, music by Robert Kessler) (Judy Guyll), "A Dramatized Message" (lyric and music by Paul Nassau) (Grover Dale, Joy Lynne Sica, Margaret Hall, Joe Ross, Virginia Vestoff, Jack Kauflin, Charles Nelson Reilly) "The Poet Is Cornered" (sketch by David Panich) (Paul Dooley) "Too Many Questions" (lyric and music by Paul Nassau) (Jack Kauflin) "E MC2" (sketch by David Panich) (Charles Nelson Reilly, Grover Dale) "Problem" (lyric by Dennis Marks, music by Alan Friedman) (Joe Ross), "A La Carte" (sketch by Martin Charnin) (Grover Dale, Jack Kauflin, Judy Guyll) "You're My Man" (lyrics by Martin Charnin, music by Robert Kessler) (Joy Lynne Sica) "Individuals" (lyric by Herb Hartig, music by Jerry Alters) (Charles Nelson Reilly, Grover Dale, Jack Kauflin) "Bard to Verse" (sketch by David Panich) (Paul Dooley), "The Three Faces of Sam" (sketch by Abe Goldsmith and Jerry Goodman) (Virginia Vestoff, Charles Nelson Reilly, Joe Ross) "Oh Say, Can You See?" (lyric and music by Martin Charnin and Robert Kessler) (Margaret Hall, Joy Lynne Sica) "Love Is" (lyric and music by Martin Charnin) (Grover Dale, Judy Guyll, Virginia Vestoff), "The End" (lyric by Martin Charnin, music by Robert Kessler) (Company)

NOTES—*Fallout* opened the night following the premiere of *Chic* (see entry), and it, too, was a failure. Brooks Atkinson in the *New York Times* noted the revue's material was thin and lacked a point of view; he found that the "trifling and inconclusive" evening offered "no great surge of originality" because its creators had "nothing" to say.

But there were many interesting names in the revue, including Charles Nelson Reilly in another Off Broadway appearance (Atkinson praised his "attractive personality"). And Grover Dale and Virginia Vestoff's names would soon be appearing frequently in the credits for Off Broadway and Broadway musicals. Martin Charnin would be heard from, too, most notably as the lyricist of *Annie* (1977). Paul Nassau was an interesting composer who unfortunately never found success on Broadway. His three book musicals had a total of forty-five performances: *Happy Town* (1959, 5 performances), *A Joyful Noise* (1966, 12 performances), and *The Education of H*y*m*a*n K*a*p*l*a*n** (1968, 28 performances).

In the program, "Oriental" wasn't listed by that title, but was instead spelled in Japanese.

"Clandestine" and "Oriental" were later used in *Pieces-of-Eight* (1959; see entry), but only the latter was recorded on that show's cast album (the former may have been added to *Pieces-of-Eight* sometime during the revue's run).

473 **Falsettoland.** THEATRE: Playwrights Horizons; transferred to the Lucille Lortel Theatre on September 16, 1990; OPENING DATE: June 28, 1990; PERFORMANCES: 215; BOOK: William Finn and James Lapine; LYRICS: William Finn; MUSIC: William Finn; DIRECTION: James Lapine; SCENERY: Douglas Stein; COSTUMES: Franne Lee; LIGHTING: Nancy Schertler; MUSICAL DIRECTION: Michael Starobin; PRODUCER: Playwrights Horizons (Andre Bishop, Artistic Director; Paul S. Daniels, Executive Director)

CAST—Chip Zien (Mendel), Michael Rupert (Marvin), Danny Gerard (Jason), Stephen Bogardus (Whizzer), Faith Prince (Trina), Heather MacRae (Dr. Charlotte), Janet Metz (Cordelia, Caroline)

The action occurs in 1981.

The musical was presented in one act.

MUSICAL NUMBERS—"Falsettoland" (Company), "About Time" (Michael Rupert), "Year of the Child" (Heather MacRae, Janet Metz, Michael Rupert, Faith Prince, Chip Zien, Danny Gerard), "Miracle of Judaism" (Danny Gerard), "The Baseball Game" (Company), A Day in Falsettoland:, "Mendel at Work" (Chip Zien), "Trina and Mendel's House" (Faith Prince, Chip Zien), "Dr. Charlotte and Cordelia's House" (Heather MacRae, Janet Metz), "Racquetball Court" (Michael Rupert, Stephen Bogardus), "Planning the Bar Mitzvah" (a/k/a "Round Tables, Square Tables") (Danny Gerard, Faith Prince, Chip Zien, Michael Rupert), "Everyone Hates His Parents" (Chip Zien, Danny Gerard), "What More Can I Say?" (Michael Rupert), "Something Bad Is Happening" (Heather MacRae, Janet Metz), "More Racquetball" (Michael Rupert, Stephen Bogardus), "Holding to the Ground" (Faith Prince), "Days Like This" (Company), "Canceling the Bar Mitzvah" (Faith Prince, Chip Zien, Danny Gerard), "Unlikely Lovers" (Michael Rupert, Stephen Bogardus, Janet Metz, Heather MacRae), "Another Miracle of Judaism" (Danny Gerard), "You Gotta Die Sometime" (Stephen Bogardus), "Jason's Bar Mitzvah" (Company), "What Would I Do?" (Michael Rupert, Stephen Bogardus)

NOTES—With *Falsettoland*, William Finn brought his "Marvin Trilogy" to a close. See entries for *In Trousers* and *March of the Falsettos* for more information about the first two musicals. (Finn later combined *March of the Falsettos* and *Falsettoland* into *Falsettos*, which opened on Broadway on April 29, 1992, for a run of 487 performances.)

Falsettoland takes place a short time after the action in *March of the Falsettos*, and continued with the story of Marvin, his former wife Trina, their son Jason, and Marvin's lover Whizzer. The musical also dealt with Marvin's new psychiatrist (Dr. Charlotte, and her lover, Cordelia) as well as Trina's new husband, Mendel, who was Marvin's former psychiatrist. In this the final musical of the trilogy, AIDS intrudes into Marvin's life by taking Whizzer. The program notes indicate "Marvin is left with nothing except the possibility of a relationship with his son." In his liner notes for the cast album released by DRG Records (CD # 12601), Andre Bishop, the Artistic Director of Playwrights Horizons, wrote that the musical "doesn't preach or proselytize," but one wonders why Finn felt compelled to write a cruel and gratuitous lyric about Nancy Reagan ("meanest and thinnest of the first ladies").

Falsettoland was published by Samuel French, Inc., in 1995, in a volume which included the scripts of both *March of the Falsettos* and *Falsettoland* (the volume is titled *Falsettos*). The scripts of all three musicals in the "Marvin Trilogy" were published as *The Marvin Songs* by The Fireside Theatre in an undated (but possibly 1991) edition. On July 16, 1998, *Falsettoland* was briefly revived Off Off Broadway by the National Asian American Theatre at the Dim Sum Theatre for twenty-nine performances with an all Asian-American cast.

474 **Fame on 42nd Street.** THEATRE: Little Shubert Theatre; OPENING DATE: November 11, 2003; PERFORMANCES: 264; BOOK: Jose Fernandez; LYRICS: Jacques Levy; MUSIC: Steve Margoshes; DIRECTION: Drew Scott Harris; CHOREOGRAPHY: Lars Bethke; SCENERY: Norbert U. Kolb; COSTUMES: Paul Tazewell; LIGHTING: Ken Billington; MUSICAL DIRECTION: Eric Barnes; PRODUCERS: Richard Martini, Allen Spivak, and Joop van den Ende/Dodger Stage Holding, by arrangement with Father Fame Foundation; Larry Magid, Adam Spivak, Lee Marshall, and Joe Marsh, Associate Producers

CAST—Christopher J. Hanke (Nick Piazza), Sara Schmidt (Serena Katz), Jose Restrepo (Jose [Joe] Vegas), Nicole Leach (Carmen Diaz), Q. Smith (Mabel Washington), Jenna Coker (Grace "Lambchops" Lamb), Cheryl Freeman (Miss Ester Sherman), Dennis Moench (Schlomo Metzenbaum), Shakiem Evans (Tyrone Jackson), Peter Reardon (Mr. Myers), Nancy Hess (Ms. Greta Bell), Gannon McHale (Mr. Sheinkopf), Michael Kary (Goodman "Goody" King), Emily Corney (Iris Kelly); Ensemble: Angela Brydon, Alexis Carra, Ryan Christopher Chotto, David Finch, David Garcia, Jesse Nager, Jennifer Parsinsen, Dawn Noel Pignuola, Eduardo Rioseco, Enrico Rodriguez, Danita Salamida, Erika Weber

SOURCE—The 1980 MGM film *Fame*.

The action occurs during the period 1980-1984 at New York's High School for the Performing Arts.

The musical was presented in two acts.

NOTES—*Fame on 42nd Street* began life as the popular 1980 film *Fame*, which in turn became a long-running television series shown on NBC during the 1982-1983 season and then in first-run syndication from 1983 through 1987. (As of this writing, the 1980 film is scheduled to be re-made by MGM in an updated version which is set for release in Summer 2008; reportedly, some of the songs from the original film will be retained for re-make.)

In October 1988, *Fame* was first produced on the stage at the Coconut Grove Playhouse in Miami. From there, the musical was produced throughout the United States as well as in London (at the Cambridge Theatre on June 27, 1995; recorded by Really Useful/Polydor Records [CD # 529109-2]) and other foreign venues (there was even a Swedish cast recording [released by Polydor on CD # 517-957-2]). There was also a 1999 American cast recording (released by DRG Records [CD # 19010]) from a touring production. All stage productions have incorporated the film's Academy Award-winning title song (lyric by Dean Pitchford, music by Michael Gore).

There always seemed to be rumors that *Fame* would open on Broadway, but it took fifteen years for the musical to finally reach New York (as *Fame on 42nd Street*), and when it did it played at an Off Broadway theatre for a little over eight months. Perhaps *Fame* waited too long to open in New York; by 2003, its zeitgeist had probably run its course. Had the musical played in New York in the late 1980s it might have enjoyed a much longer run.

The musical told the story of show business wannabes attending New York City's High School of Performing Arts located on West 46th Street (its last graduating class was in 1984; at that time it merged with the High School of Music and Art and relocated to Lincoln Center as LaGuardia High School).

The song list below is from the first stage production at the Coconut Grove Playhouse (song titles are followed by the names of the characters who performed the songs):

ACT ONE—"Pray I Make P.A." (Ensemble), "Hard Word" (Ensemble), "I Want to Make Magic" (Nick), "Can't Keep It Down" (Joe, Boys), "Tyrone's Rap" (Tyrone), "Let's Play a Love Scene" (Serena), "There She Goes!"/"Fame" (lyric by Dean Pitchford, music by Michael Gore), "Bring on Tomorrow" (Schlomo, Carmen), "The Teachers' Argument" (Teachers), "Like Carmen, Not Me!" (Lambchops), "Shake the Foundation" (Ensemble)

ACT TWO—"I Want to Make Magic" (reprise) (Nick, Serena, Ensemble), "Sugar Blues" (Mabel, Girls), "Think of Meryl Streep" (Serena), "Dancin' on the Sidewalk" (Tyrone, Ensemble), "These Are My Children" (Miss Sherman), "Lemme Out" (Joe), "In L.A." (Carmen), "Let's Play a Love Scene" (Nick, Serena), "Bring on Tomorrow" (reprise) (Ensemble)

475 **Fame Takes a Holiday.** THEATRE: La Mama Experimental Theatre Club (ETC); OPENING DATE: October 26, 2000; PERFORMANCES: Unknown; BOOK: Cassandra Danz, Mary Fulham, and Warren Leight; LYRICS: Cassandra Danz, Mary Fulham, Warren Leight, and Marc Shaiman; MUSIC: Tracy Berg, Dick Gallagher, Cliff Korman, and Marc Shaiman; DIRECTION: Mary Fulham; Barbara Allen, Assistant Director; CHOREOGRAPHY: Barbara Allen;

SCENERY: Gregory John Mercurio; COSTUMES: Ramona Ponce; LIGHTING: David Adams; MUSICAL DIRECTION: Dick Gallagher; PRODUCERS: La Mama Experimental Club (ETC) and Watson Arts

CAST—Abigail Gampel (Dee Dee), Deborah Lacy (Lavender), Susan Murphy (Crystal), Mary Purdy (Polly)

The musical was presented in two acts.

NOTES—In the early 1980s, the High-Heeled Women was a popular five-woman cabaret troupe who performed in such venues as the 13th Street Theatre and Mickey's 2. The act (subtitled "An Evening of Ovarian Humor") included sketches and songs.

In 2000, two of the troupe's founders, Cassandra Danz and Mary Fulham, returned in a four-woman musical about a women's comedy troupe and its problems when one of the members (ominously named Crystal) becomes hell-bent on her own success and thus undermines the quartet of comediennes. Both acts of the musical took place both onstage and backstage at two different cabaret performances.

Bruce Weber in the *New York Times* found the evening "difficult to resist," and he singled out two songs. One, "Je Ne Regrout Rien" (music by Dick Gallagher), was a spoof of Edith Piaf in which a cleaning woman sings of her pride in being about to grout so well. The other, "Girls, Girls, Girls" (the musical's opening number with music by Marc Shaiman and lyric by Shaiman, Cassandra Danz, Mary Fulham, and Warren Leight), had a frothy" melody and a "flirty" lyric which accompanied a parody of 1930s film extravaganzas in the style of Busby Berkeley.

Weber said the entire number was a "delight." Warren Leight had written the touching drama *Side Man* (1998) about musicians at the end of the Big Band era.

476 Fanny Hill. THEATRE: Theatre at St. Peter's Church/York Theatre Company; OPENING DATE: February 14, 2006; PERFORMANCES: 32; BOOK: Ed Dixon; LYRICS: Ed Dixon; MUSIC: Ed Dixon; DIRECTION: James Brennan; SCENERY: Michael Bottari and Ronald Case; COSTUMES: Michael Bottari and Ronald Case; LIGHTING: Phil Monat; MUSICAL DIRECTION: Tara Chambers; PRODUCER: York Theatre Company (James Morgan, Producing Artistic Director)

CAST—Nancy Anderson (Fanny Hill), Christianne Tisdale (Phoebe Davis), Patti Allison (Mrs. Brown), Tony Yazbeck (Charles Waneigh), Emily Skinner (Ensemble), Gina Ferrall (Ensemble), David Cromwell (Ensemble), Adam Monley (Ensemble), Michael J. Farina (Ensemble)

SOURCE—The novel *Fanny Hill* by John Cleland (published in two installments in 1748 and 1749).

The musical was presented in two acts.

ACT ONE—Overture (Orchestra, Nancy Anderson), "Lancashire" (Ensemble), "On the Road" (Ensemble), "Seeing London" (Ensemble), "Going to Mrs. Brown's" (Patti Allison), "House of Joy" (Cousins, Patti Allison), "Croft's Serenade" (David Cromwell, Nancy Anderson), "Welcome to London" (Emily Skinner, Nancy Anderson), "Sailor's Song" (Sailors, Tony Yazbeck), "The Most Heavenly Creature" (Tony Yazbeck, Robbers), "I Have Never Been So Happy" (Tony Yazbeck, Nancy Anderson), "Marriage Song" (Tony Yazbeck, Nancy Anderson), "Phoebe's Song" (Christianne Tisdale, Gina Ferrall, Emily Skinner), "The Weeping Song" (Nancy Anderson, Ensemble)

ACT TWO—Entr'acte (Patti Allison, Gina Ferrall, Christianne Tisdale, Emily Skinner, Sailor), "The Card Game" (Patti Allison, Gina Ferrall, Christianne Tisdale, Emily Skinner), "Tea Service" (Patti Allison, Cousins), "Honor Lost" (Nancy Anderson), "A Little House in the Country" (Nancy Anderson, Ensemble), "My Only Love" (Nancy Anderson, Tony Yazbeck), "Every Man in London" (Patti Allison), "Big" (Nancy Anderson, Adam Monley), "I Came to London" (Nancy Anderson), "Pleasure Dance" (Ensemble), "Goodbye" (Nancy Anderson, Ensemble), "Storm" (Nancy Anderson, Tony Yazbeck, Ensemble), Finale (Ensemble)

NOTES—Based on the ribald eighteenth-century novel, the musical version of *Fanny Hill* had been first produced on August 5, 1999, by the Goodspeed Opera House, East Haddam, Connecticut, in its Chester, Connecticut, theatre; for this production, Nancy Anderson created the title role, which she would later perform in the Off Broadway production. Songs heard in this version but not in the New York production were "Falwell," "I Wish Her All the Best," "Back Home," "Pleasure Dance," and "Mrs. Brown's House" (the latter may have been heard in New York as "Going to Mrs. Brown's").

In reviewing the Off Broadway production, Jeffrey Eric Jenkins in *The Best Plays Theatre Yearbook 2005-2006* noted the evening was "lively" and "clever." Neil Genzlinger in the *New York Times* found the musical about as "family friendly as a show full of phallic jokes can be." He felt the evening was "enjoyable enough," but observed that Fanny's story wasn't all that "compelling" and thus needed more "over the top" humor, such as the sequence in which Tony Yazbeck delivered an entire song ("The Most Heavenly Creature") while being mugged. Genzlinger also praised a number of other songs, including "Honor Lost," "My Only Love," and "Every Man in London."

477 A Fantastic Fricassee. THEATRE: Greenwich Village Theatre; OPENING DATE: September 11, 1922; PERFORMANCES: Unknown

NOTES—*A Fantastic Fricassee* was an evening of vaudeville turns. Alexander Woollcott in the *New York Times* reported that much of the evening consisted of two ballet sequences presented under the "deleterious" influence of the Ballet Russe, and he noted that the dancers were not particularly "constructed, endowed or trained" for their "moist and inclement" ballets. He was equally unimpressed with two playlets done in the Grand Guignol style. But Woollcott was quite taken by Rene Bufano's marionettes (who enacted a "delightfully facetious" tale about Orlando Furioso) and by singer Robert Edwards (who performed several "charming" numbers, including one in which he sang of "Greenwich Village flappers in their dirty batik wrappers").

478 The Fantasticks (1960). "A New Musical." THEATRE: Sullivan Street Playhouse; OPENING DATE: May 3, 1960; PERFORMANCES: 17,162; BOOK: Tom Jones; LYRICS: Tom Jones; MUSIC: Harvey Schmidt; DIRECTION: Word Baker; CHOREOGRAPHY: Lathan Sanford; SCENERY: Ed Wittstein; COSTUMES: Ed Wittstein; LIGHTING: Ed Wittstein; MUSICAL DIRECTION: Julian Stein; PRODUCER: Lore Noto in association with Sheldon Baron, Dorothy Olim, and Robert Alan Gold

CAST—Jerry Orbach (The Narrator [El Gallo]), Rita Gardner (The Girl [Luisa]), Kenneth Nelson (The Boy [Matt]), William Larsen (The Boy's Father [Hucklebee]), Hugh Thomas (The Girl's Father [Bellomy]), "Thomas Bruce" a/k/a Tom Jones (The Old Actor [Henry]), George Curley (The Man Who Dies [Mortimer]), Richard Stauffer (The Mute), Jay Hampton (The Handyman)

SOURCE—The 1894 play *The Romanesques* by Edmund Rostand.

The musical was presented in two acts.

ACT ONE—Overture, "Try to Remember" (Jerry Orbach), "Much More" (Rita Gardner), "Metaphor" (Kenneth Nelson, Rita Gardner), "Never Say No" (Hugh Thomas, William Larsen), "It Depends on What You Pay" (Jerry Orbach, Hugh Thomas, William Larsen), "Soon It's Gonna Rain" (Kenneth Nelson, Rita Gardner), "Rape Ballet" (Company), "Happy Ending" (Company)

ACT TWO—"This Plum Is Too Ripe" (Kenneth Nelson, Rita Gardner, Hugh Thomas, William Larsen), "I Can See It" (Kenneth Nelson, Jerry Orbach), "Plant a Radish" (Hugh Thomas, William Larsen), "Round and Round" (Jerry Orbach, Rita Gardner, Company), "They Were You" (Kenneth Nelson, Rita Gardner), "Try to Remember" (reprise) (Jerry Orbach)

NOTES—Much has been written about *The Fantasticks*, the Olympus (if that's the precise word for this small musical) of Off Broadway musicals. But Olympian it is, because when the term "Off Broadway musical" is used, *The Fantasticks* is the musical which immediately comes to mind. Its marathon run of 17,162 performances (all at the Sullivan Street Theatre), its numerous U.S. and foreign productions, its saga of the-show-which-receives-middling-reviews-but-nonetheless-parlays-itself-into-a-hit, have all been told before. Indeed, there's an entire book about the show (*The Amazing Story of The Fantasticks/America's Longest-Running Play* by Donald C. Farber and Robert Viagas [1991; the revised edition was published in 2005 by Limelight Editions]) as well as a documentary film by Eli Kabillo (*Try to Remember: The Fantasticks*) which was released in 2003 by Zeitgeist Films (the DVD was released by Zeitgeist [# Z-1061]).

For the record, Brooks Atkinson in the *New York Times* was for the most part enchanted with *The Fantasticks*. In his opening night review, he praised the "grace and humor" of Harvey Schmidt's music, the "entrancing" staging of Word Baker, and the actors who performed with an "artlessness that is winning." Atkinson was particularly intrigued by the musical's combination of the harlequinade, the masque, and characters inspired by the stories of Pierrot and Columbine. He found the first act "fresh and sweet," but noted when the second act's mood turned to disillusionment, the musical lost some of its magic. Nevertheless, he admitted his reservations were "ungrateful," and he wondered if the intrinsic nature of the plot worked against preserving the enchanting tone of the first act. Among the fascinating facts about *The Fantasticks* is that it was originally envisioned as a big Broadway musical (called *Joy Comes to Dead Horse*). When the show's concept was pared down and its title changed to *The Fantasticks*, the then one-act musical had its world premiere at Mildred Dunnock's Barnard Summer Theatre at the Minor Latham Playhouse on the Barnard campus on August 4, 1959. Susan Watson created the role of The Girl, Crayton Rowe was The Boy, and Jonathan Farwell was The Narrator. Two songs in this version ("O Have You Ever Been to China?" and "I Have Acted Like a Fool") were dropped by the time the show was expanded into two acts for the Off Broadway production the following spring. The former song can be heard as a bonus track (performed by Harvey Schmidt) on the cast album of the 2006 Off Broadway revival (see entry) which was recorded by Ghostlight Records (CD # 8-4415); the latter is included in the collection *Lost in Boson II* (Varese Sarabande Records CD # VSD-5485).

Another song, "Come on Along," wasn't used, but later appears to have been considered for the team's first Broadway musical *110 in the Shade* (1963); the number eventually came into its own when it was used in Schmidt and Jones' 1997 revue *The Show Goes On* (see entry).

On October 18, 1964, a television version of *The Fantasticks* was produced on NBC's *Hallmark Hall of Fame*. Susan Watson, who created the role of The Girl for the Barnard production but didn't play the role Off Broadway, here reprised her original role for television. John Davidson was The Boy, Ricardo Montalban was The Narrator, and Bert Lahr and

Stanley Holloway were the Fathers. In 2008, Susan Watson recorded three songs ("Never Say No," "Soon It's Gonna Rain," and "They Were You") from *The Fantasticks* for her priceless collection of songs by Jones and Schmidt (*Earthly Paradise* [Nassau Records CD # 96598]). On September 7, 1961, *The Fantasticks* opened in London, where it bombed. It lasted only forty-four performances (Terrence Cooper played The Narrator, Peter Gilmore, The Boy, and Stephanie Voss, The Girl). The fanciful musical didn't go over well with British audiences, just as London's long-running *Salad Days* (see entry) didn't connect with New Yorkers. For years there was talk of a film version, and, finally, in 1995 the film was made. But it sat on the shelf for five years, and not until 2000 was it distributed to a few theatres in a very limited release. Later that year it was also released on DVD by MGM Home Entertainment (# 1001533). The film actually works rather well, considering that it "opens up" the elegant simplicity of the stage version; but it's a reasonably entertaining film if one accepts it on its own terms.

The Off Broadway cast album was released by MGM Records (LP # E387200; issued on CD by Decca Broadway [# 314-543-665-2]); and in 1964 the script was published by the Drama Book Shop. In 1973, the script was republished (by Drama Book Specialists/Publishers) along with Jones and Schmidt's *Celebration*, a fascinating failure which played on Broadway for three months in 1969 (it would probably have worked better in a small Off Broadway theatre than in a Broadway house). In 1990, Applause Books published a thirtieth "anniversary edition" of the script which was chockfull of extras (which included articles and photographs).

Over the years there's been only minor tinkering with the original script. To appease the politically correct police, the "Rape Ballet" was re-conceived and became "Abductions (And So Forth)" (a/k/a "The Abduction Ballet") even though the word "rape" was used in the context of its original meaning (to seize, to carry away) and had nothing to do with forced sexual activity. And for a later touring production with Robert Goulet, the song "A Perfect Time to Be in Love" was added.

Incidentally, the iconic artwork logo for *The Fantasticks* was designed by Harvey Schmidt, the musical's composer.

The score for *The Fantasticks* contains two numbers which became major standards ("Try to Remember" and "Soon It's Gonna Rain") and two ("Much More" and "They Were You") which became minor ones. The only Off Broadway score closest in popularity to *The Fantasticks* is probably *Hair* (1967; see entry), which enjoyed a number of hit songs in the late 1960s.

Soon after the opening of *The Fantasticks*, Tom Jones, Harvey Schmidt, and Word Baker collaborated on another musical, a revue called *New York Scrapbook*. Instead of being produced on stage, the revue appeared on television as part of the *Play of the Week* series, and was apparently shown sometime in late 1960. A few of *Scrapbook*'s songs were later heard in the team's 1997 Off-Broadway revue *The Show Goes On* (see entry).

In 2006, just four years after its marathon run of 42 years, *The Fantasticks* was revived Off Broadway (but not at its old home; in the intervening years, the Sullivan Street Theatre had been razed to make way for a condominium); see entry for information about the revival.

Besides the original cast album, there have been a number of other recordings of the score: a 1973 Tokyo cast recording (sung in Japanese; HMI Records CD # HMI-1006); a 1992 "Japan Tour Cast Recording" (sung in English with a cast which included Robert Goulet as the Narrator, Tom Jones as the Old Actor, and Harvey Schmidt at the piano; DRG Records CD # 19005); a 2000 King's College, Wimbleton, cast album released by Jay Records (CD # CDJAY-8007); and *The Fantasticks in Jazz*, a mostly instrumental version of the score by the Trotter Trio released by Fynsworth Alley Records (CD # FA-1203-SE). There were no soundtracks issued of the television and film adaptations.

479 The Fantasticks (2006).

THEATRE: Snapple Theatre Center; OPENING DATE: August 23, 2006; PERFORMANCES: 628; BOOK: Tom Jones; LYRICS: Tom Jones; MUSIC: Harvey Schmidt; DIRECTION: Tom Jones; CHOREOGRAPHY: Janet Watson; SCENERY: Ed Wittstein; COSTUMES: Ed Wittstein; LIGHTING: Mary Jo Dondlinger; MUSICAL DIRECTION: Dorothy Martin; PRODUCERS: Steven Baruch, Richard Frankel, Marc Routh, and Thomas Viertel

CAST—"Thomas Bruce" a/k/a Tom Jones (Henry), Leo Burmester (Hucklebee), Santino Fontana (Matt), Sara Jean Ford (Luisa), Burke Moses (El Gallo), Robert R. Oliver (Mortimer) Douglas Ullman, Jr. (The Mute), Martin Vidnovic (Bellomy)

NOTES—This revival of the longest-running musical in the history of Off Broadway was produced less than five years after the original production had closed.

See entry for original 1960 production for more information, including song list. The revival included a politically correct title ("The Rape Ballet" became "The Abduction Ballet").

The revival was recorded by Ghostlight Records (CD # 8-4415) and included a bonus track of "O Have You Ever Been to China?," sung by Harvey Schmidt; the song was originally intended to be heard in the sequence for which "Round and Round" was eventually written.

480 Fashion (1974; Don Pippin).

"A New Style Musical Comedy." THEATRE: McAlpin Rooftop Theatre; OPENING DATE: February 18, 1974; PERFORMANCES: 94; BOOK: Anthony Stimac; LYRICS: Steve Brown; MUSIC: Don Pippin; DIRECTION: Anthony Stimac; CHOREOGRAPHY: "Additional musical staging" by Gene Kelton; SCENERY: Robert U. Taylor; COSTUMES: Bieff-Herrera; LIGHTING: Spencer Mosse; MUSICAL DIRECTION: Susan Romann; PRODUCER: H. Scott Lucas

CAST—Mary Jo Catlett (Evelyn/Mrs. Tiffany), Sydney Blake (Jean/Millinette), Susan Romann (Edwina/Frankson), Sandra Thornton (Rita/Seraphina Tiffany), Ty McConnell (Richard/Count Jolimaitre), Henrietta Valor (Nan/Adam Trueman), Jan Buttram (Pat/Mr. Antony Tiffany), Rhoda Butler (Suzanne/Joseph Snobson), Joanne Gibson (Marion/Gertrude), Holland Taylor (Kim/Colonel Howard)

SOURCE—The 1845 play *Fashion* by Anna Cora Mowatt.

The action occurs during "Nippy Fall 1973" in a high fashion living room on Long Island, the home of Evelyn and Allen Rich. The musical was presented in two acts.

ACT ONE—"Rococo Rag" (Mary Jo Catlett, Girls), "You See Before You What Fashion Can Do" (Ty McConnell, Mary Jo Catlett, Sandra Thornton), "It Was for Fashion's Sake" (Jan Buttram), "The Good Old American Way" (Henrietta Valor, Jan Buttram), "What Kind of Man Is He?" (Joanne Gibson), "My Daughter The Countess" (Mary Jo Catlett), "Take Me" (Ty McConnell, Sandra Thornton), "Why Should They Know About Paris?" (Ty McConnell, Sydney Blake), "I Must Devise a Plan" (Company)

ACT TWO—"Meet Me Tonight" (Company), "My Title Song" (Mary Jo Catlett, Company), "A Life Without Her" (Henrietta Valor), "My Daughter The Countess" (reprise) (Mary Jo Catlett), "My Title Song" (reprise) (Company)

NOTES—The 1974 production of *Fashion* was the second Off Broadway musical adaptation of Anna Cora Mowatt's play; see entry for *Fashion*, or *Life in New York*, the 1959 version. A third version of the material, *Yankee Ingenuity*, was produced in regional theatre (for more information, see entry for *Fashion*, or *Life in New York*).

For the 1974 adaptation, the musical was set in the present. A program note explained that the setting of the musical, the living room of Evelyn and Allen Rich's Long Island home, is also the headquarters of the Long Island Masque and Wig Society, an organization devoted to the ideal of the preservation of early American drama. The actresses in the musical not only played the ladies in the Society who are presenting a revival of the play *Fashion*; they also played the roles of the female and male characters in their revival of *Fashion* (with the one exception of Ty McConnell, who played their director as well as the character of Count Jolimaitre).

The musical had been previously produced Off Off Broadway at the Greenwich Mews Theatre on December 6, 1973.

The Off Broadway production of *Fashion* received generally favorable reviews, and it's surprising it lasted only three months. The team of Anthony Stimac, Don Pippin, and Steve Brown had been previously represented Off Broadway in *The Contrast* (1972) and later wrote *The Cast Aways* (1975)/*Castaways* (1977); see entries for these musicals, which, like *Fashion*, were based on early American plays. The trio of Stimac, Pippin, and Brown showed great promise, but, unfortunately, all three of their musicals were failures and they never again wrote together as a team. Among the highlights of their score for *Fashion* was "The Rococo Rag" and "My Title Song" (the latter was a self-described homage to Jerry Herman).

Don Pippin had been the musical director for such Broadway hits as *Irma La Douce* (1961), *Oliver!* (1963), and *Applause* (1970), and would continue in this role (and as vocal director) for a number of musicals, including *Mack & Mabel* (1974), *A Chorus Line* (1975; see entry), and *La Cage Aux Folles* (1983).

In 1994, a regional production of *Fashion* was recorded by Original Cast Records (CD # OCR-9492), with Mary Jo Catlett recreating her role of Evelyn/Mrs. Tiffany. The recording included two songs not in the original production ("You're Out of Fashion" and "Candlelight Ballet") as well as a few songs from *The Contrast* and *Castaways*.

The script of *Fashion* was published by Samuel French, Inc., in 1974.

481 Fashion, or Life in New York (1959; Deems Taylor).

"A Comedy with Music." THEATRE: Royal Playhouse; OPENING DATE: January 20, 1959; PERFORMANCES: 50; BOOK: (Credited to) Anna Cora Mowatt (NOTE: There was no program credit for the musical adaptation.) Lyrics: Uncredited; MUSIC: (Compiled and Arranged by) Deems Taylor; DIRECTION: David Fulford; CHOREOGRAPHY: Rhoda Levine; SCENERY: Donald Bailey Tirrell; COSTUMES: Maganini; LIGHTING: Donald Bailey Tirrell; MUSICAL DIRECTION: William Hess; PRODUCERS: David Fulford and William Dempsey

CAST—ENID MARKEY (Mrs. Tiffany), Dee Victor (Prudence), Margot Hand (Millinette), Rosina Fernhoff (Gertrude), JUNE ERICSON (Seraphina Tiffany), Carolee Campbell (Miss Proudacre), Marietta Abel (Mrs. Tiffany's Harpist), WILL GEER (Adam Trueman), Frederic Warriner (Count Jolimaitre), Jonathan Abel (Colonel Howard), William Swetland (Mr. Tiffany), Al Corbin (T. Tennyson Twinkle), Francis Dux (Augustus Fogg), Stanley Jay (Snobson), Stephen Daley (Zeke)

SOURCE—The 1845 play *Fashion* by Anna Cora Mowatt.

The musical was presented in five acts (the program didn't designate division of acts; songs are listed in performance order).

MUSICAL NUMBERS—"Jim Along Josie" (Stephen Daley), "Croquet" (June Ericson, Al Corbin), "Call Me Pet Names" (June Ericson, Frederic Warriner), "Come, Birdie, Come" (Rosina Fernhoff), "The Independent Farmer" (Will Geer, Company), "Kemo Kimo" (Stephen Daley), "The Gipsy's Warning" (Margot Hand), "Take Back the Heart" (Will Geer), "We Met" (June Ericson), "Walking Down Broadway" (Enid Markey, Gentlemen), "Down by the Riverside" (Jonathan Abel), "Not for Joe" (Stanley Jay), Finale (Company)

NOTES—*Fashion*, or *Life in New York* was based on Anna Cora Mowatt's successful 1845 comedy of the same title which spoofed Mrs. Tiffany, who is determined to be fashionable, no matter the cost. The Off Broadway musical seems to have been directly inspired by Brian Hooker's 1924 adaptation of the play, which was also seen Off Broadway (at the Provincetown Playhouse for a long run of 235 performances). According to John Corbin's review of the 1924 production in the *New York Times*, Hooker shortened the original play and accentuated its "archaic absurdities"; further, with the aid of Deems Taylor, Hooker's version included a dozen songs from the period in which the musical took place. While the 1959 musical didn't credit Hooker for the script (Mowatt was credited), it nonetheless included twelve songs arranged by Deems Taylor, presumably the same ones heard in the 1924 version.

During the Boston tryout of the 1959 revival, the role of Count Jolimaitre was played by James Coco; the role of Miss Proudacre by Rhoda Levine; the role of the Gertrude by Joyce Ebert; and role of Mr. Tiffany by Humphrey Davis. In Boston, the show's title was *Fashion!, or Life in New* York. The exclamation point was dropped for the New York production. *The Burns Mantle Yearbook/The Best Plays of 1958-1959* singled out "Walking Down Broadway" as the musical highlight of the show. This song is probably the same "Walking Down Broadway" which was later heard in *Hijinks!* (see entry; written in 1868, the song's lyric is credited to William Lingard and its music to Charles E. Pratt). *Fashion* surfaced again in a different Off Broadway adaptation which opened in 1974 and which ran for ninety-four performances (see entry). In 1976, there was a third musical version, *Yankee Ingenuity*, with music by Jim Wise, the composer of *Dames at Sea* (1968; see entry), and book and lyrics by Richard Bimonte; this production, which never played in New York, was seen on April 22, 1976, for twenty-nine performances at the Meadow Brook Theatre in Rochester, Michigan, as part of the Oakland University Professional Theatre Program. The cast included Max Showalter (a/k/a Casey Adams), and the script was published by Samuel French, Inc., in 1977.

482 Fat Tuesday.

THEATRE: Lepercq Space/ Brooklyn Academy of Music; OPENING DATE: March 7, 1976; PERFORMANCES: Unknown; BOOK: Roger Furman; LYRICS: Dee Robinson; MUSIC: Dee Robinson; DIRECTION: Roger Furman

NOTES—The Off Off Broadway musical *Fat Tuesday* took place in a New Orleans' brothel. The musical was apparently produced at both the New Heritage Repertory Theatre and the Brooklyn Academy of Music during the 1975-1976 season.

This production is not to be confused with *Fat Tuesday (And All That Jazz!)*, an all-dance musical set in New Orleans during Mardi Gras. Produced by the Tennessee Performing Arts Foundation, the musical was seen for four performances at the Wolf Trap Farm Park for the Performing Arts in Vienna, Virginia, beginning on June 14, 1977. It was conceived and developed by Wesley O. Brustad, Allan Jaffe, and Arthur Hall, and it featured the Olympia Brass Band from Preservation Hall and the Arthur Hall Afro-Amerian Dance Ensemble.

483 Fearless Frank.

"A New Musical." THEATRE: Princess Theatre; OPENING DATE: June 15, 1980; PERFORMANCES: 12; BOOK: Andrew Davies; LYRICS: Andrew Davies; MUSIC: Dave Brown; DIRECTION: Robert Gillespie; CHOREOGRAPHY: Michael Vernon; SCENERY: Martin Tilley; COSTUMES: Carrie F. Robbins; LIGHTING: Ruth Roberts; MUSICAL DIRECTION: Michael Rose; PRODUCERS: David Black and Robert Fabian in association with Oscar Lewenstein and Theodore P. Donahue, Jr.

CAST—NIALL TOIBIN (Frank Harris), Alex Wipf (French Waiter, Headmaster, Kendrick, Lord Folkestone, Whistler), Valerie Mahaffey (Secretary, School Girl, Jessie, Lily), Kristen Meadows (Nellie, Kate, Laura), Steve Burney (Tobin, Whitehouse, Smith, Chapman, Oscar Wilde), Ann Hodapp (Nursemaid, Actress, Bootblack, Topsy, Newsboy, Enid), Olivier Pierre (Cowboy, Carlyle, Mr. Clapton, deMaupassant, Dowson), Evalyn Baron (Mrs. Mayhew, Mrs. Clapton, Mrs. Clayton). The company also played the following characters: School Boys, New Yorkers, Hotel Guests, Cowboys, Cows, Indians, A Crowd, Newsboys, Strollers, Opera Chorus, Harris Detractors, and Harris Praisers.

The action occurs in 1921 in Nice and in the mind of Frank Harris.

The musical was presented in two acts.

ACT ONE—"The Man Who Made His Life Into a Work of Art" (Niall Toibin, Girls), "Nora, The Nursemaid's Door" (Valerie Mahaffey), "The Examination Song, or Get Me on That Boat" (Alex Wipf, Steve Burney, and Niall Toibin), "Halted at the Very Gates of Paradise (A Song of Frustration)" (Niall Toibin, Girls), "Come and Help Yourself to America, or Frank in the Melting Pot" (Company), "Dandy Night Clerk, or How to Get On in the Hotel Trade" (Company), "Riding the Range (A Song of the Old West)" (Company), "Oh, Catch Me, Mr. Harris, 'Cause I'm Falling for You!" (Kristen Meadows, Ann Hodapp, Valerie Mahaffey, Evalyn Baron, and Niall Tobin), "The Greatest Man of All" (Niall Toibin)

ACT TWO—"My Poor Wee Lassie (A Scottish Lament)" (Olivier Pierre), "My Own, or True Love at Last" (Niall Toibin, Kristen Meadows, Evalyn Baron, and Olivier Pierre), "Evening News (A Song of Success)" (Company), "Le Maitre de la Conte, or Maupassant Tells All" (Olivier Pierre), "Oh, Mr. Harris, You're a Naughty, Naughty Man!" (Niall Toibin, Evalyn Baron), "Great Men, Great Days, or The King of the Café Royal" (Niall Toibin), "Free Speech, Free Thought, Free Love" (Ann Hodapp, Niall Toibin, Company), "Mr. Harris, It's All Over Now!" (Niall Toibin, Company), "Fearless Frank" (Company)

NOTES—The musical's subject was Frank Harris (1856[?]-1931), the Victorian writer, critic, and editor, who had a lecherous eye for the women and a critical acumen for appreciating unknown writers (such as Oscar Wilde and George Bernard Shaw). The musical was presented as a series of music hall vignettes in which the older Harris looks back on his life and times; it was apparently produced under a Middle Broadway contract.

The critics weren't impressed. Frank Rich in the *New York Times* noted that *Fearless Frank* offered one of the wittiest books of the season, but felt the material itself lacked the ingredients for success. Given the dispiriting reviews (Don Nelsen in the *New York Daily News* said the musical "runs two hours ... two hours too long") and the obscurity of the subject (could one in a hundred-thousand theatergoers identify Frank Harris?), the show was doomed.

The work had previously been seen on the BBC, apparently as a non-musical biography. It was later developed for the musical stage, opening in London at the King's Head Theatre Club, where it was mildly successful. *Flesh, Flash and Frank Harris*, an Off Off Broadway non-musical play about Frank Harris, was produced by Shelter West at the Marquee Theatre on October 27, 1983, and in two slightly separated engagements played a total of thirty-seven performances. Written by Paul Stephen Lim, the play utilized three actors to play Harris at different stages of his life.

484 Feathertop.

"A Musical." THEATRE: WPA Theatre; OPENING DATE: October 17, 1984; PERFORMANCES: 33; BOOK: Bruce Peyton; LYRICS: Skip Kennon; MUSIC: Skip Kennon; DIRECTION: Susan H. Schulman; CHOREOGRAPHY: Michael Lichtefeld; SCENERY: Edward T. Gianfrancesco; COSTUMES: David Murin; LIGHTING: Craig Evans; MUSICAL DIRECTION: Sand Lawn; PRODUCER: WPA Theatre (Kyle Renick, Artistic Director)

CAST—Alexandra [Alix] Korey (Rigby), David Barron (Justice Groutt), Charles Bari (Dickon), Stephen Bogardus (Lord Feathertop), Laura Dean (Polly), Jason Graae (Tom Fulham)

SOURCE—Nathaniel Hawthorne's 1852 short story "Feathertop: A Moralized Legend" (which appeared in the volume of short stories *Twice-Told Tales*).

The action occurs in the Colony of Massachusetts during spring of the middle 1700s.

The musical was presented in two acts.

ACT ONE—"The New World" (Company), "Here I Am" (Charles Bari), "The Incantations" (Alexandra Korey), "They Had to Change" (Jason Graae, Laura Dean), "Spring Day" (Stephen Bogardus), "Home" (David Barron, Laura Dean), "One, Two, Three" (Stephen Bogardus, Laura Dean, Alexandra Korey, Charles Bari), "Better" (Alexandra Korey), "Happily the Days Are Running By" (Company)

ACT TWO—"Alleluia" (David Barron, Charles Bari, Laura Dean, Jason Graae, Stephen Bogardus), "Marvelous, Curious, and Strange" (Stephen Bogardus), "The New World" (reprise) (Alexandra Korey), "Something Different" (Jason Graae), "It's Only the Best Yet" (Stephen Bogardus, Laura Dean), "The Last Incantation" (Alexandra Korey)

NOTES—Nathaniel Hawthorne's short story "Feathertop: A Moralized Legend" told the tale of a witch who brings a scarecrow to life in order to cause problems for various mortals. But once Feathertop experiences human feelings, he happily becomes a mortal. (Percy MacKaye's touching 1911 play *The Scarecrow*, which is somewhat similar in theme to Hawthorne's story, is told through the prism of tragedy.)

Frank Rich in the *New York Times* was less than impressed by the production, and felt the authors wrote the musical only for "the exercise of writing a musical." He noted the "sweet-voiced" Stephen Bogardus played the title role as if he were "a song-and-dance Elephant Man," and said Alexandra Korey's witch was "so angrily righteous" that he feared she and the authors were planning a musical version of Hawthorne's *The Scarlet Letter*. An earlier musical adaptation of Hawthorne's short story, also called *Feathertop*, was produced for television by ABC on October 19, 1961, starring Jane Powell, Hugh O'Brian, Hans Conried, Cathleen Nesbitt, and Anthony Teague. Mary Rodgers and Martin Charnin's score was charming, and the cast album received limited distribution by Mars Candy Records (LP # LB-2931). In 2006, the University of Texas presented an operatic version of Hawthorne's story; titled *The Scarecrow*, the libretto and music were by Joseph Turrin. Incidentally, MacKaye's *The Scarecrow* was adapted into a musical as *Lord Scarecrow*. It opened at Brandeis University's Spingold Theatre on April 22, 1975, and played there for eight performances. The book and lyrics were by Charles Kondek, and the music was composed by Gregg Saeger.

485 Fermat's Last Tango. THEATRE: The Theatre at Saint Peter's Church/The York Theatre Company; OPENING DATE: December 6, 2000; PERFORMANCES: 30; BOOK: Joanne Sydney Lessner; LYRICS: Joanne Sydney Lessner and Joshua Rosenblum; MUSIC: Joshua Rosenblum; DIRECTION: Mel Marvin; CHOREOGRAPHY: Janet Watson; SCENERY: James Morgan; COSTUMES: Lynn Bowling; LIGHTING: John Michael Deegan; MUSICAL DIRECTION: Milton Granger; PRODUCER: The York Theatre Company (James Morgan, Artistic Director)

CAST—Gilles Chiasson (Carl Friedrich Gauss, Reporter), Edwardyne Cowan (Anna Keane), Mitchell Kantor (Pythagoras, Reporter), Jonathan Rabb (Pierre de Fermat), Chris Thompson (Daniel Keane), Christianne Tisdale (Euclid, Reporter), Carrie Wilshusen (Sir Isaac Newton, Reporter)

The action occurs in 1993-1994 in a conference hall, an attic, and "points heavenward."

The musical was presented in one act.

MUSICAL NUMBERS—Prologue (Gilles Chiasson, Mitchell Kantor, Christianne Tisdale, Carrie Wilshusen, Jonathan Rabb), "Press Conference I" (Gilles Chiasson, Mitchell Kantor, Christianne Tisdale, Carrie Wilshusen, Chris Thompson), "You're a Hero Now" (Edwardyne Cowan, Chris Thompson), "The Beauty of Numbers" (Chris Thompson), "Tell Me Your Secret" (Chris Thompson, Jonathan Rabb), "Sing We to Symmetry" (Gilles Chiasson, Mitchell Kantor, Christianne Tisdale, Carrie Wilshusen), "Welcome to the AfterMath" (Gilles Chiasson, Mitchell Kantor, Christianne Tisdale, Carrie Wilshusen, Chris Thompson, Jonathan Rabb), "Your Proof Contains a Hole" (Gilles Chiasson, Mitchell Kantor, Christianne Tisdale, Carrie Wilshusen, Jonathan Rabb, Chris Thompson), "I Dreamed" (Chris Thompson, Edwardyne Cowan), "Press Conference II" (Chris Thompson, Edwardyne Cowan, Gilles Chiasson, Mitchell Kantor, Christianne Tisdale, Carrie Wilshusen), "My Name" (Jonathan Rabb), "All I Want for My Birthday" (Edwardyne Cowan), "The Game Show" (Jonathan Rabb, Chris Thompson, Gilles Chiasson, Mitchell Kantor, Christianne Tisdale, Carrie Wilshusen), "Math Widow" (Edwardyne Cowan), "I'll Always Be There (Fermat's Last Tango)" (Jonathan Rabb, Chris Thompson, Edwardyne Cowan), "The Relay Race" (Giles Chiasson, Mitchell Kantor, Christianne Tisdale, Carrie Wilshusen), "I'm Stumbling" (Chris Thompson), "Oh, It's You" (Chris Thompson, Mitchell Kantor), "The Beauty of Numbers" (Chris Thompson, Edwardyne Cowan), "Press Conference III" (Gilles Chiasson, Mitchell Kantor, Chrisitanne Tisdale, Carrie Wilshusen, Chris Thompson, Jonathan Rabb)

NOTES—*Fermat's Last Tango* was a fascinating and unusual musical which revolved around mathematics; it was inspired by Andrew Wiles, a Princeton University mathematics professor who in 1993 offered proof of a 300-year-old math theory first proposed by Pierre de Fermat (1601-1665), who is generally credited as the father of modern calculus, especially differential calculus. The cast recording was released by Original Cast Records (CD # OC-6010), and the liner notes explained that Fermat had notated in the margin of a textbook his discovery of the proof of a particular theorem, but the space in the margin was too small for him to explain. Hence, for three centuries mathematicians tried to prove the theorem, and it wasn't until 1993 that Wiles offered proof (in a 200-page solution which had taken him seven years to complete). Wiles later learned there was one flaw in his solution, but in 1995 he presented corrected and irrefutable proof of his solution.

(Oddly enough, during the same season in which *Fermat's Last Tango* opened, mathematicians were also the subject of David Auburn's Broadway play *Proof*, which won the Pulitzer Prize for Drama as well as the Tony Award for Best Play.)

486 Festival. "A Zany New Musical." THEATRE: City Center Downstairs; OPENING DATE: May 16, 1979; PERFORMANCES: 5; BOOK: Stephen Downs and Randal Martin; additional book and special material by Bruce Vilanch; LYRICS: Stephen Downs and Randal Martin; MUSIC: Stephen Downs; DIRECTION: Wayne Bryan; CHOREOGRAPHY: Stan Mazin; SCENERY: George Gizienski; COSTUMES: Madeline Ann Graneto; LIGHTING: George Gizienski; MUSICAL DIRECTION: David Spear; PRODUCERS: Roger Berlind, Franklin R. Levy, and Mike Wise in association with Kip Richard Krones and Leslie Moonves; presented in association with LBN Company

CAST—MICHAEL RUPERT (Troubador, Henchman, Captain, King of Carthage), Bill Hutton (Aucassin), Michael Magnusen (Count Garin de Beaucaire), Robin Taylor (The Would-Be Bride, Aucassin's Warrior, Shepherdess, Pirate, Gypsy), John Windsor (Count Bougars de Valence, Sheperd, Pirate), Roxann Parker (Viscountess, Pirate, Gypsy), Maureen McNamara (Nicolette), Lindy Nisbet (Valence's Warrior, Pirate, Gypsy Queen), Leon Stewart (Oxherd, Pirate); Sons of King (Michael Magnusen, Leon Stewart, John Windsor); NOTE: At selected performances, Tina Johnson played the roles usually performed by Robin Taylor.

SOURCE—The anonymous thirteenth-century French chantefable *Aucassin and Nicolette*.

The action occurs in an abandoned amusement park.

The musical was presented in one act.

MUSICAL NUMBERS—Overture (Orchestra), "Our Song" (Michael Rupert, Company), "Ballad of Oh"/"For the Love" (Michael Rupert, Company), "Beata, Biax (Beautiful, Beautiful)" (Bill Hutton), "Prelude to War"/"War" (Michael Magnusen, John Windsor, Bill Hutton, Maureen McNamara, Robin Taylor, Lindy Nisbet), "Just Like You" (Michael Magnusen, Bill Hutton, Michael Rupert), "Special Day" (Maureen McNamara), "The Time Is Come" (Michael Rupert, Maureen McNamara, Bill Hutton), "Roger the Ox" (Leon Stewart), "When the Lady Passes" (Bill Hutton, Robin Taylor, John Windsor), "Gifts to You" (Maureen McNamara, Bill Hutton), "The Escape" (Quintet) (Company), "Pirates Song" (Michael Rupert, Ensemble), "I Can't Remember" (Michael Rupert, Michael Magnusen, Leon Stewart, John Windsor, Maureen McNamara), "One Step Further" (Roxann Parker, Robin Taylor, Maureen McNamara, Lindy Nisbet), "Let Him Love You" (Roxann Parker, Maureen McNamara), "The Ceremony" (Company), "Unfinished Song" (Michael Rupert), Finale ("Our Song" [reprise]) (Company)

NOTES—Based on the medieval tale *Aucassin and Nicolette*, *Festival* was a pleasant if minor evening, with a nice if unremarkable score. Like the ragtag players of *Godspell* (see entry) who cavorted in what appeared to be an abandoned playground, *Festival* utilized the concept of a carnival troupe performing the story of the legendary lovers in an abandoned amusement park or playground. But *Festival* was gone after five performances, and despite its being a natural for school and community theatre, it seems to have disappeared. Its major weakness was a tendency to emphasize coy and cutesy stage business. For some reason, musicals set in medieval times bring out the twee factor in writers, composers, and directors. The Broadway musical *Tricks* (1973) fell into this trap, and even Bob Fosse occasionally let obvious and silly effects creep into his otherwise sleek and ironic *Pippin* (1972).

Festival originally premiered in Los Angeles in September 1976 as *Aucassin and Nicolette*, with book, lyrics, and music by Stephen Downs. As *Festival*, a revised version (with Randal Martin credited as co-lyricist and book writer, and with extra book and special material credits by Bruce Vilanch) opened in Los Angeles in January 1979, and then later played in San Francisco and Washington, D.C. During its tryout, *Festival*'s cast included Gregory Harrison in the leading role of the Troubador and Stephanie Zimbalist as Nicolette. By the time the musical reached D.C., Maureen McNamara was playing Nicolette; and by the New York opening, Michael Rupert had assumed the role of the Troubador. During the tryout, the show was subtitled "A Musical Mischief," but for New York the subtitle was changed to "A Zany New Musical."

During the tryout, the musical was presented in two acts (the first act ended with "The Escape"), and the following songs were dropped prior to New York: "You Should've Been There," "Older Is Better," "Oh, Dear!," "In Toreolore" ("Toreolore Fight Song"), "A Father to Be," and "Through Love's Eyes."

The cast recording was released by Original Cast Records (LP # OC-7916; Robin Taylor and Tina Johnson alternated performances during the run, but both are heard on the album), and the script was published by Samuel French, Inc., in 1983 (the latter included a new song for the Troubador, "Why Do You Weep?").

In 2000, another musical version of the source material opened in regional theatre; titled *Nicolette and Aucassin*, the book and lyrics were by Peter Kellogg and the music by David Friedman.

487 The Festival of Regrets.

NOTES—See entry for *Central Park*.

488 Fiesta in Madrid. THEATRE: City Center Theatre; OPENING DATE: May 28, 1969; PERFORMANCES: 23; TEXT ADAPTATION: Tito Capobianco; original text by Tomas Breton; MUSIC: Tomas Breton; DIRECTION: Tito Capobianco; Elena Denda, Associate Director; CHOREOGRAPHY: Teresa; SCENERY: Jose Varona; David Mitchell, Associate Set Designer; COSTUMES: Jose Varona; LIGHTING: Hans Sondheimer; MUSICAL DIRECTION: Odon Alonso; Choral Direction by Martinez Palomo; PRODUCER: City Center of Music and Drama, Inc. (Norman Singer, General Administrator)

CAST—Chavo Ximenez (Photographer), NICO CASTEL (Don Hilarion), Alfonso Manosalvas (Don Sebastian), Nino Garcia (Don Pepe), CLARAMAE TURNER (Sena Rita), FRANCO IGLESIAS (Julian), ISABEL PENAGOS (Susana), TERESA (Teresa), KAY CREED (Casta), Antonia Rey (Tia Antonia), MURIEL GREENSPON (First Maid, First Little Sailor), Roberto Lorca (Grenadier), Luis Olivares (Grenadier), Manolo Rivera (Grenadier), Dan Kingman (Policeman), Harry De Dio (Juggler); Singing Ensemble: Arlene Adler, Marilyn Armstrong, Renee Herman, Suzy Hunter, Diana Kehrig, Donna Owen, Hanna Owen, Frances Pavlides, Sandra Jean Schaeffer, Henrietta Valor, Maria West, Marie Young, Ron Bentley, George Bohachevsky, Don Carlo, Tony Darius, Harris Davis, Joseph Galiano, Nino Garcia, Don Henderson, Douglas Hunnikin, Karl Krause, Raymond Papay, Dick Park; Dancers: Martha Calzado, Deardra Correa, Andrea Del Conte, Lilana Morales, Juana Ortega, Dini Roman

SOURCE—The 1894 zarzuela *La Verbena de la Paloma* by Tomas Breton.

The zarzuela was presented in two acts.

ACT ONE—Overture (Preludio), "Fiesta in Madrid" (Chorus, Dancers), "Times Have Changed (Los Tiempos Han Cambiado)" (Nico Castel, Alfonso Manosalvas, Nino Garcia), "I Also Have a Heart (Tambien Yo, Tego Mi Corazoncito)" (Franco Iglesias, Claramae Turner), "The Tanantula" (Isabel Penagos, Friends), "Blondes and Brunettes, I Like Them All (Las Rubias y Las Morenas)" (Nico Castel), "On a Girl's Hard Life (Pobre Chica, La Que Tiene Que Servir)" (lyric by J. Perez, music by Chueca and Valverde) (Maids), "Patio Espanol" (music by R. Chapi) (Dancers), "Flamenco Song

(Canto Flamenco)" (Kay Creed, Antonia Rey, Isabel Penagos, Chorus, Dancers), "The Grenadiers (Los Granaderos)" (Roberto Lorca, Luis Olivares, Manolo Rivera), "O, What a Lovely Evening (Que, Hermosa Noche Me Espera)" (Nico Castel, Kay Creed, Isabel Penagos, Antonia Rey, "Forget the Girl, Once and for All (Olivida esa Muchacha para Siempre)" (Claramae Turner, Franco Iglesias), "Where Are You Going Wearing That Shawl from Manila? (Donde vas con Manton de Manila)" (Isabel Penagos, Franco Iglesias), "The Fight (La Pelea)" (Isabel Penagos, Kay Creed, Antonia Rey, Franco Iglesias, Claramae Turner, Nico Castel, Dan Kingman, Chorus, Dancers)

ACT TWO—Prelude (Preludio), "The Streets of Madrid (Las Calles de Madrid)" (lyric by J. Perez, music by Chueca and Valverde) (Chorus), "Who Cares for Love? (Que Te Importa Que No Venga)" (Isabel Penagos), "The Barquilleros (Los Barquilleros)" (lyric by V. Sevilla and Carreno, music by J. Serrano) (Chorus, Dancers), "Danza Espanola" (music by Gimenez) (Dancers), "Three Little Sailors (Los Marineritos)" (lyric by J. Perez, music by Chueca and Valverde) (Soloists, Chorus), "Mazurka" (Chorus, Dancers), "The Best Women in the World (Las Mejores Mujeres del Mundo)" (lyric by Perrin and Palacios, music by J. Ileo) (Claramae Turner), "The Milord's Waltz (Caballero de Gracia)" (lyric by J. Perez, music by Chueca and Valverde) (Nico Castel), "The Second Fight (La Pelea)" (Claramae Turner, Nico Castel, Franco Iglesias, Kay Creed, Isabel Penagos, Antonia Rey, Dan Kingman, Chorus, Dancers), "You Are the Only One for Me (Tu Eres Ese)" (lyric by Shaw and Silva, music by R. Chapi) (Isabel Penagos, Franco Iglesias), "Fiesta in Madrid" (reprise) (Soloists, Chorus, Dancers)

NOTES—*Fiesta in Madrid* might have been under a Broadway contract or a modified variation thereof (or possibly under an Off Broadway contract); to be as inclusive as possible, I've included the work in this survey of Off Broadway musicals.

The zarzuela was adapted from Tomas Breton's *La Verbena de la Paloma*, and it appears that unless otherwise noted, all lyrics and music were by Breton (songs from other zarzuelas were interpolated into the production in order to expand the evening into two acts).

Fiesta in Madrid told the story of a wealthy apothecary who is infatuated with two young women; their aunt is determined that he will marry one of them.

Harold C. Schonberg in the *New York Times* found the evening entertaining, "with no sex, no problems, no Big Issues," and noted the evening's mission was to ensure that the audience had a "good, relaxing time." The cast included two opera singers, Claramae Turner and Muriel (Costa) Greenspon. The former had appeared as Nettie Fowler in the 1956 film version of *Carousel*, and the latter appeared in the occasional Off Broadway musical before making her mark with the New York City Opera, the company with whom she was most associated.

For more information about zarzuelas, see entry for *Ole!*

489 The 5th Season. THEATRE: Eden Theatre; OPENING DATE: October 12, 1975; PERFORMANCES: 122; BOOK: Luba Kadison; LYRICS: Dick Manning; Yiddish adaptation of lyrics by Isaac Dogim; MUSIC: Dick Manning; DIRECTION: Joseph Buloff; CHOREOGRAPHY: Sophie Maslow; SCENERY: Jeffrey B. Moss; COSTUMES: Jeffrey B. Moss; LIGHTING: Bob McCarthy; MUSICAL DIRECTION: Renee Solomon; PRODUCERS: Harry Rothpearl and Jewish Nostalgic Productions, Inc.

CAST—Elias Patron (Mr. Katz), Gerri-Ann Frank (Shelly), Raquel Yossiffon (Laurie), David Carey (Perl), JOSEPH BULOFF (Max Pincus), STAN PORTER (Benny Goodwin), Evelyn Kingsley (Frances Goodwin), Gene Barrett (Marty Goodwin), Miriam Kressyn (Miriam Oppenheim), Jack Rechtzeit (Mr. Lewis), Models (Franceska Fischler, Cathy Carnevale, Barbara Joan Frank)

SOURCE—The 1953 play *The Fifth Season* by Sylvia Regan.

The action occurs at the present time in a Seventh Avenue fashion showroom.

The musical was presented in two acts.

ACT ONE—"Believe in Yourself" (Stan Porter, Raquel Yossiffon), "My Son, The Doctor" (Stan Porter, Evelyn Kingsley, Gene Barrett), "Goodbye" (Stan Porter, Raquel Yossiffon), "The Fifth Season" (Ensemble)

ACT TWO—"Friday Night" (Joseph Buloff, Miriam Kressyn), "Mom! You Don't Understand!" (Gene Barrett, Evelyn Kingsley), "How Did This Happen to Me" (Stan Porter), "From Seventh Avenue to Seventh Heaven" (Stan Porter, Ensemble)

NOTES—Sylvia Regan's 1953 Broadway comedy *The Fifth Season* is a perfect example of the forgotten hit. The comedy itself was roundly dismissed by the critics, but they wrote valentines to its star, Menasha Skulnik. As a result, the play ran for 645 performances, but after the mid-1950s it all but disappeared until the musical version, *The 5th Season*, was produced. Since the musical wasn't a hit, both it and its source play haven't been heard from again.

The title referred to the five seasons of the garment industry ... Spring, Summer, Fall, Winter, and the Slack season (and "slack" doesn't refer to women's leisure apparel).

The lyric for "Friday Night" was written by Luba Kadison.

As of this writing, Regan's 1940 play *Morning Star*, which starred Molly Picon and played on Broadway for sixty-three performances, is reportedly being adapted into an opera.

490 Final Solutions. THEATRE: Felt Forum/ Madison Square Garden; OPENING DATE: March 11, 1968; PERFORMANCES: 1; BOOK: Jan Hartman; LYRICS: Jan Hartman; MUSIC: Jacques Belasco; DIRECTION: Gene Lasko; CHOREOGRAPHY: Valerie Bettis; COSTUMES: Coordinated by Claire Ferraris; LIGHTING: Kenetic Light Art (Jackie Cassen and Rudi Stern); MUSICAL DIRECTION: Harry Fuchs; PRODUCER: Ziv Kolitz; the production was sponsored by the American League for Russian Jews

CAST—Marian Seldes (The Woman), Tony Lo Bianco (The Poet), John Heffernan (Chorus Leader), Leonard Cimino (Voice of Tyranny), Bruce Kimes (Voice of Tyranny II), Joanne Grillo, Geula Gill; Dancers: Ze'eva Cohen, Laura Gleen, Lorry May, Edward DeSoto, Edward Effron, Phillip Filiato, Louis Garcia, Jim May; Chorus: Members of the Neighborhood Playhouse School of Theatre

NOTES—*Final Solutions*, a musical pageant about the plight of Jews in the present-day U.S.S.R., was presented for one performance only. Irving Spiegel in the *New York Times* quoted the aim of the American League for Russian Jews (which sponsored the evening): "To aid Jews in the Soviet Union [to] gain their rights to live as Jews, culturally and religiously" and "to emigrate if they so desire." Through the eyes of a young Jewish poet (played by Tony Lo Bianco) who is on trial in Russia, the pageant traced the history of attempts by despots to practice genocide on the Jewish race. Further, the pageant hailed three key years in recent Jewish history: 1948 (the establishment of Israel as a home for the Jewish people), 1956 (the Israeli conquest of the Sinai Peninsula), and 1967 (Israel's victory during the Six-Day War).

491 A Fine and Private Place. THEATRE: Theatre at St. Peter's Church/The York Theatre Company; OPENING DATE: April 27, 2006; PERFORMANCES: 29; BOOK: Erik Haagensen; LYRICS: Erik Haagensen; MUSIC: Richard Isen; DIRECTION: Gabriel Barre; SCENERY: James Morgan; Scott DelaCruz, Projections; COSTUMES: Pamela Scofield; LIGHTING: Jeff Croiter; MUSICAL DIRECTION: Milton Granger; PRODUCER: The York Theatre Company (James Morgan, Artistic Director)

CAST—Joseph Kolinski (Jonathan Rebeck), Gabriel Barre (Raven), Glenn Seven Allen (Michael Morgan), Christiane Noll (Laura Durand), Evalyn Baron (Gertrude Klapper), Larri Rebega (Campos)

SOURCE—The 1960 novel *A Fine and Private Place* by Peter S. Beagle.

The action occurs in a cemetery in the Bronx.

The musical was presented in two acts.

ACT ONE—Prologue (Joseph Kolinski), "I'm Not Going Gently" (Glenn Seven Allen), "Much More Alive" (Joseph Kolinski), "You Know What I Mean" (Evalyn Baron), "A Fine and Private Place" (Christiane Noll, Glenn Seven Allen), "As Long as I Can" (Glenn Seven Allen, Christiane Noll), "Stop Kidding Yourself" (Joseph Kolinski, Evalyn Baron), "The Telepathetique" (Glenn Seven Allen, Christiane Noll), "What Did You Expect?" (Christiane Noll), "Let Me Explain" (Glenn Seven Allen), "It's None of My Business" (Evalyn Baron, Joseph Kolinski), "Quartet" (Glenn Seven Allen, Christiane Noll, Joseph Kolinski, Evalyn Baron)

ACT TWO—"What Should I Do?" (Evalyn Baron, Christiane Noll, Joseph Kolinski, Glenn Seven Allen), "Close Your Eyes" (Christiane Noll), "Argument" (Joseph Kolinksi, Evalyn Baron), "No One Ever Knows" (Evalyn Baron), "Because of Them All" (Glenn Seven Allen, Christiane Noll), "Much More Alive" (reprise) (Joseph Kolinski), "Do Something" (Christiane Noll, Glenn Seven Allen, Joseph Kolinski), "How Can I Leave Here?" (Joseph Kolinski)

NOTES—Based on Peter S. Beagle's 1960 novel *A Fine and Private Place*, the musical dealt with characters both living and dead, and how they come to grips with their respective realities.

The musical had first been produced on August 3, 1989, at the Goodspeed Opera House's Norma Terris Theatre in Chester, Connecticut, and then on January 24, 1990, was produced by the American Stage Company at Fairleigh Dickinson University's Becton Theatre. In his review of the New York production, Neil Genzlinger in the *New York Times* felt the "modest" story was only "serviceable," and noted "a few sterling songs" would give the musical the dramatic weight necessary to propel its story forward. But he could single out only one song, "Close Your Eyes," which was "beautifully delivered" by Christiane Noll.

As of this writing, the cast recording of the musical is scheduled to be released by Jay Records during Spring 2008, and the script was published by Samuel French, Inc., in 1992).

The musical's title is derived from the poem "To His Coy Mistress" by Andrew Marvell (1621-1678): "The grave's a fine and private place/But none, I think, do there embrace."

492 Finkel's Follies. THEATRE: John Houseman Theatre; transferred to the Westside Theatre/ Downstairs on January 30, 1992; OPENING DATE: December 15, 1991; PERFORMANCES: 65; MATERIAL ADAPTED BY Robert H. Livingston; LYRICS: Phillip Namanworth; MUSIC: Elliot Finkel; DIRECTION: Robert H. Livingston; CHOREOGRAPHY: James J. Mellon; SCENERY: Mimi Maxmen; COSTUMES: Mimi Maxmen; LIGHTING: Bob Bessoir; MUSICAL DIRECTION: Mike Huffman; PRODUCER: Eric Krebs

CAST—Mary Ellen Ashley, Fyvush Finkel, Avi Ber Hoffman, Laura Turnbull

The revue was presented in two acts.

ACT ONE—"Yiddish Vaudeville Tonight" (Company), "Dallas" (Fyvush Finkel, Avi Ber Hoffman), "How It All Began" (Fyvush Finkel, Company), "Mom, I Want to Be in Yiddish Vaudeville" (Laura Turnbull), "Togetherness" (Laura Turnbull, Mary

Ellen Ashley, Fyvush Finkel), "You Were Meant for Me" (Fyvush Finkel, Mary Ellen Ashley), "A Look Back" (Fyvush Finkel, Company), "A Kliene Soft Shoe" (Fyvush Finkel, Laura Turnbull), "The Landlord" (Avi Ber Hoffman, Laura Turnbull, Fyvush Finkel), "Ringa Zinga" (Mary Ellen Ashley), "Tankhum" (by Solomon Golub) (Fyvush Finkel), "Mi-Komash Melon (What Is the Meaning?)" (by A. Reisen and N.L. Saslavsky) (Avi Ber Hoffman), The Genuine Article (Company): "Rozinkes Mit Mandlen (Raisins and Olives)" (by Abraham Goldfaden), "Di Greene Kuzeene (My Little Cousin)" (by Abe Schwartz), "Yossel, Yossel (Joseph, Joseph)" (by Nellie Casman), "Ich Hob Dich Tzufil Lieb (I Love You Too Much)" (music by Alexander Olshanetsky), "Belz (Wonderful Girl of Mine)" (music by Alexander Olshanetsky)

ACT TWO—"It Happened One Night" (Avi Ber Hoffman, Laura Turnbull, Fyvush Finkel), "Vaudeville, Kosher Style" (Mary Ellen Ashley, Avi Ber Hoffman, Laura Turnbull), "Not on the Top" (by Abe Ellstein) (Fyvush Finkel), "That Something Special" (Avi Ber Hoffman, Laura Turnbull), "The Farewell" (Fyvush Finkel, Laura Turnbull, Avi Ber Hoffman), The Shawl (Mary Ellen Ashley): "Vee Zenen Meine Zibn Gute Yur (Where Are My Seven Good Years?)" (by David Meyerowitz), "Oy Mama" (lyric by Molly Picon, music by Abe Ellstein) "Rozinkes Mit Mandlen" (reprise), "The Fiddle," "Tzi Tsu Zein Ich Zein Du? (Why Do I Have To Be Here?)," "These Are the Jokes" (Company), "Auditions" (Company), "Odenemya" (Avi Ber Hoffman), "The Golden Wedding" (Fyvush Finkel, Mary Ellen Ashley), "Abi Tsu Zein Mit Dir (As Long as I'm with You)" (Fyvush Finkel, Mary Ellen Ashley), Finale (Company)

NOTES—The revue was a salute to old-time Yiddish vaudeville and starred Fyvush Finkel. In 1996, Finkel returned in what was essentially a one-man revue, *Fyvush Finkel* (see entry) which was later revived in an Off Off Broadway production in 1997.

493 Fire of Flowers. THEATRE: Provincetown Playhouse; OPENING DATE: January 29, 1976; PERFORMANCES: 38; LYRICS: Peter Copani; MUSIC: Peter Copani, David McHugh, Lawrence Pitilli, Christian Staudt, Bob Tuthill, and Ed Vogel; DIRECTION: Don Signore; SCENERY: Richard Harper; LIGHTING: Richard Harper; MUSICAL DIRECTION: Ed Vogel; PRODUCER: The Peoples Performing Company, Inc.

CAST—Larry Campbell, Sylvia Miranda, Val Reiter, Gwen Sumter

The revue was presented in one act.

MUSICAL NUMBERS—"Today Will Be" (Company), "Keep Hope Alive" (Company), "Poppy Fields" (Val Reiter), "A Special Man" (Gwen Sumter), "If Jesus Walked" (Company), "Instant Hate" (Val Reiter), "One of Us" (Sylvia Miranda), "I Need to Know" (Larry Campbell), "In the Name of Love" (Company), "I'm Afire" (Gwen Sumter), "God Is in the People" (Larry Campbell, Company), "A Lover's Dream" (Val Reiter, Sylvia Miranda), "Who Can Say?" (Larry Campbell, Gwen Sumter), "Strawberries, Pickles and Ice Cream" (Sylvia Miranda), "Down on Me" (Larry Campbell), "The Blind Junkie" (Gwen Sumter, Company), "Riot" (Val Reiter, Company), "I Love the Sun" (Sylvia Miranda, Company), "Pairs of One" (Larry Campbell, Val Reiter), "Verily, Verily" (Sylvia Miranda, Gwen Sumter), "More Than Love" (Gwen Sumter, Company), "Make Them Hate" (Val Reiter, Sylvia Miranda), "Street Jesus" (Company), "L'America Ha Fato per Te" (Sylvia Miranda), "Love Comes and Goes" (Val Reiter), "Drug Free" (Larry Campbell, Company), "Wait and See" (Gwen Sumter), "When We Are Together" (Company), "God Is in the People" (reprise) (Company)

NOTES—Thirteen songs in the short-lived revue *Fire of Flowers* by Peter Copani had been previously heard in *Street Jesus* (1974; see entry)" "Today Will Be," "A Special Man," "If Jesus Walked," "One of Us," "God Is in the People," "Who Can Say?," "Strawberries, Pickles and Ice Cream," "Down on Me," "Riot," "Make Them Hate," "Street Jesus," "L'America Ha Fato per Te," and "Wait and See." Moreover, for the later *New York City Street Show* (1977; see entry) Copani used eight of these songs again ("A Special Man," "If Jesus Walked," "One of Us," "God Is in the People," "Who Can Say?," "Strawberries, Pickles and Ice Cream," "Make Them Hate," and "Wait and See").

In reviewing *Fire of Flowers*, Clive Barnes in the *New York Times* found the *Jacques Brel* wannabe revue "diffuse and defunct," and noted the evening had a "certain pretentiousness about it that is surely justifiably unendearing."

494 The Fireman's Flame. "A Musical Melodrama." THEATRE: American Music Hall; OPENING DATE: October 9, 1937; PERFORMANCES: 204; BOOK: John Van Antwerp; LYRICS: Ted Fetter; MUSIC: Richard Lewine; DIRECTION: Morgan Lewis (?); CHOREOGRAPHY: Morgan Lewis; SCENERY: Eugene Dunkel; COSTUMES: Kermit Love; MUSICAL DIRECTION: Al Evans; PRODUCERS: John and Jerrold Krimsky

CAST—Alan Handley (Napoleon Markham), Anna Erskine (Miss Snodgrass), Julie Hartwell (Miss Cabot), Ben Cutler (Harry Howard), Harry Meehan (Mose), Isham Keith (Nozzle), Cynthia Rogers (Mrs. Howard, Daphne Vanderpool), Rose Lieder (Jenny), Phillip Bourneuf (Adolphus Vanderpool), Grace Coppin (Vesta Violet), Sellwyn Myers (Bedlington), Bruce Gordon (Bowery B'Hoy), George Spelvin (Policeman), George Stinchfeld (Rensselaer), Lee Burke (Mayor Wickham), Fire Belles (Anna Erskine, Margaret Ballentine, Eleanora Dixon, Jo Ann Lee, Julie Hartwell, Honey Sinclaire, Christie Gillespie), Red Heart and Bluebird Volunteers (Lee Burke, Bruce Gordon, George Stinchfeld, Sellwyn Myers, James Hayes, Remington Olmstead)

The musical was presented in three acts.

ACT ONE—"Hose Boys" (Bluebird Boys and Red Heart Boys), "The Fireman's Flame" (Christie Gillespie, Ensemble), "Fire Belles Gallop" (The Pony Ballet) (Fire Belles), "Doin' the Waltz" (Grace Coppin, Ensemble), "We're Off" (Bluebird Boys), (Between Acts One and Two: Olios [Harry Meehan, the Irish Thrush, and the Singing Waitresses, Dale Carter, Audrey Edmonds, Mildred Kent, Mary Thomas, Dorothy White, Helen Spina, Virginia Deane, Wilma Davis)

ACT TWO—"Do My Eyes Deceive Me" (Elizabeth Love, Ben Cutler, Ensemble), "Mother Isn't Getting Any Younger" (Harry Meehan), "It's a Lovely Night on the Hudson River" (Ben Cutler, Elizabeth Love, Ensemble), (Between Acts Two and Three: Unidentified song performed by the Singing Waitresses.)

ACT THREE—"I Like the Nose on Your Face" (Rose Lieder, Isham Keith, Ensemble), Finale (Ensemble)

NOTES—The American Music Hall followed up its previous success *Naughty-Naught '00* (see entry) with another hit, *The Fireman's Flame*. The tongue-in-cheek melodrama dealt with Villain Napoleon Markham and Hero Harry Howard who belong, respectively, to the "aristocratic" Red Hearts volunteer fire brigade and the "democratic" Bluebirds brigade. Both are in love with Daphne Vanderpool, the ward of the millionaire Adolphus Vanderpool. Napolean tries various nefarious schemes to win the hand of Daphne, including an attempt to set fire to the Vanderpool mansion, but not only does Harry save the day, it also turns out he's the long-lost son of Mr. Vanderpool.

John Van Antwerp, the musical's book writer, was in fact co-producer Jerrold Krimsky.

The script was published by Samuel French, Inc., in 1938.

See entry for *Naughty-Naught '00* for more information concerning the musical melodramas which played at the American Music Hall.

The song "Mother Isn't Getting Any Younger" was interpolated into the 1946 revival of *Naughty-Naught'00* (see entry).

495 The First Emperor. THEATRE: Metropolitan Opera House; OPENING DATE: December 21, 2006; PERFORMANCES: 9; LIBRETTO: Tan Dun and Ha Jin; MUSIC: Tan Dun; DIRECTION: Zhang Yimou; Wang Chaoge, Co-Director; CHOREOGRAPHY: Dou Dou Huang; SCENERY: Fan Yue; COSTUMES: Emi Wada; LIGHTING: Duane Schuler; MUSICAL DIRECTION: Tan Dun; PRODUCER: The Metropolitan Opera CAST—Placido Domingo (Emperor Qin Shi Huang), Michelle DeYoung (Shaman), Paul Groves (Gao Jianli), Hao Jiang Yian (General Wang), Susanne Mentzer (Mother of Yueyang), Haijing Fu (Chief Minister), Wu Hsing-Kuo (Yin-Yang Master), Danrell Williams (Guard), Dou Dou Huang (Principal Male Dancer), Qi Yao (Zheng Player)

The opera was presented in two acts.

NOTES—Not only was *The First Emperor* a world premiere, it was also the first time in his thirty-eight years at the Met that Placido Domingo appeared in a world premiere there, creating the title role of Emperor Qin Shi Huang. In order to unite China, the emperor decides the nation needs an anthem, and chooses a childhood friend, Gao Jianli, to compose it. But Gao Jianli, who secretly resents the emperor and blames him for his mother's death, has an affair with the emperor's headstrong daughter who is engaged to the emperor's confidant, General Wang. The princess ultimately kills herself (in what the *New York Times*' critic Anthony Tommasini cited as possibly "the longest farewell aria" in the history of opera ["which is saying something"]), and after Gao Jianli poisons the general, he proceeds to bite off his own tongue. Tommasini noted Tan Dun's "undeniable artistry" produced "exotic" harmonies and "enticing" vocal lines, but overall the score was an "enormous disappointment" in its "long, arching and slow" melodic lines which went "on and on" and led him to think "Oh, no, not again" when Domingo began yet another aria "of ponderously arching lyricism." Tommasini mentioned the opera lasted three hours and twenty minutes (with one intermission), and in his review in the *Washington Post*, Philip Kennicott suggested the opera be trimmed by about one hour. Kennicott also felt the music was too often merely "functional," doing the basic job of storytelling. But he praised Tan Dun's use of percussive effects, which were often "novel."

In December 2006 the Met began an ambitious experiment in which live performances were simulcast in high-definition broadcasts in selected movie theatres. *The First Emperor* was shown on January 13, 2007.

496 First Lady Suite. THEATRE: Susan Stein Shiva Theatre/The Joseph Papp Public Theatre; OPENING DATE: December 15, 1993; PERFORMANCES: 15; LYRICS: Michael John LaChiusa; MUSIC: Michael John LaChiusa; DIRECTION: Kirsten Sanderson; CHOREOGRAPHY: Janet Bogardus; SCENERY: Derek McLane; COSTUMES: Tom Broecker; LIGHTING: Brian MacDevitt; MUSICAL DIRECTION: Alan Johnson; PRODUCER: The New York Shakespeare Festival (George C. Wolfe, Producer; Jason Steven Cohen, Managing Director; Rosemarie Tichler and Kevin Kline, Associate Producers)

CAST—Carolann Page (Eleanor Roosevelt, Evelyn Lincoln [Personal Secretary of John F. Kennedy]), Carol Woods (Hick [Lorena Hickok]), Maureen Moore (Amelia Earhart, Jacqueline Kennedy), David Wasson (Bess Truman, Ike [Dwight D. Eisenhower], A Presidential Aide), Debra Stricklin (Margaret Truman, Ike's Chauffer [Kay Summersby], Mary Gallagher [Personal Secretary to Jacqueline Kennedy]), Alice Playten (Mamie [Mary Geneva Doud Eisenhower], Lady Bird Johnson), Priscilla Baskerville (Marian Anderson)

NOTES—*First Lady Suite* was an evening of four short one-act musicals (*Eleanor Sleeps Here*, *Olio*, *Where's Mamie?*, and *Over Texas*) about four First Ladies. Alternately poignant and humorous, the four musicals dealt with how the First Ladies (and other women in their lives) balance their public personas and their private lives.

A production of *First Lady Suite* by the Blank Theatre Company in Los Angeles was recorded in 2002 by PS Classics Records (CD # PS-206); the script was published by Dramatists Play Service, Inc., in 1995.

The musical was the first of two by Michael John LaChiusa which were produced during the 1993-1994 season; six weeks after the New York premiere of *First Lady Suite* at the Public, his musical *Hello Again* opened at Lincoln Center (see entry).

First Lady Suite marked the second time in less than three years that Amelia Earhart appeared as a character in an Off Broadway musical (under very different circumstances, she had been seen two seasons earlier in *Song of Singapore* [1991; see entry, which also discusses another musical about Earhart and also one which saluted female pilots in song]); the production also marked the second appearance of the character of Bess Truman in these pages (see entry for *The Buck Stops Here!* [1983]). The published script of *First Lady Suite*, the Blank Theatre Company's production (and recording), and presumably other productions of the musical offered a reordered presentation of the four musicals (*Over Texas*, *Where's Mamie?*, *Olio*, and *Eleanor Sleeps Here*); it appears that *Olio* wasn't included in the Blank Theatre's production, and the sequence isn't on the PS Classics'recording.

Where's Mamie? and *Over Texas* had been originally developed at the Ensemble Studio Theatre.

The following is a list of the four musicals in the order in which they were presented in New York.

Eleanor Sleeps Here. The action occurs in Amelia Earhart's Lockheed Electra in 1936. "This Is the Beginning" (Carolann Page, Carol Woods, Maureen Moore), "Eleanor's Room" (Carol Woods), "Wingwalk" (Carol Woods, Carolann Page, Maureen Moore), "Eleanor's Hand" (Carol Woods), "If the DAR Wants to Support Rearmament" (Carolann Page, Maureen Moore, Carol Woods), "When Eleanor Smiles" (Carol Woods), "Eleanor's Letter" (Carol Woods, Carolann Page), "Eleanor Sleeps Here" (Carol Woods), "Miss Hickok, I Must Ask You to Come Back Inside" (Maureen Moore, Carol Woods), "Great Ladies" (Amelia Earhart), "Look at Washington!" (Carolann Page, Carol Woods, Maureen Moore)

Olio. The action occurs at the Christian Democratic Mothers and Daughters Luncheon in 1950. "Won't You Lay Me to Rest in Ole Missoura" (Debra Stricklin)

Where's Mamie? The action occurs in Ike and Mamie Eisenhower's bedroom, the White House, in 1957. "This Is the Worst Birthday" (Alice Playten), "Where's Mamie?" (Alice Playten), "My Husband Was an Army Man" (Alice Playten), "Melba, Gloria" (Priscilla Baskerville, Alice Playten), "To Algiers!" (Alice Playten, Priscilla Baskerville), "Algiers" (Alice Playten, Priscilla Baskerville, David Wasson, Debra Stricklin), "Kidnapping" (Alice Playten, Priscilla Baskerville, Debra Stricklin, David Wasson), "Old Rules Are Old Rules" (Alice Playten, David Wasson), "Tomorrow I Will Love You More" (David Wasson, Alice Playten, Priscilla Baskerville, Debra Stricklin), "Bluer Than Blue" (David Wasson, Alice Playten, Priscilla Baskerville)

Over Texas. The action occurs on board Air Force One en route from Fort Worth to Love Field, Dallas, Texas, on November 22, 1963. "Always Something" (Debra Stricklin, Carolann Page), "Over Texas" (Debra Stricklin), "Ladies ... Tea?" (David Wasson, Debra Stricklin, Carolann Page), "Four More Years" (Debra Stricklin, Carolann Page), "Caroline" (Debra Stricklin, Carolann Page), "Kitty Cat Nap" (Maureen Moore, Debra Stricklin, Alice Playten), "The Smallest Thing" (Maureen Moore, Debra Stricklin), "What What?" (Debra Stricklin, Carolann Page), "This Is What We Are" (Carolann Page, Debra Stricklin), "Mary Gallagher, You're Needed" (David Wasson, Debra Stricklin, Carolann Page)

497 Five After Eight. "A Musical Entertainment." THEATRE: Cubiculo Theatre; OPENING DATE: November 27, 1979; PERFORMANCES: Unknown; BOOK: Richard Morton; LYRICS: Michael Bitterman; MUSIC: Michael Bitterman; DIRECTION: Michael Pearthree; CHOREOGRAPHY: Michael Pearthree; SCENERY: Frank Kelly; COSTUMES: Dolores Gamba; LIGHTING: Paul Lindsay Butler; MUSICAL DIRECTION: Ron Williams

CAST—Sally Funk, James Paul Handakas, Dena Olstad, Arthur Alan Sorenson, Barbara Walker

The musical was presented in two acts.

ACT ONE—"Closing Song" (Company), "Spirit Song" (Company), "What I'm Looking For" (Sally Funk, Barbara Walker), "A Quartet with a Smile" (Company), "I Know You're Here, Jeannine" (Dena Olstad), "You Better Watch Out for Me" (Sally Funk, Dena Olstad, Barbara Walker), "It's Not Working Out" (Dena Olstad), "If We Spent Our Lives in a Fishbowl" (Arthur Alan Sorenson, Barbara Walker), "Nothing Can Stand in My Way" (Sally Funk)

ACT TWO—"We're Not Who We Think We Are" (Company), "Unanswered Questions" (Company), "If There's Anything Left of Us" (James Paul Handakas, Barbara Walker), "That's What Love Does to Me" (Dena Olstad), "25 Years" (Barbara Walker), "Still Here with Me" (Arthur Alan Sorenson), "Besancon" (Sally Funt), "The Perfect Imbalance"(James Paul Handakas, with Arthur Alan Sorenson and Barbara Walker), "What Is Funny" (Arthur Alan Sorenson), New York Finale ("How Can You Write a Song About Manhattan When They've All Been Written Before?") (Company)

NOTES—This Off Off Broadway musical dealt with a group of young performers who recently appeared together in a long-running Off Broadway musical. The plot followed their private and professional lives.

James Atlas in the *New York Times* found the "rather hectic show" less a book musical than a "succession of random cabaret sketches," and noted the choreography was "familiar but lively" and the music "more inventive" than the lyrics. He added that during the finale, he found himself agreeing with the cast when they sang out, "Enough's enough."

The "New York Finale" sequence included parodies of "Manhattan" (from *The Garrick Gaities* [First Edition], 1925; lyric by Lorenz Hart, music by Richard Rodgers); "How About You" (1942 film *Babes on Broadway*; lyric by Arthur Freed, music by Burton Lane); "New York, New York" (*On the Town*, 1944; lyric by Betty Comden and Adolph Green, music by Leonard Bernstein); "Lullaby of Broadway" (1935 film *Gold Diggers of 1935*; lyric by Al Dubin, music by Harry Warren); and "Another Hundred People" (*Company*, 1970; lyric and music by Stephen Sondheim).

The cast recording was released by Original Cast Records (LP # OC-8027); the song titles are taken from the recording.

498 Five A.M. Jazz.

NOTES—See entry for *That Five A.M. Jazz.*

499 Five Course Love. "A Lip-Smacking Musical Comedy." THEATRE: Minetta Lane Theatre; OPENING DATE: October 16, 2005; PERFORMANCES: 70; BOOK: Gregg Coffin; Marge Betley, Dramaturg; LYRICS: Gregg Coffin; MUSIC: Gregg Coffin; DIRECTION: Emma Griffin; CHOREOGRAPHY: Mindy Cooper; SCENERY: G.W. Mercier; COSTUMES: G.W. Mercier; LIGHTING: Mark Barton; MUSICAL DIRECTION: Fred Tessler; PRODUCERS: Geva Theatre Center (Mark Cuddy, Artistic Director) and Five Course Love Company, LLC

CAST—Heather Ayers (Barbie, Sofia, Gretchen, Rosalinda, Kitty), John Bolton (Matt, Gino, Klaus, Guillermo, Clutch), Jeff Gurner (Dean, Carlo, Heimlich, Ernesto, Pops), Erin Maguire (Offstage Singer), Billy Sharpe (Offstage Singer)

The action occurs in five different restaurants "on one fateful night" in the present time.

The musical was presented in one act.

MUSICAL NUMBERS—"A Very Single Man" (John Bolton), "Dean's Old-Fashioned All-American Down-Home Bar-B-Que Texas Eats" (Jeff Gurner), "Jumpin' the Gun" (Heather Ayers, John Bolton), "I Loved You When I Thought Your Name Was Ken" (Heather Ayers), "Morning Light" (Jeff Gurner, John Bolton), "If Nicky Knew" (Heather Ayers, Jeff Gurner, John Bolton), "Give Me This Night" (John Bolton, Heather Ayers), "Nicky Knows" (Heather Ayers, Jeff Gurner, John Bolton), "Shetler-Lied" (Jeff Gurner), "'No' Is a Word I Don't Fear" (Heather Ayers), "Der Bumsen-Kratzentanz" (John Bolton, Jeff Gurner, Heather Ayers), "Risk Love" (John Bolton, Jeff Gurner), "Gretchen's Lament" (Heather Ayers), "The Ballad of Guillermo" (Jeff Gurner, John Bolton), "Come Be My Love" (Heather Ayers, John Bolton), "Pick Me" (Jeff Gurner, John Bolton), "The Blue Flame" (Jeff Gurner, Heather Ayers), "True Love at the Star-Lite Tonight" (John Bolton, Heather Ayers, Jeff Gurner), "It's a Mystery" (John Bolton, Heather Ayers), "Medley" (Jeff Gurner, John Bolton), "Love Looking Back at Me" (Heather Ayers)

NOTES—Perhaps "Did You Move?," the second sequence of *Contact* (see entry), inspired *Five Course Love*, a revue-like musical which looked at love from the perspective of five different restaurant settings (a barbeque hangout, an upscale Italian restaurant, a German restaurant, a Mexican cantina, and a diner). Neil Genzlinger in the *New York Times* had reservations concerning the slim plot and its occasional tastelessness, but had high praise for the three performers, John Bolton, Jeff Gurner, and Heather Ayers (as for the latter, he felt her "potentially star-making" performance "might make Kristin Chenoweth want to check the rearview mirror"). He also liked Gregg Coffin's "zippy" score and Mindy Cooper's "daffy" choreography.

The amusing script was published by Dramatists Play Service, Inc., in 2007. The cast album is scheduled for release by Little Spaceman Music Records in 2009.

The musical was first presented at the Geva Theatre Center in Rochester, New York, on June 16, 2004.

500 Five Points. THEATRE: AMAS Repertory Theatre; OPENING DATE: April 15, 1982; PERFORMANCES: 16; BOOK: Laurence Holder; LYRICS: John Braden; MUSIC: John Braden; DIRECTION: William Michael Maher; CHOREOGRAPHY: Keith Rozie; SCENERY: Tom Barnes; COSTUMES: Gabriel Berry; LIGHTING: Gregg Marriner; MUSICAL DIRECTION: Steve Oirich; PRODUCER: AMAS Repertory Theatre (Rosetta LeNoire, Founder and Artistic Director; Gary Halcott, Administrator and Business Manager; Jerry Lapidus, Administrator)

CAST—Larry Campbell (Pete Williams), Marjorie Gayle Edwards (Ensemble), Joseph Fugett

(William Henry Lane [a/k/a Juba), J. Herbert Kerr, Jr. (Johnnie Night), Robert Lydiard (Jack Diamond), Cynthia McPherson (Ethel Myrrh), Valois Mickens (Ensemble), Nicky Paraiso (Fong), Tonya Pinkins (Arnabelle), Rochelle Parker (Lena), Bertin Rowser (Ensemble), Robert Vaucresson, Jr. (Ensemble)

The action occurs in the Five Points district of New York City during the 1840s.

NOTES—Five Points was a notorious slum district in New York City; in 1863, it was the site of the Civil War draft riots, which were the subject of the 1968 Broadway musical *Maggie Flynn* as well as Martin Scorsese's 2002 film *Gangs of New York*. The general area of Five Points was also known as the Tenderloin, itself the subject of a 1960 musical by Sheldon Harnick and Jerry Bock.

The Off Off Broadway musical *Five Points* followed the true-life story of Juba, a Black dancer who performed in the Tenderloin. Frank Rich in the *New York Times* reported that Juba was the first Black entertainer to receive billing above Whites, and that Juba combined both both Irish and African-American dancing into "lightning-fast routines that were entirely new." But despite a "spirited" production which included "sweet melodies" composed by John Braden and "exuberantly performed" challenge-dances choreographed by Keith Rozie, Rich felt the musical was one of missed opportunities. It eschewed the "grittier" aspects of Juba's life and times, and instead relied on the tried-and-true clichés of typical show-business biographies. As *Juba* (by John Braden, Laurence Holder, William Elliott, and Richard Weinstock, and directed by John Vaccaro), an earlier version of the musical had been seen Off Off Broadway at La Mama Experimental Theatre Club (ETC) on March 2, 1978. *Five Points* marked one of the earliest New York appearances by Tonya Pinkins (earlier in the season she had appeared in the original Broadway production of Stephen Sondheim's *Merrily We Roll Along*).

501 Fixed. "A Musical." THEATRE: Theatre of the Riverside Church; OPENING DATE: November 26, 1977; PERFORMANCES: 28; BOOK: Robert Maurice Riley; LYRICS: Gene Bone and Howard Fenton; additional lyrics by Langston Hughes; MUSIC: Gene Bone and Howard Fenton; DIRECTION: George Faison; CHOREOGRAPHY: George Faison; SCENERY: David Chapman; COSTUMES: Victor Capecce; LIGHTING: Chenault Spence; MUSICAL DIRECTION: Thom Edlun; PRODUCER: Theatre of the Riverside Church (Anita L. Thomas, Artistic Director)

CAST—J. Edward Adams (Randolph Moore), Miriam Burton (Molly Darby), Harold Dumont (Edward Lee Watson), Mel Grayson (The Dealer), Patricia Hayling (Gladys Brown), Ray Anthony Jones (Eddie Watson, Jr.), Urylee Leonardos (Flora Watson), Ilene Lewis (Mailou Starr), Crystal Lilly (Frankie), Stuart Mabray (Mr. McDowd), Barbara Montgomery (Barcelona Starr), Janette Moody (Minnie Buford), Gwendolyn Strand (Marie Buford), Flo Wiley (Mrs. McDowd, Violet), Margo Williams (Anne Coleman

The action occurs in Detroit, Michigan, during Christmas 1939.

The musical was presented in two acts.

ACT ONE—"Fixed" (Barbara Montgomery, Company), "Nickolodean Holiday" (Orchestra), "Why Is It I Just Don't Belong" (Ilene Lewis), "Fixed" (reprise) (Barbara Montgomery), "I'm a Lonesome Woman" (Barbara Montgomery), "Happy Tomorrow" (Janette Moody, Gwendolyn Strand), "Ballad of the Oak Tree" (Harold Dumont, Urylee Leonardos), "What I Hope For and What I Get" (Urylee Leonardos), "Preference" (Harold Dumont), "Flattery Will Get You Nowhere" (Crystal Lilly), "Not So Easy" (David Weatherspoon), "A.T.F.D." (J. Edward Adams, Beauty Parlor Clientele)

ACT TWO—"No Crystal Stair" (Miriam Burton, Company), "Madam & The Numbers Runner" (J. Edward Adams, Miriam Burton), "My Star" (Patricia Hayling, Company), "On the Heavenly Side" (Janette Moody, Margo Williams), "See Me as a Man" (Harold Dumont, Ray Anthony Jones), "Heaven" (Barbara Montgomery, Ilene Lewis, J. Edward Adams, Company), "Fixed" (reprise) (Company)

NOTES—The Off Off Broadway musical *Fixed* took place during the 1939 Christmas season in a Detroit beauty parlor, and dealt with the shop's owner and an assortment of her friends and relatives. Mel Gussow in the *New York Times* noted the story was "commonplace and derivative," but praised the score, which had "bounce and energy" and was "liltingly" played. He singled out "A.T.F.D." ("All Time Favorite Doll"), a "high-stepping" "knockout" number. Considering what the musical had going for it (a strong score, imaginative choreography, "stylish" direction, and a strong cast in "excellent" voice), Gussow noted that it was just the "banal" book of *Fixed* which needed "fixing."

The musical included seven songs based on lyrics by Langston Hughes: "Happy Tomorrow," "Ballad of the Oak Tree," "Preference," "No Crystal Stair," "Madam & the Numbers Runner," "On the Heavenly Side," and "Heaven."

502 Floyd and Clea Under the Western Sky. THEATRE: Playwrights Horizons; OPENING DATE: December 5, 2006; PERFORMANCES: 16; BOOK: David Cale; LYRICS: David Cale; MUSIC: Jonathan Kreisberg and David Cale; DIRECTION: Joe Calarco; SCENERY: David Korins; COSTUMES: Anne Kennedy; MUSICAL DIRECTION: Jonathan Kreisberg; PRODUCER: Playwrights Horizons (Tim Sanford, Artistic Director; Leslie Marcus, Managing Director; William Russo, General Manager)

CAST—David Cale (Floyd Duffner), Mary Faber (Clea Johnson)

The action occurs in the present in Lubbock, Texas, Great Falls, Montana, Austin, Texas, and Los Angeles.

The musical was presented in two acts.

ACT ONE—"burntangel@aol.com" (David Cale), "One Foot in the Real World" (David Cale), "I Dread the Night" (David Cale), "Greedy" (Mary Faber), "Safety Net" (David Cale), "I'll Be Your Secret" (Mary Faber), "Can I Stay Awhile?" (David Cale), "Linger Awhile" (David Cale), "Help's on the Way" (Mary Faber), "White Cowboy Hat" (David Cale)

ACT TWO—"A Simple Life" (David Cale), "White Cowboy Hat" (reprise) (Mary Faber), "Would You Give a Damn?" (Mary Faber), "Left Hook" (David Cale, Mary Faber), "(We're in It for) The Long Haul" (David Cale, Mary Faber)

NOTES—The two-character musical *Floyd and Clea Under the Western Sky* dealt with the apparent non-romantic relationship between two singer-songwriters. The forty-something Floyd is an alcoholic living in a Studebaker, his career on the skids; Clea, a young woman in her twenties, helps him get on his feet. Later, she find stardom, but becomes addicted to drugs. Now it's time for Floyd to help her.

Frank Scheck in the *New York Post* found the book "thin" and the central relationship never quite convincing; but he nonetheless felt there was "genuine warmth" in the evening and he liked the "tuneful, country-infused" score. Christopher Isherwood in the *New York Times* felt the book sometimes lost its way when "sweetness and sentiment" took over, but he praised the "fine" score which included "sly parodies of country-western staples." He singled out the "thumping rhythm" of "(We're in It for) The Long Haul," a "rollicking" and "quick-witted take-off" on a he-said-she-said country number.

A program note indicated the character of "Floyd" was inspired by David Cale's performance as "Studebaker" in the 2000 film *The Slaughter Rule*, written and directed by Alex and Andrew Smith.

The musical's world premiere occurred in April 2005 at the Goodman Theatre in Chicago.

503 Floyd Collins. THEATRE: Playwrights Horizons; OPENING DATE: March 3, 1996; PERFORMANCES: 25; BOOK: Tina Landau; LYRICS: Adam Guettel; additional lyrics by Tina Landau; MUSIC: Adam Guettel; DIRECTION: Tina Landau; SCENERY: James Schuette; COSTUMES: Melina Root; LIGHTING: Scott Zielinski; MUSICAL DIRECTION: Ted Sperling; PRODUCER: Playwrights Horizons (Tim Sanford, Artistic Director; Leslie Marcus, Managing Director; Lynn Landis, General Manager)

CAST—Christopher Innvar (Floyd Collins), Stephen Lee Anderson (Bee Doyle), Rudy Roberson (Ed Bishop), Jesse Lenat (Jewell Estes), Don Chastain (Lee Collins), Cass Morgan (Miss Jane), Theresa McCarthy (Nellie Collins), Jason Danieley (Homer Collins), Martin Moran (Skeets Miller), Michael Mulheren (H.T. Carmichael), Brian d'Arcy James (Cliff Roney, Reporter), Matthew Bennett (Dr. Hazlett, Reporter), James Bohanek (Reporter, Con Man)

The action occurs during the period January 30-February 16, 1925, in Barren County Kentucky, at Bee Doyle's farm.

The musical was presented in two acts.

ACT ONE—"The Ballad of Floyd Collins" (Jesse Lenat, Theresa McCarthy, Jason Danieley, Cass Morgan, Don Chastain, Martin Moran, Stephen Lee Anderson), The Call: "The Call"/"It Moves" (lyric by Adam Guettel and Tina Landau)/Time to Go (Christopher Innvar), "'Tween a Rock an' a Hard Place" (Rudy Roberson, Jesse Lenat, Stephen Lee Anderson), "Lucky" (Theresa McCarthy, Cass Morgan), "Daybreak" (lyric by Adam Guettel and Tina Landau) (Jason Danieley, Christopher Innvar), "I Landed on Him" (lyric by Adam Guettel and Tina Landau) (Martin Moran), "Blue Eyes" (Christopher Innvar), "Heart an' Hand" (Cass Morgan, Don Chastain), "The Riddle Song" (lyric by Adam Guettel and Tina Landau) (Jason Danieley, Christopher Innvar)

ACT TWO—"Is That Remarkable?" (Company [except Christopher Innvar), "The Carnival" (Company), "Through the Mountain" (Theresa McCarthy), "Git Comfortable" (Jason Danieley), "Floyd" (Christopher Innvar), "The Dream" (Company) "How Glory Goes" (Christopher Innvar)

NOTES—*Floyd Collins* told the true story of a Kentucky cave explorer who became hopelessly trapped in the passageway of a cave 150 feet underground. For three weeks his plight turned into a media circus when reporters, barkers, and others exploited his tragedy; when the rescuers finally reached him, he had been dead for three days.

With its richly melodic score and memorable lyrics by Adam Guittel (the son of Mary Rodgers and the grandson of Richard Rodgers) and Tina Landau, *Floyd Collins* was one of the finest lyric works seen in New York during the past forty years; its only equals were the original production of *Candide* (1956; see entry for the 1973 revival), *Follies* (1971), and *The Voyage* (1992; see entry). *Floyd Collins* told a compelling and dramatic story; it was brilliantly directed and performed; and accompanying it was one of the greatest scores in the history of American musical theatre. (And perhaps *Meet John Doe*, with lyrics by Eddie Sugarman and music by Andrew Gerle, is the most exciting and original theatre score since *Floyd Collins*; based on Frank Capra's classic 1941 film, the musical as of this writing hasn't enjoyed a full-fledged New York production, although it was produced in concert format for one performance in 2004 at the New York Theatre Music Festival.)

As John Simon has noted, the score of *Floyd Collins* was composed in three distinct "movements"; most of the establishing first-act songs were written in what might be termed Broadway bluegrass ("The Ballad of Floyd Collins," "Lucky," "Heart an' Hand," "The Riddle Song"); once the outside world of the media begins to exploit the tragedy, Guittel offered the witty, old-time Broadway pizzazz of "Isn't That Remarkable?"; and, finally, when Floyd Collins realizes that only death will release him from the cave, the music reached an elegiac purity of heart-breaking intensity ("How Glory Goes").

The score was beautifully preserved in a lavish recording by Nonesuch Records (CD # 79434-2), and the script was included in the anthology *The New American Musical* (edited by Wiley Hausam) which was published by the Theatre Communications Group in 2003. "How Glory Goes" was later recorded by Audra McDonald and served as the title of her collection of theatre and film music (Nonesuch Records [CD # 79580-2).

The published script omitted "'Tween a Rock an' a Hard Place" ("Where a Man Belongs" was substituted). *Floyd Collins* was first seen at the 1994 American Music Theatre Festival in Philadelphia where it premiered on April 13; the production included some cast members (Jason Danieley, Theresa McCarthy, Stephen Lee Anderson, Nick Plakias) who appeared in the New York premiere two years later (for the Philadelphia world premiere, the title role was performed by Jim Morlino and the role of Miss Jane by Mary Beth Peil).

504 Fly Blackbird. THEATRE: Mayfair Theatre; OPENING DATE: February 5, 1962; PERFORMANCES: 127; BOOK: C. Jackson and James Hatch; LYRICS: C. Jackson and James Hatch; MUSIC: C. Jackson and James Hatch; DIRECTION: Jerome Eskow; CHOREOGRAPHY: Talley Beatty; SCENERY: Robert Soule; COSTUMES: Robby Campbell; LIGHTING: Jules Fisher; MUSICAL DIRECTION: Gershon Kingsley; PRODUCER: Helen Jacobson

CAST—Avon Long (William Piper), Elwood Smith (Police Officer Jonsen), Paul Reid Roman (Lodge Member, Paul), Gilbert Price (Lodge Member, Roger), Jack Crowder (Lodge Member, Paul), Jim Bailey (Lodge Member, Lou), William Sugihara (Lodge Member, George), Robert Guillaume (Carl), Mary Louise (Josie), Thelma Oliver (Susie), Chele Abel (Gladys), Micki Grant (Camille), Gail Ziferstein (Gail), Glory Van Scott (Big Betty), Michael Kermoyan (Mr. Crocker), Helon Blount (Police Matron Jonsen)

The action occurs in New York City at the present time.

The musical was presented in two acts.

ACT ONE—"Everything Comes to Those Who Wait" (Avon Long, Paul Reid Roman, Gilbert Price, Jack Crowder, Jim Bailey, William Sugihara), "Now" (Students), "Big Betty's Song" (Glory Van Scott, Students), "I'm Sick of the Whole Damn Problem" (Michael Kermoyan, Avon Long), "Who's the Fool?" (Avon Long), "Right Way" (Avon Long), "Couldn't We" (Mary Louise, Robert Guillaume), "The Housing Cha-Cha" (Students), "Natchitoches, Louisiana" (Helon Blount, Elwood Smith), "Fly Blackbird" (Thelma Oliver, Students), "The Gong Song" (Thelma Oliver, Glory Van Scott, William Sugihara), "Rivers to the South" (Robert Guillaume, Jack Crowder, Students)

ACT TWO—"Lilac Tree" (Mary Louise, Robert Guillaume, Students), "Twilight Zone" (Helon Blount, Elwood Smith), "The Love Elixir" (Troupe), "Mister Boy" (Michael Kermoyan, Jack Crowder, Troupe), "Old White Tom" (Robert Guillaume, Troupe), "Natchitoches, Louisiana" (reprise) (Helon Blount, Elwood Smith), "Who's the Fool?" (reprise) (Avon Long), "Wake Up" (Robert Guillaume, Mary Louise, Company)

NOTES—*Fly Blackbird* is an historical musical, the first one on Broadway or off, to use the struggle for civil rights as the core of its plot. The story dealt with a group of students (Black, White, Chinese) who plan to travel South to join other civil rights groups in their demand for equal rights. (At one point, the students are arrested in Washington Square, and when they're booked at a police station, each one gives "Blackbird" as his or her last name.)

Milton Esterow in the *New York Times* found the work "provocative and exhilarating," and noted that even with a few minor flaws the musical had "warmth, humor and wit." He mentioned one bit of dialogue in which a Black says the hour is 2:00 C.T. and goes on to explain, "That's colored time. We're just a little bit behind everybody else." Esterow also singled out a dream sequence in which a White prison matron dreams of a snake-oil salesman who peddles an elixir which can put Blacks in their "proper" place; for this sequence, a Black (Robert Guillaume) who drinks the elixir is thus transformed into a racial stereotype who, in straw hat and oversized bow tie, goes down on one knee and sings "Old White Tom."

The musical had an interesting cast, from veteran Avon Long, who had been in musicals since the 1930s and who would continue performing well into the 1970s with a final starring role in the long-running *Bubbling Black Sugar* (1975; see entry for the Off Off Broadway production), to newcomer Micki Grant, who later wrote and starred in her own Off Broadway musical, the long-running *Dont Bother Me I Cant Cope* (1972; see entry). Gilbert Price, Jack Crowder, and Michael Kermoyan would have brief but memorable moments in other musicals, and Robert Guillaume would find his greatest success in television.

The cast recording was released by Mercury Records (LP # OCS-6206). There had been an earlier (1961) production of the musical in Los Angeles, and it was recorded on Imaginate Records (LP # V-13786).

505 Fly with Me. THEATRE: McMillin Theatre/Columbia University; OPENING DATE: April 22, 1980; PERFORMANCES: 6; BOOK: Milton Kroopf and Phillip Leavitt; adapted by Michael Numark; LYRICS: Lorenz Hart; additional lyrics by Oscar Hammerstein II and Richard Rodgers; MUSIC: Richard Rodgers; DIRECTION: Clint Atkinson; Sonya Baevsky, Assistant Director; CHOREOGRAPHY: Dennis Dennehy; Jim Clark, Assistant Choreographer; SCENERY: Phyllis Carlin; COSTUMES: Susan Leaming; LIGHTING: Mark Weingartner; MUSICAL DIRECTION: Howard Shanet; PRODUCER: Columbia University's Center for Theatre Studies; produced for Columbia University by Andrew B. Harris

CAST—Avi Simon (Professor), Marci Pliskin (Mrs. Houghton), Cheryl Suzanne Horowitz (Emmy), Daniel Frank (Jimmy), Steven Katz (Ming Boy), Annie Laurita (Tsu Tsan), Rod McLucas (Andre), Joshua Worby (Harvey; at alternate performances, the role was performed by Steven Arenson), Johanna Melamed (Ethel), Francis Larson (Mr. Larrimore), Joseph Kissane (Dean); Students of the University (Jeffrey Benson, Jackie Bernard, Mark A. Berti, Simone Couture, Helene Anne Fluhr, Ruth Goodman, Robert Greenwald, Ginny Grunfeld, Jon Hutcheson, Kelly Ivie, Lisa Kaplan, John C. Liderbach, Betty Liu, Diana Lustgarten, Nancy Maras, Steve Miller, Tara Munjee, Erika Pardes, Peggy Sullivan, Amanda Werth, Roxana Xenia-Ortiz); the Columbia University Orchestra; and members of the Columbia football team

The action occurs in 1970 at Futuristic College, Bolsheviki U., on an island ruled by the Soviets.

The musical was presented in two acts.

ACT ONE—Overture (Orchestra), Opening Chorus ("Gone Are the Days") (Avi Simon, Students), "A Penny for Your Thoughts" (Cheryl Suzanne Horowitz, Daniel Frank), "Another Melody in F" (Marci Pliskin, Chorus), "Working for the Government" (Avi Simon, Rod McLucas, Joshua Worby, Steven Katz), "Inspiration (The Futurist Love Song)" (Marci Pliskin, Cheryl Suzanne Horowitz, Johanna Melamed, Daniel Frank, Joshua Worby, Rod McLucas, Chorus), "Don't Love Me Like Othello" (Marci Pliskin, Francis Larson), "Dreaming True" (Cheryl Suzanne Horowitz, Daniel Frank), "Peek in Pekin'" (Steven Katz, Annie Laurita), "A College on Broadway" (Daniel Frank, Chorus), Finale ("Call Me Andre") (Ensemble)

ACT TWO—"Moonlight and You" (Daniel Frank, Chorus), "Always Room for One More" (lyric by Oscar Hammerstein II) (Daniel Frank, Chorus), "Peek in Pekin'" (reprise) (Steven Katz, Annie Laurita), "If You Were You" (David Frank, Cheryl Suzanne Horowitz), "Kid, I Love You" (Joshua Worby, Johanna Melamed), "The Third Degree of Love" (Francis Larson, Girls), "Gunga Dhin" (Rod McLucas, Chorus), "Twinkling Eyes" (lyric by Richard Rodgers) (Annie Laurita), Finale (Ensemble)

NOTES—*Fly with Me*, Columbia University's 1920 varsity show, played at the Astor Hotel's Grand Ballroom for four days beginning on March 24, 1920. It was the second collaboration between Richard Rodgers and Lorenz Hart (their musical *You'd Be Surprised* had opened earlier in the year); later that year, they were heard on Broadway for the first time in the musical *Poor Little Ritz Girl*, and their legendary partnership lasted until 1943, when Hart died within a week of the opening of their final collaboration, a revised version of their 1927 Broadway hit *A Connecticut Yankee*. *Fly with Me* also included two songs with lyrics by Oscar Hammerstein II, who in 1943 became Rodgers' collaborator with *Oklahoma!*; their partnership lasted until 1960, when Hammerstein died. Their final collaboration was *The Sound of Music* (1959).

Columbia University presented its revival of *Fly with Me* almost sixty years to the day of the original's premiere. The 1920 musical took place in the future, in 1970, on a Soviet-run island off the coast of the United States. Russian politics threaten to separate two young lovers, but all ends well when the hero and heroine not only marry but also see the Soviet empire overturned by the force of romantic love.

The revival was scheduled to be recorded by New World Records, but was instead recorded by Original Cast Records (LP # OC-8023). The script was published by the Dramatic Publishing Company in 1980.

The revival didn't include "Weaknesses," which had been heard in the original production and was one of the two songs in the score with lyrics by Hammerstein.

Eleven years after the opening of *Fly with Me*, Oscar Hammerstein II was associated with another musical which dealt with young people and Communism. *Free for All* dealt with a group of college students who decide to test socialist theories; it opened at the Manhattan Theatre on September 8, 1931, and played for just fifteen performances. One of its leads was Don Tomkins, who in 1927 was one of the performers who introduced the "Varsity Drag" in *Good News*; some thirty-five years later, he was back on Broadway in another show-stopping routine when he and Lucille Ball cavorted through "What Takes My Fancy" in *Wildcat* (1960).

506 Follies Burlesque '67. THEATRE: Players Theatre; OPENING DATE: May 3, 1967; PERFORMANCES: 16; BOOK: Stanley Richman; LYRICS: Stanley Richman; MUSIC: Sol Richman; DIRECTION: Dick Richards; CHOREOGRAPHY: Paul Morokoff; COSTUMES: S. Binder; LIGHTING: Ricardo; PRODUCERS: Richman-Maurer-Richards

CAST—Libby Jones, Mickey Hargitay, Claude Mathis, Count Gregory, Joe Tempo, Cathy Collins, Bill Drew, Frank Silvano, Julie Taylor, Toni Karrol, and Les Belles de Paree

The action occurs in Paris.

The musical was presented in two acts.

ACT ONE—"Burlesque Is a Stamping Ground" (Company), "Parisian Street Scene"/"Oooh Lah Lah" (Company), "The Title" (Count Gregory, Frank Silvano, Libby Jones), "Exotic" (Julie Taylor), "The Transformer" (Cathy Collins, Mickey Hargitay, Claude Mathis, Libby Jones), "Exotic Dance Team" (Toni Karrol, Dick Richards), "Comedy in Stripping" (Cathy Collins), "The Stand-In" (Mickey Hargitay, Frank Silvano, Bill Drew), "Scratch-My-Back" (Cathy Collins, Girls)

ACT TWO—"The Rabbit Habit" (Cathy Collins, Joe Tempo, Girls), "The More I Hold You" (Frank Silvano), "Buono Notte" (Frank Silvano), "Tappin' In" (Bill Drew), "Tell Me" (Libby Jones), "Exotic" (reprise) (Julie Taylor), "The Spiritual" (Frank Silvano, Girls), "Crazy House" (Claude Mathis, Mickey Hargitay, Cathy Collins, Girls), "Libby" (Libby Jones), Finale (Company)

NOTES—Ann Corio hit the jackpot with her long-running (in New York and on tour) burlesque revue *This Was Burlesque*, and her success inspired a number of Off Broadway imitators, most if not all of which lost money (see Appendix J for a list of the burlesque musicals discussed in this book).

What distinguished *Follies Burlesque '67* from others of its ilk was that it presented burlesque and revue numbers in the format of a book show (in this case, burlesque types visiting Paris). But it closed quickly anyway, after playing just two weeks during the first half of May. The producers announced the revue would reopen at the Bert Wheeler Theatre on June 2, but the production (which was to have included two new cast members, Linda Terry and Erin Adair) was cancelled prior to giving any performances there.

However, in Fall 1968 the musical resurfaced on tour as *Follies Burlesque '69*, starring Denise Darcel and Mickey Hargitay as well as Count Gregory (who, along with Hargitay, had appeared in the Off Broadway production). For the touring version, the book was jettisoned and the revival was billed as "A Musical Extravaganza Glorifying Burlesque." At least five numbers were retained for the revival ("Exotic," "Scratch-My-Back," "The Rabbit Habit," "The Spiritual," and "Crazy House") and one, "Burlesque Is a Place to Learn the Ropes," may have been a revised version of "Burlesque Is a Stamping Ground."

507 The Follies of 1910. "A Nostalgic Musical Extravaganza." THEATRE: Carnegie Hall Playhouse; OPENING DATE: January 14, 1960 (NOTE: Program indicates opening date was January 14 as does both an article and a review in the *New York Times*; other sources indicate the opening was on January 12.); PERFORMANCES: 14; SKETCHES: Albert Moritz; additional material and dialogue by Francis Swann; LYRICS: Albert Moritz; MUSIC: Albert Moritz; additional music by Joseph Liebman and Don Isenman; DIRECTION: Saul Swimmer; CHOREOGRAPHY: Jim Russell; SCENERY: Leo Meyer; COSTUMES: Jerry Boxhorn; MUSICAL DIRECTION: Don Isenman; PRODUCERS: Ken Williams in association with Gayle-Swimmer-Anthony

CAST—JUNE L. WALKER (Vinnie Peters, Princess, Miss Eva Lillianora, Heloise, Clara Dipping), DOUG ROGERS (Bub Frazingo, Paul De Wolfe, Captain, Phil Strong, Abelard, George Spelvin), LIZ WILLIAMS (Gigi D'Or, Gypsy, Carla Dipping), JOAN DAVENPORT (Trilby Frazingo, Cordelia Lotus Skinder, A Radical, Mama Robinson), ALBERT MORITZ (The Great Frustro, Papa Robinson, Don Hart), SUSAN WATSON (Little Ellie Tanglewood, Elsie Robinson, Bar Customer), Tommy Finnan III (Buz Frazingo, Escort of Gigi D'Or, Assistant to Cordelia Lotus Skinder, Sailor, First Peasant, Escort of Miss Eva Lillianora, Bar Customer), Joanne Leeman (Assistant to The Great Frustro, Chinese Girl, Hildie Robinson, Second Peasant), Michael Fesco (Bud Frazingo, Escort of Gigi D'Or, An Inebriate, Kurt Robinson, Escort of Miss Eva Lillianora, Bartender), Rhoda Levine (Chinese Girl, Lisa Robinson), Don Price (Escort of Gigi D'Or, Sailor, Escort of Miss Eva Lillianora), Jack Finnegan (Escort of Gigi D'Or, A Radical, Prince, Escort of Miss Eva Lillianora, Policeman), Nan Courtney (Assistant to The Great Frustro, A Radical, Bessie Robinson, Bar Customer), Manuel J. Fernandez (An Inebriate, Bar Customer), KATHY BARR (Miss Virginia Tanglewood, The Girl in the Dressing Gown, Miss Clara Throgg), Ken Williams (The Entrepreneur), Kay Reid (Card Girl) The revue was presented in two acts.

ACT ONE—Overture ("A selection of the latest popular melodies which will be heard in this programme"), 1. The Entrepreneur (Ken Williams, Kay Reid) 2. The Great Frustro (Albert Moritz, Joanne Leeman, Nan Courtney), 3. Miss Virginia Tanglewood, Little Ellie Tanglewood:, "Touch'd by Romance" (Kathy Barr), "Oh, Brother" (Susan Watson), "Diamond Jubilee" (Kathy Barr, Susan Watson; danced by Michael Fesco, Don Price, Tommy Finnan III, Manuel J. Fernandez, Jack Finnegan, Rhoda Levine, Nan Courtney, Joanne Leeman), 4. The Five Flying Frazingos (Michael Fesco, Tommy Finnan III, Doug Rogers, Joan Davenport) 5. La Belle Gigi D'Or and Her Escorts: "Paree" (Michael Fesco, Tommy Finnan III, Jack Finnegan, Don Price), "Boule, Boulevard" (Liz Williams), "The Kremlin Krawl" (Liz Williams, Michael Fesco, Don Price), 6. Tragedienne-Pantomimiste Cordelia Lotus Skinder (Joan Davenport, Tommy Finnan III), 7. Vinnie Peters and Paul De Wolfe, Songs, Dances and Patter:, "D*I*X*I*E" (June L. Walker, Paul De Wolfe), "Ivy Covered Cottage" (June L. Walker, Paul De Wolfe), "Third Avenue" (June L. Walker, Paul De Wolfe), 8. The Girl in the Dressing Gown (Kathy Barr):, "Gone on That Guy," 9. The Swiss Robinson Family, Angelic Voices Too Sweet for Words:, "Climb That Mountain" (Albert Moritz, Joan Davenport, Susan Watson, Joanne Leeman, Nan Courtney, Rhoda Levine, Michael Fesco), "Flower Scent Song" (Michael Fesco), "The Easter Bunny Polka" (Albert Moritz, Joan Davenport, Susan Watson, Joanne Leeman, Nan Courtney, Rhoda Levine, Michael Fesco), 10. The San Quentin Opera Company Presents the 5000th Performance of *Through the Red Mill with Rose Marie* by Herbert Victor:, "Tomorrow" (Liz Williams), "Calcamania" (Soldiers [performers not credited]), "Drinking Song" (Company), "Fiesta" (Company), "Love, Love, Oh See Now" (June L. Walker)

ACT TWO—11. Phil Strong & Don Hart, The Broadway Boys, Including "The Seaside Spectacle": "Hello, Hello" (Doug Rogers, Albert Moritz), "Down by the Sea Shore" (The Company of "The Seaside Spectacle" [performers not credited]), "Cool Cape May" (Doug Rogers, Albert Moritz), 12. Miss Eva Lillianora:, "Someday There'll Be Some One Up There with the Man in the Moon" (June L. Walker), 13. The "Ben Hur" Spectacle/The Chariot Race: "Sunshine" (June L. Walker, Doug Rogers), 14. Miss Clara Throgg:, "Pacific Street" (Kathy Barr), 15. The Dipping Sisters:, "Together" (June L. Walker, Liz Williams), 16. George Spelvin:, "The New Soft Shoe" (Doug Rogers), 17. Grand Finale: Fourth of July in Cape May:, "There's a Grand Flag Flyin'" (Company), "I'm the Boy Who Owns the Lights on Broadway" (The Man [performer not credited]), 18. Finale (reprises) ("A summary and happy recollection of some of the foot-tapping melodies heard in *The Follies of 1910* for your homeward-bound pleasure")

NOTES—*The Follies of 1910*, a nostalgic spoof of old-time vaudeville-styled entertainments, was supposedly an actual revue being produced at the Cape May Opera House in 1910. Even the large, almost poster-sized program for the show was fringed with advertisements, similar to ads placed on the prosceniums of vaudeville stages to hawk the products of various advertisers. Louis Calta in the *New York Times* noted that Off Broadway seemed to be in the midst of a trend of nostalgic musicals and revues which looked to the past for their inspiration (*Little Mary Sunshine* had opened two months before, and the long-running revival of *The Boy Friend* had just closed). But Calta felt *The Follies of 1910* was a "weak parody of yesteryear," and said the evening was "a bit too precocious and rehearsed." Further, the revue was too "sprawling," and therefore it lacked a "humorous point of view."

And Calta wondered what the sketch "The Swiss Family Robinson" was doing in the show since it came closer to lampooning *The Sound of Music* (which had opened on Broadway two months earlier) than anything seen on the old two-a-day circuit. "The Swiss Family Robinson" was in fact the first of two spoofs of *The Sound of Music* seen in New York during the 1959-1960 season; the Broadway revue *From A to Z*, which premiered three months after *The Follies of 1910* opened, offered "The Sound of Schmaltz" and the Klaptrap Family. (*From A to Z* was gone in less than three weeks, but is notable for the Broadway debuts of a number of talents [Woody Allen, Jerry Herman, and Fred Ebb].)

Calta felt the parody "Through the Red Mill with Rose Marie" was more in keeping with the revue's period, and he also singled out such songs as "Ivy Covered Cottage," "Third Avenue," and "Someday There'll Be Someone Up There with the Man in the Moon."

Calta also found time to praise cast member Kathy Barr, who had injured her elbow prior to the opening; but "in the true tradition of the theatre," she performed with one arm in a sling. The revue closed within two weeks, but Susan Watson soon distinguished herself in Broadway musicals. She had created the role of The Girl (Luisa) in the pre-Off Broadway version of Tom Jones and Harvey Schmidt's *The Fantasticks* in 1959 (see entry for the 1960 Off Broadway production), and later recreated her role for the 1964 television adaptation. And just months after appearing in *The Follies of 1910*, she created the role of Kim in the original Broadway production of *Bye Bye Birdie*; she also appeared in *Ben Franklin in Paris* (1964), *A Joyful Noise* (1966), Jones and Schmidt's *Celebration* (1969), and performed the title role in the 1971 long-running hit revival of *No, No, Nanette*. In 2008, *Earthly Paradise*, her collection of songs by Jones and Schmidt, was released on CD.

508 The Food of Love.

NOTES—See entry for *Central Park*.

509 For Love or Money. "A Musical Entertainment." THEATRE: Circle Repertory Company Theatre; OPENING DATE: March 29, 1977; PERFORMANCES: 9; LYRICS: Jay Jeffries; MUSIC: Jason McAuliffe; DIRECTION: Susan Lehman; CHOREOGRAPHY: Kathie Kallaghan; SCENERY (AND COSTUMES?): Michael Massee; MUSICAL DIRECTION: Daniel Glosser; PRODUCER: Circle Repertory Company Projects in Progress (Marshall W. Mason, Artistic Director; Steven Gomer, Program Director)

CAST—Kate Kelly, Ken Kimmons, Sharon Madden, Jason McAuliffe

The revue was presented in one act (song assignments unknown).

MUSICAL NUMBERS—"Other Alternatives," "Geography," "That Happy Melody," "Brief Encounter," "Confessional," "Where Have I Been All My Life?," "Snap Decision," "Taboo or Not Taboo," "Counterpoint," "Mamma's Cooking," "Living Love"

NOTES—The revue *For Love or Money* was produced under an Off Off Broadway contract. "Where Have I Been All My Life?" was later heard in the 1983 revue *London Days and New York Nights* (see entry).

510 For the Snark Was a Boojum, You See. "A Musical Play." THEATRE: The Nat Horne Musical Theatre; OPENING DATE: August 20, 1977; PERFORMANCES: Unknown; BOOK: Jeff Duteil; LYRICS: Jeff Duteil and Lewis B. Carroll; MUSIC: Stan Smith; DIRECTION: Ron Wachholtz; CHOREOGRAPHY: Peter Westerhoff; SCENERY: Rockland Mers; COSTUMES: Becky Wachholtz and Lori Leeka; LIGHTING: Rockland Mers; MUSICAL DIRECTION: Carter Leeka and Scott Smith; PRODUCER: Ron Wachholtz

CAST—Becky Wachholtz (White Rabbit), Greg Howard (Mad Hatter), Heidi Anderson (Cheshire Cat), Carter Leeka (John Tenniel), Chuck Schallenberg (Lewis B. Carroll [The Rev. Charles Lutwidge Dodson]), Ed Havlovic (Christopher Pidgeon), Shelley Myers (Agnes Raikes, Ruth), Karen Bailey (Miss Williams, Pub Patron), Rockland Mers (Father, Barkeep), Margie Hamm (Queen of Hearts, Pub Patron), Denise LaCroix (Mrs. Liddell), Bob Phillips (Dean Liddell), Jerry Dale Widholm (Bishop Wilberforce), Katie Higgins (Ellen Terry), Joyce Bolton (Duchess), George Pausel (King of Hearts), David Brandt (The Reverend Drake, Edward Godwin), Robin Edwards (The Reverend Hartlage, Robert, Pub Patron), Mike Nemec (Alfred Lord Tennyson, Pub Patron), Bob Wilson (Hallam Tennyson), Nancy Wagner (Mrs. Drake, Pub Patron), Joni Skelton (Alice Liddell), Jill Hoel (Laura), Lori Leeka (Pub Patron, Delivery Girl), Sherri Schallenberg (Caterpillar)

The action occurs during the spring, around 1871, in Oxford, England.

The musical was presented in two acts.

ACT ONE—Overture (Orchestra), "Mr. Tenniel, Reverend Dodgson, Lewis Carroll" (Wonderland Characters, Carter Leeka, Chuck Schallenberg), "Wonderland" (Chuck Schallenberg, Shelley Myers), "Wonderland Theme" (Orchestra), "Tarts" (lyric by Lewis B. Carroll) (Becky Wachholtz), "The Woman in Me" (Katie Higgins), "A Friendly Little Game"/ "Gossip" (Wonderland Characters, Company), "Behave" (lyric by Lewis B. Carroll) (Chuck Schallenberg), "I Want Real" (Katie Higgins), "Two People" (Chuck Schallenberg)

ACT TWO—"Wonderland March" (Orchestra), "Tarts" (reprise) (Wonderland Characters), "Mr. Tenniel, Reverend Dodgson" (reprise) (Chuck Schallenberg, Carter Leeka), "Matilda Jane" (lyric by Lewis B. Carroll) (Chuck Schallenberg, Katie Higgins, Ed Havlovic), "Home from the Sea" (Joni Skelton), "I Want Real" (reprise) (Katie Higgins), "Waking Up Alone" (Chuck Schallenberg, Joel Hoel, Ed Havlovic, Company), "The Children, They Grow Up" (Chuck Schallenberg), "Mr. Tenniel" (reprise) (Chuck Schallenberg), "Dedication" (lyric by Lewis B. Carroll) (Chuck Schallenberg), "Wonderland Theme" (Orchestra)

NOTES—The musical *For the Snark Was a Boojum, You See*, was first presented by the Nettle Creek Players, Inc., a theatre group located in Indiana; the Off Off Broadway production played for a limited engagement.

Although some of the characters in the musical were from Lewis B. Carroll's 1865 novel *Alice's Adventures in Wonderland*, the musical itself wasn't an adaptation of Carroll's masterpiece; it was instead a musical about events and people in his life.

For a list of *Alice* adaptations both on Broadway and off, see entry for *Alice with Kisses* as well as Appendix K.

511 Forbidden Broadway. THEATRE: Palsson's Supper Club; OPENING DATE: May 4, 1982; PERFORMANCES: 2,332; CONCEPT AND PARODY LYRICS: Gerard Alessandrini; DIRECTION: Jeff Martin; LIGHTING: Steven Adler; PRODUCER: Playkill Productions, Inc.; MUSICAL DIRECTION: Fred Barton

CAST—Gerard Alessandrini, Fred Barton, Bill Carmichael, Nora Mae Lyng, Chloe Webb

The revue was presented in one act.

MUSICAL NUMBERS—"I'm Glad I Don't Act Anymore" (music by Frederick Loewe) (Gerard Alessandrini, Nora Mae Lyng), "Forbidden Broadway" (Company), "I Want to See It" (music by Marvin Hamlisch) (Wendee Winters), "You Must See Evita" (music by Andrew Lloyd Webber) (Gerard Alessandrini), "Woman of the Year" (music by John Kander) (Nora Mae Lyng), "Almost Like 1948" (music by Frederick Loewe) (Gerard Alessandrini, Nora Mae Lyng), "You Really Should See Amadeus" (music by Wolfgang Amadeus Mozart [?]) (Bill Carmichael), "How About You?" (music by Burton Lane) (Gerard Alessandrini, Chloe Webb), "Has Anyone Here Seen Patti?" (music by Andrew Lloyd Webber) (Gerard Alessandrini), "Don't Cry for Me, Barbra Streisand" (music by Andrew Lloyd Webber) (Nora Mae Lyng), "It Is a Glorious Thing to Be Kevin Kline" (music by Arthur Sullivan) (Gerard Alessandrini), "Oh There Is Not One Maiden Fair Who Does Not Flutter at My Beauty" (music by Arthur Sullivan) (Bill Carmichael, after Rex Smith), "Poor Warbling Star" (music by Arthur Sullivan) (Nora Mae Lyng), "There Are Worse Shows I Could Do" (music by Jim Jacobs and Warren Casey), (Chloe Webb), "Sets" (music by Harry Warren) (Gerard Alessandrini), "I'll Learn a New Song Tomorrow" (music by Charles Strouse) (Chloe Webb), "Kids Are the Only Ones Who Get Work Today" (music by Charles Strouse and Marvin Hamlisch) (Company), "Too Many Sondheims" (music by Stephen Sondheim) (Fred Barton), Merman-Martin Medley: "Everything's Coming Up Merman" (music by Jule Styne) (Nora Mae Lyng), "A Cockeyed Vocalist" (music by Richard Rodgers) (Chloe Webb), "An Old-Fashioned Ballad" (music by Irving Berlin) (Nora Mae Lyng, Chloe Webb) "I've Grown Accustomed to This Show" (music by Frederick Loewe) (Gerard Alessandrini), "I'm One of the Girls Who Sings Like a Boy" (music by John Kander) (Nora Mae Lyng), "I'm Jim Dale" (music by Cy Coleman) (Bill Carmichael), "I'm Entertainment" (music by Arthur Schwartz) (Chloe Webb, after Ann Miller), "Do I Shave?" (music by Richard Rodgers) (Gerard Alessandrini), "Casting Director, Casting Director, Give Me a Part" (music by Jerry Bock) (Chloe Webb, Nora Mae Lyng, Bill Carmichael), "Ambition" (music by Jerry Bock) (Gerard Alessandrini, Company), Sondheim Encore: "Waiting Around for the Sondheim Show" (music by Stephen Sondheim) (Company), Finale: "Forbidden Broadway" (Company)

NOTES—*Forbidden Broadway*, a mad-cap send-up of current Broadway hits and performer, has become as synonymous with Off Broadway as *The Fantasticks* (see entry). In one form or another, the revue has been around for over a quarter-century, and even when it disappears for a season or two, it always resurfaces in a new edition. Long may it reign!

For the revue's material, Gerard Alessandrini rewrote the lyrics of songs from recent Broadway shows, and his new lyrics spoofed the latest shows and performers. The composers always cooperated by allowing Alessandrini to use their music, and Broadway celebrities enjoyed being the targets of Alessandrini's arrows; in fact, being spoofed in an edition of *Forbidden Broadway* was almost as good as having your caricature on Sardi's wall or your likeness drawn by Hirschfeld.

The original edition of *Forbidden Broadway* opened at Palsson's on January 15, 1982, as an Off Off Broadway production, and on May 4, the revue, still at Palsson's, became an official Off Broadway production. During its original run (1982-1987), the revue introduced updated material, and ran for a total of 2,332 performances. During the Off Off Broadway run, playgoers received their very own "Forbidden Playbill." Later, during the regular Off Broadway run, they got an edition of "Playkill."

A "West End Edition" of the revue was seen in London at the Fortune Theatre on March 2, 1989.

The first cast album was released by DRG Records in 1984 (LP # SBL-12585). As new editions opened, DRG released seven more cast albums: *Forbidden Broadway Volume 2* (CD # 12599), *Forbidden Broadway Volume 3* (CD # 12609), *Forbidden Broadway Strikes Back!* (CD # 12614), *Forbidden Broadway Cleans Up Its Act!* (CD # 12616), *Forbidden Broadway 2001: A Spoof Odyssey* (CD # 12627), *Forbidden Broadway Special Victims Unit* (CD # 12629), and *Forbidden Broadway: Rude Awakening* (CD # 12632). A recording of *Forbidden Hollywood* was released by Varese Sarabande Records (CD # VSD-5669). After the original 1982-1987 run of 2,332 performances (which included new editions in 1983, 1985, 1986, and 1987), the following new editions of the revue opened: *Forbidden Broadway 1988* (September 15, 1988; 534 performances; during the run the title was changed to *Forbidden Broadway 1989*); *Forbidden Broadway 1990* (January 23, 1990; 576); *Forbidden Broadway 1991½* (June 20, 1991; 237; during the run a special *Forbidden Christmas* was presented for 56 performances from November 19, 1991, to January 5, 1992); *Forbidden Broadway 1992* (April 6, 1992; 304; during part of the run the revue's title was changed to *The Best of Forbidden Broadway—10th Anniversary Edition*); *Forbidden Broadway 1993* (January 12, 1993; 288; between *Forbidden Broadway 1992* and *Forbidden Broadway 1993*, a special *Forbidden Broadway Featuring Forbidden Christmas* was presented from December 1—27, 1992); *Forbidden Broadway 1994* (November 11, 1993; 62); *Forbidden Broadway Strikes Back!* (October 17, 1996; 850); *Forbidden Broadway Cleans Up Its Act!* (November 17, 1998; 754); *Forbidden Broadway 2001: A Spoof Odyssey* (November 18, 2000; 552); *Forbidden Broadway: 20th Anniversary Celebration* (February 25, 2002; 983); *Forbidden Broadway Summer Shock!* (July 5, 2004; 83); *Forbidden Broadway: Special Victims Unit* (December 16, 2004; 816); *Forbidden Broadway: The Roast of Utopia* (June 13, 2007; 85 performances [estimated]); and *Forbidden Broadway: Rude Awakening* (September 23, 2007; still playing as of December 31, 2007). *Forbidden Hollywood* was originally produced in California, and opened Off Broadway on March 10, 1996, for 225 performances. Also see Appendix S for a complete list of the *Forbidden Broadway* entries. In 2009, *Forbidden Broadway: Behind the Mylar Curtain* was published by Applause Books; the book by Gerard Alessandrini (with Michael Portantiere) covered the history of the *Forbidden Broadway* series (and includes over 100 forbidden parody lyrics!).

512 Forbidden Broadway 1988. THEATRE: Theatre East; OPENING DATE: September 15, 1988; PERFORMANCES: 534; CONCEPT AND PARODY LYRICS: Gerard Alessandrini; DIRECTION: Gerard Alessandrini; CHOREOGRAPHY: Roxie Lucas; COSTUMES: Erika Dyson; PRODUCERS: Jonathan Sherer; Arthur B. Brown and Chip Quigley, Associate Producers

CAST—Toni DiBuono, Philip Fortenberry, Roxie Lucas, David B. McDonald, Michael McGrath

NOTES—The original production of *Forbidden Broadway* enjoyed a marathon run of 2,332 performances (during the run, revised versions of the revue were introduced on October 27, 1983, January 29, 1985, June 11, 1986, and June 26, 1987). With *Forbidden Broadway 1988*, the revue returned with a completely new edition (during the run, the title was changed to *Forbidden Broadway 1989*).

The revue included three songs with lyrics and music by Gerard Alessandrini ("Forbidden Broadway

88," "Who Do They Know?," and "The Phantom of the Musical").

For a list of all *Forbidden Broadway* series, see entry for original 1982 production; also see Appendix S for a complete list of the *Forbidden Broadway* editions.

513 Forbidden Broadway 1990. THEATRE: Theatre East; OPENING DATE: January 23, 1990; PERFORMANCES: 576; CONCEPT AND PARODY LYRICS: Gerard Alessandrini; DIRECTION: Gerard Alessandrini; COSTUMES: Erika Dyson; PRODUCER: Jonathan Scharer; Chip Quigley, Associate Producer

CAST—Susanne Blakeslee. Philip Fortenberry, Jeff Lyons, Marilyn Pasekoff, Bob Rogerson

The revue was presented in two acts.

NOTES—Gerard Alessandrini's latest edition of *Forbidden Broadway* played for well over a year.

In the program (the *Playkill*), Alessandrini thanked various Broadway lyricists and composers (Stephen Sondheim, Jerry Bock and Sheldon Harnick, John Kander and Fred Ebb, Charles Strouse and Martin Charnin, and others) for allowing him to use their songs for his parodies (he also thanked "Terry Hands and the R.S.C." for permission to use the English language!).

The revue included three original songs by Alessandrini ("Forbidden Broadway 90," "Who Do They Know?," and "The Phantom of the Musical").

For a list of the *Forbidden Broadway* series, see entry for the 1982 edition; also see Appendix S.

514 Forbidden Broadway 1991. THEATRE: Theatre East; OPENING DATE: June 20, 1991; PERFORMANCES: 237; CONCEPT AND PARODY LYRICS: Gerard Alessandrini; DIRECTION: Gerard Alessandrini; Phillip George, Assistant Director; COSTUMES: Erika Dyson; MUSICAL DIRECTION: Brad Ellis; PRODUCERS: Jonathan Scharer; Chip Quigley, Associate Producer

CAST—Mary Denise Bentley, Susanne Blakeslee, Brad Ellis, Herndon Lackey, Jeff Lyons

The revue was presented in two acts.

NOTES—The latest edition of the long-running spoof included three songs from the 1990 edition ("Who Do They Know?," "The Phantom of the Musical," and an updated "Forbidden Broadway 1991 ½"). Among the take-offs were "If I Sing It Slower" (a nod to Topol's performance in *Fiddler on the Roof*), "I Ham What I Ham" (George Hearn's performance in *La Cage Aux Folles*), and "Somewhat Overindulgent" (Mandy Patinkin in *anything*); other send-ups included "Grim Hotel," "I'm Asian, Too," and "Liza One Note."

During the latter part of the run, a special *Forbidden Christmas* edition was presented from November 19, 1991, to January 5, 1992, for a total of fifty-six performances (cast members were Susanne Blakeslee, Brad Ellis, Leah Hocking, Herndon Lackey, and Michael McGrath).

For a list of the *Forbidden Broadway* series, see entry for the 1982 edition; also see Appendix S.

515 Forbidden Broadway 1992. THEATRE: Theatre East; OPENING DATE: April 6, 1992; PERFORMANCES: 304; CONCEPT AND PARODY LYRICS: Gerard Alessandrini; DIRECTION: Gerard Alessandrini; Phillip George, Assistant Director; COSTUMES: Erika Dyson; MUSICAL DIRECTION: Brad Ellis; PRODUCERS: Jonathan Scharer; Chip Quigley, Associate Producer

CAST—Brad Ellis, Leah Hocking, Alix Korey, Michael McGrath, Patrick Quinn

The revue was presented in two acts.

NOTES—During part of its run, this edition seems to have been temporarily titled *The Best of Forbidden Broadway—10th Anniversary Edition*.

For a list of all the *Forbidden Broadway* series, see entry for the 1982 edition; also see Appendix S.

516 Forbidden Broadway 1993. THEATRE: Theatre East; OPENING DATE: January 12, 1993; PERFORMANCES: 288; CONCEPT AND PARODY LYRICS: Gerard Alessandrini; DIRECTION: Gerard Alessandrini; Phillip George, Assistant Director; COSTUMES: Erika Dyson; MUSICAL DIRECTION: Brad Ellis; PRODUCERS: Jonathan Scharer; Chip Quigley, Associate Producer

CAST—Susanne Blakeslee, Brad Ellis, Dorothy Kiara, Brad Oscar, Craig Wells

The revue was presented in two acts.

NOTES—The revue included such numbers as "Guys and Dolls (I Know I've Seen This Show Before)," "Fugue for Scalpers," and "Crazy for You (Replaceable You)." Marla Maples, Mandy Patinkin, Tommy Tune, and Michael Crawford were among the performers who were eviscerated, er, that is, spoofed.

Between the closing of the show's predecessor *Forbidden Broadway 1992* and the opening of the 1993 edition, a special holiday edition (*Forbidden Broadway Featuring Forbidden Christmas*) opened on December 1, 1992, and played through December 27. For a list of the *Forbidden Broadway* series, see entry for the 1982 edition; also see Appendix S.

517 Forbidden Broadway 1994. THEATRE: Theatre East; OPENING DATE: November 11, 1993; PERFORMANCES: 62; CONCEPT AND PARODY LYRICS: Gerard Alessandrini; DIRECTION: Gerard Alessandrini; CHOREOGRAPHY: Susanne Blakeslee and Craig Wells; COSTUMES: Alvin Colt; MUSICAL DIRECTION: Brad Ellis; PRODUCERS: Jonathan Scharer; Chip Quigley, Associate Producer

CAST—Susanne Blakeslee, Brad Ellis, Brad Oscar, Christine Pedi, Craig Wells

The revue was presented in two acts.

NOTES—The latest visit of the Off Broadway perennial was subtitled the "Take-No-Prisoners" edition.

For a list of the *Forbidden Broadway* series, see entry for the 1982 edition; also see Appendix S.

518 Forbidden Broadway Cleans Up Its Act! THEATRE: Stardust Theatre; OPENING DATE: November 17, 1998; PERFORMANCES: 754; CONCEPT AND PARODY LYRICS: Gerard Alessandrini; DIRECTION: Phillip George and Gerard Alessandrini; CHOREOGRAPHY: Phillip George; SCENERY: Bradley Kaye; COSTUMES: Alvin Colt; LIGHTING: Marc Janowitz; MUSICAL DIRECTION: Matthew Ward; PRODUCERS: John Freedson, Harriet Yellin, and Jon B. Platt in association with Steve McGraw, Nancy McCall, Peter Martin, Gary Hoffman, Jerry Kravat, and Masakazu Shibaoka

CAST—Bryan Batt, Lori Hammel, Edward Staudenmayer, Kristine Zbornik

The revue was presented in two acts.

NOTES—The latest edition in the *Forbidden Broadway* series ran just short of two full years. This time around, the targets included *Ragtime* (*Gagtime*), *Chicago* ("Glossy Fosse"), the recent revival of *The Sound of Music* ("Find Mary Martin"), Mandy Patinkin ("Super-Frantic-Hyper-Active-Self-Indulgent-Mandy"), and Ann Miller ("I'm Still Weird"; [Miller had recently appeared in a regional revival of *Follies*]).

The cast album was released by DRG Records (CD # 12616).

For a list of the *Forbidden Broadway* series, see entry for the 1982 edition; also see Appendix S.

519 Forbidden Broadway: The Roast of Utopia (2007). THEATRE: 47th Street Theatre; OPENING DATE: June 13, 2007; PERFORMANCES: 96; CONCEPT AND PARODY LYRICS: Gerard Alessandrini; DIRECTION: Gerard Alessandrini; Phillip George, Co-Director; SCENERY: Megan K. Halpern; COSTUMES: Alvin Colt; LIGHTING: Marc Janowitz; MUSICAL DIRECTION: David Caldwell (Piano)

CAST—Jared Bradshaw, Erin Crosby, Janet Dickinson, James Donegan

NOTES—This retrospective revue included a few new spoofs (including *The Coast of Utopia* and *LoveMusik*).

For a list of the *Forbidden Broadway* series, see entry for the 1982 edition; also see Appendix S.

520 Forbidden Broadway: Rude Awakening (2007). THEATRE: 47th Street Theatre; OPENING DATE: October 2, 2007; PERFORMANCES: 200; CONCEPT AND PARODY LYRICS: Gerard Alessandrini; DIRECTION: Phillip George and Gerard Alessandrini.; SCENERY: Megan K. Halpern; COSTUMES: Alvin Colt; LIGHTING: Marc Janowitz; MUSICAL DIRECTION: David Caldwell (Piano); PRODUCERS: John Freedson, Harriet Yellin, and Jon B. Platt

CAST—Jared Bradshaw, Janet Dickinson, Valerie Fagan, Michael West

NOTES—The latest entry in Gerard Alessandrini's *Forbidden Broadway* series spoofed such recent musicals and plays as *Spring Awakening*, *Legally Blonde*, the revival of *Grease*, and *Frost/Nixon*.

Frank Scheck in the *New York Post* praised the "scathing yet affectionate" revue, and noted that *Spring Awakening* was spoofed in "hilarious fashion" ("the more pretentious the show, the more ammunition it gives Alessandrini"). There were also digs at Raul Esparza's performance in the recent *Company* revival, at David Hyde-Pierce in *Curtains* (this sequence mocked the worship of television stars who visit Broadway), and even *The Little Mermaid*, which had not yet opened on Broadway when *Forbidden Broadway: Rude Awakening* premiered. Scheck had special praise for 91-year-old costumer designer Alvin Colt; his creations were the "real stars" of the evening, and his "uproarious" wigs and costumes got laughs "before anyone wearing them even says a word."

The cast recording (subtitled the "25th Anniversary Edition") was released by DRG Records (CD # 12632); the CD not only included selections from *Forbidden Broadway: Rude Awakening* (such as the 2006 Broadway revival of *Les Miserables* ["Even More Miserables"] and "The Be-Littled Mermaid"), it also included previously recorded but unreleased tracks (nay, forbidden tracks!) from earlier *Forbidden Broadway* editions, including such numbers as "Chicago — Give 'Em the Old Star Replacement" and "Sour Charity."

For a list of the *Forbidden Broadway* series, see entry for the 1982 edition; also see Appendix S.

521 Forbidden Broadway: Special Victims Unit. THEATRE: Douglas Fairbanks Theatre; transferred to the 47th Street Theatre on June 24, 2005; OPENING DATE: December 16, 2004; PERFORMANCES: 816; CONCEPT AND PARODY LYRICS: Gerard Alessandrini; DIRECTION: Gerard Alessandrini and Phillip George; CHOREOGRAPHY: Phillip George; SCENERY: Megan K. Halpern; COSTUMES: Alvin Colt; LIGHTING: Marc Janowitz; MUSICAL DIRECTION: David Caldwell; PRODUCERS: John Freedson, Jon B. Platt, and Harriet Yellen; Gary Hoffman, Jerry Kravat, and Masakazu Shibaoka, Associate Producers

CAST—Ron Bohmer, Christine Pedi, Jason Mills, Jennifer Simard, David Caldwell (Piano)

The revue was presented in two acts.

NOTES—This version eviscerated the latest Broadway musicals (and revivals), such as *Mamma Mi-diocre*, *The Boy Who's Odd* (Peter Allen and *The Boy from Oz*), *Fiddler with No Jew*, and *La Cage Aw Ful*. The revue also tweaked PBS and its tributes to

Broadway in *Julie Andrews PBS—The American Musical: The Next Hundred Years*.

The cast album was recorded by DRG Records (CD # 12629).

For a list of the *Forbidden Broadway* series, see entry for the 1982 edition; also see Appendix S.

522 Forbidden Broadway Strikes Back! THEATRE: Triad Theatre; OPENING DATE: October 17, 1996; PERFORMANCES: 850; CONCEPT AND PARODY LYRICS: Gerard Alessandrini; DIRECTION: Gerard Alessandrini; Phillip George, Associate Director; CHOREOGRAPHY: Phillip George; SCENERY: Bradley Kaye; COSTUMES: Alvin Colt; MUSICAL DIRECTION: Matthew Ward; PRODUCERS: John Freedson, Harriet Yellin, and Jon B. Platt; Steve McGraw, Nancy McCall, Peter Martin, and Masakazu Shibaoka, Associate Producers

CAST—Bryan Batt, Donna English, David Hibbard, Christine Pedi

The revue was presented in two acts.

NOTES—The Off Broadway perennial continued its merry spoofs of the current Broadway scene. Among the targets in this edition were the Disneyfication of Broadway (the song "Be Depressed" was set to the music of "Be Our Guest"); the onslaught of merchandising at Broadway shows ("Cameron Mackintosh—My Souvenir Things"); Ethel Merman (as she might have attacked *Sunset Blvd.*); *Rent* (*Rant*); and the Patti LuPone-Glenn Close *Sunset Blvd.* casting brouhaha ("Glenn Close But No Cigar—As If She Never Played This Part"). The cast album was recorded by DRG Records (CD # 12614).

For a list of the *Forbidden Broadway* series, see entry for the 1982 edition; also see Appendix S.

523 Forbidden Broadway Summer Shock! THEATRE: Douglas Fairbanks Theatre; OPENING DATE: July 5, 2004; PERFORMANCES: 83; CONCEPT AND PARODY LYRICS: Gerard Alessandrini; DIRECTION: Gerard Alessandrini, with Phillip George; SCENERY: Bradley Kay and Megan K. Halpern; COSTUMES: Alvin Colt; LIGHTING: Marc Janowitz; PRODUCERS: John Freedson, Harriet Yellin, and Jon B. Platt

CAST—David Benoit, Valerie Fagan, Jennifer Simard, Michael West

The revue was presented in two acts.

NOTES—This was the "summer shock" edition of the Off Broadway perennial revue.

For a list of the *Forbidden Broadway* series, see entry for the 1982 edition; also see Appendix S.

524 Forbidden Broadway: 20th Anniversary Celebration. THEATRE: Douglas Fairbanks Theatre; OPENING DATE: February 25, 2002; PERFORMANCES: 983; CONCEPT AND PARODY LYRICS: Gerard Alessandrini; DIRECTION: Gerard Alessandrini; Phillip George, Co-Director; CHOREOGRAPHY: Phillip George; SCENERY: Bradley Kaye; COSTUMES: Alvin Colt; MUSICAL DIRECTION: Brad Ellis (Piano); PRODUCERS: John Freedson, Harriet Yellin, and Jon B. Platt

CAST—Donna English, Michael West, Ben Evans, Valerie Fagan

The revue was presented in two acts.

NOTES—For a list of the *Forbidden Broadway* series, see entry for the 1982 edition; also see Appendix S.

525 Forbidden Broadway 2001: A Spoof Odyssey. THEATRE: Stardust Theatre; transferred to the Douglas Fairbanks Theatre on May 8, 2001; OPENING DATE: November 18, 2000; PERFORMANCES: 552; CONCEPT AND PARODY LYRICS: Gerard Alessandrini; DIRECTION: Phillip George and Gerard Alessandrini; CHOREOGRAPHY: Phillip George; SCENERY: Bradley Kaye; COSTUMES: Alvin Colt; MUSICAL DIRECTION: Brad Ellis; PRODUCERS: John Freedson, Harriet Yellin, and Jon B. Platt in association with Steve McGraw, Nancy McCall, Peter Martin, Gary Hoffman, Jerry Kravat, and Masakazu Shibaoka

CAST—Felicia Finley, Danny Gurwin, Tony Nation, Christine Pedi

The revue was presented in two acts.

NOTES—The latest of the *Forbidden Broadway* entries spoofed current-running shows (*Saturday Night Fever* was *Saturday Night Fiasco*); various performers (Patti LuPone ["Being LuPone" was set to the music of "Being Alive"]); and Stephen Sondheim (singing "'The Ev'rybody Loves Me But Nobody Will Produce Me' Blues"). The cast recording was released by DRG Records (CD # 12627).

For a list of the *Forbidden Broadway* series, see entry for the 1982 edition; also see Appendix S.

526 Forbidden Hollywood. THEATRE: Triad Theatre; OPENING DATE: March 10, 1996; PERFORMANCES: 225; CONCEPT AND PARODY LYRICS: Gerard Alessandrini; DIRECTION: Gerard Alessandrini and Phillip George; CHOREOGRAPHY: Gerard Alessandrini and Phillip George; Roxie Lucas, Additional Choreography; SCENERY: Bradley Kaye; COSTUMES: Alvin Colt; MUSICAL DIRECTION: Fred Barton; PRODUCERS: John Freedson, Harriet Yellin, and Jon B. Platt in association with Steve McGraw, Nancy McCall, and Peter Martin

CAST—Fred Barton, Tom DiBuono, Michael McGrath, Christine Pedi, Lance Roberts

The revue was presented in two acts.

NOTES—This time around, the *Forbidden Broadway* crowd skewered the sacred cows of Hollywood.

The revue had previously been produced at the Coronet Theatre in Los Angeles, and a recording of that production (with cast members Suzanne Blakeslee, Brad Ellis, Jason Graae, Gerry McIntyre, and Christine Pedi) was released by Varese Sarabande Records CD # VSD-5669).

Among the Hollywood victims in this round-up were Ann-Margret ("Bye Bye Thirty"), Audrey Hepburn ("Dub Me"), Liza Minnelli ("Mein Film Career"), and Sharon Stone ("Rawhide") as well as such films as *South Pacific* ("Blurry Hues") and *Waterworld* ("I'll Blow the Budget of *Waterworld*").

For a list of the *Forbidden Broadway* entries, see entry for the 1982 edition; also see Appendix S.

527 Forever Plaid. "The Heavenly Musical." THEATRE: Steve McGraw's; OPENING DATE: May 20, 1990; PERFORMANCES: 1,811; DIALOGUE: Stuart Ross; LYRICS: See song list for credits; MUSIC: See song list for credits; DIRECTION: Stuart Ross; Larry Raben, Assistant Director; SCENERY: Neil Peter Jampolis; COSTUMES: Debra Stein; LIGHTING: Jane Resiman; MUSICAL DIRECTION: James Followell; PRODUCERS: Gene Wolsk in association with Allen M. Shore and Steven Suskin

CAST—Stan Chandler (Jinx), David Engel (Smudge), Jason Graae (Sparky), Guy Stroman (Francis)

The action occurs on the night of February 9, 1964.

The revue was presented in two acts (division of acts unknown; musical numbers weren't listed in the program; the following list of songs is taken from the cast album, and performer's name indicates who was the lead vocalist for the number).

MUSICAL NUMBERS—"Three Coins in the Fountain" (from 1954 film *Three Coins in the Fountain*; lyric by Sammy Cahn, music by Jule Styne) (Guy Stroman), "Gotta Be This or That" (lyric and music by Sunny Syklar)/"Undecided" (lyric and music by Sid Robin and Charles Shavers) (Jason Graae), "Moments to Remember" (lyric and music by Al Stillman and Robert Allen) (Stan Chandler), "Crazy 'Bout Ya' Baby" (lyric and music by Pat Barrett and Rudi Maugeri) (Guy Stroman), "No Not Much" (lyric and music by Al Stillman and Robert Allen) (Stan Chandler), "Perfidia" (lyric and music by Milton Leeds and Alberto Dominguez) (Jason Graae), "Cry" (lyric and music by Churchill Kohlman) (Stan Chandler), "Sixteen Tons" (lyric and music by Merle Travis) (David Engel), "Chain Gang" (lyric and music by Sam Cooke) (Guy Stroman), A Tribute to Mr. C.: "Sing to Me, Mr. C." (lyric and music by Charles Ray)/"Dream Along with Me" (lyric and music by Carl Sigman)/"Catch a Falling Star" (lyric by Paul Vance, music by Lee Pockriss) (Jason Graae), Caribbean Plaid: "Kingston Market" (lyric and music by Irving Burgie) (Stan Chandler)/"Jamaica Farewell" (lyric and music by Irving Burgie) (David Engel, Jason Graae)/"Matilda, Matilda" (lyric and music by Harry Thomas) (Guy Stroman), "Heart and Soul" (lyric by Frank Loesser, music by Hoagy Carmichael) (Guy Stroman), "Lady of Spain" (lyric and music by Robert Hargreaves, Tolchard Evans, Stanley J. Damerell, and Henry Tinsley) (Stan Chandler), "Scotland the Brave" (traditional) (Company), "Shangri-La" (lyric and music by Carl Sigman, Matt Malneck, and Robert Maxwell) (Company), "Rags to Riches" (lyric and music by Richard Adler and Jerry Ross) (David Engel), "Love Is a Many Splendored Thing" (1955 film *Love Is a Many Splendored Thing*; lyric by Paul Francis Webster, music by Sammy Fain) (Company)

NOTES—The earlier revues *Beehive*, *Suds*, and *The Taffetas* (see entries) celebrated "girl groups" of the 1950s and 1960s; with *Forever Plaid*, the guy groups finally had their day with this likable revue with performances in the style of the Four Aces, the Four Freshman, the Four Lads, the Ames Brothers, and other guy groups of that ilk. The back story of the revue concerned four guys who meet in high school in 1956 and dream of becoming a popular singing group. Despite changing musical styles, the guys adhere to their standards of harmonized crooning while wearing dinner jackets and bow ties, and they perform at weddings, proms, and country club socials. On February 9, 1964, they finally get their big chance, an engagement at the Airport Hilton Cocktail Bar (The Fusel-Lounge). Unfortunately, on their way to the gig, the guys are killed in an accident when their car is hit by a school bus carrying Catholic teens to Manhattan to see the Beatles make their U.S. television debut on *The Ed Sullivan Show* (the teens emerged unscathed, and hopefully were able to get to the Ed Sullivan Theatre in time to see the Beatles perform).

But through the miracle of cosmic forces, the guys briefly return to life in order to perform and record their show. *Forever Plaid* is that show, and its RCA Victor cast recording is that album (CD # 60702-2-RC)! (But if ever a musical cried out for an LP release, it was *Forever Plaid*; the nostalgic CD cover proudly boasts that the recording is in "Living Stereo.")

Forever Plaid previously played in such Off Off Broadway venues as the Westbank Café, the American Stage Company, and the Wisdom Bridge Theatre. A "pre-taped" film version was released in 2009.

528 Fortuna. "A Musical Comedy." THEATRE: Maidman Playhouse; OPENING DATE: January 3, 1962; PERFORMANCES: 5; BOOK: Arnold Weinstein; LYRICS: Arnold Weinstein; MUSIC: Francis Thorne; DIRECTION: Directed by Arnold Weinstein; staged by Glen Tetley; SCENERY: William Ritman; COSTUMES: Willa Kim; LIGHTING: William Ritman; MUSICAL DIRECTION: Jack Lee; PRODUCERS: Sam Cohn and John Wulp in association with Julia Miles

CAST—Gabriel Dell (Fortuna), Jane Connell (Christina), Blaire Stauffer (Ricci), Honey Sanders (Mrs. de Angelo), Benjamin Hayeem (Mr. de Angelo), Ed Powell (Druggist), Ted Beniades (Smystero), Pat Birch (Constance), Morrie Pierce (Waiter,

Baron), Jake Dengel (Mr. Guiseffi), Harry Singleton (Doctor), Gene Massimo (Vendor), Jerry de Luise (Policeman)

SOURCE—The play *Fortuna Con 'F' Maiuscula* by Eduardo de Filippo and Armando Curcio.

The action occurs at the present time in and about Fortuna's tenement dwelling in Naples.

The musical was presented in two acts (song assignments unknown).

ACT ONE—"A Deal," "Someone Such as Me," "Checking the Facts," "Call Him Papa," "So What? Why Not!," "The Ice House Fire," "O Stomach of Mine, We Eat!," "Police!"

ACT TWO—"Angelica," "Speak in Silence," "Premeditated Luck," "Speech," "What a Lovely Dream," "Million Goes to Million," "Premeditated Luck" (reprise)

NOTES—*Fortuna* was a quick flop, but many interesting names were associated with it, including William Ritman (scenery and lighting), Willa Kim (costumes), and future Broadway choreographer Pat Birch. And *Fortuna* gave a few lucky theatergoers another opportunity to see the always welcome Jane Connell. The cast album was released by Owl Records (LP # ORLP-4).

Fortuna dealt with a small-time crook (Fortuna, played by Gabriel Dell) who becomes involved in a small-time forgery scheme, thus outwitting himself when it turns out he's on the cusp of inheriting a fortune.

Arthur Gelb in the *New York Times* found the musical a pale imitation of *The Threepenny Opera*, and reported that the script's sense of humor resorted to offstage rumblings when a character sang "O Stomach of Mine, We Eat!" Further, when another character realizes a recently-purchased fountain pen is ersatz, he exclaims, "This is the end of a beautiful penship."

Gelb noted the musical's opening scene used "stylized mime movements" which seemed to indicate that the director (Glen Tetley) had some interesting ideas about how to stage the work. But Gelb quickly added that Tetley was unable to overcome the "strained and strident hodgepodge" of "tedious banality." He concluded by asking that they "bring back" *The Threepenny Opera* and "take *Fortuna* away!" And *Fortuna* was indeed taken away, after five performances.

As for Jane Connell, Gelb said he hoped the "droll" comedienne would someday find a vehicle worthy of her "pixie talents."

Eduardo de Filippo was a popular Italian playwright, but his work never found success in New York. *Fortuna* didn't find fortune, and Broadway translations of his plays also failed. Two adaptations of *Filumena Marturano* were quick flops (F. Hugh Herbert's *The Best House in Naples* [1956] played for three performances and *Filumena* [1980] lasted for thirty-two). Another of his plays was adapted by Keith Waterhouse and Willis Hall, but *Saturday Sunday Monday* (1974) played for only twelve performances.

With the failures of *The Decameron* (1961; see entry) and *Fortuna*, this might be an appropriate time to examine the theatre's "Italian Curse." An inordinate number of musicals (and straight plays, too, for that matter) have taken place (wholly or partially) in Italy, and for the most part all have flopped. Here's a partial list of the failed musicals: *Fioretta* (1929, 111 performances); *The Venetian Glass Nephew* (1931, 8 performances); *Music Hath Charms* (1934, 25 performances); *Saluda* (1934, 39 performances); *Caviar* (1934, 20 performances); *Swingin' the Dream* (1939, 13 performances); *Glad to See You* (1944; closed prior to Broadway opening); *The Firebrand of Florence* (1945, 43 performances); *A Lady Says Yes* (1945, 87 performances); *The Liar* (1950, 12 performances); *Buttrio Square* (1952, 7 performances); *Shuffle Along of 1952* (1952, 4 performances); *Ankles Aweigh* (1955, 176 performances); *Candide* (1956, 73 performances; see entry for 1973 revival); *Portofino* (1958, 3 performances); *The Decameron* (1961, 39 performances; see entry), *Bravo Giovanni* (1962, 76 performances); *Rugantino* (1964, 28 performances); *Something More!* (1964, 15 performances); *Do I Hear a Waltz?* (1965, 220 performances); *Royal Flush* (1965; closed prior to Broadway opening); *La Strada* (1969, one performance); *Sensations* (1970, 16 performances; see entry); *Comedy* (1972; closed prior to Broadway opening); *A Musical Merchant of Venice* (1975, 12 performances; see entry); *Boccaccio* (1975, 8 performances, see entry); *Carmelina* (1979, 17 performances); *Not Tonight, Benvenuto!* (1979, one performance; see entry); *Francis* (1981, 30 performances; see entry); *Mandrake* (1984, 20 performances; see entry); *Whores of Heaven* (1987, 14 performances; see entry for *Mandrake*); *Shylock* (1987, 10 performances [estimated]; see entry); *Troubadour* (1990, 16 performances; see entry); *White Widow* (1993, 13 performances; see entry); *Passion* (1994, 280 performances); and *The Green Bird* (both 1996 [see entry] and 2000 productions, 15 and 56 performances respectively). There are just a handful of successful musicals which have taken place in Italy: *A Funny Thing Happened on the Way to the Forum* (1962, 964 performances); *Two Gentlemen of Verona* (1971, 627 performances; see entry); and *Nine* (1982, 739 performances); and it appears the recent *The Light in the Piazza* (2005, 504 performances) escaped the jinx. Further, as of this writing the jury is out on *The Glorious Ones* (see entry); the musical received generally favorable reviews and a cast album is scheduled for release in mid–2008; on the other hand, the production closed after its scheduled run at Lincoln Center, and there seems to be no Broadway transfer in the offing.

(Of course, *Kiss Me Kate* [1948, 1,070 performances] takes place entirely in *Baltimore*.)

Even non-musicals set in Italy haven't been successful; using the year 1945 as a benchmark, there have been at least twenty-two flops set in Italy and only two hits (*A Bell for Adano* [1945, 304 performances] and *The Time of the Cuckoo* [1952, 263 performances]).

Besides The Italian Curse and the most famous of all theatre curses (The Curse of "The Scottish Play"; actually, the name of the play *Macbeth* may be mentioned, but just not in the premises of a theatre), there are a number of other theatre curses: The New Orleans Curse (see entry for *Basin Street*), The Silent-Movie Making Curse (see entry for *Theda Bara and the Frontier Rabbi*), The Adelphi Theatre Curse (see entry for *Nellie*), The Carmen Mathews Curse (see entry for *Sunday in the Park with George*), The Joey Faye Curse (see entry for *Lyle*), The Alexander H. Cohen Curse (see entry for *Lyle*), and The Hot-Air Balloon Curse (see entry for *Nellie*). In these instances, the locale, the subject matter, the theatre, the performers, the producer, and sometimes even the scenery itself were more than likely to bring bad luck to their productions.

529 41 in a Sack. THEATRE: 41st Street Theatre; OPENING DATE: March 25, 1960; PERFORMANCES: 45; WRITTEN BY: Shai K. Ophir; MUSIC: Martin Roman; DIRECTION: Shai K. Ophir; production supervised by Barry Hyams; CHOREOGRAPHY: Uncredited; probably by Shai K. Ophir; COSTUMES: Supervised by Brachah Klausner

CAST—SHAI K. OPHIR, Nira Paaz, Sol Backar, Barbara Loden

The revue was presented in two acts.

ACT ONE—Prologue (Shai K. Ophir, with Barbara Loden), "Family Farewell" (Shai K. Ophir), "Between Me and Myself" (Shai K. Ophir, with Nira Paaz), "American in Paris" (Shai K. Ophir), "Bistro" (Shai K. Ophir), "Ode to Love" (Shai K. Ophir, with Barbara Loden), "Gentlemen's Duel" (Shai K. Ophir, with Sol Backar), "Narcissus" (Shai K. Ophir, with Barbara Loden)

ACT TWO—"Gladiators" (Shai K. Ophir, with Sol Backar), "Gazelles" (Shai K. Ophir, with Nira Paaz), "Tiger" (Shai K. Ophir, with Barbara Loden), "Not My Day" (Shai K. Ophir), "Nightmare" (Shai K. Ophir, with Barbara Loden), "Movie" (Shai K. Ophir), "Voyeur and His Conscience" (Shai K. Ophir, with Nira Paaz), "Beggar and Poet" (Shai K. Ophir), "Cigarets" (Shai K. Ophir), "Flamenco Dancer" (Shai K. Ophir)

NOTES—Appropriately enough, Shai K. Ophir's *41 in a Sack* played at the 41st Street Theatre. It was a curious little revue, apparently autobiographical in nature and presented in a mixture of mime, dance, and spoken word. Lewis Funke in the *New York Times* singled out "Gazelles," "Narcissus," and "Flamenco Dancer," and praised Ophir as a performer of "perceptive intelligence, a wry sense of humor and an eye for the ridiculous."

Although he "conceived," wrote, directed, and starred in the production, Ophir's American career went nowhere (according to the program notes, he was "a fighting fifth generation Sabrah" who was popular in Israel and in Europe, and who, in 1957, was "the star performer before 4,000 members and dignitaries of the United Nations General Assembly in New York"). Barbara Loden later created the role of Maggie (the "Marilyn Monroe" character) in Arthur Miller's *After the Fall* (1964).

530 Four Below. THEATRE: The Downstairs Room Opening Date: March 4, 1956; PERFORMANCES: 256 (estimated); SKETCHES, LYRICS, AND MUSIC: Michael Brown, Kenward Elmslie, Murray Grand, Tom Jones, Stan Keen, Bud McCreery, Claibe Richardson, Harvey Schmidt, and William Sheidy; DIRECTION: John Heawood; MUSICAL DIRECTION: Murray Grand; PRODUCERS: Julius Monk and Irving Haber in association with Murray Grand and John Heawood

CAST—Dody Goodman, Jack Fletcher, Gerry Matthews, June Ericson

NOTES—Not much information has surfaced about *Four Below*, the first of Julius Monk's "numerical" revues (see list at the end of this entry for titles). (For some reason, Monk started his series with the fourth numeral, and ignored the first three.)

Four Below must have been something special, because it played five months and inaugurated an eleven-year series of clever revues, all helmed by Monk, who, in a fascinating introduction to the published script of his revue *Baker's Dozen* (Random House, 1964; see entry), described the genesis of his cabaret shows, which began in 1944.

Four Below was presented at The Playgoers, a nightclub located at West 51st Street and Sixth Avenue. The Playgoers consisted of two rooms, the larger Downstairs Room, where the revues were performed, and, upstairs, a street-level bar. During the run of *Four Below*, Monk annexed the upstairs bar where he presented such entertainers as Blossom Dearie and Tammy Grimes.

In 1958, upon notification that the building in which the The Playgoers was housed was going to be demolished, Monk was forced to relocate. He found a townhouse on West 56th Street (the former home of department store mogul Sam Wanamaker), and fashioned it into two separate cabaret venues, the Upstairs at the Downstairs and the Downstairs at the Upstairs. Wanamaker's former home was itself celebrated in song in a later Upstairs at the Downstairs revue produced not by Monk but by Rod Warren, whose own series of "sporting title" revues played there when Monk relocated to the Plaza Hotel in 1962. "Mr. Wanamaker's Home" (lyric by Michael McWhinney and Rod Warren, music by Rod Warren) first appeared in Warren's revue *...And in This Corner* (1964) and then later in his *The Playoffs of*

Mixed Doubles (1967) (see entries). On July 22, 1958, Alice Ghostley opened the Downstairs room; and on October 11, 1958, the Upstairs room (on the second floor, in what had been the townhouse's dining, morning, and drawing rooms) opened with *Demi-Dozen* (see entry), which played for over 500 performances. Monk continued his cabaret revues at this location until 1961, with *Ten-ish, Anyone?* (see entry). The Upstairs Room was designed by Ed Wittstein and Bob Miller, and it was their décor which served as the background scenery for the revues which played there.

On October 18, 1962, Monk settled in at the Plaza Hotel when *Dime a Dozen* (see entry) opened at the PLaza 9- Room (as in a telephone number beginning PL-9). (One name considered for the new venue had been Upstage at the Downstage.) The room had previously been a supper club called the Rendez-Vous, and prior to 1947 it had been known as the Plaza Grill. Monk and other producers continued to offer revues and musicals at the venue until the early 1970s.

Two of *Four Below's* numbers have surfaced. The first, "Candygram Song," was written by Kenward Elmslie (lyric) and Claibe Richardson (music). The team later wrote the Broadway musical *The Grass Harp* (1971), a lyric version of Truman Capote's novella and play; it closed after one week, but its memorable score assured the musical almost instant cult status among lovers of Broadway music. The cast album was recorded by Ben Bagley's Painted Smiles Record label; Bagley not only continued with his "revisited" series of obscure Broadway songs, but he also occasionally recorded shows such as *The Grass Harp* as well as studio cast recordings (Rodgers and Hart's 1938 musical *Too Many Girls*).

The other number is "Third Avenue El" (lyric and music by Michael Brown) which appeared in no less than three revues within a three-year period. After first being heard in *Four Below*, it was interpolated into the score of *The Littlest Revue* (see entry) two months later, and was recorded for that show's cast album. The song was later reprised in Monk's revue *Demi-Dozen* (1958; see entry) and appeared on that show's cast album as well. This sweetly nostalgic song about the passing of a New York City landmark resonates more than ever today, and is particularly touching in its wish that vanished New York sites might always be with us, if not in concrete and steel, then at least in memory.

Monk's revues, like Bagley's and Rod Warren's, were written for sophisticated, educated, well-heeled audiences. The revues were of an era in which fashionable theatre-goers sought out satiric, topical revues presented in chic venues, and the writers, performers, and audiences all seemed to be involved in conspiratorial enjoyment of songs and sketches about the foibles and mores of the day, subjects which film and television barely touched upon. A few years after the musical revue became an established part of the Off Broadway scene, the improvisational revues came along, and for the better part of the 1960s they too became synonymous with Off Broadway theatre. These revues also spoofed trends and cultural landmarks of the era, but their particular forte was political satire.

But by the late 1960s, the culture was dumbing down, and perhaps chic musical and clever improvisational revues were seen as elitist in a theatrical culture which was quick to embrace rock and other forms of protest musicals. So by 1970 the heyday of these revues was over.

But for a little more than a decade Off Broadway offered classic entertainments with the cozy and chic revues of Monk, Bagley, and Warren as well as the legendary improvisational revues of the Second City, the Committee, the Premise, the Stewed Prunes, and other groups. Monk produced a total of fifteen revues in New York during the period 1956-1967: *Four Below* (1956), *The Son of Four Below* (1956), *Take Five* (1957), *Demi-Dozen* (1958), *Pieces-of-Eight* (1959), *Four Below Strikes Back* (1959), *Dressed to the Nines* (1960), *Seven Come Eleven* (1961), *Ten-ish, Anyone?* (1961), *Dime a Dozen* (1961), *Seven Come Eleven* (Second Edition; 1963), *Baker's Dozen* (1964), *Bits and Pieces XIV* (1964), *Pick a Number XV* (1965), and *4 in Hand* (1967); see separate entries for each revue; also see Appendix Q.

531 Four Below Strikes Back. "A Competitive Charade." THEATRE: Downstairs at the Upstairs Opening Date: September 24, 1959; PERFORMANCES: Unknown; SKETCHES: Herbert Hartig and Lois Korey; LYRICS: Louis Botto, Michael Brown, Ronny Graham, Tom Jones, Walter Marks, Bud McCreery, John Meyer, Edward C. Redding, William Roy, Bruce Williamson, and G. Wood; MUSIC: Michael Brown, Bud McCreery, Walter Marks, John Meyer, Ronny Graham, Edward C. Redding, William Roy, Bruce Williamson, and G. Wood; DIRECTION: Julius Monk; MUSICAL DIRECTION: Robert Colston and Paul Trueblood on the Plural Pianos; PRODUCER: Julius Monk

CAST—Nancy Dussault, George Furth, Cy Young, Jenny Lou Law

The revue was presented in two acts.

ACT ONE—Overture and Opening (lyric and music by Bud McCreery) (Company); "Leave Your Mind Alone" (lyric and music by Ronny Graham) (Nancy Dussault, Cy Young) "Mr. X" (sketch by Herbert Hartig and Lois Korey) (Jenny Lou Law, George Furth) "It's a Wonderful Day to Be Seventeen" (lyric and music by Tom Jones and Ronny Graham) (Nancy Dussault) "The Castro Tango!" (lyric and music by Bruce Williamson) (Jenny Lou Law, George Furth); "Charlie Chan" (lyric and music by William Roy) (Nancy Dussault) "The Sitwells" (sketch by Bud McCreery) (Jenny Lou Law, Cy Young, George Furth) "Merry-Go, Merry-Go-Round" (lyric and music by G. Wood) (Jenny Lou Law) "Jefferson Davis Tyler's General Store" (lyric and music by Edward C. Redding) (Nancy Dussault, Company)

ACT TWO—"Four Seasons" (lyric and music by Louis Botto and William Roy) (Company) "Speak No Love" (lyric and music by Edward C. Redding) (Cy Young) "The Constant Nymphet" (sketch by John Meyer) (Jenny Lou Law, Nancy Dussault) "Man Tan" (lyric by Ronny Graham, music by William Roy) (Jenny Lou Law) "Lola Montez" (lyric and music by Michael Brown) (Nancy Dussault, Cy Young) "Family Fallout Shelter" (lyric and music by Bruce Williamson) (George Furth) "Literary Time" (sketch by Tom Jones) (Cy Young, Jenny Lou Law) "Love, Here I Am" (lyric and music by Walter Marks) "Payola" (lyric by Bruce Williamson, music by William Roy) (Company)

NOTES—A week after *Pieces-of-Eight* opened at the Upstairs Room, Julius Monk produced *Four Below Strikes Back* for the Downstairs Room. The songs and sketches are based on information from the cast album, which was released by Offbeat Records (LP # O-4017).

The revue spoofed politics ("The Castro Tango!"), the Cold War ("Family Fallout Shelter"), current scandals ("Payola"), nostalgia ("Charlie Chan"), current trends and fads ("Man Tan" and a new Manhattan restaurant ["Four Seasons"]), and literary types ("The Sitwells," "Literary Time," and "The Constant Nymphet"). The latter was particularly amusing in its spoof of Francoise Sagan; in this case, the authoress is a twelve-year-old *enfant terrible* from Queens whose sexy novel *Au Revoir, Papa* is a best-seller. There was even a song about "Lola Montez" (for a full-length musical about her, see entry for *Lola*).

The cast included Nancy Dussault, who made her Broadway debut the following year in *Do Re Mi* (1960). In *Four Below Strikes Back*, she sang "Love, Here I Am," a ballad with lyric and music by Walter Marks, and in 1964, she was one of the leads in Marks' Broadway musical *Bajour*. "Love, Here I Am" was later heard in Monk's 1965 revue *Bits and Pieces XV*.

George Furth later wrote the books of several musicals (including the iconic *Company* [1970]) and a few plays [most notably *Twigs* in 1971]).

"Jefferson Davis Tyler's General Store" was previously heard in *Take Five* (1957; see entry) and *Tongue and Cheek* (1958), a revue which never played in New York. "Merry-Go, Merry-Go-Round" was later heard in *Baker's Dozen* (see entry) as "Merry-Go-Round."

For a complete list of Julius Monk's revues, see entry for *Four Below*; also see Appendix Q.

532 Four Faces East. THEATRE: The Roundtable/King Arthur's Room; OPENING DATE: May 16, 1963; PERFORMANCES: Unknown

CAST—Carl Esser, Bob Shane, Fiddle Viracola, Phoebe Wray

NOTES—*Four Faces East* received a rave from the *New York Times*. Paul Gardner found the satiric revue "as bright as sunshine ... a light, summery entertainment" with a cast "who can take a song and send it sailing, like a balloon, into the sky." Gardner indicated the revue wasn't improvised and didn't contain material about such well-worn topics as the Kennedys. Instead, the deadpan material focused on such topics as civil defense, film stars, matrimony, the New York State Liquor Authority, and the mania of Americans to be heroes in whatever they do. Gardner also singled out a clever song (by Theodore James) which dealt with a little boy learning how to read (the song seems to be an amusing first-cousin to Noel Coward's "The Little Ones' ABC" from *Sail Away* [1961]).

533 4 Guys Named Jose ... and Una Mujer Named Maria! THEATRE: Blue Angel Theatre; OPENING DATE: September 18, 2000; PERFORMANCES: 191; BOOK: Dolores Prida; LYRICS AND MUSIC: By various writers; DIRECTION: Susana Tubert; CHOREOGRAPHY: Maria Torres; SCENERY: Mary Houston; COSTUMES: Tania Bass; LIGHTING: Aaron Spivey; MUSICAL DIRECTION: Oscar Hernandez; PRODUCERS: Enrique Iglesias and Dasha Epstein

CAST—Philip Anthony, Henry Gainza, Lissette Gonzalez, Allen Hidalgo, Ricardo Puente

The revue was presented in two acts.

ACT ONE—*Feel It*: "Guantanamera," "Linda Quisqueya," "Piel Canela," "Mexico Lindo y Querido," "Perfidia" (lyric and music by Alberto Dominguez, English lyric by Milton Leeds); *Then & Now Medley*: "I Make My Money with Bananas," "Babalu," "Tito's Timbales," "La Bamba" (traditional; in the 1950s, the song was again popularized, this time in a version by Ritchie Valens), "Black Magic Woman," "Bidi, Bidi, Bom, Bom," "Bailamos," "Livin' la Vida Loca," "Macarena," "La Cumbancha (Oiga Usted)"; *Nonsense Songs*: "Burundanga," "Corazon de Melon," "Mambo Fuego," "Las Mulatas del Cha Cha Cha," "Amor, Amor," "Te Quiero Dijiste (Magic Is the Moonlight)," "Besame Mucho" (original Spanish lyric and music by Consuelo Velaquez; popular English lyric by Sunny Skylar), "Quien Sera (Sway)"/"Quizas, Quizas, Quizas (Perhaps, Perhaps, Perhaps)," "Es Mentiroso"

ACT TWO—Entr'acte, *La Mansiera*: "Muchachita Borincana"; *Nostalgia Medley*: "En Mi Viejo San Juan," "Santiago," "Veracruz," "Nostalgia Habanera," "Mi Tierra," "Rhythm Divine"; *Maria Medley*: "Maria Bonita," "Maria Elena," "Maria la O," "Un, Dos, Tres, Maria"; *Piensa en Mi*: "Gracias a la Vida," "La Murga de Panama"; *Bang Bang*: "Oye Como Va," "I Like It Like That"

NOTES—The revue-like musical *4 Guys Named*

Jose...and Una Mujer Named Maria! dealt with a quartet of Latino men who hope to counteract prejudice against Latinos by producing a revue of popular Latino songs in Omaha during the middle of winter. At the last minute, a girl singer joins their group, and the five performers present an evening of Latino-styled music. Ben Brantley in the *New York Times* found the show "chipper" and "very likable," and he praised the "strong individual presence" of each singer. Further, he liked the "jauntily choreographed" sequences devised by Maria Torres. But he noted that one left the show thinking less about "cultural identity" than about the evening's "irresistible rhythms."

The revue was recorded by DRG Records (CD # 12991); the song titles are taken from the recording.

534 4 in Hand. "All New Déjà Vu Revue." THEATRE: PLaza 9- Room; OPENING DATE: November 1967; PERFORMANCES: Unknown; DIRECTION: "Directed by" Julius Monk; "staged by" Frank Wagner; CHOREOGRAPHY: Frank Wagner; MUSICAL DIRECTION: Robert Colston

CAST—Terry O'Mara, Rex Robbins, Liz Sheridan, Mary Louise Wilson, Alex Wipf; Robert Colston and Otis Clements at the Plural Pianos; Baldwin Bergersen at the Singular Piano; PRODUCER: Julius Monk

NOTES—*4 in Hand* was another entry in Julius Monk's series of topical revues; it seems to have been a retrospective revue of sorts, although it included at least two new numbers ("Take a Trippie with a Hippie" and "That New-Time Religion," both with lyrics and music by June Reizner).

Later in the run, *4 in Hand* 's cast of five were reduced to four (Lesley Stewart, Alex Wipf, Mary Jo Gillis, and John Svar)

For a complete list of Julius Monk's revues, see entry for *Four Below*; also see Appendix Q.

535 Fourth Avenue North. "A Revue." THEATRE: Madison Avenue Playhouse; OPENING DATE: September 27, 1961; PERFORMANCES: 2; SKETCHES, LYRICS, AND MUSIC: George Allen, Michael Batterberry, Gene Bertoncini, Gene Bone, William H. (Bill) Borden, C.B. Bryan, Don Brockett, Martin Charnin, Richard Craven, Robert Dennis, Walter Dwyer, Howard Fenton, Shippen Geer, Murray Grand, Leslie Harnley, Rory Harrity, James Harvey, Bart Howard, Bob (Robert) Kessler, Tom LeGrady, Glen Mallin, Charles S. Marvin, Joanne Pasquineli, Bob Randell, Dan Rustin, Chilton Ryan, and Cy Walter; DIRECTION: Michael Batterberry; staging by Michael Batterberry and Tilda Morse; CHOREOGRAPHY: Tilda Morse; SCENERY: Joseph Stell; COSTUMES: John Pratt, Lotte Doria; LIGHTING: Joseph Stell; MUSICAL DIRECTION: Leslie Harnley; PRODUCERS: Michael Batterberry and Shippen Geer

CAST—Clint Anderson, Bob Carey, Barre Dennen, Rory Harrity, Eugenie Hunt, Linda Lavin, Alice Nunn, Gerrianne Raphael, Sylvia Shay, Wayne Storm

The revue was presented in two acts (sketch and song assignments unknown).

ACT ONE—"Fourth Avenue North" (lyricist unknown, music by Charles S. Marvin), "Sunrise Semester," "Love at an Auction" (lyric and music by Murray Grand), "White Russian New Year" (lyric and music by Tom LeGrady), "Jenny" (lyric by Cy Walker, music by Chilton Ryan), "Doorman" "Let's Have a Party" "Martin's Coming Up" "Mr. Corbett" (lyric by Charles S. Marvin, composer unknown), "T-Party" "Thank God for the Civil War" "March," "So Long as He Loves You" (lyric and music by Bart Howard), "Musak," "H.M.S. Brownstone" (sketch by Rory Harrity and Richard Craven), "Lonely Man" (lyric by Glen Mallin, music by George Allen; title may have been "Lonely Heartache, Lonely Man"), "The Medium" "Park Avenue Rapid Transit"

ACT TWO—"Happy House" "Hold Me" (lyric by Shippen Geer, composer unknown), "Lenox Hill Laundramat" "Beauty Treatment" (lyric by Martin Charnin, music by Bob Kessler), "A Cleaner N.Y." "Not So Easy" "To the Dentist" "Christmas Trees" (lyric by Richard Craven, music by Leslie Harnley), "Troubador" (lyric by Walter Dwyer and James Harvey, music by Gene Bertoncini), "Let's Not Go Away This Summer" (lyric and music by Bill Borden), "Long Time No See" "Open Air Market" "The Director" "Institute for Psychodrama" (by Robert Dennis; this sequence was probably a sketch), Finale

NOTES—Louis Calta's review of *Fourth Avenue North* in the *New York Times* lamented that the twenty-five contributors of the revue's thirty-two numbers were "unable to rise above the adequate." He listed the revue's tired targets (including Muzak, snooty doormen, high society, mass psychotherapy), and was able to single out only two numbers: "Sunrise Semester" (in which Kennedy and Nixon quarrel over the merits of Park Avenue) and "Happy House" (a "wry, slovenly comic and adolescently indifferent but tuneful" song in the tradition of Elvis Presley).

"H.M.S. Brownstone" was later used in Julius Monk's revues *Dime a Dozen* (1962) and *Bits and Pieces XIV* (1964); see entries.

Fourth Avenue North was the second of three short-running flops to open during the latter half of September 1961; its cast members included Linda Lavin, who would be heard from again in many happier circumstances, and Gerrianne Raphael, who was a frequent Off Broadway visitor.

536 The Fourth Wall. THEATRE: Theatre East; OPENING DATE: September 4, 1968; PERFORMANCES: 141; MATERIAL: Created by the performers; DIRECTION: Jeremy Stevens; SCENERY: Kent Broadhurst; PRODUCERS: Jay H. Fuchs in association with Barry Diamond

CAST—Kent Broadhurst, James Manis, Bette-Jane Raphael, Jeremy Stevens, Marcia Wallace

The revue was presented in one act.

NOTES—*The Fourth Wall* was an improvisational revue; Dan Sullivan in the *New York Times* reported that some of the material consisted of set pieces developed in rehearsal, but most of the sketches "were worked out on the floor" in front of the audience. Sullivan stated he would have trouble finding a rhyme for "moon" if he were in front of an audience, and so noted he was in "superst:itious awe" of performers who were "experts in the dangerous art of winging it."

He particularly praised a sequence in which a word (or words) suggested by an audience member was then developed by the company into an impromptu skit. In the case of the word "computer," Kent Broadhurst ("looking WASPish") and Marcia Wallace ("looking waspish") worked up a scene in which they are matched by a computer dating service; but eventually Wallace is exposed as a computer in female drag. The cover of the program indicated the revue's title was *The 4th Wall*, but the program's title page gave the revue's name as *The Fourth Wall*.

Marcia Wallace later sparkled as the dizzy receptionist on the CBS television series *The Bob Newhart Show*. In her program bio for *The Fourth Wall*, she noted that at age seven she was cast as the Virgin Mary in a nativity play, but she modestly brushed off this achievement as "little more than type-casting."

537 Fourtune. "A Different New Musical." THEATRE: Actors' Playhouse; OPENING DATE: April 27, 1980; PERFORMANCES: 241; BOOK: Bill Russell; LYRICS: Bill Russell; MUSIC: Ronald Melrose; DIRECTION: Ron Troutman; CHOREOGRAPHY: Troy Garza; SCENERY: Harry Silverglat; COSTUMES: Coordinated by Joan Culkin; LIGHTING: Michael Newton-Brown; MUSICAL DIRECTION: Janet Hood; PRODUCER: Jonathan Scharer

CAST—Ken Arthur (Brad), Gail Hebert (Tracy), Barbara Richardson (Madelaine), Justin Ross (Roscoe)

The musical was presented in two acts.

ACT ONE—Prologue/"Four Part Harmony" (The Group), "Rich and Famous" (The Group), "Women in Love" (Gail Hebert, Barbara Richardson, with Ken Arthur and Justin Ross), "Fantasy" (Ken Arthur, Gail Hebert), "Funky Love" (Justin Ross, Barbara Richardson), "No One Ever Told Me Love Would Be So Hard" (Gail Hebert), "I'd Rather Be a Fairy Than a Troll" (Justin Ross), "Complications" (The Group)

ACT TWO—"On the Road" (The Group), "What Do I Do Now?" (Ken Arthur), "Making It" (Barbara Richardson, with Ken Arthur and Justin Ross), "I'll Try It Your Way" (Gail Hebert, Justin Ross), "Fortune" (Ken Arthur, The Group)

NOTES—Despite a run of almost eight months, *Fourtune* has now completely disappeared. According to the musical's flyer, the story dealt with "four wild and talented people on their way to stardom"; the plot also examined their romantic goings-on, much of it same-sex related (the flyer noted that the musical's "happy ending" will "keep you out of the Army!").

John Corry in the *New York Times* noted that but for the open bisexuality of the musical's plot, the evening itself was really no different from an old MGM musical with Judy Garland and Mickey Rooney. But he reported that "probably without meaning to" the musical marked the "maturity" of the gay musical because it wasn't a polemic and it wasn't campy. Instead, the musical assumed that "promiscuity is good for you" and that "homosexuality is a lot of laughs."

Corry felt the book was "sappy," but he liked the "literate" lyrics by Bill Russell and the music by Ronald Melrose. He singled out "I'll Try It Your Way" ("interesting jazz"), "Women in Love" ("funny double-entendre"), and the "bittersweet-comic" "I'd Rather Be a Fairy Than a Troll" (a "wonderful moment" for Justin Ross, who performed it).

Ronald Melrose had previously written two Harvard Hasty Pudding musicals, including *Tots in Tinseltown*.

538 Foxy. THEATRE: 14th Street Y; OPENING DATE: December 5, 2000; PERFORMANCES: 16; BOOK: Ian McLellan Hunter and Ring Lardner, Jr.; LYRICS: Johnny Mercer; MUSIC: Robert Emmett Dolan; DIRECTION: Thomas Mills; CHOREOGRAPHY: Thomas Mills; LIGHTING: Shuhei Seo; MUSICAL DIRECTION: Robert Felstein; PRODUCERS: *Musicals Tonight!* and Mel Miller

CAST—Marvin Einhorn (Rottingham), Jessica Frankel (Brandy), Andrew Gitzy (Buzzard), Natasha Harper (Celia), Rob Lorey (Doc), Michael Mendiola (Stirling), George Pellegrino (Ben), Rudy Robertson (Foxy), David Sabella (Bedrock), Jay Brian Winnick (Shortcut); Ensemble: Amy Barker, Brian Cooper, Lawrence Cummings, James Flynn, Jason Levinson, Juliette Morgan, Marni Raab, Jennifer Scheer

SOURCE—The 1606 play *Volpone, or The Fox* by Ben Jonson.

The action occurs in the Yukon, Canada, in 1896.

The musical was presented in two acts.

ACT ONE—Prologue (Rob Lorey), "Respectability" (Rudy Roberson, Jay Brian Winnick, Andrew Gitzy, David Sabella), "Many Ways to Skin a Cat" (Rob Lorey, Rudy Roberson), "Rollin' in Gold" (Company), "Money Isn't Everything" (Rob Lorey, Rudy Roberson), "Larceny and Love" (Jessica Frankel, Rob Lorey), "S.S. Commodore Ebenezer McAfee III" (Ensemble), "The Honeymoon Is Over" (Jessica

Frankel, Natasha Harper), "Talk to Me, Baby" (George Pellegrino, Natasha Harper), "This Is My Night To Howl" (Ensemble), "Bon Vivant" (Rudy Roberson, Ensemble)

ACT TWO—"It's Easy When You Know How" (Rob Lorey), "Run, Run, Run Cinderella" (Natasha Harper), "Talk to Me, Baby" (reprise) (George Pellegrino), "I'm Way Ahead of the Game" (Jessica Frankel, Rob Lorey), "The Letter of the Law" (Michael Mendiola, Ensemble), "In Loving Memory" (Rob Lorey, Jay Brian Winnick, Andrew Gitzy, David Sabella), Finale (Company)

NOTES—Like the *Encores!* (see entry) and *Musicals in Mufti* series, *Musicals Tonight!* revisits neglected musicals, and *Foxy* was a more than welcome choice. The original production's two tryout engagements were presented some seventeen months apart. With Bert Lahr in the title role and Larry Blyden as the con artist Doc, *Foxy* premiered in Alaska, where the musical took place. The first tryout opened on July 2, 1962, at the Palace Grand Theatre in Dawson City in the Yukon, and closed there the following month. But on January 13, 1964, a revised version surfaced at the Fisher Theatre in Detroit, this time under the aegis of David Merrick and with Lahr and Blyden returning in the leads. The musical then opened at the Ziegfeld Theatre on February 18, and despite generally good notices for the show and rave reviews for Lahr (who won the Tony Award for Best Actor in a Musical), the musical played for just seventy-two performances. (Richard Watts, Jr., in the *New York Post* said of Lahr that the "master buffoon is in top form ... his leers and his ruttish noises have never been funnier"; and Walter Kerr in *New York Herald Tribune* felt that Lahr "should be preserved like a fine old wine, or in one, it doesn't matter which ...he is beginning to carbonate.")

Legend has it that Merrick wasn't all that interested in keeping *Foxy* on the boards because the month before it opened another Merrick production premiered, Jerry Herman's *Hello, Dolly!*, and Merrick's energies were directed into parlaying *Dolly* into a national and worldwide phenomenon. But this story doesn't quite ring true. Merrick was the consummate showman, and surely if he thought *Foxy* had a chance, he would have put more money into it and kept it running. But perhaps his instincts told him the musical would never emerge as a blockbuster, and maybe he felt even Lahr's performance wouldn't keep the show afloat.

So *Foxy* quietly disappeared, and didn't even leave behind a cast album (RCA Victor Records was scheduled to record it [# LOC-1089 and # LSO-1089 were assigned to the album]). However, in the 1970s S.P.M. Records (LP # CO-4636) released an album of a live performance from the Broadway production, and while the sound isn't always clear, the recording is a valuable one because it allows us to hear what the Broadway production sounded like and it gives us a chance to savor Lahr and Blyden's delicious performances.

The *Musicals Tonight!* production was a special treat because the revival was recorded by Original Cast Records (CD # OC-6026). The Robert Emmett Dolan and Johnny Mercer score offers a variety of delights: Foxy's "Bon Vivant," one of the funniest comedy songs in the musical theatre canon; Doc's sly and conspiratorial and insinuating "It's Easy When You Know How"; a lovely ballad, "Talk to Me, Baby"; and a haunting blues number, "I'm Way Ahead of the Game."

The CD omitted one song from the Broadway production ("A Case of Rape," which can be heard on the live recording) and included three songs not heard on Broadway ("Respectability," "The Letter of the Law," and "The Honeymoon Is Over"); "The Letter of the Law" had been performed in the Dawson City production. Songs heard during the Dawson City tryout but which weren't used in the Broadway production were: "Share and Share Alike," "A Child of the Wild," "The Power of Love," "Take It from a Lady," "Life's Darkest Moment," "Till It Goes Outta Style," and "The Letter of the Law." Songs in the Detroit tryout which weren't heard in New York were "Celia's First Essay" and "Shivaree."

For an operatic treatment of the story, see entry for *Volpone* (which also discusses other stage adaptations of the material).

For another adventuresome entry in the invaluable *Musicals Tonight!* series, see entry for Harold Rome's *That's the Ticket!* Also, see entries for *Musicals in Mufti* and *Musicals Tonight!*

539 Francis. "A New Musical." THEATRE: The Common/The Theatre at St. Peter's Church; OPENING DATE: December 22, 1981; PERFORMANCES: 30; BOOK: Joseph Leonardo; LYRICS: Kenny Morris; MUSIC: Steve Jankowski; DIRECTION: Frank Martin; SCENERY: Neil Bierbower; COSTUMES: Martha Kelly; LIGHTING: Thomas Bowen; MUSICAL DIRECTION: Larry Esposito; PRODUCER: The Praxis Group

CAST—JOHN DOSSETT (Francis Bernadone), K.C. Wilson (Old Rufino), Lloyd Battista (Pietro Bernadone, Pope Innocent III), Tanny McDonald (Lady Pica Bernadone), Donna Murphy (Clare de Favorone), Kenny Morris (Leo), Cris Groenendaal (Bernard de Quintavalle), Ron Lee Savin (Father Silvestro), Paul Browne (Juniper), Whitney Kershaw (Agnes), Deborah Bendixen (Pacifica), Tom Rolfing (Elias Bombarone of Cortono)

The action occurs during the twelfth century in Umbria, a province of central Italy.

The musical was presented in two acts.

ACT ONE—"Miracle Town" (Ensemble), Bedtime Stories:, "The Legend of Old Rufino" (Tanny McDonald), "The Legend of King Arthur" (Lloyd Battista), "Serenade" (John Dossett, Donna Murphy), "Canticle of Pleasure" (Ensemble), "I'm Ready Now!" (John Dossett), "The Fire in My Heart" (John Dossett), "Ballet for San Damiano" (Women), "For the Good of Brotherhood" (Brothers), "The New Madness" (John Dossett, Ensemble), "Bidding the World Farewell" (John Dossett, Donna Murphy)

ACT TWO—"Oh, Brother!" (Brothers), "All the Time in the World" (Donna Murphy), "All the Time in the World" (reprise) (Donna Murphy, Tanny McDonald), "Walking All the Way to Rome" (Ensemble), "Two Keys" (Lloyd Battista), "The Road to Paradise" (Tom Rolfing, Brothers), "Francis" (Donna Murphy, Kenny Morris), "The Legend of Old Rufino" (reprise) (Tanny McDonald), "Praises to the Sun! (Canticle of Our Brother Sun)" (Ensemble)

NOTES—This short-lived musical was about Saint Francis of Assisi, who, on his deathbed, looks back on the events of his life.

Mel Gussow in the *New York Times* found *Francis* full of "musical platitudes" and stereotyped characters, and noted that while some might find the evening "uplifting," for others it would "be a slow road to Rome." He singled out two songs, "Oh, Brother!," a "peppy chorus," and "All the Time in the World," the latter "sweetly" sung by Donna Murphy.

Besides Donna Murphy, the cast of *Francis* included Cris Groenendaal and John Dossett, both of whom would become familiar faces in future Broadway and Off Broadway musicals. For another musical about the subject, see entry for *Troubadour*.

540 Frank Gagliano's City Scene.
NOTES—See entry for *City Scene*.

541 Frankenstein. "A New Musical." THEATRE: 37 Arts Theatre; OPENING DATE: November 1, 2007; PERFORMANCES: 45; BOOK: Jeffrey Jackson; original story adaptation by Gary P. Cohen; LYRICS: Jeffrey Jackson; MUSIC: Mark Baron; DIRECTION: Bill Fennelly; CHOREOGRAPHY: Kelly Devine; SCENERY: Kevin Judge; Michael Clark, Projection Design; COSTUMES: Emily Pepper; LIGHTING: Thom Weaver; MUSICAL DIRECTION: Stephen Purdy; PRODUCERS: Gerald Goehring, Douglas C. Evans, Michael F. Mitri, and David S. Stone in association with Barbara and Emery Olcott CAST—Aaron Serotsky (Captain Robert Walton, A Blind Man), HUNTER FOSTER (Dr. Victor Frankenstein), Eric Michael Gillett (Alphonse Frankenstein), Becky Barta (Caroline Frankenstein), Struan Erlenborn (William Frankenstein), Mandy Bruno (Justine Moritz), Jim Stanek (Henry Clerval), CHRISTIANE NOLL (Elizabeth Lavenza), STEVE BLANCHARD (A Condemned Man, The Creature), Casey Erin Clark (Agatha), Nick Cartell (Ensemble), Leslie Henstock (Ensemble), Patrick Mellen (Ensemble)

SOURCES—The 1818 (revised, 1831) novel *Frankenstein*; or, *The Modern Prometheus* by Mary Shelley.

The action occurs during the late eighteenth-century in Geneva, Switzerland, Ingolstadt, Germany, and various locales throughout Europe and the Arctic.

The musical was presented in two acts.

ACT ONE—Prelude (Aaron Serotsky, Hunter Foster, Company), "A Golden Age" (Company), "Amen" (Steve Blanchard, Hunter Foster, Company), "Birth to My Creation" (Hunter Foster), "The Hands of Time" (Christiane Noll, Jim Stanek, Mandy Bruno, Struan Erlenborn), "Your Father's Eyes" (Eric Michael Gillett), "The Creature's Tale" (Steve Blanchard), "The Waking Nightmare" (Steve Blanchard), "The Music of Love" (Aaron Serotsky, Casey Erin Clark, Company), "Why?" (Struan Erlenborn, Mandy Bruno, Steve Blanchard, Hunter Foster, Company), "The Proposition" (Hunter Foster, Steve Blanchard)

ACT TWO—"A Happier Day" (Company), "The Modern Prometheus" (Hunter Foster, Jim Stanek, Steve Blanchard), "The Hands of Time" (reprise) (Christiane Noll, Hunter Foster), "The Workings of the Heart" (Christiane Noll, Hunter Foster, Company), "An Angel's Embrace" (Steve Blanchard), "The Workings of the Heart" (reprise) (Hunter Foster), "Your Father's Eyes" (reprise) (Eric Michael Gillett), "These Hands" (Steve Blanchard), "The Chase" (Hunter Foster, Company), "The Coming of the Dawn" (Hunter Foster), "Amen" (reprise) (Steve Blanchard, Hunter Foster), "The Sorrow Born of Dreams" (Company)

NOTES—*Frankenstein* was at least the third musical adaptation inspired by the famous novel by Mary Shelley. In 1986, the Off Broadway production *Have I Got a Girl for You!* (see entry) was loosely based on the 1935 film *The Bride of Frankenstein* and other horror films of that genre, and in 2007, just one week after *Frankenstein*'s opening, Mel Brooks' *Young Frankenstein*, an adaptation of his 1974 film, premiered on November 8 at the Hilton (formerly the Ford Center for the Performing Arts) Theatre (with Shuler Hensley playing Frankenstein's monster, who famously sings Irving Berlin's "Puttin' on the Ritz" in white tie and tails). Hunter Foster played the role of Dr. Victor Frankenstein in *Frankenstein*, and his sister Sutton Foster played the role of Inga in *Young Frankenstein* (in a pre-opening online article for *Playbill*, Kenneth Jones noted that "You can smell the photo op even now"). In his review of *Frankenstein* for the *New York Times*, Christopher Isherwood quoted a line from the musical ("I passed a night of unmingled wretchedness"), and noted he could well relate to the sentiment because he found the evening "drably earnest" and "wearying to the point of silliness." As for the Creature, he indicated it was hunky with "hairless pecs and buzz cut," and "would probably be a man magnet on a Saturday night in Chelsea." Frank Scheck in the *New York Post* found the musical "deadly dull" with a "ponderous" score, and, he, too, noted that the leather-clad Creature was hunky. Scheck mentioned that with his "bared chest and six-pack abs," the Creature didn't let the mere fact of being dead cause him to cut down on his exercise routine. In 2003, a concept recording of *Frankenstein* was released by Curio Productions, Inc., Records (unnumbered CD); curiously, for this production Shuler Hensley also played the creature. The CD, which included twenty-three musical sequences, was a self-described soundtrack from a workshop film of the production; the film was in effect a demo for the musical (and was available on VHS and DVD on a limited, request-only basis).

Songs heard on the CD which weren't used in the stage production were: "Misguided Mission," "The Lab," "Dear Victor," "Once Upon a Time," "Music Is Love," "The Brides," "What Have You Done?," and "A Father's Love." The CD included two songs, "A Blessed Day" and "This Golden Age," which were probably heard on the stage as "A Happier Day" and "A Golden Age." The remaining songs on the CD (all of which were heard in the Off Broadway production) were "Amen," "Birth to My Creation," "The Creature's Tale" (parts one and two), "The Modern Prometheus," "The Workings of the Heart," "Why?," "The Chase," and "The Coming of the Dawn."

The cast recording was released by Ghostlight Records (CD # 8-8001).

Another (non-musical) adaptation of the material opened (and closed) on Broadway at the Palace Theatre on January 4, 1981, in an adaptation by Victor Gialanella. Awash in special effects and spectacular scenery, the play was reportedly at the time the most expensive non-musical to open in Broadway history. For the play, Keith Jochim performed the role of "The Creature."

542 Free Fall. "An Evening of Parody, Irony and Satire." THEATRE: Upstairs at the Downstairs; OPENING DATE: March 20, 1969; PERFORMANCES: 72 (estimated); SKETCHES: Warren Burton, Bud Cort, Frank Giordano, Jay Jeffries, Steve Nelson, James Rusk, and Rod Warren; LYRICS: Dan Almagor, David Finkle, Alan Foster Friedman, Brandon Maggart, Lance Mulcahy, and Rod Warren; MUSIC: Alan Foster Friedman, Brandon Maggart, Lance Mulcahy, Rod Warren, and Bill Weeden; DIRECTION: Ronny Graham; CHOREOGRAPHY: Bruce Becker; COSTUMES: Bernard Johnson; LIGHTING: Larry Carter; MUSICAL DIRECTION: Jerry Goldberg; PRODUCER: Rod Warren, in association with Bill Weeden and David Finkle

CAST—Warren Burton, Bud Cort, Patti Deutsch, Judy Engles, Brandon Maggart

The revue was presented in two acts.

ACT ONE—"What Kind of Life Is This?" (lyric by David Finkle, from the original Hebrew by Dan Almagor; music by Bill Weeden) (Company) "Street Scene" (sketch by Rod Warren) (Patti Deutsch, Judy Engles) "The Anti-Establishment Rag" (lyric and music by Rod Warren) (Company), "Peaceful Coexistence" (sketch by Steve Nelson) (Brandon Maggart, introducing Judy Engles for "PEACE") "The Jug Song" (lyric and music by Brandon Maggart) (Brandon Maggart) "Let It All Hang Out" (sketch by Frank Giordano) (Patti Deutsch, Bud Cort) "The Moon Song" (lyric by David Finkle, music by Bill Weeden) (Warren Burton, Bud Cort, Brandon Maggart) Patti Deutsch for "PEACE" "The Flight of the Wasp" (lyric and music by Rod Warren) (Warren Burton), "Just Rapping" (lyric by David Finkle, music by Bill Weeden) (Company), Warren Burton for "PEACE," "Nothing Sacred" (sketch by Warren Burton and Jay Jeffries) (Company)

ACT TWO—"Breathes There a Man with Soul So Dead?" (lyric and music by Rod Warren) (Company) Brandon Maggart for "PEACE," "Generation Gap" (sketch by James Rusk) (Warren Burton, Brandon Maggart, with Patti Deutsch, Judy Engles), "That Switched-On Feeling" (lyric by David Finkle, music by Bill Weeden) (Patti Deutsch) "Classified Information" (sketch by Bud Cort) (Judy Engles, Bud Cort) "The Tribute" (lyric and music by Alan Foster Friedman) (Company) "Bye the Time" (lyric and music by Brandon Maggart) (Brandon Maggart) Bud Cort for "PEACE," "Chanson Francais" (lyric and music by Lance Mulcahy) (Warren Burton) "L'After Lines" (sketch by Warren Burton) (Company) Finale (Company)

NOTES—Sadly, this was the twelfth and last of Rod Warren's revues (for a complete list of his revues, see entry for *...And in This Corner* or Appendix R). For the final entry, he was joined by Ronny Graham, who directed the revue and who was himself a major name from the golden age of the Off Broadway revue.

Free Fall's title was indeed prophetic. With the demise of the classic Upstairs/Downstairs-styled revues, New York was never to know another long-running series of topical evenings performed in classy surroundings by tuxedoed actors and gowned actresses, all of whom offered up the latest round of satiric songs and sketches by a virtual stock company of talented sketch writers, lyricists, and composers.

543 Frere Jacques. THEATRE: Theatre 802; OPENING DATE: June 6, 1968; PERFORMANCES: 13; BOOK: Gerald Singer; LYRICS: Gerald Singer; MUSIC: Gerald Singer; DIRECTION: Richard Balin; MUSICAL DIRECTION: Harry Goodman; PRODUCER: Singer Productions, Inc.

CAST—Joe Disraeli (Jacques, a/k/a John Friedman), David Tabor (Brother David), Nina Dova (Aunt Emma Goldman), Pamela Hall (Julie Goldman), Michael Makman (Stanley Goldman), Sy Cohen (Uncle Samuel Goldman), Douglas Fisher (Percy Johnson), Carolyn Dahl (Joanne Harvey)

The action occurs in Brooklyn at the present time.

The musical was presented in two acts (division of acts and song assignments unknown; songs are listed in performance order).

MUSICAL NUMBERS—"Cum Deum," "Philosophy," "I Remember," "A Kiss Is a Poem," "Keep the Cool," "Smile and Be Gracious," "Frere Jacques Rock," "You Can't Judge the World," "The Love of a Woman," "Julie," "The Heffley & Browne Secretarial School"

NOTES—The perhaps only slightly farfetched plot of *Frere Jacques* dealt with a nice Jewish boy who, after being raised in Tibet by Jesuit monks, returns to his family in Brooklyn and becomes a famous rock 'n' roll star.

According to Vincent Canby in the *New York Times*, Theatre 802 was "a tiered dining room" located in the area of the Verrazano Bridge in Brooklyn (audience members could order food and drinks before the performance and during intermission). Despite the Brooklyn location, the musical was produced under a standard Off Broadway contract (Canby referred to *Frere Jacques* as an "off off Second Avenue" production). As for the musical itself, Canby felt the "vanity" production had the "wobbly look of an amateur theatrical."

544 Frimbo. "A New Musical." THEATRE: The musical was performed at Grand Central Station on Terminal Tracks 39 to 42; OPENING DATE: November 9, 1980; PERFORMANCES: 1; BOOK: John L. Haber; LYRICS: Jim Wann; MUSIC: Howard Harris; DIRECTION: John L. Haber; SCENERY: Karl Eigsti with Fred Buchholz; COSTUMES: Patricia McGourty; LIGHTING: Fred Buchholz; MUSICAL DIRECTION: Howard Harris; PRODUCERS: Dodger Productions, John L. Haber, and Louis Busch Hager

CAST—RICHARD B. SHULL (E.M. Frimbo), Larry Riley (Conductor), Trio (Pattie D'Arcy, Pauletta Pearson, Cass Morgan), Deborah May (Guest Vocalist [Contessa]), The Band: Peter Poacquadio, Trumpet; Peter Ecklund, Trumpet; Britt Woodman, Tenor and Bass Trombone; Ralph Olsen, Alto Saxophone and Clarinet; Art Bressler, Tenor Saxophone and Bass Clarinet; Lenny Klinger, Baritone and Soprano Saxophones; Matt Glaser, Violin; Stephen Roane, Bass; Bill Ward, Drums; Edwin Rodregues, Percussion; Howard Harris, Piano)

SOURCE—The 1974 book *All Aboard with E.M. Frimbo: World's Greatest Railroad Buff* by Rogers E.M. Whitaker and Anthony Hiss.

"The train will be an express, without a layover" (that is, one act, no intermission!).

MUSICAL NUMBERS—"The Frimbo Special" (The Band), "The Ballad of Frimbo" (Larry Riley, Company), "The Train" (Company), "Train Walking" (Larry Riley, Company), "Trains or Me" (Richard B. Shull, Pattie D'Arcy, Pauletta Pearson, Cass Morgan), "Going Home" (Richard B. Shull), "Lady by Choice" (Deborah May, Company), "On a Train at Night" (Richard B. Shull, Deborah May), "I Hate Trains" (Pattie D'Arcy, Pauletta Pearson, Cass Morgan, The Band), "Mambo Frimbo" ("Club Car" and Company), "The Mileage Millionaire" (Richard B. Shull, Company), "Gone Everywhere But Home" (Deborah May), "Siberia" (Pattie D'Arcy, Pauletta Pearson, Cass Morgan, The Band), "Ode to Steam" (Larry Riley, Company), "That's the Way to Make It Move" (Larry Riley, Company), "Names of the Trains" (Company), "Ballad of Frimbo" (reprise) (Larry Riley, Company)

NOTES—No Off Broadway musical ever premiered in such a bizarre venue as *Frimbo*. Its first and last performance took place at Grand Central Station, in the area of Tracks 39-42. Because the musical was about trains, the setting was at least appropriate. Even the program was in keeping with the theme, since it was in the shape and form of a railroad timetable. During previews, the musical was presented in two acts ("There will be a ten minute layover for refreshments at Seward"). However, by opening night the musical was presented in one act, there had been considerable reshuffling of songs (one, "Hey Stranger," was left on the tracks), and there were some cast changes as well. Mel Gussow in the *New York Times* reported that "short of Walter Matthau," Richard B. Shull was a fine choice for the title role. But Gussow noted the musical "chugged along with starts and stops," and indicated it was an "amiable oddity if you happen to be catching a train in Grand Central Station, but it's not a necessary excursion." Gussow singled out one number, "Names of the Trains" (a "flavorful patter song").

"Train" musicals don't seem to have much success in New York. Besides the one-performance *Frimbo*, the Off Broadway *A Bistro Car on the CNR* (see entry) was another train wreck. Further, Broadway's glorious art deco operetta *On the Twentieth Century* (1978) played for 460 performances without turning a profit, and *Starlight Express* (1987), which had a long and financially profitable run in London, lost money in its Broadway production despite an almost two-year run. And the 1994 Off Off Broadway musical *American Enterprise* (about George M. Pullman) lasted just two weeks (see entry).

545 From Brooks, with Love. "A New Musical." THEATRE: The Harold Clurman Theatre; OPENING DATE: March 30, 1983; PERFORMANCES: 4; BOOK: Wayne Sheridan; LYRICS: Wayne Sheridan; MUSIC: George Koch and Russ Taylor; DIRECTION: William Michael Maher; CHOREOGRAPHY: Robin Reseen; SCENERY: Tom Barnes; COSTUMES: Carol H. Buele; LIGHTING: Paul Sullivan; MUSICAL DIRECTION: Jim Fradrich; PRODUCER: Joseph L. Runner

CAST—Ralph Anthony (Jerry Wakefield), Gillian Walke (Lynn Pennington), Fred Bishop (Brendan Adams), Gwen Arment (Marjorie Morgan), Richard Sabellico (Rocco Sanducci), Geraldine Hanning (The Countess), Ken Seiter (Alan Perkins), Peter Blaxill (Harold Nettleton, Esq.)

The action occurs on the main floor and in the employees' lounge of one of New York's exclusive clothiers; the time is 8:59 A.M. to 5:30 P.M. on July 3.

The musical was presented in two acts.

ACT ONE—"The Main Floor" (Ralph Anthony, Gillian Walke, Fred Bishop, Gwen Arment, Richard Sabellico), "I'll Be Someone Someday" (Fred Bishop, Gwen Arment), "Brendan's Dream" (Fred Bishop, Ralph Anthony, Richard Sabellico, Ken Seiter, Gillian Walke, Gwen Arment, Geraldine Hanning), "Shopping" (Geraldine Hanning, Fred Bishop, Gwen Arment, Gillian Walke), "Marjorie's Dream" (Gwen Arment, Richard Sabellico, Ken Seiter, Fred Bishop, Peter Blaxill), "Love Is a Feeling" (Ralph Anthony, Fred Bishop), "The Service" (Geraldine Hanning, Peter Blaxill), "The Customer's Nightmare (*Eggs*)" (Geraldine Hanning, Peter Blaxill, Gwen Arment, Fred Bishop, Richard Sabellico, Ken Seiter, Gillian Walke), "Showbiz" (Ralph Anthony, Gwen Arment), "Rocco's Dream (*Security*)" (Richard Sabellico, Gwen Arment, Fred Bishop, Ken Seiter, Gillian Walke), "It's Nice" (Fred Bishop, Gwen Arment)

ACT TWO—"Unemployment" (Gwen Arment, Gillian Walke), "A New Kind of Husband" (Richard Sabellico, Fred Bishop), "Let's Go" (Richard Sabellico, Gillian Walke), "Lynn's Dream" (Gillian Walke, Richard Sabellico, Peter Blaxill, Geraldine Hanning), "Will They Remember" (Gwen Arment), "We'd Like to Go Back" (Geraldine Hanning, Peter Blaxill), "It's Nice" (reprise) (Fred Bishop, Gwen Arment), "Jerry's Dream ('Move Over, You Guys')" (Ralph Anthony, Richard Sabellico, Ken Seiter, Gillian Walke, Gwen Arment), "Will They Remember" (reprise) (Gwen Arment), "Move Over, You Guys" (reprise) (Ralph Anthony)

NOTES—*From Brooks, with Love*, an Off Off Broadway musical about an exclusive clothing store, didn't last a full week, but sounds somewhat ambitious. It told its story through songs as well as five dream (and one nightmare) sequences. This was the second musical to open in March 1983 which dealt with the garment trade (see entries for *The Rise of David Levinsky*).

546 From My Hometown. THEATRE: Gramercy Theatre; OPENING DATE: July 22, 2004; PERFORMANCES: 36; BOOK: Lee Summers, Ty Stephens, and Herbert Rawlings, Jr.; LYRICS: Lee Summers, Ty Stephens, and Will Barrow; MUSIC: Lee Summers, Ty Stephens, and Will Barrow; DIRECTION: Kevin Ramsey; CHOREOGRAPHY: Kevin Ramsey and Leslie Dockery

Scenery and Projections: Matthew Myhrum; COSTUMES: Deborah A. Cheretun; LIGHTING: Aaron Spivey; MUSICAL DIRECTION: Stacey Penson; PRODUCERS: Lee Summers in association with Leonard Soloway and Steven M. Levy

CAST—Kevin R. Free (Memphis), Andre Garner (Detroit), Rodney Hicks (Philly)

The musical was presented in one act.

NOTES—*From My Hometown* was about three aspiring Black rhythm-and-blues entertainers (from Detroit, Memphis, and Philadelphia) who go to New York to seek fame and fortune. The musical had originally premiered at the Milwaukee Repertory Theatre in April 1998, and was later produced Off Off Broadway on June 19, 2003, by the Amas Musical Theatre.

In reviewing the Off Broadway production, Lawrence Van Gelder in the *New York Times* reported that the musical offered almost forty songs during the one-act ninety-minute evening, and noted that the "all-too-familiar" story "meant well" and "sometimes it does very well indeed."

547 From Renoir—to Reagan. "A Kabaretistic Kaleidoscope." THEATRE: The 3 Muses Theatre; OPENING DATE: March 3, 1982; PERFORMANCES: 20; TEXT AND LYRICS: Herbert Nelson; MUSIC: Herbert Nelson; PRODUCERS: Mina Carvi-Bozza and Guild Media

CAST—HERBERT AND EVA NELSON

The revue was presented in one act (all material performed by Herbert and Eva Nelson).

MUSICAL NUMBERS—"At the Chat Noir," "To Err Is Human," "A Freudian Slip," "The Story of Nelly O.," "Dada 1982," "The Fabulous Twenties," "Falling in Love Again" (from 1930 film *The Blue Angel*; English lyric by Sammy Lerner, music by Frederick Hollander), "By Brecht and Weill," "The Ballad of Louis," "The Ism Song," "The Cabaret Dies—The Cabaret Lives," "...And the Pursuit of Happiness," "More on the Same Subject," "March in the Right Direction," "Genetic Engineering," "The Kleptomaniac," "Genius at Work," "It's Gonna Rain!," "Leak Something to Me...," "The Evening News," "The Geisha Song," "The Late News," "$ $ $...," "Pick Me a Flower"

NOTES—The Off Off Broadway revue *From Renoir-to Reagan* was a self-described "Kabaretistic Kaleidoscope" and "An American Experience—in the European Tradition." Herbert and Eva Nelson had previously performed at the 3 Muses Theatre during Fall 1980 in their revue *...And the Pursuit of Happiness!*

548 From the Second City. THEATRE: Eastside Playhouse; OPENING DATE: October 14, 1969; PERFORMANCES: 31; MATERIAL: Written and improvised by the cast; DIRECTION: David Lynn; MUSIC: Fred Kaz; "Flower Song" lyric by Sandy Holt; SCENERY: Steven Holmes; LIGHTING: Gary Harris; PRODUCERS: Bernard Sahlins; Arts and Leisure Corp. Production

CAST—J.J. Barry, Murphy Dunne, Martin Harvey Friedberg, Burt Heyman, Pamela Hoffman, Ira Miller, Carol Robinson

NOTES—*From the Second City*, the ninth Second City revue to play Off Broadway, borrowed its name from the edition which had played on Broadway in 1961 (see entry for *Seacoast of Bohemia* for a list of all Second City productions which played in New York; also see Appendix T).

Clive Barnes in the *New York Times* found the material "bright and generally witty" and the performers fresh; his only regret was that the evening was generally tame and lacked "genuine, corrosive satire."

Throughout the 1960s, the Second City presented satiric, improvisatory revues to enthusiastic and receptive audiences. But as the decade wound down, the runs got shorter and shorter, and the1969 offering could muster only one month of performances. The previous season had seen the last of the Rod Warren's Upstairs at the Downstairs revues, and now the dwindling months of 1969 saw the beginning of the end of the Second City revues (there would be two more, in 1971 and in 1984). There would be other topical and improvisatory revues in Off Broadway's future (and, indeed, one of the latter proved highly popular), but for all purposes the era of intelligent, satiric, and topical entertainments for educated audiences was over. In their place came endless rock and other protest musicals and revues, all of which had their brief moment before disappearing as well. And when they were gone, it's unlikely anyone mourned their passing the way audiences did for the demise of the Bagley/Monk/Warren and Second City revues.

549 Frozen Roses. "A Theatrical Collage." THEATRE: The Entermedia's Second Story Theatre; OPENING DATE: May 2, 1984; PERFORMANCES: 20 (estimated); BOOK: August Armstrong; LYRICS: Mark Stewart; MUSIC: Mark Stewart; DIRECTION: August Armstrong; CHOREOGRAPHY: Michele Ribble; LIGHTING: Kimberly Foos; MUSICAL DIRECTION: Mark Stewart; PRODUCER: Street Magic Theatre

CAST—Joe Baer (The Men), Virginia Ferri (The Women)

NOTES—The program for the Off Off Broadway musical *Frozen Roses* indicated it was "about men and women." As Beatrice Lillie once said, "Too much plot."

There was no regular song listing in the program, but four songs were referenced: "Forever and Always," "Don't Blame Me," "The Dream Song," and "Only for One Night," the latter credited to Mark Stewart and Cathy Shields.

Sometime after the production closed, the musical was presented Off Broadway at the Colonnades Theatre (opening date and number of performances unknown); it was produced by Street Magic Theatre in association with Phil Werbel and Mikel Carvin, and was subtitled "A Serious Musical Comedy." Joe Baer and Virginia Ferri reprised their original roles, and August Armstrong and Mark Stewart were again the respective director and musical director. The musical was presented in two acts, and included the following songs: "I Have a Friend," "Sex Education," "The Telephone Song," "Going Out Tonight," "Necking," "College Cartoons," "Who Needs Love?," "Only for One Night," "Forever and Always," "Don't Blame Me!," "The Woman's Song," "The Father's Song," "Frozen Roses," "Touche," "There Was a Time," and "I Have a Friend" (reprise). "The Dream Song," which had been heard in the earlier Entermedia production, wasn't included in the second production, and the program didn't credit Mark Stewart and Cathy Shields with "Only for One Night."

550 Fun City. THEATRE: Jan Hus Playhouse; OPENING DATE: March 6, 1968; PERFORMANCES: 31; SKETCHES: David Rogers; special material by Fred Silver, Nelson Garringer, Jay Jeffries, Franklin Underwood, and Norman Martin; LYRICS: David Rogers; Mel Edwards and Dee Robinson (Mel 'n' Dee); MUSIC: James Reed Lawlor; Mel Edwards and Dee Robinson (Mel 'n' Dee); DIRECTION: David Rogers; SCENERY: Sal Tinnerello, Richard Burnside; COSTUMES: Frank Page, Michael Landi; with "special thanks" to the Good Will Shops; LIGHTING: David Anderson; MUSICAL DIRECTION: James Reed Lawlor; PRODUCER: Jack Irving

CAST—MR. LYNNE CARTER, Joan Porter, Ted Tinling, and introducing Mel Edwards and Dee Robinson (Mel 'n' Dee)

The revue was presented in two acts.

NOTES—The revue *Fun City* underwent considerable changes during its one-month run (at least four different insert lists of songs and sketches were included in programs during the brief run). The list below is taken from an insert included in the program for the second week of the run, and thus may represent the "final" version of the revue. Whenever possible, the names of the performers impersonated by Lynne Carter are noted in capital letters.

The insert also lists just four performers in the cast (Lynne Carter, Cari Stevens [who isn't listed in the regular program], and Mel 'n' Dee [Mel Edwards and Dee Robinson, who are credited for writing most of their material]; at one point during the run, Joan Porter and Ted Tinling left the production).

ACT ONE—Overture (Trio [James Reed Lawlor, piano; Averill Pollard, bass; and Ralph Jones, drums]), "Fun City" (lyric by David Rogers, music by James Reed Lawlor) (Mel 'n' Dee), "Have Piano and Hanky...Will Travel" (Lynne Carter) (impersonation of HILDEGARDE.), "The Old Gray Mayor He Ain't What He Used to Be" (Mel 'n' Dee), "A Tragic

Queen" (Lynne Carter) (HERMIONE GINGOLD), "Everything Leads Me to You" (Mel 'n' Dee), "Miss Subways" (Lynne Carter), "Bits of Nonsense" (Cari Stevens, Mel 'n' Dee), "Where the Elite Meet—Carnegie Hall" (Lynne Carter) (MOLLY PICON), "Would You Believe Me" (Mel 'n' Dee), "Manners" (Lynne Carter) (EARTHA KITT), "Louder! I Can't Hear You When the Philharmonic's Playing on Sheep Meadow" (Mel 'n' Dee), "Goodness Had Nothing to Do with It" (Lynne Carter) (MAE WEST)

ACT TWO—"Sudden Beauty" (Lynne Carter) (MARLENE DIETRICH), "I Adore You" (Mel 'n' Dee), "A Bunny's Mother" (Lynne Carter), "Orange Juice" (Cari Stevens), "Dear John—Help!" (Lynne Carter) (TALLULAH BANKHEAD), "Try, Try, Try" (Mel 'n'Dee), "Concert Reading at Town Hall" (Lynne Carter), "Smoking" (Cari Stevens), "A Gem of a Pearl" (Lynne Carter, Mel 'n' Dee) (PEARL BAILEY), "Fun City" (Company)

MORE NOTES—Lynne Carter's evening of female impersonations lasted only a month, and, as mentioned above, many sketches, impersonations, and songs were dropped during the run. Among the numbers which appear to have been in the show at one point or another are: "A Voice That Will Ring Forever" (ETHEL MERMAN), "(M) Is for the Money Things She Gave Me," "Cover Girl" (PHYLLIS DILLER), "Brooklyn Interlude" (lyric and music by Joel Herron), "Manners," "Going Highbrow" (BETTE DAVIS), "Hot Data," "As Long as You're Covered," "Madison Avenue Jingle," "Birth of a Nation," "Movies Are Your Best Entertainment," "Everybody Leaves Somebody Some Crime," and "Make Me a Match" (another PEARL BAILEY impersonation). It seems unlikely that the impersonations of Ethel Merman, Phyllis Diller, and Bette Davis were completely dropped, and so they may have appeared in the revue under different titles (such as the Pearl Bailey sketch, which was changed from "Make Me a Match" to "A Gem of a Pearl").

Richard F. Shepard in the *New York Times* praised Lynne Carter as "an extraordinarily gifted female impersonator ... if your taste runs to female impersonators," and he singled out one sequence in which Carter, impersonating Marlene Dietrich, discusses her new recording, which consists entirely of applause. He also liked the two "personable" young couples (Joan Porter and Ted Tinling, and Mel Edwards and Dee Robinson) who sang numbers which spoofed New York City life. But Shepard felt the revue was somewhat overstuffed with songs and sketches ("enough is too much already"), and suggested some of the material might have been more effective had it been developed before being performed in front of a live audience. And, like so many Off Broadway revues, he indicated the evening would have been more at home in a nightclub than in a theatre. Lynne Carter returned in 1971 for a special one-performance engagement which was presented at Carnegie Hall (see entry for *It's Lynne Carter*).

551 Funeral March for a One-Man Band. THEATRE: Westbeth Theatre; OPENING DATE: May 14, 1978; PERFORMANCES: 12; PLAY: Ron Whyte (conceived in collaboration with H. Thomas Moore); LYRICS: Robert Satuloff; MUSIC: Mel Marvin; DIRECTION: Leonard Peters; SCENERY: Salvatore Tagliarino; COSTUMES: Carol Oditz; LIGHTING: Paul Gallo; MUSICAL DIRECTION: John McKinney; PRODUCER: Westbeth Theatre Center

CAST—Dwight Schultz (Michael), Thomas Toner (Mr. Chrisolde, Dad), June Squibb (Head Nurse, Mom), Rob DeRosa (Tiny, Jamie), Dennis Boutsikaris (Mike), Ellen Barber (Joanna)

The action occurs in the present time in a room at a New York City hospital.

The play with music was presented in two acts.

NOTES—The Off Off Broadway play *Funeral March for a One-Man Band* included songs by Robert Satuloff and Mel Marvin.

552 Funny Feet. THEATRE: Lamb's Theatre; OPENING DATE: April 21, 1987; PERFORMANCES: 103; DIRECTION: Bob Bowyer; "Creative Supervision" by Art Wolff; CHOREOGRAPHY: Bob Bowyer; SCENERY: Lindsay W. Davis; COSTUMES: Lindsay W. Davis; LIGHTING: Arden Fingerhut; PRODUCERS: Nancy E. Diamond in association with Hieronymus Foundation, Inc., and Universal Artists Management, Inc.

CAST—Wilton Anderson (Philippe, A Molotov Brother, X, Ray, Welcoming Committee, A Helping Hand), Matthew Baker (A Molotov Brother, Beam, Host), Bob Bowyer (A New Yorker, Baby Bobby, Older Man, Mr. Green, Mourner, Security), Veronica Castonguay (Jeannine, Mother, Simone, Brenda Sue, A Molotov Brother, A Paracomic, Welcoming Committee, Hostess), Sandra Chinn (Natasha Roach, Playmate, Younger Woman, Z, The Dearly Departed), Irene Cho (Organism II, Betti Li), Martha Connerton (Rhoda Fernandez, Goldie, Older Woman, Danseuse, Hostess), Amy Flood (Madelaine, Bobbi-Jo, Danseuse, Hostess), Zane Rankin (Rudolph Roach, Seymour Fernandez, Organism I, Younger Man, Sting, A Paracomic, Premier Danseur, A Party Giver), D. Kevin Rhind (Jacques, Father, Eduardo, A Molotov Brother, Y, Haze, Man, Welcoming Committee, Host)

The revue was presented in one act.

MUSICAL NUMBERS—"Black Cockroach Pas de Deux" (from "Grand Tarantella for Piano and Orchestra" by Louis Moreau Gottschalk [reconstructed by Hershey Kay]) (Bob Bowyer, Zane Rankin, Sandra Chinn), "Jacques and Jeannine" ("What I Did for Love," from 1975 musical *A Chorus Line* [see entry], lyric by Edward Kleban, music by Marvin Hamlisch) (D. Kevin Rhind, Veronica Castonguay), "Baby Bobby's Backyard" ("Meditation" from 1894 opera *Thais* by Jules Massenet) (Bob Bowyer, D. Kevin Rhind, Sandra Chinn, Veronica Castonguay) "La Stampa de Feeta" ("Malaguena" by Ernesto Lecuona) (Zane Rankin, Martha Connerton), "Les Jazz Chics" ("I Hear a Symphony," lyric and music by Eddie Holland, Lamont Dozier, and Brian Holland) (D. Kevin Rhind, Wilton Anderson, Veronica Castonguay, Amy Flood), "Duet for Mating Organisms" ("Adagio for Strings, Opus 11" by Samuel Barber) (Zane Rankin, Irene Cho) "Molotov Brothers" ("Hungarian Dance No. 5" by Johannes Brahms) (Wilton Anderson, Matthew Baker, Veronica Castonguay, D. Kevin Rhind), "Remembrance Waltz" ("Nocturne" by Frederic Chopin) (Martha Connerton, Bob Bowyer, Sandra Chinn, Zane Rankin), "The Buttercups" ("You Are My Friend," lyric and music by Patti LaBelle, Budd Ellison, and Armstead Edwards) (Irene Cho, Veronica Castonguay, Amy Flood, Wilton Anderson, Bob Bowyer, D. Kevin Rhind, Martha Connerton, Zane Rankin, Matthew Baker), "Pas de Trois pour la Psychologie Contemporaine" ("Piano Concerto #2 in C Minor, Opus 18 (2nd Movement, Adagio Sostenuto" by Serge Rachmaninoff) (Wilton Anderson, D. Kevin Rhind, Sandra Chinn), "Smile" ("Send in the Clowns," from 1973 musical *A Little Night Music*, lyric and music by Stephen Sondheim) (D. Kevin Rhind, Veronica Castonguay, Zane Rankin), "Faux Pas de Trois" ("Waltz" from 1859 opera *Faust* by Charles Francois Gounod) (Zane Rankin, Martha Connerton, Amy Flood), "The Big Ballet in the Sky" ("Adagio in G Minor for Strings" by Johann Someri; "Hallelujah Chorus" by George Frederic Handel; and "The Beloved Choruses") (Sandra Chinn, Bob Bowyer, Wilton Anderson, Veronica Castonguay, D. Kevin Rhind, Zane Rankin, Matthew Baker, Amy Flood), Bows ("That's Entertainment" from 1953 film *The Band Wagon*, lyric by Howard Dietz, music by Arthur Schwartz) (Company)

NOTES—Bob Bowyer's dance revue *Funny Feet* spoofed professional dancing in all its forms (ballet, ballroom, Broadway, modern dance), all set to prerecorded music.

Stephen Holden in the *New York Times* found "The Buttercups" the evening's highlight, a "rhapsodically amusing" blend of Disney and Motown into an "irresistibly sunny fantasy of floral wellbeing." He also had praise for Bowyer's "wickedly funny" spoof of "exhibitionistic" pop dancing styles and his ribbing of "psychologically tormented" modern dance.

553 Further Mo'. THEATRE: The Village Gate/Downstairs; OPENING DATE: May 17, 1990; PERFORMANCES: 174; CONCEIVED AND WRITTEN BY Vernel Bagneris

Lyrics and Music by various lyricists and composers (not credited in the program); DIRECTION: Vernel Bagneris; CHOREOGRAPHY: Pepsi Bethel; SCENERY: Charles McClennahan; COSTUMES: Joanne Clevenger; LIGHTING: John McKernon; MUSICAL DIRECTION: Orange Kellin; PRODUCERS: Norzar Productions, Inc., and Michael Frazier

CAST—James "Red" Wilcher (Theatre Owner), Topsy Chapman (Thelma), Vernel Bagneris (Papa Du), Frozine Thomas (Ma Reed), Sandra Reaves-Phillips (Big Bertha), The New Orleans Blue Serenaders

The action occurs at the Lyric Theatre in New Orleans in 1927.

The musical was presented in two acts.

ACT ONE—"Shake It and Break It" (The New Orleans Blue Serenaders), "Messing Around" (Topsy Chapman, Vernel Bagneris, Frozine Thomas), "Sweetie Dear" (Topsy Chapman, Vernel Bagneris), "Salty Dog" (Frozine Thomas), "One Hour Mama" (Sandra Reaves-Phillips), "Mississippi Mud" (Vernel Bagneris, Topsy Chapman, Frozine Thomas), "Wild Women" (Frozine Thomas), "Sweet Man" (Topsy Chapman), "Positively No (Construction Gang)" (Sandra Reaves-Phillips, Vernel Bagneris), "Had to Give Up Gym" (Frozine Thomas, Topsy Chapman), "Trouble in Mind" (Sandra Reaves-Phillips), "Pretty Doll" (The New Orleans Blue Serenaders), "Here Comes the Hot Tamale Man" (Company)

ACT TWO—"Boogie Woogie" (The New Orleans Blue Serenaders), "Come On In" (Company), "My Man" (Topsy Chapman), "Don't Advertise Your Man" (Sandra Reaves-Phillips), "Baby, Won't You Please Come Home" (Sandra Reaves-Phillips, Frozine Thomas, Topsy Chapman), "Funny Feathers" (Vernel Bagneris), "Clarinet Marmalade" (The New Orleans Blue Serenaders), "West Indies Blues" (Frozine Thomas, Sandra Reaves-Phillips, Topsy Chapman), "Boot It Boy" (Vernel Bagneris), "Alabamy Bound" (Topsy Chapman, Frozine Thomas, Vernel Bagneris), "Home Sweet Home" (Topsy Chapman, Sandra Reaves-Phillips), "Hot Times in the Ole Town Tonight" (Company)

NOTES—*Further Mo'* was Vernel Bagneris' sequel to his enormously successful *One Mo' Time!* (see entry). In the new revue-cum-musical, the same characters from the previous musical were again appearing in New Orleans at the Lyric Theatre in yet another revue, and the evening alternated between backstage goings-on and songs presented in performance on the stage of the Lyric Theatre.

Although Stephen Holden in the *New York Times* found the evening "rollicking," the new work played for a disappointing 174 performances (its predecessor ran for 1,372 performances). Holden mentioned that while the book "fizzles," the music "sails," and noted that those who sought a more "high-style" version of similar material would do well to get tickets for *Black and Blue*, a revue which was currently playing on Broadway. But he concluded that while *Further Mo'* wasn't as "ambitious as its uptown cousin," it nonetheless offered "hot music, steamy atmosphere and lowdown fun."

554 The Future. THEATRE: Judson Poets' Theatre; OPENING DATE: March 25, 1974; PERFORMANCES: 24 (estimated); BOOK: Al Carmines; LYRICS: Al Carmines; MUSIC: Al Carmines; DIRECTION: Al Carmines; CHOREOGRAPHY: Dan Wagoner; SCENERY: Elwin Charles Terrel 2nd Costumes: Ira Siff and Mary Christine Barth; LIGHTING: David J. Dean; MUSICAL DIRECTION: Al Carmines (?); PRODUCER: The Judson Poets' Theatre

CAST—Cast included David Pursley, Essie Borden, Ira Siff, Lee Guilliatt, and Reathel Bean

NOTES—This Off Off Broadway musical *The Future* took a look at life in 2048. According to Mel Gussow in the *New York Times*, Carmines' "future" was a frozen and emotionless one, and he apparently intended the sermon-like evening to be a cautionary tale to remind his audience that manners, values, and emotions are necessary for a fulfilled existence. If Carmines' book was somewhat random and gratuitous, Gussow praised his score, which included "four or five of the composer's most vibrant songs" (Gussow singled out "The Rediscovery of the Eunich" and "Survey of Western Culture"). Besides the principals, the cast included a large chorus (Gussow noted they were "multitudinous" in number).

555 Fyvush Finkel/From Second Avenue to Broadway. "A Musical Comedy Gift." THEATRE: John Houseman Theatre; OPENING DATE: December 22, 1996; PERFORMANCES: 16; LIGHTING: Robert Bessoir; MUSICAL DIRECTION: Ian Finkel; PRODUCER: Eric Krebs

CAST—FYVUSH FINKEL, Ian Finkel, The Finkel Orchestra

The revue was presented in two acts (the program didn't designate division of acts).

MUSICAL NUMBERS—Bie Mir Overture, "Bumble Bee Freilach," Yiddish Theatre Klezmer Medley, "Finkel & Son," Songs in My Mother Tongue and in English, "As Long as I'm with You" (lyric and music by Elliot Finkel and Philip Namenworth), "Mambo Jambo," Gershwin Tribute, "In the Barrel House," "Not on the Top," "If I Were a Rich Man" (from *Fiddler on the Roof*, 1964; lyric by Sheldon Harnick, music by Jerry Bock), "I'm Glad I'm Not Young Anymore" (1958 film *Gigi*; lyric by Alan Jay Lerner, music by Frederick Loewe), "L'Chaim (To Life)" (*Fiddler on the Roof*, 1964; lyric by Sheldon Harnick, music by Jerry Bock)

NOTES—After appearing in this evening of Broadway and Yiddish songs, Fyvush Finkel returned the following season in an Off Off production of the revue, which played for eleven performances at Town Hall beginning on December 25, 1997; the revival, which included all material from the 1996 production (as well as a medley of Christmas and Hanukah songs), was produced by Eric Krebs (Bruce Roberts was Associate Producer).

For another revue with Finkel, see entry for *Finkel's Follies*.

556 The Game Is Up (First Edition). "A New Musical Revue." THEATRE: Upstairs at the Downstairs; OPENING DATE: September 29, 1964; PERFORMANCES: 260; SKETCHES: R.G. Brown, Dee Caruso, Bill Kaufman, Paul Koreto, Bill Levine, Joan Rivers, Les Roberts, Hap Schlein, Treva Silverman, and Rod Warren; LYRICS: Richard Blair, Alan Friedman, Michael McWhinney, John Meyer, Les Roberts, James Rusk, Frank Underwood, and Rod Warren; MUSIC: Alan Friedman, John Meyer, Jerry Powell, Les Roberts, James Rusk, Ted Simon, Frank Underwood, and Rod Warren; DIRECTION: Jonathan Lucas; CHOREOGRAPHY: Jonathan Lucas (?); SCENERY: Tom Harriss; MUSICAL DIRECTION: Daniel Strickland and Michael Cohen at the twin pianos; PRODUCER: Rod Warren

CAST—Richard Blair, R.G. Brown, Virgil Curry, Judy Knaiz, Marian Mercer, Carol Morley

The revue was presented in two acts.

ACT ONE—"The Game Is Up" (lyric and music by Rod Warren) (Company) "Sunday Television" (lyric and music by Rod Warren) (Judy Knaiz, Carol Morley, Richard Blair, Virgil Curry) "Supermarket" (sketch by Rod Warren) (Richard Blair, Virgil Curry) "Freedom" (lyric and music by Frank Underwood) (Judy Knaiz, Carol Morley) "Uncle Sam Wants Who?" (lyric by Howard Liebling, music by Marvin Hamlisch) (Richard Blair), "Ding Dong Cocktail Party" (sketch by Les Roberts) (Judy Knaiz, Carol Morley, Richard Blair, R.G. Brown) "What's in a Name?" (lyric and music by Les Roberts) (Judy Knaiz, Marian Mercer, Carol Morley) "76 Foolish Things" (lyric and music by Les Roberts) (R.G. Brown) "Tinsel" (lyric and music by John Meyer) (Judy Knaiz, Richard Blair, R.G. Brown, Virgil Curry), "Trio Con Brio" (lyric by Bruce Williamson, music by Blair Weille) (Carol Morley, Richard Blair, R.G. Brown), "Job Interview" (sketch by Joan Rivers and Treva Silverman) (Judy Knaiz, Marian Mercer) "Hip Hooray" (lyric and music by James Rusk) (Company)

ACT TWO—"Tokyo, Mon Amour" (lyric and music by Rod Warren) (Company) "Forgotten Words" (lyric and music by Rod Warren) (Marian Mercer, Virgil Curry) "Keep 'Em Flying" (sketch by Bill Kaufman and Paul Koreto) (Judy Knaiz, Carol Morley, Richard Blair, R.G. Brown, Virgil Curry), "The Loves in My Life" (lyric by Nino Banome, music by Julian Stein) (Marian Mercer), "I'm the Girl" (lyric and music by Alan Friedman) (Judy Knaiz, Richard Blair), "The Doll Song" (lyric and music by James Rusk) (Carol Morley) "Speed Typists" (sketch by R.G. Brown) (Marian Mercer, R.G. Brown) "Adam Clayton Powell" (lyric and music by Rod Warren) (Virgil Curry), "Hello, Columbus" (sketch by Hap Schlein) (Company), Finale: "The Game Is Up" (lyric and music by Rod Warren) (Company)

NOTES—*The Game Is Up* was the second of Rod Warren's revues at the Upstairs at the Downstairs, and, like the successful *...And in This Corner* (1964; see entry) which preceded it, it, too, had a long run (260 performances for the first edition; plus two other editions, both in 1965; see entries).

In keeping with the tradition of the Upstairs revues, *The Game Is Up* spoofed topical trends (the emergence of the discotheque) and current politics (Adam Clayton Powell).

Richard F. Shepard in the *New York Times* liked the "charming" company and found the material "breezy, tuneful, often funny ... a steady run of chuckles punctuated by some belly laughs." He singled out a number of sequences, including the songs "Forgotten Words" (a laundry list of "departed" words, such as "Idlewild," "el," and "lend-lease") and "76 Foolish Things" (a one-man spoof of *The Music Man* [1957]).

It appears that some numbers in the above song list may not have been heard on opening night and were added during the run (such as "Uncle Sam Wants Who?," "Trio Con Brio," and "The Loves in My Life") while others were added during the run and then later dropped (for example, "Eye on New York," sketch by Dee Caruso and Bill Levine, performer[s] unknown; "Beth," lyric by Richard Blair, music by Ted Simon, performer[s] unknown; "Discotheque," lyric and music by Rod Warren, performer[s] unknown; and "Love's Labour Lost," lyric by Michael McWhinney, music by Jerry Powell, performer[s] unknown). "The Doll Song" and "Love's Labour Lost" were also heard in the retrospective revue *Below the Belt* (1966; see entry), and the latter can be heard on that revue's cast album. "Trio Con Brio" had first been heard in *Tour de Four* (see entry).

"Uncle Sam Wants Who?" was the first song by Marvin Hamlisch to be heard in a New York musical. "Tokyo, Mon Amour" had been previously heard in *...And in This Corner* (1964; see entry).

For a complete list of Rod Warren's revues, see entry for *...And in This Corner*; also see Appendix R.

557 The Game Is Up (Second Edition). "A New Musical Revue." THEATRE: Upstairs at the Downstairs; OPENING DATE: March 11, 1965; PERFORMANCES: 132; SKETCHES: Dee Caruso, Bill Kaufman, Paul Koreto, Bill Levine, Gayle Parent, Les Roberts, Hap Schlein, Kenny Solms, and Rod Warren; LYRICS: Howard Liebling, John Meyer, Les Roberts, James Rusk, Frank Underwood, and Rod Warren; MUSIC: Marvin Hamlisch, John Meyer, Les Roberts, James Rusk, Daniel Strickland, Frank Underwood, and Rod Warren; DIRECTION: Jonathan Lucas; with staging by Sandra Devlin for the second edition; CHOREOGRAPHY: Jonathan Lucas (?); SCENERY: Tom Harriss; MUSICAL DIRECTION: Daniel Strickland and Michael Cohen at the twin pianos; PRODUCER: Rod Warren

CAST—Richard Blair, R.G. Brown, Virgil Curry, Judy Knaiz, Marian Mercer, Carol Morley

The revue was presented in two acts.

ACT ONE—"The Game Is Up" (lyric and music by Rod Warren) (Company) "Sunday Television" (lyric and music by Rod Warren) (Judy Knaiz, Carol Morley, Richard Blair, Virgil Curry) "Anna Maria" (sketch by Dee Caruso) (Marian Mercer, R.G. Brown), "Freedom" (lyric and music by Frank Underwood) (Judy Knaiz, Carol Morley) "Supermarket" (sketch by Rod Warren) (Richard Blair, Virgil Curry) "Radio City Music Hall" (lyric and music by Rod Warren) (Judy Knaiz, Marian Mercer, Carol Morley) "Ding Dong Cocktail Party" (sketch by Les Roberts) (Judy Knaiz, Carol Morley, Richard Blair, R.G. Brown), "Doris" (lyric by Howard Liebling, music by Marvin Hamlisch) (Richard Blair, with Judy Knaiz, Carol Morley) "76 Foolish Things" (lyric and music by Les Roberts) (R.G. Brown) "Tinsel" (lyric and music by John Meyer) (Judy Knaiz, Richard Blair, R.G. Brown, Virgil Curry) "Discotheque" (lyric and music by Rod Warren) (Carol Morley, Richard Blair, R.G. Brown), "Eye on New York" (sketch by Dee Caruso and Bill Levine) (Marian Mercer, Virgil Curry) "Hip Hooray" (lyric and music by James Rusk) (Company)

ACT TWO—"The Great Society Waltz" (lyric and music by Rod Warren) (Company), "Forgotten Words" (lyric and music by Rod Warren) (Marian Mercer, Virgil Curry) "Keep 'Em Flying" (sketch by Bill Kaufman and Paul Koreto) (Judy Knaiz, Carol Morley, Richard Blair, R.G. Brown, Virgil Curry), "The Jean Harlow Story" (lyric by Rod Warren, music by Daniel Strickland) (Marian Mercer) "Where There's Smoke" (sketch by Les Roberts) (Judy Knaiz, Richard Blair) "The Doll Song" (lyric and music by James Rusk) (Carol Morley) "American Express—Italian Style" (sketch by Kenny Solms and Gayle Parent) (Marian Mercer, R.G. Brown) "Adam Clayton Powell" (lyric and music by Rod Warren) (Virgil Curry) "Hello Central Park" (sketch by Hap Schlein) (Company), Finale: "The Game Is Up" (lyric and music by Rod Warren) (Company)

NOTES—This was the second edition of Rod Warren's successful revue, which ran for 260 performances the first time around (see entry). New numbers for this edition were: "Anna Maria," "Radio City Music Hall," "Doris" (Marvin Hamlisch's second contribution to the series), "The Great Society Waltz," "Eye on New York," "Where There's Smoke," "American Express—Italian Style," "Hello Central Park," and the timely "The Jean Harlow Story" (1965 saw two competing films on the subject).

"Doris," "Eye on New York," and "The Great Society Waltz" also appeared in the retrospective revue *Below the Belt* (1966; see entry), and the latter song appears on that revue's cast album; "The Great Society Waltz" also was heard in *The Playoffs of Mixed Doubles* (see entry).

A third edition of *The Game Is Up* opened later in the year (see entry).

For a complete list of Rod Warren's revues, see entry for *...And in This Corner*; also see Appendix R.

558 The Game Is Up (Third Edition). "A New Musical Revue." THEATRE: Downstairs at the Upstairs; OPENING DATE: June 15, 1965; PERFORMANCES: 228; SKETCHES: Dee Caruso, Bill Kaufman, Paul Koreto, Bill Levine, Gayle Parent, Les Roberts, Kenny Solms, and Rod Warren; LYRICS: Linda Ashton, Lesley Davison, Alan Friedman, Michael McWhinney, John Meyer, Franklin (Frank) Underwood, and Rod Warren; MUSIC: Michael Cohen, Lesley Davison, Alan Friedman, Marvin Hamlisch, John Meyer, Franklin (Frank) Underwood, and Rod Warren; DIRECTION: Sandra Devlin; SCENERY: Tom Harriss; MUSICAL DIRECTION: Daniel Strickland at the singular piano; PRODUCER: Rod Warren

CAST—Betty Aberlin, Richard Blair, R.G. Brown, Ruth Buzzi, Linda Lavin

The revue was presented in two acts.

ACT ONE—"The Game Is Up" (lyric and music by Rod Warren) (Company) "(Daytime) Sunday Television" (lyric and music by Rod Warren) (Betty Aberlin, Ruth Buzzi, Richard Blair) "Eye on New York" (sketch by Dee Caruso and Bill Levine) (Linda Lavin, R.G. Brown) "Freedom" (lyric and music by Franklin [Frank] Underwood) (Betty Aberlin, Ruth Buzzi), "Discotheque" (lyric and music by Rod Warren; choreography by R.G. Brown) (Linda Lavin, Richard Blair, R.G. Brown) "Tinsel" (lyric and music by John Meyer) (Ruth Buzzi "and parts of" Richard Blair and R.G. Brown), "Camp" (lyric and music by Rod Warren) (Betty Aberlin, Ruth Buzzi, Linda Lavin) "76 Foolish Things" (sketch by Les Roberts) (R.G. Brown, Company) "Counterpoint" (lyric and music by Alan Friedman) (Linda Lavin, Richard Blair), "Keep 'Em Flying" (sketch by Bill Kaufman and Paul Koreto) (Company) "I Like the Job" (lyric by Linda Ashton, music by Michael Cohen) (Betty Aberlin) "Suburbia Square Dance" (lyric by Michael McWhinney, music by Rod Warren) (Company)

ACT TWO—"The Great Society Waltz" (lyric and music by Rod Warren) (Company) "Resale Shop" (sketch by Rod Warren) (Betty Aberlin, Linda Lavin) "Lady Bird" (lyric and music by Lesley Davison) (Ruth Buzzi, R.G. Brown) "Doris" (lyric by Howard Liebling, music by Marvin Hamlisch) (Richard Blair, Company) "American Express—Italian Style" (sketch by Kenny Solms and Gayle Parent) (Betty Aberlin, R.G. Brown) "The Day the Peace Action Broke Out" (lyric and music by Rod Warren) (Linda Lavin) "International Monopoly" (sketch by Rod Warren) (Company), Finale: "The Game Is Up" (lyric and music by Rod Warren) (Company)

NOTES—For its third edition, *The Game Is Up* moved Downstairs; the combined run for the three editions was 620 performances (see entries for the first two editions).

The new numbers for this edition were: "Camp," "Counterpoint," "I Like the Job," "Suburbia Square Dance," "Resale Shop" (a/k/a "Gentlemen's Resale Shop"), "Lady Bird," "The Day the Peace Action Broke Out," and "International Monopoly." "Camp," "Suburbia Square Dance," "Gentlemen's Resale Shop," "Lady Bird," and "International Monopoly" were also heard in the retrospective revue *Below the Belt* (1966; see entry), and "Camp," "Suburbia Square Dance," and "International Monopoly" can be heard on that revue's cast album; besides being first heard in *The Game Is Up* and then later in *Below the Belt*, "Suburbia Square Dance" was also used in *Hark!* (see entry) and was recorded for its cast album. "Camp" and "I Like the Job" were later heard in *The Playoffs of Mixed Doubles* (see entry). "Lady Bird" had first been heard a month earlier in *That Thing at the Cherry Lane*, and then was later used in Rod Warren's *Below the Belt*; see entries.

For a complete list of Rod Warren's revues, see entry for *...And in This Corner*; also see Appendix R.

559 A Game of Chance.
NOTES—See entry for *Three by One*.

560 The Games. THEATRE: Brooklyn Academy of Music; OPENING DATE: October 9, 1984; PERFORMANCES: Unknown; TEXT: Meredith Monk and Ping Chong; MUSIC: Meredith Monk; DIRECTION: Meredith Monk and Ping Chong; PRODUCER: The Next Wave Festival

CAST—The cast included Meredith Monk

NOTES—Presented as part of the Next Wave Festival, *The Games* had first premiered the previous year in West Berlin.

Mel Gussow in the *New York Times* described the performance piece as "Orwellian and Olympian" in its examination of games (everything from children's games to board games to war games), and he praised Monk's "throbbingly evocative score."

561 The Garden of Earthly Delights (1984). THEATRE: St. Clement's Theatre; OPENING DATE: November 20, 1984; PERFORMANCES: Unknown; DIRECTION: Martha Clarke; COSTUMES: Jane Greenwood; LIGHTING: Paul Gallo; PRODUCERS: Music Theatre Group/Lenox Arts Center (Lyn Austin, Producing Director), The New York Shakespeare Festival (Joseph Papp, Producer), and Robert de Rothschild CAST—Felix Blaska, Martha Clarke (or Lila York), Robert Faust, Marie Fourcaut, Eugene Friesen, Margie Gillis, Bill Ruyle, Steven Silverstein, Polly Stryon, Tim Wengerd

SOURCE—The production was inspired by Hieronymous Bosch's painting *The Garden of Earthly Delights* (painted 1505-1510).

The dance-theatre piece was performed in four parts (*Eden*, *The Garden*, *The Seven Sins*, and *Hell*) without an intermission.

NOTES—The dance-theatre piece *The Garden of Earthly Delights* had been previously performed in an incomplete version, and the 1984 Off Off Broadway production was the first time the complete work had been produced. The piece was directed and conceived by Martha Clarke, and was created in collaboration with Robert Barnett, Felix Blaska, Robert Faust, Marie Fourcaut, Margie Gillis, and Polly Styron; the music was by Richard Peaslee, in collaboration with Eugene Friesen, William Ruykem and Steven Silverstein.

The work was inspired by Flemish painter Hieronymous Bosch's painting *The Garden of Earthly Delights* which depicted both the sensual pleasures of mankind on Earth and the punishments awaiting him in Hell. The work was revived Off Broadway on May 15, 1987, at the Minetta Lane Theatre where it played for 120 performances, and was again revived at the same theatre on October 21, 2008.

For other works by Martha Clarke, see entries for *Vienna: Lusthaus* (1986), *The Hunger Artist* (1987), *Miracola d'Amour* (1988), *Belle Epoque* (2004), and *Kaos* (2006).

562 Gauguin in Tahiti. "A Musical Drama." THEATRE: Church of the Holy Trinity; OPENING DATE: December 2, 1976; PERFORMANCES: Unknown; BOOK: Wendy Erdman; LYRICS: Wendy Erdman Music: Teiji Ito and Wendy Erdman; DIRECTION: Jean Erdman; CHOREOGRAPHY: Jean Erdman; SCENERY: Frank Marsico; COSTUMES: Linda Letta; LIGHTING: Frank Marsico; MUSICAL DIRECTION: Teiji Ito; PRODUCER: The Theatre of the Open Eye (Jean Erdman, Artistic Director)

CAST—KEVIN O'CONNOR (Paul Gauguin), Sheila Grenham (Mette), Kathy Paulo (Teha'amana, Anna, Terika), John Genke (French Governor, Pissarro, Charles Morice, Pastor Vernier), John FitzGibbon (Priest, Vincent Van Gogh, August Strindberg, Gendarme Charpillet), William Hao (Prince Tati, Tioka), Valerie Hammer (Aline [Gauguin's Mother], Aline [Gauguin's Daughter]), Ari Darom (Peddler), Esther Jane Chaves (Streetwalker), Wendy Erdman (Café Singer), Marie Alailima (Tahataua), Renee Ane (Vaeoho), Amador Joaquin (Teiki); Ensemble of Dancers and Singers: Marie Alailima, Renee Ane, Esther Jane Chaves, Ari Darom, Leslie Dillingham, Valerie Hammer, William Hao, Amador Joaquin, Kathy Paulo, Jean Erdman

The musical about Paul Gauguin (1848-1903) was presented in three acts (*The Dream*, *The Reality*, and *The Resolve*).

NOTES—The Off Off Broadway musical centered around Paul Gauguin's life in Tahiti and Hivaoa.

The musical premiered in Honolulu in September 1976, and was later seen at the Queen Elizabeth Playhouse in Vancouver beginning on October 12, 1976. Mel Gussow in the *New York Times* praised the "currency and imagination" of the musical's choreography, score, and scenic design as well as Kevin O'Connor's performance in the title role. But he felt the script let the show down, and noted that too often O'Connor's dialogue consisted of announcements and labels, as if he were giving the audience a "progress report." Further, there was too much name-dropping, and thus the characters of Vincent Van Gogh, August Strindberg, and Pablo Picasso became distracting "straw figures."

This was a period in which many Off and Off Off Broadway plays and musicals focused on the lives of famous painters: the plays *Cassatt* (1980; Mary Cassatt); *Van Gogh!* (1976) and *Vincent* (1981); *Whistler* (1981; James McNeill Whistler); and Steve Martin's delightful 1995 comedy *Picasso at the Lapin Agile*, which took a fanciful look at Pablo Picasso and Albert Einstein in their early days when they were nobodies and just hung around the café Lapin Agile. (And now we know: One of the characters in the play is the first to utter the immortal word "*Einstein*" in a derisive tone to someone, the someone in this case being no less than Einstein himself.) As for musicals, besides *Gauguin in Tahiti*, Stephen Sondheim's *Sunday in the Park with George* (George Seurat) opened in 1983 (see entry) and was seen on Broadway the following year. On November 15, 1986, Gian-Carlo Menotti's opera *Goya*, based on the life of Francisco Goya, had its world premiere at the Kennedy Center's Opera House for five performances; Placido Domingo sang the title role (the opera was later revised in 1991). Coincidentally, in 1989 another musical about Goya's life, titled *Goya ...A Life in Song*, was released on a lavish studio cast album by CBS Records, Inc., which touted the album as an "introductory selection of songs from a forthcoming new stage musical" which was "expected" to open on Broadway in 1990. The lyrics and music were by Maury Yeston, and, in another coincidence, Domingo sang the title role (other singers on the recording were Dionne Warwick, Gloria Estefan, and Richie Havens). On September 26, 1993, the opera *El Greco* was performed Off Off Broadway for sixteen performances at Playhouse 91; the libretto was by Bernardo Solano and the music by William Harper; the direction was by Tom O'Horgan, the scenery by Robin Wagner, and Daryl Henriksen played the title role. Further, in 2004, Signature Theatre, in Arlington, Virginia, offered the world premiere of *The Highest Yellow* (Van Gogh); the lyrics and music were by Michael John LaChiusa and the book was by John Strand (Marc Kudisch played Van Gogh, and the cast included Jason Danieley and Judy Kuhn). During 2006 and 2007, Off Off Broadway offered four productions of another musical about Gauguin, George Fischoff's *Gauguin/Savage Light* (see entry).

Moreover, Off Off Broadway offered the musical *Toulouse* in 1981, and Off Broadway offered another musical on the same subject in 1985, *Times and Appetites of Toulouse-Lautrec* (see entries). London also offered two musicals about Lautrec, *Bordello* in 1974 and *Lautrec* in 2000. Further, *Jane Avril*, a play about one of Toulouse-Lautrec's models, opened Off Broadway at the Provincetown Playhouse on June 22, 1982, for forty performances; written by Jane Marla Robbins (who also played the title role), the play included among its cast of characters Toulouse-Lautrec, who was played by Kevin O'Connor (who had portrayed Gauguin in *Gauguin in Tahiti*).

The opera *Later That Same Evening* is based on five paintings by Edward Hopper (*Hotel Room* [1931], *Hotel Window* [1955], *Automat* [1927], *Room in New York* [1932], and *Two on the Aisle* [1927]). With text by Mark Campbell and music by John Musto, the opera premiered at the University of Maryland in November 2007 and was given at the National Gallery of Art in Washington, D.C., the following month (as of this writing, the work has yet to be seen in New York); Ethan Watermeier and Jenna Lebherz were the leads. According to Lavanya Ramanathan in the *Washington Post*, the opera is a series of interconnected stories which take place during a single night, and the vignettes depict "the simultaneous disappointment, isolation and hopefulness that drive New York."

563 Gauguin/Savage Light. "A Musical Sketchbook." THEATRE: Abington Theatre; OPENING DATE: November 8, 2006; PERFORMANCES: 64 (estimated); BOOK: George Fischoff; LYRICS: George Fischoff; MUSIC: George Fischoff; DIRECTION: Michael Ormond; MUSICAL DIRECTION: George Fischoff; PRODUCER: George Fischoff

CAST—Jeff Nardone (Paul Gauguin), Joseph Martin Guidera (Tioka), Sylvianne Chebance (Mette), Jennifer Sanchez (Tehura), Kelly Dynan (Peasant Girl, Others), Mick Bleyer (Vincent Van Gogh, Others)

The musical was presented in one act.

MUSICAL NUMBERS—"Tupapau" (Jennifer Sanchez), "El Dorado" (Jeff Nardone), "Money" (Jeff Nardone, Mick Bleyer), "Family Obligation" (Jeff Nardone, Sylvianne Chebance), "With Love" (Mick Bleyer, Kelly Dynan), "I Wore It for My Love" (Kelly Dynan), "Ridiculous" (Kelly Dynan), "Savage Light" (Paul Nardone), "Man Who Makes Human Beings" (Mick Bleyer, Kelly Dynan), "Only Dreams" (Jeff Nardone, Jennifer Sanchez), Finale: "Savage Light" (reprise) (Company)

NOTES—George Fischoff's Off Off Broadway musical *Gauguin/Savage Light* was first seen at Theatre Row for four weeks during Spring 2006; the musical was then produced for eight weeks at the Abington Theatre in November of that year; during Summer 2007, the musical was produced at the Roy Arias Theatre for four weeks, and then on September 26, 2007, the musical reopened there. The musical was also seen Off Off Broadway in late Spring 2008. The script is scheduled for publication by Samuel French, Inc., in 2009, and the cast recording was released by Original Cast Records (CD # 6208).

For another musical about Paul Gauguin, see entry for *Gauguin in Tahiti*.

Fischoff has written the scores for the Off Broadway musical *The Prince and the Pauper*, the Off Off Broadway *Bingo!*, and the regional theatre production *Sayonara* (see entries). Fischoff also wrote the score for the 1971 Broadway musical *Georgy*; for the better part of a decade, a studio cast album of the ingratiating score has been announced for release (as of this writing, we're still waiting for it!).

564 Gay Company. "A Try-Sexual Musical Revue." THEATRE: The Little Hippodrome; OPENING DATE: October 29, 1974; PERFORMANCES: 244; "ADDITIONAL DIALOGUE" by Les Barkdull; LYRICS: Fred Silver; MUSIC: Fred Silver; DIRECTION: Sue Lawless; SCENERY: Michael J. Hotopp and Paul de Pass; COSTUMES: Coordinated by Laura Thompson; LIGHTING: Cheryl Thacker, "Associate Lighting Designer"; MUSICAL DIRECTION: John Franceschina; PRODUCER: The Little Hippodrome

CAST—Candice Earley, Rick Gardner, Cola Pinto, Gordon Ramsey, Robert Tananis

The revue was presented in two acts.

ACT ONE—"Welcome" (Company), "Beginners Guide to Cruising (Pilgrim's Primer)" (Gordon Ramsey, Robert Tananis, Rick Gardner), "A Special Boy" (Candice Earley), "Handsome Stranger" (Cola Pinto), "True Confessions" (Rick Gardner, Robert Tananis, Gordon Ramsey, Candice Earley), "Where There's Smoke" (Rick Gardner, Robert Tananis, Gordon Ramsey, Cola Pinto), "I Met My Love" (Robert Tananis), "Lament (of a Decoy Cop)" (Gordon Ramsey), "Phantom of the Opera" (Company)

ACT TWO—"Your Home Away from Home" (Gordon Ramsey, Company), "Two Strangers" (Candice Earley), "Remembrances" (Gordon Ramsey, Cola Pinto), "Days of the Dancing Are Gone" (Robert Tananis), "I've Just Been to a Wedding" (Cola Pinto, Rick Gardner, Gordon Ramsey, Robert Tananis), "If He'd Only Been Gentle" (Rick Gardner), "Freddy Liked to Fugue" (a/k/a "Freddie's Fugue") (Candice Earley, Robert Tananis, Rick Gardner, Gordon Ramsey), Finale (Company)

NOTES—Fred Silver's *Gay Company* played at the Little Hippodrome, which was advertised as "New York City's First Dinner Theatre!" Later in the season, a revised version of the revue opened at Upstairs at Jimmy's as *In Gay Company*, where it played for less than two weeks, and in 1980 the revue returned as *Gay Company Revisited* (see entries).

A few years later, new material was added for a touring version of the revue, which was took its title from the second entry in the series and was subtitled "A Musical Revue for (Almost) Everyone!"; *In Gay Company* played in such cities as Washington, D.C., Chicago, and Los Angeles. A program from the Washington production included the following songs: "(I'm Just a) Small Town Boy," "At the Symphony Concert," "The Classified Ad," "The Fireman's Song," "(You Really) Ought to Get (Be) Married," "The Mattachine Society Masquerade," and "The Gregorian Chant," and "The WASP Blues" (the latter had originally been heard in Silver's 1979 revue *Sterling Silver* [see entry] as "The White Anglo-Saxon Protestant Blues" [a/k/a "Blues"]).

There were no New York cast recordings of any of the three related musicals, but later a cast album was released by WEB Records (LP # OC-111) of the Los Angeles production of *In Gay Company* which opened at the Backlot Theatre on March 22, 1984. It included a number of songs from the various New York productions as well as material added for the tour (including "Mugged to Mazoursky"); the album included such numbers as "Up on Your Toes," "At the Theatre" (probably a revised version of "At the Symphony Concert"), "I'm in Love with a Boy," and "Sondheim." The recording also included five songs ("The Age of Elegance," "Wooing in the Woods," "[It's] Closing Time," "Someone in My Life," and "Freddie's Fugue" [a/k/a "Freddy Liked to Fugue"]) which had first been heard in *Sterling Silver*; "The Age of Elegance" had also been heard in the Off Broadway revue *Jane White, Who?...* (1980; see entry).

565 Gay Company Revisited. THEATRE: Gene Frankel Theatre; OPENING DATE: August 8, 1980; PERFORMANCES: Unknown; LYRICS: Fred Silver; MUSIC: Fred Silver; DIRECTION: Miriam Fond; CHOREOGRAPHY: Miriam Fond; SCENERY: Vittorio Capecce; COSTUMES: Van Ramsey; LIGHTING: Andrea Wilson; MUSICAL DIRECTION: Wes McAfee; PRODUCER: The Gene Frankel Theatre (Gene Frankel, Artistic Director)

CAST—Hal Davis, Arne Gundersen, Michael McAssey, James Scopeletis, Susan Elizabeth Scott

NOTES—This Off Off Broadway production was the third edition of the *Gay Company* revues. For more information, see separate entries for *Gay Company* (1974) and *In Gay Company* (1975).

566 Gay Divorce (1960). THEATRE: Cherry Lane Theatre; OPENING DATE: April 3, 1960; PERFORMANCES: 25; BOOK: Dwight Taylor; LYRICS: Cole Porter; MUSIC: Cole Porter; DIRECTION: Gus Schirmer, Jr.; CHOREOGRAPHY: Joan Mann; SCENERY: Helen Pond, Herbert Senn; COSTUMES: Ann Roth; LIGHTING: Charles Levy; MUSICAL DIRECTION: Fred Werner, Jr.; PRODUCERS: Noel Behn and The New Princess Company

CAST—Adele Aron (Doris), Gaylynn Baker (Iris), Jeanne Rogers (Claire), Kathi Dean (Vivian), Kay Brower (Joyce), Sigyn (Sonia), MARY JANE DOERR (Barbara), EMORY BASS (Teddy), FRANK ALETTER (Guy), Tony Aylward (Bellboy), BEATRICE ARTHUR (Hortense), SKEDGE MILLER (Waiter), JUDY JOHNSON (Mimi), ARNY JOHNSON (Tonetti), Charles Davisson (Octavius Pratt)

The action occurs in 1932 at a seaside hotel, somewhere in England.

The musical was presented in two "reels."

REEL 1—"Salt Air" (The Girls), "After You, Who?" (Frank Aletter), "A Picture of Me Without You" (Mary Jane Doerr, Emory Bass), "I'm in Love" (Judy Johnson), "Most Gentlemen Don't Like Love" (Beatrice Arthur, The Girls), "Rap Tap on Wood" (Mary Jane Doerr, The Girls), "Night and Day" (Frank Aletter, Jane Johnson), "How's Your Romance?" (Arny Freeman, The Girls)

REEL 2—"Take Me Back to Manhattan" (Beatrice Arthur, The Girls), "It Might Have Been" (Jane Johnson), "I've Got You on My Mind" (Frank Aletter, Jane Johnson), "I Happen to Be in Love" (Mary Jane Doerr, The Girls), "Mr. and Mrs. Fitch" (Beatrice Arthur), "You're in Love" (Frank Aletter, Jane Johnson, Arny Freeman), Finale (Company)

NOTES—*Gay Divorce* was a revival of the hit Cole Porter musical which opened on Broadway on November 29, 1932, at the Ethel Barrymore Theatre, for 248 performances; the production also marked Fred Astaire's final Broadway appearance. Astaire reprised his role in the 1934 film version (opposite Ginger Rogers) which was titled *The Gay Divorcee*. For the film, only "Night and Day" was retained from the Broadway production (the film offered new songs, some by the team of Mack Gordon and Harry Revel, others by Con Conrad and Herb Magidson; the latter team contributed "The Continental," which was the first song to win the Academy Award).

Arthur Gelb in the *New York Times* was unimpressed with the "sad, sad" revival, but praised designers Helen Pond and Herbert Senn for their "ingenuity" in creating the sets and costumes, all of which were in black and white (with only occasional scenes in "glorious" color). He also noted that Beatrice Arthur was "a kind of brunette Elaine Stritch."

The songs retained for the Off Broadway revival were: "Salt Air," "After You, Who?," "Night and Day," "How's Your Romance?," "I've Got You on My Mind," "Mr. and Mrs. Fitch," and "You're in Love." Not included were "Why Marry Them?," "I Still Love the Red, White and Blue," and "What Will Become of Our England?"

The following songs were interpolated into the revival from other stage and film musicals by Cole Porter: "A Picture of Me Without You" (*Jubilee*, 1935); "I'm in Love" (*Fifty Million Frenchmen*, 1929); "Most Gentlemen Don't Like Love" (*Leave It to Me!*, 1939); "Rap Tap on Wood" (1936 film *Born to Dance*); "Take Me Back to Manhattan" (*The New Yorkers*, 1930); "It Might Have Been" (1943 film *Something To Shout About*; written for, but not used in, the film); and "I Happen to Be in Love" (1939 film *The Broadway Melody of 1940*; written for, but not used in, the film).

Columbia Records was to have recorded the revival's cast album (OL-5490, KOS-2023), which was cancelled due to the show's brief run.

A curious bit of casting trivia can be found in the show's listing in *Theatre World Season 1959-1960*. There are two production photographs accompanying the show's credits, one of Jimmy (a/k/a Jimmie) Thompson and Evelyn Ward, the other of Frank Aletter and Jane Johnson. Thompson and Ward didn't appear in the revival (except perhaps in preview performances), and were replaced by Aletter and Johnson; and yet the photo of Thompson and Ward was inadvertently included in the volume.

If Jimmy Thompson had appeared in *Gay Divorce* and *if* the cast album had been recorded, it would have been a rare opportunity to hear his singing voice. He had earlier been seen in two MGM musicals. In *Singin' in the Rain* (1952), he appeared in the "Beautiful Girls" production number, speaking the narration (it's unclear if his singing voice was used for the song itself). In *Brigadoon* (1954), he "sang" "I'll Go Home with Bonnie Jean" (he was dubbed by John Gustafson). In 1956, he was one of the crew members in the science fiction classic *Forbidden Planet* (see entry for the spoof *Return to the Forbidden Planet*).

Gay Divorce was revived Off Off Broadway in 1987 (see entry)

567 Gay Divorce (1987). THEATRE: Kaufman Theatre; OPENING DATE: February 24, 1987; PERFORMANCES: 39; BOOK: Dwight Taylor, Kenneth Webb, and Samuel Hoffenstein; BOOK ADAPTATION by Robert Brittan; LYRICS: Cole Porter; MUSIC: Cole Porter; DIRECTION: Robert Brink; CHOREOGRAPHY: Helen Butleroff; SCENERY: James Morgan; COSTUMES: Patricia Adshead; LIGHTING: Jeffrey Schissler; MUSICAL DIRECTION: David Schaefer; PRODUCER: Martin R. Kaufman

CAST—Paul V. Ames (Teddy Egbert), Ray DeMattis (Robert), Oliver Woodall (Guy Holden), Steven Minning (Porter), Leonard Drum (Waiter), Peggy Taphorn (Doris), Kristie Hannum (Iris), Gina Trano (Vivian), Christine Gradl (Gladys), Karen Ziemba (Barbara Wyndham), Diane Findlay (Hortense Howard), Debra Dickinson (Mimi Pratt), Joaquin Romaguera (Rudolfo Tonetti), Richard Lupino (Octavius Pratt)

The action occurs in the 1930s, in London and at the Ritz Hotel in South England.

The musical was presented in two acts.

ACT ONE—"After You, Who?" (Oliver Woodall), "Please Don't Make Me Be Good" (Karen Ziemba, Peggy Taphorn, Christine Gradl, Gina Trano, Kristie Hannum), "Salt Air" (Karen Ziemba, Paul V. Ames), "Why Shouldn't I?" (Debra Dickinson), "Pets" (Diane Findlay), "A Weekend Affair" (Ray DeMattis, Peggy Taphorn, Christine Gradl, Gina Trano, Kristie Hannum), "After You, Who?" (reprise) (Oliver Woodall), "Night and Day" (Oliver Woodall, Debra Dickinson), "How's Your Romance?" (Joaquin Romaguera, Peggy Taphorn, Christine Gradl, Gina Trano, Kristie Hannum)

ACT TWO—"My Cozy Little Corner in the Ritz" (Leonard Drum, Peggy Taphorn, Christine Gradl, Gina Trano, Kristie Hannum), "I'm in Love Again" (Debra Dickinson), "I've Got You on My Mind" (Oliver Woodall, Debra Dickinson), "You Do Something to Me" (Karen Ziemba, Paul V. Ames), "I Love Only You" (Joaquin Romaguera), "My Cozy Little Corner in the Ritz" (reprise) (Leonard Drum, Peggy Taphorn, Christine Gradl, Gina Trano, Kristie Hannum), "Mr. and Mrs. Fitch" (Diane Findlay), "A Weekend Affair" (reprise) (Ray DeMattis, Peggy Taphorn, Christine Gradl, Gina Trano, Kristie Hannum), "You're in Love" (Joaquin Romaguera, Oliver Woodall, Debra Dickinson), "Night and Day" (reprise) (Oliver Woodall, Debra Dickinson)

NOTES—This Off Off Broadway revival of Cole Porter's 1932 hit Broadway musical *Gay Divorce* had been also been produced Off Broadway in 1960 (see entry).

For the 1987 revival, the following numbers were retained from the original 1932 production: "After You, Who?," "Salt Air," "Night and Day," "How's Your Romance?," "I've Got You on My Mind," "Mr. and Mrs. Fitch," and "You're in Love"; also included were "A Weekend Affair," which had been written for the original 1932 production but wasn't used, and "I Love Only You," which was written for the 1933 London production.

Songs interpolated into the revival from other of Cole Porter's musicals were: "You Do Something to Me" (*Fifty Million Frenchmen*, 1929), "Please Don't Make Me Be Good" (dropped during the tryout of *Fifty Million Frenchmen*, 1929), "Why Shouldn't I?" (*Jubilee*, 1935), "Pets" (written for, but not used in, *Let's Face It!*, 1941), "My Cozy Little Corner at the Ritz" (*Hitchy-Koo of 1919*), and "I'm in Love Again" (added after opening to *Greenwich Village Follies*, 1924).

The revival's cast included future Tony Award winner Karen Ziemba as well as Joaquin Romaguera, who is best remembered for creating the role of Pirelli in the original 1979 Broadway production of *Sweeney Todd/The Demon Barber of Fleet Street*.

568 Gemini the Musical.

NOTES—See entry for *The New York Musical Theatre Festival*.

569 Gentlemen, Be Seated! THEATRE: New York City Center; OPENING DATE: October 10, 1963; PERFORMANCES: 3; BOOK: Jerome Moross and Edward Eager; LYRICS: Edward Eager; MUSIC: Jerome Moross; DIRECTION: Robert Turoff; CHOREOGRAPHY: Paul Draper; Bob Bernard, Assistant Choreographer; SCENERY: William Pitkin; COSTUMES: Henry Heymann; MUSICAL DIRECTION: Emerson Buckley; PRODUCER: The New York City Center of Music and Drama

CAST—DICK SHAWN (Mr. Interlocutor, Mr. Brady), Avon Long (Mister Tambo), Charles Atkins (Mister Bones), ALICE GHOSTLEY (The Comedienne: The Dowager, Belle Boyd, Dorothea Dix), Carol Brice (The Contralto, Harriet Tubman, Amanda), William McDonald (Johnny Reb), Richard Fredricks (Billy Yank), June Card (Southern Girl), Mary Burgess (Northern Girl), Bernard Addison (Mister Banjo), Richard Krause (Character Actor: The Senator, The General, The Pinkerton Man, Mr. Brady's Assistant), PAUL DRAPER (Mister Taps), Charlotte Povia (Ermyntrude, Nurse), David Smith (Farmer McLean), Michele Hardy (Florida Cotton); the following cast members also played Minstrels, Waltzers, Spectators, and Slaves: Bob Bernard (Horse, Drill Team Member), Rec Russel (Horse, Drill Team Member), Kellis Miller (Soldier, Another Soldier), Don Henderson (Soldier), John Tormey (Drill Team Member), Bob Ellis (Drill Team Member), Don Yule (Another Soldier), Joyce Miko (Girl, Nurse), Beverly Evans (Girl, Nurse), Candida Pilla (Nurse) The musical was presented in two acts.

ACT ONE—"Grand March" (Avon Long, Charles Atkins, Chorus, William McDonald, Richard Fredricks, June Card, Mary Burgess), "In the Sunny Old South" (Dick Shawn, Avon Long, Charles Atkins, Chorus), "The Freedom Train" (Carol Brice), "Waltzing in the Shadow" (Dick Shawn, William McDonald, Richard Fredricks, Chorus), "Fare You Well" (June Card, William McDonald, Mary Burgess, Richard Fredricks), "Why Ain't We Got a Dome?" (Avon Long, Charles Atkins, Dick Shawn), "Tap Dance Drill" (Paul Draper, Men's Dance Ensemble), "O, the Picnic at Manassas" (Alice Ghostley, Richard Krause, Charlotte Povia), "Mocking Bird" (June Card), "Shiloh" (William McDonald, Men's Chorus), "The Ballad of Belle Boyd (Belle Boyd's Back in Town)" (Ladies' Chorus) "I Spy" (Alice Ghostley), "It's the Witching Hour by the Old Water Tower" (Men's Chorus, Alice Ghostley), "I'm a Pinkerton Man" (Richard Krause), "Belle Boyd, Where Have You Been?" (Ladies' Chorus), "Mancipation" (Avon Long, Charles Atkins, Carol Brice), "Pardon, Ma'am" (performer[s] unknown), "Look Who I Am, Surprise, Surprise!" (performer[s] unknown), "This Isn't a Gentlemen's War Anymore" (Dick Shawn), "The Contraband Ball" (Alice Ghostley, June Card, Charles Atkins, Avon Long, Richard Fredricks, Chorus), "O, Miss Walkaround, Come Walking Out with Me" (Dick Shawn, Alice Ghostley, Richard Fredricks, Avon Long, Charles Atkins, June Card, Company)

ACT TWO—"Gentlemen, Be Seated" (Dick Shawn), "It's Quiet on the Potomac Tonight" (Avon Long, Charles Atkins), "The Ballad of Stonewall Jackson" (William McDonald, Men's Chorus), "Mr. Brady Takes a Photograph" (performer[s] unknown), "I'm Mathew P. Brady, the Camera Man" (Dick Shawn, Richard Krause), "Miss Dorothea Dix" (Alice Ghostley, Joyce Miko, Candida Pilla, Beverly Evans, Charlotte Povia, Dick Shawn), "I Can't Remember" (Mary Burgess), "From Atlanta to the Sea" (Richard Fredricks, Carol Brice, Chorus), "What Has Become of Beauty?" (Dick Shawn), "Have You Seen Him, Did He Pass This Way?" (Carol Brice), Grand Finale: "This Was the War, What Did It Do for Me and You? ... Didn't It, Did It?" (Company)

NOTES—*Gentlemen, Be Seated!* is one of the most ambitious of all musicals. Using the framework of a traditional minstrel show, the musical told the story of the Civil War (including Appomattox, Andersonville, and the Emancipation Proclamation) as well as a variety of historical characters (such as Abraham Lincoln, Matthew Brady, and Belle Boyd). Harold C. Schoenberg in the *New York Times* felt that the opening sequence of the musical promised "something unusual—perhaps even a new concept of American opera," but lamented that too often the show lapsed into "slick musical comedy." However, he praised the "pure minstrel" opening and ending sequences of the musical, and also singled out such songs as "The Ballad of Belle Boyd," "All Quiet on the Potomac" ("a very nice spoof" delivered by Avon Long and Cholly Atkins), and "This Isn't a Gentleman's War" (a "fresh and likable" soft-shoe routine for Dick Shawn in which Shawn lamented that it isn't a gentleman's "woah any moah"). With music by Jerome Moross, the composer of one of America's greatest musicals, *The Golden Apple* (see entry), this virtually sung-through musical deserves another hearing. The early 1960s was an exciting period for Off Broadway musicals, with one ambitious musical after another opening (and, unfortunately, quickly closing). See entries for *The Tiger Rag* and *Meet Peter Grant*.

A note in the program for *Gentlemen, Be Seated!* indicated "Mr. Brady Takes a Photograph" was the only fictionalized sequence in the musical. The authors stated the number was their own explanation of a "peculiar gap in the otherwise remarkably complete photographic documentation" of the Civil War by Matthew Brady and his assistant.

Two songs from the musical ("Fare You Well" and "I Can't Remember") were recorded on *Windflowers*, a priceless collection of songs by Moross which was released by PS Classics (CD # 03607-01022).

The program didn't list individual musical numbers; the above list is taken from Richard C. Norton's invaluable *A Chronology of American Musical Theatre*.

Incidentally, Schonberg noted that on opening night Dick Shawn and Alice Ghostley were "nearly lost to posterity" when "the stagehands pulled a prop from under them too soon," leaving Shawn "tottering" on a ladder and Ghostley "suspended" in a trapdoor. But like the "troupers" they were, the two saved themselves "by a neat bit of acrobatics."

570 George M. Cohan Tonight! THEATRE: Irish Repertory Theatre; OPENING DATE: March 9, 2006; PERFORMANCES: 77; BOOK MATERIAL: Chip Deffaa; LYRICS: All lyrics by George M. Cohan (unless otherwise noted in list of musical numbers); MUSIC: George M. Cohan; DIRECTION: Chip Deffaa; CHOREOGRAPHY: Jon Peterson; SCENERY: James Morgan; COSTUMES: David Toser; LIGHTING: Mary Jo Dondlinger; MUSICAL DIRECTION: Sterling Price-McKenney; PRODUCER: Irish Repertory Theatre (Charlotte Moore, Artistic Director; Ciaran O'Reilly, Producing Director)

CAST—Jon Peterson

The revue was presented in two acts (division of acts unknown; all songs performed by Jon Peterson; the songs are listed in performance order).

MUSICAL NUMBERS—"Hello, Broadway!" (from *Hello, Broadway!*, 1914)/"Give My Regards to Broadway" (*Little Johnny Jones*, 1904), "The Man Who Owns Broadway" (*The Man Who Owns Broadway*, 1909; lyric revisions by Chip Deffaa), "Night Time" (*The Governor's Son*, 1906), "Musical Moon" (*The Little Millionaire*, 1911; additional lyric by Chip Deffaa), "Ireland: My Land of Dreams" (*The Voice of McConnell*, 1918), "I'm Saving Up to Buy a Home for Mother" (source unknown), "Josephine" (source unknown)/"Oh, You Wonderful Girl" (*The Little Millionaire*, 1911), "The Dancing Master" (source unknown; lyric by Jerry Cohan), "Until My Luck Comes Rolling Along" (source unknown), "The Hinkey Dee" (a/k/a "When You Do the Hinky Dee") (*Little Nellie Kelly*, 1922), "Harrigan" (*Fifty Miles from Boston*, 1908), "You Won't Do Any Business If You Haven't Got a Band" (source unknown; lyric revisions by Chip Deffaa), "My Father Told Me" (source unknown; lyric by Chip Deffaa), "I Was Born in Virginia" (a/k/a "Virginia") (*George Washington, Jr.*, 1906), "Forty-Five Minutes from Broadway" (*Forty-Five Minutes from Broadway*, 1906; lyric revisions by Chip Deffaa), "I'm Awfully Strong for You" (*The Yankee Prince*, 1908), "Oh! You Beautiful Girl" (probably a variation of "Oh, You Wonderful Girl," which had been introduced in *The Little Millionaire*, 1911; lyric revisions by Chip Deffaa)/"I Want the World to Know" (source unknown), "Goodbye Flo" (perhaps "I Say, Flo" from *The Yankee Prince*, 1908; lyric revision by Chip Deffaa), "I Want to Hear a Yankee Doodle Tune" (possibly from *Mother Goose*, 1903), "The Fatal Curse of Drink" (source unknown; lyric by Chip Deffaa [based on "traditional material," according to the program), "The Yankee Doodle Boy" (a/k/a "I'm a Yankee Doodle Dandy") (*Little Johnny Jones*, 1904), "Mary's a Grand Old Name" (*Forty-Five Minutes from Broadway*, 1906; lyric revision by Chip Deffaa), "You're a Grand Old Flag" (originally titled "The Grand Old Rag"; from *George Washington, Jr.*, 1906), "Over There" (independent song), "Sweet Popularity" (a/k/a "Popularity") (*Running for Office*, 1903)/"I'm a Popular Man" (*The Honeymooners*, 1907; lyric revision by Chip Deffaa), "Drink with Me" (*The Talk of New York*, 1907)/"Did Ya Ever Have One of Those Days" (source unknown; lyric by Chip Deffaa), "I Love Everyone in the (This) Wide, Wide World" (*The Governor's Son*, 1906)/"I'm True to Them All" (source unknown; lyric revision by Chip Deffaa), "All-American Sweetheart" (source unknown; lyric by Chip Deffaa, music by George M. Cohan and Chip Deffaa), "Josephine" (reprise), "I Won't Be an Actor No More" (source unknown; music and title by George M. Cohan, lyric by Chip Deffaa), "Life's a Funny Proposition, After All" (*Little Johnny Jones*, 1906), "All Aboard for Broadway" (*George Washington, Jr.*, 1906; additional lyric by Chip Deffaa)/"Give My Regards to Broadway" (reprise; lyric revision by Chip Deffaa)

NOTES—*George M. Cohan Tonight!* was a one-man solo show which starred Jon Peterson.

George M. Cohan (1878-1942), performer, lyricist, composer, book writer, and producer, was one of the stalwarts of early twentieth-century musical theatre; today, his works have all but disappeared from the musical stage, but many of his songs (such as "Give My Regards to Broadway," "The Yankee Doodle Boy" (a/k/a "I'm a Yankee Doodle Dandy"), "You're a Grand Old Flag," and "Over There") are standards in the American songbook.

A 1982 Broadway revival of Cohan's *Little Johnny Jones* (1906) lasted for just one performance, but *George M!*, a 1968 Broadway musical about Cohan's life, played for 427 performances (without turning a profit). *George M!* suffered from a confused book and a miscast Joel Grey in the title role, but Joe Layton's choreography for "Popularity" is one of the best Broadway dance numbers of the era. The cast album of *George M!* is better than the show, and it makes for wonderful listening.

Ghostlight Records released the cast recording of *George M. Cohan Tonight!* (CD # 791558-441024). A program note indicated that the recorded voice over the theatre's sound system, which welcomed the audience to the show and which asked them to silence their cell phones, was the voice of Jennie Cohan Ross, Cohan's great-granddaughter.

571 Gertrude Stein's First Reader. "A New Musical. THEATRE: Astor Place Theatre; OPENING DATE: December 15, 1969; PERFORMANCES: 40; TEXT: Gertrude Stein (adapted by Ann Sternberg); MUSIC: Ann Sternberg; DIRECTION: Herbert Machiz; SCENERY: Kendall Shaw; LIGHTING: Patrika Brown; MUSICAL DIRECTION: Ann Sternberg; PRODUCERS: John Bernard Myers in association with Bob Cato CAST—Michael Anthony, Joy Garrett, Frank Giordano, Sandra Thornton, Ann Sternberg (piano)

SOURCE—The 1946 collection of stories *The First Reader* by Gertrude Stein.

The revue was presented in two acts.

ACT ONE—"Sunshine" (Company), "Wildflowers" (Company), "A Dog" (Company), "Writing Lesson" (Joy Garrett, Sandra Thornton), "Johnny and Jimmy" (Frank Giordano, Michael Anthony), "The Blackberry Vine (A Play)" (Company), "Big Bird" (Ann Sternberg), "The Three Sisters Who Are Not Sisters (A Murder Mystery)" (Company), "Be Very Careful" (Company)

ACT TWO—"New Word" (Company), "Jenny" (Sandra Thornton), "How They Do, Do" (Joy Garrett), "Soldier" (Michael Anthony), "Baby Benjamin" (Frank Giordano), "Wildflowers" (reprise) (Company), "In a Garden (A Mini-Opera)" (Michael Anthony, Joy Garrett, Frank Giordano), "Be Very Careful" (reprise) (Company)

NOTES—Clive Barnes in the *New York Times* noted that Al Carmines had found "the right musical voice" for Stein in *In Circles* (see entry), and so he was disappointed with the "cheerfully arch" music by Ann Sternberg in the children-oriented revue *Gertrude Stein's First Reader*. He noted the cast confused innocence with the "sticky radiance" of "child-like television commercials," and suggested the musical be retitled *Gertrude Stein Meets Charlie Brown and Loses*. Barnes lamented that the musical was not "Gertrude Stein at her Gertrude Steinest." The musical was recorded by Polydor Records (LP # 24-7002).

572 Get Thee to Canterbury. "A Medieval Happenynge." THEATRE: Sheridan Square Playhouse; OPENING DATE: January 15, 1969; PERFORMANCES: 20; BOOK: Jan Steen and David Secter; LYRICS: David Secter; MUSIC: Paul Hoffert; DIRECTION: Jan Steen; CHOREOGRAPHY: Darwin Knight; SCENERY: James F. Gohl; COSTUMES: Jeanne Button; LIGHTING: Michael Davidson; MUSICAL DIRECTION: Jerald B. Stone; PRODUCER: David Secter

CAST—Will B. Able (Carpenter), Norman Allen (Priest), Al Cohen (Summoner), Walker Daniels (Geoffrey Chaucer), Michael Harrison (John), Travis Hudson (Wife of Bath), Marc Jordan (Miller), John Mintun (Pardoner), Paul Renault (Allan), Shev Rodgers (Host), Shoshanna Rogers (Prudence), Tom Sinclair (Friar); Minstrels (Jerald B. Stone, Salli Parker, Fred Ehnes, Jeff Bartlett)

SOURCE—Geoffrey Chaucer's collection of stories *The Canterbury Tales* (written between 1387 and 1400).

The musical was presented in two acts.

ACT ONE—"Get Thee to Canterbury" (Company), "The Journey" (Shev Rodgers), "Take a Pick" (Company), "Death Beware" (Tom Sinclair, Al Cohen, Norman Allen), "Buy My Pardons" (John Mintun), "Dreams" (Shev Rodgers, Travis Hudson), "Canter Banter" (Al Cohen), "Day of Judgement I" (Company), "Ballad of Sir Topaz" (Walker Daniels)

ACT TWO—"Bottom's Up" (Will B. Able, Norman Allen, Al Cohen, Walker Daniels, Michael Harrison, Marc Jordan, John Mintum, Paul Renault, Shev Rodgers, Tom Sinclair), "A Simple Wife" (Travis Hudson), "Shadows" (Paul Renault, Shoshanna Rogers), "Day of Judgement II" (Company), "Alison Dear" (Walker Daniels), "Where Are the Blossoms?" (Will B. Able), "On the Relative Merits of Education & Experience" (Marc Jordan, Michael Harrison, Paul Renault), "Everybody Gets It in the End" (Company), The Prologue (Walker Daniels)

NOTES—Chaucer's *The Canterbury Tales* as a "medieval happenynge"? Only in the 1960s!

As the musical fates would have it, two adaptations of Chaucer's work turned up during the 1968-1969 season, and both were flops (Clive Barnes in the *New York Times* noted there were "flying Chaucers" everywhere that season). *Get Thee to Canterbury*, the Off Broadway adaptation, lasted less than three weeks, and a Broadway production, titled *Canterbury Tales*, played three months (the latter was briefly revived Off Broadway in 1980; see entry). Both musicals originated in other countries: *Get Thee to Canterbury* was first seen in Canada as a mostly straight, non-musical play, and *Canterbury Tales*, which opened in London in 1968, was a long-running hit, eventually playing there for 2,080 performances. Barnes felt the evening of "mildly tasteful vulgarity" lacked a strong score and book. The music was like a "millstone round the show's neck" and reminded him of some of the "duller and more forgettable hymns in the English hymnal." And the book was too "waggish, having little genuine Chaucerian flavor." But he praised the "attractive" cast, which included Walker Daniels, who had created the leading role of Claude in the first productions of *Hair* at the Public Theatre and the Cheetah (see entries) but didn't make the trip to Broadway with that iconic musical. In *Get Thee to Canterbury*, he appeared as Chaucer, but after this he seems to have vanished from the New York stage.

For another lyric adaptation of Chaucer's work, see entry for *The Canterbury Pilgrims*, which opened at the Metropolitan Opera in 1917.

573 Get Used to It! "A New Musical Revue." THEATRE: The Glines; OPENING DATE: March 22, 1992; PERFORMANCES: 78; LYRICS: Tom Wilson Weinberg; MUSIC: Tom Wilson Weinberg; DIRECTION: Tom Wilson Weinberg; CHOREOGRAPHY: Jack Matter; SCENERY: Edmond Ramage; COSTUMES: Cantanese/Lauze; LIGHTING: Tracy Dedrickson; MUSICAL DIRECTION: Wayne Barker; PRODUCER: The Glines

CAST—Sebastian Herald, John O'Brien, Todd Whitley, Wayne Barker (Piano)

MUSICAL NUMBERS (number of acts and song assignments unknown; songs are listed in performance order)—"No Opening Number," "Get Used to It," "Who's That Man?," "Hymn," "My Leviticus," "Three-Letter Word," "Friends in High Places," "I'll Call You Lover," "Bat Boy," "Breaking the Penal Code with You," "Who Did Langston Love?," "Colorblind Blues," "Experts," "Public Service Announcement," "How We Get the News," "What a Gift," "Means to an End," "Can't Wait"

NOTES—This Off Off Broadway revue about gay life was released on a studio cast recording by Aboveground Records (CD # AR-106-CD). The musical appears to have been previously performed at the Courtyard Playhouse earlier in the month, opening there on March 4, 1992.

574 **The Ghosts of Versailles.** "A Grand Opera Buffa." THEATRE: Metropolitan Opera House; OPENING DATE: December 19, 1991; PERFORMANCES: 7; LIBRETTO: William M. Hoffman; MUSIC: John Corigliano; DIRECTION: Colin Graham; CHOREOGRAPHY: Debra Brown; SCENERY: John Conklin; COSTUMES: John Conklin; LIGHTING: Gil Wechsler; MUSICAL DIRECTION: James Levine; Samuel Cristler (Stage Orchestra Conductor); PRODUCER: The Metropolitan Opera

CAST—*The Ghosts*: Teresa Stratas (Marie Antoniette), Jane Shaulis (Elegant Woman in a Hat [the Past Glory of France]), James Courtney (Louis XVI), Richard Drews (Marquis), Three Gossips (Betsy Norden, Kitt Reuter-Foss, Wendy Hoffman), An Opera-Going Quartet of French Aristocrats (Lauren Flanigan, Sondra Kelly, Michael Best, Kevin Short), Hakan Hagegard (Pierre-Augustin Caron de Beaumarchais); *The Players*: Gino Quilico (Figaro), Judith Christin (Susanna), Peter Kazaras (Count Almaviva), Renee Fleming (Rosina), Tracy Dahl (Florestine), Neil Rosenshein (Leon), Graham Clark (Patrick Honore Begearss), Wilbur Pauley (Wilhelm), Stella Zambalis (Cherubino), Ara Berberian (Suleyman Pasha), Dean Badolato (The Pasha's Page), Philip Cokorinos (English Ambassador), Marilyn Horne (Samira), Midhat Serbagi (Egyptian Violinist), Three Muscovite Traders (David Bernard, Steven Combs, John Darrenkamp), John Horton Murray (Man with a Ladder), Howard Bender (Man with Lather on His Face), Andrij Dobriansky (The Other Man), Two Women with Babies (Theresa Cincione, Korliss Uecker), Four Other Women with Children (Loretta di Franco, Janet Hopkins, Lynda Keith, Mary Ann McCormick), Ladies of the Town (Hilda Harris, Linda Thompson), Two Bailiffs (Ken Chester, Andrea Velis)

SOURCE—Suggested by *Le Mere Coupable* by Pierre-Augustin Caron de Beaumarchais

The action occurs "in a world beyond time," both in the present as well as in the autumn of 1793, in Marie Antoinette's theatre in the Petit Trianon, Versailles.

The opera was presented in two acts.

NOTES—The world premiere of *The Ghosts of Versailles* was commissioned by the Met in order to celebrate its one-hundredth anniversary.

The program notes explained that the opera occurred "in a world beyond time," a space inhabited by French aristocrats (including Marie Antoinette, who is haunted by her death and refuses to accept the grisly destiny that was her end) who were executed during the French Revolution. The ghost of playwright Beaumarchais, who is in love with Marie Antoinette, writes a play which will alter destiny and allow her to escape her fate. At one point, Beaumarchais must enter into his own play in order to resolve political issues which have arisen among the characters. And then suddenly the ghost characters and the characters of Beaumarchais' play as well as Beaumarchais himself are thrust into the past, back to the Paris of the French Revolution where they find themselves in attendance at Marie Antoinette's trial. Ultimately, Marie Antoinette accepts her fate, however unjust it may have been, and she and Beaumarchais are united in heaven. In his review for the *New York Times*, Bernard Hollin wrote that the opera threw operatic conventions on its ear: it was happily "subversive" in its "vaudeville and Saturday-cartoon humor," an operatic world where the orchestra suddenly played kazoos and Marilyn Horne danced the hoochy-koochy. *Newsweek* noted that the score could sound "eerie ... like a misty November afternoon," and yet could also abound in "coloratura vaudeville." One character in the opera acknowledged all the strange goings-on by singing, "This is not opera! Wagner is opera!"

The opera was released on videocassette by Deutsche Grammophon (# 44-072-530-3) as well as on laser disc, and in January 1992 it was shown on public television. The script was published by G. Schirmer, Inc., in 1991.

The Ghosts of Versailles is scheduled to be revived at the Met in 2010, with Kristin Chenoweth to sing the role of Samira (first sung by Marilyn Horne in the world premiere).

575 **Gift of the Magi** (1975). THEATRE: Players Theatre; OPENING DATE: December 1, 1975; PERFORMANCES: 48; BOOK: Ronnie Britton; LYRICS: Ronnie Britton; MUSIC: Ronnie Britton; DIRECTION: M.T. Knoblauh; SCENERY: Michael Dulin; COSTUMES: Neil Cooper; LIGHTING: Jerryn Michaels; MUSICAL DIRECTION: James Fradrich; PRODUCERS: Wayne Clark and Joseph Tiraco in association with Larry J. Pontillo

CAST—Mary Saunders (Her), Paige O'Hara (Della), Bill March (Jim), William Brockmeier (Him)

SOURCE—O. Henry (William Sydney Porter)'s short story "The Gift of the Magi," which first appeared in the short story collection *The Big City*.

The action occurs in Greenwich Village in December 1906.

The musical was presented in two acts.

ACT ONE—"The Magi Waltz" (Orchestra), "There You Go Again" (Mary Saunders), "The Gift" (Paige O'Hara), "Della's Desire" (Mary Saunders), "Mr. James Dillingham Young" (Bill March, Paige O'Hara), "Day After Day" (Bill March), "Kids Are Out" (Bill March, Paige O'Hara), "Sullivan Street Flat" (Jim March, Paige O'Hara, William Brockmeier, Mary Saunders), "The Beautiful Children" (Paige O'Hara), "You'd Better Tell Her!" (William Brockmeier), "Washington Square" (Bill March), "Till Tomorrow" (William Brockmeier, Mary Saunders, Bill March, Paige O'Hara)

ACT TWO—Entr'acte (Orchestra), "Quiet Morning" (William Brockmeier, Mary Saunders), "Brave You" (Paige O'Hara), "A Penny Saved" (Paige O'Hara), "Day After Day" (reprise) (Paige O'Hara), "I've Got Something Better" (Bill March), "Pretty Lady" (Bill March, Paige O'Hara, William Brockmeier, Mary Saunders), "He Did It, She Did It!" (William Brockmeier, Mary Saunders), "Make Him Think I'm Still Pretty" (Paige O'Hara), Finale (Bill March, Paige O'Hara, William Brockmeier, Mary Saunders)

NOTES—*Gift of the Magi*, a musical version of O. Henry's famous Christmas short story "The Gift of the Magi," barely lasted beyond the holiday season. The critics weren't particularly impressed with the adaptation, and, in truth, the six-page short story wasn't all that suitable for a full-length two-act musical. The musical was briefly revived Off Off Broadway on December 19, 1978, by the People's Performing Company.

An earlier adaptation of the material was produced Off Off Broadway in 1972 as *The Blue Magi* (see entry).

Another adaptation (Mark St. Germain and Randy Courts' *The Gifts of the Magi*; see entry) was later produced at the Lamb's Theatre in 1984 and was presented there for a number of years during the Christmas holiday season; this version was based on two short stories by O. Henry ("The Gift of the Magi" and "The Cop and the Anthem").

As *Gift of the Magi*, a one-hour television musical version of O. Henry's story was produced by CBS on December 9, 1958, with lyrics and music by Richard Adler. Sally Ann Howes and Gordon MacRae starred, and the supporting cast included Allen Case, Tammy Grimes, and Bibi Osterwald. The television soundtrack album was released by United Artists Records (LP # 5013).

As *The Gift of the Magi*, another musical version of the story premiered on December 1, 1981, at the Actors' Theatre of Louisville; the book, lyrics, and music were by Peter Ekstrom, and the script was published by Samuel French, Inc., in 1984.

576 **The Gifts of the Magi** (1984). THEATRE: Lamb's Theatre; OPENING DATE: December 3, 1984; PERFORMANCES: 34; BOOK: Mark St. Germain; LYRICS: Mark St. Germain and Randy Courts; MUSIC: Randy Courts; DIRECTION: Christopher Catt; CHOREOGRAPHY: Piper Pickrell; SCENERY: Michael C. Smith; COSTUMES: Hope Hanafin; LIGHTING: Heather Carson; MUSICAL DIRECTION: Steve Alper; PRODUCER: The Lamb's Theatre Company (Carolyn Rossi Copeland, Executive Director)

CAST—Brick Hartney (City Man), Lynne Wintersteller (City Woman), Michael Brian (Willy Porter), Jeff McCarthy (Jim Dillingham), Leslie Hicks (Della Dillingham), Bert Michaels (Soapy Smith)

SOURCE—The short stories "The Gift of the Magi" (which first appeared in the short story collection *The Big City*) and "The Cop and the Anthem" by O. Henry (William Sidney Porter).

The action occurs in New York City from December 23 through December 25, 1905.

The musical was presented in one act.

MUSICAL NUMBERS—"Light Our Way" (possibly Brick Hartney and Lynne Wintersteller), "The Gifts of the Magi" (Michael Brian, Company), "Christmas Is to Blame" (Jeff McCarthy, Leslie Hicks), "How Much to Buy My Dream?" (Jeff McCarthy), "The Restaurant" (Bert Michaels, Brick Hartney, Lynne Wintersteller), "Who Needs Presents" (performer[s] unknown), "Bum Luck" (Bert Michaels, Jeff McCarthy), "Greed" (Company), "Pockets" (Michael Brian), "The Same Girl" (Leslie Hicks)

NOTES—Mark St. Germain and Randy Courts' *The Gifts of the Magi* was the second recent musical adaptation of O. Henry's famous short story (see entry for *Gift of the Magi*, Ronnie Britton's version of the material). The new version, which opened at the Lamb's Theatre, also incorporated another O. Henry short story, "The Cop and the Anthem."

With the exception of 1991, the Lamb's Theatre version was presented annually for a limited run during each Christmas season from 1984 through 1992, usually as an Off Off Broadway production. But according to *Best Plays/Theatre Yearbook of 1990-1991*, the 1990 production was a "full" Off Broadway production (with some performances during that engagement presented as dinner theatre).

During the musical's eight seasons at the Lamb's, various performers played in the production, and at one point the names of the characters "City Man" and "City Woman" were changed to "City Him" and "City Her." Over the years, the song "Who Needs Presents" was deleted and three songs ("Jim and Della," "Once More," and "The Gift of Christmas") were added. The opening number, "Light Our Way," may have been later re-written as "Star of the Night."

A cast album of sorts was released on an unnamed (and unnumbered) label; the CD included a few cast members (Scott Waara, Sarah Knapp, Gordon Stanley) who had performed in the musical at one point or another during the show's run at the

Lamb's. The script was published by Dramatists Play Service, Inc., in 1995.

An earlier adaptation of the material was produced Off Off Broadway in 1972 as *The Blue Magi* (see entry) As *Gift of the Magi*, a one-hour television musical version of O. Henry's story was produced by CBS on December 9, 1958, with lyrics and music by Richard Adler. Sally Ann Howes and Gordon MacRae starred, and the supporting cast included Allen Case, Tammy Grimes, and Bibi Osterwald. The television soundtrack album was released by United Artists Records (LP # 5013).

As *The Gift of the Magi*, a musical version of the story premiered on December 1, 1981, at the Actors' Theatre of Louisville; the book, lyrics, and music were by Peter Ekstrom, and the script was published by Samuel French, Inc., in 1984.

577 The Gilded Cage. "A Turn-of-the-Century Musical." THEATRE: The Production Company; OPENING DATE: January 9, 1983; PERFORMANCES: 19; BOOK: James Milton; LYRICS: Additional lyrics by James Milton; recitatives by Polly Pen (see song list for other credits); MUSIC: Arranged by Polly Pen (see song list for credits); DIRECTION: James Milton; CHOREOGRAPHY: Marcia Milgrom Dodge; COSTUMES: Amanda J. Klein; LIGHTING: Debra J. Kletter; MUSICAL DIRECTION: Polly Pen; PRODUCER: The Production Company (Norman Rene, Artistic Director; Abigail Franklin, Managing Director)

CAST—Marianne Tatum (Evelyn Nesbit), Tom McKinney (Stanford White), Robert Stillman (Harry K. Thaw), Paula Sweeney (Mimi), Susan Blommaert (Lulu), Marilyn Firment (Kitty), Polly Pen (Pinkie, at the piano)

The musical was presented in one act.

MUSICAL NUMBERS—"There's a Broken Heart for Every Light on Broadway" (lyric and music by Johnson and Fischer) (Company), "Always Do as People Say You Should" (from *The Fortune Teller*, 1898; lyric by Harry B. Smith, music by Victor Herbert) (Marianne Tatum), "You Naughty, Naughty Men" (lyric and music by Kennick and Bicknell) (Paula Sweeney, Susan Blommaert, Marilyn Firment, Marianne Tatum), "Little Birdies Learning How to Fly" (lyric and music by Morton and Kerker) (Tom McKinney, Chorus), "Put on Your Tatta, Little Girlie" (lyric and music by Leigh) (Tom McKinney, Chorus), "A Bird in a Gilded Cage" (lyric by Arthur J. Lamb, music by Harry von Tilzer) (Marianne Tatum), "Take Back Your Gold" (lyric and music by Pritzkow and Rosenfeld) (Paula Sweeney), "(A Woman Is Only a Woman, but) A Good Cigar Is a Smoke" (*Miss Dolly Dollars*, 1905; lyric by Harry B. Smith, music by Victor Herbert) (Susan Blommaert, Tom McKinney), "(I Ain't Never Done Nothing to) Nobody" (*Ziegfeld Follies of 1910*; lyric and music by Axel Rogers and Bert Williams) (Paula Sweeney, Susan Blommaert, Marilyn Firment, Marianne Tatum), "She Was One of the Early Birds" (lyric and music by O'Connor) (Robert Stillman), "Je Ne Sais Pa Pa" (lyric and music by Fischer and Coleman) (Robert Stillman, Marianne Tatum, Chorus), "She Is More to Be Pitied Than Censured" (lyric and music by Davis) (Polly Pen, Marianne Tatum), "Sawing a Woman in Half" (lyric and music by Silverman and Swift) (Tom McKinney, Robert Stillman, Marianne Tatum), "In the Baggage Car Ahead" (lyric and music by Davis) (Marilyn Firment), "Waitin' for the Evening Mail" (lyric and music by Baskette) (Robert Stillman), "Kiss a Lonely Wife" (lyric and music by Fisher and Emmerich) (Paula Sweeney, Susan Blommaert, Marilyn Firment, Marianne Tatum), "Absinthe Frappe" (*It Happened in Nordland*, 1904; lyric by Glen MacDonough, music by Victor Herbert) (Marianne Tatum), "There's a Broken Heart for Every Light on Broadway" (reprise) (Company)

NOTES—The story of Evelyn Nesbit, Stanford White, and Harry K. Thaw is a peculiarly American one (like that of Baby Doe, Horace Tabor, and Augustus Tabor; see entry for *The Ballad of Baby Doe*) which seems more fictional than real. But fiction could never compete with the lives of these three almost legendary figures.

In turn-of-the-century New York City, the teenaged Evelyn Nesbit was considered by many the most beautiful woman in America; in fact, she was the inspiration for Charles Dana Gibson's Gibson Girl drawings. She joined the cast of the most popular musical in New York, *Florodora* (1900), and, as one of the Florodora Sextette, sang the show's most famous number, "Tell Me, Pretty Maiden (Are There Any More at Home Like You?)." (Florodora, incidentally, wasn't the name of the musical's heroine, but was an island in the Philippines where the musical took place.) Nesbit drew the attention of the middle-aged Stanford White, the country's prominent architect (among his iconic buildings was Pennsylvania Station) and a leading figure in New York society. The two began an affair which often took place in White's hideaway on West 24th Street; the top floor of the townhouse was two stories high, and a red velvet swing was installed there for Nesbit, who would swing as high as she could, and would try to kick a paper Japanese parasol which hung from the ceiling (some accounts indicate she tried to kick a section of the ceiling where there was a painted moon).

In the meantime, Nesbit and John Barrymore (who was a newspaper cartoonist at the time, and who later became the famous actor) had an affair (some sources indicate an aborted child was the result of their union), and she later met, and married, Harry K. Thaw, a young millionaire from Pittsburgh whose family had made its fortune in coal, railroads, and other interests. Thaw was insanely jealous of White and Nesbit's affair, and blamed White for seducing Nesbit. The unluckiest of stars were in alignment on the night of June 25, 1906, when Thaw and Nesbitt, as well as White, were in attendance for the opening of a new musical, *Mamzelle Champagne*. As the cast members performed a number ("I Could Love a Million Girls"), Thaw left his seat, walked over to where White was seated, and shot him to death. The ensuing trial was a sensation, arguably the most famous trial in American history up to that time. Thaw was eventually acquitted, and divorced Nesbit. She tried her hand at show business but never had any real success (the character of Susan Alexander in the 1941 film *Citizen Kane* was reportedly inspired by her). Nesbit saw her life story filmed (as *The Girl in the Red Velvet Swing*, 1955), and even posed for pictures with Joan Collins, who portrayed her in the film. Thaw died in 1947; most of his years were spent in and out of institutions of one sort or another (prisons, sanitariums, mental hospitals). However, Nesbit lived until 1966, and using the dates of the premieres of musical comedies as a reference point to measure the length of time she lived after White's murder, consider that the murder occurred during the opening night performance of *Mamzelle Champagne* in 1906, and that Nesbit died in January 1966, the month when *Sweet Charity* opened on Broadway.

The Nesbit-White-Thaw triangle was a major part of E.L. Doctorow's 1975 novel *Ragtime*, which was filmed in 1981. It's fascinating to compare how the films *The Girl in the Red Velvet Swing* and *Ragtime* treated the story.

There's certainly a musical in all this; but the almost epic story deserves more than the one paltry number assigned to it in the vastly overrated stage musical of Doctorow's novel (*Ragtime* opened on Broadway in 1996).

By using authentic turn-of-the-century songs to wryly comment upon the action, *The Gilded Cage* seems to have touched upon just the right note for its interpretation of the story. With a rave review from John S. Wilson in the *New York Times* (who noted that although the show's title suggested "veneer," the musical was "pure gold"), the Off Off Broadway musical seemed poised for a successful future. But after its brief run it was never heard from again.

578 The Girl from Wyoming. "A Musical Melodrama." THEATRE: American Music Hall; OPENING DATE: October 29, 1938; PERFORMANCES: 86; BOOK: John Van Antwerp; LYRICS: Ted Fetter; MUSIC: Richard Lewine; DIRECTION: Robert Ross; CHOREOGRAPHY: John Pierce and Grace Rolland; SCENERY: Eugene B. Dunkel; COSTUMES: Peggy Clark; PRODUCERS: John and Jerrold Krimsky

CAST—Philip Huston (Ben Longwood), Nellie Thorne (Mrs. Longwood), Billy M. Greene (Sheriff Peters), Tony Kraber (Sleepy), Duncan Baldwin (Rusty), George Petrie (Marcy Desmond), Donald MacDonald (Alkali), June Walker (The Girl from Wyoming), Anne Hunter (Chiquori), James Russo (Pedro), Jack Goldie (Bartender), Cow Belles (Ruth Mann, Jackie Susanne, Polly Smiley, Mary La Roche, Sherrand Pollard, Irene Mann), Cow Hands (Bruce Gordon, Walter Reed Smith, Alfred Brower, Norman Barcliff, Duncan Baldwin, Jack Riley), Singing Cowgirls (Audrey Edmonds, Pauline Meadows, Mildred Kent, Daphne Picard, Lorna Miller, Dorothy Knox, Terry Fay, Eleanor Morrison, Ann Cleverie, Helen Johnson)

The musical was presented in three acts.

ACT ONE—"Boston in the Spring" (Philip Huston, Graduates), "Ride Cowboy Ride" (Cowboys and Cowgirls), "Hats Off" (George Petrie, Donald MacDonald, Billy M. Greene, Cowboys), "Manuelo" (Anne Hunter), "The Dying Cowboy" (Donald MacDonald, George Petrie, Billy M. Greene, Tony Kraber), (Between Acts One and Two: Olio or Specialty)

ACT TWO—"Lullaby of the Plain" (Cowboys), "Our Home" (Philip Huston, June Walker, Company), "Stay East, Young Man" (Cowboys and Cowgirls), "Boston in the Spring" (reprise) (Boston Girls), (Between Acts Two and Three: Olio or Specialty)

ACT THREE—"Kickin' the Corn Around" (Company), Finale (Company)

NOTES—*The Girl from Wyoming*, the last new offering at the American Music Hall, wasn't as successful as its predecessors (see entry for *Naughty-Naught '00* for more information about the musical melodramas which played at the venue).

The Girl from Wyoming told the story of a Harvard boy from Boston who goes West to recover the family fortune. He becomes involved with a number of cowboys, prospectors, a dastardly villain, and a beautiful, mysterious girl (the title character) whom he marries (and it doesn't hurt that she's the long-lost daughter of a millionaire and will inherit thirty million dollars).

While Brooks Atkinson in the *New York Times* felt the most recent spoof at the American Music Hall wasn't up to *Naughty Naught '00*, he noted the latest "rowdy-dowdy" was "written and acted with the tongue, tonsils, larynx and both feet in the cheek" and had "appropriate tunes." He concluded that since the offering was a "hoot-and-hiss" musical, criticism should hold its "solemn tongue."

The script was published by Samuel French, Inc., in 1941.

579 The Girl Who Was Plugged In.

NOTES—See entry for *Weird Romance* (1992), an evening which was comprised of two one-act musicals, *The Girl Who Was Plugged In* and *Her Pilgrim Soul*.

580 Girls, Girls, Girls. THEATRE: The Other Stage/The Public Theatre; OPENING DATE: September 30, 1980; PERFORMANCES: 6; BOOK: Marilyn Suzanne Miller; LYRICS: Marilyn Suzanne Miller; MUSIC: Cheryl Hardwick; DIRECTION: Bob Balaban; CHOREOGRAPHY: Graciela Daniele; SCENERY: Akira Yoshimura; James E. Mayo, Associate Set Designer; COSTUMES: Karen Roston; LIGHTING: Arden Fingerhut; MUSICAL DIRECTION: Cheryl Hardwick; PRODUCER: The New York Shakespeare Festival (Joseph Papp, Director)

CAST—Valri Bromfield (Woman in Jeans), Frances Conroy (Woman in Skirt), Anne DeSalvo (Woman in Jeans), Judith Ivey (Woman in Overalls); Jay O. Sanders

The musical was presented in one act (song assignments unknown).

MUSICAL NUMBERS—Opening, "The Betty Song," "High School," "Vickie Lawrence," "Punk," "Frances' Ballad," "Lovers," "Credit Card," "Divorce," "Planet of No Thigh Bulge," "Street Lady," "Man/Woman," "Val's Ballad"

NOTES—*Girls, Girls, Girls*, a feminist musical from the Public Theatre, didn't last a full week. The names of its characters seem like a parody of the characters' names in another feminist Pappfest, *For Colored Girls Who Have Considered Suicide/When the Rainbow Is Enuf* (1977).

In his review for the *New York Times*, Frank Rich noted that the talented cast was stuck with lame material which never really analyzed women. Instead, the evening centered around references to television shows (*Good Morning, America, The Bob Newhart Show, The Merv Griffin Show*, etc.) and their sponsors (Bic pens, Mister Coffee, etc.). Rich noted the musical's frame of reference centered around television to such an extent that it seemed "as if no other reality exists."

581 Give My Regards to Leicester Square. "An Affectionate Salute to English Music Hall." THEATRE: Theatre Off Park; OPENING DATE: November 21, 1979; PERFORMANCES: 13; DIRECTION: Clif Dowell; CHOREOGRAPHY: Helen Baldassare; COSTUMES: Bob Thompson; MUSICAL DIRECTION: Dean Burris (?); PRODUCER: Richard Bennett

CAST—Dean Burris (Maestro Cecil Beauchamp), Bruce Vernon Bradley (Tom Tinsley), Neal Arluck (Dan Leno, Bijou, Tennyson, Ernie Mayne), Clif Dowell (Emile Clare, Dame Wilkie Bard, O'Gorman), Helen Baldassare (Marie Lloyd, Bella, Vesta Tilley), Lynn Gerb (Victoria Monks, Vesta Victoria); The McQueen Quartet (Clif Dowel, Neal Arluck, Helen Baldassare, Lynn Gerb); West End Temperance Society (Entire Company)

The action occurs at the Prince of Wales Music Hall, London, in 1904.

The revue was presented in three acts.

ACT ONE—"God Save the King" (Dean Burris), "She Told Me to Meet Her at the Gate" (Neal Arluck, Bruce Vernon Bradley), "Music Hall Shakespeare" (Clif Dowell), "She's Going There Every Night" (Helen Baldassare), "Give My Regards to Leicester Square" (Lynn Gerb), "I Want to Sing in Opera" (Clif Dowell), "Nursie, Nursie" (Helen Baldassare, Neal Arluck), "Lady Love" (Clif Dowell, Neal Arluck, Helen Baldassare, Lynn Gerb), "The Aerialist, Leotard" (performer unknown)

ACT TWO—"Pantomine (A Melodrama with a Moral for Our Time)"/"We've Been Chums for Fifty Years" (Company)

ACT THREE—"Henery the Eighth, I Am" (Helen Baldassare), "And Her Golden Hair Was Hanging Down Her Back" (Neal Arluck, Clif Dowell), "And It's Alright in the Summertime" (Lynn Gerb), "What I Want Is a Proper Cup of Coffee" (Neal Arluck), Grand Finale (Company)

NOTES—A month earlier, *One Mo' Time!* (see entry) offered authentic Black vaudeville; with *Give My Regards to Leicester Square*, Off Off Broadway presented an evening of authentic British music hall.

During the two-week run, Joanna Seaton assumed some of the female roles (Bella, Victoria Monks, and Vesta Victoria). Ernest Lehrer, who was not listed in the program, may have appeared as the Aerialist Leotard, the legendary trapeze artist who died at age 28, but not before inspiring the song "(The Daring Young Man on) The Flying Trapeze" as well as lending his name to a piece of clothing previously known as "tights."

582 The Glorious Age. "A Light Look at the Dark Ages." THEATRE: Theatre Four; OPENING DATE: May 11, 1975; PERFORMANCES: 9; BOOK: Cy Young; LYRICS: Cy Young; MUSIC: Cy Young; DIRECTION: John-Michael Tebelak; CHOREOGRAPHY: "Special Movement" by Dick Stephens; SCENERY: Stuart Wurtzel; COSTUMES: Jennifer von Mayrhauser; LIGHTING: Barry Arnold; MUSICAL DIRECTION: Robert W. Preston; PRODUCERS: Jane Manning and Carol McGroder in association with Wendell Minnick

CAST—Stuart Pankin (Blacksmith, Student, Hunchback Man, Crusader, Bear), George Riddle (Doctor, Town Crier, Student, Crusader), Clyde Laurents (Scientist, Student, Relic Seller, Crusader), Susan Willis (Madame Duncan, Crusader), Barry Pearl (Theologian Number One, Merchant, Professor, Commissioner), Paul Kreppel (Theologian Number Two, Merchant, Professor, Commissioner), Laurie Faso (Theologian Number Three, Merchant, Professor, Commissioner, Crusader), Robin Wesley (Henrietta, Student), D'Jamin Bartlett (Liana, Student, Crusader), Carol Swarbrick (Drum Girl, Student, Commissioner's Wife, Crusader), W.M. Hunt (Peter the Crusader, Student), Don Scardino (Matthew, Crusader) The action occurs in and around a town square during the Glorious Age.

The musical was presented in two acts.

ACT ONE—"Glorious Age" (Company), "Teach the Children" (Susan Willis, Robin Wesley), "Stay on the Path" (Robin Wesley, Stuart Pankin, George Riddle, Carol Swarbrick, D'Jamin Bartlett, Clyde Laurents, W.M. Hunt), "Mother Love" (Susan Willis, Don Scardino), "People Like You" (performer[s] unknown; possibly D'Jamin Bartlett), "Relic Seller Theme" (Clyde Laurents), "Theologian Theme" (Barry Pearl, Paul Kreppel, Laurie Faso), "The Turn My Life Is Taking" (D'Jamin Bartlett), "Rah, Rah" (Barry Pearl, Paul Kreppel, Laurie Faso), "Whoop De Doo" (W.M. Hunt, Clyde Laurents, Barry Pearl, Paul Kreppel, Robin Wesley, Stuart Pankin, Carol Swarbrick, Laurie Faso, George Riddle, D'Jamin Bartlett, Susan Willis, Don Scardino), "Must Be a Witch in Town" (Company)

ACT TWO—"Everyone Should Play a Musical Instrument" (Carol Swarbrick, Stuart Pankin, Company), "Theologian Theme" (reprise) (Barry Pearl, Paul Kreppel, Laurie Faso), "Relic Seller Theme" (reprise) (Clyde Laurents), "The Future Looks Promising" (W.M. Hunt), "Maybe There's a Place" (Don Scardino), "La La La" (Company), "Child of the Shade" (D'Jamin Bartlett, Don Scardino)

NOTES—Cy Young had written the book, lyrics, and music for *That Hat!* (1964; see entry), a one-performance flop which nonetheless included the song "Draw Me a Circle," which became a minor standard. He performed similar duties with *The Glorious Age*, which played for just a little over one week and then quietly disappeared. Like *Ride the Winds* (see entry), perhaps the medieval setting and characters of *The Glorious Age* verged too deeply into *Pippin* (1972) territory. Clive Barnes in the *New York Times* noted that despite the musical's description of being a "light look at the dark ages," the proceedings at Theatre Four were "heavy, heavy, heavy." He remarked that the mix of Crusaders, witches, "and that kind of nonsense" offered up a "ramshackle" evening, a "broken *Crucible*" and "a bit of *The Fairy Queen*" which "intended to be as bright as cheerful as *Once Upon a Mattress*." But instead of a mattress, the musical offered a "leaking waterbed." Barnes found Cy Young's book, lyrics, and music the "three main drawbacks" of the evening, and he noted that John-Michael Tebelak's staging fell back on the "waggish-cartoon" devices he had previously used in his direction of the original production of *Godspell* (see entry).

During previews, the song "All About the Plum" (sung by D'Jamin Bartlett and the Company) was dropped, and replaced by "People Like You."

583 The Glorious Ones. THEATRE: The Mitzi E. Newhouse Theatre/Lincoln Center; OPENING DATE: November 5, 2007; PERFORMANCES: 72; BOOK: Lynn Ahrens; LYRICS: Lynn Ahrens; MUSIC: Stephen Flaherty; DIRECTION: Graciela Daniele; CHOREOGRAPHY: Graciela Daniele; SCENERY: Dan Ostling; COSTUMES: Mara Blumenfeld; LIGHTING: Stephen Strawbridge; MUSICAL DIRECTION: David Holcenberg; PRODUCER: Lincoln Center Theatre (Andre Bishop and Bernard Gersten, Directors)

CAST—Marc Kudisch (Flaminio Scala), David Patrick Kelly (Pantalone), Natalie Venetia Belcon (Columbina), Julyana Soelistyo (Armanda Ragusa), John Kassir (Dottore), Erin Davie (Isabella Andreini, Jeremy Webb (Francesco Andreini, Comic Servant)

SOURCE—The 1974 novel *The Glorious Ones* by Francine Prose.

The action occurs in Italy during the late 1500s "and beyond" (the original novel was set in the early 1600s).

The musical was presented in one act.

MUSICAL NUMBERS—Prologue: "The Glorious Ones" (Marc Kudisch, The Glorious Ones), "Making Love" (Natalie Venetia Belcon, Marc Kudisch, Troupe), "Pantalone Alone" (David Patrick Kelly), "The Comedy of Love" (David Patrick Kelly, Julyana Soelistyo, Troupe), Scenario: "The Madness of Columbina" (The Glorious Ones), "The Glorious Ones" (reprise) (Marc Kudisch, Jeremy Webb), "Madness to Act" (Marc Kudisch), "Absalom" (Jeremy Webb), "The Invitation to France" (John Kassir), "Flaminio Scala's Historical Journey to France" (The Glorious Ones), "Three Lazzi" (The Glorious Ones), "Armanda's Tarantella" (Julyana Soelistyo, Men), "Improvisation" (Marc Kudisch), "The World She Writes" (Erin Davie), "Opposite You" (Jeremy Webb, Erin Davie), "My Body Wasn't Why" (Natalie Venetia Belcon), Scenario: "The Madness of Isabella" (The Glorious Ones," "Flaminio Scala's Ominous Dream" (Marc Kudisch, Troupe), "The World She Writes" (reprise) (Jeremy Webb), "Rise and Fall" (John Kassir, Troupe), "The Moon Woman" (A Play) (The Glorious Ones), "The Glorious Ones" (reprise) (Marc Kudisch), "I Was Here" (Marc Kudisch), "Armanda's Sack" (Julyana Soelistyo, Troupe), Finale: "The Comedy of Love" (The Glorious Ones)

NOTES—Because it was set in Italy and dealt with commedia dell'arte types, *The Glorious Ones* seemed to have two strikes against it, since musicals set in Italy (see entry for *Fortuna*) and musicals which use commedia dell'arte techniques (see entries for *The Green Bird* and *Smile, Smile, Smile*) almost always seem doomed to failure. So when *The Glorious Ones* was announced for production, a veritable hush fell over the theatre world and bets were placed on the musical's odds for artistic and commercial success. The New York reviews for *The Glorious Ones* were mixed, but Lynn Ahrens and Stephen Flaherty's score was generally well received. Further, the musical's cast album was released by Jay Records (CD # CDJAY-1407). But when the show played out its limited engagement at Lincoln Center, it didn't transfer to another theatre for an extended run. So it looks as though the jury is out on whether or not *The Glorious Ones* is an "official" success. But certainly the release of the cast album and the fact the musical requires a small cast will work in its favor in regard to a possible future in regional and community theatre. Charles Isherwood in the *New York Times* noted the evening was "short on narrative thrust" and occasionally moved "haphazardly" between scenes taking place on and off stage. But he liked Ahrens and Flaherty's "trunkful of well-made songs," and singled out "Armanda's Tarantella" as the show's "most delightful" number, "a rollicking parade of double-entendres." The headline of Frank Scheck's review in the *New York Post* proclaimed the musical was "not so glorious," and he felt the "extensive examples" of commedia dell'arte became tiresome and the "relentless procession" of songs became "numbing." Steve Suskin in *Variety* noted the plot never really got going until some fifty minutes into the one hour and forty minute evening, and thus felt it was "way too late to win over" most of the audience. He observed that Ahren and Flaherty's score was "well-crafted," but like some of their other musicals it was "self-sabotaged" by their choice of material.

For his performance as Flaminio Scala, Marc Kudisch received yet another set of glowing reviews. This busy New York (and regional theatre) performer boasts an impressive array of both stage and recorded performances, and he's a worthy successor to Alfred Drake. One hopes he'll soon find the breakthrough role in a hit musical to ensure his place in musical theatre.

The Glorious Ones had first been produced at the Pittsburgh Public Theatre/O'Reilly Theatre on April 27, 2007.

584 Gloryday.

NOTES—See entry for *See What I Wanna See.*

585 Go Fight City Hall. "A Musical Play."

THEATRE: Mayfair Theatre; OPENING DATE: November 2, 1961; PERFORMANCES: 77; BOOK: Harry Kalmanowich; LYRICS: Bella Mysell; MUSIC: Murray Rumshinsky; DIRECTION: Menachem Rubin; CHOREOGRAPHY: Henrietta Jacobson; SCENERY: Henrietta Jacobson; COSTUMES: Possibly by Henrietta Jacobson; PRODUCERS: Irving Jacobson, Julius Adler

CAST—Bruce Adler (Julius), Roberta Lean (Flora), Menachem Rubin (Abraham), Irving Jacobson (Naftuia), Fyvush Finkel (Nathan), Rose Rosenzweig (Mrs. Mirkin), Mae Schoenfeld (Miriam), Henrietta Jacobson (Jennie), Julius Adler (Benjamin Glick), David Ellin (Julius, as an adult), Anne Winters (Flora, as an adult)

The action occurs in the home of Abraham Ginsburg in Brooklyn from 1948 to 1961.

NOTES—*Go Fight City Hall* was a Yiddish-American musical which dealt with a widow (Henrietta Jacobson), her suitor and later husband (Irving Jacobson), and an assortment of her family and friends. Milton Esterow in the *New York Times* found the evening "broad and folksy, thick and sudsy," and concluded that Yiddish theatre was in "good shape." He had particular praise for the "superb" clowning of the Jacobsons.

A Tikva Records album (LP # T-72) included songs from both *Go Fight City Hall* and *Bei Mir Bistu Schoen* (see entry).

586 Goblin Market.

THEATRE: Circle in the Square Downtown; OPENING DATE: April 13, 1986; PERFORMANCES: 89; ADAPTATION: Polly Pen and Peggy Harmon Lyrics: Christina Rossetti; MUSIC: Polly Pen (For other lyric and music credits, see song list); DIRECTION: Andre Ernotte; CHOREOGRAPHY: Ara Fitzgerald; SCENERY: William Barclay; COSTUMES: Muriel Stockdale and Kitty Leach; LIGHTING: Phil Monat; MUSICAL DIRECTION: Lawrence Yurman; PRODUCERS: Ken Marsolais, Patricia Daily, and James Scott in association with Mark Beigelman, Lois Deutchman, and Paulette Haupt; a Vineyard Theatre production

CAST—TERRI KLAUSNER (Laura), ANN MORRISON (Lizzie)

The action occurs in Victorian England.

SOURCE—The poem "Goblin Market" (which appeared in the book of poetry *Goblin Market and Other Poems*, published in 1862) by Christina Rossetti.

The musical was presented in one act.

MUSICAL NUMBERS—"Come Buy, Come Buy," "We Must Not Look," "Mouth So Charmful" (lyric by Theodore Baker, music by Antonio Lotti), "Do You Not Remember Jeanie," "Sleep, Laura, Sleep" (lyric by Christopher Morgenstern; translated by Max Knight), "The Sisters" (music by Johannes Brahms), "Some There Are Who Never Venture" (lyric by John Gay, additional lyric by Polly Pen and Peggy Harmon), "Mirage" (music by Charles Ives), "Passing Away," "Here They Come," "Like a Lily," "Lizzie, Lizzie, Have You Tasted," "The Sisters" (reprise), "Two Doves"

NOTES—Set in Victorian England, *Goblin Market* was an unusual musical which dealt with two sisters (Laura and Lizzie) who revisit the home of their youth; there they reenact childhood games from the perspective of adulthood, including a world of goblins who sell luscious if poisonous fruits. Laura tastes the forbidden fruit, and almost dies; but she's saved by Lizzie, who had gone into the woods to buy fruit from the goblins as an antidote.

The work, which has been interpreted as an allegory of Victorian sexual repression, was first presented as an Off Off Broadway production at the Vineyard Theatre in 1985 for fifty-eight performances.

The cast album was released by That's Entertainment Records (LP # TER-1144), and the script was published by Dramatists Play Service, Inc., in 1987.

On November 11 and 12, 2007, the Vineyard Theatre presented an anniversary concert reading of the musical, and Terri Klausner and Ann Morrison returned to recreate their original roles. They were joined by Lawrence Yurman, the work's original musical director.

Polly Pen was single-handedly keeping the Victorian era alive in the Off and Off Off Broadway musical, either as a performer or a writer (see entries for *Charlotte Sweet*, *The Gilded Cage*, and *Once on a Summer's Day*). She also wrote the book, lyrics, and music for *Christina Alberta's Father*; based on the novel by H.G. Wells, the musical opened Off Off Broadway at the Vineyard Theatre on May 13, 1993, and played for nineteen performances (see entry).

587 God Bless Coney. "A Musical."

THEATRE: Orpheum Theatre; OPENING DATE: May 3, 1972; PERFORMANCES: 3; BOOK: John Glines; LYRICS: John Glines; MUSIC: John Glines; DIRECTION: Bob Schwartz; SCENERY: Don Tirrell; COSTUMES: Margaretta Magnini; LIGHTING: William Mintzer; MUSICAL DIRECTION: Robert Rogers; PRODUCER: Paul B. Reynolds

CAST—Bill Hinnant (Homer), Ann Hodapp (Christine), Marcia Lewis (Toula), William Francis (Father William), Liz Sheridan (Bertie), Johnny La Motta (Maxie)

The action occurs at Coney Island on July 14, 1964.

The musical was presented in two acts.

ACT ONE—Overture: "Subway to Coney Island" (Orchestra), "Seagulls" (Bill Hinnant, Ann Hodapp), "Throw Out the Lifeline" (William Francis, Marcia Lewis), "Love Life" (Marcia Lewis, Bill Hinnant, Ann Hodapp), "Eight-Horse Parlay" (Marcia Lewis, Liz Sheridan, William Francis, Bill Hinnant), "Man and Wife" (Marcia Lewis), "Goodbye Hives" (Liz Sheridan, Marcia Lewis, Ann Hodapp, Bill Hinnant), "He Looked at Me" (Liz Sheridan), "The Coney Island" (Johnny La Motta, Company)

ACT TWO—"Intermission Rag" (Orchestra), "Here We Are" (Bill Hinnant, Ann Hodapp), "God Bless All the Misfits" (William Francis), "Music Hall Medley" (See notes below) (Liz Sheridan, Johnny La Motta, Company), "Here Comes the Rabbi" (Company), "God Bless Coney" (Company), "Here We Are" (reprise) (Bill Hinnant, Ann Hodapp)

NOTES—The short-running *God Bless Coney* dealt with a young lifeguard who plans to commit suicide at Coney Island during a fireworks display on Bastille Day. Mel Gussow in the *New York Times* felt the "tinkly" music would be appropriate for the cocktail hour, the lyrics would be "better if hummed," and the book "should be remaindered." He noted that one of the musical's low points concerned a priest who gets hives when he eats ham, discovers he's really Jewish and is allergic to ham, and then decides to become a rabbi. The stage was covered in sand, and at one point the priest is discovered chest-deep in the sand, hoping it will cure his hives. Gussow wondered what a "deep-sand cure would do for this whimsical musical."

In the "Music Hall Medley" sequence, three songs (not by Glines) were used: "I Do Like to Be Beside the Seaside," lyric and music by John A. Glover-kind and Lewis Ilda; "Any Old Iron" (public domain); and "Don't Dilly Dally on the Way," lyric and music by Charles Collins and Fred W. Leight (with new lyric by Dick Manning).

A special word about Liz Sheridan: She was an occasional Off Broadway and Broadway visitor (including Michael Bennett's *Ballroom* [1978]), but she is perhaps now best remembered for her relationship with James Dean during the period of his brief Broadway career in the early 1950s; she examined their relationship in her 2000 book *Dizzy & Jimmy: My Life with James Dean: A Love Story*, which was published by Regan Books.

588 God Bless You, Mr. Rosewater.

THEATRE: Entermedia Theatre; OPENING DATE: October 14, 1979; PERFORMANCES: 49; BOOK: Howard Ashman; LYRICS: Howard Ashman; ADDITIONAL LYRICS by Dennis Green; MUSIC: Alan Menken; DIRECTION: Alan Menken; CHOREOGRAPHY: Mary Kyte; SCENERY: Edward T. Gianfrancesco Costumes: David Graden; LIGHTING: Craig Evans; MUSICAL DIRECTION: David Friedman; PRODUCERS: Edith Vonnegut in association with Warner Theatre Productions, Inc., and Mark Gasarch

CAST—Ed Vannuys (Thurmond McAllister), Jonathan Hadary (Norman Mushari), Frederick Coffin (Eliot Rosewater), Janie Sell (Sylvia Rosewater), John Towey (Psychiatrist, Fireman, Writer, Allen [and other unidentified roles]), Will Hussung (Senator Lister Ames Rosewater). Alan David-Little (Jerome, Kid, Fireman, Sergeant Boyle [and other unidentified roles]), Anne Desalvo (Mary Moody, Blanche, Jane Jasper [and other unidentified roles]), Charles C. Welch (Delbert Peach, Fireman [and other unidentified roles]), Elizabeth Moore (Diana Moon Glampers), Peter J. Saputo (Noyes Finnerty, Fireman, Fred Rosewater [and other unidentified roles]), Holly Villaire (Dawn Leonard, Hostess, Caroline Rosewater [and other unidentified roles]), David Christmas (Charley Warmergran, Arthur Garvey Ulm, Fireman [and other unidentified roles]), Pierre Epstein (Kilgore Trout)

SOURCE—The 1965 novel *God Bless You, Mr. Rosewater*, or *Pearls Before Swine* by Kurt Vonnegut. The action occurs in various states throughout the country, and the time is "not very long ago."

The musical was presented in two acts.

ACT ONE—"The Rosewater Foundation" (Frederick Coffin, Ensemble [Applicants and Foundation Staff]), "Dear Ophelia" (Frederick Coffin), "Thank

God for the Volunteer Fire Brigade" (Frederick Coffin, Ensemble [Texas Volunteer Fire Department]), "Mushari's Waltz" (Jonathan Hadary), "Thirty Miles from the Banks of the Ohio"/"Look Who's Here" (Frederick Coffin, Ensemble [Citizens of Rosewater County]), "Cheese Nips" (Janie Sell, Ensemble [Citizens of Rosewater County]), "The Rosewater Foundation" (reprise) (David Christmas, Anne Desalvo, Frederick Coffin), "Since You Came to This Town" (Elizabeth Moore, Anne Desalvo, Charles C. Welch, Holly Villaire, Alan David-Little, Ensemble [Citizens of Rosewater County])

ACT TWO—"A Poem by William Blake" (Anne Desalvo), "Rhode Island Tango" (Peter J. Saputo, Holly Villaire, Jonathan Hadary), "Eliot...Sylvia" (Janie Sell, Frederick Coffin), "Plain, Clean, Average Americans" (Jonathan Hadary, Peter J. Saputo, Holly Villaire, Ensemble [Americans]), "A Firestorm Consuming Indianapolis" (Frederick Coffin), "Dear Ophelia" (reprise) (Janie Sell), "I, Eliot Rosewater" (Frederick Coffin, Ensemble [Citizens of Rosewater])

NOTES—*God Bless You, Mr. Rosewater* was first seen in a showcase production on May 17, 1979, at the WPA Theatre; most of the cast transferred when the musical opened at the Entermedia a few months later (for this production, Janie Sell replaced Mimi Turque in the role of Sylvia Rosewater). One number ("Oughta Build a Statue") from the showcase was dropped for the Off Broadway production.

Based on the sophomoric book by Kurt Vonnegut, the basic storyline actually made for an interesting libretto, and coupled with Alan Menken's fascinating and quirky score ("Cheese Nips," "A Firestorm Consuming Indianapolis," "Rhode Island Tango"), the musical should have had a long run. But it was gone in six weeks, and in a period when many cast albums of Off Broadway shows with less-interesting scores were released (such as *Piano Bar* [1978], *The Housewives' Cantata* [1980], and *I Can't Keep Running in Place* [1981]), it's a shame Menken's exciting and theatrical score went unrecorded.

Dennis Blake wrote the lyrics for "Dear Ophelia," "Thank God for the Volunteer Fire Brigade," "Since You Came to This Town," and "Rhode Island Tango."

A 1981 production at Arena Stage in Washington, D.C., omitted "A Poem by William Blake." For this revival, Frederick Coffin reprised his role of Eliot Rosewater (Barbara Andres played Sylvia). The Arena cast also included Don Liberto, an almost legendary performer among musical theatre aficionados; he appeared in the original productions of a number of Broadway and Off Broadway musicals. The script, which was published by Samuel French, Inc., in 1980, included "A Poem by William Blake."

The musical was briefly revived by the York Theatre Company on April 1, 2005, as part of its *Musicals in Mufti* presentations (see entry for more information about the series).

589 God Is a (Guess What?). "A Morality Play with Music." THEATRE: St. Marks Playhouse; OPENING DATE: December 17, 1968; PERFORMANCES: 32; BOOK: Ray McIver; LYRICS: Ray McIver; MUSIC: Coleridge-Taylor Perkinson; DIRECTION: Michael A. Schultz; CHOREOGRAPHY: Louis Johnson; SCENERY: Edward Burbridge; COSTUMES: Bernard Johnson; LIGHTING: Marshall Williams; MUSICAL DIRECTION: Margaret Harris; PRODUCER: The Negro Ensemble Company

CAST—Arthur French (First End Man), David Downing (Second End Man), Julius W. Harris (Jim), Theodore Wilson (Officer), Clarice Taylor (Reba), William Jay (Boy), Frances Foster (Lady), Graham Brown (Voice, Bla-Bla), Allie Woods (A Man), Judyann Jonsson (First Extraordinary Spook), Hattie Winston (Second Extraordinary Spook), Rosalind Cash (Third Extraordinary Spook), Esther Rolle (Cannibal), Norman Bush (Priest), Mari Toussaint (Acolyte)

The action occurs "here and now."

The musical was presented in one act.

MUSICAL NUMBERS—"A Mighty Fortress" (Chorus), "The Lynch-Him Song" (Arthur French, David Downing), "The Sonny-Boy Slave Song" (Norman Bush, William Jay, Mari Toussaint, Theodore Wilson), "The Black-Black Song" (Chorus, David Downing, Arthur French), "The Golden Rule Song" (Arthur French, David Downing), "God Will Take Care" (Norman Bush, William Jay, Mari Touissant, Theodore Wilson), "The Darkies Song" (David Downing, Arthur French), "The Sit Down Song" (Rosalind Cash, Judyann Jonsson, Hattie Winston, Allie Woods), "The Lynchers' Prayer" (Company)

NOTES—*God Is a (Guess What?)*, a musical about a would-be lynching which is prevented by the deus ex machina Himself, used the structure of an old-fashioned minstrel show to tell its story.

Dan Sullivan in the *New York Times* found the evening part minstrel show, part morality play, part nightclub revue, part sermonette, and all of it "hard to bag" and "nervous as a squirrel." Sullivan noted the work was somewhat of an updated take on *The Green Pastures*, and reported the musical's examination of Black and White relations (and confrontations) was "much too black and white for sustained dramatic interest." But he found the direction "bright" and "lively," the cast "snazzy," the costumes "witty," and Coleridge-Taylor Perkinson's score "full of impish echoes of practically everybody, but maintaining a jauntiness all its own."

Of the cast members, Esther Rolle later found success on television, and Rosalind Cash became a minor cult figure of sorts as the star of a series of so-called blaxploitation films in the 1970s.

And the answer to the question posed in musical's title: God Is a (Black Man).

590 God's Trombones (1960).
NOTES—See entry for *Shakespeare in Harlem.*

591 God's Trombones (1975). THEATRE: Church of St. Paul and St. Andrew; OPENING DATE: April 11, 1975; PERFORMANCES: 12; TEXT: James Weldon Johnson; DIRECTION: John Barracuda; CHOREOGRAPHY: Juliet Seignious; SCENERY: Linda Day; COSTUMES: Linda Day; LIGHTING: Phillip Almquist; MUSICAL DIRECTION: J. Hamilton Grandison; PRODUCER: AMAS Repertory Theatre, Inc. (Rosetta LeNoire, Founder and Artistic Director)

CAST—Dorothea Anderson, John Barracuda, Pamela Carpenter, Joe Crawford, Mary Cunningham, Michael Ebbin, Mel Edmondson, Juanita Greene, Katherine Kelly, John LeGros, Dee Dee Levant, John McCurry, Fran Salisbury, Juliet Seignious, Barbara Sloane, Joseph Smith, Tad Truesdale, Pauline Weekes, Carlton Williams

SOURCE—The 1922 book *God's Trombones* by James Weldon Johnson (the book is a collection of his sermons).

The musical was presented in one act (song assignments unknown).

MUSICAL NUMBERS—"He Brought Me Out," "Prayer," "Ol' Time Religion," "Sweet Hour of Prayer," "My God Looked Down," "There Comes a Time," "Young Man, Young Man," "Death Come to My House," "Soon-ah Will Be Done," "Steal Away," "Weep Not," "Noah," "The Ol' Ark's A-Moverin'," "Fire, Fire," "Take My Mother Home," "Were You There," "Let My People Go," "See the Sign of Judgment," "In Dat Great Gittin' Up Mornin'," "Work On, Pray On"

NOTES—The Off Off Broadway musical *God's Trombones* was based on the collection of sermons written by James Weldon Johnson (1871-1938) which was originally published in 1922.

For other adaptations of the work, see entries for *Shakespeare in Harlem* (1960); *Trumpets of the Lord* (Vinnette Carroll's 1963 version which also played on Broadway in 1969); and two adaptations of Carroll's version which played Off Off Broadway in 1989 (as *God's Trombones!*) and 1997 (as *God's Trombones*). The 1975 production doesn't seem to be based on Carroll's version, and neither does a 1982 production which played at Town Hall for three performances beginning on April 16. Another adaptation of the material was Tad Truesdale's *Godsong*, which was presented Off Off Broadway, first at Amas Repertory Theatre on March 4, 1976, and then at La Mama Experimental Theatre Club (ETC) on April 23, 1976, and on December 30, 1976.

592 God's Trombones! (1989). THEATRE: Theatre of the Riverside Church; OPENING DATE: October 4, 1989; PERFORMANCES: 45; ADAPTATION: Writer unknown (possibly Vinnette Carroll?); DIRECTION: Woodie King, Jr.; CHOREOGRAPHY: Dianne McIntyre; SCENERY: Llewellyn Harrison; COSTUMES: Judy Dearing; LIGHTING: William H. Grant, III; MUSICAL DIRECTION: Grenoldo Frazier; PRODUCER: New Federal Theatre, Inc. (Woodie King, Jr.)

CAST—Lex Monson (The Rev. Bradford Parham), Theresa Merritt (The Rev. Sister Rena Pinkston), Rhetta Hughes (Sister Odessa Jackson), Trazana Beverley (The Rev. Sister Marion Alexander), Cliff Frazier The Rev. Ridgley Washington), Jackson Family (Deborah Blackwell-Cook, Sabrynaah Pope, Don Corey Washington)

SOURCE—The 1922 book *God's Trombones* by James Weldon Johnson (the book is a collection of his sermons).

The musical was presented in two acts (division of acts and song assignments unknown).

MUSICAL NUMBERS—Prelude, "So Glad I'm Here," "Twelve Gates," "Sweet Hour of Prayer," "Amen," "Lord, Don't Move This Mountain," "Trombones Ensemble," "In Shady Green Pastures," "How Great Thou Art," "Didn't It Rain," "Just a Little Walk with Jesus," "I'm Coming Home, Dear Lord," "Hush," "He'll Understand," "Were You There," "Swing Low Sweet Chariot," "How I Got Over," Finale

NOTES—Although she doesn't seem to have been credited, the 1989 Off Off Broadway production *God's Trombones!* may have been a revised version of Vinnette Carroll's *Trumpets of the Lord*, her adaptation of *God's Trombones*, James Weldon Johnson's collection of sermons which was published in 1922. *Trumpets of the Lord* was first produced Off Broadway in 1963 (see entry) and was later seen on Broadway in 1969. The revised *Trumpets* was also revived Off Off Broadway in 1997 (as *God's Trombones*); see entry.

For other musical adaptations of *God's Trombones*, see entries for *Shakespeare in Harlem* (1960) and a 1975 Off Off Broadway adaptation titled *God's Trombones* (which doesn't seem to be based on Carroll's version). There was also a version which was presented at Town Hall on April 16, 1982, for three performances (and which also doesn't seem to be based on Carroll's adaptation). Further, *Godsong*, an adaptation of *God's Trombones*, was presented Off Off Broadway, first at Amas Repertory Theatre on March 4, 1976, and then at La Mama Experimental Theatre Club (ETC) on April 23, 1976, and on December 30, 1976.

593 God's Trombones (1997). THEATRE: Tribeca Arts Center; OPENING DATE: February 5, 1997; PERFORMANCES: 5; ADAPTATION: Vinnette Carroll; DIRECTION: Woodie King, Jr.; CHOREOGRAPHY: Kathleen Sumler; COSTUMES: Vassie Welbeck-Browne; LIGHTING: Antoinette Tynes; MUSICAL DIRECTION: Paul Vincent Hendricks; PRO-

DUCERS: Tribeca Performing Arts Center and National Black Touring Circuit

CAST—Trazana Beverley (the Rev. Sister Marion Alexander), Todd Davis (the Rev. Ridgely Washington), Cliff Frazier (Character Name Unknown), Theresa Merritt (the Rev. Sister Rena Pinkston), Joseph A. Walker (the Rev. Bradford Parhan), Debbie Blackwell-Cook (Sister Odessa Jackson), Sabrynaah Pope, Don Corey Washington, Ernest Witherspoon

SOURCE—The 1922 book *God's Trombones* by James Weldon Johnson (the book is a collection of his sermons).

The musical was presented in two acts (no song list available; see separate entry for *Trumpets of the Lord*).

NOTES—The Off Off Broadway production *God's Trombones* was a revised version of Vinnette Carroll's *Trumpets of the Lord*, her adaptation of *God's Trombones*, James Weldon Johnson's collection of sermons which was published in1922. *Trumpets of the Lord* was first produced Off Broadway in 1963 (see entry), and was later seen on Broadway in 1969. As *God's Trombones!*, Carroll's revised version was also seen Off Off Broadway in 1989 (see entry).

For other musical adaptations of *God's Trombones*, see entries for *Shakespeare in Harlem* (1960) and a 1975 Off Off Broadway adaptation titled *God's Trombones* (which doesn't seem to be based on Carroll's version). There was also another version of the work which was presented at Town Hall on April 16, 1982, for three performances (and which also doesn't seem to have been based on Carroll's version). Further, *Godsong*, an adaptation of *God's Trombones* by Tad Truesdale, was presented Off Off Broadway, first at Amas Repertory Theatre on March 4, 1976, and then at La Mama Experimental Theatre Club (ETC) on April 23, 1976, and on December 30, 1976.

594 Godsong.

NOTES—See entry for *Shakespeare in Harlem*.

595 Godspell (1971).

"A Musical." THEATRE: Cherry Lane Theatre; transferred to the Promenade Theatre on August 17, 1971; OPENING DATE: May 17, 1971; PERFORMANCES: 2,124; BOOK: John-Michael Tebelak; LYRICS: Stephen Schwartz; MUSIC: Stephen Schwartz; DIRECTION: John-Michael Tebelak; COSTUMES: Susan Tzu; LIGHTING: Lowell B. Achziger; MUSICAL DIRECTION: Stephen Schwartz; PRODUCERS: Edgar Lansbury, Stuart Duncan, and Joseph Beruh; Charles Haid, Associate Producer

CAST—Lamar Alford, Peggy Gordon, David Haskell, Joanne Jonas, Robin Lamont, Sonia Manzano, Gilmer McCormick, Jeffrey Mylett, Stephen Nathan, Herb Simon

SOURCE—The Gospel According to St. Matthew.

The musical was presented in two acts.

ACT ONE—"Tower of Babble" (Company), "Prepare Ye the Way of the Lord" (David Haskell, Company), "Save the People" (Stephen Nathan, Company), "Day by Day" (Robin Lamont, Company), "Learn Your Lessons Well" (Gilmer McCormick), "Bless the Lord" (Joanne Jonas), "All for the Best" (Stephen Nathan, David Haskell), "All Good Gifts" (Lamar Alford, Company), "Light of the World" (Company)

ACT TWO—"Learn Your Lessons Well" (reprise) (Lamar Alford), "Turn Back, O Man" (Sonia Manzano, Company), "Alas for You" (Stephen Nathan), "By My Side" (Peggy Gordon, Gilmer McCormick, Company), "We Beseech Thee" (Jeffrey Mylett, Company), "On the Willows" (Band), Finale (Company)

NOTES—*Godspell* ("gospel") is one of the most successful of all Off Broadway musicals, running 2,124 performances. The musical toured extensively, and settled in for long runs in many cities. On June 22, 1976, it opened on Broadway at the Broadhurst Theatre for 527 performances (Don Scardino was Jesus, and the company included Robin Lamont of the original Off Broadway company). The London production (with Jeremy Irons in the role of Judas [created by David Haskell in the Off-Broadway production]) opened at the Wyndham's Theatre on November 17, 1971, and played for 1,128 performances. The 1973 film version was released by Columbia Pictures and starred Victor Garber as Jesus; the film's cast included many original cast members (David Haskell, Robin Lamont, Gilmer McCormack) as well as a new song, "Beautiful City." The musical was revived at the Lamb's Theatre on June 12, 1988, for 225 performances, and then on August 2, 2000, it was revived at the Theatre at Saint Peter's Church for seventy-seven performances (see entries). As of this writing, *Godspell* is scheduled to be revived on Broadway during Summer 2008.

Bell Records released the New York (LP # BELL-1102) and London (LP # BELLS-203) cast albums as well as the film soundtrack (LP # BELL-1118). Other recordings of the score include the 1971 Australian cast album (Lewis Young Productions Records LP # SFL-934486); a 1993 studio cast recording by That's Entertainment Records (CD # CDTER-1204) with a cast which included John Barrowman and Ruthie Henshaw ("Beautiful City" was included on the recording); a 1994 "UK Cast Recording for the 90's" on Playback Records (CD # GSCD-01) which also included "Beautiful City"; and a studio cast album performed by The Last Galaxie (General American Records LP # GAR-11312).

The musical was first presented at Café La Mama. The loosely structured, almost revue-like book dealt with the story of Jesus, as told in the Gospel According to Saint Matthew. The presentation had a slightly improvised quality, with mime-like clowns and ragtag hippies rendering the Biblical story against the backdrop of an abandoned children's playground.

Stephen Schwartz' score was in a soft-rock mode, and there were several outstanding numbers, including the soft-shoe shuffle "All for the Best" and the honky-tonkish "Turn Back, O Man," as well as "Day by Day," the show's best-known song and one of the most popular and enduring show tunes of the era. (One number in the score, "By My Side," was not by Schwartz; its lyric was by Jay Hamburger, and its music by Peggy Gordon.)

Despite his extraordinary successes, Schwartz has been continuously underestimated by critics and theatre buffs; it seems only audiences enjoy his musicals. *Godspell*, in its initial Off Broadway and Broadway runs, totaled 2,651 performances; his first Broadway musical, *Pippin* (1972), played for 1,944 performances; and *The Magic Show* (1974) for 1,920. He also contributed lyrics to Leonard Bernstein's *Mass* (1971; see entry). Thereafter followed a lean period in which his musicals (either on Broadway, in regional theatre, or in London) never quite made it (including his finest work, *The Baker's Wife*, which closed prior to its Broadway opening in 1976; see entry for the Off Off Broadway production). However, Schwartz soon found his way again, winning two Oscars, for "Colors of the Wind" (from Disney's *Pocahontas* [1995; lyric by Schwartz and music by Alan Menken]) and "When You Believe" (*The Prince of Egypt* [1998; lyric and music by Schwartz]). He returned to Broadway in 2003 with *Wicked*, one of the most successful musicals in the history of Broadway and which seems primed to run longer than the combined New York performances of *Godspell*, *Pippin*, and *The Magic Show*.

596 Godspell (1988).

THEATRE: Lamb's Theatre; OPENING DATE: June 12, 1988; PERFORMANCES: 225; BOOK: John-Michael Tebelak; LYRICS: Stephen Schwartz; MUSIC: Stephen Schwartz; DIRECTION: Don Scardino; SCENERY: Alison Campbell; COSTUMES: David C. Woolard; LIGHTING: Phil Monat; MUSICAL DIRECTION: Steven M. Alper; PRODUCER: The Lamb's Theatre Company (Carolyn Rossi Copeland, Producing Director)

CAST—Trini Alvarado, Anne Bobby, Bill Damaschke, Laura Dean, Angel Jemmott, Eddie Korbich, Mia Korf, Robert McNeill, Harold Perrineau, Jr., Jeffrey Steefel

SOURCE—The Gospel According to St. Matthew.

The musical was presented in two acts.

NOTES—This revival of *Godspell* played over six months, and was directed by Don Scardino, who had played the role of Jesus in the musical's 1976 Broadway production. For song list and more information about the musical, see entry for the original 1971 production.

597 Godspell (2000).

THEATRE: The Theatre at Saint Peter's Church; OPENING DATE: August 2, 2000; PERFORMANCES: 77; BOOK: John-Michael Tebelak; LYRICS: Stephen Schwartz; MUSIC: Stephen Schwartz; DIRECTION: Shawn Rozsa and RJ Tolan; CHOREOGRAPHY: Ovi Vargas; SCENERY: Kevin Lock; COSTUMES: William Ivey Long and Bernard Grenier; LIGHTING: Herrick Goldman; MUSICAL DIRECTION: Dan Schachner; PRODUCER: NET Theatrical Productions

CAST—Shoshana Bean, Tim Cain, Catherine Carpenter, Will Erat, Barrett Foa, Lucia Giannetta, Capathia Jenkins, Chad Kimball, Leslie Kritzer, Eliseo Roman

SOURCE—The Gospel According to St. Matthew

The musical was presented in two acts.

NOTES—This Off Broadway revival of *Godspell* included "Beautiful City," which Stephen Schwartz had written for the 1973 film version. The revival had been seen earlier in the year in an Off Off Broadway production at Third Eye Rep, opening on February 25 and playing for approximately sixty-four performances.

For song list and more information about the musical, see entry for the original 1971 production.

598 Gogo Loves You.

THEATRE: Theatre de Lys; OPENING DATE: October 9, 1964; PERFORMANCES: 2; BOOK: Anita Loos; LYRICS: Gladys Shelley; MUSIC: Claude Leveillee; DIRECTION: Fred Weintraub; CHOREOGRAPHY: Marvin Gordon; SCENERY: Kert Lundell; COSTUMES: Alfred Lehman; LIGHTING: Jules Fisher; MUSICAL DIRECTION: Everett Gordon; PRODUCER: Fredana Productions

CAST—Stanley Suter (Hortense), Gene Lindsey (Bert), Walter "Dutch" Miller (Papa Potasse), JUDY HENSKE (Gogo), ARNOLD SOBOLOFF (Count Stanislaus de la Ferronniere), DOROTHY GREENER (Mme. Bernoux), Janet Lee Parker (Amelia), Ted Chapman (LaBaume), Ray Hausen (Racinet): Dancers: JoAnn Lehmann, Nomi Mitty, Rosemarie Ocasio, Donna Smith, Peter Hamparian, Jim Hovis

SOURCE—Based on a French play (author unknown) titled *L'Ecole des Cocottes*.

The action occurs in Paris.

The musical was presented in two acts.

ACT ONE—"Parnasse" (Sandy Suter), "Bazoom" (Judy Henske, Gene Lindsey, Chorus), "Prima Donna" (Judy Henske, Arnold Soboloff), "He Can, I Can" (Judy Henske, Janet Lee Parker), "Gogo" (Arnold Soboloff), "There Is No Difference" (Judy Henske, Dorothy Greener), "Keep in Touch" (Gogo, Gene Lindsey), "My Uncle's Mistress" (Gene Lindsey, Chorus), "Happy Love Affair" (Janet Lee Parker, Dorothy Greener, Chorus), "Tell Me the Story of Your Life" (Arnold Soboloff), "Tell Me the Story of Your Life" (reprise) (Judy Henske)

ACT TWO—"Woman Makes the Man" (Roy Hausen, Ted Chapman), "Life Is Lovely" (Ted Chapman), "College of L'Amour" (Arnold Soboloff), "Savoir Faire" (Judy Henske, Chorus), "Quelle

Heure Est-Il?" (Judy Henske, Gene Lindsey), Finale (Company)

NOTES—Lewis Funke in the *New York Times* noted that *Gogo Loves You* "does not stand still. It goes downhill all the way." The two-performance flop about the training of a Parisian cocotte was New York's final chance to see Dorothy Greener, the unique clown who always seemed to find herself in failures. *Gogo Loves You* was also Gladys Shelley's last musical. She's best remembered as the lyricist of *The Duchess Misbehaves* (1946), one of Broadway's legendary flops.

Anita Loos would be heard from one more time, in *Cheri*, her 1959 Broadway adaptation of Colette's stories about the son of a cocotte. Cheri, incidentally, was the name of the cocotte's son (played by Horst Buchholz), not the name of a middle-aged woman (Kim Stanley) who loves him and who shares his mother's profession.

The song "Happy Love Affair" (sung by Judy Henske) was dropped during previews.

599 Going Hollywood. "A Musical Comedy"; Date of Workshop: 1983; BOOK: Joe Leonardo and David Zippel; LYRICS: David Zippel; MUSIC: Jonathan Sheffer; DIRECTION: Peter Mark Schifter; CHOREOGRAPHY: Onna White; Jim Taylor, Associate Choreographer; MUSICAL DIRECTION: Edward Strauss; PRODUCERS: Michael Frazier and the Shubert Organization; Donna Tomas, Associate Producer

CAST—Jerry Highland (Peter Evans), Robert Blumenfeld (Stage Manager, Rudolph Kammerling), Joel Blum (Buddy, Page), Christine Ebersole (May Daniels), Harvey Evans (George Lewis), Clifford Fearl (Porter), Dolores Gray (Helen Hobart), Virginia Seidel (Susan Walker), Kurt Knudson (Herman Glogauer), Tarry Caruso (Florabel Leigh), Aileen Savage (Phyllis Fontaine), Jane Connell (Miss Leighton), Freyda Thomas (Miss Chasen, Third Announcer), Timothy Jerome (Lawrence Vail), Trooper (Rin-Tin-Tin), John Remme (Flick), Claude Tessier (Designer), Michael Hayward-Jones (Bishop), Gene Varrone (Cyril Fonsdale), Kevin Marcum (First Announcer), Jack Magradey (Second Announcer), Keith Savage (Fourth Announcer); "The Columbus Quartet" was played by Clifford Fearl, Michael Hayward-Jones, Eric Johnson, and Gene Varrone (the Quartet also played the roles of the Flunkies and the Porters); Ensemble: Gretchen Albrecht, Joel Blum, Tarry Caruso, Candy Cook, Candy Darling, Terri Homberg, Merilee Magnuson, Jack Magradey, Kevin Marcum, Jerry Mitchell, John Remme, Aileen Savage, Keith Savage, Brian Sutherland, Claude Tessier, Freyda Thomas, Candace Tovar, Karen Ziemba

SOURCE—The 1930 play *Once in a Lifetime* by George S. Kaufman and Moss Hart.

The workshop was presented in two acts.

ACT ONE—"Waiting in the Wings" (Christine Ebersole, Company), "Gotta Go West" (Peter Evans, Company), "Waiting in the Wings" (reprise) (Christine Ebersole), "If I Could Dance with You" (Peter Evans, Christine Ebersole), "Hollywood Rhythm" (Dolores Gray, Company), "Made for the Movies" (Harvey Evans, Virginia Seidel), "Give 'Em What They Want" (Kurt Knudson, Clifford Fearl, Michael Hayward-Jones, Eric Johnson, Gene Varrone, Peter Evans), "Talk, Talk, Talk" (Jane Connell, Dolores Gray), "Talk, Talk, Talk" (reprise) (Christine Ebersole, Company), "We Don't Talk Anymore" (Christine Ebersole, Peter Evans), "Talk, Talk, Talk" (reprise) (Timothy Jerome), "You Know Who" (Peter Evans, Christine Ebersole, Harvey Evans), "You Know Who" (reprise) (Peter Evans, Christine Ebersole, Harvey Evans, Virginia Seidel)

ACT TWO—"I Never Let It Ruin My Day" (Dolores Gray, Company), "I Reach for a Star" (Peter Evans), "This Darling Industry" (Timothy Jerome), "Today I'm Smiling Rainbows" (Harvey Evans, Company), "Gingham and Orchid"s (Gene Varrone, Virginia Seidel, Company), "Another Mister Right" (Christine Ebersole), "I Never Let It Ruin My Day" (reprise) (Dolores Gray), "This Darling Industry" (reprise) (Timothy Jerome, Christine Ebersole), "Today I'm Smiling Rainbows" (reprise) (Kurt Knudson), Finale (Company)

NOTES—For what seemed the better part of the 1980s, *Going Hollywood* was always being announced for a future Broadway season. But except for this lavish workshop, the musical version of *Once in a Lifetime*, George S. Kaufman and Moss Hart's classic 1930 spoof of the film industry, never materialized. Occasionally one or another of the musical's songs was heard, most notably the jazzy torch song "Another Mister Right," which was recorded by Barbara Cook and was often part of her concert repertoire. "Another Mister Right" (as well as "I Reach for a Star") were later heard in the 1983 revue *It's Better with a Band*, an evening of songs with lyrics by David Zippel (see entry).

Going Hollywood would have been an interesting companion piece to *On the Twentieth Century*, the 1978 musical which was also based on a classic stage comedy from the early 1930s about show business types (in this case, the 1932 *Twentieth Century* by Ben Hecht and Charles MacArthur).

600 The Golden Apple (1954). THEATRE: Phoenix Theatre; OPENING DATE: March 11, 1954; PERFORMANCES: 48; BOOK: John LaTouche; LYRICS: John LaTouche; MUSIC: Jerome Moross; DIRECTION: Norman Lloyd; CHOREOGRAPHY: Hanya Holm; SCENERY: William and Jean Eckart; COSTUMES: Alvin Colt; LIGHTING: Klaus Holm; MUSICAL DIRECTION: Hugh Ross; PRODUCERS: The Phoenix Theatre (T. Edward Hambleton and Norris Houghton)

CAST—KAYE BALLARD (Helen), BIBI OSTERWALD (Lovey Mars), Geraldine Viti (Mrs. Juniper), PORTIA NELSON (Miss Minerva Oliver), Nola Day (Mother Hare), PRISCILLA GILLETTE (Penelope and Circe), Dean Michener (Menelaus), STEPHEN DOUGLASS (Ulysses), David Hooks (Theron), Jerry Stiller (Mayor Juniper), JONATHAN LUCAS (Paris), JACK WHITING (Hector Charybdis); The Heroes: Frank Seabolt (Captain Mars), Marten Sameth (Ajax), Crandall Diehl (Agamemmon), Maurice Edwards (Nestor), Murray Gitlin (Bluey), Don Redlich (Thirsty), Peter De Mayo (Silas), Barton Mumaw (Homer), Robert Flavelle (Diomede), Julian Patrick (Achilles), Larry Chelsi (Patroclus), Garry Gordon (Doe MacCahan); The Local Girls: Sara Bettis, Dorothy Etheridge, Nelle Fisher, Dee Harless, Janet Hayes, Lois McCauley, Ann Needham, Joli Roberts, Jere Stevens, Tao Strong, Helen Ahola; The Local Boys: Santa Anselmo, Bob Gay, Charles Post, Arthur Schoep

SOURCES—Homer's epic poems (written between the eighth and sixth centuries B.C.) *The Iliad* and *The Odyssey* (with an emphasis on the latter). The action occurs in the State of Washington between 1900 and 1910.

The musical was presented in two acts.

ACT ONE—"Nothing Ever Happens in Angel's Roost" (Kaye Ballard, Bibi Osterwald, Geraldine Viti, Portia Nelson), "Mother Hare's Séance" (Nola Day), "My Love Is On the Way" (Priscilla Gillette), "The Heroes Come Home" (Company), "It Was a Glad Adventure" (Stephen Douglass, The Heroes), "Come Along, Boys" (The Heroes, Ensemble), "It's the Going Home Together" (Stephen Douglass, Priscilla Gillette), "Mother Hare's Prophecy" (Nola Day), "Helen Is Always Willing" (The Heroes), "The Church Social" (The Heroes, Ensemble), "Introducin' Mr. Paris" (Bibi Osterwald, Geraldine Viti, Portia Nelson, Nola Day, Jonathan Lucas), "Lazy Afternoon" (Kaye Ballard, Jonathan Lucas), "The Departure for Rhododendron" (Company)

ACT TWO—"My Picture in the Papers" (Kaye Ballard, Jonathan Lucas, Male Ensemble), "The Taking of Rhododendron" (Stephen Douglass, Jack Whiting, Jonathan Lucas), "Hector's Song" (Jack Whiting), "When We Were Young" (Priscilla Gillette), "Store-Bought Suit" (Stephen Douglass), "Calypso" (Geraldine Viti), "Scylla and Charybdis" (Dean Michener, Jack Whiting), "By Goona-Goona Lagoon" (Bibi Osterwald), "Doomed, Doomed, Doomed" (Portia Nelson), "Circe, Circe" (Priscilla Gillette, Geraldine Viti, Ensemble), "Ulysses' Soliloquy" (Stephen Douglass), "The Sewing Bee" (Priscilla Gillette, Kaye Ballard, Portia Nelson, Geraldine Viti, Bibi Osterwald, Suitors, Stephen Douglass), "We've Just Begun" (Stephen Douglass, Priscilla Gillette)

NOTES—*The Golden Apple* received rapturous reviews from the critics and from discerning audience members. New York had never seen a sung-through musical (no dialogue, and all songs written in rhymed couplets) set to a pastiche of march, ragtime, calypso, cakewalk, vaudeville routines, and other forms of American popular music. Moreover, the production was genuinely offbeat and quirky (the character of Paris is only partially dressed, and is a non-singing, all-dancing character).

Within weeks of its Off Broadway opening, *The Golden Apple* transferred to Broadway at the Alvin (now Neil Simon) Theatre on April 20, 1954, for a (disappointing) run of 125 performances. But it was nonetheless a landmark production: It was the first Off Broadway musical to transfer to a Broadway theatre; the first Off Broadway musical to be awarded the New York Drama Critics' Circle Award for Best Musical (heretofore, all winners in this category, such as *Carousel* [1945], *Brigadoon* [1947], *South Pacific* [1949], and *Guys and Dolls* [1951] were musicals which had originated on Broadway); and the first Off Broadway musical to be published in a hardback edition (by Random House in 1954).

When *The Golden Apple* transferred to Broadway, there were a few changes in its casting and score. For Broadway, Shannon Bolin played the role of Mrs. Juniper (Geraldine Viti, who originated the role Off Broadway, remained with the production, as standby for Bolin); Martha Larrimore replaced Nola Day in the role of Mother Hare; and Martin Keane replaced Larry Chelsi in the role of Patroclus. Moreover, for Broadway, the song "When We Were Young" was re-titled "Windflowers"; Ulysses and Penelope's due "We've Just Begun" was replaced by "The Tirade"; and a traditional finale was added (a reprise of "It's the Going Home Together").

Despite its being one of the gems of the American musical stage, *The Golden Apple* has been scandalously neglected (but ones of its songs, the haunting and shimmering "Lazy Afternoon," has become a something of a standard). The musical has never been revived on Broadway, and is virtually ignored by regional theatres and opera companies as well as those institutions which specialize in concert adaptations of musicals. One hopes that *The Golden Apple* will someday be produced by the New York City Opera or by *Encores!* (see entry) and that such a production will lead to a complete recording of the score.

The Golden Apple was briefly revived Off Broadway in 1962 (see entry), and on March 23, 1990, it was seen Off Off Broadway for twenty-three performances when it was presented by the York Theatre Company.

It's one of the theatre's greatest losses that Jerome Moross, here the composer of one of the greatest scores ever written for an American musical, virtually disappeared from the stage (with the exception of one more musical, the equally ambitious *Gentlemen, Be Seated!*, which was produced Off Broadway in 1963; see entry). However, he enjoyed a successful career composing background scores for films, most notably *The Big Country* (1958) and *The Cardinal* (1963). A special note regarding the Broadway cast recording: because the musical was sung-through, only a two or three LP set could have included all the music. But RCA Victor released the recording on one LP (# LOC-1014), which was speeded up in order to include as much music as possible. As a result, some numbers on the recording are heard at a faster speed than they were sung in the theatre, and the effect is occasionally jarring. Within a few years of its release, the album was deleted from the RCA catalogue, but the rights to the recording were purchased by Elektra Records, which re-released the LP in the early 1960s (# EKL-5000). At one point the rights to the album reverted to RCA, which in the 1990s issued the score on CD (# 09026-68934-2).

For other versions of Homer's epic poems, see entries for *Sing Muse!*, *Helen*, and *La Belle Helene*.

601 The Golden Apple (1962).

THEATRE: York Playhouse; OPENING DATE: February 12, 1962; PERFORMANCES: 112; BOOK: John LaTouche; LYRICS: John LaTouche; MUSIC: Jerome Moross; DIRECTION: Robert Turoff; CHOREOGRAPHY: Nelle Fisher; SCENERY: Bill Hargate; COSTUMES: Bill Hargate; LIGHTING: Jules Fisher; MUSICAL DIRECTION: Philip Fradkin; PRODUCERS: Dorothy Olim, George Krone

CAST—ROBERTA MACDONALD (Helen), JANE CONNELL (Lovey Mars), SYLVIA SHORT (Mrs. Juniper), PEGGY LE ROY (Miss Minerva Oliver), JULIA ROSS (Mother Hare), JAN MCART (Penelope), Gabor Morea (Menelaus), The Heroes (Todd Butler, Captain Mars; Bill Oliver, Ajax; Scott Ray, Agamemnon; Jay Foote, Nestor; John Holmes, Jr,, Diomede; Stephen [Steve] Elmore, Achilles; Ken Corday, Patroclus; Dick Latessa, Doc Maccahan), STAN PAGE (Ulysses), MICHAEL DOMINICO (Paris), Lynne E. Albert (Figurehead), SWEN SWENSON (Hector Charybdis), Lynne E. Albert (Townswoman), Harriet All (Townswoman), Nancy Fenster (Townswoman), Janet McCall (Townswoman), Lois Ann Oaks (Townswoman), Marcia Shaw (Townswoman), Dave Anderson (Townsman), Buddy Mann (Townsman), John Philibert (Townsman), Jerry Powell (Townsman)

SOURCES—Homer's epic poems (written between the eighth and sixth centuries B.C.) *The Iliad* and *The Odyssey* (with an emphasis on the latter).

The action occurs in the State of Washington between 1900 and 1910.

The musical was presented in two acts.

NOTES—Just eight years after its premiere, *The Golden Apple* was briefly revived Off Broadway (the program didn't list individual musical numbers; for list of songs, see entry for the original 1954 production).

Among the revival's cast members was Stephen (Steve) Elmore, who in the late 1960s appeared in one of the biggest Off Broadway hits (*Dames at Sea* [1968; see entry]); with Tamara Long, he memorably introduced that show's sultry beguine (of romantic, exotic Pensacola, Florida). His most famous role is probably that of Paul (whom Amy didn't want to marry today) in the original production of *Company* (1970).

Another cast member in the revival was Swen Swenson, who had appeared in many Broadway productions, including *Destry Rides Again* (1959) and *Wildcat* (1960), both of which featured Michael Kidd's choreography. In 1962, he found his signature song in *Little Me's* "I've Got Your Number," a slithering male-striptease showstopper with a knockout lyric (by Carolyn Leigh), vampy music (by Cy Coleman), and sizzling choreography (by Bob Fosse). In the Off Broadway retrospective dance revue *The American Dance Machine* (see entry), Swenson reprised the memorable number.

The revival also included an early appearance by Dick Latessa, who became a welcome presence in Off Broadway and Broadway musicals; four decades after he appeared in *The Golden Apple*, he was still going strong, winning a Tony Award for Best Performance by a Featured Actor in a Musical for *Hairspray* (2002). *The Golden Apple* was later revived Off Off Broadway by the York Theatre Company; the production opened on March 23, 1990, and played for twenty-three performances.

602 Golden Bat.

"A Japanese Rock Musical." THEATRE: Sheridan Square Playhouse; OPENING DATE: July 21, 1970; PERFORMANCES: 152; BOOK: Yutaka Higashi; LYRICS: Yutaka Higashi; MUSIC: Itsuro Shimoda; DIRECTION: Yutaka Higashi; SCENERY: Kenkichi Sato; COSTUMES: Kiyoko Chiba; LIGHTING: Barry Arnold; MUSICAL DIRECTION: Itsuro Shimoda; PRODUCERS: Kermit Bloomgarden and Arthur Cantor

CAST—Yukiko Kobayashi, Kyoichi Nagakura, Reiko Nagai, Shoichi Saito, Sukae Kato, Sansho Shinsui, Yasunori Saito, Jun Arakawa, Setsuko Nakagawa, Nonoru Mine, Kenkichi Sato, Yoshie Matsuno

The musical was presented in one act.

MUSICAL NUMBERS—I. *Japan*: Introduction (Yukiko Kobayashi), "America, America"/"Extra, Extra" (Setsuko Nagagawa), "American Flag" (Kenkichi Sato), "Goeika (Song of Invocation and Supplication)" (performer[s] unknown), "Ba-Ba-Ba (A Song for Fun)" (performer[s] unknown), "Home" (Setsuko Nakagawa), "I Like Girls" (Noboru Mine); II. *The Pacific*: "Western Movies" (Yasunori Saito), "Soliloquy (Look Over There)" (Yasunori Saito), "North-Northwest" (performer[s] unknown); III. *American Rock*: "American Rock" (performer[s] unknown), "Encountering America (A Vaudeville Interlude)" (Reiko Nagai, Jun Arakawa, Shoichi Saito, Setsuko Nakagawa), "Strike! America" (Kyoichi Nagakura), "Rock, Crane's Town" (performer[s] unknown), "Looking Over My Life" (Shoichi Sato), Background Music/"Indus River," "Peace (Cries from Asia and Prayers for Peace)" (performer[s] unknown), "I Like"/"Love! Love! Love!" (performer[s] unknown), "For Whom?" (Troupe), "Mawari Toro (Revolving Lantern)" (Saka Kato), "Kid's World (Temari)" (Yukiko Kobayashi), "Background Song (Warabe-Uta)" (performer[s] unknown), "Soliloquy" (Yukiko Kobayashi), "Hana Wa (Song of Flowers)" (performer[s] unknown), "Namu Amida Butsu" (performer[s] unknown), "Medeta, Medeta (Festival Song)" (Kenkichi Sato), "Japanese Lesson" (Kenkichi Sato); IV. *Matsuri*: Matsuri" (Yukiko Kobayashi), "Okage, Okage!" (performer[s] unknown), "Affirmation of Life" (Sakae Kato), "Hana, Yuki, Kaze (Flower, Snow, Wind)" (performer[s] unknown), "Final Declaration" (Reiko Nagai)

NOTES—Although *Golden Bat* was credited with a book writer, it was an evening of sketches, songs, and dances, all set to a rock score. Yes, the rock musical was ubiquitous, even taking root in other countries. The musical had been previously produced in Japan by the Tokyo Kid Brothers (a theatre group) and then in New York by the Café La Mama.

A program note indicated the title was derived from a popular Japanese comic strip character, who, like the phoenix, rises from the ashes.

The program also explained that the title is a symbol of "matsuri," which is the "hopes, dreams and will of the young generation." Note the era's obsession with youth (and the supposed wisdom of youth). *Hair* and *The Me Nobody Knows* (see entries) had a similar message, and in fact many rock musicals pandered to baby boomers and credited them with special wisdom not found in anyone over the age of thirty.

Walter Kerr in the *New York Times* found the evening "warm and moth-like and altogether winning," and noted that the "angry, sometimes skipping vaudeville" of the young and rebellious performers was based on their desire to be free of traditional theatrical styles (Kerr also noted that the forms and styles of rebellion were becoming very "conventional" these days). Kerr felt the evening could have been shortened, but he nonetheless liked the performers and found the score "pleasant"; he further remarked that rock music in the theatre was more and more making "compromises" with traditional theatre music and so in effect often sounded like pastiche.

603 Golden Boy.

"The New Musical." THEATRE: Billie Holiday Theatre; OPENING DATE: June 7, 1984; PERFORMANCES: Unknown; BOOK: Leslie Lee; LYRICS: Lee Adams; MUSIC: Charles Strouse; DIRECTION: Jeffrey B. Moss; CHOREOGRAPHY: Louis Johnson; SCENERY: Felix E. Cochren; COSTUMES: Charles Schoonmaker; LIGHTING: Tim Phillips; MUSICAL DIRECTION: Thom Birdwell; PRODUCERS: Marjorie Moon in association with Jerry Kravat/ Nelle Adams

CAST—Obba Babatunde (Joe Wellington), Kyme S. Hersi (Denise), Wade T. Pretlow Goss (Boxer, Bernie, Sam, Reporter), Ivson Polk (Boxer, Youth, Handler), Brian Evaret Chandler (Boxer, Youth, Referee), Dwayne Phelps (Boxer, Youth, Carlos), Bruce Hawkins (Boxer, Ronnie, Doctor), James A. Johnson (Boxer, Youth, Reporter, Handler), Don Billett (Tom Moody), James Randolph (Eddie Prince), Leata Galloway (Lorna Moon), Ebony Jo-Ann (Emma Wellington), Lisa Dawn Cave (Joe's Fan, Teenager, Widow), Marcia James (Joe's Fan, Schoolgirl, News Reporter), Michael Rivera (Oscar Lopez)

SOURCE—The 1964 musical *Golden Boy* (book, Clifford Odets and William Gibson, lyrics by Lee Adams, and music by Charles Strouse) which was based on the 1937 play *Golden Boy* by Clifford Odets.

The musical was presented in two acts.

ACT ONE—*The Manly Art*: "Nightsong" (Obba Babatunde), "Workout" (Wade T. Pretlow Goss, Ivson Polk, Brian Evaret Chandler, Dwayne Phelps, Bruce Hawkins, James A. Johnson), "Everything's Great" (James Randolph, Leata Galloway), "This Is the Life" (James Randolph, Wade T. Pretlow Goss, Ivson Polk, Brian Evaret Chandler, Dwayne Phelps, Bruce Hawkins, James A. Johnson, Obba Babatunde, Leata Galloway, Don Billett), "Gimme Some" (Ebony Jo-Ann, Obba Babatunde), "Hey, Joe" (Company), "Winners" (Leata Galloway, Obba Babatunde), "Lorna's Here" (Leata Galloway), "Don't Forget 127th Street" (Obba Babatunde, Company), "Golden Boy" (Leata Galloway)

ACT TWO—*This Is the Life*: "Colorful" (Obba Babatunde, James Randolph), "I Want to Be with You" (Obba Babatunde, Leata Galloway), "Stick Around" (Michael Rivera, Obba Babatunde), "Winners" (reprise) (Obba Babatunde), "Everything's Lovely in the Morning" (Ebony Jo-Ann, Obba Babatunde)

NOTES—Despite its 569-performance run, the 1964 Broadway musical *Golden Boy* wasn't a financial success. The Off Off Broadway revival offered a new book (by playwright Leslie Lee, whose 1975 drama *The First Breeze of Summer* transferred to Broadway after an Off Broadway run). His adaptation didn't include the mixed racial romance depicted in the 1964 script (in which Joe Wellington was Black and Lorna Moon, White); in Lee's version, both Wellington and Moon were Black.

Five numbers from the original Broadway production were omitted from the revival: "The Road Tour," "Can't You See It?," "No More," "The Fight," and, most surprisingly, "While the City Sleeps," not only the score's best song but arguably the finest song in the Strouse and Adams catalogue.

The revival included three new songs, "Winners," "Everything's Lovely in the Morning," and "Hey, Joe"; for the latter, Weldon Irvine was credited with additional lyrics.

The script for the original Broadway production was published by Atheneum in 1965, and the original Broadway cast recording was released by Capitol Records (LP # VAS-2124; the CD was issued by Broadway Angel Records [# ZDM-7243-5-65024-2-0).

In December 2007, Michael Riedel reported in his column *On Broadway* for the *New York Post* that a Broadway revival of *Golden Boy* was in the offing, possibly to star Usher, who had made an impression in 2006 when he played the role of Billy Flynn in the revival of *Chicago*. (Incidentally, Riedel's immensely amusing and informative bi-weekly columns are must-reads for the latest in New York theatre news.)

604 The Golden Land. "A Joyous New Musical." THEATRE: Second Avenue Theatre; OPENING DATE: November 11, 1985; PERFORMANCES: 277; TEXT: Zalmen Mlotek and Moishe Rosenfeld; LYRICS: See song list for credits; MUSIC: See song list for credits; DIRECTION: Jacques Levy; CHOREOGRAPHY: Donald Saddler; SCENERY: Lindsey Decker; COSTUMES: Natasha Landau; LIGHTING: John McLain; MUSICAL DIRECTION: Donald Saddler; PRODUCERS: Sherwin M. Goldman, Moishe Rosenfeld, and Westport Productions, Inc.; William Twohill, Associate Producer

CAST—Bruce Adler, Phyllis Berk, Joanne Borts, Avi Hoffman, Marc Krause, Neva Small, Sonia Hagalili (Voice of the Grandmother)

The revue was presented in two acts.

ACT ONE—*Arrival:* "Mir Forn Kayn Amerike (We're Going to America, Good-Bye, Mother Russia)" (music by Arnold Perlmutter and Herman Wohl), "Vi Shver S'iz Tsu Sheyden (How Hard to Leave Old Homes)" (music by Arnold Perlmutter and Herman Wohl), "Troyerik Zayn Darf Men Nit (Why Be Sad?)" (music by Arnold Perlmutter and Herman Wohl), "Amerike, Hurrah for Onkl Sem! (America, What a Name!)" (music by Arnold Perlmutter and Herman Wohl), "Ellis Island (Ellis Island, So Awesome and Cold)" (lyric and music by Solomon Shmulewitz), "Lozt Ayayn (Let Us In)" (lyric by Jaffe, music by Joseph Rumshinsky), "Give Me Your Tired, Your Poor" (words by Emma Lazarus, music by Max Helfman), *The New City:,* "Vatch Your Step!" (Yiddish lyric by Sam Lowenworth, English lyric by Zalmen Mlotek, Moishe Rosenfeld, and Jacques Levy, music by Joseph Rumshinsky), "Gebentsht Iz Amerike (Blessed Is America)" (English lyric by Jacques Levy, Moishe Rosenfeld, and Zalmen Mlotek, music by Arnold Perlmutter and Herman Wohl), "Fonye Ganev (Ivan the Czar, The Rouge)" (folksong), "Koyft a Tsaytung! (Buy, Read a Paper!)" (lyric and music by Simkhe Schwartz), "Dem Peddlers Brivele (The Peddler's Letter)" (lyric by Yankl Brisker, music by Ziske Feigenbaum and Jacob Leiserowitz), "A Brivele Der Mamen (A Letter to Mother)" (lyric and music by Solomon Small-Smulewitz), "Lekha Doydi, Ya Riboyn Olam, Sholem Aleykhem, Gut Vokh" (Parts of the Sabbath ritual [Zmiro]); *Labor:* "Fifty-Fifty" (Yiddish lyric by Louis Gilrod, English lyric by Jacques Levy, Zalmen Mlotek, Moise Rosenfed, and Bruce Adler), music by Joseph Rumshinsky), "Shnel Loyfn Di Reder (The Wheels Turn Quickly)" (lyric by David Edelshtat, music by Lazar Weiner), "Motl Der Opereyter (Motl the Operator)" (lyric and music by Chaim Tauber) "Arbeter Froyen (Working Women)" (lyric and music by David Edelshtat), "Rebel Girl" (lyric and music by Joe Hill), "Ballad of the Triangle Fire" (lyric and music by Ruth Rubin), "Mamenyu, or Elegy on the Triangle Fire Victims" (lyric by Anshel Schorr, music by Joseph Rumshinsky), "Bread and Roses" (lyric by James Oppenheim, music by Caroline Kohlsaat); *Citizenship:* "Lebn Zol Kolombus! (Long Live Columbus)" (Yiddish lyric by Louis Gilrod, English lyric by Jacques Levy, music by Arnold Perlmutter and Herman Wohl), "Three Cheers for Yankee Doodle!" (lyric by Louis Gilrod, music by Arnold Perlmutter and Herman Wohl), "Yenki Doodl Fort Uptown (Yankee Doodle Rides Uptown)" (parody), "Di Fon Fun Frayhayt (The Flag of Freedom)" (lyric by Louis Gilrod, music by Arnold Perlmutter and Herman Wohl), "Zi Vet Kumen Fun Di Berg (She'll Be Coming from the Mountains)" (parody), "Amerike, Hurrah for Onkl Sem" (reprise)

ACT TWO—*Downtown-Uptown:* Entr'acte, "Fun Downtown-Uptown (From Downtown, We Move Uptown)" (Yiddish lyric by Boris Thomashefsky, English lyric by Chana Mlotek, Jacques Levy, Zalmen Mlotek,and Moishe Rosenfeld, music by Joseph Rumshinsky), "Ikh Bin a Border Bay Mayn Vayb (I Am a Boarder at My Wife's House)" (Yiddish lyric and music by Rubin Doctor, English lyric by Bruce Adler), "When Rosie Lived on Essex Street" (lyric and music by Addison Burkhardt), "Ovinu Malkeynu" (ancient litany for the High Holy Days); *The Early Yiddish Theatre:* "Got un Zayn Mishpet Iz Gerekht (God and His Judgement Are Right)" (lyric by Louis Gilrod, music by David Meyerovitch), "Yo, Vu Nemt Men Di Eydes (Where Shall We Find the Witnesses?)" (lyric and music by Abraham Goldfaden), "The Wedding" (traditional melodies), "Ikh Breng Aykh a Grus Fun Di Trenches (I Bring You Greeting from the Trenches)" (lyric and music by Isidore Lillian; sequence included an excerpt from "Over There" by George M. Cohan); *Film and Radio:* "Steam, Steam, Steam" (lyric and music by Sam Lowenwirth), "Joe and Paul's" (lyric and music by Sholom Secunda), "Levine and His Flying Machine" (English lyric by Saul Bernie, Yiddish lyric by Joseph Tanzman, music by Sam Coslow), "Kum Leybke Tantsn (Come Dance, Leybke)" (lyric and music by Mordecai Gebirtig), "The Yidisha Charleston" *The Depression:,* "Vu Nemt Men Parnose? (How Do I Make a Living?)" (lyric and music by David Meyerovitch), "Brother, Can You Spare a Dime?" (from *Americana*, 1932; lyric by E.Y. Harburg, music by Jay Gorney), "Gebentsht Iz Amerike (Blessed Is America)" (reprise); *Yiddish Theatre Benefit:* "Abi Gezunt (As Long As You're Healthy)" (lyric by Molly Picon, music by Abraham Ellstein), "S'iz Kayle Gevorn (Everything Is Spoiled)" (lyric and music by Menashe [Menasha] Skulnik), "Papirosn (Buy Cigarettes)" (Yiddish lyric and music by Herman Yablokoff, English lyric by Jacques Levy), "Rumenye, Rumenye (Rumania)" (Yiddish lyric and music by Aaron Lebedeff, English lyric by Bruce Adler), "Yidl Mitn Fidl (Yiddle with His Fiddle)" (Yiddish lyric by Itsik Manger and Sholomo Carlbach, English lyric by Jacques Levy, music by Abraham Ellstein); *Rebirth:* "Briderlekh Tayere (Dear Brothers, Help)" (lyric and music by Abe Schwartz), "Am Yisroel Khay!" (lyric by M. Knapheis, music by S. Beresovsky)

NOTES—*Tintypes* (see entry) was a revue about the European immigrant experience; *The Golden Land* concentrated on Eastern European Jewish immigration to "Amerike." The revue had been previously seen Off Off Broadway at the Norman Thomas Theatre in 1984 and then later in regional theatre. The 1984 Off Off Broadway production included a cast of five (Bruce Adler, Phyllis Berk, Joanne Borts, Avi Hoffman, and Betty Silberman); by the time of the 1985 Off Broadway production, Silberman was no longer with the musical, and Marc Krause and Neva Small had joined the other four cast members. The Off Broadway program didn't include a song list; the list above is taken from the Off Off Broadway program (the songs were sung in Yiddish, English, and a mixture of both languages). The Off Broadway production was recorded by Golden Land Records, Inc. (LP # GL-001); for the recording, Stuart Zagnit replaced Avi Hoffman, and two extra singers were added (Jacob Ehrenreich and Ellen Gould). The recording also included a booklet with lyrics.

Clive Barnes in the *New York Post* found the revue one of "shining simplicity and wonderful effectiveness ... [a] heart-warming yet passionate show." He also found the cast "terrific."

For *My Place in the World*, Neva Small's luminous 2004 collection of mostly Broadway and Off Broadway songs (Small Penny Enterprises, LLC [CD # NS-2211]), she included one song from *The Golden Land* ("Papirosn [Buy Cigarettes]").

At least five songs were added to the 1985 production: "Oy, I Like Him!," based on "Oy, I Like She," Yiddish lyric by Jacob Jacobs, English lyric by Jacques Levy, music by Alexander Olshanetsky; "A Khulem (A Dream)," Yiddish folk song with lyric by Jacques Levy, Salmen Mlotek, and Moishe Rosenfeld; "Show You Care!," Yiddish folk song with lyric by Chana Mlotek, Jacques Levy, Zalmen Mlotek, and Moise Rosenfeld; "Mayn Yiddishe Meydele (My Jewish Girl)," lyric by Ansel Schorr, music by Sholom Secunda; and "Belz, Mayn Shtetele Belz (Belz, My Little Town of Belz)," Yiddish lyric by Jacob Jacobs, English lyric by Zalmen Mlotek and Moise Rosenfeld, music by Jacob Jacobs.

The Second Avenue Theatre (previously the Phoenix, Eden, and Entermedia) had originally opened in 1926 as the Yiddish Art Theatre, and it was appropriate that *The Golden Land* played at the venue which had been the heart of American-Yiddish theatre during its heyday.

605 The Golden Screw. "A Folk-Rock Musical." THEATRE: Provincetown Playhouse; OPENING DATE: January 30, 1967; PERFORMANCES: 40; BOOK: Tom Sankey; LYRICS: Tom Sankey; MUSIC: Tom Sankey; DIRECTION: James Grove; SCENERY: C. Murawski; COSTUMES: Possibly by C. Murawski; MUSICAL DIRECTION: David Lucas; PRODUCERS: Pandora Productions in association with Delancey Productions

CAST—TOM SANKEY, Janet Day (Sankey) (Grandma, Millie, Betty, Susy), Patrick Sullivan (Red Sharpe, Poet), Murray Paskin (Ben); musicians: Jack Harper (Guitarist), The Inner Sanctum (Kevin Michael, Lead Guitar; Gerry Michael, Drums; Vince Taggart, Rhythm Guitar, Frank Thumhart, Bass Guitar)

The musical was presented in two acts.

ACT ONE—"Little White Dog," "Bad Girl," GRANDMA (Janet Day), "New Evaline," WASHINGTON HIGH SCHOOL (Murray Paskin, Patrick Sullivan), "2000 Miles," THE COSTUME (Murray Paskin), "Jesus Come Down," UNEMPLOYMENT OFFICE—MILLIE (Murray Paskin, Janet Day), "You Won't Say No," BEN AND BETTY (Murray Paskin, Janet Day), "The Beautiful People," RED SHARPE'S LAMENT (Patrick Sullivan), "I Heard My Mother Crying," NEWPORT FOLK FESTIVAL (Murray Paskin, Janet Day, Patrick Sullivan), "I Can't Make It Anymore"

ACT TWO—"Trip Tick Talking Blues," SUSY (Janet Day), "Can I Touch You?," SIMON SAYS (Murray Paskin), "That's Your Thing, Baby (It's Not Mine)," BACKSTAGE (Patrick Sullivan, Janet Day), "I Can't Remember," COCKTAIL PARTY (Murray Paskin, Janet Day, Patrick Sullivan), "(Here I Am on the) Bottom End of Bleecker Street," POET (Patrick Sullivan), "Flippin' Out!," "Little White Dog" (reprise)

NOTES—*Hair* (see entry) is incorrectly cited as the first rock musical; but it is *The Golden Screw* which holds that (dubious) distinction. *The Golden Screw* opened nine months before *Hair*, and its program cover identifies the work as a "folk-rock musical." Prior to its production at the Provincetown Playhouse, the musical had been presented in a June 1966 workshop at the Theatre Genesis at St. Marks-

Church-in-the-Bouwerie with the same cast (but a different director, Robert Siegler). In September 1966, the musical re-opened at the Theatre Genesis, and then finally played at a regular Off Broadway theatre in January 1967.

The book-musical-cum-revue was about a folk singer whose success almost destroys him; he retains his principles by rejecting the commercialization of his talent.

The staging was somewhat unusual. On one side of the stage were three non-singing performers (Janet Day, Patrick Sullivan, and Murray Paskin) who enacted scenes from the folk singer's story; on the other side were Tom Sankey (who performed all vocals), Jack Harper on guitar, and a quartet of musicians called The Inner Sanctum. (One of the clichés of the Off Broadway rock musical was that the musicians were never called the "orchestra" or the "band"; instead, most rock musicals gave its orchestra a bizarre name, in keeping with the names of popular rock groups of the era, such as the Strawberry Alarm Clock, and, yes, the Harpers Bizarre.) The non-musical and musical scenes took turns telling the story. (In the above listing, the book sequences are capitalized.)

Tom Sankey proved to be an interesting performer-writer-composer, but was never heard from again. It was a shame, because many of his songs were likable and inventive (perhaps the score's highlight is "Bottom End of Bleecker Street"), and he held promise as a lyricist and composer of musicals.

Critic Edward Sothern Hipp generally praised Sankey's score, and also thanked him because "not one of his ballads is a protest song, not one assails the draft system, not one calls for retreat from Vietnam."

During the mid and late 1960s, many mainstream musicals toyed with rock music, the beat/hippie counter-culture, and, occasionally, the anti-war song, and thus one such token song would appear in otherwise traditional scores: "The Rhythm of Life" (*Sweet Charity*, 1966); "You Are Not Real" (*The Apple Tree*, 1966); "Well, It Ain't" (*The Mad Show*, 1966; see entry); "Weary Near to Dyin'" (*Henry Sweet Henry*, 1967); "Maman" (*Mata Hari*, 1967; see entries for *Mata Hari* and *Ballad for a Firing Squad*); "It Ain't Us Who Makes the Wars" (*Billy*, 1969); and "Momma, Look Sharp" (*1776*, 1969). After *The Golden Screw* and *Hair*, full-fledged rock musicals had their brief day in the musical theatre sun. Some would say sunset, and would cite *Hair* (and rock musicals in general) as the beginning of the end of musical theatre, but *Hair* marked a major turning-point in the history of musical theatre, and not because of its rock music (see entry for *Hair* and its importance as one of the first concept musicals).

For such an obscure musical, *The Golden Screw* nonetheless left an impressive record of its existence. The cast album was released by Atlantic Records (LP # ATCO-33-208); the Theatre Genesis version of the script (as *The Golden Screw*, or *That's Your Thing, Baby*) was published in the 1968 Bantam Books anthology *The New Underground Theatre* (edited by Robert L. Schroeder); and on October 18, 1966, the Theatre Genesis production was taped for New York City's "educational" Channel 13. It's unclear if the musical was actually shown (perhaps its then-controversial subject matter was considered inappropriate for television). Moreover, it's uncertain if a tape of the production still exists; if it does, it would be a unique historical record of early Off Broadway (along with the television versions of *Simply Heavenly* and *...And in This Corner* [see entries]).

606 Golf: The Musical. "A Musical Round in 18 Songs." THEATRE: John Houseman Theatre; OPENING DATE: November 19, 2003; PERFORMANCES: 159 (estimated); SKETCHES: Michael Roberts; LYRICS: Michael Roberts; MUSIC: Michael Roberts; DIRECTION: Christopher Scott; CHOREOGRAPHY: Christopher Scott; SCENERY: James Joughin; COSTUMES: Bernard Grenier; LIGHTING: Aaron Spivey; MUSICAL DIRECTION: Ken Lundie; PRODUCER: Eric Krebs

CAST—Joel Blum, Trisha Rapier, Christopher Sutton, Sal Viviano

The revue was presented in two acts.

ACT ONE—*The Front Nine*: "Life's Unanswerable Questions" (sketch)/"A Show About Golf" (Company), "That's How You Play Golf" (Company), "Scratch Golfer" (Joel Blum, Trisha Rapier), "Plaid" (Sal Viviano, Company), "The Golfer's Psalm"/"Tiger Woods" (Christopher Sutton, Company), "A Great Lady Golfer" (Trisha Rapier, Company), "Let's Bring Golf to the Gulf" (Company)

ACT TWO—*The Back Nine*: "My Husband Is Playing Around" (Trisha Rapier), "Golfing Museum" (Christopher Sutton), "The Road to Heaven" (Joel Blum, Sal Viviano), "No Blacks, No Chicks, No Jews" (Christopher Sutton, Sal Viviano), "Big Bertha" (Joel Blum), "Golf's Such a Naughty Game" (Trisha Rapier), "Presidents and Golf" (Joel Blum, Sal Viviano, Christopher Sutton), "The Beautiful Time" (Sal Viviano), "I'm Going Golfing Tomorrow" (Company)

NOTES—Based on a concept by Eric Krebs, this amiable revue looked at the game of golf from various points of view (the die-hard players, the golf widow, even from social and political angles).

Neil Genzlinger in the *New York Times* said the "hilarious" evening turned "mindlessness and predictability into art forms"; he noted that the revue was so "obvious and shameless" that one could actually feel oneself getting "stupider" as one watched it (but he quickly noted, "It feels great"). Genzlinger singled out a number of sequences, including "A Great Lady Golfer," "The Beautiful Time," and "The Road to Heaven" (the latter in which Bob Hope joins Bing Crosby for a "heavenly tee-off").

The sketch and song titles listed in *Theatre World 2003-2004*, the script (published by Samuel French, Inc., in 2005), and the cast album (released by Eric Krebs Productions, Inc; CD # 81430-00004) are at variance with one another. The above list is taken from the cast album, and the following information is from *Theatre World* and the script: *Theatre World* includes "The History of Golf," "Who Plays Celebrity Golf?," "The Ballad of Casey Martin," and "Pro Shop Polyphony"; and the script includes the sketches "It's Not My Fault," "Hook and Slice/Golfing Newscast," "The Rope Gag," "Golf Detective," and "The Putting Competition." It's likely all the sketches were included in the revue, and perhaps one or more of the sequences listed in *Theatre World* were included as well.

It appears *Golf* may have been under an Off Off Broadway contract for the month or so after it began performances on October 8, 2003, at the John Houseman Theatre, and that regular Off Broadway performances began on November 19. The estimated 159 performances include only those of the Off Broadway run.

Because of the nature of the revue, some material dealt with topical issues; the script included a website for information regarding updates for jokes of a time-sensitive nature.

607 Gone Missing. THEATRE: Barrow Street Theatre; OPENING DATE: June 24, 2007; PERFORMANCES: 194; TEXT: Steven Cosson; ADDITIONAL TEXT by Peter Morris; LYRICS: Michael Friedman; MUSIC: Michael Friedman; DIRECTION: Steven Cosson; CHOREOGRAPHY: Jim Augustine; SCENERY: Takeshi Kata; COSTUMES: Sarah Beers; LIGHTING: Thomas Dunn; MUSICAL DIRECTION: Andy Boroson; PRODUCERS: Scott Morfee and Tom Wirtshafter in association with The Civilians (Kyle Gordon, Producing Director; Steven Cosson, Artistic Director)

CAST—The Civilians (Emily Ackerman, Damian Baldet, Jennifer R. Morris, Stephen Plunkett, Robbie Collier Sublett, Colleen Werthmann)

The musical was presented in one act.

MUSICAL NUMBERS—"Gone Missing" (Company), "The Only Thing Missing Is You" (Emily Ackerman), "La Bodega" (Stephen Plunkett, Damain Baldet, Robbie Collier Sublett), "Hide & Seek" (Colleen Werthmann), "I Gave It Away" (Emily Ackerman, Jennifer R. Morris, Colleen Werthmann), "Ich Traumt Du Kamst An Mich" (Damiam Baldet), "Lost Horizon" (Robbie Collier Sublett), "Etch a Sketch" (Jennifer R. Morris, Company), "Stars" (Company)

NOTES—The Civilians, a theatrical group specializing in storytelling through songs and sketches, had first presented *Gone Missing* Off Off Broadway in 2001. The new edition was a revised and expanded version of the earlier work, and it dealt with things "gone missing" in one's life, everything from keys and pets, to people, faith, and even one's mind ... not to mention Atlantis (the revue wondered how an entire continent could get itself lost).

Charles Isherwood in the *New York Times* found the "delightful" revue "fresh, breezy and very funny ... a perfect summer entertainment" with "witty pastiche songs" by Michael Friedman. But Isherwood quickly noted that the lighthearted aspects of the revue didn't mean it had nothing to say; indeed, he pointed out that under the revue's "wry" exterior was a "mournful" realization of the "transience of life's pleasures." Besides the above-listed numbers, the program credited the sequence "Interview with Dr. Palinurus" to Peter Morris, and indicated that additional interviews were contributed by Quincy Bernstine, Matthew Francis, Winter Miller, and Charlie Schroeder. "Teri's Theme" was composed by Andy Boroson. The cast recording was released by Ghostlight Records (CD # 8-4426) and included a brief prologue sequence ("Things I Have Lost," performed by Robbie Collier Sublett).

608 Good Luck. THEATRE: Anderson Yiddish Theatre; OPENING DATE: October 17, 1964; PERFORMANCES: 117; BOOK: Chaim Tauber and Louis Freiman; LYRICS: Jacob Jacobs; MUSIC: Sholom Secunda; DIRECTION: Max Perlman; SCENERY: Arthur Aronson; PRODUCER: Jacob Jacobs

CAST—Gita Galina (Zisel), Thelma Mintz (Regina), Rose Greenfield (Sarah), Seymour Rechtzeit (Dr. Edelman), Susan Walters (Goldele), Jacob Jacobs (Usher-Leml Navel), Miriam Kressyn (Esther Margulis), Bruce Adler (Danny), Max Perlman (Yosel Soloveitchik), Fyvush Finkel (Barry Jonah)

The action takes place in Miami.

NOTES—The musical *Good Luck* was presented mostly in Yiddish, and concerned the romances of two couples, one young, one middle-aged. Richard F. Shepard in the *New York Times* noted that while the evening wasn't a *Fiddler on the Roof* (which had opened on Broadway three weeks earlier), it nonetheless had "pleasant settings, music and cast," all of which made the musical "as soft as a fresh bagel to the tried and true friends of Jewish vaudeville." He singled out a number of the cast members, including old-time favorite Fyvush Finkel ("an expert laugh-maker") in the role of "Barry Jonah from Arizona."

609 The Good Soldier Schweik. THEATRE: New York City Center; OPENING DATE: April 23, 1958; PERFORMANCES: 3 (estimated); LIBRETTO: Lewis Allan; MUSIC: Robert Kurka; DIRECTION: Carmen Capalbo; CHOREOGRAPHY: Robert Joffrey; SCENERY: Andreas Nomikos; special sketches for screen projections by David Stone Martin; COSTUMES: Ruth Morley; LIGHTING: Lee Watson; MU-

SICAL DIRECTION: Julius Rudel; PRODUCER: New York City Opera

CAST—George S. Irving (A Gentleman of Bohemia, Colonel von Zillergut), Norman Kelley (Joseph Schweik), Mary Lesawyer (Mrs. Muller), Chester Watson (Palivec, General von Schwartzburg), Jack De Lon (Bretschneider, Army Chaplain), Arthur Newman (Police Officer, Sergeant), Keith Kaldenberg (Guard, Mr. Wendler), Five Prisoners (Robert Ruddy, William Zakariasen, Robert Atherton, George Del Monte, Edward Ghazal), Howard Fried (First Psychiatrist, Sergeant Vanek), Chester Ludgin (Second Psychiatrist, First Doctor, Voditchka), Joshua Hecht (Third Psychiatrist), Robert Ruddy (Second Doctor), Peter Sliker (A Consumptive), Four Malingerers (William Elliott, William Zakariasen, John Dennison, Edward Ghazal), Emile Renan (Army Doctor, Fox [a dog], Mr. Kakonyi), Ruth Kobart (The Baroness von Botzenheim), David Atkinson (Lieutenant Henry Lukash), Helen Baisley (Katy Wendler), Naomi Collier (Madame Kakonyi); Dancers (Dianne Consoer, Gloria Gustafson, Marie Paquet, Francoise Martinet, Brunhilda Ruiz, Gerald Arpino, Nels Jorgensen, Vicente Nebreda, John Neff)

SOURCE—The 1923 novel *The Good Soldier Schweik* by Jaroslav Hasek.

The action occurs in Prague and on the Austrian-Hungarian border in 1914.

The opera was presented in two acts.

ACT ONE—Overture (Orchestra), Prologue: "Dami a Pani!" (George S. Irving), "So They Killed Ferdinand!" (Mary Lesawyer, Norman Kelley), "We're Having a Very Fine Summer" (Jack De Lon, Chester Watson, Norman Kelley), "Pantomime Dance," "Good Evening, Gentlemen" (Norman Kelley, Arthur Newman), "Good Evening, Ev'rybody, It's Been a Lovely Day" (Norman Kelley, Chester Watson, Robert Ruddy, William Zakariasen, Robert Atherton, George Del Monte, Edward Ghazal), "We're All in a Hell of a Mess" (Norman Kelley, Chester Watson), "It's Great Fun" (Norman Kelley, Keith Kaldenberg), "The Ego and the Id" (Howard Fried, Chester Ludgin, Joshua Hecht, Norman Kelley), "I Never Felt So Good Before" (Norman Kelley), "Furiant" (dance), "Achtung!" (Chester Ludgin), "Who Will Go to the War When It Comes?" (Norman Kelley), "Have They Ever Examined the State of Your Mind?" (Chester Ludgin, Robert Ruddy, Norman Kelley), "Mrs. Muller!" (Norman Kelley, Mary Lesawyer), "Oh, the Gen'rals" (Norman Kelley), "To Belgrade!" (Norman Kelley, Ensemble)

ACT TWO—Prelude: "March," "O-o-oh!" (Peter Sliker, Chester Watson, William Elliott, Norman Kelley), "Just Look at Me" (William Elliott, William Zakariasen, John Dennison, Edward Ghazal), "Achtung!" (Howard Fried, William Elliott, Chester Ludgin, William Zakariasen, Chester Watson, Norman Kelley) "Aha, Rheumatism!" (Chester Ludgin, Norman Kelley, Howard Fried), "Baroness von Botzenheim" (Howard Fried, Ruth Kobart, Norman Kelley, William Elliott, William Zakariasen, John Dennison, Edward Ghazal, Chester Ludgin), "I Always Thought the Army" (Norman Kelley, William Elliott, William Zakariasen, John Dennison, Edgar Ghazal, Howard Fried), "Okay, Let's Pray!" (Jack De Lon, Norman Kelley, William Elliott, William Zakariasen, John Dennison, Edgar Ghazal), "Why Bless My Soul" (Jack De Lon, David Atkinson), "Well, Schweik, How'd Things Go Today?" (David Atkinson, Norman Kelley, Emile Renan, Helen Baisley), "Fox! Fox! Come Here Boy" (George S. Irving, David Atkinson, Norman Kelley, Keith Kaldenberg, Helen Baisley), "Sextet" (George S. Irving, David Atkinson, Keith Kaldenberg, Norman Kelley, Helen Baisley, Emile Renan), "So You Let One of Our Trunks Get Stolen" (David Atkinson, Norman Kelley, [and unknown performer]), "What Happened?" (Passengers [and unknown performers]), "Dear Madame" (David Atkinson), "Come In!" (David Atkinson, Norman Kelley), "Schweik!" (Chester Ludgin, Norman Kelley), "Fill Up and Drink Up" (Ensemble), "Polka," "Sixteen Soprony, Madame Kakonyi" (Chester Ludgin, Emile Renan, Naomi Collier), "Well, Schweik" (David Atkinson, Norman Kelley), "Wait for the Ragged Soldiers" (Soldiers), "Now We Go to the Right" (Howard Fried, Norman Kelley), "I'll Take a Quiet Road" (Norman Kelley), "Schweik, Schweik" (George S. Irving)

NOTES—According to Howard Taubman in the *New York Times*, the title character of Robert Kurka's operatic adaptation of Jaroslav Hasek's satiric novel *The Good Soldier Schweik* is an "amiable fool" caught up in the horrors of World War One. But this eternal if simple Everyman is a survivor, and through him we see the follies and absurdity of war. Taubman noted the opera was episodic, but nonetheless found the evening "a stylized, lively, often slapstick-ing commentary ... at its brightest it is diverting, knockabout lyric theatre." For the half-century following its New York premiere, the opera has enjoyed some one-hundred productions worldwide, including two with the Chicago Opera Theatre, one of which led to a lavish 2-CD recording in 2001 by Cedille Records (# CDR-90000-062). Cedille must be commended for making such an obscure opera available; the invaluable album reveals a jaunty, melodic score which matches the comic libretto (the song list above is derived from the song sequences listed on the CD; the original New York City Opera program didn't list individual song numbers).

The original production included a few familiar names from musical theatre (George S. Irving, David Atkinson, Ruth Kobart).

A sad note in the program referred to the untimely death (by leukemia) in December 1957 of the opera's young composer, Robert Kurka. He knew he didn't have long to live, and so during his final days in the hospital he hurried in vain to complete the orchestrations for the opera; based on Kurka's notes in the vocal score, Hershy Kay was able to complete the orchestrations for the opera's final scenes. Ironically, Jaroslav Hasek, the author of the original novel upon which the opera was based, also died at a young age and was never able to finish the complete series of novels he envisioned about his title character.

According to the CD's liner notes, librettist Lewis Allan was a pseudonym for Abel Meeropol, who had written the song "Strange Fruit" and who had adopted the sons of Julius and Ethel Rosenberg.

610 A Good Swift Kick. THEATRE: Variety Arts Theatre; OPENING DATE: July 29, 1999; PERFORMANCES: 13; LYRICS: John Forster; MUSIC: John Forster; DIRECTION: Paul Kreppel; CHOREOGRAPHY: Murphy Cross; SCENERY: Kenneth Foy; COSTUMES: Marian Hale; LIGHTING: Jason Kantrowitz; MUSICAL DIRECTION: John DiPinto; PRODUCERS: Sandy Faison, Chase Mishkin, Steven M. Levy, and Leonard Soloway

CAST—D'Monroe, Wanda Houston, David Naughton, Jim Newman, Elisa Surmont

The revue was presented in one act (song assignments unknown; songs are listed in performance order).

MUSICAL NUMBERS—"In the Closet," "Tone Deaf," "The PAC Man," "Helium," "Legacy," "One Billion Little Emperors," "Whole," "The Ballad of Robert Moses," "Fusion," "Way Down Deep," "A Mismatch Made in Hell," "Spores," "Bye Bye Future," "The Big Mac Tree," "The Tragique Kingdom," "Entering Marion," "Nothing Ventured, Nothing Lost," "Virtual Vivian," "Codependent with You," "Passing"

NOTES—Ben Brantley in the *New York Times* reported the would-be satiric revue *A Good Swift Kick* had "the cutting edge of a melting ice-cream sandwich." Its barbs were too perky, it avoided the sarcastic, and as a result the evening offered obvious and safe humor in order to ensure that no audience member "would feel left out by insider hipness." Brantley noted that "cautious satire" is by its very nature "self-defeating." Brantley indicated the revue's idea of humor rested on such notions as gays in the military drilling to the sound-off of "Judy, since you went away/Life is not a cabaret" and the opening in France of a Disneyesque theme park, the existential and morose "Tragique Kingdom."

A Good Swift Kick had been previously produced at Goodspeed Opera House.

611 Goodbye Tomorrow. THEATRE: Central Arts Cabaret; OPENING DATE: March 23, 1973; PERFORMANCES: 9 (estimated); BOOK: Sue Brock; LYRICS: Sue Brock; MUSIC: Carl Friberg; DIRECTION: Anthony Stimac; SCENERY: "Set Elements" by Plasticity; COSTUMES: Robert Pusilo; LIGHTING: C. Murawski; MUSICAL DIRECTION: Carl Friberg; PRODUCER: Central Arts Cabaret (Albert L. DuBose, Director)

CAST—Patti Perkins (Mary), Bob Spencer (Joe), Raymond Thorne (The Man), Carl Friberg (Chorus), Clive Kennedy (Chorus), Barbara Wheeler (Chorus)

NOTES—The Off Off Broadway musical *Goodbye Tomorrow* was performed over three consecutive weekends.

612 The Gorey Details. "A Musicale." THEATRE: The Century Center for the Performing Arts; OPENING DATE: October 16, 2000; PERFORMANCES: 65; TEXT: Edward Gorey; MUSIC: Peter Matz; DIRECTION: Daniel Levans; CHOREOGRAPHY: Daniel Levans; SCENERY: Jesse Poleshuck (apparently based on designs by Edward Gorey); COSTUMES: Martha Bromelmeier; LIGHTING: Craig Kennedy; MUSICAL DIRECTION: Bruce W. Coyle; PRODUCERS: Ken Hoyt and Kevin McDermott in association with Brent Peek

CAST—Alison Crowley, Allison DeSalvo, Matt Kuehl, Daniel C. Levine, Kevin McDermott, Ben Nordstrom, Liza Shaller, Clare Stollak, Christopher Youngsman

SOURCE—Various writings by Edward Gorey.

The revue was presented in two acts (song assignments unknown).

ACT ONE—"The Narrator," "Q.R.V.," "The Frozen Man," "The Disrespectful Summons," "The Weeping Chandelier," "The Doubtful Guest," "The Forty-Seven Questions," "The Deranged Cousins," "The Woeful Waking," "The Blue Aspic"

ACT TWO—"The Nursery Frieze," "The Object Lesson," "The Wuggly Ump," "Gin," "The Insect God," "The Unknown Vegetable," "The Inanimate Tragedy," "The Admonitory Hippopotamus," Finale

NOTES—This short-lived revue based on Edward Gorey's writings and drawings was one of a number of productions based on Gorey's work which appeared in New York over the years. Bruce Weber in the *New York Times* found the evening generally amusing in its presentation of Gorey's purposely arch and peculiar humor. Kevin McDermott assumed the role of the evening's narrator ("Ogdred Weary," an anagram for Edward Gorey), and he and the cast conveyed the "fervor of happy cultists" who were thoroughly attuned to Gorey's "alternative world." Weber also noted that Peter Matz' score was "appropriately jingly in a Halloween mode."

Amphigorey, an early version of *The Gorey Details* (with music by Peter Golub), opened Off Broadway at the Perry Street Theatre in 1994 (see entry).

On October 30, 1978, Broadway offered the revue *Gorey Stories* (which played for just one performance at the Booth Theatre).

613 Gorilla Queen. "A Play." THEATRE: Martinique Theatre; OPENING DATE: April 24, 1967;

PERFORMANCES: 64; PLAY: Ronald Tavel; LYRICS: Al Carmines; MUSIC: Al Carmines; DIRECTION: Lawrence Kornfeld; SCENERY: Jerry Joyner; COSTUMES: Linda Sampson; LIGHTING: John P. Dodd and Deborah Lee; PRODUCER: Paul Libin

CAST—Jo Ann Foreman (Venus Fly Trap), George Harris II (Brute), Selena Williams (Mais Oui), Paula Shaw (Karma), James Hilbrandt (Clyde), Quinn Halford (Taharahnugi White Woman), David Kerry Heefner (Chimney Sweep), Eddie McCarti (Sister Carries), Barbara Ann Camp (Paulet), Norman Thomas Marshall (Queen Kong), Harry Tavel (Intern); Glitz Ionas played by Adrienne De Antonio, Mary Duke, Norman R. Glick, John Harrill, George Harris III, Dick Lipkin, and Norman Soifer

The play was presented in two acts.

NOTES—Although not a musical, *Gorilla Queen* included a few songs by Al Carmines (including "Frickadellin,'" "Cockamanie," "Pyromania," and "Ay Yi Yi"). The program also credited Robert Cosmos Savage with music for the production. With its premise of a gorilla-queen-goddess (played by a male actor) worshipped by men; with characters who sported such names as Venus Fly Trap, Mais Oui, and Taharahnugi White Woman; with lyrics which included such lines as "One bwana/Two bwana/ Three bwana, four"; and with dialogue which somehow managed to explain that *Ben Hur* should not have been titled *Ben Him* because *Ben Hur* was really the story of Ben Gay, *Gorilla Queen* was not an exercise in stark realism. Prior to its Off Broadway production, *Gorilla Queen* had first been produced Off Off Broadway at the Judson Poets' Theatre on March 10, 1967. The script was included in the collection *The Best of Off Off-Broadway* (edited by Michael Smith and published by E.P. Dutton & Co. in 1969).

With its camp-infused outlook, the production was probably typical of the semi-underground theatre of the era, and a revival would probably make for a fascinating time-capsule of 1960s fringe theatre.

614 The Gospel According to Al.

"A Musical Celebration of Al Carmines' Twenty Years in Theatre." THEATRE: Wonderhorse Theatre; OPENING DATE: October 14, 1982; PERFORMANCES: 12; LYRICS: Al Carmines; MUSIC: Al Carmines; DIRECTION: William Hopkins; CHOREOGRAPHY: Carmela Guiteras; SCENERY: Peter Harrison; COSTUMES: Vincente Criado; LIGHTING: Craig Kennedy; MUSICAL DIRECTION: James Laev; PRODUCER: TRG Repertory Company (Marvin Kahan, Producer)

CAST—Cathleen Axelrod, Georgia Creighton, Paul Farin, Kate Ingram, Tad Ingram

The revue was presented in one act.

MUSICAL NUMBERS—"Sometimes the Sky Is Blue" (from *Religion*, 1973) (Tad Ingram, Company), "The Good Old Days" (*W.C.*, 1971) (Company), "It's a Man's World" (*The Bonus Army*, 1976) (Cathleen Axelrod, Georgia Creighton), "My Old Man" (*The Bonus Army*, 1976) (Tad Ingram), "A Woman Needs Approval Now and Then" (*Why I Love New York*, 1975) (Georgia Creighton), "It's Nice to Cuddle in a Threesome" (*Joan*, 1972) (Cathleen Axelrod, Kate Ingram, Paul Farin), "New Boy in Town" (*The Faggot*, 1973) (Paul Farin), "Ordinary Things (Homage to Gertrude Stein and Alice B. Toklas)" (*The Faggot*, 1973) (Cathleen Axelrod, Kate Ingram), "Disposable Woman" (*The Faggot*, 1973) (Georgia Creighton), "Coca Cola Girl" (*The Life of a Man*, 1972) (Kate Ingram, Company), "Montgomery Moon" (*A Look at the Fifties*, 1972) (Paul Farin, with Kate Ingram, Cathleen Axelrod, and Georgia Creighton), "Dummy Juggler" (Homage to W.C. Fields) (*W.C.*, 1971) (Tad Ingram), "I'm Peculiar That Way" (*A Look at the Fifties*, 1972) (Georgia Creighton), "I Am My Beloved" (*Song of Songs*, 1971) (Cathleen Axelrod), "I Forget and I Remember" (words by Gertrude Stein) (*The Making of Americans*, 1972) (Paul Ingram), "Nostalgia" (*Sacred and Profane Love*, 1975) (Georgia Creighton), "Fifty Years of Making People Laugh" (*W.C*, 1972) (Company), "Forgiveness" (Cathleen Axelrod), "I'm Innocence" (Kate Ingram), "The World Is Yours" (*The Songs of Mao Tse-Tung*, 1971) (Company), "God Bless Us All" (Company)

NOTES—This Off Off Broadway evening consisted of a collection of songs written by Al Carmines during the previous dozen or so years; most were from his musicals, but it appears a few were written independent of any particular production. In a program note, Carmines wrote that the songs in the production were "neither a complete catalogue nor even typical of my composing career. They are songs that touch something mysterious in my heart that makes me go on composing. There are cheerful songs, ribald ones, dirges, songs of love, of hate, of jealousy and despair. All the things that I know about being human."

For two decades, Carmines' melody machine never stopped. But, unfortunately, after *The Gospel According to Al*, there would be little in the way of new music from him (see entry for *Exhalations*, which appears to be his last produced musical). For whatever reasons, during the early 1980s he seems to have turned his energies away from composing. However, in 1982 he became the pastor of the Trinity-Rauschenbusch Memorial United Church of Christ, and was active in its ministry until the time of his death in 2005.

Carmines is all but forgotten today. His musicals were never produced on Broadway, and his biggest hit was *Promenade* (1969; see entry), which ran for 259 performances; further, as of this writing it appears the cast recordings of his musicals and revues are no longer in print. But his quirky, melodic scores are a wonder, and for those fortunate enough to know his musicals from productions or recordings, Carmines will always be a major figure in the history of the Off Broadway musical. Al Carmines is the quintessential Off Broadway composer.

615 The Gospel at Colonus.

THEATRE: Apollo Theatre; OPENING DATE: October 25, 2004; PERFORMANCES: 12; BOOK: Lee Breuer; LYRICS: Lee Breuer and Bob Telson; MUSIC: Bob Telson; DIRECTION: Lee Breuer; SCENERY: Alison Yerxa; COSTUMES: Ghretta Hynd; LIGHTING: Jason Boyd; MUSICAL DIRECTION: Bob Telson; PRODUCERS: Washington Mutual in association with Dovetail Productions

CAST—Charles S. Dutton (The Messenger), The Blind Boys of Alabama (featuring Clarence Fountain (Oedipus), Earl F. Miller (Theseus), The Legendary Soul Stirrers: Willie Rogers, Ben Odom, Lloyd Moore, Gene Stewart (Choragos), Jevetta Steele (Ismene), Bernardine Mitchell (Antigone), J.D. Steele (Choir Director), Sam Butler (Balladeer), Jay Caldwell (Creon), Kevin Davis (Polyneices), Carolyn Johnson-White (Choir Soloist), Jose Johnson (The Acolyte), Chorus (The Abyssinian Baptist and Institutional Radio Choirs)

SOURCES—The play *Oedipus at Colonus* (written circa 406 B.C.) by Sophocles in the translation by Robert Fitzgerald; the musical also incorporated passages from two other plays by Sophocles, *Oedipus Rex* (428 B.C.) and *Antigone* (written circa 441 B.C.), in the translations by Dudley Fitts and Robert Fitzgerald.

The action occurs in a Black Pentecostal church.

The musical was presented in two acts.

ACT ONE—"The Welcome" and "Quotations" (Charles S. Dutton), The Invocation: "Live Where You Can" (Jevetta Steele, Choir), "Recapitulation from *Oedipus the King*" (*Oedipus Rex*) (Bernardine Mitchell, Charles S. Dutton), "Oedipus and Antigone Enter Colonus" (Bernardine Mitchell, Charles S. Dutton), "Ode to Colonus: Fair Colonus" (Willie Rogers)/"Stop, Do Not Go On" (Sam Butler, The Blind Boys of Alabama, The Legendary Soul Stirrers), Choral Dialogue: "Who Is This Man?" (Jay Caldwell, Jimmy Carter, Charles S. Dutton, The Blind Boys of Alabama), Ismene Comes to Colonus: "How Shall I See You Through My Tears?" (Jevetta Steele, The Blind Boys of Alabama), "Narrative of Ismene" (Bernardine Mitchell), "Chorus Questions Oedipus" (Jay Caldwell, Charles S. Dutton, The Blind Boys of Alabama), The Prayer: "A Voice Foretold" (The Blind Boys of Alabama, Sam Butler, J.D. Steele), Oedipus Is Welcomed at Colonus: "Peroration" (Earl F. Miller), "Jubilee: No Never" (The Legendary Soul Stirrers, The Blind Boys of Alabama, Choir), "Creon Comes to Colonus: Come Home" (Jay Caldwell, Ushers), "Seizure of the Daughters" (Jay Caldwell, Ushers), Oedipus Curses Creon: "Evil Kindness"/"You'd Take Him Away" (The Blind Boys of Alabama, Choir, Jay Caldwell, Charles S. Dutton), Choral Ode: "Numberless Are the World's Wonders" (J.D. Steele, Jevetta Steele, Choir)

ACT TWO—Oedipus Laments: "Lift Me Up" (The Blind Boys of Alabama), Polyneices's Testimony and Supplication: "Evil" (Sam Butler), "Oedipus's Curse" (Kevin Davis, Charles S. Dutton, The Blind Boys of Alabama), "Stand by Me"/"You Break My Heart" (Heroes), Poem: "Love Unconquerable" (Bernardine Mitchell), "Preaching with Tuned Response" (Charles S. Dutton, The Blind Boys of Alabama), Special Effect: "Ah, Heaven's Height Has Cracked!," "The Teachings" (Charles S. Dutton, Earl F. Miller), The Descent of Oedipus: "Oh Sunlight of No Light" (Bernardine Mitchell, Jevetta Steele, Sam Butler)/"Eternal Sleep" (Willie Rogers, The Legendary Soul Stirrers), "Mourning" (Bernardine Mitchell, Earl F. Miller, Jevetta Steele), Doxology, the Paeon: "Lift Him Up" (Carolyn Johnson-White, Choir), "The Sermon" (Charles S. Dutton), Closing Hymn: "Now Let the Weeping Cease" (The Legendary Soul Stirrers, Choir), "Benediction" (Charles S. Dutton)

NOTES—Set in a Black Penetcostal church, *The Gospel at Colonus* was a re-telling of Sophocles' tragedy in which the aged Oedipus, who has suffered and repented for sins he committed in innocence, finds spiritual redemption at the time of his death.

The musical had first been performed as a work-in-progress at the ReCherChez Studio for the Avant-Garde Performing Arts at the Washington Square United Methodist Church on December 23, 1981. It was later presented at the Carey Playhouse/Brooklyn Academy of Music on November 8, 1983, in two slightly separated engagements for a total of thirty performances, and the Broadway premiere occurred at the Lunt-Fontanne Theatre on March 24, 1988, for sixty-one performances. For both the Brooklyn and Broadway engagements, Morgan Freeman played the role of the Messenger.

In 1984, a cast recording of the 1983 Brooklyn production was released by Warner Brothers Records (LP # 1-25182) and in 1988 Elektra/Nonesuch Records (LP # 9-79191-1) released the cast recording of a 1985 production which was performed at the American Music Theatre Festival in Philadelphia. (Freeman appears on the second recording.) In 1985, the musical was shown on public television as part of the *Great Performances* series, and this version, which included Morgan Freeman in its cast, was released on videocassette.

616 Graham Crackers.

"An Untraditional Revue." THEATRE: Upstairs at the Downstairs; OPENING DATE: January 23, 1963; PERFORMANCES: 286; SKETCHES: Woody Allen, Ronald Axe, David Axelrod, Dee Caruso, Bruce Hart, Herbert Hartig, William Levine, Eliza Ross, and Peter Salamando; LYRICS: David Axelrod, Ronny Graham, Bill Lacey, Carolyn Leigh, Richard Maltby, Jr., John Meyer, Edna St. Vincent Millay, and James Rusk Music:

Cy Coleman, Ronny Graham, Bill Lacey, John Meyer, Sam Pottle, James Rusk, and David Shire; DIRECTION: Ronny Graham; CHOREOGRAPHY: Lee Becker; MUSICAL DIRECTION: David Shire; PRODUCER: Ronny Graham

CAST—Bill McCutcheon, Bob Kaliban, Mona Abboud, McLean Stevenson, Anita Darian, Pat Stanley (or Ann Fraser; see below)

The revue was presented in two acts (sketch and song assignments unknown).

ACT ONE—"Facts and Figures" (lyric by Richard Maltby, Jr., music by David Shire), "To Tell the Truth" (sketch by Dee Caruso and William Levine), "The Time of the Cuckold" (lyric and music by Ronny Graham), "Psychological Warfare" (sketch by Woody Allen) "Crossword Puzzle" (lyric by Richard Maltby, Jr., music by David Shire), "The Sound of Muzak" (lyric by Richard Maltby, Jr., music by David Shire) "The Word to the Action" (sketch by Ronald Axe), "Sidney" (lyric and music by Bill Lacey) "Street Scene" (sketch by David Axelrod and Bruce Hart) "Summer in New York" (lyric and music by James Rusk), "Circa 1929" (sketch by Dee Caruso and William Levine) "Ask a Foolish Question" (sketch by Herbert Hartig) "Lovely Light" (lyric by Edna St. Vincent Millay and Richard Maltby, Jr., music by David Shire) "Immigration, Please" (sketch by Eliza Ross) "Treble" (lyric and music by James Rusk) "Gelber Meets the Wolfgang" (libretto by David Axelrod, music by Sam Pottle)

ACT TWO—"Saturday Night" (lyric by David Axelrod, music by Sam Pottle) "Next Week: David and the Goliaths" (sketch by Dee Caruso and William Levine) "A Doodlin' Song" (lyric by Carolyn Leigh, music by Cy Coleman), "Letter Suite" (sketch by Dee Caruso and William Levine), "A Love Song" (lyric by Richard Maltby, Jr., music by David Shire) "Always Autumn" (lyric by Richard Maltby, Jr., music by David Shire), "A Bedtime Story" (sketch by Herbert Hartig) "Memorabilia" (lyric and music by John Meyer) "A La What?" (sketch by Peter Salamando), "Come Join the Party" (lyric by Richard Maltby, Jr., music by David Shire)

NOTES—Ronny Graham's revue played for almost six months, and included a sketch by Woody Allen and no fewer than seven songs by Richard Maltby, Jr., and David Shire. Their "Crossword Puzzle" was later heard in *Starting Here, Starting Now* (1977; see entry) and was recorded for that revue's cast album; and "The Sound of Muzak" was included in their 1989 revue *Closer Than Ever* (see entry) and can be heard on the cast album for that show.

Graham Crackers appears to have been an amusing evening, and the sketch "Immigration, Please" sounds particularly intriguing.

The Best Plays of 1962-1963 indicates that Pat Stanley was "replaced" by Ann Fraser, and so it's unclear if the former was in the revue on opening night; she may have left the show prior to the opening, or shortly thereafter. Ken Bloom's *American Song* includes Fraser (but not Stanley) in the cast list.

After Julius Monk settled into the Plaza for the continuation of his revues, the Upstairs at the Downstairs was utilized once by Ben Bagley (*No Shoestrings*; 1962; see entry) and once by Ronny Graham. Perhaps each intended to present a series of revues at the venue; if so, the plans never reached fruition. But in 1964 Rod Warren's highly successful *...And in This Corner* (see entry) opened at the Upstairs at the Downstairs, and it ushered in a five-year series of twelve "sporting title" revues which he produced there (see Appendix R). (Incidentally, Warren's final revue, *Free Fall* [1969; see entry] was directed by Graham.)

617 The Grand Music Hall of Israel.

THEATRE: Felt Forum; OPENING DATE: January 4, 1973; PERFORMANCES: 15; DIRECTION: Jonathan Karmon; CHOREOGRAPHY: Jonathan Karmon; COSTUMES: Lydia Punkus Ganay; MUSICAL DIRECTION: Rafi Paz; PRODUCERS: Madison Square Garden Productions and Hy Einhorn

CAST—Shoshana Damari, Ron Eliran, Myron Cohen, Ariela, The Marganiot, The Tal U'Matar, The Karmon Israel Dancers and Singers

The revue was presented in two acts (division of acts and sketch and song assignments unknown; the sketches and songs are listed in performance order).

MUSICAL NUMBERS—"Israeli Rhapsody," The Marganiot, "The Fishermen of Kineret," The Tal U'Matar, "A Night on the Gilboa Mountains," Ron Eliran, "A Panorama of Hassidic Life," "The Mediterranean Flavor," Ariela, "Fire on the Mountains," Shoshana Damari, "Holiday in the Kibbutz"

NOTES—Jonathan Karmon had previously presented four Israeli revues on Broadway: *Karmon Israeli Dancers* (1963), *The Grand Music Hall of Israel* (1968), *The New Music Hall of Israel* (1969), and *To Live Another Summer, To Pass Another Winter* (1971). The 1973 Off Broadway production of *The Grand Music Hall of Israel* included old and new material. His sixth and final New York revue, *Don't Step on My Olive Branch*, opened Off Broadway in 1976 (see entry).

To Live Another Summer was recorded by Buddah Records (LP # 95004); a flavor of the other revues can be sampled on two recordings by Vanguard Records (*Folk Songs* [VRS-9048] and *Songs of the Sabras* [VRS-9060]), both of which include songs and dance music by the Karmon Israeli Dancers and Singers.

The 1967 Parisian production of *The Grand Music Hall of Israel* was recorded by London International Records (LP # SW-99463).

618 The Grand Street Follies (1922; First Edition).

THEATRE: Neighborhood Playhouse; OPENING DATE: June 13, 1922; PERFORMANCES: 12; CHOREOGRAPHY: Albert Carroll; COSTUMES: Alice Beer and Polaire Weissmann; PRODUCER: The Neighborhood Playhouse; MUSICAL DIRECTION: Lily M. Hyland (?)

CAST—Helen Arthur, Michel Barroy, Albert Carroll, Eleanor Carroll, Sol Friedman, Whitford Kane, Irene Lewisohn, Lily Lubell, Aline MacMahon, Philip Mann, Junius Matthews, Esther Mitchell, Agnes Morgan, Adrienne Morrison, John Francis Roche, Ann Schmidt, Blanche Talmud, Paula Trueman, Dan Walker, Polaire Weissmann

The revue was presented in two acts.

NOTES—This revue was the first of seven *Grand Street Follies* which were produced from 1922 to 1929. The first five in this series of satiric revues (1922, 1924, 1925, 1926, and 1927) were produced Off Broadway at the Neighborhood Playhouse (see entries for the 1924, 1925, 1926, and 1927 editions); the 1927 edition transferred to Broadway, and the final two editions (1928 and 1929) opened directly on Broadway.

The 1922 edition apparently played out its limited engagement on a subscription series. According to Richard C. Norton's *A Chronology of American Musical Theatre*, except for the song "Personality" (lyric and music by Albert Carroll), songs weren't listed in the program. However, besides a prologue ("In the Beginning"), Norton cites the following sequences in the first act: "The Mattress House," "The Color Organ," "The Royal Damn Fango, or All Change Places," "Making Light of Day," "The Green King, or the Vicious Circle"; and, for the second act, "As Far as Thought Can Reach: So Sorry" and an epilogue ("The Tragedy of an Elderly Gentleman").

619 The Grand Street Follies (1924; Second Edition).

THEATRE: Neighborhood Playhouse; OPENING DATE: May 20, 1924; PERFORMANCES: 172; SKETCHES: Agnes Morgan; LYRICS: Agnes Morgan; MUSIC: Lily Hyland and Don Walker; DIRECTION: John F. Roche; CHOREOGRAPHY: Albert Carroll; SCENERY: Aline Bernstein; COSTUMES: Aline Bernstein; PRODUCER: The Neighborhood Playhouse

CAST—Helen Arthur, George Bratt, Albert Carroll, Edgar Kent, Florence Levine, Lily Lubell, Aline MacMahon, Junius Matthews, Esther Mitchell, Agnes Morgan, Adrienne Morrison, Betty Prescott, Edmond Rickett, John Francis Roche, Joanna Roos, John Scott, Bertha Tuite, Dan Walker, Martin Wolfson, Ensemble (Sophie Bernsohn, Sol Friedman, Edla Frankau, George Heller, Grace D. Hooper, Sophie Hurwitz, Edmond Kent, Philip Mann, Ella Markowitz, Evan Mosher, William Stahl, Hadra Spelvin, Polaire Weissmann, Joanna Roos, Ann Schmidt, Paula Trueman)

The revue was presented in two acts.

NOTES—See entry for the 1922 edition for a complete list of all the revues in the *Grand Street Follies* series. Also see entries for the 1922, 1925, 1926, and 1927 editions.

According to Richard C. Norton's *A Chronology of American Musical Theatre*, the following sequences were in the first act: "Opening Remarks," "Prologue," "The Shewing-Up of Jo Leblanco," "Not So Long, Long Ago," "Sinfonica Domestica Triangula (Suite: Town and Country)," "Play the Queen, or Old Irish Poker"; for the second act, "A Business Conference," "Who Killed the Ghost?," "An English Favorite," "The South Sea Islands According to Broadway," "A Recital at Town Hall," "Epilogue: The Verdict," and "Finale."

Perhaps the highlight of the revue was "The South Sea Islands According to Broadway" (lyric by Agnes Morgan, music by Dan Walker), a parody of the Broadway hit *Rain* (1922). Ann Schmidt played "Gilded Gilda" in the sequence.

Chorus member George Heller later created the role of the "Legend Singer" in the 1933 Broadway premiere of *The Threepenny Opera* and introduced the song "The Legend of Mackie Messer."

620 The Grand Street Follies (1925; Third Edition).

THEATRE: Neighborhood Playhouse; OPENING DATE: May 18, 1925; PERFORMANCES: 148; SKETCHES: Agnes Morgan; LYRICS: Agnes Morgan; MUSIC: Lily Hyland; CHOREOGRAPHY: Albert Carroll; SCENERY: Russel Wright; COSTUMES: Russel Wright and Aline Bernstein; PRODUCER: The Neighborhood Playhouse

CAST—Vera Allen, Helen Arthur, Michael Barroy, William Beyer, George Bratt, Albert Carroll, Edla Frankau, George Heller, George Hoag, Otto Hulicius, Zita Johann, Whitford Kane, Edgar Kent, Irene Lewisohn, Marc Loebell, Lily Lubell, Ian McClaren, Lewis McMichael, Helen Mack, Philip Mann, Junius Matthews, Harold Minjer, Esther Mitchell, Mae Noble, Madeline Ross, Dorothy Sands, Ann Schmidt, J. Blake Scott, Lois Shore, Sadie Sussman, Blanche Talmud, Thomas Tilton, Paula Trueman, Allen Vincent, Dan Walker, Polaire Weissmann The revue was presented in three acts.

NOTES—See entry for the 1922 edition for a complete list of all the revues in the *Grand Street Follies* series. Also see entries for the 1922, 1924, 1926, and 1927 editions.

According to Richard C. Norton's *A Chronology of American Musical Theatre*, the following sequences were in the first act: "A Committee Meeting," "They Knew What They Wanted Under the Elms," "At Ciro's," "Americana," "The Duncan Sisters ("Broadway Mammy Blues"), "What Price Morning-Glories?"; for Act Two, "Mr. and Mrs. Guardsman" and "Gala Performance of the Opera"; for Act Three, "The Midnight Show."

"Mr. and Mrs. Guardsman" was a spoof of the Lunts and dealt with the perils of a married couple performing together. Two sketches parodied recent

Broadway hits: "They Knew What They Wanted Under the Elms" (*They Knew What They Wanted* and *Desire Under the Elms*, both 1924) and "What Price Morning-Glories?" (*What Price Glory?*, 1924). Zita Johann is perhaps best remembered as the modern-day Egyptian beauty whom Boris Karloff believed was the reincarnation of an Egyptian princess in the 1932 classic horror film *The Mummy*.

621 The Grand Street Follies (1926; Fourth Edition).

THEATRE: Neighborhood Playhouse; OPENING DATE: June 15, 1926; PERFORMANCES: 55; SKETCHES: Agnes Morgan; LYRICS: Agnes Morgan, Theodore Goodwin, Arthur Schwartz, and Robert Simon; MUSIC: Lily Hyland, Arthur Schwartz, Randall Thompson, and Walter Haenschen; DIRECTION: Agnes Morgan; CHOREOGRAPHY: Irene Lewisohn, Albert Carroll, and Blanche Talmud; SCENERY: Aline Bernstein; COSTUMES: Aline Bernstein; LIGHTING: Albert Hawkes; MUSICAL DIRECTION: Howard Barlow; PRODUCER: The Neighborhood Playhouse

CAST—Vera Allen, Helen Arthur, William Beyer, Wesley Boynton, Grover Burgess, Albert Carroll, Frances Cowles, Jessica Dragonette, Edla Frankau, Juliette Gauthier (de la Verendrye), George Heller, George Hoag, Otto Hulicius, George Knisely, Marc Loebell, Lily Lubell, Ian Mclaren, Lewis McMichael, Harold Minjer, Agnes Morgan, Tom Morgan, Mae Noble, John F. Roche, Dorothy Sands, J. Blake Scott, Lois Shore, Sadie Sussman, Blanche Talmud, Paula Trueman

The revue was presented in two acts.

NOTES—See entry for the 1922 edition for a complete list of the revues in the *Grand Street Follies* series. Also see entries for the 1922, 1924, 1925, and 1927 editions.

According to Richard C. Norton's *A Chronology of American Musical Theatre*, the following songs and sequences were presented in the first act: "Original Eskimo Chants," "Fixed for Life," "Little Igloo for Two," "Aurory Bory Alice," "Taxi Drivers Lament," "The Discontented Bandits," "My Icy Floe," "Skating Ballet," "Reindeer Dance," and "Mrs. Feitelbaum Sees the Dybbuk"; for the second act, "Uncle Tom's Cabin," "Ice Mazurka," "At the Eskimo Neighbor Playhouse," "Beatrice Lillie at the North Pole," "Beatrice Lillie Ballad," "At the Gilt Theatre: A Symbolic Drama," "If You Know What I Mean," "At the Ritz-Icicle," "The Polar Bear Strut," and "The Eskimo Blues."

The revue marked Arthur Schwartz' New York debut. He contributed four songs to the production: "Little Igloo for Two" (lyric by Agnes Morgan), the "Uncle Tom's Cabin" sequence (music by both Schwartz and Randall Thompson), "If You Know What I Mean" (lyric by Theodore Goodwin and Albert Carroll), and "The Polar Bear Strut" (lyric and music by Schwartz).

"At the Gilt Theatre: A Symbolic Drama" was a spoof of Theatre Guild productions.

622 The Grand Street Follies (1927; Fifth Edition).

THEATRE: Neighborhood Playhouse; OPENING DATE: May 19, 1927; PERFORMANCES: 14 (estimated); SKETCHES: Agnes Morgan; LYRICS: Agnes Morgan; MUSIC: Max Ewing; SCENERY: Aline Bernstein; COSTUMES: Aline Bernstein; MUSICAL DIRECTION: Howard Barlow; PRODUCER: The Neighborhood Playhouse

CAST—Odna Brandeis, George Bratt, Albert Carroll, William Challee, Frances Cowles, Bert Farjeon, Edla Frankau, Ralph Geddis, John Haggart, Estelle Helle, George Heller, George Hoag, Otto Hulicius, Marc Loebell, Lily Lubell, Junius Matthews, Agnes Morgan, Mae Noble, Edmond Rickett, John Francis Roche, Joanna Roos, Dorothy Sands, J. Blake Scott, Lois Shore, Sally Sussman, Blanche Talmud, Paula Trueman, Polaire Weisssman

The revue was presented in two acts.

ACT ONE—"Morning Lecture and Its Results" (Edmond Rickett, Agnes Morgan, Lois Shore), "Stars with Stripes" (lyric by Dorothy Sands and Marc Loebell) (Dorothy Sands, Marc Loebell, Otto Hulicius, John Frances Roche, George Bratt, George Hoag, J. Blake Scott, George Heller, John Haggart, Ralph Geddis, Junius Matthews, William Challee, Bert Farjeon, Paula Trueman, Lily Lubell, Blanche Talmud, Sally Sussman, Polaire Weissman, Edla Frankau, Joanna Roos, Mae Noble, Odma Brandeis, Frances Cowles, Estelle Helle), "Further Particulars": a) "La Prisonniere" (lyric by Albert Carroll, music by Max Ewing) (Paula Trueman); b) "A Lady of Sex" (Mae Noble, Ralph Geddis), "A Fiord Joke" (sketch by Albert Carroll) (Albert Carroll, Junius Matthews), "Why Girls Leave Home" (Edmond Rickett, Lois Shore, Dorothy Sands), "Three Little Maids from Broadway Town" (music by Max Ewing) (Lily Lubell [as Helen Ford], Paula Trueman [as Mary Eaton], Sally Sussman [as Mary Hay]), "Close Harmony at Detroit (A Minstrel Show)" (George Hoag, Otto Hulicius, John Francis Roche, George Heller, George Bratt, John Haggart, Junius Matthews, Odna Brandeis, Joanna Roos, Frances Cowles, Ralph Geddis, Bert Jarjeon, Blanche Talmud, Mae Noble, Polaire Weissman), "Don't Ask Her Another" (music by Max Ewing) (Edmond Rickett, Lois Shore), "It" (music by Max Ewing) (Dorothy Sands [as Elinor Glyn], Marc Loebell [John Gilbert], Paula Trueman [Lillian Gish], J. Blake Scott [Harold Lloyd], Sally Sussman [Clara Bow], William Challee [Rin-Tin-Tin], Lois Shore [Jackie Coogan], Albert Carroll [John Barrymore], Lily Lubell [Estelle Taylor], Edla Frankau [Lya de Putti], Frances Cowles Mary Astor], George Heller [Eddie Cantor]; Camera Men, Property Men, and Movie Fans: John Francis Roche, Junius Matthews, Otto Hulicius, George Hoag, Raplh Geddis, John Haggart, Bert Farjeon, Edmond Rickett, Blanche Talmud, Polaire Weissmann, Odna Brandeis, Joanna Roos)

ACT TWO—Sketch: "A Revival of Miss Ethel Barrymore in *The School for Rivals*" (Marc Loebell, Dorothy Sands, Paula Trueman, Edmond Rickett, Agnes Morgan, George Heller, Otto Hulicius, Junius Matthews, and Albert Carroll as Miss Ethel Barrymore Playing Lydia Loose), "Jazz Baby Learns Aesthetic Dancing" (choreographed by Blanche Talmud) (Blanche Talmud, Sally Sussman), "Criss-Cross-Wordless Puzzle" (by J. Blake Scott and Lily Lubell) (J. Blake Scott, Lily Lubell) "Hooray for Us!" ("A posthumous work of Gilbert and Sullivan, unearthed in the cellar of the White House during recent excavations to install heating apparatus") (Junius Matthews [as Cautious Cal, President of the *U*nited *S*ewing *A*ssociation], George Bratt, John Francis Roche, George Hoag, Otto Hulicius, Marc Loebell, George Heller, John Haggart, William Challee, Ralph Geddis), "A Bedtime Story" (music by Ralph Ewing) (Dorothy Sands [as Laura Hope Crewes], Albert Carroll), "The Real Origin of the Black Bottom" (by John Haggart and George Heller) (George Heller, John Haggart [as Miss Ducky]), "The Unknown Quantity (A Mystery Play)" (John Francis Roche, Junius Matthews, Agnes Morgan, Paula Trueman, Edla Frankau, J. Blake Scott, Otto Hulicius, Marc Loebell), "The Naughty Nineties" (music by Max Ewing) (Dorothy Sands [as Floradora Fay]), "An Official Welcome" (Mae Noble, Polaire Weissman, Ethel Frankau, Odna Brandeis, Aline Bernstein, Albert Carroll) (Sketch included song "Unaccustomed As I Am," lyric by Albert Carroll, music by Max Ewing), "The Banquet" (music by Max Ewing) (Company)

NOTES—See entry for the 1922 edition for a complete list of all the revues in the *Grand Street Follies* series. Also see entries for the 1922, 1924, 1925, and 1926 editions.

The 1927 edition (the fifth in the series) transferred to Broadway at the Little Theatre two weeks after opening at the Neighborhood Playhouse. The revue played approximately fourteen performances Off Broadway, and about 134 performances on Broadway. The last two editions of the revue (1928 and 1929) opened directly on Broadway.

The revue continued to poke fun at current events. The movies and Clara Bow were spoofed in "It"; all-star revivals of classic plays were parodied in *The School for Rivals* (which included Ethel Barrymore played by a man in drag); the President and the White House were mocked in a Gilbert and Sullivan parody called "Hooray for Us!"; and recent dance crazes were mocked in "The Real Origin of the Black Bottom" (another "drag" entry, with John Haggart as "Miss Ducky").

One number ("Three Little Maids from Broadway Town") spoofed current Broadway musical comedy stars (Helen Ford, Mary Eaton, and Mary Hay). Ford and Eaton were in currently-running Broadway musicals when the revue opened (Ford was performing the title role in Richard Rodgers and Lorenz Hart's *Peggy-Ann* [1926] and Eaton was playing the title role in *Lucky* [1927], which included music by Jerome Kern); Hay had recently appeared in a supporting role in Kern's *Sunny* (1925), which had closed a few months before the opening of *The Grand Street Follies*. "Three Little Maids from Broadway Town" was somewhat similar in nature to both "Best Loved Girls" from *Shoestring '57* (see entry), which spoofed recent Broadway and Off Broadway heroines (from *Wonderful Town* [1953], *The Threepenny Opera* [1954 and 1955; see entries], *Seventh Heaven* [1955], and *Pipe Dream* [1955]), and "Off Broadway Broads" from *Greenwich Village, U.S.A.* (1960; see entry), which spoofed the era's Off Broadway heroines (Jenny [*The Threepenny Opera*], Jane [*Leave It to Jane*, 1959], and Mary Potts a/k/a Little Mary [*Little Mary Sunshine*, 1959]).

When *The Grand Street Follies* gave its final performance at the Neighborhood Theatre, the *New York Times* covered the event, noting that the theatre officially ended its career ("with more than a few tears and heart pangs") at 11:17 P.M. on May 29, 1927. The *Times* praised the satiric group (one of the "most colorful and vital factors in the theatrical life of this city") and reported that on May 31 the revue would continue performances at Broadway's Little Theatre (on a "cooperative basis" [did the group perform under a special Broadway contract, similar perhaps to the Middle/Limited theatre agreements of the 1970s and 1980s?]). The *Times* mentioned that the final Off Broadway performance drew many "uptowners" to Grand Street, and included in the audience were Lynn Fontanne and Alfred Lunt (who themselves had been parodied in the 1925 edition's "Mr. and Mrs. Guardsman" sketch).

The sketches and songs listed above are taken from the June 6 program (the second week of the Broadway run).

623 El Grande de Coca-Cola (1986).

THEATRE: Village Gate Downstairs; OPENING DATE: January 22, 1986; PERFORMANCES: 86; MATERIAL WRITTEN by Ron House, Diz White, Alan Shearman, and John Neville-Andrews; DIRECTION: Ron House, Diz White, and Alan Shearman; CHOREOGRAPHY: Anne Gunderson; SCENERY: Elwin Charles Terrel II; LIGHTING: Judy Rasmuson; PRODUCERS: Ron Abbott, Susan Liederman, and Michael Tucker

CAST—Diz White (Consuela Hernandez), Rodger Bumpass (Juan Rodriguez), Alan Shearman (Miguel Rodriguez), Ron House (Senor Don Pepe Hernandez), Olga Merediz (Maria Hernandez)

The revue was presented in one act.

NOTES—As *El Coca-Cola Grande* (the title was changed to *El Grande de Coca-Cola* a week after the opening), the original production played for over 1,000 performances (see entry); but the revival (as *El*

Grande de Coca-Cola) had a disappointing run of less than three months. According to *The Best Plays of 1985-1986*, the revival was a "somewhat revised" version of the 1973 original.

624 Grandpa. THEATRE: Kaufmann Auditorium/92nd Street YM-YWHA; OPENING DATE: January 23, 1977; PERFORMANCES: 20; BOOK: Judith Martin; LYRICS: Judith Martin; MUSIC: Donald Ashwander; DIRECTION: John W. Lloyd, Technical Director; SCENERY: Judith Martin; COSTUMES: Judith Martin; LIGHTING: Robby Monk; PRODUCER: The Paper Bag Players (Judith Martin, Director)

CAST—Irving Burton, Judith Martin, Jeanne Michels, Virgil Roberson, Donald Ashwander

The revue was presented in one act (song assignments unknown).

MUSICAL NUMBERS—"Getting Older," "Worrying," "Stolen Sneakers," "A Long Story," "Fast Dance," "It's Just Not Fair," "Can You Tell Me What's Happened to Kurtz?," "Bubble Gum," "A Great Big Kiss," "Born Leader," "Dancing Partners," "When You're Older," "Growing Up," "Changing"

NOTES—*Theatre World 1976-1977 Season* reported that the Off Off Broadway revue *Grandpa*, which dealt with growing older, was presented for a limited run of twenty performances.

625 Grease. THEATRE: Eden Theatre; OPENING DATE: February 14, 1972; PERFORMANCES: 128; BOOK: Jim Jacobs and Warren Casey; LYRICS: Jim Jacobs and Warren Casey; MUSIC: Jim Jacobs and Warren Casey; DIRECTION: Tom Moore; CHOREOGRAPHY: Patricia Birch; SCENERY: Douglas W. Schmidt; COSTUMES: Carrie F. Robbins; LIGHTING: Karl Eigsti; MUSICAL DIRECTION: Louis St. Louis; PRODUCERS: Kenneth Waissman and Maxine Fox in association with Anthony D'Amato

CAST—Dorothy Leon (Miss Lynch), Ilene Kristen (Patty Simcox), Tom Harris (Eugene Florczyk), Garn Stevens (Jan), Katie Hanley (Marty), Adrienne Barbeau (Betty Rizzo), James Canning (Doody), Walter Bobbie (Roger), Timothy Meyers (Kenickie), Jim Borrelli (Sonny LaTierri), Marya Small (French), Carole Demas (Sandy Dumbrowksi), Barry Bostwick (Danny Zuko), Don Billett (Vince Fontaine), Alan Paul (Johnny Casino, Teen Angel), Kathi Moss (Cha-Cha Di Gregorio)

The action occurs in the 1950s.

The musical was presented in two acts.

ACT ONE—"Alma Mater" (Dorothy Leon, Ilene Kristen, Tom Harris), "Alma Mater (Parody)" (reprise) (Pink Ladies, Burger Palace Boys), "Summer Nights" (Carole Demas, Barry Bostwick, Pink Ladies, Burger Palace Boys), "Those Magic Changes" (James Canning, Burger Palace Boys, Pink Ladies), "Freddy, My Love" (Katie Hanley, Garn Stephens, Marya Small, Adrienne Barbeau), "Greased Lightin'" (Timothy Meyers, Burger Palace Boys), "Mooning" (Walter Bobbie, Garn Stephens), "Look at Me, I'm Sandra Dee" (Adrienne Barbeau), "We Go Together" (Pink Ladies, Burger Palace Boys)

ACT TWO—"Shakin' at the High School Hop" (Compnay), "It's Raining on Prom Night" (Carole Demas, Kathi Moss [Radio Voice]), "Shakin' at the High School Hop" (reprise) (Company), "Born To Hand Jive" (Alan Paul, Company), "Beauty School Dropout" (Alan Paul, Marya Small, Choir), "Alone at a Drive-In Movie" (Barry Bostwick, Burger Palace Boys), "Rock 'n' Roll Party Queen" (James Canning, Walter Bobbie), "There Are Worse Things I Could Do" (Adrienne Barbeau), "Look at Me, I'm Sandra Dee" (reprise) Carole Demas), "All Choked Up" (Carole Demas, Barry Bostwick, Company), "We Go Together" (reprise) (Company)

NOTES—*Grease* premiered at an Off Broadway Theatre (the Eden, formerly the Phoenix, was the original home of *The Golden Apple* [see entry]) and played there for four months before transferring to Broadway at the Broadhurst Theatre on June 7. According to *The Burns Mantle Yearbook/The Best Plays of 1971-1972*, the Eden run was under a Broadway contract, and so technically *Grease* wasn't an Off Broadway show. But other reference books refer to show's first four months as "Off Broadway," and so the musical is included in this volume with the caveat that it was an Off Broadway musical only in respect to its theatre's location. When *Grease* closed on Broadway, it had played a total of 3,388 performances (including the 128 performances at the Eden), making it at the time the longest-running musical in Broadway history. It was revived on Broadway at the Eugene O'Neill Theatre on May 11, 1994, and played for 1,503 performances; and on August 19, 2007, the second Broadway revival opened at the Brooks Atkinson Theatre (the casting for this revival was itself the subject of a reality television series in which hopefuls competed against one another in an *American Idol*-styled contest).

The original 1972 production launched many careers (Barry Bostwick, Adrienne Barbeau, Walter Bobbie, and Alan Paul, who was one of the original Manhattan Transfer). In 1973, the first national touring company included such future names as Judy Kaye, Marilu Henner, Jerry Zaks, and John Travolta (as Doody). For the highly popular film version released by Paramount Pictures in 1978, Travolta assumed the role of Danny Zuko and Olivia Newton-John played Sandy. (The less successful London production opened at the New London Theater on June 26, 1973, for 236 performances [some sources cite 258 performances], and featured Richard Gere in the role of Danny Zuko.)

The film version included a few new songs, including a title number with lyric and music by Barry Gibb; "Hopelessly Devoted to You" and "You're the One That I Want," lyrics and music by John Farrar; and "Sandy," lyric and music by Louis St. Louis and Scott Simon. The first three songs became hits, and were often interpolated into stage revivals of the musical.

The 1972 Broadway cast recording was released by MGM Records (LP # 1SE-34-OC) and the CD was released by Polydor Records (# 827-548-2); the film soundtrack was issued by RSO Records, Inc., on a 2-LP set (# RS-2-4002); the 1994 Broadway revival was released by RCA Victor Records (CD # 09026-62703-2), and when Brooks Shields joined the cast the CD was reissued by RCA with her tracks (# 09026-68179-2). The 2007 Broadway revival was recorded by Sony BMG Music Entertainment/Masterworks Broadway (CD # 88697-16398-2). A 1993 London revival was released by Epic Records (LP # 474632-1 and CD # 474632-2); a studio cast recording released by That's Entertainment Records (CD # CDTER-1220) included John Barrowman in the cast; and among the foreign cast recordings were a 1977 South African album released by MFP Records (LP # SRSJ-8079); a 1991-1992 season Norwegian album released by Polydor Records (CD # 513-367-2); and a 1993 Hungarian album released by Polygram Records (CD # 521520-2).

The script was published by Winter House, Ltd., in 1972, and was also included in the collection *Great Rock Musicals*, edited by Stanley Richards and published by Stein and Day in 1979. *Grease* was first produced at the Kingston Mines Theatre in Chicago in February 1971. After *Grease*, its authors, Jim Jacobs and Warren Casey, were never heard from again, as far as New York was concerned. However, in the early 1980s their musical *Island of Lost Co-eds* was produced in Chicago, and reports indicate it was a delightful spoof of the beach-blanket and jungle film genres.

626 The Great American Backstage Musical. THEATRE: Silver Lining; OPENING DATE: September 15, 1983; PERFORMANCES: 18; BOOK: Bill Solly and Donald Ward; LYRICS: Bill Solly; MUSIC: Bill Solly; DIRECTION: Bob Talmadge; CHOREOGRAPHY: Bob Talmadge; COSTUMES: George Potts; LIGHTING: Gregg Mariner; MUSICAL DIRECTION: Fred Barton; PRODUCER: Daniel and Geraldine Abrahamsen with Silver Lining

CAST—Mark Fotopoulos (Johnny Brash), Suzanne Dawson (Sylvia), Joe Barrett (Harry), Paige O'Hara (Kelly Moran), Bob Amaral (Banjo), Maris Clement (Constance Duquette)

The action occurs in New York, London, and the battlefields of Europe during the period 1942-1945.

The musical was presented in one act.

MUSICAL NUMBERS—"Backstage" (performer[s] unknown), "The Girls in Short Supply" (performer[s] unknown), "Nickel's Worth of Dreams" (performer[s] unknown), "I Got the What? (The Bug)" (Bob Amaral, Paige O'Hara, Mark Fotopoulous, Suzanne Dawson, Joe Barrett), "This Isn't Tomorrow" (performer[s] unknown), "Pie and Coffee" (Bob Amaral, Suzanne Dawson), "(You Should Be) Being Made Love To" (Maris Clement), "The Star of the Show" (Mark Fotopoulous), "When the Money Comes In" (Paige O'Hara, Chorus), "News of You" (Maris Clement, Joe Barrett), "I Could Fall in Love" (Maris Clement, Chorus), "Ba-Boom" (Mark Fotopoulous, Bob Amaral), "I'll Wait for Joe" (Suzanne Dawson), Finale (Company)

NOTES—The Off Off Broadway musical *The Great American Backstage Musical* was a mixture of show business and World War II clichés (and performed "in the style of a mid-1940's Hollywood musical," according to the published script). It made its belated New York premiere seven years after it was first produced in Los Angeles on December 2, 1976, at the Matrix Theatre; the production was subtitled "An Intimate Epic for Six Performers" and the cast included Tamara Long as Constance Duquette. The London premiere took place at the Regent Theatre on August 8, 1978 (it was subtitled "The New 40's Musical Direct from Hollywood," and the cast included Marti Webb, who played the role of Kelly Moran), and there was, among other U.S. productions, a version which played at the Goodspeed Opera House (on September 15, 1982, with a cast which included Faith Prince [as Sylvia Hotchkiss] and Pamela Blair [Kelly Moran]). The musical underwent various revisions over the years; numbers heard in earlier versions (but not in the New York production) were: "Cheerio," "Crumbs in My Bed," "On the Avenue," "Safe Home," "Going Places," and "Signature"; there was also an opening titled "Opening Number" as well as a finale titled "The End." For most productions, the musical was divided into two acts. The musical even underwent a time change (from 1942-1945 to 1939-1945).

Perhaps the most recent version of the musical is a revival which was seen in a Music Theatre of Connecticut production at the Westport Town Hall Theatre in March 1990. In reviewing this production for the *New York Times*, Alvin Klein noted that if you're looking for another variation on old musical films, "you're not likely to do much worse than this one."

One version of the script was published by Samuel French, Inc., in 1979; and AEI Records released the cast recording of the 1976 Los Angeles production (LP # AEI-1101).

627 The Great American Trailer Park Musical. THEATRE: Dodger Stages; OPENING DATE: September 27, 2005; PERFORMANCES: 80; BOOK: Betsy Kelso; LYRICS: David Nehls; MUSIC: David Nehls; DIRECTION: Betsy Kelso; CHOREOGRAPHY: Sergio Trujillo; SCENERY: Derek McLane; COSTUMES: Markas Henry; LIGHTING: Donald Holder; MUSICAL DIRECTION: David Nehls; PRODUCERS: Jean Doumanian, Jeffrey Richards, and Rick Steiner

CAST—Linda Hart (Betty), Marya Grandy (Linoleum), Leslie Kritzer (Pickles), Shuler Hensley (Norbert), Kaitlin Hopkins (Jeannie), Orfeh (Pippi), Wayne Wilcox (Leo, Duke)

The action occurs mostly in Armadillo Acres, a trailer park in Starke, Florida; some sequences occur in a local strip club and in a mall in Oklahoma City.

The musical was presented in one act.

MUSICAL NUMBERS—"This Side of the Tracks" (Linda Hart, Leslie Kritzer, Marya Grandy, Shuler Hensley, Kaitlin Hopkins, Orfeh), "One Step Closer" (Linda Hart, Leslie Kritzer, Marya Grandy, Shuler Hensley, Kaitlin Hopkins), "The Buck Stops Here" (Orfeh, Linda Hart, Leslie Kritzer, Marya Grandy), "It Doesn't Take a Genius" (Linda Hart, Leslie Kritzer, Marya Grandy, Shuler Hensley, Orfeh, Kaitlin Hopkins), "Owner of My Heart" (Kaitlin Hopkins, Shuler Hensley), "The Great American TV Show" (Linda Hart, Leslie Kritzer, Marya Grandy, Orfeh, Shuler Hensley), "Flushed Down the Pipes" (Kaitlin Hopkins, Linda Hart, Leslie Kritzer, Marya Grandy), "Storm's A-Brewin'" (Linda Hart, Leslie Kritzer, Marya Grandy, Orfeh, Kaitlin Hopkins, Shuler Hensley), "Road Kill" (Wayne Wilcox, Linda Hart, Leslie Kritzer, Marya Grandy), "But He's Mine"/"It's Never Easy" (Orfeh, Shuler Hemsley, Kaitlin Hopkins), "That's Why I Love My Man" (Linda Hart, Leslie Kritzer, Marya Grandy), "Panic" (Kaitlin Hopkins), Finale (Company)

NOTES—Set mostly in a trailer park in northern Florida, the amusingly titled *The Great American Trailer Park Musical* centered on an agoraphobic wife whose husband is pursued by the town's newcomer, a stripper on the lam.

Christopher Isherwood in the *New York Times* found the tongue-in-cheek musical "bright but flimsy," "busy but doggedly inert," and "mostly a loose assemblage of gags poking mildly malicious fun at ... white trash." But he praised the game cast (especially Leslie Kritzer) and the "appealing if not markedly original score."

The lively score was recorded by Sh-K-Boom Records (CD # 7915586051-2), and the script was published by Dramatists Play Service, Inc., in 2006.

During previews (in which the musical was presented in two acts), the songs "Do Nuthin' Day," "Bill Billy's No-Tell Motel," and "Immobile in My Mobile Home" were deleted. As for the latter, the title alone makes it sound like a worthy candidate for a future CD of lost Off Broadway songs.

The musical had first been produced at Theatre Three for seven performances on September 28, 2004, as part of the 2004 New York Musical Theatre Festival.

628 The Great Gatsby. THEATRE: Metropolitan Opera House; OPENING DATE: December 20, 1999; PERFORMANCES: 8; LIBRETTO: John Harbison; popular song lyrics by Murray Horwitz; MUSIC: John Harbison; DIRECTION: Mark Lamos; CHOREOGRAPHY: Robert La Fosse; SCENERY: Michael Yeargan; COSTUMES: Jane Greenwood; LIGHTING: Duane Schuler; MUSICAL DIRECTION: James Levine

CAST—Daisy Buchanan (Dawn Upshaw), Susan Graham (Jordan Baker), Dwayne Croft (Nick Carraway), Mark Baker (Tom Buchanan), Richard Paul Fink (George Wilson), Lorraine Hunt (Myrtle Wilson), Matthew Polenzani (Radio Singer, Band Vocalist), Jerry Hadley (Jay Gatsby), Jennifer Dunley (Tango Singer), William Powers (Meyer Wolfshiem), Frederick Burchinal (Henry Gatz), LeRoy Lehr (Minister); Chorus of Party-Goers

SOURCE—The 1925 novel *The Great Gatsby* by F. Scott Fitzgerald.

The action occurs in Long Island and New York City during the mid-1920s.

The opera was presented in two acts.

NOTES—From a note in the program: "*The Great Gatsby* was commissioned by the Metropolitan Opera to commemorate the 25th anniversary of the debut of James Levine."

John Harbison's adaptation of F. Scott Fitzgerald's masterpiece was faithful to its source, perhaps too faithful according to Bernard Holland, who reviewed the work in the *New York Times* after its world premiere (opera "should not be allowed to treat great writing with too much respect"). Indeed, the opera was sometimes too reverential to its source material and probably the libretto should have completely re-imagined the novel for the lyric stage.

However, Harbison rightly noted that *The Great Gatsby* is about more than just the doomed love affair between Gatsby and the shallow Daisy, and that Nick Carraway (who is sometimes overlooked in his "narrator" role) is the second most important character in the novel; thus Harbison gave important stage time to Nick. Daisy is in many respects a secondary character, and it might have been interesting (and daring on Harbison's part) if he'd shaped Daisy's role into a supporting one, relegating her to some extent as one of the crowd of superficial people surrounding Gatsby and Nick. Unfortunately, Harbison dwelt too much on her (particularly in the second act, when she occasionally seemed to dominate the proceedings).

Harbison's elegant and melodic score included many fine sequences, including a brilliant opening quintet (for Daisy, Jordan, Nick and Tom) and an aria for Daisy ("Where Is the Old Warm World?"). Further, Murray Horwitz provided lyrics for a series of songs in the party sequences; this pastiche (particularly the foxtrot "Dreaming of You") evoked the popular music of the Jazz Age and in its way served to mirror the conflicts and emotions of the main characters.

The Great Gatsby returned to the Met in 2002 for four more performances in a reportedly revised version which shortened the opera by about twenty minutes. Even so, the opera still seemed to drag in its final scenes and could have done with more trimming (particularly the "Daisy" scene in the second act).

Unfortunately, *The Great Gatsby* wasn't recorded or shown on public television; however, the January 1, 2000, performance was broadcast on radio. The libretto was published by G. Schirmer, Inc., in 1999.

629 The Great MacDaddy (1974). "A Dramatic Musical Odyssey." THEATRE: St. Marks Playhouse; OPENING DATE: February 12, 1974; PERFORMANCES: 72; BOOK: Paul Carter Harrison; LYRICS: Paul Carter Harrison; MUSIC: Coleridge-Taylor Perkinson; DIRECTION: Douglas Turner Ward; CHOREOGRAPHY: Dianne McIntyre; SCENERY: Gary James Wheeler; COSTUMES: Mary Mease Warren; LIGHTING: Ken Billington; MUSICAL DIRECTION: Unknown; PRODUCER: The Negro Ensemble Company, Inc. (Douglas Turner Ward, Artistic Director; Robert Hooks, Executive Director; Frederick Garrett, Administrative Director)

CAST—David Downing (MacDaddy), Al Freeman, Jr. (Scag, Photographer, Skull, Sheriff, Scarecrow, Humdrum), BeBe Drake Hooks (Old Woman, Mother Faith), Adolph Caesar (Deacon Jones, Dude, Skeleton, Bartender, Mr. Middlesex), Marjorie Barnes (Young Woman, Song), Graham Brown (Wine, Old Grandad, Poppa, Blood Leader), Martha Short-Goldsen (Momma, Mrs. Middlesex), Sati Jamal (Shine, Niggertoe, Red), Hattie Winston (Leionah), Charles Weldon (Skuleton, Jackle, Stagolee), Victor Willis (Signifyin' Baby), Howard Porter (Cowboy, Dude, Benny), Alton Lathrop (Eagle), Freda T. Vanterpool (Red Woman, Tree, Dance), Alvin Ronn Pratt (Blood Son, Jackie), Omar Clay (Drum); Community Members (Phylicia Ayers-Allen, Dyane Harvey)

The action begins in the 1930s during Prohibition. The musical was presented in two acts.

Individual musical numbers weren't listed in the program; however, the acts and scenes were divided as follows:

ACT ONE—Primal Rhythm — Los Angeles, Beat One — Nevada Desert, Beat Two — Las Vegas

ACT TWO—Beat Three — Arizona Dog Races, Beat Four — Texas, Beat Five — Arkansas, Beat Six — St. Louis, Beat Seven — Louisiana, Terminal Rhythm — South Carolina, Terminal Coda — Los Angeles

NOTES—A program note indicated that while the action for *The Great MacDaddy* began in the 1930s during Prohibition, the succeeding scenes (or "beats") didn't conform to strict time sequences, and thus moments freely progressed forward and backward in time. For the play's purposely disjointed structure, time served merely as a series of transitional "beats" in the play's chronology of events.

The Great MacDaddy was inspired by the African story-telling technique advanced by Amos Tutuola in his novel *The Palm Wine Drinkard*.

The musical's free-form, unstructured narrative confused the critics, but most felt the evening was highly theatrical and the music lively. The story depicted MacDaddy's surreal odyssey across America, searching for his long-lost friend Wine (who died, but has nonetheless left his coffin) while always being pursued by Scag (a symbol of all Whites, and portrayed by Al Freeman, Jr., who played all the White characters).

Clive Barnes in the *New York Times* noted that the "very funny, scabrous, entertaining" musical was sometimes confusing ("Don't try to find a purpose in everything. Ride with it") but that the "attractive" score and the "bounce and flair" of the choreography smoothed over some of the more puzzling aspects of the libretto.

In 1995, the script was published in the collection *Classic Plays from the Negro Ensemble Company* (Paul Carter Harrison and Gus Edwards, editors).

In 1977 the musical was revived by The Negro Ensemble Company for an additional fifty-six performances (see entry).

630 The Great MacDaddy (1977). THEATRE: Theatre de Lys; OPENING DATE: April 5, 1977; PERFORMANCES: 56; BOOK: Paul Carter Harrison; LYRICS: Paul Carter Harrison; MUSIC: Coleridge-Taylor Perkinson; DIRECTION: Douglas Turner Ward; CHOREOGRAPHY: Dianne McIntyre; SCENERY: William Ritman; COSTUMES: Arthur McGee; LIGHTING: Sandra L. Ross

CAST—Charles Weldon (MacDaddy), Bill Mackey (Scag, Photographer, Skull, Sheriff, Scarecrow, Humdrum), Barbara Montgomery (Old Woman, Momma, Mother Faith), Norman Jacob (Deacon Jones, Cowboy), Carol Maillard (Young Woman, Song, Niggertoe), Charles Brown (Young Man, Signifyin' Baby), Graham Brown (Wine, Old Grandad, Soldier), Reyno (Shine, Blood Son), Lynn Whitfield (Leionah), Frankie R. Faison (Skulleton, Stagolee/Scagolee), Carl Gordon (Skulleton, Bartender, Mr. Middlesex), Joella Breedlove (Dance), Charliese Drakeford (Mrs. Middlesex), Dennis Williams (Eagle); Community Members (Joella Breedlove, Charliese Drakeford, Frankie R. Faison, Kenneth Frett, Carl Gordon, Jennifer Jarrett, Reyno, Maggie Stewart, Freda T. Vanderpool, Dennis Williams); Fast Life Dudes (Charles Brown, Kenneth Frett, Norman Jacob, Reyno, Dennis Williams); Four Jackles (Charles Brown, Carl Gordon, Frankie R. Faison, Norman Jacob); Beast of Prey (Joella Breedlove, Kenneth Frett), Spirit of Woe (Charles Brown, Graham Brown, Frankie R. Faison, Kenneth Frett, Norman Jacob, Reyno)

NOTES—For more information, see entry for the original 1974 production.

631 Great Scot! "The Exciting New Musical." THEATRE: Theatre Four; OPENING DATE: November 10, 1965; PERFORMANCES: 38; BOOK: Mark Conradt and Gregory Dawson; LYRICS: Nancy Leeds; MUSIC: Don McAfee; DIRECTION: Charles Tate; CHOREOGRAPHY: Joyce Trisler; SCENERY: Herbert Senn and Helen Pond; COSTUMES: Patton Campbell; LIGHTING: Theda Taylor; MUSICAL DIRECTION: Joseph Raposo; PRODUCERS: Scotia Productions in association with Edward H. Davis

CAST—ALLAN BRUCE (Robert Burns), JOLEEN FODOR (Jean Armour), JACK EDDLEMAN (McGurk, Creech, Old Elder), CHARLOTTE JONES (Heather, Duchess of Montrose, Fish Monger), CASH BAXTER (Gilbert, the Reverend Dillingham, Duke of Montrose), CHARLES HUDSON (James Armour, Duffy), ARTHUR WHITFIELD (Jamie), Thomas Boyd (MacCohen, Constable, Bishop), Charles Burks (MacIntosh, Sailor, Town Elder), Shirley Caballero (Maggie, Mackerel, Lady Louise Glenpatrick), Ginger Gerlach (Agnes McGurk, Lady Cynthia), Mary Jo Gillis (Allison, Lucy), Anita Maye (Clarinda), Lois Ann Saunders (Lorna, Salmon), Dale Westerman (Jock, Town Elder), Camelot Guinevere (Jennie)

The action occurs in Scotland between the years 1783 and 1784.

The musical was presented in two acts.

ACT ONE—"You're the Only One" (Allan Bruce, unidentified performers, Ensemble), "Great Scot" (Allan Bruce, unidentified performers, Ensemble), "We'll Find a Dream Somewhere" (Allan Bruce), "He's Not for Me" (Joleen Fodor), "She's Not for Me" (reprise) (Allan Bruce, Joleen Fodor, Ensemble), Dance (Arthur Whitfield, Ensemble), "That Special Day" (Joleen Fodor, unidentified performer, Allan Bruce, Ensemble), "Brandy in Your Champagne" (Charlotte Jones, Jack Eddleman), "I'm Gonna Have a Baby" (Allan Bruce, Ensemble), "Original Sin" (Charles Hudson, Jack Eddleman, Charles Burks, Dale Westerman), "I'll Still Love Jean" (Allan Bruce), "Where Is That Rainbow" (Allan Bruce, Joleen Fodor)

ACT TWO—"Princes' Street" (Ensemble), "You're the Only One" (reprise) (Allan Bruce, Ensemble), "Happy New Year" (Allan Bruce, Ensemble), "The Big-Bellied Bottle" (Charles Hudson, Charlotte Jones, Allan Bruce, Ensemble), "He Knows Where to Find Me" (Joleen Fodor), "Where Does a Man Begin?" (Allan Bruce), "What a Shame" (Ensemble), "I Left a Dream Somewhere" (Allan Bruce), Finale: "We're Gonna Have a Wedding" (Allan Bruce, Joleen Fodor, Ensemble)

NOTES—*Great Scot!*, a musical version of the life of Scottish poet Robert Burns, lasted barely a month. If the song titles are any indication, the musical was a re-telling of the poet's life. But Lewis Funke in the *New York Times* reported the musical was probably one of the "most sumptuous" ever seen Off Broadway (the décor was by Herbert Senn and Helen Pond, and the costumes were designed by Patton Campbell), and he found Don McAfee's score "bountiful" with many songs "rich in melody." Alas, the book was the culprit. It lacked imagination and the "essential buoyancy to lift [the musical] beyond the mechanical and plodding." And the title character was written in "one-dimensional" fashion.

632 The Green Bird. THEATRE: New Victory Theatre; OPENING DATE: March 7, 1996; PERFORMANCES: 15; BOOK: Carlo Gozzi; translated by Albert Bermel and Ted Emery; LYRICS: Carlo Gozzi, Albert Bermel, David Suehsdorf; MUSIC: Elliot Goldenthal; DIRECTION: Julie Taymor; SCENERY: Christine Jones; Julie Taymor, Co-Designer; Masks and Puppet Designs by Julie Taymor; COSTUMES: Constance Hoffman; LIGHTING: Donald Holder; MUSICAL DIRECTION: Richard Martinez; PRODUCERS: The New 42nd Street Inc. and Theatre for a New Audience

CAST—Trellis Stepter (Brighella), Andrew Weems (Pantalone, Voice of Calmon), Didi Conn (Smeraldina), Ned Eisenberg (Truffaldino), Myriam Cyr (Barbarina), Sebastian Roche (Renzo), Bruce Turk (Green Bird), Kristine Nielsen (Ninetta), Derek Smith (Tartaglia), Priscilla Shanks (Tartagliona, Statue of Treviso), Lee Lewis (Pompea), Erico Villanueva); Singing Apples (Sophia Salguero [Soloist], Didi Conn, Myriam Cyr), Servants (Kristine Nielsen, Sophia Salguero, Erico Villanueva), Musicians (Liz Knowles, Bill Ruyle, Bruce Williamson), Puppeteers (David Barlow, Stephen Kaplin, Katherine Profeta, Peggy Sullivan, Kathleen Tobin)

SOURCE—The 1765 play *The Green Bird* by Count Carlo Gozzi.

The play with music was presented in two acts.

NOTES—Count Carlo Gozzi's classic commedia dell'arte *The Green Bird* was seen during the inaugural season of the New Victory Theatre, a 499-seat Off Broadway house which had originally opened on September 27, 1900, as the Republic Theatre.

The musical version of the story told the tale of Renzo and Barbarina, twins of King Tartaglia, supposedly killed at birth but secretly rescued by a poor sausage-seller and his wife. Ultimately, the twins are reunited with their mother, Queen Ninetta.

The Off Broadway production included two sequences of original music by Elliot Goldenthal ("Nygma Variations" and "Mr. E's"), and the work was notable for its scenery and costumes, particularly the masks and puppet designs by Julie Taymor.

The musical later opened on Broadway at the Cort Theatre on April 18, 2000, for fifty-six performances. The Broadway production credited "additional text" to Eric Overmeyer, and while the program didn't list specific song titles, it credited the lyric of "Oh Foolish Heart" to David Suehsdorf. The Broadway cast recording was released by DRG Records (CD # 12989).

The following list of songs and other musical sequences is taken from the cast recording: "Truffaldino's Sausage Shop," "O Greedy People (The Apples That Sing)," "Tartaglia's Lament," "The Bickering," "Calmon, King of Statues," "Joy to the King," "Ninetta's Hope," "Renzo and Pompea Duet," "Barbarina's Lament," "The Waters That Dance," "Serpentina's Garden," "Under Bustle Funk," "Green Bird Descent," "The Magic Feather," "The King's Lament," "Accordions" and "Palace Rhumba," Prologue ("Radio Waves"), "Acids and Alkalis," "Apple Aria Instrumental," "O Foolish Heart"

633 The Green Heart. THEATRE: Variety Arts Theatre/Manhattan Theatre Club; OPENING DATE: April 10, 1997; PERFORMANCES: 30; BOOK: Charles Busch; LYRICS: Rusty Magee; MUSIC: Rusty Magee; DIRECTION: Kenneth Elliott; CHOREOGRAPHY: Joey McKneely; SCENERY: James Noone; COSTUMES: Robert Mackintosh; LIGHTING: Kirk Bookman; MUSICAL DIRECTION: Joe Baker; PRODUCER: Manhattan Theatre Club (Lynne Meadow, Artistic Director; Barry Grove, Executive Producer; Michael Bush, Associate Artistic Director; Victoria Bailey, General Manager)

CAST—Jay Russell (Manager, Rutherford), David Andrew Macdonald (William Graham), Alison Fraser (Uta), Elizabeth Ward (Edith, Lydia), Tim Salamandyk (Minister, Santiani), Karen Trott (Henrietta Lowell), Jeff Edgerton (Harvey), John Ellison Conlee (McPherson), Julie J. Hafney (Molly, Clara), Karyn Quackenbush (Estelle), Ruth Williamson (Mrs. Tragger), Lovette George (Ruby), Don Goodspeed (Dallas)

SOURCE—A short story by Jack Ritchie.

The action occurs in the present, in New York City, Dutchess County, and the Adirondacks.

The musical was presented in two acts.

ACT ONE—"Our Finest Customer" (Jay Russell, David Andrew Macdonald, Ensemble), "I'm Poor" (David Andrew Macdonald), "Picture Me" (Alison Fraser), "Henrietta's Elegy" (Karen Trott), "I Can't Recall" (Karen Trott), "Til Death Do They Part" (Ensemble), "Tropical Island Breezes" (Ensemble), "An Open Mind" (David Andrew Macdonald), "The Easy Life" (Ruth Williamson, Ensemble), "The Easy Life" (reprise) (Ruth Williamson), "Get Used to It" (John Ellison Conlee), "Get Used to It" (reprise) (Company)

ACT TWO—"Why Can't We Turn Back the Clock?" (Karen Trott, David Andrew Macdonald, Ensemble), "Horns of an Immoral Dilemma" (David Andrew Macdonald, Alison Fraser, Karen Trott), "Ornithology" (Ensemble), "The Green Heart" (Karen Trott), "The Green Heart" (reprise) (David Andrew Macdonald), "I'm the Victim Here" (Alison Fraser, Ruth Williamson, John Ellison Conlee), "I'm Poor" (reprise) (David Andrew Macdonald), "What's It Gonna Take (To Make It Clear Across the Lake)?" (David Andrew Macdonald, Alison Fraser, Ruth Williamson, John Ellison Conlee, Karen Trott), "The Green Heart" (reprise) (David Andrew Macdonald, Karen Trott, Ensemble)

NOTES—*A New Leaf*, the 1971 film version of Jack Ritchie's short story about a wealthy botanist who is pursued by, and then married to, a shallow and penniless playboy who plans to murder her, was an underrated black comedy directed and written by Elaine May, who also starred in it along with Walter Matthau (comics Jack Weston, George Rose, Doris Roberts, James Coco, David Doyle, and Renee Taylor rounded out the cast list). May was terrific as the clueless botanist who tried to decide if her greatest wish (to discover a new species of plant life) was her *hope* ... or her *dream*.

If the film was largely unappreciated (even May disowned it), the musical version of the material (*The Green Heart*, which was based on Ritchie's short story, not the film adaptation) was even more so. After its brief run, it seems to have completely disappeared. But Jeffrey Sweet in *The Best Plays of 1996-1997* said the musical was "an underappreciated gem, campy yet sweet ... a generally delightful work." Ben Brantley in the *New York Times* felt the musical never took wing until its secondary characters took over, and he wrote valentines to Alison Fraser and Ruth Williamson as two off-the-wall villainesses who prove that "you don't have to be a man to be a female impersonator."

The script was published by Samuel French, Inc., in 1999. In her collection *A New York Romance* (released by Original Cast Records CD # OC-9534), Alison Fraser recorded the musical's title song.

634 Green Pond. "A Musical." THEATRE: Westside Theatre; OPENING DATE: December 7, 1977; PERFORMANCES: 16 (estimated); BOOK: Robert Montgomery; LYRICS: Robert Montgomery; MUSIC: Mel Marvin; DIRECTION: David Chambers; SCENERY: Marjorie Kellogg; COSTUMES: Marjorie Kellogg; LIGHTING: Arden Fingerhut; MUSICAL DIRECTION: Mel Marvin; PRODUCER: Chelsea Theatre Center (Robert Kalfin, Artistic Director; Michael David, Executive Director)

CAST—Stephanie Cotsirilos (Liz), Christine Ebersole (Dana), Stephen James (Sam), Richard Ryder (Frank)

The action occurs on the South Carolina coast during Summer 1976.

The musical was presented in two acts (song assignments not listed in program).

ACT ONE—"Green Pond," "Pleasant Company," "Daughter," "I Live Alone," "The Eyes of Egypt," "How We Get Down"

ACT TWO—"Alligator Meat," "Priceless Relics," "Woman to Woman," "Brother to Brother," "Hurricane," "Hard to Love," "On the Ground at Last"

NOTES—Before transferring to the Westside Theatre, *Green Pond* first played at the Brooklyn

Academy of Music, where it opened on November 22 and played for approximately sixteen performances. The musical was originally produced by Stage South, a program of the South Carolina Arts Commission.

The musical dealt with two couples vacationing on the South Carolina coast. Richard Eder in the *New York Times* noted that the evening lacked characterization, motivation, and plot development. Instead, in typically 1970s fashion, the musical analyzed the "feelings" of its characters, and Eder reported they weren't real people but "merely attitudes" which moped, talked, and sang about feelings. They also sat around and drank mint juleps and ate roasted alligator meat. Eder said Mel Marvin's score was at its best in the title number and in "Hard to Love," the latter a "lovely song" which was performed "most beautifully" by Stephanie Cotsirilos. He also mentioned a rather curious number ("The Eyes of Egypt") in which various countries of the world were likened to specific areas of the human anatomy.

A program note indicated that the alligator meat used in the production was by courtesy of Long John Silver's Seafood Shoppe on Columbus Avenue.

635 The Greenwich Village Follies (1919).

"A Revusical Comedy of New York's Latin Quarter." THEATRE: Greenwich Village Theatre; OPENING DATE: July 15, 1919; PERFORMANCES: 232; SKETCHES AND LYRICS: Philip Bartholomae and John Murray Anderson; MUSIC: A. Baldwin Sloane; DIRECTION: John Murray Anderson; SCENERY: Charles B. Falls; COSTUMES: Shirley Barker; PRODUCER: The Bohemians, Incorporated

CAST—See individual numbers for names of performers

The revue was presented in two acts.

ACT ONE—Prologue: "The Green Line" (Susanne Morgan, Charles Derickson, William Foran, Robert Edwards, James Watts), "Before the Curtain" (Jane Carroll, Homer Rosine, Willard Ward, Warner Gault, Edgar Thornton), "Greenwich Village Quartette" (William Foran, Robert Edwards, Billlie Holbrook, Rita Zalmani), "The Greenwich Village Theatre" (Harry K. Morton, Arjamand, Dorothy Clay, Anna Mae Clift, Doris Faithful, Alden Gay, Virginia Lee, Rita Marshall, Irene Marcellus, Billie Weston, Bessie McCoy Davis), "The Stolen Melody" (Bessie McCoy Davis, Harry K. Morton, Charles Derickson, Irene Olsen), "I Want a Daddy" (Irene Olsen, Charles Derickson, Rita Zalmani), Bobby Edwards, "In Java"/"My Little Javanese" (Jane Carroll, Ada Forman, Arjamand, Dorothy Clay, Anna Mae Clift, Doris Faithful, Alden Gay, Virginia Lee, Rita Marshall, Billie Weston), Ted Lewis, The Jazz King, "Godiva's Gambol"/"Red as the Rose" (Irene Olsen, Cynthia Perot, Billie Holbrook, Robert Edwards, Susanne Morgan, Harry K. Morgan, James Watts), "Danse Classique" (James Watts), "Adagio" (James Watts, Rex Story), "Tony Sarg" (Bessie McCoy Davis, Irene Olsen, Babette Busey, Virginia Curtis, Jacqueline Delaine, Helen Frances, Ruth Weeks, Olga Ziceva, William Foran, Robert Edwards, Billie Holbrook, Rita Zalmani), "The Critic's Blues" (Harry K. Morton)

ACT TWO—"Up in the Air" (Charles Derickson), "I've a Sweetheart in Each Star" (Charles Derickson, Billie Holbrook, Arjamand, Jane Carroll, Dorothy Clay, Anna Mae Clift, Doris Faithful, Virginia Lee, Reta Marshall, Billie Weston, Olga Ziceva, Irene Mathews), "A Street in Greenwich Village" (James Watts, Rex Story), "The Cameo"/"The Message of the Cameo" (Bessie McCoy Davis), "The Dream Lovers" (Edgar Thornton, Homer Rosine, Willard Ward, Warner Gault, Babette Busey, Jacqueline Delaine, Helen Frances, Virginia Lee, Rita Marshall, Ruth Weeks), "Passe-Pied" (Olga Ziceva, Virginia Curtis, Billie Holbrook), Cecil Cunningham, "Marguerite's Backyard" (Susanne Morgan, William Foran, Edgar Thornton, James Watts)Jack Wilson and Frank Hearst, "The Floating Cabaret" (Bessie McCoy Davis, Harry K. Morton, William Foran), "I'm the Hostess of a Bum Cabaret" (Bessie McCoy Davis, Harry K. Morton, Susanne Morgan, Irene Olsen, Charles Derickson, Robert Edwards), "I'm Ashamed to Look the Moon in the Face" (Harry K. Morton, Arjamand, Dorothy Clay, Anna Mae Clift, Doris Faithful, Alden Gay, Virginia Lee, Reta Marshall, Irene S. Mathews, Billie Weston, Cynthia Perot)

NOTES—With *The Greenwich Village Follies*, John Murray Anderson ushered in a series of eight revues which lasted until 1928. Following the success of the 1919 edition, Anderson offered a second one in 1920 (see entry), which transferred to Broadway. From then on, the six subsequent revues in the series (1921, 1922, 1923, 1924, 1925, and 1928) all opened on Broadway. An unsigned review in the *New York Times* reported the revue needed rearranging, cutting, and revision, and noted the show barely succeeded in wrapping up by midnight. Further, the reviewer noted that the program didn't correctly list the sketches and songs as performed on opening night. But for all that, the critic nonetheless praised the cast, costumes, scenery (the latter made "an impression not to be forgotten"), and "several tuneful pieces" (the reviewer singled out "I Want a Daddy," "My Little Javanese," and "I'm the Hostess of a Bum Cabaret"). He also praised James Watts, who excelled in "a number of he-feminine parts" and was the "outstanding funmaker of the frolic."

636 Greenwich Village Follies.

THEATRE: New Follies Theatre; transferred to the Gate Theatre on September 8, 1976, and then to the Cricket Theatre on November 11, 1976; OPENING DATE: June 10, 1976; PERFORMANCES: 444; SKETCHES: Ronnie Britton; LYRICS: Ronnie Britton; MUSIC: Ronnie Britton; DIRECTION: Production "supervised" by Ronnie Britton; COSTUMES: Kapton; LIGHTING: Steve Loew; MUSICAL DIRECTION: Max Lifchitz; PRODUCERS: Donald Elliott in association with Erehwon Productions

CAST—Linda David, Lance Marcone, Danny Freedman, Gregory Cook, Jacqueline Carol, Ronaeld Smith, Philippe de Brugada, Marissa Lyon

The revue was presented in two acts.

ACT ONE—Overture, Introduction (performer[s] unknown), "Greenwich Village Follies" (Company), "Let Me Sing!" (Linda David), "Hello, New York" (performer unknown), "Le Grand Rape" (Company), "You Show Me Yours" (Jacqueline Carol, other performer unknown), "Quartet for Losers" (Lance Marcone, Linda David, Two other performers unknown), "Nude with Violin" (performer[s] unknown), "We Wanna Star" (Jacqueline Carol, Linda David, other performer unknown), "Rock 'n' Roll Star" (Lance Marcone), "Long Ago, or Yesterday?" (performer unknown), "I've Been in Love" (performer[s] unknown), "Most Unusual Pair" (performer[s] unknown)

ACT TWO—"Melody of Manhattan" (Lance Marcone, two other performers unknown), "Merry-Go-Round" (Linda David), "Bicentennial March" (Company), "Look at Me" (Lance Marcone), "That Girl with the Curls" (four performers unknown), "Ole Soft Core" (performer[s] unknown), "Ballet Erotique" (Lance Marcone, performer unknown, Company), "The Expose" (two performers unknown), "Garbage-Ella" (Linda Marcone), "Pandora" (Jacqueline Carol), Finale (Company)

NOTES—Six months after the short-run of his *Gift of the Magi* (1974; see entry), Ronnie Britton returned with *Greenwich Village Follies*, which appears to have been a combination salute-to-New-York-City and soft-porn revue.

During the run, some sequences were added ("High School Hi-Jinks," "Mimi," "Mimi and the Beggar," "Mimi???," and "Isn't It Fun and Gay?") and some were dropped ("Nude with Violin," "I've Been in Love," and "Most Unusual Pair"). There was also considerable re-ordering of the songs and sketches.

"Garbage-Ella" had been earlier heard in the children's musical *Twanger* (see entry).

637 The Greenwich Village Follies of 1920.

"A Revusical Comedy of New York's Latin Quarter." THEATRE: Greenwich Village Theatre; transferred to Broadway at the Shubert Theatre on on September 20 (for approximately 193 performances); OPENING DATE: August 30, 1920; PERFORMANCES: 24 (estimated)

"The Dialogue" (Sketches): Thomas J. Gray; LYRICS: John Murray Anderson and Arthur Swanstrom; MUSIC: A. Baldwin Sloane; DIRECTION: John Murray Anderson; SCENERY: Robert E. Locher; Persian Setting by James Reynolds; COSTUMES: Robert E. Locher; Fourteenth-Century Russian Costumes by James Reynolds Musical Direction: Charles Previn; PRODUCERS: The Bohemians, Inc. (A.L. Jones and Morris Green, Managing Directors)

CAST—See song listing below

The revue was presented in two acts.

ACT ONE—Prologue: "The Pawn Shop" (Maurice Quinlivan, Harriet Gimbel, Mary Lewis, Olive Brower, Howard Marsh, Florence Browne, James Clemons, Bernice Elmore, Constance Farber, Irene Farber, Frank Crumit, Dorothy Arnold, Alden Gay, Doris Green, Anna Mae Clift, Vera Carleton), "'Set' in Silver: The Naked Truth" (Frank Crumit); the sequence included The Models/The Art Students/The Batik Girls/Le Torso (Eugene Fosdick, Edward Graham, Maurice Quinlivan, Allen Joslyn, Harriet Gimbel, Delores Edwards, Dorothy Hadley, Doris Green, Harriet Tator, Dorothy Arnold, Florence Browne, Vera Carleton, Bernice Elmore, Olive Brower, Anna Mae Clift, Jay Brennan, Bert Savoy, Alden Gay), "Just Sweet Sixteen" (Howard Marsh, Mona Celete); the sequence included Vera Carleton, Loretta Morgan, Dorothy Hadley, Florence Browne, Bernice Elmore, Sybil Stokes, Harriet Haig, Delores Edwards, Olga Ziceva, Margaret Davies, Doris Green, Anna Mae Clift, Olive Brower, Dorothy Arnold, Marie Tudar, Irene Coffman, Mildred Mann, Eugenie Young, Frances Mann, Edith Slack, Constance Farber, Irene Farber), "I'll Be Your Valentine" (ballet music for the "Valentine Pas de Deux" by Charles Previn) (Mary Lewis, Howard Marsh; the sequence included Mildred Mann, Harriet Gimbel, Margaret Davies, Olga Ziceva, Frances Mann, Marie Tudar, Irene Coffman, Eugenie Young, Edith Slack, Ivan Bankoff, Mlle. Phebe, Allen Joslyn, Eugene Fosdick, Pee Wee Myers, Ford Hanford), "Come to Bohemia" (Howard Marsh; the sequence included Harriet Tator, Anna Mae Clift, Harriette Haig, Vera Carleton, Helen Le Von, Olive Brower, Bernice Elmore, Florence Browne, Doris Green, Delores Edwards, Alden Gay, Dorothy Arnold, Mary Lewis, Harriet Gimbel, Jay Brennan, Bert Savoy), "The Mad Hatters" (Frances Mann, Margaret Davies), "Snap Your Fingers at Care" (lyric by B.G. [Buddy] DeSylva, music by Louis Silvers) (Frank Crumit, Mary Lewis; danced by James Clemons), "A Broadway Cinderella" (lyric by Ballard MacDonald, music by Harry Carroll) (Constance Farber), "The Song of the Samovar" (Howard Marsh, Mona Celete); the sequence included Martha Throop, Eugene Fosdick, Edward Graham, Maurice Quinlivan, Allen Joslyn, Ivan Bankoff, Mlle. Phebe, Irene Coffman, Marie Tudar, Edith Slack, Frances Mann, Eugenie Young, Mildred Mann, Alden Gay, Bernice Elmore, Florence Browne), "Tam" (Frank Crumit, Ensemble)

ACT TWO—"In Front of the Screens" (Howard Marsh, Hap Hadley), "The Sandwich Girls" (Sybil Stokes, Florence Browne, Anna Mae Clift, Blanche

Clark, Loretta Morgan, Harriet Haig), "Krazy Kat's Ball" (Harriet Gimbel, Mildred Mann, Margaret Davies), "Divertissement" (Collins and Hart), "Before the Music Motif Curtain" (Frank Crumit), "Tsin" (Howard Marsh); the sequence included Blanche Clark, Sybil Stokes, Harriet Haig, Olga Ziceva, Loretta Morgan, Vera Carleton, Dorothy Hadley, Florence Browne), "Parfum d'Amour" (Mary Lewis); the sequence included Edward Graham, Olive Brower, Doris Green, Dorothy Arnold, Bernice Elmore, Delores Edwards, Alden Gay, Harriet Tator, Anna Mae Clift), The Dance (Margaret Severn), "'Set'" in Silver (Venita Gould), "'Set'" in Silver (special material by Bert Kalmer and Harry Ruby) (Bert Savoy and Jay Brennan), "The Golden Carnival"/"Valse Empire" (Doris Green, Allen Joslyn, Mary Lewis, Eugene Fosdick, Anna Mae Clift, Edward Graham, Florence Browne, Maurice Quinlivan, Margaret Severn), "The Greenwich Village Carnival" (Martha Throop, Howard Marsh), "Dance Guignole" (James Clemons), "Resume" (Company)

NOTES—This was the second of eight editions of John Murray Anderson's *Greenwich Village Follies*. The first edition (see entry) and the second edition opened Off Broadway (three weeks after opening Off Broadway, the second edition transferred to Broadway at the Shubert Theatre); the six subsequent revues (1921, 1922, 1923, 1924, 1925, and 1928) opened on Broadway.

The song sequence is taken from a touring version of the production, and includes "A Broadway Cinderella" (which was added during the Broadway run).

Among the revue's cast members was Howard Marsh, who created leading roles in the three longest-running musicals of the 1920s. In 1921, he appeared in *Blossom Time* (576 performances); in 1924, he was the original Prince Karl Franz in *The Student Prince in Heidelberg* (608 performances); and in 1927 was Gaylord Ravenal in *Show Boat* (572 performances). Also in the cast was Allen (Allan) Joslyn, later Allyn Joslyn, who had a long stage, screen, and television career. His most famous role was that of Mortimer Brewster in the original Broadway production of *Arsenic and Old Lace* (1941). Mortimer, a drama critic who doesn't seem to particularly care for the theatre (when a character says he should be fair to the plays he reviews, he asks whether the plays are fair to him), discovers that his sweet old aunts have a bad habit of adding a little something extra to their elderberry wine (for the film version, which was released in 1944, Cary Grant played the role of Mortimer).

638 Greenwich Village, U.S.A.

"A New Musical Revue." THEATRE: One Sheridan Square; OPENING DATE: September 28, 1960; PERFORMANCES: 87; SKETCHES: Frank Gehrecke; LYRICS: Jeanne Bargy, Frank Gehrecke, and Herb Corey; MUSIC: Jeanne Bargy; DIRECTION: Burke McHugh, Allen Hodshire (sketches); "entire production under the supervision of" Burke McHugh and Allen Hodshire; SONG DIRECTION AND CHOREOGRAPHY: Jim Russell; SCENERY: Robert Soule; COSTUMES: Nilo; LIGHTING: Jules Fisher; MUSICAL DIRECTION: Carl Janelli; PRODUCER: Allen Hodshire; Richard Barlow, Associate Producer

CAST—Jack Betts, Saralou Cooper, Pat Finley, Judy Guyll, Dawn Hampton, James Harwood, Jane A. Johnston, Burke McHugh, James Pompeii, Ken Urmston

The revue was presented in two acts.

ACT ONE—"Greenwich Village, U.S.A." (Company) "It's a Nice Place to Visit" (Burke McHugh), "Life Isn't Easy, Agnes" (Judy Guyll, Ken Urmston) "Ladies of the House" (Pat Finley, Dawn Hampton, Jane A. Johnston), "How Can Anyone So Sweet" (James Pompeii) "Sunday Brunch" (Company), "Time to Call It Quits" (Jack Betts) "Convention Results" (Burke McHugh, Dawn Hampton), "Love Me" (Saralou Cooper, Judy Guyll, James Pompeii, Ken Urmston), "How About Us Last Nite" (Jack Betts, Jane A. Johnston) "Theatre in the Round" (Judy Guyll, Pat Finley, James Harwood, Jack Betts, James Pompeii) "Brownstone" (Dawn Hampton) "BLT" (Pat Finley, James Harwood) "Village Vignette" (Jack Betts, Jane A. Johnston) "Love's Melody" (Saralou Cooper, James Harwood), "Village Lad" (Jack Betts), "That's How You Get Your Kicks" (Burke McHugh, Saralou Cooper, Pat Finley, Judy Guyll, Dawn Hampton) "Miss Hi-Fie" (Jane A. Johnston), "Living Pictures" (Company)

ACT TWO—"N.Y.U." (Pat Finley, Judy Guyll, Dawn Hampton, James Harwood, Jane A. Johnston, Burke McHugh, James Pompeii, Ken Urmston) "Take Me Away" (Saralou Cooper) "Four Seasons" (performer not credited) (See NOTES.), "Birth of a Beatnik" (Ken Urmston) (this dance solo was "especially conceived by Jim Russell"), "Off Broadway Broads" (Pat Finley, Judy Guyll, Jane A. Johnston) "It Has Everything" (Saralou Cooper, James Harwood), "Shopkeepers Trio" (Burke McHugh, James Pompeii, Ken Urmston), "Espresso House" (Jane A. Johnston, James Harwood) "Baby You Bore Me" (Jack Betts, Judy Guyll) "Week-End Shopping" (Saralou Cooper, Pat Finley, James Pompeii, Ken Urmston) "Petition" (Jack Betts, Pat Finley, Judy Guyll, James Harwood, Jane A. Johnston, James Pompeii) "Tea Party" (Saralou Cooper) "Movie Fan" (James Harwood) "What Do They Know About Love Uptown" (Pat Finley, Ken Urmston, Judy Guyll, James Pompeii) "It Pays to Advertise" (Jane A. Johnston), "We Got Love" (Dawn Hampton), "When the Village Goes to Sleep" (James Harwood) Finale ("Save the Village!") (Company)

NOTES—The long-forgotten revue *Greenwich Village, U.S.A.* holds a distinction of sorts: it was the second musical to be released on more than one LP. *The Most Happy Fella* (1956) had been released by Columbia Records on a 3-LP set, and *Greenwich Village, U.S.A.* was released on two LPs by 20th Fox MasterArts (# TCF-105-2), making it the most complete recording of a revue from its era.

Lewis Funke in the *New York Times* wasn't particularly taken with this "grab-bag little entertainment," which, in his opinion, lacked a point of view. But he liked the performers and a few of the songs and sketches, including Jane A. Johnston, "who succeeds in bringing down the house" in the "real low-down" number "Miss Hi-Fie," and Dawn Hampton, who "cuts loose" in "We Got Love," which he described as "a piece of hot jazz."

Perhaps the revue's highlight is "Off Broadway Broads," a send-up of the heroines (and the actresses playing them) of three then-current Off Broadway musicals (Jenny [*The Threepenny Opera*, 1954 and 1955; see entries], Jane [*Leave It to Jane*, 1959; see entry], and Mary a/k/a Mary Potts [*Little Mary Sunshine*, 1959; see entry]). Funke noted that Pat Finley, Judy Guyll, and Jane A. Johnston performed the song with "enchanting gusto." For more information about similar songs, see entries for *The Grand Street Follies* (1927, Fifth Edition) and its song "Three Little Maids from Broadway Town," which saluted three musical comedy stars of the mid-1920s, and *Shoestring '57* and its song "Best Loved Girls," which spoofed the leading ladies of four Broadway and Off Broadway musicals of the mid-1950s.

"Ladies of the House" was the second Off Broadway song of the year about the Village's House of Detention for Women. *Parade* (see entry) had earlier covered the same territory in "Save the Village" (a/k/a "Bless This House").

Overall, the revue was a harmless and generally mild look at Village life (although, at one point, a Village character says, "I'm Larry, I work in leather"), and in many respects the revue is a time capsule of life in 1960, with references to various topical benchmarks of the period (beatniks, cold water pads, espresso bars, Jack Kerouac, leotards, kooks, Metrical, folk singing, poetry readings, bongos, hi-fi sets, the Kennedys, and ... the cha-cha-cha).

Speaking of the Kennedys, for *Merrily We Roll Along* (1981), Stephen Sondheim wrote a parody of early Off Broadway revue material in the song "Bobby and Jackie and Jack," a song supposedly sung in an authentic 1960 Off Broadway revue called *Frankly Frank* (a revue no doubt similar to *Greenwich Village, U.S.A.*). The song, in part, mocks the cultural pretentiousness of Jacqueline Kennedy, who wants opera singer Galina Vishnevskaya to sing at the White House (Jackie notes that "just pronouncing her name is refreshing enough") and who wants to paint the White House cream. *Greenwich Village, U.S.A.*, which opened five weeks before the 1960 Presidential election, actually *did* spoof Jackie Kennedy's pretensions. In "Sunday Brunch," we're told if Kennedy is elected, Jackie will probably want to paint the White House black because it's such a chic color.

The score also included a catchy ballad in "How About Us Last Nite." In 1960, show music was still part of the nation's mainstream music, and so it's surprising this breezy, upbeat love song never met with any kind of popularity.

Incidentally, "Four Seasons" appears to have been dropped during the show's run (to be replaced by "Dining Out," performed by James Pompeii), although it's possible the number could have undergone a title change.

639 Greetings from Yorkville.

"A New Musical." THEATRE: Soho Playhouse; OPENING DATE: October 4, 2007; PERFORMANCES: 35; BOOK: Anya Turner; LYRICS: Anya Turner and Robert Grusecki; MUSIC: Robert Grusecki; DIRECTION: Thommie Walsh; SCENERY: Jesse Poleshuck; COSTUMES: Dona Granata; LIGHTING: Natasha Katz; MUSICAL DIRECTION: Robert Grusecki (Piano); PRODUCER: Who Knows Productions

CAST—Anya Turner (Anya), Robert Grusecki (Robert)

The action occurs in "the present, and everything leading up to it," and takes place in an apartment in the Yorkville section of Manhattan, in a television studio in New Jersey, in a Manhattan cabaret called Restaurant Row, and in a supper club in Peoria.

The musical was presented in two acts (all songs were performed by Anya Turner and Robert Grusecki).

ACT ONE—"Greetings from Yorkville," "Secret Song," "Ordinary People," "Robert's Song," "Showcases," "It's Called a Piano," "The Farmer and His Wife," "Showcases" (reprise), "So You're Not from New York," "What a Lovely Thing," "Destiny," "Clara Drum"

ACT TWO—"Musical Comedy Dream," "I Know You Too Well," "Not as I Was"/"All Out of Tune," "Happy," "Just Lucky I Guess," "The Road," "Hole-in-the-Head Blues," "Handle Me with Care," "Iowa Summer," "Greetings from Yorkville" (reprise), "Life Is Good"

NOTES—*Greetings from Yorkville* was a look at songwriters Anya Turner and Robert Grusecki and their show-business aspirations. The two live in the Yorkville section of Manhattan, and the revue dealt with their lives and songs. Anne Midgette in the *New York Times* said the evening was an essentially "glorified cabaret" act, but she quickly noted that the songs were "quite good" and that Turner and Grusecki were "genuinely likable." She also found Turner to be "a lovely singer with a clear, low voice tinged with a whiskeyish burr."

Incidentally, "The Farmer and His Wife" ("Greeny Sod") was a Sondheim spoof. The evening also included a medley of songs from Turner and Grusecki's proposed musical version of *Much Ado About Nothing.*

640 Grendel. THEATRE: New York State Theatre; OPENING DATE: July 11, 2006; PERFORMANCES: 4; LIBRETTO: Julie Taymor and J.D. McClatchy; MUSIC: Elliot Goldenthal; DIRECTION: Julie Taymor; CHOREOGRAPHY: Angelin Preljocaj; SCENERY: George Tyspin; COSTUMES: Constance Hoffman; MUSICAL DIRECTION: Steven Sloane

CAST—Eric Owens (Grendel), Denyce Graves (Dragon), Jay Hunter Morris (Beowulf), Richard Croft (The Shaper), Laura Claycomb (Wealtheow), Desmond Richardson (Beowulf [as dancer])

SOURCE—The 1971 novel *Grendel* by John Gardner.; PRODUCER: The Lincoln Center Festival

NOTES—Based on the Anglo-Saxon legend of the hero Beowulf who slayed the dragon Grendel, the opera, which was based on John Gardner's novel, told the story from the dragon's perspective.

The opera's world premiere occurred on May 27, 2006, with the Los Angeles Opera, and the New York premiere followed less than three months later as part of the tenth anniversary of the Lincoln Center Festival.

Even before its Los Angeles premiere, the opera made news because of a recalcitrant piece of scenery. A wall, weighing eighteen tons and reaching a height of forty-eight feet, refused to work, and the world premiere had to be postponed for a few days. But for the New York premiere, Anthony Tommasini's first words in his *New York Times*' review were, "The wall works!"

Tommasini reported the huge production employed twenty singers, a chorus of sixty, twenty dancers, and a large orchestra. But he found fault with the "convoluted and amorphous ... pretentious and hokey" work. He noted the confusing libretto ("loaded down with philosophical mumbo-jumbo"), the extravagant scenery, and "needlessly layered music" obscured the story. As for Elliott Goldenthal's score, he found some of it derivative and some of it "vocally punishing" for the performers; but he praised a few sequences, including a "razzle-dazzle jazz" passage and "a nifty episode of clanking percussion."

For another lyric version of the Beowulf legend, see entry for *Beowulf.*

641 Grey Gardens. THEATRE: Playwrights Horizons; OPENING DATE: March 7, 2006; PERFORMANCES: 63; BOOK: Doug Wright; LYRICS: Michael Korie; MUSIC: Scott Frankel; DIRECTION: Michael Greif; CHOREOGRAPHY: Jeff Calhoun; Jodi Moccia, Associate Choreographer; SCENERY: Allen Moyer; COSTUMES: William Ivey Long; LIGHTING: Peter Kaczorowski; MUSICAL DIRECTION: Lawrence Yurman; PRODUCER: Playwrights Horizons (Tim Sanford, Artistic Director; Leslie Marcus, Managing Director; William Russo, General Manager)

CAST—Mary Louise Wilson (Edith Bouvier Beale), Christine Ebersole ("Little" Edie Beale, Edith Bouvier Beale), Bob Stillman (George Gould Strong), Michael Potts (Brooks, Sr., Brooks, Jr.), Sarah Hyland (Jacqueline Bouvier), Audrey Twitchell (Lee Bouvier), Sara Gettelfinger ("Little" Edie Beale), Matt Cavenaugh (Joseph Patrick Kennedy, Jr., Jerry), John McMartin (J.V. "Major" Bouvier, Norman Vincent Peale)

SOURCE—The 1976 documentary film *Grey Gardens* (directed by David and Albert Maysles).

The action in the prologue and in act two occurs in 1973 at Grey Gardens, East Hampton, Long Island, New York; the action in act one occurs in July 1941 at Grey Gardens.

The musical was presented in two acts.

PROLOGUE—"Toyland" (Mary Louise Wilson)

ACT ONE—"The Five-Fifteen" (Christine Ebersole, Bob Stillman, Michael Potts, Sarah Hyland, Audrey Twitchell), "Body Beautiful Beale" (Bob Stillman, Christine Ebersole, Michael Potts, Sara Gettelfinger, Sarah Hyland, Audrey Twitchell, Matt Cavenaugh), "Mother, Darling" (Sara Gettelfinger, Christine Ebersole, Bob Stillman), "Better Fall Out of Love" (Matt Cavenaugh, Sara Gettelfinger), "Being Bouvier" (John McMartin, Michael Potts, Sarah Hyland, Audrey Twitchell, Sara Gettelfinger), "Hominy Grits" (Christine Ebersole, Bob Stillman, Sarah Hyland, Audrey Twitchell), "Peas in a Pod" (Sara Gettelfinger, Christine Ebersole), "Drift Away" (Bob Stillman, Christine Ebersole), "The Five-Fifteen" (reprise) (Christine Ebersole), "Tomorrow's Woman" (Sara Gettelfinger, Sarah Hyland, Audrey Twitchell), "Daddy's Girl" (Sara Gettelfinger), "The Telegram" (Sara Gettelfinger, Christine Ebersole), "Being Bouvier" (reprise) (John McMartin, Sarah Hyland, Audrey Twitchell), "Will You?" (Christine Ebersole)

ACT TWO—"The Revolutionary Costume for Today" (Christine Ebersole), "The Cake I Had" (Mary Louise Wilson), "Entering Gray Gardens" (Company), "The House We Live In" (Christine Ebersole, Company), "Jerry Likes My Corn" (Mary Louise Wilson, Christine Ebersole), "Around the World" (Christine Ebersole), "Will You?" (reprise) (Mary Louise Wilson, Christine Ebersole), "Choose to Be Happy" (John McMartin, Company), "Around the World" (reprise) (Christine Ebersole), "Another Winter in a Summer Town" (Christine Ebersole, Mary Louise Wilson), "Peas in a Pod" (reprise) (Mary Louise Wilson, Christine Ebersole)

NOTES—Based on David and Albert Maysles' cult classic 1976 documentary film of the same name, *Grey Gardens* examined the lives of Jacqueline Kennedy's aunt, Edith Bouvier Beale, and her cousin, "Little" Edie Beale, both of whom were discovered living in squalor in their decaying 28-room mansion in East Hampton during the 1970s. In his *2007 Movie Guide*, Leonard Maltin noted the film would have been better served if some perspective had been given to the earlier lives of the two women. The musical did just that. While its second act took place during the period depicted in the film, the first act showed their lives in the 1940s, a period of glamour, money, and even the promise of Little Edie marrying Joseph Kennedy, Jr. (In the first act, Christine Ebersole played the role of Edith Bouvier Beale, and the role of young "Little" Edie was played by Sara Gettelfinger; in the second act, Mary Louise Wilson was Edith Bouvier Beale, and Ebersole was "Little" Edie.)

The musical was a sensation Off Broadway, and Ben Brantley in the *New York Times* pronounced Ebersole's performance as "one of the most gorgeous ever to grace a musical." He found her a "pearl of incalculable price" in a musical which "is, at best, costume jewelry." Despite his reservations about the musical itself, the show's buzz virtually guaranteed a transfer to Broadway, which occurred on November 2, 2006, when the musical opened at the Walter Kerr Theatre. But *Grey Gardens* never quite connected with mainstream audiences, and so the show closed after a disappointing 307 performances with a reported loss of five million dollars.

The score was attractive, and perhaps its outstanding song was the affecting "Another Winter in a Summer Town."

For the Broadway version, five numbers were deleted ("Toyland," "Body Beautiful Beale," "Better Fall Out of Love," "Tomorrow's Woman," and "Being Bouvier"), and three were added ("The Girl Who Has Everything," "Goin' Places," and "Marry Well"). The Off Broadway cast recording which was released in 2006 on PS Classics Records (CD # PS-642) included the five eventually-deleted numbers, and in an unusual move, the label withdrew the recording from its catalogue upon its release of the Broadway cast album (also CD # PS-642) in 2007. The new recording included the three new numbers; a new ending sequence; a previously unrecorded song ("The Telegram"); and newly recorded versions of other songs in the score (such as "Mother, Darling," "Peas in a Pod," and "Daddy's Girl"). The CD cover of the new recording reflected the Broadway artwork ("Little" Edie with mirror) rather than the Off Broadway artwork which was used for the Off Broadway playbill and recording (the ravaged stone cupid and "Little" Edie in furs). To hear the "complete" score of *Grey Gardens*, one must have both albums.

For their performances in the musical, Christine Ebersole and Mary Louise Wilson won the respective 2007 Tony Awards for Best Actress in a Musical and Best Featured Actress in a Musical. William Ivey Long also won, for Best Costume Design for a Musical. Of the twenty-four Tony Awards given in 2007, eleven were given to two musicals which had originated Off Broadway (three to *Grey Gardens* and eight to *Spring Awakening* [see entry]).

The script was published by Applause Theatre & Cinema Books in 2007, and an acting edition was published by Dramatists Play Service, Inc., in 2008.

In 2007, *Grey Gardens: from East Hampton to Broadway*, Albert Maysles' documentary film about the making of the musical, was released.

642 Groucho: A Life in Revue. THEATRE: Lucille Lortel Theatre; OPENING DATE: October 8, 1986; PERFORMANCES: 254; TEXT: Arthur Marx and Robert Fisher; DIRECTION: Arthur Marx; David Storey, Assistant Director; SCENERY: Michael Hotopp; COSTUMES: Baker Smith; LIGHTING: Richard Winkler; MUSICAL DIRECTION: Brian Hurley; PRODUCERS: Louis C. Blau, with Dennis D. Hennessy, Stockton Briggle and Richard Carrothers; John Wilner, Executive Producer; Nancy and Ronnie Horowitz, Co-Producers; Helen Henderson and Howard Pechet, Associate Producers

CAST—Frank Ferrante (Groucho Marx), Les Marsden (Chico Marx, Harpo Marx), Faith Prince (The Girls), Rusty Magee (Deckhand)

The revue was presented in two acts (*The Early Years* and *The Later Years*).

NOTES—*Groucho: A Life in Revue* took place in the memory of Groucho Marx (1890-1977), and offered episodes from his life and career as well as various jokes and songs associated with him, including "Hooray for Captain Spaulding" (*Animal Crackers*, lyric by Bert Kalmar, music by Harry Ruby; stage, 1928; film, 1930) and "Lydia, The Tattooed Lady" (1939 film *At the Circus*; lyric by E.Y. Harburg, music by Harold Arlen). Arthur Marx, the director and co-author, was Groucho's son. With Robert Fisher, the revue's co-author, Arthur Marx had written the long-running 1965 Broadway comedy *The Impossible Years.*

Groucho: A Life in Revue was recorded by Original Cast Records (CD # OCR-9498), and the script was published by Samuel French, Inc., in 1988. The revue opened in London on September 16, 1987, at the Comedy Theatre (Frank Ferrante reprised his role of Groucho).

Minnie's Boys, a musical about Groucho Marx, his brothers, and his mother, opened on Broadway in 1970.

643 Groundhog. THEATRE: Manhattan Theatre Club/Stage II; OPENING DATE: April 14, 1992; PERFORMANCES: 40; LYRICS: Elizabeth Swados; MUSIC: Elizabeth Swados; DIRECTION: Elizabeth Swados; SCENERY: G.W. Mercier; COSTUMES: G.W. Mercier; LIGHTING: Natasha Katz; MUSICAL DIRECTION: Ann Marie Milazzo; PRODUCER: Manhattan Theatre Club (Lynne Meadow, Artistic Director; Barry Grove, Managing Director)

CAST—Stephen Lee Anderson (Dr. R.T. Ebney, Others), Anne Bobby (Gila), Bill Buell (Judge Alex

T. Waldman, Others), Gilles Chiasson (Zoe, Others), Nora Cole (Georgette Bergen), Ula Hedwig (D.A. Randall), Ann Marie Milazzo (Weatherperson, Others), Lauren Mufson (Sandy, Others), Daniel Neiden (Mayor of New York, Others), Suzan Postel (Lauree, Others), David Schechter (Fez, Others), Tony Scheitinger (Fez, Others), Michael Sottile (Danilo Chelnik)

The action occurs in New York City during the mid-1980s.

The musical was presented in two acts.

ACT ONE—"Weather Report # 1" (Meteorologists), "Cooper Square" (David Schechter, Street People), "Project Heal" (Daniel Neiden, Company), "One More Day" (David Schechter, Company), "Willard Scott" (David Schechter, Anne Bobby), "Abduction" (Company), "Weather Report # 2" (Ann Marie Milazzo), "Street People" (Anne Bobby, Street People), "Groundhog Is Going to Trial" (Street People), "My Movie of the Week" (Bill Buell, Company), "Who Will It Be?" (Anne Bobby), "Flight to Health" (Street People), "Bellevue and the Judge" (Ula Hedwig, Nora Cole), "Testimony" ('Dr. Chang,' 'Dr. Schloss' [performers unknown]), "Experts" (David Schechter, Company), "This Isn't How I Imagined a Trial to Be" (David Schechter, Company), "Just Trust Me" (Anne Bobby, David Schechter), "Yes/No" (Anne Bobby, David Schechter), "Flight to Health" (reprise) (Street People), "Doctor's Canon" ('Dr. Davidkoff,' 'Jakes' [performers unknown], Anne Bobby, 'Green' [performer unknown]), "Bill and Willa" ('Bill Dajurian,' 'Willa Dajurian' [performers unknown]), "Danilo's Rap" (Michael Sottile), "Sweet Bitter Candy" (David Schechter, Anne Bobby, Company)

ACT TWO—"Hey Groundhog" (David Schechter, Company), "Why Did I Forget?" (Anne Bobby, David Schechter, Company), "Ten Year Blues" (David Schechter), "Harmonica Man" (David Schechter), "Weather Report # 3" (Stephen Lee Anderson, Suzan Postel), "If I Am Released" (David Schechter, Company), "Closing Arguments" (Nora Cole, Ula Hedwig, David Schechter), "The Judge's Decision" (Bill Buell, Company), "Battle Hymn of Groundhog" (David Schechter, Company), "Groundhog Has Won" (Street People), "Lawyer's Lament" (Ula Hedwig, Nora Cole, Company), "Open the Door" (Anne Bobby, Company), "Groundhog Is Becoming Important" (Street People), "Hearing Voices" (Company), "Pay Phone" (Anne Bobby, David Schechter, Company), "Hearing Voices" (reprise) (Company), "ACLU" (David Schechter, Company), "Rewrite Your Own Story" (Company), "Hymn to Spring" (David Schechter, Company), "Weather Report # 4" (Ann Marie Milazzo, Lauren Mufson, Suzan Postel), "What Could I Have Done?" (Anne Bobby), "Someone Is Discovering Something" (David Schechter, Anne Bobby, Company)

NOTES—Jeffrey Sweet in *The Applause/Best Plays Theatre Yearbook of 1991-1992* found Elizabeth Swados' *Groundhog* the "most daring" musical of the season; while he couldn't "pretend to have ever been a fan of Swados' song writing," he nonetheless praised the "provocative" musical, which told the touching story of a mentally-troubled homeless man (Groundhog, the title character) and his sister. Sweet reported the musical was inspired by Swados' own relationship with her brother, who ultimately died "after a life on the streets."

Jeffrey regretted that much of the evening dealt with show business when Groundhog becomes something of a celebrity when his legal issues attract the attention of the media.

Mel Gussow in the *New York Times* noted that Swados had made an "ambitious attempt at writing a musical play of Brechtian proportions," and while he didn't feel the evening was completely successful, he felt the musical's weaknesses could be easily corrected (such as shortening the musical and also avoiding a certain "tendentious" in the second act). Gussow found the score "highly eclectic," and while he noted it perhaps wasn't as melodic as some of Swados' other musicals, he said it had a "definite New York beat." *Groundhog* sounds intriguing, and it seems to be a worthy candidate for revival either Off Broadway or in regional and college theatre; further, one wishes the ambitious-sounding work had been recorded. *Groundhog* may well be the most personal and heartfelt musical written by Swados, and one hopes she will someday revisit the material.

644 Gunmetal Blues.

"A New Musical Mystery." THEATRE: Theatre Off Park; OPENING DATE: April 2 (or 4, depending on source), 1992; PERFORMANCES: 45; BOOK: Scott Wentworth; LYRICS: Craig Bohmler and Marion Adler; MUSIC: Craig Bohmler and Marion Adler; DIRECTION: Davis Hall; Patricia L. Page, Co-Musical Staging; SCENERY: Eduardo Sicangco; COSTUMES: Eduardo Sicangco; LIGHTING: Scott Zielinski; MUSICAL DIRECTION: Craig Bohmler; PRODUCER: AMAS Musical Theatre, Inc. (Rosetta LeNoire, Founder and Artistic Director; William Michael Maher, Producing Director)

CAST—Daniel Marcus (The Piano Player [Buddy Toupee in the published script]), Michael Knowles (The Barkeep), Marion Adler (The Blondes [Laura Vesper, Princess, Carol Indigo, Jenny), Scott Wentworth (The Private Eye [Sam Galahad])

The action occurs in the late 1940s or early 1950s in the Red Eye Lounge ("one of those bars at one of those hotels out by the airport") and the time is "pretty late."

The musical was presented in two acts.

ACT ONE—"Welcome to This Window" (Daniel Marcus), "Don't Know What I Expected" (Daniel Marcus, Scott Wentworth, Marion Adler), "Facts!" (Scott Wentworth), "The Well-to-Do Waltz" (performer[s] unknown), "Spare Some Change" ("Loose Change" in script) (Marion Adler), "Mansion Hill" (Scott Wentworth, Daniel Marcus), "Shadowplay" (Daniel Marcus, Scott Wentworth), "Skeletons" (Marion Adler), "The Blonde Song" (Marion Adler), "Childhood Days" (Daniel Marcus, Scott Wentworth, Marion Adler), "Take a Break" (Daniel Marcus)

ACT TWO—"Not Available in Stores!" ("Buddy Toupee—Live" in the script) (Daniel Marcus), "Gunmetal Blues" (Scott Wentworth), "I'm the One That Got Away" (Marion Adler), "Jenny" (Scott Wentworth), "Don't Know What I Expected" (reprise) (Daniel Marcus, Scott Wentworth, Marion Adler), "Put It on the (My) Tab" (Marion Adler), "The Virtuoso" (Daniel Marcus), Finale (Daniel Marcus, Scott Wentworth, Marion Adler)

NOTES—*Gunmetal Blues* was an Off Off Broadway musical mystery spoof of the hardboiled detective story/movie genre, and it came with an amusing surprise ending (the program respectfully requested audience members to not reveal the ending!). The script reads well, and it's a shame the musical never found its audience.

Stephen Holden in the *New York Times* said the evening was"diverting," and noted the score was "musically more sophisticated" than other film noir send-ups such as *City of Angels* (1989). He said the "torchy, swiveling melodies echo the moody grandeur of 40's film-noir soundtracks" (Holden's comments make one regret the score was never recorded).

The musical premiered on May 30, 1991, at the Phoenix Little Theatre, in association with the Musical Theatre of Arizona; its first professional production took place at Theater New Brunswick.

The script was published by Samuel French, Inc., in 1993 ("The Well-to-Do Waltz" wasn't included in the script; another number, "In the Penthouse," was included in the script but wasn't listed in the program). "The Blonde Song" was included in Alison Fraser's collection *A New York Romance* (Original Cast Records CD # OC-9534).

645 Gutenberg! The Musical!

THEATRE: Actors' Playhouse; OPENING DATE: January 21, 2007; PERFORMANCES: 126; BOOK, LYRICS, AND MUSIC: Scott Brown and Anthony King; DIRECTION: Alex Timbers; COSTUMES: Emily Rebholz; LIGHTING: Tyler Micoleau; MUSICAL DIRECTION: T.O. Sterrett; PRODUCERS: Trevor Brown, Ron Kastner, Terry Allen Kramer, and Joseph Smith in association with Upright Citizens Brigade Theatre

CAST—Christopher Fitzgerald (Bud Davenport), Jeremy Shamos (Doug Simon)

The musical was presented in two acts (songs were not listed in the program).

NOTES—*Gutenberg! The Musical!* was a freewheeling spoof in which two writers, Bud and Doug, perform a backers' audition for their new musical about Johann Gutenberg, the inventor of the printing press. Jason Zinoman's tongue-in-cheek review in the *New York Times* was in the form of a letter to Bud and Doug, telling them their musical was a "smashing success," and while their incorporation of the Holocaust into the plot "might not be historically accurate, I agree with Doug that it gave the show real gravitas." He also singled out Bud's first act finale, "Tomorrow Is Tonight" ("one monster of a rock ballad").

The musical had first been developed by the Upright Citizens Brigade Theatre in 2003, and an excerpt was seen at the 2005 New York Musical Theatre Festival. The world premiere took place in London in January 2006 at the Jermyn Street Theatre, and the American premiere took place at the 2006 New York Musical Theatre Festival; before transferring to Off Broadway, the musical played Off Off Broadway for six weeks at the 59E59 Theatres beginning on November 21, 2006. The script was published by Samuel French, Inc., in 2008, and the cast album is scheduled for release by PS Classics Records.

646 Haarlem Nocturne.

THEATRE: Latin Quarter; OPENING DATE: November 18, 1984; PERFORMANCES: 49; TEXT: Andre De Shields and Murray Horwitz; LYRICS: See song list for credits; MUSIC: See song list for credits; DIRECTION: Andre De Shields and Murray Horwitz; SCENERY: David Chapman; COSTUMES: Jean-Claude Robin; LIGHTING: Marc B. Weiss; MUSICAL DIRECTION: Marc Shaiman; PRODUCERS: Barry and Fran Weissler; Alecia Parker, Associate Producer

CAST—ANDRE DE SHIELDS, Debra Byrd, Ellia English, Marc Shaiman, Freida Williams

The revue was presented in one act.

MUSICAL NUMBERS—"Love in the Morning" (lyric and music by Steven Lemberg) (Andre De Shields, Ladies), "Wishful Thinking" (lyric and music by Kenny Moore, Marti McCall, and Zedrick Turnbough) (Andre De Shields, Ladies), "New York Is a Party" (lyric by Robert I, music by Marc Shaiman) (Andre De Shields, Ladies) "Jungle Hip Hop" (lyric and music by Andre De Shields) (Andre De Shields, Ladies), "Sweet Dreams (Are Made of This)" (lyric by D.A. Stewart, music by Annie Lennox) (Ladies), "What Becomes of the Broken Hearted" (lyric and music by W. Witherspoon, P. Riser, and J. Dean) (Andre De Shields, Ladies), "Love's Sad Glance" (lyric by Ula Hedwig, music by Marc Shaiman) (Ladies), "Secret Love" (lyric by Alex Brown, music by Kenny Moore) (Debra Byrd, Ladies), "Say It Again" (lyric and music by Denis Andreopoulos) (Freida Williams, Ladies), "Heads or Tails" (lyric and music by Denis Andreopoulos) (Andre De Shields, Ladies), "Hit the Road, Jack" (lyric and music by Percy Mayfield) (Ellia English,

Andre De Shields, Ladies), "Waterfaucet Blues" (traditional blues adapted by Micki Grant) (Ellia English), Streetcorner Symphony: "Release Yourself" (lyrics by Larry Graham, composer unknown) (Andre De Shields, Ladies), "Bad Boy" (lyric and music by Lil Armstrong) (Andre De Shields, Ladies), "Symphony Rap" (lyric and music by Andre De Shields) (Andre De Shields, Ladies), "Mary Mack" (traditional children's song) (Andre De Shields, Freida Williams, Ladies), Pastiche (sung by the Ladies; this sequence included songs [specific titles not listed in the program] by the following lyricists and composers: Alan Bergman, Marvin Hamlisch, Marilyn Keith, Eddie Holland, Brian Holland, Lamont Dozier, Jeff Barry, Ellie Greenwich, Phil Spector, Rudy Clark, Cynthia Weil, Barry Mann, Bob Feldman, Gerald Goldstein, Richard Gottehrer, George Morton, Gene Pitney, Tony Powers, Carole King, Gerald Coffin, Florence Green, Luther Dixon, Burt Bacharach, Hal David, Ronald Mack, George Harrison, Robert Bateman, Freddie Gorman, Burt Russell, Thomas Elliot, Andrew Lloyd Webber, Trevor Nunn), "Sermon" (lyric and music by Murray Horwitz and Andre De Shields) (Andre De Shields), "Haarlem Nocturne" (lyric by Dick Rogers, music by Earl Hagen) (Ladies), "Louie" (lyric and music by Marc Shaiman) (Andre De Shields, Marc Shaiman, Ladies), "B.Y.O.B." (lyric and music by Andre De Shields) (Andre De Shields, Ladies), "Now Is the Time" (lyric and music by Andre De Shields) (Andre De Shields, Ladies)

NOTES—*Haarlem Nocturne*, which seems to have been produced under a Middle or Limited Broadway contract, was yet another in a long cycle of revues which celebrated Harlem nightlife.

The short-running revue is notable for a few songs by Marc Shaiman, who later was the composer and co-lyricist of the long-running Broadway musical *Hairspray* (2003). Shaiman was also the revue's musical director and pianist, and as a warm-up for the evening he played a medley of theme songs from old television shows. *The Christian Science Monitor* found Shaiman "indispensable," and Clive Barnes in the *New York Post* noted he resembled "a pixie-like Liberace without the chandelier" (but didn't Liberace perform with candelabra?). Shaiman's "New York Is a Party" had been earlier heard in his 1983 musical *Dementos* (see entry). The revue had previously been produced at La Mama E.T.C. by special arrangement with Black Goat Entertainment.

The revue opened at the newly restored and newly re-named Latin Quarter; the venue had originally been the site of the fabled Latin Quarter nightclub, but in later years had been known as the 22 Steps and the Princess Theatre.

647 The Haggadah (1980).

"A Passover Cantata." THEATRE: LuEsther Hall/The Public Theatre; OPENING DATE: March 31, 1980; PERFORMANCES: 64; WORDS: Elizabeth Swados (narration adapted from texts by Elie Wiesel); MUSIC: Elizabeth Swados; DIRECTION: Elizabeth Swados; SCENERY: Julie Taymor; COSTUMES, MASKS, PUPPETRY: Julie Taymor; LIGHTING: Arden Fingerhut; MUSICAL DIRECTION: Unknown; PRODUCER: The New York Shakespeare Festival (Joseph Papp, Director)

CAST—Roger Babb, Suzanne Baxtresser, Shami Chaikin, Craig Chang, Victor Cook, Keith David, John B. Farrell, Patrick Jude, Alisha Kahlil, Esther Levy, John S. Lewandowski, Martha Plimpton, Martin Robinson, David Schechter, Kate Schmitt, Zvee Scooler, Ira Siff, Kerry Stubbs, Deborah Anne Wise

SOURCES—"Moses: Portrait of a Leader" from *Messengers of God: Biblical Portraits and Legends* by Elie Wiesel; portions of the *Haggadah*; the Old Testament; and poetry of Gabriela Mistral, Kadia Molodowsky, and Elie Wiesel (all Elie Wiesel material translated by Marian Wiesel).

The revue was presented in one act.

MUSICAL NUMBERS—"The Four Questions" (Craig Chang, Martha Plimpton), "Prelude" (Zvee Scooler), "Pesach Has Come to the Ghetto" (Suzanne Baxtresser), "The Narration" (Suzanne Baxtresser, Patrick Jude, Shami Chaikin, David Schechter, Company), "Slave Chant" (Esther Levy, Zvee Scooler, Company), "God Faithful" (Shami Chaikin), "By the Waters of Babylon" (Keith David, Patrick Jude, Company), Narration (Alisha Kahlil, Craig Chang, Company), "Shepherd Song" (Company), "The Burning Bush" (Company, Keith David, Martin Robinson, Craig Chang), Narration (Suzanne Baxtresser, Company), "Pharoah's Chant"—"Sorcerer's Dance" (Martin Robinson, Craig Chang, Roger Babb, Alisha Kahlil, John B. Farrell, John S. Lewandowski, Company), "Why Hast Thou Done Evil to These People?" (Alisha Kahlil, Shami Chaikin, Company), "The Plagues" (Company), "Death of the Firstborn" (Zvee Scooler, Martha Plimpton, Craig Chang, Roger Babb, John S. Lewandowski, Company), "Look at the Children" (Shami Chaikin), "We Are All Dead Men" (Ira Siff), "The Puppet Rebbe" (Kate Schmidt, Ira Siff, John B. Farrell, Suzanne Baxtresser, Deborah Anne Wise, David Schechter, Roger Babb, Patrick Jude), Narration (Company), "Dayenu Chant" (Esther Levy, Company), "Crossing the Red Sea" (Company), "Who Is Like Unto Thee" (Alisha Kahlil, Company), Narration (Company), "Three Midrash" (Roger Babb, Suzanne Baxtresser, David Schechter), "Country That Is Missing" (Company), "A Midrash" (Suzanne Baxtresser), "The Golden Calf" (Keith David, Alisha Kahlil, David Schechter, Roger Babb, Company), "God of Mercy" (Keith David, Patrick Jude, Suzanne Baxtresser), "Ten Commandments" (Zvee Scooler, Company), Narration (Suzanne Baxtresser, Craig Chang, Martha Plimpton, Victor Cook, Kerry Stubbs, Company), "Hebrew Benediction" (Ira Siff, Company), "The Death of Moses" (Craig Chang, Shami Chaikin, Company), "A Blessing" (Shami Chaikin, Company), "Elijah" (Zvee Scooler, Shami Chaikin, Esther Levy), "Song of Songs" (Victor Cook, Kerry Stubbs, Martha Plimpton, Craig Chang)

NOTES—The program notes explained that the text for the seder (a family religious service which takes place around a dinner table) is based upon the *Haggadah*, a text with prayers, songs, and discussion which occur during the service. A number of versions of the *Haggadah* exist, some in the traditional Hebrew and others of an ecumenical bent, which actually incorporate poetry and songs of other cultures.

The Haggadah returned to the Public a year later for another limited run (see entry).

The Haggadah marked the first major New York appearance of Julie Taymor, who created the musical's scenery, costumes, masks, and puppets. In 1996, she created the wondrous designs for one of the biggest hits in Broadway history, *The Lion King*; her creative genius was the only memorable aspect of an evening otherwise lacking in strong book, lyrics, and music. In 1994, she created fascinating designs for the interesting and rather touching *Juan Darien*; in 1999, her Broadway venture *The Green Bird* was a short-running (and expensive) failure; and in 2006 she directed the opera *Grendel*, which was seen at the Met (see entries for these productions). One hopes Taymor's next Broadway musical will have a book and score which matches her scenic and directorial talents. The script of *The Haggadah* was published by Samuel French, Inc., in 1982.

648 The Haggadah (1981).

"A Passover Cantata." THEATRE: LuEsther Hall/The Public Theatre; OPENING DATE: April 14, 1981; PERFORMANCES: 72; WORDS: Elizabeth Swados (narration adapted from texts by Elie Wiesel); MUSIC: Elizabeth Swados; DIRECTION: Elizabeth Swados; SCENERY: Julie Taymor Costumes, Masks, Puppetry: Julie Taymor; LIGHTING: Arden Fingerhut; PRODUCER: The New York Shakespeare Festival (Joseph Papp, Director)

CAST—Richard Allen, Anthony B. Asbury, Shami Chaikin, Craig Chang, Victor Cook, Sheila Dabney, Jossie de Guzman, Michael Edward-Stevens, Onni Johnson, Sally Kate, Esther Levy, Larry Marshall, Steven Memel, Martin Robinson, David Schechter, Peter Schlosser, Zvee Scooler, Ira Siff, Louise Smith, Kerry Stubbs

NOTES—For more information about *The Haggadah*, see entry for the original 1980 production. For the return engagement, there was one change in the musical numbers. The song "Country That Is Missing" from the 1980 production was dropped, and a new song was substituted ("Song of Waiting," sung by Larry Marshall and Company).

649 Hair (October 1967).

THEATRE: Anspacher Theatre/The Public Theatre; OPENING DATE: October 29, 1967; PERFORMANCES: 49; BOOK: Gerome Ragni and James Rado; LYRICS: Gerome Ragni and James Rado; MUSIC: Galt MacDermot; DIRECTION: Gerald Freedman; SCENERY: Ming Cho Lee; COSTUMES: Theoni V. Aldredge; LIGHTING: Martin Aronstein; MUSICAL DIRECTION: John Morris; PRODUCER: Joseph Papp (New York Shakespeare Festival, The Public Theatre)

CAST—Jonelle Allen (Dionne), Ed Crowley ("Dad"), Walker Daniels (Claude), Steve Dean (Woof), Sally Eaton (Jeannie), Marijane Maricle ("Mom"), Jill O'Hara (Sheila), Shelley Plimpton (Crissy), Gerome Ragni (Berger), Arnold Wilkerson (Hud), Susan Batson (Susan), Linda Compton (Linda), Suzannah Evans (Suzannah), Lynda Gudde (Lynda), Jane Levin (Louise), Alma Robinson (Alma), Warren Burton (Charlie), Thommie Bush (Thommie), William Herter (Bill), Paul Jabara (Paul), Bob Johnson (Bob), Edward Murphy, Jr. (Jim)

The action occurs at the present time in New York City, mostly in the East Village.

The musical was presented in two acts.

ACT ONE—"Red, Blue, and White" (Marijane Maricle, Ed Crowley), "Ain't Got No" (Walker Daniels, Gerome Ragni, Steve Dean, Arnold Wilkerson, Company), "I Got Life" (Walker Daniels, Marijane Maricle), "Air" (Sally Eaton, Shelley Plimpton, Jonelle Allen), "Going Down" (Gerome Ragni, Company), "Hair" (Walker Daniels, Gerome Ragni, Company), "Dead End" (Jill O'Hara, Company), "Frank Mills" (Shelley Plimpton), "Where Do I Go" (Walker Daniel, Company)

ACT TWO—"Electric Blues" (Suzannah Evans, Linda Compton, Paul Jabara), "Easy to Be Hard" (Suzannah Evans, Linda Compton, Paul Jabara, Company), "Manchester" (Walker Daniels), "White Boys" (Jonelle Allen, Susan Batson, Alma Robinson), "Black Boys" (Linda Compton, Shelley Plimpton, Suzannah Evans), "Walking in Space" (Company), "Aquarius" (Company), "Good Morning Starshine" (Jill O'Hara, Company), "Exanaplanetooch" (Walker Daniels, Jill O'Hara) "The Climax" (Jill O'Hara)

NOTES—*Hair* was an immediate sensation, and after its initial production at the Public Theatre it quickly moved uptown to another Off Broadway theater, the Cheetah (see entry). On April 29, 1968, a slightly revised version opened on Broadway at the Biltmore Theatre for a run of 1,750 performances. The London production, which opened at the Shaftesbury Theatre on September 27, 1968, ran even longer, for 1,998 performances.

Hair told the story of counter-culture types who protest war, mock traditional American values, take drugs, indulge in casual sex, and, in general, stand for everything that loses you votes in the Red States. Like its almost-counterpart *Rent* (1996; see entry), the piece was dated almost as soon as it opened, but the combination of hit songs (*Hair* was probably the last musical to get major radio play), the frisson of its anti-establishment stance, its vulgarity, and, on Broadway, its gratuitous nude scene, all helped to catapult *Hair* into the zeitgeist. The musical's greatest strength was Galt MacDermot's melodic score. Without his music, *Hair* would no doubt have gone the way of *Salvation* [1969], *Touch* [1970], *Soon* [1971], and other forgotten rock musicals.

RCA Victor Records released both the Off Broadway (LP # LSO-1143) and Broadway (LP # LSO-1150) cast albums, and a later LP reissue (# 1150-1-RC) included previously unreleased material ("Going Down" and "Electric Blues"). Further, the 1988 CD release of the Broadway cast album included five previously unreleased songs ("I Believe in Love," "Ain't Got No" [reprise], "Manchester England" [reprise], "Walking in Space" [reprise], and "The Bed"), and in 2003 RCA released a "deluxe" 2-CD edition of the score (# 82876-56085-2), which included both the Off Broadway and Broadway cast albums; the set included all previously released tracks as well as three previously unreleased tracks from the 1967 production (an "Opening" sequence, "Red Blue and White" [which became "Don't Put It Down" for the Broadway version], and "Sentimental Ending" [a finale which wasn't listed in the Off Broadway production's program]). Besides the above, RCA Victor released *DisinHAIRited* (LP # LSO-1163; later issued on CD by RCA Records/Arkiv Music CD # 05095), a collection of songs written or projected for the Off Broadway and Broadway productions as well as songs written especially for the recording; among the singers on the album were James Rado, Gerome Ragni, Galt MacDermot, Melba Moore, Susanna Norstrand, Donnie Burks, and Leata Galloway; the songs included "One-Thousand-Year-Old Man," "So Sing the Children on the Avenue," "Manhattan Beggar," "Mr. Berger," "I'm Hung," and "Mess O'Dirt." Other recordings include: a British studio cast recording (Polydor Records LP # 583-043); the French cast album (Philips Records LP # 844-987-BY); the Japanese cast album (RCA Victor Records LP # LSO-1170); and a 2004 concert version (a benefit recording for the Actors' Fund of America) released by Ghostlight Records (CD # 1968-2). There was also a recording of the songs called *Hair Styles* by the Terminal Barbershop (Atco Records LP # SD-33-301).

The script was published by Pocket Books in 1969, and was also included in the collection *Great Rock Musicals*, edited by Stanley Richards and published by Stein and Day in 1979.

But except for MacDermot's music, *Hair* had little staying power. Its 1977 Broadway revival closed within weeks, and the 1979 film version released by United Artists was weak (the 2-LP soundtrack album was issued by RCA Victor Records # CBL2-3274). The work quickly became a period piece, and, because of its weak book, its cardboard characters, and its generally repetitious lyrics (unimaginative lyrics were the bane of the rock musical), the work is more likely to be remembered for its then-shocking nudity and for being a "rock musical." (On September 22, 2007, the musical was revived briefly for three special concert performances, which were presented free at the Delacorte Theatre; the production was directed by Diane Paulus, and in 2009 transferred to Broadway in a hit production which won the Tony Award for Best Musical Revival (the cast album was released by Ghostlight Records CD # 8-4467.) *Hair: Let the Sunshine In*, a documentary film about the iconic musical, was released in 2009.

But *Hair* actually has an important place in the history of the musical: it was the first successful concept musical. While there had been concept musicals before (such as the 1948 Broadway musical *Love Life*), with *Hair* the concept musical took on new life and paved the way for *Company* (1970), *Follies* (1971), *Mass* (1971; see entry), *A Chorus Line* (1975; see entry), and *Pacific Overtures* (1976; see entry for 1984 Off Broadway revival).

With the concept musical, the story and characters were subjugated to the mood, atmosphere, and overall point of view of the particular production (the vaguely unhappy singles and married couples seeking *Company* in modern Manhattan; the loss of youth and ideals in *Follies*; a priest's loss of faith while celebrating *Mass*). All forces (book, lyrics, music, direction, choreography, visual design, and performances) were fashioned into a narrative which usually embraced a generally abstract point of view which didn't necessarily wrap up the plot with a neat, clear-cut ending.

650 Hair (December 1967). "The American Tribal Love-Rock Musical." THEATRE: Cheetah Theatre; OPENING DATE: December 22, 1967; PERFORMANCES: 45

NOTES—With its transfer to the Cheetah Theatre, *Hair* played an additional few weeks Off Broadway before opening on Broadway at the Biltmore Theatre on April 29, 1968.

The Off Broadway cast album was released by RCA Victor, and when the musical opened on Broadway, it was recorded again by RCA. These two recordings were followed by a number of cast and studio albums (see entry for the Anspacher production for more information). *Hair* was probably the most recorded musical since *My Fair Lady* (1956) and *Fiddler on the Roof* (1964).

For the Cheetah engagement, the musical was presented in one act, and Frank Metzler replaced Martin Aronstein as the show's lighting designer. There were various cast member changes: Steve Curry replaced co-writer Gerome Ragni (Berger); Susan Anspach replaced Jill O'Hara (Sheila); and Gale Dixon replaced Shelley Plimpton (Crissy).

When the show opened on Broadway, it was again performed in two acts. Tom O'Horgan was now the director; Robin Wagner the scenic designer; Nancy Potts designed the costumes; and Jules Fisher was the show's (third) lighting designer. Julie Arenal was credited with the choreography.

For Broadway, Ragni was back in his original role of Berger, and Shelley Plimpton returned as Crissy; Walker Daniels was replaced by co-writer James Rado (Claude); Lynn Kellogg replaced Susan Anspach (Sheila); and Diane Keaton and Melba Moore had joined the cast.

Fifteen new songs were added for Broadway: "Donna," "Hashish," "Sodomy," "Colored Spade," "I Believe in Love," "Initials," "My Conviction," "Hung," "Don't Put It Down," "Hare Krishna," "Abie Baby," "Prisoners in Niggertown," "What a Piece of Work Is Man," "The Bed," and "The Flesh Failures." Four songs from the Off-Broadway production were dropped ("Red, Blue and White," "Dead End," "Exanaplanetooch," and "Climax"). "Aquarius," the score's most enduring song, was moved from its original late-second-act spot to become the musical's opening number.

The critics generally fell over themselves with rave (and perhaps unconsciously condescending) reviews. One writer gushed over the musical's depiction of hippie joy and anger (as though only hippies experienced such emotions); and for some critics the show's emphasis on non-conformity was an automatic plus (as if non-conformity was a badge of honor). But it was the show's narrow point of view, its more-sensitive-than-thou sanctimoniousness, which eventually did it in, relegating it to being little more than a time-capsule of a superficial, self-congratulatory lifestyle, of a period when restraint and good taste became shibboleths. What is best about *Hair* is Galt MacDermot's ingratiating score; further, the musical is noteworthy for being the first successful concept musical (for more information, see entry for the Anspacher Theatre production).

651 Halala! THEATRE: Douglas Fairbanks Theatre; OPENING DATE: February 12, 1986; PERFORMANCES: 31; BOOK: Welcome Msomi; LYRICS: Welcome Msomi; MUSIC: Welcome Msomi; DIRECTION: Welcome Msomi; CHOREOGRAPHY: Thuli Dumakude; LIGHTING: Whitney Quesenbery; PRODUCER: Eric Krebs; an Izulu Dance Theatre production

CAST—Thuli Dumakude, Lorraine Mahlangu, Mandla Msomi, Seth Sibanda, Linda Tshabalala, Michael Xulu

The musical was presented in one act.

MUSICAL NUMBERS—"Drums Communicate a Warm Welcome," Introduction (Mandla Msomi), "Personal Experiences" (Michael Xulu, Thuli Dumakude), "Koze Kubenini (Until When)" (Seth Sibanda, Lorraine Mahlangu), "Sonqoba (We Shall Conquer)" (Thuli Dumakude), "Sivuk'ekuseni (A Demonstration)," "Inside a Prison Cell" (Seth Sibanda), "Bayakhala (They Mourn)" (Thuli Dumakude), "The Halala Song" (Michael Xulu, Linda Tshabalala, Thuli Dumakude, Mandla Msomi, Lorraine Mahlangu), "Celebration"/"Boot Dance," "Izigubhu (Drums Speak)," "Isangoma (The Diviner)," "Zasho (A Celebration)"

NOTES—*Halala!* (*Congratulations!*), a Zulu musical performed in English, had its world premiere in the Off Broadway production. The musical dealt with political and racial problems in modern-day South Africa.

Mel Gussow in the *New York Times* felt the evening was at its most exuberant in the songs and dances. Otherwise, the musical was "fragmented" and its "simplistic attitude" didn't avoid "sloganeering"; further, he noted that the work was more in the nature of a concert than a musical play.

652 Half-Past Wednesday. "A New Musical." THEATRE: Orpheum Theatre; OPENING DATE: April 6, 1962; PERFORMANCES: 2; BOOK: Anna Marie Barlow; LYRICS: Robert Colby and Nita Jonas; MUSIC: Robert Colby; ADDITIONAL LYRICS AND MUSIC by Robert Colby; DIRECTION: Hal Raywin; CHOREOGRAPHY: Gene Bayliss; SCENERY: Lloyd Burlingame; COSTUMES: Robert Fletcher; LIGHTING: Jules Fisher; MUSICAL DIRECTION: Julian Stein; PRODUCERS: Hal Raywin and Jerome Rudolph (Parthenon Productions)

CAST—DAVID WINTERS (Playing a character whose name is comprised of notes from the musical scale, and who is in actuality Rumpelstiltskin), Holly Sherwood (Fittlebee), CHARLES C. WELCH (The Miller), AUDRE JOHNSTON (Erelda), DOM DE LUISE (The King), SEAN GARRISON (The Prince); The People of the Kingdom and Palace Attendants: Marie-Antoinette, Lorraine Bergstrom, Yvonne Carroll, Henrietta Valor, Mark Barkan, Robert (Bob) Fitch, Jay Gerber, William Kennedy

SOURCE—The Brothers Grimm fairy tale "Rumpelstiltskin."

The musical was presented in two acts.

ACT ONE—Overture, "Give 'Em a Lollipop and..." (Holly Sherwood, David Winters), "I've Got a Goose" (Charles C. Welch, Audre Johnston, The People of the Kingdom) "What's the Fun of Being King (If the King Is Poor?)" (Dom De Luise) "(You're the) Sweet Beginning" (Sean Garrison, Audre Johnston) "Who? Where? What?" (David Winters) "Spinning Song" (David Winters, Audre Johnston) "Jumpin' Jehosephat" (Dom De Luise, Charles C. Welch, Audre Johnson, The People of the Kingdom), "If You Did It Once" (Dom De Luise, Charles C. Welch, Sean Garrison, Audre Johnston, The People of the Kingdom) "How Lovely, How Lovely" (Sean Garrison, Audre Johnston) "Spinning Song" (reprise) (David Winters, Audre Johnston)

ACT TWO—"Ladies in Waiting" (Dom De Luise, The Palace Attendants), "(You're the) Sweet Beginning" (reprise) (Audre Johnson, Sean Garrison, The Palace Attendants), "Grandfathers (Ev'ry Baby's Best

Friend)" (Dom De Luise, Charles C. Welch), "To Whit—To Whoo" (David Winters) "What's the Name of What's-His-Name?" (David Winters) "If-If-If-If" (Charles C. Welch, Sean Garrison, Dom De Luise, Audre Johnston), "Companionship" (David Winters), "We Know a Secret Secret" (Dom De Luise, Sean Garrison, Charles C. Welch, Audre Johnston, The Palace Attendants)

NOTES—*Half-Past Wednesday* opened on April 6, 1962, and closed the next day, giving a total of two performances. On April 28, it re-opened, giving four more performances, for a grand total of six.

Half-Past Wednesday lacked the spark which made another fairy tale adaptation a hit (see entry for *Once Upon a Mattress*). Perhaps this version of the "Rumpelstiltskin" tale was neither-nor, not quite a children's musical, and yet not tongue-in-cheek enough for adults. Louis Calta in the *New York Times* noted the "uninteresting and innocuous" evening had the "bothersome precociousness" of a college show but might work as a children's musical. Calta noted that one or two of the cast members had "remarkable talent," and singled out Dom De Luise's "droll" performance as the king. Surprisingly, there was a cast recording (its title was *Half-Past Wednesday* and *Rumpelstiltskin*) on Columbia/Harmony Records (LP # HS-14560), which included many of the songs performed in the production; on the album, in place of Charles C. Welch (as the Miller), chorus member Robert Fitch sang the duet "Grandfathers" (with Dom De Luise).

For another musical about Rumpelstiltskin, see entry for *A Spinning Tale* (1990).

653 Hamelin. "A Musical Tale from Rats to Riches." THEATRE: Circle in the Square Downtown; OPENING DATE: November 10, 1985; PERFORMANCES: 33; BOOK: Richard Jarboe, Harvey Shield, and Matthew Wells; LYRICS: Richard Jarboe and Harvey Shield; MUSIC: Richard Jarboe and Harvey Shield; DIRECTION: Ron Nash; CHOREOGRAPHY: Jerry Yoder; SCENERY: Steven Rubin; COSTUMES: Mark Bridges; LIGHTING: Rick Belzer; MUSICAL DIRECTION: Madelyn Rubenstein; PRODUCERS: Craig Anderson; Jan Jalenak and Golden Rose Productions, Inc., Associate Producers

CAST—Scott Fless (Lech), Patrick Hamilton (The Piper), G. Wayne Hoffman (The Mayor), Steven Jacob (Rudolph), Andrew Kraus (Jigger, Otto), Liz Larsen (Gilda), Jodi Mitchel (Gretrude), Erica L. Paulson (Chigger, Utta)

SOURCE—The fairy tale *The Pied Piper of Hamelin*.

The action occurs on a street in Hamelin on the afternoon of June 26, 1284.

The musical was presented in two acts.

ACT ONE—"We're Rats" (Scott Fless, Company), "The Mayor Doesn't Care" (Steven Jacob, Liz Larsen, The Rats), "Doing My Job" (G. Wayne Hoffman, Jodi Mitchel), "Rat Trap" (Company), "Easy for Me" (Patrick Hamilton, Company), "What a Day" (Patrick Hamilton, The Kids), "Paradise" (Patrick Hamilton, Liz Larsen, Steven Jacob), "Charismatic" (Scott Fless, G. Wayne Hoffman, Jodi Mitchel), "Better Keep Your Promise" (G. Wayne Hoffman, Jodi Mtchel, Scott Fless, The Rats), "Follow the Music Man" (Patrick Hamilton, Company)

ACT TWO—"Feel the Beat" (Patrick Hamilton, The Kids), "Serving the People" (G. Wayne Hoffman, Jodi Mitchel, Liz Larsen, Steven Jacob), Mother (Liz Larsen), "Gold" (G. Wayne Hoffman, Jodi Mitchel, Company), "I'll Remember" (Patrick Hamilton, Liz Larsen, Steven Jacob), "You've Outstayed Your Welcome" (Company), "Follow the Music Man" (reprise) (Patrick Hamilton), "Paradise" (reprise) (Company)

NOTES—Set to rock music, *Hamelin* told the familiar story of the Pied Piper. The public wasn't interested, and the musical was gone after four weeks.

With the uptown *Cats* comfortably settled in the Winter Garden Theatre for (almost) "now and forever," Mel Gussow in the *New York Times* credited the creators of *Hamelin* for not titling their musical *Rats* (although he noted that the word was part of the musical's subtitle). (Three years earlier, there *had* been a musical called *Rats* [see entry]). Gussow reported that one of *Hamelin*'s songs ("I'll Remember") evoked memories of a certain song from *Cats*, and other songs ("Follow the Music Man" and "Gold") reminded him of numbers from *The Music Man* and *Oliver!* Further, Gussow found the direction "derivative" and the book "illogical" and too dependent on anachronisms. He also commented that the jokes were of the "stale cheese" variety.

The musical had been previously produced Off Off Broadway by Musical Theater Works.

654 Hamlet of Stepney Green. "A Fable with Music." THEATRE: The Cricket Theatre; OPENING DATE: November 13, 1958; PERFORMANCES: 166; BOOK: Bernard Kops; LYRICS: Bernard Kops; MUSIC: Robert Procter; DIRECTION: Joe O'Brien; CHOREOGRAPHY: Allen Baker; SCENERY: Herbert Senn, Helen Pond; COSTUMES: Connie Baxter Lighting: Richard Nelson; PRODUCERS: Joe O'Brien, Rhett Cone

CAST—Blanche Marvin (Chava Segal), Michael Gorrin (Sam Levy), Menachem Rubin (Solly Segal), Dino Narizzano (David), Jeanette Roony (Essie Levy), Clarence Hoffman (Mr. Stone), Miriam Phillips (Mrs. Stone), Amnon Kabatchnik (Mr. Green), Maurice Edwards (Mr. Black), Harold Hernan (Mr. White); Peggy Cone, Carole Cone, Robin Chaikin, Peter Chaikin, Valerie Munda, Geoffrey O'Brien (Children's Voices)

The action occurs at the present time in Stepney Green, a once elegant section of London's East End, about two miles from St. Paul's. The musical was presented in three acts.

ACT ONE—"Beggars Can't Be Choosers" (Michael Gorrin, Dino Narizzano, Menachem Rubin), "Sky, Sky" (Children's Voices, Dino Narizzano), "When Your Hair Has Turned to Silver" (Clarence Hoffman), "Over the Hill There Stands a Lady" (Children's Voices, Dino Narizzano), "Sky, Sky" (reprise) (Children's Voices)

ACT TWO—"Woe Is Me" (Dino Narizzano, Michael Gorrin), "Oy, Yoy" (Michael Gorrin, Dino Narizzano), "Yiddisher Father" (Dino Narizzano), "Listen, Davey" (Jeanette Roony), "Mr. White, Mr. Black, Mr. Green" (Harold Hernan, Maurice Edwards, Amnon Kabatchnik)

ACT THREE—"Poor Jenny" (Children's Voices), "The Second Time Is Always Nicer" (Menachem Rubin, Jeanette Roony, Men), "Life" (Dino Narizzano), "A Singer I Must Be" (Dino Narizzano), "Now You're Married" (Children's Voices), "I Am the Boy" (Company)

NOTES—*The Hamlet of Stepney Green* (with article), a modern-day retelling of William Shakespeare's *Hamlet*, had originally been seen in London at the Lyric Opera House, Hammersmith, on July 15, 1958, for thirty-one performances. In reviewing the Off Broadway production *Hamlet of Stepney Green* (without article), Brooks Atkinson in the *New York Times* said he wasn't sure what Bernard Kops was "getting at" in this self-described fable which looked at *Hamlet* from the perspective of a Jewish herring merchant and his son who live in London's East End. If the writing and performances had been incompetent, Atkinson felt he could have dismissed the work. But for the most part he liked the script, found the characterizations "attractive," and the songs (which added to the evening's general air of "mystification") were "as pleasant as the dialogue." Further, he found "everything" in the musical "carefully done," including a "first-rate" setting by Herbert Senn and Helen Pond and performances "above" the standard he was accustomed to seeing Off Broadway. Moreover, he noted that Joe O'Brien had directed the work "conscientiously." But for all this, Atkinson still couldn't glean what Kops had in mind when he wrote the play with music, and he concluded that the evening was a "mystery" to him.

The play with music was published by Penguin Books in 1959, and in 1964 reappeared in a collection titled *Penguin Plays*. The published script described the work as "A Sad Comedy with Some Songs."

The London program, the Off Broadway program, and the script didn't list individual song titles. The above song list represents "best-guess" titles for the lyrics of the untitled songs which appear in the script, and the New York program was referenced to identify which cast members would have performed the songs.

Incidentally, for New York, Mrs. Levy's first name was "Essie," but the London program and the script identified her as "Bessie." Moreover, Mrs. Segal is identified as "Hava" in the London program and the script, but in New York her name was "Chava."

Further, the New York program identified Robert Procter as the composer, but the London program indicated the songs were set to traditional Jewish melodies. Presumably Procter adapted traditional music for the theatre songs.

Hamlet of Stepney Green was the third production to open in New York within a sixteen-month period which offered a modern-day adaptation of *Hamlet*. The other two were *Cue for Passion* (1958) by Elmer Rice (his final play) and *The Tumbler* (1960) by Benn W. Levy, both of which had short runs on Broadway.

655 Hang Down Your Head and Die. "A Musical Entertainment." THEATRE: Mayfair Theatre; OPENING DATE: October 18, 1964; PERFORMANCES: 1; DIRECTION: Braham Murray; CHOREOGRAPHY: Braham Murray; SCENERY: Fred Voelpel; James Taylor, Assistant; COSTUMES: Fred Voelpel; MUSICAL DIRECTION: Jonathan Anderson; PRODUCER: Marion Javits

CAST—The Men (Michael Berkson, Ben Bryant, Jordan Charney, David Garfield, Charles Gray, Robert Jackson, George Marcy, Paul Michael, James Rado, Gerome Ragni, Remak Ramsey); The Women (Virginia Mason, Jenny O'Hara, Jill O'Hara, Teri Phillips, Ria Tawney, Nancy Tribush)

The revue was presented in two acts.

ACT ONE—"There's Gonna Be a Commission" (by Robert Hewison and Vashti Bunyan) (Virginia Mason, Company; choreographed by Virginia Mason), "I Want Gas" (by David Wood) (Gerome Ragni, with Ben Bryant, David Garfield, James Rado, Remak Ramsey), "Sam Hall" (traditional) (George Marcy, Company), "Tripe Seller's Lament" (lyric, traditional; music by Iwan Williams) (Gerome Ragni), "An Innocent Man Is Never Hanged" (by David Wood) (Michael Berkson, James Rado, Remak Ramsey), "Tin Cap" (by Jonathan Anderson) (Jenny O'Hara, Jill O'Hara), "Hanging Johnny" (traditional) (Michael Berkson, Ben Bryant, David Garfield, Remak Ramsey), "Geordie" (traditional) (Ben Bryant, Jill O'Hara)

ACT TWO—"Alcatraz" (by David Wood) (George Marcy, The Girls), "Hang Down Your Head and Die" (by Lanny Meyers) (Robert Jackson), "The English Way to Die" (by David Wood) (James Rado, Remak Ramsey), "Ballad for Christmas" (by Greg Stephens) (Ben Bryant, Jenny O'Hara), "Jack Ketch" (by Greg Stephens) (Michael Berkson, George Marcy), "Gallows Pole" (traditional; arranged by Iwan Williams) (Gerome Ragni, with George Marcy, Jill O'Hara, Ben Bryant, Jenny O'Hara, Nancy Tribush), "The Magic Number" (by David Wood) (Paul Michael, David Garfield, The Girls), "A Long Way from Home" (by Greg Stephens) (George

Marcy), "Brother Men" (words by Francois-Villon; music by Iwan Williams) (Dickson Reed), "The Show's the Thing" (by David Wood) (Company)

NOTES—From a program note for *Hang Down Your Head and Die*: "This production was first seen at Oxford University and subsequently at the Comedy Theatre, London, [and] was conceived as a group presentation, utilizing the special talents of all those concerned with the production. In reworking this revue for America, we have attempted to retain this same principle. The recorded opinions used in the production represent as fair a cross-section as possible of a series of sidewalk interviews made in London and New York."

The revue was against capital punishment, and Howard Taubman in the *New York Times* noted that while death by hanging is swift, the revue "made a long evening of it." The revue never relented in its "tiresome" tirade against capital punishment, and Taubman felt he was being "bludgeoned" and "pounded ... in a torture chamber." Despite the fervent beliefs of its writers, he felt the revue wasn't entertaining in its single-minded obsession of its subject. He even noted that efforts to encourage audience members to sing along during a particular number was marred by the "almost hysterical" behavior of the cast members.

The London production had opened during the 1963-1964 theatre season, and played for forty-four performances.

Perhaps not surprisingly, the New York version of the revue played for just one performance, and is now best remembered for its cast. Gerome Ragni and James Rado later wrote the book and lyrics for *Hair* (1967; see entry), and, along with Jill O'Hara, they also appeared in the production. O'Hara introduced "Good Morning Starshine" in *Hair*, and later originated the role of Fran Kubelik in *Promises, Promises* (1968), introducing "Knowing When to Leave" and, with Jerry Orbach, the lovely duet "I'll Never Fall in Love Again." Her sister Jenny appeared in *The Fig Leaves Are Falling* (1969). Remak Ramsey became one of the busiest actors in New York, delighting audiences over the decades with his wry, understated performances in dramas and comedies as well as the occasional musical.

656 Hang on to the Good Times. "A Musical Revue." THEATRE: Manhattan Theatre Club at City Center Theatre (The Space at City Center Theatre); OPENING DATE: January 22, 1985; PERFORMANCES: 40; SCRIPT: Gretchen Cryer; LYRICS: Gretchen Cryer; MUSIC: Nancy Ford; DIRECTION: Richard Maltby, Jr.; CHOREOGRAPHY: Kay Cole; SCENERY AND PROJECTIONS: James Morgan; COSTUMES: Karen Gerson; LIGHTING: Mary Jo Dondlinger; MUSICAL DIRECTION: Cheryl Hardwick; PRODUCER: Manhattan Theatre Club (Lynne Meadow, Artistic Director; Barry Grove, Managing Director)

CAST—Terri Klausner, Cass Morgan, Don Scardino, Charlaine Woodard

The revue was presented in two acts.

ACT ONE—"You Know My Music" (Company), "Woman on the Run" (Don Scardino, Company), "Joy" (Terri Klausner), "Do Whatcha Gotta Do" (Cass Morgan, Company), "Too Many Women in My Life" (Don Scardino, Company), "You Can Kill Love" (Terri Klausner, Cass Morgan, Charlaine Woodard), "She's My Girl" (Don Scardino, Terri Klausner, Company), "Dear Tom" (Cass Morgan), "You Can Never Know My Mind" (Charlaine Woodard), "Big Bill Murphy" (Company), "Changing" (Charlaine Woodard, Company), "Happy Birthday" (Company)

ACT TWO—"Katydid" (Company), "Goin' Home with My Children" (Terri Klausner, Company), "Mary Margaret's House in the Country" (Charlaine Woodard, Company), "White Trash Motel" (Don Scardino, Company), "Last Day on the Job" (Cass Morgan, Company), "The News" (Company), "Rock Singer" (Company), "Put in a Package and Sold" (Terri Klausner, Company), "Blackberry Wine" (Cass Morgan), "Old Friend" (Don Scardino), "Hang on to the Good Times" (Company)

NOTES—A program note indicated all songs in the revue *Hang on to the Good Times* were written by Gretchen Cryer and Nancy Ford between 1967 and 1980. About half the numbers had been heard in their musicals, and the others had been performed by them in concerts and on recordings.

"Woman on the Run," "She's My Girl," "Changing," "Goin' Home with My Children," and "Mary Margaret's House in the Country" were from the Broadway musical *Shelter* which opened in 1973 and played for thirty-one performances. "Katydid" was from *Now Is the Time for All Good Men* (1967) and "Dear Tom," "Put in a Package and Sold," and "Old Friend" were from *I'm Getting My Act Together and Taking It on the Road* (1978) (see entries). The latter number is one of the superior theatre songs of the 1970s.

Frank Rich in the *New York Times* said the "strained" evening of "saccharine sensibility" offered lyrics "laced" with "psychobabble" and often predictable rhymes; further, the orchestrations made the music sound "more repetitious than it actually is." He also noted that the revue's characters were "unfailingly enlightened," and the male contingent so "well-meaning and sensitive" they could make Phil Donahue seem like a "cad."

657 Hank Williams: Lost Highway. "The Music and Legend of Hank Williams." THEATRE: Little Shubert Theatre; OPENING DATE: March 26, 2003; PERFORMANCES: 132; BOOK: Randal Myler and Mark Harelik; LYRICS: Hank Williams; MUSIC: Hank Williams; DIRECTION: Randal Myler; SCENERY: Beowulf Boritt; COSTUMES: Robert Blackman; LIGHTING: Don Darnutzer; MUSICAL DIRECTION: Dan Wheetman; PRODUCERS: Cindy and Jay Gutterman, Kardana-Swinsky Productions, Inc, Jerry Hamza, Sony/ATV Music Publishing LLC, in association with Manhattan Ensemble Theatre

CAST—JASON PETTY (Hank Williams), Michael W. Howell (Tee-Tot), Juliet Smith (Waitress), Margaret Bowman (Mama Lilly), Stephen G. Anthony (Hoss), Myk Watford (Jimmy [Burrhead]), Drew Perkins (Leon [Loudmouth]), Michael P. Moran (Fred "Pap" Rose), Tertia Lynch (Audrey Williams), Russ Wever (Shag)

The action occurs from the hills of rural southern Alabama to the stage of the Grand Ole Opry.

The musical was presented in two acts.

ACT ONE—"This Is the Way I Do" (Michael W. Howell), "Message to My Mother" (Jason Petty), "Thank God" (Jason Petty, Margaret Bowman, Company), "WPA Blues" (Jason Petty), "Long Gone Lonesome Blues" (Michael W. Howell, Jason Petty), "Settin' the Woods on Fire" (Jason Petty, Stephen G. Anthony, Myk Watford, Drew Perkins, Russ Wever), "Sally Goodin'" (Drew Perkins), "Honky Tonk Blues" (Jason Petty, Stephen G. Anthony, Myk Watford, Drew Perkins, Russ Wever), "I'm Tellin' You" (Tertia Lynch, Stephen G. Anthony, Myk Watford, Drew Perkins, Russ Wever), "I Can't Help It (If I'm Still in Love with You)" (Jason Petty, Stephen G. Anthony, Myk Watford, Drew Perkins, Russ Wever), "I'm So Lonesome I Could Cry" (Michael W. Howell), "Jambalaya (On the Bayou)" (Jason Petty, Stephen G. Anthony, Myk Watford, Drew Perkins, Russ Wever), "Move It On Over" (Jason Petty, Stephen G. Anthony, Myk Watford, Drew Perkins, Russ Wever), "Mind Your Own Business" (Jason Petty, Stephen G. Anthony, Myk Watford, Drew Perkins, Russ Wever), "Lovesick Blues" (Jason Petty, Stephen G. Anthony, Myk Watford, Drew Perkins, Russ Wever)

ACT TWO—"The Blood Done Sign My Name" (Michael W. Howell), "Happy Rovin' Cowboy" (Jason Petty, Stephen G. Anthony, Myk Watford, Drew Perkins, Russ Wever), "I'm Gonna Sing, Sing, Sing" (Jason Petty, Tertia Lynch, Stephen G. Anthony, Myk Watford, Drew Perkins, Russ Wever), "Long Gone Lonesome Blues" (reprise) (Jason Petty, Michael W. Howell, Stephen G. Anthony, Myk Watford, Drew Perkins, Russ Wever), "Way Downtown" (Stephen G. Anthony, Myk Watford, Drew Perkins, Russ Wever), "I'm So Lonesome I Could Cry" (reprise) (Jason Petty), "I'm a Run to the City of Refuge"/"A House of Gold" (medley) (Michael W. Howell, Stephen G. Anthony, Myk Watford, Drew Perkins, Russ Wever), "Hey, Good Lookin'" (Jason Petty, Stephen G. Anthony, Myk Watford, Drew Perkins, Russ Wever), "I Saw the Light" (Jason Petty, Stephen G. Anthony), "Lost Highway" (Jason Petty, Michael W. Howell), "Your Cheatin' Heart" (Jason Petty, Stephen G. Anthony, Myk Watford, Drew Perkins, Russ Wever), "I Saw the Light" (reprise) (Company)

NOTES—The musical used the songs of Hank Williams (1923-1953) to tell the story of his short, meteoric life. The script was published by Dramatists Play Service, Inc., in 2004, and the cast album was recorded by Fynsworth Alley Records (CD # 302-062-190-2). In the production, and on the recording, the song "Hey, Good Lookin'" was purposely performed by Jason Petty in a shaky, hesitant style to denote Williams' freefall into drugs and alcohol. However, the recording also includes a bonus track of Petty performing the song in a straightforward version.

The musical premiered at the Denver Center Theatre Company on April 19, 1987, with co-author Mark Harelik in the title role; it was later produced in Nashville, Cleveland, and other cities, and was first seen in New York in an Off Off Broadway production at the Manhattan Ensemble Theatre on December 19, 2002.

Randal Myler, who directed and co-wrote the book for *Hank Williams: Lost Highway*, was associated with three other Off Broadway musicals which looked at the lives and careers of pop singers (see entries for *Dream a Little Dream* [The Mamas and The Papas], *Almost Heaven: Songs of John Denver*, and *Love, Janis* [Joplin]).

658 Hannah...1939. THEATRE: Vineyard Theatre; OPENING DATE: May 31, 1990; PERFORMANCES: 46; BOOK: Bob Merrill; LYRICS: Bob Merrill; MUSIC: Bob Merrill; DIRECTION: Douglas Aibel; CHOREOGRAPHY: Tina Paul; SCENERY: G.W. Mercier; COSTUMES: James Scott; LIGHTING: Phil Monat; MUSICAL DIRECTION: Stephen Milbank; PRODUCER: Vineyard Theatre (Douglas Aibel, Artistic Director; Barbara Zinn Krieger, Executive Director; Jon Nakagawa, Managing Director)

CAST—Julie Wilson (Hannah Schuler), Tony Carlin (Lieutenant Kurt Wald), Richard Thomsen (Commandant Baumann), Yusef Bulos (Janos), Patti Perkins (Luba), Lori Wilner (Toby), Deirdre Lovejoy (Mina), Leah Hocking (Vera), Allan Heinberg (Reuben), Mary Setrakian (Paulina), Mark Ankeny (Jules), Nicolette Salas (Leah), Kathleen Mahoney-Bennett (Young Hannah), Leigh Beery (Gerte Baumann), Paul Klementowicz and Kirk Lombard (German Soldiers)

The action occurs in a dress factory in Prague from March 1939 to December 1939.

The musical was presented in two acts (the program didn't credit song assignments).

ACT ONE—Opening (Julie Wilson, Company), "Ah, Our Germans" (Julie Wilson, Company), "No Give, No Take" (Julie Wilson, Tony Carlin), "The Pearl We Called Prague" (Yusef Bulos, Patti Perkins, Company), "Martina" (Tony Carlin, Julie Wilson), "Pretty"/"Kissed on the Eyes" (Julie Wilson, Tony

Carlin, Kathleen Mahony-Bennett), "Things Will Be Different" (performer[s] unknown), "Wear a Little Grin" (Orchestra), "We Dance" (Neva Small, Leigh Berry), "Hannah Will Take Care of You" (Julie Wilson, Yusef Bulos, Patti Perkins)

ACT TWO—"Radio Dance" (Company), "Someday" (Lori Wilner, Company), "Gentle Afternoon" (Leigh Berry, Julie Wilson), "So Good to See You" (Kathleen Mahony-Bennett, Tony Carlin), "Who Is Hannah?" (Julie Wilson), "Someday" (reprise) (Lori Wilner, Company)

NOTES—Bob Merrill's *Hannah ...1939* told the grim story of Hannah Schuler, a Jewish woman who runs a dress factory in Prague in the late 1930s. When Nazi occupiers commandeer the factory for the manufacturing of uniforms, Hannah tries to cooperate and comes to believe she's been able to reach accord, and mutual respect, with them. All too late, she realizes terrorists can't be accommodated, and she's taken away to a death camp.

But for all its somber story, Mel Gussow in the *New York Times* felt the musical never truly reflected the drama of its time and place. He noted that often the Prague of *Hannah...1939* was more reminiscent of the Budapest of *She Loves Me* (1963) than the Berlin of *Cabaret* (1966), and remarked that some of Bob Merrill's "pretty tunes" would be more at home in his musicals *Take Me Along* (1959) and *Carnival!* (1961). But he praised Julie Wilson's performance, and said her "stylish embodiment" of Hannah offered "Chanel-like self-assurance" and "quiet elegance."

The above song list is taken from information on the original cast album, which was recorded by That's Entertainment Records (CD # CDTER-1192) almost two years after the musical had closed. For the recording, Peter Frechette sang the role of Lieutenant Kurt Wald and Ann Talman the role of Young Hannah. "Things Will Be Different" was performed in previews, but may have been dropped by opening night. "Different" wasn't included on the recording, but two other deleted numbers were ("Sew a Button" and "Learn About Life").

"Sew a Button" had originally been introduced by Neva Small (and a factory chorus) in *The Prince of Grand Street*, which closed during its pre-Broadway tryout in 1978. Small also appeared in *Hannah...1939*.

659 Hannah Senesh.

THEATRE: Cherry Lane Theatre; OPENING DATE: April 10, 1985; PERFORMANCES: 161; PLAY: David Schechter; DIRECTION: David Schechter; SCENERY: Jennifer Gallagher; COSTUMES: David Woolard; LIGHTING: Vivian Leone; PRODUCERS: William Ross and Perry Bruskin in association with Daniel Neiden in a Writers Theatre production

CAST—Lori Wilner (Catherine, Hannah Senesh), John Fistos (Young Man), David Schechter (Voice of George Senesh)

SOURCE—The diaries and poems of Hannah Senesh, translated by Marta Cohn and Peter Hay (originally developed by Dafna Soltes).

The play was presented in one act.

NOTES—David Schechter's virtually one-character play *Hannah Senesh* (which included incidental songs and background music) told the true story of a 22-year-old Jewish Hungarian woman who left her home in Palestine in order to rescue Hungarian Jews from the Nazis. She became a freedom fighter in Europe, but eventually was captured, tortured, and executed by the Gestapo in 1944.

Schechter's play was developed in collaboration with Lori Wilner, and had been previously seen Off Off Broadway during the summer of 1984.

The production included the following musical numbers: "The Rainbow Song" (lyric and music by Steven Lutvak), "Eli, Eli" (words by Hannah Senesh, music by D. Zehavi), "Blessed Is the Match" (words by Hannah Senesh, music by Steven Lutvak), "Soon" (lyric and music by David Schechter), "Shtil De Nacht" (lyric by Hirsh Gilk, composer unknown), "Zog Nit Keyn Mol" (lyric by Hirsch Gilk, music by Dimitri Pokrass), and "One, Two, Three" (words by Hannah Senesh, music by Elizabeth Swados).

660 Happy End.

THEATRE: Brooklyn Academy of Music; OPENING DATE: March 8, 1977; PERFORMANCES: 56; BOOK: "Dorothy Lane" (a pseudonym for Elisabeth Hauptmann, Bertolt Brecht's secretary; the book was probably also written by Brecht himself); adapted from the original German by Michael Feingold; LYRICS: Bertolt Brecht; adapted from the original German by Michael Feingold; MUSIC: Kurt Weill; DIRECTION: Michael Posnick; CHOREOGRAPHY: Patricia Birch; SCENERY: Robert U. Taylor; COSTUMES: Carrie F. Robbins; LIGHTING: Jennifer Tipton; MUSICAL DIRECTION: Roland Gagnon; PRODUCERS: Chelsea Theatre Center (Robert Kalfin, Artistic Director; Michael David, Executive Director; Burl Hash, Productions Director) and Michael Harvey

CAST—*The Gang*—Christopher Lloyd (Bill Cracker), Benjamin Rayson (Sam "Mammy" Wurlitzer), Tony Azito (Dr. Nakamura ["The Governor"]), John A. Coe (Jimmy Dexter ["The Reverend"]), Robert Weil (Bob Marker ["The Professor"]), Raymond J. Barry (Johnny Flint ["Baby Face"]), Grayson Hall (A Lady in Gray ["The Fly"]), Donna Emmanuel (Miriam); *The Army*—Shirley Knight (Lieutenant Lillian Holiday ["Hallelujah Lil'"]), Liz Sheridan (Major Stone), Joe Grifasi (Captain Hannibal Jackson), Prudence Wright Holmes (Sister Mary), Alexandra Borrie (Sister Jane), Bob Gunton (Brother Ben Owens); *The Fold* (Kristin Jolliff, Frank Kopyc, Tom Mardirosian, Martha Miller, Victor Pappas); David Pursley (A Cop)

The action occurs in Chicago during December 1915.

The musical was presented in three acts.

ACT ONE—Prologue (Company), "The Bilbao Song" (Tony Azito, Raymond J. Barry, Christopher Lloyd, The Gang), "Lieutenants of the Lord" (Shirley Knight, The Army), "March Ahead" (The Army), "The Sailors' Tango" (Shirley Knight)

ACT TWO—"Brother, Give Yourself a Shove" (The Army, The Fold), "Song of the Big Shot" (Tony Azito), "Don't Be Afraid" (Alexandra Borrie, The Army, The Fold), "In Our Childhood's Bright Endeavor" (Joe Grifasi), "The Liquor Dealer's Dream" (Joe Grifasi, Tony Azito, Alexandra Borrie, The Army, The Fold)

ACT THREE—"The Mandalay Song" (Benjamin Rayson, The Gang), "Surabaya Johnny" (Shirley Knight), "Song of the Big Shot" (reprise) (Christopher Lloyd), "Ballad of the Lily of Hell" (Grayson Hall), "The Happy End" (finale) (Company)

NOTES—Bertolt Brecht and Kurt Weill's *Happy End* premiered in Germany under its English title, opening in Berlin on September 2, 1929, at the Theatre am Schiffbauerdamm, almost a year to the day of the premiere of *The Threepenny Opera* (see entries) at the same theatre. In fact, the two works also shared the same director (Erich Engel), set designer (Caspar Neher), and conductor (Theo Mackeben). Among the cast members of the original German production were Carola Neher (Lillian), Oskar (Oscar) Homolka (Bill), Helene Weigel (A Lady in Grey), and Peter Lorre (Dr. Nakamura).

Set in Chicago, the story dealt with a local Salvation Army unit which tries to reform a group of gangsters. Ultimately, the gang merges with the Army members, and the group moves to one of Chicago's wealthiest neighborhoods; both the gang and the Salvation Army members agree that it is the rich who are most in need of their respective services.

Like *The Rise and Fall of the City of Mahagonny* (see entry), the opening night of the original production of *Happy End* met with controversy. The cynical ending led to a riot in the theatre, and the police were called in. Moreover, the critics were generally dismissive of the work; but the musical was kept alive over the decades because of its memorable songs, and finally some thirty years after the Berlin premiere a recording of the score (which included Lotte Lenya in the role of Lillian) was released by Columbia Records (LP # OL-5630 and # OS-2032). In 2006, a production by the American Conservatory Theatre in a translation by Michael Feingold was recorded by Ghostlight Records (CD # 7915584418-2).

It was Feingold's translation which had earlier been used for the New York premiere of *Happy End*, which took place at the Brooklyn Academy of Music on March 8, 1977, with Shirley Knight in the role of Lillian. The production temporarily closed on April 3 after playing thirty-two performances, and when it resumed on April 12, Meryl Streep had assumed the role of Lillian; further, the production had been re-directed by Robert Kalfin. After playing twenty-four more performances at the Brooklyn Academy of Music (for a total of fifty-six), the musical then transferred to Broadway at the Martin Beck (now Al Hirschfeld) Theatre on May 7, 1977, where it played for seventy-five additional performances, closing on July 10; during the musical's final weeks, Streep was no longer with the production, and the role of Lillian was played by Janie Sell, the 1977 revival's third Lillian. Because the musical had never before been performed in New York, the revival received a Tony Award nomination for Best Musical (its competitors were *Annie* and *I Love My Wife*).

661 The Happy Hypocrite.

"A Fairy Tale for Tired Men." THEATRE: Bouwerie Lane Theatre; OPENING DATE: September 5, 1968; PERFORMANCES: 17; BOOK: Edward Eager; LYRICS: Edward Eager; MUSIC: James Bredt (Additional material by Tony Tanner.); DIRECTION: Tony Tanner; SCENERY: Michael Horen; COSTUMES: Deidre Cartier; LIGHTING: Jules Fisher; MUSICAL DIRECTION: Richard J. Leonard; PRODUCER: Arete Spero

CAST—Howard Girven (Cheapside), Keith Cota (Shoreditch), Rose Roffman (Mistress Bow), John Aman (Lord George Hell), Kevin O'Leary (Lord Follard Follard), Rosemarie Heyer (La Gambogi), George Feeney (The Merry Archer), Joan Kroschell (Jenny Mere), Edward J. McPhillips (Aeneas Aeneas)

SOURCE—The 1900 play *The Happy Hypocrite—A Fairy Tale for Tired Men* by Sir Max Beerbohm.

The action occurs in England during the Regency Era.

The musical was presented in one act.

MUSICAL NUMBERS—"Street Song" and Opening (Howard Girven, Keith Cota, Rose Roffman), "Deep in Me" (Rosemarie Heyer, John Aman), "The Amorous Arrow" (Rose Roffman), "Echo Song" (Joan Kroschell), "Miss Mere" (John Aman), "Mornings at Seven" (John Aman), "The Song of the Mask" (Edward J. McPhillips, John Aman), "Deep in Me" (reprise) (Rosemarie Heyer), "Almost Too Good to Be True" (John Aman, Joan Kroschell), "Wedding Pantomime" (Company), "Don't Take Sides" (Howard Girvin, Keith Cota, Rose Roffman), "Almost Too Good to Be True" (reprise) (John Aman, Joan Kroschell, Howard Girvin, Keith Cota, Rose Roffman), "Hell Hath No Fury" (Rosemarie Heyer, Howard Girvin, Keith Cota, Rose Roffman), "I Must Smile" (John Aman), "Once, Only Once" (Rosemarie Heyer, Ensemble), "The Face of Love" (Joan Kroschell, John Aman, Ensemble)

NOTES—*The Happy Hypocrite*, a musical adaptation of the Max Beerbohm play, was presented as a spoof of operettas. As Dan Sullivan in the *New York Times* noted, all the proper and "charmingly dated" conventions of operetta were in place (a slightly tainted hero, a pure heroine, an evil mistress, and a mysterious mask-maker), and the tone was just right ("smiling, but in earnest"). But he felt the writers couldn't match the quality of the original play, and he found fault with the "embarrassing" and "banal" lyrics and the "featureless" music. Further, the production was "vocally shabby," a fatal sin for an operetta. Sullivan concluded the evening looked like "a very expensive Hallmark Christmas card," but wasn't sure if that was "enough."

662 Happy with the Blues. "The Music of Harold Arlen." THEATRE: Cabaret/Manhattan Theatre Club; OPENING DATE: May 3, 1978; PERFORMANCES: 28; LYRICS: See song list for credits; MUSIC: Harold Arlen; DIRECTION: Julianne Boyd; CHOREOGRAPHY: Otis A. Sallid; MUSICAL DIRECTION: Vicki Helms Carter; PRODUCER: Manhattan Theatre Club (Lynne Meadow, Artistic Director; Barry Grove, Managing Director; Stephen Pascal, Associate Artistic Director)

CAST—Jean Andalman, Barbara Andres, Stephen James, Sarilee Kahn, Orrin Reiley

The revue was presented in two acts.

ACT ONE—"Get Happy" (from *Nine-Fifteen Revue*, 1930; lyric by Ted Koehler) (Company), "On the Swing Shift" (1942 film *Star Spangled Rhythm*; lyric by Johnny Mercer) Sarilee Kahn, Stephen James, Jean Andalman, Orrin Reiley), "I'm Doin' It for Defense" (1942 film *Star Spangled Rhythm*; lyric by Johnny Mercer) (Sarilee Kahn, Orrin Reiley), "Hooray for Love" (1948 film *Casbah*; lyric by Leo Robin) (Barbara Andres), "Last Night When We Were Young" (lyric by E.Y. Harburg; song written independent of a musical production, 1935) (Stephen James), "It's Only a Paper Moon (If You Believed in Me)" (*The Great Magoo*, 1932; lyric by Billy Rose and E.Y. Harburg) (Barbara Andres, Orrin Reiley), "Tess's Torch Song" (1943 film *Up in Arms*; lyric by Ted Koehler) (Jean Andalman, Company), "Happy as the Day Is Long" (*Cotton Club Parade*, 1933; lyric by Ted Koehler) (Stephen James), "Waitin'" (*House of Flowers*, 1954; lyric by Truman Capote and Harold Arlen) (Barbara Andres, Jean Andalman, Sarilee Kahn), "One Man Ain't Quite Enough" (*House of Flowers*, 1954; lyric by Truman Capote and Harold Arlen) (Barbara Andres, Jean Andalman), "A Sleepin' Bee" (*House of Flowers*, 1954; lyric by Truman Capote and Harold Arlen) (Sarilee Kahn), "So Long, Big Time" (lyric by Dory Langdon Previn; independent song, 1963) (Orrin Reiley), "Leavin' Time" (*St. Louis Woman*, 1946; lyric by Johnny Mercer) (Company), "Ding Dong! The Witch Is Dead!" (1939 film *The Wizard of Oz*; lyric by E.Y. Harburg) Company)

ACT TWO—"Sweet and Hot" (*You Said It*, 1931; lyric by Jack Yellen) (Company), "You'll Do" (*You Said It*, 1931; lyric by Jack Yellen) (Barbara Andres, Orrin Reiley), Down and Out Medley: "One for My Baby" (1943 film *The Sky's the Limit*; lyric by Johnny Mercer) (Stephen James), "Accentuate the Positive" (1944 film *Here Come the Waves*; lyric by Johnny Mercer) (Barbara Andres), "I Gotta Right to Sing the Blues" (*Earl Carroll Vanities* [Tenth Edition], 1932; lyric by Ted Koehler) (Jean Andalman), "I Wonder What Became of Me" (*St. Louis Woman*, 1946; lyric by Johnny Mercer) (Sarilee Kahn), "Down with Love" (*Hooray for What!*, 1937; lyric by E.Y. Harburg), (Orrin Reiley), "The Man That Got Away" (1954 film *A Star Is Born*; lyric by Ira Gershwin) (Barbara Andres), "Lydia, The Tattooed Lady" (1939 film *At the Circus*; lyric by E.Y. Harburg), (Orrin Reiley, Stephen James), "Take It Slow, Joe" (*Jamaica*, 1957; lyric by E.Y. Harburg) (Jean Andalman)/"This Is Only the Beginning" (1934 film *Let's Fall in Love*; lyric by Ted Koehler) (Orrin Reiley), "Blues in the Night" (1941 film *Blues in the Night*; lyric by Johnny Mercer) (Orrin Reiley), "Gotta Have Me Go with You" (1954 film *A Star Is Born*; lyric by Ira Gershwin) (Sarilee Kahn), "Ridin' on the Moon" (*St. Louis Woman*, 1946; lyric by Johnny Mercer) (Stephen James), "Napoleon" (*Jamaica*, 1957; lyric by E.Y. Harburg) (Company), "The Morning After" (lyric by Dory Langdon Previn; independent song, 1962) (Barbara Andres), "Stormy Weather" (*Cotton Club Parade*, 1933; lyric by Ted Koehler) (Jean Andalman), "Ain't It De Truth" (*Jamaica*, 1957; lyric by E.Y. Harburg) (Company)

NOTES—Harold Arlen's wonderful songs rank with the best from Broadway and Hollywood, and his body of work is happily well-known. So the Manhattan Theatre Club's Off Off Broadway revue *Happy with the Blues* was probably superfluous. But, then again, any excuse to hear Arlen's music will do, and this particular evening offered an interesting mix of evergreens and esoterica.

On the heels of such successful tributes as *Side by Side by Sondheim* (1977) and the Manhattan Theatre Club's own *Ain't Misbehavin'* (1978; see entry), virtually every prominent lyricist and composer received tribute-revues during this era, with no doubt each and every producer praying for another cash cow like *Ain't Misbehavin'*.

For another Harold Arlen tribute, see entry for *The Harold Arlen Songbook*.

663 Hard Job Being God. "A New Rock Musical." THEATRE: Edison Theatre; OPENING DATE: May 15, 1972; PERFORMANCES: 6; BOOK: Uncredited (Tom Martel?); LYRICS: Tom Martel; MUSIC: Tom Martel; DIRECTION: Bob Yde; CHOREOGRAPHY: Lee Theodore; SCENERY: Ray Wilke; COSTUMES: Mary Whitehead; LIGHTING: Patrika Brown; MUSICAL DIRECTION: Roy Bittan; PRODUCERS: Bob Yde in association with Andy Wiswell

CAST—Gini Eastwood (Sarah, Jacob's Wife, Slave, Pharaoh's Soldier, Moabite, Judean, Susanna), Stu Freeman (Jacob's Son, Moses, Moabite, David), Tom Martel (God), Anne Sarofeen (Slave, Pharoah's Soldier, Ruth, Judean, Shepherd), John Twomey (Abraham, Jacob, Pharoah, Moabite, Judean, Amos)

SOURCE—Various books of the Old Testament

The musical was presented in one act.

MUSICAL NUMBERS—"Anytime, Anywhere" (Tom Martel, Company), "Wherever You Go" (Gini Eastwood, John Twomey), "Famine" (John Twomey, Gini Eastwood, Stu Freeman), "Buy a Slave" (Egyptian Slave Merchants), "Prayer" (Gini Eastwood, Anne Sarofeen), "Moses' Song" (Stu Freeman, John Twomey), "The Ten Plagues" (John Twomey, Gini Eastwood, Anne Sarofeen, Stu Freeman), "Passover" (Gini Eastwood, Anne Sarofeen, John Twomey, Stu Freeman) "The Eleven Commandments" (Stu Freeman, Gini Eastwood, Anne Sarofeen), "Tribes" (Hebrew Women, Tribes), "Ruth" (Gini Eastwood, John Twomey, Anne Sarofeen), "Festival" (Judeans), "Hail, David" (Judeans, Stu Freeman), "A Very Lonely King" (Stu Freeman), "Battle" (performer[s] unknown), "You're On Your Own" (Hebrews, Tom Martel), "A Psalm of Peace" (Gini Eastwood, Hebrews), "I'm Countin' on You" (Tom Martel, John Twomey), "Shalom L'chaim!" (Hebrews), "Amos Gonna Give You Hell" (Anne Sarofeen), "What Do I Have to Do?" (Tom Martel, Company)

NOTES—*Hard Job Being God* jumped on the rock/religious musical bandwagon, but fell off after six performances.

Clive Barnes in the *New York Times* remarked there were many New Testament-based musicals (*Jesus Christ Superstar*, *Godspell*, even Handel's *Messiah)*, and so it was time the Old Testament was represented. But *Hard Job Being God*'s "quick run-through" of the Old Testament was "simplistic, naïve and distasteful," with "bathetic" and "puerile" lyrics to boot. As for the music, Barnes found it "unmemorable but attractive" in a Muzak kind of way, and noted that when "I noticed it I liked it." A studio/cast album was released by GWP Records (LP # ST-2036), which included printed lyrics for many of the songs.

664 Hard Sell. THEATRE: The Other Stage/The Public Theatre; OPENING DATE: January 11, 1980; PERFORMANCES: 11; SKETCHES: Roger Director and Murray Horwitz, with additional material by Mimi Kennedy, Ted Mann, Herb Sargent, and Wendy Wasserstein; LYRICS: Murray Horwitz; MUSIC: John Lewis; DIRECTION: Murray Horwitz; CHOREOGRAPHY: Sammy Dallas Bayes; SCENERY: Barry Robison; COSTUMES: Pegi Goodman; LIGHTING: Gail Dahl; MUSICAL DIRECTION: John Lewis; PRODUCER: The New York Shakespeare Festival (Joseph Papp, Director; Jason Steven Cohen, Production Supervisor)

CAST—Seth Allen, Murray Horwitz, Andrea Martin, Carolyn Mignini, Steve Vinovich

The revue appears to have been presented in one act (sketch and song assignments not identified in program).

MUSICAL NUMBERS—"Hard Sell," "Soho" (lyric by John Lewis), "Keeping Posted," "How'm I Doin'," "Great Leap Forward," Total Entertainment News:, "Afghanistan," "Iowa," "Redlining," "Editorial," "Stocks-Sports-Weather," SKETCHES, "Cook American" (by Mimi Kennedy and Wendy Wasserstein), "Evelyn Woods" (by Mimi Kennedy, Roger Director, and Murray Horwitz), "Martha Graham" (by Roger Director, Murray Horwitz, and Ted Mann), "Smoke Detector" (by Ted Mann and Murray Horwitz), "Danny DeLuca" (by Mimi Kennedy and Murray Horwitz), "David Garth" (by Herb Sargent and Murray Horwitz)

NOTES—According to Mel Gussow in the *New York Times*, the revue *Hard Sell*, a spoof of "media hype" and "salesmanship," was "scattershot" and "ineffectual," and he concluded that *Hard Sell* was "no sale." However, he found John Lewis' music "breezy," and singled out Andrea Martin ("an intense little imp") in the skit "Martha Graham Learn to Dance Schools," a spoof of modern dance. The revue marked an early appearance by Wendy Wasserstein. Unfortunately, she seems destined to join Joseph Kramm, William Inge, Paul Zindel, Jason Miller, and a few other Pulitzer Prize-winning playwrights whose plays haven't aged all that well.

665 A Hard Time to Be Single. "A New Musical Revue." THEATRE: Don't Tell Mama; OPENING DATE: October 1, 1990; PERFORMANCES: Unknown; LYRICS: Brian Gari; MUSIC: Brian Gari

CAST—Larry Victor, Janet Kirker, Angela Warren, Michael Massey

MUSICAL NUMBERS—(number of acts unknown [probably one act]; songs are listed in performance order): "Those Who Want the Best" (Company), "I'm at My Best in Love" (Angela Warren), "Portfolio Girl" (Larry Victor), "Obsessed" (Michael Massey), "I Think Too Much of the Future" (Janet Kirker), "Sweet Words Don't Scare My Lady" (Michael Massey, Larry Victor), "Working Woman" (Larry Victor), "I Want Your Boyfriend" (Janet Kirker), "Don't Give Up Your Key" (Angela Warren), "Face to Face" (Michael Massey), "Am I Supposed to Be Mad Today?" (Larry Victor, Janet Kirker), "It Had to Happen Sometime" (Michael Massey, Angela Warren), "Only One Person's Opinion" (Janet Kirker), "If Our Songs Still Make It" (Michael Massey, Angela Warren), "A Hard Time to Be Single" (Company), "Friends for Life" (Angela Warren, Janet Kirker), "Connected Forever" (Angela Warren), "Some Things Don't Have to End" (Company)

NOTES—The revue *A Hard Time to Be Single* was recorded by Original Cast Records (CD # OC-913). The recording included a bonus track, "A Child Should Live Forever," performed by Tammy Quinn, who had replaced Janet Kirker during the revue's run. "A Child Should Live Forever" wasn't from the revue, and had been written for a benefit performance for the Eddie Cantor Fund for Children with AIDS. Jana Robbins' collection of Gari's songs (*Jana Robbins/Face to Face* [released by Original Cast Records CD # OC915]) included three songs from the revue ("Face to Face," "Only One Person's Opinion," and "I've Got a Boyfriend Now" [the latter had been deleted from the production]). Brian Gari had been represented on Broadway with his musical *Late Nite Comic*, which opened in 1987 for four performances; it was recorded by Original Cast Records (CD # OC-8843). Two songs from *Late Nite Comic* ("Obsessed" and "It Had to Happen Sometime") were later used in *A Hard Time to Be Single* and were recorded on the latter's cast album. In 2006, Gari wrote an account of the making of the musical (*We Bombed in New London/The Inside Story of the Broadway Musical 'Late Nite Comic'* [BearManor Media]). In 2007, a "20th Anniversary Edition" of *Late Nite Comic*'s score was released by Original Cast Records (CD # 0315).

666 Hard to Be a Jew (Shver Tzu Zine a Yid) (1973; Sholom Secunda). THEATRE: Eden Theatre; OPENING DATE: October 28, 1973; PERFORMANCES: 161; BOOK: Joseph Buloff and David Licht; LYRICS: Yitzchok Perlov; MUSIC: Sholom Secunda; DIRECTION: David Licht; CHOREOGRAPHY: Pearl Lang; SCENERY: Jeffrey B. Moss; COSTUMES: Jeffrey B. Moss; LIGHTING: Tom Meleck; MUSICAL DIRECTION: Renee Solomon; PRODUCERS: Harry Rothpearl and Jewish Nostalgic Productions, Inc.

CAST—Zvee Scooler (Rabbi Levi Halpern [Narrator]), STAN PORTER (Ivan Ivanovitch Ivanov), David Carey (Misha Greenboym), Elia Patron (Yakov Fratkin), BRUCE ADLER (Hershko Shneyerson), Bernardo Hiller (Sioma Shapiro), Miriam Kressyn (Sarah Shapiro), Raquel Yossiffon (Betty Shapiro), JOSEPH BULOFF (David Shapiro), Shmulik Goldstein (Ketzele Katz), Jack Rechtzeit (Police Captain), Tom Melcek (Policeman); Students, Waitresses, Guests (Richard Arbacj, Jocqulyn Buglisi, Christine Dakin, Scott D. Morrow, Joe Stephen, Patrick Suzeau, Marcus Williamson)

SOURCE—The 1920 play *Hard to Be a Jew* by Sholom Aleichem.

The action occurs in a "big city" in Czarist Russia during 1913 and 1914.

The musical was presented in two acts.

ACT ONE—"Gaudeamus Igitur" (traditional) (Students), "Romance" (Stan Porter), "Tchort Vasmi (To Hell with It!)" (Stan Porter, David Carey, Students), "Yiddishe Tzores" (Stan Porter, Bruce Adler, David Carey, Elia Patron), "Tchaikovsky Romance" (Stan Porter), "Shver Tzu Zine A Yid" (Stan Porter, Bruce Adler, David Carey, Elia Patron), "Slavite" (Bernardo Hiller, Ensemble), "Russian Waltz" (Ensemble)

ACT TWO—"Candle Blessing" (Miriam Kressyn, Raquel Yossiffon), "Duet" (Stan Porter, Bruce Adler), "Kiddush" (Elia Patron, Ensemble), "Chad"/"Gad"/"Yo" (Ensemble), "Am Yisroel Chai (Jewish People Will Live On)" (Ensemble)

NOTES—*Hard to Be a Jew* told the tale of a Jew and a Christian Russian who exchange identities in Czarist Russia. The musical played for two slightly separated engagements during the season (a total of 161 performances).

According to Richard F. Shepard in the *New York Times*, the "disquieting" story of racial and religious prejudice was nonetheless "a bouncy, tasteful comedy ... a sparkling new Yiddish musical."

Cast member and co-book writer Joseph Buloff had appeared in the original 1943 production of *Oklahoma!*; he created the role of the peddler Ali Hakim and introduced "It's a Scandal! It's a Outrage!" In 1983, another musical version (titled *It's Hard to Be a Jew*) was presented Off Off Broadway (see entry), and, in 1984, a non-musical version of Aleichem's story was presented Off Off Broadway.

667 Hark! "The New Musical." THEATRE: Mercer-O'Casey Theatre; OPENING DATE: May 22, 1972; PERFORMANCES: 152; LYRICS: Robert Lorick; MUSIC: Dan Goggin and Marvin Solley; DIRECTION: Darwin Knight; SCENERY: Chenault Spence; COSTUMES: Danny Morgan; LIGHTING: Chenault Spence; MUSICAL DIRECTION: Sande Campbell; PRODUCER: Robert Lissauer

CAST—Dan Goggin, Marvin Solley, Elaine Petricoff, Danny Guerrero, Sharron Miller, Jack Blackton

The revue was presented in two acts.

ACT ONE—Prologue: "Hark"; "Take a Look"; "George"; "Hip Hooray for America" (Company). Part I: *The Cycle Begins*: "Smart People" (Company), "What D'ya Wanna Be?" (Elaine Petricoff, Danny Guerrero, Company), "Six Little Kids" (Dan Goggin, Marvin Solley), "Icarus" (Marvin Solley, Elaine Petricoff, Company), "Sun Down" (Sharron Miller), "Conversation Piece" (Elaine Petricoff, Jack Blackton, Danny Guerrero, Sharron Miller), "The Outstanding Member" (Danny Guerrero, Company), "How Am I Doin', Dad?" (Company), "All Good Things" (Danny Guerrero), "Molly" (Dan Goggin, Marvin Solley), "Smart People" (reprise) (Company), "In a Hundred Years" (Company)

ACT TWO—Part II: *The Cycle Continues*: "It's Funny About Love" (Company), "Coffee Morning" (Jack Blackton), "Suburbia Square Dance" (Dan Goggin, Marvin Solley, Company), "I See the People" (Jack Blackton, Dan Goggin, Marvin Solley), "Pretty Jack" (Sharron Miller), "Big Day Tomorrow" (Danny Guerrero), "Lullaby" (Elaine Petricoff), "Here's to You, Mrs. Rodreguez" (Dan Goggin, Marvin Solley), "Early Sunday" (Company), "I See the People" (reprise) (Company), "What's Your Sign, Mr. Simpson?" (Elaine Petricoff, Sharron Miller), "All Good Things" (reprise) (Dan Goggin), "A Dying Business" (Danny Guerrero, Company), "Waltz with Me, Lady" (Marvin Solley), Epilogue (Company)

NOTES—*Hark!* was generally well-received by the critics, and it's surprising the revue didn't last longer than five months (like *Dont Bother Me, I Cant Cope* [see entry], it would probably have benefited from playing in a nightclub venue).

Despite its title, the revue wasn't one of the many religious-themed musicals of the period; *Hark!* was instead a collection of easy-going songs about life in the United States, everything from funerals and vasectomies to love and dancing. Clive Barnes in the *New York Times* found the evening a "happy excursion" which "swings with the pulse of today," and he enjoyed the performers and the score.

The cast album was recorded on a two-LP set (# STK-1015/16/17/18), with a note stating the album was recorded "for demonstration purposes only ... not for sale"; but for a time the album was generally available through various outlets which specialized in the sale of theatre-music recordings.

The score included three numbers not by Goggin, Solley, and Lorick: "A Dying Business" (lyric by Fred Ebb, music by Norman L. Martin), "Suburbia Square Dance" (lyric and music by Rod Warren and Michael McWhinney), and "Hip Hooray for America" (lyric and music by Jim Rusk). All three were recorded on the cast album. ("Suburbia Square Dance" was heard in three Off Broadway revues, and was recorded on two cast albums. Before being used in *Hark!* and recorded for its cast album, the song had first been introduced in the third edition of Rod Warren's *The Game Is Up* [1965; see entry] and was later in Warren's 1966 revue *Below the Belt* [see entry]; it can be heard on the latter's cast album.)

Two years after its New York run, *Hark!* surfaced as *Something for Everybody's Mother*, which briefly toured (but never played New York) and was recorded by Theatre Archives Records (LP # JGR-300). The new album included seven songs, two from the earlier production ("Hark" and "In a Hundred Years") and five new ones ("Starsong," "Everybody's Gone to California," "Too Bad (Too Soon)," "Psalm," and "A Mishandled Tribute (to the Nixon Administration)." "(A) Conversation Piece" was later heard in *A One-Way Ticket to Broadway* (see entry).

668 Harlem Song. "A New Musical." THEATRE: Apollo Theatre; OPENING DATE: August 6, 2002; PERFORMANCES: 146; TEXT: George C. Wolfe; ORIGINAL MUSIC: Zane Mark and Daryl Waters; DIRECTION: George C. Wolfe; CHOREOGRAPHY: Ken Roberson; SCENERY: Riccardo Hernandez; COSTUMES: Paul Tazewell; LIGHTING: Jules Fisher and Peggy Eisenhauer; MUSICAL DIRECTION: Zane Mark; PRODUCERS: John Schreiber, Margo Lion/Jay Furman, Daryl Roth, Morton Swinsky, Color Mad, Inc., and Charles Flateman, Executive Producer, in association with Sony Music, Arielle Tepper, Whoopi Goldberg, The Apollo Theatre Foundation, and Herb Alpert; Mark Krantz, David Goodman, and Frank Wildhorn, Co-Producers; Gwen Gilliam and Gail Goldstein, Associate Producers

CAST—Rosa Evangelina Arredondo, Renee Monique Brown, Gabriel A. Croom, B.J. CROSBY, Rosa Curry, Randy A. Davis, QUEEN ESTHER, DeLandis McClam, Sinclair Mitchell, Zoie Morris, DanaShavonne Rainey, Stacey Sargent, DAVID ST. LOUIS, Keith Lamelle Thomas, Charles E. Wallace

The revue was presented in one act.

MUSICAL NUMBERS—Opening (David St. Louis, B.J. Crosby, Gabriel A. Croom, Randy A. Davis, Charles E. Wallace); *Strollin'*: "Well Alright Then" (lyric and music by Jimmie Lunceford) (Queen Esther, with Rosa Evangelina Arredondo, Renee Monique Brown, Gabriel A. Croom, Rosa Curry, Randy A. Davis, DeLandis McClam, Sinclair Mitchell, DanaShavonne Rainey, Stacey Sargent, Keith Lamelle Thomas); *Slummin'*: "Drop Me Off at Harlem" (lyric and music by Duke Ellington and Nick Kenny) (Rosa Curry, with David St. Louis, Gabriel A. Croom, Randy A. Davis, Sinclair Mitchell, Stacey Sargent, Keith Lamelle Thomas), "Tarzan of Harlem" (lyric and music by Irving Mills, Henry Nemo, and Lupin Fein) (Queen Esther, with Rosa Evangelina Arredondo, Renee Monique Brown, Rosa Curry, DanaShavonne Rainey) "Shakin' the Africann" (lyric by Ted Koehler, music by Harold Arlen; additional lyric by George C. Wolfe) (Keith Lamelle Thomas, Gabriel A. Croom, Randy A. Davis, DeLandis McClam, Sinclair Mitchell), "For Sale" (lyric and music by Clarence Williams and Henry Troy) (B.J. Crosby, Charles E. Wallace), "Drop Me Off at Harlem" (reprise) (Company); *Migration*: "Take the 'A' Train" (lyric by Billy Strayhorn, music by Duke Ellington) (Rosa Evangelina Arredondo, Gabriel A. Croom, Charles E. Wallace); *Depresssion*: "Doin' the Niggerati Rag" (lyric by George C. Wolfe, music by Zane Mark) (Queen Esther, Gabriel A. Crooms, Rosa Curry, Randy A. Davis, Sinclair Mitchell, Stacey Sargent, Keith Lamelle Thomas), "The Hungry Blues" (lyric by Langston Hughes, music by James P. Johnson) (B.J. Crosby, Randy A. Davis), "Miss Linda Brown" (lyric and music by Alvin Cowens) (Rosa Curry); *Eviction*: "Here You Come with Love" (lyric and music by Jo Trent, Harry Tobias, and Neil Moret) (Queen Esther); *Visions*: "Time Is Winding Up" (lyric and music by Zane Mark and Daryl Waters?) (David St. Louis, Keith Lamelle Thomas, Stacey Sargent, Charles E. Wallace); *The Brown Bomber*: "King Joe" (lyric and music by William "Count" Basie and Richard Wright) (Queen Esther, B.J. Crosby), "A Fable of Rage in the Key of Jive" (by George C. Wolfe, Zane Mark, and Daryl Waters; set to music of "Apple Honey" by Woody Herman) (David St. Louis, Company); *Main Drag of Many Tears*: "Dream Deferred" (lyric by Langston Hughes, music by Zane Mark) (Queen Esther), "Shake" (lyric and music by Sam Cooke; additional lyric by George C. Wolfe) (David St. Louis, Rosa Curry, Stacey Sargent, Ensemble), "Tree of Life" (lyric and music by Pamela Warrick-Smith) (B.J. Crosby, Company)

NOTES—Like the hit revue *Bubbling Brown Sugar* (see entry), *Harlem Song* was yet another journey to old-time Harlem, but this time around not all that many theatergoers wanted to take the trip. The revue hung on for a few months, and then finally gave up, but apparently not without a fight. It appears that work on the show continued throughout the run; the song list in *The Best Plays of 2002-2003* (which reflects what numbers were performed on opening night); the song list from an undated program; and numbers from the cast album released by Columbia Records (CD # CK-86886) all contain contradictory information about which songs were performed. For example, the program lists "Late One Night," a Spanish version of "Take the 'A' Train" ("Coje el 'A' Train"), "Uptown Jazzmen," and "One Word," but none of these appear in the opening-night list of songs in *Best Plays* (but they appear on the cast album); on the other hand, the cast album includes "Here Comes My Daddy," which isn't listed in *Best Plays* or the program.

669 The Harold Arlen Songbook.

THEATRE: Stage 73; OPENING DATE: February 28, 1967; PERFORMANCES: 41; LYRICS: See song list for credits; MUSIC: Harold Arlen; DIRECTION: Robert Elston; LIGHTING: Tony Quintavalla; MUSICAL DIRECTION: George Taros; PRODUCERS: Ray Ramirez and Robert Elston

CAST—Pamela Hall, Jerry Holmes, Marcia Mohr, Ray Ramirez, Major Wiley

The revue was presented in two acts.

ACT ONE—Opening (specific songs in this sequence not identified in the program; see notes below for songs performed in the opening sequence as well as in the various medley sequences) (Company), "Little Biscuit" (from *Jamaica*, 1957; lyric by E.Y. Harburg) (Ray Ramirez), Medley (specific songs in this sequence not identified in the program) (Company), "Let's Take a Walk Around the Block" (*Life Begins at 8:40*, 1934; lyric by E.Y. Harburg and Ira Gershwin) (Marcia Mohr), "In the Shade of the New Apple Tree" (*Hooray for What!*, 1937; lyric by E.Y. Harburg) (Jerry Holmes), Medley (specific songs in this sequence not identified in the program) (Company), "Ridin' on the Moon" (*St. Louis Woman*, 1946; lyric by Johnny Mercer) (Ray Ramirez), "Out of This World" (1945 film *Out of This World*; lyric by Johnny Mercer) (Pamela Hall), "We're Off to See the Wizard" (1939 film *The Wizard of Oz*; lyric by E.Y. Harburg) (Company), Medley (specific songs in this sequence not identified in the program) (Company), "Bubbles" (1962 film *Gay Purr-ee*; lyric by E.Y. Harburg) (Company), "The Merry Old Land of Oz" (1939 film *The Wizard of Oz*; lyric by E.Y. Harburg) (Major Wiley), "Push de Button" (*Jamaica*, 1957; lyric by E.Y. Harburg) (Company), "I Wonder What Became of Me" (*St. Louis Woman*, 1946; lyric by Johnny Mercer) (Pamela Hall), "So Long, Big Time" (lyric by Dory Langdon Previn; independent song, 1963) (Ray Ramirez), "The Man That Got Away" (1954 film *A Star Is Born*; lyric by Ira Gershwin) (Marcia Mohr), "For Ev'ry Man There's a Woman" (1948 film *Casbah*; lyric by Leo Robin) (Jerry Holmes), "Anyplace I Hang My Hat Is Home" (*St. Louis Woman*, 1946; lyric by Johnny Mercer) (Major Wiley)

ACT TWO—Medley (specific songs in this sequence were not identified in the program) (Company), "T,morra, T,morra" (*Bloomer Girl*, 1944; lyric by E.Y. Harburg) (Major Wiley), "Love Held Lightly" (*Saratoga*, 1959; lyric by Johnny Mercer) (Pamela Hall), "(Love Is) A Game of Poker" (*Saratoga*, 1959; lyric by Johnny Mercer) (Jerry Holmes), "It's Only a Paper Moon (If You Believed in Me)" (*The Great Magoo*, 1932; lyric by E.Y. Harburg and Billy Rose) (Marcia Mohr), "I Had Myself a True Love" (*St. Louis Woman*, 1946; lyric by Johnny Mercer) (Pamela Hall), "House of Flowers" (*House of Flowers*, 1954; lyric by Truman Capote and Harold Arlen) (Ray Ramirez), "Willow in the Wind" (lyric by E.Y. Harburg; independent song) (Jerry Holmes), Medley (specific songs in this sequence were not identified in the program) (Company)

NOTES—*The Harold Arlen Songbook* was yet another in the ever-growing trend of songwriter-tribute revues.

Besides the above-listed songs, the following were also performed in the revue, as part of the opening and in the various medley sequences: "Accentuate the Positive" (1944 film *Here Come the Waves*; lyric by Johnny Mercer), "Andiamo" (1951 film *Mr. Imperium*; lyric by Dorothy Fields), "Between the Devil and the Deep Blue Sea" (*Rhyth-mania*, 1931; lyric by Ted Koehler), "Blues in the Night" (1941 film *Blues in the Night*; lyric by Johnny Mercer), "Come Rain or Come Shine" (*St. Louis Woman*, 1946; lyric by Johnny Mercer), "Ding Dong! The Witch Is Dead!" (1939 film *The Wizard of Oz*; lyric by E.Y. Harburg), "Down with Love" (*Hooray for What!*, 1937; lyric by E.Y. Harburg), "The Eagle and Me" (*Bloomer Girl*, 1944; lyric by E.Y. Harburg), "The Farmer's Daughter" (*Bloomer Girl*, 1944; lyric by E.Y. Harburg), "Fun to Be Fooled" (*Life Begins at 8:40*, 1934; lyric by E.Y. Harburg and Ira Gershwin), "Get Happy" (*Nine-Fifteen Revue*, 1930; lyric by Ted Koehler), "God's Country" (*Hooray for What!*, 1937; lyric by E.Y. Harburg), "Gotta Have Me Go with You" (1954 film *A Star Is Born*; lyric by Ira Gershwin), "Happiness Is a Thing Called Joe" (1943 film *Cabin in the Sky*; lyric by E.Y. Harburg), "He Loved Me Till the All-Clear Came" (1942 film *Star-Spangled Rhythm*; lyric by Johnny Mercer), "Hooray for Love" (1948 *Casbah*; lyric by Leo Robin), "The Horse Won't Talk" (1962 film *Gay Purr-ee*; lyric by E.Y. Harburg), "I Don't Think I'll End It All Today" (*Jamaica*, 1957; lyric by E.Y. Harburg), "I Gotta Right to Sing the Blues" (*Earl Carroll Vanities*, 1932; lyric by Ted Koehler); "I Love a Parade" (*Rhyth-mania*, 1931; lyric by Ted Koehler), "Ill Wind" (*Cotton Club Parade*, 1934; lyric by Ted Koehler), "It's a New World" (1954 film *A Star Is Born*; lyric by Ira Gershwin), "It Was Good Enough for Grandma" (*Bloomer Girl*, 1944; lyric by E.Y. Harburg), "I've Got the World on a String" (*Cotton Club Parade*, 1932; lyric by Ted Koehler), "Legalize My Name" (*St. Louis Woman*, 1946; lyric by Johnny Mercer), "Let's Fall in Love" (1934 film *Let's Fall in Love*; lyric by Ted Koehler), "Let's Take the Long Way Home" (1944 film *Here Come the Waves*; lyric by Johnny Mercer), "Like a Straw in the Wind" (source unknown; lyric by Ted Koehler), "Lose That Long Face" (1954 film *A Star Is Born*; lyric by Johnny Mercer), "Love Is Love Anywhere" (1934 film *Let's Fall in Love*; lyric by Ted Koehler), "Lydia, the Tattooed Lady" (1939 film *At the Circus*; lyric by E.Y. Harburg), "My Shining Hour" (1943 film *The Sky's the Limit*; lyric by Johnny Mercer), "One for My Baby" (1943 film *The Sky's the Limit*; lyric by Johnny Mercer), "Right as the Rain" (*Bloomer Girl*, 1944; lyric by E.Y. Harburg), "Someone at Last" (1954 film *A Star Is Born*; lyric by Ira Gershwin), "Stormy Weather" (*Cotton Club Parade*, 1933; lyric by Ted Koehler), "That Old Black Magic" (*Star-Spangled Rhythm*, 1944; lyric by Johnny Mercer), "Things" (*Life Begins at 8:40*, 1934; lyric by E.Y. Harburg and Ira Gershwin), "Two Ladies in De Shade of De Banana Tree" (*House of Flowers*, 1954; lyric by Truman Capote and Harold Arlen), "When the Sun Comes Out" (independent song; lyric by Ted Koehler), "What Can You Say in a Love Song?" (*Life Begins at 8:40*, 1934; lyric by E.Y. Harburg and Ira Gershwin), "What's Good About Goodbye" (1948 film *Casbah*; lyric by Leo Robin), "A Woman's Prerogative" (*St. Louis Woman*, 1946; lyric by Johnny Mercer).

For another Harold Arlen tribute, see entry for *Happy with the Blues*.

670 Haroun and the Sea of Stories.

THEATRE: New York State Theater; OPENING DATE: October 31, 2004; PERFORMANCES: 4; LIBRETTO: James Fenton; MUSIC: Charles Wuorinen; DIRECTION: Mark Lamos; CHOREOGRAPHY: Sean Curran; SCENERY: Riccardo Hernandez; COSTUMES: Candice Donnelly; MUSICAL DIRECTION: George Manahan; PRODUCER: The New York City Opera

CAST—Heather Buck (Haroun), Wilbur Pauley (Mali), Peter Strummer (Rashid), Joel Sorensen (Snooty Buttoo), Ethan Herschenfeld (Butt the Hoopoe), Ryan McPherson (Iff)

SOURCE—The 1990 novel *Haroun and the Sea of Stories* by Salman Rushdie.

NOTES—The world premiere of *Haroun and the Sea of Stories* was based on Salman Rushdie's novel, which was a plea for artistic self-expression. The title character goes to the Sea of Stories and there meets an adversary who hopes to destroy all stories because he can't control what they say.

In his review for the *New York Times*, Anthony Tommasini praised James Fenton's whimsical libretto of "punchy clarity ... one of the most streamlined and gently poetic librettos in some time." And while he praised parts of Charles Wuorinen's score (there were "brilliant, even ingenious" aspects to the music), he felt that too often the overly complex score "distracts from and deadens" the story.

671 The Harpies.

NOTES—See entry for *The Blitzstein Project*.

672 Harry Ruby's Songs My Mother Never Sang.

THEATRE: UpStage/Manhattan Theatre Club; OPENING DATE: June 9, 1981; PERFORMANCES: 12; LYRICS AND MUSIC: Unless otherwise noted, all lyrics by Bert Kalmar and all music by Harry Ruby; DIRECTION: Paul Lazarus; CHOREOGRAPHY: Douglas Norwick; SCENERY: Jane Thurn; COSTUMES: Christa Scholtz; LIGHTING: F. Mitchell Dana; MUSICAL DIRECTION: Michael S. Roth; PRODUCER: Manhattan Theatre Club (Lynne Meadow, Artistic Director; Barry Grove, Managing Director)

CAST—Indira Christopherson, Peter Frechette, I.M. Hobson

The revue was presented in one act (song assignments weren't identified in the program).

MUSICAL NUMBERS—Overture: "The Real McCoys" (Theme and Variation) (theme song from the CBS television series *The Real McCoys*) (Orchestra), "Hello, I Must Be Going" (part of the "Hooray for Captain Spalding!" sequence in *Animal Crackers* [stage, 1928; film, 1930]), "The Songs My Mother Used to Sing to Me" "A Tulip Told a Tale," "My Dream of the South of France" "Timbuctoo" "Father's Day" "The Three Little Fishes" "Fight on for Tannenbaum"/"Get Off the Pot" "There's a Place Called Omaha, Nebraska" (lyric by Groucho Marx, music by Harry Ruby) "Thinking of You" (from *The Five O'Clock Girl*, 1927), "My Love Is Waiting" "Love Is Like a Rose" "Nevertheless" "(We're Four of the Three)" Musketeers (*Animal Crackers*, 1928), "Whoopee!" "Hold Me Thusly" (lyric and music by Harry Ruby), "A Streetcar Is a Horsecar" (lyric and music by Harry Ruby), "There's a Girl in the Heart of Wheeling, West Virginia" (lyric and music by Harry Ruby), "Show Me a Rose" "He's Not an Aristocrat" (lyric and music by Harry Ruby), "Three Little Words" (1930 film *Check and Double Check*)

NOTES—Most musical theatre reference books examine in detail the lyricists and composers of the golden age of the American musical, but for some reason such names as Harry Ruby (1895-1974), Bert

Kalmar, Sigmund Romberg, Victor Herbert, Rudolf Friml, and the team of B.G. (Buddy) DeSylva, Lew Brown, and Ray Henderson are generally ignored. Off Off Broadway made the effort to remember Harry Ruby (and his frequent collaborator, Bert Kalmar) in *Harry Ruby's Songs My Mother Never Sang*, an evening of mostly unfamiliar songs, many of which were written independent of musical productions. (Also see entry for the 1977 Off Broadway musical *The Cockeyed Tiger*, which interpolated a few Ruby and Kalmar songs into its score.)

Frank Rich in the *New York Times* felt that Ruby's intrinsically zany material never quite found its voice, and instead of "big laughs" the revue received "mild chuckles." But he praised the performers, and singled out I.M. Hobson, who clearly understood the "particular spirit" of Ruby's songs.

673 Harvey Milk. THEATRE: The New York State Theatre; OPENING DATE: April 4, 1995; PERFORMANCES: Unknown; LIBRETTO: Michael Korie; MUSIC: Stewart Wallace; DIRECTION: Christopher Alden; CHOREOGRAPHY: Ross Perry; SCENERY: Paul Steinberg; COSTUMES: Gabriel Berry; LIGHTING: Jeff Davis; MUSICAL DIRECTION: Christopher Keene; PRODUCER: The New York City Opera

CAST—Robert Orth (Harvey Milk), Raymond Very (Dan White, Man in Trenchcoat, Cop), Gidon Saks (George Moscone, Horst Brauer, Teamster), Bradley Williams (Scott Smith, Closet Lover), Juliana Gondek (Dianne Feinstein, Mama, Hooker), Ron Baker (Messenger, Mintz, Empress), Robynne Redmon (Anne Kronenberg, Beard), Randall Wong (Henry Wong, Closet Lover), Matthew Cavenaugh (Young Harvey Milk), Kathryn H. Cavenaugh (Medora), San Francisco City Supervisors (John Lankston, Barbara Shirvis, Shane Kim, Geraldine McMillan, Don Yule, Jonathan Green, Stephen Bryant, William Ledbetter)

The action occurs in New York City and in San Francisco.

The opera was presented in three acts.

ACT ONE—"Yitgadel" (Chorus, Mama, Sampled Voice of Dianne Feinstein, Young Harvey), "Bravo Bravo"/"Who Are These Men?" (Men at the Opera, Young Harvey), "Like Chocolate, Soldier?" (Men in the Park, Men in the Park, Young Harvey, Mama), "An Angel Will Go Before You" (Women's Chorus), "Harvey" (Closet Lovers, Mintz, Beard, Horst, Harvey, Cop), "Closets Are a Necessary Fact of Life" (Harvey, Closet Lovers, Beard, Horst, Mintz, Cop), "Poor Dear Is Beside Himself" (Mintz, Closet Lovers, Beard, Horst, Harvey, Cop), "You Don't Have to Stand There" (Scott, Harvey), "Who Are These Men?" (reprise)/"My Forefathers" (Men at the Opera, Harvey, Concentration Camp Inmates, Horst), "From Dust We Come" (Chorus), "Cops and Mafia Out of the Bars!" (Drag Queens, Cops, Dykes, Chorus, Scott), "We Are the Stonewall Girls!" (Drag Queens, Chorus), "Out of the Closets and Into the Streets!" (Rioters), "Out of the Closets"/"Remember the Moment" (Rioters, Chorus, Harvey, Scott)

ACT TWO—"This Used to Be a Nice, Normal Neighborhood" (Hooker, Dan White), "This Used to Be an Old Irish Neighborhood" (Dan White), "Macho!" (Castro Clones, Lavender Menace, Arrivals, Politicos, Empress, Vietnam Vet, S and M's, Cleveland, Anne, Doctor), "I Come from Woodmere, Long Island!" (Voice of Harvey on Tape, Politicos, Scott, Chorus), "I Met Harvey Like Most People Did" (Anne, Harvey, Three TV Reporters, Wong, Teamster, Medora, Mother, Old Ladies, Mailman, Blue Collar), "The Milk Train!" (Anne, Wong, Teamster, Mother, Old Ladies, Mailman, Blue Collar, Chorus, Three TV Reporters, Medora), "Scott? Are You Asleep?" (Harvey, Scott), "The Haircut" (Orchestral Interlude), "Faggots!" (Chorus), "What We Have Here Is Not What It Seems" (Dan White, Harvey), "Thank You, San Francisco!" (Mayor Moscone, Harvey), "Thank You, San Francisco!" (Chorus, Harvey)

ACT THREE—"I Can Live with That!' (Eight City Supervisors, Harvey), "These Are the Corridors of Power" (Dianne Feinstein, Dan White), "The Issue of the Floor Is"/"Not in My Backyard!" (Dianne Feinstein, Dan White, Harvey, Supervisors), "Next on the Agenda"/"Good-bye, Judy Garland" (Dianne Feinstein, Harvey), "All in Favor?"/"Aye!" (Dianne Feinstein, Supervisors, Harvey, Mayor Moscone), "I Can't Take This Anymore!" (Dan White), "Dan, You Idiot"!/"Easy Harvey—Don't Push" (Dianne Feinstein, Anne, Wong, Scott, Harvey, Dan White, Mayor Moscone), "He's Back!"/"A Man Is Allowed to Change His Mind" (Power Brokers, Dan White, Harvey, Dianne Feinstein, Mayor Moscone), "Time Out! Did I Just Hear What I Heard?" (Harvey, Mayor Moscone, Dan White), "Bravo! Bravo!" (Chorus, Scott, Harvey, Dan White), "Harvey. Come Home"/"Mama. There Are Things" (Mama, Harvey), "Go Ahead, Fire Me, George" (Dan White, Mayor Moscone, Voice of Harvey Milk, Harvey), "When I Heard, I Was in a State of Shock" (Wong, Chorus, The Messenger, Anne, Scott)

NOTES—*Harvey Milk* was one of a number of operas produced during the era which were based on either recent headlines or the lives of celebrities. Besides *Harvey Milk*, *Nixon in China*, *X (The Life and Times of Malcolm X)*, and *The Death of Klinghoffer* (see entries) dealt with news events, and *Marilyn* (see entry) and *The Dream of Valentino* examined the lives of film stars. Harvey Milk was a gay San Francisco politician who, along with the city's mayor, was murdered by a fellow politician in 1978.

The world premiere of *Harvey Milk* took place at the Houston Grand Opera in 1995. Reviewing the City Opera premiere for the *New York Times*, Bernard Holland described the piece as a "docu-opera with music" and noted the conflict between Harvey Milk and Dan White came across as "one set of ideas killing another ... [the opera] offers not people but photographs of people." He also found the music "not so much composed as collected ... nothing is original or personal."

The opera was recorded on a 2-CD set by Teldec Records (# 0630-15856-2; the list of the musical sequences is taken from the recording).

In 1986, Broadway had seen *Execution of Justice*, Emily Mann's docu-drama about the trial following the 1978 murders. Although it played for just twelve performances, the drama was selected by *The Burns Mantle Theatre Yearbook* as one of the ten best plays of its season.

674 A Haunted Deconstruction of Nathaniel Hawthorne's *The House of the Seven Gables*.

NOTES—See entry for *The House of the Seven Gables*.

675 Have I Got a Girl for You! "The Frankenstein Musical." THEATRE: Second Avenue Theatre; OPENING DATE: October 29, 1986; PERFORMANCES: 78; BOOK: Joel Greenhouse and Penny Rockwell; LYRICS: Dick Gallagher; MUSIC: Dick Gallagher; DIRECTION: Bruce Hopkins; CHOREOGRAPHY: Felton Smith; SCENERY: Harry Darrow; Illusions by Ben Robinson; COSTUMES: Kenneth M. Yount; LIGHTING: Jeffrey Schissler; MUSICAL DIRECTOR: Michael Rice Producers: Heide Mintzer, George Grec, Frank Laraia, and David Singer in association with Gary H. Herman; Robert De Rothschild, Associate Producer

CAST—Gregory Jbara (The Monster), Walter Hudson (Baron John Von Frankenstein), Semina De Laurentis (Nurse Mary Phillips), Angelina Fiordellisi (Elke), J.P. Dougherty (Doctor Pretorius), Ritamarie Kelly (A Little Peasant Girl, A Blind Peasant Girl), Dennis Parlato (Igor), "?" (The Bride of Frankenstein)

The action occurs a long time ago in a Bavarian forest just east of Hollywood.

The musical was presented in two acts.

ACT ONE—"The Peasants' Song" (Ensemble), "Don't Open the Door" (Mary's Protectors), "Always for Science" (Semina De Laurentis), "Hollywood" (J.P. Dougherty, Ensemble), "Girlfriends for Life" (Angelina Fiordellisi, Semina De Laurentis), "The Monster's Song" (Gregory Jbara), "I Love Me" (Walter Hudson, Semina De Laurentis), "Have I Got a Girl for You" (J.P. Dougherty, Dennis Parlato, Gregory Jbara)

ACT TWO—"Mary's Lament" (Semina De Laurentis), "The Opera" (Company), "Something" (The Bride), Finale (Company)

NOTES—Taking place "a long time ago in a Bavarian forest just east of Hollywood," *Have I Got a Girl for You!* was a spoof of such classic horror films as *The Bride of Frankenstein* (1935). It sounds amusing, but it ran just a little over two months and was never heard from again. Prior to its Off Broadway production, the musical had been seen Off Off Broadway at the Inroads Theatre where it opened on February 10, 1985, and played for sixteen performances. Stephen Holden in the *New York Times* reported that the plot concerned Frankenstein's obsession with creating the "ultimate Hollywood goddess" by assembling the body parts of famous screen actresses; further, an "ill-fated" pajama party thrown by Greta Garbo provides the "requisite final ingredients" to concoct the last word in Hollywood Bombshell. Semina De Laurentis played the role of Nurse Mary, and Holden described her as a "young Imogene Coca" and a "pint-sized, bug-eyed, young Edith Bunker" with a "goofy ear-to-ear overbite." To add to the internal mad logic of the musical, Nurse Mary's head is deemed the perfect one to be attached to the body of Frankenstein's glamorous creation.

Adding to all the merry nonsense was a subplot involving Frankenstein's original monster (played by Gregory Jbara) who roams through the Hollywood hills and encounters peasants with disconcerting resemblances to Shirley Temple and Joan Rivers.

Holden noted the evening was a "free-for-all collection of television skits" which was "stitched" together by an "amusing satirical premise," one which blended traditional musical comedy and stylized camp. He singled out one song, the "pseudo-operatic" "Always for Science," sung by De Laurentis.

During the Off Broadway run, the song "Don't Open the Door" was deleted. Also, the opening number ("The Peasants' Song") was replaced by another opening chorus ("Bavaria's Hot Tonight") which, however, might have been the same song with a new title. Not to be confused with Irving Cooper's *Have I Got a Girl for You!*, a comedy which played on Broadway for one performance in 1963. For another musical inspired by Mary Shelley's novel, see entry for *Frankenstein*.

676 Have I Got One for You. "A New Musical." THEATRE: Theatre Four; OPENING DATE: January 7, 1968; PERFORMANCES: 1; BOOK: Jerry Blatt and Lonnie Burstein; LYRICS: Jerry Blatt and Lonnie Burstein; MUSIC: Jerry Blatt; DIRECTION: Roberta Sklar; SCENERY: John Conklin; COSTUMES: John Conklin; LIGHTING: Peter Hunt; MUSICAL DIRECTION: Alan Marlowe; PRODUCER: Harlan P. Kleiman

CAST—The Animals (Gloria DeHaven, Gertrude, Mother Toad; Ted Pugh, Joshua; Dick O'Neill, Marcello; Peter Roark, Mole; Fred Osin, Mole; Michael Schroeder, Mole; Ellen Shade, Butterfly; Alma Marshak, Butterfly; Mary Crawford, Butterfly); The People (Anne Kaye, Thumby; John Michael King (Prince); Men and Women of the Court played by Peter Roark, Fred Osin, Michael

Schroeder, Ellen Shade, Alma Marshak, Mary Crawford)

ACT ONE—"The Toad's Lament") Gloria DeHaven), "Chapter One" (Company), "Fly Away" (John Michael King, Anne Kaye, Men of the Court, Butterflies), "It's Comin' True" (Anne Kaye), "Have I Got a Girl for You" (Gloria DeHaven, Ted Pugh), "Imagine Me" (Ted Pugh, Anne Kaye), "Ode to Marcello" (The Moles), "Livin' in a Hole" (Dick O'Neill, Gloria DeHaven, Moles), "The Chicken Song" (Gloria DeHaven, Moles), "I Should Stay" (Ted Pugh), "My Dream Is Through" (Anne Kaye, Butterflies)

ACT TWO—"What a Bore" (John Michael King, Men and Women of the Court), "A Nice Girl Like You" (Gloria DeHaven, Anne Kaye), "So It Goes" (Gloria DeHaven), "The Getaway Quintet" (Anne Kaye, Ted Pugh, Gloria DeHaven, Dick O'Neill, Moles), "¾ Drag" (Men and Women of the Court), "The Presentation" (John Michael King, Anne Kaye, Men and Women of the Court), Finale (Company)

NOTES—An adult musical fairy tale about animals and human royalty, the twee musical *Have I Got One for You* went belly-up on opening night. Clive Barnes in the *New York Times* noted that ten minutes after the show opened, "it was apparent that they hadn't." The story dealt with a girl named Thumby who dreams that one day her prince will come; unfortunately, when he arrives she realizes he's a cad. Meanwhile, Gertrude (a toad played by Gloria DeHaven) is determined that Thumby will marry her son, Joshua, who is of course also a toad. And with an assist from Marcello, a mole, Gertrude sees Thumby and Joshua happily wed.

Barnes found the musical "labored and so unfunny, so lacking in focus, shape or purpose, that the fairy tale is grimm, and the music grimmer." However, he singled out one number ("So It Goes") in which Gertrude looks back on her past with "vigorous nostalgia." *Have I Got One for You* was to have been recorded by ABC-Paramount Records, but the recording was cancelled due to the show's brief run. A privately recorded cast album of a live performance was issued on LP by an unnamed label (# 272).

The musical was one of the few opportunities for New York to see the vastly-underrated Gloria DeHaven, a lovely and ingratiating performer who was always a welcome film presence. She appeared in a number of MGM musicals (such as *Two Girls and a Sailor* [1944; her and June Allyson's charming rendition of "Sweet and Lovely" is one of the most memorable moments in MGM musicals] and *Summer Holiday* [1948]).

677 He Who Gets Slapped. THEATRE: New York City Center; OPENING DATE: April 12, 1959; PERFORMANCES: 2; LIBRETTO: Bernard Stambler; MUSIC: Robert Ward; DIRECTION: Michael Pollock Scenery: Andreas Nomikos; COSTUMES: Andreas Nomikos; MUSICAL DIRECTION: Emerson Buckley; PRODUCER: The New York City Opera Company

CAST—Norman Kelley (Count Mancini), Regina Sarfaty (Zinida), David Atkinson (Pantaloon), Lee Venora (Consuelo), Frank Porretta (Benzano), Emile Renan (Baron Regnard), Paul Dooley (Polly), Phil Bruns (Tilly), Chester Ludgin (Briquet), Will B. Able

SOURCE—The 1916 play *He Who Gets Slapped* by Leonid Andreyev.

The action occurs in a European circus at the end of the nineteenth century.

The opera was produced in three acts.

NOTES—Leonid Andreyev's play *He Who Gets Slapped* dealt with an embittered and unhappy married man who becomes a circus clown. He falls in love with the young bareback rider of the circus, but when he discovers her father is forcing her into marriage with a scoundrel, the clown murders her and kills himself.

Robert Ward and Bernard Stambler's operatic version of the material (which had previously been produced in New York in 1956 as *Pantaloon* [see entry]), softened the ending. Howard Taubman in the *New York Times* had reviewed the original production as well as the revival, and he noted the opera's more optimistic ending "is not death but a touch of happiness and a measure of resignation."

Taubman had been impressed by the opera in 1956, and he again had praise for the work. He felt the libretto had "considerable theatrical worth," and wrote that Ward's "melodic material flows in abundance" and "is laid out agreeably for the human voice." Further, Ward's music gave the story a "personal dimension." For the 1959 production, the opera's title reverted to its source material; besides the change of title, the opera probably underwent other revisions as well.

As *Pantaloon, He Who Gets Slapped*, the opera was briefly revived Off Off Broadway on January 18, 1978, at the Encompass Theatre.

In 1971, another lyric version of Andreyev's play opened Off Off Broadway as *Nevertheless, They Laugh* (see entry). It starred David Holliday as the clown and Bernadette Peters as the young bareback rider.

678 Head Over Heels. THEATRE: Harold Clurman Theatre; OPENING DATE: December 15, 1981; PERFORMANCES: 22; BOOK: William S. Kilborne, Jr., and Albert T. Viola; LYRICS: William S. Kilborne, Jr.; MUSIC: Albert T. Viola; DIRECTION: Jay Binder; CHOREOGRAPHY: Terry Rieser; SCENERY: John Falabella; COSTUMES: John Falabella; LIGHTING: Jeff Davis; MUSICAL DIRECTION: Herbert Kaplan; PRODUCERS: Aristotle Productions; Leonard Soloway and Allan Francis, Executive Producers; Joseph M. Sutherin, Associate Producer

CAST—John Cunningham (Punchinello), Dennis Bailey (Harlequin), Elizabeth Austin (Columbine), Charles Michael Wright (Pierrot), Gwyda Donhowe (Nurse)

SOURCE—The play *The Wonder Hat* (circa 1925) by Kenneth Sawyer Goodman and Ben Hecht.

The action occurs on a moonlit evening.

The musical was presented in two acts.

ACT ONE—"New Loves for Old" (John Cunningham, Elizabeth Austin, Charles Michael Wright), "Perfection" (Elizabeth Austin, Gwyda DonHowe, John Cunningham), "I'm in Love" (Dennis Bailey), "Aqua Vitae" (John Cunningham, Gwyda DonHowe), "Nowhere" (John Cunningham, Dennis Bailey), Finaletto (Company)

ACT TWO—"Castles in the Sand" (Elizabeth Austin, Gwyda DonHowe), "As If" (Elizabeth Austin), "Could He Be You?" (John Cunningham, Gwyda DonHowe), "Lullabye to Myself" (Charles Michael Wright), Finale (Company)

NOTES—Based on *The Wonder Hat*, an obscure play by Kenneth Sawyer Goodman and Ben Hecht (the latter was the co-author of the classic *The Front Page* [1928]), *Head Over Heels* became an even more obscure musical. It had originally been produced in regional theater as *Harlequinade*. Mel Gussow in the *New York Times* noted the musical's "childlike charm" tried for a *Fantastick* effect, but fell short. The story dealt with Punchinello's magic (including a hat which renders the wearer invisible), and how his potions work their spells on various sets of lovers. Gussow remarked that children (and adults "with a sweet tooth") might enjoy the evening, but otherwise "cynics stand forewarned." However, he had praise for "several melodic" second-act songs, and singled out "Could He Be You?," a "catchy comedy duet" for John Cunningham and Gwyda Donhowe.

The script was published by Samuel French, Inc., in 1983.

679 Heat Lightning. "The Musical." THEATRE: Kirk Theatre; OPENING DATE: March 5, 2003; PERFORMANCES: Unknown; BOOK: George Griggs and Paul Andrew Perez; LYRICS: George Griggs; MUSIC: George Griggs; DIRECTION: Jeremy Dobrish; CHOREOGRAPHY: Tesha Buss; SCENERY: Leo T. Van Allen; COSTUMES: Rachel Attridge; LIGHTING: Thom Weaver; MUSICAL DIRECTION: George Griggs; PRODUCER: Steve Griggs

CAST—Sean Fri (Seth), Laura Marie Duncan (Cris), Jackie Seiden (Fury), Coleen Sexton (Aurora), Jennifer Waldman (Fury)

The action takes place in a middle-class American suburb during the present time.

The musical was presented in one act.

NOTES—*Heat Lightning* was presented Off Off Broadway. The program didn't list musical numbers.

The story seems to have been inspired by the story of Cephalus and Procris, one of the tales in Ovid's *Metamorphoses*. The plot dealt with a wannabe rockstar who is torn between his wife and girlfriend. Neil Genzlinger in the *New York Times* noted that "plotwise" the musical didn't have much. But he liked the "pretty punchy" songs and the "talented" company.

680 Hedwig and the Angry Inch. THEATRE: Jane Street Theatre; OPENING DATE: February 14, 1998; PERFORMANCES: 857; BOOK: John Cameron Mitchell; LYRICS: Stephen Trask; MUSIC: Stephen Trask; DIRECTION: Peter Askin; CHOREOGRAPHY: Jerry Mitchell; SCENERY AND PROJECTIONS: James Youmans; COSTUMES: Fabio Toblini; LIGHTING: Kevin Adams; PRODUCERS: Alice's Enterprises, The Westside Theatre, and J.B.F. Producing Corp.; Eric Osbun and Terry Byrne, Associate Producers

CAST—John Cameron Mitchell (Hedwig [Tommy Gnosis]), Miriam Shor (Yitzhak); Cheater (the orchestra): Scott Bilbrey, Bass, Vocals; David McKinley, Drums; Stephen Trask, Keyboards, Guitar, Vocals; Chris Weilding, Guitar, Vocals

The action occurs in a Manhattan riverside fleabag hotel ballroom.

The musical was presented in one act.

MUSICAL NUMBERS—"Tear Me Down," "The Origin of Love," "Sugar Daddy," "Angry Inch," "Wig in a Box," "Wicked Little Town," "The Long Grift," "Hedwig's Lament," "Exquisite Corpse," "Wicked Little Town" (reprise), "Midnight Radio"

NOTES—*Hedwig and the Angry Inch* wasn't a would-be edgy show which ultimately let down the audience with its tameness; it *was* edgy, and with its tawdry ambience, its highly praised performance by John Cameron Mitchell (who also wrote the book), and its powerfully charged rock score, the musical played over two years. The musical's strongest number was the affecting "Wig in a Box"; with its plaintive, seductive melody and its touching yet comic lyric, it's one of the best theatre songs of the 1990s. (The number is also an interesting companion piece to Jerry Herman's "A Little More Mascara" [from the 1983 Broadway musical *La Cage Aux Folles*]; both character songs share the same philosophy, albeit in very different styles.) The musical was presented as a rock music concert/stand-up comedy performance given by Hedwig ("the internationally ignored song stylist") and his/her band Cheater in the rundown ballroom of a seedy Manhattan waterfront hotel.

Hedwig used to be an East German man named Hansel, who fell in love with Luther, an American GI who promised to take him to the United States if he had a sex-change operation. But instead of a sex change, Hansel was short-changed when the operation was botched. When Hedwig is abandoned by Luther, Hedwig starts writing songs and eventually takes up with Tommy Speck, who steals Hedwig's music and becomes an international rock star. Hedwig is determined to stalk Tommy and perform her cabaret act near the stadiums where his rock concerts play. Tonight, while Tommy performs across the river in a sold-out concert at Giants Stadium, Hedwig's comic irony reveals the innate toughness which allows her to ride out life's vagaries and disappointments ("I'm the new Berlin Wall. Try and tear me down!").

The musical had previously been produced Off Off Broadway at the Westbeth Theatre Center on March 9, 1997, for seventeen performances.

The script was published by the Overlook Press in 2000, and later by Dramatists Play Service, Inc., in 2003. The cast album was released by Atlantic Records (CD # 83160-2). In 2001, Mitchell both starred in and directed the entertaining and innovative film version, which was released by New Line Cinema and which included three new songs ("Nailed," "Freaks," and "In Your Arms Tonight"). The soundtrack was released on Hybrid Records (CD # HY-20024-2), and the film was released on DVD by New Line Home Entertainment (# N-5401).

Another album, *Wig in a Box*, was released by Off Records (CD # OFF-994); it included songs from the stage production and film version ("The Origin of Love," "Angry Inch," "The Long Grift," "Sugar Daddy," "Freaks," "Wicked Little Town" [both the "Hedwig" and "Tommy Gnosis" versions], "Nailed," and "Wig in a Box," "Tear Me Down," "Hedwig's Lament," "Exquisite Corpse, "Midnight Radio") as well as songs inspired by the musical ("City of Women" and "Milford Lane").

The musical was produced in London beginning on September 19, 2000, at the Playhouse Theatre.

A program note indicated *Hedwig* was the inaugural production of the Jane Street Theatre, which had originally opened in 1907 as a boarding house for seamen (in 1912, some of the surviving crew of the *Titanic* lodged there); at one point in its history, Herman Melville reportedly worked at the front desk. In later years, the space was the site of many nightclubs and theatres, including the Theatre for the New City.

A revival of *Hedwig* had been scheduled to open Off Broadway in October 2007 at the Zipper Theatre, but as of this writing the revival has either been postponed or permanently cancelled.

681 The Heebie Jeebies. "A Musical Tribute to the Boswell Sisters." THEATRE: Westside Arts Theatre/Downstairs; OPENING DATE: June 16, 1981; PERFORMANCES: 37; SCRIPT: Original idea by Mark Hampton; written by Mark Hampton and Stuart Ross; Vet Boswell, script and production advisor; DIRECTION: Stuart Ross; CHOREOGRAPHY: Stuart Ross; Terry Riser, Associate Choreographer; SCENERY: Michael Sharp; COSTUMES: Carol Oditz; LIGHTING: Richard Winkler; MUSICAL DIRECTION: Howard A. Roberts (?); PRODUCERS: Spencer Tandy, Joseph Butt, and Peter Alsop, produced in association with Dale Ward and Doug Cole

CAST—Memrie Innerarity, Audrey Lavine, Nancy McCall

The revue was presented in two acts.

ACT ONE—"The Heebie Jeebies," "Spend an Evening in Caroline," "Sentimental Gentleman from Georgia," "Nights When I'm Lonely," "St. Louis Blues" (lyric and music by W.C. Handy), "I'm Gonna Cry," "Dinah" (lyric by Sam M. Lewis and Joe Young, music by Harry Akst), "That's How Rhythm Was Born," "We're on the Highway to Heaven," The California Melodies Hour:, "We Gotta Put the Sun Back in the Sky," "Life Is Just a Bowl of Cherries" (from *George White's Scandals* [Eleventh Edition], 1931; lyric by B.G. [Buddy] DeSylva and Lew Brown, music by Ray Henderson) "Sing a Little Jingle," "Crazy People" (lyric by Edgar Leslie, music by James V. Monaco), "Nothing Is Sweeter Than You," "When I Take My Sugar to Tea" (lyric by Irving Kahal and Pierre Norman, music by Sammy Fain)

ACT TWO—"The Music Goes 'Round and Around" (lyric and music by Red Hodgson, Ed Farley, and Mike Riley), "Let Yourself Go" (1936 film *Follow the Fleet*; lyric and music by Irving Berlin), "You Oughta Be in Pictures" (lyric by Edward Heyman, music by Dana Suesse), "Rock 'n' Roll," "These Foolish Things (Remind Me of You)" (1936 British musical *Spread It Around*; lyric by Eric Maschwitz [Holt Marvell], music by James Strachey and Harry Link), "Until [Till] the Real Thing Comes Along" (original lyric by Mann Holiner [revised lyric by Sammy Cahn], music by Alberta Nichols and Saul Chaplin), "Darktown Strutters Ball" (1917; lyric and music by Sheldon Brooks), "Minnie the Moocher's Wedding Day" (lyric by Ted Koehler, music by Harold Arlen; *Cotton Club Parade* [Eleventh Edition], 1932), "Goin' Home," "Shout, Sister, Shout" (lyric and music by Clarence Williams), "The Object of My Affection" (lyric and music by Pinky Tomlin, Coy Poe, and Jimmie Grier), "Everybody Loves My Baby" (lyric and music by Jack Palmer and Spencer Williams), "The Heebie Jeebies" (reprise)

NOTES—The short-lived revue *The Heebie Jeebies* was a tribute to Martha, Connee, and Vet Boswell, a sister trio who were famous in the 1920s and early 1930s (the group disbanded in 1936). Until then, they had enjoyed successful vaudeville, concert, radio, and recording careers, and even appeared in a few films. Martha died in 1958, Connee in 1976. At the time of the production of *The Heebie Jeebies*, Vet was alive, and she was credited as the revue's script and production advisor.

The general understudy for the production was Mary-Cleere Haran, who later became one of the luminaries of the New York cabaret scene.

682 Helen. THEATRE: The AMAS Repertory Theatre; OPENING DATE: November 30, 1978; PERFORMANCES: 12; BOOK: Lucia Victor; LYRICS: Johnny Brandon; MUSIC: Johnny Brandon; DIRECTION: Lucia Victor; CHOREOGRAPHY: Bernard Johnson; SCENERY: Michael Meadows; COSTUMES: Lindsay Davis; LIGHTING: Paul Sullivan; MUSICAL DIRECTION: Danny Holgate; PRODUCER: The AMAS Repertory Theatre (Rosetta LeNoire, Founder and Artistic Director)

CAST—Jean Dushon, Chuck Patterson, Fran Salisbury, Newton Winters, Rob Barnes, Jamil K. Garland, Gerri Griffin, Pauletta Pearson, Kevin John Gee, James Moody, Paul Dinotto, Charlie J. Rodriguez, Amy Pivar, Joella Breedlove, Trudy Miller, Diane Wilson, Darnell Williams, Charles "CB" Murray, Carol Jean Lewis, John Russell

MUSICAL NUMBERS—(division of acts and song assignments unknown; songs are listed in performance order): "Nothing Ever Happens in Greece," "Come On and Dance," "Somethin's Doin'," "Bring It On Home," "Bite Your Tongue," "There Are Ways of Gettin' Things Done," "Diplomacy," "You've Got It," "Do Us a Favor," "Dance of the Golden Apple," "Helen," "Hold On Tight," "Do What You Must," "Somebody Touched Me," "You Never Know the Mind of a Woman," "Good or Bad," Finale

NOTES—*Helen* was based on the legend of Helen of Troy. For information on the definitive musical based on the material, see entry for *The Golden Apple*. Also see entries for *Sing Muse!*, an amusing version of the legend set in modern times, and for *La Belle Helene*, an adaptation of Jacques Offenbach's 1865 operetta. *Helen* shared a similar opening-song title with *The Golden Apple*; perhaps "Nothing Ever Happens in Greece" was Johnny Brandon's homage to the Jerome Moross and John LaTouche classic and its opening number "Nothing Ever Happens in Angel's Roost."

Helen was the second of three musicals by Brandon which were produced Off Off Broadway during the 1978-1979 season (see entries for *Ain't Doin' Nothin' But Singin' My Song* and *Suddenly the Music Starts*).

683 Hello Again. "A New Musical." THEATRE: The Mitzi E. Newhouse Theatre/Lincoln Center; OPENING DATE: January 30, 1994; PERFORMANCES: 65; BOOK: Michael John LaChiusa; LYRICS: Michael John LaChiusa; MUSIC: Michael John LaChiusa; DIRECTION: Graciela Daniele; CHOREOGRAPHY: Graciela Daniele; SCENERY: Derek McLane; COSTUMES: Toni-Leslie James; LIGHTING: Jules Fisher and Peggy Eisenhauer; MUSICAL DIRECTION: David Evans; PRODUCER: Lincoln Center Theatre (Andre Bishop and Bernard Gersten, Directors)

CAST—Donna Murphy (The Whore), David A. White (The Soldier), Judy Blazer (The Nurse), Michael Park (The College Boy), Carolee Carmello (The Young Wife), Dennis Parlato (The Husband), John Cameron Mitchell (The Young Thing), Malcolm Gets (The Writer), Michele Pawk (The Actress), John Dossett (The Senator)

SOURCE—The 1900 play *La Ronde* by Arthur Schnitzler.

The action occurs from the 1900s to the present.

The musical was presented in one act.

MUSICAL NUMBERS—1) The Whore and the Soldier (Around 1900): "Hello Again" (Donna Murphy, David A. White), 2) The Soldier and the Nurse (1940s): "Zei Gezent" (Carolee Carmello, John Cameron Mitchell, Michele Pawk), "I Gotta Little Time" (David A. White), "We Kiss" (David A. White and Judy Blazer, with Carolee Carmello, Malcolm Gets, John Cameron Mitchell, Michele Pawk, Dennis Parlato), 3) The Nurse and the College Boy (1960s): "In Some Other Life" (Judy Blazer, Michael Park), 4) The College Boy and the Young Wife (1930s): "Story of My Life" (Michael Park and Carolee Carmello, with John Dossett, John Cameron Mitchell, Dennis Parlato, David A. White), 5) The Young Wife and the Husband (1950s): "At the Prom" (John Cameron Mitchell), "Ah, Maien Zeit!" (Michele Pawk), "Tom" (Carolee Carmello), 6) The Husband and the Young Thing (1910s): "Listen to the Music" (Dennis Parlato and John Cameron Mitchell, with Michele Pawk), 7) The Young Thing and the Writer (1970s): "Montage" (Malcolm Gets, Ensemble), "Safe" (John Cameron Mitchell), "The One I Love" (Malcolm Gets, John Cameron Mitchell), 8) The Writer and the Actress (1920s): "Silent Movie" (Malcolm Gets), 9) The Actress and the Senator (1980s): "Rock with Rock" (David A. White), "Angel of Mercy" (Judy Blazer), "Mistress of the Senator" (Michele Pawk, John Dossett, Ensemble), 10) The Senator and the Whore (the Present and the Past): "The Bed Was Not My Own" (John Dossett, Donna Murphy), "Hello Again" (reprise) (Donna Murphy, David A. White, Judy Blazer, Michael Park, Carolee Carmello, Dennis Parlato, John Cameron Mitchell, Malcolm Gets, Michele Pawk)

NOTES—Loosely based on Arthur Schnitzler's 1900 play *La Ronde* (which was also the basis for the 1969 Off Broadway musical *Rondelay* [see entry]), *Hello Again* was a series of interlocking vignettes about ten couples seeking love throughout the twentieth century (but their stories weren't told in strict chronological order). John Lahr in the *New Yorker* complained that the "postmodern musical" struck a "sour antiromantic pose, in which love never finds a way" and he wasn't particularly impressed with Michael John LaChiusa's score ("the old guard worked hard to make songs look easy ... [LaChiusa] works to make the songs look hard"). On the other hand, David Patrick Sterns in *USA Today* found the musical "innovative" and "stylish," and said it reached "an eloquence few shows have achieved since Stephen Sondheim's *Company*."

The cast recording was released by RCA Victor Records (CD # 09026-62680-2), and the script was published by Dramatists Play Service, Inc., in 1995.

For information about other musicals based on

works by Schnitzler, see entries for *Bon Voyage* and *Rondelay*.

Six weeks prior to the opening of *Hello Again* at Lincoln Center, LaChiusa's musical *First Lady Suite* (see entry) had premiered at the Public Theatre. And during the 1999-2000 theatre season, he again enjoyed the rare achievement of seeing two of his musicals produced in New York during the same season, *Marie Christine* at Lincoln Center and *The Wild Party* on Broadway (for an Off Broadway adaptation of *The Wild Party* [which opened almost concurrently with LaChiusa's version], see entry).

684 Hello, Charlie. THEATRE: Yiddish Anderson Theatre; OPENING DATE: October 23, 1965; PERFORMANCES: 129; BOOK: H. Kalmanowitch; LYRICS: Jacob Jacobs; MUSIC: Maurice Rauch; DIRECTION: Max Perlman; CHOREOGRAPHY: Michael Aubrey; PRODUCER: Jacob Jacobs

CAST—Leon Liebgold (Benjamin Lichtenstein), Susan Walters (Lilly), Rick Grayson (Milton Kleinstein), Seymour Rexsite (Jack), Gita Galina (Fanny), Jacob Jacobs (Chaim Ber Zeitlin), Max Perlman (Charlie Zeitlin), Chayele Rosental (Molly), Miriam Kressyn (Miriam Rappaport), Anna Jacobowitz (Frumeh), Thelma Mintz (Jeanette); Ensemble of Dancers: Michael Aubrey, Lisa Berg, Cathy Haas, Enid Hart, David DeMarie, David Marcus

NOTES—*Hello, Charlie* was the 1965-1966 season's Jewish-American Off Broadway musical. By the mid-1960s, almost every season offered at least one such Broadway or Off Broadway musical. But by the early 1970s the genre was close to becoming extinct. However, the Jewish Repertory Theatre, which was founded in 1974, made its mark by presenting both classic and new Jewish-themed plays and musicals for over a quarter-century. Its mission ensured that the rich tradition of Jewish theatre had a venue in New York. Another important company which offered many seasons of Jewish theatrical fare was the American Jewish Theatre.

As for *Hello, Charlie*, Richard F. Shepard in the *New York Times* noted that while the evening offered "generically the same show, same cast, same audience" of previous Yiddish musicals, the tradition was nonetheless "a pleasant eternal verity." The plot (which had something to do with family bloodlines) offered both old and new jokes, a cast of seasoned comics, young dancers, and songs "winging up to the rafters."

685 Hello Muddah, Hello Fadduh! "The Allan Sherman Musical." THEATRE: Circle in the Square Downtown; OPENING DATE: December 5, 1992; PERFORMANCES: 235; BOOK: Douglas Bernstein and Rob Krausz; LYRICS: Allan Sherman; MUSIC: Allan Sherman; additional music by Albert Hague; DIRECTION: Michael Leeds; CHOREOGRAPHY: Michael Leeds; SCENERY: Michael E. Downs; COSTUMES: Susan Branch; LIGHTING: Howard Werner; MUSICAL DIRECTION: David Evans; PRODUCERS: Diane F. Krausz, Jennifer R. Manocherian, and David A. Blumberg

CAST—Stephen Berger (Doctor, Mohel, Morty, Myer, Choir, Phil, Robbie, Mr. Bloo, Store Clerk, Policeman, Lenny), Tovah Feldshuh (Mother, Louise, Esther, Carlotta, Choir, Sheila, Sophie, Doris), Jason Graae (Intern, Nun, Baby, Barry, Rose), Paul Kreppel (Father, Mr. Kalodner, Leonard, Principal, Harvey, Goldfarb, Shirley, Boyfriend, Nat), Mary Testa (Nurse, Sarah)

The action occurs in a Florida retirement community.

The musical was presented in two acts.

ACT ONE—"Opening Goulash" (Company), "Sarah Jackman" (Jason Graae, Mary Testa), "Won't You Come Home, Disraeli?" (Mary Testa, Tovah Feldshuh), "Sir Greenbaum's Madrigal" (Jason Graae, Stephen Berger), "Good Advice" (Paul Kreppel, Company), "I Can't Dance" (Jason Graae, Tovah Feldshuh), "Kiss of Myer" (Stephen Berger, Tovah Feldshuh, Mary Testa), "Hello Muddah, Hello Fadduh" (Jason Graae), "No One's Perfect" (Company), "One Hippopotami" (Jason Graae, Mary Testa), "Phil's Medley" (Stephen Berger), "Harvey and Sheila" (Paul Kreppel, Tovah Feldshuh, Company)

ACT TWO—"Shake Hands with Your Uncle Max" (Company), "Here's to the Crabgrass" (Jason Graae, Mary Testa), "Shine On, Harvey Bloom" (Stephen Berger, Company), "Mexican Hat Dance" (Tovah Feldshuh, Company), "Grow, Mrs. Goldfarb" (Paul Kreppel), "Jump Down, Spin Around" (Paul Kreppel, Company), "Crazy Downtown" (Mary Testa, Jason Graae), "Did I Ever Really Live?" (music by Albert Hague) (Jason Graae), "Like Yours" (music by Albert Hague) (Jason Graae, Mary Testa), "Down the Drain" (music by Albert Hague) (Paul Kreppel, Tovah Feldshuh, Stephen Berger), "The Ballad of Harry Lewis" (Company)

NOTES—Allan Sherman had died in 1973; *Hello Muddah, Hello Fadduh!* strung together some of his songs into a loose revue-like musical set in a Florida retirement community.

Sherman's one Broadway musical (for which he wrote book and lyrics) was the 1969 four-performance flop *The Fig Leaves Are Falling*, with music by Albert Hague. *Hello Muddah, Hello Fadduh!* included three songs from that show ("Did I Ever Really Live?," "Like Yours," and "Down the Drain").

The script was published by Samuel French, Inc., in 1994.

The revue was revived on August 2, 2001, at the Triad Theatre for 124 performances.

686 Hello Out There. THEATRE: Brander Matthews Theatre/Columbia University; OPENING DATE: May 27, 1954; PERFORMANCES: Unknown; LIBRETTO: Jack Beeson (from William Saroyan); MUSIC: Jack Beeson; DIRECTION: Felix Brentano; SCENERY: Paul Morrison; MUSICAL DIRECTION: Willard Rhodes; PRODUCERS: Columbia University Opera Workshop (sponsored by the Alice M. Ditson Fund)

CAST—Lena Gabrieli, Stephanie Turash, Ralph Farnsworth, Marvin Worden, Lorenzo Herrera

SOURCE—The 1942 play *Hello, Out There* by William Saroyan.

The action occurs in a jail in Matador, Texas.

The opera was presented in one act.

NOTES—William Saroyan's one-act play *Hello Out There* dealt with Photo Finish, a man unjustly accused of rape. While in his prison cell, he calls "Hello, out there" to no one in particular, and to his surprise he's answered by a young woman who works in the prison. The girl falls in love with Photo Finish (and perhaps he with her), and they plan his escape. But when the accuser's husband realizes his wife lied about the rape, he kills Photo Finish in order to protect his wife's reputation. At the end of the play, the girl is alone in the prison and calls out "Hello, out there."

Jack Beeson's chamber opera had its world premiere at Columbia University on a double bill with Lehman Engel's *Malady of Love* (see entry). In his review for the *New York Times*, Olin Downes had reservations about Beeson's score but admitted the music had a "dramatic feeling ... the curve of sensuous melody ... and capacity for orchestral accentuation and atmosphere." He felt that Beeson had a "manifest gift" for composing and should go on writing operas.

The opera was later recorded by Desto Records on a one-LP set (# D-451/DST-6251). For the recording, John Reardon sang Photo Finish, and both Lenya Gabriele ("Lena Gabrieli" in the *New York Times'* review) and Marvin Worden reprised their original roles.

The opera was revived Off Off Broadway by the Encompass Theatre on February 17, 1980.

687 Her Pilgrim Soul.

NOTES—See entry for *Weird Romance* (1992), an evening which was comprised of two one-act musicals, *The Girl Who Was Plugged In* and *Her Pilgrim Soul*.

688 Her Talking Drum. THEATRE: American Place Theatre; OPENING DATE: June 14, 1987; PERFORMANCES: 16; MATERIAL ADAPTED by Vinie Burrows and Lenwood O. Sloan; MUSIC CREATED AND PERFORMED by Madeleine Yayodele Nelson; DIRECTION: Lenwood O. Sloan; SCENERY: Brian Martin; COSTUMES: Judy Dearing; LIGHTING: Steven R. Jones; PRODUCER: American Place Theatre (Wynn Handman, Director; Julia Miles, Associate Director)

CAST—Vinie Burrows, Madeleine Yayodele Nelson, Kim Staunton, Hattie Winston

The revue was presented in one act.

NOTES—*Her Talking Drum*, a revue with music, created portraits of Black women from all over the world.

See entries for Vinie Burrows' *Walk Together Children* (1968 and 1972) which dealt with the Black experience in America from the times of slavery to the modern era.

Burows returned on June 16, 1992, with *Sister! Sister!*, a one-woman show which played at the Vineyard Theatre for sixteen performances; it reopened Off Off Broadway at the American Place Theatre on October 29, 1992, and played there for twenty performances (*Theatre World 1992-1993 Season* described it as "a collage of women's voices from around the world").

689 Here Lies Jenny. THEATRE: Zipper Theatre; OPENING DATE: May 27, 2004; PERFORMANCES: 92; TEXT: Roger Rees; LYRICS: See song list for credits; MUSIC: Kurt Weill; DIRECTION: Roger Rees; CHOREOGRAPHY: Ann Reinking; SCENERY: Neil Patel; COSTUMES: Kaye Voyce; LIGHTING: Frances Aronson; MUSICAL DIRECTION: Leslie Steifelman; PRODUCERS: Maria Di Dia, Kathryn Frawley, Hugh Hayes, Martin Platt, and the Zipper Theatre with the Green Moon Gang

CAST—BEBE NEUWIRTH (Jenny), Gregory Butler (Jim), Ed Dixon (George), Shawn Emamjomeh (John), Leslie Steifelman (The Piano Player)

The revue was presented in one act (song assignments unknown).

MUSICAL NUMBERS—"A Boy Like You" (from *Street Scene*, 1947; lyric by Langston Hughes), "The Army Song" (a/k/a "The Recruiting Song" and "The Kanon Song") (*The Threepenny Opera*, 1928; original German lyric by Bertolt Brecht; English lyric by Roger Rees and Eric Elice), "Barbara's Song" (a/k/a "The Barbara Song" and "Barbara Song") (*The Threepenny Opera*, 1928; original German lyric by Bertolt Brecht; English lyric by Marc Blitzstein), "Berlin im Licht-Song" (independent song, 1928; original German lyric by Kurt Weill), "Bilbao Song" (*Happy End*, 1929; original German lyric by Bertolt Brecht; English lyric by Michael Feingold), "Children's Game ("Fat, Fat, the Water Rat" and "Catch Me If You Can")" (*Street Scene*, 1947; lyric by Langston Hughes), "Don't Be Afraid" (*Happy End*, 1928; original German lyric by Bertolt Brecht; English lyric by Michael Feingold), "In Meinem Garten" (from song cycle *Ofrah's Lieder*, 1916; German lyric based on Hebrew poem by Jehuda [Judah] Halevi; English lyric by Steven Blier), "In Our Childhood's Bright Endeavor" (*Happy End*, 1928; original German lyric by Bertolt Brecht; English lyric by Michael Feingold), "Je ne t'Aime Pas" (independent song, 1934; original French lyric by Maurice Magre), "Marterl (Memorial Tablet)" (*Das*

Berliner Requiem; original German lyric by Bertolt Brecht), "Oh Heavenly Salvation" (*The Rise and Fall of the City of Mahagonny*, 1930; original German lyric by Bertolt Brecht; English lyric by Arnold Weinstein), "Pimp's Ballad" (*The Threepenny Opera*, 1928; original German lyric by Bertolt Brecht; English lyric by Michael Feingold), "The Saga of Jenny" (*Lady in the Dark*, 1941; lyric by Ira Gershwin) "Song of Ruth" (*Der Weg der Verheissung* [*The Road of Promise* a/k/a *The Eternal Road*], 1937; original German lyric by Franz Werfel), "Song of the Big Shot" (*Happy End*, 1929; original German lyric by Bertolt Brecht; English lyric by Michael Feingold) "I'm a Stranger Here Myself" (*One Touch of Venus*, 1943; lyric by Ogden Nash), "Surabaya Johnny" (*Happy End*, 1929; original German lyric by Bertolt Brecht; English lyric by Michael Feingold), "Susan's Dream" (*Love Life*, 1948; lyric by Alan Jay Lerner), "The Tale of the Soldier's Wife" (a/k/a "Ballade vom Soldatenweib") (independent song, 1942; original German lyric by Bertolt Brecht; this song was the last collaboration between Weill and Brecht; English lyric by Eric Salzman), "Youkali: Tango Habanera" (background music heard in *Marie Galante*, 1934; the music was set to a lyric by Roger Fernay in 1946; for *Here Lies Jenny*, the number was apparently performed without a lyric)

NOTES—As of this writing, *Here Lies Jenny* is the most recent in the long history of Off and Off Off Broadway revues devoted to the music of Kurt Weill (for more information about Kurt Weill-related musicals and revues, see entry for the 1963 edition of *The World of Kurt Weill in Song*; also see Appendix O). In 2007, Broadway offered a revue-like musical of many of Weill's songs; focusing on the relationship of Kurt Weill and Lotte Lenya, *LoveMusik* opened at the Biltmore Theatre on May 3, 2007, for sixty-one performances. It was directed by Hal Prince and starred Michael Cerveris and Donna Murphy.

Note that the lyric for the song "In Meinem Garten" was based on the words of the twelfth-century Spanish poet Judah Halevy, who was the subject of the 1983 Off Off Broadway musical *My Heart Is in the East* (see entry).

690 Herringbone. "A Musical." THEATRE: Playwrights Horizons; OPENING DATE: June 30, 1982; PERFORMANCES: 46; BOOK: Tom Cone; LYRICS: Ellen Fitzhugh; MUSIC: Skip Kennon; DIRECTION: Ben Levit; CHOREOGRAPHY: Theodore Pappas; SCENERY: Christopher Nowak; COSTUMES: Karen Matthews; LIGHTING: Frances Aronson; MUSICAL DIRECTION: Skip Kennon; PRODUCER: Playwrights Horizon (Andre Bishop, Artistic Director; Paul Daniels, Managing Director)

CAST—Skip Kennon (Thumbs DoBois), DAVID ROUNDS (Herringbone, Arthur, Louise, Grandmother, George, Lawyer, Nathan Mosely, Howard, Lou, Dot)

SOURCE—A play by Tom Cone.

The musical was presented in two acts.

ACT ONE—"Herringbone" (David Rounds [as Herringbone]), "Not President, Please" (David Rounds [as George]), "Uncle Billy" (David Rounds [as Arthur]), "God Said" (David Rounds [as Arthur]), Finaletto:, "Little Mister Tippy Toes" (David Rounds [as George]), "George" (David Rounds [as Louise]), "The Cheap Exit" (David Rounds [as Ensemble])

ACT TWO—"What's a Body to Do?" (David Rounds [as Herringbone]), "The Chicken and the Frog" (David Rounds [as Lou]), "Lily Pad Tango" (David Rounds [as Herringbone, Lou, and George]), "A Mother" (David Rounds [as Herringbone]), "Lullabye" (David Rounds [as George]), Three Waltzes:, "Tulip Print Waltz" (David Rounds [as George, Dot, and Lou]), "Ten Years" (David Rounds [as Lou]), "¾ for Three" (David Rounds [as Lou, George, and Dot]), "Herringbone" (reprise) (David Rounds [as Herringbone])

NOTES—In *Herringbone*, David Rounds starred in the title role of the one-man musical (with an assist from Skip Kennon, the composer, at the piano), which had been produced in Chicago the previous year by the St. Nicholas Theatre Company, opening on September 23, 1981. Based on word of mouth from Chicago, *Herringbone* seemed poised to become the next big Off Broadway hit. When the musical reached New York, the critics generally liked it and were particularly impressed with David Rounds' virtuoso performance as Herringbone (and nine other characters). But after a few weeks at Playwrights Horizons, the musical closed. A cast album wasn't recorded, and the work was seldom heard from again (the musical has occasionally surfaced in regional theatre with such performers as Joel Grey and B.D. Wong in the title role).

The bizarre plot told the Depression-era saga of George Herringbone, an eight-year-old Southern boy who is possessed by the spirit of a vaudevillian named Lou. In life, Lou was a dancing midget (professionally known as Frog) who was murdered by his partner, Chicken. Once in control of Herringbone, Lou pushes the boy into a show business career. Lou and George fight over the "rights" to the adult Herringbone, and finally reach a truce in which Herringbone is guided into vaudeville, and then movie, superstardom. In his *New York Times*' review, Frank Rich described *Herringbone* as *Gypsy* (1959) rewritten by the authors of the film *Whatever Happened to Baby Jane?* (1962) and *Sybil* (a 1976 made-for-television movie), and *Newsweek* reported the dialogue as a cross between Tennessee Williams and Edward Gorey, with a score reminiscent of Kurt Weill and Stephen Sondheim. Don Nelsen in the *Daily News* noted that David Rounds' performance reminded him of Lawrence Olivier's virtuoso turn in John Osborne's 1957 British play *The Entertainer* (which was seen on Broadway with Olivier in 1958), and said that while *Herringbone* was not in the league of *The Entertainer*, "to mention Rounds in the same sentence as Olivier is no travesty." (For more information about *The Entertainer*, see entry for its Off Broadway revival.)

Herringbone's title referred not only to the leading character's name, but also to the weave of his suit; one of musical's themes was the weaving back and forth between show business and real life.

During the Chicago run, two numbers were dropped ("Sneaky Little Fella" and "The Act: I Can't Get You Out of My Mind").

691 Hey, Love. "The Songs of Mary Rodgers." THEATRE: Eighty Eights; OPENING DATE: March 24, 1993; PERFORMANCES: 15; LYRICS: See song list for credits; MUSIC: Mary Rodgers; DIRECTION: Richard Maltby, Jr.; COSTUMES: David C. Woolard; MUSICAL DIRECTION: Patrick S. Brady; PRODUCER: Music-Theatre Group (Lyn Austin, Producing Director; Diane Wondisford, General Director)

CAST—Karen Mason, Marcus Lovett, Mark Waldrop

NOTES—*Hey, Love*, a welcome Off Off Broadway tribute to Mary Rodgers, later opened at Rainbow and Stars on September 3, 1996, as *Three of Hearts: The Songs of Mary Rodgers*. The latter production, which featured Faith Prince, Mark Waldrop (who had appeared in the original 1993 version), and Jason Workman, played for forty performances and was recorded by Varese Sarabande Records as *Hey, Love* (CD # VSD-5772). The Rainbow and Stars' production included the following songs: "I'm Looking for Someone" (from *The Mad Show*, 1966; lyric by Marshall Barer), "An Opening for a Princess" (*Once Upon a Mattress*, 1959; lyric by Marshall Barer), "Shy" (*Once Upon a Mattress*, 1959; lyric by Marshall Barer), "O, Mistress Mine" (independent song; lyric by William Shakespeare) "Show Me" (a version of "Don't Laugh," originally heard in *Hot Spot* [1963]; lyric by Martin Charnin and Stephen Sondheim; additional lyric by Richard Maltby, Jr.; music by Mary Rodgers and Stephen Sondheim), "(You'd Like) Nebraska" (*Hot Spot*, 1963; lyric by Martin Charnin)/"Normandy" (*Once Upon a Mattress*, 1959; lyric by Marshall Barer), "The Boy from..." (*The Mad Show*, 1966; lyric by Stephen Sondheim), "Once I Had a Friend" (lyric and music by Mary Rodgers and Stephen Sondheim; written in the 1950s for an unproduced version of *The Lady or the Tiger*), "At the Same Time" (lyric by John Forster; written for an [unproduced?] musical version of Mary Rodgers' book *Freaky Friday*), "Hey, Love" (*Hot Spot*, 1963; lyric by Martin Charnin), "Happily Ever After" (*Once Upon a Mattress*, 1959; lyric by Marshall Barer), "Love Is on Parade" (independent song; lyric by Mark Waldrop), "Don't Take My Word for It" (*Hot Spot*, 1963; lyric by Martin Charnin; unclear if the song was ever performed in *Hot Spot*; not listed in tryout or Broadway programs), Medley: "In a Little While" (*Once Upon a Mattress*, 1959; lyric by Marshall Barer)/"Something Old, Something New" (lyric by Mary Rodgers; from an unproduced musical based on *The Courtship of Miles Standish*)/"Yesterday I Loved You" (*Once Upon a Mattress*, 1959; lyric by Marshall Barer), "Double or Nothing" (independent song, 1996; lyric by Mark Waldrop), "Who Knows?"/"I'll Know" (*Hot Spot*, 1963; original lyric ["Who Knows?"] by Martin Charnin and Stephen Sondheim, music by Mary Rodgers and Stephen Sondheim; new lyric ["I'll Know"] by Mark Waldrop; unclear if "Who Knows?" was ever performed in *Hot Spot*; not listed in tryout or Broadway programs), "Something Known" (written in late 1960s for an unproduced musical version of Carson McCullers' *The Member of the Wedding*; in 1967, the musical had been announced for a 1968 Broadway production; lyric by Marshall Barer; for more information, see entry for *F. Jasmine Addams*, another musical adaptation of McCullers' play), "Like Love" (independent song; lyric by Richard Maltby, Jr.)

MORE NOTES—The Rainbow and Stars' production also included "In Every Bedtime Story," "Back Here at Square One," and "Three of Hearts" (sources unknown; these songs may have been written independent of any production).

In his liner notes for the cast album, Mark Waldrop wrote that "The Boy from..." is considered by many to be one of the funniest songs ever written. Indeed, "The Boy from..." and Tom Jones and Harvey Schmidt's "Statehood Hula" (from *Demi-Dozen*; see entry) may well be the two greatest comedy songs in American musical theatre (and both came from Off Broadway musicals).

For more information about *Once Upon a Mattress* and *The Mad Show*, see entries.

692 Hey, Ma...Kaye Ballard. THEATRE: Promenade Theatre; OPENING DATE: February 27, 1984; PERFORMANCES: 62; DIALOGUE: Kaye Ballard; LYRICS: See song list for credits; MUSIC: See song list for credits; DIRECTION: Susan H. Schulman; SCENERY: Linda Hacker; COSTUMES: William Ivey Long; LIGHTING: Ruth Roberts; MUSICAL DIRECTION: Robert Billig; PRODUCERS: Karl Allison and Bryan Bantry

CAST—KAYE BALLARD

The revue was presented in two acts (all songs performed by Kaye Ballard).

ACT ONE—"Up There" (lyric and music by David Levy and Leslie Eberhard), "Someone Special" (lyric and music by David Schaefer and Joseph Connolly), "Nana" (lyric and music by Jerry Goldberg and Danny Saks), "You Made Me Love You" (lyric and music by James Monaco and Joe McCarthy), "Thinking of You" (from *The Five O'Clock Girl*, 1927; lyric by Bert Kalmar, music by Harry

Ruby) "Supper Club" (lyric and music by David Levy and Leslie Eberhard), "Without a Song" (*Great Day!*, 1929; lyric by Billy Rose and Edward Eliscu, music by Vincent Youmans), "Nobody But You" (*La, La, Lucille*, 1919; lyric by Arthur Jackson and B.G. [Buddy] DeSylva, music by George Gershwin), "Teeny Tiny" (lyric and music by Kaye Ballard, Marshall Baerer [Barer], and David Walker), "Hey, Ma" (lyric and music by David Levy and Leslie Eberhard)

ACT TWO—"Down There" (reprise), "Lazy Afternoon" (*The Golden Apple*, 1954; lyric by John LaTouche, music by Jerome Moross), "Always, Always You" (*Carnival!*, 1961; lyric and music by Bob Merrill), "Hey, Ma" (reprise), "You Don't Need It" (lyric and music by David Levy and Leslie Eberhard), "Down in the Depths (on the 90th Floor)" (*Red, Hot and Blue!*, 1936; lyric and music by Cole Porter), "Cookin' Breakfast (for the One I Love)" (1929 film *Be Yourself*; lyric and music by Henry Tobias and William [Billy] Rose), "Old Tunes" (lyric by Lee Adams, music by Charles Strouse), "All the Magic Ladies" (lyric and music by David Levy and Leslie Eberhard)

NOTES—With the abrupt cancellation of *Bodo* (see entry), *Hey, Ma...Kaye Ballard* was quickly booked into the Promenade Theatre. The revue was a retrospective of sorts in which Kaye Ballard looked back on her fascinating career. It was a pleasant evening, but probably musical theatre buffs would have appreciated more songs from shows she had appeared in rather than new material especially written for the revue and numbers from musicals not associated with her. Surely there could have been room for "Take Off the Coat" (from *That's the Ticket!*, 1948; see entry), "Monday Morning Blues" (*Reuben Reuben*, 1955 [introduced by Allen Case in the musical]), and "Go in the Best of Health" (*Molly*, 1973).

During her Broadway career, Kaye Ballard appeared in just one certifiable hit, *Carnival!* (1961). However, she was also in the original cast of one of the greatest American musicals, *The Golden Apple* (1954; see entry), introducing "Lazy Afternoon," one of the finest of musical theatre ballads. Despite its short run, the musical has achieved legendary cult status (and got Ballard a *Life* magazine cover). She also appeared in a number of flops, three of them closing prior to New York: Harold Rome's *That's the Ticket!* (in which she introduced the sultry seduction number "Take Off the Coat"); Marc Blitzstein's *Reuben Reuben*, another musical which has taken on cult status due to its great score; and *Royal Flush* (1965). *Pleasure Dome* didn't even close out of town; instead, the 1956 revue never got out of rehearsals (a few flyers were distributed prior to the scheduled Washington, D.C., tryout at the National Theatre). Ballard appeared in the Broadway revue *The Beast in Me* (1963), which was a sequel of sorts to *A Thurber Carnival* (1960), but it lasted only four performances. And *Molly*, based on Gertrude Berg's popular radio series *The Goldbergs* and her play *Me and Molly* (1948), lasted only sixty-eight performances. Ballard also appeared Off Broadway in *The Decline and Fall of the Entire World as Seen Through the Eyes of Cole Porter Revisited* (1965; see entry) in which she sang "Down in the Depths (on the 90th Floor)." In 1962 she appeared in a New York City Center revival of *Wonderful Town*, and during the long run of the 1981 Broadway revival of *The Pirates of Penzance* (see entry for the 1980 Off Broadway production) she succeeded Estelle Parsons in the role of Ruth.

Hey, Ma...Kaye Ballard had a cast album of sorts. DRG Records released *Kaye Ballard/Hey, Ma!* as part of its cabaret series, and the CD included five numbers from the revue (CD # 91408).

Kaye Ballard returned to Off Broadway on May 16, 1988, in her revue *Kaye Ballard...Working 42nd Street at Last!* (see entry).

693 Hi, Paisano! "A Musical."

THEATRE: York Playhouse; OPENING DATE: September 30, 1961; PERFORMANCES: 3; BOOK: Ernest Chambers; LYRICS: June Carroll; MUSIC: Robert Holton; DIRECTION: Vassili Lambrinos; CHOREOGRAPHY: Vassili Lambrinos; SCENERY: Mario Vanarelli; COSTUMES: James Bidgood; LIGHTING: Dom Poleo; MUSICAL DIRECTION: Joseph Stecko; PRODUCER: Arron Gardner

CAST—DAVID CANARY (Dino), Greta Aldene (Hostess, American Girl in Yellow), Eric Kelly (First Officer, Cop, Jim), John Wilson (Second Officer, Melvin), Bob Milanese (Third Officer, Orville, Waiter), MARIE SANTELL (Teresa), JAMES CRESSON (Vernon), Mimi Alexander (Landlady), PAULA WAYNE (Sheila), GRAHAM JARVIS (Spanos), Ronny Johnson (Johnny), Myrna Danen (American Girl in Red), Yvonne Carroll (American Girl in Green), JORIE REMUS (Margo), John Wallace (Bergdorf Floorwalker)

The action occurs in and around New York City at the present time.

The musical was presented in two acts.

ACT ONE—"What Is Your Name?" (Greta Aldene, Eric Kelly, John Wilson, Bon Milanese, Ensemble), "Cubes and Abstracts" (Marie Santell), "Dino Repetti" (David Canary), "Office Under the Sky" (Paula Wayne, James Cresson), "Hi, Paisano" (Company), Ballet (Company), "Time We Talked" (David Canary, Marie Santell), "Dino's in Love" (Paula Wayne, James Cresson), "Faith" (Graham Jarvis, David Canary), "Cubes and Abstracts" (reprise) (David Canary), "Sounds of Silence" (David Canary), "Girl He Adores" (Paula Wayne), "It Happens Every Day" (David Canary, James Cresson, Boys), "Born in America" (Myrna Danen, Greta Aldene, Yvonne Carroll), "Teresa" (David Canary), "Carousel" (Company)

ACT TWO—"Reason to Marry" (David Canary, James Cresson, Boys), "Dozen Husbands" (Jorie Remus), "Born in America" (reprise) (Paula Wayne), "Over Forty" (Jorie Remus), "Time We Talked" (reprise) (David Canary, Marie Santell), "Table Tango" (David Canary, Jorie Remus), "I Know What He's Up To" (Marie Santell), "Let Me Drown" (Marie Santell), Finale (Company)

NOTES—*Hi, Paisano!* was a short-lived musical about the adventures of a young Italian immigrant (David Canary) in New York City. Lewis Funke in the *New York Times* found the evening an "artless bouillabaisse" (an "uninventive" book, "lame" jokes, "so-so" music, and "less than so-so" lyrics).

Some of the cast members (Paula Wayne, Graham Jarvis, James Cresson) later enjoyed brief Broadway careers, leaving behind fondly remembered performances on various cast albums.

694 La Hija de Rappaccini.

NOTES—See entry for *Rappaccini's Daughter*.

695 Hijinks! "A Musical Entertainment."

THEATRE: Cheryl Crawford Theatre/Chelsea Theatre Center; OPENING DATE: December 17, 1980; PERFORMANCES: 39; BOOK: Robert Kalfin, Steve Brown, and John McKinney; LYRICS: See song list for credits; MUSIC: See song list for credits; DIRECTION: Robert Kalfin; CHOREOGRAPHY: Larry Hayden; SCENERY: Sandro La Ferla; COSTUMES: Elizabeth P. Palmer; LIGHTING: Paul Everett; MUSICAL DIRECTION: Michael O'Flaherty; PRODUCERS: Chelsea Theatre Center (Robert Kalfin, Producing Director; A. Harrison Cromer, Managing Director), The Fisher Theatre Foundation, and Roger L. Stevens

CAST—Jeannine Taylor (Madame Trentoni, alias Aurelia Johnson), Joseph Kolinski (Captain Jinks), Michael Connolly (Clyde Fitch, *Times* Reporter, Papa Belliarti), Sal Basile (Policeman, *Sun* Reporter), Randall Easterbrook (Charlie, *Herald* Reporter), Scott Ellis (Gussie, *Tribune* Reporter), Christopher Farr (Peter), Evalyn Baron (Sailor, Fraulein Hochspits), Elizabeth Devine (Sailor, Mrs. Maggitt), Elaine Petricoff (Sailor, Mrs. Pettitoes), Michael O'Flaherty (Piano Player, Detective), Marian Primont (Mrs. Greenborough, Mrs. Jinks), Bruce Conner (Sailor), Elyot Chase (Monkey), Sarah Lowman (Jenny)

SOURCE—The 1904 play *Captain Jinks of the Horse Marines* by Clyde Fitch.

The action occurs in 1872 in New York City, on the landing dock of the Cunard Steamship Company and the Brevoort House.

The musical was presented in three acts.

ACT ONE—"Love's Old Sweet Song" (lyric by G. Clifton Bingham, music by J.L. Molloy, c. 1882) (Company), "Take Them Away, They'll Drive Me Crazy" (lyric and music by Henry Clay Work, 1871) (Joseph Kolinski, Randall Easterbrook, Scott Ellis, Company), "If You've Only Got a Moustache" (lyric by George Cooper, music by Stephen C. Foster, 1864) (Randall Easterbrook, Company), "Dad's a Millionaire" (lyric and music by Henry Clay Work, 1867; additional lyric by Steve Brown) (Scott Ellis, Company), "Walking Down Broadway" (lyric by William Lingard, music by Charles E. Pratt, 1868) (Joseph Kolinski, Randall Easterbrook, Scott Ellis), "The Star-Spangled Banner" (lyric by Francis Scott Key to the music of "To Anacreon in Heaven," 1814) (Jeannine Taylor, Company), "Home Sweet Home" (lyric and music by John Howard Payne, 1830) (Jeannine Taylor, Michael Connolly, Sal Basile, Randall Easterbrook, Scott Ellis, Company), "A Mother's Smile" (lyric by Mary E. Hewitt, music by W.V. Wallace, 1859) (Joseph Kolinski), "The Hour for Thee and Me" (lyric and music by Stephen C. Foster, 1852) (Jeannine Taylor, Joseph Kolinski, Company), "Captain Jinks of the Horse Marines" (lyric and music by William Lingard, 1869) (Randall Easterbrook, Scott Ellis, Company)

ACT TWO—"Will You Love Me in December as You Do in May?" (lyric by J.J. Walker, music by Ernest Ball, 1905) (Company), "Champagne Charlie" (lyric by George Leybourne, music by Alfred Lee, 1887; additional lyric by Steve Brown) (Randall Easterbrook, Scott Ellis, Company), "Shew! Fly, Don't Bother Me" (music by Frank Campbell, 1869; song used as incidental music in this part of the musical), "Last Rose of Summer" (traditional song, used in the opera *Martha* [1847], music adapted by Fredrich von Flotow) (Jeannine Taylor), "Those Tassels on Her Boots" (lyric and music by Robert Cooms, 1870) (Joseph Kolinski, Company), "Beautiful Dreamer" (lyric and music by Stephen C. Foster, 1864) (Joseph Kolinski), "Wilt Thou Be Gone, Love?" (lyric by William Shakespeare [from *Romeo and Juliet*], music by Stephen C. Foster) (Jeannine Taylor, Joseph Kolinski), "A Boy's Best Friend Is His Mother" (lyrics by Harry Miller, music by J.P. Skelly, 1884; additional lyric by Steve Brown) (Marian Primont, Jeannine Taylor, Company), "Then You'll Remember Me" (lyric by Alfred Bunn, music by M.W. Balfe; from the operetta *The Bohemian Girl*, 1843) (Joseph Kolinski), *La Traviata* Waltzes (music by Giuseppi Verdi, from the opera *La Traviata*, 1853) (dance) (Elaine Petricoff, Evalyn Baron, Elizabeth Devine)

ACT THREE—"Silver Threads Among the Gold" (lyric by Eben E. Rexford, music by H.P. Danks, 1873) (Company), "That Gal Is a High Born Lady" (lyric and music by Barney Fagan, 1896; new lyric by Steve Brown) (Christopher Farr, Joseph Kolinski, Company), "Whispering Hope" (lyric and music by Septimus Winner, 1863) (Joseph Kolinski, Marian Primont, Company), "Poor Kitty Popcorn (or, The Soldier's Pet)" (lyric and music by Henry Clay Work, 1866) (Jeannine Taylor, Company), "The Mermaid's Evening Song" (lyric by J.E. Carpenter, music by S. Glover, 1858) (Elaine Petricoff, Evalyn Baron, Elizabeth Devine), "Auld Lang Syne" (traditional Scottish song; the well-known lyric was adapted by

Robert Burns) (Company), "Goodbye, My Lady Love" (lyric and music by Joseph E. Howard, 1904) (Randall Easterbrook, Scott Ellis, Company), "Then You'll Remember Me" (reprise) (Joseph Kolinski, Jeannine Taylor), "Captain Jinks of the Horse Marines" (reprise) (Joseph Kolinski, Company), "Wait 'Til the Sun Shines, Nellie" (lyric by Andrew E. Sterling, music by Harry von Tilzer, 1905) (Company)

NOTES—The musical *Hijinks!* was based on Clyde Fitch's successful early twentieth-century play *Captain Jinks of the Horse Marines*, which dealt with the romance between a successful European opera star and the title character. But it turns out that diva Madame Trentoni is actually an American girl from Trenton, New Jersey.

Mel Gussow in the *New York Times* found the evening a "convivial entertainment" and praised the two leads, Joseph Kolinski and Jeannine Taylor, both of whom had "strong voices and amiable personalities." Gussow reported the musical's cast included three dogs, two birds, and one monkey, and he noted that two of the dogs were late for the opening night performance; he wondered if their late entrances had anything to do with their being offended because only the monkey received program credit.

Hijinks! was the third lyric adaptation of Fitch's play. The first was the 1925 Broadway musical *Captain Jinks* (book by Frank Mandel, lyrics by B.G. [Buddy] DeSylva and Laurence Schwab, music by Lewis E. Gensler and Stephen Jones) which opened on September 8 and played for almost six months at the Martin Beck (now Al Hirschfeld) Theatre. The second adaptation, *Captain Jinks of the Horse Marines* (subtitled "A Romantic Comedy in Music"), was an opera which premiered on September 20, 1975, at the Lyric Theatre in Kansas City, Missouri. The libretto was by Sheldon Harnick and the music by Jack Beeson (it was recorded on a 2-LP set by RCA Victor [# ARL2-1727]).

Hijinks! marked yet another early American play in which Steve Brown had a part in adapting into a musical (see entries for *The Contrast*, *Fashion* [1974 version], *The Cast Aways/Castaways*).

Speaking of *Fashion*, the 1959 musical version (*Fashion, or Life in New York*) included a song titled "Walking Down Broadway" which *The Burns Mantle Yearbook* cited as the show's musical highlight. The song is probably the same "Walking Down Broadway" which was heard in *Hijinks!* The script of *Hijinks!* was published by Samuel French, Inc., in 1982.

696 Hillbilly Women. THEATRE: The Actors Studio; OPENING DATE: February 6, 1979; PERFORMANCES: 15; BOOK: Elizabeth Stearns; LYRICS: Clint Ballard, Jr.; MUSIC: Clint Ballard, Jr.; DIRECTION: Peter Bennett; CHOREOGRAPHY: Robert (Bob) Fitch; Pauline Fitch, Choreographic Coordinator; Terry Rieser, Choreography Assistant Scenery: Hugh Landwehr; COSTUMES: Coordinated by Penny Davis; LIGHTING: Leslie Spohn; PRODUCERS: The Actors Studio (Lee Strasberg, Artistic Director; Carl Schaeffer, Executive Producer) and Lee Pucklis, Associate Producer

CAST—Jacqueline Knapp (Della), Katherine Squire (Siddy), Sharon Goldman (Sharleen), Janet Ward (Jewel), Susan Peretz (Sue Ellen), Lois Smith (Denise), Robin Howard (Ada)

SOURCE—The 1973 book *Hillbilly Women* by Kathy Kahn. The action occurs in the present at Blue Ridge Enterprises, a factory in Macaysville, Georgia.

The musical was presented in one act (song assignments unknown)

MUSICAL NUMBERS—"Lay a Little Love on Me," "Which Side Are You On" (traditional), "Hillbilly Hambone," "Amazing Grace" (traditional), "Crocodile Lounge," "Hillbilly Women Go Home," "Damned If You Do," "Jubilee," "Livin'"

NOTES—A few weeks after the Off Off Broadway production closed, *Hillbilly Women* (a play with music about Appalachian women) was performed with the New York cast at the Long Wharf Theatre. For this production, two songs ("The Way It Never Was" and "Miner's Life" [the latter a traditional number]) were added.

Note that Off Broadway and Broadway stalwart Bob Fitch choreographed the musical.

697 The Hired Man. THEATRE: 47th Street Theatre; OPENING DATE: November 10, 1988; PERFORMANCES: 33; BOOK: Melvyn Bragg; LYRICS: Howard Goodall; MUSIC: Howard Goodall; DIRECTION: Brian Aschinger; CHOREOGRAPHY: Rodney Griffin; SCENERY: Tamara Kinkman; COSTUMES: Patricia Adshead; LIGHTING: Leon Di Leone; MUSICAL DIRECTION: Ann Crawford; PRODUCER: The Heritage Project, Inc. (Brian Aschinger, Producer)

CAST—Paul Avedisian (John), Carolyn Popp (Emily), Ray Luetters (Jackson), Ray Collins (Isaac), Nick Corley (Seth), Corliss Preston (May), James O'Neill (Harry), Gloria Boucher (Sally), Bob Wilkens (Blacklock), Richard Lupino (Pennington, Vicar), Robin Smith (Landlady), David M. Beris (Josh), Christopher Boyd (Chairman, Photographer, Alec), Keith D. Cooper (Tom), Tom Freeman (Dan), Aimee M. Luzier (Bob, Mr. Stephens), Len Matheo (Joe Sharp, Alf), Larry Stotz (Recruiting Officer)

SOURCE—The 1969 novel *The Hired Man* by Melvyn Bragg.

The action occurs in various English towns from 1896 to 1919.

The musical was presented in two acts.

ACT ONE—"Song of the Hired Man" (Company), "Fill It to the Top" (Ray Collins, Nick Corley, Paul Avedisian, Ensemble), "Now for the First Time" (Carolyn Popp, Paul Avedisian), "Song of the Hired Man" (reprise) (Workers), "Work Song: It's All Right for You" (Farmers, Workers), "Who Will You Marry Then?" (Carolyn Popp, Gloria Boucher), "Time Passing" (instrumental interlude), "Get Up and Go, Lad" (Ray Collins, Paul Avedisian, Ensemble), "I Wouldn't Be the First" (Carolyn Popp, Ray Luetters), "Fade Away" (Paul Avedisian, Carolyn Popp), "Hear Your Voice" (Ray Luetters), "What a Fool I've Been" (Paul Avedisian), "If I Could" (Carolyn Popp), "Song of the Hired Man" (reprise)/"Men of Stone" (Company)

ACT TWO—"You Never See the Sun" (Corliss Preston), Interlude: "Jackson" (Instrumental Ensemble), "What Would You Say to Your Son?" (Paul Avedisian), Union Song: "Men of Stone" (reprise) (Nick Corley, Bob Wilkens, Men), Interlude: "Gathering of Soldiers" (Instrumental Ensemble), "Farewell Song" (Carolyn Popp, Paul Avedisian, Ray Collins, Corliss Preston, Ensemble), War Song: "So Tell Your Children" (Ray Collins, Paul Avedisian, Ray Luetters, Carolyn Popp, Corliss Preston, James O'Neill, Nick Corley, Soldiers), "Crossbridge Dance" (Ray Collins, Company), "No Choir of Angels" (Carolyn Popp, Paul Avedisian), "Hear Your Voice" (reprise) (Ray Luetters), "If I Could" (reprise) (Carolyn Popp), Finale: "Song of the Hired Man" (reprise) (Company)

NOTES—Melvyn Bragg, the author of the British musical's book as well as the novel upon which it was based, wrote that the life of his grandfather inspired him to write *The Hired Man*, the story of humble working men who lived during an era of British history which saw a new century and the war to end all wars.

Mel Gussow in the *New York Times* praised the musical, which had "heart and purpose" in its epic story of the common man. The plot had "detail enough for a Hardy novel," and the score was "robust, with a folkloric and choral flavor."

The musical's London premiere took place at the Astoria Theatre on October 31, 1984, where it played for 164 performances. The cast recording was released by Polydor Records (LP # POLH-18), and a 1992 British concert version of the work was released on a 2-CD set by That's Entertainment Records (# CDTER2-1189). Although the musical seems a natural for regional theatre, the only other time the work has been seen in the United States was in 2008 (when it was revived in New York for a limited engagement as part of the "Brits on Broadway" festival). The script was published by Samuel French, Ltd. (London) in 1986.

698 Hobo. "A New Musical Comedy." THEATRE: Gate Theatre; OPENING DATE: April 10, 1961; PERFORMANCES: 32; BOOK: John Dooley; LYRICS: John Dooley; MUSIC: John Dooley; DIRECTION: Rinaldo Capillupo; CHOREOGRAPHY: Ray James; SCENERY: Sonia Lowenstein; COSTUMES: Ken Starrett; LIGHTING: Richard Nelson; PRODUCER: George E. Burns

CAST—Ned Wertimer (Belcher), Kenneth Lynch, Jr. (Fancy Dan), Rita Howell (Freightcar Freda), Herbert Flyer (Barfly Bill), Otto Lohmann (Boyle), RONALD HOLGATE (Jonah), Hal Waters (Bhudda), ELMARIE WENDEL (Anguish), Jim Cade (Considine), Al Zungolo (Officer Hammerschlag), Clare Justice (Edith), Bob Lees (Georgie Keptwell), George Neighbors (Phillip Stoneheart), ELEANOR LA FORGE (Julie)

The action occurs in Boyle's Bar, on the Bowery, with a fleeting glimpse of Bleeker Street, in Greenwich Village.

The musical was presented in two acts.

ACT ONE—Prologue (Hal Waters), "Home Away from Home" (Bums), "Nuthin for Nuthin" (Otto Lohmann), "Jonah's Wail" (Ronald Holgate), "Sympathy" (Elmarie Wendel), "The Virgin Polka" (Bums, Elmarie Wendel), "Cindy" (Hal Waters), "Julie" (Ronald Holgate), "From the Moment" (Elmarie Wendel), "Bleecker Street" (Rita Howell, Kenneth Lynch, Jr., Ned Wertimer), "Jonah's Wail" (reprise) (Ronald Holgate), "Sweetness" (Ned Wertimer, Kenneth Lynch, Jr., Otto Lohmann, Jim Cade, Hal Waters, Ronald Holgate)

ACT TWO—"On the Day When the World Goes Boom" (Ned Wertimer, Rita Howell, Kenneth Lynch, Jr.), "Somewhere in Your Eyes" (Elmarie Wendel, Ronald Holgate), "From the Moment" (reprise) (Eleanor La Forge), "I Hate You" (Clare Justice, Bob Lees), "Good for Nothing" (Elmarie Wendel), "Julie" (reprise) (Eleanor La Forge, Ronald Holgate), "Little Birds" (Clare Justice, Bums), "Who Put Out the Light That Lit the Candle That Started the Fire That Started the Flame "Deep Down in My Heart" (Eleanor La Forge), "Jonah's Wail" (reprise/finale) (Company)

NOTES—*Hobo*, a fanciful look at Bowery types, was gone in a month. It featured Off Broadway perennial Elmarie Wendel, and it marked the New York debut of Ronald Holgate, who portrayed Jonah, a man who chooses the hobo life of the Bowery in order to retain his individuality. (His dilemma sounds suspiciously like the one faced by Sydney Chaplin in *Subways Are for Sleeping*, which opened on Broadway later in the year.) In his review for the *New York Times*, Howard Taubman noted the musical's targets were "bums in the Bowery, the beatniks in the Village and the idle rich on Park Avenue," and felt the implicit satire in these subjects was lost when the musical started moralizing. Nonetheless, Taubman found much to appreciate in the score, including "Bleecker Street" (which dealt with the pretensions of Villagers), "I Hate You" (an "ironic" number for a Park Avenue couple), and "several pleasant romantic tunes." Taubman also praised Holgate (who has "a big, trained bass-baritone [offering] unusually sonorous singing for Off Broadway"). Holgate soon made his mark as Miles ("I am a parade") Gloriosus in the original Broadway production of *A Funny Thing Happened on the Way to the Forum* (1962), and later won the Tony Award for

Best Featured Actor in a Musical for his rollicking portrayal of Richard Henry Lee in *1776* (1969) (his "The Lees of Old Virginia" stopped the show). In *The Grand Tour* (1979), he and Joel Grey introduced "You I Like," one of the most delightful numbers in the Jerry Herman songbook. If *Hobo* had a show-stopper, it must have been "Who Put Out the Light That Lit the Candle That Started the Fire That Started the Flame Deep Down in My Heart." Indeed, Taubman noted that "the future must be bright" for anyone who could write a blues number like this one, and said he looked forward to a "sprightly musical" in the future from the talented lyricist-composer. Unfortunately, after *Hobo*, John Dooley was never heard from again as far as Off Broadway and Broadway were concerned.

699 Holeville. THEATRE: Attic Theatre/Brooklyn Academy of Music; OPENING DATE: December 2, 1979; PERFORMANCES: 17; BOOK: Jeff Wanshel; LYRICS: Des McAnuff; MUSIC: Des McAnuff; DIRECTION: Des McAnuff; SCENERY: Heidi Landesman; COSTUMES: Carol Oditz; LIGHTING: Richard Nelson; MUSICAL DIRECTION: Curt Neishloss; PRODUCER: Dodger Theatre (Michael David, Des McAnuff, Edward Strong, and Sherman Warner, Associate Directors)

CAST—Don Scardino (Rich Forrester), John Bottoms (Sal Video), Philip Casnoff (Front Man of the Band), Saul Rubinek (Gus Quid), Deborah Rush (Mother Quid), Christopher Murney (Messrs. Frisks and McDo); and a Band of Criminals and Bums (Randy Klein, Curt Neishloss, David Rinehimer, and Steven Singer)

The musical was presented in two acts.

ACT ONE—"Movin' Day" (Don Scardino, John Bottoms, Philip Casnoff), "I Need You" (Deborah Rush), "There's Nothing Like a Clean Room to Sweep You Off Your Feet" (Saul Rubinek), "Where Do You Come From?" (Don Scardino, John Bottoms), "Where Do You Come from (They Want to Know)" (Randy Klein, Curt Neishloss, David Rinehimer, Steven Singer), "Genius" (Don Scardino, John Bottoms, Saul Rubinek, Philip Castnoff), "It's a Dog's Life" (Christopher Murney, Randy Klein, Curt Neishloss, David Rinehimer, Steven Singer)

ACT TWO—"Baby, It's a Matter of Life (All I Want to Do Is See It Through)" (Randy Klein, Curt Neishloss, David Rinehimer, Steven Singer), "There's Nothing Like a Clean Room to Sweep You Off Your Feet" (reprise) (Randy Klein, Curt Neishloss, David Rinehimer, Steven Singer), "Genius" (reprise) (Randy Klein, Curt Neishloss, David Rinehimer, Steven Singer), "All I Really Want to Do Is Dance" (Don Scardino, John Bottoms, Randy Klein, Curt Neishloss, David Rinehimer, Steven Singer), "We Are the Police" (Randy Klein, Curt Neishloss, David Rinehimer, Steven Singer), "Round and Round" (Don Scardino), "Rehabilitation in America" (Company)

NOTES—*Holeville* was described in *The Best Plays of 1979-1980* as a "sinister cartoon of terror in modern America" in which a group of hoodlums terrorize a boy scout in his home.

Mel Gussow in the *New York Times* found the production "arduous," noting that Jeff Wenshel (who had written the 1970 black comedy *The Disintegration of James Cherry*, about a boy's endless string of bad luck) offered an evening of whimsy which included one actor (Christopher Murney) portraying a dog. But Gussow mentioned he looked forward ("in relief") to the occasional musical interludes written by Des McAnuff and performed by a combo which "seems to have strayed from Brecht-Weill country." Gussow singled out the "lilting" "Another Age," which was an "attempt at another 'Aquarius.'" He also mentioned that the dog had his own solo ("It's a Dog's Life") with lyrics which were ("not surprisingly") "doggerel."

700 Hollywood Opera. "Rare musical numbers from the Vaults of Tinsel Town." THEATRE: The Ballroom; OPENING DATE: March 13, 1985; PERFORMANCES: 40; LYRICS: Barry Keating; additional lyrics by David Schechter; MUSIC: Barry Keating; SPECIAL MATERIAL by Stuart Ross; DIRECTION: Barry Keating; CHOREOGRAPHY: Stuart Ross; PUPPET DESIGNS: Perry Arthur; COSTUMES: Bosha Johnson; LIGHTING: Matthew Ehlert; MUSICAL DIRECTION: John Spalla; PRODUCERS: Wendell Minnick, Robert Smith, and Entertainment Ventures Ltd.

CAST—Camille Saviola, Mary-Cleere Haran, Perry Arthur

The revue was presented in one act (song assignments unknown).

MUSICAL NUMBERS—"Hollywood Opera," "D'Oyly Carte Blanche" (lyrics by Barry Keating and David Schechter), "Citizen Kong," "Three Phases of Eve" (lyrics by David Schechter), "Opera in 3-D," "Delle Rose's Turn," "Das Exorcist" (lyrics by David Schechter), "How Now Voyager," "Tippy's Immolation," Hollywood Opera Finale

NOTES—*Hollywood Opera*, an evening devoted to musical and operatic parodies of classic Hollywood films, sounds hysterical; what a shame it wasn't recorded. "Three Phases of Eve" demolished both *All About Eve* and *The Three Faces of Eve* (according to Stephen Holden in the *New York Times*, "three conniving understudies share the same dress"). "Tippy's Immolation" was a parody of *The Birds*, and included puppets which enacted the menacing feathered creatures. Perhaps the evening's highlight was "D'Oyly Carte Blanche," a Gilbert-and-Sullivan parody of *A Streetcar Named Desire* in which the heroine announces she's always depended on the wine lists of strangers.

Holden found the revue "lighter-than-air" and noted that it "cannily combines the formulas that have made *Forbidden Broadway* and *Little Shop of Horrors* hits."

701 Home Movies. "A New Musical Romp." THEATRE: Provincetown Playhouse; OPENING DATE: May 11, 1964; PERFORMANCES: 72; BOOK: Rosalyn Drexler; LYRICS: Rosalyn Drexler; MUSIC: Al Carmines; DIRECTION: Lawrence Kornfeld; SCENERY: Larry Siegel; COSTUMES: Judith Berkowitz; LIGHTING: Nicola Cernovich; PRODUCERS: Orson Bean Productions, Inc., in association with Judson Poets' Theater

CAST—Gretel Cummings (Mrs. Verdun), Sudie Bond (Vivienne), Barbara Ann Teer (Violet), Fred Herko (Peter Peterouter), Sheindi Tokayer (Sister Thalia), Al Carmines (Father Shenanigan), Otto Mjaanes (Charles Anduit), Jim Anderson (John the Truck Driver), George Bartenieff (Mr. Verdun)

The musical was presented in one act.

MUSICAL NUMBERS—"A Mania" (Sudie Bond), "Peanut Song" (Barbara Ann Teer), "Pents-unwreckum" (Barbara Ann Teer), "Swoop of the Moopem" (performer[s] unknown), "Birdies" (Gretel Cummings, Fredie Herko), "A Power Stronger Than Will" (Gretel Cummings, Fredie Herko), "Equipment Song" (Fredie Herko), "You Look Like Me" (Sudie Bond, Fredie Herko), "Remember When I Hated You?" (Sudie Bond), "Once You've Seen Everything" (Gretel Cummings), "Darkness Song" (George Bartenieff), "Show Me" (Al Carmines), "My Number Is Eleven" (George Bartenieff), "Boasting Song" (George Bartenieff), "I Know How You Sell It" (George Bartenieff), "Here They Come Now" (Fredie Herko), "Lower the Boom" (Gretel Cummings), "Chocolate Turkey" (Barbara Ann Teers), "Daisies" (Sudie Bond), "Do Not Bruise the Fruit" (George Bartenieff), "Stuttering Song" (Otto Mjaanes), "Pussy Cat Song" (Fredie Herko), "Seminary Song" (Sheindi Tokayer, Al Carmines), "I'm Gwine Lie Down" (performer[s] unknown), "Two Falls to a Finish" (Company)

NOTES—*Home Movies* had originally been presented at the Judson Memorial Church on March 19, 1964; as a curtain raiser to *Home Movies*, a short (non-musical) one-act play was presented, *The Bitch of Waverly Place* by Arthur Sainer. When *Home Movies* opened at the Provincetown Playhouse two months later, another short play was substituted (Rosalyn Drexler's *Softly, and Consider the Nearness*, which was billed as a "Short Subject" and followed by the "Feature," *Home Movies*).

It appears that sometime after the opening, *Softly, and Consider the Nearness* was dropped from the bill, and only *Home Movies* was presented. *The Burns Mantle Yearbook/The Best Plays of 1963-1964* described *Softly* as about a woman in love with her television set, and *Home Movies* about "the carryings-on of a lot of strange people."

Louis Calta in the *New York Times* felt the "contrived" and "far out" *Home Movies* was "virtually inaccessible" and "of questionable worth and taste." Drexler's script and Al Carmines' songs seemed bent on spoofing modern mores, but Gussow noted it was "difficult to identify the objects" being "jabbed at." Further, the humor lacked "imaginative zaniness." Al Carmines was new to Off Broadway, but would soon become a major figure in the Off Broadway musical. Although his musicals never achieved wide popularity, and none transferred to Broadway, they were offbeat, loony works peppered with irresistible music of the pastiche variety and often set to dadaesque lyrics and plots. Fortunately, a number of his musicals were recorded, and they're a testament to his unique approach to musical-theatre writing. His music was free-wheeling and daring, and his almost surreal song structures were often set to merry, circus-like melodies. Carmines often wrote his own lyrics, and would occasionally appear in his musicals (in *Home Movies*, he played the role of Father Shenanigan, and was succeeded in the part by Orson Bean, the musical's co-producer). The musical was presented in association with the Judson Memorial Church, where Carmines was a minister. Most of his musicals were produced in conjunction with the church. (For a list of Carmines' musicals which are discussed in this book, see Appendix N.)

The script of *Home Movies* (as well as *Softly, and Consider the Nearness*) was published by Random House in a collection of plays by Rosalyn Drexler titled *The Line of Least Existence and Other Plays*. (See entry for *The Line of Least Existence*.)

702 Homecoming. THEATRE: Theatre for the New City; OPENING DATE: August 1, 1986; PERFORMANCES: 16; BOOK AND LYRICS: Crystal Field, George Bartenieff, and the *Homecoming* Company; MUSIC: Mark Hardwick; DIRECTION: Crystal Field; SCENERY: Anthony Angel; COSTUMES: Animal X; Mask and Puppet Designs by Stephen Kaplin, Pamela Mayo, and Sarah Germain; MUSICAL DIRECTION: Christopher Cherney; PRODUCER: Theatre for the New City (George Bartenieff and Crystal Field, Artistic Directors)

CAST—The cast included Crystal Field, Michael David Gordon, Mark Marcante, George Bartenieff, Ben Silver, and Marie McKinney.

NOTES—According to Nan Robertson in the *New York Times*, the Off Off Broadway musical *Homecoming* dealt with a young man who, upon returning to his old neighborhood after having served "abroad," is determined to "protect and nurture" the planet.

Among the musical numbers were "The Mermaid Tap Dance," "Dance of the Developers," and "Radiation Monster Lost on the BMT " (the latter featured a twelve-foot high, three-headed "nuclear" puppet monster [three puppeteers inside the puppet were required to maneuver it]).

Robertson reported that the musical was presented free for a series of outdoor performances offered throughout the summer; the cast numbered fifty, two-thirds of whom were non-professional "neighborhood amateurs" (ages 8 to the 60s) who were given "intensive" stage training.

703 Honky-Tonk Highway. "A Mountain Musical." THEATRE: Don't Tell Mama; OPENING DATE: June 13, 1994; PERFORMANCES: Unknown; BOOK: Richard Berg; additional dialogue by Robert Nassif Lindsey; LYRICS: Robert Nassif Lindsey; MUSIC: Robert Nassif Lindsey; DIRECTION: Gabriel Barre; SCENERY: Charles E. McCarry; COSTUMES: Robert Strong Miller; LIGHTING: Carol Dorn; MUSICAL DIRECTION: Steve Steiner; PRODUCERS: Five by Five Productions; and Pamela Guthman and Jonathan D. Moll

CAST—Matthew Bennett, Kevin Fox, Erin Hill, Rick Leon, David M. Lutken, Sean McCourt, Andy Taylor; and Joyce Leigh Bowden, Jennifer F. Neuland, Steve Steiner, and Ken Triwush

The action occurs at Tucker's Roadhouse in Alton Falls, Tennessee, in 1970.

The musical was presented in two acts (song assignments unknown).

ACT ONE—"I Found a Song" "Chalhatchee," "Far-Off Lights," "Come Out and Play" "Follow Where the Music Goes," "Perfect Stranger," "Perfect Stranger" (harmonica version), "I'll Be There," "Follow Where the Music Goes" (reprise; blues version), "Baby, I Love Your Biscuits" (prerecorded), "Answer the Call," "Heartbreak Hall of Fame," "Answer the Call" (reprise)

ACT TWO—"Honky-Tonk Highway," "Mr. Money," "Dr. Love," "Daddy's Girl," "Me, Myself and I," "I'm So Happy, I Could Cry," "Easier to Sing Than Say," "Far-Off Lights" (reprise), "Music in This Mountain," "Baby, I Love Your Biscuits" (reprise; prerecorded)

NOTES—*Honky-Tonk Highway* told the tale of a legendary (albeit fictitious) country-western singer named Clint Colby. The Off Off Broadway musical takes place on the first anniversary of Clint's death when his former band members, the Mountain Rangers, reunite one last time to perform his songs and reminisce about him. Clint was known for his trademark baby-blue cowboy hat, and each time a band member puts on the hat, the band member "becomes" Clint for the moment and via flashbacks tells the story of Clint's life and career.

Each song in the musical was performed by all the cast members, often with one or two singing the lead vocals while the rest provided back-up; the cast members also played their own instruments.

The musical was later produced at the Goodspeed Opera House in 1995.

The engaging score was recorded by Boebe Records (CD # BB-111), and the script was published by Samuel French, Inc., in 1999. Four songs from the production ("Easier to Sing Than Say," "Baby, I Love Your Biscuits," "I'll Be There," and "Music in This Mountain") were also heard on *Opal, Honky-Tonk Highway, and Other Theatre Songs by Robert Nassif Lindsey* (released by Original Cast Records [CD # OC-9514]). The lyricist-composer's exact name seems to cause confusion (see entry for *Opal*), and at least one reference book which discusses *Honky-Tonk Highway* cites his name as Robert Lindsey-Nassif.

704 The Hoofers. THEATRE: Mercury Theatre; OPENING DATE: July 29, 1969; PERFORMANCES: 88; CONCEIVED AND COORDINATED by Leticia Jay; DIRECTION: Derby Wilson; COSTUMES: Angel Cheremeteff; LIGHTING: Barbara Nollman; MUSICAL DIRECTION: Tiny Grimes; PRODUCERS: The Mercury Theatre in association with Leticia Jay

CAST—Jerry Ames, Lon Chaney, Sandra Gibson, Chuck Green, Leticia Jay, Raymond Kaalund, Mabel Lee, Rhythm Red, Sandman Sims, Jimmy Slyde, Eva Turner, Tony White, Derby Wilson

The revue was presented in two acts.

ACT ONE—Overture (Tiny Grimes and His Band), "You Gotta Go Tap Dancing Tonight" (Company), Riffs and Introductions (Jimmy Slyde, Rhythm Red, Sandra Gibson, Jerry Ames, Tony White, Chuck Green, Eva Turner, Raymond Kaalund, Mabel Lee, Sandman Sims, Derby Wilson), Jimmy Slyde, Mabel Lee, Duet (Lon Chaney, Tony White), Sandman Sims, Chuck Green, Trio (Chuck Green, Jerry Ames, Rhythm Red), Raymond Kaalund, Sandra Gibson, Jerry Ames, Finale

ACT TWO—Derby Wilson, Tiny Grimes and His Band, Eva Turner, Challenge

NOTES—*The Hoofers* seems to have been an amiable evening of tap and rhythm dancing, interspersed with songs, stand-up comedy, and mime. Anna Kisselgoff in the *New York Times* remarked that the two-hour evening offered a display by some of the "best" veterans of tap dancing, and said if the "enthusiastic" opening night audience was any indication, then tap dancing might be in a for a "lively revival." She further noted that the show was a "must" for audiences interested in tap and "particularly for those who are not." An earlier version of the work was performed Off Off Broadway as *Tap Happening.*

705 Hooray!! It's a Glorious Day...And All That. "A New Musical Comedy." THEATRE: Theatre Four; OPENING DATE: March 9, 1966; PERFORMANCES: 15; BOOK: Maurice Teitelbaum and Charles Grodin; LYRICS: Ethel Bieber, Maurice Teitelbaum, and Charles Grodin; MUSIC: Arthur Gordon; DIRECTION: Charles Grodin; CHOREOGRAPHY: Sandra Devlin; SCENERY: Peter Harvey; COSTUMES: Peter Harvey; LIGHTING: Jules Fisher; MUSICAL DIRECTION: Peter Fuchs; PRODUCER: Jeff Britton

CAST—Daniel Keyes (B.K. Pfeffer), Lou David (Russell Underhand), Lois Holmes (Maggie Martyr), Laverne Burden (Miss Blossom), RONALD HOLGATE (Carl Strong), Louis Criscuolo (Muggsy), John Kane (Willie), Joan Eastman (Rose Pfeffer), Mina Kolb (Betty Plain), Joan Kroschell (Kitty Sweetness), Benny Smith (Tap Dancer), Raymond Allen (Nick, Willard Gerard Ryan), Don Emmons (Customer); Singers: Charles Burks, Joy Franz, Rosemary McNamara, Wilson Robey, William Wendt; Dancers: Pat Cope, Wilson Robey, Michael Maurer, Ann McKinley, Terry Nicholson, Lynn Simonson, Benny Smith, Jaclynn Villamil

The action occurs in New York City and Chicago at the present time.

The musical was presented in two acts.

ACT ONE—"He's a Comin'" (Ensemble), "I Hope He's Not Ashamed of Me" (Lois Holmes, Laverne Burden, Ensemble), "Happy" (John Kane, Boy Dancers), "What's a Gang Without a Guy Named Muggsy?" (Louis Criscuolo, Ronald Holgate, John Kane), "I Wish I Knew" (Mina Kolb), "He's a Comin'" (reprise) (Ensemble), "Love Was a Stranger to Me" (Joan Kroschell, Ronald Holgate), "Tap Dance" (Benny Smith), "Nasality" (Joan Eastman, Girl Dancers), "The Wonderland of Love" (Joan Kroshcell, Ronald Holgate), "The Wonderland of Love" (reprise) (Joan Kroschell)

ACT TWO—"Dear Diary" (Joan Kroschell, Mina Kolb, Ronald Holgate, Daniel Keyes, John Kane, Louis Criscuolo), "For Example" (Joan Kroschell, Mina Kolb), "Nasality" (reprise) (Joan Eastman), "It's a Glorious Day" (Joan Kroschell, Mina Kolb, Daniel Keyes, Ronald Holgate, John Kane, Louis Criscuolo,Lou David, Ensemble), "I Hope He's Not Ashamed of Me" (reprise) (Lois Holmes), "Panic Ballet" (Joan Kroschell, Mina Kolb, Lois Holmes, Joan Eastman, Laverne Burden, Daniel Keyes, Lou David, Ensemble), "Inspirational Song" (Company), "You're Gorgeous, You're Fantastic" (Mina Kolb, Daniel Keyes, The Boys), "Everything Happens for the Best" (Company)

NOTES—With Charles Grodin in charge, *Hooray!! It's a Glorious Day...And All That*, a musical which kidded musicals, must have been wonderful. Indeed, the show was ahead of its time. Today's audiences are used to "ironic" musicals in which the creators and performers are keenly aware of the musical's conventions and limitations, and in which the characters are cognizant of the fact they're appearing in a musical (examples of "ironic" musicals include *The Producers* [2001], *Urinetown* [2002; see entry], *The Musical of Musicals* [2003; see entry], *Spamalot* (2005), *[title of show]* 2006; see entry], *The Drowsy Chaperone* (2006], and *Adrift in Macao* [2007]). But Grodin & Co. did all this over forty years ago. When it was time for an inspirational song, there was a number called "Inspirational Song"; when a scene changed from an office to a park, a character wonders what happened to the office scenery; another character keeps asking when he's going to get to do his big number; during a dance sequence, a chorus boy screws up his face in mock-worry in order to fool the audience into thinking his dance steps are really tough to get through (and of course to ensure him extra applause when the dance is over).

Martin Gottfried in his *Opening Nights/Theatre Criticism of the Sixties* (G.P. Putnam's Sons, 1972) thought *Hooray* was the funniest musical he had seen in years, a "knowledgeable, witty, and marvelously accurate parody of our not-so-modern musicals, laughing them to pieces.... It is all theater-theater fun and very funny indeed." He also cited Sandra Devlin's choreography as "a show in itself," a witty homage to Michael Kidd, Bob Fosse, and Jerome Robbins which included a sly reference to the calculated repetitive movement of Broadway choreography.

Between 1966's *Hooray* and the ironic musicals of the early and mid 2000s, there was only one other ironic musical, *Smith* (1973; see entry), which told the story of a mild-mannered fellow who suddenly discovers his life has turned into a musical comedy of which he is the reluctant hero.

706 Horizons. THEATRE: Riverwest Theatre; OPENING DATE: December 19, 1984; PERFORMANCES: 21; BOOK: Jack Adolfi; LYRICS: Kathleen True; additional lyrics by Jack Adolfi; MUSIC: Carlos Davidson; additional music by Jack Adolfi; DIRECTION: Paul Eiseman; CHOREOGRAPHY: Ron Bohmer; SCENERY: Christopher Cole; M. Paige Miller, Props; COSTUMES: Susan Rosenberg; LIGHTING: Nancy Collings; MUSICAL DIRECTION: J.T. Thomas; PRODUCERS: CHS Productions, RoseAnn and Jack Adolfi in association with Riverwest Management Co.

CAST—Deborah Smith (Candi), Clayton Prince (Marvin), Jamie Lee Eisner (Lucy), Leslie Kincaid (Santa), Ron Bohmer (Keith), Sundra Jean Williams (Jo), Anthony Abbriano (Billy), Bob Ferreri (Drug Dealer, "John")

The action occurs at the present time in any major city in the United States (but specifically in New York City) and alternates between the street and the Horizons, which is a lodging for teenagers.

The musical was presented in two acts (division of acts and song assignments unknown; songs are listed in performance order).

MUSICAL NUMBERS—"I See the Light," "I See the Streetlights," "Your Time Has Come," "Turned Off to Turning On," "Ladies of the Night," "Why Can't It Be?," "Listen to the Children," "Grow Up, Little Girl," "Don't Live in Yesterday"

NOTES—*Theatre World 1984-1985 Season* described *Horizons* as a "musical drama" which dealt with teenagers' lives both on the "street" and in the Horizons, a lodging for teenagers. The production was apparently presented under an Off Off Broadway contract.

707 Horseman, Pass By. "A Musical Celebration!" THEATRE: Fortune Theatre; OPENING DATE: January 15, 1969; PERFORMANCES: 37; LYRICS: W.B. Yeats; lyrics adapted by Rocco Bufano and John Duffy; MUSIC: John Duffy; DIRECTION: Rocco Bufano; CHOREOGRAPHY: Rhoda Levine; SCENERY: Dennis Dougherty; COSTUMES: Nancy Potts; LIGHTING: Nancy Potts; MUSICAL DIRECTION: Stanley Walden; PRODUCER: John A. McQuiggan

CAST—Barbara Barrie (Intellect), Clifton Davis (Political Man), George Hearn (Imagination), Terry Kiser (Spirit), Laurence Luckinbill (Sensuality), Novella Nelson (Vanity), Maria Tucci (Timidity); and, on tape, Will Geer as The Voice

SOURCE—"The Writings and Spirit of W.B. Yeats" (1865-1939).

The revue was presented in one act.

MUSICAL NUMBERS—"What Then? (Dead Man's Tango)" (Company), "The Great Purple Butterfly" (Terry Kiser), "Brown Penny" (Laurence Luckinbill), "Girl's Song" (Barbara Barrie), "A Soldier Takes Pride in Saluting His Captain" (Clifton Davis), "Before the World Was Made" (Novella Nelson), "Last Confession" (Maria Tucci), "Mad as the Mist and Snow" (George Hearn), "Crazy Jane on the Day of Judgment" (Novella Nelson, Laurence Luckinbill, Terry Kiser), "Her Anxiety" (Novella Nelson), "Salley Gardens" (Terry Kiser), "Soulless a Faery Dies" (Maria Tucci), "A Drunken Man's Praise of Sobriety" (Company), "To an Isle in the Water" (George Hearn), "Consolation" (Company), "For Anne Gregory" (Barbara Barrie, Laurence Luckinbill), "Three Songs to the One Burden" (a/k/a "Henry Middleton") (Clifton Davis), "Final Choral Blessing" (Company)

NOTES—An evening of William Butler Yeats' poems set to rock music might have been more successful if it had toured college campuses. As it was, despite a glowing (and unsigned) review in the *New York Times*, the musical lasted little more than a month in New York.

The *Times* found the work "a lovely, lilting multimedia musical ... bright and breezy theatre that is long on imagination and talent." The *Times* noted that the musical styles ranged from rock to traditional ballad, from gospel-soul to Irish ballad, and concluded that the evening did more than its title indicated by coming across "at a full gallop."

This was the second time that Yeats' poem "Brown Penny" was used in a musical. In 1946, the poem was set to Duke Ellington's music (with the words adapted by John LaTouche) for *Beggar's Holiday*, and was introduced by Muriel Smith (who had performed the title role of *Carmen Jones* in 1943). Sometime during the run of *Beggar's Holiday*, "Brown Penny" was dropped from the score; but the song was reinstated for the musical's brief national tour.

708 Hot and Cold Heros. "A Musical Sandwich." THEATRE: 13th Street Theatre; OPENING DATE: May 9, 1973; PERFORMANCES: 16; LYRICS AND MUSIC: Islish Baldwin, George Bamford, Ronnie Britton, Arnold Borget, Jehan Clements, Tom Hawkins, Johnny Mann, Lance Mulcahy, and Robert W. Preston; SPECIAL MATERIAL: Jehan Clements, Joe Jakubowitz, Larry Meyers, Albert Poland, Joel Schapira, Ivan Todd, Vi Weiner, Ron Zarro, "and company"; DIRECTION: Joe Jakubowitz; CHOREOGRAPHY: Ivan Todd; SCENERY: R. Thomas Finch; COSTUMES: Fran Caruso; LIGHTING: Carla Blumberg (and Nancy Golladlay?); MUSICAL DIRECTION: Lee Gillespie and Mark Weiner; additional staging by Gary Weathersbee; PRODUCER: Mama Hare's Tree Company

CAST—Jehan Clements, Susan Conderman, Damien Leake, Melanie Michelle, Helena Reis, Murray I. Shactman, Monica Grignon, Ron Zarro

The revue was presented in two acts (division of acts and song assignments unknown; sketches and songs are listed in performance order).

MUSICAL NUMBERS—Intro, "New Gun in Town," "Subway," "Ode to Willie," "No Dessert," "He Is an Animal," "Name Dropping," "Ballad of Castle Maiden," "Anna Lee," "And Freedom," "Don't Tell Me Too Many Lies," "Man from Glad," "Rape," "Rock and Roll Critic," "N.E.T. and This Is Remote," "Four Eyes," "Mary Alice, Don't Say Shit," "Masks"

NOTES—The revue *Hot and Cold Heros* was produced by a company called Mama Hare's Tree, whose director was Edith O'Hara. In 1970, O'Hara's company The Plowright Players had produced *Touch* (see entry), which had celebrated communal life. According to Mel Gussow in the *New York Times*, *Hot and Cold Heros* was an "acerbic" look at life in the big city, and it covered such topics as runaways, subways, and rape (there was even a "heavyhanded" swipe at Al Carmines). Gussow felt the revue was "too unstructured," and he found it "neither hot nor cold, merely tepid."

709 Hot Dishes! THEATRE: Harry DeJur Playhouse; OPENING DATE: October 19, 1978; PERFORMANCES: 12; BOOK: Maurice Peterson; LYRICS: Maurice Peterson; MUSIC: Maurice Peterson; Grenoldo Frazier, Dance Music; DIRECTION: Irving Lee; Gary Easterling, Assistant to the Director; CHOREOGRAPHY: Irving Lee; SCENERY: Robert Edmonds; COSTUMES: Rene Lavergneau and Wia Carpenter; LIGHTING: George Grecyzlo; MUSICAL DIRECTION: Grenoldo Frazier; PRODUCER: Henry Street Settlement's New Federal Theatre (Woodie King, Jr., Producer)

CAST—Ernestine Jackson, Gia Galeano, Berniece Hall, Matthew Inge, Harold Jurkiewicz, Suzanne Klewan, James Moody, Sandra Phillips, James Patterson, Eric Riley, Besseye Ruth Scott, Andrea Suter

NOTES—The musical *Hot Dishes!* was presented under an Off Off Broadway contract.

710 Hot Grog. THEATRE: Merrymount Manhattan Theatre; OPENING DATE: October 6, 1977; PERFORMANCES: 22; BOOK: Jim Wann; LYRICS: Bland Simpson and Jim Wann; MUSIC: Bland Simpson and Jim Wann; DIRECTION: Edward Berkeley; CHOREOGRAPHY: Patricia Birch; SCENERY: James Tilton; COSTUMES: Hilary Rosenfeld; LIGHTING: James Tilton; MUSICAL DIRECTION: Jeff Waxman; PRODUCERS: The Phoenix Theatre (T. Edward Hambleton, Managing Director; Marilyn S. Miller, Executive Director; and Daniel Freudenberger, Artistic Director)

CAST—Mimi Kennedy (Anne Bonney), Patrick Hines (Governor Charles Eden), Terry O'Quinn (Calico Jack Rackham), Louis Zorich (Blackbeard [Edward Teach]), John McCurry (Caesar), Timothy Meyers (Israel Hands), Mary Bracken Phillips (Mr. Read), Homer Foil (Major Stede Bonnet), Rebecca Gilchrist (Savannah), Kathi Moss (Jamaica), Roger Howell (Lieutenant William Rhett)

The action occurs in 1718, in Coastal Carolina and on the high seas.

The musical was presented in two acts.

ACT ONE—Overture (The Band), "Seizure to Roam" (Terry O'Quinn, Company), "Got a Notion" (Mimi Kennedy, Terry O'Quinn), "Come on Down to the Sea" (Mimi Kennedy, Company), "Hot Grog" (Company), "The Pirates' Life" (Mimi Kennedy, Company), "The Difference Is Me" (Mary Bracken Phillips), "Change in Direction" (Mary Bracken Phillips, Mimi Kennedy, Company)

ACT TWO—"Heaven Must Have Been Smiling" (Mimi Kennedy, Terry O'Quinn, Company), "Hack 'Em" (Roger Howell), "Treasure to Bury"/"One of Us" (Louis Zorich, Mary Bracken Phillips, Homer Foil, John McCurry, Timothy Meyers, Terry O'Quinn), "Sea Breeze" (Mimi Kennedy, Patrick Hines), "The Chase" (The Band), "Skye Boat Song" (Mimi Kennedy, Mary Bracken Phillips, Homer Foil), "Marooned" (Terry O'Quinn, Mimi Kennedy, Mary Bracken Phillips, Homer Foil), "The Swordfight" (The Band), "The Head Song" (Louis Zorich, John McCurry, Timothy Meyers), "Drinking Fool" (Terry O'Quinn, Company), "Bound Away" (Mimi Kennedy, Company)

NOTES—With *Hot Grog*, Jim Wann and Bland Simpson traded outlaws of the Old West (see entry for *Diamond Studs*, 1975) for pirates of the early eighteenth century. The musical, which kicked off the Phoenix Theatre's twenty-fifth season, was a pleasant entertainment with attractive songs, and it seemed destined for a healthy life in regional and community theatre. But after its engagement at the Phoenix it all but disappeared.

Shortly after the opening, Louis Zorich, who played Bluebeard, was replaced by Timothy Meyer (whose role of Israel Hands was assumed by William Mesnik).

The musical was first produced at the Playmakers' Repertory Company in Chapel Hill, North Carolina, on February 19, 1976. During the show's run at the Kennedy Center's Musical Theatre Lab in March 1977, the role of Bluebeard was played by Frederick Coffin. Numbers dropped during the tryout were "Make Way," "Only a Woman," "Break Me Out," "High Summer," "Bastards Have the Best Luck," and "Heaven Must Have Been Smiling." The script was published by Samuel French, Inc., in 1980 (and included "Heaven Must Have Been Smiling").

711 Hot Klezmer. THEATRE: The Raymond J. Greenwald Theatre; OPENING DATE: March 31, 1998; PERFORMANCES: 8; MUSIC: Harold Seletsky and Mary Feinsinger; DIRECTION: Michael Leeds; CHOREOGRAPHY: Arte Phillips; SCENERY: Bruce Goodrich; COSTUMES: Bruce Goodrich; LIGHTING: Jeff Croiter; PRODUCERS: The American Jewish Theatre (Stanley Brechner, Artistic Director) in association with Carol Ostrow

CAST—Harold Seletsky (Clarinet), Hal Jeffrin (Vocal), Mary Feinsinger (Synthesizer, Vocal), Ellis Berger (Drums), Avram Pengas (Guitar, Oud, Bouzouki, Vocal), Zohar Fresco (Percussion, Drum), Peter Stan (Accordion), Julie Signitzer Krajicek (Violin), Shoshanna (Dancer)

The revue was presented in one act.

NOTES—As the title indicated, *Hot Klezmer* offered an evening of klezmer music, in this case both old songs as well as new ones (the latter written by Harold Seletsky and Mary Feinsinger). Lawrence Van Gelder in the *New York Times* noted the revue was at its best when the musicians played; when they did, the theatre was filled with "outbursts of handclapping, toe-tapping, foot-stamping fervor." Otherwise, he felt it was a mistake to have the musicians talk and assume small comic roles, and suggested that the "rousing" klezmer music should have been allowed to do all the talking.

712 Hot Sake ... with a Pinch of Salt. THEATRE: The AMAS Repertory Theatre; OPENING DATE: October 23, 1986; PERFORMANCES: 16; BOOK: Carol Baker and Lana Stein; LYRICS: Carol Baker and Lana Stein; MUSIC: Jerome I. Goldstein; DIRECTION: William Martin; CHOREOGRAPHY: Audrey Tischler; SCENERY: Frank J. Boros; COSTUMES: Howard Behar; LIGHTING: Ken Lapham; MUSICAL DIRECTION: Neal Tate; PRODUCER: The AMAS Repertory Theatre (Rosetta LeNoire, Founder and Artistic Director)

CAST—Anne Allgood (Ensemble), Carle E. Atwater (Ensemble), Wendy Baila (Alice Black), Jim Donahoe (Mr. Putnam), Laurie Katzmann (Mrs. Jacoby), Gordon Kupperstein (Ensemble), Alvin K.U. Lum (Mr. Asano), Gary Kenji Masuoka (Houseboy, Ensemble), Mary Rocco (Essie, Ensemble), Steve Steiner (Jerry Black), Marzetta Tate (Ensemble), Kirby Wahl (Ensemble), Ann Yen (Ayako, Ensemble)

SOURCE—The 1959 play *A Majority of One* by Leonard Spigelgass.

The action occurs in Brooklyn, aboard ship on the Pacific Ocean, and in Tokyo during 1959.

The musical was presented in two acts.

ACT ONE—"Fridays" (Laurie Katzmann, Ensemble), "Pictures of You" (Laurie Katzmann), "Here We Go Again" (Ensemble), "How Do You Do?" (Alvin K.U. Lum), "Another Martini" (Ensemble), "Trust No One" (Jim Donahoe), "How Was Your Day?" (Wendy Baila, Steve Steiner), "I Found a Friend" (Laurie Katzmann, Alvin K.U. Lum), "Moon Watching" (Alvin K.U. Lum)

ACT TWO—"Let the Flowers Find Me" (Alvin K.U. Lum, Ann Yen, Gary Kenji Masuoka), "Mama's Advice" (Laurie Katzmann, Wendy Baila), "All or Nothing Woman" (Wendy Baila), "Sake" (Laurie Katzmann), "What Good Does Loneliness Do?" (Alvin K.U. Lum, Laurie Katzmann), "The Embassy Sidestep" (Ensemble), "El Tango de la Embasada" (Wendy Baila, Ensemble), "You Who Have Taught Me to Love" (Steve Steiner), "Fridays" (reprise) (Mary Rocco, Ensemble), "A Nice Man Like That" (Laurie Katzmann, Mary Rocco), "How Do You Do?" (reprise) (Alvin K.U. Lum), "I Found a Friend" (reprise) (Laurie Katzmann, Alvin K.U. Lum)

NOTES—*Hot Sake...with a Pinch of Salt* was a musical version of one of Broadway's forgotten hits, *A Majority of One*, which opened in 1959 with Gertrude Berg and Cedric Hardwicke and played for 556 performances (the national tour also starred Berg and Hardwicke); Molly Picon and Robert Morley headlined the 1960 London production; and the 1962 film version starred Rosalind Russell and Alec Guinness.

The plot dealt with a Jewish widow and a Japanese widower who find romance once they overcome both their cultural differences and their personal tragedies resulting from World War II.

713 Hotel for Criminals. THEATRE: Exchange (Westbeth) Theatre; OPENING DATE: December 30, 1974; PERFORMANCES: 15; BOOK: Richard Foreman; LYRICS: Richard Foreman; MUSIC: Stanley Silverman; DIRECTION: Richard Foreman; SCENERY: Richard Foreman; COSTUMES: Whitney Blausen; LIGHTING: Richard Foreman; MUSICAL DIRECTION: Richard Gagnon; PRODUCERS: Lyn Austin, Mary Silverman, and Charles Hollerith; a Music-Theatre Performing Group Production

CAST—Ken Bell (Judex), Paul Ukena (Fantomas), Lyn Gerb (Helene), Lisa Kirchner (Irma Vep), Gene West (Gene West), Vampire Gang (Luther Enstad, M. Gaston; Robert Schlee, Alain Duchamp; Ray Murcell, Julot l'Enjoleur; Paul Ukena, Jr. (Dr. Lacloche); Parisians (Victor Abravaya, Katherine Alport, Glenn Barrett, Roxy Dawn, Steven Guimond)

The action occurs in Paris in 1902.

The musical was presented in two acts (no information available regarding musical numbers).

NOTES—With *Hotel for Criminals*, Richard Foreman and Stanley Silverman returned to Off Broadway with another of their offbeat musicals, this one a two-week limited engagement which dealt with vampires in turn-of-the-century Paris. Clive Barnes in the *New York Times* found the musical just as "strange" and "mad" as Foreman and Silverman's *Doctor Selavy's Magic Theatre* (see entry), but, unfortunately, "not nearly so engaging." The plot was a bit too "obscure" and "dense," and the score was the musical's "main merit" as well as its "chief disappointment" because it overwhelmed the evening with "a little too much" in the way of parody and pastiche.

Hotel for Criminals is interesting for the introduction of the character Irma Vep (performed by Lisa Kirchner), who, Barnes noted, was a vampiress decidedly different from another Irma from Paris, Irma La Douce (Irma Vep's name is an anagram for the word "vampire"). The character found both vampiric and theatrical immortality with the opening of Charles Ludlam's highly popular 1984 Off Broadway "penny dreadful" spoof *The Mystery of Irma Vep* (which was successful all over again in its 1998 Off Broadway revival); for Ludlam's romp, the late Lady Hillcrest was the former Irma Vep.

For more information on musicals about vampires, see entry for *Carmilla*.

714 Hotel Passionato. THEATRE: East 74th Street Theatre; OPENING DATE: October 22, 1965; PERFORMANCES: 11; BOOK: Jerome J. Schwartz; LYRICS: Joan Javits; MUSIC: Philip Springer; DIRECTION: Michael Ross; CHOREOGRAPHY: Bradford Craig; SCENERY: Paul Barnes; COSTUMES: Robert Mackintosh; LIGHTING: Paul Barnes; MUSICAL DIRECTION: Gershon Kingsley; PRODUCER: Slade Brown

CAST—PHIL LEEDS (Benoit Pinglet), JO ANNE WORLEY (Angelique Pinglet), MARIAN MERCER (Marcelle Paillardin), LEE CASS (Henri Paillardin), LINDA LAVIN (Victoire, Street Performer), PAUL SAND (Maxime, The Sandwich-Board Man, Street Performer), NED WERTIMER (Matthieu), THE KANE TRIPLETS (Yvette, LUCILLE KANE; Georgette, Baroness, JEAN KANE; Suzette, MAUREEN KANE), Lois Zetter (Flower Lady, Tart), Art Wallace (Concierge), Robert Rovin (Bellboy), Peter Maloney (Sailor), Adam Petroski (Enrico), Roger Hamilton (Inspector Boucard), Dutch Miller (Policeman)

SOURCE—The play *L'Hotel du Libre Echange* by Georges Feydeau and Maurice Desvallieres.

The action occurs in and around Paris during the spring of 1912.

The musical was presented in two acts.

ACT ONE—"Not Getting Any Younger" (Phil Leeds, Jo Anne Worley, Marian Mercer, Lee Cass, Linda Lavin, Paul Sand), "What a Curious Girl" (Paul Sand, Linda Lavin), "We'll Suffer Together" (Phil Leeds, Marian Mercer), "A Perfectly Charming Visit" (Jo Anne Worley, Phil Leeds, Ned Wertimer, Lucille Kane, Jean Kane, Maureen Kane), "You Gay Dog You!" (Phil Leeds), "Hotel Passionato" (Paul Sand), "Hotel Passionato" (reprise) (Art Wallace, Robert Rovin, Lois Zetter, Peter Maloney, Adam Petroski, Jean Kane, Paul Sand), "Don't" (Marian Mercer, Phil Leeds), "What Is This Sensation?" (Phil Leeds), "Tea-Tea-Tea" (Lucille Kane, Jean Kane, Maureen Kane), "Hot Water Bottles" (Phil Leeds, Marian Mercer, Ned Wertimer, Lucille Kane, Jean Kane, Maureen Kane, Adam Petroski, Art Wallace, Robert Rovin, Lois Zetter, Peter Maloney), "Good, Good, Good" (Lucille Kane, Jean Kane, Maureen Kane), "Hot Water Bottles" (reprise) (Company)

ACT TWO—"Tomorrow When the World Comes Crashing Down Around Our Ears" (Phil Leeds, Marian Mercer), "Marry Me" (Paul Sand, Linda Lavin), "What a Night!" (Lee Cass), "What a Night!" (reprise) (Jo Anne Worley), "The Confrontation" (Phil Leeds, Jo Anne Worley, Lee Cass, Marian Mercer, Linda Lavin), "A Perfectly Charming Visit" (reprise) (Lucille Kane, Jean Kane, Maureen Kane), "We Saw Everybody There" (Lucille Kane, Jean Kane, Maureen Kane), Finale (Company)

NOTES—Such amusing clowns as Paul Sand, Linda Lavin, Jo Anne Worley, Marian Mercer, and Phil Leeds couldn't keep *Hotel Passionato*, a farce about adulterous goings-on in a Parisian hotel, going for more than eleven performances. Lewis Funke in the *New York Times* singled out Sand for providing the musical's best performance and felt he was the only reason to savor "an otherwise boring evening" with "utterly elementary" dialogue. Funke found the score generally unmemorable, "with the exception of a few rhythmic numbers." He also mentioned a "wild interlude of operatic burlesque" which spoofed opera as well as Gilbert and Sullivan.

During the preview period, the songs "An Unbelievable Boy," "A Happy Wife," and "A Happy Man" had been performed; also, "What a Curious Girl," a duet for Sand and Lavin, had been heard as "What an Interesting Girl," a solo number for Sand. And, most importantly, during previews the song "Good, Good, Good" had been titled "Good-Good-Good."

In his program bio, Slade Brown, the producer of *Hotel Passionato*, said he would bring the hit British musical *Robert and Elizabeth* to Broadway during the 1966-1967 season (the production had premiered at the Lyric Theatre in London on October 20, 1964, running there for 948 performances). But the musical was never seen on Broadway, and the closest it ever got to New York was in a Paper Mill Playhouse production which opened in New Jersey on November 3, 1982 (the musical had been previously seen in Chicago in 1974 and in Maine in 1978).

One song from *Hotel Passionato*, "Tomorrow When the World Comes Crashing Down Around Our Ears" was later heard in *A Song Floating* (see entry), an evening of Philip Springer's songs, and it was recorded for the revue's cast album.

Later in the 1965-1966 season, Sand, Lavin, and Worley returned to Off Broadway under happier circumstances with *The Mad Show* (see entry), one of the longest running revues of the 1960s.

Hotel Passionato's source was the French farce *L'Hotel du Libre Echange*, which had been produced in London as *Hotel Paradiso* in 1956 with Alec Guinness and Irene Worth, and on Broadway in 1957 with Bert Lahr and Angela Lansbury. A 1966 film version also starred Guinness (and Gina Lollobrigida). The film's background music was composed and conducted by Laurence Rosenthal (who wrote the score for the 1967 Broadway musical *Sherry!*); the film's soundtrack was released by MGM Records LP # E/SE-4419-ST, and a later CD release by Chapter III Records (# CH-37504-2) also included the soundtrack of Rosenthal's score for *The Comedians* (1967).

715 House of Flowers. THEATRE: Theatre de Lys; OPENING DATE: January 28, 1968; PERFORMANCES: 57; BOOK: Truman Capote Lyrics: Truman Capote and Harold Arlen; MUSIC: Harold Arlen; DIRECTION: Joseph Hardy; CHOREOGRAPHY: Talley Beatty; SCENERY: Kert Lundell; COSTUMES: Richard Casler; LIGHTING: Tharon Musser; MUSICAL DIRECTION: Joseph Raposo; PRODUCERS: Saint-Subber (presented by special arrangement with Lucille Lortel Productions, Inc.)

CAST—Daniel Barrajanos (Dummer), Charles Moore (The Houngan), Yolande Bavan (Ottilie), Hope Clarke (Mamselle Tulip), Thelma Oliver (Mamselle Pansy), Josephine Premice (Madame Fleur, Old Bonaparte), Novella Nelson (Madame Tango), Carla Pinza (Senorita Maria), Tom Helmore (Lord Jamison), Bob Broadway (The Champion), Robert Jackson (Royal), Trina Parks (Woman), Walter Raines (Man)

SOURCE—Truman Capote's 1952 short story "House of Flowers."

The action occurs on an island in the Caribbean.

The musical was presented in two acts.

ACT ONE—"Two Ladies in De Shade of the Banana Tree" (Thelma Oliver, Hope Clarke), "A Sleepin' Bee" (Yolande Bavan, Thelma Oliver, Hope Clarke), "Somethin' Cold to Drink" (Josephine Premice), "Smellin' of Vanilla" (Thelma Oliver, Hope Clarke, Novella Nelson, Company), "House of Flowers" (Robert Jackson, Yolande Bavan), "Don't Like Goodbyes" (Yolande Bavan), "Jump De Broom" (lyric by Truman Capote only) (Charles Moore, Company)

ACT TWO—"Waitin'" (Thelma Oliver, Hope Clarke), "I Never Has Seen Snow" (Yolande Bavan), "Walk to De Grave" (Charles Moore, Mourners), "Woman Never Understan'" (Robert Jackson), "Madame Tango's Particular Tango" (Novella Nelson, Carla Pinza, Hope Clarke, Thelma Oliver), "What Is a Friend For?" (Tom Helmore, Josephine Premice), "A Sleepin' Bee"/"I Never Has Seen Snow" (reprises) (Robert Jackson, Yolande Bavan), "Two Ladies in De Shade of the Banana Tree" (reprise) (Thelma Oliver, Company)

NOTES—Truman Capote's charming if slight short story "House of Flowers" was a wispy mood piece, virtually plotless but heavy on atmosphere. When he and Harold Arlen wrote the musical version which premiered on Broadway in 1954, everything about the musical was just about perfect (with one fatal exception). The score was magnificent, one of the finest ever written for a musical; the lavish scenery and costumes by Oliver Messel were breathtaking; the choreography by Herbert Ross was exciting; and the almost forty-member cast was memorable (it included Pearl Bailey, Diahann Carroll, Ray Walston, Geoffrey Holder, Carmen de Lavallade, and Alvin Ailey). The fatal exception was the show's non-existent book. And although she's been vilified for overwhelming the musical with her larger-than-life persona, Pearl Bailey was obviously aware of the book's limitations, and so decided to give the customers a star-powered performance. Indeed, her take-no-prisoners approach to her role probably gave the weak book the kind of support it needed to get the audience from one glorious musical number to another. The musical lasted just five months, leaving behind a cast album which kept the show alive and which prompted the hope that one day a revival would validate the material and allow the piece to enjoy widespread acclaim (the Broadway cast album was released by Columbia Records [LP # OL-4969 and CD # SK-86857; the latter includes not only bonus material, such as the "Mardi Gras Waltz," but also expanded versions of such songs as "Slide, Boy, Slide"]). For trivia addicts: on the cast album, one of the high notes for "I Never Has Seen Snow" is actually sung by Arlen, not Diahann Carroll; listen closely, and you can hear Arlen's inserted note. Unfortunately, the 1968 Off Broadway revival (which included some new songs) wasn't able to redeem the original Broadway version. The revival offered an extremely scaled-down production with a weak book (whereas the Broadway production had offered a lavish production with a weak book). With the absence of star-power personalities, scaled-back dancers, chorus singers, and orchestra members, as well as bargain-basement settings, there was really no reason to revive the work. Clive Barnes in the *New York Times* noted the evening should have been a "big, brash, flashy, splashy Broadway musical" with a full orchestra and orchestrations, and concluded by saying the "smartest" people were those who advertised the original Broadway cast album in the Off Broadway program.

And so for almost two decades the musical virtually disappeared. But in the mid-1980s, the Denver Center Theatre Company offered a revival; and then in 1991 another revival, apparently aimed for Broadway, was produced (with Patti LaBelle in Pearl Bailey's role of Madame Fleur); although it didn't reach New York, this version offered the full original score (minus the songs which had been added to the 1968 revival). In 2003, Encores! offered a concert version (again, the complete Broadway score without the 1968 additions).

So *House of Flowers* remains a tantalizing if .... if only something could be done about its book, the show would be vindicated. But until that happens, *House of Flowers* is best enjoyed on a CD player.

The Off Broadway revival omitted several numbers from the original Broadway production ("One Man Ain't Quite Enough," "Mardi Gras," "Husband Cage," "I'm Gonna Leave Off Wearing My Shoes," "Has I Let You Down?," "Voudou," "Slide, Boy, Slide," and "Turtle Song"), and included five new and rather undistinguished songs by Capote and Arlen ("Somethin' Cold to Drink," "Jump De Broom," "Walk to De Grave," "Woman Never Understan," and "Madame Tango's Particular Tango," which was completely different from "Madame Tango's Tango," which was used in the 1954 production).

The Off Broadway revival was recorded by United Artists Records (LP # UAS-5180). Random House published the script of the revised production in 1968, and it appears to be the rarest and most collectible (and hence most expensive) of all published musical scripts. (The Holy Grail of scripts may be that of *Merrily We Roll Along*, which opened in 1981 at the Alvin [now Neil Simon] Theatre, the original home of the 1954 production of *House of Flowers*. The script of *Merrily* was scheduled for publication by Dodd, Mead, & Company, but for various reasons the publication was cancelled—but not before some half-dozen copies in uncorrected advance proofs were published in bound softback format.)

Tom Helmore, who played Mr. Jamison in the Off Broadway revival of *House of Flowers*, had appeared in the original 1945 production of Alan Jay Lerner and Frederick Loewe's *The Day Before Spring*.

Incidentally, during the run of the 1954 production, a new song, "Indoor Girl," was added for Pearl Bailey. Its lyric was by Michael Brown, who was later a frequent contributor to Off Broadway revues and who wrote a number of New York City-tribute songs which popped up in various revues over a ten-year period.

Although the score for *House of Flowers* is one of the most glorious in all musical theatre, and its overture one of the best to ever grace a musical, it's interesting that in his review of the original production in the *New York Times*, Brooks Atkinson found Arlen's music "commonplace" and his "big numbers ... second-rate Broadway or Hollywood." Further, he found the overture "uninteresting." But John Chapman in the *New York Daily News* said the production offered "the season's most fetching score," and Walter Kerr in the *New York Herald Tribune* found Arlen's score "tantalizing ... [it] takes wings with the overture itself, a magical medley," and noted that he would have been happy if the overture had been played twice.

Speaking of overtures, there are just a handful of truly memorable ones, among them *House of Flowers*, *Candide*, *Goldilocks*, *Gypsy*, *Take Me Along*, *The Fantasticks*, *Irma La Douce*, *Tenderloin* (with a trumpet solo for the ages!), *Subways Are for Sleeping*, *Funny Girl*, and *High Spirits*.

716 The House of Leather. "The Ante-Bellum Rock Musical." THEATRE: Ellen Stewart Theatre; OPENING DATE: March 18, 1970; PERFORMANCES: 1; BOOK: Frederick Gaines; LYRICS: Dale F. Menten and Frederick Gaines; MUSIC: Dale F. Menten; DIRECTION: H. Wesley Balk; SCENERY: David F. Segal; COSTUMES: Judith Cooper and James K. Shearon; LIGHTING: David F. Segal; MUSICAL DIRECTION: Dale F. Menten; PRODUCERS: William H. Semans and Richard K. Shapiro in association with Marshall Naify

CAST—Peter DeAnda (Copper), Ann Hodapp (First Woman), Kathleen Miller (Second Woman), John Kuhner (First Man), Robert Rovin (Second Man), Kia Coleman (Dixie), Beverly Wideman (Yankee), Barry Bostwick (Donny Brook), Norma Jean Wood (Mrs. Grimm), John Parriott (Butler Ramsey), Jonelle Allen (Sara Jane), Dennis Libby (Preacher); Band, Hugo (Dick Hedlund, Gus Dewey, Dick Bortolussi, George Miller)

SOURCE—A theme by Dale F. Menten.

The action occurs in Mrs. Grimm's house of prostitution in New Orleans; and Donny Brook Farm outside the city; before, during, and after the Civil War.

The musical was presented in two acts.

ACT ONE—"Swanee River Overture" (Band), "House of Leather Theme" (Band), "Sara Jane" (Abstract) (Band), "Graduates of Mrs. Grimm's Learning" (Band), "Do You Recall the House of Leather?" (Band), "Graduates of Mrs. Grimm's Learning" (reprise) (Slavers), "Copper's Creed" (Peter DeAnda), "Here I Am" (Kia Coleman, Beverly Wideman), "Do You Recall the House of Leather?" (reprise) (Band), "Mrs. Grimm" (Abstract) (Band), "Time Marches On" (Barry Bostwick, Workers, Dennis Libby), "Children's Song"/"Recess with Mrs. Grimm" (Norma Jean Wood, Students), "Steady Job" (Jonelle Allen, Dennis Libby), "Imagine You're Alive" (Barry Bostwick, Jonelle Allen), "House of Leather Theme" (reprise) (Band)

ACT TWO—"Dixie Prelude"/"The Civil War" (Band), "Armies of the Right" (Kia Coleman, Beverly Wideman, John Parriott, Civilians, Union Jack [performer unknown], Johnny Reb [performer unknown]), "Mrs. Grimm" (reprise) (Band), "God Is Black" (Jonelle Allen), "I'd Give to Her the World in Diamonds" (Barry Bostwick), "There's Love in the Country" (Barry Bostwick, Jonelle Allen), "Sara Jane" (Norma Jean Wood), "Now It's Gone, Gone, Gone" (Norma Jean Wood), "Sara Jane" (reprise) (Jonelle Allen), "Sherman's March to the Sea" (Company), "Death and Reality" (Company), "Epilogue in Suede" (Band), "Swanee River" (Company), "House of Leather Theme" (finale) (Band)

NOTES—*The House of Leather*, which was the fourth one-performance flop musical of the 1969-1970 Off Broadway season, had originally been performed at the Crawford-Livingston Theatre in St. Paul. Clive Barnes in the *New York Times* wrote that the musical dealt with Mrs. Grimm, who not only runs a house of prostitution during the Civil War era but also manages a Black-slave baby-farm as well as a factory which manufactures rifles designed to explode when fired. Barnes found the music less "rock" and more "concrete," and the direction pompous and inflated. He said the evening intended to be "stern, stark, and Brechtian," and wondered if perhaps the director had been "frightened as a baby by the Berliner Ensemble and never recovered." Barnes had good things to say about the scenery ("a series of rostra and grainily textured flats ... decoratively as fine as anything I have seen this season") and singled out three of the cast members for praise (Peter DeAnda, Jonelle Allen, and Barry Bostwick). *House of Leather* continued two interesting trends in the Off Broadway musical. There were almost twice the number of songs than the typical musical, and with the songs telling most of the story, the production was nearly sung-through. Also, the band (here called Hugo) performed some songs in counterpoint to the stage action (see entry for *The Last Sweet Days of Isaac*).

Capitol Records was to have released the original cast album, but the recording was cancelled due to the musical's brief run. However, at one point a studio cast album was recorded by a group called The Blackwood Apology (which included composer and co-lyricist Dale F. Menten) and was released by Fontana Records (LP # SRF-67591). Since the album was recorded in Minneapolis and includes material not heard in the New York production, the album was probably recorded prior to the Off-Broadway production. (The album credits the songs only to Menten; there's no mention of Frederick Gaines.) Like *Tamalpais Exchange*, *The House of Leather* album provides no clue that its material had been written for a musical; it looks like a pop record album, and, in fact, the album cover's artwork is similar in style to that of *Sgt. Pepper's Lonely Hearts Club Band*. Jonelle Allen later appeared in *The Two Gentlemen of Verona* (1971) and Barry Bostwick created the role of Danny Zuko in *Grease* (1972) (see entries for more information about these two musicals).

717 The House of the Seven Gables. THEATRE: John C. Borden Auditorium/Manhattan School of Music; OPENING DATE: December 6, 2000; PERFORMANCES: 3; LIBRETTO: Scott Eyerly; MUSIC: Scott Eyerly; DIRECTION: Linda Brovsky; SCENERY: Dipu Gupta; COSTUMES: Marie Anne Chiment; LIGHTING: Dennis Parichy; MUSICAL DIRECTION: David Gilbert; PRODUCER: The Manhattan School of Music Opera Theatre (Gordon Ostrowski, Director of Opera Studies and Productions)

CAST—James Schaffner (Clifford Pyncheon), Christianne Rushton (Hepzibah Pyncheon), Kelly Smith (Phoebe Pyncheon), Bert Johnson (Holgrave), Dominic Aquilino (Jaffrey Pyncheon), John Bischoff (Reverend), Keith Smith (Thomas Maule), Kyle Barisich (Mr. Dirkson), Ted Huffman (Mr. Hillyer), John Zuckerman (Mr. Carberg), Alex Richardson (Mr. Goss, Speaker), James Morera (Footman), Oshin Gregorian (Solicitor), Maxime Alvarez de Toledo (Lord Mayor), Kristin Reiersen (Mrs. Hillyer), Katherine Rappaport (Mrs. Dirkson), Amanda Crider (Mrs. Carberg), Vanessa Cariddi (Mrs. Goss), Eudora Brown (Lord Mayor's Wife), Evan Charney Maltby (Boy), Giuseppe Spoletini (Banker), Ghosts (Dorothy Grimley, Dawn Kasprow, Shanna Lesniak, Cameron Smith, Stanford Felix, Michael Rice, James Mendelson)

SOURCE—The 1851 novel *The House of the Seven Gables* by Nathaniel Hawthorne.

The action takes place in Salem, Massachusetts, in the mid-nineteenth century.

The opera was presented in three acts.

ACT ONE—Opening and Scene "Tell Me You Know Me," "Good Day" "Look in the Mirror" "There Once Was a King (The Song of the Rose)," Interlude and Scene, "Well, Well" "I Try to Be Like the Rose" "Why, Hepzibah," "The Mirror" "O God with Grace," "Are You All Right?"

ACT TWO—Opening and Scene "Why Should He" "Clifford, Where Are You?" "How Clear," "Lovely Is the Breeze (Quartet)" "Happy" "You Are Right" "Who Is the Man"

ACT THREE—Opening and Scene, "Here It Happened" "We Shall Discuss, "Jaffrey...Jaffrey ...," "I Now Pronounce," "Let Us Take (Quartet)"

NOTES—It's regrettable that the operatic version of *The House of the Seven Gables* seems to have disappeared since its world premiere. Writing in the *New York Times*, Allan Kozinn noted that while the opera was too lengthy and could do with some judicious pruning, he had positive comments about Scott Eyerly's score ("likable, attractively neo-Romantic"). He found the vocal lines "lyrical and shapely" and the orchestrations "beautiful ... a natural flow that suggests [Eyerly] thought carefully about the coloration and texture of every phrase." Kozinn singled out many musical sequences, including a hymn, two folk-like melodies, a "blustery" campaign song, and a motif on a Baroque harpsichord which signaled the death of a member of the Pyncheon family. Happily, the opera was recorded by Albany Records on a 2-CD set (# TROY-447; the titles of the musical sequences are taken from this recording).

On November 28, 1995, *A Haunted Deconstruction of Nathaniel Hawthorne's The House of the Seven Gables* was presented Off Off Broadway by the Tiny Mythic Theatre Company at the Here Theatre for almost four weeks. *Theatre World 1995-1996* reported that the work looked at "the last living members of a cursed New England family." The adaptation was by Elizabeth Banks, with texts by Britt Coles, David Greenspan, Anita Liberty, and Ruth Gargraff, and the music was by Matthew Pierce, Steven Day, and Stephen Streuber. The production was conceived and directed by Tim Maner. It's unclear if the work was a full-fledged musical, but since the production had three composers it seems likely that music was an integral part of the presentation.

718 The Housewives' Cantata. "A Musical." THEATRE: Theatre Four; OPENING DATE: February 18, 1980; PERFORMANCES: 24; BOOK: Willy Holtzman; LYRICS: June Siegel; MUSIC: Mira J. Spektor; DIRECTION: Rina Elisha; CHOREOGRAPHY: Rina Elisha; SCENERY: Raymond C. Recht; COSTUMES: Judy Dearing; LIGHTING: Marshall S. Spiller; MUSICAL DIRECTION: Richard A. Schacher; PRODUCERS: Cheryl Crawford and Eryk Spektor

CAST—Patti Karr (Flora), Sharon Talbot (Lily), Forbesy Russell (Heather), William Perley (Everyman, Harvey, Freddie, Sheldon, Allen, Judge, Rod)

The action occurs from 1962 to the present.

The musical was presented in three acts.

ACT ONE—Overture (Orchestra), "Dirty Dish Rag" (Patti Karr, Sharon Talbot, Forbesy Russell), "Sex" (William Perley, Sharon Talbot, Patti Karr, Forbesy Russell), "Song of the Bourgeois Beatnik" (Sharon Talbot), "Early Morning Rain" (lyric by Charline Spektor) (William Perley, Patti Karr), "Little Women" (Sharon Talbot, Patti Karr, Forbesy Russell)

ACT TWO—"Adultery Waltz" (Sharon Talbot, William Perley), "Divorce Lament" (Sharon Talbot, William Perley), "Suburban Rose" (Patti Karr), "Song of the Open Road" (Forbesy Russell), "Dirty Dish Rag" (reprise) (Sharon Talbot, Patti Karr, Forbesy Russell), "Legs" (Sharon Talbot), "M.C.P." (William Perley, Forbesy Russell, Patti Karr, Sharon Talbot)

ACT THREE—"Daughter's Lullaby" (Forbesy Russell), "Guinevere Among the Grapefruit Peels" (Forbesy Russell, Patti Karr, Sharon Talbot), "Song of the Bourgeois Beatnik" (reprise) (Sharon Talbot), "Apartment Lament" (Forbesy Russell, William Perley, Sharon Talbot, Patti Karr), "Middle Aged" (Patti Karr, Sharon Talbot, Forbesy Russell, William Perley), "Mr. Fixer" (Patti Karr), "White House Resident" (William Perley), "A New Song" (Forbesy Russell, Sharon Talbot, Patti Karr, William Perley)

NOTES—The short-lived feminist musical *The Housewives' Cantata* dealt with three sisters (Flora, Lily, and Heather) and the various men in their lives (one actor, William Perley, portrayed all the men). The musical had been produced as early as 1973, and on April 2, 1979, it was presented in workshop at the Bruno Walter Auditorium at Lincoln Center (here the three sisters were called Flora, Nora, and Dora); William Perley was also in this version, which was presented by the Stage Directors and Choreographers Workshop Foundation. The following songs heard in the workshop were dropped for the Off Broadway production: "We're the Pepsi Generation," "Liberated Song," "Bourgeois Hippie," and "Someday Blues" ("Bourgeois Hippie" and "Song of the Bourgeois Beatnik" may have been the same song with a change of title). Original Cast Records released an album of songs from the show (LP # OC-8133; the cast included Sharon Talbot from the Off Broadway production), and the liner notes indicate that over the years the authors had written almost thirty songs for the piece; on the album, the sisters are called Flora, Nora, and Dora, and the men in their lives are named Henry, Harry, and Harvey.

John Corry in the *New York Times* wanted to like the musical, but felt it tried too hard to be "determinedly sprightly" when it needed to "come down hard" and stand for something. As it was, the evening was "meringue, with hardly any crust underneath."

719 How I Survived High School. THEATRE: Jan Hus Playhouse; OPENING DATE: June 9, 1986; PERFORMANCES: 12; BOOK: E. Taubenslag; LYRICS: Bob and Alec Nemser and Charles Jones; MUSIC: Glen Slater; DIRECTION: Michael Taubenslag; CHOREOGRAPHY: Tammy Thomas; SCENERY: Jeffrey Allen; COSTUMES: Jeffrey Allen; MUSICAL DIRECTION: Michael Bergman; PRODUCER: Robert Nicholas

CAST—Joe Buffington, Scott Fried, Nancy Pothier, Orlando Powers, Eileen Tepper, Torri Whitehead

The musical was presented in two acts (division of acts and song assignments unknown; songs are listed in performance order).

MUSICAL NUMBERS—"High School," "Shy Couple," "Phone Calls," "I'm Leaving," "Wondering," "Prom Date," "By Myself," "V.D.," "Lonely," "Please Don't Tell My Father," "Where," "Afraid of Rejection," "Child Abuse," "Hi Grandma," "The Note," "Living a Dream," "Numbers," "Friendship," "Song of Youth," "Virgin," "View from the Hill," "Life"

NOTES—*How I Survived High School* seems to have been produced under an Off Off Broadway contract.

720 How to Get Rid of It. THEATRE: Astor Place Theatre; OPENING DATE: November 17, 1974; PERFORMANCES: 9; BOOK: Eric Blau; LYRICS: Eric Blau; MUSIC: Mort Shuman; DIRECTION: Eric Blau; SCENERY: Don Jensen; COSTUMES: Don Jensen; LIGHTING: Ian Calderon; MUSICAL DIRECTION: Wolfgang Knittel; PRODUCERS: 3W Productions, Inc.; Stan Swerdlow, Executive Producer

CAST—Matt Conley (Amedee Buccinioni), Carol L. Hendrick (Lady Super), Lorrie Davis (Shirley), David Vogel (Mr. Helliker), Joseph Neal (Mr. Provan), Janet McCall (Lucinda), Vilma Vaccaro (Ms. Cohen), James Doerr (Harry), Mike Dantuono (Police Sergeant O'Hanley), Edward Rodriguez (Police Sergeant Ramirez), Joe Masiell (Vietnam Veteran), Muriel Costa-Greenspon (Madeleine Buccinioni), Joseph Neal (Postman); Mushrooms (Mike Dantuono, Lorrie Davis, Carol L. Hendrick, Janet McCall, Joseph Neal, Edward Rodriguez, Vilma Vaccaro, David Vogel)

SOURCE—The 1954 play *Amedee*, or *Comments S'en Debarrasser* by Eugene Ionesco.

The action occurs during the present time in the apartment of Mr. and Mrs. Buccinioni on Barrow Street, somewhere in Greenwich Village, in New York City.

The musical was presented in two acts (division of acts and song assignments unknown; songs are listed in performance order).

MUSICAL NUMBERS—"Mind Your Business," "The Old Man Says to the Old Woman," "The Mushrooms Are Coming in Here," "Good Morning, I'll Put You Through," "At the End of a Period of Time," "Are You the Man Whose Name Is on the Paper," "Almost Everybody Suffers More Than Us," "You've Got to Get Rid of It," "Suite for a Growing Corpse," "I Am Here at the Place Where Time Began," "I Am a Vietnam Veteran," "Well, Yes, He's a Friend," "What an Evening," "Five to One," "Amedee, Amedee, It Isn't Too Late," "The Late, Late Show"

NOTES—The 1973-1974 revue *Ionescopade* (see entry) didn't do well, and neither did *How to Get Rid of It*, a musical adaptation of one Ionesco's plays. The story concerned an unhappily married couple (Matt Conley and Muriel Costa-Greenspon) whose closet contains a corpse which grows larger and larger by the day. The corpse serves as the objective correlative of their troubled marriage.

Clive Barnes in the *New York Times* felt Eric Blau got the tone all wrong for Ionesco's sensitive if surreal portrait of a failed marriage; he wrote that Ionesco had been "raped and the result is not ravishing," and he found fault with the "coarse jokes and unsubtle characterizations." He felt a major mistake was the change in the musical's setting: "Ionesco is Paris and this show tries to be Greenwich Village." For all that, Barnes had high praise for Blau and Mort Shuman's "bold and attractive" score which had "vigor and strength." He noted especially the "particularly rousing" songs given to the character of a Vietnam veteran (played by Joe Masiell).

Barnes wasn't all that taken with the musical's "anthropomorphic" mushrooms, but he seemed to like the "skeletal cartoon" of a set, and he felt the first glimpse of the ever-growing corpse was "mightily impressive."

721 How to Save the World and Find True Love in 90 Minutes. THEATRE: New World Stages; OPENING DATE: November 12, 2006; PERFORMANCES: 57; BOOK: Jonathan Karp; LYRICS: Jonathan Karp; MUSIC: Seth Weinstein; DIRECTION: Christopher Gattelli; CHOREOGRAPHY: Christopher Gattelli; SCENERY: Beowulf Boritt; COSTUMES: David Murin; LIGHTING: Jeff Croiter; MUSICAL DIRECTION: Seth Weinstein; PRODUCERS: Lawrence Anderson and The Singing Comedians

CAST—Michael McEachran (Miles Muldoon, He), Stephen Bienskie (Greek, Therapist), Natalie Joy Johnson (Greek, Yogi), Kevin Smith Kirkwood (Greek, Federal Bureaucrat), Anika Larsen (Julie Lemmon), Nicole Ruth Snelson (Violet Zipper)

The action occurs in the present.

The musical was presented in one act.

MUSICAL NUMBERS—"Only the Paranoid Survive" (Michael McEachran, Stephen Bienskie, Natalie Joy Johnson, Kevin Smith Kirkwood), "Love or Fear" (Anika Larsen, Michael McEachran), "I Want What You Want" (Michael McEachran, Nicole Ruth Snelson, Stephen Bienskie, Natalie Joy Johnson, Kevin Smith Kirkwood), "The Melon Ballet" (Company), "Julie's Prayer" (Anika Larsen, Stephen Bienskie, Natalie Joy Johnson, Kevin Smith Kirkwood), "The Voices in My Head" (Michael McEachran, Stephen Bienskie, Natalie Joy Johnson, Kevin Smith Kirkwood), "Violet's Confession" (Nicole Ruth Snelson) "Love Is" (Nicole Ruth Snelson, Anika Larsen, Natalie Joy Johnson), "Yoga Class" (Natalie Joy Johnson, Anika Larsen, Michael McEachran, Yoga Students), "I Want to Know You" (Michael McEachran, Nicole Ruth Snelson), "Read My Mind" (Stephen Bienskie, Natalie Joy Johnson, Kevin Smith Kirkwood), "It's Over, Miles" (Company), "When the Music Played" (Anika Larsen), "We Can Save the World and Find True Love" (Michael McEachran, Nicole Ruth Snelson), "Save the People" (Michael McEachran, Stephen Bienskie, Natalie Joy Johnson, Kevin Smith Kirkwood), "Oh, God"/"Read My Mind" (Company)

NOTES—This free-wheeling, friendly little musical *How to Save the World and Find True Love in 90 Minutes* dealt with a nerdy bookstore clerk who after being knocked out by Guatemalan melons during a demonstration emerges with the ability to read minds. He then becomes involved with a sexy United Nations diplomat, while all along a co-worker secretly loves him. Meanwhile, the diplomat is having a secret affair with a terrorist who has dastardly plans up his sleeve.

Anita Gates in the *New York Times* praised the musical's "untethered sense of fun," its score, and its "witty" book and lyrics. She noted this was the kind of musical in which the lyric "Oh God, why are all the good men unconscious?" makes sense, and she singled out some of the loopy dialogue (in describing her affair with the terrorist, the diplomat notes, "He was on a hunger strike, and I was on the South Beach Diet"). She also noted that the chorus morphed into such diverse characters as Condoleezza Rice and Celine Dion, and singled out Kevin Smith Kirkwood's "fabulous" turn in drag as "Bonquisha," who answers phones at the Office of Homeland Security ("Are you calling to report a threat, baby?").

The musical ran just a few weeks, but perhaps it will find an afterlife in regional and community theatre. The cast recording was released by Hy-Fy Records (CD # 001); two songs were retitled; two songs were omitted; and four added.

The work was previously seen at the 2004 New York International Fringe Festival and the 2004 New York Musical Theatre Festival.

722 How to Steal an Election. "A Dirty Politics Musical." THEATRE: Pocket Theatre; OPENING DATE: October 13, 1968; PERFORMANCES: 89; BOOK: William F. Brown; LYRICS: Oscar Brand; MUSIC: Oscar Brand; DIRECTION: Robert H. Livingston; CHOREOGRAPHY: Frank Wagner; SCENERY: Clarke Dunham; COSTUMES: Mopsy; LIGHTING: Clarke Dunham; MUSICAL DIRECTION: Bhen Lanzaroni; PRODUCERS: Stephen Mellow, Seymour Vail, and IPC

CAST—D.R. Allen, Barbara Anson, Beverly Ballard, Ed Crowley, Clifton Davis, Carole Demas, Del Hinkley, Thom Koutsoukos, Bill McCutcheon

The action occurs yesterday, today, and tomorrow in the United States of America.

The musical was presented in two acts.

ACT ONE—"The Plumed Knight" (Ed Crowley), "Clay and Frelinghuysen" (Barbara Anson, Beverly Ballard, Ed Crowley), "Get on the Raft with Taft" (Bill McCutcheon), "Silent Cal" (Barbara Anson, with Beverly Ballard, Ed Crowley, Del Hinkley, Thom Koutsoukos, Bill McCutcheon), "Nobody's Listening" (Clifton Davis), "Comes the Right Man" (Carole Demas), "How to Steal an Election" (D.R. Allen, with Ed Crowley, Del Hinkley, Thom Koutsoukos, Bill McCutcheon), "Van Buren" (Thom Koutsoukos), "Tippecanoe and Tyler, Too" (Bill McCutcheon, with Ensemble), "Charisma" (D.R. Allen), "Nobody's Listening" (reprise) (Clifton Davis), "Lincoln and Soda" (Beverly Ballard), "With Lincoln and Liberty" (Ed Crowley, Del Hinkley, Thom Koutsoukos, Bill McCutcheon), "He's the Right Man (March)" (D.R. Allen, with Ensemble)

ACT TWO—"Grant" (Ed Crowley, Del Hinkley, Thom Koutsoukos, Bill McCutcheon), "Law and Order" (Ed Crowley), "Lucky Lindy" (Barbara Anson, Beverly Ballard), "Down Among the Grass Roots" (D.R. Allen, with Ensemble), "Get Out the Vote" (Ensemble), "Mr. Might've Been" (Carole Demas, Clifton Davis), "We're Gonna Win" (Carole Demas, Clifton Davis, with Ensemble), "More of the Same" (Carole Demas, Clifton Davis)

NOTES—*How to Steal an Election* was a revue-like book musical about two young political idealists whose experience is limited to the 1968 election. "On a nonspecific satiric night" they meet Calvin Coolidge, who takes them on a surreal journey of American (dirty) politics, from Martin Van Buren's 1840 presidential campaign to a future (1972) campaign. The two young people assume that politics is and will ever be "more of the same," but Coolidge encourages them with the thought that in our democracy somehow everything always works out for the best.

The musical's fresh perspective on American politics, coupled with Oscar Brand's lively score, should have ensured it a longer run and, one would think, an occasional revival as an interesting and offbeat look at the nation's political history. But with the show's closing, it disappeared. The score was recorded by RCA Victor Records (LP # LSO-1153), and the album noted the evening was "Politics Set to Music, or The Lowdown on What's Happening Among the Grass Roots."

Richard F. Shepard in the *New York Times* reported the "mock pageant" evening utilized slides and film to tell its story, and he praised the "pertinent," "good," and "thoughtful" songs, including "The Right Man," "Down Among the Grass Roots," "Get Out the Vote," and "Mr. Might've Been" (the latter a tribute to Eugene J. McCarthy).

723 Howard Crabtree's When Pigs Fly.
NOTES—See entry for *When Pigs Fly*.

724 Howard Crabtree's Whoop-Dee-Doo!
NOTES—See entry for *Whoop-Dee-Doo!*

725 How's the House? "A Musical Entertainment." THEATRE: Park Royal Theatre; OPENING DATE: October 20 (?), 1979; PERFORMANCES: Unknown; BOOK: Tom Savage, Scott Newborn, and Barry Berg; LYRICS: Tom Savage; MUSIC: Tom Savage; DIRECTION: Scott Newborn; Susan Stroman, Assistant Director; CHOREOGRAPHY: Scott Newborn; Susan Stroman, Assistant Choreographer; SCENERY: Ernest Allen Smith; COSTUMES: Michael J. Cesario; LIGHTING: Frederick Buchholz; MUSICAL DIRECTION: Ada Janik; PRODUCERS: Lesley Savage and Bert Stratford

CAST—John Dossett (Joe), Bruce Laffey (Mr. B.), Scott Ellis (Sally's Boyfriend), Enid Blaymore (Millie), Louise Kirtland (Roberta), Nick Cantrell (Brad), Leslie Anne Wolfe (Miranda), Eileen McCabe (Lillian), Charlie Stovola (Harold), Brian Evers (Gary), Laurie Franks (Janet), Clifton Steere (Brown Suit), Stanley Sayer (Blue Suit), Rick Emery (Tuxedo), Lee Meredith (Lulu)

The musical was presented in one act.

MUSICAL NUMBERS—"My Time" (John Dossett), "Who's Who" (Company), "What I Could Have Done Tonight" (Charlie Stovola, Laurie Franks), "If I Could Be Beautiful" (Leslie Anne Wolfe), "There You Are" (Rick Emery), "Sally" (Scott Ellis), "Other People" (Laurie Franks), "Hit the Ladies" (Eileen McCabe, Leslie Anne Wolfe, Louise Kirtland, Enid Blaymore, Laurie Franks), "Is Everybody Happy?" (Brian Evers), "What's Goin' On" (Louise Kirtland, Enid Blaymore), "My Time" (reprise) (John Dossett), "Stop the Presses (Stanley Sayer, Rick Emery, Clifton Steere) Finale" (Company)

NOTES—The Off Off Broadway musical *How's the House* marked an early appearance by Susan Stroman (as the musical's co-director and co-choreographer). And among the cast members was Lee Meredith (connect the dots to find a major show-business connection between Meredith and Stroman). The musical was later revised as *Musical Chairs* (see entry).

The cast also included Scott Ellis, who later directed both *And the World Goes 'Round* (1991; see entry), a tribute revue to John Kander and Fred Ebb, and Kander and Ebb's *Steel Pier* (1997), both of which were choreographed by Stroman.

726 The Human Comedy. THEATRE: Anspacher Theatre/The Public Theatre; OPENING DATE: December 28, 1983; PERFORMANCES: 79; LIBRETTO: William Dumaresq; MUSIC: Galt MacDermot; DIRECTION: Wilford Leach; COSTUMES: Rita Ryack; LIGHTING: Stephen Strawbridge; MUSICAL DIRECTION: Tania Leon; PRODUCER: The New York Shakespeare Festival (Joseph Papp, Director)

CAST—David Lawrence Johnson (Trainman), Josh Blake (Ulysses), Bonnie Koloc (Mother), Stephen Geoffreys (Homer), Mary Elizabeth Mastrantonio (Bess), Anne Marie Bobby (Helen), Laurie Franks (Miss Hicks), Rex Smith (Spangler), Christopher Edmonds (Thief), Gordon Connell (Mr. Grogan), Daniel Noel (Felix), Delores Hall (Beautiful Music), Caroline Peyton (Mary Arena), Olga Merediz (Mexican Lady), Don Kehr (Voice of Matthew, Marcus), Lisa Kirchner (Girl), Louis Padilla (Boy), Joseph Kolinski (Toby), Kenneth Bryan (Soldier), Michael Willson (Soldier), Kathleen Rowe McAllen (A Neighbor), Leata Galloway (Diana Steed), Donna Lee Marshall (Neighbor),

Grady Mulligan (Neighbor), Vernon Spencer (Neighbor)

SOURCE—The program credited the source to William Saroyan's 1943 novel *The Human Comedy* (which was itself based on William Saroyan's 1943 Academy Award-winning screenplay).

The action occurs in a little town in California in 1943.

The musical was presented in two acts.

ACT ONE—"In a Little Town in California" (Company), "Hi Ya Kid" (David Lawrence Johnson, Josh Blake), "We're a Little Family" (Bonnie Koloc, Stephen Geoffreys, Josh Blake, Mary Elizabeth Mastrontonio), "The Assyrians" (Anne Marie Bobby, Laurie Franks), "Noses" (Stephen Geoffreys), "You're a Little Young for the Job" (Rex Smith, Stephen Geoffreys), "I Can Carry a Tune" (Stephen Geoffreys), "Happy Birthday" (Stephen Geoffreys), "Happy Anniversary" (Stephen Geoffreys, Rex Smith, Gordon Connell), "I Think the Kid Will Do" (Gordon Connell, Rex Smith), "Beautiful Music" (Delores Hall, Company), "Cocoanut Cream Pie" (Gordon Connell, Stephen Geoffreys), "When I Am Lost" (Stephen Geoffreys, Delores Hall, Company), "I Said, Oh No" (Mary Elizabeth Mastrantonio, Caroline Peyton, Olga Merediz), "Daddy Will Not Come Walking Through the Door" (Bonnie Koloc), "The Birds in the Sky" (Mary Elizabeth Mastrantonio), "Remember Always to Give" (Bonnie Koloc), "Long Past Sunset" (Don Kehr), "Don't Tell Me" (Louis Padilla, Lisa Kirchner, Family, Company), "The Fourth Telegram" (Rex Smith, Gordon Connell), "Give Me All the Money" (Christopher Edmonds, Rex Smith), "Everything Is Changed" (Stephen Geoffreys, Bonnie Koloc), "The World Is Full of Loneliness" (Bonnie Koloc), "Hi Ya Kid" (reprise) (David Lawrence Johnson, Josh Blake, Company)

ACT TWO—"How I Love Your Thingamajig" (Kenneth Bryan, D. Peter Samuel), "Everlasting" (Joseph Kolinski), "An Orphan, I Am" (Joseph Kolinski), "I'll Tell You About My Family" (Don Kehr), "I Wish I Were a Man" (Caroline Peyton), "Marcus, My Friend" (Joseph Kolinski), "My Sister Bess" (Don Kehr), "I've Known a Lot of Guys" (Leata Galloway), "Diana" (Rex Smith), "Dear Brother" (Stephen Geoffreys, Don Kehr), "The Birds in the Trees"/"A Lot of Men" (Leata Galloway, Rex Smith), "Parting" (Bonnie Koloc, Wives, Sweethearts, Mothers, Friends, Soldiers), "Mr. Grogan, Wake Up" (Stephen Geoffreys), "Hello Doc" (Rex Smith), "What Am I Supposed to Do?" (Stephen Geoffreys, Rex Smith), "Long Past Sunset" (reprise) (Bonnie Koloc, Company), "I'm Home" (Joseph Kolinksi), "Somewhere, Someone" (Mary Elizabeth Mastrontonio), "I'll Always Love You" (Caroline Peyton), "Hi Ya Kid" (reprise) (David Lawrence Johnson, Josh Blake, Company), "Fathers and Mothers (And You and Me)" (Company)

NOTES—The Off Broadway program for *The Human Comedy* didn't list individual musical numbers (the above is derived from the song titles listed in the Broadway playbill).

The sung-through musical was based on William Saroyan's *The Human Comedy*, which was first seen as a 1943 MGM film (Saroyan won the Academy Award for his screenplay). Later that year Saroyan adapted the screenplay into a novel. The musical credited the novel, not the film, as its source.

The nostalgic musical about life in small-town America during the War Forties played for a little more than two months Off Broadway, and then transferred to Broadway at the Royale (now Schoenfeld) Theatre on April 5, 1984. The production received mixed reviews from the critics, and closed after just thirteen performances. The Off Broadway program didn't list a scenic designer, but the Broadway version credited Bob Shaw.

The script was published by Samuel French, Inc., in 1985; the Broadway cast album of Galt McDermot's impressive score was first released on two audiocassettes, and then eventually on a two CD-set by Kilmarnock Records (# KIL-9702). Cass Morgan was an understudy for the role of Mother, and Donna Murphy was a swing; both singers were included in the chorus of the recording.

The evocative artwork seen on the window card of the musical's Broadway production (by Paul Davis, one of the finest artists in the field of theatre posters) was marred by a photograph of Joseph Papp, which was jarringly and unnecessarily inserted into the nostalgic drawing.

727 Hundreds of Hats. THEATRE: WPA Theatre; OPENING DATE: May 25, 1995; PERFORMANCES: 40; LYRICS: Howard Ashman; MUSIC: See song list for credits; DIRECTION: Michael Mayer; CHOREOGRAPHY: John Ruocco; SCENERY: Mark Beard; COSTUMES: Michael Krass; LIGHTING: Jack Mehler; MUSICAL DIRECTION: Helen Gregory; PRODUCER: WPA Theatre (Kyle Renick, Artistic Director; Lori Sherman, Managing Director)

CAST—John Ellison Conlee, Bob Kirsh, Philip Lehl, Amanda Naughton, Nancy Opel

The revue was presented in two acts (division of acts and song assignments unknown; songs are listed in performance order).

MUSICAL NUMBERS—"Hero" (music by Alan Menken), "In Our Hands" (from *Smile*, 1987; music by Marvin Hamlisch), "30 Miles from the Banks of the Ohio" (*God Bless You, Mr. Rosewater*, 1979; music by Alan Menken), "A Firestorm Consuming Indianapolis" (*God Bless You, Mr. Rosewater*, 1979; music by Alan Menken), "Rhode Island Tango" (*God Bless You, Mr. Rosewater*, 1979; music by Alan Menken), "Belle" (1991 film *Beauty and the Beast*; music by Alan Menken), "Skid Row Downtown" (*Little Shop of Horrors*, 1982; music by Alan Menken), "Song for a Hunter College Graduate" (*Diamonds*, 1984; music by Jonathan Sheffer), "Thank God for the Volunteer Fire Brigade" (*God Bless You, Mr. Rosewater*, 1979; music by Alan Menken), "Cheese Nips" (*God Bless You, Mr. Rosewater*, 1979; music by Alan Menken), "A Little Dental Music" (written for, but not used in, *Little Shop of Horrors*, 1982; music by Alan Menken), "Aria for a Cow" (source unknown; music by Alan Menken), "Hundreds of Hats" (*Diamonds*, 1984; music by Jonathan Sheffer), "Growing Bo" (source unknown; music by Alan Menken), "Les Poissons" (1989 film *The Little Mermaid*; music by Alan Menken), "Maria's Song" (source unknown; music by Alan Menken), "Suddenly Seymour" (*Little Shop of Horrors*, 1982; music by Alan Menken), "Since You Came to This Town" (*God Bless You, Mr. Rosewater*, 1979; music by Alan Menken), "A Day in the Life of a Fat Kid from Philly" (unfinished musical *Fatty Goes to the Opera*; music by Alan Menken), "Part of Your World" (1989 film *The Little Mermaid*; music by Alan Menken), "Somewhere That's Green" (from *Little Shop of Horrors*, 1982; music by Alan Menken) "Disneyland" (*Smile*, 1987; music by Marvin Hamlisch), "Your Day Begins Tonight" (source unknown; music by Alan Menken), "A Magician's Work" (source unknown; music by Alan Menken), "Babkak Omar Aladdin Kassim" (written for, but not used in, 1992 film *Aladdin*; music by Alan Menken), "Daughter of Prospero" (possibly written for, but not used in, 1989 film *The Little Mermaid*; music by Alan Menken), "Kiss the Girl" (1989 film *The Little Mermaid*; music by Alan Menken), "How Quick They Forget" (written for, but not used in, 1992 film *Aladdin*; music by Alan Menken), "Poor Unfortunate Souls" (1989 film *The Little Mermaid*; music by Alan Menken), "We'll Have Tomorrow" (written for, but not used in, *Little Shop of Horrors*, 1982; music by Alan Menken), "Proud of Your Boy" (written for, but not used in, 1992 film *Aladdin*; music by Alan Menken), "High Adventure" (written for, but not used in, from 1992 film *Aladdin*; music by Alan Menken), "Sheridan Square" (source unknown; music by Alan Menken), "Daughter of God" (source unknown; music by Alan Menken)

NOTES—Howard Ashman's untimely death at the age of 40 in 1991 robbed the musical theatre of a major lyricist. The tribute-revue *Hundreds of Hats* included many songs from his stage and film musicals, as well as a few "trunk" songs by him and his most frequent collaborator, Alan Menken.

Stephen Holden in the *New York Times* found the revue "aggressively zany," not particularly well-sung, and often "hysterical in its attempt to generate excitement." But the evening was a "serviceable showcase" for Ashman, who "savored the subtleties of language" even if the revue itself didn't.

Three numbers from *God Bless You, Mr. Rosewater* ("Thank God for the Volunteer Fire Brigade," "Since You Came to This Town," and "Rhode Island Tango") were credited with additional lyrics by Dennis Green. The revue took its title from a song heard in the baseball revue *Diamonds*. The song "Hundreds of Hats" is included in the collection *Unsung Musicals III* (Varese Sarabande Records CD # VSD-5769).

For more information about *God Bless You, Mr. Rosewater*, *Little Shop of Horrors*, and *Diamonds*, see entries.

728 The Hunger Artist. THEATRE: St. Clement's Theatre; OPENING DATE: February 26, 1987; PERFORMANCES: 68; TEXT: Created by Martha Clarke and the company of *The Hunger Artist*; text adapted by Richard Greenberg; MUSIC: Richard Peaslee; DIRECTION: Martha Clarke; CHOREOGRAPHY: Martha Clarke; SCENERY: Robert Israel; COSTUMES: Robert Israel; LIGHTING: Paul Gallo; PRODUCERS: The Music-Theatre Group/Lenox Arts Center (Lyn Austin, Producer-Director; Diane Wondisford and Mark Jones, Associate Producing Directors) and the John F. Kennedy Center for the Performing Arts

CAST—Rob Besserer, Brenda Currin, Anthony Holland, Jill Jaffe, David Jon, Bill Ruyle, Paola Styron

SOURCE—Various writings of Franz Kafka (1883-1924).

NOTES—Martha Clarke's Off Off Broadway theatre-dance piece *The Hunger Artist* (a/k/a *Image and Word: The Hunger Artist*) drew upon Franz Kafka's stories and letters to create a portrait of the artist, who was portrayed by Anthony Holland.

Frank Rich in the *New York Times* noted that despite a "magically choreographed" sequence by Clarke, a striking performance by Holland, "ominous" lighting, "striking" scenery, and occasional "prettily sung pastiches" of Czechoslovakian folk songs, *The Hunger Artist* never quite found its voice and thus lacked the "cumulative dramatic or intellectual momentum" of Clarke's *Vienna: Lusthaus* or the unity of *The Garden of Earthly Delights*. Too often the evening was "a fairly arbitrary grab bag of uneven sketches."

The work was originally titled *Kafka*. For theatre works by Martha Clarke see entry for *The Garden of Earthly Delights*.

729 Hydrogen Jukebox. THEATRE: Brooklyn Academy of Music; OPENING DATE: May 7, 1991; PERFORMANCES: 6; TEXT: Allen Ginsberg; MUSIC: Philip Glass; DIRECTION: Ann Carlson; SCENERY: Jerome Sirlin; COSTUMES: Jerome Sirlin; LIGHTING: Robert Wierzel; MUSICAL DIRECTION: Martin Goldray; PRODUCER: Jedediah Wheeler

CAST—James Butler (Referee), Richard Fracker (Businessman), Suzan Hanson (Cheerleader), Mary Ann Hart (Policewoman), Daryl Henriksen (Mechanic), Lynnen Yates (Waitress)

The song cycle was presented in two acts (song assignments unknown).

ACT ONE—Song # 1 from "Iron Horse," Song # 2—"Jahweh and Allah Battle," Song # 3 from "Iron Horse," Song # 4—"To P.O.," Song # 5 from "Crossing Nation"; "Over Denver Again"; "Going to Chicago"; "To Poe: Over the Planet, Air Albany-Baltimore," Song # 6 from "Wichita Vortex Sutra"

ACT TWO—Song # 7 from "Howl Part II," Song # 8 from "Cabin in the Rockies," Song # 9 from "Nagasaki Days" ("Numbers in the Red Notebook"), Song # 10—"Aunt Rose," Song # 11 from "The Green Automobile," Song # 12 from "N.S.A. [National Security Agency] Dope Calypso," Song # 13 from "Nagasaki Days" ("Everybody's Fantasy"), Song # 14—"Ayers Rock/Uluru Song" and "Throw Out the Yellow Journalists...," Song # 15—"Father Death Blues" (from "Don't Grow Old")

NOTES—*Hydrogen Jukebox* premiered in June 1990 at the Spoleto Festival U.S.A., and the limited run of six performances at the Brooklyn Academy of Music marked the work's New York debut.

The song cycle consisted of poems by Allen Ginsberg, which, according to John Rockwell in the *New York Times*, were "linked loosely on the theme of America, its potential and its failings." Rockwell noted Glass' score was "far more varied" than usual and evoked American and world folk music, including a barbershop-styled sextet. The song cycle was recorded by Elektra Nonesuch Records (CD # 9-79286-2), and included singers Richard Fracker and Mary Ann Hart and musical director Martin Goldray from the original production; the recording also included narration by Ginsberg (the song titles above are taken from the recording).

730 Hysterical Blindness and Other Southern Tragedies That Have Plagued My Life Thus Far. "A Musical of Comic Proportions!" THEATRE: Playhouse on Vandam; OPENING DATE: May 19, 1994; PERFORMANCES: 197; BOOK: Leslie Jordan; script developed by Carolyne Berry; LYRICS: Joe Patrick Ward; MUSIC: Joe Patrick Ward; DIRECTION: Carolyne Berry; CHOREOGRAPHY: Mark Knowles; SCENERY: Charles E. McCarry; COSTUMES: Wern-Ying Hwarng; LIGHTING: Phil Monat; Archie Wilson, Associate Lighting Designer; MUSICAL DIRECTION: Joe Patrick Ward; PRODUCER: Dana Matthew

CAST—LESLIE JORDAN (Storyteller), Matthew Bennett (Preacher, Buck, Commercial Director), Mary Bond Davis (Miss Bessemer, A.D. #5, Ethyl Mae, Nurse, Sister Shame, Woman at Bus Station), Terri Girvin (Pastel Griffin, A.D. #2, Twin #1, Johnnie Ruth, Girl with Dog), Blair Ross (Grandma, Twin #2, A.D. #4, Sister Swope, Therapist), Cordell Stahl (Grady, A.D. #1, Medical Specialist, Tor, Sit-Com Director), David Titus (Earl, Clerk at Bus Station, A.D. #3, Master, Stepmonster, Video Clerk)

The action occurs in Tennessee and Hollywood.

The musical was presented in two acts (the program didn't credit song assignments).

ACT ONE—Prelude (instrumental), "Long Long Way to Heaven," "Keep Smilin' Through," "God Loves the Baptist," "Precious Twins," "Pessimistic Voices, Part One," "Pessimistic Voices, Part Two," "Come Little Children," "Sing, All Ye Women of the Lord," "Precious Twins" (reprise), "Mother, May I Be Forgiven?"

ACT TWO—"A Prayer for Mama," "Keep Smilin' Through" (reprise), "The Hymn of Shame," "Ace's Revelation" (instrumental), "What a Friend We Have in Jesus" (lyric and music by George Scriven and C.C. Converse), "I'm Twirling," "The Trashy Effeminate Hoodlum," "Just the Way We're Bred," "Keep Smilin' Through" (reprise and finale), "Postlude" (instrumental)

NOTES—*The Best Plays of 1993-1994* described the loopy autobiographical musical as having to do with a young Tennessee Baptist (Leslie Jordan) coping with his mother's psychosomatic illness while simultaneously trying to break into show business. With his tongue in his cheek, Ben Brantley in the *New York Times* said the evening was a step forward in "the evolution of autobiographical theatre: the confessional gospel musical." He noted that while the material poked fun at itself, one's response to the familiar "gallery of Southern eccentrics" would depend one one's tolerance for the peculiar "charm" of the "eternally boyish, sentimental iconoclast" leading man. As for the score, Brantley remarked that Patrick Ward's contributions consisted of "slight, parodistic pastiches of songs." Shortly after the opening, one song ("Southern Ghosts") was added to the production.

731 I Can't Keep Running in Place. "A New Musical." THEATRE: Westside Arts Theatre/Cheryl Crawford Theatre; OPENING DATE: May 14, 1981; PERFORMANCES: 208; BOOK: Barbara Schottenfeld; LYRICS: Barbara Schottenfeld; MUSIC: Barbara Schottenfeld; DIRECTION: Susan Einhorn; CHOREOGRAPHER: Baayork Lee; Dennis Grimaldi, Assistant Choreographer; SCENERY: Ursula Belden; COSTUMES: Christina Weppner; LIGHTING: Victor En Yu Tan; MUSICAL DIRECTION: Robert Hirschhorn; PRODUCERS: Ray Gaspard in association with Chris Silva, Stephen Dailey, and Will Dailey

CAST—Marcia Rodd (Michelle), Helen Gallagher (Beth), Mary Donner (Mandy), Joy Franz (Eileen), Jennie Ventriss (Gwen), Bev Larson (Sherry), Evalyn Baron (Alice)

The action occurs in a loft, somewhere in Soho.

The musical was presented in two acts.

ACT ONE—"I'm Glad I'm Here" (Company), "Don't Say Yes If You Want to Say No" (Marcia Rodd, Company), "I Can't Keep Running in Place" (Joy Franz), "More of Me to Love" (Jennie Ventriss, Evalyn Baron), "I Live Alone" (Helen Gallagher), "I Can Count on You" (Evalyn Baron, Company), "I'm on My Own" (Marica Rodd)

ACT TWO—"Penis Envy" (Marica Rodd, Company), "Get the Answer Now" (Bev Larson, Company), "What If We..." (Marcia Rodd), "Almosts, Maybes and Perhapses" (Helen Gallagher), "Where Will I Be Next Wednesday Night?" (Company)

NOTES—Barbara Schottenfeld's musical *I Can't Keep Running in Place* dealt with six women who meet weekly with their psychiatrist (Marcia Rodd) for assertiveness training. Mel Gussow in the *New York Times* found the musical uneven, noting that many of the characters had "old-fashioned ladies' magazine problems." He felt their sessions were "unconvincing" as therapy and "unimaginative" as theatre. But he praised Helen Gallagher (the musical's "most valuable asset"), who sang the score's "most striking" song, "I Live Alone." He also suggested her other big number, "Almosts, Maybes and Perhapses," was "almost, maybe and perhaps" a second showstopper.

Yes, this was another musical in the style of *A Chorus Line* (see entry), and so the women talked out their problems in what amounted to a musical pity party (Gussow mentioned the evening ended with an "outpouring" of "unearned tears"). Call it *A Psychiatrist's Line*. In the years following *A Chorus Line*, it was the curse of musical theatre-going (and even non-musical theatre-going) to encounter what were essentially monologue musicals (and plays) with little in the way of character interaction and old-fashioned plots. Perhaps the most popular of the plays to embrace this conception was the 1977 feminist harangue *For Colored Girls Who Have Considered Suicide/When the Rainbow Is Enuf*, produced (of course) by Joseph Papp at the Public Theatre. This was an endless evening of wailing and whining by a group of women who seemed to exult in the role of victimhood, even as they purported to achieve growth, assertiveness, and independence. The reality is that most musicals and plays of this ilk aren't particularly revivable because good theatre comes down to characters and plots you care about. It's difficult to relate to characters who Symbolize Something, and plays with a Cause tend to grow dated very quickly. Moreover, many theatre pieces of this era were self-described "concerts" or "cantatas" or "mosaics" or "collages" or "journeys"; these terms often seemed to be an admission on the part of the writers that they could not (or would not) tackle a structured musical with character and plot development. And, except for *A Chorus Line*, most of these musicals and plays have virtually disappeared.

During the run of *I Can't Keep Running in Place*, Jill O'Hara assumed the role of the psychiatrist. The cast album was recorded by Painted Smiles Records (LP # PS-1346); for the album, Phyllis Newman sang the role of Gwen, which had been created by Jennie Ventriss. The script was published by Samuel French, Inc., in 1982 (in 1979, the musical had first been copyrighted under the title *A Woman Suspended*). The musical had first been produced Off Off Broadway at La Mama Experimental Theatre Club (ETC) on February 21, 1980.

For other "therapy" musicals, see entries for *Inside Out* (which dealt with six women who meet weekly for group therapy), *One Foot Out the Door* (about two women and one man in therapy, all trying to deal with the men in their lives), and *Sessions* (in which even the psychiatrist has issues). Also, see entry for Schottenfeld's *Sit Down and Eat Before Our Love Gets Cold*, which dealt with women living (and coping) in modern-day Manhattan.

732 I Could Go on Lip-Synching! THEATRE: Provincetown Playhouse; transferred to Theatre Off Park on November 10, 1988 Opening Date: September 15, 1988; PERFORMANCES: 22 performances at Provincetown Playhouse; an estimated 250 performances at Theatre Off Park; DIRECTION: Justin Ross; CHOREOGRAPHY: Justin Ross; SCENERY: John-Eric Broaddus; puppets by Harry Rainbow and Mike Thomas; COSTUMES: Gowns by Anthony Wong; LIGHTING: Vivian Leone; PRODUCER: Theatre-in-Limbo

CAST—JOHN EPPERSON (Lypsinka), The Enrico Kuklafraninalli Puppets

The revue was presented in one act.

NOTES—The Off Off Broadway production of *I Could Go on Lip-Synching!* marked the official debut of John Epperson's campy drag persona Lypsinka (who had first been seen during the previous season in *The Many Moods of Lypsinka* at TWEED's Fifth Annual New Works Festival). Through pre-recorded dialogue and songs, Lypsinka spoofed the American woman (especially celebrities of the Joan Crawford variety) as depicted through the mass media.

Peter Marks in the *Washington Post* called Lypsinka "the glamorous vessel for the spirits (and recorded voices) of assorted movie dames from the era when real women ... roamed the big screen." He wrote that Lypsinka's "fabulousness" had "been established so definitively that it could be cited in case law." Lypsinka returned over the years in various "evenings": Off Broadway (*Lypsinka! A Day in the Life* [1993]); and Off Off Broadway (*The Fabulous Lypsinka* [1991]; *Lypsinka! Now It Can Be Lip-Synched* [1992]; *Lypsinka! As I Lay Lip-Synching* [1995; also Off Broadway, 2003]; *Lypsinka Is Harriet Craig!* [1998]; *Lypsinka! The Boxed Set* [2001]; and *Lypsinka: The Passion of the Crawford* [2005]). Who knows what Lypsinka will offer next? (*I'll Lip-Synch Tomorrow*—??, *I Want to Lip-Synch!*—??, *Imitation of Lip-Synching*—??) Her fans are breathless with anticipation!

In an interview with the *Washington Post*, Lypsinka noted that Joan Crawford's adopted daughter Christina Crawford was "so thrilled" by his performance in *Lypsinka: The Passion of the Crawford* that she gave him a decorated wire coat hanger.

Incidentally, at an all-woman memorial tribute to Betty Comden in 2007, Lypsinka was there, lip-synching to Dolores Gray's snazzy rendition of "Thanks a Lot but No Thanks," which is one of the great moments of 1950s film musicals (from 1955 film *It's Always Fair Weather*; lyric by Betty Comden and Adolph Green, music by Andre Previn).

733 I Do! I Do! "The Musical Musical." THEATRE: Lamb's Theatre; OPENING DATE: March 28, 1996; PERFORMANCES: 68; BOOK: Tom Jones; LYRICS: Tom Jones; MUSIC: Harvey Schmidt; DIRECTION: Will MacKenzie; CHOREOGRAPHY: Janet Watson; SCENERY: Ed Wittstein; COSTUMES: Suzy Benzinger; LIGHTING: Mary Jo Dondlinger; MUSICAL DIRECTION: Tim Stella; PRODUCERS: Arthur Cantor; Dan Shaheen, Associate Producer; presented in association with Friends of the Lamb's Inc.

CAST—DAVID GARRISON (Michael), KAREN ZIEMBA (Agnes)

SOURCE—The 1951 play *The Fourposter* by Jan de Hartog.

The action occurs over a fifty-year period beginning in 1898.

The musical was presented in two acts.

ACT ONE—The Wedding: "All the Dearly Beloved" (Karen Ziemba, David Garrison), "Together Forever" (Karen Ziemba, David Garrison), "I Do! I Do!" (Karen Ziemba, David Garrison), "Goodnight" (Karen Ziemba, David Garrison), "I Love My Wife" (David Garrison), "Something Has Happened" (Karen Ziemba), "Love Isn't Everything" (Karen Ziemba, David Garrison), "Nobody's Perfect" (Karen Ziemba, David Garrison), "It's a Well-Known Fact" (David Garrison), "Flaming Agnes" (Karen Ziemba), "The Honeymoon Is Over" (Karen Ziemba, David Garrison)

ACT TWO—"Where Are the Snows?" (Karen Ziemba, David Garrison), "My Cup Runneth Over" (Karen Ziemba, David Garrison), "When the Kids Get Married" (Karen Ziemba, David Garrison), "The Father of the Bride" (David Garrison), "What Is a Woman?" (Karen Ziemba), "Someone Needs Me" (Karen Ziemba, David Garrison), "Roll Up the Ribbons" (Karen Ziemba, David Garrison), "This House" (Karen Ziemba, David Garrison)

NOTES—Jan de Hartog's *The Fourposter*, a long-running two-character play which starred Hume Cronyn and Jessica Tandy, followed the ups and downs of married couple over a fifty-year period. Its musical adaptation in 1966 (which was directed and choreographed by Gower Champion) served as an equally successful vehicle for Mary Martin and Robert Preston, and Tom Jones and Harvey Schmidt's score offered a genuine song hit ("My Cup Runneth Over") in an era when fewer and fewer show tunes achieved wide popularity. And there were other musical pleasures as well, including the feisty duet "The Honeymoon Is Over" and two memorable turns for Mary Martin, the haunting ballad "What Is a Woman?" and the comic free-for-all "Flaming Agnes." United Artists bought the rights for the film version (Champion was to direct, and Julie Andrews and Dick Van Dyke were mentioned for the leads), but the film never materialized. In the 1970s, Carol Burnett and Rock Hudson toured in an amiable revival of the musical (Burnett was especially sparkling in her pull-all-the-stops-out rendition of "Flaming Agnes"), and in the 1980s an adaptation was seen on The Entertainment Channel (with Lee Remick and Hal Linden); it was produced by RKO/Nederlander and The Entertainment Channel, and was directed by Marge Champion.

The Off Broadway revival played just a little over two months, but left behind a pleasant cast recording released by Varese Sarabande Records (CD # VSD-5730).

Among other recordings of the score are the original Broadway cast album which was released by RCA Victor Records (LP # LOC-1128 and # LS0-1128; CD # 1128-2-RC); the 1968 British cast (Ian Carmichael and Anne Rogers; RCA Victor Records LP # SF-7938); and a 1969 Tokyo cast album (Toshiba Records LP # TP-72157; HMI Records CD # HMI-113). For her priceless collection of songs by Jones and Schmidt (*Earthly Paradise*, released by Nassau Records [CD # 96598]), Susan Watson recorded a medley of three different title songs the team wrote for the musical. Further, four songs written for the musical which were either dropped during rehearsals or the tryout can be heard in the collection *Lost in Boston II* (Varese Sarabande Records CD # VSD-5485).

734 I Dreamt I Dwelt in Bloomingdale's. "An Absurd Rock Fable." THEATRE: Provincetown Playhouse; OPENING DATE: February 12, 1970; PERFORMANCES: 6; BOOK: Jack Ramer; LYRICS: Ernest McCarty; MUSIC: Jack Ramer and Ernest McCarty; DIRECTION: David Dunham; CHOREOGRAPHY: Bick Goss; SCENERY: Ed Wittstein; COSTUMES: Bloomingdale's ("by-who-else?"); LIGHTING: Jim Hardy; MUSICAL DIRECTION: Richard Maltifano; PRODUCER: Sam Levine

CAST—Tom Hull (Window Dresser), MICHAEL DEL MEDICO (Father, Bernie), LUCY SAROYAN (Naomi), Erika Petersen (Jessica, Sue), LIZ OTTO (Mother), Richard Darrow (Lenny), Linda Rae Hager (Ronnie); THE WET CLAM (Richard Maltifano, Dawn Culton, Joseph Prinzo, Ronald Jackowski, Steve Gibba)

The musical was presented in two acts (all songs were performed by The Wet Clam).

ACT ONE—"Ballad of Dry Dock Country," "Makin' Believe," "Who Will I Be?," "I Dreamt I Dwelt in Bloomingdale's," "We Didn't Ask to Be Born"

ACT TWO—"Any Spare Change?," "Brown Paper Bag," "Naomi," "I Dreamt I Dwelt in Bloomingdale's" (reprise), "Smart"

NOTES—The rock musical *I Dreamt I Dwelt in Bloomingdale's* dealt with Naomi (Lucy Saroyan, the daughter of William Saroyan), a young woman who rebels against her parents and decides to live in the famous department store. The trendy generation-gap plot had already been explored in a number of recent Broadway plays (*Generation* [1965], *The Impossible Years* [1965], *Me and Thee* [1965], *A Minor Adjustment* [1967], *Johnny No-Trump* [1967], *What Did We Do Wrong?* [1967], and *Halfway Up the Tree* [1967]), and so the musical, which had nothing new to say on the done-to-death subject, was gone within a week.

Perhaps Naomi would have had second thoughts about living in Bloomingdale's if she'd seen Stephen Sondheim's 1966 television musical *Evening Primrose*, a *Twilight Zone*–like musical about a young man who decides to live in a department store.

Every rock musical seemed to have an on-stage band with an offbeat name, and so most productions "created" a band for its purposes. The band in *I Dreamt I Dwelt in Bloomingdale's* was called The Wet Clam, and its program bio noted it was the first self-contained rock pop group to play in an Off Broadway musical. We had indeed come a long way from the traditional Broadway orchestra. Perhaps of all the orchestras heard in musicals, the one for the original production of *Girl Crazy* (1930) is the most famous. Red Nichols conducted, and among the musicians were such future legendary names as Glenn Miller, Benny Goodman, Tommy Dorsey, Gene Krupa, and Jack Teagarden.

735 I Feel Wonderful. "A New Musical Revue." THEATRE: Theatre de Lys; OPENING DATE: October 18, 1954; PERFORMANCES: 48; SKETCHES: Barry Alan Grael; LYRICS: Jerry Herman; MUSIC: Jerry Herman; DIRECTION: Jerry Herman; SCENERY: Romain Johnston; COSTUMES: Romain Johnston; LIGHTING: George Corrin; MUSICAL DIRECTION: Wally Levine; PRODUCER: Sidney S. Oshrin

CAST—Rebecca Barksdale, John Bartis, Joan Coburn, Nina Dova, Albie Gaye, Barry Alan Grael, Ed Hollerman, Janie Janivier, Bob Miller, Sherry McCutcheon, Tom Mixon, Phyllis Newman, Rita Tanno, Richard Tone

The revue was presented in two acts.

ACT ONE—Overture (Orchestra), "For the People" (Company) "Let's Fall in Love Today" (John Bartis, Phyllis Newman, Bob Miller, Albie Gaye, Barry Alan Grael) "When I Love Again" (Joan Coburn, John Bartis, Barry Alan Grael, Ed Holleman, Bob Miller, Tom Mixon "Smoke Roly Poly" (Albie Gaye) "It's Christmas Today" (Janie Janvier, Rebecca Barksdale, Richard Tone, Tom Mixon, Sherry McCutcheon, John Bartis, Phyllis Newman, Rita Tanno, Ed Holleman), "The Tea and I" (Phyllis Newman, Janie Janvier, Bob Miller, Ed Holleman, Barry Alan Grael) "Over and Over" (John Bartis, Janie Janvier, Sherry McCutcheon, Tom Mixon), "A Revue on a Stool" (Barry Alan Grael, Nina Dova, Ed Holleman, Joan Coburn Tom Mixon) "I Feel Wonderful" (Phyllis Newman, Bob Miller, Richard Tone, Sherry McCutcheon, Rita Tanno, Rebecca Barksdale)

ACT TWO—"I Feel Wonderful" (reprise) (Richard Tone, Rita Tanno, Company), "Crack in the Record" (Phyllis Newman, Bob Miller, Albie Gaye, Rebecca Barksdale, Ed Holleman, Sherry McCutcheon, Tom Mixon, Rita Tanno, Richard Tone) "Lonesome in New York" (Joan Coburn), "The Tragicale Historie of Queen Isaboo II" (Albie Gaye, Nina Dova, Barry Alan Grael) "My Love Song" (Janie Janvier, John Bartis) "Eulogy to Chlorophyl" (Nina Dova, Rebecca Barksdale, Ed Holleman, Sherry McCutcheon, Tom Mixon, Rita Tanno, Richard Tone) "Dior, Dior" (Phyllis Newman) "Jailhouse Blues" (John Bartis, Barry Alan Grael, Ed Holleman, Bob Miller, Tom Mixon) "Since Eve" (Albie Gaye), Finale (Company)

NOTES—Jerry Herman's *I Feel Wonderful* opened at the Theatre de Lys between the two runs of *The Threepenny Opera*. Herman would of course find fame as the lyricist and composer of many of the longest-running hits in Broadway musical history, as well as some of its biggest flops (many of which nonetheless achieved cult status). Herman wrote three more Off Broadway shows (see entries): two revues, *Nightcap* (1958) and *Parade* (1960), and one book musical, *Madame Aphrodite* (1961), which opened two months after his Broadway debut with *Milk and Honey*. *I Feel Wonderful* has become an obscure footnote in Herman's career, and apparently all its songs have gone unrecorded.

And Barry Alan Grael holds a special place in this book, because he's the first sketch writer for the new kind of intimate revue which would flower Off Broadway. He also had one success in his future, the highly regarded Off Broadway musical *The Streets of New York* (1963; see entry). Of the cast members in *I Feel Wonderful*, Richard Tone was later in Jerry Herman's *Parade* (1960), which Tone also choreographed. In 1961, he appeared in the Broadway flop *13 Daughters*, and with Isabelle Farrell introduced the almost legendary song "Puka Puka Pants," one of the guilty pleasures of 1960s musicals. Phyllis Newman later won the 1962 Tony Award for Best Performance by a Featured Actress in a Musical (for *Subways Are for Sleeping* [1961]). Of course, *Subways* is legendary for Producer David Merrick's ad campaign antics; but the underrated Betty Comden-Adolph Green-Jule Styne score is perhaps the best the team ever wrote together, and Michael Kidd created a series of show-stopping dances.

Brooks Atkinson in the *New York Times* found *I Feel Wonderful* "thin and monotonous," but singled out four numbers: "Over and Over" (a "pleasant romantic song"), "Dior, Dior" ("an amusing fashion satire"), "Jailhouse Blues" (a "lively" interlude in which Richard Tone performed a "whirling" dance), and the title song ("agreeable").

In an *I Feel Wonderful* program, an unknown playgoer wrote copious notes about the songs and sketches. For what it's worth, he felt "Since Eve" was the best number and "My Love Song" the least impressive. He also wrote that during the sketch "The Tragicale Historie of Queen Isaboo II," the scenery collapsed, and one quick-thinking cast member (Nina Dova) ad-libbed that it was time she moved some of the furniture.

736 I Have a Dream. THEATRE: Louis Abrons Arts for Living Center; OPENING DATE: December 19, 1985; PERFORMANCES: 24; PLAY "ADAPTED" by Josh Greenfield; DIRECTION: Woodie King, Jr.; SCENERY: Ina Mayhew; COSTUMES: Judy Dearing; LIGHTING: Richard Lew; MUSICAL DIRECTION: Lee Howard; PRODUCER: Henry Street Settlement's New Federal Theatre (Woodie King, Jr., Producer)

CAST—Dwight Witherspoon (Soloist, Ensemble), Diane Weaver (Rosa Parks, Deranged Woman, Ensemble), James Curt Bergwall (Bus Driver, John Kennedy, Robert Kennedy, Ensemble), Bruce Strickland (Martin Luther King), Herman LeVern Jones (Abernathy, Martin Luther King, Jr., A. Phillip Randolph, Ensemble), Chequita Jackson (Coretta Scott King, Ensemble)

The action occurs in America during the 1950s and 1960s.

The musical was presented in two acts.

ACT ONE—*America, 1950s*: "I Must Tell Jesus" (Dwight Witherspoon), "I Cried and I Cried" (Diane Weaver), "The Storm Is Passing Over" (Bruce Strickland, Chequita Jackson), "Standing in the Need of Prayer" (Bruce Strickland), "Thank You Lord" (Company), "Sweet Hour of Prayer" (Bruce Strickland), "His Eye Is on the Sparrow" (Diane Weaver), "We Shall Overcome" (Company), "We Shall Not Be Moved" (Company), "Freedom (Amen)" (Bruce Strickland, Company), "Jesus Is My Captain" (Company), "Lift Every Voice and Sing" (Heman LeVern Jones, Company), "Free at Last" (Dwight Witherspoon)

ACT TWO—*America, 1960s*: "Nearer My God to Thee" (Company), "Over My Head" (Chequita Jackson), "Yes, I Thank You, Thank You, Thank You" (Bruce Strickand), "I'm Going to Sit at the Welcome Table" (Company), "Amazing Grace" (Herman Levern Jones, Company), "Come Ye Disconsolate" (Dwight Witherspoon, Diane Weaver), "We Shall Overcome" (reprise) (Company), "I Will Trust in the Lord" (James Curt Bergwall), "I Woke Up This Morning with My Mind Stayed on Freedom" (Bruce Strickland, Company), "I Ain't Gonna Let Nobody Turn Me Around" (Diane Weaver, Company), "We've Come This Far by Faith" (Chequita Jackson), "It Is Well, Well with My Soul" (Bruce Strickland), "Precious Lord" (Dwight Witherspoon), "I Don't Feel No Ways Tired" (Chequita Jackson), "Abraham, Martin and John" (Dwight Witherspoon, Company)

NOTES—*I Have a Dream*, a musical about civil rights, was produced under an Off Off Broadway contract. The cast of characters included Martin Luther King, Jr., Coretta King, Rosa Parks, John Kennedy, and Robert Kennedy. The score included traditional gospel and spiritual numbers, and the text was based on writings and speeches by Martin Luther King, Jr.

An earlier version of the work had been seen on Broadway at the Ambassador Theatre, where it opened on September 20, 1976, for eighty performances (Billy Dee Williams portrayed King; late in the run, the role was assumed by Moses Gunn). The work had first been produced at Ford's Theatre in Washington, D.C., on April 5, 1976 (with Williams).

737 I Hear Music...of Frank Loesser and Friends. THEATRE: Ballroom Theatre; OPENING DATE: October 29, 1984; PERFORMANCES: 32; DIRECTION: Donald Saddler; COSTUMES: Gowns by Robert Mackintosh; LIGHTING: Gene McCann; MUSICAL DIRECTION: Colin Romoff; PRODUCER: Henry Luhrman

CAST—JO SULLIVAN, Greg Utzig, Brian Slawson, Douglas Romoff, Ed Joffe, Colin Romoff

NOTES—The revue *I Hear Music...of Frank Loesser and Friends* was an evening of songs by Frank Loesser, George Gershwin, Richard Rodgers, Kurt Weill, Stephen Sondheim, Giacomo Puccini, Jule Styne, and other composers and lyricists.

Jo Sullivan, who originated the role of Amy/Rosabella in Loesser's 1956 musical *The Most Happy Fella*, was Loesser's widow; she later appeared in the 1980 Broadway production of *Perfectly Frank*, a revue devoted to her late husband's songs. Their daughter Emily Loesser has appeared in various musicals, including the Broadway production of Andrew Lloyd Webber's *By Jeeves* (2001), and in 1989 mother and daughter appeared Off Broadway in a two-woman revue of song selections from Broadway musicals (see entry for *Together Again for the First Time*).

Jo Sullivan had also appeared in the 1958 Off Broadway musical version of John Steinbeck's *Of Mice and Men* (see entry).

738 I Love You Because. "A Modern Day Musical Love Story." THEATRE: Village Theatre; OPENING DATE: February 14, 2006; PERFORMANCES: 111; BOOK: Ryan Cunningham; LYRICS: Ryan Cunningham; MUSIC: Joshua Salzman; DIRECTION: Daniel Kutner; CHOREOGRAPHY: Christopher Gattelli; SCENERY: Beowulf Boritt and Jo Winiarski; COSTUMES: Millie B. Hiibel; LIGHTING: Jeff Croiter; MUSICAL DIRECTION: Jana Zielonka; PRODUCERS: Jennifer Maloney, Fred M. Caruso, Robert Cuillo, and GFOUR Productions in association with Jana Robbins and Sharon Carr; Jeffrey Kent, Associate Producer

CAST—Colin Hanlon (Austin Bennet), David A. Austin (Jeff Bennet), Farah Alvin (Marcy Fitzwilliams), Stephanie D'Abruzzo (Diana Bingley), Jordan Leeds (NYC Man), Courtney Balan (NYC Woman)

SOURCE—The 1813 novel *Pride and Prejudice* by Jane Austen.

The action occurs in New York City in the present day.

The musical was presented in two acts.

ACT ONE—"Another Saturday Night in New York" (Colin Hanlon, Jordan Leeds, Courtney Balan, David A. Austin, Stephanie D'Abruzzo), "Oh What a Difference" (David A. Austin, Colin Hanlon), "The Acutary Song" (Stephanie D'Abruzzo, Farah Alvin), "...But I Don't Want to Talk About Her" (Colin Hanlon, Farah Alvin), "Coffee" (Farah Alvin, Colin Hanlon), "The Perfect Romance" (Jordan Leeds, Courtney Balan), "Because of You" (Colin Hanlon, Farah Alvin), "We're Just Friends" (David A. Austin, Stephanie D'Abruzzo), "Maybe We Just Made Love" (Colin Hanlon), "Just Not Now" (Farah Alvin), "I Love You Because" (Company)

ACT TWO—"Alone" (Jordan Leeds, Courtney Balan, Farah Alvin), "That's What's Gonna Happen" (David A. Austin, Jordan Leeds, Colin Hanlon, Stephanie D'Abruzzo), "Even Though" (Farah Alvin), "But I Do" (Colin Hanlon, Farah Alvin, David A. Austin, Stephanie D'Abruzzo), "What Do We Do It For?" (Jordan Leeds, Courtney Balan, Farah Alvin, Stephanie D'Abruzzo), "Marcy's Yours" (Stephanie D'Abruzzo, David A. Austin, Colin Hanlon), "Goodbye" (Colin Hanlon), "I Love You Because" (finale) (Company)

NOTES—A very loose adaptation of Jane Austen's novel *Pride and Prejudice*, *I Love You Because* centered on Austin and Marcy, two young New Yorkers in search of romance; Marcy's best friend Diana suggests she use a mathematical formula to find the "right" man. Neil Genzlinger in the *New York Times* noted that while the musical "seems briefly in danger of drowning in predictability," the appealing characters and performers offered "an infectiously entertaining show" which is "terrific, refreshing fun," and he praised book writer and lyricist Ryan Cunningham and composer Joshua Salzman for providing an evening of "wit and zest." He also singled out David A. Austin's performance as Austin's clueless, malapropic brother. The score was recorded by PS Classics Records (CD # PS-643).

The musical made its London debut on September 16, 2007, for a limited run at the Landor Theatre.

The Broadway musical *First Impressions* was a more traditional adaptation of Austen's novel (the musical's title had actually been Austen's first choice for the novel's title). It opened at the Alvin (now Neil Simon) Theatre on March 19, 1959, for ninety-two performances and left behind a richly melodic score by Robert Goldman, Glen Paxton, and George Weiss, one of the most underrated of the era. And judging from production photographs, it must have been one of the most lavish and beautiful musicals of the 1950s (the costumes were by Alvin Colt and the scenery by Peter Larkin). A British adaptation (called *Pride and Prejudice*) doesn't seem to have been produced on the stage; but a studio cast recording was released by Dress Circle Records in the early 1990s (CD # PPCD-3); the lyrics and music were by Bernard J. Taylor, and the performers included Claire Moore, Peter Karrie, and Gay Soper. Another British adaptation (it, too, was titled *Pride and Prejudice*) surfaced during the same period, and a studio cast album was released on audiocassette.

For other Austen-inspired musicals, see entry for *The New York Musical Theatre Festival*, which references *Austentatious* and *Emma*.

739 I Love You, You're Perfect, Now Change. THEATRE: Westside Theatre/Upstairs; OPENING DATE: August 1, 1996; PERFORMANCES: 5003; BOOK: Joe DiPietro; LYRICS: Joe DiPietro; MUSIC: Jimmy Roberts; DIRECTION: Joel Bishoff; SCENERY: Neil Peter Jampolis; COSTUMES: Candice Donnelly; LIGHTING: Mary Louise Geiger; MUSICAL DIRECTION: Tom Fay; PRODUCERS: James Hammerstein, Bernie Kukoff, and Jonathan Pollard; Matt Garfield, Associate Producer

CAST—Jordan Leeds, Robert Roznowski, Jennifer Simard, Melissa Weil

The revue was presented in two acts.

ACT ONE—"Cantata for a First Date" (Company), "A Stud and a Babe" (Robert Roznowski, Jennifer Simard), "Single Man Drought" (Jennifer Simard, Melissa Weil), "Why? Cause I'm a Guy" (Robert Roznowski, Jordan Leeds), "Tear Jerk" (Jordan Leeds, Melissa Weil), "I Will Be Loved Tonight" (Jennifer Simard), "Hey, There, Single Guy/Gal" (Jordan Leeds, Jennifer Simard), "He Called Me" (Jennifer Simard, Company), "Wedding Vows" (Company)

ACT TWO—"Always a Bridesmaid" (Melissa Weil), "The Baby Song" (Jordan Leeds), "Marriage Tango" (Robert Roznowski, Melissa Weil), "On the Highway of Love" (Jordan Leeds, Company), "Waiting Trio" (Melissa Weil, Robert Roznowski, Jennifer Simard), "Shouldn't I Be Less in Love with You?" (Rober Roznowski), "I Can Live with That" (Jordan Leeds, Melissa Weil), "I Love You, You're Perfect, Now Change" (Company)

NOTES—The cutely titled *I Love You, You're Perfect, Now Change* was the little show that could. It slipped into New York at the end of the summer, an amiable Off Broadway revue-like musical which received generally favorable reviews and seemed set for a season's run and a reasonably healthy afterlife in regional and community theatre. (But not all the critics were enthusiastic. Howard Kissel in the *New York Daily News* wrote that for "some cozy little club in the Village 40 years ago, this would be passable," but for today the evening was "too thin.")

But the revue, which wryly depicted heterosexual romance in all its phases (first dates through marriage) and told its story through catchy music, amusing lyrics, and familiar-but-enjoyable sketches, clearly struck a chord with audiences and the show became one of the most successful of all Off Broadway musicals (according to the BroadwayWorld website, the musical has been performed in almost 300 cities worldwide and has grossed over 85 million dollars). Beginning on May 7, 2007, for twenty-three performances, the Shanghai Dramatic Arts Centre and Broadway Asia Entertainment's production of the musical was performed Off Broadway in Mandarin (supertitles were projected above the stage). Kenneth Jones in *Playbill* reported that just prior to their Off Broadway visit the company had performed the musical as the opening ceremony of the 2007 Beijing Theatre Festival on April 17, and that after their New York engagement, the company returned to Beijing to begin an extensive tour throughout China.

The original Off Broadway cast recording was released by Varese Sarabande Records (CD # VSD-5771).

The musical first premiered in 1995 at New Jersey's American Stage Company, and in the early summer of 1996 was produced at the Long Wharf Theatre in New Haven.

Incidentally, Joe DiPietro, the musical's book writer and lyricist, also enjoyed a long-running success (over 800 performances) with his 1998 Off Broadway comedy *Over the River and Through the Woods*. Also see entries for his 1991 revue *Love Lemmings* and his 2003 musical *The Thing About Men*, for which he wrote the book and lyrics.

740 I Paid My Dues. THEATRE: Astor Place Theatre; OPENING DATE: April 20, 1976; PERFORMANCES: 20; BOOK: Eric Blau; LYRICS: New lyrics by Eric Blau; see song list for other lyricists; MUSIC: New music (composer[s] unknown); see song list for other composers; DIRECTION: George Allison Elmer; SCENERY: Don Jensen; COSTUMES: Don Jensen; LIGHTING: Jeff Davis; MUSICAL DIRECTION: David Frank; PRODUCERS: Labor Arts Community Services Committee in association with Stuart White

CAST—Joe Morton, Christopher Cable, Tom Demenkoff, Jacqueline Reilly, Linda Rios, James Robinson, Edward Rodriguez, Wendy Wolfe, Zenobia

The revue was presented in two acts (division of acts and song assignments unknown; songs are listed in performance order).

MUSICAL NUMBERS—"I Paid My Dues," "In Good Old Colony Times," "Whiskey in the Jar," "Yankee Doodle," "Fate of John Burgoyne," "Battle of Trenton," "Young Ladies in Town," "Yankee Doodle Dandy-O," "Johnny Has Gone for a Soldier," "Blow Ye Winds," "Cape Cod Girls," "Haul on the Bow Line," "Erie Canal," "Frozen Logger," "Santy Anno," "Praties They Grow Small," "Shenandoah," "John Henry," "Doney Gal," "Red Iron Ore," "My Sweetheart's the Mule in the Mine," "Railroad Bill," "A Cowboy's Life," "The Cowboys," "Zum Gali, Gali," "Drill Ye Tarriers, Drill," "Wade in the Water," "Hushabye," "Go Down Moses," "This Train," "Oh! Freedom," "Take This Hammer," "When I'm Gone," "Pick a Bale of Cotton," "Many Thousands Gone," "Tenting Tonight," "John Brown's Body," "Battle Hymn of the Republic," "Solidarity Forever," "Dark as a Dungeon," "Sixteen Tons," "Union Maid," "Which Side Are You On," "Talking Union," "The Scabs Crawl In," "Hinky Dinky Parlez Vous," "On the Line," "You've Got to Go Down," "Roll the Union On," "Casey Jones," "Hold the Fort," "We Shall Not Be Moved," "Goin' Down the Road," "Beans, Bacon and Gravy," "Soup Song," "Brother, Can You Spare a Dime?" (from *Americana*, 1932; lyric by E.Y. Harburg, music by Jay Gorney), "Let's Have Another Cup of Coffee" (*Face the Music*, 1932; lyric and music by Irving Berlin), "When the Red, Red Robin Comes Bob, Bob, Bobbin' Along" (lyric and music by Harry Woods), "I Want to Be Happy" (*No, No, Nanette*, 1925; lyric by Irving Caesar, music by Vincent Youmans), "Agent 008," "Violet Eyes," "Ballad of Mervyn Schwartz," "Nosotros Venceremos," "A Man's a Man for All That"

NOTES—Just in time for the nation's Bicentennial, the revue *I Paid My Dues* was a celebration of American labor from colonial through modern times; it offered new songs, traditional songs, and a few numbers from Broadway musicals. Curiously, no songs were included from Harold Rome's *Pins and Needles*, the ultimate labor revue (see entries for two Off Broadway revivals).

741 I Sent a Letter to My Love. THEATRE: Primary Stages; OPENING DATE: January 18, 1995; PERFORMANCES: 34; BOOK: Jeffrey Sweet; LYRICS: Jeffrey Sweet and Melissa Manchester; MUSIC: Melissa Manchester; DIRECTION: Pat Birch; SCENERY: James Noone; COSTUMES: Rodney Munoz; LIGHTING: Kirk Bookman; MUSICAL DIRECTION: Aaron Hagan; PRODUCER: Primary Stages (Casey Childs, Artistic Director)

CAST—Lynne Wintersteller (Amy), Robert Westenberg (Stan), John Hickok (Jimmy), Bethe B. Austin (Gwen), Meagen Fay (Miss Morgan)

SOURCE—The 1975 novel *I Sent a Letter to My Love* by Bernice Rubens.

The action occurs in a small town in Ohio during 1954.

The musical was presented in two acts (division of acts and song assignments unknown; songs listed in performance order).

MUSICAL NUMBERS—Prologue, "Across the Lake," "God Never Closes a Door," "What I Am," "Lady Seeks Gentleman," "Grass Between My Toes," "Your Prince," "Very Truly Yours, Rosy Red Pants Angela" (may not be accurate title), "Perfect Timing," "Chance of You," "I Never Knew," "Someone in a Chair," "The Day I Met My Friend," "Last Night," "Change in the Air"

NOTES—Pop singer and song-writer Melissa Manchester composed the music and co-wrote the lyrics for the Off Off Broadway musical *I Sent a Letter to My Love*, which was based on the 1975 novel by Bernice Rubens (which was later filmed in 1981). The story dealt with a woman who takes care of her paralyzed brother; like Amalia and Georg in *She Loves Me* (1963), the two begin writing letters to each other through a personals column, not realizing who the other is. At one point, the sister realizes her romantic pen-pal is her brother, and, as they say, complications ensue.

Stephen Holden in the *New York Times* felt the script was "too nice," and noted there were lost opportunities for black humor and the darker psychological layers inherent in the plot. But he praised Manchester's "richly romantic score," and singled out "Lady Seeks Gentleman," which "achieves a melodic and harmonic breadth that surpasses" anything in Manchester's pop song oeuvre. Holden also mentioned "What I Am," a "desperately upbeat number" in which the siblings sing out such politically incorrect words as "cripple" and "old maid." Incidentally, Holden noted that the original novel was set Wales; the film version in France; and the musical in Ohio.

742 I Sing! THEATRE: Maverick Theatre; OPENING DATE: June 14, 2001; PERFORMANCES: Unknown; BOOK: Sam Forman, Eli Bolin, and Benjamin Salka; LYRICS: Sam Forman; MUSIC: Eli Bolin; DIRECTION: Benjamin Salka; CHOREOGRAPHY: Whitney Kroenke; SCENERY: Eric L. Renschler; COSTUMES: Steven Epstein; LIGHTING: Ben Stanton; MUSICAL DIRECTION: Vadim Feichtner; PRODUCERS: A Bebek City Allstars Production (presented by Arik Ahitov, Jeff Beil, and Samuel Franco) and The Maverick Theatre

CAST—Billy Eichner (Charlie), Jeff Juday (Nicky), Jodie Langel (Pepper), Michael Raine (Alan), Meredith Zeitlin (Heidi)

The action occurs in Manhattan at the present time.

The musical was presented in two acts.

ACT ONE—"I Sing" (Company), "I Won't Let It Happen to Me" (Jeff Juday), "A Perfect Pair" (Meredith Zietlin, Jeff Juday, Michael Raine), "Daddy's Girl" ("pre-reprise") (Meredith Zeitlin), "My Favorite Guy" (Billy Eichner, Jodie Langel), "How Do You Love a Girl Like That?" (Jeff Juday), "A Night at the Bar" (Jodie Langel, Meredith Zeitlin, Jeff Juday), "What Alan Likes" (Michael Raine), "I'm Coming Out" (Billy Eichner), "Promise Me" (Jodie Langel, Billy Eichner, Jeff Juday), "The Dressing Room Shuffle" (Michael Raine, Meredith Zeitlin), "Drinking Games" (Billy Eichner, Jodie Langel), "One Week Later" (Michael Raine), "The Old Apartment" (Meredith Zeitlin), "All the Children Sing" (Company)

ACT TWO—"It's Just a Little Awkward" (Company), "Heidi, Are You There?" (Michael Raine, Meredith Zeitlin), "More Drinking Games" (Billy Eichner, Jeff Juday, Jodie Langel), "Two Days Later"/"Daddy's Girl" (Michael Raine, Meredith Zeitlin), "Smile Through the Pain" (Billy Eichner, Michael Raine), "Starting Over" (Jodie Langel), "Charlie and Pepper" (Jodie Langel, Billy Eichner), "Good Enough" (Jeff Juday, Michael Raine, Meredith Zeitlin), "You Said You Loved Me" (Meredith Zeitlin, Jeff Juday), "Dancing Alone" (Jeff Juday), Finale (Company)

NOTES—The Off Off Broadway musical *I Sing!* dealt with the romances and friendships among a group of young twenty-something New Yorkers. Noting that the musical was written by three young graduates of Northwestern University (Eli Bolin, Sam Forman, and Benjamin Salka), Bruce Weber in the *New York Times* said the "earnest and immature" evening came right out of the "musical theater starter kit." He felt the book needed "bolstering," and noted the virtually sung-through musical could do with a few song cuts. As for the music, it was a mostly "vapid" collection of "genre songs," and he felt the lyrics were "inconsistent." But he liked one or two numbers, and singled out "A Night at the Bar" (a "cleverly staged bittersweet trio"). Overall, *I Sing!* was a "terrific senior project, but graduation has come and gone."

On October 14, 2002, the musical was presented in concert at the York Theatre, and a few days later was recorded on a 2-CD set by Jay Records (# CDJAY2-1378) with Matt Bogart, Danny Gurwin, Lauren Kennedy, Chad Kimball, and Leslie Kritzer. According to the album's liner notes, the musical's original title, *All the Children Sing*, was changed at the last minute because it might have given the impression the musical was a family show instead of "a foul-mouthed operetta about lost twenty-somethings searching for love in Manhattan."

743 I Take These Women. THEATRE: Nat Horne Theatre; OPENING DATE: March 11, 1982; PERFORMANCES: 20; BOOK: J.J. Coyle; LYRICS: Sandi

Merle; MUSIC: Robert Kole; Nathan Hurwitz, Incidental Music; DIRECTION: J.J. Coyle; SCENERY: Ernest A. Smith; COSTUMES: Guy Tanno; LIGHTING: Paul B. Fadoul; MUSICAL DIRECTION: Nathan Hurwitz; Howard Sperling, Assistant Musical Director; PRODUCER: King Stuart Productions

CAST—Jane Altman (Mary), Jean Barlow (Annie), Judi Mann (Jane), Lew Resseguie (Guy), Richard-Charles Hoh (Jim), Robert Cooner (Jack)

The action occurs during Easter time in 1970.

The musical was presented in two acts (division of acts and song assignments unknown; songs listed in performance order).

MUSICAL NUMBERS—"Adultery," "Annie's Lament," "I Am Yours," "Soliloquy," "Why," "This Is My House," "Common Sense," "I Took These Women," "Yesterday's Champagne," "Incomprehensible," "I Like Her," "You Turn Me On," "On My Own"

NOTES—*I Take These Women* was presented under an Off Off Broadway contract.

744 I Want to Walk to San Francisco. NOTES—See entry for *The Last Sweet Days of Isaac.*

745 I Want You. "A Musical Comedy." THEATRE: Maidman Playhouse; OPENING DATE: September 14, 1961; PERFORMANCES: 4; BOOK: Stefan Kanfer and Jess J. Korman; LYRICS: Stefan Kanfer, Jess J. Korman, and Joseph Crayhon; MUSIC: Stefan Kanfer, Jess J. Korman, and Joseph Crayhon; DIRECTION: Theodore J. Flicker; CHOREOGRAPHY: Rhoda Levine; SCENERY: David Moon; COSTUMES: Freida Evans; LIGHTING: Jerome Liotta; MUSICAL DIRECTION: Harold Beebe; PRODUCERS: Theodore J. Flicker, Sam W. Gelfman and Joseph Crayhon in association with David W. Carter

CAST—Al Mancini (Jerry Gray, Niccollini Fettucini), Dwight Townsend (Jackie Gray, Chinese Strongman), Vivian Clemons (A Valencia Lovely, Jackie's Girl), Nancy Junion (A Valencia Lovely), Bernard Reed (Newsboy, Hugo), Francis Dux (Doughboy, Herman), D. Bruce Rabbino (Sergeant, Mulligan's Horse, Famous World War I General), Edward Crowley (Hockenbock), Leo Bloom (Tweed), Barbara Quaney (Sally Cork), William Morris (Mulligan), David Haine (Graum, Mulligan's Horse, Lew), Joshua Shelley (Colonel Yeast, Madame Rita), K.C. Townsend (Gwen), Sally Bramlette (Mrs. Wiggins) The action occurs in New York City in 1917.

The musical was presented in two acts (song assignments unknown).

ACT ONE—"My Daddy Was Right," "I Want You," "This Is a Dollar Bill," "Perfect Man," "The Farewells," "Remarkable," "That's What the Public Wants," "Ain't It Funny," "So Long, Yesterday," "You Devil You"

ACT TWO—"Loyal American," "The Street," "Hong Kong Gong," "Perfect Man" (reprise), "Take Every Opportunity," "You Devil You" (reprise), Finale

NOTES—*I Want You* was a World War I era musical about an unscrupulous if likable con artist who hopes to make his fortune by publishing patriotic songs.

Howard Taubman in the *New York Times* reported that along with giving programs to the audience, the ushers also handed out sheet music of the show's title song. Taubman noted that if the sheet music was a "gift," then it was the only gift of the evening. He found the musical "unfunny, uninspired and unquiet."

As a precursor to a certain chandelier which flew over the heads of theatre audiences, Taubman reported that for the finale of *I Want You* a Zeppelin "flew" above the audience along the theatre's ceiling in a "triumph of technique."

746 I Will Come Back. THEATRE: Players Theatre; OPENING DATE: February 25, 1998; PERFORMANCES: 72; DIALOGUE: Timothy Gray; LYRICS: See song list for credits; MUSIC: See song list for credits; DIRECTION: Timothy Gray; J.T. O'Connor, Assistant Director; SCENERY: Leo Meyer; COSTUMES: Marc Bouwer; LIGHTING: Jen Acomb; MUSICAL DIRECTION: David K. Maiocco; PRODUCERS: New Journeys Ahead, Ltd.; Dyanne M. McNamara, Associate Producer

CAST—TOMMY FEMIA (Judy Garland), Kristine Zbornik (A Friend of Barbra)

The revue was presented in two acts.

ACT ONE—"I Will Come Back" (traditional), "La Cucaracha" (traditional), "Come On In" (lyric by Timothy Gray, music by Hugh Martin) "They Don't Write 'Em Like That Anymore" (lyric by Timothy Gray, music by Hugh Martin), "Two Is Company" (lyric by Timothy Gray, music by Hugh Martin), "Optimism" (lyric by Timothy Gray, music by Hugh Martin), "Smile" (lyric and music by John Turner, Geoffrey Parsons, and Charles Chaplin), "Zing! Went the Strings of My Heart" (*Thumbs Up!*, 1934; lyric and music by James F. Hanley), "After You've Gone" (lyric by Henry Creamer, music by J. Turner Layton), "Somewhere Out There" (lyric and music by James Horner, Barry Mann, and Cynthia Weil)

ACT TWO—"Meet Me in St. Louis" (lyric and music by Andrew B. Sterling and Kerry Mills; additional lyric by Timothy Gray), "The Boy Next Door" (1944 film *Meet Me in St. Louis*; lyric and music by Hugh Martin and Ralph Blane), "The Trolley Song" (1944 film *Meet Me in St. Louis*; lyric and music by Hugh Martin and Ralph Blane), "Rock-a-Bye Your Baby with a Dixie Melody" (*Sinbad*, 1918; lyric by Sam M. Lewis and Joe Young, music by Jean Schwartz), "Just in Time" (*Bells Are Ringing*, 1956; lyric by Betty Comden and Adolph Green, music by Jule Styne), "Happy Days Are Here Again" (1930 film *Chasing Rainbows*; lyric by Jack Yellen, music by Milton Ager), "Get Happy" (*Nine-Fifteen Revue*, 1930; lyric by Ted Koehler, music by Harold Arlen), "Over the Rainbow" (1939 film *The Wizard of Oz*; lyric by E.Y. Harburg, music by Harold Arlen), "I Will Come Back" (reprise)

NOTES—The revue *I Will Come Back* was a tribute to Judy Garland (1924-1969), who was portrayed by Tommy Femia. Anita Gates in the *New York Times* found the evening "well worth seeing," and she praised both Femia and the production's clever touches (the Gumm Sisters were portrayed by hand puppets). Gates reported that near the end of the second act, Femia was joined by Kristine Zbornik (playing "A Friend of Barbra"), and the two recreated the famous television appearance when the legend and soon-to-be-legend sang two duets ("Happy Days Are Here Again" and "Get Happy"). Gates reported that for the duets Femia couldn't match Garland's simultaneous looks of "surprise, fear, confidence, envy and determination," but noted that his efforts were "almost enough" to conjure up the "real thing."

The songs included some older ones by Hugh Martin and Ralph Blane as well as a few newer ones by the team. The number "They Don't Write 'Em Like That Anymore" was no doubt a revised version of the title song for Martin and Timothy Gray's 1972 Off Broadway revue *They Don't Make 'Em Like That Anymore* (see entry).

For another Judy Garland tribute, see entries for three productions of *Judy: A Garland of Songs*. On March 26, 1986, *Judy*, a play (with music) by Terry Wale, opened in London at the Strand Theatre; Lesley Mackie portrayed Garland.

747 I Won't Dance. "Steve Ross Sings Fred Astaire." THEATRE: Theatre at St. Peter's Church; OPENING DATE: December 12, 1991; PERFORMANCES: 70; TEXT: Steve Ross and Michael Sommers; LYRICS: See song list for credits; MUSIC: See song list for credits; SCENERY: Jean Valente; LIGHTING: Matt Berman; PRODUCER: American Cabaret Theatre (Peter Ligeti, Producing Director)

CAST—Steve Ross, Bruno David Casolari (Second Piano), Brian Cassier (Bass)

The revue was presented in two acts.

NOTES—*I Won't Dance* was a salute to Fred Astaire by one of the jewels of the New York cabaret scene, pianist and singer Steve Ross. The evening included a narrative about Astaire's life and career, and songs were selected from among the following (the songs' original sources are cited): "All of You" (from *Silk Stockings*, 1955; lyric and music by Cole Porter), "Begin the Beguine" (*Jubilee*, 1935; lyric and music by Cole Porter), "Night and Day" (*Gay Divorce*, 1932; lyric and music by Cole Porter), "Please Don't Monkey with Broadway" (film *Broadway Melody of 1940*; lyric and music by Cole Porter), "Change Partners" (1938 film *Carefree*; lyric and music by Irving Berlin), "Cheek to Cheek" (1935 film *Top Hat*; lyric and music by Irving Berlin), "A Couple of Swells" (1948 film *Easter Parade*; lyric and music by Irving Berlin), "Easter Parade" (*As Thousands Cheer*, 1933; lyric and music by Irving Berlin), "It Only Happens When I Dance with You" (1948 film *Easter Parade*; lyric and music by Irving Berlin), "Let Yourself Go" (1936 film *Follow the Fleet*; lyric and music by Irving Berlin), "Let's Face the Music and Dance" (1936 film *Follow the Fleet*; lyric and music by Irving Berlin), "The Piccolino" (1935 film *Top Hat*; lyric and music by Irving Berlin), "Puttin' on the Ritz" (1929 film *Puttin' on the Ritz*; lyric and music by Irving Berlin), "Steppin' Out with My Baby" (1948 film *Easter Parade*; lyric and music by Irving Berlin), "Top Hat, White Tie, and Tails" (1935 film *Top Hat*; lyric and music by Irving Berlin), "City of Angels" (independent song; lyric by Fred Astaire, music by Tommy Wolf), "The Continental" (1934 film *The Gay Divorcee*; lyric by Herb Magidson, music by Con Conrad), "Dancing in the Dark" (*The Band Wagon*, 1931; lyric by Howard Dietz, music by Arthur Schwartz), "I Guess I'll Have to Change My Plan" (*The Little Show*, 1930; lyric by Howard Dietz, music by Arthur Schwartz), "Dream" (lyric and music by Johnny Mercer; used in [but not specifically written for] 1955 film *Daddy Long Legs*), "I've Got a Lot in Common with You" (1943 film *The Sky's the Limit*; lyric by Johnny Mercer, music by Harold Arlen), "Something's Gotta Give" (1955 film *Daddy Long Legs*; lyric and music by Johnny Mercer), "Fascinating Rhythm" (*Lady, Be Good!*, 1924; lyric by Ira Gershwin, music by George Gershwin), "Funny Face" (*Funny Face*, 1927; lyric by Ira Gershwin, music by George Gershwin), "Oh, Lady, Be Good!" (*Lady, Be Good!*, 1924; lyric by Ira Gershwin, music by George Gershwin), "Shall We Dance" (1937 film *Shall We Dance*; lyric by Ira Gershwin, music by George Gershwin), "They All Laughed" (1937 film *Shall We Dance*; lyric by Ira Gershwin, music by George Gershwin), "They Can't Take That Away from Me" (1937 film *Shall We Dance*; lyric by Ira Gershwin, music by George Gershwin), "Flying Down to Rio" (1933 film *Flying Down to Rio*; lyric by Edward Eliscu and Gus Kahn, music by Vincent Youmans), "Orchids in the Moonlight" (1933 film *Flying Down to Rio*; lyric by Edward Eliscu and Gus Kahn, music by Vincent Youmans), "Heigh-Ho! The Gang's All Here" (*Earl Carroll Vanities*, 1930; lyric by Harold Adamson, music by Burton Lane), "Let's Go Bavarian" (1933 film *Dancing Lady*; lyric by Harold Adamson, music by Burton Lane), "I Won't Dance" (1935 film *Roberta*; lyric by Otto Harbach, Dorothy Fields, Oscar Hammerstein II, and Jimmy McHugh, music by Jerome Kern), "The Way You Look Tonight" (1936 film *Swing Time*; lyric by Dorothy Fields, music by Jerome Kern), "You Were Never Lovelier" (1942 film *You Were Never Lovelier*;

lyric by Johnny Mercer, music by Jerome Kern), "Waltz in Swing Time" (1936 film *Swing Time*; music by Jerome Kern), "My Sunny Tennessee" (*Midnight Rounders of 1921*; lyric and music by Bert Kalmar, Harry Ruby, and Herman Ruby), "Nevertheless" (independent song; lyric by Bert Kalmar, music by Harry Ruby), "So Long, Oo-Long" (independent song?; lyric by Bert Kalmar, music by Harry Ruby), "Thinking of You" (*The Five O'Clock Girl*, 1927; lyric by Bert Kalmar, music by Harry Ruby), "Three Little Words" (1930 film *Check and Double Check*; lyric by Bert Kalmar, music by Harry Ruby), "Say, Young Man of Manhattan" (*Smiles*, 1930; lyric by Harold Adamson and Clifford Grey, music by Vincent Youmans), "You're All the World to Me" (1951 film *Royal Wedding*; lyric by Alan Jay Lerner, music by Burton Lane; song originally introduced as "I Want to Be a Minstrel Man" by Eddie Cantor in 1934 film *Kid Millions*, lyric by Harold Adamson)

748 Ichabod. THEATRE: Town Hall; OPENING DATE: January 12, 1977; PERFORMANCES: 1; BOOK: Gene Traylor; LYRICS: Gene Traylor; MUSIC: Thomas Tierney; DIRECTION: Michael Montel; staged by Michel Stuart; CHOREOGRAPHY: Terri White; SCENERY: Properties designed by Robert Joyce; COSTUMES: James Edmund Brady; LIGHTING: Jeffrey Schissler; MUSICAL DIRECTION: Charles Homewood; PRODUCER: Interludes/Town Hall

CAST—TOMMY TUNE

SOURCE—The 1820 short story *The Legend of Sleepy Hollow* by Washington Irving.

The musical was presented in one act (all songs performed by Tommy Tune).

MUSICAL NUMBERS—1) *Here and Now*: "Vote for Crane (Campaign Song)"; 2) *Then and There*: "A Pleasing Land," "Sleepy Little Valley"; Lesson for the Ladies: a) "Singing (The Bird of Love)"; b) "Elocution (Repining Heart)"; c) "Dancing (The Katrina Waltz)" "Tales" in the Schoolroom: a) "Education"; b) "Aspirations"; c) "Protections"; d) "The Glory of Sleepy Hollow," "The Katrina Waltz" (reprise), "She Could Be a Lot Worse," "Brom Bones"; At the Quilting Frolic: a) "Galop"; b) "Schottische," "The Proposal"/"The Katrina Waltz" (reprise), "Just a Moment," "The Ride," "The Ghost's Turn"; 3) *Here and Now*: Finale

NOTES—*Ichabod* may well be Tommy Tune's most obscure musical theatre appearance. The one-man musical (apparently produced under an Off Off Broadway contract) played for one scheduled performance at Town Hall's series of late Wednesday afternoon "interludes" (other performers in the series included Martha Schlamme and Alvin Epstein, Tessie O'Shea, Anna Russell, Celeste Holm, and Lainie Kazan).

See entry for *Autumn's Here!* regarding other musicals based on *The Legend of Sleepy Hollow*.

749 Identical Twins from Baltimore. THEATRE: Playhouse 91; OPENING DATE: June 25, 1995; PERFORMANCES: 16; BOOK: Dan Alvy; LYRICS: Dan Alvy; MUSIC: Marc Mantell; DIRECTION: Bill Castellino; CHOREOGRAPHY: Bill Castellino; SCENERY (AND PROJECTIONS): Michael Bottari and Ronald Case; COSTUMES: Tzili Charney; LIGHTING: Mathew J. Williams; MUSICAL DIRECTION: Christopher McGovern; PRODUCER: The Electric Theatre Company in association with Peralta Productions

CAST—Rose McGuire (Madonna), Rob Roznowski (Max Pullian), T. Robert Rigott (Tony Dilema), Neil Scheifer (Manny Gelt), Colleen Durham (Fritzie), Lisa McMillan (Hedy Harlowe), Jeremy Czarniak (Cedric), Bill Whitefield (Randy Bachelor), Jill Locnikar (Sheila), Robert Cary (Baby Boy Bruce), Adriane Lenox (Jill Undergrowth), Mary Stout (Jane Undergrowth)

The action occurs in New York City and Los Angeles in the "Distant/Present."

The musical was presented in two acts (division of acts and song assignments unknown; songs are listed in performance order).

MUSICAL NUMBERS—"Take the Picture," "New York, Get Ready for Us," "Famous for Fifteen Minutes," "This Night," "One-Sided Love," "I'm on Your Side," "Movie Moguls," "Love Gets in the Way," "Everyone's Here," "Interrogation," "Another Chance," "The Girls Are Back," "I Made It to the Top," Finale

NOTES—The title almost said it all for the Off Broadway musical *Identical Twins from Baltimore*, about two identical twins from Baltimore who are determined to make it in show business. But the joke was that the twins were played by a thin, Black actress and by a "250 pounds and white" actress (the latter according to Stephen Holden in the *New York Times*, who quoted the musical's press release). But Holden felt the amusing premise lacked humor and that the book and score didn't possess the "parodistic wit and energy" needed to keep the would-be campy musical on target.

750 Idol: The Musical. THEATRE: 45th Street Theatre; OPENING DATE: August 12, 2007; PERFORMANCES: 1; BOOK: Bill Boland; LYRICS: Bill Boland and Jon Balcourt; MUSIC: Jon Balcourt; DIRECTION: Daniel Tursi; Kellie Ellis, Associate Director; CHOREOGRAPHY: Jason Bumpus and Joe Walker; SCENERY: Brian Howard; COSTUMES: Mary Rubinstein, Elaine Burt, and Theresa Burns; LIGHTING: Charles Shatskin; MUSICAL DIRECTION: Jon Balcourt; PRODUCERS: Todd Ellis and Bipolar Productions

PREVIEW CAST—Babs Rubenstein (Adrienne), Jennie Riverso (Alex), Nikita Richards (Cass), Courtney Ellis (Cicaida), Jon Balcourt (Connor), Ryan Sprague (Duncan), Joella Burt (Emily), Joe Walker (J.D.), Roy George-Thiemann (Kodi);

OPENING NIGHT CAST—Katy Reinsel (Adrienne), Jillian Giacchi (Alex), Kierstyn Sharrow (Cass), Kaitlin Mercurio (Cicaida), Philip Deyesso (Connor), Saum Eskandani (Duncan), Stephanie Robinson (Emily), Joe Walker (J.D.), Shadae Smith (Kodi), Dawn Barry (Midge) The action occurs in and around Steubenville, Ohio.

The musical was presented in two acts.

ACT ONE—"Idolize" (Company), "Small Town Blues" (Company), "Fifteen Minutes" (Company, Katy Reinsel), "Discipline" (Company, Katy Reinsel), "Chip & Dale Days" (Joe Walker, Saum Eskandani), "Prima Donna Fabulous" (Katy Reinsel), "Quakin' for Aiken" (Company), "Prima Donna Fabulous" (reprise) (Katy Reinsel)

ACT TWO—"Burnin' Hunk of Clay" (Stephanie Robinson), "Simon Says" (Kaitlin Mercurio, Shadae Smith, Jillian Giacci), "Distance" (Kierstyn Sharrow, Philip Deyesso), "Family of Misfits" (Company), "Realize" (Company, Katy Reinsel)

NOTES—*Idol: The Musical* was a spoof of those fans obsessed by the television show *American Idol*, particularly those who worshiped Clay Aiken, one of the show's finalists.

The musical made a bit of a stir during previews when the producers replaced all but one of the nine cast members (Joe Walker, as J.D., remained with the show). And by opening night the musical seems to have added a tenth character, Midge (played by Dawn Barry).

But it was all for naught, and the musical's opening night was also its closing night. According to Matthew Murray in *TalkinBroadway.com*, the evening was a "sad spectacle" which resembled a "bottom-tier Fringe Festival spoofsical that's mistakenly wangled its way uptown." And while he singled out the "bitchy" "Prima Donna Fabulous" as the score's "best" song, he noted something was wrong when you rooted for the villainess and not the heroes.

751 If Love Were All. THEATRE: Lucille Lortel Theatre; OPENING DATE: June 10, 1999; PERFORMANCES: 101; TEXT: Devised by Sheridan Morley and adapted by Leigh Lawson from the works of Noel Coward; LYRICS: Noel Coward; MUSIC: Noel Coward; DIRECTION: Leigh Lawson; CHOREOGRAPHY: Leigh Lawson; Jeffry Denman, Assistant Choreographer; SCENERY: Tony Walton; COSTUMES: Tony Walton; LIGHTING: Michael Lincoln; MUSICAL DIRECTION: Tom Fay; PRODUCERS: Julian Schlossberg, Mask Productions, Redbus, Mark S. Golub, and Bill Haber by special arrangement with the Lucille Lortel Theatre Foundation; Meyer Ackerman, Associate Producer

CAST—Twiggy (Gertrude Lawrence), Harry Groener (Noel Coward)

The revue was presented in two acts.

ACT ONE—"Someday I'll Find You" (from *Private Lives*, 1930 [London]; New York, 1931) (Harry Groener, Twiggy), "A Room with a View" (*This Year of Grace!*, 1928 [London]; New York, 1928) (Harry Groener, Twiggy), "(I'm) Mad About You" (*This Year of Grace!*, 1928 [London]; New York, 1928; song not included in New York production) (Harry Groener, Twiggy), "Don't Put Your Daughter on the Stage, Mrs. Worthington" (independent song, 1936) (Harry Groener), "Parisian Pierrot" (*London Calling!*, 1923 [London]) (Twiggy), "Mad Dogs and Englishmen" (*The Third Little Show*, 1931 [New York]; later heard in London revue *Words and Music*, 1932) (Harry Groener), "Poor Little Rich Girl" (*On with the Dance*, 1925 [London]) (Harry Groener), "Twentieth Century Blues" (*Cavalcade*, 1931 [London]) (Twiggy), "You Were There" (*To-Night at 8:30/Shadow Play*, 1936 [London]; New York, 1936) (Harry Groener, Twiggy), "Has Anybody Seen Our Ship?" (*To-Night at 8:30/Red Peppers*, 1936 [London]; New York, 1936) (Harry Groener, Twiggy)

ACT TWO—"Men About Town" (*To-Night at 8:30/Red Peppers*, 1936 [London]; New York, 1936) (Harry Groener, Twiggy), "Mad About the Boy" (*Words and Music*, 1932 [London]; opened in New York as *Set to Music* [1938]) (Harry Groener, Twiggy), "I'll Follow My Secret Heart" (*Conversation Piece*, 1934 [London]; New York, 1934; see separate entry for the Off Broadway production of *Conversation Piece*) (Twiggy), "I Like America" (*Ace of Clubs*, 1950 [London]) (Twiggy), "London Pride" (*Up and Doing* [Second Edition], 1941 [London]) (Harry Groener, Twiggy), "I'll See You Again" (*Bitter-Sweet*, 1929 [London]; New York, 1929) (Twiggy), "Younger Generation" (*Words and Music*, 1932 [London]; opened in New York as *Set to Music* [1938]; song not included in American production) (Harry Groener), "If Love Were All" (*Bitter-Sweet*, 1929 [London]; New York, 1929) (Harry Groener, Twiggy), "I'll Remember Her" (*The Girl Who Came to Supper*, 1963 [New York]/"I'll See You Again" (reprise) (Harry Groener, Twiggy)

NOTES—*If Love Were All* was a tribute to Noel Coward, with Harry Groener as Coward and Twiggy as Gertrude Lawrence; it was recorded by Varese Sarabande Records (CD # 302-066-083-2). The revue had been previously produced by Bay Street Theatre in Sag Harbor, New York, in July 1998.

For another Coward tribute, see entry for *Oh Coward!*

752 I'll Die If I Can't Live Forever. "A Stage-Struck Revue." THEATRE: The Improvisation; OPENING DATE: October 31, 1974; PERFORMANCES: 81; BOOK: "Original book concept" by Karen Johnson; additional book material by William Brooke; LYRICS: Joyce Stoner; MUSIC: Joyce Stoner; additional music by William Boswell; DIRECTION: Uncredited (Technical Director, Dale Lally); CHOREOGRAPHY: Joyce Stoner; SCENERY: Irving Milton Duke; COSTUMES: Irving Milton Duke (?); MUSICAL

DIRECTION: William Boswell; PRODUCER: Patrick Stoner

CAST—Gail Johnston (Gabrielle Schwartz [Gabby]), Maureen Maloney (Heather O'Malley), Nancy Reddon (Jenette Morrison), Don Bradford (Dan Craig), Tom Hastings (Jonathan Winslow), Michael David Laibson (Ted Thornton), Mark T. Long (Pianist)

The musical was presented in two acts.

ACT ONE—"The Opening Number" (Company), "The Improvisation" (Company), Flashback:, "Joys of Manhattan Life" (Tom Hastings, Gail Johnston, Michael David Laibson), "Where Would We Be Without Perverts?" (Company), "My Life's a Musical Comedy" (Gail Johnston, Tom Hastings), "We're Strangers Who Sleep Side by Side" (Nancy Reddon, Michael David Laibson), "The Roommate Beguine" (Maureen Maloney, Don Bradford), "A Is For" (Gail Johnston), "Take Me!" (Company), "There's Always Someone Who'll Tell You 'No'" (Tom Hastings), "Twenty-Four Hours from This Moment" (Company)

ACT TWO—"The Improvisation" (reprise) (Company), "Ode to Electricity" (Company), "I'm in Love" (Maureen Maloney), "I'm So Bored" (Company), "My Place or Yours?" (Nancy Reddon, Michael David Laibson), "Who Do We Thank!" (Company), "Let's Have a Rodgers and Hammerstein Affair" (Nancy Reddon, Maureen Maloney, Tom Hastings, Michael David Laibson), "Less Is More and More" (Gail Johnston, Don Bradford), "I Hate Football" (Nancy Reddon), "They Left Me" (Maureen Maloney), "It's Great to Be Gay" (Company), "I'll Die If I Can't Live Forever" (Company), "The Finale" (Company), "The Great White Way" (Company)

NOTES—*I'll Die If I Can't Live Forever*, which dealt with a group of actors auditioning for roles in an upcoming Broadway musical, played for three months; another musical with the same subject matter opened later in the season and ran for twelve years.

The lyric for "Let's Have a Rodgers and Hammerstein Affair" consisted entirely of phrases of songs from various R & H musicals.

The script was published by Samuel French, Inc., in 1975.

753 I'm Getting My Act Together and Taking It on the Road. THEATRE: Anspacher Theatre/The Public Theatre; transferred to Circle in the Square (Downtown) on December 16, 1978; OPENING DATE: May 16, 1978; PERFORMANCES: 1,165; BOOK: Gretchen Cryer; LYRICS: Gretchen Cryer; MUSIC: Nancy Ford; DIRECTION: Word Baker; COSTUMES: Pearl Somner; LIGHTING: Martin Tudor; PRODUCER: The New York Shakespeare Festival (Joseph Papp, Producer; Bernard Gersten, Associate Producer)

CAST—Gretchen Cryer (Heather), Joel Fabiani (Joe), Margot Rose (Alice), Betty Aberlin (Cheryl), Don Scardino (Jake)

The musical was presented in one act.

NOTES—Early during its run at the Anspacher, the program for *I'm Getting My Act Together and Taking It on the Road* included an insert which listed the following songs (with no song assignments): "Music Is My One Salvation," "Smile, Smile, Smile," "In a Simple Way I Love You," Miss America," "I'm Doing My Strong Woman Number," "Dear Tom," "How Love Is Rare, and Life Is Strange," "Somebody's Changing My Act," "Happy Birthday," and "Music Is My One Salvation" (reprise). Later, the following songs were added: "Natural High," "Old Friend," "Put in a Package and Sold," "Feel the Love," and "Lonely Lady."

In December 1978, the musical transferred to the Circle in the Square (Downtown), and a program from that month lists the following songs (and performers): "Natural High" (Gretchen Cryer, Margot Rose, Betty Aberlin, and The Liberated Man's Band [Scott Berry, Piano; Lee Grayson, Guitar; Bob George, Drums; Dean Swenson, Bass and Fiddle]), "Smile" (Gretchen Cryer, James Mellon [Jake], Betty Aberlin, Margot Rose, Scott Berry, Lee Grayson, The Band), "In a Simple Way I Love You" (Gretchen Cryer, The Band), "Miss America" (Gretchen Cryer, Margot Rose, Betty Aberlin), "Strong Woman Number" (Margot Rose, Gretchen Cryer, Betty Aberlin), "Dear Tom" (Gretchen Cryer), "Old Friend" (Gretchen Cryer), "In a Simple Way I Love You" (reprise) (James Mellon), "Put in a Package and Sold" (Gretchen Cryer, Margot Rose, Betty Aberlin), "If Only Things Was Different" (James Mellon), "Feel the Love" (Company), "Lonely Lady" (Gretchen Cryer), "Happy Birthday" (Gretchen Cryer, The Band), "Natural High" (reprise) (Company)

Gretchen Cryer and Nancy Ford had one Off Broadway failure (*Now Is the Time for All Good Men* [1967; see entry]) and one success (*The Last Sweet Days of Isaac* ([1970; see entry]), not to mention a major disaster on Broadway with their one-month-and-out *Shelter* (1972). But with *I'm Getting My Act Together and Taking It on the Road*, they enjoyed their biggest hit; however, after this musical they were seldom heard from again, never on Broadway and only occasionally Off Broadway. *I'm Getting My Act Together* seems to have disappeared, and although it hasn't aged well, it might someday qualify for revival as a period piece. As a women's liberation musical, it was fortunate to come along when it did; the zeitgeist probably allowed it a far longer run than it would have enjoyed a few years earlier or a few years later. And while the musical sang about strong women, what it really needed was a strong book and score. The weak book offered cardboard characters who were strictly from the culture of victimization. And this being the 1970s, there was endless introspective "how-do-I-feel-about-this" self-analysis. The generally mundane score had just one superior song, "Old Friend," which was one of the best theatre songs of the era. Ultimately, the flaccid book and score, along with the musical's dated outlook, have all but doomed the show from enjoying a viable afterlife; it's probably not on anyone's list of "must" revivals (but, as noted, it might someday be revived as an artifact of its era). "Lonely Lady" had lyric as well as music by Gretchen Cryer.

The cast album on Columbia Records' CSP Collectors' Series (LP # X-14885) includes Don Scardino, who had left the show by the time it transferred to the Circle in the Square (Downtown); a few months after the musical opened at the Public, Scardino was cast in the title role of *King of Hearts*, which turned out to be one of many major Broadway musical bombs of the 1978-1979 season.

The cast album of *I'm Getting My Act Together* didn't include the song "If Only Things Was Different"; but the number was included on the London cast album, which was recorded on That's Entertainment Records (LP # TER-1006).

In 1980, the script was published by both Nelson Doubleday, Inc., and Samuel French, Inc.

In 1985, the Manhattan Theatre Club presented *Hang on to the Good Times* (see entry), an evening of songs by Cryer and Ford. The revue played for forty performances and included songs from *I'm Getting My Act Together*.

On April 20, 2007, Cryer and Ford appeared together in a limited Off Off Broadway engagement called *Getting Their Act Together Again* at the 59E59 Theatres. Andrew Gans in *Playbill* noted the press release indicated the evening looked at their personal and professional lives and included "the hits (and a few of the side-splitting misses!)" of their musical theatre career.

754 The Immigrant. "A New American Musical." THEATRE: Dodger Stages; OPENING DATE: November 4, 2004; PERFORMANCES: 29; BOOK: Mark Harelik; LYRICS: Sarah Knapp; MUSIC: Steven M. Alper; DIRECTION: Randal Myler; SCENERY: Brian Webb; COSTUMES: Willa Kim; LIGHTING: Don Darnutzer; MUSICAL DIRECTION: Kimberly Grigsby; PRODUCERS: HELLO Entertainment in association with Richard G. Weinberg for Omneity Entertainment, Inc., and Jeffrey B. Hecktman; Jack I. Silvera, Associate Producer

CAST—Adam Heller (Haskell), Cass Morgan (Ima), Walter Charles (Milton), Jacqueline Antaramian (Leah)

SOURCE—The 1985 play *The Immigrant: A Hamilton County Album* by Mark Harelik.

The action occurs in Hamilton, Texas, during the period 1909-1942.

The musical was presented in two acts.

ACT ONE—OPENING: "The Stars" (Adam Heller), "A Stranger Here" (Cass Morgan, Walter Charles, Adam Heller), "Simply Free" (Adam Heller), "Changes" (Walter Charles, Adam Heller), "Travel Light" (Jacqueline Antaramian, Adam Heller), "Keep Him Safe" (Cass Morgan), "Changes" (reprise) (Adam Heller), "I Don't Want It" (Jacqueline Antaramian), Finale Act I: "The Stars" (reprise) (Adam Heller)

ACT TWO—"Take the Comforting Hand of Jesus" (Calvary Baptist Church Choir), "Padadooly" (Cass Morgan, Jacqueline Antaramian), "The Stars—Leah" (Jacqueline Antaramian), "The Sun Comes Up" (Walter Charles, Adam Heller, Cass Morgan), "Candlesticks" (Jacqueline Antaramian), "Where Would You Be?" (Adam Heller), "No Place to Go" (Adam Heller), "Take the Comforting Hand of Jesus" (reprise) (Cass Morgan), Finale Act II: "The Stars" (reprise) (Jacqueline Antaramian, Cass Morgan, Adam Heller)

NOTES—Based on the lives of his grandparents, Mark Harelik's book for *The Immigrant* told the story of the two young Russian Jews who fled the pogroms of Eastern Europe in 1909 and made new lives for themselves in rural Texas. In his introduction to the published script, Harelik noted the young couple raised their family in an environment where full observance of their religion was difficult and "all outward signs of the shtetl life they left behind were gone."

The touching story and attractive score should have enabled the musical to enjoy a longer run in New York; perhaps the work will find its place in regional and community theatre.

The script was published by Samuel French, Inc., in 2005, and the cast recording was released by Ghostlight Records (CD # 7915584404-2).

An earlier production of the musical (with the same cast which eventually played in New York) opened at the Mainstage Theatre of the Coconut Grove Playhouse in Miami during the 2001-2002 theatre season.

755 Imperfect Chemistry. "A New Musical Comedy." THEATRE: Minetta Lane Theatre; OPENING DATE: August 24, 2000; PERFORMANCES: 46; BOOK: James Racheff; story by Albert M. Tapper; LYRICS: James Racheff; MUSIC: Albert M. Tapper; DIRECTION: John Ruocco; CHOREOGRAPHED: John Ruocco; SCENERY: Rob Odorisio; COSTUMES: Curtis Hay; LIGHTING: John-Paul Szczepanski; MUSICAL DIRECTION: August Eriksmoen; PRODUCERS: Back to Back Productions; Peter Press, Executive Producer

CAST—John Jellison (Dr. Goodman, Dr. Bubinksi), Brooks Ashmanskas (Harry Lizzarde), Ken Barnett (Dr. Alvin Rivers), Amanda Watkins (Dr. Elizabeth Gibbs), Joel Carlton (Ensemble), Michael Greenwood (Ensemble), Deirdre Lovejoy (Ensemble), Sara Schmidt (Ensemble)

The action occurs in Avalon, the "most advanced research laboratory known to man."

The musical was presented in two acts.

ACT ONE—"Avalon" (Company), "Dream Come True" (Ken Barnett, Amanda Watkins), "Serious Business" (John Jellison, Brooks Ashmanskas, Ensemble), "Dream Come True" (reprise) (Ken Barnett, Amanda Watkins), "It's All Written in Your Genes" (Ken Barnett, Amanda Watkins), "Ahhhh" (Amanda Watkins), "St. Andrews" (John Jellison, Ensemble), "Leave Your Fate to Fate" (Brooks Ashmanskas), "Ahhhh" (reprise) (Ken Barnett, Amanda Watkins), "Hell to Pay" (John Jellison, Ensemble), "Dream Come True"/"Avalon" (reprises) (Ken Barnett, Amanda Watkins)

ACT TWO—"Loxagane (Avalon)" (Company), "Loxagane (Avalon)" (reprise) (Company), "Big Hair" (Brooks Ashmanskas, Ensemble), "E-Mail Love Notes" (Ken Barnett, Amanda Watkins), "Bub's Song" (John Jellison, Brooks Ashmanskas, Ensemble), "Chaos Ballet" (Company), "Avalon" (reprise) (Company)

NOTES—*Imperfect Chemistry* dealt with two genetic specialists (Alvin and Elizabeth) who discover the cure for male pattern baldness; but a somewhat distressing side effect of the cure results in de-evolution. Society begins to dumb-down, and eventually the world is all but destroyed in a nuclear holocaust. However, Adam and Eve (that is, Alvin and Elizabeth) survive the catastrophe, and on a small island where apples grow in abundance they begin to start over.

Lawrence Van Gelder in the *New York Times* noted that one of the musical's props was a super computer, and he wondered if *Imperfect Chemistry* might have been better had the computer created it. But he praised the cast and the scenery, and mentioned that the score had "bright spots" (he singled out "St. Andrews").

The cast recording was released by Original Cast Records (CD # OC-6001).

756 In Circles (1967). "A Circular Play." THEATRE: Cherry Lane Theatre; OPENING DATE: November 5, 1967; PERFORMANCES: 222; WORDS: Gertrude Stein; text adapted by Al Carmines and Lawrence Kornfeld; MUSIC: Al Carmines; DIRECTION: Lawrence Kornfeld; SCENERY: Roland Turner and Johnnie Jones; LIGHTING: Eric Gertner; PRODUCERS: A Judson Poets' Theatre Production (Produced by Franklin De Boer)

CAST—Theo Barnes (Cousins), Jacque Lynn Colton (Mildred), Elaine Summers (Mable), Lee Guilliatt (Jessie), George McGrath (George), Arlene Rothlein (Sylvia), Al Carmines (Dole), David Vaughan (Ollie), Arthur Williams (The Citizen), Nancy Zala (Lucy Armitage)

SOURCE—Various writings of Gertrude Stein (1874-1946).

The action occurs in the present.

The musical was presented in one act.

NOTES—*In Circles*, a free-form "circular play," was, according to *The Burns Mantle Yearbook/The Best Plays of 1966-1967*, "a complex arrangement of word, song and dance effects, each one conceived as describing its own circle, without conventional story or subject line." Al Carmines' catchy pastiche score included tango, waltz, ragtime, spiritual, opera, vaudeville, barbershop quartet, and other styles of music. The cast album was recorded by Avant Garde Records (LP # AV-108).

In Circles was the second of six operas by Carmines which were based on works of Gertrude Stein. See entries for *What Happened* (1963), *The Making of Americans* (1972), *Listen to Me* (1974), *A Manoir* (1977), and *Dr. Faustus Lights the Lights* (1979).

In 1968, *In Circles* was revived on a double bill with *Songs by Carmines* (for more information, see entry for 1968 production of *In Circles*).

757 In Circles (1968) and Songs by Carmines. THEATRE: Gramercy Arts Theatre; OPENING DATE: June 25, 1968; PERFORMANCES: 56

In Circles: WORDS: Gertrude Stein; text adapted by Al Carmines and Lawrence Kornfeld; MUSIC: Al Carmines; DIRECTION: Lawrence Kornfeld; SCENERY: Roland Turner and Johnnie Jones; LIGHTING: Barry Arnold; MUSICAL DIRECTION: Al Carmines; PRODUCER: A Judson Poets' Theatre Production presented by Dina and Alexander E. Racolin and Samuel J. Friedman

CAST—Theo Barnes (Cousin), Jacque Lynn Colton (Mildred), Lee Crespi (Mable), Lee Guilliatt (Jessie), George McGrath (George), Arlene Rothlein (Sylvia), Al Carmines (Dole), Andrew Roman (Ollie), Arthur Williams (The Citizen), Julie Kurnitz (Lucy Armitage)

NOTES—The evening consisted of a revival of Gertrude Stein's *In Circles* (1967; see entry, which includes a list of all six operas by Al Carmines which were based on works by Stein) and a one-man performance of Carmines singing and playing many of his own songs.

According to Dan Sullivan in the *New York Times*, the revival was a ninety-minute evening of "solid obfuscation" which was nonetheless "great fun." He also praised Carmines' "potluck score" and Lawrence Kornfeld's "superlative" direction. Corry noted that just prior to the revival's opening at the Gramercy Arts Theatre, it had been produced at the Cherry Lane Theatre (the original 1967 production had premiered at the Judson Poets' Theatre).

758 In Gay Company. "A Try-Sexual Musical Revue." THEATRE: Upstairs at Jimmy's; OPENING DATE: April 4, 1975; PERFORMANCES: 13; "ADDITIONAL DIALOGUE" by Les Barkdull; LYRICS: Fred Silver; MUSIC: Fred Silver; DIRECTION: Sue Lawless; SCENERY: John J. Hotopp and Paul de Pass; COSTUMES: John J. Hotopp and Paul de Pass (?); MUSICAL DIRECTION: John Franceschina (or possibly Dennis Buck); PRODUCER: MCB Company

CAST—Candice Earley, Rick Gardiner, Cola Pinto, Gordon Ramsey, Robert Tananis

The revue was presented in two acts.

ACT ONE—"Welcome, Welcome" (Company), "A Pilgrim's Primer (Beginner's Guide to Cruising)" (Gordon Ramsey, Robert Tananis, Rick Gardner), "A Special Boy" (Candice Earley), "Handsome Stranger" (Cola Pinto), "Ode to a Hard Hat" "Fahrenheit 451," "Loew's Sheridan Square," "Lament for a Man in Blue" (Gordon Ramsey), "Opera Buffa" (Company)

ACT TWO—"A House Is Not a Home" (Gordon Ramsey, Company), "Two Strangers" (Candice Earley), "Remembrance of Things Past" (Gordon Ramsey, Cola Pinto), "The Days of the Dancing (Are Gone)" (Robert Tananis), "I Remember Mama," "If He'd Only Been Gentle" (Rick Gardner), "Freddy Liked to Fugue" (a/k/a "Freddie's Fugue") (Candice Earley, Robert Tananis, Rick Gardner, Gordon Ramsey), "Thank You, Thank You" (Company)

NOTES—The above song listing identifies performers when possible. Although Fred Silver's revue chalked up 244 performances earlier in the season (as *Gay Company*; see entry), *In Gay Company* played less than two weeks.

The 1975 version included numbers not heard in the earlier production ("Ode to a Hard Hat," "Fahrenheit 451," "Loew's Sheridan Square," "Opera Buffa," "I Remember Mama"); other numbers seem to have undergone slight title changes (1974's "Lament" was now "Lament for a Man in Blue").

The following numbers from the 1974 production weren't used: "True Confession," "Where There's Smoke," "Phantom of the Opera," and "I've Just Been to a Wedding." "Freddie Liked to Fugue" (a/k/a "Freddie's Fugue") had originally been heard in Silver's 1979 revue *Sterling Silver* (see entry).

In 1980, the revue returned as *Gay Company Revisited* (see entry). For further information (including information about a cast recording of a 1984 tour of the revue), see entry for *Gay Company*.

759 In Praise of Death. "A New Musical Play." THEATRE: Judson Poets' Theatre; OPENING DATE: November 3, 1978; PERFORMANCES: 8; BOOK: Al Carmines; LYRICS: Al Carmines; MUSIC: Al Carmines; DIRECTION: Dan Wagoner; CHOREOGRAPHY: Dan Wagoner; COSTUMES: Michele Edwards; LIGHTING: Victor En Yu Tan; MUSICAL DIRECTION: Al Carmines (?); PRODUCER: The Judson Poets' Theatre

CAST—Emily Adams (Emily Adams), The Dead (Ann Doemland, Ann; Eileen McNutt, Eileen; John Barrett, John; Judy Murphy, Judy; Alice Bosveld, Alice), Susan Chasin (Mother), Richard Leete (Father), Karl Garlid (Arguer), Essie Borden (Lyric Spirit), Lee Guilliatt (Lyric Spirit)

NOTES—In his program notes for the Off Off Broadway musical *In Praise of Death*, Al Carmines wrote: "In September of 1977, I suffered a cerebral aneurysm. I was operated on in October for 5½ hours. I recovered, but at the price of that innocence which all of us carry until smitten in some intimate way by fate. This musical play results from that experience."

The program didn't indicate the number of acts and didn't include a list of songs, but it referenced two numbers: the music of "I Cannot Live with You" was set to words by Emily Dickinson, and the program included the lyric and music of the song "Come Drink the Fountain of Life." Tom Buckley in the *New York Times* was mostly unimpressed with the musical. He noted that Carmines "has seen the hereafter and it works," but found the overall message (death is a beginning; the dead watch over us and await our joining them; we should live life to the fullest) unsurprising, considering that Carmines was a minister. Moreover, he found it odd Carmines didn't reference a divine presence, and noted that the dead seemed to live in a "clubhouse of the Village Independent Democrats." And, for what it's worth, Buckley noted that one young man in the cast bore a "disconcerting resemblance" to Pat Boone.

In 1998, another musical was inspired by a composer's brush with death. William Finn's *A New Brain* dealt with his experience of being mistakenly diagnosed with a brain tumor (see entry).

760 In the Heights. "A New Musical." THEATRE: 37 Arts Theatre; OPENING DATE: February 8, 2007; PERFORMANCES: 181; BOOK: Quiara Alegria Hudes; LYRICS: Lin-Manuel Miranda; MUSIC: Lin-Manuel Miranda; DIRECTION: Thomas Kail; CHOREOGRAPHY: Andy Blankenbuehler; SCENERY: Anna Louizos; COSTUMES: Paul Tazewell; LIGHTING: Jason Lyons; MUSICAL DIRECTION: Alex Lacamoire; PRODUCERS: Kevin McCollum, Jeffrey Seller, and Jill Furman

CAST—Seth Stewart (Graffiti Pete), Lin-Manuel Miranda (Usnavi), Eliseo Roman (Piragua Guy), Olga Merediz (Claudia), Priscilla Lopez (Camila), John Herrera (Kevin), Janet Dacal (Carla), Andrea Burns (Daniela), Robin de Jesus (Sonny), Christopher Jackson (Benny), Karen Olivo (Vanessa), Mandy Gonzalez (Nina); Ensemble: Rosie Lani Fiedelman, Asmeret Ghebremichael, Joshua Henry, Nina LaFarga, Doreen Montalvo, Javier Munoz, Eliseo Roman, Luis Salgado, Seth Stewart, Rickey Tripp

The action occurs in the present time over the Fourth of July weekend in Washington Heights.

The musical was presented in two acts.

ACT ONE—"In the Heights" (Lin-Manuel Miranda, Company), "Fire Escape" (Mandy Gonzalez), "Benny's Dispatch" (Christopher Jackson, Mandy

Gonzalez), "It Won't Be Long Now" (Karen Olivo, Lin-Manuel Miranda, Robin de Jesus), "Plan B" (John Herrera, Priscilla Lopez, Mandy Gonzalez), "Inutil (Useless)" (John Herrera), "No Me Diga" (Andrea Burns, Janet Dacal, Karen Olivo, Mandy Gonzalez), "96,000" (Lin-Manuel Miranda, Christopher Jackson, Robin de Jesus, Karen Olivo, Andrea Burns, Janet Dacal, Company), "Paciencia y Fe (Patience and Faith)" (Olga Merediz, Company), "When You're Home" (Mandy Gonzalez, Christopher Jackson, Company), "Piragua" (Eliseo Roman), "Siempre" (Priscilla Lopez, Bolero Singer), "The Club"/"Fireworks" (Company)

ACT TWO—"Sunrise" (Mandy Gonzalez, Christopher Jackson, Company), "Hundreds of Stories" (Olga Merediz, Lin-Manuel Miranda), "Atencion" (John Herrera), "The Day Goes By" (Company), "Everything I Know" (Mandy Gonzalez), "Hear Me Out" (Christopher Jackson), "Goodbye" (Lin-Manuel Miranda, Karen Olivo), Finale (Lin-Manuel Miranda, Company)

NOTES—*In the Heights* was set in Washington Heights and revolved around the lives and loves of Latinos living in the barrio.

Charles Isherwood in the *New York Times* noted the evening was episodic and didn't offer much in the way of dramatic tension. But he felt the evening had genuine authenticity, and he praised the Latino-inflected score and the "joyous" choreography created by Andy Blankenbuehler. In all, he found the musical an "uptown *Rent*, plus some salsa fresca and without the sex, drugs and disease." Frank Scheck in the *New York Post* found the score "invigorating and fresh," the dances "sexy," and the evening "exuberant ... bursts with a vitality and freshness that overcomes its occasionally rough-hewn elements."

The musical closed after 181 performances for revisions and rewrites prior to a transfer to Broadway, where it opened on March 9, 2008, at the Richard Rodgers (formerly the 46th Street) Theatre. For Broadway, seven new songs were added (and seven numbers from the Off Broadway production were omitted). The 2-CD set Broadway cast album was released by Ghostlight Records (CD # 8-4428). In 2009, *In the Heights: Chasing Broadway Dreams*, a documentary film about the musical, was released.

761 In the Nick of Time. THEATRE: Stage 73; OPENING DATE: June 1, 1967; PERFORMANCES: 22; MATERIAL by: Barbara Fried, Charles Appel, Herb Suffrin, Lenny Stern, Sue Lawless, and Ted Pugh; DIRECTION: Earl Durham; LIGHTING: Jene Youtt; PRODUCERS: David Hedges and William B. Allen, in association with Richard Herd

CAST—Sue Lawless, Ted Pugh; musical accompaniment by Andrew Orestes Lesko

The revue was presented in two acts: Act One (Prologue) and Act Two (Epilogue), with an intermission "between the logues"

NOTES—The program for *In the Nick of Time* noted that Sue Lawless "fought her way tooth and claw up the ladder of set-backs," and Ted Pugh's bio mentioned that his "dark, statuesque good looks will tell you immediately that he hails from Anadarko, Oklahoma."

Clive Barnes in the *New York Times* liked the comic twosome, but felt much of the material let them down. However, he had high praise for two sequences. In one, he reported that Lawless was a take-no-prisoners pianist who accompanies a hapless concert singer (Pugh) who performs such songs as "Your Lips Are No-Man's Land but Mine" and "Honna-Lulu, America Loves You." But Lawless didn't just "play" the piano, she "performed," and her inspired and zany Beatrice Lillie-like antics all but reduce the tenor to little more than backdrop as she adjusts her 98-cent orchid, "painfully" peels off her long black gloves, "delicately" wipes her hands on a flowered handkerchief, and helpfully prompts the singer when she feels he may forget a lyric. Further, Barnes said she paused "portentously" each time she turned a page of her sheet music (although several sheets seem to blow away or disappear before she can turn them). In another sequence, Barnes praised a "wonderfully arrogant parody" of a "rrreally" big show at Radio City Music Hall.

762 In the Pasha's Garden. THEATRE: Metropolitan Opera House; OPENING DATE: January 24, 1935; PERFORMANCES: 3; LIBRETTO: H.C. Tracy; MUSIC: John Laurence Seymour; DIRECTION: Wilhelm Von Wymetal, Jr.; SCENERY: Frederick J. Kiesler; MUSICAL DIRECTION: Ettore Panizza; PRODUCER: The Metropolitan Opera

CAST—Helen Jepson (Helene), Frederick Jagel (Etienne), Marek Windheim (Zumbul Agha), Lawrence Tibbett (Pasha), Arthur Anderson (Shaban)

SOURCE—The story "Stamboul Nights" by H.G. Dwight.

The opera was presented in one act.

NOTES—The world premiere of *In the Pasha's Garden* appeared on a double bill with Giacomo Puccini's *La Boheme* (Ezio Pinza was Colline and Helen Gleason was Musetta).

In his review for the *New York Times*, Olin Downes indicated the original story upon which the opera was based told of a pasha who believes his wife is having an affair. He doesn't confront her, but when he becomes convinced her lover is hiding in a chest, he orders the chest to be buried. With its burial, he must put to rest his doubts about his wife's guilt or innocence (neither of which is ever established). In the opera, the pasha's eunuch confirms the wife's guilt. When the pasha confronts his wife, she denies the truth and leaves, but not before giving him a key to the trunk. Instead of opening the trunk, the pasha and the eunuch bury it in the garden, which was once a symbol of the pasha's love for his wife but which now is possibly the burial ground for her lover.

Downes felt the opera was "dramatically ineffective" and stated the piece was "not one of the best but one of the worst American operas produced hereabouts in years." The work was "tedious and inept" and its length of fifty-five minutes "became a very long time."

Downes noted that Marek Windheim's eunuch "cackled and emitted roulades," and he also complained that the words were often difficult to understand. This was a standard complaint for operas sung in English, and the problem continues to the present day. Indeed, today's "super" or sur-titles are deemed as necessary for operas performed in English as they are for non-English-sung operas.

763 In Trousers (1978). "A Musical." THEATRE: Mainstage/Playwrights Horizons; OPENING DATE: December 8, 1978; PERFORMANCES: 8; LYRICS: William Finn; MUSIC: William Finn; DIRECTION: William Finn; CHOREOGRAPHY: Marta Renzi; SCENERY: Donato Moreno; COSTUMES: Bob Wojewodski; LIGHTING: Annie Wrightson; MUSICAL DIRECTION: Michael Starobin; PRODUCER: Playwrights Horizons (Robert Moss, Producing Director; Jane Moss, Managing Director; Andre Bishop, Artistic Director)

CAST—Alison Fraser (With the Pink Shirt [Marvin's Wife]), Joanna Green (With the Blonde Hair [Marvin's High School Sweetheart]), Mary Testa (With the Sunglasses [Marvin's Teacher, Miss Goldberg]), Chip Zien (With the Sneakers [Marvin])

The action occurs in the present.

The musical was presented in one act.

MUSICAL NUMBERS—"Marvin's Giddy Seizures" (Chip Zien, Alison Fraser, Joanna Green, Mary Testa), "How the Body Falls Apart" (Alison Fraser, Joanna Green, Mary Testa), "Your Lips and Me" (Alison Fraser), "How Marvin Eats His Breakfast" (Chip Zien, Alison Fraser, Joanna Green, Mary Testa), "My High School Sweetheart" (Chip Zien, Alison Fraser, Joanna Green, Mary Testa), "Set Those Sails" (Mary Testa, with Alison Fraser and Joanna Green), "My Chance to Survive the Night" (Chip Zien), "I Am Wearing a Hat" (a/k/a "Marvin Takes a Wife") (Mary Testa, Alison Fraser, Chip Zien, Joanna Green), "A Breakfast Over Sugar" (Chip Zien, Alison Fraser), "Whizzer Going Down" (Chip Zien, Alison Fraser, Joanna Green, Mary Testa), "High School Ladies at 5 O'Clock" (Joanna Green, with Alison Fraser and Mary Testa), "The Rape of Miss Goldberg (by Marvin)" (Chip Zien, Mary Testa), "(The) Nausea Before the Game" (Chip Zien, Alison Fraser, Joanna Green, Mary Testa), "Love Me for What I Am" (Alison Fraser), "How America Got Its Name" (Chip Zien), "Marvin Takes a Victory Shower" (Chip Zien, Alison Fraser, Joanna Green, Mary Testa), "Another Sleepless Night" (Joanna Green, Mary Testa, Chip Zien, Alison Fraser), "In Trousers (The Dream)" (Chip Zien, Alison Fraser, Joanna Green, Mary Testa)

NOTES—*In Trousers* was the first of three musicals in William Finn's so-called "Marvin Trilogy," about Marvin, a gay man, his wife, son, male lover, and psychiatrist (as well as his high school sweetheart and one of his high school teachers). The Off Off Broadway musical premiered at Playwrights Horizons on December 8, 1978, for eight performances, and then re-opened there with the same cast on February 21, 1979, for an additional twenty-four performances. The production was recorded by Original Cast Records (LP # OC-7915), and the script was published by Samuel French, Inc., in 1986. A revised version later opened Off Broadway at the Second Stage in 1981, and in 1985 the musical was revived Off Broadway at the Promenade Theatre for sixteen performances (see entries). *In Trousers* and William Finn were perhaps acquired tastes, and had their fierce adherents; eventually, Finn wrote two more musicals which followed the angst and anxieties of Marvin and Company. The second, *March of the Falsettos*, opened at Playwrights Horizons in 1981, and in June 1990 the third musical, *Falsettoland*, opened there (see entries). The scripts of all three musicals in the "Marvin Trilogy" were published as *The Marvin Songs* by The Fireside Theatre in an undated (but possibly 1991) edition.

Finn eventually combined *March of the Falsettos* and *Falsettoland* into *Falsettos*, which opened on Broadway at the John Golden Theatre on April 29, 1992, for 487 performances. For this production, Michael Rupert (Marvin), Stephen Bogardus (Whizzer), and Chip Zien (Mendel) reprised their roles from earlier productions of *March of the Falsettos* and *Falsettoland*; Barbara Walsh was Trina, and Jonathan Kaplan played Jason.

Finn's musicals never attained widespread popularity, and none had marathon runs. But in 2005 he hit the jackpot with a mainstream musical, the popular Tony Award-winning *The 25th Annual Putnam County Spelling Bee* (see entry).

764 In Trousers (1981). "A Musical." THEATRE: The Second Stage; OPENING DATE: February 22, 1981; PERFORMANCES: 15; LYRICS: William Finn; MUSIC: William Finn; DIRECTION: Judith Swift; CHOREOGRAPHY: Sharon Kinney; Marta Renzi, Co-Choreographer; SCENERY: Nancy Winters; COSTUMES: Karen D. Miller; LIGHTING: Victor En Yu Tan; MUSICAL DIRECTION: Michael Starobin; PRODUCER: The Second Stage (Robyn Goodman and Carole Rothman, Artistic Directors)

CAST—Jay O. Sanders (Marvin), Kate DeZina (Marvin's Wife), Alaina Reed (Marvin's Teacher, Miss Goldberg), Karen Jablons (Marvin's High School Sweetheart)

The musical was presented in one act.

MUSICAL NUMBERS—"I Can't Sleep" (Jay O. Sanders, Kate DeZina, Alaina Reed, Karen Jablons), "A Helluva Day" (Kate DeZina), "How Marvin Eats

His Breakfast" (Jay O. Sanders, Kate DeZina, Alaina Reed, Karen Jablons), "My High School Sweetheart" (Karen Jablons, Chip Zien, Kate DeZina, Alaina Reed), "Set Those Sails" (Alaina Reed, Kate DeZina, Karen Jablons), "I Swear I Won't Ever Again" (Jay O. Sanders), "I Am Wearing a Hat" (a/k/a "Marvin Takes a Wife") (Alaina Reed, Jay O. Sanders, Kate DeZina, Karen Jablons), "Marvin's Giddy Seizures" (Jay O. Sanders, Kate DeZina, Alaina Reed, Karen Jablons), "A Breakfast Over Sugar" (Jay O. Sanders, Kate DeZina), "I'm Breaking Down" (Kate DeZina), "Whizzer Brown" (Jay O. Sanders, Kate DeZina, Alaina Reed, Karen Jablons), "High School Ladies at 5 O'Clock" (Karen Jablons), "The Rape of Miss Goldberg (by Marvin)" (A 2-Act Dialogue with Music) (Jay O. Sanders, Alaina Reed), "(The) Nausea Before the Game" (Jay O. Sanders, Kate DeZina, Alaina Reed, Karen Jablons), "Love Me for What I Am" (Kate DeZina), "How America Got Its Name" (Jay O. Sanders, Kate DeZina, Alaina Reed, Karen Jablons), "A Helluva Day" (reprise) (Kate DeZina), "Marvin Takes a Victory Shower" (Jay O. Sanders, Kate DeZina, Alaina Reed, Karen Jablons), "Goodnight" (Jay O. Sanders)

NOTES—This Off Off Broadway revival of *In Trousers* was a slightly revised version of the production which had originally premiered at Playwrights Horizons in 1978 (see entry for the original production, including information regarding all the musicals in the "Marvin Trilogy" [*In Trousers, March of the Falsettos*, and *Falsettoland*]).

765 In Trousers (1985). THEATRE: Promenade Theatre; OPENING DATE: March 26, 1985; PERFORMANCES: 16; BOOK: William Finn; LYRICS: William Finn; MUSIC: William Finn; DIRECTION: Matt Casella; SCENERY: Santo Loquasto; COSTUMES: Madeline Ann Graneto; LIGHTING: Marilyn Rennagel; MUSICAL DIRECTION: Roy Leake, Jr.; PRODUCERS: Roger Berlind, Franklin R. Levy, and Gregory Harrison

CAST—Tony Cummings (Marvin), Catherine Cox (His Wife), Sherry Hursey (His High School Sweetheart), Kathy Garrick (His Teacher [Miss Goldberg])

The action occurs in the present.

The musical was presented in one act.

MUSICAL NUMBERS—"In Trousers (The Dream)"/"I Can't Sleep" (Company), "Time to Wake Up" (Catherine Cox), "I Have a Family" (Tony Cummings), "How Marvin Eats His Breakfast" (Company), "Marvin's Giddy Seizures I" (Sherry Hursey), "My High School Sweetheart" (Company), "Set Those Sails" (Kathy Garrick, Catherine Cox, Sherry Hursey), "I Swear I Won't Ever Again" (Tony Cummings), "High School Ladies at Five O'Clock" (Sherry Hursey, Catherine Cox, Kathy Garrick), "The Rape of Miss Goldberg (by Marvin)" (Tony Cummings, Kathy Garrick), "Love Me for What I Am" (Tony Cummings, Catherine Cox), "I Am Wearing a Hat" (Sherry Hursey, Kathy Garrick), "Wedding Song" (Company), "Three Seconds" (Tony Cummings), "How the Body Falls Apart" (Catherine Cox, Sherry Hursey, Kathy Garrick), "I Feel Him Slipping Away" (Catherine Cox, with Sherry Hursey and Kathy Garrick), "Whizzer Going Down" (Tony Cummings), "Marvin's Giddy Seizures II" (Company), "I'm Breaking Down" (Catherine Cox), "Packing Up" (Tony Cummings), "Breakfast Over Sugar" (Tony Cummings, Catherine Cox), "How America Got Its Name" (Sherry Hursey, Kathy Garrick, Tony Cummings), "Time to Wake Up" (reprise) (Catherine Cox), "Scrubby Dubby" (Company), "Another Sleepless Night" (Company), "Without You"/"No Hard Feelings" (Company)

NOTES—This slightly revised Off Broadway revival of *In Trousers* marked its third New York production (see entry for the original 1978 production which opened Off Off Broadway in two slightly separated engagements in 1978 and 1979 as well as the entry for the 1981 Off Off Broadway revival). Also, see entry for the 1978 production regarding information about the "Marvin Trilogy" musicals (*In Trousers, March of the Falsettos*, and *Falsettoland*).

766 In Your Hat. "A New Intimate Musical Revue." THEATRE: The Showplace; OPENING DATE: October 13, 1957; PERFORMANCES: Unknown; LYRICS: Rick Besoyan; MUSIC: Rick Besoyan; DIRECTION: Christopher Hewett and Ray Harrison; SCENERY: Howard Barker; COSTUMES: Howard Barker; LIGHTING: Edmund Roney; MUSICAL DIRECTION: Natalie Charleston; PRODUCER: Jim Paul Eilers

CAST—KAREN ANDERS, William Graham, Kenneth McMillan, Barbara Sharma

The revue was presented in three acts.

ACT ONE—Opening Chorus (Company), "Good Morrow My Love" (Barbara Sharma), "Sur la Table" (Karen Anders), "Have You Heard I've Fallen in Love" (William Graham, Barbara Sharma), "Myrtle May's Birthday Party" (Karen Anders, Barbara Sharma), "I'm Growing Up" (Kenneth McMillan), "J. Timothy Fielding III" (Barbara Sharma), "A Madrigal" (Company)

ACT TWO—"Gems from *Little Mary Sunshine*," "Little Mary Sunshine" (William Graham, Kenneth McMillan), "Look for a Sky of Blue" (Barbara Sharma), "Once in a Blue Moon" (Karen Anders, Kenneth McMillan), "You're the Fairest Flower" (William Graham), "Colorado Love Call" (Barbara Sharma, William Graham), "Mata Hari" (Karen Anders), "Old-Fashioned Girl" (Kenneth McMillan), "Coo-Coo" (Barbara Sharma), "The Forest Rangers" (Kenneth McMillan, William Graham), "Every Little Nothing" (Karen Anders, Barbara Sharma)

ACT THREE—"Venetcia" (William Graham, Kenneth McMillan), "This Is the Life" (Karen Anders), "Hat and Cane" (Kenneth McMillan, Barbara Sharma), "Good Fer Nothin' Me" (William Graham), "Love Conquers All" (Karen Anders, Barbara Sharma), "Rock Sweet Baby" (Kenneth McMillan), "Hot Tamale Tango" (Karen Anders), "Don't You Love Everything About Show Biz" (Company)

NOTES—*In Your Hat* was Rick Besoyan's first musical, and its second act was the genesis of his successful musical spoof *Little Mary Sunshine* (1959; see entry). The entire second act of the revue was a collection of "gems" from a supposedly old musical called *Little Mary Sunshine* (Barbara Sharma was the first to play Little Mary Sunshine, alias Mary Potts). The sequence included ten songs, nine of which were heard two years later when the show was expanded into a full-length musical. One song, "Old-Fashioned Girl," which was sung by Kenneth McMillan, didn't make the transfer, but was later used in Besoyan's *Babes in the Wood* (see entry) and was performed by McMillan in that production.

For the 1959 production of *Little Mary Sunshine*, William Graham reprised his role of Captain "Big Jim" Warrington, Ray Harrison returned as the musical's director, and Howard Barker again designed the scenery and costumes. Howard Barker was also one of three co-producers for the expanded production (along with Robert Chambers and Cynthia Baer; the latter, incidentally, was Jim Paul Eiler's assistant during the run of *In Your Hat*). It appears that all the numbers in *In Your Hat* were songs; the program credits Rick Besoyan with all the material ("music and lyrics") and doesn't mention any sketches.

The Showplace opened during Fall 1958 (*In Your Hat* seems to have been its inaugural production) and it was located near 6th Street and Fourth Avenue in Greenwich Village. Jim Paul Eilers was the manager, and his venue consisted of two separate rooms: upstairs was The Showplace, a nightclub where intimate revues were presented, and downstairs was The Speakeasy, a small cocktail lounge. Apparently Eilers produced most of the revues which played The Showplace.

767 Inappropriate. THEATRE: Theatre Row Theatre; OPENING DATE: November 23, 1999; PERFORMANCES: 112; BOOK: "Co-conceived" by A. Michael DeSisto and Lonnie McNeil; LYRICS: Michael Sottile; MUSIC: Michael Sottile; DIRECTION: Ray Leeper and Michael Sottile; original direction by Lonnie McNeil; CHOREOGRAPHY: Ray Leeper; original choreography by Lonnie McNeil; SCENERY: Shane Ballard; COSTUMES: Shane Ballard; LIGHTING: S. Ryan Schmidt; MUSICAL DIRECTION: Michael Sottile; PRODUCERS: A. Michael DeSisto and Butterfly Productions

CAST—Mia Benenate, Averie Boyer, Josh Geyer, Elizabeth Irwin, Jamie Ourisman, Diane Schwartz, Sarah Seckinger, Adam Shiffman

SOURCE—The graduation books of DeSisto School alumni.

The revue was presented in one act.

MUSICAL NUMBERS—"Our World Within (Part I and Part II)" (Company), "Let Me Be the One" (Averie Boyer, Elizabeth Irwin, Company), "Dear Dad" (Diane Schwartz, Elizabeth Irwin, Sarah Seckinger, Mia Benenate), "Feels Good (Drugs)" (Company), "Real" (Diane Schwartz, Company), "A Good Boy" (Josh Geyer, Company), "I Wonder" (Averie Boyer, Elizabeth Irwin, Company), "The Dream" (Adam Schiffman, Company), "Mexico" (Diane Schwartz, Jamie Ourisman), "Kaleidoscope" (Company), "Lost" (Averie Boyer, Elizabeth Irwin, Company), "The Discovery" (Company), "Everything That You Are" (Elizabeth Irwin, Company)

NOTES—The revue *Inappropriate* was somewhat similar to *The Me Nobody Knows* (see entry); it was based on the writings of young people and dealt with their troubled relationships with parents and peers.

While Anita Gates in the *New York Times* found the evening "alternately pretentious and inarticulate," she also noted that the musical vignettes did an "excellent job" of analyzing the emotions of adolescents; she further noted that sometimes the work conjured up the "anger, hurt and exuberance" found in such musicals as *Hair* and *Rent* (see entries). Although the cast album was briefly available in such venues as the theatres where the production played, it has yet to receive a wide release.

768 The Incredible Feeling Show. "A New Musical." THEATRE: Beacon Theatre; OPENING DATE: December 26, 1979; PERFORMANCES: 10; BOOK: Elizabeth Swados; LYRICS: Elizabeth Swados; MUSIC: Elizabeth Swados; DIRECTION: Meridee Stein; CHOREOGRAPHY: Linda Reiff; SCENERY: Mavis Smith; COSTUMES: Meridee Stein; LIGHTING: Lee DeWeerdt; MUSICAL DIRECTION: Vicky Blumenthal and Sue Anderson; PRODUCER: Concert Arts Society, Inc. (Kazuko Hillyer, Director); The First All Children's Theatre (The Meri Mini Players, The Teen Company), Meridee Stein, Producer

CAST—Lichiana Amigo, Finesse Banks, Micki Barnett, Anthony Barrile, Teddy Bishop, Kim Brown, Grisha Coleman, Reneta Cuff, Lisa Daniels, Carlos Davidson, Samantha Defiris, Stephanie Dunn, Gerard Dure, Arsenia Farmer, Maria Fuentes, Bonnie Gertler, Frank Giardino, Jennifer Greenstein, Reiko Hillyer, Pamela Hyman, Raymond Jenkins, Joseph Johnson, Maurice Johnson, Jill Kern, Belkys Lopez, Diane Paulus, Glen Philipson, Julie Rapoport, Kim Raver, Jessie Richards, Debbi Roth, Martiza Santana, Shirley Santana, Velma Saunders, Lili Schlossberg, Denise Schneider, Jo Ann Schnoll, Ben Schwartz, Rodney Smith, Lauren Stauber, Nicole Sullivan, Allen Thomas, Annie Viscuso, Steven Ward (During the run of the production, the roles were rotated among members of the company.)

SOURCE—The novel *The Girl with Incredible Feeling* by Elizabeth Swados.

NOTES—Musical numbers (and division of acts) weren't listed in the program. *The Incredible Feeling Show*, which was presented for a limited engagement of ten performances, was about a little girl who discovers her feelings have disappeared and thus begins a quest to regain them.

769 **Infertility.** "The Musical That's Hard to Conceive." THEATRE: Dillon's Theatre; OPENING DATE: November 4, 2005; PERFORMANCES: 60 (estimated); BOOK: Chris Neuner; LYRICS: Chris Neuner; MUSIC: Chris Neuner; DIRECTION: Dan Foster; CHOREOGRAPHY: Michelle Yaroshko; SCENERY: Victor Whitehurst; COSTUMES: Zinda Williams; LIGHTING: Andrew Gmoser; MUSICAL DIRECTION: Albert Ahronheim; PRODUCERS: Kathryn Frawley and Chris Neuner

CAST—Erin Davie (April), Jenni Frost (Zusu), Seri Johnson (Heather), Cadden Jones (Jane), Larry Picard (Doctor), Kurt Robbins (Dick)

The action occurs in the present.

The musical was presented in one act.

MUSICAL NUMBERS—"Love Song" (Kurt Robbins, Erin Davie, Seri Johnson, Jenni Frost, Cadden Jones), "You've Got Parts" (Larry Picard, Company), "All Ya' Gotta Do Is" (Erin Davie, Company), "The Donor Dating Game" (Seri Johnson, Jenni Frost, Company), "Cricket" (Cadden Jones), "Infertile Love Song" (Erin Davie, Kurt Robbins), "I've Got Sperm in My Pocket (and I'm Talkin' to Eileen)" (Kurt Robbins), "Adoption Interrogation" (Cadden Jones), "Ain't It Great to Have a Kid?" (Company), "We Found Love Our Own Way" (Seri Johnson, Jenni Frost), "Infertile Love Song" (reprise) (Erin Davie, Kurt Robbins), "(Scene) Misconceptions" (Company), "Big Dogs Run" (Kurt Robbins, Erin Davie, Seri Johnson, Jenni Frost, Cadden Jones), "When I Have You" (Company)

NOTES—*Infertility* dealt with a number of individuals (a married couple, a single woman, and a lesbian couple) who want to have children, but who can't conceive; they ultimately learn to live their lives without children (for various reasons, adoption is apparently not an option for them).

The Off Off Broadway musical had originally been presented by the Hudson Stage Company and then was later seen at the New York International Fringe Festival. Jason Zinoman in the *New York Times* found the "harmless, insubstantial" evening "pleasing enough—fill of broad, diverting comedy" (but with a penchant for "bad metaphors").

The cast recording was released by Conception Productions (unnumbered CD).

It would be interesting to see *Infertility* performed in repertory with two other works dealing with the same general theme, David Rudkin's deeply poignant drama *Ashes*, which was produced Off Broadway in 1977, and Richard Maltby, Jr., and David Shire's 1983 Broadway musical *Baby*.

770 **Inside Out.** THEATRE: Cherry Lane Theatre; OPENING DATE: November 7, 1994; PERFORMANCES: 61; BOOK: Doug Haverty; LYRICS: Adryan Russ and Doug Haverty; MUSIC: Adryan Russ; DIRECTION: Henry Fonte; CHOREOGRAPHY: Gary Slavin; SCENERY: Rob Odorisio; COSTUMES: Gail Brassard; LIGHTING: Douglas O'Flaherty; MUSICAL DIRECTION: E. Suzan Ott; PRODUCERS: Marc Routh, Richard Frankel, and Randy Kelly; Margot Ross London and Prima K. Stephen, Associate Producers

CAST—Ann Crumb (Dena), Harriett D. Foy (Grace), Kathleen Mahoney-Bennett (Molly), Jan Maxwell (Liz), Cass Morgan (Chlo), Julie Prosser (Sage)

The musical was presented in two acts.

ACT ONE—"Inside Out" (Company), "Thin" (Kathleen Mahoney-Bennett, Julie Prosser, Cass Morgan, Jan Maxwell), "Let It Go" (Julie Prosser, Harriett D. Foy), "I Can See You Here" (Harriett D. Foy), "If You Really Loved Me" (Company), "Yo, Chlo" (Ann Crumb, Company), "If You Really Loved Me" (reprise) (Cass Morgan), "Behind Dena's Back" (Company), "No One Inside" (Ann Crumb), "Inside Out" (reprise) (Company)

ACT TWO—"Grace's Nightmare" (Harriett D. Foy, Company), "All I Do Is Sing" (Ann Crumb), "Never Enough" (Cass Morgan), "I Don't Say Anything" (Julie Prosser), "Things Look Different" (Jan Maxwell, Harriett D. Foy), "The Passing of a Friend" (Kathleen Mahoney-Bennett, Company), "Things Look Different" (Jan Maxwell, Harriett D. Foy), "Do It at Home" (Jan Maxwell, Company), "Reaching Up" (Ann Crumb, Company)

NOTES—Previously produced Off Off Broadway by the Village Theatre Company in July 1992 (as *Roleplay*) and later in regional theatre, *Inside Out* dealt with six women who meet weekly for group therapy sessions.

Stephen Holden in the *New York Times* praised the "smart, spunky" and "bright, witty" musical, noting that while it didn't always avoid "clichéd psychobabble" and "perky bromides," it nonetheless created characters who seemed like "real people with real problems." He singled out a few songs, including "No One Inside" (the evening's "show-stopper"), "Never Enough" ("wonderfully sung" by Cass Morgan), and "Yo, Chlo" (the musical's "funniest" song).

The cast album was released by DRG Records (CD # 19007-2), and the script was published by Samuel French, Inc., in 1996.

For other "therapy" musicals, see entries for *I Can't Keep Running in Place* (which dealt with six women who meet weekly for assertiveness training), *One Foot Out the Door* (about two women and a man in therapy, all trying to deal with the men in their lives), and *Sessions* (in which even the psychiatrist has issues).

771 **Instant Replay.** THEATRE: Upstairs at the Downstairs; OPENING DATE: August 6, 1968; PERFORMANCES: Unknown; SKETCHES, LYRICS, MUSIC: Rod Warren, Jay Jeffries, Steve Nelson, Bill Weeden, David Finkle, Bruce Williamson, Blair Weille, Jerry Powell, Michael Brown, Don Tucker, Alan Foster Friedman, Kenny Solms, Gayle Parent, Treva Silverman, Michael McWhinney, and Warren Burton; DIRECTION: Rod Warren; LIGHTING: Larry Carter; MUSICAL DIRECTION: Jerry Powell

CAST—Warren Burton, Jeanette Landis, Larry Moss, George Poulos, Lily Tomlin

NOTES—*Instant Replay* may have been a second edition of sorts to *Photo Finish* (see entry); if so, it would have reprised (instant replayed) many of the numbers from the earlier revue.

There would be only one more traditional Upstairs/Downstairs revue, the prophetically titled *Free Fall* (see entry), which was a collaboration between Rod Warren and Ronny Graham. After *Free Fall*, the era of the classic nightclub revue was completely over. For an almost fifteen-year period, Ben Bagley, Ronny Graham, Julius Monk, and Rod Warren had presented intimate and cosmopolitan revues for the sophisticated theatergoer. But by the late 1960s, this type of theatergoer was slowly but surely discovering that serious dramas, witty comedies, clever mysteries, traditional book musicals, and urbane revues were no longer in style, and that cruder, dumb-downed "entertainments" were more and more becoming the norm.

For a complete list of Rod Warren's revues, see entry for *...And in This Corner*; also see Appendix R.

772 **International Playgirls '64.** THEATRE: Village Theatre; OPENING DATE: May 21, 1964; PERFORMANCES: 4; SPECIAL MATERIAL: John Roeburt; DIRECTION: Martin B. Cohen; Allan Drake, Assistant Director; Peter Xantho, Production Supervisor; CHOREOGRAPHY: Bhaskar; SCENERY: Leo B. Meyers; COSTUMES: Kam Deveraux; LIGHTING: Peter Xantho; MUSICAL DIRECTION: Joe Cabot; PRODUCER: Trans-World Productions

CAST—Georgia Sothern, John Conte, Allan Drake, Miss Hollywood, Saja Lee, Morocco, The Albrights, Pamela Hayes, Mark LaRoche, Sheva Rozier, "and 12 International Beauties"

The revue was presented in two acts.

ACT ONE—Opening Production, Morocco, "Marriage License Bureau," "Japanese Production," "The Demonstrators," John Conte, "Paris Artist," Allan Drake, Production Finale

ACT TWO—Opening Production, "Magician," "Miss Hollywood," "The Mother-in-Law," John Conte, Allan Drake, Georgia Sothern, Finale

NOTES—Ann Corio hit the jackpot with her long-running *This Was Burlesque* (1962; see entry), but it was diminishing returns for other famous strip tease artists of the past who visited Off Broadway. Blaze Starr and *Burlesque on Parade* (1963; see entry) ran for one month; Georgia Sothern and her *International Playgirls '64* lasted for just four performances; and even Gypsy Rose Lee herself, in her non-burlesque, one-woman show *A Curious Evening with Gypsy Rose Lee* (1961; see entry), didn't play a full four weeks. Further, Lili St. Cyr's *The Wonderful Days of Burlesque* played the summer stock circuit in 1967, but never ventured into New York.

Despite a certain "tinseled opulence in the production numbers," Lewis Funke in the *New York Times* found *International Playgirls '64* "dreadful," "dismal," and "flat." He noted that Allen Drake endured "flopsweat" despite "working heroically," that the girls did some "so-called" stripping, and that Georgia Sothern was "hardly the Sothern of memory."

International Playgirls '64 offered not one, but two, single-named performers: Morocco and Bhaskar (the latter as the production's choreographer). Second-billed John Conte had created leading roles on Broadway in *Allegro* (1947) and *Arms and the Girl* (1950).

773 **Ionescopade.** "A Vaudeville Musical Entertainment Taken from the Works of Eugene Ionesco." THEATRE: Theatre Four; OPENING DATE: April 25, 1974; PERFORMANCES: 14; LYRICS: Mildred Kayden; MUSIC: Mildred Kayden; DIRECTION: Robert Allan Ackerman; CHOREOGRAPHY: Merry Lynn Katis; SCENERY: David Sackeroff; COSTUMES: Patricia Adshead; LIGHTING: David Sackeroff; MUSICAL DIRECTION: Ed Linderman; PRODUCERS: Kermit Bloomgarden and Roger Ailes

CAST—Joseph Abaldo, Gary Beach, Jerry Beal, Veronica Castang, Richard Crook, Connie Danese, Marion McCorry, Bob Morrisey, Stephanie Satie, Howard L. Sponseller, Jr.

SOURCE—Various plays, journals, and other writings by Eugene Ionesco (1912-1994).

The revue was presented in two acts.

ACT ONE—Ionescopade Overture (Joseph Abaldo), "Salutations" (adapted from first scene of an uncompleted play; includes characters from other Ionesco plays) (Howard L. Sponseller, Jr., Stephanie Satie, Veronica Castang, Marion McCorry, Bob Morrisey, Connie Danese), "The Two Robertas" (lyric adapated from Roberta Two's seduction speech in *Jack, or The Submission*) (Marion McCorry, Connie Danese), "Surprising People" (adapted from various conversations in the plays *The Killer* and *Rhinoceros*) (Gary Beach, Bob Morrisey), "Maid to Marry" (a full-length play, performed in its entirety) (Jerry Beal, Stephanie Satie, Veronica Castang, Richard Crook, Howard L. Sponseller, Jr.), "Fire" (adapted from poem of the same name in play *The Bald Soprano*) (Marion McCorry), "Madeleine" (adapted from a passage in Ionesco's journals) (Gary Beach), "The Cooking Lesson" (adapted from sketch originally presented in Paris in 1967) (Richard Crook), "Mother Peep" (adapted from a character in *The Killer*) (Jerry Beal, Stephanie Satie, Connie Danese, Gary Beach, Bob Morrisey), "The Leader" (a full-length play, performed in its entirety) (Howard L. Sponseller, Jr., Stephanie Satie, Jerry Beal, Bob Morrisey, Marion McCorry, Richard Crook)

ACT TWO—"Cirque-O-Pade" (Company), "The Auto Salon" (a full-length play, performed in its entirety) (Joseph Abaldo, Jerry Beal, Stephanie Satie, Connie Danese, Gary Beach, Richard Crook), "Josette" (adapted from passages in Ionesco's journals) (Gary Beach), "Bobby Watson and the Family" (these characters are referred to, but not seen, in *The Bald Soprano*) (Bob Morrisey, Howard Sponseller, Veronica Castang, Stephanie Satie, Richard Crook, Marion McCorry):, "In Time" (adapted from *Ionesco's Fragments of a Journal* and *Present Past Past Present*) (Bob Morrisey, Howard Sponseller, Veronica Castang, Stephanie Satie, Richard Crook, Marion McCorry), "Ginger Wildcat" (adapted from a passage in play *Exit the King*) (Stephanie Satie), "The Saga of the Prima Ballerina" (adapted from *Ionesco's Fragments of a Journal* and *Present Past Past Present* (Marion McCorry), "Cap-Pitulation" (Bob Morrisey, Howard Sponseller, Veronica Castang, Stephanie Satie, Richard Crook, Marion McCorry), "The Peace Conference" (source unknown) (Connie Danese, Gary Beach, Howard L. Sponseller, Jr., Jerry Beal, Richard Crook, Marion McCorrey), "Knocks" (taken from an idea suggested in Ionesco's journals) (Bob Morrisey, Connie Danese), "Flying" (adapted from *The Killer*) (Gary Beach), "Wipe Out Games" (opening scene of play *Jeux de Massacre*) (Company), Finale (Company)

NOTES—Conceived and directed by Robert Allan Ackerman, the revue *Ionescopade* consisted of short playlets and songs which were inspired by and adapted from the plays and journals of Eugene Ionesco. Mildred Kayden was credited with lyrics and music, and she may have also adapted some of the non-musical portions of the evening.

Ionesco's plays had never been particularly successful in New York (even the 1961 production of *Rhinoceros*, which starred Zero Mostel and played on Broadway for 240 performances, lost money), and so a musical revue of his writings faced an uphill battle. *Ionescopade* lost the battle after fourteen performances. Although Mel Gussow in the *New York Times* wasn't overwhelmed by the evening (more a "grab bag" than a "romp"), he nonetheless praised the cast and Kayden's "tinkling toy-soldier of a score."

"The Peace Conference" may have been performed only in previews.

The revue had first been produced Off Off Broadway by the New Repertory Company in January 1973, and then later by the same company for a run beginning on July 26, 1973.

In late 1974, another Ionesco-inspired musical failed (see entry for *How to Get Rid of It*).

774 Iphigenia in Concert.
NOTES—See entry for *The Wedding of Iphigenia* and *Iphigenia in Concert.*

775 The Irish...And How They Got That Way. THEATRE: The Irish Repertory Theatre; transferred to the Chelsea Playhouse on November 20, 1997; OPENING DATE: October 2, 1997; PERFORMANCES: 98; TEXT: Frank McCourt; LYRICS: See song list for credits; MUSIC: See song list for credits; DIRECTION: Charlotte Moore; CHOREOGRAPHY: Alexia Hess Sheehan; SCENERY: Shawn Lewis; COSTUMES: David Toser; LIGHTING: Daniel L. Walker; MUSICAL DIRECTION: Rusty Magee; PRODUCER: The Irish Repertory Theatre (Charlotte Moore, Artistic Director; Ciaran O'Reilly, Producing Director)

CAST—Terry Donnelly, Bob Green, Marian Tomas Griffin, Ciaran O'Reilly, Ciaran Sheehan

The revue was presented in two acts.

ACT ONE—"Look to the Rainbow" (from *Finian's Rainbow*, 1947; lyric by E.Y. Harburg, music by Burton Lane) (performer[s] unknown), "Those Endearing Young Charms" (lyric and music by Thomas Moore) (Ciaran Sheehan), "Holy Ground" (traditional) (Ciaran O'Reilly), "Galway Bay" (lyric and music by Arthur Colohan) (Marian Tomas Griffin), "Carrickfergus" (traditional) (Terry Donnelly), "I'll Take You Home Again, Kathleen" (lyric and music by T.P. Westendorf) (Ciaran Sheehan), "The Rose of Tralee" (lyric by C.M. Spencer, music by Charles W. Glover) (Marian Tomas Griffin), "Too-Ra-Loo-Ra-Loo-Ra" (lyric and music by J.R. Shannon) (Rusty Magee), "Come Back, Paddy Reilly" (lyric and music by Percy French) (Ensemble), "Mother Machree" (lyric by R.J. Young, music by Chauncey Olcott and E.R. Ball) (Rusty Magee), "Mrs. McGrath" (traditional) (Ciaran O'Reilly, Ensemble), "The Rare Old Times" (lyric and music by Pete St. John) (Ciaran Sheehan, Ensemble), "Fields of Athenry" (lyric and music by Pete St. John) (Marian Tomas Griffin, Ensemble), "Skibbereen" (traditional) (Ciaran Sheehan), "Shores of Amerikay" (traditional) (Ensemble), "The Anchor's Aweigh" (traditional) (Ciaran Sheehan, Marian Tomas Griffin), "No Irish Need Apply" (traditional) (Ensemble), "The Irish Washerwoman" (lyric by Charles Hansen, music by Jeremiah Duggan) (Terry Donnelly, Marian Tomas Griffin), "Erie Canal" (traditional) (Ensemble)

ACT TWO—"Give My Regards to Broadway" (*Little Johnny Jones*, 1904; lyric and music by George M. Cohan) (Ensemble), "Rings on Her Fingers" (lyric by R.P. Westen and F.J. Barnes, music by Maurice Scott), (Terry Donnelly), "Has Anybody Here Seen Kelly?" (*The Jolly Bachelors*, 1910; lyric by Raymond Hubbell, music by Glen MacDonough; NOTE: the cast album credited this song to C.W. Murphy, Will Letters, John Charles Moore, and William J. McKenna) (Marian Tomas Griffin), "Moonshiner" (traditional) (Maria Tomas Griffin, Rusty Magee), "Danny Boy" (traditional music; lyric by Fred E. Weatherby) (Ciaran Sheehan), "Who Threw the Overalls in Mrs. Murphy's Chowder?" (lyric and music by George L. Giefer) (Ciaran Sheehan, Ciaran O'Reilly), "Finnegan's Wake" (traditional) (Terry Donnelly), "Dear Old Ireland" (traditional) (Ensemble), "You're a Grand Old Flag" (*George Washington, Jr.*, 1906; lyric and music by George M. Cohan) (Ensemble), "Over There" (lyric and music by George M. Cohan) (Ensemble), "Yankee Doodle Dandy" (*Little Johnny Jones*, 1904; lyric and music by George M. Cohan) (Rusty Magee), "Johnny, I Hardly Knew Ye" (traditional) (Ensemble), "I Still Haven't Found What I'm Looking For" (lyric by Bono, music by U2), (Ensemble)

NOTES—The liner notes for the cast album of *The Irish ... and How They Got That Way* (released by Varese Sarabande Records [CD # VSD-5916]) noted the evening was "a collection of diaries, letters, newspaper clippings, musings, digressions strung together with song, poetry, lamentation." The revue opened at the Irish Repertory Theatre as an Off Off Broadway presentation, and then later transferred to the Chelsea Playhouse, where it was probably presented under an Off Broadway contract.

On the album, Donna Kane replaced Marian Tomas Griffin. The revue's opening sequence was changed sometime prior to the recording of the album. Instead of "Look to the Rainbow," the opening consisted of "The Butterfly" (uncredited) and "The Musicmakers" (lyric and music by Arthur Shaughnessy).

The Irish Repertory Theatre revived the revue three times (on June 10, 1998, for thirty-two performances; on December 28, 1999, for twenty-eight performances; and on August 28, 2001 [number of performances unknown]).

776 The Island God. Theatre: Metropolitan Opera House; OPENING DATE: February 20, 1942; PERFORMANCES: 4; LIBRETTO: Gian-Carlo Menotti; MUSIC: Gian-Carlo Menotti; DIRECTION: Lothar Wallerstein; SCENERY: Richard Rychtarik; MUSICAL DIRECTION: Ettore Panizza; PRODUCER: The Metropolitan Opera

CAST—Leonard Warren (Ilo), Astrid Varnay (Telea), Raoul Jobin (Luca), Norman Cordon (Greek God), John Carter (Fisherman's Voice)

The action occurs on an island in the Mediterranean.

The opera was performed in one act.

NOTES—The Met's production of Gian-Carlo Menotti's *The Island God* was a world premiere; three other operas by Menotti were also performed at the Met (see entries for *Amelia Goes to the Ball* and *The Last Savage* [for which he wrote both the libretti and the music] and *Vanessa* [for which he wrote the libretto]).

According to the Met's database, the opera had been "composed in Italian" as *Ilo e Zeus* (that is, the libretto had been *written* in Italian). However, the work had never enjoyed a production until its world premiere at the Met (there the original Italian libretto was translated into English by Fleming McLeisch). The database also states that following the Met's production, Menotti "withdrew the title from his catalog and sought to destroy all copies of the score."

According to Oscar Thompson's review in *Musical America*, the opera dealt with two refugees (Ilo and his wife Telea) who come upon the ruins of an ancient temple on an island in the Mediterranean. When Ilo prays to the temple's god, the god returns to his temple and demands that Ilo restore it to its former glory. In the meantime, when Telea falls in love with a local fisherman and runs away with him, Ilo believes his god has abandoned him, but soon discovers the god is actually afraid of him. The god exists because of man, and man exists because of god, and without each other both entities are for all purposes dead. When Ilo smashes the temple's altar, the god destroys him. But in doing so the god also destroys himself. He fades into oblivion because he existed only when a mortal believed in him.

In his review for the *New York Times*, Olin Downes noted that the opera was "inhibited by the essentially unemotional and undramatic nature of an impossible libretto." Downes was also unimpressed by the score, but mentioned that Menotti often wrote in a melodic vein similar to Puccini. He praised a "pleasing ditty" sung by the fisherman ("a barcarolle with a lift") as well as a lovers' duet which was the "musical climax" of the opera, a sequence "written to a text felicitously simple and evocative of image and feeling."

The one-act opera was produced on a double bill with a revival of Ruggiero Leoncavallo's *Pagliacci* (1892); Licia Albanese was Nedda.

777 It Ain't Nothin' But the Blues. "A New Musical." THEATRE: New Victory Theatre; OPENING DATE: March 26, 1999; PERFORMANCES: 16; DIALOGUE: Charles Bevel, Lita Gaithers, Randal Myler, Ron Taylor, and Dan Wheetman; LYRICS: See song list for credits; MUSIC: See song list for credits; DIRECTION: Randal Myler; CHOREOGRAPHY: Donald McKayle; SCENERY: Robin Sanford Roberts; COSTUMES: Dione H. LebHar; LIGHTING: Don Darnutzer; MUSICAL DIRECTION: Dan Wheetman; PRODUCERS: The New 42nd Street Inc. (Cora Cahan, President); a Crossroads Theatre Company production (Ricardo Kahn, Artistic Director) in association with San Diego Repertory Theatre (Sam Woodhouse, Artistic Director) and Alabama Shakespeare Theatre Festival (Kent Thompson, Artistic Director)

CAST—Charles Bevel, Gretha Boston, Carter Calvert, Eloise Laws, Gregory Porter, Ron Taylor, Dan Wheetman

The revue was presented in two acts.

ACT ONE—"Odun De" (traditional) (Company), "Niwah Wechi" (traditional) (Eloise Laws, Company), "Blood Done Signed My Name" (traditional) (Ron Taylor, Gretha Boston), "Raise Them Up Higher" (traditional) (Charles Bevel), "Danger Blues" (traditional) (Eloise Laws), "Black Woman" (traditional) (Gregory Porter), "I'm Gonna Do What the Spirit Say Do" (traditional) (Gretha Boston), "I've Been Living with the Blues" (lyric and music by Sonny Terry) (Company), "Blues Man" (lyric and music by Z.Z. Hill) (Ron Taylor), "My Home's Across the Blue Ridge Mountains" (traditional) (Carter Calvert), "'T' for Texas" (lyric and music by Jimmie Rogers) (Dan Wheetman), "Who Broke the Lock?" (traditional) (Gregory Porter, Charles Bevel), "Gabrielle" (lyric and music by Dan Wheetman) (Dan Wheetman, Ron Taylor), "Goin' to Louisanne" (lyric and music by Ron Taylor) (Ron Taylor), "My Man Rocks Me" (traditional) (Eloise Laws), "St. Louis Blues" (lyric and music by W.C. Handy) (Gretha Boston), "Now I'm Gonna Be Bad" (lyric and music by Dan Wheetman) (Carter Calvert), "Walkin' Blues" (lyric and music by Robert L. Johnson) (Charles Bevel), "Come On in My Kitchen" (lyric and music by Robert L. Johnson) (Gregory Porter), "Crossroad Blues" (lyric and music by Robert L. Johnson) (Charles Bevel), "Children, Your Line Is Dragging" (traditional; arranged by Fisher Thompson, Sr.) (Gregory Porter), "How Can I Keep from Singing" (traditional) (Carter Calvert), "I Know I've Been Changed" (traditional) (Gretha Boston), "Go Tell It on the Mountain" (traditional) (Eloise Laws), "Child of the Most High King" (traditional; arranged by Ron Taylor) (Ron Taylor, with Charles Bevel, Gregory Porter, and Dan Wheetman), "Catch on Fire" (traditional; arranged by Lita Gaithers) (Company)

ACT TWO—"Let the Good Times Roll" (lyric and music by F. Moore and S. Theard) (Ron Taylor), "Sweet Home Chicago" (lyric and music by Robert L. Johnson) (Gregory Porter, Charles Bevel), "Wang Dang Doodle" (lyric and music by Willie Dixon) (Gretha Boston, Carter Calvert, Eloise Laws), "Someone Else Is Steppin' In" (lyric and music by Denise LaSalle) (Eloise Laws), "Please Don't Stop Him"/Blues Medley (lyrics and music by Herb J. Lance and John Wallace; additional lyrics and arrangements by Lita Gaithers) (Gretha Boston), "I'm Your Hoochie Coochie Man" (lyric and music by Willie Dixon; arranged by Ron Taylor) (Ron Taylor), "Crawlin' King Snake" (lyric and music by John Lee Hooker) (Gregory Porter), "Mind Your Own Business" (lyric and music by Hank Williams, Sr.) (Dan Wheetman), "Walking After Midnight" (lyric and music by Don Hect and Alan Block) (Carter Calvert), "I Can't Stop Lovin' You" (lyric and music by Don Gibson) (Charles Bevel), "The Thrill Is Gone" (lyric and music by Roy Hawkins and Rick Darnell) (Ron Taylor), "I Put a Spell on You" (lyric and music by Jay Hawkins) (Eloise Laws), "Fever" (lyric and music by John Davenport and Eddie Cooley) (Carter Calvert), "Candy Man" (traditional) (Dan Wheetman), "Good Night, Irene" (lyric and music by Huddie Ledbetter) (Charles Bevel, Dan Wheetman), "Strange Fruit" (lyric and music by Lewis Allan) (Gretha Boston), "Someday We'll All Be Free" (lyric and music by Donny Hathaway and Edward Howard; arranged by Charles Bevel) (Charles Bevel, Gregory Porter), "Members Only" (lyric and music by Larry Addison) (Company), "Let the Good Times Roll" (reprise/finale) (Company)

NOTES—Originally produced by the Denver Center Theatre Company, the revue *It Ain't Nothin' But the Blues* was a collection of mostly blues numbers, and perhaps suffered from being too similar in style to other revues before it. After its two-week run Off Broadway, the revue transferred to the Vivian Beaumont Theatre on April 24, 1999 (and then later to the Ambassador Theatre). In reviewing the production when it transferred to the Beaumont, John Simon in *New York* concluded that the first three words of the title summed up the quality of the evening, and added that comparisons to the "wonderful" *Ain't Misbehavin'* (see entry) were "absurd." Simon noted that some (White) members of the audience clapped "like crazy" after each song, "whooping like unhinged cranes" and "shouting out 'Oh, yeah!' to prove" they "possessed soul." The revue, which somehow managed to get nominated by the Tony Nominating Committee for Best Book of a Musical, played for a total of 276 performances. The Broadway cast recording was released by MCA Records (CD # 088-112-150-2), and the script was published by Samuel French, Inc., in 2002. On August 20, 2000, the revue opened Off Off Broadway in a revised one-act version at B.B. King Blues Club for thirty-seven performances.

778 The IT Girl. THEATRE: The Theatre at Saint Peter's Church/The York Theatre Company; OPENING DATE: May 3, 2001; PERFORMANCES: 29; BOOK: Michael Small and BT McNicholl; LYRICS: BT McNicholl; MUSIC: Paul McKibbins; DIRECTION: BT McNicholl; CHOREOGRAPHY: Robert Bianca; SCENERY: Mark Nayden; Elaine J. McCarthy, Projections; COSTUMES: Robin L McGee; LIGHTING: Jeff Nellis; MUSICAL DIRECTION: Albin Konopka; PRODUCERS: The York Theatre Company (James Morgan, Artistic Director) in association with It Girl Productions, LLC

CAST—Jean Louisa Kelly (Betty Lou Spencer), Monte Wheeler (Mr. Notting, Barker, Reporter, Sailor, Trevor Pitstop), Danette Holden (Jane, Mrs. Sullivan, Mrs. Van Norman, Snake Charmer), Susan M. Haefner (Daisy, Molly, Hootchie-Kootchie), Jonathan Dokuchitz (Dancer, Brearley Chapin, Jonathan Waltham), Stephen DeRosa (Monty Montgomery), Jessica Boevers (Adela Van Norman)

SOURCE—The Paramount 1927 silent film *It* (directed by Clarence Badger), which was based on Elinor Glyn's short story "It."

The action occurs in New York City in the late 1920s.

The musical was presented in two acts.

ACT ONE—"Black and White World" (Jean Louisa Kelly, Company), "Why Not?" (Jean Louisa Kelly, Girls), "Stand Straight and Tall" (Jonathan Dokuchitz), "It" (Stephen DeRosa, Company), "Mama's Arms" (Susan M. Haefner), "What to Wear?" (Jean Louisa Kelly, Susan M. Haefner, Jessica Boevers, Danette Holden, Jonathan Dokuchitz, Stephen DeRosa), "It" (reprise) (Jonathan Dokuchitz), "A Perfect Plan" (Jessica Boevers), "Coney Island" (Jean Louisa Kelly, Jonathan Dokuchitz, Company), Act One Finale (Jessica Boevers, Company)

ACT TWO—"Woman and Waif" (Company), "Stay with Me"/"Left-Hand Arrangement" (Jonathan Dokuchitz, Jean Louisa Kelly), "Step Into Their Shoes" (Susan M. Haefner, Jean Louisa Kelly, Stephen DeRosa), "Out at Sea" (Company), "How Do You Say?" (Jean Louisa Kelly, Company), "Step Into Their Shoes" (reprise) (Jean Louisa Kelly), "You're the Best Thing That Ever Happened to Me" (Jean Louisa Kelly, Jonathan Dokuchitz), Finale (Company)

NOTES—Based on the iconic silent film *It* (which starred Clara Bow), the musical *The IT Girl* told the familiar Cinderella-like story of the shop girl who ends up marrying the boss. With its amusing book and delightful score, the musical seemed poised to transfer to a larger Off Broadway theatre or even to Broadway, but, curiously, it disappeared after its short run at the York. But the publication of the script by Samuel French, Inc., in 2004 and the release of the cast recording by Jay Records (CD # CDJAY-1365) should give the musical a long life in regional and community theatre. In reviewing the production for the *New York Times*, Bruce Weber noted the "perky" musical offered a "sprightly, savvy score" and bright performances. But he found the second act considerably weaker than the first and some of the one-liners "strikingly dull," and so suggested the musical might need "one more run through the typewriter."

The musical was first produced at the Blowing Rock Stage Company in Blowing Rock, North Carolina.

779 The Italian Straw Hat. THEATRE: Fourth Street Theatre; OPENING DATE: September 30, 1957; PERFORMANCES: 8; BOOK: Richard G. Mason and Regina Wojak; LYRICS: Mitchell Parish; MUSIC: Jacques Ibert; DIRECTION: David Ross; CHOREOGRAPHY: Ellida Geyra; SCENERY: Richard G. Mason; COSTUMES: Possibly by Richard G. Mason; MUSICAL DIRECTION: Zenon Fisdbein; PRODUCER: David Ross

CAST—Jacqueline Reed (Virginie), Robert Morea (Felix), Harrison Dowd (Vezinet), Larry Blyden (Fadinard), Carol Guilford (Anais), Gerald Price (Emile), Russell Gaige (Nonacourt), Zahra Norbo (Helene), Milton Zucker (Bobin), Virginia Hart (Clara), Gabrielle Mason (Tardoveau), Dorothy Kurilla (First Bridesmaid), Lois Robinson (Second Bridesmaid), Peter Benzoni (Achille), Elizabeth Watts (Baronesse), Lore Noto (Servant, Corporal), Mary Engel (First Guest), Babette New (Second Guest), Dorothy Dickinson (Chambermaid), Albert M. Ottenheimer (Beauperthuis), John Flood (Guard)

SOURCE—The play *Le Chapeau de Paille D'Italie* by Eugene Libiche and Marc-Michel.

MUSICAL NUMBERS—(division of acts and song assignments unknown; songs are listed in alphabetical order) "Do You Retreat?," "Gallop," "Happy Day," "I Have a Single Track Mind," "I Knew a Girl in Barcelona," "Is He Nisardi?," "It's Matrimonial Weather," "Parade," "Tho' I Had Never Meant to Tell You"

NOTES—The lyricist for *The Italian Straw Hat* was Mitchell Parish, who wrote the lyrics for many standards, including the ultimate standard, "Stardust," often cited as the most popular and most recorded ballad in the American songbook.

Note two of the musical's cast members: Lore Noto, who would go on to produce *The Fantasticks* (see entry), and Larry Blyden, a comic actor with a delightful flair for eccentric humor. Blyden later appeared in such Broadway musicals as *Flower Drum Song* (1958), *Foxy* (1964), and *The Apple Tree* (1966) as well as the Broadway comedy *Absurd Person Singular* (1974). His career was cut tragically short in 1975, when he died of injuries suffered in an automobile accident while vacationing in Europe. Although Brooks Atkinson in the *New York Times* dismissed *The Italian Straw Hat*, he praised Blyden, who "manages to suggest some sort of theatrical logic in the midst of bedlam" (the plot dealt with a bridegroom's efforts to replace his bride's straw hat, which unfortunately has been eaten by a horse).

The Italian Straw Hat would be adapted again as an Off Broadway musical when it surfaced as *That Hat!* in 1964 (see entry.) The second version of the material was an even bigger failure than the first, closing on its opening night. The work was also the basis for the 1977 opera *Il Cappello de Paglia di Firenze (The Florentine Straw Hat)* composed by film composer Nino Rota (a 2-CD set was released by BMG Records [# 74321551092]).

A new version of the classic play has been announced for production in 2009 by the Shakespeare Theatre Company in Washington, D.C. This version will be presented in a new adaptation by John Strand, with songs by Dennis McCarthy.

780 It's a Jungle Out There! THEATRE: The 78th Street Theatre Lab; OPENING DATE: December 1982; PERFORMANCES: 8 (estimated); BOOK: Michael Zettler and Shelly Altman; LYRICS: Oscar Brand; MUSIC: Oscar Brand; DIRECTION: Penelope Hirsch; SCENERY: Bill Stabile; COSTUMES: Bill Stabile (?); MUSICAL DIRECTION: Jonathan L. Segal; PRODUCER: Farr Productions

CAST—OSCAR BRAND (Oscar), Robert Ross (Dean Cash), Marnie Andrews (Monica Money), Kay Harper (Donna DeNiro)

The musical was presented in one act (song assignments weren't listed in the program; all lyrics and music were by Oscar Brand, with the exception of additional song-writing credits noted below).

MUSICAL NUMBERS—"Long Time Travelling" (a/k/a "Longtime Travelin'") (lyric and music by Oscar Brand and Paul Nassau), "The College of Reality and Pragmatism," "The Money Rolls In," "Remember the Horse," "The Joy of My Desiring" (music also by Johann Sebastian Bach), "Wonderful Country," "Everybody Talking 'Bout Heaven," "How to Steal an Election" "Get a Dog," "It's a Jungle Out There," "Where Do You Go," "Surgery," "Deductions" (music by Jerry Bock; based on original lyric by Sheldon Harnick), "Touch the Earth," "The Preppy Song," "The Game of the Name" (lyric by Shelly Altman), "Long Time Travelling" (reprise)

NOTES—The program for *It's a Jungle Out There!* indicated that Oscar Brand's Off Off Broadway revue was "satire & cabaret. It's nightclub with a twist. It's a BRAND new show."

The material included "Longtime Travelin'" from Brand's Broadway musical *A Joyful Noise* (1966) and the title song from his Off Broadway musical *How to Steal an Election* (1967; see entry).

781 It's Better with a Band. "A New Musical Revue." THEATRE: The Club Room at Sardi's; OPENING DATE: March 28, 1983; PERFORMANCES: 47; LYRICS: David Zippel; MUSIC: See song list for credits; DIRECTION: Joseph Leonardo; SCENERY: Michael J. Hotopp and Paul de Pass; COSTUMES: Cinthia Waas; LIGHTING: John Hastings; MUSICAL DIRECTION: Rob LaRocco; PRODUCER: Roger Alan Gindi, Executive Producer; Joseph Hartney, Associate Producer

CAST—Scott Bakula, Catherine Cox, Nancy LaMott, Jenifer Lewis

The revue was presented in one act.

MUSICAL NUMBERS—"It's Better with a Band" (music by Wally Harper) (Company), "The Camel Song" (music by Doug Katsaros) (Jenifer Lewis), "You'll Never See Me Run" (music by Alan Menken) (Scott Bakula), "Loud Is Good" (music by Jonathan Sheffer) (Nancy LaMott), "The Ingenue" (music by Wally Harper) (Catherine Cox), "What I Like Is You" (music by Pamala Stanley) (Catherine Cox, Nancy LaMott, Jenifer Lewis), "God's Gift" (music by Rob LaRocco) (Scott Bakula), "Why Don't We Run Away" (music by Byron Sommers) (Nancy LaMott), "Make Me a Star" (music by Bryon Sommers)/Movie Queen (music by Pamala Stanley) (Jenifer Lewis, Company), "Lullaby" (music by Doug Katsaros) (Scott Bakula), "I Can't Remember Living Without Loving You" (music by Wally Harper) (Catherine Cox), "Horsin' Around" (music by Jimmy Roberts) (Nancy LaMott), "Forget It" (music by Rob LaRocco) (Catherine Cox, Nancy LaMott, Jenifer Lewis), "I Reach for a Star" (music by Jonathan Sheffer) (Scott Bakula), "Time on Our Side" (music by Bryon Sommers) (Jenifer Lewis), "Life's Ambition" (music by Wally Harper) (Catherine Cox), "Another Mr. Right" (music by Jonathan Sheffer) (Nancy LaMott), "A Song for Myself" (music by Pamala Stanley) (Company)

NOTES—*It's Better with a Band* was a tribute-revue to David Zippel; a talented lyricist, it was often his misfortune to be associated with projects which were either short-lived or never got produced (with the exception of *City of Angels*, the long-running and award-winning Broadway musical with music by Cy Coleman). *It's Better with a Band* didn't make any waves, closing after just six weeks; in the words of cast member Catherine Cox, "It's better with an audience."

"The Camel Song" (a/k/a "The Camel's Blues") and "Lullaby" were from *Just So*, a musical adaptation of Rudyard Kipling's *Just So Stories*. The musical was eventually produced Off-Broadway for six performances in 1985 (see entry). "I Reach for a Star" and the blazing torch song "Another Mr. Right" were written for the still-unproduced *Going Hollywood*, an adaptation of George S. Kaufman and Moss Hart's *Once in a Lifetime* (1930); see entry for information about the production's workshop performance.

Barbara Cook has recorded "It's Better with a Band," "The Ingenue," and "Another Mr. Right."

782 It's Hard to Be a Jew (1983; Alexander Yampolsky). THEATRE: Folksbiene Playhouse; OPENING DATE: October 22, 1983; PERFORMANCES: 61; BOOK: Israel Beker; LYRICS: Israel Beker; MUSIC: Alexander Yampolsky; DIRECTION: Israel Beker; SCENERY: J. Ben-Miriam Costumes: Kulyk Costumes; LIGHTING: Paul McDonach; MUSICAL DIRECTION: Zalmen Mlotek; PRODUCER: The Folksbiene Playhouse (Ben Schechter, Manager; Morris Adler, Chairman)

CAST—I.W. Firestone (Shneyerson, Hersh Movshovitz), Alexander Sirotin (Ivanov, Ivan Ivanovich), Ibi Kaufman (Betty), Paula Teitelbaum (Siomke), Jack Rechtzeit (Ketzele), Zypora Spaisman (Sarah), Leon Liebgold (David), Jacob Gostinsky (Makar), Yosef Toomim (Rabbi), Jacques Brawer (Policeman)

SOURCE—The 1920 play *Hard to Be a Jew* by Sholom Aleichem.

NOTES—The Off Off Broadway musical *It's Hard to Be a Jew* was the second adaptation of Aleichem's classic Yiddish play (see entry for the 1973 Off Broadway version [*Hard to Be a Jew*]). During the 1983-1984 season, another version of Aleichem's story was produced Off Off Broadway, this time as a non-musical (Isaiah Sheffer's adaptation opened at the American Jewish Theatre on February 11, 1984, and played there for forty performances).

783 It's Lynne Carter. THEATRE: Carnegie Hall; OPENING DATE: January 20, 1971; PERFORMANCES: 1; SPECIAL MATERIAL: Fred Ebb, John Kander, Bob Lees, Dickson Hughes, Franklyn Underwood, and Lynne Carter; DIRECTION: Lynne Carter (?); "additional staging" by Jim Hoskins; COSTUMES: Mr. Bruno of New York; LIGHTING: Paul Sullivan; MUSICAL DIRECTION: Dickson Hughes; PRODUCER: Michael E. Fesco

CAST—Lynne Carter

The revue was presented in two acts.

ACT ONE—"Gorgeous," "Disney for Adults," "A Freak-Out in Feathers," "I Didn't Raise My Girl to Be a Bunny," "The Torch Song," "The Star Spot"

ACT TWO—Famous Dietrich Medley, "Shaking My Can in Front of Carnegie Hall," "Bette Davis," "Miss Pearl Bailey," "The Final Curtain"

NOTES—Lynne Carter's one-man show of female impersonations was presented for one evening only at Carnegie Hall. For another Lynne Carter revue, see entry for *Fun City* (1968; not to be confused with the 1972 Broadway comedy of the same name, which was co-written by Joan Rivers, who also starred).

784 It's Me, Sylvia! "Lived, Written and Even Sung by the Above." THEATRE: Playhouse II; OPENING DATE: April 13, 1981; PERFORMANCES: 9; BOOK: Sylvia Miles; LYRICS: Sylvia Miles; MUSIC: Galt MacDermot; DIRECTION: Arthur Sherman; SCENERY: Eugene Lee; COSTUMES: Clifford Capone; LIGHTING: Roger Morgan; MUSICAL DIRECTION: Galt MacDermot; PRODUCERS: Steven A. Greenberg; Jeffrey Madrick, Executive Producer; Liska March, Associate Producer

CAST—SYLVIA MILES

The action occurs in Sylvia Miles' apartment from Fall 1979 through the Spring 1980, "then and now."

The revue was presented in one act.

NOTES—No songs were listed in the program for *It's Me, Sylvia!*; the songs in the production were: "Please Find Me (I Really Need You to See Me Through)," "I Believe in Me," "I'm Your Space Angel," "River of Change," "I've Got to Do What I Want Today," "All I Need Is Me (I Need Me, Babe)," "This Time," "There's A Room for Me," "I'm Desperate for Your Love," "I Can't Hide My Grief No More," and "I Have Born So Much Pain."

The revue of Sylvia Miles' life and times took place in her apartment; the setting, according to the program notes, was "a genuine facsimile of the real thing, located high above Central Park and crammed full of the memorabilia and eclecticism of a unique personality."

Mel Gussow in the *New York Times* found the evening a "dreary exercise in self-exposure" accompanied by a score of "unmitigated blandness" (he suggested that Galt MacDermot "phoned it in from Staten Island"). As for Miles herself, Gussow was unimpressed with her performance, but noted at one point she waved a magic wand and thus "made several theatergoers disappear."

Despite the poor reviews and the short run of her musical, Sylvia Miles remains legendary for 1) her Oscar-nominated performance in *Midnight Cowboy* (1969), in which she memorably told Jon Voight what the Statue of Liberty was up to in Central Park; 2) her contretemps with critic John Simon (after receiving a negative review from him, she unloaded a plateful of dinner on his head at an affair they both happened to be attending); and 3) her uncanny ability to show up at almost every "in" New York event, from theatre first-nighting to restaurant- and club- openings. Hail to Sylvia, truly one of a kind!

(In regard to the memorable meeting between Sylvia Miles and John Simon, it seems to be a case of life imitating art. In the 1960 film *Please Don't Eat the Daisies* [which was based on Jean Kerr's book of humorous essays], drama critic Larry MacKay [played by David Niven] is eating in a Sardi's-like restaurant when actress Deborah Vaughn [Janis Paige] confronts him about a negative review he wrote about her; but instead of dumping a plateful of food on him, she instead slaps him [twice]).

785 It's So Nice to Be Civilized. THEATRE: AMAS Repertory Theatre; OPENING DATE: February 22, 1979; PERFORMANCES: 12; BOOK: Micki Grant; LYRICS: Micki Grant; MUSIC: Micki Grant; DIRECTION: Jeffrey Dunn; CHOREOGRAPHY: Fred Benjamin; SCENERY: Patrick Mann; COSTUMES: Bill Baldwin; LIGHTING: Paul Sullivan; MUSICAL DIRECTION: William "Gregg" Hunter; PRODUCER: AMAS Repertory Theatre (Rosetta LeNoire, Founder and Artistic Director)

CAST—Charles Berry, Karen G. Burke, David Cahn, Claudine Cassan, Jean Cheek, Kevin DeVoe, Eugene Edwards, Joey Ginza, Dwayne Grayman, Paul Harman, Sundy Leake, Carol Lynn Maillard, Brenda Mitchell, Ennis Smith, Cassie Stein, Diane Wilson

The action occurs over a weekend in late summer on Sweetbitter Street.

The musical was presented in two acts (song assignments unknown).

ACT ONE—"Step Into My World," "Wake Up, Sun," "Subway Rider," "God Help Us," "Who's Gonna Teach the Children?," "Out On the Street," "Welcome, Mr. Anderson," "Why Can't Me and You?," "When I Rise," "Up Front Behind," "Walkin' the Dog," "I Want to Be Your Congressman," "Everybody's Got a Pitch," "Terrible Tuesday," "Come Back, Baby," "Alice," "It's So Nice to Be Civilized," "The World Keeps Going Round"

ACT TWO—"Talking to People," "Old Things," "I've Still Got My Bite," "Look at Us," "Jub-Jub," "Bright Lights," "Like a Lady," "Me and Jesus," "Pass a Little Love Around"

NOTES—After its Off Off Broadway run in a showcase production at the AMAS Repertory Theatre, the revue-like musical *It's So Nice to Be Civilized* was produced on Broadway a little over a year later, opening at the Martin Beck (now the Al Hirschfeld) Theatre on June 3, 1980, and playing for eight performances.

The musical had no real plot, and was instead a collection of mild vignettes about various types living in an urban neighborhood. Reviewing the Broadway production in the *New York Times*, Mel Gussow praised Micki Grant as "a cheerful and convivial composer. Her songs are melodic representations of the winking sunburst that adorns the program." The Broadway critics were also impressed with Vivian Reed and Mabel King's performances. The Broadway production added three numbers ("Keep Your Eye on the Red," "Antiquity," and "The American Dream") and omitted seven which had been heard in the showcase version ("Up Front Behind," "Walkin' the Dog," "I Want to Be Your Congressman," "Everybody's Got a Pitch," "Come Back, Baby," "Talking to People," and "Old Things").

The musical's opening number, "Step Into My World," was later used as the title for a 1989 AMAS retrospective revue of Micki Grant's songs (see entry for *Step Into My World*).

786 It's Wilde! "A New Musical." THEATRE: Theatre East; OPENING DATE: May 21, 1980; PERFORMANCES: 7; BOOK: Burton Wolfe; LYRICS: Burton Wolfe; MUSIC: Randy Klein; DIRECTION: Burton Wolfe; CHOREOGRAPHY: Buck Heller; SCENERY: John Falabella; COSTUMES: James Corry; LIGHTING: Frances Aronson; PRODUCERS: Stages Theatrical Productions Ltd. (Herbert Acevedo, Executive Producer)

CAST—Ross Petty (Wilde), Allan Stevens (Carson), Betsy Jamison (Constance), Peter Toran (Bosie), Carol Cass (Spectator)

The action occurs in "a timeless place" as well as in a courtroom, a prison, and in Wilde's home.

The musical was presented in two acts.

ACT ONE—"Times Divine" (Company), "Two Should Be Harmonious" (Ross Petty, Betsy Jamison, Allan Stevens, Carol Cass), "I Need One Man" (Betsy Jamison), "Masses of Masses" (Company, Ross Petty), "Exquisite Passions" (Ross Petty), "Jail-House Blues" (Company), "It's Wilde!" (Company, Ross Petty), "Our Special Love" (Ross Petty, Peter Toran), "Society Means Propriety" (Allan Stevens, Ross Petty, Peter Toran, Betsy Jamison), "Poor Teddy Bear" (Company), Medley (Company), "All the Flowers Turn to Snow" (Ross Petty)

ACT TWO—"We're Back" (Company), "Reach for the Sky!" (Ross Petty), "Get Thee to Bed" (Allan Stevens, Betsy Jamison, Peter Toran, Ross Petty), "Hot Chocolate and Marshmallow" (Carol Cass), "Rape Me" (Betsy Jamison, Allan Stevens), "Love Please Stay" (Betsy Jamison), "What Do I Believe In" (Allan Stevens), "Our Special Love" (reprise) (Ross Petty, Peter Toran), "You Are My Gold" (Ross Petty, Betsy Jamison, Peter Toran), "Exquisite Passions" (reprise) (Company), "It's Wilde!" (reprise) (Company), "Reach for the Sky!" (reprise) (Company)

NOTES—Like 1972's *Dear Oscar*, which was also based on Wilde's life, *It's Wilde!* was a quick flop. Actually, the musical dealt with both Wilde's life and afterlife, and part of the musical was set in heaven, where, according to John Corry in the *New York Times*, everyone wears white outfits and looks like a "convention of vanilla ice-cream sodas." Corry reported that much of the score ran together, and noted he couldn't remember if some of the songs had been performed or not. But he singled out two, "Rape Me" ("funny, despite the title") and "You Are My Gold" ("romantic").

For more information concerning plays and musicals based on Wilde's life, see entry for *Dear Oscar*. Also see entry for *Utterly Wilde!!!*, a one-man musical biography. For musical adaptations of Wilde's work, see entries for *After the Ball* and *A Delightful Season*, both based on *Lady Windermere's Fan*; *Dorian* (which also references *Dorian Gray*, another musical adaptation of the material [both musicals opened within a month of one another in 1990]); *Dorian Gray*, another musical adaptation (which opened in 1996); and *Ernest in Love* (which also references other musical versions of *The Importance of Being Earnest*).

787 I've Got the Tune.
NOTES—See entry for *The Blitzstein Project*.

788 Jack and Jill. THEATRE: Theatre Arielle; OPENING DATE: April 27, 1993; PERFORMANCES: 4; BOOK: Bob Larimer; LYRICS: Bob Larimer; MUSIC: Hal Schaefer; DIRECTION: Miriam Fond; MUSICAL DIRECTION: Wes McAfee; PRODUCER: Thomas Sinclair

CAST—Michael Scott (Jack Miller), Julia Lema (Jill Donovan), John Steber (Brad Donovan), Marilyn J. Johnson (Ruby Donovan), Ennis Smith (Ernie Harris), Raymond Thorne (Ben Miller), Sheila Smith (Ruth Miller)

MUSICAL NUMBERS (division of acts and song assignments unknown; songs are listed in performance order)—"J-a-z-z," "First Time I Heard Ella," "Black and White People," "Woulda Coulda Shoulda," "First Time I Heard Ellington," "A Little Bit," "Old Mom and Pop Lament," "He's Waltzing You Around," "After All," "On Your Own," "In Between Gigs," Finale

NOTES—*Theatre World 1992-1993 Season* described this Off Off Broadway offering as a "jazz musical."

789 The Jack the Ripper Review. "A Dark Musical." THEATRE: Manhattan Punchline; OPENING DATE: September 18, 1979; PERFORMANCES: 21 (estimated); BOOK: Peter Mattaliano; LYRICS: Peter Mattaliano; MUSIC: Stephen Jankowski; DIRECTION: Peter Mattaliano; CHOREOGRAPHY: Janet Watson; SCENERY: Charles McCarry; COSTUMES: Janus Stefanowicz and Susan Trimble; LIGHTING: Robert Heller; MUSICAL DIRECTION: Laurence J. Esposito; PRODUCER: Ripper Productions

CAST—Michael McArthur (Man in Cape), Robin Grean (Polly Nichols), Kathi Moss (Ann Chapman), Carole Monferdini (Liz Stride), Kathrin King Segal (Kate Eddowes), Donna Trinkoff (Mary Kelly), Harold Shepard (the Reverend Barnett), Julie J. Hafner (Queen Victoria), James Seymour (Constable Alfred Meers), William Perley (Commissioner Charles Warren), Timothy Meyers (George Lusk), Ken Bonafons (Mayor-Elect James Whitehead), Christopher Coddington (Duke of Clarence), Charles Bari (Dr. Pedachenko), Robert MacCallum (Warren's Eyewitness), Jim Siatkowski (Montague John Druitt), Jon-Alan Adams (Whitehead's Eyewitness), Mary E. Baird (Jill the Ripper), Ruth Moore and Judy Soto (Barnett's Eyewitnesses)

The action occurs in London, late in the nineteenth century.

The musical was presented in two acts.

ACT ONE—"Overture to the Dance" (Five Women [performers unknown]), "Whitechapel Life" (Company), "The Gin Song" (Robin Grean, The Ladies [performers unknown]), "Annie's Waltz" (Kathi Moss), "The Royal We" (Julie J. Hafner, Ken Bonafons, William Perley, [other performer unknown]), "Rules of the Game" (Carole Monferdini, Kathrin King Segal, Timothy Meyers, Streeters), "The Princess and the Prince" (Carole Montferdini), "The Jack the Ripper Waltz" (Kathrin King Segal), "United Kingdom" (Streeters, Julie J. Hafner, West Enders)

ACT TWO—"Fear's Alive" (Timothy Meyers, Men), "The End of the World" (Donna Trinkoff, James Seymour), "The Suspects Polka" (Accusers, Suspects, Witnesses [Robert MacCullum, Jon-Alan Adams, Ruth Moore, Judy Soto], Victims), "Mary's Song" (Donna Trinkoff), "Survivors" (Company)

NOTES—As *The Jack the Ripper Review*, this Off Off Broadway musical about Jack the Ripper had been first presented at Villanova University in November 1977, and then later at the Manhattan Punchline in two engagements, one in May 1979 and the other on September 18. For a brief period in September and October 1979, New Yorkers could see two musicals about throat-slashing killers in nineteenth-century London (*Sweeney Todd/The Demon Barber of Fleet Street* had opened on Broadway a few months earlier). As *The Jack the Ripper Revue*, the musical was revived Off Off Broadway on February 14, 1991, at the Actor's Outlet.

Other musicals about Jack the Ripper are: *Jack the Ripper*, which opened in London at the Ambassadors Theatre on September 17, 1974, for 228 performances (book and lyrics by Ron Pember and Denis Demarne, and music by Ron Pember); *Jack the Ripper und die Frau Seines Herzens*, which opened in Germany on December 23, 1989 (book, lyrics, and music by Gunther Fischer and Kurt Bartsch); *Jack's Holiday* (see entry), which premiered at Playwrights Horizons on February 10, 1995, for twenty-five performances (book by Mark St. Germain, lyrics by Randy Courts and Mark St. Germain, and music by Randy Courts); and *Yours Truly, Jack the Ripper*, a 2007 regional production seen in Washington, D.C., at the Landless Theatre Company ("narrative" written by David J. Taylor, lyrics and music by Jeremy "Frogg" Moody).

790 The Jackie Wilson Story. THEATRE: Apollo Theatre; OPENING DATE: April 6, 2003; PERFORMANCES: 19; BOOK: Jackie Taylor; LYRICS: Jackie Wilson; MUSIC: Jackie Wilson (additional songs with lyrics and music by Jackie Taylor); DIRECTION: Jackie Taylor; MUSICAL DIRECTION: Jimmy Tillman and Rick Hall; PRODUCERS: Jackie Taylor and Brian Kabatznick in association with the Black Ensemble Touring Company; Douglas Gray, Associate Producer

CAST—Chester Gregory II (Jackie Wilson), Melba Moore (Eliza), Rueben D. Echoles (BB), Katrina Tate (Freda), Mark D. Hayes (Roquel "Billy" Davis), Robert L. Thomas (Carl Davis), Elfeigo N. Goodun III (Father, William Davis), Lyle Miller (Shaker, Sam Cooke, Clyde McPhatter), Tony Duwon (Shaker, Billy Ward, Reporter), Valarie Tekosky (Etta James, Harlene), Eva D. (LaVern Baker, Barbara Acklin)

The revue was presented in two acts (division of acts and song assignments unknown; songs are listed in performance order).

MUSICAL NUMBERS—"My Heart Is Crying," "I Am the Man," "We Are the Shakers," "I Ain't Had Your Woman," "When the Sun Refused to Shine," "You Can't Keep a Good Man Down," "Little-Bitty Pretty One," "Move to the Outskirts of Town,"

"Tweedle Dee," "Reet Petite," "I Can't Help It," "That's Why I Love You So," "To Be Loved," "Tennessee Waltz," "Something's Got a Hold on Me," "Lonely Teardrops," "Shake, Shake, Shake," "Doggin' Me Around," "A Woman, a Lover, a Friend," "Oh, Danny Boy," "Whispers (Getting Louder)," "The Closer I Get," "(Your Love Keeps Lifting Me) Higher and Higher," "To Be Loved" (reprise), Baby Workout, "Nightshift," "(Your Love Keeps Lifting Me) Higher and Higher" (reprise)

NOTES—Bruce Weber in the *New York Times* found the book of *The Jackie Wilson Story* "awkward and full of hokey cliches"; further, the story wasn't dramatized and was instead told via recitation in the manner of a "television-style biography." Moreover, the direction was "rudimentary" and the sets were "high schoolish." But none of this mattered, because the title role was performed by Chester Gregory II, a "unique" performer of "physical and vocal dexterity" who gave an "overflowingly charismatic performance." To add to the joy of the evening, most of the musical numbers were "terrific."

The 2002-2003 Off Broadway season offered a number of revues and musicals which paid tribute to various singers and/or lyricists and composers. Besides *The Jackie Wilson Story*, the season also saw *Hank Williams: Lost Highway* (see entry); *Dream a Little Dream* (The Mamas and the Papas; presented Off Off Broadway; see entry); *Showtune: The Words and Music of Jerry Herman* (see entry for *Tune the Grand Up! Words and Music by Jerry Herman*); *Boobs! The Musical (The World According to Ruth Wallis)* (see entry); a revival of *Jolson & Co.* (see entry for the original 1999 production); and *Dudu Fisher: Something Old, Something New* (see entry).

The limited New York engagement of *The Jackie Wilson Story* was part of a national tour by the Black Ensemble Theatre (based in Chicago).

791 Jack's Holiday. "A New Musical." THEATRE: Playwrights Horizons; OPENING DATE: March 5, 1995; PERFORMANCES: 25; BOOK: Mark St. Germain; LYRICS: Randy Courts; MUSIC: Randy Courts; DIRECTION: Susan H. Schulman; CHOREOGRAPHY: Michael Lichtefeld; SCENERY: Jerome Sirlin; COSTUMES: Catherine Zuber; LIGHTING: Robert Wierzel; MUSICAL DIRECTION: Steve Tyler; PRODUCER: Playwrights Horizons (Don Scardino, Artistic Director; Lynn Landis, General Manager; Leslie Marcus, Managing Director; Tim Sanford, Associate Artistic Director)

CAST—Swan's Players—Lauren Ward (Jennie [The Female Ingenue]), Anne Runolfsson (Sarah [The Actor Manager's Wife]), Herb Foster (Spencer [The Actor Manager]), Alix Korey (Elizabeth [The Leading Lady]), Mark Lotito (John [The Male Ingenue]), Allen Fitzpatrick (Jack [The General Utility Man]), Michael X. Martin (Edward [The Leading Man]); Greg Naughton (Will Bolger), Henry Stram (Snatchem Leese), Michael Mulheren (Humpty Jackson), Lou Williford (Gallus Mag), Nicolas Coster (Max Pierce), Dennis Parlato (Inspector Thomas Byrnes), Mark Lotito (Clubber Williams), Alix Korey (Shakespeare, Mrs. Parkhurst, Molly), Judy Blazer (Mary Healey), Anne Runolfsson (Suzy, Edith), Michael X. Martin (Samuel Shine, the Reverend Billis), Lauren Ward (Servant, Daisy), Herb Foster (the Reverend Parkhurst, Ameer Ben Ali, Sergeant Deehan) The action occurs in New York City in 1891.

The musical was presented in two acts.

ACT ONE—"Changing Faces" (Allen Fitzpatrick, Swan's Players [The Acting Company]), "City of Dreams" (Greg Naughton, Company), "Letter #1" (Allen Fitzpatrick), "Tricks of the Trade" (Nicolas Coster, Alix Korey, Company), "Tricks of the Trade" (reprise) (Michael X. Martin), "Never Time to Dance" (Allen Fitzpatrick, Alix Korey), "Letter #2" (Allen Fitzpatrick), "The Line" (Dennis Parlato, Allen Fitzpatrick), "What I Almost Said" (Greg Naughton, Judy Blazer), "The Hands of God" (Herb Foster, Michael X. Martin, Company), "Letter #3" (Allen Fitzpatrick), "You Never Know Who's Behind You" (Dennis Parlato, Allen Fitzpatrick), "What Land Is This?" (Greg Naughton, Allen Fitzpatrick, Dennis Parlato, Company), Act One Finale (Company)

ACT TWO—"Stage Blood" (Allen Fitzpatrick, Swan's Players [The Acting Company]), "Letter #4" (Allen Fitzpatrick), "If You Will Dream of Me" (Judy Blazer), "Don't Think About It" (Nicolas Coster, Lou Williford, Michael Mulheren, Henry Stram, Michael X. Martin, Allen Fitzpatrick, Lauren Ward, Anne Runolfsson, Alix Korey), "Don't Think About It" (reprise) (Michael Mulheren, Henry Stram), "All You Want Is Always" (Greg Naughton, Allen Fitzpatrick), "Pandarus' Song" (Herb Foster), "Never Time to Dance" (reprise) (Allen Fitzpatrick, Judy Blazer), Act Two Finale (Company)

NOTES—In *Jack's Holiday*, Jack the Ripper travels to New York City and takes up with an acting company; soon thereafter New York finds itself in the midst of a bloody crime wave. Ben Brantley in the *New York Times* felt the evening not only lacked fully developed characters, it also lacked suspense. But he praised Randy Courts' "elegantly sinister, period-inspired" score and was especially taken with Jerome Sirlin's scenery, which used photographs and gauzy scrims to create a "confused" world of shadow and substance. Brantley also described the evening's "greatest coup de theatre": bathed in red light, the body of a murdered prostitute is suddenly framed by a "staged-sized projection" of a newspaper's front page. In one stroke, the prostitute's death "has been transformed into a peep show" for New York's newspaper readers. The musical was one of many which dealt with the story of Jack the Ripper. For more information, see entry for *The Jack the Ripper Review* (later produced as *The Jack the Ripper Revue*).

The script of *Jack's Holiday* was published by Samuel French, Inc., in 1997.

792 Jacques Brel Is Alive and Well and Living in Paris (1968). THEATRE: Village Gate; OPENING DATE: January 22, 1968; PERFORMANCES: 1,847; COMMENTARY: Jacques Brel (translated by Eric Blau and Mort Shuman); ADDITIONAL MATERIAL: Eric Blau and Mort Shuman; LYRICS AND MUSIC: See song list for credits; lyrics translated by Eric Blau and Mort Shuman; DIRECTION: Moni Yakim; production supervised by Eric Blau; SCENERY: Henry E. Scott III; COSTUMES: Ilka Suarez; LIGHTING: James Nisbet Clark; MUSICAL DIRECTION: Mort Shuman; PRODUCER: 3 W Productions

CAST—Elly Stone, Mort Shuman, Shawn Elliott, Alice Whitfield

The revue was presented in two acts.

ACT ONE—"Marathon (Les Flamandes)" (lyric and music by Jacques Brel) (Company), "Alone" (Suel) (lyric and music by Jacques Brel) (Shawn Elliott), "Madeleine" (lyric and music by Jean Cortinovis [some sources site last name as "Corti"], Gerard [some sources cite first name as "Jerard"] Jouannest, and Jacques Brel) (Company), "I Loved (J'Aimais)" (lyric and music by Francois Rauber, Jacques Brel, and Gerard Jouannest) (Elly Stone), "Mathilde" (lyric and music by Jacques Brel and Gerard Jouannest) Mort Shuman), "Bachelor's Dance (La Bouree du Celibataire)" (lyric and music by Jacques Brel) (Shawn Elliott), "Timid Frieda (Les Timides)" (lyric and music by Jacques Brel) (Alice Whitfield), "My Death (La Mort)" (Elly Stone), "The Girls and the Dogs (Les Filles et les Chiens)" (Mort Shuman, Shawn Elliott), "Jackie (La Chanson de Jacky)" (lyric and music by Jacques Brel and Gerard Jouannest) (Mort Shuman), "The Statue (La Statue)" (lyric and music by Jacques Brel and Francois Rauber) (Shawn Elliott), "The Desperate Ones (Les Desesperes)" (lyric and music by Jacques Brel and Gerard Jouannest) (Company), "Sons Of ... (Fils De ...)" (lyric and music by Jacques Brel and Gerard Jouannest) (Elly Stone), "Amsterdam" (lyric and music by Jacques Brel) (Mort Shuman)

ACT TWO—"The Bulls (Les Toros)" (lyric and music by Jean Cortinovis, Jacques Brel, and Gerard Jouannest) (Shawn Elliott), "The Old Folks (Les Vieux)" (lyric and music by Jacques Brel, Jean Cortinovis, and Gerard Jouannest) (Elly Stone), "Marieke" (lyric and music by Jacques Brel and Gerard Jouannest) (Elly Stone), Brussels (Bruxelles) (lyric and music by Jacques Brel and Gerard Jouannest) (Company), "Fanette (La Fanette)" (lyric and music by Jacques Brel) (Shawn Elliott), "Funeral Tango (Tango Funebre)" (lyric and music by Jacques Brel and Gerard Jouannest) (Mort Shuman, Shawn Elliott), "The Middle Class (Les Bourgeois)" (lyric and music by Jean Cortinovis and Jacques Brel) (Mort Shuman, Shawn Elliott), "No, Love, You're Not Alone" (Jef) (lyric and music by Jacques Brel) (Elly Stone), "Next (Au Suivant)" (lyric and music by Jacques Brel) (Mort Shuman), "Carousel (La Valse a Mille Temps)" (lyric and music by Jacques Brel) (Elly Stone), "If We Only Have Love (Quand on N'a Que L'Amour)" (lyric and music by Jacques Brel) (Company)

NOTES—*Jacques Brel Is Alive and Well and Living in Paris* was the second Off Broadway hit to open in January 1968 (see entry for *Your Own Thing*). The original production played for almost two-thousand performances, and revivals have popped up with distressing regularity both Off and Off Off Broadway (nine so far; see entries for the 1974, 1977, 1978 [two revivals that year], 1981, 1983, 1988, 1992, and 2006 revivals). There was also a Broadway production in 1972 (which couldn't muster even two months at the relatively intimate Royale [now Schoenfeld] Theatre).

Brel's songs are a highly acquired taste. If you like your ballads bottom-lip-trembling-tremulous, then this is the revue for you. Moreover, if you have never, ever once come to the realization that one day you're going to die—!!! That wars happen—!!! That people are lonely—!!! ... then the fortune-cookie wisdom of Brel's lyrics will be an eye-opener. Yes, there was far too much naval-gazing in the songs, and, like so much of late 1960s feel-good philosophy, the show proclaimed that "if we only have love," then everything will be OK (the song belongs in the same syrup bottle with such other 1960s anthems as "People," "What the World Needs Now" ("Is love, sweet love"), "If I Ruled the World," and "If I Had a Hammer").

If anything entertaining emerged from the production, it was the gushing program notes by Nat Shapiro, who wrote that Brel was no less than the conscience of "his people," that he possessed humanism, a "fierce" integrity, and a revulsion for hypocrisy. And, oh, yes, Brel was "unbelievably honest about himself." At any rate, as a composer-tribute revue, the best that can be said for *Jacques Brel* is that it introduced relatively unfamiliar songs which weren't tied to previous book musicals. And, considering that there must have been dozens upon dozens of songs in the Brel catalogue, there was, mercifully, never a sequel, at least in the United States. There were, however, two other Brel-related musicals, both produced in London. One, *Brel*, opened at the Donmar Warehouse on December 10, 1987 (the cast included Sian Phillips), and the other, *Brel/The Life and Songs of Jacques Brel*, opened at the Theatre Museum on October 2, 1990, with a book by John Swift and Peter Gee. One is also grateful the show didn't spawn a number of similar French-based evenings of song. There were just two, in fact. On January 4, 1972, *Echoes of the Left Bank*, a revue of songs by Brel, Gilbert Becaud, Charles Aznavour, and Michel

LeGrand, briefly played at Ford's Theatre in Washington, D.C. There was also an attempt to weave together a group of Becaud's songs into a book musical; first called *Becaud Tonight*, and then later *Gabrielle*, the musical disappeared after its Washington, D.C., production in 1975, which was also presented at Ford's Theatre (with a cast which included Tammy Grimes, Laurence Guittard, Marilyn Cooper, and *Jacques Brel* stalwart, Joe Masiell). *Gabrielle* may well have been ahead of its time, for it appears to have anticipated the juke-box musical (the form which shoehorns non-show songs into a book musical, forcing the songs to carry the weight of plot, character, and atmosphere, something for which they were never intended).

Jacques Brel was released on a 2-LP set by Columbia Records (# D2S-779) which omitted "The Girls and the Dogs," "The Statue," and "The Middle Class"; however, the latter song was recorded during the cast album recording session and was added to a later CD reissue of the cast album (Sony Classical/Columbia/Legacy Records # SK-89998). The script was published by E.P. Dutton & Co., Inc., 1971, and later by Dramatists Play Service, Inc., in 2000.

A 1974 Cleveland production was recorded on a 2-LP set (by Playhouse Square Records, Inc. # PHS-CLE-2S-101), and included "The Girls and the Dogs"; and a cast album of the 1985 (?) Vancouver production (titled *Jacques Brel Lives...*), which included Leon Bibb in the cast (he had appeared in the 1983 New York revival [see entry]), was released by Jabula Records (LP # JR-38).

In 1975, a film version was released (under the aegis of the ambitious, ill-fated American Film Theatre); the film's cast included Elly Stone, Mort Shuman, Joe Masiell, and J.B. himself. The film omitted four songs ("My Death," "The Girls and the Dogs," "Fanette," and "You're Not Alone"), but included "The Statue" and "The Middle Class," both of which are on the film's soundtrack album, which was released on a 2-LP set by Atlantic Records (# SD-2-1000-0998). The cast album of the 2006 Off Broadway revival (see entry) was released by Ghostlight Records (CD # 7915584416-2).

The film added six songs: "My Childhood (Mon Enfance)" (lyric and music by Jacques Brel), "The Taxicab (Le Gaz)" (lyric and music by Jacques Brel and Gerard Jouannest), "Ne Me Quitte Pas" (lyric and music by Jacques Brel), "The Last Supper (Le Dernier Repas)" (lyric and music by Jacques Brel), "Middle Class (Les Bourgeois)" (lyric and music by Jean Cortinovis and Jacques Brel), and "Song for Old Lovers (La Chanson Des Vieux Amants" (lyric and music by Jacques Brel and Gerard Jouannest).

The 2006 Off Broadway revival included four of the six numbers added for the film ("My Childhood," "Ne Me Quitte Pas," "The Last Supper," and "Song for Old Lovers") as well as two other songs, "Le Diable (Ca Va)," apparently one of Brel's earliest songs, and "Le Moribond," here in a translation by Eric Blau and Mort Shuman called "Goodbye My Friends." Seven years before the original production of *Jacques Brel* opened, Elly Stone, on the same Village Gate stage where the Brel revue opened in 1968, appeared in *O, Oysters!!!* (1961; see entry) and performed two Brel songs, "Ne Me Quitte Pas" and "Carousels and Cotton Candy" (the later was rewritten as "Carousel" for *Jacques Brel*). It's interesting to examine the *New York Times*' review of the original production of *Jacques Brel*. Dan Sullivan said the revue's major flaw was that Brel was in Paris and not in New York. He felt if Brel could be induced to perform in the musical, the evening would find its style; otherwise, the four "attractive" performers were an "ocean" away from capturing the essence of Brel and his songs. Sullivan noted that Elly Stone tried to emulate Piaf in her gestures and only succeeded in reminding him of "a salesgirl measuring yard goods"; that Alice Whitfield tried for the "blank-eyed stare of Marcel Marceau imitating a mannequin" and instead looked "like a mannequin imitating Marcel Marceau"; and that Shawn Elliott tried for a Folies Bergeres effect but ended up "Times Square at midnight." He concluded that only Mort Shuman was at home with the material. Sullivan also mentioned that with its lack of empathy for Brel's style, the evening often seemed to be an "unconscious parody" of French chansonniers in general. SPECIAL NOTE: In later years, an article in *Playbill* magazine discussed the revue's other contributors, Francois Rauber, Gerard Jouannest, and Jean Cortinovis. They had written some of the music which was heard in *Jacques Brel*, but apparently sold their music to Brel with the understanding they would receive no program credit. But five years before his death, Brel requested that all forthcoming productions acknowledge the three with program credit. However, while later productions have not always included these acknowledgements, the LPs of the original cast and film soundtrack albums give specific credit to the other writers.

793 Jacques Brel Is Alive and Well and Living in Paris (1974). THEATRE: Astor Place Theatre; OPENING DATE: May 17, 1974; PERFORMANCES: 125; COMMENTARY: Eric Blau and Mort Shuman; LYRICS AND MUSIC: For specific credits, see song list for 1968 production; DIRECTION: Moni Yakim; SCENERY: Don Jensen; COSTUMES: Don Jensen; LIGHTING: Ian Calderon; MUSICAL DIRECTION: Mort Shuman; PRODUCERS: 3 W Productions, Inc., and Lily Turner

CAST—Jack Blackton, Barbara Gutterman, Stan Porter, Henrietta Valor

NOTES—This was the first of many (*far* too many) revivals of *Jacques Brel Is Alive and Well and Living in Paris* (for list of musical numbers and for a list of all Off and Off Off Broadway revivals of the revue, see entry for the original 1968 production).

794 Jacques Brel Is Alive and Well and Living in Paris (1977). THEATRE: Queens Theatre in the Park/Playwrights Horizons; OPENING DATE: April 8, 1977; PERFORMANCES: 13; LYRICS AND MUSIC: For specific credits, see song list for 1968 production.; DIRECTION: Stuart H. Ross; SCENERY: Stephen P. Edelstein; COSTUMES: Patricia Adshead; LIGHTING: Pat Stern; MUSICAL DIRECTION: Norman L. Berman; PRODUCER: Playwrights Horizons (Robert Moss, Executive Director)

CAST—Jonathan Ball, Peter Bartlett, Jan Buttram, Susan Cella

NOTES—This version of the perennial revue was produced for a limited engagement of thirteen performances under an Off Off Broadway contract by Playwrights Horizons. See entry for 1968 production for a list of musical numbers and for a list of all Off and Off Off Broadway revivals.

795 Jacques Brel Is Alive and Well and Living in Paris (January [?] 1978). THEATRE: Town Hall; OPENING DATE: January (?) 1978; PERFORMANCES: Unknown; LYRICS AND MUSIC: For specific credits, see song list for the 1968 production; DIRECTION: Moni Yakim; LIGHTING: James Nisbet Clark; PRODUCER: Town Hall (Lily Turner, General Manager)

CAST—ELLY STONE, JOE MASIELL, Joseph Neal, Sally Cooke

NOTES—This revival was billed as a series of tenth-anniversary performances, and included original cast member Elly Stone. For song listing and for a list of all *Jacques Brel* revivals, see entry for original 1968 production.

796 Jacques Brel Is Alive and Well and Living in Paris (February 1978). THEATRE: Park Royal Cabaret Theatre; OPENING DATE: February 16, 1978; PERFORMANCES: 4; LYRICS AND MUSIC: For specific credits, see song list for 1968 production; LIGHTING: Sal Sclafani and Chuck Robbins; MUSICAL DIRECTION: Richard A. Schacher; PRODUCER: Park Royal Hotel Cabaret Theatre

CAST—Annette Hannington, Laurie Lipson, Bruce Sherman, Tony Michael Pann

The revue was presented in two acts.

NOTES—This revival was a limited Off Off Broadway engagement of four performances. For song listing and for a list of all *Jacques Brel* revivals, see entry for original 1968 production.

797 Jacques Brel Is Alive and Well and Living in Paris (1981). THEATRE: Town Hall; OPENING DATE: February 19, 1981; PERFORMANCES: 21; LYRICS AND MUSIC: For specific credits, see song list for 1968 production; DIRECTION: Production supervised by Eric Blau, based on the original direction by Moni Yakim; MUSICAL DIRECTION: Bertha Melnik; PRODUCER: Lily Turner Attractions

CAST—Joe Masiell, Betty Rhodes, Shawn Elliott, Sally Cooke

NOTES—This revival (which may have been under an Off Off Broadway contract) included original cast member Shawn Elliott as well as *Jacques Brel* stalwart Joe Masiell. For song listing and for a list of all *Jacques Brel* revivals, see entry for original 1968 production.

798 Jacques Brel Is Alive and Well and Living in Paris (1983). THEATRE: First City Theatre; OPENING DATE: May 15, 1983; PERFORMANCES: 48; LYRICS AND MUSIC: For specific credits, see song list for 1968 production; DIRECTION: Eric Blau; SCENERY: Don Jensen; COSTUMES: Don Jensen; LIGHTING: Steve Helliker; PRODUCER: Pat Productions

CAST—Leon Bibb, Betty Rhodes, Joseph Neal, Jacqueline Reilly

The revue was presented in two acts.

NOTES—For better or for worse (depending on your tolerance for songs smug, whimsical, and full of self-importance), *Jacques Brel* is one of those shows which will never ago away. For a list of musical numbers and a summary of all Off and Off Off Broadway revivals of the revue, see entry for the original 1968 production.

799 Jacques Brel Is Alive and Well and Living in Paris (1985). THEATRE: Equity (Library) Theatre; OPENING DATE: January 3, 1985; PERFORMANCES: 30; LYRICS AND MUSIC: For specific credits, see song list for 1968 production.; DIRECTION: Stephen Bonnell; CHOREOGRAPHY: Piper Pickrell; SCENERY: J. Robin Modereger; COSTUMES: Margarita Delgado; LIGHTING: Mark DiQuinzio; MUSICAL DIRECTION: Benjamin Whiteley; PRODUCER: Equity (Library) Theatre (George Wojtasik, Managing Director)

CAST—Louise Edeiken, Richard Hilton, Jan Horvath, J.C. Sheets

NOTES—This limited-run Off Off Broadway production by the Equity (Library) Theatre was another in the steady stream of *Jacques Brel* revivals.

For a list of musical numbers and a list of all Off and Off Off Broadway productions of the revue, see entry for the original 1968 production.

800 Jacques Brel Is Alive and Well and Living in Paris (1988). THEATRE: Town Hall; OPENING DATE: January 22, 1988; PERFORMANCES: 7; LYRICS AND MUSIC: For specific credits, see song list for the 1968 production; DIRECTION: Elly Stone; CHOREOGRAPHY: Susan Osberg; SCENERY: Don Jensen; COSTUMES: Don Jensen; LIGHTING: Steve Helliker; MUSICAL DIRECTION: Jonathan Irving; PRODUCER: Reuben Hoppenstein

CAST—Karen Akers, Shelle Ackerman, Elmore James, Kenny Morris, Aileen Savage, Adam Bryant

NOTES—This Off Off Broadway revival, billed as the "International 20th Anniversary Production" of the perennial revue, was directed by original cast member Elly Stone. For song listing and for a list of all *Jacques Brel* revivals, see entry for original 1968 production.

801 Jacques Brel Is Alive and Well and Living in Paris (1992). THEATRE: Village Gate; OPENING DATE: October 18, 1992; PERFORMANCES: 131; LYRICS AND MUSIC: For specific credits, see song list for the 1968 production; DIRECTION: Elly Stone; Gabriel Barre; ADDITIONAL MOVEMENT; SCENERY: Don Jensen; COSTUMES: Mary Brecht; LIGHTING: Graeme F. McDonnell; MUSICAL DIRECTION: Annie Lebeaux; PRODUCERS: Blue Curl Productions, Inc., in association with Philis Raskind, Harold L. Strauss, and Stuart Zimberg

CAST—Gabriel Barre, Andrea Green, Joseph Neal, Karen Saunders

NOTES—This production was billed as the twenty-fifth anniversary revival, and as she did for the 1988 revival which celebrated the revue's twentieth anniversary, original cast member Elly Stone directed. This revival played at the Village Gate, home of the original production.

For song listing and for a list of all *Jacques Brel* revivals, see entry for original 1968 production.

802 Jacques Brel Is Alive and Well and Living in Paris (2006). THEATRE: Zipper Theatre; OPENING DATE: March 27, 2006; PERFORMANCES: 384; LYRICS AND MUSIC: For specific credits, see song list for 1968 production; DIRECTION: Gordon Greenberg; CHOREOGRAPHY: Mark Dendy; SCENERY: Robert Bissinger; COSTUMES: Mattie Ullrich; LIGHTING: Jeff Croiter; MUSICAL DIRECTION: Eric Svejcar; PRODUCERS: Dan Whitten, Bob and Rhonda Silver, Ken Grossman, in association with Tiger Theatricals; Kathleen Brochin, Associate Producer

CAST—Robert Cuccioli, Natascia Diaz, Rodney Hicks, Gay Marshall

The revue was presented in two acts.

NOTES—Of the nine *Jacques Brel* revivals, this production ran the longest (almost one year). It was recorded by Ghostlight Records (CD # 7915584416-2).

The revival omitted "Marathon" and "Mathilde," but included four songs which were heard in the 1975 film version ("My Childhood," "Ne Me Quitte Pas," "The Last Supper," and "Song for Old Lovers"). The revival also included "Le Diable (Ca Va)," apparently one of Brel's earliest songs, and "Le Moribund," here in a translation by Eric Blau and Mort Shuman called "Goodbye My Friends."

For a complete song list as well as a list of all *Jacques Brel* revivals, see entry for original 1968 production.

803 Jam. THEATRE: AMAS Repertory Theatre; OPENING DATE: April 24, 1980; PERFORMANCES: 14; BOOK: John Gerstad; LYRICS AND MUSIC: Various Lyricists and Composers; DIRECTION: William Mooney; CHOREOGRAPHY: Dennis J. Shearer; SCENERY: Vicki Paul; COSTUMES: Jeffrey N. Mazor; LIGHTING: Bob Scheeler; MUSICAL DIRECTION: Ernie Scott; PRODUCER: AMAS Repertory Theatre (Rosetta LeNoire, Founder and Artistic Director)

CAST—William Dillard (C.C. Frazee), Michael McCurry (George Roy), Joe Gardner (Paris Benbow, Spiffy Hagedore), David Heath (Dr. Pipick, Boots Traynor), Ernie Scott (Piano Player, Young Papa Joe, Ribs Tarkey), Harold Cromer (Chisolm, Papa Joe Bonheur), L. Edmond Wesley (Charlie Valentine), Every Hayes (Ewell, Young C.C.), Larry J. Stewart (Elliott, Bliss Baldwin), Ann Duquesnay (Bitty, Frolic Des Piaines, Spanish Agnes), Susan Beaubian (Young Frolic, Twibby), Edye Byrde (Lady Vanilla, Maidel), Claudia Shel (Cherry), Terpsie Toon (Cooky), Sharon K. Brooks (Cissy), Lois Hayes (Chooch), Cynthia Belgrave (Lily Jane), Jean Cheek (Gospel Singer); Dakeeta Grinage, Shane Johnson, Charisse Kelly

NOTES—The Off Off Broadway musical *Jam* told the story of a jazz musician who returns to New Orleans to die. Richard F. Shepard in the *New York Times* noted that while the musician does indeed die, the audience will "laugh and giggle" all the way through the "thumping and jumping" musical, an "affectionate and ebullient" show which went "bouncily and boisterously" on its merry way. He concluded that the evening was "all jazz and a yard wide and should be going places."

The score didn't include original material; instead, it offered a number of songs by W.C. Handy, Duke Ellington, Kid Ory, Percy Grainger, and (per Shepard) "that great composer Traditional." Among the songs heard during the evening were "O, Didn't He Ramble" and "Muskrat Ramble."

804 Jam on the Groove. THEATRE: Minetta Lane Theatre; OPENING DATE: November 16, 1995; PERFORMANCES: 100; TEXT: GhettOriginal Productions Dance Company; DIRECTION: GhettOriginal Productions Dance Company; CHOREOGRAPHY: GhettOriginal Productions Dance Company; SCENERY: Andrew Jackness; Murals by Ernie Vales; LIGHTING: Peter Kaczorowski; PRODUCERS: Mitchell Maxwell, Alan J. Schuster, and Margaret Selby in association with IMG; Michael Skipper, Victoria Maxwell, Co-Producers; Susan Selby, James L. Simon, Associate Producers

CAST—Peter "Bam Bam" Arizmendi, Leon "Mister Twister" Chesney, Steve "Mr. Wiggles" Clemente, "Crazy Legs," Gabriel "Kwikstep" Dionisio, Kenny "Ken Swift" Gabbert, Tamara Gaspard, Antoine "Doc" Judkins, Risa Kobatake, Adesola "D'Incredible" Osakalumi, Jorge "Fabel" Pabon, Jerry "Flow Master" Randolph, Roger "Orko" Romero, Ereine "Honey Roc Well" Valencia

The dance revue was presented in one act.

MUSICAL NUMBERS—"Concrete Jungle" (Company), "The Shadow Knows" (Kenny "Ken Swift" Gabbert, Jerry "Flow Master" Randolph), "Portrait of a Freeze" ("Crazy Legs," Kenny "Ken Swift" Gabbert, Gabriel "Kwikstep" Dionisio, Jerry "Flow Master" Randolph), "Puppet" (Steve "Mr. Wiggles" Clemente, Jorge "Fabel" Pabon), "Who's the Mac" (Company), "Janitor" (Gabriel "Kwikstep" Dionisio, Jerry "Flow Master" Randolph), "Moments" (Steve "Mr. Wiggles" Clemente, "Crazy Legs," Gabriel "Kwikstep" Dionisio, Kenny "Ken Swift" Gabbert, Adesola "D'Incredible" Osakalumi, Jorge "Fabel" Pabon), "Shaolin Temple of Hip-Hop" (Company), "Hip-Hop Ya Don't Stop" (Company), "Jam on the Groove" (Company)

NOTES—The night after *Bring in 'da Noise Bring in 'da Funk* (see entry) opened Off Broadway, *Jam on the Groove*, another similarly styled hip-hop dance revue, opened there. But apparently there was room for only one such revue in town, and so for *Jam on the Groove* there was no transfer to Broadway, no long run, no cast album, and no awards. *Jam on the Groove*'s series of dance-vignettes eschewed the often preachy political agenda of *'da Noise* and instead settled for pure entertainment. Jeffrey Sweet in *The Best Plays of 1995-1996* praised the revue's "series of jaw-dropping combinations only the terminally jaded could fail to cheer."

The GhettOriginal Productions Dance Company had been formed by members of three hip-hop troupes (Magnificent Force, Rhythm Techniques, and Rock Steady Crew).

805 James Joyce's The Dead. "A New Musical Play." THEATRE: Playwrights Horizons; OPENING DATE: October 28, 1999; PERFORMANCES: 38; BOOK: Richard Nelson; LYRICS: Conceived and adapted by Richard Nelson and Shaun Davey (see notes below); MUSIC: Shaun Davey (see NOTES below); DIRECTION: Jack Holmes and Richard Nelson; CHOREOGRAPHY: Sean Curran; SCENERY: David Jenkins; COSTUMES: Jane Greenwood; LIGHTING: Jennifer Tipton; MUSICAL DIRECTION: Charles Prince; PRODUCERS: Playwrights Horizons (Tim Sanford, Artistic Director; Leslie Marcus, Managing Director; Lynn Landis, General Manager) by special arrangement with Gregory Mosher and Arielle Tepper

CAST—Sally Ann Howes (Aunt Julia Morkan), Marni Nixon (Aunt Kate Morkan), Emily Skinner (Mary Jane Morkan), Christopher Walken (Gabriel Conroy), Blair Brown (Gretta Conroy), Brian Davies (Mr. Browne), Stephen Spinella (Freddy Malins), Paddy Croft (Mrs. Malins), Alice Ripley (Molly Ivors), John Kelly (Bartell D'Arcy), Brooke Sunny Moriber (Lily), Dashiell Eaves (Michael), Daisy Eagan (Rita, Young Julia Morkan), Daniel Barrett (Cellist), Louise Owen (Violinist)

SOURCE—The 1907 short story "The Dead" by James Joyce.

The action occurs at the Misses Morkans' annual Christmas-time party in Dublin at the turn of the twentieth century.

The musical was presented in one act.

MUSICAL NUMBERS—Prologue (Musicians), "Killarney's Lakes" (Emily Skinner, Marni Nixon, Daisy Eagan), "Kate Kearney" (Dashiell Eaves, Emily Skinner), "Parnell's Plight" (Alice Ripley, Dashiell Eaves, Christopher Walken, Blair Brown, Company), "Adieu to Ballyshannon" (Christopher Walken, Blair Brown), "When Lovely Lady" (Sally Ann Howes, Marni Nixon), "Three Jolly Pigeons" (Stephen Spinella, Brian Davies, Company), "Goldenhair" (Blair Brown, Christopher Walken), "Three Graces" (Christopher Walken, Company), "Naughty Girls" (Sally Ann Howes, Marni Nixon, Emily Skinner, Company), "Wake the Dead" (Stephen Spinella, Company), "D'Arcy's Aria" (John Kelly), "Queen of Our Hearts" (Brian Davies, Stephen Spinella, John Kelly, Dashiell Eaves), "When Lovely Lady" (reprise) (Daisy Eagan, Sally Ann Howes), "Michael Furey" (Blair Brown), "The Living and the Dead" (Christopher Walken, Company)

NOTES—*James Joyce's The Dead* played Off Broadway at Playwrights Horizons for thirty-eight performances before transferring to Broadway at the Belasco Theatre on January 11, 2000, where it played for 112 performances and won the 1999-2000 New York Drama Critics' Circle Award for Best Musical.

The action occurred at the Misses Morkans' annual Christmas party in Dublin in an early year of the twentieth century, and virtually all songs in the musical were "presentational" (that is, they were sung by the hosts and their guests as part of the festivities at the party). Only in the musical's last scene were the songs performed as "book" songs which advanced the plot (for some, this sudden shift in tone was jarring and disruptive to the narrative flow).

The haunting musical (or play-with-music) was heavy with the sense of loss and living in the past, and was perhaps best suited for an intimate Off Broadway theatre (although the Broadway transfer couldn't have played at a more appropriate house than the Belasco, which is perhaps the most haunting, if not haunted, of all Broadway theatres). A program note by the authors indicated that many of the musical's lyrics had been adapted from or inspired by various eighteenth and nineteenth century poems (by Oliver Goldsmith and other writers) as well as by an anonymous music hall song. Other lyrics were adapted from Joyce's writings, or were original. The musical's cast included many welcome names from an earlier era of the Broadway musical, including Sally Ann Howes and Brian Davies. The latter hadn't been seen on Broadway in thirty-eight years* when he created the role of Hero in the original 1962 production of *A Funny Thing Happened on the Way to the Forum* (in 1959, he had created the role of Rolf Gruber in the original production of *The Sound of Music* [with Lauri Peters he introduced "You Are Sixteen"]). Marni Nixon was another name from the past, and is of course best remembered as the singing voice of Deborah Kerr, Natalie Wood, and Audrey Hepburn in various film musicals. And "new" Broadway was represented by Emily Skinner and Alice Ripley, who had created the roles of Daisy and Violet Hilton in the memorable 1997 musical *Side Show*.

The script was published in *American Theatre* magazine and later in a hardback edition by Stage & Screen (undated, but probably 2000). A December 2004 production by the Pittsburgh Irish & Classical Theatre was recorded in a limited-edition CD (unlabeled and unnumbered with the notation that the CD was "for promotional use only. Not for sale"; there was no recording of the New York production).

*Joan Roberts (who in 1943 created the role of Laurey in *Oklahoma!*) appears to hold the record for the longest time between Broadway appearances. She appeared as Heidi Schiller in the 2001 revival of *Follies* (which had also played at the Belasco), and prior to that engagement she had last been seen on Broadway fifty-three years earlier, when in 1948 she replaced Nanette Fabray in *High Button Shoes*.

806 James Naughton: Street of Dreams. THEATRE: Promenade Theatre; OPENING DATE: February 4, 1999; PERFORMANCES: 69; SCENERY: John Lee Beatty; LIGHTING: Tharon Musser; MUSICAL DIRECTION: John Oddo; PRODUCERS: Mike Nichols; also, Julian Schlossberg, Chase Mishkin, and David Stone; The Araca Group and Meyer Ackerman, Associate Producers

CAST—James Naughton

NOTES—The evening was a one-man concert by James Naughton, who performed songs and monologues (including spoken sequences from *City of Angels*, the 1989 musical in which he appeared).

Stephen Holden in the *New York Times* said the performance was "immensely entertaining," and noted that Naughton's voice was "revelatory in its flexibility and sheer beauty." Among the songs performed were: "Star Dust" (lyric by Mitchell Parish, music by Hoagy Carmichael), "My Life Is Good" (lyric and music by Randy Newman), "She's Funny That Way (I Got a Woman, Crazy for Me)" (lyric by Richard A. Whiting, music by Neil Moret), "The Folks Who Live on the Hill" (from 1937 film *High, Wide and Handsome*; lyric by Oscar Hammerstein II, music by Jerome Kern), "Lush Life" (lyric and music by Billy Strayhorn), "Are You Lonesome Tonight?" (lyric by Roy Turk, music by Lou Handman), "I Want You to Be My Baby" (lyric and music by Jon Hendricks), "I've Been Everywhere" (lyric and music by Hank Snow), and "I'm Hip" (lyric by Dave Frishberg and music by Bob Dorough).

Naughton performed an earlier version of the concert at the Manhattan Theatre Club in June 1998.

807 Jane White, Who?... THEATRE: One Sheridan Square; OPENING DATE: January 29, 1980; PERFORMANCES: 51; WRITTEN by Jane White and Joe Masteroff; LIGHTING: Ian McKay; MUSICAL DIRECTION: Roger Leonard; PRODUCER: Saffron Ltd.

CAST—JANE WHITE; Kay Stonefelt, Drums; Michael Fleming, Bass.

The revue was presented in two acts (all songs performed by Jane White; the program didn't designate division of acts; all musical numbers were listed alphabetically).

MUSICAL NUMBERS—"After You, Who?" (from *Gay Divorce*, 1932; lyric and music by Cole Porter), "Being Alive" (*Company*, 1970; lyric and music by Stephen Sondheim), "Don't Like Goodbyes" (*House of Flowers*, 1954; lyric by Truman Capote and Harold Arlen, music by Harold Arlen), "Give Him the Oo-La-La" (*DuBarry Was a Lady*, 1939; lyric and music by Cole Porter), "God Bless the Child" (lyric and music by Billie Holiday and Arthur Herzog, Jr.), "Hallelujah, Baby!" (*Hallelujah, Baby!*, 1967; lyric by Betty Comden and Adolph Green), music by Jule Styne), "I Never Do Anything Twice" (1977 film *The Seven Percent Solution*; lyric and music by Stephen Sondheim), "I Remember" (1966 television musical *Evening Primrose*; lyric and music by Stephen Sondheim), "My Own Best Friend" (*Chicago*, 1975; lyric by Fred Ebb, music by John Kander), "My Own Space" (*The Act*, 1977; lyric by Fred Ebb, music by John Kander), "Pirate Jenny" (*The Threepenny Opera*, 1928; original German lyric by Bertolt Brecht, music by Kurt Weill; no indication which English translation was used), "Remember?" (*A Little Night Music*, 1973; lyric and music by Stephen Sondheim), "Sing Happy" (*Flora, the Red Menace*, 1965; lyric by Fred Ebb, music by John Kander), "Sono Come Tu Mi Vuoi" (lyric and music by Murri and Canfora), "Tante Helene" (anonymous), "(The) Age of Elegance" (*Sterling Silver*, 1979; lyric and music by Frederick [Fred] Silver), "That Face" (lyric and music by Bergman and Spence), "That's Him" (*One Touch of Venus*, 1943; lyric by Ogden Nash, music by Kurt Weill), "There Is a Time" (lyric and music by Charles Aznavour), "Who's That Woman?" (*Follies*, 1971; lyric and music by Stephen Sondheim)

NOTES—As indicated by the title of her one-woman show, Jane White was never a "name" performer; nevertheless, she had a varied and fascinating career in theatre (everything from Shakespeare to *Once Upon a Mattress* [1959; see entry]), television, film, and cabaret, and many theatre fans were glad to make the journey to One Sheridan Square to see her perform.

Stephen Sondheim and John Kander and Fred Ebb were the main lyricists and composers represented in an evening of mostly familiar songs, but there was one obscure and surprising choice in her repertoire, Frederick (Fred) Silver's "Age of Elegance" from the previous year's six-performance failure *Sterling Silver* (see entry); the song was later interpolated into the 1984 touring production *In Gay Company* and can be heard on the cast recording of that revue (see entry for *Gay Company* [1974] for more information).

In her revue, Jane White sang "Who's That Woman?" from *Follies*; in 2001, she appeared as Solange la Fitte in the Broadway revival of Stephen Sondheim's masterpiece and performed "Ah, Paris!"

808 Jayson. THEATRE: 45th Street Theatre; OPENING DATE: July 10, 1998; PERFORMANCES: 44; BOOK: Jeff Krell; LYRICS: Ron Romanovsky and Paul Phillips; MUSIC: Ron Romanovsky and Paul Phillips; DIRECTION: Jay Michaels; CHOREOGRAPHY: Kyle Craig; Lee Wilkins, Assistant Choreographer; SCENERY: Jim McNicholas; COSTUMES: Julia N. Van Vliet; LIGHTING: Roger Formosa; MUSICAL DIRECTION: Simon Deacon; PRODUCER: Ignite! Entertainment

CAST—Brian Cooper (Jason Callowhill), Susan Agin (Arena Stage), Craig Dawson (Robyn Ricketts), Mark Haen (Eduardo Rivera, Mr. Feldman), Jane Smulyan (Bertha Callowhill, Stella Stage), Kenny Morris (Armistice Callowhill, Stan Stage, Phelps, Rabbi, Riverdale, DiCerchio), D. Matt Crabtree and Alicia Litwin (Ensemble)

SOURCE—The comic strip *Jason* by Jeff Krell.

The action occurs in a cartoon world "remarkably similar to our own."

The musical was presented in two acts.

ACT ONE—"I May Not Be Much" (Brian Cooper), "A Friend Like Me" (Susan Agin), "I'm Here!" (Craig Dawson), "Video Boys" (Brian Cooper, Susan Agin), "My Mother's Clothes" (Craig Dawson, Brian Cooper, Susan Agin), "Always a Friend (Never a Lover)" (Susan Agin, Craig Dawson), "Baby, Take Advantage of Me" (Brian Cooper), "All We Have to Do" (Brian Cooper, Susan Agin)

ACT TWO—"The Promise of Love" (Company), "Authentic" (Craig Dawson, Brian Cooper, Mark Haen), "All You Had to Do" (Susan Agin), "Dr. Love" (Mark Haen, Company), "He Wasn't Talking to Me" (Brian Cooper), "Let's Do Lunch" (Craig Dawson, Company), "Follow Your Heart" (Brian Cooper, Susan Agin), "Success" (Brian Cooper, Susan Agin, Craig Dawson)

NOTES—Based on the gay comic strip of the same name, *Jayson* was a short-running musical which dealt with friendships and romantic relationships among gays.

Lawrence Van Gelder in the *New York Times* noted that although the musical wasn't dull, it covered all-too-familiar territory and came across as "just another routine sitcom" with "unmemorable music." But he singled out both Jim McNicholas' scenery with its "Sunday comic strip colorfulness" and Craig Dawson, who stole the show in a "display of queenly bitchiness" as Robyn Ricketts, a gay porn film producer.

809 Jazzbo Brown. "A New Musical." THEATRE: City Lights Theatre; OPENING DATE: June 24, 1980; PERFORMANCES: 44; BOOK: Stephen M. Lemberg; LYRICS: Stephen M. Lemberg; MUSIC: Stephen M. Lemberg; DIRECTION: Louis Johnson; CHOREOGRAPHY: Louis Johnson; Mercedes Ellington, Assistant Choreographer; SCENERY: Harry Lines; COSTUMES: Karen Roston and Vel Riberto; LIGHTING: Bill Mintzer; MUSICAL DIRECTION: Tod Cooper; PRODUCERS: Barbara Gittler in association with Morris Jaffe

CAST—Andre De Shields (Billy "Jazzbo" Brown), Chris Galloway (Maxine McCall), Jerry Jarrett (D.D. Daniels), Zulema (Rachael Brown), Ned Wright (the Rev. Raymond W. Brown); Chorus (The Company of the Harlem Follies): Charles Bernard, Deborah Lynn Bridges, Rodney Green, Janice "Nicki"Harrison, Dennis A. Morgan, Gayle Samuels, Wynonna Smith, Allysia C. Sneed

The action occurs in 1924 during a 48-hour period in both a Broadway theatre and a prosperous church in Harlem.

The musical was presented in two acts.

ACT ONE—Overture, "Jazzbo Brown" (Andre De Shields, Chris Calloway, Chorus), "Broadway, Broadway" (Andre De Sheilds), "I'm Bettin' on You" (Jerry Jarrett, Company), "Million Songs" (Andre De Shields, Company), "Born to Sing (Gospel)" (Choir, Zulema), "He Had the Callin'" (Ned Wright), "Bump, Bump, Bump" (Andre De Shields, Angels), "The Same Old Tune" (Andre De Shields), "When You've Loved Your Man" (Zulema), "The Best Man" (Chris Calloway), "Give Me More" (Chris Calloway, Chorus), "When I Die" (Andre De Shields, Chorus), "Million Songs" (reprise) (Andre De Shields)

ACT TWO—"Dancin' Shoes" (Andre De Shields), "Precious Patterns" (Ned Wright, Zulema), "Funky Bessie" (Chris Calloway), "Harlem Follies" (Jerry Jarrett, Chorus), "First Time I Saw You" (Chris Calloway, Andre De Shields), "The Best Man" (reprise) (Chris Calloway), "Pride and Freedom" (Zulema, Company), "Born to Sing" (reprise) (Company), "Million Songs" (reprise) (Ned Wright), "Harlem Follies" (reprise) (Chorus, Chris Calloway), "Jazzbo Brown" (reprise) (Andre De Shields, Chris Calloway, Chorus), "Take a Bow" (Andre De Shields, Company), Exit Music (Orchestra)

NOTES—*Jazzbo Brown* began preview performances on June 24, 1980; in an article dated July 31, the *New York Times* indicated the "ragtime musical" had postponed its scheduled opening night of August 7; no new opening night was announced, but the article said the musical would continue with preview performances. There doesn't seem to be any information available regarding the musical's first official performance. However, its final performance of record was on August 24. If the musical never officially opened, then June 24 serves as its first date of New York performances, and it played for a total of forty-four performances (previews as well as any regular performances).

810 Jeff Harnar Sings the 1959 Broadway Songbook. THEATRE: Oak Room/Algonquin Hotel; OPENING DATE: February 5, 1991; PERFORMANCES: Unknown; DIRECTION: Sara Louise Lazarus; MUSICAL DIRECTION: Alex Rybeck

CAST—Jeff Harnar (Vocals and Piano)

NOTES—1959 was a great year for lovers of musical theatre. The original Broadway productions of *My Fair Lady, Bells Are Ringing, West Side Story, Jamaica, The Music Man*, and *Flower Drum Song* were still running on Broadway, and 1959 itself introduced such hits as *Redhead, Once Upon a Mattress* (which opened Off Broadway and later transferred to Broadway; see entry), *Gypsy, The Sound of Music*, and *Fiorello!* And even the year's failures were notable: *Juno* left behind one of the strongest and most melodic scores of post-World War Two Broadway, and *First Impressions, Destry Rides Again, The Nervous Set, Take Me Along*, and *Saratoga* offered memorable if underrated scores.

For his salute to the Broadway musical of 1959, Jeff Harnar sang numbers from all these scores, everything from the familiar ("Tonight" from *West Side Story* and "My Favorite Things" from *The Sound of Music*) to the esoteric ("I Wish It So" from *Juno*, "A Perfect Evening" from *First Impressions*, and "The Men Who Run the Country" from *Saratoga*). He also saluted a few Off Broadway musicals from 1959 (besides *Once Upon a Mattress, The Billy Barnes Revue* and *Little Mary Sunshine* [see entries] were represented); sang a number from the two-man revue *At the Drop of a Hat*; and even threw in a song from *Li'l Abner* (that musical had closed six months before New Year's Day 1959, but its film version was released in 1959; and *Abner*'s "The Country's in the Very Best of Hands" was a perfect lyrical cousin to "The Men Who Run the Country").

But, gee, Jeff, no songs from *Happy Town*, 1959's shortest-running musical? And nothing from two other flops, *The Girls Against the Boys* and *Whoop-Up*—? The latter opened in December 1958, and played for the first five weeks of 1959; while Harnar might understandably have wished to avoid such clinkers as "Nobody Throw Those Bull" and "Caress Me, Possess Me Perfume," *Whoop-Up* did offer "Never Before," a minor but lovely ballad which never attained standard status; the song had been introduced by Julienne Marie on the stage and was later "covered" by Connie Francis on a 45 RPM single.

And Harnar didn't offer anything from the flop 1959 Off Broadway musical *Ole!* (see entry); as a result, an opportunity to hear that show's "The Belle of Ball and the Bull of the Brawl" was lost.

Jeff Harnar Sings the 1959 Broadway Songbook was recorded live at the Algonquin by Original Cast Records (CD # 916) and it belongs in everyone's cast album collection.

811 Jekyll and Hyde. THEATRE: Promenade Theatre; OPENING DATE: June 25, 1990; PERFORMANCES: 45; BOOK: David Crane and Marta Kauffman; LYRICS: David Crane and Marta Kauffman; MUSIC: Michael Skloff; DIRECTION: Jay Harnick; CHOREOGRAPHY: Helen Butleroff; SCENERY: Vaughn Patterson; COSTUMES: Ann-Marie Wright; LIGHTING: Mathew J. Williams; MUSICAL DIRECTION: Wayne Abravanel; PRODUCER: Theatreworks USA (Jay Harnick, Artistic Director; Charles Hull, Managing Director)

CAST—Christopher Scott (Henry), Eric Ruffin (Stuart), Amanda Green (Marissa, Mother), Emily Bear (Chelsea), Frederick Einhorn (Vernicker, Father)

SOURCE—The 1886 novel *Strange Case of Dr. Jekyll and Mr. Hyde* by Robert Louis Stevenson.

The action occurs in the present time in Cleveland.

The musical was presented in one act.

NOTES—The one-hour musical *Jekyll and Hyde* was presented as free summer theatre entertainment for young people. The musical updated Robert Louis Stevenson's classic novel to present-day Cleveland, and centered on a mild-mannered high school boy who, upon drinking a potion he concocted, suddenly turns into a dangerous bully. According to Stephen Holden in the *New York Times*, David Crane and Marta Kauffman's book and lyrics were successful in balancing entertainment with a cautionary lesson about the dangers of drugs, and his only complaint was that the musical came to an abrupt end and felt "frustratingly half-finished." Holden also noted that Michael Skloff contributed a "scaled-down and Americanized" Andrew Lloyd Webber-styled score. (Incidentally, Crane and Kauffman later created and wrote the phenomenally successful television series *Friends*.)

There have been at least seven other musical versions of Stevenson's novel. *After You, Mr. Hyde*, with a score by Norman Sachs and Mel Mandel, played in regional theatre in 1968, and a later 1973 television musical called *Dr. Jekyll and Mr. Hyde* included songs from *After You, Mr. Hyde* as well as new ones by Lionel Bart. In 1990, Sachs and Mandel re-wrote *After You, Mr. Hyde* as *Jekyll and Hyde*, and it was produced in regional theatre. Also in 1990, Leslie Bricusse and Frank Wildhorn's musical version of the novel, also called *Jekyll and Hyde*, opened at the Alley Theatre in Houston; the musical opened on Broadway in 1997, and despite a run of 1,543 performances, it failed to recoup its investment. In 1995, an Off Off Broadway version titled *Dr. Jekyll and Mr. Hyde* played for fourteen performances (the book and lyrics were by Brandon Long, and the music was by Roger Butterley). Further, a German musical, *Dr. Jekyll & Mr. Hyde*, appears to have been produced during the mid-1980s (the book was by Rudiger Rudolph and Clemens Cochius, and the lyrics and music were by Cochius). Although the musical was produced in Germany, it appears the work was sung in English (the song list in the program is in English, and the program includes English lyrics to three of the twenty-eight musical numbers).

In 1989, Charles Ludlam's Ridiculous Theatrical Company presented a version of Stevenson's novel; two songs from *Dr. Jekyll and Mr. Hyde* ("Eddie's Swing" and "You've Changed") can be heard on the collection *The Ridiculous Theatrical Company/The 25th Anniversary* (DRG Records CD # 6301).

812 The Jello Is Always Red. "The Cabaret Songs of Clark Gesner." THEATRE: The Theatre at Saint Peter's Church/The York Theatre Company; OPENING DATE: June 11, 1998; PERFORMANCES: 22; SKETCHES: Clark Gesner; LYRICS: Clark Gesner; MUSIC: Clark Gesner; DIRECTION: James Morgan; COSTUMES: John Carver Sullivan; LIGHTING: Brian Haynsworth; MUSICAL DIRECTION: Winston Clark; PRODUCER: The York Theatre Company (James Morgan, Artistic Director; Joseph V. De Michele, Managing Director)

CAST—Celia Gentry, Clark Gesner, Neal Young

The revue was presented in two acts.

ACT ONE—"The Jello Is Always Red" (Clark Gesner), "Hey, There, Let's All Have a Little Fun" (written for *The Dick Cavett Show* [television, 1975) (Company), "You're the One I'm For" (from *New Faces of 1968*) (Clark Gesner), "Resolution" (Neal Young), "Reflection" (*The Utter Glory of Morrisey Hall*, 1979) (Celia Gentry), "Everything I Buy Was Made in China" (Clark Gesner), "There Is Always Some More Toothpaste in the Tube" (Company), "The Diner" (sketch) (Company), "By the Sea" (*New Faces of 1968*) (Clark Gesner), "It's Very Warm in Here" (Celia Gentry), "Humpty Doo" (Clark Gesner, Neal Young), "If I Could" (*The Dick Cavett Show*, 1975) (Neal Young), "The Peanut Butter Affair" (*Bits & Pieces XIV*, 1964) (Company), "Roses" (sketch) (Clark Gesner), "Hey, Buckaroo" (Clark Gesner, Neal Young), "Where Do All the Chickens Come From" (Clark Gesner)

ACT TWO—"Bird's Song (I Like Them)" (from unproduced musical *The Adventures of Betty Boop*) ("Bird"), "Beautiful Song" (Neal Young), "Baby" (sketch) (Company), "A Proposal for Our Time" (Neal Young), "I'm No Sure" (Celia Gentry), "You Are" (*New Faces of 1968*) (Clark Gesner), "The Agent Returns" (sketch) (Clark Gesner, Neal Young), "I Love a Lad" (Celia Gentry), "Cool" (Clark Gesner), "The Chipmunk" (*Animal Fair*, 1991; produced at the Denver Theatre Center in 1991) (Neal Young), "A Bird in a Cage" (Celia Gentry), "A Dog Outside a Store" (Clark Gesner), "Alligators" (Company), "The Ending" (Company)

NOTES—The revue *The Jello Is Always Red* was the first Off Broadway visit from Clark Gesner in over thirty years. Except for *The Utter Glory of Morrisey Hall*, his one-performance Broadway flop in 1979, New York hadn't seen a full-length musical from him since 1967, when *You're a Good Man, Charlie Brown* opened and became one of the biggest successes in Off Broadway history (see entry). His career had seemed so promising. At Princeton, he contributed to musicals for the Triangle Club (such as *After a Fashion!* and *Breakfast in Bedlam*), and then later his songs were heard in the occasional Off Broadway revue (*Bits and Pieces XIV*; see entry). With the smash hit *Charlie Brown*, he seemed primed to become a major figure in Broadway musicals, but after *Charlie Brown* there were just a few songs for *New Faces of 1968*, and then *Morrisey Hall* and *The Jello Is Always Red*. He died in 2002 at the age of 64, sadly never fulfilling his early promise. *The Jello Is Always Red* was a collection of old and new material Gesner had written over the years, including songs written for his cabaret performances. The score was recorded by Harbinger Records (CD # HCD-1502).

813 Jelly Roll! "The Music and the Man." THEATRE: 47th Street Theatre; transferred to the Kaufman Theatre on April 1, 1995; OPENING DATE: August 9, 1994; PERFORMANCES: 294; BOOK: Vernel Bagneris; LYRICS: Mostly by Vernel Bagneris; MUSIC: Mostly by Vernel Bagneris; DIRECTION: Dean Irby, "Production Supervisor"; CHOREOGRAPHY: Pepsi Bethel; SCENERY: Mike Fish; LIGHTING: John McKernon; PRODUCERS: Michael and Barbara Ross in association with Susan Melman; David Melman, Associate Producer

CAST—Vernel Bagneris (Jelly Roll Morton); Morten Gunnar Larsen (Accompanist)

The revue was presented in one act.

MUSICAL NUMBERS—"Mamie Desdoume's Blues" (lyric and music by Desdoume), "Pep," "Le Miserere" (from *Il Trovatore*, 1853; music by Giuseppe Verdi), "Le Miserere" (jazz version), "Mr. Jelly Lord," "Aaron Harris," "Jelly Roll Blues," "Wolverines," "The Crave," "Winin' Boy," "If You Knew How I Love You" (lyric and music by Werac and Jelly Roll Morton), "Don't You Leave Me Here," "Alabama Bound," "Fingerbreaker," "Animule Ball," "Buddy Bolden's Blues," "Milbeburg Joys" (lyric and music by Mares and Jelly Roll Morton), "Ballin' the Jack" (lyric by Jim Burris, music by Chris Smith), "Tiger Rag" (lyric and music by LaRocca), Medley: "Sunday Sweetheart" (lyric and music by Spikes and Jelly Roll Morton)/"My Home Is in a Southern

Town"/"Nearer My God to Thee" (traditional)/ "Didn't He Ramble" (traditional)/"Sweet Substitute," "Jelly Roll Blues" (reprise)

NOTES—Two years before this one-man revue about Jelly Roll Morton (Ferdinand Joseph La Menthe) (1890-1941) opened Off Broadway, Broadway had offered *Jelly's Last Jam*, a compelling and surreal book musical starring Gregory Hines and Savion Glover as the adult and child personas of the title character.

An earlier version of *Jelly Roll!*, titled *Vernel Bagneris Presents Jelly Roll Morton: A Me-Morial*, had opened Off Off Broadway at Michael's Pub on October 13, 1992, and played there for almost a year.

814 Jericho. "A Musical Legend." THEATRE: 18th Street Playhouse; OPENING DATE: November 11, 1984; PERFORMANCES: 12; BOOK: Judy Brussell; LYRICS: Judy Brussell; MUSIC: Buck Brown; DIRECTION: Jerry Campbell; SCENERY: Bob Phillips; PRODUCER: The Greensboro Civil Rights Fund

CAST—Eugene Key (Joshua), Buck Brown (Mayor), Mark Cohen (Paul Berliner), Kate Hunter Brown (Katy Berliner), Juanda LaJoyce Holley (Sandy Johnson), Evelyn Blakey (Evelyn), Molly Stark (Johanna Berliner), Kevin Glenn (Matt Cane), Marcus Neville (Frank, Wayne), Richard Rohan (Fred, Police Chief), Mimi Wyche (Billie Jo Klyde), Larry Campbell (the Rev. Darwin Johnson)

The musical was presented in three acts (division of acts and song assignments unknown; songs are listed in performance order).

MUSICAL NUMBERS—"Spinning Song," "But I Hear," "A Decent Job," "In Good Old Colony Times," "Jericho Cotton Mill Blues," "Devoted to the Cause," "One Step at a Time," "My Son," "Song of the United Racist Front," "Song of Escape," "If It Were All True," "In Love with the Expert Red," "A Kind of Power," "Hard Times in the Mill," "Strike!," "Joshua's Rap," "Come Back to Brooklyn," "One Step Forward, Two Steps Back," "The Douglass Decree," "Gentle People," "The Necessity of Being Cruel," "Song of the Nazi Dogs," "Operation Flea," "Song of Identification," "We Have to Lead the Fight," "Nothing Left but the Rope," "Remember November Third," "Our Kids," "The Union Is Behind Us," "Jericho Massacre," "Nothing Else to Do," "We Are No Longer Strangers," "Beware the Thunder and the Light"

NOTES—*Jericho*, a musical about civil rights, was produced under an Off Off Broadway contract. Besides its twelve regular performances, the musical played one benefit performance at Symphony Space.

815 Jerico-Jim Crow (1964). THEATRE: The Sanctuary; OPENING DATE: January 12, 1964; PERFORMANCES: 31; PLAY: Langston Hughes; MUSIC: Mostly traditional songs (lyrics and music of "Such a Little King" and "Freedom Land" by Langston Hughes); DIRECTION: Alvin Ailey and William Hairston; CHOREOGRAPHY: Alvin Ailey (?); COSTUMES: Ves Harper; LIGHTING: Ves Harpre; MUSIC DIRECTION: Professor Hugh Porter; PRODUCER: Greenwich Players Inc., in co-ordination with CORE, and SNCC; a Stella Holt production; Frances Drucker, Associate Producer

CAST—GILBERT PRICE (Young Man), HILDA HARRIS (Young Girl), JOSEPH (C.) ATTLES (Old Man), ROSALIE KING (Old Woman), JAMES WOODALL (Jim Crow), DOROTHY DRAKE (Woman), The Hugh Porter Gospel Singers (Virginia Davis, Eleanor Howell, Dorothy Brazzle, Sylvia Terry, Vivian Moore, Walter Coleman, Marquette Miller, Bob Broadway, Brock Williams, Johnny Riddley, Moses Brown, Lamont Washington)

The musical was presented in one act.

MUSICAL NUMBERS—"A Meeting Here Tonight" (Ensemble), "I'm On My Way" (Joseph Attles, Ensemble), "I Been 'Buked and I Been Scorned" (Rosalie King), "Such a Little King" (Rosalie King, Hilda Harris), "Is Massa Gwine to Sell Us Tomorrow?" (Gilbert Price), "How Much Do You Want Me to Bear?" (Dorothy Drake), "Where Will I Lie Down?" (Hilda Harris, Gilbert Davis), "Follow the Drinking Gourd" (Virginia Davis), "John Brown's Body" (Ensemble), "Battle Hymn of the Republic" (Ensemble), "Slavery Chain Done Broke at Last" (Rosalie King, Hilda Harris, Ensemble), "Oh, Freedom!" (Hilda Harris), "Go Down, Moses" (Dorothy Drake), "Ezekiel Saw the Wheel" (Joseph Attles, Ensemble), "Stay in the Field" (Joseph Attles), "Freedom Land" (Gilbert Price), "God's Gonna Cut You Down" (Gilbert Price, Dorothy Drake, Ensemble), "Better Leave Segregation Alone" (James Woodall), "My Mind on Freedom" (Hilda Harris, Ensemble), "We Shall Overcome" (Gilbert Price, Hilda Harris), "The Battle of Old Jim Crow" (Ensemble), "Come and Go with Me" (Dorothy Drake, Ensemble)

NOTES—Through the use of dramatic readings as well as traditional and original songs, Langston Hughes' *Jerico-Jim Crow*, which was co-produced by Stella Holt, traced the history of racism in the United States through the eyes of six characters. Richard F. Shepard in the *New York Times* noted that a similar work, Martin B. Duberman's non-musical *In White America* (which had opened Off Broadway earlier in the season), had explored the same general subject matter. Further, Broadway later used a similar device to explore racial issues in the United States (*Hallelujah, Baby!* [1967] and *1600 Pennsylvania Avenue* [1976]). Shepard found *Jerico-Jim Crow* "rousing," and he noted that while the musical didn't provide answers to America's racial problems, it posed its questions "in thunderous letters."

In 1964, Folkways Records issued a 2-LP set of *Jerico-Jim Crow* (# FL-9671), with many of the original cast members (on the album, Micki Grant replaced Hilda Harris).

In 1968, a series of five performances of *Jerico-Jim Crow* was presented at the Greenwich Mews Theatre (see entry). The revival was dedicated to the memories of Langston Hughes and Stella Holt, both of whom had died in the interim between the two productions.

816 Jerico-Jim Crow (1968). THEATRE: Greenwich Mews Theatre/The Village Presbyterian Church and Brotherhood Synagogue; OPENING DATE: March 9, 1968; PERFORMANCES: 5; PLAY: Langston Hughes; MUSIC: Mostly traditional songs (lyric and music of "Such a Little King" and "Freedom Land" by Langston Hughes); DIRECTION: Louis Johnson (original direction by Alvin Ailey and William Hairston); LIGHTING: Ray McCutcheon Musical Direction: Professor Hugh Porter; PRODUCER: The Greenwich Mews Theatre (A Stella Holt Production)

CAST—Dion Watts (Young Man), Hilda Harris (Young Girl), Joseph (C.) Attles (Old Man), Rosalie King (Old Woman), Barney Hodges (Jim Crow), Dorothy Drake (Woman); The Hugh Porter Gospel Singers: Mary Brown, Roberta Caldwell, Eleanor Howell, Marquette Miller, Fletcher Rozier, Jon Harris, Herbert Slater, Verma Moorehead, Brock Williams

The musical was presented in one act.

MUSICAL NUMBERS—"A Meeting Here Tonight" (Ensemble), "I'm On My Way" (Joseph Attles, Ensemble), "I Been 'Buked and I Been Scorned" (Rosalie King), "Such a Little King" (Rosalie King, Hilda Harris), "Is Massa Gwine to Sell Us Tomorrow?" (Dion Watts), "How Much Do You Want Me to Bear?" (Dorothy Drake), "Where Will I Lie Down?" (Hilda Harris, Dion Watts), "Follow the Drinking Gourd" (Dorothy Drake, Ensemble), "John Brown's Body" (Ensemble), "Battle Hymn of the Republic" (Ensemble), "Slavery Chain Done Broke at Last" (Rosalie King, Hilda Harris, Ensemble), "Oh, Freedom" (Hilda Harris), "Go Down, Moses" (Dorothy Drake), "Ezekiel Saw the Wheel" (Joseph Attles, Ensemble), "Stay in the Field" (Joseph Attles), "Freedom Land" (Dion Watts), "God's Gonna Cut You Down" (Dion Watts, Dorothy Drake, Ensemble), "Better Leave Segregation Alone" (Barney Hodges), "My Mind on Freedom" (Hilda Harris, Ensemble), "We Shall Overcome" (Hilda Harris, Dion Watts), "Freedom Land" (reprise) (Hilda Harris, Dion Watts), "The Battle of Old Jim Crow" (Ensemble), "Come and Go with Me" (Dorothy Drake, Ensemble)

NOTES—The limited engagement of *Jerico-Jim Crow* (which had originally premiered in 1964 [see entry]) opened on March 9, and gave a total of five performances over a series of a few weekends. The production was dedicated to Langston Hughes and Stella Holt (the producer of the original production), both of whom had died in the interim between the two productions.

Dan Sullivan in the *New York Times* observed that some Black writers might find the musical's text "disgracefully obsequious toward the values of white middle-class America," and he felt the musical could do with more "righteous anger" and "backbone" and less "bland talk about 'brotherhood.'" But he found the music "great," and said it made one "want to jump into the aisle and dance out of the church, which is just how the show ends."

817 Jerry Herman's Parade.
NOTES—See entry for *Parade*.

818 Jerry's Girls. "A Musical Revue." THEATRE: Ted Hook's Onstage Theatre; OPENING DATE: August 17, 1981; PERFORMANCES: 101; LYRICS: Jerry Herman; MUSIC: Jerry Herman; DIRECTION: Larry Alford; CHOREOGRAPHY: Sharon Halley; SCENERY: Hal Tine; COSTUMES: Bernard Johnson; LIGHTING: Hal Tine; MUSICAL DIRECTION: Cheryl Hardwick; PRODUCER: The Bosom Buddies Company

CAST—Evalyn Baron, Alexandra (Alix) Korey, Leila Martin, Pauletta Pearson

The revue was presented in two acts.

ACT ONE—"Jerry's Girls"/"It's Today" (from *Mame*, 1966) (Company), Optimist Medley:, "Put On Your Sunday Clothes" (*Hello, Dolly!*, 1964) (Leila Martin), "Open a New Window" (*Mame*, 1966) (Company), "Chin Up, Ladies" (*Milk and Honey*, 1961) (Company), "It Only Takes a Moment" (*Hello, Dolly!*, 1964) (Pauletta Pearson), "Wherever He Ain't" (*Mack & Mabel*, 1974) (Alexandra Korey), "We Need a Little Christmas" (*Mame*, 1966) (Company), "I Won't Send Roses" (*Mack & Mabel*, 1974) (Evalyn Baron), "Tap Your Troubles Away" (*Mack & Mabel*, 1974) (Alexandra Korey), Vaudeville Medley:, "Two-a-Day" (*Parade*, 1960) (Pauletta Pearson), "Bosom Buddies" (*Mame*, 1966) (Evalyn Baron, Leila Martin), "I Wanna Make the World Laugh" (*Mack & Mabel*, 1974) (Alexandra Korey), "The Man in the Moon" (*Mame*, 1966) (Company), "So Long, Dearie" (*Hello, Dolly!*, 1964) (Pauletta Pearson), "When I'm Playin' the Palace" (*Joe Masiell Not at the Palace*, 1977) (Leila Martin), "Two-a-Day" (reprise) (Company), "The Spring of Next Year" (*Dear World*, 1969) (Evalyn Baron), "If He Walked Into My Life" (*Mame*, 1966) (Leila Martin), "Hello, Dolly!" (*Hello, Dolly!*, 1964) (Company)

ACT TWO—Movies Medley: "Just Go to the Movies" (*A Day in Hollywood/A Night in the Ukraine*, 1980; performer[s] not credited in the program, but probably sung by the entire company), "Movies Were Movies" (*Mack & Mabel*, 1974) (Pauletta Pearson), "Look What Happened to Mabel" (*Mack & Mabel*, 1974) (Alexandra Korey), "Nelson" (*A Day in Hollywood/A Night in the Ukraine*, 1980) (Evalyn Baron), "Just Go to the Movies" (reprise) (Company), "Shalom" (*Milk and Honey*, 1961) (Leila Martin), "Milk and Honey" (*Milk and Honey*, 1961)

(Evalyn Baron, Leila Martin, Pauletta Pearson), "Time Heals Everything" (*Mack & Mabel*, 1974) (Alexandra Korey), "Mame" (*Mame*, 1966) (Company), "Kiss Her Now" (*Dear World*, 1969) (Leila Martin, Pauletta Pearson), "The Tea Party" (*Dear World*, 1969) (Alexandria Korey, Evalyn Baron, Leila Martin), "And I Was Beautiful" (*Dear World*, 1969) (Evalyn Baron), "Gooch's Song" (*Mame*, 1966) (Alexandra Korey), "Before the Parade Passes By" (*Hello, Dolly!*, 1964) (Leila Martin), "I Don't Want to Know" (*Dear World*, 1969) (Pauletta Pearson). Girl Medley (Company):, "My Best Girl" (*Mame*, 1966) "It Takes a Woman" (*Hello, Dolly!*, 1964) "Hundreds of Girls" (*Mack & Mabel*, 1974), "Marianne" (*The Grand Tour*, 1979), "When Mabel Comes in the Room" (*Mack & Mabel*, 1974), "Mame" (reprise), "Hello, Dolly" (reprise), "I'll Be Here Tomorrow" (*The Grand Tour*, 1979) (Company), "Jerry's Girls" (reprise) (Company)

NOTES—Five retrospectives of Jerry Herman's songs have been heard in New York. Besides two separate engagements of *Jerry's Girls* (the 1981 Off Off-Broadway version and the 1985 Broadway engagement), there have also been the Off Off Broadway *Tune the Grand Up! Words and Music by Jerry Herman* (1978; see entry), the Broadway revue *An Evening with Jerry Herman*, which played for twenty-eight performances in 1998, and the Off Broadway *Showtune: The Words and Music of Jerry Herman*, which played for fifty-three performances in 2003 (for more information about the latter production, see entry for *Tune the Grand Up! Words and Music by Jerry Herman*). One questions the point of these productions, all of them excrescences. The musicals recycled the same basic songs, and were disappointing because they virtually ignored Herman's Off Broadway work (*I Feel Wonderful* [1954], *Nightcap* [1958], *Parade* [1960], and *Madame Aphrodite* [1961]; see entries) as well as his trunk songs. *Jerry's Girls* included just one new song (the title number) and the obscure "When I'm Playin' the Palace" (from *Joe Masiell Not at the Palace*; see entry).

Jerry's Girls included five songs from *Hello, Dolly!*, eight from *Mame*, and no less than nine from *Mack & Mabel*. It might have been better if the producer had given the Broadway cast albums of these musicals to the audience and dispensed with the production altogether.

Jerry's Girls was later revived (and slightly revised) for a national tour which began during the 1983-1984 theatre season and which starred Carol Channing, Leslie Uggams, and Andrea McArdle. The production was recorded during its Washington, D.C., engagement, and a 2-LP cast album was released by Polydor Records (# 820-207-1-Y-2). The production included one new song by Herman ("Take It All Off"). It later opened on Broadway at the St. James Theatre on December 18, 1985, and ran for 139 performances (Dorothy Loudon, Leslie Uggams, and Chita Rivera were the leads).

The script of *Jerry's Girls* was published by Samuel French, Inc., in 1988; the revised script included four songs from Herman's 1983 Broadway hit *La Cage Aux Folles*.

819 The Jewish Gypsy. THEATRE: Town Hall; OPENING DATE: October 9, 1983; PERFORMANCES: 65; BOOK: Mordechai Mandel; English translation by Bella Mysell Yablokoff; LYRICS: Moshe Sachar; MUSIC: Martin Moskowitz; ADDITIONAL MUSIC by Dan Blitenthal; DIRECTION: Michael Greenstein; CHOREOGRAPHY: Derek Wolshonak; SCENERY: Adina Reich and Abraham Mordoh; COSTUMES: Clare Gosney; MUSICAL DIRECTION: Renee Solomon; PRODUCER: Shalom Yiddish Musical Comedy Theatre, Inc. (Raymond Ariel, Producer)

CAST—David Ellin (Danilo), MARY SOREANU (Palashka), David Montefiore (Yosl), Michael Michalovic (Shloime), Sandy Levitt (Hirsh), Reizl Bozyk (Chaya), Diane Cypkin (Tzirl), Shifee Lovitt (Paya), Yankele Alperin (Sherml), Stewart Figa (Berl); Gypsies and Townspeople (Catherine Caplin, Carolyn Goor, Tara Tyrrell, Bill Badolato, Stanley Kramer, John Milne)

The action occurs in early Czarist Russia.

The musical was presented in a prologue and two acts.

PROLOGUE—Overture (Orchestra), "Ballade" (David Ellin), "Play Gypsy" (Mary Soreanu, Ensemble), "My Yiddish Gypsy" (David Montefiore, Mary Soreanu), "Lord in Heaven" (David Montefiore), "Ballade" (reprise) (David Ellin)

ACT ONE—"A Good Week" (Michael Michalovic, Ensemble), "I Don't Agree" (Reizl Bozyk, Shifee Lovitt, Yankele Alperin), "What a Pair" (Shifee Lovitt, Stewart Figa), "Bessarabia" (Mary Soreanu), "Yearning" (Mary Soreanu)

ACT TWO—"Ballade" (reprise) (David Ellin), "The Russian Waltz" (Sandy Levitt, Ensemble), "To Your Health" (Yankele Alperin, Ensemble), "Let There Be Peace" (Yankele Alperin, Reizl Bozyk), "When Love Calls" (David Montefiore), "Life Is So Beautiful" (Diane Cypkin, Sandy Levitt), "The Dream" (Mary Soreanu, David Montefiore, Ensemble), "No, No, No!" (David Montefiore), "Wish Me Luck" (Mary Soreanu), "Together" (Mary Soreanu, David Montefiore), "I Want to Be a Jewish Girl" (Mary Soreanu), Finale (Ensemble)

NOTES—This was another Jewish-themed musical which starred Mary Soreanu, who almost single-handedly was keeping old-time, traditional Jewish musicals on the boards. The Off Off Broadway production played for more than two months.

820 Jigsaw. "A New Musical." THEATRE: Tudor Room/The Commodore Hotel; OPENING DATE: April 4, 1978; PERFORMANCES: 10; SKETCHES: Jean Reavey; LYRICS: Jean Reavey; MUSIC: John Wallowitch; DIRECTION: Bertram Ross; CHOREOGRAPHY: Bertram Ross; LIGHTING: Roy Wallace; PRODUCER: Quaigh Theatre, Inc.

CAST—David Barron, Mike Dantuono, Anthony Giaimo, Nancy Harrow, Ted Richert, Theresa Saldana, Eve St. John, Sandra Zeeman

The revue was presented in two acts.

ACT ONE; OPENING—"No One, Jigsaw" (Company), "Lost" (Mike Dantuono, David Barron, Theresa Saldana, Nancy Harrow, Ted Richert), "I Know of a Place" (Sandra Zeeman), "Rue de la Solitude" (Eve St. John, Anthony Giaimo), "I Know of a Place" (reprise) (Sandra Zeeman, Mike Dantuono, Ted Richert), "Makeshift Into Elephants" (Company), "Soho" (Company), "Everyone Tells Me" (Mike Dantuono), "Telephone Song" (Theresa Saldana), "Vanilla Soda" (Company), "Red Letter Hope" (Eve St. John, Ted Richert, Nancy Harrow, Theresa Saldana, Sandra Zeeman), "Don't Cross Your Bridge" (David Barron, Anthony Giaimo, Sandra Zeeman, Theresa Saldana), "Cup" (Ted Richert, Nancy Harrow), "Under the Wonder" (Nancy Harrow, Company), "Don't Cross Your Bridge" (reprise) (Eve St. John, Theresa Saldana, Sandra Zeeman), "Rock" (David Barron, Anthony Giaimo), "She's a Big White Mouse" (Eve St. John), "The Man with a Mirror in His Hat" (David Barron), "He's a Tall Man" (Nancy Harrow, Theresa Saldana, Sandra Zeeman), "Big Belinda Fatsquat" (Mike Dantuono, Company)

ACT TWO—"Universe Song" (Ted Richert, Moon Maidens), "Upside Down" (Anthony Giaimo, Theresa Saldana), "Journey to Ever" (Mike Dantuono, David Barron, Company), "Capes" (Eve St. John, Ted Richert, Mike Dantuono, David Barron), "Fabulous Faker" (Sandra Zeeman, Mike Dantuono, Anthony Giaimo), "I Put Watches Out of Time" (Anthony Giaimo, Ted Richert, Theresa Saldana, Nancy Harrow), "Flowers" (David Barron, Sandra Zeeman), "Look, Look at Me" (Anthony Giaimo, Ted Richert, Theresa Saldana, Nancy Harrow), "Blanket Over the Sorrows of Werther" (Mike Dantuono, David Barron, Nancy Harrow, Sandra Zeeman, Eve St. John, Theresa Saldana), "Avant the Guard" (Eve St. John, Sandra Zeeman, Theresa Saldana), "The First Volume of My Life" (Ted Richert), "Marietta" (Theresa Saldana, Sandra Zeeman, Ted Richert, Anthony Giaimo), "Johnny Over There" (Nancy Harrow, Eve St. John, Theresa Saldana, Sandra Zeeman, Ted Richert), "Love Times One" (Mike Dantuono, David Barron, Ted Richert, Eve St. John, Nancy Harrow, Sandra Zeeman), "Bird" (Theresa Saldana, Anthony Giaimo), "Down the Fire Valley" (Company), "Fashions of the Day" (Anthony Giaimo, Company)

NOTES—*Jigsaw* was presented April 4 through April 10, 1978, at the Commodore Hotel (probably under an Off Off Broadway contract); it had previously been produced at the Quaigh Theatre in March 1976.

821 Jimmy and Billy. THEATRE: Westside/Upstairs; OPENING DATE: December 10, 1978; PERFORMANCES: 1; BOOK: David I. Levine; LYRICS: David I. Levine; MUSIC: David I. Levine and Pat Curtis; DIRECTION: Robert Pagent; CHOREOGRAPHY: Robert Pagent; SCENERY: James Steere; COSTUMES: Terry Leong; LIGHTING: William Anderson; MUSICAL DIRECTION: John Lesko

CAST—Richie Allen, Richard Blair, Kathy Ellen Collins, Joan Dunham, Laurie Franks, Gary Holcombe, Molly King, John Sheridan, Leayha Sturges, Dennis Warning

NOTES—Presumably somewhere in the theatre-going universe there were potential audience members for this musical about then-President Jimmy Carter and his brother Billy. If so, they had only one chance to see the production; the musical's opening night was also its closing night.

822 Jo. "A New Musical." THEATRE: Orpheum Theatre; OPENING DATE: February 12, 1964; PERFORMANCES: 63; BOOK: Don Parks and William Dyer; LYRICS: Don Parks and William Dyer; MUSIC: William Dyer; DIRECTION: John Bishop; CHOREOGRAPHY: Chele Abel and Gerald Teijelo; SCENERY: Gordon Micunis; COSTUMES: Evelyn Norton Anderson; LIGHTING: Miller-Moffatt; MUSICAL DIRECTION: Jane Douglass White; PRODUCER: Victoria Crandall

CAST—Joyce Lynn (Hannah), Judith McCauley (Beth), April Shawhan (Amy), Susan Browning (Meg), Karin Wolfe (Jo), Joy Hodges (Marmee), Paul Blake (Freddie, Editor), Myron Odegaard (Mr. Laurence), Lowell Harris (John Brooke), Salicia Smith (Sallie Gardiner, Maid), Joyce MacDonald (Harriet King), Don Stewart (Laurie), Mimi Randolph (Aunt March), Joseph Davies (Mr. March), Alan Zemel (Geordie), Jania Zozhen (Kitty), Renee Tetro (Minna), Bernard F. Wurger (Professor Bhaer), Joel Pitt (Ned Moffat), Jack Fletcher (Frank Vaughn)

SOURCE—The 1868 novel *Little Women* by Louisa May Alcott.

The action occurs in Harmony, Massachusetts, during and after the Civil War; and, in parts of Act Two, New York and Europe.

The musical was presented in two acts.

ACT ONE—"Harmony, Mass." (Townspeople), "Deep in the Bosom of the Family" (Karin Wolfe, Susan Browning, Judith McCauley, April Shawhan), "Hurry Home" (Joy Hodges, Susan Browning, Karin Wolfe, Judith McCauley, April Shawhan), "Let's Be Elegant or Die!" (Susan Browning, Karin Wolfe, Judith McCauley, April Shawhan), "Castles in the Air" (Don Stewart), "Friendly Polka" (Karin Wolfe, Don Stewart, Guests), "Time Will Be" (Lowell Harris), "What a Long Cold Winter!" (April Shawhan, Judith McCauley, Joyce Lynn, Townspeople), "Moods" (Karin Wolfe, Don Stewart), "Afraid to Fall in Love" (Karin Wolfe), "A Wedding! A Wedding!" (Judith McCauley, April Shawhan, Susan Browning, Townspeople), "I Like" (Don Stewart)

ACT TWO—"Genius Burns" (Karin Wolfe, Paul Blake), "If You Find a True Love" (Bernard F. Wurger, Children), "Nice as Any Man Can Be" (Karin Wolfe), "More Than Friends" (Don Stewart), "Taking the Cure" (Tourists, April Shawhan, Mimi Randolph, Don Stewart)

NOTES—There have been at least ten musical adaptations of *Little Women* (Broadway, Off Broadway, British versions, a television adaptation, and an opera), most of them not particularly noteworthy or successful (with the exception of the 1998 opera *Little Women* [libretto and music by Mark Adamo] which seems to have found its way into the current opera repertory; see entry). Other adaptations of the novel include six British versions, two of which were produced in London: *A Girl Called Jo* (1955) played for 141 performances and *Dear Jo* (1974) played for six weeks. The other musical versions (all titled *Little Women*) didn't play the West End (one was another 1955 adaptation, and the other three played in 1970, 1974, and 2005, the latter in a concert adaptation). In the United States, a 1958 musical version with lyrics and music by Richard Adler was produced on television by CBS on October 16, and the cast included Jeannie Carson, Florence Henderson, Margaret O'Brien, Rise Stevens, Bill Hayes, and Joel Grey (the TV soundtrack album was released by Kapp Records [LP # KL-1104]); and in 2004 a musical version played on Broadway for a few months; Maureen McGovern was in the cast, and the lyrics were by Mindi Dickstein and the music by Jason Howland (the cast album was released by Ghostlight Records [CD # 4405-2).

For *Jo*, Karin Wolfe created the title role; she also performed the title role in another failed musical, the 1973 stage adaptation of Alan Jay Lerner and Frederick Loewe's 1958 film musical *Gigi*. Another cast member, Susan Browning, would memorably sing of "Barcelona" in the original 1970 Broadway production of Stephen Sondheim's landmark musical *Company*.

But perhaps the most interesting casting in *Jo* was that of Joy Hodges (as Marmee). She had a leading role in the original 1937 production of Richard Rodgers and Lorenz Hart's *I'd Rather Be Right*, and, with Austin Marshall, introduced the standard "Have You Met Miss Jones?" She later appeared in the title role of *Nellie Bly* (1946), one of the legendary disasters of the 1940s Broadway musical, and during the run of the hit 1971 revival of *No, No, Nanette* she replaced Ruby Keeler. Hers was a fascinating career, spanning fifty decades.

There appears to be some confusion regarding which actresses played the roles of Beth and Amy on opening night. *The Burn Mantle Yearbook/The Best Plays of 1963-1964* credits Kitty Sullivan and Jodi Williams in the respective roles. However, *Theatre World/Season 1963-1964* credits Judith McCauley and April Shawhan. Further, a program from the musical's second week indicates Kitty Sullivan and April Shawhan performed the roles. In his opening night review for the *New York Times*, Howard Taubman cited Judith McCauley's "fragile" performance as Beth and indicates April Shawhan's Amy looked like a Tenniel drawing for *Alice in Wonderland*. So Taubman has the last word on who performed the roles, at least on opening night (since the program for the second week lists Kitty Sullivan's name as the actress playing Beth, it appears Judith McCauley left the show after its first week).

823 Joan. "A Musical." THEATRE: Circle in the Square (Downtown); OPENING DATE: June 19, 1972; PERFORMANCES: 64; BOOK: Al Carmines; LYRICS: Al Carmines; MUSIC: Al Carmines; DIRECTION: Al Carmines; CHOREOGRAPHY: Gus Solomons, Jr.; special choreography by David Vaughn; SCENERY: Earl Eidman; COSTUMES: Ira Siff with Joan Kilpatrick; LIGHTING: Earl Eidman; MUSICAL DIRECTION: Al Carmines; PRODUCERS: Circle in the Square (Theodore Mann, Artistic Director; Paul Libin, Managing Director) in association with Seymour Hacker

CAST—LEE GUILLIATT (Joan), Emily Adams (Mother), Sandy Padilla (Sandy, Police Matron), Phyllis MacBryde (Phyllis), Ira Siff (Ira), Teresa King (Teresa), Tony Clark (Policeman), Margaret Wright (Therapist), Essie Borden (Virgin Mary), David Vaughn (Cardinal), David McCorkle (Bishop, Social Worker), Jeffrey Apter (Rabbi), Julie Kurnitz (Mother Superior), Tracy Moore (Tracy), Al Carmines (Pianist)

The action occurs in the East Village.

The musical was presented in two acts.

ACT ONE—"Praise the Lord" (Chorus), "Come on Joan" (Tracy Moore, with Chorus), "It's So Nice to Cuddle in a Threesome" (Lee Guilliatt, Ira Siff, Tracy Moore), "Go Back" (Phyllis MacBryde, Sandy Padilla) (choreographed by Phyllis MacBryde), "They Call Me the Virgin Mary" (Essie Borden, with Lee Guilliatt), "Salve Madonna" (Chorus), "The Woman I Love" (Tracy Moore), "Spoken Aria" (Emily Adams), "Ira, My Dope Fiend" (Lee Guilliatt), "A Country of the Mind" (Ira Siff), "I Live a Little" (Essie Borden, with Chorus), "What I Wonder" (Lee Guilliatt, with Chorus)

ACT TWO—"The Religious Establishment" (David Vaughn, David McCorkle, Jeffrey Apter) (choreographed by David Vaughn), "In My Silent Universe" (Ira Siff), "Take Courage, Daughter" (Julie Kurnitz, with Chorus), "Rivers of Roses" (Chorus), "I'm Madame Margaret the Therapist" (Margaret Wright, with Chorus), (choreographed by David Vaughn), "Look at Me Joan" (Chorus), "Despair" (Teresa King), "Faith Is Such a Simple Thing" (Lee Guilliatt, with Chorus), "Praise the Lord" (reprise) (Lee Guilliatt, with Chorus)

NOTES—*Joan* was the second of three musicals produced Off Broadway (and on) during the first half of the 1970s which dealt with Joan of Arc (for more information, see entry for *The Survival of St. Joan*). Since *Joan* was by Al Carmines, the musical was a skewed and topsy-turvy approach to the famous story. Carmines described his version as "a razz-ma-tazz musical comedy" rather than a traditional religious play. Well, yes. Because in his version Joan is a Village political activist of Jewish-Presbyterian heritage who is arrested when she bombs a government building and is ultimately executed for her crime. Before she meets her preordained end, Joan becomes involved with a drug addict, a state-sponsored therapist, the religious establishment, and a bizarre meeting with the Virgin Mary on East 6th Street (Mary is a wise-cracking redhead who wears flashy clothes).

The 2-LP cast album was released by Judson Records (# JU-1001), and included extra material not heard in the Off Broadway production. During the run of the show, there was some minor tinkering with the order of the songs.

Joan had first been produced Off Off Broadway at the Judson Poets' Theatre in November 1971 for ten performances and was briefly revived there the following month for a weekend's worth of performances; the Judson engagements included more performers than were seen in the Off Broadway production.

In reviewing the December 1971 return engagement, Mel Gussow in the *New York Times* noted the musical offered one of Carmines' "most melodic" scores, and he felt the musical should be produced on Broadway or Off Broadway or even on a cross-country concert tour. One song from *Joan* ("It's So Nice to Cuddle in a Threesome") was heard in the 1982 revue *The Gospel According to Al* (see entry).

824 Joe Masiell Not at the Palace. THEATRE: Astor Place Theatre; OPENING DATE: December 11, 1977; PERFORMANCES: 23; DIRECTION: James Coco; CHOREOGRAPHY: C. Tod Jackson; SCENERY: C. Tod Jackson; COSTUMES: C. Tod Jackson; LIGHTING: James Nisbet Clark; MUSICAL DIRECTION: Christopher Bankey; PRODUCER: Lily Turner

CAST—JOE MASIELL, Debra Dickinson, Anita Ehrler, Gena Ramsel, Nancy Salis

The revue was presented in two acts (song assignments not listed in program, although apparently all numbers featured Joe Masiell and his quartet of back-up singers and dancers).

ACT ONE—"When I'm Playin' the Palace" (lyric and music by Jerry Herman; written especially for this production), "Everything" (by Holmes and Williams), "Two for the Road" (from 1967 film *Two for the Road*; lyric by Leslie Bricusse, music by Henry Mancini), "You and I" (1969 film *Goodbye, Mr. Chips*; lyric and music by Leslie Bricusse), "The Lady Is a Tramp" (*Babes in Arms*, 1937; lyric by Lorenz Hart, music by Richard Rodgers), "Io E' Te" (by Morricone and Pace), "I Don't Want to Know" (*Dear World*, 1969; lyric and music by Jerry Herman), "In My Life" (lyric and music by John Lennon and Paul McCartney), "We Were Young" (lyric and music by Joe Masiell), "If You Like the Music" (lyric and music by Pete McCann), "Here's That Rainy Day" (*Carnival in Flanders*, 1953; lyric by Johnny Burke, music by Jimmy Van Heusen), "Money, Money, Money" (lyric and music by Benny Andersson and Bjorn Ulvaeus), "Money, Money" (1972 film *Cabaret*; lyric by Fred Ebb, music by John Kander), "This Funny World" (*Betsy*, 1926; lyric by Lorenz Hart, music by Richard Rodgers) "But the World Goes 'Round" (1977 film *New York, New York*; lyric by Fred Ebb, music by John Kander)

ACT TWO—"What Now My Love" (lyric and music by Delanoe and Gilbert Becaud; English lyric by Carl Sigman), "Who" (lyric and music by Charles Aznavour; English lyric by Herbert Kretzmer), "It Will Be My Day" (lyric and music by Charles Aznavour; English lyric by Bob Morrison), "Madeleine" (lyric and music by Jacques Brel; English lyric by Mort Shuman and Eric Blau; this version first heard in *Jacques Brel Is Alive and Well and Living in Paris* [1968; see entry]), "Crazy Melody" (by Varel and Bailly; English lyric by Will Holt), "Hey, Poppa" (lyric by Fred Ebb, music by John Kander; written especially for this production)

NOTES—Joe Masiell was an Off Broadway baby who never quite made it to the big time. He was in a string of flops, both Off Broadway (*Sensations* [1970], *Leaves of Grass* [1971], *How to Get Rid of It* [1974], *A Matter of Time* [1975], *Tickles by Tucholsky* [1976]; see entries) and on (*Dear World* [1969] and *Different Times* [1972]), and was most closely associated with *Jacques Brel Is Alive and Well and Living in Paris* (1968; see entry): he was a replacement in the original Off Broadway production, and later played the role on Broadway, on tour, and in the film version. He also appeared in *Gabrielle* (1974), a regional production which attempted to graft various songs by Gilbert Becaud into a book musical. Masiell died in 1985. In his review for the *New York Times*, Richard F. Shepard noted that the Astor Place Theatre was offering a "big, buoyant and joyful sound" in which the "handsome" Masiell's "clear and big" voice melted into the "appropriate sentimentality" to suit the style of any song. Shepard said the revue "romps along in easy good humor," and concluded that the show conveyed a "sense of fun" in its "refreshing and most effective simplicity."

825 Johnny Guitar. "The Musical." THEATRE: Century Center for the Performing Arts; OPENING DATE: March 23, 2004; PERFORMANCES: 63; BOOK: Nicholas Van Hoogstraten; LYRICS: Joel Higgins; MUSIC: Joel Higgins and Martin Silvestri;

DIRECTION: Joel Higgins; CHOREOGRAPHY: Jane Lanier; SCENERY: Van Santvoord; COSTUMES: Kaye Voice; LIGHTING: Ed McCarthy; MUSICAL DIRECTION: James Mironchik; PRODUCERS: Definite Maybe Productions LLC and Mark H. Kress in association with Victoria Lang and Pier Paolo Piccoli and the Century Center for the Performing Arts; Sarah Brockus and Jeffrey Kent, Associate Producers

CAST—Jason Edwards (Quartet. Eddie, Jenks, Trio, Bill, Hank), Robb Sapp (Quartet, Turkey, Trio, The Western Singer), David Sinkus (Quartet, Tom, Bart Lonnergan, Trio, Carl), Ann Crumb (Quartet, Emma Small), Judy McLane (The Title Singer, Emma), Steve Blanchard (Johnny Guitar), Grant Norman (Sam, Ned), Ed Sala (Mr. McIvers). Robert Evan (The Dancin' Kid)

SOURCE—The 1954 Republic film *Johnny Guitar* (directed by Nicholas Ray, screenplay by Philip Yordan).

The prologue occurs in 1954; the rest of the action occurs late in the nineteenth century in New Mexico.

The musical was presented in two acts.

ACT ONE—"Johnny Guitar" (Prologue) (Judy McLane, Jason Edwards, Robb Sapp, David Sinkus, Ann Crumb), "Let It Spin" (Judy McLane, David Sinkus, Jason Edwards), "A Smoke and a Good Cup o' Coffee" (Steve Blanchard), "Branded a Tramp" (Judy McLane), "In Old Santa Fe" (Steve Blanchard, Judy McLane), "What's in It for Me?" (Robert Evans, Judy McLane), "Who Do They Think They Are?" (Ann Crumb, Ed Sala, Robb Sapp, Jason Edwards, David Sinkus), "Welcome Home" (Judy McLane)

ACT TWO—"Johnny Guitar" (reprise) (Robb Sapp, Jason Edwards, David Sinkus), "Tell Me a Lie" (Steve Blanchard), "The Gunfighter" (Robert Evans), "We've Had Our Moments" (Judy McLane, Steve Blanchard), "Bad Blood" (Judy McLane, Ann Crumb, Company), "Johnny Guitar" (reprise) (Company)

NOTES—If Nicholas Ray's 1954 western *Johnny Guitar* had dealt with two tough guys slugging it out while their wimmenfolk watched from the sidelines, it would have been just another forgotten oater today. But Ray and script writer Philip Yordan memorably reversed the roles of the sexes in what Leonard Maltin in his always-fascinating *Movie Guide* annuals calls "the screen's great kinky Western." Joan Crawford and Mercedes McCambridge played Vienna and Emma, the two toughest testosterone-filled babes the screen has ever seen, harpies on steroids who dominated a film filled with wimpering, ineffectual men, some of the blowhard variety and one, the title character, who'd rather strum his guitar than play with his gun.

When the Off Broadway musical version was announced, it seemed destined to be a sure-fire winner with its campy allure and its classic so-bad-it's-good movie pedigree. But for some reason, the musical never caught on and was gone in two months. It's hard to understand why, because Joel Higgins and Martin Silvestri's score is appealing, and Nicholas van Hoogstraten's book reads well, truly funny and with all the clichés down pat (Emma tells Vienna, "I'm going to be dancing on your grave") and with all the necessary campy accessories (a male roulette spinner tells Johnny Guitar, "That's a lot of man you're carrying in those boots, stranger"). If New York didn't embrace the musical, perhaps regional and community theatre will; this show definitely deserves a second chance.

The dance sequence "Rhapsody in Boots" and the trio "They Were on Fire" weren't listed in the program, but are in the script (published by Samuel French, Inc., in 2004) and were recorded for the cast album (released by Definite Maybe Productions Records [CD # DMCD-0401]).

Incidentally, Hoogstraten is the author of the invaluable *Lost Broadway Theatres*, a nostalgic, fascinating look at either demolished theatres (such as the Empire) or ones which are no longer active playhouses (the Mark Hellinger).

826 Johnny Johnson (1956). "A Musical Play." THEATRE: Carnegie Hall Playhouse; OPENING DATE: October 21, 1956; PERFORMANCES: Unknown; BOOK: Paul Green; LYRICS: Paul Green; MUSIC: Kurt Weill; DIRECTION: Stella Adler; CHOREOGRAPHY: Robert Joffrey; SCENERY: Wolfgang Roth; COSTUMES: Betty Coe Armstrong; LIGHTING: Wolfgang Roth; MUSICAL DIRECTION: Samuel Matlowsky; PRODUCER: Stella Adler

CAST—SIDNEY ARMUS (The Mayor, Sergeant Jackson, Second Doctor, Chief of the Allied High Command, Brother Hiram), Charles Tyner (The Village Editor, Dr. McBray, American Brigadier General, Attendant, Attendant), ROSEMARY O'REILLY (Minny Belle), Maurice Edwards (Grandpa Joe, English Premier, Brother Thomas), JAMES BRODERICK (Johnny Johnson), Jack Waltzer (Photographer, Orderly, Belgian Major General, Mr. First), Virginia McMahon (Minnie Belle's Friend), Frances Lane (Another Friend, Anguish Howington's Secretary), Jonathan Bush (Anguish Howington), Alice Winston (Aggie Tompkins, His Majesty [a King]), GENE SAKS (Private Jessel, Doctor, French Premier, Dr. Mahodan), James Moran (Sentry, Private O'Day, British Commander-in-Chief, Secretary), LOGAN RAMSEY (Captain Valentine, American Commander-in-Chief, Brother Henry), Robert Minford (English Sergeant, British Major General, Doctor), Art Alisi (Corporal George, Brother William), James Vazules (Private Fairfax, Orderly, Dr. Frewd), Edward Printz (Private Goldberg, Johann, Brother Claude), Gerald Garrigan (Private Harwood, Scottish Colonel, Field Radio Operator, Brother Theodore), James McDonald (Private Kearns, Another Field Operator, Brother Jim), Bruce Williamson (Private Svenson, Brother George), Elizabeth Parrish (French Nurse, Secretary), Joanne Linville (A Sister), Joseph Kahn (French Major General, Wee One), Edmund Gaynes (Anguish Howington, Jr.)

The action occurs a few years ago, as well as now, somewhere in America, somewhere in France, and somewhere in a house of balm.

The musical was presented in two acts.

ACT ONE—"Over in Europe" (Sidney Armus, Ensemble), "Democracy's Call" (Rosemary O'Reilly, Friends), "The Battle of San Juan Hill" (Maurice Edwards, Villagers), "Aggie's Song" (Alice Winston), "Oh, Heart of Love" (Rosemary O'Reilly), "Captain Valentine's Song" (Logan Ramsey), "The Tea Song" (Robert Minford, Soldiers), "The Rio Grande" (Gerald Garrigan)

ACT TWO—"Mon Ami, My Friend" (Elizabeth Parrish), "The Allied High Command" (Sidney Armus, Generals), "The Laughing Generals" (Generals), "Psychiatry Song" (Gene Saks), "The Asylum Chorus" (Inmates), "A Hymn to Peace" (Inmates), "Johnny's Song" (James Broderick)

NOTES—*Johnny Johnson* was the first musical Kurt Weill specifically wrote for Broadway. The 1936 anti-war musical had a somewhat jumbled plot which utilized surreal, expressionist techniques to tell the story of Johnny Johnson, a young American pacifist who finds himself fighting in France during World War II. When his anti-war stance leads him to spray high-ranking officers with laughing gas, he's committed to an insane asylum where he and other inmates believe they're part of the League of Nations. Ultimately, Johnny Johnson is released and returns home, where he makes non-aggressive children's toys as the world prepares for the next war.

The original 1936 production had a disappointing run of only two months; it was briefly revived in New York during the 1940-1941 theatre season in what appears to have been an Off Broadway production. After the 1956 Off Broadway production, the musical was seen Off Broadway in 1971, when it played for just one performance (see entry).

The script was published in hardback by Samuel French, Inc., in 1937, and in 1957 a generally complete studio cast recording was released by MGM Records (LP # E-3447; later reissued on Heliodor Records [LP # H/HS-25024]). The album was conducted by Samuel Matlowsky, and the cast included Burgess Meredith, Lotte Lenya, Evelyn Lear, and Jane Connell. Another recording, *Music for Johnny Johnson*, was released by Erato Records (CD # 0630-17870-2) in 1997.

Johnny Johnson was the second of three Kurt Weill musicals for which Samuel Matlowsky was the musical director (see entries for *The Threepenny Opera* [1954 and 1955 productions] and *The Rise and Fall of the City of Mahagonny* [1970]).

827 Johnny Johnson (1971). THEATRE: Edison Theatre; OPENING DATE: April 11, 1971; PERFORMANCES: 1; BOOK: Paul Green; LYRICS: Paul Green; MUSIC: Kurt Weill; DIRECTION: Jose Quintero; CHOREOGRAPHY: Bertram Ross; SCENERY: Peter Harvey; COSTUMES: Robert Fletcher; LIGHTING: Roger Morgan; MUSICAL DIRECTION: Joseph Klein; PRODUCERS: Timothy Gray and Robert Fletcher in association with Midge La Guardia

CAST—Ralph Williams (Johnny Johnson), Alice Cannon (Minny Belle Tompkins), Paul Michael (His Honor the Mayor, Wounded French Soldier, Pvt. Fairfax, American Commander), June Helmers (Miz Smith, French Nurse), Bob Lydiard (Photographer), Christopher Klein (Messenger), James Billings (Grandpa Joe, Wounded French Soldier, Pvt. Goldberger, Chief, Dr. Mahodan), Gordon Minard (Anguish Howington, Pvt. Harwood), Charlotte Jones (Aggie, Sister of the Organization for the Delight of Soldiers Disabled in the Line of Duty), Norman Chase (Captain Valentine), Wayne Sherwood (Doctor McBray, Wounded French Soldier, Pvt. O'Day, Scottish Colonel, German Priest), Clay Johns (Pvt. Jessell, Wounded French Soldier, Pvt. Swenson, Orderly, British Commander, Lieutenant, Military Police), Alexander Orfaly (Recruiting Sergeant, Wounded French Soldier, Cpl. George, Belgian Major General, Captain), Nadine Lewis (Goddess of Liberty), Norman Riggins (English Sergeant, Doctor, French Major General, American Priest), Bob Lydiard (Johann Lang), Entire Company (Villagers)

The action occurs in 1917 (and in the years following) in France and the United States.

The musical was presented in two acts.

ACT ONE—Introduction — Overture (Orchestra), "Over in Europe" (Paul Michael), "Democracy's Call" (Alice Cannon, Paul Michael, Company), "Up Chickamauga Hill" (James Billings), "Johnny's Melody" (Ralph Williams), "Aggie's Song" (Charlotte Jones), "Oh, Heart of Love" (Alice Cannon), "Farewell, Goodbye" (Alice Cannon), "The Sergeant's Chant" (Alexander Orfaly), "Valentine's Tango" (Norman Chase), "You're in the Army Now"— Interlude (Orchestra), "Johnny's Oath" (Orchestra), "Song of the Goddess" (Nadine Lewis), "Song of the Wounded Frenchmen" (Wayne Sherwood, Clay Johns, Alexander Orfaly, James Billings, Paul Michael), "Tea Song" (Norman Riggins, Soldiers), "Cowboy Song" (a/k/a "Oh, The Rio Grande") (Gordon Minnard), "Johnny's Dream" (Alice Cannon), "Song of the Guns" (Male Chorus), "Music of the Stricken Redeemer" (Orchestra)

ACT TWO—"Army Song" (Entr'acte), "Mon Ami, My Friend" (June Helmers), "Allied High Command" (Officers), "The Laughing Generals" (Orchestra), "The Battle" (Orchestra), Prayer: "In Times of War and Tumults" (Norman Riggins, Wayne Sherwood), "No Man's Land" (Orchestra), "Goddess of Liberty" (a/k/a "Song of the Goddess") (reprise) (Nadine Lewis), "The Psychiatry Song" (James Billings), "Hymn to Peace" (Asylum Inmates), "Johnny Johnson's Song" (Ralph Williams), "How Sweetly Friendship Binds," "Oh, Heart of Love" (reprise) (Alice Cannon), "Johnny's Melody (When Man Was First Created)" (finale) (Ralph Williams)

NOTES—Given the political unrest of the era, the anti-war musical *Johnny Johnson* must have seemed ripe for revival. But the musical closed on its opening night, and since 1971 there hasn't been another New York production. The musical was under a Limited Broadway (Middle Broadway) contract.

Despite its reputation, *Johnny Johnson* has never been all that popular with the public. The original 1936 Broadway production, which was the first musical Kurt Weill wrote specifically for New York, ran for just sixty-eight performances. The piece was briefly revived during the 1940-1941 theatre season in what appears to have been an Off Broadway production, and a 1956 Off Broadway revival had a short run as well (for more details about the musical and for the 1956 revival, see entry for that production).

828 Johnny Pye and the Foolkiller. "A Musical." THEATRE: Lamb's Theatre; OPENING DATE: October 31, 1993; PERFORMANCES: 49; BOOK: Mark St. Germain; LYRICS: Mark St. Germain and Randy Courts; MUSIC: Randy Courts; DIRECTION: Scott Harris; CHOREOGRAPHY: Janet Watson; SCENERY: Peter Harrison; COSTUMES: Claudia Stephens; LIGHTING: Kenneth Posner; MUSICAL DIRECTION: Steven M. Alper; PRODUCER: The Lamb's Theatre Company (Carolyn Rossi Copeland, Producing Artistic Director)

CAST—Daniel Jenkins (Johnny Pye), Spiro Malas (The Foolkiller), Kaitlin Hopkins (Suzy Marsh), Peter Gerety (Wilbur Wilberforce), Tanny McDonald (Mrs. Miller), Ralston Hill (Barber), Mark Lotito (Bob), Michael Ingram (Bill), Conor Gillespie (Young Johnny Pye), Heather Lee Soroka (Young Suzy Marsh)

SOURCE—The short story "Johnny Pye and the Foolkiller" by Stephen Vincent Benet.

The action occurs in Martinsville, U.S.A., and various locations during the period 1928-1995.

The musical was presented in two acts.

ACT ONE—"Another Day" (Spiro Malas, Company), "Goodbye Johnny" (Conor Gillespie, Heather Lee Soroka), "Shower of Sparks" (Spiro Malas), "Occupations" (Conor Gillespie, Heather Lee Soroka, Daniel Jenkins, Kaitlin Hopkins, Company), "Goodbye Johnny" (reprise) (Daniel Jenkins, Kaitlin Hopkins), "Handle with Care" (Peter Gerety, Kaitlin Hopkins), "The End of the Road" (Daniel Jenkins, Kaitlin Hopkins, Spiro Malas, Company), "Challenge to Love" (Daniel Jenkins, Kaitlin Hopkins, Company)

ACT TWO—"The Barbershop" (Ralston Hill, Mark Lotito, Michael Ingram), "Married with Children" (Daniel Jenkins, Kaitlin Hopkins, Company), "The Land Where There Is No Death" (Daniel Jenkins, Conor Gillespie), "Time Passes" (Spiro Malas, Company), "Challenge to Love" (reprise) (Daniel Jenkins, Kaitlin Hopkins), "Never Felt Better in My Life" (Peter Gerety, Daniel Jenkins, Ralston Hill, Mark Lotito, Michael Ingram), Epilogue ("The Answer") (Daniel Jenkins), "The End of the Road" (reprise) (Daniel Jenkins, Spiro Malas), Finale (Company)

NOTES—Based on Stephen Vincent Benet's short story of the same name, *Johnny Pye and the Foolkiller* told the story of a young man (Johnny Pye) who makes a bargain with Death (the Foolkiller): if Johnny can discover the answer to a riddle posed by the Foolkiller, Johnny will live forever. Johnny grows older and sees the eventual deaths of his wife and son; when he at last discovers the answer to Death's riddle, he foregoes eternal life and asks Death to take him so that he can join his wife and son in the hereafter. (The devil's riddle is how can a man be a human being and not a fool; the answer: only when he's dead and buried.)

Stephen Holden in the *New York Times* said the bittersweet family musical was a welcome blend of Stephen Sondheim's *Into the Woods* (1987) and Thornton Wilder's *Our Town* (1938), and he praised Mark St. Germain's "adept" book which included "spare, quirky" details to tell its folk-like story. He also was impressed with Randy Courts' score, which had a "surging sweetness" reminiscent of both Sondheim and "folk-flavored soft rock." Holden singled out three songs of "genuine narrative eloquence" ("Goodbye Johnny," "The End of the Road," and "Time Passes"). The musical had originally been produced by the Lamb's Theatre Company as a work-in-progress on March 22, 1988, for fourteen performances, and was later seen at the George Street Playhouse, Brunswick, New Jersey, in February 1990 (John Hickok was Johnny Pye, John Jellison was the Foolkiller, and Victoria Clark was Suzy, Johnny's wife).

The script was published by Dramatists Play Service, Inc., in 1994 (as *Johnny Pye*).

829 Jolson & Co. THEATRE: The Theatre at Saint Peter's Church/The York Theatre Company; OPENING DATE: December 9, 1999; PERFORMANCES: 38; BOOK: Stephen Mo Hanan and Jay Berkow; LYRICS: See song list for credits; MUSIC: See song list for credits; DIRECTION: Jay Berkow; SCENERY: James Morgan; COSTUMES: Gail Baldoni; LIGHTING: Annmarie Duggan; MUSICAL DIRECTION: Peter Larson; PRODUCER: The York Theatre Company (James Morgan, Artistic Director; Robert A. Buckley, Managing Director)

CAST—Stephen Mo Hanan (Al Jolson), Robert Ari (Barry Gray, Hirsch [later Harry], Poppa, Dockstader, Lloyd, Chuck, Colonel Webster, Harry Cohn, Morris), Nancy Anderson (Naomi Yoelson, Mae, Ethel, Josephine, Ruby Keeler, Martha, Erle)

The action occurs in December 1949 on the stage of the Winter Garden Theatre (and in various locales from Al Jolson's past).

The revue was presented in two acts (song assignments and division of acts unknown; songs are listed in performance order).

MUSICAL NUMBERS—"Swanee" (*Demi-Tasse/ Capitol Revue*, 1919; later interpolated into tour of *Sinbad* [also 1919]; lyric by Irving Caesar, music by George Gershwin), "A Bird in a Gilded Cage" (lyric by Arthur J. Lamb, music by Harry von Tilzer), "I'm Sitting on Top of the World" (*Artists and Models/ Paris Edition*, 1925; interpolated into the musical during New York run; lyric by Joe Young and Sam M. Lewis, music by Ray Henderson), "The Little Victrola" (lyric and music by Billy Murray and Norbert Roscoe), "You Made Me Love You (I Didn't Want to Do It)" (*The Honeymoon Express*, 1913 [Second Edition]; lyric by Joseph McCarthy, music by James V. Monaco), "Where Did Robinson Crusoe Go with Friday on Saturday Night?" (*Robinson Crusoe, Jr.*, 1916; lyric by Joe Young and Sam M. Lewis, music by George Meyer), "California, Here I Come" (*Bombo*, 1921; interpolated into the musical during New York run; lyric by B.G. [Buddy] DeSylva and Al Jolson, music by Joseph Meyer), "Sonny Boy" (1928 film *The Singing Fool*; lyric by Lew Brown, B.G. [Buddy] DeSylva, and Al Jolson, music by Ray Henderson), "When the Red, Red Robin Comes Bob, Bob, Bobbin' Along" (lyric and music by Harry M. Woods), "My Mammy" (*Sinbad*, 1919; interpolated into the musical's national tour; lyric by Joe Young and Sam M. Lewis, music by Walter Donaldson), "Toot Toot Tootsie! (Goodbye)" (*Bombo*, 1921; interpolated into the musical during New York run; lyric by Gus Kahn, music by Ernie Erdman and Ted Fiorito; Dan Russo may have co-composed the song), "Hello, Central, Give Me No Man's Land" (*Sinbad*, 1919; interpolated into the musical during New York run; lyric by Joe Young and Sam Lewis, music by Jean Schwartz), "Rock-a-Bye Your Baby with a Dixie Melody" (*Sinbad*, 1919; lyric by Joe Young and Sam M. Lewis, music by Jean Schwartz), "You Made Me Love You" (reprise), "April Showers" (*Bombo*, 1921; interpolated into the musical's national tour; lyric by B.G. [Buddy] DeSylva, music by Louis Silvers), "You Made Me Love You" (reprise)

NOTES—*Jolson & Co.*, a tribute-revue to Al Jolson (1883 [1886?]-1950), was one of many revues and musicals over the years about the legendary entertainer (as *Jolson and Company*, the revue was revived at the Century Center for the Performing Arts on September 29, 2002, for ninety-seven performances). Off Broadway also saw a second musical about the subject (see entry for *The Magic of Jolson!*). Another musical, *Jolson* (1978), played at the Paper Mill Playhouse and starred Clive Baldwin in the title role (the lyrics and music were by Irwin Levine and L. Russell Brown), and *Joley* (1979) played at the Northstage Theatre in Glen Cove, New York, with Larry Kert (the score included new songs with lyrics by Herbert Hartig and music by Milton DeLugg as well as standards which Jolson either introduced or popularized). In 1999, Mike Burstyn toured in *Jolson* (it's unclear if this was based on the 1978 *Jolson* or the 1996 London *Jolson*).

There have been at least two British musicals about Jolson: *The Jolson Revue* opened in 1974 and *Jolson* opened at the Victoria Palace Theatre in 1996 (the latter was recorded by First Night Records [CD # CASTCD-56]). There were two film versions about Jolson's life, *The Jolson Story* (1946) and its sequel *Jolson Sings Again* (1949); in both films, Larry Parks played the title role. The script of *Jolson & Co.* was published by Samuel French, Inc., in 1999.

830 jon & jen. "A New Musical." THEATRE: Lamb's Theatre; OPENING DATE: June 1, 1995; PERFORMANCES: 114; BOOK: Tom Greenwald and Andrew Lippa; LYRICS: Tom Greenwald; MUSIC: Andrew Lippa; DIRECTION: Gabriel Barre; SCENERY: Charles McCarry; COSTUMES: D. Polly Kendrick; LIGHTING: Stuart Duke; MUSICAL DIRECTION: Joel Fram; PRODUCER: The Lamb's Theatre Company (Carolyn Rossi Copeland, Producing Director)

CAST—Carolee Carmello (Jen), James Ludwig (John [Jen's brother], John [Jen's son])

The action occurs in the United States and Canada during the years 1952-1990.

The musical was presented in two acts.

ACT ONE—"Welcome to the World" (Carolee Carmello), "Christmas" (performer[s] unknown), "Think Big" (Carolee Carmello, James Ludwig), "Dear God" (James Ludwig), "Hold Down the Fort" (Carolee Carmello), "Timeline" (Carolee Carmello, James Ludwig), "Out of My Sight" (Carolee Carmello, James Ludwig), "Run and Hide" (Carolee Carmello, James Ludwig)

ACT TWO—"Old Clothes" (Carolee Carmello), "Little League" (James Ludwig), "Just Like You" (Carolee Carmello), "Bye Room" (Carolee Carmello), "What Can I Do?" (performer[s] unknown), "Smile of Your Dreams" (Carolee Carmello), "Graduation" (Carolee Carmello, James Ludwig), "The Road Ends Here" (Carolee Carmello), "That Was My Way" (Carolee Carmello), "Every Goodbye Is Hello" (Carolee Carmello, James Ludwig)

NOTES—The Off Off Broadway musical *john and jen* told the story of Jen, who is overly protective of her young brother John. As they grow older, their lifestyles draw them apart; Jen is a hippie who moves to Canada with her draft-dodging boyfriend, and John enlists in military service and is killed in Vietnam. When Jen's son John is born, she becomes overly protective of him as well, and is fearful of losing him, too. Soon she's no longer able to distinguish between her son and her brother, but ultimately comes to the realization that her son is an adult who must live his own life.

Stephen Holden in the *New York Times* found the evening "serious, well meaning and ultimately bland," the performers "talented," the music "melodic but not strongly tuneful," and the lyrics "direct and unpretentious." Overall, he felt the clichéd story only occasionally caught fire.

The musical was recorded by Varese Sarabande Records (VSD-5688), which omitted two songs heard on opening night ("Christmas" and "What Can I Do?") but included two others which were apparently added after the opening ("It Took Me a While" and "Talk Show").

The musical included two names which would make interesting contributions to the new American musical theatre: the musical's composer, Andrew Lippa, later wrote the score for the Off Broadway musical version of *The Wild Party* (see entry); and *jon & jen*'s orchestrator, Jason Robert Brown, was heard from later in the 1995-1996 theatre season with his song-cycle *Songs for a New World* (see entry); he later won the Tony Award for his 1998 Broadway musical *Parade*. The 1995-1996 season also introduced a third new theatre composer, Adam Guettel, whose score for *Floyd Collins* (see entry) is one of the towering achievements of modern musical theatre.

831 Jonah (Meyer Kupferman; 1966). THEATRE: American Place Theatre; OPENING DATE: January 12, 1966; PERFORMANCES: 13; BOOK: Paul Goodman; LYRICS: Paul Goodman; MUSIC: Meyer Kupferman; DIRECTION: Lawrence Kornfeld; CHOREOGRAPHY: Remy Charlip; SCENERY: Remy Charlip; COSTUMES: Remy Charlip; LIGHTING: Roger Morgan; PRODUCER: The American Place Theatre

CAST—Earle Hyman (Angel), Ruth Jaroslow (Hephzibah, Cow), Sorrell Booke (Jonah), John A. Coe (Captain, Guide), Jamil Zakkai (A Sailor, Duke), Burt Supree (Sailor, Heavenly Counselor), Jay Fletcher (Sailor, Ninevite, Heavenly Counselor), Richard Frisch (Passenger, Ninevite, Martial Singer), William Shorr (Passenger, Peasant), Stephanie Turash (Passenger, Ninevite, Coloratura), Yolande Bavan (Passenger, Singer, Worm), Larrio Ekson (Angel Helper, Ninevite), Carl Wilson (Angel Helper, Ninevite), Pamela Jones (Ninevite), Jeff Rock (Courtier), Marcia Kurtz (Duchess, Heavenly Counselor), Gretchen MacLane (Lady, Heavenly Counselor), Robert Frink (King), Aileen Passloff (Heavenly Counselor)

SOURCE—The Old Testament story of Jonah.

The musical was presented in two acts.

ACT ONE (*Jonah*)—"Leviathan" (Ensemble), "Hey, What's This?" (Ruth Jaroslow), "Sailor's Rebound" (Ensemble), "Leviathan" (reprise) (Ensemble), "Evocation" (Stephanie Turash), "Jonah's Melodrama" (Sorrell Booke), "I'll Carry You an Inch" (Sorrell Booke), "Puppet Dream" (Sorrell Booke, Earle Hyman), "Sleep Little Mouse" (Sorrell Booke), "My God Why Hast Thou Forsaken Me?" (Yolande Bavan), "Forty Days" (Ensemble)

ACT TWO (*Jonah and the King*)—"There's Nothing New Under the Sun" (Ensemble), "Miserere" (Ensemble), "Day After Day" (Richard Frisch), "The Suns That Daily Rise" (Richard Frisch, Stephanie Turash), "Angel's Ballet" (Stephanie Turash), "Madrigal" (Stephanie Turash, Yolande Bavan, Richard Frisch), "I Am a Little Worm" (Yolande Bavan), "Paradise Quintet" (Ensemble)

NOTES—The musical dramatized Jonah's life after his famous encounter with the whale. But instead of an earnest and solemn approach to the material, Paul Goodman's loopy vaudeville-styled musical told the story through the prism of Jewish life in New York City. Stanley Kauffman's review in the *New York Times* was tinged with regret for what might have been. It seems Goodman's promising approach to the familiar story never quite found its voice and wound up muted and dull when it should have been incisive and irreverent.

The songs "Forty Days," "There's Nothing New Under the Sun," "Miserere," and "Day After Day" included dance sequences. Also, in the third scene of the second act there was a dance sequence titled "Council in Heaven." For another light-hearted adaptation of the Biblical story, see entry for Elizabeth Swados' 1990 musical, also titled *Jonah*.

832 Jonah (Elizabeth Swados; 1990). THEATRE: Martinson Hall/The Public Theatre; OPENING DATE: March 20, 1990; PERFORMANCES: 8; TEXT: Elizabeth Swados; ADDITIONAL TEXT ADAPTED from the Old Testament; LYRICS: Elizabeth Swados; MUSIC: Elizabeth Swados; DIRECTION: Elizabeth Swados; CHOREOGRAPHY: Bill Castellino; SCENERY: Michael E. Downs; COSTUMES: Judy Dearing; LIGHTING: Beverly Emmons; MUSICAL DIRECTION: Michael S. Sottile; PRODUCER: The New York Shakespeare Festival (Joseph Papp, Producer)

CAST—Jake Ehrenreich (Jonah), Cathy Porter (Phyllis Jonette, Other Roles), Ann Marie Milazzo (Marguarita Jonette, Other Roles)

SOURCES—The Biblical story of Jonah; and the novel *Jonah* (circa 1925) by Robert Nathan.

The musical was presented in one act (song titles unknown).

NOTES—Stephen Holden in the *New York Times* found Elizabeth Swados' score for *Jonah* "upbeat and breezy," and noted that the music for her adaptation of I Corinthians 13 was one of her "strongest" songs, a "soaring folk-rock chorale." Holden also reported the musical used "whimsical" details in the telling of its familiar story (for example, the whale is afraid to swallow Jonah because it may choke to death). For another light-hearted look at the Biblical story of Jonah, see entry for Meyer Kupferman's adaptation, also titled *Jonah*, which played at the American Place Theatre in 1966.

833 Joseph and the Amazing Technicolor Dreamcoat. THEATRE: Entermedia Theatre; OPENING DATE: November 18, 1981; PERFORMANCES: 77; LYRICS: Tim Rice; MUSIC: Andrew Lloyd Webber; DIRECTION: Tony Tanner; CHOREOGRAPHY: Tony Tanner; SCENERY: Karl Eigsti; COSTUMES: Judith Dolan; LIGHTING: Barry Arnold; MUSICAL DIRECTION: David Friedman; PRODUCERS: Zev Bufman, Susan R. Rose, Melvyn J. Estrin and Sidney Shlenker by arrangement with the Robert Stigwood Organization and David Land; Gail Berman and Jean Luskin, Associate Producers

CAST—LAURIE BEECHMAN (Narrator), Gordon Stanley (Jacob), Robert Hyman (Reuben), Kenneth Bryan (Simeon, Butler), Steve McNaughton (Levi), Charlie Serrano (Napthali), Peter Kapetan (Issachar), David Asher (Asher), James Rich (Dan), Doug Voet (Zebulon), Barry Tarallo (Gad, Baker), Philip Carrubba (Benjamin), Stephen Hope (Judah), BILL HUTTON (Joseph), Tom Carder (Ishmaelite, Pharoah), David Ardao (Ishmaelite, Potiphar), Randon Lo (Mrs. Potiphar), Joni Masella (Apache Dancer); Women's Chorus (Lorraine Barrett, Karen Bogan, Katharine Buffaloe, Lauren Goler, Randon Lo, Joni Masella, Kathleen Rowe McAllen, Renee Warren)

SOURCE—The Biblical story of Joseph and his many-colored coat.

The musical was presented in two acts.

ACT ONE—"Jacob and Sons"/"Joseph's Coat" (Laurie Beechman, Brothers, Gordon Stanley, Bill Hutton, Women), "Joseph's Dreams" (Laurie Beechman, Bill Hutton, Brothers), "Poor, Poor Joseph" (Laurie Beechman, Brothers, Women), "One More Angel in Heaven" (Brothers), "Potiphar" (Laurie Beechman, Women, Randon Lo, David Ardao, Bill Hutton), "Close Every Door" (Bill Hutton, Women, "Go, Go, Go, Joseph" (Laurie Beechman, Barry Tarallo, Kenneth Bryan, Chorus, Bill Hutton, Men), "Pharoah's Story" (Laurie Beechman, Women)

ACT TWO—"Poor, Poor Pharoah"/"Song of the King" (Laurie Beechman, Tom Carder, Women, Men), "Pharoah's Dream Explained" (Bill Hutton, Women, Men), "Stone the Crows" (Laurie Beechman, Tom Carder, Bill Hutton, Women, Men), "Those Canaan Days" (Robert Hyman, Brothers, Joni Masella), "The Brothers Came to Egypt"/"Grovel, Grovel" (Laurie Beechman, Brothers, Bill Hutton, Women), "Who's the Thief?" (Bill Hutton, Brothers, Women), "Benjamin Calypso" (Charlie Serrano, Brothers), "Joseph All the Time" (Laurie Beechman, Bill Hutton, Brothers, Women), "Jacob in Egypt" (Bill Hutton, Brothers, Women)

NOTES—*Joseph and the Amazing Technicolor Dreamcoat* was the first produced collaboration between Tim Rice and Andrew Lloyd Webber, and it premiered on March 1, 1968, at St. Paul's School in London. The first American production opened in May 1970 at the College of the Immaculate Conception in Douglastown, Long Island. In 1973, the musical opened in London's West End, and on December 12, 1976, it was presented at the Brooklyn Academy of Music for twenty-three performances (Cleavon Little was the Narrator, David-James Carroll was Joseph, and Virginia Martin was Mrs. Potiphar); it was again produced there in December 1977 for twenty-four performances. The 1981 Off Broadway production transferred to Broadway at the Royale (now Schonefeld) Theatre on January 27, 1982, playing there for a total of 670 performances. It was recorded by Chrysalis Records (LP # CHR-1387), and is one of innumerable recordings of the popular score. A later version of the musical was released on DVD for home video.

The musical was revived on Broadway at the Minskoff Theatre on November 10, 1993, for 231 performances.

834 The Journey of Snow White. "An Opera." THEATRE: Judson Poets' Theatre; OPENING DATE: February 26, 1971; PERFORMANCES: 10 (estimated); LIBRETTO: Al Carmines; MUSIC: Al Carmines; DIRECTION: Gus Solomons, Jr.; CHOREOGRAPHY: Movement by Gus Solomons, Jr.; COSTUMES: Ira Siff and Joan Kilpatrick; LIGHTING: Earl Eidman; MUSICAL DIRECTION: Al Carmines (?); PRODUCER: The Judson Poets' Theatre

CAST—Essie Borden (Snow White), Margaret Wright (Queen I [Snow White's Mother]), Julie Kurnitz (Queen II [Snow White's Step-Mother]), David Pursley (King), Ira Siff (Mirror), John Braden (Huntsman), Lee Guilliatt (Witch I [The Singing Witch]), Phyllis Somerville (Witch II [The Speaking Witch]), Gus Solomons, Jr. (Witch III [The Dancing Witch]), Jerry Fargo (Prince I [The Opera Prince]), Reathel Bean (Prince II [The Country and Western Prince]), Marc Allen III (Prince III [The Rock and Roll Prince]); The Seven Dwarfs (Jeffrey Apter, Eric Jacobs, Teresa King, Phillip Owen, Sandy Padilla, Paul Rounsaville, David Tice); First Sopranos (Misty Barth, Genie D'Ambrosio, Carmen Hendershott, Debbie Moody, Evelyn Schneider); Second Sopranos (Jo Dean, Kathi Kirkpatrick, Sandy Miner, Nancy Stover, Cris Webb); First Altos (Marcy Doyle, Grace Goodman, Molly Heit, Karin Hoenig, Eleanor Howe, Nancy Kolodney, Lyz Kurnitz, Gay Martin, Brenda Mattox, Deborah Sweeney, Maggie Wise); Second Altos (Hjordis Anderson, Arlene Batwin, Judith Greenberg, Francoise Jeanpierre, Dodi Kenan, Carolyn Moody, Toni Signoretti, Holly Vincent); Tenors (Jan Grice, Keith Gonzales, Andrew Hanerfield, Peter Niland); Baritones (Joe Cecil, Paul Hookey, Stephen Lamb, Bill McInnis, Joseph Meyer, Lyon Phelps, Charles Richetelle, Allan Scott, Bob Small, Michael Zande); Basses (Frederick Courtney, Michael C. Lipton,

Ronald Willoughby); Toni Signoretti (Trumpet), Nancy Stover (Violin), Keith Gonzales (Harmonica)

SOURCE—The traditional fairy tale *Snow White*.

The opera was presented in two acts.

ACT ONE—Overture (Orchestra), Septet: "Introductions" (Margaret Wright, Julie Kurnitz, David Pursley, Ira Siff, John Braden, Lee Guilliatt, Phyllis Somerville, Gus Solomons, Jr., Jerry Fargo, Reathel Bean, Marc Allen III), Solo: "Goodbye. It's Time for Me to Die" (Margaret Wright), Recitative: "Marry Me. I Will" (David Pursley, Julie Kurnitz), Solo: "Every Woman Brings Something with Her" (David Pursley), Solo: "I Am an Absence" (Essie Borden), Recitative: "Come, I Will Be Your Mother" (Julie Kurnitz, Essie Borden), Trio: "I Love Myself in Two" (Julie Kurnitz, Essie Borden, Ira Siff), Solo: "Every Time I Look I See a Stranger" (Julie Kurnitz), Solo: "Kingly Duties" (David Pursley), Recitative: "Who Are You?" (Essie Borden), Solo and Dance: "When You Looked at Me for the First Time" (Ira Siff, with Essie Borden), Recitative: "Betrayed" (Julie Kurnitz, with Essie Borden and Ira Siff), Solo: "I Have a Charge to Fulfill" (John Braden), Solo: "I Hate Being Me" (Essie Borden), Chorus: "When Everything Human Has Failed You" (Animals), Solo and Chorus: "I'm Here and You're Here"/"You Be You and I'll Be Me" (Essie Borden, Animals [Soloist, Maggie Wise]), Chorus: "Creatures Go to Sleep in Peace" (Animals [Soloists, Debbie Moody and Keith Gonzales), Solo: "Night! Healing Darkness!" (Keith Gonzales), Septet: "La-La-La-La-La" (Seven Dwarfs), Septet: "What Is It?" (Dwarfs [Soloists, Sandy Padilla and Teresa King]), Septet: "Should She Stay?" (Seven Dwarfs), Solo, Septet, Chorus: "Wandering Walking Everyday" (Essie Borden, Seven Dwarfs, Animals), Septet: "Further Comments" (Julie Kurnitz, Ira Siff, David Pursley, John Braden, Lee Guilliatt, Phyllis Somerville, Gus Solomons, Jr., Jerry Fargo, Reathel Bean, Marc Allen III, Margaret Wright)

ACT TWO—Overture (Orchestra), Septet with Solo: "Scoobi-doo — Since You've Come" (Essie Borden, Seven Dwarfs), Recitative: "Spirits of Banality and Hate!" (Julie Kurnitz, Lee Guilliatt, Phyllis Somerville, Gus Solomons, Jr.), Septet Reprise: "La-La-La-La-La" (Seven Dwarfs), Solo: "A Girl Really Needs a Woman" (Lee Guilliatt), Spoken Aria: "Hi There!" (Phyllis Somerville), Dance: "Big Apple" (Gus Solomons, Jr.), Chorus: "Requiem" (Animals, Seven Dwarfs, Margaret Wright, Julie Kurnitz, David Pursley, Ira Siff, John Braden, Lee Guilliatt, Phyllis Somerville, Gus Solomons, Jr., Jerry Fargo, Reathel Bean, Marc Allen III), Solo: "I Remember a Feeling Called Love" (Margaret Wright), Aria: "Oh Mio Snow White" (Jerry Fargo), Solo: "I Am a Handsome Prince" (Reathel Bean), Solo: "Who's This Chick?" (Marc Allen III), Septet: "Three Handsome Young Princes Have Been Here" (Seven Dwarfs [Soloist, Sandy Padilla]), Solo: "I Don't Want to Be a Mirror Anymore" (Ira Siff), Recitative: "I'm Snow White — A Human Woman" (Essie Borden), Duet: "There Can Be One and There Can Be Two" (Essie Borden, A Man [performer not identified in program]), Chorus: "The Image on Our Retina Has Gone. We Go On" (Animals), Chorus: "On the Checkerboard of Time We've All Played Our Parts. But the Heart Exists in Freedom" (Margaret Wright, Julie Kurnitz, David Pursley, John Braden, Lee Guilliatt, Phyllis Somerville, Gus Solomons, Jr., Jerry Fargo, Reathel Bean, Marc Allen III), Septet: "Everything Is Only for a Little While" (Seven Dwarfs), Solos with Chorus: "Becoming Is a Lot Like Dying"; "Learning Is a Lot Like Forgetting"; "Loving Is a Lot Like Indifference"; "I Love What's Like You About Me and I Love in You What's Different from Me" (Company)

NOTES—One can safely assume Al Carmines' version of the Snow White story was probably nothing like the Disney version. The Off Off Broadway musical was revived at the Judson Poets' Theatre on March 29, 1975. In 1983, it was again revived, this time as one of two musicals presented under the umbrella title of *An Evening of Adult Fairy Tales* (see entry).

835 Joy. "A Musical Come-Together." THEATRE: New Theatre; OPENING DATE: January 27, 1970; PERFORMANCES: 208; LYRICS: Mostly by Oscar Brown, Jr.; MUSIC: Mostly by Oscar Brown, Jr.; LIGHTING: F. Mitchell Dana; PRODUCERS: Sunbar Productions; A High-John Production

CAST—OSCAR BROWN, JR., JEAN PACE (Brown), SIVUCA; Musicians: Norman Shobey, James Benjamin, Everaldo Ferrerra

The revue was presented in two acts.

ACT ONE—"Time" (lyric and music by Oscar Brown, Jr.) (Oscar Brown, Jr.), "Under the Sun" (lyric and music by Oscar Brown, Jr.) (Jean Pace), "Wimmen's Ways" (lyric and music by Oscar Brown, Jr.) (Oscar Brown, Jr.), "Funny Feeling" (lyric and music by Luis Henrique and Oscar Brown, Jr.) (Jean Pace), "If I Only Had" (lyric and music by Charles Aznavour and Oscar Brown, Jr.) (Jean Pace), "What Is a Friend?" (lyric and music by Luis Henrique and Oscar Brown, Jr.) (Oscar Brown, Jr., Sivuca, Norman Shobey), "Much as I Love You" (lyric and music by Luis Henrique and Oscar Brown, Jr.) (Oscar Brown, Jr., Sivuca, Norman Shobey), "Sky and Sea" (lyric and music by Johnny Alf and Oscar Brown, Jr.) (Sivuca), "Afro Blue" (lyric and music by Mongo Santamaria and Oscar Brown, Jr.) (Jean Pace), "Mother Africa's Day" (lyric and music by Sivuca and Oscar Brown, Jr.) (Oscar Brown, Jr., Sivuca)

ACT TWO—"A New Generation" (lyric and music by Luis Henrique and Oscar Brown, Jr.) (Oscar Brown, Jr., Jean Pace), "Brown Baby" (lyric and music by Oscar Brown, Jr.) (Jean Pace), "Funky World" (lyric and music by Oscar Brown, Jr.) (Oscar Brown, Jr.), "Nothing but a Fool" (lyric and music by Luis Henrique and Oscar Brown, Jr.) (Oscar Brown, Jr., Sivuca), "Flowing to the Sea" (lyric and music by Oscar Brown, Jr.) (performer[s] unknown), "Brother, Where Are You?" (lyric and music by Oscar Brown, Jr.) (performer[s] unknown)

NOTES—Oscar Brown, Jr.'s revue *Joy* had been originally produced in San Francisco; the Off Broadway production played six months, and RCA Victor recorded the cast album (LP # LSO-1166). (There also appears to have been a much earlier version of the revue; in 1966, Brown's *Joy 66* was performed in Chicago.)

Joy was a pleasant evening of songs by Brand, ones he either wrote individually or in collaboration with others; but like so many other Off Broadway evenings which consisted entirely of songs, the revue was slightly overwhelmed by the size of its Off Broadway house and undoubtedly would have been more comfortable in a nightclub setting. Brown had previously appeared in another evening of his songs (*Worlds of Oscar Brown, Jr.* [1967, see entry]).

Unfortunately, *Joy* and *Worlds of Oscar Brown, Jr.*, didn't include any songs from Brown's *Kicks & Co.*, which closed four days into the run of its 1961 pre-Broadway Chicago tryout (however, over the years Brown recorded a few numbers from the production). *Kicks & Co.* seems to have first been directed by Vinnette Carroll, who was replaced by Lorraine Hansberry (the latter's husband, Robert Barron Nemiroff, was one of the musical's co-producers). Burgess Meredith was Mr. Kicks (for at least one of the Chicago performances, Harold Scott played the role), who was no less than Satan himself. Satan and his sidekick Silky Satin (Al Freeman, Jr.) are involved in the pornography business (which at one point or another is equated with racism). Some twenty-five years later, a revised version of the musical resurfaced as *Kicks & Company*, where it played for five performances at Frostburg State College (Frostburg, Maryland) with Brown himself playing the role of Mr. Kicks.

836 Joyful Noise. THEATRE: Lamb's Theatre; OPENING DATE: February 17, 2000; PERFORMANCES: 44; PLAY: Tim Slover; DIRECTION: Robert Smyth; SCENERY: David Thayer; COSTUMES: Jeanne Reith; LIGHTING: David Thayer; PRODUCER: Lamb's Players Theatre (Robert Smyth, Artistic Director)

CAST—Mary Miller (Susannah Cibber), Paul Eggingon (Charles Jennens), Tom Stephenson (George Frederick Handel), Doren Elias (John Christopher Smith), Deborah Gilmour Smyth (Kitty Clive), Linda Bush (Mary Pendarves), Robert Smyth (George II), David Cochran Heath (Bishop Henry Egerton)

The action occurs in London and Leicestershire during the years 1741-1743.

The play was presented in two acts.

NOTES—The play with music dealt with the premiere of George Frederick Handel's *Messiah*. Anthony Tommasini in the *New York Times* noted the play's historical details were "essentially correct," but he reported the evening was filled with "overly broad physical comedy" and a penchant for "boisterously loud delivery" of the lines by most of the performers. As for the music heard in the production, Tommasini reported that while some of it was played on tape, other musical sequences were sung by Mary Miller and Robert Smyth. As for the "Halluleujah" chorus, it was performed by the entire company.

837 The Joys of Sex. "A Naughty New Musical." THEATRE: Variety Arts Theatre; OPENING DATE: May 12, 2004; PERFORMANCES: 39; BOOK: Melissa Levis and David Weinstein; LYRICS: Melissa Levis; MUSIC: David Weinstein; DIRECTION: Jeremy Dobrish; CHOREOGRAPHY: Lisa Shriver; SCENERY: Neil Patel; COSTUMES: David C. Woolard; LIGHTING: Donald Holder; MUSICAL DIRECTION: Steven Ray Watkins; PRODUCERS: Ben Sprecher, William P. Miller, Kenneth D. Greenblatt, and Benjamin C. Singer

CAST—Ron Bohmer (Howard Nolton, Irving), David Josefsberg (Brian Shapiro, Others), Stephanie Kurtzuba (Stephs Nolton, Others), Jenelle Lynn Randall (April Jones, Others)

The revue was presented in one act.

MUSICAL NUMBERS—"The Joys of Sex" (Company), "O' No" (Stephanie Kurtzuba), "Cup of Sugar" (Jenelle Lynn Randall, Ron Bohmer), "Intercourse on the Internet" (David Josefsberg, 'Gladys' [performer unknown]), "The First Time" (Company), "One Night Stand" (Jenelle Lynn Randall), "In the Parlor Be a Lady" ('Granny' [performer unknown], Stephanie Kurtzuba), "Twins" (Ron Bohmer, 'Twins' [Stephanie Kurtzuba, Jenelle Lynn Randall]), "In Our Fantasy" (Company), "Kinks" (David Josefsberg), "The Vault" (David Josefsberg, Ron Bohmer, Company), "The Three-Way" (Ron Bohmer), "Pandora's Box" (Stephanie Kurtzuba), "Free the Tiger" (Stephanie Kurtzuba, Ron Bohmer, Jenelle Lynn Randall), "I Need It Bad" (Company), "Fantasy Come True" (Ron Bohmer), "Not Too Nice" (David Josefsberg, Jenelle Lynn Randall), "Making Love with You" (Company), "The Joys of Sex" (reprise) (Company)

NOTES—The musical, which dealt with sex and sexual relationships, including one about a couple trying to conceive, lasted little more than a month. Anita Gates in the *New York Times* noted that although *The Joys of Sex* was sometimes "childish and inane," it was occasionally "refreshingly innocent" with a "playful attitude" towards its subject matter. Gates reported that one song in the score ("Intercourse on the Internet") was composed by Neil Ginsberg, and, in a throwback to musicals of the late 1960s and early 1970s, the musical's band sported a name (the Throbbing Threesome). Gates also noted the "blonde good looks" of cast member Ron Bohmer screamed "local TV anchor."

838 J.P. Morgan Saves the Nation. THEATRE: En Garde Arts; OPENING DATE: June 15, 1995; PERFORMANCES: 30; BOOK: Jeffrey M. Jones; LYRICS: Jeffrey M. Jones; MUSIC: Jonathan Larson; DIRECTION: Jean Randich; CHOREOGRAPHY: Doug Elkins; SCENERY: Kyle Chepulis; COSTUMES: Kasia Maimone; LIGHTING: Pat Dignan; MUSICAL DIRECTION: Jules Cohen; PRODUCER: En Garde Arts (Anne Hamburger, Founder and Producer)

CAST—James Judy (J.P. Morgan), Stephen DeRosa (Uncle Sam), Buzz Bovshow (G. Washington, Esq.), Julie Fain Lawrence (Liberty), Robin Miles (A Devil)

NOTES—En Garde Art's Off Off Broadway musical *J.P. Morgan Saves the Nation* wasn't presented in a theatre per se; as was the company's wont, the work was produced in "site specific" venues (in this case, sites were chosen which mirrored Morgan's life, such as the front of Federal Hall National Memorial, the J.P. Morgan Bank Building [the Morgan Guaranty Trust Company], and the New York Stock Exchange).

Ben Brantley in the *New York Times* said the "anti-materialist musical spectacle" was a somewhat "priggish allegory" about Morgan and his rise to financial power, and he noted the often esoteric aspects of Morgan's life and times seemed to have been created by an "earnest team of Marxist economics students."

J.P. Morgan Saves the Nation is notable because its music was by Jonathan Larson (the lyrics were by Jeffrey M. Jones). (Later in the season, Larson's *Rent* [see entry] and his untimely death became part of theatrical folklore.) Brantley praised the "peppy" score by "Jonathan M. Larson," a pastiche which ranged from ragtime to rap, and he singled out "Appetite Annie," a "music-hall hymn to capitalist hunger."

839 Juan Darien. "A Carnival Mass." THEATRE: St. Clement's Theatre; OPENING DATE: March 4, 1988; PERFORMANCES: 21; MATERIAL: Julie Taymor and Elliot Goldenthal, with text chosen and arranged by Elliot Goldenthal; MUSIC: Elliot Goldenthal; DIRECTION: Julie Taymor; SCENERY: G.W. Mercier and Julie Taymor; puppetry and masks by Julie Taymor; COSTUMES: G.W. Mercier and Julie Taymor; LIGHTING: Richard Nelson; MUSICAL DIRECTION: Richard Cordova; PRODUCER: Music-Theatre Group (Lyn Austin, Producing Director; Diane Wondisford and Mark Jones, Associate Producing Directors)

CAST—Ariel Ashwell, Renee Banks, Willie C. Barnes, Thuli Dumakude, Nicholas Gunn, Andrea Kane, Stephen Kaplin, Lawrence A. Neals, Jr., Lenard Petit, Barbara Pollitt, Irene Wiley

NOTES—Based on a tale by Horacio Quiroga, the Off Off Broadway one-act puppet-musical *Juan Darien* (later subtitled "A Carnival Mass") told the story of an orphaned jaguar cub who is nurtured by a woman whose baby has died in a plague. The cub miraculously becomes a human child (Juan Darien), but a few years after his mother dies, the local villagers discover he's really a jaguar in human form and torture him until his body is transformed back into a jaguar. Other jaguars nurse him to health, and he returns to the jungle as a jaguar, but not before he visits his mother's grave. From the blood of his wounds, Juan Darien writes his name on the cross below hers.

The haunting and mysterious tale utilized a mixture of puppets and live performers, and was distinguished by Julie Taymor's ingenious designs for both the puppets and the masks of the performers. *Juan Darien* was revived by the Music-Theatre Group at St. Clement's Theatre for an additional eighty performances beginning on December 26, 1989; and on November 24, 1996, the musical was revived at the Vivian Beaumont Theatre at Lincoln Center for forty-nine performances.

RCA Victor Records (CD # SK-62845) released a recording of the original concept version of the fable. The following numbers are heard on the CD: "Agnus Dei" (Chorus), "Lacrymosa"/"Mr. Bones' Fanfare" (Chorus, Mother), "Jaguar Cub Approach" (Mother), "Mr. Bones' Two-Step" (dance), "The Hunter's Entrance" (Hunter), "Gloria" (Chorus, Mother), "Initiation" (Mother, Chorus), "A Round at Midnight" (Villagers), "Sanctus" (Mother), "School" (Juan), "Recordare" (Mother, Juan, Chorus), "Carnaval" (Circus Barker), "Lullabye" (lyric by Elliot Goldenthal) (Streetsinger), "Trance" (lyric by Horacio Quiroga) (Juan), "Dies Irae" (Circus Barker, Chorus), "Lacrymosa II"/"Retribution" (Chorus, Juan, Mother)

840 Judy: A Garland of Songs (1974). THEATRE: Upstairs at Channel VII; OPENING DATE: May 9, 1974; PERFORMANCES: Unknown (at least 24 performances); MATERIAL by Jeffrey K. Neill; DIRECTION: Jeffrey K. Neill; SCENERY: Set Pieces and Properties by Charles Roeder; Art Décor by Richard Sachinis; COSTUMES: George Yazbek; MUSICAL ADAPTATION AND DIRECTION: Wendell Kindberg; PRODUCER: Upstairs at Channel VII

CAST—Barbara Coggin, Peter Marinos, Patricia Moline, Tim Sheahan, Norb Joerder (Narrator)

The revue was presented in one act (song assignments unknown).

MUSICAL NUMBERS—"Broadway Rhythm" (from film *Broadway Melody of 1936*; later used in film *Broadway Melody of 1938*; lyric by Arthur Freed, music by Nacio Herb Brown), "After You've Gone" (used in 1942 film *For Me and My Gal*; lyric by Henry Creamer, music by J. Turner Layton), "The Balboa" (1936 film *Pigskin Parade*; lyric and music by Sidney Mitchell and Lew Pollack), "You Made Me Love You (I Didn't Want to Do It) (Dear Mr. Gable)" (used in *Broadway Melody of 1938*; lyric by Joseph McCarthy, music by James V. Monaco; special "Gable" lyric by Roger Edens), "Zing! Went the Strings of My Heart" (from *Thumbs Up!*, 1934; used in 1938 film *Listen Darling*; lyric and music by James F. Hanley), "In Between" (1938 film *Love Finds Andy Hardy*; lyric and music by Roger Edens), Medley from film *The Wizard of Oz* (1939; lyrics by E.Y. Harburg, music by Harold Arlen), "It's a Great Day for the Irish" (1940 film *Little Nellie Kelly*; lyric and music by Roger Edens), "Minnie from Trinidad" (1941 film *Ziegfeld Girl*; lyric and music by Roger Edens), Medley from film *For Me and My Gal* (1942), "The Joint Is Really Jumpin' Down at Carnegie Hall" (1943 film *Thousands Cheer*; lyric and music by Roger Edens, Ralph Blane, and Hugh Martin), Medley from film *Meet Me in St. Louis* (1944), MGM '40s, Clown Medley, "The Man That Got Away" (*A Star Is Born*, 1954; lyric by Ira Gershwin, music by Harold Arlen), A Garland Song Book

NOTES—This Off Broadway tribute to Judy Garland (1924-1969) and her career was later seen Off Off Broadway in 1977 and 1984 (see entries).

For another tribute to Judy Garland, see entry for *I Will Come Back* (1998). On March 26, 1986, *Judy*, a play (with music) by Terry Wale, opened in London at the Strand Theatre; Lesley Mackie portrayed Garland.

841 Judy: A Garland of Songs (1977). THEATRE: Library & Museum of Performing Arts/Lincoln Center; OPENING DATE: December 19, 1977; PERFORMANCES: 3; MATERIAL by Jeffrey K. Neill; DIRECTION: Jeffrey K. Neill; PROPS: Charles W. Roeder; COSTUMES: Charles W. Roeder; LIGHTING: Denise Yaney; MUSICAL ADAPTATION AND DIRECTION: Wendell Kindberg; PRODUCER: Stage Directors and Choreographers Workshop Foundation

CAST—Barbara Coggin, Lou Corato, Peter Marinos, Mary Lynne Metternich, Jacqueline Reilly

The revue was presented in two acts (for list of songs, see entry for 1974 production).

NOTES—The Off Off Broadway revue was a musical celebration of Judy Garland (1924-1969) and her career, and played for a limited engagement of three performances. It had been earlier seen Off Broadway in 1974 and then later Off Off Broadway in 1984 (see entries). For another tribute to Judy Garland, see entry for *I Will Come Back* (1998).

842 Judy: A Garland of Songs (1984). THEATRE: All Souls Fellowship Hall; OPENING DATE: February 24, 1984; PERFORMANCES: 8; MATERIAL by Jeffrey K. Neill; DIRECTION: Jeffrey K. Neill; SCENERY: Robert Edmonds; COSTUMES: Charles W. Roeder; LIGHTING: Dorian Bernacchio; MUSICAL ADAPTATION AND DIRECTION: Wendell Kindberg; PRODUCERS: The All Souls Players, Suzanne Kaszynski, Jeffrey K. Neill, Howard Van Der Meulen

CAST—Diana Daniel, Edwin Decker, Helen Eckard, Steven Fickinger, Debra Kelman, Richard K. Smith

The revue was presented in two acts (for list of songs, see entry for 1974 production).

NOTES—The Off Off Broadway revue was a musical celebration of Judy Garland (1924-1969) and her career, and had been earlier seen Off Broadway in 1974 and Off Off Broadway in 1977 (see entries). For another tribute to Judy Garland, see entry for *I Will Come Back* (1998).

843 Julie Wilson from Weill to Sondheim. "A Concert." THEATRE: Kaufman Theatre; OPENING DATE: October 19, 1987; PERFORMANCES: 53; LYRICS: Maxwell Anderson, Marc Blitzstein, Bertolt Brecht, Michael Feingold, Ira Gershwin, Langston Hughes, Alan Jay Lerner, Ogden Nash, and Stephen Sondheim; MUSIC: Kurt Weill and Stephen Sondheim; COSTUMES: Julie Wilson's gowns by Lenore Smith; LIGHTING: Nadine Charlsen; PRODUCER: Martin R. Kaufman

CAST—JULIE WILSON, William Roy (Piano)

The revue was presented in two acts (all songs performed by Julie Wilson).

ACT ONE—*The Songs of Kurt Weill*

ACT TWO—*The Songs of Stephen Sondheim*

NOTES—In her tribute to Kurt Weill and Stephen Sondheim, cabaret singer Julie Wilson (in the words of Stephen Holden in the *New York Times*) cut an "exotic figure" that seemed "even more striking" in a theatre venue than in a nightclub.

The program didn't list individual musical numbers, but among those by Weill were "Mack the Knife" (*The Threepenny Opera*, 1928), "The Barbara Song" (*The Threepenny Opera*, 1928), "Surabaya-Johnny" (*Happy End*, 1929), "Bilbao Moon" (*Happy End*, 1929), and "September Song" (*Knickerbocker Holiday*, 1938); most surprisingly, Wilson performed the obscure "The Nina, the Pinta, the Santa Maria," a song from Weill and Ira Gershwin's ambitious 1945 film musical *Where Do We Go from Here?*

Songs by Stephen Sondheim included "Could I Leave You?" (*Follies*, 1971), "Can That Boy Foxtrot" (*Follies*, 1971; song dropped during pre-Broadway tryout), "I Never Do Anything Twice" (1976 film *The Seven-Per-Cent Solution*), and "Not While I'm Around" (*Sweeney Todd/The Demon Barber of Fleet Street*, 1979).

844 Junebug Graduates Tonight! "A Jazz Allegory." THEATRE: Chelsea Theatre Center; OPENING DATE: February 26, 1967; PERFORMANCES: 5; BOOK: Archie Shepp; LYRICS: Archie Shepp; MUSIC: Archie Shepp; DIRECTION: Robert Kalfin; CHORE-

OGRAPHY: "Movement" by Louis Johnson; SCENERY: Donn Russell; COSTUMES: Evelyn Thompson; LIGHTING: Nuckolls; PRODUCERS: The Chelsea Theatre Center (Robert Kalfin, Artistic Director; David Long, Producing Director)

CAST—Moses Gunn (Muslim), Minnie Gentry (Jessie), Rosalind Cash (Sonja), Beatrice Winde (Julia), Cynthia Belgrave (Celia), Gordon Watkins (Billy), Marilyn Chris (America), John Coe (Uncle Sam), Glynn Turman (Junebug), Brad Sullivan (Cowboy), Willie Woods (Young Man Sit-In), Dorothy Levy (First Woman Bystander), Elaine Shore (Second Woman Bystander), John Glover (Nazi), Robert Clapsaddle (Minuteman), Roger Becket (Y.A.F.-er), Ula Walker (First Woman Sit-In), Vickie Thomas (Second Woman Sit-In), Garrett Hotrich (Bystander), Bruce C. Jones (Bystander), Gene A. Dicks (Bystander), Herbert Salley (Bystander), Bobbie McCauley (Bystander)

The musical was presented in two acts.

ACT ONE—"Dispensible" (John Coe), "Interlude" (Company), "Juney Graduates Tonight" (Minnie Gentry), "Hollow Days, Mellow Days" (Minnie Gentry), "They 4-F'd My Billy" (Beatrice Winde), "You Could've Been a Big-Time Pimp" (Beatrice Winde), "I'm a Virgin" (Gordon Watkins), "Let Freedom Ring" (Glynn Turman), "I Dig Action" (Joe Coe), "Poor Foolish Frightened Boy" (Marilyn Chris)

ACT TWO—"Allah" (Moses Gunn), "Hey Now" (Company), "Scorin' Makes a Girl Seem Old" (Rosalind Cash), "Blame the Reds" (Marilyn Chris), "Procession" (performer[s]) unknown), "My Man Don't Love Me" (Rosalind Cash)

NOTES—*Junebug Graduates Tonight!* played out its limited-engagement run of five preview and five regular performances, and was never heard from again.

Dan Sullivan in the *New York Times* reported that the self-described "jazz allegory" dealt with Junebug, a young Black who will be delivering the valedictory address at his high school graduation ceremony. Junebug is torn between living the "white liberal game" or the "Black Muslim game." Sullivan felt the evening was stacked against the first choice, and, in fact, he noted the work "merely drives both sides back into their corners" and doesn't "really solve a thing."

"Procession" was composed by Walter Davis, and "Dispensable" was reassigned from the character of Uncle Sam (John Coe) to the character of the Muslim (Moses Gunn).

The musical had first been presented in October 1965 at the Chelsea Theatre Center, as one of twenty-three new plays presented there for single performances in rehearsed readings.

845 Junie B. Jones. THEATRE: Lucille Lortel Theatre; OPENING DATE: July 21, 2004; PERFORMANCES: 51; BOOK: Marcy Heisler; LYRICS: Marcy Heisler; MUSIC: Zina Goldrich; DIRECTION: Peter Flynn; CHOREOGRAPHY: Devanand Janki; Robert Tatad, Associate Choreographer; SCENERY: Luke Hegel-Cantarella; COSTUMES: Lora LaVon; LIGHTING: Jeff Croiter; MUSICAL DIRECTION: Kimberly Grigsby; PRODUCER: Theatreworks USA (Barbara Pasternack, Producer; Ken Arthur, Managing Director)

CAST—Mary Faber (Junie B. Jones), Michael McCoy (Mr. Scary, Others), Jill Abramovitz (May, Others), Keara Hailey (Lucille, Others), Adam Overett (Herb, Others), Darius Nichols (Sheldon, Others)

SOURCE—A series of children's books by Barbara Park.

The musical was presented in one act (song assignments unknown).

MUSICAL NUMBERS—"Top Secret Personal Beeswax," "Lucille Camille Chenille," "You Can Be My Friend," "Time to Make a Drawing," "Show and Tell," "Now I See," "Lunch Box," "Gladys Gutzman," "Kickball Tournament," "Sheldon Potts' Halftime Show," "When Life Gives You Lemons," "Kickball Tournament" (reprise), "When Life Gives You Lemons" (reprise), "Writing Down the Story of My Life"

NOTES—*Junie B. Jones* was a children's musical (with adults in child drag); according to *Theatre World Volume 61*, the plot dealt with typical "first grade angst-ridden situations." Lawrence Van Gelder in the *New York Times* found the production "bright" and "inventive," and noted the score was beguiling, the cast "talented," the direction "spirited," and the scenery "clever." The production was presented free as part of Theatreworks USA's commitment to bring theatre to young people.

846 The Juniper Tree (2007; Philip Glass and Robert Moran). THEATRE: Alice Tully Hall/Lincoln Center; OPENING DATE: March 20, 2007; PERFORMANCES: 1; LIBRETTO: Arthur Yorinks; MUSIC: Philip Glass and Robert Moran; MUSICAL DIRECTION: Michael Riesman

CAST—Roger Rees (Narrator), Anita Johnson (Boy), Kevin Deas (Father), Ilana Davidson (Mother), Stella Zambalis (Stepmother), Elizabeth Hillebrand (Sister); Collegiate Chorale; Orchestra of St. Luke's

SOURCE—The short story *The Juniper-Tree* by the Brothers Grimm (Jacob and Wilhelm) from their 1812 short story collection *Children's and Household Tales*.

NOTES—Based on a tale by the Brothers Grimm, the opera *The Juniper Tree* was about a boy who is murdered by his stepmother. Buried beneath a juniper tree, he later returns to life as a magical bird who comforts his father and sister and kills his stepmother.

The opera was first produced by the American Repertory Theatre in Cambridge, Massachusetts, and was later seen at the 1986 American Music Theatre Festival; the belated New York premiere occurred in 2007 in a concert version at Lincoln Center.

In reviewing the concert for the *New York Times*, Allan Kozinn wrote that Philip Glass and Robert Moran, the opera's two composers, "evenly divided" the scenes between them and noted that their individual styles "easily mesh, perhaps because each borrowed the other's themes to give the piece a unified veneer." In 1983, the story was seen Off Off Broadway in a version by Wendy Kesselman (see entry for *The Juniper Tree, A Tragic Household Tale*).

847 The Juniper Tree, a Tragic Household Tale (1983; Wendy Kesselman). THEATRE: St. Clement's Theatre; OPENING DATE: April 19, 1983; PERFORMANCES: Unknown; TEXT: Wendy Kesselman; MUSIC: Wendy Kesselman; DIRECTION: Michael Montel; SCENERY: Lawrence Casey; COSTUMES: Lawrence Casey; LIGHTING: Marilyn Rennagel; MUSICAL DIRECTION: William Schimmel; PRODUCER: Musical Theatre Group, Lenox Arts Center (Lyn Austin, Producing Director) and Playwrights' Forum (Lynda Sturner, Executive Director)

CAST—Wendy Kesselman (Narrator, Singer), Anthony Crivello (Husband, Boy), Deborah Offner (Stepmother, Marlinchen)

SOURCE—The short story *The Juniper-Tree* by the Brothers Grimm (Jacob and Wilhelm) from their 1812 short story collection *Children's and Household Tales*.

The musical was presented in one act.

NOTES—The program didn't list individual musical numbers for the Off Off Broadway production *The Juniper Tree, a Tragic Household Tale*. Based on a tale by the Brothers Grimm, the story was about a boy who is murdered by his stepmother. Buried beneath a juniper tree, he later returns to life as a magical bird who comforts his father and sister and kills the stepmother. Mel Gussow in the *New York Times* found the evening "haunting," and praised the "both dreamlike and nightmarish" stage action of the "strange story." Gussow noted the score had a "folk sensibility" to it, and mentioned that the murder of the boy was accompanied by the "slashing strokes" of a guitar in a style reminiscent of *Sweeney Todd/The Demon Barber of Fleet Street*.

Another version of the material (which music by Philip Glass and Robert Moran) was later seen in a concert production in 2007 (see entry).

848 Juno. THEATRE: Vineyard Theatre; OPENING DATE: October 18, 1992; PERFORMANCES: 29; BOOK: Joseph Stein; LYRICS: Marc Blitzstein; ADDITIONAL LYRICS by Ellen Fitzhugh; MUSIC: Marc Blitzstein; DIRECTION: Lonny Price; CHOREOGRAPHY: Joey McKneely; SCENERY: William Barclay; COSTUMES: Gail Brassard; LIGHTING: Phil Monat; MUSICAL DIRECTION: Grant Sturiale; PRODUCER: Vineyard Theatre (Douglas Aibel, Artistic Director; Barbara Zinn Krieger, Executive Director; Jon Nakagawa, Managing Director)

CAST—Anne O'Sullivan (Mrs. Madigan), Verna Jeanne Pierce (Mrs. Brady), Jeanette Landis (Mrs. Coyne), James Clow (Charlie Bentham), Dick Latessa ("Captain" Jack Boyle), Ivar Brogger (Joxer Daly), Anita Gillette (Juno Boyle), Bill Nabel (Reilly, IRA Man), Andy Taylor (Jerry Devine), Erin O'Brien (Mary Boyle), Malcolm Gets (Johnny Boyle), Stephen Lee Anderson (IRA Man), Tanny McDonald (Mrs. Tanered), Frank O'Brien (Nugent), Justin Malone, Tony Valentine

SOURCE—The 1924 play *Juno and the Paycock* by Sean O'Casey.

The action occurs in Dublin in 1921.

The musical was presented in two acts (song assignments not credited in the program).

ACT ONE—"We're Alive," "We Can Be Proud," "The Liffey Waltz," "Daarlin' Man," "Song of the Ma," "I Wish It So," "One Kind Word," "Old Sayin's," "His Own Peculiar Charm," "Old Sayin's" (reprise), "On a Day Like This"

ACT TWO—"You Poor Thing," "My True Heart," "Bird Upon the Tree," "Music in the House," "It's Not Irish," "The Liffey Waltz" (reprise), "Hymn," "Ireland's Eye," "You Poor Thing" (reprise), "Farewell, Me Butty," "For Love," "One Kind Word"/"I Wish It So" (reprises), "Where?" Finale

NOTES—Marc Blitzstein's short-lived *Juno* originally opened on Broadway on March 3, 1959; audiences had just sixteen chances to see one of the greatest of American musicals. With its expansive, opera-like score and its unrelenting drama, it was like nothing New York had seen during the 1950s. *The Golden Apple* (1954; see entry) and *Candide* (1956; see entry for 1973 Off Broadway revival) had offered equally impressive scores, but they told essentially light-hearted, satiric stories. *Juno* offered nothing but sadness and tragedy, and its ending was perhaps the bleakest in the history of American musical theatre (at best, the ending was darkly optimistic in that Juno Boyle and her daughter Mary find the courage to leave the Captain in order to make something of the rest of their lives). Otherwise, the musical, like the Sean O'Casey play upon which it was based, showed the bleakness of the human heart; its humor was bitter, and its happiest moment, when the Boyles believe they've inherited a fortune and throw a party for their friends and neighbors, turns sour when the inheritance turns out to be a misunderstanding.

Blitzstein's score was one of the best ever heard in the Broadway theatre, with richly melodic choral numbers (the brilliant opening number "We're Alive," the irresistible "Liffey Waltz," the gay dance-driven "On a Day Like This"), haunting ballads ("I

Wish It So," "One Kind Word," "For Love"), and kitschy Irish tunes ("It's Not Irish ["to deny your dear old mother"]). The score's finest moment was "Bird Upon the Tree," a "madrigally" folk-like song performed by Juno and Mary at the ill-fated party. The song told of a bird whose foot is caught in its nest during a fierce storm; but ironically the storm which imprisons the bird also frees it when the wind and the rain shake loose the bird's foot from the twigs. The song foretold the political and emotional storm which would soon sweep over the Boyle home and which would eventually free Juno (whose son Johnny, a traitor to the Irish cause, has just been killed) and Mary (now pregnant and unwed, and deserted by her lover) from the drunk and irresponsible Captain. As the curtain fell on *Juno*, audiences witnessed perhaps the most painful and bitter finale in the history of the American musical in its juxtaposition of Juno and Mary leaving their home for an unknown future as the Captain and his buddy Joxer drunkenly and obliviously sing away in a barroom.

In 1976, the musical had been briefly revived (as *Daarlin' Juno*) at the Long Wharf Theatre; directed by Arvin Brown, Joseph Stein's book was adapted by Richard Maltby, Jr., and Geraldine Fitzgerald, with additional lyrics by Maltby (Fitzgerald and Milo O'Shea portrayed Juno and the Captain, roles first created by Shirley Booth and Melvyn Douglas). The 1992 Vineyard Theatre production (in a different adaptation from the 1976 version, and with additional lyrics by Ellen Fitzhugh) gave New York its first chance to see *Juno* in almost thirty-five years. Unfortunately, despite its strong cast (Anita Gillette's masterful Juno was one of the greatest musical theatre performance of the 1990s, and Dick Latessa made a fine Captain), the production was, necessarily, small (confined scenery, modest dancing, and a small orchestra and chorus). Because *Juno* was conceived as an epic musical, a small production only diminished the sweep and grandeur of the score. Since the opera house seems the natural home for *Juno*, perhaps one day the musical will be seen at the New York City Opera. (As of this writing, *Juno* is scheduled to open on March 27, 2008, as part of *Encores!* [see entry] 2008 season.)

The Vineyard's production included three songs deleted during the original production's tryout ("His Own Peculiar Charm," "Ireland's Eye," and "Farewell, Me Butty").

October 1992 was a memorable month for lovers of Blitzstein's music. Besides the *Juno* revival at the Vineyard, the New York City Opera offered a revival of *Regina* (1949), Blitzstein's lyric adaptation of Lillian Hellman's 1939 play *The Little Foxes*.

The cast album of the original 1959 production of *Juno* was released by Columbia Records (LP # OS-2013; CD released by Fynsworth Alley Records # FA-2134); and a demo recording of Blitzstein playing and singing numbers from the production (as well as from *No for an Answer*; see entry) was released by JJA Records (LP # 19772).

849 Junon and Avos: The Hope. THEATRE: City Center; OPENING DATE: January 7, 1990; PERFORMANCES: 48; BOOK: Andrey Voznesensky; Susan Silver and Albert Todd, English Narrative; LYRICS: Andrey Voznesensky; MUSIC: Alexis Ribnikov; DIRECTION: Mark Zakharov; CHOREOGRAPHY: Vladimir Vassiliev; SCENERY: Oleg Sheintsiss; COSTUMES: Valentina Komolova; MUSICAL DIRECTION: Dimitri Kudriavtsev; PRODUCERS: Pierre Cardin; Lucy Jarvis, American Producer; by special arrangement with the Lencom Theatre in Paris and the Theatre Union of the U.S.S.R.

CAST—NIKOLAI KARACHENTZOV (Count Nikolai Rezanov), YELENA SHANINA (Conchita), Yury Naumkin (First Conjuror), Gennady Trofimov (Second Conjuror), ALEXANDER ABDULOV (Burning Heretic, Fernando Lopez, Theatrical Narrator), Ludmilla Porgina (Vision of Woman with Infant, Spanish Lady), Vladimir Shiryayev (Count Alexey Rumiantsev, The Governor of San Francisco), Vladimir Belousov (Naval Officer), Boris Chunayev (Naval Officer), Vladimir Kuznetsov (Naval Officer), Rady Ovchinnikov (Naval Officer, Interpreter), Villor Kuznetsov (Padre Abella), Irena Alfiorova (Spanish Lady), Tatiana Derbeneva (Spanish Lady), Alexandra Zakharova (Spanish Lady), Tatiana Rudina (Spanish Lady), Ludmilla Artemieva (Spanish Lady), Yury Zelenin (Conchita's Messenger), Alexander Sado (The Singing Mask); The following performers played Russian Sailors, Spaniards, Shareholders of the Russian-American Company, Monks, Chimeras, and Others: Vladislav Bykov, Victor Rakov, Alexander Sririn, Nikolai Shusharin, Alexander Karnaushkin, Igor Fokin, Andrey Leonov, Yury Zelenin, Andrey Druzhkin, Gennady Kozlov, Sergey Chonishvilli, Oleg Ruduk, Leonid Luvinsky, Leonid Gromov, Denis Karasiov; The Choir: Sopranos (Irena Musayelian, Valentina Prokhorova, Zinaida Morozova, Matalia Mishenko); Altos (Irena Kushnarenko, Valeria Zhivova, Lilia Semashko, Yelena Rudnitskaya); Tenor (Vladimir Tursky); Basses (Alexey Larin, Vladimir Prokhorov, Sergey Stepanchenko); Rock Group Araks: Sergey Rudnitsky, Keyboards; Sergey Rizhov (Bass Guitar); Sergey Berezkin (Guitar, Violin, Cello); Anatoly Abromov (Drums); Yakov Levda and Viktor Denisov (Brass Section); Alexander Sado, Nikolai Parfenyuk, Pavel Smeian (Vocals); PHILIP CASNOFF (Storyteller)

The action occurs during the period 1806-1842 in Russia and San Francisco.

The opera was performed in two acts.

NOTES—The Russian rock opera *Junon and Avos* told the story of Count Rezanov and his hope of opening trade between Russia and the United States. *Junon* and *Avos* were the names of the two schnooners Rezanov build in order to sail to America; the former ship was named after Jupiter because the planet was used by sailors for navigation, and the latter was so named because it meant hope or good luck.

Stephen Holden in the *New York Times* noted the evening was less a rock musical than an "elaborately staged pop pageant." Although he found the score generally "robust," he felt the production itself was often stiff and preachy; if *Junon and Avoes* was the Soviet Union's answer to *Hair*, then it "woefully" lacked humor and a light touch. But Holden singled out and reported in detail the evening's most theatrical and "exciting" moment, which came at the end of the first act: from the rear of the stage came "tiers of bare-chested sailors" who, on a "raked set of illuminated Plexiglas cubes," performed a gymnastic dance while singing a "lusty" anthem. Holden said the "splendidly" choreographed sequence suggested "a Soviet Socialist answer to a Bob Fosse musical." The opera was performed in Russian, with spoken narrative asides in English (by guest artist Philip Casnoff, who played the role of the Storyteller).

There was no song list in the program, but a special insert included the lyrics for six numbers: "Song of the Naval Officers," "Avos," "Song of the Wild White Rose," "Angel, Become a Woman," "Ten Years Have Passed," and "Alleluia." As *Juno and Avos*, a 2-LP Russian recording of the score was released by Meloydia (?) Records (# C60-18627-008) in 1982.

850 Just a Night Out! "A Musical Love Story." THEATRE: Top of the Village Gate; OPENING DATE: February 16, 1992; PERFORMANCES: 65; BOOK, LYRICS, AND MUSIC: Richard and Susan Turner (unless otherwise cited, all songs appear to by Richard and Susan Turner); DIRECTION: Leslie Dockery; CHOREOGRAPHY: Leslie Dockery; SCENERY: Lisa Watson; COSTUMES: Gregory Clenn; LIGHTING: Sandra Ross; PRODUCERS: The Negro Ensemble Company (Douglas Turner Ward, Artistic Director) and Turner Monarch Productions

CAST—Zenzele Scott, Messeret Stroman, Bruce Butler, Chandra Simmons, Deborah Keeling

The action occurs in a Midwestern town.

The musical was presented in two acts (division of acts and song assignments unknown; songs are listed in performance order).

MUSICAL NUMBERS—"Just a Night Out," "Just in Time" (from *Bells Are Ringing*, 1956; lyric by Betty Comden and Adolph Green, music by Jule Styne)/ "The Lady Is a Tramp" (*Babes in Arms*, 1937; lyric by Lorenz Hart, music by Richard Rodgers), "Misty" (lyric by Johnny Burke, music by Erroll Garner), "All of You" (*Silk Stockings*, 1955; lyric and music by Cole Porter), "Everything Costs Money in New York," "6' 2" and Ooh!," "Here We Go Again," "Don't Go to Strangers" (lyric and music by Redd Evans, Arthur Kent, and David Mann), "What Is She Doing Here," "I'll Be There When You Need Me," "I've Got You Under My Skin" (1936 film *Born to Dance*; lyric and music by Cole Porter), "Renee's Lament," "Let's Get One Thing Straight," "Showtime Is Mine," "That Woman Is Me," "Lovely Ladies," Finale

NOTES—*Just a Night Out!* dealt with the romances of a singing group which is performing in a small Midwestern town.

851 Just for Love. THEATRE: Provincetown Playhouse; OPENING DATE: October 17, 1968; PERFORMANCES: 6; SCRIPT AND LYRICS "devised" by: Jill Showell and Henry Comor; MUSIC: Michael Valenti; DIRECTION: Henry Comor; SCENERY: Jack Blackman; COSTUMES: Sara Brook Lighting: Jack Blackman; MUSICAL DIRECTION: George Taros; PRODUCERS: Seymour Vall in association with Investors Production Company and Maurice Rind

CAST—Jill Showell, Henry Comor, Jacqueline Mayro, Steve Perry

The revue was presented in two acts (division of acts and song assignments not listed in program; songs are listed in performance order).

MUSICAL NUMBERS—"Just for Love," "One and Twenty," "Mary Ann," "Come Live with Me," "A Birthday," "Two Strings to a Bow," "Did Not," "What Is Love," "Jenny Kissed Me," "Echo," "Bella," "Man Is For Woman Made," "So We'll Go No More A'roving," "Epitaph"

NOTES—*Just for Love* dealt with songs about love, and the lyrics were both original as well as ones adapted from various literary sources. In his *New York Times'* review, Clive Barnes noted the evening was a bland one with coy direction, tired jokes, and "faintly embarrassed" music.

The evening's composer was the talented Michael Valenti who unfortunately never found the hit vehicle to secure his place in musical theatre. He had earlier appeared as a performer in the original production of *Your Own Thing* (see entry).

RCA Victor Records was to have recorded the cast album of *Just for Love*, which was cancelled due to the revue's brief run. Two songs ("What Is Love" and "Jenny Kissed [Kiss'd] Me") were later heard in *Lovesong* (see entry).

852 Just for Openers. "A New Musical Revue." THEATRE: Upstairs at the Downstairs; OPENING DATE: November 3, 1965; PERFORMANCES: 395; SKETCHES: Fannie Flagg, Mary Hurt, Bill Kaufman, Paul Koreto, Gayle Parent, Kenny Solms, and Rod Warren; LYRICS: Larry Alexander, William Dyer, Ed Fearon, David Finkle, Alan Freidman, Michael McWhinney, John Meyer, Don Parks, Drey Shepperd, and Rod Warren; MUSIC: William Dyer, Alan Friedman, William Goldenberg, Lee Holdridge, Ed Kresley, Stephen Lawrence, Don Parks, Rod Warren, and Bill Weeden; DIRECTION: Sandra Devlin; CHOREOGRAPHY: Sandra Devlin; SCENERY: Tom Harriss; COSTUMES: Gowns by Nesha; MUSICAL DIRECTION: Michael Cohen; PRODUCER: Rod Warren

CAST—Betty Aberlin, Richard Blair, Stockton Brigel, R.G. Brown, Fannie Flagg, Madeline Kahn

The revue was presented in two acts.

ACT ONE—"Just for Openers" (lyric and music by Rod Warren) (Company), "The 'Dolly' Sisters" (lyric by Drey Shepperd, music by Ed Kresley) (Betty Aberlin, Fannie Flagg, Madeline Kahn), "Hail, Columbia" (sketch by Rod Warren) (performers unknown) "Anyone Who's Anyone" (lyric by David Finkle, music by Bill Wheeden) (Betty Aberlin, Madeline Kahn, Richard Blair, Stockton Brigel) "Where Did We Go Wrong?" (lyric by John Meyer, music by Stephen Lawrence) (Fannie Flagg, R.G. Brown) "If the Crown Fits" (sketch by Kenny Solms and Gayle Parent) (Richard Blair, Betty Aberlin, Madeline Kahn, Fannie Flagg) "America the Beautiful" (lyric by Michael McWhinney, music by Rod Warren) (Madeline Kahn) "The Waitress" (sketch by Fannie Flagg) (Fannie Flagg, Richard Blair) "New York Without Bob" (lyric and music by Alan Freidman) (R.G. Brown), "The Telephone Hang-Up" (sketch by Bill Kaufman and Paul Koreto) (Madeline Kahn, Betty Aberlin) "Adaptations" (lyric by Ed Fearon, music by Lee Holdridge) ("Most of the Company")

ACT TWO—"You're a Big Boy Now" (lyric and music by Rod Warren) (Company), "The Second-Best Man" (sketch by Rod Warren) (Betty Aberlin, Stockton Brigel, R.G. Brown) "The Matinee" (lyric by John Meyer, music by Stephen Lawrence) (Madeline Kahn, Richard Blair) "Fun in the Morning" (sketch by Fannie Flagg and Mary Hurt) (Fannie Flagg, R.G. Brown) "Mr. Know-It-All" (lyric by Larry Alexander, music by William Goldenbeg) (Richard Blair), "Let's Abolish Holidays" (lyric and music by William Dyer and Don Parks) (Company), "Space Age" (sketch by Rod Warren) (Company) Finale: "Just for Openers" (reprise) (lyric and music by Rod Warren) (Company)

NOTES—Rod Warren's revue *Just for Openers* was another long-running success, and his first to be recorded (by Upstairs at the Downstairs Records [LP # UD-37W56]).

Robert Alden in the *New York Times* found the "copper-bright" revue an evening of "infectious gaiety." He singled out a number of sketches and songs, including "New York Without Bob" (a farewell to the city's Mayor Robert Wagner); "Mr. Know-It-All" (a spoof of folk singers who lament that much of the nation's youth have to watch television on black-and-white sets); "You're a Big Boy Now" (a plea for the United Nations to grow up); and "Anyone Who's Anyone" (being Jewish is suddenly the "in" thing).

During the run, the sketch "Hail, Columbia" was dropped, and replaced by "Christmas Shopping" (sketch by Rod Warren). "Anyone Who's Anyone," "If the Crown Fits," and "The Telephone Hang-Up" also appeared the retrospective revue *Below the Belt* (1966).

For a complete list of Rod Warren's revues, see entry for *...And in This Corner*; also see Appendix R.

853 Just Libby. THEATRE: Upstage at Jimmy's; OPENING DATE: November 16, 1974; PERFORMANCES: 32; MATERIAL WRITTEN by Libby Morris and Leslie Lawson; SPECIAL MUSICAL NUMBERS WRITTEN by Bill Solly.; MUSICAL DIRECTION: Geoffrey Brawn

CAST—Libby Holman

NOTES—Canadian Libby Holman emerged in the 1960s as a singer of unusual taste and skill, and her repertoire consisted of a mixture of standards and offbeat material. She appeared as Rose in a 1976 South African revival of *Gypsy*, and the cast album of that production on Philips Records (LP # STO-774) is probably the most obscure recording of the classic score. The album includes Bonnie Langford, who reprised the role of Baby June (which she had created for the belated 1973 London premiere of the musical).

854 Just Once. "A Love Story About the Feeling of Magic." THEATRE: The Bottom Line; OPENING DATE: April 17, 1986; PERFORMANCES: Unknown; TEXT: Melanie Mintz; LYRICS: Cynthia Weil; MUSIC: Barry Mann (Some of the songs were written in collaboration with Gerry Goffin, Dan Hill, Larry Kolber, Jerry Leiber and Mike Stoller, Lionel Richie, Tom Snow, and Phil Spector.); DIRECTION: Sam Ellis; CHOREOGRAPHY: Wayne Cilento; Lisa Mordente, Assistant Choreographer; SCENERY: Michael Anania; COSTUMES: Sharon Lynch; LIGHTING: Jeffrey Schissler; MUSICAL DIRECTION: Jimmy Vivino; PRODUCERS: Allan Pepper and Stanley Snadowsky

CAST—Beth Taylor (Jesse), Eleanor McCoy (Cynthia), Doug Suvall (Jacob), Ula Hedwig (Linda), Kaz Silver (Marilyn), Earl Scooter (Alfred), Peter Neptune (Harold), Bobby Jay (Assorted Characters and Background Vocals), Vivian Cherry, Curtis King, Jr., Tanya Willoughby The action occurs in Brooklyn and Manhattan during the periods 1960-1968 and 1973-1985.

The revue was presented in two acts.

ACT ONE—"Walking in the Rain" (lyric and music by Barry Mann, Cynthia Weil, and Phil Spector) (Tanya Willoughby), "Who Put the Bomp" (lyric and music by Barry Mann and Gerry Goffin) (Peter Neptune), "Bless You" (lyric and music by Barry Mann and Cynthia Weil) (Earl Scooter), "On Broadway" (lyric and music by Barry Mann, Cynthia Weil, Jerry Leiber, and Mike Stoller) (Curtis King, Jr.), "Only in America" (lyric and music by Barry Mann, Cynthia Weil, Jerry Leiber, and Mike Stoller) (Peter Neptune), "Uptown" (lyric and music by Barry Mann and Cynthia Weil) (Tanya Willoughby), "He's Sure the Boy I Love" (lyric and music by Barry Mann and Cynthia Weil) (Vivian Cherry), "Blame It on the Bossa Nova" (lyric and music by Barry Mann and Cynthia Weil) (Kaz Silver), "I Love How You Love Me" (lyric and music by Barry Mann and Larry Kolber) (Kaz Silver), "I'm Gonna Be Strong" (lyric and music by Barry Mann and Cynthia Weil) (Earl Scooter), "Born to Be Together" (lyric and music by Barry Mann, Cynthia Weil, and Phil Spector) (Tanya Willoughby), "You've Lost That Lovin' Feeling" (lyric and music by Barry Mann, Cynthia Weil, and Phil Spector) (Curtis King, Jr., Earl Scooter)

ACT TWO—"Kicks"/"We Gotta Get Out of This Place" (lyric and music by Barry Mann and Cynthia Weil) (Peter Neptune), "New World Coming"/ "Make Your Own Kind of Music" (lyric and music by Barry Mann and Cynthia Weil) (Kaz Silver), "Sweet Freedom" (lyric and music by Barry Mann and Cynthia Weil) (Vivian Cherry), "Somewhere Down the Road" (lyric and music by Barry Mann and Tom Snow) (Earl Scooter), "Sometimes When We Touch" (lyric and music by Barry Mann and Dan Hill) (Ula Hedwig), "Here You Come Again" (lyric and music by Barry Mann and Cynthia Weil) (Kaz Silver), "He's So Shy" (lyric and music by Cynthia Weil and Tom Snow) (Tanya Willoughby), "Don't Know Much" (lyric and music by Barry Mann, Cynthia Weil, and Tom Snow) (Ula Hedwig), "Just Once" (lyric and music by Barry Mann and Cynthia Weil) (Curtis King, Jr.), "Running with the Night" (lyric and music by Cynthia Weil and Lionel Richie)(Ula Hedwig), "Never Gonna Let You Go" (lyric and music by Barry Mann and Cynthia Weil) (Vivian Cherry, Curtis King, Jr.)

NOTES—The Off Off Broadway revue-like musical *Just Once* was a tribute to Barry Mann and Cynthia Weil who together and with various collaborators wrote an amazing number of hit songs.

In 2004, Off Broadway offered *They Wrote That?* (see entry), another evening of songs by the team; this time around, Mann and Weil headed the cast.

855 Just So. "A New Musical Comedy." THEATRE: Jack Lawrence Theatre; OPENING DATE: December 3, 1985; PERFORMANCES: 6; BOOK: Mark St. Germain; LYRICS: David Zippel; MUSIC: Doug Katsaros; DIRECTION: Julianne Boyd; CHOREOGRAPHY: David Storey; SCENERY: Atkin Pace; COSTUMES: Ann Hould-Ward; LIGHTING: Craig Miller; MUSICAL DIRECTION: David Friedman; PRODUCERS: Ivan Bloch, Joanne L. Zippel, New Day Productions, and Mary Fisher Productions

CAST—ANDRE DE SHIELDS (Eldest Magician), Keith Curran (Giraffe), Teresa Burrell (Camel), Tom Robbins (Rhino), Tina Johnson (Elephant Child), Tico Wells (Leopard), Jason Graae (Man)

SOURCE—The 1902 volume of short stories *Just So Stories* by Rudyard Kipling.

The action occurs on the world's first day.

The musical was presented in two acts.

ACT ONE—"Just So" (Andre De Shields, Animals), "The Whole World Revolves Around You" (Andre De Shields, Animals, Jason Graae), "Arm in Arm in Harmony" (Jason Graae, Animals), "Chill Out!" (Andre De Shields, Jason Graae), "The Camel's Blues" (a/k/a "The Camel's Song") (Teresa Burrell), "Eat, Eat, Eat" (Tom Robbins, Jason Graae, Animals), "Desert Dessert" (Andre De Shields, Jason Graae, Animals), "Itch, Itch, Itch" (Tom Robbins), "Everything Under the Sun" (Jason Graae), "The Gospel According to the Leopard" (Tico Wells, Jason Graae, Animals)

ACT TWO—"My First Mistake" (Andre De Shields), "Shadowy Forest of Garadufi Dance" (Tico Wells, Animals), "Giraffe's Reprise" (Keith Curran), "The Answer Song" (Andre De Shields, Tina Johnson), "I've Got to Know" (Tina Johnson), "I Have Changed" (Andre De Shields, Animals), "Lullaby" (Andre de Shields)

NOTES—This musical version of Rudyard Kipling's *Just So Stories* lasted less than a week. Mel Gussow in the *New York Times* found the short (ninety-minutes, not counting intermission) evening as slow-going as Kipling's turtle. He found the anachronisms tiresome and the score "mediocre"; moreover, the way in which the performers were attired provided few clues to their animal identities.

Just So had first been produced by the Pennsylvania Stage Company in Allentown, Pennsylvania, on September 19, 1984, and the cast included Larry Marshall (as the Eldest Magician) and Bebe Neuwirth (as Leopard). Two numbers ("The Camel's Blues" and "Lullaby") had been previously heard in the 1983 Off Broadway revue *It's Better with a Band* (see entry), an evening devoted to songs with lyrics by David Zippel. The script of *Just So* was published by Samuel French, Inc., in 1986.

Another musical adaptation of *Just So Stories* was first produced in Great Britain in 1989; also titled *Just So*, the musical had book and lyrics by Anthony Drewe and music by George Stiles (a recording was released by First Night Records in 2006 [CD # CD-95] with John Barrowman and the cast of Chichester Festival Theatre production). This version was later seen at Goodspeed at Chester beginning on November 5, 1998.

The year before the Off Broadway production of *Just So*, Kipling himself was the subject of the one-man Broadway play *Kipling* by Brian Clark; the critics liked Alec McCowen in the title role, but otherwise were unimpressed with the evening; the play was gone after twelve performances.

856 Ka-Boom! "The Explosive New Musical!" THEATRE: Carter Theatre; OPENING DATE: November 20, 1980; PERFORMANCES: 71; BOOK: Bruce Kluger; LYRICS: Bruce Kluger; MUSIC: Joe Ercole; DIRECTION: John-Michael Tebelak; CHOREOGRAPHY: Lynne Gannaway; SCENERY: Ken Holamon; COSTUMES: Erica Hollmann; LIGHTING: Kirk Bookman; MUSICAL DIRECTION: John Lehman; PRODUCERS: Jim Payne in association with Sherie Seff and Bruce Kluger

CAST—Ken Ward (Matt), Fannie Whitehead (Hattie), John Hall (Tony), Andrea Wright (June), Judith Bro (Jasmine), Terry Barnes (Avery)

The musical was presented in two acts.

ACT ONE—Overture/Prologue (Orchestra), "Now We Pray" (Ensemble), "Oh, Lord" (Ensemble), "A Little Bit o' Glitter" (John Hall), "Maybe for Instance" (Judith Bro), "With a World to Conquer" (Fannie Whitehead), "Smile" (Andrea Wright), "Let Me Believe in Me" (Ken Ward), "Believe Us"/"Receive Us" (Terry Barnes, Ensemble), "A Few to Get Through" (Judith Bro), "Ballad of Adam and Eve" (John Hall, Fannie Whitehead), "Gimme a 'G'" (Andrea Wright), Finale (Ensemble), "Maybe for Instance" (reprise) (Judith Bro), "The Soft Spot" (John Hall, Judith Bro), "You Are You" (Ensemble), "The Light Around the Corner" (Ensemble)

ACT TWO—"Believe Us"/"Receive Us" (reprise) (Ensemble), "Those ABC's" (Andrea Wright, Ensemble), "Judgement Day" (John Hall, Ensemble), "Bump and Grind for God" (Fannie Whitehead, Ensemble), "Let Me Believe in Me" (reprise) (Ken Ward, Ensemble), "Let the Show Go On!" (Terry Barnes, Ensemble)

NOTES—*Ka-Boom!*, which dealt with the trials and tribulations of putting on a musical show after a nuclear holocaust, gave a whole new meaning to the word "bomb." John S. Wilson in the *New York Times* felt the music was "haunted" by *Jesus Christ Superstar*, and noted the book and lyrics were "bogged down" in their efforts to tell the story of five show-business types (a Las Vegas singer, a TV sit-com writer, a stripper, a drama student, and an ingénue who has been in countless tours of *Oklahoma!*) who are the only survivors of a nuclear holocaust. At the urging of an angel, they are encouraged to put on a "Big Show for God," *Creation, Part II.*

The cast recording was released on CYM Records (LP # 8130). The musical had originally been seen in a workshop production at the University of Maryland.

Not to be confused with *Kaboom!*, a bomb which played for one performance in 1974 (see entry).

857 Kaboom! THEATRE: Bottom Line Theatre; OPENING DATE: May 1, 1974; PERFORMANCES: 1; BOOK: Ira Wallach; LYRICS: Ira Wallach; MUSIC: Doris Schwerin; DIRECTION: Don Price; CHOREOGRAPHY: Don Price; SCENERY: Peter Harvey; COSTUMES: Lohr Wilson; LIGHTING: Timmy Harris; MUSICAL DIRECTION: Arnold Gross; PRODUCERS: Joseph Rhodes; Alice Shuman, Associate Producer

CAST—James Donahue (Grisdale), Marjorie Barnes (Griselda), Tom Matthew Tobin (Mr. Crackle, Granny, Tom), Bernice Massi (Goneril), Charles Hudson (President, Tibulonimus, Frank), Jack Blackton (Colonel Washburn), Corinne Kason (Emily)

The musical was presented in two acts (division of acts and song assignments unknown; songs are listed in performance order)

MUSICAL NUMBERS—"Supermarket," "Buying and Selling," "High School Diplomas," "Busy Lady," "Ritual," "Ave Nelson," "Velvet Vest," "Existential," "Time Was," "Mother Darling," "I'm Gonna Make It," "While They Were Sleeping," "Sex, Sex, Sex," "Is It Too Late," "On Her Own," "God Is Smiling on You"

NOTES—The revue *Kaboom!* satirized various American institutions. It was gone after its first performance, and Jack Blackton, one of its cast members, was back in another Off Broadway show two weeks later (see entry for 1974 revival of *Jaques Brel Is Alive and Well and Living in Paris*).

Howard Thompson in the *New York Times* wrote that *Kaboom!* "goes kaplunk" in dullness and vulgarity. He praised a "bubbly" mini-overture, but noted that the "fiercely cheerful" finale ("God Is Smiling on You") did not reflect what was seen on the stage of the Bottom Line Theatre.

Not to be confused with *Ka-Boom!*, which opened in 1980 (see entry).

858 Kaleidoscope. THEATRE: Provincetown Playhouse; OPENING DATE: June 13, 1957; PERFORMANCES: Unknown; SKETCHES: Lee Adams, Sig Altman, Lois Balk, Louis Botto, Mickey Deems, William Dyer, Martin Gal, Herbert Hartig, Tom Jones, David Panich, Don Parks, Herbert Reich, David Ross, and Mike (Michael) Stewart; LYRICS: Cherry Balaban, Martin Charnin, Raoul Gonzalez, Murray Grand, David Gregory, Sheldon Harnick, Herbert Hartig, Tom Jones, Don Richards, David Rogers, Kenneth Welch, and G. Wood; MUSIC: Gerald Alters, David Baker, Cherry Balaban, Elisse Boyd, Raoul Gonzalez, Marie Gordon, Sheldon Harnick, David Hollister, Robert Kessler, Harvey Schmidt, Kenneth Welch, and G. Wood; SKETCHES AND BLACKOUTS DIRECTION: Paul Mazurksy

MUSICAL NUMBERS—and Choreography: Edmund Balin; SCENERY: Lin Emery; COSTUMES: Mariana Elliott; LIGHTING: Wendy Lee; MUSICAL DIRECTION: Herbert E. Hecht; PRODUCERS: Richard D. Stainbrook and Jeanellen McKee

CAST—Mickey Deems, Wisa D'Orso, Leonard Drum, Maria Karnilova, Bobo Lewis, Penny Malone, Erin Martin, Tom Mixon, Kenneth Nelson, John Smolko

The revue was presented in two acts.

ACT ONE—Overture (Orchestra), Opening (Company) (Writer[s] not credited), "Subway" (sketch by Sig Altman) (Company) "This Is Love" (by Herbert Hecht) (Kenneth Nelson, Wisa D'Orso) "Time Flies" (sketch by David Panich) (Tom Mixon, John Smolko, Kenneth Nelson, Wisa D'Orso, Mickey Deems, Maria Karnilova, Penny Malone, Erin Martin), "Boughten Bride" (lyric and music by Cherry Balaban) (John Smolko, Erin Martin, Tom Mixon), "November in Kenya" (lyric by Martin Charnin, music by Bob Kessler) (Leonard Drum) "Father's Day" (sketch by Mickey Deems) (Mickey Deems, Erin Martin, Tom Mixon, Penny Malone, Bobo Lewis) "Lament" (lyric and music by Raoul Gonzalez) (Wisa D'Orso), "More Coffee" (sketch by Herbert Hartig and Lois Balk) (Mickey Deems, Bobo Lewis, Kenneth Nelson) "I Love Ann" (lyric by Tom Jones, music by Harvey Schmidt) (Tom Mixon, Wisa D'Orso, John Smolko), "One Helluva Bore" (lyric and music by G. Wood) (Maria Karnilova) "The Grass Is Always Greener" (sketch by Louis Botto) (Mickey Deems, John Smolko, Tom Mixon, Leonard Drum, Penny Malone), "Lady B" (lyric by David Rogers, music by Marie Gordon) (Bobo Lewis) "Supersonic" (sketch by David Panich) (Company) "All for a Dime" (SKETCH by Mickey Deems; ADDITIONAL DIALOGUE by Herb Reich) (Mickey Deems) "A House on the Ohio" (lyric and music by Ken Welch) (Tom Mixon, Erin Martin, John Smolko) "I've Got It Hidden" (lyric by Murray Grand, music by Elisse Boyd) (Penny Malone) "Trench Coat" (lyric and music by Sheldon Harnick, ballet music by Herbert Hecht) (Company)

ACT TWO—"Doin' the Finale First" (lyric by David Greggory, music by David Hollister) (Company), "Love Match" (sketch by Don Parks and William Dyer) (Kenneth Nelson, Tom Mixon, Maria Karnilova, Bobo Lewis, John Smolko, Erin Martin, Leonard Drum, Wisa D'Orso) "When I Make Up My Mind" (lyric by Sheldon Harnick, music by David Baker) (Erin Martin, Tom Mixon) "Memories" (sketch by David Panich) (Leonard Drum, Maria Karnilova, John Smolko) "The Diehards" (lyric by Don Richards, music by Jeanellen McKee) (Bobo Lewis, Mickey Deems), "Modern Artists" (sketch by Tom Jones and Martin Gal) (Leonard Smolko, Kenneth Nelson, Bobo Lewis) "Illusion" (music by Jeanellen McKee) (Kenneth Nelson, Erin Martin, Tom Mixon, John Smolko) (NOTE: Jeanelle McKee may be the song's lyricist.), "Young Nhudanycke" (lyric by Herbert Hartig, music by Gerald Alters) (Kenneth Nelson, Leonard Drum, Mickey Deems, Wisa D'Orso), "Nothing Ever Happens to Me" (sketch by Herbert Hartig and Lois Balk) (Penny Malone) "I Know Loneliness" (lyric by Tom Jones, music by Harvey Schmidt) (John Smolko) "The General" (sketch by David Panich) (Leonard Drum, Mickey Deems, John Smolko, Kenneth Nelson) "Destroy Me" (lyric by Ken Welch, music by Sol Berkowitz) (Bobo Lewis), "Baby Sitters Ball" (by Ken Welch) (Wisa D'Orso, Tom Mixon, Erin Martin, John Smolko) "Thoughteasy" (sketch by Lee Adams, Mike Stewart, and David Ross) (Mickey Deems, Bobo Lewis, Kenneth Nelson, John Smolko, Leonard Drum, Maria Karnilova, Wisa D'Orso, Tom Mixon, Erin Martin) Finale (Company)

NOTES—*Kaleidoscope* is an early Off Broadway revue, now all but forgotten. But it boasted a number of performers, writers, lyricists, and composers who would soon find major successes in both Broadway and Off Broadway musical theatre. Louis Calta in the *New York Times* found the material flat and commonplace, but it appears the revue had a certain skewed sense of humor in such numbers as "Doin' the Finale First," which was performed at the top of the second act. According to the song's logic, New York theatre audiences are notorious for rushing out of a theatre before a show is over, and so the placement of the finale in an earlier spot gives the audience a chance to hear the number.

Apparently Herbert Hartig and Lois Balk's sketch "More Coffee" was a "sequel" to their "Coffee, A Relativity," which had first been performed in *Shoestring '57* (see entry) and recorded on that show's cast album. The earlier sketch had also been performed in *Spread Eagle IV*, a 1969 Washington, D.C., revue. David Panich's sketch "Memories" was later used in the 1963 revue *Put It in Writing* (see entry).

859 Kaos. THEATRE: New York Theatre Workshop; OPENING DATE: December 4, 2006; PERFORMANCES: 31; TEXT ADAPTATION: Frank Pugliese; Giovanni Papotto, Dramaturg; MUSIC: See NOTES section below; DIRECTION: Martha Clarke; CHOREOGRAPHY: Martha Clarke; SCENERY: Scott Pask; COSTUMES: Donna Zakowska; LIGHTING: Christopher Akerlind; MUSICAL DIRECTION: Jill Jaffe, with John T. La Barbera; PRODUCER: New York Theatre Workshop (James C. Nicola, Artistic Director; Lynn Moffat, Managing Director)

CAST—Felix Blaska, Sophie Bortolussi, George de la Pena, Daria Deflorian, Vito di Bella, Lorenzo Iacona, Jim Iorio, Gabrielle Malone, Matthew Mohr, Rocco Sisto, Cristina Spina, Rebecca Wender, Robert Wersinger, Julia Wilkins

SOURCES—Four short stories by Luigi Pirandello ("L'Altro Figlio (The Other Son)," "Mal di Luna (Moon Sickness)," "Requiem," and a section of "Colloqui con i Personaggi (A Talk with the Characters)" and the 1984 telefilm *Kaos* by Paolo and Vittorio Taviani and Tonino Guerra.

The action occurs in Sicily around 1900.

The dance-piece was presented in one act.

SCENE LIST—Prologue, "L'Altro Figlio (The Other Son)," "Mal di Luna (Moon Sickness)—Part 1," "Requiem—Part 1," "Mal di Luna (Moon Sickness)—Part 2," "Requiem—Part 2," Epilogue (an excerpt from *Colloqui con i Personaggi* [A Talk with the Characters])

NOTES—For *Kaos*, Martha Clarke used movement, text, and music to interpret four short stories by Luigi Pirandello and the film *Kaos*, which was based on five short stories by Pirandello. The work was conceived, directed, and choreographed by Clarke, and the stories were adapted by Frank Pugliese. Some of the score was adapted from Italian music, and new music was composed by Jill Jaffe and John T. La Barbera; also, sections of Antonio Vivaldi's "Mandolin Concerto in C, Trio in C Minor" and Johann Sebastian Bach's "Sinfona No. 5 in E Flat Major" were heard.

The dialogue in the Off Off Broadway production was spoken in Italian, and supertitles in English were projected on the back wall of the stage. The dances told various stories of Sicilian life, including "L'Altro Figlio," about a lonely mother who has lost contact with two sons who now live in the United States; she has a third son in Sicily, but refuses to acknowledge him because he was the result of her being raped. John Rockwell in the *New York Times* found *Kaos* "affecting and intense, one of [Clarke's] better efforts ... a sparkling job ... well worth seeing." However, he felt the supertitles distracted the audience from the action; on other hand, he noted English would have "clashed egregiously with the painstakingly drawn Sicilian setting."

As *The Pirandello Project*, the piece was first seen in a workshop production at the New York Theatre Workshop in July 2003.

For a list of theatre works by Martha Clarke which are discussed in this book, see entry for *The Garden of Earthly Delights*.

860 The Karl Marx Play. THEATRE: American Place Theatre; OPENING DATE: March 16, 1973; PERFORMANCES: 32; PLAY: Rochelle Owens; LYRICS: Rochelle Owens; MUSIC: Galt MacDermot; DIRECTION: Mel Shapiro; SCENERY: Karl Eigsti; COSTUMES: Linda Fisher; LIGHTING: Roger Morgan; PRODUCER: The American Place Theatre (Wynn Handman, Director)

CAST—Linda Mulrean (Shirlee [clarinet]), Deborah Loomis (Krista [violin]), Louie Piday (Elly [cello]), Zenobia Conkerite (Trinka [guitar]), Linda Swenson (Laurie [autoharp-baritone]), Norman Matlock (Leadbelly), Leonard Jackson (Karl Marx), Randy Kim (Frederick Engels), Katherine Helmond (Jenny von Westphalen), Lizabeth Pritchett (Lenchen), Ralph Carter (Baby Johann)

The action occurs in London during the mid-nineteenth century.

The play was presented in two acts.

ACT ONE—Overture, "My Knees Are Weak" (Norman Matlock), Tavern Scene: "There Was a Hen" (Randy Kim, Girls), "O Mistress Mine" (Norman Matlock), "White Sheeting" (Norman Matlock), "Hello, Hello" (Leonard Jackson), "Jenny von Westphalen" (Katherine Helmond), "So I Give You" (Ensemble), "Dying Child" (Leonard Jackson), "Jenny Is Like an Angel" (Katherine Helmond, Girls), Interlude, "Pretty Woman" (Norman Matlock), "Tempting Salome" (Katherine Helmond), "It's Me They Talk About" (Leonard Jackson), "He Eats" (Norman Matlock, Girls), "Red Leather Wrist Watch" (Ralph Carter)

ACT TWO—"Holy Mystery" (Ralph Carter, Katherine Helmond, Girls), "Baby Johann" (Leonard Jackson), "Comes the Revolution" (Ensemble), "We Doubt You, Papa" (Ralph Carter, Norman Matlock, Randy Kim, Ensemble), "The Hand of Fate" (Norman Matlock), Finale: "World Creation" (Katherine Helmond, Chorus)

NOTES—Rochelle Owens' play-with-music *The Karl Marx Play* depicted Marx' life prior to his fame as the father of communism and the author of *Das Kapital*. Clive Barnes in the *New York Times* emphasized that Owens was concerned less with historical accuracy than with "historical inevitability" because Marx has an "historic past to eventually fulfill" since he "had" to write *Das Kapital*. Indeed, the characters in the play seem to know that Marx will eventually author an influential book, and they have a strange, almost supernatural pre-knowledge of the importance of the book he has yet to write.

Barnes felt the evening was "flawed" and "untidy" but nonetheless "rewarding." Further, he liked Galt MacDermot's "tuneful, totally appropriate score" and praised Ralph Carter in the role of Marx' son Baby Johann. Barnes noted that *The Karl Marx Play* was Carter's third appearance in a MacDermot work that season (earlier in the season, Carter had been in the short-lived Broadway productions of MacDermot's *Dude*, or *The Highway Life* and *Via Galactica*; in 1973, Carter also appeared in the long-running *Raisin*, introducing Judd Woldin and Robert Brittan's "Sidewalk Tree," one of the finest theatre songs of the era).

The songs were recorded by Kilmarnock Records (LP # KIL-72010), and included cast members from the original company (such as Norman Matlock and Ralph Carter) as well as those who performed with the European touring company (Harold Gould and Phyllis Newman).

The list of song titles is taken from the recording.

The script was published in 1974 by E.P. Dutton & Co., Inc., in *The Karl Marx Play & Others*, a collection of plays by Rochelle Owens. The script had earlier been published in a one-act version in *The Best Short Plays of 1971*, edited by Stanley Richards, and was later published by Samuel French, Inc.

861 Kaye Ballard: Working 42nd Street at Last! THEATRE: Kaufman Theatre; OPENING DATE: May 16, 1988; PERFORMANCES: 29; CREATIVE CONSULTANT: Ben Bagley; SCENERY: Jeffrey Schissler; COSTUMES: Clovis Ruffin, Grace Costumes, and Reuben Panis; LIGHTING: Jeffrey Schissler; MUSICAL DIRECTION: Arthur Siegel; PRODUCER: Martin R. Kaufman

CAST—Kaye Ballard

The revue was presented in two acts.

ACT ONE—"Don't Ask the Lady What the Lady Did Before" (from 1982 revival of *Little Me*; lyric by Carolyn Leigh, music by Cy Coleman), "Sondheim Song" (lyric and music by Barry Kleinbort), "My Son" (lyric and music by Suzanne Buhrer), "Burger Beguine" (lyric and music by Leslie Eberhard and David Levy), "The Old Soft Shoe" (*Three to Make Ready*, 1946; lyric by Nancy Hamilton, music by Morgan Lewis), "Remind Me" (1940 film *One Night in the Tropics*; lyric by Dorothy Fields, music by Jerome Kern), "Folk Song" (lyric and music by Gordon Connell), "Country Song" (lyric and music by Suzanne Buhrer), "Is That All There Is?" (written for the unproduced musical *International Wrestling Match*; lyric and music by Jerry Leiber and Mike Stoller), *The Wizard of Oz* Medley (1939 film; lyrics by E.Y. Harburg, music by Harold Arlen), "I Just Found Out" (lyric and music by Fred [Frederick] Silver), Irving Berlin Medley

ACT TWO—"I Gotta Make My Own Music" (lyric by Charlotte Kent, music by Arthur Siegel), "I Hate Spring" (lyric and music by Nancy Hamilton and Martha Caples), "Lizzie Borden" (*New Faces of 1952*; lyric and music by Michael Brown), "Love Is a Simple Thing" (*New Faces of 1952*; lyric by June Carroll, music by Arthur Siegel), "When?" (lyric and music by Barry Kleinbort), "The Tale of the Oyster" (*Fifty Million Frenchmen*, 1929 [but dropped from that production soon after the Broadway opening]; lyric and music by Cole Porter), "Paramount, Capitol and the Strand" (lyric and music by Norman Martin), "After Forty" (lyric by Dorothy Fields, music by Cy Coleman), "Yellow Flower" (a/k/a "You're My Yaller Flower") (*Ballet Ballads*, 1948; lyric by John LaTouche, music by Jerome Moross), "I Just Kissed My Nose Goodnight" (lyric and music by Mary McCarty, Buddy Pepper, and Kaye Ballard), "My City"/"You Can Be a New Yorker Too" (lyric and music by Charles Strouse), Lady Lyricists Medley, "Time, You Old Gypsy Man" (lyric by E.Y. Harburg, music by Philip Springer)

NOTES—This one-woman revue was an all-too-brief visit from the always-welcome Kaye Ballard (for another visit, see entry for *Hey, Ma ...Kaye Ballard*).

862 Kesa & Morito

NOTES—See entry for *See What I Wanna See*.

863 A Kid's Life! THEATRE: The York Theatre; OPENING DATE: December 16, 2007; PERFORMANCES: 24; BOOK: Cynthia Riddle and Peter Hunziker; LYRICS: Corey Leland; MUSIC: Corey Leland; DIRECTION: Keith Markinson; CHOREOGRAPHY: Ellie Mooney; SCENERY: Bradley Kaye; COSTUMES: Bradley Kaye; LIGHTING: Jeff Porter; PRODUCER: The York Theatre Company

CAST—Carlos (Zack), Ashley Wallace (Zoe), Mark Borum (Mr. Sullivan), Yoav Levin (Starsky [The Dog]), Jessica Blyweiss (Old Ben [The Clock]), Joshua Greenwood (Bart [The Tree]), Kaitlin Becker (Bells [The Owl])

NOTES—The children's musical *A Kid's Life!* told the story of the adventures of a boy and his dog as they journey through their hometown and meet various new friends.

864 King Mackerel & The Blues Are Running. "Songs and Stories of the Carolina Coast." THEATRE: West Bank Downstairs Theatre; OPENING DATE: February 9, 1995; PERFORMANCES: 30; LYRICS AND MUSIC: Bland Simpson and Jim Wann; ADDITIONAL MATERIAL by Jerry Leath Mills, Cass Morgan, and John Dos Passos; DIRECTION: John L. Haber; SCENERY: Fred Buchholz; COSTUMES: Fred Buchholz (?); LIGHTING: Joe Kentner; PRODUCER: West Bank

CAST—Don Dixon, Bland Simpson, and Jim Wann (The Coastal Cohorts)

The revue was presented in two acts (division of acts and song assignments unknown; songs are listed in performance order).

MUSICAL NUMBERS—"King Mackerel & The Blues Are Running," "Corncake Inlet Inn," "Food Chain" (co-written with Cass Morgan), "Timeless," "Ain't That Something?" (lyric by Jerry Leith Mills), "Rushing the Season," "Joyride," "Whose Idea Was This?," "Down by the Edge of the Sea," "Georgia Rose," "Kitty Hawk and Jockey's Ridge," "Sand Mountain Song," "Sound Side," "Shag Baby," "Maco Light," "Ethiope's Ear," "To Catch a King," "Home on the River," "A Mighty Storm," "I'm the Breeze," "Beautiful Day"

NOTES—*King Mackerel & The Blues Are Running* was a song cycle of sorts, an evening of songs and stories about life on the Carolina coast.

The Off Off Broadway musical premiered on December 8, 1985, at Rhythm Alley in Chapel Hill, North Carolina. The first New York performances were given during the fall of 1994 at the West Bank Theatre Downstairs for a total of approximately seven performances. The following winter the musical settled into a longer run of five weeks, for a total of thirty performances at the West Bank, and in 1996 briefly played at the Bottom Line Theatre and Cabaret.

The musical was recorded by Sugar Hill Records (CD # SHCD-8503), and in 1997 was shown on public television in North Carolina; during the following year the film was shown on national public television. The script was published by Samuel French, Inc., in 1998.

865 King of Schnorrers (October 1979). "A New Musical." THEATRE: Harold Clurman Theatre; OPENING DATE: October 9, 1979; PERFORMANCES: 30; BOOK: Judd Woldin; LYRICS: Judd Woldin; ADDITIONAL LYRICS by Susan Birkenhead, Herb Martin, and Amy Seidman; MUSIC: Judd Woldin; DIRECTION: Grover Dale; CHOREOGRAPHY: Grover Dale; SCENERY: Adrianne Lobel; COSTUMES: Patricia Adshead; LIGHTING: Richard Nelson; MUSICAL DIRECTION: Hank Ross; PRODUCERS: Eric Krebs and Sam Landis

CAST—Lloyd Battista (De Costa), Sophie Schwab (Deborah Da Costa), Philip Casnoff (David Ben Yonkel), Angelina Reaux (Sadie, Mrs. Grobstock, Housekeeper), Ralph Bruneau (Harry Tinker), Jerry Mayer (Mendel, Butler, Furtado), Rick McElhiney (Greenbaum, Third Counselor), Paul Binotto (Aaron, Wilkinson, Cosmetician), Ed Dixon (Isaac, Belasco, Chancellor), Thomas Lee Sinclair (Grobstock, President)

SOURCE—The 1894 novel *The King of Schnorrers* by Israel Zangwill.

The action occurs in the East End of London in 1791.

The musical was presented in two acts.

ACT ONE—"Sephardic Lullaby" (Lloyd Battista), "Petticoat Lane" (Street Peddlers), "It's Better to Give Than Receive" (Thomas Lee Sinclair, Peddlers), "Chutzpah" (lyric for chorus by Amy Seidman) (Lloyd Battista, Quartet), "I'm Only a Woman" (Sophie Schwab), "It's a Living" (lyric by Susan Birkenhead and Judd Woldin) (Philip Casnoff, Ralph Bruneau), "I Have Not Lived in Vain" (Ed Dixon), "The Fine Art of Schnorring" (Lloyd Battista), "Tell Me" (lyric by Susan Birkenhead) (Sophie Schwab), "What Do You Do?" (Philip Casnoff), "It's Over" (lyric by Herb Martin) (Street Peddlers)

ACT TWO—"Try Me" (Jerry Mayer), "Dead" (Philip Casnoff, Jerry Mayer), "Chutzpah" (reprise) (Company), "A Man Is Meant to Reason" (lyric by Susan Birkenhead and Judd Woldin) (Lloyd Battista), "Guided by Love" (Sophie Schwab), "Tell Me" (reprise) (Sophie Schwab, Philip Casnoff), "Sephardic Lullaby" (reprise) (Paul Binotto), "Each of Us" (Company), Finale (Company)

NOTES—A program note for *King of Schnorrers* explained that "schnorrer" meant "beggar," but also cautioned that "the traditional Jewish schnorrer bears little resemblance to a mendicant. He is first of all a professional who, through his generous receipt of your charity, allows you to fulfill your religious obligations to help the unfortunate. He does not ask alms ... he claims them, never hesitating to use his extensive knowledge of the Scriptures to berate the non-generous." The plot dealt with the title character, the arrogant Da Costa, his daughter Deborah, and David, a poor young man who loves her.

Richard F. Shepard in the *New York Times* said *King of Schnorrers* was a "must"; he praised it as "tunefully musical and a delightful comedy," and noted that director and choreographer Grover Dale had brought "style and joy" to the production.

The musical was first produced as *Pettycoat Lane* at the George Street Playhouse in New Brunswick, New Jersey, during the 1978-1979 season.

After the Off Broadway run, the musical transferred to Broadway under a Middle Broadway contract (see entry); it opened on November 28 and played for sixty-three performances. For the Middle Broadway run, most of the cast and credits remained the same, with the exception of Philip Casnoff, who was replaced by John Dossett. The Broadway run omitted five songs ("A Man Is Meant to Reason," "It's a Living," "Try Me," "Petticoat Lane," and "It's Better to Give Than Receive") and added one new number ("Hail to the King"); during the Broadway run, "Hail to the King" was dropped and "Petticoat Lane" and "It's Better to Give Than Receive" were reinstated. The Middle Broadway production also included "Just for Me" and "Murder," both of which had been heard at one point or another during the Off Broadway run (but apparently not on the opening night of the Off Broadway run).

In October 1985, a revised version of *King of Schnorrers* opened Off Broadway at the Douglas Fairbanks Theatre for twenty-five performances. Titled *Tatterdemalion*, the musical included six new numbers ("Ours," "Born to Schnorr," "Blood Lines," "Leave the Thinking to Men" [lyrics by Susan Birkenhead], "An Ordinary Man," and "Well Done, Da Costa"); see separate entry.

The script was published by Samuel French, Inc., in 1982 (as *Petticoat Lane*).

Judd Woldin had earlier composed the music for the long-running Broadway musical *Raisin* (1973); his attractive, powerful, and somewhat underrated score includes "Sidewalk Tree," one of the best theatre songs of the 1970s. There have been at least two other lyric adaptations of Zangwill's novel (a 1970 version presented at Goodspeed Opera House, East Haddam, Connecticut, and a 1971 version at the Gallery Theatre in Los Angeles.

866 King of Schnorrers (November 1979).

THEATRE: Playhouse Theatre; OPENING DATE: November 28, 1979; PERFORMANCES: 63; BOOK: Judd Woldin; LYRICS: Judd Woldin; ADDITIONAL LYRICS by Susan Birkenhead, Herb Martin, and Amy Seidman; MUSIC: Judd Woldin; DIRECTION: Grover Dale; CHOREOGRAPHY: Grover Dale; SCENERY: Ed Wittstein; COSTUMES: Patricia Adshead; LIGHTING: Richard Nelson; MUSICAL DIRECTION: Robert Billig; PRODUCERS: Eric Krebs and Sam Landis; Linda Canavan, Associate Producer

CAST—Thomas Lee Sinclair (Rodriquez, President), Ralph Bruneau (Harry Tinker), Jerry Mayer (Mendel, Butler, Furtado, Treasurer), Angelina Reaux (Sadie, Housekeeper), Paul Binotto (Aaron, Wilkinson, Cosmetician), Ed Dixon (Isaac, Belasco, Chancellor), Rick McElhiney (Greenbaum), Lloyd Battista (Da Costa), Sophie Schwab (Deborah Da Costa), John Dossett (David Ben Yonkel)

SOURCE—The 1894 novel *The King of the Schnorrers* by Israel Zangwill.

The action occurs in the East End of London in 1791.

The musical was presented in two acts.

ACT ONE—"Hail to the King" (Lloyd Battista, Thomas Lee Sinclair, Street Peddlers), "Chutzpah" (lyric for chorus by Amy Seidman) (Lloyd Battista, Thomas Lee Sinclair, Quartet), "I'm Only a Woman" (Sophie Schwab), "Just for Me" (John Dossett, Ralph Bruneau), "I Have Not Lived in Vain" (Ed Dixon), "The Fine Art of Schnorring" (Lloyd Battista), "Tell Me" (lyric by Susan Birkenhead) (Sophie Schwab), "What Do You Do?" (John Dossett), "It's Over" (lyric by Herb Martin) (Street Peddlers)

ACT TWO—"Murder" (Ralph Bruneau, Peddlers), "Dead" (John Dossett, Jerry Mayer), "Chutzpah" (reprise) (Company), "Guided by Love" (Sophie Schwab), "Tell Me" (reprise) (Sophie Schwab, John Dossett), "Sephardic Lullaby" (Paul Binotto), "Each of Us" (Company), Finale (Company)

NOTES—After its Off Broadway run at the Harold Clurman Theatre (which opened a month earlier; for more information, see entry for that production), *King of Schnorrers* transferred to Broadway under what appears to have been a Middle Broadway contract. Although Richard F. Shepard in the *New York Times* had given the earlier Off Broadway production a rave review (see entry), his colleague Mel Gussow wasn't so enthusiastic about the return engagement. Gussow found the musical "amiable," "middling," and "modest." But he too singled out Grover Dale's directorial and choreographic contributions. The musical was later revived Off Broadway in 1985 as *Tatterdemalion* (see entry).

Shortly after the Broadway opening, the first scene of the first act was revised. The song "Hail to the King" was dropped, and two numbers, "Petticoat Lane" and "It's Better to Give Than Receive," both of which had been heard during the Off Broadway run, were reinstated.

867 King of the Whole Damn World!

"A New Musical." THEATRE: Jan Hus Playhouse; OPENING DATE: April 14, 1962; PERFORMANCES: 43; BOOK: George Panetta; LYRICS: Robert Larimer; MUSIC: Robert Larimer; ballet music by Gershon Kingsley; DIRECTION: Jack Ragotzy; CHOREOGRAPHY: Zachary Solov; SCENERY: Jack Cornwell; COSTUMES: Rachel Mehr; LIGHTING: William Rittman; MUSICAL DIRECTION: Dobbs Franks; PRODUCER: Norman Forman

CAST—Alan Howard (Iggie), Jerry Brent (Socrates), Jackie Perkuhn (Joey), Brendan Fay Sarge), Joseph Macaulay (Maloney), Tom Pedi (Hippo), Francine Beers (Hannah Klein), Boris Aplon (Enrico Romani), Kathy Crawford (Bleecker Street Woman, Mrs. McKinney, Surgeon's Nurse), Lois Grandi (Bleecker Street Woman, Nurse Phelps, Cat Girl), David C. Jones (DeWolfe, Dr. Thorndyke), Kenneth McMillan (Leo, The Mayor), Joseph Liberatore (Bleecker Street Man), Merlin Bruce (Bleecker Street Man, Dr. Jamison), Mel Johnson (Bleecker Street Man, Surgeon), Robert Shane (Bleecker Street Man, Ambulance Driver), Bobbi Lange (Mrs. Babbson, Nurse Duffy), Floria Mari (Mrs. Romani), Sheldon Golomb (Jimmy Potts), Esther Hollis (Neighbor, Surgical Nurse), Henry Sutton (Interne), Charlotte Whaley (Willie)

SOURCES—The 1947 novel *Jimmy Potts Gets a Haircut* by George Panetta and *Comic Book*, Panetta's 1958 stage (non-musical) adaptation of the material.

The action occurs in Greenwich Village in 1940.

The musical was performed in two acts.

ACT ONE—Opening (Company), "What to Do?" (Alan Howard, Jerry Brent, Jackie Perkuhn), "Grasshop Song" (Boris Aplon, Sheldon Golomb), "Poor Little Boy" (Boris Aplon, Joseph Macaulay, Francine Beers, Kenneth McMillan, Company), "The Night Gondolfo Got Married" (Floria Mari, Boris Aplon), "King of the World" (Boris Aplon, Alan Howard), "Who's Perfect?" (Francine Beers, Tom Pedi), "Little Dog Blue" (Tom Pedi), "March You Off in Style" (Charlotte Whaley, Sheldon Golomb, Company), "The Riddle of You" (David C. Jones, Company)

ACT TWO—"How Do They Ever Grow Up?" (Francine Beers, Floria Mari, Bobbi Lange, Joseph Macauley, Tom Pedi, and one performer not credited), "What's a Mama For?" (Floria Mari, Alan Howard), "Iggie's Nightmare" (Alan Howard, Lois Grandi, Kenneth McMillan, Sheldon Golomb), "Don't Tear Up the Horse Slips" (Kenneth McMillan, Joseph Macauley), "Who's Perfect for You?" (Francine Beers), "Far Rockaway" (Tom Pedi, Francine Beers, Company), "There's Gotta Be a Villain" (Brendan Fay), "King of the World" (reprise) (Alan Howard, Company)

NOTES—The short-running musical *King of the Whole Damn World!*, which dealt with the misadventures of young boys in pre-World War II New York City, had been more successful as a straight play (*Comic Strip*, which ran Off Broadway for 156 performances in 1958). Tom Pedi played the role of Hippo in both the play and its musical adaptation.

Milton Esterow in the *New York Times* thought the saga of Jimmy Potts (who first appeared in the 1947 novel *Jimmy Potts Gets a Haircut* and then later in the afore mentioned stage adaptation *Comic Book*) was an "amusing idea" which had now become "tedious." He felt the musical version was "not much of a show," and the score, except for a handful of "rousing" songs, lacked originality.

The cast album was privately recorded, and in the 1980s was issued by Blue Pear Records (LP # BP-1017). On the album, "How Do They Ever Grow Up?," which was sung by six characters in the production, became a solo, "How Did I Ever Grow Up?" for Mr. Romani (Boris Aplon). Also heard on the cast album is "I Cry Sometimes" (for Hippo and Sarge), which isn't listed in the program.

"King of the World" was included in Jerry Orbach's collection of Off Broadway songs (see discography [Appendix B]).

868 The King's Henchman.

THEATRE: Metropolitan Opera House; OPENING DATE: February 27, 1927; PERFORMANCES: 7; LIBRETTO: Edna St. Vincent Millay; MUSIC: Deems Taylor; DIRECTION:

Wilhelm Von Wymetal; SCENERY: Joseph Urban; MUSICAL DIRECTION: Tullio Serafin; PRODUCER: The Metropolitan Opera

CAST—Lawrence Tibbett (Eadger), Edward Johnson (Aethelwold), William Gustafson (Maccus), Louis D'Angelo (Ordgar), Florence Easton (Aelfrida), Merle Alcock (Ase), George Meader (Dunstan [Archbishop of Canterbury]), Arnold Gabor (Thored), Max Bloch (Hwita, Old Man), Max Altglass (Gunner), George Cehanovsky (Cynric), Millo Picco (Wulfred), James Wolfe (Oslac, Blacksmith), Henriette Wakefield (Hildeburh), Grace Anthony (Ostharu, Fisherman's Wife), Louise Lerch (or Larch) (Godgyfu, Girl), Dorothy (or Dorothea) Flexer (Leofsydu, Woman Servant), Paolo Ananian (Saddler), Joseph Macpherson (Miller), Frederick Vajda (Fisherman), Minnie Egener (Blacksmith's Wife), Mary Bonetti (Miller's Wife) The action occurs in England early in the tenth century.

The opera was presented in three acts.

NOTES—The opera *The King's Henchman* told the story of King Eadger (Lawrence Tibbett), who sends his friend and henchman Aethelwold to Devon to escort his unseen and soon-to-be-bride Aelfrida to the court. When Aethelwold meets her, he immediately falls in love with her beauty and marries her, and sends word to Eadger that Aelfrida isn't worth marrying because of her plainness. When Eadger visits Devon, he realizes his henchman betrayed him; meanwhile, Aelfrida turns on Aethelwold when she discovers she could have been the wife of the king. Aethelwold then kills himself.

In his review for the *New York Times*, Olin Downes called *The King's Henchman* the most effective and "artistically wrought American opera that has reached the stage." He further noted that Taylor's score "proves his melodic gift, his spirit and sense of drama," and said that at the end of the opera there was a full twenty minutes of applause. Downes' review singled out many musical passages, including a "brief and brilliant orchestral prelude," a "rousing folk-song," and a love duet which made "good theatre." The opera returned for a total of ten performances during the next two seasons, and then was never again produced at the Met. Indeed, the work seems to have completely disappeared. *The King's Henchman* marked the first of five world premieres of American operas at the Met which starred Lawrence Tibbett (see entries for *Peter Ibbetson*, *The Emperor Jones*, *Merry Mount*, and *In the Pasha's Garden*). Tibbett made his debut at the Met in 1923, and performed there until 1950. He also created a leading role in *The Barrier*, an American opera which premiered on Broadway in 1950, and he succeeded Ezio Pinza in the role of Cesar during the original Broadway run of *Fanny* (1954).

869 Kiss Now. "A Musical." THEATRE: Martinique Theatre; OPENING DATE: April 20, 1971; PERFORMANCES: 4; BOOK: Maxine Klein; LYRICS: Maxine Klein; MUSIC: William S. Fischer; DIRECTION: Maxine Klein; CHOREOGRAPHY: Sandra Caprin; SCENERY: Richard Devin; COSTUMES: Nancy Adzima; LIGHTING: Richard Devin; MUSICAL DIRECTION: Herbert Kaplan; PRODUCERS: John Ramsey, William Formand, and Milan Stitt

CAST—Lloyd Bremseth, Sandra Caprin, Nancy Denning, Louise Hoven, Irving A. Lee, Susan McAneny, Lyle Pearsons, Eddie Silas

The musical was presented in one act (song assignments unknown).

MUSICAL NUMBERS—"This City Is a Kisser," "Travelin' Man," "The June Taylor," "Too Tired to Love," "Try the Sky," "Death Dance," "No Touch Mine," "Strawberry Day," "Touch Kiss," "Rodeo," "French Thing Tango," "Kabuki Rock," "Kiss Now"

NOTES—The revue-like musical *Kiss Now* dealt with monotonous episodes revolving around the concept of the word "kiss." Mel Gussow in the *New York Times* indicated that according to the musical's logic, even a body touch (such as an elbow touching an elbow) counted as a kiss; he complained that there were not all that many variations on the word, and so the evening began to "drone" on.

Because the critics and audiences kissed off the show, it was gone after four performances.

870 Kittiwake Island. THEATRE: Martinique Theatre; OPENING DATE: October 12, 1960; PERFORMANCES: 7; BOOK: Arnold Sundgaard; LYRICS: Arnold Sundgaard; MUSIC: Alec Wilder; DIRECTION: Lawrence Carra; CHOREOGRAPHY: Peter Hamilton; SCENERY: Romain Johnston; COSTUMES: Al Lehman; LIGHTING: George Corrin; MUSICAL DIRECTION: Joseph Stecko; PRODUCERS: Joseph Beruh and Lawrence Carra

CAST—Joe Lautner (Orlando Puffin), Kathleen Murray (Lydia Sparrow), G. Wood (Dr. Hobie Merganser); Girl Scholars: Caroline Worth (Kestrel Grebe), Lainie Kazan (Jenny Wren), Katharine Vaughan (Lucy Larkin), Helen Hudson (Ann Vireo), Judith Gilman (Robin O'Day), Betty Koerber (Katie Bunting); Boy Scholars: Don Liberto (Keith Brant), Tom Kaminski (Coot Johnson), David Canary (Rusty Swallow), Reid Klein (Cory Sanderling), Bob Carey (Jay Byrd), Tom Hester (Peter Bulfinch)

The action occurs on Kittiwake Island at the present time on a summer's day.

The musical was presented in two acts.

ACT ONE—"Were This to Prove a Feather in My Hat" (Joe Lautner), "It Doesn't Look Deserted to Me" (Girl Scholars), "Can This Be a Toe-Print?" (Joe Lautner), "Good Morning, Dr. Puffin" (Kathleen Murray), "I'd Gladly Walk to Alaska" (Kathleen Murray), "The Smew Song" (Joe Lautner, Kathleen Murray, Girl Scholars), "Never Try Too Hard" (Kathleen Murray), "Under a Tree" (Don Liberto, Reid Klein, David Canary, Boy Scholars), "Good Morning, Dr. Puffin" (reprise) (G. Wood), "I Delight in the Sight of My Lydia" (G. Wood), "The Bard" (Don Liberto), "Robinson Crusoe" (Don Liberto, Caroline Worth, Scholars), "Nothing Is Working Quite Right" (Joe Lautner, Kathleen Murray, G. Wood), "Never Try Too Hard" (reprise) (Kathleen Murray)

ACT TWO—"Don't Give Up the Hunt, Dr. Puffin" (G. Wood, Kathleen Murray, Joe Lautner, Scholars), "If Love's Like a Lark" (Joe Lautner, Kathleen Murray), "When One Deems a Lady Sweet" (G. Wood, Boy Scholars), "When a Robin Leaves Chicago" (Joe Lautner), "So Raise the Banner High" (Scholars), "Oceanography and Old Astronomy" (Don Liberto, Scholars), "It's So Easy to Say" (Scholars; danced by Caroline Worth and Don Liberto), "Hail, the Mythic Smew" (Scholars), Finale ("Kittiwake Island") Company)

NOTES—*Kittiwake Island* is one of the gems of American musical theatre. But like the mythic smew it sings about, it seems to have vanished. It was originally produced in summer stock in 1955 (two of its cast members included Tom Mixon and G. Wood, the latter of whom appeared in the New York production). Songs used in the 1955 version, but which weren't heard in New York, are "The Lesser Antilles," "Who Do You Think You're Kiddin'?," "Kittiwake Island," and "Good Morning, Dr. Sparrow" (the latter probably a variant of "Good Morning, Dr. Puffin").

The musical's slight story (dealing with a group of teachers and students who go to Kittiwake Island in search of the mythic smew) was told with one of the most distinctive scores ever written for the musical theatre. Wilder's music constantly surprises with its rich melodies (which often take unexpected turns, such as in "It Doesn't Look Deserted to Me"), and Sundgaard's lyrics are alternately clever and touching, and always perfect. "Nothing Is Working Out Right" is one of the best blues songs in all musical theatre, and "When a Robin Leaves Chicago" is classic American art song writing.

Howard Taubman in the *New York Times* wasn't impressed by the book, but praised the score, singling out "When One Deems a Lady Sweet," "It's So Easy to Say," "If Love's Like a Lark," and "Nothing Is Working Out Right." Taubman felt when the performers "sing and cavort, they suggest an entertainment"; but for the book portions of the musical, he suggested audiences "leave Kittiwake Island to the birds." Wilder is recognized as the foremost musicologist of American popular song. Ironically, despite his composing genius, he didn't have any popular success with his theatre music. *Kittiwake Island* was his only musical to play in New York (although he wrote background music for such Broadway plays as *The Birdcage* [1950] and *See the Jaguar* [1953], the latter marking James Dean's Broadway debut). Some of his music was heard in the 1955 revue *Once Over Lightly* (see entry), and he wrote *Nobody's Earnest*, a 1974 musical adaptation of *The Importance of Being Earnest* which never got beyond summer stock. There was also a retrospective revue of Wilder's songs (see entry for *Alec Wilder/Clues to a Life*).

Happily, the Off Broadway production of *Kittiwake Island* was recorded by Adelphi Records (LP # AD-2015/6) as a souvenir for those involved in the production, and decades later the recording was issued by Blue Pear Records (LP # BP-1003).

Incidentally, the character of Rusty Swallow was performed by David Canary ("and that's no joke, son," commented Taubman).

The libretto of the 1955 version was published by G. Schirmer, Inc., in 1955.

871 Klenosky Against the Slings and Arrows of Outrageous Fortune. THEATRE: Theatre East; OPENING DATE: September 12, 1967; PERFORMANCES: 12; BOOK: "by Life"; LYRICS: William J. Klenosky; MUSIC: William J. Klenosky; "No scenery by Klenosky"; lighting by Con Edison; PRODUCERS: "Billy K Productions in association with God"

CAST—William J. Klenosky

The revue was presented in two acts.

ACT ONE—"The Hooligan's Hop," "Ye Shall Know the Truth," "Which Can See Further, An Ant or an Eagle," "I See by the Papers," "The Making of President Fink," "The Magillah," "How to Become the Lightest Soldier in the History of the U.S. Army," "How to Get Rich Quick," "The Bald Eagle and the Hairy Canaries," "The French Fink," "A Million Dollar Fiasco," "Guggenheim's Bald Eagle," "The K-Bomb," "Khrushchev, Castro and Klenosky," "Independence Day, July 4th, 1959"

ACT TWO—"L'Audace, L'Audace et Plus L'Audace!," "A Little Moosic to Soothe the Savage," "Malaguena," "Return to Utopia," "They That Buildeth a Wall Against Man," "The World's Greatest Loser?," "The Republican Dilemma: Goldwater or Klenosky," "Lindsay Was Prettier and Taller Than Klenosky and Who's Sorry Now?," "The Loser's Dream Team," "Klenosky vs. Thaler," "No-Holds Barred Press Conference," "An American Odyssey"

NOTES—This one-man revue by one-time New York City mayoral candidate William J. Klenosky was gone in less than two weeks. Klenosky had been previously represented Off Broadway by *Utopia!* (1963; see entry), a full-fledged musical (with a cast of twenty-five) for which he wrote book, lyrics, and music (and which was also gone in less than two weeks).

Was "Return to Utopia" a sketch about his experience with the earlier musical, or was it perhaps a medley of *Utopia*'s greatest hits?

872 The Knee Plays. THEATRE: Alice Tully Hall/Lincoln Center; OPENING DATE: December 2, 1986; PERFORMANCES: 4; SCENARIO: Robert Wilson;

LYRICS: David Byrne; MUSIC: David Byrne; DIRECTION: Robert Wilson; CHOREOGRAPHY: Suzushi Hanayagi; LIGHTING: Heinrich Brunke; MUSICAL DIRECTION: Frank London; PRODUCERS: Great Performers at Lincoln Center, sponsored by the American Telephone and Telegraph Company in associate with IPA Presents, Inc. (Robert LoBianco and Jedediah Wheeler)

CAST—Matthew Buckingham (Narrator), Frank Conversano (Admiral Perry, Basket), Denise Gustafson and Suzushi Hanayagi (both performers alternated in the roles of Lion and Snow Carrier), Jeannie Hill (Knee Dancer), Carl House (Reader), Cho Kyoo Hyun (Cannon, Basket Seller), Fabrizia Pinto (Passenger, Man in Library), Saturo Shimazaki (Knee Dancer), Sanghi Wagner (Fisherman), Gail Donnerfield (lion, Woman with Umbrella, Lion); Les Miserables Brass Band

NOTES—*The Knee Plays* were thirteen short one-act plays to be presented between the acts of Robert Wilson and Philip Glass' twelve-hour epic opera *the CIVIL warS: a tree is best measured when it is down* (see entry); for the Alice Tully Hall engagement at Lincoln Center, all thirteen plays were presented in one evening, for a total length of about one-hundred minutes. Two weeks after the production at Lincoln Center, the prologue to and the complete fourth act of *the CIVIL warS* were presented at the Brooklyn Academy of Music.

Mel Gussow in the *New York Times* noted that each knee play had its own prelude, prompting him to wonder if these preludes were perhaps "elbow" plays. He reported the plays were decidedly Japanese in nature and filled with puns. On the whole, he felt the evening was about both the art of transformation (people become puppets, trees become houses, and vice versa), with things seldom what they seem to be, as well as about time and travel. He felt the audience (the "passengers") should let its "senses luxuriate in a pristine performance-art journey."

Gussow praised *The Knee Plays* as one of Wilson's "most sheerly enjoyable and accessible works," and he enjoyed David Byrne's "infectious New Orleans-style music — slow drags and street marches."

873 The Knife. THEATRE: Newman Theatre/ The Public Theatre; OPENING DATE: March 10, 1987; PERFORMANCES: 32; BOOK: David Hare; LYRICS: Tim Rose Price; MUSIC: Nick Bicat; DIRECTION: David Hare; CHOREOGRAPHY: Graciela Daniele; SCENERY: Hayden Griffin; COSTUMES: Jane Greenwood; LIGHTING: Tharon Musser; MUSICAL DIRECTION: Michael Starobin; PRODUCER: The Public Theatre (Joseph Papp, Producer; Jason Steven Cohen, Associate Producer)

CAST—Mandy Patinkin (Peter, Liz), Cass Morgan (Angela), Michael Willson (Lifeboat Collector, Guitarist), Wade Raley (Johnny), William Parry (Ralph), Tim Shew (Jeremy), Mary Elizabeth Mastrantonio (Jenny), Mary Gordon Murray (Roxanne, Nurse), Mary Testa (Sally), Louis Padilla (First Waiter), Reuben Gaumes (Kitchen Boy), Shelly Paul (Chloe), Devon Michaels (Richard), Lisa Vroman and Louisa Flaningam (Citizens Advice Bureau Workers), Ronn Carroll (G.P., Michael), Olivia Virgil Harper (Therapist), Kevin Gray (English Surgeon), Mary Gutzi (Mariachi Singer), Dennis Parlato (Dr. Bauer), Louisa Flaningam (Michael's Wife, Party Guest), Hansford Rowe (Andrew), Choir Boys (Jeremy Cummins, Reuben Gaumes, Roshi Handwerger)

The action occurs in Winchester, England, at the present time.

The musical was presented in two acts.

ACT ONE—"To Be at Sea" (Mandy Patinkin, Cass Morgan, Chorus), "Hello, Jeremy"/"Agnus Dei"/"Miserere" (Mandy Patinkin, William Parry, Tim Shew, Choir), "Between the Sheets" (Cass Morgan), "Blow Slow Kisses" (Mary Elizabeth Mastrantonio, Mary Gordon Murray, Mary Testa), "The Gay Rap" (Waiters), "Men's Eyes" (Mary Elizabeth Mastrantonio, Mandy Patinkin), "The Shape I'm In" (Mandy Patinkin), "You're Not Unique" (Mandy Patinkin, Dennis Parlato, Officials), "Macumba" (Mary Gutzi), "Someone Who Touches Me" (Mary Elizabeth Mastrantonio)

ACT TWO—"Africa" (Mandy Patinkin, Mary Elizabeth Mastrantonio), "Shadows Dance Behind You" (Mary Elizabeth Mastrantonio), "The Knife"/ "To Be at Sea" (reprise) (Dennis Parlato, Hospital Staff), "Hello Peter We're Going Out" (Cass Morgan, Mandy Patinkin, William Parry), "What Would You Do in My Place?" (Wade Raley), "When I Was a Man" (Mandy Patinkin), "At Least There Are Parties" (Guests, Mandy Patinkin, Ronn Carroll), "The Open Sea" (Mary Elizabeth Mastrantonio, Mandy Patinkin), "Ache in Acorn" (Schoolchildren), "What You Mean to Me" (Mandy Patinkin, Wade Raley)

NOTES—*The Knife*, an all-sung British musical having its world premiere at the Public, was about a man who undergoes a sex-change operation. Frank Rich in the *New York Times* noted that with the possible exception of the Public Theatre's audience, "there's no one gloomier in town" than Mandy Patinkin's character ("in a funk so thick one could cut it with a hacksaw"); moreover, the performers made a "Greek chorus seem as frivolous as a conga line." Clive Barnes in the *New York Post* rightly predicted that "this hack *The Knife* will presumably be soon forgotten"; and Howard Kissel in the *New York Daily News* found the work "too genteel, too tepid ... no more bracing or invigorating than a cup of weak tea." Another review in the *Daily News*, by Douglas Watt, said *The Knife* was "just plain dull," and noted that playwright David Hare's book "bears some of his usual gripes and pretensions." However, David Lida in *Women's Wear Daily* found the musical a "groundbreaking and unique theatrical experience" (although he noted that at the performance he attended there were several walkouts during the first act, and one audience member loudly announced that the show was "rubbish").

874 The Kosher Widow. "A Musical Play." THEATRE: Anderson Theatre; OPENING DATE: October 31, 1959; PERFORMANCES: 87; BOOK: Jacob Kalich and Louis Freiman; LYRICS: Yiddish lyrics by Molly Picon; English lyrics by Sholom Secunda; MUSIC: Sholom Secunda; DIRECTION: Jacob Kalich; CHOREOGRAPHY: Henrietta Jacobson; SCENERY: Tom Jewett; MUSICAL DIRECTION: Sholom Secunda; PRODUCERS: Irving Jacobson and Julius Adler

CAST—Jacob Kalich (Benjamin Horowitz), Anne Winters (Judy), Julius Adler (Lou), Esta Saltzman (Stella), Brucie (Bruce) Adler (Brucie), Irving Jacobson (Meyer), Molly Picon (Peppy, Dora), Muni Serebrov (Bernard), Henrietta Jacobson (Gussie), Mae Shoenfeld (Matilda)

The division of acts is unknown.

MUSICAL NUMBERS—According to Ken Bloom in the second edition of his fascinating *American Song*, the theatre program didn't list musical numbers. However, he provides the following titles of the show's songs (in alphabetical order; no information available concerning song assignments): "An Actress," "All Long Island Gossips," "The Belles of Belle Harbor," "Good Luck," "I Need You," "Israel Shall Live," "They've Gotcha on the Hutska," "To Health," "What's Destined to Be"

NOTES—Besides the above song titles, the published vocal score included two more songs ("No Greater Love" and "All I Want Baby, Is You").

Given the popularity of plays and musicals with Jewish themes, along with the built-in New York audience for such shows, it's surprising how few Off Broadway musicals during this era dealt with Jewish subject matter. In fact, besides *The Kosher Widow*, there were only a few such musicals which opened during the period (such as *Hamlet of Stepney Green* [1958], *Go Fight City Hall* [1961], *Bei Mir Bistu Schoen* [1961], and *The Stones of Jehoshaphat* [1963]; see entries). But as the seasons continued, Yiddish-American musicals appeared with more and more frequency, and with the founding of the Jewish Repertory Theatre in 1974, and later the American Jewish Theatre, New York finally had two homes where Jewish-themed plays and musicals were presented on a regular basis.

The Kosher Widow was an opportunity for theatre-goers to see their beloved Molly Picon on the boards again. In his *New York Times'* review, Louis Funke found Picon "ever-adorable," and said the musical was a "real delight ... one of the best musicals to adorn the dwindling Yiddish theatre in years." He noted that the "tuneful" score might even produce one or two hit songs. Molly Picon played two roles: a wife who left her home a dozen years before (and who has now returned to home and husband) and an actress with whom the husband has fallen in love. Funke reported the show's burning question was whether the husband should reconcile with his runaway wife or pursue his romance with the actress. In order to resolve the issue, an "applause meter" was brought on stage and the audience was asked to make the decision. Funke indicated that at the performance he attended the matter was somewhat of a toss-up, and he speculated that future audience decisions could cause schisms and feuds among families and friends in ways too "frightening to contemplate." (In 1985, audiences were also polled in order to determine the denouement of *The Mystery of Edwin Drood* [during its run the title was shortened to *Drood*]; see entry).

As a performer and writer, Molly Picon (1898-1992) enjoyed a lengthy and successful theatrical career which spanned five decades, but there was only one long-running show in her future, *Milk and Honey* (1961), which marked Jerry Herman's Broadway debut. She left the disastrous 1966 musical *Chu Chem* (dubbed *The King and Oy* by one critic; see entry for Off Off Broadway revival) during its short tryout life of five days in Philadelphia, and it was her fellow *Kosher Widow* performer Henrietta Jacobson who briefly replaced her. Picon also appeared on Broadway in the 1967 flop *How to Be a Jewish Mother*, a play with incidental songs which ran for twenty-one performances. Her final Broadway appearance was in another flop, the one-performance comedy *Something Old, Something New* (1977). A later tribute to Picon was produced in regional theatre, Off Off Broadway, and eventually Off Broadway; see entry for *Picon Pie* (2005), which starred June Gable as Picon.

Two performers in *The Kosher Widow* went on to create supporting roles in two hit musicals: Irving Jacobson was Sancho Panza in *Man of La Mancha* (1965) and Brucie (later Bruce) Adler was Bela Zangler in *Crazy for You* (1992). For his performance in *The Kosher Widow*, the fourteen-year-old Adler was praised by Funke for his "winning personality and professional stage presence."

875 Kukla, Burr and Ollie. THEATRE: Kuklapolitan Room/Hotel Astor; OPENING DATE: October 31, 1960; PERFORMANCES: 27; WRITTEN by: Burr Tillstrom; MUSIC: Jack Fascinato and Caesar Giovanni; SCENERY: William Ritman; MUSICAL DIRECTION: George Bauer; PRODUCERS: Cheryl Crawford and Joel Schenker; A Burr Tillstrom Production

CAST—Kukla, Burr, and Ollie, "in person with all the Kuklapolitans" (Miss Beulah Witch, Mme. Ophelia Oooglepuss, Mr. Oliver J. Dragon, Mr. Fletcher Rabbit, Miss Doloras Dragon, Mr. Cecil Bill, Col. R.H. Crackie, Ollie's Mother, Prown Crince, and Dragon Prep Alumni); Claiborne Cary

NOTES—A program note indicated that "Mr.

Kukla and Mr. Oliver J. Dragon, both unrestricted people, are desirous of keeping their program that way ... therefore ... there will be two intermissions surrounded by three acts of their selection."

No information in program regarding specific musical numbers.

Louis Calta in the *New York Times* found the evening a "happy one." The first act dealt with the puppets poking gentle satiric thrusts at "various foibles and established institutions," and the second act, *St. George and the Dragon*, was an operatic spoof of "wonderful make-believe" and included "admirably conceived" music. Calta reported the Kukapolitan Room was formerly the Astor Hotel's Emerald Room, and he noted the revue "came off rather well" in the "intimate" 208-seat venue.

876 The Kumquat in the Persimmon Tree. "A Vaudeville." THEATRE: Bowery Theatre; OPENING DATE: June 18, 1962; PERFORMANCES: 11; SKETCHES: William C. Curtis; LYRICS: William C. Curtis; MUSIC: Bruce Haack and Ted Pandel; DIRECTION: George Lanin; CHOREOGRAPHY: Mamie Jones; SCENERY: Charles Copenhaver; LIGHTING: Susin; PRODUCERS: George Lanin and Charles Copenhaver in association with the New York Repertory Company

CAST—Cynthia Belgrave, Caroline Culbertson, Lawrence Dukore, Marie Hoff, Helen Honkamp, Adam Kilgour, Ken Lloyd, Charles Brown

NOTES—The forgotten revue *The Kumquat in the Persimmon Tree* played for little more than a week. A self-described "vaudeville," the evening was nonetheless difficult to categorize. Louis Calta in the *New York Times* felt that William C. Curtis' would-be avant-garde piece might belong to any number of theatrical schools (the schools of the "absurd, nonsensical, or the ridiculous"); but one thing Calta was sure of, the musical "looked like the school of amalgamation," taking its inspiration from a "faculty" of such disparate professors as Franz Kafka, Jerry Lewis, Jean Genet, and Mack Sennett. While the vaudeville may have aimed to be "charmingly dotty," Calta found it a "dismal mélange," and noted that when the characters "Auntie" and "The Duchess" spoke such lines as "I knew there was going to be an awful mess" and "I'd like to forget it all if I could," he readily agreed that they were speaking the truth.

877 Kumquats. THEATRE: Village Gate Theatre; OPENING DATE: November 15, 1971; PERFORMANCES: 53; BOOK: Cosmo Richard Falcon; LYRICS: Cosmo Richard Falcon; MUSIC: Gustavo Motta; DIRECTION: Nicholas Coppola; SCENERY: Bob Olson; COSTUMES: Apparently designed by Wayland Flowers; LIGHTING: Ken Moses; MUSICAL DIRECTION: Michael Leonard; PRODUCERS: Cosmo Richard Falcon and Wayland Flowers in association with Art and Burt D'Lugoff

CAST—Wayland Flowers, Michael Alogna, Gregory Smith, James Racioppi

The revue was presented in two acts (song assignments unknown).

ACT ONE—"In the Name of Love," "Kumquats," "At the Library," "Old Hat Joke," "American Dream Girl," "Legs!," "The Evil Fairy and the Hippie," "The Wee Scotsman," "Hello, Dolly!," "The Dirty Word Waltz"

ACT TWO—"Irma's Candy Heaven," "Old Hat Joke" (reprise), "Adam and Eve," "This Is Paradise," "The Fairy and the Hard Hat," "Madame Meets a Midget," "Legs!" (reprise), "Mao Tse Tongue," "The Sensuous Woman," "The Wee Scotsman" (reprise), "The Story of Ooooh!," "In the Name of Love" (reprise)

NOTES—Although Cosmo Richard Falcon (a nom de plume?) was credited with the book, it appears that *Kumquats,* a self-described "World's First Erotic Puppet Show," was more in the nature of a revue. And while the revue certainly wasn't the first adult puppet show (see entry for *Les Poupees de Paris* [1962]), it was probably more ribald than its predecessor. Wayland Flowers' most famous puppet creation, Madame, made her Off Broadway debut in *Kumquats.* Michael Leonard, the musical director, was the composer of two mid-1960s Broadway failures, *The Yearling* (1965) and *How to Be a Jewish Mother* (1966). The former had a particularly appealing score which included such songs as "I'm All Smiles" and "Why Did I Choose You?"

878 Kuni-Leml, or The Mismatch. "A Rollicking New Musical." THEATRE: Audrey Wood Theatre; OPENING DATE: October 9, 1984; PERFORMANCES: 298; BOOK: Nahma Sandrow; LYRICS: Richard Engquist; MUSIC: Raphael Crystal; DIRECTION: Ran Avni; CHOREOGRAPHY: Haila Strauss; SCENERY: Joel Fontaine; COSTUMES: Karen Hummel; LIGHTING: Dab Kinsley; MUSICAL DIRECTION: Raphael Crystal; PRODUCERS: JRT (Jewish Repertory Theatre) and Jarick Productions, Inc.

CAST—Adam Heller (Yankl, Yasha), Jack Savage (Simkhe, Sasha), Mark Zeller (Reb Pinkhos), Barbara McCulloh (Carolina), Gene Varrone (Kalmen), Scott Wentworth (Max), Susan Friedman (Libe), Stuart Zagnit (Kuni-Leml)

SOURCE—The 1880 play *The Fanatic, or the Two Kuni-Lemls* by Avrom Goldfadn.

The action occurs in Odessa in the Ukraine during the reign of Czar Alexander II (during a time span of twenty-four hours in 1880 both before and during the holiday of Purim).

The musical was presented in two acts.

ACT ONE—"Celebrate!" (Jack Savage, Adam Heller, Mark Zeller, Barbara McCulloh), "The Boy Is Perfect" (Gene Varrone), "Carolina's Lament" (Barbara McCulloh), "The World Is Getting Better" (Jack Savage, Adam Heller, Scott Wentworth), "Cuckoo" (Scott Wentworth, Barbara McCulloh), "The Matchmaker's Daughter" (Susan Friedman), "A Meeting of the Minds" (Mark Zeller, Barbara McCulloh), Act One Finale (Company)

ACT TWO—"A Little Learning" (Mark Zeller), "Nothing Counts But Love" (Scott Wentworth, Barbara McCulloh), "What's My Name?" (Stuart Zagnit), "Purim Song" (Jack Savage, Adam Heller), "Do Horses Talk to Horses?" (Susan Friedman, Stuart Zagnit), "Lovesongs and Lullabies" (Susan Friedman, Barbara McCulloh), "Be Fruitful and Multiply" (Jack Savage, Adam Heller), Act Two Finale (Company)

NOTES—Set in Russia in 1880, *Kuni-Leml* dealt with a young woman who has set her sights on a young scholar rather than the title character, a rabbi's son whom her father wants her to marry. The plot involved impersonations and chase scenes, and the free-wheeling nature of the book along with the highly praised score allowed the musical to run almost nine months. Ron Cohen in *Women's Wear Daily* praised the "unforced air of ethnic whimsy," and urged his readers to "think of *The Fantasticks* dressed up for Purim as a piece of gefilte fish."

Prior to its transfer to Off Broadway, the musical had been seen the previous June in an Off Off Broadway version produced by the Jewish Repertory Theatre.

Kuni-Leml was revived Off Off Broadway by the Jewish Repertory Theatre on November 1, 1998, for thirty-one performances, and this production was recorded by Slider Stage Music Records (CD # SM-701). The script was published by Samuel French, Inc., in 1986.

879 A Kurt Weill Cabaret (1976). THEATRE: Edison Theatre; OPENING DATE: May 4, 1976; PERFORMANCES: 3; LYRICS: See song list for credits; MUSIC: Kurt Weill; DIRECTION: Will Holt; MUSICAL DIRECTION: William Cox

CAST—WILL HOLT, DOLLY JONAH

The revue was presented in two acts (all songs performed by Will Holt and Dolly Jonah).

ACT ONE—"Alabama Song" (from *The Rise and Fall of the City of Mahagonny*, 1930; English lyric by Bertolt Brecht) "The Ballad of the Easy Life" (*The Threepenny Opera*, 1928; original German lyric by Bertolt Brecht, English lyric by Marc Blitzstein), "The Barbara Song" (a/k/a "Barbara Song") (*The Threepenny Opera*, 1928; original German lyric by Bertolt Brecht, English lyric by Marc Blitzstein), "The Moritat" (a/k/a "Mack the Knife") (*The Threepenny Opera*, 1928; original German lyric by Bertolt Brecht; English translator unknown), "Duet" (*The Rise and Fall of the City of Mahagonny*, 1930; original German lyric by Bertolt Brecht, English translator unknown), "Tango Ballade" (*The Threepenny Opera*, 1928; original German lyric by Bertolt Brecht, English lyric by Marc Blitzstein), "Pirate Jenny" (*The Threepenny Opera*, 1928; original German lyric by Bertolt Brecht, English lyric by Marc Blitzstein), "Recruiting Song" (a/k/a "Army Song" and "Kanon Song") (*The Threepenny Opera*, 1928; original German lyric by Bertolt Brecht, English lyric by Marc Blitzstein), "Benares Song" (*The Rise and Fall of the City of Mahagonny*, 1930; English lyric by Bertolt Brecht), "Denn Wie Man Sich Bettet" (*The Rise and Fall of the City of Mahagonny*, 1930; original German lyric by Bertolt Brecht, English lyric by Will Holt), "Caesar's Death" (*The Silver Lake*, 1933; original German lyric by George Kaiser, English lyric by Will Holt)

ACT TWO—*Johnny Johnson* (specific song performed from *Johnny Johnson* [1936] is unknown; lyric by Paul Green), "My Ship" (*Lady in the Dark*, 1941; lyric by Ira Gershwin), "Speak Low" (*One Touch of Venus*, 1943; lyric by Ogden Nash), "Jenny Made Her Mind Up" ("The Saga of Jenny") (*Lady in the Dark*, 1941; lyric by Ira Gershwin) "September Song" (*Knickerbocker Holiday*, 1938; lyric by Maxwell Anderson), "It Never Was You" (*Knickerbocker Holiday*, 1938; lyric by Maxwell Anderson), "Mandalay Song" (*Happy End*, 1929; English lyric by Bertolt Brecht), "Sailor's Tango" (*Happy End*, 1929; original German lyric by Bertolt Brecht, English lyric by Will Holt), "Surabaya Johnny" (*Happy End*, 1929; original German lyric by Bertolt Brecht, English lyric by Will Holt), "Bilbao Song" (*Happy End*, 1929; original German lyric by Bertolt Brecht, English lyric by Will Holt), Finale ("Mahagonny") (unclear which song from *The Rise and Fall of the City of Mahagonny* was used; original German lyric by Bertolt Brecht, English lyric by Marc Blitzstein)

NOTES—An Off Broadway season wouldn't be complete without a visit from Kurt Weill. The 1975-1976 season offered a limited three-performance revival of *A Kurt Weill Cabaret*, which had originally been conceived and directed by Will Holt in 1963 when the revue was called *The World of Kurt Weill in Song*. See entry for that production regarding return engagement of *The World of Kurt Weill in Song* as well as productions of *A Kurt Weill Cabaret*, *Berlin to Broadway with Kurt Weill*, and other Weill productions discussed in this book; also see Appendix O.

880 A Kurt Weill Cabaret (1979). "His Broadway and Berlin Songs." THEATRE: Bijou Theatre; OPENING DATE: November 15, 1979; PERFORMANCES: 72; LYRICS: See song list for credits; MUSIC: Kurt Weill; DIRECTION: Production supervised by Billie McBride; PRODUCER: An Arthur Shafman International, Ltd. Presentation

CAST—MATHA SCHLAMME, ALVIN EPSTEIN, Steven Blier (Piano)

The revue was presented in one act.

MUSICAL NUMBERS—*His Berlin Songs:* "Moritat" ("Ballad of Mack the Knife") (from *The Threepenny Opera*, 1928; original German lyric by Bertolt Brecht, English lyric by Marc Blitzstein) (Alvin Epstein), "Barbara-Song" (*The Threepenny Opera*, 1928; original German lyric by Bertolt Brecht, English lyric by Marc Blitzstein) (Martha Schlamme), "Alabama-Song" (*The Rise and Fall of the City of Mahagonny*, 1930; English lyric by Bertolt Brecht) (Martha Schlamme, Alvin Epstein), Duet: "Herr Jakob Schmidt" (*The Rise and Fall of the City of Mahagonny*, 1930; song may have been performed in the original German; German lyric by Bertolt Brecht) (Martha Schlamme and Alvin Epstein), "Ballad of Sexual Slavery" (*The Threepenny Opera*, 1928; original German lyric by Bertolt Brecht, English lyric by George Tabori) (Alvin Epstein), "Ballad of the Pimp and the Whore" (*The Threepenny Opera*, 1928; original German lyric by Bertolt Brecht, English lyric by Marc Blitzstein) (Martha Schlamme, Alvin Epstein), "Pirate Jenny" (*The Threepenny Opera*, 1928; original German lyric by Bertolt Brecht, English lyric by Marc Blitzstein) (Martha Schlamme), "Kanonensong" (a/k/a "Army Song" and "Recruitment Song") (*The Threepenny Opera*, 1928; original German lyric by Bertolt Brecht, English version by Marc Blitzstein) (Alvin Epstein), "Soldatenweib" ("Ballad of the Soldier's Wife"; German lyric by Bertolt Brecht; composed in 1946, this song was the final collaboration between Brecht and Weill) (Martha Schlamme), "Eating" ("Essen") (*The Rise and Fall of the City of Mahagonny*, 1930; original German lyric by Bertolt Brecht, English lyric by Arnold Weinstein) (Martha Schlamme, Alvin Epstein). *His Broadway Songs:* "That's Him" (*One Touch of Venus*, 1943; lyric by Ogden Nash) (Martha Schlamme, Alvin Epstein), "September Song" (*Knickerbocker Holiday*, 1938; lyric by Maxwell Anderson) (Alvin Epstein), "The Saga of Jenny" (*Lady in the Dark*, 1941; lyric by Ira Gershwin) (Martha Schlamme, Alvin Epstein). *Back to Berlin:* "Bilbao Song" (*Happy End*, 1929; the original German lyric by Bertolt Brecht may have been performed) (Martha Schlamme), "Sailor's Tango" (*Happy End*, 1929; original German lyric by Bertolt Brecht, English lyric by Will Holt) (Alvin Epstein), "Surabaya Johnny" (*Happy End*, 1929; the original German lyric by Bertolt Brecht may have been performed) (Martha Schlamme), "The Life That We Lead" (*The Rise and Fall of the City of Mahagonny*, 1930; original German lyric by Bertolt Brecht, English lyric by Will Holt) (Martha Schlamme, Alvin Epstein), *"...And Others..."*

NOTES—During previews, Leonard Frey was replaced by Alvin Epstein.

The revival of *A Kurt Weill Cabaret* played for a total of seventy-two performances in three slightly separated engagements. It played for ten performances from November 5 through November 25, 1979, and for thirty performances from December 26, 1979, through March 4, 1980, alternating with the mime production *Mummemchanz*, which was also playing at the Bijou Theatre; the revue also occasionally presented late-evening performances. The revue later played a regular schedule of performances from May 6, 1980, through June 1, 1980 (thirty-two in all).

The revival seems to have been presented under an Off Broadway contract, although some sources list it as a Broadway production.

For more information regarding Kurt Weill retrospectives (including other productions of *A Kurt Weill Cabaret* in 1976, 1981, and 1984) as well as revivals of his musicals and operas, see entry for the 1963 production of *The World of Kurt Weill in Song*; also see Appendix O.

881 A Kurt Weill Cabaret (1981). THEATRE: Stage One/Roundabout Theatre; OPENING DATE: December 15, 1981; PERFORMANCES: 16; PRODUCER: Roundabout Theatre (Gene Feist and Michael Fried, Producing Directors)

CAST—Martha Schlamme, Alvin Epstein, Steven Blier (Piano)

NOTES—The revival of this perennial revue *A Kurt Weill Cabaret* played for two weeks. The songs were the same as those performed in the 1979 revival (see entry).

For more information regarding Kurt Weill retrospectives (including other productions of *A Kurt Weill Cabaret* in 1976, 1979, and 1984) as well as revivals of his musicals and operas, see entry for the 1963 production of *The World of Kurt Weill in Song*; also see Appendix O.

882 A Kurt Weill Cabaret (1984). "His Broadway and Berlin Songs." THEATRE: Harold Clurman Theatre; OPENING DATE: December 20, 1984; PERFORMANCES: 130; LYRICS: See song list for credits; MUSIC: Kurt Weill; LIGHTING: Kevin Rigdon; PRODUCERS: The Harold Clurman Theatre (Jack Garfein, Artistic Director) and Byron Laskey produced by special arrangement with Arthur Shafman International Ltd.

CAST—MARTHA SCHLAMME, ALVIN EPSTEIN, Harry Huff (Piano)

The revue was presented in two acts.

ACT ONE—"Moritat" ("Ballad of Mack the Knife") (from *The Threepenny Opera*, 1928; original German lyric by Bertolt Brecht, English lyric by Marc Blitzstein) (Alvin Epstein), "Barbara-Song" (*The Threepenny Opera*, 1928; original German lyric by Bertolt Brecht, English lyric by Marc Blitzstein) (Martha Schlamme), "Alabama-Song" (*The Rise and Fall of the City of Mahagonny*, 1930; English lyric by Bertolt Brecht) (Martha Schlamme, Alvin Epstein), "Herr Jakob Schmidt" (*The Rise and Fall of the City of Mahagonny*, 1930; original German lyric by Bertolt Brecht, English lyric by Marc Blitzstein) (Martha Schlamme, Alvin Epstein), "Ich Habe Gelernt" (*The Rise and Fall of the City of Mahagonny*, 1930; German lyric by Bertolt Brecht) (Martha Schlamme, Alvin Epstein), "Ballad of Sexual Slavery" (*The Threepenny Opera*, 1928; original German lyric by Bertolt Brecht, English lyric by George Tabori) (Alvin Epstein), "There Was a Time" (*The Threepenny Opera*, 1928; original German lyric by Bertolt Brecht, English lyric by Marc Blitzstein) (Martha Schlamme, Alvin Epstein), "Pirate Jenny" (*The Threepenny Opera*, 1928; original German lyric by Bertolt Brecht, English lyric by Marc Blitzstein) (Martha Schlamme), "Kanonensong" (a/k/a "Canon Song" and "Recruitment Song") (*The Threepenny Opera*, 1928; original German lyric by Bertolt Brecht, English lyric by Marc Blitzstein) (Alvin Epstein), "Soldatenweib" ("Ballad of the Soldier's Wife") German lyric by Bertolt Brecht; composed in 1946, this song was the final collaboration between Brecht and Weill) (Martha Schlamme), "Eating" ("Essen") (*The Rise and Fall of the City of Mahagonny*, 1930; original German lyric by Bertolt Brecht, English lyric by Arnold Weinstein) (Martha Schlamme, Alvin Epstein), "That's Him" (*One Touch of Venus*, 1943; lyric by Ogden Nash) (Martha Schlamme, Alvin Epstein), "The Life That We Lead" (*The Rise and Fall of the City of Mahagonny*, 1930; original German lyric by Bertolt Brecht, English lyric by Will Holt) (Martha Schlamme, Alvin Epstein)

ACT TWO—"The Saga of Jenny" (*Lady in the Dark*, 1941; lyric by Ira Gershwin) (Martha Schlamme, Alvin Epstein), "September Song" (*Knickerbocker Holiday*, 1938; lyric by Maxwell Anderson) (Alvin Epstein), "Le Roi D'Aquitaine" (*Marie Galante*, 1933; lyric by Jacques DeVal) (Martha Schlamme, Alvin Epstein), "Moon-Faced, Starry-Eyed" (*Street Scene*, 1947; lyric by Langston Hughes) (Martha Schlamme, Alvin Epstein), "It Never Was You" (*Knickerbocker Holiday*, 1938; lyric by Maxwell Anderson) (Martha Schlamme), "Tschaikowsky" (*Lady in the Dark*, 1941; lyric by Ira Gershwin) (Alvin Epstein), "Bilbao Song" (*Happy End*, 1929; the original German lyric by Bertolt Brecht may have been performed) (Martha Schlamme), "Sailor's Tango" (*Happy End*, 1929; original German lyric by Bertolt Brecht, English lyric by Will Holt) (Alvin Epstein), "Surabaya Johnny" (*Happy End*, 1929; the original lyric by Bertolt Brecht may have been performed) (Martha Schlamme), "Survival Song" (*The Threepenny Opera*, 1928; original German lyric by Bertolt Brecht, English lyric by Marc Blitzstein) (Martha Schlamme, Alvin Epstein), Finale (Martha Schlamme, Alvin Epstein)

NOTES—This was the final time Martha Schlamme and Alvin Epstein appeared in *A Kurt Weill Cabaret*. For more information regarding Kurt Weill retrospectives (including other productions of *A Kurt Weill Cabaret* in 1976, 1979 and 1981) as well as revivals of his musicals and operas, see entry for the 1963 production of *The World of Kurt Weill in Song*; also see Appendix O.

883 Ladies and Gentlemen, Jerome Kern. THEATRE: Harold Clurman Theatre; OPENING DATE: June 10, 1985; PERFORMANCES: 22; LYRICS: See song list for credits; MUSIC: Jerome Kern; DIRECTION: William E. Hunt; CHOREOGRAPHY: Valarie Pettiford; SCENERY: James Wolk; COSTUMES: David P. Pearson; LIGHTING: Dan Kotlowitz; MUSICAL DIRECTION: Janet Glazener; PRODUCER: West Dobson

CAST—Michael Howell Deane, Louise Edeiken, Milton B. Grayson, Jr., Delores Hall, Michele Pigliavento, John Scherer, Toba Sherwood, Frank Torren

The revue was presented in two acts.

ACT ONE—*Songs from the Stage*: "How'd You Like to Spoon with Me?" (from *The Earl and the Girl*, 1905; lyric by Edward Laska) (Company), "They Didn't Believe Me" (*The Girl from Utah*, 1914; lyric by Herbert Reynolds) (Milton B. Grayson, Jr.), "Till the Clouds Roll By" (*Oh, Boy!*, 1917; lyric by P.G. Wodehouse) (Company), "Go Little Boat" (*Miss 1917*, 1917; later used in *Oh, My Dear!*, 1918; lyric by P.G. Wodehouse) (Louise Edeiken), "Who?" (*Sunny*, 1925; lyric by Otto Harbach and Oscar Hammerstein II) (Michael Howell Deane, Milton B. Grayson, Jr., John Scherer, Frank Torren), "Sunny" (*Sunny*, 1925; lyric by Otto Harbach and Oscar Hammerstein II) (Company; danced by Michele Pigliavento), "Can't Help Lovin' That Man" (*Show Boat*, 1927; lyric by Oscar Hammerstein II) (Toba Sherwood), "Ol' Man River" (*Show Boat*, 1927; lyric by Oscar Hammerstein II) (Milton B. Grayson, Jr.), "Life Upon the Wicked Stage" (*Show Boat*, 1927; lyric by Oscar Hammerstein II) (John Scherer, Delores Hall, Toba Sherwood, Louise Edeiken), "Don't Ever Leave Me"/"Why Was I Born" (*Sweet Adeline*, 1929; lyrics by Oscar Hammerstein II) (Delores Hall), "She Didn't Say 'Yes'" (*The Cat and the Fiddle*, 1931; lyric by Otto Harbach) (Ensemble), "The Night Was Made for Love" (*The Cat and the Fiddle*, 1931; lyric by Otto Harbach) (Michael Howell Deane, Louise Edeiken), "I've Told Every Little Star" (*Music in the Air*, 1932; lyric by Oscar Hammerstein II) (Michele Pigliavento), "Let's Begin" (*Roberta*, 1933; lyric by Otto Harbach) (Company), "Yesterdays" (*Roberta*, 1933; lyric by Otto Harbach) (Frank Torren), "Smoke Gets in Your Eyes" (*Roberta*, 1933; lyric by Otto Harbach) (Delores Hall), "All the Things You Are" (*Very Warm for May*, 1939; lyric by Oscar Hammerstein II) (Company)

ACT TWO—*Songs from the Movies*: "I Won't Dance" (*Roberta*, 1935; lyric by Otto Harbach, Dorothy Fields, Oscar Hammerstein II, and Jimmy McHugh) (Delores Hall, John Scherer), "Lovely to Look At" (*Roberta*, 1935; lyric by Dorothy Fields and Jimmy McHugh) (Michele Pigliavento, Michael Howell Deane), "Pick Yourself Up" (*Swing Time*, 1936; lyric by Dorothy Fields) (Company), "The Way You Look Tonight" (*Swing Time*, 1936; lyric by Dorothy Fields) (Frank Torren), "A Fine Romance" (*Swing Time*, 1936; lyric by Dorothy Fields) (Company), "The Folks Who Live on the Hill" (*High,*

Wide and Handsome, 1937; lyric by Oscar Hammerstein II) (Louise Edeiken, John Scherer), "Remind Me" (*One Night in the Tropics*, 1940; lyric by Dorothy Fields) (Toba Sherwood), "The Last Time I Saw Paris" (*Lady, Be Good*, 1941; lyric by Oscar Hammerstein II) (Company), "Sure Thing" (*Cover Girl*, 1944; lyric by Ira Gershwin) (Company), "Long Ago (and Far Away)" (*Cover Girl*, 1944; lyric by Ira Gershwin) (Milton B. Grayson, Jr.), "Can't Help Singing" (*Can't Help Singing*, 1944; lyric by E.Y. Harburg) (Company), "In Love in Vain" (*Centennial Summer*, 1946; lyric by Oscar Hammerstein II) (Delores Hall), "All Through the Day" (*Centennial Summer*, 1946; lyric by Oscar Hammerstein II) (Company), "You Couldn't Be Cuter" (*Joy of Living*, 1938; lyric by Dorothy Fields) (Company)

NOTES—*Ladies and Gentlemen, Jerome Kern* was a composer-tribute revue honoring Jerome Kern; despite his glorious music, the revue managed only a three-week run. The following year, a similar tribute, *Jerome Kern Goes to Hollywood*, played on Broadway for just thirteen performances.

The revue included three songs from Kern's 1936 film musical *Swing Time*, arguably Fred Astaire and Ginger Roger's greatest film and certainly one of the best film musicals ever made. Kern and Dorothy Fields' score included the lovely ballad "The Way You Look Tonight" (which won the Academy Award for Best Song), the lively "Pick Yourself Up," and the amusing comedy song "A Fine Romance" (all of which were performed in *Ladies and Gentlemen, Jerome Kern*). The film's score also included "Bojangles of Harlem," one of the most syncopated numbers in the Kern songbook, and "Never Gonna Dance," an insinuating ballad with a haunting melody wedded to a lyric sometimes bordering on the surreal. These five songs (along with the dance number "Waltz in Swing Time") constitute one of the most memorable scores ever written for a film. And yet when he reviewed the film (which opened at the Radio City Music Hall on August 27, 1936) for the *New York Times*, Frank S. Nugent found the musical a "disappointment," and blamed Kern for offering a score which was "neither good Kern nor good swing"; he found the songs "merely adequate, or worse"—!!

884 Lady Audley's Secret. "A Melodrama."

THEATRE: Eastside Playhouse; OPENING DATE: October 3, 1972; PERFORMANCES: 7; BOOK: Douglas Seale; LYRICS: John Kuntz; MUSIC: George Goehring; DIRECTION: Douglas Seale; CHOREOGRAPHY: George Bunt; SCENERY: Alicia Finkel; COSTUMES: Alicia Finkel; LIGHTING: Lawrence Metzler; MUSICAL DIRECTION: John Cina; PRODUCERS: Haila Stoddard and Arnold H. Levy

CAST—Lu Ann Post (Phoebe), Danny Sewell (Luke), Donna Curtis (Lady Audley), Douglas Seale (Sir Michael Audley), June Gable (Alicia), Russell Nype (Capt. Robert Audley), Richard Curnock (George Talboys), Rick Atwell (Butler), Rosalin Ricci (Parlour Maid), Michael Serrecchia (Policeman), Jonathan Miele (Shepherd), Virginia Pulos (Barmaid), Dennis Roberts (Game Keeper), Joyce Maret (Shepherdess)

SOURCE—The 1862 play *Lady Audley's Secret* by Mary Elizabeth Braddon.

The action occurs in and around Audley Court as well as the interior of the Castle Inn during the nineteenth century.

The musical was presented in two acts.

ACT ONE—"The English Country Life" (Company), "A Mother's Wish Is a Daughter's Duty" (Lu Ann Post), "The Winter Rose" (Donna Curtis, Douglas Seale), "Comes a Time" (performer[s] unknown), "That Lady from Eng-a-land" (Richard Curnock, Russell Nype), "Civilized" (Russell Nype, June Gable, Donna Curtis), "Dead Men Tell No Tales" (Donna Curtis)

ACT TWO—"Pas de Deux" (perfomer[s] unknown), "An Old Maid" (June Gable), "Repose" (Donna Curtis), "The Audley Family Honor" (Donna Curtis, Russell Nype), "La-De-Da-Da" (June Gable, Douglas Seale, Donna Curtis), "I Know What I Knows" (performer[s] unknown), "How? What? Why?" (Russell Nype, Donna Curtis, Lu Ann Post), "Firemen's Quartet" (Rick Atwell, Michael Serrecchia, [the other two performers unknown]), "Forgive Her, Forgive Her" (Company)

NOTES—*Lady Audley's Secret* was an entertaining spoof of Victorian melodramas, and deserved a long and profitable run. But despite a charming score, a droll and delicious performance by Donna Curtis in the title role, and a wildly comic show-stopping performance by June Gable, the musical was gone within a week.

Clive Barnes in the *New York Times* was unimpressed with the evening, feeling it lacked a point of view and unsure if it was Victorian "pastiche or satire." As for the musical's finale ("Forgive Her, Forgive Her"), he reported that he could forgive, but it would "take until next week to forget."

The musical had been previously produced by the Goodman Theatre in Chicago and by the Washington Theatre Club. Numbers deleted prior to the Off Broadway production were "I Wait for Him" and "A Man's Home Is His Castle."

885 Lady Day: A Musical Tragedy.

THEATRE: The Brooklyn Academy of Music; OPENING DATE: October 17, 1972; PERFORMANCES: 24; BOOK: Aishah Rahman; LYRICS: Various lyricists (including Aishah Rahman for songs written especially for the production [?]); MUSIC: Archie Shepp; ADDITIONAL MUSIC by Stanley Cowell and Cal Massey; DIRECTION: Paul Carter Harrison; SCENERY: Robert U. Taylor; COSTUMES: Randy Barcelo; LIGHTING: William Mintzer; MUSICAL DIRECTION: Stanley Cowell; PRODUCER: The Chelsea Theatre Center of Brooklyn (Robert Kalfin, Artistic Director; Burl Hash, Productions Director; Michael David, Executive Director) CAST—R.T. Vessels (Contestant [Ronnie], Vi-Tone, Wino, Reporter, Guard), Don Jay (Contestant [Ricky], Vi-Tone, Wino, Buttercup, Waiter), Joe Lee Wilson (Contestant [Sonny], Vi-Tone, Wino, Beware Scat Wino, Reporter), Psyche Wanzandae (Contestant [Bullfrog]), Roger Robinson (Flim Flam, Preacher, Freddie Freedom), Rosetta Le Noire (Mother Horn, Mom), Eugene Riley (Vi-Tone, Wino, Cameraman), Cecelia Norfleet (Billie), Frank Adu (Piano Player, White Nightclub Owner, Judge, Policeman, Newsboy), Clifford Jordan, Jr. (Lester), Madge Sinclair (Fanny, Flo), Signa Joy (Anonymous White Woman, Gilly), Maxwell Glanville (Mort Shazer, Gangster), Al Kirk (Dan Sugarman, Levitt, unknown lover), Onike Lee (Cellmate, Nurse)

The action occurs "yesterday, today but not tomorrow" in the "Eye of the Black Nation."

The musical was presented in three acts ("beats").

FIRST BEAT—"My My Darling" (R.T. Vessel), "Ah Need" (Don Jay), "Tears of This Fool" (Joe Lee Wilson), "In the Spring of the Year 1915 — Raped at 10" (Roger Robinson, Don Jay, Eugene Riley, R.T. Vessels, Joe Lee Wilson), "Song of Fate" (Don Jay, Eugene Riley, R.T. Vessels, Joe Lee Wilson), "Looking for Someone to Love" (Cecelia Norfleet), "Billie's Blues" (Rosetta Le Noire)

SECOND BEAT—"He's Gone" (Rosetta Le Noire, Cecelia Norfleet, Madge Sinclair, Signa Joy), "Strange Fruit" (lyric and music by Lewis Allan) (Don Jay), "Beware Scat Song" (Joe Lee Wilson), "Blues for the Lady" (Cecelia Norfleet), "Stealin' Gold" (Don Jay, Eugene Riley, R.T. Vessels, Joe Lee Wilson), "America on Her Back" (Company), "Enough" (Madge Sinclair)

THIRD BEAT—"God Bless the Child" (lyric and music by Billie Holiday and Arthur Herzog, Jr.) (Roger Robinson, Don Jay, Eugene Riley, R.T. Vessels, Joe Lee Wilson), "No One Will Help the Lady" (Don Jay, Eugene Riley, R.T. Vessels, Joe Lee Wilson), "A Year and a Day" (Don Jay, Eugene Riley, R.T. Vessels, Joe Lee Wilson), "What Would It Be Without You" (Cecelia Norfleet), "Do You Know What It's Like" (Don Jay), "The Professional Friends Duet" (Signa Joy, Eugene Riley), "Lover Man" (Roger Robinson), "I Cried Like a Baby" (Cecelia Norfleet), "Big Daddy" (Cecelia Norfleet), "Song to a Loved One" (Company)

NOTES—*Lady Day: A Musical Tragedy* was based on the life of Billie Holiday (1915-1959), the legendary jazz singer whose drug addiction ruined her life and career; coincidentally, a film biography of Holiday's life was released during the run of the stage version (*Lady Sings the Blues*, with Diana Ross portraying Billie Holiday). The stage musical offered new songs as well as standards associated with Holiday.

The musical told its story through "beats," not scenes or acts. In 1974, *The Great MacDaddy* and *The Prodigal Sister* (see entries) also used "beats," but by the mid-1970s this mini-trend was shelved and everyone went back to scenes and acts.

Billie Holiday herself appeared on Broadway in her own revue *Holiday on Broadway*, which opened at the Mansfield (now Brooks Atkinson) Theatre on April 27, 1948, for six performances.

886 A Lady Needs a Change. "A Tribute to Dorothy Fields."

THEATRE: Cabaret/Manhattan Theatre Club; OPENING DATE: November 15, 1978; PERFORMANCES: 28; LYRICS: Dorothy Fields; MUSIC: See song list for credits; DIRECTION: Bill Gile; CHOREOGRAPHY: Graciela Daniele; Adam Grammis, Assistant Choreographer; COSTUMES: David Toser, Costume Consultant; MUSICAL DIRECTION: William Roy; PRODUCER: Manhattan Theatre Club (Lynne Meadow, Artistic Director; Barry Grove, Managing Director; Stephen Pascal, Associate Artistic Director)

CAST—Patti Allison, Kelly Bishop, Tyra Ferrell, Chip Garnett, Carolyn Mignini, Scott Robertson

The revue was presented in two acts.

ACT ONE—"I Can't Give You Anything but Love" (from *Blackbirds of 1928*; music by Jimmy McHugh) (Company), "I Must Have That Man" (*Blackbirds of 1928*; music by Jimmy McHugh) (Patti Allison, Kelly Bishop, Tyra Ferrell, Carolyn Mignini), "Welcome to Holiday Inn" (*Seesaw*, 1973; music by Cy Coleman) (Patti Allison), "Looking for Love" (independent song, 1929; music by Jimmy McHugh) (Carolyn Mignini), "I'd Rather Wake Up by Myself" (*By the Beautiful Sea*, 1954; music by Arthur Schwartz) (Kelly Bishop), "Freeze an' Melt" (independent song, 1929; music by Jimmy McHugh) (Tyra Ferrell), "Just for Once" (*Redhead*, 1959; music by Albert Hague) (Chip Garnett, Scott Robertson, Carolyn Mignini), "Remind Me" (1940 film *One Night in the Tropics*; music by Jerome Kern) (Carolyn Mignini), "Have Feet Will Dance" (1957 television musical *Junior Miss*; music by Burton Lane) (Company), "I Won't Dance" (1935 film *Roberta*; lyric by Dorothy Fields, Otto Harbach, Oscar Hammerstein II, and Jimmy McHugh; music by Jerome Kern) (Chip Garnett, Patti Allison), "Take It Easy" (1935 film *Every Night at Eight*; music by Jimmy McHugh) (Patti Allison, Kelly Bishop, Tyra Ferrell, Carolyn Mignini), "Doin' the New Low-Down" (*Blackbirds of 1928*; music by Jimmy McHugh) (Kelly Bishop), "Never Gonna Dance" (1936 film *Swing Time*; music by Jerome Kern) (Chip Garnett), "Shuffle Your Feet and Just Roll Along" (*Blackbirds of 1928*; music by Jimmy McHugh) (Patti Allison, Kelly Bishop, Tyra Ferrell, Carolyn Mignini), "Hot Feet" (independent song, 1929; music by Jimmy McHugh) (Company), "Keys to Your Heart" (*Lew Leslie's International Revue*, 1930; music by Jimmy McHugh) (Scott Robertson), "Don't Blame Me" (independent song, 1932;

music by Jimmy McHugh) (Patti Allison), "Serenade to a Wealthy Widow" (independent song, 1934; music by Reginald Forsythe) (Chip Garnett), "Singin' the Blues" (*Singin' the Blues*, 1931; music by Jimmy McHugh) (Kelly Bishop), "I'm a Broken-hearted Blackbird" (*The Vanderbilt Revue*, 1930; music by Jimmy McHugh) (Tyra Ferrell), "Blue Again" (*The Vanderbilt Revue*, 1930; music by Jimmy McHugh) (Carolyn Mignini), "I'm Feelin' Blue" (*Lew Leslie's International Revue*, 1930; music by Jimmy McHugh) (Patti Allison), "Good Bye Blues" (independent song, date unknown; music by Jimmy McHugh) (Patti Allison, Kelly Bishop, Tyra Ferrell, Carolyn Mignini)

ACT TWO—"Uncle Sam Rag" (*Redhead*, 1959; music by Albert Hague) (Company), "How's Your Uncle" (*Shoot the Works*, 1931; music by Jimmy McHugh) (Scott Robertson), "Out of Sight, Out of Mind" (independent song, date unknown; music by Oscar Levant) (Chip Garnett), "Alone Too Long" (*By the Beautiful Sea*, 1954; music by Arthur Schwartz) (Patti Allison), "There's Gotta Be Something Better Than This" (*Sweet Charity*, 1966; music by Cy Coleman) (Carolyn Mignini), "I'll Pay the Check" (*Stars in Your Eyes*, 1939; music by Arthur Schwartz) (Kelly Bishop), "Where Am I Going" (*Sweet Charity*, 1966; music by Cy Coleman) (Tyra Ferrell), "Pick Up the Pieces" (written for, but not used in, *Seesaw*, 1973; music by Cy Coleman) (Patti Allison, with Kelly Bishop, Tyra Ferrell, Carolyn Mignini), "Bojangles of Harlem" (1936 film *Swing Time*; music by Jerome Kern) (Chip Garnett), "Harlem River Quiver" (independent song, 1928; music by Jimmy McHugh) (Carolyn Mignini), "Diga, Diga, Do" (*Blackbirds of 1928*; music by Jimmy McHugh) (Company), "A Lady Needs a Change" (*Stars in Your Eyes*, 1939; music by Arthur Schwartz) (Kelly Bishop), "The Way You Look Tonight" (1936 film *Swing Time*; music by Jerome Kern) (Chip Garnett), "Exactly Like You" (*Lew Leslie's International Revue*, 1930; music by Jimmy McHugh) (Kelly Bishop), "I'm in the Mood for Love" (1935 film *Every Night at Eight*; music by Jimmy McHugh) (Patti Allison), "A Fine Romance" (1936 film *Swing Time*; music by Jerome Kern) (Kelly Bishop, Scott Robertson), "Lovely to Look At" (lyric by Dorothy Fields and Jimmy McHugh; 1935 film *Roberta*; music by Jerome Kern) (Scott Robertson, Chip Garnett), "Looking for Love" (independent song, 1929; music by Jimmy McHugh) (Carolyn Mignini), "Ride Out the Storm" (*Seesaw*, 1973; music by Cy Coleman) (Company), "On the Sunny Side of the Street" (*Lew Leslie's International Revue*, 1930; music by Jimmy McHugh) (Company)

NOTES—The Off Off Broadway revue *A Lady Needs a Change* was a welcome (and long overdue) tribute to Dorothy Fields, one of the premiere lyricists of American stage and film musicals. Her career spanned an almost fifty-year period, from the 1920s to the 1970s.

887 The Lady of the Lake. THEATRE: 92nd Street Y; OPENING DATE: October 5, 1985; PERFORMANCES: Unknown; LIBRETTO: Edward Mabley; MUSIC: Elie Siegmeister; SCENERY: Tony Castrigno; LIGHTING: Victor En Yu Tan; MUSICAL DIRECTION: Amy Kaiser; PRODUCER: Jewish Opera at the Y

CAST—James Javore, Sharon Cooner, Raymond Murcell

SOURCE—Bernard Malamud's short story "The Lady of the Lake," which first appeared in the 1958 short story collection *The Magic Barrel*.

The action occurs in Italy.

The opera was presented in one act.

NOTES—The world premiere of Elie Siegmeister's one-act opera *The Lady of the Lake* was presented on a double bill with *Angel Levine* (see entry), another world premiere by Siegmeister; the libretti for both operas were by Edward Mabley, and both operas were based on short stories by Bernard Malamud. Will Crutchfield in the *New York Times* was disappointed in the story of an American tourist and an Italian caretaker's daughter, "both of whom are concealing their identities and Jewishness" from each another. He noted the opera seemed to promise a "humorous or at least warmhearted" ending when the two would-be lovers discovered the truth about one another; but instead the ending was "harsh" and came across as an "unconvincing shock." Further, he found the music consisted of "dreary dissonance ... almost unrelieved," and the words were "rather bland and obvious."

In 1999, Naxos American Classics Records released *Scenes from Jewish Operas, Volume Two* (CD # 8-559450), which included approximately seventeen minutes' worth of music from the opera (Scene Five; Interlude; Scene Six; and Scene Seven). The recording also included music from Hugo Weisgall's opera *Esther* (see entry).

888 The Last Chance Revue. "A Cabaret." THEATRE: Ted Hook's Onstage; OPENING DATE: April 18, (1979?); PERFORMANCES: 6 (estimated); SKETCHES AND LYRICS: Boyd Graham; MUSIC: Stephen Graziano; DIRECTION: Boyd Graham

CAST—Boyd Graham, Harriet Hayward, Sarah Lindemann, Deborah Wray

The revue was presented in one act (sketch and song assignments unknown).

MUSICAL NUMBERS—"Prelude Opus One," "Fashion Show," "Tribute," "I'm So Happy for You," "We'll Get You Babes," "The Narcotic Harriet Hayward," "Waiting," "Don't Cry for Me," "Public Service Message," "Billy Boyd and His Buckeroos," "Little Girl, Big Voice," "Singer Who Moves Well," "Stinky Lindemann and the Odors," "Whoa Boy," "TNT Institute," "Cavalcade of Curtain Calls"

889 The Last Empress. THEATRE: New York State Theatre; OPENING DATE: August 15, 1997; PERFORMANCES: 12; BOOK: Mun Yol Yi; ADAPTATION BY Kwang Lim Kim; LYRICS: In Ja Yang; ADAPTATION BY Kwang Lim Kim; MUSIC: Hee Gab Kim; ADDITIONAL MUSIC by Peter Casey; DIRECTION: Ho Jin Yun; CHOREOGRAPHY: Byrung Goo Seo; SCENERY: Dong Woo Park; COSTUMES: Hyun Sook Kim; LIGHTING: Hyung O Choi; MUSICAL DIRECTION: Kolleen Park; PRODUCERS: Arts Communications Seoul Company (A-Com); Young Hwan Kim, Executive Producer; Sang Ryul Lee, Sun Mun Lee, Young il Yang, and Woo Jong Lee, Associate Producers

CAST—Wonjung Kim and Taewon Kim (alternating the role of Queen Min [Ja-Young Min]), Jae Hwan Lee (Taewongun), Hee Sung Yu (King Kojung), Hee Jung Lee (Inoue), Mu Yeol Choi (Itoh Hirobumi), Min Soo Kim (Kye Hun Hong), Sung Ki Kim (Miura Goroh), Hyun Dong Kim (Chillyunggun), Hak Jun Kim (Japanese Merchant), Do Kyung Kim (Japanese Merchant), Ho Jin Kim (Japanese Merchant), Sang Hoe Park (Japanese Merchant), Young Ju Jeong (Park), He Jung Kim (Kim), David De Witt (Weber), Mary Jo Todaro (Sontag), Anne Chun (Young Queen), Hyun Dong Kim (Prince), Tom Schmid (Foreign Envoy), Eric Morgan (Foreign Envoy), Claire Beckman (Foreign Envoy), Samantha Camp (Foreign Envoy); Chorus/Dancers: So Youn An, Geon Ryeong Bae, Eun Jung Cho, Im Su Choi, Se Hwan Choi, Jeong Ju Doh, Soon Chul Hyun, Young Ju Jeong, Woo Jeong Jeoung, Do Hyeong Kim, Hakjun Kim, Hak Muk Kim, Ho Jin Kim, Hyun Dong Kim, Soo Jin Kim, Young Ju Kim, Young Ok Kim, Min Kyeng Kwak, He Jeong Lee, Jae Gu Lee, Ji Eun Lee, Ji Youn Lee, Kyoung Woo Lee, Sung Ho Lee, Hyo Jung Moon, Sang Hoe Park, Seung Jun Seo, Hyo In Shin, Chan Youn

SOURCE—The 1994 novel *The Fox Hunt* by Mun Yol Yi.

The action of the prelude occurs in 1945 in Hiroshima; the remainder of the action occurs during the turn-of-the-twentieth-century

The opera was presented in two acts (song assignments unknown).

ACT ONE—Prelude, "Japan's Choice," "The Day We Greet the New Queen," "Taewongun's Regency," "King and Courtesans," "Your Highness Is Beautiful," "Look on Me," "Market Place," "Four Japanese Merchants," "Fight at the Market Place," "I Am Hong Kye-Hun," "A Wish for a Prince," "The Shaman," "Knock Knock"/"Song of the Soldiers," "Grow Big and Strong, Dear Prince," "You Are the King of Chosun," "Until the World Needs Me Again," "Kojong's Imperial Conference," "It's All a Scheme," "Seven Foreign Envoys," "Four Japanese," "Itoh's Ambition," "Uprising of the Old Line Units," "Military Mutiny of 1882," "Back at the Seat of Power," "I Miss You, My Dear Queen," "We Shall Return," "Wu Chang-Ching and Taewongun," "Inoue Threatens King Kojong," "Queen Min's Return," "We Shall Rise Again," "Meeting on Japan's Chosun Policy"

ACT TWO—"Dancing at the Grand Banquet," "Come Celebrate Our Reforms," "Elizabeth I of Chosun," "Negotiations at the Grand Banquet," "New Morning Is Dawning in Chosun," "Isn't It Strange, Snowflakes Are Falling," "You Shall Drink Miura's Wine," "Tripartite Intervention and the Atami House Conspiracy," "Isn't It Strange, Snowflakes Are Falling" (reprise), "Chosun Is Tangun's Land," "Miura's Audience with the King," "The French Lesson," "When the Wine Gets Cold," "Welcome, Ladies," "Ritual for Murder," "Prince and Queen," "Where Was It That We Met," "You Are My Destiny," "Take Away the Darkening Sky," "Do Not Hurt the Queen," "The Last of Hong Kye-Hun," "Queen Min Chased by the Beasts," "Find the Queen, Kill the Fox," "How Will I Live Now," "Rise, People of Chosun"

NOTES—The opera *The Last Empress*, which was sung in Korean, depicted the events in turn-of-the-twentieth-century Korea which led up to the assassination (carried out by the Japanese under the code name "Fox Hunt") of the Chosun Kingdom's last empress, the Empress Myungsung (Queen Min). The program notes indicated some saw the Queen as a visionary who led Korea into out of its "Hermit Kingdom" and into a new era. Others viewed her as manipulative and dangerous, a power-hungry matriarch who brought nothing but conflict to the kingdom.

Anita Gates in the *New York Times* noted that Queen Min was not unlike Eva Peron in her journey from humble beginnings to the highest echelons of power; and, like Peron, she was divisive and died at a young age. Gates found the opera "magnificent," and was impressed by the performances, choreography, scenery, costumes and lighting. Indeed, the décor was so spectacular that Gates mentioned it would remind theatergoers just how "satisfying real splendor can be." She also noted that the opera's final sequence ("Rise, People of Chosun") was "spectacular" and was guaranteed to raise goose bumps.

The opera had been previously performed in Seoul.

890 The Last Five Years. THEATRE: Minetta Lane Theatre; OPENING DATE: March 3, 2002; PERFORMANCES: 73; LYRICS: Jason Robert Brown; MUSIC: Jason Robert Brown; DIRECTION: Daisy Prince; SCENERY: Beowulf Boritt; COSTUMES: Beowulf Boritt; LIGHTING: Christine Binder; MUSICAL DIRECTION: Jason Robert Brown; PRODUCERS: Arielle Tepper and Marty Bell in association with Libby Adler Mages/Mari Glick and Rose/Land Productions

CAST—NORBERT LEO BUTZ (Jamie), SHERIE RENE SCOTT (Cathy)

The musical was presented in one act.

MUSICAL NUMBERS—"Still Hurting" (Sherie Rene Scott), "Jamie's Song" (Norbert Leo Butz), "See I'm Smiling" (Sherie Rene Scott), "Moving Too Fast" (Norbert Leo Butz), "A Part of That" (Sherie Rene Scott), "The Schmuel Song" (Norbert Leo Butz), "A Summer in Ohio" (Sherie Rene Scott), "The Next Ten Minutes" (Norbert Leo Butz, Sherie Rene Scott), "A Miracle Would Happen" (Norbert Leo Butz)/"When You Come Home to Me" (Sherie Rene Scott), "Climbing Uphill" (Sherie Rene Scott), "If I Didn't Believe in You" (Norbert Leo Butz), "I Can Do Better Than That" (Sherie Rene Scott), "Nobody Needs to Know" (Norbert Leo Butz), "Goodbye Until Tomorrow" (Sherie Rene Scott)/"I Could Never Rescue You" (Norbert Leo Butz, Sherie Rene Scott)

NOTES—The fascinating two-character song-cycle *The Last Five Years* was about a failed marriage; it offered an impressive, melodic score by Jason Robert Brown, and although it lasted only a few weeks, it's been frequently produced in regional and community theatre. Besides the strong score, the musical also offered a plot which was presented in a novel way. The wife's story begins with the break-up of the marriage, and then, in *Merrily We Roll Along*-like fashion, goes back in time to the couple's first meeting. However, the husband's story begins with their first meeting, and then progresses to the point of the break-up. Appropriately, the only time the two characters share the same time and space is in a brief wedding scene.

Ben Brantley in the *New York Times* noted that the plot's handling of time and space was mirrored in the score, scenic design, and direction. Through its use of "tone and tempos," Jason Robert Brown's music revealed how the two characters "live at different speeds." Further, Beowulf Borrit's scenery suggested "gravity gone haywire" and "time out of joint." Moreover, Daisy Prince's "cleanly geometric" direction ensured that the performers rarely interacted.

Brantley praised Jason Robert Brown's "sparkling" way of mixing "diverse styles" of music (everything from "Sondheimesque urbanity" to a "clever" piece reminiscent of *A Chorus Line*), and singled out "Nobody Needs to Know" as the musical's "most completely realized ballad."

The cast recording was released by Sh-K-Boom Records (CD # 4001-2).

For her collection *Lauren Kennedy/Songs of Jason Robert Brown* (PS Classics Records CD # PS-309), Kennedy recorded three songs from the production ("I Can Do Better Than That, "Goodbye Until Tomorrow," and "When You Come Home to Me"). According to the liner notes, the latter was a "throw-away moment" in the production which "if you blink, you'll miss it." For Kennedy's collection, the number was given the full treatment, like a "real standard" given "the old Nelson Riddle."

The Last Five Years is an interesting contrast to another musical view of marriage, Harvey Schmidt and Tom Jones' *I Do! I Do!* (see entry), which tells the story of a marriage over a fifty-year time span.

891 The Last Savage.

THEATRE: Metropolitan Opera House; OPENING DATE: January 23, 1964; PERFORMANCES: 7; LIBRETTO: Gian-Carlo Menotti; MUSIC: Gian-Carlo Menotti; DIRECTION: Gian-Carlo Menotti; SCENERY: Beni Montresor; MUSICAL DIRECTION: Thomas Schippers; PRODUCER: The Metropolitan Opera

CAST—Roberta Peters (Kitty), Teresa Stratas (Sardula), Lili Chookasian (The Maharanee), George London (Abdul), Nicolai Gedda (Kodanda), Morley Meredith (Mr. Scattergood), Ezio Flagello (Mararajah), Paul Franke (First Learned Man, English Tailor), Andrea Velis (Second Learned Man, First American Tailor), Clifford Harvuot (The Philosopher), William Walker (The Composer), Gerhard Pechner (The Doctor), Calvin March (The Protestant Pastor), Robert Patterson (The Catholic Priest), Arthur Graham (The Scientist), Gabor Carelli (The Poet), Norman Scott (The Second American Tailor), Carlotta Ordassy (Businesswoman), Janis Martin (The Singer), Erbert Aldridge (The Rabbi), William Dembaugh (The Orthodox Priest), Lou Marcella (The Painter), Dorothy Shawn (Woman), William McLuckey (Major-Domo)

NOTES—*The Last Savage* received its American premiere at the Met (as *Le Dernier Sauvage*, its world premiere had taken place at the Opera Comique on April 2, 1963). It appears that Gian-Carlo Menotti originally wrote the opera in Italian (as *L'Ultimo Selvaggio*) and that the world premiere was performed in French. The translation for the American production was credited to George Mead.

The opera was a satire on the noble savage (Abdul, played by George London) and his encounters with civilization, including one with a young anthropologist (Kitty, played by Roberta Peters) who falls in love with him. According to Howard C. Schonberg in the *New York Times*, London, who was costumed in an animal skin which showed off his muscles, looked like "the cover of one of those magazines on subway stands." Further, Alan Rich in the *New York Herald Tribune* noted that London "in a leopard skin, caged, munching a plastic bone, is one of the sights of the century."

The opera contrasted the frivolous fads and foibles of modern civilization with the qualities of the noble savage; ultimately, Abdul and Kitty wed, and retreat to a cave in the jungle. But Kitty has no intention of "going native": at the end of the opera she's ensured that $99,999 has been deposited at the nearest bank, and she's planning to hire gardeners to keep the jungle well-manicured and a maid to see that her tiger skins don't get ruined by moths. Further, Kitty has ordered a television, a refrigerator, and a "W.C."

Schonberg felt that Menotti's music was too wedded to nineteenth-century conventions to be able to truly satirize modern life. At its best, he felt the work was "a Broadway musical masquerading as an opera." He praised Teresa Stratas ("a diminutive bundle of temperament ... enchanting, and she sang well") and also had high praise for Beni Montresor's scenic designs. Rich said the opera was "a simply delightful evening of pure entertainment ... the music whizzes by on wings of the finest gossamer."

Some of the cast members had almost-but-not-quite careers in the Broadway musical. George London's name appeared on the first window cards of *Anya* (1966), but he never performed in the production (he was replaced by George Kermoyan). Morley Meredith (a baritone whose Met career lasted from 1962 to 1992) created the role of Joey in the first tryout performances of *The Most Happy Fella* (1956), but he was replaced by Art Lund (Morley later appeared in the short-lived 1960 Broadway musical *Christine*, and can be heard on that show's cast album). Finally, Teresa Stratas appeared in the Charles Strouse-Stephen Schwartz musical *Rags* (1986), a failure which lasted four performances but left behind a wonderful score (Stratas introduced the lovely and haunting "Blame It on the Summer Night," the score's most memorable number).

In 1964, the New York Graphic Society and the Metropolitan Opera Guild published an unusual book of the opera. Instead of a straightforward libretto, the text provided a narrative of the story which was accompanied by numerous drawings by Montresor which depicted the sets and costumes seen in the production.

892 The Last Session.

THEATRE: 47th Street Theatre; OPENING DATE: October 17, 1997; PERFORMANCES: 154; BOOK: Jim Brochu; LYRICS: Steve Schalchlin; ADDITIONAL LYRICS by John Bettis and Marie Cain; MUSIC: Steve Schalchlin; DIRECTION: Jim Brochu; SCENERY: Eric Lowell Renschler; COSTUMES: Markas Henry; LIGHTING: Michael Gottlieb; MUSICAL DIRECTION: John Kroner; PRODUCERS: Carl D. White, Jamie Cesa, Michael Alden, Jay Cardwell, Kim and Ronda Espy/Bob-A-Lew Music, and Nancy Nagel Gibbs

CAST—Bob Stillman (Gideon), Dean Bradshaw (Jim), Grace Garland (Tryshia), Amy Coleman (Vicki), Stephen Bienskie (Buddy)

The action occurs "tonight" in a recording studio (once a fallout shelter) under a house in Burbank, California The musical was presented in two acts.

ACT ONE—"Save Me a Seat" (lyric and music by Steve Schalchlin) (Bob Stillman), "The Preacher and the Nurse" (lyric and music by Steve Schalchlin) (Company), "Somebody's Friend" (lyric and music by Steve Schalchlin) (Amy Coleman, Grace Garland, Bob Stillman), "The Group" (lyric and music by Steve Schalchlin) (Amy Coleman, Grace Garland, Bob Stillman), "Going It Alone" (lyric and music by Steve Schalchlin) (Stephen Bienskie)

ACT TWO—"At Least I Know What's Killing Me" (lyric and music by Steve Schalchlin) (Bob Stillman), "Friendly Fire" (lyric and music by Steve Schalchlin and Marie Cain; this sequence included "The Cassions Are Rolling Along," "Anchors Away," "Wild Blue Yonder," and "Marine's Hymn" [traditional arrangements by Schalchlin and Cain]) (Company), "Connected" (lyric and music by Steve Schalchlin) (Bob Stillman), "The Singer and the Song" (lyric and music by Steve Schalchlin) (Grace Garland, Company), "When You Care" (lyric and music by Steve Schalchlin and John Bettis) Company)

NOTES—*The Last Session* told the story of a singer-songwriter with AIDS who decides to commit suicide after recording his last album. Despite the potential grimness of the story, Jeffrey Sweet in *The Best Plays of 1997-1998* remarked that the piece "was surprisingly upbeat ... [and] brimmed with wisecracks." Similarly, the score was strong, and "several numbers were rousers."

The cast album was released by EMG Records (CD # EMG-1004), and the script was published by Samuel French, Inc., in 1998. The script also referenced the following songs: "Preacher and the Nurse Prelude" (music by Bob Stillman), "I Will Trust in the Lord" (lyric and music by Steve Schalchlin), "Shades of Blue" (lyric and music by Steve Schalchlin and Jim Brochu), and "Edge of Night Music" (music by Bob Stillman).

The musical had been previously produced Off Off Broadway at the Curtican Theatre on May 8, 1997.

Steve Schalchlin and Jim Brochu returned in 2006 with *The Big Voice: God or Merman?* (see entry).

893 The Last Starfighter

NOTES—See entry for *The New York Musical Theatre Festival*.

894 The Last Sweet Days of Isaac.

"A 1970 Musical." THEATRE: East Side Playhouse; OPENING DATE: January 26, 1970; PERFORMANCES: 485; BOOK: Gretchen Cryer; LYRICS: Gretchen Cryer; MUSIC: Nancy Ford; DIRECTION: Word Baker; SCENERY: Ed Wittstein; COSTUMES: Caley Summers; LIGHTING: David F. Segal; MUSICAL DIRECTION: Clay Fullum; PRODUCERS: Haila Stoddard, Mark Wright, and Duane Wilder

NOTES—*The Last Sweet Days of Isaac* consisted of two one-act musicals, *The Elevator* and *I Want to Walk to San Francisco*, both of which were unconnected except for the title character. The two musicals were Cryer and Ford's first after *Now Is the Time for All Good Men* (see entry), and, unlike the earlier show, *Isaac* was a hit, running over a year. RCA Victor recorded the cast album, and Metromedia On Stage published the script. The two one-acts dealt with Isaac and two women whom he meets; in the first act, just like (Sweet) Charity and Oscar, Isaac and a young woman (Alice) meet when they're trapped in an elevator; in the second, Isaac and Ingrid meet in jail after they've been arrested during a protest. While watching television news reports of the protest, Isaac realizes he was accidentally killed while filming the protest (he was inadvertently strangled by his own tape recorder); further, he discovers that his camera recorded his death.

The musicals utilized a few songs in traditional book format, sung by the main characters. But other numbers were performed by a rock group (here called the Zeitgeist) who remained outside the main action but whose songs were heard in counterpoint to the stage action.

The surreal plot of the second half, combined with the offbeat use of the rock band, helped carry the evening along. But the show's innovations couldn't disguise the weakness of the overall writing, especially the tiresome navel-gazing characters, who, in typically 1970s fashion (and this was only the first month of 1970!), were too introspective for their own good and indulged in far too much self-analysis. The score was pleasant enough, with one superior number, the ingratiating "I Want to Walk to San Francisco"; but some of the other songs (especially "A Transparent Crystal Moment") came across as inadvertent parodies of popular songs of the day.

The Elevator, CAST—AUSTIN PENDLETON (Isaac), FREDRICKA WEBER (Ingrid), The Zeitgeist (vocals, Charles Collins, C. David Colson, Louise Heath, and John Long; musicians, Clay Fullum, George Broderick, Aaron Bell, Harry Gist, Art Betker)

The action occurs in an elevator at the present time.

MUSICAL NUMBERS—Opening (The Zeitgeist), "The Last Sweet Days of Isaac" (Austin Pendleton, The Zeitgeist), "A Transparent Crystal Moment" (The Zeitgeist, Austin Pendleton, Fredricka Weber), "My Most Important Moments Go By" (Fredricka Weber, Austin Pendleton), "Love, You Came to Me" (Fredricka Weber, Austin Pendleton, The Zeitgeist), Finale (Fredricka Weber, The Zeitgeist)

I Want to Walk to San Francisco, CAST—AUSTIN PENDLETON (Isaac), FREDRICKA WEBER (Alice), C. David Colson (Policeman), The Zeitgeist

The action occurs in two jail cells at the present time.

MUSICAL NUMBERS—"I Want to Walk to San Francisco" (The Zeitgeist), "I Can't Live in Solitary" (John Long, The Zeitgeist), "Herein Lie the Seeds of Revolution" (Charles Collins, The Zeitgeist), "Touching Your Hand Is Like Touching Your Mind" (Austin Pendleton, The Zeitgeist), "Somebody Died Today" (C. David Colson, The Zeitgeist), "Yes, I Know That I'm Alive" (Louise Heath, Fredricka Weber, Austin Pendleton, The Zeitgeist), "I Want to Walk to San Francisco" (reprise) (Austin Pendleton, Fredricka Weber, The Zeitgeist)

MORE NOTES—After the opening of *I Want to Walk to San Francisco*, three numbers were added ("I Can't Live in Solitary," "Herein Lie the Seeds of Revolution," and "Somebody Died Today"), and the songs are listed above in performance order. With the addition of the new songs, The Zeitgeist's presence was more prominent; and they even gave a brief concert at the end of the show, after the bows (it's unclear if the informal concert continued for the entire run). Incidentally, C. David Colson left the cast, to join the upcoming Broadway production of *Purlie* (he sang the short folk/protest songs which were peppered throughout the musical). The above song lists reflect the "final" score as it was eventually presented in New York. (The script, which was published by Metromedia on Stage in 1969, doesn't include the three new numbers, but they appear on the RCA Victor Records cast album [LP # LSO-1169]; the album, incidentally, was produced by Steve Schwartz.)

But "final" may not be the right word. Because in 1980, Cryer and Ford combined *The Elevator* and their failed Broadway musical *Shelter* (1973) into *Isaac & Ingrid & Michael* (Fredricka Weber returned as Ingrid, Word Baker directed, and Ed Wittstein designed the scenery). The "revisal" opened at the Center for the Arts at Purchase, New York. The plot of *Shelter* dealt in part with a writer of television commercials who lives in a television studio with a talking computer named Arthur.

Much later, a revised version of *Isaac & Ingrid & Michael* opened Off Off Broadway at the York Theatre on April 6, 1997, as *The Last Sweet Days*; it was directed by Word Baker, and Willy Falk and Ellen Foley were in the cast. A cast recording was released by Original Cast Records (under the title of *Shelter* [CD # OC-9785]). *The Last Sweet Days* included most of the numbers from *The Elevator*; and retained seven of *Shelter*'s thirteen songs ("Woman on the Run," "Changing," "It's Hard to Care," "Mary Margaret's House in the Country," "Sleep, My Baby, Sleep," "I Bring Him Sea Shells," and "She's My Girl"). Two new songs were heard in the production ("Like a River" and "Goodbye, Plastic Flowers").

The 1973 *Shelter* was recorded by Columbia Records at the time of its original production, but has never been released (it's one of about twenty original and studio cast albums recorded since the late 1940s which have never been commercially released).

The Last Sweet Days of Isaac was produced in London at the Old Vic during the 1971-1972 theatre season. The production ran for eight performances, and Bob Sherman and Julia McKenzie had the leading roles.

895 The Last Vaudeville Show at Radio City Music Hall. THEATRE: Off Center Theatre; OPENING DATE: April 27, 1978; PERFORMANCES: 12; BOOK: Stanley Seidman; LYRICS: Peter Wright; MUSIC: Peter Wright; DIRECTION: Abigail Rosen; SCENERY: Daniel Thomas Field

NOTES—The Off Off Broadway musical *The Last Vaudeville Show at Radio City Music Hall* viewed backstage life at the venerable film palace.

896 The Last Year in the Life of Reverend Martin Luther King Jr. as Devised by Waterwell: A Rock Operetta. THEATRE: Barrow Street Theatre; OPENING DATE: July 8, 2007; PERFORMANCES: 18; BOOK: The Waterwell Company; LYRICS: Lauren Cregor; MUSIC: Lauren Cregor; DIRECTION: Tom Ridgely

CAST—The cast included Rodney Gardiner (as Martin Luther King, Jr.).

NOTES—Frank Scheck in the *New York Post* found the "exhaustively titled" musical a "highly mixed" evening which included "sophomoric" humor (a scene in the Oval office between a "cussing" Lyndon Johnson and a cross-dressing J. Edgar Hoover) as well as scenes which were "powerfully moving." (The musical may have been presented under an Off Off Broadway contract.)

For another musical about the subject, see entry for *Selma*.

The British musical *King* ("A Musical Testimony") also explored the personal and public lives of Martin Luther King, Jr. The lyrics were by Maya Angelou (with additional lyrics by Alistair Beaton), and the music was by Richard Blackford. The production opened in London on April 11, 1989, at the Piccadilly Theatre (Simon Estes portrayed King), and it was recorded by London Records (CD # 424-212-2).

897 Latinos. "A New Musical." THEATRE: Intar Theatre; OPENING DATE: June 2, 1979; PERFORMANCES: 15 (estimated); BOOK: "Created by Intar's Playwrights Unit" (Lynne Alvarez, Manuel Martin, and Omar Torres); LYRICS: Manuel Martin, Eddie Ruperto, Frank Rivera, and Omar Torres; MUSIC: Eddie Ruperto and Omar Torres; DIRECTION: Emmanual Yesckas; Gloria Zelaya, Assistant to the Director; CHOREOGRAPHY: Poli Rogers and Toni Mulett; SCENERY: Lisa Frazza; COSTUMES: Kay Panthaky; LIGHTING: Ronald A. Castleman; MUSICAL DIRECTION: Angelo Cruz; PRODUCER: International Arts Relations, Inc. (Max Ferra, Director)

CAST—Vilma Almonte, Ray Arrocho, Xiomara Arriaga, Luis Arriaga, Jose Bayona, Blanca Camacho, Rafael Dantes Mercado, Georgina Feliz, Carlos Giovanni Ruiz, Barbarell Hughes, Frank Irizarry, Lauren Lumley, Manual Martinez, Millie Morales, Antoine Pagan, Evelyn Pagan, Paula Raflo, Anthony Ruiz, Francisco Rosario, Susan Rybin, Santana Jose, Carmen Torrido De Rosario

The action occurs at Kennedy Airport and different locations in Manhattan at the present time.

The musical was presented in one act.

MUSICAL NUMBERS (Some sequences in the program appear to be scenes, not songs.)—"Airport '79" (Company), "Can the Big 'A' Beat" (lyric by Manuel Martin, music by Eddie Ruperto) (Company), Maletero (Frank Irizarry), "Three Latin Tales" (Anthony Ruiz, Xiomara Arriaga, Lauren Lumley, Georgina Feliz, Ray Arrocho), "From El Barrio to Riverdale" (Rafael Dantes Mercado, Barbarell Hughes, Susan Rybin, Francisco Rosario), "Flushing Gaucho" (Antoine Pagan, Company), "Another Place—Another World" (lyric and music by Omar Torres) (Blanca Camacho, Evelyn Pagan, Santana Jose), "Mauricio and Nettie—Part I" (music by Eddie Ruperto) (Antoine Pagan, Paula Raflo), "A Mexican Experience" (Anthony Ruiz, Manuel Martinez), "Requiem for Living" (lyric by Manuel Martin, music by Omar Torres) (Anthony Ruiz, Manuel Martinez, Lauren Lumley, Jose Bayona), "Maletero" (Frank Irizarry), America Explained—"Spics" (lyric by Manuel Martin, music by Omar Torres) (Manuel Martinez, Francisco Rosario, Rafael Dantes Mercado, Luis Arriaga), A Riverdale Family—"La Mecedora" (lyric by Manuel Martin, music by Omar Torres) (Francisco Rosario, Barbarell Hughes, Rafael Dantes Mercado, Susan Rybin), "Fresh from Puerto Rico" (a/k/a "We Come from Puerto Rico") (lyric by Frank Rivera and Eddie Ruperto, music by Eddie Ruperto) (Paula Raflo, Susan Rybin, Blanca Camacho, Millie Morales, Georgina Feliz, Manuel Martinez, Anthony Ruiz, Santana Jose, Evelyn Pagan), "Guaguanco" (lyric and music by Omar Torres) (Entire Male Cast), "Ranchera of the Lonesome Women" (lyric and music by Omar Torres) (Entire Female Cast), "El Jibaro y el Politico" (Ray Arocho, Manuel Martinez), "Nettie and Mauricio—Part II" (music by Eddie Ruperto) (Paula Raflo, Antoine Pagan), "Good Morning Color Photo" (lyric Omar Torres and Eddie Ruperto, music by Eddie Ruperto) (Manuel Martinez, Anthony Ruiz, Blanca Camacho, Xiomarra Arriaga, Paula Raflo), "Luis and Susana" (Antoine Pagan, Susan Rybin), "Latin Feelings" (lyric by Manuel Martin and Lynn Alvarez, music by Eddie Ruperto) (Manuel Martinez), Finale (Manuel Martinez)

NOTES—Two different programs from the Off Off Broadway production *Latinos* contain variant spellings of the names of some of the cast members. The programs are also contradictory regarding the names of the lyricists as well as which performers sang certain numbers. The above credits are a combination of information from both programs and reflect a "best guess" for spelling and other contradictions between the two programs.

898 Laugh a Lifetime. THEATRE: Norman Thomas Theatre; OPENING DATE: October 22, 1978; PERFORMANCES: 20; SKETCHES AND LYRICS: J. Tunkeler, J. Bratt, M. Nudelman, I. Heyblum, A. Shulman, and E. Kishon; MUSIC: Hanoch Cohen, I. Lustig, and Sol Berezowsky; DIRECTION: Shimon Dzigan; MUSICAL DIRECTION: William Gunther; PRODUCER: The Lively and Yiddish Company

CAST—Shimon Dzigan, Ben Bonus, Mina Bern, Herschel Fox, Shoshana Ron

SKETCHES AND MUSICAL NUMBERS (number of acts unknown; sketch and song assignments unknown; sketches and songs are listed in performance order)—"A Face to Face Meeting," "How to Prevent a Nuclear Explosion," "A Star? No, a Bomb," "Tel-Aviv Construction Worker," "Let's Make Up," "In the Theatre Mirror," "Cave of the Patriarchs," "The Hitch-Hiker," "A Fortunate Father," "There Were Times," Finale

NOTES—The satirical Yiddish-American revue *Laugh a Lifetime* appears to have been presented under an Off Off Broadway contract.

899 Laughing Matters. THEATRE: Theatre at St. Peter's Church; OPENING DATE: May 18, 1989; PERFORMANCES: 85; PLAYLETS: Linda Wallem and Peter Tolan; LYRICS: Peter Tolan; MUSIC: Peter Tolan; DIRECTION: Martin Charnin; SCENERY: Ray Recht; COSTUMES: Jade Jobson, Costume Coordinator; Miss Wallem's costumes by Isaac Izrahi, Mr. Tolan's by Giorgio Armani; LIGHTING: Ray Recht; PRODUCERS: Zev Guber, Sanford H. Fisher, and Beluga Entertainment Corporation

CAST—Linda Wallem, Peter Tolan

The revue was presented in two acts.

ACT ONE—"Inner Thoughts: Just Before the Curtain at St. Peter's, Now," "Weird Interlude: A Good Table at a Bad Restaurant," "Labor Relations: Mom-to-Be's Old Bedroom in Naperville, Just Outside of Chicago," "Nightmare on M Street: A Personnel Office in Washington, D.C., Now," "The Gap: A Corner Booth Very Near the Orchestra at the Rainbow Room," "The Ten-Percent Solution: An 18th Floor Office at the Most Powerful Talent Agency on Earth," "Bridge Over Troubled Daughters: A Kitchen in Champagne-Urbana, 9 P.M. on a Saturday Night"

ACT TWO—"John Loves Mary: A Television Studio in Los Angeles and Elsewhere," Songs: "When You Love New York"; "Max"; and "Next Season on Broadway," "Reunion: Outside the Metropolitan Tower on 57th Street, a Rainy November Afternoon," "Back in Champagne-Urbana: Later That Night, Much Later, Much Much Later," "Inner Thoughts: Just After the Final Playlet at St. Peter's, Now"

NOTES—The revue *Laughing Matters* centered around two of Off Broadway's favorite subjects, show business and life in New York City, and it consisted of sketches and a few songs; it opened on the same night as *Showing Off*, another revue about life in Manhattan (see entry).

Except for a "delirious" comic segment in the second act ("Next Season on Broadway"), Mel Gussow in the *New York Times* found the evening only "moderately amusing." The wickedly funny sequence which Gussow praised was a spoof of musicals in the styles of Irving Berlin, Stephen Sondheim, and John Kander and Fred Ebb. The Berlin spoof dealt with his adaptation of Kafka's "Metamorphosis" and included the song "You're Not Sick, You're Just a Bug," while the Sondheim sequence could have been called "Sunday Into the Woods with George and Sweeney Todd." And "the oddest of all" was the Kander and Ebb spoof, an "upbeat" musical version of *The Iliad* "in which a Liza Minnelli-like Helen offers a high-kicking command to 'open the gates' to Troy, as if it were a Greek cabaret."

An earlier version of *Laughing Matters* had previously been produced Off Off Broadway at the Manhattan Punch Line.

900 The Laundry Hour. THEATRE: The Other Stage/The Public Theatre; OPENING DATE: August 4, 1981; PERFORMANCES: 8; SKETCHES: Mark Linn-Baker, Lewis Black, and William Peters; LYRICS: Mark Linn-Baker, Lewis Black, and William Peters; MUSIC: Paul Schierhorn; DIRECTION: William Peters; CHOREOGRAPHY: Eric Elice; LIGHTING: Gerard P. Bourcier; MUSICAL DIRECTION: Paul Schierhorn; PRODUCER: The New York Shakespeare Festival (Joseph Papp, Director)

CAST—Mark Linn-Baker, Lewis Black, Paul Schierhorn

The revue was presented in one act.

MUSICAL NUMBERS—"The Laundry Hour" (Mark Linn-Baker, Lewis Black), "The Barnyard Song" (Mark Linn-Baker), "Shooting Stars" (Mark Linn-Baker, Paul Schierhorn), "Laugh and the World Laughs" (Company)

NOTES—The revue *The Laundry Room* was in part a fond remembrance for the liberal politics of the 1960s and regret over the country's turn towards conservatism. Only at the Public Theatre.

Mel Gussow in the *New York Times* noted the cabaret-styled revue aimed for "bad taste and wild, anarchic humor," and felt it succeeded in the former (there was "some unconscionable tomfoolery about attempted assassinations") and failed in the latter ("the amusement is only intermittent"). All in all, *The Laundry Hour* was too "singleminded — 60 minutes spinning on one cycle."

901 Lazer Vaudeville. THEATRE: John Houseman Theatre; OPENING DATE: March 9, 2005; PERFORMANCES: 70; MUSIC: Jesse Manno and Max Morath; DIRECTION: Carter Brown; CHOREOGRAPHY: Cindy Marvell; SCENERY: Maia Robbins-Zust; Corey Simpson, Laser Design; COSTUMES: Jennifer Johanos; MUSICAL DIRECTION: Jesse Manno; PRODUCER: Lazer Vaudeville, Inc.

CAST—Carter Brown, Cindy Marvell, Nicholas Flair

The revue was presented in two acts.

NOTES—*Lazer Vaudeville* was the final production to play the John Houseman Theatre before it was demolished. A few weeks after the production closed at the Houseman (where it was apparently produced under an Off Off Broadway contract), it re-opened under an Off Broadway contract at the Lamb's Theatre on June 9, 2005, where it played for eighty-six performances.

The evening included juggling, acrobatics, and rope spinning.

902 Leave It to Jane. THEATRE: Sheridan Square Playhouse; OPENING DATE: May 25, 1959; PERFORMANCES: 928; BOOK: Guy Bolton and P.G. Wodehouse; LYRICS: P.G. Wodehouse; MUSIC: Jerome Kern; DIRECTION: Lawrence Carra; CHOREOGRAPHY: Mary Jane Doerr; SCENERY: Lloyd Burlingame; COSTUMES: Al Lehman; LIGHTING: George Corrin; MUSICAL DIRECTOR: Joseph Stecko; PRODUCERS: Joseph Beruh and Peter Kent

CAST—George Segal (Ollie Mitchell), Monroe Arnold (Matty McGowan), The Boys (Eddie O'Flynn, Dick; Austin O'Toole, Jimsey; Ronald Knight, Happy; Carlo Manalli, Jack; Bob Carey, Smitty; Noel Erler, Tom; Gene Bullard, Joe), Angelo Mango ("Stub" Talmadge), Josip Elic ("Silent" Murphy), Jon Richards (Peter Witherspoon), Dorothy Stinnette (Bessie Tanners), Dorothy Greener (Flora Wiggins), Al Checco (Howard Talbot), Kathleen Murray (Beruh) (Jane Witherspoon), Vince O'Brien (Hiram Bolton), The Girls (Lee Thornberry, Sally; Mitzie McWhorter, Cora; Marianne Gayle, Bertha; Lainie Levine (Kazan), Martha; Patricia Brooks, Josephine; Linda Bates, Louella; Sue Swanson, Sue); Art Matthews (Billy Bolton), Alek Primrose (Hon. Elan Hicks), Ray Tudor (Harold "Bub" Hicks)

SOURCE—The 1904 play *The College Widow* by George Ade.

The action occurs at Atwater College.

The musical was presented in two acts.

ACT ONE—"Good Old Atwater" (George Segal, Boys), "Great Big Land" (Angelo Mango, Dorothy Stinnette), "Wait Till Tomorrow" (Kathleen Murray. Boys), "Just You Watch My Step" (Angelo Mango, Dorothy Stinnette, Girls), "Leave It to Jane" (Kathleen Murray, Dorothy Stinnette, Angelo Mango, Boys, Girls), "The Siren's Song" (Kathleen Murray, Girls), Medley of College Songs (Ensemble), "There It Is Again" (Art Matthews, Lee Thornberry, Girls, Kathleen Murray), "Cleopatterer" (Dorothy Greener, Girls), "The Crickets Are Calling" (Kathleen Murray, Art Matthews, Ensemble), Finale: "Leave It to Jane" (reprise) (Ensemble)

ACT TWO—Cheers & "Good Old Atwater" (reprise) (Ensemble), "What I'm Longing to Say" (Kathleen Murray), "Sir Galahad" (Angelo Mango, Dorothy Greener, Ray Tudor), "Good Old Atwater" and "Leave It to Jane" (reprises) (Ensemble), "The Sun Shines Brighter" (Dorothy Stinnette, Angelo Mango, Girls), "I'm Going to Find a Girl" (George Segal, Angelo Mango, Ray Tudor, Girls), "Poor Prune" (Dorothy Greener), "The Sun Shines Brighter" (reprise) (Angelo Mango, Dorothy Stinnette), "Wait Till Tomorrow" (reprise) (Kathleen Murray, Art Matthews), Finale (Company)

NOTES—Although it didn't open at the Princess Theater and is thus technically not one of the legendary Princess Theater musical comedies by Jerome Kern, Guy Bolton, and P.G. Wodehouse, the original 1917 Broadway production *Leave It to Jane* was still a Princess show in style and spirit (small cast and orchestra, modest sets), and, in keeping with the intimate nature of the Princess shows, it opened at a small Broadway house (the Longacre), where it played for 167 performances.

Leave It to Jane also started a trend in college musicals. For a while, almost every decade saw at least one Broadway musical comedy about college life: *Good News* (1927), *Too Many Girls* (1939), *Best Foot Forward* (1941), *Toplitzky of Notre Dame* (1947), and *All American* (1962). The 1959 Off Broadway revival of *Leave It to Jane* was a smash, running over 900 performances. While Kathleen Murray, Angelo Mango, and most of the cast didn't become well-known, one of the cast members, George Segal, found success in films. And chorus member Lainie Levine became famous, too (as Lainie Kazan).

Murray appeared in one more Off Broadway musical, the vastly underrated *Kittiwake Island* (1960; see entry).

The cast also included Off Broadway legend Dorothy Greener, possibly the only Off Broadway performer to ever achieve true iconic status among musical theater cognoscenti. She shined in supporting roles in Off Broadway revues and musicals, but never found recognition by the general public. Her single Broadway musical appearance was in the eight-performance flop *Razzle Dazzle* (1951) which was for all purposes an Off Broadway revue in a Broadway theatre (the Arena, which later became the Edison). Most productions which played the Edison were under Off Broadway/Middle Broadway contracts, and so it's fitting that this ultimate Off Broadway performer's only musical appearance on Broadway was in a theatre which would eventually be considered an Off Broadway theatre. Dorothy Greener was also Nancy Walker's standby in the 1959 Broadway revue *The Girls Against the Boys*, and had two small roles in *My Mother, My Father and Me* (1963), which was Lillian Hellman's final play.

Thankfully, a number of Greener's Off Broadway

performances were captured on cast recordings, and so we can still sample her unique way with sketches and songs. Her performance style was probably an acquired taste (she was described as a female Wally Cox), and perhaps her specialized approach to theatre material limited her appeal to general audiences. As mentioned in these pages, her "Grace Fogerty" sketch from *Razzle Dazzle* was recorded when it was interpolated into *Shoestring '57*. "A Peach of a Life" was sung in the original 1917 production of *Leave It to Jane*, but wasn't included in the revival. Added to the revival was "Poor Prune" (for Dorothy Greener), a number which had been deleted prior to the original production's Broadway opening. Also added was "Great Big Land," a number intended for the original production but which apparently was never performed until the 1959 revival.

The Off Broadway cast album was originally released on Strand Records (LP # SL-1002; later reissued by AEI Records [LP # AEI-1143]); unfortunately, "Great Big Land" wasn't included in the recording. A later CD release by AEI Records (# AEI-CD-038) included theatre playout music from the 1959 production as well as a live performance of "A Peach of a Life" (titled "The Life of a Peach" on the CD). The CD's liner notes indicate the origin of the latter's recording is uncertain; the track may have been recorded during a rehearsal (if so, that would indicate the song had been intended for the revival, but was dropped prior to the opening) or during a live performance from a 1961 Chicago production of the show which may have included the song. The invaluable CD also includes a 1917 Victor Light Opera selection of music from *Leave It to Jane*. Incidentally, Jeanne Allen replaced Dorothy Stinnette in the role of Bessie Tanner, and so it's Allen who is heard on the cast album.

903 Leaves of Grass. "A Musical Celebration." THEATRE: Theatre Four; OPENING DATE: September 12, 1971; PERFORMANCES: 49; WORDS: Walt Whitman; adapted by Stan Harte, Jr.; MUSIC: Stan Harte, Jr.; DIRECTION: Stan Harte, Jr., and Bert Michaels; CHOREOGRAPHY: Bert Michaels; SCENERY: David Chapman; COSTUMES: David Chapman; MUSICAL DIRECTION: Karen Gustafson; PRODUCER: New Era Productions, Inc.

CAST—JOE MASIELL, Scott Jarvis, Yolande Bavan, Lynn Gerb

SOURCE—The writings of Walt Whitman (1819-1892)

The revue was presented in two acts.

ACT ONE—"Come Said My Soul" (Joe Masiell), "There Is That in Me" (Scott Jarvis), "Give Me" (Yolande Bavan, Lynn Gerb), "Song of the Open Road" (Joe Masiell, Ensemble), "Who Makes Much of a Miracle?" (Lynn Gerb, Ensemble), "Tears" (Lynn Gerb), "Twenty-Eight Men" (Scott Jarvis, Ensemble), "A Woman Waits for Me" (Joe Masiell), "As Adam" (Yolande Bavan, Ensemble), "Do You Suppose" (Scott Jarvis, Ensemble), "Enough" (Joe Masiell), "Dirge for Two Veterans" (Scott Jarvis), "How Solemn" (Lynn Gerb, Ensemble), "Oh Captain! My Captain!" (Yolande Bavan, Ensemble)

ACT TWO—"Pioneers" (Ensemble), "Song of Myself" (Ensemble), "Excelsior" (Yolande Bavan), "In the Prison" (Yolande Bavan), "Twenty Years" (Joe Maisell, Ensemble), "Unseen Buds" (Joe Maisell, Ensemble), "Goodbye, My Fancy" (Lynn Gerb), "Thanks" (Joe Maisell), "I Hear America Singing" (Ensemble)

NOTES—*Leaves of Grass* was a rare instance of an Off Broadway revue patterned after the words of a poet (in this case, Walt Whitman). But the critics were generally unimpressed and felt there was no arc to the production. They found the evening to be a scattershot collection of songs set to Whitman's poetry, presented in no particular order and lacking a framework and a unifying device.

Other Off Broadway revues based on the works of poets include *Betjemania* (Sir John Betjeman; 1980) and *Cummings and Goings* (e.e. cummings; 1984) (see entries). And of course there was a long-running British and Broadway musical about cats which was based on a volume of poetry by T.S. Eliot.

904 Leftovers. THEATRE: Astor Place Theatre; transferred to the AMDA Theatre on December 2, 1983; OPENING DATE: November 8, 1983; PERFORMANCES: 43; MATERIAL by Marcia Kimmell, Deah Schwartz, and Anne Wilford; DIRECTION: Barbara Harris, Directorial Consultant for the New York production; Kenna White, Directorial Consultant for the San Francisco production; SCENERY: Robert F. Strohmeier; COSTUMES: Tamara Melcher and Gregory Reeves; LIGHTING: Arwin Bittern; PRODUCERS: Judith Finn Haines and John Adams Vaccaro

CAST—Marcia Kimmell, Deah Schwartz, Anne Wilford

The revue was presented in one act.

NOTES—*Leftovers* was an improvisatory revue about compulsive eaters, including their problems with dieting; Mel Gussow in the *New York Times* noted the show's cast members (who were also its writers) were "variously overweight actresses" who in a "salvo of self-exposure" discuss their weight issues. In terms of "taste and humor," he found the evening a "doggy bag of table scraps."

Gussow also assumed that since Barbara Harris ("expert improviser and honored graduate of Second City") was the directorial consultant for the New York production, she could be credited for whatever "minimal merit" the cast achieved in their improvisations.

The revue had been previously produced in San Francisco and other cities.

Otis L. Guernsey, Jr., in *The Best Plays of 1983-1984* referred to *Leftovers* as a "musical revue," and while it isn't clear if there were any songs or incidental music in the production, I'm adding the revue to this book in order to be as inclusive as possible. For another evening about diet and weight-related issues, see entry for *Oh! Oh! Obesity*.

905 The Legend. THEATRE: Metropolitan Opera House; OPENING DATE: March 12, 1919; PERFORMANCES: 3; LIBRETTO: Jack Byrne; MUSIC: Joseph Carl Byrne; DIRECTION: Richard Ordynski; SCENERY: Norman Bel Geddes; MUSICAL DIRECTION: Roberto Moranzoni; PRODUCER: The Metropolitan Opera

CAST—Rosa Ponselle (Carmelita), Kathleen Howard (Marta), Paul Althouse (Stephen), Louis D'Angelo (Stackareff)

The opera was presented in one act.

NOTES—The Met offered an evening of three one-act operas, two world premieres (*The Legend* and *The Temple Dancers* [see entry for the latter]) and a revival of the previous season's world premiere, *The Robin Woman: Shanewis* (see entry).

The story of *The Legend* was a bloody one: in his review for the *New York Times*, James Gibbens Hunaker reported that Carmelita (Rosa Ponselle) stabs a man in order to save her father (who is nonetheless shot) and that she herself dies in a torrent of soldiers' bullets. Hunaker also noted that in *The Temple Dancer* one character poisons another and then in turn is killed by a god; and that the director of *Shanewis* had a "busy time sweeping up the remains of murdered humans." The *Times* concluded that morticians should leave their cards at the Thirty-Ninth Street entrance of the Metropolitan Opera House.

The *Times* wasn't particularly impressed with the two world premieres, and by the time of the evening's final offering, the revival of *Shanewis*, Hunaker said the "pleasing Indian operetta" seemed like a classic. He also mentioned that all three of the evening's operas would be more at home across the street at the Casino Theater (a traditional musical comedy house [one of its most famous tenants was the original 1926 production of *The Desert Song*]).

Hunaker also voiced the then-new, now-old complaint about operas which are performed in English: he noted that the English words were unintelligible (and added that they might as well have been sung in Choctaw).

906 Legends in Concert. THEATRE: Academy Theatre; OPENING DATE: May 10, 1989; PERFORMANCES: 22; DIRECTION: John Stuart; CHOREOGRAPHY: Inez Mourning; COSTUMES: Betty Lurenz; LIGHTING: Dennis Condon; MUSICAL DIRECTION: Kerry McCoy; PRODUCER: John Stuart

CAST—Eddie Carroll (Jack Benny), George Trullinger (Buddy Holly), Daryl Wagner (Liberace), Clive Baldwin (Al Jolson), Katie LaBourdette (Marilyn Monroe), Randy Clark (John Lennon), Julie Sheppard (Judy Garland), Donny Ray Evins (Nat King Cole), Tony Roi (Elvis Presley); Singers and Dancers (Renee Chambers, Troy Christian, Vincent D'Elia, Elena Ferrante, Debby Kole, Gary La Rosa, Michael Roberts, Marrielle Monte)

The revue was presented in two acts.

NOTES—Created, directed, and produced by John Stuart, *Legends in Concert* offered nine performers impersonating Jack Benny, Buddy Holly, Liberace, Al Jolson, Marilyn Monroe, John Lennon, Judy Garland, Nat King Cole, and Elvis Presley. Over the years, revues, musicals, and operas have been written about seven of these nine legends (Jack Benny and Liberace are still waiting for their own musical tributes).

907 Legs. "A New Musical." THEATRE: Musical Theatre Works; OPENING DATE: October 9, 1985; PERFORMANCES: 16; BOOK: Robert Satuloff; LYRICS: Robert Satuloff; MUSIC: Mel Marvin; DIRECTION: Stephen Zuckerman; CHOREOGRAPHY: Tina Paul; SCENERY: James Fenhagen; COSTUMES: Bruce Goodrich; LIGHTING: Richard Winkler; MUSICAL DIRECTION: Robert Fisher; PRODUCER: Musical Theatre Works (Anthony J. Stimac, Artistic Director)

CAST—Tom Bade (Madison DeMott, Hilary Hopkinson), Carolyn Mignini (Nan Wilcox), Ellen Foley (Hallie Malone), Karen Ziemba (Juniper Joyce), Diane Findlay (Godzillian Roth), Ken Marshall (Aldo Roth), Mary Catherine Wright (Fairy Godmother, Helvetica Olson, Yetta, Nurse Wretched), Frank Mastrocola (Zeus Mercury, Cobra Priest), Robert Ott Boyle (Cobra Priest, NGN Vice President, Sam Arnold, Legman, Rothtone), Tom Garrett (Cobra Priest, Carlisle Webb, Legman), Rob Marshall (King Cobra, Mr. Hollywood, NGN Vice President, Legman, Rothtone, Young Punk, Young Doctor)

The action occurs in New York City and Hollywood during the early 1950s.

The musical was presented in two acts.

ACT ONE—"New York Unknown" (Carolyn Mignini, Ellen Foley, Karen Ziemba, Ensemble), "Get Tough or Get Out" (Diane Findlay), "Roommates" (Carolyn Mignini, Ellen Foley, Karen Ziemba), "Madonna" (Ken Marshall), "I Lied" (Carolyn Mignini), "Co-Cobra Women" (Diane Findlay, Karen Ziemba, Robert Ott Boyle, Tom Garrett, Frank Mastrocola, Rob Marshall), "Brooklyn" (Ellen Foley), "We Got What We Wanted" (Carolyn Mignini, Ellen Foley, Frank Mastrocola, Karen Ziemba, Ken Marshall, Mary Catherine Wright, Rob Marshall)

ACT TWO—"Aldo Would Be Better Off Without You"/"Fairy Godmother's Beguine"/"See Ya in Tiajuana"/"Nothing" (Karen Ziemba, Diane Findlay, Mary Catherine Wright, Robert Ott Boyle, Rob Marshall), "Illicit Love Affair" (Carolyn Mignini,

Tom Garrett), "Ups and Downs" (Ellen Foley), "Legs" (Diane Findlay, Frank Mastrocola, Robert Ott Boyle, Tom Garrett, Rob Marshall) "Illicit Love Affair" (reprise) (Carolyn Mignini, Tom Garrett), "Weep" (Ken Marshall, Robert Ott Boyle, Rob Marshall), "Nothing" (reprise) (Ken Marshall, Karen Ziemba), Finale (Ensemble)

NOTES—The Off Off Broadway musical *Legs* had an interesting cast, including Rob Marshall, who later directed the hit film version of *Chicago* (which won six Academy Awards, including Best Picture of 2002), and Karen Ziemba, who won the 2000 Tony Award for Best Performance by a Featured Actress in *Contact* (see entry). Other performers included Ellen Foley, who created the role of the Witch during the tryout of Stephen Sondheim's *Into the Woods* (1987) and introduced one of his best songs ("Boom Crunch"); both Foley and the song were out of the musical by the time it opened on Broadway. Other cast members, such as Carolyn Mignini, Ken Marshall, and Mary Catherine Wright, appeared in a number of musicals (Broadway and Off Broadway as well as the occasional out-of-town closing).

908 Lend an Ear. THEATRE: Renata Theatre; OPENING DATE: September 24, 1959; PERFORMANCES: 94; SKETCHES: Charles Gaynor; LYRICS: Charles Gaynor; MUSIC: Charles Gaynor; DIRECTION: Jenny Lou Law; CHOREOGRAPHY: Bill Hooks; SCENERY: Warwick Brown; COSTUMES: Marion Lathrop; LIGHTING: Theda Taylor; MUSICAL DIRECTION: George Bauer; PRODUCERS: L-E Company (Stephan Slane and Jenny Lou Law)

CAST—Elizabeth Allen, Tom Cahill, AL Checco, Barbara Creed, Jack Eddleman, Robert (Bob) Fitch, Jenny Lou Law, Sherry McCutcheon, Alan Peterson, Charles Nelson Reilly, June Squibb, Fiddle Viracola, Jeff Warren, Susan Watson

The revue was presented in two acts.

ACT ONE—"After Hours" (Company), "Give Your Heart a Chance to Sing" (Barbara Creed, Jack Eddleman, Tom Cahill, Robert Fitch, Alan Peterson), "Neurotic You and Psychopathic Me" (June Squibb, Jenny Lou Law, Charles Nelson Reilly), "I'm Not in Love" (Jeff Warren, Elizabeth Allen, Robert Fitch, Alan Peterson, Tom Cahill), "Do It Yourself" (Jack Eddleman, Jenny Lou Law, Al Checco, Charles Nelson Reilly), "Friday Dancing Class" (Jeff Warren, Susan Watson, Alan Peterson, Jenny Lou Law, Jack Eddleman, Tom Cahill, Elizabeth Allen, Barbara Creed, Sherry McCutcheon, June Squibb, Robert Fitch, Fiddle Viracola),"Ballade" (Jenny Lou Law), "When Someone You Love Loves You" (Jeff Warren, Susan Watson, Sherry McCutcheon, Robert Fitch, Elizabeth Allen, Jack Eddleman, June Squibb, Tom Cahill, Fiddle Viracola); *The Gladiola Girl* (Charles Nelson Reilly, Susan Watson, June Squibb, Jack Eddleman, Robert Fitch, Elizabeth Allen, Barbara Creed, Jenny Lou Law, Fiddle Viracola, Tom Cahill, Al Checco, Alan Peterson, Jeff Warren)

The Gladiola Girl sketch included the following songs:

ACT ONE—"Join Us in a Cup of Tea" (Boys, Girls), "Where Is the She for Me?" (Charles Nelson Reilly, Girls), "I'll Be True to You" (Susan Watson, Charles Nelson Reilly), "Doin' the Old Yahoo Step" (June Squibb, Chorus), Finaletto (performers uncredited)

ACT TWO—Opening: "A Little Game of Tennis" (Boys, Girls), "In Our Teeny Little Weeny Nest" (Susan Watson, Charles Nelson Reilly), Finale (performers uncredited), "Santo Domingo" (Jeff Warren, Elizabeth Allen, Company) "I'm on the Look-Out" (Susan Watson) "Three Little Queens of the Silver Screen" (June Squibb, Elizabeth Allen, Jenny Lou Law) "Molly O'Reilly" (Barbara Creed, Alan Peterson, Jack Eddleman, Fiddle Viracola, Jeff Warren, Susan Watson), "All the World's" (Jack Eddleman, Charles Nelson Reilly, Jenny Lou Law, Al Checco) "Who Hit Me?" (Elizabeth Allen, Robert Fitch) "Words Without Song" (Jeff Warren, Jenny Lou Law, June Squibb, Al Checco, Charles Nelson Reilly, Company) Finale (Company)

NOTES—*Lend an Ear* (1948) was one of a succession of mostly successful revues which opened on Broadway in the late 1940s and early 1950s. Although this period was the last gasp of the Broadway revue, Off Broadway extended the tradition with its own series of intimate revues by such producers and writers as Julius Monk, Ben Bagley, and Rod Warren.

The original production of *Lend an Ear* was a major success, racking up 460 performances and establishing the careers of Carol Channing and Gene Nelson. Its most fondly remembered sequence was *The Gladiola Girl*, a mini-musical which spoofed musical comedies of the 1920s. No doubt *The Gladiola Girl* was the inspiration for Sandy Wilson's *The Boy Friend* (see entry). (And the year following the premiere of *Lend an Ear*, Carol Channing was back on Broadway, starring in a full-length musical comedy set in the 1920s, *Gentlemen Prefer Blondes*.)

The 1959 Off Broadway revival of *Lend an Ear* included many familiar Off Broadway names (Charles Nelson Reilly, Jenny Lou Law), and many of the cast members (Reilly, Susan Watson, Elizabeth Allen, Robert Fitch) would make their marks in a number of Broadway musicals.

Brooks Atkinson in the *New York Times* praised the revival, noting its freshness had lasted because its point of view was "sound originally." He noted that *The Gladiola Girl* was the revue's "most priceless item," and he praised its tongue-in-cheek performers, June Squibb (who kept her mouth open "to denote daring and abandon"), Susan Watson ("impossibly arch"), and Charles Nelson Reilly ("dashing" and "stalwart and grand").

Incidentally, two performers in the 1959 revival (Jenny Lou Law and Al Checco) were original cast members of the 1948 production. Law was also a co-producer of the revival. Checco is an interesting name, because he appeared in two legendary musical flops in the 1950s: *Buttrio Square* (1952), which didn't last beyond its opening week in New York, and *Reuben Reuben* (1955), which closed during its Boston tryout. And perhaps he was in *three* legendary flops: while his name isn't to be found in a number of pre-Broadway and Broadway programs for the one-week Broadway flop *Carnival in Flanders* (1953), Checco lists it among his credits in the *Lend an Ear* program. (So he *must* have been in it. Would *anyone* make that up?)

With the exception of the sketch "Power of the Press," which was replaced by another sketch ("Do It Yourself"), the revival retained all the sketches and songs from the original production. It appears "Do It Yourself" was written expressly for the revival; it isn't listed in numerous pre-Broadway, Broadway, and touring programs of the original 1948 production.

In 1961, three numbers from *The Gladiola Girl* ("Join Us in a Cup of Tea," "In Our Teeny Little Weeny Nest," and "The Yahoo Step") were included in Charles Gaynor's 1961 Broadway revue *Show Girl*, which starred Carol Channing. "Join Us in a Cup of Tea" and "The Yahoo Step" can be heard on Roulette Records' cast recording of *Show Girl* (LP # 80001; as of this writing, *Show Girl* is one of a handful of Broadway cast recordings yet to be released on CD).

The script of *Lend an Ear* was published by Samuel French, Inc., in 1971; it includes the "Do It Yourself" sketch and omits "Power of the Press."

909 Lennon. "A Musical Play." THEATRE: Entermedia Theatre; OPENING DATE: October 5, 1982; PERFORMANCES: 25; PLAY: Bob Eaton; DIRECTION: Bob Eaton; SCENERY: Peter David Gould; COSTUMES: Deborah Shaw; LIGHTING: Dennis Parichy; PRODUCERS: Sid Bernstein and Stanley Bernstein in association with Abe Margolies and Dennis Paget; The Liverpool Everyman Theatre Production

CAST—Gusti Bogok (Julia, Yoko Ono; Tambourine, Banjo), Katherine Borowitz (Mimi, Cynthia; Piano, Electric Keyboard, Synthesizer), Lee Grayson (Jeff Mohammed, George Harrison, Gerry Marsden, Tony Palma; Guitar, Drums), Vincent Irizarry (Paul McCartney, Tony Tyler, Bertrand Russell; Guitar, Bass, Piano, Drums), John Jellison (Arthur Ballard, Herr Koschmider, George Martin, Dick Gregory, Elton John, Bon Wooler; Piano, Guitar, Electric Keyboard, Synthesizer, Drums, Bass, Banjo), David Patrick Kelly (Younger John, Pierre Trudeau, Nightclub Manager; Guitar, Bass, Harmonica, Piano), Robert LuPone (Older John, Stuart Sutcliffe, Les Chadwick, Brian Epstein; Guitar, Sax, Bass, Recorder), Greg Martyn (Pete Best, Ringo Starr, Harry Nilsson, Tony Barrow, Tim Leary; Drums, Electric Keyboard, Tea Chest Bass), Bill Sadler (Pete Shotton, Alan Williams, Victor Spinetti, Arthur Janov, Andy Peebles; Guitar, Drums, Piano, Washboard)

The play with music was presented in two acts (musical numbers weren't listed in the program; all songs were apparently popular songs written by John Lennon and Paul McCartney).

NOTES—Previously produced in Great Britain, *Lennon* opened less than two years after John Lennon's murder; but the public wasn't interested, and the play with music was gone in three weeks. Frank Rich in the *New York Times* said Bob Eaton's "shapeless," "flavorless," and "dull" play lacked drama and character development, and instead told its story via "headline announcements" while its musical numbers were presented in *This Is Your Life*-styled song cues. He also noted the play had no point of view whatsoever ("unless total reverence counts as such"). Rich reported that the evening's songs included "In My Life" (the opening number), "All You Need Is Love" (the first-act finale), and "Imagine" (the second-act finale). Howard Kissel in *Women's Wear Daily* found the production shapeless as well as "tepid" and "as bland as a Linda McCartney photograph."

Thirty-three years later, another musical about the subject opened and quickly closed on Broadway (it was also titled *Lennon*). For more information about Beatles and John Lennon-related musicals, see entry for *Sgt. Pepper's Lonely Hearts Club Band on the Road*.

910 Lenny and the Heartbreakers. "A New American Opera." THEATRE: Newman Theatre/The Public Theatre; OPENING DATE: December 22, 1983; PERFORMANCES: 20; LIBRETTO: Kenneth Robins; LYRICS: Kenneth Robins, Scott Killian, and Kim D. Sherman; MUSIC: Scott Killian and Kim D. Sherman; DIRECTION: Murray Louis and Alwin Nikolais; CHOREOGRAPHY: Murray Louis and Alwin Nikolais; SCENERY: Alwin Nikolais with Nancy Winters; film sequences and computer graphic slides by John Sanborn and Mary Perillo; COSTUMES: Lindsay W. Davis; LIGHTING: Alwin Nikolais with Peter Koletzke; MUSICAL DIRECTION: James McElwaine; PRODUCER: The New York Shakespeare Festival (Joseph Papp, Producer; Jason Steven Cohen, Associate Producer)

CAST—Michael Brian or Robert Joy (Lenny), Darren Nimnicht (J.P. di Medici), Sally Williams (Alto Saint), James Wilson (Tenor Saint), Frank Nemhauser (Bass Saint), Nancy Ringham (Soprano Saint), Joanna Glushak or Sally Stotts (Angela); Dancers (Michael Blake, Janis Brenner, Betsy Fisher, Robert McWilliams, Margaret Morris, Danial Shapiro, Joanie Smith, Edward Akio Taketa)

The opera was presented in two acts (the musical numbers weren't identified in the program).

MUSICAL NUMBERS (division of acts and song

assignments unknown; songs are listed in performance order): "The First Last Supper," "The Saints Come In—Flying In," "Video Dreamboy," "Study of the Human Figure," "Video Bleeptones," "Gimme-a-Break Heartbreak," "Hockney-Blue Eyes," "Art Machine #1," "Video Enigma," "A Light Thing," "Lighter Than a Light Thing," "Dissection Section," "I'm a Rocket Tonight," "Interesting Use of Space," "De Medici Cha Cha," "Angela's Flight Drama," "Angela's Tango," "There's Art in My Revenge," "Lonely in Space," "Lenny and the Heartbreakers"

NOTES—This short-lived musical *Lenny and the Heartbreakers* was an updated look at Leonardo Da Vinci. Lenny, the title character, is commissioned to create a great work of art. Leonardo is timeless, but *Lenny* lasted less than three weeks.

The self-styled opera was, in the words of John Rockwell in the *New York Times*, a "gussied-up old American musical ... pretty old and creaky"; instead of an innovative combination of theatre, opera, musical comedy, and dance, Rockwell found the work a "mess," noting the evening's theme seemed to be that "life is tough for artists."

However, Rockwell singled out Alwin Nikolais, Murray Louis, Nancy Winters, Peter Koletzke, Lindsay W. Davis, John Sanborn, and Mary Perillo for their various contributions to the production's distinctive look.

911 Leonard Bernstein's Theatre Songs. "A Unique Musical Evening." THEATRE: Theatre de Lys; OPENING DATE: June 28, 1965; PERFORMANCES: 88; LYRICS: See song list for credits; MUSIC: Leonard Bernstein; DIRECTION: Will Holt; LIGHTING: Jules Fisher; PRODUCERS: Judith Rutherford Marechal Productions, Inc., Josephine Forrestal Productions, Inc., and Seymour Litvinoff

CAST—Trude Adams, Don Francks, Micki Grant

The revue was presented in two acts (song assignments not listed in program).

ACT ONE—"Something's Coming" (from *West Side Story*, 1957; lyric by Stephen Sondheim), "Christopher Street" (*Wonderful* Town, 1953; lyric by Betty Comden and Adolph Green), "Conversation Piece" (*Wonderful Town*, 1953; words by Betty Comden and Adolph Green), "Conga!" (*Wonderful Town*, 1953; lyric by Betty Comden and Adolph Green), "Wrong Note Rag" (*Wonderful Town*, 1953; lyric by Betty Comden and Adolph Green) "What a Waste" (*Wonderful Town*, 1953; lyric by Betty Comden and Adolph Green) "I Feel Like I'm Not Out of Bed Yet" (*On the Town*, 1944; lyric by Betty Comden and Adolph Green), "New York, New York" (*On the Town*, 1944; lyric by Betty Comden and Adolph Green), "It's Love" (*Wonderful Town*, 1953; lyric by Betty Comden and Adolph Green), "Glitter and Be Gay" (*Candide*, 1956; lyric by Richard Wilbur), "Ohio" (*Wonderful Town*, 1953; lyric by Betty Comden and Adolph Green), "A Quiet Girl" (*Wonderful Town*, 1953; lyric by Betty Comden and Adolph Green), "America" (*West Side Story*, 1957; lyric by Stephen Sondheim), "The Best of All Possible Worlds" (*Candide*, 1956; lyric by John LaTouche)

ACT TWO—"My Love" (*Candide*, 1956; lyric by John LaTouche and Richard Wilbur), "Tonight" (*West Side Story*, 1957; lyric by Stephen Sondheim) "Oh, Happy We" (*Candide*, 1956; lyric by Richard Wilbur), "Morning Sun" (*Trouble in Tahiti*, 1951; lyric by Leonard Bernstein), "Tahiti Duet" (*Trouble in Tahiti*, 1951; lyric by Leonard Bernstein), "It Must Be So" (*Candide*, 1956; lyric by Richard Wilbur), "Eldorado" (*Candide*, 1956; lyric by Lillian Hellman), "Trouble in Tahiti" (*Trouble in Tahiti*, 1951; lyric by Leonard Bernstein), "What's the Use?" (*Candide*, 1956; lyric by Richard Wilbur), "Gee, Officer Krupke" (*West Side Story*, 1957; lyric by Stephen Sondheim), "It Must Be Me" (*Candide*, 1956; lyric by Richard Wilbur), "Somewhere" (*West Side Story*, 1957; lyric by Stephen Sondheim), "Make Our Garden Grow" (Candide, 1956; lyric by Richard Wilbur), "Some Other Time" (*On the Town*, 1944; lyric by Betty Comden and Adolph Green)

NOTES—A completely superfluous composer-tribute, this revue offered absolutely nothing new for fans of Leonard Bernstein's music. The revue didn't include even one unfamiliar song from the Bernstein canon (unless one counts "It Must Be Me," the reprise version of "It Must Be So"). In fact, of the five Bernstein shows represented here (*Peter Pan* [1950] was ignored), all had been heard in New York during the preceding ten years, and so weren't exactly hidden treasures: *On the Town* had been revived Off Broadway in 1959 (see entry); *Wonderful Town* had twice played the New York City Center (in 1958 and 1963); *Trouble in Tahiti* had been produced on Broadway in 1955 (as part of *All in One*), and had been revived by the New York City Opera in 1958; *Candide* had opened on Broadway in 1956; and *West Side Story* had opened on Broadway in 1957 for 732 performances, with a return engagement in 1959 for another 249 performances (and, of course, the latter's blockbuster 1961 film version had enjoyed widespread popularity). Further, the albums of all the musicals were in print, and, in fact, one of the programs from an early performance of the revue included a full-page ad by Columbia Records which touted their available recordings of *On the Town*, *Peter Pan*, *Wonderful Town*, *Candide*, and both the cast album and soundtrack of *West Side Story*. (The MGM Records recording of *Trouble in Tahiti* was also in print at the time the revue opened.)

So one wonders: What was the purpose of this revue? All the songs were available in mostly original cast performances with full orchestra, while the revue offered three singers and a three-piece combo. But Lewis Funke in the *New York Times* reported the opening night audience (which included "Mrs. John F. Kennedy") enjoyed the "tasteful, intelligent and engaging" revue. He noted that one of the evening's highlights was a three-part version of "It's Love"; first, Trude Adams sang the number in a straightforward version; then Micki Grant performed the song in an "amusing ... all muted and impassioned" imitation of Lena Horne; and finally Don Francks "cut loose" with an "hilarious" Elvis Presley-styled version of the number.

It appears that "Conga!" may not have been heard on opening night and was added to the revue during the run.

The revue gave New Yorkers another opportunity to see Francks, who had played the title role in the disastrous and legendary *Kelly* a few months earlier. But they had to be quick, because Francks didn't remain with the revue during its brief run (he was replaced by the director, Will Holt).

Another Off Broadway tribute to Bernstein a few years later was much more adventurous in its song offerings (see entry for *By Bernstein*).

912 Let 'Em Eat Cake. THEATRE: Opera House/Brooklyn Academy of Music; OPENING DATE: March 18, 1987; PERFORMANCES: 8 (estimated); BOOK: George S. Kaufman and Morrie Ryskind; LYRICS: Ira Gershwin; MUSIC: George Gershwin; DIRECTION: Maurice Levine; SCENERY: Eduardo Sicangco; COSTUMES: Eduardo Sicangco; LIGHTING: Jeff Davis; MUSICAL DIRECTION: Michael Tilson Thomas; John McGlinn, Guest Conductor; PRODUCER: Brooklyn Academy of Music (Harvey Lichtenstein, President and Executive Director)

CAST—JACK GILFORD (Alexander Throttlebottom), LARRY KERT (John P. Wintergreen), MAUREEN MCGOVERN (Mary Turner Wintergreen), DAVID GARRISON (Kruger), PAIGE O'HARA (Trixie Flynn), Jack Dabdoub (General Adam Snookfield), George Dvorsky (Lieutenant), Louise Edeiken (Miss Benson), Merwin Goldsmith (Louis Lippman), Haskell Gordon (John P. Tweedledee), Walter Hook (Senator Robert E. Lyons), Frank Kopyc (Francis X. Gilhooley), Casper Roos (The Chief Justice), Raymond Thorne (Matthew Arnold Fulton), Mark Zimmerman (Senator Carver Jones); The New York Choral Artists (Paraders, Flunkeys, Radicals, Salesgirls, Customers, Members of the Union League Club, Soldiers, Sailors, League of Nations, Interpreters, Judges, Spectators, Committee Members)

The action occurs on "Main Street" and in New York City and Washington, D.C.

The musical was presented in two acts.

ACT ONE—"Tweedledee for President" (Ensemble), "Union Square" (David Garrison, Ensemble), "Shirts by the Millions (Orders! Orders!)" (Ensemble), "Comes the Revolution" (Jack Gilford, Ensemble), "Mine" (Larry Kert, Maureen McGovern, Ensemble), "Climb Up the Social Ladder (The New Blue D.A.R.)" (Maureen McGovern, Ensemble), "The Union League (Cloistered from the Noisy City)" (Ensemble), "On and On and On" (Larry Kert, Maureen McGovern, Ensemble), Finale Act One (Company): "I've Brushed My Teeth" (Jack Dabdoub, Ensemble), "Double Dummy Drill" (Soldiers), "The General's Gone to a Party" (Ensemble), "Mothers of the Nation" (Maureen McGovern, Ensemble), "Let 'Em Eat Cake" (Larry Kert, Ensemble)

ACT TWO—"Blue, Blue, Blue" (Ensemble), "Who's the Greatest?" (Larry Kert, Ensemble), "The League of Nations": "No Comprenez, No Capish, No Versteh!" (Larry Kert, David Garrison, League), "When Nations Come Together" (Larry Kert, League), "Why Speak of Money?" (League, Interpreters), "Team, Team, Team" (Ensemble), "No Better Way to Start a Case" (Casper Roos, Judges), "Up and At 'Em" (Judges, Girls), "Oyez! Oyez! Oyez!" (Soldiers, Spectators), "The Trial of Throttlebottom": "That's What He Did" (David Garrison, Jack Gilford, Ensemble), "I Know a Foul Ball" (Jack Gilford, David Garrison, Ensemble), "Throttle Throttlebottom" (David Garrison, Ensemble), "The Trial of Wintergreen" (Larry Kert, David Garrison, Maureen McGovern, Ensemble): "A Hell of a Hole" (Larry Kert, Committee), "It Isn't What You Did, It's What You Didn't" (David Garrison, Larry Kert, Army), "First Lady and First Gent" (David Garrison, Paige O'Hara," "Hanging Throttlebottom in the Morning" (George Dvorsky, Ensemble), "Fashion Show" (Maureen McGovern, Paige O'Hara, David Garrison, Ensemble), Finale Ultimo (Company)

NOTES—For part of its 1987 *Gershwin Gala*, the Brooklyn Academy of Music presented an unprecedented and welcome treat, a double-bill concert presentation of two political musicals by George and Ira Gershwin, *Of Thee I Sing* (1931) and its sequel *Let 'Em Eat Cake* (1933). The first half of the evening was comprised of the two acts of the former musical, and the second act of the bill the two acts of the latter. The complete performance lasted approximately three and one half hours.

For more information about *Of Thee I Sing* (including recordings, published script, revivals, and television version), see entries for both 1969 and 1987 productions.

The Brooklyn Academy of Music's revival of the two musicals was released on a 2-LP and 2-CD set by CBS Records (LP # 52M-422522 and CD # M2K-42522), and marked the first time *Let 'Em Eat Cake* had been recorded.

Let 'Em Eat Cake originally opened on Broadway at the Imperial Theatre on October 21, 1933, for ninety performances. Like most theatrical sequels (such as *Divorce Me, Darling* [1965; a sequel to *The Boy Friend*, 1953], *Bring Back Birdie* [1981; *Bye Bye Birdie*, 1960], *Annie 2: Miss Hannigan's Revenge* [1990; *Annie*, 1977], and *The Best Little Whorehouse Goes Public* [1994; *The Best Little Whorehouse in Texas*, 1978]), *Let 'Em Eat Cake* was a disappointment. The often bitter libretto found Wintergreen and Throttlebottom losing the next election to Tweedledee; because of the economic depression, Wintergreen decides to lead a revolution against Tweedledee and soon sets himself up as dictator of the proletariat (he addresses his fellow citizens as "comrades"). But soon both Wintergreen and Throttlebottom are arrested and sentenced to death. Ultimately all ends well when Wintergreen restores democracy to the United States and retires from politics to open a clothing store. But the sour tone of the proceedings even found its way into the ballad "Mine," the musical's most enduring song. Sung in counterpoint by the Wintergreens and the ensemble, Wintergreen and Mary sing of their love while the chorus makes cynical comments about their relationship.

The script was published by Alfred A. Knopf in 1933, the second such Broadway musical to be published in a hardback edition (*Of Thee I Sing* was the first), and it's interesting to note that the first six Broadway musicals to be published in hardback were all 1930s musicals dealing in one way or another with politics (*Of Thee I Sing*, *Let 'Em Eat Cake*, *Johnny Johnson*, *I'd Rather Be Right*, *The Cradle Will Rock*, and *Knickerbocker Holiday*). The Gershwins also wrote a third political musical (not related to *Of Thee I Sing* and *Let 'Em Eat Cake*). *Strike Up the Band* had first been produced in 1927, but closed during its pre-Broadway tryout; a revised version opened on Broadway at the Times Square Theatre on January 14, 1930, and played for 191 performances. The musical dealt with an international incident deriving from tainted chocolate (tainted cheese in the 1927 version).

913 Let My People Come. "A Sexual Musical." THEATRE: Village Gate; OPENING DATE: January 8, 1974; PERFORMANCES: 1167; LYRICS: Earl Wilson, Jr.; MUSIC: Earl Wilson, Jr.; DIRECTION: Phil Oesterman; CHOREOGRAPHY: Ian Naylor; LIGHTING: Centaur Productions; PRODUCER: Phil Oesterman

CAST—Christine Andersen, Tobie Columbus, Daina Darzin, Lorraine Davidson, Marty Duffy, Alan Evans, Lola Howse, Joe Jones, James Moore, Ian Naylor, Larry Paulette, Peachena, Jim Rise, Denise Connolley

The revue was presented in two acts.

ACT ONE—Opening Number (Company), "Mirror" (Lola Howse, Daina Darzin, Alan Evans), "Whatever Turns You On" (Company), "Give It to Me" (Lorraine Davidson), "Giving Life" (Lola Howse, Daina Darzin, Tobie Columbus, Denise Connolley, Alan Evans, Larry Paulette, Joe Jones, Ian Naylor), "The Ad" (James Moore), "Fellatio 101" (Denise Connolley, Students), "I'm Gay" (Joe Jones, Marty Duffy), "Linda, Georgina, Marilyn and Me" (Christine Andersen), "Dirty Words" (Company), "I Believe My Body" (Company)

ACT TWO—"The Show Business Nobody Knows" (Company), "Take Me Home with You" (Larry Paulette), "Choir Practice" (Ian Naylor, Company), "And She Loved Me" (Lola Howse, Peachena, Daina Darzin, Tobie Columbus), "Poontang" (Company), "Come in My Mouth" (Tobie Columbus), "The Cunnilingus Champion of Co. C" (Joe Jones, Larry Paulette, Christine Andersen), "Doesn't Anybody Love Anymore" (Peachena, Company), "Let My People Come" (Company)

NOTES—Mercifully, *Oh! Calcutta!* (1969; see entry) spawned only a few revues of its kind; however, one wannabe was an excrescence called *Let My People Come*, which, for all its vaunted liberation, wasn't quite liberated enough to face the critics for a formal opening night. The revue began performances on January 8, 1974, but never had an official opening. However, as the weeks went by, critics eventually began to review the musical. The show found a supportive audience, and it played Off Broadway for almost three years. Its cast album was released by Libra Records (LP # LR-1069). On August 19, 1974, the revue opened in London at the Oxford Circus Theatre for a long run.

At one point during the Off Broadway run, Earl Wilson, Jr.'s name was omitted from the credits (apparently at his request), and so it appeared that the lyrics and music had written themselves. The musical later opened on Broadway at the Morosco Theatre on July 22, 1976, and played for 106 performances. For Broadway, a scenic designer (Duane F. Mazey) was listed in the credits, and Douglas W. Schmidt was credited for the "supervision" of the sets and costumes. The Broadway production ("proudly" presented by Phil Osterman) reflected a major reordering of the songs and didn't include Peachena in the cast (but one Rozaa joined the revue, so all was not lost).

914 Let's Put on a Show! THEATRE: Irish Repertory Theatre; OPENING DATE: August 10, 2004; PERFORMANCES: 40; TEXT: Jan and Mickey Rooney; NEW LYRICS AND MUSIC: Mickey Rooney; SCENERY: James Morgan; LIGHTING: Gregory Cohen; MUSICAL DIRECTION: Sam Kriger; PRODUCER: The Irish Repertory Theatre (Charlotte Moore, Artistic Director; Ciaran O'Reilly, Producing Director) in association with Densmore Productions and Christopher Aber

CAST—Mickey Rooney, Jan Chamberlin Rooney

The revue was presented in two acts.

NOTES—In the nostalgic evening *Let's Put on a Show!*, the legendary Mickey Rooney (with his eighth wife, Jan Chamberlin Rooney) looked back on his career.

Anita Gates in the *New York Times* said Rooney still had "star power," and noted that for the first act Rooney appeared by himself (he was joined by his wife for the second). Gates reported that Rooney wrote six songs for the revue, including "The Lady's Name Was Love" (a tribute to Ava Gardner, to whom he was married in 1942 and 1943) and "Guess I'm Coming Down with the Blues." Other songs in the production included "I Remember It Well" (1958 film *Gigi*; lyric by Alan Jay Lerner, music by Frederick Lowe); "Makin' Whoopee" (*Whoopee*, 1928; lyric by Gus Kahn, music by Walter Donaldson); "Our Love Is Here to Stay" (1938 film *Goldwyn Follies*; lyric by Ira Gershwin, music by George Gershwin); "Where or When" (*Babes in Arms*, 1937; lyric by Lorenz Hart, music by Richard Rodgers); "Our Love Affair" (1940 film *Strike Up the Band*; lyric by Arthur Freed, music by Roger Edens); "It Had to Be You" (lyric by Gus Kahn, music by Isham Jones); "Crazy" (lyric and music by Willie Nelson); and "I Fall to Pieces" (lyric by Hank Cochran, music by Harlan Howard).

Gates noted that the evening concluded with a tape of Rooney and Judy Garland from a television show in early 1960s, and said the reunion was "sad and sweet for a dozen reasons."

915 Letters to Ben. "A New Musical." THEATRE: Theatre for the New City; OPENING DATE: April 1, 1982; PERFORMANCES: 12 (estimated); BOOK: Charles Choset; LYRICS: Charles Choset; MUSIC: Charles Choset; DIRECTION: Lisa Simon; CHOREOGRAPHY: Sharon Kinney; SCENERY: Joe Ray; COSTUMES: Don Sheffield; LIGHTING: Joe Ray; MUSICAL DIRECTION: Curtis Blaine; PRODUCERS: Theatre for a New City and Bartenieff/Field

CAST—Carol Harris (Beverly Stone), Jamie Beth Nathan (Paula Stone), Diane Irwin (Roz Miller), Bebe Landis (Carole Barnett-Browne), Kenneth Cortland (Tom Utley), John Gallogly (Jack MacPherson), Michael Conant (Al Heald), Perry Stephens (Arnold Whittington); Ensemble (Adrienne Doucette, Allen Hidalgo, Philip Wm. McKinley, Perry Stephens, Donna Trinkoff)

The musical was presented in one act.

MUSICAL NUMBERS—Overture ("Remember Me"), "Me So Far" (Carol Harris, Ensemble), "My Empty Bed" (Carol Harris), "Another Spring" (Bebe Landis, Ensemble), "Thank You" (Jamie Beth Nathan, Kenneth Cortland, Ensemble), "Joe Sanchez" (Diane Irwin), "Lonely Is" (John Gallogly), "Love Essay" (Carol Harris, John Gallogly, Diane Irwin, Perry Stephens), "Personals" (Carol Harris), "School Rap" (Carol Harris, Ensemble), "Hope" (Jamie Beth Nathan, Ensemble), "Favorite Words" (Carol Harris, Michael Conant), "Love Is a Sickness" (John Gallogly), "Simple Principles" (Bebe Landis, Ensemble), "Catullus Song" (Michael Conant), "Hey, World" (Kenneth Cortland, Ensemble), "Tsuris" (Diane Irwin, Ensemble), "If Only, Ben" (Carol Harris, Jamie Beth Nathan), "Live and Be Well" (Bebe Landis, Ensemble), "Catullus Song" (reprise) (Carol Harris, Michael Conant)

NOTES—*Letters to Ben* dealt with a widow who writes letters to her dead husband. Mel Gussow in the *New York Times* said the "epistolary musical" was a "stationery genre," and remarked that the disappointing evening was "saddled with soap-opera subplots." Although he felt "*Letters to Ben* should be marked 'Return to Sender,'" he noted the music "ripples with variety." The lyric of "Love Is a Sickness" was by Samuel Daniel. The lyric of the song "Remember Me" was by David Axlerod, and the music was by Sam Pottle (the Off Off Broadway production was dedicated to the latter, who had died in 1978).

916 Lies & Legends/The Musical Stories of Harry Chapin. THEATRE: Village Gate; OPENING DATE: April 24, 1985; PERFORMANCES: 79; LYRICS: Harry Chapin; MUSIC: Harry Chapin; DIRECTION: Sam Weisman; CHOREOGRAPHY: Tracy Friedman; SCENERY: Gerry Hariton and Vicki Baral; COSTUMES: Marsha Kowal; LIGHTING: Gerry Hariton and Vicki Baral; MUSICAL DIRECTION: Karl Jurman; PRODUCERS: Ken Kragen, Lewis Friedman, Albert Nocciolino, Ken Yates, Stuart Oken, Jason Brett; Richard Martini and Richard Grayson, Associate Producers

CAST—Joanna Glushak, John Herrera, Terri Klausner, Ron Orbach, Martin Vidnovic

The revue was presented in two acts.

ACT ONE—"Circle"/"Story of a Life" (Company), "Corey's Coming" (John Herrera, Company), "Salt and Pepper" (Terri Klausner, Ron Orbach, Company), "Mr. Tanner" (Joanna Glushak, Martin Vidnovic, Company), "The Rock" (Ron Orbach, Company), "Old College Avenue" (Terri Klausner), "Taxi" (John Herrera), "Get On with It" (Joanna Glushak, Ron Orbach), "Bananas" (Martin Vidnovic), "Shooting Star" (Terri Klausner), "Sniper" (Martin Vidnovic, John Herrera, Company)

ACT TWO—"Dance Band on the Titanic" (Company), "W*O*L*D*" (Martin Vidnovic), "Dogtown" (Terri Klausner, Company), "Mail Order Annie" (John Herrera, Joanna Glushak), "Odd Job Man" (Ron Orbach, Company), "Dreams Go By" (John Herrera, Joanna Glushak), "Tangled Up Puppet" (Terri Klausner), "Cat's in the Cradle" (Martin Vidnovic), "Halfway to Heaven" (Ron Orbach), "Better Place to Be" (Terri Klausner, Martin Vidnovic), "You Are the Only Song"/"Circle" (reprise) (Company)

NOTES—This revue of Harry Chapin's "musical stories" was the third such evening of Chapin's songs heard in New York. It was preceded by the 1975 Broadway revue *The Night That Made America Famous* and the 1981 Off Broadway revue *Cotton Patch Gospel* (a/k/a *Somethin's Brewin' in Gainseville*) (for more information regarding these productions, see entry for *Cotton Patch Gospel*). (Another revue, *Chapin*, was produced in Chicago in 1977.)

Two songs in the revue, "Tangled Up Puppet"

and "Cat's in the Cradle," were by both Harry Chapin and Sandy Chapin. During the run, "Winter Song" was added to the production.

The revue had been previously seen in Chicago as *Harry Chapin: Lies & Legends*, and that production was recorded on a 2-LP set by Titanic Productions Records (# T-0184). The recording included one song not heard in New York ("Oh Man, I Call You My Man"). Two members of the Chicago cast (John Herrera and Ron Orbach) were also seen in the New York production; another member of the Chicago cast, George Ball, had also been in the earlier 1977 Chicago revue *Chapin*.

917 The Life and Times of Joseph Stalin. THEATRE: The Opera House/Brooklyn Academy of Music; OPENING DATE: December 14/15, 1973 (some sources indicate the opening took place on December 15/16); PERFORMANCES: 4 (some sources indicate 7 performances); TEXT: Robert Wilson; MUSIC: Various sources; DIRECTION: Robert Wilson; CHOREOGRAPHY: Andrew de Groat

CAST—The cast was comprised of a company of 144 as well as students from New York City Public School 47 (The School for the Deaf).

The opera was presented in seven acts (no intermissions).

NOTES—*The Life and Times of Joseph Stalin* was performed for twelve hours (without intermission) between 7:00 P.M. on Friday, December 14, and 7:00 A.M. on Saturday, December 15, 1973. In his review for the *New York Times*, Clive Barnes noted that the performance ended "precisely" on schedule at 7:00 A.M.

Barnes felt the evening was less an opera than a dance piece. But since the work was the creation of the innovative and often impossible-to-pigeonhole Robert Wilson, Barnes quickly added that the piece was "not really dance" either. Further, the evening had little to do with Joseph Stalin, although Barnes reported that occasionally characters with Stalinesque mustaches and Soviet military uniforms appeared during the twelve-hour proceedings. Further, there was a ballet for sixteen ostriches, and the production included characters from earlier works by Wilson, such as Freud, King Philip of Spain, and an "unamused" Queen Victoria.

The work was essentially one of dance and pantomime and even painterly visual effects, a nonverbal theatre piece which, according to Barnes, depended largely on "visual effects, partly on camp humor, partly on the artistic power of repetition."

As for the audience, the theatre was virtually sold out for the opening performance, and Barnes estimated that by the end of the twelve-hour production there were approximately five-hundred "survivors" (the theatre seated just over 2,000). He reported that during the course of the premiere, audience members picnicked in the aisles, giggled, slept, but "mostly" watched the mesmerizing, surreal production.

918 A Life in a Dream. "A Rock Cantata." THEATRE: Cubiculo Theatre; OPENING DATE: April 3, 1974; PERFORMANCES: 10; LYRICS: Gene Rempel; MUSIC: Dave Bobrowitz; DIRECTION: Andy Thomas Anselmo; Staging by Beverly Ron and Luba Ash; COSTUMES: Christina Katz; LIGHTING: Brian Jayne and Dwight Jayne; MUSICAL DIRECTION: Dave Bobrowitz; Phil Goldberg, Assistant Musical Director; PRODUCER: The Cubiculo

CAST—The Anselmo Singers (Andy Thomas Anselmo, Norma Frances, Steve Gellar, Nancy Tate, John Harris, Carol Leslie, Jerry Rodgers, Iony L. Wormley

NOTES—*A Life in a Dream*, a self-described "rock cantata," was produced Off Off Broadway.

919 Life Is Not a Doris Day Movie. "A New Musical Revue." THEATRE: Top of the Gate/Village Gate; OPENING DATE: June 25, 1982; PERFORMANCES: 37; BOOK: Boyd Graham; LYRICS: Boyd Graham; MUSIC: Stephen Graziano; DIRECTION: Norman Rene; CHOREOGRAPHY: Marcia Milgrom Dodge; SCENERY: Mike Boak; COSTUMES: Walker Hicklin; LIGHTING: Debra J. Kletter; MUSICAL DIRECTION: Jim Cantin; PRODUCERS: Reid-Dolph Inc. (Stephen O. Reid, Producer)

CAST—Boyd Graham (Lingerie Salesman), Mary Testa (Singing Telegram Lady), Neva Small (Waitress)

The action occurs at a bus stop at dawn, on the tip of Manhattan.

The musical was presented in two acts.

ACT ONE—"Waiting for the Bus of Life" (Company), "Don't Cry for Me" (Neva Small), "Lament" (Boyd Graham), "Oh, William Morris" (Mary Testa), "The Fashion Show" (Boyd Graham), "The Last Thing That I Want to Do Is Fall in Love" (Mary Testa, Neva Small), "You'll Be Sorry" (Company), "Tribute" (Mary Testa), "Little Girl—Big Voice" (Neva Small), "I'm So Fat" (Mary Testa), "The Uh Oh Could It Be That I'm an Oh No Tango" (Boyd Graham), "The Right Image"/"The Last Chance Revue" (Company)

ACT TWO—"It's a Doris Day Morning" (Company), "Influenza" (Company), "Last Chance Series" ('Sonny and the Captain'), "Super Wasp" (Boyd Graham), "Report on Status" ('Betsy Finesse'), "A Man Who Isn't" ('Desiree'), "Geographically Undesirable" (Company), "Whoa Boy" ('Brenda and Brent'), "Junk Food Boogie" (Mary Testa, Neva Small), "Public Service Message" ('Tiffany Winerack'), "Singer Who Moves Well" (Boyd Graham), "Not Mister Right" (Mary Testa, Neva Small), "Pause for Prayer" (Company), "Cavalcade of Curtain Calls" (Company), "Think of Me" (Company)

NOTES—*Life Is Not a Doris Day Movie* was a short-running spoof of show business wannabes. In the first act, three would-be performers hope for their big break. In the second act, they strut their stuff after being given a chance to star in a show (in this act, the performers portrayed characters in a musical-within-the-musical, and for the song list it was not always possible to identify which performers played which characters in the show-within-a-show).

John Wilson in the *New York Times* wasn't impressed with Boyd Graham's book and lyrics, but noted the writer, who played a lingerie salesman in the musical, dug "deep into the Paul Lynde bag of frenzy" for "campy furor" effect. As for Stephen Graziano's music, it had a "light, rhythmic if derivative lilt." Wilson said the musical's "one touch of reality" was that the characters spent the entirety of the first act waiting for a bus.

During the run of the musical, the song "Super Wasp" appears to have been dropped.

920 The Life of a Man. "A New Musical." THEATRE: Judson Poets' Theatre; OPENING DATE: September 29, 1972; PERFORMANCES: 19; BOOK: Al Carmines; LYRICS: Al Carmines; MUSIC: Al Carmines; DIRECTION: Al Carmines (?); CHOREOGRAPHY: Dan Wagoner; LIGHTING: Suzanne Kinder; MUSICAL DIRECTION: Al Carmines (?); PRODUCER: Judson Poets' Theatre

CAST—Reathel Bean (Man), Jacque Lynn Colson (Mother), Pregnant Women (Carolyn Moody, Sandy Padilla, Maureen Sadusk, Maggie Wise), Tony Clark (Father), Frank Coppola (Enemy), John Canemaker (Friend), Philip Owens (Barker), Dorian Barth (Coca-Cola Girl), Joanna Kyd (Whore), Theo Barnes (Marx), Stu Silver (Freud), Richard Marshall (Einstein), Sailors (Frank Coppola, Danny Kreitzberg, Matthew Lipton, J. Victor Lopez), Britt Swanson (Sweetheart-Wife), Gretchen Van Aken (Woman), Businessmen (Frank Coppola, Lou Bullock, Ken Marsolais), Cleaning Women (Julie Kurnitz, Maureen Sadusk); Chorus: First Sopranos (Misty Barth, Essie Borden, Semina DeLaurentis, Maureen Sadusk, Melissa Sutphen, Marion Waits Swan, Britt Swanson); Second Sopranos (Dorian Barth, Mary Chesterman, Teresa King, Joanna Kyd, Joanne Pitcher, Barbara Sanek, Gretchen Van Aken); First Altos (Jacque Lynn Colton, Julie Kurnitz, Lyz Kurnitz, Sandy Padilla, Maggie Wise); Second Altos (Sharon Brown, MaryAnn Fahey, Alice Garrard, Lee Guilliatt, Francoise Jeanpierre, Mary Meyer, Lynne Miller, Carolyn Moody, Toni Salmere); First Tenors (Dennis Curley, Bruce Hopkins, Ira Siff); Second Tenors (Frank Coppola, Jerry Dooley, Ted Goldstein, Ken Marsolais, Bill Reynolds); Baritones (Steve Anderson, Theo Barnes, Lou Bullock, John Canemaker, George Garden, Adrian Glass, Danny Kreitzberg, J. Victor Lopez, Bill Maloney, Scott Mansfield, Richard Marshall, Bill McInnis, Harlan Mills, Alfie Nessell, Don Nute, Philip Owens, Burt Rendin, Dan Shnaider, Stu Silver, Allen Swan); Basses (Tony Clark, Matthew Lipton, Stanley Sendzimir, Ronald Willoughby); Cast for *Three's a Crowd* (A Broadway Musical): Dennis Curley (Chorus Boy), Philip Owen (Chorus Boy), Lee Guilliatt (Leading Lady), Bruce Hopkins and Bill McInnis (Children), Sandy Padilla (Pasquela), Bill Reynolds (Psychiatrist), Scott Mansfield (Jimbo), Barbara Sandek (Honey Bitch), Don Nute (Golf Instructor), Ira Siff (Sickness), Dan Shnaider (Orderly), Stanley Sendzimir (Fate)

The musical was presented in two acts.

ACT ONE—"Take Courage Heart" (Chorus), *Womb and Birth*: "Womb Chant" (Chorus), "Song of the Pregnant Women" (Jacque Lynn Colton, Carolyn Moody, Sandy Padilla, Maureen Sadusk, Maggie Wise), *Childhood and Youth*: "Lullabye" (Jacque Lynn Colton), "Father's Song" (Tony Clark), "Do You Ever?" (Reathel Bean, John Canemaker), "Bedsheets" (Jacque Lynn Colton), "Coca-Cola Girl" (Dorian Barth), "Just a Piece of Ass" (Joanne Kyd), "Tragedy Waltz" (Chorus), *Education*: "Marx" (Theo Barnes, Reathel Bean), "Freud" (Stu Silver, Reathel Bean), "Einstein" (Richard Marshall, Reathel Bean), "Chanty" (Frank Coppola, Danny Kreitzberg, Matthew Lipton, J. Victor Lopez), *Love and Marriage*: "Sally" (Britt Swanson, Chorus), "I'll Still Be Here" (Reathel Bean), "Chew Your Bitter Nails" (Chorus), "When Love Comes" (Britt Swanson), Finaletto (Reathel Bean, Britt Swanson, Chorus)

ACT TWO—"If You're a Woman" (Gretchen Van Aken), "American Business" (Frank Coppola, Reathel Bean, Lou Bullock, Ken Marsolais), "One Kind of Man" (Julie Kurnitz, Maureen Sadusk), "He's a Peculiar Guy" (Lou Bullock, Ken Marsolais), *The Middle Years*: *Three's a Crowd* (A Broadway Musical), "Welcome to Broadway" (Dennis Curley, Philip Owen), "I'm an Upper East Side Neurotic" (Lee Guilliatt), "Gordita Es Bonita" (Sandy Padilla), "Mommy We Love You" (Bruce Hopkins, Bill McInnis), "Because of You" (Lee Guilliatt, Bill Reynolds), "Now You've Been to the Big Time" (Company), "Thinking of You" (Scott Mansfield), "I'm Just a Toy" (Don Nute), *Sickness*: "Sickness" (Ira Siff), "Your Life, Oh Man" (Stanley Sendzimir, Chorus)

NOTES—The Off Off Broadway musical *The Life of a Man* literally followed the life of one man (played by Reathel Bean, a Carmines' house favorite), from birth to death; but *New York Times'* critic Mel Gussow felt the blandness of the hero mitigated against the success of the work. However, Gussow praised the songs (which "could be hits if anyone had the good sense to record them"). He noted that an interpolated mini-musical which spoofed a recent Broadway hit (*Company*) was weak (although he enjoyed Lee Guilliatt's "I'm an Upper East Side Neurotic"), but praised a clever sequence parodying nightclub performers.

The song "Coca-Cola Girl" was later heard in the 1982 revue *The Gospel According to Al* (see entry).

921 Light Opera of Manhattan (LOOM)

NOTES—In an era during which operetta had all but disappeared from the New York stage, the Light Opera of Manhattan (LOOM) offered New York audiences classic operettas for over twenty years. There were the very occasional revivals of Gilbert and Sullivan and other operettas by the New York City Opera, and Off Broadway (and later Broadway) offered a memorable revival of *The Pirates of Penzance* in 1981 (see entry). And Broadway even revived two operettas during the period, both of which were poorly received: a delightful production of *The Desert Song* (1926) in 1973, which closed after fifteen performances, and a revised version of Rudolf Friml's *The Three Musketeers* (1928) which lasted for nine performances in 1984. LOOM saw to it that operettas had a consistent home base for over twenty years, much of that time under the artistic direction of its founder William Mount-Burke; for many years, the now-demolished Eastside Playhouse was LOOM's home.

LOOM first opened in 1968 (*The Pirates of Penzance* was its first production), and it sadly closed its doors some twenty-two years later; its final production was a revival of *Babes in Toyland* in 1990.

Its 1978-1979 season was particularly noteworthy: besides such offerings as *Mlle. Modiste* (Victor Herbert), LOOM presented thirteen of Gilbert and Sullivan's fourteen operettas during this one season (most of the music for *Thespis*, their first collaboration, appears to be lost), including productions of *Utopia Unlimited* (which apparently hadn't been seen in New York since the work's 1894 American premiere) and what appears to have been the first New York production of *The Grand Duke*.

A more typical LOOM season offered a mixture of Gilbert and Sullivan and American operettas. For example, during the 1983-1984 season, a total of thirteen works were presented: *The Red Mill* (Victor Herbert), *The Desert Song* (Sigmund Romberg), *The Student Prince* (Sigmund Romberg), *The Merry Widow* (Franz Lehar), *Babes in Toyland* (Victor Herbert), *A Night in Venice* (Johann Strauss), *The Vagabond King* (Rudolf Friml), and *Rose-Marie* (Rudolf Friml and Herbert Stothart) as well as the following operettas by Gilbert and Sullivan: *The Mikado*, *H.M.S. Pinafore*, *The Pirates of Penzance*, *Princess Ida*, and *The Gondoliers*.

922 Lightin' Out.

THEATRE: Judith Anderson Theatre; OPENING DATE: December 3, 1992; PERFORMANCES: 18; BOOK: Walt Stepp; LYRICS: Walt Stepp; MUSIC: Walt Stepp and John Tucker; ADDITIONAL MUSIC by Gregory Tucker; DIRECTION: Kevin Cochran; Catherine Ulissey, ADDITIONAL MUSICAL STAGING; SCENERY: Campbell Baird; COSTUMES: Thom J. Peterson; LIGHTING: Paul Bartlett; MUSICAL DIRECTION: Robert Meffe; PRODUCER: The Dauphin Company

CAST—Gordon Stanley (Mark Twain), Robert Tate (Huckleberry Finn), Tony Fair (Jim), Karen Looze (Jane Clemens, Judith Loftus, Livy Clemens), Beth Blatt (Miss Lyons, Clara Clemens, Emmeline Grangerford), Robert Roznowski (Duke, Tom Sawyer)

The musical was presented in two acts (song assignments unknown).

ACT ONE—Overture, "Nothing Left But You," "I Got De Raff," "Mother, I Am Not a Christian," "So Says I," "Ain't No Trouble," "Fog Song," "Dat Truck Da Is Trash," "Blue Jeans and Misery," "One Sweet Chile," "Don't Take Off Your Mask in Bricksville," "Follow the Drinkin' Gourd," "I'll Be Gone to Freedom"

ACT TWO—Entr'acte, "Home Is a State of Mind," "Stephen Dowling Botts," "Every Day's an Invention of Youth," "Belle of New York," "Rip Around," "Call This a Guverment?," "It Was Kind of Lazy and Jolly," "Awful Word and Awful Thoughts," "Negro Prison Songs," "Murderer's Home," "Satan's Song," "Poor Pitiful Rascals," Finale

NOTES—The Off Off Broadway musical *Lightin' Out* dealt with both Mark Twain's life and his fictional characters, including his thoughts on the denouement of *The Adventures of Huckleberry Finn* (Huck and Jim materialize in order to reenact sequences from the novel as well as to rewrite its ending). If it hadn't been for the confusing book, D.J.R. Bruckner in the *New York Times* felt the "hummable" songs, talented cast, and "stunning" sets could have added up to a "terrific" musical. But the book was "disorderly, tentative, self-conscious and often confusing," and Bruckner said it never explained why Twain was unhappy with his original ending or why Huck and Jim's version turns out the way it does (however, Bruckner noted one aspect of the evening was quite clear: Huck and Jim's new ending is not an improvement upon the original). A revised version of the musical (as *Mark Twain's Blues*) opened Off Off Broadway in 2008 and was recorded on an unnamed and unnumbered CD.

For more information about musicals based on Twain's novels, see entries for *Livin' the Life* and *Downriver*.

923 Like Love

NOTES—See entry for *The New York Musical Theatre Festival*.

924 Liliane Montevecchi on the Boulevard.

THEATRE: Kaufman Theatre; OPENING DATE: February 15, 1988; PERFORMANCES: 64; SCENERY: Dain Marcus; COSTUMES: Michael Katz; LIGHTING: Nadine Charlsen; MUSICAL DIRECTION: Joel Silberman; PRODUCERS: Martin R. Kaufman and Jean-Claude Baker

CAST—Liliane Montevecchi

The revue was presented in two acts.

ACT ONE—*A La Carte*: "Paris Canaille," "Sweet Beginning" (from *The Roar of The Greasepaint—The Smell of the Crowd*, 1965; lyric and music by Anthony Newley and Leslie Bricusse), "Bruxelles" (lyric and music by Jacques Brel), "Le Dernier Pierrot" (lyric and music by Pierre Porte and Pascal Sevran), "Le Temps" (lyric and music by Jeff Davis and Charles Aznavour, English lyric by Gene Lees), "I Never Do Anything Twice" (1976 film *The Seven Percent Solution*; lyric and music by Stephen Sondheim), "Let's Call the Whole Thing Off" (1937 film *Shall We Dance*; lyric by Ira Gershwin, music by George Gershwin), "Tico Tico" (lyric and music by Zequinha Abreu and Aloysio Oliviera, English lyric by Ervin Drake), "It Might as Well Be Spring" (1945 film *State Fair*; lyric by Oscar Hammerstein II, music by Richard Rodgers), "Autumn Leaves" (lyric and music by Joseph Kosma and Jacques Prevert, English lyric by Johnny Mercer), "I've Got You Under My Skin" (1936 film *Born to Dance*; lyric and music by Cole Porter), "La Vie en Rose" (lyric and music by Edith Piaf and Louguy), "My Man" (*Ziegfeld Follies of 1921*; original French lyric by Albert Willemetz and Jacques Charles, English lyric by Channing Pollock, music by Maurce Yvain), "You Don't Know Paree" (*Fifty Million Frenchmen*, 1929; lyric and music by Cole Porter), "I Love Paris" (*Can-Can*, 1953; lyric and music by Cole Porter), "Ballet Barre" (lyric and music by Joel Silberman)

ACT TWO—*On the Boulevard*: "Je Cherche un Millionaire" "Formidable" (lyric and music by Charles Aznavour), "Just a Gigolo" (lyric and music by Julius Brammer, English lyric by Irving Caesar), "The Boulevard of Broken Dreams" (1934 film *Moulin Rouge*; lyric by Al Dubin, music by Harry Warren), "Bridge of Coulaincourt" (*Irma La Douce*, [1958, London; 1960, New York]; lyric by Alexandre Breffort, music by Marguerite Monnot, English lyric by Julian More, David Heneker, and Monty Norman), "Hey Jacques" (lyric and music by Eden Ahbez and Wayne Franklin), "Irma la Douce" (*Irma La Douce*, [1958, London; 1960, New York]; lyric by Alexandre Breffort, music by Marguerite Monnot, English lyric by Julian More, David Heneker, and Monty Norman), "New-Fangled Tango" (*Happy Hunting*, 1956; lyric by Matt Dubey, music by Harold Kerr), "But Beautiful" (1948 film *Road to Rio*; lyric by Johnny Burke, music by Jimmy Van Heusen), "Ne Me Quitte Pas" (lyric and music by Jacques Brel, English lyric by Rod McKuen), "I Don't Want to Know" (*Dear World*, 1969; lyric and music by Jerry Herman), "Folies Bergeres" (*Nine*, 1982; lyric and music by Maury Yeston), "Bon Soir" (lyric and music by Maury Yeston)

NOTES—Among the numbers Liliane Montevecchi performed in her one-woman revue was "Folies Bergere," which she introduced in the hit 1982 Broadway musical *Nine* and for which she won the Tony Award for Outstanding Featured Actress in a Musical.

Montevecchi returned to the Kaufman Theatre on September 11, 1996, in *Back on the Boulevard*; essentially a return engagement of the earlier production and with virtually the same material, the revue played for twenty-four performances.

925 The Line of Least Existence.

THEATRE: Judson Poets' Theatre; OPENING DATE: March 1968; PERFORMANCES: Unknown; PLAY: Rosalyn Drexler; LYRICS: Al Carmines; MUSIC: Al Carmines; DIRECTION: Lawrence Kornfeld; SCENERY: Carlos Sansegundo; COSTUMES: Ruth Sansegundo; LIGHTING: Teresa King; MUSICAL DIRECTION: Al Carmines; PRODUCER: The Judson Poets' Theatre

CAST—Eugene Heller (Pschug), George Barteniefff (Dr. Toolon-Fraak), Katherine Litz (Mrs. Toolon-Fraak), Crystal Field (Ibolya), Louis Waldon (Andy); The Feds: Reathel Bean, Peter Ferrara, Michael Mason

NOTES—*The Line of Least Existence* was a farce which centered around a psychiatrist who also happens to be a drug dealer and a pimp. Clive Barnes in the *New York Times* found the comic moments reminiscent of the Marx Brothers and W.C. Fields, but felt the production was overwhelmed by its campy sensibility. He noted Al Carmines' songs weren't up to the ones he wrote for *In Circles* (see entry), but nonetheless praised the "mean honky-tonk piano interludes" and singled out one song ("I Remember Your Warm Bottom") in which Carmines' "melodic gift rises supreme."

Most of Carmines' songs for this Off Off Broadway production were performed by an on-stage group called The Feds (which included Reathel Bean, one of Carmines' house favorites). The script had been published the year before by Random House in a collection of Rosalyn Drexler's plays titled *The Line of Least Existence and Other Plays* ("printed in hard cover ... just like Robert Anderson's," quipped Barnes). The collection also included her musical *Home Movies* (see entry), for which Carmines wrote the songs.

The songs in the script of *The Line of Least Existence* included "My Love for You Is Tres Tragique," "The End of My Eyes," "You're Not in My Bag, Baby," "Need Some Light, Doc?," "It's Green, It's Green," "I Got the Boudoir Blues," "Where Is All the Sunshine?," "He Was Too Mad," "Yeah, Yeah (Never Trust a Dancing Daughter)," "Easy Come, Easy Go," "We Got a Message, Baby," and "I'm Gonna Fly." Some songs were full-length, others very brief (titles are best-guesses). Since the script doesn't credit Carmines with the songs, it seems all the lyrics in the script were by Drexler (with no composer credit) and all the lyrics and music in the stage production represented new songs by Carmines.

926 Lingoland.

"A Musical Revue by Kenward Elmslie." THEATRE: The Theatre at Saint Peter's Church/The York Theatre Company; OPENING DATE: February 23, 2005; PERFORMANCES: 31 (estimated); LYRICS: Kenward Elmslie; MUSIC: See song list for credits; DIRECTION: James Morgan; CHOREOGRAPHY: Janet Watson; SCENERY: James Morgan; COSTUMES: Suzy Benzinger; LIGHTING: Mary Jo Dondlinger; MUSICAL DIRECTION: Matt Castle; PRODUCER: The York Theatre Company (James Morgan, Artistic Director)

CAST—Kenward Elmslie, Jane Bodle, Jason Dula, Jeanne Lehman, Steve Routman, Lauren Shealy

The revue was presented in two acts.

ACT ONE—Opening (spoken sequence with background music of "Yellow Drum" from *The Grass Harp*, 1971; music by Claibe Richardson) (Kenward Elmslie), "Lingoland" (music by Doug Katsaros) (Company), "Musicals in My Head" (monologue) (Kenward Elmslie), "Them as Has Gets" (music by Claibe Richardson) (Jason Dula, Steve Routman), "The Middle of Nowhere" (*Postcards on Parade*, 2000; music by Steven Taylor) (Jane Bodle, Lauren Shealy, Jeanne Lehman), "Touche's Salon" (spoken sequence from *Taking a Chance on Love*, 2000) (Company), "Take Me Away, Roy Rogers" (*Postcards on Parade*, 2000; music by Kenward Elmslie) (Kenward Elmslie, Jason Dula, Steve Routman), Bar Poems: "Zebra Club" (Steve Routman), "Last Chance Saloon" (Jane Bodle), "Vivi's" (Jeanne Lehman), "Cajun Vitrine: The Ballad of Aout Anni" (music by Kenward Elmslie) (Kenward Elmslie), "Kaleidoscope 1" (Jason Dula, Jeanne Lehman), "Memories" (*Miss Julie*, 1965; music by Ned Rorem) (Jane Bodle), "Bare Bones 1" (Kenward Elmslie), "Love Song" (*The Sweet Bye and Bye*, 1957; music by Jack Beeson) (Company, Matt Castle), "Harvest Parlor Game" (*Lizzie Borden*, 1966; music by Jack Beeson) (Company), "Tree-House Scene" (spoken sequence from *The Grass Harp*, 1971; music by Claibe Richardson) (Jason Dula, Steve Routman), "Chain of Love" (*The Grass Harp*, 1971; music by Claibe Richardson) (Jeanne Lehman), "Original Parkway" (*26 Bars* [date unknown]; music by Doug Katsaros) (Steve Routman, Jane Bodle, Jeanne Lehman, Lauren Shealy), "Lifeshine Ark I" (*The Sweet Bye and Bye*, 1957; music by Jack Beeson) (Jane Bodle, Jeanne Lehman, Lauren Shealy), "Bare Bones II" (Kenward Elmslie), "Cool, Cool Elbow" (written for, but not used in, *The Grass Harp*, 1971; music by Claibe Richardson) (Jane Bodle), "Sleep on Seven Flowers" (*Miss Julie*, 1965; music by Ned Rorem) (Lauren Shealy, Jason Dula), "Kaleidoscope 2" (Company), "The Oval Office" (Company), "Brazil" (written for, but not used in, *The Grass Harp*, 1971; music by Claibe Richardson) (Company)

ACT TWO—"A Telephone Call" (Kenward Elmslie), "Girl Machine" (music by Steven Taylor) (Company), "Vaudeville for Jean Harlow" (music by Andrew Gerle) (Lauren Shealy), "Bare Bones III" (Kenward Elmslie), "Who'll Prop Me Up in the Rain" (music by Kenward Elmslie) (Steve Routman, Company), "Lifeshine Ark II" (*The Sweet Bye and Bye*, 1957; music by Jack Beeson) (Jane Bodle, Jeanne Lehman, Lauren Shealy), "Floozies" (*The Grass Harp*, 1971; music by Claibe Richardson) (Jason Dula), "One Night Stand" (music by Claibe Richardson) (Jane Bodle), "Top o' Silo" (*26 Bars* [date unknown]; music by Doug Katsaros) (Jeanne Lehman, Steve Routman), "They" (music by Claibe Richardson) (Kenward Elmslie), "Yoofry" (music by Claibe Richardson) (Steve Routman), "Marry with Me" (*The Grass Harp*, 1971; music by Claibe Richardson) (Lauren Shealy), "Kaleidoscope 3" (Jeanne Lehman, Lauren Shealy, Jason Dula, Jane Bodle), Three Vermont Haikus: "September" (Jeanne Lehman), "October" (Lauren Shealy), "Harold Benched" (Kenward Elmslie), "Dark Night of My Soul" (written for, but not used in, *The Grass Harp*, 1971; music by Claibe Richardson) (Jason Dula), "Bare Bones IV" (Kenward Elmslie), "Staring" (*Lola*, 1982; music by Claibe Richardson) (Jane Bodle, Jeanne Lehman, Lauren Shealy), "Beauty Secrets" (*Lola*, 1982; music by Claibe Richardson) (Jeanne Lehman), "Love-Wise Anecdote" (Kenward Elmslie), "Yoofry" (reprise) (music by Claibe Richardson) (Steve Routman), "Love-Wise" (music by Marvin Fisher) (Lauren Shealy), "Routine Disruption" (Kenward Elmslie), "Together Forever" (Duet) (*The Seagull*, 1974; music by Thomas Pasatieri) (Jason Dula, Jane Bodle, Jeanne Lehman, Lauren Shealy), "Kaleidoscope 4" (Company), "If There's Love Enough" (*The Grass Harp*, 1971; music by Claibe Richardson) (Company), "Wrap Up" (Kenward Elmslie), Bows/Exit Music: "Yellow Drum" (*The Grass Harp*, 1971; music by Claibe Richardson) and "Lingoland" (reprise) (music by Doug Katsaros) (Orchestra)

NOTES—*Lingoland* was a welcome surprise: a revue honoring Kenward Elmslie, one of the theatre's most important lyricists and librettists. His work may be caviar to the general, but those in search of superior theatre-writing need look no further than Elmslie. He was also part of the revue's cast, and the evening included songs from his musicals and operas as well as independently written songs, poems, and other commentary.

Jay Records recorded the Off Off Broadway revue on a 2-CD set (# CDJAY-1395), and included seven bonus tracks (among them were "Cheeky Kiki" [*Postcards on Parade*, 2000; music by Steven Taylor] and a complete version of "Dark Night of My Soul" [*The Grass Harp*, 1971; music by Claibe Richardson]). The album is an indispensable part of any serious musical theatre library.

"Memories" from *Miss Julie* was part of the opera's "I'm Ready, I Have Money" sequence; "Harvest Parlor Game" from *Lizzie Borden* was from the opera's "Two Quintets" sequence; and "Together Forever" from *The Seagull* was part of the opera's "I Remember Once" sequence.

For more information on musicals by Kenward Elmslie, see entries for *Lizzie Borden*, *Lola*, *Miss Julie*, *Postcards on Parade*, *The Seagull*, *The Sweet Bye and Bye*, and *Taking a Chance on Love*.

927 The Lion and the Jewel. "An African-American Telling of an African Tale." THEATRE: The Mitzi E. Newhouse Theatre/Lincoln Center; OPENING DATE: June 3, 1980; PERFORMANCES: 8; BOOK: Wole Soyinka; LYRICS: Billy Taylor; MUSIC: Billy Taylor; DIRECTION: Mical Whitaker; CHOREOGRAPHY: Hazel S. Bryant; COSTUMES: Myrna Colley-Lee; PRODUCER: The Richard Allen Center for Culture and Art (Host Company for the International Performing Arts Festival at Lincoln Center)

CAST—Loretta Devine (Sidi), Milledge Mosley (Lakunle), Hari Dam Kaur Khalsa (First Girl, Chorus), Chiquita Ross (Second Girl, Chorus), Aisha Coley (Third Girl, Chorus), Clebert Ford (Baroka), Henry Judd Baker (Wrestler), Fran Salisbury (Sadiku), Gayle L. Turner (Favorite), Charles Douglass (Chorus, Villager, Dancer), Donald Greenhill (Chorus, Villager, Dancer), Mercie Hinton (Chorus, Villager, Dancer), Reggie Phoenix (Chorus, Villager, Dancer), Freda T. Vanterpool (Chorus, Villager, Dancer)

SOURCE—An African folk tale.

The action occurs in the late 1950s in the small African village of Ilujinle.

The musical was presented in two acts.

ACT ONE—"Arithmetic Times" (Company), "When We Are Wed" (Milledge Mosley), "The Book" (Hari Dam Kaur Khalsa, Chorus), "I Am Famous" (Loretta Devine), "Wandering Stranger" (Loretta Devine, Chorus), "Little Bird" (Loretta Devine), "Five Full Months" (Clebert Ford), "It's a Rich Life" (Fran Salisbury, Henry Judd Baker, Gayle L. Turner), "The Lion and the Jewel" (Loretta Devine), "I Wish I Led This Kind of Life" (Milledge Mosley), "Do I Improve My Lord" (Gayle L. Turner), "Lovin' Hands" (Clebert Ford), "When Ilujinle Joins the World" (Milledge Mosley, Chorus)

ACT TWO—"The Lion and the Jewel" (reprise) (Loretta Devine), "Old Man Won" (Loretta Devine), "Old Wine in New Bottle" (Clebert Ford), "Moteni" (Company)

NOTES—*The Lion and the Jewel* was performed for one week during the one-month International Performing Arts Festival at Lincoln Center in 1980. The musical was also performed for six performances at the Richard Allen Center for Culture and Art beginning on June 11, 1980.

The plot concerned a young woman from a small Nigerian village who can't decide if she should marry a school teacher with a modern outlook or a town elder who embraces the old ways. Richard F. Shepard in the *New York Times* praised the cast, the "fun" music, the "clever" lyrics, and even the "melodious" dialogue. He concluded that *The Lion and the Jewel* was "attractive theatre."

928 Listen to Me. THEATRE: Judson Poets' Theatre; OPENING DATE: October 18, 1974; PERFORMANCES: 12 Text: Al Carmines; adapted from Gertrude Stein; MUSIC: Al Carmines; DIRECTION: Lawrence Kornfeld; SCENERY: Ed Lazansky; LIGHTING: Edward M. Greenberg; MUSICAL DIRECTION: Al Carmines; PRODUCER: Judson Poets' Theatre

CAST—Theo Barnes, Essie Borden, Lou Bullock, Al Carmines, Tony Clark, Lee Guilliatt, John Kuhner, Julie Kurnitz, Katherine Litz, Trisha Long, Gretchen Van Aken, Margaret Wright

SOURCE—The 1936 play *Listen to Me* by Gertrude Stein.

The musical was presented in two acts.

NOTES—Based on Gertrude Stein's *Listen to Me*, the Off Off Broadway musical was the fourth of six which Al Carmines and Lawrence Kornfeld adapted from her works (see below). Mel Gussow in the *New York Times* described the evening as one which was essentially an exercise in word play (particularly words of one syllable); the musical also had a "deeply buried" subtext about people in pairs; moreover, it also dealt with the "dissimulating aspects" of theatre itself. Gussow found the work somewhat predictable, and noted it might have been more effective in one act. But he praised Carmines' score as "luxuriant," and remarked that the music "is undivided into songs" ("one glides into the other," thus giving the score "more cohesion than usual"). He also liked the array of musical styles (love duets, vaudeville routines, and arias). The musical gave four preview performances between October 11 and October 14.

See separate entries for five other adaptations by Carmines and Kornfeld of Stein's work: *What Happened* (1963), *In Circles* (1967), *The Making of Americans* (1972), *A Manoir* (1977), and *Dr. Faustus Lights the Lights* (1979).

929 Listen to My Heart. "The Songs of David Friedman." THEATRE: Upstairs at Studio 54; OPENING DATE: October 23, 2003; PERFORMANCES: 52; LYRICS: David Friedman; ADDITIONAL LYRICS by Scott Barnes, Robin Boudreau, Deborah Brevoort, Clarissa Dane, Kathie Lee Gifford, Peter Kellogg, Alix (Alexandra) Korey, Portia Nelson, Muriel Robinson, and Barbara Rothstein; MUSIC: David Friedman; DIRECTION: Mark Waldrop; SCENERY: Michael Anania; COSTUMES: Markas Henry; LIGHTING: Matt Berman; MUSICAL DIRECTION: David Friedman (?); PRODUCERS: Victoria Lang, Pier Paolo Piccoli, and William P. Sutter; Carol Cogan Savitsky, Associate Producer

CAST—Allison Briner, Joe Cassidy, David Friedman, Michael Hunsaker, Alix Korey, Anne Runolfsson

The revue was presented in two acts (unless otherwise noted, all lyrics by David Friedman).

ACT ONE—"Trust the Wind" (David Friedman, Company), "You're Already There" (Michael Hunsaker), "What I Was Dreamin' Of" (Anne Runolfsson), "My White Knight" (Allison Briner), "He Comes Home Tired" (lyric by Muriel Robinson) (Alix Korey) "If You Love Me Please Don't Feed Me" (lyric by Robin Boudreau and Scott Barnes) (Joe Cassidy), "I'm Not My Mother" (lyric by Muriel Robinson) (Alix Korey), "You'll Always Be My Baby" (lyric by Barbara Rothstein) (Allison Briner), "Two Different Worlds" (Michael Hunsaker, Anne Runolfsson), "Open Up Your Eyes to Love" (Company), "Live It Up" (Company), "Trick of Fate" (Joe Cassidy), "Listen to My Heart" (Company)

ACT TWO—"The Gift of Trouble" (lyric by Deborah Brevoort) (Company), "Catch Me" (Joe Cassidy), "I Can Hold You" (Michael Hunsaker), "My Simple Wish (Rich, Famous & Powerful)" (Alix Korey), "We Can Be Kind" (Anne Runolfsson), "Only My Pillow Knows" (lyric by Kathie Lee Gifford) (Allison Briner), "Nothing in Common" (lyric by Peter Kellogg) (Anne Runolfsson), "What I'd Had in Mind" (lyric by Muriel Robinson) (Michael Hunsaker), "If I Were Pretty" (lyric by Muriel Robinson) (Alix Korey), "We Live on Borrowed Time" (Allison Briner), "You're There" (lyric by Alix Korey) (Joe Cassidy), "As Long as I Can Sing" (lyric by Clarissa Dane) (Company), "Help Is on the Way" (Company), "I'll Be Here with You" (David Friedman)

NOTES—*Listen to My Heart* was an evening devoted to the songs of David Friedman. Bruce Weber in the *New York Times* noted that while Friedman's "middle-of-the-roadness" wasn't quite his cup of tea, he nonetheless found the revue "deft and unpretentious" and in style far superior to *The Look of Love* (a composer-and-lyricist tribute to Burt Bacharach and Hal David which had bombed on Broadway earlier in the year). Weber singled out "I'll Be Here with You" as the revue's most "affecting" song, and he praised Alix Korey, who did a "well-executed job" of providing the evening's comedy.

The cast recording was released on a 2-CD set by Midder Music (# MMCD-201).

In March 2007, a reading of Friedman's new musical *Goodbye and Good Luck* took place at JCC/The National Yiddish Theatre-Folksbiene; with lyrics by Muriel Robinson and starring Judy Kaye, the musical was based on a short story by Grace Paley; *Listen to My Heart* included one song from the production ("He Comes Home Tired").

Listen to My Heart also included the following numbers which had been written for other productions: "Open Your Eyes to Love" (*The Lizzie McGuire Movie*), "Trick of Fate" (from film *Trick*), "The Gift of Trouble" (*King Island Christmas*), and "Nothing in Common" (*Nicolette*).

Although the program and the cast album indicated Portia Nelson had written additional lyrics which were used in the production, no specific song was credited to her.

930 Little by Little. "A Musical About Friendship, Harmones ... and Popcorn." THEATRE: The Theatre at Saint Peter's Church/The York Theatre Company; OPENING DATE: January 21, 1999; PERFORMANCES: 41; BOOK: Annette Jolles and Ellen Greenfield; LYRICS: Ellen Greenfield and Hal Hackady; MUSIC: Brad Ross; DIRECTION: Annette Jolles; SCENERY: James Morgan; COSTUMES: John Carver Sullivan; LIGHTING: Mary Jo Dondlinger; MUSICAL DIRECTION: Vincent Trovato; PRODUCER: The York Theatre Company (James Morgan, Artistic Director; Joseph V. De Michele, Managing Director)

CAST—Liz Larsen (Woman I), Christiane Noll (Woman II), Darrin Baker (Man)

The musical was presented in one act.

MUSICAL NUMBERS—"Little by Little I" (lyric by Hal Hackaday) (Company), "Friendship and Love" (lyric by Ellen Greenfield) (Company), "Homework" (lyric by Ellen Greenfield) (Company), "Tag" (lyric by Ellen Greenfield) (Company), "Little by Little II" (lyric by Hal Hackaday) (Company), "Life and All That" (lyric by Ellen Greenfield) (Company), "Starlight" (lyric by Ellen Greenfield) (Company), "Popcorn" (lyric by Hal Hackaday) (Darrin Baker, Liz Larsen), "Just Between Us" (lyric by Ellen Greenfield) (Company), "I'm Not" (lyric by Ellen Greenfield) (Christiane Noll), "Little by Little III" (lyric by Hal Hackaday) (Company), "A Little Hustle" (lyric by Ellen Greenfield) (Company), "Rainbows" (lyric by Hal Hackaday) (Darrin Baker, Liz Larsen), "Nocturne" (lyric by Ellen Greenfield) (Liz Larsen), "Little by Little IV" (lyric by Hal Hackaday) (Company), "Yes" (lyric by Ellen Greenfield) (Company), "The Schmooze" (lyric by Hal Hackaday) (Darrin Baker, Christiane Noll), "Take My (the) World Away" (lyric by Ellen Greenfield) (Christiane Noll) "Okay" (lyric by Ellen Greenfield) (Darrin Baker), "If You Only Knew" (lyric by Ellen Greenfield) (Company), "Little by Little V" (lyric by Hal Hackaday) (Company), "If You Loved Me" (lyric by Ellen Greenfield) (Company), "I'm Not" (reprise) (lyric by Ellen Greenfield) (Christiane Noll), "Tell Me" (lyric by Ellen Greenfield) (Darrin Baker), "I Ought to Cry" (lyric by Ellen Greenfield) (Liz Larsen), "Little by Little VI" (lyric by Hal Hackaday) (Company), "So It Goes" (lyric by Ellen Greenfield) (Company), "Popcorn II" (lyric by Hal Hackaday) (Company), "I'm a Rotten Person" (lyric by Ellen Greenfield) Company), "A Journey That Never Ends" (lyric by Ellen Greenfield) (Company)

NOTES—The sung-through musical *Little by Little* told the story of a man and the two women in his life, one of whom he thinks he loves and one of whom he finally realizes is his true love.

Peter Marks in the *New York Times* felt the love triangle was "so banal" it would put "gossip-starved" beauty-parlor patrons to sleep under their hair dryers. He found the score "syrupy" and many of the songs "indistinguishable" from one another; moreover, the "interchangeable" songs were "strangely neutral." The cast album was released by Varese Sarabande Records (CD # VSD-6024), and the script was published by Samuel French, Inc., in 1999.

The musical was originally produced at the Coconut Grove Playhouse in Miami, Florida.

931 The Little Comedy

NOTES—See entry for *Romance Romance*.

932 Little Egypt

NOTES—See entry for *The New York Musical Theatre Festival*.

933 Little Fish. "A New Musical." THEATRE: 2econd (Second) Stage Theatre; OPENING DATE: February 13, 2003; PERFORMANCES: 29; BOOK: Michael John LaChiusa; LYRICS: Michael John LaChiusa; MUSIC: Michael John LaChiusa; DIRECTION: Graciela Daniele; CHOREOGRAPHY: Graciela Daniele; Maddie Ehlert, Associate Choreographer; SCENERY: Riccardo Hernandez; COSTUMES: Toni-Leslie James; LIGHTING: Peggy Eisenhauer; MUSICAL DIRECTION: Dan Lipton; PRODUCER: Second Stage Theatre (Carole Rothman, Artistic Director; Carol Fishman, Managing Director)

CAST—Jennifer Laura Thompson (Charlotte), Marcy Harriell (Kathy), Jesse Tyler Ferguson (Marco), Hugh Panaro (Robert), Lea DeLaria (Cinder), Eric Jordan Young (John Paul), Celia Keenan-Bolger (Young Girl), Ken Marks (Mr. Bunder, Bodega Man)

SOURCE—The short stories "Flotsam" and "Days" from *Transactions in a Foreign Currency* by Deborah Eisenberg.

The action occurs in New York City in 2003, with flashbacks to 1993.

The musical was presented in one act.

MUSICAL NUMBERS—"Days" (Jennifer Laura Thompson, Company), "Robert" (Jennifer Laura Thompson), "It's a Sign" (Lea DeLaria), "The Pool" (Jennifer Laura Thompson, Company), "Winter Is Here" (Jennifer Laura Thompson), "Short Story" (Hugh Panaro, Lifeguards), "Perfect" (March Harriell), "John Paul" (Jennifer Laura Thompson, Marcy Harriell), "He" (Hugh Panaro, Men), "Cigarette Dream" (Jennifer Laura Thompson, Company), "Flotsam" (Celia Keenan-Bolger), "I Ran" (Jesse Tyler Ferguson), "By the Way" (Ken Marks), "Remember Me" (Marcy Harriell), "It Feels Good" (Celia Keenan-Bolger), "Little Fish" (Jesse Tyler Ferguson), "Poor Charlotte" (Lea DeLaria), "Simple Creature" (Jennifer Laura Thompson), "In Twos and Threes" (Jennifer Laura Thompson, Company)

NOTES—*Little Fish* centered around a young woman named Charlotte who lives in New York City and is desperately trying to give up cigarettes. She looks back on her ten years in the city, and in a dream her heroine, Anne Frank, appears and sings of the dangers of flotsam in one's life (she explains that flotsam is the emotional baggage one carries and which can overwhelm and drown an individual). Charlotte finally comes to the realization she's never been comfortable with herself until she quit smoking; she's always been running away from something, and now she decides to connect with self and with friends; after all, swimming alone can be dangerous, and so maybe it's better to be a "little fish" in a pond with one's friends.

Ben Brantley in the *New York Times* found the "stylish" evening a "direct, latter-day answer" to another musical about life in Manhattan, Stephen Sondheim's *Company*. He noted the first half of the musical offered "shapely, hard-edged contours" which ultimately deteriorated into a "sentimental ... blob" during the second half; but he praised Michael John LaChiusa's "jazzy, noirsh" score of "swirling melodies," Riccardo Hernandez' "terraced, silver-toned set" (which evoked the iconic décor of Boris Aronson's designs for *Company*), and Jennifer Laura Thompson's performance in the title role ("her burnished [singing] voice lopes with bluesy suppleness").

The script was published by Dramatists Play Service, Inc., in 2003. "Cigarette Dream" was sung by Alice Ripley in her and Emily Skinner's CD collection *Skinner/Ripley Raw at Town Hall* (Kritzerland Records #KR-20011-0).

The Hollywood cast recording of Blank Theatre Company's 2007 production was released on Ghostlight Records (CD # 8-4430) with Ripley, Chad Kimball, and Gregory Jbara.

934 Little Ham. "A Harlem Jazzical." THEATRE: John Houseman Theatre; OPENING DATE: September 26, 2002; PERFORMANCES: 77; BOOK: Dan Owens; LYRICS: Richard Engquist and Judd Woldin; MUSIC: Judd Woldin; DIRECTION: Eric Riley; CHOREOGRAPHY: Leslie Dockery; SCENERY: Edward T. Gianfrancesco; COSTUMES: Bernard Grenier; LIGHTING: Richard Latta; MUSICAL DIRECTION: David Alan Bunn; PRODUCERS: Eric Krebs in association with Ted Snowdon, Martin Hummel, Entitled Entertainment, and Amas (formerly AMAS) Musical Theatre; M. Kilburg Reedy, Associate Producer

CAST—Christopher L. Morgan (Clarence), Cheryl Alexander (Lucille), Joy Styles (Opal), D'Ambrose Boyd (Larchmont), Lee Summers (Leroy), Venida Evans (Mrs. Dobson), Julia Lema (Amanda), Andre Garner (Hamlet Hitchcock Jones [Little Ham]), Monica L. Patton (Tiny Lee), Richard Vida (Louie "The Nail" Mahoney), Jerry Gallagher (Rushmore), Joe Wilson, Jr. (Jimmy), Brenda Braxton (Sugar Lou Bird), Howard Kaye (Policeman, Bradford)

SOURCE—The 1936 play *Little Ham* by Langston Hughes.

The action occurs in Harlem in 1936.

The musical was presented in two acts.

ACT ONE—"I'm Gonna Hit Today" (Company), "It's All in the Point of View" (Andre Garner), "Stick with Me, Kid" (Richard Vida), "No" (Monica L. Patton, Brenda Braxton, Joe Wilson, Jr.), "Get Yourself Some Lovin'" (Andre Garner, Monica L. Patton), "That Ain't Right" (Company), "Cuttin' Out" (Brenda Braxton, Joe Wilson, Jr.), "Room for Improvement" (Cheryl Alexander, Lee Summers), "Get Back" (Company)

ACT TWO—"Harlem, You're My Girl" (Andre Garner), "Angels" (Andre Garner, Venida Evans, Company), "Big Ideas" (Monica L. Patton), "It's a Helluva Big Job" (Company), "Wastin' Time" (Andre Garner, Monica L. Patton), "Say Hello to Your Feet" (Christopher L. Morgan, Company)

NOTES—The plot centered around Little Ham, a lovable scamp who outwits a gangster (Louie "The Nail" Mahoney) whose ambition is to control the numbers racket in Harlem.

The musical was first produced by Eric Krebs at the George Street Playhouse in New Brunswick, New Jersey, on February 20, 1987, and a revised production (subtitled "The Numbers Musical" and starring Obba Babatunde in the title role) opened at the Westport Country Playhouse in Connecticut on August 31 of that year. The musical was later Presented Off Off Broadway by the Amas Musical Theatre on November 11, 2001, almost a full year before the Off Broadway production opened.

Bruce Weber in the *New York Times* had found the Amas production "exciting" and was looking forward to the Off Broadway version. But he noted the new production at the John Houseman never quite jelled, mainly because it was playing in a theatre three times the size of the Amas and it hadn't "raised the volume of its zing" to correspond to the larger house. But he liked Judd Woldin's "spirited, jazzy" score, and singled out "Harlem, You're My Girl" (a "beautiful, Billy Strayhorn-esque ballad"), "Room for Improvement" ("a lushly gorgeous and funny duet"), and two "uptempo" numbers ("Angels" and "Say Hello to Your Feet").

Numbers deleted prior to the Off Broadway production at the John Houseman Theatre were "Hot Stuff," "Mojo," and "The Dance Contest." The script was published by Samuel French, Inc., in 2003, and a recording of the score (with some members from the Off Broadway cast) was released by EXP Records (CD # EXP1131-2).

935 Little Mary Sunshine. "A New Musical About an Old Operetta." THEATRE: Orpheum Theatre; transferred to the Players Theatre on June 21, 1961, to the Cherry Lane Theatre on March 30, 1962, and back to the Players Theatre on June 20, 1962; OPENING DATE: November 18, 1959; PERFORMANCES: 1,143; BOOK: Rick Besoyan; LYRICS: Rick Besoyan; MUSIC: Rick Besoyan; DIRECTION: Ray Harrison; CHOREOGRAPHY: Ray Harrison; SCENERY: Howard Barker; COSTUMES: Howard Barker; LIGHTING: Jim Gore (later programs credited the lighting design to Wynn Olmon); MUSICAL DIRECTION: Jack Holmes; PRODUCERS: Howard Barker, Cynthia Baer, and Robert Chambers

CAST—JOHN ANISTON (Chief Brown Bear), JOHN MCMARTIN (Cpl. "Billy" Jester), WILLIAM GRAHAM (Capt. "Big Jim" Warington), EILEEN BRENNAN (Little Mary Sunshine, a/k/a Mary Potts), ELIZABETH PARRISH (Mme. Ernestine Von Liebedich), ELMARIE WENDEL (Nancy Twinkle), Robert Chambers (Fleet Foot), Ray James (Yellow Feather), MARIO SILETTI (Gen'l Oscar Farifax, Ret.), The Young Ladies of the Eastchester Finishing School (Floria Mari, Cora; Jana Stuart, Maud; Elaine Labour, Gwendolyn; Rita Howell, Henrietta; Sally Bramlette, Mabel), The Young Gentlemen of the United States Forest Rangers (Jerry Melo, Pete; Joe Warfield, Tex; Arthur Hunt, Slim; Ed Riley, Buster; Mark Destin, Hank)

The action occurs early in the twentieth century at the Colorado Inn, high in the Rocky Mountains.

The musical was presented in two acts.

ACT ONE—"The Forest Rangers" (William Graham, Jerry Melo, Joe Warfield, Arthur Hunt, Ed Riley, Mark Destin), "Little Mary Sunshine" (Eileen Brennan, Jerry Melo, Joe Warfield, Arthur Hunt, Ed Riley, Mark Destin), "Look for a Sky of Blue" (Eileen Brennan, Jerry Melo, Joe Warfield, Arthur Hunt, Ed Riley, Mark Destin), "You're the Fairest Flower" (William Graham), "In Izzenschnooken on the Lovely Essnezook Zee" (Elizabeth Parrish), "Playing Croquet" (Floria Mari, Jana Stuart, Elaine Labour, Rita Howell, Sally Bramlette), "Swinging"/"Playing Croquet" (reprise) (Floria Mari, Jana Stuart, Elaine Labour, Rita Howell, Sally Bramlette), "How Do You Do?" (Jerry Melo, Joe Warfield, Arthur Hunt, Ed Riley, Mark Destin, Floria Mari, Jana Stuart, Elaine Labour, Rita Howell, Sally Bramlette), "Tell a Handsome Stranger" (Sextet) (Jerry Melo and Floria Mari, Joe Warfield and Sally Bramlette, Arthur Hunt and Rita Howell), "Once in a Blue Moon "(John McMartin, Elmarie Wendel), "Colorado Love Call" (William Graham, Eileen Brennan), "Every Little Nothing" (Elizabeth Parrish, Eileen Brennan), "What Has Happened?" (Finale, Act One) ("Tutti")

ACT TWO—"Such a Merry Party" (Elmarie Wendel, Jerry Melo, Joe Warfield, Arthur Hunt, Ed Riley, Mark Destin, Floria Mari, Jana Stuart, Elaine Labour, Rita Howell, Sally Bramlette), "Say 'Uncle'" (Mario Siletti, Floria Mari, Jana Stuart, Elaine Labour, Rita Howell, Sally Bramlette), "The Forest Rangers" (reprise) (Jerry Melo, Joe Warfield, Arthur Hunt, Ed Riley, Mark Destin), "Me, a Heap Big Injun" (John McMartin), "Naughty, Naughty Nancy" (Eileen Brennan, Floria Mari, Jana Stuart, Elaine Labour, Rita Howell, Sally Bramlette), "Mata Hari" (Elmarie Wendel, Floria Mari, Jana Stuart, Elaine Labour, Rita Howell, Sally Bramlette), "Do You Ever Dream of Vienna?" (Elizabeth Parrish, Mario Siletti), "A 'Shell Game'" (John McMartin, Ray James, Elmarie Wendel), "Coo Coo" (Eileen Brennan), "Colorado Love Call" (reprise) (William Graham, Eileen Brennan), Finale, Act II ("Tutti")

NOTES—One of the most successful of all Off Broadway musicals, Rick Besoyan's *Little Mary Sunshine* was a spoof of operettas, specifically those of the *Rose-Marie* (1924) variety. What made it work so well was that the performance never deteriorated into camp. Despite the demented deliriousness of Rick Besoyan's lyrics (when Little Mary is distraught, the very wise Mme. Von Liebedich consoles her with the uplifting "Every Little Nothing," enlightening Little Mary with the knowledge that life is full of precious little nothings, all of which must be treasured every day), the work was performed straight.

Louis Calta in the *New York Times* noted that with the imminent closing of the long-running Off Broadway revival of *The Boy Friend* (see entry), *Little Mary Sunshine* was poised to take its place in the genre of "intimate ... musical caricature." Calta found Besoyan an Off Broadway "threat to Noel Coward," and of the two-dozen songs he said it was difficult to single out the "best of a good lot"; he found all of them "tuneful, genteel and amiable." The evening was "delightful, lively and humorous ... an extremely well done show." The script was published by Samuel French, Inc., in 1960, and also in the December 1960 issue of *Theatre Arts* magazine. The cast album was released by Capitol Records (LP # SWAO-1240; issued on CD by Broadway Angel Records [# ZDM-0777-7-64774-2-8]; and again issued on CD by DRG Records [# 21471-90992]); three numbers were omitted from the recording: "Say 'Uncle,'" "Me, a Heap Big Injun," and "A 'Shell Game.'" The now politically incorrect "Me, a Heap Big Injun" is probably omitted from most revivals (similar to the exclusion of "I'm an Indian, Too" in current revivals of Irving Berlin's *Annie Get Your Gun* [1947]). Inexplicably, for the entire run of the show, "Me, a Heap Big Injun" was identified in programs as "Me, a Heap Big Indian," and so it shared another Irving Berlin connection: "Easter Parade," from the 1933 revue *As Thousands Cheer*, is one of Berlin's most popular songs, and, indeed, it's one of the most enduring in the entire American songbook; and yet the number was always listed in playbills as "Her Easter Bonnet." (See entry for Off Off Broadway revival of *As Thousands Cheer.*)

Little Mary Sunshine opened in London on May 17, 1962, at the Comedy Theatre with Patricia Routledge in the title role. Although the production was a failure and played for only forty-four performances, it was recorded by Pye Records (LP # NPL-18071; later issued on LP by AEI Records [# AEI-1105]; and issued on CD by DRG Records [# 13108]); the recording included "Say 'Uncle'" and "Me, a Heap Big Injun." In the early 1960s, a film version of *Little Mary Sunshine* was announced, but never happened. Then, in the 1970s, there was again talk of a film version because Flip Wilson was interested in playing the title role (!!). It, too, never materialized.

Eileen Brennan later created the role of Irene Molloy in *Hello, Dolly!* (1964) and John McMartin created memorable roles in *Sweet Charity* (1966) and *Follies* (1971). Marian Mercer was one of the actresses who succeeded Eileen Brennan, and she found fleeting fame on Broadway, winning a Tony Award for Best Featured Actress in a Musical (*Promises, Promises* [1968]). William Graham, who created the role of Captain "Big Jim" Warrington, seems to have disappeared from the New York stage after his appearance in *Little Mary Sunshine.*

Unfortunately, Besoyan never again had a stage success. His first and only Broadway musical, *The Student Gypsy*, or *The Prince of Liederkranz* (1963), lasted just sixteen performances. Eileen Brennan was the lead, and four months after the show's closing she was back on Broadway in *Hello, Dolly!*

Besoyan wrote one more musical, Off Broadway's *Babes in the Wood* (see entry), an adaptation of Shakespeare's *A Midsummer Night's Dream.* It opened in 1964, and closed after forty-five performances (the cast included Elmarie Wendel, one of the original cast members of *Little Mary Sunshine*). Besoyan died in 1970.

See entry for *In Your Hat* (1957) regarding the genesis of *Little Mary Sunshine.*

936 The Little Prince (1982; Ada Janik)

NOTES—See entry for *The Little Prince* (2005).

937 The Little Prince (1993; Rick Cummins)

NOTES—See entry for *The Little Prince* (2005).

938 The Little Prince (2005; Rachel Portman). "A Magical Opera." THEATRE: New York State Theatre; OPENING DATE: November 12, 2005; PERFORMANCES: 8; LIBRETTO: Nicholas Wright; MUSIC: Rachel Portman; DIRECTION: Production directed by Francesca Zambello; Stage Direction by Sarah Meyers; CHOREOGRAPHY: Denni Sayers; SCENERY: Maria Bjornson; COSTUMES: Maria Bjornson; LIGHTING: Rick Fisher; MUSICAL DIRECTION: Gerald Steichen; PRODUCER: The New York City Opera

CAST—Graham Phillips (The Little Prince), Stephanie Styles (The Rose), Keith Phares (The Pilot), Joshua Winograde (The King), Hanan Alatter (The Water), Jennifer Tiller (The Fox), Robert Mack (Snake), Andrew Drost (The Drunkard), Richard Byrne (The Businessman)

SOURCE—The 1943 novel *The Little Prince* by Antoine de Saint-Exupery.

The opera was presented in two acts (song assignments unknown).

ACT ONE—"The Pilot," "The Stars," "The Pilot Meets the Prince," "Sunsets," "The Prince's Planet," "The Baobabs," "On My Planet," "The Rose," "The Cranes Are Flying," "The King," "The Vain Man," "The Drunkard," "The Businessman," "The Lamplighter," "We Light Our Lamps"

ACT TWO—"The Snake," "The Rose Garden," "The Hunters," "The Fox," "The Taming," "Here's My Secret," "If We Don't Find a Well," "The Walk to the Well," "The Well," "The Time Has Come," "The Snake Returns," "It Is the Place," "Look at the Stars"

NOTES—The opera *The Little Prince* received its world premiere with the Houston Grand Opera in 2003, and the current production marked is its York premiere.

In her review for the *New York Times*, Anne Midgette found the score "functional" and "pretty," but lacking in "real melodic gift." As for the libretto, she found its "clunky rhymes" gave the large children's chorus too much to do and felt the opera could do with some judicious trimming.

The opera was televised by the BBC on November 27, 2004, and was later seen on public television in the United States. Sony Classical Records released a 2-CD set of the opera (# S2K-93924) as well as a DVD of the television production.

Another musical adaptation of the story is Alan Jay Lerner and Frederick Loewe's unjustly maligned 1974 film version. It offered a sleek, surreal production with fine performances by Richard Kiley, Gene Wilder, and Bob Fosse as well as a memorable score ("I Never Met a Rose," "Closer and Closer," "Snake in the Grass," and the title song).

Yet another lyric version of the work was *The Little Prince and the Aviator*, which closed during Broadway previews in January 1982 (book by Hugh Wheeler, lyrics by Don Black, music by John Barry); future *Rent* performer Anthony Rapp was the Little Prince, and Michael York was the aviator. There were also two Off Off Broadway musical versions of the story, both titled *The Little Prince*. The first opened on December 28, 1982, at the Harold Clurman Theatre and played for five performances (the adaptation was by Ada Janik; Charles Coleman was the Little Prince, and William Parry was the aviator); the second opened on October 6, 1993, at the 28th Street Theatre and transferred to Off Broadway status when it opened at the John Houseman Theatre for a total of seventy-nine performances (lyrics and book by John Scoullar, music by Rick Cummins).

939 Little Shop of Horrors. "A New Musical." THEATRE: Orpheum Theatre; OPENING DATE: July 27, 1982; PERFORMANCES: 2,209; BOOK: Howard Ashman; LYRICS: Howard Ashman; MUSIC: Alan Menken; DIRECTION: Howard Ashman; CHOREOGRAPHY: Edie Cowan; SCENERY: Edward T. Gianfrancesco; COSTUMES: Sally Lesser; PUPPETS: Martin P. Robinson; LIGHTING: Craig Evans; MUSICAL DIRECTION: Robert Billig; PRODUCERS: The WPA Theatre, David Geffen, Cameron Mackintosh, and The Shubert Organization

CAST—Marlene Danielle (Chiffon), Jennifer Leigh Warren (Crystal), Sheila Kay Davis (Ronnette), Hy Anzell (Mushnik), Ellen Greene (Audrey), Lee Wilkof (Seymour), Martin P. Robinson (Derelict), Franc Luz (Orin, Bernstien, Snip, Luce, and Everyone Else); Audrey II (Manipulation by Martin P. Robinson, voice by Ron Taylor)

SOURCE—The 1960 film *The Little Shop of Horrors*, directed by Roger Corman.

The action occurs in Greenwich Village.

The musical was presented in two acts.

ACT ONE—Prologue ("Little Shop of Horrors") (Marlene Danielle, Jennifer Leigh Warren, Sheila Kay Davis), "Skid Row (Downtown)" (Company), "Grow for Me" (Lee Wilkof), "Don't It Go to Show Ya Never Know" (Hy Anzell, Marlene Danielle, Jennifer Leigh Warren, Sheila Kay Davis, Lee Wilkof), "Somewhere That's Green" (Ellen Greene), "Closed for Renovations" (Lee Wilkof, Ellen Greene, Hy Anzell), "Dentist!" (Franc Luz, Marlene Danielle, Jennifer Leigh Warren, Sheila Kay Davis), "Mushnik and Son" (Hy Anzell, Lee Wilkof), "Git It!" (Lee Wilkof, Ron Taylor), "Now (It's Just the Gas)" (Lee Wilkof, Franc Luz)

ACT TWO—"Call Back in the Morning" (Lee Wilkof, Ellen Greene), "Suddenly, Seymour" (Lee Wilkof, Ellen Greene), "Suppertime" (Ron Taylor), "The Meek Shall Inherit" (Company), Finale ("Don't Feed the Plants") (Company)

NOTES—*Little Shop of Horrors*, based on the 1960 cult film *The Little Shop of Horrors*, was a black musical comedy about a man-eating plant (a horticultural Sweeney Todd, according to the *New York Times*) in a Village florist shop. The plant is lovingly nurtured by a nebbishy clerk (Lee Wilkof), who names it Audrey II, after his girlfriend Audrey (Ellen Greene). The problem with Audrey II is that it thrives on only one kind of plant food ... human blood. So Seymour does what he's got to do, and seeks out human victims to satisfy Audrey II's insatiable lust for blood, blood, and more blood. As the evening progresses, Audrey II grows larger and larger, and by the finale has taken over the space of the entire stage. Audrey II is a cross between a plant and a shark, albeit one which speaks jive and sings rhythm-and-blues.

The musical had premiered Off Off Broadway at the WPA Theatre on May 20, and when it opened at the Orpheum three months later, it received rave reviews and settled into a marathon run of over five years. The zany 1960 screenplay was cleverly adapted by Howard Ashman, and his lyrics, along with Alan Menken's catchy score, perfectly complemented the gory goings-on at the wicked little shop of horrors. And, in "Somewhere That's Green," they even managed to find a quiet, touching moment for Audrey, Seymour's hapless, doomed girlfriend.

The script was published by Nelson Doubleday, Inc., in 1982, and the cast album was released by Geffen Records (LP # GHSP-2020). Marlene Danielle had created the role of Chiffon, but on August 10, 1982, two weeks after the Off Broadway opening, Leilani Jones assumed the role, and it is Jones who is heard on the cast album.

The amusing, underrated film version was released by the Geffen Company in 1986 (with Ellen Greene repeating her stage role, as she also did in the London production of the musical) and the soundtrack was released by Geffen Records (LP # GHS-24145). The film included two new songs, "Some Fun Now" and "Mean Green Mother from Outer Space." A laser disc edition of the film included an alternate ending. There have also been many other recordings of the score, including a 1985 Icelandic cast album (HMI Records CD # 108); a 1992 Berlin cast album (*Der Kleine Horror-Laden*) released by Polydor Records (CD # 513547-3); and a 1994 British recording (C & B Records CD # LS94CD01). Two songs cut from the production can be heard in the collection *Lost in Boston IV* (Varese Sarabande CD # VSD-5768).

A Broadway revival in 2002 wasn't successful (it was recorded by DRG Records [CD # 12998]), but the musical nevertheless seems destined for eternal life in smaller venues, such as college and community theatre.

940 The Little Show and Friends. "The Intimate Revues of Dietz & Schwartz." THEATRE: All Soul's Church Theatre; OPENING DATE: April 24, 1987; PERFORMANCES: 15; SKETCHES: Howard Dietz and Charles Sherman, Moss Hart, George S. Kaufman, George S. Kaufman and Howard Dietz, William Miles and Donald Blackwell; LYRICS: Howard Dietz; MUSIC: Arthur Schwartz; DIRECTION: David McNitt; CHOREOGRAPHY: Linda Panzer; COSTUMES: Virginia Wood; LIGHTING: David Bean; MUSICAL DIRECTION: Joyce Hitchcock and David Lahm; PRODUCER: Tran William Rhodes

CAST—Patricia Berg, Jim Bumgardner, John Corker, Beth Crook, Siobhan Fallon, Nathan Gibson, Clay Guthrie, Marion Markham, Jeff Paul, Jeff Shonert, John Sullivan, Alphie Thorn, Ellen Zachos, Madeline Zeiberg

The revue was presented in two acts (division of acts and sketch and song assignments unknown; sketches and songs are listed in performance order).

SKETCHES AND SONGS—"It Better Be Good" (from *The Band Wagon*, 1931), Prologue to *The Little Show* (sketch writer unknown), "Right at the Start of It" (*Three's a Crowd*, 1930), "New Sun in the Sky" (*The Band Wagon*, 1931), "Alone Together" (*Flying Colors*, 1932), "The Pride of the Claghornes" (*The Band Wagon*, 1931; sketch by George S. Kaufman and Howard Dietz), "I See Your Face Before Me" (*Between the Devil*, 1937), "Confession" (*The Band Wagon*, 1931), "Thief in the Night" (*At Home Abroad*, 1935), "Better Luck Next Time" (source unknown), "Don't Go Away, Monsieur" (*Between the Devil*, 1937), "Something to Remember You By" (*Three's a Crowd*, 1930), "On the American Plan" (*Flying Colors*, 1932; sketch by George S. Kaufman and Howard Dietz), "Triplets" (*Between the Devil*, 1937; for background information concerning this song, see notes in entry for *That's Entertainment*), "Hoops" (*The Band Wagon*, 1931), "Lucky Seven" (*The Second Little Show*, 1930), "I Love Louisa" (*The Band Wagon*, 1931), "Haunted Heart" (*Inside U.S.A.*, 1948), "First Prize at the Fair" (*Inside U.S.A.*, 1948), "Blue Grass (of Kentucky)" (*Inside U.S.A.*, 1948), "Miserable with You" (*The Band Wagon*, 1931), "In Marbled Halls" (*Three's a Crowd*, 1930; sketch by William Miles and Donald Blackwell), "Smokin' Reefers" (*Flying Colors*, 1932), "I Guess I'll Have to Change My Plan" (*The Little Show*, 1929), "Lost in a Crowd" (source unknown), "Mother Told Me So" (*Flying Colors*, 1932), "By Myself" (*Between the Devil*, 1937), "The Still Alarm" (*The Little Show*, 1929; sketch by George S. Kaufman), "A Shine on Your Shoes" (*Flying Colors*, 1932), "Sing a Lament" (source unknown), "High and Low" (*The Band Wagon*, 1931), "Dancing in the Dark" (*The Band Wagon*, 1931), "Right at the End of It" (*Three's a Crowd*, 1930), "That's Entertainment" (1953 film *The Band Wagon*)

NOTES—Although subtitled "The Intimate Revues of Dietz & Schwartz," the Off Off Broadway revue *The Little Show and Friends* included songs from the team's book musicals as well as from the 1953 film *The Band Wagon*.

For other tributes to Dietz and Schwartz, see entries for *Dancing in the Dark* and *That's Entertainment*.

941 Little Women. THEATRE: New York State Theatre; OPENING DATE: March 23, 2003; PERFORMANCES: 5; LIBRETTO: Mark Adamo; MUSIC: Mark Adamo; DIRECTION: Rhoda Levine; SCENERY: Peter Harrison; COSTUMES: Paul Tazewell; LIGHTING: Amy Appleyard; MUSICAL DIRECTION: George Manahan; PRODUCER: The New York City Opera

CAST—Julianne Borg (Beth), Caroline Worra (Amy), Jennifer Dudley (Jo), Jennifer Rivera (Meg), Gwendolyn Jones (Alma), Chad Shelton (Laurie), Jake Gardner (Gideon), Charles Robert Stephens (Fredrich Bhaer), Daniel Belcher (John Brooke), Voices

SOURCE—The 1868 novel *Little Women* by Louisa May Alcott.

The opera was presented in two acts.

ACT ONE—"Four Little Chests All in a Row" (Voices), "Laurie!—The Very Same, Madam" (Jennifer Dudley), "Couldn't I Un-Bake the Breads"

(Jennifer Dudley), "Barristers! It's Quarter Past!" (Jennifer Dudley), "Again We Meet to Celebrate" (All, Voices), "Socks!" (Jennifer Dudley), "Supper, Half an Hour!" (Gwendolyn Jones), "Madness. No. Mania. No." (Jennifer Dudley), "Rigmarole? It's Another Game" (Daniel Belcher), "There Was a Knight, Once" (Daniel Belcher), "Oh, This Cannot Be Borne" (Jennifer Dudley), "She That Is Down Need Fear No Fall" (Julianne Borg), "Our Own Fanny Mendelssohn!" (Caroline Worra), "Mr. John Brooke, Laurie's Tutor" (Jennifer Rivera), "Long May Our Comrades Prosper Well" (Voices), "Things Change, Jo" (Jennifer Rivera), "I Understand. You're Leaving Us" (Jennifer Dudley), "Aunt? Now, I Haven't Done Any Shading Yet" (Caroline Worra), "We Stand Together on This Old—" (Gwendolyn Jones), "Jupiter Ammon! The Poetry!" (Chad Shelton), "We Stand Together on This Old/New Day" (Jennifer Rivera, Daniel Belcher, Gwendolyn Jones, Jake Gardner), "Don't Dare Suggest It, Laurie" (Jennifer Dudley)

ACT TWO—"Cockling? Cackling" ('Mr. Dashwood'), "Drizzling in New York" (Jennifer Dudley), "But That's Why I Loved It! So Lurid and Preposterous" (Jennifer Dudley), "Kennst du das Land, wo die Zitronen Bluhn?" (Charles Robert Stephens), "Do You Know the Land Where the Lemon Trees Bloom" (Charles Robert Stephens), "It's Lovely. My Father Swears by Him" (Jennifer Dudley), "She's Asked for You" (Jake Gardner), "Have Peace Jo" (Julianne Borg), "She Who Is Down Need Fear No Fall" (reprise) (Voices), "That's the Problem with Solitaire; You Always Need a King" ('Cecilia'), "My. Joy Beyond Measure, Mother!" (Jennifer Dudley), "She Sounds Very Happy. I Hope Laurie Feels the Same" (Jennifer Dudley), "You, Alone; A Mansion of Stone" ('Cecilia'), "So the Days Go By, and the Summers Fly" (Jennifer Dudley), "Let Me Look at You" (Jennifer Dudley)

NOTES—Mark Adamo's operatic version of *Little Women* was first seen in a 1998 workshop production by the Opera Studio of the Houston Grand Opera, and in 2000 the final version premiered in the company's main theatre. In his review of the New York premiere for the *New York Times*, John Rockwell noted that within three years the new opera had received thirteen productions by twenty different companies.

Rockwell was enthusiastic about the work; he praised the "amazing sureness" of the libretto, which was written in rhymed couplets of "seemingly effortless naturalness," and he found that the score mixed modernism and tonal lyricism into an effective blend which ensured that "nearly all the big moments in the opera work." He urged his readers to see the opera, which was "some sort of masterpiece."

The opera was seen on public television on August 29, 2001, and was recorded on a 2-CD set by Ondine Records (# ODE-988-2D); the list of song sequences is taken from the recording.

For information about other lyric works based on *Little Women*, see entry for *Jo*.

942 The Littlest Revue. THEATRE: Phoenix Theatre; OPENING DATE: May 22, 1956; PERFORMANCES: 32; SKETCHES: Nat Hiken and Billy Friedberg, Eudora Welty, Mike (Michael) Stewart, George Baxt, Bud McCreery, Alan Manings and Bob Van Scoyk; LYRICS: Mostly by Ogden Nash; MUSIC: Mostly by Vernon Duke; ADDITIONAL MUSIC AND LYRICS: John LaTouche, Sheldon Harnick, Lee Adams, Charles Strouse, John Strauss, Sammy Cahn, and Michael Brown; DIRECTION: Paul Lammers; CHOREOGRAPHY: Charles Weidman; SCENERY: Klaus Holm; COSTUMES: Alvin Colt

Musical Director: Will Irwin; PRODUCERS: Phoenix Theatre (T. Edward Hambleton and Norris Houghton) by arrangement with Ben Bagley ("Conceived, Cast and Assembled by Ben Bagley")

CAST—Beverley Bozeman, Joel Grey, Tammy Grimes, Dorothy Jarnac, George Marcy, Tommy Morton, Charlotte Rae, Larry Storch

The revue was presented in two acts.

ACT ONE—Opening Number ("The Littlest Revue") (lyric by John LaTouche and Kenward Elmslie, music by John Strauss) (Company), "Credit Is Due" (sketch by Allan Manings and Bob Van Scoyk) (Joel Grey) "Good Little Girls" (lyric by Sammy Cahn, music by Vernon Duke (Beverley Bozeman, Tommy Morton, George Marcy) "Give My Regards to Mott St." (sketch by Mike Stewart) (Charlotte Rae, Larry Storch, Tammy Grimes) "Second Avenue and 12th Street Rag" (lyric by Ogden Nash, music by Vernon Duke) (George Marcy, Dorothy Jarnac, Beverley Bozeman, Tommy Morton) "The Shape of Things" (lyric and music by Sheldon Harnick) (Charlotte Rae) "Madly in Love" (lyric by Ogden Nash, music by Vernon Duke) (Tammy Grimes), "Two Cents Worth of Plain" (sketch by Mike Stewart) (Joel Grey, Tommy Morton, Beverley Bozeman, Charlotte Rae), "I Lost the Rhythm" (music by Charles Strouse) (Joel Grey) "Game of Dance" (choreography by Danny Daniels; music by Sol Berkowitz; dialogue by Don Meyer) (George Marcy, Beverley Bozeman, Tommy Morton) "Diet" (sketch by Bud McCreery) (Charlotte Rae) "Vignette" (sketch by George Baxt) (Larry Storch, Tammy Grimes) "Third Avenue El" (lyric and music by Michael Brown) (Tommy Morton) "The Power of Negative Thinking" (sketch by Bud McCreery) (Company)

ACT TWO—"Fly Now, Pay Later" (lyric by Ogden Nash, music by Vernon Duke) (Tommy Morton, Dorothy Jarnac, George Marcy, Beverley Bozeman) "Beyond Reproach" (sketch by Allan Manings and Bob Van Scoyk) (Tammy Grimes, Larry Storch, Joel Grey, Charlotte Rae), "A Little Love, A Little Money—I" (Tommy Morton, George Marcy) "Far from Wonderful" (a/k/a "You're Far from Wonderful") (lyric by Ogden Nash, music by Vernon Duke) (Joel Grey, Dorothy Jarnac) "Bye-Bye Brevoort" (sketch by Eudora Welty) (George Marcy, Charlotte Rae, Tammy Grimes, Beverley Bozeman, Larry Storch, Tommy Morton, George Marcy), "Born Too Late" (lyric by Ogden Nash, music by Vernon Duke) (Tommy Morton) "Spring Doth Let Her Colours Fly" (lyric by Lee Adams, music by Charles Strouse) (Charlotte Rae, Mary Harmon, Beverley Bozeman, Tommy Morton, George Marcy) "The Man in the Gray Flannel Space Suit" (sketch by Allan Manings and Bob Van Scoyk) (Larry Storch) "Opus 9" (dance) (music by Edward Sauter) (Dorothy Jarnac) "Sumer Is Icumen In" (lyric by John LaTouche, music by Vernon Duke) (Charlotte Rae), "A Little Love, A Little Money—II" (Tommy Morton, George Marcy) "East Is East" (sketch by Nat Hiken and Billy Friedberg) (Tammy Grimes, George Marcy, Tommy Morton, Dorothy Jarnac, Mary Harmon, Joel Grey, Larry Storch, Charlotte Rae) "Love Is Still in Town" (lyric by Ogden Nash, music by Vernon Duke) (George Marcy, Dorothy Jarnac, Beverley Bozeman) "I'm Glad I'm Not a Man" (lyric by Ogden Nash, music by Vernon Duke) (Tammy Grimes) Finale (Company)

NOTES—Brooks Atkinson in the *New York Times* praised *The Littlest Revue*, noting it had "a uniformly high standard of intelligence and humor."

The revue offered mostly new songs and sketches, but a few had been written for other musicals.

According to Ken Bloom, "Good Little Girls" was originally written for, but not used in, the film *April in Paris*, which was released in 1953. Previously, it had been considered for the Broadway revue *Two's Company* 1952), but wasn't used.

"Third Avenue El" had first been heard two months earlier, in *Four Below* (see entry), and was later used in *Demi-Dozen* (1958; see entry). The song appears on the cast albums of both *The Littlest Revue* and *Demi-Dozen*.

"Born Too Late" was written for, but not used in, *Sweet Bye and Bye* (1946), which closed during its pre-Broadway tryout.

As "Summer Is a Comin' In," "Sumer Is Icumen In" was originally introduced by The Martins and the Ensemble in the three-performance Broadway flop *The Lady Comes Across* (1942). Atkinson found the number a "mischievous parody" which was performed by Charlotte Rae "with a spurious elegance that is also funny."

By all accounts, the highlight of the revue was "Spring Doth Let Her Colours Fly," Rae's devastating impersonation of opera singer Helen Traubel's Las Vegas night club act. Atkinson noted it was the "best staged sketch" of the evening.

Atkinson also singled out a "wry and enjoyable" sketch about the demolition of the Hotel Brevoort (written by Eudora Welty); a sketch about Noel Coward trying to clean up one of his plays for a television adaptation; and a "little gem" about dieting ("Diet"). Other songs and sketches kidded the space age, the State Department, Harry Belafonte, Norman Vincent Peale, and the recent film version of the play *Anastasia*.

During the run of the revue, "A Little Love, A Little Money" (Parts I and II) were deleted, and "I'm Glad I'm Not a Man" was moved to an earlier spot in the second act in order to replace Part I of "A Little Love." Added to the production during its run was the song "Modest Maid (I Love Lechery)," a number written by Marc Blitzstein which had been intended for Beatrice Lillie (who never performed it). It was sung by Charlotte Rae, and it may have been inserted into the second act, to replace the Part II sequence of "A Little Love." Rae had previously performed the song in her nightclub act at the Blue Angel, and she later recorded it on her 1955 Vanguard Records solo album.

Also added to the production was the song "Backer's Audition" (lyric by John LaTouche and Kenward Elmslie, music by John Strauss).

Eudora Welty's sketch "Bye-Bye Brevoort" was published in 1980 by Palaemon Press in a limited edition of 476 copies.

The cast album was originally released by Epic Records (LP # 3275), which was later reissued by Painted Smiles Records (LP # PS-1361); a CD was issued by Painted Smiles Records (# PSCD-112) and included two bonus tracks (rehearsal versions of "Second Avenue and 12th Street Rag" and "A Little Love, A Little Money").

943 Livin' Dolls. THEATRE: UpStage/Manhattan Theatre Club; OPENING DATE: March 9, 1982; PERFORMANCES: 56; BOOK: Scott Wittman and Marc Shaiman; LYRICS: Scott Wittman and Marc Shaiman; MUSIC: Scott Wittman and Marc Shaiman; DIRECTION: Richard Maltby, Jr.; CHOREOGRAPHY: Scott Wittman and Richard Maltby, Jr.; SCENERY: John Lee Beatty; COSTUMES: Timothy Dunleavy; LIGHTING: Pat Collins; MUSICAL DIRECTION: Marc Shaiman; PRODUCER: Manhattan Theatre Club (Lynne Meadow, Artistic Director; Barry Grove, Managing Director)

CAST—Linda Hart (Babe), Zora Rasmussen (Blabby Betty), Deborah Van Valkenburgh (Candi), Lisa Embs (Fifi), Kim Milford (Poindexter), James Rich (Paul), Tom Wiggin (Rip Curl)

The action occurs during a fabulous two-week vacation in Hawaii.

The musical was presented in two acts (division of acts and song assignments unknown [the program didn't list musical numbers]; songs are listed in performance order).

MUSICAL NUMBERS—"Waiting for Our Wave," "Love Come A-Callin'," "Girls," "A Livin' Doll," "Nobody's Valentine," "Lifesaver," "Down in the Sand," "Something Special," "Poindexter's Lament," "Round About Midnight," "Wipeout at Panic

Point," "There's a Girl," "Lost in Space," "G.I. Joe," "No Questions Asked," Finale

NOTES—Marc Shaiman and Scott Wittman's Off Off Broadway musical *Livin' Dolls* was, according to its flyer, "inspired by the beach blanket movies of the sixties. Fun, sun and surfing! Don't forget to bring your reflector." The plot dealt with three teenaged girls who vacation in Waikiki to find boyfriends. Frank Rich in the *New York Times* noted the musical was a "fastidious" re-creation of the films it spoofed, finding time to depict the ins and outs of summer romance as well as "to dance the twist or apotheosize the perfect wave." Rich liked the score, but felt that perhaps the book was too "slavish" to its film sources (there were "hair-splitting nuances" of each and every variation to be found in the clichés of the beach-blanket film genre). Rich praised John Lee Beatty's set, a large beach hamper which opened to depict both comic-book renderings of various resorts as well as two-dimensional cardboard cut-outs of hair dryers, soda bottles, and waves.

Livin' Dolls didn't go anywhere, but twenty years later Scott Wittman and Marc Shaiman hit the jackpot with *Hairspray* (2002), another musical set during the same era. (The burning question of our time: Was Rip Curl, a character in *Livin' Dolls*, Shaiman and Wittman's muse during the writing of *Hairspray*?)

944 Livin' the Life. "A New Musical." THEATRE: Phoenix Theatre; OPENING DATE: April 27, 1957; PERFORMANCES: 25; BOOK: Dale Wasserman and Bruce Geller; LYRICS: Bruce Geller; MUSIC: Jack Urbont; dance music by Genevieve Pitot; DIRECTION: David Alexander; CHOREOGRAPHY: John Butler; SCENERY: William and Jean Eckart; COSTUMES: Alvin Colt; LIGHTING: Klaus Holm; MUSICAL DIRECTION: Anton Coppola; PRODUCERS: The Phoenix Theatre (T. Edward Hambleton and Norris Houghton)

CAST—Francis Barnard (Marshall Rogers), Jack De Lon (Judge Thatcher), Earl Hammond (Mr. Dobbins), Dean Michener (Captain Mumford), Marijane Maricle (Emmy Harper), STEPHEN ELLIOTT (Muff Potter), LEE CHARLES (Jim), RONALD ROGERS (Doc Robinson), ALICE GHOSTLEY (Aunt Polly), JAMES MITCHELL (Injun Joe), RICHARD IDE (Huckleberry Finn), TIMMY EVERETT (Tom Sawyer), PATSY BRUDER (Becky Thatcher), LEE BECKER (Amy Lawrence), LOREN HIGHTOWER (Alfred Noble), Tom Hasson (Joe Harper), Kevin Carlisle (Ben Rogers), George Liker (Jeff Hollis), Edward Villella (Bill Anders), Joan Bowman (Susy Harper), Julie Oser (Mary Austin), Rettadel Tupper (Gracie Miller), Paula Waring (Jennie Daniels), Charles Queenan (George), Joe Nash (Clem), Irving Barnes (Frank), James Hawthorne-Bey (Zeke), Ida Johnson (Roxy), Audrey Vanterpool (Hannah), Jacqueline Walcott (Annie Lou), Fred Jones (Sam Harper), Doris Okerson (Emily Noble), Marvin Gordon (Andy Douglas), Annette Warren (Lila Hollis), Joyce Carroll (Nancy Rogers), Tod Jackson (Prosecutor), Dean Michener (Henry Liggett), Sylvia Dick (Adele Sims), Doris Greb (Freda Walters), Ronald Rogers (Captain Leather)

SOURCES—"Based on Mark Twain's Mississippi River Stories"; specifically, *The Adventures of Tom Sawyer* (1876) and *The Adventures of Huckleberry Finn* (1884), with an emphasis on the former. Some aspects of the musical may have also been based on Twain's *Life on the Mississippi* stories (1883).

The action occurs in and around Hannibal, Missouri, about 1850.

The musical was presented in two acts.

ACT ONE—"River Ballad" (Townspeople), "Someone" (Lee Charles, Alice Ghostley), "Whiskey Bug" (Stephen Elliott), "Livin' the Life" (Timmy Everett, Richard Ide), "Steamboat" (Timmy Everett, Richard Ide, Stephen Elliott, Lee Charles), "Take Kids" (Alice Ghostley, Marijane Maricle, Doris Okerson, Annette Warren, Joyce Carroll, "Mock Battle" (Timmy Everett, Lee Becker, Loren Hightower, Boys and Girls of the Town), "Probably in Love" (Timmy Everett), "Sunday Promenade" (Townspeople), "Don't Tell Me" (Alice Ghostley), "All of 'Em Say" (Timmy Everett, Patsy Bruder), "Late Love" (Alice Ghostley, Stephen Elliott)

ACT TWO—"Jim's Lament" (Lee Charles), "Ain't It a Shame" (Townspeople), "Supersational Day" (Minstrels and Townspeople), "Late Love" (reprise) (Alice Ghostley), "Ain't It a Shame" (reprise) (Townspeople), "Nightmare Ballet" (Timmy Everett, James Mitchell, Dancers), "MacDougal's Cave" (Townspeople), "River Ballad" (reprise) (Townspeople), Finale (Company)

NOTES—*Livin' the Life* was one of many stage, film, and television musical adaptations of Twain's *The Adventures of Tom Sawyer* and *The Adventures of Huckleberry Finn*; as of this writing, all but one (*Big River* [1985]), have met with failure and indifference (from the out-of-town closing of *Huckleberry Finn* [1902] to the recent 2001 Broadway adaptation, *The Adventures of Tom* Sawyer, which lasted only twenty-one performances).

Even when a revised version of *Livin' the Life* surfaced in regional theater in 1981, it was quickly forgotten. Re-titled *Great Big River (By the Mississippi)*, the new book was credited to Dale Wasserman (sans Bruce Geller, who had died in an airplane crash in 1978). New lyrics for *Great Big River* were written by Mike Colby, and other lyrics were credited to both Geller and Colby.

The musical numbers for *Great Big River* are as follows (* indicates lyric by Mike Colby; ** indicates lyric by both Geller and Colby; *** indicates lyric by Geller only):

ACT ONE—"By the Mississippi" (*), "Whiskey Bug" (**), "Someone," "Livin' the Life," "Steamboat," "Whiskey Bug" (Reprise), "'Tis Saturday," "Probably in Love," "Warts," "Take Kids" (**), "All of 'Em Say" (**), "Better Late Than Never" (*), "Finale Act I" (*);

ACT TWO—"Muff's Lament," "Someone" (Reprise), "Ain't It a Shame," "As Long As I'm with You" (*), "As Long As We're with You" (**), "McDougal's Cave," "Finale" (**).

Livin' the Life received a generally cool reception by the New York critics, and their lack of enthusiasm put the kibosh on the chance for a Broadway transfer. But they were in agreement about John Butler's exciting choreography, and praised "Nightmare Ballet" ("wonderfully inventive," according to John McClain in the *New York Journal-American*, and "inventive and attractive," according to Walter Kerr in the *New York Herald Tribune*) and "Supersational Day" (Kerr called it a "rollicking" cakewalk, and Richard Watts, Jr., in the *New York Post* found it "gay and invigorating"). But opinions differed on Alice Ghostley's ballad "Late Love"; McClain found it "first class," but Tom Donnelly in the *New York World-Telegram* called it "dreary." Overall, the score didn't impress the critics, with Kerr pronouncing it "somewhat nervous and fragmentary," and Brooks Atkinson in the *New York Times* finding it "thin and diffuse." Timmy Everett, who played the leading role of Tom Sawyer in *Livin' the Life*, is perhaps best remembered for his portrayal of Tommy Djilas in the film version of *The Music Man* (1962).

After *Livin' the Life*, Gelber and Urbont collaborated on one more Off Broadway musical, the charming *All in Love* (1961; see entry).

For the record, besides the five above-mentioned *Tom Sawyer/Huckleberry Finn* musicals, there have been at least twelve others: *Huck Finn*, a 1954 musical produced at Catholic University in Washington, D.C. (book, lyrics, and music by George Herman); Tom *Sawyer*, a 1956 television adaptation presented on the *U.S. Steel Hour*; two British versions (*Tom Sawyer* [1960] and *Huckleberry Finn* [1978]), neither of which played the West End; *Tom Sawyer*, a children's musical, premiered at the Goodman School of Drama's Children's Theatre at the Goodman Theatre in Chicago on October 18, 1975, for thirty three performances (the book and lyrics were by Sarah Marie Schlesinger and the music was by Michael Dansicker); another musical for children, *The Adventures of Tom Sawyer*, opened at the Magic Turtle Children's Theatre at the Dallas Theatre Center on April 8, 1978, for seven performances (the book, lyrics, and music were by Sam L. Rosen); *Huck and Jim on the Mississippi*, a regional theatre production which was seen in 1983; and a 1985 Off Off Broadway adaptation of *Huckleberry Finn* (*Downriver*; see entry). Moreover, there were also two unfinished adaptations, both titled *Huckleberry Finn*. The first was a proposed film musical to be produced by MGM. According to Hugh Fordin's *The Movies' Greatest Musicals*, the first adaptation was written in 1945, with a screenplay by Sally Benson and songs by Hugh Martin and Ralph Blane as well as by Harry Warren and Ralph Blane; a second treatment was drafted in 1950 by Donald Ogden Stewart; and a third treatment was written in 1951, with screenplay and lyrics by Alan Jay Lerner and music by Burton Lane (apparently some songs from the last treatment surfaced in the 1960 film *The Adventures of Huckleberry Finn*). The second adaptation had music by Kurt Weill and book and lyrics by Maxwell Anderson; because of Weill's death, the musical wasn't completed, but it was nonetheless adapted into a German television musical in the 1960s (the cast included Randolph Symonette, who played Huck's father). Also see entry for the Off Off Broadway musical *Lightin' Out*, which dealt with both Mark Twain's life and his fictional characters.

945 Living Color. "A Twisted Mnemonic Entertainment." THEATRE: Don't Tell Mama; OPENING DATE: March 18, 1986; PERFORMANCES: 32; LYRICS: Scott Warrender; MUSIC: Scott Warrender; DIRECTION: Susan Stroman; SCENERY: Gregory W. Galway; COSTUMES: Robert DeMora; MUSICAL DIRECTION: Brad Garside; PRODUCER: Pendleton Productions

CAST—Davis Gaines, Jason Graae, Nancy Johnston, Faith Prince

The revue appears to have been presented in one act (song assignments unknown; songs are listed in performance order).

MUSICAL NUMBERS—"Living Color," "Life Is Funny," "Reruns," "Parakeet Counselor by Day—Nightingale by Night," "Bobby Bear," "Texas Chainsaw Manicurist," "Asia Avenue," "Spirograph," "I Will See You," "Make It in L.A.," "Young Americans," "Candy Bar," "That Girl," "Mr. Potato Head," "Love for Four," "My Barbie Was the Tramp of the Neighborhood," "Waiting Game"

NOTES—The short-running Off Off Broadway revue *Living Color* included such amusing-sounding numbers as "Texas Chainsaw Manicurist" and "My Barbie Was the Tramp of the Neighborhood." But Stephen Holden in the *New York Times* found the evening generally "sour" in its depiction of self-obsessed baby boomers. He noted the revue's lowest point was a sequence ("Waiting Game") in which the performers offered up "glum, clichéd monologues" about being single, but he praised "Young Americans," a spoof of "Up with People" and the only number in the revue with "satirical bite." The revue also used television as the basic reference point for the boomers; one sequence ("That Girl") dwelt upon a woman's fantasy of being the roommate of the Marlo Thomas character on the popular television series, and another number ("Love for Four") offered a look at the loves of four television couples (Lucy and Desi, Ozzie and Harriet, etc.). Many names associated with *Living Color* would soon become familiar to New York audiences (Susan Stroman, Faith Prince, Davis Gaines, and Jason Graae).

946 The Living Premise. THEATRE: The Premise; OPENING DATE: June 13, 1963; PERFORMANCES: 163 (estimated); DIRECTION: Theodore J. Flicker and Joan Darling; SCENERY: David Moon; PRODUCER: Theodore J. Flicker

CAST—Calvin Ander, Godfrey Cambridge, Al Freeman, Jr., Jo Ann LeCompte, Diana Sands

NOTES—This edition of *The Premise* (see entry for the original edition) dealt with racial discrimination, and was performed by a cast of three Blacks and two Whites.

Richard F. Shepard in the *New York Times* found the revue "merciless, sharp and furiously funny," and noted the evening skewered White racists, Black Muslims, "lip service" liberals, and the "particularly shrill type of Negrophile" who doesn't really like Negroes but nonetheless fawns upon them. A program note stated that the majority of scenes in *The Living Premise* were created by the cast during the rehearsal period and were performed before an audience as if the scenes were based on a written script. The program also noted that a few scenes would be "spot improvisations," that is, scenes invented on the spot by the cast from suggestions by the audience.

See entry for *The New Show at the Premise* regarding the number of performances given by that revue and by *The Living Premise.* Also, see entry for the final revue in the series (*The Third Ear*).

947 Lizzie Borden. "A Family Portrait in Three Acts." THEATRE: New York City Center; OPENING DATE: March 25, 1965; PERFORMANCES: 2; LIBRETTO: Kenward Elmslie (based on a scenario by Richard Plant); MUSIC: Jack Beeson; DIRECTION: Nikos Psacharopoulos; SCENERY: Peter Wexler; COSTUMES: Patton Campbell; MUSICAL DIRECTION: Anton Coppola; PRODUCER: The New York City Opera (Julius Rudel, General Director)

CAST—Herbert Beatty (Andrew Borden), Ellen Faull (Abigail Borden), Brenda Lewis (Elizabeth [Lizzie] Andrew Borden), Ann Elgar (Margret Borden), Richard Krause (the Reverend Harrington), Richard Fredricks (Captain Jason MacFarlane); and a chorus of children and young people

SOURCE—A scenario by Richard Plant.

The action occurs in Fall River, Massachusetts, in 1892.

The opera was presented in three acts.

ACT ONE—Prelude (Orchestra), "Tolling Early in the Morning" (Children), "It Is Almost Finished"/"Lizzie" (Herbert Beatty, Brenda Lewis), "Andrew's Aria" (Herbert Beatty), "Margret's Garden Aria" (Ann Elgar), "The House Watches" (Ann Elgar)

ACT TWO—Prelude to Act II/"Abbie's Bird Song" (Ellen Faull), "Unpleasantries and Introductions" (Herbert Beatty, Brenda Lewis, Ellen Faull, Richard Krause, Richard Fredricks), "Two Quintets" (Company), "More Unpleasantness" (Company), "What Am I Forbidden Now?" (Brenda Lewis), "Lizzie's Mad Scene" (Brenda Lewis)

ACT THREE—Act III, Scene I Sequence (Herbert Beatty, Ann Elgar, Ellen Faull, Brenda Lewis, Richard Fredricks), "Jason's Song"/"Duet"/"Trio" (Richard Fredricks, Ann Elgar, Brenda Lewis), "Lizzie's Dressing Scene" (Brenda Lewis), "Bravo!" (Ellen Faull)/"The Bitch Scene" (Ellen Faull, Brenda Lewis), "Kill Time"/Scene/"Murder" (Brenda Lewis, Richard Fredricks, Herbert Beatty), "Seduction Scene" (Herbert Beatty, Brenda Lewis), "Second Murder Interlude" (Orchestra), Epilogue (Brenda Lewis, Richard Krause, Children)

NOTES—The story of Lizzie Borden (1860-1927) has taken on the patina of legend; it's one of those tales which seems more apocryphal than real. But the events actually occurred, and the two murders on that summer day in 1892 have taken on a mythic quality which has been told in novels, films, plays, ballet, and musical adaptations.

The recording by Desto Records (on a 3-LP set; # DST-6455/6/7) reveals a powerful psychological chamber opera (the recording was later issued on 2-CD set by Composers Recordings, Inc./CRI [# CRI-694], and the song list is taken from that recording). Many works about Lizzie Borden have left open the question of her guilt or innocence. But Jack Beeson and Kenward Elmslie's opera doesn't equivocate: she definitely dunnit.

While Howard Klein in the *New York Times* had certain reservations about the score ("no clear personality," but he singled out "a lively ballad ... close to Gay Nineties operetta" ["Abby's Bird Song"] and "perky" rhythms of the "hoe-down variety"), he nonetheless found the evening "gripping theatre" and felt the opera was "well worth investigating."

For a while, it seemed as though the opera had all but vanished. But a revival by Glimmerglass Opera in 1996 led *New York Times*' critic Anthony Tommasini to write that Beeson was a "true theatre composer" whose music surged "in waves of highly charged, heavily chromatic, at times atonal Expressionistic music" which at the same time evoked hymn-like tunes and Victorian parlor music. When the work was revived in 1999 by the New York City Opera, Peter G. Davis in *New York* said it was perhaps time to consider *Lizzie Borden* as a permanent part of the American operatic repertory; he praised Beeson for his flair in creating character, story, and atmosphere.

The City Opera revival was seen on public television on March 24, 1999.

"Harvest Parlor Game" (part of the overall "Two Quintets" sequence) was heard in the 2005 revue *Lingoland* (see entry) and was recorded for that show's cast album.

On September 9, 1994, another musical about the subject, also called *Lizzie Borden*, played Off Off Broadway at the Here Theatre; the lyrics and music were by Steven Cheslik-DeMeyer. In 2009, Off Off Broadway saw a revised version of this musical.

Another lyric work, also called *Lizzie Borden*, premiered on October 31, 1998, at the American Stage Company in New Jersey; its score was released on CD in 1999 by Original Cast Records (# OC-9913); Alison Frazer was Lizzie, the lyrics were by Christopher McGovern and Amy Powers, and the music by Christopher McGovern.

948 Lola. "A Musical." THEATRE: The Church of the Heavenly Rest/The York Theatre Company; OPENING DATE: March 24, 1982; PERFORMANCES: 20; BOOK: Kenward Elmslie; LYRICS: Kenward Elmslie; MUSIC: Claibe Richardson; DIRECTION: John Going; CHOREOGRAPHY: David Holdgreiwe; SCENERY: James Morgan; COSTUMES: William Schroder; LIGHTING: David Gotwald; MUSICAL DIRECTION: David Bishop; PRODUCER: The York Theatre Company (Janet Hayes Walker, Artistic Director)

CAST—*Cast in the Present*—Jane White (Lola Montez, Lizette in *The Princess of Herzogovinia*), Robert Stillman (Shosho), Tom Flagg (Fernando), Bud Nease (Augustus Follin), John Foster (Old King Zog in *The Princess of Herzogovinia*), Kevin Gray (Prince Zachary in *The Princess of Herzogovinia*), Jack Dabdoub (Johnny Southwick), The Forty-Niners (Michael Brogran, John Foster, Sean McGuirk, Shaver Tillitt), The Dandies (Kevin Gray, Joseph Giuffre, Marshall Hagins, Patrick Parker); *Cast in Lola Montez' Memories and Fantasies*—Gretchen Albrecht (Lola), Leigh Beery (Lola Lola), Jack Dabdoub (King Ludwig I of Bavaria), Bud Nease (Dujarier), Tom Flagg (Russian Viceroy), Michael Brogan (General Lipsky), Tom Flagg (Prime Minister), Lola's Mazurka Admirers, Polish Revolutionaries, Bavarian Cabinet, Bavarian Guards, and The Lolaland Lolas (Michael Brogan, John Foster, Joseph Giuffre, Kevin Gray, Marshall Hagins, Sean McGuirk, Patrick Parker, Shaver Tillitt) The action occurs in Lola's salon in Grass Valley, California, in 1850, as well as in various locales in Lola's memories and fantasies.

The musical was presented in two acts.

ACT ONE—"The Healing Chant (I)" (Robert Stillman), "Abandoned" (Jane White), "Little Old Lady in Black" (Jane White, Leigh Beery), "Spanish Mazurka" (Jane White, Gretchen Albrecht, Leigh Beery, Jack Dabdoub, Bud Nease, Lola's Admirers), "Mirrors and Shadows" (Bud Nease), "Shuffle the Cards" (Leigh Berry, Gretchen Albrecht, Jane White), "Another Soiree" (The Forty-Niners, The Dandies, Tom Flagg, Robert Stillman), "The Princess of Herzogovinia" (Kevin Gray, John Foster, Jane White), "A New Life" (Leigh Beery, The Polish Revolutionaries, Bud Nease, Michael Brogan, Tom Flagg), "Staying In" (Leigh Beery, Bud Nease), "Uncrowned Queen of Californiay" (Jack Dabdoub), "Staring" (Leigh Beery, Gretchen Albrecht, Jane White), "I Lay Alone All Winter" (Jack Dabdoub), "Dansa de la Arana" (Gretchen Albrecht), "Hooked!" (Gretchen Albrecht, Leigh Beery, Jane White), "Lola in Bavaria" (Gretchen Albrecht, Jack Dabdoub, Tom Flagg, The Cabinet, The Guards), "Do What You Do" (Jack Dabdoub, Gretchen Albrecht), "The Healing Chant (II)" (Robert Stillman)

ACT TWO—"The Whores Behind the Doors" (The Forty-Niners, The Dandies), "Beauty Secrets" (Leigh Beery), "Winter Comes in Summer" (Bud Nease), "Down Under" (Jane White, Bud Nease), "Many Happy Returns" (Jack Dabdoub, Jane White), "Oranges from Seville" (Bud Nease), "My Lola" (Jack Dabdoub, Bud Nease), "The Whip Dance" (Jane White, Gretchen Albrecht, Leigh Beery, Jack Dabdoub), "The Pledge" (The Forty-Niners, The Dandies, Jack Dabdoub), "The Palace of Pleasure" (Jane White), "Lolaland" (Jane White, Gretchen Albrecht, Leigh Beery, Jack Dabdoub, Bud Nease, Tom Flagg, The Lolaland Lolas), "Rise Up!" (Robert Stillman, Jane White)

NOTES—Lola Montez, along with Baby Doe Tabor (see entry for *The Ballad of Baby Doe*) and Evelyn Nesbit (see entry for *The Gilded Cage*), lived a life so colorful it seems more fictional than real. Kenward Elmslie's program notes for the Off Off Broadway musical provided fascinating background information about the title character. She was born in Ireland in 1818 as Marie Dolores Eliza Rosanna Gilbert; she changed her name to Lola Montez and created the persona of a mysterious dancer with vague, possibly royal, antecedents. After an affair with Franz Liszt, she later became the mistress of King Ludwig I of Bavaria, who bestowed upon her a title, and for all purposes she ruled the country until she was expelled during an uprising in 1848. She later settled in the United States, often touring in a play about her life in Bavaria. She also toured Australia, and there indulged in the occult. She died alone and in poverty at the age of 43, and is buried in Brooklyn under the name of Eliza Gilbert. In 1985, *Lola* was recorded by Painted Smiles Records (LP # PS-1335). For the recording, Judy Kaye was Lola Montez, Christine Andreas was Lola, David (-James) Carroll was Augustus Follin and Dujarier; Jack Dabdoub reprised his roles of King Ludwig and Johnny Southwick. The recording included eighteen numbers as well as a booklet of the musical's lyrics.

Two songs from *Lola* ("Staring" and "Beauty Secrets") were heard in the 2005 revue *Lingoland* (see entry) and were recorded on that show's cast album.

An earlier Australian musical had also been produced about the subject; called *Lola Montez*, the book was by Alan Burke, the lyrics by Peter Benjamin, and the music by Peter Stannard. Mary Preston created the title role. The musical was recorded by (Australian) Columbia Records (LP # 33OEX-9262 and # S33OEX-9262) and was later released on CD by Bayview Recording Company Records (# RNBW-003).

Julius Monk's revue *Four Below Strikes Back* (see entry) offered a song about the subject ("Lola Montez," lyric and music by Michael Brown); the number can be heard on the revue's cast album.

Another collaboration of Kenward Elmslie and Claibe Richardson was *The Grass Harp* (1971); based on Truman Capote's short story and play, the musical lasted for just seven performances but left behind a memorable score which was recorded by Painted Smiles Records.

949 London Days and New York Nights. THEATRE: Jason's Park Royal Theatre; OPENING DATE: October 27, 1983; PERFORMANCES: 20; LYRICS: Chuck Abbott, Henry Avery, John Paul Hudson, Jay Jeffries, Bill Jones, Kel Kaufman, Fran Landesman, and Jeff Golding; MUSIC: Jason McAuliffe; DIRECTION: Jeff Golding; CHOREOGRAPHY: Marcia Milgrom Dodge; MUSICAL DIRECTION: Rick Lewis; PRODUCERS: Jeff Golding and Marshall H. Kozinn

CAST—Nancy Johnson, Joseph Kolinski, Scott Robertson

MUSICAL NUMBERS (number of acts and song assignments unknown; songs are listed in performance order)—"London Days and New York Nights," "Yankee Doodle Londoner," "Jaywalkin'," "A Song Whose Time Has Come," "Against the Time," "I'll Sing a Different Song Tomorrow," "May the Force Be with You" "I Will Never Be the Same," "Best Way to Have the Blues," "One Night Stand," "Code of the West," "I Live in a Dive," "Half-Remembered Melody," "When Did the End Begin?," "Who's New," "A Permanent Romance," "Brief Encounter," "There's Something Worse Than Living Alone," "Ending Up Alone," "Dying a Little a Lot Alone," "Big Dreams," "Where Have I Been All My Life?," "Crystal Palaces," "Best of Friends"

NOTES—This obscure Off Off Broadway musical lasted less than three weeks. "Where Have I Been All My Life?" had earlier been heard in the 1977 revue *For Love or Money* (see entry).

950 Lone Star Love, or The Merry Wives of Windsor, Texas. "A New Musical." THEATRE: AMAS Musical Theatre; OPENING DATE: December 8, 2004; PERFORMANCES: 71 (estimated); BOOK: John L. Haber; LYRICS: Jack Herrick; MUSIC: Jack Herrick; WITH "CONTRIBUTIONS" from Michael Bogdanov, Bland Simpson, and Tommy Thompson; DIRECTION: Michael Bogdanov; CHOREOGRAPHY: Randy Skinner; SCENERY: Derek McLane; COSTUMES: Jane Greenwood; LIGHTING: Jeff Croiter; MUSICAL DIRECTION: Jack Herrick; PRODUCER: AMAS Musical Theatre (Donna Trinkoff, Producing Director); Many Ann Anderson, Executive Producer

CAST—Dan Sharkey (Colonel Joseph E. Johnson, George Page), Jay O. Sanders (Sergeant John Falstaff), Joseph Mahowald (Frank Ford), Beth Leavel (Aggie Ford), Stacia Fernandez (Margaret Anne Page), Julie Tolivar (MissAnne Page), Nick Sullivan (Sheriff Bob Shallow), Brandon Williams (Abraham Slender), Drew McVety (Doctor Caius), Harriett D. Foy (Miss Quickly), Clarke Thorell (Fenton), Kevin Bernard (Lucas), Peter Connelly (Chester), Shane Braddock/Kilty Reidy (Rugby), Stacey Harris (Consuela), Asmeret Ghebremichael/April Nixon (Grace), Dana Zihlman (Ruby): The Band: The Red Clay Ramblers (Clay Buckner [Corporal Nym], Chris Frank [Private Bardolph], and Jack Herrick [Captain Pistol), Emily Mikesell (Miss Libby), Gary Bristol (Host of the Garter Saloon), David Longworth (Sticks)

SOURCE—The play *The Merry Wives of Windsor* (circa 1597) by William Shakespeare.

The action occurs in Bentonville, North Carolina, and Windsor, Texas, in 1865.

ACT ONE—"Carry Me Home" (Mourners [Women of the Company]), "Cold Cash" (Jay O. Sanders, Band, Women), "The Ballad of Falstaff" (Dan Sharkey, Jay O. Sanders, Chris Frank, Jack Herrick, Clay Buckner), "Cattlemen" (The Men of Windsor), "Prairie Moon" (Julie Tolivar, Clarke Thorell), "Caius's Theme" (Drew McVety), "Throwdown in Windsor" (Company), "Cowboy's Dream" (Clarke Thorell, Harriett D. Foy), "Hard Times" (Chris Frank, Jack Herrick, Clay Buckner), "World of Men" (Stacia Fernandez, Beth Leavel), "By Way of Frank Ford" (Joseph Mahowald, Band), "Lone Star Love" (Company)

ACT TWO—"A Man for the Age" (Jay O. Sanders), "Count on My Love" (Clark Thorell, Julie Tolivar), "Code of the West" (Company), "Quail-Bagging" (Company), "Texas Wind" (Beth Leavel), "Wildcat Moan" (Company), "The Ballad of Falstaff" (reprise)/"Lone Star Love" (reprise) (Company), "Dance Finale" (Band)

NOTES—*Lone Star Love* was an Off Off Broadway musical adaptation of Shakespeare's *The Merry Wives of Windsor*. For another Off Off Broadway musical version of the play, see entry for *Boston Boston* (1978), which also played at AMAS (the entry also references *I Love Alice*, a musical treatment of the material which was seen in regional theatre in 1985).

In *Lone Star Love*, Sergeant John Falstaff is dishonorably discharged from the Confederate Army; but when he accidentally shoots an officer, he "borrows" his rank, pronounces himself Colonel Falstaff, and heads for Texas.

Charles Isherwood in the *New York Times*, noting that "corn and sugar" were the essential ingredients of the "cheerfully hokey production," found the evening "innocuous" and felt it tended to "dawdle when it should sprint." But he praised the "tangy" score, and singled out "Count on My Love" ("lilting" and a "real honey"). The musical had first been presented in 2001 at the Great Lakes Theatre Festival in Cleveland.

The attractive, indeed merry, score was recorded by PS Classics Records (CD # PS-531).

A revised version of the musical was scheduled to open on Broadway at the Belasco Theatre on December 3, 2007, with Robert Cuccioli, Dee Hoty, Lauren Kennedy, and Randy Quaid (the latter as Falstaff); however, the production closed during its pre-Broadway tryout in Seattle. Songs retained from the 2004 production for the revised version were: "The Ballad of (John) Falstaff," "(Texas) Cattlemen," "Prairie Moon," "Throwdown in Windsor," "Cowboy's Dream," "Hard Times," "World of Men," "Lone Star Love," "A Man for the Age," "Count on My Love," "Code of the West," "Quail-Bagging," "Texas Wind," and "Dance Finale." Songs not used in the revival were: "Carry Me Home," "Cold Cash," "Caius's Theme," "By Way of Frank Ford," and "Wildcat Moan." New songs for the 2007 version were: "Wild West Women," "Only a Fool," "Fat Men Jump," "A Fatal Dosage," "Slender's Theme," "Ask Me No Reason," "Vaquero," "Jump on the Wagon," and "Love in the Light of the Moon." "Slender's Theme" might have been a revised version of "Caius's Theme."

Of course, the definitive lyric treatment of Shakespeare's play is Verdi's 1893 opera *Falstaff*.

951 The Long Christmas Dinner. THEATRE: Juilliard Concert Hall; OPENING DATE: March 13, 1963; PERFORMANCES: 5; LIBRETTO: Thornton Wilder; MUSIC: Paul Hindemith; DIRECTION: Christopher West; SCENERY: Thea Neu; COSTUMES: Thea Neu; LIGHTING: Thomas DeGaetani; MUSICAL DIRECTION: Paul Hindemith; PRODUCER: Juilliard School of Music

CAST—Lorna Haywood (Lucia), Marilyn Zschau (Mother Bayard), John Harris (Roderick), Allan Evans (Brandon), Robert White (Charles), Geraldine McIlroy (Genevieve), Frances Riley (Leonora), Janet Wagner (Ermengarde), Calvin Koots (Sam), Lorraine Santore (Lucia II), Clifton Steere (Roderick II), Veronica Tyler (Nursemaid)

SOURCE—The 1931 play *The Long Christmas Dinner* by Thornton Wilder.

The action occurs in the Bayard home over a period of ninety years.

The opera was presented in one act.

MUSICAL SEQUENCES (song assignments unknown)—"I Was Remembering This Morning the Days When I Was a Child," "How Long Have We Been in This House?," "Here's to the Health, and Here's to the Wealth of Bayard, Brandon and Bayard," "Greetings to All," "Light Is Her Step on the Stair and the Floor," "Some Day They'll Come in That Door and Say: Good Morning, Good Morning, Mother!," "My Mother's Mother and Your Mother's Mother Were Sisters," "I Shall Hold This Tight," "All the Days Are Dark. All the Days Are Long," "Such Beautiful Snow"

NOTES—The opera *The Long Christmas Dinner* was based on a 1931 one-act play by Thornton Wilder, which, as far as I can tell, has never been professionally produced in New York. The New York premiere of Paul Hindemith's opera occurred two years after the work had first been seen in Mannheim, and was part of a Juilliard festival devoted to the German composer.

The opera revolved around various members of the Bayard family at their Christmas dinners over a ninety-year period. Harold C. Schonberg in the *New York Times* felt there was "something curiously moving" about the libretto and music of the fifty-minute opera, but noted Hindemith's music might be more appreciated by professionals than the general public. But he said Hindemith's score had dealt with every "dramatic and musical detail" of the story, and he praised a "fine" sextet.

The opera was presented on a double bill with a new production of Hindemith's ballet *The Demon*.

In his review, Schonberg mentioned another opera by Hindemith which looked at a story from an unusual time perspective. In 1927, the plot of Hindemith's *Hin und Zuruck* "went forward to a certain point — and then went backward." Besides *The Long Christmas Dinner*, three other plays by Wilder's have been set to music. In 1987, *Grover's Corners*, an adaptation of *Our Town* (1938) by Tom Jones and Harvey Schmidt, was seen in regional theatre; *The Merchant of Yonkers* (1938; revised as *The Matchmaker* [1955]) was musicalized by Jerry Herman as *Hello, Dolly!* (1964); and John Kander and Fred Ebb's lyric version of *The Skin of Our Teeth* (1942) was first seen in regional theatre as *Over & Over* (1999) and then later as *All About Us* (2007). (Leonard Bernstein, Betty Comden, and Adolph Green also wrote a few songs for an unproduced musical adaptation of *The Skin of Our Teeth*.)

952 A Look at the Fifties. THEATRE: Judson Poets' Theatre; OPENING DATE: April 1972 Performances: Unknown; BOOK: Al Carmines; LYRICS: Al Carmines; MUSIC: Al Carmines; CHOREOGRAPHY: David Vaughan, Phyllis MacBryde, and Bruce Hopkins; SCENERY: Tom Craft; COSTUMES: Ira Siff with Joan Kilpatrick; LIGHTING: Earl Eidman; MUSICAL DIRECTION: Al Carmines; PRODUCER: The Judson Poets' Theatre

CAST—Teresa King (Nan), Jeffery Apter (Paul, Cousin), Sandy Padilla (Sandy, The Cook), Margaret Wright (Auntie), Julie Kurnitz (Mother), Emily Adams (Grandmother), Don Nute (Ned), Montgomery Team — Tony Clark (Kevin Leach), Craig Kuehl (Charlie Thomas), Richard Marshall (Bobby Myerson), David McCorkle (Clovis Pickle), Allen Swan (Tommy Saunders), Bill Reynolds (Coach), Grierson Team — Steve Bancroft, Curtis Carlson, Matthew Lipton, Ken Marsolals, Tom Roderick,

Carlton Austin Lukens (Referee), Essie Borden (Lane), Alice Bosveld (Timmy Massey), Ira Siff (Sam), Marion Swan (Carol), Holly Vincent (Terry), Jane Whitehill (Betsy), Bruce Hopkins (Montgomery Drum Major), Sara Kibbey (Majorette), Brenda Mattox (Majorette), Joan Muyskens (Majorette), Lee Guilliatt (Sister Mary)

The action occurs during Spring 1956 in Montgomery, Iowa.

The musical was presented in two acts.

NOTES—One of the best musicals of the 1970s, *A Look at the Fifties* briefly played at the Judson Poets' Theatre during the 1971-1972 season as an Off Off Broadway production and in 1973 was seen at the Arena Stage in Washington, D.C. The musical was never recorded, its script was never published, and after these two productions, the musical all but disappeared (it was seen at least one more time in a production by the Seattle Repertory Theatre, where it opened at the Second Stage on June 3, 1975, and played for fourteen performances).

The following information is taken from the Arena Stage program. (While the work was part of Arena's regular subscription season, many of those associated with the production were the usual welcome suspects from Al Carmines' unofficial stock company in New York.)

The musical utilized the metaphor of the "sweet release" of high school basketball games to comment on the values and mores of small-town America in the 1950s; both at the Judson and at Arena Stage, the stages were transformed into a basketball court for the second act.

In his review for the Off Off Broadway production, Mel Gussow in the *New York Times* told his readers to forget *Grease* and *Bye Bye Birdie*, and said it was "difficult to imagine that Mr. Carmines has ever created a more enchanting show" than *A Look at the Fifties*. He found the musical "pertinent" and "intelligent," and enjoyed Carmines' spoof of the fads, styles, and values of the period (a cheerleader informs us that she is not a virgin but is still a cheerleader, and being a cheerleader is like being a virgin).

For New York, the first act was titled *BEFORE THE GAME/A Drawing Room Comedy*, and the second act was titled *TIME OUT/A Basketball Oratorio*.

THE ARENA STAGE PRODUCTION—DIRECTION: Lawrence Kornfeld; CHOREOGRAPHY: Dan Wagoner; SCENERY: Robert U. Taylor; COSTUMES: Marjorie Slaiman; LIGHTING: William Mintzer; MUSICAL DIRECTION: Susan Romann

CAST—Boni Enten (Nan), Stuart Silver (Paul), Maureen Sadusk (Sandy), Margaret Wright (Auntie, Miss Loomis), Julie Kurnitz (Mother), Don Nute (Ned), Emily Adams (Grandmother), Frank Coppola (Referee), Reathel Bean (Coach); Cheerleaders: Essie Borden, Lane (Head Cheerleader); Louisa Flaningam, Terry; Dorian Barth, Carol; Kristi Tucker, Timmey; Semina De Laurentis, Betsy; Montgomery Team (The Red/White): Michael Petro, Bobby Myerson #9; Roger Oliver, Charlie Thomas #22, Scott Stevensen, Kevin Leach #17; John Kuhner, Clovis Pickle #11; Edmund Gaynes, Tommy Saunders #24; Don Nute, Ned #13; Grierson Team (The Blue/Gold): Scott Mansfield, Scoop #18; Tom Everett, Tony #6; Rick Podell, Ken #15; Jeff Dalton, Jim #22; Michael Mullins, Moon #20); Grierson Fans: Ira Siff, Innis Anderson, E.L. James, Judith Long, Bill Reynolds, Phyllis MacBryde, Marion Swan; Bruce Hopkins (Drum Major), Lee Guilliatt (Sister Mary)

The action occurs during Spring 1956 in Montgomery, Iowa.

The musical was presented in two acts.

ACT ONE—"Dinner Is Served" (Maureen Sadusk), "How Did Freud Know?" (Boni Enten, Stuart Silver, Margaret Wright, Julie Kurnitz, Don Nute, Maureen Sadusk), "Lullaby" (Julie Kurnitz), "The Plunger"/"Scoobie Doo" (Stuart Silver, Maureen Sadusk), "Montgomery Moon" (Don Nute, with Maureen Sadusk, Julie Kurnitz, Margaret Wright), "Dissatisfied Women" (Boni Enten, Margaret Wright; the song incorporated "Jesu Joy of "Man's Desiring" (music by Johann Sebastian Bach), "It's Team Time" (Montgomery Team, Grierson Team, Reathel Bean, Frank Coppola), "National Anthem" (Company), "Montgomery School Song" (Company), "Daffodils and Mud I" (Cheerleaders), "Winning Is Half the Fun" (Michael Petro, Rick Podell, Frank Copolla, Montgomery Team, Grierson Team), "Daffodils and Mud II" (Cheerleaders), "Heroes" (Company), "Eisenhower — Grandfather to the World" (Company), "The Locker Room" (John Kuhner, Company)

ACT TWO—"Hallelujah Basketball" (Lee Guilliatt, Company), "Win for Us, Guys" (Company), "I'm Peculiar That Way" (Margaret Wright), "Innocence" (Company), "Without Rules" (Frank Coppola), "It Ain't Nice Not to Play on Your Own Turf" (Rick Podell, with Scott Mansfield, Michael Mullins, Tom Everett, Jeff Dalton), "Winning Is Half the Fun" (reprise) (Winning Team), "Benediction" (Lee Guilliatt, Company), "Montgomery Moon" (reprise) (Company)

MORE NOTES—Two songs from *A Look at the Fifties* ("Montgomery Moon" and "I'm Peculiar That Way") were heard in the 1982 revue *The Gospel According to Al* (see entry).

953 Look at Us

NOTES—See entry for *Down in the Valley/Look at Us*.

954 Look, Ma, I'm Dancin'!

THEATRE: 14th Street Y Opening Date: March 7, 2000; PERFORMANCES: 16; BOOK: Jerome Lawrence and Robert E. Lee; LYRICS: Hugh Martin; MUSIC: Hugh Martin; DIRECTION: Thomas Mills; CHOREOGRAPHY: Thomas Mills; LIGHTING: Lita Riddock; PRODUCER: *Musicals Tonight!* CAST—Jennifer Allen (Lily), Alli Barnes (Ginny), Julian Brightman (Wotan), Stephen Carter-Hicks (Ferbish, Bellhop), Ryan Duncan (Lenny), Noah Racey (Eddie), Rita Rehn (Tanya), Richard Rutz (Plancek), Sally Mae Dunn (Dusty), John Flynn (Tommy), Kelli Rabke (Snow White), Rob Lorey (Larry), Jennifer Miller (Suzy), Elise Molinelli (Ann), Edward Prostak (Luboff)

The action occurs in New York City, Joplin, Amarillo, Phoenix, Los Angeles, Des Moines, and "on tour."

The musical was presented in two acts.

NOTES—*Look, Ma, I'm Dancin'!* originally opened at the Adelphi Theatre on January 29, 1948, and played for 188 performances. It was co-directed by George Abbott and Jerome Robbins and was choreographed by Robbins; like their other dance-rich musical of the period, *Billion Dollar Baby* (1945; see entry for its revival by *Musicals in Mufti*), the work received mixed reviews, had a relatively short run (which nonetheless was profitable enough to pay back its initial investment and return a small profit), and was generally forgotten. Unlike *Billion Dollar Baby, Look, Ma, I'm Dancin'!* was recorded (by Decca Records; for more information about the cast album, see below), but like *Billion Dollar Baby* it didn't enjoy a hit song, didn't tour, wasn't produced in London, and appears to have gone unseen until the 2000 production by *Musicals Tonight!* The musical originally starred Nancy Walker, who played a brewery heiress who is determined to break into the world of ballet. In reviewing the original production, Robert Coleman in the *New York Daily Mirror* said the work was "a fast, funny, zippy musical ... destined for popularity and ducats will be scarce." However, Robert Sylvester of the *New York Daily News* noted the book "seemed to have been written (or maybe torn apart) somewhere between rehearsals and Philadelphia." And Richard Watts, Jr., in the *New York Post* found the musical "almost steadily disappointing"; further, he complained about the show's "difficult" title with "its commas, apostrophes, exclamation point and all."

The *Musicals Tonight!* revival was a welcome opportunity for new audiences to discover Hugh Martin's underrated score and for audiences familiar with the songs to enjoy them all over again.

As mentioned, unlike *Billion Dollar Baby, Look, Ma, I'm Dancin'!* enjoyed a cast album (of sorts). The album, first released by Decca Records on a 78 RPM set (# DA-637) and then on a 10" LP (# DL-5231; and then later on another LP release), was actually recorded during the pre-Broadway tryout (in anticipation of the ASCAP strike, a strike which put the kibosh on the original cast albums of a number of musicals which opened during the era, such as *Magdalena, Love Life, Where's Charley?,* and *As the Girls Go*). The recording included eight songs: "Gotta Dance, "I'm the First Girl (in the Second Row of the Third Scene of the Fourth Number)," "I'm Not So Bright," "I'm Tired of Texas," "Tiny Room," "The Little Boy Blues," "If You'll Be Mine," and "Shauny O'Shay." On stage, "I'm Not So Bright" was sung by Loren Welch, but for the album Harold Lang performed the song; again, for the stage production "Tiny Room" was sung by Welch, but for the album it was performed by Bill Shirley, who was replaced by Welch either during rehearsals or during the pre-Broadway tryout; further, "The Little Boy Blues" was performed by Virginia Gorski (later Gibson) and Don Liberto on stage, but for the recording was sung by another cast member (Sandra Deel) as well as by lyricist-composer Hugh Martin. "If You'll Be Mine" was performed on stage by Nancy Walker and six other cast members, but for the recording only Walker and Shirley are heard. "Shauny O'Shay" was performed on stage by Gorski and Liberto, but for the album Deel and the chorus sing the number.

The CD release of the 1948 cast album (by Decca Broadway Records # B0003571-02) included four bonus tracks: "Let's Do a Ballet" (sung by Loren Welch [with this number we finally get to hear his voice!], Sandra Deel, Nancy Walker, Bill Shirley, Harold Lang, and the company) was deleted during the tryout (in the liner notes for the CD, Martin mentions he later re-wrote the number, and it was heard as "The Tour Must Go On" in his 1951 Broadway musical *Make a Wish*); "Horrible, Horrible Love" (sung by Nancy Walker, Sandra Deel, and chorus), another number which was deleted during the tryout, was rewritten and used as the verse of another *Make a Wish* song, "Who Gives a Sou?"; and alternate tracks of "Gotta Dance" and "Shauny O'Shay." The *Musicals Tonight!* recording (released by Original Cast Records; unnumbered CD) included four songs not heard on the previous releases of the original cast album: "Jazz," "The New Look," "All My Life," and "The Two of Us." The CD's liner notes indicated that "The New Look" was "extensively rewritten" by Martin for the 2000 production, and that "All My Life" was an unpublished (trunk?) song by Martin.

The "'Mademoiselle Marie' Ballet" wasn't recorded for either the 1948 or 2000 albums, but can be heard on *Ballet on Broadway* (as "Mlle. Scandale Ballet"), which was released on CD by Painted Smiles Records (# PSCD-149).

The following is a list of the musical numbers from the original 1948 production (followed by the names of the original performers who introduced them):

ACT ONE—"Gotta Dance" (Harold Lang, Company), "I'm the First Girl (in the Second Row of the Third Scene of the Fourth Number)" (Nancy Walker, Corps de Ballet), "I'm Not So Bright" (Loren Welch; danced by Janet Reed and Harold Lang), "I'm Tired of Texas" (Nancy Walker, Company), "Tiny Room" (Loren Welch), "The Little Boy

Blues" (Virginia Gorski, Don Liberto), "'Mademoiselle Marie' Ballet" (music by Trude Rittman) (Nancy Walker, Corps de Ballet [including Herbert Ross and Tommy Rall])

ACT TWO—"Jazz" (Don Liberto, Nancy Walker, Company), "The New Look" (Alice Pearce), "If You'll Be Mine" (Nancy Walker, Dean Campbell, Priscilla Hathaway, Sandra Deel, Loren Welch, Alice Pearce, James Pollack), "Pajama Dance" (Company), "Shauny O'Shea" (Virginia Gorski, Don Liberto), "Pas de Deux" from *Swan Lake* (music by Peter Ilyich Tchaikovsky) (Janet Reed, Harold Lang), "The Two of Us" (Nancy Walker, Harold Lang, Chorus)

955 Look Me Up. "A Musical Revue of Nostalgia/The Years of Sophisticated Innocence." THEATRE: Plaza 9—Music Hall; OPENING DATE: October 6, 1971; PERFORMANCES: 406; CONCEPT AND BOOK: Laurence Taylor; LYRICS: See song list for credits; MUSIC: See song list for credits; DIRECTION: Costas Omero; CHOREOGRAPHY: Bob Tucker; SCENERY: James Steward Morcum; COSTUMES: Rosemary Heyer; LIGHTING: Augusto Martinez; MUSICAL DIRECTION: Horace Diaz; also, Ozzie Ray; PRODUCERS: Costas Omero in association with Rio Plaza Productions Ltd., by special arrangement with Café Chantant Ent.

CAST—Ted Agress, Zan Charisse, Kevin Christopher, Murphy Cross, Connie Day, Robin Field, Linda Gerard, Mary Lynn Kolas, Linda Kurtz, Don Liberto, Jeff Richards, Geoffrey Webb

The revue was presented in two acts.

ACT ONE—"Runnin' Wild" (from *Runnin' Wild*, 1922; lyric by Joe Grey and Lew Wood, music by A. Harrington Gibbs) (Ted Agress, Kevin Christopher, Don Liberto, Jeff Richards, Geoffrey Webb), A Song and Dance Man (Medley [songs in this sequence unknown]) (Robin Field), "Hallelujah!" (*Hit the Deck!*, 1927; lyric by Leo Robin and Clifford Grey, music by Vincent Youmans) (Company), "Get Happy" (*Nine-Fifteen Revue*, 1930; lyric by Ted Koehler, music by Harold Arlen) (Company), "Happy Feet" (1930 film *King of Jazz*, lyric by Milton Yellen, music by Howard Ager) (Don Liberto), "Someone to Watch Over Me" (*Oh, Kay!*, 1926; lyric by Ira Gershwin, music by George Gershwin) (Linda Gerard, Jeff Richards), "Makin' Whoopee" (*Whoopee*, 1928; lyric by Gus Kahn, music by Walter Donaldson) (Geoffrey Webb), "Button Up Your Overcoat" (*Follow Thru*, 1929; lyric by B.G. [Buddy] DeSylva and Lew Brown, music by Ray Henderson) (Zan Charisse, Linda Kurtz, Mary Lynn Kolas, Murphy Cross), "You Made Me Love You (I Didn't Want to Do It)" (*The Honeymoon Express*, 1913 [Second Edition]; lyric by Joseph McCarthy, music by James V. Monaco) (Connie Day, Robin Field), "Bidin' My Time" (*Girl Crazy*, 1930; lyric by Ira Gershwin, music by George Gershwin) (Ted Agress, Kevin Christopher, Jeff Richards, Geoffrey Webb), "Can't Help Lovin' That Man" (*Show Boat*, 1927; lyric by Oscar Hammerstein II, music by Jerome Kern) (Linda Gerard), "Strike Up the Band" (*Strike Up the Band*, 1927 and 1930 productions; lyric by Ira Gershwin, music by George Gershwin) (Company), (Special program note between the acts: "During the intermission the audience and the waiting personel [sic] are invited to sing along with Sam Bixby and his cousins [Don Liberto, with Robin Field and Kevin Christopher])"

ACT TWO—"Drums in My Heart" (*Through the Years*, 1932; lyric by Edward Heyman, music by Vincent Youmans) (Company), "It Had to Be You" (*The Greenwich Village Follies*, 1924; lyric by Isham Jones, music by Gus Kahn) (Linda Gerard, Jeff Richards), "If You Knew Susie" (independent song, 1925; lyric by B.G. [Buddy] DeSylva, music by Joseph Meyer) (Geoffrey Webb, Connie Day, Company), "Thinking of You" (independent song, 1926; lyric by Harry Askt, music by Walter Donaldson) (Jeff Richards), "The Best Things in Life Are Free" (*Good News*, 1927; lyric by B.G. [Buddy] DeSylva and Lew Brown, music by Ray Henderson) (Linda Gerard, Jeff Richards, Company), "Glad Rag Doll" (independent song, 1929; lyric by Jack Yellen, music by Dan Dougherty and Milton Ager) (Connie Day), "Yes, Sir, That's My Baby" (independent song, 1925; lyric by Gus Kahn, music by Walter Donaldson) (Zan Charisse, Linda Kurtz, Mary Lynn Kolas, Murphy Cross), "Baby Face" (independent song, 1926; lyric by Harry Akst, music by Benny Davis) (Ted Agress, The Girls), "Aba Daba Honeymoon" (independent song, 1914; lyric by Arthur Fields, music by Walter Donovan) (Ted Agress), "Manhattan" (*The Garrick Gaities*, 1925; lyric by Lorenz Hart, music by Richard Rodgers) (Don Liberto, Company), "How Long Has This Been Going On?" (dropped during the tryout of *Funny Face* [1927]; later used in *Rosalie* [1928]; lyric by Ira Gershwin, music by George Gershwin) (Linda Gerard), "Great Day!" (*Great Day!*, 1929; lyric by Billy Rose and Edward Eliscu, music by Vincent Youmans) (Company)

NOTES—Early in 1971, the hit Broadway revival of Vincent Youmans' *No, No, Nanette* ushered in a nostalgia craze which eventually saw a number of revivals of older musicals. *Look Me Up* was clearly a reaction to the success of *Nanette*, and in fact three songs by Youmans were included in the revue. *Look Me Up* was an upbeat affair, full of feel-good nostalgic tunes, and it ran for over 400 performances. Incidentally, Zan Charisse was the niece of musical film legend Cyd Charisse. In the 1973 London production of *Gypsy* (which starred Angela Lansbury as Mama Rose), Zan Charisse played the role of Louise, which she later reprised on Broadway the following year.

956 Look What a Wonder Jesus Has Done

NOTES—See entry for *The New York Musical Theatre Festival*.

957 Look Where I'm At! "A Musical Comedy." THEATRE: Theatre Four; OPENING DATE: March 5, 1971; PERFORMANCES: 5; BOOK: James Leasor and Gib Dennigan; LYRICS: Frank H. Stanton and Murray Semos; MUSIC: Jordan Ramin; DIRECTION: Wakefield Poole; CHOREOGRAPHY: Wakefield Poole; Frank DeSal, Associate Choreographer; SCENERY: Robert Guerra; COSTUMES: Rosemarie Heyer; LIGHTING: Robert Guerra; MUSICAL DIRECTION: Jack Lee; Mack Schlefer, Conductor; PRODUCER: Jean Marie-Lee

CAST—RON HUSMANN (Hector), MARTIN ROSS (Horrid), MARY BRACKEN PHILLIPS (Satin), ARTHUR BARTOW (Larkin), SHERRI SPILLANE (Gloria); Singers and Dancers (Yveline Baudez, Lonnie Burr, Denny Martin Flinn, Eileen Shannon, Eleanor Smith, Jennifer Williams)

SOURCE—The 1933 novel *Rain in the Doorway* by Thorne Smith.

The action occurs in the present.

The musical was presented in two acts.

ACT ONE—"Change of Scene" (Ron Hussman), "What a Day for a Wonderful Day" (Cast), "Animals" (Martin Ross, Cast), "What Are You Running From, Mister?" (Mary Bracken Phillips), "Partners" (Ron Hussman, Martin Ross, Arthur Bartow, Sherri Spillane), "Who Does She Think She Is?" (Ron Hussman), "Look Where I'm At!" (Ron Hussman, Cast), "Never, Never Leave Me" (Ron Hussman)

ACT TWO—"Money Isn't Everything, But" (Stockholders), "Party Scene" (Cast), "Company of Men" (Sherri Spillane), "The Me I Want to Be" (Mary Bracken Phillips), "Little Sparrow" (Mary Bracken Phillips), "Euphoria" ([performer unknown], Ron Hussman)

NOTES—*Look Where I'm At!* was an updated version of Thorne Smith's 1933 novel *Rain in the Doorway*. The musical centered around a man's unhappiness with both the left-wing and right-wing lifestyles of his era (his disenchantment lasted for just five performances). Clive Barnes in the *New York Times* noted the musical also dealt with a "declining" department store and two "reclining" ladies, and said the work was "a monstrously ineffectual show" which was "impossible" to recommend on any level. As an example of the show's humor, he noted that in response to the question, "Do you have a copy of Flaubert's *Madame Bovary*?," one character answered, "Yes, right on the top shelf between lesbians and necrophiliacs." But Barnes had sympathy for the engaging cast, including the "very talented" Ron Husmann and Martin Ross. (Incidentally, cast member Sherri Spillane was Mrs. Mickey Spillane.)

958 Lotta, or The Best Thing Evolution's Ever Come Up With. THEATRE: Anspacher Theatre/The Public Theatre; OPENING DATE: October 18, 1973; PERFORMANCES: 54; BOOK: Robert Montgomery; LYRICS: Robert Montgomery; MUSIC: Robert Montgomery; ADDITIONAL MUSIC by Mel Marvin; DIRECTION: David Chambers; CHOREOGRAPHY: Dennis Nahat; SCENERY: Tom H. John; COSTUMES: Nancy Adzima and Richard Graziano; LIGHTING: Roger Morgan; MUSICAL DIRECTION: Ken Guilmartin; PRODUCER: The New York Shakespeare Festival Public Theatre (Joseph Papp, Producer)

CAST—Irene Cara (Priestess), David Gunnip (Priest), MacIntyre Dixon (Bub), Paula Larke (Doctor), Bette Henritze (Trixie), Jeffrey Duncan Jones (Jeffrey Jones) (Limester), Dale Soules (Lotta), Ronald (Ron) Silver (Repairman One), R.H. Thomson (Repairman Two), John Long (Repairman Three), Richard Ramos (Tracy Shamus), Jerrold Ziman (Glenn, Overvoice), Jill Eikenberry (Mrs. Diddly, Dr. Olving), Sean Barker (Dr. Gray Medulla); Choir (Sean Barker, Irene Cara, Jill Eikenberry, David Gunnip, Paula Larke, Jerrold Ziman

The action occurs in the Eastern U.S.A., and the program noted that "Lotta was born tomorrow."

The musical was presented in one act.

MUSICAL NUMBERS—"Fetus" (Irene Cara, Choir), "Birth" (David Gunnip, Irene Cara, Dale Soules, Choir), "Science" (Choir), "No More Magic" (Jeffrey Duncan Jones, Choir, Dale Soules), "God" (Ronald Silver, R.H. Thomson, John Long), "Perfect Acts" (Dale Soules, Ronald Silver, R.H. Thomson, John Long), "Beef Stew" (Dale Soules, Choir), "Perfect Dialogue" (MacIntyre Dixon, Bette Henritze), "Lotta" (Dale Soules), "World Without Pain" (Richard Ramos, Ronald Silver, R.H. Thomson, John Long, Dale Soules, Choir), "How Do You Die?" (Irene Cara, David Gunnip), "The Human Thing" (Dale Soules, Jeffrey Duncan Jones, Choir), "Heaven" (Dale Soules, Ronald Silver, R.H. Thomson, John Long, Richard Ramos, Jeffrey Duncan Jones), Finale (Jeffrey Duncan Jones, Choir, Dale Soules, Company)

NOTES—Robert Montgomery's play *Subject to Fits* (1971) had met with critical success, but *Lotta* was found wanting in almost every department. The critics noted that the messianic and magically empowered title character of the surreal musical was born at the age of sixteen, and her mission on earth is to help others achieve perfection, understand the meaning of life, and penetrate the secret of life after death. The confused and noisy story was set to rock music, and the purposeless direction and choreography were framed against a décor of Day-Glo colors; it all seemed a lotta to do about nothing, and so the sophomoric musical was gone within a few weeks. The music for the finale sequence was composed by Mel Marvin.

The first performance of *Lotta* was given on October 18, 1973, the official press performance was on November 21, and the musical closed on December 2 (the total number of performances was fifty-four).

959 Louis. "The Musical." THEATRE: New Federal Theatre; OPENING DATE: September 18, 1981; PERFORMANCES: 12; BOOK: Don Evans; LYRICS: Don Evans; MUSIC: Michael Renzi; DIRECTION: Gilbert Moses; CHOREOGRAPHY: Billy Wilson; SCENERY: Robert Edmonds; COSTUMES: Judy Dearing; LIGHTING: Shirley Prendergast; MUSICAL DIRECTION: Neal Tate; PRODUCER: Henry Street Settlement (Woodie King, Jr., and Steven Tennen, Producers)

CAST—Tiger Haynes (Papa Jazz), Donna P. Ingram (Urchin, Cora, Sarah, Ensemble), Assata Hazell (Urchin, Flora, Ensemble), Alde Lewis, Jr. (Urchin, Ensemble), Debbie Allen (Daisy), Mel Edmondson (Willie, Ensemble), Don Jay (Bennie), Eugene Little (Man, Ensemble), Marcella Lowry (Mayann), Ken Page (Joe Oliver), Ricky Powell (Gabe), Renee Rose (Adora, Ensemble), Lynn Sterling (Sally, Ensemble, Dance Captain), Jeffrey V. Thompson (Frenchman), Andy Torres (Otis, Ensemble), Skip Waters (Buddy), Northern J. Calloway (Louis; Jimmy Maxwell cornet), Ernestine Jackson (Lil)

The musical was presented in two acts.

ACT ONE—"Lucky Day" (Northern J. Calloway, Ensemble), "Funky-Butt Hall" (Jeffrey V. Thompson, Ensemble), "I Wouldn't Have Believed It" (Ken Page), "There's Something Special" (Jeffrey V. Thompson, Ensemble), "All I Wanna Do Is Dance" (Marcella Lowry, Ensemble), "All I Wanna Do Is Dance" (reprise) (Debbie Allen), "Shimmy" (Northern J. Calloway, Debbie Allen), "Simple Melody" (Debbie Allen), "Struttin' with Some Barbeque" (Ensemble), "Georgia Peach" (Skip Waters), "Give a Damn (What You Do)" (Ken Page), "Something I'm Supposed to Do" (Northern J. Calloway)

ACT TWO—"Daisy Mae Blues" (Tiger Haynes), "Love Duet (I Like the Way He Looks)" (Ernestine Jackson, Northern J. Calloway), "Lord Have Mercy" (Tiger Haynes, Donna P. Ingram), "You Been a Good Ol' Wagon" (Donna P. Ingram), "No Time to Cry" (Debbie Allen), "No Love in Lies" (Ernestine Jackson), Finale: "Look Out to the World" (Northern J. Calloway, Ensemble)

NOTES—Despite its impressive roster of names, this Off Off Broadway musical biography of Louis Armstrong (1900-1971) didn't go anywhere. Neither did *Satchmo*, a lavish musical about Armstrong which briefly toured during Summer 1987.

960 Louisiana Summer. THEATRE: AMAS Repertory Theatre; OPENING DATE: October 28, 1982; PERFORMANCES: 16; BOOK: Robert and Bradley Wexler; LYRICS: Robert Wexler; MUSIC: Rocky Stone; DIRECTION: Robert Stark; CHOREOGRAPHY: Keith Rozie; SCENERY: Tom Barnes; Susan McClain-Moore, Animal Designer; COSTUMES: Eiko Yamaguchi; LIGHTING: Ronald L. McIntyre; MUSICAL DIRECTION: Lea Richardson; PRODUCER: AMAS Repertory Theatre (Rosetta LeNoire, Founder and Artistic Director)

CAST—Sonia Bailey (Dossie), Hal Blankenship (Boswell, Loup-Garou), Jeff Reade (Charlie, Willie), R. Michael Dayton (Grandpa Paul, Olidon), Robin Dunn (Rosalind, Voodoo Queen), Steve Fickinger (Luke), Douglass D. Frazier (Willard), Margaret Goodman (Dodie), Tracy O'Neil Heffernan (Dot), Wendy Kimball (Narrator, Older Bradley), Hans Krown (Bobby, Squeak), Garrick Lavon (Floyd, Egret), Lani Marrell (Alice), Kimberly Mucci (Bradley), Raphael Nash (James Lee, Voodoo King), Don Oliver (Louisiana Jack), Cynthia I. Pearson (Older Dossie), Kevin Ramsey (Freddie, Papa Gator), Ann Talman (Josette), Tug Wilson (Luke), Raymond Skip Zipf (Lloyd, Egret)

The action occurs in 1947 and in 1954 in Paradise, Louisiana, and in the swamps and bayous between Paradise and New Orleans.

The musical was presented in two acts (division of acts and song assignments unknown; songs are listed in performance order).

MUSICAL NUMBERS—Prologue, "Cutting in the Cane," "Silent Summer Nights," "Pictures in the Sky," "Busy Days," "Country Harmony," "Go Your Way with the Lord," "Train Song," "Cane Cutter's Ballet," "Voodoo Dance," "Lullaby of Night," "Alligator Romp," "Josette's Theme," "Louisiana Summer," "Louisiana Cajun Man," "Loup's Lament," "Black Annie," "My Friend," Epilogue

NOTES—The Off Off Broadway musical *Louisiana Summer* was another in an almost unending parade of short-running musicals set in Louisiana (for more information, see entry for *Basin Street*).

961 Love. "A New Musical Comedy." THEATRE: Audrey Wood Theatre; OPENING DATE: April 15, 1984; PERFORMANCES: 17; BOOK: Jeffrey Sweet; LYRICS: Susan Birkenhead; MUSIC: Howard Marren; DIRECTION: Walton Jones; CHOREOGRAPHY: Ed Nolfi; SCENERY: Kevin Rupnik; COSTUMES: Kevin Rupnik; LIGHTING: Ruth Roberts; MUSICAL DIRECTION: Uel Wade; PRODUCERS: Haila Stoddard, Joy Klein, and Maggie Minskoff

CAST—NATHAN LANE (Harry), STEPHEN VINOVICH (Milt), JUDY KAYE (Ellen)

SOURCE—The 1964 play *Luv* by Murray Schisgal.

The action occurs on a bridge on an October evening, and one year later.

The musical was presented in two acts.

ACT ONE—"Sincerely, Harold Berlin" (Nathan Lane), "Polyarts U" (Stephen Vinovich, Nathan Lane), "Paradise" (Stephen Vinovich, Nathan Lane), "Carnival Ride" (Stephen Vinovich, Nathan Lane), "The Chart" (Judy Kaye), "Paradise" (reprise) (Judy Kaye, Nathan Lane), "Ellen's Lament" (Judy Kaye, Nathan Lane), "Somebody" (Nathan Lane, Judy Kaye), "Yes, Yes, I Love You" (Nathan Lane, Judy Kaye), "Carnival Ride" (reprise) (Stephen Vinovich, Nathan Lane, Judy Kaye)

ACT TWO—"Love" (Judy Kaye), "What a Life!" (Judy Kaye, Stephen Vinovich), "Paradise" (reprise) (Judy Kaye, Stephen Vinovich), "Lady" (Stephen Vinovich, Judy Kaye), "If Harry Weren't Here" (Judy Kaye, Stephen Vinovich), "My Brown Paper Hat" (Nathan Lane, Judy Kaye, Stephen Vinovich), "Do I Love Him?" (Nathan Lane, Judy Kaye), "Harry's Resolution" (Nathan Lane, Judy Kaye, Stephen Vinovich), "Love" (reprise) (Judy Kaye, Stephen Vinovich), "Carnival Ride" (reprise) (Nathan Lane)

NOTES—Murray Schisgal's *Luv* is one of those forgotten hit comedies of the 1960s; like *Mary, Mary* (1961) and *Never Too Late* (1962), it's drifted into obscurity. Perhaps if the musical version had been a hit, the play would be better known today. Like the play, the musical told the story of three misfits; the plot included two suicide attempts, one attempted murder, and two unhappy marriages. But the story ends on a reasonably upbeat note, considering the wacky neurotics involved. After such "bridge"-related disasters as *Reuben Reuben* (1955; closed during its pre-Broadway tryout) and *Kelly* (1965; the legendary one-performance Broadway flop), perhaps any musical whose characters talked about jumping off bridges was asking for it. So despite the success of its source, its winning cast, and its pleasant score, the musical was a quick failure, lasting less than three weeks. Frank Rich in the *New York Times* felt the evening lacked the snap and zing of the original play, and even found some of the performances wanting. Further, he wasn't impressed with the score. He noted that while "Carnival Ride" (the musical's "most insistently reprised song") referred to love as a "roller coaster," *Love* was "mostly a creaky merry-go-round."

During previews, Harry's opening number "Don't Make Me Laugh" was replaced by "Sincerely, Harold Berlin," and during the second act a reprise of "Lady" was substituted with a reprise of the title song.

The following summer the musical was produced in summer stock as *A 'Luv' Musical*, with Stephen Vinovich reprising his role of Milt (Gary Sandy played Harry and Marcia Rodd played Ellen). For this production, Harry had a new opening number ("Harry's Dilemma").

The musical was later produced in London in 1986 as *What About Luv?*

In 1989, That's Entertainment Records recorded the score as both *What About Luv?* (the title given on the disk itself as well as on the spine of the CD's insert sleeve) and *Love* (the title given on the cover of the CD's booklet) with original cast member Judy Kaye (Simon Green was Harry, and David Green was Milt). The CD (# CDTER-1171) included new numbers (such as "How Beautiful the Night Is") as well as a bonus track of an earlier version of the second act's opening. The musical was revived for twenty-nine performances in 1991 by the York Theatre Company as *What About Luv?* (with Judy Kaye, David Green, and Austin Pendleton); see entry.

962 Love and Let Love. "A Musical Romance." THEATRE: Sheridan Square Playhouse; OPENING DATE: January 4, 1968; PERFORMANCES: 14; BOOK: John Lollos; LYRICS: John Lollos and Don Christopher; MUSIC: Stanley Jay Gelber; DIRECTION: John Lollos; CHOREOGRAPHY: Rhoda Levine; SCENERY: Barbara Miller; COSTUMES: Ynes; LIGHTING: Fred Allison; MUSICAL DIRECTION: Daniel Paget; PRODUCER: L & L.L. Company

CAST—Marcia Rodd (Viola), Tom Lacy (Captain, Priest), John Cunningham (Count Orsino), Tony Hendra (Sir Toby Belch), Susan Willis (Maria), Nic Ullett (Sir Andrew Aguecheek), Joseph R. Sicari (Feste), Virginia Vestoff (Countess Olivia), Michael O'Sullivan (Malvolio), Roy Clary (Antonio), Michael Hawkins (Sebastian), Don Moran (Officer)

SOURCE—The play *Twelfth Night* (written in either 1600 or 1601) by William Shakespeare. The action occurs in Ilyria.

The musical was presented in two acts.

ACT ONE—"I've Got a Plan" (Marian Mercer, Tom Lacy), "If She Could Only Feel the Same" (John Cunningham), "The Dancing Rogue" (Tony Hendra, Nic Ullett), "Will He Ever Know?" (Marian Mercer), "I Like It" (Virginia Vestoff), "Man Is Made for Woman" (Joseph R. Sicari, Tony Hendra, Nic Ullett), "Epistle of Love" (Susan Willis, Tony Hendra, Nic Ullett, Joseph R. Sicari), "Love Lesson" (John Cunningham, Marian Mercer), "I'll Smile" (Michael O'Sullivan)

ACT TWO—"I Will Have Him" (Virginia Vestoff, Marian Mercer), "Write Him a Challenge" (Tony Hendra, Nic Ullett), "She Called Me Fellow" (Michael O'Sullivan), "They'll Say I've Been Dreaming" (Michael Hawkins), "How Do I Know You're Not Mad, Sir?" (Joseph R. Sicari, Michael O'Sullivan), "I Like It" (reprise) (Michael Hawkins, Virginia Vestoff), "I Found My Twin" (Ensemble), "Some Are Born Great" (Ensemble)

NOTES—By one of those strange twists of theatrical fate, two Off Broadway musical adaptations of Shakespeare's *Twelfth Night* opened within the first two weeks of January 1968. The first, *Love and Let Love*, was gone in two weeks. The second, *Your Own Thing* (see entry), was a hit and ran over two years. And an even stranger twist is that Marcia Rodd, who played Viola in *Love and Let Love*, also appeared in *Your Own Thing* (playing Olivia) when its leading lady (Marian Mercer) suddenly left the show shortly after the opening. Since both *Love and Let Love* and *Your Own Thing* were recorded (the latter after Marian Mercer had left the production), Marcia Rodd's respective performances as Viola and Olivia can be heard on the cast albums of the two musicals. *Love and Let Love* was privately released as

Twelfth Night ("Love and Let Love") on Sam Fox Records (LP # X4RS-0371/2). The cast of *Love and Let Love* is interesting, with many familiar names (John Cunningham, Virginia Vestoff, and Michael O'Sullivan).

Unlike the "mod" *Your Own Thing*, *Love and Let Love* was a traditional musical adaptation of Shakespeare's comedy; its score is pleasant, if not particularly distinguished. Clive Barnes in the *New York Times* felt the evening lacked a consistency of tone, and it appears the performance, the direction, and the libretto were an unhappy combination of Shakespeare and modern musical comedy. Barnes noted the "mixture of idioms" even affected the costumes, which didn't seem to belong to any particular period, and the overall effect of the musical was that it was "styleless rather than timeless." Further, he found the score "bloodless," but singled out Malvolio's "I'll Smile" (sung by Michael Sullivan in a performance filled with "seething frenzy only lightly covering otherwise naked ambition ... vain to the point of madness").

There were two Broadway musicals based on *Twelfth Night*. Richard Adler's *Music Is* opened at the St. James Theatre on December 20, 1976; it was unaccountably rejected by the critics, and closed after only eight performances. It was a jewel of a musical, and Adler's score was a bounty of lyrical and melodic delight, including "Should I Speak of Loving You?," one of the most ravishing ballads of the era (it was exquisitely sung by Catherine Cox, who played Viola). Other highlights of the score were "Please Be Human," another lovely ballad (for Olivia, played by Sherry Mathis), and "Hate to Say Goodbye to You," a highly rhythmic duet for Antonio and Sebastian (Marc Jordan and Joel Higgins). The second Broadway adaptation was *Play On!*, which opened at the Brooks Atkinson Theatre on March 20, 1997, for sixty-one performances. Set in the "Swingin' '40s" in the "Magical Kingdom of Harlem," *Play On!* utilized Duke Ellington standards (such as "Take the 'A' Train," "Don't Get Around Much Anymore," "It Don't Mean a Thing (If It Ain't Got That Swing)," and ""I Got It Bad [and That Ain't Good]") to tell its story; the cast included Carl Anderson, Andre DeShields, Larry Marshall, and Tonya Pinkins. There was also an Off Off Broadway adaptation by Andrew Sherman and Rusty Magee; *What You Will*, which took place at the Club Illyria during World War II, opened at the Connelly Theatre on April 5, 2001, and played for seventeen performances.

963 Love and Maple Syrup. "Words and Music from Canada." THEATRE: Mercer-Hansbury Theatre; OPENING DATE: January 7, 1970; PERFORMANCES: 15; LYRICS AND MUSIC: various Canadian lyricists and composers; DEVISED AND COMPILED BY Louis Negin.; DIRECTION: Don Gillies; SCENERY: Charles L. Dunlop; LIGHTING: Barry Arnold; PRODUCERS: Ruth Kalkstein and Edward Specter Productions, by arrangement with Dorian Productions, Ltd., Louis Negin, and The National Arts Centre of Canada; Art and Burt D'Lugoff, Associate Producers

CAST—Sandra Caron, Gabriel Gascon, Judy Lander, Ann Mortifee, Louis Negin, Margaret Robertson, Bill Schustik

The revue was presented in two acts.

ACT ONE—Prologue (by Gertrude Katz) (Company), "The Gypsy" (by Gordon Lightfoot) (Ann Mortifee), "Alouette" (Company), "Mon Pays" (by Gilles Vigneault) (Gabriel Gascon), "Introduction" (by Irving Layton) (Gabriel Gascon, Margaret Robertson), "Salish Song of Longing" (Ann Mortifee), "Duet" (by Gertrude Katz) (Sandra Caron), "The Dimple" (by Stephen Leacock) (Louis Negin), "Attempt" (by A.W. Purdy) (Margaret Robertson), "Tonite Will Be Fine" (by Leonard Cohen) (Ann Mortifee, Bill Schustik, Company), "Celebration" (by Leonard Cohen) (Gabriel Gascon), "Zalinka" (by Tom MacInnes) (Margaret Robertson), "The Last Time I Saw Her Face" (Ann Mortifee), "Des Mots (Elio de Grandmont)" (Sandra Caron, Gabriel Gascon), "Bonne Entente" (by F.R. Scott) (Sandra Caron), "Emmene-moi" (by Claude Leveille) (Gabriel Gascon), "Queen Victoria" (by Leonard Cohen) (Louis Negin), "Motet" (by Irving Layton) (Company), "Imperial" (by Irving Layton) (Company), "Misunderstanding" (by Irving Layton) (Louis Negin), "A Person Who Eats Meat" (by Leonard Cohen) (Gabriel Gascon), "Springhill Mine Disaster" (Bill Schustik), "Anerca" (by Edmund Carpenter) (Margaret Robertson), "Making" Songs (Bill Schustik), "The Sculptors" (by A.W. Purdy) (Louis Negin), "Eskimo Tableaux" (Company), "Boss Man" (by Gordon Lightfoot) (Company), "Over the Pacific" (by A.W. Purdy) (Bill Schustik), "Kivkaq" (Margaret Robertson), "Etude No. X" (by Pierre Coupey) (Company)

ACT TWO—"Epilogue" (by Gertrude Katz) (Company), "Happy Stoned Song" (by Ann Mortifee) (Ann Mortifee, Company), "Dance, My Little One" (by Irving Layton) (Louis Negin), "The Sorcerer" (by A.J. Smith) (Gabriel Gascon), "Grandmere et Grandpere" (by Janice Stillway, a public school student) (Louis Negin), "Love and Maple Syrup" (by Gordon Lightfoot) (Ann Mortifee), "Hagar Shipley" (Margaret Laurence, from her novel *The Stone Angel*) (Margaret Robertson), "I Had a King" (by Joni Mitchell) (Ann Mortifee), "Bitter Green" (by Gordon Lightfoot) (Bill Schustik), "Cuckold's Song" (by Leonard Cohen) (Louis Negin), "Quand Vous Mourrez de Nos Amours" (Gabriel Gascon), "Shore Leave" (by Gertrude Katz) (Sandra Caron), "Constance Insured" (by Gertrude Katz) (Gabriel Gascon), "Anti-Romantic" (by Irving Layton) (Sandra Caron), "Oh, Canada" (by John Robert Colombo) (Louis Negin), "Proverb" (Sandra Caron), "Love at Robin Lake" (by A.W. Purdy) (Gabriel Gascon), "The Poor Little Girls of Ontario" (Ann Mortifee, Sandra Caron, Margaret Robertson), "On the Virtues of Being Canadian" (Louis Negin), "After Dark" (by Raymond Souster, from his book of poetry, *The Colour of the Times*) (Margaret Robertson), "Where the Blue Horses" (by Raymond Souster, from his book of poetry, *The Colour of the Times*) (Sandra Caron), "L'Exile" (by Francois Hertel) (Gabriel Gascon), "Un Canadian Errant" (by M.A. Gerin Lajoie) (Gabriel Gascon), "Hey, That's No Way to Say Good-bye" (by Leonard Cohen) (Company)

NOTES—*Love and Maple Syrup* (*Amour et Sucre d'Erable*) was first produced in London in January 1968, and later re-staged in Ottawa. It was an evening of English and French songs by written by Canadians (the title song was especially written for the production by Gordon Lightfoot).

Clive Barnes in the *New York Times* noted that Canada wasn't the United States, Britain, or "even" France, and "seems sad" about it. He mentioned the revue's opening number was about Canadians being "dull," and he feared the rest of the evening seemed "more justification than refutation" of that assertion. *The American Hamburger League* (see entry) and now *Love and Maple Syrup* ushered in a brief series of Canadian musicals to visit New York in the 1970s, all of them for mostly short runs (in their Canadian productions, two of them starred Brent Carver two decades before he found Tony Award-winning success on Broadway). Future Off Broadway seasons would see *Love Me, Love My Children* (1971) and *A Bistro Car on the CNR* (1978) (see entries); the former was originally produced in Canada as *Justine* and the latter as *Jubalay* in 1974 and then as *A Bistro Car* in 1979 (Brent Carver was in the original cast of *Jubalay*). In 1976, Broadway would see *Rockabye Hamlet*, which had premiered in Canada as *Kronberg: 1600* with Brent Carver as Hamlet.

964 Love in the Nick of Tyme. THEATRE: Beacon Theatre; OPENING DATE: January 16, 2007; PERFORMANCES: 8; BOOK: David E. Talbert; LYRICS: Vivian Green; MUSIC: Vivian Green; DIRECTION: David E. Talbert

CAST—Morris Chestnut, Terry Dexter, Andre Pitre, Avant, Ellia English, Trenyce, Blu Mitchell, Christi Dickerson, Jerrell Roberts, Lyn Talbert

NOTES—*Love in the Nick of Tyme*, an Off Off Broadway musical about a beauty salon owner whose business life is successful but her romantic one is not, played a limited engagement of one week before embarking on a seventeen-city national tour.

965 Love, Janis. THEATRE: Village Theatre; OPENING DATE: April 22, 2001; PERFORMANCES: 713; TEXT ADAPTATION: Randal Myler; LYRICS: See song list for credits; MUSIC: See song list for credits; DIRECTION: Randal Myler; SCENERY: Jules Fisher and Peggy Eisenhauer; Bo Eriksson, Projection Designs; LIGHTING: Jules Fisher and Peggy Eisenhauer; COSTUMES: Robert Blackman; ADDITIONAL COSTUME RE-CREATION by Michael Louis; MUSICAL DIRECTION: Sam Andrews; PRODUCERS: Jennifer Dumas, Jack Cullen, Patricia Watt, and Jeff Rosen in association with Laura Joplin and Michael Joplin; Jay and Cindy Gutterman, Co-Producers; Jennifer Taylor, Madelyn Bell Ewing, Robert Schreiber, Jamie Cesa, Carl D. White, Tom Smedes, and Scooter Weintraub, Associate Producers

CAST—Catherine Curtin (Janis Joplin [speaking role]), Andra Mitrovich and Cathy Richardson (Janis Joplin [alternating in singing role]), Seth Jones (Interviewer)

SOURCE—Inspired by the 1992 book *Love, Janis* by Laura Joplin.

The revue was presented in two acts.

ACT ONE—"Piece of My Heart" (lyric and music by Bert Berns and Jerry Ragovoy), "What Good Can Drinking Do?" (lyric and music by Janis Joplin), "Down on Me" (lyric and music by Janis Joplin), "Bye, Bye Baby" (lyric and music by Powell St. John), "Let the Good Times Roll" (lyric and music by Leonard and Shirley Goodman), "Turtle Blues" (lyric and music by Janis Joplin), "Women Is Losers" (lyric and music by Janis Joplin), "I Need a Man to Love" (lyric and music by Janis Joplin and Sam Andrew), "Summertime" (from *Porgy and Bess*, 1935; lyric by DuBose Heyward, music by George Gershwin), "Ball & Chain" (lyric and music by Willie Mae Thornton)

ACT TWO—"Mercedes Benz" (lyric and music by Janis Joplin, Michael McClure, and Bobby Neuwirth), "A Woman Left Lonely" (lyric and music by Dan Penn and S. Oldham), "Work Me, Lord" (lyric and music by Nick Gravenities), "Try (Just a Little Bit Harder)" (lyric and music by Jerry Ragovoy and Chip Taylor), "To Love Somebody" (lyric and music by Barry Gibb and Robin Gibb), "Me and Bobby McGee" (lyric and music by Fred Foster and Kris Kristofferson), "Little Girl Blue" (*Jumbo*, 1935; lyric by Lorenz Hart, music by Richard Rodgers), "Move Over" (lyric and music by Janis Joplin), "Get It While You Can" (lyric and music by Jerry Ragovoy and Mort Shuman)

NOTES—*Love, Janis* paid tribute to the blues/rock singer Janis Joplin (1943-1970). A program note indicated the entire spoken text of the revue came from Joplin herself (letters to her family as well as many press, television, and radio interviews during the period 1966-1970).

For the revue, one actress (Catherine Curtin) performed the speaking role of Joplin, and another actress the singing role (actually, two actresses, Andra Mitrovich and Cathy Richardson, alternated performances).

Anita Gates in the *New York Times* found the evening "surprisingly satisfying," and while the performers couldn't match the intensity of Joplin's singing, Gates noted the overall musical sound was authentic because Sam Andrews, the production's arranger and musical director, had been a member of Joplin's two bands (Big Brother and the Holding Company as well as the Kozmic Blues Band). Gates also noted it was somewhat disconcerting to learn that the iconic and controversial singer actually wrote letters to her mother, recommended books like *Rosemary's Baby*, and saw *Hello, Dolly!* on Broadway.

Love, Janis had been first produced by the Denver Center Theatre Company, and then was subsequently seen at the Cleveland Play House and the Bay Street Theatre in Sag Harbor, Maine.

Randal Myler, who directed *Love, Janis* and adapted it for the stage, was associated with three other Off Broadway musicals which looked at the lives and careers of pop singers (see entries for *Almost Heaven: Songs of John Denver*, *Dream a Little Dream* [The Mamas and The Papas], and *Hank Williams: Lost Highway*).

966 Love Kills

NOTES—See entry for *The New York Musical Theatre Festival.*

967 Love Lemmings.

THEATRE: The Village Gate Upstairs; OPENING DATE: April 18, 1991; PERFORMANCES: Unknown; SKETCHES: Joe DiPietro; LYRICS: Joe DiPietro and Eric Thoroman; MUSIC: Eric Thoroman; DIRECTION: Melia Bensussen; PRODUCERS: Fireball Entertainment in association with Mark May

CAST—Steve Ahern, Becky Borczon, John Daggett, Helen Greenberg

NOTES—According to Stephen Holden in the *New York Times*, Joe DiPietro and Eric Thoroman's Off Off Broadway revue *Love Lemmings* was an amusing look at "contemporary dating and mating rituals," themes which DePietro revisited in 1996 with his smash-hit revue *I Love You, You're Perfect, Now Change* (which is still playing as of December 31, 2007).

Holden singled out "Beat the Biological Clock," "Basic Dating," and "Men Who Don't Call and the Women Who Wait for Them" among twenty "viciously funny sketches," and he praised the cast, especially Helen Greenberg, whose expression reminded him of "someone who has just had a lemon twisted in her face."

Earlier versions of the revue had been seen in such venues as the West Bank Café and Steve McGraw's Supper Club.

968 Love! Love! Love!

"An All-American Musical 'Bout Love & Other Things." THEATRE: Astor Place Theatre; OPENING DATE: June 15, 1977; PERFORMANCES: 25; LYRICS: Johnny Brandon; MUSIC: Johnny Brandon; DIRECTION: Buck Heller; CHOREOGRAPHY: Buck Heller; SCENERY: Don Jensen; COSTUMES: Don Jensen; LIGHTING: Jeff Davis; MUSICAL DIRECTION: Clark McClellan; PRODUCER: Robert E. Richardson

CAST—Michael Calkins, Mel Johnson, Jr., Pat Lundy, Neva Rae Powers, Glory Van Scott

The action occurs in the U.S.A. during the present time.

The revue was presented in two acts.

ACT ONE—"The Great-All-American-Power-Driven-Engine" (Michael Calkins), "Searching for Love" (Company), "The Battle of Chicago" (Glory Van Scott), "Where Did the Dream Go" (Neva Rae Powers, Michael Calkins), "I Am You" (Mel Johnson, Jr., Michael Calkins), "Consenting Adults" (Company), "Come On In" (Neva Rae Powers, Mel Johnson, Jr.), "Preacher Man" (Mel Johnson, Jr.), "Age Is a State of Mind" (Neva Rae Powers), "Searching for Yesterdays" (Glory Van Scott), "Somewhere Along the Road" (Pat Lundy), "Reach Out" (Mel Johnson, Jr., Company), "Love! Love! Love!" (Pat Lundy, Company)

ACT TWO—"Empty Spaces" (Michael Calkins), "Look All Around You (See What's Happenin')" (Glory Van Scott), "Find Someone to Love (Song of the Soldier)" (Neva Rae Powers), "The Streets of Bed-Stuy" (Pat Lundy), "Where Did the Dream Go?" (reprise) (Mel Johnson, Jr., Glory Van Scott, Neva Rae Powers), "What Is There to Say?" (Mel Johnson, Jr.), "Mother's Day" (Michael Calkins), "Lovin'" (Pat Lundy), "What Did I Do Wrong?" (Neva Rae Powers), "Law and Order" (Glory Van Scott), "Middle-Class-Liberal-Blues" (Mel Johnson, Jr.), "Love! Love! Love!" and "Where Did the Dream Go?" (reprises) (Company)

NOTES—Johnny Brandon's *Cindy* (1964; see entry) was a mildly successful (if now forgotten) musical; but for the rest of his career even modest successes eluded him. All his remaining musicals were quick failures, including *Love! Love! Love!*, a revue which according to Richard Eder in the *New York Times* took potshots at easy and obvious targets (politicians, religion, bigots). Eder said the evening revisited "every slogan and cliché" of the previous decade, and he pronounced Brandon's lyrics "a mucilaginous mess of old underground editorials." But he found the music "fresh and appealing," and noted it overcame the "leaden" lyrics; Eder singled out "The Battle of Chicago" (a "rousing calypso strut") and "Somewhere Along the Road" (performed by Pat Lundy with a "shivering power").

969 Love Me, Love My Children.

THEATRE: Mercer-O'Casey Theatre; OPENING DATE: November 3, 1971; PERFORMANCES: 187; BOOK: Robert Swerdlow; LYRICS: Robert Swerdlow; MUSIC: Robert Swerdlow; DIRECTION: Paul Aaron; CHOREOGRAPHY: Elizabeth Swerdlow; SCENERY: "Stage form designed by" Jo Mielziner; COSTUMES: Patricia Quinn Stuart; LIGHTING: Dahl Delu; MUSICAL DIRECTION: Michael Alterman; PRODUCERS: Joel W. Schenker and Edward F. Kook

CAST—Don Atkinson, Mark Baker, Salome Bey, Jacqueline Britt, Matthew Diamond, Ed Evanko, Sharron Miller, Michon Peacock, Patsy Rahn, Chapman Roberts, Myrna Strom, Rose Mary Taylor, Suzanne Walker

The musical was presented in one act.

MUSICAL NUMBERS—"Don't Twist My Mind" (Company), "Reflections" (Chapman Roberts, Patsy Rahn), "Don't Twist Her Mind" (Rose Mary Taylor, Company), "See" (Salome Bey, Patsy Rahn, Matthew Diamond, Company), "Fat City" (Company), "Deca Dance" (Sharron Miller, Company), "Leave the World Behind" (Myrna Strom, Chapman Roberts, Suzanne Walker, Ed Evanko, Rose Mary Taylor, Company), "Don't Be a Miracle" (Company), "Face to Face" (Jacqueline Britt, Company), "Journey Home" (Salome Bey, Patsy Rahn, Michon Peacock), "Critics" (Don Atkinson, Mark Baker, Company), "Let Me Down" (Ed Evanko, Patsy Rahn, Company), "Walking in the World" (Salome Bey, Company), "North American Shmear" (Company), "Gingerbread Girl" (Chapman Roberts, Company), "Plot and Counterplot" (Company), "Do the Least You Can" (Ed Evanko, Chapman Roberts, Rose Mary Taylor, Michon Peacock, Company), "You're Dreaming" (Ed Evanko, Company), "Running Down the Sun" (Salome Bey, Patsy Rahn, Matthew Diamond), "Love Me, Love My Children" (Company), "Don't Twist My Mind" (reprise) (Company)

NOTES—*Love Me, Love My Children* was one of a number of Canadian musicals which appeared in New York during the 1970s (for more information, see entry for *Love and Maple Syrup*). It had originally been presented in Toronto as *Justine*, and played there for seven months. The Off Broadway production played almost as long (it's unclear if it recouped its investment). United Artists Records was to have recorded the Off Broadway cast album, which never materialized.

The musical dealt with a young woman who flees the culture of her middle-class life for the counterculture of the big city, where she first finds freedom, and then disappointment. Although the names of the characters weren't listed in the program, Patsy Rahn played the leading role of Justine (she and Salome Bey had also appeared in the Canadian production).

The critics praised the score, and Douglas Watt in the *New York Daily News* noted that Swerdlow was a composer, and not just a tunesmith. The score included Fifth Dimension-styled soft rock, traditional show tunes, vaudeville, waltz, Charleston, blues, ragtime, minuet, and "near classical" music. The ballad "Gingerbread Girl" was singled out by the critics, who also praised the comedy song "Critics" (which criticized the critics).

Louis Botto on NBC-4 felt the "rebel theme" in musicals such as *Love Me, Love My Children*, *Hair*, *Salvation*, and *Stomp* (see entries) was "beginning to get maudlin." Botto also praised "Critics," and noted that one of the lines in the song stated the job of critics was to "kill, kill, kill"; as far as *Love Me, Love My Children* was concerned, he said "Yes, Yes, Yes."

970 Love Sucks

NOTES—See entry for *The New York Musical Theatre Festival.*

971 Lovers.

THEATRE: Players Theatre; OPENING DATE: January 27, 1975; PERFORMANCES: 118; BOOK: Peter del Valle; LYRICS: Peter del Valle; MUSIC: Steve Sterner; DIRECTION: Steve Sterner; COSTUMES: Reve Richards; LIGHTING: Paul Sullivan; PRODUCERS: Phillip Graham-Geraci and Michael Brown

CAST—Martin Rivera (Freddie), Michael Cascone (Eddie), John Ingle (Harry), Robert Sevra (Dave), Reathel Bean (Spencer), Gary Sneed (George)

The revue was presented in two acts.

ACT ONE—"Lovers" (Company), "Look at Him" (Michael Cascone, Martin Rivera), "Make It" (John Ingle, Robert Sevra), "I Don't Want to Watch TV"/"Twenty Years" (Company), "Somebody, Somebody to Hold Me" (Robert Sevra), "Belt & Leather" (John Ingle, Robert Sevra), "There Is Always You" (Gary Sneed), "Hymn" (Company), "Somehow I'm Taller" (Michael Cascone, Gary Sneed, Company)

ACT TWO—"Role-Playing" (Gary Sneed, Reathel Bean, Martin Rivera, Michael Cascone), "Argument" (Gary Sneed, Reathel Bean), "Where Do I Go from Here?" (Martin Rivera, with Gary Sneed, John Ingle, Robert Sevra), "The Trucks" (Reathel Bean, John Ingle, Company), "Don't Betray His Love" (Gary Sneed, Company), "You Came to Me as a Young Man" (Reathel Bean), "Lovers" (reprise) (Company), "Somehow I'm Taller" (reprise) (Company)

NOTES—The program noted that *Lovers* is "The musical hit that proves IT'S NO LONGER SAD TO BE GAY." While Clive Barnes in the *New York Times* noted the "frank and often dirty" revue didn't "proselytize," he mentioned that the material was often stereotypical in its depiction of gays. He mentioned one sequence which dealt with two "belt-and-leather" types who to their dismay discover both are masochists "without a decent sadistic streak between them." He congratulated the author for not once referring to Fire Island.

Lovers ran out the season, but, like *The Faggot* (1973; see entry), its run was on the short side. For the time being, at least, gay-themed musicals were not particularly popular, and none of them could match the success of long-running gay-themed Off Broadway non-musicals, such as *The Boys in the Band* (1968; 1,000 performances).

The cast recording was released by Golden Gloves Music, Inc., Records (LP # PG-723-A/B), and included two songs not heard on opening night ("Celebrate" and "Help Him Along"), both of which may have been added during the run.

972 Lovesong. "A Musical Entertainment." THEATRE: Top of the Village Gate; OPENING DATE: October 5, 1976; PERFORMANCES: 24; LYRICS: Most lyrics adapted from the works of various writers and poets (specific credits following song titles, below); LYRIC ADAPTATIONS were by Henry Comor; ADDITIONAL LYRICS were by Edwin Dulchin, John Lewin, Kenneth Pressman, and Elsa Rael; ADDITIONAL POETRY used in the production by Dorothy Parker, Elsa Rael, Anne Sexton, Alfred, Lord Tennyson, William Shakespeare, and Edna St. Vincent Millay; MUSIC: Michael Valenti; DIRECTION: Michael Valenti (?); MUSICAL NUMBERS STAGED BY John Montgomery; CHOREOGRAPHIC ASSISTANT, Michael Perrier; SCENERY: Jack Logan; COSTUMES: Joan Mayo; LIGHTING: Martin Friedman; MUSICAL DIRECTION: David Krane; PRODUCERS: Wayne Starr in association with Thomas Hannan and Charles Kalan

CAST—Melanie Chartoff, Sigrid Heath, Ty McConnell, Jess Richards

The revue was presented in two acts.

ACT ONE—"What Is Love?" (by Sir Walter Raleigh [1522-1618]) (Company), "Did Not" (by Thomas Moore [1779-1852]) (Melanie Chartoff, Ty McConnell), "When I Was One-and-Twenty" (by A.E. Houseman [1859-1936]) (Company), "Bid Me Love" (by Robert Herrick [1591-1674]) (Company), "A Birthday" (by Christina Rossetti [1830-1894]) (Sigrid Heath), "Sophia" (by Edward Dulchin) (Jess Richards), "Many a Fairer Face" (anonymous) (Ty McConnell, Melanie Chartoff), "Maryann" (anonymous) (Sigrid Heath), "When We're Married" (by Elsa Rael) (Company), "To My Dear and Loving Husband" (by Anne Bradstreet [1612-1672]) (Sigrid Heath, Jess Richards), "I Remember" (by Thomas Hood [1799-1845]) (Jess Richards), "April Child" (by Kenneth Pressman) (Melanie Chartoff, Company), "Song" (by Thomas Lodge [1558-1625]) (Company), "What Is a Woman Like?" (anonymous) (Ty McConnell), "Let the Toast Pass" (by Richard Brinsley Sheridan [1751-1816]) (Company)

ACT TWO—"Let the Toast Pass" (reprise) (by Richard Brinsley Sheridan [1751-1816]) (Company), "Echo" (anonymous) (Company), "Open All Night" (by James Agee [1909-1955]) (Jess Richards), "A Rondelay" (by Peter Anthony Motteaux [1660-1718]) (Sigrid Heath, Jess Richards, Ty McConnell), "Just Suppose" (by Edward Dulchin) (Ty McConnell, Melanie Chartoff), "Unhappy Bella" (anonymous) (Melanie Chartoff, Company), "Young I Was" (anonymous) (Jess Richards), "Jenny Kiss'd Me" (by Leigh Hunt [1784-1859]) (Ty McConnell), "Indian Summer" (by Dorothy Parker [1893-1967]) (Melanie Chartoff), "The Fair Dissenter Lass" (by John Lewin) (Sigrid Heath), "Blood Red Roses" (by John Lewin) (Jess Richards, Company), "So, We'll Go No More A-Roving" (George Gordon, Lord Byron [1788-1824]) (Company), "An Epitaph" (by Richard Crashaw [c.1613-1649]) (Company)

NOTES—Michael Valenti's revue of love songs set to music by poets and other writers had first been produced in Toronto.

Clive Barnes in the *New York Times* felt the evening aimed to be another *Jacques Brel* but fell short because of its "totally unmemorable" score. *Lovesong* included two numbers from Valenti's 1970 Broadway musical *Blood Red Roses*, the title song and "Song of the Fair Dissenter Lass" (the latter listed in the program as "The Fair Dissenter Lass"). In both *Blood Red Roses* and *Lovesong*, Jess Richards sang "Blood Red Roses." The revue had been produced Off Off Broadway at The Showplace on July 8, 1976, with direction by Albert Harris; a few years after the revue was produced Off Broadway, its score was recorded by Original Cast Records (LP # OC-8022) with three of the original cast members (Melanie Chartoff, Sigrid Heath, and Jess Richards); Robert Manzari assumed the role created by Ty McConnell, and, curiously, it was Manzari, and not Richards, who is heard singing "Blood Red Roses" on the album. "What Is Love" and "Jenny Kiss'd [Kissed] Me" had earlier been heard in *Just for Love* (see entry); and "What Is Love" and "Just Suppose" were later heard in the 1977 production of *Mademoiselle Colombe* (see entry).

973 Lucky Stiff. "A New Musical Comedy." THEATRE: Playwrights Horizons; OPENING DATE: April 25, 1988; PERFORMANCES: 15; BOOK: Lynn Ahrens; LYRICS: Lynn Ahrens; MUSIC: Stephen Flaherty; DIRECTION: Thommie Walsh; SCENERY: Bob Shaw; COSTUMES: Michael Krass; LIGHTING: Beverly Emmons; MUSICAL DIRECTION: Jeffrey Saver; PRODUCER: Playwrights Horizons (Andre Bishop, Artistic Director; Paul S. Daniels, Executive Director)

CAST—Stephen Stout (Harry Witherspoon), Barbara Rosenblat (Mrs. Markham, Miss Thornsby, Nurse, Lady on a Train), Patty Holley (Boarder #1, Lady on a Train, Dominique du Monaco), Michael McCarty (Boarder #2, The Solicitor, Nightclub Emcee), Frank Zagottis (Boarder #3, Mr. Goldberg, French Waiter, Bellhop), Ron Faber (Uncle Anthony "Tony" Hendon), Stuart Zagnit (Dr. Vincent "Vinnie" DiRuzzio), Mary Testa (Rita La Porta), Paul Kandel (Luigi Gaudi), Julie White (Annabel Glick), Nightclub Patrons, Gamblers, Passengers, and Tourists (Ron Faber, Patty Holley, Paul Kandel, Michael McCarty, Barbara Rosenblat, Frank Zagottis)

SOURCE—The 1983 novel *The Man Who Broke the Bank at Monte Carlo* by Michael Butterworth.

The action occurs in the present in England, New Jersey, and Monte Carlo.

The musical was presented in two acts.

ACT ONE—"Something Funny's Going On" (Company), "Mr. Witherspoon's Friday Night" (Stephen Stout, Barbara Rosenblat, Patty Holley, Michael McCarty, Frank Zagottis, Passengers), "Rita's Confession" (Mary Testa, Stuart Zagnit), "Good to Be Alive" (Stephen Stout, Paul Kandel, Passengers), "Lucky" (Stephen Stout, Ron Faber), "Dogs Versus You" (Julie White, Stephen Stout), "The Phone Call" (Stuart Zagnit), "A Day Around Town Dance" (Stephen Stout, Julie White, Ron Faber, Company), "Monte Carlo" (Michael McCarty), "Speaking French" (Patty Holey, Stephen Stout, Patrons), "Times Like This" (Julie White), "Monte Carlo" (reprise) (Michael McCarty), "Fancy Meeting You Here" (Mary Testa), "Good to Be Alive" (reprise) (Gamblers)

ACT TWO—"Something Funny's Going On" (reprise) (Company), "Him, Them, It, Her" (Company), "Nice" (Julie White, Stephen Stout), "Harry's Nightmare: Welcome Back, Mr. Witherspoon" (Company), "A Woman in My Bathroom" (Stephen Stout), "Nice" (reprise) (Julie White, Stephen Stout, Mary Testa), "Confession #2" (Mary Testa, Stephen Stout, Julie White, Ron Faber), "Fancy Meeting You Here" (reprise) (Mary Testa, Ron Faber), "Good to Be Alive" (reprise) (Stephen Stout, Julie White, Company)

NOTES—*Lucky Stiff* told the amusing story of a young man who in order to inherit his uncle's fortune must take the body of the dead uncle on a vacation to Monte Carlo (the uncle has thoughtfully provided a list of things he wants to do on the trip); if the uncle is denied his vacation, his millions will go to a dog shelter. With a dead body, a dog activist, an accidental murder, and a various assortment of busy bodies, the musical had potential. But Frank Rich in the *New York Times* reported the evening was a near miss, and faulted Lynn Ahrens' shaky book. As for her lyrics, Rich found them "winning" and "delightful," and singled out the plot-driven "Him, Them, It, Her," which was "far cleverer" than the narrative. He also noted that the score by Stephen Flaherty was "professional" and "serviceably tuneful." The musical was the team's first, and Rich felt their promising future was "more in need of guidance than luck." *Lucky Stiff* has been recorded twice. In 2003, a revival by the York Theater Company was recorded by Jay Records (CD # CDJAY-1379); besides Malcolm Gets, the recording included 1988 cast members Ron Faber, Paul Kandel, Barbara Rosenblat, Mary Testa, and Stuart Zagnit; the recording also included a bonus song, "Shoes," which had been written for, but never used, in any production of the musical. In 2004, a studio cast recording was released by Varese Sarabande Records (CD # VSD-5461); it, too, included some original cast members (Paul Kandel, Barbara Rosenblat, Mary Testa) as well as Judy Blazer, Jason Graae, Debbie Shapiro Gravitt, and Evan Pappas. One song from the musical ("Times Like This") served as the title of Lynn Maxwell's CD collection of many obscure Broadway and Off Broadway songs (released by Original Cast Records # OC-8061).

974 The Lullaby of Broadway, or Harry Who? THEATRE: Boltax Theatre; OPENING DATE: November 27, 1979; PERFORMANCES: 36; SCRIPT: Judith Haskell and Mark O'Donnell; MUSIC: Harry Warren; DIRECTION: Judith Haskell; CHOREOGRAPHY: Eleanor Treiber; COSTUMES: Kevin Reid; LIGHTING: Rick Belzer; MUSICAL DIRECTION: Jeremy Harris; PRODUCER: Leonard M. Landau

CAST—Suellen Estey, Josie O'Donnell, Jess Richards, Scott Robertson

NOTES—The title of this Off Off Broadway 1979 composer-tribute revue asked *Harry Who?*, and indeed the name of Harry Warren was probably not all that well known to the general theatre-going public. The prolific composer was most closely associated with film musicals, and over the years he contributed an impressive array of standards to the American songbook, including "I Only Have Eyes for You" (1934 film *Dames*; lyric by Al Dubin); "September in the Rain" (1935 film *Stars Over Broadway*; lyric by Al Dubin); "Chattanooga Choo-Choo" (1941 film *Sun Valley Serenade*; lyric by Mack Gordon); "There Will Never Be Another You" (1942 film *Iceland*; lyric by Mack Gordon); "At Last" (1942 film *Orchestra Wives*; lyric by Mack Gordon); and "That's Amore" (1953 film *The Caddy*; lyric by Jack Brooks). He won three Academy Awards for Best Song: "Lullaby of Broadway" (1935 film *Gold Diggers of 1935*; lyric by Al Dubin); "You'll Never Know" (1943 film *Hello, Frisco, Hello*; lyric by Mack Gordon); and "On the Atchison, Topeka and the Santa Fe" (1946 film *The Harvey Girls*; lyric by Johnny Mercer). In 1980, David Merrick produced a stage version of Warren's 1933 film musical *42nd Street*, and after that Warren's name no longer elicited a question mark. The musical won the Tony Award for Best Musical, and played on Broadway for 3,486 performances; it was revived on Broadway in 2001, won the Tony Award for Best Revival of a Musical, and played for 1,524 performances.

975 Lullabye and Goodnight. "A Musical Romance." THEATRE: Newman Theatre/The Public Theatre; OPENING DATE: February 9, 1982; PERFORMANCES: 30; BOOK: Elizabeth Swados; LYRICS: Elizabeth Swados; MUSIC: Elizabeth Swados; DIRECTION: Elizabeth Swados; CHOREOGRAPHY: Ara Fitzgerald; SCENERY: David Jenkins; COSTUMES: Hilary Rosenfeld; LIGHTING: Marcia Madeira; PRODUCER: The New York Shakespeare Festival (Joseph Papp, Director; Jason Steven Cohen, Production Supervisor)

CAST—Frances Asher (Retail), Gail Boggs (Velvet Puppy), Jesse Corti (Deputy), Jossie de Guzman (Lullabye), Ula Hedwig (Stiletto), Bruce Hubbard

(Trojan), Larry Marshall (Snow), Olga Merediz (Saint), Tim Moore (Cody), Rudy Roberson (Chameleon)

The musical was presented in two acts.

ACT ONE—Prologue (Company), "Gentlemen of Leisure" (Larry Marshall, Women), "Port Authority" (Women), "I Am Sick of Love" (Larry Marshall, Jossie de Guzman), "When a Pimp Meets a Whore" (Larry Marshall, Jossie de Guzman), "Love Loves the Difficult Things" (Larry Marshall, Jossie de Guzman, Men), "In the Life" (Company), "The Moth and the Flame" (Larry Marshall, Jossie de Guzman, Women), "Why We Do It" (Women), "Wife Beating Song" (Jossie de Guzman), "You're My Favorite Lullabye" (Larry Marshall, Jossie de Guzman), "When Any Woman Makes a Running Issue Out of Her Flesh" (Company), "Now You Are One of the Family" (Larry Marshall, Jossie de Guzman, Company), "Turn Her Out" (Larry Marshall, Company), "You Gave Me Love" (Jossie de Guzman)

ACT TWO—"Let the Day Perish When I Was Born" (Jossie de Guzman, Larry Marshall), "Keep Working" (Larry Marshall, Company), "Deprogramming Song" (Jossie de Guzman), "Lies, Lies, Lies" (Jossie de Guzman, Larry Marshall), "Ladies, Look at Yourselves" (Jossie de Guzman, Women), "Don't You Ever Give It All Away" (Jossie de Guzman, Larry Marshall, Company), "Man That Is Born of a Woman" (Larry Marshall, Men), "Sub-Babylon" (Larry Marshall, Company), "Getting from Day to Day" (Larry Marshall), "Sweet Words" (Larry Marshall, Jossie de Guzman, Company), "The Nightmare Was Me" (Jossie de Guzman, Company)

NOTES—The program for *Lullabye and Goodnight* stated Elizabeth Swados had been working on the musical for three years; once it opened, the musical about pimps and prostitutes was gone in less than four weeks. Frank Rich in the *New York Times* reported the musical was essentially inspired by two songs ("Minnesota Strip" and "Song of a Child Prostitute") from Swados' earlier *Runaways* (see entry). Rich found the monotonous *Lullabye and Goodnight* a "failure," and mentioned that for every "sincere" and "anguished" song, Swados offered "at least" two more which "needlessly attitudinize or hector." He felt musical was condescending not only to its audience but to its subject matter, and noted that Swados provided "repeated authorial lectures" on how prostitution mirrors "corporate America" and "conventional male-female relationships." One of *Lullabye*'s songs was "In the Life," and the title brings to mind another musical which was long aborning and which was also about pimps and prostitutes, Cy Coleman's *The Life*, which finally opened on Broadway in 1996. Despite a year's run, *The Life* lost money, but left behind a cast album with a typically melodic Coleman score. As for its plot, there was too much of it, and had Coleman divided the story three or four ways, he no doubt could have written a cycle of musicals on the subject.

Speaking of Coleman, Rich reported that two numbers from *Lullabye and Goodnight* were restatements of "Big Spender" and "There's Gotta Be Something Better Than This," two songs from Coleman's *Sweet Charity* (1966).

976 Lulu.

"A New Musical." THEATRE: Direct Theatre; OPENING DATE: January 20, 1977; PERFORMANCES: 24 (estimated); BOOK: Ross Alexander; adapted by Allen R. Belknap; LYRICS: Gary Levinson; MUSIC: Gary Levinson; DIRECTION: Allen R. Belknap; CHOREOGRAPHY: "Additional choreography" by John Werkheiser; SCENERY: Gary R. Langley; COSTUMES: Janet Bartu and Elaine Massas; LIGHTING: Richard Winkler; PRODUCER: Direct Theatre (Allen R. Belknap, Artistic Director)

CAST—Fred Martell (Jack), D'JAMIN BARTLETT (Lulu), James Carruthers (Ludwig Schoen), Jeff Ware (Alva Schoen), Bob Del Pazzo (Dr. Goll, Alfred Hugenberg, Casti Piani), Charles Leader (Schwartz), Kermit Brown (Schigolch), Y. York (Countess Geschwitz), Peter Jason (Rodrigo)

SOURCES—The *Lulu* plays of Frank Wedekind (*Earth Spirit* [1895] and *Pandora's Box* [1902]).

The musical was presented in two acts.

ACT ONE—"My Life Is Love" (D'Jamin Bartlett, Company), "Every Afternoon at Four"/"Little Nell" (Bob Del Pazzo), "I Knew Her" (D'Jamin Bartlett, Kermit Brown), "The Perfect Woman"/"Eve" (Charles Leader), "Impressions" (D'Jamin Bartlett), "Suddenly"/"Mignon" (D'Jamin Bartlett), "The Autumn of My Life" (James Carruthers), "Stock Exchange Day" (Peter Jason, Bob Del Pazzo, Kermit Brown, Y. York), "Tell Me Who I Am" (D'Jamin Bartlett)

ACT TWO—"Pandora's Box" (D'Jamin Bartlett, Company), "The Roll of the Dice" (Bob Del Pazzo, Company; solos, Y. York, Bob Del Pazzo, Peter Jason, Jeff Ware, Kermit Brown), "Pandora's Waltz" (D'Jamin Bartlett)

NOTES—Once the Off Off Broadway musical *Lulu* played out its limited engagement, it disappeared; the musical was based on Frank Wedekind's two *Lulu* plays, *Earth Spirit* and *Pandora's Box*. Alban Berg's 1937 opera *Lulu* remains the definitive musical adaptation of the *Lulu* plays, and another memorable version of the material is the silent 1928 German film *Pandora's Box*, directed by G.W. Pabst (Louise Brooks was Lulu). One year after the Off Off Broadway musical opened, Off Broadway offered a dramatic adaptation (also called *Lulu*) of the *Lulu* plays. Produced by the Circle Repertory Theatre, the translation was by Frances Fawcett and Stephen Spender (Trish Hawkins was Lulu, and the cast included Jeff Daniels); incidental music for the production was composed by Norman L. Berman. Richard Eder in the *New York Times* found the evening a "disaster," a "jumble," and a "junkyard of theatrical effects."

977 Das Lusitania Songspiel (1976).

THEATRE: Van Dam Theatre; OPENING DATE: May 10, 1976; PERFORMANCES: 8; PRODUCER: John Rothman Productions Ltd. in association with the Direct Theatre and Dorothy Ames

NOTES—The evening consisted of a brief curtain-raiser, *Das Lusitania Songspiel*, a spoof of Brechtian cabaret (with "Swiss Family Trapp" supposedly from a musical version of *Mother Courage*), which was followed by *Titanic*, a one-act play (for more information about the latter, see below). Later in the year, on November 19, *Das Lusitania Songspiel* (sans *Titanic*) was presented Off Off Broadway at the Direct Theatre; for this production, Christopher Durang and Sigourney Weaver reprised their roles. In 1980, Durang and Weaver revisited the musical (again, without *Titanic*); see entry for this production.

Das Lusitania Songspiel ("The Theatre Songs of Bertolt Breck"). LYRICS: Various lyricists, including Christopher Durang; MUSIC: Various composers (see below); DIRECTION: Peter Mark Schifter; PIANIST: Jack Gaughan

CAST—Christopher Durang, Sigourney Weaver

MUSICAL NUMBERS—"The Frogs" (from *The Frogs*, 1974; lyric and music by Stephen Sondheim), "The Sea Gull" (*The Caucasian Chalk Circle*; lyric by Christopher Durang, music by Jack Feldman), "A Public Place" (*The Beggar's Opera*; lyric by Christopher Durang, music by Walt Jones), "Swiss Family Trapp" (*Mother Courage*; lyric by Christopher Durang, music by Walt Jones), "The Young Sailor's Lesson" (*The Measures Taken*; lyric by Christopher Durang, music by Jack Gaughan), "Song of Economic Difficulty" (*Der Mensch Ist Schlect*; lyric by Christopher Durang, music by Leon Jessel)

MORE NOTES—The program credited research to Christopher Durang and Sigourney Weaver, and "Miss Wiegel's audition piece by Wendy Wasserstein and Mr. Durang."

Titanic. PLAY by Christopher Durang; DIRECTION: Peter Mark Schifter; SCENERY: Ernie Smith; COSTUMES: Ernie Smith; LIGHTING: Mitchell Kurtz

CAST—Kate McGregor-Stewart (Victoria Tammurai), Stefan Hartman (Richard Tammaurai), Richard Peterson (Teddy Tammurai), Sigourney Weaver (Lidia), Jeff Brooks (The Captain), Ralph Redpath (Higgins)

Titanic was a black farce about imagined goings-on aboard the ill-fated maiden voyage of the "unsinkable" ocean liner.

978 Das Lusitania Songspiel (1980).

THEATRE: Vanities Theatre/Chelsea Theatre Center; OPENING DATE: January 10, 1980; PERFORMANCES: 24; WRITTEN BY Christopher Durang and Sigourney Weaver; PRODUCTION SUPERVISED BY Garland Wright; PRODUCERS: Milton Justice and Jack Heifner

CAST—SIGOURNEY WEAVER, CHRISTOPHER DURANG, Bob Goldstone (Piano)

The revue was presented in one act.

MUSICAL NUMBERS—Overture (from *The Rise and Fall of the City of Magahonny*, 1930; music by Kurt Weill), Songs from *The Frogs* (lyrics and music by Stephen Sondheim), "The Young Sailor's Lesson" (music by Jack Gaughan), "The Bouillabaisse Song" (music by Mel Marvin), "The Song of Economic Reality (or, Diamonds Are the Best Friend for a Girl)" (music by Mel Marvin), Medley of songs by Kurt Weill, "The Song of Economic Difficulty" (music by Leon Jessel)

NOTES—The revival of *Das Lusitania Songspiel* credited both Sigourney Weaver and Christopher Durang for the material (unless otherwise noted, all lyrics were by Weaver and Durang). The original production had credited only Durang.

The limited-engagement revue was performed at the Chelsea Theatre Center after performances of Jack Heifner's long-running play *Vanities* (1976), and the program thanked both the cast of *Vanities* ("for the use of their dressing room") and John Arnone, who designed the scenery for *Vanities*, for the use of his set. See entry for information about the original 1976 production of *Das Lusitania Songspiel*, which was performed with *Titanic*, a one-act play by Christopher Durang. For the 1980 revival of *Lusitania*, *Titanic* didn't make the voyage.

979 Lust.

"A Musical Romp." THEATRE: John Houseman Theatre; OPENING DATE: July 13, 1995; PERFORMANCES: 27; BOOK: The Heather Brothers; LYRICS: The Heather Brothers; MUSIC: The Heather Brothers; DIRECTION: Bob Carlton; CHOREOGRAPHY: Barry Finkel; SCENERY: Rodney Ford; COSTUMES: Rodney Ford; LIGHTING: F. Mitchell Dana; MUSICAL DIRECTION: John Johnson; PRODUCERS: Eric Krebs, Frederic B. Vogel, Anne Strickland Squadron, A Walnut Street Theatre Production; Michael Plunkett, Barry Holland, and Nancy Myers, Associate Producers

CAST—Denis Lawson (Horner), Robert McCormick (Quack), David Barron (Pinchwife), Jennifer Lee Andrews (Margery Pinchwife), Lee Golden (Sir Jasper Fidget), Judith Moore (Lady Fidget), Janet Aldrich (Mistress Dainty), Suzanne Ishee (Mistress Squeamish), Jennifer Piech (Alithea Pinchwife), A.J. Vincent (Harcourt), Dan Schiff (Dorilant), Barry Finkel (Sparkish), Servants and Townspeople (Michael Babin, Leslie Castay, James Javore)

SOURCE—The play *The Country Wife* by William Wycherly (Wycherley, according to some sources), written in either 1672 or 1673 and first published in 1675.

The action occurs in London during 1661.

The musical was presented in two acts.

ACT ONE—"Lust" (Company), "The Art of Deceiving" (Robert McCormick, Denis Lawson), "Serve the Dog Right" (Company), "I Live for Love" (Denis Lawson), "A Pox on Love and Wenching" (Denis Lawson, Robert McCormick, A.J. Vincent, Barry Finkel, Dan Schiff), "I Live for Love" (reprise) (Denis Lawson), "Somewhere Out There" (Jennifer Lee Andrews), "Ladies of Quality" (Judith Moore, Suzanne Ishee, Janet Aldrich), "Husbands Beware" (Denis Lawton, Robert McCormick, Suzanne Ishee, Janet Aldrich, Judith Moore), "Why Did You Have to Come Into My Life?" (A.J. Vincent, Jennifer Piech), "What a Handsome Little Fellow" (Company), "The Captain's Jig" (a/k/a "Tyburn Jig") (Company), "Wait and See"/"Lust" (reprise) (Company)

ACT TWO—"Lust" (reprise) (Company), "Dear Sir" (David Barron, Jennifer Lee Andrews), "Ode to the One I Love" (Denis Lawson), "China" (Lee Golden, Robert McCormick, Denis Lawson, Judith Moore, Janet Aldrich, Suzanne Ishee), "Come Tomorrow" (Jennifer Piech, A.J. Vincent, Jennifer Lee Andrews), "The Master Class" (Denis Lawson, Jennider Lee Andrews), "One of You" (Denis Lawson, Judith Moore, Janet Aldrich, Suzanne Ishee), "Vengeance" (Company), "The Master Class" (reprise) (Denis Lawson, Judith Moore, Janet Aldrich, Suzanne Ishee, Jennifer Lee Andrews), "We Thank You"/"Lust" (reprise) (Company)

NOTES—The Off Off Broadway musical *Lust* originally opened in London at the Theatre Royal Haymarket on in July 19, 1993, and its American premiere took place at the Walnut Street Theatre in Philadelphia.

Stephen Holden in the *New York Times* found the evening of sexual goings-on among the British upper-classes flat and unfunny, noting that too often the musical confused "mugging and buffoonery with focused comic energy." As for the score, it was a "thin, cheesy fusion of Purcell and early-1960's New York pop."

The New York production didn't include "A Little Time in the Country," which had been heard in London.

The script was published by Samuel French (London) in 1994.

For an earlier Off Broadway adaptation of *The Country Wife*, see entry for *She Shall Have Music* (1959); the entry also references *My Love to Your Wife*, a 1977 musical adaptation of the material which was seen in regional theatre.

980 Lyle. THEATRE: McAlpin Rooftop Theatre; OPENING DATE: March 20, 1970; PERFORMANCES: 3; BOOK: Chuck Horner; LYRICS: Toby Garson; MUSIC: Janet Gari; DIRECTION: Marvin Gordon; SCENERY: Jack Blackman; COSTUMES: Winn Morton; LIGHTING: Jack Blackman; MUSICAL DIRECTION: Robert Esty; PRODUCER: Marilyn Cantor Baker

CAST—Steve Harmon (Lyle), Joey Faye (Hector), Jack Fletcher (Mr. Grimble), Stanley Grover (Bob Primm), Ann Vivian (Joan Primm), Steven Paul (Josh Primm), Matthew Tobin (Mr. Long, Guard, Mr. Mamakos), Ellyn Harris (Secretary, European Announcer), Dick Bonelle (Policeman, Postman, Antonio, Mr. Carruthers), Noreen Nichols (European Announcer)

SOURCE—A series of children's books by Bernard Waber.

The action occurs at the present time.

The musical was presented in two acts (division of acts and song assignments unknown; songs are listed in performance order).

MUSICAL NUMBERS—"Always Leave 'Em Wanting More," "I Can't Believe It's Real," "Generation Gap," "I Belong," "Me, Me, Me," "Alternative Parking," "Try to Make the Best of It," "Loretta," "Look at Me," "Crocodiles Cry," "On the Road," "Lyle's Turn," "Suddenly You're a Stranger," "Everybody Wants to Be Remembered," "Lyle," "Things Were Much Better in the Past," "We Belong"

NOTES—*Lyle* was based on a series of children's books by Bernard Waber. Clive Barnes in the *New York Times* reported the musical would please neither children nor adults, and noted the bland book, lyrics, and music brought "the concept of nothingness to new depths." He also reported there was little in the way of costuming to indicate the title character was a crocodile; unless one had been told so, one never would have guessed it. Producer Marilyn Cantor Baker and composer Janet (Cantor) Gari were Eddie Cantor's daughters, and lyricist Toby Garson was Harry Ruby's daughter. In January 1970, the *New York Times* reported the $60,000 production had ninety-three backers, including Dick Cavett and Woody Allen. It also reported the musical was scheduled to open on March 4 (it eventually opened on March 20) and that Gene Baylis was to direct (Marvin Gordon later replaced him). During previews, the title role was played by Carleton Carpenter (Steve Harmon eventually assumed the role).

Cast member Joey Faye (1909-1997) was an amiable and impish performer (the credits of Sergio Leone's classic 1984 film *Once Upon a Time in America* list his very brief role as "Adorable Old Man") who was inordinately unlucky in his choice of musicals. Approximately 165 new musicals and revues opened on Broadway during the 1940s, thirty of them lasting for twenty or less performances. And poor Joey Faye was in three of them: *Allah Be Praised!* (1944, 20 performances); *The Duchess Misbehaves* (1946, 5 performances; Faye replaced star Jackie Gleason, who decamped during the Philadelphia tryout); and *Tidbits of 1946* (8 performances; Howard Barnes in the *New York Herald Tribune* noted the revue was "a random assortment of vaudeville canapés, with an abundance of crumbs").

Faye had earlier appeared in the 1938 revue *Sing Out the News* (105 performances); and was later seen in *Top Banana* (1951, 350 performances; although it ran for almost a year and was later filmed, the musical lost money); *Little Me* (1962, 257 performances; despite the musical's favorable reputation [which sparked two Broadway revivals], Cy Coleman and Carolyn Leigh's delightful score, and Bob Fosse's memorable choreography, the musical was a financial failure); *70, Girls, 70* (1971, 36 performances, and the shortest-running of all the John Kander and Fred Ebb collaborations); and *Grind* (1985, 79 performances). Faye was also in four musicals which closed during their pre-Broadway tryouts: *Windy City* (1946); *The Amazing Adele* (1956; the musical would have marked Tammy Grimes' Broadway debut in the title role; she had to wait a few more years before creating two title roles on Broadway [the comedy *Look After Lulu* [1959] and the musical *The Unsinkable Molly Brown* [1960]); *Strip for Action* (1956; the musical was adapted from the 1942 play *Strip for Action*, which lasted just three months [Faye had also appeared in the non-musical version]); and *Hellzapoppin'* (which starred Jerry Lewis and Lynn Redgrave and which closed in 1977; it was produced by Alexander Cohen [see below for The Alexander Cohen Curse]).

Lyle played for just three performances, and Faye's other Off Broadway musical, *The Coolest Cat in Town* (1978; see entry), for which he was top billed, lasted for only thirty-seven performances.

With fourteen musical failures on his resume, Faye could nonetheless boast of one unqualified success. He was featured in *High Button Shoes* (1947), one of the biggest hits of the late 1940s, running 727 performances. *Lyle* was the premiere attraction at the new McAlpin Roof Theatre which was located on the top floor of the McAlpin Hotel; the theatre occupied the space of what had once been the hotel's ballroom.

Charles Strouse wrote the book, lyrics, and music for his own adaptation of Waber's *Lyle* stories; Strouse's version, which was based on Waber's *The House on East 88th Street*, premiered in London at the Lyric Hammersmith on November 28, 1987; the musical was later seen in 1988 at the Empire State Institute for the Performing Arts in Albany, New York.

In regard to The Alexander Cohen Curse, Cohen is now perhaps best remembered as the producer (sometimes co-producer) of an extraordinary number of musical flops which opened over a period of fifty-two years: *Of V We Sing* (1942, 76 performances); *Bright Lights of 1944* (1943, 4 performances); *Make a Wish* (1951, 102 performances); *Courtin' Time* (1951, 37 performances); *Lena Horne and Her Nine O'Clock Revue* (closed in 1961 during its pre-Broadway tryout); *Rugantino* (1964, 28 performances); *Baker Street* (1965, 313 performances); *A Time for Singing* (1966, 41 performances); *Hellzapoppin'* (the 1967 version which starred Soupy Sales and which closed during its pre-Broadway tryout); *Dear World* (1969, 132 performances); *Prettybelle* (closed in 1971 during its pre-Broadway tryout); *Hellzapoppin'* (the Jerry Lewis version which closed in 1977 during its pre-Broadway tryout); *I Remember Mama* (1979, 108 performances [the production was Richard Rodgers' final musical]); and *Comedy Tonight* (1994, 9 performances). Sometimes theatrical curses crossed paths: Carmen Mathews appeared in two of Cohen's musicals (*Courtin' Time* and *Dear World*; for more information on "The "Carmen Mathews Curse," see entry for *Sunday in the Park with George*); Joey Faye appeared in Cohen's *Hellzapoppin'* (the 1976-1977 production); Louisiana was the setting of Cohen's *Prettybelle* (see entry for *Basin Street* regarding the many unlucky musicals which were set in either New Orleans or in Louisiana); and Italy was the setting of Cohen's *Rugantino* (for "The Italian Curse," see entry for *Fortuna*). Cohen produced two musicals which were hits. Despite its relatively short run of 127 performances, *Words and Music*, the 1974 tribute to Sammy Cahn, turned a profit. And *A Day in Hollywood/A Night in the Ukraine* opened in 1980 for a healthy run of 588 performances.

981 Lyrical and Satirical: The Music of Harold Rome. THEATRE: The Little Church Around the Corner; OPENING DATE: November 30, 1977; PERFORMANCES: 12; LYRICS: Harold Rome; MUSIC: Harold Rome; DIRECTION: Julianne Boyd; CHOREOGRAPHY: Jeff Veazey; SCENERY: Lee Mayman; COSTUMES: Rachel Kurland; LIGHTING: Boyd Masten; MUSICAL DIRECTION: Vicki H. Carter; PRODUCER: Joseph Jefferson Theatre Company, Inc.

CAST—Cris Groenendaal, Sophie Schwab, Gordon Stanley, Susan Waldman

The revue was presented in two acts.

ACT ONE—*Mostly Satirical*: "Sing Me a Song of Social Significance" (from *Pins and Needles*, 1937) (Company), "(It's) Not Cricket to Picket" (*Pins and Needles*, 1937) (Susan Waldman), "It's Better with a Union Man" (*Pins and Needles*, 1937) (Gordon Stanley, Sophie Schwab, Cris Groenendaal), "My Heart Is Unemployed" (*Sing Out the News*, 1938) (Cris Groenendaal), "Nobody Makes a Pass at Me" (*Pins and Needles*, 1937) (Sophie Schwab), "Cry, Baby, Cry" (*Pretty Penny*, 1949; closed during pre-Broadway tryout) (Gordon Stanley), "Respectability" (*Destry Rides Again*, 1959) (Sophie Schwab, Susan Waldman), The Money Medley: "The Money Song" (*That's the Ticket!*, 1948; closed during pre-Broadway tryout) (Cris Groenendaal, Company), "The Sound of Money" (*I Can Get It for You Wholesale*, 1962), (Gordon Stanley, Company), "What Good Is Love?" (*Pins and Needles*, 1937) (Sophie Schwab), "Military Life" (*Call Me Mister*, 1946) (Cris Groenendaal, Gordon Stanley), "Four Little Angels of Peace (Are We)" (*Pins and Needles*, 1937) (Company), "What Are

They Doing to Us Now?" (*I Can Get It for You Wholesale*, 1962) (Susan Waldman, Ensemble)

ACT TWO—*Mostly Lyrical*: "Love, It Hurts So Good" (*Alive and Kicking*, 1950) (Company), "I Have to Tell You" (*Fanny*, 1954) (Susan Waldman), "Fanny" (*Fanny*, 1954) (Cris Groenendaal), "A Funny Thing Happened (on My Way to Love)" (*I Can Get It for You Wholesale*, 1962) (Sophie Schwab, Gordon Stanley), "Miss Marmelstein" (*I Can Get It for You Wholesale*, 1962) (Susan Waldman), "Don Jose of Far Rockaway" (*Wish You Were Here*, 1952) (Gordon Stanley, Company), "Wish You Were Here" (*Wish You Were Here*, 1952) (Sophie Schwab, Cris Groenendaal), "Fair Warning" (*Destry Rides Again*, 1959) (Susan Waldman), "One of These Fine Days" (*Sing Out the News*, 1938) (Cris Groenendaal), "Shopping Around" (*Wish You Were Here*, 1952) (Sophie Schwab, Susan Waldman), "Restless Heart" (*Fanny*, 1954) (Gordon Stanley), "Be Kind to Your Parents" (*Fanny*, 1954) (Company), "Half-Forgotten Teddy Bear" (from Gallery Records album, 1964) (Sophie Schwab), "Like the Breeze Blows" (*The Zulu and the Zayda*, 1965) (Company)

NOTES—Harold Rome, one of Broadway's finest lyricists and composers, is all but forgotten today. Most of his works were revues, and thus are not particularly revivable, and most of his book musicals had weak libretti. With its superior score and generally strong book, *Fanny* (1954) is probably the most likely of his musicals to enjoy occasional stagings. *I Can Get It for You Wholesale* (1962) is Rome's masterpiece, but it had a generally short Broadway run and its leading character is tough and cold (and thus unlikable); as a result, *Wholesale* is most likely to be revived by small and innovative theatre companies and will probably never get the chance for another Broadway showing. The revue included songs from two of Rome's productions which never made it to New York: *That's the Ticket!* (1948) and *Pretty Penny* (1949). The former received an Off Off Broadway production in 2001 (see entry), which was released by Original Cast Records.

But the fascinating revue *Pretty Penny* remains elusive. It opened at the Bucks County Playhouse on June 20, 1949, with lyrics and music by Rome and sketches by Jerome Chodorov. It was directed by George S. Kaufman, was choreographed by Michael Kidd, and the musical direction was by Rome himself. The cast included David Burns and Carl Reiner, as well as Michael Kidd (already an established Broadway choreographer) and two future Broadway choreographers, Onna White and Peter Gennaro.

Pretty Penny included three numbers from *That's the Ticket!* ("[You Never Know] What Hit You [When It's Love]," "Gin Rummy Rhapsody," and "The Ballad of Marcia La Rue"). Two numbers from *Pretty Penny* were used in other Rome musicals: "French with Tears" and "Cry, Baby, Cry" found their way into *Alive and Kicking* (1950).

One sketch ("Death with Father") was a spoof of *Life with Father* (1939), while another ("Life of a Salesman") kidded *Death of a Salesman* (1949). Television was satirized in the sketch *Operation Television*, and Rome seems to have spoofed himself in the song "Up North American Way," a musical cousin of "South America, Take It Away" (from *Call Me Mister* [1946]).

982 Lyrics and Lyricists/Great Lyricists Remembered

NOTES—Beginning in 1970 with a tribute to E.Y. Harburg, the Music Department of the 92nd Street YM-YWHA, in cooperation with the Billy Rose Foundation, began its unique and indispensable *Lyrics and Lyricists/Great Lyricists Remembered* series, which was devoted to evenings paying tribute to lyricists of the American musical theatre. In its early years, Maurice Levine was the series' Artistic Director, and Hadassah B. Markson was the Director of the Y's Music Department.

Over the years, such lyricists as Oscar Hammerstein II and Cole Porter have been honored. Perhaps a typical example of these tributes is the one presented on May 13 and 15, 1979, which honored Otto Harbach (1873-1963). The singers, musicians, and speakers for the evening were William Harbach (Narrator), Stanley Adams (Speaker [Adams was the president of ASCAP]), Harry Danner (Singer), Sheldon Harnick (Speaker, Singer), Judith McCauley (Singer), Tom Urich (Singer), Kay Armen (Singer), and Michael Renzi (Pianist).

The tribute included twenty-eight of Harbach's songs, including such familiar ones as "The Night Was Made for Love" (from *The Cat and the Fiddle* [1931, music by Jerome Kern], sung by Harry Danner) and "Smoke Gets in Your Eyes" (*Roberta* [1933, music by Jerome Kern], sung by Kay Armen) and such esoteric numbers as "The Tickle Toe" (*Going Up* [1917, music by Louis A. Hirsch], sung by Danner, Tom Urich, and Judith McCauley) and "Something Had to Happen" (*Roberta*, sung by Urich and McCauley). Sheldon Harnick analyzed (and then sang) the lyrics of "Poor Pierrot" (*The Cat and the Fiddle*) and "Let's Begin" (*Roberta*).

In 2008, the *Lyrics and Lyricists* series will begin its thirty-eighth season with scheduled tributes to Sammy Cahn, Fred Ebb, and Carolyn Leigh.

983 Lyz!

THEATRE: Samuel Beckett Theatre; OPENING DATE: January 10, 1999; PERFORMANCES: 13; BOOK: Joe Lauinger; LYRICS: Joe Lauinger; MUSIC: Jim Cowdery; DIRECTION: John Rue; CHOREOGRAPHY: Jeni Breen and Paul Aguirre; SCENERY: Emily Gaunt; COSTUMES: Brie Rogers and Rebecca J. Wimmer; LIGHTING: Christopher Gorzelnik; PRODUCERS: Ivy Productions in association with Rakka-Thamm

CAST—Paul Aguirre (Hector), Rachel Alvarado (Maria), Jason C. Brown (Bobby), Ricky Cortez (Bugg, Athlete), Thomas E. Cunningham (Priest, Johnson), Christopher Leo Daniels (Biker, Smith), Nathan Flower (Captain Gunn), Kymberly Harris (Sheila), Andrea J. Johnson (Lampeesha), Kris Kane (Dylan), Melissa Minyard (Bella), Nanci Moy (Microphone Woman), Jill Paxton (Lyz), Christopher G. Roberts (Aktion), Bruce Sabath (Mayor), Amy Speace (Hammerwell), Scott Thomson (Aristo), Jenna Zablocki (Muffin)

SOURCE—The 411 B.C. play *Lysistrata* by Aristophanes.

The action occurs in New York City.

The musical was presented in two acts (division of acts and song assignments unknown; songs are listed in performance order).

MUSICAL NUMBERS—Prologue, "The Gods," "The Answer Is No," "Fire in the Belly," "Song of Peace," "Fanged Tango," "Women's Chants," "Battle of the Choruses," "We Can't Finish," "I'll Do Anything," "Bug Song," "Reconciliation," "We All Gotta Stand," "Kindness and Love," Finale

NOTES—The Off Off Broadway musical *Lyz!* was an updated version of Artistophanes' play *Lysistrata*, this time around set in present-day New York City.

Two Broadway musical adaptations of *Lysistrata* were failures. Despite sparkling lyrics by E.Y. Harburg (with music adapted from Jacques Offenbach) and a lavish physical production, *The Happiest Girl in the World* managed just ninety-seven performances when it opened at the Martin Beck (now Al Hirschfeld) Theatre on April 13, 1961 (Dran Seitz was Lysistrata). And the beyond-dreadful *Lysistrata* (in an adaptation by Michael Cacoyannis with forgettable incidental songs by Peter Link) lasted for eight performances when it opened at the Brooks Atkinson Theatre on November, 13 1972 (Melina Mercouri performed the title role). (See entry for *The Athenian Touch* [1964], in which the play *Lysistrata* and even Aristophanes himself figure into the plot.) For other musicals based on Aristophanes' plays, some of which are discussed in this book, see entry for *Wings* (1975).

984 Mack the Knife.

"The Life and Music of Bobby Darin." THEATRE: The Theatre at Saint Peter's Church; OPENING DATE: June 22, 2003; PERFORMANCES: 56; BOOK: Chaz Esposito and James Haddon; DIRECTION: Chaz Esposito; SCENERY: Martin Machitto; LIGHTING: John Pappas; MUSICAL DIRECTION: James Haddon; PRODUCER: Splish Splash Productions

CAST—Chaz Esposito, Larry Frenock (music)

The revue was presented in two acts.

NOTES—*Mack the Knife* wasn't a tribute to Kurt Weill; instead it saluted singer Bobby Darin (1936-1973), whose recording of the Marc Blitzstein version of Weill and Bertolt Brecht's song from *The Threepenny Opera* was one of the biggest hits of the late 1950s (see entries for information about various productions of *The Threepenny Opera*, including the long-running 1955 revival).

The evening included a number of songs popularized by Darin, including, of course, "Mack the Knife" as well as "Dream Lover" (lyric and music by Bobby Darin), "Beyond the Sea" (lyric and music by Charles Trenet and Jack Lawrence), "Things," "You're the Reason I'm Living," and "If I Were a Carpenter" (lyric and music by Tim Hardin).

Beyond the Sea, a film about Darin's life, was released in 2004; Kevin Spacey (who also directed) portrayed Darin. Although Darin is now most remembered for his hit recording of "Mack the Knife," he also found success with another show song, Jerry Bock and Sheldon Harnick's "Artificial Flowers," which was a spoof of sentimental nineteenth-century story ballads from the 1960 musical *Tenderloin*. (It's unclear if "Artificial Flowers" was in *Mack the Knife*, but the song was heard in *Beyond the Sea* and is included on the film's soundtrack album.) 1960 was another world, and during that era songs from new Broadway musicals enjoyed radio play; besides "Artificial Flowers," two other songs from *Tenderloin* were occasionally heard on the radio during Fall 1960: "Bless This Land" (just in time for the Thanksgiving season) and "First Things First" (recorded by Dakota Staton, the latter song was dropped from the musical during its pre-Broadway tryout). Besides boasting one of the best Broadway overtures ever (which includes a trumpet solo for the ages), *Tenderloin* is a cornucopia of melodic delight and lyric wit. Besides "Artificial Flowers," the score offers a galvanic opening number, "Little Old New York"; the satiric and cynical "The Picture of Happiness"; the haunting torch song "My Gentle Young Johnny"; the merry polka "Dear Friend"; and that joyous ode to capitalism, "How the Money Changes Hands."

985 Mackey of Appalachia.

THEATRE: Blackfriars' Guild; OPENING DATE: October 6, 1965; PERFORMANCES: 54; BOOK: Walter Cool; LYRICS: Walter Cool; MUSIC: Walter Cool; DIRECTION: Walter Cool; CHOREOGRAPHY: Robert Charles; SCENERY: Allen Edward Klein; COSTUMES: Alice Merrigal; LIGHTING: Allen Edward Klein; PRODUCER: Blackfriars' Guild

CAST—James Bormann (Mackey), James Batch (Jake), George Patelis (Jake), Frances Beck (Deardra), Virginia Ellyn Haynes (Deardra), Michael Murray (Odd), Christopher Smith (Odd), Tish Yousef (Emmey), Barbara Coggin (Emmey), Kay Preston (Weltha), Elizabeth Ferraro (Weltha), Frank Johnson (Happy Jack), Martin McHale (Happy Jack), Mary W. O'Malley (Loney), Rosemary Gallo (Loney), John Beyer (Buck), Soney Chriss (Buck), Allister C. Whitman (Ezria), Jerry Pearlman (Ezria), Jacqueline Page (Alice), Laura Taylor (Alice), Kathryn Martin (Maude), E. Bette Pardee (Maude), Bob Charles (Zeke)

The musical was presented in two acts.

The action occurs in Slatey Fork, West Virginia, in October 1900.

MUSICAL NUMBERS (division of acts unknown; songs are listed in performance order; for information regarding song assignments, see notes below)—"Mackey of Appalachia," "Appalachia and Mackey," "Judging Song," "I Wonder Why," "Love Me Too," "You're Too Smart," "There Goes My Gal," "Love Will Come Your Way," "It's Sad to Be Lonesome," "Slatey Fork," "How We Would Like Our Man," "Lonely Voice," "My Love, My Love," "Blue and Troubled," "My Little Girl," "We're Having a Party," "Polka a la Appalachia," "Go Up to the Mountain," "There's Got to Be Love," "We Got Troubles," "Gotta Pay," "Only a Day Dream," "Things Ain't as Nice," "Everybody Loves a Tree," "We Are Friends," Finale

NOTES—*Mackey of Appalachia* is probably the only musical which deals with government poverty programs.

Except for the roles of Mackey and Zeke, two cast members were credited for each role, and so apparently the actors alternated performances during the run.

986 The Mad Show. "A New Musical Revue." THEATRE: New Theatre; OPENING DATE: January 10, 1966; PERFORMANCES: 871; SKETCHES: Stan Hart, Larry Siegel, and Steven Vinaver; LYRICS: Marshall Barer, Larry Siegel, Stephen Sondheim, and Steven Vinaver; MUSIC: Mary Rodgers; DIRECTION: Marshall Barer; SCENERY: Peter Harvey; COSTUMES: Peter Harvey; LIGHTING: V.C. Fuqua; MUSICAL DIRECTION: Joseph Raposo; PRODUCERS: Ivor David Balding, for the The Establishment Theatre Company, Inc. (in association with Hitchcock-Balding Productions, Ltd.)

CAST—Linda Lavin, MacIntyre Dixon, Dick (Richard) Libertini, Paul Sand, Jo Anne Worley

SOURCE—Inspired by *Mad* magazine.

The revue was presented in two acts.

ACT ONE—Opening (lyric by Marshall Barer) (Linda Lavin, Jo Anne Worley, Company), "Academy Awards" (sketch by Larry Siegel and Stan Hart) (Company), "You Never Can Tell" (lyric by Steven Vinaver) (Linda Lavin, MacIntyre Dixon, Jo Anne Worley) "Interview" (sketch by Larry Siegel and Stan Hart) (MacIntyre Dixon, Dick Libertini) "Eccch" (lyric by Marshall Barer) (Company) "Saboteurs" (sketch by Larry Siegel and Stan Hart) (performer[s] unknown) "The Real Thing" (sketch by Steven Vinaver, lyric by Marshall Barer) (Paul Sand) "Babysitter" (sketch by Larry Siegel and Stan Hart) (performer[s] unknown) "Misery Is" (lyric by Marshall Barer) (Linda Lavin, MacIntyre Dixon, Paul Sand), "Handle with Care" (sketch by Larry Siegel and Stan Hart) (MacIntyre Dixon, Dick Libertini, Jo Anne Worley) "Hey, Sweet Momma" (lyric by Steven Vinaver) (performer[s] unknown) "Primers" (sketch by Larry Siegel and Stan Hart) (Paul Sand, Jo Anne Worley, Dick Libertini, Linda Lavin) "Well, It Ain't" (lyric by Larry Siegel) (Dick Libertini) "Football in Depth" (sketch by Larry Siegel and Stan Hart) (Paul Sand, MacIntyre Dixon, Dick Libertini) "Hate Song" (lyric by Steven Vinaver) (Company)

ACT TWO—"Kiddie T.V." (sketch by Larry Siegel and Stan Hart) (Company) "Looking for Someone" (lyric by Marshall Barer) (Linda Lavin, Paul Sand, Jo Anne Worley) "Hollywood Surplus" (sketch by Larry Siegel and Stan Hart) (performer[s] unknown) "The Gift of Maggie (and Others)" (lyric by Marshall Barer) (Jo Anne Worley) "T.V. Nik" (sketch by Larry Siegel and Stan Hart) (Linda Lavin, Paul Sand, Jo Anne Worley) "Zoom" (sketch by Larry Siegel and Stan Hart) (performer[s] unknown) "Snappy Answers" (sketch by Larry Siegel and Stan Hart) (performer[s] unknown) "Getting to Know You" (sketch by Larry Siegel and Stan Hart) (Paul Sand, Jo Anne Worley, Linda Lavin) "The Boy from..." (lyric by Norm Deploom a/k/a Esteban Ria Nido [Stephen Sondheim]) (Linda Lavin), "The Irving Irving Story" (sketch by Larry Siegel and Stan Hart) (Company)

NOTES—*The Mad Show* was one of the zaniest and most popular revues of the 1960s. The cast was chockfull of clowns: the quintet was comprised of two Stewed Prunes (MacIntyre Dixon and Dick Libertini), a Second City alumnus (Paul Sand), and Off Broadway madcaps Linda Lavin and Jo Anne Worley. Stanley Kauffmann in the *New York Times* found the evening "thoroughly enjoyable" and "always amusing." He praised the cast, and noted that Dick Libertini "looks and behaves like a bewigged insane beanpole." He singled such sketches as "Primers," and he liked the brief messages that were periodically flashed onto two blank comic-strip balloon cut-outs between scene changes (such as, "In case of atomic attack, the Hadassah meeting will be canceled").

The musical underwent various changes during its more than two-year run. It appears that the sketches "Saboteurs," "Babysitter," "Hollywood Surplus," "Zoom," and "Snappy Answers" as well as the song "Hey, Sweet Momma" were deleted, and that "Transistors" (a/k/a "Transistor"), a sketch performed by Jo Anne Worley and Dick Libertini, was added. And some sequences were shuffled between the two acts ("Getting to Know You" from the second to the first, "Interview" from the first to second).

Stan Hart was listed as one of the lyricists, but none of the songs in the revue are credited to him. The "Football in Depth" sketch was based on a *Mad* magazine story by Ron Axe and Sol Weinstein.

The sketch "Kiddie T.V.," an amusing look at Romper Room-styled children's television shows, kidded the teaching of diversity, with its comment that Brotherhood Week is *the one week of the year* in which you don't care about a person's color. The "Hate Song" concerned a group of children so intent on abolishing violence from the world that they intend to stamp it, sock it, shoot it, lash it, amputate it, lynch it, and "nail it to a cross." "Well, It Ain't" spoofed popular singers who rage at the misery in the world while collecting their enormous paychecks.

The revue's highlight was "The Boy from...," a spoof of the popular song "The Girl from Ipanema"; set to an irresistible Mary Rodgers' samba, Stephen Sondheim's lyric depicted the plight of a clueless young woman who can't seem to draw the attention of a certain fellow. For some mysterious reason, the tall and slender guy, who moves like a dancer, likes to wear vermilion-colored trousers, and is called "Lillian" by his friends, shows absolutely no interest in her.

The Mad Show was recorded by Columbia Records (LP # OL-6530 and # OS-2930; later issued on CD by DRG Records [# 19072]; the CD offered a re-ordered and sometimes retitled song and sketch list), and the script was published by Samuel French, Inc., in 1973.

987 Madame Aphrodite. THEATRE: Orpheum Theatre; OPENING DATE: December 29, 1961; PERFORMANCES: 13; BOOK: Tad Mosel; LYRICS: Jerry Herman; MUSIC: Jerry Herman; DIRECTION: Robert Turoff; SCENERY: David Ballou; COSTUMES: Patricia Zipprodt; LIGHTING: Lee Watson; MUSICAL DIRECTION: Peg Foster; PRODUCERS: Howard Barker, Cynthia Baer, and Robert Chambers

CAST—JACK DRUMMOND (Barney), Stephen (Steve) Elmore (Policeman, Boy), ROD COLBIN (Fifty), NANCY ANDREWS (Madame Aphrodite), June Hyer (Miss Rita LaPorte), Joyce Hines (Miss Rooney), Mona Paulee (Sister of Pity), Alice Borsuk (Girl), Ray Tudor (Mr. Musetta), Lou Cutell (Mr. Schultz), Harry Stanton (Mr. Morgan), CHERRY DAVIS (Rosemary), Kenneth Lewis (Bank Clerk)

SOURCE—The 1953 teleplay *Madame Aphrodite* by Tad Mosel.

The action occurs on a street corner, Fifty's place, and the steps of Miss Rita LaPorte's Rooming House (all of which are on Euclid Avenue), and to Madame Aphrodite's Flat, which is out beyond the sandlots near the garbage dump.

The musical was presented in two acts.

ACT ONE—Overture, "I Don't Mind" (Jack Drummond), "Sales Reproach" (Nancy Andrews, Jack Drummond), "Beat the World" (Nancy Andrews), "Miss Euclid Avenue" (Ray Tudor, Lou Cutell, Harry Stanton, Rod Colbin), "Beautiful" (Jack Drummond, Cherry Davis), "You I Like" (Jack Drummond, Nancy Andrews), "...And a Drop of Lavendar Oil" (Nancy Andrews), "The Girls Who Sit and Wait" (Cherry Davis), "Beat the World" (reprise) (Nancy Andrews)

ACT TWO—Entr'acte, "You I Like" (reprise) (Rod Colbin, Nancy Andrews), "Afferdytie" (Madame Aphrodite), "There Comes a Time" (Jack Drummond), "Miss Euclid Avenue" (reprise) (Cherry Davis, Ray Tudor, Lou Cutell, Harry Stanton), "Only Love" (Cherry Davis), "Take a Good Look Around" (Jack Drummond, Cherry Davis, Ray Tudor, Lou Cutell, Harry Stanton, Joyce Hines, Alice Borsuk, Stephen Elmore, Mona Paulee), "Beautiful" (reprise) (performers not credited)

NOTES—*Madame Aphrodite* was the fourth and final of Jerry Herman's Off Broadway musicals, and was also his first Off Broadway book musical; the others (*I Feel Wonderful* [1954], *Nightcap* [1958], and *Parade* [1960]) were revues (see entries). Two months before *Madame Aphrodite* opened Off Broadway, Herman's first full-length Broadway musical, *Milk and Honey*, had premiered (he was first heard on Broadway earlier in the year, when his song "Best Gold" was the opening number for the revue *From A to Z*, which opened at the Plymouth [now Schoenfeld] Theatre on April 20 and played for twenty-one performances [the revue also introduced Woody Allen, who contributed three sketches, and Fred Ebb, who wrote the lyrics for four songs and co-wrote the lyrics for two others]). For the course of his Broadway career, Herman wrote six more musicals, three smashes, *Hello, Dolly!* (1964), *Mame* (1966), and *La Cage Aux Folles* (1983), and three failures, two of which have become cult musicals and are frequently revived (*Dear World* [1969] and *Mack & Mabel* [1974]; the third, *The Grand Tour* [1978], has its adherents as well). There have also been two Broadway revues which highlighted his theatre music (*Jerry's Girls* [1985] and *An Evening with Jerry Herman* [1998]). He also contributed songs to a few other musicals, either officially (*A Day in Hollywood/A Night in the Ukraine* [1980]) or unofficially (*Ben Franklin in Paris* [1964]). See entries for three Off Broadway retrospectives of Herman's music (*Tune the Grand Up! Words and Music by Jerry Herman* [1978]; an early version of *Jerry's Girls* [1981]; and *Showtune: The Words and Music of Jerry Herman* [2003]).

Madame Aphrodite began life as a television drama in 1953, starring Ruth White and produced by Fred Coe. Early in 1954, Mostel and Herman began working on a musical version, but over the years they became involved in separate projects, and it wasn't until 1961 that they finally completed the musical.

Incidentally, during the 1960-1961 theater season, Mosel's first and only Broadway play, *All the Way Home*, opened. Based on James Agee's Pulitzer-Prize-winning novel *A Death in the Family*, the drama won the Pulitzer Prize as well, for Best Play. *All the Way Home* was co-produced by Fred Coe. See entry for *A Death in the Family*, an operatic adaptation of Agee's novel.

In *Madame Aphrodite*, Nancy Andrews played the title role, a con-artist cosmetician who makes phony claims to naïve women about the benefits of her beauty cream. Lewis Funke in the *New York Times* noted the concoctions in Madame Aphrodite's face cream were a "hodgepodge of irrelevant ingredients" which, truth to tell, was a "capsule criticism of the musical itself." He felt the work often came across a mixture of Gian-Carlo Menotti's *The Medium* (1947) and traditional musical comedy, and he found the book "lumbering and humorless," with a propensity to overuse the title character's malapropic comments for would-be comic effect. And while Funke thought Herman's songs didn't quite blend into the libretto, he nonetheless found them "attractive and melodious ... Mr. Herman will be heard from again." Funke singled out five songs, "Beautiful," "Only Love," "The Girls Who Sit and Wait," "Beat the World," and "...And a Drop of Lavender Oil," and noted that "Beat the World" had a "bitter current to it" and "Lavender Oil" had "the right sinister undertone."

Madame Aphrodite gave Broadway favorite Nancy Andrews a brief chance to shine and allowed her to be the first of four leading ladies who created title roles in Jerry Herman musicals (the others are Carol Channing, Angela Lansbury, and Bernadette Peters). Unfortunately, Andrews never had the breakthrough role in a classic musical, but over the years she gave memorable performances in a number of musicals (*Touch and Go* [1949], *Plain and Fancy* [1955], *Juno* [1959], *Christine* [1960], and *Little Me* [1962]) and many of her musical theatre appearances have been preserved on cast albums.

Of the songs mentioned by Funke, Cherry Davis introduced three of them. She had earlier appeared in *She Shall Have Music* and *Miss Emily Adam* (see entries), playing the title role in the latter musical. Henry Hewes in *The Burns Mantle Yearbook/Best Plays of 1958-1959* hailed her as "the Off-Broadway Gwen Vernon," but after the early 1960s she all but disappeared from the theatre scene, apparently making just one more appearance, in a 1968 Equity Library Theatre revival of *Redhead* (playing the role of Essie, which Gwen Vernon had originated on Broadway in 1959).

For the record, one of *Madame Aphrodite*'s songs ("Beautiful") was re-worked as "A Little More Mascara" for *La Cage Aux Folles*. *Madame Aphrodite*'s "You I Like" is not the same "You I Like" which was written for *The Grand Tour* (and which is that score's highlight). "The Girls Who Sit and Wait" was recorded by Leanne Masterton on her CD collection *Before the Parade Passes By/The Jerry Herman Songbook*.

988 Madeleine. THEATRE: Metropolitan Opera House; OPENING DATE: January 24, 1914; PERFORMANCES: 6; LIBRETTO: Grant Stewart; MUSIC: Victor Herbert; DIRECTION: Jules Speck; SCENERY: Joseph Novak; MUSICAL DIRECTION: Giorgio Polacco; PRODUCER: The Metropolitan Opera

CAST—Frances Alda (Madeleine), Paul Althouse (Francois), Lenora Sparkes (Nichette), Antonio Pini-Corsi (Mauprat), Andres De Segurola (Didier), Marcel Reiner (Coachman), Armin Laufer (Servant), Stefen Buckreus (Servant), Alfred Sappio (Servant)

SOURCE—An unidentified French play by A. Decourcelles and L. Thibaut.

The action occurs in Paris late in the eighteenth century.

The opera was presented in one act.

NOTES—Victor Herbert's opera *Madeleine* was the third American opera to have its world premiere at the Metropolitan (as of this writing, the Met has seen the premieres of twenty-two American operas).

According to an unsigned review in the *New York Times*, the plot dealt with Madeleine, a famous prima donna living in Paris in the late eighteenth century who can't find anyone to dine with her on New Year's Day. Her lovers, admirers, even her servants, have other plans or excuses. An unknown painter asks her to dine with him and his parents, but Madeleine declines and instead has dinner with her mother, or, rather, a portrait of her mother.

The *Times*' critic noted that Herbert could always be depended upon for a "tune," but felt that with *Madeleine* Herbert rejected old-fashioned melody and instead produced a "'conversation opera' ... in an excited and fragmentary, often disjointed manner" which used the repetition of short musical phrases. The *Times* concluded that *Madeleine* was "not a great showing for American opera."

The opera's premiere occurred on a double bill with another one-act opera, Ruggiero Leoncavallo's *Pagliacci* (1892); Enrico Caruso sang the role of Canio.

989 Mademoiselle Colombe (1977). THEATRE: Playwrights Horizons; OPENING DATE: February 7, 1977; PERFORMANCES: 2; BOOK: Albert Harris; LYRICS: Edwin Dulchin; MUSIC: Michael Valenti; DIRECTION: Albert Harris; PRODUCER: Playwrights Horizons

CAST—Candice Earley (Colombe), Robert Manzari (Julien), Naomi Riseman (Mme. Georges), Nancy Andrews (Mme. Alexandra), Norman Weiler (Chiropodist), Kristin Jolliff (Manicurist), Tad Motyka (Hairdresser), I.W. Klein (Gourette), Ty McConnell (Edouard), Richard Marr (Deschamps), Keith Perry (Poet-Mine-Own), Richard Rossomme (Gaulois), Steve Rotblatt (Stagehand), Bill Hedge (Stagehand)

SOURCE—*Mademoiselle Colombe*, the 1954 adaptation by Louis Kronenberger of Jean Anouilh's play *Colombe*.

The action occurs in a Paris theatre around 1900.

The musical was presented in two acts.

ACT ONE—"What Is Love?" (Company), "The Goddess of Love" (Robert Manzari, Naomi Riseman), "Just Suppose" (Robert Manzari, Candice Earley), "There's Only So Much I Can Give" (Nancy Andrews, Ensemble), "Moon Dear" (Keith Perry), "What Is Your Name" (Candice Earley), "More Than One Man in Her Life" (Nancy Andrews, Candice Earley, Keith Perry, I.W. Klein), "After Rehearsal" (Richard Rossomme, Keith Perry, Richard Marr, Ty McConnell, Candice Earley, Men), "The Game of Love" (Ty McConnell, Candice Earley, Ensemble)

ACT TWO—"We're a Little Nervous Tonight" (Ensemble), "The Realm of Passion" (Nancy Andrews, Richard Rossomme, I.W. Klein, Candice Earley, Ensemble), "Alone" (Candice Earley), "Years from Now" (Robert Manzari), "Georgie and I" (Nancy Andrews), "Suddenly" (Robert Manzari, Candice Earley)

NOTES—The Off Off Broadway musical adaptation *Mademoiselle Colombe*, Louis Kronenberger's 1954 translation of Jean Anouilh's play which played on Broadway with Julie Harris, was presented for two performances over a period of two weeks. The story centered on Julien's innocent young wife Colombe. When he's drafted, he entrusts her to his mother Mme. Alexandra, a famous actress. Colombe soon adapts to Parisian night life and takes on a series of lovers; when Julien returns, she has no qualms about letting him know of her new life style.

With Tammy Grimes in the role of Mme. Alexandra, a revised version of the musical briefly surfaced Off Off Broadway in 1987 (see entry). "What Is Love" and "Just Suppose" had first been heard in other Valenti musicals, the former in *Just for Love* and *Lovesong*, the latter in *Lovesong* (see entries).

990 Mademoiselle Colombe (1987). "A New Musical." THEATRE: Theatre Off Park; OPENING DATE: December 9, 1987; PERFORMANCES: 42; BOOK: Edwin Dulchin, Albert Harris, and Michael Valenti; LYRICS: Edwin Dulchin; MUSIC: Michael Valenti; DIRECTION: Albert Harris; CHOREOGRAPHY: William Fleet Lively; SCENERY: Philipp Jung; COSTUMES: Lindsay Davis; LIGHTING: Donald Holder; MUSICAL DIRECTION: Rod Derefinko; PRODUCER: Theatre Off Park, Inc. (Albert Harris, Artistic Director; Richard Salfas, Business Manager)

CAST—Joaquin Romaguera (Robinet), David Cryer (Gaulois), Michael Tartel (Deschamps), Dick Decareau (Gourette), Georgia Creighton (Mme. Georges), Robert Cooner (Stagehand), Judith McLane (Judith), Richard Stegman (Hairdresser), Lisa Vroman (Lisa), Elizabeth Walsh (Manicurist), Campbell Martin (Chiropodist), Victoria Brasser (Colombe), Keith Buterbaugh (Julien), TAMMY GRIMES (Mme. Alexandra), Tom Galantich (Edouard)

SOURCE—*Mademoiselle Colombe*, the 1954 adaptation by Louis Kronenberger of Jean Anouilh's play *Colombe*.

The action occurs in a Paris theatre around 1900.

The musical was presented in two acts.

ACT ONE—Rehearsal: "The Realm of Passion (or The Soldier's Wife)" (Company), "She's an Actress" (Georgia Creighton), "What's the Mail?" (Tammy Grimes, Dick Decareau, Company), "Only So Much I Can Give" (Tammy Grimes, Company), "Yes Alexandra, No Alexandra" (Dick Decareau, Keith Buterbaugh), "Left, Right, Left" (Tom Galantich), "Two Against the World" (Keith Buterbaugh, Victoria Brasser), "Perfect" (Michael Tartel, Joaquin Romaguera), "Moon Dear" (Joaquin Romaguera), "This Bright Morning" (Victoria Brasser), "More Than One Man in Her Life" (Tammy Grimes, with Victoria Brasser, Joaquin Romaguera, Michael Tartel, Men), "After Rehearsal" (Victoria Brasser, David Cryer, Joaquin Romaguera, Michael Tartel, Men), "And If I Told You That I Want You" (Tom Galantich, Victoria Brasser, Company)

ACT TWO—"She's an Actress" (reprise) (Georgia Creighton), "The Color Red" (Dick Decareau), "Folies Bergeres" (Keith Buterbaugh, Victoria Brasser), "Why Did It Have to Be You" (Keith Buterbaugh, Tom Galantich), Final Scene: "The Realm of Passion (or The Soldier's Wife)" (Tammy Grimes, David Cryer, Dick Decareau, Company), "Flower Shop" (Victoria Brasser), "Years from Now" (Keith Buterbaugh), "Georgie and I" (Tammy Grimes), "From This Day" (Keith Buterbaugh, Victoria Brasser)

NOTES—This Off Off Broadway musical was a revised version of the 1977 production (see entry).

Songs from the 1977 production which weren't heard in the revival were: "What Is Love?," "The Goddess of Love," "Just Suppose," "What Is Your Name," "The Game of Love," "We're a Little Nervous Tonight," "Alone," and "Suddenly."

991 Madison Avenue. "The Subliminal Musical." THEATRE: Lone Star Theatre; OPENING DATE: December 29, 1992; PERFORMANCES: 48; BOOK: Paul Streitz; LYRICS: Paul Streitz and Gary Cherpakov; MUSIC: Gary Cherpakov and Robert Moehl; DIRECTION: David C. Wright; CHOREOGRAPHY: David C. Wright; SCENERY: Chris O'Leary; COSTUMES: Brenda Burton; LIGHTING: Chris O'Leary; MUSICAL DIRECTION: Joel Maisano; PRODUCER: Paul Streitz

CAST—Randi Cooper (Women on the Move, Michelle McDermott, Sarah Laine Terrell), Jordan Church (Alice O'Connor), Bill Goodman (J. Quinby IV), Donald Fish (Bruce Singer), Nicole Sislian (Honeydew Plushbottom), Tony Rossi (Media Rep)

The musical was presented in two acts.

ACT ONE—"Women on the Move" (Randi Cooper, Jordan Church, Nicole Sislian), "A Woman at Home" (Bill Goodman, Donald Fish, Tony Rossi),

"Something for Me" (Bill Goodman, Nicole Sislian), "All a Matter of Strategy" (Bill Goodman, Donald Fish, Nicole Sislian), "Thirty Seconds" (Bill Goodman, Jordan Church), "Client Service" (Nicole Sislian), "L.A. Freeway" (Tony Rossi), "Office Romance" (Jordan Church, Donald Fish), "Typical American Consumer" (Company)

ACT TWO—"Residuals" ('Krystal and Alexis'), "Leonardo's Lemonade"/"Lennie's Lemonade"/"Leonard's Lemonade" (Donald Fish), "It's Not a Commercial, It's Art" (performer unknown), "Squeeze, Squeeze, Squeeze" ('Lemons'), "Thirty Seconds" (reprise) (Bill Goodman), "The Look" (Jordan Church, Nicole Sislian), "Upper East Side Blues" (Jordan Church), "Thirty Seconds" (reprise) (Bill Goodman), "Madison Avenue" (Jordan Church, Company)

NOTES—*Madison Avenue* was a spoof of the advertising business, including the trials and tribulations of a firm after a lemonade company's account.

The musical first opened at the Lone Star Café dinner theatre on October 31, 1992, and then transferred to Off Broadway status on December 29, 1992, at which point the venue changed its name to Lone Star Theatre.

The cast album was released by Original Cast Records (CD # OC-9699). The album included "Madison Avenue (Intro)" and omitted "A Woman at Home" and "L.A. Freeway." The CD noted that the songs "All a Matter of Strategy" and "Thirty Seconds" were by Robert Moehl, and all other songs were by Gary Cherpakov and Paul Streitz. The CD also noted that the production had been previously seen at the Nat Horne Theatre in 1984 and in London at the Water Rats Theatre in 1988.

As of this writing, the musical's script is scheduled to published by Samuel French, Inc.

992 The Madwoman of Central Park West. "An Original Musical Comedy." THEATRE: 22 Steps Theatre; OPENING DATE: June 13, 1979; PERFORMANCES: 85; BOOK: Phyllis Newman and Arthur Laurents; LYRICS: See song list for credits; MUSIC: See song list for credits; DIRECTION: Arthur Laurents; SCENERY: Philipp Jung; COSTUMES: Theoni V. Aldredge; LIGHTING: Ken Billington; MUSICAL DIRECTION: Herbert Kaplan; PRODUCERS: Gladys Rackmil, Fritz Holt, and Barry M. Brown

CAST—PHYLLIS NEWMAN

The revue was presented in two acts.

ACT ONE—"Up, Up, Up" (from unproduced musical *The Skin of Our Teeth*; lyric by Betty Comden and Adolph Green, music by Leonard Bernstein), "My Mother Was a Fortune-Teller" (lyric by Phyllis Newman, music by John Clifton), "Cheerleader" (lyric by Fred Ebb, music by John Kander), "What Makes Me Love Him" (*The Apple Tree*, 1966; lyric by Sheldon Harnick, music by Jerry Bock), "Don't Laugh" (*Hot Spot*, 1963; lyric by Martin Charnin and Stephen Sondheim, music by Mary Rodgers), "No One's Toy" (lyric and music by Joe [Joseph] Raposo)/"Women's Medley" (medley arranged by Glen Roven)

ACT TWO—"Up, Up, Up" (reprise), "Better" (lyric and music by Ed Kleban), "Don't Wish" (lyric and music by Peter Allen and Carole [Bayer] Sager), "Copacabana" (lyric and music by Bruce Sussman, Jack Feldman, and Barry Manilow), "My New Friends" (lyric and music by Leonard Bernstein), "List Song" (a/k/a "A Song of Lists") (lyric by Phyllis Newman, music by John Clifton), "My Mother Was a Fortune-Teller" (reprise)

NOTES—Phyllis Newman returned in *The Madwoman of Central Park West*, a one-woman show which was a revised version of *My Mother Was a Fortune-Teller* (see entry). It's unclear if the production was under a Broadway or an Off Broadway contract.

For the songs in the "Women's Medley" sequence, see entry for *My Mother Was a Fortune-Teller.*

Ed Kleban's "Better" had earlier been heard in *My Mother Was a Fortune-Teller* and was later included in *A Class Act* (see entry); it was recorded for the cast albums of both *The Madwoman of Central Park West* and *A Class Act.*

"Up, Up, Up" was from an unproduced musical version of Thornton Wilder's *The Skin of Our Teeth* (for other songs from this adaptation, see entry for *By Bernstein*; also see entry for *2 by 5* for information about John Kander and Fred Ebb's musical version of Wilder's play). According to David Wolf in *The TheatreMania Guide to Musical Theatre Recordings*, there was a television adaptation of *The Madwoman of Central Park West.*

The musical was also recorded (DRG Records CD # CDSL-5212).

993 The Magic of Jolson! "A Musical Portrait." THEATRE: Provincetown Playhouse; OPENING DATE: April 9, 1975; PERFORMANCES: 5; BOOK: Pearl Sieben; LYRICS: Pearl Sieben (see song list for all credits); MUSIC: Richard DeMone (see song list for all credits); DIRECTION: Isaac Dostis; SCENERY: Chuck Hoefler; LIGHTING: Ralph Madero; MUSICAL DIRECTION: Richard DeMone

CAST—NORMAN BROOKS (Al Jolson), Linda Gerard (Fanny Brice), John Medici (Eddie Cantor) The musical was presented in two acts.

ACT ONE—"Toot Toot Tootsie! (Goodbye)" (*Bombo*, 1921; interpolated into the musical during New York run; lyric by Joe Young and Sam Lewis, music by Jean Schwartz), "Street Singer" (lyric by Pearl Sieben, music by Richard DeMone), "Alabamy Bound" (lyric by B.G. [Buddy] DeSylva and Green, music by Ray Henderson), "If You Knew Susie (Like I Know Susie)" (lyric by B.G. [Buddy] DeSylva, music by Joseph Meyer), "Ma, She's Makin' Eyes at Me" (lyric by Sidney Clare, music by Con Conrad), "Where Did Robinson Crusoe Go with Friday on Saturday Night?" (*Robinson Crusoe, Jr.*, 1916; lyric by Joe Young and Sam M. Lewis, music by George Meyer), "You Made Me Love You (I Didn't Want to Do It)" (from *The Honeymoon Express*, 1913 [Second Edition]; lyric by Joseph McCarthy, music by James V. Monaco), "All My Love" (lyric and music by Al Jolson, Harry Akst, and Saul Chaplin), "Swanee" (*Demi-Tassel Capitol Revue*, 1919; later interpolated into tour of *Sinbad* [also 1919]; lyric by Irving Caesar, music by George Gershwin), "Rock-a-Bye Your Baby with a Dixie Melody" (*Sinbad*, 1919; lyric by Joe Young and Sam M. Lewis, music by Jean Schwartz), "Faces" (lyric by Pearl Sieben, music by Richard DeMone), "You Ain't Heard Nothin' Yet" (lyric and music by Al Jolson, Gus Kahn, and B.G. [Buddy] DeSylva), "My Mammy" (*Sinbad*, 1919; interpolated into the musical's national tour; lyric by Joe Young and Sam M. Lewis, music by Walter Donaldson)

ACT TWO—"I've Gotta Get Back to New York" (1933 film *Hallelujah, I'm a Bum*; lyric by Lorenz Hart, music by Richard Rodgers), "Hello, Tucky!" (lyric and music by Joseph Meyer, Hanley, and B.G. [Buddy] DeSylva), "California, Here I Come" (*Bombo*, 1921; interpolated into the musical during New York run; lyric by B.G. [Buddy] DeSylva and Al Jolson, music by Joseph Meyer), "Mah Blushin' Rosie" (lyric and music by Stromberg and Smith), "April Showers" (*Bombo*, 1921; interpolated into the musical's national tour; lyric by B.G. [Buddy] DeSylva, music by Louis Silvers), "A Goil Like Me" (lyric by Pearl Sieben, music by Richard DeMone), "I Still Love You" (lyric and music by Richard DeMone), "Makin' Whoopee" (*Whoopee*, 1928; lyric by Gus Kahn, music by Walter Donaldson), "I Could Not Get Along Without a Song" (lyric and music by Richard DeMone), "Avalon" (*Sinbad*, 1918; interpolated into the musical's national tour; song was also heard in *Bombo* [1921], either interpolated into the musical during New York run or during national tour; lyric and music by Al Jolson, B.G. [Buddy] DeSylva, and Vincent Rose), "Sonny Boy" (1928 film *The Singing Fool*; lyric by Lew Brown, B.G. [Buddy] DeSylva, and Al Jolson, music by Ray Henderson), "Give My Regards to Broadway" (*Little Johnny Jones*, 1904; lyric and music by George M. Cohan), "Anniversary Song" (lyric and music by Al Jolson and Saul Chaplin), "I'm Sitting on Top of the World" (*Artists and Models/Paris Edition*, 1925; interpolated into the musical during New York run; lyric by Joe Young and Sam M. Lewis, music by Ray Henderson), "God's Country" (lyric and music by B. Smith and H. Gillespie)

NOTES—This revue-like musical was a tribute to Al Jolson (1883 [1886?]-1950), and included new songs as well as standards which Jolson either introduced or popularized. For another Jolson tribute, see entry for *Jolson & Co.* (which also includes information on regional and London musicals about Jolson).

994 Magic on Broadway. THEATRE: Lamb's Theatre; OPENING DATE: September 29, 1996; PERFORMANCES: 334; CHOREOGRAPHY: Tiger Martina; LIGHTING: Gregory Cohen; PRODUCERS: Catco Inc. and Skyline Entertainment Inc.; Donald Spector, Executive Producer; Mary Rodas and Dee Snyder, Producers

CAST—Joseph Gabriel, Lucy Gabriel and Vincent Giordano (Magic Assistants), Romano Frediani (Juggler), Heather Rochelle Harmon, Melanie Doskocil, Kathleen Grimaldi, Karen Mascari, and Victoria Whitten (Dancers)

The revue was presented in two acts.

NOTES—*Magic on Broadway* was a long-running surprise, chalking up over 300 hundred performances; Joseph Gabriel was the magician-in-chief. On January 13, 1998, he returned with *Joseph Gabriel Magic '98*, another magic show with many of the cast members from the first production; it played at the Lamb's Theatre for a run of 131 performances.

995 Magpie. THEATRE: Players Theatre; OPENING DATE: March 9, 2007; PERFORMANCES: 29 (estimated); BOOK: Steven M. Jacobson; LYRICS: Edward Gallardo; ADDITIONAL LYRICS by Stevie Holland and Steven M. Jacobson; MUSIC: Gary William Friedman; DIRECTION: Rajendra Ramoon Maharaj; CHOREOGRAPHY: Rajendra Ramoon Maharaj; SCENERY: John Pollard; COSTUMES: Leslie Bernstein; LIGHTING: Japhy Weideman and Justin A. Partier; MUSICAL DIRECTION: Jana Zielonka; PRODUCER: Amas Musical Theatre (Donna Trinkoff, Producing Artistic Director; Rosetta LeNoire, Founder)

CAST—J. Cameron Barnett (Martinez), Kimberly Reid Dunbar (Maggie's Mother), Jessica Fields (Maggie), Jene Hernandez (Carmela), Dennis Holland (Donald Wales), Gary Lindemann (George), Joseph Melendez (Ramon), Ronny Mercedes (Ramon), Michael Murnoch (Julio), Julian Rebelledo (Miguel Hernandez), Natalie Toro (Flora Hernandez)

The action occurs in New York City in the present.

The musical was presented in two acts.

ACT ONE—Opening/"Maggie's Dream" (Jessica Fields, Joseph Melendez, Messengers, Kimberly Reid Dunbar), "You're a Good Boy" (Natalie Toro, Julian Rebelledo), "Anybody See Him Do It?" (Joseph Melendez, Messengers), "Important Papers" (Jessica Fields), "A Gypsy Girl Named Carmen" (Jessica Fields, Ronny Mercedes), "Another Day" (Jene Hernandez, Michael Murnoch, J. Cameron Barnett), "She's an Innocent" (Gary Lindemann), "Collision Course" (Jessica Fields), "Crazy Girl, Loquita" (Ronny Mercedes, Jessica Fields), "Breakdown" (Jessica Fields, Kimberly Reid Dunbar, Ronny Mercedes, Gary Lindemann)

ACT TWO—"Maggie's Opera: Oh Come to Me, My Love" (lyric by Stephen M. Jacobson) (Jessica Fields, Ronny Mercedes, Joseph Melendez, Messengers), "We Thought You'd Make Us Proud" (Natalie Toro, Julian Rebelledo, Ronny Mercedes), "Give Her Back Her Music" (Ronny Mercedes), "Dance Me 'Cross the Stream" (lyric by Stevie Holland) (Gary Lindemann, Jessica Fields), "No One Had a Clue in Santiago" (Joseph Melendez), "Remember" (Natalie Toro, Julian Rebelledo, Gary Lindemann), "Trust Your Heart" (Dennis Holland), "From Now On" (lyric by Stevie Holland) (Jessica Fields), "Ribbons of Gold" (Jessica Fields, Ronny Mercedes)

NOTES—Like *In the Heights*, which had opened earlier in the season, the Off Off Broadway musical *Magpie* offered a Latino-styled score (by Gary William Friedman). And like *Heights*, the musical dealt in part with street life in the big city, in this case ubiquitous bike messengers.

Magpie had earlier been produced as a staged reading at the 2006 New York Musical Theatre Festival.

The late Rosetta LeNoire founded Amas (Latin for "you love") in 1968, and forty years later the visionary actress and producer's dream of a multi-ethnic theatre company still exists under the directorship of Donna Trinkoff, the company's Producing Artistic Director. In an early Amas program, LeNoire wrote that the company's mission was to develop and produce new musicals and to offer a training ground for new musical theatre talent. She wrote that Amas "is dedicated to bringing *all* people — regardless of race, color, creed, religion, or national origin — together through the performing arts." Rosetta LeNoire's legacy to our national theatre is priceless.

996 Mahalia.

THEATRE: Henry Street Playhouse; OPENING DATE: May 31, 1978; PERFORMANCES: 14; BOOK: Don Evans; LYRICS: Don Evans; ORIGINAL MUSIC: John Lewis; DIRECTION: Oz Scott; CHOREOGRAPHY: Mabel Robinson; SCENERY: Richard Williams; COSTUMES: Beverly Parks; LIGHTING: Victor En Yu Tan; MUSICAL DIRECTION: Luther Henderson; PRODUCER: Carousel Group, Inc., and Lucy Productions Corp.

CAST—Nat Adderly (Red Beans), Bardell Conner (Choir), Lee Cooper (Choir, Mabel Green), Loretta Devine (Choir), Frances Foster (Aunt Duke, Potion Lady), Andrew Frierson (Choir), Fred Gripper (Choir), Edna Goode (Nightclub Inhabitant), William Hardy, Jr. (Brother Maxwell), Lola Holman (Young Mahalia), Esther Marrow (Mahalia), Gayle McKinney (Congregation), Roscoe Orman (Ike Hockinhull), Chuck Patterson (Minters Galloway), Al Perryman (Choir), Otis Sallid (Chafalaya), Rosemary Thompson (Choir), Jimmy Weaver (Nightclub Inhabitant)

SOURCE—The 1975 book *Just Mahalia, Baby* by Laurraine Goreau.

The musical was presented in two acts (division of acts and song assignments unknown; songs are listed in performance order).

MUSICAL NUMBERS—"Great Gittin' Up Morning," "When I've Done the Best I Can," "Home Folks," "That's Enough," "Didn't It Rain," "Chi Town Strut," "Gimme a Pigfoot (and a Bottle of Beer)" (lyric and music by Wesley "Socks" Wilson and Coot Grant; some sources credit only Wilson as the lyricist and composer of the song), "Leaning on the Everlasting Arms," "Chalfalaya's Ballet," "Amazing Grace," "Didn't He Ramble," "Higher Ground," "Time to Think of Myself," "Mardi Gras in Chicago," "Take My Hand, Precious Lord," "Move On Up a Little Higher," "Peace," "Blues for Minnis," "His Eye Is on the Sparrow," "Minnis in Eros," Finale

NOTES—Esther Marrow played the title role in *Mahalia*, an Off Off Broadway musical version of the life of legendary gospel singer Mahalia Jackson (1911-1972).

In 1985, *Sing, Mahalia, Sing!*, another musical version of Mahalia Jackson's life, toured nationally but never played New York. The book was by George Faison, and original lyrics and music were by Richard Smallwood, George Faison, and Wayne Davis. For this version, Jennifer Holliday played the title role (at certain performances Esther Marrow performed the role). A third musical about the subject, *Mahalia—A Gospel Musical*, opened at the Hartford Stage in Hartford, Connecticut, in August 2007; written by Tom Stolz and directed by Jeremy B. Cohen, the musical starred Frenchie Davis, a former *American Idol* contestant.

997 Make Me a Song/The Music of William Finn.

THEATRE: New World Stages; OPENING DATE: November 12, 2007; PERFORMANCES: 55; LYRICS: William Finn; MUSIC: William Finn; DIRECTION: Rob Ruggiero; SCENERY: Luke Hegel-Cantarella; COSTUMES: Alejo Vietti; LIGHTING: John Lasiter; MUSICAL DIRECTION: Darren R. Cohen; PRODUCERS: Junkyard Productions, Larry Hirschhorn, Jayson Raitt, Stacey Mindich, Jamie DeRoy, and Eric Falkenstein in association with Nick Demos and Francine Bizar, Bob Eckert, Impresario's Choice on Broadway, Barbara Manocherian and Remmel Tyndall Dickinson

CAST—Sandy Binion, D.B. Bonds, Adam Heller, Sally Wilfert

The revue was presented in one act.

MUSICAL NUMBERS—"Make Me a Song" (Adam Heller), "Heart and Music" (Company), "Hitchhiking Across America" (D.B. Bonds), "Billy's Law of Genetics" (D.B. Bonds, Company), "Passover" (Sally Wilfert), "Republicans" (Part One) (Adam Heller), "Only One" (Sandy Binion), "I'd Rather Be Sailing"/"Set Those Sails" (D.B. Bonds, Sally Wilfert), "Republicans" (Part Two) (Adam Heller), "Change" (Sandy Binion, Company), "I Have Found" (Sally Wilfert), "Republicans" (Part Three) (Adam Heller), "You're Even Better Than You Think You Are" (Company), *Falsettos* Suite (Company): "Four Jews in a Room Bitching," "A Tight-Knit Family," "Love Is Blind," "My Father Is a Homo," "Trina's Song," "March of the Falsettos," "The Year of the Child," "The Baseball Game," "Unlikely Lovers," "Falsettoland," "All Fall Down" (Sandy Binion), "Republicans" (Part Four) (Adam Heller), "Stupid Things I Won't Do" (Adam Heller), "That's Enough for Me" (Sandy Binion), "I Went Fishing with My Dad" (D.B. Bonds), "When the Earth Stopped Turning" (Adam Heller), "Anytime (I Am There)" (Sally Wilfert), "Song of Innocence and Experience" (Company), Finale (Company)

NOTES—*Make Me a Song* was a tribute-revue to William Finn, and featured songs from many of his musicals, including *Falsettos, America Kicks Up Its Heels* (and its later revised version, *Romance in Hard Times*), *A New Brain*, and *Elegies* (but not *The 25th Annual Putnam County Spelling Bee*, which was still running on Broadway when the revue opened) (see entries). Steven Suskin in *Variety* found the evening "Finntastic," and Frank Scheck in the *New York Post* said that despite the revue's "modesty" and its "no-frills" approach, it was an event no musical theatre fan would want to miss. Among the songs in the revue were "I'd Rather Be Sailing" (from *A New Brain*); "All Fall Down" (from *America Kicks Up Its Heels* and *Romance in Hard Times*), "That's Enough for Me" (*Romance in Hard Times*); and "Passover," "When the Earth Stopped Turning," and "Anytime (I Am There)" (*Elegies*). Scheck noted that "Anytime (I Am There)" was the revue's "emotional showstopper."

The evening also offered a twenty-minute mini-version of *Falsettos* (see entries for the three "Marvin" musicals [*In Trousers*, *March of the Falsettos*, and *Falsettoland*]). Other songs heard in the production included "I Went Fishing with My Dad," "Unlikely Lovers," and "Republicans" (Scheck mentioned the latter consisted of an "increasingly tired series of musical one-liners").

The revue also included "Stupid Things I Won't Do" and "I Have Found," two songs from Finn's long-aborning musical adaptation of the classic 1927 comedy *The Royal Family* by George S. Kaufman and Edna Ferber; one hopes Finn's adaptation won't go the way of a musical adaptation of another farce from that era, David Zippel and Jonathan Sheffer's *Going Hollywood* (see entry), which was based on Kaufman and Moss Hart's *Once in a Lifetime* (1930) and which never got out of workshop.

Make Me a Song had originally been produced at TheatreWorks in Hartford, Connecticut, in August 2006.

The cast recording was released on a 2-CD set by Ghostlight Records (CD # 8-4427).

Twelve songs from the revue ("Mister, Make Me a Song," "Hitchhiking Across America," "Republicans," "I'd Rather Be Sailing," "Set Those Sails," "I Have Found," "The Baseball Game," "All Fall Down," "Stupid Things I Won't Do," "That's Enough for Me," "When the Earth Stopped Turning," and "Anytime [I Am There]") were recorded for the collection *Infinite Joy/The Songs of William Finn* (RCA Victor Records CD # 09026-63766-2).

The revue is scheduled to premiere in London at the New Players Theatre on March 3, 2008, for an announced engagement of four weeks.

998 The Making of Americans (1972).

THEATRE: Judson Poets' Theatre; OPENING DATE: November 10, 1972; PERFORMANCES: Unknown; LIBRETTO: Leon Katz; MUSIC: Al Carmines; DIRECTION: Lawrence Kornfeld; SCENERY: Ed Lazansky; COSTUMES: Reve Richards; LIGHTING: Roger Morgan; MUSICAL DIRECTION: Al Carmines; PRODUCER: The Judson Poets' Theatre

CAST—Al Carmines (The Voice of Gertrude Stein), Stuart Silver (David Hersland), Maureen Sadusk (Martha Hersland, Bertha), Spence Berg (Grandmother, Miss Douner), Dorian Barth (Grandmother, Pauline), Essie Borden (Grandmother, Julia Dehning), Julie Kurnitz (Martha Hersland), Craig Kuehl (David Hersland), Margaret Wright (Fanny Hersland), Danny Kreitzberg (Photographer), David Cryer (Alfred Hersland), Gretchen Van Aken (Martha Hersland), Theo Barnes (David Hersland), Tony Clark (Henry Dehning), Lee Guilliatt (Jenny Dehning), John Canemaker (George Dehning), Jerry Fargo (Philip Redfern)

SOURCE—The 1934 book *The Making of Americans* by Gertrude Stein.

The musical was presented in three acts (the song titles were not identified in the program).

NOTES—Based on Gertrude Stein's novel of the same title, this Off Off Broadway musical was the third of six which Al Carmines and Lawrence Kornfeld adapted from her works. See entries for *What Happened* (1963), *In Circles* (1967), *Listen to Me* (1974), *A Manoir* (1977), and *Dr. Faustus Lights the Lights* (1979).

The work was a musical portrait of Stein's family history. One song ("I Forget and I Remember") from the production was included in the 1982 revue *The Gospel According to Al* (see entry).

Mel Gussow in the *New York Times* noted the adaptation was faithful to Stein's 900-page book, but he felt the script was repetitious and the dramatic action inherently inert. But he emphasized that the evening was "relieved" by Carmines' "bountiful" music. In fact, Carmines not only played the piano, he also portrayed the "Voice of Gertrude Stein," and Gussow indicated that with Carmines speaking and singing "torrents of Stein with unquenchable enthusiasm, he is a show by himself."

The musical was revived Off Off Broadway in 1985 (see entry).

999 The Making of Americans (1985). THEATRE: St. Clement's Theatre; OPENING DATE: March 5, 1985; PERFORMANCES: Unknown; LIBRETTO: Leo Katz; MUSIC: Al Carmines; DIRECTION: Anne Bogart; SCENERY: Nancy Winters and Jim Buff; COSTUMES: Nancy Winters and Jim Buff; LIGHTING: Carol Mullins; MUSICAL DIRECTION: Albin Konopka; PRODUCERS: The Music-Theatre Group/Lenox Arts Center in association with Robert Marx

CAST—Catherine Coray (Gertrude Stein, Sister Martha, Martha Hersland), Karen Evans-Kandel (Gertrude Stein, Fanny Hissen, Ms. Dounor), Myvanwy Jenn (Gertrude Stein, Grandmother Martha, Jenny Dehning, Pauline), Scott L. Johnson (Gertrude Stein, David Hersland), George McGrath (Gertrude Stein, Grandfather David, Henry Dehning, Aunt), Martin Moran (Gertrude Stein, Alfred Hersland), Joan Scheckel (Gertrude Stein, Julia Dehning), Henry Stram (Gertrude Stein, David Hersland, Sr., George Dehning, Philip Redfern)

SOURCE—The 1934 book *The Making of Americans* by Gertrude Stein.

NOTES—Based on Gertrude Stein's novel of the same title, this Off Off Broadway revival of *The Making of Americans* was one of six which Al Carmines adapted from her works (see entry for the original 1972 production for a list of all the adaptations). The opera dealt with Stein's family history, and Tim Page in the *New York Times* noted George McGrath's portrayal of her grandfather "reminded one of Jimmy Stewart gone mad." Page thought the opera lacked the magic of Stein and Virgil Thomson's *Four Saints in Three Acts* (1934), but nonetheless felt Carmines' score was "tuneful and ingratiating" and that "Stein aficionados will have to see it."

1000 Malady of Love. THEATRE: Brander Matthews Theatre/Columbia University; OPENING DATE: May 27, 1954; PERFORMANCES: Unknown; LIBRETTO: Lewis Allan; MUSIC: Lehman Engel; DIRECTION: Felix Brentano; SCENERY: Paul Morrison; MUSICAL DIRECTION: William Rhodes; PRODUCERS: Columbia University Opera Workshop (sponsored by the Alice M. Ditson Fund)

CAST—Ruth Fleming, Stephanie Turash, Warren Galgour

The opera was presented in one act.

NOTES—Lehman Engel's opera *Malady of Love* had its world premiere performance at Columbia University on a double bill with Jack Beeson's *Hello Out There* (see entry). Engel's opera was worlds away from the tragic one by Beeson, for *Malady of Love* was a lighthearted look at a young woman who takes romantic aim at a naïve and vulnerable psychoanalyst. Olin Downes in the *New York Times* reported that besides the two singing characters there were also two pantomimists who enacted the young woman's dreams and the state of her libido. Downes found the score "adroit, in the humorous or farcical vein." While the music was not "strong," it was nonetheless "neatly done and orchestrated with finesse."

1001 Mama, I Want to Sing (1980). THEATRE: AMAS Repertory Theatre; OPENING DATE: December 3, 1980; PERFORMANCES: 13; BOOK: Vy Higginsen; ADDITIONAL "STORY CONSULTATION" by Ken Wydro; LYRICS: Vy Higginsen; ADDITIONAL LYRICS by Ken Wydro; MUSIC: Richard Tee; DIRECTION: Duane L. Jones; CHOREOGRAPHY: Joseph Cohen; SCENERY: Felix E. Cochren; COSTUMES: Georgia Collins-Langhorne; LIGHTING: Sandra L. Ross; MUSICAL DIRECTION: Frederic Gripper; PRODUCER: AMAS Repertory Theatre (Rosetta LeNoire, Founder and Artistic Director)

CAST—Vanessa Bell, Steve Bland, Joe Breedlove, Richard Dow, Ann Duquesnay, Sheila Ellis, Leo Elmore, Andrew Friarson, Helena D. Garcia, Crystal Johnson, Ursuline Kairson, Tony Lawrence, Robert Melvin, Eboyn Jo-Ann Pinkney, Charlie Serrano, Tyrone Williams, Diane Wilson

The musical was presented in two acts.

NOTES—*Mama, I Want to Sing* was nothing short of a phenomenon. Three years after the Off Off Broadway musical premiered at AMAS, the musical re-opened on March 23, 1983, at the Heckscher Theatre and ran there continuously (and apparently sometimes in repertory with other productions) until 1990 (for approximately 2,400 performances), when, on March 25 of that year, a sequel opened (*Mama, I Want to Sing—Part II: The Story Continues*). A second sequel, *Born to Sing!*, opened at the Union Square Theatre on August 8, 1996, for 133 performances. See entries for these productions.

The trilogy told the story of Vy Higginsen's sister, singer Doris Troy (Doris Winter in the musical), who was the co-author and original singer of the 1960s pop hit "Just One Look." (In the 1986 touring production of the musical, Doris Troy performed the role of Mama Winter.)

The Off Off Broadway cast album was recorded live at the Heckscher Theatre on November 7 and 8, 1986, by Reach Records (LP # MWS-50000).

The song list on the cast recording, on a June 1986 program from the touring production, and on the 1995 London cast album (released by EMI Records [CD # 7243-8-33925-2-0) are at variance with one another, including songwriting credits. The list below is derived from the Off Off Broadway cast album, with other songs discussed following the listing. Since the musical's songwriting credits are often contradictory (for example, the touring program credits Rudolph V. Hawkins with the music for the song "What Do You Win When You Win?," but the London cast album credits Wesley Naylor), I've opted to be as inclusive as possible and thus have listed all the writers who have been credited by the various sources. (Although Richard Tee is credited with the music for the 1980 production at AMAS, his name doesn't seem to appear in the credits for any of the later productions of the musical.)

ACT ONE—Overture "Choir Rehearsal" (traditional), "You Are My Child" (lyric by Vy Higginsen and Ken Wydro, music by Pat Holley and Wesley Naylor) "Faith Can Move a Mountain" (lyric by Vy Higginsen and Ken Wydro, music by Rudolph V. Hawkins and Wesley Naylor), "My Faith Looks Up to Thee" (lyric probably by Vy Higginsen and Ken Wydro, composer[s] unknown), "I Don't Worry About Tomorrow" (lyric probably by Vy Higginsen and Ken Wydro, composer[s] unknown), "God Will Be" (lyric by Vy Higginsen and Ken Wydro, music by Rudolph V. Hawkins), "Gifted Is" (lyric by Vy Higginsen and Ken Wydro, music by Rudolph V. Hawkins and Doris Troy), "Mama, I Want to Sing" (lyric by Vy Higginsen and Ken Wydro, music by Pat Holley, Rudolph V. Hawkins, and Wesley Naylor)

ACT TWO—"What Do You Win When You Win?" (lyric and music by Vy Higginsen and Pat Wydro, music by Rudolph V. Hawkins and Wesley Naylor), "Precious Lord" (lyric probably by Vy Higginsen and Ken Wydro, composer[s] unknown), "Know When to Leave the Party" (lyric by Vy Higginsen and Ken Wydro, music by Pat Holley and Wesley Naylor), "The One Who Will Love Me" (lyric by Vy Higginsen and Ken Wydro, music by Rudolph V. Hawkins and Wesley Naylor), Finale Medley (lyric by Vy Higginsen and Ken Wydro, music by Rudolph V. Hawkins)

The following songs were listed in a touring production program from June 1986 and/or the London cast album: "The Treasure of Love" (lyric and music by Shapiro and Stallman); "Vy's Theme" (lyricist[s] and composer[s] unknown); "On Christ"/"Traveling Shoes" (lyricist[s] and composer[s] unknown); "We Come This Far by Faith" (lyricist[s] and composer[s] unknown); "Sermon Song" (lyric by Vy Higginsen and Ken Wydro, composer[s] unknown); "He'll (I'll) Be Your Strength" (lyric by Vy Higginsen and Ken Wydro, music by Rudolph V. Hawkins/Wesley Naylor); "And Now He's Gone" (lyric by Vy Higginsen and Ken Wydro, music by Steven Taylor); "Just One Look" (lyric and music by Doris [Payne] Troy and Carroll); "DJ Sequence" (lyric by Vy Higginsen and Ken Wydro, composer[s] unknown); "Choir Sequence" (traditional); "I Know Who Holds Tomorrow" (lyric and music by Stanphil); "I'll Do Anything" (lyric and music by Payne, Gamble, and Huff); "Take My Hand" (lyric and music by Dorsey); and "His Eye Is on the Sparrow" (traditional).

The touring production included a "Star Sequence" section which paid tribute to four singers, Dinah Washington, Lena Horne, Sarah Vaughn, and Billie Holiday (but only three songs were credited: "This Bitter Earth," lyric and music by Otis; "'T Ain't Nobody's Biz-ness If I Do," lyric and music by Porter Grainger and Everett Robbins; and "God Bless the Child," lyric and music by Arthur Herzog, Jr., and Billie Holiday; however, the London cast album listed the following four numbers for this sequence: "This Bitter Earth"; "Stormy Weather" (from *Cotton Club Parade* [Twenty-Second Edition], 1933; lyric by Ted Koehler, music by Harold Arlen); "(In My) Solitude" (lyric by Eddie DeLange, Irving Mills, and Mitchell Parrish, music by Duke Ellington); and "God Bless the Child." The musical opened in London on February 1, 1995, at the Cambridge Theatre and, as noted above, its cast recording was released by EMI Records.

As *Mama, I Want to Sing!*, a film version of the musical is scheduled for release in April 2008; produced by The Bigger Picture, the film's direction is by Charles Randolph-White, who also wrote the screenplay; the cast includes Ciara, Lynn Whitfield, Billy Zane, Patti LaBelle, and Ben Vereen. The film's soundtrack is scheduled for release by Releve Entertainment Records.

1002 Mama, I Want to Sing—Part II: The Story Continues. THEATRE: Heckscher Theatre; OPENING DATE: March 25, 1990; PERFORMANCES: Unknown; BOOK: Vy Higginsen and Ken Wydro; LYRICS: Vy Higginsen and Ken Wydro; MUSIC: Wesley Naylor; DIRECTION: Ken Wydro; CHOREOGRAPHY: Cisco Drayton; SCENERY: Charles McClennahan; LIGHTING: Marshall Williams; PRODUCERS: Reach Entertainment and Sports in association with Vy Higginsen and Ken Wydro

CAST—D'Atra Hicks, Victoria Hamilton (Doris Winter), Norwood, Richard Hartley, Pierre Cook (the Reverend Julian Simmons), Doris Troy, Lorraine Moore (Mama Winter), Kathleen Murphy-Palmer (Sister Carrie), Charles Stewart, Stewart Hartley, Boysie White (Minister of Music), Anaysha Figueroa, Knoelle Higginsen-Wydro (Little Doris), Vy Higginsen, Hazel Smith (Narrator, D.J.)

The musical was presented in two acts (song assignments unknown).

ACT ONE—"Joy, Joy, Joy"/"Great Is Thy Faithfulness," "The Spirit of Your Father," "The Lord Is Blessing Me," "Sanctify Me Holy," "Sermon Song," "You'll Never Walk Alone," "Something Pretty," "Something to Remember Me By," "When We All Get to Heaven," "We Belong Together," "Bless You, My Children"

ACT TWO—"Stay Close to the Music," "Long Distance Love," "New Life on the Planet," "Glad to Be in the Service," "Promise of the Future," "To Love Is to Serve," "Please Understand," "Where Is My

Mommy, Please?," "Alone on the Road," "Coming Back Home," Finale

NOTES—*Mama, I Want to Sing—Part II: The Story Continues* was an Off Off Broadway sequel to the long-running *Mama, I Want to Sing*, and was followed by a third musical, *Born to Sing!* (see entries). For a time during the run of *Part Two*, the first and second musicals were presented in repertory. *Part Two* was later produced on March 7, 1995, at the Paramount Theatre at Madison Square Garden for eight performances. The musical was recorded on Reach Records (CD # RRCD-00005), and included about half of the above-listed songs; the album also included two numbers not listed above ("Because He Lives" and "The Baptism Song"; these songs were later heard in the 1995 revival, the latter as "Mt. Calvary Baptism Day").

1003 Mama's Got a Job! THEATRE: Alice Tully Hall; OPENING DATE: December 26, 1979; PERFORMANCES: 10. SCRIPT: Judith Martin; LYRICS: Donald Ashwander; MUSIC: Donald Ashwander; DIRECTION: Judith Martin; PRODUCER: The Paper Bag Players (Judith Martin, Director)

CAST—Irving Burton, Pat Brodhead, James Lally, Judith Martin

NOTES—The revue was probably presented under an Off Off Broadway contract. After its initial engagement at Alice Tully Hall, the production later played at Town Hall for ten performances beginning on February 22, 1980. Judith Martin is not to be confused with the Judith Martin who is better known as Miss Manners.

1004 Man Better Man. THEATRE: St. Mark's Playhouse; OPENING DATE: July 2, 1969; PERFORMANCES: 23; BOOK: Erol Hill; LYRICS: Erol Hill; MUSIC: Coleridge-Taylor Perkinson; DIRECTION: Douglas Turner Ward; CHOREOGRAPHY: Percival Borde; SCENERY: Edward Burbridge; COSTUMES: Bernard Johnson; LIGHTING: Buddy Butler; PRODUCER: The Negro Ensemble Company

CAST—David Downing (Tim Briscoe), Graham Brown (Portagee Joe), Allie Woods (Swifty), Rosalind Cash (Inez Briscoe), Tony McKay (Hannibal), Samual Blue, Jr. (Tiny Satin), Arthur French (Crackerjack), Hattie Winston (Petite Belle Lily), Julius W. Harris (Cutaway Rimbeau), Aston Young (Aston Young), Esther Rolle (Alice Sugar), Norman Bush (Coolie), Afolabi Ajayi (Peloo), William Jay (Pogo), Damon W. Brazwell (Diable Papa), Mari Toussaint (Minee Woopsa), Frances Foster (First Village Woman), Clarice Taylor (Second Village Woman); Other Villagers: Louise Heath, Marilyn McConnie, Richard Roundtree, Lennal Wainwright, Anita Wilson

The action occurs at the turn of the century in a small village on the island of Trinidad, West Indies.

The musical was presented in three acts.

ACT ONE—"Procession" (Company), "Tiny, the Champion" (Tony McKay, Samual Blue, Jr., Company), "I Love Petite Belle" (David Downing, Company), "One Day, One Day, Congotay" (Damon W. Brazwell Mari Toussaint)

ACT TWO—"One, Two, Three" (Tony McKay, Male Villagers), "Man Better Man" (Mari Toussaint, Male Villagers), "Petite Belle Lily" (Tony McKay, Hattie Winston, Company), "Thousand, Thousand" (Hattie Winston, Company), "Me Alone" (Rosalind Cash, Company), "Girl in the Coffee" (Company), "Petite Belle Lily" (reprise) (Hattie Winston, Company)

ACT THREE—"Coolie Gone" (Rosalind Cash, Company), "War and Rebellion" (Hattie Winston, Company), "Beautiful Heaven" (Damon W. Brazwell, Mari Toussaint, Norman Bush, Afolabi Ajayi), "Briscoe, the Hero" (reprise version of "Tiny, the Champion") (Tony McKay, Company)

NOTES—*Man Better Man* appears to have been previously produced in Trinidad. The simple story told of the love of a young village boy and girl and the various villains who try to cause them trouble. Richard F. Shepard in the *New York Times* noted that by the finale boy gets girl and the villains are vanquished. Shepard found the evening a "good-humored yarn" with an "authentic folktale flavor," and he praised the lilting music (singling out "Girl in the Coffee," "Petite Lily Belle," and "Coolie Gone"), the "bouncy" choreography, and the "amiable and talented" cast. He concluded that the musical was like a cruise to the West Indies which "you can enjoy without packing."

Future blaxploitation queen Rosalind Cash had previously appeared in the Negro Ensemble Company's production of *God Is a (Guess What?)* (1968; see entry), which also had music by Coleridge-Taylor Perkinson. In *Man Better Man*, she was joined by another future film personality, Richard Roundtree, who would play the character John Shaft in a series of early 1970s blaxploitation films.

1005 Man in the Moon. THEATRE: Biltmore Theatre; OPENING DATE: April 11, 1963; PERFORMANCES: 22; BOOK: Arthur Burns; LYRICS: Sheldon Harnick; MUSIC: Jerry Bock; DIRECTION: Gerald Freedman; PRODUCERS: Arthur Cantor and Joseph Harris; a Bil and Cora Baird Marionette Theatre Production; PUPPETEERS: Frank Sullivan (Prologue, Nose Nolan, The Man in the Moon), Franz Fazakas (Jerry, Fluffy), Bil Baird (Flicker Martin, Mondo), Michael King (Sleeves), Bob Brown (Skin), Faz Korabel (Happy), Cora Baird (Chandra), Waxey Gibbous (Buz), Emil Maurer (The Giant); Assorted Moonbirds, Hi-Behinds, and Gollywhoppers (Carl Harms, George Baird, Bob Brown, Mike King)

SOURCE—A story by Bil Baird.

NOTES—This double bill of Bil Baird's puppet presentations was given in two acts. The first act, *Man in the Moon*, with lyrics by Sheldon Harnick and music by Jerry Bock, was the first of two musicals by the team which opened in April (their classic *She Loves Me* opened on Broadway at the Eugene O'Neill Theatre just a few days after the premiere of *Man in the Moon*). (According to the *New York Times*, the show's title was *A Man on the Moon*.)

The cast album of *Man in the Moon* was released by Golden Records (LP # 104) and included the full score of the show ("Look Where I Am," "Itch to Be Rich," "Worlds Apart," "You Treacherous Men," "Ain't You Never Been Afraid" and a reprise of "Worlds Apart").

The musical played either seven or twenty-two performances, depending on the source referenced (*Theatre World Season 1962-1963* credits the musical with seven, *The Burns Mantle Yearbook/The Best Plays of 1962-1963* with twenty-two).

(The second act of the production was *A Pageant of Puppetry*, which included puppets from Asia, Africa, Europe, and both Americas; the piece was accompanied by classical, folk, and popular music. *Pageant*, which also disclosed some of the marionettes' secrets, was [under variant titles] included in almost all future Bil Baird presentations.)

Paul Gardner in the *New York Times* found *Man in the Moon* a "box of holiday bon-bons," and praised the "snappy" score of the first act and the "diverting" second act which included a "rollicking" finale. Gardner also reported that after the New York engagement the Bairds were embarking on a nine-week tour of the Soviet Union; and, in an exchange program, the Seigel Obraztsov Puppet Theatre would visit the United States during the coming fall.

1006 A Man of No Importance. "A New Musical"

The Mitzi E. Newhouse Theatre/Lincoln Center; OPENING DATE: October 10, 2002; PERFORMANCES: 93; BOOK: Terrence McNally; LYRICS: Lynn Ahrens; MUSIC: Stephen Flaherty; DIRECTION: Joe Mantello; CHOREOGRAPHY: Jonathan Butterell; SCENERY: Loy Arcenas; COSTUMES: Jane Greenwood; LIGHTING: Donald Holder; MUSICAL DIRECTION: Rob Berman; PRODUCER: Lincoln Center Theatre (Andre Bishop and Bernard Gersten, Directors)

CAST—Roger Rees (Alfie Byrne), Jarlath Conroy (Father Kenny), Katherine McGrath (Mrs. Grace, Kitty Farrelly), Barbara Marineau (Miss Crowe), Patti Perkins (Mrs. Curtin), Ronn Carroll (Baldy O'Shea), Michael McCormick (Rasher Flynn, Carson), Martin Moran (Ernie Lally), Jessica Molaskey (Mrs. Patrick), Sean McCourt (Sully O'Hara), Luther Creek (Peter, Breton Beret), Faith Prince (Lily Byrne), Charles Keating (Carney, Oscar Wilde), Steven Pasquale (Robbie Fay), Sally Murphy (Adele Rice)

SOURCE—The 1994 film *A Man of No Importance* (directed by Suri Krishnamma).

The action occurs in Dublin in 1964.

The musical was presented in two acts.

ACT ONE—"A Man of No Importance" (Roger Rees, Company), "The Burden of Life" (Faith Prince), "Going Up" (Charles Keating, The St. Imelda's Players), "Princess" (Sally Murphy), "First Rehearsal" (Roger Rees, The St. Imelda's Players), "The Streets of Dublin" (Steven Pasquale, Company), "Books" (Charles Keating, Faith Prince), "Man in the Mirror" (Roger Rees, Charles Keating), "The Burden of Life" (reprise) (Faith Prince), "Love Who You Love" (Roger Rees)

ACT TWO—"Our Father" (Jessica Molaskey, Company), "Confession" (Roger Rees, Steven Pasquale, Jarlath Conroy), "The Cuddles Mary Gave" (Ronn Carroll), "Art" (Roger Rees, The St. Imelda's Players), "A Man of No Importance" (reprise) (Jessica Molaskey, Luther Creek, Sean McCourt), "Confusing Times" (Charles Keating), "Love Who You Love" (reprise) (Steven Pasquale), "Man in the Mirror" (reprise) (Charles Keating, Company), "Tell Me Why" (Faith Prince), "A Man of No Importance" (reprise) (Company), "Love Who You Love" (reprise) (Sally Murphy), "Welcome to the World" (Roger Rees)

NOTES—Based on the 1994 film of the same name (which starred Albert Finney), *A Man of No Importance* was the story of Alfie Byrne, a closeted, rather meek bus conductor who hopes to stage Oscar Wilde's *Salome* at his church's social hall but is barred from doing so when the church deems the play immoral. When the spirit of Oscar Wilde becomes his mentor, Alfie no longer denies his homosexuality and thus becomes a complete person. He meets with his theatrical troupe, and while their future is uncertain, they are all still friends who love their art, and Alfie, no longer a man of no importance, is the heart and center of the little group.

The musical was clearly a labor of love on the part of its creators, but its book and score were too mild. Some tried to make the case for "The Streets of Dublin," but even that song fell short of the mark. John Simon in *New York* noted that Terrence McNally's book stayed "staunchly faithful to the mediocrity" of the film, and found Stephen Flaherty's music "nondescript" (aiming "both a jig toward Ireland and a zag toward Broadway") and Lynn Ahrens' lyrics "conflicted." Ben Brantley in the *New York Times* wrote that audiences ready to use their handkerchiefs were "likely to find that the teardrops never fall," and he found the evening "as repressed and tentative as its hero."

During previews, "That's What I Think" was dropped.

The script was published by Stage and Screen in 2003, and the cast recording was released by Jay Records (CD # CDJAY-1369); the recording included a bonus song, "Love's Never Lost," written for, but not used in, the musical.

1007 Man on the Moon. "A New Musical." THEATRE: Little Theatre; OPENING DATE: January 29, 1975; PERFORMANCES: 5; BOOK: John Phillips; LYRICS: John Phillips; MUSIC: John Phillips; DIRECTION: Paul Morrissey; SCENERY: John J. Moore; COSTUMES: Marisa Trinder; costume design supervision by Michael Yeargan; LIGHTING: Jules Fisher; MUSICAL DIRECTION: Karen Gustafson; PRODUCERS: Andy Warhol in association with Richard Turley

CAST—Harlan S. Foss (Dr. Bomb), ERIC LANG (Ernie Hardy), Mark Lawhead (Leroy [Little Red Box]), DENNIS DOHERTY (President, King Can), GENEVIEVE WAITE (Angel), MONIQUE VAN VOOREN (Venus); Celestial Choir (Brenda Bergman, Mercury, Miss America; John Patrick Sundine, Mars; Jennifer Elder, Neptune; E. Lynn Nickerson, Pluto; Jeanette Chastonay, Saturn)

The action occurs on Earth, the Moon, and in the Canis Minor.

The musical was presented in one act.

MUSICAL NUMBERS—Prologue (Harlan S. Foss), "Boys from the South" (Eric Lang), "Midnight Deadline Blastoff" (Eric Lang), "Mission Control" (Harlan S. Foss, Eric Lang, Mark Lawhead, Dennis Doherty, Brenda Bergman), "Speed of Light" (Eric Lang, Mark Lawhead), "Though I'm a Little Angel" (Genevieve Waite), "Girls" (Dennis Doherty, Monique Van Vooren, Genevieve Waite), "Canis Minor Bolero Waltz" (Dennis Doherty, Monique Van Vooren, Genevieve Waite), "Starburst" (Genevieve Waite), "Penthouse of Your Mind" (Dennis Doherty), "Champagne and Kisses" (Monique Van Vooren), "Star Stepping Stranger"/"Convent" (Eric Lang, Genevieve Waite), "My Name Is Can" (Dennis Doherty), "American Man on the Moon" (Genevieve Waite), "Welcome to the Moon" (Company), "Sunny, Sunny Moon" (Monique Van Vooren, Harlan S. Foss), "Love Is Coming Back" (Genevieve Waite, Eric Lang), "Truth Cannot Be Treason" (Mark Lawhead), "Place in Space" (Eric Lang, Genevieve Waite), "Family of Man" (Harlan S. Foss), "Yesterday I Left the Earth" (Company), "Stepping to the Stars" (reprise) (Company)

NOTES—The critics complained about the plot of *Man on the Moon* (something to do with a mad scientist who wants to blow up the moon), and one even suggested he'd rather sit through the infamous Broadway flop *Via Galactica* (1972) again. But the critics were in general agreement about the pleasant score by John Phillips (including an unidentified torch song for Monique Van Vooren [apparently "Champagne and Kisses"]), and one critic looked forward to the cast album (which was never recorded). In 2009, Varese Sarabande Records (CD # 302-066-965-2) released a studio/original cast recording of the score.

Phillips had been the songwriter for, and one of the singers of the Mamas and The Papas; the cast included Dennis Doherty, who was at one time the lead singer for the group, and Genevieve Waite, who was Mrs. John Phillips.

During previews, Phillips played the roles of the President and King Can, and Dennis Doherty played the role of the scientist (later called Dr. Bomb). By opening night, Phillips was no longer in the cast, and his roles had been assumed by Dennis Doherty, whose role of the scientist was in turn assumed by Harlan S. Foss. Pop art icon Andy Warhol produced the musical, and at least one critic indicated the pre-show goings-on at the Little Theatre were more interesting than what occurred on stage: the opening night curtain was delayed thirty minutes for the arrival of the audience, Warhol's "in" crowd of "beautiful people." Genevieve Waite's 1974 LP recording *Romance Is on the Rise* (released by Paramour Records [# PR5088SD] and reissued in 2004 on CD by Chrome Records [# CDCD-5006]) included two songs from the musical ("American Man on the Moon" and "Love Is Coming Back").

The musical's early title had been *S-P-A-C-E*.

For an Off Broadway tribute to The Mamas and The Papas, see entry for *Dream a Little Dream*.

1008 Man with a Load of Mischief. "A New Musical." THEATRE: Jan Hus Playhouse; transferred to the Provincetown Playhouse on May 14, 1967; OPENING DATE: November 6, 1966; PERFORMANCES: 241; BOOK: Ben Tarver; LYRICS: John Clifton and Ben Tarver; MUSIC: John Clifton; DIRECTION: Tom Gruenewald; CHOREOGRAPHY: Noel Schwartz; SCENERY: Joan Larkey; COSTUMES: Volavkova; LIGHTING: Joan Larkey; MUSICAL DIRECTION: Sande Campbell; PRODUCER: Donald H. Goldman

CAST—Tom Noel (The Innkeeper), Lesslie Nicol (His Wife), Raymond Thorne (The Lord), Reid Shelton (The Man), Virginia Vestoff (The Lady), Alice Cannon (The Maid)

SOURCE—The British play *The Man with a Load of Mischief* by Ashley Dukes (which premiered on Broadway in 1925).

The action occurs in the early part of the nineteenth century at The Man with a Load of Mischief, a wayside inn in England.

The musical was presented in two acts.

ACT ONE—Overture (Orchestra), "Wayside Inn" (Tom Noel), "The Rescue" (Lesslie Nicol), "Entrance Polonaise" (Company), "Goodbye, My Sweet" (Virginia Vestoff), "Romance!" (Tom Noel, Lesslie Nicol, Raymond Thorne, Alice Cannon), "Lover Lost" (Virginia Vestoff), "Once You've Had a Little Taste" (Alice Cannon), "Hulla-Baloo-Balay" (Reid Shelton), "Once You've Had a Little Taste" (reprise) (Alice Cannon, Lesslie Nicol, Tom Noel), "Dinner Minuet" (Company), "You'd Be Amazed" (Raymond Thorne, Virginia Vestoff, Reid Shelton), "A Friend Like You" (Virginia Vestoff, Raymond Thorne), "Masquerade" (Reid Shelton), "Man with a Load of Mischief" (Virginia Vestoff), "Masquerade" (reprise) (Reid Shelton)

ACT TWO—Entr'acte (Orchestra), "What Style!" (Tom Noel), "A Wonder" (Virginia Vestoff), "Make Way for My Lady" (Reid Shelton), "Forget" (Raymond Thorne), "Any Other Way" (Lesslie Nicol, Tom Noel), "Little Rag Doll" (Alice Cannon), "Romance!" (reprise) (Virginia Vestoff), "Sextet" (Company), "Make Way for My Lady" (reprise) (Reid Shelton, Virginia Vestoff)

NOTES—*Man with a Load of Mischief*, which had originally premiered in Atlanta as *The High Life*, is one of the most fondly remembered Off Broadway musicals of the 1960s. Its memorable score includes "Masquerade" (also called "Come to the Masquerade"), one of the most hauntingly beautiful ballads in all musical theatre. The story concerned an ignored wife (Virginia Vestoff) who flirts with a nobleman (Raymond Thorne), only to find that she has fallen in love with his servant (Reid Shelton).

Dan Sullivan in the *New York Times* found the evening "perfectly charming," and he praised John Clifton's score ("fresh and quirky enough to be called contemporary ... but you can hum almost all" the songs). As for "Masquerade," he rightly felt the song should become a standard (unfortunately, it didn't), and suggested that Barbra Streisand record it (she didn't); he further noted that Reid Shelton's rendition of the ballad had the "pow!" that Carol Channing brought to *Hello, Dolly!*'s title song. Sullivan also reported that on opening night, sheet music from the score was handed out to the audience.

The cast included Off Broadway stalwarts Virginia Vestoff and Alice Cannon; and eleven years later Reid Shelton and Raymond Thorne found themselves in one of the biggest hits in Broadway history, creating the respective roles of Daddy Warbucks and FDR in *Annie* (1977).

The cast album was recorded by Kapp Records (# KRL-4508). In 2004, a new recording of the score was released by Original Cast Records (# 41117-61002), and the CD included many numbers which weren't on the original cast album (such as "Entrance Polonaise," "Dinner Minuet," "Sextet," and various reprises). For the 2004 recording, John Clifton, the musical's composer and co-lyricist, assumed the role of the Innkeeper.

The musical was produced in London during the 1968-1969 season.

1009 The Man with the Ragtime Blues. THEATRE: AMAS Repertory Theatre; OPENING DATE: October 16, 1975; PERFORMANCES: Unknown; BOOK, LYRICS, AND MUSIC: Mitch Douglas; DIRECTION: Jay Binder

CAST—Mitch Douglas; PRODUCER: AMAS Repertory Theatre (Rosetta LeNoire, Founder and Artistic Director)

NOTES—It appears that the Off Off Broadway musical *The Man with the Ragtime Blues* was a one-man show.

1010 The Man Without a Country. THEATRE: Metropolitan Opera House; OPENING DATE: May 12, 1937; PERFORMANCES: 4; LIBRETTO: Arthur Guiterman; MUSIC: Walter Damrosch; DIRECTION: Desire Defrere; SCENERY: See notes section; MUSICAL DIRECTION: See notes section; PRODUCER: The Metropolitan Opera

CAST—Arthur Carron (Lieutenant Philip Nolan), Helen Traubel (Mary Rutledge), George Rasely (Harman Blennerhassett, Fifth Midshipman, Admiral of the Algerine Fleet), Joseph Royer (Aaron Burr, Boatswain), John Gurney (Colonel Morgan, Fourth Midshipman), Nicholas Massue (Parke, Third Officer, First Midshipman), Lodovico Oliviero (Fairfax), Wilfred Engelman (Lieutenant Pinckney), George Cehanovsky (Lieutenant Reeve), Donald Dickson (Negro Boatman, Second Officer, Second Midshipman), Daniel Harris (First Officer, Third Midshipman), Five American Girls (Thelma Votipka, Maxine Stellman, Lucielle Browning, Maria Matyas, Jarna Paull); Speaking Parts: Louis D'Angelo (Commodore Stephen Decatur, Sergeant O'Neil), Norman Cordon (Captain Morris), Donald Dickson (Midshipman Denton), John Gurney (Midshipman Ahearn), Robert Nicholson (Surgeon, Captain Sedley, Fourth Officer), Ludwig Burgstaller (Private Schwartz), Lodovico Oliviero (Fifth Officer)

SOURCE—The story "The Man Without a Country" by Edward Everett Hale.

The opera was performed in two acts.

NOTES—The opera *The Man Without a Country* told the fictional story of a traitor who was involved in the plot to assassinate Aaron Burr; he's tried in a military tribunal and is condemned to forever sail the seas on a government man-of-war, never to see his native land again or to even hear the name of his country uttered by anyone. Olin Downes in the *New York Times* was reminded of another opera in which a man was condemned to sail the seas forever, Richard Wagner's *Flying Dutchman* (1843). As for the new work, Downes reported the score was "melodious but along too well-trodden paths." Further, it never went "deep" and often became "sentimental" and clichéd. But he praised the direction and performances.

The opera marked Helen Traubel's Met debut, and the cast included Norman Cordon. Traubel was best known for her Wagnerian roles, but she was "game": she later appeared in the original Broadway production of Richard Rodgers and Oscar Hammerstein II's *Pipe Dream* (1955); had her own nightclub act; and starred opposite Jerry Lewis in his best comedy, the surreal, dadaesque *The Ladies' Man* (1961). As for Cordon, in 1942 he created the title role in the Met's world premiere of Gian-Carlo Menotti's *The Island God* (see entry) and on Broadway created the role of Frank Maurrant in Kurt Weill's *Street Scene*

(1947), introducing the powerful "I Loved Her, Too" (he apparently left the production before it was recorded; his understudy, Randolph Symonette, performs the song on the cast album).

The Met's database indicates the second-act scenery for *The Man Without a Country* was designed by David Twachtman; there seems to be no record of who designed the scenery for the first act. The database also indicates Damrosch conducted the last performance of the opera during its first season of four performances; however, in his opening night review, Downes mentions that Damrosch conducted the opening night performance.

1011 Mandrake. "A New Musical." THEATRE: Soho Rep Theatre; OPENING DATE: April 13, 1984; PERFORMANCES: 20; BOOK: Michael Alfreds; LYRICS: Michael Alfreds; MUSIC: Anthony Bowles; DIRECTION: Anthony Bowles; SCENERY: Joseph A. Varga; COSTUMES: Steven L. Birnbaum; LIGHTING: David Noling; MUSICAL DIRECTION: Michael Rafter; PRODUCER: Soho Rep (Jerry Engelbach and Marlene Swartz, Artistic Directors)

CAST—Steve Sterner (Siro), Helen Zelon (Genevieve), Kim Moerer (Callimaco), Suzanne Ford (Lucrezia), Mary Rocco (Sostrata), Mary Eileen O'-Donnell (A Widow), Mary Testa (Doris), Sharon Watroba (A Chaperone), Tory Alexander (Fra Timoteo), Jeff Etjen (A Novice), Jim Denton (Nicia), Andrew Barnicle (Ligurio)

SOURCE—Niccolo Machiavelli's *Mandragola* (circa 1515).

The action occurs in Florence and covers the twenty-four hours of a summer's day in 1493.

The musical was presented in two acts.

ACT ONE—"Have You Seen...?" (Mary Rocco, Kim Moerer, Mary Eileen O'Donnell, Mary Testa, Tory Alexander, Helen Zelon, Jim Denton, Suzanne Ford, Sharon Watroba, Jeff Etjen, Steve Sterner), "One Thing After Another" (Mary Rocco, Kim Moerer, Mary Eileen O'Donnell, Mary Testa, Tory Alexander, Helen Zelon, Jim Denton, Suzanne Ford, Sharon Watroba, Jeff Etjen, Steve Sterner), "Song of Exposition" (Kim Moerer, Steve Sterner), "Whose Baby Are You?" (Helen Zelon), "Matter and Pills" (Jim Denton, Andrew Barnicle), "Give a Little Helping Hand" (Andrew Barnicle), "Waiting" (Suzanne Ford), "She Never Knew What Hit Her" (Mary Rocco, Sharon Watroba, Mary Testa), "The Waters of the Spa" (Andrew Barnicle, Mary Rocco, Suzanne Ford, Sharon Watroba, Mary Testa, Mary Eileen O'Donnell, Steve Sterner, Tory Alexander, Jim Denton, Jeff Etjen), "Mandrake" (Andrew Barnicle, Kim Moerer, Steve Sterner), "Mandrake" (reprise) (Company)

ACT TWO—"To Get It Off My Chest" (Mary Eileen O'Donnell, Tory Alexander, Jeff Etjen), "Lament to an Elephant-Woman" (Sharon Watroba), "If You Really Cared" (Kim Moerer, Helen Zelon, Steve Sterner, Mary Testa, Andrew Barnicle, Jim Denton), "The Means to an End" (Tory Alexander, Gregorians), "Widow's Testimony" (Mary Eileen O'Donnell), "Waiting" (reprise) (Kim Moerer), "Never Be a Servant" (Steve Sterner), "If Things Go Awry" (Tory Alexander, Mary Rocco, Andrew Barnicle, Jim Denton), "The Situation Changes Overnight" (Kim Moerer, Suzanne Ford), "Mandrake Hymn" (Company)

NOTES—The program called *Mandrake* a "new" Off Off Broadway musical, and while it might have been new to New York, it had actually been produced fourteen years earlier in London, where it opened at the Criterion Theatre on April 16, 1970, for twelve performances. Soho Rep's production didn't transfer to another theatre, and so after three weeks the musical was gone.

In 1974, a different musical version of the material, called *The Mandrake*, played at the Kennedy Center in Washington, D.C., as part of the American College Theatre Festival. For this version, the action was updated to the New York City of the 1890s.

And *Mandragola* ("A Renaissance Musical") was produced on radio by the Canadian Broadcasting Corporation in 1977; a recording was released that year by CBC Radio Canada Records (LP # LM-448). The book and lyrics were by Alan Gordon and the music by Doug Riley, and the cast included Don Francks (as Ligurio), who had created the title role of *Kelly* on Broadway in 1965; other performers on the recording are Mary Ann McDonald (Lucrezia; singing voice, Sharon Lee Williams); Martin Short (Callimaco; singing voice, Cal Dodd); and Andrea Martin (The Young Widow). (Another musical adaptation of the material, also titled *Mandragola*, was produced Off Off Broadway on December 3, 1976, at Solaron Productions; the translation Machiavelli was by J.R. Hale, and the book's adaptation was by Dan Held; the lyrics were by Joe Cook, and the lyrics by Pat Cook.)

Further, on March 2, 1987, *Whores of Heaven*, was another musical adaptation, and it was produced by the American Folk Theatre for fourteen performances in an Off Off Broadway presentation. The book was by David Wells and Luisa Inez Newton, and the lyrics and music were by Michael Wright (with additional lyrics by Wells, Newton, and Machiavelli). *Theatre World 1986-1987 Season* indicated the musical took place "at the point in space and time" where sixteenth-century Florence, Italy, and modern-day Little Italy in New York City "are most apt to intersect."

1012 Mandy Patinkin in Concert. THEATRE: Dodger Stages; OPENING DATE: September 20, 2004; PERFORMANCES: 25; PRODUCER: Dodger Stage Holding

CAST—Mandy Patinkin, Paul Ford (Piano)

The concert was presented in one act.

NOTES—Mandy Patinkin presented an evening of songs by such writers as Stephen Sondheim and Richard Rodgers and Oscar Hammerstein II.

Patinkin had previously performed on Broadway in three one-man concerts: *Mandy Patinkin in Concert: Dress Casual* (Helen Hayes Theatre, September 16, 1989; 49 performances); *Mandy Patinkin in Concert* (Lyceum Theatre, March 23, 1997; 17 performances); and *Mandy Patinkin in Concert: Mamaloshen* (Belasco Theatre, October 13, 1998; 28 performances); he had first performed the latter concert Off Off Broadway at the Angel Orensanz Center (a former synagogue) on July 21, 1998, for 35 performances.

1013 Manhattan Follies. "A Delightfully Different Revue." THEATRE: Persian Room/Plaza Hotel; OPENING DATE: July 1974 (July 9?); PERFORMANCES: Unknown; DIRECTION: Daniel Roussel; CHOREOGRAPHY: Neil Jones; SCENERY: Marcel Dauphinais; COSTUMES: Joseph G. Aulisi; LIGHTING: Gregory Allen Hirsch; PRODUCERS: Robert Stigwood in association with Anne Fargue and Allan Carr

CAST—Alan Hernandez, Robin Magnus, Antonio Pantojas, David Radner, Bob Ray, Michael St. Laurent, Tony Scaccia, Caleb Stonn, CRAIG RUSSELL

NOTES—Female impersonator Craig Russell headlined the drag revue *Manhattan Follies*, which played at the fabled Persian Room at the Plaza Hotel. Mae West, Diana Ross, Marlene Dietrich, Bette Midler, Ginger Rogers, Carol Channing, Tallulah Bankhead, Judy Garland, and Marilyn Monroe were among the evening's targets. Of the impersonations, Howard Thompson in the *New York Times* noted that the one of Shirley Temple was "dweadful"; that Jeanette MacDonald came across like Judy Canova; and Liza Minnelli seemed "more like a young Beulah Bondi."

1014 Manhattan Moves. THEATRE: American Place Theatre; OPENING DATE: December 17, 1992; PERFORMANCES: 45; LYRICS: See song list for credits; MUSIC: See song list for credits; DIRECTION: Michael Kessler; CHOREOGRAPHY: Michael Kessler; COSTUMES: Geff Rhian; LIGHTING: Randy Becker; PRODUCERS: M & M American Dance Theatre, Melinda Jackson, David H. Peipers, and Virginia L. Dean

CAST—Adrienne Armstrong (Ms. Biz), Kevin Gaudin (Con Eddie), Andre George (Mr. Mahvuss), El Tahra Ibrahim (Bodyworkit), Barry Wizoreck (Officer Wiz), Michael Kessler (Flash), Melinda Jackson (Star)

The action occurs in Manhattan.

The dance revue was presented in two acts.

ACT ONE—*New York Day—"The Street"*: "Manhattan Moves" (lyric and music by Michael Kessler) (pre-recorded by Michael Kessler) (Company), "Rhapsody in Blue Jeans" (music based on *Rhapsody in Blue* by George Gershwin; 1924) (Melinda Jackson, Michael Kessler, Company), "Subway" (lyric and music by John Kander and Fred Ebb, Jon Gordon, Melinda Jackson, and Michael Kessler) (Company), "Wall Street" (lyric and music by Brock Walsh and Mark Goldenberg) (pre-recorded song performed by the Pointer Sisters) (danced by Adrienne Armstrong, Barry Wizoreck, Kevin Gaudin, Andre George, El Tahra Ibrahim), "Taxi" (lyric and music by John Lennon and Paul McCartney) (pre-recorded by Bobby McFerrin) (danced by Michael Kessler, Kevin Gaudin, Barry Wizoreck, Andre George, Adrienne Armstrong, El Tahra Ibrahim), "Eat" (lyric and music by Donna Summer and Michael Omartian) (pre-recorded by Donna Summer) (Melinda Jackson, Barry Wizoreck, Kevin Gaudin, Andre George), "Faux Pas de la Dee Dah" (music by Peter Ilyich Tchaikowsky) (Company), "Lambatomy" (lyric and music by E.E. Garcia; other music by Amilcare Ponchielli) (pre-recorded by Miami Sound Machine) (Company), "Central Park" (lyric and music by M. Mainieri, B. Martin, and James Brown) (pre-recorded by Steps Ahead and James Brown) (Michael Kessler, Andre George, Barry Wizoreck, El Tahra Ibrahim, Adrienne Armstrong), "Bad News" (lyric and music by Michael Kessler) (pre-recorded by Michael Kessler) (Kevin Gaudin, Barry Wizoreck, Andre George), "Let's Face the Music and Dance" (from 1936 film *Follow the Fleet*; lyric and music by Irving Berlin) (pre-recorded by Michael Kessler) (Melinda Jackson, Michael Kessler)

ACT TWO—*New York Night—"The Stage"*: "On Broadway" (lyric and music by Barry Mann, Cynthia Weil, Jerry Leiber, and Mike Stoller) (pre-recorded by George Benson) (Company), "Panther" (theme from 1964 film *The Pink Panther*; music by Henry Mancini) (pre-recorded by Henry Mancini) (Company), "Spies" (lyric by Alan Paul, music by Jay Graydon, Alan Paul, and David Foster) (pre-recorded by the Manhattan Transfer) (Company), "Mermaid" (lyric and music by Mindy Jostyn, Jon Gordon, and Michael Kessler) (pre-recorded by Mindy Jostyn) (Melinda Jackson, Michael Kessler), "Puttin' on the Ritz" (1929 film *Puttin' on the Ritz*; lyric and music by Irving Berlin) (pre-recorded by Michael Kessler) (Adrienne Armstrong, El Tahra Ibrahim, Kevin Gaudin, Barry Wizoreck, Andre George), "Star-Spangled Breakdown" (based on "The Star-Spangled Banner," music by Francis Scott Key) (Guitar solo pre-recorded by J. Gordon) (El Tahra Ibrahim, Kevin Gaudin, Barry Wizoreck, Andre George, Adrienne Armstrong), "Rainbow" (lyric and music attributed to Harold Arlen; probably "Over the Rainbow,," lyric by E.Y. Harburg, music by Harold Arlen; from 1939 film *The Wizard of Oz*) (pre-recorded by Joan Osborne) (Michael Kessler, Melinda Jackson), "Rhapsody on Broadway" (themes from Barry Mann, Cynthia Weil, Jerry Leiber, Mike Stoller, and George Gershwin; adapted by Jon Gordon and Michael Kessler) (Company), "Manhattan Moves" (lyric and music by Michael Kessler) (pre-recorded by Michael Kessler) (Company)

NOTES—*Manhattan Moves*, a show business-themed dance revue set in New York, was choreographed by Michael Kessler. It appears that most if not all the songs were pre-recorded. Jack Anderson in the *New York Times* liked the choreography, but noted the show was "frivolous without being fun" because it offered "almost unrelievedly antic" and busy dance sequences. While these numbers made the evening "lively," they also made it "monotonous," and so Anderson praised Melinda Jackson and Kessler's "Let's Face the Music and Dance," finding Ms. Jackson "elegant" and a "welcome contrast to the prevailing jitters."

1015 Manhattan Rhythm. THEATRE: Savoy Theatre; OPENING DATE: July 21, 1982; PERFORMANCES: 24; CHOREOGRAPHY: Jon Devlin; COSTUMES: David Toser; LIGHTING: David Adams; MUSICAL DIRECTION: Richard Dimino; PRODUCER: Barbara Moore, Executive Producer

CAST—Jon Devlin and His Company: Female Dancers (Virginia Clark East, Lyn Gendron, Ann Marie Giambattista, Kim Kuhlman, Diana Laurenson, Linda Paul, Lisa Rudy, Lauren Salerno); Male Dancers (Louis Albert, Richard Loreto, Ralph Rodriguez, Steven Van Dyke); Singers (Armour Gomez, Teri Hiatt, Karyn Quackenbush, Bonnie Sue Taylor); Musicians (Babafemi, Percussion; Hank B., Drums; Andrew Brown, Trombone; Tyrone Cox, Drums; Richard Dimino, Leader Piano, Keyboards; Garrison Dow, Bass; Robert Madiou, Guitar; Vernon Jeffrey Smith, Sax; Larry Smith, Sax)

The dance revue was presented in two acts.

ACT ONE—Opening (Company); *Jazz*: "Love for Sale" (from *The New Yorkers*, 1930; lyric and music by Cole Porter) (Jon Devlin, Lisa Rudy, Ann Marie Giambattista, Diana Laurenson, Kim Kuhlman, Virginia Clark East, Steven Van Dyke, Richard Loreto, Louis Albert; Teri Hiatt, Vocal), Manhattan Rhythm Blues (Jon Devlin, Lyn Gendron), "All Blues" (Virginia Clark East, Lisa Rudy, Diana Laurenson, Lauren Salerno, Linda Paul, Kim Kuhlman, Ann Marie Giambattista (Solo), "Take Five" (Steven Van Dyke, Richard Loreto, Louis Albert), "Walkin' Sally" (Diana Laurenson, Linda Paul, Ann Marie Giambattista), *Big Band 40's*: "One O'Clock Jump"/"In the Mood" (Jon Devlin, Teri Hiatt; Bonnie Sue Taylor, Armour Gomez, Karen Quackenbush), "57 Street" (Louis Albert, Kim Kuhlman, Steven Van Dyke, Diana Laurenson, Ralph Rodriguez, Ann Marie Giambattista, Linda Paul, Lyn Gendron), *Broadway*: Crossover (Virginia Clark East), Medley (Karen Quackenbush, Ann Marie Giambattista, Lauren Salerno, Bonnie Sue Taylor, Armour Gomez, Richard Loreto, Ralph Rodriguez, Steven Van Dyke), "You Can Dance" (Teri Hiatt, Steven Van Dyke, Ralph Rodriguez), *Disco Space Fantasy*: *Star Trek* Medley/"Star Wars Cantina" (Lyn Gendron, Richard Loreto, Lauren Salerno, Louis Albert, Diana Laurenson, Ann Marie Giambattista, Lisa Rudy, Steven, Van Dyke, Ralph Rodreguez)

ACT TWO—Rock n' Roll n' Rock Medley (Company); *Latin*: Mambo/Cha-Cha/Mambo (Ann Marie Giambattista, Diana Laurenson, Virginia Clark, East, Lauren Salerno, Jon Devlin, Lyn Gendron), Merengue (Ann Marie Giambattista, Lyn Gendron, Virginia Clark East, Lauren, Salerno), "Spanish Cape" (Jon Devlin), Tango (Jon Devlin, Diana Laurenson), Samba (Company; Duo, Jon Devlin and Ann Marie Giambattista); *Country/Western*: "Hey, Good Lookin'" (*Something for the Boys*, 1943; lyric and music by Cole Porter) (Bonnie Sue Taylor), "Lady" (Armour Gomez), "9 to 5" (Karen Quackenbush), "Never Ending Love" (Company); *Top Hits*: "Guilty" (Teri Hiatt, Armour Gomez), "Physical" (Bonnie Sue Taylor, Steven Van Dyke, Ralph Rodriguez), "Out Here on My Own" (Teri Hiatt), "Fame" (Diana Laurenson, Anne Marie Giambattista, Lyn Gendron, Virginia Clark East), "Celebration" (Company)

NOTES—Virtually ignored by critics and audiences, *Manhattan Rhythm* crept in and out of town in the middle of the summer. But those who saw it witnessed a pleasant dance revue in the style of old-time television variety entertainment. It may have been a *Dancin'* (1978) wannabe, but it was nonetheless a pleasant way to spend a couple of hours.

The Savoy was the former Hudson Theatre.

1016 Manhattan Serenade. "A Musical Revue Based on the Music of Louis Alter." THEATRE: The AMAS Repertory Theatre; OPENING DATE: April 18, 1985; PERFORMANCES: 16; SCRIPT: Karen Cottrel and Alfred Heller; LYRICS: See song list for credits; MUSIC: Louis Alter; DIRECTION: Bob Rizzo; CHOREOGRAPHY: Bob Rizzo; ballets choreographed by David Anderson; SCENERY: Mina Albergo; COSTUMES: Christina Giannini; LIGHTING: Gregg Marriner; MUSICAL DIRECTION: Alfred Heller; PRODUCER: The AMAS Repertory Theatre, Inc. (Rosetta LeNoire, Founder and Artistic Director)

CAST—Michael Biondi, Cliff Hicklen, Connie Kunkle, Janice Lorraine, Luke Lynch, Richie McCall, Marie McKinney, Kelly Patterson, Mark Pennington, Michele Pigliavento, Brad J. Reynolds, Andrea Sandall, Sally Ann Swarm, Robert Torres, Carrie Wilder, Mona Yvette Wyatt, Sally Yorke

The revue was presented in two acts.

ACT ONE—Overture (Steve Bernstein, Peter Hammer, Alfred Heller), "Manhattan Serenade" (from 1944 film *Broadway Rhythm*; lyric by Harold Adamson), (Mark Pennington, Connie Kunkle), "Piano Phun"/"Lopeziana"/"Manhattan Serenade" (reprise) (featured dancers in this sequence were Michael Biondi, Janice Lorraine, and Michele Pigliavento), "Melody from the Sky" (lyric by Sidney D. Mitchell) (Sally Ann Swarm, Cliff Hicklen, Luke Lynch, Mark Pennington, Brad J. Reynolds), "Blue Shadows" (*Earl Carroll Vanities*, 1928; lyric by Ray (Raymond) Klages)/"New Love for Old Love" (lyric by Louis Alter)/"My Kinda Love" (lyric by Jo' Trent) (Connie Kunkle, Mark Pennington), "That Tired Feeling" (lyric possibly by Harry Ruskin and Leighton K. Brill)/"Throw It Out the Window" (lyric by Harry Ruskin and Leighton K. Brill)/"Blow Hot, Blow Cold" (lyric by Harry Ruskin and Leighton K. Brill) (all three songs from *Ballyhoo*, 1930) (Michele Pigliavento and Cliff Hicklen, with Connie Kunkle, Janice Lorraine, Sally Ann Swarm, Mona Yvette Wyatt), "Metropolitan Nocturne" (story by Karen Cottrell) (Kelly Patterson, Andrea Sandall), "You Turned the Tables on Me" (1936 film *Sing, Baby, Sing*; lyric by Sidney D. Mitchell) (Sally Yorke, Michael Biondi, Carrie Wilder), "Up to Your Ears in Souvenirs" (lyric by Stanley Adams) (Cliff Hicklen, Mona Yvette Wyatt, Company)

ACT TWO—Entr'acte (Steve Bernstein, Peter Hammer, Alfred Heller), "Wonderworld" (lyric by Stanley Adams) (Company; featuring tap dancers Michael Biondi, Janice Lorraine, Kelly Patterson, and Michele Pigliavento), "Autumn Night" (lyric by Stanley Adams) (Marie McKinney and Richie McCall; offstage solos by Mona Yvette Wyatt and Cliff Hicklen), "Something's Come Over Me" (lyric by Stanley Adams) (Richie McCall and Marie McKinney, with Michael Biondi, Janice Lorraine, Kelly Patterson, and Michele Pigliavento), "Dolores" (1941 film *Las Vegas Nights*; lyric by Frank Loesser) (Brad J. Reynolds, with Luke Lynch, Cliff Hicklen, and Mark Pennington), "Love Me As I Am" (lyric by Frank Loesser; the song was intended as a duet for Dorothy Lamour and Bob Hope in the 1941 film *Caught in the Draft*, but only the music was used) (Janice Lorraine, Brad J. Reynolds), "The Blues Are Brewin'" (1947 film *New Orleans*; lyric by Eddie [Edgar] De Lange) (Mona Yvette Wyatt; saxophone solo by Steve Bernstein), "Side Street in Gotham" (story by Karen Cottrell and David Anderson) (Andrea Sandall, Robert Torres, Kelly Patterson, Michele Pigliavento, Company), "Hello, Manhattan!" (A Comedy by Karen Cottrell) (Company), "Hello, Manhattan!" (lyric by Karen Cottrell) (Connie Kunkle, Cliff Hicklen, Mark Pennington, Brad J. Reynolds, Carrie Wilder, Sally Yorke), "Star Crazy" (lyric by Eddie [Edgar] De Lange) (Luke Lynch), "We Can't Go On Like This!" (lyric by Karen Cottrell) (Company), "Star Crazy" (reprise) (Luke Lynch), "We Worked the Whole Thing Out" (lyric by Karen Cottrell)/"Seeing Things" (lyric by Stanley Adams/"Manhattan Serenade" (reprise) (Company)

NOTES—The Off Off Broadway *Manhattan Serenade*, a composer-tribute revue to Broadway and Hollywood composer Louis Alter (1902-1980), was a welcome and rare chance to hear his relatively obscure music.

The dialogue and continuity were written by Karen Cottrell and Alfred Heller, and a mini-musical at the end of the second act was written by Cottrell; new lyrics for some of Alter's songs were written by Cottrell and Stanley Adams. Since it's unlikely we'll see another evening of Alter's music produced any time soon, it's regrettable that *Manhattan Serenade* wasn't recorded.

1017 A Manoir. "A New Opera." THEATRE: Judson Poets' Theatre; OPENING DATE: April 22, 1977; PERFORMANCES: Unknown; LIBRETTO: Al Carmines; MUSIC: Al Carmines; DIRECTION: Lawrence Kornfeld; SCENERY: Edward Lazansky; COSTUMES: Theo Barnes; Esther Jenkins, collaborator; LIGHTING: Gary Weathersbee; MUSICAL DIRECTION: Al Carmines Producer: The Judson Poets' Theatre

CAST—James Bryan (Man at Spotlight), Semina De Laurentis (Girl with Laurel), Bill Conway (Boy with Cap), Margaret Wright (Woman in White), Michael Petro (Naval Officer), David Tice (Curate), Katherine Litz (Lady with a Fan), Wendell Cordtz (Young Man with a Bow Tie), Essie Borden (Young Woman with a Sweater), Lee Guilliatt (Woman in a Beige Suit), Trisha Long (Woman with a Purse), Theo Barnes (Man in Dark Glasses)

SOURCE—Gertrude Stein's 1932 play *A Manoir*.

The action occurs in A Manoir, a French country estate.

The opera was presented in two acts.

NOTES—Usually the critics had high praise for Al Carmines' scores, but in the case of *A Manoir*, Peter G. Davis in the *New York Times* wasn't impressed with Carmines' "broadly eclectic, scarcely memorable show-biz tunes," and noted that as Carmines played the score he gave "the impression of making it all up" as he went along. But Davis praised the twelve-member cast and Lawrence Kornfeld's direction. Since the work emphasized character over plot, Davis was particularly impressed with the cast, all of whom conveyed the "passionate natures" of "real people who believe in themselves intensely." Individual musical sequences weren't listed in the program for the Off Off Broadway musical, which was the fifth of six musicals Carmines and Kornfeld adapted from various works by Gertrude Stein. See entries for *What Happened* (1963), *In Circles* (1967), *The Making of Americans* (1972), *Listen to Me* (1974), and *Dr. Faustus Lights the Lights* (1979).

1018 The Manson Family/Helter Five-O. "A Multimedia Music Drama." THEATRE: Lincoln Center; OPENING DATE: July 1990; PERFORMANCES: Unknown; LIBRETTO: John Moran; MUSIC: John Moran; DIRECTION: Bob McGrath; PRODUCER: Lincoln Center's *Serious Fun!* Series

CAST—The Ridge Theatre

The opera was presented in three acts.

NOTES—John Moran's *The Manson Family/Helter Five-O* was produced Off Off Broadway as part of Lincoln Center's *Serious Fun!* series, and in 1992 was recorded as *The Manson Family: An Opera* by Point/Philips Records (CD # 432-967-2) with a studio cast which included Iggy Pop. In his liner notes, Alvin Eng described the work as "an opera that is not entirely sung and does not present a clear, tragically-correct, moral ending." He further described the opera as a "montage of aria, song and monologue set against classical acoustic and experimental electronically-treated-soundscapes."

In the liner notes, Moran indicated the figures in Charles Manson's "family" were "represented in form and basic character only, to serve as empty vessels for" the opera's perspective, which didn't attempt to literally reenact the events of the 1969 murders and subsequent trial. Moran also noted his opera "is not meant to be seen as any sort of condemnation or approval, towards either side of the law."

For another musical about Charles Manson and his "family," see entry for *22 Years*. For a musical depicting Squeaky Fromme, see entry for *Assassins*.

The following list of songs is taken from the CD of *The Manson Family*:

ACT ONE—*"The Murders"*: "Night Highway #1," "Tate House" (Early Morning), "'The Prosecutor' at Death-Train Station Five" (The Tate House), SUBJECT: The Beatles

ACT TWO—*"The Family"*: "Rape Music" (Introduction to Act Two), SUBJECT: Lynette (Squeaky) Fromme, "Charlie in a Field, Forever," "Susan Atkins on Night Highway," SUBJECT: Charles Manson (at Spahn's Movie Ranch), "'Good Morning!' ... It's The Beatles"

ACT THREE—*"The Hall of Justice"*: "Raid on Spahn" (Introduction to Act Three), "Susan Atkins, on the Staircase to Justice (Leading to Night Highway)," "Night Highway," "Squeaky in a Boat," "The Family in a Courtroom ('Manson Leaps at Judge!')," "The Judge," SUBJECT: Charles (No Name) Manson

1019 March of the Falsettos. "A New Marvin Musical." THEATRE: Studio Theatre/Playwrights Horizons from April 1, 1981, to May 16, 1981 (42 performances); transferred to Mainstage Theatre/Playwrights Horizons on May 20, 1981 (through September 26, 1981) (170 performances); and then transferred to the Westside Arts Theatre/The Cheryl Crawford Theatre on October 13, 1981 (through January 31, 1982) (128 performances).; OPENING DATE: April 1, 1981; PERFORMANCES: 340; BOOK: William Finn; LYRICS: William Finn; MUSIC: William Finn; DIRECTION: James Lapine; SCENERY: Douglas Stein; COSTUMES: Maureen Connor; LIGHTING: Frances Aronson; MUSICAL DIRECTION: Michael Starobin; PRODUCER: Playwrights Horizons (Andre Bishop, Artistic Director)

CAST—Michael Rupert (Marvin), Alison Fraser (Trina), James Kushner (Jason), Stephen Bogardus (Whizzer Brown), Chip Zien (Mendel)

The musical was presented in one act.

MUSICAL NUMBERS—"Four Jews in a Room Bitching" (Company), "A Tight-Knit Family" (Michael Rupert), "Love Is Blind" (Alsion Fraser, Chip Zien, Company), "The Thrill of First Love" (Michael Rupert, Stephen Bogardus), "Marvin at the Psychiatrist" (A 3-Part Mini-Opera) (Michael Rupert, Chip Zien, James Kushner), "My Father's a Homo" (James Kushner), "Everyone Tells Jason to See a Psychiatrist" (Company), "This Had Better Come to a Stop" (Company), "Please Come to My House" (Alison Fraser, Chip Zien, James Kushner), "Jason's Therapy" (James Kushner, Chip Zien, Company), "A Marriage Proposal" (Chip Zien), "A Tight-Knit Family" (reprise) (Michael Rupert, Chip Zien), "Trina's Song" (Alison Fraser), "March of the Falsettos" (Michael Rupert, Stephen Bogardus, Chip Zien, James Kushner), "The Chess Game" (Michael Rupert, Stephen Bogardus), "Making a Home" (Alison Fraser, Chip Zien, Stephen Bogardus), "The Games I Play" (Stephen Bogardus), "Marvin Hits Trina" (Company), "I Never Wanted to Love You" (Company), "Father to Son" (Michael Rupert, James Kushner)

NOTES—*March of the Falsettos* (its original title was *The Pettiness of Misogyny* and then later *Four Jews in a Room Bitching*) was the second of three musicals in William Finn's "Marvin Trilogy" (*In Trousers, March of the Falsettos*, and *Falsettoland*). Chip Zien, who played Marvin in the trilogy's first musical, now played his psychiatrist; Alison Fraser continued in the role of Trina, Marvin's wife, and Michael Rupert and Stephen Bogardus assumed the respective roles of Marvin and Whizzer. DRG Records (LP # SBL-12581) released the cast album; the script was published by Samuel French, Inc., in 1995 as *Falsettos*, which combined *March of the Falsettos* and *Falsettoland* (see entry for the latter); Samuel French, Inc., had also published a separate edition of the script of *March of the Falsettos* in 1981. The scripts of all three musicals in the "Marvin Trilogy" were published as *The Marvin Songs* by The Fireside Theatre in an undated (but possibly 1991) edition.

See entry for the 1978 production of *In Trousers* for information regarding all productions of the "Marvin Trilogy" (*In Trousers, March of the Falsettos*, and *Falsettoland*). *March of the Falsettos* premiered in London at the Albery Theatre on March 24, 1987.

1020 Marco Polo. "An Opera Within an Opera." THEATRE: New York State Theatre; OPENING DATE: November 8, 1997; PERFORMANCES: 4; LIBRETTO: Paul Griffiths; MUSIC: Tan Dun; DIRECTION: Martha Clarke; SCENERY: Debra Booth; COSTUMES: Jane Greenwood; LIGHTING: Stephen Strawbridge; PRODUCER: The New York City Opera

CAST—Laura Tucker (Marco), Christine Abraham (Sheherazada, Mahler, Queen), Susan Botti (Water), Adam Klein (Polo), Chen Shi-Zheng (Rustichello, Li Po), Rod Neiman (Kublai Khan), Stephen Bryant (Dante, Shakespeare)

The opera was produced in one act.

MUSICAL NUMBERS—"I Have Not Told One Half of What I Saw," "No," "What a Place That Was," "Venezia Vento," "Journey—Shin Tsen," "Wayward the Air This Morning," "Listen," "The Past Goes On," "We Stood at the Harbour," "Such a Moment," "Slowly on Your Thighs," "The Sea A Sound A Thing An Animal," "S—Sksk ... Every Face a Mask," "S—Sksk ... Spilled from a Fountain," "Desert ... As Near as My Finger's End," "M–," "Silence" "I Wait," "Himalaya," "Himalaya" (dance), "Himalaya" (overtone singing), "Stone Song," "Human, a Grace Note," "Was This in the Book?," "I Have Not Told," "The Journey That Was Yours," "If Life Is Only a Dream," "Wenn Nur Ein Traum das Leben Ist," "We are Such Stuff as Dreams Are Made On," "From High," "At the Middle of the Earth," "Tsong Gou," "Death Could Not Be Colder," "Beyond the Rule of the Khan"

NOTES—This production was the New York premiere of *Marco Polo*, which had first been seen in two acts in Munich the previous year and had been recorded by Sony Records on a 2-CD set (S2K-62912); the song sequences listed above are taken from this recording.

The plot dealt with the both the spiritual journey ("Opera I") as well as the literal or physical journey ("Opera II") of Marco Polo as he travels the world and meets such figures as Shakespeare, Dante, and Gustav Mahler. Two singers portrayed the title character (one is the "real" Marco Polo [Laura Tucker], the other his memory [Adam Klein]). Writing for *New York*, Peter G. Davis found Richard Griffiths' libretto "irritatingly obscure" and felt Tan Dun's "wildly eclectic" score was a combination of Eastern and Western styles which gave "the sensation of being trapped in some kind of exotic international-airport mall." However, in his review for the *New York Times*, Patrick J. Smith praised the opera as an "extraordinary" work, a "determinedly nonlinear fantasia on words, sounds and ideas associated with travel" and with Marco Polo's journey. Smith praised the "heart-catching expressiveness" of the score, noting its baroque music offered "a variety of musical styles" representing Eastern and Western cultures.

1021 Mardi Gras! "A New Musical Spectacular." THEATRE: Jones Beach Theatre (formerly Marine Stadium and then Jones Beach Marine Theatre); OPENING DATE: June 26, 1965; PERFORMANCES: 68; BOOK: Sig Herzig; LYRICS: Carmen Lombardo and John Jacob Loeb; MUSIC: Carmen Lombardo and John Jacob Loeb; DIRECTION: Entire production supervised by Arnold Sector; staging by June Taylor; CHOREOGRAPHY: June Taylor; SCENERY: George Jenkins; COSTUMES: Winn Morton; LIGHTING: George Jenkins; MUSICAL DIRECTION: Mitchell Ayers; PRODUCER: Carmen Lombardo

CAST—DAVID ATKINSON (John Laffity, Jean Laffite, Lucky Laffity), RALPH PURDUM (George Baxter, Captain Benedict Baxter, Arnold Baxter), KAREN SHEPARD (Peggy Willard, Marguerite de Villiers, Meg), RUTH KOBART (Caroline Willard, Madame de Villiers, Carrie Nation), PHIL LEEDS (Louis Lamont, Dominique You, Louis [The Guide]), GAIL JOHNSTON (Anne, Annette, Anna), JUANITA HALL (Katie, Katherine, Marie Le Veau), James Kennon-Wilson (Dan), PETER GLADKE (Jacques), Barbara Ann Webb (Vesta), WILBUR DE PARIS (Himself), Jamie Simmons (Lulu), Keith Connes (Father Time); Singers: Girls—Katherine Barnes, Margaret Broderson, Doris Galiber, Joy Holly, Sherry Lambert, Carol Marraccini, Mary Ann Rydzeski, Jamie Simmons, Marsha Tamaroff, Betty Terrell, Elise Warner, Barbara Ann Webb, Maggie Worth; Boys—Gilbert Adkins, Eddie Carr, Peter Clark, Nino Galanti, Leslie Meadow, Donald Meyers, Richard Nieves, Adam Petroski, Herbert Pordum, Jerome Toti, Edmund Walenta, James Kennon-Wilson; Dancers: Girls—Jean Adams, Kathie Dalton, Bonnie Dwyer, Mercedes Ellington, Mimi Funes, Peggy Marie Haug, Jane Karel, Joan Paige, Patti Palumbo, Carol Perry, Lucinda Ransom, Toni Reither, Renee Rose, Geri Spinner, Paula Tennyson, Patti Watson; Boys—Fred Benjamin, Donn Bonnell, Steven Boockvor, Henry Boyer, Bob Ellis, Ted Goodridge, Ralph Hoffman, Dennis Lynch, Myron Meljie, Ed Nolfi, Dick Prescott, Gary Ramback, Doug Spingler, Kip Watson, Ron Watson, Vernon Wendorf

The action occurs in New Orleans during three time periods (1965, 1815, and 1905).

The musical was presented in two acts.

ACT ONE—Overture (Orchestra), "The Mardi Gras Waltz" (Ensemble), "I'd Know That Smile" (David Atkinson), "Mumbo Jumbo" (Juanita Hall), "We're Wanted" (Phil Leeds, David Atkinson, Peter Gladke, Pirates), "Ladies of the Ballet" (Gail Johnston, Ruth Kobart, Ladies), "Pirates' Polka" (Pirates, Ladies), "When I Take My Lady" (David Atkinson, Pirates), "When My Man Sails Home" (Juanita Hall), "We're Wanted" (reprise) (Phil Leeds, Pirates), "A Pirate's Lament" (Phil Leeds, Gail Johnston), "Someone I Could Love" (Karen Shepard, Gail Johnston), "When I Take My Lady" (reprise) (David Atkinson, Pirates), "I'd Know That Smile" (reprise) (David Atkinson, Karen Shepard), Finale (Company)

ACT TWO—Entr'acte, "Come Along Down" (Phil Leeds, Ensemble), "The Kind of a Girl" (David Atkinson, Karen Shepard), "The Kind of a Girl" (reprise) (Ralph Purdum, David Atkinson, Karen Shepard), Sequence: Wilbur de Paris and His New Orleans Jazz, "Down with Whiskey" (Ruth Kobart, Ralph Purdum, Ensemble), "The Kind of a Girl" (reprise) (David Atkinson), "We're Gonna See the Voodoo Queen" (Juanita Hall, Ensemble), "Someone I Could Love" (Karen Shepard), "Mumbo Jumbo" (reprise) (Juanita Hall), Finale (Company)

NOTES—*Mardi Gras!* told the story of John Laffity, a mild-mannered director of New Orleans' annual Mardi Gras Ball who is so engrossed with the preparations for the ball that he's in danger of losing his girlfriend. When he's given a special potion, he goes back in time to view his ancestors (in 1815, the notorious pirate Jean Lafitte, and in 1905, Lucky Laffity, a devil-may-care gambler). When he returns to the present, he's now a different man, having learned the ways of romance from his colorful forebears. (Jean Lafitte was also a major character in the 1929 musical *A Noble Rouge* [see entry]).

As with all Jones Beach musicals, the evening was rich in production values, including a pirate ship which sailed on the theatre's lagoon. Lewis Funke in the *New York Times* praised the "attractive" scenery and the "lavish and gorgeous" costumes. While he felt the story meandered (and could have done with more comedy) and the score was merely "conventional," he praised June Taylor's "energetic, gay" and "amusing" choreography.

There was no cast recording, but Decca Records released an LP (# DL-74696) of twelve instrumental selections from the musical performed by Mitchell Ayers and the Mardi Gras Strings (Ayers was the musical director for *Mardi Gras!*). The musical returned the following summer, opening on July 8, 1966, for fifty-four performances. David Atkinson, Karen Shepard, Gail Johnston, and Ralph Purdum reprised their roles, and replacing Phil Leeds, Ruth Kobart, and Juanita Hall, were, respectively, Joel Grey, Fran Stevens, and Barbara Ann Webb. For the 1966 production, Louis Armstrong and His All Stars replaced Wilbur de Paris and His New Orleans Jazz group.

Among the characters in *Mardi Gras!* was Carry Nation, who had one song, "Down with Whiskey" (for an opera about her, see entry for *Carry Nation*). The Jones Beach production is not to be confused with two other productions with the same title. The drama *Mardi Gras* by Norman Rosten closed during its pre-Broadway tryout in 1954 (the play's background music was composed by Duke Ellington). The plot had something to do with a driven mother who is determined to see her daughter crowned queen of the Mardi Gras. Despite her daughter's tuberculosis, the mother sees to it that the young woman joins the Mardi Gras parade in the pouring rain. There was also a London musical called *Mardi Gras*; it opened at the Prince of Wale's Theatre on March 18, 1976, for a money-losing run of 212 performances. The book was by Melvyn Bragg, and the lyrics and music were by Alan Blaikley and Ken Howard. Set in the New Orleans of 1917, the musical dealt with the romance of a musician (Nicky Henson) and a prostitute (Dana Gillespie). The cast album was released by EMI Records (LP # EMC-3123).

1022 Margaret Garner. THEATRE: New York State Theatre; OPENING DATE: September 11, 2007; PERFORMANCES: 7; LIBRETTO: Toni Morrison; MUSIC: Richard Danielpour; DIRECTION: Tazewell Thompson; CHOREOGRAPHY: Anthony Salatino; SCENERY: Donald Eastman; COSTUMES: Merrily Murray-Walsh; LIGHTING: Robert Wierzel; MUSICAL DIRECTION: George Manahan; PRODUCER: The New York City Opera

CAST—Tracie Luck (Margaret Garner), Gregg Baker (Robert Garner), Lisa Daltirus (Cilla), Wayne Hobbs (Auctioneer, Judge I), Timothy Mix (Edward Gaines), Laurice Simmons Kennel (Female Slave), Joel Sorenson (Casey), Maureen McKay (Caroline Gaines), Christopher Jackson (George Hancock), Gregory Harrell (Slave-Catcher), Sean Anderson (Judge II), Jeffrey Tucker (Judge III), Brea Watkins and Jordan Johnson (Garner Children)

The action occurs in 1856 in Kentucky and Ohio.

The opera was presented in two acts.

NOTES—Originally produced in May 2003 and then later in 2005 (in Detroit), the opera *Margaret Garner* told the true story of a runaway slave who murders her children rather than let them live as slaves; after her arrest and trial, she ultimately commits suicide.

Anthony Tommasini in the *New York Times* noted that Richard Danielpour's score "pulls you in," and praised the "lyrically ruminative vocal lines." But Tommasini felt the music was also "safe," "sappy," "hokey," "mawkish," and "shamelessly manipulative." However, Clive Barnes in the *New York Post* found the score "accessible and smoothly eclectic," running the gamut "from aria to Broadway, from gospel to symphony." He didn't think the work would find a place in the operatic "stratosphere," but predicted it would leave its mark in the operatic repertory.

1023 Marilyn. THEATRE: New York State Theatre; OPENING DATE: October 6, 1993; PERFORMANCES: 3; LIBRETTO: Norman Rosten; MUSIC: Ezra Laderman; DIRECTION: Jerome Sirlin; CO-DIRECTION: Paul L. King; CHOREOGRAPHY: Esperanza Galan; SCENERY: Jerome Sirlin; COSTUMES: V. Jane Suttell; LIGHTING: Jeff Davis; MUSICAL DIRECTION: Hal France; PRODUCER: The New York City Opera

CAST—Susanne Marsee (Rose), Louis Perry (Photographer), Steven Raiford (Reporter), Kathryn Gamberoni (Marilyn Monroe), William Ledbetter (Window Washer), John Lankston (First Mogul), Jonathan Green (Second Mogul), Ron Baker (Psychiatrist), Philip Cokorinos (Rick), Pamela Brotherton (Marilyn Apparition), Michael Rees Davis (Senator), Michele McBride (Vinnie)

The action occurs in 1962 during the last months of Marilyn Monroe's life.

The opera was performed in two acts.

NOTES—The critics were divided over Ezra Laderman's opera *Marilyn*. Joseph McLellan in the *Washington Post* found the opera "a powerful and memorable work of art," and cited a number of ambitious musical sequences: a trio ("I'm in a Room; the Door Is Locked"); a soprano solo with male sextet ("You're All One, You've Got the Scent of the Hunt"); a duet ("Norma? Is That You, Norma Jean?"); and a death scene ("Don't Scold Me, Momma, I'm Tired"). The *Post* praised Laderman's ability to shift between tonal music and the styles of jazz, Broadway, and film background music. On the other hand, Edward Rothstein in the *New York Times* found the evening one of "amiable lugubriousness," and felt that the libretto offered no real dramatic conflict; but he noted the score was "skillfully eclectic." The three sold-out performances seem to have been the beginning and the end of *Marilyn*, the opera. But from the critical comments, it appears the opera had much to offer in the way of interesting music. Unfortunately, there was no recording. There have been at least four other musical versions of Marilyn Monroe's life. *Hey Marilyn* opened in Canada in 1980, with lyrics and music by Cliff Jones (who had written the Broadway flop *Rockabye Hamlet*). There was also the British musical *Marilyn!*, which had a brief run in early 1983, and another musical, also titled *Marilyn*, which opened on Broadway later in the same year for a run of just sixteen performances. These three musicals weren't recorded, but in 1996 Stephanie Lawrence, who had portrayed Monroe in the London musical, recorded an album called *Marilyn—The Legend*, which included songs from the musical as well as numbers which Monroe had performed in some of her films (Carlton Sounds Records CD # 30360-00312). However, a fourth musical version, the 1993 German *Marilyn—Musical* was recorded by Edelton Records (CD # EDL-2734-2).

1024 Markheim. THEATRE: Manhattan Theatre Club; OPENING DATE: October 18, 1973; PERFORMANCES: 6; LIBRETTO: Carlisle Floyd; MUSIC: Carlisle Floyd; DIRECTION: David Shookhoff; SCENERY: Wayne Chouinard; LIGHTING: Derek Fox; MUSICAL DIRECTION: Ethan Mordden; PRODUCER: Manhattan Theatre Club (Lynne Meadow, Artistic and Executive Director)

CAST—Douglas Perry (Creach), Michael Riley (Markheim), Sarah Sager (Tess), Neil Rosenshein (Stranger)

SOURCE—The short story "Markheim" by Robert Louis Stevenson, which first appeared in the 1885 volume *The Merry Men and Other Tales and Fables*.

The opera was presented in one act.

NOTES—*Markheim*, a little-known opera by Carlisle Floyd which was based on Robert Louis Stevenson's short story of the same name, was produced Off Off Broadway by the Manhattan Theatre Club for a limited engagement of six performances.

Somewhat similar in theme to Stevenson's *Strange Case of Dr. Jekyll and Mr. Hyde*, the opera dealt with Markheim, whose villainous alter-ego commits a murder; however, the kinder and gentler side of Markheim's nature fights to save his soul.

Peter G. Davis in the *New York Times* found the libretto "talky," but felt Floyd's music was "atmospheric" and "effectively" underscored the story. He praised the "first-rate" singers" whom he found "worthier ... than what one often hears and sees on some of New York's more prestigious opera stages." He found David Shookhoff's direction "precise" and vivid, and complemented Ethan Mordden for providing a "well-played" piano accompaniment. Mordden has written numerous books on American dramas, musicals, and stage personalities, including an invaluable and highly entertaining seven-volume series which analyzes the American musical for the better part of the twentieth-century.

1025 Marlowe. "A New Rock Musical." THEATRE: Rialto Theatre; OPENING DATE: October 12, 1981; PERFORMANCES: 48; BOOK: Leo Rost; LYRICS: Leo Rost and Jimmy Horowitz; MUSIC: Jimmy Horowitz; DIRECTION: Don Price; SCENERY: Cary Chalmers; COSTUMES: Natalie Walker; LIGHTING: Mitch Acker and Rick Belzer; MUSICAL DIRECTION: Kinny Landrum; PRODUCERS: Tony Conforti presents a John Annunziato Production; co-produced by Robert R. Blume in association with Billy Gaff and Howard P. Effron

CAST—Margaret Warncke (Queen Elizabeth I), Debra Greenfield (Audrey Walsingham), Steve (Stephen F.) Hall (Captain Townsend), Raymond Serra (Archbishop Parker), John Henry Kurtz (Richard Burbage), Lennie Del Duca, Jr. (William Shakespeare), LISA MORDENTE (Emelia Bossano), PATRICK JUDE (Christopher Marlowe), Robert Rosen (Ingram Frizer); Chorus (Kenneth D. Ard, Marlene Danielle, Robert Hoshour, Renee Dulaney, Timothy Tobin, Teri Gibson, Diane Pennington, Caryn Richmond)

The action occurs in England in 1593.

The musical was presented in two acts.

ACT ONE—Prologue (Chroniclers), "Rocking the Boat" (Raymond Serra, Margaret Warncke, Steve Hall, Chorus), "Because I'm a Woman" (Lisa Mordente, Lennie Del Duca, Jr., John Henry Kurtz), "Live for the Moment" (Patrick Jude, Company), "Emelia" (Lennie Del Duca, Jr., Patrick Jude), "I'm Coming 'Round to Your Point of View" (Patrick

Jude, Lisa Mordente), "The Ends Justify the Means" (Robert Rosen, Debra Greenfield), "Higher Than High" (Patrick Jude, Lisa Mordente, John Henry Kurtz, Lennie Del Duca, Jr., Chorus), "Rocking the Boat" (reprise) (Company)

ACT TWO—Act II Prologue (Chroniclers), "Christopher" (Lisa Mordente, Chorus), "So Do I (Ode to Virginity)" (John Henry Kurtz, Chorus), "Two Lovers" (Lisa Mordente), "The Funeral Dirge" (John Henry Kurtz, Lisa Mordente, Lennie Del Duca, Jr., Robert Rosen, Steve Hall, Margaret Warncke), "Live for the Moment" (reprise) (Patrick Jude, Lisa Mordente), "Emelia" (reprise) (Patrick Jude, Lisa Mordente), "Can't Leave Now" (Patrick Jude), "Christopher" (reprise) (Lisa Mordente, Lennie Del Duca, Jr., Company), "The Madrigal Blues" (Patrick Jude, Company)

NOTES—*Marlowe* (which may have been under a Middle Broadway contract) called itself as "a new rock musical," this some ten years after musicals had all but stopped identifying themselves as new rock musicals. Fourteen years had passed since the opening of the first self-described rock musical (*The Golden Screw*, 1967; see entry).

The critics compared *Marlowe* to such disasters as *Kelly* (1965), *Rachael Lily Rosenbloom and Don't You Ever Forget It* (1973; closed during Broadway previews), *Rockabye Hamlet* (1976), and *Got Tu Go Disco* (1979). Writing in the *New York Times*, Frank Rich said the plot "left no folio undefaced." In one scene, Christopher ("Kit") Marlowe, William ("Willy") Shakespeare, and Richard Burbage get stoned on pot, thoughtfully provided to them by Sir Walter Raleigh, who in turn got it from his friend Pocahontas. In another, Queen Elizabeth I (who according to Douglas Watt in the *New York Daily News* sounded like a Ninth Avenue landlady demanding back rent from a tenant) reminds her lover to put on his codpiece. At one point, Shakespeare muses that he should have "stuck with sonnets." Finally, the recently-murdered Marlowe (wearing a silver-colored jumpsuit) appears in a cloud of dry-ice smoke and sings "The Madrigal Blues" (because he has paid his dues).

1026 The Marriage Contract. "A Comedy with Music." THEATRE: Folksbiene Playhouse; OPENING DATE: 1991-1992 Season; PERFORMANCES: Unknown; BOOK: Ephraim Kishon; Yiddish translation by Israel Beker; LYRICS: Ephraim Kishon (?); MUSIC: Ed Linderman; DIRECTION: Howard Rossen; SCENERY: Harry Lines; COSTUMES: Susan Sigrist; LIGHTING: Alan Baron; PRODUCER: The Folksbiene Playhouse of the Workmen's Circle (Ben Schechter, Managing Director; Morris Adler, Chairman)

CAST—DAVID ROGOW (Elimelech Borozovsky), ZYPORA SPAISMAN (Shifra), Shira Flam (Ayala), Richard Carlow (Robert Knall), Diane Cypkin (Yaffa Birnbaum), Sandy Levitt (Buki)

The action occurs in Tel Aviv during a spring in the early 1950s.

The play with music was presented in two acts.

NOTES—*The Marriage Contract* was presented in Yiddish with a simultaneous English translation (apparently narrated by Simcha Kruger). The play with music dealt with a seemingly lost marriage contract, the lack of which makes Elimelech and Shifra Borozovsky's marriage invalid and causes awkwardness for their daughter Ayala. But all ends well, and the program notes indicate the evening concluded with "one of the funniest phone-calls in the history of telephone communications between Israel and Mexico."

1027 Marry Me a Little. THEATRE: Actors' Playhouse; OPENING DATE: March 12, 1981; PERFORMANCES: 96; LYRICS: Stephen Sondheim; MUSIC: Stephen Sondheim; DIRECTION: Norman Rene; CHOREOGRAPHY: Don Johanson; SCENERY: Jane Thurn; COSTUMES: Oleksa; LIGHTING: Debra J. Kletter; MUSICAL DIRECTION: E. Martin Perry; PRODUCERS: Diane de Mailly in association with William B. Young

CAST—Suzanne Henry, Craig Lucas

The action occurs in an apartment house in New York City at the present time.

The musical was presented in one act (all songs performed by Suzanne Henry and Craig Lucas).

MUSICAL NUMBERS—"Two Fairy Tales" (written for, but not used in, *A Little Night Music*, 1973), "Saturday Night" (written for the unproduced Broadway musical *Saturday Night*, 1955; the musical was eventually produced Off Broadway in 2000; see entry), "Can That Boy Fox Trot!" (dropped during the tryout of *Follies*, 1971), "All Things Bright and Beautiful" (written for *Follies*, 1971; only the music was used, as background for the opening sequence of *Follies*), "Bang!" (dropped during the tryout of *A Little Night Music*, 1973), "All Things Bright and Beautiful" (Part II), "The Girls of Summer" (*The Girls of Summer*, 1956), "Uptown, Downtown" (dropped during the tryout of *Follies*, 1971), "So Many People" (*Saturday Night*, 1955), "Your Eyes Are Blue" (dropped during the tryout of *A Funny Thing Happened on the Way to the Forum*, 1962), "A Moment with You" (*Saturday Night*, 1955), "Marry Me a Little" (written for, but not used in, *Company*, 1970), "Happily Ever After" (dropped during the tryout of *Company*, 1970), "Pour Le Sport" (written for *The Last Resorts*, an unproduced musical; apparently was used in Julius Monk's 1957 revue *Take Five* [see entry]), "Silly People" (dropped during the tryout of *A Little Night Music*, 1973), "There Won't Be Trumpets" (dropped from *Anyone Can Whistle*, 1964, after its first New York preview), "It Wasn't Meant to Happen" (written for, but not used in, *Follies*, 1971)

NOTES—*Marry Me a Little* was a collection of mostly unfamiliar songs by Stephen Sondheim; in a cabaret context, the evening would have been perfect. But instead the songs were used in a book musical. Craig Lucas and Norman Rene had the precious notion of presenting the songs in a "story" about two lonely New York singles in their separate apartments (however, the apartments in essence merge together, so the two people share the same space without actually seeing one another).

This wrongheaded conceit was later used in *Sondheim Putting It Together*, another Sondheim evening of obscure and not-so-obscure songs which had been written for specific musicals and which were now being grafted into a new plot. *Sondheim Putting It Together* first opened Off Broadway (with Julie Andrews) in 1992 (see entry), and then on Broadway in 1996 (with Carol Burnett).

Marry Me a Little was recorded by RCA Victor (LP # ABL1-4159; CD # 7142-2-RG), and included two numbers dropped during the show's previews ("Who Could Be Blue" and "Little White House," both written for, but not used in, *Follies* [1971], although the former was later used as background music for the 1974 film *Stavisky*). The CD included a bonus track of "Can That Boy Fox Trot!," which was heard in the production but wasn't included on the LP release.

The musical was revived by the York Theatre Company on January 16, 1987, for twenty performances; Liz Callaway and John Jellison were in the cast.

Craig Lucas had appeared in the chorus of the original 1979 Broadway production of *Sweeney Todd/The Demon Barber of Fleet Street*.

1028 Mary. "A 1921 Musical." THEATRE: Equity (Library) Theatre; OPENING DATE: March 1, 1979; PERFORMANCES: 18 (estimated); BOOK: Otto Harbach and Frank Mandel; LYRICS: Otto Harbach; MUSIC: Louis A. Hirsch; DIRECTION: Clinton Atkinson; CHOREOGRAPHY: Dennis Dennehy; J.H. Clark, Assistant Choreographer; Clinton Atkinson and Dennis Dennehy, Musical Staging; SCENERY: Wade Giampa; COSTUMES: Jack McGroder; LIGHTING: Ruth Roberts; MUSICAL DIRECTION: Donald Chan; PRODUCER: Equity (Library) Theatre

CAST—Michael Waldron (Jack Keene), Fiona Hale (Mrs. Keene), W.M. Hunt (Tom Boyd), Nancy Meadows (Daisy), Kay Walbye (Iris), Cathy Brewer-Moore (Madeline Francis), Rick DeFilipps (Roger), Peggy Ann Zitko (Violet), Vince Rhomberg (Larry, Dancing Butler), Michael Estes (George, Dancing Butler), Debbie McLeod (Magnolia), Mark Manley (Reggie), Maryellen Landon (Lily), Bonnie Simmons (Rose), Eric Alderfer (Cleveland), Rustin Billingsly (Chester), Robin Stone (Huggins), Betsy Beard (Mary), John High (Gaston Marceau), Jay Barney (Mr. Goddard)

The action occurs in the living room and garden of Mrs. Keene's suburban home during the early 1920s.

The musical was presented in two acts.

ACT ONE—Overture (Orchestra), "That Might (May) Have Satisfied Grandma" (Michael Waldron, W.M. Hunt, Cathy Brewer-Moore, Ensemble), "That Farm Out in Kansas (Down on the Old Kansas Farm)" (Michael Waldron, Betsy Beard, Robin Stone, Michael Estes, Vince Rhomberg), "Anything You Want to Do Dear" (W.M. Hunt, Cathy Brewer-Moore), "Every Time I Meet a Lady" (John High, Ladies), "Tom Tom Toddle (Tom, Tom, Toddle)" (W.M. Hunt, Cathy Brewer-Moore, Ensemble), "The Love Nest" (Michael Waldron, Betsy Beard), "Anything You Want to Do, Dear" (reprise) (John High, Fiona Hale), Finale Act One (Michael Waldron, Betsy Beard, Ensemble)

ACT TWO—Act Two Opening (Ensemble)/Tango Specialty (Nancy Meadows, Rustin Billingsly)/"Tumbling" (Eric Alderfer), "Mary" (Betsy Beard, Men), "When the Vampire (When a Woman) Exits Laughing" (W.M. Hunt, Cathy Brewer-Moore), "Deeper" (Michael Waldron, Robin Stone, Ensemble), "Don't Fall Till (Until) You've Seen Them All" (W.M. Hunt, Ladies), "Waiting" (Betsy Beard), "Money (Money, Money, Money)" (Michael Waldron, W.M. Hunt, John High, Jay Barney), "We'll Have (Give) a Wonderful Party" (W.M. Hunt, Cathy Brewer-Moore, Ensemble), Specialty (Bonnie Simmons), Finale Act Two (Ensemble)

NOTES—With *Mary*, the Equity (Library) Theatre presented one of its most unusual productions; instead of a revival of a familiar musical (*Can-Can, Carnival!, Silk Stockings*), Equity offered a faithful revival of the one the most popular musicals of the 1920s, but one which had fallen into obscurity over the decades. The original production of *Mary* opened on October 18, 1920, at the Knickerbocker Theatre for a run of 219 performances (Janet Velie was Mary). Directed by George M. Cohan, the musical was one of the biggest hits of the period. Indeed, prior to its Broadway premiere, the musical had toured for a full year, and after its New York run there were four touring productions. A London production opened in 1921, with Evelyn Laye in the title role.

Further, its song "The Love Nest" became one of the era's biggest song hits (it later became the theme song for *The George Burns and Gracie Allen Show*). In reviewing the original production for the *New York Times*, an unidentified critic wrote that Louis A. Hirsch's songs were "consistently tuneful ... the score is studded with hummable melodies," including "The Love Nest" (an "instantaneous" hit). Further, Cohan's staging was praised for its constant use of dancers to move the story along. The *Times* noted that *Mary* was "the fastest musical comedy in town," and any weaknesses in the plot were glossed over by Cohan's "whirlwind" direction in which there were "no pauses for breath." Cohan had his dancers pour upon the stage in successive pairs, adding "speed, dash, pep, momentum, zip and all the other synonyms for movement." The reviewer praised the cast members, but ended his review by noting, "And then there are the dancers. Long live the dancers." But except for "The Love Nest," *Mary* became a forgotten hit. It never enjoyed a New York revival, and there wasn't a film version. As a result, Equity's welcome revival marked the musical's first New York visit in almost sixty years. Jennifer Dunning in the *New York Times* noted that while Otto Harbach's book was "thin and exceedingly silly," Louis Hirsch's music was "hummable." She praised the cast, choreography, scenery, and orchestra, and overall found the evening a "corny, silly and utter delight." Happily, Equity didn't add songs from other musicals, and all the numbers were performed in the order in which they had been heard in the original production. And the song "Deeper," which had been added to the musical during the original Broadway run, was included in the Equity production.

The original production's second act began with an opening chorus which was followed by "Flirtation Dance" (for the tour, the latter was replaced by "Golf Dance"). For the revival, "Tumbling" was used as part of the second-act opening (along with an opening chorus and a tango sequence); "Tumbling" may have been a dance sequence especially created for the revival, and perhaps it and the tango were in essence substitutes for the original "Flirtation" and later "Golf" dances.

Note that for the revival a few song titles underwent minor changes; the original titles are noted in parentheses in the above song listing.

Curiously, for a work which originally opened in 1920, the revival subtitled the musical "A 1921 Musical." By the way, the plot of *Mary* revolved around the world of real estate and concerned a young man who wants to build affordable mobile homes (that is, trailers). During the early engagements of its pre-Broadway tour, the musical was titled *The House That Jack Built.*

1029 Mass. "A Theatre Piece for Singers, Players and Dancers." THEATRE: Metropolitan Opera House; OPENING DATE: June 28, 1972; PERFORMANCES: 22; TEXT: from the Liturgy of the Roman Catholic Mass; English texts by Stephen Schwartz and Leonard Bernstein; MUSIC: Leonard Bernstein; DIRECTION: "Entire Production Directed" by Gordon Davidson; Production "Staged" by Gordon Davidson and Alvin Ailey; CHOREOGRAPHY: Alvin Ailey; SCENERY: Oliver Smith; COSTUMES: Frank Thompson; LIGHTING: Gilbert Hemsley, Jr.; MUSICAL DIRECTION: Maurice Peress; PRODUCERS: Roger L. Stevens and Martin Feinstein; Schuyler G. Chapin, Associate Producer

CAST—ALAN TITUS (Celebrant), DAVID CRYER (Alternate Celebrant); Singing Ensemble (John D. Anthony, Cheryl Barnes, Jacqueline Britt, Jane Coleman, David Cryer, Margaret Crowie, Ed Dixon, Leigh Dodson, Eugene Edwards, Thom Ellis, Lowell Harris, Lee Hooper, Gary Lipps, Linda Lloyd, Linda Marks, Larry Marshall, Gina Penn, John Bennett Perry, Mary Bracken Phillips, Neva Small, David Spangler, Alan Titus); The Alvin Ailey American Dance Theatre (Acolytes: Judith Jamison and Dudley Williams, Clive Thompson, Linda Kent, Kenneth Pearl, Sylvia Waters, Estelle E. Spurlock; Dancing Ensemble: Kelvin Rotardier, Sara Yarborough, Mari Kajiwara, John Parks, Hector [Jaime] Mercado, Leland Schwantes, Clover Mathis, Lynne Del Walker); The Norman Scribner Choir (Sopranos: Juanita Brown, Carol Gericke, Diane Higginbotham, Vicki Johnstone, Janet Kenney, Katherine Ray, Cynthia Richards, Diana Rothman, Sandra Willetts; Altos: Barbara Boller, Catherine Bounds, Alicia Kopfstein-Penk, Patricia George, Suzanne Grant, Raina Mann, Anne Miller, Janet Sooy, Joy Wood; Tenors: Barry Butts, David Coon, Robert Dorsey, Michael Hume, William Jones, Robert Kimball, John Madden, Robert Stevenson, Robert Whitney; Basses: Earl Baker, Glenn Cunningham, Albert deRuiter, Richard Frisch, Arphelius Paul Gatling, Charles Greenwell, Walter Richardson, Ronald Roxbury, Michael Tronzo); The Berkshire Boys' Choir (David Abell, Ben Borsch, Timothy Brown, Chris Cole, Sammy Coleman, Peter Coulianos, Thomas Ettinghausen, Liam Fennelly, Tim Ferrell, Jonathan Gram, Bruce Haynes, Richard Michael, Michael Miller, Chris Negus, Edward Rosen, Robert Rough, Miles Smith, Richard Swan, David Voorhees

The musical was presented in one act.

MUSICAL NUMBERS—I. *Devotions Before Mass*: 1) Antiphon: "Kyrie Eleison," 2) Hymn: "A Simple Song" (Alan Titus), 3) Psalm: "A New Song," 4) Responsory: "Alleluia"; II. *First Introit: Rondo*: 1) Prefatory Prayers ("Kyrie," "Asperfes," "Introibo," etc.), 2) Thrice-tripe Canon: "Dominus Vobiscum"; III. *Second Introit*: 1) "In Nomine Patris," 2) Prayer for the Congregation (Chorale: "Almighty Father"), 3) Epiphany; IV. *Confession*: 1) "Confiteor," 2) Strophe: "I Don't Know" (Gary Lipps, Linda Lloyd, David Spangler), 3) Strophe: "Easy"; V. *Meditation #1*; VI. *Gloria*: 1) "Gloria Tibi" (Alan Titus), 2) "Gloria in Excelsis," 3) Strophe: "Half of the People," 4) Strophe: "Thank You" (Lee Hooper); VII. *Meditation #2*; VIII. *Epistle*: "The Word of the Lord" (Alan Titus); IX. *Gospel-Sermon*: "God Said" (Leader: Larry Marshall); X. *Credo*: 1) "Credo in Unum Deum ...," 2) Strophe: "Non Credo" (John Bennett Perry; on Monday and Friday evenings, the song was performed by David Cryer), 3) Strophe: "Hurry" (Gina Penn), 4) Strophe: "World Without End" (Mary Bracken Phillips), 5) Stophe: "I Believe in God" (Thom Ellis); XI. *Meditation #3: De Profundis, Part One*; XII. *Offertory: De Profundis, Part Two*; XIII. *The Lord's Prayer*: 1) "Our Father ...," 2) Strophe: "I Go On" (Alan Titus); XIV. *Sanctus*; XV. *Agnus Dei*; XVI. *Fraction*: "Things Get Broken"; XVII. *Pax: Communion*: 1) "Secret Songs" (Margaret Cowie, Gary Lipps. John D. Anthony, Leigh Dodson, Ed Dixon)

NOTES—Leonard Bernstein's *Mass* is perhaps the ultimate concept musical. The framework of the piece is anchored in the ritual of the Roman Catholic Mass, which is in essence an abstract ceremony which encompasses the basic beliefs of the Church. The musical wedded the structure of the Mass into a story about a Roman Catholic priest who loses touch with his faith and his parishioners. The latter become increasingly rebellious and questioning, but through faith both the priest and the parishioners ultimately reconcile themselves to the Church and to each other. The work's muddy liberal piety and its bleeding-heart angst mitigated against a completely successful evening. The work railed at government and big business, and even worked in a song about the environment. Further, the sometimes trite lyrics weren't particularly inspiring or original (at one point, a parishioner sings that he believes in God, but does God believe in him?). Finally, at the end of the musical, and the Mass, audience members were encouraged to shake hands with each other. But one could overlook and forgive the weaknesses in the work's structure because Bernstein's thrilling and electric score was one of the best of the era, a cornucopia of musical styles which were richly melodic and inherently theatrical.

Mass was the opening event for the new John F. Kennedy Center for the Performing Arts in Washington, D.C., in September 1971, and returned there the following spring. It also played in a few cities, including a stop at the Metropolitan Opera House for its New York premiere. For the tenth anniversary of the opening of the Kennedy Center, the work returned there in a scaled-down version (Joseph Kolinski performed the role of the Celebrant, and at certain performances the role was sung by Michael Hume.)

Mass was released on a 2-LP set by Columbia Records (# M2-31008 and # M2Q-31008), and was later reissued by Sony Records on a 2-CD set (# SM2K-63089).

1030 A Mass Murder in the Balcony of the Old Ritz-Rialto. THEATRE: Elysian Playhouse; OPENING DATE: November 14, 1975; PERFORMANCES: 20; BOOK: Ed Kuczewski; LYRICS: Bill Vitale; MUSIC: Bill Vitale; dance music by Leon Odenz; DIRECTION: Bill Vitale; ADDITIONAL STAGING by Teddy Kern; CHOREOGRAPHY: Martin Rivera; SCENERY: Elmon Webb and Virginia Dancy; COSTUMES: Reve Richards; LIGHTING: Rick Claflin; PRODUCER: The Fantasy Factory

CAST—Joseph Adorante, Linda Andrews, Marc Castle, Louise Claps, Bruno Damon, Joyce Griffen, Michael Kemmerling, Ed Kuczewski, Ethel A. Morgan, Joy Venus Morton, Joan Neuman, David Noh, Oliver Rish, Martin Rivera, Bob Santucci, Ray Shelton, Prima Stephen, Claudia Tompkins, LizaGrace Vachon-Coco, Paul Vanase, Steve Wadley, Louis Zippin

The musical was presented in one act (song assignments unknown).

MUSICAL NUMBERS—"Shadow Song," "Slumming," "Homely Woman," "42nd Street," "Popcorn and Piss," "Dope," "Dope Rag," "Dope Double Time," "Let's All Go to the Lobby," "Musical Chairs," "I Got Rhythm Too," "The Old Days," "Sung-Fu," "Pictures and an Exhibition," "Savin' Souls," "Time to Go Home," "Vernon," "Anybody Wanna Buy a Little Love," "Pink Lady," "The Comic," "When You're Shot at the Movies"

NOTES—Depending on the source referenced, this obscure musical was either under an Off Broadway or an Off Off Broadway contract. Either way, it was gone in less than three weeks. And whatever happened to LizaGrace Vachon-Coco?

1031 Mata Hari. THEATRE: Theatre at Saint Peter's Church/The York Theatre Company; OPENING DATE: January 25, 1996; PERFORMANCES: 12; BOOK: Jerome Coopersmith; LYRICS: Martin Charnin; MUSIC: Edward Thomas; DIRECTION: Martin Charnin; CHOREOGRAPHY: Michele Assaf; SCENERY: James Morgan; COSTUMES: Jennifer Arnold; LIGHTING: Mary Jo Dondlinger; PRODUCER: The York Theatre Company (Janet Hayes Walker, Producing Artistic Director; James Morgan, Associate Artistic Director; Joseph V. De Michele, Managing Director)

CAST—Kirk McDonald (Young Soldier), John Antony (Pollinaire, A German Soldier, Sergeant Grindstaff), Allen Fitzpatrick (Henri LeFarge), Jack Fletcher (Major Bonnard, A Wounded Soldier), Jim Jacobson (Masson, General Delacorte, Zauberhande, Father Maurice DePre, A French Sergeant, The President of France), Tom Treadwell (Devries, Felice Duvalier, Cousin Philipe, Lt. Charlie Grant), Marguerite MacIntyre (Mata Hari), Stephanie Seeley (Tamil, A Young Lady, Michele LaFarge, A Nun at St. Lazare Prison), Robin Syke (Paulette LaFarge), Judith Thiergaard (The Countess d'Orleans, Madame DuPre), Julia K. Murney (La Pistolette, Cousin Claudine)

The musical was presented in two acts.

ACT ONE—"Gone" (Kirk McDonald), "Is This Fact?" (Allen Fitzpatrick, Officers, Jack Fletcher), "Dance at the Salon" (Marguerite MacIntyre, Stephanie Seeley), "Everyone Has Something to Hide" (Marguerite MacIntyre, Company), "How Young You Were Tonight" (Allen Fitzpatrick, Robin Skye), "I'm Saving Myself for a Soldier" (Tom Treadwell, Julia K. Murney), "The Choice Is Yours" (Marguerite MacIntyre, Allen Fitzpatrick), "Fritzie" (Kirk

McDonald, John Antony), "No More Than a Moment" (Marguerite MacIntyre), "This Is Nice" (Robin Skye, Julia K. Murney, Judith Thiergaard, Stephanie Seeley, Tom Treadwell, Jim Jacobson), "Maman" (Kirk McDonald), "Not Now, Not Here" (Marguerite MacIntyre), "Is This Fact?" (reprise) (Allen Fitzpatrick)

ACT TWO—"Hello, Yank" (Kirk McDonald, Two Old Soldiers, Two American Soldiers), "No More Than a Moment" (reprise) (Allen Fitzpatrick), "I Don't See Him Very Much Anymore" (Robin Syke), "You Have No Idea" (Marguerite MacIntyre, Allen Fitzpatrick, Officers), "This Is Nice" (reprise) (Robin Syke, Julia K. Murney, Judith Thiergaard, Stephanie Seeley, Tom Treadwell, Jim Jacobson), "What Might Have Been" (Marguerite MacIntyre), "Gone" (reprise) (Kirk McDonald)

NOTES—The production of *Mata Hari* was an Off Off Broadway revival of the 1967 flop which closed in Washington, D.C., prior to its Broadway opening. In fact, *Mata Hari* didn't even last through its scheduled Washington run. The York production closed early, too. It was scheduled to play through February 18, 1996, but instead closed on February 4, after having given 13 previews and 12 regular performances.

In between the Washington, D.C., and the York Theatre Company's productions, an Off Broadway production of the musical (called *Ballad for a Firing Squad*) quickly opened and closed in 1968 (the entry for *Ballad of a Firing Squad* includes information about the 1967 production of *Mata Hari*).

The York version included the following songs which had been heard in the original 1967 production: "Is This Fact?," "Dance at the Salon," "Everyone Has Something to Hide," "How Young You Were Tonight," "I'm Saving Myself for a Soldier," "The Choice Is Yours," "Sextet" (called "This Is Nice" in the program for the York production, but "Sextet" on the York recording), "Maman," "Not Now, Not Here," "Hello, Yank!," "I Don't See Him Very Much Anymore," and "You Have No Idea."

Numbers heard in the York version which had been written for *Ballad for a Firing Squad* were "Fritzie" and "What Might Have Been," and one new song was added for the York production ("Gone").

Numbers not used from the original 1967 production were "This Is Not a Very Nice War," "Waltz at the Salon," "Curiosity," "In Madrid," "Dance at the Café del Torro," "Interrogation and Ballet," "There Is No You," and "There Will Be Love Again." (Incidentally, "This Is Not a Very Nice War" and "Curiosity" were both dropped during the second week of the Washington run.)

Numbers not used from the 1968 Off Broadway production were "Ballad for a Firing Squad," "There Is Only One Thing to Be Sure Of," "I Did Not Sleep Last Night," and "What Then?"

As mentioned, the York revival led to a recording released by Original Cast Records (CD # OC-8600); Robin Syke sang the roles of both Mata Hari and Paulette LaFarge. Incidentally, the CD includes the poster artwork for both the 1967 and 1968 productions.

1032 A Match Made in Heaven. THEATRE: Town Hall; OPENING DATE: October 30, 1985; PERFORMANCES: 54; BOOK: Jack Rechtzeit; English translation by David Ellin; LYRICS: New lyrics by I. Alper; MUSIC: New music by Jack Rechtzeit; additional music by Alexander Lustig; DIRECTION: Yankele Alperin; CHOREOGRAPHY: Derek Wolshonak; SCENERY: Gary Prianti; COSTUMES: Clare Gosney; LIGHTING: Bernard Sauer; MUSICAL DIRECTION: Bruce W. Coyle; PRODUCERS: Yiddish Musical Theatre for New York (Raymond Ariel and Stuart Rosenberg, Producers) CAST—MONICA TESLER (Natasha), ELEANOR REISSA (Tsipke), YANKELE ALPERIN (Tzudik), Reizl Bozyk (Mintze), Stewart Figa (Berish), LEON LIEBGOLD (Pesach), Shifee Lovitt (Lida), David Ellin (Smirnov), DAVID MONTEFIORE (The Rebbe), Ben Gotlieb (Grisha Smirnov), Friends, Neighbors, Peasants, Chassidim, City Folk (Nicole Flender, Carolyn Goor, Tara Tyrrell, Dean Badolato, Anthony Bova, Jay Tramel)

The action occurs in the miller's yard in 1910.

The musical was presented in two acts.

ACT ONE—Overture (Orchestra), "Dos Yiddishe Shtetele" (Company), "Lomir Geyn a Polka Tantzn" (Monica Tesler, Eleanor Reissa), "Lubov Nye Kartoshka" (Monica Tesler, Stewart Figa), "Ich Trink in Sholof" (Yankele Alperin), "Az Der Rebbe Vill" (David Montefiore, Ensemble), "Shayles Tzim Rebb'n" (David Montefiore, Reizl Bozyk, Monica Tesler, Eleanor Reissa, Shifee Lovitt), "Yiddishkeit" (David Montefiore), "A Shiduch Fin Himmel" (David Montefiore, Eleanor Reissa), "A L'Chayim, Men Shraybt T'noyim" (Ensemble)

ACT TWO—"Lomir Freylach Zeyn" (Reizl Bozyk, Leon Liebgold, Shifee Lovitt), "In Atzind Vi Ahin" (Monica Tesler), "Mir Fur'n Kin Odess" (Shifee Lovitt, Ben Gotlieb, Friends), "Dem Rebbn's Chassene" (David Montefiore), "Nor Yiddish" (Monica Tesler, Yankele Alperin), "S'vet Zeyn a Chassene" (Ensemble), "A Beyzer Chulem" (Monica Tesler, Ensemble), Finale (Company)

NOTES—According to Richard F. Shepard in the *New York Times*, *A Match Made in Heaven* got the new Yiddish theatre season off to a "surprisingly brisk" and "pleasant pace." As for the plot ("oy, it's too complicated to simplify"), it revolved around various couples and their romantic mix-ups, including the love story of a rebbe (teacher) and a miller's daughter; but Shepard noted that "everyone ends up in the proper arms by the time the finale catches up with the plot."

The musical was presented in Yiddish with English subtitles.

Either this production (or a revival) was taped and released on videocassette by Jewish Video Library.

1033 The Matinee Kids. THEATRE: BTA Theatre; OPENING DATE: March 10, 1981; PERFORMANCES: 15; BOOK: Garry Bormet and Gary Gardner; LYRICS: Brian Lasser; MUSIC: Brian Lasser; DIRECTION: Garry Bormet and Brian Lasser; CHOREOGRAPHY: Carol Marik; SCENERY: Nancy Winters; COSTUMES: Bruce H. Brumage; LIGHTING: Ronald M. Bundt; MUSICAL DIRECTION: Laurence J. Esposito; PRODUCER: Fisher Theatre Foundation, Inc.

CAST—Karen Mason (Chris), Liz Callaway (Chrissy), Colleen Dodson (Movie Woman), Scott Baker (Movie Man), Will Jeffries (Tom), Michael Corbett (Tommy)

The musical was presented in two acts (song assignments weren't listed in the program).

ACT ONE (preceded by "Short Subjects")—Our First Feature: *Lucky Love*: "Lucky Love," "The Date," "Just to Look at Him," "A Couple of Years from Now," "Favorite Son," "Hello, Tom," "Footprints," "Hi!," "Alborada," "Lucky Love" (reprise)

ACT TWO (followed by "Coming Attractions")—Our Second Feature: *Lucky Baby*: "Lucky Baby," "Hold Me," "A Couple of Years from Now" (reprise), "First to Walk Away," "Favorite Son" (reprise), "Matinee"

NOTES—The musical, which was apparently produced under an Off Off Broadway contract, told the story of two couples, one young (Liz Callaway and Michael Corbett) and one mature (Karen Mason and Will Jeffries), who are influenced by their film idols ("Movie Man" and "Movie Woman" were portrayed by Scott Baker and Coleen Dodson). The story seems to have been told via the conventions of an old-fashioned double-feature movie, complete with short subjects and coming attractions.

For the production of *The Matinee Kids*, the Black Theatre Alliance venue was temporarily renamed the BTA Theatre.

1034 A Matter of Opinion. "A New Musical." THEATRE: Players Theatre; OPENING DATE: September 30, 1980; PERFORMANCES: 8; BOOK: Mary Elizabeth Hauer; LYRICS: Mary Elizabeth Hauer; MUSIC: Harold Danko and John Jacobson; DIRECTION: Shari Upbin; David S. Rosenak, "Production Supervisor"; CHOREOGRAPHY: Shari Upbin; SCENERY: John Arnone; COSTUMES: John Arnone; LIGHTING: Joanna Schielke; MUSICAL DIRECTION: John Jacobson; PRODUCER: Miracle Expressions, Inc.

CAST—Fantasy People (Suzanne Smartt, Ms. Easily; Charles Randolph Wright, Mr. Merrily; Vickie D. Chappell, Fantasy Child; Janet Bliss, Mrs. Gentle); Fact People (Ralph Braun, Mr. Fate; Leigh Finner, Mrs. Finished; Kate Klugman, Fact Child); The Others (Seymour Penzner, Judge; David Anchel, Hobo; Janet Bliss, Bag Lady; Andy Bey, Prophet)

The action occurs in the town square.

The musical was presented in two acts.

ACT ONE—Opening (Townspeople), "Not Every Day Can Be a Day of Shine" (Ralph Braun, Leigh Finner, Kate Klugman), "Almost Working" (Charles Randolph Wright), "No Thank You from a Mocking Sun" (Ralph Braun), "If the Sun Didn't Shine Each Day" (Janet Bliss, Charles Randolph Wright), "The Average Man" (Leigh Finner), "Free Time" (Suzanne Smartt), "Mrs. Finished Lament" (Leigh Finner), "Determination" (Suzanne Smartt, Janet Bliss), "The Hobo's Song" (David Anchel), "Shopping Bag Lady" (Janet Bliss)

ACT TWO—"Gotta Pretend" (Vickie D. Chappell), "ABC to XYZ" (Kate Klugman), "The Wanderer" (David Anchel), "The Sandman" (Janet Bliss), "Just the Facts" (Ralph Braun), "Gotta Pretend" (reprise) (Vickie D. Chappell, Charles Randolph Wright), "I Am Here" (Andy Bey), "Humanity" (Andy Bey, Vickie D. Chappell, Kate Klugman), "Matter of Opinion" (Townspeople), "Hooray for the Judge" (Townspeople)

NOTES—*A Matter of Opinion* dealt with "fantasy people" and "fact people," all of whom go to court for a ruling on which group has the correct outlook on life. The musical, with dialogue written in rhymed couplets, was gone in a week. Mel Gussow in the *New York Times* pronounced the lyrics "doggerel" and the book "dogged." He found the musical's producer, Miracle Expressions, Inc., "inaccurately named," and noted that the lyricist and book writer had written the lyrics for a projected film called *Sludge*, which he felt could serve as an alternate title for the musical itself.

1035 A Matter of Time. "A musical entertainment." THEATRE: Playhouse Theatre; OPENING NIGHT: April 27, 1975; PERFORMANCES: 1; BOOK: Hap Schlein and Russell Leib; LYRICS: Philip F. Margo; MUSIC: Philip F. Margo; DIRECTION: Tod Jackson; CHOREOGRAPHY: Tod Jackson; SCENERY: David Guthrie; COSTUMES: David Guthrie; LIGHTING: Martin Aronstein; MUSICAL DIRECTION: Arnold Gross; PRODUCER: Jeff Britton

CAST—David-James Carroll (Next), Jane Robertson (Lily), Glory Van Scott (Blaze), Joe Masiell ("D"), Carol Estey (Pansy, Candy), Miriam Welch (Tulip, Fatima), Joyce Nolen (Rose, Cynthia), Leland Schwantes (Leroy, Harry), Dennis Michaelson (Mervyn), Ronnie De Marco (Harvey), Douglas Bentz (Jordon), Charlise Harris (Kate), Donald M. Griffith (Paul), Elliott Lawrence (The Flasher, The Voice of "G"), Suellen Arlen (Young Girl), Rosamond Lynn (Fifi), Linda Willows (Louise), The Flames (Carol Estey, Rosamond Lynn, Miriam Welch), The Furies (Douglas Bentz, Ronnie De Marco, Leland Schwantes)

The action occurs on December 31, 1975.

The musical was presented in two acts.

ACT ONE—"Me God, Please God" (David-James Carroll, Jane Robertson, Glory Van Scott, Pray-ers), "It's Not Easy Being Next" (David-James Carroll), "The Ritual" (Hellpersons), "Welcome to Hell" (Hellpersons), "Purgatory U." (Glory Van Scott), "Snake" (Joe Masiell), "If This Were My World" (Joe Masiell), "A Matter of Time" (David-James Carroll), "This Moment" (Donald M. Griffith), "A Matter of Time" (reprise) (David-James Carroll), "Don't Let Me Bother You" (Glory Van Scott, Joe Masiell), "Oh, What a Wonderful Plan" (Joe Masiell and "D"'s Company), Act One Finale (Jane Robertson, Glory Van Scott, David-James Carroll, Joe Masiell, The Heavenly Choir)

ACT TWO—"Sex Is a Spectator Sport" ("D"'s Company), "A Matter of Time" (reprise) (David-James Carroll), "Winner" (Joe Masielle, Carol Estey, Rosamond Lynn, Miriam Welch, Douglas Bentz, Ronnie De Marco, Leland Schwantes), "It Will Be My Day" (Joe Masiell), "Time Is a Travellin' Show" (David-James Carroll), "I Can Give You Music" (Donald W. Griffith, David-James Carroll), "This Is Your Year 1976" (David-James Carroll, Joe Maisell, "D"'s Company, Glory Van Scott), "The Devil in Your Eyes" (Joe Masiell), "Purgatory U." (reprise) (Glory Van Scott), "Oh, World" (David-James Carroll), "I Am the Next" (David-James Carroll, The New Year's Revelers)

NOTES—The plot of *A Matter of Time* dealt with time standing still: December 31, 1975, refuses to become January 1, 1976. The musical itself opened on April 27, 1975, and never saw April 28, 1975. Clive Barnes in the *New York Times* reported the $200,000 production was "horrible, most horrible," with "bad and unmemorable" lyrics, music which was even "worse" and a book which was the "worst of the lot."

1036 Maybe I'm Doing It Wrong (1982).

"A Musical Entertainment." THEATRE: Astor Place Theatre; OPENING DATE: March 14, 1982; PERFORMANCES: 33; LYRICS: Randy Newman; MUSIC: Randy Newman; DIRECTION: Joan Micklin Silver; CHOREOGRAPHY: Eric Elice; SCENERY: Heidi Landesman; COSTUMES: Hilary Rosenfeld; LIGHTING: Fred Buchholz; MUSICAL DIRECTION: Michael S. Roth; PRODUCER: Raphael D. Silver

CAST—Mark Linn-Baker, Patti Perkins, Larry Riley, Deborah Rush

The revue was presented in one act.

MUSICAL NUMBERS—"Sigmund Freud's Impersonation of Albert Einstein in America" (Band), "My Old Kentucky Home" (Company), "Birmingham" (Mark Linn-Baker, Larry Riley), "Political Science" (Deborah Rush, Patti Perkins), "It's Money That I Love" (Company), "Jolly Coppers on Parade" (Deborah, Company), "Caroline" (Company), "Simon Smith and the Amazing Dancing Bear" (Mark Linn-Baker), "Love Story" (Larry Riley, Deborah Rush), "Tickle Me" (Patti Perkins, Mark Linn-Baker), "Maybe I'm Doing It Wrong" (Company), "The Debutante's Ball" (Company), "Burn On" (Patti Perkins), "Pants" (Mark Linn-Baker), "God's Song (That's Why I Love Mankind)" (Larry Riley), "They Just Got Married" (Company), "A Wedding in Cherokee County" (Larry Riley, Patti Perkins), "Yellow Man" (Company), "The Girls in My Life (Part I)" (Mark Linn-Baker, Deborah Rush), "Rider in the Rain" (Mark Linn-Baker, Company), "Mama Told Me Not To Come" (Deborah Rush, Company), "Old Man" (Patti Perkins), "Lonely at the Top" (Company), "Mr. President (Have Pity on the Working Man)" (Company), "Sail Away" (Larry Riley, Company), Theme from *Ragtime* (film, 1981) (Band), "Marie" (Larry Riley), "I Think It's Going to Rain Today" (Patti Perkins), "Let's Burn Down the Cornfield" (Larry Riley, Mark Linn-Baker), "Davy the Fat Boy" (Company), "You Can Leave Your Hat On" (Mark Linn-Baker), "Rollin'" (Deborah Rush), "Short People" (Company), "I'll Be Home" (Patti Perkins, Company), "Dayton, Ohio 1903" (Company)

NOTES—An earlier version of the revue *Maybe I'm Doing It Wrong* had been presented the previous year for 17 performances (see entry for *Randy Newman's Maybe I'm Doing It Wrong*, which also includes information about other musicals based on Newman's songs). Also, *The Middle of Nowhere* (1988; see entry) used Newman's songs (many of which were heard in the two *Maybe I'm Doing It Wrong* revues) within the framework of a book musical.

1037 Mayor.

"The Musical." THEATRE: Top of the Gate/The Village Gate; OPENING DATE: May 13, 1985; PERFORMANCES: 185; SKETCHES: Warren Leight; LYRICS: Charles Strouse; MUSIC: Charles Strouse; DIRECTION: Jeffrey B. Moss; CHOREOGRAPHY: Barbara Siman; SCENERY: Randy Barcelo; COSTUMES: Randy Barcelo; LIGHTING: Richard Winkler; MUSICAL DIRECTION: Michael Kosarin; PRODUCERS: Martin Richards, Jerry Kravat, and Mary Lea Johnson with the New York Musical Company; Sam Crothers, Associate Producer

CAST—Lenny Wolpe (The Mayor), Douglas Bernstein, Marion Caffey, Keith Curran, Nancy Giles, Ken Jennings, Ilene Kristen, Kathryn McAteer

SOURCE—The 1982 book *Mayor: An Autobiography* by Edward I. Koch (with William Rauch).

The revue was presented in two acts.

ACT ONE—"Mayor" (Lenny Wolpe) (song), "You Can Be a New Yorker Too!" (Keith Curran, Douglas Bernstein, Marion J. Caffey, Company) (song), "Board of Estimate" (Lenny Wolpe, Kathryn McAteer, Ilene Kristen, Ken Jennings, Marion J. Caffey) (sketch), "You're Not the Mayor" (Kathryn McAteer, Ken Jennings, Marion J. Caffey) (song), "Mayor" (reprise) (Lenny Wolpe) (song), "The Four Seasons" (Kathryn McAteer, Ilene Kristen, Ken Jennings) (sketch), "March of the Yuppies" (Douglas Bernstein, Keith Curran, Nancy Giles, Company) (sketch), "The Ribbon Cutting: Hootspa" (Note: Chutzpah) (Lenny Wolpe, Keith Curran, Ken Jennings) (sketch and song), "Alternate Side" (Kathryn McAteer) (song), "Isn't It Time for the People" (Marion J. Caffey, Ilene Kristen, Keith Curran) (song), "What You See Is What You Get" (Nancy Giles, Lenny Wolpe, Company) (song)

ACT TWO—"In the Park" (Marion J. Caffey, Company) (sketch), "Ballad" (Keith Curran, Ilene Kristen) (song), "I Want to Be the Mayor" (Douglas Bernstein) (song), On the Telephone (Lenny Wolpe, Kathryn McAteer) (sketch), Subway: "The Last 'I Love New York' Song" (Kathryn McAteer, Ken Jennings, Ilene Kristen, Marion J. Caffey, Douglas Bernstein, Keith Curran, Nancy Giles) (sketch and song), "Ballad" (reprise) (Lenny Wolpe) (song), Testimonial Dinner: "Good Times" (Lenny Wolpe, Douglas Bernstein, Nancy Giles, Ilene Kristen, Keith Curran, Ken Jennings, Marion J. Caffrey) (sketch and song), "We Are One" (a/k/a "I'll Never Leave You") (Marion J. Caffrey, Kathryn McAteer, Keith Curran, Ilene Kristen) (song), "How'm I Doin'?" (Lenny Wolpe, Company) (song), "My City" (Company) (song)

NOTES—There had been two Broadway musicals about New York City mayors, the long-running Pulitzer Prize-winning hit about Fiorello H. LaGuardia (*Fiorello!*, 1959) and the flop musical about James J. Walker (*Jimmy*, 1969). The Off Broadway revue *Mayor*, about the then-current New York City Mayor Edward I. Koch, wasn't as successful as *Fiorello!*, but neither was it a fast flop like *Jimmy*.

The revue had a thin storyline which was virtually abandoned in favor of sketches, songs, and blackouts, many of which were less about the mayor and more about life in New York ("You Can Be a New Yorker Too!," "The Last 'I Love New York' Song," "My City," and "We Are One," the last about the homeless) and fads and foibles of the day ("March of the Yuppies"). The lyric for the second act reprise of the title song was by the revue's sketch writer Warren Leight, who later wrote the hit *Side Man* (1998).

During previews, *Mayor* was presented in one act, and one song ("Everyone Tells Me So") was dropped. During the run, the sketch "The Four Seasons" and the song "Isn't It Time for the People" were deleted, and two sketches ("Critics" and "Coalition") were added.

The cast album was recorded by New York Music Company Records (LP # NYM-21).

On October 23, 1985, the revue transferred to the Latin Quarter for an additional 70 performances (perhaps under a Middle Broadway contract).

1038 The Me Nobody Knows (1970).

THEATRE: Orpheum Theatre; OPENING DATE: May 18, 1970; PERFORMANCES: 208; BOOK: Stephen M. Joseph; LYRICS: Will Holt; ADDITIONAL LYRICS by Herb Schapiro as well as by unidentified school children; MUSIC: Gary William Friedman; DIRECTION: Robert H. Livingston; CHOREOGRAPHY: Patricia Birch; SCENERY: Clarke Dunham; MEDIA DESIGN AND PHOTOGRAPHY: Stan Goldberg and Mopsy; COSTUMES: Patricia Quinn Stuart; LIGHTING: Clarke Dunham; MUSICAL DIRECTION: Edward Strauss; PRODUCERS: Jeff Britton in association with Sagittarius Productions, Inc.

CAST—Melanie Henderson (Rhoda), Laura Michaels (Lillian), Jose Fernandez (Carlos), Irene Cara (Lillie Mae), Douglas Grant (Benjamin), Beverly Ann Bremers (Catherine), Gerri Dean (Melba), Paul Mace (Donald), Northern J. Calloway (Lloyd), Carl Thoma (Clorox), Kevin Lindsay (William), Hattie Winston (Nell)

SOURCE—*The Me Nobody Knows: Children's Voices from the Ghetto*, a 1969 book of writings by school children (edited by Stephen M. Joseph). See notes below.

The revue was presented in two acts.

ACT ONE—"Dream Babies" (Gerri Dean), "Light Sings" (Kevin Lindsay, Company), "This World" (Company), "Numbers" (Company), "What Happens to Life" (Laura Michaels, Northern J. Calloway), "Take Hold the Crutch" (Hattie Winston, Company), "Flying Milk and Runaway Plates" (Douglas Grant, Company), "I Love What the Girls Have" (Paul Mace), "How I Feel" (Beverly Ann Bremers, Jose Fernandez), "If I Had a Million Dollars" (Company)

ACT TWO—"Fugue for Four Girls" (Irene Cara, Beverly Ann Bremers, Laura Michaels, Hattie Winston), "Rejoice" (Carl Thoma), "Sounds" (Hattie Winston, Beverly Ann Bremers), "The Tree" (Jose Fernandez), "Robert, Alvin, Wendell and Jo Jo" (Melanie Henderson, Laura Michaels, Irene Cara, Kevin Lindsay), "Jail-Life Walk" (Paul Mace, Northern J. Callaway, Carl Thoma, Jose Fernandez), "Something Beautiful" (Melanie Henderson), "Black" (Douglas Grant, Carl Thoma, Irene Cara, Northern J. Calloway, Gerri Dean, Hattie Winston, Melanie Henderson, Kevin Lindsay), "The Horse" (Northern J. Calloway), "Let Me Come In" (Company), "War Babies" (Northern J. Calloway)

NOTES—A program note indicated the book *The Me Nobody Knows* was a collection of writings by New York City school children between the ages of seven and eighteen, all of whom attended schools in Bedford-Stuyvesant, Harlem, Jamaica, Manhattan, and the Youth House in the Bronx.

The lyrics of "Fugue for Four Girls," "Rejoice," "The Horse," and "War Babies" were poems presented exactly as written by various school children, and the lyrics of "Dream Babies," "This World," and "Something Beautiful" were written by Herb Schapiro. All other lyrics were written by Will Holt.

The musical played Off Broadway for approximately six months (208 performances), and then transferred to Broadway on December 18, 1970, where it played for 378 performances, first at the Helen Hayes Theatre and then at the Lyceum. Some Broadway record books give the total number of Broadway performances as 586, but that number is incorrect because it includes the 208 Off Broadway performances. The program indicates that *The Me Nobody Knows* presents "children's voices from the ghetto. In their struggle lies their hope, and ours. They are the voices of change." Clearly, the musical was well-intentioned, but it had a slightly preachy tone and often seemed too self-aware, sometimes working too hard in its attempt to capture the innocence it tried to convey. The work would have been more effective had it been presented at schools and colleges, or as a program on educational television; the musical was in fact televised in the 1980s (on the Showtime Channel). The musical doesn't seem to have had much of an after-life, although one of its songs, "Light Sings," was the inspiration for a ballet in 1978, and the dance piece had a certain popularity. It was first presented at T.O.M.I. on March 3, 1978, and was directed by Keith Levenson. Later productions (including an engagement at the Kennedy Center) credited the choreography to Patricia Birch, and included eight songs from *The Me Nobody Knows*: "Dream Babies," "This World," "Something Beautiful," "I Love What the Girls Have," "How I Feel," "If I Had a Million Dollars," "Let Me Come In," and "Light Sings."

The cast album of *The Me Nobody Knows* was recorded by Atlantic Records (LP # 1566), and the script was published by Metromedia on Stage (script undated). A London production opened during the 1972-1973 season, and the musical was briefly revived Off Broadway in 1984 (see entry).

In 1994, Gary William Friedman and Herb Schapiro wrote another revue based on young people's writings (see entry for *Bring in the Morning*). Earlier, Friedman and Will Holt collaborated on a revue inspired by the writings of older people (see entries for *Turns* [1980] and *Taking My Turn* [1983]).

1039 The Me Nobody Knows (1984). THEATRE: South Street Theatre; OPENING DATE: April 5, 1984; PERFORMANCES: 16; ADAPTATION by Robert H. Livingston and Herb Schapiro; LYRICS: Will Holt; ADDITIONAL LYRICS by Herb Schapiro as well as by various unidentified school children; MUSIC: Gary William Friedman; DIRECTION: Robert H. Livingston; CHOREOGRAPHY: Rael Lamb; SCENERY: John Falabella; COSTUMES: John Falabella; LIGHTING: Jeff Davis; MUSICAL DIRECTION: Jefrey Silverman

CAST—Sonia Bailey (Rhoda), Tisha Campbell (Lillian), Jose Martinez (Carlos), Kia Joy Goodwin (Lillie), Donald Acree (Benjamin), Jessie Janet Richards (Catherine), Pamela Harley (Melba), Jaison Walker (Lloyd), Stephen Fenning (Donald), Keith Amos (Clorox), Deborah Smith (Nell)

SOURCE—*The Me Nobody Knows: Children's Writings from the Ghetto*, a 1969 book of writings by school children (edited by Stephen M. Joseph).

The musical was presented in two acts.

NOTES—This Off Off Broadway production of *The Me Nobody Knows* was a revival of the long-running 1971 musical (see entry for information about that production, including titles of songs).

Alvin Klein in the *New York Times* felt the "tepid" fourteen-year-old musical wasn't "all it used to be," and noted the work now offered a "rather insulated, almost quaint view" of how teenagers survive in tenement neighborhoods.

1040 The Meehans. "A New Musical." THEATRE: Theatre for the New City; OPENING DATE: May 28, 1981; PERFORMANCES: Unknown; BOOK: Charles Choset; LYRICS: Charles Choset; MUSIC: Sam Pottle; DIRECTION: Peter Napolitano; CHOREOGRAPHY: Ronald Dabney; SCENERY: EllenMarie Jervey; COSTUMES: Ira Barber; LIGHTING: Joe Ray; MUSICAL DIRECTION: Ernest Lehrer; PRODUCER: Theatre for the New City and Bartenieff/Field

CAST—Howard Pinhasik (Michael Meehan), Donna Pelc (Lorraine Meehan), Bonnie Horan (Katherine Mary Meehan [Kitty]), Jesse Cline (Father Frank Burke), David Berk (Captain DeBlasio), Frank Torren (Lt. Thomas Corcoran), John Gallogly (Officer Thompson), Richard Alpers (Officer Gorman), Charles Del Vecchio (Officer O'Malley), Gary Di Mauro (Officer Santiago), Joe Duquette (Sergeant Callahan), Kathi McGunnigle (Officer Scull), Debbie Petrino (Officer Casey), Jesse L. Stokes (Officer Cox), Bar Patrons (Wally Alvarez, Christine Dhimos, Curtis Sykes, Amanda Rotardier), Musicians (Adam Snyder, Martin Wright, Mike Mulvey)

The musical was presented in one act.

MUSICAL NUMBERS—"It Isn't Easy" (Donna Pelc), "Points" (Joe Duquette, John Gallogly, Richard Alpers, Charles Del Vecchio, Gary Di Mauro, Kathi McGunnigle, Debbie Petrino, Jesse L. Stokes), "It's a Beautiful World" (John Gallogly), "An Even Chance" (Howard Pinhasik), "I'm Not in Love with You" (Donna Pelc, Howard Pinkasik), "The Scum of the Earth (Papa Was Right)" (Debbie Petrino, Joe Duquette, Jesse L. Stokes, Charles Del Vecchio, Richard Alpers), "More Love" (Ensemble), "Oh, Lorraine" (Howard Pinhasik), "Lorraine's Tape" (Donna Pelc), "The New School, The Old School" (David Berk, Frank Torren), "It's a Beautiful World" (reprise) (John Gallogly), "Partners" (Kathi McGunnigle), "Everything Changes" (Jesse Cline), "Trio" (Howard Pinhasik, Donna Pelc, Jesse Cline), "Back Off" (Donna Pelc), "Unmanly" (Gary Di Mauro, John Gallogly, Richard Alpers, Charles Del Vecchio, Kathi McGunnigle, Debbie Petrino, Jesse L. Stokes), "Take Care" (Donna Pelc, Howard Pinhasik)

NOTES—Although Mel Gussow in the *New York Times* had some minor reservations about the "hard-boiled"(but with a "somewhat soft center") Off Off Broadway musical *The Meehans*, he was generally enthusiastic about it and particularly liked the "unusual" subject matter of "blue-collar" types (he noted how few musicals dealt with them, and indicated only *The Pajama Game* [1954] and *Working* [1978] came to mind).

He praised the "musical freshness" of the score by Charles Choset and the late Sam Pottle, singling out a number of songs, including "two-fisted musical paeans to pragmatism, sung to a barrelhouse, gang's-all-here beat" and "It's a Beautiful World," one of Pottle's "sweetest melodies." Further, he liked the "emotionally charged" number "Lorraine's Tape," in which a wife (Donna Pelc) details her marital problems; "Trio," a "musical three-way discord" with the wife (Pelc), her husband (Howard Pinhasik), and a police-force priest (Jesse Cline) trying to deal with a family dispute and an attempted reconciliation; and a pas de deux for two "hefty but graceful" bar patrons. *The Meehans* is a musical which seems worthy of reexamination, and from Gussow's comments it appears the score would make a enjoyable recording.

An interesting footnote to this obscure musical is that its program artwork was designed by artist Sean Scully, who also designed the artwork for *Letters to Ben* (1982; see entry), another musical which was produced by the Theatre for the New City; after these early ventures, it appears Scully never returned to theatre artwork.

1041 Meet Peter Grant. THEATRE: Folksbiene Theatre; OPENING DATE: May 10, 1961; PERFORMANCES: Unknown; BOOK: Elliot Arluck; LYRICS: Elliot Arluck; MUSIC: Ted Harris; DIRECTION: Roger Sullivan; SCENERY: John Braden; COSTUMES: Mary Ann Reed; LIGHTING: John Braden; MUSICAL DIRECTION: Edward Johnson; PRODUCER: Lee Bergman

CAST—Frank Vohs (Salesman), David Hartman (The Devil), Chet Sommers (Peter Grant), Jety Herlick (Amelia Grant), Nancy Junion (Karen Grannick), Irene Clark (Susan), Ewel Cornett (Windy), Tobi Reynolds (Girl), Paula Coonen (Sally Benton)

SOURCE—The play *Peer Gynt* by Henrik Ibsen (written in 1867 and first produced in 1876).

NOTES—Like *The Tiger Rag* (see entry), *Meet Peter Grant* was one of the more ambitious Off Broadway musicals of its era. Louis Calta in the *New York Times* described the musical as *Oklahoma!* rewritten by Henrik Ibsen, and quickly added that the unlikely merger was not at all a bad idea. Calta indicated the musical "has strived mightily and earnestly to make something new, fresh and lively" in its adaptation of Ibsen's difficult play *Peer Gynt*, which was now set in the American Midwest. Calta praised the score (singling out "If You Have a Dream," "Are You for Real," "Like a Man," and "Memories") and concluded by saying the production was "felicitous ... a venture worth seeing." Chet Sommers was also praised for his performance in the title role. Calta felt his singing voice and stage presence was excellent, and noted he had a physique suitable for Li'l Abner. But Sommers was never again seen in a New York musical.

Edvard Grieg had composed incidental music for the original 1876 production of *Peer Gynt*, and this music was later heard in *Song of Norway* (1944).

Another lyric adaptation, titled *Peer Gynt*, opened on August 4, 1974, for fifteen performances at the Missouri Repertory Theatre/University of Missouri; based on Christopher Fry's adaptation of Johann Fillinger's translation of the play, the musical's book was by Adrian Hall and Richard Cumming, and the lyrics and music were by Cumming.

1042 Memphis Is Gone. "A New Play with Music." THEATRE: St. Clement's; OPENING DATE: January 28, 1977; PERFORMANCES: Unknown; PLAY: Richard (Dick) Hobson; LYRICS: Richard (Dick) Hobson; MUSIC: Richard (Dick) Hobson; DIRECTION: Robert Allan Ackerman; SCENERY: Eric Head; COSTUMES: Bobby Wojewodski; LIGHTING: Arden Fingerhut; MUSICAL DIRECTION: Arden Fingerhut; PRODUCERS: Stephanie Copeland and Peter Henderson

CAST—Kevin O'Connor (Jasmine), William Snikowski (Dr. Stone, Deputy Digs, Jimmy Deaser), Jean DeBaer (Mrs. Keening, Rebecca Wells, Maggie Jo), John Kellogg (Moon), Thom Schuyler (Guitarist, Singer in Gray), Bill Swiggard (Guitarist, Singer in Brown), Robert Pararozzi (Harmonica)

The action occurs in the spring and fall during the present time, and also thirteen years earlier.

The play was presented in two acts.

ACT ONE—"Memphis Is Gone," "Shine Moon" (theme), "Moon and Me," "The High Road," "Cornbean Pie," "The Old Lonesome Stranger," "What're You Doin'?," "Call Me Jasmine," "The Mayor of Memphis," "He Is Coming"

ACT TWO—"I'll Die Laughing," "When Maggie Died"/"Shine Moon" (reprise), "Nine Lives Blues," "The Mayor of Memphis" (reprise), "Maggie's Chant" (theme), "Transportation," "Call Me Jasmine" (theme), "Stray Cat" "Maggie's Chant" (reprise), "Maggie's Chant" (theme), "Memphis Is Gone" (theme), "Judgment," "Memphis Is Gone" (theme)

NOTES—*Memphis Is Gone* had been previously produced at the Theatre for the New City, first on April 19, 1975, and then later in September of that year. It appears Susan Gregg directed these first two productions.

Like Sheba, the titular dog of William Inge's first Broadway play *Come Back, Little Sheba* (1950),

Memphis is another pooch who has taken off for parts unknown.

Mel Gussow in the *New York Times* described the Off Off Broadway musical as a "hitchhike through hoboland," and found the simplistic characterizations of derelicts a bit too cloying and sentimental. But he praised the score, which was for the most part sung by an on-stage combo and not by the main characters themselves.

1043 Memphis Store-Bought Teeth. "A New Musical." THEATRE: Orpheum Theatre; OPENING DATE: December 29, 1971; PERFORMANCES: 1; BOOK: E. Don Alldredge; LYRICS: D. Brian Wallach; MUSIC: William Fisher; DIRECTION: Marvin Gordon; SCENERY: Robert O' Hearn; COSTUMES: William Pitkin; LIGHTING: George Vaughn Lowther; MUSICAL DIRECTION: Rene Weigert; PRODUCER: D. Brian Wallach

CAST—Jerry Lanning (Traveller), J.J. Jepson (William), Alice Cannon (Jennifer), Travis Hudson (Fanny Crabtree), Evelyn Brooks (Ora Lee MacNew), Lloyd Harris (Greely MacNew, Judge Garmony), Sherill Price (Elmira Boone), Hal Robinson (Preacher Potter) The action occurs in Sunflower, Alabama, in July Present and Memory Past.

The musical was presented in one act.

MUSICAL NUMBERS—"Quiet Place" (J.J. Jepson), "It's Been a Hard Life" (Evelyn Brooks, Travis Hudson), "Where Have I Been" (Jerry Lanning), "The Lord Bless and Keep You" (Hal Robinson, Evelyn Brooks, Travis Hudson, Sherill Price, Lloyd Harris, Jerry Lanning), "Quiet Place" (reprise) (J.J. Jepson, Alice Cannon), "Fanny Dear" (Sherill Price, Travis Hudson), "My Final Fling" (Evelyn Brooks), "When I Leave" (Jerry Lanning, J.J. Jepson), "That's What a Friend's For" (Evelyn Brooks, Travis Hudson, Sherill Price), "Nothing Seems the Same" (Jerry Lanning, Alice Cannon, J.J. Jepson), "My Final Fling" (reprise) (Hal Robinson, Travis Hudson, Evelyn Brooks, Sherill Price), "That's What a Friend's For" (reprise) (Hal Robinson, Evelyn Brooks), "Something You Really Want" (J.J. Jepson, Alice Cannon), "Nicest Part of Me" (Travis Hudson), "Fanny Dear" (reprise) (Travis Hudson, J.J. Jepson), "Something to Hold On To" (Jerry Lanning)

NOTES—*Memphis Store-Bought Teeth* dealt with an older man (Jerry Lanning) who returns to his small town and looks back on his youthful self (J.J. Jepson) acting out his romantic involvements of fifteen years earlier. The musical was one of the 1971-1972 Off Broadway season's two single-performance failures. Noting that the musical took place in Sunflower, Alabama, in a time of "July Present and Memory Past," Mel Gussow in the *New York Times* felt that while the authors may have believed they "were in Inge country playing *The Fantasticks*," they were "really in limbo." He found the music "bland to the point of disappearance," the lyrics "banal," and the dialogue "wretched enough to set even store-bought teeth on edge." Gussow explained that if he correctly understood the offstage action, the musical's title had something to do with a pair of dentures owned by a character named Preacher Potter (Hal Robinson). His dentures were retrieved from a fire by a lovesick widow, but by the musical's end another fire consumes a different widow as well as the preacher himself, but, thankfully, not the dentures.

1044 Men and Dreams. THEATRE: Theatre de Lys; OPENING DATE: September 6, 1966; PERFORMANCES: 63; MIME SEQUENCES created by: Claude Kipnis; MUSIC: Noam Sheriff; SCENERY: Amiram Shamir; COSTUMES: Dinah Kipnis; LIGHTING: Marshall Spiller; PRODUCERS: Luben Vichey (Vichey Attractions, Inc.) by arrangement with Lucille Lortel Productions

CAST—Claude Kipnis, Sascha World, Robert World (The Israeli Mime Theatre)

The revue was presented in two acts.

ACT ONE—Introduction, "The Hobo (Dreams of a Parisian Hobo)," "Eve and the Serpent (Story of an Apple)," "The Village (Recollections of a Jewish Village)," "Fantasy in Wax (The Thief and the Mannequin)," "The Hooligan (When a Bad Boy Kills Time)," "The Cabinet Minister (His Excellency Spends a Weekend as a Commoner Member in His Kibbutz)"

ACT TWO—"The Lifeguard (on a Crowded Beach)," "The Bottle (Fantasy on Alcohol)," "Main Street (in Tel Aviv — or Anywhere)," "Jacob and the Angel (Man's Fight Against Divine Power)," "The Bus (in Israel)," Finale

NOTES—The three-person mime revue *Men and Dreams* had previously been presented in Israel and other countries. Harry Gilroy in the *New York Times* praised the revue's star, Claude Kipnis, and said his mime characterizations "are so universal that he is funny anywhere." Gilroy also noted the "special charm" of Kipnis' ability to find humor "in the land and among the people who have known so much tragedy."

1045 Men Women and why it won't work. THEATRE: The Theatre at Mama Gail's; OPENING DATE: October 22, 1975; PERFORMANCES: 12; BOOK: June Siegel and Miriam Fond; LYRICS: June Siegel; MUSIC: David Warrack; DIRECTION: Miriam Fond; CHOREOGRAPHY: Miriam Fond; SCENERY: Dan Leigh; COSTUMES: Danny Morgan; LIGHTING: Deanna Greenwood; MUSICAL DIRECTION: John R. Williams; PRODUCER: Charles Leslie

CAST—Ann Hodapp (Elaine Desmond), Arne Gundersen (Art Desmond), Leila Holiday (Jill Callen), Charles Maggiore (Al Callen), Gail Oscar (Phyllis Gelman), Garrett M. Brown (Herb Kessler), Barbara Lea (Kay Windsor)

The action occurs in the city and the suburbs at the present time.

The musical was presented in two acts.

ACT ONE—"What Do We Do?" (Company), "A Weekend at the Club" (Company), "Brand New Wall-to-Wall Day" (Company), "Desire Under the Elmsford Country Club Oaks" (Company), "Temporary Woman Blues" (Gail Oscar), "Let's Spend an Hour" (Arne Gundersen, Gail Oscar), "Have a Career" (Barbara Lea), "It's Great to Be Single Again" (Ann Hodapp), "Background Music" (Garrett M. Brown), "Morris" (Leila Holiday), "Let's Spend an Hour" (reprise) (Charles Maggiore, Arne Gundersen), "Background Music" (reprise) (Gail Oscar), "Wild Kingdom" (Leila Holiday, Ann Hodapp)

ACT TWO—"What Do (What Would) We Do?" (reprise) (Company), "Capitalist Beguine" (Charles Maggiore, with Arne Gundersen, Garrett M. Brown), "Lonely Woman" (Barbara Lea, with Charles Maggiore, Arne Gundersen, Garrett M. Brown), "Men Are Never Lonely" (Charles Maggiore, Arne Gundersen, Garrett M. Brown), "It's Love! So What?" (Ann Hodapp, Leila Holiday, Gail Oscar, Barbara Lea), "It's Really Easy Baking Bread" (Leilia Holiday, Barbara Lea, Gail Oscar), "The Best of Both Possible Worlds" (Charles Maggiore, Garrett M. Brown), "People Are Up for Grabs" (Ann Hodapp, with Leila Holiday, Gail Oscar, Barbara Lea), Faceless Clock (Arne Gundersen), "The Best of Both Possible Worlds" (reprise) (Arne Gundersen, Charles Maggiore, Garrett M. Brown), "People Are Up for Grabs" (reprise) (Ann Hodapp, Leila Holiday, Gail Oscar, Barbara Lea), "Milles Fountain" (Arne Gundersen, Ann Hodapp), "Take Me-Find Me" (Gail Oscar, Garrett M. Brown), Finale (Company)

NOTES—This cutely titled musical (with a few amusing song titles) was presented for a limited engagement in what appears to have been a workshop of sorts; after the production closed, it was never heard from again. Lyricist and co-book writer June Siegel would later return in *The Housewives' Cantata* (1980; see entry).

1046 Menopause: The Musical. THEATRE: Theatre Four; transferred to Playhouse 91 on September 26, 2002; OPENING DATE: April 4, 2002; PERFORMANCES: 1,724; BOOK: Jeanie Linders; LYRICS: Parody lyrics by Jeanie Linders; see song list for credits of original lyricists; MUSIC: See song list for credits; DIRECTION: Kathleen Lindsey; CHOREOGRAPHY: Patty Bender; SCENERY: Jesse Poleshuck; COSTUMES: Martha Bromelmeier; LIGHTING: Michael Gilliam; MUSICAL DIRECTION: Corinne Aquilina; PRODUCERS: Mark Schwartz and TOC Productions in association with Brent Peek

CAST—Joy Lynn Matthews (Power Woman), Mary Jo McConnell (Soap Star), Joyce A. Presutti (Earth Mother), Carolann Page (Iowa Housewife)

The action occurs at Bloomingdale's in New York City during the present time.

The revue was presented in one act.

MUSICAL NUMBERS—Overture (Band), "Change, Change, Change" (parody of "Chain of Fools"; lyric and music by Don Covay) (Company), "I Heard It" (parody of "I Heard It Through the Grapevine"; lyric and music by Norman Whitfield and Barry Strong) (Joy Lynn Matthews, Mary Jo McConnell), "Sign of the Times" (parody of "A Sign of the Times"; lyric and music by Anthony Peter Hatch) (Joyce A. Presutti, Carolann Page), "Stayin' Awake"/"Night Fever" (parodies of "Stayin' Alive" and "Night Fever"; lyric and music by Maurice, Barry, and Robin Gibb; from 1977 film *Saturday Night Fever*) (Company), "My Husband Sleeps Tonight" (parody of "The Lion Sleeps Tonight"; lyric and music by Hugo Pereti, Luigi Creatore, George David Weiss, and Albert Stanton) (Joyce A. Presutti, Company), "Drippin' and Droppin'" (parody of "Wishin' and Hopin'"; lyric by Hal David, music by Burt Bacharach) (Joyce A. Presutti), "I'm Flashing" (parody of "I'm Sorry"; lyric and music by Thomas Bell and William Hart) (Joy Lynn Matthews), "The Great Pretender" (parody of "The Great Pretender"; lyric and music by Buck Ram) (Joy Lynn, Carolann Page, Company), "Sane and Normal Girls" (parody of "California Girls"; lyric and music by Brian Wilson and Mike Love)/"Thank You Doctor" (parody of "Help Me Rhonda"; lyric and music by Brian Wilson and Mike Love) (Company), "Lookin' for Food" (parody of "Lookin' for Love in All the Wrong Places"; lyric and music by Wanda Mallette, Bob Morrison, and Patti Ryan) (Mary Jo McConnell, Carolann Page, Company), "Please Make Me Over" (parody of "Don't Make Me Over"; lyric by Hal David, music by Burt Bacharach), "Beauty" (parody of "Beauty Is Only Skin Deep"; lyric and music by Eddie Holland and Norman Whitfield) (Company), "Puff, My God, I'm Draggin'" (parody of "Puff, the Magic Dragon"; lyric by Lenny Lipton, music by Pete Yarrow) (Joyce A. Presutti), The Work-Out Medley: "The Fat Gram Song" (parody of "The Shoop Shoop Song"; lyric and music by Rudy Clark) (Joy Lynn Matthews, Company), "My Thighs" (parody of "My Guy"; lyric and music by Smokey Robinson) (Carolann Page, Company), "Don't Say Nothing Bad About My Body" (parody of "Don't Say Nothing Bad About My Baby"; lyric and music by Gerry Goffin, music by Carole King) (Mary Jo McConnell, Company), "I'm No Babe, Ma!" (parody of "I Got You Babe"' lyric and music by Sonny Bono) (Company), "Good Vibrations" (parody of "Good Vibrations"; lyric by Mike Love and Brian Wilson, music by Brian Wilson) (Joyce A. Presutti, Mary Jo McConnell) "What's Love Got to Do with It" (parody of "What's Love Got to Do with It"; lyric by Terry Britten, music by Graham Lyle) (Joy Lynn Matthews, Company), "Only You" (parody of "Only You"; lyric and music by Buck Ram and Ande Rand) (Carolann Page, Company), "New Attitude" (parody of "New

Attitude"; lyric and music by Sharon Robinson, Jonathan Gilutin, and Bunny Hall) (Company), "This Is Your Day!" (parody of "YMCA"; lyric and music by Jacques Marali, Henri Belolo, and Victor Willis) (Company)

NOTES—*Menopause: The Musical*, a revue about women in their middle years, was an unexpected hit, running four years Off Broadway and becoming a staple in regional and community theatre. Jeanie Linders wrote the script, and she set her lyrics to popular songs from the period of the 1950s-1980s.

The revue had first been produced in Orlando, Florida, on March 28, 2001, and its cast album was released by Menomusic Records (unnumbered CD); the song titles are taken from the recording.

For another revue on the same subject, see entry for *We're Still Hot!*, which opened in 2005, but had first been produced as *Menopositive! The Musical* in Vancouver in 1998.

A similar musical, *Hot Flashes*, was produced in regional theatre in 2002; its cast recording was released by Rose City Records on an unnumbered CD; the revue included original songs (mostly by Kate Finn and Rick Weiss), but, like *Menopause: The Musical*, some songs offered new lyrics set to the music of popular hits ("I Am Woman" became "I Am Woman, Hear Me Snore").

1047 Merry Mount. THEATRE: Metropolitan Opera House; OPENING DATE: February 10, 1934; PERFORMANCES: 9; LIBRETTO: Richard L. Stokes; MUSIC: Howard Hanson; DIRECTION: Wilhelm Von Wymetal, Jr.; CHOREOGRAPHY: Rosina Gailli; SCENERY: Jo Mielziner; MUSICAL DIRECTION: Tullio Serafin; PRODUCER: The Metropolitan Opera

CAST—Arnold Gabor (Faint-Not Tinker), James Wolfe (Samoset), Irra Petina (Desire Annable), Giordano Paltrinieri (Jonathan Banks), Lawrence Tibbett (Wrestling Bradford), Gladys Swarthout (Plentiful Tewke), Louis d'Angelo (Praise-God Tewke), Alfredo Gandolfi (Myles Brodrib), Helen Gleason (Peregrine Brodrib), Lillian Clark (Love Brewster), Henriette Wakefield (Bridget Crackston), Marek Windheim (Jack Prence), Gota Ljungberg (Lady Marigold Sandys), George Cehanovsky (Thomas Morton), Edward Johnson (Sir Gower Lackland), Millo Picco (Jewel Scooby), Max Altglass (Puritan), Pompilio Malatesta (Puritan), Rita De Leporte (Dancer)

SOURCE—The short story "The Maypole of Merry Mount" by Nathaniel Hawthorne.

The action occurs in Massachusetts on a Sunday in May 1625.

The opera was presented in four acts.

NOTES—The cautious announcement that *Merry Mount* was a "world operatic premiere" was undoubtedly because the opera had been previously presented in concert form at Ann Arbor, Michigan, the previous year. But for all purposes the Met production was a world premiere.

The story contrasted the dour and religious New England Puritans with visiting British cavaliers who embrace a more "pagan" lifestyle. Wrestling Bradford (Lawrence Tibbett), Merry Mount's preacher, constantly fights against sin and temptation, and although he wants to marry Plentiful Tewke (Gladys Swarthout), she's repelled by his obsessions and his suppressed lustfulness. When Bradford meets Lady Marygold, one of the visiting cavaliers, he's attracted to her and proposes marriage, which she scorns. He attempts to rape her, and when her fiancé tries to protect her, Bradford murders him. In a dream, Bradford signs a pact with the devil in exchange for giving him Marygold. When he awakens, Indians have attacked Merry Mount and have burned it. When the villagers see the mark of Satan on Bradford's brow, they stone him, and, with Marygold in his arms, Bradford rushes into the flames.

Olin Downes' review in the *New York Times* praised much of Hanson's atmospheric score, which included hymn-like sequences as well as maypole dance music (the production apparently included more dancing than usual for a Met production), but he also noted that the music "treads water and marks time." Further, he felt the opera was weak in its characterizations and noted that Bradford wasn't a particularly sympathetic leading character.

With its theme of sexual frankness, Downes mentioned that the audience for the premiere (as well as the "on the air" audience [the first performance was broadcast on radio]) heard "some terms of Elizabethan frankness and vigor."

The libretto had been published in 1932 by Farrar & Rinehart, Inc.; a note in the libretto indicated the opera would be produced at the Met during the 1932-1933 season (of course, it was actually produced during the 1933-1934 season). The libretto was published in three acts (the Met's production was presented in four acts). A few weeks before the Met's premiere, Tibbett recorded an aria from *Merry Mount*, "'Tis an Earth Defiled," which can be heard in the collection *Lawrence Tibbet, Baritone*, which is part of *The Stanford Archive Series*; the 2-CD recording was released by Delos Records (# 5500).

In 1950, Tibbett appeared in the Broadway opera *The Barrier*, and later replaced Enzo Pinza during the run of *Fanny* (1954). The *Merry Mount* company also included two other singers who appeared in Broadway musicals. Helen Gleason was the lead in the 1941 flop *Night of Love*, which lasted for just eight performances, and Irra Petina appeared in a number of musicals, most of them failures. Petina was in one long-running hit (*Song of Norway*, 1944; 860 performances) as well as in a string of fast-closing flops (*Magdalena*, 1948; 88 performances; *Hit the Trail*, 1954; 4 performances; *Candide*, 1956; 73 performances; and *Anya*, 1965; 16 performances). Of course, she's best remembered for *Candide*, in which she created the role of the Old Lady and introduced "I Am Easily Assimilated." For more information about *Candide*, see entry for the Off Broadway revival.

Tibbett appeared in six films between 1930 and 1936, including *The Rogue Song* (1930; based on Franz Lehar's 1910 operetta *Gypsy Love*) and *New Moon* (1930; the first film version of Oscar Hammerstein II and Sigmund Romberg's 1928 Broadway musical *The New Moon*). In 1931, he appeared in *The Prodigal*, singing "Without a Song" (lyric by Edward Eliscu and Billy Rose, music by Vincent Youmans), which had first been heard in the short-running 1929 Broadway musical *Great Day!* In *The Cuban Love Song* (also 1931), he introduced the attractive title song (sung by both his younger and older self on a split screen, Tibbett performed the number as a baritone and as a tenor); the film also introduced "The Peanut Vendor," first sung by Lupe Velez, and then later reprised by Tibbett. Gladys Swarthout never appeared in a Broadway musical, but, like Tibbett, she enjoyed a brief film career, appearing in five films between 1936 and 1939.

1048 Miami. "A New Musical." THEATRE: Playwrights Horizons; OPENING DATE: January 1, 1986; PERFORMANCES: 39; BOOK: Wendy Wasserstein; LYRICS: Bruce Sussman and Jack Feldman; MUSIC: Jack Feldman; DIRECTION: Gerald Gutierrez; CHOREOGRAPHY: Larry Hyman; SCENERY: Heidi Landesman; COSTUMES: Ann Hould-Ward; LIGHTING: Richard Nelson; MUSICAL DIRECTION: David Bishop; PRODUCER: Playwrights Horizons (Andre Bishop, Artistic Director; Paul S. Daniels, Executive Director; James F. Priebe, Managing Director)

CAST—Royana Black (Cathy Maidman), Fisher Stevens (Jonathan Maidman), Phyllis Newman (Helen Maidman), Stephen Pearlman (Sam Maidman), John Aller (Maitre d', Carlos de Goya), David Green (Vic Barry), Marcia Lewis (Kitty Katz), Chevi Colton (Erma Goldman), Cleve Asbury (Dirk, Waiter, Renaldo, Boy #2), Bill Badolato (Andy, Boy #1, Waiter), Catherine Wolf (Vita Weinstein), John Cunningham (Ted Fine), Jane Krakowski (Denise Fine), Joanna Glushak (Annette de Goya), Molly Wassermann (Nanette, Girl #2), Mary Anne Dorward (Yvette, Mrs. Cohen, Girl #1), Larry Keith (Murray Murray), Jerry Mayer (Luis Hernandez)

The action occurs in Miami Beach during Christmas Week 1959.

The musical was presented in two acts.

ACT ONE—"Miami" (Marcia Lewis, Bill Badolato, Cleve Asbury, Company), "Wait for Me" (Fisher Stevens), "Wait for Me" (reprise) (Royana Black), "The Wonderful World of Wearables" (Joanna Glushak, Molly Wassermann, Mary Anne Dorward), "Morning in Madrid" (Joanna Glushak), "Tiger, Tiger" (Molly Wassermann), "Galaxy Girl" (Mary Anne Dorward), "Perfect" (Fisher Stevens, Jane Krakowski), "The Words We Whisper Cha-Cha" (John Aller, Joanna Glushak), "Dance Night" (Company), "Girls Like Me" (Marcia Lewis, Larry Keith), "The Catherine Maidman Show" (Royana Black), "Puilly Fuisse" (Fisher Stevens), "You Could Do Worse" (Fisher Stevens, Royana Black, Stephen Pearlman, Phyllis Newman), "Miami" (reprise) (Marcia Lewis, Company)

ACT TWO—"Happy New Year, Darling" (Chevi Colton, Cleve Asbury, Phyllis Newman, Mary Anne Dorward, Catherine Wolf, Marcia Lewis, and unknown performer), "The Bitter and the Sweet" (Phyllis Newman), "Uh-Huh" (Fisher Stevens, Jane Krakowski, Sunbathers), "The Rehearsal" (Marcia Lewis, Bill Badolato, Cleve Asbury, John Aller, Joanna Glushak), "Wait for Me" (reprise) (Fisher Stevens, Royana Black), "Mambo Ensembo" (Company)

NOTES—*Miami* played for thirty-nine workshop performances at Playwrights Horizons from January 1 to February 2, 1986; it never officially opened, and after the workshop the musical disappeared. It sounds intriguing: a satiric book by Wendy Wasserstein which was apparently about Jewish New Yorkers vacationing in Miami Beach during the Christmas holiday season of 1959. And there seems to have been a subplot about the garment business as well. Further, the musical included such cut-ups as Phyllis Newman, Marcia Lewis, and Jane Krakowski. Plus there were pastiches of 1950s cha-chas and mambos. How could this show have gone wrong? A decade earlier, Wasserstein had been associated with Playwrights Horizons in another musical (for which she wrote the book and lyrics); it also disappeared after its scheduled workshop performances (see entry for *Montpelier Pizazz*).

1049 The Middle of Nowhere. THEATRE: Astor Place Theatre; OPENING DATE: November 20, 1988; PERFORMANCES: 24; BOOK: Tracy Friedman; LYRICS: Randy Newman; MUSIC: Randy Newman; DIRECTION: Tracy Friedman; CHOREOGRAPHY: Tracy Friedman; SCENERY: Loren Sherman; COSTUMES: Juliet Polcsa and Loren Sherman; LIGHTING: Phil Monat; MUSICAL DIRECTION: Jonny Bowden; PRODUCERS: Frank Basile, Lewis Friedman, Tom O. Meyerhoff, and Albert Nocciolino

CAST—Roger Robinson (Joe), Vondie Curtis-Hall (G.I.), Michael Arkin (Salesman), Diana Castle (Girl), Tony Hoylen (Redneck)

The action occurs in a bus depot somewhere on the back roads of Louisiana in 1969.

The musical was presented in one act (song assignments unknown).

MUSICAL NUMBERS—"I Think It's Going to Rain Today," "Simon Smith," "Yellow Man," "Davy the Fat Boy," "Political Science," "Lonely at the Top," "Lover's Prayer," "Old Kentucky Home," "Tickle Me," "Maybe I'm Doing It Wrong," "They Just Got Married," "Short People," "Song for the Dead," "Baltimore," "I'm Different," "It's Money

That I Love," "Sigmund Freud's Impersonation," "Sail Away," "You Can Leave Your Hat On," "Old Man," "Marie," "Rednecks," "Mr. President," "Louisiana 1927"

NOTES—The short-lived book musical *The Middle of Nowhere* used two-dozen pre-existing songs by Randy Newman to tell the story of stranded travelers in a bus station in Louisiana in 1969 who find themselves transported into a surreal minstrel show dealing with racial and other social issues. Jeffrey Sweet in *The Best Plays of 1988-1989* praised the musical's concept and its "unified and unsettling vision of America"; he found the piece "inventively staged and choreographed" and impressively cast. But the musical was gone in three weeks, and so it never had much time to find its audience.

See entry for *Randy Newman's Maybe I'm Doing It Wrong* for more information on other musicals which used Newman's songs.

1050 Millicent Montrose. "A Musical Fable." THEATRE: Wings Theatre Company; OPENING DATE: Late 1980s (1987?); PERFORMANCES: Unknown; BOOK: Bill Solly; LYRICS: Bill Solly; MUSIC: Bill Solly; DIRECTION: Bill Solly; CHOREOGRAPHY: Jeffery Corrick; SCENERY: Edmond Ramage; COSTUMES: Alan Michael Smith; LIGHTING: Edmond Ramage; MUSICAL DIRECTION: Davy Temperley; PRODUCER: Wings Theatre Company (Jeffery Corrick, Artistic Director)

CAST—Dennis Holly (Sheridan Montague, Sheriff), Lisa Spackman (Bridget, Sink [Fashion Show Model], Housewife [Fashion Show Model]), Liana Harris (Millicent Montrose), Curt Mitchell Buckler (Travis, Back Legs), Anne Fisher (The Lady of the Desert Sand, Table [Fashion Show Model], Back Legs), John Banta (Idra), Robert Grader (Policeman, Back Legs, Ensemble), Jeffrey Rose (Ken), David Fobair (Anchor Man, Back Legs, Ensemble), Catherine Parrinello (Clothes-line [Fashion Show Model], Ensemble), Laurie Whitten (TV [Fashion Show Model], Chair [Fashion Show Model], Ensemble), Leslie Darwin (Lampshade [Fashion Show Model], Ensemble) The action occurs in the present in Manhattan "and other places."

The musical was presented in two acts.

ACT ONE—"The American Clothes of Millicent Montrose" (Dennis Holly, Liana Harris, Company), "Wasn't Easy" (Liana Harris), "El Kazar" (Anne Fisher, Chorus), "Back Legs" (John Banta), "Brilliant!" (Curt Mitchell Buckler, Lisa Spackman, Reporters), "Look Who's Here" (Liana Harris), "Lady of the Desert Sand" (Jeffrey Rose), "How Do You Get to the Desert?" (Liana Harris, John Banta), "We're Off!" (John Banta, Liana Harris), "Starring Me" (Lisa Spackman, Curt Mitchell Buckler), "Don't Go Back to Baltimore" (Jeffrey Rose, John Banta, Liana Harris), Finale (Company)

ACT TWO—"Brilliant!" (reprise) (Curt Mitchell Buckler, Lisa Spackman, Dennis Holly, Catherine Parrinello, Laurie Whitten, Leslie Darwin, Anne Fisher), "There Is No Avenue" (Anne Fisher), "Phantasmagoria at the Caravanserai" (John Banta, Anne Fisher, Jeffrey Rose, Ensemble), "The Fashion Show" (Lisa Spackman, Catherine Parrinello, Laurie Whitten, Leslie Darwin, Anne Fisher), "Look Who's Here" (reprise) (Chorus, Anne Fisher, Jeffrey Rose, Dennis Holly), "My Favorite Mirage" (John Banta, Ensemble), "Pretty Like You Do" (Jeffrey Rose), "El Kazar" (reprise) (sung by characters 'Laura' and 'Colin' [performers not identified in program]), "Let's Hear It for the Kid" (Liana Harris), Finale (Company)

NOTES—The musical was produced under an Off Off Broadway contract.

1051 A Millionaire in Trouble. THEATRE: Town Hall; OPENING DATE: January 16, 1980; PERFORMANCES: 55; BOOK: Moshe Tamir; adapted by Michael Greenstein; LYRICS: Yankele Alperin; MUSIC: Alexander Lustig; DIRECTION: Yankele Alperin; CHOREOGRAPHY: Felix Fibich; COSTUMES: Joni Rudesill ("Wardrobe"); Adolpho ("Suits"); Equity (Library) Theatre ("Costumes"); SCENERY: Equity Library Theatre ("Props") Musical Direction: Renee Solomon; PRODUCER: Shalom Yiddish Musical Comedy Theatre

CAST—Chaim Levin (Philip), Diane Cypkin (Goldele), Bernardo Hiller (Teddy), Yakov Bodo (Simon Oppenheim), Solo Moise (Harry Fishbein), Moishe Rosenfeld (Attorney Green), Raquel Yossiffon (Emma Shayn), Paul Czolczynski (Yukel Kishke), Chayele Ash (Esther Shayn)

SOURCE—The Yiddish play *Hard to Be a Pauper* by Sidney Wolf.

The musical was presented in two acts (division of acts and song assignments unknown; songs are listed in performance order).

MUSICAL NUMBERS—"Promises and Love," "How Do You Do," "A Happy Life," "Many Trades," "Mother Son," "Drunkenness" ("Shikeres"), "Longing," "Mazel Tov," "Hard to Be a Pauper"

NOTES—*A Millionaire in Trouble* was probably produced under a variation of an Off Off Broadway contract.

Richard F. Shepard in the *New York Times* reported that the familiar but pleasant plot centered on a man who returns to New York from Israel when he discovers he's going to inherit a fortune; along the way, he meets a bum with whom he trades places for one year. Further, the musical offered a surprise ending. Shepard noted the evening teemed with amiable stock types, including a "quintessential" Jewish mother ("whose idea of a match is one made in the safe-deposit-box"), a lawyer, a valet, a gold-digger, and a "Zeppo Marx"-like straight romantic lead. Shepard singled out "Shikeres" ("Drunkenness") as a "funny and good" song.

1052 Mimi le Duck. "A Nouveau Musical." THEATRE: New World Stages; OPENING DATE: November 6, 2006; PERFORMANCES: 30; BOOK: Diana Hansen-Young; LYRICS: Diana Hansen-Young; MUSIC: Brian Feinstein; DIRECTION: Thomas Caruso; CHOREOGRAPHY: Matt West; SCENERY: John Arnone; COSTUMES: Ann Hould-Ward; LIGHTING: David Lander; MUSICAL DIRECTION: Chris Fenwick; PRODUCERS: Mango Hill Productions LLC and Aruba Productions LLC in association with Marie Costanza and Paul Beattie

CAST—Annie Golden (Miriam), Marcus Neville (Peter), Allen Fitzpatrick (Ernest Hemingway), Ken Jennings (Gypsy), Robert DuSold (Claude), Eartha Kitt (Madame Vallet), Tom Aldredge (Ziggy), Candy Buckley (Clay); Idaho Choir, Ancestors, and the Paris House were performed by members of the cast

The action occurs in the present in Ketchum, Idaho, and in Paris.

The musical was presented in two acts.

ACT ONE—"Ketchum, Idaho" (Ketchum Choir), "Gray" (Annie Golden), "Paris Is a City" (Ken Jennings), "22 Rue Danou" ('The House'), "A Thousand Hands" (Allen Fitzpatrick), "Why Not?" (Robert DuSold, Ancestors), "It's All About" (Eartha Kitt, Annie Golden), "Empty or Full" (Tom Aldredge, Annie Golden), "Everything Changes" (Eartha Kitt), "There Are Times in Life" (Candy Buckley, Annie Golden), "Don't Ask" (Candy Buckley), "Get Outta Here, Peter" (Annie Golden, Marcus Neville), "Is There Room?" (Annie Golden, Marcus Neville)

ACT TWO—"The Green Flash" (Allen Fitzpatrick), "My Mother Always Said" (Annie Golden), "The Only Time We Have Is Now" (Tom Aldredge), "Cozy Dreams Come True" (Marcus Neville, Robert DuSold, Ken Jennings), "Paris Is a City" (reprise) (Ken Jennings), "Peter's Reprise" (Marcus Neville), "All Things New" (Eartha Kitt), "The Garden Is Green" (Annie Golden), "There Is Room" ("Is There Room?") (Annie Golden, Marcus Neville, 'The House')

NOTES—*Mimi le Duck* told the tale of Miriam, a restless middle-aged housewife who lives in Ketchum, Idaho, where Ernest Hemingway committed suicide; there she paints pictures of ducks for mass-production sales. Spurred on by the ghost of Hemingway, Miriam leaves Idaho for Paris in order to find herself and, like Mamie, a sung-about character in the 1949 Broadway musical *Gentlemen Prefer Blondes*, she becomes Mimi ("Mamie Is Mimi" is one of the most ingratiating songs in the Jule Styne songbook). According to Zachary Pincus-Roth in a *Playbill* website article, once in Paris Miriam/Mimi comes upon Parisian types "familiar to anyone who's ever seen *La Boheme*, *Gigi* or *An American in Paris*."

Neil Genzlinger in the *New York Times* had high praise for the legendary Eartha Kitt, but was unimpressed with the rest of the musical. He felt the score and the book were based on "the kinds of bromides found in women's magazines," and he assumed "44-year-old duck-painting housewives" were "the target audience" for the musical.

During previews, the song "Red" was cut (or perhaps its title was changed to "Gray"); also, "Wild Dreams Come True" was changed to "Cozy Dreams Come True."

The musical was first seen in 2004 at the Adirondack Theatre Festival in Glens Falls, New York, and then later at the New York International Fringe Festival in 2004 where it played a limited engagement.

During the run of the Off Broadway production, an unlabeled and unnumbered sampler CD of four songs performed by original cast members was distributed to the audience; the songs were: "My Mother Always Said" (Annie Golden), "A Thousand Hands" (Allen Fitzpatrick), "Don't Ask" (Candy Buckley), and "Is There Room?" ("There Is Room") (Annie Golden and Marcus Neville).

1053 MindGames. THEATRE: Westside Theatre/Downstairs; OPENING DATE: November 17, 1997; PERFORMANCES: 237; MATERIAL: Marc Salem; SCENERY: Ray Recht; LIGHTING: Chris Dallos; PRODUCERS: Anita Waxman, Richard Richenthal, and Jeffrey Ash

CAST—Marc Salem

The revue was presented in one act.

NOTES—"Mentalist" Marc Salem's evening of mind-reading tricks ran through the season, and on December 3, 2001, he returned with *Marc Salem's Mind Games, Too*, which played at The Duke at 42nd Street Theatre for forty-eight performances. Lawrence Van Gelder in the *New York Times* found *MindGames* "good, old-fashioned family fun," and noted Salem was a "genial, quick-witted ... busy thief of thoughts." The revue was originally set for a limited run, but was extended and played through the season. A few weeks after the opening, Rick Lyman in the *Times* reported that the show's producers announced they would give a certified check for $100,000 to anyone who could prove Salem used "electronic devices, hidden cameras or unseen assistants." Further, the producers said they would earmark an additional $50,000 to be given to the winner's charity of choice.

1054 Ministry of Progress. THEATRE: Jane Street Theatre; OPENING DATE: March 4, 2004; PERFORMANCES: 30; BOOK: Kim Hughes; LYRICS AND MUSIC: John Beltzer, Sara Carlson, Philip Dressinger, Ted Eyes, Alex Forbes, Kathy Hart, Kim Hughes, Gary Levine, Christian Martirano, Jeremy Schonfeld, and Tony Visconti; DIRECTION: Kim Hughes; SCENERY: Adriana Serrano; COSTUMES: Fabio Toblini; LIGHTING: Jason Kantrowitz; MUSICAL DIRECTION: Christian Martirano; PRODUCER: Terry E. Schnuck

CAST—Jason Scott Campbell, Brian J. Dorsey, Tyne Firmin, Gary Maricheck, Jennifer McCabe, Maia A. Moss, Julie Reiber, Stacey Sargeant, Richard E. Waits, Christian Whelan

SOURCE—A radio play by Charles Morrow.

The revue was presented in one act.

NOTES—The short-lived revue-like musical *Ministry of Progress* spoofed modern bureaucracy, and centered on a young man who has surreal encounters with a number of bureaucrats when he tries to have them correct various errors on his driver's license.

Neil Genzlinger in the *New York Times* reported that the musical had begun life as a radio play in the 1980s. He noted the score often felt "random and tacked on," but singled out one number, "Come On Angel." He also reported that Maia A. Moss produced the evening's "most memorable moment: a cleavage revelation that brought gasps" from the audience.

1055 Miracolo d'Amore. THEATRE: Newman Theatre/The Public Theatre; OPENING DATE: June 29, 1988; PERFORMANCES: 47; CREATED by Martha Clarke and the Company; MUSIC: Richard Peaslee; DIRECTION: Martha Clarke; SCENERY: Robert Israel; COSTUMES: Robert Israel; LIGHTING: Paul Gallo; PRODUCERS: The New York Shakespeare Festival (Joseph Papp, Producer) in association with the Spoleto Festival U.S.A. as part of the First New York International Festival of the Arts

CAST—Peter Becker, Rob Besserer, Felix Blaska, Marshall Coid, Larrio Ekson, Marie Fourcaut, Alexandra Ivanoff, David Jon, John Kelly, Francine Landes, Nina Martin, Adam Rogers, Paola Styron, Elisabeth Van Ingen, Nina Watt

NOTES—*The Best Plays of 1988-1989* reported that Martha Clarke's *Miracolo d'Amore* used imagery from commedia dell'arte to depict sexual conflicts.

Frank Rich in the *New York Times* reported the work was an unusual one for Clarke because it contained no dancing. Instead, he described the evening as a beautiful "spare-no-expense spectacle" with a "melodic pastiche of a score" which looked at all aspects of love between men and women. But Rich noted the work seemed "to contract and evaporate" as he watched it, and suggested the subject of love was too general to be successful under the circumstances; he believed Clarke was more successful when she concentrated on specific subjects, such as Bosch's painting *The Garden of Earthly Delights* and the decadence of a civilization in *Vienna: Lusthaus*.

For a list of theatre works by Martha Clarke which are discussed in this book, see entry for *The Garden of Earthly Delights*.

1056 Mirette. THEATRE: Theatre at St. Clement's Church/The York Theatre Company; OPENING DATE: December 16, 2005; PERFORMANCES: 5 (estimated); BOOK: Elizabeth Diggs; LYRICS: Tom Jones; MUSIC: Harvey Schmidt; DIRECTION: Drew Scott Harris; MUSICAL DIRECTION: Matt Castle; PRODUCER: The York Theatre Company (James Morgan, Artistic Director)

CAST—Susan Cella, Robert Cuccioli, Ed Dixon, Davis Duffield, Joyce Franz, Patti Murin, Anthony Santelmo, Kelly Sullivan, Maggie Watts

SOURCE—The 1992 novel *Mirette on the High Wire* by Emily Arnold McCully.

The action occurs in Madame Gateau's hotel in Paris in the 1890s.

The musical was presented in two acts.

NOTES—First produced by the Goodspeed Opera House at the Norma Terris Theatre in Chester, Connecticut, Tom Jones and Harvey Schmidt's *Mirette* received its first New York production by the York Theatre Company as part of its *Musicals in Mufti* series (see entry).

The Chester production opened on August 1, 1996, and was directed by Drew Scott Harris, who later directed the *Mufti* production; the scenery for the Chester production was designed by James Morgan, the Artistic Director for the York Theatre Company, which produces the *Mufti* series. For Chester, the role of Mirette was performed by Kelly Mady; the cast also included Steve Barton. The musical numbers in the 1996 production were as follows: ACT ONE—"Madame Gateau's Colorful Hotel," "I Like It Here," "Someone in the Mirror," "Irkutsk," "Practicing," "Learning Who You Are," "Keep Your Feet Upon the Ground," "Learning Who You Are" (reprise), "If You Choose to Walk Upon the Wire," "She Isn't You"; ACT TWO—"The Great Bellini," "Sometimes You Just Need Someone," "Madame Gateau's Desolate Hotel" (reprise), "The Great Bellini" (reprise), "Practicing" (reprise), "Sometimes You Just Need Someone" (reprise), "The Show Goes On."

The Show Goes On, a 1997 tribute-revue to Tom Jones and Harvey Schmidt, took its title from one of the songs in *Mirette*'s score, and the number can be heard on the revue's cast album (see entry).

1057 The Misanthrope. THEATRE: Anspacher Theatre/The Public Theatre; OPENING DATE: October 5, 1977; PERFORMANCES: 63; BOOK, LYRICS, AND MUSIC: See notes below. DIRECTION: Bill Gile; CHOREOGRAPHY: Rachel Lampert; SCENERY: Bill Stabile; COSTUMES: Carrie F. Robbins; LIGHTING: Arden Fingerhut; MUSICAL DIRECTION: Allen Shawn; PRODUCERS: The New York Shakespeare Festival (Joseph Papp, Director; Bernard Gersten, Associate Producer)

CAST—John McMartin (Alceste), John Bottoms (Philinte), Arthur Burghardt (Oronte), Virginia Vestoff (Celimene), William Parry (Basque), Deborah Rush (Eliante), Ed Zang (Clitandre), Seth Allen (Acaste), Walt Gorney (Guard), Helen Gallagher (Arsinoe), Joshua Mostel (Dubois)

SOURCE—The 1666 play *Le Misanthrope, ou l'Atrabilaire Amoureaux* by Jean-Baptiste Poquelin (Moliere).

The action occurs in Celimene's house in Paris.

The musical was presented in five acts (with one intermission between Acts Three and Four).

ACT ONE—Symphonie" (*) (Orchestra), Allemande—"Be Witness to My Madness" (*) (Company), Air—"Where in the World?" (***) (John McMartin), Bouree—"The Art of Pleasing Me" (*) (John McMartin), "Sonnet" (**) (Arthur Burghardt, John Bottoms, John McMartin), Old Love Song—"Paris" (**) (John McMartin)

ACT TWO—"Double" (**) (Virginia Vestoff, John McMartin), Gavotte—"He Loves to Make a Fuss" (*) (Virginia Vestoff, Seth Allen, Ed Zang), Passepied—"Lovers Manage" (*) (Deborah Rush), "Waltz" (*) (Company)

ACT THREE—Caprice—"Madam" (*) (Helen Gallagher), Gigue—"The Other Day I Went to an Affair" (*) (Virginia Vestoff), Bagatelle—"We Women" (*) (Helen Gallagher)

ACT FOUR—Menuet I—"Substitute" (*) (Deborah Rush), Menuet II—"Second Best" (*) (John Bottoms, Deborah Rush), Air—"I Love You More" (*) (John McMartin, Virginia Vestoff), Burlesca—"Things Are Most Mysterious" (*) (Joshua Mostel)

ACT FIVE—Courante—"Altogether Too Outrageous" (*) (Virginia Vestoff), Tocatta—"How Dare You?" (***) (Helen Gallagher), Loure—"I Confess" (*) (Virginia Vestoff), Rondo—"Be Witness to My Madness" (*) (performer[s] unknown)

NOTES—This musical version of the classic play by Moliere underwent a series of major changes during its brief run at the Public Theatre. Early programs credited Richard Wilbur with the verse translation (presumably including all lyrics) and Margaret Pine with the music. No director was listed, and Paul Hecht played the role of Oronte. (In a September 7, 1977, article about the production, the *New York Times* reported that Leonardo Shapiro would be the director of the musical.) The musical was originally set to begin performances on October 4, but the first performance was on October 5; the press performance was on November 22; and the final performance was on November 27. Richard Eder in the *New York Times* noted that when the producers finally decided to invite the critics for the November 22 performance, it was clearly for the "obituaries." By the time of the press performance, the musical had a completely new set of songs (perhaps no other musical has undergone such a major transformation in so short a time). Richard Wilbur's name was no longer in the program (however, some reference sources credit him with the musical's book and lyrics; perhaps his translation of the play was still utilized). Bill Gile was credited with direction, and Arthur Burghardt assumed the role of Oronte. The program credited the songs to Jobriath Boone (*), Margaret Pine (**), and Arthur Bienstock (***). See song list above for specific credits.

For the record, the following songs were listed in the program at the beginning of the preview period (presumably all had lyrics by Richard Wilbur, and all music was by Margaret Pine): "No, I Include All Men," "Hope," "The King Song," "Why Am I Doomed to Love You?," "Gossip," "Love, As a Rule," "I'm Not the Sort of Fool," "The Flame of Friendship," "The Other Day," "I Believe in Frankness," "When a Beloved Hand," "Ah Traitress!," "Madam," "So, After All the Letters," "Reproach Me Freely," and "Woman."

Eder said the adaptation "blurred and coarsened" Moliere, and he found fault with the "noisy, slapstick" style of the performance. He even criticized the "extremely ugly set," and noted that the classical French furniture looked as if it were on consignment. He felt the only performers to emerge unscathed from the wreckage were John Bottoms and Deborah Rush, and mentioned that their musical sequence ("Substitute" and "Second Best") offered the only "genuine charm" in an otherwise "mediocre" score. The 1977-1978 season offered another musical which was based on a play by Moliere (see entry for *Monsieur de Pourceaugnac*). Also see entries for *'Toinette* (1961) and *Show Me Where the Good Times Are* (1970), both of which were based on Moliere's *The Imaginary Invalid*; and see entry for *The Amorous Flea* (based on *The School for Wives*).

1058 Mis-Guided Tour. "A New Musical Revue." THEATRE: Downtown Theatre; OPENING DATE: October 12, 1959; PERFORMANCES: 56; SKETCHES: James Allen Reid; LYRICS: James Allen Reid; MUSIC: Shirley Botwin, Margaret Foster, Jane White, Blair Weille, and James Reid; DIRECTION: James Allen Reid; CHOREOGRAPHY: Charles Nicoll Scenery: Robert E. Verberkmoes; COSTUMES: Robert E. Verberkmoes; MUSICAL DIRECTION: Margaret Foster

CAST—Leo Bloom, (Ruth) Buzzi, Barbara Evans, Charles Floyd, Michael Fesco, Jane Judge, Roberta MacDonald, Maureen McNalley, Bryan O'Byrne, Jean Sincere

The revue was presented in two acts.

ACT ONE—"Am I Late?" (music by Shirley Botwin) (Charles Floyd, Barbara Evans, Michael Fesco, Maureen McNalley, Leo Bloom, Jane Judge, Buzzi, Roberta McDonald, Jean Sincere) "Better Safe Than Sorry" (Bryan O'Byrne) "The Family Plan" (Jane Judge, Leo Bloom, Charles Floyd, Barbara Evans) "Maiden's Voyage" (music by Margaret Foster) (Jean Sincere) "Djibuti!" (Robert McDonald, Bryan O'Byrne, Leo Bloom, Maureen McNalley) "Copenhagen, Denmark" (music by Margaret Foster) (Barbara Evans, Michael Fesco) "Second Deck Diplomacy" (Leo Bloom, Roberta MacDonald) "Now Isn't That Lovely?" (music by Blair Weille)

(Buzzi, Barbara Evans, Michael Fesco, Jane Judge, Maureen McNalley, Leo Bloom, Roberta MacDonald, Bryan O'Byrne, Charles Floyd) "Alice in Italy" (Jean Sincere) "Who Are You?" (music by Jane White) (Michael Fesco, Roberta MacDonald) "Lower Deck Diplomacy" (Leo Bloom, Jane Judge) "Transplant" (music by Shirley Botwin) (Leo Bloom) "Take a Ride" (music by James Reid) (Jane Judge, Barbara Evans, Bryan O'Byrne) "Alice in Spain" (Jean Sincere), "I Am" (music by James Reid) (Maureen McNalley), "Take a Chance on Me" (music by Margaret Foster) (Barbara Evans, Charles Floyd) "Shandu Mishoo-Ganah" (sketch by Leo Bloom) (Leo Bloom, Buzzi) "Alice on the Matterhorn" (Jean Sincere), "Le Folly Bergere" (music by Margaret Foster) (Bryan O'Byrne, Roberta MacDonald, Jane Judge, Maureen McNalley, Barbara Evans)

ACT TWO—"Romance on the High Seas" (Buzzi), "At Least We Can Say We've Been There" (music by Margaret Foster) (Michael Fesco, Bryan O'Byrne, Maureen McNalley, Charles Floyd, Barbara Evans, Leo Bloom, Buzzi, Jane Judge, Roberta McDonald) "Alice in Africa" (Jean Sincere) "Nomad" (music by James Reid) (Jane Judge), "Try Try Again" (Leo Bloom, Maureen McNalley) "Port of Debarkation" (Bryan O'Byrne, Buzzi), "Another Bumper Crop" (music by Margaret Foster) (Charles Floyd, Maureen McNalley, Roberta MacDonald, Barbara Evans, Michael Fesco, Leo Bloom, Bryan O'Byrne) "Two Bags" (music by Shirley Botwin) (Buzzi, Jane Judge), "We Is Wonderful" (music by Jane White) (Michael Fesco, Charles Floyd, Maureen McNalley, Barbara Evans), "Desert Incident" (performer[s] not credited) "First Ones There" (Buzzi, Roberta MacDonald, Bryan O'Byrne), "Alice Back Home" (Jean Sincere) "Go! Go! Go!" (music by James Reid) (Company)

NOTES—Broadway enjoyed two notable revues about travel, so why not Off Broadway too? *At Home Abroad* (1935) and *Inside U.S.A.* (1948), both with scores by Howard Dietz and Arthur Schwartz, were hits (although a song in their 1961 musical *The Gay Life* asked, "Why Go Anywhere at All?"). Certainly *Mis-Guided Tour* went nowhere at all. It ran for less than two months, and faded into obscurity. Louis Calta in the *New York Times* found the revue "fundamentally undistinguished ... devoid of wit, urbanity and good comic sense." However, he singled out a "melodious and touching" song, "Who Are You?," and he found the sketch "Shandu Mishoo-Ganah" a bit of "inspired tomfoolery."

Most of the revue's cast is now forgotten (although the name Leo Bloom certainly strikes a familiar note). And Buzzi (literally, one name ... Buzzi) later found success on the television show *Laugh-In* (but that was after she added a first name and became Ruth Buzzi); Calta reported he didn't want to overlook the young woman who "frugally" called herself Buzzi, and said she had "the quality of a Nancy Walker." Kaye Ballard was once advised by an astrologist to change her name (or, at least, alter it, and so she did, for a brief period), and so perhaps Buzzi consulted an astrologist, too. She made a wise choice, because performers with one name just don't seem to find their permanent niche on the New York stage (paging Lilo, Yuriko, Bhaskar, Morocco, Despo, Sivuca, Peachena, Rozaa, Asia, Daffi, and others). Yes, in the nightclubs there was Hildegarde, but, after all, she was incomparable.

1059 Miss Chicken Little

NOTES—See entry for *An Evening of Adult Fairy Tales*, which consisted of two musicals, *Miss Chicken Little* and a revival of Al Carmines' *The Journey of Snow White* (and for more information on the latter, see entry for original production).

1060 Miss Emily Adam. "A New Musical Comedy."

THEATRE: Theatre Marquee; OPENING DATE: March 29, 1960; PERFORMANCES: 21; BOOK: James Lipton; LYRICS: James Lipton; MUSIC: Sol Berkowitz; DIRECTION: Paul E. Davis; CHOREOGRAPHY: Alex Palermo; SCENERY: Joseph Weishar; COSTUMES: Gene Barth; LIGHTING: Paul Saitta; MUSICAL DIRECTION: Liza Redfield; PRODUCERS: Paul E. Davis and Stanley G. Weiss in association with Winthrop Palmer

CAST—CHERRY DAVIS (Emily Adam), FRANCIS DUX (Pandroid), BETTY LOW (Zephyr in "Storm Ballet," Tutor, Obedian, Eminex), ALEX PALERMO (Pink Bus Driver, Coutouier, Sanitation Man, Coco), BOB (Robert) FITCH (Lightning in "Storm Ballet," Grey Bus Driver, Second Sanitation Man, Steroid), MAURICE EDWARDS (Salvage Officer, Teacher, Obedian, The Doctor), ROBERT SHANE (Zerex, The Boy), Susan Blythe (Tree in "Storm Ballet," Obedian, Helia), Sherry Lambert (Zephyr in "Storm Ballet," Obedian, Castle Gardener), Frank Mangan (Obedian, Drearian [Chuckles]), Angela McNeil (Winifrex, Bobo), Richard (Dick) Latessa (Obedian, Castle Gardener), Reni Cooper (Zephyr, Castle Gardener, Persona)

SOURCE—The short story "Rosemary and the Planet" by Winthrop Palmer.

The musical was presented in two acts.

ACT ONE—Overture (Orchestra), "Home" (Cherry Davis), "Storm Ballet" (Ensemble), "Oh, the Shame" (Francis Dux), "Name: Emily Adam" (Cherry Davis, Maurice Edwards), "All Aboard" (Bob Fitch, Cherry Davis, Alex Palermo), "Obedian March" (Ensemble), "It's Positively You" (Alex Palermo, Cherry Davis), "Once Upon a Time" (Cherry Davis), "Talk to Me" (Cherry Davis), "Love Is" (Cherry Davis, The Obedians), "Love Is" (reprise) (Cherry Davis, Robert Shane), Ultivac (Ensemble)

ACT TWO—Overture (Orchestra), "All Aboard" (reprise) (Cherry Davis, Francis Dux, Alex Palermo), "Fun" (Ensemble), "Dear Old Friend" (Cherry Davis), "According to Plotnik" (Maurice Edwards), "Dear Old Friend" (reprise) (Francis Dux), "I" (Ensemble), "Your Valentine" (Cherry Davis), "At the Ball" (Ensemble), "Dear Old Friend" (reprise) (Cherry Davis), "Home" (reprise) (Robert Shane), "Homeward" (Cherry Davis, Robert Shane)

NOTES—*Miss Emily Adam* told the story of a young girl ("charmingly" played by Cherry Davis, according to Brooks Atkinson in the *New York Times*) who rebels against her parents' rules (such as their insistence that she hang up her clothes). So when she meets an alien named Pandroid, she's more than happy to travel to his planet; but once there, she discovers that all emotion has been eliminated. In the second act, she travels to another alien land; here she finds its citizens dividing their time between having fun and consulting psychiatrists. But if the musical's final song "Homeward" is any indication, Emily (like Dorothy, another girl who wanted to leave home and travel somewhere far away) decides that home is where she belongs.

Atkinson was charmed by the first act, and found James Lipton's libretto "amusing" and Sol Berkowitz' score "full of pleasant melodies in a decorous style." But the second act was "too close to reality to seem ironic," and he felt that here the book was "labored." Further, while he acknowledged the score "maintains its civility and is perhaps increasingly inventive, the songs do not spring so spontaneously out of the story" in the second act.

Miss Emily Adam was Bob (a/k/a Robert and Robert E.) Fitch's third performance in an Off Broadway musical during the 1959-1960 season (see entries for *Lend an Ear* and *The Crystal Heart*). He was a tried-and-true Off Broadway and Broadway reliable, and during the course of his career created roles in some two-dozen Broadway and Off Broadway musicals, including *Tenderloin* (1960), *Sherry!* (1967), *Promises, Promises* (1968), and *Coco* (1969). In 1977, he got his big show-stopping moment in a Broadway blockbuster, creating the role of Rooster in the original production of *Annie*, and, along with Dorothy Loudon and Barbara Erwin, he slinked and strutted and belted out the joys of living on "Easy Street." In 2007, he appeared in the *Encores!* production of Stephen Sondheim's *Follies*, and Ben Brantley in the *New York Times* said he "loved the giddy, rubber-limbed dancing" of Fitch and Anne Rogers in "Bolero d'Amour" (Rogers had created the role of Polly in the original 1954 London production of *The Boy Friend*).

Another notable cast member in *Miss Emily Adam* was Richard (Dick) Latessa. He, too, remained active on Broadway and Off Broadway for decades, and like Fitch is always a welcome presence. In 2002, Latessa won a Tony Award for Best Featured Actor in a Musical for *Hairspray*. Lipton and Berkowitz' next musical opened on Broadway. Unfortunately, like *Miss Emily Adam*, *Nowhere to Go but Up* (1962) was a failure, lasting only nine performances. Lipton's second and last Broadway musical (with music by Laurence Rosenthal) was *Sherry!* (1967). Based on *The Man Who Came to Dinner* (1939), *Sherry!* played for a disappointing sixty-five performances, but its pleasant and tuneful score was preserved on a studio cast album which was released in 2004. Lipton was later the interviewer/host of the popular television series *Inside the Actors' Studio*.

1061 Miss Gulch Returns! "The Wicked Musical."

THEATRE: The Duplex; OPENING DATE: August 12, 1985; PERFORMANCES: 200 (estimated); TEXT: Fred Barton; LYRICS: Fred Barton; MUSIC: Fred Barton

CAST—Fred Barton (Almira Gulch); PRODUCER: Fred Bracken (?)

The revue was presented in one act.

MUSICAL NUMBERS—"Take Me, Please," "You're the Woman I Want to Be," "I'm a Bitch," "Born on a Bike" ("with all due respect to Leonard Gershe [who wrote "Born in a Trunk" for the 1954 film *A Star Is Born*]), "Pour Me a Man," "You Can't Have Everything" (from 1937 film *You Can't Have Everything*; lyric by Mack Gordon, music by Harry Revel), "Everyone Worth Taking" (Part I), "It's Not My Idea of a Gig," "Miss Gulch's 'Take Me, Please'," "Don't Touch Me," "I'm Your Bitch," "I Poured Me a Man," "Give My Best to the Blonde," "Everyone Worth Taking" (Part II), "Take Me, Please"/"Born on a Bike" (reprises/finale)

NOTES—Eighteen years before Stephen Schwartz' musical *Wicked* (2003) provided the back story of such *Wizard of Oz* characters as The Wicked Witch of the West, Glinda, and the Wizard himself, Steve Barton's Off Off Broadway revue *Miss Gulch Returns!* (subtitled "The Wicked Musical") told a similar back story, that of poor, misunderstood Almira Gulch, "the dog-snatching, bicycle-riding, basket-wielding, spiteful spinster-next-door who had it in for Dorothy's little Toto"; according to the cast album's liner notes (released by Gulch Mania Productions [LP # MGR-5757]), Miss Gulch was never given the opportunity to give *her* side of the story, and thus the revue set out to answer such burning questions as why she disliked little girls and their dogs, why she liked to ride bikes, and what happened to her after that iconic tornado.

In Margaret-Hamilton drag, Steve Barton gave us the inside scoop on Miss Gulch, including the fact that "I'm a Bitch" (her only song in the 1939 film *The Wizard of Oz*) was left on the cutting room floor in order to make room for a sappy little song about rainbows and lemon drops which was sung by Judy Garland, the film's alleged star. On the liner notes of her cast album, Miss Gulch noted that listeners would no doubt enjoy her other exciting recordings: *Miss Gulch in Love*; *Almira ... Always*; *Miss Gulch Sings the Larry Grossman Songbook*; *The Miss Gulch*

Christmas Album; and *Gulchy-Gulchy-Goo! (Songs for Children).*

Fred Barton occasionally returned to the role of Miss Gulch, including a special encore performance at the Actors' Playhouse which was given on January 25, 1993.

Barton was also the musical director for the original production of *Forbidden Broadway* (see entry).

1062 Miss Havisham's Fire. THEATRE: The New York State Theatre; OPENING DATE: March 23, 1979; PERFORMANCES: Unknown; LIBRETTO: John Olon-Scrymgeour; MUSIC: Dominick Argento; DIRECTION: H. Wesley Balk; CHOREOGRAPHY: Dorothy Frank Danner; SCENERY: John Conklin; COSTUMES: John Conklin; LIGHTING: Gilbert V. Hemsley, Jr.; MUSICAL DIRECTION: Julius Rudel; PRODUCER: The New York City Opera

CAST—Rita Shane (Aurelia Havisham [Recluse]), Gianna Rolandi (Aurelia Havisham [Young Woman]), Susanne Marcee (Estella Drummie [Young Woman]), Lorna Wallach (Estella Drummie [Young Girl]), Alan Titus (Phillip Pirrip [Pip as Young Man]), Robert Sapolsky (Phillip Pirrip [Pip as Young Boy]), Elaine Bonazzi and Martha Shell (Grace-Helen Broome [Nanny]), Richard Cross (Jagger), Ralph Bassett (Examiner), John Lankston (Bentley Drummie), Paul Ukena (Old Orlick [as Caretaker]), James Brewer (Old Orlick [as Young Man]), William Ledbetter (Pumplechook), Rosemarie Freni (Sarah Pocket), Martha Thigpen (Camilla Pocket), Kathleen Heglerski (Georgiana Pocket), Jonathan Green (Raymond Pocket), Reflections of Miss Havisham (Laura Harth, Judith-Mari Jarosz, Zola Long), Guests at Assembly Ball (Robert Brubaker, James Brewer, Lee Bellaver, Sally Lambert, Jean Rawn), Gwenlynn Little (First Maid), Eunice Hill (Second Maid)

SOURCE—The novel *Great Expectations* (first published in serial form during 1860 and 1861) by Charles Dickens.

The opera was presented in two acts.

NOTES—The production of *Miss Havisham's Fire* marked the seventeenth world premiere by the New York City Opera, and the program included the following note about the new work: "Being an Investigation Into the Unusual and Violent Death of Aurelia Havisham on the Seventeenth of April in the Year Eighteem Hundred and Sixty." The opera was based upon only those chapters in Charles Dickens' *Great Expectations* which dealt with Miss Havisham. Harold C. Schonberg in the *New York Times* noted that the past and the present intermingled as the investigation into Miss Havisham's death alternated with flashbacks which told her sad story. Schonberg said the concept was "interesting," but found Dominick Argento's score "featureless" and "neutral"; he felt the music lacked "a strong personality ... the opera rapidly dissolves into a mass of gray matter." He also noted the evening offered "what may be the longest mad scene in the literature [of opera], and it seems to go on forever."

In 1981, John-Olon Scrymgeour and Argento offered a chamber-opera version of the story. As *Miss Havisham's Wedding Night*, the work was a one-woman opera (with two silent roles) in which Miss Havisham (again sung by Rita Shane) recalls her wedding day and wonders how her life might have turned out if she had married. In this version, the concept of the investigation was eliminated as was the intermingling of characters from past and present.

1063 Miss Julie. THEATRE: New York City Center; OPENING DATE: November 4, 1965; PERFORMANCES: Unknown; LIBRETTO: Kenward Elmslie; MUSIC: Ned Rorem; DIRECTION: Nikos Psacharopoulos; SCENERY: Will Steven Armstrong; COSTUMES: Patton Campbell; MUSICAL DIRECTION: Robert Zeller; PRODUCER: The New York City Opera

CAST—Marguerite Willauer (Miss Julie), Donald Gramm (John), Elaine Bonazzi (Christine), Richard Krause (Niels), Betsy Hepburn (Wildcat Boy), Don Yule (Stableboy), Young Couple (Nico Castel and Joan Summers)

SOURCE—The 1888 play *Miss Julie* by August Strindberg.

The opera was presented in two acts.

ACT ONE—Introduction and Chorus, "Sleep on Seven Flowers," "Wind Around Me," "Miss Julie's Taken Leave," "Dance with Me, John," "John Is Your Sweetheart," "How Strange You Are," "Sometimes I Dream," "Christopher, Pass the Warm Wine," "Put That Down," "I've Never Seen the Back," "Be My Love," "Promise"

ACT TWO—Introduction, "Each Sin Brings," "We Have to Go Away," "If We Catch the Next Train," "You Gave Your Word of Honor," "Sweet Jesus What a Mess," "I'm Ready, I Have Money," "How Much Money," "Butcher, Why Didn't You Kill Me?," "Protect Me from Him," "In a Pretty New Dress," "It's a Sound Idea," "I'll Tell Stable," "A Carriage, You Hear It?," "Pretend You're Him," "You're Tired of Dancing"

NOTES—The world premiere of *Miss Julie*, Ned Rorem's operatic version of August Strindberg's classic play, was cooly received by the *New York Times*. Harold C. Schonberg noted the essentially two-character opera offered a "long duologue" in which the two main characters "spend an interminable amount of time discussing their psyches." The inward analysis inhibited much in the way of action and dramatic tension and led to a "polite and innocuous" evening. Further, Schonberg found Rorem's score "bland, lacking in profile or distinction" and his vocal lines ("a sort of parlando") "terribly boring."

As part of a 2003 "Roremania" festival honoring the composer on his eightieth birthday, *Miss Julie* was performed by the Curtis Opera Theatre in Philadelphia; the production was released on a 2-CD set by the invaluable Albany Records (# TROY-761/62); the song sequences listed above are taken from the recording. Thanks to Albany Records, perhaps this fascinating psychological chamber opera will become better known and will receive more productions by companies willing to explore neglected modern American operas.

Two sequences from the opera, "Sleep on Seven Flowers" and "I'm Ready, I Have Money," were heard in the 2005 revue *Lingoland* (see entry), the latter as "Memories"; both were recorded for that show's cast album.

1064 Miss Truth. THEATRE: Apollo Theatre; OPENING DATE: June 5, 1979; PERFORMANCES: 16; BOOK: Glory Van Scott; LYRICS: Glory Van Scott; MUSIC: Glory Van Scott; ADDITIONAL MUSIC by Louis Johnson and Thom Birdwell; DIRECTION: Louis Johnson; CHOREOGRAPHY: Louis Johnson; SCENERY: Louis Johnson; COSTUMES: Alice E. Carter and Judy Dearing; LIGHTING: Gary Harris; MUSICAL DIRECTION: Thom Bridwell; PRODUCER: Apollo Theatre

CAST—Glory Van Scott (Sojourner Truth), Christopher Pierre (Narrator), Phoebe Redmond (Cleaning Lady), Loretta Abbott (Dancer), Lloyd McNeill (Flutist), Syrena Irvin (Slave Dancer), Charles LaVont Williams (Slave Dancer, Charles, Butler), Pat Lundy (Pat), Herbert Lee Rawlings, Jr. (Slave), Loretta Devine (Loretta), Candice Graig (Little Girl)

Number of acts and song assignments unknown (musical probably presented in one act; songs are listed in performance order).

MUSICAL NUMBERS—"Disco," "Miss Truth," "Children Are for Loving," "I Sing the Rainbow," "(I'm a) Self-Made Woman," "My Religion (Makes Me Feel All Over)," "Do Your Thing, Miss Truth," "(It Is Your) Shame," "This Is a Very Special Day," "Freedom Diet," "Lift Every Voice and Sing"

NOTES—The title character of *Miss Truth* was Sojourner Truth (1797-1883), the nineteenth-century civil rights and women's rights pioneer. But with such song titles as "Disco" and "Do Your Thing, Miss Truth," it appears the Off Off Broadway musical took artistic license with Truth and her era in an attempt to make the story more "relevant."

The musical had been previously produced Off Off Broadway at the Nat Horne Theatre on September 15, 1978, for thirty-two performances.

An early (1971) version of the script was divided into four "sections," but the musical may have been intended for presentation in one act.

1065 Miss Waters, to You. THEATRE: AMAS Repertory Theatre; OPENING DATE: February 24, 1983; PERFORMANCES: 16; BOOK: Loften Mitchell; DIRECTION: Billie Allen; CHOREOGRAPHY: Keith Rozie; SCENERY: Tom Barnes; COSTUMES: Jeff Mazor; LIGHTING: Gregg Marriner; MUSICAL DIRECTION: Luther Henderson; PRODUCER: AMAS Repertory Theatre (Rosetta LeNoire, Founder and Artistic Director)

CAST—Jeff Bates (Duke Ellington, Walt Maxton), Donna Brown (Pearl Wright), Keith David (Earl Dancer, Narrator), Robin Dunn (Young Lady), Douglas Frazier (Buddy, Bartender), Yolanda Graves (Maggie Hill), Lucille Harley (Momweez), Luther Henderson (Fletcher Henderson), Mary Louise (Ethel Waters), Ronald Mann (Milton Starr, Irving Berlin), Devron Minion (Nugent, Man, Young Man), Denise Morgan (Bessie Smith, Young Woman), Stanley Ramsey (Sporty-O-Tee, Eddie Matthews), Melodee Savage (Jo Hill), Angela Sprouse (Sally Anderson), Leon Summers, Jr. (Cab Calloway, Braxton), Carole Sylvan (Vi, Woman), Ed Taylor (Joe, Bob White, Professor), Lee Winston (Charles Bailey, Jr., Gumm)

The action occurs in various cities in the life of Ethel Waters from 1917 to 1960.

The musical was presented in two acts.

NOTES—With perhaps the exception of some new music by Luther Henderson, the score for the Off Off Broadway musical *Miss Waters, to You* was comprised of songs associated with Ethel Waters (1896-1977) during her long and illustrious career. The musical was the second one about Ethel Waters which was produced by AMAS. See entry for *Sparrow in Flight* (1978), which includes information about Waters' career. Further, Waters was the subject of *Sweet Mama Stringbean*, a play with music which opened Off Off Broadway in 2008.

1066 Mr. Montage. "A New Musical-Comedy-Revue." THEATRE: West Side Theatre; OPENING DATE: 1958; PERFORMANCES: Unknown; SKETCHES: Dick DeBartol; see song list for additional credits; LYRICS AND MUSIC: See song list for credits; DIRECTION: Ray McDonough; CHOREOGRAPHY: Marion Hunter and Rob Speller (see song list for specific credits); SCENERY: John H. Bos; COSTUMES: Joe Codori; LIGHTING: John H. Bos; MUSICAL DIRECTION: Ron Brown; PRODUCERS: Dick DeBartol; Susan McDonald, Associate Producer

CAST—Dick DeBartol, Susan McDonald, Bill Wheless, Lynn Hodgkiss, Jesse Oliver, Pat Pearson, Eugene Heller, Mimi Bowen-Roberts, Bill Farley, Roberta Marshall, Rob Speller, Paulette Attie, Martin Azarow, Marion Hunter, Dennis McLaughlin, Ken Thomas, Ann Carter, Joan Feldman, Paul Moran, Jim Harrison, Susan Menden

The revue was presented in two acts.

ACT ONE—"We, We, We" (lyric by Peter Beagle, music by Ron Brown; choreography by Marion Hunter) (Company), "Once Is Enough" (lyric by Ernie Chambers, music by George Linsenmann;

choreography by Marion Hunter) (Joan Feldman, with Ken Thomas, Jesse Oliver, Rob Speller, Jim Harrison), "Birthstone of the Death Squad" (sketch by Martin Azarow) (Eugene Heller, Mimi Bowen-Roberts, Susan McDonald, Martin Azarow, Paul Moran, Bill Farley), "You Said So Yourself" (lyric by Ernie Chambers, music by George Linsenmann; choreography by Rob Speller) (Bill Wheless, Paulette Attie, Singers and Dancers), "Elip-Parcs" (sketch by Dick DeBartol; choreography by Rob Speller) (Dick DeBartol, Martin Azarow, Susan McDonald, Bill Farley, Joan Feldman, Eugene Heller), "When You Talk to a Lady Like Me" (sketch by Dick DeBartol) (Mimi Bowen-Roberts), "Stage Manager's Song" (lyric by Peter Beagle, music by Ron Brown) (Bill Wheless, Singers and Dancers), "The Method" (sketch by Al DuMais) (Joan Feldman, Eugene Heller, Bill Farley, Martin Azarow), "Where Were You" (lyric by Peter Beagle, music by Ron Brown; choreography by Marion Hunter) (Susan McDonald, Dennis McLaughlin, Roberta Marshall), "Song Writer's Awards" (sketch by Dick DeBartol) (Dick DeBartol, MC), a) "My Only Love" (lyric by Peter Beagle, music by Ron Brown) (Bill Wheless, Paul Moran, Jesse Oliver, Dennis McLaughlin, Bill Farley), b) "Until" (lyricist and composer not credited in program) (Paulette Attie), c) "Zut Alors" (lyric and music by Jim Kohn; choreography by Rob Speller) (Bill Wheless, Roberta Marshall, Ann Carter), "Happy Lament" (sketch by Dick DeBartol) (Mimi Bowen-Roberts), "Man Alone Blues" (lyric by Peter Beagle, music by Ron Brown; choreography by Marion Hunter) (Bill Wheless, Roberta Marshall, Ken Thomas, Ann Carter, Jim Harrison, Rob Speller, Jesse Oliver, Martin Azarow, Dancers)

ACT TWO—"Empire City Music Hall" (lyric by Dick DeBartol, music by Ron Brown; choreography by Rob Speller) (Company), "The Natives Are Restless" (lyric by Peter Beagle, music by Ron Brown) (Bill Wheless, Dennis McLaughlin), "Tax Time, USA" (lyric by Dick DeBartol, music by Ron Brown) (Bill Farley, Dick DeBartol, Susan McDonald, Mimi Bowen-Roberts, Eugene Heller, Paulette Attie, Singers and Dancers), "The Urge to Merge" (lyricist and composer not credited in program; choreography by Rob Speller) (Pat Pearson, Ken Thomas, Rob Speller), "Gunze, Gunze, Gunze" (sketch by John Owen) (Mimi Bowen-Roberts, Ann Carter, Paul Moran, Martin Azarow, Eugene Heller, Rob Speller), "I'd Do It All Over" (lyric by Peter Beagle, music by Ron Brown) (Lynn Hodgkiss, Bill Farley), "Jet Ace" (sketch by Dick DeBartol) (Dennis McLaughlin, Martin Azarow, Lynn Hodgkiss, Dick DeBartol, Eugene Heller), "Sing a Song of Octopi" (lyric by Ernie Chambers, music by George Linsenmann) (Jesse Oliver), "One Night of Loneliness" (sketch by Dick DeBartol) (Susan McDonald), "The Dancing Bandannas" (lyric by Peter Beagle, music by Ron Brown; choreography by Marion Hunter) (Ken Thomas, Ann Carter, Rob Speller, Roberta Marshall, Jesse Oliver, Jim Harrison), "PTA" (sketch by Dick DeBartol) (Joan Feldman, Martin Azarow, Roberta Marshall, Ann Carter, Lynn Hodgkiss, Bill Farley, Susan McDonald, Pat Pearson, Mimi Bowen-Roberts), "In the Mist of the Night" (lyric and music by Shirley Menden; choreography by Marion Hunter) (Shirley Menden, Roberta Marshall, Jesse Oliver, Ann Carter, Jim Harrison), "Tran-Quil" (sketch by Dick DeBartol) (Dick DeBartol), "Assault Me" (lyric by Peter Beagle, music by Ron Brown) (Joan Feldman), "New York": a) Opening (Company), b) "Subway" (choreography by Marion Hunter), c) "Manhattan Is My Favorite Rendezvous" (lyric by Peter Beagle, music by Ron Brown) (Dennis McLaughlin), d) "Take Me to Central Park" (Pat Pearson, Joan Feldman, Susan McDonald, Mimi Bowen-Roberts, Jesse Oliver, Jim Harrison, Paul Moran, Ken Thomas, Bill Farley, Paulette Attie), e) "Chinese Cha, Cha, Cha" (lyric and music by Harold Cummings) (Lynn Hodgkiss, Roberta Marshall, Ann Carter), f) "Manhattan Is My Favorite Rendezvous" (reprise) (Company)

In the program, the final number in the production was listed as "No Finale."

NOTES—A note in the program for the obscure revue *Mr. Montage* credited Peter Beagle for the lyrics and Ron Brown for the music of "Hang Up Your Children"; but the number wasn't in the program's song list.

1067 Mr. President. THEATRE: Douglas Fairbanks Theatre; OPENING DATE: August 2, 2001; PERFORMANCES: Unknown; NEW BOOK: Gerard Alessandrini; NEW LYRICS: Gerard Alessandrini; MUSIC: Irving Berlin; DIRECTION: John Znidarsic and Gerard Alessandrini; CHOREOGRAPHY: John Znidarsic and Gerard Alessandrini; SCENERY: *Forbidden Broadway* set design by Bradley Kaye; set pieces for *Mr. President* designed by Bryan Johnson; COSTUMES: Alvin Colt; Joseph McFate, Associate Costume Design; LIGHTING: Marc Janowitz; MUSICAL DIRECTION: Paul Katz; PRODUCERS: Forbidden Broadway; John Freedson and Harriet Yellin

CAST—Jono Mainelli (Irving Berlin), Clif Thorne (George Shrub, Jr.), Michael West (Al Bore, Will Fenton), Amanda Naughton (Flora Shrub), Whitney Allen (Chillary Fenton), Eric Jordan Young (Coalhouse Power), Stuart Zagnit (Dick Brainy, Barbara Shrub); Various media and political personalities played by the entire company

The musical was presented in two acts.

NOTES—The original *Mr. President* opened on Broadway on October 20, 1962, at the St. James Theatre, and ran for 265 performances. Its lyrics and music were by Irving Berlin, and the book by Howard Lindsay and Russel Crouse. The musical opened in New York with reportedly the highest advance sale in Broadway history up to that time and seemed poised to become a long-running hit. But the reviews were poor, and many felt the show was too tame for its own good. Sadly, the musical was Irving Berlin's last new Broadway show (but for the 1966 revival of *Annie Get Your Gun* he came up with the showstopper "An Old-Fashioned Wedding").

Gerard Alessandrini took his *Forbidden Broadway*-approach to the musical, updating most of Irving Berlin's songs with new lyrics and adding all-new characters, such as George Schrub, Jr., Chillary Clinton, Al Bore, and Dick Brainy. According to the program, the new *Mr. President* "was conceived, rewritten, and politically corrected" by Alessandrini.

Donald Lyons in the *New York Post* felt that Berlin "must be turning in his grave — not at the irreverence, but at the tastelessness of it all." Ben Brantley in the *New York Times* noted the production lacked freshness, and "despite the liveliness of the ever-game cast," "the dust of déjà vu" permeated the evening. Brantley mentioned that Alessandrini hoped *Mr. President* would be the first in a series of *Gongcores* (a la the *Encores!* presentations) devoted to revisiting flop musicals. However, as of this writing, *Mr. President* remains the first and the last in the *Gongcores* series.

The musical used Irving Berlin songs (some not from the original production of *Mr. President*), a few with their original lyrics, others with mostly new lyrics by Alessandrini (in the style of his *Forbidden Broadway* series [see entry]).

The following songs from the original production were for the most part sung with their original lyrics: "Empty Pockets Filled with Love," "I'm Gonna Get Him," "Let's Go Back to the Waltz," "Is He the Only Man in the World?," "Don't Be Afraid of Romance," and "This Is a Great Country." Also used (with a minimum of topical updates) were the following non-*Mr. President* songs: "God Bless America," "Let's Face the Music and Dance" (from 1936 film *Follow the Fleet*), "Now It Can Be Told" (1938 film *Alexander's Ragtime Band*), and "Be Careful, It's My Heart" (1942 film *Holiday Inn*).

The following songs from the original 1962 production were used with mostly new lyrics by Alessandrini: "Mr. President" ("Opening," a/k/a "Not the Kennedys"; this song may have been performed in both its original version and in its revised version by Alessandrini), "The Secret Service Makes Me Nervous," "It Gets Lonely in the White House," "In Our Hide-Away," "The First Lady," and "The Washington Twist." Other non-*Mr. President* songs used which had mostly new lyrics were "Only for Republicans/Only for New Democrats" (based on "Only for Americans" from *Miss Liberty* [1949]), "Shakin' the Chads Away" (based on "Shaking the Blues Away" from *Ziegfeld Follies of 1927*), "This Is My Army" (based on "This Is the Army, Mr. Jones" from *This Is the Army* [1942]), and "It's All Showbiz, Kid" (original source unknown).

The musical was presented in repertory with *Forbidden Broadway*.

Incidentally, some of the music for "Is He the Only Man in the World?" had originally been used in "Where Is the Song of Songs for Me?" from the 1928 film *Lady of the Pavements*.

The original 1962 production of *Mr. President* was recorded by Columbia Records (LP # KOS-2270; the CD was issued by Sony Broadway Records [# SK-48212]).

1068 misUnderstanding Mammy: The Hattie McDaniel Story. THEATRE: Theatre 5; OPENING DATE: February 7, 2007; PERFORMANCES: 16; PLAY: Joan Ross Sorkin; DIRECTION: David Glenn Armstrong; Daniel Haley, Associate Director; SCENERY: Robert Monaco; COSTUMES: Amy Elizabeth Bravo; LIGHTING: Jenny Granrud; MUSICAL DIRECTION: Lance Horne; PRODUCER: Emerging Artists Theatre

CAST—Capathia Jenkins (Hattie McDaniel)

The action of the play occurs at the Motion Picture Country Home and Hospital in Woodlands Hills, California, in 1952, and in the mind and memory of Hattie McDaniel (1895-1952).

NOTES—*misUnderstanding Mammy: The Hattie McDaniel Story*, an Off Off Broadway play with music about the iconic actress Hattie McDaniel, depicted her last days in a hospital before she succumbed to cancer. She looks back on her Hollywood career (she was the first Black performer to win an Academy Award, for her performance as Mammy in the 1939 film *Gone with the Wind*), including the overwhelming criticism she endured when she was accused of accepting film roles which were supposedly degrading to her and to her race. The play included sequences from her career in nightclubs, prior to her Hollywood fame. Incidentally, although McDaniel's film roles were mostly in dramas and comedies, she appeared in a major Hollywood musical, *Thank Your Lucky Stars* (1943), in which she sang "Ice Cold Katy" (lyric by Frank Loesser, music by Arthur Schwartz). McDaniel was also the subject of another Off Off Broadway musical (*Hattie... What I Need You to Know!* [2008]).

1069 Mixed Doubles. THEATRE: Upstairs at the Downstairs; OPENING DATE: October 19, 1966; PERFORMANCES: 428; SKETCHES: John Boni, Marshall Brickman, Sid Davis, Bill Kaufman, and Paul Koreto; LYRICS: Gene Bissell, David Finkle, Tony Geiss, Michael McWhinney, John Meyer, June Reizner, James Rusk, Drey Shepard, Franklin Underwood, and Rod Warren; MUSIC: Johann Sebastian Bach, Gene Bissell, Michael Cohen, Ed Kresley, Steven Lawrence, Jerry Powell, June Reizner, Richard Robinson, James Rusk, Franklin Underwood, Rod Warren, and Bill Weeden; DIRECTION: Robert Audy; production supervised by Rod Warren; CHOREOGRAPHY: Robert Audy; LIGHTING: Richard Mensoff;

Musical Direction: Michael Cohen; Producer: Upstairs at the Downstairs

Cast—Judy Graubart, Madeline Kahn, Larry Moss, Robert Rovin, Janie Sell, Gary Sneed

The revue was presented in two acts.

Act One—"Mixed Doubles" (lyric by Rod Warren, music by Johann Sebastian Bach) (Company), "New York Is a Festival of Fun" (lyric and music by Gene Bissell) (Madeline Kahn, Janie Sell, Robert Rovin, Gary Sneed), "The Honeymooners" (sketch by Marshall Brickman) (Judy Graubart, Larry Moss) "Questions" (lyric by Drey Shepard, music by Ed Kresley) (Madeline Kahn, Robert Rovin, Gary Sneed) "Mixed Marriages" (lyric by David Finkle, music by Bill Weeden) (Janie Sell, Larry Moss) "Man with a Problem" (sketch by John Boni) (Judy Graubart, Robert Rovin) "Walter Kerr" (lyric by Michael McWhinney and Rod Warren, music by Rod Warren) (Gary Sneed), "Sartor Sartoris" (lyric and music by Franklin Underwood) (Larry Moss, Robert Rovin) "Fashion Show" (sketch by Sid Davis) (Madeline Kahn, Judy Graubart, Gary Sneed) "Bon Voyeur" (lyric and music by James Rusk) (Larry Moss) "Ronald Reagan" (lyric by Drey Shepard, music by Ed Kresley) (Judy Graubart, Madeline Kahn, Janie Sell), "More Questions" (reprise) (Judy Graubart, Madeline Kahn, Larry Moss, Robert Rovin), "Physical Fitness" (lyric and music by James Rusk) (Janie Sell) "Spoleto" (lyric by Michael McWhinney, music by Jerry Powell) (Company)

Act Two—"And a Messenger Appeared" (lyric and music by Gene Bissell) (Madeline Kahn, Company), "Brittania Rules" (lyric by Rod Warren, music by Jerry Powell) (Judy Graubart) "Brief Encounter" (sketch by Bill Kaufman and Paul Koreto) (Madeline Kahn, Janie Sell, Robert Rovin, Gary Sneed) "Friendly, Liberal Neighborhood" (lyric and music by June Reizner) (Larry Moss, Robert Rovin, Gary Sneed) "Still More Questions" (reprise) (Judy Graubart, Madeline Kahn, Larry Moss, Gary Sneed) "Holden and Phoebe" (lyric by Michael McWhinney, music by Michael Cohen) (Judy Graubart, Robert Rovin), "In Old Chicago" (a/k/a "Das Chicago Song") (lyric by Tony Geiss, music by Michael Cohen) (Madeline Kahn) "Civilian Review Board" (sketch by Michael McWhinney) (Janie Sell, Gary Sneed) "Bobby the K" (lyric by Michael McWhinney, music by Richard Robinson) (Robert Rovin) "And a Few More Questions" (reprise) (Performed by "most of the company"), "Best Wishes" (lyric by John Meyer, music by Steven Lawrence) (Company)

Notes—*Mixed Doubles* was the seventh in Rod Warren's string of successful revues, and it included the obligatory New York City song (here, "New York Is a Festival of Fun"), the usual political numbers ("Ronald Reagan," "Bobby the K," "Friendly, Liberal Neighborhood," "Mixed Marriages"), as well as the spoofs of modern mores and foibles ("Bon Voyeur," "Fashion Show"). There was even a song about critic Walter Kerr.

Madeline Kahn introduced "In Old Chicago" (a/k/a "Das Chicago Song"), a spoof of Bertolt Brecht and Kurt Weill. She later sang the number in *New Faces of 1968*, and it can be heard on both the cast albums of *Mixed Doubles* (a 2-LP set released by Upstairs at the Downstairs Records [# UD-37W56] which also includes songs from *Below the Belt* [1966; see entry]) and *New Faces of 1968* (Warner Brothers Records LP # 2551).

The song "Spoleto" had earlier been heard in the 1963 revue *New York Coloring Book* (see entry).

The Playoffs of Mixed Doubles (see entry) was for all purposes a second edition of *Mixed Doubles*, and included five numbers from the earlier revue ("New York Is a Festival of Fun," "Mixed Marriages," "Fashion Show," "And a Messenger Appeared," and "Holden and Phoebe").

For a complete list of Rod Warren's revues, see entry for *...And in This Corner*; also see Appendix R.

1070 Mo' Tea, Miss Ann? Theatre: AMAS Repertory Theatre; Opening Date: February 18, 1981; Performances: 15; Book: Bebe Coker; Lyrics: Bebe Coker; Music: Leander Morris; Direction: Denny Shearer; Choreography: Denny Shearer; Scenery: Lisa Cameron; Costumes: Vickie McLaughlin; Lighting: Mark Diquinzio; Musical Direction: Ernie Scott; Producer: AMAS Repertory Theatre (Rosetta LeNoire, Founder and Artistic Director)

Cast—Jimmy Almistad, Suzanne Buffington, Jay Aubrey Jones, Joy Kelly, Boncellia Lewis, Charles Muckle, Herb Quebec, Zoe Walker, Juanita Walsh, Carmiletta Wiggins, Alonzo G. Reid, Sundy Leigh Leake

Notes—*Mo' Tea, Miss Ann?* was an Off Off Broadway musical.

1071 Moby Dick. Theatre: Paul Mazur Theatre/The York Theatre Company; Opening Date: February 2, 1986; Performances: 16; Libretto: Mark St. Germain; Music: Doug Katsaros; Direction: Thomas Gardner; Scenery: James Morgan; Costumes: Sheila Kohoe; Lighting: Mary Jo Dondlinger; Musical Direction: Doug Katsaros; Producers: The York Theatre Company (Janet Hayes Walker, Producing Director; Molly Pickering Grose, Managing Director) in association with It's the Gling, Inc.

Cast—Richard Bowne (Boomer, Bildad, Mapple), Steven Blanchard (Captain of *Jeroboam*, Bunger, Sailor), Victor Cook (Pip), Ed Dixon (Captain Ahab), Michael Ingram (Stubb), Dennis Parlato (Starbuck), Buddy Rudolph (Ishmael), Gordon Stanley (Peleg, Captain of *Rachael*), John Timmons (Elijah, Carpenter, Sailor), Louis Tucker (Queequeg)

Source—The 1851 novel *Moby-Dick; or, The Whale* by Herman Melville.

Act One—"The Sea" (Company), "The Sermon" (Richard Bowne, Company), "The Sea" (reprise) (Buddy Rudolph), "What Makes Ye Go a Whaling?" (Gordon Stanley, Buddy Rudolph, Richard Bowne), "Morning to Ye" (John Timmons, Buddy Rudolph), "Ahab" (Buddy Rudolph, Gordon Stanley), "Aft Ye"/"Setting Sail" (Dennis Parlato, Richard Bowne, Gordon Stanley, John Timmons, Crew), "The Doubloon" (Ed Dixon, Dennis Parlato, Company), "Eight Bells" (Victor Cook, Sailors), "Stand by Me" (Ed Dixon, Dennis Parlato), "Stubb's Song" (Ed Dixon, Michael Ingram), "The Whiteness" (Buddy Rudolph, Dennis Parlato, Michael Ingram), "Stubb's Song" (reprise) (Dennis Parlato, Michael Ingram), "Every Morning" (Dennis Parlato), "The *Jeroboam*" (Ed Dixon, Crew, Steven Blanchard, performer unknown), "The Will" (Louis Tucker, Buddy Rudolph), "The First Hunt" (Company), "Pip's Song" (Victor Cook)

Act Two—"The Doubloom" (reprise)/"The White Whale" (Company), "Thou Venerable Head" (Ed Dixon), "Boomer and Bunger" (Ed Dixon, Richard Bowne, Steven Blanchard, Buddy Rudolph), "Queequeg Dying" (Buddy Rudolph, Ed Dixon, Louis Tucker, Michael Ingram, Dennis Parlato), "Ahab's Cabin" (Ed Dixon, Dennis Parlato), "Ahab and the Carpenter" (Ed Dixon, John Timmons), "My Boy" (Gordon Stanley, Ed Dixon, Louis Tucker, Buddy Rudolph, Michael Ingram), "I Will Stay with You" (Ed Dixon, Victor Cook), "Mild, Mild Day" (Dennis Parlato, Ed Dixon, Gordon Stanley), "The Final Chase" (Company), Epilogue (Buddy Rudolph)

Notes—The sung-through musical *Moby Dick* was, like *Pequod/The Next Voyage* (see entry), one of many lyric adaptations of Herman Melville's works (for more information, see entry for *Bartleby*). Mel Gussow in the *New York Times* felt the adaptation was too small-scaled, and suggested a full-fledged operatic version or a *Nicholas Nickleby*-styled treatment would serve the material better. He felt much of the score had vigor, and singled out "I Will Stay with You" (a revival number which "rocks the deck of the Pequod"), "The Sermon" (a "rousing hymn"), "Every Morning" (an "affecting" ballad), a whaler's chorus, and several soliloquies for Ahab.

A dramatic adaptation of *Moby Dick* by Orson Welles was produced in London in 1955 for twenty-five performances (with Welles) and on Broadway in 1962 for thirteen (with Rod Steiger).

1072 Mod Donna. "A Space-Age Musical Soap." Theatre: The Public Theatre; Opening Date: April 24, 1970; Performances: 56; Book: Myrna Lamb; Lyrics: Myrna Lamb; Music: Susan Hulsman Bingham; Direction: Joseph Papp; Choreography: Ze-eva Cohen; Costumes: Milo Morrow; Lighting: Martin Aronstein; Musical Direction: Liza Redfield; Dorothea Freitag, conductor; Producer: The New York Shakespeare Festival

Cast—April Shawhan (Donna), Sharon Laughlin (Chris), Larry Bryggman (Jeff), Peter Haig (Charlie); Chorus of Women: Ellen Barber, Jani Brenn, Katharine Dunfee, June Gable, Deloris Gaskins, Liz Gorrill, Zora Margolis, Maureen Mooney, Madge Sinclair

The musical was presented in two acts.

Act One—Overture: "Trapped," "Earthworms" (Chorus of Women), "The Incorporation" (Sharon Laughlin, Larry Bryggman), "Invitation" (April Shawhan, Chorus), "All the Way Down" (Chorus), "The Deal" (Sharon Laughlin, Larry Bryggman, April Shawhan, Chorus), "Liberia" (Chorus), "The Morning After" (Sharon Laughlin, Larry Bryggman, April Shawhan), "Charlie's Plaint" (Peter Haig, Chorus), "Creon" (Chorus), "The Worker and the Shirker" (April Shawhan, Peter Haig), "Food Is Love" (Chorus), "First Act Crisis" (Sharon Laughlin, April Shawhan)

Act Two—Overture: "Astrociggy," "Second Act Beginning" (April Shawhan, Sharon Laughlin, Larry Bryggman, Chorus), "Hollow" (Sharon Laughlin, April Shawhan, Chorus), "Seduction Second Degree" (Sharon Laughlin, Larry Bryggman), "Panassociative" (Sharon Laughlin, Chorus), "Earth Dance" (Chorus), "Trinity" (April Shawhan, Sharon Laughlin, Chorus), "Trapped" (reprise) (April Shawhan, Chorus), "Astrociggy" (reprise) (April Shawhan, Chorus), "Special Bulletin" (April Shawhan, Sharon Laughlin), "Take a Knife" (Sharon Laughlin), "The Second Honeymoon" (April Shawhan, Larry Bryggman), "Jeff's Plaints" (Larry Bryggman, Chorus), "Incantation" (Chorus), "Beautiful Man" (Chorus), "Sacrifice" (April Shawhan, Sharon Laughlin, Larry Bryggman, Peter Haig), "Now!" (Chorus), "Beautiful Man" (reprise) (Chorus), "We Are the Whores (Liberation Song)" (Chorus)

Notes—*Mod Donna* was the third protest musical of the Public Theatre's 1969-1970 season (see entries for *Stomp* and *Sambo*), and was the first women's liberation musical (Off Broadway would offer a few such book musicals and revues over the next few seasons; in fact, Black, gay, and feminist musicals were a cottage industry of sorts throughout the 1970s; see appendices for lists of musicals in these categories). *Mod Donna* saw women as victims, and despite its politically correct viewpoint, it didn't attract enough theatergoers for more than a seven-week run. Clive Barnes in the *New York Times* found the musical "a very mixed evening," but nonetheless seemed to generally admire the work. He described the musical as "based on life" but not "particularly lifelike" in its story of a rich couple (Chris and Jeff) who become involved with a young woman (Donna, played by April Shawhan) who subsequently becomes pregnant by Jeff. When Donna refuses Chris and Jeff's proposal to adopt her baby, they show Donna's husband Charlie pictures of her in bed with Jeff, and so Charlie murders Donna. Barnes indicated the musical depicted the "arrogance" of males and said the two male characters were depicted as "tyrannical fools." The show was not recorded, but the script was published in a monthly political magazine as well as in a collection of Myrna Lamb's plays (*The Mod Donna and Scyklon Z/Plays of Women's Liberation*). In the *Introduction* to the collection, Lamb seems to say that the point of women's liberation is to free women from the institution of marriage: marriage is "death," marriage is "punishment," marriage is "approval shit," marriage is what is wrong with the world ("fuck marriage," she concludes). Actually, her catalogue of the wrongs perpetrated against women comes across as a male chauvinist's parody of feminist writing.

1073 Momix. THEATRE: City Center; OPENING DATE: October 28, 1997; PERFORMANCES: 8; MATERIAL: Created by the Momix Company (Moses Pendleton, Artistic Director); DIRECTION: Bruce Goldstein; LIGHTING: Howell Binkley; PRODUCERS: ICM Artists, Inc., and City Center

CAST—Tim Acito, Erin Elliott, Claire Kaplan, P.I. Keohavong, Suzanne Lampl, Yasmine Lee, Cynthia Quinn, Brian Simerson

The revue was presented in two acts.

ACT ONE—"Jonas et Latude" (choreography by Sandy Chase, Brian Sanders, and Moses Pendleton; prop design by Cynthia Quinn; costumes by Kitty Daly; music by Vivaldi) (Tim Acito, Brian Simerson), "The Wind-Up" (choreography by Moses Pendleton; music ["Spirit of the Forest"] by Martin Cradick) (Cynthia Quinn), "TUU" (choreography by Tim Acito, Solveig Olsen, and Moses Pendleton; costumes by Cynthia Quinn; music ["TUU"] by TUU) (Tim Acito, Suzanne Lampl), "Spawning" (choreography by Moses Pendleton, Lisa Giobbi, Dianne Howarth, and Cynthia Quinn; music ["Mercy Street"] by Peter Gabriel) (Suzanne Lampl, Yasmine Lee, Cynthia Quinn), "Underwater Study #5" (created by Brian Sanders; music by Art of Noise) (Tim Acito), "White Widow" (choreography by Moses Pendleton and Cynthia Quinn; costume by Cynthia Quinn; song, "The World Spins," lyric by David Lynch, music by Angelo Badalerenti) (Cynthia Quinn), "Skiva" (choreography by Moses Pendleton and Company; music by King Sunny Ade and His African Beats) (Tim Acito, Yasmine Lee)

ACT TWO—"Table Talk" (choreography by Moses Pendleton and Kaul Baumann; music, "Safe from Harm" by R. Del Naja, A. Vowles, and G. Marshall) (Tim Acito), "Orbit" (choreography by Erin Elliott and Moses Pendleton; music from Feed Your Head, compiled by Michael Dog) (Erin Elliott), "Sputnik (Fellow Traveler)" (directed by Moses Pendleton, assisted by Tim Acito, Ezra Caldwell, Lorin Campolattaro, Claire Kaplan, P.I. Keohavong, Suzanne Lampl, Yasmine Lee, Cynthia Quinn, Brian Sanders, and Brian Simerson; music ["Diamante"] by Brenda Perry and Lisa Gerard) (Tim Acito, Claire Kaplan, P.I. Keohavong, Suzanne Lampl, Yasmine Lee, Cynthia Quinn, Brian Simerson), "E.C." (choreography by Moses Pendleton and Company; music by Laraaji, Vena, and Moses Pendleton) (Company)

NOTES—*Momix* was a performance piece of dance, movement, and illusion created by the Momix Company. The group had toured extensively in the United States and throughout the world; for the current production, the number "Sputnik (Fellow Traveler)" was a world premiere. According to Anna Kisselgoff in the *New York Times*, Moses Pendleton (Momix's artistic director and co-founder of the Pilobolus Dance Theatre) created a "gloriously wacky show" of choreography "for those who hate choreography," and the evening brought "Christmas in October."

1074 Moms. THEATRE: Astor Place Theatre; OPENING DATE: August 4, 1987; PERFORMANCES: 152; BOOK: Ben Caldwell; LYRICS: Grenoldo Frazier; MUSIC: Grenoldo Frazier; DIRECTION: Walter Dallas; SCENERY: Rosario Provenza; COSTUMES: Judy Dearing; LIGHTING: Robert Wierzel; PRODUCERS: The Moms Company in association with Paul B. Berkowsky; James Pulliam, Associate Producer

CAST—Grenoldo Frazier (Luther, Pianist, Others), Carol Dennis (Anna Mae, Dresser, Sister), Clarice Taylor (Jackie "Moms" Mabley)

The action occurs in 1970, "before and after."

The musical was presented in two acts.

NOTES—The musical *Moms* was a tribute to comedienne Jackie "Moms" Mabley (1894-1975); Clarice Taylor played the title role; the lyrics and music were by Grenoldo Frazier, and the book was by Ben Caldwell. Earlier in the year, on February 4, another work about the subject (also called *Moms* and also starring Clarice Taylor) had opened Off Off Broadway at the Hudson Guild Theatre for twenty-eight performances; the play was written by Alice Childress and the lyrics and music were by Childress and her husband Nathan Woodard. Further, both productions shared the same director as well as the same scenic, costume, and lighting designers. Moreover, besides Taylor, Grenoldo Frazier had also appeared in the earlier production. Upon the opening of the second *Moms*, Mel Gussow in the *New York Times* reported an authorship dispute, with Childress alleging the second play was "essentially" hers; on the other hand, Taylor stated the second play (with a book by Ben Caldwell) was not based on the earlier play. Gussow noted a "complicating factor" in the matter was that much of the material for both plays was derived from Mabley herself and not from Taylor and the two playwrights. It's unclear how the dispute was resolved, but the second musical continued its run and went on to play for about five months.

On March 2, 2005, Taylor revisited "Moms" Mabley in her Off Off Broadway play *Jackie "Moms" Mabley and Her Ladies*, which opened at the Producers Club.

1075 Mona. THEATRE: Metropolitan Opera House; OPENING DATE: March 14, 1912; PERFORMANCES: 4; LIBRETTO: Brian Hooker; MUSIC: H.W. Parker; DIRECTION: Loomis Taylor; SCENERY: Paul Paquereau; MUSICAL DIRECTION: Alfred Hertz; PRODUCER: The Metropolitan Opera

CAST—Louise Homer (Mona), Rita Fornia (Enya), Herbert Witherspoon (Arth), William Hinshaw (Gloom), Albert Reiss (Nial), Lambert Murphy (Caradoc), Putnam Griswold (The Roman Governor of Britain), Riccardo Martin (Quintus), Basil Ruysdael (Old Man)

The opera was presented in three acts.

NOTES—*Mona* is virtually forgotten today, but it holds an important place in the history of American opera because it was the first such opera to have its world premiere at the Met (as of this writing, twenty-two American operas have had their world premieres with the company). Two years earlier, *The Pipe of Desire* (see entry) had been presented by the Met, and as such was not only the first American opera to be seen there, it was also the company's first opera to be performed in English. But *The Pipe of Desire* wasn't a world premiere; it had been performed in Boston in 1906.

Mona told the story of a young woman who seems destined by the gods to deliver the British people from Roman rule. But she learns too late that had she followed her heart and married the man she loved (who is half-British and half-Roman), she would have fulfilled her destiny.

Reviewing the world premiere of the opera, the unsigned reviewer in the *New York Times* wrote that Brian Hooker's libretto was "fine," "beautiful," and "the work of a poet," but noted it wasn't particularly dramatic. Further, the *Times*' reviewer felt H.W. Parker's music was deemed wanting; despite Parker's "remarkable musicianship," the reviewer found the score "bleak and austere," offering a "stern and unbending mood" which, like the libretto, wasn't dramatic. However, the reviewer noted that Parker used a musical device which "so far as we know, is his own": that is, Parker used different musical keys for each character, thus giving each one his or her own special musical identity.

1076 Money. "A Musical Play for Cabaret." THEATRE: Upstairs at the Downstairs; OPENING DATE: July 9, 1963; PERFORMANCES: 214; BOOK: David Axelrod and Tom Whedon; LYRICS: David Axelrod and Tom Whedon; MUSIC: Sam Pottle; DIRECTION: Ronny Graham; SCENERY: Peter Harvey; COSTUMES: Mr. Williams; LIGHTING: George Curley; MUSICAL DIRECTION: Sam Pottle; PRODUCER: Ronny Graham (?)

CAST—David Rounds (Harry Clay), Barbara Quaney (Cynthia Burgess), Jon Stone (Bernie Bartok, George Coe (Mr. Mann)

The musical was presented in two acts.

ACT ONE—"She Just Walked In" (David Rounds, Ensemble), "A Man with a Problem" (Barbara Quaney, David Rounds, Jon Stone), "Beautiful Day" (Company), "Commitment" (Company), "How Can I Tell?" (Barbara Quaney)

ACT TWO—"San Fernando" (David Rounds, Jon Stone, George Coe), "Give a Cheer" (Jon Stone), "The Philanthropist's Progress" ("A Cautionary Cantata") (Company): 1) Aria (Barbara Quaney), 2) Recitative and Duet (David Rounds, Barbara Quaney), 3) Scene (George Coe, David Rounds), 4) Grand Trio (Barbara Quaney, David Rounds, George Coe), 5) Finaletto (George Coe, Barbara Quaney), 6) Arietta (David Rounds), 7) Scene and Finale (David Rounds, George Coe, Jon Stone, Barbara Quaney), "Who Wants to Work?" (Company)

NOTES—This forgotten "musical play for cabaret" seems to have been titled both *$* and *Money*. Paul Gardner in the *New York Times* praised the "extremely bright — and frequently hilarious — lyrics," and noted "Give a Cheer" was the outstanding song of the evening. Gardner was also glad to see a book musical at the Upstairs at the Downstairs, and felt the story (about a rich young man looking for love and happiness among the common folk) was a welcome change from revues which dealt with such "passé" topics as the Kennedys, Barry Goldwater, and the Common Market. The musical's cast included David Rounds who gave a memorable performance in the Broadway chiller *Child's Play* (1970), for which he won a Tony Award for Best Featured Actor in a Play. He also appeared in the title role of the ambitious Off Broadway musical *Herringbone* (see entry).

Money had been previously produced in Cleveland, and the following songs were dropped prior to the New York opening: "Cuyahoga," "Domus Sur Pampas," and "I Hate the Avant Garde."

The script was published by Dramatists Play Service, Inc., in 1964.

1077 Monsieur de Pourceaugnac. THEATRE: Hartley Theatre; OPENING DATE: March 1978; PERFORMANCES: Unknown; BOOK: Members of the Theatre Illustre Company; LYRICS: Tony Schulman; MUSIC: Howard Harris; DIRECTION: Jerry Heymann; Debra Bick, Assistant Direction; CHOREOGRAPHY: Lauren Persichetti; SCENERY: Set Design by Mike Schomaker; Scene Design by Jack Wikoff; COSTUMES: Louise Martinez; LIGHTING: Mike Schomaker Producer: Theatre Illustre

CAST—Lisa Loomer (Julia), Tony Calabro (Sbrigani), Margaret McGuire (Lucette, Apothecary), Arthur Erickson (Oronte, Lawyer), John Foley (Eraste), Dorian Barth (Nerine), Robert Trebor

(Doctor Maldefesse, Lawyer), Homer Foil (Monsieur de Pourceaugnac)

SOURCE—The 1669 play *Monsieur de Pourceaugnac* by Jean-Baptiste Poquelin (Moliere).

The musical was presented in two acts.

ACT ONE—"Here Tonight Off-Broadway" (Company) "Who But You?" (Dorian Barth, Tony Calabro), "Anticipation Blues" (John Foley [Back-Up Vocal: Blake Travis]), "Fantasy for a Fool" (instrumental; piano solo), "Call on a Veteran" (Tony Calabro, John Foley), "What Is This Malady?" (Homer Foil, Margaret McGuire, Robert Trebor), "I Go by the Book" (Arthur Erickson, Robert Trebor), "Pullin' the Wool" (Dorian Barth, Tony Calabro)

ACT TWO—Prelude to Act II (instrumental reprise), "My Ordeal" (Tony Calabro), "Passionate Pourceaugnac" (Lisa Loomer), "Liaisons Dangereuses (A Common Conjugal Problem)" (Margaret McGuire, Homer Foil, Company), "It's Capital" (Arthur Erickson, Robert Trebor), "Tantalize" (Dorian Barth), "This Is a Real, Slow Drag" (Homer Foil), "Invitation to a Hanging" (Dorian Barth, Lisa Loomer, Margaret McGuire), "Feelin' Bleu" (Arthur Erickson), Grand Finale (instrumental), "Suite Limousine" (instrumental)

NOTES—The plot dealt with a pair of young lovers who thwart the girl's father, who wants her married to a rich man, Monsieur de Pourceaugnac.

The Off Off Broadway musical was recorded by Broadway Baby Records (LP # BBD-789); the song titles are taken from the recording, which also included a pamphlet with the lyrics.

Monsieur de Pourceaugnac was the season's second musical adaptation of a play by Moliere (see entry for *The Misanthrope*). Also see entries for *'Toinette* (1961) and *Show Me Where the Good Times Are* (1970), both of which were based on Moliere's *The Imaginary Invalid*; and see entry for *The Amorous Flea* (based on *The School for Wives*).

1078 Month of Sundays. "A New Musical." THEATRE: Theatre de Lys; OPENING DATE: September 16, 1968; PERFORMANCES: 8; BOOK: Romeo Muller; LYRICS: Jules Bass; MUSIC: Maury Laws; DIRECTION: Stone Widney; SCENERY: Robert T. Williams; COSTUMES: Sara Brook; LIGHTING: Joan Larkey; MUSICAL DIRECTION: Irv Dweir; PRODUCERS: Arthur Rankin, Jr., and Jules Bass, by special arrangement with Lucille Lortel Productions, Inc.

CAST—Gil Robbins (Carrousel Jones), Pamela Hall (Emmy Pleasant), John Bennett Perry (Henry), Allen Swift (Ponce Packard, First Announcer), Amanda Trees (Decibelle), Joe Morton (Jesse), Martha Schlamme (Olga Trischkovnova), Dan Resin (Herman Higgens), Patti Karr (Miss Unit [Gwen]), Tex Antoine (Second Announcer)

SOURCE—The play *The Great Git-Away* by Romeo Muller.

The action occurs around and about and aboard the rather remarkable house of Carrousel Jones.

The musical was presented in two acts.

ACT ONE—"How Far Can You Follow" (Pamela Hall, Gil Robbins), "I Won't Worry" (Gil Robbins, Pamela Hall, John Bennett Perry), "Communicate" (Allen Swift, John Bennett Perry, Pamela Hall, Gil Robbins), "Part of the Crowd" (Joe Morton, Pamela Hall), "We Know Where We've Been" (Company), "Summer Love" (Gil Robbins), "Who Knows Better Than I" (Joe Morton, Pamela Hall), "Words Will Pay My Way" (Martha Schlamme), Finale—Act One (Company)

ACT TWO—"Elbow Room" (Company), "My First Girl" (John Bennett Perry), "Flower I Don't Need You Anymore" (Amanda Trees), "I Won't Worry" (reprise) (Company), "It's Out of Our Hands" (Patti Karr, Dan Resin), "The Wedding" (Company), Finale—Act Two (Company)

NOTES—The fanciful musical *Month of Sundays* dealt with a group of people whose floating house is towed by a whale to a paradise prior to an apocalyptic flood.

Clive Barnes in the *New York Times* complained that the evening suffered from "an excess of fantasy over sense," and noted that "whimsy flowed ...like a flood and submerged all in sight." The plot was an idea "gone hopelessly adrift" and it never made "relevant landfall." Barnes indicated the music was "unmemorable yet modestly pleasing ... the country-flavored score has a certain lyric charm," and noted that the "strong-voiced" Patti Karr played "a secretary with a computer-heart of gold."

During previews the following songs were dropped: "The Way Things Are," "Month of Sundays," "I've Been Away Too Long," and "Man Has to Do What He Thinks Is Right."

The musical had been previously produced at the Tyrone Guthrie Theatre in Minneapolis.

Month of Sundays is sometimes confused with *A Month of Sundays*, which closed during its pre-Broadway tryout during the 1951-1952 season (its book and lyrics were by Burt Shevelove [with additional lyrics by Ted Fetter] and the music was by Albert Selden). Curiously, *A Month of Sundays* also took place on board a sailing vessel (in this case, the S.S. *Happiness*).

1079 Montpelier Pizazz. THEATRE: Playwrights Horizons; OPENING DATE: June 15, 1976; PERFORMANCES: 5; BOOK: Wendy Wasserstein; LYRICS: Wendy Wasserstein; MUSIC: David Hollister; DIRECTION: Donald Warfield; SCENERY: Nancy Winters and Donald Warfield; COSTUMES: V. Jane Suttell; LIGHTING: William D. Anderson; PRODUCER: Playwrights Horizons, Inc. (Robert Moss, Executive Director; Philip Himberg, Producing Director)

CAST—Bess Armstrong, Jonathan Charnas, Peggy Harner, Bonnie Hellman, Gayle Kelly Landers, Jill Medow, Nancy New, Debbe Renee, Charles Ryan, Harris Shore, Sally Sockwell, Jeffrey Spolan, Elizabeth Stockhammer, Federick Stone

NOTES—The Off Off Broadway musical *Montpelier Pizazz* (according to *The Best Plays of 1976-1977*) or *Montpelier Pa-Zazz* (according to *Theatre World 1976-1977 Season*) was an early work by noted playwright Wendy Wasserstein, who would later be associated with Playwrights Horizons in another musical, *Miami* (1986; see entry), which, like *Montpelier Pizazz/Pa-Zazz*, didn't go anywhere after its scheduled workshop performances.

1080 The Moon Dreamers. "Like a Floorshow in Hell." THEATRE: Ellen Stewart Theatre; OPENING DATE: December 8, 1969; PERFORMANCES: 24; PLAY: Julie Bovasso; DIRECTION: Julie Bovasso; Raymond Bussey, Associate Director; CHOREOGRAPHY: Raymond Bussey; SCENERY: Bernard X. Bovasso; COSTUMES: Randy Barcelo; LIGHTING: John P. Dodd; MUSICAL DIRECTION: LaMar Alford; PRODUCERS: Peter Moreau, Herschel Waxman, and Maury Kanbar

CAST—Louis Ramos (Soldier), Alan Wynroth (Soldier), Alan Harvey (Soldier). Chris Christian (Stockbroker), Carl Wilson (Stockbroker), Wes Williams (Stockbrocker), Vincenza DiMaggio (The Bride), Constantine Poutous (The Tourist, The Squaw), Laura Simms (The Gold Star Mother, Geisha), Ching Yeh (Zen Buddhist), Evan Ritter (The Indian), Tom Rosica (Rene Utray), Jane Sanford (Sandra), Zina Jasper (Mimi), LaMar Alford, Maria D'Elia, and Ella Luxembourg (The Doublemint Opera Trio), Jean David (The Mother), Ted Henning (The Lawyer), Leonard Hicks (The Doctor), Reigh Hagen (Salvation Army Singer), Alex Beall (Mick), LaMar Alford (Mack), Herve Villechaize (The Chief of Police), Elayne Barat (Bubu), Douglas Stone (Apple Boy), John Bacher and Lanny Harrison (Two Dancing Swells), Raymond Bussey (Strange Fruit Dancer), Fred Muselli (The Groom), Alan Harvey (The Father), Daffi (Ira), Louis Ramos (The Man at the End), Maria D'Elia, Roberta Hammer, and Diedre Simone (Ziegfeld Nurses and Hula Girls), Janda Lee, Mossa Ossa, and Ella Luxembourg (Flappers, Vamps, and Dance Hall Girls), John Bacher, Chris Christian, and Reigh Hagen (Dancehall Boys, Dappers), William Pierce, Carl Wilson, and Lawrence Sellars (Sheiks, Space Boys), Elayne Barat, Lanny Harrison, Constantine Poutous, Douglas Stone, Robert Ullman, Steven Verakus, and Dennis Sokal (Chorus of Constantly Present People)

NOTES—The program for Julie Bovasso's campy *The Moon Dreamers*, which was the inaugural production of the Ellen Stewart Theatre, didn't denote division of acts, and listed only one song ("Jesus Christ," lyric and music by Bovasso). But the evening included dances and other songs.

The window card proclaimed the forty-member production (which included cast members Mossa Ossa and Daffi) was "the largest show ever presented Off-Broadway," and besides describing the evening "like a floorshow in hell," the window card also noted the work was "a demonic American saga with funky music and a truly rotten chorus" (the program credited seven cast members as a "chorus of constantly present people"). Originally produced Off Off Broadway at the Café La Mama, *The Moon Dreamers* was a campy, bemused look at American life, including the nation's ability to send a man to the moon and back and yet unable to resolve its internal social problems.

Clive Barnes in the *New York Times* wrote that he suspected rather than knew what the play was about. He indicated the hero was "perhaps" an astronaut recently returned from the moon who might be three men (soldiers from the Civil War, World War I, and World War II). The plot also included "a most peculiar murder mystery" with diminutive Herve Villechaize as a chief of police prone to dress like Napoleon (Villechaize's program bio stated he was he was three feet and ten inches tall). Further, other characters danced to the "Tiger Rag" as the three-soldier chorus looked on in "accusation" at all the "frivolity" happening around them. Barnes noted the evening had "funny" and "liberating" moments of "bizarre" humor, but felt Bovasso "is so liberated that her work is almost a free-fall." Indeed, he felt the evening was sometimes too cute and too irritating in its "high regard" for "amateurism" and its lack of professionalism and pointed satire. The poster artwork of *The Moon Dreamers* is one of the earliest from noted artist David Byrd, who later created the iconic artwork for the original 1971 production of *Follies* (over the years, he designed new poster art work for various revivals of Stephen Sondheim's monumental musical) as well as for a number of other plays and musicals, including *Godspell* (1971; see entry) and *The Grand Tour* (1979).

Incidentally, on the window card and on the program's cover, the show's title is given as *The Moon Dreamers*; but the title page of the program gives the title as *The Moondreamers*.

1081 Moon Walk. THEATRE: New York City Center; OPENING DATE: November 28, 1970; PERFORMANCES: 8; BOOK: Betty Jean Lifton; LYRICS AND MUSIC: The Open Window; DIRECTION: Hal Wicke; CHOREOGRAPHY: Anne Wilson; SCENERY: Visuals by Group II; COSTUMES: Jack McGroder; PRODUCER: City Center of Music and Drama (Norman Singer, General Director)

CAST—Tommy Breslin (Jimmy), Annie Abbott (Granny, Moonmoth, Old Woman of the Universe), Ronald Dennis (Buddy), Ann Hodapp (Linda), James Barbosa (Moonblowfoofoo), Roberta Rodin (Moonbeam), Ralph Santinelli (Moonosaur), Jerry DiGiacoma (Galaxy); Dancers: Lindsay Ann Crouse,

Jim Gates, David Gleaton, Stephanie Satie, Paul Wittenborn

The musical was presented in one act.

MUSICAL NUMBERS (all songs were performed by The Open Window)—"Ready to Go," "Moon Walk," "Moonblowfoofoo," "Sea of Tranquility," "Millions of Envelopes," "Making the Moonmoth Laugh," "Grand Tour of the Planets," "On Moonrock Mountain," "Moonrock Candy Freak-Out," "Love Song to a Monster," "Earth Fall," Finale

NOTES—The Off Off Broadway science-fiction musical *Moon Walk*, which dealt with three children who take a trip to the moon, was presented at City Center for a limited engagement of eight performances. The fantasy had earlier been performed at the Electric Circus in December 1969.

Mel Gussow in the *New York Times* found the story "conventional," and noted the program indicated the musical was appropriate for children in the five-to-eleven-year-old range (Gussow felt "the younger the better"). But he found the style of the musical interesting because it "physically" involved the children in the audience with the action on stage (in what today would be termed an interactive production).

1082 More Than You Deserve. THEATRE: Newman Theatre/The Public Theatre; OPENING DATE: November 21, 1973; PERFORMANCES: 63; BOOK: Michael Weller; LYRICS: Michael Weller and Jim Steinman; MUSIC: Jim Steinman; DIRECTION: Kim Friedman; CHOREOGRAPHY: Scott Salmon; SCENERY: Miguel Romero; COSTUMES: Lowell Detweiler; LIGHTING: Martin Aronstein; MUSICAL DIRECTION: Steve Margoshes; PRODUCER: The New York Shakespeare Festival Public Theatre

CAST—Leata Galloway (Nurse, Nin Hua), Maybeth Hurt (Nurse, Uncle Remus), Steve Collins (Nathan, Herbie, Pilot), Graham Jarvis (Dr. Smith, Sgt. Price), Seth Allen (Luke, Lance Moriarity), Larry Marshall (Mike, Brown, Gerald Moore), Meat Loaf (Perrine, Rabbit), Kim Milford (Wiley, Trout), Tom Leo (Owlsy, Joe), Edward Zang (Costucci, Lt. Maddox), Justin Ross (Spooky 1, Vietnamese), Eivie McGehee (Spooky 2, Vietnamese, Radioman), Terry Kiser (Melvin), Fred Gwynne (Maj. Michael Dillon), Kimberly Farr (Fiona Markhan), Ronald (Ron) Silver (Gen. Chet Eastacre), Dale Soules (Vietnamese)

The action occurs in Vietnam at the present time.

The musical was presented in two acts.

ACT ONE—"Give Me the Simple Life" (Larry Marshall, Meat Loaf, Kim Milford, Company), "Could She Be the One" (Fred Gwynne, Kimberly Farr), "Where Did It Go?" (Seth Allen), "Come with Me ... We Know Love" (Leata Galloway, Seth Allen), "Mama You Better Watch Out for Your Daughter" (Kim Milford, Larry Marshall, Kimberly Farr), "O, What a War" (Fred Gwynne, Ronald Silver, Graham Jarvis, Edward Zang), "More Than You Deserve" (Meat Loaf, Company), "Song of the City of Hope" (Leata Galloway, Kim Milford, Fred Gwynne, Kimberly Farr)

ACT TWO—"To Feel So Needed" (Leata Galloway, Kimberly Farr), "Go, Go, Go Guerillas" (Ken Marshall, Seth Allen, Ronald Silver), "What Became of the People We Were?" (Kimberly Farr, Terry Kiser), "If Only" (Fred Gwynne, Kimberly Farr), "Midnight Lullabye" (Leata Galloway), "Song of the Golden Egg" (Kim Milford, Company), Finale (Company)

NOTES—With almost depressing regularity, Joseph Papp produced musical after musical diatribe from his perch at the Public Theatre. These all seemed to be angry, unstructured rock musicals with anti-establishment views which espoused the fashionable causes of the day (feminist, Black, environmental, anti-war). One wonders the point, because almost all were failures, with short runs and little in the way of critical or general audience acclaim. Virtually all these special-interest musicals disappeared after their brief runs at the Public (even *Hair* [see entry], the one successful musical in this group, quickly became a period piece; today, its strength lies in Galt MacDermot's melodic score and not in the musical's now quaint anti-establishment message). *More Than You Deserve* is a perfect case in point. It was another anti-war rock musical, this one superimposing the form of the traditional military-themed play or musical (here, *South Pacific* [1949], with specific references to Nellie Forbush, Bloody Mary, and Liat) against an actual historical event (the My-Lai massacre, which occurred in South Vietnam on March 16, 1968). The critics noted the musical also borrowed attitudes from the novel *Catch-22* (1962) and the 1970 film *MASH*. Further, the unstructured, free-wheeling plot emphasized the sexual obsessions of the characters (for example, "Nellie Forbush," here a reporter, is gang-raped by a group of American soldiers, enjoys the experience, and becomes a nymphomaniac; and "Bloody Mary" sells "Liat" to the platoon).

Richard Watts in the *New York Post* "hated" the musical and said it lacked an "excuse for its existence." Further, Martin Gottfried in *Women's Wear Daily* called it "trash." But Kevin Sanders on WABC-TV7 found the evening "audacious and challenging" and made the improbable suggestion that if a musical like *More Than You Deserve* had opened five years earlier, the Vietnam War might have ended sooner.

Michael Weller, the musical's librettist and co-lyricist, had written the vastly overpraised *Moonchildren* (1970), the first of a number of drearily introspective plays and films which centered around naval-gazing baby boomers.

More Than You Deserve wasn't the last musical to deal with the My-Lai massacre. In 1975, the Broadway "rock opera" *The Lieutenant* explored the event (but only for nine performances).

The first performance of *More Than You Deserve* was given on November 21, 1973, the official press performance was on January 3, 1974, and the musical closed on January 13 (the total number of performances was sixty-three).

1083 Morning Sun. "A New Play with Music." THEATRE: Phoenix Theatre; OPENING DATE: October 6, 1963; PERFORMANCES: 9; BOOK: Fred Ebb; LYRICS: Fred Ebb; MUSIC: Paul Klein; DIRECTION: Daniel Petrie; CHOREOGRAPHY: Donald Saddler; SCENERY: Eldon Elder; COSTUMES: Patricia Zipprodt; LIGHTING: Eldon Elder, Martin Aronstein; MUSICAL DIRECTION: John Strauss; PRODUCER: The Phoenix Theatre (T. Edward Hambleton and Martin Tahse)

CAST—BERT CONVY (Rome), PATRICIA NEWAY (Mother), David Aguilar (Halleck), DANNY LOCKIN (Thad), Ave Maria Megna (Mary), Sammy Bayes (Robert, Jailor), Nancy Cheevers (Mrs. Peabody), Elizabeth Wullen (Virginia), DAVID THOMAS (Mr. Haskins), Nancy Haywood (Sarah), Kitty Sullivan (Emily), Jan Tanzy (Margaret), Joan August (Elvira), WILL MACKENZIE (John Atzel), CAROLE DEMAS (Melissa), Stuart Hodes (Alex), Richard Hermany (Mr. Simpson), Michael Maurer (Will)

SOURCE—A story by Mary Deasy.

The action occurs in the Southwestern United States in 1870.

The musical was presented in two acts.

ACT ONE—"Morning Sun" (Bert Convy), "This Heat" (Patricia Neway), "Tell Me Goodbye" (Bert Convy, Patricia Neway), "New Boy in Town" (Townspeople), "Good as Anybody" (Bert Convy, Will Mackenzie), "Mr. Chigger" (Patricia Neway, Ave Maria Megna, Danny Lockin, David Aguilar), "Pebble Waltz" (Danny Lockin), "Follow Him" (Patricia Neway), "Missouri Mule" (David Thomas; danced by Townspeople), "Square Dance" (Townspeople), "Seventeen Summers" (Carole Demas, Ave Maria Megna), "It's a Lie" (Patricia Neway, David Thomas)

ACT TWO—"My Sister-in-Law" (Carole Demas, Danny Lockin, Ave Maria Megna, David Aguilar), "Why?" (Patricia Neway), "That's Right!" (Nancy Haywood, Stuart Hodes, Joan August, Townspeople), "Morning Sun" (reprise) (Bert Convy), "For Once in My Life" (Danny Lockin), "Thad's Journey" (Danny Lockin), "All the Pretty Little Horses" (Patricia Neway), "I Seen It with My Very Own Eyes" (Townspeople)

NOTES—*Morning Sun* was a dour fable about a rigid, unforgiving woman (Patricia Neway) who eventually has the tables turned on her when her son (Bert Convy) is killed for a crime he didn't mean to commit. Howard Taubman in the *New York Times* found the book "pretentious and empty" and "deeply tinged by what passes for psychologizing." But he had much praise for the score, singling out six songs, including a "lovely American folksong" ("All the Pretty Little Horses"), a "wry ensemble" ("Missouri Mule"), and an "inventive" waltz ("Pebble Waltz"). Further, he noted "That's Right!" was "a choice example of the shrewd uses to which rhythm" can be used; he reported that the song employed lyrics chanted to the beats of a drum by the townspeople, and as the tempo accelerated, the "mob spirit being whipped up is swiftly and forcefully conveyed." Taubman's tantalizing comments about the score make one regret a cast album was never issued. The musical marked one of Fred Ebb's earliest New York appearances (he had made his Broadway debut three years earlier in *From A to Z* [1960], for which he contributed lyrics for five songs, four of which had music composed by Paul Klein, his *Morning Sun* collaborator); Ebb would of course soon form one of the musical theatre's most enduring partnerships when he teamed up with John Kander. *Morning Sun* cast member Bert Convy later created roles in the original Broadway productions of *Fiddler on the Roof* (1964) and Kander and Ebb's *Cabaret* (1966).

Patricia Neway, who had appeared in the original Broadway productions of *The Consul* (1950) and *The Sound of Music* (1959; as the Mother Abbess, she introduced the standard "Climb Every Mountain"), here again created a "mother" role (see entry for *Tale for a Deaf Ear*). And tucked away in the show's credits was Ave Maria Megna, who had appeared on Broadway in *Greenwillow* (1960) with her brother John Megna. In that memorable but short-lived musical, John Megna received the kind of raves most performers can only dream about. He next appeared in the key role of Rufus, the little boy who lost his father, in Tad Mosel's Pulitzer Prize-winning drama *All the Way Home* (1961), which was based on John Agee's novel *A Death in the Family* (1958), which had won the Pulitzer Prize for fiction. Master Megna also made his mark as Dill, the eccentric little boy in the film *To Kill a Mockingbird* (1962). *Morning Sun* cast member Carole Demas appeared in the tryouts of *No, No, Nanette* (1971) and *The Baker's Wife* 1976), only to be replaced by Susan Watson and Patti LuPone, respectively. But Demas was in one of the biggest hits in musical theatre history when she created the role of Sandy in the original production of *Grease* (1972; see entry).

Fred Ebb's program bio mentioned his two forthcoming Broadway musicals (both of which were never produced), *Simon Says* and *Golden Gate*. For the former, he was both lyricist and co-librettist (Paul Klein composed the music, and Lionel Wilson was the co-librettist). For *Golden Gate*, Ebb was the lyricist and John Kander the composer (Richard Morris wrote the book); if the latter had been produced, it would have been the first Kander and Ebb musical seen on Broadway. Instead, the team's

Broadway debut was two years away, with *Flora, the Red Menace* (1965).

An unknown (and obviously unhappy) theatergoer scribbled these notes in a *Morning Sun* program: "Dull ... big fat unoriginal ... slow-moving ... pretentious is not a strong enough word ... unoriginal ... hackneyed ... old-hat ... no musical surprises ... can sometimes predict next note ... scene changes clumsy ... dances very athletic and noisy."

1084 Most Men Are. THEATRE: Theatre Off Park; OPENING DATE: February 3, 1995; PERFORMANCES: 6; BOOK: Stephen Dolginoff; LYRICS: Stephen Dolginoff; MUSIC: Stephen Dolginoff; DIRECTION: Daniel Simmons; SCENERY: Graphics by Linda Thomas; LIGHTING: Jeffrey Zeidman; MUSICAL DIRECTION: Stephen Dolginoff; PRODUCERS: SDD Productions in conjunction with Betty and Harold Levitt, and Kathleen Ruen

CAST—James Heatherly (Scott), Joel Carlton (Russ), Terrance Flynn (Larry), Mark Peters (Jack)

The action occurs in New York City at the present time.

The musical was performed in one act (song assignments unknown).

MUSICAL NUMBERS—Overture, "You Won't Die Alone," "Not That Strong," "Scott, He Can Still Hear You," "What If," "Daddy's Playboy Magazines," "Something Bound to Begin," "The Perfect Place on Christopher Street," "I Couldn't Care Less," "Never Disappointed Him," "Potential," "Steal My Thunder," "We Could Rent a Movie," "Away," "When I Come Home at Night," "Gotta Get Outta Here," "Most Men Are," "Better Not to Know," "My Body," "Urban Legend," "Maybe Some Weekend"

NOTES—According to the liner notes of the musical's studio cast album released by Original Cast Records (CD # OC-9532), *Most Men Are* told the story of Russ, who has just lost his lover Scott to AIDS. Russ invites both Scott's unbending father Jack and estranged brother Larry to an impromptu memorial service, and in flashbacks the sung-through musical revealed the relationships between the four men and how the three survivors come to terms with themselves and with one another. The musical played Off Off Broadway for a limited engagement after having been developed by the Under One Roof Theater Company.

The studio cast album was a collection of highlights from the score, and was sung by David Gurland, Roger Seyer, and Michael Patrick Walker. The ten songs heard on the album were: "You Won't Die Alone," "Daddy's Playboy Magazines," "What If," "Something Bound to Begin," "The Perfect Place on Christopher Street," "We Could Rent a Movie," "Most Men Are," "Better Not to Know," "Urban Legend," and "My Body."

1085 Mother Goose Go-Go. "A Rock-Folk Musical Revue for Children." THEATRE: Helen Hayes Theatre; OPENING DATE: 1969-1970 Season; PERFORMANCES: Unknown; BOOK: Adaptation of Mother Goose rhymes by Jim Eiler; LYRICS: Jim Eiler; MUSIC: Jim Eiler and Jeanne Bargy; DIRECTION: Jim Eiler; MUSICAL DIRECTION: Jeanne Bargy; PRODUCERS: Leonard Goldberg and Ken Gaston; A Prince St. Players Ltd. Production

SOURCE—Traditional Mother Goose Rhymes

CAST—GEORGIA CREIGHTON (Mother Goose), Robert Anderson, Ronald Dennis, Jim Eiler, Nathylin Flowers, Fred Grades, Joyce Griffen, Charlotte Marcheret

The revue was presented in two acts.

ACT ONE—"Hello, Little Chillin'!" (Georgia Creighton, Company), "Games" (Company), "Little Boy Blue" (Georgia Creighton), "Song of Sixpence" (Ronald Dennis), "Cambrick Shirt" (Robert Anderson, Fred Grades, Charlotte Marcheret, Joyce Griffen), "Twinkle Little Star" (Nathylin Flowers), "Civilization and the Nursery Rhyme" (Company)

ACT TWO—"Yankee Doodle" (Fred Grades), "Mother Goose Almanac" (Company), "Aiken Drum" (Jim Eiler), "Hickerie, Dickerie, Dock" (Georgia Creighton), "Spider and the Fly" (Joyce Griffen, Ron Dennis), "I Saw a Ship" (Charlotte Marcheret, Robert Anderson), "Love Everybody" (finale) (Company)

NOTES—*Mother Goose Go-Go*, which starred Georgia Creighton in the title role, was a revue-like musical for children originally produced in 1968 by the Prince Street Players, who performed the work in public parks throughout the New York City area. The musical was also briefly seen on Broadway in two separate engagements during the 1969-1970 season. It first played at the now demolished Helen Hayes Theatre, probably sometime in late fall or early winter between the theatre's bookings of the revival of *Three Men on a Horse* (October 1969) and Art Buchwald's comedy *Sheep on the Runway* (January 1970). (The above cast and other credits, including the song list, are taken from an undated program from the engagement at the Helen Hayes Theatre.)

It seems likely the musical was produced at the Hayes shortly after the closing of *Three Men on a Horse*, because Leonard Goldberg and Ken Gaston were the co-producers of both *Three Men on a Horse* and *Mother Goose Go-Go*. The musical's second engagement took place in late March and early April 1970 (the specific dates may have been March 27 through April 5) at the Edison Theatre.

Although the revue played at one regular Broadway theatre (the Hayes) and one which often presented Middle Broadway productions (the Edison), the cast may or may not have been under Broadway contracts; if they were under Broadway contracts, the revue was definitely a "Broadway musical," but it seems more likely the production was offered under an Off Broadway or Middle Broadway contract. I don't know of any reference books which include the musical in their Broadway and Off Broadway seasonal surveys and discussions, and so adding *Mother Goose Go-Go* to this book gets the musical "on the record." A revised version of the musical was later telecast on CBS as a limited series (the number of episodes are unknown); this adaptation apparently starred Georgia Creighton in the title role and was called *The Mother Goose Assembly*. In 1986, the Detroit Institute of Arts Youtheatre commissioned a revised and updated version of the piece called *A Pocketful of Rhymes* (which is licensed by Music Theatre International under that name).

For more information about Georgia Creighton, see entry for *The Penny Friend*.

1086 The Mother of Us All (1947). "An Opera." THEATRE: Brander Matthews Hall/Columbia University; OPENING DATE: May 7, 1947; PERFORMANCES: 4 (estimated); TEXT: Gertrude Stein; Scenario by Maurice Grosser; MUSIC: Virgil Thomson; DIRECTION: John Taras; SCENERY: Paul du Pont; COSTUMES: Paul du Pont; MUSICAL DIRECTION: Otto Luening; Jack Beeson, Assistant Conductor; PRODUCERS: Columbia Theatre Associates of Columbia University in Co-operation with the Columbia University Department of Music

CAST—Dorothy Dow (Susan B. Anthony), Belva Kibler (Anne), Hazel Gravell (Gertrude S.), Robert Grooters (Virgil T.), Bertram Rowe (Daniel Webster), William Horne (Jo the Loiterer), Carlton Sunday (Chris the Citizen), Ruth Krug (Indiana Elliott), Carolyn Blakeslee (Angel More), Teresa Stich (Henrietta M.)

The action occurs in the nineteenth century in the United States.

The opera was presented in three acts.

NOTES—*The Mother of Us All* was the second operatic collaboration between Virgil Thomson and Gertrude Stein; in 1934, their abstract opera *Four Saints in Three Acts* had premiered on Broadway. *The Mother of Us All*, which premiered at Columbia University in 1947, was more traditional than the first, with a libretto which if not linear was nonetheless centered around a narrative (albeit a loose one) and a central character (including many anachronistic ones).

The opera told the story of Susan B. Anthony (1820-1906) and her struggle for women's rights, including the right to vote. The opera's freewheeling sense of time introduced historical figures as major characters, such as Daniel Webster, John Adams, Thaddeus Stevens, Ulysses S. Grant, and musical comedy star Lillian Russell; most if not all had never met Anthony. In fact, some of the historical figures could never have met: Adams and Russell shared a musical sequence together, but Adams had died in 1848, a full thirteen years before Russell was born. Further, Grant sang of Dwight D. Eisenhower, who became president almost a hundred years after Grant left office. The opera also included characters based on friends of the composer and the librettist, and, indeed, even Thomson and Stein were actual characters in the opera (as "Virgil T." and "Gertrude S.").

While the opera focused on Anthony and her quest for women's rights, the Nineteenth Amendment (which gave women the right to vote) didn't become part of the Constitution until 1920, fourteen years after her death. In the final moments of the opera, Anthony asks the ultimate question, which was more important, the cause itself or her lifelong commitment to it? Like the voyagers in Philip Glass' opera *The Voyage* (see entry), for which the voyage itself is as important as the ultimate discovery of new worlds, Anthony concludes that her commitment to her vision is just as liberating as the actual attainment of her quest.

In reviewing the opera's first performance, Olin Downes in the *New York Times* praised the score, often a pastiche of American-styled music (such as hymns, waltzes, marches, and ballads), but wondered if this "very literary" opera would find a permanent place in the American operatic repertoire. The liner notes for the sparkling 1976 Santa Fe Opera's 2-LP recording on New World Records (# NW-288) indicate a resounding "yes" to Downes' query: during the first thirty years following the opera's premiere, it received over 1,000 performances in almost 200 different productions.

See entry for information concerning a 1983 revival of the opera.

(Another production of the opera was seen in New York at the Guggenheim Museum on November 26, 1972, for seventeen performances.)

In 1981, Off Off Broadway offered another musical about the subject; *Susan B!* (lyrics by Ted Drachman and music by Thomas Tierney) opened at the Martin Theatre on November 29 for eight performances.

1087 The Mother of Us All (1983). THEATRE: Lenox Arts Center/Saint Clement's Episcopal Church; OPENING DATE: May 15, 1983; PERFORMANCES: Unknown; LIBRETTO: Gertrude Stein; MUSIC: Virgil Thomson; DIRECTION: Stanley Silverman; SCENERY: Power Boothe; COSTUMES: Lawrence Casey; LIGHTING: William Armstrong; MUSICAL DIRECTION: Richard Cordova; PRODUCER: Music-Theatre Group (Lyn Austin, Producing Director)

CAST—Carmen Pelton (Susan B. Anthony), Linn Maxwell (Anne, Indiana Elliot), Ruth Jacobson (Gertrude S.), Richard Frisch (Virgil T., Indiana Elliot's Brother), Harris Poor (Daniel Webster), John Vining (Jo the Loiterer, Donald Gallup), James Javore (Chris the Citizen, Thaddeus Stevens, Ulysses S. Grant), Paula Seibel (Angel More, Lillian Russell), Avery J. Tracht (John Adams), Kate Hurney (Constance Fletcher) The opera was presented in two acts.

NOTES—This Off Off Broadway revival of the Virgil Thomson and Gertrude Stein opera *The Mother of Us All* was later produced in Stockbridge, Massachusetts, and at Wolf Trap in Vienna, Virginia.

For more information about the opera, see entry for the original production, which premiered on May 7, 1947, at Columbia University.

The opera was also revived at the Guggenheim Museum on November 26, 1972, for seventeen performances.

1088 Mourning Becomes Electra. "A Lyric Tragedy." THEATRE: Metropolitan Opera House; OPENING DATE: March 17, 1967; PERFORMANCES: 6; LIBRETTO: Henry Butler; MUSIC: Marvin David Levy; DIRECTION: Michael Cacoyannis; SCENERY: Boris Aronson; COSTUMES: Boris Aronson; MUSICAL DIRECTION: Zubin Mehta; PRODUCER: The Metropolitan Opera

CAST—Evelyn Lear (Lavinia Mannon), John Reardon (Orin Mannon), Marie Collier (Christine Mannon), Sherrill Milnes (Captain Adam Brant), John Macurdy (General Ezra Mannon), Ron Bottcher (Captain Peter Niles), Lilian Sukis (Helen), Raymond Michalski (Jed)

SOURCE—The 1931 trilogy *Mourning Becomes Electra* (*Homecoming*, *The Hunted*, and *The Haunted*) by Eugene O'Neill.

The opera was presented in three acts.

NOTES—For its inaugural season in its new home at Lincoln Center, the Metropolitan commissioned two new American operas. The first, Samuel Barber's *Antony and Cleopatra* (see entry), had met with disappointment; but *Mourning Becomes Electra*, Martin David Levy's lyric treatment of Eugene O'Neill's trilogy, was more enthusiastically received, and was revived there the following season. In reviewing the world premiere, Harold C. Schonberg in the *New York Times* reported that Henry Butler's libretto had stripped O'Neill down to a "digest version," but he nonetheless felt Butler had retained the essential power of both O'Neill's trilogy and the Greek myths upon which the trilogy was based.

As for Levy's music, Schonberg said it was "hard" to describe, being background and yet not background music; being neither modern nor traditional; being neither melodious nor non-melodious. He wrote that the melody didn't "sing or say anything"; and while musical phrases went "up and down in melodic patterns," there was actually "little" in the way of melody. Overall, he found the score "impersonal," "neutral," and "nondescript," and concluded that except for the music everything about the opera was "convincing." He noted that perhaps only a Wagner or a Berg could have successfully set O'Neill's trilogy to music. The opera appears to have undergone revisions in 1998 and in 2003.

1089 Movie Buff. THEATRE: Actors' Playhouse; OPENING DATE: March 14, 1977; PERFORMANCES: 21; BOOK: Hiram Taylor; LYRICS: Hiram Taylor and John Raniello; MUSIC: John Raniello; DIRECTION: Jim Payne; CHOREOGRAPHY: Jack Dyville; SCENERY: Jimmy Cuomo; COSTUMES: Carol Wenz; LIGHTING: Jo Mayer; MUSICAL DIRECTION: Donald G. Jones; PRODUCER: Free Space Ltd.

CAST—Charlie Scatamacchia (Spirit of the 1930s), Jim Richards (Mike Williams), Deborah Carlson (Joanne Simpson), Nora Cole (Velma), Nancy Rich (Sally Smith), Mark Waldrop (Tom), Marianna Doro (Mildred [Gloria De Wilde]), Keith Curran (Robert Robbins [Butch])

The action occurs in New York City during the present.

The musical was presented in two acts.

ACT ONE—"Silver Screen" (Charlie Scatamacchia, Jim Richards), "Something to Believe In" (Nora Cole, Deborah Carlson, Nancy Rich), "Movietown, U.S.A." (Nancy Rich, Deborah Carlson, Nora Cole, Mark Waldrop), "You Are Something Very Special" (Jim Richards, Deborah Carlson), "Where Is the Man" (Marianna Doro), "Movie Stars" (Jim Richards), "May I Dance with You?" (Nora Cole, Mark Waldrop, Nancy Rich), "Tell a Little Lie or Two" (Mark Waldrop, Keith Curran, Nora Cole, Deborah Carlson)

ACT TWO—"Song of Yesterday" (Charlie Scatamacchia), "The Movie Cowboy" (Keith Curran), "Reflections in a Mirror" (Deborah Carlson), "All-Talking, All-Singing, All-Dancing" (Deborah Carlson, Company), "Coming Attractions" (Jim Richards, Charlie Scatamacchia), "Tomorrow" (Deborah Carlson, Company), "Song of Yesterday" (reprise) (Charlie Scatamacchia), "Silver Screen" (reprise) (Charlie Scatamacchia, Jim Richards)

NOTES—*Movie Buff* was an affectionate look at movie musicals of the 1930s from the perspective of the present. It didn't excite critics and audiences, and so it was gone in less than three weeks.

Clive Barnes in the *New York Times* thought the evening would amuse only those who are "so far into camp that they are practically scoutmasters." The plot dealt with audience members in a modern-day movie theatre who are whisked away by the "Spirit of the 1930s" to re-live the golden age of movie musicals (Barnes remarked that "if you can believe that you can believe anything"). But he liked the "tuneful" music, particularly "Where is the Man?," a "burnt-out" torch song with "definite, sleazy charms." And while he commented that Hiram Taylor wrote the "horrendous" book, he also noted that Taylor was the co-writer of the "vastly superior" lyrics.

1090 Mud Donahue and Son

NOTES—See entry for *The New York Musical Theatre Festival*.

1091 The Muffled Report. THEATRE: Strollers Theatre-Club; OPENING DATE: April 8, 1964; PERFORMANCES: 92; SKETCHES: Peter Cook and John Bird; PRODUCERS: Peter Cook and John Krimsky

CAST—Jeremy Geidt, John Bird, David Battley, Eleanor Bron, Carole Simpson The revue was presented in two acts.

ACT ONE—"Introductory Remarks," "Doctor's Office," "There Will Never Be Another You," "Investigation of Police Brutality," "Trafalgar Square," "A Fly-By-Night Affair," "The General Election," "I Guess I'll Have to Change My Plans," "The Liberal Campaign," "The Stabbing Campaign," "The Election Returns," "Looney Bin Administration," "Harold Wilson Honors Sir George Muffle," "The Queen and the New Order"

ACT TWO—"News Report," "How Now Frau Brown?," "General DeGaulle's Agent," "Mrs. Lady Bird," "British Defense Minister Peter Thornycroft," Finale

NOTES—*The Muffled Report* was the third Establishment revue presented in New York within fifteen months (see entries for the 1963 and 1964-1964 editions, both titled *The Establishment*).

Milton Esterow in the *New York Times* found the revue "terribly, terribly funny ... a real rouser" in its jibes at (mostly) British targets (Britain, by the way, isn't located near any hostile countries, "except possibly France") and the occasional swipe at the colonies (the Republican convention headquarters is located in Saigon).

1092 Murder in the Old Red Barn. THEATRE: American Music Hall; OPENING DATE: February 1, 1936; PERFORMANCES: 337; BOOK: John Latimer; LYRICS: Original lyrics by John LaTouche; see song list for other lyricists; MUSIC: Original music by Richard Lewine; see song list for other composers; SCENERY: Frank Ambos and Stephen Golding; PRODUCERS: Harry Bannister and John Krimsky in association with Lucius Beebe

CAST—M. Manisoff (Tim Robbin), RICHARD RAUBER (William Corder), STAPLETON KENT (Marten), MARIANNE COWAN (Maria Marten), ROBERT VIVIAN (Ishmael), Gertrude Keith (Anne Marten), JUDITH ELDER (Dame Marten), Alfred L. Rigali (First Barker), HARRY MEEHAN (Second Barker), LESLIE LITOMY (Pharosee), George Jones (Mark), George Spelvin (Servant); other specialty acts are listed below

The musical was presented in three acts.

ACT ONE—Interlude, "The Cancan Volunteers" (Ann Suter, The American Music Hallettes), "When Irish Eyes Are Smiling" (lyric by Chauncey Olcott and George Graff, Jr., music by Ernest R. Ball) (Harry Meehan), "Not on Your Tintype" (Leslie Litomy), Pope and Johnson (Jugglers)/The Washboard Musicians

ACT TWO—Interlude, Soubrette de Resistance, Ann Suter, "Skating in the Bois" (The Comets)

ACT THREE—"Don't Throw Me Out of the House, Father" (The American Music Hallettes), "That Quartet" (George Jones, Aubrey Pringle, Johnny Burns, Al Duke) (sequence included "Annie Laurie," "White Wings," "A Bicycle Built for Two," and "Down Went McGinty"), The Six Danwills (Gymnasts), Finale: "Happy Days Are Here Again" (from 1930 film *Chasing Rainbows*; lyric by Jack Yellen, music by Milton Ager) (Company)

NOTES—The American Music Hall was a new theatre fashioned from a dilapidated building which had originally been a church before being converted into a movie theatre. When the venue became home for live theatre, it was decorated in the style of a Gay Nineties' beer hall and for a few years a series of old-fashioned musical melodramas were produced there (see entry for *Naughty-Naught '00* [1937] for more information). The cast, credits, and song listing of *Murder in the Old Red Barn* are derived from Richard C. Norton's invaluable *A Chronology of American Musical Theatre*.

1093 Murder in 3 Keys. "A Trilogy of Terror and Suspense." THEATRE: Cherry Lane Theatre; OPENING DATE: Unknown (1956?); PERFORMANCES: Unknown; TEXTS OF THE THREE MUSICALS: Erik Chisholm; MUSIC: Erik Chisholm; DIRECTION: Nelson Sykes; SCENERY: Joseph Braswell; COSTUMES: Joseph Braswell; MUSICAL DIRECTION: Rex Wilder; PRODUCER: Punch Opera, Inc.

The musical trilogy was presented in three acts.

NOTES—*Murder in 3 Keys* was an evening of three short musicals, all of which dealt with murder. Erik Chisholm wrote the libretto and composed the music for the original first act mini-opera *Black Roses*. The musicals for the second and third acts, *Dark Sonnet* and *Simoon*, were based on the respective plays by Eugene O'Neill and August Strindberg, and both were adapted by Chisholm, who also set them to music.

Black Roses, the first act in the trilogy, was a mini-opera murder mystery; set in a London flat in the 1920s during a birthday party, the opera dealt with a murderer who crashes the party, confesses to his crime, and to his dismay discovers the party guests don't take him seriously. The cast members were as follows: Harriet Hill (Alice), Martha Moore (Mary), John Miller (Bertie), Willard Pierce (Charlie), Carolyn Burns (Annabella), Fred Patrick (Sam), and Charles Oliver (Joe).

The second act, *Dark Sonnet*, was based on *Before Breakfast*, a 1916 mono-drama by Eugene O'Neill. Set in Greenwich Village, the one-woman musical centered around the daily pre-breakfast harangues, complaints, and insults of a nagging wife

(Mrs. Rowland, performed by Ellen Brehm) to her (off-stage) husband. He finally responds to her endless tirades by cutting his throat.

The third act, *Simoon*, was based on a play by August Strindberg. It took place in Algeria in 1900 during a sand storm, and told the story of two men who avenge the death of one of their friends. The piece was performed by Jane Craner (Biskra), John Miller (Yusuf), Richard Roussin (Guimard), and Harriet Hill (Voice).

1094 Music-Hall Sidelights. THEATRE: Lion Theatre; OPENING DATE: October 19, 1978; PERFORMANCES: 24; BOOK: Jack Heifner; LYRICS: Jack Heifner; MUSIC: John McKinney; DIRECTION: Garland Wright; CHOREOGRAPHY: Randolyn Zinn; SCENERY: John Arnone; COSTUMES: David James; LIGHTING: Frances Aronson; PRODUCER: Lion Theatre Company (Gene Nye, Producing Director; Larry Carpenter, Managing Director)

CAST—Kim Ameen (La Tou Tou, Little Jady), Kathy Bates (Colette), Wanda Bimson (Lise Damoiseau, Giseal), Tony Campisi (Dog Trainer, Sultan), Janice Fuller (Ida, Gribiche's Mother), Jane Galloway (Bastienne, Gitanette), John Guerrasio (Marcel, Starvling), Jennifer Jestin (Misfit, Rita), Barbara LeBrun (Carmen Brasero), James McLure (Brague, Pierrot), Susan Merson (La Rousalika, Gribiche), Gene Nye (Compere)

SOURCE—The 1913 novel *L'Envers du Music-Hall* by Colette.

The musical was presented in two acts.

NOTES—The Off Off Broadway musical *Music-Hall Sidelights*, with book and lyrics by Jack Heifner, was based on Colette's *L'Envers du Music-Hall*, and featured Kathy Bates as Colette; the cast also included Jane Galloway and Susan Merson. In 1976, Bates, Galloway, and Merson had created the roles of the three cheerleaders in Heifner's hugely popular Off Broadway comedy *Vanities*, which ran for 1,785 performances. For other musicals based on Colette's life and writings, see entries for *Colette* and *Colette Collage*.

1095 Music, Music (1951). THEATRE: Provincetown Playhouse; OPENING DATE: August 14, 1951; PERFORMANCES: 5; LYRICS: Lorenzo Fuller; MUSIC: Lorenzo Fuller; PRODUCER: Joyce Slone

CAST—Shirley King, Betty George, Jimmy Merrick, Ronnie Kane, Judy Peters, Lynn Lyons, Marilyn Raphael, Dick Lavel

The revue was presented in one act.

MUSICAL NUMBERS—"Sometime" (Shirley King), "Smoke Gets in Your Eyes" (from *Roberta*, 1933; lyric by Otto Harbach, music by Jerome Kern) (Betty George), "Ol' Man River" (*Show Boat*, 1927; lyric by Oscar Hammerstein II, music by Jerome Kern) (Jimmy Merrick), "A Thing Like This" (Ronnie Kane), "Love Does" (Judy Peters), "A Slow Summer" (Lynn Lyons), "Embraceable You" (*Girl Crazy*, 1930; lyric by Ira Gershwin, music by George Gershwin) (Marilyn Raphael), "Music, Music" (Dick Lavel), "Music, Music" (reprise/finale) (Company)

NOTES—Although the program for *Music, Music* credited Lorenzo Fuller, some of the songs were standards by George Gershwin and Jerome Kern. The revue played out its limited engagement of five performances at the Provincetown Playhouse before embarking upon a short summer tour. "A Thing Like This" was later used in *The World's My Oyster* (see entry).

1096 Music! Music! "A Cavalcade of American Music." THEATRE: City Center 55th Street Theatre; OPENING DATE: April 11, 1974; PERFORMANCES: 37; TEXT: Alan Jay Lerner; LYRICS: See song list for credits; MUSIC: See song list for credits; DIRECTION: Martin Charnin; CHOREOGRAPHY: Tony Stevens; SCENERY: David Chapman; COSTUMES: Theoni V. Aldredge; LIGHTING: Martin Aronstein; MUSICAL DIRECTION: John Lesko; PRODUCERS: The City Center of Music and Drama, Inc. (Norman Singer, Executive Producer; Producers for City Center, Robert P. Brannigan and Chuck Eisler) and Alvin Bojar

CAST—GENE NELSON, LARRY KERT, KAREN MORROW, DONNA MCKECHNIE, ROBERT GUILLAUME, Will MacKenzie, Gail Nelson, Ted Pritchard, Arnold Soboloff, Russ Thacker; Singing and Dancing Ensemble: Renee Baughman, Trish Garland, Denise Mauthe, Michon Peacock, Tom Offt, Michael Radigan, Yolanda R. Raven, Freda Soiffer, Thomas (Thommie) J. Walsh

The revue was presented in two acts (song assignments unknown).

ACT ONE (1895-1941)—"Basin Street Blues" (lyric and music by Spencer Williams), "When the Saints Go Marching In" (traditional), "The Merry Widow Waltz" (from *The Merry Widow*, 1906; original German lyric apparently by Victor Leon and Leo Stein, English lyricist unknown; music by Franz Lehar), "Yankee Doodle Dandy" (*Little Johnny Jones*, 1906; lyric and music by George M. Cohan), "Over There" (1918; lyric and music by George M. Cohan), "I Didn't Raise My Boy to Be a Soldier" (lyric and music by Alfred Bryan and Al Piantadosi), "How Ya Gonna Keep 'Em Down on the Farm?" (lyric by Sam Lewis and Joe Young, music by Walter Donaldson), "Hinky Dinky Parlay Voo" (lyric and music by Al Dubin, Irving Mills, Jimmy McHugh, and Julian Dash), "Look for the Silver Lining" (*Sally*, 1921; lyric by B.G. [Buddy] DeSylva, music by Jerome Kern), "Bill" (*Show Boat*, 1927; lyric by P.G. Wodehouse, music by Jerome Kern), "Yes, Sir, That's My Baby" (lyric by Gus Kahn, music by Walter Donaldson), George Gershwin Medley: "Fascinating Rhythm" (*Funny Face*, 1927; lyric by Ira Gershwin), "Somebody Loves Me" (*George White's Scandals of 1924*; lyric by B.G. [Buddy] DeSylva and Ballard MacDonald), "The Babbitt and the Bromide" (*Funny Face*, 1927; lyric by Ira Gershwin), "Funny Face" (*Funny Face*, 1927; lyric by Ira Gershwin), "(I'll Build a) Stairway to Paradise" (*George White's Scandals of 1922*; lyric by Ira Gershwin and B.G. [Buddy] DeSylva), "The Man I Love" (lyric by Ira Gershwin; song was dropped during tryout of *Lady, Be Good!*, 1924; was used in the 1927 version of *Strike Up the Band*, which closed during, its pre–Broadway tryout; and was considered for, but not used in, *Rosalie*, 1928) "Oh, Lady Be Good" (*Lady, Be Good!*, 1924; lyric by Ira Gershwin), "Someone to Watch Over Me" (*Oh, Kay!*, 1927; lyric by Ira Gershwin), "Manhattan" (*The Garrick Gaities of 1925*; lyric by Lorenz Hart, music by Richard Rodgers), "The Girl Friend" (*The Girl Friend*, 1925; lyric by Lorenz Hart, music by Richard Rodgers), "Stouthearted Men" (*The New Moon*, 1928; lyric by Oscar Hammerstein II, music by Sigmund Romberg), "Lucky Lindy" (lyric and music by Abel Bauer and L. Wolfe Gilbert), "Brother, Can You Spare a Dime?" (*Americana*, 1932; lyric by E.Y. Harburg, music by Jay Gorney), "I'll See You Again" (*Bitter Sweet*, 1929 [London; also New York, later in the same year]; lyric and music by Noel Coward), "Great Day" (*Great Day!*, 1928; lyric by Edward Eliscu and Billy Rose, music by Vincent Youmans), "Stormy Weather" (*Cotton Club Revue of 1933*; lyric by Ted Koehler, music by Harold Arlen), "Bess, You Is My Woman Now" (*Porgy and Bess*, 1935; lyric by Ira Gershwin and DuBose Heyward, music by George Gershwin), "I Loves You, Porgy" (*Porgy and Bess*, 1935; lyric by Ira Gershwin and DuBose Heyward, music by George Gershwin), "Hooray for Hollywood" (film *Hollywood Hotel*, 1937; lyric by Johnny Mercer, music by Richard A. Whiting), "Lullaby of Broadway" (film *Golddiggers of 1935*; lyric by Al Dubin, music by Harry Warren)

ACT TWO (1941–1974)—"In the Mood" (lyric by Andy Razaf, music by Joe Garland), "There Are Such Things" (lyric and music by George W. Meyer, Abel Baer, and Stanley Adams), "The White Cliffs of Dover" (lyric and music by Walter Kent and Nat Burton), Medley of songs from *Oklahoma!* (1943; lyrics by Oscar Hammerstein II, music by Richard Rodgers), "Call Me Mister" (*Call Me Mister*, 1946; lyric and music by Harold Rome), "The Composers' Song" (a recitation written by Alan Jay Lerner), Rock and Roll Recitation, "Whiffenpoof Song" (a parody), Medley of songs from *My Fair Lady* (1956; lyrics by Alan Jay Lerner, music by Frederick Loewe), Medley of songs from *West Side Story* (1957; lyrics by Stephen Sondheim, music by Leonard Bernstein), Dance sequences from *The Music Man* (1957), *Camelot* (1960), *Bye Bye Birdie* (1960), and *Gypsy* (1959), Medley of songs from *Hello, Dolly!* (1964; lyrics and music by Jerry Herman), Medley of songs from *Fiddler on the Roof* (1964; lyrics by Sheldon Harnick, music by Jerry Bock), "Abraham, Martin and John" (lyric and music by Dick Holler), "Maman" (*Mata Hari*, 1967; closed during pre-Broadway tryout; lyric by Martin Charnin, music by Edward Thomas), "I Believe in Music" (lyric and music by Mac Davis)

NOTES—During the period of the nation's Bicentennial, a number of quickly forgotten revues appeared, all of which celebrated American music in somewhat slapdash fashion (it isn't quite clear why Noel Coward's "I'll See You Again" appeared in *Music! Music!* because the song is one of the most famous ballads ever introduced in a *British* musical [*Bitter-Sweet*, 1929]; similarly, "The Merry Widow Waltz" is one of the most famous songs to emerge from *Austrian* operetta). New York saw another such short-lived revue, *A Musical Jubilee*. It opened on Broadway in 1975 for ninety-two performances, and its cast included Larry Kert, an alumnus of *Music! Music!* And in 1975, Washington, D.C., saw a similar revue, *Sing America Sing*, which was choreographed by Tony Stevens, who performed a similar duty for *Music! Music!*

1097 Musical Chairs. "A New Musical." THEATRE: Rialto Theatre; OPENING DATE: May 14, 1980; PERFORMANCES: 14; BOOK: Barry Berg, Ken Donnelly, and Tom Savage; LYRICS: Tom Savage; MUSIC: Tom Savage; DIRECTION: Rudy Tronto; Susan Stroman, Assistant Choreographer; CHOREOGRAPHY: Rudy Tronto; SCENERY: Ernest Allen Smith; COSTUMES: Michael J. Cesario; LIGHTING: Peggy Clark; MUSICAL DIRECTION: Barry H. Gordon; PRODUCERS: Lesley Savage and Bert Stratford

CAST—RON HOLGATE (Joe Preston), Eileen McCabe (Matty), Douglas Walker (Stage Manager), Scott Ellis (Sally's Boyfriend), Enid Blaymore (Millie), GRACE KEAGY (Roberta), Randall Easterbrook (Brad), Leslie-Anne Wolfe (Miranda), PATTI KARR (Lillian), BRANDON MAGGART (Harold), JESS RICHARDS (Gary), JOY FRANZ (Janet), Edward Earle (Brown Suit), Tom (Tommy) Breslin (Blue Suit), Rick Emery (Tuxedo), LEE MEREDITH (Valerie Brooks)

The action occurs in a partial area of the orchestra section of an Off Broadway theatre on the opening night of the play *Forest of Shadows*.

The musical was presented in two acts.

ACT ONE—Overture (Orchestra), "Tonight's the Night" (Company), "My Time" (Ronald Holgate), "Who's Who" (Company), "If I Could Be Beautiful" (Leslie-Anne Wolfe, Boys), "What I Could Have Done Tonight" (Brandon Maggart, Joy Franz), "There You Are" (Rick Emery), "Sally" (Scott Ellis, Company), "Other People" (Joy Franz), "My Time" (reprise) (Ron Holgate), "Hit the Ladies" (Patti Karr, Ladies)

ACT TWO—"Musical Chairs" (Rick Emery, Tom Breslin, Edward Earle), "Suddenly Love" (Jess Richards), "Better Than Broadway" (Enid Blaymore, Grace Keagy), "Every Time the Music Starts" (Randall Easterbrook, Company), "There You Are" (reprise) (Rick Emery, Ron Holgate, Lee Meredith), "My Time" (reprise) (Ron Holgate)

NOTES—*Musical Chairs* told its story from the perspective of a cross-section of the audience attending the opening night of an Off Broadway play called *Forest of Shadows*. Included in the audience are the play's author, a few critics, and other assorted opening-night types. After seeing *Musical Chairs*, Frank Rich in the *New York Times* said *Reggae* was no longer the worst musical of the season (a "musical confusion" [according to Mel Gussow in his review for the *Times*], *Reggae* had opened two months earlier and had played for twenty-one performances). *Reggae* holds a special place in theatrical lore because during the opening night performance the theatre's sound system picked up signals from a radio station; as a result, first-nighters got to watch the new musical *and* to hear sportscaster Marv Albert give a play-by-play description of an ongoing Knicks game. Given the trite dialogue and lyrics of *Musical Chairs* (the lyrics included "some memorable lulus"), Rich suggested the producers of *Musical Chairs* should consider broadcasting the Mets' games or even "the collected hits of Jerry Vale" over the Rialto's sound system.

As *How's the House?* (see entry), *Musical Chairs* had been previously produced Off Off Broadway at the Park Royal; the musical was based on an original story concept by Larry P. Pontillo.

Ronald Holgate and Grace Keagy left the production midway through the musical's two-week run, and were replaced by Tom Urich and Helon Blount. Original Cast Records released the cast album (LP # OC-2084), which includes Urich and Blount in the roles created by Holgate and Keagy. The script was published by Samuel French in 1982.

1098 A Musical Merchant of Venice. THEATRE: Roundabout Theatre/Stage Two; OPENING DATE: June 4, 1975; PERFORMANCES: 12; BOOK: William Shakespeare; LYRICS: Tony Tanner; MUSIC: Jim Smith; DIRECTION: Tony Tanner; SCENERY: Sandro LaFerla; COSTUMES: Dwayne Moritz; LIGHTING: Lewis Mead; PRODUCERS: Roundabout Theatre Company (Gene Feist, Producing Director; Michael Fried, Executive Director); David Guc, Associate Producer

CAST—Gary Beach (Lorenzo), Rudy Hornish (Antonio), Cara-Duff McCormick (Portia), Mary Ann Robbins (Jessica), Danny Sewell (Shylock), Albert Verdesca (Duke), Sel Vitella (Arragon), John Thomas Waite (Gratiano), Phylis Ward (Nerissa), Mark Winkworth (Bassanio); Chorus: Michael Bright, Linda diDario, Nancy Donovan, Jack Godby, Sara Maylond, Theresa Saldana

SOURCE—The play *The Merchant of Venice* by William Shakespeare (written between 1594 and 1597).

NOTES—The musical was presented in a workshop production for a limited engagement of twelve performances. For another musical version of *The Merchant of Venice*, see entry for *Shylock*.

1099 The Musical of Musicals. "The Musical!" THEATRE: The Theatre at Saint Peter's Church/The York Theatre Company; transferred to Dodger Stages on February 10, 2005; OPENING DATE: December 16, 2003; PERFORMANCES: 512; BOOK: Eric Rockwell and Joanne Bogart; LYRICS: Joanne Bogart; MUSIC: Eric Rockwell; DIRECTION: Pamela Hunt; CHOREOGRAPHY: Pamela Hunt; SCENERY: James Morgan; COSTUMES: John Carver Sullivan; LIGHTING: Mary Jo Dondlinger; PRODUCER: The York Theatre Company (James Morgan, Artistic Director; Louis Chiodo, Managing Director)

CAST—Joanne Bogart, Craig Fols, Lovette George, Eric Rockwell

The evening of five musicals was presented in two acts (with an intermission between the third and fourth musical).

NOTES—*The Musical of Musicals* was an evening of five mini-musicals, each one utilizing the same basic plot and written in the styles of Richard Rodgers and Oscar Hammerstein II, Stephen Sondheim, Jerry Herman, Andrew Lloyd Webber, and John Kander and Fred Ebb. Musicals have spoofed themselves over the years. In fact, less than a year after *Oklahoma!* opened, the 1944 Broadway musical *Jackpot* included a parody of Agnes de Mille with its dance number "Grist for De Mille." The first half of the second act of London's *Songbook* (1979; seen in New York in 1981 as *The Moony Shapiro Songbook*) kidded Rodgers and Hammerstein with its on-target spoof of an imaginary 1954 musical called *Happy Hickory*; the spoof included "vocal gems" from the production, two "trunk" songs, and the title song as performed in the 1956 international tour which played in Tel Aviv and Moscow. In 1977, Off Off Broadway offered *North Atlantic* (see entry), a full evening's spoof of Rodgers and Hammerstein. In 1982, the revue *Corkscrews* (see entry) included a mini-spoof of Sondheim's musicals (*Psychotic Overtures*). Further, such musicals as *Hooray!! ... It's a Glorious Day and All That* (1966), *Smith* (1973), and *Urinetown* (2001) kidded the overall genre (see entries).

But *The Musical of Musicals* went one step further, and presented a set of five mini-musicals spoofing the sacred cows of musical theatre. All five musicals used the same basic plot (heroine is threatened with eviction by evil landlord, and hero must come to the rescue), and then dressed up that plot in the songs and styles of the composers and lyricists being kidded. In *Corn!*, the Rodgers and Hammerstein spoof, the hero-cowboy-farmer Big Willy sings "I'm in love with a beautiful hoe"; in *A Little Complex*, the evil landlord evicts his tenants by slashing their throats (and when criticized for making an unseemly comment, he replies "A funny thing happened on the way to decorum").

The cast of four (Joanne Bogart, Craig Fols, Lovette George, and Eric Rockwell [Bogart and Rockwell had also written the musical]) played the characters in all five musicals, as well as the chorus. A program note indicated all "really good" actors never appear in the chorus "unless it turns out that, well, they have to. And then they do so only grudgingly." The five mini-musical spoofs were as follows:

Corn! (In the style of Richard Rodgers and Oscar Hammerstein II):

CAST—Craig Fols (Big Willy), Lovette George (June), Eric Rockwell (Jidder), Joanne Bogart (Mother Abby)

MUSICAL NUMBERS—"Oh, What Beautiful Corn" (Craig Fols), "I Couldn't Keer Less About You" (Lovette George), "I Don't Love You" (Craig Fols), "Follow Your Dream" (Joanne Bogart), "Dream Ballet" (Company), "Sowillyquey" (Craig Fols), "Clam Dip" (Chorus), "Daylight Savings Time" (Chorus), "Corn Finale" (Company)

A Little Complex (In the style of Stephen Sondheim)

CAST—Eric Rockwell (Jitter), Lovette George (Jeune), Craig Fols (Billy), Joanne Bogart (Abby)

MUSICAL NUMBERS—"Welcome to the Woods" (Chorus), "The Ballad of Jitter" (Chorus), "Jitter's Oath" (Eric Rockwell), "Birds" (Lovette George), "Getting Away with Murder" (Eric Rockwell), "Billy-Baby"/"A Melody?" (Lovette George, Craig Fols), "Stay with Me" (Eric Rockwell, Lovette George, Craig Fols), "We're All Gonna Die" (Joanne Bogart), "Complex Finale" (Chorus)

Dear Abby! (In the style of Jerry Herman):

CAST—Joanne Bogart (Auntie Abby), Lovette George (Junie Faye), Craig Fols (William), Eric Rockwell (Mr. Jitters)

MUSICAL NUMBERS—"Dear Abby" (Chorus), "Take My Advice and Live" (Joanne Bogart, Chorus), "Show Tune" (Craig Fols, Lovette George), "Did I Put Out Enough?" (Joanne Bogart), "Dear Abby Finale" (Chorus)

Aspects of Junita (in the style of Andrew Lloyd Webber):

CAST—Lovette George (Junita), Craig Fols (Bill), Eric Rockwell (Phantom Jitter), Joanne Bogart (Abigail Von Schtarr)

MUSICAL NUMBERS—"Aspects of Juanita"/Prologue (Craig Fols, Chorus), "I've Heard That Song Before" (Lovette George), "Opera Scena" (Company), "Sing a Song" (Eric Rockwell), "Junita's Recitative" (Lovette George), "Go Go Go Go Junita" (Chorus), "We Never Talk Anymore" (Craig Fols, Lovette George), "A Sense of Entitlement"/"Second Opera Scena" (Chorus, Lovette George), "Over the Top" (Joanne Bogart), "Chandelier Scena" (Craig Fols, Lovette George, Eric Rockwell), "Aspects Finale" (Company)

Speakeasy (in the style of John Kander and Fred Ebb)

CAST—Eric Rockwell (Jitter), Lovette George (Juny), Craig Fols (Villy), Joanne Bogart (Fraulein Abby)

MUSICAL NUMBERS—"Hola, Aloha, Hello" (Eric Rockwell), "Juny with a 'J'" (Lovette George), "Color Me Gay" (Craig Vols), "Just Don't Pay" (Chorus), "Easy Mark" (Joanne Bogart), "Round and Round" (Lovette George, Chorus)

The evening ended with a finale, "Done," in which the audience is described as "screaming for the exit."

The musical played a total of 512 performances at two theatres (The Theatre at Saint Peter's Church and Dodger Stages) which included two lengthy hiatus periods.

The script was published by Samuel French, Inc., in 2005, and the cast recording was released by Jay Records (CD # CDJAY-1376).

1100 Musicals in Mufti

NOTES—The York Theatre Company, which is under the direction of James Morgan (Producing Artistic Director), Brian Blythe (Associate Artistic Director), and Nancy P. Barry (Developmental Director), is a vibrant and invaluable theatre company which not only produces new musicals (many of which are discussed in these pages, such as *After the Fair*, *Fermat's Last Tango*, *The Jello Is Always Red*, *Lingoland*, *No Way to Treat a Lady*, *Taking a Chance on Love*, and *Prodigal*) but also revives neglected musicals under its *Musicals in Mufti* series (that is, musicals presented "in everyday clothes, without all the trappings of a large production"). *Musicals in Mufti* along with *Encores!* and *Musicals Tonight!* (see entries) offer theatergoers the opportunity of seeing about a dozen lost (or at least rarely produced) musicals during each theatre season.

During the years, the York has produced over sixty concert revivals of musicals which for one reason or another have gone by the wayside. Some, like *Wish You Were Here*, were hits in their time, but now are generally forgotten; others, like *Greenwillow*, were failures on Broadway but are deserving of revival because of their superior scores; still others, like *Mata Hari*, were never produced in New York, having closed during their pre-Broadway tryouts; some, such as *Mirette*, have been produced only in regional theatre and have not been seen in New York; and a few, such as *I and Albert*, have been produced in London but not in New York. The following is a partial list of some of the musicals resurrected by the York in the *Musicals in Mufti* series (each musical is followed by the names of its lyricist and composer; the year in which the original production opened; and the number of performances of the original run): *Bajour* (lyrics and music by Walter Marks; 1964, 218 performances), *Beggar's Holiday* (lyrics by John LaTouche, music by Duke Ellington; 1946, 111 performances), *Billion Dollar Baby* (lyrics by Betty Comden and Adolph Green, music by Morton Gould; 1945, 219 performances), *Carmelina* (lyrics by Alan Jay Lerner, music by Burton Lane; 1979, 17 performances), *Carmen Jones* (lyrics by Oscar Hammerstein II, music by Georges Bizet; 1943, 502 performances), *Celebration* (lyrics by Tom Jones, music by Harvey Schmidt; 1969, 109 performances), *Darling of the Day* (lyrics by E.Y. Harburg, music by Jule Styne; 1968, 32 performances), *The Day Before Spring* (lyrics by Alan Jay Lerner, music by Frederick Loewe; 1945, 167 performances), *Fanny* (lyrics and music by Harold Rome; 1954, 888 performances), *The Girl Who Came to Supper* (lyrics and music by Noel Coward; 1963, 112 performances), *God Bless You, Mr. Rosewater* (lyrics by Howard Ashman, music by Alan Menken; 1979, 49 performances), *Golden Boy* (lyrics by Lee Adams, music by Charles Strouse; 1964, 569 performances), *The Good Companions* (lyrics by Johnny Mercer, music by Andre Previn; London, 1974; 252 performances), *The Grass Harp* (lyrics by Kenward Elmslie, music by Claibe Richardson; 1971, 7 performances), *Greenwillow* (lyrics and music by Frank Loesser; 1960, 95 performances), *I and Albert* (lyrics by Lee Adams, music by Charles Strouse; London, 1972; 120 performances), *It's a Bird ... It's a Plane ... It's Superman* (lyrics by Lee Adams, music by Charles Strouse; 1966, 129 performances), *Johnny Johnson* (lyrics by Paul Green, music by Kurt Weill; 1936, 68 performances), *Jumbo* (lyrics by Lorenz Hart, music by Richard Rodgers; 1935, 233 performances), *Kelly* (lyrics by Eddie Lawrence, music by Moose Charlap; 1965, 1 performance), *Lucky Stiff* (lyrics by Lynn Ahrens, music by Stephen Flaherty; 1988, 15 performances), *Mata Hari* (lyrics by Martin Charnin, music by Edward Thomas; closed during pre-Broadway tryout in 1967), *Mirette* (lyrics by Tom Jones, music by Harvey Schmidt; produced in regional theatre in 1998), *Onward Victoria* (lyrics by Charlotte Anker and Irene Rosenberg, music by Keith Herrmann; 1980, 1 performance), *Regina* (lyrics and music by Marc Blitzstein; 1949, 56 performances), *Rex* (lyrics by Sheldon Harnick, music by Richard Rodgers; 1976, 48 performances), *70, Girls, 70* (lyrics by Fred Ebb, music by John Kander; 1971, 36 performances), *Weird Romance* (lyrics by David Spencer, music by Alan Menken; 1992, 50 performances), *Wish You Were Here* (lyrics and music by Harold Rome; 1952, 598 performances), For the 2007-2008 season, *Musicals in Mufti* offered a deserving salute to legendary librettist Joseph Stein, who wrote the books for *Plain and Fancy* (lyrics by Arnold B. Horwitt, music by Albert Hague; 1955, 461 performances [the book was co-written with Will Glickman]); *Mr. Wonderful* (lyrics and music by Jerry Bock, Larry Holofcener, and George Weiss; 1956, 383 performances [the book was co-written with Will Glickman]); *Juno* (lyrics and music by Marc Blitzstein; 1959, 16 performances); *Take Me Along* (lyrics and music by Bob Merrill; 1959, 448 performances [the book was co-written with Robert Russell); and *Fiddler on the Roof* (lyrics by Sheldon Harnick, music by Jerry Bock; 1964, 3,242 performances). The *Mufti* tribute presented four of Stein's musicals: *The Baker's Wife* (lyrics and music by Stephen Schwartz; closed during its pre-Broadway tryout in 1976); *The Body Beautiful* (lyrics by Sheldon Harnick, music by Jerry Bock; 1958, 60 performances); *So Long, 174th Street* (lyrics and music by Stan Daniels; 1976, 16 performances; the musical was based on Stein's hit comedy *Enter Laughing*, which opened on Broadway in 1963 and played for 419 performances); and *Zorba* (lyrics by Fred Ebb, music by John Kander; 1968, 305 performances).

The 1998 *Musicals in Mufti* production of the 1945 musical *Billion Dollar Baby* (see entry) led directly to the musical's first recording (by Original Cast Records CD # OC-4304); and *Mufti's* 2003 production of *Lucky Stiff* was recorded by Jay Records (CD # CDJAY-1379) (see entry for the 1988 production of *Lucky Stiff*).

1101 Musicals Tonight!

NOTES—Founded in 1998 by Mel Miller, its Producer and Artistic Director, *Musicals Tonight!*, like *Encores!* and *Musicals in Mufti* (see entries), is dedicated to presenting short-run revivals of mostly neglected musicals. The following musicals have been presented by the company (after the date of each musical are the names of the lyricist and composer; the year in which the original production opened; and the number of performances for the original runs): *The Beauty Prize* (lyrics by P.G. Wodehouse, music by Jerome Kern; London, 1923; 213 performances), *By the Beautiful Sea* (lyrics by Dorothy Fields, music by Arthur Schwartz; 1954, 270 performances), *Cabin in the Sky* (lyrics by John LaTouche, music by Vernon Duke; 1940, 156 performances), *Chee-Chee* (lyrics by Lorenz Hart, music by Richard Rodgers; 1928, 31 performances), *The Chocolate Soldier* (lyrics by Stanislaus Stange, music by Oscar Strauss; 1909, 296 performances), *Dearest Enemy* (lyrics by Lorenz Hart, music by Richard Rodgers; 1925, 286 performances), *Drat! The Cat!* (lyrics by Ira Levin, music by Milton Schafer; 1965, eight performances), *Face the Music* (lyrics and music by Irving Berlin; 1932, 165 performances), *Fifty Million Frenchmen* (lyrics and music by Cole Porter; 1929, 254 performances), *Foxy* (lyrics by Johnny Mercer, music by Robert Emmett Dolan; 1964, 72 performances), *Gay Divorce* (lyrics and music by Cole Porter; 1932, 248 performances), *Girl Crazy* (lyrics by Ira Gershwin, music by George Gershwin; 1930, 272 performances), *The Girl Friend* (lyrics by Lorenz Hart, music by Richard Rodgers; 1926, 301 performances) *Goldilocks* (lyrics by Joan Ford and Jean and Walter Kerr, music by Leroy Anderson; 1958, 161 performances), *Good News* (lyrics by B.G. [Buddy] DeSylva and Lew Brown, music by Ray Henderson; 1927, 551 performances), *Have a Heart* (lyrics by P.G. Wodehouse, music by Jerome Kern; 1917, 76 performances), *The High Life* (originally produced as *The Gay Life* in 1961; 113 performances) (lyrics by Howard Dietz, music by Arthur Schwartz), *I Married an Angel* (lyrics by Lorenz Hart, music by Richard Rodgers; 1938, 338 performances), *Jubilee* (lyrics and music by Cole Porter; 1935, 169 performances), *King of Hearts* (lyrics by Jacob Brackman, music by Peter Link; 1978, 48 performances), *Lady, Be Good!* (lyrics by Ira Gershwin, music by Ira Gershwin; 1924, 330 performances), *Leave It to Me!* (lyrics and music by Cole Porter; 1938, 307 performances), *Let It Ride!* (lyrics and music by Jay Livingston and Ray Evans; 1961, 68 performances), *Let's Face It!* (lyrics and music by Cole Porter; 1941, 547 performances), *Look, Ma, I'm Dancin'!* (lyrics and music by Hugh Martin; 1948, 188 performances), *Love from Judy* (lyrics by Jack [Timothy] Gray and Hugh Martin, music by Hugh Martin; London, 1952; 594 performances), *Mademoiselle Modiste* (lyrics by Henry Blossom, music by Victor Herbert; 1905, 202 performances), *Meet Me in St. Louis* (lyrics and music by Hugh Martin and Ralph Blane; film version released in 1945; first produced on the stage in 1960 in regional productions; first produced on Broadway in 1989 for 253 performances), *My Favorite Year* (lyrics by Lynn Ahrens, music by Stephen Flaherty; 1992, 37 performances), *The New Yorkers* (lyrics and music by Cole Porter; 1930, 168 performances), *Oh, Lady! Lady!!* (lyrics by P.G. Wodehouse, music by Jerome Kern; 1918, 219 performances), *Primrose* (lyrics by Desmond Carter, music by George Gershwin; London, 1924; 255 performances), *The Roar of the Greasepaint—The Smell of the Crowd* (lyrics and music by Leslie Bricusse and Anthony Newley; 1965, 232 performances), *So Long, 174th Street* (lyrics and music by Stan Daniels; 1976, 16 performances), *Stop! Look! Listen!* (lyrics and music by Irving Berlin; 1915, 105 performances), *That's the Ticket!* (lyrics and music by Harold Rome; closed during pre-Broadway tryout in 1948), *Watch Your Step!* (lyrics and music by Irving Berlin; 1914, 175), The 2006-2007 season of *Musicals Tonight!* saluted veteran performer George S. Irving with five musicals: *Ernest in Love* (lyrics by Anne Croswell, music by Lee Pockriss; 1960, 111 performances; for *Musicals Tonight!*, Irving played the role of Lady Bracknell); *The Happy Time* (lyrics by Fred Ebb, music by John Kander; 1968, 268 performances; in the original 1968 production, Irving played the role of Philippe Bonnard, the eldest son; for the *Musicals Tonight!* revival, he played the role of Louis Bonnard, the father); *Irene* (lyrics by Joseph McCarthy, music by Harry Tierney; 1919, 670 performances; revived on Broadway in 1973 for 594 performances; Irving appeared in the 1973 revival, winning the Tony Award for Best Supporting Actor in a Musical for his role as Madame Lucy); *Me and My Girl* (lyrics by Douglas Furber and L. Arthur Rose, music by Noel Gay; London, 1937, 1,646 performances; New York, 1986, 1,420 performances; in the Broadway production, Irving performed the role of Sir John Tremayne); and *Shinbone Alley* (lyrics by Joe Darion, music by George Kleinsinger; 1957, 49 performances; for the Broadway production, Irving performed the role of Big Bill). The *Musicals Tonight*! tribute to George S. Irving was a deserving salute to this legendary Broadway veteran who since 1943 has performed in over twenty Broadway and Off Broadway musicals as well as numerous comedies and dramas. Irving appeared in the original productions of three musicals by Richard Rodgers (*Oklahoma!* [1943], *Me and Juliet* [1953], and *I Remember Mama* [1979]), and was also in the original Broadway productions of *Call Me Mister* (1946), *Along Fifth Avenue* (1949), *Gentlemen Prefer Blondes* (1949), *Two's Company* (1952), *Bells Are Ringing* (1956), *Irma La Douce* (1960), *Bravo Giovanni* (1962), *Tovarich* (1963), *Anya* (1965), and *Copperfield* (1981). He was in the 1983 Broadway revival of *On Your Toes* and in Al Carmines' 1969 Off Broadway musical *Promenade* as well as the original productions of two plays by Gore Vidal, *Romulus* (1962) and *An Evening with Richard Nixon and ...* (1972). Irving appeared in ten other Broadway productions, and was also in the ill-fated tryout of Harold Rome's *That's the Ticket!* (when *Musicals Tonight!* resurrected this rarity, Irving was among the revival's cast members).

Three productions from the *Musicals Tonight!* series have been recorded: *Foxy*, *Look, Ma, I'm Dancin'!*, and *That's the Ticket!* (see entries).

1102 My Heart Is in the East.

"A New Musical." THEATRE: Jewish Repertory Theatre; OPENING DATE: May 28, 1983; PERFORMANCES: 23; BOOK: Linda Kline; LYRICS: Richard Engquist; MUSIC: Raphael Crystal; DIRECTION: Ran Avni; ADDITIONAL STAGING by Haila Strauss; SCENERY: Jeffrey Schneider; COSTUMES: Karen Hummel; LIGHTING: Phil Monat; MUSICAL DIRECTION: Raphael Crystal; PRODUCER: The Jewish Repertory Theater (Ran Avni, Artistic Director)

CAST—Steve Sterner (Benjamin, Captain, Chief Rabbi), John M. Towey (Judah Halevy), Nancy Mayans (Mazal, Keturah), Adam Heller (Issac, Emir, Aaron), Angelina Reaux (Tamar, Turkha, Zipporah), Dave DeChristopher (Simon, Halfan), Susan Victor (Muna, Midwife, Shifra)

The action occurs in Cordoba, Spain; at sea; and in Egypt in 1140.

The musical was presented in two acts.

ACT ONE—"That's How It Is" (John M. Towey, Ensemble), "The Pen" (John M. Towey), "That's How It Is" (reprise) (Steve Sterner), "After I Go to Sleep" (Angelina Reaux), "First Things First" (Adam Heller, Steve Sterner, Dave DeChristopher), "First Things First" (reprise) (John M. Towey), "Stars of the Morning" (Nancy Mayans), "Neighbors" (Angelina Reaux, Nancy Mayans), "Another April" (John M. Towey, Angelina Reaux), "The Kuzari" (Steve Sterner, Ensemble [Rabbi, Angel, King, Philosopher, Priest, Mullah), "Camellias" (Angelina Reaux), "Word Game" (Adam Heller, John M. Towey), "My Heart Is in the East" (John M. Towey)

ACT TWO—"Baggage" (John M. Towey), "Beautiful Storm" (John M. Towey, Sailors, 'Abu Jafar'), "Stars of the Morning" (reprise) (John M. Towey), "Take a Little Time" (Adam Heller, Nancy Mayans, John M. Towey, Angelina Reaux, Rabbi), "Take a Little Time" (reprise) (Dave DeChristopher), "Why, Love?" (Susan Victor, John M. Towey), "Now Is All I Have" (John M. Towey), "My Heart Is in the East" (reprise) (Company), "Stars of the Morning" (Company)

NOTES—The Off Off Broadway musical *My Heart Is in the East* was based on the life and times of Judah Halevy, a poet who lived in twelfth-century Spain. Richard F. Shepard in the *New York Times* noted that the "awkwardly simplistic" vignette-like book was weak, and felt the story never matched the passion of the central character, a poet whose writings expressed "his passion for Zion" and "his yearning to visit Jerusalem." But Shepard said the score was "something else," and he praised Raphael Crystal's bright music and Richard Engquist's "clever" lyrics, singling out three songs ("After I Go to Sleep," "First Things First," and "Take a Little Time").

1103 My Life with Albertine. "A New Musical." THEATRE: Playwrights Horizons; OPENING DATE: March 13, 2003; PERFORMANCES: 22; BOOK: Richard Nelson; LYRICS: Richard Nelson and Ricky Ian Gordon; MUSIC: Ricky Ian Gordon; DIRECTION: Richard Nelson; CHOREOGRAPHY: Sean Curran; SCENERY: Thomas Lynch; COSTUMES: Susan Hilferty; LIGHTING: James F. Ingalls; MUSICAL DIRECTION: Charles Prince; PRODUCERS: Playwrights Horizons (Tim Sanford, Artistic Director; Leslie Marcus, Managing Director; William Russo, General Manager); Ira Weitzman, Associate Producer

CAST—Brent Carver (The Narrator), Chad Kimball (Marcel), Kelli O'Hara (Albertine), Donna Lynne Champlin (Grandmother, Francoise), Emily Skinner (Mlle. Lea), Caroline McMahon (Andree), Brooke Sunny Moriber (Rosemonde), Paul Anthony McGrane (The Pianist), Laura Woyasz (Mlle. Lea's Girlfriend), Nicholas Belton/Jim Poulos/Paul S. Schaefer (Three Young Men)

SOURCE—The "Albertine" sections of Marcel Proust's *Remembrance of Things Past* (the overall title for his seven-volume series of novels written between 1913-1927).

The action occurs at a private theatre in an apartment in Paris in 1919.

The musical was presented in two acts.

ACT ONE—"It Is Too Late" (Kelli O'Hara), "Balbec-by-the-Sea" (Chad Kimball, Brent Carver, Bathers, Strollers), "Lullabye" (Donna Lynne Champlin), "Ferret Song" (Kelli O'Hara, Caroline McMahon, Brooke Sunny Moriber, Chad Kimball), "My Soul Weeps" (Kelli O'Hara), "The Prayer" (Chad Kimball, Donna Lynne Champlin, Company), "Talk About the Weather" (Chad Kimball, Donna Lynne Champlin, Company), "The Different Albertines" (Brent Carver, Chad Kimball), "My Soul Weeps" (reprise) (Emily Skinner, Caroline McMahon, Brooke Sunny Moriber, Laura Woyasz, Company), "But What I Say" (Brent Carver, Chad Kimball, Kelli O'Hara), "Song of Solitude" (Brent Carver)

ACT TWO—"I Want You" (Emily Skinner), "I Need Me a Girl" (Kelli O'Hara, Company), "Sometimes" (Brent Carver, Chad Kimball), "But What I Say" (reprise) (Brent Carver, Chad Kimball, Kelli O'Hara), "Sometimes" (reprise) (Emily Skinner, Caroline McMahon, Brooke Sunny Moriber), "Ferret Song" (reprise) (Kelli O'Hara, Chad Kimball, Caroline McMahon), "The Street" (Chad Kimball, Company), "The Different Albertines" (reprise) (Brent Carver, Chad Kimball), "The Letters" (Kelli O'Hara, Chad Kimball, Brent Carver, Donna Lynne Champlin, Company), "It Is Too Late" (reprise) (Brent Carver), "If It Is True" (Kelli O'Hara)

NOTES—In 1999, Richard Nelson adapted James Joyce's short story "The Dead" for the musical stage (see entry for *James Joyce's The Dead*); with *My Life with Albertine*, he turned to another "difficult" writer, Marcel Proust, adapting segments from his epic *Remembrance of Things Past*.

The musical focused on the elder Marcel (played by Brent Carver, as the Narrator) looking back on his youthful self (Chad Kimball) and his infatuation with the elusive Albertine (Kelli O'Hara).

The musical was somewhat cooly received by the critics (Charles Isherwood in *Variety* found it "static and choppy ...ultimately pedantic"), but Ben Brantley in the *New York Times* noted that Ricky Ian Gordon's score offered glimpses "of a Proustian fluidity of feeling and form," and singled out the opening sequence which "seems to swirl with regret, romance, fear, and, yes, a sense of lost time."

The impressive and evocative score was recorded by PS Classics Records (CD # PS-313).

1104 My Lucky Day. "Yiddish American Musical." THEATRE: Second Avenue Theatre; OPENING DATE: Early 1950s (?); PERFORMANCES: Unknown; BOOK: Louis Freiman; LYRICS: Jacob Jacobs; MUSIC: Joseph Rumshinsky; DIRECTION: Louis Freiman; CHOREOGRAPHY: Felix Sadoski; SCENERY: Michael Saltzman; PRODUCERS: Irving Jacobson and Edmund Zayenda

CAST—SELMA KAYE (Mary Nelson), MIRIAM KRESSYN (Evelyn), Lucy Gehrman (Dora), Gustave Berger (Dr. Bernard Edelman), EDMUND ZAYENDA (George Prince), IRVING JACOBSON (Meyer Yoina), YETTA ZWERLING (Tzippe), MAE SCHOENFIELD (Fannie), Esta Saltzman (Annie), David Lubritsky (Jerry), Moe Zaar (Arthur), Charles Cohan (Marcel), Israel Mandell (Policeman)

1105 My Mama the General. THEATRE: Burstein Theatre; OPENING DATE: October 9, 1973; PERFORMANCES: 111; BOOK: Eli Shagi (translated from the Hebrew by Moshe Sachar); English narration by Lillian Lux; LYRICS AND MUSIC: Nurit Hirsch and Lillian Lux; DIRECTION: Israel Valin; CHOREOGRAPHY: Baruch Blum; SCENERY: Van; MUSICAL DIRECTION: Elliot Finkel; PRODUCER: Israel Valin

CAST—Natalie Rogers (Narrator), PESACH BURSTEIN (Binstock [Papa]), JAIME LEWIN (Sgt. Shmuli), Gerri-Ann Frank (Hedvah), LILLIAN LUX (Mama [Zelda]), Baruch Blum (Lt. Arik), William Gary (Colonel). The action occurs during the Six Day War at a tank division on the Suez Canal., The musical was presented in two acts.

ACT ONE—"Galicianer Cabellero" (Pesach Burstein), "Shalom Suez" (Lillian Lux), "Kalt Vi Ize (Cold as Ice)" (Duet) (Baruch Blum, Gerri-Ann Frank), "Mine Zien (My Son)" (Soliloquy) (Lillian Lux)

ACT TWO—"Look at Mama, the General!" (Duet) (Pesach Burstein, Lillian Lux), "Ch'ob Zich Areinge-Dreit (How Did I Get Into This?)" (Pesach Burstein), "Kimen Vet der Sholom (Peace Will Come)" (Finale) (Ensemble)

NOTES—*My Mama the General*, the long-running Israeli hit musical about a Jewish mother who fights in the Six-Day War, managed a run of over three months; at the time of its New York production, the musical was in its third year in Israel. Richard F. Shepard in the *New York Times* noted the musical often had "charm" and comic moments, but felt that recent political realities of the Middle East had a dampening effect on the evening. He wrote that in peacetime, a military setting could make for "high humor," but in time of war, "it hurts too much to laugh." He emphasized that while the musical "really wants to be liked," the "frightening headlines" of the day prevented him from enjoying the "merriment" of the plot, which dealt with the titular mama who visits her son at the Suez Canal and becomes involved in combat "high-jinks."

The program cover referenced the musical's title as *Mein Mama der General*, but the program's title page gave the title as *My Mama the General*.

It appears that early in the run Natalie Rogers was the production's narrator.

The Burstein Theatre had been formerly known as the Bert Wheeler Theatre and the Carter Theatre.

1106 My Mother Was a Fortune-Teller. THEATRE: Hudson Guild Theatre; OPENING DATE: May 5, 1978; PERFORMANCES: 24; LYRICS: See song list for credits; MUSIC: See song list for credits; DIRECTION: Arthur Laurents; CHOREOGRAPHY: Elizabeth Keen; SCENERY: Philipp Jung; COSTUMES: Bill Kellard; LIGHTING: Toni Golden; MUSICAL DIRECTION: Herbert Kaplan

CAST—PHYLLIS NEWMAN

The revue was presented in two acts.

ACT ONE—"My Mother Was a Fortune-Teller" (lyric by Phyllis Newman, music by John Clifton), South American Medley (arranged by John Clifton), "Woman in the Moon" (lyric by Barbra Streisand, music by Kenny Asher), "My Mother Was a Fortune-Teller" (reprise), "What Makes Me Love Him" (from *The Apple Tree*, 1966; lyric by Sheldon Harnick, music by Jerry Bock), "Don't Laugh" (*Hot Spot*, 1963; lyric by Martin Charnin and Stephen Sondheim, music by Mary Rodgers), "No One's Toy" (lyric and music by Joe [Joseph] Raposo), Woman's (Women's) Medley

ACT TWO—"Some People" (*Gypsy*, 1959; lyric by Stephen Sondheim, music by Jule Styne), "Better" (lyric and music by Edward [Ed] Kleban), "Don't Wish" (lyric and music by Peter Allen), "Copacabana" (lyric and music by Barry Manilow), "Wait Till You See Her" (*By Jupiter*, 1942; lyric by Lorenz Hart, music by Richard Rodgers; for more information about this song, see entry for *By Jupiter*), "Come in from the Rain" (lyric and music by Carole [Bayer] Sager, Melissa Manchester, and Robert Turner), "Not Easy Being Green" (lyric and music by Joe Raposo), "List Song" (a/k/a "A Song of Lists") (lyric by Phyllis Newman, music by John Clifton)

NOTES—The one-woman show *My Mother Was a Fortune-Teller* starred Phyllis Newman, a delicious performer who never appeared in enough musicals, on Broadway or off. For *Subways Are for Sleeping* (1961), she won the Tony Award for Best Featured Actress in a Musical, and her performance should have been taped for posterity. Her deliriously funny portrayal of a daffy eccentric was the embodiment of musical comedy grandeur; by sheer goodwill, magnetism, and inspired comic skill, she owned every inch of the St. James' stage and the audience never took its eyes off her.

One of the songs in *Fortune-Teller* was the haunting "What Makes Me Love Him," a song she performed when she spelled Barbara Harris for matinee performances in Sheldon Harnick and Jerry Bock's *The Apple Tree* (1966). Another song, Ed Kleban's "Better," was later used in *A Class Act* (see entry) and was recorded on that show's cast album.

The "Women's Medley" was a sequence of fifteen songs (most of them from Broadway musicals) which allegedly were sexist and demeaning to women. The songs were: "I Enjoy Being a Girl" (*Flower Drum Song*, 1958; lyric by Oscar Hammerstein II, music by Richard Rodgers); "The Girl That I Marry" (*Annie Get Your Gun*, 1946; lyric and music by Irving Berlin); "Thank Heaven for Little Girls" (1958 film *Gigi*; lyric by Alan Jay Lerner, music by Frederick Loewe); "I Say a Little Prayer" (lyric by Hal David, music by Burt Bacharach); "Homework" (*Miss Liberty*, 1949; lyric and music by Irving Berlin); "Try a Little Tenderness" (lyric by Harry Woods, Jimmy Campbell, and Reginald Connelly, music by Harry Woods); "Happy to Keep His Dinner Warm" (*How to Succeed in Business Without Really Trying*, 1961; lyric and music by Frank Loesser); "I'm Having His Baby"; "Everybody Ought to Have a Maid" (*A Funny Thing Happened on the Way to the Forum*, 1962; lyric and music by Stephen Sondheim); "Pretty Women" (*Sweeney Todd/The Demon Barber of Fleet Street*, 1979; lyric and music by Stephen Sondheim); "There Is Nothin' Like a Dame" (*South Pacific*, 1949; lyric by Oscar Hammerstein II, music by Richard Rodgers); "A Hymn to Him" (*My Fair Lady*, 1956; lyric by Alan Jay Lerner, music by Frederick Loewe); "My Lord and Master" (*The King and I*, 1951; lyric by Oscar Hammerstein II, music by Richard Rodgers); "You Are Woman" (*Funny Girl*, 1964; lyric by Bob Merrill, music by Jule Styne); and "A Woman Is a Sometime Thing" (*Porgy and Bess*, 1935; lyric by DuBose Heyward, music by George Gershwin).

One year later, *My Mother Was a Fortune-Teller* reappeared in a revised version (as *The Madwoman of Central Park West* [see entry]; that version was recorded by DRG Records [CD # CDSL-5212]).

1107 My Old Friends. "A New Musical." THEATRE: Orpheum Theatre; OPENING DATE: January 12, 1979; PERFORMANCES: 100; BOOK: Mel Mandel and Norman Sachs; LYRICS: Mel Mandel and Norman Sachs; MUSIC: Mel Mandel and Norman Sachs; DIRECTION: Philip Rose; CHOREOGRAPHY: Bob Tucker; SCENERY: Leon Munier; COSTUMES: George Drew; LIGHTING: Leon Munier; MUSICAL DIRECTION: Larry Hochman; PRODUCER: Larry Abrams

CAST—Allen Swift (Catlan), Leslie Barrett (Fineberg), Robert Weil (Slocum), Norberto Kerner (Arias), Grace Carney (Mrs. Polianoffsky), Maxine Sullivan (Mrs. Cooper), Sylvia Davis (Heloise Michaud), Peter Walker (Peter Schermann), Brenda Gardner (Mrs. Stone), Fred Morsell (A Carpenter; Gettlinger)

The action occurs in the present at the Golden Days Retirement Hotel.

The musical was presented in one act.

MUSICAL NUMBERS—"I'm Not Old" (Residents), "My Old Friends" (Peter Walker), "For Two Minutes" (Robert Weil, Norberto Kerner, Allen Swift, Leslie Barrett), "What We Need Around Here" (Peter Walker, Sylvia Davis), "Oh, My Rose" (Peter Walker), "I Bought a Bicycle" (Leslie Barrett, Residents), "The Battle at Eagle Rock" (Sylvia Davis, Residents), "Dear Jane" (Residents), "The Only Place for Me" (Residents), "I Work with Wood" (Peter Walker, Robert Weil), "Mambo '52" (Norberto Kerner, Maxine Sullivan), "A Little Starch Left" (Maxine Sullivan), "Our Time Together" (Sylvia Davis), "You've Got to Keep Building" (Peter Walker)

NOTES—*My Old Friends*, a well-meaning musical about senior citizens, lasted barely more than three months. Other musicals of the period which dealt almost exclusively with older people were *70, Girls, 70* (1971), which was the shortest-running of all John Kander and Fred Ebb's musicals; *Antiques*, a 1973 Off Broadway musical which lasted just one week; and Off Broadway's *Taking My Turn* (1982; see entry) which played for a year.

My Old Friends was notable in marking the welcome return of Maxine Sullivan, whose rendition of "Loch Lomond" was a popular hit song of the late 1930s. She also starred in *Swingin' the Dream* (1939), introducing (along with Louis Armstrong and other performers) "Darn That Dream," one of the finest ballads ever heard in a Broadway musical.

My Old Friends had first been produced Off Off Broadway at La Mama Experimental Theatre Club (ETC) on November 24, 1978. The Off Broadway production transferred to Broadway on April 12, 1979, opening at the 22 Steps Theatre for fifty-three performances, apparently under a Middle Broadway contract. On May 1, 1985, the musical was revived Off Off Broadway by the American Jewish Theatre for a total of thirty-six performances; Maxine Sullivan was again in the cast, and she was joined by such performers as Imogene Coca and King Donovan.

Two songs in the score ("I Bought a Bicycle" and "Our Time Together") had first been heard in Mel Mandel and Norman Sachs' musical *After You, Mr. Hyde*, their adaptation of Robert Louis Stevenson's *The Strange Case of Dr. Jekyll and Mr. Hyde*, which played in regional theatre in 1968. The two songs were heard again in a 1973 television adaptation, *Dr. Jekyll and Mr. Hyde*, which starred Kirk Douglas; the television version also included songs by Lionel Bart (in 1990, Mandel and Sacks revised the musical, and, as *Jekyll & Hyde*, it played at the George Street Playhouse in New Brunswick, New Jersey). The script of *My Old Friends* was published by Samuel French, Inc., in 1980.

1108 My Wife and I. "A Family Musical." THEATRE: Theatre Four; OPENING DATE: October 10, 1966; PERFORMANCES: 8; BOOK: Bill Mahoney; LYRICS: Bill Mahoney; MUSIC: Bill Mahoney; DIRECTION: Tom Ross Prather; CHOREOGRAPHY: Darwin Knight; SCENERY: Robert Green; LIGHTING: Robert Green; MUSICAL DIRECTION: James Reed Lawlor; PRODUCER: Katydid Productions

CAST—HELON BLOUNT (Katie), ROBERT R. WAIT (Charlie), Carol-Leigh Jensen (Susan), Denise Nordon (Angie), Debbie Thomas (Barbara), Greg Stone (Andy), Karen Schuck (Patsy), ED (EDWARD) PENN (Michael), Ron Leath (Danny)

The action occurs in Michael's home and on a street outside, in 1939 ("the time before television").

The musical was presented in two acts.

ACT ONE—"Confusion" (Company), "Busy, Busy Day" (Ed Penn, Helon Blount), "They've Got to Complain" (Ed Penn), "My Wife and I" (Ed Penn), "Pay, Pay, Pay" (Ed Penn, Girls), "I've Got a Problem" (Karen Schuck), "Busy, Busy, Busy" (reprise) (Ed Penn, Helon Blount), "It's Pouring" (Helon Blount), "I'll Come By" (Ron Leath, Carol-Leigh Jensen), "Dad Got Girls (Instead of Boys)" (Greg Stone), "Baltimore" (Robert R. Wait, Greg Stone)

ACT TWO—"The Principle of the Thing" (Robert R. Wait), "Please God" (Karen Schuck), "I Really Love You" (Carol-Leigh Jensen), "I'll Try to Smile" (Helon Blount), "Family Tree" (Ed Penn, Robert R. Wait), "Why Grow Up" (Helon Blount), "My Wife and I" (reprise) (Ed Penn)

NOTES—Bill Mahoney wrote the book, lyrics, and music for the one-week flop *My Wife and I*. Dan Sullivan in the *New York Times* called the musical a "limp string of situation-comedy clichés" which dealt in part with a harried father who discovers his teenaged daughter is dating the son of a business rival. Sullivan wrote that *My Wife and I* was "a bad, bad musical ... it's so bad that it's bad."

The program notes indicated that Mr. Mahoney, not content with his current accomplishment, was now setting his sights on his next project, the building of his own radio station. One hopes the radio station was more successful than *My Wife and I*.

1109 The Mystery of Edwin Drood. "A Musical." THEATRE: Delacorte Theatre/The Public Theatre; OPENING DATE: August 4, 1985; PERFORMANCES: 24; BOOK: Rupert Holmes; LYRICS: Rupert Holmes; MUSIC: Rupert Holmes; DIRECTION: Wilford Leach; CHOREOGRAPHY: Graciela Daniele; SCENERY: Bob Shaw; COSTUMES: Lindsay W. Davis; LIGHTING: Paul Gallo; MUSICAL DIRECTION: Michael Starobin; PRODUCER: The New York Shakespeare Festival (Joseph Papp, Producer, Jason Steven Cohen, Associate Producer)

CAST—(NOTE—The musical was presented as a play-within-a-play about a troupe of English music hall performers who are in a musical version of Dickens' novel; following each cast member's name is the name of the music hall performer, which in turn is followed by the name of the character being played by the music hall performer; e.g., Howard McGillin played music-hall performer Mr. Clive Pagent, who plays the character of "John Jasper" in the troupe's musical adaptation of Dickens' novel.); George Rose (The Chairman [Mr. William Cartwright]; Mr. James Hitchens/Major Thomas Sapsea), Howard McGillin (Mr. Clive Paget/John Jasper), Larry Shue (Mr. Wilfred Barking-Smythe/the Reverend Mr. Crisparkle), Betty Buckley (Miss Alice Nutting/Edwin Drood), Patti Cohenour (Miss Deirdre Peregrine/Rosa Bud), Judy Kuhn (Miss Isabel Yearsley/Alice, One of the Succubae), Donna Murphy (Miss Florence Gill/Beatrice, One of the Succubae), Jana Schneider (Miss Janet Conover/Helena Landless), John Herrera (Mr. Victor Grinstead/Neville Landless), Jerome Dempsey (Mr. Nick Cricker/Durdles), Don Kehr (Master Robert Bascomb/Deputy), Cleo Laine (Miss Angela Prysock/The Princess Puffer), Nicholas Gunn (Mr. Harry Sayle/A Lascar), Brad Miskell (Mr. Montague Pruitt/A Thugee), Robert Grossman (Mr. James Throttle/Client of Princess Puffer, Harold, Stage Manager, Barkeep), Herndon Lackey (Mr. Alan Eliot/Client of Princess Puffer, Julian), Frances Landes (Miss Gwendolen Pynn/One of the Succubae), Karen Giombetti (Miss Sarah Cook/One of the Succubae), Stephen Glavin (Mr. Christopher Lyon/Statue), Charles Goff (Mr. Brian Pankurst/Portrait, Horace), Joe Grifasi (Mr. Phillip Bax/Bazzard), "???????" (Dick Datchery), Citizens of Cloisterham (Karen Giombetti, Stephen Glavin, Charles Goff, Nicholas Gunn, Robert Grossman, Judy Kuhn, Herndon Lackey, Francine Landes, Brad Miskell, Donna Murphy)

SOURCE—The unfinished 1870 novel *The Mystery of Edwin Drood* by Charles Dickens.

The action occurs during Summer 1873 at London's Music Hall Royale.

The musical was presented in two acts.

ACT ONE—"There'll Be England Again" (George Rose, Company), "A Man Could Go Quite Mad" (Howard McGillin), "Two Kinsman" (Betty Buckley, Howard McGillin), "Moonfall" (Patti Cohenour), "A British Subject" (John Herrera and Larry Shue, with Howard McGillin), "Moonfall" (reprise) (Patti Cohenour and Jana Schneider, with Judy Kuhn and Donna Murphy), "I Wouldn't Say No" (Jerome Dempsy, Don Kehr, George Rose, with Ensemble), "The Wages of Sin" (Cleo Laine), "Jasper's Vision" ('Shades of Jasper and Drood, Succubae, Satyr'), "No Good Can Come with Bad" (John Herrera, Betty Buckley, Patti Cohenour, Jana Schneider, Larry Shue, George Rose), "Ceylon" (Jana Schneider, John Herrera, Larry Shue, with Ensemble), "Perfect Strangers" (Betty Buckley, Patti Cohenour), "Both Sides of the Coin" (Howard McGillin and George Rose, with Company), "The Name of Love"/"Moonfall" (reprise) (Patti Cohenour and Howard McGillin, with Company)

ACT TWO—"Settling Up the Score" ('??????' and Cleo Laine, with Ensemble), "Off to the Races" (Jerome Dempsey, Cleo Laine, and Don Kehr, with Ensemble), "Don't Quit While You're Ahead" (Company), "The Garden Path to Hell" (Cleo Laine), "The Conclusion"

NOTES—*The Mystery of Edwin Drood* opened during the summer at the Delacorte Theatre in Central Park for a limited run of three weeks, and then re-opened on Broadway at the Imperial Theatre on December 2 for a run of 608 performances (during the run the title was shortened to *Drood*). Most of the original cast transferred to Broadway; one notable addition to the Broadway cast was Rob Marshall (who played Mr. Christopher Lyon).

For the Broadway run, three songs ("There'll Be England Again," "A British Subject," and "I Wouldn't Say No") were dropped and one ("There You Are") was added.

Charles Dickens died before finishing his novel, and so it's not known which character he intended to be the murderer of Edwin Drood. The musical was written as a play-within-a-play in which an English music hall company is performing a musical version of the Dickens' novel. At each performance of the musical, the audience was asked to vote ito determine which of seven suspects murdered Edwin Drood and which character is actually Dick Datchery. Alternate endings, each with specific musical sequences, were written, and the appropriate one was performed according to the votes of the audience.

The critics generally liked the musical (while Linda Winer in *USA Today* found it "tiresome," Frank Rich in the *New York Times* said it was "an enjoyable, entertaining evening" and Howard Kissel in *Women's Wear Daily* noted the offering was "as pleasurable an evening as Broadway has seen in years"). Rupert Holmes' clever score was highly praised, and two ballads ("Moonfall" and "Perfect Strangers") were singled out. Nelson Doubleday, Inc., published the script in 1986 (which included some forty-two pages of alternate endings). The Broadway cast album was recorded by Polydor Records (LP # 827-969-1-Y-2), and included two alternate endings; a later CD release by Varese Sarabande Records (# VSD-5597) included three alternate endings; and another CD release (by PolyGram Records [# G-827-969-2-Y-1]) included all seven endings. The musical was later performed in London; and a CD of the 1994 Australian cast was released on GEP Records (CD # GEP-9401) with all seven endings. The collection *Lost in Boston* (I) (Varese Sarabande Records CD # VSD-5475) includes two songs cut from the score ("An English Music Hall" and "Evensong").

1110 Naked Boys Singing! THEATRE: Actors' Playhouse; later transferred to Theatre 4, the John Houseman Theatre, the 47th Street Theatre, the Julia Miles Theatre, and New World Stages/Stage 4. "A New Musical Revue"; OPENING DATE: July 22, 1999; PERFORMANCES: Still playing as of December 31, 2007; LYRICS: See song list for credits; MUSIC: See song list for credits; DIRECTION: Robert Schrock; CHOREOGRAPHY: Jeffry Denman; SCENERY: Carl D. White; COSTUMES: Carl D. White; LIGHTING: Aaron Copp; MUSICAL DIRECTION: Stephen Bates; PRODUCERS: Jamie Cesa, Carl D. White, Hugh Hayes, Tom Smedes, and Jennifer Dumas

CAST—Sean McNally, Daniel C. Levine, Adam Michaels, Tim Burke, Tom Gualtieri, Trance Thompson, Glenn Seven Allen, Jonathan Brody

The revue was presented in two acts.

ACT ONE—"Gratuitous Nudity" (lyric and music by Stephen Bates; additional lyric by Robert Schrock and Mark Winkler; additional music by Shelly Markham) (Company), "The Naked Maid" (lyric and music by David Pevsner) (Sean McNally), "Bliss" (lyric and music by Marie Cain) (Daniel C. Levine, Company), "Window to Window" (lyric and music by Rayme Sciaroni) (Adam Michaels), "Fight the Urge" (lyric by David Pevsner, music by David Pevsner and Rayme Sciaroni) (Sean McNally, Daniel C. Levine, Tim Burke, Company), "Robert Mitchum" (lyric by Mark Winkler, music by Shelly Markham) (Tom Gualtieri, Company) "Jack's Song" (lyric by Jim Morgan, music by Ben Schaechter) (Company)

ACT TWO—"Members Only" (lyric by Stephen Bates and Robert Schrock, music by Stephen Bates) (Trance Thompson, Glenn Seven Allen, Jonathan Brody, Company), "Perky Little Porn Star" (lyric and music by David Pevsner) (Daniel C. Levine), "Nothin' But the Radio On" (lyric by Mark Winkler, music by Shelly Markham) (Glenn Seven Allen, Company), "Kris, Look What You've Missed" (lyric by Robert Schrock, music by Stephen Bates) (Jonathan Brody), "Music Addiction" (lyric and music by Mark Savage) (Tim Burke, Company), "The Entertainer" (lyric and music by Trance Thompson and Perry Hart) (Trance Thompson, Company), "Window to Window" (reprise) (Sean McNally), "Window to the Soul" (lyric and music by Stephen Bates) (Sean McNally, Adam Michaels, Trance Thompson, Jonathan Brody), Finale/"Naked Boys Singing!" (lyric and music by Stephen Bates) (Company)

NOTES—*Naked Boys Singing!* was the title, but presumably the customers didn't come for the songs. As of this writing, the revue is still playing (on a reduced schedule of four performances a week at New World Stages/Stage 4).

The revue had originally been produced on March 28, 1998, at the Celebration Theatre in Los Angeles; the cast recording of that production was released by Café Pacific Records (CD # CPCD-1210).

TLA Releasing filmed a Los Angeles production of the revue, which was released in 2007 (later in the year, the DVD was issued [# TLAD-187]). Jeannette Catsoulis in the *New York Times* noted that few films would benefit so much from "the eventual consolations of 'pause' and 'zoom.'" Further, Lou Lumenick in the *New York Post* indicated the film's eventual DVD release would "eliminate the need for opera glasses" and would allow "for freeze-framing."

1111 Natalia Petrovna. THEATRE: New York City Center; OPENING DATE: October 8, 1964; PERFORMANCES: Unknown; LIBRETTO: William Ball; MUSIC: Lee Hoiby; DIRECTION: William Ball; SCENERY: Howard Bay; COSTUMES: Patton Campbell; MUSICAL DIRECTION: Julius Rudel; PRODUCER: The New York City Opera

CAST—Maria Dornya (Natalia Petrovna), John Reardon (Belaev), John McCollum (Arcady), Sandra Darling (Vera), Patricia Brooks (Lisavetta), Jack Harrold (Doctor), Muriel (Costa) Greenspon (Anna Simyoneva), Richard Cross (Rakitin), Richard Krause (Bolisov), Anthony Rudel (Kolia)

SOURCE—The 1850 play *A Month in the Country* by Ivan Turgenev.

The opera was presented in two acts.

NOTES—The world premiere of *Natalia Petrovna* dealt with a married woman and the three men who love her (her husband and two suitors). In his review for the *New York Times*, Harold C. Schonberg criticized William Ball's libretto for its one-dimensional characterizations. He also found fault with Ball's fleshing out a minor character (Anna Simyoneva, played by Muriel Greenspon) for (unfunny) comic relief. He further faulted the delineation of the title character; in the original play, she was to be pitied for her dilemma; for the opera, he felt she was an unsympathetic and scheming figure. But Schonberg had praise for Hoiby's score ("his style is simple, romantic, traditional and cosmopolitan") and singled out a duet ("Nightingale and Meadow Lark") and a late second-act octet.

Hoiby later revised the opera (which also enjoyed a new title, that of the play upon which it was based), and a 2004 production by the Manhattan School of Music and Opera Theatre to celebrate the opera's fortieth anniversary was recorded live on a 2-CD set by Albany Records (# TROY-747-748), an invaluable company which has recorded many obscure American operas. The song titles below are derived from that recording.

ACT ONE—"Two Hearts," "Let's Go Out," "Dear Lady" (Aria), "Who Is This Paragon?," "Oh, Terrible Lady" (Aria), "Ooh...Forgive Me," "If You Want to Learn," "You've Never Seen" (Aria) (Note—This sequence includes the "Nightingale and Meadow Lark" duet.), "Ladies and Gentlemen," "That Smile," "You Sent for Me?" (Duet), "These Children Are in Love"

ACT TWO—Prelude, "They're Waiting for You," "Your Wife and I," "Good, We Can Be Alone," "There's No Need," "Your Accusations" (Aria), "Come Back Here!," "Sir, I've Decided," "Natasha!" (Octet), "No One Can Know," "Incredible!"

1112 The National Lampoon Show. THEATRE: New Palladium; OPENING DATE: March 2, 1975; PERFORMANCES: 180; MATERIAL AND LYRICS by the cast, and "overlooked" by Sean Kelly; MUSIC: Paul Jacobs; DIRECTION: Martin Charnin; production supervised by Dale Anglund; COSTUMES: Coordinated by Patricia Britton; LIGHTING: Lowell Sherman; MUSICAL DIRECTION: Paul Jacobs; PRODUCER: Ivan Reitman

CAST—John Belushi, Brian Doyle-Murray, Bill Murray, Gilda Radner, Harold Ramis

The revue was performed in one act (the program didn't list songs and sketches).

NOTES—The successful *National Lampoon's Lemmings* (1973; see entry) was followed by another satiric evening, *The National Lampoon Show*. The first revue had introduced John Belushi and Chevy Chase; Belushi returned for the current edition, and the remarkable cast for the new revue also included Bill Murray, Gilda Radner, and Harold Ramis, all of whom later made their marks on television and in films. Mel Gussow in the *New York Times* indicated the revue "sets new boundaries for impropriety" (one sketch depicted Gilda Radner as a victim of a gang rape who calmly asks her assailants about their qualifications). He praised a song about white-collar criminals who are "forced to live like kings" in jail, and enjoyed Bill Murray's ode to the mundane reasons for living in New York. He also singled out John Belushi's impersonations of Truman Capote and Marlon Brando. (Belushi doing Capote must have been a classic of its kind.)

In 1986, one more edition in the series opened (*National Lampoon's Class of '86* [see entry]).

1113 National Lampoon's Class of '86. THEATRE: Village Gate Downstairs; OPENING DATE: May 22, 1986; PERFORMANCES: 53; SKETCHES: Andrew Simmons (Head Writer), John Belushi, Chevy Chase, Stephen Collins, Lance Contrucci, Christopher Guest, Dave Hanson, Matty Simmons, Michael Simmons, Larry Sloman; also, Rodger Bumpass, Veanne Cox, Annie Golden, John Michael Higgins, Tommy Koenig, and Brian Brucker O'Connor; LYRICS: See song list for credits; MUSIC: See song list for credits; DIRECTION: Jerry Adler; CHOREOGRAPHY: Nora Brennan; SCENERY: Daniel Proett; COSTUMES: Nancy Konrardy; LIGHTING: Robert Strohmeier; PRODUCERS: Michael Simmons and Jonathan Weiss; a Matty Simmons-John Heyman production

CAST—Rodger Bumpass, Veanne Cox, Annie Golden, John Michael Higgins, Tommy Koenig, Brian Brucker O'Connor

The revue was presented in two acts (sketch and song assignments unknown).

SKETCHES—"Paradise Lost," "Eating Out," "Honey, I Have Something to Tell You," "Five Minutes," "Tasty Fresh," "The Jumper," "Living Well," "Death & Apartment Rentals," "Solid God," "Publishing," "Arrivederci Vito," "Out of the Closet," "Oval Office," "The Psychiatrist"

MUSICAL NUMBERS—"Cocaine" (lyric and music by Jim Mentel and Larry Sloman), "Yuppie Love" (lyric by Richard Levinson, music by Richard Levinson and Will Etra), "They Lost the Revolution" (lyric and music by Richard Levinson; lyric of reprise version by Michael Sansonia), "My Bod Is for God" (lyric and music by Jeff Mandel and Phil Proctor), "I've Got It" (lyric and music by Michael Garin),

"The President's Dream" (lyric and music by Michael Sansonia), "Don't Drop the Bomb" (lyric by Richard Levinson, music by Richard Levinson and Will Etra), "Apartheid Love" (lyric by Jan Kirschner, Brian Brucker O'Connor, and Michael Sansonia, music by Michael Sansonia, Robert Bond, Paul Guzzone, and Stuart Ziff), "The Ticker" (lyric and music by Michael Sansonia)

NOTES—*National Lampoon's Class of '86* was the least successful of the three satirical *Lampoon* revues to play Off Broadway (see entries for *National Lampoon's Lemmings* [1973] and *The National Lampoon Show* [1975]).

Despite its short run, the revue's material seems to have been fresh and edgy. At one point, we're informed that if Mama Cass had shared her sandwich with Karen Carpenter, they'd both be alive today. Further, the sketch "Tasty Fresh" dealt with the making of a television commercial for a feminine deodorant (writing in the *New York Times*, J.D.R. Bruckner said the sequence was "so tasteless and obscene it is bound to offend everyone"); another sketch, "Solid God," spoofed televangelists and a born-again Madonna, who was also spoofed by Annie Golden in the song "My Bod Is for God." Another highlight was a yuppie on trial; accused of being unassuming and modest, he's brought down by Prosecutor Perrier Mason who then strips him of his power tie.

1114 National Lampoon's Lemmings. "A Satirical Joke-Rock Mock-Concert Musical Comedy Semi-Revue Theatrical Presentation." THEATRE: Village Gate; OPENING DATE: January 25, 1973; PERFORMANCES: 350; SKETCHES AND LYRICS: David Axelrod, Anne Beatts, Henry Beard, John Boni, Tony Hendra, Sean Kelly, Doug Kenny, and P.J. O'Rourke (and members of the cast); MUSIC: Paul Jacobs and Christopher Guest; DIRECTION: Tony Hendra; SCENERY: Production Arts Studio; COSTUMES: Laurie Hudson; LIGHTING: Beverly Emmons; MUSICAL DIRECTION: Paul Jacobs; PRODUCER: Tony Hendra

CAST—John Belushi (Woodshuck Announcer, Joe Cocker, Bass), Chevy Chase (Debbie, Hell's Angel, Drums), Garry Goodrow (Voice of Deteriorata, School Principal, Incarnate Starlight), Christopher Guest (Four-Eyes, Christ, Bob Dylan), Paul Jacobs (Musical Director, Piano, Guitar), Mary-Jenifer Mitchell (Mary Magdeline, Pat Nixon, Joan Baez), Alice Playten (Winkie, Judy Agnew, Mick Jaggar)

SOURCE—"The spirit and sometimes the letter of" the *National Lampoon* magazine.

The revue was presented in two acts (the program didn't list individual songs and sketches).

NOTES—With a cast of clowns which included John Belushi, Chevy Chase, Christopher Guest, and Alice Playten, the satiric revue *National Lampoon's Lemmings* was one of a number of hit revues which opened during the 1972-1973 season. Mel Gussow in the *New York Times* indicated the first act suffered from a case of the "puerilities" ("tasteless" need not be "brainless"), but said the second act "mercifully" found its wit in a "wicked" parody of the rock music world (which included Alice Playten's "devastating" impersonation of Mick Jagger as well as an extended sequence about the "Woodchuck Festival of Peace, Love and Death"). The cast album (titled *National Lampoon Lemmings*, featuring "Music from the Original Show and More") was released by Banana/Blue Thumb Records (LP # BTS-6006), and the liner notes described the show as "a satirical joke-rock mock-concert musical-comedy semi-revue theatrical presentation, or none of the above."

The album included the following sequences: "Stage Announcements" (performed by John Belushi), "Lemmings' Lament" (by Paul Jacobs and Sean Kelly), "Positively Wall Street" (by Paul Jacobs, Sean Kelly, and Christopher Guest), "Weather Person" (performed by Garry Goodrow), "Pizza Man" (by Sean Kelly, Christopher Guest, and Tony Hendra), "Colorado" (by Sean Kelly, Christopher Guest, and Tony Hendra; performed by Chevy Chase), "Richie Havens" (performed by Christopher Guest), "Crowd Rain Chant," "Papa Was a Running-Dog Lackey of the Bourgeoisie" (by Paul Jacobs and Tony Hendra), "All-Star Dead Band," "Highway Toes" (by Sean Kelly and Christopher Guest), "Hell's Angel" (performed by Chevy Chase), "Farmer Yassir" (performed by Garry Goodrow), "Lonely at the Bottom" (by Paul Jacobs and John Belushi), "Megagroupie," and "Megadeath" (by Paul Jacobs and Sean Kelly; lead singer, John Belushi).

The following season the revue toured (with direction by John Belushi, and a cast which included Belushi and Chevy Chase); the tour's program credited music to Paul Jacobs, Christopher Guest, and Zal Yanovsky; lyrics to Sean Kelly, John Belushi, and Zal Yanovsky; and words (sketches) to David Alexrod, Tony Hendra, Sean Kelly, Henry Beard, "and the cast" (Hendra was an editor of the *National Lampoon* magazine).

Two more *National Lampoon* revues were seen in New York: *The National Lampoon Show* (1975) and *National Lampoon's Class of '86* (1986); see entries. In 2007, Reuters' website reported the series would return to New York during the 2007-2008 season (but this time around on Broadway) as *National Lemmings Comedy Troupe Presents America 2.0* (the website noted the new revue would include a "Michael Vick" character who promotes a new dog food).

1115 Naughty-Naught '00. "A Musical Drama of Life at Yale." THEATRE: American Music Hall; OPENING DATE: January 23, 1937; PERFORMANCES: 173; BOOK: John Van Antwerp; LYRICS: Ted Fetter; additional lyrics by Charles Alan; MUSIC: Richard Lewine; DIRECTION: Morgan Lewis; CHOREOGRAPHY: Morgan Lewis; SCENERY: Eugene Dunkel; COSTUMES: Eaves and Kermit Love; MUSICAL DIRECTION: Howard Johnson; PRODUCERS: John and Jerrold Krimsky

CAST—Alexander Clark (P. DeQuincy Devereux), Percy Helton (Spunky), Bartlett Robinson (Frank Plover), Leslie Litomy (Jack Granville), Phil Eppens (Stub), Howard Fischer (Fred), Eleanor Phelps (Claire Granville), Alan Handley (Jim Pawling), Lee Berkman (Joe), Douglas Rowland (Tom), Harry Meehan (Bartender), Isham Keith (Tough), Gerrie Worthing (Cathleen), Howard Sullivan (Pugsy), Kermit Love (A Student), Gibson Girls (Eleanora Dixon, Anna Erskine, Julie Hartwell, Jane Hammond, Barbara Hunter, Lucille Rich)

The action occurs at Yale University and in various locales in New Haven.

The musical was presented in three acts.

ACT ONE—"Goodbye, Girls, Hello, Yale" (Freshmen), "Naughty-Naught" (Seniors), "Love Makes the World Go Round" (Eleanor Phelps, Bartlett Robinson, Chorus)

ACT TWO—"Love Makes the World Go Round" (reprise) (Eleanor Phelps), "Zim Zam Zee" (Gerrie Worthing, Men), "Pull the Boat for Eli" (Students, Girls)

ACT THREE—Finale (Company)

NOTES—With *Naughty-Naught '00* (which later shortened its title to *Naughty-Naught*), the American Music Hall began a series of three old-time musical melodramas, all with books by John Van Antwerp, lyrics by Ted Fetter, and music by Richard Lewine. The musicals were produced by John and Jerrold Krimsky (the latter was "John Van Antwerp"), and the presentations were in a style which encouraged the audience members to hiss the villains (while they ordered another round of beer). The other two musicals in the series were *The Fireman's Flame* (1937) and *The Girl from Wyoming* (1938) (see entries).

The above song titles are taken from the script published by Metromedia On Stage (the undated script is titled *Naughty-Naught*); the script advised that the performers should play their parts "straight" and not "show that they are in on the joke." In his *A Chronology of American Musical Theatre*, Richard C. Norton cites an early edition of the published script (by Viking Press), and notes that the second act ended with an "olio" sequence ["Coney-by-the-Sea"]).

Naughty-Naught was briefly revived on January 24, 1939, for forty-two performances and on October 19, 1946, for twenty-one performances (see entry for the latter production).

The three musicals in the series are early examples of Off Broadway spoofs of melodramas (for similar shows, see entries for *Will the Mail Train Run Tonight?* and *The Drunkard*).

1116 Naughty-Naught '00 (1946). THEATRE: Old Knickerbocker Music Hall; OPENING DATE: October 19, 1946; PERFORMANCES: 17; BOOK: John Van Antwerp; LYRICS: Ted Fetter; MUSIC: Richard Lewine; DIRECTION: Ted Fetter; CHOREOGRAPHY: Ray Harrison; SCENERY: Kermit Love; COSTUMES: Robert Moore; LIGHTING: Kermit Love; MUSICAL DIRECTION: Richard Lewine; PRODUCERS: Paul Killiam in association with Oliver Rea

CAST—John Cromwell (P. de Quincy Devereux), Teddy Hart (Spunky), Leonard Hicks (Frank Plover), Kenneth Forbes (Jack Granville), Shepard Curelop (Stub), King Taylor (Fred), Ottilie Kruger (Claire Granville), Marshall Jamison (Jim Pawling), Roy Wolvin (Joe), Len Smith, Jr. (Tom), George Spelvin (Bartender), Virginia Barbour (Cathleen), L.A. Nicoletti (Pugsy), Naughty-Naught Girls (Aza Bard, Helen Franklin, Dorothy Hill, Rhoda Johannson, Diane Renay, Mildred Roane), Myrtle Dunedin (Unicyclist Extraordinary), Maxine and Bobby (A Man and His Dog), Ullaine Malloy (Aerialist Supreme)

The action occurs in and around New Haven.

The musical was presented in three acts (division of acts and song assignments unknown).

MUSICAL NUMBERS—"Goodbye Girls, Hello Yale," "Naughty-Naught," "Mother Isn't Getting Any Younger," "When We're in Love," "Zim Zam Zee," "Coney-by-the-Sea," "What's Good About Good Morning?," "Pull the Boat for Eli," "Just Like a Woman"

NOTES—The 1946 production of *Naughty-Naught '00* was a brief attempt to revive the musical melodrama spoofs offered during the late 1930s by the producing team of John and Jerrold Krimsky and the writing team of John Van Antwerp (Jerrold Krimsky), Ted Fetter, and Richard Lewine. But a run of just over two weeks for *Naughty-Naught '00* quashed any chances for revivals of *The Fireman's Flame* and *The Girl from Wyoming* (see entries). For more information about the Krimsky-Antwerp-Fetter-Lewine spoofs, see entry for the original production of *Naughty-Naught '00*.

The current revival omitted "Love Makes the World Go Round" and added three new numbers ("When We're in Love," "What's Good About Good Morning?," and "Just Like a Woman"). The revival also interpolated "Mother Isn't Getting Any Younger," which had first been heard in *The Fireman's Flame*.

1117 Nellie. THEATRE: Greenwich Street Theatre; OPENING DATE: May 22, 1997; PERFORMANCES: 10; BOOK: Bernice Lee; LYRICS: Jaz Dorsey and Bernice Lee; MUSIC: Jaz Dorsey; DIRECTION: Scott Pegg; CHOREOGRAPHY: Andrea Andresakis; SCENERY: Nadine Charlsen; COSTUMES: Bill Lewk; LIGHTING: Nadine Charlsen; MUSICAL DIRECTION: James Mironchik; PRODUCERS: Villar-Hauser Theatre Company & Works by Women in association with Marnee May

CAST—Jeanine Serralles (Nellie Bly), Timothy Estin (Cockerill), Garrison Phillips (Pulitzer), Veronica Burke (Mrs. Cochrnae), John Quilty (Chester, Bobby, Inmate), John Sacco (Charles, Albert, Prisoner, Inmate), George Cambus (Reporter, Madden, Judge, Phelps), Lorca Peress (Anna Schuiltz, Nurse, Inmate), Jerry Rago (Cochrane, Reporter), Oliver Buckingham (Simon, Reporter), Jane Lowe (Mrs. Galbertson), Charlotte Parsons (Cleaning Woman, Nurse), Sara Jo (Newsboy, Nurse), Jessica Bowen (Newsboy)

The action occurs in New York City and in Pittsburgh during the 1890s.

The musical was presented in two acts (division of acts and song assignments unknown; songs are listed in performance order).

MUSICAL NUMBERS—"Nellie, Don't Go," "Been There, Done That," "Alone," "What Choices Are Left for Me?," "Why Did Ya Go?," "Come Luv," "Papa's Song," "Always Remember," "Mexico," "Check It Out," "Gettin' Ready for Love," "Happy Am I," "We Don't Waste Food," "You Are There," "Easy Breezy," "Woman Who Acts Like a Man," "Mother of the Bride," "Away with Age," "Could I?," "Nellie Paves the Way," "Still Be Me?," "International Reporters' Song," "Look at Me!," "And I Know"

NOTES—The Off Off Broadway musical *Nellie* was based on the life of Nellie Bly (1867-1922), the legendary reporter who in November 1889 and under the sponsorship of the *New York World* set off to go around the world in seventy-five days in order to beat the (fictional) record held by Phileas Fogg, the leading character of Jules Verne's novel *Around the World in Eighty Days* (serialized in 1872 and published in 1873). (Phileas had a competitor in Dick Fix, and in the 1946 Broadway musical *Nellie Bly*, Nellie's nemesis was one Phineas T. Fogarty. But all ended well, and Nellie not only beat Phileas Fogg's record, she also bested her own goal by going around the world in seventy-two days.)

Nellie apparently told its story from a feminist perspective, and if some of the song titles (such as "Been There, Done That" and "Check It Out") are any indication, from an anachronistic perspective as well. The musical was revived Off Off Broadway two seasons later, opening on June 5, 1999, at the Lamb's Theatre for nine performances. This time around, Becky Little played the title role, and new songs added for this version were "Take My Bouquet," "Baiting of Nellie," "We Wish," and "We Women Will Have a Say."

As for the Broadway musical about the journalist, *Nellie Bly* opened at the Adelphi Theatre on January 21, 1946, and played for just sixteen performances. The lyrics were by Johnny Burke and the music by Jimmy Van Heusen, and the musical marked the seventh and final teaming of the legendary duo of William Gaxton and Victor Moore (they had earlier appeared together in *Of Thee I Sing* [1931], *Let 'Em Eat Cake* [1933], *Anything Goes* [1934], *Leave It to Me!* [1938], *Louisiana Purchase* [1940], and *Hollywood Pinafore* [1945]). Joy Hodges, who with Austin Marshall had introduced "Have You Met Miss Jones?" in Richard Rodgers and Lorenz Hart's 1937 musical *I'd Rather Be Right*, played the title role (she replaced Marilyn Maxwell, who left the show during the Philadelphia tryout). In his review for the *New York Sun*, Ward Morehouse wrote that *Nellie Bly* "lags, drags and fairly crawls" during its "long, long" trip around the world ... "a costly, cumbersome, and completely lifeless show."

Perhaps *Nellie Bly* was done in by two theatre curses, The Hot-Air Balloon Curse and The Adelphi Theatre Curse.

It seems to be a rule that musicals which include hot-air balloons in their scenery inevitably fail: besides *Nellie Bly*, another musical which opened during the 1945-1946 season, Cole Porter's *Around the World in Eighty Days* (which was based on Verne's novel and which also opened at the Adelphi Theatre [four months after *Nellie Bly*'s two-week run]), played for seventy-five performances (and was the shortest-running of all of Porter's Broadway musicals). Moreover, two musicals from the 1953-1954 season also employed hot-air balloons, and both were financial failures. Despite its glorious score, *The Golden Apple* (see entry), which opened Off Broadway on March 1, 1954, and subsequently transferred to Broadway at the Alvin (now Neil Simon) Theatre, played for a total of just 125 performances. And *By the Beautiful Sea*, which opened on April 8, 1954, at the Majestic Theatre, closed in the red after 270 performances. The score is vastly underrated by most theatre buffs, but it's worth noting that Brooks Atkinson in the *New York Times* found Arthur Schwartz' music "melodious," and singled out no less than six songs; he praised the overall score as "good picnic song numbers." In 1963, another lyric adaptation of Verne's novel (here titled *Around the World in 80 Days*; see entry) opened at Jones Beach, and returned there the following summer. After these two productions, the musical was never seen again. Paul Gardner in the *New York Times* reported that the musical's hot-air balloon (called Brigitte) cost $22,000 and was imported from France for the occasion. Brigitte could sail 100 feet across the length of the theatre's lagoon and up to a height of 100 feet. Fritz Weaver was called upon to ascend in the balloon during two sequences, one in which he was joined by Robert Clary and Elaine Malbin. But unlucky combinations of wind gusts, rain, and one technical miscalculation caused major problems. During one rehearsal, the balloon hit part of the stage set and "popped." For another rehearsal, the balloon narrowly missed a telephone pole and the theatre's lighting tower, and yet another time the balloon landed in the lagoon itself. At one rehearsal, the stalwart Weaver climbed back into the balloon's basket, only to find himself in a ride which was "jerky, windy, bumpy." Weaver later told Gardner that Elaine Malbin was reluctant to perform in the balloon unless it ascended no more than twenty-five feet, but Weaver was hoping "we can talk her into going all the way" up. Finally, the hot-air balloon flop *Ben Franklin in Paris* opened on October 27, 1964, at the Lunt-Fontanne Theatre for 215 performances; its song "A Balloon Is Ascending" became the official anthem for the annual cast reunions of all hot-air-balloon musicals.

And, as mentioned, both *Nellie Bly* and *Around the World* both played at the Adelphi Theatre, which William Gaxton once famously called "the dump of dumps."

The theatre opened in 1928 as the Craig, and was renamed three times, as the Adelphi in 1934; the 54th Street in 1958; and the George Abbott in 1965. Moreover, for two periods in the early 1940s it was briefly renamed (as the Radiant Center [!!] in 1940 and as the Yiddish Arts Theatre in 1943), but both times the theatre's name soon reverted to the Adelphi.

Located on West 54th Street near Seventh Avenue (152 West 54th Street, to be precise), the theatre's location was deemed a drawback since it wasn't in the heart of the theatre district. Besides, *Nellie Bly* and *Around the World*, many more musicals flopped at the unlucky theatre (although at least one, *Street Scene*, is one of the greatest of American musicals and eventually found its home in the opera house): *Jonica* (1930, 40 performances); *The Well of Romance* (1930, 8 performances); *Swing It* (1937, 36 performances); *A Hero Is Born* (1937, 50 performances); *Sing for Your Supper* (1939, 60 performances); *Allah Be Praised!* (1944, 20 performances); *Robin Hood* (1944 revival, 15 performances); *Carib Song* (1945, 36 performances); *The Girl from Nantucket* (1945, 12 performances); *The Duchess Misbehaves* (1946, 5 performances); *Street Scene* (1947, 148 performances); *Music in My Heart* (1947, 124 performances); *Hilarities* (1948, 14 performances); *Portofino* (1958, 3 performances; Walter Kerr in the *New York Herald Tribune* noted that he couldn't say it was the "worst musical *ever* produced because I've only been seeing musicals since 1919"); *Happy Town* (1959, 3 performances); *13 Daughters* (1961, 28 performances); *Kwamina* (1961, 32 performances); *The Student Gypsy*, or *The Prince of Liederkranz* (1963, 16 performances); *What Makes Sammy Run?* (1964, 540 performances; yes, even at 540 performances [which made *Sammy* the second-longest-running musical to play the theatre], the musical still failed to pay back its initial investment); *La Grosse Valise* (1965, 7 performances); *Darling of the Day* (1968, 32 performances); *Buck White* (1969, 7 performances; the musical starred Cassius Clay, a/k/a Mohammed Ali); and *Gantry* (1970, one performance; and the final production to play the theatre before it was demolished).

Successful musicals were indeed a rarity at the Adelphi, and if a hit actually opened there, it soon transferred to a more desirable theatre. *On the Town*, for example, opened in 1944 for a run of 462 Broadway performances, but of its thirteen months on Broadway only five were spent at the Adelphi. And *No Strings* (1962, 580 performances), which played for almost seventeen months on Broadway, stayed at the theatre for just under seven months, and so while it had the longest Broadway run of any musical to open at the theatre, most of that run was at the Broadhurst Theatre. And *No Strings* didn't even want the Adelphi/54th Street. An early window card indicated it would open at Mark Hellinger (home of the original production of *My Fair Lady*); but when *My Fair Lady* posted its closing notice, ticket sales picked up and the musical opted to keep running at the Hellinger for a while (*My Fair Lady* eventually transferred to both the Broadhurst and the Broadway before closing), and thus *No Strings* was forced into the Adelphi/54th Street. The theatre also enjoyed a modest hit in *Look, Ma, I'm Dancin'!* (see entry for the musical's revival as part of the *Musicals Tonight!* series), which opened in 1948; despite its run of 188 performances, it nonetheless turned a profit.

When the Adelphi wasn't hosting a flop or when it wasn't saying goodbye to a hit show which transferred to a more desirable theatre, it sometimes booked long-running musicals from other theatres, shows which were now on their last legs (such as *Damn Yankees* and *Bye Bye Birdie*).

A bright spot in the Adelphi Theatre's life occurred in 1955 and 1956 when the theatre was home to the CBS television series *The Honeymooners*; all of the "classic 39" episodes were filmed live there. For photographs of the Adelphi and other lost theatres, see Nicholas van Hoogstraten's indispensable *Lost Broadway Theatres* (published by Princeton Architectural Press in 1991 [updated and expanded edition published in 1997]).

1118 Neva Small: Not Quite an Ingenue. "A Musical Celebration of Life On and Off the Stage." THEATRE: Actor's Temple Theatre; OPENING DATE: August 23, 2007; PERFORMANCES: 11; DIRECTION: Pamela Hall; MUSICAL DIRECTION: Don Rebic; PRODUCERS: Edmund Gaynes, Pamela Hall, and Louis S. Salamone; Letty Simon, Associate Producer

CAST—NEVA SMALL

NOTES—*Neva Small: Not Quite an Ingenue* was a one-woman show in which Neva Small performed songs mostly associated with her Broadway and Off Broadway musical career, including her role as Chava in the 1971 film version of *Fiddler on the Roof*.

The evening included a medley of songs by Hoagy Carmichael as well as a medley from *Fiddler*; "My Funny Valentine" (from *Babes in Arms*, 1937);

"A Cockeyed Optimist" (*South Pacific*, 1949); "The Girl with Too Much Heart" (dropped from *Henry, Sweet Henry*; 1967); "I Go On" (*Mass*, 1971 [see entry]); "How Sweet Is Peach Ice Cream" (*F. Jasmine Addams*, 1971 [see entry]); and "Job Application" (dropped from *Ballroom*, 1978). In his review for *Talk Entertainment.com*, Oscar E. Moore reported he hadn't seen Small perform since *Henry, Sweet Henry* in 1967, and noted that she looked "like a million bucks." He found her a "charmer," and praised her voice and personality.

A delightful cast recording of the production was released by Small Penny Enterprises Records (unnumbered CD).

Small's *Neva Small/My Place in the World* (released by Small Penny Enterprises Records CD # NS-2211) belongs in the collection of anyone who loves theatre music. The CD is one of the most luminous and enchanting theatre recordings in years.

1119 Nevertheless, They Laugh. "A New Musical." THEATRE: Lamb's Theatre; OPENING DATE: March 24, 1971; PERFORMANCES: 5; BOOK: LaRue Watts; LYRICS: LaRue Watts; MUSIC: Richard Lescsak; DIRECTION: Tod Jackson; CHOREOGRAPHY: Tod Jackson; Lynn Simonson, Assistant Choreographer; SCENERY: Mark Ivancic; COSTUMES: Peter Joseph; LIGHTING: Beverly Emmons; MUSICAL DIRECTION: William R. Cox; PRODUCER: The Lamb's Club

CAST—David Holliday (He), Bernadette Peters (Consuelo), Marilyn Child (Zinida), Bill Starr (Jackson), Lu Leonard (Jezebel), Michael Byrne (Papa Briguet), Dick Korthaze (Mancini), Craig Yates (Bezano), Charles Caron (Baron Regnard), Gordon Fearing (A Gentleman), Terry Nicholson (Ernestine), J.J. Coyle (Dodo), Diane Ball (Helene), Anne Piacentini (Sylvette), Dennis Edenfield (Hugo); Roustabout Clowns (Robert Middleton, Peter Loffredo, Allayne Johnson)

SOURCE—The 1916 play *He Who Gets Slapped* by Leonid Andreyev.

The action occurs in a European circus at the end of the nineteenth century.

The musical was presented in two acts.

ACT ONE—"You Must Forget" (Bill Starr, Lu Leonard, Michael Byrne, Dick Korthaze, Circus Performers), "The Clown" (David Holliday), "No One Will Know" (Marilyn Child, Michael Byrne, David Holliday), "Can You Love" (Marilyn Child), "The Baron" (Lu Leonard, Diane Ball, Anne Piacentini, Terry Nicolson), "Believe" (Charles Caron, Bernadette Peters), "Nevertheless, They Laugh" (David Holliday, Michael Byrne, Bill Starr, Lu Leonard, Circus Performers), "One Simple Song" (Marilyn Child), "I Don't Understand It" (Bernadette Peters), "Consuelo" (David Holliday), "More Than You" (David Holliday)

ACT TWO—"Freaks" (Gordon Fearing, Bill Starr, Lu Leonard, Terry Nicholson, Dennis Edenfield, David Holliday, Circus Performers), "Soliloquy" (Bernadette Peters), "Once and For All" (Craig Yates), "More Than Me" (David Holliday), "Everything Fine" (Michael Bryne, Marilyn Child, Circus Performers), "I Charmed the Wine" (David Holliday, Bernadette Peters), "You Must Forget" (reprise) (Circus Performers)

NOTES—The Off Off Broadway musical *Nevertheless, They Laugh* was produced by the Lamb's Club for a limited engagement of five performances, and is probably the most obscure of all Bernadette Peters' appearances (even the one-performance Broadway drama *Johnny No-Trump* [1967] and the out-of-town flop musical *W.C.* [1971] are better known).

Based on Leonid Andreyev's play *He Who Gets Slapped*, the plot dealt with an embittered, unhappily married man who becomes a circus clown. He falls in love with the bareback rider of the circus, but when he discovers her father is forcing her into marriage with a scoundrel, the clown murders her and then kills himself.

Nevertheless, They Laugh was the second lyric adaptation of Andreyev's play; in 1956, Robert Ward's *Pantaloon* was an operatic adaptation of the material, and in 1959 a revised version of the opera (now using the title of the original play) was produced by the New York City Opera (see entries for both *Pantaloon* and *He Who Gets Slapped*).

Peters had earlier appeared in another circus musical, the one-performance Broadway flop *La Strada* (1969); after *La Strada* and *Nevertheless, They Laugh*, don't look for Peters to show up in revivals of *Jumbo* (1935), *Are You with It?* (1945), *Carnival!* (1961), and *Barnum* (1980).

Carnival! also dealt with an embittered circus performer who loves a naïve young woman who works there (but at least Paul doesn't murder Lili). (Come to think of it, the young Peters would probably have made a great Lili. The character and the songs are greatly suited to her performance style.)

Eight months after the production closed, Louis Calta in the *New York Times* reported that *Nevertheless, They Laugh* would open on Broadway in January 1972. The article stated the $200,000 production, directed by Tony Tanner and starring David Holliday, would be presented by Les Schecter and Barbara Schwel (no mention of who would portray Consuelo, the role originally created by Bernadette Peters). The Broadway production never materialized.

1120 The New Bozena. "A Slacker Vaudeville." THEATRE: Cherry Lane Theatre; OPENING DATE: October 31, 1996; PERFORMANCES: 74; DIRECTION: Rainn Wilson; SCENERY: Chris Muller; COSTUMES: Melissa Toth; LIGHTING: Adam Silverman; PRODUCERS: Falstaff Presents (Michael Winter, and Rachel Colbert, Producers); Taylor Reinhart, Associate Producer

CAST—David Costabile (Ramon), Michael Dahlen (Spiv Westenberg), Kevin Isola (Revhanavaan Sahaanahanadaan)

The revue was presented in one act.

NOTES—*The Best Plays of 1996-1997* described the revue *The New Bozena* as a series of clowning skits and demonstrations in the post-modern style. Apparently the evening's highlight was a sequence titled *Winter Is the Coldest Season*, a spoof of Eastern European drama.

Peter Marks in the *New York Times* said the "uneven" evening was like a work-in-progress which had not yet found its "distinctive voice." He noted that the revue's title came from the name of a waitress who worked in a diner frequented by the cast members.

1121 A New Brain. THEATRE: The Mitzi E. Newhouse Theatre/The Lincoln Center Theatre; OPENING DATE: June 18, 1998; PERFORMANCES: 78; BOOK: William Finn and James Lapine; LYRICS: William Finn; MUSIC: William Finn; DIRECTION: Graciela Daniele; CHOREOGRAPHY: Graciela Daniele; SCENERY: David Gallo; COSTUMES: Toni-Leslie James; LIGHTING: Peggy Eisenhauer; MUSICAL DIRECTION: Ted Sperling; PRODUCER: The Lincoln Center Theatre (Andre Bishop and Bernard Gersten, Directors)

CAST—Malcolm Gets (Gordon Michael Schwinn), Mary Testa (Lisa), Liz Larsen (Rhoda), Kristin Chenoweth (Waitress, Nancy D.), Chip Zien (Mr. Bungee), Michael Mandell (Richard), John Jellison (Dr. Jafar Berensteiner), Keith Byron Kirk (The Minister), Christopher Innvar (Roger Delli-Bovi), Penny Fuller (Mimi Schwinn)

The musical was presented in one act.

MUSICAL NUMBERS—Prologue: "Frogs Have So Much Spring (The Spring Song)" (Malcolm Gets), "The Specials Today (Calamari)" (Malcolm Gets, Liz Larsen, Kristin Chenoweth, Chip Zien), "911 Emergency" (Michael Mandell, Kristin Chenoweth, John Jellison, Liz Larsen, Keith Bryon Kirk, Mary Testa), "I Have So Many Songs" (Malcolm Gets), "Heart and Music" (Keith Byron Kirk, Malcolm Gets; with Liz Larsen, Mary Testa, Penny Fuller, Christopher Innvar, Kristin Chenoweth, Michael Mandell, John Jellison), "There's Trouble in His Brain" (John Jellison, Penny Fuller), "Mother's Gonna Make Things Fine" (Penny Fuller, Malcolm Gets), "Be Polite to Everybody" (Chip Zien), "I'd Rather Be Sailing" (Christopher Innvar, Malcolm Gets), "Family History" (Kristin Chenoweth, Michael Mandell, Penny Fuller), "Gordo's Law of Genetics" (Kristin Chenoweth, John Jellison, Keith Byron Kirk, Liz Larsen, Michael Mandell, Mary Testa), "And They're Off" (Malcolm Gets with Kristin Chenoweth, John Jellison, Keith Byron Kirk, Liz Larsen, Michael Mandell, Mary Testa), "Roger Arrives" (Mary Testa, Liz Larsen, Penny Fuller, Christopher Innvar, Malcolm Gets), "Just Go" (Malcolm Gets, Christopher Innvar), "Operation Tomorrow" (Michael Mandell), "Poor, Unsuccessful and Fat" (Michael Mandell, Malcolm Gets, Chip Zien), "Sitting Becalmed in the Lee of Cuttyhunk" (Malcolm Gets, Kristin Chenoweth, Penny Fuller, John Jellison, Keith Byron Kirk, Liz Larsen, Christopher Innvar, Michael Mandell, Mary Testa), "Craniotomy" (John Jellison, Kristin Chenoweth, Malcolm Gets, Keith Byron Kirk), "An Invitation to Sleep in My Arms" (Malcolm Gets, Christopher Innvar, Liz Larsen, Penny Fuller), "Change" (Mary Testa), "Yes" (Malcolm Gets, Chip Zien; with Kristin Chenoweth, John Jellison, Keith Byron Kirk, Liz Larsen), "In the Middle of the Room" (Malcolm Gets, Penny Fuller), "I Am the Nice Nurse" (Michael Mandell), "Throw It Out" (Penny Fuller), "A Really Lousy Day in the Universe" (Mary Testa, Christopher Innvar), "Brain Dead" (Malcolm Gets, Christopher Innvar), "Whenever I Dream" (Liz Larsen, Malcolm Gets), "Eating Myself Up Alive" (Michael Mandell, with Kristin Chenoweth, John Jellison, Keith Byron Kirk, Mary Testa), "The Music Still Plays On" (Penny Fuller), "Don't Give In" (Chip Zien, with Malcolm Gets, Christopher Innvar, Liz Larsen, Penny Fuller), "You Boys Are Gonna Get Me in Such Trouble"/"I Feel Like I'm Sailing" (Michael Mandell, Christopher Innvar, Malcolm Gets), "The Homeless Lady's Revenge" (Mary Testa, Malcolm Gets, Christopher Innvar), "Time" (Christopher Innvar, Malcolm Gets), "Time and Music" (Keith Byron Kirk, Malcolm Gets, Company), "I Feel So Much Spring" (Malcolm Gets, Mary Testa, Keith Byron Kirk, Company)

NOTES—In the program notes for *A New Brain*, William Finn wrote that one week after winning the Tony Award in 1992 for *Falsettos*, he was hospitalized with what a doctor mistakenly diagnosed as an inoperable brain tumor. The musical was "an attempt to recreate what it was like during those five weeks in June and the beginning of July when I thought I was going to die, and didn't." The sung-through musical (in which Malcolm Gets played the leading role) was perhaps padded with extraneous material, but Finn nonetheless composed a fascinating and welcome score.

The script was published by Samuel French, Inc., in 1999, and the cast album was recorded by RCA Victor Records (CD # 09026-63298-2); for the recording, the role of Roger (created by Christopher Innvar on the stage) was sung by Norm Lewis.

Twenty years earlier, Al Carmines' Off Off Broadway musical *In Praise of Death* (see entry) dealt with a subject similar to the one depicted in *A New Brain*; in 1977, Carmines underwent an operation for a cerebral aneurysm, and his 1978 musical was inspired by the results of that experience ("I recovered, but at the price of that innocence which all of us carry until smitten in some intimate way by fate").

1122 New Cambridge Circus. THEATRE: Square East; OPENING DATE: January 14, 1965; PERFORMANCES: 78; MATERIAL: Tim Brooke-Taylor, David Hatch, John Cleese, Bill Oddie, Jean Hart, John Cameron, Graham Chapman, and the "Clap Hands" Company; MUSIC: Bill Oddie; LIGHTING: Peter Ness

CAST—Tim Brooke-Taylor, David Hatch, John Cleese, Bill Oddie, Jean Hart

NOTES—This was the new edition of *Cambridge Circus*, with a slightly scaled-down cast (and with four returning members of the original group). No information available on specific sketches and songs (see entry for *Cambridge Circus* [1964] for more information).

Harris Gilroy in the *New York Times* (who noted the evening lacked animals but included accents) felt the evening worked better Off Broadway than on. He liked a sequence which poked fun at popular culture (we're told that "folk music" is when "rich college students get together to sing about poverty"), and he praised John Cleese, who"dominated" his skits with his "talent for portraying innate cruelty."

1123 New Cole Porter Revue

NOTES—See entry for *The Decline and Fall of the Entire World as Seen Through the Eyes of Cole Porter Revisited* (December 1965 edition).

1124 New York City Street Show. THEATRE: Actors' Playhouse; OPENING DATE: April 28, 1977; PERFORMANCES: 20; BOOK: Peter Copani; LYRICS: Peter Copani; MUSIC: Peter Copani; ADDITIONAL MUSIC by Christian Staudt, David McHugh, and Ed Vogel; DIRECTION: Peter Copani; CHOREOGRAPHY: Charles Goeddertz; SCENERY: Jim Chestnut; LIGHTING: Richard Harper; MUSICAL DIRECTION: Steven Oirich; PRODUCERS: Peter Copani and Victor Papa; A People's Performing Company Production

CAST—Bob Acaro (Sergio), Eva Charney (Meri), Rob DeRosa (Jesus), Florie Freshman (Anita), Hubert Kelly (Vernon), Deborah Malone (Xena), Theresa Saldana (Gina), Richard Woods (Bob)

The musical was presented in one act.

MUSICAL NUMBERS—"American Dream" (music by David McHugh) (Company), "Who Can Say" (Theresa Saldana, Deborah Malone), "God Is in the People" (Bob Acaro, Rob DeRosa, Company), "A Special Man" (Florie Freshman), "Strawberries, Pickles and Ice Cream" (Eva Charney), "Hail, Hail" (Theresa Saldana, Company), "Kung Fu" (Hubert Kelly, Richard Woods), "One of Us" (Deborah Malone), "When You Are Together" (music by David McHugh) (Bob Arcaro, Richard Woods), "If Jesus Walked" (Company), "Bad But Good" (Company), "Make Them Hate" (Company), "Corruption" (Theresa Saldana), "Wait and See" (music by Peter Copani and Ed Vogel) (Deborah Malone), "Hanging Out" (Richard Woods, Company), "Love Is Beautiful" (Company)

NOTES—*New York City Street Show* was yet another recycled version of Peter Copani's *Street Jesus* (1974; see entry), which had previously been rewritten as *Fire of Flowers* (1976; see entry). Eight songs in *New York City Street Show* ("A Special Man," "If Jesus Walked," "One of Us," "God Is in the People," "Who Can Say?," "Strawberries, Pickles and Ice Cream," "Make Them Hate," and "Wait and See") had first been heard in *Street Jesus* and then later in *Fire of Flowers*. And four other songs from *Street Jesus* (which had not been used in *Fire of Flowers*) were also heard in *New York City Street Show*: "Bad But Good," "Hail, Hail," "Corruption," and "Love Is Beautiful." In the productions of *Street Jesus* and *Fire of Flowers,* "Wait and See" appears to have been credited solely to Peter Copani; however, for *New York City Street Show*, the song is credited to both Copani and Ed Vogel.

1125 New York Coloring Book. THEATRE: Café Society; OPENING DATE: April 2, 1963; PERFORMANCES: 84; LYRICS: Michael McWhinney; MUSIC: Jerry Powell; DIRECTION: Bill Penn; production supervised by Yvette Schumer; CHOREOGRAPHY: Bill Miller; PRODUCER: Jan Wallman

CAST—Gloria Bleezarde, Ronnie Hall, Barbara Gilbert, Ronny Whyte

The revue was presented in two acts (song assignments unknown).

ACT ONE—"Café Society," "S-E-X," "When Will They Finish New York?," "The Big Walk," "The Gal Who Took the Minutes," "A Family Affair," "Silent Spring," "Souvenirs," "Old Miss," "On My Own," "Spoleto"

ACT TWO—"My Friends, the Celebrities," "Everything for Roz," "The Bunny's Lament," "Low Fidelity," "Will My Real Love Please Stand Up," "Rocky on the Rocks" (Ronny Whyte), "Beyond the Binge, I Want to Get Off," "Time and Time Again," "No Sign of the Times," "Coloring Book"

NOTES—Given many of the sprightly song titles, *New York Coloring Book* sounds like a delightful revue. Milton Esterow in the *New York Times* reported the evening was "bright" and "fresh," and singled out "Beyond the Binge, I Want to Get Off" (which dealt with the British invasion of Broadway) and "Rocky on the Rocks" (a song about Nelson Rockefeller, which was performed by Ronny Whyte). "Rocky" re-surfaced later in the year in the industrial revue *All About Life*, and was again sung by Whyte, who also recorded the number for the cast album of *All About Life* (unidentified label; # XTV-89424/5).

"Everything for Roz" appears to have been a lament that Rosalind Russell seemed to snag roles in almost every film version of a Broadway show (*Picnic, A Majority of One, Five Finger Exercise, Gypsy,* and, in a reversal of the usual practice, she even reprised her stage role of *Auntie Mame*). For the record, in 1967 she appeared in two more film versions of stage productions (*Oh, Dad, Poor Dad, Mama's Hung You in the Closet and I'm Feelin' So Sad* and *Rosie!*, which was adapted from *The Good Soup*).

"Spoleto" was later heard in *Mixed Doubles* (1966; see entry) and can be heard on that show's cast album. "(New York) Coloring Book" was later heard in *That Thing at the Cherry Lane* (see entry).

1126 The New York Musical Theatre Festival

NOTES—The New York Musical Theatre Festival (NYMF) is a musical theatre junkie's dream. Since 2004, the company has produced some thirty musicals over a three-week period during the fall at various New York theatres. Kris Stewart is the company's executive director and Isaac Robert Hurwitz its executive producer. Their website for NYMF sums up the festival's theatrical mission: "Musicals must be heard." As a result, every year new musical theatre writers are given the opportunity to see their musicals staged before an audience.

Among NYMF's productions have been *Altar Boyz, The Great American Trailer Park Musical, Gutenberg! The Musical!*, and *[title of show]* (see entries), all of which eventually transferred to open-end runs in Off and Off Off Broadway.

The 2007 festival was presented over thirty musicals during the period September 17-October 7, 2007, including *Austentatious, Bernice Bobs Her Mullet, The Brain from Planet X, Emma, Gemini The Musical, The Last Starfighter, Like Love, Little Egypt, Look What a Wonder Jesus Has Done, Love Kills, Love Sucks, Mud Donahue & Son, Platforms, The Rockae, Such Good Friends, Tully (In No Particular Order), Unlock'd, with Glee*, and *The Yellow Wood* (for the Festival's production of *Roller Derby*, see entry for John Braden's *The Derby* [1980]):

Austentatious. BOOK: Matt Board, Jane Caplow, Kate Galvin, Luisa Hinchliff, and Joe Slabe; LYRICS AND MUSIC: Matt Board and Joe Slabe; DIRECTION: Mary Catherine Burke; CHOREOGRAPHY: Rhonda Miller

CAST—Stephanie D'Abruzzo (Sam), Stephen Bel Davies (Dominic), Stacey Sargeant (Emily), Amy Goldberger (Lauren), Paul Wyatt (Blake), George Merrick

NOTES—The cutely titled *Austentatious* dealt with an amateur theatrical group putting on a new stage adaptation of Jane Austen's *Pride and Prejudice* (1813). For another musical loosely based on the novel, see entry for *I Love You Because* (this entry also references *First Impressions*, a 1959 musical adaptation of the novel). Also see entry below for *Emma*, which is based on Austen's 1816 novel.

Bernice Bobs Her Mullet. BOOK, LYRICS, AND MUSIC: Joe Major; DIRECTION: Andy Sandberg; CHOREOGRAPHY: Shea Sullivan

CAST—Cast included Garrett Long (Bernice), Ann Morrison (Bernice's Mother, Bernice's Aunt), Hollie Howard (Marjorie), Brandon Wardell (Warren), Nick Cearley (Otis), Jeff Hill (Draycott), Katrina Rose Dideriksen

SOURCE—The 1920 short story "Bernice Bobs Her Hair" by F. Scott Fitzgerald

NOTES—F. Scott Fitzgerald's 1920 short story "Bernice Bobs Her Hair" was updated to the present in this musical version by Joe Major which dealt with trailer-park types, including the title character, who hopes to leave the world of the trailer park and find her place in society (in Little Rock, Arkansas!). Paul Menard in *BackStage.com* felt the evening was "little more than a musical episode of *The Beverly Hillbillies*," but he singled out a few songs, including "The Gospel According to Draycott" ("rousing"), "You Pull It Off Nicely" (a "catty duet"), and "Hate Yourself" (which illustrated Major's "ability to pen incisively sarcastic lyrics with genuine comic payoff"). Among the other songs in the score were "Eau Claire" and "I Wanna Be in Little Rock."

The musical was performed at the Julia Miles Theatre.

The Brain from Planet X. BOOK: Bruce Kimmel and David Wechter; LYRICS AND MUSIC: Bruce Kimmel; DIRECTION: Bruce Kimmel; CHOREOGRAPHY: Adam Cates

CAST—Amy Bodnar (Joyce), Benjamin Clark (Narrator), Paul Downs Colaizzo (Rod), Rob Evan (Fred Bunson), Merrill Grant (Donna), Cason Murphy (Zubrick), Barry Pearl (The Brain), Alet Taylor (Yoni)

NOTES—*The Brain from Planet X* took place in 1958, and told of two teenagers who must save the San Fernando Valley, if not the entire Planet Earth, from alien invaders. David Sheward in *BackStage.com* noted that Bruce Kimmel's score contained "snappy" numbers, and singled out Adam Cates' choreography in "The Brain Tap." The musical played at the Acorn Theatre.

Emma. BOOK: Joel Adlen; LYRICS: Joel Adlen; MUSIC: Joel Adlen; DIRECTION: Terry Berliner

CAST—Leah Horowitz (Emma), John Patrick Moore (Knightley), Kara Boyer (Harriet), Ben Roseberry, Terry Palasz, Jessie Lawder, Brenda Jean Foley, Dan Guller, Tiffany Diane Smith, Gael Schaefer, Brett Macias, Tiffan Borelli, John Wiegand

SOURCE—The 1816 novel *Emma* by Jane Austen.

NOTES—*Emma* was NYMF's second Jane Austen-inspired musical (see *Austentatious*). The musical opened at the Acorn Theatre for five performances.

Robert Windeler in *Backstage.com* was generally unimpressed with the adaptation, and found the score merely "serviceable." But he singled out three songs, the title number, "If I Loved You Less," and "A Country Dance (Will You Dance with Me?)."

For more information about Jane Austen-inspired musicals, see above entry for *Austentatious*; also see separate entry for *I Love You Because*.

Gemini the Musical. BOOK: Albert Innaurato; LYRICS: Charles Gilbert; MUSIC: Charles Gilbert; DIRECTION: Mark Robinson

CAST—Dan Micciche (Francis Geminiani), Joel Blum (Fran), Ryan Reid (Randy), Bethe Austin (Lucille), Kirsten Bracken (Judith), Jonathan Kay (Herschel), Linda Hart (Bunny)

NOTES—Albert Innaurato's 1977 play *Gemini* was a long-running hit, playing 1,788 performances; it was later filmed in 1980 as *Happy Birthday, Gemini*. The musical version seen at NYMF was scripted by Innaurato, and it appears the musical had first been produced in 2004.

The story dealt with Francis Geminiani on his twenty-first birthday, and looked at his problems with both his family and his sexual identity.

Dan Bacalzo in *TheaterMania* felt the musical version offered "mixed results"; on the plus side, the libretto strengthened the relationship between with Francis and his father, but Bacalzo also noted that some of the musical numbers fell flat." He praised the score's best song ("Trolley"), which was sung by a minor character, and he also liked "Good People" and "Concrete."

The musical was presented at the Acorn Theatre.

The Last Starfighter. BOOK: Fred Landau; LYRICS: Skip Kennon; MUSIC: Skip Kennon; DIRECTION: Elizabeth Lucas; CHOREOGRAPHY: David Eggers; SCENERY: Anne Goelz; COSTUMES: Mark Richard Caswell; LIGHTING: Herrick Goldman

SOURCE—The 1984 film *The Last Starfighter* (screenplay by Jonathan Betuel).

The action occurs during Spring 1983 in a Sierra Nevada trailer park.

CAST—Danny Binstock (Alex Rogan), Joseph Kolinski (Centauri), Don Mayo (Otis Wright), Nora Blackall (Maggie), Janet Carroll (Granny), Adinah Alexander (Mrs. Rogan), Tom Treadwell (Enduran), Mary Ellen Ashley, Michael Cone, Jesse J.P. Johnson, Jonathan Richard Sandler, Ryan Jesse, Natalie Hall, Sean Montgomery, Jessica Blair

NOTES—Like the film upon which it was based, *The Last Starfighter* dealt with a teenage boy who lives in a Sierra Nevada trailer park and suddenly finds himself fighting battles in a faraway galaxy.

The musical had earlier been seen Off Off Broadway at the Storm Theatre on October 15, 2004, and that production was recorded by Kritzerland Records (CD # KR-20010-4); the songs on the CD included "Starlite Starbrite," "Somebody, Somewhere, Something," "A Place Like This," "Little Did We Know (The Game)," "Things Change," "Out of This World," "Star League Anthem," "Father to Son," "Love Is Like Water," "To Make a Hero," "Zandozan!," "To Make a Hero" (reprise), "Spring Break," "Reach Out," "Caves of the Heart (The Battle)," and "Finale." Joseph Kolinski had created the role of Centauri in the original production and on the recording, and reprised the role for the NYMF revival (William Parry was Otis in the original production).

The NYMF production opened at The Theatre at St. Clements on September 28, 2007, for seven performances.

Like Love. BOOK: Barry Jay Kaplan; LYRICS: Barry Jay Kaplan; MUSIC: Lewis Flinn; DIRECTION: Lisa Rothe; SCENERY: Sean Tribble; COSTUMES: Christina Bullard

CAST—Jon Patrick Walker (He), Emily Swallow (She), Danielle Ferland (Love, Others)

NOTES—*Like Love* dealt with a man and woman who agree to meet weekly for sexual encounters; they also agree to share nothing about their lives, not even their names. Dan Bacalzo in *TheaterMania* felt the premise somewhat backfired because the audience never really got to know the characters. But he praised Lewis Flinn's "rich, diverse score" which "beautifully" blended such idioms as jazz, Latin, soft pop, and traditional Broadway.

Little Egypt. "An Unexpected Love Story"; BOOK: Lynn Siefert; LYRICS: Gregg Lee Henry; MUSIC: Gregg Lee Henry; DIRECTION: Lisa James; SCENERY: Lex Liang; COSTUMES: Vicki Sanchez; LIGHTING: Brian Gale; MUSICAL DIRECTION: Robert Martin

CAST—Lisa Akey (Bernadette), Gregg Lee Henry (Watson), Jenny O'Hara (Faye), Sara Rue (Celeste), Raphael Sbarge (Victor), Lee Wilkof (Hugh)

The action occurs in Little Egypt, Illinois, in the early 1980s.

NOTES—Originally produced in workshop at the Matrix Theatre in Los Angeles, *Little Egypt* told the story of three couples seeking romance in Little Egypt, Illinois. Ron Cohen in *BackStage* felt the book was undramatic and at times unbelievable. But he praised Gregg Lee Henry's "quite infectious" score, an amalgamation of "country-flavored melodies with catchy blues and boogie-woogie rhythms."

The production opened at the Acorn Theatre on September 27, 2007, for six performances.

Look What a Wonder Jesus Has Done. BOOK: Walter Robinson; LYRICS: Walter Robinson; MUSIC: Walter Robinson; DIRECTION: Hilary Adams; CHOREOGRAPHY: Robert Bianca; SCENERY: Lara Fabian

CAST—Horace V. Rogers (Denmark Vesey), Tyrone Grant (Pastor Grant), Selena Nelson (Rose), CJ Palma (Prosser), Tamara Robinson (Chloe), David Andrew Anderson (Colonel Moore)

NOTES—*Lord What a Wonder Jesus Has Done* told the true story of Denmark Vesey, a free Black who plotted an 1822 rebellion against Charleston slave owners. Matthew Murray in *Talkin' Broadway* noted the "gospel opera" was heavy on "soulful and true" gospel numbers sung in a church, but felt they "flattened" emotions which should be "electrically charged." He noted that the "out-of-church" sequences cried out for musical interpretation.

One song, "Answer My Prayer," was written by Livingston Taylor and Carol Bayer-Sager.

The musical was presented at The Theatre at St. Clements.

Love Kills. "An Emo Rock Musical." BOOK, LYRICS, AND MUSIC: Kyle Jarrow; DIRECTION: Jason Southerland; SCENERY: James Williston

CAST—Cast included Eli Schneider (Charlie), Marisa Rhodes (Caril Ann), John Hickock (Sheriff Merle Karnopp), Deirdre O'Connell (Gertrude O'-Connell)

NOTES—Based on a true story about two teenagers who went on a killing spree in 1958, *Love Kills* juxtaposed the love of the two teenagers with that of a sheriff and his wife. Jerry Portwood in *BackStage.com* praised Kyle Jarrow's score, and noted that while the evening sometimes felt like "being at a rock concert for misunderstood teens," the contrast between the two couples "transcends juvenile anguish."

Dan Bacalzo in *TheaterMania* praised such songs as "Love Will Never Die" ("a terrific 1950s-style tune") and "When I Could Feel," and while he felt the evening was "compelling," he also noted it was sometimes "uneven"; but he concluded that overall the musical was "vibrant and exciting." The musical was presented at the 45th Street Theatre.

The story upon which the musical was based had earlier inspired two films, *Badlands* (1973) and *Natural Born Killers* (1994).

Love Sucks. BOOK: Stephen O'Rourke; LYRICS: Stephen O'Rourke; MUSIC: Brandon Patton; DIRECTION: Andy Goldberg

CAST—Cast included Nicholas Webber (Big Joe), Rebecca Hart (Patti), Jason Wooten (Johnny), Heather Robb (Kate)

SOURCE—The 1595 (possibly 1596) play *Love's Labour's Lost* by William Shakespeare.

NOTES—*Love Sucks*, a very updated adaptation of Shakespeare's *Love's Labour's Lost*, pitted two rock groups against one another, a four-man band called The Molotovs and a four-woman band called The Guttersnipes. Andy Propst in *TheatreMania* liked the musical, and noted it moved "with swift energy befitting a storytelling rock concert ... with some revisions [the musical] could be completely lovable." Propst singled out two songs in the "punk, hard rock score" ("Let's Do It Now" and "Love Ain't So Bad").

A earlier musical adaptation of Shakespeare's comedy was seen in regional theatre as *Love's Labour's Lost*; the musical was produced by the Folger Library Theatre Group in Washington, D.C., on April 23, 1974, with book and lyrics by David Vando and music by Bryan Williams (the cast included Martin Vidnovic, Meg Bussert, Richard Kind, and Frank Coppola).

Mud Donahue & Son. BOOK: Jeff Hochhauser; LYRICS: Jeff Hochhauser and Bob Johnston; MUSIC: Bob Johnston; DIRECTION: Lynne Taylor-Corbett; CHOREOGRAPHY: Lynne Taylor-Corbett

CAST—Karen Murphy (Mud Donahue), Shonn Wiley (Jack Donahue)

SOURCE—The autobiography *Letters of a Hoofer to His Ma* by Jack Donahue.

The action occurs during the early part of the twentieth century.

NOTES—The two-character musical *Mud Donahue & Son* dealt with vaudeville and musical comedy star Jack Donahue (1892-1930) and his mother Mud, who opposed his dreams of becoming a dancer. Donahue's Broadway appearances included roles in the original Broadway productions of *Ziegfeld Follies of 1920*, *Sunny* (1925) and *Rosalie* (1928). He received top billing in the 1929 hit *Sons o' Guns*, which played for 295 performances. Sadly, Donahue died the following year. Matthew Murray in *Talkin' Broadway* noted that the musical, based on letters from Jack Donahue to his mother, was often an "epistolary bore." But he singled out two dance sequences ("The Shadow" and "The Tap Drunk"), and praised the latter "as fine an expression ... of the storytelling powers of dance that's been seen on NYMF—or most other New York stages—this year."

Besides the two above-mentioned numbers, Dan Bacalzo in *TheatreMania* also praised "My Son, I Know," "So the Old Dog Has Come Home," "French Kiss," and "Vaudeville Man."

The musical opened at the 45th Street Theatre for seven performances. It was revived by the York Theatre in 2008 (as *My Vaudeville Man!*, which is scheduled for a CD release).

Platforms

NOTES—*Platforms* was a "dance narrative musical" conceived by Holly-Anne Ruggiero and Delaney Britt Brewer. The cast included Deborah Yates (who had created the role of the The Girl in the Yellow Dress in *Contact* [see entry]), Ted Levy, Albert Blaise Cattafi, Donielle Janora, Matt Anctil, Matthew Steffens, Monette McKay, Ron Nahass, Trevor Downey, Zachary Denison, and Eric Rubbe.

The musical was presented at The Theatre at St. Clement's.

The Rockae. BOOK: Peter Mills and Cara Reichel; LYRICS: Peter Mills; MUSIC: Peter Mills; DIRECTION: Cara Reichel; COSTUMES: David Withrow; CHOREOGRAPHY: Marlo Hunter

CAST—Cast included Michael Cunio (Dionysus), Mitchell Jarvis (King Pentheus), Gordon Stanley (Cadmus), Meghan McGeary (Agave), Matt DeAngelis

SOURCE—The 406 B.C. play *The Bacchae* by Euripides.

NOTES—Euripides' *The Bacchae* here became *The Rockae*, and it told the same story of Dionysus, who, furious at not being recognized as a god, brings horror and tragedy to Thebes. Andy Propst in *Theatre-*

Mania wrote that that the evening was like an "adrenaline-filled rock concert," and he noted that Michael Cunio (as Dionysus) looked the part of a rock star ("an impressively seductive figure ... in rocker's pants that look painted on"). Propst praised the score, the "vocally powerful" performances, and the "animalistic intensity" of the overall production.

Other lyric adaptations of *The Bacchae* include two operas, *Revelation in the Courthouse Park* (1960), libretto and music by Harry Partch, and *The Bassarids* (1965), libretto by W.H. Auden and Chester Kallman, music by Hans Werner Henze.

Roller Derby

NOTES—See entry for John Braden's *The Derby* (1980).

Such Good Friends. BOOK: Noel Katz; LYRICS: Noel Katz; MUSIC: Noel Katz; DIRECTION: Marc Bruni; CHOREOGRAPHY: Wendy Seyb; SCENERY: Jeff Hinchee; Teresa Hall ("Props Master"); LIGHTING: Jim Milkey; MUSICAL DIRECTION: Michael Horsley

CAST—Liz Larson (Dottie Francis), Brad Oscar (Gabe Fisher), Jeff Talbott (Danny Factor), Dirk Lumbard (Donald McMahon), Lynne Wintersteller (Vivian March), Joshua Campbell, Michael Thomas Holmes, Shannon O'Bryan, Laura Jordan, Blake Whyte

NOTES—*Such Good Friends* took place in New York during the 1950s and was set against the early days of television and the investigations by the House Committee on Un-American Activities. The musical dealt with four friends, a television actress, a writer, a director, and a choreographer, all of whom struggle to put on a weekly television variety show and who are ultimately called upon to testify in the HUAC hearings.

Don Bacalzo in *TheatreMania* felt the musical was uneven but indicated its weaknesses were "fixable." He praised such songs as "You're a Red," "My Name Is Mud," and "Little Sister." The musical opened at the Julia Miles Theatre.

Tully (In No Particular Order). BOOK: Joshua William Gelb; LYRICS: Stephanie Johnstone; MUSIC: Stephanie Johnstone and Joshua William Gelb; DIRECTION: Joshua William Gelb

CAST—Cast included Adam Hose (Tully), Kate Rockwell (Clodia Beautee), Evan Jay Newman (Julie), Autumn Hurlbert (Quinn), David McGee (Cal), Austin Miller (Claude), Owen O'Malley (Rufus)

NOTES—*Tully (In No Particular Order)* was an ambitious musical which dealt with no less than the Roman poet Catullus (84 B.C.-54 B.C.), who, having lost his memory, uses his poems as clues and reference points to piece together the picture of his life. Dan Bacalzo in *TheaterMania* felt the characters were "flatly" written and he wasn't particularly impressed with the evening. But he noted the score contained "haunting" melodies, including "The Loving of You." He also liked "The Door Song" ("very funny"), "Bob" ("amusing"), and "Forever" (a "sly" look at love and marriage). While the script made references to ancient Rome, Bacalzo indicated the evening utilized "contemporary" language and a modern sensibility.

Unlock'd. BOOK: Sam Carner; LYRICS: Sam Carner; MUSIC: Derek Gregor; MUSICAL DIRECTION: Eric Svejcar

CAST—Sarah Jane Everman (Belinda), Jackie Burns (Clarissa), Christopher Gunn (Edwin), Alison Cimmet, Maria Couch, Mary Catherine McDonald, Darryl Winslow, Christopher Totten, William Thomas Evans

SOURCE—Alexander Pope's poem *The Rape of the Lock* (first published in 1712; expanded version published in 1714).

NOTES—Based on Alexander Pope's poem *The Rape of the Lock*, Sam Carner and Derek Gregor's musical *Unlock'd* received a rave review from Matthew Murray in *Talkin' Broadway*. He praised the "sparkling comic operetta" as "one of the most ravishing musicals of 2007," and noted the music was "resplendent" and the lyrics "sumptuously romantic" (he singled out the "creamy, complex harmonies" of "Hampton Court").

With Glee. BOOK: John Gregor; LYRICS: John Gregor; MUSIC: John Gregor; DIRECTION: Ryan Mekenian; CHOREOGRAPHY: Billy Griffin

CAST—Greg Kenna (Nathaniel), Ryan Speakman (Sam), Justin Bellero (Scott), Dan Lawler (Clay), Kevin Michael Murray (Kip), Michael J. Miller, Elizabeth Kerins

NOTES—*With Glee* dealt with life in a boys' boarding school. Matthew Murray in *Talkin' Broadway* noted the musical deftly avoided being retro and hip as well as square. Instead, the work embraced "traditional musical-writing know-how unapologetically and honestly." The result was "one of the most ingratiating shows of the year," and Murray praised the story ("told without irony") and performances ("without affectation"). Further, Gregor's score was a "marvel of unadorned simplicity," and Murray singled out "Bad School Kids" (an "irresistible" opening number), "If You Want to Be a Vanderberg" (a Gilbert and Sullivan spoof), "Normal," "Worcester," and "Gaul Was Divided Into Three Parts."

The musical was presented at the 45th Street Theatre for five performances

The Yellow Wood. BOOK, LYRICS, AND MUSIC: Michelle Elliott and Danny Larsen; DIRECTION: B.D. Wong

CAST—Jason Tam (Adam), Yuko Takara (Gwen), Randy Blair (Casserole), Caissie Levy

NOTES—*The Yellow Wood* dealt with a Korean-American family, including a teenager (played by Jason Tam) with Attention Deficit Disorder who tries to go a full day without taking Ritalin. Dan Bacalzo in *TheaterMania* noted that the musical needed development in some areas, but felt there was "definite potential" in its unusual story; he singled out two songs, "Door/Window" and "Tater Tot Cassrole."

1127 The News in Review

NOTES—See entry for *Newsical*.

1128 Newsical.

"All the Stuff That's Fit to Spoof." THEATRE: Upstairs at Studio 54; OPENING DATE: October 7, 2004; PERFORMANCES: 215; SKETCHES: Rick Crom; LYRICS: Rick Crom; MUSIC: Rick Crom; DIRECTION: Donna Drake; CHOREOGRAPHY: Donna Drake; SCENERY: Peter P. Allburn; COSTUMES: David Kaley; LIGHTING: Michael Flink; MUSICAL DIRECTION: Ed Goldschneider; PRODUCERS: Fred M. Caruso in association with Gary Maffei, Barry Fisher, and Jesse Adelaar

CAST—Kim Cea, Todd Alan Johnson, Stephanie Kurtzuba, Jeff Skowron

The revue was presented in two acts (division of acts and song assignments unknown).

MUSICAL NUMBERS—"Everyone's Full of #%it," "Dubya We Love Ya," "Felt Up at the Airport," "What About Me," "I Must Have Been Stoned," "My Political Opinion," "Arnold and the Kennedys," "I Just Came to Say, 'I'm Gay'," "Martha Stewart: The Musical," "Prozac, Ritalin, TrimSpa," "Too Much Botox," "Dr. Phil," "Not the Man I Married," "Hooters Air," "America Online," "Anna Nicole," "I Am an Animal," "Michael and Peter," "Nobody Messes with Liza," "Denial"

NOTES—*Newsical* was a musical revue which spoofed politics (James McGreevey, Arnold Schwarzenegger, the Clintons, John Kerry, Dubya), personalities (Anna Nicole Smith, Liza Minnelli, Dr. Phil, Martha Stewart), and various aspects of modern life (Botox, airport security).

Lawrence Van Gelder in the *New York Times* noted one could order drinks at Upstairs at Studio 54, but they weren't necessary because *Newsical* "makes it possible to get high on hilarity." He said the evening of "witty" lyrics and music was "fast, funny and irreverent" and it "zestfully ... skewered" celebrities; the cast members created an "asylum of inflated personalities, reducing them to their asinine essence." As a result, the audience saw Barbra Streisand "waxing lyrical about politics" and Anna Nicole Smith "making a spectacle of herself."

The cast album was released by NEWSical Records (CD # 25346-80922); the song titles are taken from the CD.

An earlier musical somewhat similar in style to *Newsical* was *The News in Review* ("The Musical Scoop"), which opened at Del's Down Under/Delsomma's Restaurant on July 23, 1992. Written by Nancy Holson, the evening offered new lyrics to standard songs, all of which commented on topical events (Ross Perrot sings "Billion Dollar Baby"; the ousted Mikhail Gorbachev sings "The Party's Over"; and Jerry Brown performs "Aquarius"). Other figures spoofed during the evening included Ronald Reagan, Clarence Thomas, Ted Kennedy, Bill Clinton, Leona Helmsley, Barbara Walters, Larry King, Geraldo Rivera, Sister Souljah, and Gennifer Flowers. The revue was directed by Terry Long, the musical direction was by Stephen A. Sasloe, and the cast included Monique Lareau, Jack Plotnick, Richard Rowan, Linda Strassler, and Stan Taffel. Lawrence Van Gelder in the *New York Times* found the company "talented," and noted that the politicians of the era were indeed doing something about the economy because they were giving employment to the creators and performers of topical revues.

1129 Newyorkers.

THEATRE: City Center Stage II/Manhattan Theatre Club; OPENING DATE: March 27, 2001; PERFORMANCES: 16; LYRICS: Glenn Slater; MUSIC: Stephen Weiner; DIRECTION: Christopher Ashley; CHOREOGRAPHY: Daniel Pelzig; SCENERY: Derek McLane; COSTUMES: David C. Woolard; LIGHTING: Ken Billington; MUSICAL DIRECTION: Robert Billig; PRODUCER: Manhattan Theatre Club (Lynne Meadow, Artistic Director; Barry Grove, Executive Producer)

CAST—Stephen DeRosa (Stephen), Jerry Dixon (Jerry), Jesse Tyler Ferguson (Jesse), Pamela Isaacs (Pamela), Liz Larsen (Liz), Priscilla Lopez (Priscilla)

The revue was presented in one act (song titles not available).

NOTES—*Suburb* (see entry), which opened earlier in the month, dealt with life in the suburbs, *Newyorkers* with life in the city.

Bruce Weber in the *New York Times* liked the amiable revue with its "glib and generally prickly" lyrics about New York City life (including such obvious targets as non-English-speaking taxi drivers, yuppies, and "tyrannical" co-op boards). He particularly enjoyed "Today's Special," a look at trendy restaurants, and "Tall Quiet Guy," sung by the Statue of Liberty to the Empire State Building. He was also amused by "No Hurry at All," in which a Starbucks' "counter girl" takes her time and makes her yuppie customers wait for their all-important lattes. Weber was especially taken with "Manhattan 4 A.M.," a non-satiric song which was a "romantic paean" to the city in the hours just before dawn; he said the song floated "like a pretty balloon" (the number might work well in a medley with "My Time of Day" [*Guys and Dolls*]).

1130 Nicol Williamson's Late Show.

THEATRE: Eastside Playhouse; OPENING DATE: June 26, 1973; PERFORMANCES: 30; LIGHTING: Jene Youtt; MUSICAL DIRECTION: Ray Kane; PRODUCER: Norman Twain

CAST—Nicol Williamson

The revue was presented in one act.

NOTES—In his revue *Nicol Williamson's Late Show*, Williamson sang and read poetry at the Eastside Playhouse after his evening performances in the title role of the Broadway revival of *Uncle Vanya* (he also performed the revue after Sunday matinees). He was accompanied by a six-piece combo.

The writers, lyricists, and composers represented in the revue were: e.e. cummings, Samuel Beckett, Dylan Thomas, T.S. Eliot, Dorothy Parker, T.A. Daly, John Betjeman, E.B. White, Spike Mulligan, William Shakespeare, Carl Lee Perkins, Hoagy Carmichael, Kris Kristofferson, Tim Hardin, Johnny (John) Dankworth, Kurt Weill and Marc Blitzstein, John Killigrew, Jimmy Webb, Jimmy McHugh and Dorothy Fields, Barry Robbins and Maurice Gibb, J.P. Richardson, and Fred Neil.

It's interesting to note that Williamson chose to read from Sir John Betjeman, the Poet Laureate of Great Britain who was probably completely unknown in the United States. Betjeman's writings were later adapted into a British musical revue, which played Off Broadway in 1980 (see entry).

In 1976, Williamson appeared in a full-fledged Broadway musical, the deadly dull *Rex* (which is now best remembered for an impromptu contretemps between Williamson and a cast member during a curtain call).

1131 A Night in Venice. "A Romantic Extravaganza." THEATRE: The New Jones Beach Marine Stadium; OPENING DATE: June 26, 1952; PERFORMANCES: Unknown; BOOK: Book adapted by Ruth and Thomas Martin; LYRICS: Lyrics adapted by Ruth and Thomas Martin; MUSIC: Johann Strauss; music adaptation by Thomas Martin; DIRECTION: Jack Donohue; CHOREOGRAPHY: James Nygren; SCENERY: Raoul Pene du Bois; COSTUMES: Raoul Pene du Bois; MUSICAL DIRECTION: Thomas Martin; PRODUCER: Michael Todd

CAST—Jimmy Casanova (Pappacoda), Thomas (Tibbett) Hayward (Mario), David Kurlan (Senator Bartoldi), Arthur Newman (Senator Lorenzo), Kenneth Schon (Senator Del Aqua), Nola Fairbanks (Ciboletta), Michael Roberts (Centurio), Norwood Smith (Caramello), Larry Laurence (Larry Laurence later changed his name to Enzo Stuarti; Francesco), Jack Russell (Duke), Guen Omeron (Barbara), Rose Perfect (Agrippina), Betty Stone (Serafina), Laurel Hurley (Nina), Gloria Gilbert (The Dancer), Rosita Royce (The Dove Fancier); Singing Ensemble: Sopranos—Jennie Andrea, Betsy Bridge, Sara Carter, Olga Christie, Kathy Collin, Lola Fisher, Fredericka Fondo, Nell Foster, Teresa Gannon, Marie Gibson, Teresa Gray, Ruth Kelly, Ethel Kerner, Helena Lawrence, Mary Le Sawyer, Helen Oliver, Edith Terry, Adrian Wadsworth, Julie Williams, Betty Winsett, Elinor Winter, Sara Bettis, Matilda Broadman, Elinor Daniels, Lori Dew, Gloria Eisner, Ethel Greene, Katherine Harvey, Dorothy Juden, Sally Moore, Frances Paige, Noell Peloquin, Dorothy Shawn, Dorothy Siegfried, Betty Stone, Maria Yauger, Maria Yavne; Baritones—Harold Bertelson, Charles Booth, Walter Brandin, Donald Dewhirst, Philip Douglass, John Trydel, Carl Honzack, Henry Lawrence, Steve Manning, James Morris, Tom Powell, Michael Roberts, Howard Shaw, Carlos Sherman, Bob Trehy, John Trehy, John Zadorzny, Alan Lowell, Francis Manachino; Tenors—Max Alperstein, Glenn Biggam, Bill Carlson, Matthew Farrugio, Frank Finn, James Galvin, Duke Giddens, Norman Giffin, William Golden, Joe Gregory, Kurt Kessler, Charles Kuestner, Alfred Morgan, Roland Miles, Bernard Ratshin, Abram Tamres, Deloyd Tibbs, Norman Warwick, Benjamin Wilkes; Dancing Group: Boys—John Aristedes, Hubert Bland, Alfredo Corvino, Peter Deign, Phil Gerard, Tex Hightower, John Kelly, Joseph Layton, Gerald Leavitt, Carl Luman, Donald Martin, Lee Murray, Louis Shaw, Jim Smith; Girls—Estelle Aza, Virginia Barnes, Ann Barney, Janet Cowan, Wilma Curley, Cathryn Damon, Lorna Del Maestro, Louise Ferrand, Penny Green, Maria Harriton, Ruby Herndon, Emilika Hulovo, Audrey Kearne, Natasha Kelepovska, Joan Kruger, Zoya Meyer, Sally McRoberts, Barbara Michaels, Irene Minor, Zebra Nevins, Christy Peterson, Lucille Ricker, Kirsten Valbor, Nikki Willis, Doris Wright

The action occurs in Venice "some time ago."

The musical was presented in two acts.

ACT ONE—Overture (Orchestra), "Now the Day Is Done" (Chorus), "Spaghetti Song" (Jimmy Casanova, Chorus), "Market Song" (Nola Fairbanks, Vendors), "A Lovable Fellow" (Norwood Smith, Chorus), "Tarantella" (Norwood Smith, Chorus and Dancing Ensemble), "'Marrying' Duet" (Nola Fairbanks, Norwood Smith), "With Festive Pride" (Chorus), "We Always Get Our Man" (Guen Omeron, Senators' Wives), "Quintet" (Jack Russell, Guen Omeron, Nola Fairbanks, Jimmy Casanova, Laurel Hurley), "Gondola Song" (Thomas Tibbett Hayward) "Trio" (Kenneth Schon, Guen Omeron, Jimmy Casanova), "Birthday Serenade" (Singing Ensemble), "Gondola Duet" (Thomas Tibbett Hayward, Singing Ensemble), "Wine, Women and Song" (Dancing Ensemble), "Bells of St. Mark's" (Singing Ensemble), "Polka Furioso" (a/k/a "Fireworks Gallop") (Dancing Ensemble)

ACT TWO—"Ni-nana Waltz" (Thomas Tibbett Hayward, Laurel Hurley, Singing Ensemble), "Pigeons of San Marco" (Rosita Royce, Women's Singing Ensemble), Ballet (Gloria Gilbert, Dancing Ensemble), "Don't Speak of Love to Me" (Nola Fairbanks), "Now That We Are Alone" (a/k/a "Duet") (Nola Fairbanks, Jack Russell), "There's Nothing Like a Spree" (Norwood Smith, Jimmy Casanova, Men's Ensemble), "I Can't Find My Wife" (Kenneth Schon, Men's Singing Ensemble), "Women Are Here to Stay" (Norwood Smith, Jack Russell, Thomas Tibbett Hayward, Laurel Hurley, Nola Fairbanks, Guen Omeron), Finale (Entire Company)

NOTES—*A Night in Venice* was the premiere attraction at the new Marine Stadium at Jones Beach, Long Island. The mammoth theatre cost four million in 1952 dollars and seated 8,206; besides huge turntables and a large orchestra pit, the outdoor theater also boasted a large lagoon which was located between the audience and the stage. (The theatre was later re-named the Jones Beach Marine Theatre.)

During the summer seasons, the theatre presented both new and old musicals. Besides the revised version of *A Night in Venice*, four new musicals premiered there (see entries for *Arabian Nights*, *Paradise Island*, *Around the World in 80 Days*, and *Mardi Gras!*). Among the revivals produced at Jones Beach were *Show Boat* (1956; 1957; 1976), *Song of Norway* (1958 and 1959), *Hit the Deck* (1960), *South Pacific* (1968; 1969), *The Sound of Music* (1970; 1971; 1980), *The King and I* (1972), *Carousel* (1973), *Fiddler on the Roof* (1974), *Oklahoma!* (1975), *Finian's Rainbow* (1977), *Annie Get Your Gun* (1978), *The Music Man* (1979), *Damn Yankees* (1981).

A Night in Venice was a new adaptation by Ruth and Thomas Martin of Johann Strauss' operetta *Eine Nacht in Venedig*, which premiered in Berlin in 1883 (the original libretto was written by F. Zell and Richard Genee); the American premiere occurred on April 26, 1884, at Daly's Theatre, where it played for thirty-three performances. (The 1929 musical of the same name, which opened at the Shubert Theatre on June 29 for 175 performances, was a revue which except for its title and location bore no relation to the operetta.)

In reviewing the premiere attraction at the Marine Stadium, Brooks Atkinson in the *New York Times* found Strauss' score "succulent" but felt the conventional operetta situations (romantic tomfoolery during carnival time) were "not quite so comforting." He praised the "excellent" cast and Raoul Pene du Bois' "capacious and handsome" scenic designs (which included Venetian streets and palaces), but was less than impressed with the new venue, which he said was "awkward and unresponsive" to the demands of traditional theatre. He complained about the lagoon, noting it divided the audience from the performers which such a "separation" that it was "almost a divorce." And he noted one could barely see the faces of the performers.

But Atkinson mentioned that Mike Todd, the musical's producer, obeyed his "showman instinct," and so at one point a performer fell into the lagoon with all his clothes on. Further, the first act ended with a "lively" fireworks display.

Note that the dancing ensemble included Cathryn Damon as well as future Broadway choreographer Joseph (Joe) Layton.

The cast album was released by Everest Records (LP # SDBR-3028; CD # EVC-9036); Larry Laurence (who later changed his name to Enzo Stuarti) had played the role of Francesco on opening night, but for the recording he sang the role of Pappacoda (which had been performed by Jimmy Casanova on opening night).

A Night in Venice was revived at Jones Beach the following summer.

As mentioned above, *South Pacific* was twice seen at Jones Beach, and as of this writing the classic musical is playing in previews at Lincoln Center's Vivian Beaumont Theatre for an announced run of March 1 through June 15, 2008 (with an official opening on April 3). In some quarters, the musical is being touted as the "first" New York revival, and while the production might be the "first" revival in a regular Broadway theatre, the musical has been previously seen in six New York City revivals, for a total of 248 performances. The original production closed on Broadway on January 16, 1954, and a little more than a year later it was produced at New York City Center for fifteen performances. This was followed by three more City Center productions: 1957, for twenty-three performances (with Juanita Hall recreating her original role of Bloody Mary [incidentally, Allen Case was Cable]); 1961, for twenty-three performances (Allyn Ann McLerie was Nellie Forbush, William Chapman was De Becque, and Rosetta LeNoire was Bloody Mary); and 1965, for fifteen performances (Betsy Palmer was Nellie Forbush and Ray Middleton was De Becque).

After the four City Center revivals, the musical was seen in two productions at Lincoln Center, the venue where the 2008 revival opened. In 1967, the Music Theatre of Lincoln Center presented *South Pacific* at the New York State Theatre for 104 performances. Florence Henderson was Nellie Forbush and Giorgio Tozzi was De Becque (for the 1958 film version, Rossano Brazzi's singing voice had been dubbed by Tozzi). The 1967 production boasted a cast of thirty-nine (one less than the 2008 cast) and was recorded by Columbia Records. The musical was again seen at Lincoln Center's New York State Theatre when it was produced by the New York City Opera in 1987 (the production included some alternates, and among the cast members seen in this version were Susan Bigelow [Nellie Forbush], Cris Groenendaal [Cable], Muriel Costa-Greenspon [Bloody Mary], and Tony Roberts [Billis]).

1132 Nightcap. "A New Revue." THEATRE: The Showplace; OPENING DATE: May 18, 1958; PERFORMANCES: 400; LYRICS: Jerry Herman; MUSIC: Jerry Herman; DIRECTION: Jerry Herman; CHOREOGRAPHY: Phyllis Newman; SCENERY: Hal Jacobs; COSTUMES: Nilo; LIGHTING: Bud Nichols; MUSICAL DIRECTION: Apparently by Jerry Herman Producer: Jim Paul Eilers

CAST—See notes below.

The revue was presented in two acts.

ACT ONE—Overture (Orchestra), Opening (Company), "Why Don't They Believe Me" (Jane

Romano), "Confession to a Park Avenue Mother (I'm in Love with a West Side Girl") (Charles Nelson Reilly), "I Wish I Could Say" (Kenneth Nelson, Fia Karin), "My Type" (Jane Romano), "Wrong Kind of Man" (Fia Karin), "(A) Jolly Theatrical Season" (Jane Romano, Charles Nelson Reilly), "As for the Future, I'll Dance" (Kenneth Nelson), "That Revue" (Company)

ACT TWO—"Show Tune in 2/4" (a/k/a "There Is No Tune Like a Show Tune" and "Show Tune") (Company), "Number 1 on Your Hit Parade" (Charles Nelson Reilly), "Your Good Morning" (Kenneth Nelson, Fia Karin), "The Producer Didn't Hire Me" (Jane Romano), "Nice Running Into You" (Fia Karin), "Naughty Forty-Second Street" (Charles Nelson Reilly, Jane Romano, Kenneth Nelson), "Washington Square" (Kenneth Nelson, Fia Karin), "In the Sack" (Jane Romano), Finale (Company)

NOTES—*Nightcap* had a performance schedule of ten shows a week.

It appears that all the sequences in the revue were songs, and sketches weren't part of the presentation. During the run, at least seven performers were seen in the four-person revue, which had two male roles and two female roles. While there's no confusion as to who performed the male roles (Charles Nelson Reilly and Kenneth Nelson), reference books don't agree about who performed the female roles on opening night (incidentally, both *Best Plays* and *Theatre World* didn't include the revue in their summaries of the 1957-1958 season, and a review of *Nightcap* doesn't appear in the archives of the *New York Times*).

In his *American Song*, Ken Bloom indicates Rita Gardner and Bobo Lewis were the female leads, but in *Show Tunes*, Steven Suskin indicates Fia Karin and Estelle Parsons were. Further, an undated *Nightcap* program lists Fia Karin and Jane Romano. And in his book *Jerry Herman: Poet of the Showtune*, Stephen Citron states that Rita Gardner, Estelle Parsons, and Bobo Lewis were cast replacements. So it well may be that Fia Karin and Jane Romano were with the production on opening night, and so for the song listing above, I've opted to use the program's cast list (Karin and Romano). "Show Tune in 2/4" (a/k/a "There Is No Tune Like a Show Tune" and "Show Tune") was later heard in *Parade* (1960) as "Show Tune" (see entry), and Jerry Herman later re-wrote the song as "It's Today" for the Broadway production of *Mame* (1966).

Other numbers first heard in *Nightcap* and later used in *Parade* were: "Confession to a Park Avenue Mother (I'm in Love with a West Side Girl)," "Your Good Morning," "Naughty Forty-Second Street," and "A Jolly Theatrical Season." The latter was a *Forbidden Broadway*-styled tribute to the Broadway scene, and was a particular delight; it merrily catalogued the gloomy plots of current Broadway plays and musicals, including *West Side Story* (1957), which, according to Herman's amusing lyric, was nothing but a series of laughs, right down to the finale when the hero gets shot in the stomach.

"A Jolly Theatrical Season" in many ways defines the difference between Stephen Sondheim's and Jerry Herman's approach to musical theatre and what they consider "appropriate" subject matter for a Broadway musical. The matter came to a head in 1984, when both had strikingly different Broadway musicals competing for the Tony Award (Herman, *La Cage Aux Folles*, Sondheim, *Sunday in the Park with George*; see entry for the latter). (Both musicals took place in France, and the setting was just about all they had in common.) When he accepted his Tony Award for *La Cage*, Herman said he was glad old-fashioned musicals were popular; his comment was interpreted as a slap at Sondheim, although Herman denied he meant any disrespect.

"A Jolly Theatrical Season" was included in, and was the title of, an LP of comedy songs from Broadway and Off Broadway musicals sung by Robert Morse and Charles Nelson Reilly in 1962 (Capitol Records # T-1862; DRG Records CD # 19101); the previous year the two had appeared in the hit Broadway musical *How to Succeed in Business Without Really Trying*.

Two years after they appeared in *Nightcap*, Rita Gardner and Kenneth Nelson created the roles of the Girl (Luisa) and Boy (Matt) in *The Fantasticks* (1960) (see entry). And forty-eight years after appearing in *Nightcap*, Rita Gardner's solo CD *Try to Remember* (Harbinger Records CD # HCD-2202) was released. Subtitled "A Look Back at Off-Broadway," the CD included two songs from *Nightcap* ("There Is No Tune Like a Show Tune" and "Your Good Morning") as well as songs from *The Fantasticks* and *Parade*. Gardner dedicated the CD "to the memory of my dear friend Kenneth Nelson." Kenneth Nelson was in the original Broadway productions of the musicals *Seventeen* (1951) and *Lovely Ladies, Kind Gentlemen* (1970), creating the respective roles of Willie Baxter and Sakini. He later relocated to London and enjoyed a successful career there. But his most famous roles were the two he originated Off Broadway; besides the role of the Boy (Matt) in *The Fantasticks*, he created the role of Michael, the host of one of the theatre's most notorious birthday parties, in *The Boys in the Band* (1968).

A few days after the opening of *Nightcap*, Sam Zolotow in the *New York Times* reported that Frank (Loesser) Productions, Inc., would be involved in Leonard Sillman's "next" edition of *New Faces* and that six songs from *Nightcap* had been optioned for the new revue. But almost four years went by before New York saw another *New Faces*, and when the 1962 edition opened it didn't include any of Herman's songs.

1133 Nightclub Cantata. THEATRE: Top of the Gate; OPENING DATE: January 9, 1977; PERFORMANCES: 145; LYRICS: Elizabeth Swados; other writers identified following titles of musical numbers; MUSIC: Elizabeth Swados; DIRECTION: Elizabeth Swados; SCENERY: Patricia Woodbridge; COSTUMES: Kate Carmel; LIGHTING: Cheryl Thacker; MUSICAL DIRECTION: Judith Fleisher (?); PRODUCERS: Charles Hollerith, Jr., and Rosita Sarnoff present The Music-Theatre Performing Group/Lenox Arts Center Production (Lyn Austin and Mary D. Silverman, Artistic Directors)

CAST—Karen Evans, Rocky Greenberg, Paul Kandel, JoAnna Peled, Shelley Plimpton, David Schechter, Elizabeth Swados, Mark Zagaeski

The revue was presented in one act.

MUSICAL NUMBERS—"Things I Didn't Know I Loved" (lyrics by Nazim Hikmet) (Company), "Bestiario" (lyrics by Pablo Neruda) (Company), "Bird Chorus" (Company), "Bird Lament" (Elizabeth Swados), "Ventriloquist & Dummy" (lyrics by Elizabeth Swados and Judith Fleisher) (David Schechter, Karen Evans, Mark Zagaeski, Shelley Plimpton), "The Applicant" (lyric by Sylvia Plath) (Karen Evans), "To the Harbormaster" (lyrics by Frank O'Hara) (Rocky Greenberg), "Adolescents" (children's writings from *Male & Female Under 18* by Eve Merriam and Nancy Larrick) (Rocky Greenberg, Karen Evans), "Indecision" (lyric by Elizabeth Swados) (Company), "Dibarti" (lyric by David Avidan) (JoAnna Peled, Mark Zagaeski), "In Dreams Begin Responsibilities" (lyric by Delmore Schwartz) (Company), "Are You with Me?" (lyrics by Elizabeth Swados) (Shelley Plimpton), "Raga" (David Schechter, Company), "Waking This Morning" (lyric by Muriel Rukeyser) (Shelley Plimpton, Karen Evans, Elizabeth Swados, JoAnna Peled), "Pastrami Brothers" (Mark Zagaeski, Rocky Greenberg, David Schechter, Paul Kandel), "The Ballad of the Sad Café" (lyric by Carson McCullers) (JoAnna Peled, Karen Evans), "Isabella" (lyric by Isabella Leitner) (JoAnna Peled, Company), "Waiting" (lyric by Elizabeth Swados) (Rocky Greenberg, Karen Evans, David Schechter, JoAnna Peled), "The Dance" (lyric by Elizabeth Swados) (JoAnna Peled, Company), "On Living" (lyric by Nazim Hikmet) (Company)

NOTES—Elizabeth Swados' dreary revue *Nightclub Cantata* somehow managed to hang on for almost five months, and was even produced at a few regional theatres, such as Arena Stage in Washington, D.C.

In a program note, "Bird Chorus" is described as "a variety of sounds to evoke the feelings of birds," and it might indeed be said that one hasn't really lived until one sits in a theatre and hears and watches actors making bird calls to one another. (Paging Rima!) Another number, "Bird Lament," supposedly expressed "the feelings of a bird caught between air and earth." The revue used the words of various writers as inspiration for the musical numbers, including Nazim Hikmet (1902-1963), a Turkish poet described in a regional production's program as a "genuine Marxist," and Pablo Neruda (1904-1973), a Chilean whom the program noted was "a member of the Central Committee of the Communist Party" in that country. For the revue's regional productions, the number "Albatross Ramble" (by Brian Patton) was added.

The script was published by Dramatists Play Service, Inc., in 1979.

1134 Nightingale. "A New Opera." THEATRE: The First All Children's Theatre; OPENING DATE: April 25, 1982; PERFORMANCES: Unknown; LIBRETTO: Charles Strouse; MUSIC: Charles Strouse; DIRECTION: Meridee Stein; Linda Reiff, Associate Director; CHOREOGRAPHY: Linda Reiff; SCENERY: Oliver Smith; COSTUMES: Christine Andrews; LIGHTING: Victor En Yu Tan; PRODUCER: The First All Children's Theatre (Meridee Stein, Director)

CAST—John Schuck, Special Guest Artist; and The First All Children's Theatre (ACT) Company (roles were rotated throughout the run of the production): Marina Arkelian, Ellen Barnett, Debbie Bluestone, Dena Bluestone, Lada Boder, Kim Brown, John Carrie, Robert DeDea, Debra Dehass, Doreen DeLise, Liz Devivo, Gerard Dure, Carrie Englander, Annette Farrington, Michael Feigin, Jofka Foreman, Kimberly Gambino, Karl Gaskin, Masai Glushanok, Jenny Golden, Samaria Graham, Helena Green, Kerrie Gross, Lynne Kolber, Michelle League, Kathleen Manousos, Edie Ogando, Carl Payne, Victoria Platt, Wendy Rockman, Ben Schwartz, Lianna Sugarman, Cathy Trien, Annette Verdolino, Ian Wagreich, Steven Ward, Fiona Williams

SOURCE—The fairy tale *The Emperor and the Nightingale* by Hans Christian Andersen.

The opera was presented in two acts (the program didn't list musical numbers and didn't identify specific performers [who rotated in their roles]).

ACT ONE—Prologue (Orchestra), "Perfect Harmony" (Company), "Perfect Harmony" (reprise) (The Emperor), "Why Am I So Happy?" (The Maid), "Take Us to the Forest"/"Who Are These People?" (Company, The Nightingale), "Never Speak Directly to an Emperor" (Palace Guards), "Nightingale" (Company), "The Emperor Is a Man" (The Maid), "I Was Lost" (The Emperor, The Nightingale)

ACT TWO—Entr'acte (Orchestra), "Charming" (Two Peacocks), "A Singer Must Be Free" (The Nightingale), "The Mechanical Bird" (Company, The Mechanical Bird), "Please Don't Make Me Hear That Song Again" (Company, The Mechanical Bird), "Rivers Cannot Flow Upwards" (The Maid, The Nightingale), "Death Duet" (Death, The Emperor, The Maid, The Nightingale), "We Are China"/Finale (The Nightingale, Company)

NOTES—John S. Wilson in the *New York Times*

praised the "charming and whimsical" opera *Nightingale*; he enjoyed Charles Strouse's lyrics and music; Oliver Smith's "striking" décor, Christine Andrews' costumes of "dazzling" colors, and Meridee Stein's "perceptive" staging. The story told of a nightingale who charms a world-weary king and ultimately saves him from death. And, in keeping with the tradition of all proper fairy tales, the king finds love (with a palace maid), and so he, the maid, and the nightingale live happily ever after.

Later in the year, on December 18, *Nightingale* opened in London at the Lyric Theatre, Hammersmith; the cast included Sarah Brightman, who performed the title role.

The British cast album was released on LP by That's Entertainment Records (# TER-1031), and the audio cassette release (# ZC-TED-1031) included approximately thirty-five minutes of extra material. The song list is taken from information on the album.

1135 Nightmare Alley. "A Musical Drama." THEATRE: Theatre 3; OPENING DATE: November 16, 1996; PERFORMANCES: 15; BOOK: Jonathan Brielle; LYRICS: Jonathan Brielle; MUSIC: Jonathan Brielle; DIRECTION: Danny Herman; CHOREOGRAPHY: Danny Herman; SCENERY: Michael Hotopp; COSTUMES: Catherine Zuber; LIGHTING: Gene Lenehan; MUSICAL DIRECTION: Phil Reno; PRODUCERS: Primary Stages Company and The Directors Company

CAST—Willy Falk (Stan), Vicki Fredrick (Zeena, Mrs. Peabody), Sarah E. Litzsinger (Molly Cahill), Nick Jolley (Clem), Ken Prymus (Pete), Evan Thompson (Ezra, Marshall), Silvia Aruj (Science Girl), Carolyn Campbell (Science Girl), Victoria Lecta Cave (Science Girl), Nancy Lemenager (Science Girl), Jonas Moscartolo (Major Mosquito)

SOURCE—The 1946 novel *Nightmare Alley* by William Lindsay Gresham.

The action occurs in the 1930s.

The musical was presented in two acts (division of acts and song assignments unknown; songs listed in performance order).

MUSICAL NUMBERS—Opening/"Ten in One," "Someday Sometime," "Tough Cookies," "Questions," "Kid," "Molly Interlude," "Shuffle the Cards," "Whatever It Takes," "Lucky Heart," "Human Nature," "This Is Not What I Had Planned," "Science," "The Code," "Indecent Exposure," "All Will Come to You," "Cross That River," "Caroline," "Hit 'Em Where It Hurts," "Nobody Home," "I Still Hear It All," "Don't You Love to Watch What People Do," "Unpredictable You," "Get Her to Do It," "Nightmare Alley," "Song of the Road"

NOTES—The musical was based on William Lindsay Gresham's 1946 novel *Nightmare Alley*, which was memorably filmed in 1947 in what was Tyrone Power's greatest screen performance.

The story told the saga of a con man who ultimately ends up as a geek in a carnival's side show.

1136 Nightsong. "A Musical Mosaic." THEATRE: Village Gate Downstairs; OPENING DATE: November 1, 1977; PERFORMANCES: 35; LYRICS: Ron Eliran; MUSIC: Ron Eliran; DIRECTION: Dan Early; SCENERY: Harry Silverglat; COSTUMES: Ron Whitehead and Margot Miller; LIGHTING: Jo Mayer; MUSICAL DIRECTION: Jaroslav (Yaron) Jakubovuc; PRODUCER: Irwin Steiner

CAST—Ron Eliran, Holly T. Lipton, Diane Sorel, Joy Kohner

The revue was presented in two acts (division of acts and song assignments unknown; songs listed in performance order).

MUSICAL NUMBERS—"Looking at Us," "My Land," "Dusty Roads," "Butterfly Child," "I Hear a Song," "Come with Me," "Who Am I?," "Nightsong," "Lady Vagabond," "Music in the City," "Come, Elijah, Come," "Grain of Sand," "All in the Name of Love," "Sweet Fantasy," "Have a Little Fun," "Moments by the Sea," "Young Days," "It Was Worth It," "I Believe"

NOTES—*Nightsong* was yet another Off Broadway evening of loosely-connected songs. And, like many revues of its ilk, *Nightsong* went nowhere.

John S. Wilson in the *New York Times* noted that singer and lyricist-composer Ron Eliran had a popular following at a Greenwich Village club called El Avram, where he was known for his Israeli songs. With *Nightsong*, Eliran offered a "musical mosaic" of songs which in structure was reminiscent of *Jacques Brel Is Alive and Well and Living in Paris* (which had premiered at the Village Gate almost a decade earlier). But in both content and performance, Wilson found the evening more similar in style to Anthony Newley than Jacques Brel. The revue also emphasized some Nashville-styled numbers (such as "Dusty Roads," which evoked John Denver). For Wilson, the highlight of the revue was "Lady Vagabond" (a "catchy tune" with a "driving momentum" reminiscent of big band, swing-era music). Some songs in the revue had earlier been heard in Eliran's 1976 musical *Don't Step on My Olive Branch* (see entry).

1137 Nine Rivers from Jordan. THEATRE: New York State Theatre; OPENING DATE: October 9, 1968; PERFORMANCES: Unknown; LIBRETTO: Denis Johnston; MUSIC: Hugo Weisgall; DIRECTION: Vlado Habunek; SCENERY: Will Steven Armstrong; COSTUMES: Jane Greenwood; MUSICAL DIRECTION: Gustav Meier; PRODUCER: The New York City Opera

CAST—William Brown (Lieutenant Jean l'Aiglon), William Ledbetter (Father Matteo Angelino), Joshua Hecht (Sergeant Abe Goldberg), John Lankston (Major Mark Lyon), Will Roy (Captain Reverend Lucius Bull), Julian Patrick (Private Don Hanwell), Eileen Schauler (Salt Woman, The Pieta, Woman D.P.), John Stewart (Andrew, the Highlander), Paul Huddleston (Copperhead Kelly), David Clements (Otto Suder), Joaquin Romaguera (Dead Man), Kellis Miller (Little Jim Clap), Raymond Gibbs (Popper Johnny), Nico Castel (Tom Tosser), Raymond Papay (Simple Simon), Michael Devlin (Sergeant Pete Fisher)

The opera was presented in three acts.

NOTES—In his review in the *New York Times* of the world premiere of Hugo Weisgall's new opera *Nine Rivers from Jordan*, Harold C. Schonberg noted that during the course of the three-act evening the opera lost many audience members, and that after the second act there were rows of empty seats.

The confusing plot, which dealt with a soldier who allows a prisoner of war to escape, covered a litany of moral issues. God becomes involved in the soldier's dilemmas and it seems at the end of the opera the soldier has become a new Christ. Schonberg noted that one could spend "hours" trying to sort out all the opera's religious parallels and allegories. He also mentioned the opera had the distinction of being the first one to use "naked" four-letter words in its libretto. But he assured the easily shocked that they need not worry: as was typical of most operas sung in English, the words were "98 per cent unintelligible."

1138 Nite Club Confidential. "The Night Club Musical." THEATRE: The Ballroom Theatre; OPENING DATE: May 10, 1984; PERFORMANCES: 165; BOOK: Dennis Deal; NEW SONGS: Dennis Deal and Albert Evans; DIRECTION: Dennis Deal; SCENERY: Christopher Cole; COSTUMES: Stephen Rotondaro; LIGHTING: Richard Latta; MUSICAL DIRECTION: Joel Raney; PRODUCERS: CHS Productions and Greentrack Entertainment Ltd. in association with Sidney L. Shlenker, Joseph Stein, Jr., and Barbara M. Friedman

CAST—Stephen Berger (Buck Holden), Tom Spiroff (Sal), Denise Nolin (Dorothy Flynn), Steve Gideon (Mitch Dupre), Fay DeWitt (Kay Goodman); Musicians (Joel Raney, Leader/Piano; Rudolph Bird, Bongos; Matthew Patuto, Drums; Faun Stacy, Bass)

The action occurs in a night club during the Eisenhower Era.

The musical was presented in two acts.

ACT ONE—"Nite Club" (lyric and music by Dennis Deal and Albert Evans) (Ensemble), "Comment Allez-Vous?" (lyric and music by Murray Grand) (The High Hopes), "Something's Gotta Give" (from 1955 film *Daddy Long Legs*; lyric and music by Johnny Mercer) (Fay DeWitt, The High Hopes), "Love Isn't Born, It's Made" (1943 film *Thank Your Lucky Stars*; lyric by Frank Loesser, music by Arthur Schwartz) (Fay DeWitt, Stephen Berger), "Comment Allez-Vous?" (reprise) (The High Hopes), "Goody, Goody" (lyric by Johnny Mercer, music by Matt Malneck) (The High Hopes), "Goody, Goody" (reprise) (The High Hopes), "Nothing Can Replace a Man" (*Ankles Aweigh*, 1955; lyric by Dan Shapiro, music by Sammy Fain) (Denise Nolin), "I Thought About You" (lyric by Johnny Mercer, music by Jimmy Van Heusen) (Stephen Berger), "Put the Blame on Mamie" (lyric and music by Dennis Deal and Albert Evans) (Fay DeWitt, The High Hopes), "Dorothy's 'Opener'" (lyric and music by Dennis Deal and Albert Evans) (Denise Nolin), "The Canarsie Diner" (lyric and music by Dennis Deal and Albert Evans) (Denis Nolin, The High Hopes), "Saturday's Child" (lyric by Phyllis McGinley, music by Baldwin Bergersen) (Denise Nolin), "Bonjour" (lyric and music by Dennis Deal and Albert Evans) (Fay DeWitt, The High Hopes), "French with Tears" (lyric and music by Harold Rome; originally from *Pretty Penny*, which closed during its pre-Broadway tryout in 1949; later used in *Alive and Kicking*, 1950) (Fay DeWitt), "That Old Black Magic" (1943 film *Star-Spangled Rhythm*; lyric by Johnny Mercer, music by Harold Arlen) (Denise Nolin, The High Hopes)

ACT TWO—"Crazy New Words" (lyric and music by Dennis Deal and Albert Evans) (Steve Gideon), "Black Slacks" (lyric and music by Joseph Bennett and Jimmy Denton) (Tom Spiroff), "Something's Gotta Give" (reprise) (Denise Nolin), "The Long Goodbye" (lyric and music by Dennis Deal and Albert Evans) (Fay DeWitt), "Nite Club" (reprise) (Stephen Berger, Ensemble), "Ev'rybody's Boppin'" (lyric and music by Jon Hendricks) (The New High Hopes), "Cloudburst" (lyric and music by Jon Hendricks, Leroy Kirkland, and Jimmy Harris) (The New High Hopes), "The Other One (Darling)" (lyric by June Carroll, music by Arthur Siegel) (Fay DeWitt), "Yodelin' Dixieland" (lyric and music by Wally Schmied and Fred Rauch) (Tom Spiroff, Steve Gideon, Denise Nolin), "Dressed to Kill" (lyric and music by Dennis Deal and Albert Evans) (Fay DeWitt), "Dead End Street" (lyric and music by Dennis Deal and Albert Evans) (Fay DeWitt, Ensemble)

NOTES—According to the cast album (which was released by The Confidential Recording Company [the LP was unnumbered]), the revue-like musical *Nite Club Confidential* was set in the "glamorous world of 50's clubs and lounges" and exposed the story of "a young singing group and an aging chanteuse, caught in a web of music, martinis and murder." Earlier in the season the musical had played Off Off Broadway at the Riverwest Theatre for forty-eight performances.

To add to the Fifties' flavor, the musical (but not the cast album) included "Nothing Can Replace a Man," a song from *Ankles Aweigh* (1955), generally regarded as one of the worst musicals to open on Broadway during that decade and perhaps second only to *Portofino* (1958) in mediocrity. "Put the Blame on Mamie" is not to be confused with "Put the Blame on Mame" (lyric by Doris Fisher, music by Allan Roberts), the song famously introduced by Rita Hayworth in the 1946 film *Gilda*.

In later productions of the musical, the following songs were added (all by Dennis Deal and Albert Evans): "He Never Leaves His Love Behind," "All Man," and "The Strip/Club Au Revoir." Dennis Deal, incidentally, was the arranger for many songs on Ben Bagley's series of *Revisited* albums, all of which celebrated obscure numbers from Broadway musicals.

1139 Nixon in China. THEATRE: Opera House/Brooklyn Academy of Music; OPENING DATE: December 4, 1987; PERFORMANCES: Unknown; LIBRETTO: Alice Goodman; MUSIC: John Adams; DIRECTION: Peter Sellars; CHOREOGRAPHY: Mark Morris; SCENERY: Adrianne Lobel; COSTUMES: Dunya Ramicova; LIGHTING: James F. Ingalls; MUSICAL DIRECTION: Edo De Waart (conducting the Orchestra of St. Luke's); PRODUCERS: The Brooklyn Academy of Music (Harvey Lichtenstein, President and Executive Director) in association with the Houston Grand Opera, the John F. Kennedy Center for the Performing Arts, De Nederlandse Opera, and the Los Angeles Music Center Opera Association

CAST—Sanford Sylvan (Chou En-lai), James Maddalena (Richard Nixon), Thomas Hammons (Henry Kissinger), Mari Opatz (Nancy T'ang), Stephanie Friedman (Second Secretary to Mao), Marion Dry (Third Secretary to Mao), John Duykers (Mao Tse-tung), Carolann Page (Pat Nixon), Trudy Ellen Craney (Chiang Ch'ing), Steven Ochoa (Hung Ch'ang-ch'ing), Heather Toma (Wu Ching-hua), Ensemble (Christopher Arneson, Todd Thomas, Frank Curtis, Barry Craft, Sharon Daniels, Judy Berry), Dancers (Homer Avila, Miguel Aviles, Pamela Giardino, Michael Ing, Andrew Pacho, Cristina Perera, Pamela Semmler, Kelly Slough)

The action occurs in Peking, China, in February 1972.

The opera was presented in three acts.

ACT ONE—Act One, Scene One Beginning, "Soldiers of Heaven Hold the Sky," "The People Are the Heroes Now," "Landing of the Spirit of '76," "Your Flight Was Smooth, I Hope?," "News Has a Kind of Mystery," Act One, Scene Two Beginning, "You Know We'll Meet with Your Confrere the Democratic Candidate If He Should Win," "You've Said That There's a Certain Well-Known Tree," "Founders Come First, Then Profiteers," "We No Longer Need Confucius," "Like the Ming Tombs," Act One, Scene Three Beginning, "Ladies and Gentlemen, Comrades and Friends," "Mr. Premier, Distinguished Guests," "Cheers"

ACT TWO—Act Two, Scene One Beginning, "Oh What a Day I Thought I'd Die!," "Whip Her to Death!," "Tropical Storm," "Flesh Rebels," "I Have My Brief," "It Seems So Strange," "I Am the Wife of Mao Tse-tung"

ACT THREE—Act Three, Scene One Beginning, "Strange Men You Cannot Satisfy," "I Am No One," "The Maos Dance," "Sitting Around the Radio," "Let Us Examine What You Did," "When I Woke Up," "I Have No Offspring," "I Can Keep Still," "After That the Sweat Had Soaked My Uniform," "Peking Watches the Stars," "You Won at Poker," "I Am Old and I Cannot Sleep"

NOTES—John Adams' monumental opera *Nixon in China* was given its world premiere on October 22, 1987, by the Houston Grand Opera. The opera was first seen in New York a few weeks later at the Brooklyn Academy of Music.

Like Stephen Sondheim's *Pacific Overtures* (1976; see entries for Off Broadway productions), which dealt with the "opening" of Japan by Commodore Matthew Galbraith Perry in 1853, Adams' opera dealt with President Richard Nixon's historic 1972 visit to China, a visit which marked the first step in the reestablishment of political ties between the two nations.

Adams' melodic minimalist score, Alice Goodman's terse libretto (written in couplets), and Adrianne Lobel's striking, deceptively simple scenery (such as the setting which depicted Air Force One/The Spirit of '76 on the runway) all combined to make the opera memorable, and *Nixon in China* seems destined to become one of the enduring operas of the twentieth century.

In reviewing the New York premiere, John Rockwell in the *New York Times* noted the work was "a stirring creation, full of charm and wit, and, in the end, beauty ... this [opera is] likely to last." Rockwell wrote that Adams' music "is his finest yet," and that Goodman's libretto struck "a lovely balance between caricature, ironic sentimentality and more deeply felt truths."

The opera was recorded on a 3-LP and 3-CD set by Elektra Nonesuch Records (LP # 9-79177-1 and CD # 9-79177-2); the titles of the musical sequences are taken from the recording. The opera was later shown on public television.

1140 No for an Answer. "An Opera." THEATRE: Mecca Auditorium; OPENING DATE: January 5, 1941; PERFORMANCES: 3; LIBRETTO: Marc Blitzstein; MUSIC: Marc Blitzstein; DIRECTION: William E. Watts; Manuel Manisoff, Assistant Director; COSTUMES: Maxine Geiser; MUSICAL DIRECTION: Marc Blitzstein; PRODUCER: A Committee (James D. Proctor, Chairman)

CAST—Charles Polacheck (Cutch), Martin Wolfson (Nick Kyriakos), Ben Ross (Emanuel), Eda Reis (Gertie Phorylles), Norma Green (Francie), Hester Sondergaard (Gina Tonieri), Charles Mendick (Alex), Martin Ritt (Steve), Curt Conway (Bulge), Ellen Merrill (Mery), George Fairchild (Club Member), Olive Deering (Clara Carver Chase), Lloyd Gough (Paul Chase), Robert Simon (Joe Kyriakos), Alfred Ryder (Max Kraus), Carol Channing (Bobby), Coby Ruskin (Jimmy), Bert Conway (Mike), Martin Andrews (First Cop), Paul Kwartin (Second Cop, Waiter), Carlton H. Bentley (Customer, A Monktowner, Board Supervisor), Rupert Pole (A Monktowner, Commissioner of Public Safety), Ben Yaffee (Filling Station Attendant); Chorus (Members of Diogenes Club, People at Demonstration, People in Pillbox Bar): Martin Andrews, Arthur Atkins, Carlton H. Bentley, George Fairchild, Anna Handzlik, Nettie Hadary, Agnes Ives, Adele Jerome, Dorothy Johnson, Michael Kozak, Paul Kwartin, Emily Marsh, Elaine Perry, Rupert Pole, Marion Rudley, Diana Selzer, Leonard Stocker

The action occurs in and around the Diogenes Social Club at Crest Lake, a summer resort in the eastern United States; the time is mid-September 1939, after the summer season is over.

The opera was presented in two acts.

ACT ONE—"The Song of the Bat" (Charles Polacheck, Chorus), "Take the Book" (Charles Polacheck), "Gina" (Hester Sondergaard), "Secret Singing" (Lloyd Gough, Olive Deering), "Dimples" (Coby Ruskin, Carol Channing), "Fraught" (Carol Channing, Coby Ruskin), "Francie" (Robert Simon, Norma Green), "No for an Answer" (Chorus)

ACT TWO—"Penny Candy" (Curt Conway), "Mike" (Bert Conway), "The Purest Kind of Guy" (Curt Conway), "Nick" (Martin Wolfson), "Make the Heart Be Stone" (Ensemble), "No for an Answer" (reprise) (Martin Wolfson, Ensemble)

NOTES—Like his 1937 "labor opera" *The Cradle Will Rock* (see entry), Marc Blitzstein's left-wing opera *No for an Answer* was similar in style to *Cradle* and other agit-prop theatrical polemics of the 1930s. Indeed, the new work was in a sense a companion piece to *Cradle* in that it dealt with conflicts between labor and management, specifically workers at a summer resort who rebel over their working conditions and are inspired by Joe Kyriakos, a union organizer fresh out of prison. But the workers are thwarted by management in their attempt to unionize, and ultimately management and the police murder Joe and burn down the social club where the workers meet.

The opera was presented on three consecutive Sunday nights at the Mecca Auditorium (later the New York City Center), and except for two special performances at the Circle in the Square on April 18 and 25, 1960, the work has apparently never again been produced. It's particularly odd that the original production didn't ultimately transfer to Broadway, because Brooks Atkinson in the *New York Times* gave the musical a near rave review. He found the evening "very exciting" and "dramatically staged," and noted that Blitzstein's "joyous and dramatic" score "remarkably succeeded" in giving life to the characters and story. Atkinson further noted that recent years had seen "no better example" of how the power of music could create characters through song. It was a "frank, vital and occasionally electric" work (which was also so far to the left it was "practically horizontal") in which Blitzstein, "hewing close to the party line," had written a musical drama which "aroused enthusiasm for the theatre." *No for an Answer* is indeed distinguished by Blitzstein's always-intriguing music, and it's particularly interesting to compare "Make the Heart Be Stone" to "Where" (in which "hearts o' stone" are asked to give way to "hearts of flesh") from *Juno* (1959), Blitzstein's final Broadway musical (see entry for an Off Off Broadway production of *Juno*).

The musical is also memorable for introducing New York audiences to Carol Channing (in the role of Bobby, a nightclub performer); it was also the second American musical to receive a full-fledged cast recording (the first was *The Cradle Will Rock*) when Keynote Records released a 78 RPM set of the score. The recording was first released on LP by Theme Records (# 103), then by JJA Records (LP # JJA-19772A/B), and then later by AEI Records (LP # AEI-1140; CD # AEI-CD-031). Although Robert Simon created the role of Joe Kyriakos, on the recording the role is sung by Michael Loring.

The program for the musical didn't list song sequences; the above song list is taken from the two LP releases. In his *Mark the Music/The Life and Work of Marc Blitzstein* (published by St. Martin's Press in 1989, and which is perhaps the finest of theatrical biographies), Eric A. Gordon cites two other songs from the opera, "Hymn of Hate" and "Weep for Me."

1141 The No-Frills Revue. THEATRE: Cherry Lane Theatre; OPENING DATE: November 25, 1987; PERFORMANCES: 207; SKETCHES: Michael Abbott, Martin Charnin, Ronny Graham, Thomas Meehan, and Sarah Weeks; all other dialogue and segues by Martin Charnin, Douglas Bernstein and Denis Markell; LYRICS: Michael Abbott, Stephen M. Alper, Douglas Bernstein, Craig Carnelia, Martin Charnin, Sally Fay, David Finkle, Ronny Graham, Michael Leeds, Denis Markell, Bill Weeden, and Sarah Weeks; MUSIC: Michael Abbott, Howard Arlen, Craig Carnelia, Martin Charnin, Sally Fay, David Finkle, Ronny Graham, Marvin Hamlisch, Brian Lasser, Bill Weeden, and Sarah Weeks; DIRECTION: Martin Charnin; CHOREOGRAPHY: Frank Ventura; SCENERY: Evelyn Sakash; COSTUMES: Perry Ellis; LIGHTING: Clarke W. Thornton; MUSICAL DIRECTION: David Gaines; PRODUCERS: Del Tenney, David H. Peipers, and Beam One, Ltd.; Anthony J. Stimac, Associate Producer

CAST—Adinah Alexander, Sasha Charnin, Clare Fields, Stephani Hardy, Sarah Knapp, Andre Montgomery, Lynn Paynter, Justin Ross, Bob Stillman

The revue was presented in one act.

SKETCHES AND MUSICAL NUMBERS—"The No-Frills Revue" (dialogue, lyric, and music by Martin

Charnin) (Company), "Stools" (lyric and music by Martin Charnin) (Company), "Yma Dream" (sketch by Thomas Meehan) (Adinah Alexander, Clare Fields), "Privacy" (lyric and music by Craig Carnelia) (Stephani Hardy, Justin Ross), "My Reunion Prayer" (lyric and music by Bill Weeden, David Finkle, and Sally Fay) (Company), "Being with Me" (lyric by Michael Leeds, music by Brian Lasser) (Sarah Knapp), "Someone's Got to Do It" (dialogue, lyrics, and music by Michael Abbott, Sarah Weeks, and Martin Charnin) (Andre Montgomery, Company), "A Brand New Hammer" (lyric and music by Bill Weeden, David Finkle, and Sally Fay) (Andre Montgomery, Sarah Knapp, Lynn Paynter, Bob Stillman), "We Have to Sing This Song" (lyric and music by Douglas Bernstein and Denis Markell) (Sasha Charnin, Company), "I Know Where the Bodies Are Buried" (lyric and music by Martin Charnin) (Lynn Paynter, Adinah Alexander), "The Nine Supreme Chords" (chords by Steven M. Alper, dialogue by Martin Charnin) (Company), "Tippy-Tappy" (lyric by Martin Charnin, music by Marvin Hamlisch) (Company), "Bud, Lou and Who?" (sketch by Thomas Meehan) (Adinah Alexander, Lynn Paynter, Stephani Hardy), "Come On, Midnight" (lyric by Martin CHarnin, music by Harold Arlen) (Adinah Alexander, Sasha Charnin, Clare Fields, Stephani Hardy, Sarah Knapp, Lynn Paynter, Bob Stillman), "Yes! We Have the Manuscripts" (by Ronny Graham and Martin Charnin, music by Ronny Graham; costumes for sequence by Amanda J. Klein): "First Musical" (Sasha Charnin, Andre Montgomery, introduced by Clare Fields; "Second Musical" (Adinah Alexander, Justin Ross, introduced by Lynn Paynter); "Third Musical" (Sarah Knapp, Bob Stillman, Justin Ross, Company, introduced by Stephani Hardy), "It Hasn't Been Easy" (lyric and music by Bill Weeden, David Finkle, and Sally Fay) (Company)

NOTES—*The No-Frills Revue* had been previously produced Off Off Broadway by Musical Theatre Works at the CSC Theatre on October 8, 1987, for sixteen performances. Numbers heard in that production which weren't used in the Off Broadway engagement were: "The Group (First Session)" (sketch by Archie T. Tridmorten), "Small Things Come in Small Packages" (sketch by Michael Abbott), "Pax de Don't" (sketch by Martin Charnin, music by Kirk Nurock), "A Vicious Cycle" (lyric and music by Howard Danziger), "We Know Why You're Here!" (lyric and music by Bill Weeden, David Finkle, and Sally Fay), "The Group (Second Session)" (sketch by Archie T. Tridmorten), "I Luv You" (lyric and music by Michael Leeds), "Runnin' with the Brat Pack" (lyric and music by Ron Melrose), and "In the Quiet of Your Arms" (lyric and music by Martin Charnin).

"Yes! We Have the Manuscripts" was a spoof of three musicals, including *Fiddler on the Roof* as written by Noel Coward as well as Martin Charnin and Thomas Meehan's own *Annie* as written by Stephen Sondheim.

"Stools" had been previously heard in *Upstairs at O'Neals'* (see entry), and was recorded on that show's cast album by Painted Smiles Records (LP # PS-1344).

"Privacy" was recorded for the collection *Pictures in the Hall/Songs of Craig Carnelia* (released by Original Cast Records [CD # OC-914]).

1142 No Shoestrings. THEATRE: Upstairs at the Downstairs; OPENING DATE: October 11, 1962; PERFORMANCES: 66; SKETCHES: Louis Botto, Dee Caruso, Herb Hartig, Bill Levine, Michael McWhinney, and Peter Meyers; LYRICS: Francis Essex, Barry Alan Grael, Lawrence (Larry) Grossman, Arthur McRae, Bud McCreery, Michael McWhinney, Peter Meyers, Stanley Meyers, Treva Silverman, Richard Waring, and Rod Warren; MUSIC: Richard Addinsell, Ronald Cass, Richard Chodosh, Lawrence (Larry) Grossman, Stephen Lawrence, Bud McCreery, John Pritchard, Arthur Siegel, Rod Warren, and Richard Wernick Direction: Ben Bagley; "staged" by Robert Haddad; CHOREOGRAPHY: Robert Haddad; COSTUMES: Dick Granger; MUSICAL DIRECTION: Dorothea Freitag; PRODUCER: Ben Bagley

CAST—Danny Carroll, Jane Connell, Larry Holofcener, Bill McCutcheon, Patti Regan, June Squibb

The revue was presented in two acts (sketch and song assignments unknown).

ACT ONE—"It's a Great Little World" (lyric by Peter Meyers, music by Ronald Cass) "This Year of Disgrace" (lyric by Peter Meyers, music by Ronald Cass) "The Dark Lady of the Senates" (lyric by Peter Meyers, music by John Pritchard), "Fun and Games" (lyric and music by Bud McCreery) "The Thing That Johnny Did" (lyric by Michael McWhinney, music by Arthur Siegel) "Suburban Lullaby" (lyric by Barry Alan Grael, music by Richard Wernick) "Instant Biographies" (sketch by Louis Botto), "Heavenly Body" (lyric by Michael McWhinney, music by Arthur Siegel), "Hoffa Love Is Better Than None" (lyric by Michael McWhinney, music by Arthur Siegel) "I've Been True to Myself" (lyric by Barry Alan Grael, music by Richard Chodosh) "That Isn't Done" (lyric by Treva Silverman, music by Stephen Lawrence) "Eye on New York" (sketch by Dee Caruso and Bill Levine) "Lac Des Scenes" (lyric by Peter Meyers and Stanley Meyers; music arranged by Ronald Cass, from themes of Peter Ilych Tchaikovsky) "The Vagabond Student" (sketch and lyric by Peter Meyers, music by John Pritchard)

ACT TWO—"The Two Miss Browns" (lyric by Arthur McRae, music by Richard Addinsell), "Little Girl Blues" (lyric by Michael McWhinney, music by Arthur Siegel), "Taken at Her Word" (sketch by Peter Meyers) "An American Tragedy" (sketch by Michael McWhinney), "A Pawn for Wernher von Braun" (lyric and music by Lawrence [Larry] Grossman) "1600 Pennsylvania Avenue" (lyric and music by Rod Warren) "Lollipop Lane" (lyric and music by Bud McCreery) "Three to the Bar" (sketch by Herb Hartig) "Time to Say Goodnight" (lyric by Richard Waring and Francis Essex, music by John Pritchard)

NOTES—*No Shoestrings* was the last of Ben Bagley's four original Off Broadway revues (and, in keeping with his "shoestring" titles, the revue acknowledged Richard Rodgers' then currently-running Broadway musical *No Strings*). Arthur Gelb in the *New York Times* said the revue was "about 75 per cent successful, which is good enough." He also indicated some of the lines in the revue had been borrowed from a Washington, D.C., cabaret revue, The Uniquecorn.

Gelb noted there were a few "dull" numbers, including a "tiresome" song about the Kennedy family ("a joke being done to death in nightclubs all over the country"). But he singled out for praise a number of sequences, including "The Vagabond Student" (an "hilarious" operetta spoof); an unidentified sketch [probably "Taken at Her Word"] parodying the best-seller *Born Free* (Jane Connell, portraying the author of a book about a lion in Kenya, notes that the lion ate the cook, an unfortunate incident which will nonetheless add welcome dramatic impact to Chapter 13); and another unidentified sequence ["Little Girl Blues"?] in which Bill McCutcheon portrayed a "younger-than-springtime" Richard Rodgers who "gloatingly dismisses all his collaborators."

The revue was the first to play at the Upstairs at the Downstairs after Julius Monk set up shop at the Plaza Hotel (see entry for *Dime a Dozen* regarding the lawsuit filed against Monk in regard to his departure from Upstairs/Downstairs as well as his lawsuit against both Upstairs/Downstairs and Bagley).

The revue was originally titled *Ben Bagley's First Edition*, and so it seems Bagley planned to produce a series of revues at the venue. But there were to be no more original Bagley revues, although he later produced two editions of an Off Broadway revue devoted to the songs of Cole Porter (*The Decline and Fall of the Entire World as Seen Through the Eyes of Cole Porter Revisited*, both 1965; see entries for both editions). But from the mid-1960s onward, Bagley's energies were devoted to recording his *Revisited* series of obscure show songs.

In 1970, the Equity Library Theatre produced a limited run of *Ben Bagley Shoestring Revues*, which contained highlights from his earlier revues. It was directed and choreographed by Miriam Fond, with special choreography by Bick Goss.

Among the contributors to *No Shoestrings* was Lawrence (Larry) Grossman, who would have an interesting musical theatre career; even though his Broadway musicals had short runs, they nonetheless produced a number of distinguished theatre songs. Barry Alan Grael and Richard Chodosh teamed up the following year for *The Streets of New York* (see entry), one of the most fondly remembered Off Broadway musicals of the 1960s. According to Ken Bloom's *American Song*, "The Story of Alice" (lyric by Larry Holofcener, music by Jerry Bock) was added during the run. The song, incidentally, had first been heard in the 1955 Broadway revue *Catch a Star!* and was later used in the second edition of *Seven Come Eleven* (see entry).

Bloom also cites a few numbers from London revues which seem to have been added to *No Shoestrings* during its run and then later dropped: "The Ballad of Beauregard Green," "Don't Let (Get) Me Down," "Mr. Henderson," and "Good Book and Lyrics." The first was by Peter Myers, Ronald (Ronnie) Cass, and Dick Vosburgh, and was originally introduced as "The Ballad of Basher Green" in *The Lord Chamberlain Regrets...!* (1961), and can be heard on that revue's London cast album; similarly, "Don't Let Me Down" (by Lionel Harris, Stanley Myers, and John Pritchett) is from *The Lord Chamberlain* (but doesn't appear on the London cast album); "Mr. Henderson" (by Ronald [Ronnie] Cass) appears to be from either *For Amusement Only* (1956) or *For Adults Only* (1958) (possibly the former, since the song doesn't appear in the latter's program); and "Good Book and Lyrics" (by Ronald [Ronnie] Cass) had been heard in *Intimacy at 8:30* (1954). Bloom also indicates "It's Time to Say Goodnight" (lyric by Francis Essex and music by John Pritchard) was in the revue (it originally appeared in *The Lord Chamberlain*, although a program and the cast album don't include the number).

For the opening night of *No Shoestrings*, other numbers from London revues were heard, and these may or may not have been dropped during the run: like "The Ballad of Beauregard (Basher) Green," both "It's a Great Little World" and "Lac Des Scenes" were also from *The Lord Chamberlain Regrets* and can be heard on the London cast album (the former as "Great Little World"); "The Two Mrs. Browns" was from *Living for Pleasure* (1958) and apparently appeared in that revue in a sequence with the overall title "The Pretty Miss Brown" (and can be heard on the London cast album as "The Pretty Miss Brown"); and "The Vagabond Student" was from *For Amusement Only* (1956).

Other numbers which were apparently added and then dropped during the run were "Billy Sol Estes" (lyric and music by Louis Botto) and "Cinema I and Cinema II" (lyric and music by Michael McWhinney) as well as the aforementioned "The Story of Alice."

Rod Warren's "1600 Pennsylvania Avenue" was later performed in *Tour de Four* (see entry).

1143 No Way to Treat a Lady (1987). THEATRE: Hudson Guild Theatre; OPENING DATE:

May 27, 1987; PERFORMANCES: 28; BOOK: Douglas J. Cohen; LYRICS: Douglas J. Cohen; MUSIC: Douglas J. Cohen; DIRECTION: Jack Hofsiss; Robert Jess Roth, Assistant Director and Dramaturg; CHOREOGRAPHY: Christopher Chadman; Linda Haberman, Assistant Choreographer; Fight Choreography by John Curless; SCENERY: David Jenkins; COSTUMES: Michael Kaplan; LIGHTING: Beverly Emmons; MUSICAL DIRECTION: Uel Wade; PRODUCER: Hudson Guild Theatre (Geoffrey Sherman, Producing Director; James Abar, Associate Director)

CAST—Stephen Bogardus (Christopher "Kit" Gill), Peter Slutsker (Morris Brummell), June Gable (Mother [Flora], Mrs. Sullivan, Carmelia, Alexandra, Sadie), Liz Callaway (Sarah Stone)

SOURCE—The 1964 novel *No Way to Treat a Lady* by William Goldman.

The action occurs in New York City.

The musical was presented in two acts.

ACT ONE—"Five More Minutes" (Stephen Bogardus, Peter Slutsker), "A Very Funny Thing" (Stephen Bogardus), "So Far, So Good" (Liz Callaway, Peter Slutsker), "Safer in My Arms" (Stephen Bogardus), "I've Been a Bad Boy" (Peter Slutsker, Stephen Bogardus), "I've Been a Bad Boy" (reprise) (June Gable, Stephen Bogardus), "The First Move" (Stephen Bogardus, Liz Callaway, Peter Slutsker), "I Hear Humming" (June Gable, Peter Slutsker), "Five More Minutes" (reprise) (Peter Slutsker), "Killer on the Line" (Peter Slutsker), "The Next Move" (Liz Callaway), "Whose Hands Are These" (Peter Slutsker), "You're Getting Warmer" (Stephen Bogardus, Peter Slutsker)

ACT TWO—"Front Page News" (Stephen Bogardus, Liz Callaway, Peter Slutsker, June Gable), "Female Encounters" (Peter Slutsker), "Once More from the Top" (Stephen Bogardus), "One of the Beautiful People" (Liz Callaway), "Still" ('Joleen,' Stephen Bogardus), "Sarah's Touch" (Peter Slutsker), "I've Noticed a Change" (Stephen Bogardus, June Gable, Liz Callaway), "A Close Call" (Peter Slutsker), "So Far, So Good" (reprise) (Liz Callaway, Peter Slutsker)

NOTES—*No Way to Treat a Lady* was based on William Goldman's entertaining novel; its 1968 film version was a highly underrated black comedy-mystery with George Segal, Lee Remick, Rod Steiger, and Eileen Heckart, the latter two giving amusing, over-the-top performances.

The Off Off Broadway musical was a worthy successor to the book and film, but never quite found the success it deserved despite regional theatre productions and a London mounting at the Arts Theatre on August 3, 1998 (with Donna McKecknie).

Happily, a revised 1996 Off Off Broadway production (see entry) was recorded by Varese Sarabande Records (CD # VSD-5815), and the script of this version was published by Samuel French, Inc., in 1999.

1144 No Way to Treat a Lady (1996). THEATRE: Saint Peter's Church/The York Theatre Company; OPENING DATE: December 22, 1996; PERFORMANCES: 42; BOOK: Douglas J. Cohen; LYRICS: Douglas J. Cohen; MUSIC: Douglas J. Cohen; DIRECTION: Scott Schwartz; CHOREOGRAPHY: Daniel Stewart; SCENERY: James Morgan; COSTUMES: Yvonne De Moravia; LIGHTING: Mary Jo Dondlinger; MUSICAL DIRECTION: Wendy Bobbitt; PRODUCER: The York Theatre Company (Janet Hayes Walker, Producing Artistic Director; James Morgan, Associate Artistic Director; Joseph V. De Michele, Managing Director)

CAST—Adam Grupper (Morris Brummell), Alix (Alexandra) Korey (Flora, Alexandra, Carmella, Mrs. Sullivan, Sadie), Paul Schoeffler (Christopher "Kit" Gill), Marguerite MacIntyre (Sarah Stone)

SOURCE—The 1964 novel *No Way To Treat a Lady* by William Goldman.

The action occurs in New York City in 1970.

The musical was presented in two acts.

ACT ONE—"I Need a Life" (Adam Grupper, Paul Schoeffler, Marguerite MacIntyre), "Only a Heartbeat Away" (Paul Schoeffler, Alix Korey), "So Far, So Good" (Adam Grupper, Marguertie MacIntyre), "Safer in My Arms" (Paul Schoeffler, Alix Korey), "I've Been a Bad Boy"/"What Shall I Sing?" (Paul Schoeffler, Adam Grupper, Alix Korey), "The First Move" (Adam Grupper, Paul Schoeffler, Marguerite MacIntyre), "I Hear Humming" (Alix Korey, Adam Grupper), "I Need a Life" (reprise) (Adam Grupper), "I'm Having Lunch with Sarah" (Adam Grupper, Paul Schoeffler), "So Far, So Good" (reprise) (Marguerite MacIntyre) "You're Getting Warmer" (Paul Schoeffler, Adam Grupper)

ACT TWO—"Front Page News" (Paul Schoeffler, Adam Grupper, Marguerite MacIntyre, Alix Korey), "So Much in Common" (Marguerite MacIntyre, Alix Korey, Adam Grupper), "Front Page News"/"What Shall I Sing?" (reprises) (Paul Schoeffler), "One of the Beautiful People" (Marguerite MacIntyre), "Still" (Alix Korey, Paul Schoeffler), "I Have Noticed a Change"/"Morris Life"/"Once More from the Top" (Paul Schoeffler, Marguerite MacIntyre, Alix Korey, Adam Grupper), "What Shall I Sing?" (reprise) (Alix Korey), "So Far, So Good" (reprise) (Adam Grupper, Marguerite MacIntyre)

NOTES—This Off Off Broadway production was a revised version of *No Way to Treat a Lady* (see entry for the 1987 version).

Numbers not used from the 1987 production were "Five More Minutes," "A Very Funny Thing," "Killer on the Line," "Whose Hands Are These," "Female Encounters," "Sarah's Touch," and "A Close Call." Songs added for the new production were "I Need a Life," "Only a Heartbeat Away," "What Shall I Sing?," "I'm Having Lunch with Sarah," "So Much in Common," and "Morris Life."

Other songs heard in various productions of the musical were "Dance Until We Drop" and "Ladykiller."

Douglas J. Cohen's delightful musical enjoyed a sparkling production from the York Theatre Company, and Alix Korey was especially memorable in her multiple roles (including the dizzy, dance-mad Carmella, whose cha-cha partner died three days ago, an event she remembers "like it was yesterday").

The York production was recorded by Varese Sarabande Records (CD # VSD-5815); and the script was published by Samuel French, Inc., in 1999.

1145 A Noble Rogue. "A Musical Melodrama." THEATRE: Gansevoort Theatre; OPENING DATE: August 19, 1929; PERFORMANCES: 9; BOOK: Kenyon Scott; LYRICS: Kenyon Scott; MUSIC: Kenyon Scott; DIRECTION: Adrian S. Perrin and Paul Gilmore; CHOREOGRAPHY: Adrian S. Perrin and J.R. O'Neil; SCENERY: Joseph Allen Physioc; MUSICAL DIRECTION: Jack Press; PRODUCER: Adrian S. Perrin

CAST—R.A. Rose (Jules Le Blanc), Cecil Carol (Celeste Beauregard), Frank Howson (Colonel Mulford), Melba Marcelle (Senorita Velasquez), Esteban Cerdan (Grambo), Nanette Flack (Mme. Le Blanc), Robert Hobbs (Major Villere), Gordon Richards (Captain Lockyer), MARGUERITE ZENDER (Virginia Mulford), Helen Heed (Evalina), ROBERT RHODES (Jean Lafitte), William Balfour (Captain Dominque You), Alfred Heather (Captain O'Shaughnessy), Jimmie Carr (Alphonse), Andre Borice (Francois), Marie La Verni (Rina), Irma Friend (Louise, Ensemble), Barry Devine (Senor Antonio), Lioner Sainer (Rancher); Ensemble: Claudia Tyce, Julie La Chane, Evelyn Hamilton, Kay Harkins, Betty Howson, Florence Fields, Viola Pye, Elsie Melvin, Beulah Yorkin, Madeline Levy, Hortense Hector, Lucy Barbaro, Margaret Collins, Harry Shapiro, Billy Nation, Jack Greenburg, John Arcelo, Jay Altman, Carmelo Amora, Fred Armerson, Billy Gallagher, Emmett Anderson

The action occurs in New Orleans and on the Island of Grand Terre, Baratarian Bay, Louisiana, in 1814.

The musical was presented in two acts.

NOTES—The Off Broadway musical *A Noble Rouge* was the first presentation at the new Gansevoort Theatre; the venue had been known as the Grove Street Theatre, and during the previous season it had been home to "that band of professional insurgents," the New Playwrights (this according to the unsigned reviewer in the *New York Times*, who even gave his readers directions to the theatre: Go one block south of the Sheridan Square subway station, and then take a turn to your right on Grove Street).

As for the musical, the critic was basically unimpressed with Kenyon Scott's "slow, overconventional" book (which dealt with the romance of a "noble rouge" of a pirate and a New Orleans belle) and "early nineteenth century" lyrics. But he had moderate praise for the score. He also remarked that the evening's most "modern touch" was the inclusion of two young effeminate men into the cast of characters (but he noted that "effeminate young men have long been fixtures of Broadway comedy").

The reviewer mentioned that after the performance, night club specialties were offered in the Persian Gardens, an entertainment venue located above the theatre.

Jean Lafitte was also a major character in the 1965 musical *Mardi Gras!* (see entry).

1146 Non Pasquale. "A Pop Opera." THEATRE: Delacorte Theatre/The Public Theatre; OPENING DATE: August 9, 1983; PERFORMANCES: 32; LIBRETTO: Nancy Heikin and Anthony Giles; MUSIC: Gaetano Donizetti; music adapted by William Elliott, from original arrangements and orchestrations by Tito Schipa, Jr., and Gianni Marchetti; ADDITIONAL ORCHESTRATIONS AND MUSIC COORDINATION by Roy Moore; DIRECTION: Wilford Leach; CHOREOGRAPHY: Margo Sappington; SCENERY: Bob Shaw and Wilford Leach; COSTUMES: Nan Cibula; LIGHTING: Jennifer Tipton; MUSICAL DIRECTION: William Elliott; PRODUCER: The New York Shakespeare Festival (Joseph Papp, Director; Jason Steven Cohen, Associate Producer)

CAST—Joe Grifasi (Trumpet), Joe Masiell (Malatesta), Ron Leibman (Don Pasquale), Maureen Sadusk (Piccola), Kipp Tozzi (Ernesto), Carol Dennis (Nina), Susan Goodman (Pinta), Marcie Shaw (Santa Maria), Priscilla Lopez (Norina), James Rich (Cousin Alfredo), Ernesto Gasco (Cousin Cesario); Pasquale's Servants, Norina's Relatives, and Townspeople (Kevin Berdini, Joyce Leigh Bowden, Katharine Buffaloe, Charlotte d'Amboise, Christopher d'Amboise, Carol Dennis, Bruce Falco, Ernesto Gasco, Susan Goodman, N.A. Klein, Paul Nunes, Caroline Peyton, Joe Pichette, James Rich, Kathy Robinson, David Sanders, Alan Sener, Charlie Serrano, Marcie Shaw, Lauren Tom, Michael Willson)

SOURCE—The 1843 opera *Don Pasquale* (music by Gaetano Donizetti and libretto by Gaetano Donizetti and Giovanni Ruffini).

PROGRAM NOTE—"This production was freely adapted from the RCA Italy recording of *Er Dom Pasquale*, originally conceived by Tito Schipa, Jr., with Gianna Marchetti, Roberto Bonanni, and William Hernandez, which was produced in Rome, Italy by RCA."

The opera was presented in two acts.

ACT ONE—"The House of Don Pasquale" (Joe Grifasi, Ron Leibman, Maureen Sadusk, Joe Masiell, Ensemble), "Holy and Innocent" (Joe Masiell), "Just Like a Young Man" (Ron Leibman, Maureen Sadusk), "The Duchess Song" (Ron Leibman, Kipp Tozzi), "Always" (Kipp Tozzi), "Love Must Be Delicato" (Priscilla Lopez), "Pazzo" (Priscilla Lopez, Carol Dennis, Susan Goodman, Marcie Shaw, Ensemble), "Recitativo" (Joe Masiell), "Ah, Sweet Revenge" (Priscilla Lopez, Joe Masiell), "Subito (Nearer to the Lire)" (Carol Dennis, Susan Goodman, Marcie Shaw, Priscilla Lopez, Joe Masiell, Ensemble), "From the Convent"/"She's a Virgin" (Priscilla Lopez, Joe Masiell, Ron Leibman, Maureen Sadusk), "The Wedding Ceremony" (Joe Grifasi, Joe Masiell, Ron Leibman, Maureen Sadusk, Priscilla Lopez), "The What On Earth Is Going On Tango" (Kipp Tozzi, Ron Leibman, Joe Masiell, Priscilla Lopez, Maureen Sadusk, Servants), "Permission" (Priscilla Lopez, Ron Leibman, Joe Masiell, Maureen Sadusk), "We Need a Few More Servants" (Priscilla Lopez, Ron Leibman, Servants, Ensemble), "Si, Signora" (Joe Pichette, Servants, Ensemble), "Oh, What a Wedding!" (Ensemble)

ACT TWO—"We Must Talk" (Ron Leibman, Priscilla Lopez), "Poor Don Pasquale" (Priscilla Lopez, Rob Leibman), "Lullaby" (Ron Leibman, Priscilla Lopez, Carol Dennis, Susan Goodman, Marcie Shaw, Beaux), "Softly, Softly to the Garden" (Joe Masiell, Ron Leibman, Joe Grifasi, Ensemble), "Fight to the Death" (Ernesto Gasco, Joe Masiell, Joe Grifasi, Ron Leibman, Ensemble), "Serenade" (Kipp Tozzi, Ensemble), "Tell Me You Love Me" (Kipp Tozzi, Priscilla Lopez), "If Only" (Ron Leibman), "This Is Norina?" (Ron Leibman, Joe Masiell, Ensemble), "La Morale" (Joe Masiell, Joe Grifasi), Finale ("Bravo, Bravo") (Ensemble)

NOTES—*Non Pasquale*, a pop version of Donizetti's opera *Don Pasquale*, was presented free in Central Park at the Delacorte Theatre. During the first half of the 1980s, Joseph Papp experimented with older musical works. He hit the jackpot with *The Pirates of Penzance* (see entry), but *Non Pasquale* and a new version of *La Boheme* (which opened at the Anspacher Theatre in 1984 with Linda Ronstadt and David [James] Carroll) went nowhere; see entry.

Mel Gussow in the *New York Times* found *Non Pasquale* "hectic" instead of "hysterical," and noted that in order to "Sid Caesarize" an Italian opera, the spoof must be "short and hilarious." But instead the evening was "full-length and scattershot," with no discernible style. Further, "several" scenes misfired, and the creators of the new work completely "mislaid their collective sense of humor."

1147 North Atlantic. "A Brand-New Musical Comedy." THEATRE: The Gene Frankel Theatre and Media Center; OPENING DATE: January 16, 1977; PERFORMANCES: Unknown; BOOK: Michael Colby; LYRICS: Michael Colby and Jim Fradrich; MUSIC: Jim Fradrich; DIRECTION: Clinton Atkinson; CHOREOGRAPHY: Dennis Dennehy; Svetlana McLee, Assistant Choreographer; MUSICAL NUMBERS: staged by Dennis Dennehy and Clinton Atkinson; SCENERY: Vicki Paul; COSTUMES: Jack McGroder; LIGHTING: Sara Schrager; MUSICAL DIRECTION: Bill Brohn; Robert Plowman, Conductor; PRODUCER: Gene Frankel Theatre and Media Center

CAST—Eskimo Men and Boys (Ted Williams, J.H. Clark, Mark Manley, Rick Emery), Eskimo Women and Girls (Marilyn Hiratzka, Mary Ann Taylor), Susan Bigelow (Honey Snodgrass), Lori Tan Chinn (Melanie Fong), Deborah Moreno (Essie Norton), Julie Kurnitz (Eskimo Annie), Alvin Lum (Nanook), Stratton Walling (Sir William Littlewood), Dennis Hearn (Sandy Shore), Rick Emery (Robert Littlewood), Mary Ann Taylor (Sister Bettina/Ballet), J.H. Clark (Johnny Joe/Ballet)

The action occurs somewhere in the North Atlantic sometime after World War II.

The musical was presented in two acts.

ACT ONE—Overture (Orchestra), "Happier Side" (Susan Bigelow, Lori Tan Chinn), "Happier Side" (reprise) (Susan Bigelow, Lori Tann Chinn, Deborah Moreno), "Where the Hell Is Annie?" (Eskimo Men), "Something Special" (Julie Kurnitz), "Before I Fall" (Susan Bigelow, Eskimo Men), "Now Is Here" (Deborah Moreno, Lori Tan Chinn, Alvin Lum, Julie Kurnitz, Eskimos), "Duo Thoughts" (Susan Bigelow, Stratton Walling), "I Held a Hope" (Stratton Walling), "The Sleigh with the Cream Colored Team" (Dennis Hearn, Lori Tan Chinn), "Sign Song" (Susan Bigelow, Eskimo Children), "There's a Rainbow at the End" (Deborah Moreno), "Raising an Igloo" (Dennis Hearn, Deborah Moreno, Lori Tan Chinn, Susan Bigelow, Alvin Lum, Julie Kurnitz, Eskimo Men and Women), "Solo Thoughts" (Stratton Walling)

ACT TWO—Entr'acte (Orchestra), "Happier Side" (reprise) (Alvin Lum, Susan Bigelow, Children), "Erase Him" (Susan Bigelow, Lori Tan Chinn, Deborah Moreno), "Ya Won't Complain" (Dennis Hearn, Lori Tan Chinn), "North Atlantic" (Company), "Who'd Have Guessed It?" (Susan Bigelow, Stratton Walling), "Deep in My Mind" (Susan Bigelow), Ballet (Company), "Reindeer Moss" (Alvin Lum, Susan Bigelow, Deborah Moreno, Dennis Hearn, Julie Kurnitz, Lori Tan Chinn, Rick Emery, Eskimos), Finale (Company)

NOTES—*North Atlantic*, an Off Off Broadway spoof of Rodgers and Hammerstein musicals (and 1950s musicals in general), was twenty years ahead of its time. It might have enjoyed a long run in later years, when audiences were more accepting of "ironic" musicals.

With characters named Eskimo Annie and such song titles as "Duo Thoughts," "Solo Thoughts," "Deep in My Mind," "Now Is Here," "The Sleigh with the Cream Colored Team," "Raising an Igloo," and "Erase Him," it's clear that Michael Colby and Jim Fradrich had Rodgers and Hammerstein and post World War II musicals down pat.

The showcase played January 8 through January 22, 1977, with an official opening night of January 16. An LP of the musical was privately recorded.

1148 Northern Boulevard. THEATRE: The AMAS Repertory Theatre; OPENING DATE: February 14, 1985; PERFORMANCES: 16; BOOK: Kevin Brofsky; LYRICS: Carleton Carpenter; MUSIC: Carleton Carpenter; DIRECTION: William Martin; CHOREOGRAPHY: Dennis Dennehy; SCENERY: Tom Barnes; COSTUMES: Judy Dearing; LIGHTING: Deborah Tulchin; MUSICAL DIRECTION: James Steven Mironchik; PRODUCER: The AMAS Repertory Theatre, Inc. (Rosetta LeNoire, Founder and Artistic Director)

CAST—Audrei-Kairen (Mrs. Golden, Mrs. McSherry), Morgan MacKay (Jerry Simon), Alice Cannon (Roslyn Simon), Regina Reynolds Hood and Jose de la Cuesta (Time-Changers), Kelly Sanderbeck (Dorothy Fisher), Luke Lynch (Donald Gelbert, Young Man), Miriam Miller (Celia Gelbert), Art Ostrin (Saul Gelbert), Kelley Paige (Margo Fields, Connie Simon), Curtis Le Febvre (George Fisher, Michael Simon), Brian Noodt (Michael Simon as a boy, Modke Simon), Dolores Garcia (Mrs. D'Angelo, Mrs. Hernandez), Rosetta LeNoire (Mrs. Washington)

The action occurs in New York on Northern Boulevard and in Simon's Delicatessen during the years 1941-1981.

The musical was presented in two acts.

ACT ONE—"Get Up and Dance" (Morgan Mackay, Alice Cannon), "He Loves Her" (Art Ostrin, Miriam Miller), "Half a World Away" (Alice Cannon), "Plus One" (Alice Cannon), "Growing" (Art Ostrin), "Northern Boulevard" (Kelly Sanderbeck), "Living in Luxury" (Morgan Mackay, Alice Cannon), "Half a World Away" (reprise) (Morgan Mackay)

ACT TWO—"Master, Master" (Luke Lynch, Curtis Le Febvre), "Priorities" (Alice Cannon), "A Silvery Song" (Curtis Le Febvre, Company), "Fathers and Sons" (Morgan Mackay), "Let's Not Miss the Boat" (Art Ostrin, Rosetta LeNoire), "Let's Not Miss the Boat" (reprise) (Art Ostrin, Rosetta LeNoire), "He Loves Her" (reprise) (Morgan Mackay, Alice Cannon), "Whoa, Baby" (Kelly Sanderbeck), "Northern Boulevard" (reprise) (Morgan Mackay, Alice Cannon)

NOTES—Carleton Carpenter, the lyricist and composer of the Off Off Broadway musical *Northern Boulevard*, is perhaps best remembered for his supporting roles in a number of fondly remembered MGM musicals and comedies of the early 1950s; his most memorable screen moment occurred when he and Debbie Reynolds performed "Aba Daba Honeymoon" in *Two Weeks with Love* (1950).

Northern Boulevard marked the first time in which AMAS founder and artistic director Rosetta LeNoire appeared in an AMAS production.

1149 Not-So-New Faces of '82. "An Evening of Wanton Mischief and Songs." THEATRE: Westside Mainstage; OPENING: December 15, 1982; PERFORMANCES: 16; SKETCHES, LYRICS, AND MUSIC: Brenda Bergman, Lynne Bernfield, Michael Colby, Michael Feingold, Mark Hampton, Gerald Markoe, Alan Menken, Jim Morgan, Scott Oakley, Bob Ost, Ronald Reagan, Jim Ricketts, Terry Rieser, Scott Robertson, Stuart Ross, Paul Ruben, Schreier/Roth, William Shakespeare, Paul Trueblood, David Zippel, and the cast; DIRECTION: Stuart Ross; CHOREOGRAPHY: Edmond Kresley; SCENERY: Jim Stewart; LIGHTING: Jeffrey McRoberts; MUSICAL DIRECTION: Jonny Bowden; PRODUCERS: Actors Producing Company (Joan Montgomery, Executive Producer); Joanne Zippel, Associate Producer

CAST—Nancy Ringham, Scott Robertson, Carole Schweid, Mary Testa, William Thomas, Jr., Margery Cohen, George Bohn

The revue was presented in two acts (division of acts and sketch and song assignments unknown).

MUSICAL NUMBERS—"Not-So-New Faces," "Schizophrenia 101A," "Ask the Doctor," "Summer's Breeze," "Nobody Knows That It's Me," "Night of the Living Preppies," "Hollywood Has Got Her," "Mom, I've Got Something to Tell You," "The Boyfriend," "Christmas Tree," "P.M. With Lufa," "Princess Di," "The News," "Edie," "E.T.," "Portman Kick," "Cell of the Well-to-Do," "Rosie," "The Dancer and the Dance," "Amyl, You're Back," "French Tickler," "Special Guest Spot," "Last Call," "Dueling Neurotics," "Baby, You Give Good Heart," "New Face in Town," "Friends Like You"

NOTES—Sporting songs and sketches with titles like "Night of the Living Preppies" and "Dueling Neurotics," the Off Off Broadway revue *Not-So-New Faces of '82* sounds as though it might have been amusing; among the revue's contributors were Alan Menken and David Zippel (not to mention Ronald Reagan and William Shakespeare). After its initial two-week run, the revue re-opened on March 17, 1983, for sixteen performances at the Century Center. For the second engagement, Nancy Ringham, Mary Testa, and William Thomas, Jr., returned, and they were joined by Barry Preston.

A year later, on April 5, 1984, the revue returned in a new edition; see entry for *Not-So-New Faces of '84*.

1150 Not-So-New Faces of '84. THEATRE: Upstairs at Greene Street; OPENING DATE: April 5, 1984; PERFORMANCES: 24; SKETCHES, LYRICS, AND MUSIC: Robin Batteau, Abra Bigham, David Buskin, Michael Feingold, Ellen Fitzhugh, Larry Grossman, Jay Jeffries, Jason McAuliffe, Alan Menken, Scott Oakley, Bob Ost, Jim Ricketts, Stuart Ross, Joel Saltzman, Michael Sartor, David Sinkler, Karen Trott, and David Zippel; DIRECTION: Stuart Ross; CHOREOGRAPHY: Edmond Kresley; COSTUMES: Carol Wenz; LIGHTING: Jeffrey McRoberts; MUSICAL DIRECTION: John Spalla

CAST—Nancy Ringham, John Spalla, Mary Testa, William Thomas, Jr.

NOTES—This short-running Off Off Broadway revue *Not-So-New Faces of '84* included many interesting names among its contributors (Ellen Fitzhugh, Larry Grossman, Alan Menken, David Zippel) and cast members (Nancy Ringham, Mary Testa).

See entry for *Not-So-New Faces of '82*, an earlier edition of the revue.

1151 Not Tonight, Benvenuto! "A Bawdy New Comedy Musical." THEATRE: Carter Theatre; OPENING DATE: June 5, 1979; PERFORMANCES: 1; BOOK: Virgil Engeran; LYRICS: Virgil Engeran; MUSIC: Virgil Engeran; DIRECTION: Jim Payne; CHOREOGRAPHY: Robin Reseen; SCENERY: James Morgan and Peter A. Scheu; COSTUMES: Sherri Bucks; LIGHTING: Jesse Ira Berger; MUSICAL DIRECTION: Steve Freeman; PRODUCERS: Jim Payne and Virgil Engeran with the Broadway-Times Theater Company

CAST—Paul Alessi (Officer, Giovanni, Caruso), Nelia Bacmeister (Statue, Wench), Ada Berry (Aida), Daniel Fortier (Beggar, Poodidicci, Judge), Christopher Hensel (Benvenuto Cellini), Shelly Herrington (Statue, Madeline), Cynde Lauren (Statue, Mother), Jonathan Luks (Willie, Sailor), Marion Markham (Statue, Bounty Hunter), Michael Mitorotondo (Leonardo, Monk, Sentry), Sharon Murray (Madonna, Mother Superior), Roger Noonan (Federico), Gene Stilwell (Bobo), Paula Ward (Diana), Ron Wyche (Suitor, Narrator)

The action occurs in Florence, Italy, in 1524.

The musical was presented in two acts (division of acts and song assignments unknown; songs are listed in performance order).

MUSICAL NUMBERS—"How Do You Do," "Can't Make Love Without You," "Why Do I Love Bennie?," "Who Can Control the Human Heart," "Diana," "Lullaby," "Funeral Procession," "Poppin'," "This Is Our World," "Now I Lay Me Down to Sleep," "Search for Diana," "Gonna Get Right Some Day," "Together," "Wedding Ball"

NOTES—A flyer for *Not Tonight, Benvenuto!* reassured potential theatergoers that while the settings and costumes were of the sixteenth century, "the dialogue, music and attitudes are today. The show contains rock and disco numbers and is just plain *fun*!" The fun lasted for just one performance.

Not Tonight, Benvenuto! was the third failed musical about Benvenuto Cellini. *The Dagger and the Rose* (1928) closed during its tryout in Atlantic City (book by Isabel Leighton, lyrics by Edward Eliscu, and music by Eugene Berton), and *The Firebrand of Florence* (1945) lasted just a few weeks (but Ira Gershwin's witty lyrics and Kurt Weill's sweeping, often operatic score is one of the best ever written for the musical theatre). The only lyric work on the subject which has enjoyed success is Hector Berlioz' 1838 opera *Benvenuto Cellini*.

1152 Not While I'm Eating. "A Revue." THEATRE: Madison Avenue Playhouse; OPENING DATE: December 19, 1961; PERFORMANCES: 2; SKETCHES: Arthur Sherman; ADDITIONAL SKETCHES by Herbert Hartig; LYRICS: Arthur Sherman; MUSIC: Arthur Siegel; DIRECTION: Warren Enters; CHOREOGRAPHY: Tom Panko; SCENERY: Charles A. Brandon; COSTUMES: Stanley Simmons; LIGHTING: Richard Nelson; MUSICAL DIRECTION: Milton Greene; orchestra conducted by Philip Della-Penna; PRODUCER: David Silberman, Jr.

CAST—Wisa D'Orso, Hal Buckley, Judd Jones, Douglas Robinson, William Skipper, Buzz Halliday, Irene Perri

The revue was presented in two acts (song assignments unknown).

ACT ONE—"Not While I'm Eating," "I've Got a Man on the Moon," "Moonshot," "Cave Art," "What Good Are You?," "A House Divided," "The Organization Man," "Take the Picture First," "Oh, Sell Me, Pretty Maiden," "Arpeggio," "Golden Eagle," "Two for the Telephone," "Hero Worship," "Atlanta Has Fallen," "Letter of the Law"

ACT TWO—"Gold Rush in the Sky," "Parade Rest," "The Redemption of Ebenezer Scrooge," "A Minute, A Minute," "I Want," "School Board," "My Heart's a Marionette," "Buy American," "The Good Old Days," "The Writer," "What Did You Put in That Look?," "How Jolly Our Folly," Finale

NOTES—The revue *Not While I'm Eating*, with a score by the talented and underrated Arthur Siegel, lasted for just two performances. Louis Calta in the *New York Times* found it "astonishingly inept," and criticized the stale material (as with so many revues of the period, Khrushchev and television commercials were among the tired targets).

1153 Now. THEATRE: Cherry Lane Theatre; OPENING DATE: June 5, 1968; PERFORMANCES: 22; SKETCHES: George Haimsohn; LYRICS: George Haimsohn; MUSIC: John Aman. (Additional material by Barry Manilow, Steve Holden, John Kuntz, Sue Lawless, Marty Panzer, and Gerald Smith.); DIRECTION: Marvin Gordon; CHOREOGRAPHY: Unknown; SCENERY: Jack Robinson; visuals designed by Staging Techniques; theatre décor by A Bird Can Fly Shop; COSTUMES: Betsey Johnson & Michael Mott for Paraphernalia; The Different Drummer; LIGHTING: Skip Palmer; light machines by The Electric Garden; MUSICAL DIRECTION: Barry Manilow; PRODUCERS: PF Co. and John H. Beaumont

CAST—John Aman, Frank Andre, Lauree Berger, Rosalind Harris, Sue Lawless, Ted Pugh

The action occurs "now" and "here."

The revue was presented in one act.

MUSICAL NUMBERS—"Come Along with Us" (Company), "You Get Me High" (John Aman, Sue Lawless, Frank Andre, Lauree Berger, Rosalind Harris), ("Bobby Baby" [Cheerleaders]; dropped during previews; see notes below), "Space Idiocy" (Frank Andre, Ted Pugh), "Come Along with Us" (reprise) (Company), "Room Service" (sketch by Gerald Smith) (John Aman, Sue Lawless), "Save a Sinner Tonight" (Ted Pugh, Congregation), "Randy Girls" (Ted Pugh, Frank Andre, Lauree Berger, John Aman), "Lonely Are They" (lyric by John Aman) (Frank Andre), "Sex Can Be Funny" (Sue Lawless, Lauree Berger, Rosalind Harris, Ted Pugh, Frank Andre, John Aman), "Come Along with Us" (reprise) (Company), "Drill Team" (Ted Pugh, Sue Lawless), "Acre of Grass" (Farmers and Farmerettes), "Sidney" (Rosalind Harris), "Peonies" (Ted Pugh, Sue Lawless), "Flower Children" (lyric by John Aman) (Sue Lawless, Friends), "Cinderella" (sketch by John Kuntz) (Company), "The Third Lady" (lyric by Marty Panzer, music by Barry Manilow) (Ted Pugh), "Hello Hubert" (John Aman, Lauree Berger), "U.S. Patent Office" (sketch by Sue Lawless) (Frank Andre, Ted Pugh), "Leather Love" (lyric by John Aman) (Sue Lawless), "Minimal" (Company), "Acrobats" (Ted Pugh, Sue Lawless), "Speed Kills" (Frank Andre), "Climb Up Here with Daddy on the Boom Boom" (lyric by Steve Holden) (John Aman, Rosalind Harris, Frank Andre), "Beautiful People" (Company), "California Style" (lyric by John Aman) (Lauree Berger), "Dark Horse" (Company), "Now" (lyric by John Aman) (Company)

NOTES—With *Now*, Sue Lawless and Ted Pugh were back in another flop revue which now seems like a fascinating time capsule of its era. The evening included swipes at such Broadway hits as *Marat/Sade* (the play's complete title was *The Persecution and Assassination of Marat as Performed by the Inmates of the Asylum of Charenton Under the Direction of the Marquis de Sade*), *Hair*, and *Rosencrantz and Guildenstern Are Dead*; Robert F. Kennedy; Andy Warhol's film *The Chelsea Girls*; and (to show that some subjects are still current almost four decades later) strange-acting astronauts. In its quest to be as timely as possible, the revue also offered a dollop of male nudity.

Now opened on the evening of June 5; because Robert F. Kennedy had been shot during the night of June 4-June 5 (he died on June 6), the song about him ("Bobby Baby") which had been performed during preview performances was eliminated (the above song list places the number in the slot where it was performed during previews). Dan Sullivan in the *New York Times* indicated the omission of the song "was an oasis of good taste in a wasteland of bad."

As mentioned, the revue also spoofed Andy Warhol, who three days earlier (on June 3) had also been shot. Despite the murder attempt which almost took his life, the sequence about him ("Randy Girls") remained in the revue (Sullivan noted that the show's "respect for the fallen goes only so far").

"Bobby Baby" was the second song deleted from a musical because of the assassination of a member of the Kennedy family. The Fall 1963 tryout of Noel Coward's *The Girl Who Came to Supper* included "Long Live the King (If He Can)," a number about political assassination. After November 22, the song was permanently dropped from the score.

Although *Now* lasted for less than three weeks, George Haimsohn, its sketch writer and lyricist, had better luck later in the year with *Dames at Sea* (see entry), which he co-authored.

1154 Now Is the Time for All Good Men. "A Musical." THEATRE: Theatre de Lys; OPENING DATE: September 26, 1967; PERFORMANCES: 112; BOOK: Gretchen Cryer; LYRICS: Gretchen Cryer; MUSIC: Nancy Ford; DIRECTION: Word Baker; SCENERY: Holly Haas; COSTUMES: Jeanne Button; LIGHTING: Carol Rubinstein; MUSICAL DIRECTION: Stephen Lawrence; PRODUCERS: David Cryer and Albert Poland; presented by Special Arrangement with Lucille Lortel Productions, Inc.

CAST—Sally Niven (Sarah Larkin), Judy Frank (Eugenie Seldin), David Cryer (Mike Butler), Donna Curtis (Tooney), David Sabin (Albert McKinley), Margot Hanson (Betty Brown), Regina Lynn (Esther Mason), Art Wallace (Herbert Heller), John Bennett Perry (Bill Miller), Murray Olson (Jasper Wilkins), Anne Kaye (Ramona), Steve Skiles (Tommy)

The action occurs in Bloomdale, Indiana, at the present time.

The musical was presented in two acts.

ACT ONE—"We Shall Meet in the Great Hereafter" (Company), "Quittin' Time" (Donna Curtis, Margot Hanson, Regina Lynn), "What's in the Air?" (David Cryer), "Keep 'em Busy, Keep 'em Quiet" (John Bennett Perry, David Sabin, Regina Lynn, David Cryer, Margot Hanson, Sally Niven, Murray Olson, Art Wallace), "Tea in the Rain" (Sally Niven), "What's a Guy Like You Doin' in a Place Like This?" (Judy Frank), "Halloween Hayride" (Margot Hanson, Donna Curtis, Regina Lynn, John Bennett Perry, Murray Olson, Steve Skiles, Anne Kaye), "Campfire Songs" (Margot Hanson, John Bennett Perry, Regina Lynn, Murray Olson, Donna Curtis, Steve Skiles, Anne Kaye), "See Everything New" (David Cryer, Sally Niven), "All Alone" (David Cryer), "He Could Show Me" (Sally Niven), "Washed Away" (Donna Curtis, Regina Lynn, David Sabin, Sally Niven, Art Wallace, Murray Olson, John Bennett Perry, Steve Skiles, Anne Kaye), "Stuck-Up" (Judy Frank), "My Holiday" (Sally Niven, David Cryer), "On My Own" (Steve Skiles, Anne Kaye), "On My Own" (reprise) (Steve Skiles, David Cryer)

ACT TWO—"It Was Good Enough for Grandpa" (Company), "A Simple Life" (David Sabin, Sally Niven), "A Star on the Monument" (Art Wallace, John Bennett Perry, Murray Olson, Steve Skiles), "Rain Your Love on Me" (David Cryer, Sally Niven),

"Stuck-Up" (reprise) (Judy Frank), "There's Goin' to Be a Wedding" (Art Wallace, Donna Curtis, Steve Skiles, Anne Kaye, Margot Hanson, John Bennett Perry, Regina Lynn, Murray Olson), "On My Own" (reprise) (Steve Skiles, Anne Kaye, David Cryer, Art Wallace)

NOTES—The original title of *Now Is the Time for All Good Men* was *What's in the Wind*.

"Quittin' Time" and "What's in the Air?" were dropped shortly after the opening.

The script was published by Samuel French, Inc. (in an undated edition), and included "What's in the Air?" as well as songs which may not have been heard in the New York production ("Katydid" [which was part of the "Campfire Songs" sequence] and "Down Through History"); the script didn't include "On My Own." The cast album was recorded by Columbia Records (LP # OS-3130 and # OL-6730; a CD was later issued by DRG Records [# 19046]).

This was a message-musical about an ex-convict draft-dodger who masquerades as a school teacher in a small Midwestern town. Given the liberal tone of the piece, the draft dodger was depicted as a hero and most of the conservative inhabitants of the small town were caricatured as small-minded bigots. (For some reason, left-wing tolerance of diverse viewpoints never seems to extend to those who embrace conservative beliefs [also see entry for *Hair*, which opened a month after *Now Is the Time for All Good Men*]).

Now Is the Time for All Good Men was revived by the Equity Library Theatre on April 29, 1971, for fourteen performances in a revised and updated production (this version included "What's in the Air?," "Katydid," and "Down Through History").

Nancy Ford and Gretchen Cryer's musicals might have been more entertaining if they'd had stronger books; moreover, Cryer's lyrics were often pedestrian, and Ford's music all too often came across as soft-rock Muzak. Although *Now Is the Time* was a flop, they later collaborated on two long-running Off-Broadway successes, *The Last Sweet Days of Isaac* (1970) and *I'm Getting My Act Together and Taking It on the Road* (1979) (see entries), both of which were hampered by seriously weak scripts; but the former had an appealing score ("I Want to Walk to San Francisco" was an exceptionally ingratiating and melodic number) and the latter included one of the best theatre songs of its era ("Old Friend"). Their one Broadway musical, *Shelter* (1972), closed within a month.

1155 Nunsense (1985). THEATRE: Cherry Lane Theatre; transferred to the Sheridan Square Playhouse on February 27, 1986, and then later to the Douglas Fairbanks Theatre; OPENING DATE: December 12, 1985; PERFORMANCES: 3,672; BOOK: Dan Goggin; LYRICS: Dan Goggin; MUSIC: Dan Goggin; DIRECTION: Dan Goggin; CHOREOGRAPHY: Felton Smith; SCENERY: Barry Axtell; LIGHTING: Susan A. White; MUSICAL DIRECTION: Michael Rice; PRODUCERS: The Nunsense Theatrical Company in association with Joseph Hoesl and Bill Crowder

CAST—Marilyn Farina (Sister Mary Cardella), Vicki Belmonte (Sister Mary Hubert), Christine Anderson (Sister Robert Anne), Semina De Laurentis (Sister Mary Amnesia), Suzi Winson (Sister Mary Leo)

The action occurs in the present time at Mt. Saint Helen's School Auditorium in Hoboken, New Jersey.

The musical was presented in two acts.

ACT ONE—"Welcome" (Marilyn Farina), "Nunsense Is Habit-Forming" (Company), "Opening Remarks" (Marilyn Farina, Vicki Belmonte), "A Difficult Transition" (Company), "The Quiz" (Semina De Laurentis), "Benedicite" (Suzi Winson), "The Biggest Ain't the Best" (Suzi Winson, Vicki Belmonte), "Playing Second Fiddle" (Christine Anderson), "Taking Responsibility" (Marilyn Farina), "So You Want to Be a Nun" (Semina De Laurentis), "A Brilliant Idea" (Company), "A Word from the Reverend Mother" (Marilyn Farina), "Turn Up the Spotlight" (Marilyn Farina), "Lilacs Bring Back Memories" (Marilyn Farina, Vicki Belmonte, Suzi Winson, Semina De Laurentis), "An Unexpected Discovery" (Marilyn Farina), "Growing Up Catholic" (Company)

ACT TWO—"Robert to the Rescue" (Christine Anderson), "Growing Up Catholic" (reprise) (Christine Anderson, Suzi Winson, Vicki Belmonte, Semina De Laurentis), "We've Got to Clean Out the Freezer" (Company), "A Minor Catastrophe" (Company), "Just a Coupla Sisters" (Marilyn Farina, Vicki Belmonte), "Soup's On (The Dying Nun Ballet)" (Suzi Winson), "Baking with the BVM" ('Sister Julia, Child of God'), "Playing Second Fiddle" (reprise) (Christine Anderson), "I Just Want to Be a Star" (Christine Anderson), "The Drive-In" (Christine Anderson, Semina De Laurentis, Suzi Winson), "A Home Movie" (Company), "I Could've Gone to Nashville" (Semina De Laurentis), "Gloria in Excelsis Deo" (Company), "Closing Remarks" (Marilyn Farina, Company), "Holier Than Thou" (Vicki Belmonte, Company), "Nunsense Is Habit-Forming" (reprise) (Company)

NOTES—*Nunsense* became one of Off Broadway's biggest hits, running 3,672 performances and inspiring a number of sequels. As *The Nunsense Story* (see entry), the musical had first been seen Off Off Broadway in March 1984 at The Duplex Cabaret Theatre. For the Off Broadway version, the musical was substantially revised.

The plot dealt with a group of nuns who've lost fifty-two of their order to the unfortunate effects of food poisoning by one of their nun-chefs (Sister Julia, Child of God). In order to raise money to bury their dead, they started a greeting card business, but their profits enabled them to bury only forty-eight sisters (the remaining four bodies are in the convent's deep freezer). The sisters come upon the idea of giving a variety show in order to raise the necessary funds for the remaining burials. *Nunsense* is the talent show performed in order to raise those funds. (For a happy denouement, Sister Mary Amnesia remembers who she is: Sister Mary Paul, who had won the Publishers' Clearing House Sweepstakes, and so now the sisters will have all the money they'll ever need.)

It appears that shortly after the opening, "An Unexpected Discovery" was dropped and "Tackle That Temptation with a Time-Step" was added.

The cast album was recorded by DRG Records (LP # SBL-12589; CD # CDSBL-12589), and the script was published by Samuel French, Inc., in 1994. The 1987 British production was recorded by That's Entertainment Records (LP # TER-1132; issued on CD by Jay Records [# CDJAY-1255]), and included Honor Blackman in the cast. A Zurich cast recording (*Nonnsense*) was released by EMU Records (LP # 90188), and a Slovak production (*Mnisky*) was issued by EMI Records (CD # 7243-5-23197-2-5). The musical was shown on the Arts and Entertainment Network channel in 1993, with Rue McClanahan as Sister Mary Cardella (Regina), the Reverend Mother Superior. Original cast members Semina De Laurentis (Sister Mary Amnesia) and Christine Anderson (Sister Robert Anne) reprised their roles for the cable telecast, which was later released on videocassette and DVD by Image Entertainment (DVD # ID-4587-DLDVD).

For a list of all *Nunsense*-related musicals, see entry for *The Nunsense Story*.

1156 Nunsense (1995). THEATRE: The Triad; OPENING DATE: November 17, 1995; PERFORMANCES: 55; BOOK: Dan Goggin; LYRICS: Dan Goggin; MUSIC: Dan Goggin; DIRECTION: Dan Goggin; CHOREOGRAPHY: Felton Smith; SCENERY: Barry Axtell; LIGHTING: Paul Miller; MUSICAL DIRECTION: Michael Rice; PRODUCERS: The Triad and The *Nunsense* Theatrical Company in association with Joseph Hoesl, Bill Crowder, Jay Cardwell, Peter Martin, and Nancy and Steve McGraw

CAST—Nancy E. Carroll (Sister Mary Regina), Jennifer Perry (Sister Mary Hubert), Lin Tucci (Sister Robert Anne), Robin Taylor (Sister Mary Amnesia), Kim Galberaith (Sister Mary Leo)

NOTES—This was a brief revival of the long-running (3,672 performances) crowd-pleaser; for more information, including a list of musical numbers, see entry for the original *Nunsense*. For a list of all *Nunsense*-related musicals, see entry for *The Nunsense Story*.

1157 Nunsense A-Men! THEATRE: 47th Street Theatre; OPENING DATE: June 23, 1998; PERFORMANCES: 231; BOOK: Dan Goggin; LYRICS: Dan Goggin; MUSIC: Dan Goggin; DIRECTION: Dan Goggin; CHOREOGRAPHY: Felton Smith; SCENERY: Barry Axtell; LIGHTING: Richard Latta; MUSICAL DIRECTION: Leo P. Carusone; PRODUCERS: The Nunsense Theatrical Company in association with Joseph Hoesl, Bill Crowder, and Jay Cardwell

CAST—David Titus (Sister Mary Regina), Lothair Eaton (Sister Mary Hubert), Danny Vaccaro (Sister Robert Anne), Greg White (Sister Mary Amnesia), Doan Mackenzie (Sister Mary Leo), Tom Dwyer (Sister Mary Immaculata)

The action occurs in the present time at Mt. Saint Helen's School auditorium.

The musical was presented in two acts.

ACT ONE—Welcome (David Titus), "Nunsense Is Habit Forming" (Company), "Opening Remarks" (David Titus, Lothair Eaton), "A Difficult Transition" (Company), "The Quiz" (Greg White), "Benedicite" (Doan Mackenzie), "The Biggest Ain't the Best" (Lothair Eaton, Doan Mackenzie), "Playing Second Fiddle" (Danny Vaccaro), "Taking Responsibility" (David Titus), "So You Want to Be a Nun" (Greg White), "A Word from the Reverend Mother" (David Titus), "Turn Up the Spotlight" (David Titus), "Lilacs Bring Back Memories" (David Titus, Lothair Eaton, Doan Mackenzie, Greg White), "An Unexpected Discovery" (David Titus), "Tackle That Temptation with a Time Step" (Company)

ACT TWO—"Robert to the Rescue" (Danny Vaccaro), "Growing Up Catholic" (Danny Vaccaro, Doan Mackenzie, Lothair Eaton, Greg White), "We've Got to Clean Out the Freezer" (Company), "A Minor Catastrophe" (Company), "Just a Coupla Sisters" (David Titus, Lothair Eaton), "Soup's On (The Dying Nun Ballet)" (Doan Mackenzie), "Baking with the BVM" ('Sister Julia, Child of God'), "Playing Second Fiddle" (reprise) (Danny Vaccaro), "I Just Want to Be a Star" (Danny Vaccaro), "The Drive-In" (Danny Vaccaro, Greg White, Doan Mackenzie), "A Home Movie" (Company), "I Could've Gone to Nashville" (Greg White), "Gloria in Excelsis Deo" (Company), "Closing Remarks" (David Titus, Company), "Holier Than Thou" (Lothair Eaton, Company), "Nunsense Is Habit Forming" (reprise) (Company)

NOTES—It was probably inevitable that the hugely popular *Nunsense* (see entry) would find its way back to New York in a drag version. *Nunsense A-Men!* was a revival of sorts (it included a few revisions), and played over six months. A "national cast recording" was released by Nunsense, Inc., Records (CD # 37101-24803).

For a list of all *Nunsense*-related musicals, see entry for *The Nunsense Story*.

1158 The Nunsense Story. "An Unconventional Musical." THEATRE: Duplex Cabaret Theatre; OPENING DATE: March 1984; PERFORMANCES: Unknown; BOOK: Steve Hayes; LYRICS: Dan Goggin; MUSIC: Dan Goggin; DIRECTION: Felton Smith; CHOREOGRAPHY: Felton Smith Lighting: Clay Coury; MUSICAL DIRECTION: Lenny Babbish; PRODUCER: T.L. Boston

CAST—Marilyn Farina (Sister Mary Cardelia), Helen Baldassare (Sister Ralph Marie), John Hatchett (Sister Ann Arbor, Brother John), Suzanne Hevner (Sister Mary Amnesia), Steve Hayes (Father Norman D. Dumbrowski)

The musical was presented in two acts.

ACT ONE—"Nunsense Is Habit-Forming" (Company), "Exposition" (Marilyn Farina), "A Difficult Transition" (Company), "The Manicurist" (Steve Hayes), "The Exercise" (Suzanne Hevner), "True Confessions" (Steve Hays, John Hatchett), "The Hairdresser" (Helen Baldassare, Marilyn Farina), "The Vineyard" (John Hatchett), "So You Want to Be a Nun?" (Suzanne Hevner, Marilyn Farina), "Roughly Speaking" (Steve Hayes, Marilyn Farina), "We're the Nuns to Come To" (The Rolling Tombstones), "A Word from Reverend Mother" (Marilyn Farina), "The Nun and the Restless" (Suzanne Hevner, Helen Baldassare), "A Message from the Backer" (Marilyn Farina)

ACT TWO—"We've Got to Clean Out the Freezer" (Company), "The Love of My Life" (Steve Hayes), "The Cook" ('Sister Julia, Child of God'), "A Chorus Nun" (Helen Baldassare), "The Flickers" (John Hatchett, Suzanne Hevner, Helen Baldassare), "The Wayward Wimple" (John Hatchett, Marilyn Farina), "Annie Green" (Helen Baldassare), "Angeline" (John Hatchett, Suzanne Hevner, Helen Baldassare), "Seven Dominicans" (Company), "My Story" (Suzanne Hevner), "A Hat and Cane Song" (Company)

NOTES—*The Nunsense Story* opened Off Off Broadway, and was an early version of the enormously successful musical *Nunsense* (see entry). It told the story of the nuns of the Little Order of Hoboken, "affectionately known throughout New Jersey as the Little Hobos."

As *Nunsense*, the revised musical opened Off Broadway at the Cherry Lane Theatre on December 12, 1985, and ran for 3,672 performances. The new version was considerably different from *The Nunsense Story*. The characters of Father Norman D. Dumbrowksi and Brother John were eliminated, and no longer was one of the nun's roles played by a man in nun drag (but 1998's *Nunsense A-Men!* revisited this notion; see entry).

Further, the new version dropped a dozen numbers (including such jolly-sounding titles as "The Nun and the Restless," "A Chorus Nun," "The Wayward Wimple," and "A Hat and Cane Song"), and more than a dozen new ones were added. "A Hat and Cane Song" was later used in *Nunsense 2: The Sequel* (1994; see entry).

In all, five *Nunsense* musicals have been seen in New York: *The Nunsense Story* (1984); *Nunsense* (1985), the revised version of *The Nunsense Story*; *Nunsense 2: The Sequel* (1994); a 1995 revival of *Nunsense*; and *Nunsense A-Men!* (1998; the all-male version). See entries for all productions.

Nunsense and *Nunsense 2: The Sequel* were recorded by DRG Records, and *Nunsense A-Men!* was released by Nunsense Inc., Records (for more information, see entries).

Nunsense and *Nunsense 2: The Sequel* were later televised on the Arts and Entertainment Network, and were released on videocassette and DVD by Image Entertainment (for more information, see entries). Rue McClanahan, who wasn't in the original casts of either production, appeared in the televised versions, as did such *Nunsense* stalwarts as Semina De Laurentis and Christine Anderson.

The *Nunsense* franchise has continued with new installments which have played throughout the United States (but not in New York):

During the 1997-1998 theatre season, *Nunsense/The Jamboree* (a/k/a *Nunsense 3*) opened at the Grand Ole Opry in Nashville, and was recorded live at the January 21, 1998, performance by DRG Records (CD # 12623); Vicki Lawrence played Sister Mary Amnesia, and the songs included "Mini-Pearls of Wisdom" and "A Cowgirl from Canarsie." The production was later televised for cable (in late 1998?); for the DVD version (released by Lance Entertainment, Inc., # KOC-DV-6628), Lawrence reprised her role of Sister Mary Amnesia, and Rue McClanahan guest-starred as Mother Superior.

On October 16, 1998, *Nuncrackers* ("The Nunsense Christmas Musical") opened in Minneapolis at the Chanhassan Theatre, and the cast recording was first released by Nunsense Inc., Records (CD # N-400) and then by DRG Records (CD # 12624); the songs included "Twelve Days Prior to Christmas" and "Jesus Was Born in Brooklyn." The production was later televised (in 2001?), and along with Rue McClanahan (who wasn't in the original 1998 cast), the television version included a guest appearance by John Ritter; the television production was released on DVD by White Star Video (# D-3083). On September 19, 2002, *Meshuggah-Nuns!* ("The Ecumenical Nunsense") opened at the Chanhassen Theatre in Minneapolis, and was recorded by Nunsense Inc., Records (CD # 60662-57422). In this version, the Little Sisters are on a cruise; except for the actor playing Tevye, the cast of the cruise ship's production of *Fiddler on the Roof* becomes ill, and so the Little Nuns and the Jewish actor put on their own show. The songs included "Contrition (A Song of Guilt)," "Three Shayna Maidels," and "Matzo Man." On March 18, 2005, *Nunsensations!* ("The Nunsense Vegas Revue") opened at the Chanhassen Theatre in Minneapolis, and was recorded by Nunsense Inc., Records (CD # 60662-51952); a DVD was released in 2007 by Nunsense, Inc. (# 37101-30970). The songs included "What Plays in Vegas," "Hollywood 'n' Vinyl," "T & A," and "What's Black and White with Her Money on Red?"

The 1987 British production of *Nunsense* was recorded by That's Entertainment Records (LP # TER-1132; the CD was issued by Jay Records [# CDJAY-1255]) and starred Honor Blackman. The 1990 Zurich cast album (*Nonnsense*) was released by EMU Records (LP# 90188), and a 1999 Slovak cast recording was issued as *Mnisky* ("Americka Muzikalova Komedia") by EMI Records (CD # 7243-5-23197-2-5). On May 9, 2007, the Campbell Theatre in Martinez, California, began a year-round series of revivals of the *Nunsense* musicals in its Willow Cabaret, which also includes a *Nunsense* museum of memorabilia from productions of all the *Nunsense*-related musicals.

SPECIAL NOTE—Some sources cite the Duplex Cabaret Theatre as the first venue where *The Nunsense Story* played; other sources cite the Baldwin Theatre. It's possible that during the initial run of *The Nunsense Story* (before it was revised and later opened Off Broadway as *Nunsense*) the musical played at both theatres.

1159 Nunsense 2: The Sequel. "The Second Coming ...." THEATRE: Douglas Fairbanks Theatre; OPENING DATE: October 31, 1994; PERFORMANCES: 149; BOOK: Dan Goggin; LYRICS: Dan Goggin; MUSIC: Dan Goggin; DIRECTION: Dan Goggin; CHOREOGRAPHY: Felton Smith; SCENERY: Barry Axtell; LIGHTING: Paul Miller; MUSICAL DIRECTION: Michael Rice; PRODUCER: Twice Blessed Company, Inc.

CAST—Nancy E. Carroll (Sister Mary Regina [The Reverend Mother]), Terri White (Sister Mary Hubert), Carolyn Droscoski (Sister Robert Anne), Susan Emerson (Sister Mary Leo), Semina De Laurentis (Sister Mary Amnesia)

The action occurs in the present time in the auditorium of Mt. St. Helen's School.

The musical was presented in two acts.

ACT ONE—Overture (The School Band), "Jubilatedo" (Company), "Nunsense, the Magic Word" (Company), "Winning Is Just the Beginning" (Company), "The Prima Ballerina" (Susan Emerson), "The Biggest Still Ain't the Best" (Terri White, Susan Emerson), "I've Got Pizzazz" (Carolyn Droscoski), "I've Got Pizzazz" (reprise) (Nancy E. Carroll), "The Country Nun" (Semina De Laurentis), "Look Ma, I Made It" (Nancy E. Carroll), "The Padre Polka" (Terri White, Susan Emerson, Semina De Laurentis), "The Classic Queens" (Nancy E. Carroll, Terri White), "A Hat and Cane Song" (Company)

ACT TWO—"Angeline" (Carolyn Droscoski), "We're the Nuns to Come To" (Terri White, Carolyn Droscoski, Semina De Laurentis, Susan Emerson), "What Would Elvis Do?" (Nancy E. Carroll, Terri White), "Yes, We Can" (Susan Emerson, Semina De Laurentis, Carolyn Droscoski), "I Am Here to Stay" (Carolyn Droscoski), "What a Catastrophe" (Terri White, Carolyn Droscoski, Semina De Laurentis, Susan Emerson), "No One Cared Like You" (Semina De Laurentis), "Gloria in Excelsis Deo" (Company), "There's Only One Way to End Your Prayers" (Terri White, Company), "Nunsense, the Magic Word" (reprise) (Company)

NOTES—This sequel to the long-running (3,672 performances) hit *Nunsense* (see entry) took place six weeks after the action of the first musical. Again, the Little Sisters of Hoboken are presenting another benefit in the auditorium of Mt. St. Helen's School. "A Hat and Cane Song" had originally been heard in *The Nunsense Story* (see entry).

The sequel, which was originally produced at the Seven Angels Theatre in Waterbury, Connecticut, on November 20, 1992, ran a disappointing 149 performances, and during the run (from January 10-January 31, 1995) the original *Nunsense* played a total of seven performances in repertory with the sequel. A cast album of *Nunsense 2* was released by DRG Records (CD # 12608) from the Waterbury production (which included Semina De Laurentis in the cast); and the musical was later shown on the Arts and Entertainment Network (with Rue McClanahan and De Laurentis); it was released on videocassette and DVD by Image Entertainment (DVD # ID-9494-DLDVD). Despite the short run of *Nunsense 2: The Sequel*, other *Nunsense*-inspired musicals would follow. For more information, see entry for *The Nunsense Story*.

1160 Nymph Errant. THEATRE: Equity Library Theatre; OPENING DATE: March 11, 1982; PERFORMANCES: 32; BOOK: Romney Brent; LYRICS: Cole Porter; MUSIC: Cole Porter; DIRECTION: Clinton J. Atkinson; CHOREOGRAPHY: Dennis Dennehy; musical staging by Dennis Dennehy and Clinton J. Atkinson; SCENERY: Johniene Papandreas; COSTUMES: Marie Anne Chiment; LIGHTING: Scott Pinkney; MUSICAL DIRECTION: Donald Sosin; PRODUCER: Equity Library Theatre

CAST—Nancy Meadows (Winnie, Feliza), Susan Berkson (Edith Sanford, Clare), Enid Rodgers (Aunt Ermyntrude Edwards, Miss Pratt), Barry Ford (the Rev. Malcolm Pither, Mr. Pappas), Josie Lawrence (Betha), Joanna Seaton (Joyce Arbuthnot-Palmer), Diane Drielsma (Henrietta Bamberg), Gerry McCarthy (Madeleine St. Maure), Kathleen Mahoney-Bennett (Evangeline Edwards), George Gitto (Andre de Croissant), Lili Arbogast (Madame Arthur), Philip Galbraith (Hercule), Larry Grey (Alexei), Michael Vita (Count Ferdinand von Hohenadelborn-Mantalini), Lynne Charney (Clarissa Parks), Rick DeFilipps (Frenchman, Manfredo), P.J. Galbraith (Pierre Fort), Michael Ashton (Pedro Hermanos), Molly Wassermann (Bessie, Zuleika), Avril Gentles (Mrs. Samuel Lee Bamberg), Steven J. Parris (Constantine Koumoundourpolis), Lee Sloan (Kassim), Ric Stoneback (Ali), Boncellia Lewis (Haidee Robinson), Joe Hart (Ben Winthrop), Bob Riley (Joe); Ensemble: Lili Arbogast, Michael Ashton, Susan Berkson, Rick DeFilipps, Diane Drielsma, Philip Galbraith, P.J. Galbraith, Eva Grant, Josie Lawrence, Andrea Lee, Nancy Meadows, Joanna Seaton, Lee Sloan, Ric Stoneback, Cynthia Thole, Barbara Tobias, Molly Wassermann

SOURCE—The 1932 novel *Nymph Errant* by James Laver.

The action occurs over a period of one year throughout Europe and Middle East.

The musical was presented in two acts.

ACT ONE—"Coffee" (Diane Drielsma, Josie Lawrence, Kathleen Mahoney-Bennett, Gerry McCarthy, Joanna Seaton), "Experiment" (Enid Rodgers, Girls), "It's Bad for Me" (Kathleen Mahoney-Bennett, George Gitto), "Neauville-Sur-Mer" (Michael Ashton, P.J. Galbraith, Eva Grant, Molly Wassermann, Ensemble), "The Cocotte" (Lynne Charnay), "You're Too Far Away" (Larry Grey), "How Could We Be Wrong?" (Kathleen Mahoney-Bennett, Larry Grey), "They're Always Entertaining" (Lili Arbogast, Michael Ashton, Susan Berkson, Rick DeFillips, Philip Galbraith, P.J. Galbraith, Molly Wassermann, Ensemble), "Casanova" (a/k/a "Cazanova") (Diane Drielsma and Avril Gentles, with Eva Grant, Andrea Lee, Nancy Meadows, Cynthia Thole, Barbara Tobias), "Nymph Errant" (Kathleen Mahoney-Bennett)

ACT TWO—"Ruins" (Ensemble), "Greek Dance" (Rick DeFilipps [Lead], Michael Ashton, Philip Galbraith, P.J. Galbraith, Eva Grant, Andrea Lee, Nancy Meadows, Cynthia Thole, Barbara Tobias, Lili Arbogast, Molly Wassermann), "Harem Dance" (Kathleen Mahoney-Bennett [Lead], Lili Arbogast, Susan Berkson, Eva Grant, Josie Lawrence, Andrea Lee, Nancy Meadows, Cynthia Thole, Barbara Tobias), "The Physician" (Kathleen Mahoney-Bennett), "Solomon" (Boncellia Lewis), "Back to Nature with You" (Kathleen Mahoney-Bennett, Joe Hart), "Plumbing" (Joe Hart), "Tiller Routine" (Lili Arbogast, Susan Berkson, Andrea Lee, Joanna Seaton, Cynthia Thole, Molly Wassermann), "Georgia Sand" (Josie Lawrence [Lead], Lili Arbogast, Michael Ashton, Rick DeFillips, Eva Grant, Nancy Meadows, Barbara Tobias), "Si Vous Aimez Les Poitrines" (Gerry McCarthy [Lead], Lili Arbogast, Diane Drielsma, Joanna Seaton, Molly Wassermann, Rick DeFillips, Michael Ashton, Andrea Lee [Persian Poitrine], Cynthia Thole [Javanese Poitrine], Barbara Tobias [Chinese Poitrine], Eva Grant [Hindoo Poitrine]), "Experiment" (reprise) (Kathleen Mahoney-Bennett)

NOTES—With its revival of Cole Porter's 1933 West End musical *Nymph Errant*, the Equity Library Theatre offered one of its most important productions, for here was a major musical by a major composer, a work which had never before been produced in the United States. The risqué musical dealt with a young woman determined to lose her virginity, and the picaresque plot followed her sexual adventures over the period of one year as she travels throughout Europe and the Middle East. Gertrude Lawrence originated the role in London, where the musical opened at the Adelphi Theatre for a run of 154 performances (the original cast also included Elisabeth Welch and David Burns, and most of the choreography was created by Agnes de Mille).

Because of its relatively short run, the musical wasn't produced in New York, but, surprisingly, Twentieth Century-Fox bought the film rights, and in the late 1930s the company announced a film version would star Alice Faye. Considering the plot, it's hard to believe the film could have been anywhere near faithful to its source, but one can easily imagine Alice Faye's sultry, throaty voice doing full justice to "How Could We Be Wrong?" In the 1960s, Fox again announced a film version, this time with Julie Andrews in the lead. This too was never made, but in 1968 Fox released *Star!*, Gertrude Lawrence's film biography, with Andrews portraying Lawrence; in the film, Andrews sang "The Physician."

With Equity's production, New York finally got to see the most elusive of all Cole Porter musicals. John S. Wilson in the *New York Times* found the book "thin and dated," but he praised the score, one of Porter's "best."

The revival interpolated "Coffee," which had been written by Porter in the early 1930s for an unproduced musical called *Ever Yours*. Also, "You're Too Far Away," which had been dropped during the pre-London tryout of *Nymph Errant*, was used in the Equity revival. For the London production, the song "Neauville-Sur-Mer" was followed by "Beach Ball Dance" and "Ruins" was followed by a dance number called "Carefree Caryatides." The New York production included a "Greek Dance" following "Ruins" and also added "Harem Dance" and "Tiller Routine." Further, during the run of the London production the song "Georgia Sand" was dropped and "Cazanova" was added; for New York, both numbers were included (the latter as "Casanova").

During the run of the original production, a number of songs were recorded by the original cast. Lawrence recorded "Experiment," "It's Bad for Me," "How Could We Be Wrong?," "The Physician," and the title song, and Welch recorded "Solomon." A 1989 concert production of the musical at Drury Lane was recorded live and released by EMI Records (CD # CDC-7-54079-2); the cast included Elisabeth Welch (singing "Solomon" a full forty-nine years after she first introduced it), Andrea McArdle, Kaye Ballard, Larry Kert, Maureen McGovern, Lisa Kirk, Liliane Montevecchi, Alexis Smith, and Patrice Munsel (curiously, the recording included a number of performers playing the title role). The recording included "Sweet Nudity," which had been dropped during the rehearsal period of the original production; also included was "My Louisa," which had been written for (but apparently not used in) the 1929 London production of *Wake Up and Dream* (the musical was also produced on Broadway later in the same year); the song was later apparently intended for, but not used in, *Nymph Errant*.

A revised version of the musical was seen at the Chichester Festival Theatre on August 5, 1999, with a new script by Steve Mackes and Michael Whaley. The script was published by Samuel French, Inc., in 2001, and includes a number of interpolations: "They All Fall in Love" (1929 film *The Battle of Paris*); "You'd Be So Nice to Come Home To" (1943 film *Something to Shout About*); "The Great Indoors" (*The New Yorkers*, 1930); "At Long Last Love" (*You Never Know*, 1938); and "When Love Comes Your Way" (originally intended for the unproduced musical *Ever Yours*, the song was performed during the pre–London tryout of *Nymph Errant*, and was eventually heard in *Jubilee* [1935]).

1161 O Marry Me! "A New Musical." THEATRE: Gate Theatre; OPENING DATE: October 27, 1961; PERFORMANCES: 21; BOOK: Lola Pergament; LYRICS: Lola Pergament; MUSIC: Robert Kessler; DIRECTION: Michael Howard; SCENERY: Herbert Senn and Helen Pond; COSTUMES: Sam Morgenstern; LIGHTING: Herbert Senn and Helen Pond; MUSICAL DIRECTION: Lowell Farr; PRODUCER: Lily Turner

CAST—JAMES HARWOOD (Tony Lumpkin), JOE SILVER (Squire Hardcastle), MURIEL GREENSPON (Mrs. Hardcastle), Ken Golden (Little Aminidab), Maurice Edwards (Diggory), Christopher Marsh (Roger), Caroline Rausch (Pimple), Sylvia O'Brien (Bridget), Frank Echols (Dick Muggins, Sir Charles Marlow), CHEVI COLTON (Kate Hardcastle), ELLY STONE (Constance Neville), Paul Bain (Stingo), Judith Burkette (Bett Bouncer), TED VAN GRIETHUYSEN (Young Marlow), LEONARD DRUM (George Hastings)

SOURCE—The 1773 play *She Stoops to Conquer* by Oliver Goldsmith.

The action occurs during the spring of 1806 in a small English village.

The musical was presented in two acts.

ACT ONE—"I Love Everything That's Old" (Joe Silver), "Time and Tide" (Joe Silver, Muriel Greenspon, Ensemble), "The Kind of Man" (Chevi Colton), "The Kind of Man" (reprise) (Chevi Colton) "Ale House Song" (James Harwood, Paul Bain, Ensemble), "Proper Due" (James Harwood), "Be a Lover" (Ted Van Griethuysen, Leonard Drum), "Perish the Baubles" (Elly Stone, Leonard Drum), "The Meeting" (Chevi Colton, Ted Van Griethuysen), "Fashions" (Muriel Greenspon, Leonard Drum), "Fashions" (reprise) (Muriel Greenspon, James Harwood), "Say Yes, Look No" (Chevi Colton, Elly Stone, Muriel Greenspon, Caroline Rausch, Sylvia O'Brien)

ACT TWO—Prelude: "Let's All Be Exactly and Precisely What We Are" (Ensemble), "The Braggart's Song" (Ted Van Griethuysen, Chevi Colton), "O Marry Me!" (Chevi Colton), "Betrayed" (Muriel Greenspon, Elly Stone, Leonard Drum, Ted Van Griethuysen, James Harwood), "O Marry Me!" (reprise) (Chevi Colton), "Motherly Love" (Muriel Greenspon, James Harwood), "Morality" (Joe Silver), Finale (Company)

NOTES—*O Marry Me!* was another Off Broadway adaptation of a classic play; but despite its pleasant score, it wasn't successful. Arthur Gelb in the *New York Times* felt that only half of the musical was "pleasant and gay," the half which featured Elly Stone, Leonard Drum, and Ted van Griethuysen. He noted that the trio "carried the show, and whether by accident or design, has been given the best numbers to sing." With *O Marry Me!*, Elly Stone continued in her succession of flop Off Broadway musicals, but *Jacques Brel Is Alive and Well and Living in Paris* (1968; see entry) was in her future. Joe Silver also found success (in plays such as *Lenny* [1971]). As for Leonard Drum, he wrote the book, lyrics, and music for *The Kid from Philly*, a musical version of George Kelly's classic 1924 comedy *The Show-Off*. Sam Zolotow in the *New York Times* reported the musical was set to open on Broadway in March 1963, but the musical was never produced. Perhaps the most interesting performer in *O Marry Me!* was Muriel (Costa-) Greenspon, here making her New York debut. Occasionally established opera singers made forays into musical theatre (Ezio Pinza, *South Pacific* [1949] and *Fanny* [1954]; Lawrence Tibbett, *The Barrier* [1950]; Cesar Siepi, *Bravo Giovanni* [1962] and *Carmelina* [1979]), but there were also those future opera stars whose careers began in musicals, such as Costa-Greenspon, who would have a distinguished opera career, particularly with the New York City Opera, the company most associated with her. She also returned to musicals, when she played the Old Lady in New York City Opera revivals of *Candide* (see entry). (Other opera stars who started in musicals: Evelyn Lear, who made her debut in Marc Blitzstein's *Reuben Reuben* [1955], which closed in Boston prior to Broadway, and Placido Domingo, who in the late 1950s appeared in the chorus and in minor roles in American musicals produced in Mexico City. He can be heard on the Mexico City cast albums of *Mi Bella Dama* [*My Fair Lady*] and *La Peli Roja* [*Redhead*], as part of the quartet of "Wouldn't It Be Loverly?" in the former and as a soloist in "Two Faces in the Dark" in the latter.)

O Marry Me! was recorded at the time of its Off Broadway production, but wasn't commercially issued until the 1980s (by Blue Pear Records LP # BP-1016).

The musical was produced in Great Britain on June 18, 1963, at the Theatre Royal, Windsor, with a cast which included Patricia Bredin, Richard Easton, and Tony Tanner. Three songs were added for this version ("Servants Madrigal," "Come What May," and "A Man Must Choose"). The script was published in Great Britain by Chappell & Co. Ltd. in 1965.

The Two Roses, a 1904 Broadway musical adaptation of *She Stoops to Conquer*, was also a failure, closing after twenty-nine performances.

1162 O, Oysters!!! "A Revue." THEATRE: Village Gate; OPENING DATE: January 26, 1961; PERFORMANCES: 104; SKETCHES: Eric Blau; ADDITIONAL MATERIAL: Bill Heyer; LYRICS: Eric Blau; MUSIC: Doris Schwerin; ADDITIONAL MUSIC: Jacques Brel, Harold Beebe, and Danny Meehan; DIRECTION: William Francisco; CHOREOGRAPHY: Don Marsh; SCENERY: Paul Sylbert; COSTUMES: Paul Sylbert; LIGHTING: Paul Sylbert; MUSICAL DIRECTION: Harold Beebe; PRODUCERS: Art D'Lugoff, Eric Blau

CAST—Elly Stone, Zale Kessler, Louise Troy, Bill Heyer, Danny Meehan, Jon Voight

The revue was presented in two acts (sketch and song assignments unknown).

ACT ONE—"O, Oysters!," "I'm Afraid," "Big Names, Big News," "Fable of Chicken Little," "Keep Off the Grass," "Fable of Emperor and Nightingale," "Dasvadanya" (Jon Voight, Zale Kessler), "Fable of the Nightingale and the Immigration Officer," "$29.50," "Ne Me Quitte Pas" (Elly Stone), "Marching Song"

ACT TWO—"Edgar's Hoedown," "Fable of the Moth and the Flame," "Squeek," "Least of All Love," "Fable of the Analyst and the Nightingale," "Twelve Days of Christmas," "Fable of the Third Little Pig," "Carousels and Cotton Candy" (Elly Stone)

NOTES—Howard Taubman in the *New York Times* noted the revue *O, Oysters!!!* offered much that was "fresh and delightful." He singled out "Dasvadanya," in which Kennedy (Jon Voight) and Khrushchev (Zale Kessler) "trade gentle digs in a nonchalant song-and-dance style"; "Marching Song," an invocation to World War III; "Edgar's Hoedown," a square dance which comments "gaily and wickedly" on J. Edgar Hoover's longevity with the FBI; and $29.50," which dealt with take-home-pay after deductions. Another number ("Squeek") dealt with Fidel Castro. A continuing thread throughout the revue was the use of six fable-like sequences for general commentary ("Fable of Chicken Little," "Fable of Emperor and Nightingale," "Fable of the Nightingale and the Immigration Officer," "Fable of the Moth and Flame," "Fable of the Analyst and the Nightingale," and "Fable of the Third Little Pig"); Taubman reported the connecting theme of the fables was that of Chicken Little's assertion that the sky is falling.

This revue was gone in three months, but it made its mark. Of the cast members, Voight, found film stardom and an Academy Award, as did the show's designer, Paul Sylbert, who was the production designer for many hit films (*One Flew Over the Cuckoo's Nest* [1974], *Heaven Can Wait* [1978, for which he won an Academy Award], and *Kramer vs. Kramer* [1979] as well as one notorious flop, *Ishtar* [1987]). Voight had understudied and eventually performed the role of Rolf during the original New York run of *The Sound of Music* (1959), and then appeared somewhat regularly on New York stages throughout the decade. Besides *O, Oysters!!!*, he performed the role of Rodolpho in the 1965 long-running (780 performances) Off Broadway revival of *A View from the Bridge* (see entry for operatic adaptation) and was seen on Broadway in Frank D. Gilroy's *That Summer—That Fall* (1967). From there, he found his breakthrough role in the 1969 film *Midnight Cowboy*, which won the Academy Award for Best Film, and he gave memorable performances in a number of other films, including *Deliverance* (1972), *Conrack* (1974; see entry for musical adaptation), and *Coming Home* (1978, for which he won the Academy Award for Best Actor). Recently, he's appeared in the series of successful *National Treasure* films. With stage and screen careers on his resume, it would seem Voight could add television, if he so desired; his occasional appearances on *Fox and Friends* reveals an incredibly ingratiating and witty personality, and he brings to mind the halcyon days of early television talk shows of the Jack Paar and Dave Garroway variety.

Eric Blau, who conceived *O, Oysters!!!* and was its co-producer and major contributor, later co-produced and co-translated many of Belgian composer-lyricist Jacques Brel's songs for what would become one of the most successful revues in Off Broadway history, *Jacques Brel Is Alive and Well and Living in Paris* (1968; see entry). Perhaps Brel's "La Valse a Mille Temps" (called "Carousels and Cotton Candy" in *O, Oysters!!!*) inspired Blau to develop the revue which became *Jacques Brel*. "Carousels and Cotton Candy" was sung by Elly Stone (who also sang another Brel song in *Oysters!!!*, "Ne Me Quitte Pas"), and the song reappeared in *Jacques Brel*, this time as "Carousel," and was again sung by Elly Stone, who can be heard performing it on *Jacques Brel*'s original cast album. Oddly enough, between the engagements of *O, Oysters!!!* and *Jacques Brel Is Alive and Well and Living in Paris*, the song was also heard on Broadway as "Days of the Waltz" (lyric by Will Holt) in Lawrence Roman's *P.S. I Love You*, a forgotten comedy from 1964 which played for twelve performances. Well, not quite forgotten. Almost forty-five years after the show's closing, the play's memorable poster artwork (by one Chava) was included in a 2008 calendar of reproductions of twelve window cards released by Pomegranate Press from the window card and poster collection of the Library of Congress; not only was the artwork for *P.S. I Love You* included for the month of December 2008, it was also featured on the calendar's cover.

1163 O Say Can You See! "An Affectionate Look at a Hollywood Musical of the 1940's." THEATRE: Provincetown Playhouse; OPENING DATE: October 8, 1962; PERFORMANCES: 32; BOOK: Bill Conklin and Bob Miller; LYRICS: Bill Conklin and Bob Miller; MUSIC: Jack Holmes; DIRECTION: "Production Staged" by Ray Harrison; "Book Directed" by Cynthia Baer; CHOREOGRAPHY: Ray Harrison; SCENERY: Jack H. Cornwell; COSTUMES: Jane Kip Stevens; LIGHTING: Jules Fisher; MUSICAL DIRECTION: Jack Holmes; PRODUCERS: The Greenville Company; Aaron Goldblatt, Associate Producer

CAST—JOEL WARFIELD (Joey Armstrong), NICOLAS COSTER (Ronnie Winterhamm), PAUL B. PRICE (Brooklyn), JOYCE KERRY (Veronica Van Whitney), ELMARIE WENDEL (Gladys Applebee), JAN CHANEY (Lt. Betty Smith), Richard Neilson (Agent), Thomas Gaines (Sergeant Duke), T.J. Halligan (General Ulysses S. Smith), Lee Delmer (Squad Member), Mike Douglas (Squad Member), Jerry Mattison (Squad Member), Sally Ackerman (Girl), Sallie Brinsmade (Girl), Marcia Rodd (Girl), Carolyn Wilmshurst (Girl)

The action occurs during the War Forties.

The musical was presented in two acts.

ACT ONE—"The Freedom Choo Choo Is Leaving Today" (Company), "Dreamboat from Dreamland" (Nicolas Coster, Harmonaires), "The Dogface Jive" (Thomas Gaines, Lee Delmer, Mike Douglas, Jerry Mattison), "Us Two" (Jan Chaney, T.J. Halligan), "Take Me Back to Texas" (Jan Chaney, Sally Ackerman, Sallie Brinsmade, Marcia Rodd, Carolyn Wilmshurst), "Doughnuts for Defense" (Elmarie Wendel), "Canteen Serenade" (Company), "These Are Worth Fighting For" (Joel Warfield, Nicolas Coster, Paul B. Price), "Someone a Lot Like You" (Jan Chaney, Joel Warfield), "Veronica Takes Over" (Joyce Kerry), "Buy Bonds, Buster, Buy Bonds" (Nicolas Coster, Company)

ACT TWO—"Chico-Chico Chico-Layo Tico-Tico Pay-Pa-Payo Buena Vista de Banana by-the-Sea" (Elmarie Wendel), "Us Two" (reprise) (Jan Chaney, T.J. Halligan), "Flim Flam Flooey" (Joyce Kerry, Sally Ackerman, Sallie Brinsmade, Marcia Rodd, Carolyn Wilmshurst), "Someone a Lot Like You" (reprise) (Joel Warfield), "When the Bluebirds Fly All Over the World" (Jan Chaney, Joel Warfield), "Just the Way You Are" (Elmarie Wendel, Paul B. Price), "My G.I. Joey" (Jan Chaney), "O Say Can You See!" (Company)

NOTES—Two weeks after *Sweet Miani* (see entry) spoofed South Sea Island movies, *O Say Can You See!* offered a send-up of War Forties movie musicals. Both shows lasted about a month, but at least the latter left a cast album. It was recorded in 1962, but wasn't released until the 1970s (by Sunbeam Music, Inc., Records [LP # XTV-87195-6]); it later was issued on CD by AEI Records (# AEI-CD-034).

The score for *O Say Can You See!* is delightful, and perhaps its two best numbers are "Someone a Lot Like You," a sweet ballad with an undertone of aching melancholy, and "Just the Way You Are," a wacky tongue-twisting tribute to the Betty Hutton-styled songs of the era. The CD added "Us Two" and its reprise, both of which were deleted during the show's run but which were later recorded by other performers.

In 1972, a revised version of *O Say Can You See!* opened Off Broadway. Now titled *Buy Bonds, Buster*, it shuttered after one performance (see entry). The following numbers were written for *Buy Bonds, Buster*: "Pearl," "So Long for Now," "Tan 'n' Fit," "The Woogie Boogie," "Now and Then," "Hat Crossover," and, last but not least, "The Master Race Polka." Carried over from *O Say Can You See!* were "The Freedom Choo Choo Is Leaving Today," "Dreamboat from Dreamland," "Us Two," "Doughnuts for Defense," "Canteen Serenade," "These Are Worth Fighting For," "Buy Bonds, Buster, Buy Bonds," "Chico Chico Chico-Layo Tico-Tico Pay-Pa-Payo Buena Vista de Banana by-the-Sea," "When the Bluebirds Fly All Over the World," "My G.I. Joey," and "O Say Can You See!" Omitted were "The Dogface Jive," "Take Me Back to Texas," "Veronica Takes Over," "Flim Flam Flooey," and, unaccountably, the score's two best numbers, "Someone a Lot Like You" and "Just the Way You Are."

Retro musicals dealing with the World War II era never had much luck on Broadway or off. Both *O Say Can You See!* and *Buy Bonds, Buster* failed, and in 1971 Goodspeed Opera House offered *Hubba Hubba*, which seems to have gone nowhere after its East Haddam, Connecticut, engagement.

1971 also saw Richard M. and Robert B. Sherman's *Victory Canteen*, which never got beyond regional theater; its star was an authentic 1940s presence, Patty Andrews, of the Andrews Sisters. The Sherman Brothers later started from scratch with another musical about the era, *Over Here!* (1974). Despite Will Holt's witty book, a catchy score, a fascinating cast (this time with two authentic stars from the World War II era [Patty and Maxene Andrews] as well as many future stars [Ann Reinking, John Travolta, Treat Williams, Marilu Henner]), just-right Technicolor-bright scenery and costumes, and dazzling choreography, *Over Here!* didn't last a full year on Broadway and apparently lost a good deal of its investment. Incidentally, Janie Sell, who had earlier appeared in *Hubba Hubba*, played the "third" Andrews Sister in *Over Here!* and won a Tony Award for Best Featured Actress in a Musical for her riotous portrayal of Mitzi (who turns out to be a Nazi!). Mitzi is exposed as a spy because she knows all the words of the "Star Spangled Banner" (as another character points out, no *real* American knows the words of the second verse of the national anthem).

The vastly underrated, surreal *Swing* (1980) fared even worse, closing during its pre-Broadway tryout (it had its own Betty Hutton tribute in "A Girl Can Go Wacky"); see entry for *Dream Time*, an Off Broadway version of *Swing*.

1164 Of Mice and Men (1958; Alfred Brooks). "A New Musical Drama." THEATRE: Provincetown Playhouse; OPENING DATE: December 4, 1958; PERFORMANCES: 37; BOOK: Ira J. Bilowit and Wilson Lehr; LYRICS: Ira J. Bilowit; MUSIC: Alfred Brooks; DIRECTION: Jerome Eskow; CHOREOGRAPHY: "Dance movement" by Zoya Leporska; SCENERY: Charles A. Brandon; COSTUMES: Charles A. Brandon; LIGHTING: Charles A. Brandon; MUSICAL DIRECTION: Samuel Matlowsky; PRODUCERS: Ira J. Bilowit in association with Unicorn Productions

CAST—LEO PENN (George), ART LUND (Lennie), Lorrie Bentley (Waitress), JOHN F. HAMILTON (Candy), John Marriott (Crooks), Tom Noel (Carlson), Tony Kraber (Slim), Kenny Adams (Whit), Byrne Piven (Curley), JO SULLIVAN (Curley's Wife)

SOURCES—John Steinbeck's novel and play *Of Mice and Men* (both 1937).

The action occurs "yesterday" in California. The musical was presented in two acts.

ACT ONE—"Nice House We Got Here" (Art Lund), "No Ketchup" (Art Lund), "We Got a Future" (Leo Penn, Art Lund), "Nice House We Got Here" (reprise) (Leo Penn, Art Lund), "Buckin' Barley" (Ranchhands), "Curley's Wife" (Ranchhands), "Wanta, Hope to Feel at Home" (Jo Sullivan), "Lemme Tell Ya" (John F. Hamilton), "Just Someone to Talk To" (Jo Sullivan), "Dudin' Up" (Ranchhands), "Nice Fella" (Leo Penn, Tony Kraber), "Why Try Hard to Be Good" (Jo Sullivan)

ACT TWO—"Never Do a Bad Thing" (Art Lund), "We Got a Future" (reprise) (Leo Penn, Art Lund), "Is There Someplace for Me" (John F. Hamilton), "A Guy, A Guy, A Guy" (Leo Penn), "Strangely" (Jo Sullivan), "Candy's Lament" (John F. Hamilton), "We Got a Future" (reprise) (Leo Penn, Art Lund)

NOTES—Louis Calta in the *New York Times* felt the musical version of John Steinbeck's novel and play *Of Mice and Men* never matched the "distinction" of the source material, and he found the score lacking "the necessary passion, grandeur and breadth" to tell the tragic story of the mentally retarded vagrant Lennie, his friend George, and the unhappy wife of the farmer for whom they work. The role of the waitress was eliminated during the run, and the song "Candy's Lament" was deleted. The musical proved to be a short-lived reunion for Jo Sullivan and Art Lund, who had memorably created the roles of Amy/Rosabella and Joey in the original Broadway production of *The Most Happy Fella* (1956). A more successful musical version of the material was Carlisle Floyd's affecting 1970 opera *Of Mice and Men* (libretto also by Floyd); see entry. Unlike so many American operas which seem to disappear almost immediately after their premieres, the opera is still produced. Two Broadway adaptations of Steinbeck's work have failed. Despite its wonderful score by Richard Rodgers and Oscar Hammerstein II, *Pipe Dream* (1955), based on *Sweet Thursday,* was the team's shortest-running Broadway musical; thankfully, the score was preserved on the cast album issued by RCA Victor. And Robert Waldman and Alfred Uhry's *Here's Where I Belong*, a 1968 adaptation of *East of Eden*, played for just one performance. There has also been an operatic adaptation of Steinbeck's 1950 novel and play *Burning Bright.* With libretto and music by Frank Lewin, *Burning Bright* premiered at Yale University in November 1993; the opera was recorded on a 2-CD set by Albany Records.

On February 10, 2007, Ricky Ian Gordon's operatic setting of Steinbeck's 1939 novel *The Grapes of Wrath* premiered at the Minnesota Opera. Mark Swed in the *Los Angeles Times* praised Michael Korie's "strong, literate" libretto and noted that Gordon had a "limitless reserve" of song for the hapless but ever hopeful Joad family; he felt Gordon's "great achievement" was to merge the musical worlds of Broadway and the opera house.

1165 Of Mice and Men (1983; Carlisle Floyd). THEATRE: New York State Theatre; OPENING DATE: October 13, 1983; PERFORMANCES: Unknown; TEXT: Carlisle Floyd; MUSIC: Carlisle Floyd; DIRECTION: Frank Corsaro; SCENERY: Robert O'-Hearn Musical Direction: Christopher Keene; PRODUCER: The New York City Opera

CAST—Cast members included Robert Moulson (Lennie), Lawrence Cooper (George), James Stith (Candy), Carol Gutknecht (Curley's Wife), Robert McFarland (Slim)

SOURCE—The 1937 novel and play *Of Mice and Men* by John Steinbeck.

The action occurs in Salinas Valley, California, in the 1930s.

The opera was performed in three acts.

NOTES—The belated premiere of Carlisle Floyd's impressive operatic setting of John Steinbeck's *Of Mice and Men* occurred thirteen years after it had been originally scheduled to open at the New York City Opera in 1970. Instead, the world premiere occurred on January 22, 1970, at the Seattle Opera. From there, *Of Mice and Men* was produced by such companies as the Central City Opera and the Houston Grand Opera. The New York premiere finally took place in 1983, when the opera was produced by the New York City Opera; the cast included Robert Moulson (who had created the role of Lennie for the world premiere in Seattle). The work has since been revived by the New York City Opera.

In reviewing the New York premiere, Donal Henahan in the *New York Times* felt the score was "feeble" and for the most part employed music as a "mood-setter." He also felt the opera was a "paean" to male-bonding and was a "fiercely antifemale tract." He added that rather than the opera he wished that the 1939 film version of Steinbeck's story had been shown. He further noted that in one sequence a brown dog ("unnamed in the program") stole a scene "just by wagging its tail." In 2003, Albany Records released a 2-CD set of the opera, performed by the Houston Grand Opera (# TROY-621/22).

1166 Of Thee I Sing. "The Pulitzer Prize 30's Musical." THEATRE: New Anderson Theatre; OPENING DATE: March 7, 1969; PERFORMANCES: 21; BOOK: George S. Kaufman and Morrie Ryskind; LYRICS: Ira Gershwin; MUSIC: George Gershwin; DIRECTION: Marvin Gordon; CHOREOGRAPHY: Michael C. Penta; SCENERY: Bob Olson; COSTUMES: James Bidgood; LIGHTING: William Marshall; MUSICAL DIRECTION: Leslie Harnley; PRODUCER: Musical Heritage Productions

CAST—Edward Penn (Senator Robert E. Lyons), Sandy Sprung (Frances X. Gilhooley), Jeannie Johnson (Chambermaid, Tourist, Ensemble), William Martel (Matthew Arnold Fulton), John Aman (Senator Carver Jones), Lloyd Hubbard (Alexander Throttlebottom), Hal Holden (John P. Wintergreen), Katie Anders (Diana Devereaux), Danny Franklin (Sam Jenkins), Joyce Orlando (Emily Benson), Joy Franz (Mary Turner), Bob Freschi (The Chief Justice, Ensemble), Richard Stack (The Guide, The Doctor, Ensemble), Gayle Swymer (Tourist, Ensemble), Larry Whiteley (The French Ambassador), Dorothy Lister (Scrubwoman, Ensemble), Ronald Dennis (The Senate Clerk, Ensemble), Joan Ashlyn (Ensemble), Linda Larsen (Ensemble), Robert Yarri (Ensemble)

Most of the action occurs in Washington, D.C. The musical was presented in two acts.

ACT ONE—"Wintergreen for President" (Company), "Because" (Katie Anders, Danny Franklin, Ensemble), Finaletto for Scene Three (Hal Holden, Katie Anders, the Committee, Ensemble), "Love Is Sweeping the Country" (Danny Franklin, Joyce Orlando, Ensemble), "Of Thee I Sing" (Hal Holden, Joy Franz, Ensemble), Finale for Act One (Company)

ACT TWO—"Hello, Good Morning" (Danny Franklin, Joyce Orlando, Ensemble), "Who Cares?" (Hal Holden, Joy Franz, the Committee, Male Ensemble), "The Illegitimate Daughter"; Finaletto for Scene One (French Entourage, Larry Whiteley, Hal Holden, Joy Franz, Katie Anders, Ensemble), "Love Is Sweeping the Country" (reprise) (Joy Franz, Hal Holden), "The Illegitimate Daughter" (reprise); "Jilted" (Larry Whiteley, Katie Anders, Ensemble), "Mary's Announcement" (Joy Franz, Ensemble), "Posterity" (Hal Holden, Joy Franz, Company), "Trumpeter, Blow Your Golden Horn" (Joyce Orlando, Danny Franklin, Female Ensemble), Finale (Company)

NOTES—The Gershwins' classic score for *Of Thee I Sing* should have ensured the revival a much longer run. Perhaps the tenor of the times wasn't favorable towards this genial political satire, which eschewed trendy anti-war and other "relevant" updates.

The musical dealt with John P. Wintergreen's campaign for the presidency, including an Atlantic City beauty contest to pick the winner of First Lady, whom Wintergreen pledges to marry. His campaign slogan is "love," and although Diana Devereaux wins the contest, Wintergreen falls in love with Mary Turner, whom he marries. This sets off an international incident when it's revealed Diana is of French ancestry; Wintergreen's marriage to Mary is considered a slap in the face to France.

Of Thee I Sing was the first musical to win the Pulitzer Prize for drama, and the original production, which opened on December 26, 1931, at the Music Box Theatre, ran for 441 performances; William Gaxton was Wintergreen; Victor Moore, Throttlebottom; Lois Moran, Mary; and Grace Brinkley, Diana Devereaux. A return engagement on May 15, 1933, at the Imperial Theatre played for thirty-two performances (Gaxton and Moore reprised their original roles; Harriette Lake [Ann Sothern] was Mary; and Betty Allen, Diana Devereaux). The 1952 Broadway revival, which opened on May 5 at the Ziegfeld Theatre, ran for seventy-two performances, and a limited engagement of the musical and its sequel, *Let 'Em Eat Cake* (1933; see entries for both productions) opened at the Brooklyn Academy of Music in 1987. There have been three recordings of the score. The 1952 Broadway revival was recorded by Capitol Records (LP # S-350; issued on CD by Broadway Angel Records [# ZMD-2435-65025-2-9] and then later by DRG Records [19024]); Jack Carson was Wintergreen; Paul Hartman, Throttlebottom; Betty Oakes, Mary; and Lenore Lonergan, Diana Devereaux. It seems Victor Moore was set to reprise his Throttlebottom for the 1952 revival, but instead Paul Hartman appeared in the role; if Moore had been in the production, the cast album would have preserved his classic performance for posterity. A 1972 CBS television adaptation was released Columbia Records (LP # S-31763); Carroll O'Connor was Wintergreen; Jack Gilford, Throttlebottom; Cloris Leachman, Mary; and Michele Lee, Diana Devereaux. The 1987 revival by the Brooklyn Academy of Musical was issued on a 2-LP and 2-CD set by CBS Records (LP # S2M-422522; CD # M2K-42522); Larry Kert was Wintergreen; Jack Gilford, Throttlebottom; Maureen McGovern, Mary; and Paige O'Hara, Diana Devereaux. (Both the 1952 Broadway revival and the 1972 television version interpolated "Mine," which had originally been introduced in *Let 'Em Eat Cake*).

Of Thee I Sing's script was published by Alfred A. Knopf in 1932, and was the first Broadway musical to be printed in hardback book format; the script was later published in a softback acting edition by Samuel French, Inc, and in the hardback collection *Ten Great Musicals of the American Theatre* (Chilton Book Company, 1973; edited by Stanley Richards).

See entry for the Brooklyn Academy of Music's revival.

1167 Of Thee I Sing (1987). THEATRE: Opera House/Brooklyn Academy of Music; OPENING DATE: March 18, 1987; PERFORMANCES: 8 (estimated); BOOK: George S. Kaufman and Morrie Ryskind; LYRICS: Ira Gershwin; MUSIC: George Gershwin; DIRECTION: Maurice Levine; SCENERY: Eduardo Sicangco; COSTUMES: Eduardo Sicangco; LIGHTING: Jeff Davis; MUSICAL DIRECTION: Michael Tilson Thomas; John McGlinn, Guest Conductor; PRODUCER: Brooklyn Academy of Music (Harvey Lichtenstein, President and Executive Director)

CAST—JACK GILFORD (Alexander Throttlebottom), LARRY KERT (John P. Wintergreen), MAUREEN MCGOVERN (Mary Turner), PAIGE O'HARA (Diana Devereaux), Jack Dabdoub (French Ambassador), George Dvorsky (Sam Jenkins, Clerk), Louise Edeiken (Miss Benson, Mrs. Fulton), Merwin Goldsmith (Louis Lippman), Walter Hook (Senator Robert E. Lyons), Frank Kopyc (Francis X. Gilhooley), Casper Roos (The Chief Justice), Raymond Thorne (Matthew Arnold Fulton), Mark Zimmerman (Senator Carver Jones); The New York Choral Artists (Paraders, Flunkeys)

The action occurs on "Main Street" and in Atlantic City, New York City, and Washington, D.C. The musical was presented in two acts.

ACT ONE—"Wintergreen for President" (Ensemble), "Who Is the Lucky Girl to Be?" (Paige O'Hara, Ensemble), "The Dimple on My Knee" (Paige O'Hara, Ensemble), "Because, Because" (Ensemble), "Exit Atlantic City Scene" (Paige O'Hara, Larry Kert, Ensemble), Finaletto Act I, Scene IV, "Never Was There a Girl So Fair" (Ensemble), "Some Girls Can Bake a Pie" (Larry Kert, Paige O'Hara, Ensemble), "Love Is Sweeping the Country" (George Dvorsky, Louise Edeiken, Ensemble), "Of Thee I Sing" (Larry Kert, Maureen McGovern, Ensemble), Finale Act I (Company), "A Kiss for Cinderella" (Larry Kert, Ensemble)

ACT TWO—"Hello, Good Morning" (Geroge Dvorsky, Louise Edeiken, Ensemble), "Who Cares?" (Larry Kert, Maureen McGovern, Ensemble), "The Illegitimate Daughter" (Larry Kert, Maureen McGovern, Paige O'Hara, Jack Dabdoub, Ensemble), "The Senator from Minnesota" (Jack Gilford, Ensemble), "The Senate" (Jack Gilford, Paige O'Hara, Larry Kert, Maureen McGovern, Jack Dabdoub, Ensemble), "Jilted" (Paige O'Hara, Ensemble), "Posterity Is Just Around the Corner" (Larry Kert, Maureen McGovern, Ensemble), "Trumpeter Blow Your Golden Horn" (Ensemble), Finale Ultimo (Company)

NOTES—For part of its 1987 *Gershwin Gala*, the Brooklyn Academy of Music presented an unprecedented and welcome treat, a double-bill concert presentation of two political musicals by George and Ira Gershwin, *Of Thee I Sing* (1931) and its sequel *Let 'Em Eat Cake* (1933). The first half of the evening was comprised of the two acts of the former musical, and the second act of the bill the two acts of the latter. The complete performance lasted approximately three and one half hours.

Of Thee I Sing was a satire of American politics, and dealt with John P. Wintergreen's campaign for the presidency, including an Atlantic City beauty contest to pick the winner of First Lady, whom Wintergreen pledges to marry. His campaign slogan is "love," and although Diana Devereaux wins the contest, Wintergreen falls in love with Mary Turner, whom he marries. This sets off an international incident when it's revealed Diana is of French ancestry; Wintergreen's marriage to Mary is considered a slap in the face to France. The merry musical played for over a year and was the first musical to win the Pulitzer Prize.

For more information about *Of Thee I Sing* (including recordings of the score), see entry for the 1969 Off Broadway revival. For more information about *Let 'Em Eat Cake*, see entry.

The Brooklyn Academy of Music's revival was recorded on a 2-LP and 2-CD set by CBS Records (LP # 52M-422522 and CD # M2K-42522), and while *Of Thee I Sing* had enjoyed earlier recordings, the revival marked the first one for *Let 'Em Eat Cake*. Moreover, the recording preserved Jack Gilford's second performance as Vice President Alexander Throttlebottom; he had earlier performed the role in a 1972 television version which had also been recorded (see entry for 1969 Off Broadway revival for more information).

The Gershwins also wrote a third political musical (not related to *Of Thee I Sing* and *Let 'Em Eat Cake*). *Strike Up the Band* had first been produced in 1927, but closed during its pre-Broadway tryout; a revised version opened on Broadway at the Times Square Theatre on January 14, 1930, and played for 191 performances. The musical dealt with an international incident involving tainted chocolate (tainted cheese in the 1927 version).

1168 Oh! Calcutta! (1969). "An Entertainment with Music." THEATRE: Eden Theatre; OPENING DATE: June 17, 1969; PERFORMANCES: 704; SKETCHES: Samuel Beckett, Jules Feiffer, Dan Greenburg, John Lennon, Jacques Levy, Leonard Melfi, David Newman and Robert Benton, Sam Shepard, Clovis Trouille, Kenneth Tynan, and Sherman Yellen; production "devised" by Kenneth Tynan; LYRICS: The Open Window; MUSIC: The Open Window; DIRECTION: Jacques Levy; CHOREOGRAPHY: Margo Sappington; SCENERY: James Tilton; projected media design by Gardner Compton and Emile Ardolino; still photography by Michael Childers; COSTUMES: Fred Voelpel; LIGHTING: David Segal; PRODUCERS: Hillard Elkins in association with Michael White and Gordon Crowe

CAST—Raina Barrett, Mark Dempsey, Katie Drew-Wilkinson, Boni Enten, Bill Macy, Alan Rachins, Leon Russom, Margo Sappington, Nancy Tribush, George Welbes; The Open Window (Robert Dennis, Peter Schickele, and Stanley Walden)

The revue was presented in two acts.

ACT ONE—Prologue, "Taking Off the Robe" (Company), "Oh! Calcutta!" (Company), "Dick and Jane" (Alan Rachins, Nancy Tribush), "Suite for Five Letters" (Dear Editor) (Mark Dempsey, Katie Drew-Wilkinson, Boni Enten, Nancy Tribush, George Welbes), "Will Answer All Sincere Replies" (Bill Macy, Leon Russom, Margo Sappington, Nancy Tribush), "Paintings of Clovis Trouille" (The Open Window), "Jack and Jill" (Boni Enten, George Welbes), "Delicious Indignities" (Mark Dempsey, Katie Drew-Wilkinson), "Was It Good for You Too?" (Raina Barrett, Mark Dempsey, Boni Enten, Bill Macy, Alan Rachins, Nancy Tribush)

ACT TWO—"Much Too Soon" (Company), "One on One" (Margo Sappington, George Welbes), "Rock Garden" (Leon Russom, Bill Macy), "Who: Whom" (Mark Dempsey, Katie Drew-Wilkinson, Nancy Tribush), "Four in Hand" (George Welbes, Leon Russom, Alan Rachins, Bill Macy), "Coming Together, Going Together" (Company)

NOTES—*Hair* (see entry) had introduced brief nudity on a dimly-lit stage, and so it was only a matter of time before full-fledged nudity became commonplace in the theatre. *Oh! Calcutta!* became the first mainstream musical to present full-length scenes of full-monty nudity on a brightly lit stage.

But *Oh! Calcutta!* was a hopelessly inept bit of pretentious nonsense, which didn't even have the courage to be openly pornographic. Surely even sleazy "adult" films of the era had more integrity than this smarmy and puerile revue, whose very own writers wouldn't own up to their specific contributions.

The wonder of *Oh! Calcutta!* is that it was actually taken seriously by many critics and theatergoers. But, then, this was an era in which one film critic wrote that he was glad to hear more and more four-letter words in mainstream films. So with standards going out the window, how could *Oh! Calcutta!* have failed to be a hit? During previews, material was also credited to Maria Irene Fornes, Bruce Jay Friedman, David Mercer, Edna O'Brien, and Tennessee Williams. Either their contributions were gone by opening night, or perhaps their sketches remained but they didn't want any general program credit. The sequences "I'll Shoot Your Dog If You Don't" and "Anybody Out There Want It?" were dropped during previews.

Oh! Calcutta! played for 704 performances Off Broadway, and then in 1971 transferred to Broadway at the Belasco Theatre for an additional 606 performances. In 1976, it was revived at the Edison Theatre and played for 5,959 performances (see entry). It marathon run was attributed to non-English-speaking tourists who could nevertheless "understand" the show. The cast album was released by Aidart Records (LP # AID-9903); other recordings include the original Australian cast (RCA Camden Records [LP # INTS-1178]) and an album of songs from the revue titled *Oh! Calcutta! And the Best of Salvation* (Polydor Records LP # 2371-103]; see entry for *Salvation*. The script was published by Grove Press, Inc., in 1969. A film version, released by Tigon Films in 1972 and directed by Jacques Levy, was later issued on DVD. A London production which opened during the 1970-1971 season enjoyed a long run.

1169 Oh! Calcutta! (1976). THEATRE: Edison Theatre; OPENING DATE: September 24, 1976; PERFORMANCES: 5,959; DIRECTION: Jacques Levy; CHOREOGRAPHY: Margo Sappington; SCENERY: James Tilton; COSTUMES: Kenneth M. Yount; LIGHTING: Harry Silverglat; MUSICAL DIRECTION: Stanley Walden; PRODUCERS: Hillard Elkins, Norman Kean, and Robert S. Fishko

CAST—Haru Aki, Jean Andalman, Bill Bass, Dorothy Chansky, Cress Darwin, John Hammil, William Knight, Cy Moore, Pamela Pilkenton, Peggy Jean Waller

NOTES—The revival of *Oh! Calcutta!* enjoyed a marathon run, which was attributed in part to the attendance of large numbers of non-English-speaking tourists who could nevertheless "understand" the show. See entry for the original production for a list of musical numbers. Many of the original numbers were heard in the revival, although they underwent a certain amount of re-ordering.

There were five new sequences ("Clarence," "Spread Your Love Around," "Love Lust Poem," "Playin'," and "Dance for George" [the latter dedicated to the memory of George Welbes, who had appeared in the original production]). For the revival, four sequences were omitted (the title song, "Dick and Jane," "Who: Whom," and "Four in Hand"). Although Samuel Beckett was credited as a contributor to the original production, his name wasn't included in the revival's credits; further, Leonore Kandel was a new contributor to the revue. The Open Window (Robert Dennis, Peter Schickele, and Stanley Walden) was credited for the music in the 1969 production as well as the revival (however, the revival also credited separate [but unidentified] musical contributions by Stanley Walden and Jacques Levy).

For the first few months of its run, the revival alternated with *Me and Bessie* (which had opened at the Ambassador Theatre in 1975 and which later transferred to the Edison). According to *Best Plays*, *Oh! Calcutta!* sometimes played under a Middle (or Limited) Broadway contract, and occasionally gave ten performances a week (two more than the standard Broadway contract).

1170 Oh Coward! "A New Musical Comedy Revue." THEATRE: New Theatre; OPENING DATE: October 4, 1972; PERFORMANCES: 294; TEXT: Noel Coward; LYRICS: Noel Coward; MUSIC: Noel Coward; DIRECTION: Roderick Cook; SCENERY: Helen Pond and Herbert Senn; MUSICAL DIRECTION: Rene Wiegert; PRODUCER: Wroderick Productions

CAST—Barbara Cason, Roderick Cook, Jamie Ross

The revue was presented in two acts.

ACT ONE—Introduction: "The Boy Actor" (Barbara Cason, Jamie Ross, Roderick Cook), Oh Coward! (songs in this sequence sung by Barbara Cason, Jamie Ross, Roderick Cook): "Something to Do with Spring" (from *Words and Music*, 1932 [London]; opened in New York as *Set to Music* [1938]) "Bright Young People" (*Cochran's 1931 Revue* [London]), "Poor Little Rich Girl" (*On with the Dance*, 1925 [London]), "Ziegeuner" (*Bitter Sweet*, 1929 [London]; New York, 1929), "Let's Say Goodbye" (*Words and Music*, 1932 [London]; opened in New York as *Set to Music* [1938]) "This Is a Changing World" (*Pacific 1860*, 1946 [London]) "We Were Dancing" (*To-Night at 8:30/We Were Dancing*, 1936 [London]; New York, 1936), "Dance, Little Lady" (*This Year of Grace!*, 1928 [London]; New York, 1928), "A Room with a View" (*This Year of Grace!*, 1928 [London]; New York, 1928), "Sail Away" (*Ace of Clubs*, 1950 [London]; also used in *Sail Away*, 1961 [New York], 1962 [London]); England: "London Pastoral" (Jamie Ross), "That Is the End of the News" (*Sigh No More*, 1945 [London]) (Barbara Cason, Roderick Cook), "The Stately Homes of England" (*Operette*, 1938 [London]) (Jamie Ross, Roderick Cook), "London Pride" (*Up and Doing* {Second Edition], 1941 [London]) (Barbara Cason); Family Album: "Auntie Jessie" (possibly "Jessie Hooper" from *Charlot's Revue* [1924], London; New York [1926] as *Charlot's Revue of 1926*) (Roderick Cook), "Uncle Harry" (independent song, 1944; later added to *Pacific 1860* [1946], London) (Babara Cason, Jamie Ross); Music Hall: Introduction (Roderick Cook), "Chase Me, Charlie" (*Ace of Clubs*, 1950 [London]) Barbara Cason), "Saturday Night at the Rose and Crown" (*The Girl Who Came to Supper*, 1963 [New York]) (Barbara Cason, Jamie Ross, Roderick Cook), "Island of Bolamazoo" (*Operette*, 1938 [London]) (Jamie Ross), "What Ho, Mrs. Brisket!" (*The Girl Who Came to Supper*, 1963 [New York]) (Roderick Cook), "Has Anybody Seen Our Ship?" (*To-Night at 8:30/Red Peppers*, 1936 [London]; New York, 1936) (Barbara Cason, Jamie Ross, Roderick Cook), "Men About Town" (*To-Night at 8:30/Red Peppers*, 1936 [London]; New York, 1936) (Jamie Ross, Roderick Cook), "If Love Were All" (*Bitter Sweet*, 1929 [London]; New York, 1929) Barbara Cason); Travel: "Too Early or Too Late" (Roderick Cook), "Why Do the Wrong People Travel?" (*Sail Away*, 1961 [New York]; London, 1962) (Barbara Cason, Jamie Ross), "The Passenger's Always Right" (*Sail Away*, 1961 [New York]; London, 1962) (Barbara Cason, Jamie Ross, Roderick Cook), "Don't Put Your Daughter on the Stage, Mrs. Worthington" (independent song, 1936) (Barbara Cason, Jamie Ross, Roderick Cook)

ACT TWO—"Mad Dogs and Englishmen" (*The Third Little Show*, 1931 [New York]; later heard in London revue *Words and Music* [1932], which opened in New York as *Set to Music* [1938]) (Barbara Cason, Jamie Ross, Roderick Cook); A Marvelous Party: "The Party's Over Now" (*Words and Music*, 1932 [London]); opened in New York as *Set to Music* [1938]) (Roderick Cook); Design for Dancing: "Dance, Little Lady" (*This Year of Grace!*, 1928 [London]; New York, 1928) (Barbara Cason, Jamie Ross, Roderick Cook), "You Were There" (*To-Night at 8:30/Shadow Play*, 1936 [London]; New York, 1936) (Jamie Ross); Theatre: "Three White Feathers" (*Words and Music*, 1932; opened in New York as *Set to Music* (1938)] (Barbara Cason, Roderick Cook), "The Star" (Jamie Ross), "The Critic" (Roderick Cook), "The Elderly Actress" (Barbara Cason); Love: "Gertie" (Roderick Cook), "Loving" (Jamie Ross), "I Am No Good at Love" (dropped during the tryout of *Sail Away*, 1961 [New York]) (Roderick Cook), "Sex Talk" (Jamie Ross), "A Question of Lighting" (Jamie Ross, Barbara Cason), "Mad About the Boy" (*Words and Music*, 1932 [London]; opened in New York as *Set to Music* [1938]) (Barbara Cason); Women: Introduction (Roderick Cook), "Nina" (independent song, early 1940s; later used in *Sigh No More*, 1945 [London]) (Jamie Ross), "Mrs. Wentworth-Brewster" (Roderick Cook), "World Weary" (introduced in the New York production of *This Year of Grace!*, 1928) (Barbara Cason, Jamie Ross, Roderick Cook), "Let's Do It" (1940s; Noel Coward wrote a parody of the song written by Cole Porter for *Paris*, 1928 [New York]; Porter's song was also included in the London revue *Wake Up and Dream* [1929]) (Barbara Cason, Jamie Ross, Roderick Cook); Finale: "Where Are the Songs We Sung?" (*Operette*, 1938 [London]) (Jamie Ross), "Someday I'll Find You" (*Private Lives*, 1930 [London]; New York, 1931) (Roderick Cook), "I'll Follow My Secret Heart" (*Conversation Piece*, 1934 [London]; New York, 1934; see entry for the Off Broadway production of *Conversation Piece*) (Barbara Cason), "If Love Were All" (reprise; from *Bitter Sweet*, 1929 [London]; New York, 1929) (Barbara Cason, Jamie Ross, Roderick Cook), "Play, Orchestra, Play" (*To-Night at 8:30/Shadow Play*, 1936 [London]; New York, 1936) (Barbara Cason, Jamie Ross, Roderick Cook), "I'll See You Again" (*Bitter Sweet*, 1929 [London]; New York, 1929) (Barbara Cason, Jamie Ross, Roderick Cook)

NOTES—*Oh Coward!* was a classy and intimate revue sung by Barbara Cason, Jamie Ross, and Roderick Cook, three expert interpreters of Noel Coward. The evening was all the more welcome because Coward's work, although familiar, wasn't overexposed. As a result, the revue played almost three-hundred performances, and a 2-LP cast album was released by Bell Records (LP # BELL-9001). The script was published by Doubleday & Company, Inc., in 1974, and a film version for television, produced by Columbia Pictures, was shown in March 1980. The tribute returned in a cabaret version in June 1981 for an Off Off Broadway engagement at Ted Hook's On Stage (with Terri Klausner, Russ Thacker, and Dalton Cathey); a Broadway engagement opened at the Helen Hayes Theatre on November 16, 1986, for fifty-six performances (with Roderick Cook, Catherine Cox, and Patrick Quinn); and on February 16, 1999, the revue was revived Off Off Broadway by the Irish Repertory Theatre for forty-two performances. As *A Noel Coward Revue*, or *To Sir, with Love*, the revue premiered at the Theatre-in-the-Dell in Toronto on May 19, 1970. During the original run of the revue at the New Theatre, a gala performance was held on January 14, 1973, in honor of Coward, who attended the performance. According to the program notes in the Off Off Broadway 1981 revival, it was Coward's last public appearance and the last show he ever saw. He died six weeks later.

The non-musical sequences of the revue were taken from various writings by Coward, including his plays *The Young Idea* (1923 [London]), *Private Lives* (1930 [London], 1931 [New York]), *Shadow Play* (the short play was part of *To-Night at 8:30*, 1936 [London], 1936 [New York]), and *Present Laughter* (1939 [London], 1946 [New York]); his book of poetry, *Not Yet the Dodo and Other Verses* (1967); one of his autobiographies (*Present Indicative* [1937]); and excerpts from his short stories.

Another Off-Broadway tribute to Coward was produced in 1999 (see entry for *If Love Were All*).

In 1972, there was also a London revue which paid tribute to Coward's songs. *Cowardy Custard* opened at the Mermaid Theatre with a cast which included Patricia Routledge; it was recorded on a 2-LP set by RCA Records (LSO-6010).

1171 Oh, Johnny. "A New Musical." THEATRE: Players Theatre; OPENING DATE: January 10, 1982; PERFORMANCES: 1; BOOK: Paul Streitz; LYRICS: Paul Streitz and Gary Cherpakov; (*) indicates lyric by Gary Cherpakov only; MUSIC: Gary Cherpakov; DIRECTION: Alan Weeks; CHOREOGRAPHER: Alan Weeks; SCENERY: Jim Chestnutt; COSTUMES: Gene Galvin; LIGHTING: Toni Goldin; MUSICAL DIRECTION: Robert Marks; PRODUCERS: Paul Streitz; Stephen Harausz, Associate Producer

CAST—Michael Crouch (Johnny), Brad Miskell (Gopher), The *Oh Johnny* Trio (Sally Yorke, Janet Donohue, Katherine Lench), Jerry Coyle (Colonel Granger Sitright), Christine Toy (The White Lotus), Janet Wong (One China), Joey Ginza (General Ko), The Soldiers (David C. Wright, Robert Kellett, Clayton Davis), Nazig Edeards (Lili)

The action occurs "a long time ago, when this country was much younger than it is today."

The musical was presented in two acts.

ACT ONE—"'I Love a Man with a Uniform On' Polka" (*) (Sally Yorke, Janet Donohue, Katherine Lench), "Ten Thousand Feet in the Air" (Michael Crouch, Brad Miskell), "Business as Usual" (*) (Joey Ginza, Christine Toy, Janet Wong), "Boost the Morale"/"Win the War for Lili" (Nazig Edwards, Sally Yorke, Janet Donohue, Katherine Lench, Brad Miskell), "Johnny Is the Man for Me" (Sally Yorke, Janet Donohue, Katherine Lench), "The Mission" (Jerry Coyle, Michael Crouch, Brad Miskell), "Song of the Orient" (Christine Toy), "Cowboy's Burning Desire" (Brad Miskell, Michael Crouch), "Ten Thousand Feet in the Air" (reprise) (Brad Miskell), "Dance Around the World with Me" (Michael Crouch)

ACT TWO—"I'd Love to Be in Love with You" (Sally Yorke, Janet Donohue, Katherine Lench), "Can't Can't" (*) (Nazig Edwards, Jerry Coyle), "Oh, Johnny" (*) (Michael Crouch), "Ancient Oriental Custom" (*) (Janet Wong, Brad Miskell), "Oh, Johnny" (reprise) (*) (Michael Crouch, Company), "Why Am I Afraid To Love" (*) (Christine Toy), "Ten Thousand Feet in the Air" (reprise) (Michael Crouch, Brad Miskell), "Soldier Boy" (Sally Yorke, Janet Donohue, Katherine Lench), "Boogie Bug" (*) (Company)

NOTES—Originally produced Off Off Broadway at the Off Center Theatre, *Oh, Johnny*, a spoof of the War Forties, was the only musical of the 1981-1982 Off Broadway season to play just one performance. Clive Barnes in the *New York Post* noted the musical's only original touch was the omission of an exclamation point in its title.

During previews, Brad Miskell succeeded Mark Frawley in the role of Gopher.

Prior to the musical's Off Broadway opening, the producer issued a promotional 7" LP which included five numbers from the show ("'I Love A Man with a Uniform On' Polka," "Ten Thousand Feet in the Air," "I'd Love to Be in Love with You," "Dance Around the World," and "Boogie Bug").

1172 Oh, Kay! THEATRE: East 74th Street Theatre; OPENING DATE: April 16, 1960; PERFOR-

MANCES: 89; BOOK: Guy Bolton and P.G. Wodehouse; LYRICS: Ira Gershwin and P.G. Wodehouse; MUSIC: George Gershwin; DIRECTION: Bertram Yarborough; CHOREOGRAPHY: Dania Krupska; SETTINGS: Don Jensen; COSTUMES: Pearl Somner; LIGHTING: Richard Nelson; MUSICAL DIRECTION: Dorothea Freitag; PRODUCERS: Bly Productions (Leighton K. Brill, Fred'k Lewis, Jr., and Bertram Yarborough)

CAST—Rosemarri Sheer (Phil), Linda Lavin (Izzy), Penny Fuller (Polly), Francesca Bell (Jean), Lynn Gay Lorino (Odile), Sybil Scotford (Molly), EDDIE PHILLIPS (Larry Potter), MURRAY MATHESON (Earl of Blandings), BERNIE WEST (McGee), James Sullivan (Chauffer, Assistant to Revenue Officer), DAVID DANIELS (Jimmy Winters), EDITH BELL (Constance), MIKE MAZURKI (Revenue Officer), MARTI STEVENS (Kay), LEN MENCE (Judge Appleton)

The action occurs in and around Jimmy Winters' home in Easthampton in 1927.

The musical was presented in two acts.

ACT ONE—"The Woman's Touch" (Girls), "The Twenties Are Here to Stay" (Murray Matheson, Eddie Phillips, Bernie West), "Home" (David Daniels), "Stiff Upper Lip" (Bernie West, Murray Matheson), "Maybe" (David Daniels, Marti Stevens), "The Pophams" (Murray Matheson, Girls), "Do, Do, Do" (David Daniels, Marti Stevens), "Clap Yo' Hands" (David Daniels, Company)

ACT TWO—"Someone to Watch Over Me" (Marti Stevens), "Fidgety Feet" (Eddie Phillips, Girls), "Stiff Upper Lip" (reprise) (Bernie West, David Daniels), "You'll Still Be There" (David Daniels, Marti Stevens), "Someone to Watch Over Me" (reprise) (Marti Stevens), "Little Jazz Bird" (Eddie Phillips, Girls; danced by Eddie Phillips, Lynn Gay Lorino), "Oh, Kay, You're Okay (Oh, Kay!)" (Eddie Phillips, Bernie West, Marti Stevens, Girls), "Little Jazz Bird" (reprise) (Murray Matheson, Linda Lavin), Finale (Company)

NOTES—*Oh, Kay!* was the month's second revival of an earlier hit Broadway musical, and it fared a little better than *Gay Divorce*, running almost three months and getting its own cast album (20th Fox MasterArts [LP # FOX-4003], later reissued on Stet Records [LP # DS-15017]).

Oh, Kay! originally opened on Broadway at the Imperial Theatre on November 8, 1926, with Gertrude Lawrence in the title role. The musical played for 256 performances.

Songs retained for the Off Broadway revival were: "The Woman's Touch" (lyric by Ira Gershwin); "Don't Ask" (lyric by Ira Gershwin; for revival, a new lyric, called "Home," was written by P.G. Wodehouse); "Maybe" (lyric by Ira Gershwin); "Do, Do, Do" (lyric by Ira Gershwin); "Clap Yo' Hands" (lyric by Ira Gershwin); "Someone to Watch Over Me" (lyric by Ira Gershwin); "Fidgety Feet" (lyric by Ira Gershwin);"Dear Little Girl" (lyric by Ira Gershwin; for revival, a new lyric, called "You'll Still Be There," was written by P.G. Wodehouse); and "Oh, Kay!" (here called "Oh, Kay, You're Okay"; lyric by Ira Gershwin).

Interpolated into the revival were the following songs by George Gershwin: "The Twenties Are Here to Stay" (new lyric by P.G. Wodehouse for the song "When Toby Is Out of Town"; original lyric by Desmond Carter, which appeared in 1924 London production of *Primrose*); "Stiff Upper Lip" (lyric by Ira Gershwin, from 1937 film *A Damsel in Distress*); "The Pophams" (new lyric by P.G. Wodehouse for the song "The Mophams"; original lyric by Desmond Carter, which appeared in *Primrose*); and "Little Jazz Bird" (lyric by Ira Gershwin, from 1924 Broadway production of *Lady, Be Good!*). Of the four songs with new lyrics by P.G. Wodehouse, the program credited him with three, omitting his credit for "Home," which was the new lyric for "Don't Ask."

Two songs from the original 1926 production were not used in the revival ("Bride and Groom" and "Heaven on Earth").

Despite its glorious score, *Oh, Kay!* has never been successfully revived. The Off Broadway production was a failure, and in 1978 a lavish production of the musical cancelled its Broadway engagement, after tryouts in Toronto and Washington, D.C. In 1990, David Merrick mounted a Broadway revival, which opened at the Richard Rodgers (formerly the 46th Street) Theatre and lasted for only seventy-seven performances. A re-vamped production opened at the Lunt-Fontanne Theatre the following April, and closed there after sixteen previews.

Lewis Funke in the *New York Times* felt that except for the classic score, the Off Broadway revival didn't provide "a fully satisfying entertainment" (but he singled out David Daniels, the production's "best casting ... good-looking ... good voice"); he suggested the Columbia studio cast album (see below) was "easier on the pocketbook" than tickets for the production.

The score was recorded in the 1950s on a delightful studio cast album (the singers included Barbara Ruick, Jack Cassidy, and Allen Case) issued by Columbia Records (LP # OS-2550 and OL-7050; released on CD by Sony Classical/Columbia/Legacy Records # SK-60703). And in 1995 Nonesuch Records released the most complete recording of the score (CD # 79361-2) with a cast which included Dawn Upshaw, Kurt Ollmann, and Patrick Cassidy. Further, in 1978 a recording of the score was part of the Smithsonian American Musical Theatre Series (released by RCA Special Products Records LP # DPL1-0310), and it included original cast performances by Gertrude Lawrence and duo pianists Victor Arden and Phil Ohman as well as solo piano recordings of Gershwin himself playing numbers from the score.

1173 Oh Me, Oh My, Oh Youmans.

THEATRE: Wonderhorse Theatre; OPENING DATE: January 14, 1981; PERFORMANCES: 20 Lyrics: See notes below; MUSIC: Vincent Youmans; DIRECTION: Darwin Knight; SCENERY: Bob Philips; COSTUMES: Andrew Marlay; LIGHTING: Eric Cornwell; MUSICAL DIRECTION: Sand Lawn; PRODUCERS: New World Theatre and Jane Stanton

CAST—Jo Ann Cunningham, Todd Taylor, Sally Woodson, Ronald Young

The revue was presented in two acts.

NOTES—Conceived by Darwin Knight and Tom Taylor, the revue *Oh Me, Oh My, Oh Youmans* was a tribute to Vincent Youmans and presented songs from his Broadway musicals *Two Little Girls in Blue* (1921; lyrics by Arthur Frances [Ira Gershwin]); *Wildflower* (1923; lyrics by Otto Harbach and Oscar Hammerstein II); *Mary Jane McKane* (1923; lyrics by Oscar Hammerstein II and William Cary Duncan); *Lollipop* (1924; lyrics by Zelda Sears); *No, No, Nanette* (1925; lyrics by Otto Harbach and Irving Caesar); *Oh Please!* (1926; lyrics by Anne Caldwell); *Hit the Deck!* (1927; lyrics by Leo Robin and Clifford Grey); *Rainbow* (1928; lyrics by Oscar Hammerstein II); *Great Day!* (1929; lyrics by Billy Rose and Edward Eliscu); *Smiles* (1930; lyrics by Harold Adamson and Clifford Grey); *Through the Years* (1932; lyrics by Edward Heyman); and *Take a Chance* (1932; lyrics by B.G. [Buddy] DeSylva). The revue also included songs from *A Night Out* (1925; lyrics by Irving Caesar and Clifford Grey), which closed prior to Broadway; and songs from the 1933 film *Flying Down to Rio* (lyrics by Edward Eliscu and Gus Kahn).

1174 Oh! Oh! Obesity.

THEATRE: Louis Abrons Arts for Living Center; OPENING DATE: June 7, 1984; PERFORMANCES: 15; BOOK: Gerald W. Deas; "SCRIPT COLLABORATION": Bette Howard; LYRICS: Gerald W. Deas; MUSIC: Gerald W. Deas; DIRECTION: Bette Howard; CHOREOGRAPHY: Ronn Pratt; SCENERY: May Callas; COSTUMES: Vicki Jones; LIGHTING: Zebedee Collins; MUSICAL DIRECTION: John McCallum; PRODUCER: Henry Street Settlement's New Federal Theatre (Woodie King, Jr., Producer; Michael Frey, Executive Director)

CAST—Sandra Reaves-Phillips (Fat Momma), Karen Langerstrom (Ms. Knosh), Reginald Veljohnson (Fat Daddy), Stuart D. Goldenberg (Blimpie), Mennie F. Nelson (Fatsie), Kent C. Jackman (Dr. Do-Nothin'); Jacqueline Bird, Regina Reynolds Hood, and Erica Arlis Smith alternated in the role of the Nurse; they also performed the roles of Three Pretty Girls, Church Sisters, and Chorus

The musical was presented in two acts.

ACT ONE—"Oh! Oh! Obesity" (Sandra Reaves-Phillips, Reginald Valjohnson, Stuart D. Goldenberg, Mennie F. Nelson, Karen Langerstrom), "I Don't Eat a Thing" (Sandra Reaves-Phillips, Kent C. Jackman), "You've Got to Stay Real Cool" (Sandra Reaves-Phillips, Karen Langerstrom) "HamSome" (Reginald Valjohnson), "You're Gonna Need Somebody" (Sandra Reaves-Phillips), "If De Boot Don't Fit You Can't Wear It" ('Maintenance Man'), "Jellybread Falls on Jellyside Down" (Karen Langerstrom, Mennie F. Nelson), "I'm Fat" (Reginald Valjohnson, Sandra Reaves-Phillips)

ACT TWO—"Everybody Wants to Be a Star" (Mennie F. Nelson, Stuart D. Goldenberg), "Gym Jam Boogie (Come Jam with Us)" (Company), "I Fried All Night Long" (Company), "Oh! Oh! Obesity" (reprise) (Company)

NOTES—The Off Off Broadway musical *Oh! Oh! Obesity* dealt with those who are diet-challenged; perhaps someday it will be produced in repertory with the Broadway comedies *My Fat Friend* (1974) and *More to Love* (1998) (the latter was subtitled "A Big Fat Comedy") and the Off Broadway revue *Leftovers* (see entry).

1175 Oh, Say Can You See L.A.

THEATRE: Actors' Playhouse; OPENING DATE: February 8, 1968; PERFORMANCES: 14

NOTES—*Oh, Say Can You See L.A.* was the overall title of two one-act plays by John Allen. The curtain-raiser was a non-musical, *The Other Man*; the second play, *Oh, Say Can You See L.A.*, concerned four disreputable vaudevillians, and included four songs with lyrics by Allen and music by Albert Hague. Dan Sullivan in the *New York Times* indicated the quartet were similar to Archie, the sleazy title character of John Osborne's *The Entertainer* (see entry), but noted that while the conceit of vaudevillians symbolizing Western decadence was fresh when Osborne introduced Archie a decade earlier, the premise was now looking "pretty thin." But Sullivan praised the "cute" music by Hague, which included tributes to "God, Mother Country, and, of course, Love."

Oh, Say Can You See L.A..; PLAY: John Allen; LYRICS: John Allen; MUSIC: Albert Hague; DIRECTION: John Allen; CHOREOGRAPHY: Vernon Lusby; SCENERY: Boyd Dumrose; COSTUMES: Possibly by Boyd Dumrose; PRODUCERS: Richard Lerner, Frances Drucker, and Gilberto Zaldivar

CAST—George Welbes (Sonny), GEORGE VOSKOVEC (Pop), Glenn Kezer (Uncle Charlie), Alan Manson (Harold)

The action occurs "here" in the present time.

The four songs included in the play were "We're Happy," "The Old Family Album," "God Bless Our Boys," and "Love, Love, Love."

1176 Oil City Symphony.

THEATRE: Circle in the Square Downtown; OPENING DATE: November 5, 1987; PERFORMANCES: 626; LYRICS: See song list for credits; MUSIC: See song list for credits; DIRECTION: Larry Forde; SCENERY: Jeffrey Schissler; LIGHTING: Natasha Katz; PRODUCERS: Lois Deutchman, Mary T. Nealon, and David Musselman; Thomas DeWolfe and George Gordon, Jay H. Fuchs, and A. Joseph Tandet, Associate Producers

CAST—Mike Craver, Mark Hardwick, Debra Monk, Mary Murfitt

The revue was presented in two acts.

ACT ONE—"Count Your Blessings" (Company), "Czardus" (Mary Murfitt, Mark Hardwick), "Musical Moments" A Classical Selection (including "Anvil Chorus") (Company), A Popular Selection (including "In-A-Gadda-Da-Vida" [lyric and music by Doug Ingle]) (Company), "Ohio Afternoon" (lyric by Mike Craver, music by Mark Hardwick and Debra Monk) (Debra Monk), "Baby, It's Cold Outside" (from 1949 film *Neptune's Daughter*; lyric and music by Frank Loesser) (Company), "Beaver Ball at the Bug Club" (lyric by Mike Craver, music by Mark Hardwick and Debra Monk) (Company), "Beehive Polka" (lyric by Debra Monk, music by Mike Craver, Mark Hardwick and Debra Monk) (Mary Murfitt, Company), "Musical Memories" "A Patriotic Fantasy" (Company)

ACT TWO—"Dueling Keyboards," "Introductions," "Iris" (lyric and music by Mike Craver) (Mike Craver), "The End of the World" (lyric by Sylvia Dee, music by Arthur Kent), "A Tribute," "Coaxing the Ivories" (a/k/a "Coaxing the Piano"; music by Zev Confrey) (Company), "Bus Ride" (lyric by Mike Craver, music by Mark Hardwick and Debra Monk) (Company), "In the Sweet Bye and Bye" (Company), "My Ol' Kentucky Rock and Roll Home" (lyric by Mike Craver, music by Mark Hardwick and Debra Monk) (Mark Hardwick, Company)

NOTES—*Oil City Symphony* took place in a high school gymnasium where four graduates are honoring a former teacher with a musical tribute of polkas, patriotic music, and popular songs. On the liner notes for the cast recording (released on DRG Records [LP # SBL-12594; CD # CDSBL-12594]), the performers wrote that the musical was based on their "collective experiences in the creative environment of small towns where we grew up: community activities, schools, churches, families, friendships, and all those music lessons!"

The musical's premiere took place at the Doo Wap Club in New York City on May 12, 1986, and then played in regional theatres in Dallas and Baltimore.

While not in its song listing, the New York program nonetheless indicated the following songs were performed (some of these are also heard on the cast album): "Getting Acquainted" (lyric and music by Mary Murfitt), "Dear Miss Reeves" (lyric by Mike Craver, music by Mark Hardwick and Debra Monk), "Dizzy Fingers" (lyric and music by Zev Confrey), and "The *Exodus* Song" (from the 1960 film *Exodus*; lyric by Charles E. Pat Boone, music by Ernest Gold). The cast album also included: "The Hokey Pokey," "Sleigh Ride," "The Christmas Medley," and "The Summer Medley."

1177 Old Bucks and New Wings.

"A Musical." THEATRE: Mayfair Theatre; OPENING DATE: November 5, 1962; PERFORMANCES: 8; BOOK: Harvey Lasker; LYRICS: Harvey Lasker; MUSIC: Eddie Stuart; DIRECTION: Harvey Lasker; CHOREOGRAPHY: Buster Burnell; SCENERY: Owen Ryan ("Design Consultant"); COSTUMES: Phyllis Uziel ("Costume Coordinator"); MUSICAL DIRECTION: Gerald Alfonso; PRODUCER: Harvey Lasker (Musivaude Productions)

CAST—Mark Stuart (Editor), Barry Frank (Bob Gordon), Carol Perea (Sophie), Phil Black (Jack Winters), Mickie Rogers (Miss Vaudeville); Vaudeville Stars: Gus Van, Flip Wilson, Harland Dixon, Mary Mon Toy, Rex Weber, Al Tucker, Bobby Ephram, Tom Patricola, Jr.; The Honey Girls: Sherry Bamber, Meredith Evans, Lores Mann, Carol Perea, Kathryn Doby, Marlena Lustik, Beverly Ann Paulsen, Cathi Schopp; The Boys: Phil Black, Ray Chabeau, Barry Frank, Ted Lambrinos, Mary Stuart

The musical was presented in two acts (song assignments unknown).

ACT ONE—Prologue, "Our Business Is News," "Get the News," "So, So Sophie," "That Was Your Life," "Keith's, Pantages & Loews," "Vaudeville," "That Day Will Come"

ACT TWO—"Get the News," "Sweet Memories," "You Made It Possible, Dear," "It Could Be Calais," "Stand Up and Cheer," "Let's Bring Back Showbusiness"

NOTES—The book-musical-cum-revue *Old Bucks and New Wings* was about the heyday of vaudeville; it featured a few names from the past (Gus Van, Smith and Dale, Harland Dixon, Rex Weber) as well as a new one which a few years later found brief fame on television (Flip Wilson).

Howard Taubman in the *New York Times* warned his readers to avoid *Old Bucks and New Wings* if they wished to preserve their fond memories of the golden age of vaudeville. He said the new musical blackened the name of vaudeville, and pronounced the evening "drab," "ineffectual," and "pathetic."

1178 The Oldest Trick in the World

NOTES—See entry for *Double Entry* (1961), an evening which was comprised of two one-act musicals, *The Bible Salesman* and *The Oldest Trick in the World*.

1179 Ole!

"A Zarzuela." Theatre: Greenwich Mews Theatre; Opening Date: March 18, 1959; Performances: 35; Book: Mary Lynn Whitman (from an English adaptation by Tracey Samuels and Max Leavitt and from a translation of the Spanish text by Dr. Daniel de Guzman); based on the original by Federico Romero and Guillermo Fernandez Shaw; Lyrics: Mary Lynn Whitman (from an English adaptation by Tracey Samuels and Max Leavitt and from a translation of the Spanish text by Dr. Daniel de Guzman); additional lyrics by Hubert Creekmore, Robert Molnar, and Paula Zwane; Music: Federico Moreno Torroba; Direction: Max Leavitt; Choreography: Ruthanna Boris; Scenery: Robert Fletcher; Costumes: Robert Fletcher; Lighting: Bernie Joy; Producers: The Village Presbyterian Church and The Brotherhood Synagogue, by arrangement with Lemonade Opera, Inc.

CAST—Ruth Kobart (Manuela), Evelyn Joyce (Concha), Robert Goss (El Chalina), Osvaldo Baez (Placido), Victoria Flores (Lolita), Lloyd Harris (Don Epifanio), Paula Zwane (Venustiana), Florence Rochelle (Rosario), Edmund Rose (Jose Maria), Ann Nelson (Mercedes), Maria Melendez (Pilar), Gino Conforti (Tin-Tan), Olga Villa Lobos (Ascencion), Marc Victor (Segismundo), Chris Mahan (El Extrano)

SOURCE—The zarzuela *La Chulapona* by Frederico Romero, Guillermo Fernandez Shaw, and Frederico Moreno Torroba.

The musical was presented in two acts.

ACT ONE—"Press a Dress" (Ruth Kobart, Evelyn Joyce, Robert Goss), "Isabel" (Robert Goss, Ensemble), "La Chulapona" (Ruth Kobart), "Mazurka (El Pelele)" (Ensemble), "Good Morning, My Dove" (Ruth Kobart, Florence Rochelle, Edmund Rose), Entr'acte: "Girls of Madrid" (Evelyn Joyce), "The Old Habanera" (Florence Rochelle, Edmund Rose), "Fiesta Brava" (Paula Zwane, Ensemble), "In the Hills of Andalusia" (Lloyd Harris), "The Belle of the Ball and the Bull of the Brawl" (Paula Zwane, Lloyd Harris), Finale: "Free for All" (Ensemble)

ACT TWO—"Ballad of the Stag" (Osvaldo Baez, Victoria Flores, Evelyn Joyce), "Love Is a Game" (Robert Goss), "Schottische" (Edmund Rose, Ensemble), Entr'acte: "Amoroso" (Ruth Kobart), "Own a Chulapona" (Robert Goss, Edmund Rose, Lloyd Harris), "Forgive Me" (Florence Rochelle), "Ole!" (Company)

NOTES—From a program note: "ZARZUELA: A typically Spanish musical stage piece. Generally, of a comic nature with customs, fashions, operas, plays, novels, and political situations reproduced, satirized and burlesqued."

Ross Parmenter in the *New York Times* found *Ole!* "lively," and he praised the score, "a succession of agreeable tunes" which included a mazurka, several habaneras, and some flamenco numbers. He noted that Federico Moreno Torroba, born in 1891 and "perhaps the most noted zarzuela composer still living," was in the audience for the premiere and was called to the stage during the curtain calls.

During the short run, Olga Villa Lobos was succeeded by Joyce Rittenberg. Other cast members included Ruth Kobart and Gino Conforti. Ruth Kobart created two memorable roles in two classic Broadway musicals during the 1961-1962 season: Miss Jones in *How to Succeed in Business Without Really Trying* (1961) and Dominia in *A Funny Thing Happened on the Way to the Forum* (1962). Clearly, musicals with long titles brought her more luck than ones with short titles.

Gino Conforti created small but memorable roles in three classic Broadway musicals in three consecutive years: he was the violinist who *didn't* create a romantic atmosphere in *She Loves Me* (1963); he was the character of The Fiddler in *Fiddler on the Roof* (1964); and he was the little barber who went his merry way in *Man of La Mancha* (1965).

The song listing and song assignments are not from an opening night program, but from one which was issued sometime during the show's one-month run. On opening night, the sequence of musical numbers in the first act was apparently different from performances later in the run (although the second act remained unchanged), and is as follows: "Press a Dress," "Isabel," "Girls of Madrid," "Good Morning, My Dove," "La Chulapona," "El Pelele," "In the Hills of Andalusia," "The Habanera and the Handkerchief" (possibly an early version of "The Old Habanera"), "Fiesta Brava," "The Belle of the Ball and the Bull of the Brawl," and "Free for All." The great tragedy of *Ole!* is that its short run killed any chance for a cast album, and thus show music buffs were forever deprived of the opportunity to hear "The Belle of the Ball and the Bull of the Brawl."

For another zarzuela, see entry for *Fiesta in Madrid*.

1180 Olio

NOTES—See entry for *First Lady Suite*.

1181 Olympus on My Mind.

"A New Musical." THEATRE: Lamb's Theatre; OPENING DATE: July 15, 1986; PERFORMANCES: 207; BOOKS: Barry Harman; LYRICS: Barry Harman; MUSIC: Grant Sturiale; DIRECTION: Barry Harman; CHOREOGRAPHY: Pamela Sousa; SCENERY: Chris Stapleton; COSTUMES: Steven Jones; LIGHTING: Fabian Yeager; PRODUCERS: Harve Brosten and Mainstage Productions, Ltd., in association with "Murray the Furrier"

CAST—The Chorus: Peter Kapetan (Tom), Andy Spangler (Dick), Keith Bennett (Horace), Elizabeth Austin (Delores); MARTIN VIDNOVIC (Jupiter, a/k/a Jove and Zeus; Amphitryon), Jason Graae (Mercury), Peggy Hewett (Charis), Emily Zacharias (Alcmene), Lewis J. Stadlen (Sosia), "George Spelvin" (Amphitryon; played by Martin Vidnovic)

SOURCE—The legend of Amphitryon (specifically the version written by Heinrich von Kleist in 1807).

The action occurs during a 41-hour day in the ancient city of Thebes, Greece.

The musical was presented in two acts.

ACT ONE—"Welcome to Greece" (Peter Kapetan, Andy Spangler, Keith Bennett, Elizabeth

Austin), "Heaven on Earth" (Martin Vidnovic [as Jupiter], Emily Zacharias, Peter Kapetan, Andy Spangler, Keith Bennett, Elizabeth Austin), "The Gods on Tap" (Elizabeth Austin, Martin Vidnovic [as Jupiter], Jason Graae, Peter Kapetan, Andy Spangler, Keith Bennett), "Surprise!" (Lewis J. Stadlen), "Wait 'Til It Dawns" (Jason Graae), "I Know My Wife" (Martin Vidnovic [as Amphitryon]), "It Was Me" (Lewis J. Stadlen), "Back So Soon?" (Martin Vidnovic [as Amphitryon], Lewis J. Stadlen, Peter Kapetan, Andy Spangler, Keith Bennett, Elizabeth Austin), "Wonderful" (Emily Zacharias), "At Liberty in Thebes" (Peggy Hewett, Peter Kapetan, Andy Spangler, Keith Bennett, Elizabeth Austin), "Jupiter Slept Here" (Company)

ACT TWO—"Back to the Play" (Peter Kapetan, Andy Spangler, Keith Bennett, Elizabeth Austin), "Don't Bring Her Flowers" (Jason Graae), "Generals' Pandemonium" (Martin Vidnovic [as both Jupiter and Amphitryon], Lewis J. Stadlen, Peter Kapetan, Andy Spangler, Keith Bennett, Elizabeth Austin), "Heaven on Earth" (reprise) (Lewis J. Stadlen, Peggy Hewett), "Olympus Is a Lonely Town" (Martin Vidnovic [as Jupiter]), "A Star Is Born" (Elizabeth Austin, Company), Final Sequence (Martin Vidnovic [as Jupiter and Amphitryon], Emily Zacharias, Jason Graae, Peggy Hewett, Lewis J. Stadlen, Peter Kapetan, Andy Spangler, Keith Bennett, and Elizabeth Austin), "Heaven on Earth" (reprise) (Martin Vidnovic, Emily Zacharias, Company)

NOTES—Based on the Amphitryon legend (which was also the source of Cole Porter's 1950 Broadway musical *Out of This World*), *Olympus on My Mind* was a jovial and light-hearted farce about that "wild and crazy god" Jupiter (who fires off thunderbolts because he's unable to handle rejection). Jupiter decides to leave Olympus for Thebes; while there, he hopes to have a fling with a mortal woman while disguised as her husband Amphitryon. (A subplot of the musical-within-the-musical reveals that the three-man chorus suddenly finds it has a fourth member, Delores, a talent-challenged ex-chorine whose husband Murray the Furrier just happens to be one of the musical's backers. Throughout the musical, Delores models Murray's furs, despite the fact they're not in keeping with the musical's setting.)

In his review for the *New York Post*, Clive Barnes praised the musical as "a good-natured and very enjoyable burlesque spin-off" of such musicals as *The Boys from Syracuse* (1938; see entry for 1963 revival) and *A Funny Thing Happened on the Way to the Forum* (1962). In reviewing the piece for the *New York Times*, Stephen Holden found in Grant Sturiale's "bubbly" score a suggestion of Richard Rodgers and Lorenz Hart "with a pop-rock undertow." He praised such numbers as "Heaven on Earth" ("mock bombastic"), "Wonderful" (a "soaring waltz"), "A Star Is Born" (a "swivelling kick-line number"), and "Olympus Is a Lonely Town" (a "mopey pesudo-saloon song").

The musical had first been produced Off Off Broadway on May 21, 1986, at the Actors' Outlet. With the exceptions of Faith Prince (Delores) and Ron Raines (Jupiter/Amphitryon), all the cast transferred when the production moved to Off Broadway.

Shortly after the production opened Off Broadway, the song "Love — What a Concept" was added to the first act (for Jupiter and Mercury), and the title of "Don't Bring Her Flowers" was changed to "Something of Yourself (Don't Bring Her Flowers)."

In 1987, That's Entertainment Records (LP # TER-1131) released a recording with many members from the Off Broadway cast (the recording included the new number "Love — What a Concept"). The script was published by Samuel French, Inc., in 1987.

One of the most popular plays based on the Amphitryon legend was S.N. Behrman's adaptation of Jean Giraudoux's *Amphitryon 38* (1937) which starred Lynn Fontanne and Alfred Lunt (the title came from Giraudoux' estimation that his was the 38th play to have been based on the legend).

1182 On the Lam. THEATRE: Theatre for the New City; OPENING DATE: January 10, 1985; PERFORMANCES: Unknown; BOOK: Georg Osterman; LYRICS: Georg Osterman; MUSIC: Jeffrey Marke; DIRECTION: John Albano; SCENERY: Bill Wolf; COSTUMES: Gabriel Berry; LIGHTING: Howard Theis; PRODUCER: Theater for the New City (George Bartenieff and Crystal Field, Artistic Directors)

CAST—George Bartenieff (Dephila, Sammy), David McCorkle (Gorgo), Robert Schelhammer (Cosmo), Crystal Field (Sorrita), Mark Marcante (Bing), Todd Charles (Martini), Margaret Miller (Tillie), Joe Pichette (Copper, Sister Sanitatious), Marlene Hoffman (Sister Agnes), Florence Peters (Sister Paulita, Candy), Lola Pashalinski (Zena), Jeff Mont (Waiter), Todd Stockman (Ventriloquist)

NOTES—Mel Gussow in the *New York Times* reported that the Off Off Broadway musical *On the Lam* dealt with the mishaps of three untalented vaudevillians who become involved with an assortment of show-business wannabes, including an embezzling former nun. Gussow noted that the musical's book writer and lyricist was Georg Osterman, an actor who had appeared in Charles Ludlam's Ridiculous Theatre Company, and while *On the Lam* attempted to recycle the style of Ludlam's farces, the book for the new musical was "lame." But Gussow said the score possessed a "certain freshness" in its evocations of 1930s music, and he singled out "Sorrita's Turn" and "Clepto Lover." With Crystal Field's "ingenuous song styling" in the former number, Gussow felt she'd be an adornment in both a real nightclub as well as in the one depicted in the musical itself. As for Lola Pashalinski, Gussow said she earned center stage in "Clepto Lover," a "lowdown blues."

1183 On-the Lock-In. THEATRE: LuEsther Hall/The Public Theatre; OPENING DATE: April 14, 1977; PERFORMANCES: 62; BOOK: David Langston Smyrl; LYRICS: David Langston Smyrl; MUSIC: David Langston Smyrl; DIRECTION: Robert Macbeth; SCENERY: Karl Eigsti; COSTUMES: Grace Williams; LIGHTING: Victor En Yu Tan; MUSICAL DIRECTION: George Stubbs; PRODUCERS: The New York Shakespeare Festival (Joseph Papp, Producer; Bernard Gersten, Associate Producer)

CAST—David Langston Smyrl (Houndog), Manuel Santiago (Frankie), Harold Cromer (Mess Hall), Billy Barnes (Home Boy), Henry Baker (Jerry), Thomas M. Brimm II (Dude), Erza Jack Maret (Rock), Leon Thomas (The Guard), Alan Weeks (Jazz), Henry Bradley (Small Times), Don Jay (Abdu)

The action occurs in a prison.

The musical was presented in one act.

MUSICAL NUMBERS—"Whatever It Happens to Be" (Company), "Dry Mouth with No Water" (Alan Weeks, Company), "Born To Lose" (Leon Thomas, Company), "Sister Paradise" (David Langston Smyrl, Company, "Peace Will Come" (Don Jay, with Alan Weeks, Henry Baker, Ezra Jack Maret), "Circumstances" (Thomas M. Brimm II, Company), "42nd St. Blues" (Harold Cromer), "Talkin' Blues" (David Langston Smyrl), "Marlene" (Henry Bradley), "Alone" (Billy Barnes)

NOTES—*On-the Lock-In* was a bleeding-heart look at prisoners who smugly inform the audience members that they too are in a prison. (Perhaps audience members who sat through the "aimless, wearisome" evening [according to Douglas Watt in the *New York Daily News*] felt they were indeed in a kind of prison.) The book, lyrics, and music were by David Langston Smyrl, who, according to Watt, had "a long way to go in all three directions." Mel Gussow in the *New York Times* felt the musical should have "remained in workshop," although he noted the musical's premise had "possibilities." However, while Gussow praised the "lively" music, he found the book "almost nonexistent" and the lyrics banal.

Perhaps the musical should have been called *A Prisoners' Line*, because, like the Public Theatre's successful show-business musical, an off-stage voice summoned the prisoners on stage, one by one, so that each could tell his particular story. The public, if not the Public, would have none of it, and so after two months *On-the Lock-In* was metaphorically sent up the river to the big (Cain's ware)house.

As *On the Lock-In*, the revue had been previously seen Off Off Broadway at the Combination Cabaret in October 1976.

1184 On the Swing Shift. "A Boogie-Woogie Opera." THEATRE: DownStage/Manhattan Theatre Club; OPENING DATE: March 20, 1983; PERFORMANCES: 37; LYRICS: Sarah Schlesinger; MUSIC: Michael Dansicker; DIRECTION: Martin Charnin; CHOREOGRAPHY: Janie Sell; SCENERY: Tony Straiges; COSTUMES: Jess Goldstein; LIGHTING: Arden Fingerhut; MUSICAL DIRECTION: Janet Glazener; PRODUCER: Manhattan Theatre Club (Lynne Meadow, Artistic Director; Barry Grove, Managing Director)

CAST—Kay Cole (Vera), Valerie Perri (Dot), Ann-Ngaire Martin (Maisie)

The action occurs in an aircraft factory during the day shift, Monday through Friday of April 1943.

The musical was presented in one act (song assignments weren't listed in the program).

MUSICAL NUMBERS—"Morning," "Row 10, Aisle 6, Bench 114," "We Got a Job to Do," "There's a War Going On," "Bond Sequence," "Killing Time," "When Tomorrow Comes," "I'm Someone Now," "Something to Do Tonight," "Night on the Town," "Chorale," "Evening"

NOTES—This overlooked Off Off Broadway mini-"boogie-woogie" opera about women working on the swing-shift in a defense plant sounds interesting. But after its limited run at the Manhattan Theatre Club, it disappeared.

1185 On the Town (1959). THEATRE: Carnegie Hall Playhouse; OPENING DATE: January 15, 1959; PERFORMANCES: 70; BOOK: Betty Comden and Adolph Green; LYRICS: Betty Comden and Adolph Green; MUSIC: Leonard Bernstein; DIRECTION: Gerald Freedman; CHOREOGRAPHY: Joe Layton; SCENERY: Jac Venza; COSTUMES: Joe Codori; PRODUCERS: Nancy Elliott Nugent in association with Ulysses Productions

CAST—John Smolko (First Workman, Uperman, Party Boy, Ballet Boy), Joe Bova (Chip), WILLIAM HICKEY (Ozzie), HAROLD LANG (Gabey), Esther Horrocks (Flossie, Musical Comedy Girl), Carol Sue Shaer (Flossie's Friend, Second Musician), Jim Moore (Bill Poster, First Musician), Marlene Dell (Little Old Lady, Girl Dancer), Mitchell Jason (Announcer, Pitkin W. Bridgework), Wisa D'Orso (Ivy), PAT CARROLL (Hildy), Tom Mixon (Figment, Aesthete), Evelyn Russell (Claire), Leonard Drum (Actor, M.C., Athlete), Jere Admire (Boy Dancer, Soldier, Bimmy), Essie Jane Coryell (Maude P. Dilly), Gubi Mann (Lucy Schmeeler), Judith Dunford (Girl), Patsi King (Diana Dream), Bob Darnell (Policeman)

SOURCES—An idea by Jerome Robbins; and the ballet *Fancy Free* (1944; choreography by Jerome Robbins and music by Leonard Bernstein).

The action occurs in and around New York City during the War Forties.

The musical was presented in two acts.

ACT ONE—"I Feel Like I'm Not Out of Bed Yet" (John Smolko), "New York, New York" (Harold

Lang, William Hickey, Joe Bova), "New York, New York Dance" (Marlene Dell, Judith Dunford, Esther Horrocks, Patsi King, Carol Sue Shaer, Jere Admire, Leonard Drum, Leonard Drum, Tom Mixon, Jim Moore, John Smolko), "Miss Turnstiles (Dance)" (Wisa D'Orso, Mitchell Jason, Marlene Dell, Judith Dunford, Esther Horrocks, Patsi King, Carol Sue Shaer, John Smolko, Jere Admire, Jim Moore, Tom Mixon, Leonard Drum), "Come Up to My Place" (Pat Carroll, Joe Bova), "Carried Away" (Evelyn Russell, William Hickey), "Lonely Town" (Harold Lang), "Lonely Town Dance" (Harold Lang, Marlene Dell, Esther Horrocks, Carol Sue Shaer), "Carnegie Hall Pavanne" (Wisa D'Orso, Essie Jane Coryell), "Do-Do-Re-Do" (Boys, Girls), "I Can Cook, Too" (Pat Carroll, Joe Bova), "Lucky to Be Me" (Harold Lang, Boys, Girls), "Times Square Ballet" (Harold Lang, Pat Carroll, Evelyn Russell, William Hickey, Joe Bova, Boys, Girls)

ACT TWO—"So Long, Baby" (Marlene Dell, Judith Dunford, Esther Horrocks, Patsi King, Carol Sue Shaer), "I'm Blue" (Patsi King), "So Long, Baby" (reprise) (Judith Dunford, Esther Horrocks, Carol Sue Shaer), "You Got Me" (Harold Lang, Pat Carroll, Evelyn Russell, William Hickey, Joe Bova), "So Long, Baby" (reprise) (Marlene Dell, Judith Dunford), "I Understand" (Mitchell Jason, Gubi Mann), "Coney Island Dream Ballet" (Harold Lang, Wisa D'Orso, Boys, Girls), "Some Other Time" (Pat Carroll, William Hickey, Evelyn Russell, Joe Bova), "The Real Coney Island" (Wisa D'Orso, Jere Admire), Finale (Company)

NOTES—This was a remarkably full-bodied revival of *On the Town*, but unfortunately it didn't run very long. It included a cast of twenty, and retained most of the song and dance sequences from the original production, which had first opened at the Adelphi Theatre on December 28, 1944, and played for 462 performances. But *On the Town* has been cursed ever since the curtain fell on the original Broadway production. The show's national tour quickly faltered, and while the entertaining 1949 film version was faithful to the spirit, plot, and dances of the original, it retained just three songs ("I Feel Like I'm Not Out of Bed Yet," "New York, New York," and "Come Up to My Place"); a few pleasant if lackluster numbers were added to the film (lyrics by Betty Comden and Adolph Green, music by Roger Edens).

Moreover, the show's belated 1963 London debut was a flop, running just fifty-three performances (it opened on May 30 at the Prince of Wales Theatre, and its cast included Elliott Gould as Ozzie), and its two major Broadway revivals were failures as well. The first Broadway revival opened on October 31, 1971, at the Imperial Theatre, where it played for seventy-three performances; the cast included Bernadette Peters, Phyllis Newman, Ron Husmann, Donna McKechnie, Remak Ramsey, and Marilyn Cooper. The 1998 revival opened at the Gershwin Theatre on November 19, 1998, and played for sixty-five performances. The 1998 revival had first been seen in a 1997 production at the Delacorte Theatre in Central Park, where it played for twenty-five performances (see entry). In fact, all major revivals of *On the Town* (Broadway, Off Broadway, and London) have collapsed within two months of their openings.

Incidentally, the lyric for "I Can Cook, Too" is credited to Comden and Green as well as by Bernstein, who dabbled with lyrics throughout his career (including *Peter Pan* [1950], *Candide* [1956], and *West Side Story* [1957]). Evelyn Russell, who played Claire, and Joe Layton, the production's choreographer, were later married.

Jere Admire, who appeared in minor roles in this production, may well be (along with Ron Schwinn) the male chorus-boy equivalent of Mary Ann Niles, who seemed to be the eternal Broadway chorus girl. And while we're on the subject, have you noticed that Tom Mixon seems to be in just about every other early Off Broadway musical? He could well be the poster boy for the ultimate, if unknown, Off Broadway musical performer. Apparently he was on Broadway just once, in the role of Sir Studley, when *Once Upon a Mattress* transferred to Broadway in late 1959. (In the original Off Broadway production [see entry], which opened earlier in 1959, he created the role of Sir Luce.) It seems appropriate that Mixon's one and only Broadway show originated Off Broadway.

There have been numerous recordings of *On the Town*. Decca Records (LP # DL-8030) released an album which included seven songs from the production (with an original/studio cast which included Betty Comden, Adolph Green, Nancy Walker, and Mary Martin) as well as seven numbers from *Lute Song*, a curious bit of chinoiserie which opened on Broadway in 1946 with Mary Martin and Yul Brynner. The 1949 film soundtrack surfaced on Show Biz Records (LP # 5603); the London cast album was released by CBS Records (LP # SAPG-60005); and Stet Records released a London studio cast album which included mostly songs from the film version (LP # DS-15029). There was also a recording by Deutsch Grammophon Records (CD # 437-516-2) of a live 1993 concert version of the score; this was the era of "crossover" show music recordings, and thus the CD included both opera (Frederica von Stade, Thomas Hampson, Samuel Ramey, Evelyn Lear) and Broadway/London (David Garrison, Tyne Daly, Cleo Laine) performers. Further, in 1996 Jay Records released a 2-CD set of the complete score (# CDJAY2-1231), which included dance music, the overture, the entr'acte, and exit music as well as such esoterica as "Pitkin's Song." But perhaps the most delightful recording of *On the Town* was released by Columbia Records in 1960 (LP # OL-5540 and # OS-2028); the sparkling album, which includes original cast (Betty Comden, Adolph Green, Nancy Walker, Cris Alexander) and studio cast (John Reardon) members, was later reissued at various times on LP and CD, and its most recent CD release by Sony Classical/Columbia/Legacy Records (# SK-60538) includes an overture conducted by Lehman Engel and three dance sequences with Bernstein conducting the New York Philharmonic. (This recording also offers one of the Great Show Album Mysteries: no one seems to know who sang "I Feel Like I'm Not Out of Bed Yet" for the recording's opening sequence.)

The script wasn't published until 1997, when it appeared in the collection *The New York Musicals of Comden & Green* (Applause Books), which also included the scripts of *Wonderful Town* (1953) and *Bells Are Ringing* (1956), both of which had been previously published in editions by Random House. Alas, the team's very New York musical *Subways Are for Sleeping* (1961) wasn't included in the volume.

1186 On the Town (1997). THEATRE: Delacorte Theatre/The Joseph Papp Public Theatre; OPENING DATE: August 1, 1997; PERFORMANCES: 25; BOOK: Betty Comden and Adolph Green; LYRICS: Betty Comden and Adolph Green; MUSIC: Leonard Bernstein; DIRECTION: George C. Wolfe; CHOREOGRAPHY: Eliot Feld; SCENERY: Adrianne Lobel; COSTUMES: Paul Tazewell; LIGHTING: Paul Gallo; MUSICAL DIRECTION: Kevin Stites; PRODUCER: The New York Shakespeare Festival (George C. Wolfe, Producer; Rosemarie Tichler, Artistic Director; Anne F. Zimmerman, Managing Director; Wiley Hausam and Bonnie Metzgar, Associate Producers)

CAST—Luiz-Ottavio Faria (Workman, Miss Turnstyle Announcer), Leslie Feagan (Quartet, Waldo Figment), Blake Hammond (Quartet, Mr. S. Uperman, Master of Ceremonies), Jesse Means, II (Quartet, Policeman), Glenn Turner (Quartet, Subway Bill Poster, Rajah Bimmy), Robert Montano (Ozzie), Jesse Tyler Ferguson (Chip), Jose Llana (Gabey), Linda Mugleston (Flossie, Carnegie Hall Woman), Chandra Wilson (Flossie's Friend, Mannequin, Carnegie Hall Woman), Mary Testa (Little Old Lady, Madame Maude P. Dilly), Ivy Fox (Mannequin, Diamond Eddie Girl), Keri Lee (Mannequin, Diamond Eddie Girl), Joanne McHugh (Mannequin, Diamond Eddie Girl), Nora Cole (Miss Turnstile Announcer, Carnegie Hall Woman, Diana Dream, Dolores Dolores), Sophia Salguero (Ivy Smith), Lea DeLaria (Hildy Esterhazy), Kate Suber (Claire DeLoone), Nickemil Concepcion (Primitive Man), Margaux Zadikian (Primitive Woman, Diamond Eddie Girl), Patricia Tuthill (Pas de Deux Dancer, Diamond Eddie Girl), Jassen Virolas (Pas de Deux Dancer), Jonathan Freeman (Pitkin W. Bridgework), Annie Golden (Lucy Schmeeler), Rachel Alvarado (Diamond Eddie Girl); Dance Ensemble: Rachel Alvarado, Andy Blankenbuehler, Nickemil Concepcion, Karl DuHoffman, Ivy Fox, Darren Gibson, Clay Harper Jackson, Keri Lee, Joanne McHugh, Patricia Tuthill, Jassen Virolas, Margaux Zadikian; The People of New York: Nora Cole, Luiz-Ottavio Faria, Leslie Feagan, Annie Golden, Blake Hammond, Jesse Means, II, Linda Mugleston, Mary Testa, Glenn Turner, Chandra Wilson

SOURCES—An idea by Jerome Robbins; and the ballet *Fancy Free* (1944; choreography by Jerome Robbins and music by Leonard Bernstein).

The action occurs in and around New York City during the War Forties.

The musical was presented in two acts.

ACT ONE—"I Feel Like I'm Not Out of Bed Yet" (Luiz-Ottavio Faria, Leslie Feagan, Blake Hammond, Jesse Means, II, Glenn Turner), "New York, New York" (Jose Llana, Jesse Tyler Ferguson, Robert Montano, Company), "Gabey's Coming" (Robert Mantano, Jesse Tyler Ferguson, Jose Llana, Ivy Fox, Keri Lee, Joanne McHugh, Chandra Wilson), "Presentation of Miss Turnstiles" (Nora Cole, Luiz-Ottavio Faria, Sophia Salguero, Dance Ensemble), "Come Up to My Place" (Lea DeLaria, Jesse Tyler Ferguson), "Carried Away" (Kate Suber, Robert Mantano, Nickemil Concepcion, Margaux Zadikian), "Lonely Town" (Jose Ilana, Dance Ensemble), "Carnegie Hall Pavane" (Sophie Salguero, Mary Testa, Nora Cole, Linda Mugleston, Chandra Wilson), "Lucky to Be Me" (Jose Ilana, Chorus), "I Understand" (Jonathan Freeman), "I Can Cook, Too" (Lea DeLaria), "Times Square Ballet" (Company)

ACT TWO—"So Long, Baby" (Rachel Alvarado, Ivy Fox, Keri Lee, Joanne McHugh, Patricia Tuthill, Margaux Zadikian), "I Wish I Was Dead" (Nora Cole), "I Wish I Was Dead" (reprise) (Nora Cole), "Ya Got Me" (Lea DeLaria, Kate Suber, Robert Montano, Jesse Tyler Ferguson), "I Understand" (reprise) (Jonathan Freeman, Annie Golden), "Subway Ride" (Jose Ilana, The People of New York), "Imaginary Coney Island" (Jose Ilana, Sophia Salguero, Dance Ensemble), "Some Other Time" (Kate Suber, Lea DeLaria, Robert Mantano, Jesse Tyler Ferguson), "The Real Coney Island" (Glenn Turner), "I Feel Like I'm Not Out of Bed Yet" (reprise) (Luiz-Ottavio Faria), "New York, New York" (reprise) (Company)

NOTES—This revival of *On the Town* gave free performances in Central Park for most of August 1997; the expectation that the musical would then transfer to Broadway at some point during the season was scotched due to a certain coolness on the part of the critics towards Eliot Feld's choreography and for some of George C. Wolfe's casting choices.

By the time the revival finally made it to Broadway some fifteen months later (at the Gershwin Theatre, where it opened on November 19, 1998, for sixty-five performances), Feld had bowed out, and some of the leads had been replaced. But the result was a disappointing evening of pleasantly adequate choreography (by Keith Young) for a musical which should have been suffused with show-stopping dances; further, some of the leads were bland. What saved the evening was the galvanic performance of Lea DeLaria as Hildy, the role first created by Nancy Walker in the original 1944 production. DeLaria gave a sterling comic performance, and it's Broadway's loss that it has never capitalized on this capital clown. Besides DeLaria, Mary Testa and Annie Golden provided what little fun there was in the decidedly unexciting revival. The musical was nice to look at, however; Adrianne Lobel's clever sets utilized the look of old-time nostalgic postcards to create the ambience of little old New York.

For more information about *On the Town*, see entry for the 1959 Off Broadway revival.

1187 Once Around the City. THEATRE: Second Stage Theatre; OPENING DATE: July 10, 2001; PERFORMANCES: 16; BOOK: Willie Reale; LYRICS: Willie Reale; MUSIC: Robert Reale; DIRECTION: Mark Linn-Baker; CHOREOGRAPHY: Jennifer Muller; SCENERY: Adrianne Lobel; COSTUMES: Paul Tazewell; LIGHTING: Donald Holder; PRODUCERS: Second Stage Theatre (Carole Rothman, Artistic Director; Mark Linn-Baker, 2001 Artistic Director; Carol Fishman, Managing Director; Alexander Fraser, Executive Director) in association with Ron Kastner and Robert Boyett

CAST—William Parry (Charlie, Brandebaine), Anna Stone (Phyllis, Eve), Peter Jay Fernandez (Luis), Patrick Garner (John), Joe Grifasi (Mario), Brandy Zarle (Elizabeth), Harry Althaus (Nicky), John Bowman (Ernie), Michael Potts (Rudy), Geoffrey Nauftts (Hank), Anne Torsiglieri (Margaret, Dolores), Michael Mandell (Bill), Michael Magee (David), Jane Bodle (Gwen), Sandra Shipley (Mrs. Merkin)

The musical was presented in two acts.

NOTES—The musical dealt with an heiress who's cheated out of her home when she turns it into a shelter for homeless men. After two weeks, the show itself was homeless.

1188 Once Around the Sun. "Life on the B Side." THEATRE: Zipper Theatre; OPENING DATE: August 11, 2005; PERFORMANCES: 66; BOOK: Kelly Overbey; LYRICS: Robert Morris, Steven Morris, and Joe Shane; MUSIC: Robert Morris, Steven Morris, and Joe Shane; DIRECTION: Jace Alexander; CHOREOGRAPHY: Taro Alexander; SCENERY: Beowulf Borritt; COSTUMES: Daniel Lawson; LIGHTING: Jason Lyons; MUSICAL DIRECTION: Henry Aronson; PRODUCERS: Sibling Entertainment and URL Productions in association with Maffei Productions

CAST—Asa Somers (Kevin), Caren Lyn Manuel (Skye, Fred), Kevin Mambo (Ray, Waldo), Jesse Lenat (Dave, Guy), Wes Little (Richie), John Hickok (Lane), Maya Days (Nona)

The musical was presented in two acts (division of acts and song assignments unknown; songs are listed in performance order).

MUSICAL NUMBERS—"It's All Music," "First Dance," "Life Is What You Make of It," "You're My Lullaby," "Let Go," "And That's Your Life," "Fool Like Me," "Once Around the Sun," "Lucky Day," "G-I-R-L," "Missing You, My Friend," "Something Sentimental," "Love and Live On," "Just Another Year"

NOTES—Jeffrey Eric Jenkins in *The Best Plays Theater Yearbook 2005-2006* noted that the plot of *Once Around the Sun* dealt with the familiar one of an artist (in this instance, a musician) who must choose between having popular success or staying true to himself. This seems to be a conflict which particularly affects characters in plays and musicals, and is perhaps second only to those plots in which a conflicted heroine must choose between the stalwart but dull male or the irresponsible but exciting one. A 7" promo CD of four songs (and one reprise) was released by Solace Productions, LLC, and included mostly original cast performances (the songs were "It's All Music," "Fool Like Me," "Love and Live On," and the title song).

1189 Once I Saw a Boy Laughing... "A Story/A Musical." THEATRE: Westside Theatre; OPENING DATE: February 21, 1974; PERFORMANCES: 5; PLAY: Scott Mansfield; LYRICS: Scott Mansfield; MUSIC: Scott Mansfield; DIRECTION: Gail Mansfield; SCENERY: David Chapman; COSTUMES: Ann Kelleher; LIGHTING: Martin Aronstein; MUSICAL DIRECTION: Jon Randall Booth; PRODUCERS: Lawrence E. Davis in association with Jolandrea Productions, Inc.

CAST—Scott Mansfield (Paul), Dennis Simpson (Johnny), Russ Thacker (Billy), Michael Glenn-Smith (Wilson), Rick Warner (Philips), Jerry Plummer Chesnut (Tompkins)

The action occurs in a piece of land in nowhere.

The play was presented in two acts.

NOTES—The opening night playbill of *Once I Saw a Boy Laughing...* cites February 24 as the play's opening, but most sources give February 21. The drama with music moved up the date of its opening to the 21st, and February 24 was actually the show's closing night.

Eight songs were included in the play: "Gee, I Got the Blues" (sung by the entire company; the remaining numbers were not identified by character), "So Long Suzanne/A Song for Boni," "Lonely as the Wind," "Morning Child," "Once I Saw a Boy Laughing," "Again, My Friend," and "Why." (Six orchestrators were credited: Lee Norris, Wally Harper, Ron Frangipane, Ron Kristy, Stephen Metcalf, and Peter Howard.)

The surreal play dealt with six soldiers; at least five are killed off, one by one, by an unseen enemy in an unidentified war.

Clive Barnes in the *New York Times* noted the boy of the evening's title might have been laughing, but Barnes couldn't imagine what he found funny. He said the play by Scott Mansfield had virtually no story, and its dialogue consisted of "wisecracks." He further noted that Mansfield's sister Gail was the show's director and that Mansfield himself had the "courage" to act in it.

1190 Once on a Summer's Day. THEATRE: Ensemble Studio Theatre; OPENING DATE: December 7, 1984; PERFORMANCES: 26; BOOK: Arthur Perlman; LYRICS: Arthur Perlman; MUSIC: Jeffrey Lunden; DIRECTION: John Henry Davis; CHOREOGRAPHY: Elizabeth Keen; SCENERY: Philipp Jung; COSTUMES: Donna Zakowska; LIGHTING: Michael Orris Watson; MUSICAL DIRECTION: Ronald Clay Fullum; PRODUCER: Ensemble Studio Theatre (Curt Dempster, Artistic Director; David S. Rosenak, Managing Director)

CAST—Kimi Morris (Alice Liddell), Martin Moran (The Mad Hatter), David Purdham (Charles Dodgson), Carolyn Mignini (Older Alice, Mrs. Liddell), Nicholas Wyman (The Caterpillar), Mimi Wyche (The Duchess), Polly Pen (The White Rabbit), David Green (Robinson Duckworth)

The action occurs in Victorian England over a thirty-year period.

The musical was presented in two acts.

ACT ONE—Prologue/"Once on a Summer's Day" (Martin Moran, David Purdham, Mimi Wyche, Nicholas Wyman, Polly Pen, Kimi Morris), "Don't Depend on Watches, My Friend" (Martin Moran), "The Angles of Geometry" (David Purdham, Nicholas Wyman, Kimi Morris), "Wonderland" (Mimi Wyche, David Purdham, Kimi Morris, Nicholas Wyman, Martin Moran, Polly Pen), "Fairy Child" (Martin Moran, Polly Pen), "No" (Mimi Wyche), "The Music Box" (Orchestra and Fantasy Characters)

ACT TWO—"See What Mr. Dodgson Gave Me" (Carolyn Mignini [?]), "The Tea Party" (Martin Moran, Nicholas Wyman, Polly Pen, Mimi Wyche, David Purdham, Kimi Morris), "Wonderland" (reprise) (Kimi Morris, Carolyn Mignini, Martin Moran, Nicholas Wyman, Mimi Wyche, Polly Pen), "Jabberwocky" (Polly Pen), "The Equation Cannot Be Solved" (David Purdham), "The Trial" (Company), "Rules Shall Not Be Broken" (David Purdham)

NOTES—The Off Off Broadway musical *Once on a Summer's Day* was inspired by Lewis B. Carroll's *Alice's Adventures in Wonderland* (1865); for more information regarding musicals based on this novel or on Carroll's *Through the Looking Glass* (1872), see entry for *Alice with Kisses* (also see Appendix K). Most of the *Alice* adaptations were more or less straightforward versions of Carroll's books, but *Once on a Summer's Day* and *For the Snark Was a Boojun, You See* (1977; see entry) explored the relationship between Lewis B. Carroll (a/k/a Charles Lutwidge Dodgson) and Alice Liddell, the little girl who was the inspiration for his masterpiece. Further, both musicals used the Wonderland characters to serve as a kind of ghostly Greek chorus to comment on the action. *Once on a Summer's Day* was produced in two slightly separated engagements at the Ensemble Studio Theatre, first on December 7, 1984, for twenty-six performances, and then on January 10, 1985, for thirty-one performances. The musical was then announced for a regular Off Broadway production at the Westside Arts Center/Cheryl Crawford Theater beginning on March 1, 1985, but at the last minute the production was cancelled because of financing problems. However, the programs had been printed, and one which has surfaced shows that a few casting changes had been intended for the aborted Off Broadway production. For Off Broadway, The Mad Hatter was to have been played by Todd Graff; for The Caterpillar, Ken Jennings; and for Charles Dodgson, Nicholas Wyman (who had played The Caterpillar during the Off Off Broadway production). For the Off Broadway production, the opening number of the second act, "See What Mr. Dodgson Gave Me" (apparently sung by the older Alice), was replaced by "I Close My Eyes" (for the same character).

An advertisement for the Off Broadway production appeared in the *New York Times* without Ken Jennings' name (apparently he hadn't yet signed a contract when the advertisement went to press), but his name appears in the program for the cancelled production.

1191 Once on This Island. THEATRE: Playwrights Horizons; OPENING DATE: May 6, 1990; PERFORMANCES: 24; BOOK: Lynn Ahrens; LYRICS: Lynn Ahrens; MUSIC: Stephen Flaherty; DIRECTION: Graciela Daniele; CHOREOGRAPHY: Graciela Daniele; SCENERY: Loy Arcenas; COSTUMES: Judy Dearing; LIGHTING: Allen Lee Hughes; MUSICAL DIRECTION: Stephen Marzullo; PRODUCER: Playwrights Horizons (Andre Bishop, Artistic Director; Paul S. Daniels, Executive Director)

CAST—Jerry Dixon (Daniel), Andrea Frierson (Erzulie), Sheila Gibbs (Mama Euralie), La Chanze (Ti Moune), Kecia Lewis-Evans (Asaka), Afi McClendon (Little Ti Moune), Gerry McIntyre (Armand), Milton Craig Nealy (Agwe), Nikke Rene (Andrea), Eric Riley (Papa Ge), Ellis E. Williams (Tonton Julian)

SOURCE—The 1985 novel *My Love, My Love, or The Peasant Girl* by Rosa Guy.

The action occurs on an island in the French Antilles.

The musical was presented in one act.

MUSICAL NUMBERS—"We Dance" (Storytellers), "One Small Girl" (Sheila Gibbs, Ellis E. Williams, Afi McClendon, Storytellers), "Waiting for Life" (La Chanze, Storytellers), "And the Gods Heard Her

Prayer" (Kecia Lewis-Evans, Milton Craig Nealy, Eric Riley, Andrea Frierson), "Rain" (Milton Craig Nealy, Storytellers), "Pray" (La Chanze, Ellis E. Williams, Sheila Gibbs, Guard, Storytellers), "Forever Yours" (La Chanze, Jerry Dixon, Eric Riley), "The Sad Tale of the Beauxhommes" (Gerry McIntyre, Storytellers), "Ti Moune" (Sheila Gibbs, Ellis E. Williams, La Chanze), "Mama Will Provide" (Kecia Lewis-Evans), "Waiting for Life" (reprise) (La Chanze), "Some Say" (Storytellers), "The Human Heart" (Andrea Frierson, Storytellers), "Pray" (reprise) (Storytellers), "Some Girls" (Jerry Dixon), "The Ball" (Nikki Rene, Jerry Dixon, La Chanze, Storytellers), "Forever Yours" (reprise) (Eric Riley, La Chanze, Andrea Frierson, Storytellers), "A Part of Us" (Sheila Gibbs, Afi McClendon, Ellis E. Williams, Storytellers), "Why We Tell the Story" (Storytellers)

NOTES—*Once on This Island* dealt with a group of islanders who wait out a storm by enacting a fable about a poor island girl who has the misfortune to fall in love with a rich man's son, who scorns her by marrying another. As Howard Kissel so succinctly put it in the *New York Daily News*, the jilted heroine does the only logical thing: "She turns into a tree"; he further noted that the musical aimed for "folk" and came out "fake." And Jan Stuart in *New York Newsday* found the score "cuddly ... alternately soporific and soothing ... you'll want to suck your thumb." On the other hand, Frank Rich in the *New York Times* said the musical had the "integrity" of a "genuine" fairy tale, and he praised Stephen Flaherty's "lush, melodic" score.

The musical transferred to Broadway at the Booth Theatre on October 18, 1990, and played for 469 performances. RCA Victor Records issued the cast album (CD # 60595-2-RC), which was recorded between the Off Broadway and Broadway engagements. A London production opened at the Island Theatre on September 28, 1994, and its cast album was issued by That's Entertainment Records (CD # CDTER-1224). Both recordings included sequences not listed in the New York program ("Ti Moune's Dance" and "When We Are Wed"; and the London album also included "Discovering Daniel"). The collections *Lost in Boston* (I) (Varese Sarabande Records CD # VSD-5475) and *Lost in Boston III* (Varese Sarabande Records CD # VSD-5563) offer cut songs from the score.

1192 Once Over Lightly. THEATRE: Barbizon-Plaza Theatre; OPENING DATE: March 15, 1955; PERFORMANCES: Unknown; SKETCHES: Melvin (Mel) Brooks, Philip Loeb, Zero Mostel, Aaron Rubin, and Ira Wallach; LYRICS: Marshall Barer and William Engvick; MUSIC: Dean Fuller, Murray Grand, Samuel Matlowsky, Ralph Strain, and Alec Wilder; DIRECTION: Stanley Prager; CHOREOGRAPHY: Lee Becker; SCENERY: Warwick Brown; COSTUMES: Warwick Brown; LIGHTING: Warwick Brown (?); MUSICAL DIRECTION: Peter Matz; PRODUCERS: Cuadro Productions (Nola Chilton, John Howell, Lee Nemetz, and Yale Wexler)

CAST—ZERO MOSTEL, SONO OSATO, JACK GILFORD, Jamie Bowers, June Ericson, Joe Lautner, George Mills, Victor Reilley, Joe Sargent, Royce Wallace, Patricia Wilkes

The revue was presented in two acts.

ACT ONE—Opening (lyric by Marshall Barer, music by Dean Fuller) (Jack Gilford, Company) "The Actor" (sketch by Melvin Brooks) (Zero Mostel, Joe Lautner, Joe Sargent) "Mobile, A Fascination" (music by Samuel Matlowsky) (Sono Osato), "Shake Hands with a Millionaire" (lyric by Marshall Barer, music by Ralph Strain) (Joe Sargent, Victor Reilley, George Mills, Joe Lautner, Jamie Bowers, Royce Wallace, June Ericson), "The Man and the Telephone" (sketch by Melvin Brooks) (Jack Gilford) "I Got Lucky" (lyric by Marshall Barer, music by Dean Fuller) (Patricia Wilkes, Royce Wallace, June Ericson) "Foreign Affairs" (sketch by Ira Wallach) (Joe Sargent, Zero Mostel, Joe Lautner, Jack Gilford, Patricia Wilkes) "Here Beside Me" (lyric by William Engvick, music by Alec Wilder) (June Ericson, Victor Reilley, Jamie Bowers, George Mills "Love on the Moon" (sketch by Ira Wallach) (Zero Mostel, Patricia Wilkes), "It's Silk, I Feel It" (lyric by Marshall Barer, music by Dean Fuller) (Patricia Wilkes, Royce Wallace, June Ericson) "Peter Pan" (Sono Osato, Jamie Bowers) "Benedictine" (lyric by Ira Wallach, music by Murray Grand) (Jack Gilford, Joe Lautner) "Melvin" (A Nine-Minute Menotti) (lyric by Marshall Barer, music by Dean Fuller) (Joe Lautner, Patricia Wilkes, Zero Mostel)

ACT TWO—"An Interview" (sketch by Philip Loeb and Zero Mostel) (Zero Mostel, Jack Gilford), "Bop-A-Bye" (lyric by Marshall Barer, music by Ralph Strain) (June Ericson, Victor Reilley, Sono Osato, George Mills, Jamie Bowers, Royce Wallace) "It's All in the Mind" (sketch by Aaron Rubin) (Joe Sargent, Zero Mostel, Jack Gilford) "I'll Dance You" (lyric by Marshall Barer, music by Dean Fuller) (Joe Lautner, Jamie Bowers, Victor Reilley, George Mills, Royce Wallace, June Ericson, Joe Sargent) "The Dog, the Cat, the Squirrel" (sketch by Melvin Brooks) (Zero Mostel, Victor Reilley, Sono Osato, Jack Gilford), "Roller Coaster Blues" (lyric by Marshall Barer, music by Dean Fuller) (Royce Wallace, Victor Reilley, Jamie Bowers, George Mills), "From the Cradle to the Grave" (sketch by Zero Mostel, music by Samuel Matlowsky) (Zero Mostel) "Cosmic Incident" (sketch by Ira Wallach) (Performer[s] uncredited), "Three Impressions" (inspired by William Steig's "The Rejected Lovers"): "Mama Mama" (Jamie Bowers); "To Hell with It, I'm Going to Have Fun" (Sono Osato); "Is This Really the End?" (Sono Osato, Company), "The Lecture" (sketch by Melvin Brooks) (Zero Mostel, Jack Gilford) "Warm Winter" (lyric by Marshall Barer, music by Dean Fuller) (Patricia Wilkes, Royce Wallace, June Ericson), "The Osteopathy Rag" (lyric by William Engvick, music by Alec Wilder) (Sono Osato, Zero Mostel, Jack Gilford), Finale (Company)

NOTES—*Once Over Lightly* is one of the most obscure Off Broadway musicals. In her fascinating autobiography *Distant Dances* (Alfred A. Knopf, 1980), Sono Osato discusses the revue and indicates its run was very brief. She remembers noting the sparse audiences and her urge to ask everyone to sit together so the performers could play to one group. Osato created the role of Miss Turnstiles in the original 1944 Broadway production of *On the Town*, and also appeared in the original Broadway productions of *One Touch of Venus* (1943) and *Ballet Ballads* (1949); see entries for the Off Broadway revivals of *On the Town* and *Ballet Ballads*.

Despite their short run in *Once Over Lightly*, Mostel and Gilford enjoyed a long-running Broadway success in *A Funny Thing Happened on the Way to the Forum* (1962). In 1967 Mel Brooks and Mostel made comic history with *The Producers*.

Brooks Atkinson in the *New York Times* had high praise for Mostel's antics, and singled out a number of sketches, songs, and dances (including Osato's Japanese re-telling of the Peter Pan story and the "fuguelike" song "I Got Lucky").

Once Over Lightly's program listed twenty-six numbers, and, in order to shorten the length of the evening, some may have been dropped after the opening. This assessment is based on a program in which an unknown theatergoer heavily marked out eight numbers (of course, maybe he just didn't like them): "Mobile, A Fascination," "Shake Hands with a Millionaire," "Love on the Moon," "Roller Coaster Blues," "From the Cradle to the Grave," "Cosmic Incident," "The Lecturer," and "Warm Winter."

Once Over Lightly isn't to be confused with the Broadway musical of the same name, which opened at the Alvin (now Neil Simon) Theatre on November 19, 1942, for six performances. This was a musical comedy treatment of Gioacchino Rossini's 1816 opera *The Barber of Seville,* and in his *Theatre Book of the Year 1942-1943*, George Jean Nathan provided a sample of the lyrics: "I'm the well-known barber of Seville who gets in everybody's hair."

1193 Once Upon a Mattress. "A New Musical." THEATRE: Phoenix Theatre; OPENING DATE: May 11, 1959; PERFORMANCES: 216; BOOK: Jay Thompson, Marshall Barer, and Dean Fuller; LYRICS: Marshall Barer; MUSIC: Mary Rodgers; DIRECTION: George Abbott; CHOREOGRAPHY: Joe Layton; SCENERY: William and Jean Eckart; COSTUMES: William and Jean Eckart; LIGHTING: Tharon Musser; MUSICAL DIRECTION: Hal Hastings; PRODUCERS: The Phoenix Theatre (T. Edward Hambleton and Norris Houghton) and William and Jean Eckart

CAST—HARRY SNOW (Minstrel), Jim Maher (Prince), Chris Karner (Princess, Lady Mabell), Gloria Stevens (Queen, Lady Beatrice), ROBERT WEIL (Wizard), Mary Stanton (Princess Number Twelve), Dorothy Aull (Lady Rowena), Patsi King (Lady Merrill), JOE BOVA (Prince Dauntless), JANE WHITE (The Queen), Luce Ennis (Lady Lucille), ANNE JONES (Lady Larkin), Jerry Newby (Sir Studley), JACK GILFORD (The King), MATT MATTOX (Jester), ALLEN CASE (Sir Harry), CAROL BURNETT (Princess Winnifred), David Neuman (Sir Harold), Tom Mixon (Sir Luce), Ginny Perlowin (Nightingale of Samarkand), Dorothy D'Honau (Lady Dorothy), Christopher Edwards (Sir Christopher), Howard Parker (Lord Howard), Dorothy Frank (Lady Dora), Dan Resin (Sir Daniel), Jim Stevenson (Sir Steven), Julian Patrick (Lord Patrick)

SOURCE—The 1835 fairy tale "The Princess and the Pea" by Hans Christian Andersen.

The musical was presented in two acts.

ACT ONE—"Many Moons Ago" (Harry Snow, Court), "An Opening for a Princess" (Joe Bova, Anne Jones, Knights, Ladies), "In a Little While" (Anne Jones, Allen Case), "In a Little While" (reprise) (Anne Jones, Allen Case), "Shy" (Carol Burnett, Jerry Newby, Knights, Ladies), "The Minstrel, the Jester and I" (Jack Gilford, Harry Snow, Matt Mattox), "Sensitivity" (Jane White, Robert Weil), "Swamps of Home" (Carol Burnett, Joe Bova, Matt Mattox), "Normandy" (Harry Snow, Matt Mattox, Jack Gilford, Anne Jones), "Spanish Panic" (Jane White, Knights, Ladies), "Song of Love" (Joe Bova, Carol Burnett, Knights, Ladies)

ACT TWO—"Quiet" (Matt Mattox, Knights, Ladies), "Happily Ever After" (Carol Burnett), "Man to Man Talk" (Jack Gilford, Knights, Ladies, Joe Bova), "Very Soft Shoes" (Matt Mattox, Knights, Ladies), "Yesterday I Loved You" (Allen Case, Anne Jones), "Lullaby" (Ginny Perlowin), Finale (Entire Court)

NOTES—Of the Phoenix Theatre's first five musicals, *Once Upon a Mattress* was its first hit. The Phoenix would continue producing plays and musicals for many more decades, and perhaps one of its highlights was the 1962 premiere of one of the greatest of American dramas, Frank D. Gilroy's shamelessly neglected *Who'll Save the Plowboy?* But during the company's early years, there would be just one more new musical, the 1963 Off Broadway failure *Morning Sun* (see entry).

Once Upon a Mattress was the show which catapulted Carol Burnett to stardom. Unfortunately, she would create only one more musical role in New York, the 1964 failure *Fade Out-Fade In*. Her film appearances failed to capture her unique comic flair, and it was on television where she flowered: her long-running variety show resembled musical revues with skits which often spoofed popular culture. After a 216-performance run at the Phoenix, *Mattress* opened on Broadway at the Alvin (now Neil Simon)

Theatre on November 11, 1959, and from there it transferred three times, to the Winter Garden, the Cort, and finally to the St. James, making it the only musical to play in five different New York theatres during its initial run and certainly establishing its place in the record books as New York's Most Traveled Musical. The Broadway performances totaled 244, giving the show a combined Off Broadway and Broadway run of 460 performances. During the last weeks of its Broadway run, Ann B. Davis (who, like Burnett, would later enjoy television immortality [in *The Brady Bunch*]) played the role of Winnifred.

The show was an amiable spoof of the classic fairy tale "The Princess and the Pea," and included many amusing conceits: the King's role was a non-speaking one, and he "spoke" only in mime; the interviews with the princesses (to find out who was the most delicate) were staged in the manner of a television quiz show ("Would you repeat the question, please?"); and Winnifred's establishing song, "Shy," was not quietly sung by Burnett, but was belted all the way to the back balcony.

Despite the lack of a hit song to help establish the show in the public mind, *Once Upon a Mattress* became a staple in stock, regional, college, and high school theatres, due, no doubt, to the amusing book, amiable score, and variety of colorful characters. With her delightful score, Mary Rodgers (Richard Rodgers' daughter) revealed talent and skill in her first professionally produced musical. Indeed, talent runs in the family: Mary Rodgers' son, Adam Guettel, is the composer-lyricist of *Floyd Collins* (1996; see entry), one of the finest theatre scores of recent decades. He also composed the lovely score for the highly regarded *The Light in the Piazza* (2005).

Mattress has been produced for television three times (1964, December 12, 1972, and 2005). Burnett appeared in all three productions, in the first two recreating her role of Winnifred, and in the third playing the role of the Queen. For the 1964 and 1972 versions, Jack Gilford and Jane White also reprised their original roles. The 1964 television version also included one new song, "Under a Spell." The 2005 version was released on DVD by Disney/Buena Vista Home Entertainment (# 39254).

The one Broadway revival, in 1996, failed after 187 performances. It was a beautifully designed production, which took on the bold colors of the illustrations for a book of fairy tales, and, for the most part, it was well cast. But the miscasting of Sarah Jessica Parker as Winnifed doomed the revival; the usually amiable actress was strangely tentative, and lacked the eccentric and gutsy approach which the role demanded (Lea DeLaria would have been a natural for this larger-than-life role).

The London production was a failure, opening at the Adelphi Theatre on September 20, 1960, and playing for only thirty-one performances. Jane Connell was Winnifred, and her quirky, welcome brand of comedy was preserved on the London cast album which was released by HMV Records (LP # CLP-1410; later reissued by Stet Records [LP # DS-15026]).

The Off Broadway cast album was originally released on Kapp Records (LP # KLD-7004 [reissued on KRS-5507]), and the 1996 Broadway revival on RCA Victor Records (CD # 09026-68728-2). When MCA Classics Records reissued the 1959 cast album on CD (# MCAD-10768), the release included two previously unreleased tracks of original cast performances: "Quiet" (Jane White and Ensemble) and "Lullaby" (Ginny Perlowin). These numbers are also heard on the revival's recording. The script was published in the July 1960 issue of *Theatre Arts* magazine.

Once Upon a Mattress was originally produced as one-act musical called *The Princess and the Pea* at Camp Taminent, an adult summer camp in the Poconos.

When the musical was produced at the Phoenix, a number in the first act was dropped during previews ("Up and Away," sung by Harry Snow and Matt Mattox), and there was some minor repositioning of first-act songs once the number was eliminated. When the show opened on Broadway later in the year, there were some changes in the cast, most notably Will Lee replacing Jack Gilford as the King and Jerry Newby replacing Matt Mattox as the Jester. Jerry Newby, who had performed in role of Sir Studley during the Phoenix engagement, played the role of the Jester on Broadway, and busy Off Broadway performer Tom Mixon, who played Sir Luce at the Phoenix, moved up to the role of Sir Studley for Broadway. There were also a few cast members in supporting roles who were replaced for Broadway; at the Phoenix, the names of the actors' characters were variations of their own first or last names, and when those actors didn't transfer to Broadway, the actors who replaced them found that their characters' names were variations of their own (i.e., at the Phoenix, Lord Howard was played by Howard Parker, on Broadway, Lord Casper was played by Casper Roos).

For the record, *Once Upon a Mattress* has a certain place in the history of color-blind casting. Jane White, who played the (White) Queen, was Black. She later told Dan Sullivan in the *New York Times* that audience members didn't seem to think about her race, only the character she was portraying, and "that's the way it should be."

1194 One and One.

"A New Musical Comedy." THEATRE: Bert Wheeler Theatre; OPENING DATE: April (?) 1978; PERFORMANCES: Unknown; BOOK: Fred Bennett and Richard O'Donnell; LYRICS: Dianne Adams and Richard O'Donnell; MUSIC: Dianne Adams and Richard O'Donnell; DIRECTION: Jim Payne; CHOREOGRAPHY: Roger Braun; SCENERY: Bruce Monroe; COSTUMES: Mary Mola; LIGHTING: Lisa Grossman; MUSICAL DIRECTION: Dianne Adams; PRODUCER: Broadway-Times Theatre Company, Inc.

CAST—Marla Miller (Reporter, Danny [USO Girl]), Larry Weston (Old Mutt), Linda Kerns (Nurse Kramer, Sarge), Peter Boynton (Mutt Majeski, Desk Clerk, Sailor), Alan Nicholson (Jeff O'Riely, Bellhop), Karen Kruger (Julie Allyn, USO Girl), Jerry Richkin (Zimon, Solider), Scott Bodie (Peter Lerman, M.C. Soldier)

The musical was presented in two acts.

ACT ONE—"Where Is That Man?" (Marla Miller, Peter Boynton, Alan Nicholson), "One and One" (Larry Weston, Alan Nicholson), "B-A-R-B-E-R" (Marla Miller, Jerry Richkin, Larry Weston, Alan Nicholson), "If You Can Prove I'm in Love" (Karen Kruger), "On the Road Again" (Alan Nicholson, Larry Weston, Karen Kruger), "Montage" (Karen Kruger, Larry Weston, Alan Nicholson), "Opening Night" (Alan Nicholson, Larry Weston, Karen Kruger), "Dancer" (Alan Nicholson, Karen Kruger), "Cupid's Arrow" (Larry Weston, Karen Kruger), "If You Can Prove I'm in Love" (reprise) (Karen Kruger, Alan Nicholson, Larry Weston)

ACT TWO—"Ya Gotta Be Female" (Karen Kruger, Larry Weston, Alan Nicholson), "All You Need Is Confidence" (Scott Bodie, Karen Kruger), "Opening Night" (reprise) (Larry Weston, Alan Nicholson), "Jeff's Song" (Alan Nicholson), "Military Man" (Linda Kerns, Alan Nicholson, Company), "Looking to the Sky" (Larry Weston), "Lonely Song and Dance Man" (Larry Weston)

NOTES—*One and One* kicked off the Broadway-Times Theatre Company, Inc., a short-lived venture dedicated to the production of new musicals. *One and One* was later followed by *Success*, *Shelley*, and *Not Tonight, Benvenuto!* (see entries).

A program note indicated *One and One* was about two friends bound together by their love of the stage and their love for another; the evening was described as an "Old Style" musical with a "contemporary flair" which included music in the styles of swing and honky-tonk, and a storyline "right out of the MGM era."

1195 One Foot Out the Door.

THEATRE: Trocadero Cabaret at Don't Tell Mama; OPENING DATE: March 5, 1993; PERFORMANCES: 41; BOOK: Stephen Dolginoff; LYRICS: Stephen Dolginoff; MUSIC: Stephen Dolginoff; DIRECTION: Cheryl Katz; PRODUCER: SDD Productions

CAST—Laurie Alyssa Myers (Shelley), Kyle Dadd (Bryan), Elizabeth Richmond (Marissa), Patrick Peterson (Therapist, Eddie, Tom, Phil)

The musical was presented in one act.

MUSICAL NUMBERS—Overture (Orchestra), "Therapy" (Laurie Alyssa Myers, Kyle Dadd, Elizabeth Richmond), "The Night That I Met Phil" (Kyle Dadd), "Here I Am" (Elizabeth Richmond), "Barbie and Ken" (Laurie Alyssa Myers), "What He'd Say" (Laurie Alyssa Myers, Patrick Petertson, Kyle Dadd), "Eddie's Always Here" (Patrick Peterson, Elizabeth Richmond), "Therapy—Part 2" (Laurie Alyssa Myers, Kyle Dadd, Elizabeth Richmond), "One Foot Out the Door" (Laurie Alyssa Myers, Kyle Dadd, Elizabeth Richmond), "Penalty" (Laurie Alyssa Myers, Patrick Peterson), "Barbie and Ken" (reprise) (Laurie Alyssa Myers, Kyle Dadd, Elizabeth Richmond), "House on Coney Island" (Elizabeth Richmond), "Like the Skyline" (Laurie Alyssa Myers, Kyle Dadd, Elizabeth Richmond), "My Deepest Thoughts" (Kyle Dadd, Patrick Peterson), "Therapy—Part 3" (Laurie Alyssa Myers, Kyle Dadd, Elizabeth Richmond), "When I'll Miss Him" (Elizabeth Richmond, Laurie Alyssa Myers), "Conclusions" (Laurie Alyssa Myers, Kyle Dadd, Elizabeth Richmond)

NOTES—The Off Off Broadway musical *One Foot Out the Door* dealt with Shelley, Marissa, and Bryan, two women and one man in group therapy, all of whom are unable to deal with the men in their lives (the roles of their men were performed by the actor who also played the role of the therapist).

The cast album was released on an unnamed and unnumbered label; Joel Carlton, who succeeded Patrick Peterson in the role of the therapist, was heard on the album, which omitted one song performed in the production ("Not Anymore"). For other "therapy" musicals, see entries for *I Can't Keep Running in Place* (which dealt with six women who meet weekly for assertiveness training), *Inside Out* (about six women who meet for therapy sessions), and *Sessions* (in which even the psychiatrist has issues).

1196 One for the Money Etc.

"A Musical Revue." THEATRE: Eastside Playhouse; OPENING DATE: May 24, 1972; PERFORMANCES: 23; SKETCHES: Nancy Hamilton; LYRICS: Nancy Hamilton; MUSIC: Morgan Lewis; DIRECTION: Tom Panko; CHOREOGRAPHY: Tom Panko; SCENERY: Fred Voelpel; COSTUMES: Fred Voelpel; LIGHTING: Judy Rasmuson; MUSICAL DIRECTION: Peter Howard; PRODUCER: Charles Forsythe

CAST—Pamela Adams, Georgia Engel, Joy Garrett, Douglas Houston, Geoff Leon, Pat Lysinger, Charles Murphy, Liz Otto, Edward Penn, Jess Richards

The revue was presented in two acts.

ACT ONE—"An Ordinary Family" (Company) (*), "Post-Mortem" (Ed Penn, Liz Otto, Charles Murphy, Jess Richards, Douglas Houston) (***), "Teeter Totter Tessie" (Joy Garrett) (*), "I Only Know" (Charles Murphy, Pat Lysinger, Jess Richards) (*), "The Guess-It Hour" (Geoff Leon, Charles Murphy, Pamela Adams, Ed Penn, Georgia Engel) (**), "Born for Better Things" (Joy Garrett, Ed

Penn) (***), "Wisconsin, or Kenosha Canoe" (Company) (***)

ACT TWO—"If It's Love" (Company) (***), "The Russian Lesson" (Joy Garrett, Pat Lysinger, Georgia Engel, Liz Otto) (***), "The Old Soft Shoe" (Douglas Houston, Jess Richards, Geoff Leon) (***), "A House with a Little Red Barn" (Company) (**), "How High the Moon" (Jess Richards) (**), "The Story of the Opera" (Pat Lysinger, Ed Penn, Georgia Engel) (*), "Goodnight Mrs. Astor" (Company) (**)

NOTES—The rather awkwardly titled revival was a collection of sketches and songs from three fondly remembered Broadway revues written by Nancy Hamilton and Morgan Lewis, *One for the Money* (1939; 132 performances), *Two for the Show* (1940; 124 performances), and *Three to Get Ready* (1946; 327 performances).

Howard Thompson in the *New York Times* found the revival "charming," and he was grateful the material hadn't been updated; the evening was "pleasant, clean, tuneful and smiling" (Thompson asked if the evening was "Square?," and his answer was "You bet!").

"An Ordinary Family" was a spoof of *You Can't Take It with You* (1937), and "Wisconsin, or Kenosha Canoe" was one of the earliest examples of a parody of a Rodgers and Hammerstein musical. "How High the Moon" is the most famous song to emerge from the three revues, and it remains one of the most melodic and ethereal ballads ever written for the theatre.

The revue had been seen earlier in the season in an Equity Library Theatre production at the Master Theatre, opening on January 13, 1972.

A collection of twenty-five sketches and songs from the three revues was published by Samuel French, Inc., in 1952 under the title *Three to One.*

(*) FROM *ONE FOR THE MONEY*
(**) FROM *TWO FOR THE SHOW*
(***) FROM *THREE TO GET READY*

1197 One Man Band. "A New Musical." THEATRE: South Street Theatre; OPENING DATE: June 12, 1985; PERFORMANCES: 38; BOOK: James Lecesne; LYRICS: Marc Elliot and Larry Hochman; MUSIC: Marc Elliot; DIRECTION: Jack Hofsiss; CHOREOGRAPHY: Kay Cole, Choreographic Associate; SCENERY: Lawrence Miller; COSTUMES: William Ivey Long; LIGHTING: Natasha Katz; PRODUCERS: Willa Shalit and Robert Levithan; Edward P. Carroll, Dale Anderson, and Lois Deutchman, Associate Producers

CAST—JAMES LECESNE (Art, Mary Kay, Madame Butarde, Walter, Pops, Rocky, Rose), The Women (Kay Cole, Judy Gibson, Vanessa Williams), Debra Barsha (Piano Woman)

The musical was presented in one act.

MUSICAL NUMBERS—Overture (Orchestra), "Hey Lady" (James Lecesne, Kay Cole, Judy Gibson, Vanessa Williams), "Somewhere Out There" (James Lecesne, Kay Cole, Judy Gibson, Vanessa Williams), "Moonlight" (James Lecesne), "One Silk Shirt" (James Lecesne), "Atlantic City" (James Lecesne, Kay Cole, Judy Gibson, Vanessa Williams), "Moonlight" (reprise) (Kay Cole, Judy Gibson, Vanessa Williams), "Singin' a Song" (James Lecesne, Kay Cole, Judy Gibson, Vanessa Williams), "Female Animal" (James Lecesne, Kay Cole, Judy Gibson, Vanessa Williams), "The Perfect Life" (James Lecesne), "One Man Band" (James Lecesne, Kay Cole, Judy Gibson, Vanessa Williams), "Atlantic City" (finale) (Debra Barsha, Kay Cole, Judy Gibson, Vanessa Williams), "Singin' a Song" (reprise) (James Lecesne), "One Man Band" (reprise) (Company)

NOTES—The Off Off Broadway musical *One Man Band* was essentially a one-man musical in which James Lecesne played Art, a midwestern farmer who travels across the United States in search of his runaway wife Adelle (whom he never finds); Lecesne also played the roles of various people he meets on his travels. The musical included three back-up singers (including former Miss America 1984, Vanessa Williams) and a "Piano Woman" (Debra Barsha).

D.J.R. Bruckner in the *New York Times* was highly impressed with the unusual musical, a "tour of romantic devotion that is shamelessly satisfying." He praised Lecesne's virtuoso performance and said the "clarity, wit and speed" of Jack Hofsiss' direction ensured that every aspect of the production (scenery, costumes, lighting, choreography, and sound) contributed to a "witty" but not "overdone" evening which told a "funny little story." Bruckner also praised the score, including "Singin' a Song," "Female Animal," and "One Silk Shirt" (the latter "as elusive and lovely as many an old operetta aria").

In 1992, Original Cast Records (CD # OC-9212) released an album of the musical, with Lecesne recreating his original roles. The CD included three songs not heard in the Off Off Broadway production ("Have You Seen My Wife?," "When the Cows Come Home," and "Have Your Party Now"), and omitted two numbers ("Hey Lady" and "Female Animal"). The liner notes indicated that over the years the musical played in such New York venues as The Ballroom, The Duplex, Don't Tell Mama, and Upstairs at Greene Street.

1198 One Mo' Time! "An Evening of Black Vaudeville." THEATRE: Village Gate Downstairs; OPENING DATE: October 22, 1979; PERFORMANCES: 1,372; DIRECTION: Vernel Bagneris; Dean Irby, Additional Staging; SCENERY: Elwin Charles Terrel II; COSTUMES: Joann Clevenger; LIGHTING: Joanna Schielke; PRODUCERS: Art D'Lugoff, Burt D'Lugoff, and Jerry Wexler in association with Shari Upbin

CAST—Sylvia "Kuumba" Williams (Bertha), Thais Clark (Ma Reed), Topsy Chapman (Thelma), Vernel Bagneris (Papa Du), John Stell (Theatre Owner); The New Orleans Blue Serenaders (Lars Edegran, Piano/Co-Director; Orange Kellin, Clarinet/Co-Director; John Robichaux, Drums; William Davis, Tuba; Jabbo Smith, Trumpet

The action occurs at the Lyric Theatre in New Orleans in 1926.

The revue was presented in two acts (the musical numbers weren't listed in the program; the list below is taken from the cast album; song assignments are unknown).

ACT ONE—"Down in Honky Tonk Town" (lyric and music by Charles McCarron and Chris Smith), "Kiss Me Sweet" (lyric and music by A.J. Piron and Steve J. Lewis), "Miss Jenny's Ball" (lyric and music by Reed), "Cake Walkin' Babies from Home" (lyric and music by Chris Smith, Henry Todd, and Clarence Williams), "I've Got What It Takes" (lyric and music by Clarence Williams and Hezekiah Jenkins), "C.C. Rider" (lyric and music by Rainey and Arrant), "The Graveyard" (lyric and music by Clifford Hayes), "He's Funny That Way" (a/k/a "She's Funny That Way [I Got a Woman, Crazy for Me]"; lyric by Neil Moret, music by Richard A. Whiting), "Kitchen Man" (lyric and music by Andy Razaf and Alex Bellenda), "Wait Till You See My Baby Do the Charleston" (lyric and music by Clarence Williams, Clarence Todd, and Rousseau Simmons)

ACT TWO—"Love" (lyric and music by Jabbo Smith), "Louise" (from 1929 film *Innocents of Paris*; lyric by Leo Robin, music by Richard A., Whiting), "New Orleans Hop Scop Blues" (lyric and music by George W. Thomas), "Everybody Loves My Baby" (lyric and music by Jack Palmer and Spencer Williams), "You've Got the Right Key but the Wrong Keyhole" (lyric and music by Clarence Williams and Eddie Green), "After You've Gone" (lyric by Henry Creamer, music by J. Turner Layton), "My Man Blues" (lyric and music by Bessie Smith), "Papa De Da Da" (lyric and music by Spencer Williams, Clarence Todd, and Clarence Williams), "Muddy Waters" (lyric and music by Peter de Rose, Harry Richman, and Jo Trent), "There'll Be a Hot Time in the Old Town Tonight" (lyric and music by Theodore A. Metz)

NOTES—*One Mo' Time!*, the longest-running musical of the 1979-1980 Off Broadway season, was conceived and directed by Vernel Bagneris, who also appeared in it. The revue offered a re-creation of a typical 1920s Black vaudeville show; in this instance, Bertha Williams and her touring company are at the Lyric Theater in New Orleans to perform their vaudeville show *One Mo' Time!* John Corry in the *New York Times* thought the "onstage" sequences of the evening worked, especially when the band was playing; but he found the "backstage" plot "embarrassing" and somewhat "offensive" when the performers played racial stereotypes (as though everyone associated with the musical had forgotten that "Amos and Andy are dead"). Corry also noted the performers attacked the songs with "dreadful force," all the more dreadful because they were miked (as a result, "authenticity" flew out the window). The cast recording was released by Warner Brothers Records (LP # HS-3454), and the script was published by Samuel French, Inc., in 1979.

During the runs of both the New York production and the touring company, various songs were deleted and others added. Among the added songs were "The Darktown Strutters' Ball," "Muskrat Ramble," "Black Bottom," "Yes, Yes," and "Tiger Rag."

A sequel of sorts called *Further Mo'* opened in 1990 at the Village Gate Downstairs, and played for just 174 performances (see entry). A 2002 Broadway revival of *One Mo' Time!* was also a disappointment, running for only twenty-one performances.

1199 One More Song/One More Dance. THEATRE: Joyce Theatre; OPENING DATE: December 21, 1983; PERFORMANCES: 14; DIRECTION: Grover Dale; CHOREOGRAPHY: Grover Dale; SCENERY: Lawrence Miller; COSTUMES: Albert Wolsky; LIGHTING: Richard Nelson; MUSICAL DIRECTION: Joel Silberman; PRODUCER: Lee Gross Associates, Inc.

CAST—ANN REINKING (Ann), Gary Chryst (Gary), Gregory Mitchell (Gregory), Brian Sutherland (Brian), Stephen Jay (Stephen), Jeff Calhoun (Jeff), Robert Warners (Robert)

NOTES—*One More Song/One More Dance*, a ballet musical with songs, was created by Grover Dale. The characters included a show dancer, a ballet teacher, a tap dancer, a choreographer, and "a dancer who discovers he can write." Barbara Schottenfeld was credited with contributing "special material" to the evening.

The program didn't list individual songs and dances, and didn't indicate the number of acts.

One year later, Ann Reinking returned to the Joyce Theatre in another dance musical (see entry for *Ann Reinking...Music Moves Me*).

1200 1000 Airplanes on the Roof. "A Science Fiction Music Drama." THEATRE: Beacon Theatre; OPENING DATE: December 14, 1988; PERFORMANCES: 8; LIBRETTO: David Henry Hwang; MUSIC: Philip Glass; DIRECTION: Philip Glass; MOVEMENT: Mary Ann Kellogg; SCENERY AND PROJECTIONS: Jerome Sirlin; WARDROBE: Winsome McKoy; LIGHTING: Robert Wierzel; MUSICAL DIRECTION: Martin Goldray; PRODUCERS: The Real Events Company, Robert LoBianco, and Jedediah Wheeler

CAST—The Philip Glass Ensemble (Martin Goldray, Jon Gibson, Jack Kripi, Dora Ohrenstein, Richard Peck, Phillip Bush, Dan Dryden, Bob Bielecki, and Patrick O'Connell [as "M"])

The opera was performed in one act.

MUSICAL NUMBERS—"1000 Airplanes on the

Roof," "City Walk," "Girlfriend," "My Building Disappeared," "Screens of Memory," "What Time Is Grey," "Labyrinth," "Return to the Hive," "Three Truths," "The Encounter," "Grey Cloud Over New York," "Where Have You Been Asked the Doctor," "A Normal Man Running"

NOTES—*Frimbo* (see entry), a musical about trains, premiered at Grand Central Station (Tracks 39 to 42), and *1000 Airplanes on the Roof* had its world premiere at the Vienna International Airport (Hanger # 3) on July 15, 1988. The American premiere of David Henry Hwang and Philip Glass' "musical monodrama" took place at Philadelphia's American Music Theatre Festival on September 22, 1988, and the New York premiere occurred three months later at the Beacon Theatre.

The opera dealt with "M" (Patrick O'Connell), a man who may have been abducted by space aliens.

In writing about Philip Glass in the *New York Times*, James Rockwell noted that his "best music remains some of the most impressive of our time," but for *1000 Airplanes on the Roof* Rockwell felt the music was too deferential to Hwang's text. Instead, Rockwell said the evening's most impressive features were the "dazzling" scenic designs by Jerome Sirlin.

The script was published by Peregrine Smith Books in 1989, and a recording of the opera was released by Virgin Records America, Inc. (CD # V2-86106).

1201 One Two Three Four Five. THEATRE: City Center Stage II/Manhattan Theatre Club; OPENING DATE: November 10, 1987; PERFORMANCES: 24; BOOK: Larry Gelbart; LYRICS: Maury Yeston; MUSIC: Maury Yeston; DIRECTION: Gerald Gutierrez; CHOREOGRAPHY CONSULTANT: Jerry Mitchell; DESIGN CONSULTANT: James D. Sandefur; LIGHTING: Michael R. Moody; MUSICAL DIRECTION: Tom Fay; PRODUCER: Manhattan Theatre Club (Lynne Meadow, Artistic Director; Barry Grove, Managing Director)

CAST—Lewis J. Stadlen (Romer), Alice Playten (Cynia), Jonathan Hadary (Dick), Mary Gordon Murray (Taradee), William Youmans (Kol), Vicki Lewis (Maylis), Beatrice Winde (Bmmhe), Liz Callaway (Arielle), Davis Gaines (Avi), Ann Harada (Noma), Mary Chesterman (Shopkeeper), Linda Kerns (Mrs. N), Jon Ehrlich (Avi's Son), Neal Ben-Ari (Pheti), James Judy (Ptapateepa)

SOURCE—The first five Books of the Bible.

The action begins in the Garden of Eden and goes "through roughly the next 2,000 years."

The musical was presented in two acts.

ACT ONE—"In the Beginning" (Company), "Prayer" (Company), "In the Town" (Lewis J. Stadlen, Company), "Family" (Davis Gaines), "Make Way" (Company), "One for a Rainy Day" (Mary Gordon Murray, Vicki Lewis, Alice Playten, Company), "This Is the End" (Lewis J. Stadlen), "The Flood," "You're There Too" (Jonathan Hadary), "The Second Creation" (William Youmans, Vicki Lewis, Company), "Now and Then" (Liz Callaway, Davis Gaines), "Baby at 110" (Company), "New Words" (Davis Gaines), "The Nileside Cotillion" (Company)

ACT TWO—"There Was a Place" (Jonathan Hadary, William Youmans), "Feet" (Company), "No Man's as Wonderful" (Liz Callaway), "No Women in the Bible" (Alice Playten, Vicki Lewis, Mary Gordon Murray, Liz Callaway, Beatrice Winde), "When Will It End?"/"Prayer" (reprise) (Mary Gordon Murray, Vicki Lewis, Alice Playten), "Three Steps Forward" (Davis Gaines, Company), "I Won't Cross Over" (Davis Gaines), "New Words"/"In the Town" (reprises) (Davis Gaines, Company)

NOTES—Maury Yeston's Off Off Broadway musical *One Two Three Four Five*, which looked at mankind over a period of 2,000 years, was presented for three weeks by Playwrights Horizons as a work-in-progress; despite two revivals in regional theatre (each with a different title), the musical disappeared and never enjoyed a recording. As *History Loves Company*, a revised version of the material briefly surfaced in Chicago at Marriott's Lincolnshire Theatre in 1991; subtitled "A Musical Fable," this adaptation added two songs ("The Family Tree" and "If Avi Isn't Avi"). Later, another revised version, this one titled *In the Beginning*, was produced in regional theatre. Both *History Loves Company* and *In the Beginning* never saw New York productions. The remarkable cast of *One Two Three Four Five* included Lewis J. Stadlen, Alice Playten, Jonathan Hadary, Mary Gordon Murray, Vicki Lewis, Liz Callaway, and Davis Gaines; at least one source indicates Lauren Mitchell and Mary Testa were in the cast, but their names aren't included in a program dated November 10-29, 1987. The song "New Words" can be heard on *Unsung Musicals* (I) (Varese Sarabande Records CD # VSD-5462).

Yeston made his Broadway debut in 1982 with *Nine*, a brilliant score for which he won the Tony Award (Richard Coe in the *Washington Post* felt that *Nine* boasted the best theatre score since Leonard Bernstein's *Candide* [1956]), but except for some material he contributed to *Grand Hotel* (1989), Yeston didn't return to Broadway until 1997, with his memorable score for the long-running *Titanic* (which won him another Tony Award).

1202 A One-Way Ticket to Broadway. THEATRE: Donnell Theatre; OPENING DATE: 1980 (?); PERFORMANCES: Unknown; LYRICS: Robert Lorick; MUSIC: Dan Goggin; DIRECTION: Ed Brazo; SCENERY: Bonnie Westberg; COSTUMES: Bonnie Westberg (?); PRODUCER: Layne R. Alexander

CAST—Katie Anders, Beth Fowler, Dan Goggin, Ann Hodapp, Elaine Petricoff, Marvin Solley

MUSICAL NUMBERS (number of acts unknown)—"A One-Way Ticket to Broadway"/"A Tough Town" (Company), "A Conversation Piece" (Katie Anders, Company), "Starsong" (Ann Hodapp), "The Fifth from the Right ..." (lyric by Dan Goggin) (Ann Hodapp), "Where Is the Rainbow?" (lyric by Dan Goggin) (Marvin Solley), "Mister Producer" (Elaine Petricoff), "Everybody's Gone to California" (Company), "My Bio Is Blank" (Elaine Petricoff, Company)/"A Little Bit of B.S." (lyric by Dan Goggin) (Katie Anders), "The Lady on the Piano" (Beth Fowler), "Play Away the Blues" (lyric by Dan Goggin) (Dan Goggin, Company), "Lullabye" (Elaine Petricoff), "Rhumba Rita" (Company), "Ho-Hum" (Marvin Solley), Finale (Company)

NOTES—The Off Off Broadway revue-like musical *A One-Way Ticket to Broadway* focused on a group of show-business wannabes. A revised version of the material surfaced as *Balancing Act* (see entry) in 1992 and it included five songs from *A One-Way Ticket to Broadway*. "A Conversation Piece" had been heard in the 1972 revue *Hark!* (see entry).

The cast album was released by Theatre Archives Records (LP # TA-8001); the song titles are taken from the recording.

1203 Only Fools Are Sad. THEATRE: Edison Theatre; OPENING DATE: November 22, 1971; PERFORMANCES: 144; BOOK: Dan Almagor (based on old Hassidic stories and parables); translated by Shimon Wincelberg and Valerie Arnon; LYRICS: Dan Almagor (translated by Robert Friend); MUSIC: Yohanan Zarai and Girl Aldema (derived from Hassidic songs); DIRECTION: Yossi Yzraely; SCENERY: Dani Karavan (supervised by Herbert Senn); COSTUMES: Ruth Dar (supervised by Helen Pond); LIGHTING: Yehiel Orgal (supervised by Robert Brand); PRODUCER: Yaacov Agmon

CAST—Galia Ishay, Danny Litanny, Don Maseng, Shlomo Notzan, Michael Noy, Aviva Schwarz

The revue was presented in two acts.

ACT ONE—"Once There Was a Melody" (Company) "Isaac, the Baker (The Treasure)" (Danny Litany, Michel Noy, Galia Ishay) "A Merry Melody" (Company), "Berl, the Tailor (Opening a New Account)" (Don Maseng, Shlomo Notzan) "The Promise That Was Kept" (Danny Litanny) "Don't Suck the Bones" (Danny Litanny) "Eat, Lord, and Enjoy" (Michal Noy) "Tell Me What the Rain Is Saying" (Aviva Schwarz) "Don't Sell It Cheap" (Shlomo Nitzan) "A Drinking Song" (Don Maseng) "The Ten Ruble Note" (Shlomo Nitzan) "Kol, Rinah Vish'ah" (Company), "Gedaliah, the Tar Maker" (Aviva Schwarz, Shlomo Nitzan, Danny Litanny)

ACT TWO—"The Goat" (Don Maseng, Michal Noy, Galia Ishay) "Forest, Forest" (Michal Noy), "Smoking on the Sabbath" (Shlomo Nitzan) "Bim-Bam-Bom" (Company) "Waiting for the Messiah" (Michal Noy, Don Maseng) "Haim, the Goose-Herder" (Galia Ishay) "Getzl, the Shoemaker (Aleph ... Beth)" (Danny Litanny) "The Rabbi Who Promised to Wait" (Shlomo Nitzan) "A Letter to the Rabbi" (Don Maseng) "Angel, Angel" (Galia Ishay) "Only Fools Are Sad" (Aviva Schwarz), "Avreymele Melamed" (Danny Litanny, Shlomo Nitzan, Don Maseng) "A Sabbath Song" (Shlomo Nitzan), "And God Said Unto Jacob" (Danny Litanny)

NOTES—*Only Fools Are Sad* had been originally produced in Tel Aviv in October 1968 as *Ish Hassid Haya* (*Once There Was a Hassid*), and that production was recorded by AP Records (LP # AP-332). The revue was anthology of old Hassidic tales, fables, and songs which were told and sung in Yiddish in Eastern Europe during the eighteenth and nineteenth centuries.

Clive Barnes in the *New York Times* found the revue a "gentle celebration" which was "endearing and happy." He noted that you didn't have to be Jewish to enjoy the show, but, in honesty, "a touch of Jewish blood" wouldn't hurt, especially in understanding a joke about the difference between citrons and lemons. During the pre-New York tryout, the following numbers were dropped from the production: "Veha'er Eineinu (Carlenbach)," "The Hassid's Dilemna [sic, Dilemma]," "Avinu Malkeinu" "The Beggar and the Rabbi," and "Hoshia et Amecha."

1204 Opal. "A Musical Adventure." THEATRE: Lamb's Theatre; OPENING DATE: March 12, 1992; PERFORMANCES: 63; BOOK: Robert Nassif Lindsey; LYRICS: Robert Nassif Lindsey; MUSIC: Robert Nassif Lindsey; DIRECTION: Scott Harris; CHOREOGRAPHY: Janet Watson; SCENERY: Peter Harrison; COSTUMES: Michael Bottari and Ron Case; LIGHTING: Don Ehman; MUSICAL DIRECTION: Joshua Rosenblum; PRODUCER: The Lamb's Theatre Company (Carolyn Rossi Copeland, Producing Director)

CAST—Reed Armstrong (Narrator), Mimi Bessette (The Girl That Has No Seeing [Selena]), Eliza Clark or Tracy Spindler (alternating performers in the role of Opal [Francoise]), Louisa Flaningam (The Mamma [Mrs. Potter]), Mark Goetzinger (The Man That Wears Gray Neckties [Andrew Givens], Angel Father), Sarah Knapp (Narrator), Alfred Lakeman (Narrator), Judy Malloy (Narrator), Marni Nixon (Sadie McKibben), Pippa Winslow (The Thought-Girl with the Far-Away Look in Her Eyes, Angel Mother)

SOURCE—The childhood diary of Opal Whiteley (a/k/a Francoise D'Orleans).

The action occurs in a lumber camp in Oregon in 1904.

The musical was presented in one act.

MUSICAL NUMBERS—"Make Earth Glad" (Eliza Clark/Tracy Spindler, Pippa Winslow, Mark Goetzinger, Reed Armstrong, Sarah Knapp, Alfred Lakeman, Judy Malloy), "Angel Mother, Angel Father" (Eliza Clark/Tracy Spindler, Pippa Winslow, Mark Goetzinger, Reed Armstrong, Sarah Knapp, Alfred Lakeman, Judy Malloy), "To Conquer the Land" (Company), "Sears and Roebuck Wedding Band"

(Mark Goetzinger, Eliza Clark/Tracy Spindler), "Search for a Sign" (Marni Nixon, Eliza Clark/Tracy Spindler), "Little Lamb" (lyric by William Blake) (Eliza Clark/Tracy Spindler, Reed Armstrong, Sarah Knapp, Alfred Lakeman, Judy Malloy), "Night of Shooting Stars" (Company), "Opal" (Mimi Bessette), "To Conquer the Land" (reprise) (Company), "Angel Mother, Angel Father" (reprise) (Eliza Clark/Tracy Spindler), "Someone" (Pippa Winslow, Mimi Bessette), "The Locket" (Louisa Flaningam), "Everybody's Looking for Love" (Mark Goetzinger, Company), "Why Do I See God?" (Marni Nixon)

NOTES—Adapted from the diaries of Francoise D'Orleans (a/k/a Opal Whiteley), a French orphan, the Off Off Broadway musical *Opal* depicted her life in an Oregon lumber camp in 1904.

D.J.R. Bruckner in the *New York Times* said *Opal* was a "splendid little musical" which captured the "enchanting strangeness" of Whiteley's diaries. He noted the score was "lovely" and included "many memorable songs," and concluded the musical was a "rare achievement" which in many respects was better than its source material.

The script was published by Samuel French, Inc., in 1993, and a combination original cast (Eliza Clark, Marni Nixon)/studio cast album (Rachel York, Emily Skinner, book writer-lyricist-composer Robert Nassif Lindsey) was released by Original Cast Records (CD # OC-9636). The recording included three songs which were apparently not heard in the New York production ("Just Beyond the Horizon," "Gentleman Pig," and "What Might Have Been"). Four songs from the production were heard on *Opal, Honky-Tonk Highway, and Other Theatre Songs by Robert Nassif Lindsey* ("Sears and Roebuck Wedding Band," "Someone," "Everybody's Looking for Love," and "Why Do I See God?"), which was released by Original Cast Records (CD # OC-9514).

NOTE—The cast/studio album credits the lyricist and composer's name as Robert Lindsey Nassif; the compilation album gives his name as Robert Nassif Lindsey; and the published script cites *two* names (Robert Nassif Lindsey and Robert Lindsey Nassif). In the program of the 1985 musical *Tropicana* (see entry), he was identified as Robert Nassif, and at least one reference source for *Honky-Tonk Highway* cited his name as Robert Lindsey-Nassif. This confusion will probably last for as long as books about musical theatre are written, no doubt perplexing twenty-second-century theatre buffs who will be puzzled enough that Lucille Ball's only Broadway musical wasn't *Redhead* and that *Fanny* wasn't the show about Fanny Brice.

1205 Open Heart. THEATRE: Cherry Lane Theatre; OPENING DATE: March 17, 2004; PERFORMANCES: 48 (estimated); BOOK: Robby Benson; LYRICS: Robby Benson; MUSIC: Robby Benson; DIRECTION: Matt Williams; CHOREOGRAPHY: Luis Perez; SCENERY: Michael Brown; COSTUMES: Ann Hould-Ward; LIGHTING: Ken Billington; MUSICAL DIRECTION: Kevin Farrell

CAST—Robby Benson, Karla DeVito (Benson), Stan Brown

The musical was presented in one act.

NOTES—*Open Heart* was a semi-autobiographical evening by Robby Benson which dealt with an entertainer who has a heart condition (Benson had undergone two heart surgeries).

Neil Genzlinger in the *New York Times* noted that while the evening was "a bit of a vanity project," the ninety-minute musical had some "good" songs and comic-timing. He mentioned the "lively" direction and the "amusing" set, and noted that one number ("delivered to great effect by" Benson and Stan Brown) dealt with the most obvious phrases people supposedly say when they are about to die. Genzlinger also noted that while Benson was just six years old when Anthony Newley's *Stop the World—I Want to Get Off* opened on Broadway in 1962, Benson must have been an "absorbent child," because in style and substance *Open Heart* was a "direct descendant" to Newley's musical and his character Littlechap. The script was published by Samuel French, Inc., in 2006.

1206 Open Season at the Second City. THEATRE: Square East; OPENING DATE: January 22, 1964; PERFORMANCES: 90; SCENES AND DIALOGUE: Created by the Company; DIRECTION: Paul Sills and Arnold Weinstein; MUSIC: Tom O'Horgan; PRODUCERS: Bernard Sahlins and Paul Sills

CAST—Barbara Harris, Severn Darden, Bob Dishy, Dick Schaal, Avery Schreiber, Ben Keller

The revue was presented in two acts (sketch and song assignments unknown).

ACT ONE—"Roadside Rest," "The Applicant," "Doctor's Orals," "High School Prom," "The Truckdriver," "How to Get Out of a Taxi," "Aid to Vietnam," "Kabuki Parody," "The Voting Machine"

ACT TWO—Improvisations (on themes suggested by the audience)

NOTES—*Open Season at the Second City* was the fifth Second City revue to play Off Broadway. Milton Esterow in the *New York Times* noted that the revue's sketches and blackouts were "wildly funny" and the performers "irresistible." He singled out "The Truckdriver," in which Bob Dishy and Richard Schaal portrayed two tired truck drivers trying to stay awake (Dishy was a "pure joy" in his efforts to drive, eat a sandwich, drink a beer, and smoke a cigarette, all at the same time). Esterow also praised "Roadside Rest"; set in a diner in the South, the sketch asked the burning question of whether or not the North and the South could ever learn to communicate with one another (Dishy was the Northerner, and Barbara Harris played a Southern-accented waitress). Other sequences spoofed Kabuki theatre, government aid to South Vietnam, folk songs, opera, philosophy professors, and voting machines.

(Some sources give January 13 as the revue's opening night, but the *New York Times* indicated the opening was on January 22.)

For a complete list of the Second City revues which were presented in New York, see entry for *Seacoast of Bohemia*; also see Appendix T.

1207 Opening Night. THEATRE: AMAS Repertory Theatre; OPENING DATE: April 21, 1983; PERFORMANCES: 15; BOOK, LYRICS, AND MUSIC: Corliss Taylor-Dunn and Sandra Reaves-Phillips; DIRECTION: William Michael Maher; CHOREOGRAPHY: Mabel Robinson; SCENERY: Larry Fulton; COSTUMES: Judy Dearing; LIGHTING: Gregg Marriner; MUSICAL DIRECTION: Grenoldo; PRODUCER: AMAS Repertory Theatre (Rosetta LeNoire, Founder and Artistic Director)

CAST—Julia Collins (Jill, Preacher, Secretary), Leslie Dockery (Pepper, Young Mother, Heavenly Choir), Adam Hart (Askind, Musician, Rabbi), Eddie Jordan (Vodnoff, Joe, Policeman), Kashka (Satin, Ted, Preacher, Ambassador), Amy Lachinsky (Roz, Hooker, Choir), Larry Lowe (Steve, Artist, Choir), Becky Woodley (Dutchess, Bag Lady), Bob McAndrew (Sid, Choir), Adjora Faith McMillan (Leslie), Marishka Shanice Phillips (Young Sarai, Denise, Skar), Chauncey Roberts (Hilary, Hustler), Michael Anthony Roberts (Lucivious, Carl, Student), Avery Sommers (Sarai), Dan Strayhorn (Errol), Sandra Courtney Williams (Young Leslie, Kim, Hooker)

The action occurs in New York City at the present time.

The musical was presented in two acts (division of acts and singing assignments unknown; songs are listed in performance order).

MUSICAL NUMBERS—"Mr. Playwright," "I Don't Have a Name," "Mommy Says," "You're My Friend," "New Beginnings," "Song of Praise," "Hanging Around," "Get Thee Behind Me," "New York City Cock Roach Blues," "We're Almost There," "How Many Rainbows," "The Man I Want to Be," "Take a Chance," "Cause a Sensation," "Nobody's Blues," "Keep Holding On," "I Love the Dance," "If We Can't Lick 'Em, Join 'Em," "Opening Night," "Let Me Show You a New Way to Love"

NOTES—The musical *Opening Night* was presented under an Off Off Broadway contract.

1208 Options. "A Musical Choice." THEATRE: Circle Repertory Theatre; OPENING DATE: July 11, 1985; PERFORMANCES: 2; BOOK: Walter Willison; LYRICS: Walter Willison; MUSIC: Jefrey Silverman; DIRECTION: Walter Willison; CHOREOGRAPHY: Brenda Bufalino; SCENERY: Ron Placzek; COSTUMES: Robert Turturice; LIGHTING: Mal Sturchio; PRODUCERS: Jeffrey Betancourt Productions, Inc., and March Adrian Fedor

CAST—Walter Willison (The Writer), Jefrey Silverman (The Composer), Jo Anna Rush (The Red-Headed Woman), Richard B. Schull (Voice)

A program note indicated there "may" be one intermission.

MUSICAL NUMBERS—"Livin' on Dreams" (Walter Willison), "We Have Loved Forever" (Walter Willison), "Something More" (Walter Willison), "Life Don't Always Work Out" (Jo Anna Rush), "Perfect Strangers" (Walter Willison), "Private Secretary" (Walter Willison, Jo Anna Rush, Jefrey Silverman), "I Went an' Found Myself a Cowboy" (Jo Anna Rush), "Diff'rent" (Walter Willison), "Ev'rybody's Gotta Eat" (Jefrey Silverman), "The Front Page" (Walter Willison), "Bubbles in the Bathtub" (Jo Anna Rush), "A Good Ol' Mammy Song" (Walter Willison), "Rainbow" (Walter Willison), "The Man at the Piano" (Jo Anna Rush), "Andrew Jackson James Tyrone" (Jefrey Silverman), "Chinatown" (Jo Anna Rush), "Mos'ly Love" (Walter Willison), "Options" (Walter Willison)

NOTES—*Options* was about a lyricist and composer collaborating on a new musical. The songs included numbers from other works by Walter Willison and Jefrey Silverman: their 1982 Off Broadway revue *Broadway Scandals of 1928* (see entry), their Santa Monica revue *Front Street Gaieties*, and the film *Fantasies*.

D.J.R. Bruckner in the *New York Times* felt the "lightweight" revue had its "moments," and he liked Silverman's pastiche score. He noted that during the five weeks between the time *Options* was first announced for a New York production and the opening night itself, the musical had dropped one character, added another, and "abandoned" its original story line. Resulting from this confusion was an "innocent evening" of cabaret strung together with fifteen "very loosely connected" songs.

Numbers previously heard in *Broadway Scandals of 1928* were "(Blowing) Bubbles in the Bathtub," "A Good Ol' Mammy Song," and "The Man at the Piano." The following numbers were from *Front Street Gaieties*, and can be heard on that revue's Santa Monica cast album released by AEI Records (LP # AEI-1133; the revue wasn't produced in New York): "Life Don't Always Work Out," "Mostly Love," and "I Went Out and Found Myself a Cowboy." There's no information available concerning which songs in *Options* had been previously heard in the film *Fantasies*. According to Leonard Maltin's *2007 Movie Guide*, a film titled *And Once Upon a Love* was filmed in 1973 and later released in 1981 as *Fantasies*; its cast included a sixteen-year-old Kathleen Collins (later known as Bo Derek), and the plot concerned the efforts to make over a Greek Island into a tourist attraction.

According to the program notes of *Options*, Silverman wrote a musical version of William Inge's 1955 play *Bus Stop* titled *Perfect Strangers* (the musical has apparently never been produced), and the song in *Options* called "Perfect Strangers" may well be the adaptation's title song. For another musical version of *Bus Stop*, see entry for *Cherry*.

Options had first been produced at the 1985 William Inge Festival in Independence, Kansas.

1209 Orwell That Ends Well. THEATRE: Village Gate Downstairs; OPENING DATE: March 1, 1984; PERFORMANCES: 110; MATERIAL: The Original Chicago Second City Company; MUSIC: Fred Kaz; DIRECTION: Bernard Sahlins; PRODUCERS: Bernard Sahlins and Art D'Lugoff; A Second City Production; Joyce Sloane, Associate Producer

CAST—The Original Chicago Second City Company (Meagan Fay, Mike Hagerty, Isabella Hofmann, John Kapelos, Richard Kind, Rick Thomas)

The revue was presented in two acts.

ACT ONE—"Reunion" (Company), "Job Interview" (Meagan Fay, Rick Thomas), "Rendezvous" (Company), "Editorial" (Meagan Fay), "Nothingness and Being" (Richard Kind, Mike Hagerty), "Culture Quiz" (Rick Thomas), "Oh America!" (Company), "Personals" (Meagan Fay, John Kapelos), "Pirates" (Company)

ACT TWO—"Bernardin" (Rick Thomas), "Love Story" (Meagan Fay, John Kapelos, Richard Kind), "Oh Chicago!" (Company), "Double Exposure" (Isabella Hoffman, Rick Thomas, John Kapelos), "Domesticity" (Isabella Hoffman, Richard Kind), "Home Study" (Mike Hagerty, Meagan Fay, Richard Kind), "The Uses of Television" (Rick Thomas, John Kapelos, Meagan Fay, Isabella Hoffman), "Growing Up" (Meagan Fay, Isabella Hoffman), "Margaret Thatcher" (Isabella Hoffman, Rick Thomas), "Who Gives a Damn" (Company)

NOTES—Almost fifteen years had passed since a Second City revue had been seen in New York. *Orwell That Ends Well* arrived, appropriately, in 1984, and played for three months; it seems to have been more structured and less improvised than its predecessors. It was the eleventh, and last, Second City revue to play in New York (see entry for *Seacoast of Bohemia* for a complete list of the Second City revues which were presented in New York; also see Appendix T).

Frank Rich in the *New York Times* noted the revue was no doubt "the 65th" Second City visit to New York. He found the evening "uneven but jolly," and singled out a number of sequences. Perhaps the revue's highlight was a sketch in which Mother Teresa is a guest on a television talk show where she falls victim to "show-biz exploitation"; Rich said the humor was so "sharp" it evoked Nathaniel West's "phantasmagoric" *The Day of the Locust.* Rich also praised Meagen Fay, a "standout" who may be the "next" Elaine May and who also evoked memories of Barbara Harris, another "wonderful" Second City performer.

1210 Our Sinatra. "A Musical Celebration." THEATRE: Blue Angel Theatre; transferred to the Reprise Room at Dillon's; OPENING DATE: December 19, 1999; PERFORMANCES: 1,096; LYRICS: See song list for credits; MUSIC: See song list for credits; DIRECTION: Kurt Stamm; entire production supervised by Richard Maltby, Jr.; SCENERY: Troy Hourie; LIGHTING: Jeff Nellis; PRODUCERS: Jack Lewin and Scott Perrin

CAST—Eric Comstock, Christopher Gines, and Hilary Kole

The revue was presented in two acts.

ACT ONE—"These Foolish Things (Remind Me of You)" (from British musical *Spread It Around*, 1936; lyric by Holt Marvell [Eric Maschwitz], music by Jack Strachey and Harry Link) (Company), "Where or When" (*Babes in Arms*, 1937; lyric by Lorenz Hart, music by Richard Rodgers) (Christopher Gines), "Come Rain or Come Shine" (*St. Louis Woman*, 1946; lyric by Johnny Mercer, music by Harold Arlen) (Hilary Kole), "I Like to Lead When I Dance" (1964 film *Robin and the Seven Hoods*; lyric by Sammy Cahn, music by Jimmy Van Heusen) (Eric Comstock), "A Lovely Way to Spend an Evening" (1944 film *Higher and Higher*; lyric by Harold Adamson, music by Jimmy McHugh) (Company), "I Fall in Love Too Easily" (1945 film *Anchors Aweigh*; lyric by Sammy Cahn, music by Jule Styne) (Christopher Gines), "Time After Time" (1947 film *It Happened in Brooklyn*; lyric by Sammy Cahn, music by Jule Styne) (Hilary Kole), "All the Way" (1957 film *The Joker Is Wild*; lyric by Sammy Cahn, music by Jimmy Van Heusen) (Eric Comstock), "(Love Is) The Tender Trap" (1955 film *The Tender Trap*; lyric by Sammy Cahn, music by Jimmy Van Heusen) (Hilary Kole), "From Here to Eternity" (lyric and music by Bob Wells and Fred Karger) (Christopher Gines), "You're Sensational" (1956 film *High Society*; lyric and music by Cole Porter) (Eric Comstock), "Well, Did You Evah?" (*DuBarry Was a Lady*, 1939; lyric and music by Cole Porter; song was also interpolated into 1956 film *High Society*) (Company), "My Kind of Town (Chicago Is)" (1964 film *Robin and the Seven Hoods*; lyric by Sammy Cahn, music by Jimmy Van Heusen) (Company), "As Long as There's Music" (1944 film *Step Lively*; lyric by Sammy Cahn, music by Jule Styne) (Company), "Nice 'n' Easy" (lyric by Marilyn and Alan Bergman, music by Lew Spence) (Christopher Gines, Hilary Kole), "I'm a Fool to Want You" (lyric and music by Jack Wolf, Joel Herron, and Frank Sinatra) (Hilary Kole), "Everything Happens to Me" (lyric by Tom Adair, music by Matt Dennis) (Eric Comstock), "Day In—Day Out" (lyric by Johnny Mercer, music by Rube Bloom) (Eric Comstock, Hilary Kole), "Ol' Man River" (*Show Boat*, 1927; lyric by Oscar Hammerstein II, music by Jerome Kern; sung by Sinatra in 1946 film *Till the Clouds Roll By*) (Christopher Gines), "Without a Song" (*Great Day!*, 1929; lyric by Billy Rose and Edward Eliscu, music by Vincent Youmans) (Company)

ACT TWO—"One for My Baby (and One More for the Road)" (*The Sky's the Limit*, 1943; lyric by Johnny Mercer, music by Harold Arlen) (Eric Comstock), "Angel Eyes" (lyric by Earl K. Brent, music by Matt Dennis) (Hilary Kole), "In the Wee Small Hours of the Morning" (lyric by Bob Hilliard, music by David Mann) (Eric Comstock), "It Never Entered My Mind" (*Higher and Higher*, 1940; lyric by Lorenz Hart, music by Richard Rodgers) (Hilary Kole), "Last Night When We Were Young" (lyric by E.Y. Harburg, music by Harold Arlen) (Christopher Gines), "At Long Last Love" (*You Never Know*, 1938; lyric and music by Cole Porter) (Company), "How Do You Keep the Music Playing?" (lyric by Alan and Marilyn Bergman, music by Michel Legrand) (Christopher Gines), "I've Got the World on a String" (*Cotton Club Parade*, 1932; lyric by Ted Koehler, music by Harold Arlen) (Hilary Kole), "To Love and Be Loved" (1959 film *Some Came Running*; lyric by Sammy Cahn, music by Jimmy Van Heusen) (Eric Comstock), "The One I Love (Belongs to Somebody Else)" (lyric by Gus Kahn, music by Isham Jones) (Eric Comstock), "I Have Dreamed" (*The King and I*, 1951; lyric by Oscar Hammerstein II, music by Richard Rodgers) (Hilary Kole), "If You Are But a Dream" (lyric and music by Moe Jaffe, Jack Fulton, and Nat Bonx) (Christopher Gines), "The Song Is You" (*Music in the Air*, 1932; lyric by Oscar Hammerstein II, music by Jerome Kern) (Company), "Day by Day" (lyric by Sammy Cahn, music by Alex Stordahl and Paul Weston) (Christopher Gines), "Night and Day" (*Gay Divorce*, 1932; lyric and music by Cole Porter) (Hilary Kole), "The Way You Look Tonight" (*Swing Time*, 1936; lyric by Dorothy Fields, music by Jerome Kern) (Eric Comstock), "They Can't Take That Away from Me" (*Shall We Dance*, 1937; lyric by Ira Gershwin, music by George Gershwin) (Hilary Kole), "Guess I'll Hang My Tears Out to Dry" (*Glad To See You!*, 1944; musical closed during its pre-Broadway tryout) (Christopher Gines), "I'll Never Smile Again" (1941 film *Las Vegas Nights*; lyric and music by Ruth Lowe) (Company), "Come Fly with Me" (lyric by Sammy Cahn, music by Jimmy Van Heusen), (Eric Comstock), "East of the Sun (and West of the Moon)" (from the 1935 Princeton University Triangle Club musical *Stags at Bay*; lyric and music by Brooks Bowman) (Christopher Gines, Hilary Kole), "Fly Me to the Moon (In Other Words)" (lyric and music by Bart Howard) (Hilary Kole), "The Lady Is a Tramp" (*Babes in Arms*, 1937; lyric by Lorenz Hart, music by Richard Rodgers; sung by Sinatra in 1957 film *Pal Joey*) (Christopher Gines), "Luck, Be a Lady" (*Guys and Dolls*, 1950; lyric and music by Frank Loesser) (Eric Comstock), "Here's That Rainy Day" (*Carnival in Flanders*, 1953; lyric by Johnny Burke, music by Jimmy Van Heusen) (Hilary Kole), "All or Nothing at All" (lyric by Jack Lawrence, music by Arthur Altman) (Christopher Gines), "I've Got You Under My Skin" (1936 film *Born To Dance*; lyric and music by Cole Porter) (Eric Comstock), "High Hopes" (1959 film *A Hole in the Head*; lyric by Sammy Cahn, music by Jimmy Van Heusen) (Eric Comstock, Hilary Kole), "The Best Is Yet to Come" (lyric by Carolyn Leigh, music by Cy Coleman) (Christopher Gines), "I've Got a Crush on You" (*Treasure Girl* [1928]; later used in the 1930 version of *Strike Up the Band*; lyric by Ira Gershwin, music by George Gershwin) (Hilary Kole), "All My Tomorrows" (lyric by Sammy Cahn, music by Jimmy Van Heusen) (Eric Comstock), "How Little We Know (How Little It Matters)" (lyric by Carolyn Leigh, music by Philip Springer) (Christopher Gines, Hilary Kole), "Witchcraft" (lyric by Carolyn Leigh, music by Cy Coleman) (Christopher Gines, Hilary Kole), "I Get a Kick Out of You" (*Anything Goes*, 1934; lyric and music by Cole Porter) (Eric Comstock), "Saturday Night (Is the Loneliest Night of the Week)" (lyric by Sammy Cahn, music by Jule Styne) (Eric Comstock), "Strangers in the Night" (1966 film *A Man Could Get Killed*; lyric and music by Charles Singleton, Eddie Snyder, and Bert Kaempfert) (Christopher Gines, Eric Comstock), "Come Dance with Me" (lyric by Sammy Cahn, music by Jimmy Van Heusen) (Eric Comstock, Hilary Kole), "I Won't Dance" (1935 film *Roberta*; lyric by Dorothy Fields, Jimmy McHugh, Otto Harbach, and Oscar Hammerstein II, music by Jerome Kern) (Eric Comstock, Hilary Kole), "Summer Wind" (lyric by Johnny Mercer, music by Henry Mayer) (Christopher Gines), "The Second Time Around" (1960 film *High Time*; lyric by Sammy Cahn, music by Jimmy Van Heusen) (Hilary Kole), "Young at Heart" (1954 film *Young at Heart*; lyric by Carolyn Leigh, music by Johnny Richards) (Company), "You Make Me Feel So Young" (1946 film *Three Little Girls in Blue*; lyric Mack Gordon, music by Joseph Myrow) (Company), "My Way" (lyric and music by Paul Anka and Jacques Revaux) (Company), "The Song Is You" (reprise) (Company), "Put Your Dreams Away (for Another Day)" (lyricist and composer unknown) (Company)

NOTES—This musical tribute to Frank Sinatra (1915-1998), was a surprise hit, running over 1,000 performances; it was produced at Birdland on November 20, 2003, for an additional 133 performances, and then later at Feinstein's at the Regency. It was revived on November 20, 2007, at the Songbook Theatre (located at the Broadway Comedy Club) for almost two months (the cast included Christopher Gines, Harmony Keeney, and Elliot Roth). *Our Sinatra* had originally been produced at the Algonquin Hotel's Oak Room in August 1999.

Stephen Holden in the *New York Times* found the revue "intelligent, witty and highly musical," and he praised the evening for concentrating on Sinatra the singer and not on the details of Sinatra's life (he was happy to report the evening never once referred to the Rat Pack, the Kennedys, and Mia Farrow).

"East of the Sun (and West of the Moon)" is unique; it appears to be the only standard to emerge from a college musical; it was introduced in the 1935 Princeton University Triangle Club show *Stags at Bay*; the lyric and music were by Brooks Bowman.

Another Sinatra tribute, *Frank/A Life in Song*, was produced in Toronto with Tom Burlinson in the title role (Burlinson was the voice of the young Sinatra in the television mini-series *Sinatra*.)

1211 Over Texas

NOTES—See entry for *First Lady Suite*.

1212 Oy Mama! Am I in Love! THEATRE: Town Hall; OPENING DATE: November 28, 1984; PERFORMANCES: 55; BOOK: Moshe Blum; LYRICS: Yakov Alper; MUSIC: Ed Linderman; DIRECTION: Michael Greenstein; CHOREOGRAPHY: Derek Wolshonak; SCENERY: Gary Prianti; COSTUMES: Mary Marsciano; LIGHTING: Paul McDonagh; MUSICAL DIRECTION: Barry Levitt; PRODUCER: The Shalom Yiddish Musical Comedy Theatre (Raymond Ariel, Producer)

CAST—David Ellin (Leybl Resnick, Mr. Green), Shifra Lerer (Sure Feyge), Tara Tyrrell (Malkele [as a child]), MARY SOREANU (Malkele [as an adult]), Yankele Alperin (Fayvish), Michael Michalovic (Moishe, Morris Bittman), Reizl Bozyk (Zeesl, Suzy), Alec Timerman (Simchele), Stewart Figa (Sidney [Simchele as an adult]), MAX PERLMAN (Meir Mordche Bittman), Sandy Levitt (George, Pesach), Eleanor Reissa (Millie), Barbara Niles (Annie Lyman), Ensemble, Students, Friends, Immigrants, Factory Workers (Catherine Caplin, Carolyn Goor, Elisa Heinsohn, Tara Tyrrell, Nick Harvey, Stanley Kramer, David Reitman, Alec Timerman)

The action occurs in Poland in 1905 and in New York City in 1923.

The musical was presented in two acts.

ACT ONE—Overture (Orchestra), "Adon Olam" (David Ellin, Choir), "Zollst Mich Gedenk'n" (Tara Tyrrell, Alec Timerman), "Ich Dank Eich Mein Liebe Fraynt" (Stewart Figa, Family, Friends), "Veit! Veit!" (Immigrants), "Hello, Hello America!" (Mary Soreanu, Immigrants), "Oy Mama! Bin Ich Farleebt!" (Mary Soreanu, Immigrants), "Ch'hob Moyre Derfar" (Eleanor Reissa, Sandy Levitt), "Mazel Bruche" (Mary Soreanu, Shifra Lerer, Yankele Alperin, Michael Michalovic, Reizl Bozyk, Max Perlman, Eleanor Reissa, Sandy Levitt), "Vi Erlich Rein" (Mary Soreanu, Stewart Figa), "Tatenyu" (Mary Soreanu), "Mazel Bruche" (reprise) (Mary Soreanu, Wedding Guests)

ACT TWO—Entr'acte (Orchestra), "Beep! Beep! Di Liebe Kimt" (Stewart Figa, Barbara Niles, Sandy Levitt, Eleanor Reissa, Friends), "Azoy Gich" (Shifra Lerer, Max Perlman), "Gevalt! Vus Vet Zein Der Sof?" (Reizl Bozyk, Michael Michalovic, Max Perlman, Yankele Alperin, Shifra Lerer), "Lebedeff Der Melich (The Songs of Aaron Lebedeff)" (Mary Soreanu), "Zollst Mich Gedenk'n" (reprise) (Mary Soreanu, Stewart Figa, Tara Tyrrell, Alec Timerman), "Kish Im In Derfrish Im" (Yankele Alperin, Mary Soreanu), "Nemt Eich a Man" (Mary Soreanu, Eleanor Reissa), Finale (Company)

NOTES—*Oy Mama! Am I in Love!* marked another visit by Mary Soreanu, who was single-handedly keeping old-fashioned Yiddish musicals alive in New York. The musical was at least partially spoken and sung in Yiddish (Bella Mysell Yablokoff was credited with the English translation), and it marked the first time the company used simultaneous electronic subtitles in English for its non--Yiddish-speaking audience members.

The lyric and music for the title song was by Abraham Ellstein. The musical may have been under an Off Off Broadway contract.

1213 Pacific Overtures (March 1984). THEATRE: Church of the Heavenly Rest/The York Theatre Company; OPENING DATE: March 27, 1984; PERFORMANCES: 20; BOOK: John Weidman; ADDITIONAL BOOK MATERIAL: Hugh Wheeler; LYRICS: Stephen Sondheim; MUSIC: Stephen Sondheim; DIRECTION: Fran Soeder; CHOREOGRAPHY: Janet Watson; SCENERY: James Morgan; COSTUMES: Mark Passerell; LIGHTING: Mary Jo Dondlinger; MUSICAL DIRECTION: James Stenborg; PRODUCER: The York Theatre Company (Janet Hayes Walker, Producing Director)

CAST—Ernest Abuba (Reciter, Shogun, Jonathan Goble, Emperor Meiji), Tony Marino (Lord Abe, First Officer of the USS Powhatan), Henry Ravelo (John Manjiro), Thomas Ikeda (Third Councillor, Merchant's Mother, Shogun's Physician, Madam, Noble, Japanese Merchant), Tom Matsusaka (Shogun's Mother, Fisherman, Imperial Priest), Eric Miji (Second Councillor, Thief, Soothsayer, Warrior, Russian Admiral, British Sailor), Kevin Gray (Kayama Yesaemon), Lester J.N. Mau (Tamate, Shogun's Wife, French Admiral), Ronald Yamamoto (Merchant, Sumo Wrestler, Geisha), Allan Tung (Merchant's Wife, Confucian, Geisha, Noble, Fencing Master's Daughter), John Bantay

(Merchant's Son, Commander Perry, Geisha), Tim Ewing (Observer, Shogun's Companion, First Officer of USS Powhatan, Sumo Wrestler, British Admiral, British Sailor), John Baray (Observer, Sumo Wrestler, Old Man, American Admiral), Francis Jue (Confucian, Geisha, Boy, Dutch Admiral, British Sailor), Khin-Kyaw Maung (Second Office of USS *Powhatan*, Story Teller, Fencing Master, Old Samurai, Samurai), Stagehands (Gerri Igarashi, Gayln Kong, Khin-Kyaw Maung, Diane Lam, Jennifer Lam)

The action occurs in Japan in July 1853 and "from then on."

The musical was presented in two acts.

ACT ONE—"The Advantages of Floating in the Middle of the Sea" (Ernest Abuba, Company), "There Is No Other Way" (Lester J.N. Mau, Tim Ewing, John Baray), "Four Black Dragons" (Tom Matsusaka, Eric Miji, Ernest Abuba, Townspeople), "Chrysanthemum Tea" (Ernest Abuba, Tom Matsusaka, Lester J.N. Mau, Eric Miji, Tim Ewing, Thomas Ikeda, John Baray, Priests), "Poems" (Kevin Gray, Henry Marino), "Welcome to Kanagawa" (Thomas Ikeda, Girls), "Someone in a Tree" (John Baray, Ernest Abuba, Francis Jue, Eric Miji), "Lion Dance" (John Bantay)

ACT TWO—"Please Hello" (Tony Marino, Ernest Abuba, John Baray, Tim Ewing, Francis Jue, Eric Miji, Lester J.N. Mau), "A Bowler Hat" (Kevin Gray, Henry Ravelo), "Pretty Lady" (Eric Miji, Tim Ewing, Francis Jue), "Next" (Ernest Abuba, Company)

NOTES—This was the first New York revival of Stephen Sondheim's problematic yet fascinating 1976 musical *Pacific Overtures*, which played on Broadway for a disappointing 193 performances. The Off Off Broadway production at the York was later seen Off Broadway, opening at the Promenade Theatre on October 12, 1984, for 109 performances (see entry). Many members from the York production were also in the Promenade revival. The musical was also revived on Broadway by the Roundabout Theatre Company at Studio 54 on December 4, 2004, for sixty-nine performances.

The musical dealt with the "opening" of Japan by Commodore Perry, and the magnificent score includes "Chrysanthemum Tea," "Someone in a Tree," "Please Hello," and "A Bowler Hat," songs which represent Sondheim at his peak (which is another way of saying they are among the greatest songs ever written for the musical theatre).

No production of *Pacific Overtures* has enjoyed a long run and financial success. And no production can ever match the scenic grandeur of the original.

The original Broadway cast album was released by RCA Victor Records (LP # ARL-1-1367; CD # RCD1-4407), and the script was published by Dodd, Mead & Company in 1976. The brief national tour of the original Broadway production was taped and later shown on Japanese television.

The score was also recorded by the English National Opera, which produced the musical in 1987 (the 2-LP set was released by That's Entertainment Records [LP # TER2-1151]; it was also released on CD [# CDTER2-1152]). The musical's Broadway revival by the Roundabout Theatre Company at Studio 54 on December 2, 2004, was also recorded (by PS Classics [CD # PS-528).

1214 Pacific Overtures (October 1984). THEATRE: Promenade Theatre; OPENING DATE: October 25, 1984; PERFORMANCES: 109; BOOK: John Weidman; ADDITIONAL BOOK MATERIAL: Hugh Wheeler; LYRICS: Stephen Sondheim; MUSIC: Stephen Sondheim; dance music by Daniel (Danny) Troob; DIRECTION: Fran Soeder; CHOREOGRAPHY: Janet Watson; SCENERY: James Morgan; COSTUMES: Mark Passerell; ADDITIONAL COSTUMES: Eiko Yamaguchi; LIGHTING: Mary Jo Dondlinger; MUSICAL DIRECTION: Eric Stern; PRODUCERS: The Shubert Organization and McCann & Nugent

CAST—Ernest Abuba (Reciter), Tony Marino (Lord Abe), Chuck Brown (Shogun's Mother, British Admiral), Tom Matsusaka (Imperial Priest), Ray Contreras (Warrior, British Solider), Kevin Gray (Kayama Yesaemon), Timm Fujii (Tamate, British Sailor), Ronald Yamamoto (Merchant, Sumo Wrestler), John Caleb (John Manjiro, Fisherman, French Admiral), Tim Ewing (Thief), Thomas Ikeda (Madam, Russian Admiral), John Bantay (Commander Perry), John Baray (Old Man, American Admiral), Francis Jue (Boy, Dutch Admiral, British Sailor), Allan Tung (Fencing Master's Daughter), Proscenium Servants (Gerri Igarashi, Gayln Kong, Diane Lam, Christine Toy)

The action occurs in Japan in July 1853 and "from then on."

The musical was presented in two acts.

NOTES—This Off Broadway revival of *Pacific Overtures* had first been seen the previous spring in a production by the York Theatre Company in an Off Off Broadway production. For song listing and more information about other New York productions of the work, see entry for the earlier version.

1215 Pageant. THEATRE: Blue Angel Theatre; OPENING DATE: May 2, 1991 Performances: 462; BOOK: Bill Russell and Frank Kelly; LYRICS: Bill Russell and Frank Kelly; MUSIC: Albert Evans; DIRECTION: Robert Longbottom; CHOREOGRAPHY: Robert Longbottom; Tony Parise, Co-Choreographer; SCENERY: Daniel Ettinger; COSTUMES: Gregg Barnes; LIGHTING: Timothy Hunter; MUSICAL DIRECTION: James Raitt; PRODUCER: Robert Scharer; Chip Quigley, Associate Producer

CAST—Randl Ash (Miss Bible Belt), David Drake (Miss Deep South), Russell Garrett (Miss Texas), Joe Joyce (Miss Industrial Northeast), John Salvatore (Miss West Coast, Miss Glamouresse 1990), Dick Scanlan (Miss Great Plains), J.T. Cromwell (Frankie Cavalier)

The musical was presented in one act (song assignments unknown).

MUSICAL NUMBERS—"Natural Born Females," "Something Extra," The Talent Competition: Miss Texas (Texan Medley), Miss Great Plains ("I Am the Land"), Miss Deep South ("Salute to Dixie"), Miss West Coast ("The Seven Ages of Me" [Martha Graham dance spoof]), Miss Industrial Northeast ("Classical Fantasia"), Miss Bible Belt (I'm Banking on Jesus"), "It's Gotta Be Venus," "Girl Power," "Good Bye," "Miss Glamouresse"

NOTES—*Pageant* was about a beauty contest sponsored by a cosmetics firm. A group of finalists is vying for the title of "Miss Glamouresse 1991," and the musical's conceit was to have all the contestants played by men in drag. As the evening progresses, the audience gets to know the finalists through interviews (one tells us she "personally attended Macy's Thanksgiving Day parade") and talent competitions, including one in which the contestants give advice to call-ins on a beauty-crisis hotline (when a caller complains of not being pretty, Miss Bible Belt tells the caller to be grateful God has given her eyes to see her ugliness).

The audience was given selection sheets to write in its choices for best in "Evening Gown," "Beauty Crisis Call," "Talent," and "Swimsuit" competitions (and the audience was even invited to compare its choices with the final determinations of the judges!).

The musical had been previously produced Off Off Broadway at the Riverwest Theatre on November 1, 1986, for forty-five performances. In that production, the gals were vying for the title of "Miss Glamouresse 1987," and the musical included the following songs not heard in the 1991 version: "We're on Our Way," "Beauty Work," "We're Going Back Now," "A Pretty Life," and an overall sequence titled "One Smile at a Time" (which included the numbers "Don't Be Afraid," "More Than a Woman," and "Pageant Days — Nightie Nights").

The cast recording of the 1997 Australian production was released on Polydor Records (CD # 5371562); the script was published by Samuel French, Inc., in 1998.

The musical was produced in London beginning on August 1, 2000, at the Vaudeville Theatre.

For more information on "beauty contest" musicals of the period, see entry for *Pretty Faces*.

1216 Pahokee Beach. THEATRE: Playhouse 46; OPENING DATE: November 15, 1983; PERFORMANCES: 10; BOOK: Leo Rost; LYRICS: Jimmy Horowitz; MUSIC: Jimmy Horowitz; DIRECTION: Georgia McGill; SCENERY: Ernest Allen Smith; COSTUMES: Vern Yates; LIGHTING: Susan Roth; MUSICAL DIRECTION: Jeff Bates; PRODUCERS: The Lifecatchers Company, The Long Island Theatre Company, and Jimmy Wisner

CAST—Sylvia Davis (Mrs. Entemans), Nancy Deering (Sarah), Ted Forlow (George), Curt Harpel (Lance), Kyle-Scott Jackson (Chez), Joe Muligan (Chris), Chris Seiler (Woody), Terry Urdang (Lisa)

The action occurs at the present time in a beach town.

The play with music was presented in two acts.

NOTES—The Off Off Broadway play *Pahokee Beach* included incidental songs (no song titles available).

1217 Pantaloon. THEATRE: Juilliard School Theatre; OPENING DATE: May 17, 1956; PERFORMANCES: 3; LIBRETTO: Bernard Stambler; MUSIC: Robert Ward; DIRECTION: Felix Brentano; SCENERY: Frederick Kiesler; MUSICAL DIRECTION: Rudolph Thomas; PRODUCERS: Columbia Theatre Associates in cooperation with the Columbia University Opera Workshop; the Columbia University Department of Music

CAST—Paul Ukena (Panaloon), Regina Sarfaty (Zinida), James Norbert, Norman Myrvik, Richard Ballard, Stephen Harbachick

SOURCE—The 1916 play *He Who Gets Slapped* by Leonid Andreyev.

The action occurs in a European circus at the end of the nineteenth century.

The opera was presented in three acts.

NOTES—Leonid Andreyev's play *He Who Gets Slapped* dealt with an embittered, unhappily married man who becomes a circus clown. He falls in love with the young bareback rider of the circus, but when he discovers her father is forcing her into marriage with a scoundrel, the clown murders her and kills himself. Surprisingly, *Pantaloon*, the operatic version of the material, softened the ending; but Howard Taubman in the *New York Times* noted that Robert Ward and Bernard Stambler's adaptation made a good case for a more optimistic resolution of the story, and he noted the work held his attention and engaged his sympathies. He also said the opera bolstered his hopes that one day the United States would have "its own operatic repertory."

Pantaloon was Ward's first opera; in 1959, he and Stambler revised the work, and the new version (titled *He Who Gets Slapped*) was produced by the New York City Opera (see entry). As *Pantaloon, He Who Gets Slapped*, the opera was briefly revived Off Off Broadway on January 18, 1978, at the Encompass Theatre.

In 1971, another lyric version of Andreyev's play opened Off Off Broadway; it was titled *Nevertheless, They Laugh* (see entry) and starred David Holliday and Bernadette Peters.

1218 Parade (a/k/a Jerry Herman's Parade). "A Musical Revue." THEATRE: Players Theatre; OPENING DATE: January 20, 1960; PERFORMANCES: 95; SKETCHES: Jerry Herman; LYRICS: Jerry Herman; MUSIC: Jerry Herman; DIRECTION: Jerry Herman; CHOREOGRAPHY: Richard Tone; SCENERY: Gary Smith; COSTUMES: Nilo; LIGHTING: Jules Fisher; MUSICAL DIRECTION: Jerry Herman; PRODUCER: Lawrence N. Kasha

CAST—DODY GOODMAN, Fia Karen, Charles Nelson Reilly, Lester (Les) James, RICHARD TONE

The revue was presented in two acts.

ACT ONE—"Gypsy Dance" (Company), "Bless This House" (Dody Goodman) (Song later retitled "Save the Village") "(Keep) Your Hand in Mine" (Lester James, Fia Karen) "Confession to a Park Avenue Mother (I'm in Love with a West Side Girl)" (Charles Nelson Reilly) "(I Was Born to Do) The Two-a-Day" (Richard Tone), "Hail the TV Commercial" (Company), "The Last Rockette" (Dody Goodman) "The Antique Man" (Lester James) "Just Plain Folks" (Dody Goodman, Charles Nelson Reilly) "(I'll Make Sure My Head Is Clearer) The Next Time I Love" (Fia Karen, Lester James) "Naughty Forty-Second Street" (Company), "How Hollywood Actresses Find Their Names (Part I)" (Charles Nelson Reilly, Dody Goodman), "We Put the Music" (Company)

ACT TWO—"Show Tune" (a/k/a "There Is No Tune Like a Show Tune" and "Show Tune in 2/4 Time") (Company) "Paris, I'm Prepared" (Dody Goodman), "Your Good Morning" (Lester James, Fia Karen) "Tenement Scene" (Dody Goodman) "Get Off My Lawn" (Charles Nelson Reilly) "Where's Boris" (Dody Goodman, Richard Tone), "Another Candle" (Fia Karen) "Truth and Consequences" (Charles Nelson Reilly, Lester James, Fia Karen) "Maria in Spats" (Dody Goodman) "The Audition" (Richard Tone) "How Hollywood Actresses Find Their Names (Part II)" (Charles Nelson Reilly, Fia Karen) "A Jolly Theatrical Season" (Dody Goodman, Charles Nelson Reilly) "Parade" (Company)

NOTES—In his review of *Parade* for the *New York Times*, Brooks Atkinson was somewhat cool to Jerry Herman's contributions ("Jerry-one-note"), but praised the "dazed lark" Dody Goodman. Atkinson noted the revue was produced more in the style of "Little Broadway than Off Broadway," and reported the settings were of a "simple, modish elegance" and the costumes were "in luxurious good taste." The revue was originally recorded on Kapp Records (LP # 7005), and some four decades after the LP release it was reissued by Decca Broadway Records (CD # 440-064-738-2). Five songs in *Parade* had originally been heard in *Nightcap* (1958; see entry): "Show Tune," "Confession to a Park Avenue Mother (I'm in Love with a West Side Girl)," "Your Good Morning," "Naughty Forty-Second Street," and "A Jolly Theatrical Season." A brief melody heard in *Parade*'s overture was later recycled by Jerry Herman for *Mack & Mabel* (1974) as "I Wanna Make the World Laugh." The music for this sequence is from *Parade*'s first act finale ("We Put the Music"), a song which wasn't recorded for the album.

As it was in *Nightcap*, "A Jolly Theatrical Season" was again a highlight. This time around Charles Nelson Reilly was joined by Dody Goodman, and the song was updated to reflect the gloomy plots of current plays and musicals (*Juno*'s "great charm was" the notion of the Tommy Rall character sporting a hook where "his arm was").

Another memorable song was Dody Goodman's "Maria in Spats," a spoof of temperamental opera diva Maria Callas and her notorious clashes with opera managers and fellow singers; the song suggested the only theatre in which the "dispossessed Aida" might be welcome is the Palace. The song "Bless This House" (a/k/a "Save the Village") was a tribute to the Village's House of Detention for Women, and during the following season another Off Broadway musical, *Greenwich Village, U.S.A.*, offered up another song on the same subject ("Ladies of the House"); see entry. And when those Village types Holly Golightly and Mag Wildwood sang about "The Home for Wayward Girls" in *Holly Golightly/Breakfast at Tiffany's* (1966), perhaps they were thinking of a "house" not unlike the one celebrated in "Bless This House" and "Ladies of the House."

During the run, "Hail the TV Commercial" and "Where's Boris" were deleted; in place of the latter, "The Wrong Bedroom" was added for Dody Goodman and Richard Tone.

For a production of the revue which played in California, the following songs were added: "Nice Running Into You," "Peace," and "Skip the Opening Number."

Three months to the day of *Parade*'s opening, Jerry Herman made his Broadway debut; his song "Best Gold" was the opening number of the revue *From A to Z*, which premiered at the Plymouth (now Schoenfeld) Theatre on April 20, 1960, for twenty-one performances (the revue also introduced Woody Allen, who contributed three sketches to the evening, and Fred Ebb, who wrote the lyrics of four songs and co-wrote the lyrics of two others).

1219 Paradise! "A New Musical Comedy." THEATRE: Mainstage Theatre/Playwrights Horizons; OPENING DATE: September 28, 1985; PERFORMANCES: 14; BOOK: George C. Wolfe; LYRICS: George C. Wolfe; MUSIC: Robert Forrest; DIRECTION: Theodore Papas; CHOREOGRAPHY: Theodore Papas; SCENERY: James Noone; COSTUMES: David C. Woolard; LIGHTING: Frances Aronson; MUSICAL DIRECTION: David Loud; PRODUCER: Playwrights Horizons (Andre Bishop, Artistic Director; Paul S. Daniels, Managing Director)

CAST—The Coupes — Janice Lynde (Grace), Stephen Vinovich (Dan), Danielle Ferland (Caddy), Ben Wright (Toddie); The Mahaneyheyans — Tommy Hollis (Heath), Charlaine Woodard (Local)

The action occurs this weekend, on an ocean and island.

The musical was presented in two acts.

ACT ONE—"This Could Be the End" (Janice Lynde, Stephen Vinovich, Danielle Ferland, Ben Wright), "The Rubber Plant Song" (Tommy Hollis), "We're Needed Here" (Janice Lynde, Stephen Vinovich), "Take Me Away" (Charlaine Woodard), "Something's Gonna Happen Really Strange Tonight" (Danielle Ferland), "On Mahaneyheya"

(Charlaine Woodard), "Doom Is Due at Dawn" (Charlaine Woodard, Janice Lynde, Stephen Vinovich, Danielle Ferland, Ben Wright), "With the Dawn" (Danielle Ferland, Stephen Vinovich, Charlaine Woodard), "Mama Will Be Waiting with the Dawn" (Janice Lynde), "This Must Be the End" (Tommy Hollis, Danielle Ferland, Stephen Vinovich, Janice Lynde)

ACT TWO—"Welcome to Paradise" (Tommy Hollis), "Atlanta" (Danielle Ferland), "Welcome to Paradise Part II" (Tommy Hollis), "Inside" (Ben Wright), "Who Is This Woman" (Danielle Ferland, Janice Lynde), "Secrets Men Should Know" (Stephen Vinovich), "The Last Paradise" (Charlaine Woodard, Tommy Hollis, Ben Wright), "Dear Diary"/"The Uncle Dan Song" (Danielle Ferland, Stephen Vinovich, Janice Lynde), "The Last Paradise" (reprise) (Charlaine Woodard, Tommy Hollis), "You've Got to Let Go" (Ben Wright, Danielle Ferland), "This Is Not the End" (Janice Lynde, Stephen Vinovich, Danielle Ferland, Ben Wright)

NOTES—*Paradise* was a would-be satiric musical about a "vile" family from Atlanta marooned on a tropical island, and their attempts to ruin the paradise they've found. Writing in *The Best Plays of 1985-1986*, Jeffrey Sweet noted that George C. Wolfe's "contempt" for his characters was so great that Sweet wondered how Wolfe could expect the audience to care about them. Mel Gussow in the *New York Times* said *Paradise* was like a "ticket to purgatory," and noted that the "forgettable farrago" was a "fizzle" which lacked imagination.

The musical played for only two weeks; during its preview period, Jerry Lanning was replaced by Stephen Vinovich.

1220 Paradise Gardens East
NOTES—See entry for *City Scene*.

1221 Paradise Island. "A Hawaiian Musical Fantasy." THEATRE: Jones Beach Marine Theatre; OPENING DATE: June 22, 1961; PERFORMANCES: 75; BOOK: Carmen Lombardo and John Jacob Loeb; book adapted by Francis Swann; LYRICS: Carmen Lombardo and John Jacob Loeb; MUSIC: Carmen Lombardo and John Jacob Loeb; DIRECTION: Book directed by Francis Swann; entire production supervised by Arnold Spector; CHOREOGRAPHY: June Taylor; SCENERY: George Jenkins; COSTUMES: Winniford Morton; LIGHTING: Peggy Clark; MUSICAL DIRECTION: Pembroke Davenport; PRODUCER: Guy Lombardo

CAST—John Piilani Watkins (Piilani), NORMAN ATKINS (King Kekoa), ELAINE MALBIN (Princess Hokunani), HONEY SANDERS Melemele), Children of the Island (Debra Ann Andrade, Jacqueline Ben, Kathy Gore, Alice Miller, Georgia Miller, Lucille Miller, Leland O'Connor, Milton Olmos, Shay'anne Osaki), Robert Penn (Diamond Head Charlie), WILLIAM GAXTON (Alexander J. Dodd), ARTHUR TREACHER (Oliver Perkins), JACK WASHBURN (Larry Dodd), Tom Noel (Skipper, Senator), Lillian Bozinoff (Mahualani), Joe Kekanoho (Kau-Kau), Lester Janus (Wiki; apparently at some performances, the role was performed by Stanley Janus), RALPH PURDUM (Bomarc Barnstable), Elsa Raven (Miss Emily Fleetwood), Harold Gary (O'Grady, Second Senator), GUY LOMBARDO AND HIS ROYAL CANADIANS, Ralph Vucci (Bellboy), Peter Gladke (High Priest), Nat Horne (Kahuna Dancer), Ray Gilbert (Kahuna Dancer), Fisaga Taoni Fanene (Fire Dancer), Alii Noa (Fire Dancer), Nalani Keale (Ritual Dancer), Sonny Kekuewa (Ritual Dancer), Dukie Kuahulu (Ritual Dancer), THE TOY BOYS, Singers: Girls—Nancy Anco, Lillian Bozinoff, Elena Doria, Martha Flowers, June Genovese, Doris Galiber, Maggie Goz, Helena Jackman, Marion Lauer, Miriam Lawrence, Mary Louise, Lispet Nelson, Mary Ann Rydzeski, Wanda Saxon, Karyn Styne, Lynn Wendell; Boys—Kenny Adams, Irving Barnes, Walter P. Brown, Eugene Edwards, Thomas Edwards, Harry Goz, Richard Hermany, Robert Lenn, Paul Michael, Jack Rains, Michael Roberts, Casper Roos, John J. Smith, Feodore Tedick, Ralph Vucci, Edmund Walenta; Dancers: Girls—Diana Baffa, Francine Bond, Connie Burnett, Rosalind Corn, Gloria Gabriel, Marion Jim, Mary Jane Moncrieff, Candy Reola, Pat Trott, Barbara Wallach, Mary Zahn; Boys—Kalani Cockett, Paul Eden, Al Fiorella, Ray Gilbert, Peter Gladke, Terry Green, Nat Horne, Myron Howard, Clyde Laurents, Adolph Sambogna; THE JOHN PIILANI WATKINS GROUP (Debra Ann Andrade, Patricia Andrade, Paulette Andrade, Jacqueline Ben, George Dayag, Euwilde Doo, Emanuel Duarte, Josephine Duarte, Fisaga Taoni Fanene, Kathy Gore, Carolee Kia, Silva Meinert, Albert Miller, Alice Miller, Georgia Miller, Lucille Miller, John Morris, Leland O'Connor, Milton Olmos, Shay'anne Osaki, Arvillie Ann Reed, Peter Sataraka, Leonard Soares, Priscilla Young

The action occurs on Niihau and Honolulu, Hawaii, in February and March of 1959.

The musical was presented in two acts.

ACT ONE—Overture (Orchestra), "A Happy Hukilau" (Honey Sanders, Natives), "Once Upon a Time"/"Hokunani's Prayer" (Elaine Malbin), "The Coconut Wireless" (Honey Sanders, Natives), "My World and Your World" (Jack Washburn, Elaine Malbin), "The Menehune" (Children, Arthur Treacher), "Hokunani" (Jack Washburn), "Luau Chant" (Norman Atkins, Natives), "What Could Be More Romantic" (William Gaxton), ""Niihau Hula" (John Piilani), "Paradise Island" (Norman Atkins, Natives), "The Invasion": "With a Yo Ho Heave Ho"; "We're in a Race"; "Miss Emily Fleetwood" (Harold Gary, Sailors), "My World and Your World" (reprise) (Company)

ACT TWO—"It's a Great Day for Hawaii" (Citizens of Honolulu, Guy Lombardo and His Royal Canadians), "I'll Just Pretend" (Elaine Malbin," "I'll Just Pretend" (Duet Reprise) (Jack Washburn, Elaine Malbin), "Never Any Time to Play" (Children, Honey Sanders, Arthur Treacher), "Beyond the Clouds" (Norman Atkins, Elaine Malbin), "Ceremonial Chant" (Natives), "Ceremonial March" (Orchestra), "Paradise Island" (Reprise Finale) (Company)

NOTES—*Paradise Island* (the title page of the souvenir program referred to the title as *The Legend of Paradise Island*) dealt with a stuffy businessman (William Gaxton) and his son who are shipwrecked on an Hawaiian island; the humor derived from the contrast of the Americans and the "natives," and the romantic aspects of the plot dealt with the love of the businessman's son and the princess of the island. Louis Calta in the *New York Times* found the musical "visually spectacular," and mentioned in particular a "towering" waterfall which produced over seven-hundred gallons of water a minute from a height of one-hundred feet. Further, there were "massive" cliffs which rose to "dizzying" heights, and a volcano erupted, replete with smoke and lava. However, Calta noted the dialogue was "embarrassingly dull" and the score only "fair-to-middling." He felt the best sequence in the musical was an appearance by Guy Lombardo and His Royal Canadians in which they played a medley of standard songs ("Humoresque," "Far Away Places," "When the Saints Come Marching In," and "Hawaiian Wedding Song").

It appears that at one point or another during the run, the song "Now the Time Has Come" was added for the finale.

The musical returned the following summer, opening on June 27, 1962, for sixty-eight performances. All the principal performers reprised their roles for the production, with the exception of Elaine Malbin, who was replaced by Joy Clements.

The 1961 and 1962 productions of *Paradise Island* marked the end of William Gaxton's distinguished career (he died in 1963). Virtually unknown today, he was one of the major leading men of the musical's golden age. (It appears there are no recordings of his singing voice, and of his few film roles his most accessible appearance is in a supporting and non-singing role in the 1943 film version of *Best Foot Forward*.) Gaxton starred in a number of Broadway musicals, and either in solos or duets introduced songs by Richard Rodgers and Lorenz Hart, George and Ira Gershwin, Cole Porter, and Irving Berlin, many of which went on to become standards: *A Connecticut Yankee* (1927; "Thou Swell"); *Fifty Million Frenchmen* (1929; "You Do Something to Me"); *Of Thee I Sing* (1931; "Of Thee I Sing, Baby," "Who Cares?"); *Let 'Em Eat Cake* (1933; "Mine"); *Anything Goes* (1934; "All Through the Night" and "You're the Top"); *Leave It to Me!* ("From Now On" and "Far Away"); and *Louisiana Purchase* (1940; "Fools Fall in Love" and "Outside of That, I Love You"). Speaking of leading men, a number of male leads who came upon the Broadway scene either during the World War II era or shortly after it; they all had semi-operatic voices and all were of the stalwart variety. While they never became as well-known as Ethel Merman, Mary Martin, and Carol Channing, three of them enjoyed popularity: Alfred Drake, John Raitt, and Richard Kiley. With three smash hit musicals on his resume ([*Oklahoma!* [1943], *Kiss Me, Kate* [1948], and *Kismet* [1953]), Drake's name was familiar enough to become a punch line on an episode of *I Love Lucy*. John Raitt created roles in two hits (*Carousel* [1945] and *The Pajama Game* [1954]), and even reprised his role in the latter for the 1957 film version. Richard Kiley was in the original Broadway productions of *Kismet* (1953), *Redhead* (1959), and *No Strings* (1962); and in 1965 he created the title role in *Man of La Mancha*. Kiley also appeared in non-musicals, and was occasionally seen on television [including a major role in the 1983 miniseries *The Thorn Birds*]).

And while Stephen Douglass wasn't as well-known as the above trio, no one seems to forget about him or to confuse him with other male leads of the era. He was the original Joe Hardy in *Damn Yankees* (1955), and was one of the leads in the legendary Off Broadway (and later Broadway) musical *The Golden Apple* (1954; see entry). He also appeared in a number of the era's musicals, including *Make a Wish* (1951), *Rumple* (1957), and *110 in the Shade* (1963). Except for *Rumple*, all his Broadway appearances were preserved on cast albums. (John Cullum was another leading man of the post-World War II era, winning two Tony Awards for Best Actor in a Musical; for more information, see entry for *Urinetown*.) But four other leading men, David Brooks, Lawrence Brooks, David Atkinson, and Wilbur Evans, are forgotten today, and even musical theatre buffs sometimes tend to confuse them with one another (because the quartet includes two Brooks and two Davids, perhaps it's understandable).

All four were associated in one way or another with Sigmund Romberg's final three Broadway musicals; two were in musicals by Arthur Schwartz; two performed in *Man of La Mancha* during its original New York run; two were in different New York productions of *Brigadoon*; two were associated with *Trouble in Tahiti*; and there were also connections with Cole Porter and Dorothy Fields. And three of them appeared in, or directed, Off Broadway musicals.

David Brooks was the leading man in two musical hits of the mid-1940s, Harold Arlen and E.Y. Harburg's *Bloomer Girl* (1944), in which he introduced "Evalina" and "Right as the Rain," and Alan Jay Lerner and Frederick Loewe's *Brigadoon* (1947). In the latter, he introduced "The Heather on the Hill" as well as one of the most enduring ballads in musical theatre, "Almost Like Being in Love." His performances in these two musicals were preserved on the original cast albums.

Brooks next played the leading role of Billy the Kid in the 1946 musical *Shootin' Star*, which closed prior to Broadway.

He also took part in one of the most memorable weeks in the history of musical theatre. On June 14, 1952, as part of the Festival of the Creative Arts at Brandeis University (which had seen the premiere of Leonard Bernstein's *Trouble in Tahiti* two nights before), Brooks performed the role of Macheath /Mack the Knife in Marc Blitzstein's new translation of Bertolt Brecht and Kurt Weill's *The Threepenny Opera* (see entries for the 1954 and 1955 Off Broadway productions). At the time, the musical was relatively obscure, and its only Broadway production, in 1933, had been a fast flop, lasting only twelve performances. But Blitzstein's version institutionalized the work as one of the seminal works of musical theatre, and the 1955 Off Broadway production played for 2,611 performances.

And, in an interesting connection between David Brooks and David Atkinson, at one point during the six-year run of the 1955 production of *The Threepenny Opera*, Atkinson performed the role of Macheath for seven months.

Brooks next appeared with Jack Cassidy and Alice Ghostley in the innovative 1954 Off Broadway musical *Sandhog* (see entry). In 1954, Brooks was also cast in Sigmund Romberg's final musical, *The Girl in Pink Tights*, but was replaced by David Atkinson during the show's tryout. Maybe this is another reason the Two Davids tend to be confused with one another.

Brooks directed the 1962 Off Broadway musical *The Banker's Daughter* (see entry), and he created roles in three more musicals: Irving Berlin's *Mr. President* (1962), Noel Coward's *The Girl Who Came to Supper* (1963), and *Park* (1970). (For some reason, no one ever refers to the latter as Lance Mulcahy's *Park*.)

Brooks also appeared in non-musicals, including the comedy *The Sunday Man* (1964), which was somewhat similar in plot to another 1964 comedy, *Any Wednesday*. He was also in the 1971 Off Broadway revival of Saul Bellow's *The Last Analysis*. In the latter, he came across as a dapper performer of elan and panache (come to think of it, these are adjectives one usually associates with Alfred Drake).

Lawrence Brooks starred in one of Broadway's biggest hits of the 1940s, *Song of Norway* (1944). He created the leading role of Edvard Grieg and introduced "Strange Music," the musical's most enduring song. Adapted by Robert Wright and George Forrest and based on Greig's music, when *Song of Norway* closed after 844 performances it was the fourth longest-running book musical in the history of Broadway. But Brooks' next musical, Sigmund Romberg's *My Romance* (1948), played for less than three months (rumor has it that the show was privately recorded, and that since the 1940s the master tapes have been filed away in a prominent theatre archive).

Brooks then appeared in *Buttrio Square* (1952), which ran for only seven performances; with *Hit the Trail* (1954) and *Portofino* (1958), *Buttrio Square* is on the short list of contenders for the worst musical of the 1950s (and being set in Italy certainly didn't help *Buttrio Square* and *Portofino* [see Appendix U for The Italian Curse]).

Brooks went on to replace Don Ameche in Cole Porter's *Silk Stockings* (1955) during the show's Broadway run, and in 1961 he was standby for Alfred Drake in *Kean* (lyrics and music by Wright and Forrest).

Brooks enjoyed a final success when he appeared in the 1962 Off Broadway musical *Riverwind* (1962), which played for 443 performances and was recorded by London Records (unfortunately, John Jennings' memorable score has never been released on CD). After *Riverwind*, Jennings was never heard from again; this was a great loss for the American musical, because if *Riverwind* is any indication, the man had lyrical and musical talent to spare.

Brooks had three prominent songs in *Riverwind*: an affecting solo, "I'd Forgotten How Beautiful She Could Be"; a duet, the Strauss-like "Pardon Me While I Dance "; and a quartet, the exquisite "Wishing Song." The latter is more than just the highlight of Jennings' wonderful score; "Wishing Song" is so perfect that it belongs in the uppermost echelons of musical theatre writing.

Brooks' final Broadway appearance was in a supporting role in the two-week failure *Anya* (1965), a musical version of *Anastasia*. Brooks thus began and ended his career in musicals by Wright and Forrest both of which were adapted from the music of earlier composers (in this case, the music for *Anya* was adapted from themes by Sergei Rachmaninoff).

David Atkinson's first musical was Arthur Schwartz and Howard Dietz' *Inside U.S.A.* (1948); he appeared in the pre-Broadway run of the revue and introduced its most enduring standard, the ethereal "Haunted Heart." Over a half-century later, the ballad is still popular: It was the theme song for the 1999 film *The End of the Affair*, and it was the title of opera singer Renee Fleming's CD collection of popular songs (released in 2005). Moreover, Linda Dahl's *Haunted Heart: A Biography of Susannah McCorkle* looks at the life (and tragic death) of one of our greatest cabaret singers.

For reasons which remain unclear, Atkinson was replaced by John Tyers during the tryout of *Inside U.S.A.*, and so it was Tyers who actually introduced "Haunted Heart" to Broadway audiences. But Atkinson's departure from the show must have been amicable, because at one point during the Broadway run he replaced Tyers, and so Atkinson got to sing "his" song on Broadway after all, albeit not on opening night.

In 1952, Atkinson created the role of Sam in Bernstein's one-act opera *Trouble in Tahiti* in the aforementioned arts festival at Brandeis University. For years afterward Atkinson would return to this role, via recording and live performance.

Atkinson and Tyers crossed career paths again, for besides their "Haunted Heart" connection, they also shared *Trouble in Tahiti*. In 1955, *Tahiti* premiered on Broadway as one-third of *All in One*, a three-act evening of dance (in various styles, with music by different composers), drama (Tennessee Williams' *27 Wagons Full of Cotton*), and music (*Tahiti*). Tyers played Sam in the Broadway production, and so despite Atkinson's having introduced "Haunted Heart" in *Inside U.S.A.* and Bernstein's arias and duets in *Tahiti* (including the locker-room aria, "There's a Law About Men..."), it was Tyers who officially introduced these numbers to Broadway audiences.

(And for another Two Davids connection, it was David Brooks who directed the Broadway production of *Trouble in Tahiti*.)

Atkinson next appeared in *The Girl in Pink Tights* (1954), when he replaced David Brooks during the tryout. Although the musical wasn't a success, it was recorded, and thus Atkinson's "Lost in Loveliness," a minor but pleasant ballad (and the closest thing to a popular song in the entire score) was preserved.

After *Pink Tights*, Atkinson appeared opposite Carol Channing in the 1955 failure *The Vamp* (lyrics by John LaTouche and music by James Mundy), which was a spoof of silent-movie making (see Appendix U for The Silent Movie-Making Curse). RCA Victor owned the cast album rights, but poor reviews and a brief run put the kibosh on the recording.

And to add further confusion regarding the Two Davids, Atkinson appeared in a 1957 revival of *Brigadoon* at City Center, playing the role originally created by David Brooks. Some audience members may have assumed they were seeing a reprise of an original cast performance.

Atkinson was in fact a frequent visitor to City Center: He appeared opposite Kitty Carlisle in a 1956 revival of *Kiss Me, Kate* as well as in revivals of *Annie Get Your Gun* in 1958, *Say, Darling* in 1959, and *The Cradle Will Rock* in 1960 (see entries for various Off Broadway productions of the latter). He also appeared in City Center's Theatre-in-the-Park revival of *Can-Can* in 1959.

Atkinson also reprised his role of Sam in a New York City Opera revival of *Trouble in Tahiti* in 1958, and, as mentioned, for seven months he played the role of Macheath/Mack the Knife during the marathon Off-Broadway run of *The Threepenny Opera*.

At the City Opera, Atkinson also appeared in *The Good Soldier Schweik* and *He Who Gets Slapped* (see entries).

Atkinson appeared in the Off Broadway musical *All in Love* (see entry); happily, the charming score was recorded by Mercury Records. Later, during two separate New York runs of *Man of La Mancha* (the original production which ran from 1965 to 1971, and a 1972 revival), Atkinson performed the title role of Cervantes/Don Quixote, either as a replacement or as an alternate; he also toured with the production (in the tour which starred Jose Ferrer, Atkinson played the role of Dr. Carrasco).

It was in fact Atkinson who performed the title role at *La Mancha*'s final Broadway performance on June 26, 1971. Incidentally, the last performance included a brace of former Broadway leading men; besides Atkinson, both Ray Middleton and Robert Rounseville were there (both were original cast members of the production and had created the respective roles of The Innkeeper and The Padre in 1965).

Middleton had created roles in Broadway musicals for a period of over thirty years (*Roberta* [1933], *Knickerbocker Holiday* [1938], *Annie Get Your Gun* [1946], *Love Life* [1948], and *Man of La Mancha* [1965]), and Rounseville had of course created the title role in the original Broadway production of *Candide* (1956); he also appeared as Mister Snow in the 1956 film version of *Carousel*.

Like David Brooks, Wilbur Evans appeared in two smash hits of the mid-1940s, Cole Porter's *Mexican Hayride* (1944) and Sigmund Romberg and Dorothy Fields' *Up in Central Park* (1945).

In *Mexican Hayride*, Evans introduced Porter's glorious "I Love You," and the critics praised both the song and Evans' thrilling rendition. Burton Rascoe in the *New York World-Telegram* said the song "touches the heart and spine — hummable, singable, catchy, exciting — a hit song not of the show, but of the year."

In *Up in Central Park*, Evans introduced "Close as Pages in a Book" (the musical's hit song), "When She Walks in the Room," "It Doesn't Cost You Anything to Dream," "The Big Back Yard," and the especially lovely "April Snow."

Evans' powerful baritone can be heard on the original cast albums of both shows.

Evans' next role was probably one of the most coveted of the era. He was chosen to create the role of Emile De Becque opposite Mary Martin for the London premiere of Richard Rodgers and Oscar Hammerstein II's *South Pacific*, which opened at the Drury Lane on November 1, 1951. It was thus Evans who introduced "Some Enchanted Evening" and "This Nearly Was Mine" to London audiences.

In 1954, Evans appeared opposite Shirley Booth in Arthur Schwartz and Dorothy Fields' *By the Beautiful Sea*, and he introduced the musical's almost-hit song "More Love Than Your Love." His performance was preserved on the show's original cast album.

Like David Atkinson, Evans ended his Broadway

career by appearing in *Man of La Mancha* during its original Broadway run, as one of many performers who replaced Richard Kiley. Evans also toured with the production, playing the role of The Innkeeper in the tour which starred Jose Ferrer.

1222 Paris Lights. "The All-Star Literary Genius Expatriate Revue/A Musical Celebration in Their Own Words." THEATRE: The American Place Theatre; OPENING DATE: January 11, 1980; PERFORMANCES: 23; BOOK: Developed and Adapted by Michael Zettler; based on an idea by William Russo, developed by Michael Zettler and George Ferencz; LYRICS: By the writers portrayed in the revue; MUSIC: William Russo; ADDITIONAL MUSIC: Michael Ward; DIRECTION: George Ferencz; CHOREOGRAPHY: Jane Summerhays; SCENERY: Bill Stabile; COSTUMES: Kathleen Smith and Sally Lesser; LIGHTING: Laura Rambaldi; MUSICAL DIRECTION: Michael Ward; PRODUCER: The American Place Theatre (Wynn Handman, Director; Julia Miles, Associate Director)

CAST—Trisha Long (Gertrude Stein), Margery Cohen (Alice B. Toklas, Edna St. Vincent Millay), James York (Ernest Hemingway), Jane Summerhays (Sylvia Beach, Zelda Fitzgerald), Nicholas Wyman (James Joyce, F. Scott Fitzgerald), Stephen Mellor (Harry Crosby, John "Buffy" Glassco), John David Westfall (Robert McAlmon, Jimmy Charters), Rhetta Hughes (Josephine Baker, Kiki), Christopher Murray (Charles Lindbergh)

The action occurs in Paris during the 1920s.

The musical was presented in two acts.

ACT ONE—"Haschich Fudge" (by Alice B. Toklas) (Margery Cohen), "Three Poems" ("First Fig"; "Thursday"; "Mariposa") (by Edna St. Vincent Millay) (Margery Cohen), "I Blow My Nose" (by F. Scott Fitzgerald) (John David Westfall), "mr. youse" (by e.e. cummings) (Rhetta Hughes), "Lifting Belly" (by Gertrude Stein) (Trisha Long, Ensemble), "Oh, Your Mother Is in Bed" (by Ted Parramore) (Jane Summerhays, Nicholas Wyman, Ensemble), "who knows if the moon's a balloon" (by e.e. cummings) (Rhetta Hughes), "you shall above all things"(by e.e. cummings) (James York, Margery Cohen), "Literary Jam/Jam/Band Jam, 'JAM'" (by F. Scott Fitzgerald) (Trisha Long, John David Westfall, Nicholas Wyman, Stephen Mellor, Margery Cohen, Rhetta Hughes, Jane Summerhays)

ACT TWO—"The Jewel Stairs' Grievance" (by Ezra Pound) (Rhetta Hughes), "Three Poems" (reprise) (Margery Cohen, John David Westfall, Stephen Mellor), "Let Her Be" (by Gertrude Stein) (Nicholas Wyman, Trisha Long, John David Westfall, Margery Cohen), "Dance of Exhaustion"/"Jam" (reprise) (danced by Jane Summerhays, Nicholas Wyman), "I Have Been Heavy" (by Gertrude Stein) (Trisha Long), "If I Could Tell You" (by W.H. Auden) (Jane Summerhays)

NOTES—*Paris Lights* sounds interesting; it was a loosely structured book musical about expatriate writers and celebrities living in Paris in the 1920s, and for the most part all the dialogue and lyrics were taken from the writings of the authors portrayed in the script. Thomas Lask in the *New York Times* found the evening somewhat repetitious and noted that "tedium ... set in early." But he said William Russo's score was "jazzy" with a "strong 20's flavor," and he singled out "Lifting Belly" and "Let Her Be."

The musical was yet another visit by Gertrude Stein and Alice B. Toklas; for some three decades, plays and musicals about these two (as well as adaptations of Stein's works for the stage) were almost as frequent as Kurt Weill-related revues and musicals.

1223 Paris '31. THEATRE: AMAS Musical Theatre; OPENING DATE: November 2, 1989; PERFORMANCES: 22; BOOK: John Fearnley; LYRICS: Cole Porter; MUSIC: Cole Porter; DIRECTION: John Fearnley; CHOREOGRAPHY: Robert Longbottom; SCENERY: Jane Sablow; COSTUMES: Kathryn Wagner; MUSICAL DIRECTION: William Roy; PRODUCER: AMAS Musical Theatre (Rosetta LeNoire, Founder and Artistic Director)

CAST—Thelma Carpenter, Zellie Daniels, Kevin John Gee, Nancy Groff, Randy Hills, Sebastian Hobart, Michael McAssey, Debbie Petrino, Brian Quinn, Monte Ralstin, Pamela Shaddock, Jeffrey Solis, Betty Winsett, Ellen Zachos

NOTES—The Off Off Broadway musical *Paris '31* took place in a Parisian nightclub called Toni's Paris. The musical used standards by Cole Porter to tell its story.

1224 A Party with Betty Comden and Adolph Green. "An Intimate Revue." THEATRE: Cherry Lane Theatre; OPENING DATE: November 10, 1958; PERFORMANCES: Approximately 5 (on consecutive Monday nights)

CAST—Betty Comden and Adolph Green (with Peter Howard at the piano)

The production transferred to Broadway at the John Golden Theatre on December 23, 1958, for thirty-eight performances, and re-opened there on April 16, 1958, for an additional forty-four performances.

Betty Comden and Adolph Green performed their own material, all of it derived from their revues and book musicals. The information below reflects the Broadway production's credits and musical numbers. Producer: The Theatre Guild, by special arrangement and in association with Town Productions, Inc., as originally presented by JJG Productions under the supervision of Gus Schirmer, Jr.; Décor and Lighting: Marvin Reiss

On Broadway, the revue was presented in three acts.

(Unless otherwise noted, all lyrics and sketches by Betty Comden and Adolph Green)

ACT ONE—The Performers: Opening ("I Said Good Morning") (music by Andre Previn) (Written for, but not used in, film *It's Always Fair Weather* [1955]), The Revuers — Night Club Act (sketches by The Revuers, comprised of Betty Comden, Judy Tuvim [Holliday], John Frank, Alvin Hammer, and Adolph Green), 1. Movie Ads, 2. The Reader's Digest, 3. The Screen Writers, 4. The Banshee Sisters, 5. *The Baroness Bazooka* (see note below)

ACT TWO—The Performer-Writers: *On the Town* (1944) (music by Leonard Bernstein: "New York, New York," "Lonely Town," "Lucky to Be Me," "Come Up to My Place," "(I Get) Carried Away," *Billion Dollar Baby* (1945) (music by Morton Gould): "Bad Timing," "Broadway Blossoms," *Good News* (1948 film) (music by Roger Edens): "The French Lesson," *Two on the Aisle* (1951) (music by Jule Styne): "If" (a/k/a "If You Hadn't, But You Did"), "Catch Our Act at the Met," "He'll Never Know"

ACT THREE—The Writer-Performers: *Wonderful Town* (1953) (music by Leonard Bernstein): "A Hundred Easy Ways to Lose a Man," "Ohio," "Wrong Note Rag," "A Quiet Girl," "It's Love," *Peter Pan* (1954) (music by Jule Styne): "Oh, My Mysterious Lady," "Captain Hook's Waltz," "Never Never Land," "Once Upon a Time and Long Ago," "*A Show*" (music by Saul Chaplin): "Inspiration" (see notes, below), *Say, Darling* (1958) (music by Jule Styne): Comden and Green performed a medley of songs from the musical (exactly which numbers are unknown, but possibly two were "Dance Only with Me" and "Something's Always Happening by the River," both of which were mildly popular during the run of *Say, Darling*), *Bells Are Ringing* (1956) (music by Jule Styne): "Just in Time," "The Party's Over"

NOTES—*The Baroness Bazooka*, an operetta spoof written and performed by The Revuers, had originally appeared in the pre-Broadway tryout of *My Dear Public* (1942), in which The Revuers played themselves. The show closed prior to Broadway, but was re-mounted the following year (sans The Revuers and their material).

The musical referred to as "*A Show*" in the third act was *Bonanza Bound*, a 1947 musical with book and lyrics by Comden and Green and music by Saul Chaplin; among the cast members was Green himself. The show closed during its pre-Broadway tryout, but surprisingly was recorded by RCA Victor (which never released the album; however in the 1970s the cast album surfaced on a pirated LP release). In *A Party*, Comden and Green performed one song from *Bonanza Bound*, "Inspiration" (which, in the original show, was introduced by Green and his then-wife Allyn Ann McLerie).

In 1977, Comden and Green brought their party back to Broadway (for ninety-two performances). This time around they added material written during the years following the original production, including songs from *Do Re Mi* (1960) and *Subways Are for Sleeping* (1961).

The above song listing is taken from information in the Broadway playbill of *A Party*, from Richard C. Norton's *A Chronology of American Musical Theatre*, and from the cast album by Capitol Records (LP # SWAO-1197). The 1977 revival was also recorded (by Stet Records on a 2-LP set [# S2L-5177]).

1225 Passing Strange. THEATRE: The Anspacher Theatre/The Public Theatre; OPENING DATE: May 14, 2007; PERFORMANCES: 56; BOOK: Stew; LYRICS: Stew; MUSIC: Stew and Heidi Rodewald; DIRECTION: Annie Dorsen; CHOREOGRAPHY: Karole Armitage, "Movement Coordinator"; SCENERY: David Korins; COSTUMES: Elizabeth Hope Clancy; LIGHTING: Kevin Adams; MUSICAL DIRECTION: Heidi Rodewald; PRODUCER: The Public Theatre (Oskar Eustis, Artistic Director; Mara Manus, Executive Director); Bill Bragin, Peter DuBois, and Mandy Hackett, Associate Producers; produced in association with Berkeley Repertory Theatre (Tony Taccone, Artistic Director; Susan Medak, Managing Director)

CAST—De'Adre Aziza (Edwina, Marianna, Sudabey), Daniel Breaker (Youth), Eisa Davis (Mother), Colman Domingo (Mr. Franklin, Joop, Mr. Venus), Chad Goodridge (Hugo, Christophe, Terry), Rebecca Naomi Jones (Sherry, Renata, Desi), Stew (Narrator)

The musical was presented in two acts (song titles weren't listed in the Off Broadway program; the song list below, and song assignments, are based on information in the Broadway *Playbill*).

ACT ONE—Prologue ("We Might Play All Night") (Stew, Heidi Rodewald, Band), "Baptist Fashion Show" (Stew, Ensemble), "Blues Revelation"/"Freight Train" (Stew, Ensemble), "Arlington Hill" (Stew), "Sole Brother" (Daniel Breaker, Chad Goodridge, Rebecca Naomi Jones), "Must've Been High" (Stew), "Mom Song" (Stew, Eisa Davis, Ensemble), "Merci Beaucoup, M. Godard" (Stew, Stewardesses), "Amsterdam" (Ensemble), "Keys" (De' Adre Aziza, Daniel Breaker, Stew), "We Just Had Sex" (Daniel Breaker, De'Adre Aziza, Rebecca Naomi Jones), "Stoned" (Daniel Breaker, Stew)

ACT TWO—"May Day" (Stew, Ensemble), "Surface" (Colman Domingo), "Damage" (Stew, Rebecca Naomi Jones, Daniel Breaker), "Identity" (Daniel Breaker), "The Black One" (Stew, Ensemble), "Come Down Now" (Heidi Rodewald, Rebecca Naomi Jones), "Work the Wound" (Daniel Breaker, Stew), "Passing Phase" (Daniel Breaker, Stew), "Love Like That" (Stew, Heidi Rodewald)

NOTES—For *Passing Strange*, the single-named Stew wrote the book and lyrics, co-composed the music (with Heidi Rodewald), and played the role of the narrator, who looks back on his life and the young man he used to be (Daniel Breaker). The musical told the story of a disaffected Black youth growing up in Los Angeles who eventually finds his voice in music. According to Charles Isherwood in the *New York Times*, the evening "defies generic categories" such as the concert and the traditional book musical in its "bitingly funny ... bracingly inventive" telling of the Black experience in the United States. The score covered a range of musical styles (minstrel, Europop, punk, Gilbert and Sullivan, Kurt Weill, even a "smidgen" of *My Fair Lady*).

The musical transferred to Broadway, opening at the Belasco Theatre on February 28, 2008, for 165 performances. The cast album was released by Ghostlight Records (CD # 8-4429), and in 2009 a film version was released. The script was published by Applause Books in 2009.

1226 The Passion of Alice. "A Musical Trip Through Wonderland." THEATRE: Greenwich Mews Theatre; OPENING DATE: Summer 1977; PERFORMANCES: Unknown (according to the musical's flyer, the production was booked for "A Summer Run" [seven performances a week]); BOOK: Jocko Richardson, Ken Cory, and Sean Kalliel; LYRICS: Jocko Richardson, Sean Kalliel, and Gary Richmond; MUSIC: Gary Richmond; DIRECTION: Ken Cory; CHOREOGRAPHY: Lenny Pass; SCENERY: Alexis Dickinson-Cargasacchi; COSTUMES: Carmen Torenzo, Sean Kalliel, and Alexis Dickinson-Cargasacchi; LIGHTING: Martin Chafkin; MUSICAL DIRECTION: Richard Schacher

CAST—Vicki Guarino (Alice), Cynthia Cobb (Ellie, White Queen), Rene Roy (White Rabbit), David Boyd (Caterpillar), Sal Piro (Cheshire Cat, Humpty Dumpty), Gary Reed (Maximillian Snail), Doug Bradford (Mad Hatter), Anthony Monti (March Hare), Sona Vogel (Church Mouse), Alan Hemingway (Knave of Hearts), Beth Ratzer (Queen of Hearts), Lenny Pass (Tart One), Robert Cohen (Tartuffe), Arthur D'Alessio (Tart Three)

SOURCE—The 1865 novel *Alice's Adventures in Wonderland* by Lewis B. Carroll.

The musical was presented in two acts.

ACT ONE—Overture (Orchestra), "Just Flowers" (Cynthia Cobb, Vicki Guarino), "Other Possibilities" (Company), "I'm the Guy" (Rene Roy), "Changes" (David Boyd), "Curiouser and Curiouser" (Vicki Guarino), "Charmingly Insane" (Sal Piro, Lenny Pass, Arthur D'Alessio, 'Third Tart'), "You Gotta Believe" (Gary Reed, Company)

ACT TWO—"Choices" (Vicki Guarino), "Tea for Three" (Doug Bradford, Anthony Monti, Vicki Guarino, Sona Vogel), "I'm Just a Knave" (Alan Hemingway), "Royal Flush" (Beth Ratzer, Lenny Pass, Arthur D'Alessio, Unidentified Performer), "Get Alice" (Company), "Choices" (reprise) (Vicki Guarino, Cynthia Cobb)

NOTES—Like so many musical adaptations of *Alice's Adventures in Wonderland*, the Off Off Broadway musical *The Passion of Alice* went nowhere. For a list of other *Alice* adaptations, see entry for *Alice with Kisses*; also see Appendix K.

1227 The Passion of Jonathan Wade. THEATRE: New York City Center; OPENING DATE: October 11, 1962; PERFORMANCES: 2; LIBRETTO: Carlisle Floyd; MUSIC: Carlisle Floyd; DIRECTION: Allen Fletcher; SCENERY: Will Steven Armstrong; COSTUMES: Ruth Morley; MUSICAL DIRECTION: Julius Rudel; PRODUCER: New York City Opera

CAST—Norman Treigle (Judge Brooks Townsend), Phyllis Curtin (Celia Townsend), Linda Newman (Young Girl), Jeffrey Meyer (Young Boy), Richard Fredricks (Confederate Soldier), Harry Theyard (Lieutenant Patrick), Theodor Uppman (Colonel Jonathan Wade), Miriam Burton (Nicey), Paul Ukena (J. Tertius Riddle), Frank Porretta (Lucas Wardlaw), Norman Kelley (Ely Pratt), Patricia Brooks (Amy Pratt), Ron Bottcher (Union Soldier), Thomas Paul (Rector), Arthur Graham (Union Leaguer, First Carpetbagger), Eugene Brice (A Senator), Andrew Frierson (Judge Bell), David Smith (Second Carpetbagger), Mal Scott (Driver); Four Young Boys (Vaughn Eubler, Ainsley Sigmond, Robert Hawkins, Mal Scott)

NOTES—Carlisle Floyd's opera *The Passion of Jonathan Wade* seems to have disappeared during the thirty years following its premiere. Although Carlisle radically revised the opera in 1991, the revision appears to have had little afterlife, either. The plot, about a Union officer in the post-bellum South, his marriage to a Southern girl, and his ultimate undoing because of his ideals, sounds colorful and intriguing. But Ross Parmenter in the *New York Times* felt the tragedy of the title character wasn't carefully delineated, and further noted that Floyd's music was more successful in its love story than in its depiction of the era's historical events. For example, for the wedding scene Parmenter praised an aria and duet as haunting and melodious, and noted these sequences were the opera's strongest moments. On the other hand, when the wedding was interrupted by a Ku Klux Klan raid, he found the music "feeble."

1228 Patch, Patch, Patch. "A Musical Entertainment." THEATRE: West Bank Café; OPENING DATE: August 7, 1979; PERFORMANCES: 28 (estimated); LYRICS: Alan Menken; MUSIC: Alan Menken; DIRECTION: Norman L. Berman; ADDITIONAL STAGING: Janis Roswick; MUSICAL DIRECTION: Alan Menken; PRODUCERS: Lawrence Kraman, Scott Shukat, and Larry Weiss

CAST—Alice Cannon, Michael Glenn-Smith, Patti Perkins, Chip Zien

The revue was presented in two acts.

ACT ONE—"Patch, Patch, Patch" (Company), "Lovers" (Company), "Find Her" (Chip Zien), "Rosalie Murchison" (Alice Cannon), "Yankee Man" (Patti Perkins), "Easy" (Michael Glenn-Smith), "Nice Day" (Patti Perkins, Michael Glenn-Smith), "Knock at the Door" (Alice Cannon), "Three in a Hospital Room" (lyric by Muriel Robinson) (Patti Perkins), "Harry's a Rat" (Alice Cannon, Patti Perkins), "Thirty Little Aspirins" (Company)

ACT TWO—"Answering Machine" (Patti Perkins, Michael Glenn-Smith, Chip Zien), "Margaret" (lyric by Muriel Robinson) (Alice Cannon), "You & I & Love" (Alice Cannon, Chip Zien), "Cautiously Optimistic" (Company), "Trendell Terry" (Michael Glenn-Smith), "Life Can Pass You By" (Chip Zien), "It Starts Over Here" (Michael Glenn-Smith, Chip Zien), "Snow Song" (Company), "Pink Fish" (Michael Glenn-Smith), "Juan" (lyric by Robert Joseph) (Patti Perkins, Company), "Sailing On" (lyric by Dean Pitchford) (Chip Zien, Company), "Patch, Patch, Patch" (reprise) (Company)

NOTES—The Off Off Broadway revue *Patch, Patch, Patch* arrived two months before Alan Menken's first book musical (*God Bless You, Mr. Rosewater*; see entry) opened Off Broadway. The revue dealt in part with baby boomers who suddenly realize they're over thirty and are getting older. Mel Gussow in the *New York Times* singled out a number of sequences, including the 'inventive" song "Answering Machine"; "Snow Song" (it "could be sung for warmth around a fireside on a cold night"); and "Pink Fish" (a "lowdown country-western spoof" about a cowboy's first encounter with bagels and lox). Gussow noted that much of Menken's score had the kind of "lilt" often associated with Tom Jones and Harvey Schmidt, and he said some of the acerbic lyrics were reminiscent of Stephen Sondheim. "Yankee Man" and "Margaret" had been earlier heard in the 1977 revue *The Present Tense* (see entry).

1229 Paul Bunyan. THEATRE: Brander Matthews Hall/Columbia University; OPENING DATE: May 5, 1941; PERFORMANCES: 6 (estimated); BOOK: W.H. Auden; MUSIC: Benjamin Britten; DIRECTION: Milton Smith; MUSICAL DIRECTION: Hugh Ross

CAST—Young Trees (Ellen Huffmaster, Jane Weaver, Marlowe Jones, Ben Carpens), Three Wild Geese (Harriet Greene, Augusta Dorn, Pauline Kleinhesselink), Mordecai Bauman (Narrator), Milton Warchoff (The Voice of Paul Bunyan), Walter Graf (Cross Crosshaulson), Leonard Stocker (John Shears), Clifford Jackson (Sam Sharkey), Eugene Bonham (Ben Benny), Ernest Holcombe (Jen Jenson), Lewis Pierce (Pete Peterson), Ben Carpens (Andy Anderson), Lumberjacks (Alan Adair, Elmer Barber, Arnold Jaffe, Marlowe Jones, Charles Snitow, Robert Zeller, W. Fredric Piette, Thomas Flynn, Joseph Harrow), Henry Bauman (Western Union Boy), Bliss Woodward (Hel Helsen), William Hess (Johnny Inkslinger), Pauline Kleinhesselink (Fido), Harriet Greene (Moppet), Augusta Dorn (Poppet), The Defeated (Ben Carpens, Eugene Bonham, Adelaide Van Wey, Ernest Holcombe)

The opera was presented in two acts.

ACT ONE—Introduction, Prologue, "First Ballad Interlude," "Bunyan's Greeting," "Lumberjacks' Chorus," "Bunyan's Welcome," "Quartet of Swedes," "Western Union Boy's Song," "Cooks' Duet," "Animal Trio," "Bunyan's Goodnight (I)," "Exit of Lumberjacks," "The Blues: Quartet of the Defeated," "Bunyan's Goodnight (II)," "Second Ballad Interlude," "Food Chorus," "Chorus Accusation," "Slim's Song," "Bunyan's Return," "Inkslinger's Song," "Entrance of Chorus," "Tiny's Entrance," "Tiny's Song," "Inkslinger's Regret," "Bunyan's Goodnight (III)"

ACT TWO—"Bunyan's Good Morning," "Shears' Song," "Bunyan's Warning," "Farmers' Song," "Farmers' Exit," "The Mocking of Hel Helson," "Fido's Sympathy," "Cats' Creed," "The Fight," "Love Duet," "Mock Funeral March," "Hymn," "Third Ballad Interlude," "The Christmas Party," "Western Union Boy," "Chorus," "Bunyan's Farewell," "Litany"

NOTES—*Paul Bunyan* is one of the treasures of modern American opera. Its official opening night (May 5, 1941) followed a preview performance which had been seen the previous evening. The opera played for one week, and then seems to have completely disappeared until it was produced again in 1976 (an appropriate year for the public to revisit one of the masterworks of American musical theatre). In 1998, the opera was first performed by the New York City Opera, and that production was seen on public television on April 22, 1998. Moreover, there are now three recordings of the work. The times have finally caught up with *Paul Bunyan*.

Benjamin Britten's music is like nothing he ever composed; it's more in the style of a musical, and, in an article he wrote for the *New York Times* before the 1941 world premiere, W.H. Auden referred to *Paul Bunyan* as an operetta. Perhaps *Paul Bunyan* defies neat classification: it's not quite an opera, a musical comedy, or an operetta. In his prescient review for the *New York Times*, Olin Downes noted that both *Paul Bunyan* and *The Cradle Will Rock* (see entry) showed a "development nearly upon us" in which English-language opera can be "free from the stiff tradition of either grand or light opera." He felt the new works were "refreshing" in their flexible and modern treatment of the traditional opera.

The work is indeed a happy combination of opera and musical comedy, and its quirky notions (a chorus of singing trees and the fact that Paul Bunyan never physically appears in the opera and is heard only as an off-stage voice) were probably too strange for 1941. Similarly, the work's concept was perhaps difficult for some audiences and critics to grasp at the time: Paul Bunyan represents the force of physical nature which must exist when a country is young; but when a country matures and physical nature is conquered, a Paul Bunyan is no longer needed; once he bids farewell, it's up to man to master the art of his emotional, or human, nature.

The brilliant 1998 New York City Opera production revealed a work whose time has come; this concept musical with its offbeat way of telling a story was fresh and exciting. Auden once told the author he seldom went to the opera because ticket prices were too high; but if he had lived to see the City Opera's production of *Paul Bunyan*, he might well have wanted to attend all the performances. The work attests to his and Britten's vision; theirs was an iconoclastic work which turned the notions of 1941 opera and musical comedy upside down. They had in essence created the first concept musical and they used techniques which defied the era's conventions of musical-theatre story-telling.

The song sequences listed above are taken from the 2-CD set released by Virgin Classics Records (# VCD-7-59249-2).

1230 The Payoff. THEATRE: Columbia College Theatre; OPENING DATE: Late 1970s (?); PERFORMANCES: Unknown; BOOK: Lawrence Bommer; LYRICS: Denise DeClue; MUSIC: William Russo; DIRECTION: Paul Hough; SCENERY: Mary Griswald and John Paoletti; COSTUMES: Zulma Valdez; LIGHTING: Mary M. Badger; MUSICAL DIRECTION: Jim Sellers; PRODUCER: Columbia College Theatre Music Center (Sheldon Patinkin, Chairman)

CAST—William E. Esbrook (Eugene), David Gethmann (Nick Booth), Chuck Hall (Dr. Daniel Rutledge), Kay C. Reed (Cleo), Diane Tabor (Helen), Gretchen Wasserman (Rachel Rutledge), Donna Pieroni (Chorus), Jerrold St. Jorge (Chorus), Bridget Taylor (Chorus), Tom A. Viveiros (Chorus)

1231 Peace. "A New Musical." THEATRE: Astor Place Theatre; OPENING DATE: January 17, 1969; PERFORMANCES: 192; BOOK: Tim Reynolds; LYRICS: Tim Reynolds; some lyrics adapted by Al Carmines; MUSIC: Al Carmines; DIRECTION: Lawrence Kornfeld; CHOREOGRAPHY: For character of Peace, choreography by Arlene Rothstein; Hermes' choreography and cakewalk choreographed by David Vaughan; SCENERY: Unknown; Beetle and Mask designed by Ralph Lee; "other properties" designed by Jerry Hardin; COSTUMES: Nancy Christofferson; LIGHTING: Roger Morgan; MUSICAL DIRECTION: Al Carmines (at the piano); with John Kaye (percussion); PRODUCERS: Albert Poland and Franklin De-Boer

CAST—Julie Kurnitz (Mother, a/k/a Lisa), George McGrath (Father, a/k/a Rastus), Reathel Bean (Trygaeus), Essie Borden (Trygaeus' Daughter, Mortal), Ann Dunbar (Trygaeus' Daughter, Mortal), David Vaughan (Hermes), David Pursley (War), Dave Tice (Gen. Disorder), Jeffrey Apter (Mortal), Craig Kuehl (Mortal), Margot Lewitin (Mortal), Dallett Norris (Mortal), Arlene Rothlein (Peace), Margaret Wright (Prosperity), Lee Crespi (Abundance)

SOURCE—The 421 B.C. play *Peace* by Aristophanes.

The action occurs on Earth and in Heaven.

The musical was presented in two acts.

ACT ONE—"Father's Lament" (George McGrath), "The Ballad of Baby Trygaeus" (Julie Kurnitz, Reathel Bean), "Our Last Noble Attempt" (Julie Kurnitz, George McGrath, Reathel Bean), "Oh, Daddy, Daddy!" (Essie Borden, Ann Dunbar, Reathel Bean), "Heavenly Sustenance" (Julie Kurnitz, George McGrath, Essie Borden, Ann Dunbar, Reathel Bean), "All the Gods Have Gone Away" (David Vaughan, Reathel Bean), "Plumbing" (David Pursley, David Tice), "I Want to See Peace Again" (Jeffrey Apter, Essie Borden, Ann Dunbar, Craig Kuehl, Margot Lewitin, Dallett Norris), "Just Let Me Get My Hands on Peace Again" (Jeffrey Apter, Essie Borden, Ann Dunbar, Craig Kuehl, Margot Lewitin, Dallett Norris), "Just Can't Help It" (Jeffrey Apter, Essie Borden, Ann Dunbar, Craig Kuehl, Margot Lewitin, Dallett Norris), "Don't Do It, Mr. Hermes" (Jeffrey Apter, Essie Borden, Ann Dunbar, Craig Kuehl, Margot Lewitin, Dallett Norris), "Peace Ballet" (Arlene Rothlein), "Things Starting to Grow Again" (Jeffrey Apter, Essie Borden, Ann Dunbar, Craig Kuehl, Margot Lewitin, Dallett Norris, Margaret Wright, Lee Crespi)

ACT TWO—"Muse, Darling, Muse" (Margaret Wright, Company), "Up in Heaven" (Company), "My Name's Abundance" (Lee Crespi, Company), "You've Got Yourself a Bunch of Woman" (Margaret Wright, Company), "Peace Anthem" and "Cakewalk" (Company; "Cakewalk" danced by David Vaughan and Arlene Rothlein), "Sacrifice (Poor Mortals)" (Arlene Rothlein, Company), "Just Sit Around" (Company), "Summer's Nice" (Julie Kurnitz, Company), "Oh, Beautiful" (Margaret Wright, Company)

NOTES—Musical numbers weren't listed in the program. The song list above is derived from the songs in the published script, which noted that the play's style "lies somewhere between Ancient Greece and the East Village."

Peace was a typical Al Carmines' romp, and it saw the beginning of his stock company of sorts, a group of knowing performers (such as Julie Kurnitz and Reathel Bean) who were perfect foils for the typically skewed and dadaesque outlook of his musicals. With Carmines' infectious music, a loopy script based on Aristophanes' comedy (in which Peace visits Earth), a politically correct anti-war outlook, and Tim Reynolds' zany lyrics (one of which warns that a scrambled psyche could find one in a play by Rochelle Owens or Tom Eyen, and "Albee, Eddie Albee might make you a star"), *Peace* received favorable reviews and ran for almost a half-year. Lawrence Van Gelder in the *New York Times* praised Carmines' "melodic sorcery," and noted the evening satirized "hippies, homosexuals and hatemongers" and didn't spare the Pentagon, Sicilians, and the critics, either.

Because of their often surreal style and outlook, Carmines' musicals understandably never ran for more than a few weeks or months. They may have been caviar to the general, but for those theatregoers looking for offbeat musical theatre fare, Carmines' frequent musical offerings were a welcome alternative to the mostly bland offerings on Broadway in the late 1960s and early 1970s.

Peace was recorded by Metromedia Records (LP # MP-3001), and the script was published by Metromedia On Stage (the script didn't provide year of publication). The cast album reflects slightly different song titles from the ones in the script.

The musical was originally presented at the Judson Memorial Church Theatre on November 1, 1968. Al Carmines (that is, the Rev. Alvin Carmines) was an associate minister of the church and was director of its arts program.

For more information about musicals based on comedies by Aristophanes, see entries for *Wings* (1975) and *Lyz!*

1232 The Peanut Man, George Washington Carver. THEATRE: AMAS Repertory Theatre; OPENING DATE: October 15, 1980; PERFORMANCES: 15; BOOK: Melvin Hasman; LYRICS: Melvin Hasman; MUSIC: Melvin Hasman; DIRECTION: Regge Life; CHOREOGRAPHY: Andy Torres; SCENERY: Bob Phillips; COSTUMES: Amanda Klein; LIGHTING: Mark Diquinzio; MUSICAL DIRECTION: William Gregg Hunter; PRODUCER: The AMAS Repertory Theatre, Inc. (Rosetta LeNoire, Founder and Artistic Director)

CAST—Mel Johnson, Jr. (George Washington Carver), Lance Roberts (Preacher, Ensemble), Sharon K. Brooks (Mary Carver, Ensemble), Christopher Stewart (Moses, Ensemble), Kevin Gruden (Bently, Ensemble), Steve Fertig (Blacksmith, Ensemble), Marsha Perry (Cook, Ensemble), Barbara Warren-Cooke (Miss Liston, Ensemble), Judy Soto (Cafeteria Director, Ensemble), Leon Summers, Jr. (Booker T. Washington, Ensemble), Susan Beaubian (Norene Davis), Jean Cheek (Evangelist, Ensemble), Cliff Terry (Dr. Peterson, Ensemble)

The action occurs during the period 1860-1937 in Alabama, Missouri, Kansas, and Iowa, including such sites as the campus of Tuskeegee Institute.

The musical was presented in two acts.

ACT ONE—Overture (The Band), "Here Comes the Peanut Man" (Ensemble), "Beautiful Is Black" (Sharon K. Brooks), "Night Riders" (Jean Cheek, Ensemble), "Workin' Thru School" (Ensemble), "Beautiful Is Black" (reprise) (Mel Johnson, Jr.), "Little Flower" (Mel Johnson, Jr., Barbara Warren-Cooke), "Fun, Food, and Fellowship" (Mel Johnson, Jr.), "Gonna Teach Our Brothers" (Mel Johnson, Jr., Leon Summers, Jr.)

ACT TWO—"Grow Where You're Planted" (Mel Johnson, Jr., Students), "Walkin'" (Leon Summers, Jr., Farmers), "You Can Tell a Book" (Susan Beaubian), "Turn to Him" (Mel Johnson, Jr., Ensemble), "There's Good News Tonight" (Mel Johnson, Jr., Ensemble), "I Love a Man" (Susan Beaubian), "Bones" (Jean Cheek), Finale (Ensemble)

NOTES—The biographical musical about George Washington Carver was produced Off Off Broadway. The song "Night Riders" was written by Carl Maultsby.

1233 Pendragon. THEATRE: City Center; OPENING DATE: October 25, 1995; PERFORMANCES: 3; BOOK, LYRICS, AND MUSIC: Peter Allwood, Joanna Horton, Jeremy James Taylor, and Frank Whately; DIRECTION: Joanna Horton, Jeremy James Taylor, and Frank Whately; PRODUCTION DESIGN: Alison Darke; LIGHTING: Richard House; MUSICAL DIRECTION: Peter Allwood; PRODUCER: The National Youth Music Theatre (Jeremy James Taylor, Artistic Director), supported by Andrew Lloyd Webber

CAST—Nick Saich (Uther Pendragon, Sir Malaigaunce), Shula Keyte (Ygraine), Kyriacos Messios (The Merlin), Neil Abrahamson (Priest), Louise Potter (Nurse), Hayley Gelling (Young Morgan Le Fay), Hannah Spearritt (Young Guinevere), Sheridan Smith (Young Elaine), Richard Stacey (Young Arthur Pendragon), James Hoare (Sir Kay), Tom Chambers (King Pellinore), Sonell Dadral (Will), Hugo Sheppard (Thomas), Lara Pulver (Kelemon), Irfan Ahmad (Monk), Helen Power (Raven), Daniel Beckett (Matt), Joshua Deutsch (Luke), Katie Wilson (Older Morgan Le Fay), Timothy Fornara (Older Arthur Pendragon), Angharad Reece (Lady Angharad), Michelle Thomas (Lady Alice), Sarah McMillan (Lady Margaret), Adam Knight (Gawain), Maurice MacSweeney (Sir Caradoc), Rebecca Lock (Older Guinevere), Charlotte Hoare (Older Elaine), Reuben Jones (King Leodegraunce), Tom Sellwood (King Lot of Orkney), Edmund Comer (Ulfius), Christian Coulson (Sir Gaynor), Paul Cattermole (Sir Lancelot)

The action occurs in Britain during the Dark Ages.

The musical was presented in two acts.

NOTES—*Pendragon* was based on various Arthurian legends, and emphasized the early life of King Arthur Pendragon. The musical had been previously presented in England by the National Youth Music Theatre, a British company of young actors and musicians in the 17-20 age group. The production was part of an American tour which also included a revival of *The Threepenny Opera* (see entry for the 1995 version).

Lawrence Van Gelder in the *New York Times* found the evening "visually splendid" and noted that one of the evening's highlights was a "stirringly mimed and choreographed battle."

1234 **Penn & Teller.** THEATRE: Westside Arts Theatre/Downstairs; OPENING DATE: April 18, 1985; PERFORMANCES: 666; MUSIC: "Ambient Music" by Yma Sumac; DIRECTION: "Production Supervised" by Art Wolff; SCENERY: John Lee Beatty; LIGHTING: Dennis Parichy; PRODUCERS: Richard Frankel and Ivy Properties, Ltd.

CAST—Penn Jillette and Teller

The revue was presented in two acts.

ACT ONE—"Casey at the Bat," "Ball Routine," "Coin Routine," "Knife Routine," A Card Trick, "Cups & Balls" ("Cups and Balls Suite" by James S. Campbell, Jr.), "Suspension," "East Indian Needle Mystery," "Quote of the Day"

ACT TWO—"Spooky Stuff" (instrumental), "Bacteria," "Domestication of Animals" ("performance art"), "Mofo, the Psychic Gorilla," "How We Met," "Shadows," "10 in 1"

NOTES—This was an evening of magic and comedy by the popular team of Penn Jillette and Teller (the latter is billed by one name); the long-running revue played for 666 performances.

See separate entry for their 1991 revue *Penn & Teller Rot in Hell.*

The team later returned in another evening (also titled *Penn & Teller*), which opened at the Beacon Theatre on June 6, 2000, for a limited engagement of eight performances.

1235 **Penn & Teller Rot in Hell.** THEATRE: John Houseman Theatre; OPENING DATE: July 30, 1991; PERFORMANCES: 203; MATERIAL: Penn Jillette and Teller; MUSIC: "Ambient Music" by Yma Sumac; DIRECTOR OF COVERT ACTIVITIES: Robert P. Libbon; DIRECTOR OF INTERNAL AFFAIRS: Ken "Krasher" Lewis; SCENERY: John Lee Beatty; COSTUMES: Peter J. Fitzgerald; LIGHTING: Dennis Parichy; PRODUCERS: Richard Frankel, Thomas Viertel, Steven Baruch, Tim Jenison, and Paul Montgomery; Marc Routh, Associate Producer

CAST—Penn Jillette, Teller; Carol Perkins, Special Guest

The revue was presented in two acts.

ACT ONE—"Casey at the Bat," "A Card Trick," "Liftoff to Love"/"Ripoff of Love" (sketch by Gary Stockdale, Penn Jillette, and Teller; performed by Gary Stockdale), "Fakir Tricks," "Quotation of the Day," "Houdini Tricks"

ACT TWO—"Mofo, the Psychic Gorilla," "By Buddha This Duck Is Immortal!," "Burnin' Luv" (music by Gary Stockdale), "Shadows," "King of Animal Traps"

NOTES—Some of the material had been previously performed in Penn and Teller's 1985 Off Broadway revue *Penn & Teller* (see entry) and their Broadway revue *Penn & Teller: The Refrigerator Tour*, which opened on April 3, 1991, at the Eugene O'Neill Theatre and played for 103 performances.

1236 **The Penny Friend.** THEATRE: Stage 73; OPENING DATE: December 26, 1966; PERFORMANCES: 32; BOOK: William Roy; LYRICS: William Roy; MUSIC: William Roy; DIRECTION: Benno D. Frank; CHOREOGRAPHY: Lou Kristofer; SCENERY: Ben Shecter; COSTUMES: Possibly by Ben Shecter; LIGHTING: Robert L. Steele; PRODUCER: Thomas Hammond

CAST—Michael Wager (Charles Bodie), Jamie Ross (Policeman; apparently also played role of David), Charlotte Fairchild (Kate Bodie), Bernadette Peters (Cinderella), Bill Drew (Mr. McGill), John Senger (Mr. Jennings), Georgia Creighton (Mrs. Maloney), Terry Forman (Maudie), Sherill Price (Lady), Dewey Golkin (George), Jeffrey Golkin (Hans), Jimmy Rivers (Invite)

SOURCE—The 1916 play *A Kiss for Cinderella* by James M. Barrie.

The musical was presented in two acts.

ACT ONE—"The Penny Friend" (Ensemble), "She Makes You Think of Home" (Michael Wager), "Who Am I, Who Are You, Who Are We?" (Michael Wager), "Mrs. Bodie" (Bernadette Peters), "I Am Going to Dance" (Bernadette Peters), "Feet" (Bernadette Peters), "She Makes You Think of Home" (reprise) (Jamie Ross), "The Great Unknown" (Bernadette Peters), "The Penny Friend" (reprise) (Georgia Creighton, Bill Drew, John Senger), "How Doth the Apple Butterfly" (Bernadette Peters), "The Diagnostician" (Charlotte Fairchild)

ACT TWO—"Won't You Come to the Party" (Ensemble), "The Grand Parade" (Ensemble), "A Very Full and Productive Day" (Bernadette Peters, Michael Wager, Jamie Ross, Charlotte Fairchild), "The Penny Friend" (reprise) (Michael Wager, Bernadette Peters), "The World Today" (Charlotte Fairchild, Jamie Ross), "The Great Unknown" (reprise) (Charlotte Fairchild), "The Penny Friend" (reprise) (Ensemble)

NOTES—Although she had been active in professional theatre (*This Is Goggle*, a play which closed prior to Broadway in 1958; the 1959 revival of *The Most Happy Fella* at New York City Center; and a touring production of *Gypsy*), Bernadette Peters made her first major New York stage appearance in *The Penny Friend.* Despite the show's run of just one month, she didn't remain with the musical, and was succeeded by Alice Borden.

William Roy was an interesting composer who never seemed to find success with his musicals. *Maggie*, his only Broadway musical, played for just five performances in 1953, and *The Penny Friend*, his only full-length Off Broadway musical, lasted for thirty-two. However, his songs were sometimes heard in Off Broadway revues of the era.

Georgia Creighton, who played the role of Mrs. Maloney, is a fascinating figure. Virtually unknown to the general public, she appeared in a number of legendary flop Broadway musicals in the 1960s: *The Conquering Hero* (1961), *Donnybrook!* (1961), *Anyone Can Whistle* (1964), *Kelly* (1965), and *Skyscraper* (1965). In 1996, she appeared in the world premiere of Andrew Lloyd Webber's *Whistle Down the Wind*, which opened and closed in Washington, D.C. (Indeed, with *Anyone Can Whistle* and *Whistle Down the Wind* on her resume, she should whistle only at her own risk.) She was also seen in the title role of *Mother Goose Go-Go* (see entry).

She was also one of the nuns in the 1992 film *Sister Act* (along with other obscure Broadway performers, such as Ruth Kobart and Susan Browning).

Georgia Creighton and Bernadette Peters have more in common than just *The Penny Friend.* Along with Madonna, they are the only performers in the world to have introduced both Stephen Sondheim and Webber songs to the public. Madonna introduced two Oscar-winning songs, Sondheim's "Sooner or Later" (*Dick Tracy* [1990]) and Webber's "You Must Love Me" (*Evita* [1996]). (Besides Madonna, six other singers have introduced two or more Oscar-winning songs: Bing Crosby, Doris Day, Judy Garland, Bob Hope, Maureen McGovern, and Frank Sinatra.) Peters of course starred in the original Broadway productions of Sondheim's *Sunday in the Park with George* (1984; see entry) and *Into the Woods* (1987) and introduced Webber's *Song and Dance* to American audiences in its 1985 Broadway premiere.

And Creighton, as part of the chorus in *Anyone Can Whistle* and *Whistle Down the Wind*, introduced new Sondheim and Webber material (and in fact she was one of the lead singers in the latter's "Safe Haven" sequence).

Creighton and Peters also share an *Anyone Can Whistle* connection because Peters appeared in a 1995 concert adaptation of the legendary musical at Carnegie Hall.

Further, they both appeared in original productions of Al Carmines' musicals. Peters co-starred (opposite Mickey Rooney) in Carmines' 1971 musical *W.C.* (about the life and times of W.C. Fields), which closed during its pre-Broadway tryout. Creighton appeared in such Carmines' musicals as *T.S. Eliot: Midwinter Vigil(ante)* (1981; see entry), and was also in the Carmines' retrospective revue *The Gospel According to Al* (1982; see entry), which included three songs from *W.C.* Bernadette Peters played the Cinderella character in *The Penny Friend*, and would return to the fairy tale two more times, first as the Witch in *Into the Woods* and then in the third (1997) television adaptation of Richard Rodgers and Oscar Hammerstein II's *Cinderella* (playing the Wicked Stepmother).

1237 **People Are Wrong!** THEATRE: Vineyard Theatre; OPENING DATE: November 4, 2004; PERFORMANCES: 46 (estimated); LYRICS: Julia Greenberg and Robin Goldwasser Music: Julia Greenberg and Robin Goldwasser; DIRECTION: David Herskovits; CHOREOGRAPHY: Jody Ripplinger; SCENERY: G.W. Mercier; COSTUMES: Mattie Ullrich; LIGHTING: Lenore Doxsee Musical Director: Jeremy Chatzky and Joe McGinty; PRODUCERS: Target Margin Theatre (David Herskovits, Artistic Director; Darren Critz, Managing Director); Vineyard Theatre (Douglas Aibel, Artistic Director; Jennifer Garvey-Blackwell, Executive Director); John Flansburgh, Associate Producer

CAST—Todd Almond (Mikey), Chris Anderson (Chainsaw Dick), David Driver (Xanthus), John Flansburgh (Russ), Robin Goldwasser (Joyce), Erin Hill (Terry), Maggie Moore (The Vision), Connie Petruk (Katie), Tricia Scotti (Olivia)

The musical was presented in one act.

MUSICAL NUMBERS—"I Know What I Saw" (Chris Anderson), "Car Alarms" (John Flansburgh, Erin Hill), "The Meeting Song" (John Flansburgh, Erin Hill, Chris Anderson, Robin Goldwasser, Disciples), "How Our Garden Grows—Fall" (John Flansburgh, Erin Hill), "At the Agway" (Disciples), "The Wedding" (John Flansburgh, Erin Hill), "Perennials" (Robin Goldwasser), "Enter Xanthus" (Company), "Xanthus Saves" (Robin Goldwasser, John Flansburgh, Erin Hill), "The Hayride" (David Driver, John Flansburgh, Erin Hill, Chris Anderson), "Makeout Moon" (Erin Hill, Robin Goldwasser, John Flansburgh, Chris Anderson), "Love's Too Mild a Word" (David Driver), "Dear Old Plants" (John Flansburgh, Erin Hill, David Driver, Disciples), "How Our Garden Grows—Spring" (John Flansburgh, Erin Hill), "Elizabeth X. Oliphant" (John Flansburgh, Erin Hill, Disciples), "Wooden Sign" (Chris Anderson, David Driver), "How Do I Tell You?" (Chris Anderson), "Dimension 6 Rock" (David Driver, Maggie Moore, Disciples), "Gravel's Coming with Us" (David Driver, Disciples), "Sometimes I Look at Him"/"The Bill" (Robin Goldwasser, Chris Anderson, David Driver), "2 x 2" (Company), "Xanthus, I'm Getting Nervous" (David Driver, Robin Goldwasser), "Jesus Christ, Xanthus Fucked Us" (John Flansburgh, Erin Hill, David Driver), "What World Do You Live In?" (John Flansburgh, Erin Hill, David Driver), "You'll Regret a Killing Spree" (Disciples, David Driver, Chris Anderson), "I Know What You Saw" (Robin Goldwasser), "People Are Wrong!" (Company), "Go It Alone Song" (David Driver), "Enter X. Oliphant" (Company), "Everlasting Vibe" (David Driver, Maggie Moore, Disciples), "The Beyond Ballet" (Company)

NOTES—*People Are Wrong!* dealt with a New York couple who buy a weekend retreat in order to escape from the pressures of city life. But they get more than they bargained for when their landscaper turns out to be a New Age priest who intends to build a launching pad on their front lawn so that he and his disciples can return to their home planet. ("And you thought your contractor was a nightmare?," asked Charles Isherwood in the *New York Times*.)

Isherwood liked the "off-kilter" characters, and found much to praise in a score which offered "lilting folk balladry, driving electric-guitar romps and rockabilly hoedowns." While he felt the expansive score became somewhat "repetitive" in its "narrative content," he nonetheless felt the energetic cast performed with a "friendly, let's-put-on-a-rock-musical spirit."

1238 People Be Heard. THEATRE: Mainstage Theatre/Playwrights Horizons; OPENING DATE: September 23, 2004; PERFORMANCES: 22; PLAY: Quincy Long; LYRICS: Quincy Long (?); MUSIC: Michael Roth; DIRECTION: Erica Schmidt; CHOREOGRAPHY: Peter Pucci; SCENERY: Christine Jones; COSTUMES: Michelle R. Phillips; LIGHTING: Michael Lincoln; MUSICAL DIRECTION: Michael Roth and Tarshis; PRODUCER: Playwrights Horizons (Tim Sanford, Artistic Director; Leslie Marcus, Managing Director; William Russo, General Manager)

CAST—Conrad John Schuck (Don Mesner), Dashiell Eaves (Jim Schuler, Refik), Laura Heisler (Pam, Danny Delaney, Cindy), Guy Boyd (Earl Frye), Kathy Santen (Linda Vobiato, Candy), Funda Duval (Rita Dell Delaney), Brian Hutchison (Russell Delaney, Voice of Ekaraxu, Bernie Redman, Dr. Mueller), Annie Golden (Margo, Ekaraxu, Melanie Gilfert, Dr. Schottenstein, Helen McMichaels, Mother Wit)

The action occurs in Middle America at the present time.

The musical was presented in two acts.

NOTES—*The Best Plays Theatre Yearbook 2004-2005* said the plot of *People Be Heard* dealt with a stripper (from the Wiggle Room) who joins a school board in semi-rural America "and becomes the progressive voice of reason." Charles Isherwood in the *New York Times* found the comedy with songs a "tedious, malfunctioning evening" with various subplots (including a "distasteful" one about child molestation). He also noted that one subplot dealt with a child's nightmares about invaders from outer space, and was bemused that the "fully staged" nightmares bore a striking resemblance to 1950s sci-fi movies. As for the incidental songs, Isherwood mentioned they appeared at "unpredictable intervals" with little in the way of "dramatic logic." Isherwood concluded that the only time the evening reached "daffy comic heights" was when Annie Golden took over the stage (she was "perfection" in her various cameo roles).

1239 People Is the Thing That the World Is Fullest Of. "A New Musical Revue." THEATRE: Bil Baird Theatre; OPENING DATE: February 20, 1967; PERFORMANCES: 117; SCRIPT: Written by "Diverse Hands"; MUSIC: Buster Davis; DIRECTION: Burt Shevelove; SCENERY: William Steven Armstrong (Design Consultant); COSTUMES: Fania Sullivan and Marianne Harms; LIGHTING: Peggy Clark (Lighting Consultant); MUSICAL DIRECTION: Alvy West; PRODUCERS: The American Puppet Arts Council, Inc. (Arthur Cantor, Executive Producer)

CAST (PUPPETEERS)—Bil Baird, Cora Baird, Frank Sullivan, Franz Fazakas, Carl Harms, Jerry Nelson, Phyllis Nierendorf, Robin Kendall, Byron Whiting

The revue was presented in two acts.

ACT ONE—Overture, "People, People" (music by Buster Davis), "It's a Sin to Tell a Lie," "Asia," "Conformity," "Slugger Ryan," "Man and Woman," "Science Fiction," "Bill Bailey," "Lover," "Old Abe Lincoln Had a Farm" (music by Buster Davis)

ACT TWO—Overture, "Pollution," Bil Baird, "Africa," "Words," "Saloon Talk," "The Family Danced," "Crazy, Man, Crazy," "In the Beginning, God...," "The Population Explosion"

NOTES—With *People Is the Thing That the World Is Fullest Of*, followed by a production of *Davy Jones' Locker* later in the season, Bil Baird inaugurated an annual series of puppet revues and musicals at his new theatre on Barrow Street (the Bil Baird Theatre was also called the Bil Baird Marionette Theatre).

People is unique among Baird's puppet musicals in that it was written for adults, not children. An unsigned review in the *New York Times* reported that the evening was often a "routine hash of satirical attitudes" one might see in a Julius Monk revue. Accordingly, the satirical targets included such subjects as birth control, pollution, and the "problem" of Lincoln Center (in a parody of Leonard Bernstein's discussions about music, we're told that "Culture abounds here. It teems"). The reviewer wasn't particularly impressed with the material, but noted there were two sequences which approached "genius." One, "Science Fiction," was a dance for "geometry-book figures" which recalled the film *Fantasia*; the other, "Words," found letters of the alphabetic rearranging themselves in surreal combinations which was "pure Steinberg in motion."

During the run of *Winnie the Pooh* (which opened in late 1967; see entry), *People Is the Thing That the World Is Fullest Of* was briefly revived for six performances.

Although the program credited Buster Davis with two songs, presumably he contributed other music to the revue. Premiere Records released recordings of the songs.

After the opening, a few sequences were repositioned, and two were dropped ("Crazy, Man, Crazy" and "In the Beginning, God...").

This was Will Steven Armstrong's second association with a puppet-related musical (he designed the scenery for the 1961 Broadway musical *Carnival!*).

1240 The People Who Could Fly. THEATRE: South Street Theatre; OPENING DATE: August 2, 1989; PERFORMANCES: 41; ADAPTATION: Joe Hart; DIRECTION: Joe Hart; Jackie Gill, Assistant Director; SCENERY: Ron Cadry (Kadri?); COSTUMES: Vickie Esposito; LIGHTING: Cris Gorzelnick (Gorzelik?); PRODUCERS: Eric Krebs and the Warp and Woof Theatre Company

CAST—Rich Biano, Heide Brehm, Michael Calderone, Caprice Cosgrove, John Dimaggio, Jacqueline Gregg, Jennifer Krasnansky, Chris Petit, Anne Shapiro, Steve Siegler, Kristina Swedlund, Scott Wasser

The revue was presented in two acts.

NOTES—*The People Who Could Fly* was a dance and theatre piece for children by the Warp and Woof Theatre Company's Shoestring Players. The evening offered six tales from India, Majorca, Scotland, Haiti, Japan, and the ante-bellum South.

D.J.R. Bruckner in the *New York Times* noted that adaptor and director Joe Hart was an "ingenious storyteller," and said each sequence in the revue was "spare, eloquent and often very funny." Among the folk tales was one from India about an "addled" potter who confuses a tiger with a donkey and thus captures the "surprised" beast. Bruckner concluded that the two hours of "theatrical magic" seemed to fly by in a "few moments of happy dreaming."

The revue was later produced for nine performances at Town Hall beginning on December 26, 1989.

1241 Pepper Mill. "An Intimate Revue." THEATRE: Chanin Auditorium; OPENING DATE: January 5, 1937; PERFORMANCES: 6; SKETCHES AND LYRICS: W.H. Auden, Klaus Mann, Erich Muehsam, Ernst Toller, Edwin Denby and Erika Mann; the English translation of German material was by John LaTouche; MUSIC: Magnus Henning, Aaron Copeland, Peter Kreuder, Herbert Murril, and Werner Kruse; DIRECTION: Therese Giehse; SCENERY: Anton Refregier; PRODUCER: F.C. Coppicus

CAST—Performers included Erika Mann, Therese Giehse, Lotte Goslar, Wallace Rooney, Sybele Schloss, John LaTouche, and John Beck

SKETCHES AND SONGS (division of acts and sketch and song assignments unknown)—"Children's Song" (lyric by Erika Mann), "Cold" (lyric by Erika Mann), "Demagogue" (lyric by W.H. Auden and Ernest Toller, music by Aaron Copeland), "Doctor's Orders," "Especially for Mr. Winterbottom," "Famous People of the Week" (lyric and music by Edwin Denby, Erika Mann, and Klaus Mann), "The Gangster of the Puppet Show," "The Little Revolutionary" (lyric by John LaTouche and Erich Muehsam, music by Werner Kruse), "The Lorelei" (lyric and music by John LaTouche and Klaus Mann), "The Ski Teacher" (lyric by Erika Mann and Klaus Mann, music by Peter Kreuder), "Spies" (lyric by W.H. Auden and Ernst Toller, music by Herbert Murril), "Stupidity Talks," "The Yodeler"

NOTES—According to Brooks Atkinson in the *New York Times*, the Off Broadway version of the German musical revue *Pepper Mill* "hath lost most of its savor" in its Americanized adaptation. Atkinson reported that the revue had been first seen in Munich three years earlier, and during the ensuing years the production had been performed in Europe 1,034 times (the New York premiere marked the revue's 1,035th performance). But the revue managed just six performances in New York. Atkinson noted the revue crossed the Atlantic with the "friendliest" of intentions, but felt the material and the performers were nowhere near as "crisp" as the "miniature" Chanin Auditorium in which the revue was presented (it was located on the fiftieth floor of the Chanin Building, located at 122 East 42nd Street).

For New York, the revue added extra material and a few American performers (John LaTouche, who appeared in the production, provided English translations and new adaptations of material previously heard in Europe). Atkinson remarked that when the revue was "ground out," it offered a number of ballads, a yodeler who did not yodel, and an occasional "wry grimace" at Hitler. Erika Mann (who contributed some of the lyrics to the revue and who was also its hostess) was the daughter of the writer Thomas Mann.

Besides LaTouche, other contributors to the revue included W.H. Auden and Aaron Copeland.

The list of songs and sketches is from Ken Bloom's *American Song*.

1242 Pequod/The Next Voyage. "A New Play." THEATRE: Mercury Theatre; OPENING DATE: June 29, 1969; PERFORMANCES: 1; PLAY: Roy S. Richardson; INCIDENTAL MUSIC AND LYRICS: Mildred Kayden; DIRECTION: Burt Brinckerhoff; SCENERY: David F. Segal; COSTUMES: Joseph G. Aulisi; LIGHTING: David F. Segal; PRODUCERS: William W. Rippner in association with Sumac Productions Corp.

CAST—James Seymour (Jim), John Caffin (John), Sharon Klaif (Sharon), Merrylen Sacks (Merrylen), Arleen Wetzel (Arleen), Gary Sandy (Youth), Dorothy Lyman (Director's Assistant), JOHN TILLINGER (Director), Bella Jarrett (Wife), Jason Miller (Pip), Robert Eckles (Boomer), Don Lochner (Dr. Bunger), Kelly Wood (Mary), John Mahon (Stub), John Randolph Jones (Carpenter), RICHARD KRONOLD (Captain Ahab), Jeff David (Starbuck), Lloyd Hollar (Queequeg)

The action occurs on the stage of the theater at the present time.

The play was presented in one act.

NOTES—*Pequod/The Next Voyage* was a play-within-a-play, utilizing Herman Melville's *Moby-Dick*; or, *The Whale* (1851) as the basis of its story. As she did with *City Scene* (see entry), Mildred Kayden wrote incidental songs for the production (specific titles weren't listed in the program).

During previews, the roles of Marilyn (played by Marilyn McConnie) and Gary (played by Gary Sandy) were eliminated; by opening night, Gary Sandy had replaced James Hornbeck in the role of Youth.

Anna Kisselgoff in the *New York Times* found the "somewhat earnest" evening "so fragmentary that clarity is sacrificed." The confusing script also tried to make Melville relevant to the late 1960s, and thus the evening touched upon such issues as race relations. For more information about lyric adaptations of Melville's writings, see entry for *Bartleby*; also see entry for *Moby Dick*, an Off Off Broadway musical. A dramatic adaptation of *Moby Dick* by Orson Welles was produced in London in 1955 for twenty-five performances (with Welles) and on Broadway in 1962 for thirteen (with Rod Steiger). *Pequod* included an early acting appearance by Jason Miller, whose 1972 play *That Championship Season* won the Pulitzer Prize for Drama.

1243 Personals. "A Musical Revue." THEATRE: Minetta Lane Theatre; OPENING DATE: November 24, 1985; PERFORMANCES: 265; SKETCHES: David Crane, Seth Friedman, and Marta Kauffman; LYRICS: David Crane, Seth Friedman, and Marta Kauffman; MUSIC: William Dreskin, Joel Phillip Friedman, Seth Friedman, Alan Menken, Stephen Schwartz, and Michael Skloff; DIRECTION: Paul Lazarus; CHOREOGRAPHY: D.J. Giagni; SCENERY: Loren Sherman; COSTUMES: Ann Hould-Ward; LIGHTING: Richard Nelson; MUSICAL DIRECTION: Michael Skloff; PRODUCERS: John-Edward Hill, Arthur MacKenzie, Jon D. Silverman in association with Fujisankei Communications Group

CAST—Jason Alexander (Louis and Others), Laura Dean (Kim and Others), Dee Hoty (Claire and Others), Jeff Keller (Sam and Others), Nancy Opel (Louise and Others), Trey Wilson (Typesetter and Others)

The revue was presented in two acts.

ACT ONE—"Nothing to Do with Love" (music by Stephen Schwartz) (Company), "After School Special" (music by William Dreskin) (Jason Alexander, Company), "Mama's Boys" (music by Seth Friedman and Joel Phillip Friedman) (Dee Hoty, Laura Dean, Trey Wilson, Company), "A Night Alone" (music by Michael Skloff) (Jeff Keller, Jason Alexander, Dee Hoty, Trey Wilson), "I Think You Should Know" (music by Seth Friedman and Joel Phillip Friedman) (Laura Dean, Jeff Keller), "Second Grade" (music by Michael Skloff) (Jeff Keller, Jason Alexander, Trey Wilson, Company), "Imagine My Surprise" (music by William Dreskin) (Dee Hoty), "I'd Rather Dance Alone" (music by Alan Menken) (Company)

ACT TWO—"Moving in with Linda" (music by Stephen Schwartz) (Jeff Keller, Company), "A Little Happiness" (music by Seth Friedman and Joel Phillip Friedman) (Trey Wilson), "I Could Always Go to You" (music by Alan Menken) (Dee Hoty, Nancy Opel), "The Guy I Love" (music by William Dreskin) (Nancy Opel, Jason Alexander), "Michael" (music by William Dreskin) (Laura Dean), "Picking Up the Pieces" (music by Seth Friedman and Joel Phillip Friedman) (Jason Alexander, Trey Wilson), "Some Things Don't End" (music by Stephen Schwartz) (Company)

NOTES—*Personals* was a light-hearted revue of sketches, monologues, and songs, all of which revolved around lonely-heart types seeking romance through personal classified ads. The revue contained bright lyrics, and included three songs with music by Stephen Schwartz and two by Alan Menken.

Frank Rich in the *New York Times* said the "misconceived" revue offered "unfailingly mirthless" sketches, and he noted the subject matter of personal ads wasn't enough to fill out the evening. He found "Moving in with Linda" (with music by Schwartz) the revue's "cleverest" song, and mentioned "Nothing to Do with Love" (also with music by Schwartz) echoed no less than two songs in Stephen Sondheim's *Company* (1970). Rich also remarked that the evening's décor evoked Boris Aronson's set for the iconic Sondheim musical.

An early version of the revue had been first produced at the Laurie Theatre at Brandeis University for five performances beginning on November 28, 1979. The book and lyrics for this production were credited to David Crane, Seth Jonathan Friedman, and Marta F. Kauffman, and the music to William F. Dreskin, Joel Phillip Friedman, and Seth Jonathan Friedman. Only one song ("Michael") was retained for Off Broadway; other numbers heard in the Brandeis production were "Anybody Out There," "Widower," "Harry," "The Bars," "51st Street/Lexington Ave. Station," "Lovers in My Eyes," "...Or More," "This One," "Not Asking Too Much," "Lonely Women," "The Quartet," "I Go Down Easy," "15 Words," and "I Met a Man."

The revue was later seen in London in 1998, and the cast album of that production was released by Jay Records (CD # CDJAY-1319). The script was published by Samuel French, Inc., in 1987.

David Crane and Marta Kauffman were later the creators and writers of the phenomenally successful television sitcom *Friends*.

1244 The Pet Shop. THEATRE: The Lexington Avenue Young Men's and Young Women's Hebrew Association; OPENING DATE: April 14, 1958; PERFORMANCES: 2; LIBRETTO: Claire Nicolas; MUSIC: Vittorio Rieti; SCENERY: Richard Rychtarik; MUSICAL DIRECTION: Carl Bamberger; PRODUCER: Mannes College of Music

CAST—Joan Wall (Mrs. Camouflager), Sheila Braidech (Trixy), Edward Ericksen (Mr. Canicular), Dogs (Paula Saperstein, Christine Berl, Carol Herbert)

The action occurs in a pet shop in New York City.

The opera was produced in one act.

NOTES—The evening consisted of three one-act operas, two world premieres (*The Pet Shop* and Ned Rorem's *The Robbers* [see entry]) and a revival of Georg Philipp Telemann's *Pimpinone* (1725).

In his review for the *New York Times*, Ross Parmenter had high praise for *The Pet Shop*, which dealt with a New York society woman who wants to buy a dog to match the gown she'll wear in a fashion show. She's accompanied by her daughter, who falls in love with the shop's owner. Parmenter found the music "cheerful, pretty and witty ... composed with an expert hand." He noted that three of the opera's characters were dogs; they were portrayed by three women "whose only vocal contribution consisted of barking."

1245 Pete 'n' Keely. THEATRE: John Houseman Theatre; OPENING DATE: December 14, 2000; PERFORMANCES: 96; BOOK: James Hindman; LYRICS: Original lyrics by Mark Waldrop; see song list for other credits; MUSIC: Original music by Patrick S. Brady; see song list for other credits; DIRECTION: Mark Waldrop; CHOREOGRAPHY: Keith Cromwell; SCENERY: Ray Klausen; COSTUMES: Bob Mackie; LIGHTING: F. Mitchell Dana; MUSICAL DIRECTION: Patrick S. Brady; PRODUCERS: Steve Asher, David W. Unger, and Avalon Entertainment; Joel C. Cohen, Associate Producer

CAST—Sally Mayes, George Dvorsky

The action occurs on stage during a live telecast from NBC television studios in New York City in 1968.

The musical was presented in two acts.

ACT ONE—"It's Us Again" (lyric and music by Sid Feller and Rick Ward) (George Dvorsky, Sally Mayes), "Lover" (from 1932 film *Love Me Tonight*; lyric by Lorenz Hart, music by Richard Rodgers) (George Dvorsky, Sally Mayes), "Kid Stuff"/"Daddy" (lyric and music by Bobby Troup) (Keely), "Besame Mucho" (original Spanish lyric and music by Consuelo Velazquez; English lyric by Sunny Skylar) (George Dvorsky, Sally Mayes), "This Could Be the Start of Something Big" (lyric and music by Steve Allen) (George Dvorsky, Sally Mayes), "Battle Hymn of the Republic" (lyric and music by Julia Ward Howe) (George Dvorsky, Sally Mayes), "Secret Love" (1953 film *Calamity Jane*; lyric by Paul Francis Webster, music by Sammy Fain) (George Dvorsky, Sally Mayes), "Have You Got a Lot to Learn" (George Dvorsky, Sally Mayes), "Swell Shampoo Song" (George Dvorsky), "Still" (George Dvorsky, Sally Mayes), "The Cross Country Tour" (medley of "city" and "state" songs) (George Dvorsky, Sally Mayes)

ACT TWO—*Tony 'n' Cleo* Scene: "Hello Egypt" (George Dvorsky, Sally Mayes), "Bernice, I Don't Believe You" (George Dvorsky), "Tony 'n' Cleo" (George Dvorsky, Sally Mayes), "Fever" (lyric and music by John Davenport and Eddie Cooley) (George Dvorsky), "Black Coffee" (lyric by Paul Francis Webster and Sonny Burke, music by Paul Francis Webster and Sonny Burke) (Sally Mayes), "Too Fat to Fit" (George Dvorsky, Sally Mayes), "Lover, Come Back to Me" (*The New Moon*, 1928; lyric by Oscar Hammerstein II, music by Sigmund Romberg) (George Dvorsky), "Love" (1946 film *Ziegfeld Follies*; lyric and music by Ralph Blane and Hugh Martin), "Wasn't It Fine" (George Dvorsky, Sally Mayes), "It's Us Again" (reprise) (George Dvorsky, Sally Mayes), "That's All" (lyric and music by Alan Brandt and Bob Haymes)

NOTES—*Pete 'n' Keely* was an amusing revue-like musical about a famous singing duo who underwent a bitter divorce; now, in 1968, they are appearing together (live!) in a television show, "The Pete and Keely Reunion Special." The musical presented their TV special in real time, including time-outs for station breaks and commercials (thus allowing the spatting twosome more time to argue). During the program, they tout their sponsor ("If Swell [Shampoo] can get [us] back together, think what it can do for your split ends") and even sing a few songs from their flop Broadway musical *Tony 'n' Cleo* (a "musical version of Shakespeare's immortal drama, *Anthony and Cleopatra*").

The musical combined both standards as well as new songs (by Mark Waldrop and Patrick S. Brady), and Fynsworth Alley released the cast recording (CD # 302-062-1222).

The script, published by Samuel French, Inc., in 2002, noted: "Think Steve & Eydie with the antagonism of Sonny and Cher, plus a dash of Carol Lawrence and Robert Goulet. Lucille Ball and Desi Arnaz are also a useful point of reference."

1246 Peter and the Wolf (1971). THEATRE: Bil Baird Theatre; OPENING DATE: December 18, 1971; PERFORMANCES: 131; PRODUCERS: The American Puppet Arts Council (Arthur Cantor, Executive Producer); a Bil Baird's Marionettes Production

NOTES—*Peter and the Wolf* was based on Serge Prokofiev's work of the same name; for the puppet musical, his score was adapted and arranged by Paul Weston, who also wrote incidental music for the production. The book was by A.J. Russell, the lyrics by Ogden Nash, and the direction by Gordon Hunt. The scenery was by Howard Mandel. The musical was presented in two acts, with the following cast: Peter Baird (Duck, Crow, Turtle), Pady Blackwood (Beaver, Crow, Wolf's Speaking Voice, Hunter), Olga Felgemacher (Rabbit, Peter) Merry Florshem (Person in Forest), George S. Irving (Wolf's Singing Voice), John O'Malley (Owl, Crow), Frank Sullivan (Mouse, Weasel, Grandpa, Hunter), Bill Tost (Wolf,

Bird, Squirrel, Humphrey's Singing Voice), Byron Whiting (Humphrey's Speaking Voice, Dog, Crow, Cat, Hunter).

Clive Barnes in the *New York Times* said he thought he hated puppets, but after seeing *Peter and the Wolf* he was "converted" by the "totally enchanting" and "absolutely miraculous" evening. He concluded that Bil Baird's rendering of the famous story was "quite possibly the best show in New York for children to take their parents to."

As usual, *Bil Baird's Variety* was part of the production.

Peter and the Wolf was revived by Bil Baird in 1974 (see entry).

1247 Peter and the Wolf (1974). THEATRE: Bil Baird Theatre; OPENING DATE: December 6, 1974; PERFORMANCES: 77; PRODUCERS: The American Puppet Arts Council (Arthur Cantor, Executive Director)

NOTES—*Peter and the Wolf* had been originally produced by the company in 1971 (see entry); the revival was directed by Paul Leaf; the musical direction was by Alvy West; lighting, by Carl Harms; and scenery, Howard Mandel. The book was by A.J. Russell, lyrics by Ogden Nash, and the music adapted from Serge Prokofiev (with incidental music by Paul Weston). The cast was as follows: Peter Baird (Owl, Weasel, Duck, Hunter, Crow), Rebecca Bondor (Mouse, Bird), Tim Dobbins (Grandpa, Crow, Beaver), Olga Felgemacher (Peter, Rabbit, Cat, Hunter, Bee), Steven Hansen (Humphrey, Frogs), William Tost (Wolf, Hunter, Squirrel); for the character of the Wolf, its singing voice was that of George S. Irving; the singing voice of Humphrey was William Tost.

The musical was accompanied by another visit of *Holiday on Strings*, which celebrated the Christmas season and other winter holidays.

1248 Peter and Wendy. THEATRE: New Victory Theatre; OPENING DATE: February 1, 1997; PERFORMANCES: 20; PLAY: Liza Lorwin; MUSIC: Johnny Cunningham; DIRECTION: Lee Breuer; PUPPETRY DIRECTION: Jane Catherine Shaw and Basil Twist; SCENERY AND PUPPET DESIGNS: Julie Archer; ADDITIONAL PUPPET DESIGNS: Walter Stark, Stephen Kaplin, Basil Twist, and Jane Catherine Shaw; COSTUMES: Sally Thomas; LIGHTING: Julie Archer; MUSICAL DIRECTION: Johnny Cunningham; PRODUCERS: The New 42nd Street Inc.; a Mabou Mines Prodution (Liza Lorwin, Producer)

CAST—Karen Kandel (Narrator); Puppeteers (Basil Twist, Jane Catherine Shaw, Sam Hack, Sarah Provost, Jessica Smith, Jenny Subjack, Lute Ramblin')

SOURCE—The 1911 novel *Peter Pan* by James M. Barrie (not his 1904 play *Peter Pan*).

The puppet play with music was presented in two acts.

NOTES—Peter Marks in the *New York Times* found *Peter and Wendy* a "beguiling" version of James M. Barrie's famous story, and noted there was so much "vitality and originality" in the new puppet-show adaptation that the somewhat familiar tale became "reborn." He praised the clever script, direction, and scenery, and noted that when the Darling children flew off to Neverland, their journey was depicted by "empty bedclothes flapping in the breeze" ("the most balletic representation of flying laundry you're ever likely to witness on a New York stage"). Marks' only quibble with the evening was its length, and he suggested the prologue and conclusion be trimmed in order to make the musical more manageable for young children.

1249 Peter Ibbetson. THEATRE: Metropolitan Opera House; OPENING DATE: February 7, 1931; PERFORMANCES: 10; LIBRETTO: Constance Collier and Deems Taylor; MUSIC: Deems Taylor; DIRECTION: Wilhelm Von Wymetal; SCENERY: Joseph Urban; MUSICAL DIRECTION: Tullio Serafin; PRODUCER: The Metropolitan Opera

CAST—Edward Johnson (Peter Ibbetson), Lawrence Tibbett (Colonel Ibbetson), Lucrezia Bori (Mary), Marion Telva (Mrs. Deane), Ina Bourskaya (Mrs. Glyn), Angelo Bada (Achille), Leon Rothier (Duquesnois), Louis D'Angelo (Chaplain of Newgate Prison), Giordano Paltrinieri (Charlie), Millo Picco (Guy), Marek Windheim (Footman), Phradie Wells (Diana), Grace Divine (Madge), Philine Falco (Victorine), Minnie Egener (Sister of Charity), Alfredo Gandolfi (Manservant, Turnkey), George Cehanovsky (Prison Governor), Marie Schmidt (Mimsi Seraskier), Ella Eckert (Gogo Pasquier): People of the Dream: Claudio Frigerio (Pasquier), Santa Biondo (Marie), Aida Doninelli (Mme. Seraskier)

SOURCE—The 1917 play *Peter Ibbetson* by John N. Raphael (which was based on the 1891 novel of the same name by George du Maurier).

The opera was presented in three acts.

NOTES—*Peter Ibbetson* had its world premiere at the Met; based on the famous novel and play (which had also been filmed), the tragic story dealt with the unhappy and lonely life of Peter Ibettson, who murders his uncle when he discovers the man is actually his father. He's sent to prison for life, and there he dreams of his happy childhood; those dreams sustain him until the moment of his death. His predicament was not unlike that of a character in another lyric piece: Molina, the prisoner in *Kiss of the Spider Woman* (1993), also indulges in fantasies in order to emotionally escape from his literal prison.

In the original Broadway production, John Barrymore played the title role, Lionel Barrymore was the uncle, and Constance Collier was the adult Mimsi, who had been Peter's sweetheart when he was a little boy. It was Collier who had adapted John N. Raphael's script into an acting version, and it was her adaptation which Deems Taylor used as the source of his libretto. On opening night, Collier was in the audience, along with many notables (Irving Berlin, Antoinette Perry, Edna Ferber, Harpo Marx), some of whom paid $100 for a pair of tickets to the lavish production (which included an orchestra of *ninety*, an on-stage band of *thirty* musicians, and *105* chorus members). Despite the excitement surrounding the premiere, the opera quickly faded from sight. In his review in the *New York Times*, Olin Downes generally dismissed the music as "incidental," and noted it didn't reveal character and psychological development. Another *New York Times* writer reported that during the murder scene, Lawrence Tibbett suffered "a badly cut hand in the excitement of his own murder." The writer also mentioned that Deems Taylor had earlier considered adapting Elmer Rice's *Street Scene* into an opera (Kurt Weill would of course do so in 1947).

See entry for the Off Off Broadway production of Ricky Ian Gordon's *Dream True/My Life with Vernon Dexter*, another lyric adaptation of *Peter Ibbetson*.

1250 The Petrified Prince. "A New Musical." THEATRE: Martinson Hall/The Joseph Papp Public Theatre; OPENING DATE: December 18, 1994; PERFORMANCES: 32; BOOK: Edward Gallardo; LYRICS: Michael John LaChiusa; MUSIC: Michael John LaChiusa; DIRECTION: Harold Prince; CHOREOGRAPHY: Rob Marshall; SCENERY: James Youmans; COSTUMES: Judith Dolan; LIGHTING: Howell Binkley; MUSICAL DIRECTION: Jason Robert Brown; PRODUCER: The New York Shakespeare Festival (George C. Wolfe, Producer; Jason Steven Cohen, Managing Director; Rosemarie Tichler and Kevin Kline, Associate Producers)

CAST—Alexander Gaberman (Prince Samson), Mal Z. Lawrence (King Maximillian, Abbe Sebastian, Fernando [King of the Gypsies]), Candy Buckley (Queen Katarina), Gabriel Barre (Franz), Timothy Jerome (Cardinal Pointy), Robert Blumenfeld (Judge Schied), George Merritt (General Petschul), Ralph Byers (Pope Pius VII), Marilyn Cooper (Mama Chiaramonte), Loni Ackerman (Roberta), Geoffrey Blaisdell (General Montesquieu), Alan Braunstein (Napoleon), Jane White (Madame Paulina), Daisy Prince (Elise), Judith Moore (Nursemaid); Ensemble (Wendy Edmead, Amy N. Heggins, Darren Lee, David Masenheimer, Dana Moore, Judith Moore, Troy Myers, Casey Nicholaw, Cynthia Sophiea, Mark Anthony Taylor, Sally Ann Tumas)

SOURCE—An unproduced screenplay by Ingmar Bergman.

The action occurs in Slavonia in 1807.

The musical was presented in two acts.

ACT ONE—"Move" (Alexander Gaberman, Company), "There Are Happy Endings" (Candy Buckley, Mal Z. Lawrence), "His Family Tree" (Timothy Jerome, Robert Blumenfeld, George Merritt, Courtiers), "The Easy Life" (Candy Buckley), "Abbe's Appearance" (Mal Z. Lawrence), "Samson's Thoughts" (Alexander Gaberman), "Pointy's Lament" (Timothy Jerome, Statues), "A Woman in Search of Happiness" (Loni Ackerman, Mal Z. Lawrence, Gypsies), "Napoleon's Nightmare" (Alan Braunstein), "Dormez-Vous" (Geoffrey Blaisdell, George Merritt), "One Little Taste" (Jane White, Brothel Girls), "Never Can Tell" (Daisy Prince), "Look Closer, Love" (Daisy Prince), "Stay" (Alexander Gaberman, Daisy Prince), Finale: "Move" (reprise) (Candy Buckley, Company)

ACT TWO—"Move" (reprise) (Candy Buckley, Company), "Without Me" (Candy Buckley, Palace Guards), "The Animal Song" (Daisy Prince), "Samson's Epiphany" (Alexander Gaberman), "Fernando's Suicide" (Mal Z. Lawrence), "The Easy Life" (reprise) (Candy Buckley), "The Easy Life" (reprise) (Daisy Prince), "Addio, Bambino" (Marilyn Cooper, Ralph Byers), "Roberta's Passion Play" (Loni Ackerman, Mal Z. Lawrence), "What the Prince Is Saying" (Daisy Prince, Company), "I Would Like to Say" (Alexander Gaberman, Daisy Prince), Finale (Company)

NOTES—Harold Prince's lavish production of *The Petrified Prince* was, in the words of Jeffrey Sweet in *The Best Plays of 1994-1995*, "dazzling icing on an unbaked cake." The title character, Samson, is in line for the throne of his politically troubled country. But Samson has psychological issues which have rendered him mute, and since he's been in a virtually autistic state for his entire life, Sweet wondered why Prince and the musical's creators felt an audience should believe Samson is qualified to overcome his political rivals and run his country. Further, Ben Brantley in the *New York Times* remarked that the musical had no consistency in its book, score, and direction, and that the evening wavered between cynicism and sentimentality (he felt the musical went through more personality changes than Sally Fields' performance in the 1976 television movie *Sybil*).

As for Michael John LaChiusa's score, Brantley felt it was a comedown from *First Lady Suite* and *Hello Again* (see entries), the lyricist-composer's previous efforts. He found the songs a mix of "basic Broadway pastiche" from the school of *Godspell* (see entry) and *Pippin*, and noted that one song sounded like a reject from Stephen Sondheim's *Anyone Can Whistle*.

The Petrified Prince played one month at the Public, and then seems to have completely disappeared.

1251 Pets! "A New Musical." THEATRE: Theatre East; OPENING DATE: July 27, 1995; PERFORMANCES: 68; SKETCHES: See song list for credits; LYRICS: See song list for credits; MUSIC: See song list for credits; DIRECTION: Helen Butleroff; CHOREOGRAPHY: Helen Butleroff; SCENERY: Holger; COSTUMES: Gail

Cooper-Hecht; LIGHTING: Phil Monat; MUSICAL DIRECTION: Albert Ahronheim; PRODUCERS: Leahy Productions in association with Arthur B. Brown

CAST—Michelle Azar, Barbara Broughton, Christopher Harrod, Christopher Scott, Jennifer Simard

The revue was presented in two acts.

ACT ONE—"Pets" (lyric by Alison Hubbard, music by Kim Oler) (Company), "Take Me Home with You" (lyric and music by Thomas Tierney) (Company), "Don't Worry 'Bout Me" (lyric by Dan Kael, music by Ben Schaechter) (Christopher Scott, Barbara Broughton), "I Walk Ze Dogs" (lyric by June Siegel, music by Jimmy Roberts) (Jennifer Simard), "Just Do It Without Me" (lyric by Jane Brody Zales, music by Thomas Tierney) (Christopher Harrod), "Cat in the Box" (music by Harry Tierney) (Christopher Scott), "There's a Bagel on the Piano" (lyric by Faye Greenberg, music by Ben Schaechter) (Jennifer Simard), "Perpetual Care" (lyric by Adele Ahronheim, music by Ben Schaechter) (Michelle Azar, Christopher Scott), "Cool Cats" (lyric by Alison Hubbard, music by Kim Oler) (Barbara Broughton, Christopher Scott, Christopher Harrod, Jennifer Simard), "Dear Max" (lyric by Marion Adler and Carolyn Sloan, music by Carolyn Sloan) (Michelle Azar), "First Cat" (introduction written by Thomas Edward West; lyric and music by Harry Tierney) (Company)

ACT TWO—"What About Us?" (lyric by Richard Engquist, music by Raphael Crystal) (Company), "Peculiar" (lyric by Dan Kael, music by Ben Schaechter) (Christopher Scott, Michele Azar), "Bonus #1" (sketch by Greer Woodward) (Barbara Broughton), "Franklin" (lyric by Faye Greenberg, music by Ben Schaechter) (Jennifer Simard), "Mice of Means" (lyric by Dan Kael, music by Ben Schaechter) (Michelle Azar, Christopher Harrod, Christopher Scott), "Bonus #2" (sketch by Greer Woodward) (Barbara Broughton), "Night of the Iguana" (lyric by Alison Hubbard, music by Kim Oler) (Christopher Scott, Michelle Azar, Jennifer Simard), "Bonus #3" (sketch by Greer Woodward) (Barbara Broughton), "If You Can Stay" (lyric by Greer Woodward, music by Rick Cummins) (Barbara Broughton), "All in a Day's Work" (lyric and music by Thomas Tierney) (Company), "Pets" (lyric by Alison Hubbard, music by Kim Oler) (Company)

NOTES—*Pets!* was a tribute to household pets. Ben Brantley in the *New York Times* found the revue an exercise in the obvious, and noted that a "relentless trickle of sunny blandness" ran through it. In fact, he said the evening's "innocuousness" could lead an audience member to start wondering if he had picked up the dry cleaning. Brantley reported that at the end of the revue a kitten and puppy were brought on stage as candidates for adoption. Despite their "frightened and confused" demeanors, Brantley said they came across as "charming and complex," and noted the revue itself "did not benefit from the comparison." The revue had been previously seen Off Off Broadway at the Judith Anderson Theatre on March 24, 1993, for sixteen performances.

1252 The Phantom Tollbooth. THEATRE: Workshop Theatre/Sarah Lawrence College; OPENING DATE: May 8; (year unknown; possibly 1976); PERFORMANCES: 2; BOOK: Jane Hubbard; LYRICS: Jack Z. Tantleff, Jane Hubbard, and Bob Thiele; MUSIC: Bob Thiele; DIRECTION: Jane Hubbard; Jack Z. Tantleff, Assistant Director; CHOREOGRAPHY: Jack Z. Tantleff and Jane Hubbard; Tap Choreography by Kathy Wallach (Lisa Ward and Susan Green, Assisants); Light Ballet choreographed by Martha Gehman; SCENERY: Jane Hubbard; COSTUMES: Jean Chase; MUSICAL DIRECTION: Bob Thiele

CAST—Hillary Bailey, Lori Barenfeld, Bill Barnes, Marie-Elizabeth Broady, Camila Bryce-Laporte, Cannon, Jean Chase, Marty Fluger, Carrie Frazier, Martha Gehman, Harris Gruson, Amanda Gulla, Patricia Henritze, John Hughes, Ronny Remeny, Ana Roth, Carla Salls, Mary Slattery, Kathy Wallach, Lisa Ward, Cindy Weintraub, Britt Westberg

SOURCE—The 1961 book *The Phantom Tollbooth* by Norton Juster.

The musical was presented in two acts (song assignments weren't identified in the program).

ACT ONE—"Milo's Discontent," "Tick Behind Tock," "Wordsworth," "Faintly Macabre's Song," "It Goes Without Saying," "Ordinary Boy," "The Light Ballet" (music excerpted from *The Firebird Suite* by Igor Stravinsky)

ACT TWO—"A Dog Is a Man's Best Friend"/"A Man Is a Dog's Best Friend," "The Soundkeeper's Song," "Have We Got a Number for You," "I'll Never Make It to the Top," "I'm the Trivium," "Rhyme and Reason," "Over and Over"

NOTES—Norton Juster's popular children's book *The Phantom Tollbooth* (about a boy who encounters a surreal world where letters and numbers are at war with one another) was adapted into a film in 1969; this workshop production was also performed Off Off Broadway at the Henry Street Settlement Playhouse on November 19, 1977.

In the mid-1990s, an operatic version of Juster's book was written, with libretto by Juster and Sheldon Harnick, lyrics by Harnick, and music by Arnold Black. Apparently because of Black's death, the work was never produced. But Jane Horwitz in the *Washington Post* reported that in 2000 Juster and Harnick received permission from Black's widow to readapt the opera into a musical comedy; as a result, they deleted the recitative portions of work, simplified the lyrics, and reshaped the vocal arrangements for traditional musical comedy singing. In November 2007, the production received its world premiere at the Kennedy Center Family Theatre. Celia Wren in the *Washington Post* found the musical almost as "witty and buoyant" as the novel upon which it was based, and she praised Black's "richly textured score" and the "deadpan drollery" of Harnick's lyrics. This production was recorded by the Kennedy Center and MTI on an unnamed and unnumbered CD.

1253 Philemon. THEATRE: Portfolio Studio; OPENING DATE: April 8, 1975; PERFORMANCES: 48; BOOK: Tom Jones; LYRICS: Tom Jones; MUSIC: Harvey Schmidt; DIRECTION: Lester Collins; COSTUMES: Charles Blackburn; MUSICAL DIRECTION: Ken Collins; PRODUCER: Portfolio Productions

CAST—Michael Glenn-Smith (Andos), Virginia Gregory (Marsyas), Drew Katzman (Servillus), Dick Latessa (Cockian), Leila Martin (Wife), Howard Ross (Commander), Kathrin King Segal (Kiki)

SOURCE—The musical was suggested by a paragraph in the book *Masques, Mimes and Miracles* by Allardyce Nicholl.

The action occurs in Antioch in 287 A.D.

The musical was presented in two acts.

ACT ONE—"Within This Empty Space" (Company), "The Streets of Antioch" (Dick Latessa, Howard Ross), "Gimme a Good Digestion" (Dick Latessa, Kathrin King Segal), "Don't Kiki Me" (Kathrin King Segal, Dick Latessa), "I'd Do Almost Anything to Get Out of Here and Go Home" (Dick Latessa, Howard Ross), "He's Coming" (Prisoners), "Antioch Prison" (Prisoners), "Name: Cockian" (Dick Latessa, Company)

ACT TWO—"I Love Order" (Howard Ross, Company), "My Secret Dream" (Michael Glenn-Smith, Dick Latessa, Company), "I Love His Face" (Virginia Gregory, Dick Latessa), "Sometimes" (Dick Latessa, Prisoners), "The Protest" (Company), "The Nightmare" (Dick Latessa, Company), "Love Suffers Everything" (Leila Martin), "The Confrontation" (Dick Latessa, Howard Ross, Company), "Love Suffers Everything" (reprise) (Company), "Within This Empty Space" (reprise) (Company)

NOTES—*Philemon* was the first full-fledged Off Broadway musical written by Tom Jones and Harvey Schmidt since the premiere of *The Fantasticks* (1960; see entry) fifteen years earlier. In the interim, three of their musicals had been produced on Broadway: *110 in the Shade* (1963), a modest hit at the time, but which over the years has become something of a standard in the musical theatre repertoire; *I Do! I Do!* (1966; see entry for Off Broadway revival), a hit with Mary Martin and Robert Preston; and *Celebration* (1969), a fascinating failure which was an interesting mixture of ritualistic, early theatre forms and old-fashioned show business (it should probably have played Off Broadway in a small theatre).

Jones and Schmidt had organized their Portfolio Studio to develop new musicals, and among the shows produced there were *Celebration*, *Philemon*, *The Bone Room*, and *Portfolio Revue* (see entries for *The Bone Room* and *Portfolio Revue*). While it appears *Philemon* was developed at Portfolio, it may have also been produced there for a few performances beginning on January 3, 1975, before it reopened in April of that year.

Philemon told the story of Cockian, a down-and-out clown who is persuaded by a Roman commander to impersonate the Christian leader Philemon. Cockian is placed in jail with members of the imprisoned Christian underground in order to infiltrate the group and discover their political secrets. However, once Cockian comes to know the Christian prisoners, he is transformed by their faith, refuses to betray them, and dies a martyr for the Christian cause.

The musical received good reviews, but didn't play beyond its scheduled run. Happily, the melodic score was recorded by Gallery Records (LP # OC-1), which included a new song for the character of the Wife ("The Greatest of These" instead of "Love Suffers Everything"), and the album identified three songs in "The Confrontation" sequence ("How Free I Feel," "Oh, How Easy to Be Scornful," and "Come with Me").

Philemon was taped by Hollywood Television Theatre, and on October 7, 1976; it was shown on public television (Dick Latessa recreated his role of Cockian).

The musical received two Off Off Broadway revivals, one on January 11, 1991, for twenty-three performances by the York Theatre Company, and the other on October 7, 1999, for thirteen performances at the 28th Street Theatre.

1254 Phoenix '55. "A New Musical Revue." THEATRE: Phoenix Theatre; OPENING DATE: April 23, 1955; PERFORMANCES: 97; SKETCHES: Ira Wallach; LYRICS: David Craig; MUSIC: David Baker; ballet music by John Morris; DIRECTION: Marc Daniels; CHOREOGRAPHY: Boris Runanin; SCENERY: Eldon Elder; COSTUMES: Alvin Colt; LIGHTING: Klaus Holm; MUSICAL DIRECTION: Buster Davis; PRODUCERS: The Phoenix Theatre (T. Edward Hambleton and Norris Houghton)

CAST—NANCY WALKER, GEMZE DE LAPPE, BILL HEYER, LOUISE HOFF, HARVEY LEMBECK, MARGE REDMOND, ELISE RHODES, JOSHUA SHELLEY, ELTON WARREN, Bob Bakanic, Shellie Farrell, Jerry Fries, Jay Harnick, Dick Korthaze, Ralph McWilliams, Cynthia Price, Rain Winslow

SOURCE—"The idea for this revue was conceived by Nicholas Benton and Stark Hesseltine" (program note).

The revue was presented in two acts.

ACT ONE—Opening (sketch by David Craig) (Louise Hoff) "It Says Here" (Bob Bakanic, Gemze de Lappe, Shellie Farrell, Jerry Fries, Jay Harnick, Kenneth Harvey, Bill Heyer, Dick Korthaze, Ralph

McWilliams, Cynthia Price, Marge Redmond, Elise Rhodes, Joshua Shelley, Elton Warren, Rain Winslow), "Tomorrow Is Here" (Nancy Walker, Harvery Lembeck, Company) "Handy Man Around the House" (Louise Hoff, Marge Redmond, Joshua Shelley) "All Around the World" (Elise Rhodes, Bill Heyer) "First Prize" (Harvey Lembeck, Kenneth Harvey, Nancy Walker, Cynthia Price, Marge Redmond, Rain Winslow, Jay Harnick) "Never Wait for Love" (Elton Warren, Gemze de Lappe, Ralph McWilliams, Shellie Farrell, Jerry Fries, Rain Winslow, Bob Bakanic), "Down to the Sea" (Nancy Walker) "Utter Ecstasy" (Harvey Lembeck, Rain Winslow, Louise Hoff, Marge Redmond) "The Trap" (Kenneth Harvey, Nancy Walker, Boris Runanin, Harvey Lembeck, Rain Winslow, Company) (libretto by Ira Wallach; although his name is not on the credits' page of the *Playbill* or in "Who's Who in the Cast" section of the *Playbill*, the *Playbill* credits Boris Runanin, who choreographed this spoof of the New Age angst school of modern ballet, as participating in this number as the character "The Young Dreamer")

ACT TWO—"This Tuxedo Is Mine!" (Bill Heyer, Bob Bakanic, Jerry Fries, Rain Winslow, Shellie Farrell), "The Ingenue" (Joshua Shelley, Harvey Lembeck, Elise Rhodes, Nancy Walker) "Just Him" (sketch by David Craig) (Bill Heyer, Elise Rhodes) "The Charade of the Marionettes" (Elton Warren, Gemze de Lappe, Ralph McWilliams, and George Spelvin [apparently Nancy Walker], listed in the program as "Clown" playing "A Clown") "A Funny Heart" (Nancy Walker), "Suburban Retreat" (Louise Hoff, Joshua Shelley) "Upper Birth" (Kenneth Harvey, Nancy Walker, Harvey Lembeck, Bob Bakanic, Jay Harnick) Finale (Company)

NOTES—Unless otherwise noted, all sketches by Ira Wallach.

Originally titled *Tobasco*, *Phoenix '55* had a disappointing run and is chiefly remembered today for Nancy Walker's wildly comic performance. In the "The Ingenue," she played a character named Chickie Popjoy; in another sketch, she parodied Geraldine Page's performance in *The Rainmaker* (1954); and she shined in a spoof of Edward R. Murrow's TV interviews, a sketch which Walter Kerr in the *New York Herald Tribune* described as "five or six minutes of hysteria." She also made an impression singing a torch song, "A Funny Heart."

Although she was one of the musical theatre's greatest clowns, Walker never quite found the leading role in a smash, classic musical. She sparkled in her first two Broadway hits, playing supporting roles in *Best Foot Forward* (1941) and *On the Town* (1944), the latter her last major success. *Look, Ma, I'm Dancin'!* (1948) was a modest hit (it paid back its investment and apparently returned a small profit even though it played for just 188 performances), but her other musicals were financial failures (through no fault of her own, because critics and audiences always adored her): *Barefoot Boy with Cheek* (1947, 108 performances), *Along Fifth Avenue* (1949, 180 performances), *A Month of Sundays* (1951; closed during its pre-Broadway tryout), *Phoenix '55*, *Copper and Brass* (1957, 36 performances), and *Do Re Mi* (1960; despite glowing reviews and a run of 400 performances, the show closed in the red). Incidentally, Walker's husband, David Craig, was the lyricist for both *Phoenix '55* and *Copper and Brass* (David Baker was also the composer for the latter). The New York run of *Phoenix '55* was followed by a short tour (both *The Golden Apple* and *Phoenix '55* were the first two Off Broadway musicals to tour, abeit briefly [*The Threepenny Opera* didn't tour until 1961]); the tour included Nancy Walker, Harvey Lembeck, and other original cast members, along with a few replacements, including Peggy Cass and Jo Wilder.

Five sketches ("Handy Man Around the House," "First Prize," "Utter Ecstasy," "The Ingenue," and "Upper Birth") were published by Samuel French, Inc., in 1957 under the revue's title.

Despite the revue's status as an Off Broadway musical, 1956 Tony Award nominations went to Nancy Walker for Best Actress in a Musical (the other nominees were Carol Channing for *The Vamp* [1955] and Gwen Vernon, who was the winner for her performance as Lola in *Damn Yankees* [1955]) and to Boris Runanin for Best Choreography (he was actually nominated for both *Phoenix '55* and *Pipe Dream* [1955]; the winner was Bob Fosse for *Damn Yankees*). For other Off Broadway performers who were 1956 Tony Award nominees and/or winners, see entry for the 1954 production of *The Threepenny Opera*.

1255 Photo Finish. "A Satirical Revue." THEATRE: Upstairs at the Downstairs; OPENING DATE: March 8, 1968; PERFORMANCES: Unknown; SKETCHES: Alan Foster Friedman, Steve Nelson, Drey Shepperd, Treva Silverman, Lily Tomlin, and Rod Warren; LYRICS: William Dyer, David Finkle, Alan Foster Friedman, Michael McWhinney, Don Parks, Drey Shepperd, Jay Thompson, and Rod Warren; MUSIC: William Dyer, Alan Foster Friedman, Ed Kresley, Lance Mulcahy, Don Parks, Jerry Powell, Jay Thompson, Rod Warren, and Bill Weeden; DIRECTION: Ed Kresley; production supervised by Rod Warren; CHOREOGRAPHY: Ed Kresley; LIGHTING: Larry Carter; MUSICAL DIRECTION: Edward Morris; PRODUCER: The Upstairs at the Downstairs (Rod Warren)

CAST—Warren Burton, Jerry Clark, Jeanette Landis, Steve Nelson, Lily Tomlin, Victoria Wyndham

The revue was presented in two acts.

ACT ONE—Overture (Orchestra), "Our Family Album" (lyric by David Finkle, music by Bill Weeden) (Company), "Boom" (lyric and music by Alan Foster Friedman) (Jeanette Landis, Victoria Wyndham, Warren Burton, Jerry Clark), "The Family Affair" (sketch by Drey Shepperd) (Lily Tomlin, Jerry Clark, Warren Burton) "In Italics" (lyric by Drey Shepperd, music by Ed Kresley) (Company), "To Russia with Love" (lyric by Rod Warren, music by Jerry Powell) (Jeanette Landis, Steve Nelson) "I Thought I Was All Alone" (lyric and music by William Dyer and Don Parks) (Victoria Wyndham) "The Motherland" (sketch by Drey Shepperd) (Jeanette Landis, Lily Tomlin) "Fight, Team, Fight" (lyric by Rod Warren, music by Rod Warren and Jerry Powell) (Victoria Wyndham, Warren Burton, Jerry Clark), "I Don't Feel Anything" (lyric by David Finkle, music by Bill Weeden) (Jeanette Landis, Jerry Clark) "Westchester Cathedral" (sketch by Steve Nelson) (Victoria Wyndham, Steve Nelson), "Angelus" (lyric by Michael McWhinney, music by Lance Mulcahy) (Warren Burton, Jerry Clark, Steve Nelson) "Candid Candidates" (sketch by Alan Foster Friedman) (Company), "America First" (lyric by Drey Shepperd, music by Ed Kresley and Rod Warren) (Company)

ACT TWO—"International Set" (lyric by Rod Warren and Drey Shepperd, music by Ed Kresley) (Company), "London Dierriere" (sketch by Rod Warren) (Jeanette Landis, Warren Burton, Jerry Clark) "Rodgers and Hart" (lyric and music by Alan Foster Friedman, with additional vocal arrangement by Rod Warren) (Lily Tomlin, Victoria Wyndham, Jerry Clark, Steve Nelson) "Tabulation" (sketch by Treva Silverman) (Victoria Wyndham, Warren Burton), "Beautiful People" (sketch by Lily Tomlin) (Lily Tomlin; introduced by Steve Nelson) "While the Iron Is Hot" (lyric and music by Rod Warren) (Jeanette Landis, Victoria Wyndham, Warren Burton, Steve Nelson), "It Seems We've Stood and Talked" (sketch by Drey Shepperd) (Lily Tomlin, Jerry Clark) "Love Themes" (lyric and music by William Dyer, Don Parks, and Jay Thompson) (Jeanette Landis, Company) "For a Little While" (lyric and music by Rod Warren) (Jerry Clark) "Our Crowd" (lyric by Michael McWhinney and William Dyer, music by William Dyer) (Company), Finale: "Our Family Album" (reprise) (Company)

NOTES—One sequence in *Photo Finish*, "It Seems We've Stood and Talked," sounds particularly amusing. Described in the program as "Nichols fall as they May," this sketch was about the famous performing team (here spoofed by Lily Tomlin and Jerry Clark) and may have been the highlight of the revue. Vincent Canby in the *New York Times* felt the "occasionally amusing" evening had a number of "low points." But he was full of praise for Tomlin, "a bright, fresh musical comedy talent" who was the result of a "lunar conjunction" between Beatrice Lillie and Dracula's daughter, and said she "may well be headed for the big time."

For a complete list of Rod Warren's revues, see entry for *...And in This Corner*; also see Appendix R.

1256 Piaf. "A Remembrance." THEATRE: The Playhouse; OPENING DATE: February 14, 1977; PERFORMANCES: 24; PLAY David Cohen; LYRICS: See song list for credits; MUSIC: See song list for credits; DIRECTION: Lee Rachman; SCENERY: Ralph Alswang; COSTUMES: Robert Troie; LIGHTING: Ralph Alswang; MUSICAL DIRECTION: John Marino; PRODUCERS: Michael Ross and Eddie Vallone

CAST—Gregory Salata (Theo Sarapo), Edmund Lynbeck (Louis Leplee), Lou Bedford (Marcel Cerdan), JULIETTE KOKA (Edith Piaf), Douglas Andros (Loulou Barrier), Donald Hampton (Henri, A Young Doctor)

The play with music was presented in two acts (song assignments not identified, but probably most songs were performed by Juliette Koka).

ACT ONE—"Padam" (lyric and music by Norbert Glanzberg and Henri Contet), "Bal Dans Ma Rue" (lyricist and composer unknown), "L'Etranger" (lyric by Robert Malleron, music by Marguerite Monnot) "Bravo Pour Le Clown" (lyric and music by Henri Contet and Louiguy), "Mon Dieu" (lyric and music by Charles Dumont and Michel Vaucaire), "L'Accordioniste" (lyric and music by Michel Emer), "Mon Menage a Moi" (lyric by Jean Constantin, music by Norbert Glanzberg), "Milord" (lyric by G. Moustaki, music by Marguerite Monnot)

ACT TWO—"La Vie En Rose" (lyric by Edith Piaf, music by Louiguy), Medley: "Les Trois Cloches" (lyric and music by J. Villard and B. Reisfeld); "Under Paris Skies (Sous le Ciel de Paris)" (lyric and music by Jean Drejac and Hubert Giraud); "La Goulante du Pauvre Jean" (lyric by P. de Lange [and possibly R. Roulaud], music by Marguerite Monnot), "Hymne a L'Amour" (lyric by Edith Piaf, music by Marguerite Monnot), "La Foule (Carnival)" (lyric and music by Michel Rivgauche, Charles Dumont, and possibly A. Cabral), "Les Blouses Blanches (The Ones in White)" (lyric by Michel Rivgauche, music by Marguerite Monnot), "Non, Je Ne Regrette Rien" (lyric and music by Charles Dumont and Michel Vaucaire)

NOTES—Here was yet another evening about Edith Piaf. Juliette Koka portrayed Piaf in this production, and would do so again in 1993 when she appeared in *Piaf... Remembered* (see entry; for more information regarding Off Broadway and Broadway productions about Edith Piaf, see entry for *Dear Piaf*).

1257 Piaf ... Remembered. THEATRE: Theatre Arielle; transferred to the 45th Street Theatre on July 6, 1993; OPENING DATE: June 16, 1993; PERFORMANCES: 175; CONCEIVED: Juliette Koka, with additional dialogue by Janet Alberti and Milli Janz; LYRICS: See song list for credits; MUSIC: See song list for credits; MUSICAL DIRECTION: John Marino; PRODUCERS: Michael and Barbara Ross

CAST—Juliette Koka

The revue was presented in one act (songs performed by Juliette Koka).

MUSICAL NUMBERS—"Padam" (lyric and music by Norbert Glanzberg and Henri Contet), "Bravo Pour le Clown" (lyric and music by Henri Contet and Louiguy; English lyric by D. Cohen), "L'Etranger" (lyric by Robert Malleron, music by Marguerite Monnot; English lyric by D. Cohen), "L'Accordioniste" (lyric and music by Michael Emer; English lyric by D. Cohen), "Mon Dieu" (lyric and music by Charles Dumont and Michel Vaucaire), "La Foule (Carnival)" (lyric and music by Charles Dumont, Michel Rivgauche, and possibly A. Cabral), "L'Homme a la Moto" (lyric and music Jerry Leiber, Mike Stoller, and J. Drejac), "Roulez Tambours" (lyric by Edith Piaf, music by Francis Lai; English lyric by D. Marino), "Mon Menage a Moi" (lyric by Jean Constantin, music by Norbert Glanzberg), "La Vie en Rose" (lyric by Edith Piaf, music by Louiguy), "Hymne a l'Amour" (lyric by Edith Piaf, music by Marguerite Monnot; English lyric by G. Parsons), Medley: "Les Trois Cloches" (lyric and music by J. Villard and B. Reisfeld)/"Sous le Ciel de Paris" (lyric and music by Jean Drejac and Hubert Giraud; English lyric by Kim Gannon)"/La Goulante du Pauvre Jean" (lyric by P. de Lange [and possibly R. Roulaud], music by Marguerite Monnot), "Le Diable de la Bastille" (lyric and music by Charles Dumont and P. de Lange; English lyric by D. Marino), "C'est Toujours la Meme Histoire" (lyric and music by D. White and Henri Contet), "Le Droit d'Aimer" (lyric by R. Nyel, music by Francis Lai; English lyric by M. Sedwick and Juliette Koka), "A Quoi Ca Sert l'Amour" (lyric and music by Michel Emer), "Les Blouses Blanche (The Ones in White)" (lyric by Michel Rivgauche, music by Marguerite Monnot; English lyric by D. Cohen), "Milord" (lyric by G. Moustaki, music by Marguerite Monnot), "Non, Je Ne Regrette Rien" (lyric and music by Charles Dumont and Michel Vaucaire; English lyric by Hal Davis [Hal David?])

NOTES—See entry for *Dear Piaf* regarding Broadway, Off Broadway, and Off Off Broadway productions about Edith Piaf, including *Piaf*, which, like *Piaf ... Remembered*, starred Juliette Koka.

1258 Piano Bar. "A Musical." THEATRE: Westside Chelsea Theatre; OPENING DATE: June 8, 1978; PERFORMANCES: 125; BOOK: Doris Willens and Rob Fremont; LYRICS: Doris Willens; MUSIC: Rob Fremont; DIRECTION: Albert Takazauckas; CHOREOGRAPHY: Nora Peterson; SCENERY: Michael Massee; COSTUMES: Michael Massee; LIGHTING: Gary Porto; MUSICAL DIRECTION: Joel Silberman; PRODUCERS: Lantern Productions; Charles W. Gould, Associate Producer

CAST—Jim McMahon (Bartender), Kelly Bishop (Julie), Joel Silberman (Prince), Richard Ryder (Walt), Steve Elmore (Ned), Karen De Vito (Debbie)

The action occurs at Sweet Sue's Piano Bar in the Murray Hill section of Manhattan; the time is Happy Hour, on a rainy Tuesday in March of this year ("whatever year this is").

The musical was presented in two acts.

ACT ONE—"Intro" (Joel Silberman), "Sweet Sue's" (Company), "Today" (Company), "Pigeon-Hole Time" (Steve Elmore), "Congratulations" (Karen De Vito), "Believe Me" (Richard Ryder, Kelly Bishop), "Tango" (Kelly Bishop, Richard Ryder), "Everywhere I Go" (Karen De Vito), "Dinner at the Murklines'" (Steve Elmore), "Scenes from Some Marriages (The People Gone)" (Company), "Personals" (Joel Silberman), "Nobody's Perfect" (Company)

ACT TWO—"One Two Three" (Company), "Greenspons" (Karen De Vito), "Moms and Dads" (Company), "Meanwhile, Back in Yonkers" (Kelly Bishop), "Walt's Truth" (Richard Ryder), "New York Cliché" (Karen De Vito, Steve Elmore), "It's Coming Back to Me" (Kelly Bishop, Richard Ryder), "Tomorrow Night" (Joel Silberman), "Closing" (Joel Silberman)

NOTES—Any musical about married, divorced, and single New Yorkers begged comparison with Stephen Sondheim's *Company* (1970), and *Piano Bar* didn't measure up to that iconic, ground-breaking master work. An almost sung-through musical with little in the way of dialogue, *Piano Bar* needed a strong score to get past the clichés it depicted; but unfortunately its music was bland and its lyrics ordinary. There was even a song about the impersonality of New York, which *Company*'s "Another Hundred People" had done to perfection. Further, in *Company* a husband spoke of his wife and of how he's "scared she'll stay"; *Piano Bar* told us that "no one stays." Moreover, the musical seemed to be vaguely imitating another Harold Prince-directed musical, *Cabaret* (1966), which was also set in a watering hole. According to the script of *Piano Bar*, which was published by Samuel French, Inc., in 1978, the bar's piano player (named Prince!) "controls the mood of the evening" (although certainly not to the extent of the M.C. in *Cabaret*). The published script reflected a change of title for one song ("Walt's Truth" became "Alas, Alack").

The musical had previously been presented in a showcase production at the Shirtsleeve Theatre, where it was subtitled "A Happy Hour Musical"; it opened there on February 9, 1978, and played for twelve performances. The production included two cast members who didn't transfer with the show to Off Broadway: Christopher (Chris) Callan as Julie and Dan Ruskin as Prince. The number "If Only" wasn't held over for the Off Broadway production.

The cast album was released by Original Cast Records (LP # OC-7812). Beginning with Offbeat Records in the 1950s, and continuing with Blue Pear, DRG, Fynsworth Alley, Sh-K-Boom, Ghostlight, and Original Cast Records, a vast number of Off Broadway scores have been preserved because of these innovative companies.

1259 Pick a Number XV. THEATRE: PLaza 9- Room; OPENING DATE: October 14, 1965; PERFORMANCES: 400; SKETCHES: William F. Brown, Robert Elliott, Tony Geiss, and Ted James; LYRICS: William F. Brown, Lesley Davison, David Finkle, Nelson Garringer, Clark Gesner, Howard Liebling, Tom Jones, Walter Marks, June Reizner, Claibe Richardson, and Fred Tobias; MUSIC: Lesley Davison, Clark Gesner, Stanley Lebowsky, Walter Marks, Shamus O'Connor, June Reizner, Claibe Richardson, Harvey Schmidt, Fred Silver, and Bill Weeden; DIRECTION: Julius Monk; CHOREOGRAPHY: Frank Wagner; LIGHTING: Chester Morss; MUSICAL DIRECTION: Robert Colston; PRODUCER: Thomas Hammond

CAST—Lee Beery, Rex Robbins, Bill Hinnant, Nancy Parell, Liz Sheridan, John Keatts, Elizabeth Wilson, John Svar

SKETCHES AND MUSICAL NUMBERS (division of acts and sketch and song assignments unknown)—"Pick a Number XV" (dialogue and lyric by William F. Brown, music by Stanley Lebowsky), "The Good Old Days" (lyric by David Finkle, music by Bill Weeden) "Checkbooks and All That" (sketch by Ted James) "Happiness Is a Bird" (lyric and music by Claibe Richardson) "Pop Song" (lyric and music by Lesley Davison) "Live from New York" (sketch by William F. Brown), "The New Menace" (lyric and music by June Reizner) "The Plaza's Going Native" (lyric by Fred Tobias, music by Stanley Lebowsky) "Coney Island" (lyric by Nelson Garringer, music by Fred Silver) "Peyton Place Forever" (sketch by Tony Geiss), "On the Weekend" (lyric by Fred Tobias, music by Stanley Lebowsky) "New York Is a Summer Festival" (lyric by Tom Jones, music by Harvey Schmidt) "Love, Here I Am" (lyric and music by Walter Marks), "The Kicker" (sketch by Robert Elliott), "Almost a Love Song" (lyric and music by Clark Gesner) "McNamara's Band" (lyric by Howard Liebling, music by Shamus O'Connor) "Signs of the Seasons" (lyric and music by June Reizner), "Wonderland Revisited" (sketch by William F. Brown) "The Saga of Killer Joe" (lyric by Nelson Garringer, music by Fred Silver) "Societus Magnificat: An Oratorio" (lyric and music by Clark Gesner)

NOTES—This long-running Julius Monk revue *Pick a Number XV* continued the tradition of spoofs of New York ("New York Is a Summer Festival," which had been introduced in *Demi-Dozen* [see entry]) and politics ("McNamara's Band" and "Societus Magnificat: An Oratorio"). There also appears to have been a sketch about Joe Namath ("The Kicker"). "Love, Here I Am" had been previously heard in *Four Below Strikes Back* (1959; see entry).

For a complete list of Julius Monk's revues, see entry for *Take Five*; also see Appendix Q.

1260 Picon Pie. THEATRE: Lamb's Theatre; OPENING DATE: February 17, 2005; PERFORMANCES: 121; PLAY: Rose Leiman Goldemberg; DIRECTION: Pamela Hall; SCENERY: Matthew Maraffi; COSTUMES: Laura Frecon; LIGHTING: Graham Kindred; MUSICAL DIRECTION: Steven Sterner; PRODUCERS: Merriewold Enterprises, Edmund Gaynes, and Nancy Bianconi

CAST—June Gable (Molly Picon), Stuart Zagnit (Jacob "Yonkel" Kalich)

The play with music was presented in two acts.

NOTES—*Picon Pie* celebrated Molly Picon (1898-1992), the beloved Yiddish theatre and Broadway star who was a fixture of New York theatre for over fifty years (for more information about her, see entry for *The Kosher Widow*.) The play with music had first premiered at the Santa Monica Playhouse on April 6, 2002, and before its Off Broadway opening it had been performed Off Off Broadway at the DR2 Theatre beginning on July 15, 2004, for an estimated 200 performances.

1261 Pieces-of-Eight. "A Piratic Parodic." THEATRE: Upstairs at the Downstairs; OPENING DATE: September 17, 1959; PERFORMANCES: Unknown; SKETCHES: Dave Axelrod, Elisse Boyd, Bill Dana, Bruce Hart, Bud McCreery, and John Meyer; LYRICS: Martin Charnin, David Davenport, Dennis Marks, and Bruce Williamson; MUSIC: Alan Friedman, Bart Howard, Bob (Robert) Kessler, Claibe Richardson, William Roy, Rod Warren, and William Roy; DIRECTION: Buddy Schwab; PRODUCER: Julius Monk; MUSICAL DIRECTION: William Roy and Carl Norman "at the Plural Pianos"

CAST—Ceil Cabot, Del Close, Jane Connell, Gordon Connell, Gerry Matthews, Estelle Parsons

The revue was presented in two acts.

ACT ONE—Overture and "Gala Opening" (lyric and music by Bud McCreery) (Company) "Happiness Is a Bird" (lyric and music by Claibe Richardson) (Ceil Cabot, Gerry Matthews) "And Then I Wrote..." (lyric by David Davenport, music by William Roy) (Del Close) "Radio City Music Hall" (lyric and music by Rod Warren) (Jane Connell, Estelle Parsons, Ceil Cabot) "Miss Williams" (sketch by Elisse Boyd) (Jane Connell) "The Uncle Bergie Evans Show" (sketch by Dave Axelrod and Bruce Hart) (Estelle Parsons, Jane Connell, Ceil Cabot, Del Close, Gerry Matthews) "Oriental" (lyric by Martin Charnin, music by Bob Kessler) (Ceil Cabot) "Ardent Admirer" (sketch by John Meyer) (Jane Connell), "Steel Guitars and Barking Seals" (sketch by Bud McCreery) (Company)

ACT TWO—"Election Spectacular" (sketch by Bud McCreery) (Company) "Seasons' Greetings" (lyric and music by Rod Warren) (Ceil Cabot), "A Name of Our Own" (lyric by Dennis Marks, music Alan Friedman) (Del Close, Gerry Matthews, Gordon Connell) "M'Lady Chatterley" (lyric by Bruce Williamson, music by William Roy) (Jane Connell) "Farewell" (lyric and music by William Roy) (Gerry Matthews), "The Night the Hurricane Struck" (sketch by Bud McCreery) (Ceil Cabot, Jane Connell, Gordon Connell, Gerry Matthews) "Everybody Wants to Be Loved" (lyric and music by Bart Howard) (Estelle Parsons) "A Conversation Piece" (sketch by Bill Dana) (Estelle Parsons, Del Close, Gordon Connell, Gerry Matthews) Final Reprise (Company)

NOTES—The song and sketch listing is taken from the cast album released by Offbeat Records (# 0-4016).

The cast of *Pieces-of-Eight* included Monk's usual suspects, with the addition of future Academy Award-winner Estelle Parsons. Two numbers, "Oriental" and "Clandestine," with lyrics by Martin Charnin and music by Bob Kessler, had been previously heard in *Fallout* (1959; see entry); "Clandestine" may have been added sometime during the run of *Pieces-of-Eight* since only "Oriental" is on the cast album.

"The Appian Way" (lyric and music by Bud McCreery) and "The Holy Man and the New Yorker" (lyric by Tom Jones, music by Harvey Schmidt) may also have been added after the opening (the latter had been previously heard in *Demi-Dozen* [1958; see entry]). For a complete list of Julius Monk's revues, see entry for *Four Below*; also see Appendix Q.

1262 Pigjazz

NOTES—See entry for *Pigjazz, II.*

1263 Pigjazz, II. THEATRE: Actors' Playhouse; OPENING DATE: November 16, 1981; PERFORMANCES: 30; SKETCHES, LYRICS, AND MUSIC: Gretchen Alan Aurthur, Glenn Kramer, Michael (James) Nee, and Stephen Pell; DIRECTION: Michael Nee; SCENERY: Dorian Vernacchio; COSTUMES: Muriel Stockdale; LIGHTING: Dorian Vernacchio; MUSICAL DIRECTION: Paul Sklar; PRODUCERS: Michael (James) Nee and Pigjazz Productions, Ltd.

CAST—Gretchen Alan Aurthur, Glenn Kramer, Michael (James) Nee, Stephen Pell; Paul Sklar, Piano

The revue was presented in two acts.

ACT ONE—*The Life:* Overture (Paul Sklar) "When You're Not the Same" (Company) "I Have No Name" (Gretchen Alan Aurthur) "Miya Sama Dinah Shore" (Gretchen Alan Authur), "The Hollywood Piece" (Company) "Did You Notice?" (Michael [James] Nee) "The POW-MIA Benefit Show" (Stephen Pell, Company), "The Street Act" (Company) "Phantom Affair" (Glenn Kramer) Pastiche of the First Pigjazz: "Don't Feed the Animals" (Glenn Kramer, Stephen Pell, Michael [James] Nee) "Gumby Gets a Nose" (Gretchen Alan Aurthur), "Pain(e)" (Michael [James] Nee) "Beetle Bailey, Won't You Please Come Home" (Company) "One-Faced Woman" (Stephen Pell) "An American Cripple Need Not Stand for the Star-Spangled Banner" (Glenn Kramer) "Yankle Deedan Doodah Rag" (Paul Sklar) "Chez Adams (The Washingtons Come Too)" (Company), "The 'E' Medley" (Company)

ACT TWO—*The Times:* "Love Is a Crazy Thing" (Michael [James] Nee, Company) "I Just Want to Be Happy" (Michael [James] Nee) "Yes, Yes, Yes" (Gretchen Alan Aurthur) "Bad Bar Bebop" (Company) "Job Hunting in Sodom" (Glenn Kramer) "It's the Loneliness, I Think" (Stephen Pell), "East Indian Love Call" (Michael [James] Nee, Company) "Too Hot to Handel" (Paul Sklar) "The Movie Guide to Love" (Stephen Pell, Company), "Cheatin'" (Gretchen Alan Aurthur), "One-Faced Woman Turns the Other Cheek"/"I Only Want the Best" (Stephen Pell), "Dead Bride-To-Be" (Glenn Kramer), "The L.I. Van Gogh Blue Period Gavotte" (Stephen Pell, Gretchen Alan Aurthur) "The 'Real' People's Party" (Company) "Foster Children" (Company), "'Thank God' Chorus Reprise" (Company)

NOTES—Yes, there was an earlier *Pigjazz*, and it opened on January 22, 1974, at the Nighthouse; described as a vaudeville, the first production was directed by Michael James Nee (as Michael Nee, he directed, co-wrote, co-starred, and co-directed the second production, *Pigjazz, II*), and the original cast of *Pigjazz* featured Bella Darvonne,, Danny Corcoran, Frodo Godeaux, and Ivory Snow. In case there were those who didn't remember the first production, *Pigjazz, II* helpfully included a medley of songs from the earlier revue.

1264 Pilgrim's Progress. "A Musical Drama." THEATRE: Gate Theatre; OPENING DATE: March 20, 1962; PERFORMANCES: 8; BOOK: Edwin Greenberg; LYRICS: Edwin Greenberg; MUSIC: Edwin Greenberg; DIRECTION: Ted Vermont; CHOREOGRAPHY: Graeme Carlton; SCENERY: Domingo A. Rodriguez; COSTUMES: Edward Myers; LIGHTING: Domingo A. Rodriguez; MUSICAL DIRECTION: Russ Case; musical conductor, Bob Hess; PRODUCER: Vincent (possibly Normen) Tourag

CAST—Francis Bernard (the Reverend Will), Michael Davis (Sir Paul), Stanley Sayer (Master Andrew), Don Gunderson (John Bunyan), Larry Hankin (The Seducer), Richard Marr (The Murderer), Frank Vohs (The Thief), Elliot Levine (The Drunkard), Felix Munso (The Idealist), Walter Blocher, Jr. (The Gaoler), Morrie Peirce (The Lord Mayor), Delmar Roos (Miss Carol)

The action occurs in an English dungeon.

The musical was presented in three acts (division of acts and song assignments unknown; songs are listed in performance order).

MUSICAL NUMBERS—"The Ballad of Bedford Gaol," "A B C," "Giza-on-the-Nile," "Blackest of Tresses," "Capital of the World" "Husband of Mine," "Take My Hand in Friendship," "The Voice of God," "What Do They Care?," "I'm Feeling Better All the Time," "Prisoner's Lullaby," "The Girls Who Sell Orangeade," "The Tomorrow Waltz," "My Daughter, My Angel," "Sing Out in the Streets"

Notes—*Pilgrim's Progress* was a one-week failure about a famous writer (John Bunyan) who is imprisoned. Three years later, a musical about another famous imprisoned writer (Miguel de Cervantes) would do much better.

Louis Calta in the *New York Times* called *Pilgrim's Progress* a "mish-mash," and noted that one lyric commented that "some in the audience wish they were prisoners, too"; Calta said the lyric "could not have been more gratuitous."

1265 Pimpernel! THEATRE: Gramercy Arts Theatre; OPENING DATE: January 7, 1964; PERFORMANCES: 3; BOOK: William Kaye; LYRICS: William Kaye; MUSIC: Mimi Stone; DIRECTION: Malcolm Black; CHOREOGRAPHY: Sandra Devlin; SCENERY: Lloyd Burlingame; COSTUMES: Sonia Lowenstein; LIGHTING: Lloyd Burlingame; MUSICAL DIRECTION: Robert Rogers; PRODUCERS: Gerald Krone and Dorothy Olim

CAST—Richard Marr (Jellyband, Comte de Tournay), Gelia Heinemann (Sally), Buff Shurr (Sir Anthony Dewhurst), John Cunningham (Sir Andrew Ffoulkes), Jane Lilig (Comtesse de Tournay, French Grandmother), Jeanne Devine (Suzanne Tournay), Dick Latessa (First Spy), Francis Dux (Second Spy), David Daniels (Sir Percy Blakeney), Leila Martin (Lady Marguerite Blakeney), John Canemaker (Armand St. Juste), William Larsen (Chauvelin), Budd Mann (Porteous), Stephen Pearlman (Brogarde), Joan Kenley (French Mother)

SOURCE—The 1905 novel *The Scarlet Pimpernel* by Baroness Emma (Emmuska) Orczy (the non de plume for Mrs. Montague Maclean Barstow, born Emma Magdalena Rosalia Maria Josefa Barbara Orczy).

The action occurs in England and France.

The musical was presented in two acts (song assignments unknown).

ACT ONE—"This Is England," "Dangerous Game," "A La Pimpernel," "Le Croissant," "Touch of Paris," "Everything's Just Divine," "A Woman," "Le Bon Mot," "As If I Weren't There"

ACT TWO—"Liberty, Equality & Fraternity," "Love of Long Ago," "What a Day for Me," "I'm Seeing Things," "Sing, Jacques, Sing," "I'm Seeing Things" (reprise), "Nose Ahead," "Touch of Paris" (reprise), Finale

NOTES—Lewis Funke in the *New York Times* observed that *Pimpernel!* was "schizoid" in its "disconcerting" tendency to mix both romantic and farcical elements in its adaptation of the famous novel. Funke noted that much of the evening dwelt on mock heroics, derring-do, and a buffoonish villain who actually winked at the audience when he was about to do something dastardly. On the other hand, the score was in the romantic tradition of *The Desert Song* (1926), including one unidentified number which sounded like Russian folk music.

The three-performance flop included many familiar names (David Daniels, John Cunningham, Leila Martin, Dick Latessa, and even Stephen Pearlman, who later appeared in the 1969 one-performance Broadway flop *La Strada* opposite Bernadette Peters). David Daniels is frequently mentioned in these pages, and he seems to have been in nothing but flops. But he was in one Broadway hit, *Plain and Fancy* (1955), in which he and Gloria Marlowe introduced the hit song "Young and Foolish."

Perhaps a successful musical of *The Scarlet Pimpernel* is not to be. Even the long-running (772 performances) version which opened on Broadway in 1997 lost money. Moreover, in the early 1970s another musical version (also called *Pimpernel*, with a book by Kerry Gardner and Liam Sullivan and lyrics by Liam Sullivan) was apparently written with Broadway in mind (Albert Hague was approached to compose the music), but the adaptation never got off the ground.

1266 Pinocchio. THEATRE: Bil Baird Theatre; OPENING DATE: December 15, 1973; PERFORMANCES: 134; PRODUCERS: The American Puppet Arts Council (Arthur Cantor, Executive Producer); a Bil Baird Marionette Production

CAST—Peter Baird (Alex; Harlequin; Policeman), Olga Felgemacher (Pinocchio), Jonathan E. Freeman (Mr. Fireball, Peirrot, Policeman, Mrs. Bluestone), Sean O'Malley (Cat; Numerous Fish), Bill Tost (Geppetto, Magistrate), and Byron Whiting (Fox, Carlos, Columbine). The singing voice of Mrs. Bluestone was Marcia Rodd, and the singing voice of Carlos was Robert Gorman.

NOTES—Based on the classic Italian fairy tale by Carlo Collodi, *Pinocchio* was a new addition to Bil Baird's repertory. The two-act puppet musical's book was by Jerome Coopersmith, the lyrics by Sheldon Harnick, and the music by Mary Rodgers. It was directed by Lee Theodore, the musical direction was by Alvy West, the scenery by Howard Mandel, and lighting by Peggy Clark.

The singing voice for Pinocchio was Margery Gray (Mrs. Sheldon Harnick, who memorably sang the word "shame" throughout the show-stopping "The Picture of Happiness" from *Tenderloin* [1960], with lyrics by Harnick). *Pinocchio*'s director Lee Theodore was another alumnus of *Tenderloin* (she was one of that musical's principal dancers.) Harnick and *Pinocchio*'s book writer Jerome Coopersmith had previously collaborated on *Baker Street* (1965 [Harnick and Jerry Bock had contributed a few songs to this production]) and *The Apple Tree* (1966).

Mel Gussow in the *New York Times* reported that the "ingenious" musical mixed both puppets and live actors in a fresh re-telling of the familiar story which included urban children, a social worker, and a Puerto-Rican cricket named Carlos. Gussow noted that Geppetto's workshop was full of talking and singing tools and that the score was "sprightly." The musical also offered some unusual visual angles; Geppetto was performed by an actor, but in "long-distance shots" a puppet was used. Further, Pinocchio was performed by a puppet, but, again, in those "long-distance shots," a smaller Pinocchio puppet was employed.

Bil Baird's Variety also accompanied the bill.

1267 Pins and Needles (1967). THEATRE: Roundabout Theatre; OPENING DATE: May 19, 1967; PERFORMANCES: 214; SKETCHES: Joseph Schrank; LYRICS: Harold Rome; MUSIC: Harold Rome; DIRECTION: Gene Feist; CHOREOGRAPHY: Larry Life; SCENERY: I. Milton Duke; COSTUMES: Costume supervision by Rose Fedorin Musical Direction: Mary Chaffee; PRODUCER: The Roundabout Theatre

CAST—Zaida Coles, Loretta Long, Ellen March, Susan Stevens, Elaine Tishler, Joe Abramski, Richard Allan, David Baker, John Byrd, Roger Lawson, Larry Life

The revue was presented in two acts (song assignments unknown).

ACT ONE—"Sing Me a Song of Social Significance," "Four Little Angels of Peace," "Chain Store Daisy," "(It's) Not Cricket to Picket," "I've Got the Nerve to Be in Love," "One Big Union for Two," "Bertha the Sewing Machine Girl," "What Good Is Love?," "Back to Work"

ACT TWO—"Sunday in the Park," "G-Man," "Status Quo," "I've Got the Nerve to Be in Love" (reprise), "Cream of Mush," "Nobody Makes a Pass at Me," "Doing the Revolutionary," "Mene Mene Tekel"

NOTES—The original 1937 production of *Pins and Needles* was a long-running hit, playing 1,108 performances; when it closed, it was the longest-running musical in Broadway history (a temporary record, because *Hellzapoppin'* [1938] was right around the corner with an eventual run of 1,404 performances). The 1,108 performance run is somewhat misleading because the revue played in two small theatres (the Princess and the Windsor). Compared to the larger theatres (the 46th Street [now Richard Rodgers] and the Winter Garden) where *Hellzapoppin'* played, the Princess was less than a quarter of their size and the Windsor about half. The left-wing revue was produced by the International Ladies' Garment Workers Union, and the cast was comprised of its members. During the run, the title was at times slightly altered (*New Pins and Needles*, for example) as the show underwent various "editions" (songs and sketches were deleted, added, or revised in order to keep up with current events).

The Roundabout revival was the first for the musical, and the production retained many of the revue's most fondly-remembered numbers. The revival played for over two-hundred performances, and a decade later Roundabout would produce another successful production of the revue (see entry).

In 1963, a studio cast recording of *Pins and Needles* was released by Columbia Records (LP # OS-2210; CD # CK-57380).

In 1966, an adaptation of the revue was telecast.

On February 26, 1976, songs from *Pins and Needles* were performed at Manhattan Theatre Club's Cabaret; the cast included Jonathan Hadary and Margery Cohen.

1268 Pins and Needles (1978). THEATRE: Roundabout Theatre/Stage One; OPENING DATE: May 30, 1978; PERFORMANCES: 225; SKETCHES: Arthur Arent, Marc Blitzstein, Emanuel Eisenberg, Charles Friedman, and David Gregory; LYRICS: Harold Rome; MUSIC: Harold Rome; DIRECTION: Milton Lyon; CHOREOGRAPHY: Haila Strauss; SCENERY: Scott Johnson; COSTUMES: Donna Meyer; LIGHTING: Scott Johnson; MUSICAL DIRECTION: Philip Campanella; PRODUCER: The Roundabout Theatre Company (Gene Feist and Michael Fried, Producing Directors)

CAST—Phyllis Bash, Trudy Bayne, David Berman, Richard Casper, Daniel (Danny) Fortus, Randy Graff, Robin Hoff, Tom Offt, Dennis Perren, Elaine Petricoff

The revue was presented in two acts.

ACT ONE—"Sing Me a Song of Social Significance" (Company), "It's Not Cricket to Picket" (Elaine Petricoff), "I've Got the Nerve to Be in Love" (Trudy Bayne, David Berman), "Call It Un-American" (Richard Casper, Tom Offt, Daniel Fortus), "Papa Don't Love Mama Anymore" (Randy Graff, Robin Hoff, David Berman, William Green, Dennis Perren), "Room for One" (Elaine Petricoff), "Sunday in the Park" (David Berman, Randy Graff, Tom Offt, Robin Hoff, Dennis Perren, Phyllis Bash, Richard Casper, Trudy Bayne, Elaine Petricoff, Daniel Fortus), "I'm Just Nuts About You" (Trudy Bayne, Daniel Fortus), "What Good Is Love" (Phyllis Bash), "Doing the Reactionary" (Randy Graff, Richard Casper, Robin Hoff, Tom Offt, Trudy Bayne), "Chain Store Daisy" (Randy Graff), "Back to Work" (Company)

ACT TWO—"It's Better with a Union Man" (Dennis Perren, Elaine Petricoff, David Berman, Tom Offt), "When I Grow Up (I Wanna Be a G-Man)" (a/k/a "The G-Man Song") (Daniel Fortus), "F.D.R. Jones" (Dennis Perren, Phyllis Bash, Company), "Nobody Makes a Pass at Me" (Elaine Petricoff), "One Big Union for Two" (Trudy Bayne, Richard Casper), "Mene, Mene, Tekel" (Phyllis Bash, David Berman, Randy Graff, Robin Hoff, Tom Offt, Dennis Perren), "We're the Ads" (Daniel Fortus, Richard Casper), "Status Quo" (Dennis Perren, Richard Casper, Tom Offt, Robin Hoff, Trudy Bayne), "We Sing America" (Dennis Perren, Company)

NOTES—In 1967, the Roundabout had presented a long-running revival of Harold Rome's left-wing revue *Pins and Needles* (for more information about the revival as well as the original 1937 production, see entry). The 1978 revival bested the 1967 production, running a week longer.

The 1937 production went through various editions, and in order to keep the revue's topics timely, new material was constantly added to the show. Both Roundabout revivals were highlights from the various editions of the original production.

The 1978 revival interpolated "F.D.R. Jones," which had originally been heard in Rome's 1938 Broadway revue *Sing Out the News*.

1269 The Pipe of Desire. THEATRE: Metropolitan Opera House; OPENING DATE: March 18, 1910; PERFORMANCES: 3; LIBRETTO: George E. Barton; MUSIC: Frederick S. Converse; DIRECTION: Kurt Stern; MUSICAL DIRECTION: Alfred Hertz; PRODUCER: The Metropolitan Opera

CAST—Louise Homer (Naoia), Riccardo Martin (Iolan), Clarence Whitehill (Old One), Lenora Sparkes (Sylph), Lillia Snelling (Undine), Glenn Hall (Salamander), Herbert Witherspood (Gnome)

The opera was presented in one act.

NOTES—*The Pipe of Desire* was not a world premiere production for the Met (the opera had been first seen in Boston in 1906), but it holds two distinctions: it was the first time an opera by an American composer had been produced at the Met and it was the first time an opera had been performed there in English.

The plot seems to have centered on a groom who defies convention by gazing upon his bride the day before their wedding (a natural thing to do, just like playing a pipe [or flute] is natural); but his folly leads to tragedy. An unsigned reviewer for the *New York Times* noted that this seemingly small transgression shouldn't necessarily bring on disaster and destruction. Perhaps the piece was too symbolic for its own good; further, the reviewer felt the libretto was confused and failed to kindle any interest on the viewer's part ("a great dearth of action upon the stage of any dramatic sort"), but he nonetheless praised Converse's music ("poetical and often beautiful ... it has dramatic force and suggestion"). The reviewer also noted that despite being sung in English, the performers had "little success in making their words understood ... [often] little or nothing of the text was intelligible." (This became a standard complaint which to this day haunts virtually all operas performed in English.)

The Pipe of Desire (which was presented on a double bill with Ruggiero Leoncavallo's *Pagliacci* [1892]) seems to have disappeared after its three performances at the Met.

1270 The Pirates of Penzance, or The Slave of Duty. THEATRE: Delacorte Theatre/The Public Theatre; OPENING DATE: August 5, 1980; PERFORMANCES: 30; BOOK: W.S. Gilbert; LYRICS: W.S. Gilbert; MUSIC: Arthur Sullivan; DIRECTION: Wilford Leach; CHOREOGRAPHY: Graciela Daniele; SCENERY: Bob Shaw, Jack Chandler, and Wilford Leach; COSTUMES: Patricia McGourty; LIGHTING: Jennifer Tipton; MUSICAL DIRECTION: William Elliott; PRODUCER: The New York Shakespeare Festival (Joseph Papp, Producer)

CAST—Kevin Kline (The Pirate King), Stephen Hanan (Samuel), Rex Smith (Frederic), Patricia Routledge (Ruth); Major-General Stanley's Daughters (Robin Boudreau, Maria Guida, Nancy Heikin, Bonnie Simmons); Alexandra Korey (Edith), Marcie Shaw (Kate), Wendy Wolfe (Isabel), Linda Ronstadt (Mabel), George Rose (Major-General Stanley), Tony Azito (The Sergeant); Pirates and Police (Dean Badolato, Mark Beudert, Brian Bullard, Walter Caldwell, Keith David, Tim Flavin, G. Eugene Moore, Joseph Neal, Walter Niehenke, Joe Pichette, Barry Tarallo, Michael Edwin Willson)

The musical was presented in two acts.

ACT ONE—"Pour, O Pour the Pirate Sherry" (Kevin Kline, Stephen Hanan, Rex Smith, Pirates), "When Frederic Was a Little Lad" (Patricia Routledge), "Oh, Better Far to Live and Die" (Kevin Kline, Pirates), "Oh, False One, You Have Deceived Me!" (Patricia Routledge, Rex Smith), "Climbing Over Rocky Mountain" (Daughters), "Stop, Ladies, Pray!" (Rex Smith, Daughters), "Oh, Is There Not One Maiden Breast" (Rex Smith, Daughters), "Poor Wandering One" (Linda Ronstadt, Daughters), "What Ought We to Do?" (Marcie Shaw, Wendy Wolfe, Daughters), "How Beautifully Blue the Sky" (Linda Ronstadt, Rex Smith, Daughters), "Stay, We Must Not Lose Our Senses" (Rex Smith, Daughters, Pirates), "Hold, Monsters!" (Linda Ronstadt, Stephen Hanan, George Rose, Daughters, Pirates), "I Am the Very Model of a Modern Major-General" (George Rose, Ensemble), "Oh, Men of Dark and Dismal Fate" (Ensemble)

ACT TWO—"Oh, Dry the Glistening Tear" (Linda Ronstadt, Daughters), "Then Frederic" (George Rose, Rex Smith), "When the Foeman Bares His Steel" (Tony Azito, Linda Ronstadt, Police, Daughters), "Now for the Pirates' Lair!" (Rex Smith, Kevin Kline, Patricia Routledge), "When You Had Left Our Pirate Fold" (Patricia Routledge, Rex Smith, Kevin Kline), "My Eyes Are Fully Open" (Rex Smith, Patricia Routledge, Kevin Kline), "Away, Away! (My Heart's On Fire)" (Patricia Routledge, Kevin Kline, Rex Smith), "All Is Prepared" (Patricia Routledge, Rex Smith), "Stay, Frederic, Stay!" (Linda

Ronstadt, Rex Evans), "Sorry Her Lot" (Linda Ronstadt), "No, I Am Brave" (Linda Ronstadt, Tony Azito, Police), "When a Felon's Not Engaged in His Employment" (Tony Azito, Police), "A Rollicking Band of Pirates We" (Pirates, Tony Azito, Police), "With Cat-Like Tread, Upon Our Prey We Steal" (Pirates, Police, Stephen Hanan), "Hush, Hush! Not a Word" (Rex Smith, Pirates, Police, George Rose), "Sighing Softly to the River" (George Rose, Ensemble), Finale (Ensemble)

NOTES—This successful summer revival of *The Pirates of Penzance* soon transferred to Broadway, where it opened at the Uris (later Gershwin) Theatre on January 8, 1981, and played for 772 performances, a New York record for a Gilbert and Sullivan operetta. Most of the Delacorte cast transferred to Broadway, with the major exception of Patricia Routledge, who was replaced by Estelle Parsons in the role of Ruth. Two songs were interpolated into the revival: "My Eyes Are Fully Open" (from *Ruddigore*, 1887) and "Sorry Her Lot" (*H.M.S. Pinafore*, 1878).

The Broadway production was recorded on a 2-LP set by Elektra Records (VE-601), and the musical was filmed in 1983 by Universal with most of the original Broadway principals (for the film, Angela Lansbury portrayed Ruth).

The Pirates of Penzance was the only Gilbert and Sullivan operetta to have its world premiere in the United States. The musical was produced on December 31, 1879, at the Fifth Avenue Theatre, where it played for slightly more than three months (a successful run for the era).

1271 Platforms

NOTES—See entry for *The New York Musical Theatre Festival.*

1272 Play That on Your Old Piano.

"A Comedy." THEATRE: Renata Theatre; OPENING DATE: October 14, 1965; PERFORMANCES: 2; PLAY: Dan Blue; DIRECTION: John Gerstad; CHOREOGRAPHIC CONSULTANT: Joan Gainer; SCENERY: William Rittman; COSTUMES: Noel Taylor; LIGHTING: Roger Johnson; PRODUCERS: Gilbert Bledsoe and Maxwell Silverman

CAST—Parker McCormick (Myra Scott), Dennis Scott (Henry Scott), Martin Rudy (Calvin Scott), Richard Barrie (Neil Scott), Alfred Dennis (Mike Figaro), Gaylord C. Mason (Al Wind), Sylvia Miles (Molly Wind), Sy Travers (Julian Heifetz), Viola Swayne (Mary Melody), Harold Herman (Mr. Glick)

The action occurs in September 1934 in Chicago.

The play was presented in three acts.

NOTES—Gone after just two performances, *Play That on Your Old Piano* was a comedy with incidental songs, including a title song by Eddy Chalfin and Mike Hoberman and "The Sidewalk Piano Rag" (and other incidental music) by Gaylord C. Mason.

Lewis Funke in the *New York Times* reported that the self-described comedy dealt with a family coping with the death of a son, a promising musician. Through machinations by the son's two younger brothers, the mother comes to believe that her son's ghost is orchestrating the family's destiny (which apparently includes the desire of one of the remaining sons to appear on Major Bowes' radio program). "Some fun," noted Funke about the plot. He also said the evening's only "bright" spot was the knowledge that the curtain would eventually come down so he could "get out" of the theatre.

1273 The Playoffs of Mixed Doubles.

"A Revue." THEATRE: Downstairs at the Upstairs; OPENING DATE: Unknown (possibly during the latter half of the 1966-1967 theatre season); PERFORMANCES: Unknown; SKETCHES: Sid Davis, Michael McWhinney, Treva Silverman, and Rod Warren; LYRICS: Linda Ashton, Gene Bissell, David Finkle, Irma Jurist, Michael McWhinney, Robert Milrad, Tom Pasle, James Rusk, and Rod Warren Music: Gene Bissell, Michael Cohen, Irma Jurist, Robert Milrad, Lance Mulcahy, Tom Pasle, James Rusk, Rod Warren, and Bill Weeden; DIRECTION: Rod Warren; CHOREOGRAPHY: Janie Sell; MUSICAL DIRECTION: Daniel Strickland; PRODUCER: Rod Warren

CAST—Gary Crabbe, Judy Graubart, Madeline Kahn, Larry Moss, Janie Sell

The revue was presented in two acts.

ACT ONE—"Playoffs Opening" (lyric by Rod Warren, music by Robert Milrad and Rod Warren) (Company) "New York Is a Festival of Fun" (lyric and music by Gene Bissell) (Madeline Kahn, Janie Sell, Gary Crabbe, Larry Moss) "The Defection" (sketch by Rod Warren) (Judy Graubart, Gary Crabbe) "Mixed Marriages" (lyric by David Finkle, music by Bill Weeden) (Janie Sell, Larry Moss) "The Golden Age of Smut" (lyric by Michael McWhinney, music by Lance Mulcahy) (Gary Crabbe) "Camp" (lyric and music by Rod Warren; choreography by Sandra Devlin) (Judy Graubart, Madeline Kahn, Janie Sell) "Semper, Semper" (lyric and music by Robert Milrad) (Gary Crabbe, Larry Moss), "Fashion Show" (sketch by Sid Davis) (Madeline Kahn, Larry Moss) "I Like the Job" (lyric by Linda Ashton, music by Michael Cohen) (Judy Graubart) "And a Messenger Appeared" (lyric and music by Gene Bissell) (Madeline Kahn, Company)

ACT TWO—"The Great Society Waltz" (lyric and music by Rod Warren) (Company) "Token Gesture" (lyric and music by Tom Pasle) (Larry Moss) "American Civil Liberties Union" (sketch by Michael McWhinney) (Janie Sell, Gary Crabbe) "Holden and Phoebe" (lyric by Michael McWhinney, music by Michael Cohen) (Judy Graubart, Larry Moss), "Miss Versatility" (lyric and music by James Rusk) (Janie Sell ["and her escorts"]) "Shambles" (lyric and music by Irma Jurist) (Madeline Kahn), "The Envelope, Please" (sketch by Treva Silverman and 'Déjà Vu') (Company) Finale: "Mr. Wanamaker's Home" (lyric by Michael McWhinney and Rod Warren, music by Rod Warren) (Company)

NOTES—While *Mixed Doubles* (1967; see entry) continued to play Upstairs, *The Playoffs of Mixed Doubles*, which opened Downstairs, was a second edition of sorts as well as a retrospective revue, and included numbers from earlier revues as well as a few new ones. Numbers in *Playoffs* which had first been heard in *Mixed Doubles* were "New York Is a Festival of Fun," "Mixed Marriages," "Fashion Show," "And a Messenger Appeared," and "Holden and Phoebe."

"The Great Society Waltz" was from the second edition of *The Game Is Up* (see entry), and also appeared in *Below the Belt* (see entry). "Camp" and "I Like the Job" first appeared in the third edition of *The Game Is Up* (see entry), and the former was also heard in *Below the Belt.* "Mr. Wanamaker's Home" and "The Envelope, Please" were from *...And in This Corner* (see entry) and the latter was also heard in *Below the Belt.* New to this edition were "The Defection," "The Golden Age of Smut," "Semper, Semper," "Token Gesture," "American Civil Liberties Union," and "Miss Versatility."

For a complete list of Rod Warren's revues, see entry for *...And in This Corner*; also see Appendix R.

1274 The Plot Against the Chase Manhattan Bank.

THEATRE: Theatre East; OPENING DATE: November 26, 1963; PERFORMANCES: 15; SKETCHES: Carl Larsen, David Dozer, Ernest Leongrande, Lawrence B. Eisenberg, and Betty Freedman; LYRICS: Frank Spiering, Jr.; MUSIC: Richard R. Wolf; DIRECTION: Tom Gruenwald; CHOREOGRAPHY: Karen Kristin, Bick Goss; SCENERY: Robert T. Williams; COSTUMES: Sylvia Kalegi; MUSICAL DIRECTION: Joe Bousard; PRODUCER: Eaton Associates

CAST—Renee Gorsey, Fred Jackson, Doyle Newberry, Liz Otto, Joan Shepard, Brian Watson

The revue was presented in two acts (sketch and song assignments unknown).

ACT ONE—"Let the Play Begin," "Goat Play," "There's Nothing Left to Give Away," "Our Little Family," "Freedom Riders," "Reach Out and Touch Her," "The Director," "Only Fool," "The Plot Against the Chase Manhattan Bank," "The Hour Is Ripe," "The Seal"

ACT TWO—"He She We," "No Exit," "Pamplona," "The Clocks," "The Three Horsemen of the Metropolis," "Only Two Allowed," "Josephine," "Thoughts by a River," "Almost Real," "The Closing"

NOTES—The revue *The Plot Against the Chase Manhattan Bank* ran for less than two weeks. Louis Calta in the *New York Times* found the material flat and glum, if not downright bizarre (one confusing sketch dealt with an *extremely* dysfunctional family in which a man is murdered by his mother and sister while his father takes home movies of the event). Another sketch dealt with an expectant mother and her husband, both of whom are hoping that the blessed event will result in a baby goat.

Calta singled out "Almost Real" as "a good romantic number"; it was a duet between two store mannequins (perhaps they were first cousins to the characters in Stephen Sondheim's 1966 *Twilight Zone*-like television musical *Evening Primrose*, which also dealt with department-store mannequins).

1275 The Polish Mime Theatre.

THEATRE: Beacon Theatre; OPENING DATE: February 23, 1976; PERFORMANCES: 5; ADAPTATION: Henryk Tomaszewski; MUSIC: Zbigniew Karnecki; DIRECTION: Henryk Tomaszewski; Jerzy Koztowski, Assistant Director; CHOREOGRAPHY: Henryk Tomaszewski; SCENERY: Kasimierz Wisniak; COSTUMES: Wladyslaw Wigura; LIGHTING: Kazimierz Doniec; MUSICAL DIRECTION: Mieczyslaw Gawronski; PRODUCER: Kazuko Hillyer

CAST—Danuta Kisiel Drzewinska (Empress Phylissa), Ewa Czekalska (Major Domo), Anatol Krupa (Page), Janusz Pieczuro (Marquis, Arranger), Jerry Reterski (Ludovica, Illusionist), Jerzy Stepniak (Napoleon the Greater, Stunt Man), Jerzy Koztowski (Max-Pipifax, Juggler), Marek Olesky (Mr. Adison, Tamer), Czeslaw Bielski (Dark-Skinned), Ryszard Staw (Rappo Eugene, Athlete), Elzbieta Orlow (Molly), Zygmunt Rozlach (Hidalla, Hypnotist), Krzysztof Szwaja (Medium), Feliks Kudakiewicz (Black Angel, Motorcyclist), Wojciech Hankiewicz (White Angel, Guitarist), Zbigniew Zukowski (Court Physician); Grayzyna Bielawska (Maid of Honor), Urszula Hosiej (Maid of Honor), Julian Hasiej (Courtier), Marek Olesky (Courtier), Zbigniew Papis (Courtier), Zygmunt Rozlach (Courtier); Members of Ludovico's Company: Wojciech Hankiewicz, Wojciech Misiuro, Feliks Kudakiewicz, and Krzysztof Szwaja; Members of Napoleon's Company: Andrzej Musiat and Zbigniew Zukowski; Hidalla's Company: Julian Hasiej and Jerzy Stepniak

NOTES—Although the evening was generically titled *The Polish Mime Theatre*, the visiting production from Poland was actually based on Frank Wedekind's fairy tale "Die Kaiserin von Neu Funland" ("The Menagerie of the Empress Phylissa"). Clive Barnes in the *New York Times* reported that the 95-minute story was told in mime and dance and went "from worse to disaster." The story had something to do with a princess who apparently must defeat all suitors who pursue her, and Barnes felt the evening was a "parade of outmoded sexist attitudes" which were offered with "indifferent and even smudgy clarity." For another musical based on a work by Wedekind, see entry for *Spring Awakening.*

1276 A Political Party. THEATRE: 41st Street Theatre; OPENING DATE: September 26, 1963 Performances: 8; SKETCHES: Jean Anne and C.D. Bryan; LYRICS: Jean Anne, Shirley Grossman, Pierce Rollins, Daniel Ruslander, and Gwen Gibson Schwartz; MUSIC: Shirley Grossman, Herschel Horowitz, Tony Mataresse, Kurt Moss, Sidney Schwartz, and Bob Vigoda; DIRECTION: Arch Lustberg; CHOREOGRAPHY: Gloria Contreras, Penelope Hunter; COSTUMES: Jean Anne; MUSICAL DIRECTION: Daniel Ruslander; PRODUCER: Arch Lustberg

CAST—Jean Anne, Bill Holter, Arch Lustberg, Daniel Ruslander

The revue was presented in two acts (sketch and song assignments unknown).

ACT ONE—"Washington Is Your Home" (lyric by Daniel Ruslander, music by Kurt Moss), "A Tour of Washington," "PEnnslyvania 1600" (lyric by Gwen Gibson Schwartz, music by Sidney Schwartz), "An Office in the White House," "Where the Mona Lisa Was Hung," "An Important Announcement," "This Is the Premier," "A Rilly Great Shew" (lyric by Pierce Rollins, music by Herschel Horowitz), "Under Secretary" (lyric and music by Shirley Grossman), "Rent-a-crowd," "Mississippi U," "Where Is the News?" (lyric by Pierce Rollins, music by Herschel Horowitz), "Project Moon Shot," "News Flash," "The Culture Twist" (lyric by Gwen Gibson Schwartz, music by Sidney Schwartz), "Thy Neighbor and Thy Shelter" (lyric and music by Shirley Grossman), "Youth Speaks Out," "The Medicare Rock" (lyric and music by Shirley Grossman), "The Rocky Road to the White House" (lyric and music by Shirley Grossman), "Little Black Tshombe," "Hootenanny with Peter, Paul and Irving" (lyric by Jean Anne, music by Bob Vigoda)

ACT TWO—"Filibuster" (lyric by Jean Anne, music by Tony Matraresse), "Cocktail Party Types" (lyric by Jean Anne, music by Tony Matarese), "The Ins and the Outs" (lyric by Jean Anne, music by Bob Vigoda), "Friendship for Dulles," "The Red Visitors" (lyric and music by Shirley Grossman), "Lady Bird Fly Away Home," "*V*ery *I*nfluential *P*oliticos" (lyric by Jean Anne, music by Bob Vigoda), "News Flash," "Father, Dear Father, Stop Testing" (lyric and music by Shirley Grossman), "Cuba Si Yanqui No" (lyric by Jean Anne, music by Bob Vigoda), "Minorities Is No Damn Good" (lyric and music by Shirley Grossman), "The Ballad of Federal City" (lyric by Jean Anne, music by Bob Vigoda), "Avant Garbage," "A Tour of the World," "The Church of Birch" (lyric by Jean Anne, music by Bob Vigoda), "Exuent Omnes"

NOTES—This short-lived political revue offered topics which are still timely ("Filibuster" and "The Medicare Rock"), but some of the material appears to have been a bit too obvious ("Minorities Is No Damn Good"). And, of course, the revue spoofed the Kennedys and Khrushchev.

A Political Party had originated in Washington, D.C., and Lewis Funke in the *New York Times* felt much of the revue's humor probably played better in the nation's capitol where the "members of the tribe" could enjoy "in" references to topics which were tantamount to a "family joke."

1277 Political Theatre Songs. THEATRE: Judson Poets' Theatre; OPENING DATE: July 29, 1976; PERFORMANCES: Unknown; LYRICS: Al Carmines; MUSIC: Al Carmines

CAST—Essie Borden, Lee Guilliatt, Lou Bullock, Margaret Wright

NOTES—With the 1976 presidential election some three months away, Al Carmines' Off Off Broadway revue *Political Theatre Songs* was a timely one.

1278 Polly (1925). THEATRE: Cherry Lane Theatre; OPENING DATE: October 10, 1925; PERFORMANCES: Unknown; BOOK: John Gay; LYRICS: John Gay; MUSIC: "From Old English Airs"; DIRECTION: Gordon Davis and William Rainey; SCENERY: William Mullen

CAST—Edmund Forde (Ducat), William Rainey (Morano Macheath), Richard Abbott (Vanderbluff), Pirates (Orda Creighton, Michael Kilborn, William Burke, Oscar Amundeen), David d'Arcy (Chief Pohetohee), Charles Trout (Cawwawkee), William Broderick (First Footman), Marion Cowen (Second Footman), Dorothy Brown (Polly), Maude Allan (Mrs. Ducat), Jeanne Owen (Diana Trapes), Geneva Harrison (Jenny Diver), Women of Jamaica (Eunice Osborne, Kathryn Mulholland, Zoe Barry, Grace Searles, Margot Andre, Helen White)

The opera was presented in three acts.

NOTES—*Polly*, John Gay's sequel to *The Beggar's Opera* (see entry), was written in 1729; but because the work was political in nature (with some of its satire aimed at Prime Minister Horace Walpole), the work wasn't produced until forty-five years after Gay's death. The first London performance took place on June 19, 1777, at the Haymarket Theatre. The 1925 production at the Cherry Lane marked the work's New York premiere.

In the sequel, Macheath, Polly, and friends are now living in the West Indies; Macheath is a pirate, and Polly a prostitute.

The *New York Times* gave the production a rave, noting that "the Pirates scored a 'homer' ... without censors or Senators to say them nay." The anonymous reviewer wrote that "melody flowed ... like a rare wine of authentic vintage flavor" and of the musical's forty songs, the audience demanded encores of "Who'll Sing Me an Air," "Honor Calls Me from Her Charms," "If Husbands Sit Unsteady," "Virtue's Treasure," "Madam, Alas! I Am Wholly Undone," "Laugh, Boys, Laugh," "Sleep, O Sleep," "Wait Until You Spy the Charmer," "When Horns Proclaim," and "These Twain Linked Forever."

The *Times* noted that in keeping with the atmosphere and the era of *Polly*, the Cherry Lane Theatre dispensed with cubist drawings on its walls and instead opted for candles ("courtesy of Mr. Edison"). In 1975, the Chelsea Theatre Center of Brooklyn revived *Polly* for thirty-two performances (Stephen D. Newman was Macheath, Betsy Beard was Polly, and Patricia Elliott was Jenny Diver; the score was "newly realized" by Mel Marvin); see entry for the production.

1279 Polly (1975). THEATRE: Brooklyn Academy of Music; OPENING DATE: April 29, 1975; PERFORMANCES: 32; TEXT: John Gay; "freely adapted" by Robert Kalfin; MUSIC: Popular music of the 1700s; score "newly realized" by Mel Marvin; DIRECTION: Robert Kalfin; CHOREOGRAPHY: Elizabeth Keen; SCENERY: Robert U. Taylor; COSTUMES: Carrie F. Robbins; LIGHTING: William Mintzer; MUSICAL DIRECTION: Clay Fullum; PRODUCER: The Chelsea Theatre Center of Brooklyn (Robert Kalfin, Artistic Director; Michael David, Executive Director; Burl Hash, Productions Director)

CAST—Stephen D. Newman (Poet, Morano [alias Macheath]), Roy Brocksmith (First Player, Old Woman Cook, LaGuerre), Alexander Orfaly (Second Player, Culverin), Prudence Wright Holmes (Third Player, Flimzy, Old Woman Maid, Indian Wife), Patricia Elliott (Signora Crochetta, Jenny Diver), John Long (Fourth Player, Capstern, Indian), Lucille Patton (Diana Trapes), Edward Zang (Mr. Ducat), Betsy Beard (Polly Peachum), Mary Ellen Ashley (Damaris, Indian Wife), Fran Stevens (Mrs. Ducat), Ruff Ruff (Reginald), Igors Gavon (First Footman, Vanderbluff), Brent Mintz (Second Footman, Dagger, Indian), Robert Manzari (Messenger Indian), George F. Maguire (Hacker), Brian James (Cutlace, Indian), Richard Ryder (Cawwawkee), William J. Coppola (Pohetohee) The action occurs in the West Indies.

The opera was presented in three acts (the program didn't include a list of musical numbers).

NOTES—*Polly*, John Gay's sequel to *The Beggar's Opera*, was written in 1729, but because of the political nature of the work it wasn't produced during his lifetime. The London premiere finally took place in 1777, forty-five years after Gay's death. The work was first performed in New York in 1925 (see entry), and it wasn't until the current 1975 revival that the musical was again seen by New York audiences. The Chelsea Theatre Center of Brooklyn had previously revived *The Beggar's Opera* in 1972 (see entry), and that production later transferred to Manhattan for an extended run.

1280 Pomegranada. "An Operatic Camp." THEATRE: Judson Poets' Theatre; OPENING DATE: March 4, 1966; PERFORMANCES: Unknown; LIBRETTO: H.M. Koutoukas; MUSIC: Alvin (Al) Carmines; DIRECTION: H.M. Koutoukas; MUSICAL DIRECTION: Alvin Carmines; PRODUCER: Sanford L. Smith

CAST—Michael Elias (Unicorn, Adam), Burton Supree (Butterfly), Margaret Wright (Pomegranate), David Vaughan (Peacock), Julie Kurnitz (Eve), Alvin Carmines (Celestial Voice); Flowers (Julie Kurnitz, Meredith Monk, Sandy Padilla)

NOTES—The opera *Pomegranada* occurs on the day after Adam and Eve were banished from the Garden of Eden. Annoyed with Eve, Adam throws away her mirror, which is later found by three inhabitants of Pomegranada, a magic land just outside the Garden of Eden. When Pomegranate, Butterfly, and Peacock see themselves in the mirror, they fall in love with their images and battle over possession of the mirror. Ultimately, the three realize their narcissistic obsessions were sinful, and, like Adam and Eve, they, too, are punished: Butterfly will know only one brief day of enjoying flowers, Peacock will be doomed to eternal preening, and Pomegranate will know only "bitter-beauty."

The Off Off Broadway production was recorded by Patsan Records (LP # PS-1101).

1281 Pomp Duck and Circumstance. THEATRE: Salon Zazou; OPENING DATE: October 11, 1995; PERFORMANCES: 147; CREATED BY Hans-Peter Wodarz; ARTISTIC DIRECTION: Michel Dallaire; Stephane Laisne, Assistant Director; CHOREOGRAPHY: Ross Coleman; COSTUMES: Dea Valmonte, Max Dietrich, Jurgen Blume, and Nameck Gaud; LIGHTING: Jason Kantrowitz; MUSICAL DIRECTION: Rudi Mauser; PRODUCER: MGM Grand (Dieter Esch, Producer)

CAST—"Restaurant Staff" (Performers)—Denis H. Jaquillard (Ferdinand de Belair [Restaurateur]), Jean Michel Coll (Maurice Fatale [Head Chef]), Lutz Joe (Herr Lutz [Waiter]), Francine Leonard (Miss Linda), Matthias Krahnert (Matthias [Waiter]), Eduard Kaufmann (Gusti [Wine Steward]), Hassan Celik (Hassan [Waiter]), Franziska Traub (Rosa [Chamber Maid]), Nathalie Tarlet (Juliette [Waitress]), Arnd D. Schimkat [Waiter Trainee]); Acrobats and Other Performers—Timothy Tyler (Mr. P.P. [Restaurant Host]), Corey Shank (Sophie Clutch [Waitress]), Mark C. Colli (Conc [Waiter]), Ramon Saez (Ramon [Bartender, Magic Man]), Danielle Trepanier (Pierette [Waitress]), Tim Ward (Ben Johnson [Journalist]), Sabine Hettlich (Jessica); Other Performers—Les Barons Karamazoff (Sergej Karamazoff, Zoran Madzirov, Martin Gjakonovski), The Daidalos Brothers, Boxers (Christian Mrozek, Ronald Siegmund), The Chair Man (Vassili Dementchoukov), Mouvance—Carmen on the Trapeze (Helene Turcotte, Luc Martin)

NOTES—*Pomp Duck and Circumstance* offered up an unusual Off Broadway dish: an elaborate revue which combined elements of the traditional musical revue and the circus plus cast members who performed the roles of a restaurant staff. And there was a real restaurant staff as well, which prepared a gourmet dinner for the audience members. Jeffrey Sweet in *The Best Plays of 1995-1996* praised the "beguiling" revue, which he dubbed a "restaurantical." Further, while he laid no claim to being a food critic, he noted he "would have happily indulged in seconds had they been available."

Pomp Duck and Circumstance played almost six months, and then according to Sweet it moved on to Las Vegas where it was scheduled to take up long-term residence.

In 2004, another "restaurantical" opened; see entry for *Chef's Theatre: A Musical Feast.*

1282 Poor Little Lambs. THEATRE: The Common/The Theatre at St. Peter's Church; OPENING DATE: March 14, 1982; PERFORMANCES: 73; PLAY: Paul Rudnick; DIRECTION: Jack Hofsiss; SCENERY: David Jenkins; COSTUMES: William Ivey Long; LIGHTING: Beverly Emmons; PRODUCER: Raymond Crinkley

CAST—Bronson Pinchot (Stu Arnstine), Albert Macklin (Ricky Hocheiser), David Naughton (Davey Waldman), Kevin Bacon (Frank Wozniak), Miles Chapin (Jack Bayliss Hayes), William Thomas, Jr. (Ike Ennis), Gedde Watanabe (Itsu Yoshiro), Page Moseley (Drew Waterman Reed), Blanche Baker (Claire Hazard)

The action occurs during the current academic year at Yale University, New Haven, Connecticut.

The play was presented in two acts.

ACT ONE—"Mother of Man" (lyric and music by Brian Hooker and Seth Bingham), "When My Sugar Walks Down the Street" (lyric and music by Gene Austin and Jimmy McHugh), "I Married an Angel" (from *I Married an Angel*, 1938; lyric by Lorenz Hart, music by Richard Rodgers), "Bright College Years" (lyric and music by H.S. Durand and Carl Wilhelm), "Love for Sale" (*The New Yorkers*, 1930; lyric and music by Cole Porter), "Undertaker" (traditional), "Boola" (lyric and music by Allan M. Hirsch), "Bingo (Bingo Eli Yale)" (Yale football song, 1910; lyric and music by Cole Porter), "Good Night, Poor Harvard" (lyric and music by Douglas S. Moore)

ACT TWO—"Down the Field" (lyric and music by C.W. O'Connor and Stanleigh P. Friedman), "Bull Dog" (Yale football song, 1911; lyric and music by Cole Porter), "We're Saving Ourselves for Yale" (lyric and music by David M. Lippincott), "When the Summer Moon Comes 'Long" (lyric and music by Cole Porter), "You'll Have to Put a Nightie on Aphrodite" (lyric and music by Walter Donaldson, Samuel [Sam] Lewis, and Joseph Young), "Love Never Went to College" (*Too Many Girls*, 1939; lyric by Lorenz Hart, music by Richard Rodgers), "The Whiffenpoof Song" (lyric by Meade Minnegerode and George S. Pomeroy [adapted from a verse by Rudyard Kipling], music attributed to Tod B. Galloway)

NOTES—The play with music *Poor Little Lambs* was about a female student who attempts to join the all-male Whiffenpoof singing group at Yale. The cast included up-and-coming actor Kevin Bacon, whose breakthrough film *Diner* was just about to be released, and whose immortality was assured a few years later with the six-degrees-of-separation game about him.

The Whiffenpoofs were founded in 1908; their name comes from a description of a fantasy fish in Victor Herbert's operetta *Little Nemo* (1908).

According to *The Complete Lyrics of Cole Porter*, "When the Summer Moon Comes 'Long" (a/k/a "Under the Summer Moon") is one of the two oldest surviving songs by Porter; it appears to have been written during his freshman year at Yale (1909-1910).

1283 Pop. THEATRE: Players Theatre; OPENING DATE: April 3, 1974; PERFORMANCES: 1; BOOK: Larry Schiff and Chuck Knull; LYRICS: Larry Schiff and Chuck Knull; MUSIC: Donna Cribari; ADDITIONAL MUSIC: Larry Schiff; DIRECTION: Allen R. Belknap; CHOREOGRAPHY: Ron Spencer; SCENERY: Pat Gorman; COSTUMES: Pat Gorman; LIGHTING: Hallam B. Derx; MUSICAL DIRECTION: Donna Cribari; PRODUCERS: Brad Gromelski in association with William Murphy III

CAST—Frank W. Kopyc (Learsenpower, King of Hio), Anna Gianiotis (Gonerilla), Lois Greco (Cindelia), Karen Magid (Ignoreagan), Frank Juliano (The Fool), Stephan Dunne (Albaduke), T. Galen Girvin (Cornwallass), Dennis Ferden (Kent, Viceroy of Vice), Bill Nightingale (Fudmondhanderlick, Leader of the Young White), Richard Forbes (Coponout), Larry Lowe (Oswald), Dolores Elena Garcia and Lyman Jones (Longhairs)

SOURCE—The play *King Lear* (written circa 1605) by William Shakespeare.

The action occurs yesterday and today.

The musical was presented in two acts (division of acts and song assignments unknown; songs listed in performance order).

MUSICAL NUMBERS—"Hail Hio," "Guess What from Guess Who?," "Here I Go Bananas!," "Love Is...," "Friends," "Locker of Love," "Cindelia," "Heroes," "No One Listens," "Her Song," "Hollow Faces," "See the Light," "Dad," "Revolution Now," "We Shall Release You," "Wedding Song"

NOTES—*Pop*, a musical version of *King Lear*, popped in and out after just one performance. Clive Barnes in the *New York Times* remarked that some bad musicals you "mourn," others you "pity," and still others you "writhe at." He noted that *Pop* "was a writher through and through." The musical attempted to modernize Shakespeare's play with references to President Nixon and a sequence which Barnes described as a "tasteless" parody of the shootings at Kent State University. Further, Barnes quoted a sample of the lyrics ("love and teargas is in the air" and "the rusty, lusty locker of love"), and then asked, "Whatever happened to 'Springtime for Hitler'?" The mid-1970s were not particularly kind to musical adaptations of Shakespeare. In early 1976, the late and unlamented *Rockabye Hamlet* bombed on Broadway after six performances, and later that year *Music Is*, a stylish and melodic adaptation of *Twelfth Night*, closed after five.

1284 Poppie Nongena. THEATRE: St. Clements; transferred to the Douglas Fairbanks Theatre on March 27, 1983; OPENING DATE: January 12, 1983; PERFORMANCES: 131; PLAY: Sandra Kotze and Elsa Joubert; MUSIC: Original music by Sophie Mgcina (other music in the production was traditional, and was arranged by Mgcina); DIRECTION: Hilary Blecher; SCENERY: Jon Ringbom; COSTUMES: Shura Cohen; LIGHTING: William Armstrong; PRODUCER: Edward Miller

CAST—Thuli Dumakude (Poppie), Sophie Mgcina (Ouma Hannie, Ma Lena), Seth Sibanda (Mosie), Tsepo Mokone (Plank), Fana Kekana (Jakkie; The Preacher), Lowell Williams (Pengi; A Suitor; Stone), Maggie Soboil (Mrs. Constantia, Mrs. Scobie, Mrs. Retief, Mrs. Swanepoel, Narrator), Alex Wipf (Policeman, Pass Official, Mr. Green)

SOURCE—The 1980 novel *The Long Journey of Poppie Nongena* by Elsa Joubert.

The action occurs between 1949 and 1972 in South Africa.

The play was presented in two acts.

NOTES—The play with music *Poppie Nongena* was a true story about a woman living in South Africa during apartheid (for the book upon which the play was based, her real name was changed to Poppie Rachel Nongena). The program didn't list individual musical numbers; the list below is taken from the cast album issued on CD by Hannibal Records (# HNCD-1351). It appears that "U Jehova: Poppie Uzubale" ("Wedding Song"), "Makoti ("Train Song," a/k/a "Travelling Song"), and "Liza Lisi Dinga"("Hymn," a/k/a "Second Hymn") had original music by Sophie Mgcina, and that the remainder of the score was traditional music adapted by her.

MUSICAL NUMBERS (division of acts and song assignments unknown)—"Amen," "Taru Bawo ("Prayer")/"Wenzeni Na," "U Jehova: Poppie Uzubale" ("Wedding Song"), "Makoti" ("Train Song"), "Lalasana ("Lullaby"), "Jerusalem," "Nkosi Sikelela Lafrica" ("Anthem"), "Zisana Abantwane," "Bantwana Besikolo," "Liza Lisi Dinga" ("Hymn"), "Mampondo Mse," "Taru Bawo" ("Prayer") (reprise)

As *The Long Journey of Poppie Nogena*, the musical had previously been produced at the Music Theatre Group/Lenox Arts Center in March 1982.

1285 The Portable Pioneer and Prairie Show. THEATRE: Theatre of the Riverside Church; OPENING DATE: February 7, 1997; PERFORMANCES: 23; BOOK: David Chambers; LYRICS: David Chambers and Mel Marvin; MUSIC: Mel Marvin; DIRECTION: Lori Steinberg; CHOREOGRAPHY: Cynthia Khoury; SCENERY: Ann Keehbauch; COSTUMES: Sue Gandy; LIGHTING: Deborah Dumas; MUSICAL DIRECTION: Greg Pliska; PRODUCER: The Melting Pot Theatre Company

CAST—Leenya Rideout (Karin Andersson), Sean McCourt (Paul Andersson), David M. Lutken (Karl Andersson), Larry Cahn (Tyrone Pendergast), Susan Emerson (Cordelia Crosby), Samuel D. Cohen (Johnny Slade), Rebecca Rich (Redeye Annie)

The action occurs in Minnesota during the late 1800s.

The musical was presented in two acts.

NOTES—*The Portable Pioneer and Prairie Show* was an evening devoted to the playlets, songs, and dances performed by traveling musical and dramatic troupes which fanned across the Midwestern United States during the late 1800s.

The musical had first been produced in the mid-1970s by the Guthrie Theatre in Minneapolis, and in February 1975 it was seen at Ford's Theatre in Washington, D.C.

It later played in New York as part of the Manhattan Theatre Club's Musical Development Project; it opened on March 19, 1985, for eight performances, and the cast included Donna Murphy (as Cordelia) and Mary Catherine Wright (as Karin); the latter had also appeared in the 1975 production at Ford's Theatre.

The musical was an entertaining and instructive evening about early American theatre (specifically, early American regional theatre); the 1975 production included a "moral didactic" playlet about the evils of drink ("Don't Stain Your Lips, Daddy"); a Black (Hills) comedy sequence ("The Deadwood Book of Numbers"); and such songs as "Speak to the Earth," "Fashion Is the Talk of the Day," "Dancin' Sam and His Dalmatian Dog Fanny," "Starving to Death on the Government Claim," and "Guardians of This Land."

1286 Portfolio Revue. THEATRE: Portfolio Theatre; OPENING DATE: December 6, 1974; PERFORMANCES: 12; LYRICS: Tom Jones; MUSIC: Harvey Schmidt; CHOREOGRAPHY: Janet Kerr; COSTUMES: Charles Blackburn; PRODUCERS: Drew Katzman, Portfolio Studio, and John Schak

CAST—David Cryer, Jeanne Lucas, Kathrin King Segal, Tom Jones, Harvey Schmidt

NOTES—*Portfolio Revue* included both familiar and obscure songs by Tom Jones and Harvey Schmidt, and Mel Gussow in the *New York Times* found the evening an "eminently engaging" way to visit the lyricist and composer. He noted that Jones said "Mister Off- Broadway" was the team's "most dated" song because its allusions were to a very specific time in Off Broadway history. Gussow also said the title song for the unproduced film version of *I Do! I Do!* was a "glorious" number which was superior to the one heard in the Broadway production (the number isn't listed below, but was obviously included in the revue; the evening also included another *I Do! I Do!* title song [a waltz version for a proposed mid-1960s television adaptation of the musical]).

According to Ken Bloom's *American Song*, the following numbers were heard in the Off Off Broadway production *Portfolio Revue*: "(At the) Music Hall" (from *Colette*, 1982; closed during pre-Broadway tryout), "Autumn Afternoon" (apparently written for, but not used in, the 1982 version of *Colette*), "The Bouilloux Girls" (*Colette*, 1971 [Off Broadway version]; see entry), "Celebration" (*Celebration*, 1969), "Dance Hall Saturday Night" (written for, but not used in, the 1963 Broadway musical *110 in the Shade*), "Earthly Paradise" (*Colette*, 1971 [Off Broadway version]; see entry), "Everyone Looks Lonely" (1960 television musical revue *New York Scrapbook*), "Femme du Monde" (*Colette*, 1971 [Off Broadway version]; see entry), "Fifty Million Years Ago" (written for, but not used in, the 1969 Broadway musical *Celebration*) "Flaming Agnes" (*I Do! I Do!*, 1966; see entry for Off Broadway revival), "Fliberty Jibits" (written for, but not used in, the 1963 Broadway musical *110 in the Shade*) "Follow Along with Me" (*Joy*, an unproduced musical version of *Romeo and Juliet* [apparently *Joy Comes to Dead Horse*, an earlier, unproduced musical which eventually evolved into *The Fantasticks*; see entry]), "A Freshman Song" (source unknown), "(Gonna Be) Another Hot Day" (*110 in the Shade*, 1963), "Growing Older" (*Colette*, 1982; closed during pre-Broadway tryout), "His Love" (apparently written for, but not used in, the 1982 version of *Colette*), "The Holy Man and the New Yorker" (originally heard in 1958 Off Broadway revue *Demi-Dozen* and later used in 1959 Off Broadway revue *Pieces-of-Eight*; see entries), "The Honeymoon Is Over" (*I Do! I Do!*, 1966; see entry for Off Broadway revival), "I Can Dance" (written for, but not used in, the 1963 Broadway musical *110 in the Shade*), "I Do! I Do! Waltz" (written for an unproduced television version of 1966 Broadway musical *I Do! I Do!*; see entry for Off Broadway revival), "I Know Loneliness Quite Well" (1960 television musical revue *New York Scrapbook*), "Isn't That a Wonderful Way to Die?" (1975 Off Off Broadway musical *The Bone Room*; see entry), "Love Is Not a Sentiment" (apparently written for, but not used in, the 1982 version of *Colette*), "Melisande" (*110 in the Shade*, 1963), "Mister Off-Broadway" (1958 Off Broadway revue *Demi-Dozen*; see entry), "My Cup Runneth Over" (*I Do! I Do!*, 1966; see entry for Off Broadway revival), "Not My Problem" (*Celebration*, 1969), "Now I'm Back in New York City" (1960 television musical revue *New York Scrapbook*), "A Seasonal Sonata" (1958 Off Broadway revue *Demi-Dozen*; see entry), "Simple Little Things" (*110 in the Shade*, 1963), "Thank Them for Your Love" (source unknown), "Try to Remember" (1960 Off Broadway musical *The Fantasticks*; see entry), "Wandrin' Child" (music from the 1972 film *Bad Company*; lyric written for the production of *Portfolio Revue*), "Wassail" (source unknown), "A Well-Known Fact" (*I Do! I Do!*, 1966; see entry for Off Broadway revival)

1287 Portrait of Jennie. "A New Musical." THEATRE: New Federal Theatre; OPENING DATE: November 26, 1982; PERFORMANCES: 7; BOOK: Enid Futterman and Dennis Rosa; LYRICS: Enid Futterman; MUSIC: Howard Marren; DIRECTION: Dennis Rosa; CHOREOGRAPHY: Dennis Rosa; SCENERY: Michael H. Yeargan; COSTUMES: Charles Schoonmaker; LIGHTING: Jeff Davis; MUSICAL DIRECTION: Uel Wade; PRODUCER: Henry Street Settlement's New Federal Theatre (Woodie King, Jr., Producer)

CAST—Stratton Walling (Older Eben), Brent Barrett (Eben), Maggie O'Connell (Jennie, as a Little Girl), Paul Milikin (Mr. Mathews), Jean Barker (Miss Spinney), Karen Lynn Dale (Jennie, as a Young Girl), David Wohl (Gus), Brian Phipps (Mr. Moore), John-Bedford Lloyd (Arne), Donna Bullock (Jennie, as a Young Woman); Chorus (Marcia Brushingham, Nancy Cameron, Ann Deblinger, Marion Hunter, Marilyn O'Connell, Patricia Roark, Greg Anderson, John Caleb, Bob Freschi, Bobby Grayson, Robert W. Laur, James van Treuren, Martin van Treuren, Bob Wrenn)

SOURCE—The 1940 novel *Portrait of Jennie* by Robert Nathan.

The action occurs at the Metropolitan Museum of Art in New York City at the present time, as well as in New York City and Truro in 1938.

The musical was presented in two acts.

ACT ONE—Prologue (Stratton Walling, Brent Barrett, Chorus), "Winter of the Mind" (Brent Barrett, Stratton Walling), "Where I Come From" (Maggie O'Connell), "Hammerstein's Music Hall" (Maggie O'Connell), "My City" (Brent Barrett, Chorus), "Wish" (Karyn Lynn Dale, Brent Barrett), "Alhambra Nights" (Brent Barrett, Men's Chorus), "Secrets" (Karyn Lynn Dale), "Portrait of Jennie" (Brent Barrett)

ACT TWO—"A Green Place" (Donna Bullock, Brent Barrett), "Remember Today" (Donna Bullock), "Paris" (Donna Bullock, Brent Barrett), "Time Stands Still in Truro" (Brent Barrett, Chorus), "I Love You" (Donna Bullock, Brent Barrett), Epilogue (Brent Barrett, Stratton Walling, Chorus)

NOTES—Despite its having won the Richard Rodgers Award, this workshop production of Robert Nathan's novel *Portrait of Jennie*, a charming fantasy of a girl lost in time and her ghostly meetings with a disenchanted artist, went nowhere; it seems a shame, because the book and its haunting 1948 film version seem naturals for musical adaptation. But in his *New York Times*' review, Mel Gussow criticized the piece as "a dusty artifact of the 1940's." He found Howard Marren's music "lush" if derivative, and said Enid Futterman's lyrics were akin to "greeting cards on parade." He praised "Alhambra Nights" as the score's most "zestful" song.

1288 Postcard from Morocco. "An Opera." THEATRE: Encompass Theatre; OPENING DATE: October 18, 1979; PERFORMANCES: Unknown; TEXT: John Donahue; MUSIC: Dominick Argento; DIRECTION: Nancy Rhodes; PRODUCER: Encompass Theatre (Nancy Rhodes, Artistic Director; Roger Cunningham, Producer)

CAST—Jane Garzo, Barbara Eubanks, Ruth Elmore, Joseph Porrello, William Pell, Ron Edwards, Joseph Warner, Julie Pasqual, James Rainbow

The action occurs in Morocco in 1914.

The opera was presented in one act.

NOTES—*Postcard from Morocco* was a ninety-minute one-act opera which (in the words of John Donahue, the librettist) occurred in a place "like a memory ... like an old postcard from a foreign land." The plot concerned a group of seven travelers waiting for a train in a railroad station "in Morocco or some place, hot and strange." While waiting, and as they are entertained by a surreal puppet play as well as an Algerian orchestra, each traveler holds on to his or her suitcase, to protect the secret of its contents. According to Donahue, each suitcase contains a symbolic "small part" of each traveler's secrets and dreams (or lack thereof). When the group embarks on the next phase of their travels, the faces of the Algerian orchestra members "seem to have seen it all before and will see it again."

The opera was first produced by Center Opera of Minnesota in 1972, and that production was recorded on a 2-LP set by Desto Records (# DC-7137/7138). The libretto was published by Boosey & Hawkes in 1972.

The Off Off Broadway production by the Encompass Theatre appears to have been the opera's New York premiere.

1289 Postcards on Parade. "A Musical Play." THEATRE: The Theatre at St. Peter's Church/ The York Theatre Company; OPENING DATE: April 14, 2000; PERFORMANCES: 6; BOOK: Kenward Elmslie; LYRICS: Kenward Elmslie; MUSIC: Steven Taylor; DIRECTION: Clayton Phillips; CHOREOGRAPHY: Andy Blankenbuehler; SCENERY: James Morgan; COSTUMES: Lynn Bowling; LIGHTING: Mary Jo Dondlinger; MUSICAL DIRECTION: Jack Aaronson; PRODUCER: The York Theatre Company (James Morgan, Artistic Director; Robert A. Buckley, Managing Director

CAST—Jennifer Allen, John Hillner, Mark Lotito, Randy Redd

NOTES—*Postcards on Parade* appears to have never officially opened, and so its six performances may have been previews.

The unusual musical dealt with three gatherings of postcard collectors and dealers in Narragansett, Rhode Island, Miami Beach, and Wichita over a period of nine months. The meetings provide a surreal framework in which postcard images morph into song-and-dance routines. Further, the musical kidded musical comedy conventions; one song ("Regina, La Postcard Queen of La Breeze Marina"), performed by a lip-synching drag queen, was a spoof of Stephen Sondheim's "I'm Still Here" ("Did backrooms and strip joints/I went frontally nude").

In 1993, seven years prior to the New York production, the script was published by Bamberger Books in a limited edition of 800 copies; and in 1998 a CD of highlights was released by Harbinger Records (# HCD-1604); the recording's cast included Kenward Elmslie, Steven Taylor, and Cass Morgan. The "Postcard Queen" sequence was first published in *New American Writing #11*, and "Heavenly Junket," a section of Act I, Scene 3, was first published in *Conjunctions #21*.

Two songs from *Postcards on Parade* ("The Middle of Nowhere" and "Take Me Away, Roy Rogers") were later heard in the 2005 revue *Lingoland* (see entry) and were recorded on that show's cast album. "Cheeky Kiki" was intended for *Postcards on Parade*, but wasn't used; however, it's included as a bonus track on the *Lingoland* recording.

The list below is a combination of song titles from both the script and the recording of *Postcards on Parade*:

ACT ONE—"Postcards on Parade," "Queen Victoria's Benediction," "I Remember," "Picture Postcard Poifect," "P-P-P-Pain," "Come On Down to the Ostrich Farm (Part I)," "Busy Busy Busy Correspondence Card," "The Klutzenhoffer Jingle," "Moments in Time," "Busy Busy Busy Correspondence Card" (reprise), "The Middle of Nowhere," "Suicide Rap," "Hav-A-Havana," "I Don't S-M-O-K-E Sermonette," "Hav-A-Havana"/"I Don't S-M-O-K-E Sermonette" (reprises), "Come On Down to the Ostrich Farm (Part II)," "Changes," "Biddlebury Gap," "Fun and Games," ["Cheeky Kiki"; not used in the New York production], "Fun and Games" (reprise)

ACT TWO—"Uranian Besieged," "One Day at a Time," "Come On Down to the Ostrich Farm (Part III)," "Serenity and Baby and Me," "Seventeen Years of Living Hell," "Take Me Away, Roy Rogers" (music by Kenward Elmslie), "Regina, La Postcard Queen of La Breeze Marina," "One Day at a Time" (reprise), "It's a Good Life," "Envoi," "Postcards on Parade" (reprise)

1290 Potholes. "A New Musical." THEATRE: Cherry Lane Theatre; OPENING DATE: October 9, 1979; PERFORMANCES: 15; BOOK: Elinor Guggenheimer; LYRICS: Elinor Guggenheimer; MUSIC: Ted Simons; DIRECTION: Sue Lawless; CHOREOGRAPHY: Wayne Cilento; SCENERY: Kenneth Foy; COSTUMES: Ann Emonts; LIGHTING: Robby Monk; MUSICAL DIRECTION: Steven Oirich; PRODUCERS: Roger Hess; Sheila Tronn Cooper, Associate Producer

CAST—Jill Cook, Brandon Maggart, Carol Morley, Cynthia Parva, Lee Roy Reams, Joe Romagnoli, J. Keith Ryan, Samuel E. Wright

The revue was presented in two acts.

ACT ONE—"Lost New York" (Brandon Maggart), "Welcome" (Company), "Back on the Street" (Brandon Maggart), "Back on the Street" (reprise) (Carol Morley, Lee Roy Reams, Samuel E. Wright, Brandon Maggart), "Mad About" (Cynthia Parva), "Can You Type?" (Lee Roy Reams, Cynthia Parva), "Madison Avenue" (Jill Cook, Carol Morley, Samuel E. Wright, Lee Roy Reams), "Ropin' Dogies" (J. Keith Ryan, Carol Morley, Samuel E. Wright, Brandon Maggart, Lee Roy Reams), "Just Sit Back" (Jill Cook, J. Keith Ryan), "Wall Street" (Lee Roy Reams, Brandon Maggart, Cynthia Parva), "Young and Agile" (Carol Morley, Samuel E. Wright), "City Hall" (Company)

ACT TWO—Entr'acte (Orchestra), "Back on the Street" (reprise) (Jill Cook), "Back on the Street" (reprise) (Lee Roy Reams), "St. Patrick's Day Parade" (Company), "Starved" (Cynthia Parva, J. Keith Ryan, Jill Cook, Lee Roy Reams, Samuel E. Wright), "Suddenly She Was There" (J. Keith Ryan), "Meter Maid" (Carol Morley), "Network" (Samuel E. Wright, Lee Roy Reams), "Sound and Light" (Jill Cook, Company), "Looking for Someone" (Cynthia Parva, Carol Morley), "Watch Out for the Bump" (Jill Cook, Cynthia Parva), "Typical New Yorkers" (Company), "Mad About" (reprise) (Cynthia Parva, J. Keith Ryan), "Lost New York" (reprise) (Brandon Maggart, Company)

NOTES—*Potholes*, a loosely-connected string of songs about New York, had book and lyrics by Elinor Guggenheimer, who had been a member of the New York City Planning Commission and then later served as New York's Commissioner of the Department of Consumer Affairs. Mel Gussow in the *New York Times* noted that *Potholes* took only bland "pot shots" at urban issues when more acerbic ones were needed. However, he praised Sue Lawless' clever direction, and singled out a "sweet ballad" called "Looking for Someone." Gussow recalled that another recent New York City official had an interest in theatre (as mayor, John V. Lindsay had made a cameo appearance at one performance of *Seesaw* [1973]), and Gussow wondered if New York City's then-current Mayor Edward Koch might someday write a musical. Koch didn't, but Charles Strouse wrote one about him (see entry for *Mayor* [1985]).

1291 Potluck! THEATRE: Delacorte Theatre/The Public Theatre; OPENING DATE: July 7, 1966; PERFORMANCES: 52; DIRECTION: Lotte Goslar and Bernard Gersten; CHOREOGRAPHY: Bob Fosse and Eddie Gasper, Lotte Goslar, Donald McKayle, and Alwin Nikolais; COSTUMES: Mel Cabral; LIGHTING: Martin Aronstein; PRODUCERS: The New York Shakespeare Festival (Joseph Papp, Producer) in association with the City of New York; a Rebekah Harkness Foundation Dance Festival Matinee Production; William Ritman, Executive Producer; and Bernard Gersten, Associate Producer

CAST—Bob Haygood (Folksinger), Lou Zeldis (Clown), Hermes Franqui (Boy); Dancers: Alberta Barry, Hope Clarke, Neatha Collins, Charlotte Mitzenmacher, Sara Rudner, Brent Hickman, David Krohn, Rod Rodgers, Dudley Williams

The revue was presented in one act.

MUSICAL NUMBERS—"Greetings," "Hello! Hello!," "Hermes Finds a Friend," "Excerpt from 'Galaxy'," "For Feet Only," "Songs," "The Rich Man's Frug" (from *Sweet Charity*, 1966; music by Cy Coleman), "The Great Waltz," "The Happy Washerwoman," "Ashcan," "More Songs," "Hurry, Hurry," "Goodbye! Hello!"

NOTES—*Potluck!* was a song-and-dance revue for children. The numbers included "The Rich Man's Frug" from *Sweet Charity*, which had opened on Broadway a few months earlier. Since Bob Fosse and Eddie Gasper are both listed in the choreography credits for *Potluck!*, and since Gasper was a dancer in *Sweet Charity* (and one of the lead dancers in the "Frug" number on Broadway), it's likely Gasper recreated Fosse's "Frug" choreography for its use in *Potluck!*

1292 Pouff. THEATRE: La Vie En Rose; OPENING DATE: February 1976; PERFORMANCES: Unknown; DIRECTION: Peter Jackson; CHOREOGRAPHY: Peter Jackson

CAST—Cast included Peter Jackson (Emcee), Brian Peterson, Michele Frascoli, Rodney Pridgen

NOTES—Howard Thompson in the *New York Times* reported that *Pouff*, a "spangled, helter-skelter" revue, had taken up residence at La Vie En Rose (the new name for the supper club Little Hippodome) when its old venue, The Blue Angel, had burned down.

Thompson said the revue included "near nudity" (in which even the supper club's waiters peeled down), female impersonations, dances (the evening's "hit" was a "frenzied" can-can), and chorus girls swinging on trapezes (he also noted that new material had been added for the engagement at La Vie En Rose, and that additional new material was forthcoming). Further, Thompson reported that after the show the audience could take over the stage for disco dancing!

1293 Les Poupees de Paris (The Dolls of Paris). THEATRE: Krofft Theatre (The York Playhouse); OPENING DATE: December 11, 1962; PERFORMANCES: 172 (estimated); DIRECTION: Sid Krofft and Marty Krofft; SCENERY: Nicky Nadeau; ADDITIONAL SCENERY: Rolf Roediger; COSTUMES: Bill Campbell; other costumes and head dresses designed by Faye Buckley; PUPPET DESIGN: Tony Urbano; LIGHTING: Larry Kenyon; PRODUCERS: Sid Krofft and Marty Krofft in association with Nat Hart

The revue was presented in seven acts.

ACT ONE—Ouverture: L'Orchestre Continental Dirige par Pierre Landeau, Prologue: Les Beautees de Paris ("Paris Beauties")—Paulette, Heather, Toni, La Belle dans Son Bain et Son Admirateur Mr. Charlie McCarthy ("The Beauty in Her Bath and Her Admirer"), a) Le Palais de Crystal ("Crystal Palace"), Le Chic de Paris ("The Chic of Paris"), Les Modeles: "Le Can Can," b) Sensation de Paris—Jacqueline Conrad, La Piste de Vraie Glace ("The Ice Stage")

ACT TWO—Une Nuit d'Horreur ("A Night of Horror"), a) "Conte Dracula" b) La Chambre des Tortures ("Torture Chamber"), c) Le Docteur et Sa Creature ("The Doctor and His Creation"), d) La Danse Macabre ("The Skeletons' Dance"), e) La Fille et La Chauve Souris—Miss Pamela ("The Girl and the Bat")

ACT THREE—Juggler Extraordinaire: Eric Campo

ACT FOUR—Mr. Showmanship et Sa Compagnie, a) Directement Apres Son Engagement Triomphal a La Scala de Milan (Directly following her triumphal engagement at La Scala in Milan)—Mme. Jenkins Foster, b) "The Great One" Avec Les Sirenes et Leur "Fascinating Rhythme" (The Mermaids and Their Fascinating Rhythm)—Mlles. Etoile de Mer—Ondine—Coquillage et Mme. La Pieuvre

ACT FIVE—L'Amour Exotique—Les Efluves de L'Est ("Scented Winds of the East"), a) Les Oiseaux ("The Birds"), La Cascade Geante ("The Waterfall"), b) "Les Danseuses de Bali," c) Les Amants ("The Lovers") Antoinette et Lamas, La Piscine ("The Swimming Pool"), La Pluie ("Rain"), d) Le Cortege de Mariage ("The Marriage Procession")

ACT SIX—"Pick Up" Rue Pigalle, Josephine et Salvador, a) Une Viste a "La Boite de Chocolats" ("A Visit to the Chocolate Box"), b) The Caramels ("The Caramels"), c) "Les Poupees Twist"

ACT SEVEN—Fetes Royales a Versailles, a) La Fille Aux Chandeliers ("The Girl of the Chandeliers"), b) Le Rideau Des Bijous ("The Curtain of Jewels"), c) Les Dames De La Cour ("The Ladies of the Court"), d) Maurice Chevalier, e) Mme. Du Barry—Mlle. Mae West, Les Feux d'Artifice ("The Fireworks"), Les Fontaines ("The Fountains"), Fin

NOTES—The program for *Les Poupees de Paris* was in French, but, thankfully, it included English translations which were extremely helpful in understanding the revue (for example, "Le Palais de Crystal" meant "The Palace of Crystal" and "Une Nuit d'Horreur" meant "A Night of Horror").

Another amusing aspect of the program was its inclusion of an insert which noted that for the current performance (due to an "accident regrettable") one puppet (Miss Jacqueline Conrad) would be replaced by another (Mlle. Desiree). (Alas, these unwelcome and ubiquitous inserts now seem to confetti the floors of every Broadway theatre. But don't throw away those inserts: You never know when one will be worth saving, such as those placed in the playbills of certain early performances of *The Pajama Game* in 1954: some indicated that "At this performance the role of GLADYS will be played by SHIRLEY MACLAINE" and others indicated that "Because of an injury to MISS CAROL HANEY'S foot, some of the dancing assigned her will be done at this performance by MISS SHIRLEY MACLAINE."

The puppet show premiered in Hollywood at the Krofft Theatre (which borrowed the space formerly known as P.J.'s, a nightclub now converted into a theatre for the run of the show) in October 1961, and a 1962 edition played at the Seattle World's Fair.

The Off Broadway edition played at the York Playhouse, which was temporarily renamed the Krofft Theatre during the revue's New York run.

The show was pre-recorded, and included the voices of many celebrities. A program note thanked those performers who lent their voices to the puppets: Jackie Gleason, as himself; Maurice Chevalier, as himself; Edgar Bergen, for Charlie McCarthy; Liberace, Mr. Showmanship; Mae West, Mlle. Du Barry; Edie Adams, Mme. Jenkins Foster; Jane Kean, Josephine; Andre Phillipe, Salvadore; Paul Free, for many of the puppet voices; Annie Farge, Prologue and Girl in Her Bath; Diane Du Bois, Prologue; Judi Meredith, Au Revoir.

On April 22, 1964, a revised edition of the revue opened at the New York World's Fair. Sammy Cahn and James Van Heusen contributed songs for this production, which was recorded by RCA Victor Records (LP # LOC/LSO-1090; the album included the voices of Pearl Bailey, Milton Berle, Cyd Charisse, Annie Farge, Gene Kelly, Liberace, Jayne Mansfield, Tony Martin, Phil Silvers, Loretta Young, and Edie Adams).

When *Avenue Q* opened on Broadway in 2003 after its Off Broadway run (see entry), there was much talk about its being a daring adult puppet musical. But *Les Poupees de Paris* had mined this territory four decades earlier (which proves there's not much new under the theatrical sun), albeit in a production which eschewed the preachy grandstanding of *Avenue Q* and which was more tasteful and family-friendly (although the cover for the souvenir program of *Les Poupees de Paris* warned that it was for "ADULTS ONLY"—!!). A second adult puppet musical (with Wayland Flowers and Madame) opened Off Broadway in 1971 (see entry for *Kumquats*).

Further, in the Nothing-New-Under-the-Theatrical-Sun Department (Part Two), *Les Poupees de Paris* included a spoof of Florence Foster Jenkins (here called "Mme. Jenkins Foster"), the clueless socialite who became legendary for her inadequate singing. Over forty years later, Judy Kaye portrayed Jenkins in the Off Broadway (and later Broadway) production of *Souvenir* (2005; see entry).

1294 Power. THEATRE: Playbox Studio; OPENING DATE: 1973-1974 Season; PERFORMANCES: Unknown; BOOK: Peter Copani; LYRICS: Peter Copani; MUSIC: David McHugh; DIRECTION: Don Signore; SCENERY: Richard Harper and Don Signore; COSTUMES: Richard Harper and Don Signore; LIGHTING: Peter Matusewitch; MUSICAL DIRECTION: Chris Staudt; PRODUCER: The Peoples Performing Company

CAST—Emelise Aleandri (Opal Jewel), George Gugleotti (Tony Esposito), Richard Harper (Dick Ruby), John Ronan (David Goldman), Kathy Wells (Nancy)

The musical was presented in one act.

MUSICAL NUMBERS—"Advanced Civilizations" (Company), "Waiting" (George Gugleotti), "Busy" (Company), "Pieces of Paper" (Kathy Wells, George Gugleotti, John Ronan, Company), "You Have To" (John Ronan, George Gugleotti, Kathy Wells, Company), "A Secret" (Kathy Wells, George Gugleotti, John Ronan, Company), "Like Her or Not" (George Gugleotti), "Assassination" (John Ronan), "Rats & People" (George Gugleotti, John Ronan, Company), "American Dream" (George Gugleotti, John Ronan), "Happy Me" (Kathy Wells), "American Dream" (reprise) (George Gugleotti, John Ronan, Company), "Optimistic" (Kathy Wells, George Gugleotti, John Ronan, Company), "Power Play" (Company), "Happy Ending" (George Gugleotti, John Ronan, Kathy Wells, Company), "We Are" (Kathy Wells, George Gugleotti, John Ronan, Company), "God Bless" (Company)

NOTES—*Power*, with lyrics and music by Peter Copani, was probably produced under an Off Off Broadway contract by the Peoples Performing Company, a small theatre group which lasted for a few years in the early and mid 1970s. See entries for Copani's *Street Jesus* (1974), *Fire of Flowers* (1976), and *New York City Street Show* (1977), all of which appear to have been the same musical.

1295 The Premise. THEATRE: The Premise; OPENING DATE: November 22, 1960; PERFORMANCES: 1,255; DIRECTION: Theodore J. Flicker; SCENERY: Dave Moon; PRODUCERS: Theodore J. Flicker in association with David W. Carter and Allan H. Mankoff

CAST—Theodore J. Flicker, Thomas Aldredge, Joan Darling, George Segal

SKETCHES (number of acts unknown)—"A Great Scientific Discovery" (Joan Darling, Theodore H. Flicker), "Coffee Shop Scene" (Thomas Aldredge, George Segal, Theodore J. Flicker), "Red China" (Thomas Aldredge, George Segal, Joan Darling), "Patent Office Scene" (Theodore J. Flicker, Thomas Aldredge), "Auto Suggestion" (Joan Darling, Thomas Aldredge), "Ham—The Chimpanzee in Space" (George Segal, Theodore J. Flicker, Thomas Aldredge), "If Winter Comes" (Joan Darling, George Segal), "Case History of a Strike" (Theodore J. Flicker, Joan Darling), "A Place in the Sun" (Joan Darling, George Segal), "On Segregation" (Thomas Aldredge, Theodore J. Flicker, George Segal), "The Chess Story" (Joan Darling, George Segal), News Item: "President Kennedy Hurt His Head While Leaning Over to Pick Up Some of Caroline's Toys That Were Scattered About the White House" (Thomas Aldredge, Joan Darling), "When Women Were Slaves" (Theodore J. Flicker, Joan Darling), "The First Men on the Moon" (George Segal, Thomas Aldredge, Theodore J. Flicker), "A Famous TV Interview" (Theodore J. Flicker, Thomas Aldredge, George Segal)

NOTES—The above list of sketches for *The Premise* is based on information from the cast album, which was released by Vanguard Records (LP # VRS-9092). Note the typically Sixties themes running throughout: Kennedy, Communism, outer space, segregation, women's liberation, television commercials, and television interview shows.

The Premise was an improvisational revue; based upon suggestions from the audience, the cast performed topical skits. After a lengthy run of over three years, *The Premise* adjusted its format and reopened with a new edition called *The New Show at the Premise*, which was immediately followed by *The Living Premise* (see entries). The final edition in the series was *The Third Ear* (1964; see entry).

A note in the program for *The Living Premise* stated that its revues utilized three improvisational techniques: the first, "spot improvisations," were scenes invented on the spot by the cast, from suggestions given by the audience; the second were improvisations invented during intermission and which were based on suggestions given by the audience during the previous act; and the third were scenes invented by the cast during the rehearsal period and performed in front of the audience as if the scenes were based on a written script. The program for *The Living Premise* noted its improvisations were primarily from the third technique, but that several "spot improvisations" were included.

Further, another program note indicated some improvisations were "taken from the best and most interesting suggestions supplied during previous performances." The program asked the audience "to supply the place, the thing, the issue, or the circumstance," and then the cast would "supply the satire." A note in another *Premise* program indicated that the topics for the evening, which would be announced by the cast, were "mostly up to you."

In 1971, *The Proposition*, an improvisational revue similar in style to *The Premise*, opened Off Broadway for 1,109 performances (see entry).

1296 Preppies. "A New Musical." THEATRE: Promenade Theatre; OPENING DATE: August 18, 1983; PERFORMANCES: 52; BOOK: David Taylor and Carlos Davis; LYRICS: Gary Portnoy and Judy Hart Angelo; MUSIC: Gary Portnoy and Judy Hart Angelo; DIRECTION: Tony Tanner; CHOREOGRAPHY: Tony Tanner; SCENERY: David Jenkins; COSTUMES: Patricia McGourty; LIGHTING: Richard Winkler; MUSICAL DIRECTION: Jeff Lodin; PRODUCERS: Anthony Fingleton and Carlos Davis

CAST—Tudi Roche (Bitsy Wingate, Mrs. Atwater), Karyn Quackenbush (Steffie Palmer), Michael Ingram (Joe Pantry), David Sabin (Parker Richardson Endicott III, Admissions Officer, Head Master, Majordomo, Mr. Bonifacio, Bishop), Beth Fowler (Marie Pantry), Tom Hafner (Lawyer, Jinks Deerborn), Dennis Bailey (Botsworth Norvil Bogswater II, Bogsy [Botsworth Norvil Bogswater III]), Bob Walton (Cotty [Parker Richardson Endicott IV]), Kathleen Rowe McAllen (Muffy [Angelica Livermore Atwater]), John Scherer (Bookie Bookbinder), James Gedge (Skipper Seabrook, Mr. Atwater), Susan Dow (Lallie deForest)

The action occurs during a period of twenty-one years, from New York to Maine to New Haven ("and points in between").

The musical was presented in two acts.

ACT ONE—"People Like Us" (Company), "The Chance of a Lifetime" (David Sabin, Michael Ingram, Beth Fowler, Tom Hafner), "One Step Away" (Beth Fowler), "Summertime" (Company), "Fairy Tales" (Bob Walton, Kathleen Rowe McAllen, Dennis Bailey, Company), "The Parents' Farewell" (Company), "Bells" (Company), "Moving On" (Company)

ACT TWO—"Summertime" (reprise) (Preppy Boys), "Our Night" (Kathleen Rowe McAllen, Bob Walton, Company), "We've Got Each Other" (Michael Ingram, Beth Fowler), "Gonna Run" (Bob Walton), "No Big Deal" (Company), "Worlds Apart" (Bob Walton, Kathleen Rowe McAllen), "Bring on the Loot" (Dennis Bailey, Company), "People Like Us" (reprise) (Company), Finale (Company)

NOTES—The musical was a feeble effort to satirize the preppy culture; audiences weren't particularly interested in the subject, and so the musical folded within two months.

Mel Gussow in the *New York Times* reported that for one of *Preppies'* production numbers there were nine blazers on stage, and he quickly noted that a musical must be more "than a back-to-school fashion catalogue." Gussow further noted that whatever the musical had to say about American WASP culture had been better said by A.J. Gurney and S.J. Perelman. The plot followed the life of Parker Richardson Endicott IV (a/k/a "Cotty") from his "crucial kindergarten interview" through graduation from Yale, and centered around his quest to inherit a huge trust fund. While Gussow found the book disappointing, he felt the score offered occasional pleasures and singled out "We've Got Each Other" and "Bring on the Loot." The script was published by Samuel French, Inc., in 1984, and the "caste" album was recorded by Alchemy Records (LP # AL-1001-D).

1297 The Present Tense. "An Evening of Comedy and Song." THEATRE: Park Royal Theatre; OPENING DATE: October 4, 1977; PERFORMANCES: 24; SKETCHES: Stephen Rosenfield, Haila Strauss, Ralph Buckley, and Jeff Sweet (Head Writer) as well as the cast (see below); LYRICS AND MUSIC: Allen Cohen, Bob Joseph, Alan Menken, Muriel Robinson, Don Siegal, Jeff Sweet, and Lee S. Wilkof; DIRECTION: Stephen Rosenfield; Haila Strauss, Assistant Director; SCENERY: Paul DePass; COSTUMES: Paul DePass; LIGHTING: John Fishback; MUSICAL DIRECTION: Skip Kennon; PRODUCERS: Roger Ailes and John Fishback with The Comedy Club; Norma Ferrer, Associate Producer

CAST—Barbara Brummel, Chris Carroll, Jim Cyrus, Lianne Kressin, Michael Nobel, Lee S. Wilkof

The revue was presented in one act.

MUSICAL NUMBERS—"Cautiously Optimistic" (by Alan Menken) (Company), "Yankee Man" (by Alan Menken) Barbara Brummel, Jim Cyrus, Lee S. Wilkof, Chris Carroll, Michael Nobel), "Margaret" (by Alan Menken and Muriel Robinson) (Lianne Kressin), "Come to Cuba" (by Don Siegel) (Lee S. Wilkof, Company), "Song for a Crowded Cabaret" (by Jeff Sweet) (Chris Carroll), "The Carter Song" (by Allen Cohan) (Jim Cyrus), "Love Me or Leave Me" (by Don Siegel) (Barbara Brummel), "Man on a Subway" (by Don Siegel and Bob Joseph), "Possum Pie" (by Lee S. Wilkof) (Lee S. Wilkof), "Sklip, Dat, Doobee" (by Don Siegel) (Company)

NOTES—The short-lived revue *The Present Tense* is notable for introducing Alan Menken. His stage musicals (*Little Shop of Horrors* [1983; see entry], *Beauty and the Beast* [1994]) and film musicals (*The Little Mermaid* [1989], *Beauty and the Beast* [1991], *Aladdin* [1992]) have been extraordinarily successful, and even his less popular musicals (such as *God Bless You, Mr. Rosewater* [1979; see entry] and *Weird Romance* [1992; see entry]) are fascinating. "Yankee Man" and "Margaret" were later heard in the 1979 revue *Patch, Patch, Patch* (see entry).

Five years after appearing in *The Present Tense*, Lee Wilkof created the role of Seymour in Menken's *Little Shop of Horrors*.

Wilkof, incidentally, received a rave from Richard Eder in his review of *The Present Tense* for the

New York Times. Eder in fact devoted four paragraphs to Wilkof and his hilarious performance. Otherwise, the evening was an "amiable mediocrity" with a few high spots, including one in which a Sarah Lawrence senior informs us that she took a college course in "walking." Another course combined religion and cooking, and her term paper was on the subject of "Jesus's Favorite Casseroles." Eder reported that *The Present Tense* was the first production to play the Park Royal Theatre; a "creaky" elevator ride took the audience to the cabaret theatre, which was located on the sixteenth floor of an apartment house on West 73rd Street.

1298 Pretty Faces. THEATRE: Actors Outlet Theatre; OPENING DATE: October 21, 1990; PERFORMANCES: 49; BOOK: Robert W. Cabell; LYRICS: Robert W. Cabell; MUSIC: Robert W. Cabell; DIRECTION: Gene Foote; CHOREOGRAPHY: Gene Foote; SCENERY: Peter Rogness; COSTUMES: George Bergeron; LIGHTING: Clifton Taylor; MUSICAL DIRECTION: Jim Mironchik; PRODUCER: Tommy DeMaio

CAST—Lynn Halverson (Monique), Ron Meier (Jimmy), Michael Winther (Carter). Kathleen Rosamond Kelly (Bobby-Joy), Amy Jo Phillips (Daphne), Heather Ann Stokes (Patricia), Amy Ryder (Pleasure), Margaret Dyer (Paulette), Liz Leisek (Deloris), Charles Mandracchia (Roger)

The action occurs in the present during rehearsals for the "Miss Global Glamour Girl" pageant as well as onstage and backstage during the pageant itself.

The musical was presented in two acts.

ACT ONE—"Taking Chances" (Ron Meier, Girls), "42-32-42 (Soliloquies #1)" (Girls), "How Do You Like Your Men" (Liz Leisek, Girls), "42-32-42 (Soliloquies #2)" (Girls), "Furs, Fortune, Fame, Glamor" (Amy Jo Phillips), "Sleep Walkers Lament #1" (Lynn Halverson, Charles Mandracchia), "Too Plump for Prom Night" (Heather Anne Stokes, Girls), "Heartbreaker" (Lynn Halverson, Michael Winther), "What's Missing in My Life" (Lynn Halverson), "Sleep Walkers Lament #2" (Ron Meier, Girls), "Pretty Faces" (Charles Mandracchia), "Daddy Doesn't Care" (Amy Ryder), "Sleep Walkers Lament #3" (Company), "Solo for the Telephone" (Margaret Dyer), "Waiting for the Curtain" (Michael Winther, Ron Meier, Company)

ACT TWO—"Global Glamor Girls" (Charles Mandracchia), "Woman That I Am" (Lynn Halverson), "Purple Hearted Soldiers" (Amy Jo Phillips), "Song for Jesus" (Kathleen Rosamond Kelly), "Are You the One" (Michael Winther, Kathleen Rosamond Kelly), "On with the Show" (Lynn Halverson, Amy Ryder), "Tears and Tears Ago" (Amy Ryder), "What Is Missing in My Life" (Lynn Halverson, Charles Mandracchia), "This Moment Is Mine" ('The Finalist' [the winner of the contest]), "42-32-42" (reprise) (Girls)

NOTES—*Pretty Faces* was the first of three musicals to open within an eight-month period which dealt with beauty contests. *Pretty Faces* was about finalists hoping to be selected "Miss Global Glamour Girl"; it was followed in May 1991 by *Pageant* (see entry), about a beauty contest to select "Miss Glamouresse 1991" (all the beauty contestants were performed by men in drag); and in June 1991 *Prom Queens Unchained* (see entry) offered a look at teenage girls in the 1950s vying for the title of queen of their high school prom. Actually, the spiritual granddaddy of these three musicals was probably the 1975 film *Smile*, which spoofed teenage beauty contests and was in fact the basis for Marvin Hamlisch and Howard Ashman's 1986 Broadway musical *Smile*. *Smile* played for only forty-eight performances, but left behind an appealing (and underrated) score, including an irresistibly melodic and jaunty title song, one of the best of its kind.

1299 Pretzels. "A New Revue." THEATRE: Theatre Four; OPENING DATE: December 16, 1974; PERFORMANCES: 120; SKETCHES: Jane Curtin, Fred Grandy, and Judy Kahan; LYRICS: John Forster; MUSIC: John Forster; DIRECTION: Patricia Carmichael; SCENERY: Fred Wurtzel Costumes: Clifford Capone; LIGHTING: Ken Billington; MUSICAL DIRECTION: John Forster Producers: Burry Fredrik and Walter Boxer present a Phoenix Theatre Production

CAST—Jane Curtin, John Forster, Timothy Jerome, Judy Kahan

The revue was presented in two acts.

ACT ONE—"Pretzels" (Company), "Unemployment" (Jane Curtin, Timothy Jerome, Judy Kahan), "Take Me Back" (Timothy Jerome), "Cosmetology" (Judy Kahan, Jane Curtin), "Sing and Dance" (Judy Kahan, Timothy Jerome), "Wild Strawberries" (Jane Curtin, Timothy Jerome), "Jane's Song (My Fish and I)" (Jane Curtin), "The Waitress" (Judy Kahan, Timothy Jerome), "The Cockroach Song" (John Forster, Timothy Jerome, Judy Kahan)

ACT TWO—"Richie and Theresa" (Jane Curtin, Timothy Jerome), "Classical Music" (John Forster), "Monologue" (Judy Kahan), "Tim Vander Beek" (Jane Curtin, Timothy Jerome, Judy Kahan), "Loehmann's" (Jane Curtin, Judy Kahan), "The Reunion" (Company)

NOTES—"Modest" and "mild-mannered" were words the critics used to describe *Pretzels*, and, in general, they liked the revue's clever way with sketches and songs dealing with modern city life, such as the nasty salesgirl at the cosmetics counter and the pretentious wolf who tries to pick up girls at cocktail parties with talk of Ingmar Bergman films. One sketch dealt with a rube who failed to get through tractor-trailer school, and another examined Mozart's frustration in not being able to write a hit song.

The revue had originally been produced by the Phoenix Theatre in the 1974 Sideshow Series and then in the summer season at East Hampton. The script was published by Samuel French, Inc., in 1975.

Jane Curtin, Judy Kahan, and John Forster had been part of the original production of the long-running revue *The Proposition* (1971; see entry).

1300 Prime Time. THEATRE: The AMAS Repertory Theatre; OPENING DATE: April 9, 1987; PERFORMANCES: 16; BOOK: R.A. Shiomi; LYRICS: Johnny Brandon; MUSIC: Johnny Brandon; DIRECTION: Marvin Gordon; CHOREOGRAPHY: Marvin Gordon; Loretta Abbott, Associate Choreographer; SCENERY: Vicki Davis; COSTUMES: Vicki Davis; LIGHTING: David Segal; MUSICAL DIRECTION: Joyce Brown; PRODUCER: The AMAS Repertory Theatre, Inc. (Rosetta LeNoire, Founder and Artistic Director)

CAST—Elly Barbour (Dr. Amy Klein), George Constant (Mr. Parker), Marcia Dadds (Suzanne), Debra Dauria (Ensemble), Kevin John Gee (John Kobayashi), Rommel Hyacinth (Ensemble), Valerie Lau-Kee (Vicki Lee), Jun Nagara (Ensemble), Eric Riley (Phil Short), Eddie Simon (James Wilson, Ensemble), Patricia Ward (Ensemble), Helena-Joyce Wright (Della), Peter Yoshida (Charley Kobayashi)

The action occurs in New York City in the present.

The musical was presented in two acts.

ACT ONE—"The Six O'Clock News" (Kevin John Gee, Company), "Prime Time" (Eric Riley), "A Blond in Bed" (Kevin John Gee, Marcia Dadds, Female Ensemble), "Make Way for One More Dream" (Valerie Lau-Kee, Peter Yoshida), "It's a Jungle Out There" (Kevin John Gee, Company), "Health Club Rap" (Eric Riley, Ensemble), "Inside the Inside of Another Person's Mind" (Elly Barbour), "Somethin' 'Bout Love" (Helena-Joyce Wright), "A Very Good Night" (Kevin John Gee), "Get Off My Back" (Eric Riley, Kevin John Gee)

ACT TWO—"A Reason for Living" (Elly Barbour, Peter Yoshida), "Nobody Ever Hears What I've Got to Say" (Marcia Dadds, Kevin John Gee), "You Blow Hot and Cold" (Helena-Joyce Wright, Eric Riley), "Make Way for One More Dream" (reprise) (Kevin John Gee, Eric Riley, Valerie Lau-Kee, Helena-Joyce Wright), "A Reason for Living" (reprise) (Kevin John Gee, Valerie Lau-Kee, Peter Yoshida, Elly Barbour), "Leading My Own Parade" (Kevin John Gee, Company), "Prime Time" (reprise) (Company)

NOTES—*Prime Time* was the second of two Off Off Broadway musicals by Johnny Brandon which were produced during the 1986-1987 season (see entry for *Back in the Big Time*).

Prime Time dealt with a young Japanese-American television news writer who finds prejudice at WAKO-TV. Stephen Holden in the *New York Times* said the evening brought to mind the "gee-whiz" style of MGM musicals from the 1940s, and noted Brandon's "sentimental musical razzle-dazzle" offered a "brash potpourri" of songs which were the most "polished" aspect of the evening.

1301 Prime Time Prophet. THEATRE: Players Theatre; OPENING DATE: June 10, 1993; PERFORMANCES: 54; BOOK: Randy Buck; LYRICS: Kevin Connors; MUSIC: Kevin Connors; DIRECTION: Kevin Connors; SCENERY: Don Jensen; COSTUMES: David Robinson; LIGHTING: John Michael Deegan; MUSICAL DIRECTION: David Wolfson; PRODUCER: The Prophet Company Limited

CAST—Beth Glover (Ginger), Marcus Maurice (Max), David Brand (B.L., Tina Rae Tanner), Jonathan Hadley (Tim Christy), Janet Aldrich (Jennifer McCune)

The musical was presented in two acts.

ACT ONE—"The Devil to Pay" (Marcus Maurice, Beth Glover), "Hot Shot" (David Brand), "The Award" (Jonathan Hadley), "Saved!" (David Brand, Marcus Maurice, Beth Glover), "Heavenly Party" (Jonathan Hadley, David Brand, Marcus Maurice, Beth Glover), "Expect a Miracle" (Marcus Maurice, Beth Glover), "Expect a Miracle" (reprise) (Jonathan Hadley, Marcus Maurice, Beth Glover), "So Help Me God" (Janet Aldrich), "Homesick for Hell" (Marcus Maurice, Beth Glover, David Brand), "Leap of Faith" (Company), "Step Into the Light" (Jonathan Hadley, Janet Aldrich), "Diva Supreme" (Jonathan Hadley, Marcus Maurice, Beth Glover)

ACT TWO—"Tina Seeks Solace" (David Brand, Marcus Maurice, Beth Glover), "Tips from Tina" (David Brand, Janet Aldrich), "Necessarily Evil" (Jonathan Hadley, Janet Aldrich, Marcus Maurice, Beth Glover), "Expect a Miracle" (reprise) (Marcus Maurice, Beth Glover), "How Does She Do It?" (Marcus Maurice, Beth Glover), "Tina's Finest Hour" (David Brand), "Armageddon" (David Brand, Company), "Step Into the Light" (reprise) (Jonathan Hadley, Company), Epilogue/Finale (Company)

NOTES—The short-lived musical *Prime Time Prophet* satirized televangelists, and dealt with the Devil, who comes to earth in drag as an evangelist named Tina Rae Tanner (Stephen Holden in the *New York Times* said Tina Rae resembled a "giant drag caricature of Vicki Lawrence"). Tina Rae's mission is to seduce and corrupt Tim Christy, the country's only uncorrupted televangelist. Holden found the score a mixture of "Broadway pop" and "Las Vegas glitz," and noted that while the musical covered overly familiar territory, there was still enjoyment to be had because the show's humor was "taken to campy, trashy extremes." He concluded that the "raunchy" evening would be amusing to those not easily offended.

1302 The Prince and the Pauper (1963; George Fischoff). "A New Musical." THEATRE: Judson Hall Playhouse; OPENING DATE: October 12, 1963; PERFORMANCES: 158; BOOK: Verna Tomasson;

LYRICS: Verna Tomasson; MUSIC: George Fischoff; DIRECTION: David Shanstrom; entire production under the supervision of Robert Bruce Holly; CHOREOGRAPHY: Bick Goss; SCENERY: Norman Womack; COSTUMES: Norman Womack; MUSICAL DIRECTION: George Fischoff; PRODUCER: Joseph Beinhorn

CAST—Robert McHaffey (Hugo, Prince Edward), Joe Bousard (John Canty), Joan Shepard (Tom Canty, Urchin), Budd Mann (Smitty), Carol Blodgett (Prince Edward), Flora Elkins (Lady Anne), John Davidson (Miles Hendon)

SOURCE—The 1882 novel *The Prince and the Pauper* by Mark Twain.

The action occurs in London around 1500.

The musical was presented in one act.

MUSICAL NUMBERS—Overture, "Garbage Court Round" (Joan Shepard, Joe Bousard, Budd Mann, Robert McHaffey), "In a Story Book" (Joan Shepard), "I've Been A-Begging" (Joan Shepard, Robert McHaffrey), "Why Don't We Switch?" (Carol Blodgett, Joan Shepard), "Do This, Do That" (Joan Shepard), "The Prince Is Mad" (Robert McHaffey), "Oh, Pity the Man" (Joe Bousard, Budd Mann), "With a Sword in My Buckle" (John Davidson), "Ev'rybody Needs Somebody to Love" (John Davidson, Carol Blodgett), "The Tree and the Sun" (Flora Elkins, John Davidson), "King Foo-Foo the First" (Joan Shepard, Budd Mann, Joe Bousard, Robert McHaffey), "Coronation Song" (Orchestra), Finale (Company)

NOTES—The program for *The Prince and the Pauper* didn't list individual numbers; the song list above is based on songs and performance credits from the cast album, which was recorded by London Records (LP # AM-28001).

The Prince and the Pauper was a children's musical, and a program note mentioned that children in the audience were invited backstage after the performance to meet the cast members.

George Fischoff's score was pleasant (as was his only Broadway score, the four-performance failure *Georgy* [1971], a musical version of the 1966 film *Georgy Girl*).

On opening night, Budd Mann played the role of Smitty, and Robert McHaffrey played the roles of Hugo and Lord Hertford. For the album, Mann played Hugo, and McHaffrey played Smitty and Lord Hertford.

Later in the season, John Davidson made his Broadway debut in *Foxy* (1964).

The Prince and the Pauper was also the basis for an Off Broadway adaptation which opened in 2002 (see entry). Another musical version (also titled *The Prince and the Pauper*) was produced in regional theatre; it opened at the 5th Avenue Theatre in Seattle on November 29, 2001; the book was by Ivan Menchell, and the lyrics and music were by Marc Elliot and Judd Woldin, with additional lyrics by Menchell. Further, *A Million Grains of Sand*, a British musical adaptation of Twain's novel, opened in 2007.

1303 The Prince and the Pauper (2002; Neil Berg). "A New Musical." THEATRE: Lamb's Theatre; OPENING DATE: June 16, 2002; PERFORMANCES: 194; BOOK: Bernie Garzia and Ray Roderick; LYRICS: Neil Berg and Bernie Garzia; MUSIC: Neil Berg; DIRECTION: Ray Roderick; SCENERY: Dana Kenn; Ken Larson, Associate Set Designer; COSTUMES: Sam Fleming; LIGHTING: Eric T. Haugen; MUSICAL DIRECTION: John Glaudini; PRODUCERS: The Lamb's Theatre (Carolyn Rossi Copeland, Executive Producer); Marian Lerman Jacobs; and Leftfield Productions; Kathleen Kelly, Producing Associate

CAST—Dennis Michael Hall (Prince Edward), Gerard Canonico (Tom Canty), Rob Evan (Miles, Charlie, Patch), Stephen Zinnato (Hugh Hendon, Stache), Rita Harvey (Lady Edith, Karyn), Michael McCormick (John Canty, King Henry, Castle Cook), Sally Wilfert (Mary Canty, Maggie), Robert Anthony Jones (Hermit, Grammar Canty, Dresser), Allison Fischer (Lady Jane, Jamie, Nan), Wayne Schroeder (Pike, Guard Sergeant), Aloysius Gigl (Father Andrew, Woody, Soldier, Mr. Ferguson, Richard, Guard), Kathy Brier (Annie)

SOURCE—The 1882 novel *The Prince and the Pauper* by Mark Twain.

The action occurs in London during the reign of King Henry VIII.

The musical was presented in two acts.

ACT ONE—"The Prince Is Coming" (Ensemble), "Touch My Hand" (Ensemble), "Father Andrew's Lesson" (Aloysius Gigl, Gerard Canonico), "Thrill of Adventure" (Gerard Canonico, Dennis Michael Hall), "The King of Offal Court" (Michael McCormick, Robert Anthony Jones, Gerard Canonico), "Almost Home" (Rob Evan), "If I Were You" (Gerard Canonico, Dennis Michael Hall), "The Prince Is Mad" (Ensemble), "The Lesson"/"Fortune" (Michael McCormick, Stephen Zinnato, Gerard Canonico), "If This Is Love" (Allison Fischer, Rita Harvey), "Simple Boy" (Robert Anthony Jones, Ensemble), "London Bridge" (Dennis Michael Hall)

ACT TWO—"Let's Toast" (Wayne Schroeder, Ensemble), "If I Were You" (reprise) (Gerard Canonico, Dennis Michael Hall), "My Father Was Right" (Dennis Michael Hall, Rob Evan, Robert Anthony Jones), "The Trials of Tom" (Gerard Canonico, Ensemble), "Montage (I Was Blind)" (Stephen Zinnato, Rita Harvey), "Twilight" (Rob Evan), "Montage (Now I See)" (Rob Evan, Dennis Michael Hall, Gerard Canonico, Robert Anthony Jones, Sally Wilfert, Stephen Zinnato, Rita Harvey), "The Coronation" (Ensemble), Epilogue (Ensemble), "Thrill of Adventure" (reprise) (Ensemble)

NOTES—This musical version of Mark Twain's novel *The Prince and the Pauper* played over six months in two slightly separated engagements for a total of 194 performances, and then returned the following season, opening at the Lamb's Theatre on June 4, 2003, for an additional 102 performances. The script was published by Samuel French, Inc., in 2005, and the cast album was recorded by Jay Records (CD # CDJAY-1368); the album included a bonus track of "Lonely," a song not used in the production.

For another Off Broadway musical adaptation of Twain's novel, see entry for the 1963 production (which also includes information about other lyric versions of the work).

1304 Privates on Parade. THEATRE: Christian C. Yegen Theatre; OPENING DATE: August 22, 1989; PERFORMANCES: 64; PLAY: Peter Nichols; LYRICS: Peter Nichols; MUSIC: Denis King; DIRECTION: Larry Carpenter; CHOREOGRAPHY: Daniel Pelzig; SCENERY: Loren Sherman; COSTUMES: Lindsay W. Davis; LIGHTING: Marcia Madeira; MUSICAL DIRECTION: Philip Campanella; PRODUCER: Roundabout Theatre Company (Gene Feist, Artistic Director; Todd Haimes, Producing Director)

CAST—Jim Fyfe (Private Steven Flowers), Ross Bickell (Cpl. Len Bonny), Jim Dale (Acting Captain Terri Daniels), Gregory Jbara (Flight-Sergeant Kevin Cartwright), John Curry (Lance Cpl. Charles Bishop), Edward Hibbert (Leading Aircraftman Eric Young-Love), Donna Murphy (Sylvia Morgan), Donald Burton (Sgt.-Maj. Reg Drummond), Simon Jones (Major Giles Flack), Tom Matsusaka (Lee), Stephen Lee (Cheng)

The action occurs in 1948 in Singapore and districts of Malaya.

The play with music was presented in two acts.

ACT ONE—"S.A.D.U.S.E.A." (Company), "Les Girls" (Jim Fyfe, Gregory Jbara), "Danke Schon" (Jim Dale, John Curry, Ross Bickell, Edward Hibbert, Gregory Jbara), "Western Approaches Ballet" (Donna Murphy, Jim Dale, John Curry, Gregory Jbara), "The Little Things We Used to Do" (Jim Dale, Edward Hibbert, Gregory Jbara, John Curry, Ross Bickell, Jim Fyfe), "Black Velvet" (John Curry, Gregory Jbara, Edward Hibbert, Ross Bickell), "The Prince of Peace" (Company), ACT TWO—"Could You Please Inform Us" (Jim Dale), "Privates on Parade" (Company), "The Latin American Way" (Jim Dale, Gregory Jbara, Edward Hibbert), "Sunnyside Lane" (John Curry, Ross Bickell), "Sunnyside Lane" (reprise) (Company)

NOTES—Peter Nichols' play with music *Privates on Parade* was about an aging gay female impersonator who is part of a special entertainment team (S.A.D.U.S.E.A., Song and Dance Unit, South East Asia) which presents military revues for British servicemen serving in Singapore in the late 1940s. All the songs in the musical were part of the revue sequences within the play.

The play was originally seen in London at the Aldwych Theatre on February 17, 1977, and the cast recording was released on EMI Records (LP # EMC-3233); Denis Quilley played the lead, a role he reprised in the 1982 film version which was directed by Michael Blakemore (who also directed the original British stage production). The script was published by Faber & Faber in 1977 as well as by Samuel French, Inc. The play was first seen in the United States in regional theatre, and the Roundabout production marked the New York premiere.

The British production included two numbers not heard in the New York version ("The Movie to End Them All" and "Better Far Than Sitting This Life Out"); "Les Girls" wasn't heard in the British production.

1305 Prizes. "A New Musical." THEATRE: AMAS Musical Theatre; OPENING DATE: April 26, 1989; PERFORMANCES: 20; BOOK: Raffi Pehlivanian; LYRICS: Charles DeForest; MUSIC: Charles DeForest; DIRECTION: Lee Minskoff; CHOREOGRAPHY: Margo Sappington; SCENERY: Jane Sablow; COSTUMES: Robert MacKintosh; LIGHTING: Beau Kennedy; MUSICAL DIRECTION: Ned Ginsburg; PRODUCER: AMAS Musical Theatre (Rosetta LeNoire, Founder and Artistic Director)

CAST—Bruce Barbaree, Nick Corley, Natania Cox, Peter Ermides, Luther Fontaine, Martron Gales, Nancy Groff, Paul Hoover, Dexter Jones, Allen Walker Lane, Heidi Mollenhauer, Kari Nicolaisen, Doug Okerson, Rita Renha, Troy Rintala, Mary Stout, Darcy Thompson, Karen Ziemba

NOTES—The Off Off Broadway musical *Prizes* included future Tony Award-winning Karen Ziemba in its cast.

1306 Prodigal. THEATRE: The Theatre at Saint Peter's Church/The York Theatre Company; OPENING DATE: March 12, 2002; PERFORMANCES: 24; BOOK: Dean Bryant; LYRICS: Dean Bryant; MUSIC: Mathew Frank; DIRECTION: James Morgan; SCENERY: James Morgan; COSTUMES: Daniel Lawson; LIGHTING: Edward Pierce; MUSICAL DIRECTION: Mathew Frank; PRODUCER: The York Theatre Company (James Morgan, Artistic Director)

CAST—Christian Borle (Kane Flannery, Zach Marshall), Kerry Butler (Maddy Sinclair), Alison Fraser (Celia Flannery), David Hess (Harry Flannery), Joshua Park (Luke Flannery), Mathew Frank (Pianist)

The action occurs in Australia during the present time.

The musical was presented in one act.

MUSICAL NUMBERS—Overture (Pianist), "Picture Postcard Place" (Joshua Park, Alison Fraser, David Hess, Christian Borle), "Happy Families" (Joshua Park, Alison Fraser, Christian Borle, David Hess), "Picture Postcard Place" (reprise) (Alison

Fraser, Joshua Park, Christian Borle, David Hess), "Run with the Tide" (Joshua Park), "Brand New Eyes" (Kerry Butler), "Brand New Eyes" (reprise) (Joshua Park, Kerry Butler), "When I Was a Kid (Part One)" (Kerry Butler, Christian Borle, Joshua Park), "When I Was a Kid (Part Two)" (Joshua Park), "My Boy" (David Hess, Alison Fraser, Christian Borle, Joshua Park), "Out of Myself" (Christian Borle, Joshua Park), "Set Me Free" (Christian Borle, Joshua Park), "Epiphany" (Joshua Park, Alison Fraser, David Hess, Kerry Butler), "Happy Families" (reprise) (Alison Fraser), "Love Them and Leave Them Alone" (Alison Fraser), "Where Does It Get You?" (Joshua Park, Alison Fraser), "Maddy's Piece" (Kerry Butler), "Lullaby" (David Hess), Finale (Joshua Park, Kerry Butler, Alison Fraser, David Hess)

NOTES—Set in Australia, *Prodigal* was based on the Biblical story of the prodigal son; in this case, Luke, the prodigal son, is gay, and he leaves his small town of Eden for the big city life of Sydney. There he loses all sense of responsibility, takes drugs, and loses his lover Zach as well as his best friend, a young woman named Maddy. He returns to Eden, and ultimately reconciles with Maddy, whom his parents have invited for a visit. Luke decides to return to Sydney with her, older and more mature than the boy who originally set out to see the world.

Neil Genzlinger in the *New York Times* felt the story was "ho-hum" with nothing much new to say. Further, he felt the score veered between the musical comedy style of *Stop the World, I Want to Get Off* and the Broadway opera sound of Andrew Lloyd Webber. As a result, the music was occasionally "frustrating," although it "had its moments." Genzlinger praised the scene-setting opening number ("Picture Postcard Place") which was "cleverly" staged by James Morgan and incorporated "deliberate choreographic clichés." Genzlinger also mentioned that *Prodigal* appeared to be the first Australian musical ever produced in the United States.

As *Prodigal Son*, the musical was first seen in Australia as a workshop production in September 1999; it was then produced at a small theatre in Melbourne in January 2000, and six months later received a regular commercial run there. The Australian cast album was released by Prodigal Sun Records, and the York cast recording was released by Jay Records (CD # CDJAY-1370).

1307 The Prodigal Sister. "A New Black Musical." THEATRE: Theatre de Lys; OPENING DATE: November 25, 1974; PERFORMANCES: 40; BOOK: J.E. Franklin; LYRICS: J.E. Franklin and Micki Grant; MUSIC: Micki Grant; DIRECTION: Shauneille Perry; CHOREOGRAPHY: Rod Rodgers; SCENERY: C. Richard Mills; COSTUMES: Judy Dearing; LIGHTING: C. Richard Mills (?); MUSICAL DIRECTION: Neal Tate; PRODUCERS: Woodie King, Jr., by special arrangement with Lucille Lortel Productions, Inc.

CAST—Paula Desmond (Jackie), Frances Salisbury (Mother), Esther Brown (Mrs. Johnson), Ethel Beatty (Sissie, Prostitute, Third Employment Girl), Leonard Jackson (Jack), Louise Stubbs (Essie, Baltimore Bessie), Saundra McClain (Lucille, Dowah), Kirk Kirksey (Slick, Pallbearer), Frank Carey (the Reverend Wynn, Employment Man), Joyce Griffen (Hot Pants Harriet, Dowah, First Employment Girl), Victor Willis (Dr. Patten, Caesar, Jackie's Boyfriend), Judy Dearing (Jackie's Spirit, First City Girl, Second Employment Girl, First Country Girl), Yolanda Graves (Second Prostitute, Second City Girl), Larry Lowe (Dowah, First Policeman, City Man, Country Boy), Rael Lamb (Second Policeman, Second City Man, Second Country Boy)

SOURCE—The Biblical story of the Prodigal Son.

The musical was presented in one act.

MUSICAL NUMBERS—"Slip Away" (Paula Desmond, Saundra McClain, Joyce Griffen, Larry Lowe), "Talk, Talk, Talk" (Frances Salisbury, Esther Brown, Saundra McClain, Joyce Griffen, Larry Lowe), "Ain't Marryin' Nobody" (Paula Desmond, Saundra McClain, Joyce Griffen, Larry Lowe), "If You Know What's Good for You" (Paula Desmond), "First Born" (Frances Salisbury, Ethel Beatty), "Woman Child" (Frances Salisbury, Paula Desmond), "Big City Dance" (Company), "If You Know What's Good for You" (reprise) (Paula Desmond), "Employment Office Dance" (Company), "Sister Love" (Kirk Kirksey), "Hot Pants Dance" (Joyce Griffen, Company), "Remember Caesar" (Victor Willis), "Superwoman" (Saundra McClain), "Flirtation Dance" (Paula Desmond, Victor Willis, Joyce Griffen), "Look at Me" (Ethel Beatty), "I Been Up in Hell" (Paula Desmond, Company), "Thank You Lord" (Frank Carey, Company), "Remember" (Paula Desmond), "Celebration" (Company), "The Prodigal Has Returned" (Company), "Celebration" (reprise) (Company)

NOTES—Originally produced by the New Federal Theatre (an Off Off Broadway company), *The Prodigal Sister* was an updated Black retelling of the Biblical story of the Prodigal Son. The entire story was told in rhymed couplets.

Jackie, a naïve girl from Georgia, becomes pregnant, moves to Baltimore, finds a job in a coffin factory (which is a front for drug sellers and prostitutes), becomes an indentured servant, and gets trapped in a coffin which is luckily shipped to her hometown, where she's reunited with her family. (One critic noted the baby is never mentioned again, apparently having been lost somewhere in the plot.)

The script was published by Samuel French, Inc., in 1975.

Compared with her *Dont Bother Me, I Cant Cope* (1972; see entry), Micki Grant's musical was considered a disappointment. It played just over a month, never to be heard from again.

Like *Lady Day: A Musical Tragedy* and the two productions of *The Great MacDaddy* (see entries), *The Prodigal Sister* was told in "beats," not scenes. Was this a conscious effort to start a trend? If so, it went nowhere.

1308 The Prodigal Son. "A Gospel Song-Play." THEATRE: Greenwich Mews Theatre; OPENING DATE: May 20, 1965; PERFORMANCES: 141; BOOK: Langston Hughes; LYRICS: Marion Franklin and Langston Hughes; MUSIC: Billy Eaton, Marion Franklin, Langston Hughes, and Jobe Huntley Direction: Vinnette Carroll; CHOREOGRAPHY: Syvilla Fort; SCENERY: Peter Wingate; COSTUMES: Eve Gribben; LIGHTING: James Gore; MUSICAL DIRECTION: Marion Franklin; PRODUCERS: Greenwich Players, Inc. (a Beverly Landau, Stella Holt, and Henrietta Stein production)

CAST—DOROTHY DRAKE (Sister Lord), ROBERT PINKSTON (Brother Callius), PHILIP A. STAMPS (Prodigal Son), JOSEPH (C.) ATTLES (Exhorter), Ronald Platts (Father), Clayton Corbin (Minister), JEANNETTE HODGE (Mother), Glory Van Scott (Jezebel), Marion Franklin (Brother John), Johnny Harris (Brother Alex), Jean Perry (Sister Anna), Sylvia Terry (Sister Waddy), Teddy Williams (Brother Jacob), Jeffrey Wilson (Brother Joseph), Hattie Winston (Sister Fatima)

The musical was presented in one act.

MUSICAL NUMBERS—"Wade in the Water" (traditional) (Dorothy Drake, Ensemble), "Take the Lord God" (traditional) (Robert Pinkston), "Rock with Jezebel" (lyric by Langston Hughes, music by Billy Eaton) (Glory Van Scott), "I Look Down the Road" (traditional) (Dorothy Drake), "Devil, Take Yourself Away" (lyric by Langston Hughes, music by Jobe Huntley) (Joseph Attles), "How Am I'm Gonna Make It?" (lyric and music by Langston Hughes) (Dorothy Drake), "When I Touch His Garment" (lyric by Langston Hughes, music by Jobe Huntley) (Dorothy Drake, Ensemble), "Devil, Take Yourself Away" (reprise) (lyric by Langston Hughes, music by Jobe Huntley) (Joseph Attles, Sylvia Terry, Glory Van Scott, Ensemble), "You Better Take Time To Pray" (lyric and music by Langston Hughes) (Robert Pinkston, Ensemble), "Done Found My Lost Sheep" (traditional) (Jeannette Hodge), "Come on in the House" (traditional) (Joseph Attles, Robert Pinkston, Dorothy Drake, Ensemble)

NOTES—*The Prodigal Son*, a self-described "gospel song-play" based on the Biblical story, was one of two plays presented on the bill. The evening's curtain raiser was the first professional American production of Bertolt Brecht's 1936 play *The Exception and the Rule* (translated by Eric Bentley).

The Prodigal Son underwent major changes following its opening. "Feast at the Welcome Table" and "I'm Waiting for My Child" (both traditional) were heard on opening night, but were eventually dropped from the production (although the latter was reinstated later in the run). In some programs, "Two Wings" was listed, but this may be "Fly Away (Wings)," another traditional number (if the latter, it was performed by Robert Pinkston and the Ensemble).

Interpolated during the run were "Oh Lord, Come by Me Here" (for Robert Pinkston and Ensemble) (traditional), and three numbers with lyrics and music by Marion Franklin: "Good Night" (Robert Pinkston and Ensemble), "Look at the Prodigal Son" (Sylvia Terry and Ensemble), and "Son, Get Off This Road" (Jeannette Hodge, Dorothy Drake, and Sylvia Terry).

At some point during the run, Vinnette Carroll, the production's director, played the role of the Exhorter.

Curiously, there seems to have been no songs assigned to the title character.

1309 Professionally Speaking. THEATRE: The Theatre at Saint Peter's Church; OPENING DATE: May 22, 1986; PERFORMANCES: 37; LYRICS AND MUSIC: Peter Winkler, Ernst Muller, and Frederic Block; DIRECTION: Tony Tanner; SCENERY: Robert Alan Harper; COSTUMES: P. Chelsea Harriman; LIGHTING: Barry Arnold; MUSICAL DIRECTION: Bruce W. Coyle; PRODUCERS: Frederic Block and Irving Welzer in association with Kate Harper

CAST—Marilyn Pasekoff, Dennis Bailey, Hal Davis, Meg Bussert, David Ardao, Kathy Morath

The revue was presented in two acts.

ACT ONE—"The Doctor's Out Today" (Marilyn Pasekoff), "Malpractice" (Dennis Bailey), "Patient's Lament" (Hal Davis, Dennis Bailey, Meg Bussert, David Ardao), "Three Doctors' Wives" (Kathy Morath, Meg Bussert, Marilyn Pasekoff), "A Doctor's Prayer" (David Ardao, Kathy Morath), "Guadalajara" (David Ardao, Meg Bussert), "Gastrointestinal Rag" (Dennis Bailey, Kathy Morath, Marilyn Pasekoff), "Sibling Rivalry" (David Ardao, Kathy Morath), "The Lawyer's Out Today" (Marilyn Pasekoff), "Malpractice II" (Hal Davis), "The Equitable Distribution Waltz" (Dennis Bailey, Meg Bussert), "Malpractice" (reprise) (David Ardao, Hal Davis), "Portia's Plan" (Marilyn Pasekoff), "Lawyerman" (David Ardao, Meg Bussert, Dennis Bailey), "What Price Have I Paid?" (Hal Davis, Kathy Morath), "I Professionisti" (Company), "First, Let's Kill All the Lawyers" (Company)

ACT TWO—"The Teacher's Out Today" (Marilyn Pasekoff), "The Best Part-Time Job in Town" (Hal Davis), "Emmy-Lou, Lafayette and the Football Team" (Hal Davis), "Tamara, Queen of the Nile" (Kathy Morath, Dennis Bailey, Hal Davis, David Ardao), "Stupidly in Love" (Dennis Bailey, Meg Bussert), "I Hate It" (Marilyn Pasekoff), "Mathematical Quartet" (Meg Bussert, Marilyn Pasekoff, Hal Davis, Dennis Bailey), "Remember

There Was Me" (David Ardao), "Who the Hell Do These Wise Guys Think They Are?" (Hal Davis, Marilyn Pasekoff, Dennis Bailey), "Over the Hill" (Company), Finale (Company)

NOTES—*Professionally Speaking*, a revue which satirized doctors, psychiatrists, receptionists, lawyers, teachers, gardeners, waitresses, and janitors, was a fast flop, but any musical which offered songs with such titles as "The Gastrointestinal Rag" and "The Equitable Distribution Waltz" couldn't have been all bad. The revue had been previously produced Off Off Broadway in early 1984 (at Griswold's Cabaret, which was located in Theatre Three), and then later in regional theatre that same year. In her review of the 1984 production for the *New York Times*, Leah H. Frank noted the evening was "crisp, biting and often very funny" in its examination of the "often uneasy" relationships between professionals and their clients. She singled out a number of songs, including "I Professionisti" (an "elaborate operatic parody"). Numbers heard in the 1984 productions which weren't used in the 1986 version were "By Degrees," "Better Than You," "Rapport," "My Day," "Maudie," and "Let Them Win." "I'm Leaving Today" may have been another title for "Guadalajara," and "Remember Me" an earlier title for "Remember There Was Me."

Professionally Speaking was similar in subject to the 1978 Broadway revue *Working*, although the latter was a somewhat more serious and earnest look at the American worker and it focused on the blue rather than the white collar.

1310 Prom Queens Unchained. THEATRE: Village Gate; OPENING DATE: June 30, 1991; PERFORMANCES: 57; BOOK: Stephen Witkin; LYRICS: Larry Goodsight; MUSIC: Keith Herrmann; DIRECTION: Karen Azenberg; CHOREOGRAPHY: Karen Azenberg; SCENERY: Bob Phillips; COSTUMES: Robert Strong Miller; LIGHTING: Nancy Collings; MUSICAL DIRECTION: Stuart Malina; PRODUCERS: PQU Productions Inc.; Ric Kirby, Associate Producer

CAST—Don Crosby (Mr. Kelty, Roy Mackelroy), Ron Kurowski (Mr. Sloan, Mr. McIssac, Mr. Cornelius, Miss Carlson, Mr. Turk), James Heatherly (Grant Cassidy), Dana Ertischek (Cindy Mackelroy), Sandra Purpuro (Louise Blaine), Susan Levine (Carla Zlotz), David Phillips (Frank "Switch" Dorsey), Mark Edgar Stephens (Eddy "Wheels" Stevenson, Minka Lasky), Ilene Bergelson (Brenda Carbello), Mark Traxler (Richie Pomerantz), Becky Adams (Violet O'Grady), Gary Mendelson (Myron "Hicky" Greenberg), Connie Ogden (Sherry Van Heusen), David Brummel (Mr. Pike, Mario Lanza), Natasha Baron (Venulia), Pamela Lloyd (Mrs. Glick, Bunny Mackelroy)

The action occurs during Spring 1959.

The musical was presented in two acts.

ACT ONE—Overture (Band), "Down the Hall" (Don Crosby, Company), "That Special Night" (Students), "Dustbane: The Ballad of Minka" (Don Crosby, Mark Traxler, James Heatherly, David Phillips, Mark Edgar Stephens, Gary Mendelson), "Eat the Lunch" (Company), "Most Likely" (Mark Traxler, Dana Ertischek, Glee Club), "The Venulia"/"Seeing Red" (Natasha Baron, David Phillips, Students), "That Special Night" (reprise) (Company)

ACT TWO—"The Perfect Family" (Company), "Corsage" (Pamela Lloyd, Dana Ertischek, James Heatherly, Gary Mendelson, Mark Edgar Stephens), "Seeing Red" (reprise) (David Phillips), "Squeeze Me in the Rain" (Susan Levine, Mark Edgar Stephens, Dana Ertischek, Ron Kurowski, Pamela Lloyd, Mark Traxler), "Going All the Way" (Dana Ertischek, Susan Levine, Connie Ogden, Sandra Purpuro), "Sherry's Theme" (Company), "Give Your Love" (Company)

NOTES—*Prom Queens Unchained* told the saga of four high school girls vying for the title of prom queen during the 1950s (the prom's theme, incidentally, is "Alaska—Our Frozen Friend").

Stephen Holden in the *New York Times* said the evening didn't let nostalgia get in the way of "non-stop comic silliness" and "slapstick" comedy, and he noted the musical grew "steadily loopier" until it finally became " permanently and deliriously unhinged" when a nerdy teenager who died (death by stumbling as he left his woodshop class) comes back to life as a Mario Lanza type. The musical even managed to work into its plot the Communist Menace, flying saucers, and the 1958 film *The Fly*. The script was published by Samuel French, Inc., in 1992.

For more information on "beauty contest" musicals of the period, see entry for *Pretty Faces*.

1311 Promenade. "A New Musical." THEATRE: Promenade Theatre; OPENING DATE: June 4, 1969; PERFORMANCES: 259; BOOK: Maria Irene Fornes; LYRICS: Maria Irene Fornes; MUSIC: Al Carmines; DIRECTION: Lawrence Kornfeld; SCENERY: Rouben Ter-Arutunian; COSTUMES: Willa Kim; LIGHTING: Jules Fisher; MUSICAL DIRECTION: Susan Romann; PRODUCERS: Edgar Lansbury and Joseph Beruh

CAST—Ty McConnell (105), Gilbert Price (106), Pierre Epstein (Jailer), Madeline Kahn (Servant), Margot Albert (Miss I, Viola), Carrie Wilson (Miss O), Alice Playten (Miss U), Marc Allen III (Mr. R), Glenn Kezer (Mr. S), Michael Davis (Mr. T), Edmund Gaynes (Waiter), Florence Tarlow (Rosita), Art Ostrin (Dishwasher), George S. Irving (Mayor), Shannon Bolin (Mother)

The musical was presented in two acts.

ACT ONE—"Promenade Theme" (Orchestra), "Dig, Dig, Dig" (Ty McConnell, Gilbert Price), "Unrequited Love" (Margot Albert, Carrie Wilson, Alice Playten, Marc Allen III, Glenn Kezer, Michael Davis, Madeline Kahn, Edmund Gaynes, Ty McConnell, Gilbert Price), "Isn't That Clear" (Glenn Kezer, Ensemble), "Don't Eat It" (Ensemble), "Four" (Margot Albert, Carrie Wilson, Alice Playten, Marc Allen III, Glenn Kezer, Michael Davis, Madeline Kahn, Edmund Gaines, Ty McConnell, Gilbert Price, Art Ostrin), "Chicken Is He" (Florence Tarlow), "A Flower" (Margot Albert), "Rosita Rodriguez: Serenade" (George S. Irving), "Apres Vous I" (Ty McConnell, Gilbert Price, Pierre Epstein), "Bliss" (Madeline Kahn, Ty McConnell, Gilbert Price, Ensemble), "The Moment Has Passed" (Carrie Wilson), "Thank You" (Art Ostrin), "The Clothes Make the Man" (Madeline Kahn, Ty McConnell, Gilbert Price), "The Cigarette Song" (Madeline Kahn, Ty McConnell, Gilbert Price), "Two Little Angels" (Shannon Bolin, Ty McConnell, Gilbert Price), "The Passing of Time" (Ty McConnell, Gilbert Price), "Capricious and Fickle" (Alice Playten), "Crown Me" (Madeline Kahn, Ty McConnell, Gilbert Price)

ACT TWO—"Mr. Phelps" (Art Ostrin), "Madeline" (Art Ostrin), "Spring Beauties" (Ensemble), "Apres Vous I" (reprise) (Ensemble), "A Poor Man" (Ty McConnell, Gilbert Price), "The Finger Song" (Marc Allen III), "Little Fool" (Michael Davis, Ensemble), "Czardas" (Madeline Kahn, Margot Albert), "The Laughing Song" (Ensemble), "A Mother's Love" (Shannon Bolin), "Listen, I Feel" (Madeline Kahn), "I Saw a Man" (Shannon Bolin), "All Is Well in the City" (Ty McConnell, Gilbert Price, Ensemble)

NOTES—*Promenade* may not only be Al Carmines' best score, it's also one of the best scores ever written for the musical theatre. Carmines' hurdy-gurdy tunes, often wrapped in operatic, coloratura flourishes, are perfectly wedded to the surreal, dadaesque lyrics by Maria Irene Fornes. The result is a cornucopia of rich melodies and baroque lyrics (and deliciously arch dialogue) which told the story of two escaped convicts (named 105 and 106) who meet an assortment of self-absorbed strangers in their travels through a city where both metaphorical and emotional bargains cost you much more than they're worth. Among the score's highlights: the joyous ode to "Unrequited Love"; the aria "Listen, I Feel"; the art song "I Saw a Man"; and the anthem "All Is Well in the City."

During previews, "Why Not" was deleted.

The cast album was recorded by RCA Victor Records (LP # LSO-1161; CD # 09026-63333-2); by the time the album was recorded, Madeline Kahn had left the show, and her role was performed by Sandra Schaeffer. Three songs from the musical were included on *Songs from W.C. and Other Theatre Songs of Al Carmines* (CD # OC-9483): "Promenade Theme," "I Saw a Man," and "Capricious and Fickle," the latter two sung by Alice Playten (who had introduced "Capricious and Fickle" in the original production).

The musical had been first presented in a shorter version at the Judson Poets' Theatre on April 9, 1965, and the script for that production was published in the collection *The New Underground Theatre*, published by Bantam Books in 1968 and edited by Robert J. Schroeder. The full-length script of the 1969 version was first published by Metromedia On Stage in an undated edition, and in 1979 the script was unaccountably included in the collection *Great Rock Musicals*, edited by Stanley Richards and published by Stein and Day (if *Promenade* is a rock musical, then so are *Plain and Fancy*, *Redhead*, and *Camelot*). The musical was revived for a limited engagement of sixteen performances on October 11, 1983, at the Theatre Off Park.

The colorful, saucy artwork for *Promenade*'s window card was designed by Tom Morrow, one of the outstanding artists in the field of theatre poster art. His memorable designs included *Auntie Mame* (1956), *Candide* (1956), *Oh Captain!* (1958), *Requiem for a Nun* (1959), *Redhead* (1959), *The Girls Against the Boys* (1959), *The Pink Jungle* (1959; closed prior to Broadway), *The Unsinkable Molly Brown* (1960), *Wildcat* (1960), *Take Her, She's Mine* (1961), *Venus at Large* (1962), *Lorenzo* (1963), *She Loves Me* (1963), *Alfie!* (1964), *Fiddler on the Roof* (1964), *Skyscraper* (1965), *Cabaret* (1966), *The Deer Park* (1967), *Hellzapoppin' '67* (1967; closed prior to Broadway), *Loot* (1968), *George M!* (1968), *Zorba* (1968), *Show Me Where the Good Times Are* (1970), *Lovely Ladies, Kind Gentlemen* (1970) *Twigs* (1971), *One for the Money Etc.* (1972), *Lorelei* (1974), *So Long, 174th Street* (1976), and *Grind* (1985).

Promenade was the first production to play the Promenade Theatre and the Promenade Theatre took its name from its first production. There's something rather whimsical and circular about that, not unlike the plot of the musical.

SPECIAL NOTE—In February 2008, James C. Nicola, the Artistic Director of the New York Theatre Workshop, announced that beginning with the 2008-2009 season the theatre would present *Encores!*-like concert revivals of three Off Broadway musicals each season. As of this writing, *Promenade* and *The Wedding of Iphigenia and Iphigenia in Concert* (see entry) have been announced for the first season, with a third musical still to be selected. Since Al Carmines is the quintessential Off Broadway composer, it seems only fitting that *Promenade* will inaugurate the new series.

1312 The Proposition (1968). THEATRE: The Bitter End; OPENING DATE: April 19, 1968; PERFORMANCES: 2; SKETCHES: Jeremy Leven; MUSIC: Unknown (possibly by Jeremy Leven); DIRECTION: Jeremy Leven; MUSICAL DIRECTION: John Forster; PRODUCER: Levendell Productions

CAST—Lori Heineman, Fred Grandy, Karen Meyn, Paul Jones, Ken Tigar

SKETCHES AND SONGS (division of acts and sketch and song assignments unknown)—"Five Characters in Search of a White House," "Kissinger," "Little People's Concert," "Ethnos in Song," "Felony," "Progressive Education," "Bleh," "Fenordin," "This Week in the Arts," "Kennedy Cantata," "Prostretics," "Nuclear Chef," "Wedding Night," "Angry Afro-American Artists' Institute," "Euclid's Elemental," "Bombs," "Trap the Traitor," "Raleigh," "Repoz," "The Death of God," "Milton Cross at the Met," "Nu?," "On the Scene," "Poetry"

NOTES—The revue *The Proposition* was presented for a limited run of two performances; The Proposition company was located in Boston, and their New York visit was a showcase for their satiric brand of humor (unlike another Boston troupe, which was also called The Proposition [which appeared in New York in 1971 and 1978; see entries], the current Proposition didn't offer improvisational comedy).

Richard F. Shepard in the *New York Times* found the showcase "witty, not constantly biting," but nonetheless "often funny and pertinent." He singled out the sketch "The Death of God" (the funeral is telecast live from the Vatican, and Bobby Kennedy announces he hopes to finish the work "He" has begun); a spoof of Leonard Bernstein's classical-music television concerts for young children (he analyzes "Hickory Dickory Dock"); and a parody of "inane" folk music ("A little bird is a little bird because it is small").

1313 The Proposition (1971). THEATRE: Gramercy Arts Theatre; moved to the Mercer-Shaw Arena on April 28, 1971; OPENING DATE: March 24, 1971; PERFORMANCES: 1,109; CONCEIVED AND DIRECTED BY Allan Albert; PRODUCERS: Manon Enterprises, Ltd., and Propositions, Inc.

CAST—Jane Curtin, Munson Hicks, Judy Kahan, Paul Kreppel, Josh Mostel, Karen Welles; Danny Troob (piano), Gualberto Pillich (bass)

The revue was presented in two acts.

NOTES—*The Proposition* came to New York by way of Boston. The Proposition was originally formed in Cambridge, Massachusetts, in 1968, and when the improvisational revue opened Off Broadway, the Boston production was in its fourth year.

The improvisations were based on suggestions from the audience (the program provided general topics on various categories, such as fictional characters, major playwrights, fairy tales, controversial issues, etc.). The first act's improvisations were non-musical; the second act was comprised completely of musical improvisations. Clive Barnes in the *New York Times* reported that at the performance he attended one improvisation on a drama about incest was given in the styles of Aristophanes, Noel Coward, Tennessee Williams, and Edward Albee, and a movie about a love triangle set against the background of a tennis match was given in the styles of French, Swedish, British, and Italian film directors.

The revue played for nearly two-and-a-half years, and briefly returned in 1978 (see entry). An unrelated revue, also called *The Proposition* and also from Boston with a group of players who called themselves The Proposition, had been seen in New York in 1968 (see entry); that troupe presented satiric sketches and songs and didn't perform improvisational material.

1314 The Proposition (1978). THEATRE: Actors' Playhouse; OPENING DATE: May 3, 1978; PERFORMANCES: 24; DIRECTION: Allan Albert; LIGHTING: Dick Williams; MUSICAL DIRECTION: Robert Hirschhorn, John Lewis, and Donald Sosin; PRODUCERS: The Proposition Workshop, Inc. (Allan Albert, Artistic Director; Carol Lawhon, Managing Director)

CAST—Raymond Baker, Anne Cohen, Timothy Hall, Deborah Reagan

The revue was presented in two acts.

NOTES—The improvisational company The Proposition was formed in Cambridge, Massachusetts, in 1968; it was first seen Off Broadway in 1971 for 1,109 performances (see entry). The 1978 visit was a disappointment, running only three weeks. Despite its being a staple of Off Broadway entertainment throughout the 1960s, improvisational theatre's heyday was long over. Perhaps the sudden surge in the popularity of comedy clubs was an indirect response to the demise of improvisational theatre. Comedy clubs became the only venue to offer topical humor with a certain amount of spontaneity and with a loose improvisational style.

At the time of the 1978 Off Broadway production, The Proposition was based in Stockbridge, Massachusetts, at the Berkshire Theatre Festival. Another group, also called The Proposition and also from Boston, had been seen in New York in 1968; this troupe presented satiric sketches and songs and didn't perform improvisational material.

1315 The Provincetown Follies. "An Intimate Revue." THEATRE: Provincetown Playhouse; OPENING DATE: November 3, 1935; PERFORMANCES: 63; "BOOK" (SKETCHES): George K. Arthur, Frederick Herendeen, Stanley Holloway, Gwynn Langdon, Barrie Oliver, and Mary Schaeffer; LYRICS: Sylvan Green, Frederick Herendeen, Stanley Holloway, and Gwynn Langdon; MUSIC: Sylvan Green and Dave Stamper; DIRECTION: Lee Morrison; CHOREOGRAPHY: Mary Read; SCENERY: John Plumer Ludlum; PRODUCER: The Greenwich Musical Guild, Inc.

CAST—Beatrice Kay, Billy Greene, Wood Hawkins, Phyllis Austen, Cyril Smith, Eileen Graves, Barrie Oliver, Marie Alvarez, Theodore Stanhope, The Bernays, Mary Read's Girls (Jane Prescott, Evelyn Clarke, Suzanne Jane, Dolly Zollo, Yvette Andre, Peggy Burke, Elinore Warnock, Helen Moss, Valerie Valenne, Marge Zollo), The London Four, The Bernays

The revue was presented in two acts.

ACT ONE—Barrie Oliver, "MacDougal Street" (lyric and music by Sylvan Green) (Beatrice Kay, Billy Greene, Wood Hawkins, Phyllis Austen, Cyril Smith, Eileen Graves, Barrie Oliver, "The Dancing Debutantes" (Mary Read's Girls), "Contest Winner" (Barrie Oliver, Marie Alvarez), "Keeping the Man" (Barrie Oliver), "A Spanish Shawl" (lyric by Gwynn Langdon, music by Sylvan Green) (Phyllis Austen, Mary Read's Girls), "Jui-Jitsu" (sketch by George K. Arthur) (Barrie Oliver, Theodore Stanhope, Billy Greene, Beatrice Kay), "Feeling Good"/"Heat Wave" (the latter with lyric and music by Irving Berlin) (Performers unidentified in program), "Riverman" (sketch by Mary Schaeffer) (Wood Hawkins, The London Four, Mary Read's Girls), "The Last Train" (Theodore Stanhope, Billy Greene), "New Words to an Old Love Song" (lyric by Frederick Herendeen, music by David Stamper) (Phyllis Austen, Wood Hawkins, Solo Dancers [Yvette Andre, Valerie Valenne], Mary Read's Girls), "Albert" (lyric by Stanley Holloway, music by Sylvan Green) (Cyril Smith), "Porky Done His Best" (lyric by Frederick Herendeen, music by Sylvan Green) (Beatrice Kay, Wood Hawkins, Billy Greene, The London Four, Barrie Oliver, Phyllis Austen, Mary Read's Girls)

ACT TWO—"Rain Over Manhattan" (sketch by Arthur Jones) (Phyllis Austen, The London Four, Jane Prescott, Mary Read's Girls), "I'm a Professional Now" (sketch by Sylvan Green) (Beatrice Kay), "Hell" (Cyril Smith, Billy Greene, Marie Alvarez), "Rhythm Made a Success of Me" (Barrie Oliver, Mary Read's Girls), "Dancing Dream" (sketch by Mary Schaeffer) (Wood Hawkins, The Bernays), "Waterloo" (sketch by Stanley Holloway) (Cyril Smith), "Night Club" (lyric by Frederick Herendeen, music by Dave Stamper) (Theodore Stanhope, Beatrice Kay), "She's in Again" (Marie Alvarez); this sequence included "Garbo" (Barrie Oliver) and "Rhythm in My Bones" (Barrie Oliver, Mary Read's Girls), "Children's Sour" (sketch by Sylvan Green and Beatrice Kay) (Eileen Graves, Billy Greene, Beatrice Kay), "Push Over for Love" (Barrie Oliver), "Red Sails in the Sunset" (Phyllis Austen, Barrie Oliver, Beatrice Kay, Wood Hawkins, Billy Greene, Marie Alvarez, Cyril Smith, Eileen Graves, The London Four, Mary Read's Girls)

NOTES—This short-lived revue *The Provincetown Follies* included in its cast Beatrice Kay, who later became known as the "Park Avenue Hillbilly."

The program didn't always identify specific writers of the sketches. The evening included spoofs of recent Broadway shows (*Porgy and Bess* [which had premiered a month before the revue opened] was kidded in "Porky Done His Best," and Lillian Hellman's play *The Children's Hour* [1934] was satirized in "Children's Sour"). The revue included a sequence titled "Red Sails in the Sunset," which may have been a spoof of the popular song (lyric by Jimmy Kennedy, music by Hugh Williams).

The *New York Times'* reviewer (identified as "J.K.H.") found the evening a bit of "trial-and-error," explaining that the "error" was the show, which was a "trial" to the audience.

1316 Pudding Lane. "A Musical Play." THEATRE: St. Bart's Playhouse; OPENING DATE: September 29, 1982; PERFORMANCES: 10; BOOK, LYRICS, AND MUSIC: Robert Bowman and Tony Pole; DIRECTION: Christopher Biggins; SCENERY: Jack Stewart; COSTUMES: Richard Wellington; LIGHTING: Bob Bessoir; MUSICAL DIRECTION: Tony Pole; PRODUCERS: Performing Arts Cultural Exchange (the Rev. Andrew J.W. Mullins, Director), St. Bartholomew's Church (The Rev. Thomas Dix Bowers, Rector), St. Bartholomew's Community Club (the Rev. William D. Roberts, Director), and The St. Bart's Players (Nell Robinson, Artistic Director)

CAST—Rosemary Ashe (Jenny), Robert Farrant (Lord George Darkfield), Michael Scholes (Jack Oakley), Paddie O'Neil (Poll), Leo Dolan (Jem Flashbuck), Alan Leith (Tony, Samuel Pepys), Peter Durkin (Nick, John Evelyn), Brian Johnston (Ned), Chuck Gemme (Bob), Avril Gaynor (Nell), Maggie Henderson (Meg), Verity Anne Meldrum (Rosie), Christine Macrie (Bess), Maryellen Conroy (Marge), Julia Clegg (Susan), Robert McBain (King Charles II), Richard Bitsko (Captain Burgoyne), John Daines (Guard)

The action occurs in London in 1666.

The musical was presented in two acts.

ACT ONE—Overture/Prologue, "London Town" (Company), "If My Love You'll Be" (Robert Farrant), "I Don't Give a Damn for You" (Rosemary Ashe), "Love Has Arrived" (Michael Scholes, Men), "Nothing Can Possibly Change the Fact" (Michael Scholes, Men), "At Last I Feel My Heart Awaking" (Rosemary Ashe), "You Gotta Keep Making Ends Meet" (Paddie O'Neil, Company), "I Really Think That Poverty Is Wrong" (Robert Farrant), "Pudding Lane" (Paddie O'Neil, Michae Scholes, Company), "Today Is Love" (Michael Scholes, Rosemary Ashe), "Three Serving Wenches" (Paddie O'Neil, Women), "Lucky" (Paddie O'Neil)

ACT TWO—"It's All Because of the Fire" (Leo Dolan, Company), "Put It All Down in the Diary" (Alan Leith, Peter Durkin), "Look at What We're Saving from the Blaze" (Leo Dolan, Men), "What Is Liberty?" (Michael Scholes), "They've Taken My Man Away" (Rosemary Ashe), "Court Minuet," "We Place Our Faith in Good King Charles' Hands" (Alan Leith, Robert McBain, Paddie O'Neil, Rosemary Ashe, Michael Scholes), "Today Is Love" (reprise) (Rosemary Ashe, Michael Scholes), "The Tale of Pudding Lane" (Robert McBain, Paddie

O'Neil, Rosemary Ashe, Michael Scholes, Alan Leith, Peter Durkin, Leo Dolan, and Robert Farrant)

NOTES—The Off Off Broadway musical *Pudding Lane* was seen at St. Bart's Playhouse in St. Bartholomew's Church, and had been produced in London earlier in the year by St. Bartholomew's sister church, All Hallows by the Tower Church.

The musical dealt with a "city on fire" (that is, the Great Fire of London in 1666, which started in a bakery on Pudding Lane), and Richard F. Shepard in the *New York Times* reported the plot dealt with a young baker's assistant who is accused of starting the fire.

1317 Pump Boys and Dinettes. THEATRE: Colonnades Theatre; OPENING DATE: October 1, 1981; PERFORMANCES: 112; LYRICS: Jim Wann; for other credits, see song list Music: Jim Wann; for other credits, see song list Direction: By cast members; CHOREOGRAPHY: By cast members; SCENERY: Doug Johnson; LIGHTING: Fred Buchholz; PRODUCERS: Dodger Productions, Louis Busch Hager, Marilyn Strauss, Kate Studley, Warner Theatre Productions, Inc., and Max Weitzenhoffer

CAST—John Foley (Jackson), Mark Hardwick (L.M.), Debra Monk (Prudie Cupp), Cass Morgan (Rhetta Cupp), John Schimmel (Eddie), Jim Wann (Jim)

The revue was presented in two acts.

ACT ONE—"Highway 57" (Company), "Takin' My Time" (lyric and music by Spider John Koerner, additional lyric by John Foley) (John Foley, Mark Hardwick, John Schimmel, Jim Wann), "Who Will the Next Fool Be" (lyric and music by Charlie Rich) (Mark Hardwick), "Menu Song" (lyric and music by Cass Morgan and Debra Monk) (Cass Morgan, Debra Monk), "The Best Man (I Never Had)" (Debra Monk), "Fisherman's Prayer" (John Foley, Mark Hardwick, John Schimmel, Jim Wann), "Catfish" (lyric and music by Jim Wann and B. Simpson) (John Foley, Mark Hardwick, John Schimmel, Jim Wann), "Mamaw" (Jim Wann), "Be Good or Be Gone" (Cass Morgan), "Drinkin' Shoes" (lyric and music by Mark Hardwick, Cass Morgan, and Debra Monk) (Company)

ACT TWO—"Pump Boys" (John Foley, Mark Hardwick, John Schimmel, Jim Wann), Mona (John Foley), "T.N.D.P.W.A.M." (a/k/a "The Night Dolly Parton Was Almost Mine") (Mark Hardwick), "Tips" (lyric and music by Debra Monk and Cass Morgan) (Debra Monk, Cass Morgan), "Sisters" (lyric and music by Cass Morgan) (Cass Morgan, Debra Monk), "Vacation" (Company), "No Holds Barred" (lyric and music by Jim Wann and Cass Morgan) (Company), "Farmer Tan" (Mark Hardwick, Cass Morgan, Debra Monk), "Highway 57" (reprise) (Company), "Closing Time" (Company)

NOTES—*Pump Boys and Dinettes* was a concert-styled revue in which the boys from the gas station and the "dinettes" from the Double Cupp diner across the street present an evening of songs for the locals, including a raffle. The revue had been previously produced Off Off Broadway at the Westside Arts Theatre on July 10, 1981, for twenty performances; two songs in that production ("The Blade" and "All the Good Things," both by Jim Wann) were not used in the Off Broadway production.

After transferring to the Colonnades Theatre in October and playing there for three months, the show moved to the Princess Theatre on February 4, 1982, and ran for 573 performances (it's unclear if the Princess Theatre engagement was under a regular Broadway contract or a Middle Broadway contract). Jim Wann had been active in musical theatre since the mid-1970s, and had a minor success with *Diamond Studs* (1975; see entry); with *Pump Boys and Dinettes* he enjoyed a solid hit.

For the Princess Theatre engagement, three new songs were added ("Taking It Slow" [lyric and music by John Foley, Mark Hardwick, John Schimmel, and Jim Wann], "Serve Yourself" [lyric and music by Jim Wann] and "Caution: Men Cooking" [lyric and music by Debra Monk, Cass Morgan, Jim Wann, and John Foley], and three were deleted ["Takin' My Time," "Who Will the Next Fool Be," and "Catfish"]), the scenery was credited to Doug Johnson and Christopher Nowak, and the costumes to Patricia McGourty.

The cast recording was released by CBS Records (LP # FM-37790), and included "Catfish"; the script was published by Samuel French, Inc., in 1982. The revue was televised on NBC.

1318 Put It in Writing. "The New Musical Revue." THEATRE: Theatre de Lys; OPENING DATE: May 13, 1963; PERFORMANCES: 24; SKETCHES: Jay Thompson and David Panich Lyrics: William Angelos, David Bimonte, Martin Charnin, Fred Ebb, Jim Evering, Alan Kohan, Jay Thompson, Bud McCreery, Steven Vinaver, and G. Wood; MUSIC: Robert (Bob) Kessler, Alan Kohan, Norman Martin, Bud McCreery, Steven Vinaver, Jim Wise, and G. Wood; DIRECTION: Bill Penn; CHOREOGRAPHY: Joyce Trisler; SCENERY: Peter Harvey; COSTUMES: Audre; LIGHTING: Gene Tunezi; MUSICAL DIRECTION: Gordon Connell; PRODUCERS: Lucille Lortel Prod'ns., Inc., and Arthur Cantor, by arrangement with The Happy Medium

CAST—Buzz Halliday, Barbara Gilbert, Bill Hinnant, Brandon Maggart, Jack Blackton, Kit Smythe, Will MacKenzie, Linda Harris, Peter Sands, Jane Connell

The revue was presented in two acts.

ACT ONE—"Literary Cocktail Party" (sketch by David Panich; lyric and music by Bud McCreery) (Company), "I Hope You're Happy" (lyric and music by Fred Ebb and Norman Martin) (Bill Hinnant), "Trilogy" (lyric and music by Bud McCreery) (Kit Smythe, Barbara Gilbert, Jane Connell, Will MacKenzie, Jack Blackton, Peter Sands), "Give 'Em a Kiss" (lyric and music by G. Wood) (Bill Hinnant, Brandon Maggart) "Cut Movie Songs" (lyric and music by Fred Ebb and Norman Martin, Jim Evering and Jay Thompson) (Company), "The Case of the Hum-Drum Killer" (sketch, lyric and music by Jay Thompson) (Buzz Halliday, Kit Smythe, Jack Blackton, Will MacKenzie, Brandon Maggart) "Memories" (sketch by David Panich) (Jane Connell, Jack Blackton, Bill Hinnant), "The Ayes of Texas" (lyric and music by Fred Ebb and Norman Martin) (Barbara Gilbert, Kit Smythe, Brandon Maggart) "Daisy" (lyric and music by G. Wood) (Jane Connell, Linda Harris) "Lordy, the Flies" (lyric and music by Steven Vinaver) (Barbara Gilbert, Will MacKenzie) "The People's Choice" (lyric and music by Fred Ebb and Norman Martin) (Bill Hinnant, Brandon Maggart) "What's Cooking?" (lyric and music by Fred Ebb and Norman Martin) (Company)

ACT TWO—"Top of the List" (lyric and music by Jay Thompson) (Jane Connell, Buzz Halliday, Kit Smythe, Jack Blackton, Will MacKenzie) "Youngest President" (lyric and music by Martin Charnin and Robert Kessler) (Bill Hinnant) "The Astronaut" (sketch by David Panich) (Barbara Gilbert, Brandon Maggart) "Emmy Lou" (lyric and music by Fred Ebb and Norman Martin) (Jane Connell, Bill Hinnant, Jack Blackton, Will McKenzie), "Stock Report" (lyric and music by Fred Ebb and Norman Martin) (Kim Smythe), "Progressive Education" (sketch by David Panich) (Buzz Halliday, Jane Connell, Bill Hinnant, Jack Blackton) "Arty" (lyric and music by David Bimonte and Jim Wise) (Barbara Gilbert), "Plot Luck" (sketch by Jay Thompson) (Brandon Maggart, Will MacKenzie, Peter Sands) "What Kind of Life Is That?" (lyric and music by Fred Ebb and Norman Martin) (Jane Connell, Barbara Gilbert, Buzz Halliday) "Put It in Writing" (lyric and music by Alan Kohan) (Jack Blackton), "Walking Down the Road" (lyric and music by William Angleos and Alan Kohan) (Company)

NOTES—Chicago's own version of "Off Broadway" was The Happy Medium, an intimate playhouse which opened with a successful revue, *Happy Medium*, which played for 102 weeks. It was followed by *Put It in Writing*, which was the only Happy Medium revue to play in New York. Unfortunately, and despite its cast (which included Jane Connell and Bill Hinnant), the revue played just three weeks.

Howard Taubman in the *New York Times* noted that many of the evening's satiric targets weren't worth the bother, and lacked bite. But he praised the song "Emmy Lou," Fred Ebb and Norman Martin's "envenomed valentine" to the South. Jane Connell played Emmy Lou, a Mississippi belle in blonde braids being courted by three suitors (in song they ask "Who's gonna take you to the lynchin' Saturday night, Emmy Lou?") who can't come up with anything "lethal enough to amuse her sadistic taste."

Taubman also liked another Fred Ebb and Norman Martin contribution, "The Ayes of Texas," a "sardonically bouncy" song about Billy Sol Estes. But Taubman drew the line at "I Hope You're Happy" (also by Ebb and Martin), a sequence in which the revue was "wrong" to be timely. The song dealt with then Governor Nelson Rockefeller's new marriage, and Taubman found the number "innocuous [but] somewhat uncomfortable," noting there were some subjects which a revue "would be wise to abjure."

Numbers which appeared in the Chicago production, but which weren't used in New York were: "Do Kids Go Steady?" (lyric by Fred Tobias, music by Charles Strouse); "Marquee for Twofers' (sketch by Richard Maury); "The Habit Waltz" (lyric and music by Fred Ebb and Norman Martin); "The Psychiatrist" (sketch by David Panich); "Democratic Sport" (by G. Wood); "Check List" (by Jay Thompson); and "Decisions" (lyric and music by William Angelos and Alan Kohan). Panich's sketch "Memories" was used in both *Put It in Writing* and in the 1957 revue *Kaleidoscope* (see entry).

1319 A Quarter for the Ladies Room. "A Musical Eyeview." THEATRE: Village Gate; OPENING DATE: November 12, 1972; PERFORMANCES: 1; LYRICS: Ruth Batchelor; MUSIC: John Clifton and Arthur Siegel; DIRECTION: Darwin Knight; SCENERY: David R. Ballou; COSTUMES: Miles White; LIGHTING: Lee Watson; MUSICAL DIRECTION: Karen Gustafson; PRODUCER: Philip R. Productions, Inc.

CAST—Helon Blount (The Attendant), Paula Cinko (The Angel), Norma Donaldson (The Harlot), Judy MacMurdo (The Mistress), Benay Venuta (The Wife)

The action occurs in a ladies' room the present time (as time stands still).

The musical was presented in one act (song assignments unknown).

MUSICAL NUMBERS—"First Quarter," "Turn Around," "Incomplete," "Married Man," "Gemini," "Number One Man," "My Hero's Grenades," "Talk About the Men," "Feel at Home," "My Lover and His Wife," "Incest and Apples," "Baby Dolls," "The Princess," "Nice Ladies," "Woman Power," "Whatshisname," "Butterfly's Lament," "When Will the Music Be Gone," "The Kind of Guy," "Epitaph," "When the Time Comes," "Why Don't I Leave Him," "Talk to Me," "Last Quarter"

NOTES—The one-performance flop *A Quarter for the Ladies Room* had no dialogue and was sung-through; it dealt with four women (and a powder room attendant) who complain incessantly about the men in their lives, all to a score of "high grade Muzak" (according to Joseph H. Mazo in *Women's*

Wear Daily) and often tasteless lyrics (Douglas Watt in the *New York Daily News*). Kevin Sanders on WABC-TV noted he had never been in a ladies' room, and rejoiced at his good fortune.

1320 Queen of Hearts (1998). THEATRE: Grove Street Playhouse; OPENING DATE: October 5, 1998; PERFORMANCES: 20; BOOK: Stephen Stahl; LYRICS: Claudia Perry; MUSIC: Claudia Perry; DIRECTION: Christopher Casoria; CHOREOGRAPHY: Marian Akana; SCENERY: Robert F. Wolin; COSTUMES: Dale A. Beverly; LIGHTING: Scott Davis; MUSICAL DIRECTION: Charles Eversole; PRODUCER: Marilyn Majeski

CAST—Sophia Abbasi (Young Diana), Eddie Barton (Prince Harry), Debi Clydesdale (Raine Spencer, Camilla Parker-Bowles), Mitch Ellis (Adrian, Earl Charles Spencer), J.P. Hartman (Prince William), Juliet Grinnel Howe (Mary Ann), Jon Himell (James), Margot McGuire (Grace, Woman), Kendra Munger (Princess Diana), Tony Sicuso (Dodi), James A. Walsh (Prince Charles)

The musical was presented in two acts (division of acts and song assignments unknown; songs are listed in performance order).

MUSICAL NUMBERS—"Way of the World," "Who You Are," "The Hamley Catalog," "Backbone of Steel," "Circle Round," "Nothing Ever Happens to Me," "Black Tie Waltz," "The Greatest Show," "Look at the Camera," "A Fairy Tale Come True," "Her Royal Highness," "Future King of England," "Pay Your Royal Dues," "Moment to Moment," "The Spare to the Heir," "The Walls Are Closing In," "Time to Let Go," "The New Me," "Queen of Hearts," "Back to My Babies," "You're My World," "It's My Time," Finale

NOTES—*Queen of Hearts* was an Off Off Broadway musical about Princess Diana, and included such songs as "Pay Your Royal Dues," "The Spare to the Heir," and "Back to My Babies." According to *Theatre World 1998-1999 Season*, the writers had "creative differences" concerning the production, and so later in the season their "approved" version of *Queen of Hearts* opened (see entry).

A one-woman musical about the subject, *Diana, De Musical*, opened in the Netherlands in 2000; the production, which starred Vera Mann, was recorded by Universal Classics and Jazz Records (CD # 013-658-2). Another musical, *Charles and Diana*, was produced Off Off Broadway during Summer 2005 at the Midtown International Theatre Festival; the book and music were by Lewis Papier, and the lyrics were by Mary Sullivan Struzi.

1321 Queen of Hearts (1999). THEATRE: Harold Clurman Theatre; OPENING DATE: March 26, 1999; PERFORMANCES: 13; BOOK: Stephen Stahl; LYRICS: Claudia Perry; MUSIC: Claudia Perry; DIRECTION: Stephen Stahl; CHOREOGRAPHY: Phil LaDuca; SCENERY: Rob Wolin; COSTUMES: Terry Leong; LIGHTING: Scott Davis; MUSICAL DIRECTION: Allan Kashkin; PRODUCERS: Wayne Trevisani and Ira Lippy

CAST—Sharon Alexander (Raine), Derin Altay (Grace), Jules Bartkowski (Harry), Paula Leggett Chase (Diana), Annie Edgerton (Camilla), Tom Henry (James), Bill Quinlan (Earl Spencer), Anthony Santelmo, Jr. (Sir W. Frost), Tom Schmid (Dodi), Jenny Lee Stern (Maryann), Christian Stuck (William), James A. Walsh (Charles), Julia Yorks (Young Diana)

The action occurs in England during the period 1978-1999.

The musical was presented in two acts (division of acts and song assignments unknown; songs are listed in performance order).

MUSICAL NUMBERS—Overture, "Who You Are," "Way of the World," "Backbone of Steel," "Circle Round," "Chat & Tea," "Nothing Ever Happens to Me," "Black Tie Waltz," "Someone to Love," "Greatest Show on Earth," "Look at the Camera," "Fairy-Tale Come True," "Her Royal Highness," "Future King of England," "Things Will Never Be the Same," "Pay Your Royal Dues," "Moment to Moment," "The Spare to the Heir," "Increasingly Messy," "The Walls Are Closing In," "Time to Let Go," "Teach Me How," "You're My World," "It's My Time," "Queen of Hearts," Finale

NOTES—*Theatre World 1998-1999 Season* reported that the writers of *Queen of Hearts*, the Off Off Broadway musical about Princess Diana, had "creative differences" concerning the production of the musical which been seen earlier in the season (see entry). They "approved" the second version, which still included the characters of Diana, Charles, Camilla, and Dodi as well as the songs "Pay Your Royal Dues" and "The Spare to the Heir" (but "Back to My Babies" was dropped this time around). For information about other musicals based on Diana's life, see entry for the first production.

1322 Queens Boulevard (the musical). THEATRE: The Peter Norton Space/Signature Theatre Company; OPENING DATE: December 2, 2007; PERFORMANCES: 37; BOOK: Charles Mee; LYRICS AND MUSIC: See notes below; DIRECTION: Davis McCallum; CHOREOGRAPHY: Peter Pucci; SCENERY: Mimi Lien; Joseph Spirito, Video Design; COSTUMES: Christal Weatherly; LIGHTING: Marcus Doshi; MUSICAL DIRECTION: Matt Castle; PRODUCER: Signature Theatre Company (James Houghton, Founding Artistic Director; Erika Mallin, Executive Director)

CAST—Amir Arison (Vijay), Michi Barall (Shizuko), Satya Bhabha (DJ), Marsha Stephanie Blake (Doctor 3, Esther), Bill Buell (Patrick, Bartender, Bather 1, Bob, Detective), Demosthenes Chrysan (Doctor 1, Cabbie 2, Bather 3, Giorgio, Rabbi, Criminal 3), Geeta Citygirl (Vivian, Doctor 5), Emily Donahoe (Katya, Colleen), William Jackson Harper (Flower Seller, Doctor 2, Cabbie 1, Criminal 1), Jodi Lin (Mimi), Arian Moayed (Abdi), Debargo Sanyal (Paan Beedi Guy, Bather 2, Doctor 4, Criminal 2), Jon Norman Schneider (Aly, Cabbie 3), Ruth Zhang (Min, Jenny)

SOURCE—The musical was inspired by the Kathi-Kali play *The Flower of Good Fortune* by Kottayan Tampuran; and working with the dramaturgical collaboration of Tom Damrauer, the musical also incorporated texts from Homer, James Joyce, among others.

The action occurs on Queens Boulevard in Queens, New York.

The musical was presented in one act.

NOTES—Inspired by the classical Indian dance-drama *The Flower of Good Fortune*, *Queens Boulevard (the musical)* told the story of a groom who searches all over Queens Boulevard for the mythical Flower of Heaven, which he wants to present to his bride as a wedding gift.

Frank Scheck in the *New York Post* found the "outlandish extravaganza" a "multicultural stew." He noted the musical's attempt to utilize a diverse number of cultures to tell its story was "less organic than merely showoff-y." A program note indicated the musical included songs by Shoukichi Kina, Ann Malik and Craig Pruess, Benny Anderson, Bjorn Ulvaeus, and Stig Anderson, Rizwan-Muazzam Qawwali, Akhenaton, Maya Arulpragasam and Richard X, John Lalit, and traditional Okinawan, Iranian, and Irish folk songs. (The songs by Shoukichi Kina were "Jing Jing," "Hana No Kajimaya," and "Subete No Hito No Kokoro Ni Hanna O.")

Not to be confused with the 1997 Off Broadway gay comedy *Queens Blvd.* by Paul Corrigan.

1323 Quilters. "A New Musical." THEATRE: Jack Lawrence Theatre; OPENING DATE: September 25, 1984; PERFORMANCES: 24; TEXT: Molly Newman and Barbara Damashek; LYRICS: Barbara Damashek; MUSIC: Barbara Damashek; DIRECTION: Barbara Damashek; SCENERY: Ursula Belden; COSTUMES: Elizabeth Palmer; LIGHTING: Allen Lee Hughes; PRODUCERS: The Denver Center for the Performing Arts, The John F. Kennedy Center for the Performing Arts, The American National Theatre Academy, and Brockman Seawell

CAST—Lenka Peterson (Sarah), The Daughters (Evalyn Baron, Marjorie Berman, Alma Cuervo, Lynn Lobban, Rosemary McNamara, Jennifer Parsons), Musicians, Daughters, and Sons (Emily Knapp Chatfield, Melanie Sue Harby, John S. Lionarons, Joseph A. Waterkotte, Catherine Way)

SOURCE—The 1977 book *The Quilters: Women and Domestic Art: An Oral History* by Patricia J. Cooper and Norma Bradley Allen.

The revue was presented in two acts (song assignments were not credited in the program).

ACT ONE—"Pieces of Lives" (first four lines of the song were from "The Quilt" by Dorothy MacFarlane), "Rocky Road," "Little Babes That Sleep All Night" (lyric from *Our Homes and Their Adornments* by Almon C. Varney), "Thread the Needle," "Cornelia," "Are You Washed in the Blood of the Lamb?" (words by E.A. Hoffman), "The Butterfly," "Pieces of Lives" (reprise), "Green, Green, Green," "The Needle's Eye" (the chorus is from the lyric of a traditional folk song)

ACT TWO—"Hoedown" (traditional), "Quiltin' and Dreamin'," "Pieces of Lives" (reprise), "Every Log in My House" (first line of the song by Elinore Pruitt Stewart), "Land Where We'll Never Grow Old" (words by J.C. Moore), "Who Will Count the Stitches?," "The Lord Doesn't Rain Down Manna," "Dandelion" (lyric by Clara J. Denton from the poem "Blooming in the Fall"), "Everything Has a Time," "Hands Around"

NOTES—Using dance, mime, sketches, monologues, and even occasional *Story Theatre* techniques, *Quilters* was an earnest and well-intentioned revue which depicted American pioneer women who told the stories of their lives and times through the crafting of quilts. Unfortunately, the women depicted in the piece were too generic, and the work lacked a firm narrative perspective. Frank Rich in the *New York Times* noted the characters were "so bloodlessly sketched" that it was impossible to care about them, and he concluded that *Quilters* was "threadbare."

The Best Plays of 1984-1985 categorized the revue as a Broadway show, but *Theatre World 1984-1985 Season* included it as part of its Off Broadway round-up. Since the revue was produced under a Middle Broadway contract, it's considered an Off Broadway musical for the purposes of this book.

The script was published by Dramatists Play Service, Inc., in 1986.

1324 R Shomon

NOTES—See entry for *See What I Wanna See*.

1325 Radiant Baby. "A Musical." THEATRE: Newman Theatre/The Public Theatre; OPENING DATE: March 2, 2003; PERFORMANCES: 25; BOOK: Stuart Ross; LYRICS: Unless otherwise noted, all lyrics by Stuart Ross and and Debra Barsha; MUSIC: Debra Barsha; DIRECTION: George C. Wolfe; CHOREOGRAPHY: Fatima Robinson; SCENERY: Riccardo Hernandez; COSTUMES: Emilio Sosa; LIGHTING: Howell Binkley; MUSICAL DIRECTION: Kimberly Grigsby; PRODUCER: The Public Theatre (George C. Wolfe, Producer; Mara Manus, Executive Director)

CAST—Anny Jules (Mikayla), Gabriel Enrique Alvarez (Jake, Maurice), Remy Zaken (Rini), Kate Jennings Grant (Amanda), Keong Sim (Tseng Kwong Chi), Daniel Reichard (Keith Haring), Aaron Lohr (Carlos), Michael Winther (Mr. Haring), Julee

Cruise (Mrs. Haring, Andy Warhol), Curtis Holbrook and Billy Porter (Two Incredibly Hot and Sleazy New York Men), Angela Robinson (Diva Woman), Billy Porter (Diva Man), Julee Cruise/Tracee Beazer/Celina Carvajal (Miss RN and the IVs), Tracee Beazer (Singer on the Radio), Christopher Martinez (Break Dancer), Julee Cruise/Billy Porter/Angela Robinson/Michael Winther (The Media/Critics/Journalists), Celina Carvajal/Rhett G. George/Christian Vincent (Pop Girl and Her Boys), Tracee Beazer/Celia Carvajal/Julee Cruise/Rhett G. George/Curtis Holbrook/Christopher Livsey/Christopher Martinez/Jermaine Montell/Billy Porter/Angela Robinson/Christian Vincent/Michael Winther (Business People, Prom Couples. New Yorkers, Club 80 Patrons, S.V.A. Students, Graffiti Artists, Celebrities, Gallery Owners, Art Patrons, Bath Boys, Police)

SOURCE—The 1991 book *Keith Haring: The Authorized Biography* by John Gruen.

The action occurs mostly in New York City during the period 1978-1990, with a flashback sequence to Kutztown, Pennsylvania, in 1963.

The musical was presented in two acts.

ACT ONE—"This Is the World"/"Faster Than the Speed of Life" (Anny Jules, Gabriel Enrique Alvarez, Remy Zaken, Kate Jennings Grant, Keong Sim, Ensemble), "Draw and Move" (lyric by Ira Gasman, Stuart Ross, and Debra Barsha) (Daniel Reichard, Anny Jules, Gabriel Enrique Alvarez, Remy Zaken, Ensemble), "Spirit of the Line" (Michael Winther, Daniel Reichard), "Prom Dreams"/"Get Me to New York" (Daniel Reichard, Anny Jules, Gabriel Enrique Alvarez, Remy Zaken, Ensemble), "The Journals" (Daniel Reichard, Ensemble), "New York Makes Me" (lyric by Ira Gasman, Stuart Ross, and Debra Barsha) (Curtis Holbrook, Billy Porter, Daniel Reichard), "Wei Yi Shu Xian Sheng" (Keong Sim, Daniel Reichard, Lounge Lizard Slut, June/Ward Slut, Patrons of Club 80), "Paradise"/"Instant Gratification" (Angela Robinson, Billy Porter, Julee Cruise, Tracee Beazer, Celina Carvajal, Daniel Reichard, Ensemble), "If It Can't Be Love" (Tracee Beazer, Daniel Reichard, Aaron Lohr), "Normal Day" (Kate Jennings Grant), "Taggin'" (Ensemble), "Spirit of the Line" (reprise)/"Chalk Dust Man" (Company)

ACT TWO—"Flavor of the Week" (lyric by Ira Gasman, Stuart Ross, and Debra Barsha) (Company), "Developing" (Keong Sim, Kate Jennings Grant, Anny Jules, Gabriel Enrique Alvarez, Remy Zaken), "Flavor of the Week (Part 2)" (Company), "Hot Tomato Soup" (Daniel Reichard, Julee Cruise, Ensemble), "I Really Loved You" (lyric by Ira Gasman) (Aaron Lohr), "Draw Me a Door" (Daniel Reichard), "Dear Mr. Haring" (Gabriel Enrique Alvarez), "Faster Than the Speed of Life" (Daniel Reichard, Company), "Paradise" (reprise) (Company), "Quartet" (lyric by Ira Gasman, Stuart Ross, and Debra Barsha) (Daniel Reichard, Keong Sim, Kate Jennings Grant, Aaron Lohr), "Stay" (Daniel Reichard, Keong Sim, Kate Jennings Grant, Aaron Lohr, Company)

NOTES—*Radiant Baby* told the story of pop artist Keith Haring, who died of AIDS in 1990 when he was thirty years old. Set against the hedonistic nightlife of New York City in the 1980s, the musical depicted Haring's beginnings, his rise to fame, his lovers, and his early death. All this was accompanied by the rather coy use of three children who portrayed a kind of streetwise Greek chorus (the 1970 Broadway musical *Cry for Us All* employed a similar device). Ben Brantley in *The New York Times* felt the musical was "paralyzed" by its desire to cover too much ground, and he noted the creators seemed "overwhelmed" by their goal of presenting both portraits of Haring and of the 1980s. Charles Isherwood in *Variety* found *Radiant Baby* "frenetic but vacuous," and noted the score was mostly "undistinguished"; but he singled out "Hot Tomato Soup," a vaudeville-styled duet between Haring and another pop art icon, Andy Warhol (here played by a woman in male drag). The musical was later produced on March 1, 2006, at the Cap 21 Theatre as part of the Barbara Wolff Monday Night Reading Series.

1326 Radio Gals.

THEATRE: John Houseman Theatre; OPENING DATE: October 1, 1996; PERFORMANCES: 40; BOOK: Mike Craver and Mark Hardwick; LYRICS: Mike Craver and Mark Hardwick; MUSIC: Mike Craver and Mark Hardwick; DIRECTION: Marcia Milgrom Dodge; CHOREOGRAPHY: Marcia Milgrom Dodge; SCENERY: Narelle Sissons; COSTUMES: Michael Krass; LIGHTING: Joshua Starbuck; PRODUCERS: Elliot Martin and Ron Shapiro in association with Lee Mimms and Amick Bryam; Marjorie Martin, Associate Producer

CAST—Carole Cook (Hazel C. Hunt), M. (Michael) Rice (Miss Mabel Swindle), P.M. (Mike) Craver (Miss Azilee Swindle), Emily Mikesell (America), Klea Blackhurst (Rennabelle), Rosemary Loar (Gladys Fritts), Matthew Bennet (O.B. Abbott); the entire cast also comprised the musical group "The Hazelnuts"

The action occurs in May during the late 1920s ("well before 'The Crash'") in the parlor of Hazel C. Hunt's home in Cedar Ridge, Arkansas.

The musical was presented in two acts.

ACT ONE—"The Wedding of the Flowers" (Carole Cook), "Sunrise Melody" (Carole Cook, Emily Mikesell, Klea Blackhurst, P.M. Craver), "Aviatrix Love Song" (Emily Mikesell), "Horehound Compound I" (The Hazelnuts), "If Stars Could Talk" (Rosemary Loar, Klea Blackhurst, Emily Mikesell), "When It's Sweetpea Time in Georgia" (P.M. Craver), "Dear Mr. Gershwin" (Klea Blackhurst), "The Tranquil Boxwood" (Rosemary Loar), "Faeries in My Mother's Flower Garden" (Rosemary Loar), "Horehound Compound II" (The Hazelnuts), "A Fireside, a Pipe and a Pet" (Matthew Bennett, Rosemary Loar), "Edna Jones, The Elephant Girl" (The Hazelnuts), "Paging the Ether"/"Play Gypsies, Play" (Carole Cook)

ACT TWO—"Royal Radio" (Emily Mikesell, Klea Blackhurst, M. Rice, P.M. Craver), "Weather Song" (Klea Blackhurst, Emily Mikesell, M. Rice, P.M. Craver), "Buster, He's a Hot Dog Now" (choreography by Mike Craver) (M. Rice, P.M. Craver), "Why Did You Make Me Love You?" (Matthew Bennett), "Kittens in the Snow" (The Hazelnuts), "Old Gals Are the Best Pals After All" (Carole Cooke, M. Rice, P.M. Craver), "A Gal's Got to Do What a Gal's Got to Do" (Carole Cooke), The NBC Broadcast (The Hazelnuts): "Horehound Compound III," "Whispering Pines," "The Wedding of the Flowers" (reprise), "Queenie Take Me Home with You," "Royal Radio" (The Hazelnuts)

NOTES—*Radio Gal*'s script (published by Samuel French, Inc., in 1997) and cast album (released by Varese Sarabande Records [CD # VSD-5604]) noted that in the early days of radio before the U.S. Department of Commerce cracked down on them, there were many independent "mom and pop" radio stations which "wave jumped" from channel to channel to whatever frequencies might have clear broadcast space. The musical was inspired by an incident involving Aimee Semple MacPherson, who operated an illegal independent radio station in Los Angeles; when Herbert Hoover (then the Secretary of Commerce) sent an inspector to close down the station, MacPherson reportedly eloped with the inspector on his motorcycle. (For information on musicals about MacPherson, see entry for *Sister Aimee.*)

Radio Gals told the story of Hazel C. Hunt, who operated her own independent radio station (WGAL) and presented news, weather, local announcements, and entertainment (courtesy of her group, The Hazelnuts).

Two of her Hazelnuts were M. Rice and P.M. Craver (Michael Rice and Mike Craver, the latter one of the musical's co-writers); traditionally, their roles (of Miss Mabel Swindel and Miss Azilee Swindle) have been performed by men in drag.

The published script credits Craver and Mark Hardwick as the collaborators on the songs, with the exception of four written solely by Craver ("If Stars Could Talk," "Dear Mr. Gershwin," "Royal Radio," and "Weather Song").

The critics were becoming weary of Off Broadway musicals which gently kidded country and western music, and perhaps that's why *Radio Gals* lasted only five weeks. A few critics cited similar musicals such as *Pump Boys and Dinettes*, *Oil City Symphony*, and *Cowgirls* (indeed, Craver and Hardwick had already mined this minor genre; the two had collaborated on songs for *Oil City Symphony*, and Hardwick was one of *Pump Boys'* writers). Donald Lyons in *The Wall Street Journal* found the humor "sweet and bland" and occasionally campy (but noted the camp humor was not as "out" as the material in *When Pigs Fly* [see separate entry]). Lyons concluded by recommending the musical to those who miss Ma and Pa Kettle and Judy Canova. Lawrence Van Gelder in the *New York Times* noted that despite the "tissue-thin" plot and characters, *Radio Gals* was a "lively, cheery, nostalgia-dipped musical."

The musical had been previously produced by the Arkansas Repertory Theater in Little Rock on March 18, 1993.

1327 A Rag on a Stick and a Star.

THEATRE: Theatre Row Theatre; OPENING DATE: September 10, 1992; PERFORMANCES: 1 (estimated); BOOK: Eric Blau; LYRICS: Eric Blau; MUSIC: Elliot Weiss; DIRECTION: Richard Ziman; CHOREOGRAPHY: Shaelyn Ament; SCENERY: Don Jensen; COSTUMES: Traci Di Gesu; LIGHTING: Graeme McDonnell; MUSICAL DIRECTION: Woody Regan; PRODUCER: Merry Enterprises Theatre

CAST—William Youmans (the Reverend Hechler), Daniel Neiden (Dori/Herzl), Courtenay Collins (Julie), David Pevsner (Newlinski), Jeff Gardner (Bokov), Steve Irish (Lueger, Others), Catherine Dupuis (Lulu, Others), Adriana Maxwell (Party Guest, Others), Shaelyn Ament (Queen Victoria, Others), Hart MacCardell-Fossel (Child)

The musical was presented in two acts (division of acts and singing assignments unknown; songs are listed in performance order).

MUSICAL NUMBERS—"Oh Lead Us Now," "Oh Vienna," "Wishing for a Victory," "Farewell Soft Life," "Appearances," "A Rag on a Stick and a Star," "On the Way Home to the Old Land," "Let's Play the Game," "Actress on the Stage," "Abdullah," "In the Wildest Dream," "I'm a Very Patient Man," "When It Grows Dark My Lord," "All My Anguish and My Sorrow," "We Have Come So Far," "A World Without Us," "Let Them Bleed," "What Happened Here?," "This Is My Promise," "Do You Know What the Children Were Doing Today?," "There Is a Bird," "We Are Dancing in the Temple"

NOTES—The Off Off Broadway musical *A Rag on a Stick and a Star* was about Theodore Herzl (a/k/a Dori) (1860-1904), who is considered the father of Zionism and who was convinced that without a state of their own the Jewish people could not survive.

Six years earlier, in 1986, the musical had been seen as *Dori* (see entry) for a special one-performance concert version at the Cathedral Church of St. John the Divine. The concert had presented highlights from the score, and its cast included Douglas Fairbanks, Jr. (as the production's narrator), Joseph Neal (Dori), and Gary Krawford (Newlinksi).

In a program note for *Dori*, its producer Reuben Hoppenstein said he hoped to see the musical mounted on Broadway in 1987. But *Dori* was never seen on Broadway, and its revised 1992 Off Off

Broadway version, *A Rag on a Stick and a Star*, seems to have closed after its first performance.

Songs heard in *Dori* which were carried over for the revised version were "Oh Vienna" (in *Dori*, the song was titled "O Vienna Waltz"), "On the Way Home to the Old Land," "In the Wildest Dream," "Appearances," "Let's Play the Game," "A World Without Us," "Do You Know What the Children Were Doing Today?," and "Dancing in the Temple."

Songs dropped for the revised version were "Intrigue," "I Won't Be Home for a Long, Long Time," "Papa Is a Traveller," "Diaspora," "Kishinev," and "The Promise" (however, the latter may have been heard in *A Rag on a Stick and a Star* as "This Is My Promise"). The prologue from *Dori* may have been retitled "Oh Lead Us Now" for the revised version.

Broadway had earlier seen a dramatic version of Herzl's life; titled *Herzl*, the play by Dore Schary and Amos Elon opened at the Palace Theatre on November 30, 1976, and played for eight performances (Paul Hecht performed the title role). *Herzl* was Schary's final play.

1328 Rags/Children of the Wind. THEATRE: American Jewish Theatre; OPENING DATE: December 2, 1991; PERFORMANCES: 59; BOOK: Joseph Stein; LYRICS: Stephen Schwartz; MUSIC: Charles Strouse; DIRECTION: Richard Sabellico; Andrew Volkoff, Assistant Director; CHOREOGRAPHY: Richard Sabellico; Matt Zarley and Debra Henry, Assistant Choreographers; SCENERY: Jeff Modereger; COSTUMES: Gail Baldoni; LIGHTING: Tom Sturge; MUSICAL DIRECTION: Vincent Trovato; PRODUCER: American Jewish Theatre (Stanley Brechner, Artistic Director; Lonny Price, Associate Artistic Director)

CAST—Rachel Black (Rosa, Landlady, Shopper, 14th Street Ballet Dancer, Sophie, Striker), Ann Crumb (Rebecca), Jonathan Kaplan (David), Philip Hoffman (Avram, Hamlet, Big Tim), Crista Moore (Bella), Jan Neuberger (Rachel, Ophelia, Mrs. Sullivan), David Pevsner (Doctor, Saul, 14th Street Ballet Dancer, Nathan), Robert Tate (Guard, Immigrant, Editor, Klezmer Musician, O'Leary, 14th Street Ballet Dancer, Striker), Alec Timerman (Ben, 14th Street Ballet Dancer)

The action occurs en route to and in New York City around 1910.

The musical was presented in two acts.

ACT ONE—"Children of the Wind" (Ann Crumb), "If We Never Meet Again" (Ann Crumb, Crista Moore), "Yankee Boy" (Alec Timerman, Crista Moore, Jonathan Kaplan), "Greenhorns" (Company), "Brand New World" (Ann Crumb, Crista Moore, Jonathan Kaplan), "Penny a Tune" (Company), "Easy for You" (David Pevsner, Ann Crumb), "Hamlet" (Company), "Blame It on the Summer Night" (Ann Crumb), "For My Mary" (Alec Timerman), "Rags" (Crista Moore, Philip Hoffman, Ann Crumb)

ACT TWO—"If We Never Meet Again" (reprise) (Ann Crumb, Crista Moore), "Uptown" (David Pevsner, Ann Crumb), "Cherry Street Café" (Rachel Black), "Sound of Love" (Alec Timerman, Jonathan Kaplan, Crista Moore, Ann Crumb), "Three Sunny Rooms" (Jan Neuberger, Philip Hoffman), "Wanting" (Ann Crumb, David Pevsner), "What's Wrong with That?" (Philip Hoffman, David Pevsner, Ann Crumb), "Dancing with the Fools" (Ann Crumb), Finale (Company)

NOTES—As *Rags*, the musical was first seen on Broadway in 1986 for a shockingly brief run of just four performances; the stellar cast included Teresa Stratas, Larry Kert, Dick Latessa, Terrence Mann, Lonny Price, Judy Kuhn, and Marica Lewis. The sprawling and overly familiar story of Jewish immigrants living in New York City during the early 1900s probably worked against the musical, but its strong score by Stephen Schwartz and Charles Strouse (which includes the haunting ballad "Blame It on the Summer Night," one of the finest theatre songs of the era) will no doubt ensure occasional revivals of the work by adventurous theatre groups.

The Off Off Broadway revival by the American Jewish Theatre was a revised version of the musical. The following songs in the Broadway production were omitted from the revival: "I Remember," "On the Fourth Day of July," "In America," "Democratic Club Dance," "Prayer," and "Bread and Freedom." Added to the revival were "If We Never Meet Again" and "Cherry Street Café" (the latter had been heard during the original production's pre-Broadway tryout in Boston). The revival's "Hamlet" was no doubt a new title for "Hard to Be a Prince," which was in the original Broadway production.

The Broadway cast album was released by Sony Records (CD # SK-42657).

1329 Rain. THEATRE: Alice Tully Hall/Lincoln Center; OPENING DATE: February 2003; PERFORMANCES: Unknown; LIBRETTO: Richard Owen; MUSIC: Richard Owen; MUSICAL DIRECTION: Richard Owen, Jr.; PRODUCER: Camerata New York

CAST—Lynn Owen (Sadie Thompson), Marc Embree (the Reverend Davidson), Catherine Kelly (Mrs. Davidson), Adina Aaron (Mrs. McPhail), David Gordon (Dr. McPhail), Robert Hoyt (Trader Horn), Ronnita Miller (Mrs. Horn), Sailors and Natives (Eric Burkhardt, Michael Cole, Michael Szwejbka, Peter Zuspan)

SOURCE—Somerset Maugham's short story "Miss Thompson."

The action occurs in San Francisco, on board the S.S. *Sonoma*, and on the island of Pago-Pago.

The opera was performed in two acts.

ACT ONE—"Sadie's Blues," "Davidson's Aria Condemning Sin," "The McPhails' Dialog," "Arrival at Pago-Pago," "Sadie Arrives," "The Ladies 'Sizing-Up' Trio and Dialog," "Mrs. McPhail's Aria About the Fishermen," "Sadie and the Sailors," "Sadie and Davidson's First Confrontation," "Mrs. Davidson's Denunciation of Dancing," "Davidson's Attempt to Break Up Sadie's Party," "Mr. Horn Warns Sadie," "Sadie's Sympathy Fails with Mrs. Davidson," "Davidson Speaks of Reforming Sadie," "Davidson Fails in the Final Quartet"

ACT TWO—"Horn's Aria of Distress," "Sadie's Ordered Deported," "Davidson Approves the Deportation," "Sadie's Lament," "Mrs. Horn's Sad Vocalise and McPhails' Duet," "Sadie and Davidson's Confrontation," "Mrs. McPhail's Aria of Shame and Davidson's Vision," "Sadie's 'Always Running' Aria," "Sadie/Davidson Duet," "Mrs. Davidson's Aria of Distress," "Davidson's Explanation and Aria," "Sadie and Davidson Go for a Walk," "Mrs. Horn's Lament" (reprise) and "Sadie's Prayer Aria," "Davidson's Reassurance," "Davidson Returns to Sadie's Room," "Davidson's Body Is Discovered"; "Mrs. Davidson Awakes to Reality and Sadie Turns Her," "Gramophone on Full Blast Denouncing All Men"

NOTES—Richard Owen's opera is the latest in a fascinating history of dramatic and lyric adaptations of Somerset Maugham's famous story of Sadie Thompson. *Rain* was recorded on a 2-CD set by Albany Records (# TROY-623/24), an innovative and invaluable company which is almost single-handedly ensuring that modern operas are recorded (further, the company has also released a fascinating series of recordings devoted to early American operettas). (The above list of song and dialogue sequences for *Rain* is taken from the recording.) Maugham's short story "Miss Thompson" was first adapted for the stage as *Rain* by John Colton and Clemence Randolph in 1922 when it was given a legendary performance by Jeanne Eagels and played on Broadway for 648 performances; it was revived on Broadway with Tallulah Bankhead in 1935 (incidentally, the playbill cover appears to be the first issued in color). In 1944, *Sadie Thompson*, a musical version with lyrics by Howard Dietz and music by Vernon Duke, played on Broadway for less than two months. It starred June Havoc (replacing Ethel Merman, who left during rehearsals), and its memorable if underrated score includes the haunting "Sailing at Midnight"; thanks to another innovative record company (Original Cast Records), a studio cast recording of the score was released in 2002 (Melissa Errico was Sadie). In 1952, the Broadway revue *Two's Company* (lyrics by Ogden Nash and music by Vernon Duke) included a mini-musical version of *Rain* called "Roll Along, Sadie" (Bette Davis was Sadie); Duke didn't use any music from his 1944 version for the "Roll Along, Sadie" sequence. The cast recording was released by RCA Victor (# LOC-1009). In 1972, *Rain* was revived Off Broadway (Antonia Rey was Sadie, and, in the role of one of the sailors, a very young John Travolta), and in 1984 the work was again revived Off Broadway (Sabra Jones was Sadie).

Rain was filmed four times (all versions had different titles). The first was *Sadie Thompson*, a 1928 silent version with Gloria Swanson, and the second was *Rain*, a 1932 release with Joan Crawford. In 1946, an all-Black film version was seen; titled *Dirty Gertie from Harlem U.S.A.*, Francine Everett played "Gertie La Rue." In 1953, an underrated adaptation of the material appeared when the fourth film version was released; as *Miss Sadie Thompson*, Rita Hayworth gave a memorable performance in this semi-musical remake which had lyrics by Allan Roberts and Ned Washington and music by Lester Lee. The film's four songs were "A Marine, A Marine, A Marine" (a/k/a "Marine Song"), "Hear No Evil," "The Heat Is On," and "Blue Pacific Blues." "The Heat Is On" is one of the most torrid dance numbers ever captured on film, and the overlooked "Blue Pacific Blues" is one of the best film songs of the era. The film's soundtrack was released on a 10" LP by Mercury Records (# MG-25181).

Richard Owens' operatic treatment is the most recent adaptation of the material.

1330 Rainbow. "A New Musical." THEATRE: Orpheum Theatre; OPENING DATE: December 18, 1972; PERFORMANCES: 48; BOOK: James Rado and Ted Rado; LYRICS: James Rado; MUSIC: James Rado; DIRECTION: Joe Donovan; SCENERY: James Tilton; COSTUMES: Nancy Potts; LIGHTING: James Tilton; MUSICAL DIRECTION: Steven Margoshes; PRODUCERS: James Rado and Ted Rado in association with Richard Osorio

CAST—Gregory V. Karliss (Man), Philip A.D. (Jesus), Patricia Gaul (Stripper, Ms. Friendstrangle), Rudy Brown (Dr. Banana), Camille (Mother), Michael D. Arian (Father), Meat Loaf (Buddah), Elinor Frye (Opera), Dean Compton (President), Marie Santell (First Lady), Stephen Scharf (President's Child), Marcia McClain (President's Child), Bobby C. Ferguson (Wizard), Kay Cole (Girl), Janet Powell (Twin Girl); Rainbow Band

The musical was presented in two acts.

ACT ONE—"Who Are We" (Rainbeams [entire company?]), "Love Me Love Me Dorothy Lamour La Sarong" (Rainbeams), "Fruits and Vegetables" (Rainbeams), "Welcome Banana" (Rudy Brown, Rainbeams), "Questions Questions" (Patricia Gaul), "Song to Sing" (Kay Cole, Rainbeams), "My Lungs" (Gregory V. Karliss, Rainbeams), "You Got to Be Clever" (Kay Cole, Rainbeams), "What Can I Do for You" (Janet Powell), "Tangled Tangents" (Gregory V. Karliss, Rudy Brown, [and unknown performer]), "Oh I Am a Fork" (Camille, Michael D. Arian, Rainbeams), "People Stink" (Michael D. Arian, Rainbeams), "Guinea Piggin" (Camille, Rainbeams), "Give Your Heart to Jesus" (Rainbeams), "Joke a Cola" (Rainbeams), "Mama Loves You" (Camille, Michael D. Arian, Gregory V. Karliss, Philip A.D., Rainbeams), "I Want to Make You Cry" (Gregory V.

Karliss, Janet Powell), "I Am a Cloud" (Rainbeams), "A Garden for Two" (Gregory V. Karliss, Kay Cole, Rainbeams), "Starry Cold Night" (Kay Cole, Janet Powell, Rainbeams), "Bathroom" (Camille, Michael D. Arian, Gregory V. Karliss), "O.K., Goodbye" (Gregory V. Karliss, Camille, Michael D. Arian), "Deep in the Dark" (Gregory V. Karliss, Bobby C. Ferguson), "You Live in Flowers" (Gregory V. Karliss, Rainbeams), "I Don't Hope for Great Things" (Gregory V. Karliss, Rainbeams)

ACT TWO—"Globligated" (Kay Cole, Janet Powell, Gregory V. Karliss), "Be Not Afraid" (Gregory V. Karliss, Rainbeams), "Obedience" (Dean Compton), "Ten Days Ago" (Dean Compton, Rainbeams), "Oh, Oh, Oh" (Marie Santell, Philip A.D.), "Moosh, Moosh" (Dean Compton, [performers unknown]), "The Man" (Kay Cole, Janet Powell), "The World Is Round" (Dean Compton, Patricia Gaul, Gregory V. Karliss), "Stars and Bars" (Dean Compton, [performers unknown]), "Cacophony" (Gregory V. Karliss, Rainbeams), "Groovy Green Man Groovy" (Kay Cole, Janet Powell, Gregory V. Karliss, Stephen Scharf, Marcia McClain), "Heliopolis" (Gregory V. Karliss, Rainbeams), "I Am Not Free" (Gregory V. Karliss, Dean Compton), "We Are the Clouds" ([performer unknown], Rainbeams), "How Dreamlike" (Dean Compton, Gregory V. Karliss, Rainbeams), "Somewhere Under the Rainbow" (Gregory V. Karliss, Rainbeams), "Star Song" (Gregory V. Karliss, Rainbeams)

NOTES—It took two acts and forty-two songs to tell James and Ted Rado's story; *Rainbow* dealt with a young soldier who died in Vietnam and now travels through the universe seeking knowledge and peace. Or something like that. Perhaps the unnamed wanderer was Claude, the hero of *Hair* (see entry) who died in Vietnam in that earlier musical (which was co-authored by James Rado). The script wasn't very coherent, but Clive Barnes in the *New York Times* found the musical "joyous and life-assertive," and said the "brilliant" and melodic score music was "sweet and fresh," and "full of the most astonishing variety." He also praised the lyrics with their "bizarre zaniness" and "bouncy zest."

A revised version of *Rainbow*, which briefly toured the following year, didn't clarify the plot. In fact, the piece came across as a concert-styled collection of minor but charming songs which were attached to an almost non-existent story. The revisal, which starred James Rado and was titled *The Rainbow Rainbeam Radio Roadshow* (subtitled *Heavenzapopin'*), retained twenty-six songs from *Rainbow*, and included two new ones ("Hold Me Hug Me Squeeze Me and Take Me Along" and "We Are the Rainbeams").

1331 The Rainbow Rape Trick.

"A Musical." THEATRE: Bert Wheeler Theatre; OPENING DATE: April 13, 1975; PERFORMANCES: 4; BOOK: Greg Reardon; LYRICS: Greg Reardon and Ann K. Lipson; MUSIC: Ann K. Lipson; DIRECTION: Robert Davison; CHOREOGRAPHY: Robin Raseen; SCENERY: Francis Pezza; COSTUMES: Mary Ann Tolka; LIGHTING: Chaim Gitter; MUSICAL DIRECTION: Elliot Ames; PRODUCER: Hyperion Productions

CAST—Bob Bosco (Billy Redfeather), Vincent Millard (Randy McGee), Patrick O'Sullivan (Tim McGee), Lois Hathaway (Peggy McGee), Deidre Lynn (Ruth Robbins), John Blanda (Abie), Anthony Dileva (Clovis Taylor), Jerry Rodgers (Marcus Schmidt), Joseph Tripolino (Hugo Caporello), Jeremy Stockwell (Michael Taylor), Jean Greer (Minerva Taylor), John Blanda (Gen. Merryweather, Rainbow Village Assassin)

The action occurs in the future in Rainbow Village.

The musical was presented in two acts (division of acts and song assignments unknown).

MUSICAL NUMBERS—"Zip Community," "Free," "Itch to Be a Witch," "Most Confused Prince," "Stay with Me," "Northchester," "Democracy Is Lunacy," "Little Blue Star," "Crush on You," "'Tis of Thee," "Love Me, Baby!," "Three Fierce Men," "Divorce, Of Course," "Act Like a Villager," "Empty World of Power," Finale

NOTES—This obscure musical was gone in less than a week.

1332 The Rajah's Ruby

NOTES—See entry for *Three by One*.

1333 Ram in the Thicket.

THEATRE: Judith Anderson Theatre; OPENING DATE: August 31, 1994; PERFORMANCES: 24; BOOK: Bill Johnson and Michael Criss; LYRICS: Steve Rue and Michael Criss; MUSIC: Steve Rue; DIRECTION: L. Keith White; CHOREOGRAPHY: Jamie Waggoner; COSTUMES: Jerri L. White; MUSICAL DIRECTION: Steve Rue; PRODUCER: Mid-America Artist Showcase, Inc. (MAASh)

CAST—Richard C. Barnes (God), Steve Frazier (Abraham), Charleen Ayers (Woman), Dennis Yadon (Male Pharisee, Meshach), Jerri L. White (Female Pharisee), Chad Frisque (David, Shadrach), Julieanne Stapleton (Sarah), Stuart Gray (Isaac); Dancers (Jamie Waggoner, Nicole-Capri Wallace, Anemone White)

SOURCE—Stories from the Bible (both Old and New Testaments).

The action occurs "now" in "the Bible."

The musical was presented in two acts.

ACT ONE—"Blood Religion" (Chad Frisque), "Solitary Star" (Steve Frazier), "The Promise" (Robert C. Barnes), "The Shadrach and Meshach Show" (Steve Frazier, Dennis Yadon, Chad Frisque, Dancers), "The Jonah Cliché" (Robert C. Barnes, Steve Frazier), "Let's Do the Confessional" (Steve Frazier), "Trying to Get Back on My Feet Again" (Charleen Ayers), "Trying to Get Back on My Feet Again" (reprise) (Robert C. Barnes, Charleen Ayers, Steve Frazier), "Smelly Demon Swine" (Dennis Yadon, Jerri L. White, Company), "Who Is This Man?" (Charleen Ayers, Robert C. Barnes), "A Mother with Sons" (Company), "You Call This a Promise?" (Charleen Ayers, Robert C. Barnes)

ACT TWO—"Together So Long" (Julieanne Stapleton, Steve Frazier), "It's All in the Family" (Robert C. Barnes, Company), "Out on My Own" (Stuart Gray), "Sin Ballet" (Stuart Gray, Jamie Waggoner, Anemone White, Chad Frisque), "Just as I Am" (Stuart Gray), "King David" (Company), "Lullaby" (Robert C. Barnes), "Life of an Innocent Child" (Chad Frisque), "The Promise Broken" (Dennis Yadon, Jerri L. White, Robert C. Barnes, Charleen Ayers, Julieanne Stapleton, Chad Frisque, Steve Frazier), "Trying to Get Back on My Feet Again" (reprise) (Charleen Ayers, Robert C. Barnes), "Blood Religion" (reprise) (Chad Frisque, Company), Finale (Company)

NOTES—*Ram in the Thicket* sounds like an interesting mélange of Old and New Testament stories told from a modern perspective (which included such topics as abortion and AIDS).

1334 Randy Newman's Maybe I'm Doing It Wrong (1981).

THEATRE: The Production Company Theatre; OPENING DATE: April 13, 1981; PERFORMANCES: 17; LYRICS: Randy Newman; MUSIC: Randy Newman; DIRECTION: Joan Micklin Silver; CHOREOGRAPHY: Ara Fitzgerald; SCENERY: Heidi Landesman; COSTUMES: Oleksa; LIGHTING: Debra J. Kletter; PRODUCER: The Production Company (Norman Rene, Artistic Director; Caren Harder (Managing Director)

CAST—Mark Linn-Baker, Patti Perkins, Deborah Rush, Treat Williams

The revue was presented in two acts (division of acts and song assignments unknown).

MUSICAL NUMBERS—"My Old Kentucky Home," "Birmingham," "Political Science," "Jolly Coppers on Parade," "Caroline," "Maybe I'm Doing It Wrong," "Simon Smith and the Amazing Dancing Bear," "The Debutante's Ball," "Love Story," "Tickle Me," "It's Money That I Love," "God's Song (That's Why I Love Mankind)," "Sail Away," "Yellow Man," "Rider in the Rain," "Rollin'," "You Can Leave Your Hat On," "Old Man," "Davy the Fat Boy," "Marie," "Short People," "I'll Be Home," "Dayton, Ohio 1903"

NOTES—The short-lived 1981 Off Off Broadway revue *Randy Newman's Maybe I'm Doing It Wrong* was a collection of songs by Randy Newman, and was the first of many musicals using Newman's songs. As *Maybe I'm Doing It Wrong*, it re-opened the following year in an Off Broadway production for yet another short run (see entry). The new version had one cast substitution (Larry Riley for Treat Williams) and offered more songs (all the numbers from the 1981 production plus twelve others).

Perhaps the revue was twenty years too early; if the material had been fashioned into a jukebox musical, with the pre-existing songs grafted into a storyline, it might have been a hit. On the other hand, maybe not. Because in 1988 *The Middle of Nowhere* (see entry) used two-dozen of Newman's songs (many of which had been previously heard in the two *Maybe I'm Doing It Wrong* revues) in a book musical which lasted only three weeks.

Another musical with assorted songs by Newman, *The Education of Randy Newman*, was produced by the South Coast Repertory in Costa Mesa, California, on May 26, 2000. Earlier, a British revue, *Trouble in Paradise/A Musical Celebration of the Songs of Randy Newman*, was seen at Theatre Royal Stratford East during the mid-1980s.

1335 Rap Master Ronnie.

"A Partisan Revue." THEATRE: Top of the Gate/Village Gate; OPENING DATE: October 3, 1984; PERFORMANCES: 49; LYRICS: Gary Trudeau; additional lyrics by Elizabeth Swados; MUSIC: Elizabeth Swados; DIRECTION: Caymichael Patten; CHOREOGRAPHY: Ronni Stewart; SCENERY: Neil Peter Jampolis; COSTUMES: David Woolard; LIGHTING: Anne Militello; MUSICAL DIRECTION: John Richard Lewis; PRODUCER: Rosita Sarnoff

CAST—Reathel Bean, Catherine Cox, Ernestine Jackson, Mel Johnson, Jr., Richard Ryder

The revue was presented in one act.

MUSICAL NUMBERS—"The Assistant Undersecretary of State for Human Rights" (Catherine Cox), "The Class of 1984" (Reathel Bean, Catherine Cox, Mel Johnson, Jr., Richard Ryder), "Cheese" (Mel Johnson, Jr.), "The Empire Strikes First" (Company), "Facts" (Catherine Cox), "The Majority" (Company), "New Years in Beirut, 1983" (Richard Ryder), "Nine to Twelve" (Reathel Bean, Mel Johnson, Jr., Richard Ryder), "O, Grenada" (Ernestine Jackson, Mel Johnson, Jr.), "One More Study" (Catherine Cox, Ernestine Jackson), "Rap Master Ronnie" (Company), "The Round Up" (Reathel Bean, Mel Johnson, Jr.), "Self Made Man" (Richard Ryder, Company), "Something for Nothing" (With Appreciation to Mayfair Music Hall) (Company), "Take That Smile Off Your Face" (Ernestine Jackson), "Thinking the Unthinkable" (Company), "You're Not Ready" (Reathel Bean, Catherine Cox)

NOTES—The liner notes of the cast album for the Los Angeles production of the anti-President Ronald Reagan and anti-Republican revue *Rap Master Ronnie* (released by AEI Records [LP # AEI-1177]) mentioned that political entertainments ran the risk of preaching to the converted. The brief New York run of six weeks indicated the "converted" were not all that interested in seeing the revue; perhaps the weak lyrics and even weaker music doomed the show. The revue underwent a considerable reordering of its material during the short run, and by November (when President Reagan was reelected by a forty-nine-state margin) Catherine Cox and Ernestine Jackson were no longer in the cast (they were replaced by Virginia Sandifur and Claire Bathe).

In the revue, President Reagan was played by Reathel Bean, whose program bio indicated he was starting work on his impersonation of Walter Mondale. After November 4, it's unclear where he performed his Mondale impressions.

Although there was no New York cast album, Bean "and the Doonesbury Break Crew" recorded an LP of the title song (both a long and a short version) which was released on Silver Screen Records (# SSR-115).

The revue was later shown on cable television.

1336 Rappaccini's Daughter (La Hija de Rappaccini). THEATRE: John C. Borden Auditorium/Manhattan School of Music Opera Theatre; OPENING DATE: Spring 1997; PERFORMANCES: Unknown; LIBRETTO: Juan Tovar; MUSIC: Daniel Catan; DIRECTION: Linda Brovsky; MUSICAL DIRECTION: Eduardo Diazmunoz; PRODUCER: Manhattan School of Music

CAST—Julian Rebolledo (Dr. Baglioni), David Alan Marshall (Dr. Rappaccini), Brandon Jovanovich (Giovanni), Natalie Levin (Isabela), Olivia Gorra (Beatriz), Flowers (Noelle Barbera, Karen Frankenstein, Tamara Hummel, Christine Nuki, Nancy Maria Balach, Heather Johnson)

SOURCE—The 1844 short story "Rappaccini's Daughter" by Nathaniel Hawthorne; and a play by by Octavio Paz.

The action occurs in Padua, Italy.

The opera was presented in two acts.

ACT ONE—Preludio/Opening Scene, "El Mar," "Aqui, Senor," "Que Aire," "Belladonna," "Cuant Union," "Beatriz," "Lo Que Tiene," "Yo Es Hora," "Nunca," "Beatriz"

ACT TWO—Introduction/Opening Scene, Interlude, "Cuanta Calma," "Oh, Beatriz," "Senor Doctor," "Ya Duele," "Espero No," "Dime," "Entonces," "Hija Mia," "Que Es?"

NOTES—The opera *Rappaccini's Daughter* was composed by Daniel Catan, a Mexican composer, and its libretto was written in Spanish (by Juan Tovar). The world premiere took place in Mexico City in 1991, and the opera was first produced in the United States in 1994 by the San Diego Opera. In 1997, the innovative Manhattan School of Music offered the New York premiere of the work. The production was sung in Spanish and was recorded on a 2-CD set by Newport Classic Records (# NPD-85623/2).

The opera was a re-telling of Nathaniel Hawthorne's famous short story about Dr. Rappaccini's garden of beautiful, if poisonous, plants; once picked, the plants wither and die. Rappaccini's daughter Beatriz is also beautiful, and also toxic; she has been fed poison all her life, and her touch is deadly. Giovanni, a young student, falls in love with her, but her touch infects him and dooms him to death. Beatriz meanwhile tries to leave the poisonous garden, only to die there at the foot of a tree. Her and Giovanni's dreams of love transform the garden, and their spirits live there among the beautiful flowers.

An earlier operatic treatment of the story was composed by Michael Cohen, whose musical *Yours, Anne* opened Off Broadway in 1985 (see entry for the latter). Cohen's *Rappaccini's Daughter* was produced prior to the run of *Yours, Anne*, and was seen at the O'Neill Center and the Minnesota Opera Company.

1337 Rats. "A Musical Revue *Not* Based on a Book by T.S. Eliot." THEATRE: Van Buren Theatre; OPENING DATE: October 18, 1982; PERFORMANCES: 12; BOOK: Roy Doliner; LYRICS: Roy Doliner; MUSIC: Vivian Krasner; DIRECTION: Don Swanson; CHOREOGRAPHY: Don Swanson; COSTUMES: Bronwyn O'Shaughnessy; PRODUCER: Tom O'Shea

CAST—Roy Doliner (Bernie), Yvette Freeman (Yolanda), Gerry Martin (Shirley), George Merritt (Ralph), Ken Ward (Algernon)

The musical was presented in two acts (song assignments weren't credited in program).

ACT ONE—"Does Broadway Need Some More Rats?," "Acting and Hustling," "Rodents" (music by Jule Styne), "The Night I Bit John Simon," "Mr. Sondheim" (music by Pat Ballard), "Never Have a Book," "Never Left Home" (lyric by Vivian Krasner), "We Ate the Money" (music by Harry Warren)

ACT TWO—"Under the Spotlight," "Test Tube Baby" (music by Stephen Sondheim), "Write About Me," "Chrastine" (music by Charles Strouse), "The Rat-A-Tat-Tap," "Like Liza Does," "I'd Know How to Be Big," Cheese Medley, "What Broadway Needs Is More Rats" (reprise)

NOTES—With the success of *Cats* (1982), it was inevitable there would be spoofs utilizing other animals. The Off Off Broadway musical *Rats* sounds like cheesy fun; any show with song titles such as "Does Broadway Need Some More Rats?," "The Night I Bit John Simon," "The Rat-A-Tat-Tap," "We Ate the Money," "Like Liza Does," and "Cheese Medley" couldn't have been all bad. Apparently the rat character "Algernon" was a nod to the titular mouse in Charles Strouse's *Charlie and Algernon*, which had a brief run on Broadway in 1980.

The 1983-1984 Off Broadway season offered *Dogs*, and the 1995-1996 season *Pets!* (see entries).

1338 Ready or Not. "A Dramatic Musical." THEATRE: INTAR Theatre; OPENING DATE: April 23, 1987; PERFORMANCES: 16; BOOK: Michael Smit; LYRICS: Michael Smit; MUSIC: Michael Smit; DIRECTION: Tim Vode; CHOREOGRAPHY: Keith Michael; SCENERY: Stephen Caldwell; COSTUMES: C. Jane Epperson; LIGHTING: Dennis W. Moyes; MUSICAL DIRECTION: Paul L. Johnson; PRODUCER: The City Troupe (Tim Vode, Artistic Director)

CAST—Michael DeVries (Robert Dennison), Mark Roland (Steven Dennison), Pamela McLernon (Jenny), Colleen Fitzpatrick (Lauren Harper), Melinda Tanner (Maggie Potter), Alie Smith (Mary Ellen), Charles Hettinger (Frank Dekker), Nick Locilento (George Dekker, Ensemble), Suzanne Hevner (Tina Dekker, Ensemble), Robert Tiffany (Cab Schneider, Ensemble), Gail Titunik (Mrs. Schneider, Ensemble), Kirsten Lind (Ensemble), Greg Hellems (Ensemble), Marianne Ferrari (Ensemble), Jody Abrahams (Ensemble) The action occurs in the early 1950s in Maisonville, a small town near the Great Lakes.

The musical was presented in two acts (division of acts and song assignments unknown; song list in performance order).

MUSICAL NUMBERS—"Watery Blue," "They're Going Sailing," "A Way of Showing I Love You," "Does He Think of Her," "The Arrangement," "Daddy," "Prayer Chain," "The Samba," "Quartet," "From Here to Here," "Villains of History," "Grandfather Clock in the Hall," "It Didn't Used to Be This Way," "Am I Nuts," "The Lake," "State Fair," "Lord We Thank Thee," "Aeronautics Revelation," "Ready or Not," "I Have to Tell You," "Take the Boat," "I Knew I Could Fly," "The Fog," "Jenny," Finale

NOTES—*Ready or Not* was produced under an Off Off Broadway contract.

1339 Real Life Funnies. THEATRE: Upstage/Manhattan Theatre Club; OPENING DATE: January 27, 1981; PERFORMANCES: 35; SCRIPT: Material "reported" by Stan Mack; adapted by Howard Ashman; based on an idea by Lawrence Kraman; LYRICS: Alan Menken; MUSIC: Alan Menken; DIRECTION: Howard Ashman; CHOREOGRAPHY: Douglas Norwick; LIGHTING: Frances Aronson; MUSICAL DIRECTION: Larry Hochman; PRODUCER: Manhattan Theatre Club (Lynne Meadow, Artistic Director; Barry Grove, Managing Director)

CAST—Pamela Blair, Gibby Brand, Merwin Goldsmith, Janie Sell, Dale Soules, Chip Zien

SOURCE—The comic strip *Real Life Funnies* by Stan Mack.

The revue was presented in one act.

MUSICAL NUMBERS—"Real Life Funnies" (Company), "Is It Art?" (Company), "I Love Your Brains" (Janie Sell, Gibby Brand, Merwin Goldsmith, Chip Zien), "Pleasantly Plump" (Dale Soules, Gibby Brand), "Lifted" (Dale Soules, Company), "Someday" (Merwin Goldsmith, Company), "People Collecting Things" (Janie Sell), "Ah Men" (Pamela Blair), "Every Thursday Night" (Company), "Divorce Has Brought Us Together" (Pamela Blair, Chip Zien), "The Way of My Father" (Chip Zien), "Someone to Come Home with Me Tonight" (Company), "Real Life Funnies" (reprise) (Company)

NOTES—A program note for the Off Off Broadway satiric revue *Real Life Funnies* indicated all dialogue "has been overheard, reported and guaranteed verbatim by Stan Mack," who created the comic strip *Real Life Funnies* for *The Village Voice*. *Real Life Funnies* was an early work by Alan Menken (who wrote both the lyrics and music for the revue) and Howard Ashman (who directed). Frank Rich in the *New York Times* reported that throughout the evening an electric sign above the stage read "Attention: All Dialogue Reported Verbatim," and after every joke, the sign would light up. But Rich found the "next-to-no laughs" revue a tired retread of such typically urban topics as apartment hunting, group-encounter sessions, Hare Krishna types, and Madison Avenue. He felt there was nothing here that Jules Feiffer's cartoons hadn't done better two decades earlier. Further, he found the lyrics "repetitive" and the music "primitive." He also noted the score's penultimate number ("Someone to Come Home with Me Tonight") was reminiscent of "Being Alive," the final song in Stephen Sondheim's iconic Manhattan musical *Company* (1970).

1340 Really Rosie. THEATRE: Chelsea Theatre Center/Upstairs; transferred to the American Place Theatre on November 26, 1980; OPENING DATE: October 14, 1980; PERFORMANCES: 274; BOOK: Maurice Sendak; LYRICS: Maurice Sendak; MUSIC: Carole King; DIRECTION: Patricia Birch; CHOREOGRAPHY: Patricia Birch; SCENERY: Maurice Sendak; scenery supervised by Douglas W. Schmidt; COSTUMES: Maurice Sendak; costumes supervised by Carrie Robbins; LIGHTING: John Gleason; MUSICAL DIRECTION: Joel Silberman; PRODUCERS: John H.P. Davis and Sheldon Riss in association with Alexander S. Bowers and The Chelsea Theatre Center

CAST—TISHA CAMPBELL (Rosie), April Lerman (Kathy), Joe LaBenz IV (Alligator), Wade Raley (Johnny), B.J. Barie (Pierre), Jermaine Campbell (Chicken Soup), Matthew Kolmes (Lion); Neighborhood Kids: Lara Berk, Ruben Cuevas, Matthew Kolmes; Mothers: Alison Price, Bibi Humes

SOURCES—The books *The Sign on Rosie's Door* (1960) and *The Nutshell Library* (1962) by Maurice Sendak.

The action occurs at the present time on Avenue P in Brooklyn.

The musical was presented in one act.

MUSICAL NUMBERS—Overture (Orchestra), "Really Rosie" (Tisha Campbell), "Simple Humble Neighborhood" (Tisha Campbell), "Alligators All Around" (Joe LaBenz IV, Company), "One Was Johnny" (Wade Raley), "Pierre" (B.J. Barie, Company), "Screaming and Yelling" (Tisha Campbell, Company), "The Awful Truth" (April Lerman, Wade Raley, Joe LaBenz IV, B.J. Barie), "Very Far Away"

(Company), "Avenue P" (Tisha Campbell), "Chicken Soup with Rice" (Company)

NOTES—*Really Rosie* was a musical adaptation of two of Maurice Sendak's books, and had originally been produced as a 1975 cartoon musical for television (the soundtrack recording was released on Ode Records [LP # SP-77027/SP-77053/54-PE-34955]).

The stage adaptation was first seen at the Musical Theatre Lab at the Kennedy Center; the New York cast album was recorded by Caedmon Records (LP # TRS-368), and the script was published by Samuel French, Inc., in 1985.

The musical apparently pleased children, but at least one adult found it too knowing and too calculated. The show's "big" number, "Chicken Soup with Rice," was annoyingly repetitive, in the style of a non-stop jingle for a television commercial.

Frank Rich in the *New York Times* felt the "padded" evening went "wildly wrong" in its push to be "cute, silly and harmless," and said it inadvertently represented the kind of "bland" children's entertainment that Sendak had been trying to wipe out during his career.

Further, Rich noted the musical's "irritating cuteness" even offered an alphabet song ("Alligators All Around") which made him long for "The Little Ones' ABC" (a nasty little parody of children's songs which the immortal Elaine Stritch memorably growled in Noel Coward's 1961 musical *Sail Away*).

1341 The Rebbitzen from Israel.

THEATRE: Mayfair Theatre; OPENING DATE: October 10, 1972; PERFORMANCES: 168; BOOK: Pesach Burstein; LYRICS: Lili Amber; MUSIC: Lili Amber; DIRECTION: Pesach Burstein; CHOREOGRAPHY: Yona Aloni; SCENERY: Peter Achilles; MUSICAL DIRECTION: Elliot Finkel; PRODUCER: Moishe Baruch

CAST—Janece Martel (Alice Goldenthal), Pesach Burstein (Abraham Goldenthal), Bernard Sauer (Shimon), Gene Barrett (Robert Goldenthal), Rina Ellis (Edna Goldenthal), Lillian Lux (Mirele Shapiro), David Carey (Moishele Shapiro), Art Raymond (Voice of Art Raymond)

SOURCE—An unidentified play by L. Freiman.

The musical was presented in two acts (division of acts and song assignments unknown; song list in performance order).

MUSICAL NUMBERS—"Yeverechecha," "Yehi Rutzoin," "Oy Der Pesach Pesach," "Where Were You?," "I'm in Love," "Traditional Seder," "I Should Live So," "Love Is International," "Ladies Should Be Beautiful," "I Wish It Was Over," "Tel-Aviv," Finale

NOTES—The 1972-1973 Off Broadway season offered three musicals with Jewish subject matter (two book musicals and a revue). Besides *The Rebbitzen from Israel*, the season also saw *Yoshe Kalb* (1972) and *The Grand Music Hall of Israel* (1973); see entries.

1342 Rebecca, The Rabbi's Daughter.

"A Yiddish Musical Comedy." THEATRE: Town Hall; OPENING DATE: November 4, 1979; PERFORMANCES: 84; BOOK: William Siegel; LYRICS: Lyricist unknown (possibly William Siegel?); MUSIC: Abraham Ellstein; additional music by Alexander Lustig; DIRECTION: Michael Greenstein; CHOREOGRAPHY: Felix Fibich; SCENERY: Adina Reich; COSTUMES: Joni Rudesill; also by Adina Reich (?); MUSICAL DIRECTION: Renee Solomon; PRODUCERS: Shalom Musical Comedy Theatre, Raymond Ariel, David Carey, and Theo Roller

CAST—David Ellin (Gabbai), David Carey (Yosele), Fay Nicoll (Julia), Mary Soreanu (Rivkele, Rebecca), Reizl Bozyk (Dvoyreh), Shifra Lerer (Sossl), Yankele Alperin (Zelig), Eleanor Reissa (Soorele), Solo Moise (Yukl), Karol Latowicz (Lawyer Butch), Fibisch; Dancers: Shamus Murphy, Shelly Pappas, Jim Sayger, Dafna Soltes

The musical was presented in two acts (division of acts and song assignments unknown; songs are listed in performance order).

MUSICAL NUMBERS—Prologue, "My Dreams," "Everyone Has a Right to Love," "Rivkele Dem Rebns," "Forget Me Not," "Once It Was Different," "When a Jew Sings," "How Good Is It," "Chassene," "I Want to Be a Bride," "You Are My Solace," "Hollywood," "Potpourri," "Couplet," "Charleston"

NOTES—*Rebecca, the Rabbi's Daughter* was a revised version of the musical which had originally been seen in Yiddish theatre in the 1920s.

Richard F. Shepard in the *New York Times* reported the story was about a rabbi's *grand*daughter ("really," Shepard assured us) and her love for a cantor's son who finds success in Hollywood. Shepard said the musical had "remarkable freshness," and concluded by saying "a l'chaim to all hands and let's have another round."

1343 The Red Blue-Grass Western Flyer Show.

"A Grand Ole Opry Musical Play." THEATRE: Theater at St. Clement's/The Musical Theatre Lab of St. Clement's; OPENING DATE: May 2, 1975; PERFORMANCES: 12; BOOK: Conn Fleming; LYRICS: Conn Fleming; MUSIC: Clint Ballard, Jr.; DIRECTION: Robert Brewer; Joe Bricking, Assistant to the Director; CHOREOGRAPHY: Dennis Grimaldi; Baayork Lee, Assistant to the Choreographer; SCENERY: John Falabella; COSTUMES: Bill Kellard and Michele Reisch; LIGHTING: Barley Harris; PRODUCER: The Musical Theatre Lab at St. Clement's

CAST—Maurice Copeland (Big Emmit Childress), Kate Wilkinson (Hattie Cox), Conrad McLaren (Arlen), Barbara Coggin (Dolly), Kate Kellery (Emma Lou), Robert Polenz (Scotty Young), Larry Swansen (George D. Hay), Forbesy Russell (Swing Dancer); Lookout Mountain Dancers (Terry Brown, Karen Crossley, Stephen deGhelder, Ellen Manning, John Scoullar, Debbie Woodhouse); Southern Sunshine Singers (Elinor Ellsworth, Helen Hoffman, Michael David Laibson, Dan Kruger, Carmen Peterson, Gerard Wagner); Brother Bill and the Black Bottom Boys (Mike Falk, Dick Frank, Steve Mack, Jeff Waxman)

The action occurs in an apartment in a northern city as well as on the stage of the Grand Ole Opry.

The musical was presented in two acts.

MUSICAL NUMBERS—(the list below is from a program of the 1977 Goodspeed Opera House production; names of characters follow song titles; see notes below)

ACT ONE—Opening (George D. Hay, The Southern Sunshine Singers), "Blue-Grass Dreamers" (Big Emmit, Company), "A Very Young Man" (Big Emmit), "The Old Folks at Home" (Hattie, Big Emmit, Arlen, Dolly, The Southern Sunshine Singers), "Hattie's Time" (Hattie), "I Never Sing a Song" (Emma), "I Wanna Be a Country Music Singer" (Scotty, The Southern Sunshine Singers, The Look-Out Mountain Dancers), "The Gate in the Road" (Big Emmit, Company)

ACT TWO—"The Sally Bright Self-Risin' Flour Song" (George D. Hay, Big Emmit, Scotty, The Southern Sunshine Singers), "I Don't Know How to Be My Daddy's Father" (Arlen), "When the Record Player's On" (Scotty, The Southern Sunshine Singers), "Listenin' to the Grand Ole Opry" (Company), "Don't Change the Way You Love Me" (Dolly), "As We Go Along" (Big Emmit, Emma), "Blue-Grass Dreamers" (reprise) (Company)

NOTES—The musical *The Red Blue-Grass Western Flyer Show* had been previously produced Off Off Broadway on December 11, 1972, for one performance at The New Dramatists, Inc.

After its limited Off Off Broadway engagement at the Musical Theatre Lab of St. Clement's on May 2, 1975, the musical re-surfaced two years later as part of Goodspeed's 1977-1978 season, opening on August 16, 1977. Among the cast members of that production was Bob Gunton, two years away from his most famous role of Juan Peron in the original Broadway production of *Evita* (1979). The Goodspeed version was directed by John Cullum.

In a refreshing change of pace, the musical depicted Country-Music-Star wannabes rather than Broadway-Star wannabes.

1344 The Red Horse Animation.

THEATRE: Lepercq Space/Brooklyn Academy of Music; OPENING DATE: May 6, 1976; PERFORMANCES: 4; TEXT: Lee Breuer; MUSIC: Philip Glass; DIRECTION: Lee Breuer; LIGHTING: Jene Highstein; PRODUCERS: The Brooklyn Academy of Music; a Mabou Mines Production

CAST—JoAnne Akalaitis, Ruth Maleczech, David Warrilow

NOTES—In describing *The Red Horse Animation*, *Theatre World 1975-1976 Season* indicated this early work by Philip Glass was about "the process and procedure of a creative act—animating an image of a red horse." The photo on page 104 in *Theatre World* seems to provide a good visual on how the "horse" was animated.

The Off Off Broadway production was presented for a limited engagement of four performances.

1345 The Red Sneaks.

THEATRE: Perry Street Theatre; OPENING DATE: June 28, 1989; PERFORMANCES: 23; BOOK: Elizabeth Swados; LYRICS: Elizabeth Swados; MUSIC: Elizabeth Swados; DIRECTION: Elizabeth Swados; CHOREOGRAPHY: Arthur Fredric and the Company; SCENERY: G.W. Mercier; COSTUMES: G.W. Mercier; LIGHTING: M.L. Geiger; PRODUCER: Theatre for a New Audience (Jeffrey Horowitz, Artistic and Producing Directcor)

CAST—Shawn Benjamin, Valerie Monique Evering, Donald "Shun" Faison, Dedre Guevara, Kenny Lund, Raquel Richard, James Sheffield-Dewees, Teresina Sullo

SOURCE—The short story "The Red Shoes" by Hans Christian Anderson.

The action occurs in the present in New York City.

The musical was presented in one act.

MUSICAL NUMBERS—"Bye Baby Bye" (Company), "One Rare Pair of Red Sneaks" (Company), "Material Universe" (Company), "Sad and Lonely Child" (Company), "Don't You Come Inside My Head" (Dedre Guevara, Company), "Red Sneaker Rap, Part I" (Company), "Red Sneaker Rap, Part II" (Company), "You Don't Have To" (Valerie Evering), "Look at Me" (Dedre Guevara, Shawn Benjamin, Company), "You Can't Have Anything" (Company), "I Like You, I Love You" (Donald "Shun" Faison), "Power" (Company), "The Action Never Stops" (Company), "The Action Never Stops" (reprise) (Company), "I Like How We All Dance Together" (Company), "Stand Up" (Donald "Shun" Faison, Company), "Rush of Speed" (Company), "Sneaker Prison" (Shawn Benjamin), "I Want to Be Free of This Dream" (Teresina Sullo), "I Can't Stop" (Company), "Who Will Bring Her Home" (Donald "Shun" Faison, Company)

NOTES—*The Red Sneaks* was inspired by Hans Christian Anderson's classic short story "The Red Shoes." Anderson's story was also the inspiration for the classic 1948 film *The Red Shoes* and for two Broadway musicals. *The Red Shoes* (1993), Jule Styne's final musical, was a huge financial failure, lasting just five performances; but its thrilling choreography and lavish production values were memorable. *Hot Feet* (2006) lost a fortune, too, but managed to hang on for a few weeks.

"Red Sneaker Rap, Part I" and "Sneaker Prison" were written by Shawn Benjamin; "Red Sneaker Rap, Part II" was written by Donald Faison.

After its initial Off Off Broadway run, *The Red*

Sneaks reopened for another engagement later in the summer. Stephen Holden in the *New York Times* reported the musical was an expanded version of a section of Swados' *Swing*, which had been seen two years earlier at the Brooklyn Academy of Music. Holden noted Swados' "perky bare-bones songs" had an "unaffected animation." Her plot ("such as it is") dealt with a teenage girl who lives in a welfare hotel. She's given a pair of red shoes by a satan-like character who tells her the shoes can grant her every wish, but eventually the girl dies ("the exact circumstances ... are not spelled out"). In her notes for the script which was published by Samuel French, Inc., in 1991, Elizabeth Swados complained that in theatre productions young people were forced to perform as "pea pods or banana splits" in plays which "are totally irrelevant ... in this decade of America's confusion." She wrote that *The Red Sneaks* was her attempt to create a work which "reflected the urgency of our times."

1346 The Red White and Black. "A Musical Roll Call." THEATRE: Players Theatre; OPENING DATE: March 30, 1971; PERFORMANCES: 1; SKETCHES: Eric Bentley; LYRICS: Eric Bentley; MUSIC: Brad Burg; DIRECTION: Eric Bentley; SCENERY: Mil Mikeulewicz; COSTUMES: Margaret Tobin; LIGHTING: Robert Engstrom; MUSICAL DIRECTION: Brad Burg; PRODUCER: Donald Goldman

CAST—Pamela Adams, Sofia Adoniadis, Antonio (Tony) Azito, Rob Farkas, Phil Patterson, Marilyn Sokol, Bill Sweeney; rock band, The History of Russia

The revue was presented in one act.

NOTES—This left-wing political revue *The Red White and Black* had previously been produced Off Off Broadway at the Café La Mama (La Mama Experimental Theatre Club [ETC]); the production was billed as a "patriotic demonstration," and was directed by John Dillion. When the revue reached Off Broadway, its first night was also its last. Clive Barnes in the *New York Times* listed a catalogue of the revue's topics (everything from Vietnam to "anti-Black-Pantherism") and concluded that Eric Bentley's targets were predictably easy ones which preached to the converted. Eric Bentley had earlier been associated with another political revue (see entry for *D.M.Z. Revue*).

1347 Reefer Madness. THEATRE: Variety Arts Theatre; OPENING DATE: October 7, 2001; PERFORMANCES: 25; BOOK: Kevin Murphy and Dan Studney; LYRICS: Kevin Murphy; MUSIC: Dan Studney; DIRECTION: Andy Fickman; CHOREOGRAPHY: Paula Abdul; SCENERY: Walt Spangler; COSTUMES: Dick Magnanti; LIGHTING: Robert Perry; MUSICAL DIRECTION: David Manning; PRODUCERS: James L. Nederlander and Verna Harrah in association with Nathaniel Kramer and Terry Allen Kramer and Dead Old Man Productions

CAST—Gregg Edelman (Lecturer), Christian Campbell (Jimmy), Kristen Bell (Mary), Robert Torti (Jack, Jesus), Michele Pawk (Mae), Erin Matthews (Sally), Roxane Barlow (Placard Girl), John Kassir (Ralph), Andrea Chamberlain (Ensemble), Jennifer Gambatese (Ensemble), Paul Leighton (Ensemble), Michael Seelbach (Ensemble)

SOURCE—The 1936 film *Reefer Madness* (directed by Louis Gasnier).

The action occurs in the "Good Ol' USA" during 1936.

The musical was presented in two acts.

ACT ONE—"Reefer Madness!" (Gregg Edelman, Company), "Romeo and Juliet" (Christian Campbell, Kristen Bell), "The Stuff" (Michele Pawk), "Down at the Ol' Five-and-Dime" (Gregg Edelman, Christian Campbell, Robert Torti, Company), "Jimmy Takes a Hit" (Erin Matthews, Christian Campbell, Robert Torti, Michele Pawk, John Kassir, Gregg Edelman), "The Orgy" (Company), "Lonely Pew" (Kristen Bell), "Listen to Jesus, Jimmy" (Robert Torti, Company), "Lullabye" ('Sally's Baby'), "Dead Old Man" (Christian Campbell, Company), Act One Finale (Company)

ACT TWO—"Jimmy on the Lam" (Kristen Bell, Christian Campbell, John Kassir, Erin Matthews, Michele Pawk, Company), "The Brownie Song" (Christian Campbell, Company), "Down at the Ol' Five-and-Dime" (reprise) (Gregg Edelman), "Little Mary Sunshine" (John Kassir, Kristen Bell), "Romeo and Juliet" (reprise) (Christian Campbell, Kristen Bell), "Murder" (Company), "The Stuff" (reprise) (Michele Pawk, Robert Torti), "Listen to Jesus, Jimmy" (reprise) (Robert Torti, Christian Campbell, Company), "Tell 'Em the Truth" (Company), "Reefer Madness!" (reprise) (Gregg Edelman, Company)

NOTES—The 1936 film *Reefer Madness* was a hilarious, overwrought sermon on the evils of marijuana: just one puff could lead a teenager to insanity, death, or maybe even worse. The tongue-in-cheek musical must have seemed a natural for Off Broadway, but it closed after just three weeks.

The musical had first been produced on April 30, 1999, at the Hudson Backstage Theatre in Los Angeles, and starred Christian Campbell (who also appeared in the Off Broadway production); the Los Angeles cast recording was released by Madness Records (CD # MO-753) and included two bonus tracks, "We Know Best" (a number cut from the show) and "Weather Changes" (from *Valley of Kings*, another musical by the authors).

In 2004, the musical was televised on Showtime, and a DVD was released by Showtime Entertainment (# SHO-1156-D). Again, Christian Campbell was Jimmy, and Kristen Bell reprised her role of Mary from the Off Broadway production. The television cast also included Neve Campbell, Alan Cumming, Ana Gasteyer, and Steven Weber. In 2008, Ghostlight Records (CD # 8-4432) released a 2-CD set which included the cast album of the Los Angeles production as well as the Showtime soundtrack.

1348 A Reel American Hero. THEATRE: Rialto Theatre; OPENING DATE: Production played preview performances from March 25 to March 29, 1981; previews had been scheduled through April 8, and the opening night was to have been on April 9; PERFORMANCES: 5 previews; BOOK: Judy GeBauer and Burt Vinocur; LYRICS: Gerald Paul Hillman, Stephanie Peters, Judy DeBauer, and N.T. Hillman; MUSIC: Gordon Kent, Stephanie Peters, N.T. Hillman, and Roger Neil; DIRECTION: Nancy Tribush Hillman; CHOREOGRAPHY: George Bunt; SCENERY: Harry Silverglat Darrow; COSTUMES: Carol Wenz; LIGHTING: Giles Hogya; lighting supervision by Harry Silverglat Darrow; MUSICAL DIRECTION: Roger Neil; PRODUCER: Gerald Paul Hillman

CAST—Vidya Kaur (Ruby), Peter Newman (Louis), Roxanne White (Chorine), Jess Richards (Dick), Hillary Bailey (Lili)

The musical was presented in two acts.

ACT ONE—"I Want to Be Somebody" (lyric by Gerald Hillman, music by Gordon Kent) (Company), "What's Gone Wrong" (lyric by Gerald Hillman, music by Gordon Kent) (Company), "Garter Song" (lyric by Gerald Hillman and Stephanie Peters, music by Stephanie Peters) (Hillary Bailey), "Lili Is a Lady with a Suitcase Up Her Sleeve" (lyric by Gerald Hillman, music by Gordon Kent) (Peter Newman), "Ratta Tat Tat" (lyric by Gerald Hillman, music by Gordon Kent) (Company), "Sugar Daddy Blues" (lyric by Gerald Hillman and Judy GeBauer, music by Stephanie Peters) (Roxanna White), "Dance with Me" (lyric and music by Stephanie Peters) (Roxanna White, Jess Richards), "You Mustn't Eat People" (lyric and music by N.T. Hillman) (Vidya Kaur), "Monster Medley" (music by Gordon Kent and Stephanie Peters) (Company), "Snow White, My Daughter" (lyric by Gerald Hillman, music by Gordon Kent) (Jess Richards), "Tempus Fugit" (music by Gordon Kent) (Company), "I Want to Be Somebody" (reprise) (lyric by Gerald Hillman, music by Gordon Kent) (Company)

ACT TWO—"The Movie Game of Make Believe" (lyric and music by Stephanie Peters) (Vidya Kaur, Company), "Chan Ballet" (music by Roger Neil) (Company), "The Gunfighter" (lyric by Gerald Hillman, music by Gordon Kent) (Company), "My Sargeant Doesn't Look Like Big John Wayne" (lyric by Gerald Hillman, music by Gordon Kent) (Company), "Fly Eagle Fly" (lyric by Stephanie Peters, music by Gordon Kent) (Company), "I'll Be Waitin'" (lyric by Gerald Hillman and Stephanie Peters, music by Stephanie Peters) (Roxanne White, Vidya Kaur, Hillary Bailey), "Here's a Love Song" (lyric and music by Stephanie Peters) (Peter Newman, Vidya Kaur, Jess Richards), "Hero Time" (lyric by Gerald Hillman, music by Gordon Kent) (Company), Finale (lyric by Gerald Hillman, music by Gordon Kent) (Company)

NOTES—*A Reel American Hero* was another show business musical; it took place during the 1930s and 1940s, and even included two characters named Ruby and Dick. The musical, which didn't make it out of previews, may have been produced under a Middle Broadway contract.

The *New York Times* reported that for preview performances (which were scheduled from March 25 through April 8 [the musical was scheduled to officially open on April 9, but it closed prematurely in previews on March 29]) all tickets for the musical were sold for either 60 cents (adults) or 30 cents (children). Of the 8,000 tickets available, 6,500 were sold on the first day the box office opened.

During its showcase production at the Chareeva Playhouse, the musical was titled *The World of Black and White*.

1349 Religion. "A New Oratorio." THEATRE: Judson Poets' Theatre; OPENING DATE: October 26, 1973; PERFORMANCES: 16; WORDS: Al Carmines; MUSIC: Al Carmines; DIRECTION: Al Carmines; CHOREOGRAPHY: Tedrian Chizik and Marcia Loring; SCENERY: Elwin Charles Terrel II and T.E. Mason; COSTUMES: Ira Siff; LIGHTING: Gary Weathersbee; MUSICAL DIRECTION: Al Carmines (?); PRODUCER: The Judson Poets' Theatre

CAST—Emily Adams (Mother), Al Carmines (Song Leader), Reuben Schafer (God), Jimmy Sutton (Blonde Angel), J. Victor Lopez (Brunette Angel), Nancy Stover (Violin Angel), John Harbaugh (Viola Angel), Sid Smith (Trumpet Angel), Alice Bosveld (Tambourine Angel), James Calvert (Man), Jimmy B. Hopson (Serpent), Joan Montgomery (Woman), Paul Rounsaville (Jesus), Sandy Padilla (Mary Magdelene), Ellen Maris (Mistress of Ceremonies), Grace Carney (Mrs. Thomas Sutphin), Danny Kreitzberg (Robert Grayson), Semina De Laurentis (Betty Jean Atkins), Clarence Taylor (Clarence Baker), Phyllis MacBryde (Binnie Herschbarger), Connie Campbell (Linda Johnson), Marion Swan (Queen), Alice Garrard (Princess), Jayson Atkins (Death-Dealing Stranger), Dorian Barth (Shaker Woman), Misty Barth (Mary Baker Eddy), Albert Poland (Pope Pius XII), Tom Kindle (Billy Sunday), Margaret Wright (The Seeker), Esteban Chalbaud (Satan), Michael Mullins (Beelzebub), Lynn Oliver (Satan's Woman Lover), Tormented Souls (Daniel Battles, Innocence; Matthew Lipton, Anguished Sex; Sharon Brown, Disappointed in Love; Dalton Cathey, Good Guy; Dameon Fayad, Successful Model; Sharon Jane Wyler, Laughing Lady), David Ruppe (Seminary Student), Terry Burke (Sex), Bill Maloney (Weeping), Trisha Long (Motherhood), William Rowett (Hunger), First Sopranos (Misty Barth, Alice Bosveld, Joan Cunningham, Semina De Laurentis, Ina Gillers, Phyllis MacBryde, Lynn Oliver, Nancy Stover, Melissa Sutphen, Marion Swan), Second Sopranos (Emily Adams, Dorian Barth, Joyce Beebe, Erika Bro, Mary Chesterman, Lucille A. Frisa, Garland Harris, Ellen Maris, Joanne Morris, Susan Wideman), First Altos (Kim Ameen, Connie Campbell, Grace Carney, Shirley Chetter, Jenny Glasgow, Grace Goodman, Trisha Long, Marcia Loring, Joan Montgomery, Judy Noble, Sandy Padilla, Barbara Sandek, Sharon Jane Wyler), Second Altos (Linda Bernstein, Sharon Brown, Audrey Dawson, Alice Garrard, Francoise Jeanpierre, Michele Arlette Katz, Lynne Miller, Judy Oney, Margaret Wright), First Tenors (Daniel Battles, Robert Calvert, Esteban Chalbaud, Max Hager, Richard Roberts, Raymond Yucis), Second Tenors (John Harbaugh, Jimmy B. Hopson, Danny Kreitzberg, Michael Mullins, Bill Roulet, Clarence Taylor), Baritones (Jayson Atkins, Terry Burk, Ed Campbell, Dalton Cathey, Tedrian Chizik, Dameon Fayad, Colin Garrey, Stephen Holt, Ken Hughes, Tom Kindle, Mark Kirkham, Frank Levandoski, J. Victor Lopez, Bill Maloney, Roger McIntyre, Albert Poland, John Reid, Burt Rendin, Paul Rounsaville, David Ruppe, Reuben Schafer, Sid Smith, Jimmy Sutton, Jim Swaine, Ron Tolson), Basses (Peter Hamlin, Ron Hill, Matthew Lipton, William Rowett, Ronald Willoughby)

The action occurs in a Shaker meeting house.

The oratorio was presented in a prologue and three acts.

Prologue (Ronald Willoughby, Colin Garrey)

ACT ONE—*Worship:* "I Believe in a New World" (Chorus, Emily Adams, Al Carmines, Joan Montgomery [Soloist]), "Heaven" (Reuben Schafer, Jimmy Sutton, J. Victor Lopez, Nancy Stover, John Harbaugh, Sid Smith, Alice Bosveld), "Exhortation" (Peter Hamlin), "I Seek Him Here, I Seek Her There" (Chorus), "Exhortation" (reprise) (Barbara Sandek), "The Garden" (Robert Calvert, Jimmy B. Hopson, Joan Montgomery, Reuben Schafer), "The Jesus-Mary Game" (Paul Rounsaville, Sandy Padilla), "The Pageant of Plantagenet County" (Ellen Maris, Grace Carney, Danny Kreitzberg, Semina De Laurentis, Clarence Taylor, Phyllis MacBryde, Connie Campbell, Marion Swan, Alice Gerrard, Jayson Atkins), "The Name of God" (Mark Kirkham, Chorus)

ACT TWO—*Hell:* "Limbo" (Misty Barth, Albert Poland, Tom Kindle), "Purgatory" (Margaret Wright), "Hell" (Esteban Chalbaud, Michael Mullins, Lynn Oliver, Tormented Souls)

ACT THREE—*Mother:* "When the Saints Come Home" (Chorus), "Apostasy" (David Ruppe), "Sermon" (Emily Adams), "Time Passes So Quickly" (Chorus), "Impulses Under Religion" (Terry Burk, Bill Maloney, Trisha Long, William Rowett), Finale (Company)

NOTES—Al Carmines' oratorio *Religion*, set in a Shaker meeting house, presented the religious perspective of the Shakers. A program note for the Off Off Broadway production indicated the Shakers worshipped "through dances and visions, songs and trances. They regarded Mother Ann Lee, their founder, as an incarnate visitation of God. They lived communal and celebate lives." But Mel Gussow in the *New York Times* noted that although the evening was a musical about religion, it was also a musical by Carmines, and thus the work had his "distinctive mark of impudence and irreverence" (for example, in a scene with God, Adam, Eve, and the Serpent, Eve wryly comments that there are three men against a woman). Meanwhile, God ("a skeptical Jewish intellectual in a beret") complains that before the Fall, all music was "atonal and absolutely lovely," but what came after was, alas, only "melody."

Gussow singled out "I Believe in a New World" (a "rafter-reverberating" opening number) and "God Don't Like No Fat People," a "jubilant" song which was performed by "Carmines and the other overweight members of the cast" in the "Impulses Under Religion" sequence.

The 1982 revue *The Gospel According to Al* (see entry) included the song "Sometimes the Sky Is Blue," which it credited to *Religion* but which doesn't appear in the latter's program. The cast of *Religion* included both names from past and future musicals. Grace Carney (along with Sybil Bowan and Broadway immortal Susan Johnson) had introduced "Mr. Flynn" in the 1961 Broadway musical *Donnybrook!* Julian Mitchell in *Theatre Arts* found the song "rousingly vulgar" and noted that Carney and Bowan were "two awful warnings of what would have happened if Toulouse-Lautrec had ever seen the inside of a Dublin bar." In 1985, Semina De Laurentis created the role of Sister Mary Amnesia in the long-running Off Broadway hit *Nunsense* (see entries for various versions of the revue).

1350 Rendez-vous with Marlene.

THEATRE: 47th Street Theatre; OPENING DATE: December 14, 1995; PERFORMANCES: 24; BOOK: Torrill; LYRICS: See song list for credits; MUSIC: See song list for credits; DIRECTION: Frank Corsaro; SCENERY: Bruce Goodrich; COSTUMES: Wong, Goff, Rodriguez; LIGHTING: Bruce Goodrich; MUSICAL DIRECTION: Stan Freeman; PRODUCERS: Jerry Hammer and Pat DeRosa in association with Harold J. Newman; Jim Ellis, Associate Producer

CAST—Torrill

The play with music was presented in two acts (division of acts unknown; all songs were performed by Torrill).

MUSICAL NUMBERS—"Falling in Love Again" (from 1930 film *The Blue Angel*; English lyric by Sammy Lerner, music by Frederick Hollander), "Illusions" (lyric and music by Frederick Hollander), "Lola-Lola" (from 1930 film *The Blue Angel*; lyric by R. Leibman, music by Frederick Hollander, English lyric by Sammy Lerner), "Jonny" (1933 film *Song of Songs*; lyric and music by Frederick Hollander; English lyric by Edward Heyman), "You're the Cream in My Coffee" (*Hold Everything*, 1928; lyric by B.G. [Buddy] DeSylva and Lew Brown, music by Ray Henderson), "Das Lied Ist Aus" (lyric and music by Young, Stolz, Reisch, and Robinson; English lyric by Torrill), "Wer Wird Denn Weinen" (lyric and music by Hirsch and Hirsch Rebner; English lyric by Torrill), "The Laziest Gal in Town" (1927; lyric and music by Cole Porter; later used in 1950 film *Stage Fright*), "You Go to My Head" (lyric by J. Fred Coots, music by Haven Gillespie), "When the World Was Young" (lyric by Angela Vannier, music by M. Phillipe Gerard; English lyric by Johnny Mercer), "Look Me Over Closely" (lyric and music by M. Miller and T. Gilkyson), "Makin' Whoopee" (from *Whoopee*, 1928; lyric by Gus Kahn, music by Walter Donaldson), "Quand L-Amour Meurt" (lyric and music by Robin and Cremieux), "I've Grown Accustomed to His Face" (*My Fair Lady*, 1956; lyric by Alan Jay Lerner, music by Frederick Loewe), "The Boys in the Backroom" (a/k/a "See What the Boys in the Backroom Will Have"; 1939 film *Destry Rides Again*; lyric by Frank Loesser, music by Frederick Hollander), "Go 'Way from My Window" (lyric and music by J.J. Niles), "You Little So-and-So" (1932 film *Blonde* Venus; lyric by Leo Robin, music by Sam Coslow), "Honeysuckle Rose" (lyric by Andy Razaf, music by Thomas [Fats] Waller), "Lili Marlene" (lyric by Hans Liep, music by Norbert Schultze; English lyric by John Turner and Tommy Connoer [some sources give latter's name as Tommie Connor]), "Mutter Hast Du Mir Vergeben" (lyric and music by Niemen, Grau, and Marlene Dietrich; English lyric by Torrill), "Well, All Right, Okay, You Win" (lyric and music by Sidney Wych and Mayme Watts), "Just a Gigolo" (lyric by Julius Brammer, music by Leonello Casucci; English lyric by Irving Caesar)

NOTES—The solo revue *Rendez-vous with Marlene* starred Norwegian singer and actress Norrill as the legendary Marlene Dietrich (1901-1992). On April 11, 1999, Pam Gems' play with music *Marlene* opened on Broadway for twenty-five performances; Sian Phillips portrayed Dietrich, and a cast album was released by First Night Records (CD # 1791-2). Gems also wrote *Piaf*, the play with music about Edith Piaf which opened in Britain in 1978 and on Broadway in 1981.

A popular German "musical-revue" about Dietrich, Alois Haider and Martin Flossmann's *Marlene/Ein Mythos mit Musik*, played throughout Germany in the 1980s, and a revised version of the revue premiered in Britain as a book musical on October 30, 1990, at the Northcott Theatre in Exeter. Titled *Falling in Love Again*, the musical was by Laurence Roman (not to be confused with the American playwright Lawrence Roman) and the program noted it was "suggested" by Flossman's earlier work.

On October 1, 1999, James Beaman portrayed Dietrich in the Off Off Broadway solo performance piece *Black Market Marlene: A Dietrich Cabaret*; the evening, which recreated a typical Dietrich performance, opened at Judy's Chelsea Cabaret and played for eight performances.

1351 Rent.

THEATRE: New York Theatre Workshop; OPENING DATE: October 29, 1994; PERFORMANCES: 7; BOOK: Jonathan Larsen; LYRICS: Jonathan Larsen; additional lyrics by Billy Aronson; MUSIC: Jonathan Larsen; DIRECTION: Michael Greif; SCENERY: Angela Wendt; COSTUMES: Angela Wendt; LIGHTING: Blake Burba; MUSICAL DIRECTION: Tim Weil; PRODUCER: New York Theatre Workshop (James C. Nicola, Artistic Director; Nancy Kassak Diekmann, Managing Director; Christopher Grabowski, Associate Artistic Director; Esther Cohen, General Manager)

CAST—Anthony Rapp (Mark Cohen), Tony Hoylen (Roger Davis), Pat Briggs (Tom Collins), Mark Setlock (Angel Dumott Schunard), Sarah Knowlton (Maureen Johnson), Shelley Dickinson (Joanne Jefferson), Daphne Rubin-Vega (Mimi Marquez), Michael Potts (Benjamin Coffin III), Erin Hill (Blockbuster Rep); also, Deirdre Boddie-Henderson, Gilles Chiasson, Sheila Kay Davis, John Lathan, Jesse Sinclair Lenat

SOURCE—The 1896 opera *La Boheme* by Giacomo Puccini.

The action occurs in the present in the East Village.

The musical was presented in two acts (song assignments unknown).

ACT ONE—"Message #1," "Rent," "Cool"/"Fool," "Today for You"/"Business," "Female to Female," "He Says," "Right Brain," "Light My Candle," "Christmas Bells," "Message #2," "Another Day," "Santa Fe," "I'll Cover You," "Will I?," "Over It," "Over the Moon," "La Vie Boheme," "I Should Tell You," "Message #3"

ACT TWO—"Seasons of Love," "Out Tonight," "Message #4," "Without You," "Message #5," "Contact," "Goodbye Love," "Real Estate," "Open Road," "Message #6," Finale

NOTES—Jonathan Larson's *Rent* was a politically correct modern-day version of Puccini's *La Boheme* which asked audiences to sympathize with characters who, as Jeffrey Sweet pointed out in *The Best Plays of 1995-1996*, are "not particularly engaging ... [they] are almost constantly angry and depressed with ... easy disdain for the so-called normal world"; these politically correct characters are of course "good-hearted and wise" as compared to the musical's "normal" characters. It was this smugness which has probably dated the musical; indeed, when the 2005 film version was released, some film critics felt the piece was clearly of its era (the mid-1990s) and had not aged well.

After its one-week Off Off Broadway "studio production" at the New York Theatre Workshop in 1994, the musical returned there for another Off Off Broadway workshop on January 26, 1996, for twelve performances; and it reopened there on February 13 under an Off Broadway contract for fifty-six performances. For the 1996 productions, Anthony Rapp and Daphne Rubin-Vega re-created their roles of Mark Cohen and Mimi Marquez; among the additions to the cast were Adam Pascal (Roger Davis), Taye Diggs (Benjamin Coffin III), and Idina Menzel (Maureen Johnson). On January 25, the day of the musical's first public preview before the official January 26 opening of the workshop engagement, Jonathan Larsen died of an aortic aneurysm at the age of thirty-five. He never lived to see the success of his long-gestating musical, and like Gower Champion's death just hours before the opening night of his long-running *42nd Street* (1980), Larson's untimely death became part of theatrical lore.

Rent opened at the Nederlander Theatre on April 29, 1996, for a marathon run of 5,123 performances. It won the Pulitzer Prize and a slew of other awards. The Broadway cast album was released on a 2-CD set by Dreamworks Records (# DRMD2-50003), and the soundtrack was released by Sony Records (CS # 49455-2). The script was published in 1997 by HarperCollins in a lavish coffee-table-styled edition. The script was also included in a volume of libretti titled *The New American Musical* (Wiley Hausam, editor), published by Theater Communications Group in 2003. The script was published in another edition in 2008 (*Rent: The Complete Book and Lyrics of the Broadway Musical* [Applause Theatre and Cinema Books]). The musical was produced in London, and was revived there on October 15, 2007, as *Rent Remixed* (the production was scheduled to play for six months, but closed after four). A film version of the musical's final Broadway performance (*Rent/Filmed Live on Broadway*) was released on DVD (Sony Pictures #29791).

In 2006, Anthony Rapp, who created the role of Mark Cohen, wrote *Without You: A Memoir of Love, Loss, and the Musical 'Rent'* (published by Simon & Schuster Paperbacks); the book chronicled deeply personal events in Rapp's life as well as a discussion of his involvement in *Rent*, beginning with the first production in 1994. Incidentally, Rapp created the role of the Little Prince in the Broadway musical *The Little Prince and the Aviator*, which closed during previews at the Alvin (now Neil Simon) Theatre in January 1982. For comparison purposes of the songs in the original Off Off Broadway production, the following is a list of the songs heard on Broadway (with the names of the Broadway cast members):

ACT ONE—"Tune Up"/"Voice Mail #1" (Anthony Rapp, Adam Pascal, Kristen Lee Kelly, Jesse L. Martin, Taye Diggs), "Rent" (Company), "You Okay Honey?" (Wilson Jermaine Heredia, Jesse L. Martin), "One-Song Glory" (Adam Pascal), "Light My Candle" (Adam Pascal, Daphne Rubin-Vega), "Voice Mail #2" (Byron Utley, Gwen Stewart), "Today 4 U" (Wilson Jermaine Heredia), "You'll See" (Taye Diggs, Anthony Rapp, Jesse L. Martin, Adam Pascal, Wilson Jermaine Heredia), "Tango: Maureen" (Anthony Rapp, Fredi Walker), "Life Support" (Rodney Hicks, Timothy Britten Parker, Company), "Out Tonight" (Daphne Rubin-Vega), "Another Day" (Adam Pascal, Daphne Rubin-Vega, Company), "Will I?" (Company), "On the Street" (Company), "Santa Fe" (Jesse L. Martin, Company), "We're Okay" (Fredi Walker), "I'll Cover You" (Wilson Jermaine Heredia, Jesse L. Martin), "Christmas Bells" (Company), "Over the Moon" (Idina Menzel), "La Vie Boheme"/"I Should Tell You" (Company), ACT TWO—"Seasons of Love" (Company), "Happy New Year"/"Voice Mail #3" (Daphne Rubin-Vega, Adam Pascal, Anthony Rapp, Idina Menzel, Fredi Walker, Jesse L. Martin, Wilson Jermaine Heredia, Kristen Lee Kelly, Aiko Nakasone, Taye Diggs), "Take Me or Leave Me" (Idina Menzel, Fredi Walker), "Without You" (Adam Pascal, Daphne Rubin-Vega), "Voice Mail #4" (Aiko Nakasone), "Contact" (Company), "I'll Cover You" (reprise) (Jesse L. Martin, Company), "Halloween" (Anthony Rapp), "Goodbye, Love" (Anthony Rapp, Daphne Rubin-Vega, Adam Pascal, Idina Menzel, Fredi Walker, Jesse L. Martin, Taye Diggs), "What You Own" (Byron Utley, Anthony Rapp, Jesse L. Martin, Taye Diggs, Adam Pascal), "Voice Mail #5" (Aiko Nakasone, ["Mimi's Mom"—performer unknown], Byron Utley, Kristen Lee Kelly), Finale/"Your Eyes" (Adam Pascal)

1352 The Return of the Second City in "20,000 Frozen Grenadiers." THEATRE: Square East; OPENING DATE: April 21, 1966; PERFORMANCES: 29; SKETCHES: Improvised by Sandra Caron, Bob (Robert) Klein, Judy Graubart, David Steinberg, and Fred Willard; MUSIC: William Mathieu and Will Holt; DIRECTION: Sheldon Patinkin; PRODUCER: Bernard Sahlins

CAST—Sandra Caron, Bob (Robert) Klein, Judy Graubart, David Steinberg, Fred Willard

NOTES—*The Return of the Second City in "20,000 Frozen Grenadiers"* was the eighth Second City revue to play Off Broadway (see entry for *Seacoast of Bohemia* for a complete list of the Second City revues which played in New York; also see Appendix T). The series was clearly fading in popularity; the latest edition couldn't manage a full month of performances.

Stanley Kauffmann in the *New York Times* found the revue "moderately diverting," but noted that too much of the revue's satire ("atomic disaster, folk songs, war movies, phony liberalism") was familiar and formulaic. He singled out a spoof of *The Rise and Fall of the City of Mahagonny* as the highlight of the evening. This was the second of two *Mahagonny* spoofs seen Off Broadway in the 1960s (see entry for *Signs Along the Cynic Route* [1961], which transplanted the setting of the opera to Hollywood in "The Rise & Fall of the City of Movieville"). Both *Mahagonny* spoofs were presented years before the opera itself was first produced in New York in 1970 (see entry).

The revue had originally opened in Chicago on May 14, 1963, as *20,000 Frozen Grenadiers,* or *There's Been a Terrible Accident at the Factory.*

1353 Return to the Forbidden Planet. THEATRE: Variety Arts Theatre; OPENING DATE: October 13, 1991; PERFORMANCES: 245; BOOK: Bob Carlton; LYRICS: See song list for credits; MUSIC: See song list for credits; DIRECTION: Bob Carlton; SCENERY: Rodney Ford; COSTUMES: Sally J. Lesser; Ariel's Costume Design by Adrian Rees; LIGHTING: Richard Nelson; MUSICAL DIRECTION: Kate Edgar; PRODUCERS: Andre Ptaszynski and Don Taffner

CAST—Robert McCormick (Captain Tempest), Steve Steiner (Dr. Prospero), Gabriel Barre (Ariel), Louis Tucci (Cookie), Julee Cruise (Science Officer), James H. Wiggins, Jr. (Bosun Arras), Mary Ehlinger (Navigation Officer), Erin Hill (Miranda), James Doohan (Chorus), Rebecca Ptaszynski (The Infant Miranda), Allison Briner (Ensign Betty Will), Chuck Tempo (Petty Officer Axel Rhodes), David LaDuca (Ensign Harry Saul Spray), Michael Rotondi (Ensign Dane G. Russ)

SOURCES—The 1956 film *Forbidden Planet* (which in turn was loosely based on William Shakespeare's play *The Tempest* [1611]).

The action occurs in 2024 on D'Illyria, The Forbidden Planet.

The musical was presented in two acts.

ACT ONE—"Wipeout" (lyric and music by Patrick Connolly, Robert Berryhill, James Fuller, and Ronald Wilson) (Company) "It's a Man's World" (lyric and music by James Brown and Betty Newsome) (Julee Cruise, Robert McCormick), "Great Balls of Fire" (lyric and music by Otis Blackwell and Jack Hammer) (Space Crew), "Don't Let Me Be Misunderstood" (lyric and music by Gloria Caldwell, Sol Marchus, and Bennie Benjamin) (Steve Steiner), "Good Vibrations" (lyric and music by Brian Wilson and Mike Love) (Robert McCormick, Gabriel Barre, Crew), "The Shoop Shoop Song" (lyric and music by Rudy Clark) (Louis Tucci, James H. Wiggins, Jr.), "I'm Gonna Change the World" (lyric and music by Eric Burdon) (Robert McCormick, Gabriel Barre, Steve Steiner), "Why Must I Be a Teenager in Love?" (lyric and music by Doc Pomus and Mort Shuman) (Erin Hill, Company), "Young Girl" (lyric and music by Jerry Fuller) (Robert McCormick, Company) "She's Not There" (lyric and music by Rod Argent) (Louis Tucci), "Shakin' All Over" (lyric and music by Johnny Kidd) (Robert McCormick, Erin Hill, Steve Steiner), "Gloria" (lyric and music by Van Morrison) (Company)

ACT TWO—"Gloria" (reprise) (Company), "Don't Let Me Be Misunderstood" (reprise) (Julee Cruise), "Who's Sorry Now?" (lyric and music by Bert Kalmar, Harry Ruby, and Ted Snyder) (Gabriel Barre), "Tell Her" (lyric and music by Bert Russell) (Company), "She's Not There" (underscoring), "It's a Man's World" (reprise) (underscoring), "Oh, Pretty Woman" (lyric and music by Roy Orbison and Bill Dees), "It's a Man's World" (underscoring), "Robot Man" (lyric and music by Sylvia Dee and George Goehring) (Erin Hill, Gabriel Barre), "Shake, Rattle and Roll" (lyric and music by Charles Calhoun) (Louis Tucci, Crew), "Gloria" (underscoring), "Go Now" (lyric and music by Larry Banks and Milton Bennett) (Julee Cruise), "Don't Let Me Be Misunderstood" (underscoring), "Only the Lonely" (lyric and music by Roy Orbison and Joe Melson) (Louis Tucci, James H. Wiggins, Jr., Crew), "Born to Be Wild" (lyric and music by Mars Bonfire) (Robert McCormick, James H. Wiggins, Louis Tucci), "Mister Spaceman" (lyric and music by Roger McGuinn) (Erin Hill, Company) "The Monster Mash" (lyric and music by Bobby Pickett and Leonard Capizzi) (Steve Steiner, Company), "Great Balls of Fire" (reprise) (Louis Tucci)

NOTES—*Return to the Forbidden Planet*, a spoof of science-fiction films of the 1950s, seemed to be one of those sure-fire musicals which would enjoy a long run; but it was gone well before the end of the theatre season.

The dialogue was an amusing amalgamation of uninspired 1950s-styled sci-fi movie dialogue set to a kind of warped Shakespearean blank verse ("If thou neglect'st or dost unwillingly/What I command, I'll put you in the brig"). An air of camp pervaded the production (the heroine Miranda is "would-be homecoming queen and virgin"; Ensign Betty Will is the spaceship's "entertainment officer"; and Ensign Harry Saul Spray is the ship's "esthetics control and beauty maintenance officer"). And all of this was set to pop tunes of the 1950s and 1960s.

The musical had first been produced in London at the Cambridge Theatre on September 18, 1989. The London cast album was released by V Records (LP # V-2631) and included three numbers not heard in New York ("Ain't Gonna Wash for a Week," "The Young Ones," and "We Gotta Get Out of This Place"). The script was published by Samuel French, Inc., in 1998.

1354 Reunion. "A Play with Music." THEATRE: Cubiculo Theatre; OPENING DATE: May 12, 1978; PERFORMANCES: 12; BOOK: Melvin H. Freedman and Robert Kornfeld; LYRICS: Melvin H.

Freedman and Robert Kornfeld; MUSIC: Ron Roullier; additional music by Carly Simon and Lucy Simon; DIRECTION: Jeffrey K. Neill; CHOREOGRAPHY: Jeffrey K. Neill; SCENERY: Dale Engle; COSTUMES: Chas W. Roeder; LIGHTING: Christopher Peabody; MUSICAL DIRECTION: Wendell Kindberg (?); PRODUCER: Sally E. Parry

CAST—Wendell Kindberg (Piano Player), Peter A. Rivera (Drummer), Lou Corato (John Donnelly), Eleanor Reissa (Sue Wolczek), Beverly Wideman (Roseann Campbell), David Schall (David Lerman), Geraldine Hanning (Cynthia Parker), Howard Hagan (Kevin Donnelly), Brian Watson (Avery McGraw)

The action occurs in the Student/Faculty Lounge off the main hallway to the auditorium on the third day of the rehearsal for the reunion show; the time is Spring 1978.

The musical was presented in two acts.

ACT ONE—"Today" (Lou Corato, Eleanor Reissa, Geraldine Hanning, David Schall, Beverly Wideman), "I'm All It Takes to Make You Happy" (Lou Corato, Eleanor Reissa), "Young Dreams" (Geraldine Hanning, David Schall), "A World I'll Make for Me" (Eleanor Reissa, Lou Corato), "Today" (reprise) (David Schall, Geraldine Hanning, Beverly Wideman), "Childhood"/"Golden Days" (Beverly Wideman, David Schall, Geraldine Hanning, Howard Hagan, Lou Corato, Eleanor Reissa), "Got to Sing Me a Song" (Lou Corato, Eleanor Reissa)

ACT TWO—"Got to Sing Me a Song" (reprise) (Lou Corato), "Reunion" (Lou Corato, Eleanor Reissa, Beverly Wideman, David Schall, Brian Watson, Geraldine Hanning), "I'm Gonna Make It" (Brian Watson, Lou Corato, Eleanor Reissa), "That Moment Is Now" (Geraldine Hanning, David Schall), "Give Me Love" (David Schall, Geraldine Hanning, Beverly Wideman, Eleanor Reissa), "All My Yesterdays" (Lou Corato, Eleanor Reissa), "The Great Wind" (Beverly Wideman, Eleanor Reissa, Lou Corato), "A World I'll Make for Me" (reprise) (Beverly Wideman)

NOTES—*Reunion* was a showcase production which opened at The Cubiculo Theatre, playing there for twelve performances; after that, it was never heard from again. Carly Simon composed the music for "I'm All It Takes to Make You Happy," and her sister Lucy Simon composed the music for "All My Yesterdays."

1355 Rhinegold. THEATRE: Playwrights Horizons; OPENING DATE: March 29, 1975; PERFORMANCES: 8; BOOK: Barry Keating and Jim Steinman; LYRICS: Barry Keating; MUSIC: Jim Steinman; DIRECTION: Barry Keating; CHOREOGRAPHY: Barry Keating; SCENERY: Calvin Churchman; COSTUMES: Bosha Johnson; LIGHTING: Jim Chaleff; MUSICAL DIRECTION: Jez Davidson; PRODUCER: Playwrights Horizons (Robert Moss, Executive Director)

CAST—Johanna Albrecht, George Ayer, Alan Braunstein, Sarah Harris, Mary Hendrickson, Pat Lavelle, Lester Malizia, Howard Meadow, Edwin Owens, Ellen Parks, Chuch Ritchie, Tim Sheahan, Frank Thompson, Ron Van Lieu

1356 Richard Farina: Long Time Coming and a Long Time Gone. THEATRE: Fortune Theatre; OPENING DATE: November 17, 1971; PERFORMANCES: 7; TEXT AND SONGS: Writings, poems, and songs by Richard Farina (adapted by Nancy Greenwald); DIRECTION: Robert Greenwald; SCENERY (AND COLLAGE): Richard Hammer and Patrick Sullivan; COSTUMES: Joyce and Jerry Marcel; LIGHTING: John Dodd; MUSICAL DIRECTION: Arthur Miller; PRODUCERS: Free Flow Productions and Jay K. Hoffman

CAST—Richard Gere (Richard), Vicki Sue Robinson (Richard's Lady), Penelope Milford (Judith), Charles Weldon (Thomas), Jessica Harper (Ann), Brendan Hanion (Harold), Michael Lewis (Orchestra)

The revue was presented in one act (song assignments unknown).

MUSICAL NUMBERS—"Comments," "Pack Up Your Sorrows," "Celebration for a Gray Day," "Reflections on a Crystal Wind," "The Field Near the Cathedral at Chartres," "Nothing Poem," "Joy 'Round My Brain," "An End to a Young Man," "Another Country," "Passing of Various Lives," "House Un-American Activities Blues Dream," "Breaking the Travel Ban," "Morgan the Pirate," "Juan Carlose Rosenbloom," "The Falcon," "November Elegy," "All the World Has Gone By," "Hard Loving Loser," "One Way Ticket," "Monterey Fair," "Birmingham Sunday," "The Dream Song of J. Alfred Kerouac," "St. Vincent's Isle," "Somber Wind," "Kings Die Easy," "Raven Girl," "Children of Darkness"

NOTES—Richard Farina (1937-1966) was a minor figure in 1960s politically-oriented folk music; in the musical, he was portrayed by Richard Gere (in one of his earliest New York performances). Farina's anti-establishment protest writings included songs, poetry, and one novel, *Been Down So Long It Looks Like Up to Me* (1966). He died in a motorcycle accident in 1966, and had the revue been produced shortly after his death, it might have enjoyed a longer run. At it was, the 1971 revue didn't last more than a week. Clive Barnes in the *New York Times* found the evening tedious, unexciting, and "about as dramatic as a glee club that has lost its joy." He found the music a "dated echo" of Bob Dylan, and said Nancy Greenwald's adaptation of Farina's work was "strictly anti-theatrical." Barnes concluded that boredom couldn't be reviewed, it could only be reported.

1357 Ricky Jay & His 52 Assistants. THEATRE: Second Stage Theatre; OPENING DATE: February 2, 1994; PERFORMANCES: 110; MATERIAL: Ricky Jay; DIRECTION: David Mamet; SCENERY: Kevin Rigdon; LIGHTING: Jules Fisher; PRODUCERS: Second Stage Theatre (Carole Rothman, Artistic Director; Suzanne Schwartz Davidson, Producing Director); Carol Fishman, Associate Producer

CAST—Ricky Jay

NOTES—Directed by no less than playwright David Mamet, *Ricky Jay & His 52 Assistants* was a one-man magic show which included some audience participation (Ricky Jay's "52 Assistants" were a deck of playing cards).

1358 Ride the Winds. "A New Musical." THEATRE: Bijou Theatre; OPENING DATE: May 16, 1974; PERFORMANCES: 3; BOOK: John Driver; LYRICS: John Driver; MUSIC: John Driver; DIRECTION: Lee D. Sankowich; CHOREOGRAPHY: Jay Norman; SCENERY: Samuel C. Ball; COSTUMES: Samuel C. Ball; LIGHTING: Jeff Davis; MUSICAL DIRECTION: Robert Brandzel; PRODUCERS: Berta Walker and Bill Tchakirides

CAST—Irving Lee (Mushasi), Sab Shimono (Yamada), Ernesto Gonzalez (Sensei [Honored Teacher] Takuan), Nate Barnett (Joshu), Chip Zien (Inari), Tom Matsusaka (Banzo), Fanny Cerito Assoluta (Ya Ta), Elaine Petricoff (Lan), Marion Jim (Toki), Alexander Orfaly (Oda), Laura May Lewis and John Gorrin (Tellers); Priests, Kendo Students, and Soliders (Kenneth Frett, John Gorrin, Richard Loreto, Ken Mitchell)

The action occurs in a feudal country in the Far East, around a monastery along a mountain road.

The musical was presented in two acts.

ACT ONE—"Run, Musashi, Run" (Company), "The Emperor Me" (Irving Lee), "The Gentle Buffoon" (Nate Barnett, Chip Zien), "Those Who Speak" (Irving Lee, Nate Barnett, Chip Zien), "Flower Song" (Ernesto Gonzalez, Elaine Petricoff, Nate Barnett, Ensemble), "You're Loving Me" (Irving Lee), "Breathing the Air" (Marion Jim), "Remember That Day" (Ernesto Gonzalez, Sab Shimono), "Tengu" (Ensemble)

ACT TWO—"Ride the Winds" (Company), "Are You a Man" (Elaine Petricoff), "Ride the Winds" (reprise) (Company), "Every Days" (Elaine Petricoff, Marion Jim, Inari Priests), "Loving You" (Elaine Petricoff, Irving Lee), "Pleasures" (Alexander Orfaly), "Someday I'll Walk" (Irving Lee), "That Touch" (Elaine Petricoff), Finale (Company)

NOTES—*Ride the Winds* dealt with a young man who aspires to be a Samurai, but discovers what he really wants out of life is to live peacefully with the girl he loves. New York had already seen a variation of this story when it was called *Pippin* (1972), and so it wasn't interested in another saga of a young man trying to find himself during medieval times. As a result, *Ride the Winds* was blown away after three performances. Other musicals which covered similar territory were *The Glorious Age* (which quickly opened and closed during the1974-1975 season) and *Bodo* (which never got out of rehearsals during the 1983-1984 season); see entries. *Ride the Winds* caused a certain amount of controversy because of one of its casting choices. The musical was picketed by the Oriental Actors of America, who protested because a Black actor (Irving Lee) was cast as the young Japanese man. When *Ride the Winds* opened, John Driver, its author, lyricist, and composer, was appearing on Broadway as a performer in the delightful (and underrated) *Over Here!*

1359 Der Ring Gott Farblonjet (1977). "A Masterwork." THEATRE: Truck and Warehouse Theatre; OPENING DATE: April 27, 1977; PERFORMANCES: 78; BOOK: Charles Ludlam; LYRICS: Charles Ludlam; MUSIC: Jack McElwaine; DIRECTION: Charles Ludlam; SCENERY: Charles Ludlam; COSTUMES: Charles Ludlam; LIGHTING: Richard Currie; PRODUCERS: The Ridiculous Theatrical Company (Charles Ludlam, Artistic Director)

CAST—Adam Macadam (Twoton [Nobody of the Gods]), Robert Reddy (Donner [God of Thunder], Rosseweisse), Stephen Holt (Froh [God of Rain, Sun, Fruits], Schwertleita), Georg Osteman (Loge [God of Fire and Lies], Siegmund, Bear), Ethyl Eichelberger (Fricks [Goddess of Lawful Wedlock], Gunther), Suzanne Peters (Freia [Goddess of Youth and Beauty], Grimgerde), Black-Eyed Susan (Eartha [The Earth Mother], Sieglinda, Gutruna), Everett Quinton (Flosshilde, Ninny), Beverly Brown (Woglinde, Helmvige, Bird), Ericka Brown (Welgunde, Valtrauta), John D. Brockmeyer (Fasdolt, Siegfried), Richard Currie (Fafner, Hagen, Hunding [A Gesundheit]), Bill Vehr (Alverruck), Lola Pashalinski (Brunnhilda), Janine Day (Gerthilda), Denise Day (Ortlinda), Debra Crane (Siegruna); Norns (Everett Quinton, Beverly Brown, Ericka Brown); Vassals and Heathen Onlookers (Robert Grindstaff, Randy Buck, Suzanne Peters, Stephen Holt, Robert Reddy, Debra Chase)

SOURCES—Richard Wagner's four-part opera cycle *Der Ring des Nibelungen* (*Das Rheingold* [1854], *Die Walkure* [1856], *Siegfried* [1871], and *Gotterdammerung* [1874]) as well as other versions of the saga, including ones by Henrick Ibsen and Frederick Nietzsche.

The musical was presented in four acts (songs weren't listed in the program).

NOTES—Charles Ludlam's Ridiculous Theatrical Company produced this madcap version of the *Ring* saga. And any musical which includes "Heathen Onlookers" in its cast of characters deserves a special award. The work was revived at the Charles Ludlam Theatre on March 27, 1990, for forty-eight performances; for the revival, the four acts were titled *Das Reingold*; *The Dyke Bikers at Helgeland*; *Siegfried*; and *Gotterdammerung (Ring Damns Gods)*.

In his review of the 1990 production, Mel Gussow in the *New York Times* felt the revival was tighter and more cohesive than the original version, and noted that the musical "is the funniest 'Ring' cycle one is likely to see." He enjoyed the motley assortment of characters, including *Elephant Man*-like giants; a dragon; Eartha the Earth Mother; a vegetarian "Arnold Schwarzenegger-like" Siegfried; and Gott himself, who positively dotes on his divine divinity. For the revival, Mark Bennett composed the score, which Gussow found a mixture of Wagner's *Das Rheingold* and "the music for a sudsy beer commercial." One number from this production, "Valkyrie Dance & Song," was included on the collection *The Ridiculous Theatrical Company/The 25th Anniversary* (DRG Records CD # 6301). The script was published by Samuel French, Inc.

For another spoof of the *Ring*, see entry for *Das Barbecu*.

1360 The Rise and Fall of the City of Mahagonny. THEATRE: Anderson Theatre; OPENING DATE: April 28, 1970; PERFORMANCES: 8; LIBRETTO: Bertolt Brecht (adapted by Arnold Weinstein); MUSIC: Kurt Weill; DIRECTION: Carmen Capalbo; SCENERY: Robin Wagner; COSTUMES: Ruth Morley; LIGHTING: Thomas Skelton; MUSICAL DIRECTION: Samuel Matlowsky; PRODUCERS: Carmen Capalbo and Abe Margolies in association with Atlantic Recording Corporation

CAST—Evan Thompson (Commentator), Val Pringle (Trinity Moses), Jack De Lon (Fatty), ESTELLE PARSONS (Leocadia Begbick), BARBARA HARRIS (Jenny), Alan Crofoot (John Hancock Schmidt), Bill Copeland (Alaska Wolf Joe), Don Crabtree (Billy Bankboo), FRANK PORRETTA (Jimmy Mallory), Rock Group (Louis St. Louis, Richard Apuzzo, Howard Wyeth, Jon Huston), Samuel Matlowsky (Referee), Ray Camp (Camera Man), Clint Elliot (Camera Man), Richard Miller (Toby Higgins), Kenneth Frett (Bellhop), James Hobson (Bellhop), Gordon Minard (Bellhop), Tracy Moore (Bellhop), Girls of Mahagonny (Holly Hamilton, Sayrah Hummel, Anne Kaye, Lani Miller, Jacqueline Penn, Veronica Redd, Lou Rodgers, Adrienne Whitney), Men of Mahagonny (Rudy Challenger, Jack Fletcher, Jimmy Justice, Keith Kaldenberg, Richard Miller, Alex Orfaly)

The action occurs in a desert, on the outskirts of Mahagonny, and in the city of Mahagonny.

The opera was presented in three acts (individual songs weren't listed in the program).

NOTES—Brecht and Weill's opera *The Rise and Fall of the City of Mahagonny* is perhaps the towering masterwork of twentieth-century musical theatre. Bitter and cynical, and yet overflowing with alternately lyrical and jazzy music, it told the story of Mahagonny, a "city of nets," created for man's pleasure. When Mahagonny is spared the wrath of a hurricane, it appears to be a sign from God (not that anyone in Mahagonny believes in God) that the city is indestructible and eternal, and so the citizens indulge in the pleasures of food, drink, sex, and sports. In Mahagonny, everything is allowed ... except for the one unforgivable sin of not having money. The hero Jimmy Mallory is therefore found not guilty of a death for which he was responsible, but when he can't pay his bills, he's executed. The opera was first presented as *Mahagonny* (a/k/a *Mahagonny Songspiel*) in 1927 in Baden-Baden (with Lotte Lenya as "Jessie"); instead of a straightforward plot, the presentation was a series of interconnected songs dealing with the citizens of Mahagonny and their sins; when God becomes appalled by the citizens' behavior, He condemns them to Hell; but the people of Mahagonny refuse to obey Him, insisting they already live in Hell. Mahagonny is so corrupt that God Himself steers clear of it.

Brecht and Weill expanded the work into a full-length opera, and in 1930 *Aufstieg und Fall der Stadt Mahagonny* premiered in Leipzig (with Mali Trummer in the leading role, now named "Jenny").

The 1970 Off Broadway production marked the opera's New York premiere, and because both the original director (Carmen Capalbo) and musical director (Samuel Matlowsky) of the long-running Off Broadway revival of *The Threepenny Opera* (see entries for 1954 and 1955 productions) were again in place, there was great hope that *Mahagonny* would find similar success. Mel Gussow in the *New York Times* reported that in 1956 Capalbo had originally announced that *Mahagonny* would open in New York during Fall 1957 (Marc Blitzstein had even completed a first draft of the adaptation). But because of duel copyright ownerships of the opera (a publishing company owned the European rights, and Lotte Lenya and Brecht's wife and son owned the American rights), the production never got off the ground. Once the legal issues involving the copyright were resolved, ten years had gone by; Capalbo then hired Arnold Weinstein to adapt and translate the work (Blitzstein had been murdered in 1964). For the role of Jenny, Gussow reported that, among others, Cher, Grace Slick, Dusty Springfield, and Dionne Warwick were approached. Further, a number of actors were considered for the role of Jimmy Mallory, including Robert Redford, Richard Harris, and Mick Jagger. Finally, Henry Madden was signed, although it appears he left during rehearsals and thus was long gone by the first preview performance; he was replaced by Mort Shuman, then by Bill Copeland, and finally by Frank Porretta (see below).

But the long-gestating American production never quite jelled, and the preview period was extended, was extended again, and then was extended yet again, finally playing sixty-nine preview performances, at the time a record for an Off Broadway production (the capitalization for the opera was $350,000, another Off Broadway record for the era). During the preview period, audiences saw no less than three actors perform the pivotal role of Jimmy Mallory: the above-mentioned Mort Shuman (who had recently appeared in the successful *Jacques Brel Is Alive and Well and Living in Paris* [see entry]), Bill Copeland (Shuman's understudy, who briefly replaced him), and then Frank Porretta.

The production utilized Brecht's famous "alienation" effects in updated and clever ways. For example, television cameramen were often on stage, and as they filmed scenes, those scenes were simultaneously projected "live" on large screens arranged across the stage.

Besides the orchestra, there was a four-piece "rock" band situated in one of the boxes, stage left. In truth, the band's arrangements were more honky-tonk-piano than rock, and thus seemed at home in Mahagonny. The sudden if welcome intrusions by the band added to the sense of theatre, and Brecht would probably have approved of the device (it appears the use of the rock band may have all but been abandoned by opening night, leaving just Louis St. Louis and his piano up there in the box).

At a preview performance, Mort Shuman seemed the perfect vocal and physical embodiment of Jimmy, and one couldn't quarrel with his performance; Estelle Parsons may have been vocally challenged by the role of the Widow Begbick, but she was nonetheless a caustic and chilling presence; as Jenny, Barbara Harris gave her third magnificent New York musical theatre performance in five years, but after the eighth and final regular performance of *Mahagonny*, she was never again seen on the New York stage (for more information about Barbara Harris' career, see entry for *Seacoast of Bohemia*).

Happily, the Off Broadway production paved the way for the heretofore obscure opera, and during the following years various opera companies throughout the country included it in their repertory, performing the piece in either German or in English. And while the Metropolitan Opera and the Washington Opera's productions were welcome and were excitingly sung and played, they didn't have the intense theatricality of the Off Broadway version. The Washington Opera's production premiered on December 15, 1972, in a translation by Arnold Weinstein and Lys Symonette, and the Metropolitan Opera's production (which premiered on November 11, 1979) used a translation by David Drew and Michael Geliot (incidentally, Drew is the author of the fascinating and indispensable *Kurt Weill/A Handbook*, published by the University of California Press in 1987). Some sources indicate the Off Broadway revival used a shortened title (*Mahagonny*), but the full title appears on three different preview programs as well as on the final program, not to mention the mock-up for the Atlantic Records cast album (which was never recorded).

A 3-LP recording of the opera (in German) was released by Columbia Records (# K3L-243) in 1958 (Lotte Lenya was Jenny), and was later issued on a 2-CD set by CBS Records (# M2K-77341). Another recording (also in German) was released on a 2-CD set by Capriccio Records (# 10-160/61). Further, the original *Mahagonny Songspiel* was released by Capriccio Records (CD # 60-028-1); the CD also included included Weill's *The Seven Deadly Sins* [1933]).

There are at least two publications of the script. One, published in 1969 by Theodore Presser Company, was in a translation by Arnold Weinstein and Lys Symonette. The second appeared in 1976 by David R. Godine, Publisher, in a translation by W.H. Auden and Chester Kallman.

A revival (in German) at the Salzburg Festival in 1998 was released on home video by Kultur Video (videocassette # 2078 and DVD # D2078); Catherine Malfitano was Jennie and Jerry Hadley was Jimmy. A 2007 revival by the Los Angeles Opera was shown on public television's *Great Performances* series on December 17, 2007; the translation was by Michael Feingold, and the cast included Audra MacDonald (Jenny), Patti LuPone (Leocadia Begbick), and Anthony Dean Griffey (Jim Mahoney/Jimmy Mallory, here Jimmy McIntyre); James Conlon conducted and John Doyle directed. This production was released on DVD (EuroArts # 2056258).

1361 The Rise of David Levinsky (1983). THEATRE: American Jewish Theatre; OPENING DATE: March 12, 1983; PERFORMANCES: 48 (estimated); BOOK: Isaiah Sheffer; LYRICS: Isaiah Sheffer; MUSIC: Bobby Paul; DIRECTION: Sue Lawless; CHOREOGRAPHY: Bick Goss; SCENERY: Kenneth Foy; COSTUMES: Richard Hornung; LIGHTING: Phil Monat; MUSICAL DIRECTION: Lanny Meyers; PRODUCER: The American Jewish Theatre (Stanley Brechner, Artistic Director)

CAST—Larry Keith (Levinsky), Lawrence Raiken (Maximum Max), Clarke Evans (Huntington, Shlank, Mannheimer), Marilyn Sokol (Mrs. Dienstog, Mrs. Noodleman), Avi Hoffman (David), Sylvia Danzig (Mother, Becky), Norman Golden (Reb Shmerl, Mr. Diamond), Mickey Hartnett (Neighbor, Sadie, Customer), Eva Charney (Matilda, Ruchel, Gussie), Glenn Rosenblum (Naphtali, Getzel), Paul Harman (Gitelson), Elias Tray (Big Mottel, Policeman), Rosalind Harris (Dora), Jerry Matz (Bender), Robert Ott Boyle (Chaikin)

SOURCE—The 1917 novel *The Rise of David Levinksy* by Abraham Cahan.

The action occurs between 1883 and 1910.

The musical was presented in two acts.

ACT ONE—"Who Is This Man?" (Larry Keith), "Five Hundred Pages" (Avi Hoffman), "Learning" (Sylvia Danzig, Avi Hoffman), "Letter Fantasy: Grand Street" (Eva Charney, Glenn Rosenblum, Norman Golden), "In America" (Avi Hoffman, Paul Harman, Other Immigrants), "The Boarder" (Marilyn Sokol), "Transformation" (Avi Hoffman, Shop People and Others), "Sharp" (Lawrence Raiken, Elias Tray, Clarke Evans, Glenn Rosenblum), "Two of a Kind" (Rosalind Harris), "Hard Times" (Avi Hoffman), "Credit Face" (Larry Keith, Avi Hoffman), "Five Hundred Garments" (Larry Keith, Avi Hoffman)

ACT TWO—"Ready Made" (Paul Harman, Eva Charney, Robert Ott Boyle, Shopworkers), "The Garment Trade" (Ensemble, Larry Keith), "Welcome to the Merry-Go-Round" (Paul Harman, Robert Ott Boyle, Eva Charney, Jerry Matz), "Just...Like... Me" (Lawrence Raiken, Rosalind Harris, Larry Keith), "The Shopping Waltz" (Marilyn Sokol, Larry Keith, Lawrence Raiken, Eva Charney, Mickey Hartnett, Sylvia Danzig), "Bittersweet" (Rosalind Harris), "Survival of the Fittest" (Larry Keith), "Time to Live" (Larry Keith), "Build a Union" (Eva Charney, Paul Harman, Jerry Matz, Robert Ott Boyle, Shopworkers), "After All" (Lawrence Raiken, Friends), "Who Is This Man?" (reprise) (Larry Keith, Avi Hoffman), "In America" (reprise) (Larry Keith, Avi Hoffman, Company)

NOTES—Based on Abraham Cahan's novel, the Off Off Broadway musical *The Rise of David Levinsky* told the story of David Levinksy, a young Jewish immigrant who gives up his dream of a scholarly life in order to become one of the moguls of the garment industry; Avi Hoffman played the young David, Larry Keith the older David. The musical was the first of two which opened in March 1983 and took place in the world of the garment industry (see entry for *From Brooks, with Love*). (But Harold Rome's underrated 1962 Broadway musical *I Can Get It for You Wholesale* probably remains the definitive musical about Seventh Avenue.)

In 1987, a revised version of the musical opened at the John Houseman Theatre for thirty-one performances (see entry). Sue Lawless was again the director, and Avi Hoffman reprised his role of young David. Larry Kert played the older David, and Bruce Adler was Gitelson. Songs from the 1983 production which weren't used in the 1987 version were "Learning," "Ready Made," "Welcome to the Merry-Go-Round," "Time to Live," and "After All." New songs were "Little Did I [We] Know," "Some Incredible Guy," "Be Flexible," "A Married Man," and "A View from the Top."

The script of the 1987 production was published by Samuel French, Inc., in 1988.

1362 The Rise of David Levinsky (1987). THEATRE: John Houseman Theatre; OPENING DATE: January 12, 1987; PERFORMANCES: 31; BOOK: Isaiah Sheffer; LYRICS: Isaiah Sheffer; MUSIC: Bobby Paul; DIRECTION: Sue Lawless; SCENERY: Kenneth Foy; COSTUMES: Mimi Maxmen; LIGHTING: Norbert U. Kolb; MUSICAL DIRECTION: Lanny Meyers; PRODUCER: Eric Krebs

CAST—Larry Raiken (Maximum Max, Reb Shmerel, Diamond), W.M. Hunt (Huntington, Manheimer), David Vosburgh (Blitt, Big Muttel, Moscowitz), Jack Kenny (Chaiken, Naphtali, Little Getzel), Eleanor Reissa (Dora), LARRY KERT (Levinsky), Arthur Howard (Shlankie, Bender), AVI HOFFMAN (David), Jean Kauffman (Model, Matilda, Gussie, Rosie), Bruce Adler (Gitelson), Rende Rae Norman (Model, Argentine Ruchel, Becky), Lynne Wintersteller (Model, Shopgirl, Sadie), David Kener (Peddler, Strike Worker), Wendy Baila (Shopgirl, Strike Worker)

SOURCE—The 1917 novel *The Rise of David Levinsky* by Abraham Cahan.

The action occurs during the period 1883-1910.

The musical was presented in two acts.

ACT ONE—"Who Is This Man?" (Larry Kert), "Five Hundred Pages" (Avi Hoffman), "Grand Street" (Jean Kaufmann, Jack Kenny, Larry Raiken, Avi Hoffman), "In America" (Avi Hoffman, Immigrants), "The Boarder" (Judith Cohen), "The Transformation" (Avi Hoffman, David Vosburgh, Barber Shop People), "Quartet: Sharp" (Larry Raiken, Arthur Howard, David Vosburgh, Jack Kenny), "Two of a Kind" (Eleanor Reissa), "Little Did I Know" (Larry Kert), "Hard Times" (Avi Hoffman, Larry Kert), "Two of a Kind" (reprise) (Eleanor Reissa), "Credit Face" (Larry Kert, Avi Hoffman), "Five Hundred Garments" (Avi Hoffman, Larry Kert)

ACT TWO—"The Garment Trade" (Ensemble, Larry Kert), "Some Incredible Guy" (Bruce Adler), Trio: "Just...Like...Me" (Larry Raiken, Eleanor Reissa, Larry Kert), "Be Flexible" (Avi Hoffman), "A Married Man" (Judith Cohen, Larry Raiken, David Vosburgh, Rende Rae Norman, Jean Kauffman, Lynne Winterseller, Larry Kert), Duet: "Little Did We Know" (Larry Kert, Eleanor Reissa), "Bittersweet" (Eleanor Reissa, Larry Kert), "Survival of the Fittest" (Larry Kert), "A View from the Top" (Larry Kert, Avi Hoffman), "In America" (reprise) (Larry Kert, Avi Hoffman, Ensemble)

NOTES—See entry for the 1983 Off Off Broadway production of *The Rise of David Levinsky*, which includes information regarding differences in the musical numbers for both productions. For the 1987 version, Avi Hoffman reprised his role of the young David, and was joined by Larry Kert as the older David (played by Larry Keith in 1983).

During the years between the Off Off Broadway and Off Broadway productions of *David Levinsky*, the 1986 Broadway musical *Rags* had opened (and quickly closed). (See entry for the Off Off Broadway production of *Rags*.) Critics reviewing the Off Broadway production of *David Levinsky* noted that both it and *Rags* were both musicals about Jewish immigrants in New York City at the turn-of-the-century and that Larry Kert's Levinsky was similar to the role he played in *Rags*. (The critics also mentioned the revue *The Golden Land* [see entry] covered similar territory.)

In his review of *The Rise of David Levinsky* for the *New York Times*, Stephen Holden wrote that *Rags* "failed to make coherent drama" of its story of European Jewish immigrants, but felt that *David Levinsky* offered a "sober, historically detailed version of a familiar saga." John Beaufort in the *Christian Science Monitor* noted *David Levinsky* "is the show that *Rags* might have been."

Holden further praised Kert's performance ("wary and understated in the first act, volcanic in the second").

The 1987 version of *The Rise of David Levinsky* had been previously seen at the George Street Playhouse in New Brunswick, New Jersey, in April 1986. The musical was the first production to play at the John Houseman Theatre.

1363 The River. "A Musical Revelation." THEATRE: Promenade Theatre; OPENING DATE: January 13, 1988; PERFORMANCES: 41; LYRICS: Peter Link; MUSIC: Peter Link; DIRECTION: Michael Shawn; CHOREOGRAPHY: Michael Shawn; Paul Nunes, Assistant Choreographer; SCENERY: William Barclay; COSTUMES: David Dille; LIGHTING: Phil Monat; MUSICAL DIRECTION: Ronald P. Metcalf; PRODUCERS: William P. Suter and Donald V. Thompson; William Spencer Reilly, Executive Producer; Douglas A. Love, Associate Producer

CAST—Jenny Burton (Woman #2), Carol Dennis (Woman #1), Valerie K. Eley (Woman #3), Lawrence Hamilton (Man #1), Stephanie Renee James (Woman #4), Danny Madden (High Priest; Man #3), Ray Stephens (Man #2)

The revue was presented in two acts.

ACT ONE—*The Heavens:* "Genesis" (Danny Madden), "Circle" (Company), *Rainfall:* "Didn't It Rain" (song in public domain; additional lyric and music by Peter Link) (Valerie K. Eley, Women), *One Drop Alone:* Interlude I: "One Drop Alone" (Danny Madden), "Put the Fire Out" (Jenny Burton, Women), "Wanderin' in the Wilderness" (Men), "A Still Small Voice" (Carol Dennis), *The Stream:* Interlude II: "The Stream" (Danny Madden, Carol Dennis, Company), "Lead Me to the Water" (Carol Dennis, Company), "Don't It Feel Good" (Jenny Burton, Company), *The River:* Interlude III: "The River's in Me" (Danny Madden), "The River" (translation of the Nigerian chant sequence in this song is by Babatunde Olatunji) (Valerie K. Eley, Company), *The Waterfall:* Interlude IV: "The Waterfall" (Danny Madden), "Run River Run" (Company), "Over the Edge" (Ray Stephens, Company)

ACT TWO—*The Mire:* Interlude V: "Wallowing in the Mire" (Danny Madden), "Burnin' Up" (Company), "This Is All I Ask" (Lawrence Hamilton), "Carnival" (Company), "Love Runs Deeper Than Pride" (Jenny Burton), "Love Runs Deeper Than Pride" (reprise) (Company), *The Sea:* Interlude VI: "The Sea" (Danny Madden), "Revelation" (lyric adapted from the *Book of Revelation*) (Company), *Ascension:* "Take Me Up" (Jenny Burton, Company)

NOTES—Peter Link's song cycle *The River* dealt with water in its various literal forms (the human body, rain, streams, rivers, waterfalls, the sea) and how the cycle of water (which falls from the sky, nutures earth, and then returns to the sky) mirrors the life cycle of Man.

The critics were generally unimpressed with the concert-styled musical. Don Nelsen in the *New York Daily News* noted that "these waters are troubled," and Allan Wallach in *New York Newsday* said the evening "runs aground on the shoals of an insistent message and an earthbound approach." However, Mel Gussow in the *New York Times* noted that while "hydrophobes should avoid" the musical, "others are likely to join in the exultation."

A program note thanked Lawrence Hamilton for his choreography in "Lead Me to the Water," "The River," and "Don't It Feel Good" (he adapted the choreography for the latter song from the original choreography by Michael Shawn when the musical was first produced by the Triplex at Borough of Manhattan Community College/CUNY).

During previews, "Mandala" and "All Around the World" were dropped.

1364 Riverwind. THEATRE: Actors' Playhouse; OPENING DATE: December 12, 1962; PERFORMANCES: 443; BOOK: Joseph Benjamin; LYRICS: John Jennings; MUSIC: John Jennings; DIRECTION: Adrian Hall; CHOREOGRAPHY: Ronnie Fields; MUSICAL NUMBERS—staged by Phil Landi; SCENERY: Robert Soule; COSTUMES: Robert Soule; LIGHTING: Jules Fisher; MUSICAL DIRECTION: Joseph Stecko; PRODUCER: The Bushe Company

CAST—Lovelady Powell (Virginia), Brooks Morton (Burt), Dawn Nickerson (Jenny Farrell), Helon Blount (Mrs. Farrell), Martin J. Cassidy (John Stone), Elizabeth Parrish (Louise Sumner), LAWRENCE BROOKS (Dr. Fred Sumner)

SOURCE—A story by John Jennings.

The action occurs in the present, at Riverwind (a "tourist rest") in Indiana, on the banks of Wabash River.

The musical was presented in two acts.

ACT ONE—"I Cannot Tell Her So" (Martin J. Cassidy), "I Want a Surprise" (Dawn Nickerson), "Riverwind" (Elizabeth Parrish), "American Family Plan" (Lovelady Powell, Brooks Morton), "Wishing Song" (Lawrence Brooks, Dawn Nickerson, Martin J. Cassidy, Elizabeth Parrish), "American Family Plan" (reprise) (Lovelady Powell, Brooks Morton), "Pardon Me While I Dance" (Lawrence Brooks, Dawn Nickerson), "Wishing Song" (reprise) (Brooks Morton, Martin J. Cassidy), "Sew the Buttons On" (Helon Blount, Dawn Nickerson), "Riverwind" (reprise) (Elizabeth Parrish)

ACT TWO—"Almost, But Not Quite" (Lovelady Powell, Brooks Morton), "A Woman Must Think of These Things" (Elizabeth Parrish), "I Love Your Laughing Face" (Helon Blount, Martin J. Cassidy), "A Woman Must Never Grow Old" (Helon Blount, Elizabeth Parrish), "I'd Forgotten How Beautiful She Could Be" (Lawrence Brooks, Dawn Nickerson), "Sew the Buttons On" (reprise) (Lovelady Powell, Brooks Morton)

NOTES—The score of *Riverwind* is one of the best written for 1960s musical theatre, on Broadway or off. Newcomer John Jennings wrote a variety of songs which depicted the romantic and personal problems of the staff and visitors staying at Riverwind, a small "tourist rest" in Indiana: a bouncy "wanting" song for the young heroine ("I Want a Surprise"); three haunting ballads ("I Cannot Tell Her So, "I Love Your Laughing Face," and "I'd Forgotten How Beautiful She Could Be"); two amusing comedy numbers ("Almost, But Not Quite" and "American Family Plan"); a bluesy "A Woman Must Thing of These Things"); the Straussian "Pardon Me While I Dance"; and, in the "Wishing Song" quartet, one of the most exquisite numbers ever heard on the musical stage. The "Wishing Song" is a model of an intelligent, character-driven lyric matched to haunting, enchanting music.

Riverwind played for over a year, but despite his distinguished score, John Jennings was never heard from again. But the cast album was recorded by London Records (LP # AM-48001), and although it's never been released on CD, the LP is must-listening for anyone seriously interested in musical theatre.

The musical was revived by the Equity Library Theatre on May 3, 1973, for nineteen performances (Helon Blount reprised her role of Mrs. Farrell).

Leading man Lawrence Brooks had starred in one of the biggest Broadway hits of the 1940s: He created the leading role of Edvard Grieg in *Song of Norway* (1944) and introduced "Strange Music," the score's most enduring song. When *Norway* closed, it was the third longest-running book musical in Broadway history. Brooks' next musical was Sigmund Romberg's *My Romance* (1948), and in 1952 he starred in one of Broadway's most notorious flops, *Buttrio Square*. He replaced Don Ameche during the original run of *Silk Stockings* (1955), and in 1961 was Alfred Drake's standby in *Kean*.

1365 The Road to Hollywood. THEATRE: Theatre Guinevere; OPENING DATE: March 13, 1984; PERFORMANCES: 42; BOOK: Michael Pace; LYRICS: Michael Pace and Rob Preston; MUSIC: Rob Preston; DIRECTION: Word Baker; CHOREOGRAPHY: Lynnette Barkley; SCENERY: Kate Edmunds; COSTUMES: Sally J. Lesser; LIGHTING: Debra J. Kletter; MUSICAL DIRECTION: Rob Preston; PRODUCER: The Production Company (Norman Rene, Artistic Director; Abigail Franklin, Managing Director) by special arrangement with Norman Twain

CAST—Michael Pace (Beau Hartman), Gary Herb (Tappy Butler), Baby Goofy (Himself), Haskell Gordon (Mister Fritz), Kay Cole (Babs), D. Peter Samuel (Dick), Maggie Task (Queen Minnie of Loumania), Bebe Neuwirth (Princess Dorothy), Camille Saviola (Diva Rita), Scott Fless (Frankie), Ron Lee Savin ("Shiny" Eisenberg)

The action occurs at a rotary club in Springfield, Illinois, in January 1941, as well as on a road outside Chicago and later at the Calmer House Hotel in Chicago.

The musical was presented in a prologue and two acts.

PROLOGUE—Overture (Orchestra), "I Can't Sit Still" (Gary Herb, Michael Pace)

ACT ONE—"56 Cities" (Gary Herb, Michael Pace), "Schleppin'" (Gary Herb, Michael Pace), "Welcome to the Calmer House" (Haskell Gordon, Kay Cole, D. Peter Samuel), "Loumania" (Maggie Task, Bebe Neuwirth, Company), "Talent" (Kay Cole, Gary Herb), "Hey, Kid" (Michael Pace, Bebe Neuwirth), "The Beast in Me" (Camille Saviola), "Hot Ice" (Camille Saviola, Scott Fless)

ACT TWO—"Don't Spill the Beans" (Kay Cole, Michael Pace, Gary Herb), "Mr. Flatfoot" (Kay Cole), "I've Got My Eye on You" (D. Peter Samuel), "When the Right One Comes Along" (Maggie Task), "When the Right One Comes Along" (reprise) (Bebe Neuwirth), "Opening Night" (Company), "I Don't Care" (Haskell Gordon) "I Can't Sit Still" (reprise) (Gary Herb, Michael Pace), "Frankie's Return" (Scott Fless), "She's a Star" (D. Peter Samuel), Finale (Company)

NOTES—Just about everybody's favorite *I Love Lucy* episode is the one in which she tries to break into show business, and plots about show-business wannabes seem to be the most popular theme for writers of musicals. In the case of the Off Off Broadway musical *The Road to Hollywood*, the story dealt with two entertainers (Gary Herb and Michael Pace) who hope to make it big in Hollywood. The book was patterned after the *Road* film comedies which starred Bing Crosby and Bob Hope, and Bebe Neuwirth played one of the three leading ladies (the others were Nora Mae Lyng and Kay Cole). Mel Gussow in the *New York Times* noted the musical missed an opportunity by not designating one of the actresses for the "Dorothy Lamour" role. But he found the evening "amiable," and singled out one cast member, Baby Goofy, who played himself. This "standout" performer (a canine of the "terrier persuasion") had a role so "demanding" he made Sandy in *Annie* "look like a walk-on." Further, Gussow reported that Baby Goofy "repeatedly" stole scenes with a range of expressions from "deadpan to hangdog," and during the curtain calls the pooch looked "longingly" at the audience, obviously expecting his well-deserved applause.

1366 Roadside. "A New Musical." THEATRE: The Theatre at Saint Peter's Church/The York Theatre Company; OPENING DATE: November 29, 2001; PERFORMANCES: 29; BOOK: Tom Jones; LYRICS: Tom Jones; MUSIC: Harvey Schmidt; DIRECTION: Drew Scott Harris; SCENERY: James Morgan; COSTUMES: Suzy Benzinger; LIGHTING: Mary Jo Dondlinger; MUSICAL DIRECTION: John Mulcahy

CAST—Jennifer Allen (Miz Foster), Ryan Appleby (Red Ike), G.W. Bailey (Pap Raider), Steve Barcus (Black Ike), Tom Flagg (Neb), James Hindman (Amos K. Buzzey Hale), Julie Johnson (Hannie Raider), Jonathan Beck Reed (Texas), William Ryall (The Verdigree Marshall)

SOURCE—The 1930 play *Roadside* by Lynn Riggs.

The action occurs in the Oklahoma Territory during the early 1900s.

The musical was presented in two acts.

ACT ONE—"Uncle Billy's Travellin' Family Show" (G.W. Bailey, Company), "Roadside" (G.W. Bailey, James Hindman, Julie Johnson, Ryan Appleby, Steve Barcus), "Here Am I" (Julie Johnson, James Hindman), "I Don't Want to Bother Nobody" (Jonathan Beck Reed, G.W. Bailey, Ryan Appleby, Steve Barcus), "Smellamagoody Perfume" (Julie Johnson, Jonathan Beck Reed), "Smellamagoody Perfume" (reprise) (Julie Johnson), "Lookin' at the Moon" (Ryan Appleby, Steve Barcus), "I'm Through with You" (Julie Johnson, Jonathan Beck Reed), "Peaceful Little Town" (Tom Flagg, Jennifer Allen), "I Toe the Line" (William Ryall, Jonathan Beck Reed, Tom Flagg, Jennifer Allen), "I'm Through with You" (reprise) (Julie Johnson, Jonathan Beck Reed, Tom Flagg, Jennifer Allen)

ACT TWO—Entr' acte (Band), "Back to Our Story" (G.W. Bailey, Ryan Appleby, Steve Barcus), "Personality Plus" (James Hindman), "Another Drunken Cowboy" (Jonathan Beck Reed), "The Way It Should Be" (G.W. Bailey, Jonathan Beck Reed), "My Little Prairie Flower" (Ryan Appleby, Steve Barcus), "All Men Is Crazy" (Julie Johnson), "Ain't No Woman But You" (Jonathan Beck Reed, Julie Johnson), "Borned" (Jonathan Beck Reed), "Wild and Reckless" (Jonathan Beck Reed, Company), "Peaceful Little Town" (reprise) (Tom Flagg, Jennifer Allen, James Hindman, William Ryall), "The Way It Should Be" (reprise) (Jonathan Beck Reed, Julie Johnson, Company), "Roadside" (reprise) (Company)

NOTES—*Roadside* was the first completely new Harvey Schmidt and Tom Jones musical seen in New York in seventeen years, when *Colette Collage* (see entry) had premiered in 1983 (the latter was of course based on *Colette* [see entry], a 1971 play with incidental songs, as well as the full-fledged musical *Colette* which closed during its pre-Broadway tryout in 1982). Between 1983 and 2001, a second *Colette Collage* had opened in 1991 as well as a revival of *I Do! I Do!* in 1996 and a production of the Schmidt and Jones' tribute/anthology revue *The Show Goes On* in 1997 (see entries). And in 1992, a revival of *110 in the Shade* was presented by the New York City Opera. But Schmidt and Jones' two new musicals, *Grover's Corners* (1987) and *Mirette* (1998), never got beyond their regional productions, and so *Roadside* was a welcome event. (*Mirette* was later seen in New York in 2005 [see entry] as part of the York Theatre's *Musicals in Mufti* series [see entry]). *Roadside* was based on the 1930 play of the same name by Lynn Riggs, whose *Green Grow the Lilacs* opened on Broadway the following year (*Lilacs* was of course the basis for Richard Rodgers and Oscar Hammerstein II's 1943 musical *Oklahoma!*). The play *Roadside* lasted for only eleven performances, and in 1950 it was revived on Broadway as *Borned in Texas*, playing for just eight performances.

The story dealt with a free-spirited drifter who wins the heart of a small town girl in the mid-West (shades of *110 in the Shade*); but despite a winning score by Schmidt and Jones, *Roadside* didn't become another *Oklahoma!* or even another *110 in the Shade*.

The musical was recorded by Jay Records (CD # CDJAY-1366).

The musical was first presented in Irving, Texas, by the Lyric Stage on February 17, 2001, at the Irving Arts Center's Dupree Theatre. The production included two songs not heard in the New York version ("The One for Me" and "Down in the Switch").

1367 The Robber Bridegroom. THEATRE: St. Clement's Church; OPENING DATE: November 4, 1974; PERFORMANCES: 6; BOOK: Alfred Uhry; LYRICS: Alfred Uhry; MUSIC: Robert Waldman; DIRECTION: Gerald Freedman; CHOREOGRAPHY: Don Redlich; LIGHTING: Gary Porto; PRODUCERS: The Musical Theatre Lab at St. Clement's; Stephanie Copeland, Executive Producer; Steven Woolf, Project Producer; the musical was a joint project of The Stuart Ostrow Foundation and St. Clement's

CAST—Susan Berger (Salome), William Brenner (Third Landlord, Indian), Rhonda Coullet (Rosamund), John Getz (Mike Fink), Cynthia Herman (Airie, Raven), Raul Julia (Jaimie Lockhart), Dana Kyle (Indian), Carolyn McCurry (Second Landlord, Goat's Mother), Bill Hunnery (First Landlord, Big Harp), Thomas Oglesby (Robber, Indian), Trip Plymale (Goat), Ernie Sabella (Little Harp), David Summers (Robber, Indian), Steve Vinovich (Clement Musgrove)

SOURCE—Eudora Welty's 1942 novella *The Robber Bridegroom.*

The action occurs in and around Rodney, Mississippi, "in legendary times" (the 1790s).

The musical was presented in one act.

NOTES—Prior to its two Broadway productions, *The Robber Bridegroom* was first seen Off Off Broadway in 1974 for a limited-engagement of six performances; for this world premiere, Raul Julia and Rhonda Coullet created the roles of Jamie Lockhart and Rosamund; Lockhart is a charming robber who becomes romantically involved with Rosamund, the daughter of a rich planter.

One year later, the musical was presented on Broadway at the Harkness Theatre, opening on October 7, 1975, and playing for a limited engagement of fifteen performances (the musical was one of four productions offered by The Acting Company over a period of four weeks). Kevin Kline played Jamie Lockhart, and Patti LuPone was Rosamund.

A year later, on October 9, 1976, the musical returned to Broadway at the Biltmore Theatre for 145 performances. For this production, Barry Bostwick was Jamie Lockhart and Rhonda Coullet recreated her original role of Rosamund. Bostwick won the Tony Award for Best Actor in a Musical; up against him was Raul Julia, the original Jamie, who was nominated for his performance as Mack the Knife in the revival of *The Threepenny Opera*.

The 1976 production was recorded by CBS Records in their "Collectors Series" (LP # P-14589), and the script was published by Drama Books Specialists in 1978.

The following is a list of musical numbers from the 1976 production (following the song titles are the names of the characters who performed the numbers):

MUSICAL NUMBERS—"Once Upon the Natchez Trace" (Jamie Lockhart, Roamund, Salome, Clemment Musgrove, Little Harp, Big Harp, Goat, Company), "Suddenly the Day Looks Sunny" (Jamie Lockhart), "Two Heads" (Big Harp, Little Harp), "Steal with Style" (Jamie Lockhart), "Rosamund's Dream" (Rosamund), "The Pricklepear Bloom" (Salome), "Nothin' Up" (Rosamund), "Deeper in the Woods" (Company), "Riches" (Clemment Musgrove, Jamie Lockhart, Salome, Rosamund), "Little Piece of Sugar Cane" (Jamie Lockhart, Rosamund, Company), "Love Stolen" (Jamie Lockhart), "Poor Tied Up Darlin'" (Little Harp, Goat), "Mean as a Snake" (Raven, Company), "Goodbye Salome" (Company), "Sleepy Man" (Rosamund), "Where Oh Where Is My Baby Darlin'?" (Jamie Lockhart, Clemment Musgrove, Rosamund, Company), "Pass Her Along" (Company), "Wedding Ceremony" (Gerry G. Summers), Finale (Jamie Lockhart, Company)

The 1975 production included one song ("The Real Mike Fink") which wasn't heard in the 1976 version (the 1976 version included many songs which hadn't been in the 1975 production).

1368 The Robbers. THEATRE: The Lexington Avenue Young Men's and Young Women's Hebrew Association; OPENING DATE: April 14, 1958; PERFORMANCES: 2; LIBRETTO: Ned Rorem; MUSIC: Ned Rorem; MUSICAL DIRECTION: Carl Bamberger; PRODUCER: Mannes College of Music

CAST—Daniel Caruso, Robert Schmorr, Jerold Siena

The opera was produced in one act.

NOTES—The evening consisted of three one-act operas, two world premieres (*The Pet Shop* [see entry] and *The Robbers*) and a revival (Georg Philipp Telemann's *Pimpinone* [1725]).

Ross Parmenter in the *New York Times* indicated *The Robbers*, an early work by Ned Rorem, was inspired by Chaucer's *The Pardoner's Tale*. The opera begins with three men committing a murder for gold; but they never enjoy the spoils of their crime because their greed causes them to destroy each other. Parmenter complained about the work's "gruesome" plot, but noted Rorem's score had "attractively lyric moments," including a "good" male trio.

1369 The Robin Woman: Shanewis. THEATRE: Metropolitan Opera House; OPENING DATE: March 23, 1918; PERFORMANCES: 5; LIBRETTO: Nelle Richmond Eberhart; MUSIC: Charles Wakefield Cadman; DIRECTION: Richard Ordynski; SCENERY: James Fox (Act One) and Norman Bel Geddes (Act Two); COSTUMES: Norman Bel Geddes; MUSICAL DIRECTION: Roberto Moranzoni; PRODUCER: The Metropolitan Opera

CAST—Sophie Braslau (Shanewis), Kathleen Howard (Mrs. Everton), Marie Sundelius (Amy Everton), Paul Althouse (Lionel), Thomas Chalmers (Philip), High School Girls (Marie Tiffany, Cecil Aden, Phyllis White, Veni Warwick), Angela Gorman (Indian Girl), Old Indians (Angelo Bada, Pietro Audisio, Max Bloch, Mario Laurenti)

The action occurs in California and Oklahoma.

The opera was presented in two acts.

NOTES—The two-act, one-hour opera *The Robin Woman: Shanewis* had its world premiere at the Met on a bill with two other short pieces, the ballet *The Dance in Place Congo* (another world premiere; see entry) and a revival of Franco Leoni's opera *L'Oracolo* (1905). All three works took place in the United States: *Shanewis* in California and Oklahoma, *Congo* in the bayous around New Orleans, and *L'Oracolo* in San Francisco.

Much of Charles Wakefield Cadman's score was inspired by authentic American Indian songs; the libretto told the story of Shanewis, a young Indian woman who is part of a love triangle. Scenic designer Norman Bel Geddes made his Met debut with this production, and an unsigned review in the *New York Times* noted that his second act scenery for an Oklahoma Indian reservation gave "a feeling of limitless open-air, of vastness and mystery, of mirage that is part of the true Western landscape."

1370 Robin's Band. THEATRE: AMAS Musical Theatre; OPENING DATE: April 14, 1988; PERFORMANCES: 16; BOOK: Jerome Eskow and Anthony Abeson; LYRICS: Maija Kupris; MUSIC: Maija Kupris; DIRECTION: Anthony Abeson; CHOREOGRAPHY: Rodney Nugent; SCENERY: Jeffrey Miller; COSTUMES: David Mickelsen; LIGHTING: Kathy Kaufmann; MUSICAL DIRECTION: David Wolfson; PRODUCER: AMAS Musical Theatre (Rosetta LeNoire, Founder and Artistic Director)

CAST—Liz Amberly, Peg Boas, Melissa DeSousa, Kecia Lewis-Evans, Wayne Gordy, Jeffrey Harmon, Gregory Harvey, Kelly Hinman, Carl H. Jaynes, Herb Lovelle, John McCurry, Vince Morton, Luis Ramos, Experience Robinson, Al Rodriguez, Jill Romero

NOTES—According to the flyer for the Off Off Broadway musical *Robin's Band*, the updated story of Robin Hood and his Merry Men took place in the not-too-distant future when a group of "spirited" individuals (led by Robin and his rock and roll band) strive to protect not only their cultural heritage but also the environment. When they come upon a patch of greenery (Sherwood Forest), they are determined to protect it from the encroaching jungle of steel, concrete, and plastic.

1371 The Rockae

NOTES—See entry for *The New York Musical Theatre Festival.*

1372 Roller Derby

NOTES—See entries for the *The New York Musical Theatre Festival* and for *The Derby* (1980; composed by John Braden).

1373 Rollin' on the T.O.B.A. "A Tribute to the Last Days of Black Vaudeville." THEATRE: 47th Street Theatre; OPENING DATE: January 28, 1999; PERFORMANCES: 45; CONCEIVED BY Ronald "Smokey" Stevens and Jaye Stewart; additional material by Irvin S. Bauer; excerpts from Langston Hughes' *Simple* stories; LYRICS: See song list for credits; MUSIC: See song list for credits; DIRECTION: Ronald "Smokey" Stevens and Leslie Dockery; CHOREOGRAPHY: Leslie Dockery; SCENERY: Larry W. Brown; COSTUMES: Michele Reisch; LIGHTING: Jon Kusner; MUSICAL DIRECTION: David Alan Bunn; PRODUCERS: John Grimaldi, Ashton Springer, and Frenchmen Productions, Inc.

CAST—Jeffrey V. Thompson (Stewart), Rudy Roberson (Stevens), Sandra Reaves-Phillips (Bertha Mae Little)

The action occurs on the T.O.B.A. circuit in 1931.

The revue was presented in two acts.

ACT ONE—Overture (Orchestra), "Rollin' on the T.O.B.A." (lyric and music by Ronald "Smokey" Stevens, Sandra Reaves-Phillips, Chapman Roberts, Benny Key, and David Alan Bunn) (Rudy Roberson, Jeffrey V. Thompson, Sandra Reaves-Phillips), "Livin' Ragtime" (lyric and music by David Alan Bunn, Rudy Roberson, and Jeffrey V. Thompson) (Rudy Roberson, Jeffrey V. Thompson), "Evolution" (by Flournoy Miller and Aubrey Lyles) (Rudy Roberson, Jeffrey V. Thompson), "Ugly Chile" (lyric and music by Clarence Williams) (Rudy Roberson, Jeffrey V. Thompson), "Travelin' Blues" (lyric and music by Ronald "Smokey" Stevens, Sandra Reaves-Phillips, Chapman Roberts, and Benny Key) (Sandra Reaves-Phillips), "Lincoln West" (lyric and music by Gwendolyn Brooks) (Jeffrey V. Thompson), "The Liar (Staggolee)" (lyric and music by Gwendolyn Brooks) (Jeffrey V. Thompson), "Sexy Blues" (lyric and music by Sandra Reaves-Phillips, Chapman Roberts, and Ronald "Smokey" Stevens) (Sandra Reaves-Phillips), "Toast to Harlem" (by Langston Hughes) (Rudy Roberson, Jeffrey V. Thompson), "You've Taken My Blues and Gone" (by Langston Hughes) (Sandra Reaves-Phillips), "Huggin' and Chalkin'" (lyric and music by Kermit Goell and Clancey Hayes) (Rudy Roberson), "Car Crash" (by Flournoy Miller and Aubrey Lyles) (Rudy Roberson, Jeffrey V. Thompson), "Broken Dialog" (by Flournoy Miller and Aubrey Lyles) (Rudy Roberson, Jeffrey V. Thompson), "Conversationalization" (by Flournoy Miller and Aubrey Lyles) (Rudy Roberson, Jeffrey V. Thompson), "My Handy Man Ain't Handy No More" (from *Blackbirds of 1930*; lyric by Andy Razaf, music by Eubie Blake) (Sandra Reaves-Phillips), "(I Ain't Never Done Nothing to) Nobody" (added to *Ziegfeld Follies of 1910*; lyric and music by Alex Rogers and Bert Williams) (Jeffrey V. Thompson), "The Poker Game" (by Bert Williams; sketch included "Black and Tan Fantasy," music by Duke Ellington) (Rudy Roberson), "After You've Gone" (lyric by Henry Creamer, music by J. Turner Layton) (Rudy Roberson, Jeffrey V. Thompson, Sandra Reaves-Phillips)

ACT TWO—Entr'acte (Orchestra), "Bill Robinson Walk" (by Bill "Bojangles" Robinson) (Rudy Roberson), "Freddie and Flo" (by Butterbeans and Suzie) (Rudy Roberson, Jeffrey V. Thompson), "A Good Man Is Hard to Find" (lyric and music by Eddie Green) (Jeffrey V. Thompson), "Take Me As I Am" (lyric and music by Sandra Reaves-Phillips) (Sandra Reaves-Phillips), "One Hour Mama" (lyric and music by Porter Grainger) (Sandra Reaves-Phillips), "Million Dollar Secret" (by Helen Humes) (Sandra Reaves-Phillips), "Take Me As I Am" (reprise) (Sandra Reaves-Phillips), "Simple on Integration" (by Langston Hughes) (Rudy Roberson), "Soul Food" (by Langston Hughes) (Jeffrey V. Thompson, Sandra Reaves-Phillips), "Banquet in Honor" (by Langston Hughes) (Rudy Roberson), "The Chess Game" ("Funeral March of the Marionettes" by Charles Guonod used in sketch) (Rudy Roberson, Jeffrey V. Thompson), "I'm Still Here" (by Langston Hughes) (Rudy Roberson, Jeffrey V. Thompson, Sandra Reaves-Phillips), "Trouble in Mind" (by Richard Jones) (Sandra Reaves-Phillips), "Rollin' on the T.O.B.A." (reprise/finale) (Rudy

Roberson, Jeffrey V. Thompson, Sandra Reaves-Phillips)

NOTES—*Rollin' on the T.O.B.A.* was perhaps too late in its telling of the story of the last days of Black vaudeville: the long-running hit revue *One Mo' Time!* (see entry) had already been there.

The revue had been seen at AMAS Musical Theatre on June 23, 1998, for sixteen performances; and after the Off Broadway run at the 47th Street Theatre, the revue transferred to Broadway (with a slightly reordered song and sketch sequence, and with additional material) at the Kit Kat Club at Henry Miller's Theatre on March 24, 1999, for fourteen performances.

"T.O.B.A." were the initials for "Theatre Owners' Booking Association," but Blacks who were booked by the association referred to it as "Tough on Black Asses."

1374 Roman Fever. THEATRE: Manhattan School of Music Opera Theatre; OPENING DATE: December 2001; PERFORMANCES: Unknown; LIBRETTO: Roger Brunyate; MUSIC: Robert Ward; DIRECTION: Robin Guarino; SCENERY: Narelle Sissons; COSTUMES: Kaye Voyce; LIGHTING: Jane Cox; MUSICAL DIRECTION: David Gilbert; PRODUCER: Manhattan School of Music

CAST—Dorothy Grimley (Alida Slade), Erin Elizabeth Smith (Grace Ansley), Eudora Brown (Barbara Ansley), Amy Shoremount (Jenny Slade), Maxime Alvarez de Toledo (Waiter)

SOURCE—The 1934 short story "Roman Fever" by Edith Wharton.

The action occurs in Rome in 1927.

The opera was presented in one act.

MUSICAL SEQUENCES—"It's Still the Most Beautiful City" "Yes, and Your Barbara," "Sounds Pretty Risky," "Ah, Febbre Perniciosa," "Well, Tell Us More," "Bells, Bells!," "My, Dear, You're Down," "Oh, Mrs. Slade," "High in the Sky," "They're Here!," "The Forum Looks Dark," "Yes, I Horrify You," "I Remember"

NOTES—Robert Ward's opera *Roman Fever* was first produced at Duke University in 1993, and its New York premiere by the Manhattan School of Music took place in 2001.

The plot dealt with two former acquaintances, both widows, who happen to be vacationing in Rome at the same time with their "flapper" daughters; the opera looked back on the two widows' romantic involvement with the same man when they visited Rome twenty years earlier and how that brief entanglement still has repercussions two decades later. With *Roman Fever*, the Manhattan School of Music continued to offer obscure American operas to New York audiences, and happily (and like so many of their productions) the opera was recorded (by Albany Records [CD # TROY-505]).

1375 Romance in Hard Times. THEATRE: The Newman Theatre/The Public Theatre; OPENING DATE: December 28, 1989; PERFORMANCES: 6; BOOK: William Finn; LYRICS: William Finn; MUSIC: William Finn; DIRECTION: David Warren; CHOREOGRAPHY: Marcia Milgrom Dodge; SCENERY: James Youmans; COSTUMES: David C. Woolard; LIGHTING: Peter Kaczorowski; MUSICAL DIRECTION: Ted Sperling; PRODUCER: The New York Shakespeare Festival (Joseph Papp, Producer; Jason Steven Cohen, Associate Producer)

CAST—Lillias White (Hennie), Lawrence Clayton (Harvey), Cleavant Derricks (Boris), Alix (Alexandra) Korey (Zoe), Ray Gill (Polly), Amanda Naughton (Older Handcuffed Sister), Stacey Lynn Brass (Younger Handcuffed Sister), Michael Mandell (Gus), Peggy Hewett (Eleanor Roosevelt), Harmonizing Fools, Radio Announcers, Supreme Court Justices, Prisoners and Celebrities (Rufus Bonds, Jr., Victor Trent Cook, Melodee Savage, John Sloman, James Stovall), Victor Trent Cook (The Kid); in certain sequences, John Sloman portrayed Babe Ruth; Melodee Savage, Shirley Temple; Rufus Bonds, Jr., Bojangles Robinson; and James Stovall, Franklin Roosevelt

The action occurs in a soup kitchen in New York City during the Great Depression.

The musical was presented in two acts.

ACT ONE—"Harvey" (Lillias White), "Standing in Line" (Ray Gill, Amanda Naughton, Stacey Lynn Brass, Harmonizing Fools, Michael Mandell, Alix Korey), "I'll Get Out of Here" (Cleavant Derricks), "Harvey Promised to Change the World" (Lawrence Clayton, Lillias White, Cleavant Derricks, Harmonizing Fools), "The Supreme Court Saved from Fire" (James Stovall, Supreme Court Justices [including Rufus Bonds, Jr., as the Chief Justice]), "Red Faces at the Kremlin" (Ray Gill, Amanda Naughton, Stacey Lynn Brass, Alix Korey), "Charity Quartet" (Amanda Naughton, Stacey Lynn Brass, Alix Korey, Michael Mandell), "Lovesong" (Lillias White, Cleavant Derricks, Lawrence Clayton), "Charity Quartet" (reprise) (Amanda Naughton, Stacey Lynn Brass, Alix Korey, Michael Mandell), "Eleanor Roosevelt: A Discussion of Soup" (Peggy Hewett, Alix Korey, Everyone), "I Never Said I Didn't Love You" (Lawrence Clayton), "You Got Me Crazy" (Cleavant Derricks, Lillias White, Everyone), "That's Enough for Me" (Lillias White), "Places I Fainted from Hunger"/"Time Passes" (Ray Gill, Everyone), "All Fall Down" (Alix Korey), "The Good Times Are Here" (Lillias White, Cleavant Derricks, Peggy Hewett, Everyone)

ACT TWO—"Feeling Rich" (Alix Korey, Michael Mandell, Ray Gill, Amanda Naughton, Stacey Lynn Brass, Harmonizing Fools), "Hold My Baby Back" (Lillias White), "Hennie Soup" (Peggy Hewett, Lillias White, Michael Mandell, Everyone), "Thinking About You" (Cleavant Derricks, Lillias White), "I Don't Want to Feel What I Feel" (Lillias White), "The Prosperity Song" (Peggy Hewett, Michael Mandell, Amanda Naughton, Stacey Lynn Brass, Ray Gill, Alix Korey), "A Gaggle of Celebrities" (Lillias White, John Sloman, Melodee Savage, Rufus Bonds, Jr.), "I'll Get You Out of My Life" (Cleavant Derricks, Lillias White), "How Could You Do This to Someone Who Robbed for You? (Prison Music)" (Amanda Naughton, Stacey Lynn Brass, Michael Mandell, Alix Korey, Ray Gill, Peggy Hewett, Cleavant Derricks), "Blame It on These Times" (Cleavant Derricks), "You Can't Let Romance Die" (Victor Trent Cook), "Gus' Triumph (One Verse)" (Michael Mandell), "The Last Can of Hennie Soup" (Alix Korey, Ray Gill, Amanda Naughton, Stacey Lynn Brass), "That's Enough for Me Duet" (Lillias White, Cleavant Derricks), Finale (Everyone)

NOTES—William Finn's *Romance in Hard Times* was a radically revised version of *America Kicks Up Its Heels* (see entry), which had been seen at Playwrights Horizons in 1983 for twenty-eight preview performances before canceling its official opening.

Unlike *America Kicks Up Its Heels*, the setting for *Romance in Hard Times* took place entirely in a New York soup kitchen, and most of the characters were Black. There were just two holdovers from the 1983 production (Peggy Hewett and Alix Korey), and only three songs were carried over ("Red Faces in the Kremlin," "Eleanor Roosevelt: A Discussion of Soup," and "All Fall Down"). In an article by Marilyn Stasio in the *New York Times*, Finn indicated the new production was set entirely in the 1930s and omitted a parallel story about homeless people in the 1980s.

But for all the changes, *Romance in Hard Times* fared poorly at the Public: it was gone in less than a week. After its failure, Finn completely gave up on his Depression-soup-kitchen project.

By the end of the preview period, it's unclear who was performing the role of Polly (either Ray Gill or J.P. Dougherty); further, at one point or another during the musical's brief run, the following songs were apparently performed: "Harvey," "Goodbye," and "You've Got Me Grinding My Teeth."

1376 Romance Language. THEATRE: Playwrights Horizons; OPENING DATE: November 14, 1984; PERFORMANCES: 52; PLAY: Peter Parnell; LYRICS: Jack Eric Williams; MUSIC: Jack Eric Williams; DIRECTION: Sheldon Larry

"Saloon Movement": Marcia Milgrom Dodge; SCENERY: Loren Sherman; COSTUMES: Sheila McLamb; LIGHTING: Jeff Davis; MUSICAL DIRECTION: Jack Eric Williams; PRODUCER: Playwrights Horizons (Andre Bishop, Artistic Director; Paul Daniels, Managing Director)

CAST—Al Carmines (Walt Whitman), Jon Matthews (Huckleberry Finn), Steve Ryan (Dan'l, Lt. Varnum), Frances Conroy (Louisa May Alcott), Hechter Ubarry (Kooloo, Raincloud), William Duell (Alcott, Lonesome Charley), Cynthia Harris (Charlotte Cushman), Marcia Lewis (Emma Stebbins, Ellen Emerson, Dancehall Girl), Marc Castle (Tommy, Mme. Nash), Ben Siegler (Autie Reed), Emily Dickinson (Valerie Mahaffey), Philip Pleasants (Ralph Waldo Emerson, Mitch Bouyer), William Converse-Roberts (Henry David Thoreau, George Armstrong Custer), John Noonan (Tom Sawyer), Carroll L. Cartwright (Bloody Knife), Townspeople, Cavalry, Cowboys, Barpeople, Indians (Larry Attile, Janet Borrus, Laurence Gleason, Glenn Karant, Greg Pake, David Warshofsky)

The action occurs in 1876.

The play was presented in two acts.

NOTES—In a program note for *Romance Language*, Peter Parnell explained that his play dealt with such Transcendentalists as Emily Dickinson, Henry David Thoreau, and Ralph Waldo Emerson (all of whom "pushed the literary frontier") as well as such historical figures as George Armstrong Custer (who "pushed the geographical and political" frontiers). The plot concerned actual as well as fictional relationships among the principals, but Parnell noted the events were not what "might" have happened or what he would "like" to have happened, but what "could ONLY" have happened in a nineteenth-century America as seen through a twentieth-century perspective when the "sexual frontier is our newest horizon." Frank Rich in the *New York Times* stated Parnell was a "bold writer with an abundant vision" and Ron Cohen's in *Women's Wear Daily* said the play was "a smashingly funny, bravura piece of theatre." But *Romance Language* seems to have disappeared once its limited engagement ended at Playwrights Horizons.

Jack Eric Williams contributed incidental songs to the production. He appeared as Beadle Bamford in the original Broadway production of *Sweeney Todd/The Demon Barber of Fleet Street* (1979) and introduced "Ladies in Their Sensitivities" and the numbers in the "Parlor Songs" sequence. In *Elegies* (see entry), William Finn paid tribute to Williams in the song "The Ballad of Jack Eric Williams (and Other 3-Named Composers)."

Al Carmines appeared in *Romance Language*, and later in the season he read passages from the play in his one-man revue *Carmines Sings Whitman Sings Carmines* (see entry).

1377 Romance Romance. "Two New Musicals" (*The Little Comedy* and *Summer Share*). THEATRE: Actor's Outlet Theatre; OPENING DATE: November 16, 1987; PERFORMANCES: 37; BOOK: Barry Harman; LYRICS: Barry Harman; MUSIC: Keith Herrmann; DIRECTION: Barry Harman; CHOREOGRAPHY: Pamela Sousa; SCENERY: Steven Rubin; COSTUMES: Steven Jones; LIGHTING: Craig Miller; MUSICAL DIRECTION: Kathy Sommer; PRODUCERS:

Actor's Outlet Theatre (Eleanor Segan, Executive Director; Ken Lowstetter, Artistic Director) by special arrangement with Harve Brosten and Jay S. Bulmash

SOURCES—*The Little Comedy* was based on the short story by Arthur Schnitzler (translated by George Edward Reynolds) and *Summer Share* was based on the 1898 play *Le Pain de Menage* by Jules Renard (translated by Max Gulack)

The Little Comedy takes place in Vienna around 1900.

CAST—Dennis Parlato (Alfred Von Wilmers), Alison Fraser (Josefine Weninger), Robert Hoshour ("Him"), Deborah Graham ("Her")

MUSICAL NUMBERS—"The Little Comedy" (Dennis Parlato, Alison Fraser), "Goodbye, Emil" (Alison Fraser), "It's Not Too Late" (Dennis Parlato, Alison Fraser), "Great News" (Dennis Parlato, Alison Fraser), "Oh, What a Performance!" (Dennis Parlato, Alison Fraser), "I'll Always Remember the Song" (Dennis Parlato, Alison Fraser), "Happy, Happy, Happy" (Dennis Parlato), "Women of Vienna" (Dennis Parlato), "Yes, It's Love" (Alison Fraser), "A Rustic Country Inn" (Dennis Parlato, Alison Fraser), "The Night It Had to End" (Alison Fraser), "The Little Comedy" (finale) (Dennis Parlato, Alison Fraser), *Summer Share* takes place in the Hamptons in August of the current year.

CAST—Robert Hoshour (Lenny), Deborah Graham (Barb), Dennis Parlato (Sam), Alison Fraser (Monica)

MUSICAL NUMBERS—"Summer Share" (Company), "Romantic Notions" (Deborah Graham, Robert Hoshour), "A Confession" (Dennis Parlato), "Friendships Like Ours" (Company), "When It Happens" (Alison Fraser), "Plans A & B" (Alison Fraser, Robert Hoshour), "Let's Not Talk About It" (Dennis Parlato, Deborah Graham), "So Glad I Married Her" (Company), "How Did I End Up Here?" (Alison Fraser), "Words He Doesn't Say" (Dennis Parlato), "My Love for You" (Robert Hoshour, Deborah Graham), "Now" (Alison Fraser), "Romantic Notions" (reprise) (Company)

NOTES—*Romance Romance* was an evening of two Off Off Broadway musicals, *The Little Comedy* (based on a short story by Arthur Schnitzler) and *Summer Share*, both of which looked at love and romance from the perspective of Vienna in 1900 and the Hamptons in the present. The musical was remounted for Broadway on May 1, 1988; it opened at the Helen Hayes Theatre for 297 performances. For this production, Scott Bakula assumed the roles of Alfred Von Wilmers and Sam. MCA Records released the cast album (LP # MCA-6252), and the script was published in two editions in 1989 (a special hardback edition by The Fireside Theatre and an acting edition by Samuel French, Inc.); the musical was also shown on cable television.

For the Broadway production, the songs in *The Little Comedy* remained the same. For *Summer Share*, "Romantic Notions" was dropped ("Think of the Odds" was substituted); also deleted were "Friendships Like Ours" and "When It Happens"; added were "Moonlight Passing Through a Window" and a title song (sung by the company and also heard in the production in a recorded version by an uncredited Nell Carter); and one number from *The Little Comedy* ("It's Not Too Late") was reprised (this was the only song the two musicals shared).

In his review of the Broadway production, Walter Goodman in the *New York Times* praised Keith Herrmann's score ("a pseudo-fin de siecle lilt in the first act" and a "pop-rock beat" in the second) and noted that while the current Broadway season was awash in "pretentiousness," *Romance Romance* was "delightfully small scale, the scale on which most of us live." For information about other musicals based on works by Schnitzler, see entries for *Bon Voyage* and *Rondelay*.

1378 A Romantic Detachment. THEATRE: Musical Theatre Works; OPENING DATE: 1986; PERFORMANCES: 16; BOOK: Russell Treyz; LYRICS: John Clifton; MUSIC: John Clifton; DIRECTION: Russell Treyz; CHOREOGRAPHY: Russell Treyz; SCENERY: John Falabella; COSTUMES: John Falabella; LIGHTING: Clarke W. Thornton; MUSICAL DIRECTION: Robert Grusecki; PRODUCER: Musical Theatre Works (Anthony J. Stimac, Artistic Director; Michael Jones, Managing Director)

CAST—Nancy Ringham (Abigail Gowens), Victoria Forster (Marguerita Hernandez), Richard Bowne (Stephen Evans), Bjorn Johnson (Sergeant Hanafin), Alex Santoriello (Corporal Xenarios), Glenn Mure (Corporal Beauvais), Mark Baker (Corporal Rodriguez), Dennis Parlato (Captain Carlisle), Reathel Bean (Jesse Gowens)

SOURCE—The 1950 play *Captain Carvallo* by Denis Cannan.

NOTES—The program for the Off Off Broadway musical *A Romantic Detachment* didn't include song titles or information concerning the musical's locale or its division of acts.

A Romantic Detachment was based on Denis Cannan's play *Captain Carvallo*, which enjoyed a half-year's run in London in 1950; the plot used the conventions of bedroom farce to comment on war and other serious subjects. The British production was produced and directed by Laurence Olivier, and the cast included Diana Wynyard, James Donald, and Peter Finch. In late 1950, the play was scheduled for a New York production, but closed in Cleveland during its pre-Broadway tryout; the cast included Katherine Cornell, John Buckmaster, and Cedric Hardwicke.

1379 Rondelay. "A New Musical." THEATRE: Hudson West Playhouse; OPENING DATE: November 5, 1969; PERFORMANCES: 11; BOOK: Jerry Douglas; LYRICS: Jerry Douglas; MUSIC: Hal Jordan; DIRECTION: William Francisco; CHOREOGRAPHY: Jacques d'Amboise; SCENERY: Raoul Pene du Bois; COSTUMES: Raoul Pene du Bois; LIGHTING: Neil Peter Jampolis; MUSICAL DIRECTION: Karen Gustafson; PRODUCERS: Rick Hobard, in association with Martin Hodas and James Jennings

CAST—Barbara Lang (The Whore), Terence Monk (The Soldier), Carole Demas (The Parlor Maid), Peter York (The Student), Louise Clay (The Young Wife), Dillon Evans (The Professor), Barbara Minkus (The Sweet Thing), Shawn Elliott (The Poet), Gwyda Don Howe (The Diva), Paxton Whitehead (The Count); Chorus Girls (Andrea Fulton, Betty Lynn, Maureen Maloney, Susan Schevers), Chorus Boys (Brown Bradley, John Kordel, Stephen Lehew, Terrence McKerrs)

SOURCE—The 1900 play *La Ronde* by Arthur Schnitzler.

The action occurs in Vienna in 1905 and 1906.

The musical was presented in two acts.

ACT ONE—"Rondelay" (The Lovers), "Lovers of the Lamplight" (Barbara Lang), "One Hundred Virgins" (Terence Monk, His Buddies), "Angel Face" (Terence Monk, Barbara Lang), "Tonight You Dance with Me" (The Lovers), "Easy" (Terence Monk, His Buddies), "The First Kiss" (reprise) (Carole Demas), "Afterward" (Carole Demas, Terence Monk), "The First Kiss" (Carole Demas, Barbara Lang), "She Deserves Me" (Peter York), "Closer" (Peter York, Carole Demas), "Honor" (Peter York, His Fellow Students), "The Answer (The No Song)" (Louise Clay), "Failure" (Peter York, Louise Clay), "Success" (Peter York), "The Days of My Youth" (Dillon Evans), "I've Got a Surprise for You" (Dillon Evans, Louise Clay), "Reidhof's" (The Waiters), "Champagne" (Barbara Minkus), "Dessert" (Barbara Minkus, Dillon Evans, The Waiters), "Masquerade" (Barbara Minkus, Dillon Evans, Barbara Lang, The Revelers, The Waiters)

ACT TWO—"Masquerade" (reprise) (Shawn Elliott, Barbara Minkus, The Revelers), "When Lovers Fall in Love" (Shawn Elliott, Barbara Minkus), "What You Are" (Barbara Minkus), "A Castle in India" (Shawn Elliott), "Back to Nature" (Barbara Minkus, Shawn Elliott), "Back to Nature" (reprise) (Shawn Elliott, Peasants), "Saint Genesius" (Gwyda Don Howe), "Opera Star" (Shawn Elliott), "Not So Young Love" (Gwyda Don Howe, Shawn Elliott), "Auf Weidersehen" (Gwyda Don Howe, Shawn Elliott), "Auf Weidersehen" (reprise) (Gwyda Don Howe, Chorus Boys), "Gusto" (Paxton Whitehead), "Happy Ending" (Gwyda Don Howe, Paxton Whitehead), "I'll Show You the World Tonight" (Barbara Lang, Paxton Whitehead, The Lovers), "Reflections" (Paxton Whitehead), "Before Breakfast" (Paxton Whitehead, Barbara Lang), "Give and Take" (Barbara Lang), "Rondelay" (reprise) (Barbara Lang, The Lovers)

NOTES—With thirty-nine separate song sequences, *Rondelay*, which was based on Arthur Schnitzler's play *La Ronde*, appears to have been a sung-through musical, but this novelty didn't help; the circular musical which revolved around a series of love affairs in turn-of-the-twentieth-century Vienna was gone in less than two weeks. *Rondelay* was the first presentation at the Hudson West Playhouse, a new cabaret theatre located in the Henry Hudson Hotel. Clive Barnes in the *New York Times* liked neither the musical ("no charm, wit, style or atmosphere... [the score] sounded vilely sub-Weill") nor the theatre ("surely one of the most uncomfortable and ugliest in the world"). In 1994, Off Broadway offered another version of *La Ronde*. Called *Hello Again*, Michael John LaChiusa's adaptation played for two months at Lincoln Center (see entry).

Besides *Rondelay* and *Hello Again*, there have been at least three other musicals based on works by Schnitzler. For information about *Anatol* and *The Gay Life*, see entry for *Bon Voyage*; also see entry for *Romance Romance* for information about the one-act musical *The Little Comedy*.

1380 Rosa. "A Musical Play." THEATRE: St. Clement's Theatre; OPENING DATE: May 10, 1978; PERFORMANCES: 12; BOOK: William Archibald; LYRICS: William Archibald; MUSIC: Baldwin Bergersen; DIRECTION: Pat Carmichael; CHOREOGRAPHY: Roger Preston-Smith; SCENERY: Daniel Thomas Field; COSTUMES: Danny Morgan; LIGHTING: Curt Ostermann; MUSICAL DIRECTION: Robert Colston; PRODUCER: Wendell Minnick; Phillip Moser, Associate Producer

CAST—Victoria Wyndham (Rosa), Jill Harwood (Maid, Mrs. Guernsey), Nancy Lipner (Maid, Elsie), Marnie Mosiman (Maid), Kathleen Swan (Maid), Elizabeth Torgersen (Housekeeper, Maid), Ted Houck (Footman, Chef, Bert), Betty Wragge (Mrs. Fricker), John Deyle (Dad, Fishmonger), Steve Vinovich (Henry), Everett McGill (Lord Riverton), Donald C. Moore (Edward, Prince of Wales)

SOURCE—An unidentified play by Brenda Forbes.

The action occurs in London between 1893 and 1933.

The musical was presented in two acts.

ACT ONE—"Rosa" (Steve Vinovich), "Be Kind to the Young" (Betty Wragge), "Time Goes Faster" (Performer[s] unidentified), "The Herb Song" (Jill Harwood, Nancy Lipner, Marnie Mosiman, Kathleen Swan), "I Am Royal" (Donald C. Moore), "A Place of My Own" (Victoria Wyndham), "Fame" (Victoria Wyndham), "Rosa" (Steve Vinovich), "Perfection" (Victoria Wyndham), "Where's My Love A-Wonderin'?" (Steve Vinovich), "Let Us Charm Each Other" (Victoria Wyndham, Everett McGill), "The Fish Soup Song" (Jill Harwood, Nancy Lipner, Marnie Mosiman, Kathleen Swan)

ACT TWO—"Peace Celebration Music" (Orchestra), "Be Kind to the Young" (reprise) (Victoria Wyndham, Nancy Lipner), "From the Bottom of the Sea" (John Deyle), "Oh, How We Love You, Mrs. Cornwall" (Jill Harwood, Nancy Lipner, Marnie Mosiman, Kathleen Swan), "A Place of My Own" (reprise) (Victoria Wyndham), "Dear Friend" (Victoria Wyndham), "Before It's Too Late" (Victoria Wyndham), "Rose" (reprise) (Steve Vinovich), "Fame" (reprise) (Victoria Wyndham)

NOTES—*Rosa* was a showcase production which featured book and lyrics by William Archibald and music by Baldwin Bergersen, the team who had written the exquisite score for *The Crystal Heart* (1960; see entry). They also collaborated on *Carib Song*, a Broadway failure in 1946 which nonetheless has an appealing score. The musical was based on the life of Rosa Lewis (1867-1952), the British chef who owned the legendary Cavendish Hotel in London (located at 82 Jermyn Street at Duke Street). Her life story was also the inspiration for *The Duchess of Duke Street*, which was shown on public television in 1976 and 1977.

Archibald, who had died in 1970, also wrote the brittle, stylized drama *The Cantilevered Terrace* which was briefly produced Off Broadway in 1961. Perhaps the only post-World War II play which matches it in terms of abstract, surreal dialogue is Jane Bowles' *In the Summer House*, which was seen on Broadway in 1953.

1381 The Rothschilds. THEATRE: American Jewish Theatre; OPENING DATE: February 25, 1990; PERFORMANCES: 64 (estimated); BOOK: Sherman Yellen; LYRICS: Sheldon Harnick; MUSIC: Jerry Bock; DIRECTION: Lonny Price; CHOREOGRAPHY: Michael Arnold; SCENERY: E. David Cosier, Jr.; COSTUMES: Gail Brassard; LIGHTING: Betsy Adams; MUSICAL DIRECTION: Grant Sturiale; PRODUCER: American Jewish Theatre (Stanley Brechner, Artistic Director; Lonny Price, Associate Artistic Director)

CAST—Allen Fitzpatrick (Prince William of Hesse, Joseph Fouche, Herres, Prince Metternich), Nick Corley (Guard, First Vendor, Jacob Rothschild), Mike Burstyn (Mayer Rothschild), Evan Ferrante (First Urchin, Young Nathan Rothschild), Hal Goldberg (Second Urchin, Young Solomon Rothschild), Etan or Josh Ofrane (Third Urchin, Young Jacob Rothschild), Sue Anne Gershenson (Gutele Rothschild), David Cantor (Second Vendor, Second Banker, Amshel Rothschild), Joel Malina (Third Vendor, Kalman Rothschild), Ted Forlow (Budurus), Ray Wills (First Banker, Solomon Rothschild, Skeptic), Adam Paul Plotch (Young Amshel Rothschild), Bob (Robert) Cuccioli (Nathan Rothschild), Leslie Ellis (Hannah Cohen)

SOURCE—The 1960 book *The Rothschilds* by Frederic Morton.

The action occurs in the Frankford Ghetto, the Hessian and Austrian Courts, London, and Aix-La-Chapelle.

The musical was presented in two acts.

ACT ONE—"Pleasure and Privilege" (Allen Fitzpatrick, Ensemble), "One Room" (Sue Anne Gershenson, Mike Burstyn), "He Tossed a Coin" (Mike Burstyn, Ensemble), "Sons" (Mike Burstyn, Adam Paul Plotch, Hal Goldberg, Evan Ferrante, Etan or Josh Ofrane), "Everything" (Sue Anne Gershenson, Bob Cuccioli, David Cantor, Ray Wills, Nick Corley, Joel Malina), "Rothschilds and Sons" (Mike Burstyn, Ray Wills, David Cantor, Bob Cuccioli, Nick Corley, Joel Malina), "Allons" (Allen Fitzpatrick, Grenadiers), Finale Act One: "Rothschilds and Sons"/"Sons" (reprises) (Sue Anne Gershenson, Family)

ACT TWO—"The British Free Enterprise Auction" (a/k/a "Give England Strength") (Allen Fitzpatrick, Bob Cuccioli, Mike Burstyn, Ensemble), "This Amazing London Town" (Bob Cuccioli, Ensemble), "They Say" (Bob Cuccioli, Ensemble), "I'm in Love! I'm in Love!" (Bob Cuccioli, Leslie Ellis), "In My Own Lifetime" (Mike Burstyn), "Have You Ever Seen a Prettier Little Congress?" (Allen Fitzpatrick), "Bonds" (Allen Fitzpatrick, Bob Cuccioli, Nick Corley, Ray Wills, Joel Malina, Ensemble)

NOTES—The American Jewish Theatre's Off Off Broadway production of *The Rothschilds* quickly transferred to Off Broadway at the Circle in the Square Downtown on April 27, 1990, where it played for almost one year (379 performances). The original Broadway production had opened on October 19, 1970, at the Lunt-Fontanne Theatre where it ran for 507 performances. The original Broadway cast album was released by Columbia Records (LP# S-30337; later issued on CD by Sony Broadway Records [# #SK-30337]), and the script was published by Metromedia On Stage (dated 1970, but probably published in 1971 or 1972).

The Rothschilds is a problematic musical, a sort of *Fiddler on the Roof* in reverse; this time around, the Jewish family in question gets rich (and richer), and instead of a family of five daughters, there are five sons.

Sherman Yellen probably did all that could have been done with such a sprawling story line, and his clever touches helped unify the almost epic-like canvas upon which the Rothschild story was told (a brilliant *Gypsy*-like stroke of stage magic in which the Rothschild boys are instantly transformed into adults as well as the device of having one actor portray all the powerful establishment figures); but all too often the libretto told its up-from-rags tale in by-the-numbers fashion. Jerry Bock and Sheldon Harnick's score suffered from a duel personality. When the songs dealt with stock situations ("One Room," "Everything," "This Amazing London Town," "I'm in Love! I'm in Love!"), the score seemed ordinary (albeit ordinary Bock and Harnick was still superior to most Broadway fare). But when the team explored the corridors of European cultural and financial power, their songs were among the best heard on Broadway during the era. Indeed, great theatre writing doesn't get any better than "Pleasure and Privilege," "They Say," "Have You Ever Seen a Prettier Little Congress?," "Stability," and "Bonds" (curiously, the revival seems to have eliminated "Stability," although perhaps it was included in the "Congress" sequence).

Sadly, the 1970 Broadway production of *The Rothschilds* marked the end of Bock and Harnick's partnership; rumors of backstage tryout politics apparently soured the former from composing for the commercial theatre, and so New York was never again to see another new Bock musical. Athough Harnick continued writing, he unfortunately never matched the successes he enjoyed with Bock (*Fiorello!* [1959], *She Loves Me* [1963], and *Fiddler on the Roof* [1964]). But these four scores, along with *The Body Beautiful* (1958), *Tenderloin* (1960), and *The Apple Tree* (1966), constitute a body of work which ensures their place in the highest echelon of American musical theatre. (See entry for Bock and Harnick's 1963 puppet musical *Man on the Moon*.)

In late 1972, Twentieth Century–Fox announced in *Variety* that its film version of *The Rothschilds* was forthcoming; but the "exciting musical motion picture" never materialized.

1382 The Roumanian Wedding. THEATRE: Town Hall; OPENING DATE: October 21, 1981; PERFORMANCES: Unknown; BOOK: Moshe Schorr; English narration written by Bela Maisel Yablokoff; LYRICS: Peretz Sandler; MUSIC: "Additional songs" by Mordechay Gebirtig; Musical numbers adapted and coordinated by Yankele Alperin; DIRECTION: Michael Greenstein; CHOREOGRAPHY: Felix Fibich; SCENERY: Adina Reich; COSTUMES: Renee Gladstein; MUSICAL DIRECTION: Renee Solomon; PRODUCERS: Shalom Yiddish Musical Comedy Theatre, Inc., and Raymond Ariel and David Carey

CAST—Harry Peerce (Motkeh), Linda Carelle (Rochele), Eleanor Reissa (Chanele), MARY SOREANU (Dvoyreh), DAVID ELLIN (Sholem Hersh), Sandy Levitt (Shimon), LEON LIEBGOLD (Keezler), YANKELE ALPERIN (Shloymeh Yoyneh), DAVID CAREY (Yisroel) REIZL BOZYK (Mariashah), Marek Warszawski (Dayen), Leah Post (Zahara); Chorus/Boys and Girls of the Town (Shelly Pappas, Torri Campbell, Laurie Crochet, Charles Haack, Jospeh Rich, James Vogel); The Fibich Dance Ensemble

The action occurs around 1900 in a small village in Roumania.

The musical was presented in two acts.

ACT ONE—Overture (Orchestra), "Geendikt Iz Der Tog (Peasants Return from Work)" (Ensemble), "Dvoyreh" (Mary Soreanu, Ensemble), "Dvoyreh Fun Rumeynie (Serba)" (Mary Soreanu, Ensemble), "Ich Lib Dich (I Love You)" (Sandy Levitt, Eleanor Reissa), "Gvald Ich Vil Es (I Want It!)" (Mary Soreanu, Harry Peerce), "Mayn Rochele" (David Carey, Linda Carelle), "Chassene Hobn Iz Doch Zeyer Git (Marriage Is a Good Thing)" (Mary Soreanu, Harry Peerce, David Carey, Linda Carelle, Sandy Levitt, Eleanor Reissa), "Blimelech Tzvey (Two Flowers)" (David Carey, Linda Carelle)

ACT TWO—"Roumeynishe Libe (Roumanian Love)" (Mary Soreanu), "Kinder Yohrn (Childhood Years)" (David Carey), "Huliet Huliet Kinderlech (Children, Enjoy Yourselves)" (Leah Post), "Wedding Dance" (Ensemble), "Ich Bin Gerecht (I'm Right)" (Yankele Alperin), "Mach Es Motkeh Noch Amol (Motkeh, Do It Again)" (Mary Soreanu)

NOTES—Roumanian-born Mary Soreanu starred in *The Roumanian Wedding*, a new version of an old Yiddish musical which included just enough English to help non-Yiddish-speaking audiences understand the plot.

Soreanu was a frequent visitor to Off Off Broadway during this era, and starred in a number of Yiddish musicals. Richard F. Shepard in the *New York Times* said she was a "captivating personality in any language" and noted she had "carved her niche" in current-day New York productions of old and new Yiddish musicals.

Shepard found *The Roumanian Wedding* "lighthearted and happy" and "most engaging." The plot dealt with a rich businessman who wants to marry the daughter of his manager, but she is interested in someone else. Eventually, the manager's niece (Soreanu) manages to set aright all the romantic goings-on. Shepard also noted the score will "keep you humming," and said the book "rides through waves of very singable melody."

1383 R.S.V.P. "A New Musical Revue." THEATRE: Theatre East; OPENING DATE: August 24, 1982; PERFORMANCES: 127; LYRICS: Rick Crom; MUSIC: Rick Crom; DIRECTION: Word Baker and Rod Rodgers; SCENERY: Carleton Varney; COSTUMES: Jerry Hart; LIGHTING: Dan Fabrici; MUSICAL DIRECTION: Glen Kelly; PRODUCERS: Pierrot Productions (Roz Cole and Peter Malatesta)

CAST—Christopher Durham, John Fucillo, Lianne Johnson, Julie Sheppard, John Wyatt

The revue was presented in two acts.

ACT ONE—"Tacky Opening" (Company), "Oh, Fine!" (Company), "Back Home" (Christopher Durham), "Recital" (Company), "Reunion" (Julie Sheppard), "Oh What a Lovely View" (Lianne Johnson, John Fucillo), "It's Tough to Be a Man" (Christopher Durham, John Fucillo, John Wyatt), "Is There a Straight Man in the House" (Julie Sheppard), "Sing Along" (Company), "Oh, Fine!" (reprise) (Company)

ACT TWO—"Guardian Angels" (Christopher Durham, Company), "I Don't Mind Being Funny" (John Fucillo), "It's Happening" (Lianne Johnson),

"A Quiet Kind of Love" (Lianne Johnson, John Wyatt), "Moral Majority" (Company), "Close That Show" (John Fucillo, John Wyatt), "Urban Allegro" (Company), "Tacky Closing" (Company)

NOTES—The program indicated *R.S.V.P.* was to be "part of a continuum in musicalized New York topicality as evinced in Julius Monks' [sic] Cabaret concept of the 50's and 60's." But it was not to be. *R.S.V.P.* was the first and last edition in the series.

1384 **Runaways.** THEATRE: Martinson Hall/ The Public Theatre; OPENING DATE: February 21, 1978; PERFORMANCES: 80; TEXT: Elizabeth Swados; all English-Spanish translations by Jossie De Guzman; LYRICS: Elizabeth Swados; MUSIC: Elizabeth Swados; DIRECTION: Elizabeth Swados; CHOREOGRAPHY: The director acknowledged the ideas and help of the performers in the "dancing choreography"; SCENERY: Douglas W. Schmidt and Woods Mackintosh; COSTUMES: Hilary Rosenfeld; LIGHTING: Jennifer Tipton; MUSICAL DIRECTION: Elizabeth Swados (?); PRODUCERS: The New York Shakespeare Festival (Joseph Papp, Director; Bernard Gersten, Associate Producer)

CAST—Bruce Hlibok (Hubbell), Anthony Imperato (A.J.), Diane Lane (Jackie), Jossie De Guzman (Lidia), Trini Alvarado (Melinda), Nan-Lynn Nelson (Nikki Kay Kane), Randy Ruiz (Manny), Jon Matthews (Eddie), Bernie Allison (Sundar), Venustra K. Robinson (Roby), David Schechter (Lazar), Evan Miranda (Eric), Jonathan Feig (Iggy), Karen Evans (Deidre), Leonard (Duke) Brown (EZ), Ray Contreras (Luis), Mark Anthony Butler (Mex-Mongo), Kate Schellenbach (Jame), Lorie Robinson (Interpreter for Hubbell); Chorus (Sheila Gibbs, Toby Parker); Judith Fleisher (Piano and Toy Piano), John Schimmel (String Bass) Leopoldo F. Fleming (Congas, Timbales, Bongos, Bells, Sirens, Others), David Sawyer (Trap Set, Triangle, Glass, Ratchet), Patience Higgins (Saxophones, Flutes), Elizabeth Swados (Guitar)

The revue was presented in two acts.

ACT ONE—"You Don't Understand" (improvised by Bruce Hlibok) (Bruce Hlibok), "I Had to Go" (Anthony Imperato, John Schimmel), "Parent/Kid Dance" (Company), "Appendectomy" (Diane Lane), "Where Do People Go" (Company), "Footsteps" (Spanish argument improvised by Jossie De Guzman and Randy Ruiz) (Nan-Lynn Nelson, John Schimmel, Jossie De Guzman, Randy Ruiz), "Once Upon a Time" (Jossie De Guzman, Company), "Current Events" (Jon Matthews), "Every Now and Then" (Bernie Allison, Company), "Out on the Street" (improvised by Bruce Hlibok) (Bruce Hlibok, Lorie Robinson), "Minnesota Strip" (Venustra K. Robinson), "Song of a Child Prostitute" (Diane Lane, Jossie De Guzman, Randy Ruiz, Ray Contreras), "Christmas Puppies" (Nan-Lynn Nelson), "Lazar's Heroes" (improvised by David Schechter) (David Schechter), "Find Me a Hero" (David Schechter, Company), "Scrynatchkielooaw" (Nan-Lynn Nelson), "The Undiscovered Son" (Evan Miranda, Judith Fleisher), "I Went Back Home" (Jonathan Feig, Diane Lane), "This Is What I Do When I'm Angry" (Karen Evans), "The Basketball Song" (Leonard [Duke] Brown, Company; Dance [Ray Contreras]), Spoons (Randy Ruiz), "Lullaby for Luis" (Jossie de Guzman, Ray Contreras, Patience Higgins, Company), "We Are Not Strangers" (Evan Miranda, Company)

ACT TWO—"In the Sleeping Line" (improvisations by Anthony Imperato, Venustra K. Robinson, Diane Lane, David Schechter, Vincent Stewart, Jossie De Guzman, Randy Ruiz) (Company), "Lullaby from Baby to Baby" (Trini Alvarado, Bruce Hlibok, Karen Evans), "Tra Gog Vo In Dein Whole (I Will Not Tell a Soul)" (David Schechter, Bruce Hlibok), "Revenge Song" (Company), "Enterprise" (Karen Evans, Nan-Lynn Nelson, Mark Anthony Butler, Company), "Mr. Graffiti" (Mark Anthony Butler), "Sometimes" (Venustra K. Robinson, David Schechter, Company), "Clothes" (Jonathan Feig), "Where Are Those People Who Did *Hair*" (David Schechter, Karen Evans), "The Untrue Pigeon" (Nan-Lynn Nelson), "Senoras De La Noche" (Jossie De Guzman, Randy Ruiz, Nan-Lynn Nelson), "We Have to Die?" (Karen Evans), "Appendectomy II" (Diane Lane, Trini Alvarado), "Let Me Be a Kid" (Company), "To the Dead of Family Wars" (Karen Evans), "Problem After Problem" (Bruce Hlibok, Lorie Robinson), "Lonesome of the Road" (Ray Contreras, Bernie Allison, Company)

NOTES—*Runaways* was a dreary offering by Elizabeth Swados, this one a loosely connected "collage" about runaway children from broken and "solid" families as well as children who perhaps weren't necessarily runaways but were just unmotivated and directionless. The meandering program notes revealed well-meaning if confused intentions. If some of the runaways were from "solid" families (and thus were presumably *with* their families), then they weren't runaways. But perhaps the semantics of the word "runaways" meant more to Swados. Who knows, maybe all of us are Symbolic Runaways. The ages of the cast were eleven through the early twenties, and if "some of the cast *are* runaways" (according to Swados' program notes), it's curious that of the nineteen cast members, seventeen seem to have had a certain amount of professional theatre and show business experience, on television (public broadcasting and *The Mike Douglas Show*), in Public Theatre productions (*Landscape of the Body* [1977], *The Cherry Orchard* [1977], and *Agamemnon* [1977]), and in formal theatre training and exposure (the Lee Strasberg Institute, the Boston Repertory Theatre, Washington D.C.'s Arena Stage).

The critics were generally kind to the show and its intentions, but some chastised its loose and rambling structure (by giving each runaway his or her vignette in speech or song, the show could have been titled *A Runaway Line*) and its tendency to find easy and obvious answers to the social issues it raised. But audiences weren't fooled. When the piece moved to Broadway at the Plymouth (now Schoenfeld) Theatre on May 13, 1978, it mustered only 199 showings.

This was indeed becoming the age of the vignette-musical. The night after *Runaways* opened on Broadway, a similar musical opened, this one about American factory and other workers, *Working* (or, perhaps more appropriately, *A Workers' Line*). In his review of Swados' 1982 musical *Lullabye and Goodnight* (see entry), Frank Rich in the *New York Times* noted that the new work was essentially an expanded version of two songs from *Runaways* ("Minnesota Strip" and "Song of a Child Prostitute").

The Broadway cast album of *Runaways* (and, for that matter, *Working*) was recorded by Columbia Records (LP # JS-35410). The script was published by Bantam Books in 1979, and in 1980 by Samuel French, Inc. As *Runaways: In Concert*, the musical was presented for one performance on March 25, 2007, at Joe's Pub. According to Andrew Gans in *Playbill*, the production was an updated version that had been reworked by Rodney Hicks.

1385 **Russell Patterson's Sketchbook.** "A Revue." THEATRE: Maidman Playhouse; OPENING DATE: February 6, 1960; PERFORMANCES: 3; SKETCHES: Les Kramer, Rube Goldberg, Otto Soglow, and Irwin Hansen; LYRICS: Les Kramer, Floria Vestoff, Gladys Shelley, Fred Heider, George Blake, and Tom Romano; MUSIC: Ruth Cleary Patterson; DIRECTION: Hudson Faussett; CHOREOGRAPHY: Nelle Fisher; SCENERY: William Ritman; COSTUMES: William Ritman; LIGHTING: William Ritman; MUSICAL DIRECTION: Ruth Cleary Patterson; PRODUCERS: Hudson Faussett and Russell Patterson, in association with H. Pierson Mapes

CAST—Jerry Bergen, Michael Dominico, Phyllis Ford, Margaret Gathright, Anita Gillette, Jan Leighton, Ralph Lowe, Marlene Manners, Gaby Monet, Jen Nelson, Beau Nelson, Betty Secino, Diane Shalet, Artie Palmer

The revue was presented in two acts (sketch and song assignments unknown).

ACT ONE—"The Forty-Second Street Philharmonic," "We Know What You Want and We Got It" (lyric by Floria Vestoff) "That's Why I'm Here Tonight" (lyric by Les Kramer) "Welcome," "Brief Encounter," "Artistic Confusion" "Starting from Scratch" "Dancing to the Rhythm of the Rain Drops" (lyric by Gladys Shelley) "Magician Makes Good," "Home, Sweet Home" "An Echo of Greco," "All's Right on the Left Bank," "I Want to Take 'Em Off for Norman Rockwell" (lyric by Les Kramer) "An Old Shade of the Moulin Rouge," "A Son of the Beach" "May in Manhattan" (lyric by Tom Romano), "La Calinda" (lyric by Gladys Shelley)

ACT TWO—"Paramus, New Jersey, U.S.A." "Singing Wheels" (lyric by Fred Heider), "The Canary" "This Is What I Got for Not Listening to My Mother" (lyric by Floria Vestoff) "Let's Not Get Married" (lyric by George Blake and Les Kramer), "What's the Name of the Hotel" "Interview with a Movie Star" "An Old Japanese Custom," "Scratched," "My First Love" (lyric by Fred Heider) "Gratitude" "Dig That Mummy," "Sweet Charity" (lyric by Les Kramer), "Midnight in the Museum," "When the Wings of the Wind Take Me Home" (lyric by Les Kramer), "Wonderful Way of Life" (lyric by Les Kramer, Floria Vestoff) "C'Est Fini"

NOTES—Louis Calta in the *New York Times* noted that *Russell Patterson's Sketchbook* was the premiere attraction at the Maidman Theatre. He referred to a program note which indicated Irving Maidman's new theatre (located on West 42nd Street between Eighth and Ninth Avenues in the former Bank of the United States building) would be "the first gesture" in restoring 42nd Street to its former grandeur. Calta praised the "luxurious appointments" of the plush theatre and said he only wished the new revue had been "equally endowed." He found the most of the material "undistinguished," and concluded that nothing could help the "fragment like quality" of the evening. With its short run of three performances, the revue denied most theatergoers the opportunity of hearing such songs as "I Want to Take 'Em Off for Norman Rockwell" and "Dig That Mummy."

Irving Maidman's vision of a restored 42nd Street would take almost forty years to be realized, but it was worth the wait, if only to see the glorious New Amsterdam Theatre reborn after spending almost sixty years in virtual theatrical oblivion, either dark or as a movie theatre.

An interesting aspect of *Sketchbook* is that it marked the return of Gladys Shelley, who was the lyricist and co-librettist for one of the most notorious Broadway flops of the 1940s, *The Duchess Misbehaves* (1946). This legendary dud had something to do with a modern-day mensch who dreams he is Francisco Goya. Jackie Gleason had played the role during the show's pre-Broadway tryout, but luckily managed to hurt his ankle, and thus couldn't perform. And so Joey Faye went on for the five New York performances (see entry for *Lyle* regarding The Joey Faye Curse). Vernon Rice, writing in the *New York Post*, predicted the show "will Goya way soon" and said that Shelley's book and lyrics were "about as unsubtle and distasteful ... as heard this season." Shelley was later heard on Broadway in 1957, when her lovely, semi-standard "How Did He Look?" (music by Abner Silver) was interpolated into the short-running revue *Mask and Gown*, which featured female impersonator T.C. Jones. After *Mask and*

Gown, Shelley would be heard from one more time: she wrote the lyrics for the two-performance Off Broadway flop *Gogo Loves You* (1964; see entry). *Sketchbook* marked the first New York appearance of Anita Gillette. Like Susan Watson, who had made her Off Broadway debut two weeks earlier in *Follies of 1910* (see entry), Gillette and Watson became the Ingenues of Choice for musicals during the next decade.

Their career paths crossed in *Carnival!* (1961), when each performed the leading role of Lili at various times during the show's run. They also appeared in early Broadway musicals by Charles Strouse and Lee Adams: Watson created the role of high-schooler Kim in the original production of *Bye Bye Birdie* (1960), and Anita Gillette appeared in Strouse and Adams' "college" musical *All American* (1962). Watson also appeared in the original Broadway productions of *Ben Franklin in Paris* (1964), *A Joyful Noise* (1966), Harvey Schmidt and Tom Jones' *Celebration* (1969), and played the title role in the hit revival of *No, No, Nanette* (1971). In 1959, Watson created the role of The Girl (Luisa) in the original pre-Off Broadway production of *The Fantasticks* (see entry) when it premiered at Barnard College, and she reprised the role for the 1964 NBC telecast of the musical.

Gillette appeared in Irving Berlin's *Mr. President* (1962), *Jimmy* (1969), and perhaps the most famous Broadway flop of them all, the one-nighter *Kelly* (1965). She also appeared in the original productions of two hit comedies, Woody Allen's *Don't Drink the Water* (1966) and Neil Simon's *Chapter Two* (1977).

For the record, the credits for the lyrics in the above song list are taken from the second edition of Ken Bloom's invaluable *American Song* (the first edition is also worth tracking down for Bloom's witty, informative comments about many of the musicals covered in his book).

1386 Ruthless! "The Musical." THEATRE: Players Theatre; OPENING DATE: May 6, 1992; PERFORMANCES: 302; BOOK: Joel Paley; LYRICS: Joel Paley; MUSIC: Marvin Laird; DIRECTION: Joel Paley; SCENERY: James Noone; COSTUMES: Gail Cooper-Hecht; LIGHTING: Kenneth Posner; MUSICAL DIRECTION: Marvin Laird; PRODUCERS: Kim Lang Lenny, Wolfgang Bocksch, and Jim Lenny; a Musical Theatre Works production (Anthony J. Stimac, Artistic Director)

CAST—Joel Vig (Sylvia St. Croix), Donna English (Judy Denmark, Ginger DelMarco), Laura Bundy (Tina Denmark), Susan Mansur (Myrna Thorn, Reporter), Joanne Baum (Louise Lerman, Eave), Denise Lor (Lita Encore)

The action in act one occurs in Small Town, U.S.A., at the present time; Act two occurs in New York City four years later.

The musical was presented in two acts.

ACT ONE—"Tina's Mother" (Donna English), "Born to Entertain" (Laura Bundy), "Talent" (Joel Vig), "To Play This Part" (Laura Bundy), "(Teaching) Third Grade" (Susan Mansur), "The Lippy Song" (Performer[s] unknown; probably Laura Bundy), "Where Tina Gets It From" (Donna English, Joel Vig), "Kisses and Hugs" (Laura Bundy, Donna English), "Tina, My Daughter" (Donna English), "I Hate Musicals" (Denise Lor), "Angel Mom" (Laura Bundy, Joel Vig, Donna English)

ACT TWO—"Eave's Song" (Joanne Baum), "Look at Me" (Performer[s] unknown), "Ruthless!" (Donna English, Joel Vig, Laura Bundy)

NOTES—An amusing combination of *Gypsy, All About Eve,* and *The Bad Seed, Ruthless!* was a fun-loving evening about a bratty child actress named Tina Denmark who will do anything to succeed in show business, including the death ("strangulation by jump rope," noted Stephen Holden in the *New York Times*) of one of her rivals for the starring role in the school play *Pippi in Tahiti.* At one point, Tina is even sentenced to the Daisy Clover School for Psychopathic Ingenues. Holden singled out the "candy-striped" settings by James Noone and the "fluorescent" costumes by Gail Cooper-Hecht, and suggested they evoked a "world in which all values" are reduced to a child's "intoxication of show-business glory as experienced in a grade-school pageant."

The role of Sylvia St. Croix, show biz agent *extraordinaire,* was performed by a male actor (Joel Vig); a few weeks after the musical opened, a "real" Sylvia (Miles) performed the role.

Soon after the opening, the musical underwent various changes, including the deletion of four songs ("The Lippy Song," "Tina, My Daughter," "Eave's Song," and "Look at Me") and the addition of four others ("The Pippi Song" [for Louise], "A Penthouse Apartment" [for Eave], "It Will Never Be That Way Again" [for Ginger], and "Parents and Children" [for Ginger and Tina]). ("Eave's Song" and "A Penthouse Apartment" were probably the same number.)

The script was published by Samuel French, Inc., in 1995; and a 1993 Los Angeles production was recorded by Varese Sarabande Records (CD # VSD-5476); the recording included "Unkie's Muncle," a pre-recorded song used as exit music.

Ruthless! had first been produced as a one-act Off Off Broadway musical by Musical Theatre Works on October 16, 1991, for twelve performances; three numbers from that version weren't used in the Off Broadway production ("Tap Shoes," "My Poodle Puddles," and "Sleep Now, My Child").

1387 Sacred and Profane Love. THEATRE: Judson Poets' Theatre; OPENING DATE: February 1975; PERFORMANCES: Unknown; BOOK: Al Carmines; LYRICS: Al Carmines; MUSIC: Al Carmines; DIRECTION: Al Carmines; CHOREOGRAPHY: Katherine Litz; SCENERY: Jimmy Cuomo; COSTUMES: Michele Edwards; LIGHTING: Steve Graff; MUSICAL DIRECTION: Al Carmines; PRODUCER: The Judson Poets' Theatre

CAST—Essie Borden, Lou Bullock, Terence Burk, Alice Carey, Eric Ellenburg, Lee Guilliatt, Philip Owens, Elly (Ellie) Schadt, David Tice, Beverly Wideman

NOTES—Mel Gussow in the *New York Times* reported that the message of the Off Off Broadway revue-like *Sacred and Profane Love* was that love comes in many guises and can be found in unlikely places. Although he praised Al Carmines' "soaring" melodies, Gussow felt this was an "intermediary" work which would have to do until the next "real" Carmines' musical came along (which based on his "past productivity" should be "any minute").

Gussow noted the inspiration for the musical came from such sources as "The Song of Solomon," "The Book of Ruth," *The Confessions of St. Augustine,* Yeats, Shakespeare, and Elizabeth Barrett Browning. But despite such august sources, the musical also found time to offer one number about a football hero and his "homosexual tendencies" and another about a bachelor's life with his cat. Gussow reported that Carmines had various works-in-progress, including musical versions of Shakespeare's *Richard III* and *Measure for Measure* as well as a musical titled *Brighten the Corner* (the latter probably *not* a lyric adaptation of John Cecil Holm's 1945 Broadway comedy of the same name). At any rate, it appears all three musicals were never produced.

One song from the production ("Nostalgia") was included in the 1982 revue *The Gospel According to Al* (see entry).

1388 Safari 300. THEATRE: Mayfair Theatre; OPENING DATE: July 12, 1972; PERFORMANCES: 17; DRAMATIC MATERIAL: Tony Preston; DIRECTION: Hugh Gittens; CHOREOGRAPHY: Larl Becham; additional choreography by Phil Black; SCENERY: Bob Olsen; COSTUMES: Lee Lynn; LIGHTING: David Adams; MUSICAL DIRECTION: Scat Wilson; PRODUCER: Richie Havens

CAST—Tad Truesdale, Onike Lee, Joyce Griffen, Fredi Orange, Grenna Whitaker, Larl Becham, Earnest Andrews, Holly Hamilton, Andre Robinson, Dorian Williams

The revue was presented in two acts.

MUSICAL NUMBERS (division of acts and song assignments unknown; song list is in performance order)—"Dombaye," "Singing Drums," "Adunde," "Royal Court Dance," "Little Black Baby," "Slave Auction," "Black Rape," "Sage," "O Negros Bahianos," "Johnny Too Bad," "World Keeps Turnin'," "Waiting Song," "Voodoo," "Baron Samedi," "Soon I'll Be Done," "This Little Light," "Cakewalk," "Song of Sorrow," "Goin' to Chicago," "Song of Troubles," "Cotton Club Revue," "1950's Singing Group," "1960's Twist," "Younger Men Grow Older," "My Children Searching," "Prayer," "Size Places," "Doin' It by the Book," "Get It Together," "Oratorio," "The Man and His Message," "What Have We Done," "Hallucinations," "It's Rainin'," "Rock 1975," "Return to Africa," "Akiwawa"

NOTES—For a while it seemed every Off Broadway season offered a revue which explored the Black experience from slavery to modern times; the 1972-1973 season's contribution was *Safari 300.* Conceived by Tad Truesdale, some of the sequences in the revue were traditional numbers, while others were written specifically for the production. Howard Thompson in the *New York Times* said the revue "worked brilliantly," and while the show included some "deadwood" numbers, it also became "blazingly dynamic and alive" in others.

1389 Saga. THEATRE: Wonderhorse Theatre; OPENING DATE: April 19, 1979; PERFORMANCES: 12; BOOK: Kelly Hamilton; LYRICS: Kelly Hamilton; MUSIC: Kelly Hamilton; DIRECTION: Neal Newman; CHOREOGRAPHY: Colleen Heffernan; SCENERY: Terrence B. Byrne; COSTUMES: Susan Cox; LIGHTING: John Vetere; MUSICAL DIRECTION: Bruce W. Coyle; PRODUCERS: Neal Newman; Maximilian St. James, Assistant Producer

CAST—Mara Beckerman, Stephen Bogardus, Tony Calabro, Paul Canestro, Ellyn Gale, Daryl Hunt, Scott Hunt, Jay Aubrey-Jones, Karen Longwell, Deborah MacHale, Megan McPherson, Teresa Parente, Stacy Peppell, Barbara Porter, Angelena Reaux, Tianna Schlittne, Sharon Talbot, David Sloan, Mark Wolff

NOTES—*Theatre World 1978-1979 Season* noted that the Off Off Broadway production of *Saga* was the "World Premiere of an American Folk Opera." The work dealt with the settlement of the American West, and among its cast members were Angelina Reaux and Stephen Bogardus.

Allen Hughes in the *New York Times* said the opera received a "smartly realized premiere" and was "charmingly" produced. He noted the expansive narrative was helped by three "Weavers of Legend" who served as a Greek chorus, and noted that a sequence set in New Orleans (which depicted a slave auction as well as evocations of a minstrel show and the Mardi Gras) was the evening's "most effective" number.

1390 Sail Away. THEATRE: Joan and Sanford I. Weill Recital Hall/Carnegie Hall; OPENING DATE: November 3, 1999; PERFORMANCES: 10; BOOK: Noel Coward; LYRICS: Noel Coward; MUSIC: Noel Coward; DIRECTION: Gerald Gutierrez; MUSICAL DIRECTION: Ben Whitelay; PRODUCER: Carnegie Hall

CAST—Jonathan Freeman (Joe, Ali), ELAINE STRITCH (Mimi Paragon), Bill Nolte (Elmer Candijack), Anne Allgood (Maimie Candijack), Paul Iacono (Alvin Lush), Alison Fraser (Mrs. Lush), Herb

Foster (Sir Gerard Nutfield), Gina Ferrall (Lady Nutfield), Jerry Lanning (Johnny Van Mier), Jane White (Mrs. Van Mier), James Patterson (Barnaby Slade), Jane Connell (Mrs. Sweeney), Gordon Connell (Mr. Sweeney), Marian Seldes (Elinor Spencer Bollard), Andrea Burns (Nancy Foyle), Passengers, Stewards, etc. (Danny Burstein, Tony Capone, Dale Hensley, Jennifer Kathryn Marshall, Bill Nolte), The Little Ones (Tanya Desko, Paul Iacono, Alexandra Jumper), Phyllis Gutierrez (Adlai)

The action occurs on board the S.S. *Coronia* and in various ports of call.

The musical was presented in two acts.

ACT ONE—"Come to Me" (Elaine Stritch, Stewards), "Sail Away" (Jerry Lanning), "Come to Me" (reprise) (Elaine Stritch), "Sail Away" (reprise) (Jerry Lanning, Company), "Where Shall I Find Him?" (Andrea Burns), "Beatnik Love Affair" (James Patterson), "Later Than Spring" (Jerry Lanning), "The Passenger's Always Right" (Jonathan Freeman, Stewards), "Useful Phrases" (Elaine Stritch), "Where Shall I Find Her?" (reprise) (James Patterson), "Go Slow, Johnny" (Jerry Lanning), "The Little Ones' ABC" (Elaine Stritch, Tanya Desko, Paul Iacono, Alexandra Jumper), "You're a Long, Long Way from America" (Elaine Stritch, Company)

ACT TWO—"The Customer's Always Right" (Jonathan Freeman, Arabs), "Something Very Strange" (Elaine Stritch), "Ballet (Italian Interlude)," "Don't Turn Away from Love" (Jerry Lanning), "Bronxville Darby and Joan" (Gordon Connell, Jane Connell), "When You Want Me" (Andrea Burns, James Patterson), "Later Than Spring" (reprise) (Elaine Stritch), "When You Want Me" (reprise) (Company), "Why Do the Wrong People Travel?" (Elaine Stritch)

NOTES—For Noel Coward's centenary, the limited-engagement revival of *Sail Away* in concert was a welcome surprise considering the musical hadn't been successful in its original Broadway and later London productions. The musical had first opened at the Broadhurst Theatre on October 3, 1961, and despite Coward's delightful score and a bouquet of critical valentines to Elaine Stritch as the harried seen-it-all social director of a luxury cruise ship, the musical played for a disappointing 167 performances. The London production opened at the Savoy Theatre in June 1962 with Stritch reprising her leading role, and while this version ran longer (252 performances), it too lost money. The score was recorded three times (the New York and London casts as well as a recording of the songs by Coward himself). The original Broadway cast album was released by Capitol Records (LP # SWAO-1643); was later reissued by Broadway Angel Records (CD # ZDM-0777-7-64759-2-9); and then again reissued, this time by DRG Records (CD # 19083); the latter reissue also included Coward's recordings of the songs. The London cast album was released by Stanyan Records (LP # 10027), and it was issued on CD by Fynsworth Alley Records (# 302-062-179-2). Coward's recording of the score were first released by Capitol Records (LP # SW-1667), which, as mentioned, was also included on the DRG release of the Broadway cast album.

An earlier version of the title song had appeared in Coward's 1950 London musical *Ace of Clubs*, and "Go Slow, Johnny" is a lyrical cousin to Coward's "Wait a Bit, Joe" from his 1945 London musical revue *Sigh No More*. "Bronxville Darby and Joan" was interpolated into the concert although it wasn't in the original New York production (it had been introduced in the London version).

1391 Saint Joan of the Stockyards. THEATRE: Encompass Theatre; OPENING DATE: May 24, 1978; PERFORMANCES: 20; TEXT: Naomi Replansky; translated from the original German by Bertolt Brecht; MUSIC: Paul Kazanoff; electronic music by George Quincy; DIRECTION: Jan P. Eliasberg; SCENERY: Tracy Killam; COSTUMES: Sally Lesser and Kathleen Smith; LIGHTING: Nick Hallick; MUSICAL DIRECTION: Miriam Charney; PRODUCER: Encompass Theatre (Nancy Rhodes, Artistic Director; Roger Cunningham, Producer); produced in association with Epic Construction Company

CAST—Valda Aviks (Martha), Ron Faber (Pierpont Mauler), Rick Friesen (Lennox), Barbara Hariday (Worker), Laurie Williams Howard (Clerk), David Keith (Cridle), Paul Ladenhelm (Mulberry), Joan MacIntosh (Worker), Christopher McCann (Detective), Joanne Pattavina (Buyer), Esther Rivlin (Graham), Robert Schlee (Gloomb), Joel Stevens (Worker) Will Patton

SOURCE—The play *Saint Joan of the Stockyards* by Bertolt Brecht (written between 1929 and 1931).

NOTES—The Off Off Broadway *Saint Joan of the Stockyards* was a self-described operetta based on Bertolt Brecht's satiric play *Die Heilise Johanna der Schlachthofe*, which found Brecht back in *Happy End* territory (see entry) with its Chicago location and a heroine (Joan Dark) who works for the Salvation Army (for the musical, it appears that the title character was also called Martha). Thomas Lask in the *New York Times* likened the musical to a "floundering ship" which sank Brecht, the play, the actors, and the audience. Lask indicated that Brecht's satiric thrusts were completely blunted by a production which had the "subtlety of a rock concert and the fine edge of a dynamite blast."

It appears that at one point during the run, Will Patton was in the cast.

Except for a radio telecast in 1932, it seems the play was never produced during Brecht's lifetime.

1392 Saints. THEATRE: Good Shepherd-Faith Church; OPENING DATE: June 30, 1976; PERFORMANCES: 10; BOOK: Merle Kessler; LYRICS: Merle Kessler; MUSIC: William Penn; DIRECTION: Edward Berkeley; CHOREOGRAPHY: Nora Peterson; MUSICAL DIRECTION: Bob Goldstone; PRODUCER: Musical Theatre Lab (Steve Kimball, Project Producer)

CAST—Jane Altman (Martha Harris), Dennis Bailey (Zeke), Ralph Bruneau (Elia Hancock), Yusef Bulos (Dr. MacIntire, Judge), Joanna Churgin (Cindie), Kathryn Cordes (Ann), Jill Eikenberry (Amy), Dann Florek (Will, Stone), Robin Groves (Ruthie, Mrs. Stone), Deborah Johnson (Loretta, Boo), Heather Lupton (Sarah), Bob Picardo (Ollie), Dean Pitchford (Badger Cleese), Nick Plakias (Aaron), Steve Pudenz (Pa, Governor), Terry Quinn (Joseph Tucker), Marti Rolph (Jemima), Tom Tofel (Eben, Mr. Seymour)

The musical was presented in two acts (division of acts and song assignments unknown; song list is in performance order).

MUSICAL NUMBERS—"I Am the Sign," "In the Sweet By and By," "Mama Lazarus," "I Can't Walk on Water," "The Old Rabbit Hole," "What Will Daddy Say?," "Stand by Me," "It's Hard I Know," "O My Soul," "Remember Love," "Death Comes Like a Thief," "Bastard for the Lord," "Night Is a Weapon," "The Ladies Come from Baltimore," "The Years Are Burning," "I Believe in Survival," "See the River Flow," "Let It Fall," "This Darkness," "Sweet Jesus, Blessed Savior"

NOTES—*Saints*, a religious-themed Off Off Broadway musical, played a limited engagement of ten performances. The cast included Jill Eikenberry, Dean Pitchford, Terry Quinn, and Marti Rolph.

1393 Salad Days. THEATRE: Barbizon-Plaza Theatre; OPENING DATE: November 10, 1958; PERFORMANCES: 80; BOOK: Julian Slade and Dorothy Reynolds; LYRICS: Julian Slade and Dorothy Reynolds; MUSIC: Julian Slade; DIRECTION: Barry Morse; CHOREOGRAPHY: Alan and Blanche Lund; SCENERY: Murray Laufer; COSTUMES: Clare Jeffrey; LIGHTING: David Hays; MUSICAL DIRECTION: Wilson Stone

CAST—Powys Thomas (Tramp, Butterfly Catcher, Police Inspector, Tom Smith), Barbara Franklin (Jane), Walter Burgess (Troppo, Barman), Richard Easton (Timothy/Tim), Gillie Fenwick (Mr. Dawes, Colonel, Chelsea Pensioner, Augustine Williams), Helen Burns (Aunt Prue, Fern, Rowena, Salvation Army Lass, Charmian, Spinster), Norma Renault (Lady Raeburn, Charlady, Tarty Lady, Asphinxia ["and other arms"], Spinster, Marguerite), Jack Creley (Bishop, Uncle Clam, Sailor, Night-Club Manager, Reporter, Uncle Zed), Mary Savidge (Mrs. Dawes, Heloise, Arty Lady, Hearty Lady, Spinster, Anthea), Eric Christmas (P.C. Boot, Drunk, Ambrose Gusset, Electrode), June Sampson (Manicurist, Bather, Ballet Girl, Fiona), Tom Kneebone (Fosdyke, Nigel Danvers, Chimney Sweep)

The action occurs at a university as well as in London, mainly in areas of Hyde Park and Kensington Gardens.

The musical was presented in two acts.

ACT ONE—Overture (Orchestra): "The Dons' Chorus" (a/k/a "The Things That Are Done by a Don") (The Dons, Barbara Franklin, Richard Easton), "We Said We Wouldn't Look Back" (Barbara Franklin, Richard Easton), "Find Yourself Something to Do" (Gillie Fenwick, Mary Savidge, Helen Burns, Richard Easton), "I Sit in the Sun" (Barbara Franklin), "Look At Me!" (Richard Easton, Barbara Franklin), "Look At Me!" (reprise) (People in the Park), "Hush-Hush" (Jack Creley, Tom Kneebone, Richard Easton), "Out of Breath" (Other People in the Park)

ACT TWO—"Cleopatra" (Jack Creley), "Sand in My Eyes" (Norma Renault), "It's Easy to Sing" (Barbara Franklin, Richard Easton, Tom Kneebone), "Let's Take a Stroll Through London" (Helen Burns, Eric Christmas, Walter Burgess), "We're Looking for a Piano" (More People in the Park), "The Time of My Life" (Barbara Franklin), "The Saucer Song" (Jack Creley, Richard Easton, Barbara Franklin, Eric Christmas), "We Don't Understand Our Children" (Gillie Fenwick, Norma Renault)

NOTES—*Salad Days* opened in London at the Vaudeville Theatre on August 5, 1954, and enjoyed a marathon run of 2,283 performances. Its New York run of ten weeks was a disappointment, but perhaps the plot, about a magical piano which can set people to dancing, was too twee for American tastes. Brooks Atkinson in the *New York Times* found the score pleasant enough, but noted the goings-on were "coy and gauche"; he further noted the musical's "amateur horseplay" worked against any inherent humor in the script.

The Off Broadway production was the only major American staging of the musical, but the score can be sampled on a number of recordings (see below). (Perhaps the outstanding number is the wistful "We Said We Wouldn't Look Back.") There were two additional musical sequences in the London production, following "We Don't Understand Our Children": a reprise of "Look at Me" (as "Oh, Look at Me!") for the Ensemble and a reprise of "We Said We Wouldn't Look Back" for Timothy and Jane. Although these numbers weren't listed in the Off Broadway program, they may have been performed.

The script was published by Samuel French (London) in 1961. The original British cast album was issued by Oriole Records (LP # MG-20004; also on Embassy Records LP # EMB-31046) and later on three CD releases: Sony West End Records (# SMK-66176), Sepia Records (# SEPIA-1061), and Must Close Saturday Records (# MCSR-3031); the latter recording included an excerpt of a live performance from the original London production. A 1976 British revival was recorded (That's Entertainment Records LP # TER-1018; Showstoppers Records CD # M-2-0759), and EMI Classics Records released a new

"40th Anniversary Recording" (CD # 7243-5-55200-2-9).

1394 The Salad of the Mad Café. THEATRE: Masque Theatre; OPENING DATE: March 31, 1964; PERFORMANCES: 16; WRITTEN BY: Danny Logan; DIRECTION: Danny Logan; SCENERY: Jim Rule; COSTUMES: Rita Bottomley; LIGHTING: Jim Rule; MUSICAL DIRECTION: Donald Chan; PRODUCERS: Ray Salerno and Danorm Productions

CAST— Danny Logan, Marguerite Davis, Susan Murphy, Mark Malone, Norman Farber

The revue was presented in two acts (sketch and song assignments unknown).

ACT ONE— Opening, "A Cocktail Party," "Dallas," "The Auditions," "Apartment for Rent," "Marlon of the Plaza," "The Salad of the Mad Café," "Makin' Whoopee," "Rolf Hochhuth Speaks," "Academy Awards," "The Suicide," "The Zulu Stomp"

ACT TWO—"Not Tonight," "This Was the Week That Wasn't," "Judy!," "DeGaulle," "Boy and Girl at the Movies," "Maggie," "Miss America," "A Poem," "Ann Devine," "Rex and Julie," "The Les Less Show," The Finale — A Medley of Current Hits

NOTES— Louis Funke in the *New York Times* found the topical revue *The Salad of the Mad Café* a "screamingly unfunny effort," with lame and often obvious targets (such as television, Judy Garland, and Charles de Gaulle). However, Funke praised the cast ("pleasant, as is usual in these cases") which performed (as is usual in these cases) "as though a Hollywood contract will be waiting at the curtain's fall." Alas, there was no Hollywood future for the five performers in *The Salad of the Mad Café*. But the revue sure had a great title.

1395 Salvation (March 1969). THEATRE: Village Gate; OPENING DATE: March 11, 1969; PERFORMANCES: 200 (estimated); BOOK: Peter Link and C.C. Courtney; LYRICS: Peter Link and C.C. Courtney; MUSIC: Peter Link and C.C. Courtney; DIRECTION: Peter Link and C.C. Courtney; SCENERY: Judy Fisher; COSTUMES: Stockyard of Grove Street; LIGHTING: Ed Fitzgerald (and Judy Fisher?); PRODUCER: Big Sandy Productions

CAST— C.C. Courtney, Edloe, Chapman Roberts, Marta Heflin, Joe Morton, Annie Rachel; The Nobody Else (musicians): Kirk Nurock, Igor Beruk, Charlie Brown, Eric Cohen, Wayne Fritchie

The musical was presented in one act.

MUSICAL NUMBERS—"Salvation" (C.C. Courtney, Company), "In Between" (Marta Heflin), "1001" (Chapman Roberts), "I Let the Moment Slip By" (Annie Rachel), "Daedalus" (Edloe), "Deuteronomy XVII Verse 2" (Joe Morton), "Forever" (Chapman Roberts, Joe Morton), "Footloose Youth and Fancy Free" (Chapman Roberts, Marta Heflin), "Let's Get Lost in Now" (Joe Morton, Company), "Stockhausen Potpourri" (Company), "If You Let Me Make Love to You Then Why Can't I Touch You" (Company), "Back to Genesis" (Company)

NOTES—*Salvation*, a self-described "enacted rock concert," played for over 200 performances, and in the fall reopened in a revised, expanded version (see entry). At least during its first weeks, the musical was performed on Tuesday, Wednesday, and Thursday evenings at 11:30; it appears that later the concert-like revue settled in for a regular eight-performance-week schedule.

Lawrence Van Gelder in the *New York Times* found the satire "sometimes sophomoric," but he liked the evening's "infectious reverence for music, lyrics and showmanship." He concluded by saying this is "one late show worth staying up for."

1396 Salvation (September 1969). "The New Rock Musical." THEATRE: Jan Hus Theatre; OPENING DATE: September 24, 1969; PERFORMANCES: 239; BOOK: Peter Link and C.C. Courtney; LYRICS: Peter Link and C.C. Courtney; MUSIC: Peter Link and C.C. Courtney; DIRECTION: Paul Aaron; CHOREOGRAPHY: Kirk Posin; SCENERY: Joan Larkey; COSTUMES: Joan Larkey; MUSICAL DIRECTION: Kirk Nurock; PRODUCER: David Black

CAST— Yolande Bavan (Ranee), Peter Link (Farley), C.C. Courtney (Monday), Joe Morton (Mark), Boni Enten (Boo), Annie Rachel (Diedre), Marta Heflin (Betty Lou), Chapman Roberts (LeRoy); Band: Nobody Else

The musical was presented in one act.

MUSICAL NUMBERS— Overture (Band), "Salvation" (C.C. Courtney, Yolande Bavan, Annie Rachel, Joe Morton, Marta Heflin), "In Between" (Marta Heflin, Annie Rachel, Yolande Bavan, Chapman Roberts), "1001" (Chapman Roberts), "Honest Confession Is Good for the Soul" (C.C. Courtney, Boni Enten, Peter Link, Company), "Ballin'" (Company), "Let the Moment Slip By" (Annie Rachel), "Gina" (Joe Morton, Peter Link, Company), "Stockhausen Potpourri" (Company), "If You Let Me Make Love to You Then Why Can't I Touch You" (Company), "There Ain't No Flies on Jesus" (Company, with vocal improvisations by Chapman Roberts, Peter Link, Joe Morton), "Deadalus" (Yolande Bavan), "Deuteronomy XVII Verse 2" (Joe Morton, Marta Heflin, with Yolande Bavan, Boni Enten, Annie Rachel), "For Ever" (Chapman Roberts, Joe Morton, with Marta Heflin, Yolande Bavan, Boni Enten, Annie Rachel), "Footloose Youth and Fancy-Free" (Boni Enten, Chapman Roberts), "Schwartz" (Company), "Let's Get Lost in Now" (Joe Morton, Company), "Back to Genesis" (Company), "Tomorrow Is the First Day of the Rest of My Life" (Peter Link, Company)

NOTES— The original production of *Salvation* (see entry) opened just a year after *Hair* (see entry) had transferred to Broadway, and already rock musicals were becoming tiresome. The expanded Off Broadway version of *Salvation* included all twelve songs from the original production and added five new ones. The score included "If You Let Me Make Love to You Then Why Can't I Touch You," which achieved brief popularity, but the mildly pleasant music couldn't compensate for a weak, revue-like storyline and trite lyrics.

Peter Link soon began writing solo efforts, but wasted his time composing pleasant if derivative background music (for the 1972 Public Theater production of *Much Ado About Nothing*) or incidental songs (for the ghastly *Lysistrata* [1972]). When he finally wrote a full-length Broadway musical, the 1978 flop *King of Hearts*, his score fell short of the mark, and for the most part he seems to have disappeared after that effort (except for an occasional Off Broadway foray, such as *The River* [see entry]).

Capitol Records released the *Salvation* cast album (LP # SO-337), and years later the recording was reissued first by Broadway Angel Records (CD # ZDM-7243-5-65170-2-8) and then by DRG Records (CD # 19087). The reissues included three previously-unreleased numbers from the generally forgettable score ("Overture," "Footloose Youth and Fancy Free," and "Schwartz"). Ironically, no extra material was found for the reissues of such Capitol Records cast albums as *The Music Man* (1957), *Sail Away* (1961), *The Gay Life* (1961), *Funny Girl* (1964), and other superior Broadway scores.

Mio International Records (LP # MUS-5009) released an album of songs from the score which included "Lost in the Catacombs," a number which may have been dropped during rehearsals or previews of one or the other of the two *Salvation* productions. Annie Rachel's program bio included an amusing in-joke; she listed *Half a Sixpence* [1965], *Hallelujah, Baby!* [1967] ... and *Springtime for Hitler* among her credits. (Had she been one of the chorus members in the "Springtime for Hitler" sequence in *The Producers* [1967] when it was filmed at the now-demolished Playhouse Theatre?)

During the run, Bette Midler replaced Marta Heflin, and her program bio mentioned her performance in the Off Off Broadway *Cinderella Revisited*, which, she noted, was a musical "for nine-year-old gay boys."

1397 Sambo. "A Black Opera with White Spots." THEATRE: The Public Theatre; OPENING DATE: December 12, 1969; PERFORMANCES: 37; BOOK: Ron Steward; LYRICS: Ron Steward; MUSIC: Ron Steward; DIRECTION: Gerald Freedman; SCENERY: Ming Cho Lee, Marjorie Kellogg; COSTUMES: Milo Morrow; LIGHTING: Martin Aronstein; MUSICAL DIRECTION: Neal Tate; PRODUCER: The New York Shakespeare Festival

CAST— Ron Steward (Sambo), Camille Yarbrough (Tiger), Rob Barnes (Tiger), Jenny O'Hara (Tiger), Robert La Tourneaux (Tiger), Sid Marshall (Tiger), Henry Baker (Tiger), Gerri Dean (Untogether Cinderella), Janice Lynne Montgomery (Miss Sally Muffat), Kenneth Carr (Little Boy Blue), George Turner (Jack Horney), Hattie Winston (Bo Peep)

The action occurs "here" at the present time.

The musical was presented in two acts.

ACT ONE—"Sing a Song of Sambo" (Ron Steward), "Hey Boy" (Camille Yarbrough, Rob Barnes, Jenny O'Hara, Robert La Tourneaux, Sid Marshall, Henry Baker), "I Am Child" (Ron Steward, Friends), "Young Enough to Dream" (Ronn Steward, Company), "Mama Always Said" (Camille Yarbrough, Rob Barnes, Jenny O'Hara, Robert La Tourneaux, Sid Marshall, Henry Baker, Hattie Winston, Kenneth Carr, Janice Lynne Montgomery, George Turner, Gerri Dean), "Baddest Mammyjammy" (Ron Steward, Company), "Sambo Was a Bad Boy" (Company), "Pretty Flower" (Company), "I Could Dig You" (Ron Steward, Gerri Dean), "Do You Care Too Much" (Company), "Be Black" (Company, with Henry Baker, Camille Yarbrough), "Let's Go Down" (Kenneth Carr, Janice Lynne Montgomery, Hattie Winston, George Turner)

ACT TWO—"Astrology" (Company), "The Eternal Virgin" (Hattie Winston), "Boy Blue" (Kenneth Carr), "The Piscean" (Janice Lynne Montgomery), "Aries" (George Turner), "Untogether Cinderella" (Gerri Dean), "Peace Love and Good Damn" (Ron Steward), "Come on Home" (George Turner, Company), "Black Man" (Company), "Get an Education" (Camille Yarbrough), "Ask and You Shall Receive" (Jenny O'Hara, Robert La Tourneaux), "Son of Africa" (Ron Steward, Company), "I Am a Child" (reprise) (Ron Steward, Company)

NOTES—*Sambo* was the second of the Public's three protest musicals during the 1969-1970 season (see entries for *Stomp* and *Mod Donna*). The opera dealt in episodic fashion with a Black man's sense of alienation in a world of "white spots." Mel Gussow in the *New York Times* felt the piece was rather pretentious and not fully realized; he noted the Sambo myth was only occasionally referenced and that the libretto never followed through on the famous story. Gussow indicated the opera's earlier subtitle ("A Nigguh Opera with Motown Sound as Told by The Supremes to Doris Day") was intriguing. (Did the original concept propose to the tell the story of Sambo to a White audience through forms of stylized popular Black music?) *Sambo* closed after five weeks, but the following summer a revised version was presented by the New York Shakespeare Festival Mobile Theatre. The musical played in public parks and playgrounds in New York City's five boroughs beginning on July 14, for a total of twenty-two performances; the earlier version didn't seem to credit a choreographer, but the revised musical credited Tommy Jonsen with the choreography. Howard Thompson in the *New York Times* reported that the new version was a one-hour "streamlined condensation" of the original production, and instead of twelve performers, there were seven (including two from the original cast [Ron Steward and George Turner]) and fifteen of the original twenty-four songs were retained. Thompson said the score was "rich" and "rhythmical," and singled out three songs ("Black Man," "I Could Dig You," and "Pretty Flower," the latter the evening's "loveliest melody").

1398 Sancocho. THEATRE: LuEsther Hall/The Public Theatre; OPENING DATE: March 28, 1979; PERFORMANCES: 7; BOOK: Ramiro (Ray) Ramirez; LYRICS: Jimmy Justice and Ramiro (Ray) Ramirez; MUSIC: Jimmy Justice and Ramiro (Ray) Ramirez; DIRECTION: Miguel Godreau; CHOREOGRAPHY: Miguel Godreau; SCENERY: Frank J. Boros; COSTUMES: Frank J. Boros; LIGHTING: Nananne Porcher; MUSICAL DIRECTION: Jimmy Justice; PRODUCER: The New York Shakespeare Festival (Joseph Papp, Director)

CAST—Hector Jaime Mercado (Raul Sanchez), Dan Strayhorn (Don, Janitor, Rudolph Davis III), Jerry Griffin (Ed), Arturo Rafael Puerto (Papi), Ramiro (Ray) Ramirez (Saguita, Mr. Sanchez), Guillermo Gonzalez (The Cabasa Player), Pamela Pilkenton (Bag Lady, Oggun [The God in Green, The Fourth God], Miss Tucker, Nun), Stephen DeGhelder (Mr. Brown, Flasher, Jerry Fleischer, Priest, Orunla [The Sixth God), Antonio Iglesias (Junkie, Flag Vendor, Eleggua [The Third God]), M.W. Reid (Black Dude, Chango [The Black God, The Second God], Bubba, Witch Doctor), Kenneth Frett (Guard, Announcer), Bryan Nicholas (Hippie, Hot Dog Man), Marzetta Jones (Bible Lady), Avery Sommers (Mattie, Carrie), Terri Lombardozzi (Hooker, Late Student, Oshun [The Fifth God]), Ellis Williams (Drunk, Chief, the Reverend McCook), Ka-Ron Brown (Valerie McCook, The Chief's Daughter), Teresa Yenque (Mrs. Sanchez), Ramon Franco (Young Raul Sanchez), Beth Shorter (Obatala [The God in White, The First God], Mrs. Mapp), Haru Aki (Yemaya [The God in Blue, The Seventh God], Miss Conley), Cintia Cruz (Margarita, The Singer, La Prena), Fred C. Mann III (Half Percenter [A Slave Trader]), Russell Blake (Toro), Jimmy Justice (Angel), Mario Rivera (Mario); Kenneth Frett and Marzetta Jones (Pit Singers)

The action occurs in the mid-1960s to the present time, in New York City.

The musical was presented in two acts.

ACT ONE—"The First Jam Session" (Hector Jaime Mercado, Dan Strayhorn, Ramiro [Ray] Ramirez, Jerry Griffin, The Band), "The Rhythm of the Line" (Company), "You Can Beat the System" (Hector Jaime Mercado, Marzetta Jones, Bryan Nichols, Avery Sommers, M.W. Reid, Terri Lombardozzi, The Company), "The Arrival" (Ramiro [Ray] Ramirez, Teresa Yenque, Ramon Franco), "The Purification" (Ramiro [Ray] Ramirez, Teresa Yenque, Ramon Franco, Guillermo Gonzalez, Beth Shorter, Pamela Pilkenton, Haru Aki, M.W. Reid), "My Country 'Tis of Thee" (Avery Sommers, Guillermo Gonzalez, Students), "The Slave Scene" (M.W. Reid, Ellis Williams, Cintia Cruz, Pamela Pilkenton, Stephen DeGhelder, Ka-Ron Brown, Fred C. Mann III, Company), "Ay Mi Dio" (Cintia Cruz, Stephen DeGhelder, Company), "Get Off on Somebody Else" (Avery Sommers, Company)

ACT TWO—"The Second Jam Session" (Hector Jaime Mercado, Russell Blake, Dan Strayhorn, Ramiro [Ray] Ramirez, Arturo Rafael Puerto, Jimmy Justice, Mario Rivera, The Band), In the Disco: "Give Me the Love" (Hector Jaime Mercado, Ka-Ron Brown, Company), "The Singer" (Dan Strayhorn, with Kenneth Frett and Avery Sommers), "The Chair Dance" (Company), "I Don't Want to Hear No But, But, But" (Ellis Williams, Ka-Ron Brown), "Las Siete Potencias and Despoho" (Hector Jaime Mercado, Beth Shorter, M.W. Reid, Antonio Iglesias, Pamela Pilkenton, Terri Lombardozzi, Stephen DeGhelder, Haru Aki, Guillermo Gonzalez), "The Love Duet" (Hector Jaime Mercado, Ka-Ron Brown), "Danza and Danzon" (Company), "Touch Me" (Company), "Sancocho" (Company), "The Going Out" (The Band)

NOTES—The Public Theatre's *Sancocho* dealt with the assimilation of Puerto Ricans into New York City, and for a change compared Puerto Rican culture with Black, not White, culture; as an added fillip, the plot centered around a *Romeo and Juliet*-styled love affair between a young Puerto Rican (Hector Jaime Mercado) and a Black (Ra-Kon Brown).

The critics praised the score and the spectacular dancing; however, they found fault with the book, and Douglas Watt in the *New York Daily News* noted that while the word "sancocho" meant "stew," in the context of the episodic book, the word must mean "mishmash." But there was a clear consensus that if the book were reshaped, the musical might be another *A Chorus Line* (see entry). The critics indicated the score and the choreography were too good to vanish, and so it seemed the musical would surely resurface in a revised version. But, like the Public's *The Umbrellas of Cherbourg* (see entry), which also opened during the 1978-1979 season, *Sancocho* was seen only downtown, and never found its way to Broadway. It seems a shame, for *Sancocho* appears to be a hidden treasure among 1970s musicals.

A few months before the musical's premiere, Carol Lawson in the *New York Times* reported that Joseph Papp announced the production would be directed by Mike Nichols; however, Miguel Godreau directed (and choreographed) the musical. Lawson also reported that *Sancocho* "grew out of " an earlier play by Ramiro (Ray) Ramirez called *Mondongo*, which had been produced by the Public Theatre two years earlier as part of its Mobile Theatre unit (*Mondongo* had also been produced at the New Federal Theatre in May 1976).

1399 Sandhog. "A Ballad in Three Acts." THEATRE: Phoenix Theatre; OPENING DATE: November 29, 1954; PERFORMANCES: 48; BOOK: Waldo Salt; LYRICS: Waldo Salt; MUSIC: Earl Robinson; DIRECTION: Howard da Sylva; CHOREOGRAPHY: Sophie Maslow; SCENERY: Howard Bay; COSTUMES: Toni Ward; LIGHTING: Howard Bay; MUSICAL DIRECTION: Ben Steinberg; PRODUCERS: The Phoenix Theatre (T. Edward Hambleton and Norris Houghton), by special arrangement with Rachel Productions (Howard da Sylva and Arnold Perl)

CAST—Kids (Sandy, David Winters; Small Fry, Eliot Feld; Girl with a Ball, Betty Ageloff; Ring Leader, Yukiro; Red, Muriel Mannings), John Carter (Air Lock Foreman), David Hooks (Night Shift Foreman), Leon Bibb (Sam on the Stick), Mordecai Bauman (Henderson), Robert De Cormier (Policeman), Douglas Collins (Bill Cayton), JACK CASSIDY (Johnny O'Sullivan), Paul Ukena (Fred Burger), Michael Kermoyan (Joe Novak), Rodester Timmons (Andy Cayton), DAVID BROOKS (Tim Cavanaugh), BETTY OAKES (Katie O'Sullivan), Gordon Dilworth (Sharkey), ALICE GHOSTLEY (Sheila Cavanaugh), Mary Kane (Mary Novak), Mareda Gaither (Ginny Cayton), Sandhogs and Sandhogs' Wives (Stephanie Scourby, Mitzi Wilson, Doree Simmons, Peter Maravell, Elliot Freeman)

SOURCE—The 1908 short story "St. Columba and the River" by Theodore Dreiser.

The action occurs at the North River Tunnel Works and the surrounding neighborhood in downtown New York in the late 1880s.

The musical was presented in three acts.

ACT ONE—"Come Down" (Chorus), "Some Said They Were Crazy" (Chorus), "Stand Back" (Robert De Cormier), "Hey Joe" (Kids), "Johnny's Cursing Song" (Jack Cassidy), "Come and Be Married" (Betty Ageloff), "Johnny-O" (Jack Cassidy, Betty Oakes), "Good Old Days" (Gordon Dilworth, Kids), "Song of the Bends" (David Brooks, Paul Ukena, Michael Kermoyan, Rodester Timmons), "By the Glenside" (Alice Ghostley), "High Air" (Chorus), "Work Song" (David Brooks, Paul Ukena, Leon Bibb), "28 Men" (Chorus)

ACT TWO—"Sandhog Song" (Mordecai Bauman, Chorus, Kids), "Sweat Song" (David Brooks), "Fugue on a Hot Afternoon in a Small Flat" (David Brooks, Jack Cassidy, Alice Ghostley, Betty Oakes), "T-w-i-n-s" (Quartet: David Brooks, Paul Ukena, Rodester Timmons, Michael Kermoyan), "Katie O'Sullivan" (Quartet: David Brooks, Paul Ukena, Rodester Timmons, Michael Kermoyan; Gordon Dilworth, Kids), "Johnny-O" (reprise and counter melody) (Jack Cassidy, Betty Oakes), "28 Men" (reprise) (Chorus), "High Air" (reprise) (Chorus), "Some Said They Were Crazy" (reprise) (Chorus), "Sing Sorrow" (Chorus), "You Want to Mourn" (Alice Ghostley, Stephanie Scourby, Mitzi Wilson, Doree Simmons)

ACT THREE—"Ma, Ma, Where's My Dad?" (Kids' song and dance), "Greathead Shield" (Douglas Collins, Kids), "Waiting for the Men" (Alice Ghostley, Mary Kane, Mareda Gaither), "28 Men" (Reprise) (Chorus), "Greathead Shield" (reprise) (Leon Bibb), "Ring Iron" (Chorus), "Johnny's Cursing Song" (reprise) (Jack Cassidy), "Stand Back" (Chorus, Robert De Cormier), "Johnny-O" (reprise and counter melody) (Jack Cassidy, Betty Oakes), "Oh, Oh, Oh, O'Sullivan" (Paul Ukena, Rodester Timmons, Michael Kermoyan, Douglas Collins), Finale: "Sandhog Song" (Chorus)

NOTES—Theodore Dreiser based his short story "St. Columba and the River" on an actual event which took place in 1905 under the East River during the construction of the tunnels for the New York subway system. According to the liner notes of the fascinating *Sandhog* recording (see information below), a tunnel worker (or "sandhog" [the Johnny O'Sullivan role in the musical, played by Jack Cassidy]) was working in the highly compressed air of a subway tunnel when he was suddenly blown through the roof of the tunnel and then continued to catapult upwards as his body forced its way up through the river bottom above the subway tunnel. He then continued shooting upward through the depths of river, when, suddenly and miraculously, he emerged on the water's surface, relatively unscathed.

Sandhog was the second musical produced by the Phoenix, and although it received some respectable reviews, it closed after its limited Off Broadway engagement. The Phoenix had lost money on the Broadway transfer of *The Golden Apple* (see entry), and it didn't want to risk another financial loss, especially since *Sandhog*, like its predecessor, was another esoteric musical, virtually sung-through and with unusual subject matter. So for *Sandhog* there was no Broadway transfer, no cast album, no published script, and certainly no awards. Today the work is forgotten, and what a pity, because of all 1950s musicals (Off Broadway and on), *Sandhog* is at the top of the list of those deserving re-discovery. With one of the most ambitious scores in all musical theatre, *Sandhog* deserves a second chance by opera companies, regional theatres, and groups which specialize in concert adaptations (such as *Encores!* [see entry]).

In 1956, the Vanguard Recording Society released a composer-and-lyricist demo (VRS-9001) of many of the musical numbers (Earl Robinson sang and played the piano, and Waldo Salt narrated). The recording reveals a highly melodic score, with superb lyrics. "Johnny-O" is an achingly beautiful ballad; "Fugue on a Hot Afternoon in a Small Flat" is a brilliant piece of theatre writing; and other songs, such as "Sweat Song," "Song of the Bends," and "Johnny's Cursing Song," are incisive numbers.

1400 The Sap of Life. "A Musical." THEATRE: One Sheridan Square; OPENING DATE: October 2, 1961; PERFORMANCES: 49; BOOK: Richard Maltby, Jr., in collaboration with William Francisco; LYRICS: Richard Maltby, Jr.; MUSIC: David Shire; DIRECTION: William Francisco; SCENERY: John Conklin; COSTUMES: John Conklin; LIGHTING: Peter Hunt; MUSICAL DIRECTION: Julian Stein; PRODUCER: Quartet Productions (Lewis Lloyd, Mary Jean Parson, and William Francisco)

CAST— Kenneth Nelson (Andrew), Jerry Dodge (Horatio), Jack Bittner (Oscar, Their Father, The Boss), Dina Paisner (Jessie, Their Mother), Patricia Bruder (Ruthanne, The Neighbor's Girl), Lilian Fields (Dot, The Old Aunt), Lee Powell (Sally Ann, Another Neighbor's Girl)

The action occurs in the present, at Home and in the City.

The musical was presented in two acts.

ACT ONE—"Saturday Morning" (Kenneth Nelson, Jerry Dodge), "Farewell, Family" (Kenneth Nelson, The Family), "Charmed Life" (Kenneth Nelson, Jerry Dodge), "Fill Up Your Cup with Sunshine" (The Office Family), "Good Morning" (Patricia Bruder, Kenneth Nelson), "Watching the Big Parade Go By" (Jerry Dodge), "The Love of Your Life" (Kenneth Nelson, Jerry Dodge, The Family)

ACT TWO—"A Hero's Love" (Kenneth Nelson, Patricia Bruder), "Children Have It Easy" (Kenneth Nelson, Lilian Fields), "She Loves Me Not" (Jerry Dodge, Lee Powell, Kenneth Nelson), "Mind Over Matter" (Jack Bittner), "Time and Time Again" (Patricia Bruder), Finale (Kenneth Nelson, The Family)

NOTES— The short-lived *The Sap of Life* marked the New York debut of the team of Richard Maltby, Jr., and David Shire, who, unfortunately, never found much in the way of popular success in their collaborations. The musical dealt with Andrew (Kenneth Nelson), a young man who leaves home to find his way in the big city. Once there, he finds a job in which his co-workers mysteriously resemble all the family members he left behind in his small hometown (his parents have concocted a plan in which his office "family" are in effect his actual family). Howard Taubman in the *New York Times* felt the musical wasn't all that confusing if one ignored naturalism and embraced the "fantasy" of the libretto. He noted that the plot wasn't always successful, but when it worked it had "appealing quality and taste." Further, he found the direction and the performances in keeping with the "non-realistic mood" of the piece and said Maltby and Shire's score was "the most attractive element" of the evening (a score "unusually ingenious and sophisticated," numbers of "touching refinement and shining verve"). Two of Maltby and Shire's musicals, *How Do You Do I Love You* (1967) and *Love Match* (1968), closed prior to Broadway; and their two musicals to reach New York, *Baby* (1983) and *Big* (1996), were failures. Their greatest successes together were Off Broadway retrospectives of their music. *Starting Here, Starting Now* (1977; see entry), which included one number from *The Sap of Life* ("Watching the Big Parade Go By"), played for three months and enjoyed a long life in regional theatre. *Closer Than Ever* (1989; see entry) played for almost three-hundred performances and was their longest-running New York musical (the revue included one song from *The Sap of Life*, "She Loves Me Not"). Both revues, as well as *Baby* and *Big*, were recorded.

Maltby had considerable success elsewhere. He conceived and directed *Ain't Misbehavin'* (1978; see entry); he directed and wrote the American adaptation as well as additional lyrics for Andrew Lloyd Webber's *Song and Dance* (1985); and he co-scripted and wrote the English lyrics for *Miss Saigon* (1989, London; 1991, New York).

The Sap of Life was first seen at the Adams Memorial Theater in Williamstown, Massachusetts, on August 22, 1961, and the cast members included Ken Kercheval (Andrew), James Bateman (Horatio), and Charles Kimbrough (Oscar, Their father, and The Boss). Numbers included in this production which were deleted prior to New York were "The Willowart Family Song," "Hanky-Panky," "Go Through the Motions," and "Andrew's Verse."

The Off Broadway production was recorded, but according to the liner notes for the cast album released by Blue Pear Records, for many years the score was available only on tape; it wasn't until the Blue Pear release that the score was made available on LP (# BP-1002). Numbers on the LP which aren't in the New York program are "Arrival in the City" and "Introduction, Act Two."

1401 Sarafina! THEATRE: The Mitzi E. Newhouse Theatre/Lincoln Center Theatre; OPENING DATE: October 25, 1987; PERFORMANCES: 81; TEXT: Mbongeni Ngema; MUSIC: Mbongeni Ngema and Hugh Masekela; DIRECTION: Mbongeni Ngema; CHOREOGRAPHY: Mbongeni Ngema (?); Ndaba Mhlongo, Additional Choreography; SCENERY: Sarah Roberts; COSTUMES: Sarah Roberts; LIGHTING: Mannie Manim; PRODUCERS: Lincoln Center Theatre (Gregory Mosher, Director; Bernard Gersten, Executive Director) presents a Committed Artists production

CAST— Pat Mlaba (Colgate), Lindiwe Dlamini (Teaspoon), Dumisani Dlamini (Crocodile), Congo Hadebe (Silence), Nhlanhla Ngema (Stimela Sase-Zola), Mhlathi Khuzwayo (S'Ginci), Leleti Khumalo (Sarafina), Baby Cele (Mistress It's a Pity); Other Students (Khumbuzile Dlamini, Ntomb'Khona Dlamini, Lindiwe Hlengwa, Zandile Hlengwa, Sibiniso Khumalo, Cosmas Mahlaba, Thandani Mavimbela, Nonhlanhla Mbambo, Linda Mchunu, Mubi Mofokeng, Nandi Ndlovu, Thandekile Nhlanhla, Pumi Shelembe, Kipizane Skweyiya, Thandi Zulu

The action occurs in Morris Isaacson High School in South Africa.

The musical was presented in two acts (song assignments unknown).

ACT ONE— Overture, "Zibuyile Emasisweni (It's Finally Happening)," "Niyayibona Lento Engiybonayo (Do You See What I See?)," "Sarafina," "The Lord's Prayer," "Yes! Mistress It's a Pity," "Give Us Power," "Afunani Amaphoyisa eSoweto (What Is the Army Doing in Soweto?)," "Nkosi Sikeleli'Afrika," "Freedom Is Coming Tomorrow"

ACT TWO— Entr'acte, "Excuse Me Baby"; "Please If You Don't Mind Baby"; "Thank You," "Talking About Love," "Meeting Tonight," "We Are Guerrillas," "Uyamemeza Ungoma," "We Will Fight for Our Land," "Mama," "Sechaba," "Isizwe (The Nation Is Dying)," "Kilimanjaro," "Africa Burning in the Sun," "Stimela Sasezola," "Olayithi (It's All Right)," "Bring Back Nelson Mandela," "Wololo!"

NOTES— The musical *Sarafina!* was first produced in Johannesburg in June 1987 and dealt with a group of South African high school students performing a play about Black political issues in their nation (apartheid, Nelson Mandela, the Soweto uprising).

The musical transferred to Broadway on January 28, 1988, where it played at the Cort Theatre for 597 performances. The cast recording was released by RCA Victor Records (LP # 9307-1-RC). A film version (as *Sarafina! The Sound of Freedom*) was released by Miramax in 1992, and its soundtrack was issued by Qwest/Warner Brothers Records (CD # 9-45060-2).

During previews at Lincoln Center, "Love Thy Neighbor" and "Market Place" were deleted.

1402 Sarita. THEATRE: INTAR Theatre; OPENING DATE: January 18, 1984; PERFORMANCES: 35; BOOK: Maria Irene Fornes; LYRICS: Maria Irene Fornes; MUSIC: Leon Odenz; DIRECTION: Maria Irene Fornes; SCENERY: Donald Eastman; COSTUMES: Gabriel Berry; LIGHTING: Anne E. Militello; MUSICAL DIRECTION: Leon Odenz; PRODUCER: International Arts Relations (Max Ferra, Artistic Director; Dennis Ferguson-Acosta, Managing Director)

CAST— Blanca Camacho (Yeye), Sheila Dabney (Sarita), Carmen Rosario (Fela), Rodolfo Diaz (Fernando), Michael Carmine (Julio), Tom Kirk (Marc), Juan Vega (Jose)

The action occurs in the South Bronx from 1939 to 1949.

The musical was presented in two acts.

ACT ONE—"He Was Thinking of You" (Blanca Camacho), "I'm Pudding" (Sheila Dabney), "Holy Spirit, Good Morning" (Sheila Dabney, Blanca Camacho), "I'm Lonely" (Rodolfo Diaz, Carmen Rosario, Sheila Dabney), "A Woman Like You" (Carmen Rosario), "Lo Que Me Gusta a Mi" (Performer[s] unknown), "You Are Tahiti" (Tom Kirk)

ACT TWO—"A Little Boo Boo" (Sheila Dabney, Carmen Rosario), "To Ochun" (Juan Vega, Rodolfo Diaz, Chorus), "His Wonderful Eye" (Tom Kirk), "Here Comes the Night" (Sheila Dabney, Michael Carmine), "Papi No" (Sheila Dabney), "The Letter" (Tom Kirk, Blanca Camacho, Sheila Dabney)

NOTES— The slightly revised script of the Off Off Broadway musical *Sarita* was published in 1986 by PAJ Publications in the volume *Maria Irene Fornes/Plays*. In the script, the song "Lo Que Me Gusta a Mi" is omitted; the character of Marc is identified as "Mark"; the song "To Ochun" is titled "Ofe Isia"; and the role of Jose (which seems to have been performed by Juan Vega in the stage production) is renamed Juan (and an actor named Bambu now credited with playing the role).

1403 Saturday Night. THEATRE: 2econd Stage Theatre; OPENING DATE: February 17, 2000; PERFORMANCES: 45; BOOK: Julius J. Epstein; LYRICS: Stephen Sondheim; MUSIC: Stephen Sondheim; DIRECTION: Kathleen Marshall; CHOREOGRAPHY: Kathleen Marshall; SCENERY: Derek McLane; COSTUMES: Catherine Zuber; LIGHTING: Donald Holder; MUSICAL DIRECTION: Rob Fisher; PRODUCER: Second Stage Theatre (Carole Rothman, Artistic Director; Carol Fishman, Managing Director; Alexander Fraser, Executive Director)

CAST— Michael Benjamin Washington (Ted), Kirk McDonald (Artie), Greg Zola (Ray), Joey Sorge (Dino), Christopher Fitzgerald (Bobby), Andrea Burns (Celeste), Clarke Thorell (Hank), David Campbell (Gene), Frank Vlastnik (Pinhead), Rachel Ulanet (Mildred), Donald Corren (Vocalist, Mr. Fletcher), Michael Pemberton (Plaza Attendant, Clune), Lauren Ward (Helen), David A. White (Mr. Fisher, Waiter, Lieutentant), Natascia A. Diaz (Florence, Dakota Doran)

SOURCE— The unproduced play *Front Porch in Flatbush* by Julius J. Epstein and Philip G. Epstein.

The action occurs in pre-Depression 1929 in both Brooklyn and Manhattan.

The musical was presented in two acts.

ACT ONE— Overture (Orchestra), "Saturday Night" (Michael Benjamin Washington, Kirk McDonald, Greg Zola, Joey Sorge), "Class" (David Campbell, Clarke Thorell, Andrea Burns, Christopher Fitzgerald, Michael Benjamin Washington, Kirk McDonald, Joey Sorge), "Delighted, I'm Sure" (Andrea Burns, Rachel Ulanet, Clarke Thorell, Christopher Fitzgerald, Michael Benjamin Washington, Kirk McDonald, Greg Zola, Joey Sorge), "Love's a Bond" (Donald Corren), "Isn't It?" (Lauren Ward), "In the Movies" (Michael Benjamin Washington, Kirk McDonald, Greg Zola, Joey Sorge, Clarke

Thorell, Andrea Burns, Rachel Ulanet), "Exhibit A" (Christopher Fitzgerald), "A Moment with You" (David Corren, David Campbell, Lauren Ward), "Saturday Night" (reprise) (Michael Benjamin Washington, Kirk McDonald, Greg Zola, Joey Sorge), "Gracious Living Fantasy" (David Campbell, The Gang), "Montana Chem." (Michael Benjamin Washington, Kirk McDonald, Greg Zola, Joey Sorge, Clarke Thorell, Andrea Burns), "So Many People" (Lauren Ward, David Campbell), "One Wonderful Day" (Andrea Burns, Clarke Thorell, Christopher Fitzgerald, Rachel Ulanet, Natascia A. Diaz, Michael Benjamin Washington, Kirk McDonald, Greg Zola, Joey Sorge)

ACT TWO—Entr'acte (Orchestra), "Saturday Night" (reprise) (Michael Benjamin Washington, Kirk McDonald, Greg Zola, Joey Sorge), "I Remember That" (Clarke Thorell, Andrea Burns), "'Love's a Bond' Blues" (Natascia A. Diaz), "All for You" (Lauren Ward), "That Kind of Neighborhood" (Clarke Thorell, Andrea Burns, Rachel Ulanet, Natascia A. Diaz, Christopher Fitzgerald, Michael Benjamin Washington, Kirk McDonald, Greg Zola, Joey Sorge), "What More Do I Need?" (David Campbell, Lauren Ward, Clarke Thorell, Andrea Burns, Rachel Ulanet, Natascia A. Diaz, Christopher Fitzgerald, Michael Benjamin Washington, Kirk McDonald, Greg Zola, Joey Sorge, Michael Pemberton, David A. White), "One Wonderful Day" (reprise) (Company)

NOTES—Written in 1954 and based upon an unproduced play called *Front Porch in Flatbush* by Julius J. Epstein and Philip G. Epstein, *Saturday Night* was scheduled to be produced by Lemuel Ayers during the 1955-1956 Broadway season in what would have been Stephen Sondheim's Broadway debut. Among Ayers' credits was his scenery for the original Broadway production of *Oklahoma!* in 1943; and besides designing the scenery and costumes for the original Broadway production of *Kiss Me, Kate* in 1948, he was also that musical's co-producer. And with Howard Koch, the Epstein brothers had written the script for the 1942 film *Casablanca*, winning the Academy Award for Best Screenplay. *Saturday Night* was poised for a tryout in New Haven beginning on September 12, 1955, but with Ayers' untimely death on August 14, 1955, the production was cancelled. In 1959, the musical was again announced for production, this time around under the aegis of Jule Styne and Joseph Kipness; further, Bob Fosse was hired as director and choreographer. The musical seems to have been originally announced for the 46th Street (now Richard Rodgers) Theatre, but ultimately the 54th Street Theatre was booked for a January 21, 1960, opening. But in August 1959 the production was cancelled for the second time. Sam Zolotow in the *New York Times* reported that Styne and Kipness announced the show's capitalization would be returned to the backers, and their suspect explanation for the cancellation was that there "were extreme difficulties in casting the major roles." But perhaps a little more light was shed upon the matter when Zolotow reported there were "complications" with Sondheim, the latter of whom "acknowledged there had been problems, but refused to discuss them." Zolotow added that those associated with the show wouldn't predict if the musical would later be produced "under more favorable circumstances." (With the cancellation of *Saturday Night*, the 54th Street Theatre quickly booked *Happy Town*; it lasted for three performances, and was the shortest-running musical of the 1959-1960 season.) Like the unproduced play upon which it was based, *Saturday Night* also seemed destined to never know a staged production (but songs from the score occasionally surfaced in various Sondheim tributes and compilation recordings). However, in 1997, some forty-two years after it had first been announced for production, the musical finally enjoyed a staging when it was produced by the Bridewell Theatre Company in London. Theatregoers finally had a chance to see the most elusive of Sondheim's musicals.

The London production was followed by the 1999 American premiere in Chicago by the Pegasus Players of Chicago (in a somewhat revised version which included two new songs written by Sondheim especially for the production ["Montana Chem" and "Delighted, I'm Sure"]), and in 2000 the musical was finally seen in New York.

Both the London and New York productions were recorded (the former on First Night Records [CD # CD-65; also issued by First Night/RCA Victor Records CD # 09026-633182], the latter on Nonesuch Records [CD # 79609-2]); the Nonesuch recording included "Montana Chem." and "Delighted, I'm Sure."

Saturday Night told the story of a group of young people who dream of becoming rich in pre-Depression New York City. The slight story didn't get in the way of a host of charming songs, including the comic "In the Movies," the satiric "Love's a Bond," and the haunting ballad "All for You."

1404 Saturn Returns: A Concert. THEATRE: LuEsther Hall/The Joseph Papp Public Theatre; OPENING DATE: March 31, 1997; PERFORMANCES: 16; LYRICS: Adam Guettel; MUSIC: Adam Guettel; DIRECTION: Tina Landau; SCENERY: James Schuette; COSTUMES: James Schuette; LIGHTING: Blake Burba; MUSICAL DIRECTION: Ted Sperling; PRODUCER: The New York Shakespeare Festival (George C. Wolfe, Producer; Rosemarie Tichler, Artistic Producer; Mark Litvin, Managing Director; Wiley Hausam and Bonnie Metzgar, Associate Producers)

CAST—Vivian Cherry, Lawrence Clayton, Annie Golden, Jose Llana, Theresa McCarthy, Bob Stillman

The song-cycle was presented in one act.

MUSICAL NUMBERS—"Saturn Returns: The Flight" (Company), "Icarus" (Bob Stillman, Jose Llana, Company), "Migratory V" (Theresa McCarthy), "Jesus the Mighty Conqueror" (lyric adapted from *The Temple Trio* [Hymn Edition, 1886]) (Lawrence Clayton, Vivian Cherry, Jose Llana, Bob Stillman), "Pegasus" (lyric by Ellen Fitzhugh) (Bob Stillman, Annie Golden, Theresa McCarthy), "Children of the Heavenly King" (lyric adapted from *The Temple Trio* [Hymn Edition, 1886]) (Vivian Cherry), "At the Sounding" (lyric adapted from *The Temple Trio* [Hymn Edition, 1886]) (Vivian Cherry, Lawrence Clayton, Jose Llana, Theresa McCarthy), "Build a Bridge" (Bob Stillman), "Sisyphus" (lyric by Ellen Fitzhugh) (Jose Llana, Company), "Life Is But a Dream" (Vivian Cherry), "Every Poodle" (Company), "Hero and Leander" (Jose Llana), "Come to Jesus" (Theresa McCarthy, Bob Stillman), "How Can I Lose You" (Annie Golden), "The Great Highway" (Theresa McCarthy, Company), "There's a Land" (lyric adapted from *The Temple Trio* [Hymn Edition, 1886]) (Company), "There's a Shout" (lyric adapted from *The Temple Trio* [Hymn Edition, 1886]) (Vivian Cherry), "Awaiting You" (Lawrence Clayton), "Saturn Returns: The Return" (Company)

NOTES—In his program and album liner notes for the song-cycle *Saturn Returns: A Concert*, Adam Guettel wrote that the title referred to the completion of Saturn's 29-year cycle around the Sun. For Guettel, the planet's journey was indicative of a time for personal reassessment, for ascertaining what one has done with one's life during that cycle. He noted the songs emanated from stories and myths as well as from a hymnal he found in a used book shop, and he said if anything linked the songs together is was the frame of the words "I want," the desire of Man "to transcend earthly bounds, to bond with something or someone greater." Stephen Holden's perceptive analysis of the work is worth noting. Writing in the *New York Times*, he praised the "majestic" song cycle, "a kaleidoscopically heady musical-theatre piece in which Gabriel Faure meets Stevie Wonder." The "unifying element" in the score was Guettel's "transcendent overarching melodic gift that" unifies the "often clashing inner voices of" the songs; further, his "long-lined melodies ... are as unpredictable as they are unabashedly romantic."

Guettel's rich score was released by Nonesuch Records as *Myths and Hymns* (CD # 79530-2), and the album included original cast members as well as Audra MacDonald, Mandy Patinkin, and Guettel himself. The recording omitted "Jesus the Mighty Conqueror," "Build a Bridge," "Life Is But a Dream," and "Every Poodle," and added one number, "Link."

The song cycle was originally produced as *Myths and Hymns* at the New Lyric Festival in Northampton, Massachusetts, in 1996.

1405 Satyagraha. THEATRE: Brooklyn Academy of Music; OPENING DATE: November 6, 1981; PERFORMANCES: Unknown; LIBRETTO: Philip Glass and Constance De Jong (text adapted from the *Bhagavad-Gita*).; MUSIC: Philip Glass; DIRECTION: Hans Nieuwenhuis; SCENERY: Robert Israel; COSTUMES: Robert Israel; LIGHTING: Richard Riddell; MUSICAL DIRECTION: Christopher Keene

CAST—Claudia Cummings (Miss Schlesen), Iris Hiskey (Mrs. Naidoo), Douglas Perry (Gandhi), Donald Miller (Rustomji), David Anchel (Krishna), Perry Singer (Tolstoy), John Grayson (Martin Luther King, Jr.), Linda Nichols (Mrs. Kasturbai), Bruce Hall Parsi (Mr. Kallenbach), Rhonda Liss Lord (Mrs. Alexander), Terry Bowers (Prince Arjuna), Justo Sanchez (Rabindranath Tagore); The Brooklyn Philharmonia; Artpark Opera Chorus

The opera was presented in three acts.

NOTES—*Satyagraha*, which dealt with Mohandas (Mahatma) Karamchand Gandhi, was one of Philip Glass' three "portrait" operas (see entries for *Einstein on the Beach* [1976] and *Akhnaten* [1984]). Roughly translated, the title means passive resistance to, or civil disobedience against, unfair laws.

The world premiere of *Satyagraha* occurred on September 5, 1980, at the Netherlands Opera in Rotterdam. The Brooklyn Academy of Music's production followed the work's American premiere during Summer 1981 at Artpark in Lewiston, New York. As of this writing, the opera is scheduled to receive its first Metropolitan Opera performances beginning on April 11, 2008, for six performances.

The opera was sung in Sanskrit, and its text was taken from the *Bhagavad-Gita*, the ancient Hindu sacred text. Donal Henahan in the *New York Times* felt the opera presented a "cardboard" Gandhi rather than a real human being, and he found fault with Glass' score (its "chief aim seems to be to induce the drugged, trancelike state that lies beyond boredom"). A 3-CD recording was released by Sony Masterworks Records, and Image Entertainment released a DVD of a live 1983 German production.

1406 Savion Glover/Downtown (1998). THEATRE: Variety Arts Theatre; OPENING DATE: May 19, 1998; PERFORMANCES: 51; CHOREOGRAPHY: Savion Glover and Cast Members; COSTUMES: Virginia Webster; LIGHTING: Michael Baldassari; PRODUCERS: Dodger Endemol Theatricals and Maniactin Productions in association with KISS FM

CAST—Savion Glover and NYOT (Not Your Ordinary Tappers): Ayodele Casel, Abron Glover, Chance Taylor, Jason Samuels, Omar Edwards, Ted L. Levy; Musicians: Eli Fountain, Tommy James, Gregory Jones, Patience Higgins

NOTES—The dance revue *Savion Glover/Downtown* offered improvisational and impromptu dances, and thus no two performances were the same. During the run, the revue included a few guest artists (Gregory Hines, Dinae Walker, and Yvette Glover).

Savion Glover returned the following season in another *Downtown* revue which appears to have been more structured than the first one (see entry).

1407 Savion Glover: Downtown (1999). THEATRE: Variety Arts Theatre; OPENING DATE: April 20, 1999; PERFORMANCES: 72; DIRECTION: Savion Glover; CHOREOGRAPHY: Savion Glover; COSTUMES: Virginia Webster; LIGHTING: Mike Baldassari; MUSICAL DIRECTION: Eli Fountain; PRODUCERS: Dodger Theatricals in association with Maniactin Productions Inc.

CAST—Savion Glover and NYOT (Not Your Ordinary Tappers): Ayodele Casel, Omar Edwards, Abron Glover, Jason Samuels; Reg E. Gaines (Poetry Reader)

MUSICAL NUMBERS—"Love of Money" (Savion Glover, Company), "Thievery!" (Savion Glover, Company), "Milestones" (Savion Glover), "Quick Thoughts from AG!" (Abron Glover), "Bof Booof" (Savion Glover, Company), "At This Moment" (Ayodele Casel), "Sentimental Mood" (Savion Glover), "The Track" (Savion Glover, Company), "Sheik & E" (Savion Glover, Company), "Air Jordans" (Savion Glover, Reg E. Gaines), "All Blues Jam" (Savion Glover, Company), "Murder" (Jason Samuels), "Caravan" (Savion Glover), "Some Killa Sh*" (Reg E. Gaines), "Silk Suits" (Savion Glover, Company), "Incog-Negroes" (Savion Glover, Company), "Swing a Li'l Funk Into Gang" Gang (Savion Glover, Company), "Ain't Nobody" (Savion Glover, Company), "Forget.me.knots" (Reg E. Gaines, Savion Glover, Company)

NOTES—In 1998, the dance revue *Savion Glover/Downtown* (see entry) was an evening of improvisational, impromptu dances. The 1999 edition (*Savion Glover: Downtown*) was more structured, and included scheduled, pre-choreographed performances; however, a few sequences were impromptu. This revue is also known as *Savion Glover/Downtown: Live Communication.*

1408 Say It with Music. THEATRE: Lincoln Center Library Theatre; OPENING DATE: December 26, 1979; PERFORMANCES: 4; LYRICS: Irving Berlin; MUSIC: Irving Berlin; DIRECTION: Jeffrey K. Neill; CHOREOGRAPHY: Jeffrey K. Neill (?); Suzanne Kaszynski; COSTUMES: Charles W. Roeder ("Costumes and Props"); Sy Robin ("Millinery"); MUSICAL DIRECTION: Wendell Kindberg; PRODUCER: Stage Directors and Choreographers Workshop Foundation

CAST—Richard P. Bennett, Sean McNickle, Mimi Moyer, Ken Seiter, Rima Starr, Karen Stefko

NOTES—*Say It with Music*, a tribute revue to Irving Berlin, was presented for a limited engagement of four performances, probably under an Off Off Broadway contract. The revue was created by Jeffrey K. Neill, and the music was adapted by Wendell Kindberg.

1409 Say When. THEATRE: Plaza 9 Theatre; OPENING DATE: December 4, 1972; PERFORMANCES: 7; BOOK: Keith Winter; LYRICS: Keith Winter; MUSIC: Arnold Goland; DIRECTION: Zoya Leporska; CHOREOGRAPHY: Zoya Leporska; SCENERY: William James Walt; COSTUMES: Leila Larmon; LIGHTING: Clarke W. Thornton; MUSICAL DIRECTION: Marc Pressel; PRODUCER: Walter Rosen Scholz

CAST—Bill Berrian, Andrea Duda, Michael Miller, Gerrianne Raphael, Anita Darian, Don Kyle, Sharron Miller, Michael Misita, Terrance McKerrs

NOTES—No list of song titles available.

Say When dealt with a magazine editor who compares life in the 1970s to his youth during the 1920s.

Clive Barnes in the *New York Times* felt the only possible answer to the musical's title was to say "never," and he suggested the Plaza Hotel's current tenant "could drive people to the Waldorf-Astoria in droves." He concluded by asking Julius Monk to return to the Plaza.

1410 Sayonara. THEATRE: Paper Mill Playhouse; OPENING DATE: September 16, 1987; PERFORMANCES: Unknown; BOOK: William Luce; LYRICS: Hy Gilbert; MUSIC: George Fischoff; DIRECTION: Robert Johanson; CHOREOGRAPHY: Susan Stroman; SCENERY: Michael Anania; COSTUMES: David Toser and Eiko Yamaguchi; LIGHTING: Brian MacDevitt; MUSICAL DIRECTION: Ted Kociolek; PRODUCER: The Paper Mill Playhouse (Angelo del Rossi, Executive Producer; Robert Johanson, Artistic Director)

CAST—RICHARD WHITE (Major Lloyd Gruver [Ace]), KEVIN SWEENEY (Private Joe Kelly), Eda Seasongood (Miriam Webster), Christopher Wynkoop (General Mark Webster), Colleen Fitzpatrick (Eileen Webster), Tony Gilbert (Colonel Calhoun Craford), Mark Zimmerman (Captain Mike Bailey), Ako (Fumiko), Jeffrey Brocklin (Consul), MIHO (Katsumi), Zoie Lam (Makino Girl), Valerie Lau-Kee (Makino Girl), Brent Black (AP), Robert Hoshour (AP), Yung Yung Tsuai (Takarazuka Teacher), JUNE ANGELA (Hana-ogi), Suzen Murakoshi (Flower Vendor); Takarazuka Girls, American Military Personnel, and People of Japan: Brent Black, Jeffrey Brocklin, Lyd-Lyd Gaston, Deborah Harada, Robert Hoshour, Norman Wendall Kauahi, Mia Korf, Zoie Lam, Valerie Lau-Kee, Setsuko Maruhashi, Yoshiko Matsui, Matthew McClanahan, Suzen Murakoshi, Hiroko Nagatsu, Kumiko Nakajima, Joanna Pang, Christine Toy, Yung Yung Tsuai, Kevin B. Weldon, Chris Wheeler, Sylvia Yamada

SOURCE—The novel *Sayonara* by James A. Michener.

The action occurs in April and July of 1952, in Korea and Japan.

The musical was presented in two acts.

ACT ONE—"Born to Fly" (Richard White), "When I'm with Her" (Kevin Sweeney, Richard White), "House in Arlington" (Colleen Fitzpatrick), "Song of the Seasons" (Miho, Kevin Sweeney), "L'Amour" (Mark Zimmerman, Richard White, Company), "Takarazuka Girl" (Miho, Takarazuka Girls), "Dance of the Fans" (Ako, Takarazuka Girls), "Taiko Drums" (June Angela, Takarazuka Girls), "Oh, What Joy to Be Free" (June Angela), "Here, Really Here" (Richard White, June Angela)

ACT TWO—"Tanabata" (June Angela, Ako, Company), "Night of Love" (Company), "Night of Love" (reprise) (Richard White, June Angela, Kevin Sweeney, Miho), "Reflections" (Richard White), "When I'm with Her" (reprise) (Kevin Sweeney), "House in Arlington" (reprise) (Colleen Fitzpatrick), "Japanese and Proud to Be" (June Angela, Richard White), "Song of the Seasons" (reprise) (Miho, Kevin Sweeney), "Where You Go" (June Angela), "Where You Go" (reprise) (June Angela)

NOTES—The Paper Mill Playhouse, the State Theatre of New Jersey which is located in Millburn, New Jersey, is noted for its revivals of musicals and plays. *Sayonara* was an unusual event for the venue, because it marked the world premiere of a lavish new musical based on James A. Michener's best-selling novel (which in 1957 was made into a popular film, with a title song by Irving Berlin).

The story dealt with interracial romance between American servicemen and Japanese women during the Korean War. In reviewing the musical for *Variety*, Roda noted the evening offered "splendor and seductiveness," saying the look of the production was a "joy and a jewel." But the reviewer noted it needed re-focusing, especially in the first 30 minutes of the first act. As for the lyrics, while they were occasionally "obvious and derivative," they were at their best in the romantic numbers. As for George Fischoff's score, it was "plaintive and lyrical," particularly when it incorporated "Oriental" motifs.

Alvin Klein in the *New York Times* wrote that the musical was a "spectacle with a soul," but felt the book had an "inner life" which never merged with the structure of the musical numbers. When *Sayonara* returned to the New York area in 1994 at the Westchester Broadway Theatre (in the interim, the musical had been seen in Houston, Seattle, and other cities), Klein reported that the show had been "75 percent changed" since its 1987 premiere. But he felt the musical, which had once shown "substance," had now devolved into "shadow." He concluded that after two lives, *Sayonara* now had to begin searching for a third. As for Fischoff's score, Klein singled out the title song and "Where You Go," and he noted that the Takarazuka sequences had less prominence in the second version. For other musicals by George Fischoff, see entries for *The Prince and the Pauper* (1963), *Bingo!*, and *Gauguin/Savage Light.* Fischoff's only Broadway musical, *Georgy*, opened in 1971, and was based on the popular 1966 film *Georgy Girl.* Although it played for just four performances, it left behind a delightful score.

1411 Says I, Says He. THEATRE: Marymount Manhattan Theatre; OPENING DATE: February 15, 1979; PERFORMANCES: 22; PLAY: Ron Hutchinson; DIRECTION: Steven Robman; CHOREOGRAPHY: Tom Cashin; SCENERY: David Jenkins; COSTUMES: Dona Granata; LIGHTING: Spencer Mosse; MUSICAL DIRECTION: Mick Moloney; PRODUCERS: The Phoenix Theatre (T. Edward Hambleton, Managing Director; Daniel Freudenberger, Artistic Director)

CAST—Jeanne Ruskin (Bella Phelan), Brian Dennehy (Pete Hannafin), Joe Grifasi (Mich Phelan), Christine Baranski (Maeve Macpherson), Andrew Davis (Jigger Hannafin), Sylvia Short (Landlady, May, Birdie), George Taylor (Lodger, Carradine, Hughes, Sam); The Band (The Irish Tradition: Bill McComiskey, Accordion; Brendan Mulvihill, Fiddle; and Andy O'Brien, Guitar and Vocals)

The action occurs in the present time in both Ulster and London.

The play with music was presented in two acts.

NOTES—Ron Hutchinson's *Says I, Says He* was a play which included incidental music (apparently all traditional Irish pieces), and it was performed by The Irish Tradition, an Irish band based in Washington, D.C. The play dealt in somewhat comic fashion with the political troubles between Britain and Ireland, but, as pointed out by Richard Eder in the *New York Times*, the evening never took sides by identifying Protestants and Catholics and instead concentrated on the futility of violence. While Eder felt the play was sometimes confusing in its lack of specifics, he nonetheless noted it was "engrossing and stimulating," and he praised both Hutchinson's "great talent" (with "wit and theatrical energy to spare") and the "splendid" and "first-rate" performances. The musical included Irish reels and religious songs, and Eder singled out Christine Baranksi's "Black Velvet Band," which she performed with "thrilling concentration."

1412 Scandal. THEATRE: Stage One; OPENING DATE: October 16, 1980; PERFORMANCES: 20 (estimated); BOOK: Robert Terry; LYRICS: Robert Terry; MUSIC: MacRae Cook and Robert Terry; DIRECTION: Loi Leabo and John W. Wilson; SCENERY: Roger Paradiso; COSTUMES: Kathleen Blake; LIGHTING: Gary Harris; MUSICAL DIRECTION: MacRae Cook; PRODUCERS: Delaware Heritage; a Special Project of RBT Productions Inc.

CAST—Katherine Wright (Victoria C. Woodhull), Bob Cooper, Jr. (Henry Ward Beecher), Mary Clifford (Libbie Tilton), Rufus Norris (Doc Claflin, Attorney Evarts), Elizabeth Torgersen (Tennessee Claflin), David de Berry (Theodore Tilton), David Vogel (Commodore Vanderbilt, John Martin, Judger Neilsen), Dina Paisner (Susan B. Anthony), Lauren

Scott (Catherine Beecher), Jean De Mers (Harriet B. Stowe), Maggie Hogan (Isabella B. Hooker, Maybelle), Frank Anderson (Anthony Comstock, Attorney Fullerton)

The action occurs in New York and Brooklyn in the 1870s.

The musical was presented in two acts.

ACT ONE—"On a Boat to Somewhere" (Katherine Wright), "O God Our Hearts Are Like the Trees" (Congregation), "A Thimbleful of Believin'" (Rufus Norris), "Good, Clean Brooklyn" (Congregation), "Principles" (David de Berry, Katherine Wright, Elizabeth Torgersen, Rufus Norris), "Principles" (reprise) (Katherine Wright, Elizabeth Torgersen, Men), "Suffragettes March," "A Harmless Peccadillo" (Bob Cooper, Jr., Mary Clifford), "A Harmless Peccadillo" (reprise) (Elizabeth Torgersen, David Vogel, Katherine Wright, and 'Vickie's Lovers'), "Imagine the Audacity!" (Lauren Scott, Jean De Mers), "A Moment to Live" (Katherine Wright, David de Berry), "I Should Fall Through the Floor" (Bob Cooper, Jr.), "Scandal" (Company)

ACT TWO—"England Is Lovely" (David Vogel), "Do Something Every Day for Jesus" (Frank Anderson, 'The Bluenose Brigade'), "Lamps" (Katherine Wright), "Lamps" (reprise) (Dina Paisner, Suffragettes), "Standing with Henry!" (Lauren Scott, Jean De Mers, Maggie Hogan, Men), "An Honorary Colonel" (Elizabeth Torgersen), "This One Thing I'll Do" (Katherine Wright), "On a Boat to Somewhere" (reprise) (Katherine Wright)

NOTES—The heroine of *Scandal* was feminist Victoria Woodhull, who ran for the United States presidency five times. The musical dealt with her involvement in the Henry Ward Beecher adultery trial in 1875; she had had an affair with the man who accused Beecher of infidelities, and it appears Woodhull herself may have had an affair with Beecher.

Reviewing the showcase production for the *New York Daily News*, Don Nelsen found the musical a "bright, snappy, old-fashioned rouser" with "sprightly and melodious" music and "often devilishly sly" lyrics. But the musical never went anywhere. There were at least three other musicals about Victoria Woodhull, and they too floundered. Beginning in the late 1960s, *Vicky for President* was for many years always being announced for the "next" Broadway season (at one point, Carol Channing was mentioned for the lead). The musical was never produced. In 1976, *Winner Take All* closed during its pre-Broadway tryout; Patricia Morison played Victoria Woodhull and Janet Blair was Tennessee Claflin; the book, lyrics, and music were by Russell Hunter.

And a month after *Scandal* closed, *Onward Victoria*, a Broadway musical about Woodhull, opened (and closed) on December 14, 1980, at the Martin Beck (now Al Hirschfeld) Theatre; the book and lyrics were by Charlotte Anker and Irene Rosenberg, and the music was by Keith Herrmann (Jill Eikenberry was Victoria Woodhull and Beth Austin was "Tennie" Claflin). The cast recording for *Onward Victoria* reveals a rather sprightly if somewhat conventional score. And one of its most maligned songs, "Beecher's Defense," must be defended. Despite its somewhat tasteless and anachronistic lyric, the music is highly theatrical: it is lyrical, melodic, and dramatic, with all sorts of hidden surprises in its orchestration.

For the record, Victoria's *Scandal* isn't to be confused with another *Scandal*, the Michael Bennett musical that never was. Announced for production in the mid-1980s, it was to have been directed and choreographed by Bennett, with lyrics and music by Jimmy Webb and book by Treva Silverman. According to *Variety*, the musical was to examine contemporary romantic relationships. There had been four workshops, two of them simultaneously produced. For the Broadway production, which was scheduled to open at the Mark Hellinger Theatre, the "technologically complex" scenery was to have been designed by Robin Wagner, the costumes by Theoni V. Aldredge, and the lighting by Tharon Musser. Treat Williams and Swoozie Kurtz were to have been the leads.

1413 The Scarf. THEATRE: New York City Center; OPENING DATE: April 5, 1959; PERFORMANCES: 3; LIBRETTO: Harry Duncan; MUSIC: Lee Hoiby; DIRECTION: Kirk Browning; SCENERY: Rouben Ter-Arutunian; COSTUMES: Rouben Ter-Arutunian; MUSICAL DIRECTION: Russell Stanger; PRODUCER: The New York City Opera Company

CAST—Patricia Neway (Miriam), John Druary (Reuel), Richard Cross (The Postman)

SOURCE—The short story "The Scarf" by Anton Chekhov

The opera was presented in one act.

NOTES—Lee Hoiby's *The Scarf* had its world premiere at the Spoleto Festival in June 1958; the following April saw the work's first New York performance. In his review of the opera for the *New York Times*, Howard Taubman praised the "tightly written libretto ... a shocker with a surprise ending." As for the score, Taubman applauded Hoiby's "long, arching melody" and "old-fashioned" arias which nonetheless didn't interrupt the dramatic action for vocal showpieces; he noted the music had "insistent forward momentum" which built to a "powerful climax."

The opera was performed on a double bill with a revival of Douglas Moore's *The Devil and Daniel Webster* which had originally been produced on Broadway at the Martin Beck (now Al Hirschfeld) Theatre in 1939.

1414 Scrambled Feet. THEATRE: Village Gate Upstairs; OPENING DATE: June 11, 1979; PERFORMANCES: 831; SKETCHES, LYRICS, AND MUSIC: John Driver and Jeffrey Haddow; DIRECTION: John Driver; SCENERY: Ernest Allen Smith; COSTUMES: Kenneth M. Yount; LIGHTING: Robert F. Strohmeier; MUSICAL DIRECTION: Jimmy Wisner; PRODUCERS: John Adams Vaccaro and Jimmy Wisner in association with Ciro A. Gamboni

CAST—Evalyn Baron, John Driver, Jeffrey Haddow, Roger Neil, Hermione (the duck)

The revue was presented in two acts.

ACT ONE—"Haven't We Met?" (Ensemble), "Going to the Theatre" (Ensemble), "P.T. Playwriting Kit" (Ensemble), "Makin' the Rounds" (Ensemble), "Agent" (Jeffrey Haddow, John Driver [piano]), "Composer/Hung-Up Tango" (Roger Neil, Evalyn Baron), "No Small Roles" (John Driver, Voice of Jeffrey Haddow), "Stanislaw" (John Driver, Jeffrey Haddow, Roger Neil), "Only One Dance" (Roger Neil, John Driver [piano]), "More Than Love" (Roger Neil, John Driver [piano]), "Good Connections" (John Driver, Jeffrey Haddow, Roger Neil [piano]), "Olympics" (Ensemble), "Theatre-Party Ladies" (John Driver, Jeffrey Haddow, Roger Neil, Evalyn Baron [piano])

ACT TWO—"Guru" (Jeffrey Haddow), "Party Doll" (Ensemble), "Love in the Wings" (Evalyn Baron, Roger Neil), "Huns/British" (Jeffrey Haddow, John Driver Evalyn Baron [piano]), "Sham Dancing" (Ensemble), "Improv/EDT" (Ensemble), "Have You Ever Been on the Stage?" (Evalyn Baron, John Driver [piano]), "Advice to Producers" (Ensemble), "One Happy Family" (Ensemble)

NOTES—*Scrambled Feet*, which had originally been seen Off Off Broadway at the Shirtsleeve Theatre in December 1976, was a satiric look at show business, and was the longest running musical of the 1979-1980 Off Broadway season, playing over two years. It was recorded by DRG Records (LP # DRG-6105), and the script was published by Samuel French, Inc, in 1983. The critics enjoyed the revue, including the sketch "P.T. Playwriting Kit," which spoofed the pretensions of the holy cows over at the Public Theatre (for the published script, the sketch was slighted altered and was titled the "Avant Garde Playwrighting Kit"). In order for you to get your work produced (with "public funds"), the kit will give you a "phony mystique and bogus charisma" which will "turn your meaningless tripe into a crock of art." The invaluable kit includes a gypsy headband, a box of cockroaches, a Bolshevik dwarf, that "old standby, the blind war veteran," and a copy of Elizabeth Swados' "greatest hits" (in the published script, a copy of Samuel Beckett's greatest hits). As for the P.T. "secret ... theatre handshake," it has nothing to do with the writer's hand firmly grasping the producer's hand; instead, it has to do with the writer getting on his knees and kissing the producer's posterior. The sketch "Answering Machine" was dropped prior to the opening; added during the run was "She Gives Me More Than Love" (by John Driver and Jimmy Wisner).

The program bio for Hermione, the duck, noted that prior to *Scrambled Feet* she had appeared at the Delancy Poultry Market. But fame can be fleeting, and so despite taking to the stage like a duck takes to water (and adorning the program, poster and album artwork with her portrait), Hermione was replaced by Buster for the 1984 television version of the revue.

The 1984 telecast included three original cast members (John Driver, Jeffery Haddow, and Roger Neil), with Madeleine Kahn replacing Evalyn Baron. It was directed by John Driver (the Associate Director was Len Dell'Amico); the musical director was Roger Neil; and Jonathan Statharis and Richard A. Carey were the producers (Archer King was co-producer). The videocassette was released by RKO Home Video and RKO/Nederlander (# RKO-1011).

1415 Seacoast of Bohemia. THEATRE: Square East; OPENING DATE: January 10, 1962; PERFORMANCES: 258; SCENES AND DIALOGUE: Created by the Company and by "Contributing Associates" (David Shepherd, Roger Bowen, and The Audience); MUSIC: William Mathieu; DIRECTION: Paul Sills and Alan Arkin; SCENERY: Larry Klein; LIGHTING: Gary and Timmy Harris; PRODUCERS: Bernard Sahlins, Howard Alk, and Paul Sills

CAST—Howard Alk, Alan Arkin, Severn Darden, Andrew Duncan, Barbara Harris, Lynda Segal, Eugene Troobnick, Garry Sherman (Piano)

The revue was performed in two acts (sketch and song assignments not credited in the program).

ACT ONE—"Nightclub Interview," "Candid Camera," "Vend-A-Buddy," "Colonel Clevis in West Berlin," "The Question Song," "Met's Vets," "Abduction from the Ladder"

ACT TWO—"Happy Birthday," "Clothes Make the Man," "No, George, Don't," "Khrushchev-Kennedy Interview," "Pagan Place," "The Girls in Their Summer Dresses"

NOTES—According to the liner notes of *Second City* cast albums and notes in various programs, the group which eventually became known as the Second City was founded in the early 1950s when Paul Sills, Eugene Troobnick, Howard Alk, Severn Darden, Andrew Duncan, Elaine May, and Mike Nichols met during their years at the University of Chicago and performed there at the University's theatre. Later, with David Shepherd, they formed the Playwrights Theatre Club, where they were joined by Barbara Harris. Shepherd, and later Bernard Sahlins, organized and produced the Compass Players, an improvisational group which played at local Chicago night clubs. Sahlins also formed the Studebaker Theatre Company where the Compass Players performed (they also continued to perform under the aegis of Paul Sills in nightclub venues). The Compass Players eventually disbanded, but Nichols and May found immediate success in New York, and Shelley Berman, another comedian who had joined the group, became popular in nightclubs and on television (he also appeared in the short-running 1962 Broadway musical *A Family Affair*).

In 1959, the Compass Players re-grouped as the Second City, and the troupe included Paul Sills and Mina Kolb as well as composer-pianist William Mathieu. The group opened in December 1959 and was an immediate sensation. They performed in two venues, their nightclub-cabaret and their nightclub-theatre. They also formed a school and workshop which trained other actors in the group's performing philosophy. Essentially, the Second City material was developed by Sills, Shepard, and the performers; while the sketches were improvisational in nature, they were nonetheless rehearsed and edited. Some of the skits were also based on suggestions from the audience. The nature of the development of the improvisations eventually created a repertory of short (originally improvised) scenes which had been developed through careful rehearsals and editing; the "essence" of the scenes (if not necessarily the specific lines of dialogue) became part of the repertoire, but if these scenes "died" in actual performance, the audience was then asked for suggestions. *Seacoast of Bohemia* was the first of eleven Second City revues presented Off Broadway between 1962 and 1984. Prior to *Seacoast*, the troupe had been seen on Broadway in *From the Second City*, which played for three months in 1961. Except for Mina Kolb, who was replaced by Lynda Segal (a former Stewed Prune; see entry for *Stewed Prunes*), all the members of the Broadway edition transferred downtown. Most of the revues were performed at the Square East, where the ambience of a small Off Broadway theatre was just right for the troupe's brand of improvisational satire.

Arthur Gelb in the *New York Times* warned theatergoers that the "not to be missed" *Seacoast of Bohemia* was "flamboyant, fresh, exuberant and witty." He singled out such sketches as "Vend-a-Buddy" (for a nickel, a machine will speak "platitudinous words of hollow comfort" to you); a purported scene from the musical *Irma La Douce* (which was censored "even in Italy"); a sketch in a chic men's clothing store; and a Khrushchev-Kennedy interview ("a combination of premeditated characterization and spontaneous dialogue" [Khrushchev notes that if his wife were young, thin, and rich, she, too, could be like Jacqueline Kennedy]). The latter sketch was so popular it was held over for the next Second City revue, *Alarums and Excursions*.

Besides *Seacoast of Bohemia*, the other ten Off Broadway revues in the *Second City* series (see entries for details; also see Appendix T) were *Alarums and Excursions* (1962; 619 performances); *To the Water Tower* (1963; 210 performances); *When the Owl Screams* (1963; 141 performances); *Open Season at the Second City* (1964; 90 performances); *The Wrecking Ball* (1964; 126 performances); *A View from Under the Bridge* (1964; 94 performances); *The Return of Second City in "20,000 Frozen Grenadiers"* (1966; 29 performances); from *the Second City* (1969; 31 performances); *Cooler Near the Lake* (1971; 26 performances); and *Orwell That Ends Well* (1984; 110 performances). Incidentally, the titles of the Second City revues were virtually meaningless, and in their way they "defined" the series, just as Ben Bagley (the word "shoestring"), Julius Monk (numerical references), and Rod Warren (sporting references) used unified titles to distinguish their revues.

It appears that one sketch from the 1961 Broadway edition was used in *Seacoast of Bohemia* ("No, George, Don't").

There were two Second City cast albums, *Comedy from the Second City* (LP # OCS-6201 and # OCM-2201) and from *the Second City* (LP # OCS-6203 and # OCM-2203), both released by Mercury Records. The first album was recorded live from a January 19, 1961, performance at the Second City Cabaret Theatre in Chicago ("No, George Don't" was among the sketches); the second was the cast album from the 1961 Broadway production.

No discussion of the Second City would be complete without mentioning Barbara Harris. An original member of the company, she performed in the Broadway edition of the revue as well as in three Off Broadway editions (*Seacoast, When the Owl Screams*, and *Open Season at the Second City*). She also appeared in the Phoenix Theatre production of Arthur Kopit's *Oh Dad, Poor Dad, Mamma's Hung You in the Closet and I'm Feelin' So Sad* (1962); in the first Broadway production of Bertolt Brecht's *Mother Courage and Her Children* (1963); and in William Bolcom's *Dynamite Tonight* (1964; see entry). She starred in two Broadway musicals, *On a Clear Day You Can See Forever* (1965) and *The Apple Tree* (1966); for the latter, which consisted of three one-act musicals, Harris won the Tony Award for Best Actress in a Musical. She later appeared in the 1970 Off Broadway production of *The Rise and Fall of the City of Mahagonny* (see entry), which marked the New York premiere of the Bertolt Brecht-Kurt Weill opera and which was her final appearance in New York. In 1969, she had directed the short-lived Broadway play *The Penny Wars*, and she later withdrew from two productions. Her name was on the early window cards and flyers for the 1972 premiere of Arthur Miller's *The Creation of the World and Other Business*, in which she was to play Eve (she had created an earlier Eve, in "The Diary of Adam and Eve," which was the first act of *The Apple Tree*), but she withdrew from the production prior to its first preview at the Kennedy Center. And her name was in the first newspaper advertisements for the Off Broadway revue *Sills & Company*. (1986; see entry); by the time the second round of ads appeared, her name was no longer in the cast listing. She was also credited as "Directorial Consultant" for the 1983 New York production of the revue *Leftovers* (1983; see entry).

Except for perhaps Beatrice Lillie, the musical stage probably never saw a comedienne the equal of Barbara Harris. Her comic timing was fresh, and seemed born of the moment; when you watched her, you felt the script was just her starting point. Her voice and body seemed to morph into a performance style which, while clearly rooted in script and character, nevertheless achieved a hang-loose, of-the-moment quality. Other performers "froze" their characterizations, but with Harris you felt that each performance was newly minted. Indeed, her fumbling way with a cigarette in *On a Clear Day*, her Oscar acceptance speech in "Passionella" (the third act of *The Apple Tree*), and her sincerely insincere brush-off to Jimmy Mahoney in *Mahagonny* brought a Second City improvisational sensibility to her performances, a unique style seldom seen before or since on the musical stage.

1416 The Seagull. THEATRE: Manhattan School of Music; OPENING DATE: December 11, 2002; PERFORMANCES: 2; LIBRETTO: Kenward Elmslie; MUSIC: Thomas Pasatieri; DIRECTION: Mark Harrison; MUSICAL DIRECTION: David Gilbert; PRODUCER: Manhattan School of Music Opera Theatre

CAST—Raymond Ayers (Constantine), Amy Gough (Arkadina), Amy Shoremount (Nina), Matthew Worth (Trigorin), Keri Behan (Masha), Maxime Alvarez de Toledo (Sorin), Alvaro Vallejo (Doctor Dorn), Isai Jess Munoz (Medvedenko), Thomas Pertel (Shamrayeff), Sarah Kraus (Pauline), Chorus: Sopranos (Hadley Combs, Yu Jung Chung, Kristina Sharron), Altos (Nicole Warner, Sarah Heltzel, John Gaston), Tenors (Tim Farrell, Nick Tamagna, Christian Reinert), Basses (Charles Clayton, Benjamin de la Fuente, Kwang-Mo Goo)

SOURCE—The 1896 play *The Seagull* by Anton Chekhov.

The opera was produced in three acts.

ACT ONE—Overture (Orchestra), "You Always Wear Black" (Isai Jess Munoz), "By Ten Last Night" (Maxime Alvarez de Toledo), "Two French Grenadiers" (Maxime Alvarez de Toledo), "My Play Is Full of Visions" (Raymond Ayers), "Alas, the Stage" (Thomas Pertel), "I Am Alone" (Amy Shoremount), "Summer Love" (Voices)

ACT TWO—Interlude (Orchestra), "Be Honest, Dr. Dorn" (Amy Gough), "Are You Alone?" (Raymond Ayers), "Sometimes a Mania" (Matthew Worth), "Haven't You Had Enough?" (Matthew Worth), "Odd or Even?" (Amy Shoremount), "I Remember Once" (Raymond Ayers), "If Ever You Need Me" (Matthew Worth)

ACT THREE—Interlude (Orchestra), "How Black the Garden" (Isai Jess Munoz), "Excellent Idea for a Story" (Maxime Alvarez de Toledo), "Dead Words" (Raymond Ayers), "Late Last Night" (Amy Shoremount), "I Must Go" (Amy Shoremount), "Mother Mustn't Know" (Raymond Ayers), "Sleep" (Amy Gough)

NOTES—Thomas Pasatieri's *The Seagull* received its world premiere at the Houston Grand Opera on July 5, 1974 (among the original cast members were Frederica Von Stade, Evelyn Lear, and John Reardon). The work was later revised in 2004. In the meantime, the opera received its New York premiere in 2002 by the Manhattan School of Music Opera Theatre. In her review for the *New York Times*, Anna Midgette noted that while the opera "doesn't break new ground ... it is also unexceptional in a good sense: a viable entertainment." The production was recorded on a 2-CD set by Albany Records (# TROY-579/580); the titles of the musical sequences are taken from this recording. Original Cast Records, as well as such companies as Offbeat, Painted Smiles, DRG, Fynsworth Alley, Sh-K-Boom, and Ghostlight, are invaluable for their commitment to record Off Broadway revues and musicals, and Albany Records is their equivalent for the recordings of American operas. The company has done a remarkable job of preserving the legacy of modern American opera. One sequence from the opera ("I Remember Once") was heard in the 2005 revue *Lingoland* (see entry); as "Together Forever," it was recorded for the revue's cast album. Also, see entries for *Beware the Jubjub Bird* and *Birds of Paradise*, both of which dealt with theatre companies presenting revivals of *The Seagull*. (The entry for *Beware the Jubjub Bird* also references *Gulls*, another musical based on *The Seagull*.)

1417 The 2nd Greatest Entertainer in the Whole Wide World. THEATRE: Promenade Theatre; OPENING DATE: June 2, 1977; PERFORMANCES: 78, Comedy material written by Dick Shawn; SCENERY: Akira Yoshimura; LIGHTING: Marilyn Rennagel; PRODUCER: Kenneth D. Laub

CAST—Dick Shawn

NOTES—This one-man show was an evening of comedy and songs performed by Dick Shawn, a Broadway performer who never quite found the success he deserved. He was one of the replacements for Zero Mostel in the original Broadway production of *A Funny Thing Happened on the Way to the Forum* (1962), and in the 1965 return engagement of *Fade Out-Fade In* (1964) he succeeded Jack Cassidy. He was in a number of Broadway flops, including *I'm Solomon* (1968) and *A Musical Jubilee* (1975) as well as the fascinating *Home Again* (1979), a/k/a *Home Again, Home Again*, a Cy Coleman musical which closed during its pre-Broadway tryout. He also appeared in the Off Broadway production of Jerome Moross' innovative *Gentlmen, Be Seated!* (1963; see entry). Shawn is perhaps best remembered for his role in the original film version of *The Producers* (1967), playing the hippy-dippy character who lands the role of Adolf Hitler in *Springtime for Hitler*.

In 1987, while performing in *The 2nd Greatest Entertainer* in Los Angeles, Shawn collapsed on stage and died.

1418 The Second Shepherd's Play. THEATRE: The Brook; OPENING DATE: December 15, 1976; PERFORMANCES: Unknown; BOOK: Steve Kitsakos; LYRICS: Steve Kitsakos; MUSIC: Steve Kitsakos; DIRECTION: Tony Napoli; PRODUCER: The Gap Company (Tony Napoli, Artistic Director)

CAST—Myra Quigley (The Lamb), Greg Cesario (Gib), Joel Stevens (Coll), Doug Holsclaw (Daw), Richard Woods (Mak), Karen Haas (Gill), Deborah Tilton (Angel), Natalia Chuma (Mary)

The action occurs in Palestine but "is geographically set on the Moors of England."

It appears the musical was performed in one act.

MUSICAL NUMBERS—"The Problems of a Shepherd" (Greg Cesario, Joel Stevens, Doug Holsclaw), "Why Should I Wait for a Prophet?" (Karen Haas), "Watch Through the Night"/"If He's Really Sly" (Richard Woods, Joel Stevens, Doug Holsclaw, Greg Cesario), "Lamb Stew Tonight" (Richard Woods), "Palestine" (Greg Cesario, Joel Stevens, Doug Holsclaw), "He's the Child, the Child I Bore" (Richard Woods, Doug Hosclaw, Karen Haas, Company), "Palestine: Follow the Star" (Deborah Tilton, Company), "Ballad in Bethelem" (Natalia Chuma), "Hail, Hallelujah" (Deborah Tilton, Natalia Chuma, Company), "Sign of the Times" (Company)

NOTES—The Off Off Broadway musical *The Second Shepherd's Play* was based on a series of medieval plays of unknown authorship which seem to have been first presented during the late 1300s. The musical dealt with three unhappy shepherds who have both work and family problems. Once an angel tells them to follow a star to Bethlehem and they come upon Mary and the Infant Jesus, they realize their lives are changed forever, and for the better.

The musical was recorded by Broadway Babies Records (LP # BBD-774).

1419 The Secret Annex. THEATRE: Playhouse 91; OPENING DATE: September 8, 1995; PERFORMANCES: 16; BOOK: Robert K. Carr; LYRICS: Robert K. Carr; MUSIC: William Charles Baton; DIRECTION: Dom Ruggiero; SCENERY: Ellen Waggett (and Christopher Landy?); COSTUMES: Tracy Dorman; MUSICAL DIRECTION: Edward R. Conte and Jeffrey Buchsbaum; PRODUCER: The Secret Annex LLC

CAST—Lydia Gladstone (Edith Frank), Don Frame (Otto Frank), Rhonda Merritt (Margot Frank), Patricia Ann Gardner (Anne Frank), Steve Robbins (Mr. Van Pels), Nancy Ward (Mrs. Van Pels), Kevin Berthiaume (Lars Peters), Jan Austell (Mr. Kleinman), Karin Reed Bamesberger (Marleuse), Jim Straz (Sargent), Glen Badyna (Peter Van Pels), Reggie Barton (Dr. Pfeffer), Ingrid Olsen (Clerk), Joseph DiGennaro (Ensemble), Julie Halpern (Ensemble), Carse David Parker (Ensemble)

The action occurs during World War II in the Frank family home as well in the secret annex.

The musical was presented in two acts (division of acts and song assignments unknown).

MUSICAL NUMBERS—"Montage," "We Are God's Forgotten People," "Recitative," "Forever Friends," "War," "Knights and Kings," "Lullaby," "Day and Night," "The Final Hour," "Pieces of My Life," "Anne's Song," "Evening Prayer," "World Beyond the Pane," "Peas," "Mother's Love," "These Four Walls," "On My Side," "My Darling, Close Your Eyes," "Summer Afternoons," "Living in New York," "Man I've Become," "Power of Dreams," Finale

NOTES—The Off Off Broadway musical *The Secret Annex* told the familiar story of Anne Frank. For another musical on the subject, see entry for the 1985 Off Broadway production *Yours, Anne* (which also references *I Am Anne Frank* [a revised version of *Yours, Anne*] and a Spanish operatic adaptation of Anne Frank's *Diary*). Coincidentally, both *Yours, Anne* and *The Secret Annex* opened at the same theatre, Playhouse 91.

1420 The Secret Life of Walter Mitty. "A New Musical." THEATRE: Players Theatre; OPENING DATE: October 26, 1964; PERFORMANCES: 96; BOOK: Joe Manchester; additional dialogue by Mervyn Nelson; LYRICS: Earl Shuman; MUSIC: Leon Carr; DIRECTION: Mervyn Nelson; CHOREOGRAPHY: Bob Arlen; SCENERY: Lloyd Burlingame; COSTUMES: Al Lehman; LIGHTING: Lloyd Burlingame; MUSICAL DIRECTION: Joseph Stecko; PRODUCERS: Joe Manchester in association with J.M. Fried

CAST—MARC LONDON (Walter Mitty), LORRAINE SERABIAN (Agnes Mitty), Susan Lehman (Maude), CHRISTOPHER NORRIS (Penninah), RUDY TRONTO (Harry), CATHRYN DAMON (Willa), CHARLES RYDELL (Irving), Lette Rehnolds (Ruthie), EUGENE ROCHE (Fred Gorman), Rue McClanahan (Hazel), Edmund Belson (Insurance Broker), Peter DeMaio (Real Estate Salesman), Christian Grey (Travel Agent), Caroline Worth Darnell (Adelaide), Nick Athas (McMillan); Cameo roles played by Nick Athas, Edmund Belson, Caroline Worth Darnell, Peter DeMaio, Christian Grey, Susan Lehman, Rue McClanahan, Lette Reynolds

SOURCE—James Thurber's 1936 short story "The Secret Life of Walter Mitty."

The action occurs in autumn of the present time in Waterbury, Connecticut, as well as in the everyday and secret life of Walter Mitty.

The musical was presented in two acts.

ACT ONE—Prologue: "The Secret Life" (Company), "The Walter Mitty March" (Company), "By the Time I'm Forty" (Marc London), "Walking with Peninnah" (Marc London and Christopher Norris), "Drip, Drop, Tapoketa" (Company), "Aggie" (Marc London), "Don't Forget" (Marc London, Lorraine Serabian), "Marriage Is for Old Folks" (Cathryn Damon), "Hello, I Love You, Goodbye" (Eugene Roche, Marc London, Rudy Tronto), "Marriage Is for Old Folks" (reprise) (Unknown; probably Caroline Worth Darnell, Susan Lehman, Rue McCanahan, Lette Rehnolds), "Willa" (Charles Rydell), "Confidence" (Rudy Tronto, Marc London, Cathryn Damon, Company)

ACT TWO—"Two Little Pussycats" (Marc London, Cathryn Damon), "Fan the Flame" (Cathryn Damon), "She's Talking Out" (Company), "By the Time I'm Forty" (reprise) (Marc London, Cathryn Damon, Rudy Tronto, Company), "You're Not" (Marc London, Lorraine Serabian), "Aggie" (reprise) (Lorraine Serabian), "Lonely Ones" (Marc London, Cathryn Damon, Eugene Roche, Rudy Tronto, Charles Rydell), "The Walter Mitty March" (reprise) (Company), Epilogue: "The Secret Life" (reprise) (Company)

NOTES—With the built-in popularity of Thurber's short story, *The Secret Life of Walter Mitty* should have had a long Off Broadway run and an even longer life in regional theater. But perhaps the pleasant but rather banal score is what prevented the adaptation from enjoying widespread popularity.

Lewis Funke in the *New York Times* liked the enthusiastic cast, but felt the evening itself was a "hodge-podge product" with a few "pleasant" tunes and not much in the way of wit. He concluded that Walter Mitty's dreams were "generally mirthless" and more in the way of "mild hallucination" than full-fledged fantasy.

The cast album was recorded by Columbia Records (LP # OS-2720 and # OS-6320), and the script was published by Samuel French, Inc., in 1968. The script reflects various changes in the score (for example, "By the Time I'm Forty" [a/k/a "Now That I Am Forty"] was dropped from the first act, and was sung only in the second act; and the reprise of "Marriage Is for Old Folks" was cut). "Two Little Pussycats" was originally sung by Marc London and Cathryn Damon, but sometime after the opening the song was reassigned to Rue McClanahan and Lette Rehnolds (who perform it on the cast album). The script also reflects this song's reassignment.

The musical was revived by Equity Library Theatre on January 11, 1973, for nineteen performances.

Cathryn Damon was a somewhat unappreciated tried-and-true theatre veteran who appeared in musicals and non-musicals on and off Broadway for almost three decades. Rue McClanahan's greatest popularity was on television, but she appeared in many stage productions, including *MacBird!* (1967), in which she created the role of Lady MacBird. Forty years after *The Secret Life of Walter Mitty*, she was back in a musical, appearing on Broadway as Madame Morrible when she succeeded Carole Shelley in *Wicked* (2003).

Leon Carr is perhaps best known as the composer of one of the most famous television commercial jingles of them all ("See the USA in Your Chevrolet").

1421 Secrets Every Smart Traveler Should Know. THEATRE: Triad Theatre; transferred to the IBIS Theatre on November 25, 1998; OPENING DATE: October 30, 1997; PERFORMANCES: 953; SKETCHES: Barry Creyton and Stan Freeman; Barry Kleinbort (sketch contributor?); LYRICS: Douglas Bernstein, Francesca Blumenthal, Michael Brown, Lesley Davison, Stan Freeman, Murray Grand, Glen Kelly, Jay Leonhart, and Denis Markell; MUSIC: Douglas Bernstein, Michael Brown, Lesley Davison, Addy Fieger, Stan Freeman, Murray Grand, Glen Kelly, Jay Leonhart, and Denis Markell; DIRECTION: Patrick Quinn; Matthew Lacey, Assistant; SCENERY: Rui Rita; Jeff Nellis, Associate; COSTUMES: David Brooks; LIGHTING: Rui Rita; Jeff Nellis, Associate; MUSICAL DIRECTION: Stan Freeman; PRODUCERS: Scott Perrin; Peter Martin, Nancy McCall, and Steve McGraw, Associate Producers

CAST—James Darrah, Kathy Fitzgerald, Stan Freeman, Jay Leonhart, Liz McConahay, Michael McGrath

SOURCE—Fodor's 1997 guide *Wendy Perrin's Secrets Every Smart Traveler Should Know*.

The revue was presented in two acts (division of acts unknown).

SKETCHES AND MUSICAL NUMBERS—"Secrets Every Smart Traveler Should Know" (lyric and music by Lesley Davison) (Company), "Travel Secrets" (sketch by Barry Creyton) (Company), "Naked in Pittsburgh" (lyric and music by Lesley Davison) (James Darrah), "Reservations" (sketch by Barry Creyton) (Michael McGrath, Kathy Fitzgerald), "Star Search" (lyric and music by Stan Freeman) (Liz McConahay), "Customs" (lyric and music by Jay Leonhart) (Jay Leonhart), "Hertz" (lyric and music by Lesley Davison) (Michael McGrath, Liz McConahay), "This Is Your Captain Speaking" (sketch by Stan Freeman) (Stan Freeman), "See It Now" (lyric and music by Stan Freeman) (Company), "Acapulco" (lyric by Francesca Blumenthal, music by Addy Fieger) (Kathy Fitzgerald), "Salzburg" (lyric and music by Stan Freeman) (Company), "Private Wives" (sketch by Barry Creyton) (James Darrah, Liz McConahay), "Me and Margherita" (lyric and music by Jay Leonhart) (Jay Leonhart), "Red Hot Lava" (lyric and music by Murray Grand) (Michael McGrath, James Darrah, Kathy Fitzgerald), "I Get Around" (sketch or song by Barry Kleinbort) (Liz McConahay), "Seeing America First" (lyric and music by Lesley Davison) (Michael McGrath, Kathy Fitzgerald),

"Paradise Found" (lyric and music by Stan Freeman) (Stan Freeman), "The French Song" (lyric and music by Glen Kelly) (Liz McConahay, Kathy Fitzgerald), "She Spoke Spanish" (lyric and music by Michael Brown) (Michael McGrath), "Honey, Sweetie, Baby" (lyric and music by Douglas Bernstein and Denis Markell) (Michael McGrath, Kathy Fitzgerald, James Darrah), "Home" (lyric and music by Michael Brown) (Company)

NOTES—This long-running revue *Secrets Every Smart Traveler Should Know* spoofed the vagaries of travel.

Stephen Holden in the *New York Times* found the "witty" evening a kind of "arch early-1960's-style musical-comedy revue," and singled out a number of songs and sketches, including: "Customs," a "hilarious" song and the "high point" of the revue; "Paradise Found," which describes the "decidedly limited pleasures" of vacationing in Uzbekistan; "Salzburg," which deals with "overdosing on Mozart"; and "Private Wives," a Noel Coward spoof in which "Elyot Chase" informs his ex-wife that his new partner is a man.

"Travel Secrets," "Reservations," and "This Is Your Captain Speaking" were brief sketches used throughout the revue. By the time RCA Victor Records released a cast recording (CD # 09026-63503-2), only one original cast member (Jay Leonhart) was still with the show, and, if the album is any indication, the songs and sketches underwent considerable reordering during the revue's run.

Other numbers heard in the production were the songs "What Did I Forget?," "Buffet," "Please, Mr. Trailways, Take Me Away," and "Aging Planes," and the sketch "Border Guard." Also used were "Margie and Me," "Shots," and "Traveling Light" (it's unclear if these were songs or sketches).

The revue marked a welcome return for a number of lyricists and composers from the early days of the Off Broadway revue (Michael Brown, Lesley Davison, and Murray Grand).

1422 See What I Wanna See. THEATRE: Anspacher Theatre/The Public Theatre; OPENING DATE: October 30, 2005; PERFORMANCES: 41; LYRICS: Michael John LaChiusa; MUSIC: Michael John LaChiusa; DIRECTION: Ted Sperling; CHOREOGRAPHY: Jonathan Butterell; SCENERY: Thomas Lynch; COSTUMES: Elizabeth Caitlin Ward; LIGHTING: Christopher Akerlind; MUSICAL DIRECTION: Chris Fenwick; PRODUCERS: The Public Theatre (Oskar Eustis, Artistic Director; Mara Manus, Executive Director); Peter DuBois, Mandy Hackett, and Steven Tabakin, Associate Producers

CAST—Marc Kudisch (Morito, The Husband, A CPA), Aaron Lohr (The Thief, A Reporter), Idina Menzel (Kesa, The Wife, An Actress), Henry Stram (The Janitor, A Priest), Mary Testa (The Medium, Aunt Monica)

SOURCE—The stories of Ryunosuke Akutagawa (as translated by Takashi Kojima).

The evening consisted of three musicals in two acts; *Kesa & Morito, Parts 1 & 2* were presented at the beginning of each act; *R Shomon* was presented in the first act; and *Gloryday* was presented in the second.

The action occurs in Japan during the medieval era (for *Kesa & Morito, Parts 1 & 2*), in New York City in 1951 (for *R Shomon*), and during the present time in New York City (for *Gloryday*).

ACT ONE—*Kesa & Morito, Part 1:* "Kesa" (Idina Menzel); *R Shomon:* "The Janitor's Statement" (Henry Stram), "The Thief's Statement"/"She Looked at Me" (Aaron Lohr), "See What I Wanna See" (Idina Menzel), "Big Money" (Aaron Lohr, Marc Kudisch), "The Park" (Aaron Lohr, Idina Menzel), "You'll Go Away with Me" (Aaron Lohr), "Murder" (Aaron Lohr), "Best Not to Get Involved" (Henry Stram), "The Wife's Statement" (Idina Menzel), "Louie" (Idina Menzel), "The Medium and the Husband's Statement" (Henry Stram, Mary Testa, Marc Kudisch), Quartet: "You'll Go Away with Me" (reprise) (Marc Kudisch, Idina Menzel, Aaron Lohr, Mary Testa), "No More" (Idina Menzel, Aaron Lohr, Mary Testa, Marc Kudisch), "Simple As This" (Marc Kudisch, Mary Testa), "Light in the East"/Finale Act 1 (Company)

ACT TWO—*Kesa & Morito, Part 2:* "Morito" (Morito); *Gloryday:* "Confession"/"Last Year" (Henry Stram, Mary Testa), "The Greatest Practical Joke" (Mary Testa), "First Message" (Henry Stram), "Central Park" (Marc Kudisch), "Second Message" (Henry Stram, Idina Menzel), "Coffee" (Idina Menzel), "Gloryday" (Company), "Curiosity"/"Prayer" (Aaron Lohr, Idina Menzel, Marc Kudisch, Henry Stram), "Feed the Lions" (Henry Stram, Marc Kudisch, Idina Menzel), "There Will Be a Miracle" (Mary Testa), "Prayer" (reprise) (Henry Stram, Idina Menzel, Marc Kudisch, Aaron Lohr), "Rising, Up"/Finale Act 2 (Company)

NOTES—With *See What I Wanna See*, Michael John LaChiusa continued to push the boundaries of musical theatre with his ambitious use of sung-through music which perfectly complemented his often circular, dream-like plots. His scores for such Off Broadway productions as *See What I Wanna See* as well as *First Lady Suite* and *Hello Again* (see entries) offer some of the most exciting and groundbreaking music in today's lyric theatre. His two Broadway musicals *Marie Christine* (1999) and *The Wild Party* (2000) were burdened with cumbersome books, but his intricate and expansive scores for these works explored story, character, and atmosphere in richly musical terms.

See What I Wanna See consisted of three musicals, *Kesa & Morito*, *R Shomon*, and *Gloryday*. *Kesa & Morito* was presented in two parts, with each part presented at the beginning of each act; set in medieval Japan, part one finds Kesa singing of her affair with Morito, an affair which she has confessed to her husband. Morito begins to make love to her, and as he puts his hands around her neck, she reveals a knife which she raises in order to plunge into his back. The second part takes place concurrently with the first part; this time, Morito sings of his affair with Kesa, and, as he begins to make love to her, he places his hands on her neck, revealing his intention to strangle her.

The second musical, *R Shoman*, also told its story from different perspectives; in this case, the musical was inspired by *Rashomon*, in which the audience is presented with radically different accounts of the same basic story. Set in a film noirish New York City during 1951, *R Shoman* (the film *Rashomon* has just opened, and one character notes the letter "a" is missing from the movie theatre's marquee) offered various versions about a rape and murder in Central Park. Based on Akutagawa's story "The Dragon," *Gloryday*, the third musical, was set in present day New York. After the terrorist attacks of September 11, 2001, a priest loses his faith and perpetrates a terrible hoax: He announces that Christ will appear in Central Park. When thousands of the faithful gather in the park to witness the miracle, the priest tells them he made up the story. When a storm comes up, the crowds disperse, and, alone in the park, the priest actually sees the miracle which he promised. But because he was the only person to see Christ, no one believes him. His lie "was for everyone," but the truth was only for himself. Now that the miracle has given him the truth, what does he do with it?

Ben Brantley in the *New York Times* felt the *Kesa & Morito* sequences were "forcibly shoehorned" into the evening, and found *R Shomon* "an icy abstraction" (although he praised "Simple As This" and the quintet finale). He was impressed with *Gloryday*, and praised LaChiusa's score, noting that the characters "blossom into individuals whose timbres and cadences identify them" as much as their physical traits. He praised Marc Kudisch (his roles in "Broadway behemoths" didn't afford him the opportunity to strut his voice with such "variety and penetration"), and he found Mary Testa "superb." Frank Scheck in the *New York Post* singled out the "rousing" title song from *Gloryday* as well as "the scene-stealing" Mary Testa.

The script was published by Dramatists Play Service, Inc., in 2008, and the cast album was released by Ghostlight Records (CD # 7915584408-2).

As *R Shoman*, the musical had first been produced by the Williamstown Theatre Festival in Williamstown, Massachusetts, for fourteen performances beginning on July 21, 2004.

1423 Selma. THEATRE: Louis Abron Arts for Living Center/Henry Street Settlement's New Federal Theatre; OPENING DATE: February 16, 1984; PERFORMANCES: 15; BOOK: Thomas Isaiah Butler; LYRICS: Thomas Isaiah Butler; MUSIC: Thomas Isaiah Butler; DIRECTION: Cliff Roquemore; CHOREOGRAPHY: Charles LaVont Williams; COSTUMES: Judy Dearing; LIGHTING: William H. Grant III; MUSICAL DIRECTION: Neal Tate; PRODUCER: Henry Street Settlement's New Federal Theatre (Woodie King, Jr., Producer; Barbara Tate, Director, Arts for Living Center; Michael Frey, Executive Director)

CAST—Cora Lee Day (Mama Sweets), Rita Graham-Knighton (Coretta, Ensemble), Ernie Banks (the Reverend Abernathy), Sherrie Strange (Rosa Parks), Thomas Isaiah Butler (Martin), Pamala Tyson (Miss Anne, Church Sister, Ensemble), Michael French (Bus Driver, Ensemble), Ronald Wyche (Woody), George E. Morton III (Tillman), James Curt Bergwall (the Reverend Graetz), Pat Franklin (Jackie, Ensemble), J. Lee Flynn (Sheriff Barnside, Ensemble), Paul M. Luksch (Deputy, Ensemble), Cynthia I. Pearson (Teacher), Joyce Griffen (Child), Levern (Man with T.V.), Jonathan Carroll (Drunk, Black Panther), Charles LaVont Williams (Black Panther)

The action occurs in the 1960s in various cities and towns, including Selma, Alabama, Memphis, Tennessee, Montgomery, Alabama, Washington, D.C., and Los Angeles, California.

The musical was presented in two acts.

ACT ONE—Overture (Orchestra), "Nature's Child" (Company; Levern, solo), "Working in the Name of King" (Company; George E. Morton III, solo), "Celebration" (Cora Lee Day, Rita Graham-Knighton, Sherrie Strange, Ernie Banks, Pamala Tyson, George E. Morton III), "Martin, Martin" (Rita Graham-Knighton), "Nigger Woman" (Michael French, Sherrie Strange, Pamala Tyson, Passengers), "Precious Memories" (Thomas Isaiah Butler), "The Time Is Now" (Thomas Isaiah Butler, Rita Graham-Knighton), "Wash Your Sins Away" (Thomas Isaiah Butler, Church Members), "Pull Together" (Ernie Banks, Ronald Wyche, Thomas Isaiah Butler, Church Members), "You're My Love" (Rita Graham-Knighton), "Isn't It Wonderful" (George E. Morton III, Church Members), "Freedom, Liberation" (Ernie Banks, Church Members), "Jesus Christ" (Sherrie Strange, Church Members), "Where's That Martin Boy" (J. Lee Flynn, Company), "Do You Lie?" (J. Lee Flynn, James Curt Bergwall, Company), "Pick Up Your Weapon" (Ronald Wyche), "Boycott Trial Song" (Judge [performer unknown], Thomas Isaiah Butler, District Attorney [performer unknown], Company), "I Can Feel Him" (Company)

ACT TWO—"When Will It End" (James Curt Bergwall), "Klansmen Song" (Grand Dragon [performer unknown], Klansmen [Various Performers]), "Hallelujah Day" (George E. Morton III, Pamala Tyson), "Prison Song" (Ronald Wyche, Prisoners), "Higher" (Ernie Banks, Prisoners), "I Hate Colored People" (Deputy #2 [performer unknown]), "Children of Love" (Cynthia I. Pearson, Joyce Griffen,

Other Performers), "Poison Hiding" (George E. Morton III), "Burn" (Ronald Wyche, Rioters), "Listen to Me Jesus" (Thomas Isaiah Butler), "Selma" (Company; Sherrie Strange, solo), "We Shall Overcome" (Company), "Celebration" (reprise) (Company)

NOTES—The Off Off Broadway civil rights musical *Selma* included in its cast of characters such figures as Martin Luther King, Jr., Coretta Scott King, and Rosa Parks. In the mid-1970s, *Selma* was produced in Los Angeles and other cities, and a 2-LP cast recording was released by Cotillion Records in 1976 (# SD-2-110-0998). Among the numbers heard on the album but not in the New York production were "Garbage," "I've Been Up to the Mountain Top," "We Don't Stand a Chance," "Are You Ready," "We'll Stand by You," "I Am Worried," "Sensitive Situation," "We Will Move," and "I Have a Dream."

For another musical about Martin Luther King, Jr., see entry for *The Last Year in the Life of Reverend Dr. Martin Luther King Jr. as Devised by Waterwell: A Rock Operetta.*

Also, the 1990 British musical *King* ("A Musical Testimony") dealt with the private and public life of the subject; the musical was recorded by London Records (CD # 425-212-2). The lyrics were by Maya Angelou (with additional lyrics by Alistair Beaton), and the music was by Richard Blackford.

1424 Sensations. THEATRE: Theatre Four; OPENING DATE: October 25, 1970; PERFORMANCES: 16; BOOK: Paul Zakrzewaki; LYRICS: Paul Zakrzewaki; MUSIC: Wally Harper; DIRECTION: Jerry Dodge; SCENERY: William and Jean Eckart; COSTUMES: Jeanne Button; LIGHTING: Beverly Emmons; MUSICAL DIRECTION: Jack Lee; PRODUCERS: John Bowab and Charles Celian

CAST—Paulette Attie (Lady Capulet), Arthur Bartow (The Friar), Judy Gibson (Juliet), Joe Masiell (Lord Montague), Ron Martin (Tybalt), James Ray (Lord Capulet), Marie Santell (Lady Montague), John Savage (Romeo), Bruce Scott (Mercutio)

SOURCE—The 1594 play *Romeo and Juliet* by William Shakespeare.

The action occurs in Verona.

The musical was presented in two acts.

ACT ONE—"Lonely Children" (Judy Gibson, Bruce Scott, John Savage, Ron Martin), "Sensations" (Judy Gibson), "Good Little Boy" (John Savage, Company), "The Beginning" (Bruce Scott), "What Kind of Parents" (Marie Santell, Paulette Attie), "Power" (Joe Masiell), "Up and Down" (John Savage, Judy Gibson, Ron Martin, Bruce Scott), "Friar's Tune" (Arthur Bartow, John Savage, Judy Gibson, Bruce Scott, Ron Martin), "Oh, My Age" (James Ray, Paulette Attie), "Sensations" (reprise) (John Savage), "Outracing Light" (Ron Martin), "War Is Good Business" (Company), "The Kill" (Bruce Scott), "Lying Here" (Company)

ACT TWO—"Middle Class Revolution" (James Ray, Paulette Attie, Joe Masiell, Marie Santell), "I'll Stay, I'll Go" (John Savage), "Queen Mab" (Bruce Scott), "I Cannot Wait" (Judy Gibson), "Sounds" (James Ray, Paulette Attie, Joe Masiell, Marie Santell), "No Place for Me" (John Savage), "Morning Sun" (John Savage, Judy Gibson), "In Nomine Dei" (Company), Finale (James Ray, Paulette Attie, Joe Masiell, Marie Santell)

NOTES—Set in Verona, and with the characters retaining Shakespeare's names, *Sensations* was nevertheless an updated version of *Romeo and Juliet*, with rock music, an integrated leading couple, drugs, violence, and apparently one anti-war song. Mel Gussow in the *New York Times* said the musical's attitude was "antiromatic"; Friar Tuck comes across like a junkie when he give a potion to Juliet; scenes with both Romeo and Juliet's parents are performed as soap opera; another scene was performed in the style of a silent film; Lord Capulet is impotent; and Mercutio and Tybalt are having an affair (moreover, Mercutio is apparently attracted to Romeo). Yet despite these trendy trappings, Gussow noted the score itself offered "pure and lovely" and "beautiful" love songs. *Sensation*'s "Lying Here" and "I Cannot Wait" reminded him of *West Side Story*'s "Tonight" and "Maria," and "not to the former's disadvantage."

Wally Harper was a conductor and dance music arranger, and *Sensations* was his only full-fledged New York musical. From the mid-1970s until his death in 2004, he was Barbara Cook's pianist and arranger for her concert and nightclub appearances as well as her recordings.

Mercury Records was to have recorded the cast album, which was cancelled due to the musical's brief two-week run.

1425 Serenade. THEATRE: Teatro La Tea; OPENING DATE: December 1, 2007; PERFORMANCES: 12; BOOK: Rachel Sheinkin; LYRICS: Rachel Sheinkin; MUSIC: Nils Olaf Dolven; DIRECTION: April Nickell; CHOREOGRAPHY: Luis Salgado; SCENERY: Tobin Ost; COSTUMES: Andrea Varga; LIGHTING: Herrick Goldman; MUSICAL DIRECTION: Jared Stein; PRODUCER: Jaradoa (Just a Roomful of Artists Doing Outreach And) Theatre Company

CAST—Joshua Henry, Anika Larsen, Sara Andreas, Ron Bagden, Anton Briones, Joe Donohoe, Mindy Dougherty, Michael Fielder, Chris Harbur, Amanda Hunt, Adam Kaokept, Nicole Lewis, Mario Martinez, Kelly McCreary, Eileen Rivera, Robb Sapp, Cara Samantha Scherker, Alison Solomon

NOTES—The Off Off Broadway musical *Serenade* dealt with a newcomer's adventures in the big city.

1426 Sgt. Pepper's Lonely Hearts Club Band on the Road. "A Rock Spectacle." THEATRE: Beacon Theatre; OPENING DATE: November 17, 1974; PERFORMANCES: 66; LYRICS AND MUSIC: John Lennon and Paul McCartney; produced conceived and adapted by Robin Wagner and Tom O'Horgan; DIRECTION: Tom O'Horgan; SCENERY: Robin Wagner; COSTUMES: Randy Barcelo; LIGHTING: Jules Fisher; MUSICAL DIRECTION: Gordon Lowry Harrell; PRODUCERS: Robert Stigwood in association with Brian Avnet and Scarab Productions; Peter Brown, Executive Producer

CAST—ALLAN NICHOLLS (Jack), WILLIAM PARRY (Sledge), B.G. GIBSON (Claw), TED NEELEY (Billy Shears), ALAINA REED (Lucy), Walter Rivera (Flattop), David Patrick Kelly (Sun Queen, Lovely Rita, Polythene Pam, Sgt. Pepper), KAY COLE (Strawberry Fields), Hammeroids (Blake Anderson, Edward Q. Bhartonn, Arlana Blue, Ron Capozzoli, Michael Meadows, Stoney Reece, Jason Roberts)

The musical was presented in two acts.

ACT ONE—Opening (Orchestra), "Sgt. Pepper's Lonely Hearts Club Band" (Allan Nicholls, William Parry, B.G. Gibson), "With a Little Help from My Friends" (Ted Neeley, Allan Nicholls, William Parry, B.G. Gibson), "Nowhere Man" (Allan Nicholls, William Parry, B.G. Gibson), "With a Little Help from My Friends" (reprise) (Ted Neeley, Allan Nicholls, William Parry, B.G. Gibson), "Lucy in the Sky with Diamonds" (Alaina Reed, Ted Neeley, Allan Nicholls, William Parry, B.G. Gibson), "I Want You" (Ted Neeley, Alaina Reed, Allan Nicholls, William Parry, B.G. Gibson), "Come Together" (Alaina Reed, Walter Rivera, Friends), "Nowhere Man II" (Allan Nicholls, William Parry, B.G. Gibson), Sun Queen (Company), "Lovely Rita" (David Patrick Kelly, Ted Neeley, Allan Nicholls, William Parry, B.G. Gibson, Alaina Reed), "Polythene Pam" (David Patrick Kelly, Ted Neeley, Allan Nicholls, William Parry, B.G. Gibson, Alaina Reed), "She Came in Through the Bathroom Window" (Allan Nicholls, with William Parry and B.G. Gibson), "You Never Give Me Your Money" (Ted Neeley, David Patrick Kelly, Allan Nicholls, William Parry, B.G. Gibson, Alaina Reed), "Lovely Rita" (reprise) (Ted Neeley, David Patrick Kelly, Allan Nicholls, B.G. Gibson, Alaina Reed), "Her Majesty" (Ted Neeley), "A Day in the Life" (Ted Neeley), "She's Leaving Home" (B.G. Gibson, with Allan Nicholls and William Parry), "Strawberry Fields Forever" (Kay Cole, Ted Neeley), "Getting Better" (Ted Neeley, Kay Cole, Allan Nicholls, William Parry, B.G. Gibson)

ACT TWO—Opening (Orchestra), "Because" (Ted Neeley, Kay Cole), "When I'm Sixty-Four" (Ted Neeley, Kay Cole), "Because" (reprise) (Ted Neeley, Kay Cole), "Good Morning, Good Morning" (Allan Nicholls, William Parry, B.G. Gibson), "Being for the Benefit of Mr. Kite" (Allan Nicholls, William Parry, B.G. Gibson, Alaina Reed), "Oh Darling" (Kay Cole), "Fixing a Hole" (Ted Neeley), "Oh Darling" (reprise) (Kay Cole), "Being for the Benefit of Mr. Kite II" (Allan Nicholls, William Parry, B.G. Gibson), "Mean Mr. Mustard" (Alaina Reed), "Maxwell's Silver Hammer" (Allan Nicholls, William Parry, B.G. Gibson), "Being for the Benefit of Mr. Kite III" (Allan Nicholls, William Parry, B.G. Gibson), "Carry That Weight" (Allan Nicholls, William Parry, B.G. Gibson), "Golden Slumbers" (Ted Neeley), "Carry That Weight" (reprise) (Allan Nicholls, William Parry, B.G. Gibson), "The Long and Winding Road" (Ted Neeley), "Get Back" (David Patrick Kelly, Ted Neeley, Alaina Reed, Allan Nicholls, William Parry, B.G. Gibson), "Sgt. Pepper's Lonely Hearts Club Band" (reprise) (Company), "The End" (Company)

NOTES—It's a mystery why anyone would pay to see a musical in which various performers sing well-known Beatles' songs; a more authentic, and certainly less expensive, experience would be to buy and play the original Beatles' recordings. In the case of *Sgt. Pepper's Lonely Hearts Club Band on the Road*, theatergoers weren't interested, and the musical lasted for only two months. However, another such revue, *Beatlemania*, was a success; it opened on Broadway in 1977, and unaccountably played for over 1,000 performances. Moreover, the British musical *John, Paul, George, Ringo...and Bert* opened at the Lyric Theatre on August 15, 1974, and played for 418 performances; Willy Russell's script included songs by John Lennon and Paul McCartney as well as by George Harrison, and the score also offered a few songs by Russell and other writers (the cast recording was released by RSO Records (LP # 2394-141-SUPER). The musical's lead singer was Barbara Dickson, who in 1983 created the role of Mrs. Johnstone in Russell's affecting and long-running hit musical *Blood Brothers*.

But, in general, playgoers have not embraced all-things-Beatles. Besides the failure of *Sgt. Pepper*, two musicals, both titled *Lennon*, were quick flops. The 1982 Off Broadway *Lennon* (see entry) lasted less than a month, and a different *Lennon*, which opened on Broadway in 2005, also had a brief life. In 1987, *Elvis & John* opened in Germany; an evening of two one-act musicals, one dealt with Elvis Presley, the other with Lennon (for more information regarding Presley-related musicals, see entry for *Elvis Mania*).

1427 Serious Bizness. THEATRE: O'Neals' 43rd Street Cabaret; OPENING DATE: September 26, 1983; PERFORMANCES: 189; SKETCHES: Jennifer Allen, David Babcock, Don Perman, and Winnie Holzman; MUSIC: David Evans; DIRECTION: Phyllis Newman; SCENERY: Loren Sherman; COSTUMES: Cynthia O'Neal; LIGHTING: Mal Sturchio; MUSICAL DIRECTION: Frederick Weldy; PRODUCERS: Jill Larson and Marisa Smith; Jeffrey Matthews, Associate Producer

CAST—David Babcock, Jill Larson, Don Perman, Nealla Spano

The revue was presented in two acts (sketch and song assignments unknown).

ACT ONE—"Equity Announcement Opening," "Komedy Kupboard I," "Fun with Your Doohinkus," "Can't Stand to Sing" (song), "Strange Little Man," "Maid of Honor," "Doing the Work," "Jesus Likes Me" (song), "Apres Ski," "Mr. Tornado I," "Bebe Perdu," "Swingle Songsters," "Great Explanations"

ACT TWO—"Mr. Tornado II," "My Baby" (song), "Di-a-wham," "Men at Work," "Gutter of Love" (song), "Mr. Tornado III," "Graveyard Rap," "Say Your Goodbyes," "Sexy!" (a/k/a "I Don't Find You Sexy Anymore") (song), "Komedy Kupboard" (reprise)

NOTES—The comedy revue *Serious Bizness* included a few songs, which are notated above. *Serious Bizness* had been previously produced in the American Humorists series at the American Place Theatre.

Frank Rich in the *New York Times* generally liked the evening, which attempted to recreate the style of earlier, fabled New York revues, such as those produced by Julius Monk. While he found the material not always "consistently clever," he happily noted that the humor didn't reference television. He singled out David Babcock, the revue's "distinctive performer," and mentioned he enjoyed a "wicked confession ditty" titled "I Don't Find You Sexy Anymore."

Rich reported that the show's press spokesman indicated that while Phyllis Newman was listed in the program as the director, she had withdrawn before the opening and had been succeeded by Barnet Kellman.

The script was published by Samuel French, Inc., in 1984.

1428 Sessions. "A New Musical." THEATRE: Peter Jay Sharp Theatre; OPENING DATE: June 10, 2007; PERFORMANCES: 77; BOOK: Albert Tapper; LYRICS: Albert Tapper; MUSIC: Albert Tapper; DIRECTION: Steven Petrillo; CHOREOGRAPHY: Steven Petrillo; SCENERY: Peter Barbieri, Jr.; COSTUMES: Peter Barbieri, Jr.; LIGHTING: Deborah Constantine; MUSICAL DIRECTION: Fran Minarik; PRODUCERS: Algonquin Theatre Productions and Ten Grand Productions

CAST—Bertilla Baker (Mrs. Murphy), Amy Bodnar (Leila), Al Bundonis (Baxter), David Patrick Ford (Dylan), Scott Richard Foster (George Preston), Jim Madden (Mr. Murphy), Kelli Maguire (Sunshine), Trisha Rapier (Mary), Matthew Shepard (Dr. Peterson), Ed Reynolds Young (The Voice)

The musical was presented in two acts.

ACT ONE—"I'm Only Human" (Matthew Shepard, Ed Reynolds Young), "Wendy" (Scott Richard Foster), "Above the Clouds" (Kelli Maguire, Scott Richard Foster, Jim Madden, Bertilla Baker, Matthew Shepard, Trisha Rapier, David Patrick Ford), "I'm an Average Guy" (David Patrick Ford), "Feels Like Home" (Trisha Rapier), "Breathe" (Amy Bodnar), "The Murphy's Squabble" (Bertilla Baker, Jim Madden, Kelli Maguire, Scott Richard Foster, Matthew Shepard, Trisha Rapier, David Patrick Ford), "If I Could Just Be Like Pete" (Scott Richard Foster, Amy Bodnar, Matthew Shepard), "I Saw the Rest of My Life" Amy Bodnar, Matthew Shepard)

ACT TWO—"You Should Dance" (Matthew Shepard, Kelli Maguire, Bertilla Baker, Jim Madden, Al Bundonis, David Patrick Ford), "This Is One River I Can't Cross" (Trisha Rapier, Matthew Shepard), "Living Out a Lie" (Scott Richard Foster, Matthew Shepard), "I Never Spent Time with My Dad" (Al Bundonis), "Suddenly Somehow" (Matthew Shepard), "I Just Want to Hold You for a While" (Bertilla Baker, Jim Madden), "The Sun Shines In" (Kelli Maguire, David Patrick Ford, Bertilla Baker, Jim Madden, Scott Richard Foster, Al Bundonis), "I Will Never Find Another You" (Amy Bodnar), Finale: "You Should Dance" (reprise)/"I'm Only Human" (Company)

NOTES—*Sessions* dealt with a psychiatrist and the problems of his patients in group therapy. The psychiatrist also has issues, which he discusses with *his* therapist, an unseen character ("The Voice").

Frank Scheck in the *New York Post* found the book "formulaic," the score "undistinguished," and the tone of the show "jarringly inconsistent" (from "vulgar humor" to tragedy).

During previews, the song "I've Become My Father" was deleted, and it appears that "It's All on the Record" and "There Should Be Love" were deleted in previews or early in the run. Original Cast Records released the cast album (CD # OC-6220). The musical was revived at the Algonquin Theatre in 2009.

For other "therapy" musicals, see entries for *I Can't Keep Running in Place* (six women who meet weekly in group therapy), *Inside Out* (six women in therapy), and *One Foot Out the Door* (two women and one man in therapy, all trying to deal with the men in their lives).

1429 The Seven. THEATRE: New York Theatre Workshop; OPENING DATE: February 12, 2006; PERFORMANCES: 31; LYRICS: Will Power; MUSIC: Will Power; additional music by Will Hammond and Justin Ellington; DIRECTION: Jo Bonney; CHOREOGRAPHY: Bill T. Jones; SCENERY: Richard Hoover; Kelly Bray, Reese Hicks, Richard Hoover, Frank Luna, and Robi Silvestri, Projections; COSTUMES: Emilio Sosa; LIGHTING: David Weiner; MUSICAL DIRECTION: Daryl Waters; PRODUCERS: New York Theatre Workshop (James C. Nicola, Artistic Director; Lynn Moffat, Managing Director) in association with the Public Theatre

CAST—Edwin Lee Gibson (Oedipus, Laius), Benton Greene (Eteocles), Jamyl Dobson (Polynices), Tom Nelis (Right Hand), Flaco Navaja (Tydeus), Uzo Aduba (Second Woman, Amphiarus), Shawtane Monroe Bowen (Third Man, Hippomedon), Amber Efe (D.J.), Manuel Herrera (First Man, Eteoclus), Flaco Navaja (Tydeus), Postell Pringle (Second Man, Capaneous), Pearl Sun (First Woman, Parthenopaeus), Charles Turner (Aeschylus)

SOURCE—The 467 B.C. play *Seven Against Thebes* by Aeschylus.

The musical was presented in two acts.

NOTES—*The Best Plays Theatre Yearbook 2005-2006* indicated *The Seven* used hip-hop music to wed Aeschylus to a "postmodern sensibility." Despite winning the Lucille Lortel Award for Best Musical, the work doesn't seem to have been heard from after its one-month run. Charles Isherwood in the *New York Times* said the rap adaptation was "frisky and funny" in its irreverent "in your face" and "yo mama" treatment of the classic tragedy, one in which Oedipus is dressed in "flashy pimp regalia" and the traditional Greek chorus is often told to "shut up." *The Seven* brings to mind earlier musical adaptations of Greek tragedy which were produced by the Public Theatre (which was a co-producer of *The Seven*), such as *Blood* and *The Wedding of Iphigenia/Iphigenia in Taurus* (see entries).

1430 Seven Come Eleven. "A Gaming Gambol." THEATRE: Upstairs at the Downstairs; OPENING DATE: October 5, 1961; PERFORMANCES: Unknown; SKETCHES: William F. Brown and Robert Elliott; LYRICS: Marshall Barer, Michael Brown, Lesley Davison, Robert Elliott, Bruce Geller, Jack Holmes, William Roy, Maxwell Siegel, Rod Warren, and G. Wood; MUSIC: Michael Brown, Lesley Davison, Jack Holmes, William Roy, Ralph Strain, Jack Urbont, Rod Warren, and G. Wood; DIRECTION: Julius Monk; staged by Frank Wagner; CHOREOGRAPHY: Frank Wagner; MUSICAL DIRECTION: William Roy and Carl Norman at the Plural Pianos; PRODUCER: Julius Monk

CAST—Philip Bruns, Ceil Cabot, Rex Robbins, Steve Roland, Donna Sanders, Mary Louise Wilson

ACT ONE—Opening: "Seven Come Eleven" (lyric and music by William Roy) (Company) "This Is New York" (lyric and music by Jack Holmes) (Ceil Cabot, Rex Robbins, Steve Roland) "The Jackie Look" (lyric and music by Lesley Davison) (Ceil Cabot) "Suddenly, Last Tuesday" (sketch by William F. Brown) (Rex Robbins, Donna Sanders) "I Found Him" (lyric by Bruce Geller, music by Jack Urbont) (Donna Sanders) "School Daze" (lyric and music by Michael Brown) (Company) "Forbidden Tropics" (lyric and music by G. Wood) (Mary Louise Wilson) "New York Has a New Hotel" (lyric and music by Michael Brown) (Company)

ACT TWO—"Captain of the Pinafores" (lyric and music by Rod Warren) (Steve Roland) "Alma Whatsa Mater" (lyric and music by Lesley Davision) (Company) "Sick" (lyric by Maxwell Siegel, music by William Roy) (Philip Bruns), "Don't You Feel Naked Not Drinking?" (sketch by Robert Elliott) (Mary Louise Wilson, Rex Robbins) "I Flew to Havana Last Wednesday" (lyric and music by Michael Brown) (Ceil Cabot) "Umbilicus Undulatus" (lyric by Robert Elliott, music by William Roy) (Rex Robbins) "Christmas Long Ago" (lyric by Marshall Barer, music by Ralph Strain) (Donna Sanders, Steve Roland) "John Birch Society" (lyric and music by Michael Brown) (Company), "The Princess and the Toad" (sketch by William F. Brown, incidental music by William Roy) (Company), Finale: "Seven Come Eleven" (lyric and music by William Roy) (Company)

NOTES—Julius Monk's witty revues continued with the successful "gaming gambol" *Seven Come Eleven*, which was followed by a second edition in 1963 (see entry).

The revue opened within the first year of the Kennedy Administration, and some numbers were political in nature: Ceil Cabot wanted to emulate the First Lady in "The Jackie Look"; "Alma Whatsa Mater" was a send-up of the Peace Corps; and the hoe-down "John Birch Society" spoofed far right-wing ideologues (who will be content only when Red Skelton is exposed). Other numbers commented upon the New York scene ("This Is New York" and "New York Has a New Hotel," the latter Michael Brown's latest entry in his continuing catalogue of songs about Manhattan) while another ("Don't You Feel Naked Not Drinking?") dealt with a strict teetotaler who won't remove her wrap because the needle marks on her arm might show.

"Captain of the Pinafores," a Gilbert-and-Sullivan styled ditty about an ever-so-chic fashion designer who "majored in chintz," was feyly portrayed by Steve Roland. And "Sick" was an amusing look at far-out so-called comedians who dwelt on sordid and tasteless topics.

A month before *All in Love* (see entry) opened, its song "I Found Him" was introduced in *Seven Come Eleven*, and the number appears on the cast albums of both shows.

In the Times-How-They-Have-Changed Department, the song "I Flew to Havana Last Wednesday" made merry of an airplane hi-jacking.

In his *New York Times'* review, Arthur Gelb reported the evening's highlight was "The Princess and the Toad," a spoof of Method acting. Considering that the topic had been endlessly satirized, Gelb was all the more impressed with the "originality and élan" of the sketch (which, incidentally, took place in "New York, 19"). Ceil Cabot portrayed the princess (who "majored in myth at Vassar") and Philip Bruns was a Method actor transformed into a toad because he took one of his acting assignments too literally. Gelb praised Bruns, saying his performance "might be envied by Marcel Marceau."

The following songs may have been performed in the revue: "The Poet Aster Is Cornered" (lyric by

Martin Charnin, music by John Kesner [John Kessler?, or perhaps Robert [Bob] Kessler, Charnin's occasional collaborator] and "Stock on the Rocks" (lyric and music by Jacques Urbont).

The cast album of *Seven Come Eleven* was released by Columbia Records (LP # 55477/8).

For a complete list of Julius Monk's revues, see entry for *Four Below*; also see Appendix Q.

1431 Seven Come Eleven (Second Edition). THEATRE: Upstairs at the Downstairs; OPENING DATE: August 1963 (specific date unknown); PERFORMANCES: Unknown; SKETCHES: Writers Unknown; LYRICS: Jerry Bock, Louis Botto, June Carroll, Stan Daniels, Jack Holmes, Ray Jessel, Jack Johnson, John Meyer, Peter Myers, and Paul Rosner; MUSIC: Ronald Cass, Stan Daniels, Jack Holmes, Larry Holofcener, Ray Jessel, Jack Johnson, John Meyer, Arthur Siegel, and Thomas Wagner; DIRECTION: Ben Bagley and Jonathan Lucas; CHOREOGRAPHY: Jonathan Lucas; PRODUCERS: Arthur Siegel and Julius Monk

CAST—Sudie Bond, Hal Buckley, Ralph Roberts, Cy Young, Myra de Groot

The revue was presented in two acts (division of acts and sketch and song assignments unknown).

MUSICAL NUMBERS—"After Burton, Who?" (lyric by Louis Botto, music by Arthur Siegel), "Auf Weidersehen" (lyric by Stan Daniels, music by Ray Jessel), "Ave Maria" (lyric and music by Jack Johnson), "Before and After" (lyric and music by Jack Holmes), "Bring Out the Beast in Me" (lyric by Robert Gold, music by Dolores Claman), "How to Succeed in Business Without Really Trying" (lyric by Louis Botto, music by Arthur Siegel), "Open Bright" (lyric and music by John Meyer), "Simple Tune" (lyric and music by Jack Holmes), "The Story of Alice" (lyric by Larry Holofcener, music by Jerry Bock), "This Is New York" (lyric and music by Jack Holmes), "Time for Another Affair" (lyric by Paul Rosner, music by Thomas Wagner), "Tune to Take Away" (lyric by Peter Myers, music by Ronald Cass), "We Miss Ike" (lyric by Peter Myers, music by Ronald Cass), "We Want You to Be the First Ones to Know" (lyric by June Carroll, music by Arthur Siegel)

NOTES—"This Is New York" was a carry-over from the first edition of *Seven Come Eleven*; "The Story of Alice" had been previously heard in both the Broadway revue *Catch a Star!* (1955) and in *No Shoestrings* (1962; see entry); and "We Want You to Be the First Ones To Know" had been introduced in *New Faces of 1962* (as "I Want You to Be the First To Know"; four other songs from *New Faces* had been heard in the 1962 Off Broadway revue *The Cats' Pajamas* [see entry]). "Bring Out the Beast in Me" had earlier been heard as "The Beast in Me" in the London revue *Pieces of Eight*, which opened at the Apollo Theatre on September 23, 1959; the song can be heard on the cast album of that revue. For a complete list of Julius Monk's revues, see entry for *Four Below*; also see Appendix Q.

1432 Sex Tips for Modern Girls. THEATRE: Susan Bloch Theatre; transferred to Actors' Playhouse on December 19, 1986; OPENING DATE: October 5, 1986; PERFORMANCES: 198; SKETCHES: "Collectively created" by Edward Astley, Susan Astley, Kim Seary, John Sereda, Hilary Strang, Christine Willes, and Peter Eliot Weiss; LYRICS: John Sereda; MUSIC: John Sereda; DIRECTION: Susan Astley; SCENERY: Original design by Pearl Bellesen; set adaptation by Llewellyn Harrison; COSTUMES: Pearl Bellesen; LIGHTING: Llewellyn Harrison; MUSICAL DIRECTION: John Sereda; PRODUCERS: RayWaves Productions/Raymond L. Gaspard; a Touchstone Theatre Production; Alan Harrison and Sharon and Bruce Miller, Associate Producers

CAST—Kim Seary (Dot), Christine Willes (Helen), Hilary Strang (Alyss), Edward Astley (The Men)

The revue was presented in two acts (the program didn't credit song assignments).

ACT ONE—"Ordinary Women," "Motherload," "Go for It," "Who Will Be There," "Easy for Them to Say," "Baby, Baby," "Penis Envoy"

ACT TWO—"Up to My Tits in Water," "Victim of Normality," "Oh! K-Y Chorale (or Beyond the Labia Majora)," "More and More"

NOTES—First performed in 1984, the Canadian revue *Sex Tips for Modern Girls* purported to be a "piece of theatre that would speak from a woman's point of view."

Stephen Holden in the *New York Times* felt the evening was "little more than a glorified rap session" with a "flimsy" score. While he singled out one or two songs, he noted that overall the revue was "lost in the wilderness between self-help and show business." Holden also mentioned that the revue was not related to a then recently-published book by Cynthia Heimel titled *Sex Tips for Girls*. The song "Up to My Tits in Water" was by Kim Seary and Adrian Smith, and "Penis Envoy" had additional lyrics by Gary Fisher.

The Canadian cast performed for the first forty-one performances; when the revue transferred to the Actors' Playhouse, an American cast (Julie Ridge, Laura Turnbull, Briana Burke, and Alan Harrison) assumed the roles.

1433 Sextet. "A New Musical." THEATRE: Bijou Theatre; OPENING DATE: March 3, 1974; PERFORMANCES: 9; BOOK: Harvey Perr and Lee Goldsmith; LYRICS: Lee Goldsmith; MUSIC: Lawrence Hurwit; DIRECTION: Jered Barclay; CHOREOGRAPHY: Jered Barclay; SCENERY: Peter Harvey; COSTUMES: Zoe Brown; LIGHTING: Marc B. Weiss; MUSICAL DIRECTION: David Frank; PRODUCERS: Balemar Productions and Lawrence E. Sokol

CAST—Robert Spencer (David), John Newton (Paul), Mary Small (Fay), Harvey Evans (Kenneth), Dixie Carter (Ann), Jerry Lanning (Leonard)

The action occurs in an apartment in New York City at the present time.

The musical was presented in one act.

MUSICAL NUMBERS—"Nervous" (Company), "What the Hell Am I Doing Here?" (John Newton), "Keep on Dancing" (Robert Spencer, Harvey Evans, Mary Small, John Newton), "Spunk" (Mary Small, Robert Spencer, Harvey Evans), "Visiting Rights" (Dixie Carter), "Going-Staying" (Company), "I Wonder" (Dixie Carter, Mary Small), "Women and Men" (Jerry Lanning, Robert Spencer, Harvey Evans), "I Love You All the Time" (Jerry Lanning), "Keep on Dancing" (reprise) (Company), "Hi" (Harvey Evans), "It'd Be Nice" (Mary Small), "Roseland" (Company), "How Does It Start?" (Robert Spencer), "Roseland" (reprise) (Company)

NOTES—Any musical set in modern-day Manhattan which dealt with married and unmarried couples was sure to be compared to Stephen Sondheim's *Company* (1970), and, indeed, *Sextet* was (one of its songs was actually titled "Going-Staying"). Douglas Watt in the *New York Daily News* pronounced *Sextet* "a poor man's *Company*," and Martin Gottfried called it "Son of *Company*," but not in a disparaging way. The always perceptive Gottfried found *Sextet* "a mostly terrific musical ... ambitious ... clever ... funny and unusual and fine." The musical sounds fascinating, especially in the way it told its story. Gottfried described a "non-linear" approach to the plot in which the conversations were "layered": one character spoke to a second character who in turn "responds to a third who reacts to a fourth."

The song "Roseland," was highly praised, and was apparently an homage to *Follies* (1971). Of the cast members, Dixie Carter was singled out for her performance.

1434 Sh-Boom! "The New Fifties Musical." THEATRE: The AMAS Repertory Theatre; OPENING DATE: April 11, 1986; PERFORMANCES: 16; BOOK: Eric V. Tait, Jr.; LYRICS: Eric V. Tait, Jr.; MUSIC: Willex Brown and Eric V. Tait, Jr.; DIRECTION: Stuart Warmflash; CHOREOGRAPHY: Audrey Tischler; SCENERY: Janice Davis; COSTUMES: Candace Warner; additional costumes by Howard Behar; LIGHTING: Eric Thomann; MUSICAL DIRECTION: Loni Berry; PRODUCER: The AMAS Repertory Theatre, Inc. (Rosetta LeNoire, Founder and Artistic Director)

CAST—Michael Accardo (Half Note, Chuckle), Anthony Barone (Chico, Zircon), Toni-Maria Chalmers (Charlene), Sarah Clark (Diane), Barbara Warren-Cooke (Miss McIntosh), Ruthann Curry (Mrs. Antiamore), Deborah Davis (Grace), Anthony Dowdy (Danny, Chuckle), Gregory Harvey (Chip), Reginald Hobbs (Tony C., Zircon), Sue Judin (Dolores), Michael Kostroff (Teddy, Half Note), Jill Kotler (Jill Antiamore), Daniel Neusom (Sandman, Zircon, Billy), Peter J. Saputo (Mr. Antiamore), Julia Simpson (God, Mrs. Johnson), Crist Swann (Bob, Half Note), Casey Williams (Sheila, Grandmother)

The action occurs in a lower-middle-class urban high school in New York during 1954.

The musical was presented in two acts.

ACT ONE—"Sh-Boom" (lyric and music by James W. Edwards, Carl Feaster, Claude Feaster, James Keyes, and Floyd McRae) (Ensemble), "The Merengue" (instrumental) (Dancers), "Sh-Boom" (reprise) (Michael Accardo, Michael Kostroff, Crist Swann), "Sh-Boom" (reprise) (Reginald Hobbs, Deborah Davis, Crist Swann), "The One You Love" (Deborah Davis), "Honey Love" (lyric and music by Jean Gerald and Clyde McPhatter) (Anthony Barone, Reginald Hobbs, Daniel Neusom), "A Shortage of Me" (Girls, Gregory Harvey), "What Good's a Mambo?" (Barbara Warren-Cooke, Girls, Gregory Harvey, Reginald Hobbs), "The One You Love" (reprise) (Reginald Hobbs), "And That Was Puerto Rico" (Peter J. Saputo, Barbara Warren-Cooke), "Baby, Sweet Baby" (Toni-Maria Chalmers, Crist Swann), "Brown-Eyed Girl" (Reginald Hobbs), "Sh-Boom" (reprise)/"The Merengue" (reprise) (Ensemble, Dancers)

ACT TWO—"Hush Now" (Casey Williams), "Communication" (Julia Simpson, Back-Up Singers), "Beautiful People" (Julia Simpson, Reginald Hobbs, Crist Swann), "A Thousand Miles Away" (lyric and music by James Sheppard)/"Daddy's Home" (lyric and music by James Sheppard) (Toni-Maria Chalmers, Daniel Neusom, Sarah Clark, Jill Kotler, Sue Judin), "In the Still of the Night (I'll Remember)" (lyric and music by Fred Parris) (Anthony Barone, Reginald Hobbs, Daniel Neusom), "Get a Job" (Michael Kostroff, Michael Accardo, Anthony Dowdy), "Do You Know?" (Deborah Davis, Jill Kotler, Ensemble), "Sh-Boom" (reprise) (Company)

NOTES—Like *Grease* (see entry), the plot of the Off Off Broadway musical *Sh-Boom!* dealt with high-school students during the early days of the rock and roll era; the story seems to have centered around rival high-school singing groups. The musical included a few authentic songs of the period. One, "Come Go with Me" (lyric and music by Clarence Quick), wasn't in the program's song list, but was credited elsewhere in the program; another number ("Get a Job") might have been written especially for the production or it could have been an interpolation of the song "Get a Job" which was a hit during the late 1950s [the program didn't credit a lyricist or composer]).

1435 Shades of Harlem. "A Cotton Club Cabaret Musical." THEATRE: Village Gate/Downstairs; OPENING DATE: August 21, 1984; PERFORMANCES: 258; CREATED BY: Jeree Palmer; "ADDI-

TIONAL CONCEPTS" BY Frank Owens; DIRECTION: Mical Whitaker; CHOREOGRAPHY: Ty Stephens; SCENERY: Linda Lombardi; COSTUMES: Sharon Alexander; LIGHTING: Robert Strohmeier; MUSICAL DIRECTION: Frank Owens; PRODUCERS: Tony Conforti and Jerry Saperstein in association with Brian Winthrop; Howard Effron, Robert Roth, Richard Scarlato, and Hank Thomas, Associate Producers; Sal Surace and George Tassone, Executive Producers

CAST—BRANICE MCKENZIE, JEREE PALMER, TY STEPHENS, The Harlem Renaissance Ladies (Ludie Jones, Juanita Boisseau, Alice Wilkie), The Renaissance Girls (Sheila Barker, Doris Bennett, Melanie Daniels, Alyson Lang), Frank Owens (Band Leader and Pianist)

The action occurs in a nightclub in Harlem during the 1920s.

The revue was presented in two acts.

ACT ONE—"Shades of Harlem" (lyric by Ty Stephens and Jeree Palmer, music by Frank Owens) (Ty Stephens, Branice McKenzie, Jeree Palmer, Renaissance Girls), "Take the 'A' Train" (lyric by Billy Strayhorn, music by Duke Ellington) (Ty Stephens), "I Love Harlem" (lyric by Ty Stephens and Jeree Palmer, music by Frank Owens) (Ty Stephens), "Sweet Georgia Brown" (lyric and music by Ben Bernie, Maceo Pinkard, and Kenneth Casey) (Renaissance "Ladies and Renaissance" Girls), "Madame Albert K. Johnson" (lyric by Langston Hughes, composer unknown) (Jeree Palmer), "You've Got the Right Key but the Wrong Keyhole" (lyric and music by Clarence Williams and Eddie Green) (Jeree Palmer), "Satin Doll" (lyric by Billy Strayhorn and Johnny Mercer, music by Duke Ellington) (Ty Stephens), "I Got It Bad (and That Ain't Good)" (lyric by Paul Francis Webster, music by Duke Ellington; from 1941 musical *Jump for Joy* [closed prior to Broadway]) (Branice McKenzie), "Black Coffee" (lyric by Paul Francis Webster, music by Sonny Burke) (Ty Stephens), "The Jitterbug" (music by Frank Owens) (Ty Stephens, Sheila Barker), "Harlem Hop" (lyric by Ty Stephens and Frank Owens, music by Frank Owens) (Company)

ACT TWO—"At a Georgia Camp Meeting" (music by Kerry Mills) (Renaissance Girls), "If You Wanna Keep Your Man" (lyric by Ty Stephens and Branice McKenzie, music by Branice McKenzie) (Branice McKenzie, Jeree Palmer), "Diga, Diga, Do" (from *Blackbirds of 1928;* lyric by Dorothy Fields, music by Jimmy McHugh) (Ty Stephens, Renaissance Girls) "Stowaway" (lyric and music by Ty Stephens) (Ty Stephens, Renaissance Girls), "I'm Just Simply Full of Jazz" (lyricist unknown, music by Eubie Blake) (Jeree Palmer), "My Man" (*Ziegfeld Follies of 1921*; original French lyric [as "Mon Homme"] by Albert Willemetz and Jacques Charles, English lyric by Channing Pollock, music by Maurice Yvain) (Branice McKenzie), "On the Sunny Side of the Street" (*Lew Leslie's International Revue*, 1930; lyric by Dorothy Fields, music by Jimmy McHugh) (Ty Stephens, Branice McKenzie, Jeree Palmer, Frank Owens), "Body and Soul" (*Three's a Crowd*, 1930; lyric by Edward Heyman, Robert Sour, and Frank Eyton, music by John [Johnny] Green) (Ty Stephens), "I Got Rhythm" (*Girl Crazy*, 1930; lyric by Ira Gershwin, music by George Gershwin) (Renaissance Ladies, Renaissance Girls), "Perdido" (lyric by Ervin Drake and Hans Lengsfelder, music by Juan Tizol) (Ludie Jones); at certain performances, this number was substituted with "It Don't Mean a Thing (If It Ain't Got That Swing)"; lyric by Irving Mills, music by Duke Ellington; performed by Juanita Boisseau, "God Bless the Child" (lyric and music by Billie Holiday and Arthur Herzog, Jr.) (Jeree Palmer), Finale: "Shades of Harlem" (reprise) (Company)

NOTES—Using a mixture of old and new songs, *Shades of Harlem* was supposedly a recreation of a Cotton Club Show of the 1920s. Unfortunately, it was too similar in style to other Black revues of the era which also took place in the 1920s or 1930s and which traded heavily on nostalgia (the earlier *Bubbling Brown Sugar* [1976; see entry] had also recreated a Cotton Club-styled revue). And no less than five songs used in *Shades of Harlem* had also been heard in either *Bubbling Brown Sugar* or *Sophisticated Ladies* (1981). Mel Gussow in the *New York Times* found the revue "summerweight," and while he liked the "amiable" evening, he noted it didn't match *Ain't Misbehavin'* (see entry) and other similar musical anthologies of the era.

1436 Shakespeare in Harlem. "A Theatrical Portrait." THEATRE: 41st Street Theatre; OPENING DATE: February 9, 1960; PERFORMANCES: 32; PRODUCERS: Howard Gottfried and Robert Glenn, by arrangement with the New York Chapter of ANTA; Wilhelmina Clement, Associate Producer

NOTES—The evening consisted of two one-act plays with music, *God's Trombones* and *Shakespeare in Harlem*. The former was based on James Weldon Johnson's *God's Trombones*, a collection of his sermons which was published in 1922. For other adaptations of *God's Trombones*, see entry for Vinnette Carroll's *Trumpets of the Lord*, which opened Off Broadway in 1963 (and was seen on Broadway in 1969). Two revised versions of Carroll's adaptation were performed Off Off Broadway in 1989 (as *God's Trombones!*) and in 1997 (as *God's Trombones*); see entries. Also see entry for a 1975 adaptation of Johnson's sermons which was seen Off Off Broadway as *God's Trombones* (which doesn't seem to be based on Carroll's version). There was also a production of the work presented at Town Hall on April 16, 1982, for three performances (which also doesn't appear to be based on Carroll's version). Further, *Godsong*, an adaptation of *God's Trombones* by Tad Truesdale, was presented Off Off Broadway, first at Amas Repertory Theatre on March 4, 1976, and then at La Mama Experimental Theatre Club (ETC) on April 23, 1976, and on December 30, 1976. The March production was directed by Truesdale, and the cast included Ernie Adano, Ruth Brisbane, Leslie Foglesong, Dee Dee Lavant, and Rudy Lowe.

ACT ONE—*God's Trombones* Text: James Weldon Johnson; adapted by Robert Glenn; MUSIC: Robert Cobert; DIRECTION: Robert Glenn; CHOREOGRAPHY: Jay Riley, Choreographic Consultant; SCENERY: Robert L. Ramsey; COSTUMES: Robert L. Ramsey; LIGHTING: Robert L. Ramsey; MUSICAL DIRECTION: Robert Cobert

CAST—Frederick O'Neal (The Preacher); The Congregation played by Ted Butler, Frank Glass, Alma Hubbard, Calden Marsh, John McCurry, Jay Riley, Isabel Sanford, Royce Wallace, Richard Ward

MUSICAL NUMBERS—"The Creation" (Ted Butler), "The Temptation" (Members of the Congregation), "Noah and the Ark" (Richard Ward, Members of the Congregation), "The Prodigal Son" (Jay Riley, Frank Glass, Royce Wallace, Congregation), "Let My People Go" (Ted Butler, John McCurry, Isabel Sanford), "The Judgment" (Members of the Congregation, Ted Butler)

ACT TWO—*Shakespeare in Harlem*; TEXT: Langston Hughes; adapted by Robert Glenn; MUSIC: Robert Cobert; MUSICAL CONTINUITY: Margaret Bonds; SCENERY: Robert L. Ramsey; COSTUMES: Robert L. Ramsey; LIGHTING: Robert L. Ramsey; MUSICAL DIRECTION: Robert Cobert

CAST—Jay Riley (Narrator), John McCurry (Blues Man, Preacher), Alma Hubbard (Alberta K. Johnson), Ted Butler (Old Man), Calden Marsh (Young Man), Frank Glass (Cat, Killer Boy), Richard Ward (Sick Man, Bartender), Isabel Sanford (Girl in Bar), Royce Wallace (Chippie)

The action occurs in Harlem at the present time. Song titles weren't listed in the program. On February 3, 1977, the AMAS Repertory Theatre presented the Off Off Broadway production *Come Laugh and Cry with Langston Hughes*, a new version of *Shakespeare in Harlem* which was adapted by Rosetta LeNoire and Clyde Williams.

1437 Shakespeare's Cabaret (1980; 1981). THEATRE: Colonnades Theatre Lab; OPENING DATE: February 1, 1980; PERFORMANCES: 40; LYRICS: William Shakespeare; MUSIC: Lance Mulcahy; DIRECTION: Michael Lessac; MUSICAL DIRECTION: Donald G. Jones; PRODUCERS: Colonnades Theatre Lab (Michael Lessac, Artistic Director; Robert N. Lear, Executive Producer)

CAST—Alan Brasington, Maureen Brennan, Mel Johnson, Jr., Patti Perkins, Roxanne Reese, Keith R. Rice, Peter Van Norden

SOURCE—Adaptations from the writings of William Shakespeare (1564-1616).

The revue was presented in two acts.

ACT ONE—"If Music and Sweet Poetry Agree" (from *The Passionate Pilgrim*) (Ensemble), "How Should I Your True Love Know?" (*Hamlet*) (Alan Brasington), "Come Live with Me and Be My Love" (*The Passionate Pilgrim*) (Mel Johnson, Jr.), "If I Profane" (*Romeo and Juliet*) (Peter Van Norden, Maureen Brennan), "Tell Me, Where Is Fancy Bred?" (*The Merchant of Venice*) (Ensemble), "The *Venus and Adonis* Suite" (First Meeting; The Chase; The Seduction; The Rejection; The Hunt; Final Parting) (Patti Perkins, Mel Johnson, Jr.), "What Thou See'st When Thou Dost Awake" (*A Midsummer Night's Dream*) (Ensemble), "Come Away, Death" (*Twelfth Night*) (Keith R. Rice), "Why Should This a Desert Be?" (*As You Like It*) (Performer[s] unknown), "All That Glisters Is Not Gold" (*The Merchant of Venice*) (Maureen Brennan, Patti Perkins, Roxanne Reese), "Crabbed Age and Youth" (*The Passionate Pilgrim*) (Alan Brasington)

ACT TWO—"If Music Be the Food of Love" (*Twelfth Night*) (Alan Brasington), "Fathers That Wear Rags" (*King Lear*) (Roxanne Reese), "Epitaph for Marina" (*Pericles*) (Keith R. Rice, Patti Perkins), "Will You Buy Any Tape?" (*The Winter's Tale*) (Maureen Brennan), "Shall I Compare Thee to a Summer's Day?" (Sonnet 18) (Mel Johnson, Jr.), "Come Unto These Yellow Sands" (*The Tempest*) (Ensemble), "Lawn as White as Driven Snow" (*The Winter's Tale*) (Ensemble), "The Phoenix and the Turtle" (*The Phoenix and the Turtle*) (Alan Brasington, Maureen Brennan, Peter Van Norden), "I Am Saint Jacques' Pilgrim" (*All's Well That Ends Well*) (Ensemble), "The Willow Song" (*Othello*) (Patti Perkins), "Pyramus, Arise" (*A Midsummer Night's Dream*) (Alan Brasington), "Shepherd's Song" (*The Passionate Pilgrim*) (Peter Van Norden), "Tomorrow Is Saint Valentine's Day" (*Hamlet*) (Patti Perkins), "Rosalinde" (*Hamlet*) (Alan Brasington, Keith R. Rice, Peter Van Norden), "Then Let Me the Canakin Clink" (*Othello*) (Ensemble), Shakespeare's Epitaph and Celebration (Ensemble)

NOTES—All lyrics in the revue *Shakespeare's Cabaret* were adapted from plays and poems by Shakespeare (with the exception of "Come Live with Me and Be My Love," which was written by Christopher Marlowe and was later quoted by Shakespeare in *Twelfth Night*).

A year later, on January 21, 1981, a revised one-act version of the revue was produced for fifty-four performances at the Bijou Theatre (perhaps under a Middle Broadway contract). Two members from the 1980 cast, Alan Brasington and Patti Perkins, were joined by Michael Rupert, Catherine Cox, Larry Riley, and Pauletta Pearson. Eight numbers from the 1980 production weren't used: "How Should I Your True Love Know?," "If I Profane," "Come Away, Death," "Will You Buy Any Tape?," "I Am Saint Jacques' Pilgrim," "Pyramus, Arise," "Shepherd's Song," and "Rosalinde" (the latter from *Hamlet*) and eight songs were added: "Orpheus and His Lute" (*Henry III*), "Music with Her Silver Sound" (*Romeo and Juliet*), "Have More Than Thou Showest" (*King Lear*), "Now" (*A Midsummer Night's Dream*), "Immortal Gods" (*Timon of Athens*), "The Grave Digger's Song" (*Hamlet*), "Fear No More the Heat of the Sun" (*Cymbeline*), and "Rosalynde" (the latter from *As You Like It*).

During the five-week run of the 1980 production, there was apparently a re-ordering of the songs; further, it appears that "The *Venus and Adonis* Suite" and "Why Should This a Desert Be" weren't heard at all performances.

Reviewing the 1981 production for the *New York Times*, Frank Rich found "agreeable elements" in the revue, but noted the overall effect was bland. He felt the evening lacked both a musical and a theatrical personality, and said its structure was derived from "the clichés of nightclub acts" rather than from the content of the material.

In 1985, a sequel of sorts was produced Off Off Broadway and returned there in 1986 (see entries for these productions, both of which were titled *Sweet Will*).

1438 Sharon. THEATRE: Playhouse 91; OPENING DATE: May 12, 1993; PERFORMANCES: 15; BOOK: Geraldine Fitzgerald; LYRICS: Geraldine Fitzgerald; MUSIC: Franklin Micare; DIRECTION: Geraldine Fitzgerald; CHOREOGRAPHY: Pamela Sousa; SCENERY: Mich R. Smith; COSTUMES: Mary O'Donnell; LIGHTING: Mark F. Connor; MUSICAL DIRECTION: Bruce W. Coyle; PRODUCER: Electric Theatre Company

CAST—Arthur Anderson (Lawyer, Tom Shawn), Sinead Colreavy (Miss Dee), Mark Doerr (Neelus), Patrick Farrelly (Father Riordan), Christina Gillespie (Mague), Ken Jennings (Dinzie Conlee), Kurt T. Johns (Patrick Minogue), Michael Judd (Jack Conlee), Ruth Kulerman (Moll), John McDonough (Pats Bo Bwee), David K. Thome (Guarda Mooney, Donal Conlee), Deanna Wells (Trassie Conlee), Leslie Blumenthal (Ensemble), Tim Connell (Ensemble), Karen Faistl (Ensemble), Steven Garrett (Ensemble), Mary Beth Griffith (Ensemble)

SOURCE—The 1960 novel *Sharon's Grave* by John B. Keane.

The action occurs in New York and Ireland in 1927.

The musical was presented in two acts (division of acts and song assignments unknown; song list is in performance order).

MUSICAL NUMBERS—"For the Money," "Song of Sharon," "It's a Sin," "Rim of a Rainbow," "Hear the Birds," "I'm Blest," "Hurry, Uncle Donal," "Two Eyes," "God Bless Everyone," "Grand Man," "That's How It Goes," "Dreaming," "Hail Mary," "Let's Pretend," "Boots on the Floor," "Someone," "Forgiveness," "Never," "The Man Below," "Journey's in the Mind," "Sharon's Waltz," Finale

NOTES—The Off Off Broadway musical *Sharon* was based on Irish writer John B Keane's 1960 novel *Sharon's Grave*. The book, lyrics, and direction were by Geraldine Fitzgerald, and Ken Jennings was among the cast members.

Stephen Holden in the *New York Times* described the "elaborate musical melodrama" as "*Brigadoon* crossed with *Wuthering Heights* with a dash of *Crazy for You*." The story dealt with a Manhattan playboy who in order to inherit fifty-million dollars must live in Ireland for six months and work as a roof thatcher. While there, he meets up with the supernatural. Holden noted that the "pleasant" but "hackneyed" first act turned violent with "Gothic horror" in the second. He remarked that Jennings stole the show as a hellish fiend; "exuding a feverish, phosphorescent heat," Jennings evoked Margaret Hamilton's "nightmarish" Wicked Witch in *The Wizard of Oz*.

1439 Sharps, Flats & Accidentals. THEATRE: New Victory Theatre; OPENING DATE: November 29, 1996; PERFORMANCES: 40; MATERIAL WRITTEN BY: The Flying Karamazov Brothers; ORIGINAL MUSIC: Douglas Wieselman; DIRECTION: The Flying Karamazov Brothers; BALLET CHOREOGRAPHY: Doug Elkins; DANCE COSTUMES: Susan Hilferty; LIGHTING: Stan Pressner; PRODUCERS: The New 42nd Street Inc. (Cora Cahan, President); a Flying Karamazov Brothers Production

CAST—The Flying Karamazov Brothers: Paul Magid (Dmitri), Howard Jay Patterson (Ivan), Michael Preston (Rakitin), Sam Williams (Smerdykov); also, Peter Dansky, Tim Furst, Bliss Kolb, Barbara Karger, Doug Nelson, Randy Nelson, Robert Woodruff

The revue was presented in two acts.

ACT ONE—"Concerto in B Flat for Bassoon, First Movement" (music by Wolfgang Amadeus Mozart), "Hall of the Mountain King" (music by Edvard Grieg), "Quartet for Juggling Ensemble" (music by Howard Jay Patterson), "Begin the Beguine" (1935 musical *Jubilee*; lyric and music by Cole Porter), "Taiko" (music by Howard Jay Patterson), "Fan Dance" (music by Douglas Wieselman, with Howard Jay Patterson), "Minaret" (music by The Flying Karamazov Brothers), "Minuets from The Suites for Unaccompanied Cello" (music by Johann Sebastian Bach), "The Gamble" (music by The Flying Karamazov Brothers)

ACT TWO—"Suite in Three Movements for Diverse Juggling Instruments" (music by Howard Jay Patterson; anonymous; and W.C. Handy), "Sextette" (Domenico Gaetano Maria Donizetti's 1835 opera *Lucia di Lammermoor*) "Pas de Six" (Gioachino Rossini's 1829 opera *Guillaume Tell*), "Two Part Invention in D Minor" (music by Johann Sebastian Bach), "Minimalament" (music by Howard Jay Patterson), "Jazz" (music by The Flying Karamazov Brothers), "Symphony Number 9 (Fourth Movement excerpt)" (music by Ludwig van Beethoven), "B.P. II" (Working Title) (music by Douglas Wieselman), "Whole World" (music by Howard Jay Patterson)

NOTES—*Sharps, Flats & Accidentals* was a return visit by the comic acrobats, The Flying Karamazov Brothers, who had been last seen on Broadway in their 1994 revue *The Flying Karamazov Brothers Do the Impossible*.

1440 She Shall Have Music. "A New Musical Comedy." THEATRE: Theatre Marquee; transferred to the 41st Street Theatre on February 17, 1959; OPENING DATE: January 22, 1959; PERFORMANCES: 54; BOOK: Stuart Bishop; LYRICS: Deed Meyer (NOTE: Many sources give name as Dede Meyer); MUSIC: Deed Meyer; DIRECTION: Louis MacMillan; CHOREOGRAPHY: Tao Strong; SCENERY: Herbert Senn, Helen Pond; COSTUMES: Bernie Joy; LIGHTING: Don McGovern; MUSICAL DIRECTION: Julian Stein; PRODUCERS: Stuart Bishop, Deed Meyer, and Edwin West

CAST—SKEDGE MILLER (Foppling), IRENE PERRI (Lady Fidget), LAWRENCE CHELSI (Dorilant), LAWRENCE WEBER (Horner), CHERRY DAVIS (Peg), EDGAR DANIELS (Pinchwife), BARBARA PAVELL (Althea), BETTY OAKES (Lucy), HONEY SANDERS (Mother Catchall), MICHAEL AUBREY (Christopher), RUDY TRONTO (Lackey); Gallants, Ladies, Lackeys, Maids, and Vendors played by Rhoda Levine, Peggy Ann Watson, Barbara Quaney, Arden Anderson, Ray Morrissey, Pat Tolson, Ken Fields.

SOURCES—The play *The Country Wife* by William Wycherly (Wycherley, according to some sources), written in either 1672 or 1673 and first published in 1675; some sequences within the musical were also inspired by situations depicted in the following Restoration comedies: *The School for Scandal* by Richard Brinsley Sheridan (1777), and two plays by William Congreve, *Love for Love* (1695) and *The Way of the World* (1700).

The action occurs in London during 1680.

The musical was presented in two acts.

ACT ONE—"No True Love" (Lawrence Weber, Lawrence Chelsi, Chorus), "Here's What a Mistress Ought to Be" (Skedge Miller, Lawrence Chelsi, Lawrence Webber), "Scarlet Trimmings" (Betty Oakes, Barbara Pavell, Maids) "Someday, Maybe" (Barbara Pavell, Lawrence Chelsi) "Theatre Quadrille" (Ensemble) "Moi" (Irene Perri), "Wonder Where My Heart Is" (Betty Oakes), "Twelve O'-Clock Song" (Maids, Servants), "Who Are You" (Lawrence Weber), "Basic" (Cherry Davis, Rudy Tronto) (choreography by Fernand Nault), "Maud, the Bawd" (Honey Sanders, Ensemble)

ACT TWO—"She Shall Have Music" (Betty Oakes, Chorus) "I Live to Love" (Skedge Miller, Gallants) "Who Are You" (reprise) (Betty Oakes, Lawrence Weber), "Someday, Maybe" (reprise) (Lawrence Chelsi, Barbara Pavell), "One Sweet Moment" (Betty Oakes), "Blind Man's Buff" (Irene Perri, Ensemble), "One Sweet Moment" (reprise) (Betty Oakes), "Who Needs It" (Cherry Davis, Rudy Tronto, Pat Tolson), "If I Am to Marry You" (Lawrence Weber, Betty Oakes) Finale (Ensemble)

NOTES—*Fashion* (see entry) and *She Shall Have Music* marked the beginning of a trend in the Off Broadway musical: musical adaptations based on classic American and European plays. These adaptations had two advantages: the source material came with a built-in recognition factor for audiences, and the plays were in the public domain, thus saving producers the added expense of paying royalties.

She Shall Have Music was a financial failure, playing less than two months, and like many other Off Broadway flops, its score would normally have vanished over time. But *She Shall Have Music* had a reprieve, of sorts. In early 1963, Denison University (Granville, Ohio) produced the show, and recorded a cast album of the production (FR Records LP # FR-6205) The LP reveals a pleasant, if minor score, with one stand-out number, "Maud, the Bawd."

Among the college cast members were John Davidson (who performed the role of Dorilant) and John Kuhner (who was in the chorus). A few months after he appeared in *She Shall Have Music*, Davidson made his New York debut in the Off Broadway musical *The Prince and the Pauper* (1963; see entry), and appears on that show's cast album; the following year he made his Broadway debut in a featured role in *Foxy* (1964), and also played the role of the Boy (Matt) in NBC's 1964 television adaptation of *The Fantasticks* (see entry). John Kuhner appeared in a few Off Broadway musicals, including the original production of the New York Drama Critics' Circle Award-winning *Your Own Thing* (1968; see entry), which became, after *The Golden Apple* (see entry), the second Off Broadway musical to win the award.

For the record, during its New York preview period, two numbers, "Feign a Faint, Lady" and "I Love to Flirt with the Ladies," were deleted from the musical.

Arthur Gelb in the *New York Times* admired how the musical's cast could negotiate on a stage "not much larger than a checkerboard." As for the musical itself, he thought it was a "mixed bag" of seventeenth-century flavor and modern-day slang, and regretted the "separate elements" of the evening never merged into a "satisfactory whole." He singled out four songs for praise ("Here's What a Mistress Ought to Be," "Basic," "Who Needs It," and the title number), but found "Maud, the Bawd" an "unnerving number ... tasteless ... reminiscent of a college varsity show."

Henry Hewes in *The Burns Mantle Yearbook/The Best Plays of 1958-1959* cited Cherry Davis for her performance in *She Shall Have Music*, hailing her as the Gwen Vernon of Off Broadway. Moreover, Gelb noted she was a "sparkling, red-headed gamine ... a burgeoning Gwen Vernon." Incidentally, in 1968 Davis appeared in the Equity Library Theatre's revival of *Redhead* as Essie, the role which Vernon originated on Broadway in 1959.

For other musicals with scores by Deed Meyer, see entries for *'Toinette* and *The Stones of Jehoshaphat*.

For another musical adaptation of *The Country Wife*, see entry for *Lust* (1995). *My Love to Your Wife*, a regional adaptation of the musical, was produced on May 6, 1977, for thirty-three performances at the Ringling Museum's Court Playhouse/Mainstage at the Asolo State Theatre. The book was by Brian J. McFadden, and the lyrics and music were by John Franceschina.

1441 Sheba. "A New Musical." THEATRE: Playhouse 91; OPENING DATE: January 21, 1996; PERFORMANCES: 63; BOOK: Sharleen Cooper Cohen; LYRICS: Sharleen Cooper Cohen; MUSIC: Gary William Friedman; DIRECTION: Tony Stevens; CHOREOGRAPHY: Tony Stevens; SCENERY: Gregory Hill; COSTUMES: Jonathan Bixby; LIGHTING: Tom Sturge; MUSICAL DIRECTION: Christopher McGovern; PRODUCERS: The Jewish Repertory Theatre (Ran Avni, Artistic Director) in association with SHEBA Productions

CAST—Brent Black (Hiram), Lynda Divito (Leah), Tony Gilbert (Zadok), Jonathan Giordano (Rheoboam), Michael Goz (Benaiah), Jonathan Hadley (Shem), Cynthia Leigh Heim (Cherna), Jonathan Horenstein (Abner), Ernestine Jackson (Makela), Joe Langworth (Zaku), Rose McGuire (Maat), Elizabeth Moliter (Mizpah), Lisa Morris (Irit), Natasha Rennalls (Nadi), Michael San Giovanni (Mitra), Nandita J. Shenoy (Tiza), Joseph Siravo (Solomon), Jane Strauss (Widow Huldah), Tamara Tunie (Ni-caul, Queen of Sheba), Andrew Varela (Jeroboam), Carrie Wilshusen (Mera)

The action occurs in Jerusalem during 960 B.C.

The musical was presented in two acts.

ACT ONE—"Begging the Question" (Company), "Song of Solomon" (Joseph Siravo), "We Praise the Lord" (Chorus), "Entrance of the Sabaens" (Tamara Tunie, Joseph Siravo), "I Question You" (Tamara Tunie, Joseph Siravo, Ernestine Jackson, Company), "How Does a King Decide" (Jonathan Hadley, Jonathan Horenstein, Joseph Siravo), "You'll Be King" (Rose McGuire, Jonathan Giordano), "A Day in Jerusalem" (Jonathan Hadley, Jane Strauss, Tamara Tunie, Brent Black, Ernestine Jackson), "Water Wears the Stone" (Tamara Tunie, Women of Israel), "Opinions in Public" (Joseph Siravo, Tamara Tunie), "The Names" (Tony Gilbert, Jonathan Giordano, Tamara Tunie, Joseph Siravo), "Give and Take" (Tamara Tunie, Joseph Siravo, Advisors), "Pas de Deux" (Lisa Morris, Michael San Giovanni), "You Are the One" (Ernestine Jackson, Tamara Tunie, Joseph Siravo), "Give and Take" (reprise) (Joseph Siravo, Tamara Tunie, Advisors), "Invitation" (Michael Goz, Ernestine Jackson, Joseph Siravo, Tamara Tunie), "Night of Love" (Company)

ACT TWO—"This Is the Day"/"Shema Ysrael" (Tony Gilbert, Joseph Siravo, Male Worshippers), "Moment in the Sun" (Joseph Siravo), "Advice for a Friend" (Lisa Morris, Carrie Wilshusen, Elizabeth Moliter, Natasha Rennalls, Nandita J. Shenoy, Lynda Divito, Ernestine Jackson, Cynthia Leigh Heim), "Who Is This Man"/"Woman to Me" (reprise) (Tamara Tunie, Joseph Siravo), "The Announcement" (Company), "God of Our Fathers" (Tony Gilbert, Ernestine Jackson, Worshippers), "Mysteries" (Tamara Tunie, Michael San Giovanni, Lisa Morris), Ballet (Company), "The Warning" (Company), "Child of Mine" (Tamara Tunie, Ernestine Jackson, Jane Strauss), "Come with Me" (Rose McGuire, Tamara Tunie, Joseph Siravo, Jonathan Hadley, Jonathan Giordano), "Begging the Question" (reprise) (Andrew Varela, Michael Goz, Tony Gilbert, Joseph Siravo, Company), "Solomon Decide" (Company), "You Fill My Arms" (Tamara Tunie, Joseph Siravo, Company)

NOTES—Apparently presented under an Off Broadway contract by the Jewish American Theatre, *Sheba* told the familiar Biblical story of Solomon and Sheba, but with a twist, as this Sheba was somewhat of a modern-day feminist. Lawrence Van Gelder in the *New York Times* said the "eye-catching" musical was "opulently operatic and intelligent," and noted the evening didn't stint on "passionate love, infidelity, jealousy and revenge."

The cast recording was released by Original Cast Records (CD # OC-8701).

1442 The Sheik of Avenue B. "The Ragtime and Jazz Era Comedy Revue." THEATRE: Town Hall; OPENING DATE: November 22, 1992; PERFORMANCES: 54; DIALOGUE: Isaiah Sheffer; LYRICS: See song list for credits; MUSIC: See song list for credits; DIRECTION: Dan Siretta; CHOREOGRAPHY: Dan Siretta; SCENERY: Bruce Goodrich; COSTUMES: Deirdre Burke; LIGHTING: Robert Bessoir; MUSICAL DIRECTION: Lanny Meyers; PRODUCER: Mazel Musicals (Lawrence Toppall, Alan & Kathi Glist)

CAST—Paul Harman (Don Gonfalon), Judy Premus (Becky Barrett), Jack Plotnick (Kevin Bailey), Amanda Green (Gretta Genug [Diana Darling]), Mark Nadler (Pinky Pickles), Virginia Sandifur (Fanny Farina), Larry Raiken (Willie Wills)

The action occurs during the fall of 1932.

The revue was presented in two acts.

ACT ONE—*The Broadcast—First Segment:* Radio Program Opening: "Doin' the Neighborhood Rag" (based on "Yiddish Rag," music by Harry Von Tilzer; additional lyric by Isaiah Sheffer and Lanny Meyers) (Ensemble), "Ish-Ga-Bibble (I Should Worry)" (lyric and music by Sam M. Lewis and Leo W. Meyer, additional lyric by Isaiah Sheffer and Lanny Meyers) (Larry Raiken, Ensemble), "Matinee Girl" (lyricist and composer unknown) (Judy Premus, with Mark Nadler and Paul Harman), "That's an Egg Cream!" (sketch [?] by Isaiah Sheffer and Lanny Meyers) (Virginia Sandifur, with Judy Premus, Larry Raiken, Paul Harman, Mark Nadler, Michele Ragusa), "Nathan, Nathan, What Are You Waitin' For?" (lyricist and composer unknown) (Amanda Green, with Paul Harman, Virginia Sandifur, Mark Nadler, Jack Plotnick, Michele Ragusa), "Serenade Me, Sally, with a Ragtime Tune" (lyric and music by Joe Young and Bert Grant) (Jack Plotnick, Virginia Sandifur), "Rosie Rosenblatt, Stop the Turkey Trot" (lyricist and composer unknown) (Paul Harman; danced by Michele Ragusa and Jack Plotnick), "My Yiddisha Colleen" (from touring production of *Ziegfeld Follies of* 1910; lyric by Leon Edwards, music by Edward Madden) (Jack Plotnick), "Becky, Stay in Your Own Backyard" (lyric and music by Norman and Young; additional lyric by Lanny Meyers) (Paul Harman, Judy Premus, Mark Nadler, Virginia Sandifur, Amanda Green, Michele Ragusa), "Jake the Ball Player" (lyric and music by Irving Berlin) (Larry Raiken), "Nize Baby" (lyric and music by Mac Rutchild and Lennie Whitcup) (Virginia Sandifur, Mark Nadler, Michele Ragusa, Ensemble), "Sam, You Made the Pants Too Long" (lyric and music by Sam M. Lewis and Lew Young; song also attributed to Sam M. Lewis, Milton Berle, and Fred Whitehouse [lyrics] and Isham Jones [music]) (Amanda Green, with Mark Nadler and Jack Plotnick; Larry Raiken with Judy Premus, Michele Ragusa, and Virginia Sandifur)

ACT TWO—*The Broadcast—Second Segment:* "Yiddisha Charleston" (lyric and music by Fred Fischer and Billy Rose) (Michele Ragusa, Jack Plotnick, Ensemble), "Doin' the Neighborhood Rag" (reprise) (Ensemble), "Ish-Ga-Bibble" (reprise) (Ensemble), "Yiddisha Nightingale" (lyric and music by Irving Berlin) (Paul Harman), "Abie and Me and the Baby" (lyric and music by Harry Von Tilzer and Lew Brown, with Fanny Brice) (Judy Premus, Ensemble), "Cohen Owes Me $97" (lyric and music by Irving Berlin) (Virginia Sandifur and Mark Nadler, with Paul Harman, Jack Plotnick, Amanda Green, and Michele Ragusa), "Change Your Immigrant Ways" (composer unknown; based on "Roll Your Yiddisha Eyes," lyric by Isaiah Sheffer) (Amanda Green), "Yiddisha Luck and Irisha Love" (Kelly and Rosenbaum, That's Mazel-Toff) (lyric and music by Alfred Bryan and Fred Fischer) (Virginia Sandifur, Judy Premus), "A Rabbi's Daughter" (lyric and music by Charles K. Harris) (Larry Raiken, Paul Harman, Amanda Green, Ensemble Quartet), "Since Henry Ford Apologized to Me" (touring production of *Rufus LeMaire's Affairs*, 1927 [titled *LeMaire's Affairs/Second Edition*]; lyric by Billy Rose and Ballard MacDonald, music by David Stamper) (Mark Nadler), "Whose Izzy Is He?" (lyric and music by Lew Brown, Bud Green, and Murray Sturm, additional lyric by Lanny Meyers) (Female Quartet: Judy Premus, Amanda Green, Virginia Sandifur, Michele Ragusa), "East Side Moon" (lyric and music by Sam M. Lewis and Leo Meyer, new lyric by Isaiah Sheffer) (Virginia Sandifur), "The Shiek of Avenue B" (music by Harry Ruby, lyric by Bert Kalmar) (Larry Raiken, Company)

NOTES—*The Sheik of Avenue B* was supposedly an authentic radio broadcast of the Blue Radio Network's hit show *Town Hall Tonight*; the first and second acts were the first and second segments of the broadcast. The cast of *The Sheik of Avenue B* played performers on the radio show.

Lawrence Van Gelder in the *New York Times* said the evening moved briskly, but lacked a point of view; further, while the musical had a certain "value" as entertainment history, it lacked a "soul." *The Best Plays of 1992-1993* included the revue as part of the Broadway season, and *Theatre World 1992-1993 Season* categorized it as an Off Broadway production. Because it played Town Hall, the musical was likely under an Off Broadway contract.

1443 Shelley. THEATRE: Carter Theatre; OPENING DATE: January 1979; PERFORMANCES: Unknown; BOOK: Morna Murphy; LYRICS: Percy Bysshe Shelley; MUSIC: Ralph Martell; DIRECTION: Morna Murphy; SCENERY: B. Monroe; COSTUMES: Michael Casey; LIGHTING: Stephen Graham; PRODUCER: Broadway-Times Theatre Comapny, Inc. (Jim Payne, Artistic Director)

CAST—Michael Mariani (The Writer), Percy Bysshe Shelley (Keith Benedict), Cynthia Smith (Lady Elizabeth Shelley), Allan Manning (Lord Byron), Emilie Roberts (Harriet Shelley), Robert James (Thomas Hogg), Jane McCormick (Mary Shelley)

The action occurs in the present time, in The Writer's imagination.

The musical appears to have been presented in two acts, with a break between "Ode to the West Wind" and "With a Guitar (To Jane)."

ACT ONE—"To a Skylark" (Michael Mariani), "How Thou Art Changed" (lyric taken from *Prometheus Unbound*) (Cynthia Smith), "The Name of God" (lyric taken from *Queen Mab*) (Keith Benedict), "Gentleness, Virtue" (lyric taken from *Prometheus Unbound*) (Cynthia Smith), Death (Allan Manning), "While Yet a Boy" (lyric taken from "Hymn to Intellectual Beauty") (Keith Benedict), "In Secret Chambers" (lyric taken from *Queen Mab*) (Allan Manning), "The Fountains Mingle" (lyric taken from "Love's Philosophy") (Emilie Roberts), "To Thirst and Find No Fill" (Emilie Roberts), "Whose Is the Love" (lyric taken from "To Harriet") (Keith Benedict), "When the Lamp Is Shattered" (Emilie Roberts), "Ode to the West Wind" (Michael Mariani)

ACT TWO—"With a Guitar" (lyric taken from

"To Jane") (Michael Mariani), "Ozymandias" (Robert James), "You Will See Hogg" (lyric taken from "Letter to Maria") (Allan Manning), "To the People of England" (Robert James), "War" (Keith Benedict), "One Word Is Too Often Profaned" (Robert James), "Alas, Good Friend" (lyric taken from "Lines to a Reviewer") (Allan Manning), "There Was a Woman" (lyric taken from "Revolt of Islam") (Michael Mariani), "Adonais" (lyric taken from "On the Death of Keats") (Jane McCormick), "My Dearest Mary" (Keith Benedict), "Music, When Soft Voices Die" (Jane McCormick), "Never More" (lyric taken from "A Lament") (Keith Benedict), "To a Skylark" (reprise) (Company)

NOTES—The Off Off Broadway musical *Shelley* was produced by the short-lived Broadway-Times Theatre Company, Inc. All lyrics for the production were taken from the writings of Percy Bysshe Shelley (1792-1822); some lyrics were adapted from longer poems (sources are provided, following song titles).

The musical was the first of the season's two Off Off Broadway musicals about the poet; see entry for *Duel*, which dealt with both Shelley and Lord Byron.

1444 Shockheaded Peter. "A Junk Opera." THEATRE: New Victory Theatre; OPENING DATE: October 14, 1999; PERFORMANCES: 15; ADAPTATION: Julian Bleach, Anthony Cairns, Graeme Gilmour, Tamzin Griffin, and Jo Pocock; LYRICS: Adapted from Heinrich Hoffman by Martyn Jacques; MUSIC: The Tiger Lillies (Adrian Huge, Martyn Jacques, and Adrian Stout); DIRECTION: Phelim McDermott and Julian Crouch; SCENERY: Julian Crouch and Graeme Gilmour; COSTUMES: Kevin Pollard; LIGHTING: Jon Linstrum; MUSICAL DIRECTION: Martyn Jacques; PRODUCERS: The New 42nd Street Inc. (Cora Cahan, President); a Cultural Industry Project (Michael Morris, Director), produced in collaboration with West Yorkshire Playhouse (Jude Kelly, Artistic Director) and Lyric Theatre Hammersmith (Sue Storr, Chief Executive; Neil Bartlett, Artistic Director); Rachel Feuchtwang, Associate Producer

CAST—Julian Bleach, Anthony Cairns, Graeme Gilmour, Tamzin Griffin, Jo Pocock

SOURCE—The nineteenth-century book *The Struwwelpeter* (*Slovenly Peter*) by Heinrich Hoffmann.

The musical was performed in one act.

MUSICAL NUMBERS—"The Struwwelpeter Overture," "The Story of Cruel Frederick," "The Dreadful Story About Harriet and the Matches," "Bully Boys," "The Story of the Man That Went Out Shooting," "Snip Snip," "Augustus and the Soup," "Fidgety Phil," "Johnny Head-in-Air," "Flying Robert," "Shockheaded Peter"

NOTES—Previously produced in Great Britain on March 27, 1998, at the West Yorkshire Playhouse in Leeds, *Shockheaded Peter* was performed by live actors and puppets. The gruesome, gory, and politically incorrect tales (in which Very Bad Things Happen to Bad Children) were adapted by the group The Tiger Lillies from the stories of the nineteenth-century writer Heinrich Hoffman, and the songs were set to mesmerizing Kurt Weill-ish music performed in high falsetto.

A British cast recording was released by NVC Arts Records (CD # 3984-26522-2); the above song titles are taken from the CD. During the period of the 1999 New York production, the Tiger Lillies performed at the PS122 performance space; the concert was filmed for DVD release by Kultur Video (# D-4097) as *Shockheaded Peter and Other Songs from the Tiger Lillies/Live in Concert in New York*, and included a few songs from the musical ("Snip Snip" [about a boy who bites his fingernails; don't ask what happens to him]), "The Dreadful Story About Harriet and the Matches," "Flying Robert," and "The Story of Cruel Frederick"). *Shockheaded Peter* was first seen in the United States at the Wexner Center for the Arts in Columbus, Ohio, on September 22, 1999. The musical was revived in New York at the Little Shubert Theatre on February 22, 2005, for 112 performances.

1445 The Shoemaker and the Peddler. "A Musical Drama." THEATRE: East 74th Street Playhouse; OPENING DATE: October 14, 1960; PERFORMANCES: 43; BOOK: Armand Aulicino; LYRICS: Armand Aulicino; MUSIC: Frank (Gaskin) Fields; DIRECTION: Lee Nemetz; CHOREOGRAPHY: Sophie Maslow; SCENERY: David Ballou; COSTUMES: David Ballou; LIGHTING: Lee Watson; MUSICAL DIRECTION: Richard Cumming; PRODUCER: Jullis Productions

CAST—James Tolken (Frank), Marilyn Jewett (Signora), Don Page (Tony), Pat Palin (Kathy), Millie Meitz (Millie), George Patelis (Detective), Ted Bloecher (First Policeman), Don Meyers (Second Policeman), Oliver Berg (Warden), Haig Chobanian (Guard), James Bosotina (Nick), JOSE DUVAL (Bart), ANITA DARIAN (Wife), Elinor Miller (Sister), Lenn Harten (Third Policeman), Shirley Norris (Filomena), Chet London (Rodolfo); Dancers: Mark Ryder, Martin Morginsky, Stanley Berke, Beatrice Seckler, Miriam Pandor, Carol Bender

The action occurs in a large American city.

The musical was presented in two acts.

ACT ONE—"Headlines" (Dancers), "Ah, Hum; Oh, Hum" (Chorus), "Vedi La Vita (Look at Life)" (Jose Duval, James Bosotina), "Quartet" (Joe Duval, James Bosotina, Anita Darian, Elinor Miller), "Wide-Awake Morning" (Chorus, Dancers), "Fish Song" (Jose Duval), "Naughty Bird Tarantella" (Chorus) "Childhood Lullaby" (Anita Darian, Jose Duval, Chorus), "The Robbery" (Dancers), "Is This the Way?" (Jose Duval, James Bosotina)

ACT TWO—"Headlines" (reprise) (Dancers), "Sometimes I Wonder" (James Bosotina), "Remember, Remember" (Anita Darian, James Bosotina), "Mio Fratello (My Brother)" (Elinor Miller), "The Nightmare" (Dancers, Chorus), "The Letter" (Jose Duval, James Bosotina), "Goodbye, My City" (Jose Duval, James Bosotina), "Guilty!" (Anita Darian)

NOTES—*The Shoemaker and the Peddler* was based on the controversial trial of Nicola Sacco and Bartolomeo Vanzetti (here, they are called Nick and Bart). The two men (perhaps inadvertently involved with a terrorist group dedicated to overthrowing the United States Government) may or may not have been involved in a murder and robbery which occurred in 1920, but they were ultimately arrested, tried, convicted, and executed for the crimes.

Howard Taubman in the *New York Times* indicated the evening was "a high-flying mixture of lyric theatre and poetic drama" which nonetheless lost its way due to a certain softness in its approach (it lacked "dramatic confrontation" and was overly solemn); further, the dialogue was in written in rhyme and apparently undermined the effectiveness of the story. However, Taubman had high praise for Frank Fields's score which he found "more elaborate" than was usual for a musical ("long-breathed tunes mingle a legitimately Italianate vein with the beat of American jazz") and he praised Fields' orchestrations for their "hard-driving impact."

One of the musical's cast members, Anita Darian, was Larry Kert's sister.

As *Sacco-Vanzetti!*, a revised version of the musical was seen at the Equity Library Theatre beginning on February 7, 1969, for fifteen performances.

At the time of his murder in 1964, Marc Blitzstein was working on an operatic version of the Sacco and Vanzetti case.

There have been at least two non-musical versions of the material. Robert Noah's *The Advocate* was seen in summer stock at the Buck's Country Playhouse in New Hope, Pennsylvania, on June 11, 1962, and *Sacco and Vanzetti*, by Marketta Kimbrell, was seen Off Off Broadway in September 1976 at the New York Street Theatre Caravan.

1446 Shoemakers' Holiday. "A New Musical Comedy." THEATRE: Orpheum Theatre; OPENING DATE: March 3, 1967; PERFORMANCES: 6; BOOK: Ted Berger; LYRICS: Ted Berger; MUSIC: Mel Marvin; DIRECTION: Ken Costigan; CHOREOGRAPHY: Myrna Galle; SCENERY: Robert Conley; COSTUMES: Whitney Blausen; LIGHTING: Duwico; MUSICAL DIRECTION: Elman Anderson; PRODUCERS: Ken Costigan in association with R. Robert Lussier

CAST—Tom Urich (Troubador), TOM LACY (Simon Eyre), Sue Lawless (Margery), JERRY DODGE (Firk), Penny Gaston (Jane), GARY OAKES (Raph), Marcia Wood (Flossie Frigbottom), Lana Caradimas (Madge Mumblecrust), Lynn Martin (Cicely Bumtrinket), Judy Knaiz (Sybil), Gail Johnston (Rose), Garnett Smith (Lacy), John Keller (Oteley), George Cavey (Lincoln), Robert Ronan (Hammon)

SOURCE—The 1599 play *The Shoemakers' Holiday*, or *The Gentle Craft* by Thomas Dekker.

The action occurs in London during the sixteenth century.

The musical was presented in two acts.

ACT ONE—"Cold's the Wind" (Tom Urich), "What Do We Care If It Rains" (Tom Lacy and Company, Sue Lawless), "A Poor Man at Parting" (Gary Oakes, Penny Gaston), "Who Gives a Hey" (Judy Knaiz, Gail Johnston, John Keller, Robert Ronan), "Where Is the Knight for Me" (Gail Johnston), "When a Maid Wears Purple Stockings" (Judy Knaiz), "Down a Down, Down Derry" (Tom Lacy, Company), "What Do We Care If It Rains" (reprise) (Tom Lacy, Penny Gaston), "Gather Ye Rose Buds" (Jerry Dodge, Judy Knaiz), "Ribbons I Will Give Thee" (Garnett Smith, Jerry Dodge, Judy Knaiz), "My Lovely Lad" (Penny Gaston, Gary Oakes), "What Do We Care If It Rains" (reprise) (Tom Lacy, Company)

ACT TWO—"Trowl the Bowl" (Company), "The Wonder of a Kingdom" (Gary Oakes), "The Recipe for Husbandry" (Sue Lawless, Tom Lacy, Lynn Martin, Marcia Wood, Lana Caradimas), "The Shaking of the Sheets" (Company), "Would That I" (Gail Johnston, Penny Gaston), "Everything Is Tinglin'" (Jerry Dodge), "What a Life" (Tom Lacy, Sue Lawless, Jerry Dodge, Judy Knaiz, Tom Urich, Company)

NOTES—Based on Thomas Dekkers' classic comedy (which had been most recently seen in New York in 1938 in an adaptation by Orson Welles and John Houseman which was also directed by Welles), *Shoemakers' Holiday* focused on a young man who disguises himself as a shoemaker's apprentice in order to court a girl whose father opposes the match. As for the shoemaker himself, he becomes the Lord Mayor of London.

Dan Sullivan in the *New York Times* found that "by Off Broadway standards" the musical was "bouncy, good-looking and sometimes fun"; but measured against Dekker's play, the work seemed "shoddy." He didn't care for Mel Marvin's score ("competent but predictable"), but praised the "bright" choreography and the costumes (which resembled "clothes that people actually might have worn").

Prior to its brief run in New York, *Shoemakers' Holiday* played at the Playhouse on the Mall, in Paramus, New Jersey, during the last two weeks of February.

Like many of his contemporaries (such as Peter Link, Lance Mulcahy, and Michael Valenti), Mel Marvin had the misfortune to be associated with a number of short-running musicals; thus he never enjoyed a breakthrough hit to ensure his place in musical theatre.

Three months after *Shoemakers' Holiday* closed, another lyric version of Dekker's play opened. As *The Shoemakers' Holiday*, the musical premiered at the Tyrone Guthrie Theatre/Minnesota Theatre Company on June 1, 1967, with music by Dominick Argento; apparently the lyrics were adapted by Argento from the text of the original play, and additional lyrics were by Herbert Pilhofer. The cast included Len Cariou, Grace Keagy, and Lee Richardson.

1447 Shoestring '57. "A New Revue." THEATRE: Barbizon-Plaza Theatre; OPENING DATE: November 5, 1956; PERFORMANCES: 119; SKETCHES: Mostly by Lee Adams, Kenward Elmslie, Herb Hartig, Tom Jones, Arthur MacRae, and Bud McCreery; LYRICS: Mostly by Norman Gimbel, Sheldon Harnick, Carolyn Leigh, Paul Rosner, Harvey Schmidt, Mike (Michael) Stewart, and G. Wood; MUSIC: David Baker, Moose Charlap, Shelley Mowell, Claibe Richardson, Philip Springer, and Charles Strouse; DIRECTION: Paul Lammers; CHOREOGRAPHY: Danny Daniels; SCENERY: William Riva; COSTUMES: Jeanne Partington; MUSICAL DIRECTION: Dorothea Freitag; PRODUCERS: Ben Bagley in association with Edwin H. Morris

CAST—John Bartis, Fay De Witt, Dody Goodman, Dorothy Greener, Patricia Hammerlee, Maybin Hewes, Diki Lerner, Charlie Manna, George Marcy, Paul Mazursky, Bud McCreery, Mary Ellen Terry

The revue was presented in two acts.

ACT ONE—"For Critics Only" (lyric by Mike Stewart, music by Shelley Mowell) (Company), "What's a Show" (lyric by Mike Stewart, music by Shelley Mowell) (Charlie Manna) "Queen of Spain" (lyric by Tom Jones, music by Harvey Schmidt) (Dorothy Greener, Maybin Hewes, Diki Lerner), "Two Way Play" (sketch by Arthur Macrae) (John Bartis, Paul Mazursky, Dody Goodman, Fay De Witt, Charlie Manna) "Tea Chanty" (sketch by Harvey Schmidt) (Dorothy Greener, John Bartis, Bud McCreery) "The Wild Blue" (lyric by Lee Adams, music by Charles Strouse) (Charlie Manna, Diki Lerner) "Stitch in Time" (ballet conceived by Danny Daniels, music by Moose Charlap) (George Marcy, Mary Ellen Terry, Maybin Hewes, Diki Lerner, Paul Mazursky) "At Twenty-Two" (lyric by Tom Jones, music by Harvey Schmidt) (John Bartis) "Toothloose in Rome" (sketch by Kenward Elmslie and Paul Rosner) (Paul Mazursky, Fay De Witt, Dorothy Greener), "Love Is a Feeling" (lyric by Norman Gimbel, music by Moose Charlap) (John Bartis, George Marcy) "The Rochelle Hudson Tango" (lyric by Paul Rosner, music by Claibe Richardson) (Dody Goodman, Paul Mazursky) (staged by Mavis Ray) "Renoir, Degas, Toulouse-Lautrec" (lyric and music by Bud McCreery) (Fay De Witt) "The Art of the Mime" (sketch by Kenward Elmslie) (Dody Goodman, Dorothy Greener, Mary Ellen Terry, Diki Lerner) "Don't Say You Like Tchaikowsky" (lyric by Paul Rosner, music by Claibe Richardson) (Patricia Hammerlee, Paul Mazursky, Bud McCreery, Fay De Witt) "The Song of the Queen Bee" (sketch by E.B. White) (Dody Goodman). Note—During the run, this sketch was replaced by "Creepytime Down South (Cribnotes for a Certain SRO)" (sketch by Herb Hartig) (Dody Goodman) (This sketch is also known as "Tennessee Williams' Notes for a Certain S.R.O.") "Sweet Belinda" (sketch by Arthur MacRae, music by Richard Addinsell) (Paul Mazursky, Dorothy Greener, Charlie Manna, Diki Lerner, Bud McCreery, Fay De Witt, Patricia Hammerlee, Mary Ellen Terry, John Bartis)

ACT TWO—"Doop-De-Doop" (sketch by Harvey Schmidt) (Diki Lerner, Maybin Hewes, Mary Ellen Terry, Fay De Witt, George Marcy, Paul Mazursky), "Lament on Fifth Avenue" (lyric by Paul Rosner, music by Claibe Richardson) (Fay De Witt, Dody Goodman, Patricia Hammerlee, John Bartis, Diki Lerner, Paul Mazursky, Bud McCreery) "I'm Gonna Be Rich" (lyric and music by G. Wood) (Charlie Manna) "Coffee (A Relativity)" (sketch by Herbert Hartig and Lois Balk) (Paul Mazursky, Patricia Hammerlee, Bud McCreery, George Marcy, Mary Ellen Terry), "Best Loved Girls" (lyric by Sheldon Harnick, music by David Baker) (Dody Goodman, *Wonderful Town* Girl; Patricia Hammerlee, *Seventh Heaven* Girl; Mary Ellen Terry, *Threepenny Opera* Girl; Fay De Witt, *Pipe Dream* Girl) (Note: Dody Goodman and Patricia Hammerlee had appeared in the respective original productions of *Wonderful Town* and *Seventh Heaven*.) "Always One Day More (Death of a Ballad)" (lyric by Carolyn Leigh, music by Philip Springer) (John Bartis, George Marcy, Diki Lerner), "Can You See a Girl Like Me in the Role" (lyric by Max Showalter, music by William Howe) (Dorothy Greener) "The Trouble with Miss Manderson" (sketch by Alan Melville) (Dody Goodman, Bud McCreery) "The Arts" (lyric by Lee Adams, music by Charles Strouse) (Mary Ellen Terry, Dorothy Greener, Fay De Witt, Patricia Hammerlee) "Family Trouble" (lyric by Anthony Chalmers, music by Leopold Antelme) (Dody Goodman, Bud McCreery) "Revival" (sketch by Arthur MacRae) (John Bartis, George Marcy, Dorothy Greener, Charlie Manna, Paul Mazursky, Dody Goodman), "Paradiddle" (ballet conceived by Danny Daniels, music by Ronnie Free, dialogue by Don Meyer) (George Marcy, Maybin Hewes, Diki Lerner, Mary Ellen Terry), "I Just Slipped Away from My Wedding" (sketch by Bud McCreery) (Dody Goodman) "On a Shoestring" (lyric and music by G. Wood) (Company)

NOTES—*Shoestring '57* is particularly noteworthy because of the amazing number of distinguished writers, lyricists, and composers represented in the revue, many of whom reached the pinnacle of success in musical theatre. Ben Bagley is the producer who gave many of them their first New York hearing. Of the cast members, Paul Mazursky found fame as the director of a number of well-known and well-received films, including *Bob and Carol and Ted and Alice* (1969) and *Harry and Tonto* (1974).

Among the revue's highlights was a song about New York traffic (in "Lament on Fifth Avenue." we're told that "Fifth Avenue buses never go out alone") and a sketch parodying the plays of Tennessee Williams. In the latter, Dody Goodman portrayed a faded Williams heroine who (while managing to work in many of the titles of Williams' plays into her monologue) reminisces about her family, including her grandfather's "husband," who was known as "the Oscar Wilde of the Delta."

The song "Best Loved Girls" celebrated the heroines of recent Broadway and Off Broadway musicals; see entries for *The Grand Street Follies* (1927, Fifth Edition) and *Greenwich Village U.S.A.* (1960) for songs in a similar vein.

Apparently the ballad "Always One Day More (Death of a Ballad)" wasn't completely performed. As the song progressed, the singer was slowly wrapped in white cloth in mummy-like fashion by two cast members, and so the singer was prevented from finishing the number.

During the run, "Grace Fogerty," a sketch by Mike Stewart, was added to the program, and was performed by Dorothy Greener, who had originally introduced it on Broadway in the flop 1951 revue *Razzle Dazzle*. Another *Razzle Dazzle* number, the song "What's a Show," was also used in *Shoestring'57*. Both are heard on the *Shoestring '57* cast album, which was recorded by Offbeat Records (LP # 0-4012) a year after the show's closing. The album included a combination of original cast members (Dody Goodman, Dorothy Greener, Fay de Witt, John Bartis) and studio cast members (Beatrice Arthur, G. Wood). Later reissues of the album on Painted Smiles Records (LP # PS-1362 and CD # PSCD-130) included additional material, including a sequence taped during the show's dress rehearsals. It wasn't until 1962, with *No Shoestrings* (see entry), that another Ben Bagley revue was seen in New York.

Like some material in *Shoestring Revue*, a few numbers in *Shoestring '57* found their way into *Joy Ride* (which closed prior to New York) and *Medium Rare* (the successful Chicago revue). One of *Shoestring '57*'s numbers was used in *Joy Ride* ("Can You See a Girl Like Me in the Role?"), and three were heard in *Medium Rare* ("Coffee, A Relativity" "The Arts," and "Two Way Play").

"Coffee, a Relativity" was later heard in a 1969 Washington, D.C., revue, *Spread Eagle IV*, and was performed by Georgia Engel, Ralph Strait, John Hillerman, and Sue Lawless. The first of the series of *Spread Eagle* topical revues was produced by the Washington Theatre Club in 1966. Its artistic director was Davy Marlin-Jones, and under his helm the now-defunct company was D.C.'s closest equivalent to Off Broadway theatre.

A special note about G. Wood (a/k/a G Wood and George Wood): He was a frequent contributor to Off Broadway, either as a writer, composer, or performer. See entry for his 1971 musical version of *F. Jasmine Addams*, an Off Broadway adaptation of Carson McCuller's *The Member of the Wedding* (1951).

1448 Shoestring Revue. THEATRE: The President Theatre; OPENING DATE: February 28, 1955; PERFORMANCES: 100; SKETCHES: Lee Adams, David Baker, Ronny Graham, Sheldon Harnick, Arthur MacRae, Richard F. Maury, William Putch, and Mike (Michael) Stewart; LYRICS: June Carroll, Norman Gimbel, Ronny Graham, Sheldon Harnick, Bruce Kirby, Bud McCreery, Mike Stewart, and Ken Welch; MUSIC: David Baker, Sheldon Harnick, Bud McCreery, Shelley Mowell, Arthur Siegel, Charles Strouse, Ken Welch, Alec Wilder, and G. Wood; DIRECTION: Christopher Hewett; "Production Devised and Supervised by Mr. Bagley"; CHOREOGRAPHY: Dania Krupska; SCENERY: Carter Morningstar; COSTUMES: Carter Morningstar; MUSICAL DIRECTION: Charles Strouse; PRODUCERS: Ben Bagley in association with Mr. and Mrs. Judson S. Todd

CAST—Dorothy Greener, Maxwell Grant, Rhoda Kerns, Arte Johnson, Dody Goodman, Arthur Partington, Beatrice Arthur, Mel Larned, Joan Bowman, Peter Conlow, Chita Rivera, John Sharpe

The revue was presented in two acts.

ACT ONE—Introduction (Maxwell Grant), "Man's Inhumanity" (lyric by Mike Stewart, music by Charles Strouse) (Arte Johnson, Arthur Partington, John Sharpe, Peter Conlow, Beatrice Arthur, Joan Bowman, Dody Goodman, Rhoda Kerns, Chita Rivera, Dorothy Greener) "Fresh & Young" (sketch by Ronny Graham) (Mel Larned, John Sharpe, Peter Conlow) "Hamlet, Prince of Skaters" (sketch by Arthur Macrae) (Arthur Partington, Maxwell Grant, Arte Johnson [Hamlet], Beatrice Arthur [Ophelia]), "Inevitably Me (Young People's Soiree, 1870)" (lyric and music by Ken Welch) (Arthur Partington, Joan Bowman, Chita Rivera, Mel Larned, John Sharpe, Rhoda Kerns, Peter Conlow) "Someone Is Sending Me Flowers" (lyric by Sheldon Harnick, music by David Baker) (Dody Goodman, John Sharpe) "Inside Inside" (sketch by Mike Stewart) (John Sharpe, Maxwell Grant, Mel Larned) "Garbage" (lyric and music by Sheldon Harnick) (Beatrice Arthur, Arthur Partington, Chita Rivera) "Roller Derby" (sketch by Mike Stewart) (Dorothy Greener) "Paducah" (lyric by Mike Stewart, music by Shelley Mowell) (Peter Conlow) "Bitter Licci Nuts" (sketch by William Putch) (Chita Rivera, Arthur Partington, John Sharpe, Maxwell

Grant, Beatrice Arthur) "Wabash 4-7473" (lyric by Bruce Kirby, music by G. Wood) (Mel Larned) "Medea in Disneyland" (sketch and lyric by Sheldon Harnick, music by Lloyd Norlin) (Arthur Partington, Dorothy Greener, Dody Goodman, Peter Conlow, Mel Larned, Maxwell Grant, Beatrice Arthur, Arte Johnson, Chita Rivera, John Sharpe, Rhoda Kerns, Arthur Partington)

ACT TWO—"Entire History of the World in Two Minutes and Thirty-Two Seconds" (lyric by Mike Stewart, music by Charles Strouse) (Mel Larned, Chita Rivera, Peter Conlow, Joan Bowman, Maxwell Grant, Rhoda Kerns, Arthur Partington, John Sharpe) "In Bed with the Reader's Digest" (sketch by Richard F. Maury) (Maxwell Grant, John Sharpe) "Mink, Mink, Mink" (lyric and music by Bud McCreery) (Dorothy Greener, Chita Rivera, Beatrice Arthur) "New to Me" (lyric by Bud McCreery, music by Ken Welch) (Mel Larned, John Sharpe, Arthur Partington, Joan Bowman, Rhoda Kern) "Nobody's Doin' It Dance" (lyric and music by Bud McCreery) (Dorothy Greener, Arthur Partington) "Couldn't Be Happier" (sketch by Bud McCreery) (Beatrice Arthur) "A Million Windows and I" (lyric by Norman Gimbel, music by Alec Wilder) (Mel Larned) "Epic (or, I'll Be Glad When You're Dead You Roskolnikov You)" (sketch by Lee Adams and Mike Stewart) (Chita Rivera, Maxwell Grant) "Three Loves" (lyric by Mike Stewart, music by Charles Strouse) (Peter Conlow) Entr'acte (Chita Rivera, John Sharpe), "Group Analysis" (sketch by Richard F. Maury) (Mel Larned, Beatrice Arthur, Peter Conlow, Dody Goodman, Chita Rivera, Arthur Partington, John Sharpe) "Things Are Going Well Today" (lyric by June Carroll, music by Arthur Siegel) (Rhoda Kerns, John Sharpe, Joan Bowman, Chita Rivera, Arthur Partington, Peter Conlow) "The Sea Is All Around Us" (lyric by Sheldon Harnick, music by David Baker) (Arte Johnson) "Fresh and Young" (lyric and music by Ronny Graham) and Finale (Company)

NOTES—Ben Bagley put the Off Broadway revue on the map with a series of three revues which opened within a period of twenty months (*Shoestring Revue* as well as *Shoestring '57* and *The Littlest Revue* [see entries]). Bagley had an almost prescient knack for choosing writers, composers, and performers who would Go Places. And his series of revues defined the genre of the Off Broadway revue. His "sassy" (a truly benbaglian word) revues were the essence of what savvy theatergoers grew to expect of intimate Off Broadway evenings: humorous, topical sketches, amusing, often wry songs, and knowing, clever performers who put over sketches and songs in intimate theatre and cabaret settings. *Shoestring Revue* included many names which found future fame: cast members Chita Rivera, Arte Johnson, Dody Goodman, and Beatrice Arthur (the latter between her two engagements in *The Threepenny Opera*; see entries), and writers and composers such as Sheldon Harnick, Charles Strouse, Lee Adams, and Mike Stewart. (For trivia addicts: the writer of the sketch "Bitter Licci Nuts" was William Putch, Jean Stapleton's husband.)

During the revue's three-month run, Jane Connell was a cast replacement, as was Mary Ann Niles, who had once been married to Bob Fosse. Mary Ann Niles defined the role of the eternal and ultimate Chorus Girl who never became famous but always seemed to find work in the next Broadway or Off Broadway musical.

Shoestring Revue offered a number of memorable songs and sketches. In Sheldon Harnick's "Garbage," Beatrice Arthur lampooned torch songs (her former boyfriend's treatment of her was "beyond the pale"), and, in a amusing sketch, Arthur protested a bit too much to a former boyfriend, insisting she "Couldn't Be Happier" that he's found a new love (in fact, Arthur says his fiancé has a special glow ... a glow resulting, no doubt, from the fact she's always lit). Another amusing sequence told the Medea story as presented by Walt Disney. The revue's highlight was unquestionably Harnick and David Baker's "The Sea Is All Around Us." Arte Johnson introduced the song, which dealt with the greenhouse effect on a water-logged Manhattan, now a Runyonland of grunion, where gefilte-fishing is common and where crosstown submarines take passengers to the Tavern *in* the Green.

The revue was recorded on Offbeat Records (LP # 4011); later LP (# PS-1360) and CD (# PSCD-129) reissues (as *Shoestring Revues*) on Bagley's Painted Smiles label included extra material. In the mid-1960s, Bagley found a second career producing recordings which "revisited" major Broadway composers and lyricists. The albums in his *Revisited* series were forerunners of many later recordings which examined the works of major musical theatre writers, either in compilation format or in reconstructed studio cast recordings.

The songs "Laddie" (lyrics and music by Jim Mahoney) and "Kings and Queens" (lyric by June Carroll, music by Arthur Siegel) as well as the sketch "Our Garden" (writer unknown) were apparently added to the production during its run (and may have been heard in *Shoestring '57* as well). Performances of "Laddie" (sung by Fay de Witt) and "Our Garden" (performed by Dody Goodman) have turned up on later releases of the *Shoestring Revue* and *Shoestring '57* cast albums. "Laddie" was also recorded by Jerry Orbach in his LP of songs devoted to the Off Broadway musical (see discography [Appendix B]).

In 1958, the pre-Broadway tryout of the revue *Joy Ride* opened in Los Angeles, and included five numbers from *Shoestring Revue*: "Man's Inhumanity," "Roller Derby," "Medea in Disneyland," "In Bed with the Reader's Digest," and "Group Analysis" (among the performers in "Man's Inhumanity" were Joel Grey, Bernie West, and Barbara Nichols). Dorothy Greener, Conrad Janis, and Will Holt were among the other cast members. The revue closed in 1959, prior to its Broadway engagement.

Chicago had its own "Off Broadway" theatre, the Happy Medium. In 1960, the revue *Medium Rare* opened (among its cast members were Jean Arnold and Bob Dishy), and it included seven numbers from *Shoestring Revue*: "Man's Inhumanity," "Garbage," "Medea in Disneyland," "In Bed with the Reader's Digest," "Mink, Mink, Mink," "Couldn't Be Happier," and "Group Analysis." One Happy Medium revue was seen in New York when *Put It in Writing* opened Off-Broadway in 1963 (see entry).

The following is a complete list of Ben Bagley's Off Broadway revues (see entries; also see Appendix P): *Shoestring Revue* (1955), *The Littlest Revue* (1956), *Shoestring '57* (1956), *No Shoestrings* (1962), *The Decline and Fall of the Entire World as Seen Through the Eyes of Cole Porter Revisited* (1965), and the latter's second edition, *The Decline and Fall of the Entire World as Seen Through the Eyes of Cole Porter Revisited* (a/k/a *New Cole Porter Revue)* (1965). On October 15, 1970, the Equity Library Theatre offered *Ben Bagley's Shoestring Revues*, an evening of highlights from Bagley's classic revues. The Off Off Broadway production opened at the Master Theatre for a limited engagement of twenty-two performances.

1449 The Shop on Main Street. "A New Musical." THEATRE: Jewish Repertory Theatre; OPENING DATE: January 2, 1986; PERFORMANCES: 27; BOOK: Bernard Spiro; LYRICS: Bernard Spiro; MUSIC: Saul Honigman; DIRECTION: Fran Soeder; CHOREOGRAPHY: Janet Watson; SCENERY: James Leonard Joy; puppets created by Jane Stein; COSTUMES: Mardi Philips; LIGHTING: Phil Monat; MUSICAL DIRECTION: Norman Weiss; PRODUCERS: The Jewish Repertory Theatre (Ran Avni, Artistic Director; Leonard M. Cohen, Associate Director) by special arrangement with Tanrydoon Productions, Ltd., and Dolph Browning

CAST—Chuck Brown (Narrator, Piti Bachi, Joseph Katz, Various Townspeople), Gregg Edelman (Tono Brtko), Olga Talyn (Eveline), Nancy Callman (Rose), Kenneth Kantor (Marcus), Lawrence Weber (Kuchar), Lilia Skala (Mrs. Lautman), The Commissaries (John Roccosalva and Agatha Balek), Razzle (Cognac)

SOURCE—The 1965 film *The Shop on Main Street*, screenplay by Ladislav Grosman.

The action occurs in the town of Savinov in Eastern Czechoslovakia during mid-June 1942.

The musical was presented in two acts.

ACT ONE—"Piti's Song" (Chuck Brown, Ensemble), "Brtko, Tono Brtko" (Gregg Edelman), "The Shop on Main Street "(Kenneth Kantor, Olga Talyn, Nancy Callman, Gregg Edelman), "The Chatter of an Old, Old Woman" (Lilia Skala), "Mark Me Tomorrow" (Gregg Edelman), "Someone to Do For" (Gregg Edelman, Lilia Skala), "Noon Sunday Promenade" (Ensemble)

ACT TWO—"Market Day" (Gregg Edelman, Three Women Customers, Lilia Skala), "Shainele" (Lilia Skala, Lawrence Weber, Greg Edelman), "Better Days" (Nancy Callman, Kenneth Kantor), "Who Are They to Me?" (Gregg Edelman)

NOTES—The Off Off Broadway musical *The Shop on Main Street* was based on the successful 1965 Czechoslovakian film (which won the Academy Award for Best Foreign Film). Set in Czechoslovakia during World War II, the story dealt with a persecuted, elderly Jewish woman who loses her button shop, and the young man who takes it over for her under his name.

Walter Goodman in the *New York Times* found the book "wordy and obvious" and the lyrics trite. But he said the score offered some "pleasurable" and "affecting" moments, and singled out "Better Days" and "I Feel Like a Woman." Goodman reported that for part of the evening, puppets were utilized to represent townspeople and to add "emphasis" to certain scenes (perhaps the use of puppets was a wry commentary on how innocent people became unwitting pawns for Nazi tyranny?).

Although Lawrence Weber was listed in the program (as Kuchar), it appears that on opening night the character was portrayed by John Newton. Weber had appeared in a number of failed Broadway musicals in the late 1940s and early 1950s (*My Romance* [1948], *The Liar* [1950], and *Hazel Flagg* [1953]).

1450 Shout! "The Mod Musical." THEATRE: The Julia Miles Theatre; OPENING DATE: July 27, 2006; PERFORMANCES: 157; MOD MUSINGS AND GROOVY GAB BY: Peter Charles Morris and Phillip George; LYRICS: See song list for credits; MUSIC: See song list for credits; DIRECTION: Phillip George; CHOREOGRAPHY: David Lowenstein; SCENERY: David Gallo; COSTUMES: Philip Heckman; LIGHTING: Jason Lyons; MUSICAL DIRECTION: Bradley Vieth; PRODUCERS: Victoria Lang and P.P. Piccoli, Brent Peek, and Mark Schwartz; Patricia Melanson, eBroadwayPlays/Pat Addiss, Robin Gurin, Associate Producers

CAST—Marie-France Arcilla (Blue Girl), Erin Crosby (Yellow Girl), Julie Dingman Evans (Orange Girl), Erica Schroeder (Green Girl), Denise Summerford (Red Girl), Carole Shelley (Voice of Gwendolyn Holmes), Holter Graham (Voice of the Magazine)

The action occurs in London during the "Swingin' '60s."

The program didn't indicate the number of acts or the titles of the musical numbers; the list below is derived from the songs on the cast album (which didn't credit specific song assignments).

MUSICAL NUMBERS—Medley: "England Swings" (lyric and music by Roger Miller)/"'Round Every Corner" (lyric and music by Anthony Peter Hatch)/"I Know a Place" (lyric and music by Anthony Peter Hatch), Medley: "I Only Want to Be with You" (lyric by Ivor Raymonde, music by Mike Hawker)/"Tell the Boys" (lyric by Mitch Murray, music by Peter Robin Callander), "How Can You Tell" (lyric and music by Chris Andrews), "Wishin' and Hopin'" (lyric by Hal David, music by Burt Bacharach) "One Two Three" (lyric and music by Leonard Borisoff, Lamont Dozier, Brian Holland, Edward J. Holland, John Madera, and David White), "To Sir, with Love" (from 1967 film *To Sir, with Love*; lyric by Mark London, music by Donald [Don] Black), "Don't Sleep in the Subway" (lyric by Jackie Trent, music by Anthony Peter Hatch), "Son of a Preacher Man" (lyric by Ronnie Stephen Wilkins, music by John David Hurley), "James Bond Theme" (music by John Barry)/"Goldfinger" (1964 film *Goldfinger*; lyric by Leslie Bricusse and Anthony Newley, music by John Barry), "You Don't Have to Say You Love Me" (lyric and music by P. Donaggio, Vito Pallavicini, Vicky Wickham, S.N. Bell, and Napier), "Diamonds Are Forever" (1971 film *Diamonds Are Forever*; lyric by Donald [Don] Black, music by John Barry), "Puppet on a String" (lyric by Bill Martin, music by Phil Coulter), Medley: "Georgy Girl" (1966 film *Georgy Girl*; lyric by Dion O'Brien, music by Jim Dale)/"Windy" (lyric and music by Ruthann Friedman), "Who Am I?" (lyric and music by Anthony Peter Hatch), "Don't Give Up" (lyric by Jackie Trent, music by Anthony Peter Hatch), "I Just Don't Know What to Do with Myself" (lyric by Hal David, music by Burt Bacharach), "These Boots Are Made for Walkin'" (lyric and music by Lee Hazelwood), "I Couldn't Live Without Your Love" (lyric and music by Anthony Peter Hatch) Medley: "You're My World" (lyric by Gino Paoli, music by Umberto Bindi)/"All I See Is You" (lyric by Gerald Clive Westlake, music by Benjamin Weisman), "Those Were the Days" (lyric and music by Eugene Raskin), "Shout!" (lyric by Ronald Isley and Rudolph Isley, music by Kelly O. Isley, Jr.), "Goin' Back" (lyric by Gerald Coffin, music by Carole King), "Downtown" (lyric and music by Anthony Peter Hatch)

NOTES—*Shout!* was a tribute to British "girl" singers, and the revue's program thanked Petula Clark, Dusty Springfield, Lulu, Sandy Shaw, Shirley Bassey, Cilla Black, "and all the singing birds of swinging London for inspiring us with timeless music." The revue's five singers were identified by the colors of their costumes, and the songs were framed around quizzes, advertisements, and letters to advice columnists. The cast album was released by Rhino Records (CD # R2-74791).

The revue was developed in association with Amas Musical Theatre, and had been previously seen at the Duplex in New York in 2000 and at the Raymond F. Kravis Center for the Performing Arts in West Palm Beach, Florida. The musical was also performed at the Jermyn Street Theatre in London prior to its opening at the Julia Miles Theatre.

During the middle and late 1980s, Off Broadway had seen a spate of "girl" and "girl group" tribute-revues (see entries for *Beehive*, *Suds*, and *The Taffetas*), and *Shout!* was a belated addition to this mini-genre. *Forever Plaid* (see entry) was a "guy group" tribute.

1451 The Show Goes On. "A Portfolio of Theatre Songs by Tom Jones and Harvey Schmidt." THEATRE: The Theatre at St. Peter's Church; OPENING DATE: December 17, 1997; PERFORMANCES: 88; LYRICS: Tom Jones; MUSIC: Harvey Schmidt; DIRECTION AND MUSICAL STAGING: Drew Scott Harris; CHOREOGRAPHY AND MUSICAL STAGING: Janet Watson; SCENERY: James Morgan; COSTUMES: Suzy Benzinger; LIGHTING: Mary Jo Dondlinger; PRODUCER: The York Theatre Company (James Morgan, Artistic Director; Joseph V. De Michele, Managing Director)

CAST—JoAnn Cunningham, Tom Jones, Emma Lampert, J. Mark McVey, Harvey Schmidt

The revue was presented in two acts.

ACT ONE—"Come On Along" (written for, but not used in, *The Fantasticks*; 1960) (Tom Jones, Harvey Schmidt), "Try to Remember" (*The Fantasticks*; 1960) (Emma Lampert, J. Mark McVey, JoAnn Cunningham), "Mr. Off-Broadway" (*Demi-Dozen*; 1958) (Tom Jones, Harvey Schmidt), "Everyone Looks Lonely" (1960 television musical *New York Scrapbook*) JoAnn Cunningham), "I Know Loneliness Quite Well" (1960 television musical *New York Scrapbook*) (J. Mark McVey), "The Story of My Life" (1960 television musical *New York Scrapbook*) (Emma Lampert), "The Holy Man and the New Yorker" (*Demi-Dozen*; 1958) (Tom Jones, Harvey Schmidt), "(It's Gonna Be) Another Hot Day" (*110 in the Shade*; 1963) (JoAnn Cunningham, Emma Lampert, J. Mark McVey), "I Can Dance" (written for, but not used in, *110 in the Shade*; 1963) (Emma Lampert), "Dessau Dance Hall" (written for, but not used in, *110 in the Shade*; 1963) (JoAnn Cunningham), "Flibberty-Gibbet" (written for, but not used in, *110 in the Shade*; 1963) (JoAnn Cunningham, Emma Lampert), "Melisande" (*110 in the Shade*; 1963) (J. Mark McVey), "Simple Little Things" (*110 in the Shade*; 1963) (JoAnn Cunningham), "I Do! I Do!" (*I Do! I Do!*; 1966) (Company), "I Do! I Do! (I Do Adore You)" ("Thirties" Version; not used in the 1966 production) (Emma Lampert, "I Do! I Do! (Who Loves to Touch You?)" (written for proposed film version of *I Do! I Do!*) (JoAnn Cunningham, J. Mark McVey), "The Honeymoon Is Over" (*I Do! I Do!*; 1966) (Company), "My Cup Runneth Over" (*I Do! I Do!*; 1966) (Company)

ACT TWO—"Celebration" (*Celebration*; 1969) (Company), "Orphan in the Storm" (*Celebration*; 1969) (Emma Lampert), "Survive" (*Celebration*; 1969) (J. Mark McVey), "Under the Tree" (*Celebration*; 1969) (JoAnn Cunningham, J. Mark McVey), "Fifty Million Years Ago" (*Celebration*; 1969) (JoAnn Cunningham, Emma Lampert, J. Mark McVey), "Decorate the Human Face" (*Colette Collage*; 1983) (JoAnn Cunningham), "Where Did It Go?" (*Celebration*; 1969) (J. Mark McVey), "Isn't That a Wonderful Way to Die?" (*The Bone Room*; 1975) (Tom Jones, Harvey Schmidt), "The Room Is Filled with You" (*Colette*; 1982) (JoAnn Cunningham), "Time Goes By" (*Grover's Corners*; 1987; produced only in regional theatre) (J. Mark McVey), "Goodbye, World" (*Grover's Corners*; 1987; produced only in regional theatre) Emma Lampert), "The Show Goes On" (*Mirette*; first produced in regional theatre in 1996; later presented in 2005 [see entry] as part of the *Musicals in Mufti* series [see entry]) (Company)

NOTES—*The Show Goes On* was a welcome tribute-revue to Tom Jones and Harvey Schmidt, who also appeared in the production. The revue included a great many obscure songs, including two from the team's *Grover's Corners*; based on Thornton Wilder's 1938 play *Our Town*, the musical was seen only in regional theater and never played in New York. Unfortunately, the cast album of *The Show Goes On* (released by DRG Records [CD # 19008]) didn't include the two songs.

See individual entries for more information about *The Bone Room*, *Demi-Dozen*, *The Fantasticks*, *I Do! I Do!*, *Mirette*, *Portfolio Revue*, and the various *Colette* musicals.

1452 Show Me Where the Good Times Are. "A New Musical." THEATRE: Edison Theatre; OPENING DATE: March 5, 1970; PERFORMANCES: 29; BOOK: Lee Thuna; LYRICS: Rhoda Roberts; MUSIC: Kenneth Jacobson; DIRECTION: Morton Da Costa; CHOREOGRAPHY: Bob Herget; SCENERY: Tom John; COSTUMES: Gloria Gresham; LIGHTING: Neil Peter Jampolis; MUSICAL DIRECTION: Karen Gustafson; PRODUCERS: Lorin E. Price, in association with Barbara Lee Horn

CAST—Arnold Soboloff (Aaron), Gloria LeRoy (Rachel), Neva Small (Annette), Cathryn Damon (Bella), John Bennett Perry (Maurice), Christopher Hewett (Kolinsky), Edward Earle (Rothstein), Mitchell Jason (Dr. Perlman), Michael Berkson (Thomas Perlman), Renee Orin (Madame Schwartz); Men and Women of the East Side (Austin Colyer, Kevin Daly, Denny Martin Flynn, Lydia Gonzalez, Maria Hero, Peggy Hewett, Sara Louise, Donna Monroe, James E. Rogers, Peter Sansone)

SOURCE—The 1666 play *Le Malaide Imaginaire* (*The Imaginary Invalid*) by Jean-Baptiste Poquelin (Moliere).

The action occurs in the bedroom of Aaron's house on Henry Street in New York City, and various places on the lower East Side; the time is Spring 1913.

The musical was presented in two acts.

ACT ONE—"How Do I Feel?" (Arnold Soboloff, Gloria LeRoy, Neva Small, Cathryn Damon), "He's Wonderful" (Neva Small, Gloria LeRoy), "Look Up" (Neva Small, Gloria LeRoy, Cathryn Damon, John Bennett Perry, Company), "Show Me Where the Good Times Are" (Cathryn Damon, Company), "You're My Happiness" (Arnold Soboloff, Cathryn Damon), "Café Royale Rag Time" (Company), "Staying Alive" (Christopher Hewett, Gloria LeRoy), "One Big Happy Family" (Arnold Soboloff, John Bennett Perry, Cathryn Damon, Neva Small, Gloria LeRoy, Christopher Hewett, Mitchell Jason, Michael Berkson)

ACT TWO—"Follow Your Heart" (Cathryn Damon, Ladies), "Look Who's Throwing a Party" (Arnold Soboloff, Guests), "When Tomorrow Comes" (John Bennett Perry), "One Big Happy Family" (reprise) (Mitchell Jason), "The Test" (Arnold Soboloff, Gloria LeRoy, Christopher Hewett), "I'm Not Getting Any Younger" (Cathryn Damon, '& Her Fellas'), "Who'd Believe?" (Arnold Soboloff), Finale: "Processional"/"Staying Alive" (reprise)/"Show Me Where the Good Times Are" (reprise) (Arnold Soboloff, Cathryn Damon, Company)

NOTES—*Show Me Where the Good Times Are* was performed under a Middle Broadway contract; depending on the source referenced, the musical is categorized as either a Broadway or an Off Broadway production.

The musical was the second failed Off Broadway adaptation of Moliere's play; the first, *'Toinette* (1961; see entry), played one month, as did *Show Me Where the Good Times Are*.

'Toinette retained the Parisian setting of Moliere's original, but updated the action to 1961. *Show Me Where the Good Times Are* was set in the New York City of 1913 in a Jewish neighborhood on the lower East Side.

Rhoda Roberts and Kenneth Jacobson borrowed the show's title, and the title song, from a number in their failed musical version of William Inge's *Picnic* (1953); called *Hot September*, it closed in Boston in 1965. You couldn't blame them from going into their trunk, because the song was a hum-dinger, an old-fashioned show tune in the Jerry Herman tradition. In fact, the musical *Show Me Where the Good Times Are* was sometimes quite reminiscent of Herman and *Hello, Dolly!* (1964), especially in scenes at the Café Royale and in the number "I'm Not Getting Any Younger," in which Bella and "her fellas" (like Dolly and her waiters) celebrate the fact that life must be lived because "there's life in the old girl yet."

RCA Victor was to have recorded the cast album (it had also been scheduled to record *Hot September*), but due to the show's brief run, the album was cancelled. The title song can be heard on a pirated LP edition of *Hot September*, which was taken from a live Boston performance. Thirty-four years after the closing of *Show Me Where the Good Times Are*, one of its cast members, Neva Small, recorded the title song for her CD collection *Neva Small/My Place in the World*; the selections are mostly from shows associated with her career (Broadway, Off Broadway, and one out-of-town closing), and the CD (released by Small Penny Enterprises, LLC, Records [# NS-2211]) is indispensable for those seeking memorable if generally obscure theatre music.

Samuel French, Inc., published the script of *Show Me Where the Good Times Are* in 1970.

A revised version of the musical was presented by the Jewish Repertory Theatre on June 13, 1993, for fifteen performances; the cast included Roslyn Kind, Robert Ari, Lauren Mitchell, Tim Ewing, and Gabriel Barre. Six songs were added to the score: "Bella's Plaint," "Good Intentions," "Is That a Woman?," "Something Special," "Wish Me a Happy Birthday," and "The Examination."

Roberts and Jacobson enjoyed two popular song hits in the late 1950s ("Put a Light in the Window" and "Swinging Shepherd's Blues"), but unfortunately they were unable to find success on the musical stage.

For other musical adaptations of Moliere's comedies, see entries for *The Amorous Flea*, *The Misanthrope*, *Monsieur de Pourceaugnac*, and the aforementioned *'Toinette*.

1453 The Showgirl. THEATRE: Town Hall; OPENING DATE: October 24, 1982; PERFORMANCES: 60; BOOK: Samuel Steinberg; English narration by Roz Regalson; LYRICS: Nellie Casman; lyrics and new musical numbers by Yankele Alperin; MUSIC: Nellie Casman; additional music by Alexander Lustig; DIRECTION: Michael Greenstein; CHOREOGRAPHY: Yankele Kaluski; SCENERY: Lydia Pincus-Gani (executed by Abraham Mordoh); COSTUMES: George Vallo; MUSICAL DIRECTION: Renee Solomon; PRODUCER: Shalom Yiddish Musical Comedy Theatre, Inc.

CAST—MARY SOREANU (Mme. DuBois, Bella, Fifi, Drunkard), Karol Feldman (Oscar Lampert), Lydia Saxton (Jenny, Narrator), Shifra Lerer (Serkeh), Yankele Alperin (Itzik), Adrian Mandel (Sol), Reizl Bozyk (Frimeh), Michael Michalovic (Nisan), David Carey (Fred), David Ellin (Iser), Karol Latowicz (Naftoli), Hallie Lightdale and Orly Jaffe (Jenny, as a child); Chorus (Fashion Models, Bella's Friends, Hassidim, Cabaret Patrons, Hoodlums, etc.): Laura Boerum, Toni Campbell, Sherry Charney, Charles Haack, Irit Hertzog, Rony Houta, James Vogel

The action occurs in Brooklyn and in Paris during the years 1945, 1925, and 1934.

The musical was presented in two acts.

ACT ONE—Overture (Orchestra), "Pardon, Mayn Her (Excuse Me, Sir)" (Lydia Feldman, Adrian Mandel), "Kinderishe Seychi (Childishness)" (Mary Soreanu, Lydia Feldman), "A Yiddish Lied (A Jewish Song)" (Reizl Bozyk, Michael Michalovic), "Haynt iz Yomtev (Today Is a Holiday)" (Yankele Alperin, Shifra Lerer), "Purim" (Mary Soreanu, Ensemble), "Ich Vel Eybik Dich Gedenken (I'll Always Remember You)" (Mary Soreanu, David Carey), "Shteytl" (Ensemble), "Ch'hob Lib Teater (I Love the Theatre)" (Mary Soreanu)

ACT TWO—"Femme Fatale" (French Medley) (Mary Soreanu), "Ich Vel Vartnoyf Dir (I Will Wait for You)" (David Carey), "Abi Gezint (Just a Little Bit of Health)" (Yankele Alperin), "Finif Sent (Five Cents)" (Mary Soreanu), Finale (Ensemble)

NOTES—This Off Off Broadway nostalgic musical *The Showgirl* was performed in Yiddish with occasional English narration. The plot dealt with the adventures of Mme. DuBois (Mary Soreanu) who, as a young woman known as Bella, led a controversial life as a showgirl in a Paris cabaret.

Richard F. Shepard in the *New York Times* said the evening was "heartwarmingly familiar" in its evocation of early Yiddish musical theatre, and he praised Soreanu's "remarkable range of musical and comic styles."

1454 Showing Off. THEATRE: Steve McGraw's; OPENING DATE: May 18, 1989; PERFORMANCES: 172; SKETCHES, LYRICS, AND MUSIC: Douglas Bernstein and Denis Markell; DIRECTION: Michael Leeds; CHOREOGRAPHY: Michael Leeds; SCENERY: Joseph Varga; COSTUMES: Jeanne Button; LIGHTING: Josh Starbuck; MUSICAL DIRECTION: Stephen Flaherty; PRODUCERS: Suzanne J. Schwartz and Jennifer Manocherian

CAST—Douglas Bernstein, Veanne Cox, Donna Murphy, Mark Sawyer

The revue was presented in two acts (division of acts unknown; songs and sketches are in performance order).

SKETCHES AND MUSICAL NUMBERS—"Showing Off" (Company), "72nd Street" (Company), "Native New Yorkers" (Company), "I Don't Get It" (Mark Sawyer), "S.I.P." (Company), "Showbiz Rabbi" (Douglas Bernstein), "They're Yours" (Donna Murphy, Veanne Cox), "Mightier Than the Sword" (Veanne Cox, Mark Sawyer, Donna Murphy), "Michele" (Douglas Bernstein), "Raffi: The Concert Movie" (Company), "Rental Cruelty" (Donna Murphy, Mark Sawyer), "Joshua Noveck" (Veanne Cox), "Ninas" (Company), "How Things Change" (Donna Murphy), "Take de Picture" (Company), "Old Fashioned Song" (Company)

NOTES—*Showing Off* was in the tried-and-true tradition of revues which looked at the ups and downs of life in New York City; it opened on the same evening as another revue about the same subject (see entry for *Laughing Matters*).

Richard F. Shepard in the *New York Times* said *Showing Off* was "as brisk and bright a revue as one can find," and he singled out a number of songs, including "Ninas" (a "dynamic" song about celebrities who get hidden Ninas in their caricatures by Al Hirschfeld) and "How Things Change" (Donna Murphy sang this lament about the days when one could enjoy *Amos 'n' Andy* and when one didn't worry about seal pups getting clubbed for their skins). The revue also included "Showbiz Rabbi" (who describes the High Holy Days as "the big blast and the big fast"), "Rental Cruelty" (about people who compulsively rent videocassettes), and a segment about "sophisticated" New Yorkers who wouldn't think of seeing such audience-pleasing musicals as *The Fantasticks* and *Me and My Girl*.

During the run, Donna Murphy was succeeded by Bebe Neuwirth. Steve McGraw's was formerly Palsson's.

1455 The Shrinking Bride. "A Comedy with Songs." THEATRE: Mercury Theatre; OPENING DATE: January 17, 1971; PERFORMANCES: 1; PLAY: Jonathan Levy; LYRICS: Jonathan Levy; MUSIC: William Bolcom; DIRECTION: Marvin Gordon; SCENERY: T.E. Mason; COSTUMES: Joseph G. Aulisi; LIGHTING: Molly Friedel; PRODUCERS: Tony Capodilupo and John Fink

CAST—Jake Dengel (Delano Ounce), Jack Somack (D. Norman Cates), Sully Boyar (Nat), Frank Nastasi (Vinnie), Louisa Flaningam (Allison Cates Fisch), Danny DeVito (Richie), Diane Simkin (Jeanine Cates), Joe Silver (Julius Katz), John Pleshette (Michael Fisch), Donald Symington (Sir Anthony Baer)

The action occurs in and around an estate called Tantamount Hall, on the upper Hudson River.

The play was presented in two acts.

NOTES—*The Shrinking Bride* wasn't a musical, but the comedy included incidental songs (lyrics by Jonathan Levy and music by William Bolcom). The plot dealt with a millionaire who lives in a castle on the Hudson River and his daughter, a "shrinking bride" who spends most of her time under a rug. Mel Gussow in the *New York Times* indicated the play was "overly busy" in its plot and pacing, and reported that while the program for the play indicated the evening was in three acts, only two were performed on opening night. Gussow noted that the play ended abruptly and uncertainly, "as if the play, not the bride, had shrunk." Gussow also commented that Bolcom's incidental songs might have worked better either as less (that is, relegated to background music) or more (developed into a full musical comedy score).

Among the cast members were the comics Joe Silver and Danny DeVito; Gussow singled out the latter for his "zany performance."

1456 Shylock. THEATRE: Church of the Heavenly Rest/The York Theatre Company; OPENING DATE: April 23, 1987; PERFORMANCES: 10 (estimated); LIBRETTO: Ed Dixon; MUSIC: Ed Dixon; DIRECTION: Lloyd Battista; SCENERY: Daniel Ettinger; COSTUMES: Robert W. Swasey; LIGHTING: Marcia Madeira; MUSICAL DIRECTION: Kathleen Rubbico; PRODUCER: The York Theatre Company (Janet Hayes Walker, Producing Director; Molly Pickering Grose, Managing Director)

CAST—Dennis Parlato (Antonio), Charles Pistone (Bassanio), Joel Fredrickson (Lorenzo), Ed Dixon (Shylock), Ann Brown (Jessica), Lisa Vroman (Portia), Brooks Almy (Nerissa)

SOURCE—The play *The Merchant of Venice* by William Shakespeare (written between 1594 and 1597).

The action occurs on the Piazza di San Marco in fifteenth-century Venice and on the Isle of Belmont.

The musical was presented in two acts (the musical numbers weren't listed in the program).

NOTES—*Shylock* was presented under an Off Off Broadway contract. For another musical version of *The Merchant of Venice*, see entry for *A Musical Merchant of Venice*.

1457 Sid Caesar & Company. "The Legendary Genius of Comedy." THEATRE: The Village Gate/Downstairs; OPENING DATE: June 2, 1989; PERFORMANCES: 72; PRODUCERS: Art D'Lugoff and Larry Spellman

CAST—SID CAESAR, Lee Delano, Gerrianne Raphael, Elliot Finkel Orchestra, Marilyn Sokol

The revue was presented in two acts.

ACT ONE—Overture (Elliot Finkel Orchestra), "Man Walking Down the Aisle" (Sid Caesar), "Boy at His First Dance" (Sid Caesar), "World Through the Eyes of a Baby" (Sid Caesar), "Man and Wife Arguing to the First Movement of Beethoven's Symphony" (Sid Caesar and Gerrianne Raphael), Song: "The Wicked Man" (Gerrianne Raphael), "At the Movies" (Sid Caesar, Lee Delano, Marilyn Sokol)

ACT TWO—Entr'acte (Elliot Finkel Orchestra), Medley from *Little Me* (1962; lyrics by Carolyn Leigh, music by Cy Coleman) (Marilyn Sokol, Gerrianne Raphael, Sid Caesar), "The Penny Candy Gum Machine" (Sid Caesar), Grieg Piano Concerto (Sid Caesar, Elliot Finkel), Gershwin Medley (Ian Finkel, Xylophone), "The Professor" (Sid Caesar, Lee Delano), Finale (Sid Caesar, Company)

NOTES—This revue by legendary comedian Sid Caesar played Off Broadway for nine weeks before transferring to Broadway at the John Golden Theatre for five performances beginning on November 1, 1989.

The revue's full title was apparently *From Then and Now—Sid Caesar & Company, The Legendary Genius of Comedy*, and it included sketches Caesar had performed on his hit 1950s comedy television series *Your Show of Shows* as well as a sequence of songs from his 1962 musical *Little Me*. The Broadway production (subtitled *Does Anybody Know What I'm Talking About?*) included a larger cast (minus Marilyn Sokol and Gerrianne Raphael) and new material; the *Little Me* sequence was omitted.

The Off Broadway program didn't credit a director, an author, and other creative staff; however, the Broadway production was directed by Martin Charnin (who was also credited with original songs).

In the Off Broadway production, Gerrianne Raphael sang "The Wicked Man" (which might have been "A Wicked Man," a song she introduced in *Ernest in Love* [1960]; see entry).

Mel Gussow in the *New York Times* said it was "heartening" to see Caesar performing again, and noted his "comic imagination remains sharp." But Gussow felt the evening was somewhat "formless" and was more in the nature of a nightclub appearance than a theatrical showcase.

1458 Sidd. THEATRE: Dodger Stages; OPENING DATE: March 15, 2006; PERFORMANCES: 13; BOOK: Andrew Frank; LYRICS: Andrew Frank and Doug Silver; MUSIC: Doug Silver; DIRECTION: Andrew Frank; CHOREOGRAPHY: Fran Kirmser Sharma; SCENERY: Maruti Evans; COSTUMES: Michael Bevins; LIGHTING: Chris Dallos; MUSICAL DIRECTION: Ned Paul Ginsburg; PRODUCERS: Always on the Way Productions; Fran Kirmser Sharma, Executive Producer; Joel Schonfeld, Associate Producer

CAST— Manu Narayan (Sidd), Marie-France Arcilla (Valerie, Others), Dann Fink (Willie, Others), Natalie Cortez (Mala, Others), Nicole Lewis (Lead Mystic, Others), Arthur W. Marks (Buddha, Others), Gerry McIntyre (Father, Others)

SOURCE— The 1922 novel *Siddhartha* by Hermann Hesse.

The musical was presented in two acts.

ACT ONE—"Bravest of All" (Company), "You Will Do Great Things" (Gerry McIntyre, Townspeople), "Valerie's Decision" (Marie-France Arcilla), "Standing and Waiting" (Gerry McIntyre, Manu Narayan), "The Map Song" (Manu Narayan, Marie-France Arcilla), "Let It Go" (Mystics), "Two Villagers" (Villagers), "Borders" (Manu Narayan, Marie-France Arcilla, Mystics), "Buddha's Song" (Arthur W. Marks), "Everybody Needs Something" (Dann Fink, Manu Narayan), "Happy Shop" (Natalie Cortez, Dancers), "That's Business" (Dann Fink, Manu Narayan, 'Swami' [performer unknown]), "Teach Me How to Move" (Manu Narayan, Natalie Cortez), Finale (Company)

ACT TWO—"Working Man's Shuffle" (Workers), "It Ain't Good" (Dann Fink, Manu Narayan), "Here's the Thing" (City People), "Something's Going On" (Manu Narayan, Natalie Cortez), "Fifteen Years" (Manu Narayan), "Always on the Way" (Marie-France Arcilla, Manu Narayan, Ferryman [performer unknown]), "You Are Here" (Ferryman [performer unknown], Manu Narayan), "Moving" (Merchant [performer unknown], Manu Narayan, Ferryman [performer unknown], River [performer unknown]), "Changing" (Traveler [performer unknown], Manu Narayan, Ferryman [performer unknown], River [performer unknown]), "Voices" (Buddha Followers, Manu Narayan, Ferryman [performer unknown], River [performer unknown]), "Hello, Ferryman" (Natalie Cortez, Manu Narayan, Son [performer unknown], River [performer unknown]), "Is There Anything I Can Do?" (Manu Narayan), "He Is My Son" (Ferryman [performer unknown], Manu Narayan, Son [performer unknown]), "Sidd's Enlightenment" (River [performer unknown], Manu Narayan, Ferryman [performer unknown]), Finale (Company)

NOTES—*Sidd* was a musical adaptation of Hermann Hesse's 1922 novel *Siddhartha*, about a young man who searches throughout the world for spiritual enlightenment.

Charles Isherwood in the *New York Times* said the "silly" musical mixed mysticism with wisecracks, and noted he couldn't seriously accept Sidd's descent into corruption when corruption was depicted in a dance which used every "cliché from the Bob Fosse back catalog."

1459 Sidewalkin'. THEATRE: UpStage/Cabaret/Manhattan Theatre Club; OPENING DATE: April 4, 1980; PERFORMANCES: 28; LYRICS: Jake Holmes; MUSIC: Jake Holmes; DIRECTION: Patricia Birch; CHOREOGRAPHY: Patricia Birch; SCENERY: Douglas W. Schmidt; COSTUMES: Carrie Robbins; LIGHTING: John Gleason; MUSICAL DIRECTION: Ted Irwin and John Leneham; PRODUCER: Manhattan Theatre Club (Lynne Meadow, Artistic Director; Barry Grove, Managing Director; Stephen Pascal, Associate Artistic Director)

CAST—Jake Holmes, Janie Sell, Donna Lee Marshall, Melanie Henderson, Larry Riley, Timothy Meyers, Marcelino Sanchez

The action occurs in New York City at the present time.

The revue was presented in two acts.

ACT ONE—"Sidewalks" (Jake Holmes, Company), "Lady Success" (Larry Riley), "Melody I" (Jake Holmes), "Music Business" (Donna Lee Marshall), "Melody II" (Jake Holmes), "Dealer" (Larry Riley), "Make Trixie Make" (Janie Sell), "Nada" (Larry Riley), "Monica's a Moonie" (Jake Holmes, Company), "Hey Jack" (Timothy Meyers), "Big Radio" (Donna Lee Marshall, Larry Riley, Marcelino Sanchez)

ACT TWO—"I Can Heal You" (Jake Holmes, Company), "Secret Storms" (Donna Lee Marshall, Janie Sell), "Angelita" (Marcelino Sanchez), "Johnny Blue Eyes" (Janie Sell), "Silky the Duke" (Larry Riley), "Hardcore Porn" (Timothy Meyers), "Night Wolf" (Melanie Henderson, Donna Lee Marshall, Janie Sell), "Marguerita" (Jake Holmes), "A Boy from Home" (Donna Lee Marshall), "'A' Uptown Express" (Jake Holmes, Company)

NOTES—The Off Off Broadway revue *Sidewalkin'* was about New York City street life. It played out its limited engagement at the Manhattan Theatre Club, and then disappeared.

Frank Rich in the *New York Times* found the evening "pleasant," "bland," and "pedestrian." The songs were either "plaintive" or "comic"; the former sentimentalized bag ladies and prostitutes and reminded him of "Frank Mills" from *Hair*, and the latter were Julius Monk-wannabe satiric pieces. Further, some of the numbers seemed to come from "a musty bottom drawer," and Rich noted that the time had long passed for songs about Moonies and rock groupies.

Sidewalkin' had been previously produced at the Manhattan Theatre Club a year earlier, when it opened there as *Songs from the City Streets* on March 28, 1979.

1460 Signs Along the Cynic Route. THEATRE: Actors' Playhouse; OPENING DATE: December 14, 1961; PERFORMANCES: 93; SKETCHES: Will Holt and Dolly Jonah; LYRICS: Will Holt; MUSIC: Will Holt; DIRECTION: Walt Witcover; SCENERY: Graphics by Milton Glaser; LIGHTING: Gene Tunezi; MUSICAL DIRECTION: Don Evans; PRODUCER: Precarious Productions

CAST— Will Holt (The Social Director), Dolly Jonah (The Required Blonde), Robert Barend (The Other One)

The revue was presented in two acts.

ACT ONE—"Signs," "Welcome," "Second Glances," "Bertha," "Terre Haute," "Modern Housing," "I Know You," "News Item," "Carnival," "Marriage Counsel," "The Social Director's Song," "The Rise & Fall of the City of Movieville"

ACT TWO—"Four More Shopping Days," "Second Thoughts," "Weekend," "Princeton Pastorale," "Summer Stock," "The Blonde's Song," "Discussion," "Tin Can Incantation," "Croquet," "Kulturny," "Seconds," "Till the Bird Sings," "Last"

NOTES— The program for *Signs Along the Cynic Route* stated that it was "exactly as printed — subject to change." The revue's title was one of the best ever, a skewed pun which seems to perfectly capture the flavor of the typical offbeat revue of the era. Milton Esterow in the *New York Times* noted that just before the end of the first act, Will Holt told the audience there would be a fifteen-minute intermission — and that he had counted all of them. But not to worry, the house was full when the audience returned for the second act, which, according to Esterow, was considerably better than the first. He found the three performers "fresh, gay and polished," and while there was "wit and variety" in the material, he felt the two-act evening in a regular Off Broadway theatre would have been better in a shorter version in a nightclub venue.

The revue took place in a fallout shelter and dealt with such topics as marriage and modern housing, and included a spoof of Bertolt Brecht and Kurt Weill's *The Rise and Fall of the City of Mahagonny*, here transplanted to Hollywood ("The Rise & Fall of the City of Movieville"). This was the first of two *Mahagonny* spoofs seen Off Broadway in the 1960s (see entry for *The Return of the Second City in "20,000 Frozen Grenadiers"* [1966]), and both were presented years before the opera itself was first produced in New York in 1970 (see entry). Esterow was particularly impressed with "Tin Can Incantation," an "inventive" musical number about life in New York City which was accompanied by tin cans, pots, and wooden sticks (the piece seems to be a precursor of *Stomp* [1994; see entry] and other similar performance pieces of the 1990s and 2000s).

Will Holt had a lengthy and busy career, as lyricist, librettist, composer, and occasional performer both on and off Broadway, and while he had some successes along the route, he never enjoyed the smash which would secure his place in musical theatre. It's unfortunate, because he was remarkably talented. His lyrics for *Come Summer* (1969) and *Platinum* (1978) are quite wonderful (in the latter, a 1940s-era has-been film actress looks back on a career of playing "war brides, WACs, and waifs on the run"). Holt also wrote the book for the vastly underrated *Over Here!* (1974). His greatest successes were *The Me Nobody Knows* (1971; see entry) (lyrics) and *Me and Bessie* (1975) (book).

1461 Sills & Company. THEATRE: Lamb's Theatre; OPENING DATE: June 9, 1986; PERFORMANCES: 118; DIRECTION: Paul Sills; SCENERY: Carol Sills; COSTUMES: Deborah Shaw, Costume Consultant; LIGHTING: Malcolm Sturchio; MUSICAL DIRECTION: David Evans; PRODUCERS: Thomas Viertel, Steven Baruch, Richard Frankel, and Jeffrey Joseph

CAST— Severn Darden, MacIntyre Dixon, Paul Dooley, Garry Goodrow, Gerrit Graham, Bruce Jarchow, Mina Kolb, Maggie Roswell, Rachel Sills

The revue was presented in one act.

NOTES—*Sills & Co.* was an attempt to capture the glory days of 1950s and 1960s improvisational theatre. While the revue lasted only three months, it nonetheless provided audiences a brief chance to see many cast members who were part of the Chicago and Off Broadway improvisational scene during its heyday, including Severn Darden, MacIntyre Dixon, Paul Dooley, and Mina Kolb. For the revue's basic building-block material, Viola Spolin developed the outlines of the sketches, and the audience itself provided the specifics to fill out each sequence.

During the course of the three-month run, the cast dwindled from nine to six members (MacIntyre Dixon, Gerrit Graham, Maggie Roswell, and

Rachel Sills left the revue; and Nancy McCabe-Kelly joined the cast).

Frank Rich in the *New York Times* said the evening was "on and off," but noted he was "rarely bored." He also reported that audience members in the balcony offered better suggestions than those in the orchestra, and he wondered if this had anything to do with the fact that critics were sitting downstairs.

Another legend of the improvisational revue (and of American musical theatre) was originally scheduled to appear in the production. Barbara Harris' name was included in early newspaper advertisements for the revue (billed as "Special Guest Artist"). But in later ads her name was no longer listed, and she never appeared in the production.

1462 Silverlake. "A Winter's Tale." THEATRE: New York State Theatre; OPENING DATE: March 20, 1980; PERFORMANCES: 6; BOOK: Hugh Wheeler; based on the original German text by George Kaiser; LYRICS: Lys Symonette; based on the original German text by George Kaiser; MUSIC: Kurt Weill; selections of Weill's incidental music integrated by Lys Symonette; DIRECTION: Harold Prince; CHOREOGRAPHY: Larry Fuller; SCENERY: Manuel Lutgenhorst; COSTUMES: Manuel Lutgenhorst; LIGHTING: Ken Billington; MUSICAL DIRECTION: Julius Rudel; PRODUCERS: The New York City Opera and Gert von Gontard

CAST—Harlan Foss (Johann), Robert McFarland (Dietrich), William Neill (Severin), Edward Zimmerman (Heckler), James Clark (Klaus), Norman Large (Hans), Gary Chryst (Hunger), Penny Orloff (Salesgirl), Jane Shaulis (Salesgirl), David Rae Smith (Handke), Joel Grey (Officer Olim), William Poplaski (City Inspector), Jack Harrold (Lottery Agent, Baron Laur), Richard L. Porter (Doctor), Elibeth Hynes (Fennimore), Gary Dietrich (Liveried Footman), Elaine Bonazzi (Frau von Luber), Michael Rubino (Chief), Rafael Romero (Chef), New York City Opera Chorus and Associate Chorus, New York City Opera Dancers, Character Mimes

The opera was presented in two acts.

ACT ONE—"Duet of the Woodcutters" (Harlan Foss, Robert McFarland), "Duet of the Salesgirls" (Penny Orloff, Jane Shaulis), "In the Police Station" (Unseen Chorus), "Tango" (Joel Grey), "Olim! Olim!" (Unseen Chorus), "Duet in the Hospital" (William Neill, Joel Grey), "Fennimore's Song" (Elizabeth Hynes), "The Ballad of Caesar's Death" (Elaine Bonazzi), "Severin's Revenge Aria" (William Neill), "Severin-Fennimore Duet" (William Neill, Elizabeth Hynes), Act One Finale (Chorus)

ACT TWO—"Severin in Chains" (William Neill), "First Laur and Von Luber Duet" (Elaine Bonazzi, Jack Harrold), "Friendship Duet" (Joel Grey, William Neill), "Second Laur and Von Luber Duet" (Elaine Bonazzi, Jack Harrold), Act Two Finale (Chorus, Elizabeth Hynes, Joel Grey, William Neill)

NOTES—*Silverlake* was seen in New York forty-seven years after its world premiere in Germany as *Der Silbersee* (actually, the opera enjoyed *three* premieres on the night of February 18, 1933, in Leipzig, Magdeburg, and Erfurt). The director for the Liepzig production was Detlef Sierck, who, as Douglas Sirk, directed a number of American films which bordered on soap opera but which nonetheless took on an operatic intensity in their over-the-top stories which were over-laden with symbolism and the use of blazing color (*Magnificent Obsession* [1953], *All That Heaven Allows* [1956], *Written on the Wind* [1956], and *Imitation of Life* [1959]).

In some ways, *Silverlake* was the antithesis of Kurt Weill's *The Rise and Fall of the City of Mahagonny* (see entry). After initial hostility between the opera's two main characters (Olim, a police officer [Joel Grey] and Severin, a starving homeless man [William Neill]), the two journey to Silverlake. While Mahagonny was spared when a hurricane's path was miraculously diverted, the city was nonetheless corrupt and vice-ridden. When Olim and Severin journey to Silverlake, another operatic miracle occurs. The winter suddenly turns into spring, but the ice of the lake remains frozen, and the two men walk across it in order to join their friends in a new city devoted to peace and brotherhood. The New York City Opera production was recorded on a 2-LP set (in English) by Nonesuch Records (# DB-79003), and in 1990 Capriccio Records released a 2-CD set (in the original German) (# 60011-2). The song list above is taken from the Nonesuch recording.

1463 Simoon

NOTES—See entry for *Murder in 3 Keys*.

1464 Simply Heavenly (May 1957). THEATRE: 85th Street Playhouse; OPENING DATE: May 21, 1957; PERFORMANCES: 44; BOOK: Langston Hughes; LYRICS: Langston Hughes; MUSIC: David Martin; DIRECTION: Joshua Shelley; SCENERY: Charles Brandon; LIGHTING: Norman Blumenfeld; PRODUCER: Stella Holt

CAST—Melvin Stewart (Simple), Alma Hubbard (Madame Butler), Stanley Greene (Boyd), Javotte S. Greene (Mrs. Caddy, Nurse, Party Guest), Marilyn Berry (Joyce Lane), Lawson Bates (Hopkins), Willie Pritchett (Bar Pianist), Claudia McNeil (Mamie), Charles A. McRae (Bodiddly), Allegro Kane (Character), John Bouie (Melon), Ray Thompson (Gitfiddle), Ethel Ayler (Zarita), Josephine Woods (Arcie), Charles Harrigan (John Jasper), Pierre Rayon (Big Boy)

SOURCES—Langston Hughes' short story "Simple Takes a Wife," as well as other of his *Simple* stories.

The action occurs in Harlem, U.S.A. The musical was presented in two acts.

ACT ONE—"Love Is Simply Heavenly" (Marilyn Berry), "Let Me Take You for a Ride" (Ethel Ayler, Melvin Stewart), "Broken String Blues" (Ray Thompson), "Did You Ever Hear the Blues?" (Claudia McNeil, John Bouie, Bar Guests), "John Henry" (a/k/a "I'm Gonna Be John Henry") (Melvin Stewart)

ACT TWO—"Shade and Shadows" (performer unknown), "Let's Ball Awhile" (Ethel Ayler, Ensemble), "The Men in My Life" (Ethel Ayler), "I'm a Good Old Girl" (a/k/a "Good Old Girl") (Claudia McNeil)

NOTES—*Simply Heavenly* is the first celebrated Black Off Broadway musical. It was dramatized by Langston Hughes, who based the musical on his *Simple* stories; he and composer David Martin created a short but modest and effective score (which included the haunting "Did You Ever Hear the Blues?").

After playing forty-four performances at the 85th Street Playhouse, the production transferred to Broadway on August 20, 1957, where it played for sixty-two performances. Melvin Stewart and Claudia McNeil, among others, recreated their roles for the Broadway production, and the only major cast substitution was that of Anna English, who replaced Ethel Ayler in the role of Zarita. For the Broadway production, the number "Shade and Shadows" was deleted, and two numbers were added: "When I'm in a Quiet Mood" (for Claudia McNeil and John Bouie) and "Look for the Morning Star" (for Anna English); the latter was also reprised for the show's finale, and was sung by the entire cast.

The Broadway cast recording was issued by Columbia Records (LP # OL-5240), and included two dialogue sequences from the musical, Simple's "Flying Saucer Monologue" and his "Mississippi Monologue." The recording also included two songs not heard on Broadway opening night ("Gatekeeper of My Castle" [Marilyn Berry and Melvin Stewart] and "Beat It Out, Mon" [a/k/a "Calypso—Beat It Out, Mon"] [[Duke Willliams, the character of Hopkins, and the Ensemble]]); since these numbers were written for the production, but were unused, perhaps they, along with the two spoken monologues, were included in order to fill out what would have been an inordinately short recording. In 2008, Sepia Records released the cast album on CD (# 1105); the recording included a pop version of "Did You Ever Hear the Blues?" (sung by cast member Claudia McNeil) as well as a number of bonus tracks of songs not from the musical (eight songs performed by Beatrice Reading and one by Juanita Hall).

The script was published by the Dramatists Play Service, Inc., in 1959, and includes three songs not listed in the Broadway playbill and not included in the cast album: "Deep in Love with You" (for Simple), "I Want Somebody to Come Home To" (for Joyce), and "Watermelons" (for Melon). Other numbers which were apparently written for, but not used in, the Broadway production were "The Hunter and the Hunted," "He's a Great Big Bundle of Joy," "A Sweet Worriation," and "Yankee-Dixie March."

After the Broadway closing, the show returned to Off Broadway for a two-month run at the Renata Theatre on November 8, 1957, for sixty-three performances. (See entry for this production.)

On May 20, 1958, *Simply Heavenly* opened in London at the Adelphi Theatre for a disappointing run of sixteen performances. Melvin Stewart played Simple, and Beatrice Reading was Mamie. The London version was directed and co-produced by Lawrence Harvey.

On December 7, 1959, *Simply Heavenly* was televised in a one-hour adaptation, as part of the *Play of the Week* series. Joshua Shelley repeated his direction, and Melvin Stewart, Claudia McNeil, Ethel Ayler, and Gail Fisher recreated their stage roles. Other television cast members were Frederick O'Neal (Boyd) and Earle Hyman (Hopkins). "Did You Ever Hear the Blues?" was among the numbers retained for the television version (if memory serves, four other numbers were used in the telecast: "Love Is Simply Heavenly," "Broken String Blues," "John Henry," and "Let's Ball Awhile"). With its original director, many of its original Off Broadway and Broadway cast members, its modest production values, and the fact that it was filmed during the 1950s, the seldom-seen televised version of *Simply Heavenly* is perhaps the only early Off Broadway musical captured on film, and, as such, it's the real thing, an authentic document of the look and the sound of the era's Off Broadway musicals. In 2003, *Simply Heavenly* was revived in London, to great acclaim and success. It opened at the Young Vic on March 17 of that year, and on October 25, 2004, it was produced in the West End, at the Trafalgar Studios Theatre, for a run of more than six months. It was a nominee for the 2005 Olivier Award as Outstanding Musical, and in 2005 it was recorded by First Night Records (CD # CASTCD-92).

The 2005 recording included "Watermelons," "He's a Great Big Bundle of Joy," "Deep in Love with You," and "The Hunter and the Hunted," and so between the Broadway cast album and the revival cast album, a total of sixteen songs and two monologues have been recorded from the score. The 2005 recording also includes an instrumental sequence titled "Paddy's Bar," and this may have been entr'acte music.

Stella Holt and Langston Hughes were later associated with another Black Off Broadway musical (*Jerico-Jim Crow*, 1964; see entry).

1465 Simply Heavenly (November 1957). "A New Musical Folk Comedy." THEATRE: Renata Theatre; OPENING DATE: November 8, 1957; PERFORMANCES: 63; BOOK: Langston Hughes;

LYRICS: Langston Hughes; MUSIC: David Martin; DIRECTOR: Joshua Shelley; SCENERY: Charles Brandon; LIGHTING: Norman Blumenfeld; PRODUCER: Stella Holt

CAST—Melvin Stewart* (Simple), Lillian Hayman** (Madam Butler), Stanley Greene* (Boyd), Gail Fisher** (Mrs. Caddy, Nurse, Party Guest), Dagmar Craig*** (Joyce Lane), Duke Williams**** (Hopkins), Willie Pritchett* (Bar Pianist), Miriam Burton** (Mamie), Allegro Kane* (Character), John Bouie* (Melon), Brownie McGhee (Gitfiddle), Anna English**** (Zarita), Josephine Woods* (Arcie), Charles Harrigan* (John Jasper), Franklin Mercer** (Big Boy, Cop)

SOURCE—Langston Hughes' short story "Simple Takes a Wife," as well as other of his "Simple" stories.

*Denotes performer appeared in first Off Broadway production, Broadway production, and second Off Broadway production.

**Denotes performer appeared only in second Off Broadway production.

***Dagmar Craig appeared as Mrs. Caddy in the Broadway production and as Joyce Lane in the second Off Broadway production.

****Denotes performer appeared in Broadway production and in second Off Broadway production.

The action occurs in Harlem, U.S.A.

ACT ONE—"Love Is Simply Heavenly" (Dagmar Craig), "Let Me Take You for a Ride" (Anna English, Melvin Stewart), "Broken String Blues" (Brownie McGhee), "Did You Ever Hear the Blues?" (Miriam Burton, John Bouie, Bar Characters), "I'm Gonna Be John Henry" (Melvin Stewart)

ACT TWO—"When I'm in a Quiet Mood" (Miriam Burton, John Bouie), "Look for the Morning Star" (Anna English), "Let's Ball Awhile" (Anna English, Ensemble), "The Men in My Life" (Anna English), "I'm a Good Old Girl" (Miriam Burton), "Look for the Morning Star" (reprise) (Ensemble)

NOTES—For more information, see entry for the first Off Broadway production of *Simply Heavenly*.

1466 Sing Hallelujah! "An All Singing, All Dancing Gospel Musical." THEATRE: Village Gate Downstairs; OPENING DATE: November 3, 1987; PERFORMANCES: 72; DIRECTION: Worth Gardner; SCENERY: Joseph P. Tilford; COSTUMES: Rebecca Senske; LIGHTING: Kirk Bookman; PRODUCERS: Art D'Lugoff, Lipper Productions, Inc., and Gerald Wexler Presents, Inc.

CAST—Curtis Blake, Rose Clyburn, Patricia Ann Everson, Ann Nesby, Clarence Snow

The revue was presented in two acts.

ACT ONE—"Sing Hallelujah!" (lyric and music by Donald Lawrence) (Ensemble), "Everybody Ought to Know" (lyric and music by Walter Hawkins) (Ann Nesby, Ensemble), "Good News" (traditional) (Curtis Blake, Ensemble), "We Can't Go On This Way" (lyric and music by Richard Smallwood) (Clarence Snow, Ann Nesby, Ensemble), "Safe in His Arms" (traditional) (Ann Nesby, Rose Clyburn, Ensemble), "Right Now" (lyric and music by Andre Crouch) (Clarence Snow, Ann Nesby, Ensemble), "Bright Side Somewhere" (traditional) (Clarence Snow, Curtis Blake, Richard Odom [Keyboards], Ensemble), "New World" (lyric and music by Michael Terry) (Ensemble), "Didn't It Rain" (traditional) (Rose Clyburn, Ensemble), "Hollywood Scene" (lyric and music by Andre Crouch) (Curtis Blake, Ensemble), "I'm Just Holdin' On" (lyric and music by Dorothy Love Coates) (Patricia Ann Everson, Ensemble)

ACT TWO—"Anyway You Bless" (traditional) (Ann Nesby, Ensemble), "Shut de Do'" (traditional) (Rose Clyburn, Curtis Blake, Ensemble), "Can't Nobody Do Me Like Jesus" (lyric and music by Andre Crouch) (Rose Clyburn, Ensemble), "Oh Happy Day" (traditional) (Curtis Blake, Patricia Ann Everson, Ensemble), "Couldn't Hear Nobody Pray" (traditional) (Ann Nesby, Ensemble), "Oh Mary Don't You Weep" (traditional) (Patricia Ann Everson, Ensemble), "The Question Is" (lyric and music by Marvin Winans) (Richard Odom [Keyboards], Ensemble), "No Ways Tired" (traditional) (Richard Odom [Keyboards], Ensemble), "Runnin' for Jesus" (traditional) (Ensemble), "Sing Hallelujah!" (reprise) (Ensemble)

NOTES—*Sing Hallelujah!* was a song-cycle of gospel music conceived by Worth Gardner and Donald Lawrence. Stephen Holden in the *New York Times* said the eighty-minute evening was a "non-stop, high-powered celebration" of both traditional and contemporary numbers. He noted that the "stylistic variety" and "elaborate" musical arrangements were "very exhilarating."

1467 Sing Me Sunshine! THEATRE: AMAS Repertory Theatre; OPENING DATE: February 9, 1984; PERFORMANCES: 16; BOOK: Robert E. Richardson and Johnny Brandon; LYRICS: Johnny Brandon; MUSIC: Johnny Brandon; DIRECTION: Jack Timmers; CHOREOGRAPHY: Henry Le Tang; Ellie Le Tang, Assistant Choreographer; SCENERY: Robert Lewis Smith; COSTUMES: Gail Cooper-Hecht; LIGHTING: Paul Sullivan; MUSICAL DIRECTION: Thomas Birdwell; PRODUCER: The AMAS Repertory Theatre, Inc. (Rosetta LeNoire, Founder and Artistic Director)

CAST—Sal Biagini (Roger), George Bohn (Jenkins, Reggie, Sir Horace Cholmondeley, Ensemble), Leonard Drum (Jarvis), Rod Ferrone (Claude, Footman, Ensemble), Andrea Frierson (Peg), Joanne Genelle (Mrs. Wentworth, Ensemble), Marta Hedges (Celia, Lady Cholmondeley, Ensemble), Jan Horvath (Ethel), Glenn Kramer (Hawkes, Guest, Ensemble), Mary Anne Prevost (Maid, Ensemble), Rose Roffman (Mrs. Chichestor), Scott Willis (Jerry)

SOURCE—The 1912 play *Peg O' My Heart* by J. Hartley Manners.

The action occurs in and around the Chichestor Manor House in a small country town in Hertfordshire, England, during the late spring of 1934.

The musical was presented in two acts.

ACT ONE—"The H'Elegant Homes of H'England" (Leonard Drum, Mary Ann Prevost, Rod Ferrone), "Ruined" (Rose Roffman, Jan Horvath), "A Long, Long Time" (Andrea Frierson), "When a Gentleman's Well Dressed He's Well Prepared" (Scott Willis, Friends), "Nothing Like a Friend" (Scott Willis, Andrea Frierson), "The H'Elegant Homes of H'England" (reprise) (Leonard Drum, Mary Ann Prevost, Rod Ferrone), "All Alone" (Andrea Frierson), "The Education of Peg" (Rose Roffman, Jan Horvath, Scott Willis, Andrea Frierson), "That's What Living's All About" (Andrea Frierson), "Where Is Away?" (Sal Biagini, Jan Horvath), "You Can Do It" (Andrea Frierson, Jan Horvath), "Changes" (Scott Willis), "Down My Street" (Andrea Frierson, Scott Willis, Company), "That Is What I Give to You" (Andrea Frierson, Scott Willis)

ACT TWO—"Peg" (Scott Willis), "Sing Me Sunshine" (Andrea Frierson, Company), "Sing Me Sunshine" (reprise)/"That Is What I Give to You" (reprise) (Andrea Frierson, Scott Willis), "Where Do I Stand?" (Andrea Frierson), "That Is What I Give to You" (reprise) (Andrea Frierson, Scott Willis), Finale (Company)

NOTES—Johnny Brandon's Off Off Broadway musical *Sing Me Sunshine!* was a revised version of *Peg*, his 1967 adaptation of J. Hartley Manner's classic 1912 play *Peg O' My Heart* which starred Laurette Taylor as Peg and ran for 603 performances. *Peg* had played in summer stock, and starred Eartha Kitt in the title role; the book was by Robert Emmett, and Katherine Dunham was the choreographer. Numbers from this production which weren't used in *Sing Me Sunshine!* were: "What'll It Be," "Heavens to Betsy," "She Touches My Heart," "The Right Kind of People," "Keep That Beat," and "Madam of the Manor." A note in the *Peg* program indicated that Johnny Brandon's musical *Heavens to Betsy* would "soon" open on Broadway. It never did, and it's unclear if *Heavens to Betsy* was really *Sing Me Sunshine*/*Peg* (the song "Heavens to Betsy" was a number in the 1967 production of *Peg*).

Peg O' My Heart has been the inspiration for other musicals, none of which were hits. The play was first musicalized as *Peg-O-My-Dreams*; it opened at the Jolson Theatre on May 5, 1924, and played for just thirty-two performances. Another musical version, *Peg*, opened in London at the Phoenix Theatre on April 12, 1984, and played for 146 performances; the lyrics and music were by David Heneker, best known for his *Half a Sixpence* score. The title role was played by Ann Morrison, who had created the role of Mary Flynn in Stephen Sondheim's *Merrily We Roll Along* (1981), and Sian Phillips was Mrs. Chichester. The cast album was released by That's Entertainment Records (LP # TER-1024). This version played briefly in the United States during the summer of 1987 (Ann Morrison reprised her title role, Davis Gaines was Jerry, and Jan Miner was Mrs. Chichester).

1468 Sing Muse! "A New Musical Comedy." THEATRE: Van Dam Theatre; OPENING DATE: December 6, 1961; PERFORMANCES: 39; BOOK: Erich Segal; LYRICS: Erich Segal; MUSIC: Joe Raposo; DIRECTION: Bill Penn; SCENERY: Boyd Dumrose; COSTUMES: Hal George; LIGHTING: Boyd Dumrose; MUSICAL DIRECTION: Jerry Goldberg; PRODUCER: Robert D. Feldstein

CAST—Karen Morrow (Helen), Ralph Stantley (Menelaus), Bob Spencer (Paris), Paul Michael (Achilles), Brandon Maggart (Patroklos), William Pierson (Mac)

SOURCE—Homer's epic poem *The Iliad* (written sometime between the eighth and sixth centuries B.C.).

The musical was presented in two acts.

ACT ONE—"Helen Quit Your Yellin'" (Karen Morrow, Ralph Stantley), "I Am a Travelling Poet" (Bob Spencer), "O Pallas Athene" (Bob Spencer), "Your Name May Be Paris" (Karen Morrow, Bob Spencer), "Out to Launch" (Karen Morrow), "Sing Muse!" (Karen Morrow, Bob Spencer), "You're in Love" (Karen Morrow, Bob Spencer), "The Wrath of Achilles" (Ralph Stantley, Brandon Maggart, Paul Michael), "The Wrath of Achilles" (reprise) (Ralph Stantley, Brandon Maggart, Paul Michael), "No Champagne" (Bob Spencer), "Please Let Me Read" (Ralph Stantley, Brandon Maggart, Paul Michael)

ACT TWO—"Business Is Bad" (Ralph Stantley, Brandon Maggart), "In Our Little Salon" (Karen Morrow), "Fame!" (Paul Michael, Brandon Maggart, Ralph Stantley), "Your Name May Be Paris" (reprise) (Sung by Karen Morrow), "We'll Find a Way" (Karen Morrow, Bob Spencer), "The Way" (Performer[s] not credited), Finale (Company)

NOTES—During the brief run of *Sing Muse!* there were various song changes. The following numbers were performed at one time or another: "I'm to Blame," "The Day at the Sexmockena Mambo," and "Tonight's the Flight" (all three were recorded for the cast album, which, like so many early Off Broadway musicals, was privately recorded (LP # CH-1093), and was first made available to the general public during the 1980s, thanks to Blue Pear Records [LP # BP-1004]).

And, yes, with song titles like "Helen Quit Your Yellin'," "Out to Launch," and "The Day at the Sexmockena [read: deus ex machina] Mambo," *Sing Muse!* was a light-hearted modern-day re-imagination of Homer's epic poem, and the second Off Broadway musical to be based on his work (see entry for *The Golden Apple* [1954]). (For two other Helen of Troy musicals, see *Helen* and *La Belle Helene*.)

Sing Muse! was written by Erich Segal and Joseph Raposo long before Segal found success with his novel (and film) *Love Story* and Raposo became *Sesame Street*'s composer of choice. The musical was first produced at Yale University on May 4, 1961, and the Off Broadway production later in the year ran only a few weeks. But Segal's irreverent approach to *The Iliad* and Raposo's infectious music make *Sing Muse!* one of the guilty pleasures of Off Broadway musicals. "Out to Launch" is a delightful tango; "The Wrath of Achilles" a soft shoe shuffle; "O Pallas Athene," a spoof of Elvis Presley-styled rock 'n' roll; Karen Morrow's "Tonight's the Flight," a lovely beguine; and the finale was an extended choral piece performed by the entire cast.

Sing Muse! marked the talented Karen Morrow's New York debut. She found one success, 1963's Off Broadway revival of *The Boys from Syracuse* (see entry), but her Broadway musicals were all failures (*I Had a Ball* [1964], *A Joyful Noise* [1966], *I'm Solomon* [1968], and *The Grass Harp* [1971]); Another Off Broadway musical in which she appeared (*Music! Music!* [1974]) was also unsuccessful (see entry). Fortunately, many of her musicals were recorded, and so her clarion performances were preserved.

Sing Muse! wasn't Erich Segal's last musical excursion into Homeric territory. In 1974, a lyric version of *The Odyssey* began a lengthy national tour; titled *Odyssey*, it starred Yul Brynner and Joan Diener, and the show's book and lyrics were by Segal (music by Albert Marre). By the time it reached New York on January 1, 1976, it was called *Home Sweet Homer*, and Segal had withdrawn from the show (the lyrics were now credited to Charles Burr and Forman Brown, and the book to Roland Kibbee and Marre). It was one of the worst musicals to ever reach Broadway, and, its first performance was its last. *Sing Muse!* was the first musical to play the Van Dam Theatre.

Incidentally, the year before *Sing Muse!* opened, another *Iliad*-related work had been scheduled to open in New York. Louis Calta in the *New York Times* reported that *Homer's Follies*, a spoof of *The Iliad* by Ben Copito, was scheduled for a Broadway production in February 1960. It was apparently a comedy with music, and Calta indicated the evening would be a light-hearted look at the last days of the Trojan War. But *Homer's Follies* soon dropped off the map, and never even saw a tryout production.

1469 Sinking Sinking. "A Titanic Musical." THEATRE: T.O.M.I.; OPENING DATE: 1980 (?); PERFORMANCES: Unknown; BOOK: David Csontos and Kathy Burke Hill; LYRICS: Kathy Burke Hill; MUSIC: David Csontos; DIRECTION: Edward J. Farley; CHOREOGRAPHY: Rita Hamilton; SCENERY: Ron Hiatt; COSTUMES: Denise Galonsky; LIGHTING: Ron Hiatt; MUSICAL DIRECTION: Brian Conley; PRODUCERS: Len Shendell and Tony Scioli in association with That'sa Wrap Productions, Inc.; Joffre McClung, Robbyn Peterson, and Quinton Wiles, Associate Producers

CAST—Mike Crisp (Lambert), Lisa Simon (LaRue), Paula Smith Perkins (Zazie), Gabriel Reyes (Nick Necropolis), Melinda Moore Strayhorn (Ophelia Necropolis), Joffre McClung (Lavina Khaki), Lisa O'Neill (Cecily Stunning), Bruce Pitzer (Basil Virileman), David Finck (Captain E.J. Smythe), Jennifer Ashe (Consortia Paramour), Quinton Wiles (Raoul), Brian Conley (Social Director), Sharon Ferry Connors (Sister Mary Trixie), Robbyn Peterson (Sister Mary Felicity, Rapunzel La Torres), Shannon Ryan (Birdie Tweet), R. Randy Thompson (Algernon Marmaduke), Barbara Schofield (Dementia Dalrymple), Katherine Deni (Aurora Teitz), Margarite Winer (Wanda Wonder)

The action occurs aboard the *Titanic* in April 1912.

The musical was presented in one act.

MUSICAL NUMBERS—"Hello Titanic" (Ensemble), "Azure Blue" (Bruce Pitzer, Lisa O'Neill), "Madame Z's" (Joffre McClung, Margarite Winer, Barbara Schofield), "Isn't It Great to Be Rotten" (Gabriel Reyes, Melinda Moore Strayhorn), "Oh What a Wonderful Vacation" (Brian Conley, Ensemble), "Birdie's Lament" (Shannon Ryan), "Confide in Me" (Melinda Moore Strayhorn), "Lady Anne's Chastity Belt" (Margarite Winer, Ensemble), "Someone Better Comes Along" (Bruce Pitzer, Lisa O'Neill), "LaRue's Song" (Lisa Simon), "If You're in Love" (Katherine Deni, Men), "Torture" (Lisa O'Neill, Ensemble), "Titanic Panic" (David Finck, Margarite Winer, Quinton Wiles, R. Randy Thompson, Brian Conley), "Sinking Sinking" (Ensemble)

NOTES—The Off Off Broadway musical *Sinking Sinking* utilized a theatre-of-the-absurd approach to the sinking of the *Titanic*. There have been at least two other musicals about the sinking of the ocean liner. In 1977, a Czechoslovakian musical, *The Titanic*, offered a splendidly melodic, often surreal score which was recorded by Supraphon Records (LP # 1113-2019); the book was by Juraj Herz, the lyrics by Zdenek Borovec, and the music by Bohuslav Ondracek. And the 1996 Broadway musical *Titanic* won the 1996 Tony Award for Best Musical, Best Score, and Best Book; the sweeping, epic score by Maury Yeston was recorded by RCA Victor Records (CD # 09026-69934-2).

1470 Sister Aimee. "A New Musical." THEATRE: Gene Frankel Theatre; OPENING DATE: April 17, 1981; PERFORMANCES: 13; BOOK: Worth Gardner; LYRICS: Worth Gardner; MUSIC: Worth Gardner; DIRECTION: David Holdgreiwe; CHOREOGRAPHY: David Holdgreiwe; SCENERY: J.R. Moderegger; COSTUMES: Van Ramsey; LIGHTING: Dan Farley; MUSICAL DIRECTION: Fred Barton; PRODUCER: Gene Frankel

CAST—Deb G. Girdler (Aimee Semple McPherson), Willi Kirkham (Minnie Kennedy), David Adamson (Robert Semple), Donna Sontag (Roberta Star Semple), Jack Kyrieleison (Harold Simpson McPherson), Jenifer Lewis (Louise Messnick), Eric Johnson (Judge Hardy), Ennis Smith (Monkey Abe), Jerry Bradley (Tent Salesman), Clint Vriezelaar (Whataman), Peter Moran (Rolf K. McPherson), Tom Hafner (Contractor), Pam Parker (Jury Forewoman), Sally Schwartz (Margaret Newton-Hudson), Valerie Williams (Harriet Jordan)

The musical was presented in two acts.

ACT ONE—"Sister Aimee" (Jenifer Lewis), "In the Morning" (David Adamson, Deb G. Girdler), "Preach the Good News" (Jenifer Lewis, Valerie Williams, Ensemble), "Singing Jesus" (Ensemble), "Glory Train" (Jenifer Lewis, Ensemble), "Gospel Car" (Deb G. Girdler, Ensemble), "Sister Is My Daughter" (Willi Kirkham), "Gospel Car" (reprise) (Deb G. Girdler, Ensemble), "Concrete and Steel" (Ensemble), "Lost at Sea" (Ensemble), "Joy, Joy, Joy" (Ensemble)

ACT TWO—"Sister Aimee" (reprise) (Deb G. Girdler), "Joy, Joy, Joy" (reprise) (Ensemble), "Ormiston's Blues" (performer unknown), "The New Aimee" (Jenifer Lewis, Ensemble), "Iron Furnace" (performer unknown, Ensemble), "Delicate Secrets of Love" (Clint Vriezelaar), "Jamais Encore" (Willi Kirkham), "Aimee, Slay Me" (performer unknown), "I Can Paddle My Own Canoe" (Deb G. Girdler), "In the Morning" (reprise) (Deb G. Girdler, Ensemble)

NOTES—The Off Off Broadway musical *Sister Aimee* was about the controversial (sinner or saint?) evangelist Aimee Semple McPherson (1890-1944). *Aimee*, an earlier musical about the subject (with Pamela Peyton-Wright in the title role), premiered at the Trinity Square Repertory Company, Providence, Rhode Island, on December 6, 1973, for forty-six performances; the music was by Worth Gardner, the composer of *Sister Aimee*, and the lyrics and book were by William Goyen. At least four songs from *Aimee* resurfaced in *Sister Aimee* ("Sister Is My Daughter," "Concrete and Steel," "Joy, Joy, Joy," and "Sister Aimee"). Another musical about McPherson, the one-act-was-more-than-enough *Saving Aimee*, opened in April 2007 at the Signature Theater in Arlington, Virginia, after giving a series of workshop performances at the White Plains Performing Arts Center in White Plains, New York, in October 2006. The book and lyrics were by Kathie Lee Gifford and the music by Gifford, David Pomeranz, and David Friedman. Despite Carolee Carmello's galvanic efforts to give life to the character of the enigmatic McPherson, she was defeated by an awkward script, a weak score, and unimaginative staging (the script was published in a "preview edition" by First Look Press in 2007).

For another musical about a female evangelist, see entry for Jack Beeson's opera *The Sweet Bye and Bye*, which was inspired by the life of Aimee Semple McPherson. Also see entry for *Radio Gals*. McPherson was also the subject of a song ("Sister Aimee") in *Billy Barnes' L.A.*, which opened at the Coronet Theatre in Los Angeles on October 10, 1962 (recorded by BB Records [LP # 1001]); Joyce Jameson, who was famous for her Marilyn Monroe-styled impersonations, portrayed McPherson. In her program bio for *Sister Aimee*, Jenifer Lewis noted her most recent theatre credit was the workshop of Michael Bennett's new musical *Big Dreams*, in which she had created the role of Effie Melody White (see entry for her one-woman musical *The Diva Is Dismissed*). That role was played by Jennifer Holiday when the musical was produced on Broadway later in the year as *Dreamgirls*; and, for the belated 2006 film version, Jennifer Hudson performed the role of Effie.

1471 Sisters of Mercy. "A Musical Journey Into the Words of Leonard Cohen." THEATRE: Theatre de Lys; OPENING DATE: September 25, 1973; PERFORMANCES: 15; LYRICS: Leonard Cohen; MUSIC: Leonard Cohen; additional music by Zizi Mueller; DIRECTION: Gene Lesser; SCENERY: Robert U. Taylor; COSTUMES: Carrie F. Robbins; LIGHTING: Spencer Mosse; MUSICAL DIRECTION: Zizi Mueller; PRODUCERS: Martin J. Machat, by special arrangement with Lucille Lortel Productions, Inc.

CAST—Gale Garnett, Emily Bindiger, Michael Calkins, Nicolas Surovy, Pamela Paluzzi, Rosemary Radcliffe

The revue was presented in one act.

MUSICAL NUMBERS—"Winter Lady" (Nicolas Surovy, Michael Calkins), "War Song" (Company), "Bird on a Wire" (Nicolas Surovy, Michael Calkins, Gale Garnett), "Tonight Will Be Fine" (Nicolas Surovy, Pamela Paluzzi), "Hey, That's No Way to Say Goodbye" (Emily Bindiger, Rosemary Radcliffe), "One of Us Cannot Be Wrong" (Gale Garnett), "Famous Blue Raincoat" (Emily Bindiger, Michael Calkins), "The Singer Must Die" (Emily Bindiger, Nicolas Surovy, Company), "Nancy" (Pamela Paluzzi), "Diamonds in the Mine" (Pamela Paluzzi, Company), "You Know Who I Am" (Emily Bindiger, Pamela Paluzzi, Rosemary Radcliffe, Gale Garnett) "Chelsea Song" (Nicolas Surovy, Pamela Paluzzi), "Suzanne" (Michael Calkins, Company), "Works of Charity" (Pamela Bindiger), "Love Calls You by Your Name" (Gale Garnett, Pamela Paluzzi, Emily Bindiger, Rosemary Radcliffe), "Priests" (Rosemary Radcliffe, Pamela Paluzzi, Emily Bindiger), "Dress Rehearsal Rag" (Pamela Paluzzi, Gale Garnett, Michael Calkins), "Sisters of Mercy" (Michael Calkins, Nicolas Surovy), "So, Long Marianne" (Nicolas Surovy, Emily Bindiger, Company)

NOTES—*Sisters of Mercy* was a self-described journey into the songs of Leonard Cohen, a Canadian who enjoyed a minor cult following in his heyday, thanks to a couple of his popular songs, including the whining "Suzanne" (which now comes across as a parody of folk-like ballads of the era). Clive Barnes in the *New York Times* reported that from evidence in the text, Cohen seemed "to fancy himself a lot," and noted such an attitude gave others the right to "disassociate" themselves from him. Barnes went on to say the evening was a somewhat "stylized biography" of Cohen on an "ego trip," and admitted he had the "unkind" feeling that Cohen "loves himself to distraction." Further, Barnes found Cohen's words "cute" and his music "familiar." A program note indicated the revue was producer Martin J. Machat's first theatrical venture, and Barnes said he did not "for one moment" doubt that statement. In less than two weeks, Leonard and Suzanne were gone.

1472 Sit Down and Eat Before Our Love Gets Cold. THEATRE: West Side Y Arts Center; OPENING DATE: May 3, 1985; PERFORMANCES: 11; BOOK: Barbara Schottenfeld; LYRICS: Barbara Schottenfeld; MUSIC: Barbara Schottenfeld; DIRECTION: Anthony McKay; CHOREOGRAPHY: David Storey; SCENERY: Duke Durfee; COSTUMES: Christina Weppner; LIGHTING: Rachel Budin; MUSICAL DIRECTION: David Loud; PRODUCER: American Kaleidoscope, Inc. (Joan Rice Franklin, Rebecca Dobson, Nicholas Benton, and Richard Bell, Producing Artistic Directors) in association with the West Side Y Arts Center

CAST—Bev Larson (Sue), Barbara Schottenfeld (Abby), John Wesley Shipp (Josh)

The action occurs in present-day New York City.

The musical was presented in two acts (division of acts and song assignments unknown).

MUSICAL NUMBERS—"First Child by 33," "Boy to Love," "I Don't Want Anymore Good Friends," "Legalese," "How Did I Come Across," "Losing Touch," "Simple Things," "I Don't Want to Hold Back," "Sit Down and Eat Before Our Love Gets Cold," "I'm So Happy for Her," "I Want You to Be," "Why Should We Talk," "Why Do I Only," "Revisions," "When You Find Somebody"

NOTES—*The Best Plays of 1984-1985* reported that Barbara Schottenfeld's Off Off Broadway musical *Sit Down and Eat Before Our Love Gets Cold* dealt with single women living (and coping) in New York City. Also see entry for Schottenfeld's musical *I Can't Keep Running in Place*, which dealt with six women who meet weekly for assertiveness training.

Mel Gussow in the *New York Times* reported the evening had originated as a revue, but was now expanded into a book musical (in which all dialogue was sung). Gussow liked the lyrics and music, but felt the bland book needed more work. He singled out "Revisions," in which the main character noted that in both her career and life she is a compulsive "tinkerer."

1473 Six. THEATRE: Cricket Playhouse; OPENING DATE: April 12, 1971; PERFORMANCES: 8; SKETCHES: Charles Strouse; LYRICS: Charles Strouse; MUSIC: Charles Strouse; DIRECTION: Peter Coe; SCENERY: Richard Nelson; COSTUMES: Richard Nelson (?); MUSICAL DIRECTION: Wally Harper; PRODUCER: Slade Brown

CAST—Johanna Albrecht, Lee Beery, Alvin Ing, Gail Nelson, Gilbert Price, Hal Watters

The revue was presented in one act.

MUSICAL NUMBERS—OPENING: "What Is There to Sing About" (Company), "The Garden" (Gail Nelson, Gilbert Price, Alvin Ing), "Love Song" (Gail Nelson), "Six" (Company), "Coming Attractions" (Hal Watters, Company), "The Invisible Man" (Company), "The Critic" (Alvin Ing), "Trip" (Company), "What Is There to Sing About" (reprise) (Company), "The Beginning" (Company), "The Dream" (Company)

NOTES—Charles Strouse had previously contributed music to Off Broadway revues as well as complete scores for Broadway musicals (*Bye Bye Birdie* [1960], *All American* [1962], *Golden Boy* [1964], *It's a Bird, It's a Plane, It's Superman* [1966], and *Applause* [1970]). *Six* marked the first time he wrote dialogue and lyrics as well.

The revue appears to have concentrated on serious topical matters, such as politics and the environment. It may have been too preachy, and, if so, maybe that's why it wasn't able to last beyond its first week of performances. Clive Barnes in the *New York Times* said *Six* could have been subtitled *Bye, Bye, Applause*, and that for him the most interesting aspect of the evening was watching a fellow drama critic "stolidly chewing gum in the front row."

1474 Six Characters in Search of an Author. THEATRE: New York City Center; OPENING DATE: April 26, 1959; PERFORMANCES: 2; LIBRETTO: Denis Johnston; MUSIC: Hugo Weisgall; DIRECTION: William Ball; SCENERY: Gary Smith; COSTUMES: Gary Smith; LIGHTING: Gary Smith; MUSICAL DIRECTION: Sylvan Levin; PRODUCER: The New York City Opera

CAST—Ernest McChesney (Director), Grant Williams (Tenore Buffo), Craig Timberlake (Accompanist), John Macurdy (Basso Cantante), Arnold Voketaitis (Stage Manager), Beverly Sills (Coloratura), Anita Darian (Prompter), Regina Sarfaty (Mezzo), Elizabeth Mannion (Wardrobe Mistress), Chorus of Seven Deadly Sins (Mary Lesawyer, Jennie Andrea, Les Rodgers, Rita Metzger, William Saxon, George Del Monte, Peter Sliker), Anthony Balestrieri (Another Tenor), The Characters: Paul Ukena (The Father), Robert Trehey (The Son), Adelaide Bishop (The Stepdaughter), Patricia Neway (The Mother), Ruth Kobart (Madame Pace), Marc Sullivan (The Boy), Barbara Becker (The Child)

SOURCE—The 1921 play *Six Characters in Search of an Author* by Luigi Pirandello. The opera was presented in three acts.

NOTES—The New York City Opera devoted its 1958 and 1959 spring seasons to American opera, and Howard Taubman in the *New York Times* said the world premiere of *Six Characters in Search of an Author* was "the most complex and adventurous work" seen there in the two seasons. He noted that Hugo Weisgall's score was skillful, clever, "brittle, angular, deliberately commonplace," and sometimes "expressively lyrical." The opera dealt with fictional characters who exist at the mercy of their author and the question of whether or not they are more "real" than the actors who portray them. Instead of the plot revolving around the rehearsals of a play, Weisgall invented an opera-within-an-opera (*The Temptation of St. Anthony* ... by one Hugo Weisgall) which spoofed both operatic conventions as well as the composer himself.

Taubman noted that in keeping with the mood of an opera rehearsal, Sylvan Levin, who conducted *Six Characters in Search of an Author*, wore a sport shirt "instead of the formal uniform of the maestro." Taubman also noted that Beverly Sills sang with "striking agility" and was "delightful as the feather-brained coloratura soprano."

Overall, Taubman felt the opera just missed the final touch of genius but he nonetheless recommended it to those who seek "an off-beat theatrical experience."

In 1990, the opera was recorded live from a production of the Lyric Opera Center for American Artists at the Civic Theatre in Chicago; the 2-CD set was released by New World Records (# 80454-2).

1475 Skits-Oh-Frantics! "A New Musical Revue." THEATRE: Bert Wheeler Theatre; OPENING DATE: April 2, 1967; PERFORMANCES: 17; SKETCHES: Hank Ladd; other sketch writers weren't credited in the program; LYRICS: Marvin Moore, Lee Morris, Charles Naylor, Bernie Wayne, and Ken Welch; MUSIC: Charles Naylor, Bernie Wayne, and Ken Welch; DIRECTION: Hank Ladd; CHOREOGRAPHY: Frank Westbrook; additional choreography by Patti Karr; SCENERY: Carleton Synder; COSTUMES: Eve Henriksen; LIGHTING: Carleton Snyder; MUSICAL DIRECTION: Bernie Wayne; PRODUCER: Bob Hadley in association with Thomas G. Abernethy and Freeman Parks

CAST—HANK LADD, IRVING HARMON, Bobbi Baird, Bes-Arlene, Mona Crawford, Patti Karr, Barney Martin, Robert Weill, Geene Courtney-James

The revue was presented in two acts.

ACT ONE—"Skits-Oh-Frantics or How I Found Fun in Fun City" (lyrics and music by Bernie Wayne) (Company) "Fun City" (lyric and music by Charles Naylor) (Company), "Hank Ladd" (sketch by Hank Ladd) (Hank Ladd, with Irving Harmon, Barney Martin, Robert Weil) "Ba-Boom-Ching" (lyric and music by Charles Naylor) (Bobbi Baird, Mona Crawford, Patti Karr) "Clip Joint" (sketch writer not credited) (Mona Crawford, Barney Martin, Robert Weil, Irving Harmon) "Appreciation" (lyric and music by Bernie Wayne) (Bes-Arlene) "What Is It?" (sketch by Hank Ladd) (Hank Ladd, Barney Martin, Geene Courtney-James), "Calypso" (sketch by Hank Ladd) (Hank Ladd, with Geene Courtney-James) "Love Is for the Birds" (lyric and music by Bernie Wayne) (Mona Crawford) "Pierre, The Great Lover" (sketch writer not credited) (Bobbi Baird, Robert Weil, Geene Courtney-James, Irving Harmon, Barney Martin) "Listening for Sounds I've Never Heard (Looking for Things I've Never Seen)" (lyric and music by Bernie Wayne) (Bobbi Baird), "The Courtroom Scene" (sketch writer not credited) (Barney Martin, Robert Weil, Irving Harmon, Bes-Arlene, Patti Karr), "The Blonde Under the Sheet" (lyric and music by Bernie Wayne) (Company)

ACT TWO—"The Blonde in the Bathing Suit" (sketch/song [?]; writer not credited) (Geene Courtney-James, Company) "The Girl by the Gate in Old San Juan" (lyric and music by Bernie Wayne) (Robert Weil, with Patti Karr, Barney Martin), "The Message" (sketch writer not credited) (Hank Ladd), "Wild" (lyric and music by Bernie Wayne) (Mona Crawford, Hank Ladd) "The Juggler" (sketch writer not credited) (Irving Harmon, Barney Martin) "Soliloquy in One Bar" (lyric and music by Bernie Wayne) (Patti Karr), "Rumpadee, Rumpadee" (lyric and music by Bernie Wayne) (performed by 'The Rumpadeers') "School for Music" (sketch writer not credited) (Barney Martin, Patti Karr, Robert Weil, Irving Harmon, Bes-Arlene) Finale: "Fun City" (reprise) (Company)

NOTES—Reviewing *Skits-Oh-Frantics!* in the *New York Times*, Dan Sullivan noted one thing in the revue's favor was that it was "over early"; he further remarked that the most "exciting" aspect of the revue was its exclamation point. Otherwise, he felt the material was "old stuff" which offered "the shlock of recognition."

Hank Ladd had been a minor figure in the last great period of the Broadway musical revue: he was a contributor to, and co-starred in, *Angel in the Wings* (1948), and appeared in *Along Fifth Avenue* (1949). *Skits-Oh-Frantics!* was his return to the form after spending years as a television writer for Jackie Gleason.

Patti Karr was a tried-and-true Broadway and Off Broadway favorite. She never made it to the top, but was always a welcome presence in the revues and musicals in which she appeared. Barney Martin later introduced "Mister Cellophane" in the original production of *Chicago* (1975).

Despite their being credited in the program for their "supplementary" lyrics, Marvin Moore and Lee

Morris' contributions weren't specified, nor was the "special song" attributed to Ken Welch.

Bernie Wayne, who wrote most of the revue's songs, was the composer of two well-known ballads ("Blue Velvet" and "The Magic Touch") as well as the iconic "There She Is — Miss America."

The show had one of the best revue titles ever. It was brash and silly, a skewed pun which in many ways defined the typical Off Broadway revue (another great revue title of the period was *Signs Along the Cynic Route*; see entry).

1476 Sky High. "New York's Zaniest Musical Extravaganza." THEATRE: Players Theatre; OPENING DATE: June 28, 1979; PERFORMANCES: 38; BOOK: Brian O'Hara; LYRICS: Ann Harris; MUSIC: Ann Harris; Frederic Harris, Additional Music; DIRECTION: Brian O'Hara; CHOREOGRAPHY: The Harris Sisters; SCENERY: Angel Jack; COSTUMES: Angel Jack; LIGHTING: Johnny Dodd; PRODUCERS: Hibiscus Productions and E. David Rosen

CAST— Donna Lee Betz (Sadie, Mother Nature), Richard Depasquale (The Dirty Bird), Ginger Grace (Miss America, The Cute Bird), Ann Harris (Starina), Eloise Harris (Mermaid Queen, Jayne Champagne), Jayne Ann Harris (Kitty Hauk, Sheikstress, Princess Slit Dagger), Lulu Belle Harris (Nuit, Queen Cobra), Angel Jack (Devil), Sandt Litchfield (The Ringmaster), Tom Matthews (Mrs. Gottrocks, Pierrot), Brian O'Hara (Jour), Janet "Planet" Sala (Little Girl, The Pretty Kitty)

The musical was presented in two acts.

ACT ONE— Overture (Orchestra), "Rainbow" (Brian O'Hara, Chorus), "Walk Through That Golden Gate" (Ann Harris, Donna Lee Betz), "I'm Mother Nature of You All" (Donna Lee Betz, Chorus), "She'll Get the Business in the End" (Angel Jack), "Behold the Coming of the Sun" ('The Sun Rays' [performers unknown]), "I'm Betting on You" (Brian O'Hara, Lulu Belle Harris), "One Cell" ('King Neptune' [performer unknown]), "Singing" (Cells [performers unknown]), "King Neptune" ('King Neptune' [performer unknown]), "Mermaids" (Eloise Harris, Chorus), "South American Way" (Lulu Belle Harris), "Queen Cobra" ('Candy Trio' [performers unknown]), "Fly Away" (Richard Depasquale, Ginger Grace, Jayne Anne Harris) "When He Calls Half-Hour" (Donna Lee Betz, Richard Depasquale, Ginger Grace, Jayne Anne Harris), "Birdie Follies" (Richard Depasquale, Ginger Grace, Jayne Anne Harris), "Ringmaster Song" (Sandt Litchfield), "Broadway, New York" (Brian O'Hara, Chorus), "The Clown Song" (Tom Matthews), "Let's Go to the Dogs" (Eloise Harris, Poodles [performers unknown]), "Kitty Kat Song" (Janet "Planet" Sala), "Toast of the Town" (Brian O'Hara, Company)

ACT TWO—"Au Revoir" (Ginger Grace), "Sheik Song" (Sheik [performer unknown], Jayne Anne Harris), "Opium Song" (Company), "I'm Lazy" (Tom Matthews), "Do It Yourself" (Ann Harris), "Giddyup" (Company), "Miss America" (Ginger Grace), "Hot as Hades" (Angel Jack, Jayne Anne Harris, Company), "Devil Man" (Jayne Anne Harris), "Champagne Song" (Brian O'Hara, Lulu Belle Harris), "Rainbow" (reprise) (Company), "Toast of the Town" (reprise) (Company), "Walk Through the Golden Gate" (finale) (Company)

NOTES— This short-lived book-musical-cum-revue *Sky High* was a spoof of various forms of flashy entertainment styles. But John Corry in the *New York Times* felt the evening wasn't "about" anything but itself, and "itself ... is not very interesting." He reported that the plot had "something to do" with Mother Nature (who wears a green fright wig) and Little Girl (a Betty Boop type) searching for the Golden Light, although he wasn't certain why they were doing so. (At any rate, they eventually meet the devil, who lives on Cobra Island and wears heels ["androgyny runs wild," noted Corry]). And all this was offered up in the style of Busby Berkeley, the *Ziegfeld Follies*, and old Judy Garland and Mickey Rooney movies. Corry felt the creators of the show didn't "really like" the genres it was spoofing but instead seemed to "envy" them in parodies which sometimes held "malice."

1477 Skye. "A Musical Fairy Tale." THEATRE: Library & Museum of the Performing Arts at Lincoln Center; OPENING DATE: February 1, 1971; PERFORMANCES: 3; BOOK: Avery Corman and Dan Rustin; LYRICS: Avery Corman and Dan Rustin; MUSIC: Ben Finn; DIRECTION: James Curtan; SCENERY: Donald Padgett; LIGHTING: Allison Anthorne; MUSICAL DIRECTION: Wendell Kindberg; PRODUCER: Equity Library Theatre

CAST—Jay Kirsch (Prince Mosgood), Andrew Amic-Angelo (Donald MacCutcheon), James Brochu (MacDuff), Larry Whiteley (King Peingowan), Betty Lynn (Queen Talbot), Sue Long (Princess Angeline), Larry Clinton (Uncle Bayswater)

The musical was presented in two acts (division of acts and song assignments unknown).

MUSICAL NUMBERS—"The Isle of Skye," "And More," "The Story That History Won't Tell," "Ring, Ring the Bell," "Raise Up the Flagon," "The Faerie Piper," "I'll Never Move a Mountain," "Cross Your Finger," "Showmanship," "Bridal Bouquet," "Underneath a Dragon Moon," "Someone Else Will Know," "The Wedding," "Only One Shadow," Finale

NOTES— The Off Off Broadway fairy-tale musical *Skye* was presented at Lincoln Center by the Equity Library Theatre for a limited engagement of three performances.

Mel Gussow in the *New York Times* indicated the generally agreeable musical would entertain both children and adults. The plot, which dealt with a prince who must slay a dragon before winning a princess and a kingdom, was often whimsical, and Ben Finn's score was "tuneful" (but he noted that for children the evening perhaps offered a few too many love songs). Gussow said the evening's most felicitous conceit was the "show business" dragon, a "hopelessly stagestruck" ham who is a "'singing-dancing fool' of a dragon" (portrayed by the "drily funny" James Brochu).

1478 Sleeparound Town (Songs of Puberty). THEATRE: Playwrights Horizons; OPENING DATE: March 1982; PERFORMANCES: Unknown; SPOKEN MATERIAL: Peter Parnell; LYRICS: Sarah Kernochan; MUSIC: Sarah Kernochan; DIRECTION: Thomas Hulce; CHOREOGRAPHY: Marta Renzi; SCENERY: Douglas Stein; COSTUMES: Rita Ryack; LIGHTING: Ann Wrightson; MUSICAL DIRECTION: Richard Weinstock; PRODUCER: Playwrights Horizons (Andre Bishop, Artistic Director; Paul S. Daniels, Managing Director)

CAST—Jenelle Berrien (Natalie Nan), Christine Langer (Bonny Boudreau), William Morrison (John Luke), Carl Tramon (Wayne), Jason Underwood (Henry)

The revue was presented in one act.

MUSICAL NUMBERS—"Sleeparound Town" (Company), "My Name" (Company), "The Baby Medley" (Company), "Gone to the Movies" (Jason Underwood), "The Phobia Song" (Jenelle Berrien, Company), "The Volcano" (Carl Tramon), "O! Mysterious Hole" (William Morrison), "Bonny Boudreau" (Jason Underwood), "Search Party" (William Morrison, Christine Langer), "Mr. Sloane" (Christine Langer), "Ward Off Puberty Chant" (Company), "Night Lites" (Company), "My Precious Mystery" (Jenelle Berrien), "Boys' Bunk" (William Morrison, Jason Underwood, Carl Tramon), "Panties" (Christine Langer, Jenelle Berrien), "Experience" (Carl Tramon), "John Luke Puts the Bite on Henry" (William Morrison, Jason Underwood), "Wonderful Dog" (Jason Underwood), "Nightwalk" (William Morrison, Christine Langer, Jason Underwood), "Refugees" (Company), "The Creature from the Last Offramp" (Company), "Sleeparound Town" (reprise) (Company)

NOTES— The revue-like song cycle *Sleeparound Town (Songs of Puberty)* appears to have never officially opened. And with that title, could it have attracted audiences? The evening seems to have been inspired by the Elizabeth Swados School of Musicals.

1479 Slut. THEATRE: Chernuchin Theatre; OPENING DATE: October 1, 2005; PERFORMANCES: 51; BOOK: Ben H. Winters; LYRICS: Ben H. Winters; additional lyrics by Stephan Sislan; MUSIC: Stephan Sislan; DIRECTION: Gordon Greenberg; Ryan J. Davis, Assistant Director; CHOREOGRAPHY: Warren Carlyle; SCENERY: Beowulf Boritt; COSTUMES: Anne Kennedy; LIGHTING: Jane Cox; MUSICAL DIRECTION: Eric Svejcar; PRODUCERS: A Dena Hammerstein and Pam Pariseau production for James Hammerstein Productions

CAST— Andy Karl (Adam), Mary Faber (Yesterday's News, Veronica), Kevin Pariseau (Doug, Sea Captain, Janey's Father), Harriett D. Foy (Lilly, Janey's Mother), Amanda Watkins (Janey), David Josefsberg (J-Dogg, Buddy Pendleton), Jim Stanek (Dan), Jenn Colella (Delia)

The musical was presented in two acts (divison of acts and song assignments unknown).

MUSICAL NUMBERS—"I'm Probably Not Gonna Call," "Fuel for the Fire," "Tiny Little Pieces," "Slutterday Night," "The Bravest Little Boat," "A Girl That You Meet in a Bar," "Tiny Little Pieces" (reprise), "Lower the Bar," "True Love," "The Slut of the World," "J-Dogg's Lament," "Janey's Song," "I Wouldn't Change a Thing," "One Adam at a Time," "A Girl That You Meet in a Bar" (reprise), "Slutterday Night" (reprise)

NOTES—*Slut* told the story of Adam and Delia, both dedicated to one-night-stand sex in the East Village; problems arise when Adam's doctor friend Dan falls hard for Delia. David Rooney in *Variety* said the musical "skips defiantly along on a cloud of testosterone and sophomoric humor," but lost its way in subplots dealing with Adam's wish to sail around the world in order to seduce a girl in every port and Dan's desire to cure illnesses of Third World children. But Rooney praised many "fun songs" in the score, including Harriet D. Foy's vampy "Lower the Bar," which extolled the virtues of diminished expectations.

The musical had first been seen at the 2004 New York International Fringe Festival on August 18, 2003.

1480 Smile, Smile, Smile. "A Musical Entertainment." THEATRE: Eastside Playhouse; OPENING DATE: April 4, 1973; PERFORMANCES: 7; BOOK, LYRICS, AND MUSIC: Hugo Peretti, Luigi Creatore, and George David Weiss; DIRECTION: Robert Simpson; CHOREOGRAPHY: Robert Simpson (?); SCENERY: Philip Gilliam; COSTUMES: Patricia McGourty; LIGHTING: Barry Arnold; MUSICAL DIRECTION: Bob Tarraglia (?); PRODUCER: Stuart Duncan

CAST— Bobby Lee (Arlie), Rudy Tronto (Cockalorum), Carole Joan Macho (Bibette), Diane J. Findlay (Franny), William Pierson (Professor), Chip Zien (Letch), Casey Craig (Simple), Marilyn Saunders (Gina), Joseph Neal (Giorgio), Suellen Estey (Leonora), Gary Beach (Lorenzo), Virginia Pulos (Belinda), J. Richard Beneville (Roland), Geoff Leon (Olaf), Donna Liggitt Forbes (Corrina)

SOURCE— Based on the commedia dell'arte sketch *The Great Magician* by Lawrence Carra.

The action occurs on the island of Paradise.

The musical was presented in two acts.

ACT ONE—"Haven't I Seen You Somewhere Before?" (Bobby Lee), "Paradise" (Company), "To Find True Love" (Marilyn Saunders, Joseph Neal, Suellen Esty, Gary Beach), "I'm the Cockalorum" (Rudy Tronto, Company), "A Good Old-Fashioned Revolutionary" (Diane J. Findlay, Company), "Open Your Heart" (performers unknown), "Adios" (Marilyn Saunders, Joseph Neal, Suellen Esty, Gary Beach), "Friends" (William Pierson, Casey Craig, Chip Zien), "God Bless the Fig Tree" (Diane J. Findlay), "Garland of Roses" (Bobby Lee, Rudy Tronto), "Garland of Roses" (reprise) (Suellen Esty, Gary Beach), "Buttercup" (Bobby Lee, Diane J. Findlay, Rudy Tronto, Carole Joan Macho, Company), "Smile, Smile, Smile" (Bobby Lee, Company)

ACT TWO—"Smile, Smile, Smile" (reprise) (Diane J. Findlay, Company), "It's All for the Good of the People" (Diane J. Findlay, Rudy Tronto, Company), "Magnetic" (Chip Zien), "Love Is a Fragile Thing" (Marilyn Saunders, Joseph Neal, Suellen Esty, Gary Beach), "Love Is a Pain" (Carole Joan Macho, Company), "Breakin' the Spell" (Carole Joan Macho, Diane J. Findlay, Bobby Lee, Rudy Tronto, Company), "Paradise" (reprise) (Company), "Smile, Smile, Smile" (reprise) (Company)

NOTES—*Smile, Smile, Smile* was a revised Off Broadway version of the musical *Comedy*, which had been scheduled to open at the Martin Beck (now Al Hirschfeld) Theatre on November 28, 1972, but instead closed during its pre-Broadway tryout in Boston. *Smile, Smile, Smile* was first seen in a Summer 1973 tryout at the Bucks County Playhouse in New Hope, Pennsylvania, and when it opened in New York, it lasted only seven performances. In response to the musical's title, the entirety of one review read "I didn't, I didn't, I didn't."

The musical dealt with shipwrecked survivors who come upon a strange island under the power of a magician who casts spells.

Both *Comedy* and *Smile, Smile, Smile* were to have their cast albums recorded by Bell Records, but because of the failures of both productions the recordings were cancelled.

Numbers retained from *Comedy* were: "Open Your Heart," "I'm the Cockalorum," "God Bless the Fig Tree," "Buttercup," "Smile, Smile, Smile," "Magnetic," "Love Is Such a Fragile Thing," and "Breakin' the Spell." Numbers in *Comedy* which weren't in the revival were: "Comedy," "Gotta Hang My Wash Out to Dry," "Dance Caper," "Where Is My Love," "Tarantella," and "Whirlwind Circle." *Comedy*'s song "A Friend Is a Friend" may have been rewritten as "Friends" for *Smile, Smile, Smile*.

Songs deleted from the Bucks County production were: "Sha Na Na Nay" and "Gotta Hang My Wash Out to Dry" (the latter had also been heard in *Comedy*).

Four of the cast members in *Smile, Smile, Smile* had earlier appeared in *Comedy*: Diane J. Findlay, Bobby Lee, Suellen Esty, and Marilyn Saunders.

Smile, Smile, Smile appears to be the first New York production in which Gary Beach created a role (he had earlier been a replacement in the Broadway production of *1776* [1969]).

Hugo Peretti, Luigi Creatore, and George David Weiss had previously written the pleasant score for the short-running Broadway musical *Maggie Flynn* (1968). George David Weiss co-wrote the score for the highly melodic, unappreciated Broadway failure *First Impressions* (1959), a musical version of *Pride and Prejudice*. Weiss had also written a number of pop hits in the 1950s, including "Cross Over the Bridge," "Wheel of Fortune," "What a Wonderful World," "Lullaby of Birdland," and "Too Close for Comfort" (the latter from *Mr. Wonderful*, a 1956 Broadway musical which he co-wrote).

1481 Smiling the Boy Fell Dead. "A New Musical." THEATRE: Cherry Lane Theatre; OPENING DATE: April 19, 1961; PERFORMANCES: 22; BOOK: Ira Wallach; LYRICS: Sheldon Harnick; MUSIC: David Baker; DIRECTION: "Supervised" by Theodore Mann (who replaced Word Baker, the musical's original director); SCENERY: Herbert Senn and Helen Pond; COSTUMES: Theoni V. Aldredge; LIGHTING: David Hays; MUSICAL DIRECTION: Julian Stein; PRODUCERS: Theodore Mann and George Kogel

CAST—Charles Goff (Dean Rigby, Boy), DANNY MEEHAN (Waldo Templeton), JOSEPH MACCAULAY (Lawyer Manson), Joseph Schaeffer (Boy, Cop), Heinz Neumann (Boy, Mr. Smith), LOUISE LARABEE (Eva Templeton), RUSSELL BAILEY (Squire Gatsby), JUSTINE JOHNSON (Amanda Gatsby), PHIL LEEDS (Simeon Moodis), CLAIBORNE CARY (Dorothea Gatsby), WARREN WADE (Tobias Tyler), Ted Beniades (The Bandit), Lucinda Abbey (Mrs. Moodis), Dodo Denney (Amy Graben, Miss Edna Littlewood), Gino Conforti (Moving Man), Geriane Richards (Miss Peterson); Charles Goff, Lucinda Abbey (The Martins), Joseph Schaeffer, Geriane Richards (The Johnsons), Heinz Neumann, Dodo Denney, Gino Conforti, Irene Siegfried (The Kiplingers)

The musical was presented in two acts.

ACT ONE—"Sons of Greentree" (Company), "Let's Evolve" (Danny Meehan, Charles Goff, Joseph Schaeffer, Heinz Neumann), "The ABC's of Success" (Danny Meehan, Joseph MacCauley), "If I Felt Any Younger Today" (Joseph MacCauley, Louise Larabee, Charles Goff, Lucinda Abbey, Joseph Schaeffer, Geriane Richards, Heinz Neumann, Dodo Denney, Gino Conforti, Irene Siegfried), "More Than Ever Now" (Claiborne Cary), "I've Got a Wonderful Future" (Danny Meehan), "Small Town" (Charles Goff, Lucinda Abbey, Joseph Schaeffer, Geriane Richards, Heinz Neumann, Dodo Denney, Gino Conforti, Irene Siegfried, Joseph MacCauley, Louise Larabee, Justine Johnson), "Heredity-Environment" (Phil Leeds), "The Gatsby Bridge March" (Company), "A World to Win" (Claiborne Cary, Danny Meehan), "The Wonderful Machine" (Danny Meehan, Company)

ACT TWO—"Temperance Polka" (Warren Wade, Chicago People), "Daydreams" (Danny Meehan), "Dear Old Dad" (Louise Larabee, Danny Meehan), "Me and Dorothea" (Warren Wade), "Two by Two" (Claiborne Cary, Danny Meehan), "More Than Ever Now" (reprise) (Claiborne Cary), "The ABC's of Success" (reprise) (Company)

NOTES—Sheldon Harnick was between two Broadway musicals (*Tenderloin* [1960] and *She Loves Me* [1963]) when *Smiling the Boy Fell Dead* was produced Off Broadway. According to the cast album's liner notes when it was reissued by Sunbeam Records (LP # LB-549/550; the album had been previously released in a limited pressing), Harnick and David Baker had been toying with the idea of writing a musical based on Horatio Alger stories since 1952. The musical eventually evolved into a rags-to-riches story concerning Waldo Templeton (earlier titles for the musical had been *Horatio*; *Waldo*; and *Fair-Haired Boy*), and it received its world premiere in March 1954 in Margo Jones' Theatre in Dallas, Texas, as *Horatio* (Charles Braswell created the title role). Songs in the production which weren't used in the New York version were: "Since My Life Began," "Best Loved Girls in Town," "Class of '88," "That's No Way to Live," and "When I Make Up My Mind."

Thanks to the recording, we have a chance to hear Sheldon Harnick's clever lyrics and David Martin's catchy music. Martin was a talented composer who was unlucky in his theatre ventures. *Phoenix '55* (1955; see entry), *Copper and Brass* (1957), and *Come Summer* (1969) were flops, and all went unrecorded. A studio cast album of the latter was rumored to be in the making for years, and reportedly the musical tracks had been recorded; but apparently the project has been abandoned. The score is melodic, with many memorable songs, including "Feather in My Shoe," "Come Summer," "Fine, Thank You, Fine," and "Good Time Charlie."

According to the *New York Times*, prior to the New York opening of *Smiling the Boy Fell Dead* there was the possibility Simon & Schuster was going to file a lawsuit against the musical's producers for their use of the title. The article stated that in May 1960 the firm had signed a contract with S.J. Perelman for his book of memoirs, to be titled *Smiling, the Boy Fell Dead*. But the producers of the musical held their ground, insisting they wouldn't change the title; they also noted the musical (and its title) had been in preparation for many years. Further, the line "Smiling, the Boy Fell Dead" is the final line from the poem "An Incident of the French Camp" by Robert Browning (1812-1889). Since the poem was in the public domain, and since *Smiling the Boy Fell Dead* opened as scheduled on April 19, 1961, it appears the publishing firm decided not to pursue the matter. As for Perelman, he seems to have abandoned the idea of using the title *Smiling, the Boy Fell Dead* for his memoirs (and for other writings as well).

1482 Smiling Through. THEATRE: Theatre 4; OPENING DATE: February 2, 1994; PERFORMANCES: 14; BOOK: Ivan Menchell; LYRICS: See song list for credits; MUSIC: See song list for credits; DIRECTION: Patricia Birch; Jonathan Stewart Cerullo, Associate Director; CHOREOGRAPHY: Patricia Birch; Jonathan Stewart Cerullo, Associate Choreographer; SCENERY: James Morgan; COSTUMES: Frank Krenz; LIGHTING: Craig Miller; MUSICAL DIRECTION: Tom Fay; PRODUCER: Lois Teich

CAST—Vicki Stuart (Mavis Daily), Jeff Woodman (Arthur, Frank, Norma, Penelope, Announcers)

The action occurs in London and throughout Britain during the years of World War II.

The revue was presented in two acts (song assignments unknown).

ACT ONE—"Don't Dilly Dally on the Way" (lyric and music by Charles Collins, Fred W. Leigh, and Dick Manning), "Nobody Loves a Fairy" (lyric and music by Arthur Le Clerq), "Underneath the Arches" (lyric and music by Reginald Connelly, Bud Flanagan and Joseph McCarthy), "All Our Tomorrows" (lyric and music by Jimmy Kennedy), "Wish Me Luck" (lyric by Phil Park, music by Harry Parr-Davies), "No One Believes..." (lyric and music by Desmond Carter and Noel Gray)

ACT TWO—"The Deepest Shelter in Town" (lyric and music by Leslie Julian Jones), "Dancing with My Shadow" (lyric and music by Harry Woods), "I'm Gonna Get Lit Up" (lyric and music by Hubert Gregg), "We'll Meet Again" (lyric and music by Ross Parker and Hughie Charles), "The White Cliffs of Dover" (lyric by Nat Burton, music by Walter Kent), "A Nightingale Sang in Berkeley Square" (lyric by Holt Marvell [Eric Maschwitz], music by Manning Sherwin)

NOTES—Originally produced by the Pennsylvania Stage Company and the Emelin Theatre in Mamaroneck, New York, the revue-like musical *Smiling Through* starred Vicki Stuart, who played an English music hall singer who cheers up her British audiences during the darkest days of World War II. In 1995, Stuart returned in a similar revue (see entry for *We'll Meet Again*). Between her two revues, Off Broadway saw *Swingtime Canteen*, another "British home front" revue set during World War II (see entry). And in 2007, yet another World War II "home front" revue, was seen Off Off Broadway (see entry for *When the Lights Go On Again*).

1483 Smith. "A New Musical Comedy." THEATRE: Eden Theatre; OPENING DATE: May 19, 1973; PERFORMANCES: 18; BOOK: Dean Fuller, Tony Hendra, and Matt Dubey; LYRICS AND MUSIC: Matt Dubey and Dean Fuller; DIRECTION: Neal Kenyon; CHOREOGRAPHY: Michael Shawn; Bonnie Walker, Assistant Choreographer; SCENERY: Fred Voelpel;

COSTUMES: Winn Morton; LIGHTING: Martin Aronstein; MUSICAL DIRECTION: Richard Parrinello; PRODUCERS: Jordan Hott, with Robert Anglund, Jack Millstein, Iris Kopelan, and Alexander Bedrosian

CAST—Virginia Sandifur (Melody Hazleton), DON MURRAY (Walker Smith), Mort Marshall (Ed Baggett), Carol Morley (Mrs. Smith, Irish Maid), David Horwitz (Pilot, Prompter, Vice President of Slimeroonie), Louis Criscuolo (Ralph), Renee Baughman (Island Beauty), Patricia Garland (Island Beauty, Sydney Jones), Penelope Richards (Island Beauty), Bonnie Walker (Island Beauty, The Dancing Melody), Michael Tartel (Jacques the Frenchman), William James (Policeman, Ernie), David Vosburgh (Policeman, Bruce), Guy Spaull (Chief Punitana), Don Prieur (Servant, Herbie), Ted Thurston (Sinclair Firestone), Hangers-On (Nicholas Dante, Aurelio Padron, Kenneth Henley), Singing Ensemble (Bonnie Hinson, Jacqueline Johnson, Betsy Ann Leadbetter, Shirley Lemmon, David Horwitz, William James, Don Prieur, David Vosburgh), Dancing Ensemble (Renee Baughman, Patricia Garland, Penelope Richards, Bonnie Walker, John Cashman, Nicholas Dante, Kenneth Henley, Aurelio Padron)

The action occurs at Baggett Nitrates in Tenafly, New Jersey, in the present.

The musical was presented in two acts.

ACT ONE—"Boy Meets Girl" (Ensemble), "There's a Big Job Waiting for You" (Mort Marshall, Ensemble), "There's a Big Job Waiting for You" (reprise) (Carol Morley), "To the Ends of the Earth" (Virginia Sandifur, Passengers), "Balinasia" (Renee Baughman, Patricia Garland, Penelope Richards, Bonnie Walker), "Onh-Honh-Honh!" (Michael Tartel), "Police Song" (William James, David Vosbugh), "You Need a Song" (Louis Criscuolo, Don Murray, Don Prieur, William James, David Vosburgh), "How Beautiful It Was" (Virginia Sandifur, Don Murray, Bonnie Walker), "Island Ritual" (Ensemble), "People Don't Do That" (Don Murray)

ACT TWO—"You're in New York Now" (Ensemble), "It Must Be Love" (Don Murray, Virginia Sandifur, Ensemble), "Song of the Frog" (Ted Thurston, Don Murray, Mort Marshall), "G'bye" (Virginia Sandifur), "Melody" (Don Murray, Company), "It Must Be Love" (reprise) (Don Murray, Virginia Sandifur)

NOTES—*Smith* was some thirty years ahead of its time. In 1973, the "ironic" musical barely existed. A few years earlier, Charles Grodin's *Hooray ... It's a Glorious Day and All That* (1966; see entry) didn't connect with most audiences and critics, who just didn't "get" a musical which spoofed musicals. And, unfortunately, most critics and audiences didn't "get" *Smith*, either, although Richard Watts in the *New York Post* hailed it as "one of the delights of the season" and Kevin Sanders on WABC-TV/7 found it "a bright, funny, ingenious musical." As for the score, Douglas Watt in the *New York Daily News* praised it as "catchy ... cocky, rhythmic and enlivening," in the style of Frank Loesser.

Smith told the story of Walter Smith, a staid, nerdy New Jersey botanist who discovers his life has been transformed into a musical comedy and that he is the unwilling leading man. As he explains (in a song he doesn't want to sing), it isn't normal to walk around in a "perfectly sickening baby pink spot," always looking for an exact rhyme in a world where everything is orchestrated to fast-paced timing. Further, when Smith has to make a business trip, he complains that the boarding apparatus to the plane "doesn't go anywhere" because it's just part of the stage set. (And, by the way, why is that stagehand always following him around?)

Variety reported the musical had originally been capitalized at $600,000 for a Broadway production; when that sum couldn't be raised, the musical was re-budgeted at $375,000 for Off Broadway (but the performers were paid under a full Broadway contract).

The vastly entertaining script, which was published by Samuel French, Inc., in 1973, makes a good case for *Smith* being the one of the most overlooked musicals of the 1970s, one which deserves a second chance today.

1484 Smoke on the Mountain. "A New Gospel Comedy Musical." THEATRE: Lamb's Theatre; OPENING DATE: August 14, 1990; PERFORMANCES: 368; BOOK: Connie Ray; LYRICS: See song list for credits; MUSIC: See song list for credits; DIRECTION: Alan Bailey; SCENERY: Peter Harrison; COSTUMES: Pamela Scofield; LIGHTING: Don Ehrman; MUSICAL DIRECTION: John Foley and Mike Craver; PRODUCER: The Lamb's Theatre Company (Carolyn Rossi Copeland, Producing Director)

CAST—Reathel Bean (Burl Sanders), Kevin Chamberlin (Mervin Oglethorpe), Linda Kerns (Vera Sanders), Dan Manning (Stanley Sanders), Robert Olsen (Dennis Sanders), Jane Potter (Denise Sanders), Connie Ray (June Sanders)

The action occurs in the sanctuary of the Mount Pleasant Baptist Church in Mount Pleasant, North Carolina, on a Saturday night in June 1938.

The musical was presented in two acts.

ACT ONE—"Rock of Ages" (lyric and music by Augustus Toplady and Thomas Hastings) (instrumental), "The Church in the Wildwood" (lyric and music by William S. Pitts) (Reathel Bean, Linda Kerns, Dan Manning, Robert Olsen, Jane Potter, Connie Ray), "Wonderful Time Up There" (lyric and music by Roy Lee Abernathy) (Reathel Bean, Linda Kerns, Dan Manning, Robert Olsen, Jane Potter, Connie Ray), "Build on the Rock" (lyricist and composer unknown) (Reathel Bean, Linda Kerns, Dan Manning, Robert Olsen, Jane Potter Connie Ray), "Meet Mother in the Skies" (lyricist and composer unknown) (Dan Manning, Reathel Bean) "No Tears in Heaven" (lyric and music by Robert S. Arnold) (Reathel Bean, Linda Kerns, Dan Manning, Robert Olsen, Jane Potter, Connie Ray), "Christian Cowboy" (lyric and music by Cindy Walker) (Robert Olsen, Jane Potter), "The Filling Station" (lyric and music by April Ann Nye) (Reathel Bean, Linda Kerns, Dan Manning, Robert Olsen, Jane Potter, Connie Ray), "I'll Never Die (I'll Just Change My Address)" (lyric and music by J. Preston Martinez) (Jane Potter), "Jesus Is Mine" (lyric and music by Wally Fowler and Virginia Cook) (Kevin Chamberlin, Reathel Bean, Dan Manning, Robert Olsen), Blood Medley: "Nothing But the Blood of Jesus" (lyric and music by Robert Lowry) (Reathel Bean, Linda Kerns, Dan Manning, Robert Olsen, Jane Potter, Connie Ray), "There Is Power in the Blood" (lyric and music by Lewis Jones) (Reathel Bean, Linda Kerns, Dan Manning, Robert Olsen, Jane Potter, Connie Ray), "Are You Washed in the Blood" (lyric and music by Elishe A. Hoffman) (Reathel Bean, Linda Kerns, Dan Manning, Robert Olsen, Jane Potter, Connie Ray), "There Is a Fountain Filled with Blood" (lyric and music by William Cooper) (Linda Kerns), "I'll Live a Million Years" (lyric and music by Lee Roy Abernathy) (Reathel Bean, Linda Kerns, Dan Manning, Robert Olsen, Jane Potter, Connie Ray)

ACT TWO—"I Wouldn't Take Nothing for My Journey Now" (lyric and music by Chares Goodman and Jimmie Davis) (Linda Kerns, Reathel Bean), "Everyone Home but Me" (lyricist and composer unknown) (Dan Manning), "I Wouldn't Take Nothing for My Journey Now" (reprise) (Reathel Bean, Linda Kerns, Dan Manning, Robert Olsen, Jane Potter, Connie Ray), "Angel Band" (lyric and music by J. Hascall and William B. Bradbury) (Reathel Bean, Linda Kerns, Dan Manning, Robert Olsen, Jane Potter, Connie Ray, Kevin Chamberlin), "Bringing in the Sheaves" (lyricist and composer unknown) (Kevin Chamberlin, Reathel Bean, Linda Kerns, Dan Manning, Robert Olsen, Jane Potter, Connie Ray), "Whispering Hope" (lyric and music by Alice Hawthorne) (Reathel Bean, Linda Kerns, Dan Manning, Robert Olsen, Jane Potter, Connie Ray), "Inching Along" (lyricist and composer unknown) (Reathel Bean, Linda Kerns, Dan Manning, Robert Olsen, Jane Potter, Connie Ray); Transportation Medley: "I'm Using My Bible for a Roadmap" (lyric and music by Don Reno and Charles Schroeder) (Reathel Bean, Linda Kerns, Dan Manning, Robert Olsen, Jane Potter, Connie Ray), "I'll Walk Every Step of the Way" (lyric and music by Mike Craver and Mark Hardwick) (Reathel Bean, Linda Kerns, Dan Manning, Robert Olsen, Jane Potter, Connie Ray), "I'm Taking a Flight" (lyric and music by Kathryn Boyinton) (Linda Kerns, Jane Potter, Robert Olsen), "Life's Railway to Heaven" (lyric and music by Charles D. Tillman) (Reathel Bean, Linda Kerns, Dan Manning, Robert Olsen, Jane Potter, Connie Ray), "Smoke on the Mountain" (lyric and music by Alan Bailey) (Reathel Bean, Linda Kerns, Dan Manning, Robert Olsen, Jane Potter, Connie Ray), "I'll Fly Away" (lyric and music by Albert E. Brumley) (Reathel Bean, Linda Kerns, Dan Manning, Robert Olsen, Jane Potter, Connie Ray), "When the Roll Is Called Up Yonder" (lyricist and composer unknown) (Reathel Bean, Linda Kerns, Dan Manning, Robert Olsen, Jane Potter, Connie Ray)

NOTES—*Smoke on the Mountain* takes place in a church in North Carolina during the Depression; for the Saturday night service, the Sanders Family is making its first appearance on the gospel-singing circuit in five years. The musical was "presentational," with the cast of seven performing the roles of the pastor and the six members of the Sanders family, and the theatre audience the congregation. A program note in the script published by Samuel French, Inc., in 1991 noted the characters "are not Southern caricatures or religious buffoons; they are real people."

A studio cast recording was released by Daywind Records (CD # DAY-1152-D).

Conceived by Alan Bailey, the musical was first performed by the McCarter Theatre Company in Princeton, New Jersey, in July 1988 and then later in October 1989. The Lamb's Theatre production first opened on May 12, 1990, under an Off Off Broadway contract and played for eighty-four performances. On August 14, 1990, the musical began performances under a regular Off Broadway contract and played almost a full year, for 368 performances. The work was revived there on June 18, 1998, for seventy-nine more performances.

1485 Snapshot. "A New Musical." THEATRE: Hudson Guild Theatre; OPENING DATE: January 9, 1980; PERFORMANCES: 30; LYRICS: Mitchell Bernard; MUSIC: Herbert Kaplan; DIRECTION: Thomas Gruenewald; SCENERY: James Leonard Joy; COSTUMES: Kenneth M. Yount; LIGHTING: Pat Collins; MUSICAL DIRECTION: Bruce Coyle; PRODUCER: Hudson Guild Theatre (David Kerry Heefner, Producing Director; Judson Barteaux, Managing Director)

CAST—John Cunningham (Russell), Patti Karr (Janet), Helon Blount (Frances), Kathy Morath (Denise), Robert Polenz (Philip), Elissa Wolfe (Kathie)

The musical was presented in two acts.

ACT ONE—"Snapshot" (John Cunningham), "Someday" (Robert Polenz), "Siblings" (Robert Polenz, Kathy Morath), "Normal" (Kathy Morath), "Forty-Three" (Patti Karr), "Watching the News" (John Cunningham), "Cemetery Plot" (Helon Blount, John Cunningham), "What If" (Patti Karr, John Cunningham), "Creation" (Patti Karr, John Cunningham), "Ballad of Sheldon Roth" (Elissa

Wolfe), "Point of View" (Patti Karr, Helon Blount), "Trio" (Elissa Wolfe, Patti Karr, Helon Blount), "Trio II" (Robert Polenz, John Cunningham, Kathy Morath), "My Son" (John Cunningham), "If You Run Into Bruno" (Robert Polenz), "Breakfast" (Company), "Queen of Hollywood" (Patti Karr), "Tell Me I'm Good" (Elissa Wolfe), "Another Love Song" (John Cunningham, Patti Karr)

ACT TWO—"Divorce" (Elissa Wolfe, Kathy Morath, Robert Polenz), "Temporary Thing" (Kathy Morath), "Post Card" (Robert Polenz), "Coffee" (Patti Karr, Helon Blount), "Russell's Song" (John Cunningham), "Little Girl" (Helon Blount), "Ordering the Pizza" (John Cunningham, Robert Polenz, Kathy Morath, Patti Karr, Elissa Wolfe), "Voices" (John Cunningham, Patti Karr), "Dear Death" (Elissa Wolfe), "Soon" (John Cunningham), "What Marriage Is" (Kathy Morath, Elissa Wolfe), "Something in a Birth" (Patti Karr, Robert Polenz), "Snapshots II" (Patti Karr, John Cunningham)

NOTES—The program described the sung-through musical *Snapshot* as one in which characters and plot were developed through a series of short songs (or "snapshots"), without necessarily adhering to a strict chronological format. Each "snapshot" dealt with a particular emotional moment or event (some major, some mundane) in the lives of six members of one family.

Thomas Lask in the *New York Times* noted that Mitchell Bernard's lyrics were "crisp, clear" and "verbally adroit," and Herbert Kaplan's music, "which isn't afraid to suggest classical music," varied between "simple" ballads and "weighty and dramatic" interludes. But Lask felt the overall story was too familiar, and via innumerable movies and plays he had already visited this family before.

1486 Snoopy. "The New Musical." THEATRE: Lamb's Theatre; OPENING DATE: December 20, 1982; PERFORMANCES: 152; BOOK: Charles M. Schulz Creative Associates, Warren Lockhart, Arthur Whitelaw, and Michael L. Grace; LYRICS: Hal Hackady; MUSIC: Larry Grossman; DIRECTION: Arthur Whitelaw; CHOREOGRAPHY: Marc Breaux; SCENERY: David Graden; COSTUMES: David Graden; LIGHTING: Ken Billington; MUSICAL DIRECTION: Ronald Melrose; PRODUCERS: Gene Persson in association with Paula D. Hughes, Martin Markinson, and Donald Tick, and United Media Productions (Robert Roy Metz, President); Miranda Smith, Associate Producer

CAST—Terry Kirwin (Charlie Brown), Stephen Fenning (Linus), Deborah Graham (Sally Brown), Kay Cole (Lucy), Vicki Lewis (Peppermint Patty), David Garrison (Snoopy), Cathy Cahn (Woodstock)

SOURCE—The newspaper comic strip *Peanuts* by Charles M. Shultz.

The musical was presented in two acts.

ACT ONE—Overture (Orchestra), "The World According to Snoopy" (Ensemble), "Snoopy's Song" (David Garrison, Ensemble), "Woodstock's Theme" (Orchestra), "Edgar Allan Poe" (Vicki Lewis, Kay Cole, Vicki Lewis, Deborah Graham, Stephen Fenning, Terry Kirwin), "Mother's Day" (David Garrison), "I Know Now" (Kay Cole, Deborah Graham, Vicki Lewis), "Vigil" (Stephen Fenning), "Clouds" (Ensemble), "Where Did That Little Dog Go?" (Terry Kirwin), "Dime a Dozen" (Kay Cole, Vicki Lewis, Deborah Graham, David Garrison), Daisy Hill (David Garrison)

ACT TWO—Entr'acte (Orchestra), "Bunnies" (David Garrison), "The Great Writer" (David Garrison), "Poor Sweet Baby" (Vicki Lewis), "Don't Be Anything Less Than Everything You Can Be" (Terry Kirwin, Stephen Fenning, Deborah Graham, Vicki Lewis), "The Big Bow-Wow" (David Garrison), "Just One Person" (Ensemble), Bows (Ensemble)

NOTES—While not a sequel to *You're a Good Man, Charlie Brown* (1967; see entry), *Snoopy* was clearly intended as a musical follow-up to the earlier success. But *Snoopy* never quite caught on, and despite two cast albums and a number of regional and British productions, the musical never attained the popularity of the first *Peanuts* adaptation.

Mel Gussow in the *New York Times* said David Garrison soared, but otherwise was "dogged" by the "disappointing" musical that bore his character's name. Gussow noted Larry Grossman had recently composed *A Doll's Life*, and was now dealing with a dog's life; but he felt the score was too generic and lacked a show-stopper like *Charlie Brown*'s "Suppertime." The musical was first produced in Los Angeles in 1976 as *Snoopy!!!* with Don Potter in the title role. Numbers deleted prior to New York were "Sit Up! Lie Down! Roll Over! Play Dead!" and "Friend." The cast album of that production was released on Power Exchange Records (LP # PXL-015), and included "Friend"; it was reissued on DRG Records (LP # DRG-6103). The 1983 London production was released on That's Entertainment Records (LP # TER-1073; CD # CDTER-1073), and included two new numbers ("Hurry Up Face" for Peppermint Patty and "When Do the Good Things Start" for the ensemble). Despite Larry Grossman's pleasant score, *Snoopy* was another of his many failures. He wrote consistently interesting theatre music (*Minnie's Boys*, 1970; *Goodtime Charley*, 1975; *A Doll's Life*, 1982 [see entry]; *Grind*, 1985; and *Paper Moon* [which closed during its pre-Broadway tryout in 1993 but has once or twice surfaced in regional theatre productions]) but his melodic scores were always tied to weak and/or problematic books.

1487 Social Intercourse: Pilgrim's Progress. THEATRE: The Space/New York City Center; OPENING DATE: June 9, 1982; PERFORMANCES: 12 (estimated); CONCEIVED, CHOREOGRAPHED, AND DIRECTED BY: Bill T. Jones; Arnie Zane, Assistant Director; MUSIC: Flo Brown, Johari Briggs, Rhodessa Jones, and Bill T. Jones; additional music by Joe Hannan; LIGHTING: William Yehle; MUSICAL DIRECTION: Joe Hannan; PRODUCER: The Foundation for Dance Promotion in co-operation with Arts Arcadia Associates

CAST—Dancers (Brian Arensault, Bill T. Jones, Rhonda Moore, Julio Enrique Rivera, Julie West), Vocals (Flo Brown, Johari Briggs, Rhodessa Jones), Other Performers (Homer Avila, Marie Baker-Lee, Annie Bien, Mia Borgatta, Connie Chin, Herb Dade, Michael Davis, Paul Eaddy, Kim Flowers, Erroll Grimes, Roberta Kirns, Jim Martin, Merle Matsunaga, Felicia Moseley, Amy Pivar, Bruce Regst, Sandra Sinclair, Richard Steinberg)

The dance piece was presented in four parts (Prologue, On the Square, I Believe, and Judgement)

MUSICAL NUMBERS—"Miracles" (by Bill T. Jones), "Party! Party!" (by Flo Brown), "Don't Send That Boy" (by Johari Briggs and Rhodessa Jones), "Ackabacka" (by Johari Briggs, Rhodessa Jones, and Bill T. Jones), "Felony" (by Flo Brown), "I Believe" (by Ervin Drake, Irvin Graham, Jimmy Shirl, and Al Stillman), "Judgement" (text by Bill T. Jones)

NOTES—Bill T. Jones' dance musical *Social Intercourse: Pilgrim's Progress* included new music as well as a popular inspirational song from the 1950s ("I Believe"). It was apparently presented under an Off Off Broadway contract.

Jennifer Dunning in the *New York Times* indicated the confused explanations in the program which described the evening's dances were best ignored and that instead the audience should just sit back and enjoy the four "exciting sequences of high-energy abstract dance." She noted that one piece stated it was about "the disparity between an individual living in an urban community and that individual's attempt to determine his own fate." To that, Dunning replied, "You could have fooled this viewer." But otherwise the dances by the "dynamic" choreographer and his dancers packed a "hefty wallop." In 2007, Jones won the Tony Award for Best Choreography for *Spring Awakening* (see entry).

1488 Some People, Some Other People, and What They Finally Do. "A Revue with Hardly Any Music." THEATRE: Stage 73; OPENING DATE: June 5, 1974; PERFORMANCES: 16; REVUE MATERIAL BY: Jordan Crittenden; MUSIC: Stephen Lawrence; DIRECTION: Charles Aidman; SCENERY: John Lee Beatty; COSTUMES: Reef Pell; LIGHTING: Joel Grunheim; PRODUCERS: Ruth Kalkstein and Sidney Annis; John Allen, Associate Producer

CAST—Lois Battle, Rod Browning, Jordan Crittenden, Carol Morley

NOTES—Clive Barnes in the *New York Times* noted the revue *Some People, Some Other People, and What They Finally Do* was mildly diverting "if your standards for diversion are not stratospherically high." Barnes felt the material lacked punch: one "deflationary" sketch dealt with a woman who can foretell the future (but unfortunately sees only the most trivial of events) and another ("Frozen Daiquiris") was belabored in its attempt to show that everyone is alike in bed. Barnes agreed with the revue's subtitle, but remarked that what little music there was proved to be "quite tuneful."

1489 Someone's in the Kitchen with Dinah. THEATRE: Judson Poets' Theatre; OPENING DATE: July 27, 1979; PERFORMANCES: 12; BOOK: Al Carmines; LYRICS: Al Carmines; MUSIC: Al Carmines; DIRECTION: Bob Herget; SCENERY: John Pitts; COSTUMES: Michele Edwards; LIGHTING: Victor En Yu Tan; MUSICAL DIRECTION: Al Carmines (?); PRODUCER: Judson Poets' Theatre

CAST—Essie Borden

NOTES—*Someone's in the Kitchen with Dinah* was an Off Off Broadway one-woman musical which starred Essie Borden, who, along with Lee Guilliatt and Julie Kurnitz, was one of Al Carmines' most frequent leading ladies.

1490 The Son of Four Below. THEATRE: The Downstairs Room; OPENING DATE: September 27, 1956; PERFORMANCES: Unknown; SKETCHES, LYRICS, MUSIC: Unknown; DIRECTION: Possibly John Heawood; MUSICAL DIRECTION: Murray Grand; PRODUCER: Julius Monk

CAST—Ceil Cabot, June Ericson, Jack Fletcher, Gerry Matthews

NOTES—Monk and Company followed up the success of *Four Below* (see entry) with the revue *The Son of Four Below*.

One number which has surfaced from this revue ("Guess Who Was There," lyric and music by Bud McCreery) was later used in Monk's *Demi-Dozen* (1958; see entry), and was included on that show's cast album.

For a complete list of Julius Monk's revues, see entry for *Four Below*; also see Appendix Q.

1491 Sondheim: Opening Doors. THEATRE: Zankel Hall/Carnegie Hall; OPENING DATE: October 5, 2004; PERFORMANCES: 6; LYRICS: Stephen Sondheim; MUSIC: Unless otherwise noted, all music by Stephen Sondheim; DIRECTION: David Kernan; CHOREOGRAPHY: James Scott Wise; COSTUMES: Jane Greenwood; LIGHTING: Vivian Leone; MUSICAL DIRECTION: Rob Berman; PRODUCER: Carnegie Hall (Sanford I. Weill, Chairman; Robert J. Harth, Executive and Artistic Director)

CAST—Kate Baldwin, Victoria Clark, Gregg Edelman, Jan Maxwell, Eric Jordan Young

The revue was presented in two acts (division of acts and song assignments unknown).

MUSICAL NUMBERS—"The Hills of Tomorrow" (from *Merrily We Roll Along*, 1981), "Our Time" (*Merrily We Roll Along*, 1981), "Opening Doors"

(*Merrily We Roll Along*, 1981), "Everybody Says Don't" (*Anyone Can Whistle*, 1964), "Take Me to the World" (from 1966 television musical *Evening Primrose*), "I Know Things Now" (*Into the Woods*, 1987), "Who Wants to Live in New York?" (sequence in "Opening Doors," from *Merrily We Roll Along* [1981]), "What More Do I Need?" (*Saturday Night* [written in 1954, and first scheduled for a Broadway production during the 1955-1956 season and then later during the 1959-1960 season; was finally produced in New York in 2000; see entry]), "Uptown, Downtown" (deleted during tryout of *Follies*, 1971), "Another Hundred People" (*Company*, 1970), "(They Asked Me Why) I Believe in You" (from unproduced television musical *I Believe in You*, 1956), "The Best Thing That Ever Has Happened" (*Bounce*, 2003; closed during pre-Broadway tryout), "Merrily We Roll Along" (*Merrily We Roll Along*, 1981), "A Weekend in the Country" (*A Little Night Music*, 1973), "Barcelona" (*Company*, 1970), "A Parade in Town" (*Anyone Can Whistle*, 1964), "By the Sea" (*Sweeney Todd/The Demon Barber of Fleet Street*, 1979), "Sunday" (*Sunday in the Park with George*, 1984), "Someone Is Waiting" (*Company*, 1970), "Multitudes of Amys" (written for, but not used in, *Company* [1970]), "No, Mary Ann" (from unproduced film musical *The Thing of It Is*, circa 1969), "Johanna" (*Sweeney Todd/The Demon Barber of Fleet Street*, 1979), "I Do Like You" (deleted during tryout of *A Funny Thing Happened on the Way to the Forum*, 1962), "Old Friends" (*Merrily We Roll Along*, 1981), "Side by Side by Side" (*Company*, 1970), "Putting It Together" (*Sunday in the Park with George*, 1984), "Bounce" (*Bounce*, 2003; closed during pre–Broadway tryout), "Something's Coming" (*West Side Story*, 1957; music by Leonard Bernstein), "Everything's Coming Up Roses" (*Gypsy*, 1959; music by Jule Styne), "Loving You" (*Passion*, 1994), "Not a Day Goes By" (*Merrily We Roll Along*, 1981), "So Many People" (*Saturday Night* [written in 1954, and first scheduled for a Broadway production during the 1955-1956 season and then later during the 1959-1960 season; was finally produced in New York in 2000; see entry]), "That Old Piano Roll" (written for, but not used in, *Follies* [1971]; used as background music)), "Marry Me a Little" (deleted during tryout of *Company*, 1970), "The Little Things You Do Together" (*Company*, 1970), "The Miller's Son" (*A Little Night Music*, 1973), "Goodbye for Now" (1981 film *Reds*), "I Wish I Could Forget You" (*Passion*, 1994), "Pretty Women" (*Sweeney Todd/The Demon Barber of Fleet Street*, 1979), "There's Always a Woman" (written for, but not used in, *Anyone Can Whistle* [1964]), "Ah, But Underneath" (written for 1987 London production of *Follies*), "No More" (*Into the Woods*, 1987), "No One Is Alone" (*Into the Woods*, 1987), "Being Alive" (*Company*, 1970), "With So Little to Be Sure Of" (*Anyone Can Whistle*, 1964), "Our Time" (reprise) (*Merrily We Roll Along*, 1981), "Back in Business" (1990 film *Dick Tracy*)

NOTES—*Sondheim: Opening Doors* played a limited engagement of six performances at Carnegie Hall. The concert-revue had previously been produced as *Moving On* in London at the Bridewell Theatre on July 25, 2000. Both the London and New York concerts were directed by David Kernan, who had appeared in the original London (1976) and New York (1977) productions of *Side by Side by Sondheim*. The production included two songs from *Bounce*, which had closed during its pre-Broadway tryout the previous year. Although "The Best Thing That Ever Has Happened" and the title song were welcome selections from the score, it's too bad "Isn't He Something!," one of Sondheim's most ravishing ballads, wasn't included.

The concert included video interviews with Sondheim, and the London cast album was released by Goldcrest Films International Records (CD # GF-1001-CD).

1492 Sondheim Putting It Together. THEATRE: City Center Stage I/Manhattan Theatre Club; OPENING DATE: April 1, 1993; PERFORMANCES: 59; LYRICS: Stephen Sondheim; MUSIC: Stephen Sondheim; DIRECTION: Rita McKenzie; CHOREOGRAPHY: Bob Avian; SCENERY: Robin Wagner; COSTUMES: Theoni V. Aldredge; LIGHTING: Tharon Musser; MUSICAL DIRECTION: Scott Frankel; PRODUCER: Manhattan Theatre Club (Lynne Meadow, Artistic Director; Barry Grove, Managing Director)

CAST—Julie Andrews, Stephen Collins, Christopher Durang, Michael Rupert, Rachel York

The musical was presented in two acts.

ACT ONE—"Invocation and Instructions" (from *The Frogs*, 1974) (Christopher Durang), "Putting It Together" (*Sunday in the Park with George*, 1984) (Stephen Collins, Rachel York, Michael Rupert, Julie Andrews, Christopher Durang, Scott Frankel), "Rich and Happy #1" (*Merrily We Roll Along*, 1981) (Stephen Collins, Julie Andrews, Michael Rupert, Christopher Durang, Rachel York), "Merrily We Roll Along #1" (*Merrily We Roll Along*, 1981) (Christopher Durang), "Lovely" (*A Funny Thing Happened on the Way to the Forum*, 1962) (Rachel York), "Everybody Ought to Have a Maid" (*A Funny Thing Happened on the Way to the Forum*, 1962) (Stephen Collins, Christopher Durang, Michael Rupert), Sequence (Julie Andrews, Stephen Collins, Michael Rupert, Rachel York, Christopher Durang): "Sooner or Later" (1990 film *Dick Tracy*), "I'm Calm" (*A Funny Thing Happened on the Way to the Forum*, 1962), "Impossible" (*A Funny Thing Happened on the Way to the Forum*, 1962), "Ah, But Underneath" (London production of *Follies*, 1987), "Hello, Little Girl" (*Into the Woods*, 1987) (Stephen Collins, Rachel York), "My Husband the Pig" (written for, but not used in, *A Little Night Music*, 1973)/"Every Day a Little Death" (*A Little Night Music*, 1973) (Julie Andrews, Rachel York), "Merrily We Roll Along #2" (*Merrily We Roll Along*, 1981) (Christopher Durang), "Have I Got a Girl for You" (*Company*, 1970) (Stephen Collins, Michael Rupert), "Pretty Women" (*Sweeney Todd/The Demon Barber of Fleet Street*, 1979) (Michael Rupert, Stephen Collins), "Now" (*A Little Night Music*, 1973) (Christopher Durang, Michael Rupert), "Bang!" (deleted during the pre-Broadway tryout of *A Little Night Music*, 1973) (Michael Rupert, Rachel York), "Country House" (London production of *Follies*, 1987) (Julie Andrews, Stephen Collins), "Merrily We Roll Along #3" (*Merrily We Roll Along*, 1981) (Christopher Durang), "Could I Leave You?" (*Follies*, 1971) (Julie Andrews)

ACT TWO—Entr'acte (Orchestra), "Back in Business" (1990 film *Dick Tracy*) (Company), "Rich and Happy #2" (*Merrily We Roll Along*, 1981) (Stephen Collins, Michael Rupert, Rachel York, Julie Andrews), "Night Waltzes" (*A Little Night Music*, 1973; and 1978 film version) (Christopher Durang, Michael Rupert, Julie Andrews, Rachel York, Stephen Collins): "Love Takes Time," "Remember?," "In Praise of Women," "Perpetual Anticipation," "The Sun Won't Set," "Gun Song" (*Assassins*, 1991) (Christopher Durang, Julie Andrews, Stephen Collins, Michael Rupert, Rachel York), "The Miller's Son" (*A Little Night Music*, 1973) (Rachel York), "Live Alone and Like It" (1990 film *Dick Tracy*) (Michael Rupert), "Sorry-Grateful" (*Company*, 1970) (Stephen Collins), "Sweet Polly Plunkett" (from the "Parlor Songs" sequence; *Sweeney Todd/The Demon Barber of Fleet Street*, 1979) (Julie Andrews), "I Could Drive a Person Crazy" (*Company*, 1970) (Christopher Durang, Company), "Marry Me a Little" (written for, but not used in, *Company*, 1970) (Michael Rupert), "Getting Married Today" (*Company*, 1970) (Julie Andrews, Company), "Merrily We Roll Along #4" (*Merrily We Roll Along*, 1981) (Christopher Durang), "Being Alive" (*Company*, 1970) (Stephen Collins, Michael Rupert, Julie Andrews, Rachel York), "Like It Was" (*Merrily We Roll Along*, 1981) (Julie Andrews), "Old Friends" (*Merrily We Roll Along*, 1981) (Stephen Collins), "Merrily We Roll Along #5" (*Merrily We Roll Along*, 1981) (Christopher Durang), "Putting It Together" (reprise; finale) (*Sunday in the Park with George*, 1984) (Company)

NOTES—Like *Marry Me a Little* (see entry), *Sondheim Putting It Together* was a pointless exercise in which various songs written by Stephen Sondheim for other musicals were grafted into a new plot, a song-cycle set at a party given by a wealthy couple in Manhattan. As a result, songs previously written for plot, character, and atmosphere in other Sondheim musicals were suddenly expected to tell completely different stories than the ones for which they were intended. And, like *Marry Me a Little*, *Sondheim Putting It Together* works best as a recording (in this case, a 2-CD set released by RCA Victor Records [# 09026-61729-2]) of Sondheim songs, divorced from the excess baggage of new plot and characters. The musical was notable, however, for the welcome return of Julie Andrews to the New York musical stage after more than three decades (her last appearance had been in *Camelot* [1960]).

Sondheim Putting It Together had first been seen at the Old Fire Station in Oxford, England, on January 27, 1992, and the Manhattan Theatre Club's production marked the first time the musical had been seen in the United States. At one point or another during the New York run, the songs "What Would We Do Without You?" (from *Company*) and "A Little Priest" (from *Sweeney Todd/The Demon Barber of Fleet Street*) were performed, and they can be heard on the cast album.

The musical briefly appeared on Broadway, opening at the Ethel Barrymore Theatre on November 21, 1999, for 101 performances (with Carol Burnett, George Hearn, John Barrowman, Ruthie Henshall, and Bronson Pinchot); this production was later seen on cable television and was released on DVD by Image Entertainment (# ID-3629-WRDVD).

One curious aspect of *Side by Side by Sondheim*, *Putting It Together*, and other Sondheim tributes is that not one of them has included "Rag Me That Mendelssohn March," which is the very first Sondheim song to have been performed in a professional production. It was introduced during the 1955 summer stock tour of Arthur Kober and George Oppenheimer's comedy *A Mighty Man Is He* (the program credits the song to "Steve Sondheim"). The play finally made it to Broadway five years later, when it opened at the Cort Theatre on January 6, 1960, for five performances. For New York, Sondheim's song was replaced by a similar number, "Mendelssohn March," by Sherman Edwards (nine years before his first and only musical, the long-running *1776* [1969]); the published script of *A Mighty Man Is He* includes both the lyric and the music of "Mendelssohn March," which was introduced in the Broadway production by the Nancies Kelly and Cushman. And who in the 1955 production of *A Mighty Man Is He* has the distinction of being the very first performer to introduce a Sondheim song in a professional production? None other than film legend Claudette Colbert.

1493 A Song Floating. "A New Musical." THEATRE: Westbeth Theatre Opening Date: 1993-1994 Season; PERFORMANCES: Unknown; LYRICS: See song list for credits; MUSIC: Philip Springer; DIRECTION: Babs Warden Lebowsky

CAST—Gayle Turner, Tina Stafford, David Berk, David Flynn

MUSICAL NUMBERS—"A Song Floating" (lyric by Philip Springer and Donna Barskin; 1989) (Company), "(How Little It Matters) How Little We Know" (lyric by Carolyn Leigh; 1956) (Gayle

Turner), "Moonlight Gambler" (lyric by Bob Hilliard; 1957) (David Berk), "What Became of Love" (lyric by Roy Alfred) (Gayle Turner, David Berk), "Tomorrow When the World Comes Crashing Down Around Our Ears" (lyric by Joan Javits; 1965) (Tina Stafford, David Flynn), "Change of Sky" (lyric by E.Y. Harburg; 1980) (Gayle Turner), "A Song Floating" (reprise) (Company), "Venus de Milo" (lyric by E.Y. Harburg and Philip Springer; 1953) (David Flynn), "A Face That Could Stop a Clock" (lyric by Buddy Kaye; 1964) (Tina Stafford), "The Eighth Floor" (lyric by Cathy Lynn; 1958) (David Berk), "Thief in the Night" (lyric by Richard Adler and Philip Springer; 1949) (Tina Stafford), "Santa Baby" (lyric by Joan Javits; 1953) (Gayle Turner, Tina Stafford), "Piano Players" (lyric by Donna Barskin; 1953) (Tina Stafford), "Manhattan Rhapsody" (lyric by Joan Javits, Philip Springer, Buddy Kaye, and Irwin Levine; 1966 and 1994) (Company), "Time, You Old Gypsy Man" (lyric by E.Y. Harburg; 1979) (David Berk), "Travelin' Light" (lyric by Bonny Cameryn; 1991) (Company), "Still Waters" (lyric by Bob Hilliard; 1969) (David Flynn), "Guns" (lyric by Philip Springer ad Donna Barskin; 1993) (David Berk, Gayle Turner, Tina Stafford), "Beautiful" (lyric by Donna Barskin; 1967) (Gayle Turner, Company), "Greenhouse Blues" (lyric by Philip Springer and Donna Barskin; 1993) (Gayle Turner, Tina Stafford), "Patched-Up Day" (lyric by Donna Barskin; 1967) (Tina Stafford, David Flynn), "Castle in the Air" (lyric by Joan Javits; 1958) (Gayle Turner, David Flynn), "A Song Floating" (reprise) (Tina Stafford), "Wild Cherry River" (lyric by E.Y. Harburg; 1978) (David Berk), "Travelin' Light" (reprise) (Company)

NOTES—*A Song Floating* was a welcome revue which featured the music of Philip Springer, who was an occasional contributor to the early Off Broadway revue (*Take Five*, *Shoestring '57*; see entries) and who wrote the scores for the Off Broadway musicals *Hotel Passionato* and *The Chosen* (see entries). The revue included "Tomorrow When the World Comes Crashing Down Around Our Ears," which had originally been introduced in *Hotel Passionato* by Phil Leeds and Marian Mercer.

Springer's two best-known songs are the swinging "(How Little It Matters) How Little We Know" and the saucy "Santa Baby." The former, with its irresistible melody and zesty lyric, became a standard in Frank Sinatra's definitive recording, and the saucy Christmas perennial "Santa Baby," which merrily celebrates the greed and commercialism of the holiday season, became, along with "C'Est Si Bon," one of Eartha Kitt's signature songs. "Santa Baby" was sung by Kitt when it was interpolated into the 1954 film *New Faces*, based on *New Faces of 1952*. *A Song Floating* was recorded by Original Cast Records (CD # OCR-9513); the four singers on the recording are accompanied by Springer on the piano. The song list above is taken from the recording.

1494 Song Night in the City.

"A Fantasy Cabaret." THEATRE: Orpheum Theatre; OPENING DATE: April 16, 1980; PERFORMANCES: 15; LYRICS: See song list for credits; MUSIC: See song list for credits; DIRECTION: John Braswell; SCENERY: John Braswell; LIGHTING: Phil Monat; MUSICAL DIRECTION: Karen Manno; PRODUCERS: Karen Manno in association with Andrea L. Carroad

CAST—Hillary C. Bailey, Lori Barenfeld, Bill Barnes, Doug Ingle, Jonathan Rosen, Carla Salls, Camille Tibaldeo, Susan Topping, Cindy Weintraub; The Song Night Band (Dean Block, Gene Hicks, David Nieske, Martha Obrecht)

The revue was presented in two acts.

ACT ONE—"Cooking Breakfast for the One I Love" (from 1930 film *Be Yourself*; lyric and music by Billy Rose and Henry Tobias) (Ensemble), "Our Day Will Come" (lyric and music by Bob Hilliard and Mort Garson) (Cindy Weibtraub, Ensemble), "Something's Coming Up" (lyric and music by Barry Manilow) (Jonathan Rosen, Ensemble), "The Bells" (lyric and music by Iris Bristol, Marvin Gaye, Anna Gaye, Elgie Stover, and Iris Stover) (Carla Salls), "Row, Row, Row" (*Ziegfeld Follies of 1912*; lyric by William Jerome, music by James V. Monaco) (Jonathan Rosen, Bill Barnes), "I Don't Want to Set the World on Fire" (lyric and music by Bennie Benjamin, Sol Marcus, and Eddie Seiler) (Ensemble), "Hot Stuff" (lyric and music by H. Faltemeir, K. Forsey, and P. Belotte) (Carla Salls, Ensemble), "Life on Mars" (lyric and music by David Bowie) (Bill Barnes, Dancers), "Underneath the Harlem Moon" (lyric by Mack Gordon, music by Harry Revel) (Hillary C. Bailey), "I'll Play the Fool" (lyric and music by August Darnell and Stoney Browder, Jr.) (Carla Salls, Bill Barnes, Ensemble), "Let the Good Times Roll" (lyric and music by Leonard Lee) (Camille Tibaldeo, Dancers), "Red Roses for a Blue Lady" (lyric and music by Roy C. Bennett and Sid Tepper) (Jonathan Rosen, Bill Barnes), "I Don't Want to Lose You" (lyricist and composer unknown) (Camille Tibaldeo), "Mona Lisa" (1950 film *Captain Carey, U.S.A.*; lyric by Jay Livingston and Ray Evans, music by Jay Livingston) (Jonathan Rosen [Suzanna Topping as Mona Lisa]), "Je Vous Aime" (lyric and music by Anna Sosenko) (Bill Barnes, Cindy Weintraub), "Midnight Train to Georgia" (lyric and music by Jim Weatherly) (Cindy Weintraub), "I'll Never Love This Way Again" (lyric and music by Richard Kerr and Will Jennings) (Jonathan Rosen, Dancers)

ACT TWO—"Plaisir D'Amour" (lyric and music by Martini and Giovanni) (Ensemble), "Love Story" (lyricist and composer unknown) (Jonathan Rosen), "All That Jazz" (*Chicago*, 1975; lyric by Fred Ebb, music by John Kander) (Carla Salls, Dancers), "Operator" (lyric and music by William Spivery) (Camille Tibaldeo, Ensemble), "So Into You" (lyric and music by Buddy Buie, Robert Nix, and Dean Daughtry) (Carla Salls, Dancers), "Fame" (lyric and music by David Bowie, John Lennon, and Carlos Alomar) (Bill Barnes, Ensemble), "Yellow Man" (lyric and music by Randy Newman) (Carla Salls, Lori Barenfeld, Doug Ingle, Jonathan Rosen), "Row, Row, Row" (reprise) (lyric by William Jerome, music by James V. Monaco) (Bill Barnes, Jonathan Rosen), "My Ship" (*Lady in the Dark*, 1941; lyric by Ira Gershwin, music by Kurt Weill) (Hillary Bailey, Carla Salls, Bill Barnes, Jonathan Rosen), "You Are Everything" (lyric and music by Thomas Bell and Linda Creed) (Ensemble), "Long John Blues" (lyric and music by Tommy George) (Camille Tibaldeo, Jonathan Rosen [as Dr. Long John]), "It Ain't the Meat, It's the Motion" (lyric and music by Glover Man) (Camille Tibaldeo, Jonathan Rosen), "You're the Cream in My Coffee" (*Hold Everything!*, 1928; lyric by B.G. [Buddy] DeSylva and Lew Brown, music by Ray Henderson) (Camille Tibaldeo, Jonathan Rosen), "Dim All the Lights" (lyric and music by Donna Summer) (Cindy Weintraub), "Something's Coming Up" (reprise) (lyric and music by Barry Manilow) (Jonathan Rosen, Ensemble), "The Bells" (reprise) (lyric and music by Iris Bristol, Marvin Gaye, Anna Gaye, Elgie Stover, and Iris Stover) (Carla Salls), "Cooking Breakfast for the One I Love" (reprise) (lyric and music by Billy Rose and Henry Tobias) (Ensemble), "Let It Be" (lyric and music by John Lennon) (Camille Tibaldeo, Ensemble)

NOTES—Prior to its brief run at the Orpheum Theatre, the revue *Song Night in the City* had played at the Westbeth Theatre a year earlier, opening in April 1979 in an Off Off Broadway production sponsored by the Composers Ensemble Theatre Foundation. The revue was a mixed bag of film, Broadway, disco, and pop songs.

The Westbeth production had a few different cast and band members and was presented in one act. It also included a number of songs which weren't used in the later Off Broadway version, including "I Only Have Eyes for You" (from 1934 film *Dames*; lyric by Al Dubin, music by Harry Warren), "Home Sweet Heaven" (*High Spirits*, 1964; lyric and music by Timothy Grey and Hugh Martin), and "Funny Honey" (*Chicago*, 1975; lyric by Fred Ebb, music by John Kander).

Mel Gussow in the *New York Times* noted that "lights" were the key to the evening; the stage was awash in an effect of magical lights and mirrors, all of which gave the self-styled "fantasy cabaret" the appearance of being located in "outer space." However, Gussow was more partial to the earlier and more "celestial" version of the revue, which was much shorter. Nevertheless, he praised the performers and the romantic songs, and mentioned that an established standard like "Red Roses for a Blue Lady" was so sweetly sung it was as if he had never heard it before.

1495 Song of Singapore.

"The Hot New Swing Musical"/"A Musical Adventure." THEATRE: Song of Singapore Theatre; OPENING DATE: May 23, 1991; PERFORMANCES: 459; BOOK: Allan Katz, Erik Frandsen, Robert Hipkens, Michael Garin, and Paula Lockheart; LYRICS AND MUSIC: Erik Frandsen, Robert Hipkens, Michael Garin, and Paula Lockheart; DIRECTION: A.J. Antoon; SCENERY: John Lee Beatty; COSTUMES: Frank Krenz; LIGHTING: Peter Kaczorowski; PRODUCERS: Steven Baruch, Richard Frankel, and Thomas Viertel in association with Allen Spivak and Larry Magid; Marc Routh, Associate Producer

CAST—Erik Frandsen (Spike Spauldeen; Uke, Guitar, Vocals), Michael Garin (Freddy S. Lyme; Piano, Vocals), Robert Hipkens (Hans van der Last; Trumpet, Dobro, Guitar, Vocals), Donna Murphy (Rose; Vocals), Cathy Foy (Chah Li; Vocals), Francis Kane (Inspector Marvin Kurland and other roles; Vocals), Oliver Jackson, Jr. (Kenya Ratamacue; Drums), Earl May (Taqsim Arco; Bass), Jon Gordon (Zoot DeFumee; Saxophone, Clarinet), Art Baron (T-Bone Kahanamoku; Trombone)

The action occurs in early December 1940 in Freddy's Song of Singapore Café, a nightclub on the Singapore waterfront.

The musical was presented in two acts.

ACT ONE—"Song of Singapore" (Band), "Inexpensive Tango" (Erik Frandsen), "I Miss My Home in Haarlem" (Robert Hipkens), "You Gotta Do What You Gotta Do" (Donna Murphy), "The Rose of Rangoon" (Erik Frandsen), "Necrology" (Band), "Sunrise" (Donna Murphy), "Never Pay Musicians What They're Worth" (Michael Garin), "Harbour of Love" (Francis Kane), "I Can't Remember" (Donna Murphy), "I Want to Get Off This Island"/"Harbour of Love" (reprise) (Band, Francis Kane)

ACT TWO—"Foolish Geese" (Cathy Foy), "Serve It Up" (Donna Murphy), "Fly Away Rose" (Robert Hipkens, Michael Garin, Erik Frandsen), "I Remember" (Donna Murphy, Band), "Shake, Shake, Shake" (Michael Garin, Band), "We're Rich" (Band), "Sunrise"/"Song of Singapore" (reprises) (Band)

NOTES—*Song of Singapore* was a merry bit of nonsense set in a seedy Singapore bar just before December 7, 1941. The musical offered irresistible 1940s pastiche-styled songs and a plot involving black market jewels, an amnesiac band singer ... *and* the resolution of the Amelia Earhart mystery!

Jeffrey Sweet in *The Applause/Best Plays Theatre Yearbook of 1990-1991* singled out Donna Murphy's performance as the saloon singer ("a sensationally versatile singer and a comedienne blessed with perfect timing" who gave the "season's most memorable musical theatre performance"). Mel Gussow in the *New York Times* also praised Murphy, and noted that her performance was funnier than film stars of the Dorothy Lamour variety who wandered into "movie Malaysia."

Unfortunately, when it came time for the cast album recording (released by DRG Records [CD # 19003]), Murphy was no longer with the production (her replacement, Jacquey Maltby, can be heard on the CD).

The script was published by Samuel French, Inc., in 1993. The musical had first been presented by the Playhouse Square Foundation in Cleveland, Ohio.

Gussow reported that the Song of Singapore Theatre was a "lavishly decorated club hall" (located at 17 Irving Place).

The character of Amelia Earhart also appeared in Michael John LaChiusa's *Eleanor Sleeps Here*, one of four musicals in his *First Lady Suite* (1993; see entry). Further, Earhart was the subject of *Amelia's Journey* (subtitled "A Musical Journey Through the Lives of Amelia Earhart and George Putnam"); the lyrics were by Doug Schenker and the music was by Schenker and John E. Starr, Jr. (a CD studio cast recording was released in 2008). Incidentally, *Radio Gals* (see entry) offered "Aviatrix Love Song," a salute to female pilots.

1496 Song of Songs. THEATRE: Judson Poets' Theatre; OPENING DATE: Late 1971 (?); PERFORMANCES: Unknown; LYRICS: Al Carmines; MUSIC: Al Carmines

NOTES—One song ("I Am My Beloved") from the Off Off Broadway revue *Song of Songs* surfaced in *The Gospel According to Al* (1982; see entry).

1497 Songs by Carmines

NOTES—For more information about *Songs by Carmines*, see entry for the 1968 revival of *In Circles*.

1498 Songs for a New World. THEATRE: WPA Theatre; OPENING DATE: October 26, 1995; PERFORMANCES: 27; LYRICS: Jason Robert Brown; MUSIC: Jason Robert Brown; DIRECTION: Daisy Prince; CHOREOGRAPHY: Michael Arnold; SCENERY: Stephen Olson; COSTUMES: Gail Brassard; LIGHTING: Craig Evans; PRODUCER: The WPA Theatre (Kyle Renick, Artistic Director; Lori Sherman, Managing Director)

CAST—Billy Porter, Brooks Ashmanskas, Jessica Molaskey, Andrea Burns

The revue was presented in two acts.

ACT ONE—Opening: "The New World" (Company), "On the Deck of a Spanish Sailing Ship, 1492" (Billy Porter, Company), "Just One Step" (Jessica Molaskey), "I'm Not Afraid of Anything" (Andrea Burns), "The River Won't Flow" (Company), "Stars and the Moon" (Jessica Molaskey), "She Cries" (Brooks Ashmanskas), "The Steam Train" (Billy Porter, Company)

ACT TWO—"The World Was Dancing" (Brooks Ashmanskas, Company), "Surabaya-Santa" (additional text by Kristine Zbornik) (Jessica Molaskey), "Christmas Lullaby" (Andrea Burns), "King of the World" (Billy Porter), "I'd Give It All for You" (Brooks Ashmanskas, Andrea Burns), "The Flagmaker, 1775" (Jessica Molaskey), "Flying Home" (Billy Porter, Company), "Hear My Song" (Company)

NOTES—The Off Off Broadway revue *Songs for a New World* was Jason Robert Brown's first New York hearing, and this melodic and memorable song cycle led to his first book musical, *Parade* (1998). His memorable score for *Parade* included pleasing old-fashioned songs (such as "The Old Red Hills of Home" and "Pretty Music"), incisive character numbers ("It Goes On and On"), and a dazzling concerted sequence ("The Trial"). In 2002, his impressive song-cycle *The Last Five Years* opened (see entry), and the following year he contributed a few songs to the Broadway flop *Urban Cowboy*.

Brown is currently writing a new musical based on the 1992 film *Honeymoon in Vegas*, and in 2007 he previewed two of its songs ("When You Say Vegas" and "Anywhere But Here") in an appearance which was part of Lincoln Center's American Songbook series (in reviewing the evening for the *New York Times*, Stephen Holden wrote that if the two songs were any indication of the rest of the score, then the new musical "could be a contender"). Another musical by Brown, *13*, premiered in Los Angeles at the Mark Taper Forum in January 2007 and is rumored for a Broadway production in 2008.

Songs for a New World was released by RCA Victor Records (CD # 09026-68631-2); for the recording, Ty Taylor replaced Billy Porter. For her collection *Lauren Kennedy/Songs of Jason Robert Brown* (PS Classics Records CD # PS-309), Kennedy included three songs from the production ("Christmas Lullaby," "I'd Give It All for You," and "Flying Home").

1499 Songs from an Unmade Bed. THEATRE: New York Theatre Workshop; OPENING DATE: May 24, 2005; PERFORMANCES: 20; LYRICS: Mark Campbell; MUSIC: Debra Barsha, Mark Bennett, Peter Foley, Jenny Giering, Peter Golub, Jake Heggie, Stephen Hoffman, Lance Horne, Gihieh Lee, Steve Marzullo, Brendan Milburn, Chris Miller, Greg Pliska, Duncan Sheik, Kim D. Sherman, Jeffrey Stock, Joseph Thalken; DIRECTION: David Schweizer; SCENERY: Neil Patel; COSTUMES: David Zinn; LIGHTING: Brian H. Scott; MUSICAL DIRECTION: Kimberly Grigsby; PRODUCER: New York Theatre Workshop (James C. Nicola, Artistic Director; Lynn Moffat, Managing Director)

CAST—Michael Winther

The revue was presented in one act (all songs performed by Michael Winther).

MUSICAL NUMBERS—"He Never Did That Before," "A Dinner Party," "To Sing," "Here in My Bed," "I Miss New York," "The Other Other Woman," "Our Separate Ways," "The Man in the Starched White Shirt," "Spring," "Exit Right," "The Night You Decided to Stay," "I Want to Go Out Tonight," "Perfect Finite," "Funny Gesture," "Oh, to Be Stupid Again," "Florence," "He Plays the Cello"

NOTES—*Songs from an Unmade Bed*, a one-man song cycle performed by Michael Winther, dealt with a gay man and his life in New York City. Winther also wrote the lyrics to all seventeen songs, and each lyric was set to music by a different composer.

Anne Midgette in the *New York Times* said the evening was "funny, light [and] sardonic," and eschewed a political agenda. She noted that those songs which were wry and self-mocking (such as "Florence," "A Dinner Party," and "Our Separate Ways") were more effective than the overtly emotional ones (such as "To Sing"). She singled out a number of other songs, including "Spring" ("acerbic"), "The Other Other Woman" (a send-up of Broadway), "He Never Did That Before" (a rock number), and "I Miss New York" (a torch song).

1500 Songs from the Café Escargot. "A Musical." THEATRE: The Trocadero; OPENING DATE: July 5, 1993; PERFORMANCES: 8; BOOK: Jaz Dorsey; LYRICS: Jaz Dorsey; MUSIC: Jaz Dorsey; DIRECTION: Jaz Dorsey; CHOREOGRAPHY: Ron Ben-Israel; LIGHTING: George Cameron

CAST—Shawneen Rowe (Mary Augusta DeWill), Danny Bozarth (Bud, Melodious Flow), Reginald McNeely (Little Freddy), Karron Haines (Mae Knott), Flotilla de Barge (Paces Ferry McGuire), Thom Berlin (Beverly BergBerg), Richard Johnson (Ali Ali Ali)

The musical was presented in two acts.

ACT ONE—"Café Escargot" (Ensemble), "February Weather" (Shawneen Rowe, Danny Bozarth), "Melancholy Birdsong" (Shawneen Rowe), "On the Clock on the Floor" (Shawneen Rowe), "Extraordinary Waiter" (Reginald McNeely), "Opening Day" (Shawneen Rowe, Danny Bozarth), "Rich Man's Baby" (Karron Haines), "Ain't Losin' No Sleep" (Shawneen Rowe), "Revenge Tango" (Shawneen Rowe, Reginald McNeely)

ACT TWO—"Revenge Tango" (reprise) (Ensemble), "The Escargot Song" (Karron Haines, Shawneen Rowe), "Crisis in the Kitchen" (Danny Bozarth), "Buckhead-Dunwoody Diet Brigade" (Danny Bozarth, Flotilla de Barge, Thom Berlin, Richard Johnson), "Drag Tango" (Reginald McNeely), "Like They Do" (Karron Haines, Shawneen Rowe), "Black Coffee" (Flotilla de Barge, Danny Bozarth, Thom Berlin, Richard Johnson), "Dreams" (Shawneen Rowe, Karron Haines), "The Success Song" (Shawneen Rowe)

NOTES—The campy, gaycentric Off Off Broadway musical *Songs from the Café Escargot* played a limited engagement of two performances a week throughout July 1993.

The musical dealt with Mary Augusta DeWill, the owner of the Café Escargot, her co-workers, and customers, including Melodious Flowe and Paces Ferry McGuire, two women who represented, respectively, old Atlanta money and new Atlanta money. The two women were played by male actors, one of whom was named Flotilla de Barge. Other characters included Ali Ali Ali, a "mad" international film director, Beverly BergBerg, an independent businesswoman, and Mae Knott, Mary Augusta's nemesis and a gold digger to boot.

1501 The Songs of Mao Tse-Tung. THEATRE: Judson Poets' Theatre; OPENING DATE: Circa 1971; PERFORMANCES: Unknown; LYRICS: Chairman Mao Tse-Tung; adapted by Al Carmines; MUSIC: Al Carmines; DIRECTION: "Movement" staged by Remy Charlip

CAST—Reathel Bean, David Berk, Al Carmines, Christopher Carrick, Julie Kurnitz, Florence Tarlow, Margaret Wright

NOTES—The Off Off Broadway production was based on Chairman Mao Tse-Tung's book *The Sayings of Mao Tse-Tung*, which enjoyed a brief vogue during the era.

One song ("The World Is Yours") was included in the 1982 revue *The Gospel According to Al* (see entry).

1502 Songs of Paradise. "A Pop Musical." THEATRE: The Susan Stein Shiva Theatre/The Public Theatre; OPENING DATE: January 23, 1989; PERFORMANCES: 136; BOOK: Miriam Hoffman and Rena Berkowicz Borow; LYRICS: Based on Biblical poetry by Itzik Manger; MUSIC: Rosalie Gerut; DIRECTION: Avi Hoffman; CHOREOGRAPHY: Eleanor Reissa; SCENERY: Steven Perry; LIGHTING: Anne Militello; MUSICAL DIRECTION: James Mironchik; PRODUCERS: The New York Shakespeare Festival (Joseph Papp, Director); a Joseph Papp Yiddish Theatre Production in association with YIVO Institute for Jewish Research

CAST—Adrienne Cooper, Rosalie Gerut, Avi Hoffman, David Kener, Eleanor Reissa

SOURCES—The Biblical story of Genesis and the Biblical poetry of Itzik Manger.

The musical was presented in two acts.

ACT ONE—"Di Demerung (The Twilight)" (Rosalie Gerut, Adrienne Cooper), "Khave and the Apple Tree" (Eleanor Reissa), "Odem and the Khave Duet" (Eleanor Reissa, Avi Hoffman, David Kener), "Avrum and Sore's Duet" (David Kener, Adrienne Cooper), "Hoger and the Turks" (Rosalie Gerut, Adrienne Cooper, Eleanor Reissa, Avi Hoffman), "Shir Hamaylesn (Song of Blessings)" (Company), "Hoger's Lament"/"Sore's Lullaby" (Rosalie Gerut, Company)

ACT TWO—"Yankev and Rokhl Duet" (Rosalie Gerut, Avi Hoffman), "Yosef's Tango" (Avi Hoffman, Rosalie Gerut, Adrienne Cooper), Finale: "The Farewell Song" (Company)

NOTES—*Songs of Paradise* was performed in Yiddish with a simultaneous English translation. Richard F. Shepard in the *New York Times* reported the "witty, tuneful, contemporary and traditional" revue-like evening offered a wry take on Biblical stories by infusing them with a modern sensibility. It turns out Eve was just bored with Adam, and it was this boredom which led to her encounter with the apple tree and the serpent ("and the rest is tsoris," noted Shepard). As for Cain and Abel, Shepard noted that Abel was so "irritating" that his killing was surely more in the nature of manslaughter than murder. A slightly revised version of the musical returned the following season, opening at the Astor Place Theatre for thirty-two performances beginning on November 13, 1989; a flyer for the revival noted that "The critics are kvelling/The audiences are yelling/The tickets are selling."

1503 Songs on a Shipwrecked Sofa. THEATRE: Vineyard Theatre; OPENING DATE: June 2, 1987; PERFORMANCES: 30; BOOK AND LYRICS: James Milton and Polly Pen; additional material by James Milton; MUSIC: Polly Pen; DIRECTION: Andre Ernotte; CHOREOGRAPHY: Ara Fitzgerald; SCENERY: William Barclay; COSTUMES: Muriel Stockdale; LIGHTING: Phil Monat; MUSICAL DIRECTION: Stephen Milbank; PRODUCER: The Vineyard Theatre (Douglas Aibel, Artistic Director; Barbara Zinn Kreiger, Executive Director; Gary P. Steuer, Managing Director)

CAST—Alma Cuervo (Mother), Francisco McGregor (Father), Stephen Geoffreys (Son), Ann Talman (Daughter)

SOURCE—The nonsense poems of Mervyn Peake (1911-1968).

The musical was presented in two acts (division of acts and song assignments unknown).

MUSICAL NUMBERS—"O'er Seas That Have No Beaches," "Pygmies, Palms and Pirates," "The Sunlight," "I Float," "Our Ears," "Dear Children," "The Darkness," "It Is Most Best," ""O Here It Is! And There It Is!," "Shrink," "Lean Sideways on the Wind," "The Men in Bowler Hats," "O Love! O Death! O Ecstasy!," "I Cannot Give the Reasons," "The Trouble with Geraniums," "And I Thought You Beside Me," "All Flowers That Die," "I Have My Price," "Leave the Stronger and the Lesser Things to Me," "The Threads Remain," "Out of the Overlapping," "All Flowers That Die" (finale)

NOTES—The Off Off Broadway *Songs on a Shipwrecked Sofa* was James Milton and Polly Pen's adaptation of the nonsense poems of Mervyn Peake (1911-1968), a British poet, writer, and illustrator. Mel Gussow in the *New York Times* found the musical "dramatically sedentary," and noted that Peake's lyrics were not in the class of T.S. Eliot and Christina Rossetti (the latter's poetry was the source for Pen's earlier *Goblin Market* [see entry]). Gussow said the evening had an "exceedingly high whimsy quotient," and felt *Shipwrecked Sofa* was "desperately in need of reupholstering." But he reported that Pen's music included a few "pretty" ballads.

Polly Pen always seemed to be associated with fresh and offbeat subject matter (such as *Goblin Market*), and often her musicals (and the musicals she appeared in) took place in the Victorian era.

1504 Soon. "A Rock Opera." THEATRE: Ritz Theatre; OPENING DATE: January 12, 1971; PERFORMANCES: 3; LYRICS: Scott Fagin; "adaptation" by Martin Duberman; MUSIC: Joseph M. Kookoolis and Scott Fagin; DIRECTION: Unknown; "additional staging" by Gerald Freedman; CHOREOGRAPHY: Fred Benjamin; SCENERY: Kert Lundell; COSTUMES: David Chapman; LIGHTING: Jules Fisher; MUSICAL DIRECTION: Louis St. Louis; PRODUCERS: Bruce W. Stark and Sagittarius Productions, Inc.

CAST—Barry Bostwick (Kelly), Marta Heflin (Annie), Dennis Belline (Wilson Wilson), Joseph Campbell Butler (Neil), Richard Gere (Michael), Peter Allen (Henry), Marion Ramsey (Hope), Leata Galloway (Faith), Vicki Sue Robinson (Charity), Pamela Pentony (Rita), Nell Carter (Sharon), Henry's Friends (Singer Williams, Michael Jason, John C. Nelson), Record Company Executives (Del Hinkley, Angus Cairns, Larry Spinelli, Paul Eichel), Tony Middleton (Songwriter), Pendleton Brown (Psychedelic Nurse), The musical was presented in two acts (song assignments were not listed in the program).

ACT ONE—Prologue: "Let the World Begin," "In Your Hands," "I See the Light"/"Gentle Sighs," "Roll Out the Morning," "Everybody's Running," "Henry Is Where It's At," "Music, Music," "Glad to Know Ya," "Rita Cheeta," "Henry's Dream Theme," "To Touch the Sky," "The Chase": "Everybody's Running"; "Marketing, Marketing"; "Sweet Henry Loves You"; "One More Time"; "Straight"; "Wait"

ACT TWO—"Faces, Names and Places," "Annie's Thing," "Doing the High," "Soon," "Country Store Living," "What's Gonna Happen to Me," "On the Charts," "Molecules," "So Much That I Know," "Child of Sympathy," "Frustration," "Doing the High" (reprise), "It Won't Be Long"

NOTES—*Soon* dealt with a group of pop musicians who learn the age-old show-business lesson of how success isn't all it's cracked up to be. The level of the production might be judged by the way the band was identified in the playbill; instead of listing the names of the band members under the heading of such words as "pit" or "band" or "musicians" (or, heaven forbid, "orchestra"), they were instead identified by the words "Pit-Shit."

The critics found the book lacking (in fact, Martin Gottfried in *Women's Wear Daily* called it a "disaster"), but in general they liked the score (Gottfried noted it captured "a great deal of rock's energy and lyricism"). Clive Barnes in the *New York Times* said the difficulty with *Soon* was that it was a "commercial musical" about the "horrors of musical commercialism," and felt that perhaps a "satiric" approach to the subject might have saved the evening; otherwise, he felt the score was "moderately good" but sometimes "feeble." John Schubeck on *WABC-TV7* wryly noted that the opening night audience applauded the book (a "lecture" on "avarice, hatreds and shabby values") and songs ("which virtually spit on profit and possessions"), and yet when he left the theatre he noticed "a row of limousines" was waiting for many of the audience members. What was truly amazing about *Soon* was its cast: Barry Bostwick, Richard Gere, Peter Allen, and Nell Carter, all of whom found varying degrees of success in television, music, film, and theatre.

Soon was produced under the so-called "Limited Broadway" (or Middle Broadway) contract, which allowed plays and musicals to be performed at Broadway theatres with union-approved concessions (that is, lower paychecks) which in turn allowed for lower costs on the part of producers. Therefore, in some record books *Soon* is categorized as a Broadway production and in others as an Off Broadway production. To be as inclusive as possible, the musical is part of this book (but with the caveat it could be regarded as either a Broadway or an Off Broadway musical).

1505 Sophie. "A New Musical About the Life of Sophie Tucker." THEATRE: Jewish Repertory Theatre; OPENING DATE: October 29, 1987; PERFORMANCES: 20; BOOK: Rose Leiman Goldemberg; LYRICS: Rose Leiman Goldemberg; MUSIC: Debra Barsha; DIRECTION: Louis O. Erdmann; CHOREOGRAPHY: Eugenia V. Erdmann; SCENIC DESIGN: Christian Tucker; Settings by James E. Mayo; COSTUMES: Marcy Froehlich; LIGHTING: David Weller; MUSICAL DIRECTION: Annie LeBeaux; PRODUCER: Jewish Repertory Theatre (Ran Avni, Artistic Director; Edward M. Cohen, Associate Director)

CAST—John Barilla (Phil, Flink), JUDITH COHEN (Sophie Tucker), Deborah Filler (Mama, Queen), Lorraine Goodman (Anna), Adam Heller (Papa, Ziegfeld), ERNESTINE JACKSON (Mollie), Daniel Neiden (Louie, Son), Stephen Parr (Morris Williams), Steve Sterner (Fink, Hart), Shelley Wald (Ada, Star), Rick Zieff (Irving, Gutman, Larry, George)

SOURCE—The life of Sophie Tucker (1884-1966).

The musical was presented in two acts.

ACT ONE—"Soup" (Deborah Filler), "Work" (Family), "Nice Girls Don't Do That" (Judith Cohen), "Gonna Be Somebody" (Judith Cohen), "Keep Movin'" (Judith Cohen), "De Bluebells" (Rick Zieff, Judith Cohen), "My Man" (Rick Zieff, Judith Cohen), "Don't Forget Your Mama" (Family), "Pushcart Sellers" (Judith Cohen, Girls), "Black Up" (John Barilla, Rick Zieff, Steve Sterner), "My Terms" (Judith Cohen), "We Still Love Her" (Family), "She'll Thank Me" (Shelley Wald), "Playing the Part of the Maid" (Ernestine Jackson), "Sophie's Love Song" (Judith Cohen), "This Is About Food" (Rick Zieff, Judith Cohen)

ACT TWO—"You Think It's Easy to Love Her" (Daniel Neiden), "She's Comin' to Town" (Townspeople), "How Many"/"The Looka Song" (Adam Heller, Deborah Filler), "Sophie's Waltz" (Judith Cohen, Stephen Parr), "What Do Women Want?" (Stephen Parr), "Baby Pictures" (Judith Cohen), "One Night Stands" (Judith Cohen, Girls), "Baby Pictures" (reprise) (Deborah Filler, Ernestine Jackson, Judith Cohen), "Mollie's Song" (Ernestine Jackson), "My Terms" (reprise)

NOTES—The Off Off Broadway *Sophie* was the second of three musicals New York would see about Sophie Tucker, "The Last of the Red Hot Mamas." The first, also called *Sophie*, opened on Broadway at the Winter Garden Theatre on April 15, 1963, and played for eight performances (the lyrics and music were by Steve Allen). In that version, Libi Staiger played the title role, and Rosetta LeNoire was Mollie. For whatever it's worth, the 1963 version offered a total of thirty separate musical numbers, and the 1987 production offered twenty-seven.

Sophie Tucker's third visit took place Off Broadway on May 8, 2002, with Sharon McNight's one-woman show *Red Hot Mama*. Produced by the York Theatre Company, the musical opened at the Theatre at St. Peter's for ninety-one performances. Instead of new songs, the production offered numbers from Sophie Tucker's repertoire.

In his review of the Jewish Repertory Theatre's production of *Sophie*, Walter Goodman in the *New York Times* said the musical was "intermittently enjoyable," and noted that Debra Barsha's score and Judith Cohen's "full-bodied" performance in the title role were the show's best assets. Goodman said the score's "perky period quality" was sometimes derivative but often had a "spark" which gave the show a "zip," and he singled out two blackface numbers as well as "Playing the Part of the Maid," "Pushcart Sellers," and "One-Night Stands." He felt the evening's "sweetest" song was the ballad "You Think It's Easy to Love Her."

1506 Sorry, Wrong Number. THEATRE: Sylvia and Danny Kaye Playhouse/Hunter College; OPENING DATE: May 25, 1999; PERFORMANCES: Unknown; LIBRETTO: Jack Beeson; MUSIC: Jack Beeson; DIRECTION: Charles Meryon; MUSICAL DIRECTION: Richard Marshall; PRODUCER: Center for Contemporary Opera

CAST—Patricia Dell (Mrs. Guglielmo Stevenson)

SOURCE—Lucille Fletcher's 1943 radio play *Sorry, Wrong Number*.

The action occurs in Mrs. Stevenson's home in Manhattan sometime during the 1940s.

The opera was presented in one act.

NOTES—Lucille Fletcher's successful murder mystery *Sorry, Wrong Number* was first presented as a radio play on May 25, 1943, with Agnes Moorhead creating the role of the unlucky Mrs. Stevenson. The story was later expanded for a 1948 film version which starred Barbara Stanwyck, who earned an Academy Award nomination for her performance as the murder victim. The world premiere of Jack Beeson's operatic version was presented at Hunter College in 1999.

The story dealt with a rich hypochondriac who is all alone in her Manhattan townhouse. When the wires of her phone are briefly crossed with another party, she overhears two men planning a murder which is to take place later in the evening. Slowly but surely, she realizes she's the intended victim, but by then it's too late to save herself.

In reviewing the premiere for the *New York Times*, Anthony Tommasini found the 40-minute opera's dramatic pacing "economical and sure" and liked the musical "evocations of dial tones and busy signals." He found the music "grounded in tonality but spiked with dissonance," but overall felt the score just skimmed the surface of the mystery.

The opera included eight minor characters, including telephone company staff and of course the murderer himself.

The opera was presented on a double bill with a revival of Elie Siegmeister's *Angel Levine* (see entry).

1507 Souvenir. "A Fantasia on the Life of Florence Foster Jenkins." THEATRE: The Theatre at Saint Peter's Church/The York Theatre Company; OPENING DATE: December 1, 2004; PERFORMANCES: 52; PLAY: Stephen Temperley; DIRECTION: Vivian Matalon; SCENERY: R. Michael Miller; COSTUMES: Tracy Christiansen; LIGHTING: Ann G. Wrightson; PRODUCERS: York Theatre Company (James Morgan, Artistic Director) in association with Ted Snowdon

CAST—Judy Kaye (Florence Foster Jenkins), Jack F. Lee (Cosme McMoon)

The action occurs in a supper club in Greenwich Village in 1964, returning in time to 1932 through the 1940s.

The play with music was presented in two acts.

NOTES—*Souvenir* was based on the life of Florence Foster Jenkins (1868-1944), who was portrayed by Judy Kaye in the Off Broadway musical. Convinced she had a great singing voice, Jenkins, a wealthy New York socialite, performed in public (including a sold-out house at Carnegie Hall on October 25, 1944, just a few weeks before her death), blissfully unaware that audiences were laughing at her and were not attending in order to appreciate her art. The work, a self-styled "fantasia" set in a Greenwich Village supper club twenty years after Jenkins' death, centered around Jenkins' former accompanist Cosme McMoon and his reminiscences about her.

The work didn't laugh at Jenkins. Instead, Stephen Temperley's play with music created a poignant and touching portrait of a deluded woman who nonetheless found fulfillment in the attainment of her dream (what her audiences heard was "one thing," but what Jenkins heard "was something else"). The play included a few songs, such as "Stardust" (lyric by Mitchell Parish, music by Hoagy Carmichael); "One for My Baby" (from the 1943 film *The Sky's the Limit*; lyric by Johnny Mercer, music by Harold Arlen); "Crazy Rhythm" (*Here's Howe*, 1928; lyric by Irving Caesar, music by Joseph Meyer and Roger Wolfe Kahn); "Guess I'll Hang My Tears Out to Dry" (from the 1944 musical *Glad To See You!*, which closed during its pre-Broadway tryout; lyric by Sammy Cahn, music by Jule Styne); "It All Depends on You" (lyric by B.G. [Buddy] DeSylva and Lew Brown, music by Ray Henderson; interpolated into *Big Boy*, 1925); "Violets for Your Furs" (lyric by Tom Adair, music by Matt Dennis); and "Praise the Lord and Pass the Ammunition" (lyric and music by Frank Loesser). With Judy Kaye reprising her role as Jenkins, *Souvenir* opened on Broadway at the Lyceum Theatre on October 10, 2005, and played for sixty-eight performances. (For the Off Broadway production, Cosme McMoon was performed by Jack F. Lee; for Broadway, Donald Corren.)

The script was published by Dramatists Play Service, Inc., in 2006.

In September 2005, Peter Quilter's *Glorious*, another play about Jenkins, opened in London. In 1962, Jenkins had been spoofed (as "Mme. Jenkins Foster") in the adult puppet musical revue *Les Poupees de Paris* (with the pre-recorded voice of Edie Adams); see entry.

1508 Space Trek. THEATRE: Chelsea Playhouse; OPENING DATE: February 16, 1997; PERFORMANCES: 28; BOOK: Mark Lipitz; LYRICS: Rick Crom; MUSIC: Rick Crom; DIRECTION: Vincent Sassone; Mic McCormack, Assistant Director; CHOREOGRAPHY: Karen Molnar; SCENERY: William F. Moser; COSTUMES: Carol Brys; LIGHTING: Jason Livingston; MUSICAL DIRECTION: John Bowen; PRODUCERS: Joyce M. Sarner in association with Spectrum Stage

CAST—Stephanie Jean (Ensign Bambi), Billy Sharpe (Chief Engineer Sloshy), Adam Wald (Ensign Chicks-Love), Jason Hayes (Captain Slim Quirk), Shawn Sears (Mr. Schlock), Michelle Merring (Lieutenant Yomama), Randy Lake (Dr. Moans), Hank Jacobs (Captain Christian Spike)

The action occurs on board the space ship *Merchandise.*

The musical was presented in one act.

MUSICAL NUMBERS—Opening Sequence (Jason Hayes, Crew): "Captain of the Ship" (Jason Hayes, Crew), "Shoulda Been, Coulda Been Mine" (Hank Jacobs), "The Ballad of Happy Planet" (Billy Sharpe), "Hello, Boys" (Hank Jacobs, Jason Hayes, Billy Sharpe, Randy Lake, Adam Wald, Shawn Sears), "Shoulda Been, Coulda Been Mine" (reprise) (Hank Jacobs), "The Problem with Us" (Jason Hayes, Michelle Merring), "Ensigns' Lament" (Stephanie Jean, Adam Wald), "Panic on a Planet" (Company), "Amour Time" (Company), "To Be a Captain" (Shawn Sears), "Brain Drain" (Randy Lake, Shawn Sears), "To Be a Captain (Continued)" (Hank Jacobs, Jason Hayes), "Spike's Turn" (Jason Hayes, Crew), "Got to Get a Life" (Jason Hayes, Crew), "Captain of the Ship" (reprise/finale) (Company)

NOTES—*Space Trek*, an amiable-sounding spoof of the *Star Trek* television and film franchise, was way behind the curve; the heyday of *Star Trek*-mania had long passed. The musical, which took place on the space ship *Merchandise*, was one of many science-fiction spoofs which bombed during the era.

1509 Sparrow in Flight. THEATRE: AMAS Repertory Theatre; OPENING DATE: November 2, 1978; PERFORMANCES: 12; PLAY: Charles Fuller; DIRECTION: Dean Irby; CHOREOGRAPHY: Bernard Johnson; SCENERY: Michael Meadows; COSTUMES: Bernard Johnson; LIGHTING: Paul Sullivan; MUSICAL DIRECTION: Larry Garner; PRODUCER: AMAS Repertory Theatre (Rosetta LeNoire, Founder and Artistic Director)

CAST—Ethel Ayer, Charles Brown, Charles "CB" Murray, John Martin Green, Don Paul, Amy Pivar, Kevin John Gee, Troi C. Jackson, Michelle Beteta, Cathy Orum, Pauletta Pearson, Robert Ray, James Moody, Fran Salisbury, Sandra Phillips, Lillette Harris-Jekins, William "Gregg" Hunter, Mary Louise

NOTES—Based on a concept by Rosetta LeNoire, *Sparrow in Flight* was a tribute to the legendary Ethel Waters (1896-1977); Waters' biography, *His Eye Is on the Sparrow*, had been published in 1951. Waters' many Broadway appearances included Irving Berlin's *As Thousands Cheer* (1933), in which she introduced "Heat Wave" and "Suppertime." She also appeared in Carson McCullers' play *The Member of the Wedding* (1950), and reprised her role for the 1952 film version. Earlier, in 1929, she had introduced "Am I Blue?" in the film *On with the Show*.

Waters and LeNoire had both performed the role of Petunia in *Cabin in the Sky* (see entry for the 1964 Off Broadway revival), Waters in both the original 1940 Broadway production and 1943 film version, and LeNoire in the Off Broadway revival. For the stage version, Waters introduced such songs as "Taking a Chance on Love," and for the film version introduced "Happiness Is Just a Thing Called Joe."

Richard Eder in the *New York Times* felt the evening was too "sketchy," and was less a show than a "blueprint" for one. He reported the evening included standards associated with Waters (such as "Am I Blue?"), and offered only one new song, a "lovely, lilting" title number by Johnny Brandon. Two years after the opening of the Off Off Broadway production of *Sparrow in Flight*, librettist Charles Fuller wrote the powerful Pulitzer Prize-winning play *A Soldier's Play*, which premiered Off Broadway at Theatre Four on November 20, 1981, and played for 468 performances. In 1982, AMAS presented another musical about Ethel Waters (see entry for *Miss Waters, to You*).

1510 The Special. "A New Musical." THEATRE: Jewish Repertory Theatre; OPENING DATE: October 19, 1985; PERFORMANCES: 27; BOOK: Mike Gutwillig; LYRICS: Mike Gutwillig; MUSIC: Galt MacDermot; DIRECTION: Ran Avni; CHOREOGRAPHY: Haila Strauss; SCENERY: Jeffrey Schneider; COSTUMES: Karen Hummel; LIGHTING: Dan Kinsley; MUSICAL DIRECTION: Galt MacDermot; PRODUCER: The Jewish Repertory Theatre (Ran Avni, Artistic Director; Edward M. Cohen, Associate Director)

CAST—Paul Ukena (Joe Rubinsky), Sam Stoneburner (Irving Levitt), Adam Heller (Hershie Levitt), Kenneth Bridges (Jacques Boucher), Patricia Ben Peterson (Manon Boucher), Simon Jutras (Claude Boucher), Olga Merediz (Therese Boucher), Annie Korzen (Esther Levitt), Mina Bern (Mollie Bernstein), Steve Sterner (Rabbi Wiser), Raymond Murcell (Pere LeBeau)

The action occurs in Montreal between March and August 1980.

The musical was presented in two acts.

ACT ONE—"What's So Special About a Special?" (Raymond Murcell, Steve Sterner, Company), "The Situation in Quebec" (Sam Stoneburner), "There Is an Old Tradition" (Patricia Ben Peterson), "Quebec Qui!" (Simon Jutras, Kenneth Bridges), "Non Merci!" (Olga Merediz), "Be a Mensch!" (Paul Ukena), "Longue Vie a la Famille!" (Kenneth Bridges, Olga Merediz), "Cote Saint-Jacques" (Adam Heller), "Will You Be My Yvette?" (Adam Heller, Patricia Ben Peterson), "Married Yet!" (Annie Korzen), "We Say OUI!" (Adam Heller, Patricia Ben Peterson, Simon Jutras), "J'pas Capable!" (Company)

ACT TWO—"A Ruling Is a Ruling" (Paul Ukena, Company), "It Isn't Easy to Be a Jew" (Steve Sterner), "Alleluia, Allelulia" (Raymond Murcell, Kenneth Bridges, Olga Merediz), "On My Heart" (Patricia Ben Peterson), "What Makes the Special Special" (Paul Ukena, Raymond Murcell, Steve Sterner), "A Special!" (Kenneth Bridges, Company), "What Will People Think?" (Kenneth Bridges, Annie Korzen, Sam Stoneburner, Olga Merediz), "What Will People Think?" (reprise) (Patricia Ben Peterson), "I Don't Want That You Don't Want" (Simon Jutras, Mina Bern), "Notre Pere" (Patricia Ben Peterson, Adam Heller, Company), "Shema" (Steve Sterner), "God's Favorite Choice" (Paul Ukena, Raymond

Murcell, Steve Sterner), "Raise a Glass to Love!" (Kenneth Bridges, Olga Meredíz, Annie Korzen), "Ess, Ess, Mein Kindt" (Mina Bern), "Swing Your Heart to le Bon Dieu" (Simon Jutras), Finale (Company), "A Special!" (reprise) (Company)

NOTES—A program note for Galt MacDermot's Off Off Broadway musical *The Special* indicated the inspiration for its setting came from a corner store/soda fountain/delicatessen in Montreal called Wilensky's, located there for more than fifty years. The program also noted that although Wilensky died in 1984, his legend and his "special" of the day live on.

Frank Rich in the *New York Times* reported the evening recalled *Abie's Irish Rose* in its romance between a Jewish boy and a Catholic girl (the two meet while having a "special" at the delicatessen), but noted the plot also dwelt on the Province of Quebec's 1980 separatist referendum. The two stories never quite jelled, and the amateurish book and "witless" lyrics didn't help, either. Further, because of the "hamminess" of the cast, Rich couldn't vouch that the deli was "strictly kosher." To make matters worse, Rich noted the direction all too often required the company to be on stage for "choral harmonizing," and the static staging was less *A Chorus Line* than it was "a receiving line." Yet for all this, Rich found one aspect of the evening worthy of praise: MacDermot's score, a "melodic flow" which included an "eclectic mix" of styles (such as folk music, soft rock, traditional Broadway, and calypso).

1511 Speed Gets the Poppys. "An Anti-Drug Musical Melodrama." THEATRE: Mercer-Brecht Theatre; OPENING DATE: July 25, 1972; PERFORMANCES: 7; BOOK: Lila Levant; LYRICS: Lila Levant and Lorenzo Fuller; MUSIC: Lorenzo Fuller; DIRECTION: Charles Abbott; CHOREOGRAPHY: Charles Abbott; SCENERY: Milton Duke; COSTUMES: Milton Duke; LIGHTING: Milton Duke; MUSICAL DIRECTION: Robert Esty; PRODUCER: Daffodil Productions

CAST—Robin Field (T.J. Worthyman), Edward Penn (Pendleton Poppy), Anita Keal (Priscilla Poppy), Randi Kallan (Polly Poppy), Joanna Myers (Pandy Poppy), Robert Browning (Smedley V. Speed), Raymond Cerabone (Sheriff)

The action occurs in and around the Poppys' farm in the 1890s.

The musical was presented in two acts.

ACT ONE—"What Is a Melodrama?" (Robin Field, Company), "Living Next Door to the Sun" (Edward Penn, Anita Keal, Randi Kallan, Joanna Myers), "Instant Magic" (Robert Browning), "Living Next Door to the Sun" (reprise) (Edward Penn, Anita Keal, Randi Kallan, Joanna Myers), "Caught" (Edward Penn, Anita Keal), "Whatever Happened to Tomorrow?" (Randi Kallan), "Take It from a Pal" (Robert Browning, Joanna Myers, Randi Kallan), "I'll Bring the Roses" (Robin Field, Randi Kallan), "Instant Magic" (reprise) (Robert Browning, Robin Field)

ACT TWO—"Speed Won't Get Me" (Robin Field), "He'll Bring the Roses" (reprise) (Randi Kallan), "What Real True Friends Are For" (Robin Field), "Try, Try Again" (Robin Field, Edward Penn, Anita Keal, Randi Kallan, Joanna Myers), "My Moustache Is Twitchin'" (Robert Browning), "An Old-Fashioned Chase Ballet" (Company), "Good Triumphs Over Evil" (Company)

NOTES—Using the framework of Victorian melodrama, *Speed Gets the Poppys* was an anti-drug musical for young people. Howard Taubman in the *New York Times* felt the Gay Nineties' "spearmint sermon" was a "pint-sized charmer" which provided a "healthy message ... about playing with fire." He praised the "sprightly" score, the "clever, pretty, candy-box set," and the "engaging" performers.

1512 A Spinning Tale. THEATRE: Playhouse 91; OPENING DATE: February 20, 1990; PERFORMANCES: 92; BOOK: C.E. Kemeny and A. Kemeny; LYRICS: C.E. Kemeny and A. Kemeny; MUSIC: C.E. Kemeny; DIRECTION: Jack Ross and C.E. Kemeny; CHOREOGRAPHY: Sally O'Shea; SCENERY: Mariner James Pezza; COSTUMES: Sandora Associates; LIGHTING: Kevin Connaughton; PRODUCER: Mariner James Pezza

CAST—Marianne Monroe (The Elf), Eric Ellisen (Prince Rupert), Ruth Lauricella (Page, Musette), George Lombardo (Sidney), David L. Jackins (Ralph), Sean Lawless (Henry), Karen Bianchini (Melinda), Sherrylee Dickinson (Queen Regina), Sally O'Shea (Yvette), Robert Puleo (King Maximillian)

SOURCE—The Brothers Grimm fairy tale "Rumpelstiltskin."

The musical was presented in two acts.

ACT ONE—"A Spinning Tale"/"Fall Under the Spell" (Company), "The Last Elf Aria" (Marianne Monroe), "Another Life" (Karen Bianchini, Eric Ellisen, Ruth Lauricella, Marianne Monroe), "Remember the Time" (Karen Bianchini, David L. Jackins, George Lombardo, Sean Lawless), "Hello Stranger!" (Sally O'Shea, Ruth Lauricella, George Lombardo, Sean Lawless, David L. Jackins), "Straw Into Gold" (Robert Puleo), "Locked and Secluded" (Karen Bianchini), "Spin! Spin! Spin!" (Marianne Monroe, Karen Bianchini, Sprites), "Gold! Gold!"/"I Have a Little Secret" (Robert Puleo, Sherrylee Dickinson, Karen Bianchini, Eric Ellisen), "Together as One" (Karen Bianchini, Eric Ellisen), "The Shadow" (Karen Bianchini, Marianne Monroe)

ACT TWO—"What's in a Name?" (George Lombardo, David L. Jackins, Sean Lawless, Sally O'Shea, Ruth Lauricella), "Precious to Me" (Karen Bianchini), "Never Met a Man I Didn't Like" (Sherrylee Dickinson, Sally O'Shea, Ruth Lauricella), "Ah, Sweet Youth!" (Robert Puleo), "Trust Me Tango" (Sally O'Shea, George Lombardo), "Another Life" (reprise) (Marianne Monroe), Finale: "You Get What You Give"/"Spin! Spin! Spin!" (reprise) (Company)

NOTES—Previously produced for a tour of theatres in Connecticut, *A Spinning Tale* was based on the fairy tale "Rumpelstiltskin"; for another musical version based on the Brothers Grimm story, see entry for *Half-Past Wednesday* (1962).

Stephen Holden in the *New York Times* quoted the musical's press release, which stated the musical was "targeted for an adult audience but guaranteed to entertain children." But Holden felt a more factual statement would be that the musical was "targeted for a children's audience and not guaranteed to entertain adults." He noted that for a children's musical, the evening was "slightly better than average," but felt the cast was "uneven" and the score "strictly formula fare."

1513 The Spitfire Grill. THEATRE: The Duke on 42nd Street Theatre; OPENING DATE: October 2, 2001; PERFORMANCES: 15; BOOK: James Valcq and Fred Alley; LYRICS: Fred Alley; MUSIC: James Valcq; DIRECTION: David Saint; CHOREOGRAPHY: Luis Perez; SCENERY: Michael Anania; COSTUMES: Theoni V. Aldredge; LIGHTING: Howell Binkley; MUSICAL DIRECTION: Andrew Wilder; PRODUCERS: Playwrights Horizons (Tim Sanford, Artistic Director; Leslie Marcus, Managing Director; William Russo, General Manager); Ira Weitzman, Associate Producer

CAST—Garrett Long (Percy Talbott), Steven Pasquale (Sheriff Joe Sutter), Phyllis Somerville (Hannah Ferguson), Armand Schultz (Caleb Thorpre), Mary Gordon Murray (Effy Krayneck), Liz Callaway (Shelby Thorpe), Stephen Sinclair (The Visitor)

SOURCE—The 1996 film *The Spitfire Grill* (screenplay and direction by Lee David Zlotoff)

The action occurs in rural Wisconsin in the recent past.

The musical was presented in two acts.

ACT ONE—"A Ring Around the Moon" (Garrett Long), "Something's Cooking at the Spitfire Grill" (Company), "Coffee Cups and Gossip" (Garrett Long), "Out of the Frying Pan" (Garrett Long), "Hannah Had a Son" (Liz Callaway), "When Hope Goes" (Liz Callaway), "Ice and Snow" (Armand Schultz, Steven Pasquale, Mary Gordon Murray), "Shelby's Ad" (Liz Callaway), "The Colors of Paradise" (Garrett Long, Liz Callaway), "Digging Stone" (Armand Schultz), "This Wide Woods" (Steven Pasquale, Garrett Long), "Forgotten Lullaby" (Phyllis Somerville), "Shoot the Moon" (Phyllis Somerville, Company)

ACT TWO—"Come Alive Again" (Phyllis Somerville, Company), "Forest for the Trees" (Steven Pasquale), "Wild Bird" (Liz Callaway), "Sunrise" (Garrett Long), "Shine" (Garrett Long), "Way Back Home" (Phyllis Somerville), Finale (Company)

NOTES—Based on the 1996 film of the same name, *The Spitfire Grill* told the story of an ex-convict who must adjust to her new life as a waitress in a small town.

Ben Brantley in the *New York Times* felt the musical was so "clean-cut" it made *The Music Man* look "dark and twisted." The evening's "wholesomeness" led to facile plot resolutions, characters of whom even the "meanest" are really good, and "shiny" songs which "serve as friendly signposts" in the "spiritual development" of the characters. But he praised the "gentle American vernacular charm" of the music and the "ease and simplicity" of the lyrics. The musical had been previously produced at the George Street Playhouse, New Brunswick, New Jersey, in November 2000. During New York previews, "Never Heal" was deleted and replaced by "Forgotten Lullaby." The script was published by Samuel French, Inc., in 2002, and the cast recording was released by Triangle Road Records (CD # 2836).

Phyllis Somerville played Hannah, the owner of the Spitfire Grill; her "June Allyson" in *Over Here!* (1974) was one of the guilty pleasures of 1970s musicals.

1514 Splendora. THEATRE: The American Place Theatre; OPENING DATE: November 9, 1995; PERFORMANCES: 14; BOOK: Peter Webb; LYRICS: Mark Campbell; MUSIC: Stephen Hoffman; DIRECTION: Jack Hofsiss; CHOREOGRAPHY: Robert La Fosse; SCENERY: Eduardo Sicangco; COSTUMES: William Ivey Long; LIGHTING: Richard Nelson; MUSICAL DIRECTION: Sariva Goetz; PRODUCER: Bay Street Theatre (Norman Kline, General Manager; Murphy Davis, Producer; Stephen Hamilton, Executive Director; Sybil Christopher and Emma Walton, Artistic Directors)

CAST—Evalyn Baron (Sue Ella Lightfoot), KT Sullivan (Maga Dell Spivy), Laura Kenyon (Zeda Earl Goodrich), Kathy Robinson (Agnes Pullen [A.P.]), Susan Rush (Lucille Monroe), Nancy Johnston (Jessica Gatewood), Michael Moore (Timothy John Coldridge), Ken Krugman (Brother Leggett)

SOURCE—The 1978 novel *Splendora* by Edward Swift.

The action occurs "not so long ago" in Splendora, a small town in east Texas.

The musical was presented in two acts.

ACT ONE—"In Our Hearts" (KT Sullivan, Laura Kenyon, Kathy Robinson, Susan Rush, Evalyn Baron), "How Like Heaven" (Nancy Johnston, Michael Moore), "Don't Get Me Started" (Evalyn Baron), "Pretty Boy" (Susan Rush, Laura Kenyon, Kathy Robinson), "Home"/"Say Goodnight" (Michael Moore, Nancy Johnston), "Gossip I: Poor Sad Thing..." (Susan Rush, Laura Kenyon, Kathy

Robinson), "A Hymn to Her" (Michael Moore), "Gossip II: Up at Dawn..." (Susan Rush, Laura Kenyon, Kathy Robinson), "In Small and Simple Ways" (Ken Krugman), "Gossip III: Warms My Soul..." (Susan Rush, Laura Kenyon, Kathy Robinson, KT Sullivan), "Dear Heart" (Nancy Johnston, Ken Krugman), "How Little I Know" (Ken Krugman), "Had He Kissed Me Tonight" (Nancy Johnston), "If He Knew" (Michael Moore), "Good Hearts, Rejoice" (KT Sullivan, Laura Kenyon, Kathy Robinson, Susan Rush), "What Is, Ain't" (Evalyn Baron)

ACT TWO—"Promise Me One Thing" (Nancy Johnston, Ken Krugman, Michael Moore), "I Got Faith in You" (Evalyn Baron, Michael Moore), "All the Time in the World" (Michael Moore, Nancy Johnston, Ken Krugman), "A Man Named Dewey" (KT Sullivan), "I Am Beauty" (Kathy Robinson), "Don't Get Me Started" (reprise) (Evalyn Baron), "Miss Crepe Myrtle" (Laura Kenyon, Kathy Robinson, Susan Rush, KT Sullivan), "Grateful" (Michael Moore), "My Name Is Timothy John" (Michael Moore, Laura Kenyon, Kathy Robinson, Susan Rush, KT Sullivan), "In Our Hearts" (reprise) (KT Sullivan, Laura Kenyon, Kathy Robinson, Susan Rush, Evalyn Baron)

NOTES—*Splendora* dealt with Timothy John Coldridge, who returns to his hometown of Splendora, Texas, after fifteen years. Also new in town is Jessica Gatewood, who runs the county bookmobile and has charmed all the ladies of the town with her quaint Victorian dress and ways. It turns out that Timothy John and Jessica are the same person (both characters were performed by an actor and an actress); that Brother Leggett, Splendora's assistant pastor, has fallen in love with Jessica; and that Jessica (that is, Timothy John) has fallen in love with Leggett. Timothy John finally rids himself of his Jessica persona, and Leggett comes to realize he loves Timothy John. Encouraged by Sue Ella Lightfoot, the two men run off together. Meanwhile, the townsfolk are none the wiser, and they recall in chorus the memory of Jessica, who "put the splendor back in Splendora."

Ben Brantley in the *New York Times* felt the original novel's welcome touches of malice were traded for "blatant sentimentality," and thus the musical seemed "pale, slender and determinedly quaint." He noted the musical was "Sondheim-tinted" in the sense that some songs were reminiscent of various pastiche elements in *A Little Night Music* and *Sweeney Todd/The Demon Barber of Fleet Street*. He indicated the trios (for Jessica, Timothy John, and Leggett) glimmered with "haunting intricacy," and suggested that within *Splendora* there was a "sophisticated" musical which needed more development. On February 8, 2000, the musical was revived Off Off Broadway at the Chelsea Playhouse.

The script was published by Dramatists Play Service, Inc., in 1998.

1515 Spring Awakening. THEATRE: Atlantic Theatre Company; OPENING DATE: June 15, 2006; PERFORMANCES: 54; BOOK: Steven Sater; LYRICS: Steven Sater; MUSIC: Duncan Sheik; DIRECTION: Michael Mayer; CHOREOGRAPHY: Bill T. Jones; SCENERY: Christine Jones; COSTUMES: Susan Hilferty; LIGHTING: Kevin Adams; MUSICAL DIRECTION: Kimberly Grigsby; PRODUCERS: Atlantic Theatre Company (Neil Pepe, Artistic Director; Andrew D. Hamingson, Managing Director) in association with Tom Hulce and Ira Pittelman

CAST—Lea Michele (Wendla), Mary McCann (The Adult Women), Lilli Cooper (Martha), Lauren Pritchard (Ilse), Phoebe Strole (Anna), Remy Zaken (Thea), Frank Wood (The Adult Men), Brian Charles Johnson (Otto, Reformatory Student), Jonathan B. Wright (Handschen,c Reformatory Student), Gideon Glick (Ernst, Reformatory Student), Skylar Astin (Georg, Reformatory Student), John Gallagher, Jr. (Moritz), Jonathan Groff (Mechior)

SOURCE—The 1891 play *Spring Awakening* by Frank Wedekind.

The action occurs in a provincial German town in the 1890s.

The musical was presented in two acts (songs weren't listed in the Off Broadway program; the list below is from the Broadway production).

ACT ONE—"Mama Who Bore Me" (Lea Michele), "Mama Who Bore Me" (reprise) (Girls), "All That's Known" (Jonathan Groff), "The Bitch of Living" (John Gallagher, Jr., with Boys), "My Junk" (Girls and Boys), "Touch Me" (Boys and Girls), "The Word of Your Body" (Lea Michele, Jonathan Groff), "The Dark I Know Well" (Lilli Cooper, Lauren Pritchard, with Boys), "And Then There Were None" (John Gallagher, Jr., with Boys), "The Mirror-Blue Night" (Jonathan Groff, with Boys), "I Believe" (Boys and Girls)

ACT TWO—"The Guilty Ones" (Lea Michele, Jonathan Groff, with Boys and Girls), "Don't Do Sadness" (John Gallagher, Jr.), "Blue Wind" (Lauren Pritchard), "Left Behind" (Jonathan Groff), "Totally Fucked" (Jonathan Groff, with Full Company), "The Word of Your Body" (reprise) (Jonathan B. Wright, Gideon Glick, with Boys and Girls), "Whispering" (Lea Michele), "Those You've Known" (John Gallagher, Jr., Lea Michele, Jonathan Groff), "The Song of Purple Summer" (Company)

NOTES—Based on Frank Wedekind's 1891 play of the same name, *Spring Awakening* dealt with sexual awakening among adolescents. While the musical retained the period of the 1890s, the characters had the "attitude" (and the language) of the present, and for some the juxtaposition of the two eras didn't quite work. Like *Grey Gardens* (see entry) which had opened three months earlier, the musical's buzz clearly indicated a Broadway run was inevitable, and, indeed, the musical opened at the Eugene O'Neill Theatre on December 10, 2006, for 859 performances. In 2007, the musical won eight Tony Awards, including Best Musical, Best Book, Best Score, Best Direction, Best Choreography, and Best Featured Actor in a Musical (John Gallagher, Jr.).

The Broadway cast album was released by Decca Broadway Records (CD # B0008020-02) and came with a parental advisory. The script was published by Theatre Communications Group in 2007. Further, *Spring Awakening: In the Flesh*, an "official companion" to the musical which includes the "unabridged" libretto, was published by Simon Spotlight Entertainment in 2008. As of this writing, a film version of the musical is in the offing (one of its adaptors will be Steven Sater).

1516 Squonk. "Bigsmorgasbordwunderwerk." THEATRE: Performance Space 122; OPENING DATE: June 11, 1999; PERFORMANCES: 61; "BOOK, MUSIC, MACHINERY, AND DECORATION" BY: Squonk (Jackie Dempsey, Jana Losey, Steve O'Hearn, Kevin Kornick, and T. Weldon Anderson); DIRECTION: Tom Diamond; MOVEMENT DIRECTION: Jana Losey; LIGHTING: Tim Saternow; PRODUCERS: William Repicci and Michael Minichiello; Rare Gem Productions, Michael Stoller, Cookie Centracco, and Lauren Doll, Associate Producers

CAST—Squonk (Jackie Dempsey, Jana Losey, Steve O'Hearn, Kevin Kornick, and T. Weldon Anderson)

NOTES—Like *Thwak* (see entry) which opened four days earlier, *Squonk* was a performance piece described in *The Best Plays of 1999-2000* as a "whimsical multimedia assortment of images and music." Ben Brantley in the *New York Times* said the "charmingly thought-free diversion" would sink you if you tried to make sense of it. The work created its "own little reality warp" and weaved music into the presentation as if sound "were the mother of all sensory stimuli" (and he noted the score was "New Age with a dark side"). He also commented that the décor was reminiscent of a "particularly kitschy restaurant in Little Italy after an earthquake." The revue transferred to Broadway at the Helen Hayes Theatre on February 29, 2000. While the critics had been charmed by the piece in its downtown version, they were less than enthusiastic with the uptown edition, and so the revue squonked out after just thirty-two performances.

1517 Stag Movie. "A New Musical Comedy." THEATRE: Gate Theatre; OPENING DATE: January 3, 1971; PERFORMANCES: 88; BOOK: David Newburge; LYRICS: David Newburge; MUSIC: Jacques Urbont; DIRECTION: Bernard Barrow; CHOREOGRAPHY: Doug Rogers; SCENERY: David Chapman; COSTUMES: David Toser; LIGHTING: David Chapman; MUSICAL DIRECTION: Jacques Urbont; PRODUCERS: Robert L. Steele in association with the Erani Corporation

CAST—Hy Anzell (Mike Rosenthal), Stan Weist (Marty Strauss), Renata Mannhardt (Tanya Taranovna), Tod Miller (Tommy Tucker), Brad Sullivan (Rip Cord), Adrienne Barbeau (Cookie Kovac), Moose Matthews (Arthur Jensen), Josip Elic (Cap), Shirl Bernheim (Maid)

The action occurs in a motel room near Kennedy Airport at the present time.

The musical was presented in one act.

MUSICAL NUMBERS—"Stag Movie" (Stan Weist, Hy Anzell), "Looking at the Sun" (Brad Sullivan), "I Want More Out of Life Than This" (Adrienne Barbeau, Brad Sullivan) "Grocery Boy" (Tod Miller), "Splendor in the Grass" (Tod Miller, Adrienne Barbeau), "Splendor in the Grass Ballet" (Tod Miller, Adrienne Barbeau), "It's So Good" (Adrienne Barbeau, Tod Miller), "Get in Line" (Shirl Bernheim), "Try a Trio" (Brad Sullivan, Adrienne Barbeau, Tod Miller), "Get Your Rocks Off Rock" (Brad Sullivan, Adrienne Barbeau, Tod Miller), "We Came Together" (Brad Sullivan, Adrienne Barbeau, Tod Miller), Finale (Company)

NOTES—The musical dealt with the filming of a porn movie in a motel room near Kennedy Airport. Clive Barnes in the *New York Times* reported that he found the goings-on "as appetizing and as erotic as cold mulligatawny soup laced with frozen porridge." He noted that the most diverting aspect of the evening was an ad-hoc audience demonstration by members of the Gay Liberation Front. A later article in the *Times* (by one of the musical's investors) indicated that in order to paper the house, members of the group had been invited to a performance (the one Barnes attended). But when the group became offended by the musical's attitude towards gays, they began hissing and shouting for almost thirty minutes, ultimately bringing the performance to a temporary halt until such time as the police were called to escort them from the theatre.

1518 Staggerlee. "A Rhythm and Blues Musical." THEATRE: Second Avenue Theatre; OPENING DATE: March 18, 1987; PERFORMANCES: 118; BOOK: Vernel Bagneris; LYRICS: Allen Toussaint; additional lyrics by Vernel Bagneris; MUSIC: Allen Toussaint; DIRECTION: Vernel Bagneris; CHOREOGRAPHY: Pepsi Bethel; SCENERY: Akira Yoshimura; COSTUMES: JoAnn Clevenger; LIGHTING: Allen Lee Hughes; MUSICAL DIRECTION: Allen Toussaint; PRODUCERS: John H. Williams, Ruth Mieszkuc, The Program Development Company, and The Encore A Partnership; Kirk D'Amico, Associate Producer

CAST—Vernel Bagneris (Staggerlee), Juanita Brooks (Zelita), RUTH BROWN (Elenora), Marva Hicks (June), Reginald Veljohnson (Tiny), Carol Sutton (Bertha Ann), Angeles Echols (Dolores), Christie Gaudet (Andrea), Alfred Bruce Bradley (Peat), Kevin Ramsey (Piano Player, Policeman), Bernard J. Marsh (Bone)

The action occurs at a local corner bar in the South during the late 1950s.

The musical was presented in two acts.

ACT ONE—"Iko Iko" (traditional) (Reginald Veljohnson, Company) "Night People" (lyric and music by Alan Toussaint) ('Vocalist,' Vernel Bagneris, Company), "Staggerlee" (traditional) (Juanita Brooks, Company), "Discontented Blues" (lyric by Vernel Bagneris, music by Alan Toussaint) (Ruth Brown), "With You in Mind" (lyric and music by Alan Toussaint) ('Vocalist,' Vernel Bagneris, Marva Hicks), "Big Chief" (traditional) (Reginald Veljohnson, Company), "Mardi Gras Time" (lyric by Vernel Bagneris, music by Alan Toussaint) (Vernel Bagneris, Boys), "A Pimp Like That" (lyric by Vernel Bagneris, music by Alan Toussaint) (Ruth Brown, Reginald Veljohnson, Juanita Brooks), "You Knew I Was No Good" (lyric by Vernel Bagneris, music by Alan Toussaint) (Carol Sutton, Girls), "Lover of Love" (lyric and music by Alan Toussaint) (Vernel Bagneris), "You Knew I Was No Good" (reprise) (lyric by Vernel Bagneris, music by Alan Toussaint) (Company), "Saved by Grace" (lyric and music by Alan Toussaint) (Juanita Brooks, Company)

ACT TWO—Entr'acte: "Happy Time" (lyric and music by Alan Toussaint) (Band), "Victims of the Darkness" (lyric and music by Alan Toussaint) ('Vocalist,' Vernel Bagneris, Boys), "Devil's Disguise" (lyric by Vernel Bagneris, music by Alan Toussaint) (Marva Hicks, Reginald Veljohnson, Vernel Bagneris, Alfred Bruce Bradley, Carol Sutton, Christie Gaudet), "One Monkey Don't Stop No Show" (lyric and music by Alan Toussaint) (Carol Sutton, Vernel Bagneris), "Ruler of My Heart" (lyric and music by Alan Toussaint) (Marva Hicks), "Going Down Slowly" (lyric and music by Alan Toussaint) (Vernel Bagneris, Boys), "Lighting a Candle" (lyric by Vernel Bagneris, music by Alan Toussaint) (Ruth Brown), "Knocking Myself Out" (traditional) (Juanita Brooks), "We're Gonna Do It Good" (lyric and music by Alan Toussaint) (Marva Hicks), "Let's Live It Up" (lyric and music by Alan Toussaint) (Ruth Brown), "Big Chief" (reprise) (traditional) (Company)

NOTES—*Staggerlee* told the story of a young woman (Juanita Brooks) who goes against the wishes of her mother (Ruth Brown) and thus becomes involved with a man wanted for murder (Staggerlee, played by Vernel Bagneris).

Mel Gussow in the *New York Times* said the book was so "inchoate" it almost made the book of *Starlight Express* seem "coherent." But the score (a mixture of old and new songs) and the cast (especially Ruth Brown) were enjoyable; as for the physical production, Gussow noted it looked as if it had recently weathered "a long tour on the road."

During previews, the role of "Silk" (played by Leon Williams, who also performed the role of the policeman) was eliminated, and so Kevin Ramsey, who played the role of the piano player, also played the role of the policeman. The program indicated that a character described as the "Vocalist" sang three numbers, but failed to identify the performer's name.

Although Vernel Bagneris' program bio for *Further Mo'* (1990; see entry) mentioned that a screenplay of *Staggerlee* was in preparation, a film version never materialized.

1519 Standup Shakespeare. "A Motley Musical." THEATRE: Theatre 890; OPENING DATE: April 4, 1987; PERFORMANCES: 2; WORDS: William Shakespeare; MUSIC: Ray Leslee; DIRECTION: Mike Nichols; SCENERY: John Arnone; COSTUMES: Cynthia O'Neal; LIGHTING: Mitchell Bogard; MUSICAL DIRECTION: Ray Leslee; PRODUCER: The Shubert Organization

CAST—Taborah Johnson, Kenneth Welsh, Thomas Young, Jack Bashkow, Marshall Coid, Dean Johnson, Ray Leslee

The action occurs Will's Place, a pub.

The revue was presented in two acts.

ACT ONE—"Love Is Perjured Everywhere" (from *Romeo and Juliet*) (Marshall Coid, Thomas Young, Taborah Johnson), "Come Live with Me" (Thomas Young), "Make Me a Willow Cabin" (Taborah Johnson), "Take, Oh Take" (*Measure for Measure*) (Thomas Young), "I Will Tarry" (Kenneth Welsh), "I Do Love Thee" (*A Midsummer Night's Dream*) (Kenneth Welsh), "The Chain Song" (Taborah Johnson), "O Mistress Mine" (*Twelfth Night*) (Thomas Young), "I to the World" (*The Comedy of Errors*) (Company)

ACT TWO—"When in Disgrace" (Sonnet 29) (Thomas Young), "I Know a Bank" (*A Midsummer Night's Dream*) (Ray Leslee), "Will She Not Come Again" (Thomas Young, Ray Leslee, Kenneth Welsh), "Let Me Not to the Marriage of True Minds" (Thomas Young, Kenneth Welsh), "Some Glory in Their Birth" (Thomas Young), "That Time of Year" (Kenneth Welsh), "Shall I Compare Thee" (Sonnet 18) (Taborah Johnson), "I Do Love Thee" (*A Midsummer Night's Dream*) (Thomas Young), "Love Is Perjured Everywhere" (reprise) (*Romeo and Juliet*) (Company)

NOTES—The program noted that every word ("without exception") in *Standup Shakespeare* was written by Shakespeare. Mel Gussow in the *New York Times* found the evening (which was conceived by composer Ray Leslee and directed by Mike Nichols) "felicitous," but noted the "self-conscious attempt" to spoof Shakespeare by "cavalierly" taking lines from his plays and then "purloining" them to Leslee's own purposes was sometimes "clever" but also "too whimsical for words." While Gussow thus had reservations about the "so-called book," he praised Leslee's "apt" and often jazzy score.

Gussow also noted that Shakespeare'a lyrics were "at least the equal" of T.S. Eliot, and found Shakespeare's subject (love) "more sustaining" than Eliot's (cats).

The revue had been earlier produced Off Off Broadway at the West Bank Café on April 23, 1984, and on March 18, 1994, a production of the revue at the Folger Shakespeare Library in Washington, D.C., was recorded by Bard Records (CD # BDCD-1-9509); the performers were Alison Fraser, David Margulies, and Thomas Young (the latter from the original 1987 cast), and the musicians included composer Ray Leslee. This production included about half of the material heard in New York; among the songs added for the new production were "St. Valentine's Day" (*Hamlet*), "Shallow Rivers" (*The Merry Wives of Windsor*), and "Sigh No More" (*Much Ado About Nothing*). The script of *Standup Shakespeare* was published by Dramatists Play Service, Inc., in 1998.

1520 Star Treatment. THEATRE: Lion Theatre; OPENING DATE: February 20, 1980; PERFORMANCES: 39; PLAY: Jack Heifner; LYRICS: Janis Ian; MUSIC: Janis Ian; DIRECTION: Garland Wright; SCENERY: John Arnone; COSTUMES: Frances Miksits; LIGHTING: Frances Aronson; MUSICAL DIRECTION: David Lewis; PRODUCER: Lion Theatre Company (Gene Nye, Artistic Director; Eleanor Meglio, Producing Director)

CAST—June Gable (Elaine), David Lewis (Frank), Allan Carlsen (Bill), Conan McCarty (Michael), Olana (Thomas)

The action occurs at the present time in New York City.

The play was presented in two acts.

NOTES—The Off Off Broadway play *Star Treatment* included incidental songs by Janis Ian. The plot dealt with a singer (June Gable) and the men in her life. When her lover leaves her, she picks up a young man, and although he's "twice her size" (according to John Corry in the *New York Times*) and probably less than half her age, Corry noted he seemed in "immediate danger of rape." Corry observed that Gable's character was "predatory" and "aggressive and manic," and said when her old lover walks in on her and her young pick-up, the audience might feel the two men were better suited to each other than to her. It appears that during previews the role of Bill was performed by Richard Borg.

1521 Stardust. THEATRE: Theatre Off Park; OPENING DATE: November 11, 1986; PERFORMANCES: 59; LYRICS: Mitchell Parish; MUSIC: See song list for credits; DIRECTION: Albert Harris; CHOREOGRAPHY: Patrice Soriero; SCENERY: David Jenkins; COSTUMES: Mardi Philips; LIGHTING: Ken Billington; MUSICAL DIRECTION: James Raitt; PRODUCER: Theatre Off Park (Bertha Lewis, Producing Director; Albert Harris, Artistic Director; James Randolph, Managing Director)

CAST—Michele Bautier, Maureen Brennan, Kim Criswell, Andre DeShields, Jason Graae, Jim Walton

The revue was presented in two acts.

ACT ONE—"Carolina Rolling Stone" (music by Eleanor Young and Harry D. Squires) (Jason Graae, Company), "Riverboat Shuffle" (music by Hoagy Carmichael, Dick Voynow, and Irving Mills) (Andre DeShields, Company), "Sweet Lorraine" (music by Cliff Burwell) (Jim Walton), "Sentimental Gentleman from Georgia" (music by Frank Perkins) (Michele Bautier, Maureen Brennan, Kim Criswell), "One Morning in May" (music by Hoagy Carmichael) (Maureen Brennan), "Dixie After Dark" (music by Ben Oakland and Irving Mills) (Michele Bautier, Andre DeShields, Jim Walton), "Stairway to the Stars" (music by Matt Malnick and Frank Signorelli) (Kim Criswell), "My Topic of Conversation Is You" (music by J. Fred Coots) (Jason Graae, Maureen Brennan), "Sophisticated Lady" (music by Duke Ellington and Irving Mills) (Michele Bautier), "Wealthy, Shmelthy, as Long as You're Healthy" (music by Sammy Fain) (Jason Graae), "Hands Across the Table" (music by Jean Delettre) (Michele Bautier), "You're So Indifferent" (music by Sammy Fain) (Jason Graae), "It Happens to the Best of Friends" (music by Rube Bloom) (Kim Criswell), "I Would If I Could but I Can't" (music by Bing Crosby and Alan Grey) (Jim Walton), "The Scat Song" (music by Frank Perkins and Cab Calloway) (Andre DeShields, Maureen Brennan), "Sidewalks of Cuba" (music by Ben Oakland and Irving Mills) (Kim Criswell, Jason Graae), "Evenin'" (music by Harry White) (Michele Bautier), "Deep Purple" (music by Peter DeRose) (Andre DeShields, Company)

ACT TWO—Entr'acte (Orchestra), "Moonlight Serenade" (music by Glenn Miller) (Company), "Sophisticated Swing" (music by Will Hudson) (Kim Criswell, Company), "Midnight at the Onyx" (music by Will Hudson) (Andre DeShields, Company), "Stars Fell on Alabama" (music by Frank Perkins) (Jim Walton, Maureen Brennan), "Organ Grinder's Swing" (music by Irving Mills and Will Hudson) (Andre DeShields, Jason Graae, Jim Walton), "Tell Me Why" (music by Michael Edwards and Sigmund Spaeth) (Jason Graae), "Does Your Heart Beat for Me" (music by Russ Morgan and Arnold Johnson) (Jason Graae), "Don't Be That Way" (music by Benny Goodman and Edgar Sampson) (Andre DeShields, Michele Bautier), "The Lamp Is Low" (music by Peter DeRose and Bert Shefter) (Company), "Star Dust" (music by Hoagy Carmichael) (Michele Bautier), "Belle of the Ball" (music by Leroy Anderson) (Jason Graae, Maureen Brennan), "The Syncopated Clock" (music by Leroy Anderson) (Company), "Take Me in Your Arms" (music by Fred Markush) (Maureen Brennan), "Ciao, Ciao, Bambino" (music by Domenico Modugno) (Kim Criswell), "Sleigh Ride" (music by Leroy Anderson) (Company), "Volare" (music by Domenico Modugno) (Jim Walton, Company), "Ruby" (music by

Heinz Roemheld) (Andre DeShields), "Forgotten Dreams" (music by Leroy Anderson) (Company), "Star Dust" (reprise) (Jason Graae, Company)

NOTES—*Star Dust* was a tribute to lyricist Mitchell Parish; after its Off Off Broadway run in 1986, the revue enjoyed two more productions. A Broadway version opened on February 19, 1987, at the Biltmore Theatre for 102 performances (with the Off Off Broadway cast). And during the 1989-1990 season a brief tour was mounted with a cast which included Betty Buckley, Christine Andreas, Karen Ziemba, and Hinton Battle; for some of the tour's performances, Mitchell Parish made a guest appearance; the choreography was by Donald McKayle, and the scenery and costumes were by Erte.

The touring production added "A Little Bit Older, a Little Bit Wiser" (music by Joe Harnell); and all three productions included "Your Cavalcade of Hits" theme (lyric by Jay Jeffries, music by James Raitt) and "Happy Cigarettes" theme (lyric by Peter Jablonski, music by James Raitt).

The script was published by Samuel French, Inc., in 1988.

1522 Starmites. THEATRE: Ark Theatre Opening Date: October 23, 1980; PERFORMANCES: 20; BOOK: Barry Keating; LYRICS: Barry Keating; MUSIC: Barry Keating; DIRECTION: Charles Karchmer; CHOREOGRAPHY: Edmond Kresley; SCENERY: Nina Moser; COSTUMES: Bosha Johnson; LIGHTING: Karen Singleton; MUSICAL DIRECTION: James McElwaine; PRODUCER: Ark Theatre Company

CAST—Chuck Richie, Wendy Jo Belcher, Camille, Fisher Stevens, Toby Parker, Ron Golding, Perry Arthur, Russ Kupfrian, Michael McCurry, Johanna Albrecht, Martha Horstman, Susan Shanline, Karen McIntyre, Gloria Suave, Debby Sheward

NOTES—The persistent *Starmites* has been produced six times in New York over a twenty-six-year period (in 1980, 1987, 1989, 1990, 2001, and 2006). Set in the present time on both Earth and "innerspace," the musical dealt with a teenage girl obsessed by science-fiction comic books and who dreams that she and a band of "lost boys" (the Starmites) save the world from alien invaders.

The 1980 production was presented under an Off Off Broadway contract, and the book, lyrics and music were credited to Barry Keating. Another Off Off Broadway version was produced on April 26, 1987, at Musical Theatre Works for sixteen performances; beginning with this production, the musical's book was credited to both Barry Keating and Stuart Ross. Included in the cast were Liz Larsen (Eleanor and Bizarbara) and Gabriel Barre (Trinkulus), both of whom were also in the third production, which opened on April 27, 1989, and was the first attraction at the new Criterion Center Stage Right. The musical played there for sixty performances (and appears to have been under an Off Broadway [Middle Broadway] contract at the 499-seat house). Commenting on the premiere attraction for the new theatre, Clive Barnes in the *New York Post* said the theatre was "a Right starting off with a Wrong!" Between the 1987 and 1989 productions, the musical was further developed in a version seen at the American Stage Festival in Milford, New Hampshire. *Starmites* then later opened Off Off Broadway at the Hartley House Theatre on December 14, 1990, for twenty performances; and on March 22, 2001, the musical appeared Off Off Broadway in a production at AMAS Musical Theatre for seventeen performances (as *Starmites 2001*). *Starmites* was also produced on March 29, 2006, at the Cap 21 Theatre as part of the Barbara Wolff Monday Night Reading Series.

For the 1989 production, the following songs were heard (character names follow each song title):

ACT ONE—"Superhero Girl" (Eleanor), "Starmites" (Starmites, Spacepunks), "Trink's Narration" (Trinkulus, Starmites), "Afraid of the Dark" (Spacepunk, Starmites, Eleanor, Trinkulus), "Little Hero" (Eleanor), "Attack of Banshees" (Banshees), "Hard to Be Diva" (Diva, Banshees), "Love Duet" (Spacepunk, Eleanor), "Dance of Spiritual Arousal" (Banshees, Bizarbara), Finaletto (Company)

ACT TWO—Entr'acte (Band), "Bizarbara's Wedding" (Bizarbara, Banshees), "Milady" (Spacepunk, Starmites), "Beauty Within" (Diva, Banshees), "The Cruelty Stomp" (Trinkulus, Company), "Reach Right Down" (Starmites, Diva, Banshees), "Immolation" (Eleanor, Shak Graa, Spacepunk), "Starmites"/"Hard to Be Diva" (reprises) (Divam Starmites, Banshees), Finale (Company)

(For the 1987 production, the number "Lullaby" was also heard; and "Dance of Spiritual Arousal" was titled "Festival Dance of Pleasure and Pulchritude.")

The script was published by Samuel French, Inc., in 1990, and Original Cast Records released a recording (CD # OC-8812) of the score which included Liz Larsen and Gabriel Barre (both of whom had appeared in the 1987 and 1989 productions) as well as other members of the 1989 cast (such as Victor Trent Cook, Gwen Stewart, Janet Aldrich, and John-Michael Flate); since some of the 1989 cast members (such as Sharon McNight and Brian Lane Green) weren't available when the recording was made, other performers appeared on the album. However, in her CD collection *In the Meantime* (released by Jezebel Music Records [CD # OU81SS]), Sharon McNight included her *Starmite* song "Hard to Be a Diva."

1523 Stars in Your Eyes. "A New Musical Romance." THEATRE: Cherry Lane Theatre; OPENING DATE: October 24, 1999; PERFORMANCES: 41; BOOK: Chip Meyrelles; LYRICS: Chip Meyrelles; MUSIC: Chip Meyrelles; DIRECTION: Gabriel Barre; CHOREOGRAPHY: Jennifer Paulson Lee; SCENERY: James Youmans; COSTUMES: Pamela Scofield; LIGHTING: Tim Hunter; MUSICAL DIRECTION: Georgia Stitt; PRODUCER: Tom Wirtshafter/Planetearth Partners, Inc.

CAST—James Stovall (Man in the Moon, Taylor St. Joseph), David M. Lutken (Reginald Barclay), John Braden (Charles Swanson), Christy Carlson Romano (Jo Jensen), Barbara Walsh (Annie Patterson), Heather MacRae (Helen Stevens), Crista Moore (Leigh Hunt-Smith)

The action occurs in 1962 in the towns of Milford and Bloomfield.

The musical was presented in two acts.

ACT ONE—"Endless Possibilities" (Company), "Somebody (More or Less) Likes Me" (Barbara Walsh, Heather MacRae), "Can't Say for Sure" (James Stovall), "That's What They Said" (David M. Lutken, Christy Carlson Romano, John Braden), "I'm Leigh Hunt-Smith" (Crista Moore), "Another Day" (John Braden), "Dance by Numbers" (Barbara Walsh, David M. Lutken), "Must Be Something" (Company), "Saturn Rising" (Company), "Stars in Your Eyes" (Barbara Walsh, David M. Lutken)

ACT TWO—"I've Got a Light on You" (James Stovall), "Men!" (Barbara Walsh, Heather MacRae), "Thinking the Impossible" (Company), "Ordinary Jo" (Christy Carlson Romano), "Why Do We Dance?" (Heather MacRae, David M. Lutken), "Conventional Wisdom" (James Stovall), "Can't Say for Sure" (reprise) (James Stovall), "Take Me to Heart" (David M. Lutken, Barbara Walsh), "Saturn Rising" (reprise) (Company)

NOTES—*The Best Plays of 1999-2000* reported that the plot of *Stars in Your Eyes* dealt with the Man in the Moon and his match-making activities among various people in a small town.

Peter Marks in the *New York Times* found the would-be romantic musical a "retro" and "hopelessly passe" evening awash in "sugar coating." But he noted Chip Meyrelles' score offered "pretty ditties," and he singled out the "engaging" duet "Why Do We Dance?"

1524 Starting Here, Starting Now. "A New Musical Revue." THEATRE: Barbarann Theatre Restaurant; OPENING DATE: March 7, 1977; PERFORMANCES: 120; LYRICS: Richard Maltby, Jr.; MUSIC: David Shire; DIRECTION: Richard Maltby, Jr.; CHOREOGRAPHY: Ethel Martin; COSTUMES: Stanley Simmons; MUSICAL DIRECTION: Robert W. Preston; PRODUCERS: Steve Abrams, Mary Jo Slater, and Scott Mansfield in association with Morton Schwartz

CAST—Loni Ackerman, Margery Cohen, George Lee Andrews

The revue was presented in two acts.

ACT ONE—"The Word Is Love" (Company), "Starting Here, Starting Now" (Company), "A Little Bit Off" (Margery Cohen, George Lee Andrews), "(I Think) I May Want to Remember Today" (from *Love Match*, 1968; closed during pre-Broadway tryout) (Loni Ackerman, Margery Cohen), "Beautiful" (*Love Match*, 1968) (Company), "We Can Talk to Each Other" (unproduced musical *The Girl of the Minute*) (George Lee Andrews, Margery Cohen), "(Just) Across the River" (*How Do You Do, I Love You*, 1967; closed during pre-Broadway tryout) (Company), "Crossword Puzzle" (*Graham Crackers*, 1962 [see entry]) (Loni Ackerman), "Autumn" (college musical *Cyrano*, 1958) (Margery Cohen), "I Don't Remember Christmas" (George Lee Andrews), "I Don't Believe It" (*Love Match*, 1968) (Company), "I Hear Bells" (*Love Match*, 1968) (George Lee Andrews, Company), "I'm Going to Make You Beautiful" (Margery Cohen), "Pleased with Myself" (*How Do You Do I Love You*, 1967) (Company)

ACT TWO—"Hey There Fans" (George Lee Andrews), "Girl of the Minute" (unproduced musical *Girl of the Minute*; the song was included in *New Faces of 1968*, but wasn't recorded for that revue's cast album) (Company), "A Girl You Should Know" (Loni Ackerman), "Travel" (unproduced musical *The River*) (Company), "Watching the Big Parade Go By" (*The Sap of Life*, 1961 [see entry]) (Margery Cohen), "Flair" (George Lee Andrews), "What About Today" (lyric and music by David Shire) (Loni Ackerman), "One Step" (*How Do You Do I Love You*, 1967) (Company), "Song of Me" (unproduced musical *The River*) (Margery Cohen), "Today Is the First Day of the Rest of My Life" (*Love Match*, 1968) (Loni Ackerman, Margery Cohen), "A New Life Coming" (song based on "A Charmed Life" from *The Sap of Life* [1961]) (Company)

NOTES—Earlier in the season, the Manhattan Theatre Club had presented in its Off Off Broadway cabaret theatre a limited three-week engagement of *An Evening of Theatre Songs by Maltby and Shire*. Retitled *Starting Here, Starting Now* and produced under the auspices of the Manhattan Theatre Club, the revue opened Off Broadway for a three-month engagement; it proved popular enough to be produced in other cities as well as in foreign countries.

As a team, Maltby and Shire never really enjoyed any popular successes. Thus the songs in *Starting Here, Starting Now* were relatively unknown, and the freshness of the material added to the revue's appeal. The cast members of the first production were Loni Ackerman, Margery Cohen, and Michael Tucci; the latter was replaced by George Lee Andrews when the revue moved to Off Broadway. After its opening there, the song "Barbara" was added to the score (lyric and music by Richard Maltby, Jr.), and the number was included in the RCA Victor Records cast album (LP # ABL1-2360). There was also a South African cast recording, which was released on EMI Records (LP # EMCJ[L]-11539). A 1993 London production was recorded by That's Entertainment Records (CD # CDTER-1200).

Another Maltby and Shire revue, *Closer Than Ever*, opened Off Broadway at the Cherry Lane Theatre on November 6, 1989 (see entry). And on November 24, 1998, an Off Off Broadway tribute opened at the Kaufman Theatre (as *The Story Goes On: The Music of Maltby and Shire*) for twenty-three performances (the cast members were Loni Ackerman and David Shire).

1525 Step Into My World. "Musical Revue." THEATRE: AMAS Musical Theatre; OPENING DATE: February 16, 1989; PERFORMANCES: 24; LYRICS: Micki Grant; MUSIC: Micki Grant; DIRECTION: Ronald G. Russo; CHOREOGRAPHY: Jeffrey Dobbs; COSTUMES: Mary Ann Lach; LIGHTING: Jeffrey Hubbell; MUSICAL DIRECTION: George Caldwell; PRODUCER: AMAS Musical Theatre (Rosetta LeNoire, Founder and Artistic Director)

CAST—Jennifer Bell, Jean Cheek, Ellen DeVerne, Martron Gales, Evan Matthews, George Merritt, Kenn Miller, Ellen Simms, Darius Keith Williams, Deborah Woodson

NOTES—Conceived, developed, and directed by Ronald G. Russo, the Off Off Broadway *Step Into My World* was a retrospective tribute-revue which offered songs from various musicals by Micki Grant.

The revue's title was taken from a song which had originally been heard in Grant's musical *It's So Nice to Be Civilized* (Off Off Broadway, 1979 [see entry]; also Broadway, 1980).

1526 Step Lively, Boy! THEATRE: Urban Arts Theatre; OPENING DATE: February 7, 1973; PERFORMANCES: Unknown; BOOK: Vinnette Carroll; LYRICS: Micki Grant; MUSIC: Micki Grant; DIRECTION: Vinnette Carroll; PRODUCER: Urban Arts Theatre (Vinnette Carroll, Artistic Director)

SOURCE—The 1936 play *Bury the Dead* by Irwin Shaw.

NOTES—Vinnette Carroll and Micki Grant's Off Off Broadway anti-war musical *Step Lively, Boy!* was based on Irwin Shaw's surreal 1936 Broadway play *Bury the Dead*, in which soldiers killed in battle refuse to stay buried, to the consternation of their commanders, fellow soldiers, and even their loved ones. It appears that an early version of the musical (as *Bury the Dead*) was presented Off Off Broadway at the Urban Arts Theatre during the 1970-1971 season. A few months after *Step Lively, Boy!* closed Off Off Broadway, it was produced at the New Locust Theatre in Philadelphia (on a double bill with Carroll and Grant's *Croesus and the Witch*; see entry). The cast included Martin Vidnovic, Sherman Hemsley, and Salome Bey, and the following songs were heard in the production: Prologue, Overture, "It Takes a Soldier," "Walking the Dog," "War Is Made for Generals," "Body Count," "Step Lively, Boy," "The General's Coming," "Haven't I Got Enough on My Mind," "I Ain't Had My Fill," "Our Cause Is Righteous," "That's What the Bible Say," "When Every Man Is Everyman," "The Women," "My Dear," "I Ain't Had My Fill" (reprise), "Step Lively, Boy" (reprise)

In 1982, the one-act musical was expanded into two acts, was retitled, and was produced Off Off Broadway by the Urban Arts Theatre as *The Boogie-Woogie Rumble of a Dream Deferred* (see entry; the new title was taken from the writings of Langston Hughes). The revised musical included all but two songs from *Step Lively, Boy!* ("The General's Coming" and "Haven't I Got Enough on My Mind" were omitted) and added about ten others.

1527 Sterling Silver. "A New Musical Entertainment." THEATRE: Village Gate; OPENING DATE: March 7, 1979; PERFORMANCES: 6; LYRICS: Frederick (Fred) Silver; MUSIC: Frederick Silver; DIRECTION: Sue Lawless; CHOREOGRAPHY: Bick Goss; SCENERY: Kenneth Foy; COSTUMES: David Toser; LIGHTING: Michael J. HoTopp; MUSICAL DIRECTION: Elman R. Anderson; PRODUCER: David Silberg

CAST—Roger Berdahl, Alan Brasington, Karen Jablons, Cynthia Meryl, Lee Roy Reams

The revue was presented in two acts.

ACT ONE—"Production Number" (Company), "A Matter of Position" (Cynthia Meryl), "Piano" (Karen Jablons), "Waiting in the Wings" (Company), "Love Song" (Roger Berdahl, with Karen Jablons and Cynthia Meryl), "Wooing in the Woods" (Alan Brasington, Company), "When You Are on the Coast" (Lee Roy Reams, Company), "I Do Like London" (Alan Brasington), "Very New York" (Roger Berdahl, Karen Jablons, Cynthia Meryl, Lee Roy Reams), "Mr. Ravel" (Company)

ACT TWO—"A Silver Pattern": "Rainbow, Rainbow," "A Birthday Horoscope," "Visiting Hours," "The Twelve Days After Christmas" "Biography," (Above sequence sung by the Company.), "A Simple Song" (Roger Berdahl) "A Plain Song" (Roger Berdahl, Alan Brasington, Lee Roy Reams), "Blues" (a/k/a "The White Anglo-Saxon Protestant Blues") (Karen Jablons), "Someone in My Life" (Cynthia Meryl), "(It's) Closing Time" (Alan Brasington), "Days of the Dancing" (Lee Roy Reams, with Roger Berdahl and Karen Joblons), "Age of Elegance" (Company)

NOTES—Frederick (Fred) Silver's *Sterling Silver* was another one of those Off Broadway evenings which offered a series of songs loosely connected by a theme (love, urban life, etc.). A few such song cycles (such as *Dont Bother Me, I Cant Cope* [1972; see entry]) were successful, but usually these song cycles/mosaics/collages had short runs and were quickly forgotten. John S. Wilson in the *New York Times* wasn't particularly impressed with Silver's comedy songs, but he praised a number of others, including "The Age of Elegance," which he noted had "a broad, attractively sweeping melody" and a "precise" and pointed lyric. He also enjoyed "The White Anglo-Saxon Protestant Blues" ("a twist on the traditional blues"), "A Plain Song" ("a deservedly showstopping song and dance" performed by three monks), and "I Do Like London" ("warm and unaffected"). Wilson also referred to a song ("Freddy Liked to Fugue") which wasn't listed in the program.

Sterling Silver ran less than a week, but the following season "The Age of Elegance" surfaced in *Jane White, Who?...* (1980; see entry); the song was also heard in a 1984 touring version of Silver's *Gay Company* (1974)/*In Gay Company* (1975)/*Gay Company Revisited* (1980) series (see entries for all three revues); for the 1984 tour, which was titled *In Gay Company*, five songs from *Sterling Silver* were heard (besides "The Age of Elegance," "Wooing in the Woods," "Someone in My Life," "(It's) Closing Time," and "Freddy Liked to Fugue" [here called "Freddie's Fugue"] were used); all five songs can be heard on the Los Angeles cast recording of *In Gay Company* (WEB Records LP # OC-111).

1528 Stewed Prunes. THEATRE: Circle in the Square; transferred to the Showplace on December 14, 1960; OPENING DATE: November 14, 1960; PERFORMANCES: 295; SKETCHES: The Stewed Prunes (MacIntyre Dixon, Lynda Segal, and Richard Libertini)

CAST—The Stewed Prunes (MacIntyre Dixon, Lynda Segal, and Richard Libertini)

The revue was performed in one act.

SKETCHES AND MUSICAL NUMBERS—"Sweeney Agonistes" (from T.S. Eliot) (MacIntyre Dixon, Lynda Segal, Richard Libertini), "The Nothing Doing Bar" (title from Cocteau) (Richard Libertini, MacIntyre Dixon, Lynda Segal), "Sentimental Baby, or The Speakeasy" (MacIntyre Dixon, Richard Libertini, Lynda Segal), "Old Folks Home" (Richard Libertini, MacIntyre Dixon, Lynda Segal), "The Seventh Wild Magician" (MacIntyre Dixon, Lynda Segal, Richard Libertini), "The Chanteuse" (Richard Libertini, MacIntyre Dixon, Lynda Segal), "The Concert" (Richard Libertini, MacIntyre Dixon), "The Lady of the Bookshelf" (Lynda Segal, MacIntyre Dixon, Richard Libertini), Tableaux and Dance (Lynda Segal, MacIntyre Dixon, Richard Libertini), "The Machine" (Lynda Segal, MacIntyre Dixon, Richard Libertini), "Hamlet's Soliloquy" (MacIntyre Dixon), "Trick or Treat" (Lynda Segal, MacIntyre Dixon, Richard Libertini), "Ebb Tide" (Richard Libertini), "The Nice Man" (Lynda Segal, Richard Libertini, MacIntyre Dixon), "The Red Shoes" (MacIntyre Dixon), "International Vaudevillians" (MacIntyre Dixon, Richard Libertini)

NOTES—*The Burns Mantle Yearbook/The Best Plays of 1960-1961* said the long-running *Stewed Prunes* was the most original presentation of the entire Off Broadway season. The improvisations included spoofs of nightclubs, Ingmar Bergman films, and other topics.

Lewis Funke in the *New York Times* felt the evening was "dipped in madness," and noted the "first-rate" comics offered a "sort of lunacy that has all but vanished from the theatre." But he said the revue wasn't entirely comfortable in a traditional Off Broadway theatre (especially a theatre-in-the-round like the Circle in the Square), and suggested a coffeehouse or nightclub venue would be more appropriate. Sure enough, a month after *Stewed Prunes* opened, it transferred to a cabaret theatre (the Showplace).

In 1962, a new Stewed Prunes revue (without Lynda Segal) called *The Cats' Pajamas* lasted only a month (see entry).

In the mid–1960s, MacIntyre Dixon and Richard Libertini appeared in one of the most successful Off Broadway revues of the era (see entry for *The Mad Show*).

1529 Stomp (1969). "A Multimedia Protest Rock Musical Environment Entertainment." THEATRE: Public Theatre; OPENING DATE: November 16, 1969; PERFORMANCES: 161; PRODUCER: The New York Shakespeare Festival

NOTES—*Stomp* was a self-described "multimedia protest rock musical environment entertainment" created by The Combine, a group of former University of Texas students. In his review for the *New York Times*, Clive Barnes indicated much of the revue-like evening centered around the students' feelings of alienation from their Texas community (apparently one of their major gripes was that their hippie-styled clothing "victimized" them in Texas). Barnes felt the story was bland and the score "mildly characterless"; he noted that the "communal nature" of the writing mitigated against the show's success, and that "you don't really get musicals written by committees."

The program didn't provide specific writing, acting, and other traditional credits. In two slightly separated engagements, the revue played a total of about five months. The musical was later presented in London during the 1970-1971 season for ten performances.

During the 1969-1970 theatre season, the Public Theatre offered two more protest musicals (*Sambo* [Black protest] and *Mod Donna* [feminist protest]; see entries), and these musicals are emblematic of how Joseph Papp used the resources of the Public Theatre to produce trendy, politically correct tirades, all of which preached to the converted and had little staying power (*Hair* became quickly outdated, and is now remembered for its ingratiating score by Galt McDermot; the musical is perhaps most notable for being the first successful concept musical [see entry]). It's ironic that the most popular productions to open during Papp's tenure are the show-business musical *A Chorus Line* (1975) and the 1980 revival of *The Pirates of Penzance*, which had originally premiered in 1879 (see entries); the many political diatribes Papp produced at the Public have fallen into obscurity. For the record, the Public *Stomp* is not related to the 1994 *Stomp*, a highly successful and long-running percussion performance piece which as of this writing is still playing Off Broadway (see entry).

1530 Stomp (1994). THEATRE: Orpheum Theatre; OPENING DATE: February 27, 1994; PERFORMANCES: Still playing as of December 31, 2007 Created by Luke Cresswell and Steve McNicholas; DIRECTION: Luke Cresswell and Steve McNicholas; LIGHTING: Steve McNicholas and Neil Tiplady; PRODUCERS: Columbia Artists Management, Inc., Harriet Newman Leve, James D. Stern, Morton Wolkowitz, Schuster/Maxwell, Gallin/Sandler, and Markley/Manocherian; Richard Frankel Productions/Mark Routh, Executive Producers; Fred Bracken, Associate Producer

CAST—Luke Cresswell, Nick Dwyer, Sarah Eddy, Theseus Gerard, Fraser Morrison, David Olrod, Carl Smith, Fiona Wilkes

NOTES—*Stomp*, a performance art piece in which the cast used unconventional objects to create percussion rhythms for dancing, immediately caught on with the public. As of this writing, it's the third-longest running Off Broadway musical, and by December 31, 2007, the production had played over 5,700 performances.

Stephen Holden in the *New York Times* reported the vaudeville-like evening ("with a rock-and-roll heart") was "part tap-dance ... part military drill, part swinging street festival," and said it demonstrated with "entrancing charm" the music inherent in ordinary, everyday objects (such as garbage can lids). *Stomp* was first seen at the Edinburgh Festival in Britain in 1991, and subsequently was performed on a world tour.

The dance revue inspired a short documentary film as well as an IMAX film titled *Pulse*.

STOMP Out Loud, a sequel of sorts, was shown on Home Box Office in 1997. Ten years later, on March 24, 2007, a stage version, titled *Stomp Out Loud*, opened in Las Vegas at the Planet Hollywood Hotel and Casino. Created and directed by Luke Cresswell and Steve McNicholas, the original creators of *Stomp*, the stage version offered an evening of characters interacting with one another through dance and percussion-based instruments. The revue featured a cast twice the size of the original *Stomp*, and offered new dance sequences.

The (1994) *Stomp* is not to be confused with the (1969) *Stomp* which had been produced at the Public Theatre.

1531 The Stones of Jehoshaphat. THEATRE: Rodale Theatre; OPENING DATE: December 17, 1963; PERFORMANCES: 6; BOOK: J. I. Rodale; LYRICS: Deed Meyer; MUSIC: Deed Meyer; DIRECTION: John Glines; CHOREOGRAPHY: Eleanor Chapin; SCENERY: Chuck Eisler; COSTUMES: Freida Evans; LIGHTING: Chuck Eisler; PRODUCER: J.I. Rodale

CAST—Ernie Adano (Jeduthun), R.D. Blitz (Jedidiah), John Clifton (Jonadab), Robert Hewes (Menahem), Rochelle Marek (Keturah), Robert Morea (Jehoshaphat), Prima Stefanini (Riblah), David Sigel (Slave, Soldier, Groom)

The musical was presented in two acts (division of acts and song assignments unknown).

MUSICAL NUMBERS—Opening, "A Man Who Speaks for Himself," "The Psalm of Jehoshaphat," "Riblah's Lament," "A Talk with One's Conscience" "The Stones of Jehoshaphat," "I Could Go with the Wind," "Song of the Witch," "The Jester's Tale," "The Wedding Celebration," "Beauteous Is the Bride," "Look Through the Moongate," "Jehoshaphat Makes Up His Mind," "Long Live the Greedy," Finale

NOTES—*The Stones of Jehoshaphat*, a musical about Jewish life, lasted less than a week. Its lyricist and composer was Deed Meyer, who had written the delightful score for *She Shall Have Music* (1959) as well as *'Toinette* (1961) (see entries).

1532 Stranger Here Myself. THEATRE: Susan Stein Shiva Theatre/The Public Theatre; OPENING DATE: August 11, 1988; PERFORMANCES: 19; LYRICS: See song list for credits; MUSIC: Kurt Weill; DIRECTION: Christopher Alden Scenery: Paul Steinberg; LIGHTING: Anne Militello; MUSICAL DIRECTION: Christopher Berg; PRODUCER: The New York Shakespeare Festival (Joseph Papp, Producer)

CAST—Angelina Reaux

The action occurs in a hotel room.

The revue was presented in two acts (all songs performed by Angelina Reaux).

ACT ONE—"Epitaph" (from *The Berlin Requiem*, 1929; original German lyric by Bertolt Brecht, English lyric by Michael Feingold), "Fennimore's Song" (*Silverlake*, 1933; original German lyric by George Kaiser, English lyric by Michael Feingold), "The Barbara Song" (*The Threepenny Opera*, 1928; original German lyric by Bertolt Brecht, English lyric by Marc Blitzstein), "Is It Him or Is It Me?" (*Love Life*, 1948; lyric by Alan Jay Lerner), "Prologue" (original German lyric by Bertolt Brecht, English lyric by W.H. Auden and Chester Kallmann; probably from *The Rise and Fall of the City of Mahagonny*, 1930), "Berlin in Licht-Song (Berlin in Lights)" (independent song, 1928; original German lyric by Kurt Weill, English lyric by Kim H. Kowalke), "Moon of Alabama" (*The Rise and Fall of the City of Mahagonny*, 1930; English lyric by Bertolt Brecht), "My Ship" (Childhood Dream) (*Lady in the Dark*, 1941; lyric by Ira Gershwin), "Song of the Big Shot" (*Happy End*, 1929; original German lyric by Bertolt Brecht, English lyric by Michael Feingold), "J'Attends un Navire (I Wait for a Ship)" (*Marie Galante*, 1933; original French lyric by Jacques Deval, English lyric by Michael Feingold), "Lust" (original German lyric by Bertolt Brecht, English lyric by W.H. Auden and Chester Kallmann; probably from *The Rise and Fall of the City of Mahagonny*, 1930), "Je ne t'Aime Pas (I Don't Love You)" (independent song, 1934; original French lyric by Maurice Magre, English lyric by Susan Grayson and Michael Feingold), "Remember That I Care" (*Street Scene*, 1947; lyric by Langston Hughes)

ACT TWO—"I'm a Stranger Here Myself" (*One Touch of Venus*, 1943; lyric by Ogden Nash), "Surabaya Johnny" (*Happy End*, 1929; original German lyric by Bertolt Brecht, English lyric by Michael Feingold), "Foolish Heart" (*One Touch of Venus*, 1943; lyric by Ogden Nash), "Song of Mandalay" (*Happy End*, 1929; original German lyric by Bertolt Brecht; was this translation by Michael Feingold?), "Nannas Lied" (independent song, 1939; original German lyric by Bertolt Brecht, English lyric by Kim H. Kowalke), "Lonely House" (*Street Scene*, 1947; lyric by Langston Hughes), "Le Train du Ciel (The Heaven Train)" (*Marie Galante*, 1933; original French lyric by Jacques Deval, English lyric by Michael Feingold), "Solomon Song" (*The Threepenny Opera*, 1928; original German lyric by Bertolt Brecht, English lyric by Marc Blitzstein), "Youkali: Tango Habanera" (*Marie Galante*, 1933; original French lyric by Roger Fernay, English lyric by Angelina Reaux), "Epitaph" (reprise)

NOTES—Instead of presenting Kurt Weill's songs in concert format, Angelina Reaux' solo revue-cum-book musical *Stranger Here Myself* used the tired notion of portraying a lonely, unhappy woman in a cheap hotel room who sings of her life and loves to pre-existing songs. *Blues in the Night* had already explored this conceit in two earlier productions (see entries for 1980 and 1981 versions) when it dealt with three lonely, unhappy women in their separate hotel rooms who sing of their lives and loves to pre-existing songs, and would do so again with a third production (see entry) which opened a month after *Stranger Here Myself* premiered. Further, *Marry Me a Little* (1981; see entry) was also about two lonely, unhappy people in their separate apartments who sing of their lives and loves to pre-existing songs (by Stephen Sondheim).

"Prologue" and "Lust," with lyrics by W.H. Auden and Chester Kallmann, may have been song sequences from their translation of *The Rise and Fall of the City of Mahagonny*.

Stranger Here Myself was performed in other venues, and in 1991 a 2-CD recording was issued by Koch Records (# 3-7087-2-K2) The recording included three songs which apparently were later added to new productions of the revue: "It Never Was You" (*Knickerbocker Holiday*, 1938; lyric by Maxwell Anderson); "That's Him" (*One Touch of Venus*, 1943; lyric by Ogden Nash); and "Sing Me Not a Ballad" (*The Firebrand of Florence*, 1945; lyric by Ira Gershwin).

1533 Strawberry Fields

NOTES—See entry for *Central Park*.

1534 Straws in the Wind. "A Theatrical Look Ahead." THEATRE: American Place Theatre; OPENING DATE: February 21, 1975; PERFORMANCES: 34; SKETCHES, LYRICS, AND MUSIC: Donald Barthelme, Marshall Brickman, Cy Coleman, Betty Comden and Adolph Green, Ira Gasman, Galt MacDermot, Lanny Meyers, Billy Nichols, Stephen Schwartz, and Peter Stone; DIRECTION: Phyllis Newman; Otis A. Sallid, Assistant to Director for Musical Staging; SCENERY: Peter Harvey; COSTUMES: Ruth Morley; LIGHTING: Roger Morgan; MUSICAL DIRECTION: Lanny Meyers; PRODUCER: The American Place Theatre (Wynn Handman, Director; Julia Miles, Associate Director)

CAST—Tovah Feldshuh, Carol Jean Lewis, Brandon Maggart, Josh Mostel, George Pentecost

The revue was presented in two acts (division of acts and song and sketch assignments unknown).

SKETCHES AND MUSICAL NUMBERS—Opening: "My Doctor, the Box," "Noah" (lyric and music by Stephen Schwartz), "In Which to Marry Me" (lyric by Ira Gasman, music by Galt MacDermot), "The Photographs," "The Lost Word" (lyric by Betty Comden and Adolph Green, music by Cy Coleman), "Dick's Last Tape," "Goin' Home," "Discovery of Earth...October 12, 1992," "Suffrage," "Simplified Language" (lyric by Betty Comden and Adolph Green, music by Cy Coleman), "It's Not Such a Brave New World, Mr. Huxley" (lyric by Ira Gasman, music by Galt MacDermot), "The School," "You'll Have Your Moment" (lyric and music by Billy Nichols), Finale

NOTES—According to *The Best Plays of 1974-1975*, the Off Broadway revue *Straws in the Wind* played thirty-four subscription performances and then closed prior to offering a formal opening night for the critics.

1535 Street Dreams (1984; William Eaton). THEATRE: St. Clement's Theatre; OPENING DATE: May 15, 1984; PERFORMANCES: 21; TEXT: Mitchell Ivers; MUSIC: William Eaton; DIRECTION: Peter Gennaro; CHOREOGRAPHY: Peter Gennaro; Don Bonnell, Assistant Choreographer; SCENERY: Nancy Winters; COSTUMES: Joan V. Evans; LIGHTING: Marilyn Rennagel; MUSICAL DIRECTION: Nick Diminno and Grant Sturiale; PRODUCER: Music-Theatre Group/Lenox Arts Center (Lyn Austin, Producing Director) and Jack Curtis

CAST—Ray Contreras (Lincoln), Christopher Cowley (Monkey), Ali Hernandez (Peeper), Benjamin Hernandez (Cas-Bah), Marishka Phillips (Leesha), Clayton Prince (Super-Ru), Kevin Ramsey (Calvin), Tico Wells (Prophet), Harold Williams (Bug), Lucky Williams (Jelly)

NOTES—This was the second musical of the

1983-1984 Off Off Broadway season with the title *Street Dreams* (see entry for the other production, which was a retitled [and apparently revised] version of the 1971 Broadway musical *Inner City*).

1536 Street Dreams (1984; Helen Miller). THEATRE: LaMama Experimental Theatre Club (ETC); OPENING DATE: February 2, 1984; PERFORMANCES: Unknown; LYRICS: Eve Merriman; MUSIC: Helen Miller; LIGHTING: Lance Miller; PRODUCER: LaMama Experimental Theatre Club (ETC) (Ellen Stewart, Founder; Wesley Jensby, Artistic Director)

CAST—Chiara Peacock, Stephanie Keyser, Meredith Rutledge, Rick Negron, Daniel Parker, John Braswell, Lucy Pendleton

SOURCE—The 1969 book *The Inner City Mother Goose* by Eve Merriman.

NOTES—The Off Off Broadway *Street Dreams* was a re-titled (and revised) version of the dreary "Street Cantata" *Inner City*, which played on Broadway in 1971 for ninety-seven performances. *Inner City*, which was recorded by RCA Victor Records (LP # LSO-1171), dealt with the problems of living in New York City (muggers, purse-snatchers, murderers, prostitutes, drug addicts, political corruption, poverty, failed schools, housing problems, numbers players, etc.), and Douglas Watt in the *New York Daily News* called the production a "big mistake."

The script was published by Samuel French, Inc.

During the 1983-1984 season, another musical titled *Street Dreams* opened (see entry).

1537 Street Jesus. THEATRE: Provincetown Playhouse; OPENING DATE: November 16, 1974; PERFORMANCES: 52; BOOK: Peter Copani; LYRICS: Peter Copani; MUSIC: Chris Staudt and Peter Copani; DIRECTION: Peter Copani; CHOREOGRAPHY: John Werkheiser; SCENERY: Gary Langley; COSTUMES: Gary Langley; LIGHTING: Gary Langley; MUSICAL DIRECTION: Ed Vogel

CAST—Larry Campbell, Robin Cantor, Regina Cashone, Aixa Clemente, Joe Garrambone, Michael D. Knowles, Angel Martin, Vernon Spencer, Anita Tomaino, Meri Weiner

The musical was presented in two acts (song assignments unknown).

MUSICAL NUMBERS—"Bad But Good," "The Good News," "Manufacture and Sell," "Today Will Be," "Strawberries, Pickles and Ice Cream," "Hail, Hail," "If Jesus Walked the Earth Today," "L'America Ha Fato Per Te," "Who Can Say," "Down on Me," "Wait and See," "God's in the People," "Street Jesus," "Flame of Life," "Corruption," "For the Good Times," "Special Man," Dance, "A Better Day," "Friends," "In the Name of Love," "Make Them Hate," "Riot," "One of Us," "Love Is Beautiful"

NOTES—The revue *Street Jesus* lasted less than two months. But Peter Copani didn't give up, and for his Off Broadway musicals *Fire of Flowers* (1976) and *New York City Street Show* (1977) (see entries) he recycled material first heard in *Street Jesus.*

No less than thirteen numbers from *Street Jesus* were used in *Fire of Flowers* ("Today Will Be," "Strawberries, Pickles and Ice Cream," "If Jesus Walked the Earth Today," "L'America Ha Fato per Te," "Who Can Say," "Down on Me," "Wait and See," "God Is in the People," "Street Jesus," "Special Man," "Make Them Hate," "Riot," and "One of Us"). Twelve songs from *Street Jesus* were later heard in *New York City Street Show* (eight of which had also been used in *Fire of Flowers* ["Strawberries, Pickles and Ice Cream," "A Special Man," "If Jesus Walked the Earth Today," "Who Can Say," "Wait and See," "God Is in the People," "Make Them Hate," and "One of Us"] as well as four from *Street Jesus* which hadn't been used in *Fire of Flowers* ["Bad But Good," "Hail, Hail," "Corruption," and "Love Is Beautiful"]).

In all, seventeen of the twenty-five numbers in *Street Jesus* found their way into either *Fire of Flowers* or *New York City Street Show.*

During the 1973-1974 theatre season, *Street Jesus* (on a double bill with another musical by Copani, *The Blind Junkie*) had been seen at the Greenwich Mews Theatre.

1538 Streetheat. THEATRE: 54th Street Theatre Cabaret at Studio 54; OPENING DATE: January 27, 1985; PERFORMANCES: 20; MATERIAL: Based on an original concept by Michele Assaf and Rick Atwell; LYRICS AND MUSIC: See song list for credits; DIRECTION: Rick Atwell; CHOREOGRAPHY: Rick Atwell; SCENERY: Dianna Freas and Michael Rizzo; COSTUMES: Franne Lee; LIGHTING: John McLain; PRODUCERS: Bert Straford Productions in association with Gene Cates, Doug Leeds, Christine Mortimer Biddle, and Rex Farr; Judee Wales, Associate Producer

CAST—Michael DeLorenzo (Spinner), James Arthur Johnson (Leon), Vicki Lewis (Victoria), Ron Lee Savin (The Character Man), Glenn Scarpelli (Lucky Louie), Tico Wells (Picasso); Ensemble (Bryant Baldwin, Nora Cherry, Cecila Marta, Troy Myers, Rick Negron, Daryl Richardson, Louis Ritarossi, Robin Summerfield, Jorge Vaszuez

The action occurs in New York City at the present time.

The revue was presented in one act (song assignments not credited in the program).

MUSICAL NUMBERS—"We Paint Life" (lyric and music by Rick Atwell and Perry Arthur Kroeger), "Picasso's Theme" (lyric and music by Frank Owens), "Uptown Dreamer's Express" (lyric and music by James Gregory and Rick Atwell), "Hold On" (lyric and music by Chris Darway), "To Dance Is to Fly" (lyric and music by Kyra Kaptzan), "Power" (lyric and music by Vinnie Rich and Dave Moritz), "I'm a Wow" (lyric and music by Ron Abel and Bob Garrett), "Lucky Louie" (lyric and music by Frank Owens, Rick Atwell, and Perry Arthur Kroeger), "Full Circle" (lyric and music by Laura Taylor and Charles Mortimer), "Streetheat" (lyric and music by James Gregory, Charles Mortimer, and William Hocher), "I Want a Real Man" (lyric and music by Geoff Bradford), "Sacrifice Your Body" (lyric and music by James Gregory, Charles Mortimer, and Rick Atwell), "The King Becomes a Clown" (lyric and music by Laura Taylor), "Nirvana" (lyric and music by James Gregory and Perry Arthur Kroeger), "Danger Men Working" (lyric and music by Bob Garrett and Joe Curiale), "Today I Found Me" (lyric and music by Laura Taylor), "Power" (reprise) (lyric and music by Vinnie Rich and David Moritz), "Full Circle" (reprise) (lyric and music by Laura Taylor and Charles Mortimer), "The Power Lies Within" (lyric and music by James Gregory, Joe Hudson, and Rick Atwell)

NOTES—*Streetheat* was a revue purportedly celebrating the "now" culture of the 1980s. *Best Plays* categorized the revue as a Broadway presentation, *Theatre World* considered it Off Broadway (the revue may have been under a Middle Broadway contract).

1539 The Streets of New York. "A New Musical Comedy." THEATRE: Maidman Playhouse; OPENING DATE: October 29, 1963; PERFORMANCES: 318; BOOK: Barry Alan Grael; LYRICS: Barry Alan Grael; MUSIC: Richard B. Chodosh; DIRECTION: Joseph Hardy; CHOREOGRAPHY: Neal Kenyon; SCENERY: Howard Becknell; COSTUMES: W. Thomas Seitz; LIGHTING: Howard Becknell; MUSICAL DIRECTION: Jack Holmes; PRODUCERS: Gene Dingenary and Jane Gilliland

CAST—RALSTON HILL (Gideon Bloodgood), BARRY ALAN GRAEL (Badger), Ian Brown (Captain Fairweather, Mexican, Tourist, Guest), Ken Roberts (Guide, Mexican, Tourist, Guest), DON PHELPS (Mr. Puffy), BARBARA WILLIAMS (Alida Bloodgood), Fred Cline (Edwards, Tourist, Guest), DAVID CRYER (Mark Livingstone), GAIL JOHNSTON (Lucy Fairweather), Joan Kroschell (Bridget, Maid, Tourist, Guest), Eleanor Bergquist (Kathleen, Maid, Tourist, Guest), MARGOT HAND (Mrs. Fairweather), JANET RAYMOND (Mrs. Puffy), Tom Urich (Mexican, Tourist, Guest), Ann Clements (Maid, Tourist, Guest), Robert Edwards (Police Officer, Tourist, Guest)

SOURCE—The early nineteenth-century play *Streets of New York* by Dion Boucicault.

The action occurs in New York City in the 1860s and the 1880s.

The musical was presented in two acts.

ACT ONE—Prologue (Ralston Hall, Barry Alan Grael, Ian Brown, Two Porters), "Tourist Madrigal" (Ralston Hall, Don Phelps, Ensemble), "He'll Come to Me Crawling" (Barbara Williams), "If I May" (Gail Johnston, Joan Kroschell, Ann Clements, Eleanor Bergquist), "If I May" (reprise) (David Cryer), "Aren't You Warm" (Gail Johnston, David Cryer, Margot Hand), "Where Can the Rich and the Poor Be Friends" (Margot Hand, Don Phelps, Janet Raymond, David Cryer, Gail Johnston, Ralston Hill, Two Toughs), "California" (Barry Alan Grael, Ian Brown, Ken Roberts, Tom Urich, Ralston Hill), Finale (Barbara Williams, Ralston Hill, Barry Alan Grael, Fred Cline, Ensemble)

ACT TWO—"Christmas Carol" (Don Phelps, Janet Raymond, David Cryer, Barry Alan Grael, Ralston Hill, Ensemble), "I May Blush from Anger" (performer unknown), "Arms for the Love of Me" (Gail Johnston), "Close Your Eyes" (Gail Johnston, Margot Hand, Barry Alan Grael), "Love Wins Again" (Gail Johnston, David Cryer), Finale (Company)

NOTES—*The Streets of New York* is one of the gems of the 1960s Off Broadway musical. It received enthusiastic reviews, with *Newsweek* stating it was "the brightest musical of the season and maybe next, with a lilting score" and "a contrapuntal complexity Broadway musicals never dare" (for many, "He'll Come to Me Crawling" was the show' highlight). Despite critical praise and a run of over 300 performances, the team of Barry Alan Grael and Richard B. Chodosh were never heard from again (although they continued to occasionally work on projects which never reached fruition).

The recording of *The Streets of New York* was privately pressed a few months after its opening. Like many Off Broadway musicals of the era, the recording was primarily a souvenir for cast members and others associated with the show, but many of these private recordings found their way to the general public, through sales in the theatre lobby or from the publisher of the score (in the case of *The Streets of New York*, for many years the album was available directly from Grael on an LP which was unlabeled but numbered [# SRB-450/1]). In 1995, the cast album was for the first time officially released (on CD by AEI Records [# AEI-CD-023]). The script was published by Samuel French, Inc., in 1965. In 1964, the musical was shown on pay-television by Subscription TeleVision, Inc.

Among the show's cast members was the talented David Cryer, who created leading roles in the Broadway failures *Come Summer* (1969) and *Ari* (1971) and also starred as the Red Shadow in the short-running, underrated 1973 Broadway revival of *The Desert Song*. He was married to composer Gretchen Cryer, whose credits include the Off Broadway musicals *Now Is the Time for All Good Men* (1967), *The Last Sweet Days of Isaac* (1970), and *I'm Getting My Act Together and Taking It on the Road* (1978); see entries. Joseph Hardy later directed the long-running Off Broadway musical *You're a Good Man, Charlie Brown*

(1967; see entry) and the Broadway thriller *Child's Play* (1970).

Incidentally, at some point after opening of *The Streets of New York*, the song "I May Blush from Anger" was replaced by "Laugh After Laugh" (for Alida and the Ensemble); the latter song is heard on the cast album.

Gene Dingenary, the co-producer of *The Streets of New York*, was one of the original co-founders and co-owners of Footlight Records, which opened its doors in the 1960s and happily remains open to this day (now as an Internet-only store). For decades, Footlight Records has been the store of choice for both current and out-of-print theatre- and film-related recordings.

1540 Streetsongs. THEATRE: Roundabout Theatre/Stage One; OPENING DATE: January 23, 1979; PERFORMANCES: 96; DIRECTION: Richard Maltby, Jr.; COSTUMES: Bill Walker; LIGHTING: Robert F. Strohmeier; MUSICAL DIRECTION: Stanley Wietrzychowski; VOCAL DIRECTION: Andy Thomas Anselmo; PRODUCER: The Roundabout Theatre Company, Inc. (Gene Feist and Michael Fried, Producing Directors) by special arrangement with Geraldine Fitzgerald and Alan Eichler

CAST—GERALDINE FITZGERALD; Tom Myers (Woodwinds), Greg Utzig (Guitar), Philip Campanella (Alternate Musician)

The revue was presented in two acts.

(The program didn't list musical numbers; the song list below reflects what was presented at one particular performance and no doubt is representative of the songs Geraldine Fitzgerald sang at most performances.)

ACT ONE—"Underneath the Arches" (by Reginald Connelly, Bud Flanagan, and Joseph McCarthy), "Pirate Jenny" (from *The Threepenny Opera*, 1928; original German lyric by Bertolt Brecht, music by Kurt Weill; unclear which English version was used in *Streetsongs*), "Forget-Me-Not Lane" (by Elton Box, Desmond Cox, and Paddy Roberts), "Danny Boy (Cuchulain's Lament)," "He's Funny That Way" (lyric by Richard A. Whiting, music by Neil Moret), "The Poor People of Paris" (lyric by Rene Rougaud, music by Marguerite Monnot; English lyric by Jack Lawrence), "She's Leaving Home" (lyric and music by John Lennon and Paul McCartney), "Swanee" (interpolated into the score of *Sinbad*, 1918; lyric by Irving Caesar and B.G. [Buddy] DeSylva, music by George Gershwin), "Four Green Fields" (lyric and music by Tommy Makem), "Phil the Fluter"

ACT TWO—"Lily of Laguna" (lyric and music by Leslie Stuart), "It's Not Cruel to Forget Your Ma," "Don't Cry for Me, Argentina" (*Evita*, British premiere in 1978, Broadway premiere in 1979; lyric by Tim Rice, music by Andrew Lloyd Webber), "The Pig Song," "Saturday Night at the Rose and Crown" (*The Girl Who Came to Supper*, 1963; lyric and music by Noel Coward), Pantomine Sequence: "I Believe," Impressions of Mrs. Creamer, Proprietor of the Black Lion Pub during the London blitz, "Who's This Geezer Hitler?" (*Blitz!*, 1961; lyric and music by Lionel Bart), Sing-Along Medley: "When You're Smiling" (lyric and music by Larry Shay, Mark Fisher, and Joe Goodwin), "Pack Up Your Troubles in Your Old Kit Bag" (lyric and music by Felix Powell and George Asaf), "When You're Smiling" (reprise), "The White Cliffs of Dover" (lyric by Nat Burton, music by Walter Kent)

NOTES—The great (and often overlooked) actress Geraldine Fitzgerald (her Mary Tyrone in the 1971 Off Broadway revival of *A Long Day's Journey Into Night* may well be the role's definitive performance) surprised everyone with her successful one-woman revue of "streetsongs." After its initial New York run, the revue was performed in cities throughout the United States, and was also shown on public television. One of the revue's performances at Cleveland's Great Lakes Shakespeare Festival in 1981 was recorded, and the album was released by Painted Smiles Records (LP # PS-1347). Much of the material in the 1979 production was included, as well as "Kerry Dance," "Carrick Fergus," "Smile," and "Fitzy's Rag" (the latter by Stanley Wietrzychowski, the revue's musical director and sometime pianist).

It was Geraldine Fitzgerald who first sang "Don't Cry for Me, Argentina" on the New York stage (when *Streetsongs* opened, the Broadway-bound *Evita* was ten months away from its New York premiere).

During Fall 1984, *Streetsongs* returned for a second Off Broadway engagement at the Actors' Playhouse; and later opened on April 16, 1989, at the Criterion Center Cabaret (Stage Left) for a limited engagement of six performances.

1541 Strider: The Story of a Horse. "A Play with Music." THEATRE: Chelsea Westside Theatre; OPENING DATE: May 31, 1979; PERFORMANCES: 189; PLAY: Original Russian play by Mark Rozovsky; English stage version by Robert Kalfin and Steve Brown (based on a translation by Tamara Bering Sunguroff); LYRICS: Original Russian lyrics by Uri Riashentsev; new English lyrics by Steve Brown; MUSIC: Mark Rozovsky and S. Vetkin; their music adapted by, and with new additional music composed by, Norman L. Berman; DIRECTION: Robert Kalfin and Lynne Gannaway; SCENERY: Wolfgang Roth; COSTUMES: Andrew Marley; LIGHTING: Robby Monk; MUSICAL DIRECTION: Norman L. Berman; PRODUCER: The Chelsea Theatre Center (Robert Kalfin, Producing Director)

CAST—Roger DeKoven (Vaska, Mr. Willingstone), Gordon Gould (Actor, Prince Serpuhofsky), Ronnie Newman (Actor, General Announcer), Pamela Burrell (Actor, Viazapurikha, Mathieu, Marie), Gerald Hiken (Actor, Strider), Katherine Mary Brown (Actor), Jeannine Khoutieff (Actor), Skip Lawing (Actor, Groom), Nina Dova (Actor, Gypsy), Benjamin Hendrickson (Actor, Count Bobrinksy, Darling, The Lieutenant), Igors Gavon (Actor, Feofan, Fritz), Charles Walker (Actor, Vendor), John Brownlee (Actor), Nancy Kawalek (Actor), Karen Trott (Actor, Gypsy), Tad Ingram (Actor), Evan Handler (Actor, Bet Taker), Steven Blane (Actor, Gypsy); Intermission songs performed by Nina Dova, with Karen Trott and Steven Blane

SOURCE—The 1886 short story "Kholstomer: The Story of a Horse" by Leo Tolstoy.

The play with music was presented in two acts (the program didn't list individual musical numbers).

NOTES—Based on Leo Tolstoy's 1886 short story, *Strider* was similar in theme to Anna Sewell's 1877 novel *Black Beauty* in that it depicted the life and times of one particular horse. Tolstoy used the horse as a symbol of what man experiences in his journey through life, and his story is also an allegory of the political situation in Russia during the late nineteenth century.

Strider was a popular play in Russia, and was in fact the first Russian play produced in New York under the then-new United States and Soviet Union Copyright Agreement. The critics were generally kind to the production, but certainly not overwhelmed by it, and one or two complained of the overly familiar *Story Theatre*-styled techniques used to tell the story.

The play ran for almost six months Off Broadway, for a total of 189 performances, and then transferred to Broadway, where it opened on November 21, 1979, at the Helen Hayes Theatre for 214 performances. Combining both the Off Broadway and Broadway engagements, the play ran for almost one full year in New York.

The script was published by Samuel French, Inc., in 1981.

1542 Strip! THEATRE: Village Gate; OPENING DATE: June 30, 1987; PERFORMANCES: 8; MATERIAL: Duane Mazey; LYRICS: Norman Bergman; MUSIC: Norman Bergman; DIRECTION: Phil Oesterman; PRODUCER: Phil Oesterman

CAST—John Altamura, Scott Burdick, Suzanne Cummings, Deborah Dangerfield, Beverly Hills, Donna Francis, Lat Jackson, Key Johnson, John Kasak, Markina the Amazon Woman, Lisa Randall, Michael Waldron

NOTES—The burlesque revue *Strip!* (which promised to reveal "the stripper behind the strip") was the last gasp in a long line of Off Broadway burlesque revues (see Appendix J for a complete list).

1543 Strut Miss Lizzie

NOTES—The comma-challenged *Strut Miss Lizzie* (which "Glorifies the Creole Beauty") originally opened Off Broadway on June 3, 1922, at the National Winter Garden Theatre on Hudson Street for sixteen performances. The revue soon transferred to Broadway on June 19, 1922, at the Times Square Theatre (and then to the Earl Carroll Theatre) for a total of eighty performances on Broadway. An unsigned review in the *New York Times* said the revue was "generally entertaining" but "somewhat repetitious" in its succession of songs, dances, and sketches. The reviewer noted that the evening had been deemed a "decidedly good entertainment" when it played Off Broadway. But he suspected that for Broadway the revue "suffered a little by the process of elaboration," and thus the evening could have done with some judicious pruning. He also noted that the "Creole damsels" of the chorus ranged from "dark-hued to not very dark at all," and he mentioned their scenes in the revue took place on the South Sea Islands, Southern plantations, and in restaurants.

(The information below is taken from a program from the Earl Carroll Theatre dated July 31, 1922.; LYRICS AND MUSIC: Henry Creamer and Turner Layton; DIRECTION: Henry Creamer; MUSICAL DIRECTION: Joe Jordan

CAST—HENRY CREAMER, TURNER LAYTON, Georgette Harve, The Lake Sisters, James Moore, Charles Fredericks, Hamtree Harrington, Cora Green, James Green, Bud Halliday, James Barrett, Brevard Burnett, Iris Hall, Leonard and (Eddie) Fields, Mildred Dixon, Al Moore, Willie Tyler, Carrie Edwards, Jones and Jones, Joe Henderson, Jennie Day, Lena Dukes, Lottie Ames, Jean Roundtree, Julia Aikman, Alberta Foster, Camille Barnes, Betty Page, Adelaide Jones, Minerva Lee, Mary Goodwin, Helen Dunmore, Daisy Fleming, Erma Ovington, Alberta Jones, Cornella Richardson, Ethel Taylor, Blanche Thompson, Dorothy Bellis, Wilhemena Shucraft, Madeline Yancy, Al Moore, Harry Watkins, John Gilliard, Charles Williams

The revue was presented in two acts.

ACT ONE—Spirituals (Georgette Harve, Company), "Dear Old Southland" (Georgette Harve, Company), "Buzz Mirandy" (Charles Fredericks' Creoles), "Vest Pocket Bert Williams" (sketch) (Hamtree Harrington), "Darktown Poker Club" (Hamtree Harrington), "Nobody's Gal" (Cora Green, Hamtree Harrington), Creole Alley at the Ritz: "Creole Belles" (Joe Henderson, Bud Halliday, Girls), "Dixie" (Joe Henderson, Bud Halliday), "In Yama" (Mildred Dixon, Jennie Day, Girls), "Crooning"/"Wyoming Lullaby"/"Down Yonder" (James Barrett, Charles Fredericks), "Breakin' a Leg" (Joe Henderson, Bud Halliday, Daisy Fleming, Girls), "Some Sunny Day"/"Lonesome Longing Blues" (Cora Green), "New Orleans" (Jean Roundtree, Al Moore, Company; Spanish Dancers, The Lake Sisters)

ACT TWO—"Hoola, from Coney Isle" (Cora Green, Carrie Edwards, South Sea Islanders), "Sweet Angeline" (Cora Green, James Barrett, Charles Fredericks, Joe Henderson, Bud Halliday, Creoles), "Il Trovatore" (James Green, Brevard Burnett), "When You Look in the Eyes of a Mule" (James Green), "Four Fo' Me" (Brevard Burnett), "Mandy" (Mildred Dixon, Eddie Fields, Joe Henderson, Bud Halliday, James Barrett, Charles Fredericks, Girls), Creamer and Layton, Finale (Company)

In the first act, the revue also included the sequences "Café D'Ella Lee" (with James Barrett and Charles Fredericks as "The Jazz Waiters") and "Humor in Steps" (with Leonard and Fields). The second act included "Southern Levee Types" (with Jones and Jones) and "Foreign Songs" (Georgette Harve).

During the intermission, Joe Jordan and His Velvet Band played "Ebony Rag" (music by Joe Jordan); "Bernice," a violin solo played by Willie Tyler with Joe Jordan at the piano (music by Joe Jordan]; and "At the Ball," played by Willie Tyler and the orchestra.

1544 Struttin'. "A Musical." THEATRE: AMAS Musical Theatre; OPENING DATE: February 11, 1988; PERFORMANCES: 16; BOOK: Lee Chamberlin; LYRICS: Lee Chamberlin; MUSIC: Lee Chamberlin; DIRECTION: Lee Chamberlin; CHOREOGRAPHY: Bernard J. Marsh; SCENERY: Jeffrey Miller; COSTUMES: Bernard Johnson; LIGHTING: Shirley Pendergast; MUSICAL DIRECTION: Neal Tate; PRODUCER: AMAS Musical Theatre (Rosetta LeNoire, Founder and Artistic Director)

CAST—Angelo Adkins, Jeff Bates, Josie Conte, Richard Costa, Gina Ellis, Harriett D. Foy, Jillian C. Hamilton, Dexter Jones, Shari Krikorian, David Lowenstein, Valerie Macklin, Casey McClellan, William Newhall, Roumel Reaux

The action occurs in Asbury Park, New York, Paris, and other cities during the period 1917-1940.

NOTES—The Off Off Broadway musical *Struttin'* dealt with two Black sisters who leave New Jersey for New York in order to seek fame and fortune in show business.

1545 Stupid Kids. THEATRE: Century Theatre; OPENING DATE: August 25, 1998; PERFORMANCES: 48; PLAY: John C. Russell; LYRICS: See song list for credits; MUSIC: See song list for credits; DIRECTION: Michael Mayer; CHOREOGRAPHY: Ken Roberson; SCENERY: David Gallo; COSTUMES: Michael Krass; LIGHTING: Kevin Adams; PRODUCERS: The WPA Theatre; The Shubert Organization; ABC Inc.; Scott Rudin, Roger Berlind, and Robert Fox

CAST—Shannon Burkett (Judy Noonan), James Carpinello (Jim Stark), Keith Nobbs (John "Neechee" Crawford), Mandy Siegfried (Jane "Kimberly" Willis)

The action occurs in the "the 'burbs" during the first through eighth periods, "rest of the day, day in, day out."

The play with music was presented in one act (song assignments unknown).

MUSICAL NUMBERS—"Radio Song" (lyric and music by Bill Berry, Peter Buck, and Mike Mills), "How Soon Is Now?" (lyricist and composer unknown), "Is It Really So Strange?" (lyricist and composer unknown), "The Headmaster Ritual" (lyric and music by John Marr and Steven Morrissey), "Wave of Manhattan" (lyric and music by Black Francis), "Lust for Life" (lyric and music by Iggy Pop and David Bowie), "Fall in Love with Me" (lyric and music by Iggy Pop, Hunt Sales, and Tony Sales), "Kimberly" (lyric and music by Patti Smith, Ivan Kral, and Allen Lanier), "Good Guys and Bad Guys" (lyricist and composer unknown), "Jerry's Daughter" (lyric and music by David Lowery, Jonathan Segel, Victor Krummenacher, Greg Lisher, Chris Molla, and Chris Pederson), "Take the Skinheads Bowling" (lyric and music by David Lowery, Chris Molla, Victor Krummenacher, and Jonathan Segel), "I Don't See You" (lyric and music by David Lowery, Chris Molla, and Eric Lang), "Stupid Kids" (lyric and music by Dan Sezman, Elizabeth Cox, Michael Cudahy, and Peter Rutigliano)

NOTES—*Stupid Kids*, a play with music, dealt with suburban high school kids who attend Joe McCarthy High School. The evening focused on two pairs, one popular (two "Ken and Barbie" types, according to Peter Marks in the *New York Times*), the other not (two gays).

Marks said the "peppy little satire" of high school life didn't have much in the way of a story, but noted the musical got it right in its depiction of the "insular" world of high school students and their "stylized teenspeak."

The work had been previously produced Off Off Broadway at the WPA Theatre on June 13, 1998, for twenty-eight performances.

1546 Styne After Styne. THEATRE: UpStage Cabaret/Manhattan Theatre Club; OPENING DATE: May 13, 1980; PERFORMANCES: 28; BOOK: Jonathan Reynolds; LYRICS: See song list for credits; MUSIC: Jule Styne Direction: Fritz Holt; CHOREOGRAPHY: Douglas Norwick; SCENERY: Kenneth Foy; COSTUMES: David Murin; LIGHTING: Ken Billington; MUSICAL DIRECTION: Eric Stern; PRODUCER: Manhattan Theatre Club (Lynne Meadow, Artistic Director; Barry Grove, Managing Director; Stephen Pascal, Associate Artistic Director)

CAST—Paul Hecht, Florence Lacey, Pauletta Pearson, Larry Riley, John Sheridan, Neva Small

The action occurs in a New York City rehearsal studio, some time next season.

The revue was presented in two acts.

ACT ONE—"Some People" (from *Gypsy*, 1959; lyric by Stephen Sondheim) (Florence Lacey, Pauletta Pearson, Neva Small), "Time After Time" (1947 film *It Happened in Brooklyn*; lyric by Sammy Cahn) (Larry Riley, Florence Lacey), "Never Never Land" (*Peter Pan*, 1954; lyric by Betty Comden and Adolph Green) (Pauletta Pearson), "You'll Never Get Away from Me" (*Gypsy*, 1959; lyric by Stephen Sondheim) (Neva Small), "I Met a Girl" (*Bells Are Ringing*, 1956; lyric by Betty Comden and Adolph Green) (John Sheridan), "Guess I'll Hang My Tears Out to Dry" (*Glad To See You*, which closed during its pre-Broadway tryout in 1944; lyric by Sammy Cahn) (Florence Lacey), "Give Me Five Minutes More" (lyric by Sammy Cahn; independent song) (Larry Riley), "Let It Snow! Let It Snow! Let It Snow!" (lyric by Sammy Cahn; independent song) (Pauletta Pearson), "Purple Sage in the Twilight" (source unknown) (Larry Riley), "Put 'Em in a Box" (1948 film *Romance on the High Seas*; lyric by Sammy Cahn) (Neva Small), "Saturday Night Is the Loneliest Night (of the Week)" (lyric by Sammy Cahn; independent song)"/I Fall in Love Too Easily" (1945 film *Anchors Aweigh*; lyric by Sammy Cahn) (John Sheridan), "The Christmas Waltz" (lyric by Sammy Cahn; independent song) (Florence Lacey), "The Brooklyn Bridge" (1947 film *It Happened in Brooklyn*; lyric by Sammy Cahn) (Larry Riley, Company), "Just in Time" (*Bells Are Ringing*, 1956; lyric by Betty Comden and Adolph Green) (Pauletta Pearson, Company), "I Don't Want to Walk Without You, Baby" (1942 film *Sweater Girl*; lyric by Sammy Cahn) (Neva Small, Company), "Ev'ry Street's a Boulevard (in Old New York)" (*Hazel Flagg*, 1953; lyric by Bob Hilliard) (Paul Hecht, Company), "Hallelujah, Baby!" (*Hallelujah, Baby!*, 1967; lyric by Betty Comden and Adolph Green) (Pauletta Pearson, Larry Riley), "All Is Need Is the Girl" (*Gypsy*, 1959; lyric by Stephen Sondheim) (John Sheridan), "If (If You Hadn't, But You Did)" (*Two on the Aisle*, 1951; lyric by Betty Comden and Adolph Green) (Florence Lacey), "Penniless Bums" (*Sugar*, 1972; lyric by Bob Merrill) (Larry Riley, John Sheridan), "A Butler in the Abbey" (*Darling of the Day*, 1968; lyric by E.Y. Harburg) (Paul Hecht), "Diamonds Are a Girl's Best Friend" (*Gentlemen Prefer Blondes*, 1949; lyric by Sammy Cahn) (Pauletta Pearson), "I'm Goin' Back" (*Bells Are Ringing*, 1956; lyric by Betty Comden and Adolph Green) (Neva Small), "It's a Simple Little System" (*Bells Are Ringing*, 1956; lyric by Betty Comden and Adolph Green) (Paul Hecht, Company), "Sunday" (source unknown) (Company)

ACT TWO—"People" (*Funny Girl*, 1964; lyric by Bob Merrill) (Pauletta Pearson), "Puddin' Head" (1941 film *Puddin' Head*; lyric by Eddie Cherkose and Sol Meyer) (Pauletta Pearson), "I Got a Gal I Love" (source unknown) (Larry Riley), "I Love Eggs" (1946 film *Tars and Spars*; lyric by Sammy Cahn) (John Sherdian), "Poor Little Rhode Island" (1944 film *Carolina Blues*; lyric by Sammy Cahn) (Florence Lacey), "Conchita Marquita Lolita Pepita Rosita Juanita Lopez" (1942 film *Priorities on Parade*; lyric by Herb Magidson) (Paul Hecht), "Let's See What Happens" (*Darling of the Day*, 1968; lyric by E.Y. Harburg) (Paul Hecht), "Make Someone Happy" (*Do Re Mi*, 1960; lyric by Betty Comden and Adolph Green) (Florence Lacey), "Small World" (*Gypsy*, 1959; lyric by Stephen Sondheim) (John Sheridan), "The Party's Over" (*Bells Are Ringing*, 1956; lyric by Betty Comden and Adolph Green) (Neva Small), "Independent" (*Bells Are Ringing*, 1956; lyric by Betty Comden and Adolph Green) (Larry Riley), "It's Been a Long, Long Time" (lyric by Sammy Cahn; song written independent of any production) (Pauletta Pearson), "I Said No" (1942 film *Sweater Girl*; lyric by Frank Loesser) (Neva Small), "Vict'ry (Victory) Polka" (1944 film *Jam Session*; lyric by Sammy Cahn) (Larry Riley, Florence Lacey, Pauletta Pearson, Neva Small), "I'll Walk Alone" (1944 film *Follow the Boys*; lyric by Sammy Cahn) (Florence Lacey), "Three Coins in the Fountain" (1954 film *Three Coins in the Fountain*; lyric by Sammy Cahn) (Company), "Everything's Coming Up Roses" (*Gypsy*, 1959; lyric by Stephen Sondheim) (Larry Riley), "I'm the Greatest Star" (*Funny Girl*, 1964; lyric by Bob Merrill) (Neva Small), "The Music That Makes Me Dance" (*Funny Girl*, 1964; lyric By Bob Merrill) (Florence Lacey), "Don't Rain on My Parade" (*Funny Girl*, 1964; lyric by Bob Merrill) (Pauletta Pearson), "Being Good (Isn't Good Enough)" (*Hallelujah, Baby!*, 1967; lyric by Betty Comden and Adolph Green) (John Sheridan), Finale (Company)

NOTES—In the early 1980s, there were two "tribute" revues to Jule Styne, but neither transferred to Broadway (see entry for 1982's *Vamps and Rideouts*). The program credited Jonathan Reynolds with the "book," but no one was fooled: *Styne After Styne* was still a revue. Although the Off Off Broadway piece contained mostly familiar material, it offered a welcome sampling of Styne's lesser-known film songs (such as "Puddin' Head," "Poor Little Rhode Island," and "I Said No").

1547 Suburb. THEATRE: The Theatre at Saint Peter's Church/The York Theatre Company; OPENING DATE: March 1, 2001; PERFORMANCES: 29; BOOK: David Javerbaum and Robert S. Cohen; LYRICS: David Javerbaum; MUSIC: Robert S. Cohen; DIRECTION: Jennifer Uphoff Gray; Nancy S. Chu, Assistant Director; CHOREOGRAPHY: John Carrafa; Rachel Bress, Assistant Choreographer; SCENERY: Kris Stone; COSTUMES: Jay Finnell; LIGHTING: John Michael Deegan; MUSICAL DIRECTION: Jeffrey R. Smith; PRODUCERS: The York Theatre Company (James Morgan, Artistic Director) in association with Jennifer M. Sanchez and Roberta Plutzik Baldwin

CAST—Jacquelyn Piro (Alison), James Ludwig (Stuart), Dennis Kelly (Tom), Alix (Alexandra) Korey (Rhoda), Adinah Alexander (Ensemble), Ron

Butler (Ensemble), Jennie Eisenhower (Ensemble), James Sasser (Ensemble)

The action occurs in the present time.

The musical was presented in two acts.

ACT ONE—"Directions" (Company), "Mow" (James Ludwig, Jacquelyn Piro, Ensemble), "Do It Yourself" (Dennis Kelly), "Suburb" (Ensemble), "Not Me" (Jacquelyn Piro), "Barbeque" (Ensemble), "The Girl Next Door" (Alix Korey, James Sasser, Ron Butler, James Ludwig), "Ready or Not" (James Ludwig, Dennis Kelly), "Commute" (Ensemble)

ACT TWO—"Mall" (Company), "Duet" (Jacquelyn Piro, James Ludwig), "Handy" (Alix Korey, Dennis Kelly), "Walkin' to School" (Ensemble), "Bagel-Shop Quartet" (Ensemble), "Trio for Four" (Dennis Kelly, James Ludwig, Jacquelyn Piro), "Everything Must Go" (Ensemble), "Someday" (Jacquelyn Piro, James Ludwig, Dennis Kelly, Alix Korey)

NOTES—The plot dealt with a couple who leave the city for the suburbs. Jeffrey Eric Jenkins in *The Best Plays of 2000-2001* felt the piece might have worked better "in some New Jersey bedroom community." Anita Gates in the *New York Times* said the "engaging and very promising" evening offered clever direction, "personable" performances, and a humorous book. While she noted the score was sometimes "disappointingly ordinary," she quickly added that at its best (in such songs as "Commute" and "Walkin' to School") it achieved a "Sondheimian blend of playfulness and reflection."

The cast album was released on unlabeled and unnumbered CD.

The musical had been first produced in 2000 by the Alleyway Theatre in Buffalo.

1548 Success! "A New Musical." THEATRE: Carter Theatre; OPENING DATE: February 1979 (?); PERFORMANCES: Unknown; LYRICS: Steven J. Matay; MUSIC: Steven J. Matay; DIRECTION: Marcy Davis; CHOREOGRAPHY: Kat deBlois; LIGHTING: Tim Alger; MUSICAL DIRECTION: Steve Rosenthal; PRODUCERS: Edith O'Hara and Jim Payne (Broadway Times Theatre Company, Inc.)

CAST—Laurie Brongo, Andrew Lustig, Nancy Jo Myers, Steven Cupo, Paul Wermuth

The revue was presented in one act.

MUSICAL NUMBERS—Overture (Orchestra), "Success" (Company), "Great Roles" (Paul Wermuth, Andrew Lustig), "Newest Girl in Town" (Steven Cupo, Nancy Jo Myers), "Journey's End" (Paul Wermuth), "Cattle Calls" (Company), "Dear Mr. Merrick" (Andrew Lustig), "Contracts in E Flat" (Andrew Lustig, Nancy Jo Myers, Laurie Brongo, Steven Cupo), "Off Off Broadway" (Steven Cupo, Laurie Brongo, Nancy Jo Myers), "The Closest Star" (Laurie Brongo), "The Road To" (Company), "Broadway Melody" (Company), "What Will Happen to Me" (Nancy Jo Myers), "Fame" (Paul Wermuth), "Theatre Relationships" (Andrew Lustig, Laurie Brongo, Paul Wermuth, Nancy Jo Myers), "The Old Vaudevillian" (Steven Cupo; danced by Andrew Lustig), "Theater Party" (Steven Cupo, Andrew Lustig, Company), "The Exciting Life Blues" (Nancy Jo Myers), "Broadway Melody" (reprise) (Company), "The Not So Great White Way" (Company), "If It Gives Us Nothing Else" (Company), "Something More" (Company)

NOTES—*Success!* was one of a handful of short-lived musicals presented by the Broadway Times Theatre Company, Inc. (see entries for *Shelley*, *One and One*, and *Not Tonight, Benvenuto!*)

1549 Such Good Friends

NOTES—See entry for *The New York Musical Theatre Festival.*

1550 Suddenly the Music Starts. THEATRE: The AMAS Repertory Theatre; OPENING DATE: May 3, 1979; PERFORMANCES: 12; LYRICS: Johnny Brandon Music: Johnny Brandon; CHOREOGRAPHY: Henry Le Tang; Eleanor Le Tang, Associate Choreographer; SCENERY: Patrick Mann; COSTUMES: Virginia Johnson; LIGHTING: Paul Sullivan; MUSICAL DIRECTION: Neal Tate; PRODUCER: The AMAS Repertory Theatre (Rosetta LeNoire, Founder and Artistic Director)

CAST—Mary Ellen Ashley, Jean Cheek, Debbi Dee, Kevin John Gee, George Hamilton, William "Gregg" Hunter, Kelli Kahn, Mable M. Lee, Mary Louise, Wayne McCarthy, Rozlyn Sorrell, Andy Torres

MUSICAL NUMBERS (division of acts and song assignments unknown; song list is in performance order)—"Suddenly the Music Starts," "My Home Town," "Faces in a Crowd," "Funky People," "Super Bad," "I'll Scratch Your Back," "Goodnight," "Boogie Woogie Ball," "Talk Your Feelings," "Your Love Is My Love," "Dancing Dan," "Dance! Dance! Dance!," "Whole Lotta Real Good Feeling," "Remember Someone," "Everybody's Doing the Disco," "Guides," "Stuff," "Syncopatin'" "Kansas City Blues," "Manhattan Lullaby," "One Day at a Time," "You," "It's My Turn Now," "Strolling Down Broadway," Finale

NOTES—"Syncopatin'" had been earlier heard in Johnny Brandon's 1968 musical *Who's Who, Baby?* (see entry).

Suddenly the Music Starts was the third musical by Brandon which was produced Off Off Broadway during the 1978-1979 season (see entries for *Ain't Doin' Nothin' But Singin' My Song* and *Helen*).

1551 Suds. "The Rocking 60's Musical Soap Opera." THEATRE: Criterion Center; OPENING DATE: September 25, 1988; PERFORMANCES: 81; BOOK: Melinda Gilb, Steve Gunderson, Susan Mosher, and Christine Sevec; LYRICS: See song list for credits; MUSIC: See song list for credits; DIRECTION: Will Roberson; CHOREOGRAPHY: Javier Velasco; SCENERY: Alan Okazaki; COSTUMES: Gregg Barnes; LIGHTING: Kent Dorsey; MUSICAL DIRECTION: William Doyle; PRODUCERS: Richard Redlin, Will Roberson, Bryant Scott, Norma and David Langworthy

CAST—Christine Sevec (Cindy), Melinda Gilb (Marge), Susan Mosher (Dee Dee), Steve Gunderson (Everyone Else)

The action occurs in a laundromat in the early 1960s.

The musical was presented in two acts (division of acts unknown; song assignments not credited in the program, which listed all songs alphabetically).

MUSICAL NUMBERS—"A Little Bit of Soap" (lyric and music by B. Russell), "(There's) Always Something There to Remind Me" (lyric by Hal David, music by Burt Bacharach), "Anyone Who Had a Heart" (lyric by Hal David, music by Burt Bacharach), "Are You Lonesome Tonight" (lyric and music by R. Turk and L. Handman), "Baby It's You" (lyric by Hal David, music by Burt Bacharach), "Be My Baby" (lyric and music by Jeff Barry and Ellie Greenwich), "Big Man" (lyric and music by G. Larson and B. Belland), "Birthday Party" (lyric and music by J. Madera and D. White), "Chapel of Love" (lyric and music by Jeff Barry, Ellie Greenwich, and Phil Spector), "Cindy's Birthday" (lyric and music by H. Wynn and J. Hooven), "Color My World" (lyric and music by Jackie Trent and Anthony Peter Hatch), "Dedicated to the One I Love" (lyric and music by L. Palling and R. Bass), "Do You Want to Know a Secret" (lyric and music by John Lennon and Paul McCartney), "Don't Make Me Over" (lyric by Hal David, music by Burt Bacharach), "Do Wah Diddy Diddy" (lyric and music by Jeff Barry and Ellie Greenwich), "Easier Said Than Done" (lyric and music by W. Linton and L. Huff), "The End of the World" (lyric and music by S. Dee and A. Kent), "Happy Birthday Sweet Sixteen" (lyric and music by Neil Sedaka), "Help Me Girl" (lyric and music by S. Weiss and L. English), "How Can I Be Sure" (lyric and music by F. Cavaliere and E. Brigati), "I Don't Wanna Be a Loser" (lyric and music by R. Raleigh and M. Barkan), "I Got You (I Feel Good)" (lyric and music by James Brown), "I Know a Place" (lyric and music by Anthony Peter Hatch), "I Will Follow Him" (lyric and music by A. Altman, Norman Gimbel, F. Pourcel, J. Plante, and J.W. Stole-Del Roma), "I Say a Little Prayer" (lyric by Hal David, music by Burt Bacharach), "It's My Party" (lyric and music by W. Gold, J. Gluck, H. Wiener, and S. Gottlieb), "Johnny Angel" (lyric by Lynn Duddy, music by Lee Pockriss), "(The) Loco-Motion" (lyric and music by G. Goffin and C. King), "The Letter" (lyric and music by W. Thompson), "Lollipops and Roses" (lyric and music by T. Velona), "The Look of Love" (from 1967 film *Casino Royale*; lyric by Hal David, music by Burt Bacharach), "Mystery Date" (lyric and music by J. Harvey), "Our Day Will Come" (lyric and music by M. Garson and Bob Hilliard), "Please Mr. Postman" (lyric and music by F. Gorman, R. Bateman, and Brian Holland), "Respect" (lyric and music by Otis Redding), "Reach Out in the Darkness" (lyric and music by J. Post), "Round Every Corner" (lyric and music by Anthony Peter Hatch), "Secret Agent Man" (lyric and music by J. Rivers), "Shout" (lyric and music by R. Isley, B. Isley, and O. Isley), "Tell Him (lyric and music by B. Russell), "These Boots Are Made for Walking" (lyrics and music by Lee Hazelwood), "Today I Met the Boy I'm Gonna Marry" (lyric and music by Tony Powers, Ellie Greenwich, and Phil Spector), "Town Without Pity" (1961 film *Town Without Pity*; lyric by Ned Washington, music by Dimitri Tiomkin), "Walk On By" (lyric by Hal David, music by Burt Bacharach), "We Can Work It Out" (lyric and music by John Lennon and Paul McCartney), "Where the Boys Are" (1960 film *Where the Boys Are*; lyric and music by H. Greenfield and Neil Sedaka), "Wishing and Hoping" (lyric by Hal David, music by Burt Bacharach), "Wonderful, Wonderful" (lyric and music by Sherman Edwards and B. Raleigh), "You Can't Hurry Love" (lyric and music by Brian Holland, Lamont Dozier, and Edward J. Holland), "You Don't Own Me" (lyric and music by J. Madera and D. White), "You Don't Have to Say You Love Me" (lyric and music by P. Donaggio, Vito Pallavicini, Vicky Wickham, S.N. Bell, and Napier)

NOTES—Like the revues *Beehive*, *The Taffetas* (which opened three weeks after *Suds* premiered), and the much later *Shout!* (see entries), *Suds* used popular girl-singer and girl-group songs of the 1950s and 1960s. But in the case of *Suds*, the songs weren't presented in a revue-like format like the other musicals; instead, the songs in *Suds* were used to support a slight plot about a depressed worker in a laundromat who's cheered up by guardian angels who sing old songs to her. *Suds* was an early example of a musical which took pre-existing songs and grafted them into a new plot.

The musical had been previously produced at the Old Globe Theatre in San Diego.

1552 Summer and Smoke. THEATRE: New York State Theatre; OPENING DATE: March 19, 1972; PERFORMANCES: Unknown; LIBRETTO: Lanford Wilson; MUSIC: Lee Hoiby; DIRECTION: Frank Corsaro; SCENERY: Lloyd Evans; COSTUMES: Lloyd Evans; LIGHTING: Hans Sondheimer; MUSICAL DIRECTION: Julius Rudel; PRODUCER: New York City Opera Company

CAST—Riley Kellogg (Alma [as a child]), Colin Duffy (John [as a child]), Mary Beth Peil (Alma Winemiller), J.B. Davis (the Reverend Winemiller), Zoya Leporska (Mrs. Winemiller), John Reardon (John Buchanan, Jr.), David Rae Smith (Dr.

Buchanan), Mary Cross Lueders (Rosa Gonzalez), James Cade (Papa Gonzalez), Barbara Shuttleworth (Nellie Elwell), Judith Anthony (Mrs. Bassett), John Lankston (Roger Doremus), Deborah Kieller (Rosemary), Karl Patrick Krause (Vernon), Alan Titus (Archie Kramer)

SOURCE—The 1948 play *Summer and Smoke* by Tennessee Williams.

The action occurs in Glorious Hill, Mississippi, in 1910.

The opera was presented in two acts.

NOTES—*Summer and Smoke* was Lee Hoiby's third opera to be seen at the New York City Opera. In 1959, *The Scarf* had its New York premiere with the company, and in 1964 the company presented the world premiere of *Natalia Petrovna* (see entries). *Summer and Smoke* had first been produced by the St. Louis Opera Association on June 19, 1971, with Mary Beth Peil and John Reardon in the leading roles and with direction by Frank Corsaro. All three reprised their assignments for the New York premiere of the work.

The story dealt with Alma Winemiller, a sexually repressed young woman who spurns the advances of a young and earthy doctor; by the time she comes around to embracing his outlook on life, she discovers he's no longer interested in her and has become somewhat prim and proper himself. In some ways, the play seemed a variation on Cole Porter's "I Loved Him (but He Didn't Love Me)."

Harold C. Schonberg's review in the *New York Times* noted that the expensive production, the "brilliant" cast, the "ingenious and evocative" scenery, and the period costumes were all evidence that the City Opera felt it had a potential hit. But while Schonberg praised playwright Lanford Wilson's libretto, he felt Hoiby's score emphasized the orchestra and not the voice (there was "not enough song," and the singers had few chances to "let loose"). In 1980, the Chicago Opera Theatre revived the work (Mary Beth Peil again performed the role of Alma); this production was taped for television (it was first televised in New York on June 23, 1982), and John J. O'Connor in the *New York Times* praised Hoiby's music ("a haunting tone poem"), and noted that the underlying sadness of the piece was undercut by "bright Mexican mariachi music," a "snappy marching parade," and two romantic arias.

1553 Summer Friends. THEATRE: Playwrights Horizons; OPENING DATE: February 19, 1981; PERFORMANCES: 15; LIGHTING: David N. Weiss; PRODUCER: Playwrights Horizons (Robert Moss, Producing Director; Robin J. Gold, Managing Director; Andre Bishop, Artistic Director)

CAST—Stephanie Cotsirilos

NOTES—*Summer Friends* was a one-woman evening of songs performed by Stephanie Cotsirilos; the production included songs that she, Mel Marvin, "& Friends" had written.

Gerald Guiterrez and Dorothy J. Maffei were credited as "production consultants."

1554 Summer of '42. "A New Musical." THEATRE: Variety Arts Theatre; OPENING DATE: December 18, 2001; PERFORMANCES: 47; BOOK: Hunter Foster; LYRICS: David Kirshenbaum; MUSIC: David Kirshenbaum; DIRECTION: Gabriel Barre; CHOREOGRAPHY: Gabriel Barre; Jennifer Cody, Associate Choreographer; SCENERY: James Youmans; COSTUMES: Pamela Scofield; LIGHTING: Tim Hunter; MUSICAL DIRECTION: Lynne Shankel; PRODUCERS: Mitchell Maxwell and Victoria Maxwell, Robert Eckert, James L. Simon, Michael A. Jenkins, Mark Goldberg, and Kumiko Yoshii in association with Richard Bernstein and Sibling Entertainment, Inc.; Fred H, Krones, Associate Producer

CAST—Ryan Driscoll (Hermie), Kate Jennings Grant (Dorothy), Greg Stone (Pete), Celia Keenan-Bolger (Aggie), Megan Valerie Walker (Miriam), Erin Webley (Gloria), Brett Tabisel (Oscy), Jason Marcus (Benjie), Bill Kux (Mr. Sanders, Walter Winchell)

SOURCE—The 1971 novel *Summer of '42* by Herman Raucher and the 1971 film *Summer of '42* (screenplay by Herman Raucher).

The action occurs on an island off the coast of New England during Summer 1942.

The musical was presented in two acts.

ACT ONE—Opening (Company), "Here and Now" (Ryan Driscoll, Brett Tabisel, Jason Marcus), "Will That Ever Happen to Me?" (Ryan Driscoll), "You're Gonna Miss Me" (The Girls), "Little Did I Dream" (Greg Stone, Kate Jennings Grant), "The Walk" (Ryan Driscoll, Kate Jennings Grant), "Like They Used To" (Ryan Driscoll, Kate Jennings Grant), "I Think I Like Her" (Ryan Driscoll), "The Heat" (The Girls), "The Movies" (Ryan Driscoll, Celia Keenan-Bolger, Brett Tabisel, Megan Valerie Walker), "Man Around the House" (The Girls), "Someone to Dance with Me" (Kate Jennings Grant, Ryan Driscoll)

ACT TWO—"Unfinished Business" (Brett Tabisel, Ryan Driscoll, Jason Marcus), "Make You Mine" (The Girls), "The Drugstore" (Ryan Driscoll, Bill Kux), "The Campfire" (Ryan Driscoll), "Promise of the Morning" (Kate Jennings Grant), "Oh Gee, I Love My G.I." (The Girls), "The Dance" (instrumental), Finale (Company)

NOTES—Based on the novel as well as the popular 1971 film, *Summer of '42* was a familiar coming-of-age story about Hermie, a teenage boy (Ryan Driscoll) who becomes involved with Dorothy, an older, married woman (Kate Jennings Grant).

Bruce Weber in the *New York Times* found the evening disappointing, and noted that "a little anguished adolescence ... goes a long way"; he singled out "Like They Used To" as the best song in the score. Dennis Harvey in *Variety* said the musical was a work of "engaging substance as well as considerable charm," and noted it "could prove a real regional crowdpleaser."

The musical lasted just six weeks. Its script was published by Dramatists Play Service, Inc., in 2004, and in 2007 a 2-CD recording (from a May 24, 2004, benefit performance) was released by Jay Records (# CDJAY2-1396). For the recording, Driscoll reprised his role of the young boy, and Dorothy was sung by Rachel York; original cast members heard on the recording were Celia Keenan-Bolger, Megan Valerie Walker, and Brett Tabisel, and other singers included Danielle Ferland. The CD also included two bonus tracks, "Our Story So Far" and "Losing Track of Time"; both songs were sung by the character of Dorothy, and apparently had been considered for the production at one time or another.

Summer of '42 had originally been produced by Goodspeed Musicals in Chester, Connecticut, on August 10, 2000, and was subsequently developed by Theatreworks in Palo Alto, California.

1555 Summer Share

NOTES—See entry for *Romance Romance*.

1556 Summer 69. THEATRE: Douglas Fairbanks Theatre; OPENING DATE: July 15, 1999; PERFORMANCES: 105; BOOK: Bill Van Horn, Leer Paul Leary, and Ellen Michelmore; LYRICS: See song list for credits; MUSIC: See song list for credits; DIRECTION: Bruce Lumpkin; SCENERY: John Farrell; COSTUMES: Colleen McMillan; LIGHTING: Jeffrey S. Koger; MUSICAL DIRECTION: Faser Hardin; PRODUCERS: Ira Shapiro, Robert T. Schneider, and Stuart A. Ditsky in association with Stephen Rose

CAST—E. Alyssa Claar, Jamie Hurley, Brian Maillard, Ron McClary, Kirk McGee, Anne Moore, Rik Sansone, Rachel Stern, Christine M. Williamson

The action occurs during Summer 1969.

The revue was presented in two acts.

ACT ONE—"Woodstock" (lyric and music by Joni Mitchell) (Christine M. Williamson, Jamie Hurley, Brian Maillard, Ron McClary, Kirk McGee, Anne Moore, Rik Sansone), "Summer in the City" (lyric and music by John Sebastian, Mark Sebastian, and Steve Boone) (Rachel Stern, E. Alyssa Claar, Company), "Goin' Up the Country" (lyric and music by Alan Wilson) (Rik Sansone, Brian Maillard), "Mercedes Benz" (lyric and music by Janis Joplin, Michael McClure, and Bob Neuwirth) (E. Alyssa Claar), "The Times They Are A'Changin'" (lyric and music by Bob Dylan) (Brian Maillard, Jamie Hurley, Kirk McGee, Anne Moore, Rik Sansone, Christine M. Williamson, Ron McClary), "Black Magic Woman" (lyric and music by Peter Alen Green) (E. Alyssa Claar, Brian Maillard), "Somebody to Love" (lyric and music by Darby Slick) (E. Alyssa Claar), "Teach Your Children Well" (lyric and music by Graham Nash) (Company), "I Feel Like I'm Fixin' to Die Rag" (lyric and music by Joe McDonald) (Ron McClary, Jamie Hurley, Anne Moore, Kirk McGee, Brian Maillard, Rik Sansone, Christine M. Williamson), "Find the Cost of Freedom" (lyric and music by Stephen Stills) (Rik Sansone, Brian Maillard, Ron McClary, Kirk McGee, Anne Moore, Jamie Hurley, Christine M. Williamson)

ACT TWO—"For What It's Worth" (lyric and music by Stephen Stills) (Rachel Stern, Company), "White Rabbit" (lyric and music by Grace Slick) (E. Alyssa Claar), "With a Little Help from My Friends" (lyric and music by John Lennon and Paul McCartney) (Ron McClary, E. Alyssa Claar, Rachel Stern, Company), "The Weight" (lyric and music by JR Robinson) (Rachel Stern, Company), "Piece of My Heart" (lyric and music by Bert Berns and Jerry Ragovoy) (E. Alyssa Claar), "Let's Get Together" (lyric and music by Chet Powers) (Rachel Stern, E. Alyssa Claar), "The Star-Spangled Banner" (lyric and music by Francis Scott Key) (Band), "Turn, Turn, Turn (To Everything There Is a Season)" (lyric and music by Pete Seeger) (Company), "Dance to the Music" (lyric and music by Sylvester Stewart) (Company)

NOTES—Three weeks before its Off Broadway production, *Summer 69* had been previously seen Off Off Broadway on June 24, 1999, for five performances at Theatre 80. Lawrence Van Gelder in the *New York Times* felt the evening offered "anemic" characterizations, "ineffective" projections, and an overall inability to even hint at what it was like to be living in the late 1960s. But when the songs took over, the musical was a "genuine treat," and he singled out E. Alyssa Claar (whose voice captured and channeled the "soul of the '60s" and the "essence of Woodstock").

1557 Sunday in the Park with George. THEATRE: Playwrights Horizons; OPENING DATE: July 6, 1983; PERFORMANCES: 26; BOOK: James Lapine; LYRICS: Stephen Sondheim; MUSIC: Stephen Sondheim; DIRECTION: James Lapine; SCENERY: Tony Staiges; COSTUMES: Patricia Zipprodt and Ann Hould-Ward; LIGHTING: Richard Nelson; MUSICAL DIRECTION: Paul Gemignani; PRODUCERS: Playwrights Horizons (Andre Bishop, Artistic Director; Paul Daniels, Managing Director) and the Herrick Theatre Foundation

CAST—Mandy Patinkin (George), Bernadette Peters (Dot), Carmen Mathews (Old Lady), Judith Moore (Nurse, Mrs.), Brent Spiner (Franz), Bradley Kane (Boy in the Water), Kelsey Grammer (Young Man on the Bank, Soldier), William Parry (Pervert, Boatman), Danielle Ferland (Louise), Ralph Byers (Jules), Christine Baranski (Clarissa), Kevin Marcum (Louis), Melanie Vaughan (Celeste 1), Mary Elizabeth Mastrantonio (Celeste 2), Nancy Opel (Bette), Kurt Knudson (Mr.)

SOURCES—The life of Georges Seurat and his painting "A Sunday Afternoon on the Island of La Grande Jatte."

The action occurs on a series of Sundays in 1884 and 1885, and alternates between a park on an island in the Seine just outside Paris and in George's studio in town.

NOTES—Ten months before *Sunday in the Park with George* opened on Broadway (at the Booth Theatre on May 2, 1984), a workshop production played at Playwrights Horizons for twenty-six performances in July 1983. In early performances, only the first act was presented; later in the run, the first act and part of the second act was performed. The workshop presentation included cast members who weren't in the Broadway production (for example, in the Broadway version, Barbara Byrne played the role created by Carmen Mathews in the workshop [see below]); further, Kelsey Grammer, Christine Baranski, and Mary Elizabeth Mastrantonio were in the workshop but not the Broadway production, while Cris Groenendaal, Charles Kimbrough, and Dana Ivey were in the Broadway production but not the workshop.

The Broadway production played for 604 performances and won the Pulitzer Prize for drama; the production was eventually seen on public television, and was later released on home video (laser disk, videocassette, and DVD); the most recent home video release of the musical was part of the DVD boxed set *The Stephen Sondheim Collection* by Image Entertainment (# ID-17531-MDVD). The cast album of the Broadway production was recorded by RCA Victor Records (the most recent issue, on Sony BMG Muisc Entertainment Masterworks Broadway Records, includes two bonus tracks of songs from the production [CD # 82876-68638-2]), and the script was published by Dodd, Mead & Company in 1986. The cast recording of a 2006 London production was released by PS Classics Records (CD # PS-640) with Daniel Evans and Jenna Russell in the two leading roles; the CD included a bonus track of the complete version of "The One on the Left." (Originally a complete song during some of the workshop performances, "The One on the Left" was shortened for Broadway and was in fact not even listed in the Broadway playbill. For Broadway, it was sung by the characters of George, the Soldier, Celeste #1, and Celeste #2 between "Everyone Loves Louis" and "Finishing the Hat"; the Nonesuch recording included the song in its complete version, as it was heard in some of the workshop performances.)

As of this writing, the London production of the musical is scheduled to be revived on Broadway by the Roundabout Theatre Company at Studio 54 on February 21, 2008, with London cast members Daniel Evans and Jenna Russell; Michael Crumpsty, Alexander Gemignani, Jessica Molaskey, and Mary Beth Peil are also scheduled to be in the revival.

The order of the cast listing above (as well as the list of songs below) is reflective of one of the workshop performances: "Sunday in the Park with George" (Bernadette Peters), "Yoo-Hoo!" (Bradley Kane, Kelsey Grammer, William Parry), "No Life" (Ralph Byers, Christine Baranski), "Color and Light" (Bernadette Peters, Mandy Patinkin), "Gossip" (Melanie Vaughan, Mary Elizabeth Mastrantonio, William Parry, Judith Moore, Carmen Mathews, Ralph Byers, Christine Baranski), "The Day Off" (Mandy Patinkin [as George; and as Spot and Fifi, two dogs], Judith Moore, Brent Spiner, Nancy Opel, William Parry, Kelsey Grammer, Christine Baranski, Danielle Ferland, Melanie Vaughan, Mary Elizabeth Mastrantonio), "Everybody Loves Louis" (Bernadette Peters), "Soldiers and Girls" (Kelsey Grammer, Melanie Vaughan, Mary Elizabeth Mastrantonio), "Finishing the Hat" (Mandy Patinkin), "Beautiful" (Carmen Mathews, Mandy Patinkin), "Sunday" (Company), ("Yoo-Hoo!" and "Soldiers and Girls" were dropped for the Broadway production.)

The following is a list of songs heard in the Broadway version (followed by the names of the performers):

ACT ONE—"Sunday in the Park with George" (Bernadette Peters), "No Life" (Charles Kimbrough, Dana Ivey), "Color and Light" (Bernadette Peters, Mandy Patinkin), "Gossip" (Melanie Vaughan, Mary D'Arcy, William Parry, Judith Moore, Barbara Byrne, Charles Kimbrough, Dana Ivey), "The Day Off" (Mandy Patinkin, Judith Moore, Brent Spiner, Nancy Opel, William Parry, Robert Westenberg, Melanie Vaughan, Mary D'Arcy, Dana Ivey, Danielle Ferland, Charles Kimbrough, Cris Groenendaal), "Everybody Loves Louis" (Bernadette Peters), "Finishing the Hat" (Mandy Patinkin), "We Do Not Belong Together" (Bernadette Peters, Mandy Patinkin), "Beautiful" (Mandy Patinkin, Barbara Byrne), "Sunday" (Company)

ACT TWO—"It's Hot Up Here" (Company), "Chromolume #7" (Mandy Patinkin, Bernadette Peters), "Putting It Together" (Mandy Patinkin, Company), "Children and Art" (Bernadette Peters), "Lesson #8" (Mandy Patinkin), "Move On" (Mandy Patinkin, Bernadette Peters), "Sunday" (reprise) (Company)

As mentioned above, Carmen Mathews (1914-1995) created the role of George's Mother in the workshop production, but for the Broadway version the role was performed by Barbara Byrne. If Mathews had continued with the production, *Sunday in the Park with George* would have marked her first appearance in a long-running and critically acclaimed musical. She had been performing in musicals since 1951, and all seven of them were failures: *Courtin' Time* (1951); *Zenda* (closed in 1963 during its pre-Broadway tryout); *The Yearling* (1965, three performances); *I'm Solomon* (1968, seven performances); *Dear World* (1969, 132 performances); *Ambassador* (1972, nine performances); and *Copperfield* (1981, thirteen performances). Mathews was considerably luckier in her non-musicals. The 1943 drama *Harriet* played for 377 performances, and while *My Three Angels* (1953, 342 performances) and *Holiday for Lovers* (1957, 100 performances) were financial failures, they played for a few months and were later filmed (the former in fact twice). Mathews also appeared in *Night Life* (1962, sixty-three performances), which was Sidney Kingsley's final play. She was in the original 1966 production of Edward Albee's *A Delicate Balance*, which, despite its short run of 132 performances nonetheless turned a profit; the play won the Pulitzer Prize for Drama in 1967, was filmed in 1973, and was memorably revived on Broadway in 1996 in a stunningly performed production which won the 1996 Tony Award for Best Revival of a Play.

1558 Sunset.

THEATRE: Downstairs/Village Gate; OPENING DATE: November 7, 1983; PERFORMANCES: 1; BOOK: Will Holt; LYRICS: Will Holt; MUSIC: Gary William Friedman; DIRECTION: Andre Ernotte; CHOREOGRAPHY: Buzz Miller; SCENERY: Kate Edmunds; COSTUMES: Patricia Zipprodt; LIGHTING: Robert Jared; MUSICAL DIRECTION: Donald York; PRODUCER: Diane de Mailly

CAST—TAMMY GRIMES (Lila Halliday), Ronee Blakley (Marta Gibson), Kim Milford (Danger Dan Hardin), Walt Hunter (Jamie)

The action occurs during the present time in Los Angeles.

The music was presented in two acts.

ACT ONE—"Sunset City" (Walt Hunter, Ronee Blakley, Kim Milford), "La Bamba" (Tammy Grimes), "Nothing But" (Tammy Grimes), "Funky" (Kim Milford), "Destiny" (Tammy Grimes), "Back with a Beat" (Tammy Grimes, Walt Hunter), "Standing in Need" (Ronee Blakley), "Rock Is My Way of Life" (Kim Milford, Ronee Blakley, Walt Hunter), "Sunset Dreams" (Tammy Grimes, Ronee Blakley, Walt Hunter, Kim Milford)

ACT TWO—"Rap" (Kim Milford), "Cheap Chablis" (Ronee Blakley), "Stuck on the Windshield of Life" (Walt Hunter, Ronee Blakley), "1945" (Tammy Grimes), "Retreat" (Ronee Blakley, Walt Hunter), "I Am the Light" (Kim Milford), "Moments" (Tammy Grimes), "Old Times, Good Times" (Tammy Grimes, Ronee Blakley, Kim Milford, Walt Hunter), "This One's for Me" (Tammy Grimes)

NOTES—*Sunset* was first produced in 1977 at the Studio Arena Theatre in Buffalo. It starred Alexis Smith as Lila Halliday, a former film actress hoping for a new career as a rock singer, and the director was Tommy Tune ("T. Tune" in the program). The book was credited to Louis LaRusso II.

As *Platinum* (subtitled "The Musical with a Flip-Side" and set in "the newest environmental recording studio in Hollywood"), the musical played on Broadway for a brief run in 1978, again with Alexis Smith in the lead (Joe Layton was the director and choreographer, and the book was credited to Will Holt and Bruce Vilanch). A private "live" recording of the Broadway production, made though the theatre's sound system, was briefly available for sale shortly after the Broadway run.

The overproduced Broadway version was problematic: besides being somewhat reminiscent of the film *Sunset Blvd.* (1950), the musical told the far-fetched story of a faded 1940s film star seeking success in the field of rock music (maybe a new career on stage or on television; rock music was certainly a stretch). Further, the romance between the older, classy actress and an uncouth young rock star never seemed particularly believable. What made the musical memorable were a number of first-rate songs by Will Holt and Gary William Friedman. In "Nothing But," Lila looked back on her film career with its endless roles of "war brides, WACs, and waifs on the run"; "Destiny" was an amusing number, first sung as a sultry 1940s bolero and then as "Disco Destiny" (with appropriate 1970s flourishes); "Back with a Beat" was a fascinating number in which Lila announced she was returning to show business ... but the confident lyric was undercut by tentative, uneasy, and abrupt beats in the music; "Old Times, Good Times" was a feel-good song in the tradition of Jerry Herman; the ingratiating "Movie Star Mansion" was an appealing folk-like number in which the young rock star nostalgically recalled his palmy days of the late 1960s; and "1945" was a swing number in which Lila recalled *her* heyday, when "the suit was zoot" and "every gate would gain a rep/for being hip when hip was hep." Their superior score obviously inspired Holt and Friedman to revisit the musical. Unfortunately, the revised *Sunset*, now a four-person chamber musical, didn't last beyond its first performance. However, it was recorded by That's Entertainment Records (CD # CDTER-1180). The Off-Broadway version retained the following songs from the 1978 Broadway production: "Living on Sunset" (a/k/a "Sunset" and "Sunset City"), "Nothing But," "Destiny," "Back with a Beat," "1945," "I Am the Light," "Sunset Dreams" ("Platinum Dreams" in the 1978 version), and "Old Times, Good Times" (a/k/a "Good Time Song" in the 1977 version). Numbers heard in the 1977 and 1978 productions (including the 1978 pre-Broadway tryout) which weren't used in the 1983 revisal were: "Disco Destiny," "Waltz," "Montage," "Trials and Tribulations," "I Like You," "True Music," "Movie Star Mansion," "Ride Baby Ride," "Too Many Mirrors," and "Gonna Get Hot."

New numbers for the 1983 version were "La Bamba," "Funky," "Standing in Need," "Rap" (a/k/a "Dan's Rap"), and "Cheap Chablis," and "Bug on the Windshield of Life." The latter was no doubt a revised (or at least retitled) version of "Stuck on the Windshield of Life," a number which may have been used during part of the 1977 run in Buffalo.

1559 The Sunshine Train. THEATRE: Abbey Theatre; OPENING DATE: June 15, 1972; PERFORMANCES: 224; DIRECTION: William E. Hunt; SCENERY: Philip Gilliam; LIGHTING: Philip Gilliam; MUSICAL DIRECTION: Louis Hancock; PRODUCER: Jay Sessa

CAST—The Gospel Starlets (Mary Johnson, Dottie Coley, Peggie Henry, Barbara Davis, Gladys Freeman, Clara Walker); The Carl Murray Singers (Carl Murray, Ron Horton, Ernest McCarroll, Joe Ireland, Larry Coleman)

The revue was presented in one act (song assignments unknown).

MUSICAL NUMBERS—"The Sunshine Train," "Near the Cross," "On My Knees Praying," "Wrapped, Tied, and Tangled," "Thank You, Lord," "Just Look Where I Come From," "His Eye Is on the Sparrow," "Troubled Waters," "Swing Low," "Beams of Heaven," "We Need More Love," "Jesus Loves Me," "All the World to Me," "Judgement Day," "Higher," "Come by Here," "Peace" "Stand Up for Jesus," "God Be with You"

NOTES—Conceived by William E. Hunt, *The Sunshine Train* was a program of traditional gospel music. It played until the end of the year, and was the 1972-1973 season's first long-running Off Broadway musical. Howard Thompson in the *New York Times* said the ninety-minute concert was a collection of "rhythmic, soul-felt songs in simple tribute to the Almighty," and suggested the evening could be "exactly what Fun City could use at the moment." Incidentally, he noted the Abbey Theatre (located at 136 East 13th Street) was a "small, cavelike" venue.

1560 Surf City. "The Beach Boys Musical." THEATRE: Entermedia Theatre; OPENING DATE: The musical was scheduled to open on April 9, 1985.; PERFORMANCES: 11 previews; BOOK: Danny Jacobson and Barry Vigon; LYRICS AND MUSIC: The Beach Boys; DIRECTION: Dennis Rosa; CHOREOGRAPHY: Dennis Rosa; Kathy Seng, Assistant Choreography; SCENERY: Paul de Pass; COSTUMES: Martin Pakledinaz; LIGHTING: Marc B. Weiss; MUSICAL DIRECTION: Randy Booth; PRODUCERS: Edward H. Davis, Carole J. Shorenstein, and Jack Molthen in association with CBS Productions, PACE Theatrical Group, and MTM Enterprises, Inc.

CAST—Christopher Seppe (Andy Weller), George Kmeck (Coach Trancusi), Randall Weiss (Torpedo Bill), Joie Gallo (Wendy), Kelly Meehan (Lila), Kevin Miller (Tank), David Mullen (Clutch), Gordon Lett (Sloop John), Karyn Quackenbush (Barbara Ann), Laurie McEathron (Rhonda), Bebe Gribble (Deirdre), Michael Manasseri (Chad), Doug Barden (Warren Weller), Eda Seasongood (Granny), Annie Livingstone (Caroline); The High Seas (Scott Bartlett, Craig Gilmore, Ken Lundie, David Miles, John Mack Ousley)

The musical was presented in two acts (the program didn't list musical numbers).

NOTES—*Surf City* was first announced as *Surfin' USA*, and a *New York Times*' article noted that while the show was subtitled "The New Beach Boys Musical," it wasn't based on their lives. According to Eddie Davis, one of the producers, the musical was inspired by "the idealized lifestyle of the California myth, and the feelings, spirit and fantasies epitomized by the Beach Boys music." The article indicated the musical would include twenty-five songs by the Beach Boys, including "perhaps" some new ones written especially for the show. The opening of the $1.5 million production was scheduled for March 17; but when the first newspaper ads appeared, the opening was announced for March 31, with previews beginning on March 23. Later advertisements indicated the opening night would be on April 9. The *New York Times* later reported that the producers "abruptly" suspended performances of the musical after eleven previews, that the show was going back into rehearsal, and that another opening date would be determined. But the musical never reopened, and it took twenty years for the Beach Boys to return to the New York musical stage when a collection of their songs was presented in the jukebox musical *Good Vibrations* which opened at the Eugene O'Neill Theatre on February 2, 2005, for ninety-four performances. Jeffrey Eric Jenkins in *The Best Plays Theatre Yearbook 2004-2005* called *Good Vibrations* "one of the certifiable disasters of the season," and the production reportedly lost millions of dollars.

1561 Survival. "A South African Play with Music." THEATRE: Astor Place Theatre; OPENING DATE: October 9, 1977; PERFORMANCES: 47; TEXT: Fana David Kekana, Themba Ntinga, Selaelo Dan Maredi, and Seth Sibanda; originally co-authored by Mshengu; MUSIC: Selaelo Dan Maredi; DIRECTION: Originally directed by Mshengu; additional staging for the New York production by Dean Irby; SCENERY: Clyde Kuemmerle; PRODUCERS: Clyde Kuemmerle in association with the Negro Ensemble Company

CAST—Fana David Kekana, Themba Ntinga, Selaelo Dan Maredi, Seth Sibanda

The play with music was presented in two acts.

NOTES—*Survival* was first produced by Workshop '71, a South-African-based theatre company dedicated to ensuring the artistic and human right of people of all races to perform on the stage. Four songs ("Bhula Sangoma," "Ngitshele Ngezindaba," "Khomba Khona Eduze [Days Are Getting Over],"and "Phela Malanga") were listed in the program, but more may have been performed.

Survival was revived by the New Federal Theatre in an Off Off Broadway production on January 31, 1990, for thirty performances.

1562 The Survival of St. Joan. "A Medieval Rock Opera." THEATRE: Anderson Theatre; OPENING DATE: February 28, 1971 Performances: 17; BOOK: James Lineberger; LYRICS: James Lineberger; MUSIC: Hank and Gary Ruffin; DIRECTION: Chuck Gnys; SCENERY: Peter Harvey; COSTUMES: Peter Harvey; LIGHTING: Thomas Skelton; PRODUCERS: Haila Stoddard and Neal Du Brock

CAST—F. Murray Abraham (Friar I, Villager, Corporal, Soldier, Accuser), Willie Rook (Child, Villager), Lenny Baker (Jailer, English Soldier, Villager, Philippe, Leper, Monk with Lantern, Hunter, Clerk, Penitent), Ronald Bishop (Bishop, Villager, Soldier, Servant, Nun), Richard Bright (Shepherd), Gretchen Corbett (Joan), Elizabeth Eis (Young Witch, Whore, Nun, Villager), Bill Braden (Prison Monk, Soldier, Villager, Beggar, Monk with Lantern, Hunter, Penitent), Judith Granite (Mother, Whore, Villager, Fortune Teller, Penitent), Peter Lazer (Prison Monk, Soldier, Villager, Deserter, Leper, Monk with Lantern, Hunter, Penitent), Anthony Marciona (Shepherd's Son, Leper, Tambourine Boy), Patricia O'Connell (Whore, Philippe's Mother, First Nun, Villager), Janet Sarno (Whore, Villager, Leper Woman, Nun, Penitent), Tom Sawyer (Friar II, Soldier, Blind Man, Villager, Monk with Lantern, Abbot, Executioner), Matthew Tobin (Scribe, Soldier, Monk with Lantern, Hunter, Man, Villager); songs performed by Smoke Rise (Hank Ruffin, keyboards and lead singer; Stan Ruffin, drums and lead singer), Gary Ruffin (guitar and lead singer), and Randy Bugg (bass).

The musical was presented in one act (all songs performed by the band, Smoke Rise).

MUSICAL NUMBERS—"Survival," "Back in the World," "Someone Is Dying," "Run, Run," "Back in the World" (reprise), "Prison Life," "Love Me," "Stonefire," "Country Life," "Lady of Light," "Back in the World" (reprise), "Army Life," "This Is How It Is," "Precious Mommy," "Lonely Neighbors," "Cornbread," "Cannonfire, It's Over," "This Is How It Is" (reprise), "Darkwoods Lullaby," "You Don't Know Why," "Burning a Witch," "It's Heaven"

NOTES—During the early 1970s, a mini-trend developed among a few rock musicals in which the band, instead of the main characters, performed many of the evening's songs. But with *The Survival of St. Joan*, the characters didn't sing at all; instead, every song was performed by the rock band. The out-of-town tryout took place on November 5, 1970, at Studio Arena Theatre in Buffalo, and there the band was called Ruffin; for New York, the band changed its name to the more appropriate Smoke Rise (considering what happens to the heroine of the piece). The musical's conceit was that Joan of Arc never burned at the stake (another woman took her place), and instead takes up with a farmer before eventually joining the army. Not accepted by either soldiers or civilians, she lives a solitary and religious life, until she's raped. The Church tries to find her, but local villagers, mistaking her for a witch, capture her and burn her at the stake.

Numbers deleted during the tryout were: "Living with the Devil," "How Can I Go," "I'm So Glad," and "Love Me." Later in 1971, a 2-LP cast album was released by Paramount Records (# PAS-9000) which included a booklet with all the lyrics; the deleted song "Love Me" was included on the album.

The musical was revived Off Off Broadway for a limited run of eight performances at the Bert Wheeler Theatre beginning on December 19, 1974; Naomi Robin played Joan.

The story of Joan of Arc did better in nonmusical adaptations (George Bernard Shaw's *Saint Joan* [1923] and Jean Anouilh's *L'Alouette* (*The Lark*) [1952]). Three musical versions appeared within a four-year period, and all were failures: *The Survival of St. Joan* lasted less than three weeks; the Off Broadway *Joan* (1972; see entry), two months; and Broadway's *Goodtime Charley* (1975), three months. Interestingly enough, all three musicals were recorded. For an operatic version of the story, see entry for *The Triumph of St. Joan*.

The Survival of St. Joan was the first of a series of religious-themed musicals. The popular studio cast recording of Andrew Lloyd Webber and Tim Rice's *Jesus Christ Superstar* was produced on Broadway in late 1971, and in the same year Stephen Schwartz' smash hit *Godspell* opened Off Broadway for a run of more than two-thousand performances (see entry). Schwartz had been the musical supervisor of *The Survival of St. Joan*, and was later the co-lyricist of Leonard Bernstein's *Mass*, which was the opening production at the Kennedy Center in Washington, D.C., in the fall of 1971 (*Mass* was produced at the Metropolitan Opera House in 1972; see entry). *Hard Job Being God* (1972) was another religious-themed musical which opened Off Broadway during the era (see entry). Like most theatrical trends, religious-themed musicals soon went the way of college musicals and plays inspired by disease-of-the-week television movies.

1563 Susannah. "A Musical Drama." THEATRE: New York City Center; OPENING DATE: October 19, 1956; PERFORMANCES: Unknown; TEXT: Carlisle Floyd; MUSIC: Carlisle Floyd; DIRECTION: Leo Kerz and Erich Leinsdorf; CHOREOGRAPHY: Anna Sokolow; SCENERY: Leo Kerz; COSTUMES: Leo Kerz; Women's costumes courtesy of the School of Music, Florida State University; MUSICAL DIRECTION: Erich Leinsdorf; PRODUCER: New York City Opera Company; Leo Kerz and Erich Leinsdorf

CAST—Phyllis Curtin (Susannah Polk), Jon Crain (Sam Polk), Norman Treigle (Olin Blitch), Eb Thomas (Little Bat McLean), Arthur Newman (Elder McLean), Gregory Millar (Elder Gleaton), John Druary (Elder Hays), Joshua Hecht (Elder Ott), Irene Kramarich (Mrs. McLean), Sarah Fleming (Mrs. Gleaton), Olivia Boneli (Mrs. Hays), Mignon Dunn (Mrs. Ott)

SOURCE—The Biblical story, the Apocryphal Book of Susannah.

The action occurs in the present in New Hope Valley, Tennessee.

The opera was presented in two acts.

ACT ONE—Opening Music: "It's a Hot Night for Dancin'" (Irene Kramarich, Sarah Fleming, Olivia Bonelli, Mignon Dunn, Arthur Newman), "I Am the Reverend Olin Blitch" (Norman Treigle, Arthur Newman, Gregory Millar, John Druary, Joshua Hecht, Irene Kramarich, Chorus), "Was Y'ever at Such a Nice Square Dance, Little Bat?" (Phyllis Curtin, Eb Thomas), "Ain't It a Pretty Night?" (Phyllis Curtin, Eb Thomas, Jon Crain), "Don't Go to Bed Right Yet, Sam" (Phyllis Curtiin, Jon Crain), "That Crick Oughta Be Right About Here" (Arthur Newman, Gregory Millar, John Druary, Joshua Hecht, Phyllis Curtin), "I Ain't Surprised" (Irene Kramarich, Sarah Fleming, Olivia Bonelli, Mignon Dunn, Arthur Newman, Gregory Millar, John Druary, Joshua Hecht, Phyllis Curtin), "Little Bat, What You Doin' Here?" (Phyllis Curtin, Eb Thomas), "Feeble-Minded Idjet!" (Jon Crain, Phyllis Curtin)

ACT TWO—"How Long's It Gonna Last, Sam?" (Phyllis Curtin, Jon Crain), "Are You Saved from Sin" (Congregation, Norman Treigle), "I'm Fixin' To Tell Y' 'Bout a Feller I Knowed" (Norman Treigle), "Come, Sinner, Tonight's the Night" (Congregation, Norman Treigle, Phyllis Curtin), "The Trees in the Mountains Are Cold and Bare" (Phyllis Curtin), "I'm a Lonely Man, Susannah" (Norman Treigle, Phyllis Curtin), "Hear Me, O Lord, I Beseech Thee" (Norman Treigle), "Brethren an' Sister'n" (Norman Treigle, Arthur Newman, Gregory Millar, John Druary, Joshua Hecht, Irene Kramarich, Sarah Fleming, Olivia Bonelli, Mignon Dunn, Phyllis Curtin), "Hey There, Little Robin, I'm Back Agin" (Jon Crain, Phyllis Curtin, Eb Thomas, Arthur Newman, Gregory Millar, John Druary, Joshua Hecht, Mob)

NOTES—Carlisle Floyd's *Susannah* is by all accounts the most produced American opera (apparently exceeding productions of George Gershwin's *Porgy and Bess* [1935]); according to the liner notes of a 1994 studio cast recording, the opera has enjoyed over two-hundred productions in the United States and Europe, for a total of more than seven-hundred performances. The work premiered on February 24, 1955, at Florida State University (Phyllis Curtin was Susannah, Mack Harrell, Blitch), and was first seen in New York on October 19, 1956, when it was produced by the New York City Opera (which has revived it at least three times); for the New York premiere, Phyllis Curtin reprised the title role, and Norman Treigle was Blitch. In 1999, the Metropolitan Opera included *Susannah* in its repertory for the first time.

The work was a musical response to the McCarthyism of the era, but the memorable score and its "operatic" story have long out-lived the particular political issues of its day. The opera can simply be enjoyed for its folk-like score and strong libretto.

There are two major recordings: a live performance from the New York City Opera premiere and the aforementioned 1994 studio cast recording which was released by Virgin Classics Records on a 2-CD set (# CDCB-5-45039-2-PM-613) and includes Cheryl Studer as Susannah, Samuel Ramey as Blitch, and Jerry Hadley as Sam Polk). The song titles listed above are from the liner notes of the 1994 recording (the original New York City Opera program didn't list individual numbers). Two arias from the opera ("Ain't It a Pretty Night" and "The Trees on the Mountain") have been recorded individually, and are representative of Floyd's lyric and melodic skill. Floyd's other operas include *Wuthering Heights* (1958; see entry), *The Passion of Jonathan Wade* (1962; see entry), *Of Mice and Men* (1970; see entry), *Bilby's Doll* (1976), *Willie Stark* (1981), and *Cold Sassy Tree* (2000). With its powerful libretto and score, *Of Mice and Men* has found its rightful place in the modern operatic repertory. But *Willie Stark* (based on Robert Penn Warren's 1946 novel *All the King's Men*) has yet to be produced in New York (although it was seen on public television), and doesn't seem to have made much of an impression in its few productions. This is unfortunate, because Floyd's strong libretto and expansive musical score deserve a wider hearing. The larger-than-life title role is a perfect one for the opera stage; in the original production, Timothy Nolen was a powerful Willie in a highly theatrical staging by Harold Prince. Willie's sly "The Law's Like a Single Bed Blanket" would be a welcome addition to a baritone's repertoire in either a concert or a recording of arias from modern operas.

1564 The Sweet Bye and Bye. THEATRE: Juilliard Opera Theatre; OPENING DATE: November 1957 (possibly November 22); PERFORMANCES: Unknown; LIBRETTO: Kenward Elmslie; MUSIC: Jack Beeson; DIRECTION: Frederic Cohen; CHOREOGRAPHY: Myra Kinch; SCENERY: David Hays; COSTUMES: Leo van Witsen; MUSICAL DIRECTION: Frederic Waldman; PRODUCERS: Juilliard School of Music with a grant from Columbia University's Alice M. Ditson Fund

CAST—Shirlee Emmons (Sister Rose Ora Easter), Ruth Kobart (Mother Rainey), William McGrath (Billy Wilcox); and Juilliard students performing the roles of Sister Rees, Sister Gladys, Brother Smiley, Mary Jane Ripley (The First Bather, "Miss Northern New Jersey"), Second Bather and Third Bather ("Two Good-Time Charlies"), First Beauty Judge, Two Gangsters, Gun-Moll, Two Tots (Harmony and Little Amity), and Members of the Lifeshine Flock

The action occurs in Atlantic City and New York City during the early 1920s.

The opera was produced in three acts.

NOTES—The world premiere of Jack Beeson's *The Sweet Bye and Bye* took place at Juilliard in late November 1957. The opera was later produced by the Kansas City Lyric Opera in 1974, and that production was recorded on a 2-LP set by Desto Records (# DC-7179/80). The recording notes that "The Flock of Lifeshine Ark is a fictional creation, and any resemblance to other religious groups is coincidental." The Ark's leader must be a woman who is an orphan of unknown parentage, who has no earthly ties, and who has taken the vow of chasity. While Aimee Semple McPherson wasn't named, Howard Taubman, who reviewed the world premiere for the *New York Times*, noted that older audience members would recognize her as the prototype for the opera's leading character, Sister Rose Ora Easter (for information regarding musicals about McPherson, see entry for *Sister Aimee*).

Howard Taubman found the opera an "achievement ... attractive American lyric theatre," and he had much praise for Beeson's score. Against the background of religious-oriented numbers, "several scenes are developed with power and excitement," and he noted that Beeson had "a generous lyrical gift" which included "singable" arias and "atmospheric pages ... for the chorus ... [the] orchestra is songful and colorful." He also praised Kenward Elmslie's libretto, and noted its "mordant comment" on the hypocrisy of organized religion "would have delighted a Mencken or Sinclair Lewis."

The libretto was published by Boosey & Hawkes in 1966.

Two sequences from the opera ("Love Song" and "Lifeshine Ark") were heard in the 2005 revue *Lingoland* (see entry) and were recorded for that show's cast album.

1565 Sweet Feet. "A Musical with a Happy Ending." THEATRE: New Theatre; OPENING DATE: May 25, 1972; PERFORMANCES: 6; BOOK: Dan Graham; LYRICS: Don Brockett; MUSIC: Don Brockett; DIRECTION: Don Brockett; SCENERY: James French; COSTUMES: Tom Fallon; LIGHTING: James French; MUSICAL DIRECTION: Marty Goetz; PRODUCER: Proscenium Productions, Inc.

CAST—Marty Goetz (The Piano Player), Lenora Nemetz (Rennie DuPont), Dan Graham (C.B. Seatenbourgh), Scott Burns (The Prop Boy), John Dorish (Rubulous Diamond), Bert Lloyd (Jack Ruffus), Florence Lacey (Florence Carter [Sweet Feet]), Barney McKenna (Sweet Feet's Friend)

The action occurs in a Hollywood studio during the Forgotten Forties.

The musical was presented in two acts.

ACT ONE—Opening Number (Company), "Sweet Feet" (Florence Lacey), "Falling in Love Again Boogie" (Scott Burns, The Girls), "Your Eyes Danced" (Lenora Nemetz, Bert Lloyd), "Prop-Room Ballet" (Company), "Everybody Dance" (Lenora Nemetz, Company), "Is This Love?" (Florence Lacey, Bert Lloyd), "Making a Star" (Florence Lacey, The Boys)

ACT TWO—"Making a Star" (reprise) (Florence Lacey, The Boys), "The Show Must Go On" (Florence Lacey, Barney McKenna, Company), "The Kind of a Woman" (Florence Lacey), "Boompies" (Dan Graham), "Sweet Feet" (reprise) (Bert Lloyd), Finale (Company)

NOTES—*Sweet Feet*, which dealt with moviemaking in the 1940s, didn't get beyond its first week. Howard Thompson in the *New York Times* described the evening as "excruciating" and "anemic," and mentioned that Lenora Nemetz' performance as a vamp sounded "like a cross between Donald Duck and Talluluah Bankhead." He noted that the "tapping clatter" of one of her dances "might have tilted the *Titanic*," and felt a "complete run-through" of the musical might have sunk the ship.

1566 Sweet Miani. THEATRE: Players Theatre; OPENING DATE: September 25, 1962; PERFORMANCES: 22; BOOK: Stuart Bishop; LYRICS: Ed Tyler; MUSIC: Ed Tyler; DIRECTION: Louis MacMillan; CHOREOGRAPHY: Edward Earle; SCENERY: Stuart Slade; COSTUMES: Andre; LIGHTING: Norman Finkelstien; MUSICAL DIRECTION: Robert Lenn; PRODUCER: Edmund Brophy, in association with Donald Currie

CAST—SHEILA SMITH (Miani), ISABELLE FARRELL (Turoola), LECRETIA GOULD (Turooka), Victor Pierantozzi (Tiki), Elida Jensen (George), PAUL MICHAEL (Makiti), Maury Haydn (Jeanine Winters), Shirley Dalzell (Agatha Phinster), Edward Earle (Buzz), Peter Dunlop (Lord Ronald Haversham), VIRGIL CURRY (Bart Collins)

The musical was presented in two acts.

ACT ONE—"Middle of the Sea" (Sheila Smith, Isabelle Farrell, Lecretia Gould), "Legend of the Islands" (Lecretia Gould), "Black Pearls" (Paul Michael), "Going Native" (Company), "A Honey to Love" (Maury Haydn, Victor Pierantozzi), "Sailing" (Shirley Dalzell, Company), "Not Tabu" (Isabelle Farrell, Peter Dunlop), "Maluan Moon" (Sheila Smith, Virgil Curry), "Canticle to the Wind" (Company)

ACT TWO—"Homesick in Our Hearts" (Shirley Dalzell, Maury Haydn), "Just Sit Back and Relax" (Sheila Smith), "Forever and Always" (Lecretia Gould, Paul Michael), "Turoola" (Peter Dunlop, Isabelle Farrell), "Miani" (Virgil Curry), "Black Pearls" (reprise) (Paul Michael), "Ritual of Ruku" (Maury Haydn, Isabelle Farrell, Lecretia Gould, Victor Pierantozzi), "Silvery Days" (Shirley Dalzell), "Code of the Licensed Pilot" (Virgil Curry), "Warm Breezes at Twilight" (Sheila Smith), "Far Away Island" (Company)

NOTES—*Sweet Miani*, a spoof of South Sea Island movies (particularly of the Dorothy Lamour variety), was a quick flop; but if the musical's song titles are any indication, the show must have been occasionally amusing. Howard Taubman in the *New York Times* felt the evening began promisingly: as a color film showed a blue sea and a palm-tree laden beach, the orchestra played an overture which acknowledged Puccini, Brahms, Rachmaninoff ... and Ed Tyler, the musical's composer. But the musical not only satirized South Sea Island movies (Sheila Smith in the title role played a virgin princess in dire danger of being sacrificed to the angry gods), it quickly spoofed "anything else that's handy," including operetta, calypso music, and gypsy turns. Taubman noted that "any resemblance to a musical is strictly accidental," and he found the "mangled" musical a "mishmash of elements" which included a story of "utter vacuity" and comedy of "stale witlessness."

Sheila Smith is perhaps best remembered as Meredith ("This number winded me when I was sixteen!") Lane, one of the performers in the show-stopping "Who's That Woman?" in the original production of *Follies* (1971). She was also a memorable Sweet Sue in *Sugar* (1972), introducing one of the musical's best songs, Jule Styne and Bob Merrill's "When You Meet a Man in Chicago." For a brief period she performed the title role in the original Broadway production of *Mame* (1966).

1567 Sweet Suite. THEATRE: Drifting Traffic Theatre; OPENING DATE: May 31, 1975; PERFORMANCES: Unknown; BOOK: Leonard Melfi; LYRICS: Pendleton Brown and Hayden Wayne; MUSIC: Pendleton Brown and Hayden Wayne; DIRECTION: Sande Shurin; PRODUCER: Directing Traffic (Sande Shurin, Artistic Director)

CAST—Leonard Melfi, Gwendolyn Brown, Charles Mayer Karp, Malcolm Groom, Jeff Hillock

NOTES—The book for the Off Off Broadway musical *Sweet Suite* was by playwright Leonard Melfi, who also performed in the production.

1568 Sweet Will (1985). "*Shakespeare's Cabaret* Part Two." THEATRE: Don't Tell Mama; OPENING DATE: February 2, 1985; PERFORMANCES: 20; LYRICS: William Shakespeare; MUSIC: Lance Mulcahy; DIRECTION: John Olon; MUSICAL DIRECTION: Michael Ward; PRODUCERS: David Drummond in association with Therese Orkin

CAST—Stephanie Cotsirilos, Carol Dennis, Stephen Lehew, Byron Utley, Steve Postel, Anita Ross

SOURCE—Songs adapted from the writings of William Shakespeare (1564-1616).

The revue was presented in one act.

MUSICAL NUMBERS—"Hey Ho, the Wind and the Rain" (from *Twelfth Night*) (Byron Utley), "When Icicles Hang by the Wall" (*Love's Labours Lost*) (Company), "Hark Hark, the Lark" (*Cymbeline*) (Carol Dennis), "Hey Ho, the Wind and the Rain" (reprise) (*Twelfth Night*) (Byron Utley), "Where the Bee Sucks" (*The Tempest*) (Stephanie Cotsirilos), "It Was a Lover and His Lass" (*As You Like It*) (Company), "Who Is Sylvia?" (*The Two Gentlemen of Verona*) (Stephen Lehew), "When Daisies Pied" (*Love's Labours Lost*) (Carol Dennis, Stephanie Cotsirilos), "Sigh No More" (*Much Ado About Nothing*) (Stephen Lehew, Byron Utley, Steve Postel), Selections from Shakespeare's Sonnets (Company), "O Mistress Mine" (*Twelfth Night*) (Stephanie Cotsirilos, Byron Utley, Stephen Lehew), "Sea Song" (*The Tempest*) (Stephen Lehew, Byron Utley, Steve Postel), "Over Hill, Over Dale" (*A Midsummer Night's Dream*) (Company), "Take, Oh Take Those Lips Away" (*Measure for Measure*) (Stephanie Cotsirilos, Stephen Lehew), "Full Fathom Five" (*The Tempest*) (Company), "And Will He Not Come Again?" (*Hamlet*) (Company), "Under the Greenwood Tree" (*As You Like It*) (Carol Dennis, Steve Postel), "Touch But My Lips" (*Venus and Adonis*) (Stephen Lehew, Byron Utley), "Farewell Dear Love" (*Twelfth Night*) (Stephanie Lehew, Byron Utley), "Hey Ho, the Wind and the Rain" (reprise) (*Twelfth Night*) (Byron Utley), "It Was a Lover and His Lass" (reprise) (*As You Like It*) (Company)

NOTES—*Sweet Will* was a sequel of sorts to *Shakespeare's Cabaret* which was produced Off Broadway in both 1980 and 1981 (see entry for the 1980 production for information about both versions). *Sweet Will* was also produced twice, in Off Off Broadway productions at Don't Tell Mama in 1985 and at Joann's Silver Lining Cabaret Theatre in 1986 (see entry for the 1986 production). The production at Don't Tell Mama appears to have begun preview performances on January 30 and to have officially opened on February 2 (one source cites January 30 as the official opening date). All the material in *Sweet Will* was new, and hadn't been heard in *Shakespeare's Cabaret* (with perhaps the exception of some overlapping material from "Venus and Adonis").

1569 Sweet Will (1986). THEATRE: Joann's Silver Lining Cabaret Theatre; OPENING DATE: January 5, 1986; PERFORMANCES: 9; LYRICS: William Shakespeare; MUSIC: Lance Mulcahy; DIRECTION: John Olon; CHOREOGRAPHY: Dennis Dennehy; SCENERY: Desmond Heeley ("Design Consultant"); LIGHTING: John Michael Deegan; MUSICAL DIRECTION: Michael Ward; PRODUCERS: David K. Drummond

CAST—Keith Amos, Roslyn Burrough, Stephanie Cotsirilos, Stephen Lehew; Steve Postel (Singer, Guitar), Scott Simpson (Percussion)

SOURCE—Songs adapted from the writings of William Shakespeare (1564-1616).

The revue was presented in two acts.

ACT ONE—"Hey Ho, the Wind and the Rain" (from *Twelfth Night*) (Company), "When Icicles Hang by the Wall" (*Love's Labours Lost*) (Company), "Hark! Hark! The Lark" (*Cymbeline*) (Roslyn Burrough), "Hey Ho, the Wind and the Rain" (reprise) (*Twelfth Night*) (Keith Amos), "Where the Bee Sucks" (*The Tempest*) (Stephanie Cotsirilos), "Sigh No More, Ladies" (*Much Ado About Nothing*) (Stephen Lehew, Roslyn Burrough, Keith Amos), "It Was a Lover and His Lass" (*As You Like It*) (Company), "Who Is Sylvia?" (*Two Gentlemen of Verona*) (Stephen Lehew), "When Daisies Pied" (*Love's Labours Lost*) (Stephanie Cotsirilos, Roslyn Burrough), "All That Glisters" (*The Merchant of Venice*) (Stephen Lehew, Stephanie Cotsirilos, Roslyn Burrough), *Venus and Adonis* (Company): "Anon Comes Adonis," "Thrice Fairer," "Venus and Young Adonis," "A Thousand Kisses," "I Know Not Love," "Graze on My Lips," "The Premonition," "Ah Me Poor Venus," "Adonis Leaving Venus," "If He Be Dead," "She Looks Upon His Lips," "Thus Weary of the World"

ACT TWO—"Street Cries" (*The Winter's Tale*) (Company), The Sonnets: "Shall I Compare Thee" (Keith Amos), "Some Glory in Their Birth" (Stephanie Cotsirilos), "Why Is My Verse So Barren" (Roslyn Burrough), "When My Love Swears" (Stephen Lehew), "Some Glory in Their Birth" (reprise) (Stephanie Cotsirilos), "How Heavy Do I Journey" (Keith Amos, with Stephanie Cotsirilos and Roslyn Burrough), "Absent in the Spring" (Stephen Lehew), "Some Glory in Their Birth" (reprise) (Stephanie Cotsirilos), "Who Will Believe in My Verse" (Keith Amos, Company), "O Mistress Mine" (*Twelfth Night*) (Stephanie Cotsirilos, Stephen Lehew, Keith Amos), "Come Unto These Yellow Sands" (*The Tempest*) (Roslyn Burrough, Company), "Sea Song" (*The Tempest*) (Stephen Lehew, Keith Amos), "Lo, Here the Gentle Lark" (*Venus and Adonis*) (Roslyn Burrough, Stephanie Cotsirilos), "Over Hill, Over Dale" (*A Midsummer Night's Dream*) (Company), "Now" (*A Midsummer Night's Dream*) (Company), "Take, Oh Take Those Lips Away" (*Measure for Measure*) (Stephanie Cotsirilos, with Stephen Lehew), "Full Fathom Five" (*The Tempest*) (Company), "Under the Greenwood Tree" (*As You Like It*) (Roslyn Burrough, with Steve Postel), "Farewell, Dear Love" (*Twelfth Night*) (Stephanie Cotsirilos, Keith Amos), "Hey Ho, the Wind and the Rain" (reprise) (*Twelfth Night*) (Keith Amos), "It Was a Lover and His Lass" (reprise) (*As You Like It*) (Company)

NOTES—This was the second Off Off Broadway production of *Sweet Will*, a sequel of sorts to *Shakespeare's Cabaret* which was produced in 1980 and 1981 (see entry for the 1980 production for information about both versions of *Shakespeare's Cabaret*). *Sweet Will* was first produced in an Off Off Broadway production at Don't Tell Mama in 1985 (see entry). The second Off Off Broadway production, at Joann's Silver Lining Cabaret Theatre, appears to have begun preview performances on December 26, 1985, and to have officially opened on January 5, 1986 (one source cites December 26, 1985, as the official opening date). This version, which included material not heard in the previous version of *Sweet Will*, also included songs from *Shakespeare's Cabaret*. In reviewing the 1986 production of *Sweet Will*, Stephen Holden in the *New York Times* found the mixture of Shakespeare and pop music an "awkward mismatch" and felt that the music's "swift momentum ... so insistently" hurried the revue that it didn't allow the audience enough time to "savor" Shakespeare's language.

1570 Sweethearts. "Nostalgic Musical Memories of Jeanette MacDonald and Nelson Eddy." THEATRE: Actors' Playhouse; OPENING DATE: December 7, 1988; PERFORMANCES: 54; TEXT AND CONTINUITY: Uncredited; DIRECTION: David Wolfson; COSTUMES: Josie Garner and Ethel Anderson; LIGHTING: Paul Lindsay Butler; MUSICAL DIRECTION: David Wolfson; PRODUCER: Will You Remember Me Productions

CAST—Antoinette Mille (Jeanette MacDonald), Walter Adkins (Nelson Eddy)

SOURCE—The careers of Jeanette MacDonald (1901-1965) and Nelson Eddy (1901-1967).

The musical was presented in two acts.

ACT ONE—Overture (Orchestra), "Beyond the Blue Horizon" (from 1930 film *Monte Carlo*; lyric by Leo Robin, music by Richard A. Whiting and W. Franke Harling) (Antoinette Mille), "My Own United States" (Walter Adkins), "Will You Remember" (1937 film *Maytime*; lyric by Rida Johnson Young, music by Sigmund Romberg) (Antoinette Mille, Walter Adkins), "Marsovia" (1934 film *The Merry Widow*; lyric by Lorenz Hart, music by Franz Lehar) (Antoinette Mille), Selections from 1934 film *Naughty Marietta* (music by Victor Herbert) (Antoinette Mille, Walter Adkins): "'Neath the Southern Moon" (new lyric for film by Gus Kahn), "I'm Falling in Love with Someone" (lyric by Rida Johnson Young), "Tramp! Tramp! Tramp!" (new lyric for film by Gus Kahn), "Ah! Sweet Mystery of Life" (lyric by Rida Johnson Young), "San Francisco" (1936 film *San Francisco*; lyric and music by Bronislau Kaper, Walter Jurmann, and Gus Kahn) (Antoinette Milles), "Shenandoah" (Walter Adkins), "Giannina Mia" (1937 film *The Firefly*; lyric by Otto Harbach, music by Rudolf Friml) (Antoinette Milles), Selections from 1936 film *Rose-Marie* (Antoinette Milles, Walter Adkins): "Rose-Marie" (lyric by Otto Harbach and Oscar Hammerstein II, music by Rudolf Friml), "Lak Jeem" (lyric by Otto Harbach and Oscar Hammerstein II, music by Rudolf Friml; song not used in film version), "The Mounties" (lyric by Otto Harbach and Oscar Hammerstein II, music by Rudolf Friml and Herbert Stotheart), "Indian Love Call" (lyric by Otto Harbach and Oscar Hammerstein II, music by Rudolf Friml)

ACT TWO—Entr'acte (Orchestra), "Sweethearts" (1938 film *Sweethearts*; new lyric for film by Bob [Robert] Wright and Chet [George] Forrest, music by Victor Herbert) (Antoinette Milles, Walter Adkins), "Ciribiribin" (Antoinette Milles), "While My Lady Sleeps" (1941 film *The Chocolate Soldier*; lyric by Gus Kahn, music by Bronislau Kaper) (Walter Adkins), "Farewell to Dreams" (Antoinette Milles, Wlker Adkins), "Will You Remember" (reprise) (Antoinette Milles, Walter Adkins), "Italian Street Song" (1935 film *Naughty Marietta*; lyric by Rida Johnson Young, music by Victor Herbert) (Antoinette Milles), "Cuban Love Song" (1931 film *The Cuban Love Song*; lyric by Dorothy Fields, music by Jimmy McHugh; in the film, song was introduced by Lawrence Tibbett) (Walter Adkins), "The Rogue Song" (from 1930 film *The Rogue Song*; lyric by Clifford Grey, music by Herbert Stothart; in the film, song was introduced by Lawrence Tibbett) (Walter Adkins), Selections from 1940 film *New Moon* (lyric by Oscar Hammerstein II, music by Sigmund Romberg) (Antoinette Milles, Walter Adkins): "Wanting You," "Softly, as in a Morning Sunrise," "One Kiss," "Lover, Come Back to Me," "Stout-hearted Men," Finale (Antoinette Milles, Walter Adkins)

NOTES—*Sweethearts* was a musical tribute to Jeanette MacDonald and Nelson Eddy.

Dates given are release dates for films (not dates for stage productions, if applicable).

1571 Swingtime Canteen. THEATRE: Blue Angel; OPENING DATE: March 14, 1995; PERFORMANCES: 294; BOOK: Linda Thorsen Bond, William Repicci, and Charles Busch; LYRICS: See song list for credits; MUSIC: See song list for credits; DIRECTION: Kenneth Elliott; CHOREOGRAPHY: Barry McNabb; SCENERY: B.T. Whitehill; COSTUMES: Robert Mackintosh; LIGHTING: Michael Lincoln; MUSICAL DIRECTION: Lawrence Yurman; PRODUCERS: William Repicci and Michael Minichiello in association with Ken Jillson, Robert Massimi and Patricia Greenwald; Mel Borowka, James H. Ellis, Joyce M. Sarner, and Michael Estwanik, Associate Producers

CAST—Alison Fraser (Marian Ames), Debra Barsha (Topeka Abotelli, Piano), Emily Loesser (Katie Gammersflugel), Marcy McGuigan (Jo Sterling, Drums), Jackie Sanders (Lilly McBain, Saxophone, Banjo)

The action occurs in 1944, onstage at a concert or the Eighth Air Force in London.

The revue was presented in one act.

MUSICAL NUMBERS—"Bugle Call Rag" (from 1943 film *Stage Door Canteen*; lyric and music by Jack Pettis, Billy Meyers, and Elmer Schoebel) (Company), "Accentuate the Positive" (1944 film *Here Come the Waves*; lyric by Johnny Mercer, music by Harold Arlen) (Alison Fraser, Company), "Praise the Lord and Pass the Ammunition" (lyric and music by Frank Loesser) (Alison Fraser, Company), "Hollywood Canteen" (1944 film *Hollywood Canteen*; lyric and music by Ted Koehler, Mike Jerome, and Ray Heindorf) (Alison Fraser, Emily Loesser, Jackie Sanders), Andrew Sisters Medley (Alison Fraser, Emily Loesser, Jackie Sanders): "Boogie Woogie Bugle Boy from Company 'B'" (1941 film *Buck Privates*; lyric by Don Raye, music by Hughie Prince), "Beat Me, Daddy, Eight to the Bar" (lyric and music by Don Raye, Hughie Prince, and Eleanor Sheehy), "Rhumboogie" (1940 film *Argentine Nights*; lyric by Don Raye, music by Hughie Prince), "Rum and Coca-Cola" (lyric and music by Jeri Sullivan, Paul Baron, and Morey Amsterdam), "Tico-Tico" (lyric and music by Ervin Drake and Zequinea Abreu), "Bei Mir Bistu Schoen" (lyric and music by Jacob Jacobs and Shalom Secunda, English lyric by Sammy Cahn and Saul Chaplan), "Hold Tight, Hold Tight" (lyric and music by Leonard Kent, Edward Robinson, Leonard Ware, Jerry Brandow, and Willie Spotsworth), "Three Little Fishes" (lyric and music by Saxie Dowell), "Pennsylvania Polka" (lyric and music by Lester Lee and Zeke Manners), "In the Mood" (lyric and music by Joe Garland), "Beer Barrel Polka" (lyric and music by Lew Brown, Wladimir A. Timm, Jaromir Vejvada, and Vasek Zeman), "Don't Sit Under the Apple Tree (With Anyone Else but Me)" (1942 film *Private Buckaroo*; lyric and music by Lew Brown, Charles Tobias, and Sam H. Stept), "(And) His Rocking Horse Ran Away" (1944 film *And the Angels Sing*; lyric by Johnny Burke, music by Jimmy Van Heusen) (Debra Barsha), "Thank Your Lucky Stars and Stripes" (1941 film *Playmates*; lyric by Johnny Burke, music by Jimmy Van Heusen) (Company), "Don't Fence Me In" (1944 film *Hollywood Canteen*; lyric and music by Cole Porter) (Alison Fraser, Company), "Love Isn't Born, It's Made" (1943 film *Thank Your Lucky Stars*; lyric by Frank Loesser, music by Arthur Schwartz) (Marcy McGuigan), "Daddy" (lyric and music by Bobby Troup) (Jackie Sanders), "How High the Moon" (*Two for the Show*, 1940; lyric by Nancy Hamilton, music by Morgan Lewis) (Emily Loesser), "You'll Never Know" (1943 film *Hello, Frisco, Hello*; lyric by Mack Gordon, music by Harry Warren) (Alison Fraser), "My Shining Hour" (1943 film *The Sky's the Limit*; lyric by Johnny Mercer, music by Harold Arlen) (Debra Barsha), "I'll Be Seeing You" (*Right This Way*, 1938; lyric by Irving Kahal, music by Sammy Fain) (Marcy McGuigan, Company), "Sing, Sing, Sing" (lyric and music by Louis Prima) (Company), "Keep the Home Fires Burning" (lyric and music by Ivor Novello and Lena Ford)/"Pack Up Your Troubles in Your Old Kit Bag" (lyric and music by Felix Powell and George Powell) (Jackie Sanders, Company), "I'll Be with You in Apple Blossom Time" (lyric and music by Albert von Tilzer and Neville Fleeson) (Company), "Sing, Sing, Sing" (reprise) (lyric and music by Louis Prima) (Company), "Beyond the Blue Horizon" (1930 film *Monte Carlo*; lyric by Leo Robin, music by Richard A. Whiting and W. Franke Harling)/"You're Off to See the World" (1941 film *In the Navy*; lyric by Don Raye, music by Gene de Paul) (Company)

NOTES—This musical-cum-revue *Swingtime Canteen* was given in the form of a concert for soldiers in London during World War Two.

The New York production featured Emily Loesser, whose father Frank Loesser had written some of the show's songs during the period in which the musical took place. During the run, Charles Busch joined the cast as Marion Ames (described in the script as "a lovely, classic leading lady of the silver screen who is slightly past her prime ... [such as] Irene Dunne, Greer Garson"). During the run, Maxene Andrews also joined the cast in a cameo role as herself. The script, published by Samuel French, Inc., in 1998 in a two-act version, included three more songs: "I Don't Want to Walk Without You" (1942 film *Sweater Girl*; lyric by Frank Loesser, music by Jule Styne); "A Nightingale Sang in Berkeley Square" (lyric by Eric Maschwitz, music by Manning Sherwin); and "Sentimental Journey" (lyric and music by Bud Green, Les Brown, and Ben Homer).

The *Swingtime Canteen* recording by PAPA Records (CD # HF-9798) included original cast members Alison Fraser and Emily Loesser as well as cameo guest star Maxene Andrews. The recording also featured Ruth Williamson and Mary Cleere Haran.

For other "home front" World War II revues, see entries for *Smiling Through* (1994), *We'll Meet Again* (1995), and *When the Lights Go On Again* (2007).

1572 Symphonie Fantastique. THEATRE: Dorothy B. Williams Theatre/Here Arts Center; OPENING DATE: June 5, 1998 Performances: 425 Music: Hector Berlioz; LIGHTING: Andrew Hill; PRODUCER: Here Arts Center and Barbara Busackino

CAST (Puppeteers)—Basil Twist, Oliver Dalzell, Sam Hack, Chris Hymas, Eric Jacobson, Jessica Chandlee Smith The revue was presented in one act.

NOTES—Conceived by Basil Twist, *Symphonie Fantastique* was a one-hour evening of puppetry performed underwater in a huge 500-gallon tank; the action was accompanied by all five movements of Berlioz' "Symphonie Fantastique" ("Reveries, Passions"; "A Ball"; "Scene in the Country"; "March to the Scaffold"; and "Dreams of a Witches' Sabbath").

The revue had first been presented Off Off Broadway on May 29, 1998, but a few days later quickly transferred to Off Broadway status.

Ben Brantley in the *New York Times* noted that Twist's underwater images were a visual approximation of Berlioz' music, and said the "seamless" match of music and image gave you the feeling "you had been listening with your eyes."

Symphonie Fantastique was revived at Dodger Stages on September 16, 2004, for 126 performances.

1573 Taboo in Revue. THEATRE: Palsson's; OPENING DATE: March 4, 1985; PERFORMANCES: 11; SKETCHES, LYRICS, AND MUSIC: Peggy Gordon, Robin Lamont, and Leslie Ray; DIRECTION: Michael Leeds; MUSICAL DIRECTION: Jeffrey Klitz; PRODUCER: Steve McGraw

CAST—James Gleason, Peggy Gordon, Robin Lamont, Leslie Ray

SKETCHES AND MUSICAL NUMBERS (division of acts and sketch and song assignments unknown)—"I'm Okay," "Indifference," "Live from WKGB," "Up Front," "The Box," "Celibate," "Cosmo's Angels," "Special Guy," "Working It Out," "Carter Kliner," "The Chorus," "Group Singles," "It Wasn't Me," "Beat the Clock," "Oh Helen!"

NOTES—The Off Off Broadway *Taboo in Revue* seems to have dealt with relationships (or the lack thereof) in the big city.

1574 Taboo Revue (a/k/a Timothy Gray's Taboo Revue). THEATRE: The Showplace; OPENING DATE: 1959; PERFORMANCES: Unknown; LYRICISTS: Bill Angelos, Robert A. Bernstein, Timothy Grey, Sheldon Harnick, Jerry De Bono, Lan O'Kun, and Jay Thompson; MUSIC: David Baker, Ralph Blane, Dolores Clamen, Hugh Martin, Warren B. Meyers, Lan O'Kun, Mary Rodgers, and Jay Thompson (Bill Angelos may have also contributed music to the revue); DIRECTION: Timothy Gray; CHOREOGRAPHY: Robert Haddad; SCENERY: Robert Fletcher; PRODUCERS: Robert Fletcher and Timothy Gray

CAST—Cast members included Don Crichton and Sheila Smith

MUSICAL NUMBERS (division of acts and song assignments unknown)—"Come of Age" (music by Dolores Clamen), "Counter Melody" (lyric by Marshall Barer, music by Mary Rodgers and Jay Thompson), "Cream of Mississippi" (lyric by Sheldon Harnick, music by David Baker), "Go Away" (music by Dolores Clamen), "Just Plain Will" (by Bill Angleos and Lan O'Kun; this sequence may have been a sketch), "Kaleidoscope" (music by Dolores Clamen), "Kismet Quick" (music by Dolores Clamen), "Lollipop" (lyric and music by Lan O'Kun), "Love on the Street" (lyric by Robert A. Bernstein; music possibly by Warren B. Meyers), "A Man" (music by Dolores Clamen), "Oscar" (lyric by Ralph Blane and Timothy Gray, music by Ralph Blane and Hugh Martin), "Part of Me" (lyric by Robert A. Bernstein; music possibly by Warren B. Meyers), "A Plea for Understanding" (lyric by Timothy Gray, music by Hugh Martin), "Revue Hoedown" (music by Dolores Clamen), "This Way Out" (music by Dolores Clamen),

"Triple Tango" (music by Dolores Clamen), "The Two Graces" (music by Dolores Clamen)

NOTES—The above list of songs and sketches for the obscure *Taboo Revue* (a/k/a *Timothy Gray's Taboo Revue*) is taken from Ken Bloom's *American Song*.

It appears that all songs with music by Dolores Clamen had lyrics by Warren B. Meyers.

"Counter Melody" (a/k/a "Countermelody") was later heard in the 1960 Broadway revue from *A to Z*, where it was sung by Paula Stewart and Stuart Damon. "Oscar" was later used in the 1972 revue *They Don't Make 'Em Like That Anymore* (see entry), and that production credited the song to Hugh Martin and Timothy Gray.

1575 The Taffetas. THEATRE: Cherry Lane Theatre; transferred to the Top of the Gate/The Village Gate on February 1, 1989; OPENING DATE: October 12, 1988; PERFORMANCES: 165; STORY: Rick Lewis; LYRICS: See song list for credits; MUSIC: See song list for credits; DIRECTION: Steven Harris; CHOREOGRAPHY: Tina Paul; SCENERY: Evelyn Sakash; COSTUMES: David Graden; LIGHTING: Ken Billington; MUSICAL DIRECTION: Rick Lewis; PRODUCERS: Arthur Whitelaw and James Shellenberger in association with Select Entertainment

CAST—Jody Abrahams (Donna), Karen Curlee (Kaye), Melanie Mitchell (Cheryl), Tia Speros (Peggy)

The revue was presented in two acts.

ACT ONE—"Sh-Boom" (lyric and music by Feaster, Keyes, McRae, and Edwards) (Company), "Love Is a Two-Way Street" (lyric and music by N. Sherman and J. Keller) (Company), "Mr. Sandman" (lyric and music by Pat Ballard) (Company), "The Three Bells" (lyric and music by Jean Villard and Bert Reisfeld) (Company), "I'm Sorry" (lyric and music by Self and Albritton) (Company), "Ricochet" (a/k/a "Ricochet Romance") (lyric and music by Larry Coleman, Norman Gimbel, and Joe Darion) (Jody Abrahams), "I Cried" (lyric and music by M. Elias and B. Duke) (Melanie Mitchell), "Cry" (lyric and music by Kohlman) (Tia Speros), "Smile" (lyric and music by John Turner, Geoffrey Parsons, and Charlie Chaplin) (Company), "Tonight You Belong to Me" (lyric and music by Billy Rose) (Tia Speros and Jody Abrahams) "Achoo-Cha-Cha (Gesundheit)" (lyric and music by Patrick Welch and Michel Merlo) (Company), "Mockin' Bird Hill" (lyric and music by V. Horton) (Karen Curlee, Melanie Mitchell), "You Belong to Me" (lyric and music by King, Stewart, and Price) (Company), "Happy Wanderer" (lyric and music by Malen and Ridge) (Company), "Constantinople" (lyric and music by Carlton) (Company), "My Little Grass Shack" (lyric and music by Bill Cogswell, Tommy Harrison, and Johnny Noble) (Tia Speros), "C'Est Si Bon" (lyric and music by Seelen, Betti, and Honeg) (Karen Curlee), "Sweet Song of India" (lyric and music by Kaye and Clayton) (Company), "Arrivederci Roma" (lyric and music by Sigman, Rasul, and Giovanni) (Melanie Mitchell, Jody Abrahams), "See the U.S.A. in Your Chevrolet" (lyric and music by Leon Carr and Leo Corday) (Company), "Allegheny Moon" (lyric and music by Hoffman and Manning) (Melanie Mitchell), "Tennessee Waltz" (lyric and music by Stewart and King) (Jody Abrahams), "Old Cape Cod" (lyric and music by Rathrock, Jeffrey, and Yahus) (Karen Curlee), "Nel Blue di Pinto di Blue" (a/k/a "Volare") (lyric and music by Mondugno, Migliani, and Mitchell Parish) (Company), "Around the World" (from 1956 film *Around the World in 80 Eighty Days*, 1956; lyric by Harold Adamson, music by Victor Young) (Company)

ACT TWO—"Music! Music! Music!" (lyric and music by B. Baum and S. Weiss) (Company), "You're Just in Love" (*Call Me Madam*, 1950; lyric and music by Irving Berlin) (Company), "Love Letters in the Sand" (lyric and music by Coots and Kenny) (Tia Speros), "L-O-V-E" (lyric and music by Sigler) (Melanie Mitchell), "I-M-4-U" (lyric and music by J. Melis and F. Marino) (Company), "Rag Mop" (lyric and music by J.L. Wills and D. Anderson) (Company), "You, You, You" (lyric and music by R. Mellin and L. Olias) (Tia Speros, Melanie Mitchell, Jody Abrahams), "Puppy Love" (lyric and music by Paul Anka) (Karen Curlee), "Doggie in the Window" (lyric and music by Bob Merrill) (Company), "The Hot Canary" (lyric and music by R. Gilbert and Peter Nero) (Company), "Tweedle Dee" (lyric and music by W. Scott) (Jody Abrahams), "Oop Shoop" (lyricist and composer unknown) (Karen Curlee), "Lollipop" (lyric and music by B. Ross) (Tia Speros), "Sincerely" (lyric and music by Harvey Fuqua and Harvey Freed) (Company), "Johnny Angel" (lyric by Lynn Duddy, music by Lee Pockriss) (Melanie Mitchell), "Mr. Lee" (lyric and music by Dixon and Webb) (Jody Abrahams), "Dedicated to the One I Love" (lyric and music by Lowman Pauling and Ralph Bass) (Tia Speros), "Where the Boys Are" (1960 film *Where the Boys Are*; lyric by Howard Greenfield, music by Neil Sedaka) (Karen Curlee), "I'll Think of You" (lyric and music by Noel Sherman and Clint Ballard, Jr.) (Company), "Little Darling" (lyric and music by Williams) (Company)

NOTES—Like *Beehive, Suds,* and *Shout!* (see entries), *The Taffetas* was a "girl group" revue which showcased popular songs of the 1950s and 1960s. The revue-like musical purported to be an actual telecast in which the Taffetas, an all-girl singing group from Muncie, Indiana, are making their television debut on the old DuMont television network, which went off the air during the 1954-1955 television season. (The most fascinating aspect of the musical was how the Taffetas were able to perform songs written in the late 1950s and early 1960s on a mid-1950s television show.)

The musical had originally been seen Off Off Broadway beginning on April 11, 1988, at the Westbeth Theatre/Centre Cabaret. The cast album was released by That's Entertainment Records (LP # TER-1167). For a "guy group" revue, see entry for *Forever Plaid.*

1576 Take Five. "A New Cabaret Concept." THEATRE: The Downstairs Room; OPENING DATE: October 10, 1957; PERFORMANCES: Unknown; SKETCHES: Don Adams, Dee Caruso, Ronny Graham, Bill Levine, and Steven Vinaver; LYRICS: Michael Brown, Bart Howard, Stan Keen, Carolyn Leigh, Edward C. Redding, and Steven Vinaver; MUSIC: Michael Brown, Bart Howard, Stan Keen, Philip Springer, Edward C. Redding, Jonathan Tunick, and Steven Vinaver; DIRECTION: Max Adrian and John Heawood

CAST—RONNY GRAHAM, Jean Arnold, Ceil Cabot, Ellen Hanley, Gerry Matthews

The revue was presented in two acts (there appears to have been an intermission between "The "Poet's Corner" and "Gossiping Grapevine").

ACT ONE—"Cast Call" (lyric and music by Stan Keen) (Company), "Upstairs at the Downstairs Waltz" (lyric and music by Bart Howard) (Company) "Roger, the Rabbit" (lyric and music by Steven Vinaver) (Ceil Cabot) "Night Heat!" (sketch by Dee Caruso, Don Adams, and Bill Levine) (Ronny Graham, Gerry Matthews), "Perfect Stranger" (lyric and music by Bart Howard) (Ellen Hanley) "Gristedes" (lyric by Steven Vinaver, music by Jonathan Tunick) (Jean Arnold) "The Poet's Corner" (sketch by Steven Vinaver) (Company)

ACT TWO—"Gossiping Grapevine" (lyric and music by Edward C. Redding) (Company) "Westport!" (lyric by Carolyn Leigh, music by Philip Springer) (Jean Arnold) "Witchcraft!" (lyric and music by Michael Brown) (Gerry Matthews), "The Pro Musica Antiqua" (lyric by Steven Vinaver, music by Jonathan Tunick) (Ellen Hanley) "Harry the Hipster" (sketch by Ronny Graham) (Ronny Graham) "Doing the Psycho-Neurotique" (lyric and music by Ronny Graham) (Company)

NOTES—The songs and sketches for *Take Five* are taken from information on the Offbeat Records cast album (LP # O-4013). Thanks to the imagination and foresight of this small record company, a number of early Off Broadway revues produced by Ben Bagley and Julius Monk were recorded.

One of the earliest of Julius Monk's Upstairs at the Downstairs revues, *Take Five* was filled with amusing sketches and songs. A highlight was "Night Heat!," a lampoon of television interview shows; it was written primarily by Don Adams, who found his greatest success in the 1960s television series *Get Smart*. In the sketch, a television host introduces his guest to the audience by noting that *Time* magazine praised him as a great political leader and a visionary for educational advancement in America. The interviewer then asks, "Just how long have you been a Communist?" Ronny Graham was the hapless victim of the take-no-prisoners host.

"Gristedes" was a spoof of torch songs, this one set to a beguine in which the clueless heroine, shopping in the trendy grocery store, finds and loses love by the jello display.

In "Harry the Hipster," Graham again scored, this time as a beat jazz musician (who implores his fellow artists to face east, towards Decca).

A few words about Ronny Graham (who is sometimes confused with Ronald Graham, a leading man in Broadway musicals of the late 1930s and early 1940s): Ronny Graham was a unique performer whose sly, conspiratorial way with an audience was perfect for the intimate setting of the Off Broadway revue. He was also a writer, and his sketches appeared in a number of Broadway and Off Broadway revues. He was a New Face in the 1952 edition of that revue (considered not only the best of all the *New Faces* revues, but also one of the best revues ever seen on Broadway), and he popped in and out of the Broadway scene throughout his career: as a performer in *The Tender Trap* (1954), as lyricist for the vastly underrated score for *Bravo Giovanni* (1962), as director of Broadway comedies (*Mating Dance* in 1965, *A Place for Polly* in 1970). He also appeared in the Broadway musical *Something More!* (1964), and his songs in that show ("Jaded, Degraded Am I" and "Church of My Choice") were ideally suited to his revue persona. His last appearance was in *Annie 2: Miss Hannigan's Revenge* which collapsed during its pre-Broadway tryout at the Kennedy Center in Washington, D.C., during the 1989-1990 season. But he and Dorothy Loudon made a great team, and were the only reasons to remember an otherwise sour and cheerless evening.

Ronny Graham was married to Ellen Hanley, one of his *Take Five* co-stars. In 1959, she created two supporting roles on Broadway, in *First Impressions* and *Fiorello!* When leading lady Polly Bergen left the former during its brief three-month run, Ellen Hanley replaced her.

Another fondly remembered sequence from *Take Five* was "The Pro Musica Antiqua" (lyric by Steven Vinaver and music by Jonathan Tunick), a spoof of upper-class cultural "evenings" which had first been heard in *Well I Never!* (see entry). Perhaps what's most fascinating about this number, at least from a decades-later perspective, is the cast album's liner notes about the song: "All of us who have suffered through prep school or finishing-school evenings of culture will find here our reward." There's the (probably correct) assumption that audiences for sophisticated revues of the *Take Five* variety did indeed go to prep schools and finishing schools. 1956 was emphatically another time and place.

Jonathan Tunick, the composer of "The Pro Musica Antiqua" and "Gristedes," later became Broadway's orchestrator of choice; among his notable assignments were *A Chorus Line* (1975; see entry) and the original productions of many musicals by Stephen Sondheim.

Incidentally, the pianists for this and other Monk revues were Stan Keen and Gordon Connell (Jane Connell's husband, who was an occasional performer in Broadway musicals, including the original casts of *Subways Are for Sleeping* [1961] and *Hello, Dolly!* [1964]).

Other songs apparently used in *Take Five* were "Jefferson Davis Tyler's General Store" (lyric and music by Edward C. Redding), which was later used in *Tongue in Cheek* (a 1958 revue which wasn't produced in New York) and in Monk's *Four Below Strikes Back* (1959; see entry) and "Pour Le Sport" (lyric and music by Stephen Sondheim), which had been written for an unproduced musical of the same name.

Another *Take Five* song, "Portofino" (lyric and music by Michael Brown), was also used in *Demi-Dozen* (1958; see entry), and was included on that show's cast album; Jerry Orbach included the number in his collection of Off Broadway songs (the recording erroneously attributes the song to *Dressed to the Nines*); see discography (Appendix B) for more information about Orbach's album. "Gossiping Grapevine" was also used in *Tongue in Cheek* (as "Grapevine").

Steven Vinaver's sketch "The Poet's Corner" had first been introduced in *Well I Never!*, and was later used in the Washington, D.C., revue *Spread Eagle Strikes Back* (1968).

For a complete list of Julius Monk's revues, see entry for *Four Below*; also see Appendix Q.

1577 Take It Easy. THEATRE: Judith Anderson Theatre; OPENING DATE: March 21, 1996; PERFORMANCES: 113; BOOK: Raymond Fox; LYRICS: Raymond Fox; MUSIC: Raymond Fox; DIRECTION: Collette Black; CHOREOGRAPHY: Tom Ribbink; Robin Higginbotham, Musical Staging; SCENERY: Eddie Krummins; COSTUMES: Fiona Brook; LIGHTING: Matt Berman; MUSICAL DIRECTION: William Zeffiro; PRODUCER: New Village Productions (Carol Polcovar, Artistic Director)

CAST—Emmet Murphy (John Graham), Isaac Rockoff (Fred Brown), Christian Anderson (Joe Goldman), Stephanie Kurtzuba (Susan Bradshaw), Julianna Hahn (Mary Taylor), Kristin Hughes (Becky Winslow), Carrie Pollack (Winifred Taylor), Tom Nigh (Lt. Col. Robert Davidson)

The action occurs on a college campus in 1944.

The musical was presented in two acts.

ACT ONE—Overture and "Victory March," "We're in the Army" (Isaac Rockoff, Christian Anderson, Emmet Murphy, Ensemble), "Who Cares" (Stephanie Kurtzuba), "Take It Easy" (Julianna Hahn, Isaac Rockoff, Ensemble), "An Old Time Girl" (Ensemble), "Just One More Time" (Tom Nigh, Carrie Pollack), "It's All Right" (Isaac Rockoff, Stephanie Kurtzuba), "I Think I'm Falling for You" (Christian Anderson, Kristin Hughes), "I'll Remember Spring" (Emmet Murphy, Julianna Hahn), "Funny" (Carrie Pollack), "Just One More Time" (reprise) (Carrie Pollack, Tom Nigh), "It's All Right" (reprise) (Stephanie Kurtzuba), "The Night When We Were Young" (Tom Nigh, Carrie Pollack), "Say Farewell" (Kristin Hughes, Ensemble)

ACT TWO—"Worry About the Blues Tomorrow" (Emmet Murphy, Ensemble), "The Home Front Farm Brigade" (Ensemble), "Home for Christmas" (Emmet Murphy, Julianna Hahn), "Our Yesterday" (Julianna Hahn), "It's All Right" (reprise) (Stephanie Kurtzuba), "Looking for the Sunshine" (Emmet Murphy, Julianna Hahn)

NOTES—*Take It Easy* took place in 1944 and told of the romantic escapades of three privates attending the Army Specialized Training Program at a co-ed college; the plot seems somewhat reminiscent of Alan Jay Lerner and Frederick Loewe's first Broadway musical *What's Up*, which opened in 1943 and dealt with a group of soldiers who find themselves quarantined at Miss Langley's School for Girls in Virginia when one of the co-eds develops measles.

1578 Take It from the Top (1967). THEATRE: Gramercy Arts Theatre; OPENING DATE: November 22, 1967; PERFORMANCES: 15; DIRECTION: Maurice Edwards; SCENERY: Duane Camp; LIGHTING: Duane Camp; PRODUCER: Duane Camp

CAST—Ethel (Barrymore) Colt, Rolf Barnes (Pianist)

NOTES—*Take It from the Top* was Ethel Barrymore Colt's one-woman cavalcade of songs from the American musical theatre. Richard F. Shepard in the *New York Times* reported that the revue's thirteen scenes reflected different eras of musical theatre, and for each sequence Colt wore a different outfit ("enough costume changes to put her in the class with *The Eternal Road*"). Shepard felt the evening was pleasant enough, but noted it would have been more effective as an "after-theatre entertainment" rather than as the "main event."

In the 1967 revue, Colt paid tribute to almost two-hundred years of American musical theatre (1787-1967), and in 1971 she appeared in the original production of one of its masterworks, Stephen Sondheim's *Follies*.

1579 Take It from the Top (1979). THEATRE: New Federal Theatre; OPENING DATE: January 18, 1979; PERFORMANCES: 12; WORDS: Ruby Dee; LYRICS: Ruby Dee; MUSIC: Uncredited; DIRECTION: Ossie Davis; CHOREOGRAPHY: Kimee Joyce; SCENERY: Michael Fish; COSTUMES: Judy Dearing; LIGHTING: Shirley Prendergast; MUSICAL DIRECTION: Guy Davis; PRODUCER: The Henry Street Settlement (Woodie King, Jr., Director and Producer)

CAST—Lou Myers (Prophet Willie), Ruby Dee (Angel Angeline), Ossie Davis (Almight), Jack Landron (Hallarte, Epitome), David Van Fleet (Lowen, Torn), Raymond Stough (C.B.), Kimee Joyce (Almight's Assistant, Jill, Brenda), Maurice Carlton (Bank Guard, Brother Ben, Isaiah), Walter Caldwell (Jack, Newsboy, Auctioneer), Tom McCleister (Warby, Buckie), Mariann Aaida (Jenny, Amelia), Laurie Carlos (Miz Kix), Robert Townsend (Calvin), Chequita Jackson (Deltrisha Virginelle), Rony Clanton (Norman), Pamelia Poitier (Swahilla Mae)

NOTES—Division of acts and song assignments unknown. Richard Eder in the *New York Times* indicated *Take It from the Top* had "virtually no music" except for background piano or percussion accompaniment and an occasional song. He described the "tedious" and "shapeless" plot as an "inspirational parable" along the lines of Marc Connelly's *The Green Pastures* (1930), and said that as social satire the evening had "no bite; only a noisy chewing."

1580 Take Me Along. THEATRE: Richard Allen Center for Culture and Art/Manhattan Community College; OPENING DATE: March 14, 1984; PERFORMANCES: 12; BOOK: Joseph Stein; LYRICS: Bob Merrill; MUSIC: Bob Merrill; DIRECTION: Geraldine Fitzgerald and Mike Malone; CHOREOGRAPHY: Geraldine Fitzgerald and Mike Malone; additional choreography by Dianne McIntyre; SCENERY: James Wolk; COSTUMES: Myrna Colley-Lee; LIGHTING: Toshiro Ogawa; MUSICAL DIRECTION: Frederic Gripper; PRODUCER: Richard Allen Center for Culture and Art (Shirley J. Radcliffe, Executive Producer), in association with Performing Arts Center, Inc.

CAST—Duane Jones (Nat Miller), Mary Alice (Essie Miller), Rhetta Hughes (Lily), Mario Van Peebles (Arthur Miller), Marchant Odette (Mildred Miller), Jeffrey V. Thompson (Sid), Mark Wade (Richard Miller), Robert Kya-Hill (Dave McComber), Michael Darden (Wint), Vanessa Bell (Belle), Kirk Taylor (Bartender), Sandy Williams (Muriel McComber), Olivia Ward (Mrs. McComber)

SOURCE—The 1933 play *Ah! Wilderness!* By Eugene O'Neill.

The action occurs in 1906 in Centerville, Connecticut, on July 4 and 5.

The musical was presented in two acts.

ACT ONE—Opening, "Oh, Please" (Duane Jones, Company), "Sid Ol' Kid" (Jeffrey V. Thompson, Family), "(I'm) Staying Young" (Duane Jones), "The Hurt They Write About" (Mark Wade), "I Get Embarrassed" (Jeffrey V. Thompson, Rhetta Hughes), "Take Me Along" (Jeffrey V. Thompson, Duane Jones, Family), "We're Home" (Rhetta Hughes, Mary Alice), "The Company of Men" (Jeffrey V. Thompson, Duane Jones), "That's How It Starts" (Mark Wade)

ACT TWO—"Oh, Please" (reprise) (Duane Jones, Mary Alice), "A Slight Detail (Promise Me a Rose)" (Rhetta Hughes), "(I'm) Staying Young" (reprise) (Duane Jones), "Little Green Snake" (Jeffrey V. Thompson), "The Love They Write About" (reprise of "The Hurt They Write About") (Mark Wade), "I Would Die" (Mark Wade, Sandy Williams), "I Would Die" (reprise) (Duane Jones, Mary Alice), "Take Me Along" (reprise) (Jeffrey V. Thompson, Company)

NOTES—This Off Off Broadway revival of the 1959 Broadway musical *Take Me Along* was an all-Black version, and included two new songs written especially for the production by Bob Merrill ("The Hurt [Love] They Write About" and "[In] The Company of Men").

Adapted from *Ah! Wilderness!*, Eugene O'Neill's sunniest (and most atypical) play, the original Broadway production of *Take Me Along* (which opened at the Shubert Theatre on October 22, 1959, and played for 448 performances) was, depending on the source referenced, either a hit which just barely returned its initial investment or a flop which almost recouped its capitalization. But the musical sure seemed like a hit at the time, with a Broadway run of a little more than a year, a musical sequence telecast on *The Ed Sullivan Show*, and a *Life* magazine cover. But once star Jackie Gleason left the show upon the expiration of his contract, the musical soon closed because his replacement, William Bendix, couldn't draw an audience. (This was typical of other musicals of the period; when Abbe Lane left *Oh Captain!* [1958], the show didn't last more than a week or two once Dorothy Lamour replaced her; similarly, *Once Upon a Mattress* [1959; see entry] quickly closed when Ann B. Davis replaced Carol Burnett.)

After *Take Me Along* closed on Broadway, there was no national tour, no Hollywood film, no London production. And despite its winning score (including one of the best Broadway overtures ever), there wasn't a hit song to readily identify the show to the public. But in the years following the Broadway run there were occasional summer stock productions, including a mid-1970s tour with Gene Kelly. Further, the show's title song later became well known as the jingle for an airline's television commercial.

The all-Black 1984 version probably inspired the (all-White) 1985 Broadway revival, which, unfortunately, lasted just one performance. Lacking the star power which the character of Sid demands, the Broadway revival was mildly pleasant, bordering on the bland. The 1984 version included the two above-mentioned new songs by Bob Merrill; the following songs from the original production weren't used: "For Sweet Charity (Volunteer Firemen Picnic)," "Wint's Song," "The Beardsley Ballet," "Nine O'-Clock," and "But Yours." The 1985 Broadway revival included one of the new songs written for the 1984 production ("[In] The Company of Men") as well as three new songs written especially for the 1985 version ("Knights on White Horses," "If Jesus Don't Love Ya," and "The Only Pair I've Got," the latter probably a revised version of "For Sweet Charity [Volunteer Firemen Picnic]").

For another musical version of *Ah! Wilderness!*, see MGM's problematic 1948 film *Summer Holiday* (which was actually filmed in 1946 but not released until two years later); it was directed by Rouben Mamoulian, the director of the original stage productions of *Porgy and Bess* (1935), *Oklahoma!* (1943), *Carousel* (1945), *St. Louis Woman* (1946), and *Lost in the Stars* (1949) as well as Rodgers and Hart's *Love Me Tonight* (1932), perhaps the most entertaining and inventive of all film musicals. Despite a few weak spots in the film's script, and the fact that it was severely cut prior to release, *Summer Holiday* is a beautifully crafted film, with many inventive touches, including a brilliant use of Technicolor. The Ralph Blane and Harry Warren score is vastly underrated, and includes "The Stanley Steamer," the film's best-known number. And the beautiful ballad "Spring Isn't Everything" (sung by Walter Huston) is the film's equivalent to *Take Me Along*'s equally haunting "Staying Young"; although the song was cut from the final print, it can be heard on the film's soundtrack album (Rhino Records CD # RHM2-7769).

The original Broadway cast album of *Take Me Along* was released by RCA Victor Records (LP # LSO-1050; CD # 07863-51050-2).

As of this writing, the musical is scheduled to be revived by the Irish Repertory Theatre on February 28, 2008.

1581 Taking a Chance on Love/The Lyrics & Life of John LaTouche. "A New Musical Revue." THEATRE: The Theatre at Saint Peter's Church/The York Theatre Company; OPENING DATE: March 12, 2000; PERFORMANCES: 29; LYRICS: John LaTouche; MUSIC: See song list for credits; DIRECTION: James Morgan; CHOREOGRAPHY: Janet Watson; SCENERY: James Morgan; COSTUMES: Suzy Benzinger; LIGHTING: S. Ryan Schmidt; MUSICAL DIRECTION: Jeffrey R. Smith; PRODUCER: The York Theatre Company (James Morgan, Artistic Director; Robert A. Buckley, Managing Director)

CAST—Terry Burrell, Jerry Dixon, Donna English, Eddie Korbich

The revue was presented in two acts (division of acts unknown).

NOTES—*Taking a Chance on Love* was a welcome revue honoring John LaTouche (1914-1956), one of the theatre's great lyricists. The revue was recorded by Original Cast Records (CD # OC-4444); the program didn't include a song list, and so the list below is taken from the invaluable recording (which belongs in every musical-theatre collection if for no other reason than to hear Eddie Korbich's joyous and explosive rendition of "Not a Care in World"): "Mr. Nobody" (from *Ballet Ballads*, 1948; music by Jerome Moross; from the "Lonely Willie" sequence of *Willie the Weeper*) (Company), "Nothing Ever Happens in Angel's Roost" (*The Golden Apple*, 1954; music by Jerome Moross) (Eddie Korbich), "Keep Your Nose to the Grindstone" (*The Vamp*, 1955; music by James Mundy) (Company), "Do What You Wanna Do" (*Cabin in the Sky*, 1940; music by Vernon Duke) (Donna English, Terry Burrell) "I'll Take the City" (*Banjo Eyes*, 1942; music by Vernon Duke) (Jerry Dixon, Company), "Oh, Oh, Baby" (a/k/a "Oh Baby, Gee Baby") (*Ballet Ballads*, 1948; music by Jerome Moross; from the "Sexy Willie" [a/k/a "Lover Willie"] sequence of *Willie the Weeper*) (Company), "On the Waterfront"/"Beside the Troubled Waters of the Hudson" (lyrics apparently based on music from the 1954 film *On the Waterfront*; music by Leonard Bernstein) (Jerry Dixon, Eddie Korbich), "Not a Care in the World" (*Banjo Eyes*, 1942; music by Vernon Duke) (Eddie Korbich), "The Surrealist" (nightclub material; music by John LaTouche) (Donna English); Selections from *Cabin in the Sky—A Mini-Musical* (1940; music by Vernon Duke): "Cabin in the Sky" (Terry Burrell, Jerry Dixon), "Little Poppa Satan" (doesn't appear to have been in the original 1940 production) (Eddie Korbich, Jerry Dixon), "In My Old Virginia Home (on the River Nile)" (Jerry Dixon, Terry Burrell), "Honey in the Honeycomb" (Donna English), "Love Turned the Light Out" (Terry Burrell), Finale (Company), "Taking a Chance on Love" (*Cabin in the Sky*, 1940; lyric by John LaTouche and Ted Fetter; music by Vernon Duke) (Company), "Four Little Misfits" (*The Vamp*, 1955; music by James Mundy) (Company), "Maybe I Should Change My Ways"/"Take Love Easy" (*Beggar's Holiday*, 1946; music by Duke Ellington) (Jerry Dixon, Terry Burrell), "Nail in the Horseshoe" (nightclub material; music by Johann Strauss and Wolfgang Amadeus Mozart) (Eddie Korbich); Selections from *Ballet Ballads/The Eccentricities of Davy Crockett* (1948; music by Jerome Moross): Opening (Company), "My Yellow Flower" (a/k/a "You're My Yaller Flower") (Donna English), "Ridin' on the Breeze" (Jerry Dixon), Finale (Company), "A Rainy Day" (from an unfinished and untitled musical; music by Donald Fuller) (Eddie Korbich), "Plain Words" (written for, but not used in, *Candide* [1956]; music by Leonard Bernstein) (Eddie Korbich, Donna English), "Have You Met Delilah?" (*The Vamp*, 1955; music by James Mundy) (Jerry Dixon, Eddie Korbich), "I'm Everybody's Baby" (*The Vamp*, 1955; music by James Mundy) (Terry Burrell, with Jerry Dixon and Eddie Korbich), "Windflowers" (*The Golden Apple*, 1954; music by Jerome Moross) (Donna English), "Ringaroundarosie (The Syphilis Song)" (written for, but not used in, *Candide* [1956]; music by Leonard Bernstein) (Jerry Dixon, Company), "Lazy Afternoon" (*The Golden Apple*, 1954; music by Jerome Moross) (Jerry Dixon, Eddie Korbich) "Always Through the Changing" (*The Ballad of Baby Doe*, 1956; music by Douglas Moore) (Company), A spoken sequence ("Touche's Salon") was later included in the 2005 revue *Lingoland* (see entry) and can be heard on that show's cast album. For more information on *The Ballad of Baby Doe*, *Ballet Ballads*, *Cabin in the Sky*, *Candide*, and *The Golden Apple*, see entries.

1582 Taking My Turn. "A Musical Celebration." THEATRE: Entermedia Theatre; OPENING DATE: June 9, 1983; PERFORMANCES: 345; SCRIPT: "Based on writings by people in their prime"; adapted by Robert H. Livingston; LYRICS: Will Holt; MUSIC: Gary William Friedman; DIRECTION: Robert H. Livingston; CHOREOGRAPHY: Douglas Norwick; SCENERY: Clarke Dunham; COSTUMES: Judith Dolan; LIGHTING: David F. Segal; MUSICAL DIRECTION: Barry Levitt; PRODUCERS: Richard Seader, Maurice Levine, Sonny Fox, Joanne Cummings, Arleen Kane, Anthony Kane, and Sally Sears

CAST—Mace Barrett (Eric), Marni Nixon (Edna), Victor Griffin (John), Cissy Houston (Helen), Tiger Haynes (Charles), Margaret Whiting (Dorothy), Ted Thurston (Benjamin), Sheila Smith (Janet)

The action occurs during the course of one year ... this year.

The musical was presented in two acts.

ACT ONE *Spring-Summer:* "This Is My Song" (Company), "Somebody Else" (Company), "Fine for the Shape I'm In" (Margaret Whiting, Marni Nixon, Cissy Houston), "Two of Me" (Sheila Smith), "Janet Get Up" (Company), "I Like It" (Company), "I Never Made Money from Music" (Tiger Haynes), "Vivaldi" (Marni Nixon, Company), "Do You Remember?" (Ted Thurston, Company), "In April" (Margaret Whiting), "Pick More Daisies" (Company)

ACT TWO *Fall-Winter:* "Taking Our Turn" (Company), "Sweet Longings" (Sheila Smith, Company), "I Am Not Old" (Cissy Houston), "Do You Remember?" (reprise) (Ted Thurston, Company), "The Kite" (Victor Griffin, Company), "Good Luck to You" (Mace Barrett, Company), "In the House" (Mace Barrett), "Somebody Else" (reprise) (Company), "It Still Isn't Over" (Ted Thurston, Margaret Whiting), "This Is My Song" (reprise) (Company)

NOTES—The 1980 showcase *Turns* (see entry) opened Off Broadway three years later as *Taking My Turn*. Ted Thurston and Tiger Haynes reprised their roles from the earlier production, and they were joined by such welcome Off Broadway and Broadway veterans as Sheila Smith and Victor Griffin, both of whom had created roles in the original Broadway production of *Follies* (1971), another musical which dealt with the passing of years.

In 1970, Will Holt and Gary William Friedman (with Herb Schapiro) had enjoyed a long-running success with a revue about young people (see entry for *The Me Nobody Knows*), and now they had an equally successful one which dealt with seniors; later, Friedman and Schapiro collaborated on another revue about young people (see entry for *Bring on the Morning*). *Taking My Turn* ran almost a full year; it was recorded by Broadway Limited Records (LP # BLR-1001-R) and the script was published by Samuel French, Inc., in 1984. The revue was also seen on cable television.

Mel Gussow in the *New York Times* said the "rejuvenating" evening provided "joyful entertainment," and he singled out a number of songs ("Fine for the Shape I'm In," "Sweet Longings," "It Still Isn't Over," and "Taking Our Turn").

1583 Tale for a Deaf Ear. THEATRE: New York City Center; OPENING DATE: April 6, 1958; PERFORMANCES: 3; BOOK: Mark Bucci; MUSIC: Mark Bucci; DIRECTION: Michael Pollock; SCENERY: Paul Sylbert; COSTUMES: Paul Sylbert; MUSICAL DIRECTION: Arnold Gamson; PRODUCER: The New York City Opera Company

CAST—Patricia Neway (Laura Gates), William Chapman (Tracy Gates), Beverly Bower (The Woman), Lee Venora (The Girl), Richard Cassilly (The Soldier), Arthur Newman (The Doctor)

SOURCE—One of the stories in the 1955 short story collection *The Moment Before the Rain* by Elizabeth Enright.

The action occurs in the present on a winter Sunday afternoon in the Gates' living room.

The opera was presented in one act (A Prologue, an Interlude, and an Epilogue).

NOTES—The world premiere for the opera *Tale for a Deaf Ear* had taken place at Tanglewood in 1956, and the City Opera production in 1958 marked its first New York showing. The *New York Times* reported that the plot dealt with an Italian woman of the Renaissance and a German soldier of the Thirty Years War, both of whose prayers are answered when their dead return to life (for the woman, a son, for the soldier, a brother). The role of the woman was sung in Italian, and the role of the soldier in German; despite two major characters from the past, the opera took place in the present, and the other characters sang in English.

The cast included Patricia Neway, who had created the role of Magda Sorel in the original 1950 Broadway production of Gian-Carlo Menotti's *The Consul*; in 1958 and 1959, she created no less than four "Mother" roles in New York: besides the mother in *Tale for a Deaf Ear*, she was the mother in the Broadway production of Menotti's *Maria Golovin* (1958); the mother in the New York City Opera's world premiere of Hugo Weisgall's *Six Characters in Search of an Author* (1959; see entry); and the Mother Abbess in the original 1959 Broadway production of Richard Rodgers and Oscar Hammerstein II's *The*

Sound of Music (in which she introduced "Climb Every Mountain"). And in 1963 she created the role of Bert Convy's sour, unforgiving mother in the Off Broadway musical *Morning Sun* (see entry).

William Chapman appeared in the original productions of *Candide* (1956), *Maria Golovin*, and Frank Loesser's *Greenwillow* (1960); in the latter, he and Cecil Kellaway introduced the amusing duet "The Sermon." Chapman later replaced John Cullum during the run of *Shenandoah* (1975). Lee Venora appeared in Robert Wright and George Forrest's *Kean* (1961), introducing the haunting "Willow, Willow, Willow," one of many memorable numbers from the vastly underrated score.

Tale for a Deaf Ear was presented on a double bill with a revival of Leonard Bernstein's *Trouble in Tahiti*, which had its world premiere at Brandeis University, Waltham, Massachusetts, on June 12, 1952; *Tahiti*'s Broadway premiere occurred on April 19, 1955, when the musical was presented as one-third of *All in One*, a three-act evening of dance (in various styles, by different composers), drama (Tennessee Williams' *27 Wagons Full of Cotton*), and music (*Tahiti*). An interesting bit of *Tahiti* trivia: David Atkinson created the role of Sam in the world premiere production at Brandeis, but it was John Tyers who performed the role on Broadway. So while Atkinson originated the role and was the first to sing Sam's arias and duets in *Tahiti* (including the locker room aria "There's a Law About Men"), it was Tyers who introduced the role and the songs to Broadway audiences.

And the two also share a connection with one of the loveliest songs ever heard on the Broadway stage, the ethereal ballad "Haunted Heart," from Howard Dietz and Arthur Schwartz' revue *Inside U.S.A.* (1948). Atkinson was the first to perform the song, when he introduced it during the revue's pre-Broadway tryout; but for reasons which remain unclear, Tyers assumed the role sometime during the tryout, and so when the revue opened on Broadway, it was Tyers who officially introduced "Haunted Heart." But Atkinson's departure during the tryout must have been amicable, because during the Broadway run Atkinson in turn replaced Tyers, and so Atkinson got to sing "his" song on Broadway after all, albeit not on opening night.

1584 Tales of Tinseltown. "A Movieland Musical"/"A Sardonic Satire." THEATRE: Musical Theatre Works; OPENING DATE: August 8, 1985; PERFORMANCES: 19; LIBRETTO: Michael Colby; MUSIC: Paul Katz; DIRECTION: Rick Lombardo; staging by Dennis Dennehy and Rick Lombardo; CHOREOGRAPHY: Dennis Dennehy; SCENERY: Alexander Okun; COSTUMES: Michele Reisch; LIGHTING: Jason Kantrowitz; MUSICAL DIRECTION: James Stenborg; PRODUCERS: The Director's Company/Staret (Michael Parva, Artistic Director; Victoria Lanman, Producing and Managing Director) and The Summer Directors Festival '85/Independent Project Series

CAST—Elizabeth Austin (Ellie Ash), Alison Fraser (Lulu Beauveen), Greg Mowry (Tommy Burke), Olga Talyn (Adele DeRale), Jason Graae (Elmo Green), Bob Arnold (Norman G. Nertshmertz), Nora Mae Lyng (Bertha Powell), Nat Chandler (Antonio [Tony] Toscanini)

Most of the action occurs in Hollywood during the 1930s.

The musical was presented in two acts.

ACT ONE—"Tinseltown Tattletale" (Olga DeRale, Ensemble), "I Belong to Hollywood" (Elizabeth Austin, Farmhands), "Let's Go" (Jason Graae, Elizabeth Austin), "N.G.N. Productions" (Ensemble), "The Musical Melange" (Ensemble), "Full" (Nat Chandler), "I Can Sing" (Nora Mae Lyng), "All Over the Place" (Greg Mowry, with Elizabeth Austin), "The Hollywood Sign" (Ensemble), "The Tragedy of Miss Potato Sack" (Greg Mowry), "In Broken-Promise Land" (Olga DeRale), "I Knew It!" (Bob Arnold), "Jungle Fever" (Alison Fraser, Greg Mowry, and Elizabeth Austin, with Nora Mae Lyng, Olga Talyn, and Nat Chandler), "So This Is the Movies" (Jason Graae), The Ellie Ash Medley: "Alphabet Soup" (Elizabeth Austin), "At Sea" (Greg Mowry, Elizabeth Austin), "Just Laugh It Away" (Alison Fraser, Nora Mae Lyng, Elizabeth Austin), "Hunchy" (Nat Chandler, Elizabeth Austin), "It's Mine" (Elizabeth Austin, with Alison Fraser, Nora Mae Lyng, Greg Mowry, Nat Chandler)

ACT TWO—"Oh, the Scandal!" (Olga Talyn, Ensemble), "Nobody Shtomps on My Shtudio" (Bob Arnold), "Be Good" (Alison Fraser, Ensemble), "Bad!" (Elizabeth Austin, Ensemble), "Dream of Hollywood" (Ensemble), "I'll Stand by You" (Jason Graae), "I'm Beautiful" (Nat Chandler), "Take Two" (Nora Mae Lyng, with Greg Mowry, Nat Chandler, Jason Graae, Elizabeth Austin, and Bob Arnold), "Ruin Them" (Olga Talyn), "Stars in My Eyes" (Elizabeth Austin, with Nora Mae Lyng, Nat Chandler, and Greg Mowry), "Expose" (Bob Arnold)

NOTES—The Off Off Broadway sung-through musical *Tales of Tinseltown* was a spoof of movie-making (specifically movie musicals of the 1930s), and centered on Ellie Ash (Elizabeth Austin), whose ability to imitate the voices of animals makes her a Hollywood star. D.J.R. Bruckner in the *New York Times* found the musical "ambitious," but noted the evening was sometimes "inert" and "overcomplicated." Nevertheless, Bruckner praised the "pleasant" and varied score (jazz, samba, torch, even a touch of Kurt Weill) and singled out Ellie's "Jungle Fever" (the song was "laughter from the first syllable to the last") and an "hilarious" pair of matched numbers, Alison Fraser's "Be Good" and Austin's "Bad!"

1585 Tallulah. "The Lady in Revue." THEATRE: Cheryl Crawford Theatre/Westside Arts Theatre; OPENING DATE: October 30, 1983; PERFORMANCES: 42; BOOK: Tony Lang; LYRICS: Mae Richards; MUSIC: Arthur Siegel; DIRECTION: David Holdgrive; CHOREOGRAPHY: David Holdgrive; Assistant Choreographer, William Alan Coats; SCENERY: John Falabella; production graphics by Stanley Topliff; COSTUMES: John Falabella; Helen Gallagher's gowns by Neil Bieff; LIGHTING: Ken Billington; MUSICAL DIRECTION: Bruce W. Coyle; Assistant Music Director, Jim Rice; PRODUCERS: Mark deSolla Price, John Van Ness Philip, and Leonard Soloway in association with David Susskind

CAST—HELEN GALLAGER (Tallulah Bankhead), RUSSELL NYPE (Will Bankhead), Joel Craig (John Barrymore, John Emery), Men (Tom Hafner, Eric Johnson, Ken Lundie, Patrick Parker, Clark Sterling)

The musical was presented in two acts.

ACT ONE—"Darling" (Helen Gallagher, Men), "Tallulah" (Helen Gallagher, Men), "When I Do a (Tap) Dance for You" (Helen Gallagher, Russell Nype), "Home Sweet Home" (Helen Gallagher, Men), "I've Got to Try Everything Once" (Helen Gallagher, Joel Craig), "You're You" (Helen Gallagher, Tom Hafner, Patrick Parker, Clark Sterling, Ken Lundie), "I Can See Him Clearly" (Helen Gallagher), "Tallulahbaloo" (Men), "The Party Is Where I Am" (Helen Gallagher, Men)

ACT TWO—"Stay Awhile" (Helen Gallagher, Men), "It's a Hit" (Ken Lundie, Clark Sterling, Patrick Parker, Men), "If Only He Were a Woman" (Helen Gallagher, Eric Johnson, Men), "Tallulah" (reprise) (Russell Nype), "Love Is on Its Knees" (Helen Gallagher, Eric Johnson, Men), "Don't Ever Book a Trip on the IRT" (Helen Gallagher, Men), "You Need a Lift!" (Helen Gallagher), Finale (Helen Gallagher, Men)

NOTES—A virtual one-woman musical about Tallulah Bankhead (1902-1968) with Broadway legend Helen Gallagher in the lead must have seemed a natural for an intimate Off Broadway musical. The critics loved Helen Gallagher (Clive Barnes in the *New York Post* wrote that she not only carried the show, she ran with it) and generally liked the pleasant score, but most felt the musical was too sketchy in its storytelling. Frank Rich in the *New York Times* noted that a single line of dialogue referred to Bankhead's three greatest successes (her stage hits *The Little Foxes* [1939] and *The Skin of Our Teeth* [1942] and her film *Lifeboat* [1944]), but an entire song was devoted to her face lift. Further, the musical's lack of imagination included an opening sequence in which a group of male cast members appeared in Tallulah drag (this was possibly an attempt to capitalize on the popularity of *La Cage Aux Folles*, which had opened on Broadway the previous summer).

During the brief run of the show, the second-act number "If I Were a Woman" was deleted in favor of "Tango." Further, a note in an early program indicated the song "I'm the Woman You Wanted" was part of the score (but the program didn't credit who performed the song). However, a later program indicated that the "Finale" was in fact "I'm the Woman You Wanted."

Painted Smiles Records released the cast recording (LP # PS-1348), which included both a "Tallulah Finale" as well as "I'm the Woman You Wanted" and a reprise of "It's a Hit." A later CD release (# PSCD-128) of the cast album included four songs which had been cut prior to production's opening ("It's in the Cards," "The Wrong Hat," "Stay Awhile," and "The Right One Will Ask Me to Dance") as well as "Ballet Music." The latter was dance music heard in the musical which had not been included in the original LP release.

Tallulah had opened earlier in the season at the T.O.M.I. Theatre on June 13, 1983, for twelve performances (in this production, Robert Dale Martin played the role of Will Bankhead). One song in this version ("Down Home") wasn't used when the musical re-opened Off Broadway in the fall.

On March 16, 1988, Helen Gallagher revisited Tallulah Bankhead in *Tallulah Tonight!*, which played Off Off Broadway at the American Place Theatre for twenty-two performances. The one-woman show was written by Tony Lang, and included old songs (such as "Most Gentlemen Don't Like Love" from the 1938 Broadway musical *Leave It to Me!*, lyric and music by Cole Porter) as well as new ones with lyrics by Lang and music by Bruce W. Coyle. In 1998, *Tallulah's Party*, a revised version of *Tallulah*, opened Off Off Broadway with Tovah Feldshuh in the leading role (see entry). Feldshuh also portrayed Tallulah Bankhead in *Tallulah Hallelujah!*, which opened Off Broadway at the Douglas Fairbanks Theatre on October 10, 2000, for ninety-seven performances. Written by Feldshuh (with additional material by Larry Amoros and Linda Selman) and including songs by Noel Coward, Cole Porter, and Kurt Weill, the musical depicted an impromptu appearance by Bankhead at a USO show on the evening following the premiere of her performance as Blanche DuBois in a New York revival of Tennessee Williams' *A Streetcar Named Desire* (which had opened at the New York City Center on February 15, 1956, for fifteen performances). Among the characters in the musical was Meredith Willson (portrayed by Bob Goldstone). Willson had contributed incidental music to the original stage production of *The Little Foxes*, and his "May the Good Lord Bless and Keep You" was the theme song for Bankhead's early 1950s radio program *The Big Show*.

1586 Tallulah's Party. THEATRE: The Martin R. Kaufman Theatre; OPENING DATE: March 19, 1998; PERFORMANCES: Unknown; BOOK: Bob Griffiths, Latifah Taormina, and J.D. Maria; LYRICS:

Mae Richard; MUSIC: Arthur Siegel; DIRECTION: Latifah Taormina; CHOREOGRAPHY: Jerome Vivona; SCENERY: Kent Hoffman; COSTUMES: Pascale Jutard; LIGHTING: Kent Hoffman; MUSICAL DIRECTION: Jeffrey Buchsbaum; PRODUCER: Richmond Shepard

CAST—Tovah Feldshuh (Tallulah Bankhead), Alan Gilbert (Max, Will Bankhead, Franklin P. Adams), Bobby Clark (Paul, Robert Benchley, Gerarld du Maurier), Robert Cary (Eric, Alexander Woollcott, John Emery)

The action occurs in Tullulah Bankhead's apartment in 1957 (division of acts and song assignments unknown).

MUSICAL NUMBERS—"Tallulah," "When I Do a Tap Dance for You," "I've Got to Try Everything Once," "Algonquin Anthem," "Home Sweet Home," "You're You," "The Right One Will Ask Me to Dance," "Tallulahbaloo," "The Party Is Where I Am," "Stay Awhile," "It's a Hit," "If Only He Were a Woman," "Love Is on Its Knees," "You Need a Lift, Darling," "I'm the Woman You Wanted"

NOTES—*Tallulah's Party*, with Tovah Feldshuh portraying Tallulah Bankhead, was a revised version of 1983's Off Broadway musical *Tallulah* which had starred Helen Gallagher (see entry).

The Off Off Broadway revival omitted "Darling," "I Can See Him Clearly," and "Don't Ever Book a Trip on the IRT," and added "Algonquin Anthem" and "The Right One Will Ask Me To Dance."

Feldshuh also portrayed Tallulah Bankhead in *Tallulah Hallelujah!*, which opened Off Broadway at the Douglas Fairbanks Theatre on October 10, 2000, for ninety-seven performances. Written by Feldshuh (with additional material by Larry Amoros and Linda Selman) and including songs by Noel Coward, Cole Porter, and Kurt Weill, the musical depicted an impromptu appearance by Bankhead at a USO show on the evening following the premiere of her performance as Blanche DuBois in a New York revival of Tennessee Williams' *A Streetcar Named Desire* (which opened at the New York City Center on February 15, 1956, for fifteen performances). Among the characters in the musical was Meredith Willson (portrayed by Bob Goldstone); for more information about Willson's musical associations with Tallulah Bankhead, see entry for *Tallulah*.

1587 The Taming of the Shrew.

"A Comic Opera." THEATRE: New York City Center; OPENING DATE: April 13, 1958; PERFORMANCES: 3; LIBRETTO: Vittorio Giannini and Dorothy Fee; MUSIC: Vittorio Giannini; DIRECTION: Margaret Webster; SCENERY: Watson Barratt; MUSICAL DIRECTION: Peter Hermann Adler; PRODUCER: The New York City Opera Company

CAST—John Alexander (Lucentio), Paul Ukena (Tranio), Chester Watson (Baptista), Phyllis Curtin (Katharina), Sonia Stolin (Bianca), Grant Williams (Gremio), Walter Farrell (Hortensio), John Gillaspy (Biondello), Walter Cassel (Petruchio), Keith Kaldenberg (Grumio), George Del Monte (Curtis), John Wheeler (Tailor), Arthur Newman (Vincentio), Jack De Lon (A Pedant, masquerading as Vincentio); Chorus (Servants of Baptista and Petruchio, Maids of Katharina)

SOURCE—The play *The Taming of the Shrew* (written approximately 1594) by William Shakespeare.

The action occurs in Padua, Italy.

The opera was presented in three acts.

NOTES—It was a bold and potentially foolhardy attempt on Vittorio Giannini's part to attempt a lyric adaptation of Shakespeare's *The Taming of the Shrew* so soon after the success of Cole Porter's musical comedy version, *Kiss Me, Kate* (1948). Like *My Fair Lady*, Porter's masterpiece is one of those rare musical adaptations which makes the source material come across as wanting because it lacks the songs written for the musical.

Philadelphia-born Giannini first saw his opera produced for two performances beginning on January 31, 1953, as a joint presentation by the Cincinnati Symphony and the Cincinnati Music Drama Guild. In 1954, it was televised by NBC (it was reportedly the first full-length opera seen on national television in the United States). The City Opera's production represented the New York premiere of the work.

Howard Taubman in the *New York Times* praised the work and found no need to compare it with Porter's musical. He reported that Giannini's "thoroughly enjoyable" adaptation "adorned" the opera season with the "vivacity of its spirits and the boisterousness of its laughter." He found the libretto "gay and airy," and said the score offered "crispness and point"; further, while the music moved the action along, it also paused to sing "with sentiment in a shamelessly old-fashioned way." In 1951, the opera's director Margaret Webster had directed a slapstick revival of *Shrew* at City Center; in his review for the *New York Herald-Tribune*, Otis L. Guernsey, Jr., noted she approached the script "as though Shakespeare had deliberately written it as a book for a musical comedy" (and, indeed, Webster actually had some of the performers sing snatches of a few of Porter's songs from *Kiss Me, Kate*). For the opera, Webster had a complete musical score to play with, and her direction was apparently delightful. Taubman reported that she ensured the piece was performed "as the frivolous romp it should be" and he said she staged the opera with "pace and invention."

1588 Tango Apasionado.

THEATRE: INTAR Theatre; OPENING DATE: October 28, 1987; PERFORMANCES: 56; TEXT: Graciela Daniele and Jim Lewis; LYRICS: William Finn; MUSIC: Astor Piazzolla; DIRECTION: Graciela Daniele; CHOREOGRAPHY: Graciela Daniele; SCENERY: Santo Loquasto; COSTUMES: Santo Loquasto; LIGHTING: Peggy Eisenhauer; MUSICAL DIRECTION: Pablo Zinger; PRODUCER: INTAR (Max Ferra, Artistic Director; Dennis Ferguson-Acosta, Managing Director)

CAST—Leonardo Cimino, Tina Paul, John Mineo, Gregory Mitchell, Camille Saviola, Luis Perez, Valarie Pettiford, Nicholas Gunn, Rene Caballos, Denise Faye, Norberto Carlos Simonian, Mercedes Acosta

SOURCE—The works of Jorge Luis Borges.

NOTES—The Off Off Broadway dance musical *Tango Apasionado* was one of many tango musicals which played in New York during the era. *Tango Argentino* played on Broadway in 1985 and 1999, *Tango Pasion* in 1993, and *Forever Tango* in 1997. In 1989, Graciela Daniele, Jim Lewis, William Finn, and Astor Piazolla teamed up again for the Broadway dance musical *Dangerous Games*, and Daniele and Lewis also collaborated on *Chronicle of a Death Foretold*, which played on Broadway in 1995.

1589 Tania.

THEATRE: New York Theatre Ensemble; OPENING DATE: November 5, 1975; PERFORMANCES: 30; BOOK: Mario Fratti; LYRICS: Paul Dick; MUSIC: Paul Dick; DIRECTION: Ron Nash; COSTUMES: John Reid and Dianne Charbonneau; LIGHTING: David Andrews; MUSICAL DIRECTION: Zelig Sokoll (?); PRODUCERS: New York Theatre Ensemble (Lucille Talayco, Artistic Director)

CAST—Walter George Alton (Walter), Marcy Olive (Ann), Norah Foster (Mizzie), Cynthia Haynes (Cynthia), Lee Torchia (Helen), Dennis Jones (Cinque), Norman Lewis (Bob), Akki Onyango (Akki), Jane Kerns (Diana), Marsha Bonine (Lee)

The musical was presented in two acts (division of acts and song assignments unknown).

MUSICAL NUMBERS—"To Start a Revolution," "There'll Come a Day," "Fire and Joy," "The American Dream," "I Sing a Woman," "Man in a Cage," "Hail Alma Mater," "The Wall," "The Shoot Out"

NOTES—Beginning in the 1980s, modern American opera started drawing upon recent headlines and newsmakers for inspiration (Nixon's trip to China, Leo Klinghoffer, Harvey Milk, Marilyn Monroe, Malcolm X). The Off Off Broadway musical *Tania* was about a decade ahead of the curve, and it told the story of the Patty Hearst kidnapping (the musical didn't call her by name, instead referring to her as "Cynthia" [after Cynthia Harris, the actress who played the title role]).

1590 Tap Dogs.

THEATRE: Union Square Theatre; OPENING DATE: March 16, 1997; PERFORMANCES: 182; MUSIC: Andrew Wilkie; DIRECTION: Nigel Triffitt; CHOREOGRAPHY: Dein Perry; SCENERY: Nigel Triffitt; LIGHTING: David Murray; PRODUCERS: Back Row Productions/Peter Holmes a Court and Columbia Artists Management Inc. in association with Richard Frankel and Marc Routh, by arrangement with Dein Perry and Nigel Triffitt

CAST—Billy Burke, Darren Disney, Christopher Horsey, Drew Kaluski, Jeremy Kiesman, Dein Perry, Ben Read, Nathan Sheens, Gil Stroming

The dance revue was presented in one act.

NOTES—*Tap Dogs* was an Australian tap dance revue which had been previously produced in Sydney and on a North American tour.

Peter Marks in the *New York Times* said the dancers in this "Australian beefcake tap-a-thon" preened and strutted "with the vanity of bodybuilders" and noted that two dancers stripped to the waist "for no other reason than to flash their glistening pecs." And so he wondered if a *Tap Dogs* workout video was around the corner. Marks further noted the troupe milked applause "after every musical phrase" and never let the audience forget how "arduous" their dancing was; he also mentioned they offered no "real feeling" and lacked individual personalities.

1591 Tapestry.

"The Music of Carole King." THEATRE: Union Square Theatre; OPENING DATE: February 18, 1993; PERFORMANCES: 19; LYRICS: Carole King, Gerry Goffin, T. Stern, D. Palmer, and J. Wexler; MUSIC: Carole King; DIRECTION: Jeffrey Martin; CHOREOGRAPHY: Ron Navarre; SCENERY: David Jenkins; COSTUMES: Debra Stein; LIGHTING: Peter A. Kaczorowksi; MUSICAL DIRECTION: Kathy Sommer; PRODUCERS: Rowan Joseph and Kevin Eberly, EMI Music Publishing Inc., Robert B. Shaffer and Daryl Roth in association with Shane T. Parlow and Neal Roberts; David Strong Warner, Inc., Ezecutive Producer

CAST—Lawrence Clayton, Mary Gutzi, Pattie Darcy Jones, Vanessa A. Jones, Frank Mastrone, Jim Morlino

The revue was presented in one act.

MUSICAL NUMBERS—"Music" (lyric by Carole King) (Company), "Where You Lead" (lyric by T. Stern) (Vanessa A. Jones, Company), "Sweet Seasons" (lyric by T. Stern) (Pattie Darcy Jones, Lawrence Clayton), "Been to Canaan" (lyric by Carole King) (Jim Morlino), "Up on the Roof" (lyric by Gerry Goffin) (Mary Gutzi), "Growing Away from Me" (lyric by Carole King) (Lawrence Clayton), "I Feel the Earth Move" (lyric by Carole King) (Frank Mastrone), "So Far Away"/"Home Again" (lyrics by Carole King) (Mary Gutzi, Jim Morlino), "Jazzman" (lyric by D. Palmer) (Pattie Darcy Jones), The Early Years (medley; program didn't list specific songs in this sequence; all lyrics by Gerry Gofffin) (Company), "Speeding Time" (lyric by Gerry Goffin) (Jim Morlino, with Frank Mastrone), "No Easy Way Down" (lyric by Gerry Goffin) (Mary Gutzi), "Where Does Love Go" (lyric by Gerry Goffin) (Frank Mastrone), "Beautiful" (lyric by Carole King) (Vanessa A. Jones), "Smackwater Jack" (lyric by Carole King) (Pattie Darcy Jones, Company), "Tapestry" (lyric by Carole King) (Frank Mastrone, Jim

Morlino, Company), "Will You Love Me Tomorrow" (lyric by Gerry Goffin) (Pattie Darcy Jones), "Some Kind of Wonderful" (lyric by Gerry Goffin) (Lawrence Clayton), "Natural Woman" (lyric by Gerry Goffin and J. Wexler) (Mary Gutzi, Pattie Darcy Jones, Vanessa A. Jones), "Hi De Ho" (lyric by Gerry Goffin) (Lawrence Clayton, Frank Mastrone, Jim Morlino), "Way Over Yonder" (lyric by Carole King) (Vanessa A. Jones, Lawrence Clayton), "You've Got a Friend" (lyricist unknown) (Company)

NOTES—*Tapestry*, a short-lived Off Off Broadway revue of songs by Carole King, was presented in two acts during previews. Dropped prior to the opening were the following songs: "Ride the Music" (lyric by Carole King), "It's Gonna Take Some Time" (lyric by T. Stern), "It's Too Late" (lyric by T. Stern), "Looking Out for Number One" (lyric by Carole King), "Legacy" (lyric by R. Guess), "Child of Mine" (lyric by Gerry Goffin), "Daughter of Light" (by Gerry Goffin), "Only Love Is Real" (lyric by Carole King), and "We Are All in This Together" (lyric by D. Palmer).

Stephen Holden in the *New York Times* felt the evening was a "choreographed concert" which lacked the energy of such revues as *Ain't Misbehavin'* (see entry).

1592 Tarot. THEATRE: Circle in the Square (Downtown); OPENING DATE: March 4, 1971; PERFORMANCES: 38; BOOK MATERIAL: The Rubber Duck (Joe McCord); MUSIC: Tom Constanten and Touchstone; DIRECTION: Robert Kalfin; SCENERY: Stephen Hendrickson; COSTUMES: Stephen Hendrickson; LIGHTING: Burl Hash; PRODUCERS: Richard Fields in association with William W. Rippner

CAST—Edward Barton (Hanged Man, Justice), Cassia Besson (Frog, Tree, Page of Wands), Cynthia Briggs (Eternity, Maiden), Maxine Herman (Thief, Moon, Judgment), John Kuhner (White Magician, Mystic Farmer), Renos Mandis (Old Fool, Mystic Carpenter), Joe McCord (The Fool), John Proctor Parriott (Turtle, Death, Philosopher), Frederick Rivera (Black Magician, Greed, Devil); Touchstone (Rock Combo; Jim Byers, classic guitar; Tom Constanten, electric piano; Paul Dresher, electric guitar, flute, sitar, steel pedal; Art Fayer, electric violin; Gary Hirsh, percussion; Wes Steele, bass guitar, cello)

The musical was presented in two acts.

NOTES—In *The Survival of St. Joan* (see entry), the actors didn't sing; instead, the rock group Smoke Rise performed all the songs. With *Tarot*, the actors neither spoke nor sang. The performers used mime to tell the story, and the rock group Touchstone performed the music (there were no lyrics).

The musical first premiered at the Chelsea Theatre Center at the Brooklyn Academy of Music on December 11, 1971, for thirteen performances; there were vocals in this production (sung by Yolande Bavan), and the music was performed by The Rubber Band, which included the six musicians who performed under the name of Touchstone in the Circle in the Square production. In Brooklyn, the program noted that Jerry Garcia (of the Grateful Dead rock group) would play electric lead guitar and steel pedal "when he can."

The program for the Brooklyn production indicated the music was composed by Tom Constanten as well as by Chicken Hirsch (of Country Joe and the Fish), Jerry Garcia (of the Grateful Dead), and "Wes [Steele], Art [Fayer], Paul [Dresher], Tim [last name unknown], and Others."

It appears that for the Circle in the Square production, the musical contributions by Jerry Garcia were not used, and that most of the music was by Tom Constenten (with some music by other members of the band Touchstone and at least one number co-written by Chicken Hirsch).

The "original cast mime album" (performed by Touchstone) was recorded shortly after the production closed, and was released by United Artists, Inc., Records (LP # UAS-5563). The mime-musical was about the Tarot card figure Fool and his adventures with other cards in the Tarot deck. Mel Gussow in the *New York Times* praised the music, and noted the evening was much like a silent movie accompanied by background music. He felt the presentation lacked imagination, and that the plot was weighed down by literalism. But he acknowledged the evening offered a "childishness" which would appeal to some theatergoers. As for himself, he found the musical's "simplicity" often just "simple-minded."

The following sequence of scenes is taken from the Brooklyn program:

ACT ONE *Life Before:* "The Creation of the Earth," "Reality: The Turtle Awakens the Dealer," "Appearance of the Life and Death Magicians," "Tarot," "Birth of the Hermit (God of all the Magics)," "Construction of the Death-Life-Death Mandala Bridge" and "Utopia," "Death, The Hanged Man and Eternity Take Their Places," "The Thief of Cups Looks to Death as Refuge," "Greed, Chasing the Thief, Barely Escapes Into Life and Horror," "The Heirophant (Perfection) Passes Through Utopia," "Junk Man (The Old Fool) Passes Through Utopia," "The Philosopher Encounters the Tree of Life and Transcends His Intellect," "Lunacy (The Moon) Attempts To Abort the Fool-Fetus," "The Lovers (Adolescence)," "The Fool Is Born Into Pre-Life"

ACT TWO *A Moth to the Flame:* "The Fool Is Born," "The White and Black Magicians Prepare the Fool for His Journey," "The Fool Encounters Judgement (The Establishment) and Is Saved by Justice," "The Maiden: The White Magician's Gift to the Fool," "Bones: The Magicians Foretell the Fool's Destiny," "The Mystic Carpenter Trades His Chariot to the Fool," "The Fool's Journey Through Space," "The Star (Vanity) and Phases of the Moon," "The Philosopher Tells the Fool Like It Is," "Eternity Rescues the Fool from Despair," "Intellect: War Between the Devil and the Fool," "Death March: A Last Farewell," "Limbo," "From the Cocoon to the Sun: Enlightenment," "The Turtle: Reality Returns"

1593 Tatterdemalion. "A Musical." THEATRE: Douglas Fairbanks Theatre; OPENING DATE: October 27, 1985; PERFORMANCES: 25; BOOK: Judd Woldin; LYRICS: Judd Woldin; additional lyrics by Susan Birkenhead and Herb Martin; MUSIC: Judd Woldin; DIRECTION: Eric Krebs; CHOREOGRAPHY: Mary Jane Houdina; SCENERY: Ed Wittstein; COSTUMES: Patricia Adshead; LIGHTING: Whitney Quesenbery; MUSICAL DIRECTION: Edward G. Robinson; PRODUCER: Eric Krebs

CAST—Annie McGreevey (Sadie, Mrs. Mendoza), Robert Blumenfeld (Isaac, Wilkinson, Cosmetician, Furtado), Ron Wisniski (Herschel, Belasco), Suzanne Briar (Rivka, The Housekeeper), Stuart Zagnit (David), K.C. Wilson (Mendoza), Jack Sevier (Da Costa), Tia Speros (Deborah)

SOURCE—The 1894 novel *The King of Schnorrers* by Israel Zangwill.

The action occurs in the East End of London in 1791.

The musical was presented in two acts.

ACT ONE—"Petticoat Lane" (The Peddlers), "Ours" (Jack Sevier), "Chutzpah" (K.C. Wilson, Annie McGreevey), "Tell Me" (lyric by Susan Birkenhead and Judd Woldin) (Tia Speros), "Born to Schnorr" (The Peddlers), "I Have Not Lived in Vain" (Ron Wisniski), "A Man Is Meant to Reason" (lyric by Susan Birkenhead and Judd Woldin) (Jack Sevier), "Blood Lines" (The Peddlers), "Leave the Thinking to Men" (lyric by Susan Birkenhead) (Stuart Zagnit, Tia Speros), "It's Over" (lyric by Herb Martin) (Annie McGreevy, The Peddlers)

ACT TWO—"Murder" (Annie McGreevey), "Dead" (Stuart Zagnit, Robert Blumenfeld), "A Man Is Meant to Reason" (reprise) (Jack Sevier, Stuart Zagnit), "I'm Only a Woman" (lyric by Susan Birkenhead) (Tia Speros), "An Ordinary Man" (lyric by Susan Birkenhead) (Stuart Zagnit), "Tell Me" (reprise) (Tia Speros, Stuart Zagnit), "Well Done, Da Costa" (lyric by Susan Birkenhead) (Jack Sevier), "Each of Us" (Company)

NOTES—*Tatterdemalion* was the fourth major production of Judd Woldin's musical version of the play *The King of Schnorrers*. The first was produced in January 1979 as *Pettycoat Lane* at the George Street Playhouse in New Brunswick, New Jersey; the second was seen Off Broadway as *King of Schnorrers* in October 1979 (see entry for more information, including a definition of "schnorrer"); and the third, also titled *King of Schnorrers*, opened under a Middle Broadway contract at the Playhouse Theatre in November 1979 (see entry).

Reviewing *Tatterdemalion* in the *New York Times*, Walter Goodman felt the evening was "derivative" (some aspects of the plot evoked *Fiddler on the Roof* [1964]), but he praised the cast, especially Tia Speros. He noted the musical seemed ambivalent about the leading character Da Costa, never deciding if he's "a scholar in beggar's clothing or something of a hypocritical hustler"; Goodman said it was "difficult to find him as engaging as the play requires." *Tatterdemalion* included six songs not heard in previous productions ("Ours," "Born to Schnorr," "Blood Lines," "Leave the Thinking to Men," "An Ordinary Man," and "Well Done, Da Costa"). Numbers not used in *Tatterdemalion* but which had been heard in earlier productions of the work were "Sephardic Lullaby," "It's Better to Give Than Receive," "It's a Living," "The Fine Art of Schnorring," "What Do You Do?," "Just for Me," "Hail to the King," "Try Me," and "Guided by Love."

As *Petticoat Lane*, the script was published by Samuel French, Inc., in 1981.

1594 The Tattooed Countess. THEATRE: Barbizon-Plaza Theatre; OPENING DATE: May 3, 1961; PERFORMANCES: 4; BOOK: Coleman Dowell; LYRICS: Coleman Dowell; MUSIC: Coleman Dowell; DIRECTION: Robert K. Adams; CHOREOGRAPHY: Alex Palermo; SCENERY: Robert Soule; COSTUMES: Bill Hargate; MUSICAL DIRECTION: Phil Fradkin; PRODUCERS: Dick Randall in association with Robert D. Feldstein

CAST—Al Dennis (Mr. Bierbauer), Peggy LeRoy (Mrs. Bierbauer), Janet McCall (Mrs. Fox), CHARLOTTE A. JONES (Mayme Townsend), Dick Moll (Wes Darrell), IRENE MANNING (Ella, Countess Nattatorini), TRAVIS HUDSON (Dorothy Jelliffe), JANET FOX (Lou Poore), VIRGINIA PAYNE (Anna Schmidt), Howard Claney (Mr. Johns), JOHN (JOHNNY) STEWART (Gareth Jones), CAROLYN MAYE (Lenny Coleman), Marcie Stringer (Mrs. Barnes), Jay Stern (Mr. Jackson), D.P. Smith (Mr. Achison), Art Wallace (Judge Porter), COE NORTON (Albert Colman), JUDY GUYLL (Clara)

SOURCE—The 1924 novel *The Tattooed Countess* by Carl Van Vechten.

The action occurs in Maple Valley, Iowa, in the summer of 1897.

The musical was presented in two acts.

ACT ONE—The Opening (Townspeople), "Home Town Girl" (Townsmen), "You Take Paris" (Irene Manning), "These Acres" (Irene Manning), "The Brushing Song" (Irene Manning, Janet Fox), "Advice" (Carolyn Maye, John Stewart), "Fin De Sickle" (Travis Hudson, Townspeople), "The Waterworks Madrigal" (Townspeople), "How She Glows" (John Stewart, Townsmen), "High Up" (Irene Manning), "Rolling Stone" (Irene Manning, Coe Norton), "Dusters, Goggles and Hats" (John Stewart, Townspeople), "Je M'en Fiche" (Irene Manning), "Gossip" (Townspeople), "Gossip" (reprise) (Travis Hudson, Townspeople), "Gossip" (reprise)/ "Tattooed Woman" (Travis Hudson, Townspeople), "Thoughts" and "Waltz" (Irene Manning, John Stewart), "Too Old for Love" (Irene Manning)

ACT TWO—"Gossip" (reprise) (Townspeople), "The Waterworks Madrigal" (reprise) (Townspeople), Dance (Judy Guyll), "That's Her Life" (Judy Guyll), "High Up" (reprise) (Irene Manning), "Autumn" (Carolyn Mae), "A Woman's Much Better Off Alone" (Janet Fox, Virginia Payne), "Too Young" (John Stewart), "I Can Take It" (Irene Manning), "Got To Find My Way" (John Stewart, Carolyn Mae), "Je M'en Fiche" (reprise) (Irene Manning)

NOTES—Based on Carl Van Vechten's novel *The Tattooed Countess*, this short-running musical dealt with an older woman, now a countess and an experienced woman of the world, who returns to her roots in a small town in Iowa. Howard Taubman in the *New York Times* felt the musical failed to find a consistent style and thus meandered between the sardonic and the lighthearted. He wrote that Coleman Dowell's score found is best moment in "Fin De Sickle," which was "gay and pointed." But "The Waterworks Madrigal" just missed being a "cheerful comment on group psychology," and for the most part the songs "rarely arrive[d] at fruition." Further, the book was full of "dreary romantic stereotypes," and the humor was on the level of such lines as "I spilled the beans, so now I'll go and cook them."

Irene Manning played the title role; sixteen years had passed since she had last performed on the New York stage (in Alan Jay Lerner and Frederick Loewe's *The Day Before Spring* [1945]), and *The Tattooed Countess* marked her very brief return to musical theatre. *The Tattooed Countess* was one of three recent short-running Off Broadway musicals about mature women seeking love (*The Crystal Heart* and *Valmouth* were the others [both 1960; see entries]), and John Stewart appeared in two of them (*The Crystal Heart* and *The Tattooed Countess*).

The theme of mature love enjoyed longer runs when Jerry Herman dealt with it in three successive Broadway musicals (*Milk and Honey* [1961], *Hello, Dolly!* [1964], and *Mame* [1966]).

Reference books give April 3, 1961, as the opening date of *The Tattooed Countess*; however, the correct opening date is May 3, 1961.

1595 Telecast. "A New Musical." THEATRE: St. Bart's Playhouse; OPENING DATE: February 15, 1979; PERFORMANCES: 13; BOOK: Barry Harman; LYRICS: Barry Harman; MUSIC: Martin Silvestri; DIRECTION: Barry Harman and Wayne Cilento; CHOREOGRAPHY: Wayne Cilento; SCENERY: Franco Colavecchia; COSTUMES: Kristine Haugen; LIGHTING: Jane Reisman and Neil Peter Jampolis; MUSICAL DIRECTION: John Kroner; PRODUCER: Harve Brosten

CAST—MATT LANDERS (Sammy Hart, Jr.), JOHN BARTHOLOMEW (Hugh Gallagher), JILL COREY (Molly Mabel Sweetzer), Mary Jay (Eleanor Hart Vanderwell), Robert Tananis (David Elliot Hart), Wendy Wolfe (Beatty Hart Faxon), Jana Schneider (Jamie Hart), Charles Ryan (Aaron Webster), Christopher Wynkoop (Frank Palmer), Tony Turco (Benny Rizzo), Douglas Andros (Izzie Rubin), Roger Shea (Nick), J.J. LEWIS (Rachel), Carolyn Kirsch (Andrea); The Sweethearts (Valerie Leigh Bixler, Laura McCarthy, Linda Ravinsky, Terpsie Toon); Benny's Assistants (C.A. Hutton, Janice Solia)

The action occurs in a television studio a few hours before air time; the action is continuous.

The musical was presented in two acts.

ACT ONE—"The Whole World Will Be Watching" (Matt Landers, John Bartholomew Tucker, Cast), "Don't Ask!" (J.J. Lewis), "Ordinary Guy" (Matt Landers, Mary Jay, Valerie Leigh Bixler, Laura McCarthy, Linda Ravinsky, Terpsie Toon), "Every Thursday Night" (Matt Landers, Mary Jay, Robert Tananis, Wendy Wolfe, Jana Schneider), "Izzie's Story" (Douglas Andros), "Sure of His Love" (Carolyn Kirsch, Wendy Wolfe), "The Silent Spot" (Matt Landers, Jill Corey, John Bartholomew Tucker, Family), "I've Arrived" (Jill Corey), "A Lot of Heart" (Matt Landers)

ACT TWO—"Host of Hosts" (Jana Schneider), "Something Else" (Matt Landers, J.J. Lewis), "Don't Wait Up" (Carolyn Kirsch, Valerie Leigh Bixler, Laura McCarthy, Linda Ravinsky, Terpsie Toon), "The Finale" (Matt Landers, Jill Corey, John Bartholomew Tucker, Cast), "I Caught a Glimpse of the Man" (J.J. Lewis), "In One" (Matt Landers), "I'm Nothing Without You" (Matt Landers, J.J. Lewis)

NOTES—The short-lived musical *Telecast* was about a television special honoring a famous comedian who had recently died. First-billed Jill Corey enjoyed a mildly popular recording career in the late 1950s, and later spent much of her time in summer stock and regional theatre, performing in both musicals and plays. *Telecast* was her only New York musical.

1596 The Tempest. THEATRE: New York City Center; OPENING DATE: October 11, 1956; PERFORMANCES: Unknown; LIBRETTO: Frank Martin; MUSIC: Frank Martin; DIRECTION: Leo Kerz; CHOREOGRAPHY: Anna Sokolow; SCENERY: Leo Kerz; COSTUMES: Leo Van Witsen; MUSICAL DIRECTION: Erich Leinsdorf; PRODUCER: The New York City Opera Company

CAST—Joshua Hecht (Alonso), Richard Wentworth (Sebastian), Kenneth Smith (Prospero), Gregory Millar (Antonio), Richard Cassilly (Ferdinand), Donald Gramm (Gonzalo), Rudolf Petrak (Adrian), Richard Humphrey (Caliban), Michael Pollock (Trinculo), Cornell MaNeil (Stephano), John Druary (Boatswain), Arthur Newman (Ship's Master), Priscilla Gillette (Miranda), Raimonda Orselli (Ariel)

SOURCE—The 1611 play *The Tempest* by William Shakespeare.

The opera was produced in one act.

NOTES—Frank Martin was a Swiss composer; his libretto for *The Tempest* was written in English, and the opera's world premiere occurred in Vienna in June, four months before the New York City production.

In his review for the *New York Times*, Ross Parmenter commented that the score, reminiscent of Debussy, was often "charming" and "cast a certain spell," but overall was rather "thin."

One unusual aspect of the opera was singled out by Parmenter. Martin's conception of Ariel resulted in three different dramatic approaches: Ariel was mimed by a dancer; his words were sung by a chorus; and his music was performed not by the musicians in the pit but by a small on-stage chamber orchestra. Parmenter noted Ariel's music determined the form and the atmosphere of the work, but felt the three-tiered approach to the character was "rather unoperatic." Priscilla Gillette created the role of Miranda for the New York premiere. She had a particularly distinguished career in musical theatre, creating three important roles. She was Alexandra Giddens in Marc Blitzstein's *Regina* (1949), introducing "What Will It Be" (she also was part of the "Rain Quartet"). In 1950, she was Helen in Cole Porter's *Out of This World*, and introduced three ethereal ballads ("Use Your Imagination," "I Am Loved," and "No Lover for Me") and took part in the sparkling trio "What Do You Think About Men?" And, of course, she was the original Penelope in the legendary *The Golden Apple* (1954; see entry), introducing "Windflowers."

For another musical adaptation of *The Tempest*, see entry for *Dreamstuff*.

1597 The Temple Dancer. THEATRE: Metropolitan Opera House; OPENING DATE: March 12, 1919; PERFORMANCES: 3; LIBRETTO: Jutta Bell-Ranske; MUSIC: John Adam Hugo; DIRECTION: Richard Ordynski; CHOREOGRAPHY: Rosina Galli; SCENERY: Joseph Novak; COSTUMES: Louise Musaeus; MUSICAL DIRECTION: Roberto Moranzoni; PRODUCER: The Metropolitan Opera

CAST—Carl Schlegel (Yoga), Florence Easton (Temple Dancer), Morgan Kingston (The Temple Guard), Dancers (Florence Glover, Lilyan Ogden, Jessie Rogge)

The opera was presented in one act.

NOTES—*The Temple Dancer* was one of three operas offered on the evening's bill; like *The Legend* (see entry), it was a world premiere. The two operas were joined by a revival of *The Robin Woman: Shanewis* (see entry), which had premiered during the previous season.

James Gibbens Hunaker in the *New York Times* reported that the plot dealt with a temple dancer (Florence Easton) who poisons a temple guard (Morgan Kingston) and is in turn is killed by an avenging god. (Hunaker wondered if perhaps Kingston's character was murdered because of his "chaotic phrasing.") Hunaker also noted that the opera lacked an on-stage protagonist (the character is talked about but never seen).

The Met's database indicates that some of Florence Easton's costumes had been used in a 1912-1913 production of *Die Zauberflote*.

1598 10 Million Miles. THEATRE: Linda Gross Theatre; OPENING DATE: June 14, 2007; PERFORMANCES: 30 (estimated); BOOK: Keith Bunin; LYRICS: Patty Griffin; MUSIC: Patty Griffin; DIRECTION: Michael Mayer; SCENERY: Derek McLane; COSTUMES: Michael Krass; LIGHTING: Jules Fisher and Peggy Eisenhauer; MUSICAL DIRECTION: Tim Weil; PRODUCERS: Atlantic Theatre Company (Neil Pepe, Artistic Director; Andrew D. Hamingson, Managing Director) in association with Ira Pittelman and Tom Hulce

CAST—Matthew Morrison (Duane), Irene Molloy (Molly), Mare Winningham (The Women), Skip Sudduth (The Men)

The action occurs in the present time from the southern tip of Florida to the northwest corner of New York ("with detours along the way").

The musical was presented in one act.

MUSICAL NUMBERS—"Useless Desires" (Mathew Morrison, Irene Molloy), "We Are Water" (Mare Winningham, Skipp Sudduth), "Be Careful" (Irene Molloy), "Mad Mission" (Matthew Morrison, Skipp Sudduth), "What You Are" (Matthew Morrison, Company), "One Big Love" (Irene Molloy, Company), "Kite" (Mare Winningham), "A Couple Fools" (Matthew Morrison, Irene Molloy), "Love Throws a Line" (Skipp Sudduth, Mare Winningham, Matthew Morrison, Irene Molloy), "Mary" (Irene Molloy, Company), "Making Pies" (Mare Winningham), "Icicles" (Skipp Sudduth, Matthew Morrison), "10 Million Miles" (Company), "First Star" (Matthew Morrison), "Don't Come Easy" (Irene Molloy, Matthew Morrison, Company)

NOTES—*10 Million Miles* depicted a road trip from Florida to New York State ("with detours along the way") taken by a young couple (Matthew Morrison and Irene Molloy); Mare Winningham and Skipp Sudduth portrayed a number of characters whom they meet on their journey.

The musical utilized mostly pre-existing songs by Patty Griffin to tell its story; David Rooney in *Variety* reported all the songs had been heard in earlier albums (except for "We Are Water," an unreleased track, and "A Couple of Fools" and "First Star," two songs especially written for the musical).

Despite a few reservations, Ben Brantley in the *New York Times* found the musical well worthwhile, and felt that "country back roads are well worth pursuing." He praised Mare Winningham as a performer of "depth, style and versatility" who "shifts with sublime seamlessness from feisty flash ... to ... a heartbreaking study in quiet resignation." Rooney noted that Winningham was the production's "real surprise" with a "richly expressive singing voice" and a performance which "slips effortlessly from one sensitively drawn character to the next."

Irene Molloy gave a wistful and touching performance as Swallow in the world premiere of Andrew Lloyd Webber's *Whistle Down the Wind*, which closed during its tryout in Washington, D.C., during the 1996-1997 season.

1599 Ten Nights in a Barroom. "A Musical Melodrama." THEATRE: Greenwich Mews Theatre; OPENING DATE: October 1, 1962; PERFORMANCES: 32; BOOK: John Savoca and Marcia Taradash; LYRICS: Martin Sherman; MUSIC: Stanley Silverman; DIRECTION: Robert Alvin; SCENERY: David Moon; COSTUMES: Sally Edwards; LIGHTING: David Moon; MUSICAL DIRECTION: (Possibly Christopher Butler); PRODUCER: The Greenwich Mews Players, Inc.

CAST—Barry Michlin (Joe Morgan), Annette D'Alesandro (Fanny Morgan), Catherine Pieris (Mary Morgan), David Goldstein (Simon Slade), Cleve Roller (Ann Slade), Ronald Stuart (Frank Slade), Martha Velez (Mehitable Slade), Robert Einenkel (Sample Switchel), Michel Mansson (Harvey Green), Andrew Winner (Willie Hammond), Steve Peters (Ned Hargrove), Robert Foley (Mr. Charles E. Romaine), Chuck Hover (Mr. Hargrove)

SOURCE—The play *Ten Nights in a Barroom* (circa 1858) by William W. Pratt.

The action occurs in New England around 1850.

The musical was presented in three acts (song titles unknown).

NOTES—*Ten Nights in a Barroom* was a musical adaptation of the old warhorse about the evils of demon rum.

1600 Ten Percent Revue. THEATRE: Susan Bloch Theatre; OPENING DATE: April 13, 1988; transferred to Actors' Playhouse on June 7, 1988; PERFORMANCES: 239; LYRICS: Tom Wilson Weinberg; MUSIC: Tom Wilson Weinberg; DIRECTION: Scott Green; also Joey Branden (?); CHOREOGRAPHY: Tee Scatuorchio; BACKDROP: Edwin Perez-Carrion; COSTUMES: Kevin-Robert; LIGHTING: Joshua Starbuck; PRODUCER: Laura Green

CAST—Lisa Bernstein, Valerie Hill, Trish Kane, Robert Tate, Timothy Williams

The revue was presented in two acts.

ACT ONE—"Flaunting It" (Company), "Best Years of My Life" (Company), "Threesome" (Lisa Bernstein, Valerie Hill, Trish Kane), "Wedding Song" (Company), "If I Were"/"I'd Like to Be" (Valerie Hill, Robert Tate), "Gay Name Game" (Company), "Home" (Trish Kane), "Not Allowed" (Robert Tate, Timothy Williams), "Personals" (Company), "Safe Sex Slut" (Company)

ACT TWO—"Homo Haven Fight Song" (Company), "Turkey Baster Baby" (Valerie Hill, Trish Kane), "High Risk for Afraids" (Company), "Obituary" (Timothy Williams), "And the Supremes" (Trish Kane, Company), "Before Stonewall" (Company), "Write a Letter" (Robert Tate, Company), "We're Everywhere" (Company), "Flaunting It" (reprise) (Company)

NOTES—*Ten Percent Revue* took its title from the estimation that ten percent of all Americans are gay.

Stephen Holden in the *New York Times* found the revue "venturesome in its modest way," and noted the evening was at its strongest when it dealt with such issues as homophobia and AIDS. He also praised the "brisk multistyled score," which was a "cut above the generic revue format," and he liked the way the revue emphasized humor and "musical savvy" and avoided preachiness.

During the revue's national tour, at least two songs ("Love That Dare Not Speak Its Name" and "Walk on Washington") were added to the score.

For years, the cast recording was available only on videocassette (released by Aboveground Records); in 2008, the company released a CD-R of the recording (# AR-105-CD). The recording features a slightly re-ordered song list and includes the two songs added for the tour.

1601 The Tender Land. THEATRE: New York City Center; OPENING DATE: April 1, 1954; PERFORMANCES: Unknown; LIBRETTO: Horace Everett; MUSIC: Aaron Copeland; DIRECTION: Jerome Robbins; SCENERY: Oliver Smith; COSTUMES: John Hoyt; MUSICAL DIRECTION: Thomas Schippers; PRODUCER: The New York City Opera Company

CAST—Jean Handzlik (Ma Moss), Rosemary Carlos (Laurie), Andrew Gaines (Top), Jon Crain (Martin), Norman Treigle (Grandpa), Michael Pollock (Splinters), Mary Kreste (Mrs. Splinters), Adele Newton (Beth), Teresa Gannon (Mrs. Jenks), Thomas Powell (Mr. Jenks)

The action of the opera takes place on a farm in the Midwest during the 1930s.

The opera was presented in two acts (later revised to three acts; the musical sequences listed below are taken from the 2-CD set released by Virgin Classics Limited Records [# DDD-VCD-7-9113-2]).

ACT ONE—Prelude (Orchestra), "The Front Yard of the Moss Home" (Beth, Ma Moss), "Two Little Bits of Metal" (Ma Moss), "The Arrival of the Postman" (Beth, Ma Moss, Mr. Splinters), "Opening the Package" (Beth, Ma Moss), "This Is Like the Dress I Never Had" (Ma Moss), Dance/Exit (Beth, Ma Moss), Laurie's Entrance: "Once I Thought I'd Never Grow" (Laurie), "Ma's Entrance" (Ma Moss, Laurie), "Remember the Boy That Used to Call"/Ma's Exit (Laurie, Ma Moss), "Entrance of Martin and Top" (Top, Martin), "Martin and Top Enter the Farmyard" (Martin, Top, Laurie), Duet: "We've Been North" (Martin, Top), "Grandpa Meets the Boys" (Grandpa, Top, Laurie, Martin), Trio: "A Strange May Seem Strange That's True" (Martin, Top, Grandpa), Interlude: "Martin and Top Make Horseplay," "The Invitation" (Grandpa, Laurie, Ma Moss, Top, Martin), Quintet: "The Promise of Living" (Martin, Laurie, Ma Moss, Grandpa, Top)

ACT TWO—"The Graduation Eve Supper" (Orchestra), "The Supper Ends" (Top, Mrs. Jenks, Martin, Chorus), Grandpa's Toast: "Try Makin' Peace" (Grandpa, Mr. Jenks, Chorus), Laurie's Reply: "Thank You, Thank You All" (Laurie, Grandpa, Ma Moss), "The Invitation to Dance" (Ma Moss, Top, Martin), The Dance: "Stomp Your Foot Upon the Floor" (Chorus), Dance Music/Dialogue (Ma Moss, Mr. Splinters), "Party Music Back in the House" (Martin, Grandpa, Top), Top's Song: "Oh, I Was Goin' A-Courtin'" (Top, Grandpa, Ma Moss), The Dancing Resumes (Mrs. Splinters, Top, Martin, Laurie, Grandpa), Duet: "You Dance Real Well!" (Martin, Laurie), "Laurie...You Know, Laurie" (Martin), Duet: "In Love? In Love?" (Laurie, Martin), "The Tender Land" (Laurie, Martin), "Grandpa's Confrontation" (Grandpa, Laurie, Ma Moss, Top, Martin, Mr. Splinters), "Party Farewell" (Guests)

ACT THREE—Introduction (Orchestra), Entr'acte: "Martin Alone" (Orchestra), Duet: "Laurie, Laurie" (Martin, Laurie), Martin Alone: "Daylight Will Come in Such Short Time" (Martin), Dialogue (Top, Martin), Top's Aria: "That's Crazy"/Exit of Martin and Top (Top, Martin), Interlude: "Daybreak" (Orchestra), "The Sun Is Coming Up" (Laurie), "Laurie's Farewell" (Beth, Laurie, Ma Moss), "All Thinking's Done" (Ma Moss)

NOTES—Aaron Copeland's opera *The Tender Land* received its world premiere by the New York City Opera on April 1, 1954; the opera was presented on a double bill with Gian-Carlo Menotti's *Amahl and the Night Visitors*. The headline for the opera's review in the *New York Times* referred to *The Tender Land* as a one-act opera, but in the review itself Olin Downes referred to a second act. Copeland later revised the opera, and the final version was expanded into three acts. The opera had been commissioned through the League of Composers by Richard Rodgers and Oscar Hammerstein II.

Downes noted that although the opera was conceived long before the premiere of the previous year's Pulitzer-Prize-winning drama *Picnic* by William Inge, the two works had much in common. Both were set in the American Midwest, and both dealt with two sisters who live with their mother. For *The Tender Land*, the women's placid existence is interrupted by Martin and Top, two drifters who awaken their dormant spirits (in *Picnic*, there was one drifter, Hal); in particular, the oldest sister (Laurie) falls in love with Martin (in *Picnic*, Madge runs away from her family and hometown in order to join Hal). In *The Tender Land*, Laurie and Martin plan to leave, but Martin realizes his vagabond existence wouldn't be right for Laurie, and so in the middle of the night he and Top take off "to walk in the wind ... to fly in the weather." Even though Laurie has been jilted, she decides to leave her old life behind her ("My life was here") and find a new beginning somewhere else ("I'm sure it's there").

Downes found the libretto "flimsy," but praised Copeland's score (although he found the music for the male characters more compelling than the short-changed music for the female characters). Downes also praised Oliver Smith's scenery "in the Grant Wood style" (in the coming years, the scenery for many Broadway musicals [particularly those directed by Harold Prince] would utilize the "look" of a particular painter for the show's scenery). Downes also referred to the opera's dances (presumably choreographed by Jerome Robbins, although he was credited only for the direction).

Over the years, *The Tender Land* has found its place in the repertory of modern American opera; while it has never attained the popularity of *Susannah* and *The Ballad of Baby Doe* (see entries), it has nonetheless become recognized as an important American opera, one which contains memorable music. As of this writing, the opera has enjoyed at least five recordings and one or two of its arias have been recorded separately and have also been performed in concert.

The opera was revived Off Off Broadway at the Encompass Theatre on May 12, 1977.

1602 Ten-ish, Anyone? THEATRE: Downstairs at the Upstairs; OPENING DATE: 1961; PERFORMANCES: Unknown; PRODUCER: Julius Monk

CAST—Jane Connell, Jack Fletcher

NOTES—The score included "Daisy" by G. Wood and "Thor" by Jack Holmes; the latter was also heard in *Dime a Dozen* (see entry) and was recorded on that revue's cast album.

For a complete list of Julius Monk's revues, see entry for *Take Five*; also see Appendix Q.

1603 That 5 A.M. Jazz (A double bill which included the musical *Five A.M. Jazz*). THEATRE: Astor Place Playhouse; OPENING DATE: October 19, 1964; PERFORMANCES: 94; BOOK: Will Holt; LYRICS: Will Holt; MUSIC: Will Holt; DIRECTION: Michael Kahn; CHOREOGRAPHY: Sandra Devlin; SCENERY: Lloyd Burlingame; LIGHTING: Milton Duke; MUSICAL DIRECTION: Probably Will Holt; PRODUCERS: Muriel Morse and Jay Stanwyck

CAST—Dolly Jonah (Holt) (Frances), Lester James (Warren), The Sons of the West (Musicians); Will Holt (piano), Vinnie Rogers (guitar)

The action occurs in Las Vegas at the present time.

5 A.M. Jazz was presented in one act.

MUSICAL NUMBERS—"Some Sunday" (Dolly Jonah), "Campaign Song" (Lester James, The Sons of the West), "Gonna Get a Woman" (Lester James), "The Happy Daze Saloon" (Dolly Jonah and Lester James), "The All-American Two-Step" (Dolly Jonah, Lester James, The Sons of the West), "Sweet Time" (Dolly Jonah), "Nuevo Laredo" ('A Son of the West'), "Those Were the Days" (Dolly Jonah, Lester James, The Sons of the West)

NOTES—*That 5 A.M. Jazz* was a double bill; the first act was a non-musical (*The First*, which starred James Coco, Jerry Jarrett, and Ruth Jaroslow) and the second, *Five A.M. Jazz*, was a musical about Frances and womanizing Warren, a couple who reunite briefly before Warren leaves her in order to run for the Senate and to apparently go after another woman. Lewis Funke in the *New York Times* wasn't particularly impressed with the musical, but he said the rhythm-and-blues score (with a touch of Western twang) might appeal to jazz enthusiasts.

During an earlier workshop of the production, both plays were non-musicals. *The First* was then known as *Side One* (with James Coco, Lou Gilbert, and Ruth Volner) and *5 A.M. Jazz* was titled *Side Two* (a two-character play with Dolly Jonah [Mrs. Will Holt] and Robert Elston).

1604 That Hat! THEATRE: Theatre Four; OPENING DATE: September 23, 1964; PERFORMANCES: 1; BOOK: Cy Young; LYRICS: Cy Young; MUSIC: Cy Young; DIRECTION: Dania Krupska; CHOREOGRAPHY: Dania Krupska; SCENERY: Bill Hargate; COSTUMES: Bill Hargate; LIGHTING: Patricia Collins; MUSICAL DIRECTION: Gerald Alters; PRODUCERS: Bonard Productions, in association with Katherine and Justin Sturm

CAST—Fabian Stuart (Horse, Relative), Dallas Edmunds (Horse, Relative), PIERRE OLAF (Ferdinand Goddard), JEROME COLLAMORE (Uncle Virgil), ALFRED DENNIS (Osbert Norman), MERLE LOUISE (Helene Norman), Ted August (Photographer, Relative), JOE ROSS (Casper Bernard), CARMEN ALVAREZ (Angele Bernard), ELMARIE WENDEL (Baroness de Champigny), BARBARA SHARMA (Clara), JOSE DUVAL (Emile Duval), Ann Rachel (Flower Girl, Relative), BRADFORD CRAIG (Gentleman Friend, Nisardi), Jeanna Belkin (Maybelle), JEAN DEEKS (Virginie, Countess), DAVID BEAN (Felix), LEW HORN (Theobald, Count), Joyce Maret (Head Shop Girl, Relative), John Canemaker (Jacques, Relative), JOHN TOLAND (Viscount), Louis Johnson (Jean), Beth-Lynne Low (Relative), Sandy Reed (Relative)

SOURCE—The play *Le Chapeau de Paille d'Italie* by Eugene Libiche and Marc-Michel.

The action occurs in Paris in 1895.

The musical was presented in two acts.

ACT ONE—"Exposition" (Pierre Olaf, Company), "Italian Straw Hat" (Jose Duval, Carmen Alvarez), "My Husband" (Merle Louise), "Italian Straw Hat" (reprise) (Elmarie Wendel, Jeanna Belkin), "Do a Little Exercise" (Joe Ross), "Italian Straw Hat" (reprise) (Joe Ross, Carmen Alvarez), "Draw Me a Circle" (Peter Olaf), "It's All Off" (Alfred Dennis, Pierre Olaf, Jerome Collamore, Merle Louise, Company), "Sounds of the Night" (Pierre Olaf, Merle Louise), "I Love a Man" (Carmen Alvarez, Joe Ross), Interlude (Barbara Sharma, Dallas Edmunds, Louis Johnson), "Sounds of the Day" (Carmen Alvarez, Jose Duval, Pierre Olaf), "A Tete a Tete" (dance) (David Bean, Jean Deeks), "The Apology" (Pierre Olaf), "My, It's Been Grand" (Pierre Olaf, Carmen Alvarez, Jose Duval, Alfred Dennis)

ACT TWO—"We Have Never Met" (Pierre Olaf, Barbara Sharma), "My Husband" (reprise) (Merle Louise), "Give Me a Pinch" (Elmarie Wendel, Pierre Olaf, Company), "A Pot of Myrtle" (Alfred Dennis), "The Mad Ballet" (Pierre Olaf, Company; Arabs danced by Dallas Edmunds, Louis Johnson, and Fabian Stuart), "The World of Confusion" (Pierre Olaf, Merle Louise), Finale (Company)

NOTES—This was the second time an Off Broadway musical adaptation of *Le Chapeau de Paille d'Italie* failed (see entry for *The Italian Straw Hat* [1957]).

The first performance of *That Hat!* was its last. It was a large musical, with a cast of twenty-five (including those cut-ups Elmarie Wendel, Barbara Sharma, and Carmen Alvarez), and its story was told with much more music than was typical for musicals of the period (twenty-two songs, dances, and reprises). The opening number was cleverly titled: it provided the story's background as well as reminding the audience that the musical took place during the time of the Paris Exposition. However, Howard Taubman in the *New York Times* found the book "as bare as an old, broken-down cupboard," the songs uninteresting, and the choreography derivative. One of the musical's songs, "Draw Me a Circle," became a minor pop standard.

Pierre Olaf had enjoyed a brief moment on the New York stage with two Broadway successes (*La Plume de Ma Tante* [1958], for which he and the other cast members received a special Tony Award for their performances, and *Carnival!* [1961], for which he received a Tony Award nomination for Best Featured Actor in a Musical), but after two one-performance fiascos in 1964 (besides *That Hat!*, he had starred on Broadway earlier in the year in the comedy-mystery *A Murderer Among Us*), he disappeared from the New York stage. His experience with *That Hat!* couldn't have been a happy one: Taubman reported that "he can't sing, has nothing to be funny about and is so bemused that he stumbles over his lines." Merle Louise later created roles in three of Stephen Sondheim's musicals: *Company* (1970; as Susan, who wouldn't dream of not living with her former husband); *Sweeney Todd/The Demon Barber of Fleet Street* (1979; The Beggar Woman); and *Into the Woods* (1987; various roles, including Cinderella's Mother).

1605 That Thing at the Cherry Lane. THEATRE: Cherry Lane Theatre; OPENING DATE: May 18, 1965; PERFORMANCES: 7; SKETCHES, LYRICS AND MUSIC: Mostly by Jeff Steve Harris, with additional material by Lesley Davison, Michael McWhinney, Jerry Powell, and Ira Wallach; DIRECTION: Bill Penn; SCENERY: Fred Voelpel; COSTUMES: Fred Voelpel; LIGHTING: Fred Voelpel; MUSICAL DIRECTION: Natalie Charlson; PRODUCER: Theatre 1965 (A Richard Barr Production)

CAST—John C. Becher, Gloria Bleezarde, Conard Fowkes, Ben Kukoff, Hugh Hurd, Morgan Paull, Evelyn Russell, Jo Anne Worley

The revue was presented in three acts.

ACT ONE—"The Long Song" (lyric and music by Jeff Steve Harris) (Ben Kukoff)

ACT TWO—"Beat This!" (sketch by Jeff Steve Harris) (Company; Voice of Mrs. Esterhart, Vicki Blankenship)

ACT THREE—"Lady Bird" (lyric and music by Leslie Davison) (Gloria Bleezarde, Conard Fowkes, Morgan Paull, Jo Anne Worley), "Ragtime Max" (lyric and music by Jeff Steve Harris) (Ben Kukoff), "Tears" (sketch Ira Wallach) (Evelyn Russell), "Olympics" (writer[s] and performer[s] unknown), "Scotch on the Rocks" (lyric and music by Leslie Davison) (Jo Anne Worley), "You Won't Believe Me" (lyric and music by Jeff Steve Harris) (Morgan Paull), "Minnesota" (lyric and music by Jeff Steve Harris) (John C. Becher, Evelyn Russell), "Blues" (lyric and music by Jeff Steve Harris) (Jo Anne Worley), "Safety in Numbers" (lyric and music by Michael McWhinney and Jerry Powell) (Gloria Bleezarde), "Communication" (lyric and music by Jeff Steve Harris) (Evelyn Russell, Hugh Hurd, Ben Kukoff, Conard Fowkes), "To Belong" (lyric and music by Jeff Steve Harris) (John C. Becher), "Jersey" (lyric and music by Jeff Steve Harris) (Jo Anne Worley), "The New York Coloring Book" (lyric and music by Michael McWhinney and Jerry Powell) (Company)

NOTES—Despite some interesting names in its credits and cast, the revue *That Thing at the Cherry Lane* was gone in a week. Howard Taubman in the *New York Times* reported the evening's best songs were by Michael McWhinney and Jerry Powell: "Safety in Numbers" was a satiric number about computers, and "The New York Coloring Book" was a "charmingly unpretentious" number which captured the flavor of New York life. Taubman noted the aptly titled curtain raiser "The Long Song" was "excessive" ("I mean it's long," Taubman wrote); but he praised Ben Kukoff, who "manfully" waded through the song's series of free associations (an "unrelieved chant to his invisible psychiatrist"). Taubman was also unimpressed with the sketch "Beat This!," a take-off on the television program *What's My Line?*, and he wondered if it was even possible to further satirize the well-worn subject of television panel shows.

Five numbers from Jeff Steve Harris' 1961 revue *Another Evening with Harry Stoones* (see entry) were used in *That Thing at the Cherry Lane* (at the time of *Harry Stoones*' production, Harris was billed as Jeff Harris): "To Belong," "Communication," "You Won't Believe Me," "Jersey," and "Minnesota." Another number from the earlier revue, "Ragtime," may have been heard in the current revue as "Ragtime Max," and *Harry Stoones*' "Museum Piece" was heard in *That Thing* only during previews.

During previews, T. James, Jr., was among the contributors credited with additional material. His contribution, "A B C," was dropped during previews, along with "Super Market" (by Lesley Davison), "I've Sacrificed Everything" (by Ira Wallach), and Jeff Steve Harris' aforementioned "Museum Piece." Further, during previews the second and third acts were reversed. "Lady Bird" was later used in two Rod Warren revues (*The Game Is Up* [Third Edition] and *Below the Belt*; see entries). "The New York Coloring Book" had been earlier heard in the revue with that title (see entry).

1606 That's Entertainment. "A Musical." THEATRE: Edison Theatre; OPENING DATE: April 14, 1972; PERFORMANCES: 4; LYRICS: Howard Dietz; MUSIC: Arthur Schwartz; DIRECTION: Paul Aaron; CHOREOGRAPHY: Larry Fuller; Merry Lynn Katis, Assistant Choreographer; SCENERY: David F. Segal; COSTUMES: Jane Greenwood; LIGHTING: David F. Segal; MUSICAL DIRECTION: Luther Henderson; PRODUCER: Gordon Crowe in association with J. Robert Breton

CAST—David Chaney (Greg), Jered Holmes (Richard), Judith Knaiz (Carol), Michon Peacock (Adele), Vivian Reed (Lena), Scott Salmon (Jack), Bonnie Schon (Lucille), Michael Vita (Donald), Alan Weeks (Sam)

The revue was presented in two acts.

ACT ONE—The Overture (Company); Medley: "We Won't Take It Back" (from *Inside U.S.A.*, 1948); "Hammacher Schlemmer, I Love You" (*The Little Show*, 1929); "Come, O, Come (to Pittsburgh)" (*Inside U.S.A.*, 1948) (Michon Peacock, Bonnie Schon, Scott Salmon, David Chaney), "I'm Glad I'm Single" (*The Gay Life*, 1961) (Jared Holmes), "You're Not the Type" (*The Gay Life*, 1961) and "(What's the Use of Being) Miserable with You" (*The Band Wagon*, 1931) (Judith Knaiz, Jared Holmes), "Something to Remember You By" (*Three's a Crowd*, 1930) (Judith Knaiz), "Hottentot Potentate" (*At Home Abroad*, 1935) (Vivian Reed, Alan Weeks) "Day After Day" (*Flying Colors*, 1932) and "Fly By Night" (*Between the Devil*, 1937), (Company), "Everything" (possibly "You Have Everything" from *Between the Devil*, 1937) (Jared Holmes), "Blue Grass (of Kentucky)" (*Inside U.S.A.*, 1948) (Alan Weeks), "Fatal Fascination" (*Flying Colors*, 1932) and "White Heat" (*The Band Wagon*, 1931) (Bonnie Schon), "Right at the Start of It" (*Three's a Crowd*, 1930) (Alan Weeks), "Confession" (*The Band Wagon*, 1931) (Judith Knaiz, Michael Vita), "Smokin' Reefers" (*Flying Colors*, 1932) (Vivian Reed), "How High Can a (Little) Bird Fly?" (1936 British musical *Follow the Sun*) (Scott Salmon), "Keep Off the Grass" (source unknown) (David Chaney), "I See Your Face Before Me" (*Between the Devil*, 1937) (Michael Vita, Michon Peacock), "Experience" (*Between the Devil*, 1937) (David Chaney), "Two-Faced Woman" (*Flying Colors*, 1932) (Alan Weeks), "Foolish Face" (*The Second Little Show*, 1930) (Scott Salmon), "By Myself" (*Between the Devil*, 1937) (Vivian Reed), "That's Entertainment" (1953 film *The Band Wagon*) (Michael Vita)

ACT TWO—Dance Medley: "You and the Night and the Music" (*Revenge with Music*, 1934); "Louisiana Hayride" (*Flying Colors*, 1932); "Dancing in the Dark" (*The Band Wagon*, 1931) (Company), "Triplets" (*Between the Devil*, 1937; see notes below) (Bonnie Schon, David Chaney, Jered Holmes) "High and Low" (*The Band Wagon*, 1931) (Scott Salmon), "How Low Can a Little Worm Go?" (possibly a version of "How High Can a [Little] Bird Fly"?) (Judith Knaiz), "Absent Minded" (source unknown) (Jared Holmes), "High Is Better Than Low" (*Jennie*, 1963) (Judith Knaiz, Scott Salmon), "If There Is Someone Lovelier Than You" (*Revenge with Music*, 1934) (David Chaney), "I've Made a Habit of You" (*The Little Show*, 1929) (Bonnie Schon), "I Guess I'll Have to Change My Plan" (*The Little Show*, 1929) (Alan Weeks), "New Sun in the Sky" (*The Band Wagon*, 1930) (Vivian Reed), "Farewell, My Lovely" (*At Home Abroad*, 1935) (Michon Peacock), "Alone Together" (*Flying Colors*, 1932) (Michael Vita), "A Shine on Your Shoes" (*Flying Colors*, 1932) (Company)

NOTES—Although the four-performance flop *That's Entertainment* was a composer-lyricist-tribute revue (to lyricist Howard Dietz and composer Arthur Schwartz), it was somehow deemed necessary to give each performer a character's name. The device didn't fool anybody: *That's Entertainment* was still a revue. For similar tribute revues, see entries for *Dancing in the Dark*, which honored Arthur Schwartz and was presented Off Off Broadway in 1979, and *The Little Show and Friends*, an Off Off Broadway salute to Dietz and Schwartz.

The song "Triplets" has a fascinating history. It was first sung by Clifton Webb, Patsy Kelly, and Imogene Coca in *Flying Colors* (1932), but was dropped during the pre-Broadway tryout. It resurfaced during the tryout of *At Home Abroad* (1935), when it was presented as a *solo* for Beatrice Lillie; but, again, the song was dropped prior to New York. It was finally heard on Broadway in *Between the Devil* (1937) when it was sung by The Tune Twisters (Andy Love, Jack Lathrop, and Bob Wacker), who, during the show's tryout, were called The Savoy Club Boys. The song was also heard in the 1953 MGM film *The Band Wagon*, when it was performed by Fred Astaire, Nanette Fabray, and Jack Buchanan (who had starred in *Between the Devil*). Buchanan's role in *The Band Wagon* had first been offered to Clifton Webb, and, had Webb appeared in the film, "Triplets" would have come full circle after twenty-one years because Webb had been one of the original triplets in 1932's *Flying Colors*.

1607 That's Life! THEATRE: Playhouse 91; OPENING DATE: August 1, 1994; PERFORMANCES: 292; LYRICS: Susan DiLallo, Dan Kael, Stacey Luftig, June Siegel, Glenn Slater, Carolyn Sloan, Cheryl Stern, and Greer Woodward; MUSIC: Rick Cummins, Dick Gallagher, Ben Schaechter, and Carolyn Sloan; DIRECTION: Helen Butleroff; CHOREOGRAPHY: Helen Butleroff; SCENERY: Fred Kolo; COSTUMES: Gail Cooper-Hecht; LIGHTING: Betsy Finston; MUSICAL DIRECTION: Christopher McGovern; PRODUCERS: Leahy Productions in association with Peter Breger in a Jewish Repertory Theatre Production (Ran Avni, Artistic Director; Edward M. Cohen, Managing Director)

CAST—Robert Michael Baker, David Beach, Lisa Rochelle, Cheryl Stern, Steve Sterner

The revue was presented in two acts.

ACT ONE—"More Than 5700 Years" (lyric by Dan Kael, music by Ben Schaechter) (Company), "It's Hard to Be a Patriarch Today" (lyric by Glenn Slater, music by Carolyn Sloan) (Robert Michael Baker, Steve Sterner), "Endangered Species" (lyric by June Siegel, music by Dick Gallagher) (Cheryl Stern, David Beach, Robert Michael Baker, Steve Sterner), "It's Beyond Me" (lyric by Don Kael, music by Ben Schaechter) (Lisa Rochelle), "Tap My Potential" (lyric by Susan DiLallo, music by Ben Schaechter) (David Beach, Robert Michael Baker, Lisa Rochelle, Steve Sterner), "Power Babies" (monologue by Cheryl Stern) (Robert Michael Baker), "Rhinoplasty" (lyric by Cheryl Stern, music by Dick Gallagher) (Cheryl Stern), "In a Schoolyard in Brooklyn" (lyric by Greer Woodward, music by Ben Schaechter) (Robert Michael Baker), "My Calling" (lyric by Stacey Luftig, music by Carolyn Sloan) (Cheryl Stern), "A Share of Paradise" (lyric by Greer Woodward, music by Rick Cummins) (Steve Sterner), "Mama, I Want to Sit Downstairs" (lyric by Stacey Luftig, music by Carolyn Sloan) (Lisa Rochelle), "Gorgeous Kay" (lyric Greer Woodward, music by Rick Cummins) (David Beach, Company)

ACT TWO—"We All Could Be Jewish If We Tried a Little Harder" (lyric by June Siegel, music by Rick Cummins) (Company), "Observant in My Way" (lyric by Dan Kael, music by Rick Cummins) (David Beach), "I Can Pass" (lyric by Carolyn Sloan and Cheryl Stern, music by Carolyn Sloan) (Cheryl Stern, David Beach, Robert Michael Baker, Lisa Rochelle), "The Geshrunken Meshuggena Rag" (lyric by June Siegel, music by Rick Cummins) (David Beach, Robert Michael Baker, Cheryl Stern, Steve Sterner), "Jews in Groups" (monologue by Stacey Luftig) (Lisa Rochelle), "Bei Mir Bist Du Rap" (lyric by Cheryl Stern, music by Dick Gallagher) (Robert Michael Baker, Cheryl Stern), "Fathers and Sons" (dialogue and lyric by Cheryl Stern, music by Carolyn Sloan) (Robert Michael Baker, Lisa Rochelle, Steve Sterner), "More Than 5700 Years" (reprise) (Company)

NOTES—*That's Life!* was a light-hearted look at being Jewish in America. Before opening Off Broadway for a run of 292 performances, it had been produced Off Off Broadway by the Jewish Repertory Theatre earlier in the summer. It was later revived Off Broadway at Theatre East on July 26, 1997, where it played for an additional 144 performances (for this version, the song "Fathers and Sons" was replaced by "Freedom's Song").

1608 That's the Ticket! THEATRE: 14th Street Y; OPENING DATE: April 19, 2002; PERFORMANCES: 19; BOOK: Julius J. and Philip G. Epstein; LYRICS: Harold Rome; LYRICS: Harold Rome; DIRECTION: Thomas Mills; CHOREOGRAPHY: Thomas Mills; SCENERY: Stan Pearlman/Impact Creative Group; LIGHTING: Shih-hui Wu; MUSICAL DIRECTION: Mark Hartman; PRODUCERS: *Musicals Tonight!* and Mel Miller (Marvin?)

CAST—David Staller (Alfred), Richard Bunting (Bulter, Ensemble), Edward Prostack (Greene), Michael Mendiola (Joe), Carter Calvert (Marcia), Rita Harvey (Patricia), George S. Irving (Vale-Waterhouse), Andrew Gitzy (Whyte); Ensemble: Cynthia Collins, Judy Fitzgerald, Julie La Chance, Jason Lowenthal, Laurent Nahan, Justin Roller, Shelby Rose, Christopher Talbert

The action occurs mostly in New York City.

The musical was presented in two acts.

ACT ONE—"How Peaceful Is the Evening" (Ensemble), "Looking for a Candidate" (George S. Irving), "Couplet for Alfred" (David Staller), "Fa-La-La" (David Staller, Company), "Looking for a Candidate" (reprise) (George S. Irving, Michael Mendiola, Andrew Gitzy, Edward Prostack), "Read All About It" (Ensemble), "Love Is Still Love" (Rita Harvey), "The Ballad of Marcia LaRue" (Carter Calvert, Michael Mendiola, Andrew Gitzy, Edward Prostack), "Take Off the Coat" (Carter Calvert), "The Fair Sex" (Michael Mendiola, Men), "Dost Thou" (David Staller), "The Money Song" (George S. Irving, Michael Mendiola, Andrew Gitzy, Edward Prostack), "You Never Know What Hit You—When It's Love" (Carter Calvert), "Campaign Song" (Company)

ACT TWO—"Gin Rummy Rhapsody" (George S. Irving, Michael Mendiola, Andrew Gitzy, Edward Prostack), "Cry, Baby" (a/k/a "Cry, Baby, Cry") (Rita Harvey, George S. Irving, Michael Mendiola, Andrew Gitzy, Edward Prostack), "I Shouldn't Love You"/"Dost Thou" (reprise) (Rita Harvey, David Staller), "Political Lady" (Ensemble), "A Determined Woman" (Carter Calvert, Ensemble), Finale (Company)

NOTES—Like *Foxy* (see entry), *That's the Ticket!* was another welcome entry from the innovative *Musicals Tonight!* series, which specialized in staging limited runs of obscure musicals.

The original production of *That's the Ticket!* closed prematurely during its pre-Broadway tryout at the Shubert Theatre in Philadelphia; it played there for just one week, beginning on September 24, 1948. With a wonderful score by Harold Rome, an intriguing book by Julius J. and Philip G. Epstein (who had written [with Howard Koch] the screenplay for the 1942 Oscar-winning film *Casablanca*; moreover, the Epsteins' unproduced play *Front Porch in Flatbush* was the basis for Stephen Sondheim's *Saturday Night* [see entry], and the book for that musical was by Julius J. Epstein), direction by Jerome Robbins, choreography by Paul Godkin, scenery by Oliver Smith, and costumes by Miles White, *That's the Ticket!* seemed to have all the ingredients for success. But the musical was panned by the critics, and, like *Saturday Night*, it disappeared for decades. But just as *Saturday Night* was eventually resurrected and finally made its New York debut in 2000, so did *That's the Ticket!*, which, thanks to *Musicals Tonight!*, made its belated New York premiere in 2002, some fifty-four years after the original closed in Philadelphia (and George S. Irving performed in both the 1948 and 2002 productions!).

In the musical, the Democratic and Republican parties are for once in agreement on an issue: both have mutual disdain for two other opposing political parties. When the candidate for the fourth political party, the Feudal Party, dies, its political boss Robert Vale-Waterhouse (Loring Smith in the original production and George S. Irving in the revival) has no candidate in the wings to take the dead man's place. But one night in Central Park his daughter Patricia meets a frog who materializes into a medieval knight (Alfred, Lord of Nottingwood, a/k/a Alfred the Average) wearing a suit of armor (a thousand years ago a witch had turned the knight into a frog). When Patricia brings Alfred home to meet her father, Vale-Waterhouse realizes he has at last found his replacement candidate.

Kaye Ballard played the role of Marcia LaRue, who had been a witch in the Middle Ages (and who had placed the curse on Lord Alfred) and is now a film star with designs on becoming the first female President of the United States.

Harold Rome's score was one of his best, and it

included "Take Off the Coat," a vampy, sinuous song of seduction; "The Money Song," an amusing comic number which became popular (and was later included in Robert Gottlieb and Robert Kimball's *Reading Lyrics*, a fascinating collection of lyrics published by Pantheon Books in 2000); and three particularly outstanding songs which had razor-sharp lyrics and irresistible melodies ("Gin Rummy Rhapsody," "Political Lady," and "A Determined Woman").

Despite the failure of *That's the Ticket!*, Rome was able to salvage some of its songs for future musicals. "Take Off the Coat" was used in *Bless You All* (1950); "You Never Know What Hit You—When It's Love" was used in *Pretty Penny* (1949; closed prior to Broadway) and then later in *Bless You All*; "Cry, Baby" was used in *Pretty Penny* and then later in *Alive and Kicking* (1950); and "I Shouldn't Love You" was re-written as "I Have to Tell You" for *Fanny* (1954).

Musicals Tonight! preserved the entire original score (with just one omission, the dance number "Chivalry Reel"), and the production was recorded by Original Cast Records (CD # OC-6038); for the album, "We're Going Back," the musical's first-act finale, was retitled "Campaign Song."

1609 Theatre of the Balustrade. THEATRE: Hunter College Playhouse; OPENING DATE: October 19, 1970; PERFORMANCES: 7; DIRECTION: Ladislav Fialka; PRODUCTION: Hunter College Concert Bureau and Sherman Pitluck

CAST—Josef Faita, Ladislav Fialka, Lucie Hoffmeisterova, Jiri Kaftan, Ludmilla Kovarova, Zdenka Kratochvilova, Ivan Lukes, Rudolf Papezik, Olga Przygrodska, Bozena Vechetova, Richard Weber

NOTES—Hunter College sponsored Prague's The Theatre of the Balustrade's mime comedy *Button, Button* as well as two other mime sequences, *Nine Etudes* and *Theme and Variations*. The production was scheduled for a limited engagement of seven performances, and after the New York run the company toured the United States.

Button, Button was the evening's longest piece, a mime dance-play in twelve scenes which revolved around a man who loses a gold button and becomes involved in various dreamlike episodes as he searches for it. The main performer of the piece was Ladislav Fialka, whom Mel Gussow in the *New York Times* compared to Marcel Marceau in skill if not in style. Gussow noted that Marceau was a minimalist who worked in "subtle" gestures, while Fialka used "broad, repetitive strokes and primary colors" which sometimes verged on slapstick.

1610 Theda Bara and the Frontier Rabbi. THEATRE: Jewish Repertory Theatre; OPENING DATE: January 9, 1993; PERFORMANCES: 15; BOOK: Jeff Hochhauser; LYRICS: Bob Johnston and Jeff Hochhauser; MUSIC: Bob Johnston; DIRECTION: Lynne Taylor-Corbett; CHOREOGRAPHY: Lynne Taylor-Corbett; SCENERY: Michael R. Smith; COSTUMES: Tom Reiter; LIGHTING: Tom Sturge; MUSICAL DIRECTION: Michael Rafter; PRODUCER: Jewish Repertory Theatre (Ran Avni, Artistic Director; Edward M. Cohen, Associate Director; Steven M. Levy, General Manager)

CAST—Jonathan Brody (Marv, Adolph Zukor, Cowboy), Christopher Coucill (Gordon Edwards), Frank DiPasquale (Morris Flushing, Sam Goldfish, Cowboy), Mark Frawley (D.W. Griffith, Groom, Cowboy), Jonathan Hadley (Isaac Birnbaum), Robin Irwin (Head Foremother), Jeanine LaManna (Theda Bara), Iris Lieberman (Fanny Flushing, Foremother), Ellen Margulies (Rachel Birnbaum), Rita Rehn (Irene, Foremother), Allen Lewis Rickman (Selwyn Farp)

The action occurs in Hollywood in 1927.

The musical was presented in two acts (division of acts and song assignments unknown).

MUSICAL NUMBERS—"Father, I Have Sinned," "There Are So Many Things That a Vampire Can't Do," "Frontier Rabbi," "It's Like a Movie," "Velcome to Shul," "Bolt of Love," "Sermon," "Scene with the Grapes," "Another Rabbi Outta the Hat," "There Are So Many Things That a Vampire Can Do" (reprise), "If She Came Back Again," "Waiting for the Kiss to Come," "Oh Succubus," Finale

NOTES—The title alone makes this musical sound amusing. But the Off Off Broadway musical *Theda Bara and the Frontier Rabbi* didn't go anywhere, and seems to have fallen into the trap of The Silent Movie-Making Curse, following other short-running musicals which dealt with film-making during the silent-movie era (*The Vamp* [1955, 60 performances], *Goldilocks* [1958, 161 performances], and *Mack and Mabel* [1974, 65 performances]).

Theda Bara was briefly resurrected on December 2, 2005, as part of the York Theatre Company's *Musicals in Mufti* series (see entry).

1611 They Don't Make 'Em Like That Anymore. THEATRE: Plaza 9 Music Hall; OPENING DATE: June 8, 1972; PERFORMANCES: 32; SKETCHES, LYRICS, AND MUSIC: "Mainly by" Hugh Martin and Timothy Gray; DIRECTION: Timothy Gray; SCENERY: Don Gordon; COSTUMES: E. Huntington Parker and Stephen Chandler; gowns created by Bruno Le Fantastique; LIGHTING: Beverly Emmons; MUSICAL DIRECTION: Unknown; PRODUCER: Costas Omero presents a Timothy Gray and William Justus Production

CAST—LUBA LISA, PHOEBE OTIS, Kevin Christopher, Dell Hanley, Clay Johns, Gene McCann, Paris Todd, ARTHUR BLAKE

The revue was presented in two acts.

ACT ONE—"They Don't Make 'Em Like That Anymore" (Luba Lisa, Phoebie Otis, Kevin Christopher, Dell Hanley, Clay Johns, Gene McCann, Paris Todd), "Something Tells Me" (Arthur Blake, Luba Lisa, Phoebie Otis, Kevin Christopher, Dell Hanley, Clay Johns, Gene McCann, Paris Todd), "Sorry Wrong Valley" (Arthur Blake, Clay Johns, Dell Hanley), "What's His Name" (Luba Lisa), "Once in Love with Amy" (Kevin Christopher, Luba Lisa), "Harvey" (Arthur Blake, Phoebe Otis), "Lili Marlene" (Arthur Blake, Clay Johns, Luba Lisa, Phoebe Otis, Gene McCann, Dell Hanley, Kevin Christopher), "I Lost You" (Phoebie Otis), "Mad About the Boy" (Arthur Blake, Luba Lisa, Phoebie Otis), "Swanislavsky" (Arthur Blake, Luba Lisa, Paris Todd, Kevin Christopher, Phoebie Otis, "Get Me Out of Here" (Company)

ACT TWO—"Buckle Down Winsocki" (Dell Hanley, Luba Lisa, Phoebie Otis, Clay Johns, Kevin Christopher, Gene McCann, Paris Todd), "Paradise Lost" (Arthur Blake), "Judy" (Phoebie Otis), "Drama Quartet" (Arthur Blake), "Oscar" (Luba Lisa, Kevin Christopher, Dell Hanley, Gene McCann, Paris Todd), "Sunset Boulevard" (Arthur Blake, Gene McCann, Phoebie Otis, Kevin Christopher, Dell Hanley, Paris Todd), "Frankie and Johnnies" (Arthur Blake, Kevin Christopher, Clay Johns, Gene McCann, Paris Todd), "Invisible Man" (Luba Lisa, Arthur Blake), "Silence Is Golden" (Arthur Blake, Phoebie Otis, Luba Lisa), "Show Girl"/"Disraeli"/"Victoria" (Arthur Blake), "Something Tells Me" (reprise/finale) (Company), "The Party's Over Now" (Arthur Blake)

NOTES—This short-lived revue *They Don't Make 'Em Like That Anymore* centered around impressionist Arthur Blake, who spoofed Marlene Dietrich, James Stewart, Ethel Barrymore, Noel Coward, and other celebrities. The revue included new and old material by Hugh Martin and Timothy Gray as well as various interpolations from other songwriters. The program didn't differentiate between sketches and songs.

Howard Thompson in the *New York Times* felt the Plaza was "scraping the barrel" with this "larkish lump" of a revue. He noted the sketches were "rickety" and the songs "unsparkling," and could hardly believe Martin and Gray were responsible for such material (he excepted "Oscar," which he said was "a peach of a tune" [see below for more information about the song]). Thompson also criticized female impersonator Arthur Blake (his Mae West came across like Shelley Winters) and said he'd like Luba Lisa better if she'd tone down her "calliope stridence."

Martin and Gray's "Something Tells Me" was originally heard in *High Spirits* (1964), and "Buckle Down Winsocki" was from *Best Foot Forward* (1941) (by Hugh Martin and Ralph Blane).

"Once in Love with Amy" was from *Where's Charley?* (1948), lyric and music by Frank Loesser; and "Mad About the Boy" and "The Party's Over Now" were from the London revue *Words and Music* (1932; lyrics and music by Noel Coward; the revue was produced in New York in 1938 as *Set to Music*). "Lili Marlene" was Dietrich's signature song; its lyric was written by Hans Leip in 1915, and was set to music in 1938 by Norbert Schultze.

In 1959, the song "Oscar" had been heard in *Taboo Revue* (a/k/a *Timothy Gray's Taboo Revue*; see entry); and in 1998, Martin and Gray's revue *I Will Come Back* (see entry) included the song "They Don't Write 'Em Like That Anymore," which was probably a variant title of the current revue's title song.

Paris Todd's program bio claimed he was the first male stripper to ever appear in New York.

1612 They Wrote That? THEATRE: McGinn/Cazale Theatre; OPENING DATE: February 5, 2004; PERFORMANCES: 41; LYRICS: Cynthia Weil; MUSIC: Barry Mann; DIRECTION: Richard Maltby, Jr.; CHOREOGRAPHY: Kurt Stamm; SCENERY: Neil Patel; COSTUMES: Laurie Churba; LIGHTING: Heather Carson; MUSICAL DIRECTION: Fred Mollin; PRODUCERS: CTM Productions and James B. Freydberg

CAST—Barry Mann, Cynthia Weil, Deb Lyons, Moeisha McGill, Jenelle Lynn Randall

The revue was presented in one act.

NOTES—In 1985, Off Off Broadway had offered *Just Once* (see entry), an evening of popular songs written by the Barry Mann and Cynthia Weil (and their collaborators). *They Wrote That?* offered the real thing, the duo themselves in an evening of talk about their careers as well as a selection of their hit songs (for the latter, they were joined by three other singers).

Margo Jefferson in the *New York Times* said the audience would have "a lot of fun" hearing the Mann and Weil songbook, but otherwise she felt the evening was "amazingly unshaped." She noted that because the text was superficial and never gave the audience an understanding of what shaped and drove the team, the evening might have been more successful if it had followed the "all-music, all-dance and no-talk" style of such revues as *Ain't Misbehavin'* (see entry) and *Fosse*. The revue included such songs as "You've Lost That Lovin' Feeling," "Sometimes When We Touch," "We Gotta Get Out of This Place," "Blame It on the Bossa Nova," "Make Your Own Kind of Music," "Who Put the Bomp," "On Broadway," "Just Once," "Don't Know Much," "He's So Shy," "Running with the Night," "Walkin' in the Rain," "He's the Boy I Love," "Just a Little Lovin'," and "I Love How You Love Me," all of which had been heard in *Just Once* (see entry for specific songwriting credits).

1613 The Thing About Men. THEATRE: Promenade Theatre; OPENING DATE: August 27, 2003; PERFORMANCES: 199; BOOK: Joe DiPietro; LYRICS: Joe DiPietro; MUSIC: Jimmy Roberts; DI-

RECTION: Mark Clements; CHOREOGRAPHY: Rob Ashford; SCENERY: Richard Hoover; COSTUMES: Gregory Gale; LIGHTING: Ken Billington; MUSICAL DIRECTION: Lynne Shankel; PRODUCERS: Jonathan Pollard, Bernie Kukoff, and Tony Converse in association with James Hammerstein Productions; Gregory Taft Gerard and Karen Jason, Associate Producers

CAST— Marc Kudisch (Tom), Ron Bohmer (Sebastian), Leah Hocking (Lucy), Daniel Reichard (The Man, Taxi Driver, Priest, Stylist, Maitre d', Waiter), Jennifer Simard (The Woman, Cindy, Stylist, Country Singer)

SOURCE— The 1985 film *Men...* (screenplay and direction by Doris Dorrie).

The action occurs during the summer in an American city and its suburb.

The musical was presented in two acts.

ACT ONE— Opening/"Oh, What a Man!" (Marc Kudisch, Leah Hocking, Daniel Reichard, Jennifer Simard), "No Competition for Me" (Marc Kudisch, Daniel Reichard), "Opportunity Knocking" (Marc Kudisch), "Free, Easy Guy" (Ron Bohmer, Leah Hocking), "Free, Easy Guy" (reprise) (Marc Kudisch), "Take Me Into You" (Ron Bohmer, Leah Hocking), "Because" (Leah Hocking), "The Confession" (Daniel Reichard), "The Greatest Friend" (Ron Bohmer, Marc Kudisch), "Downtown Bohemian Slum" (Company)

ACT TWO—"You Will Never Get Into This Restaurant" (Daniel Reichard), "Me, Too" (Ron Bohmer, Cindy, Daniel Reichard), "One-Woman Man" (Ron Bohmer, Daniel Reichard, Marc Kudisch), "Take Me Into You" (reprise) (Leah Hocking), "Highway of Your Heart" (Jennifer Simard), "The Better Man Won" (Marc Kudisch), "The Road to Lucy" (Marc Kudisch, Ron Bohmer, Leah Hocking), "Make Me a Promise, Thomas" (Marc Kudisch, Leah Hocking), "New, Beautiful Man" (Marc Kudisch, Ron Bohmer, Daniel Reichard, Jennifer Simard), "Time to Go Home" (Marc Kudisch), "I (You) Can't Have It All" (Company)

NOTES— Based on the German film *Men...*, *The Thing About Men* was Joe DiPietro and Jimmy Roberts' follow-up to their phenomenally successful Off Broadway revue *I Love You, You're Perfect, Now Change* (which also looked at contemporary male-and-female relationships; see entry).

The Thing About Men told the story of Tom, a man with a great job, a great wife (Lucy), and a great girlfriend (Jessica); but things go awry when he discovers Lucy has a lover (Sebastian). In order to exact revenge upon Lucy, Tom, under the guise of a man named Milo, moves in with Sebastian, and before long the two men become great friends.

Bruce Weber in the *New York Times* thought the evening began as "biting, effective social satire" but soon deteriorated into "tortuous plot contrivances"; he was also surprised by the musical's ending, which seemed to say that in order to be happy one must join the "rat race." Weber generally liked the score, and singled out "Because" ("potently bitter"), "Free, Easy Guy" ("a spirited, swaggering show tune"), and "The Better Man Won" ("rueful, ruminative ... takes some surprising melodic turns").

The amusing plot and pleasant score (recorded by DRG Records [CD # DRG-94772]) should have given the musical a longer run than six months, but presumably the musical will find a healthy life in regional and community theatre.

The songs "Because," "The Confession," "The Better Man Won," and "Time to Go Home" may have been added after the opening (all are heard on the cast album).

The musical was first produced by the 8 Street Theatre in Sacramento.

1614 The Third Ear. THEATRE: Premise Theatre; OPENING DATE: May 28, 1964; PERFORMANCES: 150; DIRECTION: Elaine May; PRODUCERS: Michael Brandman and Murray Roman in association with the Premise Rest. Corp.

CAST— Peter Boyle, Mark Gordon, Louise Lasser, Reni Santoni, Renee Taylor

The revue was presented in two acts (sketch assignments unknown).

ACT ONE—"Seduction, Literary Style," "War and Poverty," "He Who Loves Worst Loves Most," "The Mother of the Bride," "Bathos After the Funeral," "Award of the Week," "The Late Late Show" (Parody of a Romantic Movie Vintage 1935)

ACT TWO— In this act, the improvisations were based on themes suggested by the audience.

NOTES— The latest Premise revue *The Third Ear* was directed by Elaine May, who had earlier been associated with the Second City troupe. The set pieces in the first act were created by the performers, as were the "spot" improvisations in the second act (for the latter, it seems the shells of the specific scenes were devised by the performers, who then built upon and expanded the scenes when the audience suggested topics).

Brian O'Doherty in the *New York Times* praised director Elaine May ("the den mother of improvisation"), and noted the evening was often "uproarious." He mentioned that among the revue's targets was Vietnam, a subject which "looks good for another seven years" of satire. The group also demolished the notion of President Lyndon Johnson's War on Poverty.

O'Doherty mentioned that the "long low" auditorium of the Premise Theatre looked like an "outsize fin de siecle coffin" which contained the "lively" bodies of the five cast members, including Louise Lasser, who later made her mark in the title role of the tongue-in-cheek television soap opera *Mary Hartman, Mary Hartman*, where her improvisational background undoubtedly added much to the spontaneity of her long-running comic performance in that series. See entries for the other Premise revues (*The Premise*, *The New Show at the Premise*, and *The Living Premise*).

1615 This Was Burlesque (1962). "A Musical Satire." THEATRE: Casino East Theatre; OPENING DATE: March 1, 1962; PERFORMANCES: 1,509; DIRECTION: Ann Corio; CHOREOGRAPHY: Pal Brandeaux; COSTUMES: Pal Brandeaux; MUSICAL DIRECTION: Nick Francis; PRODUCER: Michael P. Iannucci in association with Milt Warner

CAST—ANN CORIO, STEVE MILLS, CONNY RYAN, CHARLEY ROBINSON, MAC DENNISON, RENI AND SUZI, MARY ALAGIA, DOLORES DUVAUGHN, MARA LYNN, The Casino Cuties (Alleen Anne, Daryl Thornton, Mesaline Marcus, Vela Ceres, Dyanne Thorne, Dee Dunsmore, June Lee Graham, Rene Cooper, Debbie Agin, Suzanne Cogan)

SOURCE— Ann Corio's recollections as told to Joe Di Mona and suggested by Eddie Jaffe.

The revue was presented in two acts.

ACT ONE— Overture; Prologue (Steve Mills, Conny Ryan, Mac Dennison, Reni and Suzi), "Hello Everybody" (Alleen Anne, Daryl Thornton, Mesaline Marcus, Vela Ceres, Dyanne Thorne, Dee Dunsmore, June Lee Graham, Rene Cooper, Debbie Agin, Suzanne Cogan), "Flirtation Scene" (Steve Mills, Conny Ryan, Ann Corio), "Ecdysiasis" (performer[s] not credited), "The Safe Scene" (Charley Robinson, Mac Dennison, Daryl Thornton [one other performer not credited]), "Dance of the Orient" (Alleen Anne, Daryl Thornton, Mesaline Marcus, Vela Ceres, Dyanne Thorne, Dee Dunsmore, June Lee Graham, Rene Cooper, Debbie Agin, Suzanne Cogan, Mac Dennison, [two other performers not credited]), Specialty (Steve Mills, Conny Ryan), "Yo-Yo" (Alleen Anne, Daryl Thornton, Mesaline Marcus, Vela Ceres, Dyanne Thorne, Dee Dunsmore, June Lee Graham, Rene Cooper, Debbie Agin, Suzanne Cogan), "Court-room Scene" (performer[s] not credited), "Simple Melody" (Alleen Anne, Daryl Thornton, Mesaline Marcus, Vela Ceres, Dyanne Thorne, Dee Dunsmore, June Lee Graham, Rene Cooper, Debbie Agin, Suzanne Cogan, Steve Mills, Conny Ryan, Daryl Thornton), "Candy Butcher" (performer[s] not credited)

ACT TWO—"Powder My Back" (Rene Cooper, with Alleen Anne, Daryl Thornton, Mesaline Marcus, Vela Ceres, Dyanne Thorne, Dee Dunsmore, June Lee Graham, Debbie Agin, Suzanne Cogan), "Fix It Scene" (Mac Dennison, Alleen Anne, Rene Cooper, [one other performer not credited]), Dolores DuVaughn, "White Cargo" (Ann Corio, Steve Mills, Conny Ryan, Mac Dennison), "Twist, Shimmy and Shake" (Alleen Anne, Daryl Thornton, Mesaline Marcus, Vela Ceres, Dyanne Thorne, Dee Dunsmore, June Lee Graham, Rene Cooper, Debbie Agin, Suzanne Cogin, [one other performer not credited]), "Hall of Fame" (Ann Corio, Daryl Thornton), "Crazy House" (Company), Finale (Company)

NOTES— *This Was Burlesque*, a nostalgic look at old-time burlesque, starred one of the most famous burlesque stars of them all, Ann Corio, who appeared in some of the sketches and also served as the revue's narrator. Corio's program bio listed her film credits (*Call of the Jungle*, *Swamp Women*, *Jungle Siren*, and *Sarong Girl*), but perhaps Delores Du Vaughn's program credits were even more impressive than Corio's: Du Vaughn's "most recent accolade" was being voted "The Girl They Would Most Like to Go Underwater With" by the U.S. sailors of the New London, Connecticut, Submarine Base.

The revue's most interesting song is "Yo-Yo," which on the Roulette Records cast recording is titled "Go and Get Yourself a Yo-Yo" (LP # R-25185). The song, with lyric and music by Albert Selden, is from the musical *The Amazing Adele*, which closed in Boston during its pre-Broadway tryout in 1956 (Tammy Grimes played the title role).

The program for *This Was Burlesque* changed often (other sequences added during the long run were "The Gun Ain't Loaded" and "The Detective"). On December 4, 1963, the show underwent considerable revision with the addition of such numbers as "Hello, New York," "The Carpenter," "Hotel de France," "Cleopatra," "Here's the Key to My Heart," "Dodger Scene," "Sutton Place," "Evolution of Dance," "Hee Haw," "Schoolroom," "Les Poules," and "Bottoms Up." A survey of a half-dozen programs from throughout the run indicate that in addition to new numbers which replaced old ones, many deleted numbers were later reinstated.

After the long Off Broadway run, the revue transferred to Broadway in 1965, playing 124 performances, and in 1970 the revue returned to Off Broadway for a run of 106 performances (see entry). Another Broadway production opened in 1981, and played for twenty-eight performances. This time around, the cast members included one "Patrick," who was billed as "The All American Male Stripper." Also in the cast were Dexter Maitland (who had appeared in the 1967 film *The Night They Raided Minsky's*) and Phil Ford (of "Phil Ford and Mimi Hines"). In 1976, a version of *This Was Burlesque* was shown on Home Box Office.

1616 This Was Burlesque (1970). THEATRE: Hudson West Theatre; OPENING DATE: February 11, 1970; PERFORMANCES: 106; DIRECTION: Richard Barstow; production "supervised" by Ann Corio; CHOREOGRAPHY: Richard Barstow; COSTUMES: Rex Huntington; LIGHTING: Steve Zwiegbaum; MUSICAL DIRECTION: Nick Francis; PRODUCER: Michael P. Iannucci

CAST— Ann Corio, Beautiful Marlene, Harry Conley, Count Gregory, Tom Dillon, Claude Mathis, Steve Mills, Frank O'Brien, Pepper Powell,

Tami Roche, Harry Ryan; and the Burley Cuties (Helen Levit, Marilyn Simon, Jinny Jasper, Vickie Daigle, Susan Stewart, Tricia Sandburg, Jennie Chandler, B.J. Hanford)

The revue was presented in two acts.

ACT ONE—Overture, "The Queen of Burlesque" (Ann Corio), "Hello Everybody" (The Burley Cuties), "Flirtation Scene" (Steve Mills, Ann Corio, Tom Dillon), "Dance L'Oriental" (The Burley Cuties), "Music Teacher" (Claude Mathis, Harry Ryan, Count Gregory, Marilyn Simon), "The Pussy Cat Girl" (Pepper Powell), "The Minnie Scene" (Harry Conley, Marilyn Simon), Special Attraction (Beautiful Marlene), "Packing the Trunk" (Steve Mills, Harry Ryan, Ann Corio, Jinny Jasper), "Minstrel Days" (Tom Dillon, The Burley Cuties), "Pantomime" (Count Gregory, Harry Ryan, Claude Mathis, Ann Corio), Mills and Dillon (Song Medley) (Steve Mills, Tom Dillon), "School Days" (Claude Mathis, Harry Ryan, Ann Corio, Helen Levit, Marilyn Simon), Feature Attraction (Tami Roche), First Act Finale (Ann Corio, Tom Dillon, Company)

ACT TWO—"Powder My Back" (Helen Levit, The Burley Cuties), "Transformer Scene" (Claude Mathis, Frank O'Brien, Pepper Powell, Harry Ryan, Helen Levit, Marilyn Simon), "Dance—Then and Now" (Tami Roche, The Burley Cuties), "White Cargo" (Steve Mills, Tom Dillon, Count Gregory, Ann Corio), "Hall of Fame" (Ann Corio), "Crazy House" (Steve Mills, Company), "Memories" (Ann Corio), Grand Finale (Company)

NOTES—Ann Corio returned in a revival of *This Was Burlesque* (see entry for original production), and while Off Broadway would still host the occasional burlesque revue, the popularity of the genre was definitely on the wan. But the burlesque revue went out in a blaze of glory with Broadway's lavish *Sugar Babies* (1979), which ran for three years. Film legends Mickey Rooney and Ann Miller gave the performances of their lives in an evening which offered old-time burlesque skits and Jimmy McHugh standards set against an array of colorful settings and costumes worthy of a classic MGM movie musical.

1617 Those Darn Kids. "A New Little Rascally Musical!" THEATRE: Theatre for the New City; OPENING DATE: October 4, 1976; PERFORMANCES: 18; Book, Lyrics, and MUSIC: Robert Dahdah and Mary Boylan; DIRECTION: Robert Dahdah (?); SCENERY: Donald L. Brooks; COSTUMES: Gene Galvin; LIGHTING: Donald L. Brooks; MUSICAL DIRECTION: David Tice; PRODUCER: Theatre for the New City/Bartenieff/Field

CAST—David Baron, Jo Drell, Dimacula Ngan, Malcolm Horton, John Johann, Jason McLane, Nailea Norvind, Jaja Pinnock, Melissa Thies, Lisa Younes

NOTES—Robert Dahdah and Mary Boylan, who had written the successful *Curley McDimple* (see entry), returned with the Off Off Broadway musical *Those Darn Kids*, which seems to be about a group of kids who take a trip into outer space.

Daddah and Boylan returned the following season with the Off Off Broadway musical *Clara Bow Loves Gary Cooper*, which opened a the Theatre for the New City on February 16, 1978, for twelve performances.

1618 Those Ringlings! "A New Musical Comedy Adventure." THEATRE: Actors' Playhouse; OPENING DATE: 1990 (?); PERFORMANCES: Unknown; BOOK: David Lewis Hammarstrom; LYRICS: David Lewis Hammarstrom; MUSIC: David Baron; DIRECTION: B.E. Rafner; CHOREOGRAPHY: Douglas Austin; SCENERY: The Theatre Company, Upland; COSTUMES: The Theatre Company, Upland; LIGHTING: John Dickey; PRODUCER: Night Music Productions

CAST—Jeffrey Rockwell (Al Ringling), Barbara Dvorett (Louise Morris Ringling), Jim Edwards (Otto Ringling), Joseph Lustig (Alf T. Ringling), Mark Barrett (Johnny Ringling), Rusty Ferracane (Charles Ringling), Hal Landon, Sr. (August Ringling), Barbara Baylis (Salome Ringling), John Dickey (Fritz), Kendal J. Taylor (Yankee Robinson, James A. Bailey), Frank Catalano (Red Pratt), Jason Harris (Hillary Hays), Linda Graves (Ginger), Craig Day (Larry Alexander), Barbara Lee Cooke (Lovie Potts), Tod Alden (Reporter), Joanne Giudici (Jennifer), Rachel Sorteberg (May)

The action occurs in various locations throughout the United States during the period 1882-1895.

The musical was presented in two acts.

ACT ONE—"Can't Stop Dreaming" (Jeffrey Rockwell), "Stranger in His World" (Barbara Dvorett), "The Five of Us" (Jeffrey Rockwell, Jim Edwards, Joseph Lustig, Mark Barrett, Rusty Ferracane, Hal Landon, Sr., Barbara Baylis), "Tonight Is the Night" (Jeffrey Rockwell, Jim Edwards, Joseph Lustig, Mark Barrett, Rusty Ferracane), "Big Wooden Shoes" (Mark Barrett), "Stranger in His World" (reprise) (Barbara Dvorett), "Silent Love" (Barbara Dvorett, Jim Edwards, Rusty Ferracane, Joseph Lustig), "Big Wooden Shoes" (reprise) (Jim Edwards), "The Circus Is Coming" (Kendal J. Taylor, Jeffrey Rockwell, Jim Edwards, Joseph Lustig, Mark Barrett, Rusty Ferracane, Ensemble), "Snake Charmer" (Barbara Dvorett), "Lifting the Leather" (Frank Catalano, Jason Harris), "Advance Man" (Mark Barrett, Linda Graves), "Without Me" (Barbara Dvorett), "The Customer Is Always Right" (Jeffrey Rockwell, Jim Edwards, Joseph Lustig, Mark Barrett, Rusty Ferracane, Barbara Lee Cooke, Ensemble), "Sunshine and Shadows" (Jeffrey Rockwell), "Welcome to the Mud" (Frank Catalano, Jeffrey Rockwell)

ACT TWO—"The Circus Is Coming" (reprise) (Jeffrey Rockwell, Jim Edwards, Joseph Lustig, Mark Barrett, Rusty Ferracane), "Sunday School Boys" (Frank Catalano, Jason Harris, Kendal J. Taylor), "Advance Man" (reprise) (Mark Barrett, Rachel Sorteberg), "If I Try" (Craig Day, Barbara Dvorett, Ensemble), "When the Season's Over" (Jeffrey Rockwell, Barbara Dvorett), "Just Let Me Dream" (Jeffrey Rockwell), "You Should See Him Now" (Jeffrey Rockwell, Jim Edwards, Joseph Lustig, Mark Barrett, Rusty Ferracane, Ensemble), "Snake Charmer" (reprise) (Barbara Dvorett), "Sunshine and Shadows" (reprise) (Jeffrey Rockwell, Barbara Dvorett), "Can't Stop Dreaming" (reprise) (Jeffrey Rockwell), "If I Try" (reprise) (Company)

NOTES—The 1980 musical *Barnum* (about P.T. Barnum) was a Broadway and international hit, and so why not a musical about the Ringling Brothers? *Those Ringlings!*, which played at the Actors' Playhouse circa 1990 as a visiting production under an Off Off Broadway contract, even managed to get James A. Bailey into the cast of characters. But, unlike *Barnum, Those Ringlings!* quickly disappeared.

1619 Those Were the Days. "The New English-Yiddish Musical Revue." THEATRE: Edison Theatre; OPENING DATE: November 7, 1990; PERFORMANCES: 130; Concept and Continuity by Zalmen Mlotek and Moishe Rosenfeld; additional material by E. Cecuona, Jacques Offenbach, Miriam Makeba, Frank Loesser, Mijos Hadjidakis, B. Towne, Bruce Adler, Robert Abelson, Mina Bern, and Eleanor Reissa; LYRICS: See song list for credits; MUSIC: See song list for credits; DIRECTION: Eleanor Reissa; CHOREOGRAPHY: Eleanor Reissa; COSTUMES: Gail Cooper-Hecht; LIGHTING: Tom Sturge; MUSICAL DIRECTION: Zalmen Mlotek; PRODUCERS: Moe Septee and Emanuel Azenberg in association with Victor H. Potamkin, Zalmen Mlotek and Moishe Rosenfeld

CAST—Bruce Adler, Eleanor Reissa, Lori Wilner, Robert Abelson, Mina Bern, The Golden Land Klezmer Orchestra; special guest appearance by Norman Atkins

The revue was presented in two acts.

ACT ONE *The Shtetl:* Overture (The Golden Land Klezmer Orchestra), Prologue: Nigunim (Melodies): "Lomir Loybn (Let Us Praise)" and "Sha Shtil (The Rabbi's Coming)" (folk songs) (Company), "Oyfn Pripetshik (At the Fireplace)" (lyric and music by M. Warshavsky) (Bruce Adler), "On a Moonlit Night" (based on a story by I.L. Peretz) (Eleanor Reissa, Lori Wilner), "Ver Der Ershter Vet Lakhn (Who Will Laugh First?)" (lyric and music by M. Gebirtig) (Eleanor Reissa, Lori Wilner), "Motele" (lyric and music by M. Gebirtig) (Robert Abelson, Eleanor Reissa), "Hudl Mitn Shtrudl (Hufl with the Shrtudl)" (lyric and music by A. Lebedeff) (Bruce Adler), "Kasrilevke Restoran (A Restaurant in Kasrilevke)" (based on a short story by Sholom Aleichem) (Bruce Adler, Robert Abelson, Mina Bern), "Di Dinst (The Maid)" (folk song) (Eleanor Reissa), "Shakakh-Mones (Gifts for Purim)" (based on a short story by Sholom Aleichem) (Eleanor Reissa, Lori Wilner), "Yosl Ber" (lyric by Itzik Manger, music, folk song) (Bruce Adler, with Lori Wilner and Eleanor Reissa), "Shabes, Shabes, Shabes (Welcoming the Sabbath)" (lyric by Ben Bonus, music by Ben Yomen) (Mina Bern), "Chelm" (Company), "Litvak/Galitsyaner" (lyric and music by Hymie Jacobson) (Bruce Adler, Eleanor Reissa), "Halevay Volt Ikh Singl Geven (I Wish I Were Single Again)" (American folk song adapted by M. Younin) (Robert Abelson, Mina Bern), "Shloymele-Malkele" (lyric and music by J. Rumshinsky) (Lori Wilner, Bruce Adler), "Mamenyu Tayere (Dear Mama)" (lyric by Mani Leib, music, folk melody; from the repertoire of Menashe Oppenheim) (Lori Wilner, Mina Bern), "Nokhumke, Mayn Zun (Nochum, My Son)" (folk song) (Robert Abelson, Bruce Adler), "Saposhkelekh (The Boots)" (folk song from research by Michael Alpert) (Eleanor Reissa), "The Wedding: Khosn-Kale Mazl Tov (Congratulations to the Bride and Groom)" (folk song); "Di Rod (The Circle)" (lyric and music by M. Warshavsky); "Der Ayznban (The Train)" (folk song); "Yoshke Fort Avek (Yoshke's Going Away)" (folk song); "Mayn Alte Heym" (from the "forbidden songs" of Soviet Jews, as recorded by David Eshet) (Company)

ACT TWO *The Music Hall:* Entr'acte (The Golden Land Klezmer Orchestra), "Those Were the Days" (lyric and music by Gene Raskin) (Eleanor Reissa, Robert Abelson), "Shpil Guitar" (Play Guitar) (Lori Wilner), "The Palace of the Czar" (lyric and music by Mel Tolkin) (Bruce Adler), "Di Mame (The Mother)" (monologue) (Mina Bern), "Yiddish International Radio Hour" (Yiddish lyrics by Chana Mlotek) (Company), Figaro's Aria (from *The Barber of Seville* [1816]) (Yiddish lyric by Robert Abelson and M. Rosenfeld, music by Gioacchino Rossini) (Robert Abelson), "My Yiddishe Mame" (lyric by Lew Pollack, music by Jack Yellen) (Eleanor Reissa), "Hootsatsa" (based on a song by Fishl Kanapoff) (Bruce Adler), "Bei Mir Bistu Schoen (To Me, You're Wonderful)" (Yiddish lyric by Jacob Jacobs, music by Sholom Secunda; English lyric by Sammy Cahn and Saul Chaplin) (Eleanor Reissa, Lori Wilner, Bruce Adler), "In an Orem Shtibele (In a Poor Little House)" (folk song) (Mina Bern), "A Khazndl Oyf Shabes (A Cantor for the Sabbath)" (folk song) (Robert Abelson), "Papirosn (Cigarettes)" (lyric and music by Bella Meisel and Herman Yablokoff) (Lori Wilner), "Yosl, Yosl" (lyric by Nellie Casman, music by Samuel Steinbeg) (Eleanor Reissa), "Rumania, Rumania" (lyric and music by A. Lebedeff and Sholom Secunda) (Bruce Adler), "Those Were the Days" (reprise) (Company)

NOTES—*Those Were the Days*, a Yiddish-English revue of traditional and popular material, was probably presented under a Middle Broadway contract.

Richard F. Shepard in the *New York Times* found the evening "a humdinger of a hum-along," and said the "musical mitzvah" was as refreshing as a glass of cold seltzer.

1620 Thoughts. "A Musical Celebration." THEATRE: Theatre de Lys; OPENING DATE: March 19, 1973; PERFORMANCES: 24; BOOK: Lamar Alford; LYRICS: Lamar Alford; additional lyrics by Megan Terry and Jose Tapla; MUSIC: Lamar Alford; DIRECTION: Michael Schultz; CHOREOGRAPHY: Jan Mickens; SCENERY: Stuart Wurtzel; COSTUMES: Joseph Thomas; "Costume Supervisor," Stanley Simmons; LIGHTING: Ken Billington; MUSICAL DIRECTION: Unknown; PRODUCERS: Arthur Whitelaw, Seth Harrison, and Dallas Alinder; presented in association with Peter Kean; presented by special arrangement with Lucille Lortel Productions, Inc.

CAST—Mary Alice, Jean Andalman, Martha Flowers, Robin Lamont, Baruk Levi, Bob Molock, Barbara Montgomery, Jeffrey Mylett, Howard Porter, Sarallen, E.H. Wright

The revue was presented in one act.

MUSICAL NUMBERS—Opening (lyric by Megan Terry) (Martha Flowers) "Blues Was a Pastime" (Barbara Montgomery, Company), "At the Bottom of Your Heart" (Robin Lamont, Jeffrey Mylett), "Ain't That Something" (Company), "Accepting the Tolls" (Howard Porter), "One of the Boys" (Howard Porter), "Trying Hard" (Barbara Montgomery), "Ain't That Something" (reprise) (Mary Alice), "Separate but Equal" (Jean Andalman, Baruk Levi, Company), "Gone" (Mary Alice, Company), "Jesus Is My Main Man" (Bob Molock, Martha Flowers, Company), "Bad Whitey" (Robin Lamont, Jean Andalman, Jeffrey Mylett, Baruk Levi), "Thoughts" (Jean Andalman), "Strange Fruit" (Barbara Montgomery), "I Can Do It Myself" (Sarallen, Company), "Shitla" (Jeffrey Mylett, Company), "Thoughts" (reprise) (Howard Porter), "Music in the Air" (Robin Lamont, Company), "Sunshine" (Mary Alice, Company), "New Song" (Howard Porter), "Day Oh Day" (Martha Flowers, Company)

NOTES—A revue-like musical about growing up as a Black preacher's son in the South, the musical had previously been produced Off Off Broadway at Café La Mama; once *Thoughts* was produced Off Broadway (by no less than five producers), the episodic musical had only three weeks to think. Perhaps such song titles as "Bad Whitey" and "Shitla" turned off potential audiences, but maybe not. (In regard to song titles, could any title have been more representative of its era than "Jesus Is My Main Man"?)

Clive Barnes in the *New York Times* praised the "touching" musical, and felt its "unpretentiousness" shouldn't work against it because *Thoughts* was "a grass roots evening for black magnolias."

During previews, the following songs were dropped (if they were in the production on opening night, they weren't listed in the program): "Walking in Strange and New Places," "Many Men Like You," and "Roofs."

1621 Three by One. THEATRE: Sullivan Street Playhouse; OPENING DATE: April 29, 1958; PERFORMANCES: 8 (estimated); LIBRETTI: Seymour Barab; MUSIC: Seymour Barab; DIRECTION: Dorothy Raedler; MUSICAL DIRECTION: Ronald Bush and Arthur Komar (Pianists)

CAST—Lorraine Phillips, Ruth Ray, Arden Anderson, Raymond Allen, Donald Slagel, Richard Krause, John J. Smith, Bruce Graham

NOTES—*Three by One* consisted of three one-act operas by Samuel Barab: *A Game of Chance*, *The Rajah's Ruby*, and *Chanticleer*. According to Ross Parmenter in the *New York Times*, *A Game of Chance* had first been performed in 1957 in Rock Island, Illinois, and was now receiving its New York premiere. The story dealt with three women knitting in a garden who wish for wealth, fame, and romance. A mysterious stranger grants their wishes, but the women come to regret that their wishes hadn't been more practical and realistic. Parmenter felt the opera was the best of the evening and praised the "pleasantly melodious" score.

The Rajah's Ruby was a world premiere, and it too dealt with people who wish for excitement in their lives. Parmenter found the music "characterless" and noted that the opera ended abruptly with no resolution.

The final opera of the evening was *Chanticleer*; based on a tale by Chaucer, the opera was described by Parmenter as "too cute" to sustain any strong musical action, but he praised an "enchanting" aria for Chanticleer as well as a duet for him and another character. The opera's world premiere had taken place in Aspen, Colorado, two years earlier, and the New York premiere actually occurred one week before the opening of *Three by One*, when the opera was performed by another company. So during the last two weeks of April, New York saw the openings of two different productions of *Chanticleer*.

The first production of *Chanticleer* had opened at the Patricia Neway Opera Workshop at the Pyramid Theatre on April 22; James Stuart (in the title role), Marion Handeren, Linda Newman, and Robert Howard were the principals; the scenery and costumes were by Louise Gutman and Tom Skelton; and the opera was directed by Patricia Neway. John Briggs reviewed the piece for the *New York Times*, and he too praised Chanticleer's solo ("it stopped the show") as well as a duet and a closing ensemble. The second production credited Seymour Barab with the libretto for *Chanticleer*, but in his review for the first production, Briggs cited M.C. Richards at the librettist. (The first production was on a double bill with Meyer Kupferman's opera *In a Garden*, which was based on a text by Gertrude Stein.)

1622 3 Guys Naked from the Waist Down. "A New Musical." THEATRE: Minetta Lane Theatre; OPENING DATE: February 5, 1985; PERFORMANCES: 160; BOOK: Jerry Colker; LYRICS: Jerry Colker; MUSIC: Michael Rupert; DIRECTION: Andrew Cadiff; CHOREOGRAPHY: Don Bondi; SCENERY: Clarke Dunham; COSTUMES: Tom McKinley; LIGHTING: Ken Billington; MUSICAL DIRECTION: Henry Aronson; PRODUCERS: James B. Freydberg, Stephen Wells, Max Weitzenhoffer in association with Richard Maltby, Jr.

CAST—Scott Bakula (Ted Klausterman), John Kassir (Kenny Brewster), Jerry Colker (Phil Kunin)

The action occurs in New York City and Southern California.

The musical was presented in two acts.

ACT ONE—"Promise of Greatness" (Scott Bakula), "Angry Guy"/"Lovely Day" (Jerry Colker), "Promise of Greatness" (reprise) (Scott Bakula), "Don't Wanna Be No Superstar I" (Scott Bakula, Jerry Colker), "Operator" (John Kassir), "Screaming Clocks (The Dummies Song)" (Scott Bakula, Jerry Colker, John Kassir), "Don't Wanna Be No Superstar II" (Scott Bakula, Jerry Colker, John Kassir), "The History of Stand-Up Comedy" (Scott Bakula, Jerry Colker, John Kassir), "Dreams of Heaven" (John Kassir), "Don't Wanna Be No Superstar III" (Scott Bakula, Jerry Colker, John Kassir), "Kamikaze Kabaret" (Scott Bakula, Jerry Colker, John Kassir)

ACT TWO—"The American Dream" (Scott Bakula, Jerry Colker, John Kassir), "What a Ride I" (Scott Bakula, Jerry Colker, John Kassir), "The 'Hello Fellas' TV Special World Tour" (Scott Bakula, Jerry Colker, John Kassir), "What a Ride II" (Scott Bakula, Jerry Colker, John Kassir), "A Father Now" (Jerry Colker), "'Three Guys Naked from the Waist Down' Theme" (Scott Bakula, Jerry Colker, John Kassir), "Screaming Clocks" (reprise) (Scott Bakula, Jerry Colker, John Kassir), "Don't Wanna Be No Superstar" (reprise) (Scott Bakula, Jerry Colker, John Kassir), "Dreams of Heaven" (reprise) (John Kassir), "I Don't Believe in Heroes Anymore" (Scott Bakula), "Promise of Greatness" (final reprise) (Scott Bakula)

NOTES—*3 Guys Naked from the Waist Down* wasn't an early version of *Naked Boys Singing!* (see entry); *The Best Plays of 1984-1985* indicated the title was show-business slang for stand-up comics.

The plot dealt with three such comics who begin their careers in Manhattan comedy clubs and eventually become superstars in a hit TV series (*Hello, Fellas*) playing undercover cops in drag. But we all know the enduring lesson from sagas about show business: Fame Isn't Always What It's Cracked Up To Be. Thus one of the trio commits suicide, and another, desperate to remain in the spotlight, sells out by performing in a retread of the earlier television success (set in Russia, *Hello, Comrade* is about an undercover CIA agent in drag). The third leaves tinsel town in order to return to his comic roots by opening an intimate comedy club in Manhattan which showcases new performers. The musical was recorded by Polydor Records (LP # 820-244-1-Y-1), and in 1989 was produced in London at the Donmar Warehouse Theatre. The Off Broadway cast album includes "A Father Now," Phil's song about the birth of his son, and the liner notes mention it was omitted from the original production. However, both *Best Plays* and *Theatre World 1984-1985 Season* include the number in their song listings; the number is also listed in a preview program; and in his opening night review for the *New York Times*, Frank Rich seems to refer to it (Phil becomes "a well-adjusted family man by means of a single, treacly song").

With its bright score and generally favorable reviews from the New York critics (in his *New York Post* review, Clive Barnes called it "one of the cleverest and funniest shows we've had in a long time"), the three-man musical seemed likely to become a long-running, audience-pleasing hit. But it was gone within a few months and seems to have all but disappeared. Another musical about stand-up comics opened on Broadway in 1987; *Late Nite Comic* played for just four performances, but left behind a recording (released by Original Cast Records [CD # OC-8843]) as well as an account of the making of the show published in 2006 by BearManor Media (*We Bombed in New London/The Inside Story of the Broadway Musical 'Late Night Comic'* by Brian Gari, the musical's lyricist and composer). In 2007, a "20th Anniversary Edition" of *Late Nite Comic*'s score was released Original Cast Records (CD # 0315); the studio cast included Liz Callaway, Mario Cantone, Jason Graae, Liz Larsen, Howard McGillin, Tony Roberts, Mary Testa, Martin Vidnovic, Sal Viviano, Karen Ziemba, and Chip Zien, and the original score was supplemented by songs deleted prior to the Broadway production or written after the show's closing.

1623 Three Mo' Tenors. THEATRE: Little Shubert Theatre; OPENING DATE: September 27, 2007; PERFORMANCES: 142; DIRECTION: Marion J. Caffey; CHOREOGRAPHY: Marion J. Caffey; SCENERY: Michael Carnahan; COSTUMES: Gail Cooper-Hecht; LIGHTING: Richard Winkler; MUSICAL DIRECTION: Keith Burton; PRODUCER: Willette Murphy Klausner

CAST—Kenneth D. Alston, Jr., Ramone Diggs, Phumzile Sojola, James N. Berger, Jr., Duane A. Moody, Victor Robertson

The revue was presented in two acts.

ACT ONE—"La Donna e Mobile" (from *Rigoletto*, 1851; words by Francesco Maria Piave, music by music by Giuseppe Verdi) (Three Mo' Tenors),

"Questa o Quella" (*Rigoletto*) (Phumzile Sojola), "Nessun Dorma" (*Turandot*, 1926; words by Giuseppe Adami and Renato Simoni, music by Giacomo Puccini) (Duane A. Moody), "Ombra Mai Fu" (*Xerxes*, 1738; words and music by George Frideric Handel) (Kenneth D. Alston, Jr.), "I Hear an Army" (words and music by Samuel Barber) (James N. Berger, Jr.), "Le Reve" (*Manon*, 1884; words by Henri Meilhac and Philippe Gille, music by Jules Massenet) (Ramone Diggs), "Ah Mes Amis" (*La Fille du Regiment*, 1840; words by Georges Henri Vernoy de Saint-Georges and Jean Francois Bayard, music by Gaetano Donizetti) (Victor Robertson), "The Three Mo' Way" (credited to *Jelly's Last Jam*, 1992; lyric by Susan Birkenhead, music by Jelly Roll Morton) (Three Mo' Tenors), "Let the Good Times Roll" (credited to *Five Guys Named Moe*, 1992; lyric and music by Fleecie Moore and Sam Theard) (Three Mo' Tenors), "Bring Him Home" (*Les Miserables*, 1987; original French lyric by Alain Boublil and Jean-Marc Natel, English lyric by Herbert Kretzmer, music by Claude-Michel Schonberg) (Ramone Diggs and Phumzile Sojola or James N. Berger, Jr., and Victor Robertson), "Make Them Hear You" (*Ragtime*, 1998; lyric by Lynn Ahrens, music by Stephen Flaherty) (Three Mo' Tenors), "I've Got to Be Me" (*Golden Rainbow*, 1968; lyric and music by Walter Marks) (Phumzile Sojola), "Being Alive" (*Company*, 1970; lyric and music by Stephen Sondheim) (James N. Berger, Jr.), "Who Can I Turn To (When Nobody Needs Me)?" (*The Roar of the Greasepaint—The Smell of the Crowd*, 1965; lyric and music by Leslie Bricusse and Anthony Newley) (Ramone Diggs), "Azure Te" (*Five Guys Named Moe*, 1992; lyric and music by Bill Davis and Don Wolf) (Victor Robertson), "This Is the Moment" (*Jekyll & Hyde*, 1997; lyric by Leslie Bricusse, music by Frank Wildhorn) (Kenneth D. Alston, Jr.), "Rain" (*Once on This Island*, 1990; lyric by Lynn Ahrens, music by Stephen Flaherty) (Duane A. Moody), South African Medley: "Circle of Life" (*The Lion King*, 1997; lyric by Tim Rice, music by Elton John)/"Dali Wam" (lyric and music by Bangani) (Phumzile Sojola with Kenneth D. Alston, Jr., and Ramone Diggs), "Minnie the Moocher" (lyric and music by Cab Calloway) (James M. Berger, Jr., with Duane A. Moody and Victor Robertson)

ACT TWO—Queen Medley: "Bohemian Rhapsody"/"I Want It All"/"We Are the Champions"/"We Will Rock You" (lyrics and music by Mercury and May) (Three Mo' Tenors), To Ray, with Love: "Don't Set Me Free" (lyric and music by Powell and Sharp)/ "Hit the Road, Jack" (lyric and music by Mayfield)/ "Georgia on My Mind" (lyric and music by Gorrell and Carmichael) (Three Mo' Tenors), "Today I Sing the Blues" (lyric and music by Lewis) (Three Mo' Tenors), "Azure Te" (reprise) (Phumzile Sojola), "Spain" (lyric and music by Corea, Jarreau, and Maren) (Victor Robertson), "I Believe in You and Me" (lyric and music by Linzer and Wolfert) (Ramone Diggs), "Superstar" (lyric and music by Russell and Bramlett)/"Let's Get It On" (lyric and music by Gaye and Townsend) (James N. Berger, Jr.), Soul Medley: "Love Train" (lyric and music by Gamble and Huff)/"My Girl" (lyric and music by Robinson and White)/"Stop Look Listen" (lyric and music by Bell and Epstein)/"Midnight Train to Georgia" (lyric and music by England)/"Heaven Must Be Missing an Angel" (lyric and music by Perren and St. Louis) (Three Mo' Tenors), New School Medley: "Yeah" (lyric and music by Bridges, Hamler, Jefferson, Phillips, Smith & Smith)/"If I Ain't Got You" (lyric and music by Keys)/"Ordinary People" (lyric and music by Legend)/"Yeah" (reprise) (Three Mo' Tenors), Spiritual Medley: "Lord How Come Me Here"/"Hush Somebody's Calling My Name"/ "Guide My Feet" (all traditional) (Three Mo' Tenors), "Noways Tired" (traditional) (Kenneth D. Alston, Jr., or Duane A. Moody), "Glorious" (lyric and music by Houghton and Munizzi) (Three Mo' Tenors), "How Sweet It Is to Be Loved by You" (lyric and music by Brian Holland, Lamont Dozier, and Edward J. Holland) (Three Mo' Tenors), "Make Them Hear You" (reprise) (Three Mo' Tenors)

NOTES—Conceived by Marion J. Caffey, *Three Mo' Tenors* (which had been touring the United States since 2001) was an evening of songs by three Black tenors who sang everything from Giuseppe Verdi to Stephen Sondheim (six different singers rotated in different combinations for each performance). In his review for *Variety*, Steven Suskin noted the revue was "not theatre, but a theatricalized concert," and suggested the evening wasn't for "traditional theatre auds." But he noted the revue *Smokey Joe's Café* (1995) managed a run of six years, and indicated *Three Mo' Tenors* might find its audience and run longer than its announced four-month engagement.

1624 Three Postcards.

"A Musical Play." THEATRE: Playwrights Horizons; OPENING DATE: May 14, 1987; PERFORMANCES: 22; BOOK: Craig Lucas; LYRICS: Craig Carnelia; MUSIC: Craig Carnelia; DIRECTION: Norman Rene; CHOREOGRAPHY: Linda Kostalik-Boussom; SCENERY: Loy Arcenas; COSTUMES: Walter Hicklin; LIGHTING: Debra J. Kletter; PRODUCER: Playwrights Horizons (Andre Bishop, Artistic Director; Paul S. Daniels, Executive Director)

CAST—Craig Carnelia (Bill), Brad O'Hare (Waiter), Jane Galloway (Big Jane), Maureen Silliman (Little Jane), Karen Trott (K.C.)

The action occurs in a restaurant.

The musical was presented in one act (song assignments unknown; the song titles weren't listed in the program, and the titles below come from *The Best Plays of 1986-1987*).

MUSICAL NUMBERS—Opening, "She Was K.C.," "What the Song Should Say," "Piano Effects," "See How the Sun Shines," "I've Been Watching You," "Collage," "Three Postcards," "The Picture in the Hall," "Cast of Thousands," "Rain," "I'm Standing in This Room"

NOTES—While *Three Postcards* was ostensibly about three women, old friends who get together over dinner in a trendy restaurant, the surreal evening told the story in a dreamlike, free-form fashion in which the women's table occasionally breaks apart into three separate tables as each drifts into her memories and fantasies (including one who fantasizes about the waiter, much as another character would later do in *Contact* [see entry]).

Writing in *Time*, William A. Henry III praised the musical's "serene, minimalist simplicity" which told its oblique story with a certain sense of "fey nuttiness" (when one woman tells the others that the waiter "hates" her, the waiter later tells her in deadpan fashion that he indeed hates her). Jeffrey Sweet's assessment in *Best Plays* was that *Three Postcards* was "first-rate," the season's most satisfying musical on or off Broadway. However, Mel Gussow in the *New York Times* found the material "ordinary," "banal," and, in its use of time, "confusing." He noted that Craig Carnelia's score was "amiable" but "seldom rising above sub-Sondheim." But he praised Loy Arcenas' décor of the trendy restaurant (the type of restaurant that's "instantly successful until it closes six months later"). He also liked Brad O'Hare's turn as a waiter who throughout the evening drily recites the endless specials which are *not* on the menu.

"The Picture in the Hall" and "Cast of Thousands" were recorded for the collection *Pictures in the Hall/Songs of Craig Carnelia* (released by Original Cast Records [CD # OC-914]), and "The Picture in the Hall" was also recorded by Sharon McNight in her collection *In the Meantime* (released by Jezebel Records [CD # OU81SS]).

On November 16, 1994, the musical was revived by the Circle Repertory Company for thirty-one performances.

1625 The 3 Travels of Aladin with the Magic Lamp.

"A New Opera." THEATRE: La Mama Experimental Theatre Club (ETC); OPENING DATE: October 13, 1982; PERFORMANCES: Unknown; LIBRETTO: Françoise Grund; MUSIC: Elizabeth Swados; DIRECTION: Françoise Grund; SCENERY: Françoise Grund; Jun Maeda and Donald Eastman, "Set Execution"; Jun Maeda and Yoshihico Tanaka, "Special Designs"; COSTUMES: Françoise Grund (?); Aline Landais, "Costume Execution"; LIGHTING: Anne Militello; PRODUCERS: LA MAMA ETC in association with the Theatres of Rennes, Orleans, Angers, and La Maison des Culture du Monde of Paris

CAST—Larry Marshall (Story Teller), Endo Suanda (Aladin), Mohammad Ghaffari (Magician, Man of China, Arrow Man, Doctor of China), Costas Charalambides (Mad Prophet), Michael Edward-Stevens (Genie, Emperor of China, Man of China), Dan Erkkila (Man of the Market, Musician), David Sawyer (Man of the Market, Percussionist), Genji Ito (Merchant, Killer of China, Musician), Sussan Deihim (Aladin's Mother, Dancer of the Market, Servant of the Princess, Slave, Fighter), Sheila Dabney (Woman of the Market, Spirit of the Earth, Servant of the Princess, Slave, Soul of Arrow Man), Youn Cho Park (Princess of China, Woman of the Market), Esther Levy (Woman of the Market, Crying Woman, Spirit of the Cavern, Servant of the Princess, Slave, Fighter), Arundhati (Woman of the Market, Spirit of the Cavern, Servant of the Princess, Slave, Fighter), Ronnie Gilbert (Cheese Seller, Spirit of the Earth, Servant of the Princess, Chief of the Slaves), Soni Moreno (Merchant, Beast of the Cavern, Servant of the Princess, Monkey, Slave, Fighter), Valois Mickens (Woman of the Market, Spirit of the Earth, Servant of the Princess, Slave, Fighter)

The opera was performed in one act.

NOTES—Elizabeth Swados' Off Off Broadway opera told the story of Aladin, so poor he's reduced to stealing oranges. But all ends well when the Emperor gives Aladin half of the Chinese empire as well as the hand of his daughter in marriage.

Mel Gussow in the *New York Times* reported that for the brief opera Swados invented a special language, and so the performers sang in what seemed to be a "collage of Eastern and African tongues" as well as a "smattering" of French and an "underpinning" of bird sounds (shades of Swados' *Nightclub Cantata*). Gussow liked the "appealing" score, but said if he could ask for three wishes on Aladin's lamp, he'd like a few more "light-hearted" songs, "understandable" lyrics, and "more imaginative" staging. The tale of Aladin (a/k/a Aladdin) first appeared in the eighteenth-century collection of stories *Arabian Nights*.

1626 The Threepenny Opera (1954).

THEATRE: Theatre de Lys; OPENING DATE: March 10, 1954; PERFORMANCES: 96; BOOK: Marc Blitzstein (adapted from the original German by Bertolt Brecht); LYRICS: Marc Blitzstein (adapted from the original German by Bertolt Brecht); MUSIC: Kurt Weill; DIRECTION: Carmen Capalbo; SCENERY: William Pitkin; COSTUMES: Bolansi; LIGHTING: Peggy Clark; MUSICAL DIRECTION: Samuel Matlowsky (Matlovsky); PRODUCERS: Carmen Capalbo and Stanley Chase

CAST—GERALD PRICE (Street Singer), LOTTE LENYA (Jenny), LEON LISHNER (Mr. J.J. Peacham), CHARLOTTE RAE (Mrs. Peacham), William Duell (Filch), SCOTT MERRILL (Macheath, a/k/a Mack the Knife), JO SULLIVAN (Polly Peacham), John Astin (Readymoney Matt), Joseph Beruh (Crookfinger Jake), Bernard Bogin (Bob the Saw), Paul Dooley

(Walt Dreary), Donald Elson (the Reverend Kimball), GEORGE TYNE (Tiger Brown), Marcella Markham (Betty), Marion Salee (Molly), Gerrianne Raphael (Dolly), Gloria Sokel (Coaxer), Chuck Smith (Smith), BEATRICE ARTHUR (Lucy Brown), Stan Schneider (First Constable), Miles Dickson (Second Constable), William Duell (Messenger)

SOURCE—The 1728 opera *The Beggar's Opera* by John Gay.

The action occurs in London during the nineteenth century.

The musical was presented in three acts.

ACT ONE—Overture (Orchestra), Prologue: "Ballad of Mack the Knife" (Gerald Price), "Morning Anthem" (Leon Lishner), "Instead-Of Song" (Leon Lishner, Charlotte Rae), "The Bide-a-Wee in Soho" (Jo Sullivan), "Wedding Song" (The Gang), "Army Song" (Scott Merrill, George Tyne, The Gang), "Wedding Song" (reprise) (The Gang), "Love Song" (Jo Sullivan, Scott Merrill), "Ballad of Dependency" (Charlotte Rae), First Threepenny Finale: "The World Is Mean" (Jo Sullivan, Leon Lishner, Charlotte Rae)

ACT TWO—"Polly's Song" (Jo Sullivan, Scott Merrill), "Ballad of Dependency" (reprise) (Charlotte Rae), "Pirate Jenny" (Lotte Lenya), "Tango-Ballad" (Lotte Lenya, Scott Merrill), "Ballad of the Easy Life" (Scott Merrill), "Barbara-Song" (Beatrice Arthur), "Jealousy Duet" (Beatrice Arthur, Jo Sullivan), Second Threepenny Finale: "How to Survive" (Scott Merrill, Charlotte Rae, Ensemble)

ACT THREE—"Useless Song" (Leon Lishner, Beggars), "Solomon Song" (Lotte Lenya), "Call from the Grave" (Scott Merrill), "Death Message" (Scott Merrill), Third Threepenny Finale: "The Mounted Messenger" (Ensemble)

NOTES—The original production of *Die Dreigroschenoper* opened in Berlin on August 31, 1928, at the Theater am Schiffbuerdamm; Harold Paulsen and Lotte Lenya created the roles of Macheath and Jenny, and Ernest Busch created the role of the Street Singer. The American premiere took place at the Empire Theatre on April 13, 1933, in an adaptation by Gifford Cochran and Jerrold Krimsky, and lasted for only twelve performances. Robert Chisholm and Marjorie Dille created the two leading roles, and George Heller was the Street Singer. Because of the production's failure, the piece fell into obscurity in the United States, and it wasn't until Marc Blitzstein's adaptation two decades later that the work found its permanent place in the repertory of American musical theatre. Further, "Mack the Knife," Blitzstein's version of the Street Singer's song "Moritat," became one of the best-known songs in all musical theatre.

Blitzstein's adaptation premiered on June 14, 1952, a part of the Festival of the Creative Arts at Brandeis University. Leonard Bernstein conducted; David Brooks, the leading man of Broadway's *Bloomer Girl* (1944) and *Brigadoon* (1947), was Macheath; and Lotte Lenya recreated her role of Jenny. (Two nights earlier, Bernstein's *Trouble in Tahiti* had premiered at the festival.)

This production led to the successful 1954 Off Broadway revival, which played for ninety-six performances at the Theater de Lys and returned there the following year for a record-breaking run of 2,611 performances (see entry for the return engagement). Lotte Lenya appeared in both productions.

The 1954 production was recorded on MGM Records (LP # 3121; released on CD by Decca Broadway Records [# 012-159-463-2] with a bonus track of Lenya singing "Mack the Knife," accompanied by Blitzstein at the piano), and became the first Off Broadway musical cast album. Technically, it's not a completely original cast album, because during the 1954 run some cast members were replaced by other performers (for example, Leon Lishner, who performed the role of Mr. Peachum on opening night, was succeeded by Martin Wolfson, and it is Wolfson who is heard on the cast recording).

Incidentally, the two Off Broadway productions were springboards for successful theatre and television careers for a number of the original cast members (Jo Sullivan, Beatrice Arthur, Charlotte Rae) and replacement cast members (Jerry Orbach, Ed Asner, Georgia Brown, Estelle Parsons). (And one replacement, Eddie Lawrence, went on to write the book and lyrics for 1965's one-performance-and-out *Kelly*, one of the most famous fiascos in the history of the Broadway musical.) Even established theatre performers appeared in the production during its marathon run, including Pert Kelton, Katharine Sergava, Dolly Haas, and James Mitchell.

In September 1961, three months before the Off Broadway production closed, a tour was mounted with Scott Merrill reprising his role of Macheath and Gypsy Rose Lee playing Jenny. Jane Connell and Richard Verney, who created the roles of Mrs. Peacham and Tiger Brown when *The Threepenny Opera* re-opened in 1955, re-created their roles for the tour. (In order to expand her role, Gypsy Rose Lee was given the Street Singer's song, "Mack the Knife"!) The disastrous tour closed permanently after two weeks of performances, and when asked to comment on the debacle, Gypsy Rose Lee said, "It was a bloodbath."

Strangely enough, while *The Threepenny Opera* has enjoyed three major Broadway revivals, not one has used Blitzstein's iconic adaptation (and, curiously, the Blitzstein translation has never been published). The 1976 revival was adapted by Ralph Manheim and John Willett (Raul Julia and Ellen Green were Macheath and Jenny; see entry for this production's return engagement); the 1989 production by Michael Feingold (Sting and Suzzanne Douglas); and the 2006 production by Wallace Shawn (Alan Cumming and Cyndi Lauper). Only a limited Broadway engagement in 1966 used Blitzstein's version, and this was a puppet version of the musical, produced by the Stockholm Marionette Theatre of Fantasy. A National Youth Music Theatre production played Off Broadway in 1995 (see entry); it's unclear which translation was used for this revival. Of all the Broadway revivals, only the 1976 version was recorded (see entry for this revival's 1977 Off Broadway production).

There have been three film versions of *Die Dreigroschenoper*. The first, filmed in Germany in 1931, was directed by G.W. Pabst and starred Lotte Lenya. The 1964 film version (which must be the most obscure film musical of the last fifty years) used Blitzstein's lyrics, and starred Curt Jurgens and Hildegarde Neff. It was conducted by Samuel Matlowsky, who was the musical director for the 1954 production; and the singing voice of Polly was that of Jo Wilder, who had succeeded Jo Sullivan in the 1955 return engagement (the soundtrack was issued by RCA Victor Records [LP # LOC-1086 and LSO-1086]). The piece was also filmed in 1989 (as *Mack the Knife*) with Raul Julia and Julia Migenes; in this adaptation, some of the lyrics were by Blitzstein (the soundtrack was issued by CBS Records, Inc. [LP # SM-45630]). (Incidentally, throughout his career Samuel Matlowsky's last name was spelled as either Matlowsky or Matlovsky; for consistency's sake, this book uses the former spelling.)

There have been numerous recordings of *The Threepenny Opera*, including one released by London Records (CD # 430-075-2-LH), with Ute Lemper as Polly. A 1994 British revival was recorded by Jay Records (CD # CDJAY-1244), in an English translation by Robert David MacDonald (the lyric translations were by Jeremy Sams). Special Note: For those who complain that the rules for Tony Award eligibility seem to change in order to accomodate the special circumstances of each particular theatre season, note that the 1956 Tony winner for a Best Featured Actress in a Musical was ... Lotte Lenya, for her role of Jenny in Off Broadway's *The Threepenny Opera*. Her Broadway competitors were Rae Allen (for her role of Gloria in Jerry Ross and Richard Adler's *Damn Yankees* [1955]), Pat Carroll (for her roles in the revue *Catch a Star!* [1955]), and Judy Tyler (Suzy in Richard Rodgers and Oscar Hammerstein II's *Pipe Dream* [1955]).

Moreover, for his role of Mack the Knife, Scott Merrill was nominated for Best Featured Actor in a Musical (the winner was Russ Brown for *Damn Yankees* [trivia buffs remember Brown for creating the title role of Don Jose O'Brien in the legendary 1941 Broadway flop *Viva O'Brien*]).

Further, for her roles in the Off Broadway revue *Phoenix '55*, Nancy Walker was nominated for Best Actress in a Musical (the winner was Gwen Vernon for *Damn Yankees*).

1627 The Threepenny Opera (1955).

THEATRE: Theatre de Lys; OPENING DATE: September 20, 1955; PERFORMANCES: 2,611; BOOK: Marc Blitzstein (adapted from the original German by Bertolt Brecht); LYRICS: Marc Blitzstein (adapted from the original German by Bertolt Brecht); MUSIC: Kurt Weill; DIRECTION: Carmen Capalbo; SCENERY: William Pitkin; COSTUMES: "Supervised by" William Pitkin; LIGHTING: Peggy Clark; MUSICAL DIRECTION: Kelly Wyatt; PRODUCERS: Carmen Capalbo and Stanley Chase, in association with Lucille Lortel

CAST—TIGE ANDREWS (Street Singer), LOTTE LENYA* (Jenny), Frederic Downs (Mr. J.J. Peacham), JANE CONNELL (Mrs. Peacham), William Duell* (Fitch), SCOTT MERRILL* (Macheath, a/k/a Mack the Knife), JO SULLIVAN* (Polly Peacham), John Astin* (Readymoney Matt), Eddie Lawrence (Crookfinger Jake), Bernie Fein (Bob the Saw), Joseph Elic (Walt Dreary), Carroll Saint (the Reverend Kimball), RICHARD VERNEY (Tiger Brown), Joan Coburn (Betty), Marion Selee (Molly), Irene Kane (Dolly), Bea Barrett (Coaxer), Rome Smith (Smith), BEATRICE ARTHUR* (Lucy Brown), Albert Valentine (First Constable), Steve Palmer (Second Constable), William Duell (Messenger)

SOURCE—The 1728 opera *The Beggar's Opera* by John Gay.

NOTES—This was the return engagement of the 1954 revival of *The Threepenny Opera* (see entry), and it played for a record-breaking 2,611 performances. The musical numbers in this production were the same as for the 1954 engagement.

* = Denotes those performers who also appeared in the 1954 production. Note the change for costume credit as well as the addition of Lucille Lortel's name as one of the producers.

1628 The Threepenny Opera (1977).

THEATRE: Delacorte Theater/The Public Theater; OPENING DATE: June 28, 1977; PERFORMANCES: 27; BOOK AND LYRICS: Ralph Manheim and John Willett; adapted from the original German by Bertolt Brecht; MUSIC: Kurt Weill; DIRECTION: Richard Foreman; SCENERY: Douglas W. Schmidt; COSTUMES: Theoni V. Aldredge; LIGHTING: Pat Collins; MUSICAL DIRECTION: Stanley Silverman; PRODUCERS: The New York Shakespeare Festival (Joseph Papp, Director)

CAST—Roy Brocksmith (The Ballad Singer), Philip Bosco (Mac the Knife [Macheath]), Ellen Greene (Jenny Towler), Jerome Dempsey (Jonathan Peachum), Tony Azito (Samuel), Ed Zang (Charles Filch), Gretel Cummings (Mrs. Peachum), Ralph Drischell (Matthew), Caroline Kava (Polly Peachum), William Duell (Jake), K.C. Wilson (Bob), Paul Ukena, Jr. (Ned), Robert Schlee (Jimmy), John Ridge (Walt), David Sabin (Tiger Brown), Marc Jordan (Smith), Penelope Bodry (Lucy Brown), Jack Eric Williams (Messenger); Beggars and Policemen (Pendleton Brown, Peter Iacangelo, George McGrath, Art Ostrin, Rick Petrucelli, Craig Rupp, Armin Shimerman, Jack Eric Williams, Ray Xifo); Whores (Barbara Andres, Nancy Campbell, Alexandra Ivanoff, Lisa Kirchner, Mimi Turque)

SOURCE—The 1728 opera *The Beggar's Opera* by John Gay.

The action occurs during the time of Queen Victoria's Coronation ("re-arranged in Brecht's imagination").

The musical was presented in three acts.

ACT ONE—"Ballad of Mac the Knife" (Roy Brocksmith, Tony Azito, Robert Schlee, Jack Eric Williams), "Peachum's Morning Hymn" (Jerome Dempsey), "'No They Can't' Song" (Jerome Dempsey, Gretel Cummings), "Wedding Song for the Less Well-Off" (Gang, Beggars), "The Cannon Song" (Philip Bosco, David Sabin, Gang), "Liebeslied" (Caroline Kava, Philip Bosco), "Barbara Song" (Caroline Kava), First Threepenny Finale: "Concerning the Insecurity of the Human State" (Caroline Kava, Jerome Dempsey)

ACT TWO—"Polly's Lied" (Caroline Kava, Philip Bosco), "Ballad of Sexual Obsession" (Gretel Cummings), "Pirate Jenny" (Ellen Greene), "Ballad of Immoral Earnings" (Ellen Greene, Philip Bosco), "Ballad of Gracious Living" (Philip Bosco), "Jealousy Duet" (Penelope Bodry, Caroline Kava), Second Threepenny Finale: "What Keeps Mankind Alive?" (Philip Bosco, Ellen Greene, Chorus)

ACT THREE—"Song of the Insufficiency of Human Endeavor" (Jerome Dempsey), "Solomon Song" (Ellen Greene), "Call from the Grave" (Philip Bosco), "Ballad in Which Macheath Begs All Men for Forgiveness" (Philip Bosco), Third Threepenny Finale (David Sabin, Marc Jordan, Jack Eric Williams, Gretel Cummings, Jerome Dempsey, Philip Bosco, Penelope Bodry, Ellen Greene, Chorus), "Ballad of Mac the Knife" (reprise) (Roy Brocksmith)

NOTES—This revival of *The Threepenny Opera* played in Central Park after almost a year's run on Broadway, where it had originally opened at the Vivian Beaumont Theatre on May 1, 1976, for 306 performances. For the Broadway production, Raul Julia had played Mack the Knife (Macheath, whose character's name was called Mac the Knife for the Delacorte production), and the cast also included C.K. Alexander (Mr. Peachum), Elizabeth Wilson (Mrs. Peachum), and Blair Brown (Lucy Brown). Many of the Broadway cast members reprised their roles for the Summer 1977 production in Central Park.

The 1976 production was recorded by Columbia Records (LP # PS-34326). The script was published in 1977 by Random House in *Collected Plays, Vol. 2* by Bertolt Brecht, and was also published singly in 1977 by Vintage Books/Random House in a special edition for the Fireside Theatre book club.

For those who collect published libretti, it's worth noting that while book club editions are generally ignored by collectors, there were actually a few scripts published *only* in book club editions (by the Fireside Theatre [later Stage & Screen] book club); thus for a few musicals, the *only* published editions (not including acting editions) are book-club-only titles (such as *Barnum, Nine, A Man of No Importance,* and *Romance Romance* [see entries for the latter two musicals]).

Other translations of *The Threepenny Opera* are no doubt more faithful to Brecht's original German than Marc Blitzstein's adaptation. But the others seem to have fallen into obscurity while Blitzstein's softened but imminently singable and theatrical version remains the most popular (and his translation of "Mack the Knife" continues to be the best version of the iconic song).

For more information about *The Threepenny Opera*, see entries for the 1954 and 1955 productions. Also see entry for a 1995 revival of the work.

This production of *The Threepenny Opera* was Philip Bosco's return to musical theater after a fifteen-year absence. He had earlier appeared in the largely non-singing role of Will Danaher in the 1961 Broadway production of *Donnybrook!* (while his character had no assigned songs, he may have taken part in some of the ensemble singing).

1629 The Threepenny Opera (1995). THEATRE: City Center; OPENING DATE: October 26, 1995; PERFORMANCES: 3; BOOK: Bertolt Brecht; LYRICS: Bertolt Brecht; MUSIC: Kurt Weill; DIRECTION: Mark Pattenden; CHOREOGRAPHY: Wendy Cook, Movement Direction; PRODUCTION DESIGN: Jason Denvir; LIGHTING: Chris Davey; MUSICAL DIRECTION: Alison Berry; PRODUCER: National Youth Music Theatre (Jeremy James Taylor, Artistic Director), supported by Andrew Lloyd Webber

CAST—Nick Dutton and Catherine Simmonds (Ballad Singers, Narrators), Tim Steeden (Jeremiah Peachum), Kate Chesworth (Mrs. Peachum), Kevin Pamplin (Filch), Laurence Taylor (Macheath), Jessica Watson (Polly Peachum), Esther Shanson (Lucy Brown), Jonathan Chesworth (Man of the Mint), James Capewell (Crook Fingered Jake), Barney Dillon (Bob the Saw), Jean-Paul Pfluger (Ned), Delroy Anderson (Jimmy Twitcher), Alex Bourne (Dreary Walter), Matthew Walton (the Reverend Kimball), David Oyelowo (Tiger Brown), Matthew Gough (Smith), Chris Swift (Constable), Tiffany Gore (Jenny Diver), Emma Sharnock (Vixen), Kelly Brett (Dolly), Johanna Hewitt (Coaxer), Carryl Thomas (Brazen), Hong-Van Laffer (Suky Tawdry), Joanna Dunn (Betty), Fiona Finlow (Divine); Beggars, Whores, Policemen (Ensemble): Delroy Atkinson, Alex Bourne, Kelly Brett, James Capewell, Jonathan Chesworth, Kate Chesworth, Barney Dillon, Joanna Dunn, Fiona Finlow, Hong-Van Laffer, David Oyelowo, Jean-Paul Pfluger, Emma Sharnock, Chris Swift, Carryl Thomas, Matthew Walton

The action occurs on the eve of a royal coronation.

NOTES—It's unclear which translation of *The Threepenny Opera* was used for the production, which was part of an American tour by the National Youth Music Theatre, a British company of young actors and musicians in the 17-20 age group. The tour also included the musical *Pendragon* (see entry) in its repertory.

For information on other productions of *The Threepenny Opera*, see entry for the 1954 production.

1630 Thrill Me: The Leopold & Loeb Story. THEATRE: Abingdon Theatre Arts Complex; OPENING DATE: July 16, 2003; PERFORMANCES: Unknown; BOOK: Stephen Dolginoff; LYRICS: Stephen Dolginoff; MUSIC: Stephen Dolginoff; DIRECTION: Martin Charnin; LIGHTING: Thom Weaver, Lighting Consultant; MUSICAL DIRECTION: Gabriel Kahane; PRODUCER: New York Midtown International Theatre Festival

CAST—Christopher Totten (Nathan Leopold), Matthew S. Morris (Richard Loeb)

The action occurs in Chicago in 1924 and at the Joliet Prison Parole Board in 1958.

The musical was presented in one act.

Prelude (Orchestra), "Why" (Christopher Totten), "Everybody Wants Richard" (Christopher Totten), "Nothing Like a Fire" (Matthew S. Morris, Christopher Totten), "A Written Contract" (Matthew S. Morris, Christopher Totten), "Thrill Me" (Christopher Totten, Matthew S. Morris), "The Plan" (Matthew S. Morris, Christopher Totten), "Way Too Far" (Christopher Totten), "Roadster" (Matthew S. Morris), "Superior" (Christopher Totten, Matthew S. Morris), "Ransom Note" (Matthew S. Morris, Christopher Totten), "My Glasses"/"Just Lay Low" (Christopher Totten, Matthew S. Morris), "I'm Trying to Think" (Matthew S. Morris, Christopher Totten), "Keep Your Deal with Me" (Matthew S. Morris, Christopher Totten), "Life Plus 99 Years"/Finale (Christopher Totten, Matthew S. Morris)

NOTES—The intriguing musical *Thrill Me* dealt with Nathan Leopold and Richard Loeb, who murdered a fourteen-year-old boy in 1924; they were defended by Clarence Darrow and escaped capital punishment. Loeb was killed in prison in 1936, and Leopold was paroled in 1958 (he died in 1971).

Thrill Me was one of many stage adaptations of the famous murder case. Patrick Hamilton's 1929 British play *Rope* (as *Rope's End*, the play was seen in New York the same year) was about a crime similar to the Leopold and Loeb case (and was filmed as *Rope* by Alfred Hitchcock in 1948). In 1957, the Broadway play *Compulsion* dealt with the subject (the production apparently used a combination of scripts by both Meyer Levin and Robert Thom), and was later filmed in 1959. In 1985, John Logan's play *Never the Sinner* opened in Chicago; in London in 1990; and finally Off Broadway in 1997. In 1992, *Swoon*, another film about the subject, was released. In 2008, David Henning's self-described docudrama *Dickie and Babe* dealt with the Leopold (Babe) and Loeb (Dickie) case; the play was presented at the Blank Theatre Company's 2nd Stage Theatre in Hollywood. Further, a ballet version (*Chicago '24*) was seen on March 5, 1964, at the Brooklyn Academy of Music when *Hal Grego-Jazz Ballets* played there for one performance. *Chicago '24* was one of four ballets seen during the evening, and it dealt with the "Dickie" Loeb and "Babe" Leopold case; the choreography was by Hal Grego (who also danced the role of "Dickie" Loeb) and the music was by Elmer Bernstein.

The Midtown International Theatre Festival's production of *Thrill Me* was recorded by Original Cast Records (CD # OC-7391). On May 26, 2005, the musical was produced by the York Theatre Company (possibly as an Off Off Broadway presentation) with Matt Bauer as Leopold and Doug Kreeger as Loeb; the production was directed by Michael Rupert, and this too was recorded by Original Cast Records (CD # OC-6158); the York production included a new song, "Afraid" (for Loeb), and was included on the second recording. The final version of the script (which included "Afraid") was published by Dramatists Play Service, Inc., in 2006.

1631 Thunder Knocking on the Door. "A New Musical." THEATRE: Minetta Lane Theatre; OPENING DATE: June 20, 2002; PERFORMANCES: 45; BOOK: Keith Glover; LYRICS: Keb' Mo' and Anderson Edwards; MUSIC: Keb' Mo' and Anderson Edwards (Additional lyrics and music by Keith Glover); DIRECTION: Oskar Eustis; CHOREOGRAPHY: Luis Perez; SCENERY: Eugene Lee; COSTUMES: Toni-Leslie James; LIGHTING: Natasha Katz; MUSICAL DIRECTION: George Caldwell; PRODUCERS: Ted Tulcin and Benjamin Mordecai in association with Mari Nakachi

CAST—LESLIE UGGAMS (Good Sister Dupree), Chuck Cooper (Jaguar Senior, Dregster Dupree), Peter Jay Fernandez (Marvell Thunder), Marva Hicks (Glory Dupree), Michael McElroy (Jaguar Dupree)

The action occurs in Bessemer, Alabama, during Fall 1966.

The musical was presented in two acts.

ACT ONE—Prologue (Company), "This House Is Built" (Company), "(Please) Believe Me" (Chuck Cooper, Leslie Uggams), "Big Money" (Michael McElroy, Leslie Uggams, Marva Hicks, Chuck Cooper), "Hold On" (Chuck Cooper, Leslie Uggams, Marva Hicks, Michael McElroy), "Stranger Blues" (Peter Jay Fernandez, Marva Hicks, Leslie Uggams), "Hurt Somebody" (Michael McElroy,

Chuck Cooper, Peter Jay Fernandez), "See Through Me" (Peter Jay Fernandez, Marva Hicks)

ACT TWO—"Way Down on the Inside" (Michael McElroy), "I'm Back" (Marva Hicks), "I Wish I Knew" (Marva Hicks, Leslie Uggams), "Motor Scooter" (Chuck Cooper, Michael McElroy), "Even When You Win, You Sometimes Lose" (Peter Jay Fernandez), "Rainmaker" (Marva Hicks, Peter Jay Fernandez), "That Ain't Right (Cuttin' Contest)" (Marva Hicks, Peter Jay Fernandez, Company), "Take on the Road" (Michael McElroy, Peter Jay Fernandez, Chuck Cooper), "Willing to Go" (Leslie Uggams), "Movin' On" (Marva Hicks, Company)

NOTES—*Thunder Knocking on the Door*, a kind of fairy tale set in Alabama in 1966, dealt with a Black family and their dealings with a supernatural being. The Dupree family encounters Marvell Thunder, a mythic (and musical) figure who was once outplayed on the guitar by one of the late Dupree family members.

Bruce Weber in the *New York Times* felt the alternately "overwritten" and "underthought" book was part sitcom humor, part "chitlins circuit," and part "flowery romanticism." The inconsistency of the musical's tone and its lack of character development led to an evening of "wasted opportunity," and Weber concluded there wasn't "much lightning to go with this *Thunder*." However, he singled out a few songs, including "See Through Me," "Rainmaker," and "Believe Me," the latter a "flirty boogie woogie" for Leslie Uggams and Chuck Cooper.

The musical had first been produced at the Alabama Shakespeare Festival on October 4, 1996, and then was later seen at Arena Stage in Washington, D.C., on November 6, 1998. Songs heard in these productions which weren't used in New York were "Guitar Story" (possibly "Hold On" in New York), "I Wish I Knew," "Born with the Blues," "I Know What You Want," and "Thinking About It."

The musical was recorded by DLP Records, but as of this writing has not been released. In 2002, a promotional "not for sale" CD was made available which included four songs from the score ("Please Believe Me" [performed by Chuck Cooper and Leslie Uggams], "See Through Me" [Peter Jay Fernandez and Marva Hicks], "That Ain't Right" [Peter Jay Fernandez and Marva Hicks], and "Movin' On" [Marva Hicks and Company]).

1632 Thwak. THEATRE: Minetta Lane Theatre; OPENING DATE: June 6, 1999; PERFORMANCES: 206; CREATED BY David Collins and Shane Dundas (The Umbilical Brothers); DIRECTION: Philip William McKinley; SCENERY: Bradley J. Mayer; LIGHTING: Josh Monroe; PRODUCERS: John Bard Manulis and Liz Heller; Metropolitan Entertainment Group (John Scher and Jeff Rowland); Arnold Engelman, Co-Producer

CAST—David Collins, Shane Dundas

The revue was presented in one act.

NOTES—The Off Broadway *Thwak* might easily be confused with the Off Off Broadway *Squonk* (see entry), or perhaps it is *Squonk* which is confused with *Thwak*. Both were performance pieces which opened within a few days of one other.

Like *Squonk*, *Thwak* was first seen Off Off Broadway (at the Westbeth Theatre Center on March 18, 1999), but while *Thwak* transferred to Off Broadway, *Squonk* bypassed that venue and went straight to Broadway (where it squonked out after thirty-two performances).

Thwak was described in *The Best Plays of 1999-2000* as an evening of "New Vaudeville clowning with acrobatics and audio presentations." In reviewing the work for its Westbeth production, Peter Marks in the *New York Times* found the one-hour revue a "wildly funny, wildly creative" piece of "inspired anarchy." Marks reported that throughout the evening the two-man cast (David Collins and Shane Dundas, a/k/a The Umbilical Brothers) used the well-worn comic shtick of two characters, one of whom is smarter than the other. The comic moments included spoofs of mimes, badly dubbed martial-arts movies, and "European visual comedy" (the joke being that two clueless German "comedians" lack even the most elementary notion of what constitutes comedy). As *Thwak!*, the performance piece was briefly revived at the New Victory Theatre on April 6, 2003.

1633 Ti-Jean and His Brothers. THEATRE: Delacorte Theatre; OPENING DATE: July 20, 1972; PERFORMANCES: 15; BOOK: Derek Walcott; LYRICS: Derek Walcott and Andre Tanker; MUSIC: Andre Tanker; additional dance music Patti Brown and George Butcher; DIRECTION: Derek Walcott; CHOREOGRAPHY: George Faison; SCENERY: Edward Burbridge; COSTUMES: Theoni V. Aldredge; LIGHTING: Martin Aronstein; MUSICAL DIRECTION: Patti Brown; PRODUCER: The New York Shakespeare Festival (Joseph Papp, Producer) in association with the City of New York

CAST—Madge Sinclair (Mother), Dennis Hines (Ti-Jean), Hamilton Parris (Frog), Elaine R. Graham (Cricket), Diane Bivens (Bird), Deborah (Debbie) Allen (Firefly), Clebert Ford (Gros-Jean), Leon Morenzie (Mi-Jean), Albert Laveau (Devil, Papa Bois, Planter), Stephannie Hampton Howard (Bolom), Renee Rose (Goat); Dancers (Members of the George Faison Universal Dance Experience): Deborah (Debbie) Allen, Gary Deloatch, Dyane Harvey, Eugene Little, Edward Love, Renee Rose, Jason Taylor, Evelyn Thomas; Singers: Margie Barnes, John Barracuda, Gail Boggs, Elaine R. Graham, Sharon Redd

The action occurs on an island in the West Indies.

The musical was presented in two acts.

NOTES—The musical *Ti-Jean and His Brothers* was presented free in Central Park's Delacorte Theatre. After the production closed there, it toured parks and playgrounds throughout the five boroughs of New York City beginning on August 9, 1972, for a total of seventeen performances.

The folk musical was a fable of the affirmation of love and hope against the forces of the evil. In particular, the title character (who apparently symbolized purity and innocence) and his brothers (one representing the physical world, the other the intellectual) encounter the devil. Clive Barnes in the *New York Times* noted the message of Derek Walcott's fable was too "emblematic" in its themes, and he felt the evening was "diluted" and lacked humanity. He mentioned the work might have been more successful if it had included more music, indicating an expanded score might have helped to shape the elements of fantasy and symbolism in Walcott's fable.

Ti-Jean and His Brothers was first seen at the Little Carib Theatre, Port of Spain, Trinidad, in 1958; the play was revived by the Trinidad Theatre Workshop in 1970, and this version included music by Andre Tanker.

The script was published by Farrar, Straus and Giroux in Derek Walcott's 1970 collection *Dream on Monkey Mountain and Other Plays*.

1634 tick, tick...BOOM! "A Musical." THEATRE: Jane Street Theatre; OPENING DATE: June 13, 2001; PERFORMANCES: 215; BOOK: Jonathan Larson; David Auburn, Script Consultant; LYRICS: Jonathan Larson; MUSIC: Jonathan Larson; DIRECTION: Scott Schwartz; CHOREOGRAPHY: Christopher Galletti; SCENERY: Anna Louizos; COSTUMES: David Zinn; LIGHTING: Kenneth Posner; MUSICAL DIRECTION: Stephen Oremus; PRODUCERS: Victoria Leacock, Robyn Goodman, Dede Harris, Lorie Cowen Levy, and Beth Smith; Ruth and Stephen Hendel, Stephen Semlitz, and Cathy Glaser, Associate Producers

CAST—Raul Esparza (Jonathan), Jerry Dixon (Michael), Amy Spangler (Susan, Karessa)

The action occurs in 1990 on "the edge of Soho."

The revue was presented in one act.

MUSICAL NUMBERS—"30/90" (Raul Esparza), "Green Green Dress" (Raul Esparza, Amy Spangler), "Johnny Can't Decide" (Raul Esparza, Amy Spangler, Jerry Dixon), "Sunday" (Raul Esparza, Diner Patrons [Jerry Dixon, Amy Spangler]), "No More" (Jerry Dixon, Raul Esparza), "Therapy" (Raul Esparza, Amy Spangler), "Play Game" (Raul Esparza), "Real Life" (Jerry Dixon), "Sugar" (Raul Esparza, 'Karessa' [Amy Spangler], Counter Guy [Jerry Dixon]), "See Her Smile" (Raul Esparza, Amy Spangler), "Come to Your Senses" ('Karessa' [Amy Spangler]), "Why" (Raul Esparza), "30/90" (reprise) (Raul Esparza), "Louder Than Words" (Raul Esparza, Jerry Dixon, Amy Spangler)

NOTES—At the time of his sudden death in 1996, Jonathan Larsen was an obscure performer-lyricist-composer and his musical *Rent* (see entry) was unknown. When *tick, tick...BOOM!* opened in 2001, *Rent* had just begun its sixth year on Broadway and Larson's untimely death had become part of theatrical folklore. *tick* was a revue-like evening of Larson's songs which were, according to *The Best Plays of 2000-2002*, "stitched together" by David Auburn from solo shows performed by Larson. Ben Brantley in the *New York Times* remarked that when viewed as a precursor to *Rent, tick, tick...BOOM!* offered "gentle fascination." But he also noted the work consisted of "self-reflective doodlings" and the thin story line exuded "familiarity." But Brantley singled out a number of songs, including "Come to Your Senses" (originally written for *Superbia*), which he felt had an "all-cylinders musical charge seldom evident" for most of the evening. During the run of the revue, "Play Game" was deleted, and didn't appear on the cast recording, which was released by RCA Victor Records (CD # 09026-63862-2). However, the CD included a bonus track of Larson singing "Boho Days" (*Boho Days* and *30/90* were earlier titles for *tick*). The script was published by Applause Theatre & Cinema Books in 2009.

1635 Tickles by Tucholsky. "A Cabaret Musical." THEATRE: Theatre Four; OPENING DATE: April 26, 1976; PERFORMANCES: 16; SKETCHES: Kurt Tucholsky; translated by Harold Poor; LYRICS: Kurt Tucholsky; translated by Louis Golden; MUSIC: Kurt Tucholsky; DIRECTION: Moni Yakim; SCENERY: Don Jensen; COSTUMES: Christina Giannini; LIGHTING: Spencer Mosse; MUSICAL DIRECTION: Wolfgang Knittel; PRODUCERS: Norman Stephens and Primavera Productions Ltd. in association with Max Weitzenhoffer

CAST—Helen Gallagher, Joe Masiell, Jana Robbins, Joseph Neal, Jerry Jarrett

The revue was presented in two acts.

ACT ONE—"The Song of Indifference" (Helen Gallagher), "Rising Expectations" (Company), "Tickles" (Jana Robbins), "Christmas Shopping" (Helen Gallagher, Joe Masiell, Jerry Jarrett), "Brown-Shirted Cowboy" (Joseph Neal), "German Evening" (Jerry Jarrett), "Transition" (Helen Gallagher), "Lovers" (Joe Masiell, Jana Robbins), "Waldemar" (Joseph Neal, Jana Robbins), "The Compromise Soft Shoe" (Helen Gallagher, Joe Masiell), "Come Avec!" (Jana Robbins, Company), "How to Get Rich" (Joseph Neal), "The King's Regiment" (Company), "Lullaby" (Helen Gallagher), "Verdun" (Joe Maisell), "War Against War" (Joe Maisell), "Waiting" (Helen Gallagher), "Follow Schmidt" (Jerry Jarrett, Company)

ACT TWO—"Anna Louisa" (Joe Masiell), "Lamplighters" (Jana Robbins, Jerry Jarrett, Joseph Neal), "Heartbeat" (Helen Gallagher), "It's Your

Turn" (Jerry Jarrett, Company), "25 Points" (Joseph Neal, Company), "Christmas Song" (Joe Masiell), "I'm Out" (Joe Masiell, Company), "General! General!" (Helen Gallagher), "To You I Gave My All" (Jana Robbins), "How That Things Are Rough" (Jerry Jarrett), "Testimony" (Joseph Neal), "Over the Trenches" (Joe Maisell, Company), "The Song of Indifference" (reprise) (Helen Gallagher), Epilogue (Company)

NOTES—Kurt Tucholsky (1890-1935) wrote material for Berlin Cabaret during the 1920s and the early 1930s; his work was a mixture of satire as well as social and political protest. Because he was Jewish, he fled Nazi Germany; in 1935 he committed suicide.

The sketches and songs heard in *Tickles by Tucholsky* were written between 1914 and 1932, and the revue represented Tucholsky's first major New York hearing. But his name and his work were too obscure for most theatregoers, and as a result the revue lasted only two weeks.

Mel Gussow in the *New York Times* noted the evening began with Helen Gallagher singing "The Song of Indifference," and he felt if the rest of the material had matched the "pungency" of this "sardonic" number, *Tickles by Tucholsky* would have been a "scorchingly evocative evening." Gussow reported that when the revue was tough and evoked the period of the 1920s and 1930s, it was at its best; but all too often the evening revolved around songs concerning "bereaved mothers and sacrificed children," and these sentimental "baby numbers" undercut the evening's effectiveness.

Gussow also reported that the revue seemed to have had its genesis in an earlier version by Louis Golden and Harry Poor called *Tucholsky!*, which had been produced at Brandeis University.

During the same period, another revue visited the era of Berlin Cabaret, and it too included songs by Kurt Tucholsky; see entry for *An Evening with Wolfgang Roth*.

Tickles by Tucholsky was Broadway legend Helen Gallagher's first Off Broadway appearance, and was yet another visit by Joe Masiell, who seemed to appear annually in either an Off Broadway revue or musical.

1636 The Tiger Rag. "A Musical Chronicle." THEATRE: Cherry Lane Theatre; OPENING DATE: February 16, 1961; PERFORMANCES: 14; BOOK: Seyril Schochen; LYRICS: Seyril Schochen; MUSIC: Kenneth Gaburo; DIRECTION: Ella Gerber; CHOREOGRAPHY: Peter Conlow; SCENERY: Robert Soule; COSTUMES: Bobb Nichols; LIGHTING: Jules Fisher; MUSICAL DIRECTION: Milton Setzer; PRODUCERS: Ira Productions and Lorin Ellington Price

CAST—Logan Ramsey (Crease), Brennan Moore (Lewis Cadman), Carlton Colyer (The Salvation Kid), Patricia Roe (Cassie McGilly), Bill Tierney (Mr. Houlighan, Old Beggar), Delos Smith (Mr. Paddy), Arthur Anderson (Mr. O'Toole, Papa Cadman, Allykan, Butler), Walter Blocher, Jr. (Mr. Houhy, Uncle Fillmore Cadman), Susan Perkins (Aunt Priscilla Cadman, Debutante, Dazzler), Inia Garbiel (Aunt Miranda Cadman, Debutante, Dazzler), Charles D. Tomlinson (Uncle Fawcett Cadman, Juvenile, Reporter), Nancy Andrews (Mother Cadman, Mme. Spig-Eye, Irish Washerwoman), John Loose (Messenger Boy, Juvenile, Reporter), Nancy Saloman (Passerby, Debutante, Dazzler), Joe Herron (Newspaper Boy, Juvenile, Reporter), Joan Anderson (Nan), Richard Mazza (Mr. Scream, Juvenile, Reporter), Dodie Marshall (Debutante, Dazzler), Jane Ross (Debutante, Dazzler), Jean Stringfellow (Debutante, Dazzler), Elaine Tara (Debutante, Dazzler), Judy Tara (Debutante, Dazzler), Jon Frosher (Juvenile, Reporter), Richard Krisher (Juvenile, Reporter), Gerald Plano (Juvenile, Reporter)
The action occurs in the 1920s, 1930s, and 1940s.

MUSICAL NUMBERS (division of acts and song assignments unknown; the songs are listed in performance order)—"We Were Born by Chance," "Cheerio, Old Boys," "Flirtation Waltz," "Honeysuckle Vine," "Flowery Waltz," "Travelling Song," "Razz-Me-Tazz-Jazz," "Tiger Rag Blues," "What Is Good for Depression," "Apache," "Slewfoot Shuffle," "Rhumba," "Tango," "Irish Washerwoman's Lament," "My Father Was a Peculiar Man"

NOTES—*The Tiger Rag* may well be one of the most ambitious musicals of its era, on the level of *The Golden Apple* (see entry) in its daring and its scope. *The Burns Mantle Yearbook/The Best Plays of 1960-1961* described it as "a modern parallel of the Oedipus legend with a touch of *Finnegan's Wake* thrown in"; Howard Taubman in the *New York Times* felt the musical would have startled Sophocles as well as Freud, and praised the work as "ambitious and bizarre" in its reimagination of the Oedipus legend as a series of vaudeville turns set to songs evocative of the 1920s, 1930s, and 1940s. Taubman found a "somber glitter" to the musical, and hailed Kenneth Gaburo's sophisticated score, an amalgam of "smooth waltzes, dark blues and teasing shuffle, rhumba and tango." But the public wouldn't come, and what is possibly one of the most daring and richly melodic works of musical theatre was gone in two weeks.

The Tiger Rag opened in an era when Off Broadway musicals could be produced for between ten and twenty thousand dollars (a typical Broadway musical of the era cost approximately $300,000). When audiences went to an Off Broadway show, they expected "small." What's notable about a musical such as *The Tiger Rag* is that by today's standards it is *big*. Broadway musicals now often have casts of no more than ten performers; *The Tiger Rag* had no less than twenty-five in the cast!

1637 Time and Again. THEATRE: City Center Stage II/Manhattan Theatre Club; OPENING DATE: January 30, 2001; PERFORMANCES: 24; BOOK: Jack Viertel; additional story material by James Hart; LYRICS: Walter Edgar Kennon; MUSIC: Walter Edgar Kennon; DIRECTION: Susan H. Schulman; CHOREOGRAPHY: Rob Ashford; SCENERY: Derek McLane; COSTUMES: Catherine Zuber; LIGHTING: Ken Billington; MUSICAL DIRECTION: Kevin Stites; PRODUCER: The Manhattan Theatre Club (Lynne Meadow, Artistic Director; Barry Grove, Executive Producer)

CAST—Melissa Rain Anderson (Bessie), Ann Arvia (Mrs. Carmody), Laura Benanti (Julia), Lewis Cleale (Si Morley), Jeff Edgerton (Felix), Eric Michael Gillett (Mr. Carmody), Gregg Goodbrod (Young Dr. Danziger), Christopher Innvar (Jake Pickering), Patricia Kilgarriff (Aunt Evie), Joseph Kolinski (Trolleyman), George Masswohl (Harriman), David McCallum (Dr. Danziger), Julia Murney (Kate), Amy Walsh (Clarissa), Lauren Ward (Emily)

SOURCE—The 1970 novel *Time and Again* by Jack Finney.

The action occurs in the present and in the New York City of 1882.

The musical was presented in two acts (not all song assignments known).

ACT ONE—"Standing in the Middle of the Road," "At the Theatre," "Who Would Have Thought It?" (Lewis Cleale, Company), "She Dies" (Lewis Cleale), "The Lady in the Harbor," "Carrara Marble" (Christopher Innvar, Eric Michael Gillett), "The Music of Love," "Who Are You Anyway?" (Laura Benanti, Julia Murney), "What of Love?" (Laura Benanti), "For Those You Love" (Joseph Kolinski, Lewis Cleale)

ACT TWO—"The Marrying Kind," "The Fire," "Time and Time Again" (Lewis Cleale, Laura Benanti), "The Right Look" (Julia Murney), "I Know This House" (Laura Benanti), Finale

NOTES—The musical *Time and Again* was based on Jack Finney's 1970 romantic science-fiction cult novel of the same name, and it dealt with a young man who is able to transport himself from the present day to the New York City of the 1880s. Once he is living in the past, he encounters both romance and intrigue.

Despite the novel's popularity, the musical never caught on (and while the book seems a natural for the screen, it's never been filmed). Ben Brantley in the *New York Times* found the evening "static and passionless," lacking "any genuine sense of wonder." He singled out a few songs, including "Who Are You Anyway?," "The Right Look," and "She Dies," the latter offering "an unexpected inkling of wit" in its observation that the heroine of the piece was dead long before the hero was even born.

A recording of the score was privately distributed.

The musical was first produced at the Old Globe Theatre in San Diego on May 4, 1996; Howard McGillin was Sy, Rebecca Luker, Julia, and Jessica Molaskey, Kate (the cast also included George Dvorsky, William Parry, Jacquelyn Piro, KT Sullivan, John Leslie Wolfe, and Joseph Kolinksi [the latter reprised his role of the Trolleyman for the New York production]); the direction was by Jack O'Brien, and Kathleen Marshall choreographed. Numbers from this production which weren't used in the New York version were "Quodlibet," "Einstein's Proposition," "When Mama Met Papa," "Monday Morning in the Mirror," "The Training," "Fairy-Tale Life," "Si's Soliloquy," "You're Mine," "Modern Romance," "The Chase," "It's Here," and "Si's Dilemma." In 1995, Finney wrote from *Time to Time*, a sequel to the original novel.

1638 Time and the Wind. "A New York Musical Revue." THEATRE: John Houseman Theatre; OPENING DATE: July 27, 1995; PERFORMANCES: 27; LYRICS: Norman Matlock; MUSIC: Galt MacDermot; DIRECTION: Louis Johnson; CHOREOGRAPHY: Louis Johnson; COSTUMES: Bernard Johnson; LIGHTING: Deborah Constantine; MUSICAL DIRECTION: Galt MacDermot; PRODUCERS: Eric Krebs and John Houseman Theatre Center in association with AMAS Musical Theatre

CAST—Johnetta Alston, Russell Brown, Carol Denise, Suzanne Griffin, Carl Hall, Chris Jackson

The action occurs in New York City.

The musical was presented in two acts (division of acts and song assignments unknown).

MUSICAL NUMBERS—"Time and the Wind," "Mais Qui," "I Came to Town," "Gentle Rain," "By the Time I Forget Her," "Now I Am Ready (Flustered)," "My Key Don't Fit the Lock," "I Am Not Gone," "There Are Times," "Should I Tell Him," "If What I Saw," "They Didn't Ask," "Quittin' Time," "What Can I Say," "I've Seen People Like Them Before," "Ah, It's Love," "When You Love Really," "Tell Her You Care," "Send Me You," "Funky Dance," "When I Was a Child," "Level with You," "I Was Taught to Love," "Flowers for Her Hair," "What You Looked Like," "I Love You," "True Love's Hand," "Wanted to Dine," "There Are Girls," "Goodbye," "According to Plan," Finale

NOTES—Galt MacDermot's Off Off Broadway musical *Time and the Wind* was a song cycle of sorts about life and relationships in New York City, specifically among three couples.

Stephen Holden in the *New York Times* noted that the self-described "New York Musical Revue" didn't especially deal with urban living; in fact, the revue lacked a point of view. Further, the actors had no characters to play. But while Holden found the lyrics "clumsy and superficial" ("nothing coherent is communicated"), he liked MacDermot's music, which made "smooth sidetracks" into tango, pop reggae, and 1950s-styled rock-and roll.

1639 Time, Gentlemen Please! (Ridgeway's Late Joys). THEATRE: Strollers Theatre-Club; OPENING DATE: November 4, 1961; PERFORMANCES: 336; SONGS: By various lyricists and composers; DIRECTION: Fred Stone; based on original direction by Don Gemmell (for London); CHOREOGRAPHY: Tony Bateman; SCENERY: Thea Neu; COSTUMES: Reginald Woolley; LIGHTING: Victor Gabriel Junquera; MUSICAL DIRECTION: Peter Greenwell; PRODUCERS: John Krimsky and The Players Theatre of London

CAST—Fred Stone (Chairman), Joan Sterndale Bennett, Sheila Bernette, Tony Bateman, Margaret Burton, Archie Harradine, Jean Rayner, Kyra Vayne, Geoffrey Webb, Jerry Terheyden

The revue was presented in three acts.

ACT ONE—"Jolly Good Luck to the Girl Who Loves a Soldier" (Tony Bateman, Margaret Burton, Geoffrey Webb), "Daddy Wouldn't Buy Me a Bow-Wow" (Sheila Bernette), "Captain Gingah" (Archie Harradine), "Just Like the Ivy I'll Cling to You" (Joan Sterdale Bennett), "Ernani! Ernani! Involami" (from 1844 opera *Ernani* by Giuseppe Verdi) (Kyra Vayne), "The Medium" (Fred Stone)

ACT TWO—"Gay Bohemia" (Margaret Burton), "Marble Arch to Leicester Square" (Joan Sterndale Bennett, with Tony Bateman, Geoffrey Webb), "Once Bit, Twice Shy" (Sheila Bernette), "The Bells" (Tony Bateman), "At the Seaside" (Company)

ACT THREE—"Who Were You with Last Night?" (Tony Bateman, Joan Rayner, Geoffrey Webb), "Little Yellow Bird" (Joan Sterndale Bennett), "Miss Julia" (Archie Harradine), "The Honeysuckle and the Bee" (Margaret Burton), "O Se Saoeste" (from 1910 opera *La Fauciulla del West* [*The Girl of the Golden West*] by Giacomo Puccini) (Kyra Vayne), "The Shooting of Dan McGrew" (Company), Chairman's Remarks and Finale

NOTES—The program for *Time, Gentlemen Please! (Ridgeway's Late Joys)* noted that the numbers in the revue would occasionally change.

From a program note: "For a quarter of a century, Players Theatre productions have appeared under the title of 'Ridgeway's Late Joys.' This title was a joking reference beginning with 'Evans' Song and Supper Rooms' in the early 19th Century. Evans had taken over the premises from a man named Joy. Peter Ridgeway was co-founder of the Players Theatre in 1937; hence 'Ridgeway's Late Joys.' 'Time, Gentlemen Please!' is the closing announcement for English pubs."

Since the late 1930s, the Players Club had been offering evenings of Victorian music hall turns, and with *Time, Gentlemen Please!* New Yorkers had the chance to sample a typical evening at a Players Club performance. After a run of two months, the first edition closed (on January 14, 1962), and on January 16 a second edition of the revue opened (see entry). The run of 336 performances represents the total number of performances for both editions. In the early 1950s, the Players Club decided to expand their repertoire by producing original musicals, the first of which was the long-running hit *The Boy Friend* (1953; see entry for Off Broadway production).

Milton Esterow in the *New York Times* found the revue "gay and saucy," a delightful evening of British "hit parade" songs from 1820-1906. He further noted that the Victorian evening of music hall entertainment included comic sequences and even a demonstration in the art of hand bell-ringing, all presided over by Fred Stone, the "chairman" of the revue who said he was bringing culture to "these occasionally United States." Esterow reported that admission cost $4.60, not including dinner (audiences could dine while they watched the show). He concluded his review by noting that the closing call ("Time, Gentlemen Please!") came all too soon for the audience. Incidentally, the pianist for the New York production of *Time, Gentlemen Please!* was Peter Greenwell, a composer of British musicals, including *The Crooked Road* (1959), which was produced under the aegis of the Players Club. Greenwell's score for *The Crooked Road* is one of the best ever written for the London musical stage. The Strollers Theatre-Club was the site of the former El Morocco nightclub.

1640 Time, Gentlemen Please! (Second Edition). THEATRE: Strollers Theatre-Club; OPENING DATE: January 16, 1962; PERFORMANCES: 336; SONGS: By various lyricists and composers; DIRECTION: Fred Stone; based on original direction by Don Gemmell (for London); CHOREOGRAPHY: Tony Bateman; SCENERY: Thea Neu; Strollers Theatre-Club décor designed by George Dunkel; COSTUMES: Reginald Woolley and James Boyce; LIGHTING: Not Credited (probably Victor Gabriel Junquera); MUSICAL DIRECTION: Fred Silver; PRODUCERS: John Krimsky and The Players Theater of London

CAST—Fred Stone (Chairman), Joan Sterndale Bennett, Sheila Bernette, Tony Bateman, Jerry Terheyden, Patricia Kelly, Archie Harradine, Margaret Burton, Jean Rayner, Geoffrey Webb

The revue was presented in two acts; the program indicated the songs in the production would be selected from the following (song assignments unknown): "Let's All Go to the Strand," "She Was Poor, But She Was Honest," "Silvery Moon," "Please Sell No More Drink to My Father," "Oh, Mr. Porter!," "Hello, Hello, Who's Your Lady Friend?," "A Pretty Pink Petty from Peter," "I'll Be Your Sweetheart," "Li Fang Fu," "Rap, Rap, Rap," "Immensikoff," "The Keys of Heaven," "Who Were You with Last Night?," "The Girl on the Stairs," "Jolly Good Luck to the Girl Who Loves a Soldier," "Just Like the Ivy I'll Cling to You," "Once Bit, Twice Shy," "The Wonderful Musician," "Miss Julia," "The Shooting of Dan McGrew," "Yip-I-Addy," "Captain Gingah," "Boating Girls," "In the Twi-Twi-Twilight," "If I Were Not Upon the Stage," "Put on Your Ta-Ta, Little Girl," "A Bird in a Gilded Cage," "And the Leaves Began To Fall," "The Ugly Duckling," "The Walrus and the Carpenter," "Rum-Tiddly-Um-Tum-Tay," "Hold Your Hand Out, Naughty Boy," "Gay Bohemia," "The Honeysuckle and the Bee," "At the Seaside," "Daddy Wouldn't Buy Me a Bow-Wow," "Marble Arch to Leicester Square," "The Bells," "Pretty Lips," "The Man Who Broke the Bank at Monte Carlo," "Little Yellow Bird," "The Polka and the Choir Boy," "Jane from Maiden Lane"

NOTES—Many songs in *Time, Gentlemen Please!* were carried over from the first edition of the revue (see separate entry); the two editions had a combined run of 336 performances.

1641 Times and Appetites of Toulouse-Lautrec. THEATRE: American Place Theatre; OPENING DATE: November 29, 1985; PERFORMANCES: 18; PLAY: Jeff Wanhel; LYRICS: Michael Feingold, based on French originals (see song list for names of French lyricists); MUSIC: See song list for credits; DIRECTION: John Ferraro; Bill Irwin, Circus and Clown Consultant; CHOREOGRAPHY: Priscilla Lopez; SCENERY: John Arnone; COSTUMES: Edi Giguere; LIGHTING: Stephen Strawbridge; MUSICAL DIRECTION: Russell Walden; PRODUCER: American Place Theatre (Wynn Handman, Director; Julia Miles, Associate Director)

CAST—Lonny Price (The Count Henri de Toulouse-Lautrec Monfa), Lezlie Dalton (Mamie, Dead Lady, Sewer-Grating, Mother Guilbert. Mathilde Tarquint d'Or), MacIntyre Dixon (Dr. Bourges, Pere Abbe, Dogmouth, Ducarre, A Doctor, Critic, Annoucer), Ron Faber (The Count Alphonse de Toulouse-Lautrec Monfa, Maurice Joyant, Vincent Van Gogh, Puffy Fellow, Olier, Lauradour), Susanna Frazer (Jane Avril, The Clowness Cha-U-Kao, Little Girl, Whore), June Gable (Yvette Guilbert, The Countess Adele Tapie de Celeyran, Something Fancy, Nini Leg-in-the-Air), Judith Hoag (Mireille, Jeanne d'Armagnac, Love-Tomato), Nicholas Kepros (Dr. Senelaigne, Jean Lorrain, Fernan Cormon, High-Class, Cheret, Tourist), Priscilla Lopez (La Goulue, Paulette), David Purdham (Aristide Bruant, Emile Bernard, Critic, Achille), Rocco Sisto (Dr. Gabriel Tapie de Celeyran, Valentin DeSosse ["The Boneless Wonder"], Louis Anquetin, Neighbor Boy, Critic), Carl Zutz (Clown, Announcer)

SOURCE—The life of Henri Toulouse-Lautrec (1864-1901).

The action occurs from November 24, 1864, to September 9, 1901, in Albi, Paris (especially Montmartre), and Chateau St. James (a lunatic asylum outside Paris).

The play with music was presented in two acts.

ACT ONE—"Freckled Fanny (Nini Peau d'Chien)" (original French lyric by Aristide Bruant, music by Aristide Bruant) (David Purdham), "Phony Jo (Le Bluffeur)" (original French lyric by Georgius, music by H. Poussique) (David Purdham), "In Saint-Lazare (A St.-Lazare)" (original French lyric by Aristide Bruant, music by Aristide Bruant) (David Purdham), "Can-Can" (dance) ("En Rev'nant de la Revue" was music used for the dance; lyric and music by L.-C. Desormes) (Priscilla Lopez, Rocco Sisto, Moulin Rouge Dancers), "A Little Anisette (Mon Anisette)" (original French lyric by L. Evrard, music by L. Evrard) (Priscilla Lopez, Rocco Sisto)

ACT TWO—"Under a Bridge at Night (Sous le Ponts de Paris)" (original French lyric by Rodor, music by Vincent Scotto) (Priscilla Lopez), "Woman (La Femme)" (original French lyric by Jules Laforgue, music by Waldteufel) (June Gable), "Madame Arthur" (original French lyric by Paul de Kock, music by Yvette Guilbert) (June Gable), "It's Not as Good as Love (Tout ca Vaut pas l'Amour)" (original French lyric by H. Trebitsch, music by Perpignan) (David Purdham, June Gable), "Mademoiselle de Paris" (original French lyric by Henri Contet, music by Paul Durand) (June Gable), "Under a Bridge at Night" (reprise) (David Purdham, June Gable), "Along the Seine (Rodeuse de Berges)" (original French lyric by Aristide Bruant, music by Aristide Bruant)

NOTES—After the success of Stephen Sondheim's *Sunday in the Park with George* in 1984 (see entry), it was probably inevitable that other French painters would become the subjects of new musicals. Sure enough, *Times and Appetites of Toulouse-Lautrec* opened the following year, but rather than using new music, the work offered authentic music of Toulouse-Lautrec's period (but with new lyrics by Michael Feingold). The script was published by Dramatists Play Service, Inc., in 1986.

On October 26, 2004, *The Highest Yellow*, a musical about Vincent Van Gogh, opened at the Signature Theatre in Arlington, Virginia. The lyrics and music were by Michael John LaChiusa, and Marc Kudisch was Van Gogh (the cast also included Jason Danieley and Judy Kuhn).

See entry for *Toulouse*, an earlier musical about Toulouse-Lautrec, which opened Off Off Broadway on September 14, 1981, at the Ukranian Hall for twelve performances. The book, lyrics, and music were by Ronnie Britton. Moreover, Off Off Broadway offered *Lautrec*, which opened on July 2, 1984, at the Riverwest Theatre for twenty performances; written by Brent Collins, the play included music by Scott Johnson; Collins played the title role, and the cast of characters included Vincent Van Gogh (performed by Robert Coles). In 2004, Toulouse-Lautrec was a central figure in Martha Clarke's *Belle Epoque* (see entry); for this production, Toulouse-Lautrec was portrayed by Mark Povinelli; further, the lyric translations for the songs in *Belle Epoque* were again by Michael Feingold.

There have been two London musicals about Toulouse-Lautrec. On April 18, 1974, *Bordello* opened at the Queen's Theatre for forty-one performances; the book was by Julian More, the lyrics by More and Bernard Spiro, and the music by Al Frisch (Henry Woolf was Toulouse-Lautrec). The cast recording was released by Rescued from Oblivion Records (LP # RFO-103). On April 6, 2000, *Lautrec* opened at the Shaftesbury Theatre; the lyrics and music were by Charles Aznavour (English lyrics by Dee Shipman), and Sevan Stephan played the title role.

Further, *Jane Avril*, a non-musical about one of Toulouse-Lautrec's models, opened Off Broadway at the Provincetown Playhouse on June 22, 1982, for forty performances; written by Jane Marla Robbins (who also performed the title role), the play included among its cast of characters Toulouse-Lautrec (performed by Kevin O'Connor, who had played another painter, Gauguin, in *Gauguin in Tahiti* [see entry]).

A number of other musicals (and plays) were based on the lives of painters; for more information, see entry for *Gauguin in Tahiti.*

1642 Timothy Gray's Taboo Revue

NOTES— See entry for *Taboo Revue.*

1643 Tintypes.

"A Musical Revue." THEATRE: The Common/The Theatre of Saint Peter's Church; OPENING DATE: April 17, 1980; PERFORMANCES: 137; LYRICS: See song list for credits; MUSIC: See song list for credits; DIRECTION: Gary Pearle; CHOREOGRAPHY: Mary Kyte; SCENERY: Tom Lynch; COSTUMES: Jess Goldstein; LIGHTING: Paul Gallo; MUSICAL DIRECTION: Mel Marvin; PRODUCERS: ANTA and Richmond Crinkley

CAST— Carolyn Mignini, Lynne Thigpen, Trey Wilson, Mary Catherine Wright, Jerry Zaks, Mel Marvin (piano)

The revue was presented in two acts (song assignments not listed in program).

ACT ONE—*Arrivals*: "Ragtime Nightingale" (lyric and music by Joseph F. Lamb; 1915), "The Yankee Doodle Boy" (a/k/a "Yankee Doodle Dandy") (from *Little Johnny Jones*, 1904; lyric and music by George M. Cohan), "Ta-Ra-Ra Boom-De-Ay!" (lyric and music by Henry J. Sayers; 1891), "I Don't Care" (lyric and music by Jean Lenox and Harry C. Sutton; 1905), "Shine On, Harvest Moon" (*Ziegfeld Follies of 1908*; lyric by Jack Norworth, music by Nora Bayes and Jack Norworth; 1908), "Come Take a Trip in My Airship" (lyric and music by George Evans and Ren Shields; 1904), "Kentucky Babe" (lyric and music by Richard H. Buck and Adam Geibel; 1896), "A Hot Time in the Old Town Tonight" (lyric and music by Joe Hayden and Theo A. Metz; 1896), "Stars and Stripes Forever" (lyric and music by John Philip Sousa; 1897); *Ingenuity and Inventions*:"Electricity" (lyric and music by Harry B. Smith and Karl Hoschna; 1905); *TR*: "El Capitan" (*El Capitan*, 1896; lyric and music by John Philip Sousa), *Wheels*: "Pastime Rag" (lyric and music by Artie Matthews; 1920), "Meet Me in St. Louis" (lyric and music by Andrew Sterling and Kerry Mills), "Daisy Bell" (lyric and music by Harry Dacre; 1892), "Waltz Me Around Again, Willie" (lyric and music by Will D. Cobb and Ren Shields; 1906), "Wabash Cannonball" (traditional; lyricist and composer unknown), "The Soldiers in the Park" (lyric and music by Aubrey Hapwood, Harry Greenback, and Lionel Monckton; 1898); *The Factory*: "Wayfaring Stranger" (traditional; lyricist and composer unknown), "Sometimes I Feel Like a Motherless Child" (traditional; lyricist and composer unknown), "Aye, Lye, Lyu Lye" (traditional; lyricist and composer unknown), "I'll Take You Home Again, Kathleen" (lyric and music by Thomas P. Westendorf; 1876), "America the Beautiful" (lyric and music by Katherine Lee Bates and Samuel Ward; 1910), "Wait for the Wagon" (traditional; lyricist and composer unknown), "What It Takes to Make Me Love You—You've Got It" (lyric and music by J.W. Johnson and James Reese Europe; 1914); *Anna Held*: "The Maiden with Dreamy Eyes" (lyric and music by J.W. Johnson and Bob Cole; 1901); "If I Were on the Stage (Kiss Me Again)" (*Mlle. Modiste*, 1905; lyric by Henry Blossom, music by Victor Herbert); *Outside Looking In*: "Shortnin' Bread" (traditional; lyricist and composer unknown); "(I Ain't Never Done Nothing to) Nobody" (added to *Ziegfeld Follies of 1910*; lyric and music by Alex Rogers and Bert Williams; 1905); *Fittin In*: "Elite Syncopations" (music by Scott Joplin; 1902); "I'm Goin' to Live Anyhow, 'Til I Die" (lyric and music by Shepard N. Edmonds; 1900)

ACT TWO—"The Ragtime Dance" (music by Scott Joplin; 1902); *Panama*: "I Want What I Want When I Want It" (*Mlle. Modiste*, 1905; lyric by Henry Blossom, music by Victor Herbert); *The Ladies:* "It's Delightful to Be Married!" (lyric and music by Anna Held and V. Scotto; 1907); "Fifty-Fifty" (lyric and music by Jim Burris and Chris Smith; 1914); "Eugenia" (lyric and music by Scott Joplin; 1905); *Rich and Poor*: "Then I'd Be Satisfied with Life" (added for the tour of *The Governor's Son*, 1901; lyric and music by George M. Cohan), "Narcissus" (lyric and music by Ethelbert Nevin; 1891), "Jonah Man" (lyric and music by Alex Rogers; 1903), "When It's All Goin' Out and Nothin' Comin' In" (lyric and music by Bert Williams and George Walker; 1902), "We Shall Not Be Moved" (traditional; lyricist and composer unknown), *Vaudeville*: "Hello, Ma Baby" (lyric and music by Joseph E. Howard and Ida Emerson; 1899), "Teddy Da Roose" (lyric and music by Ed Moran and J. Fred Helf; 1910), "A Bird in a Gilded Cage" (lyric by Arthur J. Lamb, music by Harry Von Tilzer; 1900), "Bill Bailey, Won't You Please Come Home?" (lyric and music by Hughie Cannon; 1902), "She's Getting' More Like the White Folks Every Day" (lyric and music by Bert Williams and George Walker; 1901), "You're a Grand Old Flag" (*George Washington, Jr.*, 1906; lyric and music by George M. Cohan; 1906), "The Yankee Doodle Boy" (reprise) (lyric and music by George M. Cohan; 1904), *Finale*: "Toyland" (*Babes in Toyland*, 1903; lyric by Glen MacDonough, music by Victor Herbert), "Bethena" (lyric and music by Scott Joplin; 1905), "Smiles" (lyric and music by J. Will Callahan and Lee S. Roberts; 1918)

NOTES—*Tintypes* originated at the Arena Stage in Washington, D.C., and then opened Off Broadway. It was later produced on Broadway at the John Golden Theatre in October 1980 for ninety-three performances. All three versions had a slightly different selection of songs, and a few cast members from the D.C. production didn't transfer to New York.

The revue was an attempt to create the immigrant experience from the perspective of late nineteenth- and early twentieth-century songs. However, the evening was just another empty exercise in the inglorious tradition of *The All Night Strut!* (1979; see entry) in which a collection of songs was pulled together in order to represent an era. In the case of *Tintypes*, the random order of the song presentation showed how uncreative the project was. The evening was divided into sections (*Arrivals*, *Panama*, *Vaudeville*, etc.), and many numbers could have been switched from one section to another and made little difference. For example, "America the Beautiful" was sung in *The Factory* section, but it could easily have worked in the *Arrivals* section, or even in the finale. Similarly, "Shine On, Harvest Moon" and "I Don't Care" have nothing to do with "arriving" in the United States, and might have been more effective in the *Vaudeville* section. Moreover, "I Want What I Want When I Want It," a comic song from the operetta *Mlle. Modiste*, was placed in the *Panama* section, presumably as a negative comment on U.S. government policies. *Tintypes* had its adherents, but the revue's short runs both on and off Broadway relegated the musical to an also-ran. The Los Angeles production (with the New York cast) was recorded on a 2-LP set by DRG Records (# S2L-5196); the album actually makes for pleasant background listening, and is more enjoyable than the show itself. The revue was revived Off Off Broadway at the Melting Pot Theatre Company on November 28, 2001.

1644 Tip-Toes.

THEATRE: Helen Carey Playhouse/Brooklyn Academy of Music; OPENING DATE: March 24, 1979; PERFORMANCES: 19; BOOK: Guy Bolton and Fred Thompson; LYRICS: Ira Gershwin; MUSIC: George Gershwin; DIRECTION: Sue Lawless; CHOREOGRAPHY: Dan Siretta; Larry McMillan, Assistant Choreographer; SCENERY: Not Credited; COSTUMES: David Toser; LIGHTING: Peter M. Ehrhardt; MUSICAL DIRECTION: William Cox; Gregory Dlugos, Assistant Musical Director; PRODUCER: The Brooklyn Academy of Music; produced for the Brooklyn Academy of Music by Warren Pincus

CAST—RONN ROBINSON (Stationmaster, Hodge, Detective), BOB GUNTON (Rollo Metcalf), JANA ROBBINS (Sylvia Metcalf), The Three Kayes (HASKELL GORDON [Hen Kaye], MICHAEL HIRSCH [Al Kaye], GEORGIA ENGEL [Tip-Toes Kaye]), RUSS THACKER (Steve Burton), Erik Geier (Sam Fisher), Sally O'Donnell (Miss Binnie Jones), Nicole Barth (Miss Denise Miller), Gwen Hillier Lowe (Miss Peggy Revere), Susan Danielle (Miss Lucille Wright), Dawn Le Ann Herbert (Miss Mitchell), Jill Owens (Miss Hart), Brad Witsger (Mr. Otto), Bobby Longbottom (Mr. Shay), Rodney Pridgen (Mr. Quinn), Jon Engstrom (Second Attendant at the Surf Club), David Monzione (Stewart)

The action occurs in Florida.

The musical was presented in two acts.

ACT ONE— Overture (Orchestra), "Waiting for the Train" (Ensemble), "Nice Baby" (Jana Robbins, Bob Gunton, Ensemble), "Looking for a Boy" (Georgia Engel), "Lady Luck" (Ensemble), "When Do We Dance?" (Russ Thacker, Sally O'Donnell, Nicole Barth, Jana Robbins, Ensemble), "These Charming People" (Georgia Engel, Michael Hirsch, Haskell Gordon), "That Certain Feeling" (Georgia Engel, Russ Thacker), "Sweet and Low-Down" (Michael Hirsch, Georgia Engel, Sally O'Donnell, Nicole Barth, Susan Danielle, Ronn Robinson, Ensemble), Finaletto (Company)

ACT TWO— Entr'acte (Orchestra), "Our Little Captain" (Georgia Engel, Men), "Looking for a Boy" (reprise) (Georgia Engel, Russ Thacker), "It's a Great Little World!" (Russ Thacker, Girls), "Why Do I Love You?" (Jana Robbins, Bob Gunton), "Nightie-Night!" (Georgia Engel, Russ Thacker), "Tip-Toes" (Georgia Engel, Ensemble), Finale (Company)

NOTES— George and Ira Gershwin's *Tip-Toes* premiered on Broadway at the Liberty Theatre on December 28, 1925, running there for 194 performances; Queenie Smith played the title role, Allen Kearns was Steve Burton, and Jeanette MacDonald was Sylvia Metcalf.

The musical hadn't been seen in New York until the 1979 revival, which retained all the original numbers and interpolated just one song from another Gershwin musical (Why Do I Love You?" from *Tell Me More* [1925]).

The revival had originated at Goodspeed Opera House, where it had been produced the previous year (April 11 through June 17, 1978) with Georgia Engel and Russ Thacker, who recreated their roles the following year for the New York production, which also included future Broadway director and choreographer Bobby (Robert) Longbottom in the cast.

Mel Gussow in the *New York Times* said the revival retained the "warmth and intimacy" of the Goodspeed production, and praised Engel ("a young Carol Channing") and Thacker (who has a "patent on boyishness"). He also felt the scenery and costumes formed a "creamy background for the spun-sugar romance," noting that the scenery was "like an Art Deco stroll through *Vanity Fair* and other magazines of the era." Gussow mentioned that while the program didn't credit the scenery, it nonetheless bore a "striking resemblance" to John Lee Beatty's sets for the Goodspeed production.

A recording which contained a few of the songs from the musical's 1926 British production (with Dorothy Dickson in the title role and with Allen Kearns reprising his role from the original Broadway production) was released by Monmouth Evergreen Records (LP # MES-7052; the LP also included songs from the 1926 British production of Vincent Youmans' *Wildflower* [New York, 1923]). In 2001, New World Records released a complete recording of the *Tip-Toes* score (CD # 80598-2), which was taken from a 1998 Carnegie Hall concert production (the cast included Emily Loesser, Lewis J. Stadlen, and Lee Wilkof); the CD set also contained a second CD, a studio cast recording of *Tell Me More*.

1645 [title of show]. THEATRE: Vineyard Theatre; OPENING DATE: February 26, 2006; PERFORMANCES: 156 (estimated); BOOK: Hunter Bell; LYRICS: Jeff Bowen; MUSIC: Jeff Bowen; DIRECTION: Michael Berresse; Sara Shives, Assistant Director; CHOREOGRAPHY: Michael Berresse; SCENERY: Neil Patel; Tim Mackabee, Associate Scenery Designer; COSTUMES: Chase Tyler; Matthew Sheridan, Assistant Costume Designer; LIGHTING: Ken Billington and Jason Kantrowitz; Jonathan Dunkle, Assistant Lighting Designer; MUSICAL DIRECTION: Larry Pressgrove; PRODUCER: Vineyard Theatre (Douglas Aibel, Artistic Director; Kevin McCollum and Laura Camien, Producers)

CAST—Hunter Bell (Hunter), Jeff Bowen (Jeff), Susan Blackwell (Susan), Heidi Blickenstaff (Heidi)

The action occurs in the present in New York City.

The musical was presented in one act.

MUSICAL NUMBERS—"Untitled Opening Number" (Company), "Two Nobodies in New York" (Jeff Bowen, Hunter Bell), "An Original Musical" (Hunter Bell, Jeff Bowen), "Monkeys and Playbills" (Company), "The Tony Award Song" (Hunter Bell), "Part of It All" (Hunter Bell, Jeff Bowen), "I Am Playing Me" (Heidi Blickenstaff), "What Kind of Girl Is She?" (Susan Blackwell, Heidi Blickenstaff), "Die Vampire, Die" (additional lyric and material for song by Susan Blackwell) (Susan Blackwell, Company), "Filling Out the Form" (Company), "September Song" (Company), "Secondary Characters" (Heidi Blickenstaff, Susan Blackwell), "A Way Back to Then" (Heidi Blickenstaff), "Nine People's Favorite Thing" (Company), Finale (Company)

NOTES—*[title of show]* dealt with two aspiring writers who want to create a musical for an upcoming musical theatre festival. Their only problem is what to write about, but they soon come up with the idea of writing a musical about the writing of a musical. In other words, the evening was an edgy update on the old let's-put-on-a-show musical. The title of the writers' musical, *[title of show]*, comes from the entry field on the festival's application form.

The score was bright, and included "Monkeys and Playbills," a song which managed to work in the titles of 48 musicals, many of them flops (including *Hit the Trail* [1954], *Portofino* [1958], and *Come Summer* [1969]).

The cast album was released by Ghostlight Records (CD # 7915584414-2), and included a bonus track (of the title song, "[title of show]").

[title of show] played at the Vineyard Theatre in two separate engagements, for a total of approximately 156 performances, and on July 17, 2008, opened on Broadway at the Lyceum Theatre for 102 performances.

And, yes, the musical had first been produced at a musical theatre festival (the 2004 New York Musical Theatre Festival).

1646 T.N.T. THEATRE: Players Theatre; OPENING DATE: April 22, 1982; PERFORMANCES: 6; BOOK: Richard Morrock; LYRICS: Richard Morrock; MUSIC: Richard Morrock; DIRECTION: Frank Carucci; CHOREOGRAPHY: Mary Lou Crivello; SCENERY: Ernest Allen Smith; COSTUMES: Susan J. Wright; LIGHTING: Ernest Allen Smith; MUSICAL DIRECTION: William Gladd; PRODUCER: The Dynamite Limited Partnership

CAST—Steven F. Hall (Grant), Mary Anne Dorward (Bonnie), Regis Bowman (Max), Joanne Bradley (Fran), Kenneth Boys (Bill), Mary Lou Crivello (Debbie), Bill Boss (Jonathan), Gabriel Barre (Jerry), Christine Campbell (Marie), Natalie Strauss (Gail)

The action occurs in a California college auditorium and cafeteria.

The musical was presented in two acts.

ACT ONE—"Why?" (Bill Boss, Company), "Tricephalous You" (Bill Boss, Assistants), "'Life' Is a Four-Letter Word" (Bill Boss, Assistants), "A Casual Kind of Thing" (Steven F. Hall, Mary Anne Dorward), "Previous Lives" (Bill Boss, Company, "and the past"), "Where Have I Been?" (Joanne Bradley), "Mantra" (Bill Boss, Company)

ACT TWO—"Id, Superego" (Kenneth Boys, Assistants), "Longing for Someone" (Stephen F. Hall), "I'm O.K., You're O.K." (Mary Lou Crivello), "Mass Market" (Trainees), "The Secret of Life" (Company)

NOTES—*T.N.T.* were the initials for Tricephalous Neurosyllogistic Training; the musical was a spoof of California-styled New Age cults.

It appears that by opening night, Mary Lou Crivello, the choreographer, had assumed the role of Debbie (performed by Mary Garripoli in previews).

1647 To Be or Not to Be...What Kind of a Question Is That? THEATRE: Barbizon-Plaza Theatre; OPENING DATE: October 19, 1970; PERFORMANCES: 23; SKETCHES: H. Ritterman and Zvi Reisel; LYRICS: Maz Meszel; MUSIC: Eli Rubenstein; DIRECTION: Marvin Gordon; SCENERY: Art Consultant, Ami Shamir; LIGHTING: Sally Small; MUSICAL DIRECTION: Eli Rubenstein; PRODUCERS: Henry Goldgran and Arthur V. Briskin

CAST—James Brochu, Moti Giladi, Shmulik Goldstein, Evelyn Kingsley, Denise Lor, Sarah Rubine, Yoel Sharr, Mark Stuart

The revue was presented in two acts.

ACT ONE—"Beyached" (Company), "About Israel" (Moti Giladi), "My Son the Kibutsnik" (James Brochu, Denise Lor, Moti Giladi), "The Wolf and the Lamb" (James Brochu), "Vanya" (Sarah Rubine, James Brochu), "El-Al (A Nudnik)" (Evelyn Kingsley, Shmulik Goldstein, James Brochu), "I'm in Love with a Flyer" (Evelyn Kingsley), "Inflight Nudniks" (Denise Lor), "Tilibim" (Moti Giladi), "Tel-Aviv, I Love You" (Evelyn Kingsley, Sarah Rubine), "Chasidik" (Mark Stuart, Company)

ACT TWO—"Chiribim" (Yoel Sharr, Company), "Interview with a Maid" (Evelyn Kingsley, Denise Lor), "Prisoner of War" (Yoel Sharr, Moti Giladi), "Letter from My Son" (Denise Lor), "Haifi Melody" (Moti Giladi), "Burglar" (Sarah Rubine, Shmulik Goldstein, Yoel Sharr), "The Eighth Day" (Mark Stuart), "Party" (Company)

NOTES—Like the previous season's *Unfair to Goliath* (see entry), the cutely titled Israeli revue *To Be or Not to Be...What Kind of a Question Is That?* dealt with topical matters, and like *Goliath*, the revue had a short run. There was probably a limited audience for such specialized material, but nonetheless the era saw at least one such show either on or off Broadway each season.

With the advent of the Jewish Repertory Theatre in 1974, and later the American Jewish Theatre, there would soon be an established and specialized venue for both old and new Jewish-themed plays and musicals. As for *To Be or Not to Be...*, Lewis Funke in the *New York Times* found the evening "modest" with mostly "witless" and "punchless" sketches and "ordinary" music. He felt that despite the goodwill of the performers, they couldn't overcome the "dullness" of the material.

1648 To Feed Their Hopes. THEATRE: Quaigh Theatre; OPENING DATE: February 21, 1986; PERFORMANCES: Unknown; BOOK: Elaine Kendall and Elaine Moe; LYRICS: Elaine Kendall; MUSIC: Dennis Poore; DIRECTION: Elaine Moe; CHOREOGRAPHY: Karen Soroca; Holly Hawkins, Assistant Choreographer; SCENERY: Aft, Inc.; COSTUMES: Patric McWilliams; LIGHTING: Aft, Inc.; MUSICAL DIRECTION: Dennis Poore; PRODUCER: Quaigh Theatre (Will Lieberson, Artistic Director)

CAST—Robert Boles, Mary Corcoran, Denise DeMirjian, Bob Jordan, Eleni Kelakos, Denise Morgan, Judith Thiergaard

SOURCE—The 1980 book *To Feed Their Hopes: A Book of American Women* by John Sanford.

NOTES—Based on John Sanford's book about American women, the Off Off Broadway musical *To Feed Their Hopes* was, according to Mel Gussow in the *New York Times*, a "musical pageant" which was "so diffuse" in its depiction of a group of disparate women that it lost its focus. He felt the musical's creators used a "once-over-tritely" approach in its look at a cross-section of women (including Eleanor Roosevelt, Alice Roosevelt Longworth, Mrs. Benedict Arnold, Mrs. George Armstrong Custer, Sally Hemmings, even one of Sanford's schoolteachers), but praised one of the musical's "livelier" sequences, "San Simeon Blues" (which Marion Davies sang about William Randolph Hearst).

1649 To the Water Tower. THEATRE: Square East; OPENING DATE: April 4, 1963; PERFORMANCES: 210; SCENES AND DIALOGUE: Created by the Company; MUSIC: Tom O'Horgan; DIRECTION: Paul Sills; SCENERY: Ralph Alswang; PRODUCERS: Bernard Sahlins, Howard Alk, and Paul Sills

CAST—Severn Darden, Paul Dooley, Andrew Duncan, Erin Martin, Paul Sand, Eugene Troobnick

The revue was presented in two acts (sketch and song assignments unknown).

ACT ONE—"Second City Theme Song," "Central Intelligence," "How to Sell a Fall-Out Shelter," "Camp Let-Yourself-Go," "The Truth About a Big Fish Story," "Wordless Dentistry," "Khrushchev-Kennedy Press Conference"

ACT TWO—"Looking for the Action"

NOTES—*To the Water Tower* was the third Second City revue to play Off Broadway (see entry for *Seacoast of Bohemia* for a complete list of the Second City revues which were presented in New York; also see Appendix T).

The program noted that with this production the Second City had established "a permanent outpost ... an urban renewal project for the first city." The program also stated that "everything is subject to change ... with or without notice."

The revue included another Kennedy-Khrushchev sketch as well as one about the Bay of Pigs fiasco. And the sketch about fall-out shelters was another reminder of the Cold War; it dealt with four salesmen who specialize in fall-out shelters, and Arthur Gelb in the *New York Times* predicted it will "double you up with laughter." The entire second act was devoted to an extended sketch about two fellows on the make in a Manhattan bar; Gelb noted the sequence had many "zany" segments, but felt the piece wasn't as sharp and focused as it could be.

Note that Tom O'Horgan is now associated with the group. A few years later he enjoyed a trio of directorial successes with the Broadway version of *Hair* (1968; 1,750 performances [Gerald Freedman had directed the Off Broadway version which had opened in 1967; see entry]), *Lenny* (1971; 455 performances), and *Jesus Christ Superstar* (1971; 720 performances). But O'Horgan was soon associated with a number of failures, including the Broadway musicals *Inner City* (1971; 97 performances; see entry for its Off Broadway revised version [*Street Dreams*, music by Helen Miller]), *Dude*, or *The Highway Life* (1972; 16 performances), and *Senator Joe* (which closed after three preview performances in 1989) and the plays *The Leaf People* (1975; 8 performances) and *I Won't Dance* (1981; which closed after one performance and was the final production to be performed at the Helen Hayes Theatre before it was demolished).

To the Water Tower first opened in Chicago on February 2, 1963, where it played for 182 performances.

1650 To Whom It May Concern. "A Musical Celebration." THEATRE: St. Stephen's Church; OPENING DATE: December 16, 1985; PERFORMANCES: 106; TEXT: Carol Hall; LYRICS: Carol Hall; MUSIC: Carol Hall; DIRECTION: Geraldine Fitzgerald; LIGHTING: Christina Giannelli; MUSICAL DIRECTION: Michael O'Flaherty; PRODUCERS: The Bedda Roses Company; produced by arrangement with the Williamstown Theatre Festival (Nikos Psacharopoulos, Artistic Director)

CAST—Michael O'Flaherty (Choir Master), Jennifer Naimo (The Child), Dylan Baker (The Priest), William Hardy (Grandad), Gretchen Cryer (Fay), Michael Hirsch (Bob), Carol Hall (Caroline), Louise Edeiken (Frederika), Tamara Tunie (Sister), Becky Gelke (Celia), Guy Stroman (Mike), Kecia Lewis-Evans (Deloris), Al DeCristo (Elliott), George Gerdes (The Stranger)

The action occurs in a church.

The revue was presented in one act.

MUSICAL NUMBERS—"When I Consider the Heavens" (Ensemble), "Truly My Soul" (Ensemble), "Blessed Be God" (Ensemble), "Holy God" (Carol Hall, Tamara Tunie, Al DeCristo, Michael O'Flaherty), "Miracles" (Louise Edeiken, Company), "We Were Friends" (Carol Hall, Guy Stroman), "Sandy" (Becky Gelke), "Make a Joyful Noise" (Women's Ensemble), "Ain't Nobody Got a Bed of Roses" (George Gerdes, Company), "We Believe" (Ensemble), "I'll Only Miss the Feeling" (Kecia Lewis-Evans), "My Sort Of Ex-Boyfriend" (Becky Gelke), "Jenny Rebecca" (Guy Stroman), "Skateboard Acrobats" (Tamara Tunie, Jennifer Naimo, Company), "In the Mirror's Reflection" (George Gerdes, Company), "In the Mirror's Reflection" (reprise) (Company), "Ain't Love Easy" (Gretchen Cryer, Michael Hirsch), "Walk in Love" (William Hardy, Company), "Who Will Dance with the Blind Dancing Bear" (Michael O'Flaherty, Company), "To Whom It May Concern" (Dylan Baker, George Gerdes, Company), "Walk in Love" (Ensemble)

NOTES—Carol Hall's *To Whom It May Concern* was a collection of songs sung at a church service (appropriately, the revue was presented at St. Stephen's Church); some of the numbers were performed as part of the church service, while others were introspective songs in which the churchgoers analyzed themselves as well as the place of religion in their lives.

In *The Best Plays of 1985-1986*, Jeffrey Sweet found the evening erratic, with occasional sequences of "wit and feeling" and others with all "the insight of a Hallmark card."

The revue had earlier been produced in July 1985 at the Williamstown Theatre Festival.

The script was published by Samuel French, Inc., in 1986.

Carol Hall was a talented lyricist-composer who only occasionally wrote for the theatre. In 1978, her biggest hit, *The Best Little Whorehouse in Texas* (see entry), included a number of ingratiating songs, including "Hard Candy Christmas," one of the best theatre songs of the 1970s. The musical's 1994 sequel, *The Best Little Whorehouse Goes Public*, was a huge flop; but its underrated score offered catchy music and often clever lyrics. Her fascinating musical *Good Sports* (1980) never got out of workshop, but it was a promising venture with a sprightly score and a bright cast (which included Orson Bean, June Gable, Lara Teeter, and Claudette Sutherland).

1651 Together Again for the First Time. THEATRE: Kaufman Theatre; OPENING DATE: February 27, 1989; PERFORMANCES: 30; DIRECTION: Barry Kleinbort; CHOREOGRAPHY: Donald Saddler; SCENERY: Phillip Baldwin; COSTUMES: William Ivey Long; LIGHTING: Ted Mather; MUSICAL DIRECTION: Colin Romoff; PRODUCER: Martin R. Kaufman

CAST—Jo Sullivan, Emily Loesser

The revue was presented in two acts (all songs performed by Jo Sullivan and Emily Loesser).

ACT ONE—Prologue: Introductory Frank Loesser, What's Next, "I Love To Sing-A" (from 1936 film *The Singing Kid*; lyric by E.Y. Harburg, music by Harold Arlen), "One More Kiss" (*Follies*, 1971; lyric and music by Stephen Sondheim), "Mack the Knife" (*The Threepenny Opera*, 1930; original German lyric by Bertolt Brecht, English lyric by Marc Blitzstein, music by Kurt Weill), "I Wish It So" (*Juno*, 1959; lyric and music by Marc Blitzstein), "Pack Up Your Sins and Go to the Devil" (*Music Box Revue* [Second Edition], 1922; lyric and music by Irving Berlin), "What Is There to Say?" (*Ziegfeld Follies*, 1934; lyric by E.Y. Harburg, music by Vernon Duke), "The Glamorous Life" (*A Little Night Music*, 1973; lyric and music by Stephen Sondheim), "Can't You Just See Yourself?" (*High Button Shoes*, 1947; lyric by Sammy Cahn, music by Jule Styne), What Was: The Broadway Musical

ACT TWO—A Little Gershwin, "Can You Read My Mind" (theme from 1978 film *Superman*; lyric by Leslie Bricusse, music by John Williams), "Sing Something Simple" (*The Second Little Show*, 1930; lyric and music by Herman Hupfeld), "Ev'ry Time" (*Best Foot Forward*, 1941; lyric and music by Hugh Martin and Ralph Blane), "Ev'rything I've Got" (*By Jupiter*, 1942; lyric by Lorenz Hart, music by Richard Rodgers), "Don't Let It Get You Down" (*Hold On to Your Hats*, 1940; lyric by E.Y. Harburg, music by Burton Lane), More of Loesser, Finale

NOTES—The two-woman revue *Together Again for the First Time* starred Jo Sullivan, Frank Loesser's widow, and their daughter Emily Loesser, and included songs by Loesser and other stage and film composers and lyricists. For another revue starring Jo Sullivan, see entry for *I Hear Music...of Frank Loesser and Friends*.

1652 'Toinette. "A Musical." THEATRE: Theatre Marquee; OPENING DATE: November 20, 1961; PERFORMANCES: 31; BOOK: J.I. Rodale; LYRICS: Deed Meyer; MUSIC: Deed Meyer; DIRECTION: Curt Conway; CHOREOGRAPHER: Harry Woolever; SCENERY: Stuart Bishop; COSTUMES: Joe Regan; LIGHTING: Don Sussman; MUSICAL DIRECTION: David Shire; PRODUCER: Bickerstaff Productions

CAST—Joseph George (Gaston), Logan Ramsey (Argan), Ellie Wood ('Toinette), Joelle Jons (Angelique), Tom Ingham (Cleante), Charles Kakatsakis (Dr. Purgon), Bob Randall (Thomas Diafoirus), Scottie MacGregor (Honore de Bonnefoy), Daniel Frankel (Berald), Dee Corbett (Gendarme)

SOURCE—The 1666 play *Le Malaide Imaginaire* (*The Imaginary Invalid*) by Jean-Baptiste Poquelin (Moliere).

The action occurs in 1961 in an old house in the Montmarte District of Paris as well as on the street in front of the house.

The musical was presented in two acts (song assignments unknown).

ACT ONE—"Rags," "Bonjour," "Come On Outside and Get Some Air," "Why Shouldn't I?," "A Father Speaks," "A Lullaby," "Honest Honore," "Someone to Count On," "Un, Dieux, Trois," "Fly Away," "'Toinette"

ACT TWO—"Madly in Love with You Am I," "Someone to Count On" (reprise), "Beat, Little Pulse," "Even a Doctor Can Make a Mistake," "Dr. Iatro," "Small Apartment," "Small Apartment" (reprise), "Recitative," "You're the Most Impossible Person," Finale

NOTES—Like his *She Shall Have Music* (1959; see entry), Deed Meyer's *'Toinette* was a musical adaptation of a classic play. In this case, his inspiration was Moliere's *The Imaginary Invalid*, here updated to the Paris of 1961. It lasted just two performances longer than another Off Broadway musical adaptation of the same material, *Show Me Where the Good Times Are* (1970; see entry), which was set in turn-of-the-twentieth-century New York City, and was somewhat reminiscent of *Hello, Dolly!* (1964) in its sunny score, attitude, and locale.

Howard Taubman in the *New York Times* catalogued the ways in which the creators of *'Toinette* could compensate Moliere, the actors, the audience, and the critics for the "alleged" musical comedy. As for the critics, he noted they all led rich and glamorous lives, and so money wouldn't be an appropriate way to reward them. Instead, he decided earplugs and opaque glasses would be enough to ensure that the critics could "ignore every offensive word, sound and gesture on the stage" of the Marquee Theatre.

For another musical by Deed Meyer, see entry for *The Stones of Jehoshaphat*.

For other musicals based on Moliere's comedies, see entries for *The Amorous Flea*, *The Misanthrope*, *Monsieur de Pourceaugnac*, and *Show Me Where the Good Times Are*.

1653 The Tokyo Shock Boys. THEATRE: Minetta Lane Theatre; OPENING DATE: February 19, 1997; PERFORMANCES: 63; DEVISED BY The Tokyo Shock Boys; DIRECTION: Murray Pope; MUSICAL DIRECTION: Paul Jackson; PRODUCERS: Arthur Cantor, Executive Producer; Murray Pope and Shuji Shibata, Sonny Everett and William O'Boyle, Alan Schuster and Mitchell Maxwell, Tim Woods, Associate Producers

CAST—Danna, Gyuzo, Nambu, Sango; music performed by Satoshi Nishikata

The revue was presented in one act.

NOTES—This performance piece was by the Tokyo Shock Boys (Danna, Gyuzo, Nambu, and Sango), self-styled "Samurai vaudevillians." But the Palace Theatre in the heyday of vaudeville never offered the kinds of skits seen in this revue, including one in which Gyuzo placed a live scorpion in his mouth; another in which Danna drank milk and then somehow squeezed it out of his eyes like tears; and "one that had even jaded New York jaws dropping" (wrote Jeffrey Sweet in *The Best Plays of 1996-1997*) which revolved around a toilet plunger attached to a string which in turn was tied around Nambu's testicles. For more information on this bizarre evening, see the three-quarter page discussion in *Best Plays*; Sweet deemed the evening "a category—nay, a species—all [its] own." Peter Marks in the *New York Times* found the evening "the strangest Japanese import since" — and then concluded it was "the strangest Japanese import." He noted that the "mindless monotony" included performers pulling chairs across the stage by a part of the anatomy "that was never meant for, uh, such strenuous work," and Marks commented that through the course of the performance only one organ went "pristinely untouched" (the brain). The revue had been previously produced in Japan, Australia, Canada, and Europe.

1654 Tomfoolery. "The Words and Music of Tom Lehrer." THEATRE: Top of the Gate (Upstairs)/The Village Gate; OPENING DATE: December 14, 1981; PERFORMANCES: 120; LYRICS: Tom Lehrer; MUSIC: Tom Lehrer (Tom Lehrer's songs were adapted into a theatre piece by Cameron Mackintosh and Robin Ray.); DIRECTION: Gary Pearle and Mary Kyte; SCENERY: Tom Lynch; COSTUMES: Ann Emonts; LIGHTING: Robert Jared; MUSICAL DIRECTION: Eric Stern; PRODUCERS: Cameron Mackintosh and Hinks Shimberg "in spite of" Art D'Lugoff

CAST—MacIntyre Dixon, Joy Franz, Jonathan Hadary, Donald Corren

The revue was presented in two acts.

ACT ONE—"Be Prepared" (Company), "Poisoning Pigeons" (Joy Franz, Donald Corren), "I Wanna Go Back to Dixie" (MacIntyre Dixon, Company), "My Home Town" (Donald Corren), "Pollution" (Joy Franz, McIntyre Dixon, Company), "Bright College Days" (Jonathan Hadary, Donald Corren), "Fight Fiercely, Harvard" (Jonathan Hadary, Donald Corren, MacIntyre Dixon), "The Elements" (Jonathan Hadary), "The Folk Song Army" (Company), "In Old Mexico" (Joy Franz, Company), "She's My Girl" (Donald Corren), "When You Are Old and Grey" (Company), "Wernher von Braun" (MacIntyre Dixon), "Who's Next" (Company), "I Got It from Agnes" (Jonathan Hadary), "National Brotherhood Week" (Company)

ACT TWO—"So Long Mom" (Donald Corren, Jonathan Hadary), "Send the Marines" (Company), "Hunting Song" (MacIntyre Dixon), "Irish Ballad" (Joy Franz, Company), "New Math" (Donald Corren, MacIntyre Dixon), "Silent E" (Company), "Oedipus Rex" (Joy Franz, Company), "I Hold Your Hand in Mine" (Donald Corren), "Masochism Tango" (MacIntyre Dixon), "The Old Dope Peddler" (Jonathan Hadary), "The Vatican Rag" (Company), "We Will All Go Together" (Company)

NOTES—The revue *Tomfoolery* was a collection of satiric songs written by Tom Lehrer in the 1950s and 1960s; back then, such songs as "The Masochism Tango" and "The Vatican Rag" seemed naughty and irreverent; but by the time of *Tomfoolery*'s production in the early 1980s, the songs seemed bland instead of daring, and at their best were merely quaint time capsules of a more innocent era. The musical had been first produced in London at the Criterion Theatre on June 5, 1980, and the "unoriginal cast album" for that production was recorded by MMT Records (LP # MMT-LP-001).

1655 Tommy. THEATRE: City Center 55th Street Theatre; OPENING DATE: May 3, 1972; PERFORMANCES: 31; LYRICS AND MUSIC: Pete Townshend; additional songs by Sonny Boy Williamson, John Entwistle, and Keith Moon; CHOREOGRAPHY: Fernand Nault; SCENERY: David Jenkins; COSTUMES: Francois Barbeau; LIGHTING: Nicholas Cernovitch; PRODUCER: Les Grands Ballets Canadiens (Ludmilla Chiriaeff, Founder and Director; Fernand Nault, Associate Artistic Director; Uriel G. Luft, General Manager)

CAST—ALEXANDRE BELIN/MANNIE ROWE/Vincent Warren (Tommy), HAE SHIK KIM/MANON LARIN/JANET SNYDER/Sonia Taverner (Acid Queen), LESLIE-MAY DOWNS/Reva Pincusoff/Barbara Withey (Mother), WILLIAM JOSEF/LASZLO TAMASIK (Father), RICHARD BEATY/William Josef/Renald Rabu (The Hawker), James Boyd/David Drummond/Lorne Toumine (The Lover), Maurice Lemay/Guillermo Gonzalez/Andris Toppe (Cousin Kevin), JAMES BATES/Maurice Lemay/Andris Toppe (Pin Ball Wizard), JOHN STANZEL (Uncle Ernie), Eileen Heath/Carole Landry (Sally Simpson); Dancers: Richard Bouchard, Francine Boucher, James Boyd, Lorna Cameron, Robert Dicello, Louise Dore, David Drummond, Gerry Gilbert, Guillermo Gonzalez, Eileen Heath, Barbara Jacobs, Carole Landry, Melinda Lawrence, Maurice Lemay, Helen McKergow, Conrad Peterson, Reva Pincusoff, Renald Rabu, Cathy Sharp, Richard Sugarman, Susan Taylor, Michael Thomas, Andris Toppe, Lorne Tomine, Laeleen Winchu, Barbara Withey; Note: During the run, there were alternate performers for some roles.

SOURCE—The 1969 Decca album of the rock opera *Tommy* performed by The Who.

The ballet was performed in one act.

The following song list is taken from the original 1969 album of the musical.

MUSICAL NUMBERS—Overture, "It's a Boy," "You Didn't Hear It" (a/k/a "1921"), "Amazing Journey," "Sparks," "Eyesight to the Blind" (The Hawker) (lyric and music by Sonny Boy Williamson), "Christmas," "Cousin Kevin" (lyric and music by John Entwistle), "The Acid Queen," "Underture," "Do You Think It's Alright?," "Fiddle About" (lyric and music by John Entwistle), "Pinball Wizard," "There's a Doctor" "Go to the Mirror!," "Tommy Can You Hear Me?," "Smash the Mirror," "Sensation," "Miracle Cure," "Sally Simpson," "I'm Free," "Welcome," "Tommy's Holiday Camp" (lyric and music by Keith Moon), "We're Not Gonna Take It"

NOTES—Like Andrew Lloyd Webber and Tim Rice's rock opera *Jesus Christ Superstar*, the rock opera *Tommy* was a record album before it became a full-fledged theatre work. The tiresome, overly flashy story dealt with Tommy, a catatonic boy who is stricken deaf, mute, and blind by traumatic events in his childhood. But he nonetheless becomes a champion pin ball player, is later miraculously cured of his physical afflictions, and then becomes the leader of a religious cult which eventually is discredited when Tommy's rules become too rigid.

As an album, ballet, film (which was released in 1975), and an eventual Broadway version (which opened as *The Who's Tommy* on April 22, 1993, at the St. James Theatre and played for 900 performances), *Tommy* seems to have impressed a lot of people.

For the ballet version of the work by Les Grands Ballets Canadiens, the company's dancers performed to the pre-recorded music of the album (Roger Daltrey was the lead vocalist on the album, and the role of The Hawker was sung by Sonny Boy Williamson).

Tommy was presented on a double bill which alternated between two ballets, *Ceremony* and *Hip and Straight*.

Tommy was originally released on a 2-LP set by Decca Records (# DXSW-7205; the CD was issued by MCA Records [# MCAD-11417]). The 2-LP soundtrack album was released by Polydor Records (# PD-29502), and the 2-CD Broadway cast album by RCA Victor Records (# 09026-61874-2).

1656 Tommy Tune/White Tie and Tails. THEATRE: Little Shubert Theatre; OPENING DATE: December 18, 2002; PERFORMANCES: 23; LYRICS: See song list for credits; MUSIC: See song list for credits; PROJECTION DESIGN: Wendall K. Harrington; LIGHTING: Natasha Katz; MUSICAL DIRECTION: Michael Biagi; PRODUCERS: Chase Mishkin, Leonard Soloway, Roy Furman, and Julian Schlossberg with James M. Nederlander; Robert Duva, Associate Producer

CAST—TOMMY TUNE, The Manhattan Rhythm Kings (Hal Shane, Brian Nalepka, Marc Kessler)

The revue was presented in one act.

MUSICAL NUMBERS—"Same Old Song and Dance" (lyric by Jimmy Van Heusen, music by Sammy Fain), "Tap Your Troubles Away" (*Mack & Mabel*, 1974; lyric and music by Jerry Herman), "Everything Old Is New Again" (lyric and music by Peter Allen and Carol Sager), "Puttin' on the Ritz" (1929 film *Puttin' on the Ritz*; lyric and music by Irving Berlin), "When I'm Sixty-Four" (lyric and music by Paul McCartney and John Lennon), "I'm My Own Grandpa" (lyricist and composer unknown), "Shanghai Lil" (1933 film *Footlight Parade*; lyric by Al Dubin, music by Harry Warren), "I Can't Be Bothered Now" (1937 film *A Damsel in Distress*; lyric by Ira Gershwin, music by George Gershwin), "Fascinating Rhythm" (*Lady, Be Good!*, 1924; lyric by Ira Gershwin, music by George Gershwin), "It's You" (*The Music Man*, 1957; lyric and music by Meredith Willson), "When The Midnight Choo-Choo Leaves for Alabam'" (lyric and music by Irving Berlin), "Nice Work If You Can Get It" (1937 film *A Damsel in Distress*; lyric by Ira Gershwin, music by George Gershwin), "Shall We Dance" (1938 film *Shall We Dance*; lyric by Ira Gershwin, music by George Gershwin), "They Can't Take That Away from Me" (1938 film *Shall We Dance*; lyric by Ira Gershwin, music by George Gershwin), "Nowadays" (lyric by Fred Ebb, music by John Kander)/"Hot Honey Rag" (music by John Kander) (both songs from *Chicago*, 1975)

NOTES—The revue was a welcome if brief visit from Tommy Tune, one of the stalwarts of modern musical theatre who had been absent from the New York stage since May 1994. During that month he directed and choreographed the short-lived Broadway musical *The Best Little Whorehouse Goes Public*, and on May 11, the night after *Whorehouse* opened, the "Tommy Tune Production" of a *Grease* revival premiered (produced by Barry and Fran Weissler and Jujamcyn Theatres in association with Pace Theatrical Group and TV Asahi, and directed and choreographed by Jeff Calhoun). In 1995, Tune starred in *Busker Alley* (during its tryout it was also titled *Buskers* and *Stage Door Charley*), which closed prior to Broadway (where it had been scheduled to open at the St. James theatre on November 16) because of an on-stage accident in which he broke his foot. While not perfect, *Busker Alley* was an entertaining evening and offered a charming score by Richard M. Sherman and Robert B. Sherman (happily, the score received a belated recording when a 2006 concert presentation of the musical for the benefit for the York Theatre Company was released by Jay Records [CD # CDJAY-1400]).

The above song list is taken from *The Best Plays of 2002-2003*; there was no regular song list in the program, but the program referenced various songs which may have been heard as background music or in medley format (these numbers included "A Song for Dancing," lyric by Alan and Marilyn Bergman, music by Billy Goldenberg [from *Ballroom*, 1978]), and "Maybe My Baby Loves Me," lyric and music by Robert Wright and George Forrest [*Grand Hotel*, 1989]).

1657 Tongues. THEATRE: The Other Stage/The Public Theatre; OPENING DATE: November 15, 1979; PERFORMANCES: 44; DIRECTION: Robert Woodruff; COSTUMES: Mary Brecht; LIGHTING: Beverly Emmons; PRODUCER: The New York Shakespeare Festival (Joseph Papp, Director)

NOTES—*Tongues* was a two-part play with music, a "collaboration" of Sam Shepard and Joseph Chaikin. The first play, *Savage/Love* included music by Skip Laplante, Harry Mann, and Sam Shepard, and was performed by Skip Laplante and Harry Mann. The second play, *Tongues*, had music by Sam Shepard, with music performed by Skip Laplante. Joseph Chaikin was the performer in both plays.

Shepard's extremely helpful notes in the program stated that the two pieces were an attempt to "find an equal expression between music & the actor ... connections [between the two plays] somehow arise & a story seems to be told." Mel Gussow in the *New York Times* reported the first play was essentially a love story (first meeting, courtship, and other stages of a relationship) and the second one was about death (in which "a man delivers his own last rites"). He noted the "Beckett-like" evening of "abstract essays" first seemed like "poetry set to jazz," but ultimately was like a "resplendent chamber symphony of concordant sounds." The two plays were published in the collection *Sam Shepard: Seven Plays* as well as in the 1997 collection *Sam Shepard: Plays Two*, published by Faber and Faber, Ltd.

1658 Too Jewish? "A Mensch and His Musical." THEATRE: John Houseman Theatre; OPENING DATE: January 1, 1996; PERFORMANCES: 33; TEXT: Avi Hoffman; MUSICAL DIRECTION: Ben Schaechter; PRODUCERS: John Houseman Theatre Company (Eric Krebs, Artistic Director)

CAST—Avi Hoffman

The revue was presented in one act.

MUSICAL NUMBERS—Overture, "Oyfn Pripitchik" (by Mark Warshavsky), "Oyfin Veg Shteyt a Boym" (by Itzik Manger), "Oh-Dey-Nameya" (lyric by Phillip Namanworth, music by Elliott Finkel), Yiddish Medley, "Not on the Top," "Cardova the Bronx Casanova," "I'm a Litvak, She's a Galitz," "Oom-Glick Blues," "Heym ofn Range" (lyric by M. Katz; music traditional), "# 4 Humentash Lane" (by Eli Bass), "Quiet Evening," "I Can't Wait Till You Arrive" (lyric by F. Greenberg, music by B. Schaechter, "Faith in Whom" (Yiddish lyric by Miriam Hoffman, English lyric by Sheldon Harnick, music by Jerome [Jerry] Bock)

NOTES—*Too Jewish?* was a one-man revue starring Avi Hoffman in an evening of material from Yiddish theatre. Hoffman returned in a sequel, *Too Jewish Two!*, which opened at the Jewish Repertory Theatre on April 28, 1998, and played for twenty-one performances.

The cast recordings of *Too Jewish?* and *Too Jewish Two!* were released on unnamed and unnumbered labels.

1659 Touch. "The Country-Rock Musical." THEATRE: Village Arena Theatre; transferred to the Martinique Theatre on June 1, 1971; OPENING DATE: November 8, 1970; PERFORMANCES: 422; BOOK: Kenn Long, in collaboration with Amy Saltz; LYRICS: Kenn Long; MUSIC: Kenn Long and Jim Crozier; DIRECTION: Amy Saltz; SCENERY: Robert U. Taylor (and Robert Alexander Kates?); LIGHTING: Charles Lewis (and Barry Arnold?); MUSICAL DIRECTION: David J. Rodman; PRODUCERS: Edith O'Hara in association with Robert S. Weinstein and the Two Arts Playhouse, Inc. (it appears that Albert Poland was also one of the musical's producers)

CAST—Norman Jacob (Awol), Barbara Ellis (Guiness), Kenn Long (Wyan), Phyllis Gibbs (Melissa), Gerard S. Doff (Roland), Peter J, Mitchell (Mark), Susan Rosenblum (Patti), Ava Rosenblum (Susan April), Dwight Jaybe (Alex); also, Eileen Gottermeyer, David J. Stoudnour, Cherie McDonald, Gary Graham

The musical was presented in two acts.

ACT ONE—"Declaration" (Company), "Windchild" (Company), "City Song" (Ava Rosenblum, Cherie McDonald), "Sitting in the Park" (Gerard S. Doff, Kenn Long), "I Don't Care" (Phyllis Gibbs, Company), "Goodbyes" (Norman Jacob), "Come to the Road" (Kenn Long, Ava Rosenblum, Company), "Reaching, Touching" (Barbara Ellis, Norman Jacob, Company)

ACT TWO—"Guiness, Woman" (Norman Jacob), "Susan's Song" (Ava Rosenblum), "Maxine!" (Kenn Long, Gerard S. Doff, Commune), "Quiet Country" (Gerard S. Doff, Kenn Long, Company), "Tripping" (Susan Rosenblum, Commune), "Garden Song" (Commune), "Watching" (Phyllis Gibbs), "Hasseltown" (Company), "Confrontation Song" (Commune), "Alphagenesis" (Company)

NOTES—The dreary "country-rock" musical *Touch* centered around Awol (this was 1970, and so of course Awol's name had a double meaning), panhandlers, drug addicts, an unwed mother, and others who are disillusioned with city life and thus migrate to the country in order to form a commune.

Mel Gussow in the *New York Times* found the evening a collection of fragmented vignettes, but he noted the songs were "mostly light, country and bubbly" and sometimes "even calliopic" He felt that while the musical was "modest," "artless," and "amateurish," it was nonetheless "touching."

The lyric and music of "Windchild" was by Gary Graham. Later programs listed two songs ("Cities of Light" and "Hasseltown Memorial Square Dance") which appear to be "City Song" and "Hasseltown."

Ampex Records released the cast album (LP # A-50102), and its pretentious liner notes proclaimed that *Touch* was a "classic" in the same category of *The Threepenny Opera*, *The Fantasticks*, and *Hair* (see entries). But *Touch* never approached that golden circle in terms of artistic, critical, financial, and long-running success.

1660 Toulouse. THEATRE: Ukranian Hall; OPENING DATE: September 14, 1981; PERFORMANCES: 12; BOOK: Ronnie Britton; LYRICS: Ronnie Britton; MUSIC: Ronnie Britton; DIRECTION: Ronnie Britton; CHOREOGRAPHY: Robert Speller; SCENERY: Anthony Cava; COSTUMES: Bob Thompson; LIGHTING: Nina Votolato; MUSICAL DIRECTION: Keith Ripka; PRODUCERS: Wayne Clark, Ronnie Britton, and Robert Speller

CAST—Richard Rescigno (Toulouse-Lautrec), Beverly Gold (Suzanne), Molly Stark (Mme. Jardin), Linda David (Darnelle), Faye Cameron (Yvette Guilbert), Monte Ralstin (Bourges), Susie Vaughan Raney (Claudine), Amy Ryder (Colette), Christopher LeBlanc (Gabriel), Barbara Rouse (Daphne), Valerie Adami (La Goulue), Lana Fevola (Jane Avril), Louis Baldonieri (Valentine), Louise Claps (Mimi), Gerta Grunen (Countess), Andrew Krawetz (Police Chief), Scott Wakefield (Stephen), William Kase (Joseph), Bruno Damon (Bartender), Mark Enis (Claude), James Coleman (Philippe), Michael Del Rio (Pierre), Charlotte d'Amboise (Lulu), Sandra Aldin (Marie), Clayton Sauer (Robert), Thom Stickney (Roland), Marla Kassoff (Simone), Fay Reed (Charlotte), Lory Marcosson (Belle), Schorling Schneider (Gele), Tracy Osuna (Ileana), Franck Mariglio (Marcel), Jose Andres Ocampo Cano (Jacques), Marla Graham (Fifi), Matthew Sullivan (Mircea)

The action occurs in Paris during August and October of 1891.

The musical was presented in two acts (list of musical numbers not available).

NOTES—The Off Off Broadway musical *Toulouse* was of course about Toulouse-Lautrec; the production boasted a cast of thirty-five, and included an early appearance by Charlotte d'Amboise.

For another musical about the subject, see entry for *Times and Appetites of Toulouse-Lautrec* (which references two British musicals based on the painter's life [*Bordello* and *Lautrec*], a 1984 Off Off Broadway play about the subject [also titled *Toulouse*], and *Jane Avril*, a play about one of Toulouse-Lautrec's models); also see entry for *Belle Epoque*, in which Toulouse-Lautrec is a central character. For information about other musicals which dealt with painters, see entry for *Gauguin in Tahiti*.

1661 Tour de Four. THEATRE: Writers' Stage Theatre; OPENING DATE: June 18, 1963; PERFORMANCES: 16; SKETCHES, LYRICS, AND MUSIC: John Aman, Larry Alexander and Gary Popkin, Jean Bergy and Frank Gehrecke, Albert Beach and Gratian Ouelette, Norman Brown and Hugh Taliaferro, June Carroll and Arthur Siegel, Coleman Cohen and Marty Kreiner, Carl Crow, Gerry Donovan, John McKellar and Lance Mulcahy, Ed Fearon and Lee Holdridge, Jack Johnson, Dorothy Mendoza, James Kason, Peter Saldamando, Cy Walter and Andrew Rosenthal, Rod Warren, Edwin Weinberg, and Blair Weille and Bruce Williamson; DIRECTION: Tom Eyen; COSTUMES: Edward Charles; LIGHTING: Gene Tunezi; MUSICAL DIRECTION: Natalie Charlson; PRODUCERS: Richard Everett Upton Productions, Inc., in association with Susan Eden and Tom Eyen

CAST—Lyle O'Hara, Paul Blake, Carl Crow, Carol Fox

The revue was presented in two acts (sketch and song assignments unknown; also, specific writing and composing credits unknown).

ACT ONE—"Tour de Four," "Letters," "Trio Con Brio," "Cold Turkey," "Bus Stop," "Multi-Colored Bush," "This Time Next Year," "D. and D. Rag," "What I Want to Be," "The Test," "Cooperation," "Fallout Shelter," "Ode to a Scrapbook," "Call of the Wild," "That's Why"

ACT TWO—"Whatever Happened," "That Certain Look," "Small Town Girl," "You Came from Outer Space," "Point Number," "Baby John," "Rapid Reading Rachel," "Six O'Clock," "1600 Pennsylvania Avenue," "Cuckoo Song," "Good Ole Days," "Theatres," "Hollywood Folk Song," "Beach Scene," "You Have...," "Lyle's Wedding," "Tour de Four" (reprise)

NOTES—Louis Calta in the *New York Times* noted that despite a total of twenty-nine contributors, the revue *Tour de Four* was "a tour de bore," nothing more than a "collection of songs aspiring to satirical dimensions." Further, the revue's targets were overly familiar, done-to-death topics. Perhaps the most original number was "Theatres"; according to Calta, the song's premise was that plays and musicals should be booked into theatres via an "idea-association plan" (thus the then-current Broadway comedy *A Shot in the Dark* should have been booked into the Booth Theatre). "1600 Pennsylvania Avenue" (lyric and music by Rod Warren) had previously been heard in *No Shoestrings* (see entry), and "Trio Con Brio" was later heard in the first edition of *The Game Is Up* (see entry).

1662 Tourquoise Pantomime. THEATRE: Truck and Warehouse Theatre; OPENING DATE: November 6, 1974; PERFORMANCES: 30; PRODUCTION DEVISED BY: Lindsay Kemp; DIRECTION: Lindsay Kemp; David Haughton, Assistant to the Director; John Spradbury, Stage Director CHOREOGRAPHY: Arlene Phillips; SCENERY: Lindsay Kemp; COSTUMES: Robert Anthony; LIGHTING: John Spradbury; MUSICAL DIRECTION: Henry Krieger; PRODUCERS: A Ron Link and Alan Eichler presentation of the Theatre of the Damned Production

CAST—Cast included Lindsay Kemp and the Incredible Orlando

MUSICAL NUMBERS—Overture, "The Incredible Orlando," "Circus," "Aimez-Vous Bach?," "The Flower," "Orlando at the Palais," "Adam and Eve," "The Alabatross," "Burlesque"

NOTES—*Tourquoise Pantomime* appears to have been performed in one act; the limited engagement seems to have been presented as an Off Off Broadway production.

Note that the production's musical director was Henry Krieger, the future Broadway composer (*Dreamgirls* [1981], *The Tap Dance Kid* [1983], and *Side Show* [1997], the latter boasting one of the finest scores of the 1990s).

The 1974-1975 season was an especially busy one for pantomimist Lindsay Kemp. Besides *Tourquoise Pantomime*, New Yorkers also saw *Flowers*, his program of pantomimes suggested by Jean Genet's *Notre Dame des Fleurs*; it opened on Broadway at the Biltmore Theatre on October 7, 1974, for twenty-four performances (it had earlier been seen in London, opening there on March 27, 1974). And on January

8, 1975, Kemp starred in the title role of *Salome*, his all-male adaptation of Oscar Wilde's 1896 play which opened Off Broadway at the 62 E. Fourth Street Theatre for thirty performances.

1663 Tovah: Out of Her Mind! THEATRE: Playhouse 91/Jewish Repertory Theatre; OPENING DATE: April 21, 1996; PERFORMANCES: 43; CHIEF WRITER: Larry Amoros; DIRECTION: Sara Louise Lazarus; CHOREOGRAPHY: Sara Louise Lazarus; SCENERY: Tony Walton ("Visual Consultant"); COSTUMES: William Ivey Long ("Costume Consultant"); LIGHTING: Matt Berman; MUSICAL DIRECTION: Scott Cady; PRODUCER: The Jewish Repertory Theatre (Ran Avni, Artistic Director)

CAST—Tovah Feldshuh

NOTES—In this one-woman show, Tovah Feldshuh portrayed a variety of characters, ages eight to eighty. The mostly comic monologues were occasionally interspersed with songs. While most of the offerings by the Jewish Repertory Theatre were Off Off Broadway productions, *Tovah: Out of Her Mind!* appears to have been produced under an Off Broadway contract.

The revue was recorded by Tovah Records (CD # 01). The list below is derived from the songs and sketches heard on the CD: "One Woman Show" (lyric and music by Barry Klienbart and David Levy), "No Leg to Stand On" (lyric and music by Gary Lyons), "Vilma Van Schtunkeneh" (lyric and music by Larry Amoros and Gary Lyons; song based on a character created by Tovah Feldshuh), "Shalom Santa" (lyric and music by Douglas J. Cohen and Tom Tace), "He Touched Me" (from *Drat! The Cat!*, 1965; lyric by Ira Levin, music by Milton Schafer), "The Blue Room" (*The Girl Friend*, 1926; lyric by Lorenz Hart, music by Richard Rodgers), "Just a Housewife" (*Working*, 1978; lyric and music by Craig Carnelia), "Joya Gormezano" (written by Jane Mushabac), "Cuando El Rey Nimrod" (traditional Sephardic song), "Ayloo, Loo, Loo" (lyric and music by Sidney Feldshuh), "Of Thee I Sing" (*Of Thee I Sing*, 1931; lyric by Ira Gershwin, music by George Gershwin), Gershwin Monologue (written by Tovah Feldshuh and Jack Gottlieb; based on material from Gottlieb's *Funny, It Doesn't Sound Jewish: A Study in American Popular Music*), "My One and Only" (*Funny Face*, 1927; lyric by Ira Gershwin, music by George Gershwin)/"Oh, Lady, Be Good!" (*Lady, Be Good!*, 1924; lyric by Ira Gershwin, music by George Gershwin)/"It Ain't Necessarily So" (*Porgy and Bess*, 1935; lyric by Ira Gershwin, music by George Gershwin), Gershwin Melody: "I Got Rhythm" (*Girl Crazy*, 1930; lyric by Ira Gershwin, music by George Gershwin)/"Fascinating Rhythm" (*Lady, Be Good!*, 1924; lyric by Ira Gershwin, music by George Gershwin), "Joe" (*Working*, 1978; lyric and music by Craig Carnelia), Sophie Tucker Monologue (by Larry Amoros; sequence included excerpts from Sophie Tucker's original performances)/ "I Don't Want to Get Thin" (lyric by Jack Yellin, music by Milton Ager), "Dame Victoria" (sketch by Rick Mitz; sketch based on a character created by Tovah Feldshuh), "Be Bop a Lula" (lyric and music by Gene Vincent and Sheriff Tex Davis), "If I Sing" (*Closer Than Ever*, 1989; lyric by Richard Maltby, Jr., music by David Shire), "Secret Gardens" (lyric and music by Judy Collins; special lyric by David Friedman), "Grandma Ada" (sketch by Rick Mitz; sketch based on a character created by Tovah Feldshuh), "Neverland" (*Peter Pan*, 1954; lyric by Betty Comden and Adolph Green, music by Jule Styne)

1664 Tracers. THEATRE: The Susan Stein Shiva Theatre/The Public Theatre; OPENING DATE: January 21, 1985; PERFORMANCES: 186; PLAY: Vincent Caristi, Richard Chaves, John DiFusco, Eric E. Emerson, Rick Gallavan, Merlin Marston, and Harry Stephens (with Sheldon Lettich, a contributing writer); DIRECTION: John DiFusco; SCENERY: John Falabella; COSTUMES: David Navarro Velasquez; LIGHTING: Terry Wuthrich; PRODUCERS: Joseph Papp; The Vietnam Veterans Ensemble Theatre Company (Thomas Bird, Artistic Director); Jason Steven Cohen, Associate Producer

CAST—R.J. Bonds (Professor), Lee Shepherd (Sergeant Williams), Vincent Caristi (Baby Sam), Richard Chaves (Dinky Dau), Anthony Chisholm (Habu), Josh Cruze (Doc), Brian Delate (Little John), Jim Tracy (Scooter)

The action occurs during three time periods: The Vietnam War, the period shortly thereafter, and the present time.

The play with music was presented in two acts.

ACT ONE—"Walking on a Thin Line" (lyric and music by Huey Lewis and The News [Pessis/Wells]), "Shut Out the Light" (lyric and music by Bruce Springsteen), "Fixin' to Die Rag" (lyric and music by Country Joe and the Fish), "Sympathy for the Devil" (lyric and music by Mick Jagger and Keith Richards)

ACT TWO—"Light My Fire"/"The Unknown Soldier" (lyrics and music by The Doors), "Four & Twenty Years Ago" (lyric and music by Crosby, Stills, Nash and Young), "Higher" (lyric and music by Sly and the Family Stone), "Born in the USA" (lyric and music by Bruce Springsteen), "Gimme Shelter" (lyric and music by Mick Jagger and Keith Richards), "Born Never Asked" (lyric and music by Laurie Anderson), Post-Epilogue: "Captains of Courage" (lyric and music by Brian Delate and Hal Brister)

NOTES—*Tracers*, an oral history-cum-docudrama about Vietnam veterans, was told from the perspective of the war and its aftermath. The work consisted of a collage of monologues, sketches, and semi-choreographed movement, all of which were occasionally accompanied by pre-recorded songs serving as background music. The play, which premiered in Los Angeles in 1980, was conceived by John DiFusco and was written by him and seven other Vietnam veterans (see above credits), all of whom appeared in the original production; David Berry, the author of the Vietnam drama *G.R. Point* (which opened Off Broadway in 1977 and on Broadway in 1979), served as the play's dramaturg. All the performers and writers (including Berry) were Vietnam veterans, and two of the original writers-performers (Vincent Caristi and Richard Chaves) appeared in the Off Broadway production.

In his review for the *New York Times*, Frank Rich wrote that DiFusco and Berry "artfully" assembled the vignettes and monologues into a "hallucinatory dramatic whole," and noted that despite one's personal views of the war, "we're on the side of these veterans as soon as we meet them." While Douglas Watt in the *New York Daily News* felt the material was somewhat too familiar, he nonetheless praised the play's "straight-from-the-groin" approach and its "shrewd sense of theatricality." Watts also explained the play's title (a soldier would fire tracer bullets to alert others in his platoon that he was running short of ammunition). *Tracers* was selected as a Best Play in *The Best Plays of 1984-1985*, and its script was published by Hill & Wang in 1986.

Tracers was later revived Off Off Broadway by the 29th Street Repertory Theatre on September 11, 1997, for sixteen performances.

For another Off Broadway view of American soldiers in Vietnam, see entry for *Dispatches*.

1665 The Transposed Heads. "A Tale of Passion." THEATRE: The Mitzi E. Newhouse Theatre/Lincoln Center; OPENING DATE: October 31, 1986; PERFORMANCES: 4; BOOK: Sidney Goldfarb; original novella by Thomas Mann adapted by Julie Taymor and Sidney Goldfarb; MUSIC: Elliot Goldenthal; DIRECTION: Julie Taymor; CHOREOGRAPHY: Margo Sappington, Julie Taymor, and The Company; Indian Choreography by Swati Gupte Bhise and Rajika Puri; SCENERY: "Based on a concept by" Alexander Okun; "Lightscapes" design by Caterina Bertolotto; COSTUMES: Carol Oditz; Puppets and Masks designed by Julie Taymor; LIGHTING: Marcia Madeira; MUSICAL DIRECTION: Joshua Rosenblum; PRODUCERS: Lincoln Center Theatre (Gregory Mosher, Director; Bernard Gersten, Executive Director) and American Music Theatre Festival (Marjorie Samoff, Producing Director; Eric Salzman, Artistic Director)

CAST—Yamil Borges (Sita), Scott Burkholder (Shridaman), Richard Hester (Puppeteer), Stephen Kaplin (Puppeteer), Barbara Pollitt (Puppeteer), Rajika Puri (Narrator), Byron Utley (Nanda), Erin Cressida Wilson (Puppeteer)

SOURCES—An Indian legend and the 1940 novella *The Transposed Heads* by Thomas Mann.

NOTES—*The Transposed Heads* first premiered Off Off Broadway at the Ark Theatre on May 10, 1984, and then on September 11, 1986, a revised version was produced at the American Music Theatre Festival in Philadelphia; a few weeks later, the revised production was seen in New York.

The story was based on an Indian legend about two men, one devoted to the pleasures of the mind, the other of the flesh. When they behead themselves, each head is miraculously attached to the other's body. The wife of the former, who loved both men, must now decide which man is her actual husband. In reviewing the revised production's New York premiere, Mel Gussow in the *New York Times* felt the work was more literary than theatrical. But he praised Julie Taymor's puppetry, and he liked Sidney Goldfarb's score, "twangy and percussive in the Indian manner."

1666 The Trials of OZ. THEATRE: Anderson Theatre; OPENING DATE: December 19, 1972; PERFORMANCES: 15; PLAY: Geoff Robertson; LYRICS AND MUSIC: Mick Jagger, Jordan Kaplan, John Lennon, Buzzy Linhart, Yoko Ono, and Geoff Robertson; DIRECTION: Jim Sharman; SCENERY: Mark Ravitz; COSTUMES: Joseph G. Aulisi; LIGHTING: Jules Fisher; MUSICAL DIRECTION: Bill Cunningham; PRODUCERS: Richard Scanga presents The Friends of Van Wolf Production (Ivor David Balding, Executive Producer); Cathy Cochran, Associate Producer

CAST—Harry Gold (Narrator, Vivien Berger), CLIFF DE YOUNG (Richard Neville), Dan Leach (James Anderson), Greg Antonacci (Felix Dennis), Peter Kybart (Dr. Shoofield, Dr. Haward), Dallas Alinder (George Melly, Rupert Bear), Myra Carter (Dr. Josephine Klein, Mrs. Berger, Court Officer), Gabor Morea (Professor Dworkin, Foreman of the Jury), Ginny Russell (Caroline Coon) Alek Primrose (Marty Feldman, Detective Inspector Luff), RICHARD CLARKE (Brian Leary, Q.C.), GRAHAM JARVIS (John Mortimer, Q.C.), WILLIAM ROERICK (Michael Argyle), Leata Galloway (Court Officer); The Bells of Saint Trinian's (Band)

SOURCE—The (edited) court transcripts of the twenty-seven day trial of the publishers of *Oz* magazine.

The action occurs at the Old Bailey in London in 1971.

The play with music was presented in two acts.

ACT ONE—"Oranges and Lemons" (traditional) (Company), "Rupert Bear Song" (lyricist and composer unknown) (Dallas Alinder), "If You Can't Join 'Em, Beat 'Em" (lyric and music by Buzzy Linhart) (Company), "Dirty Is the Funniest Thing I Know" (lyric and music by Buzzy Linhart) (Harry Gold, 'Rupert Bears' [performers unknown]), "Masquerade Ball" (lyric and music by Buzzy Linhart and Jordan Kaplan) (Leata Galloway)

ACT TWO—"The Love's Still Growing" (lyric and music by Buzzy Linhart) (Cliff DeYoung, Dan Leach, Greg Antonacci), "Give Me Excess of It" (lyricist and composer unknown) (Cliff De Young, Ginny Russell), "Schoolboy Blues" (lyric and music by Mick Jagger) (Harry Gold), "The Justice Game" (lyric by Geoff Robertson, music by Buzzy Linhart) (Harry Gold), "God Save Us" (lyric and music by John Lennon and Yoko Ono) (Company)

NOTES—*The Trials of OZ* was originally produced as a staged reading by the Royal Shakespeare Company in London. The play with incidental songs dealt with an actual trial in which the editors of a British magazine called *OZ* were tried on obscenity charges. In his *New York Times*' review, Clive Barnes discussed the offending issue of the magazine. The play was against censorship and in favor of freedom of expression. The evening may have been too self-important, and apparently its satire was uninspired. New York audiences weren't interested, and the work was gone within two weeks.

1667 The Triumph of St. Joan. THEATRE: New York City Center; OPENING DATE: April 16, 1959; PERFORMANCES: 2; LIBRETTO: Norman Dello Jolo; MUSIC: Norman Dello Jolo; DIRECTION: Jose Quintero; SCENERY: David Hays; COSTUMES: Ruth Morley; MUSICAL DIRECTION: Herbert Grossman; PRODUCER: The New York City Opera Company

CAST—Mack Harrell (Cauchon), Chester Watson (Father Julien), Chester Ludgin (Jailer), Lee Venora (Joan), Frank Porretta (Sentry)

The opera was produced in one act.

NOTES—The New York City Opera presented the premiere of the third version of Dello Jolo's opera *The Triumph of St. Joan*. It had first been produced at Sarah Lawrence College in 1950; a revised version was televised by NBC in 1956 (as *The Trial at Rouen*); and then a third version (with the opera's original title) was seen in New York in the current production.

Howard Taubman in the *New York Times* noted the music lacked a "fresh and dazzling illumination." But he nonetheless felt the score was the work of a "seasoned" composer whose vocal lines were "always ingratiating and often dramatic"; further, he felt the orchestra was "songful and decisive in comment ... the [musical] style is Italianate." Taubman praised Lee Venora. He wrote that she was "a fragile, moving and indomitable Joan" with a voice which had "purity of tone and assurance of style." Venora later appeared in the 1961 Broadway musical *Kean*, and her "Willow, Willow, Willow" is one of the highlights of early 1960s musicals.

For information about other lyric works inspired by the story of Joan of Arc, see entry for *The Survival of St. Joan*.

The opera was performed on a double bill with a revival of Gian-Carlo Menotti's *The Medium*, which had first been seen on Broadway in 1947.

1668 Trixie True, Teen Detective. "A New Musical." THEATRE: Theatre de Lys; OPENING DATE: December 4, 1980; PERFORMANCES: 86; BOOK: Kelly Hamilton; LYRICS: Kelly Hamilton; MUSIC: Kelly Hamilton; DIRECTION: Bill Gile; CHOREOGRAPHY: Arthur Faria; SCENERY: Michael J. Hotopp and Paul De Pass; COSTUMES: David Toser; LIGHTING: Craig Miller; MUSICAL DIRECTION: Robert (Rob) Fisher; PRODUCERS: Doug Cole, Joe Novak, Spencer Tandy, and Joseph Butt, by special arrangement with Lucille Lortel Productions, Inc.

CAST—GENE LINDSAY (Joe), Jay Lowman (Al, Wilhelm), MARILYN SOKOL (Miss Snood, Madame Olga), KATHY ANDRINI (Trixie True), Keith Rice (Dick Dickerson), Alison Bevan (LaVerne), Marianna Allen (Maxine), Keith Caldwell (Bobby)

The action occurs during the mid-1940s in the New York offices of School Publishing and in the mythical town of Cherry Hill, New Jersey.

The musical was presented in two acts.

ACT ONE—"Trixie's on the Case!" (Jay Lowman, Gene Lindsey, Marilyn Sokol, Kathy Andrini, Crooks), "This Is Indeed My Lucky Day" (Kathy Andrini), "Most Popular and Most Likely to Succeed" (Keith Rice, Keith Caldwell, Marianna Allen, Alison Bevan), "Mr. and Mrs. Dick Dickerson" (Keith Rice, Kathy Andrini), "Juvenile Fiction" (Marilyn Sokol), "Trixie's on the Case!" (reprise) (Kathy Andrini, Marianne Allen, Alison Bevan), "A Katzenjammer Kinda Song" (Marilyn Sokol, Jay Lowman), Act One Finaletto (Keith Rice, Kathy Andrini)

ACT TWO—Entr'acte (Orchestra), "In Cahoots" (Gene Lindsey, Marilyn Sokol), "The Mystery of the Moon" (Kathy Andrini), "The Secret of the Tapping Shoes" (Kathy Andrini, Marianne Allen, Alison Bevan, Keith Caldwell), "This Is Indeed My Lucky Day" (reprise) (Gene Lindsey, Keith Caldwell, Marianne Allen, Alison Bevan), "In Cahoots" (reprise) (Gene Lindsey), "Rita from Argentina" (Marilyn Sokol, Gene Lindsey), "Trixie True, Teen Detective"! (Marianna Allen, Alison Bevan, Keith Caldwell, Gene Lindsey, Keith Rice), Finale (Ensemble)

NOTES—Expectations were high for *Trixie True, Teen Detective*, a spoof of teenage-girl detective stories of the *Nancy Drew* variety.

But Frank Rich in the *New York Times* found the show "misbegotten," noting the book was "all wet," the jokes "unfunny," the score "tuneless," the choreography "lackluster," and the cast's singing "generally mediocre." But he noted that Michael J. Hotopp and Paul de Pass' scenery was "fun," "clever," and "full of surprises," and reported that with "the greatest of ease," a "sleek" Manhattan office of the 1940s broke apart to reveal a variety of settings.

The musical disappeared after less than three months, and the lack of a cast album probably doomed the show from having an afterlife. The script was published by Samuel French, Inc., in 1981.

Robert Fisher, the show's musical director, became a New York theatre fixture with his Coffee Club Orchestra and its frequent participation in the *Encores!* concert revival series (see entry). A quarter-century after its Off Broadway premiere, the musical was finally recorded when it was produced at Cabrini College (Radnor, Pennsylvania); the CD was released by Original Cast Records in 2006 (# OC-6180).

1669 Trolls. "Is Life Gay After 40?" THEATRE: Actors' Playhouse; OPENING DATE: May 19, 2005; PERFORMANCES: 70; BOOK: Bill Dyer; LYRICS: Bill Dyer; MUSIC: Dick DeBenedictis; DIRECTION: Pamela Hall; CHOREOGRAPHY: John Hoshko; SCENERY: Matthew Maraffi; COSTUMES: Karl A. Ruckdeschel; LIGHTING: Graham Kindred; MUSICAL DIRECTION: Carl Danielsen; PRODUCERS: DBD Productions in association with Edmund Gaynes and Pamela Hall

CAST—Mark Baker (Terry), Bram Heidinger (Blane), Albert Insinnia (Juan), Barry McNabb (Jo), Dale Radunz (Boomie), James Van Treuren (Michael), Christian Whelan (Phillip), Brynn Neal (Myrna)

The action occurs in West Hollywood in 1998.

The musical was presented in one act.

MUSICAL NUMBERS—"Trolls" (James Van Treuren, Mark Baker, Christian Whelan, Albert Insinnia), "Work It!" (Barry McNabb, Albert Insinnia, James Van Treuren, Mark Baker, Christian Whelan, Bram Heidinger), "Whatever Happened?" (Christian Whelan, Barry McNabb, James Van Treuren, Albert Insinnia, Mark Baker), "Will Someone Remember Me?" (Bram Heidinger, Dale Radunz), "Gay Caballeros" (Albert Insinnia, James Van Treuren, Mark Baker, Chrstian Whelan, Bram Heidinger, Dale Radunz, Barry McNabb), "If I Could Live My Life Again" (Brynn Neal, Dale Radunz), "Back in the Gay Old Days" (James Van Treuren, Mark Baker), "Duet" (Christian Whelan, Bram Heidinger), "All This and Heaven Too" (Dale Radunz), "After Time" (Company), "Trolls" (reprise) (Company)

NOTES—*Trolls* dealt with the lives and relationships of gay men over forty years old. Anita Gates in the *New York Times* praised the "glorious beginning" of the first act, in which the characters sang the title song at a party they were attending. She felt the evening had "tons of potential" and was on the verge of being a "terrific" musical. And while she found the "affecting" songs somewhat derivative, she also noted that "imitation Sondheim is better than no Sondheim at all." Gates mentioned it was difficult to figure out how old the characters were supposed to be: they fondly recalled their disco days, and also looked back on Betty Grable, the Andrews Sisters, and big-band music. Incidentally, the songs were performed to pre-recorded musical accompaniment.

1670 Tropicana. "A New Musical." THEATRE: Musical Theatre Works; OPENING DATE: May 29, 1985; PERFORMANCES: 16; BOOK: George Abbott; LYRICS: Peter Napolitano; additional lyrics by Robert Nassif (Lindsey); MUSIC: Robert Nassif (Lindsey); DIRECTION: George Abbott; CHOREOGRAPHY: Donald Saddler; SCENERY: James Noone; COSTUMES: Bruce Goodrich; LIGHTING: Clarke W. Thornton; MUSICAL DIRECTION: Lawrence W. Hill; PRODUCER: Musical Theatre Works (Anthony J. Stimac, Artistic Director)

CAST—Eugene J. Anthony (Papa Sanchez, Ghost #1), Nicholas Augustus (Roberto Mendoza), Mark Basile (Soldier, Policeman, Ricardo, Peddler, Man on Bench, Luis), Roxann Cabalero (Ana Sanchez), Constance Carpenter (Grandma), Ann Casapini (Nightclub Singer, Beggar Woman, Ghost #2), Natalie Costa (Estrella Mendoza), Christofer de Oni (Julio, Pimp, Pancho), Bert Fraser (General Zapata, Captain, Sergeant, Guide), Charles Goff (Alfredo Mendoza), T.J. Harris (Pepi Mendoza), Frank Kosik (Felipe, Ghost #3, Marine), Edmund Lyndeck (President Mendoza), LaDonna Mabry (Maria), Poli Rogers (Mama Sanchez), Lara Teeter (Bill Smith), Jon Vandertholen (Pedro, Guard, Ensemble), William Walters (Amigo, Ambassador Wright), Lynne Ann Williams (Prostitute, Chorus)

The musical was presented in two acts.

ACT ONE—"Free Our Sons" (Townswomen), "I Will Remember You" (Roxann Cabalero), "I'm Still Alive" (Roxann Cabalero, Mendoza Household), "Ancient Land" (Mendoza Household), "Ana, Goodbye" (Roxann Cabalero, Poli Rogers, Eugene J. Anthony, Lara Teeter, Townspeople), "Dark Angel" (Lara Teeter), "Street People" (Lara Teeter, Bert Fraser, Mark Basile, Christofer de Oni, Ann Casapini, Hookers, Ensemble), "Butterfly" (T.J. Harris), "The Mendoza March" (Edmund Lyndeck, T.J. Harris), "Teach Me" (Roxann Cabalero, Lara Teeter)

ACT TWO—"Lucia" (Ann Casapini), "Now I Know" (Natalie Costa), "Look At Me Go" (T.J. Harris, Constance Carpenter, Lara Teeter, Roxann Cabalero, Jon Vandertholen), "Butterfly" (reprise) (Edmund Lyndeck), "Now" (Roxann Cabalero, Lara Teeter), "A Second Chance" (Eugene J. Anthony, Ann Casapini, Frank Kosik), Finale (Company)

NOTES—The Off Off Broadway *Tropicana* appears to be George Abbott's penultimate production, his 121st. He first appeared as a performer in the 1913 Broadway play *The Misleading Lady*, and his final production was his direction of the 1987 Broadway revival of *Broadway*, which he wrote and directed in 1926.

Lyrics for "Free Our Sons," "I Will Remember You," "Ancient Land," "Dark Angel," "Teach Me," and "Now" were by Robert Nassif. The program incorrectly identified Nassif (instead of Peter Napolitano) as the lyricist for the second-act reprise of "Butterfly."

1671 Troubadour. THEATRE: Riverside Theatre; OPENING DATE: May 22, 1990; PERFORMANCES: 16; BOOK: John Martin and Bert Draesel; LYRICS: John Martin; MUSIC: Bert Draesel; DIRECTION: John Margulis; CHOREOGRAPHY: John Nunes; SCENERY: Ralph Castaldo; COSTUMES: Debbie Hall; LIGHTING: Jeff Glovsky; MUSICAL DIRECTION: Howard Kilik

CAST—Christopher Mellon (Francesco), Paul Romanello (Elias), Evan Matthews (Bernardo), Keith Clark (Leo), Drew Kelly (Juniper), Sibel Ergener (Clare), Daniel Timothy Johnson (Pietro, Cardinal Ugolino, Pope Innocent III, Syltan), Tom Tomasovic (Signor Faverone, Merchant, Friar, Papal Secretary, Saracen, Crusader), Elizabeth M. Ebel (Leper)

The action occurs in and around Assisi between the years 1205-1225.

The musical was presented in two acts (division of acts and song assignments unknown; musical numbers listed in performance order).

MUSICAL NUMBERS—"Assisi," "The Troubadour," Dance, "Who Can Benefit You Most?," "Change," "How Strange," "Troubadour of the Lord," "There Must Be Something More," "You Can't Have Me," "The Earth is the Lord's," "Organize," "The Rule"/"Called to the Simple Life," "Listen to the Voice," "An Unusual Normal," "There Is a Mystery," "Brother Mountain," "There Is a Time," "This Is the Man," "Every Day," "Jerusalem," "Soon," "I Wonder I Wonder," "And We Were One," "It Was Magnificent," "Listen to the Voice" (reprise), "The Order," "Let's Go to Tuscany," "It's Glorious," "Let There Be Books," "Once I Had a Vision," "A Great Cathedral," "Praised Be My Lord"

NOTES—The Off Off Broadway musical *Troubadour* (not to be confused with the 1978 British musical with the same title, also set in medieval times) was about the life of Saint Francis of Assisi; for another musical about the subject, see entry for *Francis*. *Troubadour* was later produced at the Ubu Repertory Theatre in June 1991. In reviewing the 1991 production, Stephen Holden in the *New York Times* noted the evening was a "Sunday school pageant with Broadway pretensions." And while he found the score a "fairly sophisticated pastiche" of Richard Rodgers and Oscar Hammerstein II via Andrew Lloyd Webber, he felt it was "terribly long-winded" (Holden reported that three-quarters of the two-and-one-half hour musical was sung). Holden also said the sight of Franciscan Brothers playing catch with papier-mache rocks in one sequence and "clomping about in ring-around-the-rosy style" in no less than two other sequences made the musical seem "simply ridiculous."

1672 Trumpets of the Lord. THEATRE: Astor Place Playhouse; transferred to One Sheridan Square on January 22, 1964; OPENING DATE: December 21, 1963; PERFORMANCES: 160; ADAPTATION: Vinnette Carroll; LYRICS AND MUSIC: Traditional gospel songs; DIRECTION: Donald McKayle; SCENERY: Ed Wittstein; COSTUMES: Norman Maxon; LIGHTING: Nicola Cernovich; MUSICAL DIRECTION: Howard Roberts; PRODUCERS: Theodore Mann in association with Will B. Sandler

CAST—Al Freeman, Jr. (the Rev. Ridgley Washington), Theresa Merritt (Henrietta Pinkston), Lex Monson (the Rev. Bradford Parham), Cicely Tyson (the Rev. Marion Alexander), Elizabeth Brown (Female Voice), Berniece Hall (Female Voice), Earl Baker (Male Voice), Bill Glover (Male Voice), William Stewart (Male Voice), Michael Hinton (Singer)

SOURCE—The 1922 book *God's Trombones* by James Weldon Johnson (the book is a collection of his sermons). The musical was performed in one act.

MUSICAL NUMBERS—"So Glad I'm Here" (Company), "Call to Prayer" (Company), "Listen Lord—A Prayer" (Lex Monson), "Amen Response" (Company), "Is His Care" (Company), "The Creation" (Lex Monson), "God Lead Us Along" (Therera Merritt), Noah Medley: "Noah Built the Ark" (Cicely Tyson), "Run Sinner Run" (Cicily Tyson, Company), "Didn't It Rain" (Berniece Hall, Company), "The Judgement Day" (Al Freeman, Jr.), "In That Great Gettin' Up Morning" (Al Freeman Jr., Company), "God Almighty Is Gonna Cut You Down" (Bill Glover, Company), Funeral Suite: "Soon One Morning" (Company), "There's a Man" (Company), "Go Down Death" (Lex Monson), "He'll Understand" (Theresa Merritt), "Were You There" (Cicely Tyson), "Calvary" (Earl Baker, Bill Glover, William Stewart), "Crucifixion" (Elizabeth Brown, Berniece Hall), Freedom Suite: "Reap What You Sow" (Company), "We Shall Not Be Moved" (Company), "We Are Soldiers" (Company), "Woke Up This Morning" (Company), "Let My People Go" (Al Freeman, Jr.), "We Shall Overcome" (Company), "Jacob's Ladder" (Company), "God Be with You"

NOTES—*Trumpets of the Lord* was Vinnette Carroll's adaptation of *God's Trombones*, a collection of sermons written by James Weldon Johnson (1871-1938) which was originally published in 1922. The musical told Biblical stories through the use of gospel and other traditional music. In 1969, the musical was briefly seen on Broadway.

For other adaptations of *God's Trombones*, see entries for *Shakespeare in Harlem* (1960) as well as two revised versions of *Trumpets of the Lord* (titled *God's Trombones!* in 1989 and *God's Trombones* in 1997), both of which were seen Off Off Broadway. Also see entry for *God's Trombones*, a 1975 Off Off Broadway adaptation which doesn't seem to be based on Carroll's version. There was also a version presented at Town Hall on April 16, 1982, for three performances (this, too, doesn't seem to have been based on Carroll's adaptation). The entry for *Shakespeare in Harlem* also references *Godsong*, an adaptation of the material by Tad Truesdale.

1673 T.S. Eliot: Midwinter Vigil(ante). THEATRE: Judson Poets' Theatre; OPENING DATE: March 20, 1981; PERFORMANCES: 16; TEXT: Al Carmines MUSIC: Al Carmines; CHOREOGRAPHY: Matthew Nash; SCENERY: George Deem; COSTUMES: George Deem; LIGHTING: Andrew Taines; PRODUCER: The Judson Poets' Theatre

CAST—Judith Elaine (Virginia, Dr. Bellman), Richard Battaglia (Eddie, Dr. Mace), Georgia Creighton (Petulia, Dr. Weatherly), Tony Calabro (Bishop, Dr. Longworth), Robert Herrig (Freddy, Dr. Fothringill), Essie Borden (Ophelia, Dr. Gilt), Blaine Brown

The action occurs at a cocktail party and at the Princeton Institute for Advanced Studies.

The musical was presented in two acts.

NOTES—Al Carmines referred to *T.S. Eliot: Midwinter Vigil(ante)* as an "opera-play." The Off Off Broadway work opened a few months before *Cats* premiered in London. *Cats* practically made Eliot a household name (something *The Waste Land* and *The Love Song of J. Alfred Prufrock* were never quite able to do).

Carmines' musical seems to have dealt in part with Eliot's intellectual journey from disillusionment to religious faith. But, as John S. Wilson noted in the *New York Times*, not understanding Carmines' musicals didn't preclude one from enjoying them. Wilson praised the "brash and buoyant" score, the "brittle" acting and singing style of the cast (he singled out Georgia Creighton and Judith Elaine), and the "crisp, unfaltering pace" of the production. Appropriately enough, the first act of the musical took place at a cocktail party.

1674 Tubes. THEATRE: Astor Place Theatre; OPENING DATE: November 17, 1991; PERFORMANCES: Still playing as of December 31, 2007; CREATED AND WRITTEN BY: Blue Man Group (Matt Goldman, Phil Stanton, and Chris Wink); Caryl Glaab, Artistic Coordinator; DIRECTION: Marlene Swartz; SCENERY: Kevin Joseph Roach; Kurisu-Chan, Computer Graphics Design; COSTUMES: Lydia Tanji and Patricia Murphy; LIGHTING: Brian Aldous; Stan Pressner, Associate Lighting Designer; PRODUCERS: Mark Dunn and Makoto Deguchi; John Rizzo, Assistant Producer; Maria Di Dia, Executive Producer

CAST—Blue Man Group (Matt Goldman, Phil Stanton, and Chris Wink); Blue Man Group Band (Larry Heinemann, Stephen March, Ian Pai)

The performance piece was presented in one act.

NOTES—The performance piece *Tubes* has been running Off Broadway since November 1991; in January and February of that year it had been performed at La Mama.

Mel Gussow in the *New York Times* said the "bald blue bullet-headed" Blue Man Group provided a "barbaric yawp of childlike pleasure" as they spoofed the art world (and performance art in particular). In one sequence, they bit into eggs filled with paint, and then proceeded to spit the paint onto canvasses in the style of Jackson Pollock. In another, they deconstructed Andrew Wyeth's "Christina's World" by zapping the figure of Christina from the painting. Gussow had a word of warning to those ticketholders who dislike audience participation: he reported that one volunteer from the audience was hung by his feet, "swabbed" with paint, and set against a canvas as if he were "a large human paintbrush."

Gussow noted that the virtually wordless evening was accompanied by a "burbling musical background."

As of this writing, a combination CD/DVD set of the Blue Man Group's most recent tour is scheduled to be released in Spring 2008 by Rhino Records; *How to Be a Megastar* will include a sequence titled "Inside the Tube," which explores the group's creative processes.

1675 Tully (In No Particular Order)

NOTES—See entry for *The New York Musical Theatre Festival*.

1676 Tune the Grand Up! Words and Music by Jerry Herman. "A New Musical Revue." THEATRE: Bruno Walter Auditorium/Lincoln Center; OPENING DATE: December 18, 1978; PERFORMANCES: 3; LYRICS: Jerry Herman; MUSIC: Jerry Herman; DIRECTION: Jeffrey K. Neill; COSTUMES: Charles W. Roeder; LIGHTING: Chris Peabody; MUSICAL DIRECTION: Wendell Kindberg; PRODUCERS: Stage Directors & Choreographers Workshop Foundation, Inc.; Sally E. Parry and Peter M. Paulino, Producers

CAST—Barbara Coggin, Lou Corato, Jim Jeffrey, Norb Joerder, Joan Kobin, Edna Manilow, Ed Penn, Maitland Peters, Lisa M. Steinman, Lynne Stuart, Joan Susswein

The revue was presented in two acts.

NOTES—This Off Off Broadway revue was a free three-performance event which celebrated the songs of Jerry Herman. It was created by Jeffrey K. Neill, who directed the revue and who apparently wrote most of the continuity. Additional dialogue was written by Mary McCartney.

The revue consisted of medleys from the following Broadway musicals by Herman: *Milk and Honey* (1961), *Hello, Dolly!* (1964), *Mame* (1966), *Dear World* (1969), and *Mack & Mabel* (1974). The revue also included a preview of his latest musical, *The Grand Tour*, which opened at the Palace Theatre three weeks later, on January 11, 1979; the number performed in *Tune the Grand Up!* ("Life Is Worth the Trouble") wasn't heard in the Broadway production.

Of Herman's four Off Broadway musicals, the revue included two songs from *Nightcap* and three from *Parade*; *I Feel Wonderful* and *Madame Aphrodite* weren't represented (see entries for all four productions). The numbers from *Nightcap* were "Show Tune" (a/k/a "There Is No Tune Like a Show Tune" and "Show Tune in 2/4 Time") and "Your Good Morning" ("Show Tune" was also heard in *Parade*). Songs from *Parade* were "(I Was Born to Do) The Two-a-Day," "(Keep) Your Hand in My Hand," and "(I'll Make Sure My Head Is Clearer) The Next Time I Love."

There have been two Broadway revue-tributes to Jerry Herman, *Jerry's Girls* (1985, 139 performances) and *An Evening with Jerry Herman* (1998, twenty-eight performances). Prior to its Broadway production, *Jerry's Girls* had previously been seen Off Off Broadway (see entry for the 1981 version). On February 27, 2003, the Off Broadway revue *Showtune: The Words and Music of Jerry Herman* opened at the Theatre at Saint Peter's Church for fifty-three performances. It covered the same basic musical territory as the other Jerry Herman tributes, and its cast included the always welcome Martin Vidnovic, who often came across as the musical theatre's equivalent to Anthony Franciosa (actually, the latter appeared in the national touring version of *Grand Hotel*, his one and only musical [Franciosa performed the role of Otternschlag]).

1677 Turns. THEATRE: The Chernuchin Theatre/The American Theatre of Actors; OPENING DATE: June 8, 1980; PERFORMANCES: 14 (estimated); SCRIPT: "Based upon the writings of people in their prime"; adapted by Robert H. Livingston; LYRICS: Will Holt; MUSIC: Gary William Friedman; DIRECTION: Robert H. Livingston; CHOREOGRAPHY: Ginger Prince; SCENERY: Clarke Dunham; COSTUMES: Sigrid Insull; LIGHTING: David F. Segal; MUSICAL DIRECTION: John Mahoney; PRODUCER: The American Theatre of Actors

CAST—Thelma Carpenter (Helen), Rita Gardner (Edna), Tiger Haynes (Charles), Michael Ingram (Rudy), Bobo Lewis (Dorothy), Fred Miller (John), Renee Orin (Janet), Malachi Throne (Eric), Ted Thurston (Ben)

The musical was presented in two acts.

ACT ONE *Spring-Summer:* "Somebody Else" (Company), "This Is My Song" (Company), "Fine for the Shape I'm In" (Bobo Lewis, Rita Gardner, Thelma Carpenter), "Two of Us" (Renee Orin), "Janet Get Up" (Company), "I Like It" (Company), "I Never Made Money from Music" (Tiger Haynes), "Vivaldi" (Rita Gardner), "Do You Remember?" (Company), "In April" (Bobo Lewis), "Pick More Daisies" (Company)

ACT TWO *Fall-Winter:* "Taking Our Turn" (Company), "I Am Not Old" (Thelma Carpenter), "Sweet Longings" (Tiger Haynes, Bobo Lewis, Fred Miller, Renee Orin), "Do You Remember?" (reprise) (Company), "The Kite" (Michael Ingram), "Good Luck to You" (Company), "In This House" (Malachi Throne), "Somebody Else" (reprise) (Company), "It Still Isn't Over" (Ted Thurston, Bobo Lewis), "This Is My Song" (finale) (Company)

NOTES—*Turns* was a collection of songs about aging, and ran for two weeks in a showcase production. Three years later, with a mostly different cast, it reopened Off Broadway as *Taking My Turn* (see entry).

In reviewing the showcase for the *New York Times*, John S. Wilson praised the score ("full of high spirits and persuasive melodies"), and he singled out Tiger Haynes' "I Never Made Money from Music" ("a joyfully sinuous waltz") and Rita Gardner's "Vivaldi" (a "rousing recollection" of hearing Vivaldi's music performed in Central Park). He also liked the contributions of Thelma Carpenter, Bobo Lewis, and Ted Thurston.

Will Holt and Gary William Friedman (with Herb Schapiro) had earlier collaborated on a revue based on the writings of young people (see entry for *The Me Nobody Knows*) and Friedman and Schapiro later collaborated on another revue about the young (see entry for *Bring on the Morning*).

1678 Tuscaloosa's Calling Me...But I'm Not Going! "THE New York Musical." THEATRE: Top of the Gate; transferred to Chelsea's Westside Theatre on December 26, 1975; OPENING DATE: December 1, 1975; PERFORMANCES: 429; SKETCHES: Bill Heyer, Hank Beebe, and Sam Dann; LYRICS: Bill Heyer; MUSIC: Hank Beebe; DIRECTION: James Hammerstein and Gui Andrisano; SCENERY: Charles E. Hoefler; COSTUMES: Rome Heyer; MUSICAL DIRECTION: Jeremy Harris; PRODUCERS: Jerry Schlossberg, Arch Lustberg, and Bruce Nelson; a Quintal Production

CAST—Len Gochman, Patti Perkins, Renny Temple

The revue was presented in two acts.

ACT ONE—"Only Right Here in New York City" (Company), "I Dig Myself" (Renny Temple), "Cold Cash" (Company) "Things Were Out" (Patti Perkins) "Central Park on a Sunday Afternoon" (Company) "New York from the Air" (Patti Perkins) "The Old Man" (Patti Perkins, Len Gochman) "Backwards" (Len Gochman), "Delicatessen" (Patti Perkins, Len Gochman, Renny Temple) "The Out-of-Towner" (Len Gochman, Renny Temple), "Everything You Hate Is Right Here" (Company)

ACT TWO—"Fugue for a Menage a Trois" (Company) "The Purse Snatch" (Patti Perkins, Renny Temple) "Poor" (Patti Perkins, Renny Temple) "Graffiti" (Company) "Singles Bar" (Patti Perkins, Renny Temple) "Astrology" (Len Gochman) "New York '69" (Company) "Tuscaloosa's Calling Me, But I'm Not Going" (Company)

NOTES—*Tuscaloosa's Calling Me...But I'm Not Going!* was a cheerful revue about life in New York City. It didn't have much of an ideological axe to grind, and thus was rewarded with the second-longest run of the 1975-1976 Off Broadway season. Mel Gussow in the *New York Times* said the evening was a "tonic for urban depression," and noted that while some of the material flagged, the music was "catchy" and the lyrics were "smoothly appliqued" to the score. Further, the three-member cast was "amiable and ingratiating." Vanguard Records released a cast album which included about half the material in the show (LP # VSD-79376). It appears that during previews "Fugue for a Menage a Trois" was titled "Suburban Fugue."

1679 Twanger. THEATRE: Van Dam Theatre; OPENING DATE: November 15, 1972; PERFORMANCES: 24; BOOK: Ronnie Britton; LYRICS: Ronnie Britton; MUSIC: Ronnie Britton; DIRECTION: Walter Ash; CHOREOGRAPHY: Ronnie Britton; COSTUMES: Owen H. Goldstein; LIGHTING: Peter Anderson; MUSICAL DIRECTION: Lee Gillespie

CAST—Andrea Noel (Garbage Ella), Nevil Martyn (Magician), Glenn M. Castello (Twanger), Sue Renee Bernstein (Phyllis Frog), Michelle Roberts (The Queen), Jess Peterson (Francis), Becky Thatcher McSpadden (Rhoda), Susane Press (Velva), Leslie Welles (Nikki), George Heusinger (Wolff), Charles Stuart (Arthur), Charles Flanagan (Kurt)

The musical was presented in two acts (division of acts and song assignments unknown; the musical numbers are listed in performance order).

MUSICAL NUMBERS—Prologue, "The Frogs Perform," "Wanna Get Married," "Five Minutes Ago," "Magic Licorice," "Phyllis Frog," "Have You Seen the Princess?," "Sneaky, Creepy Fellows," "Impossibility," "A Sister and Brother," "Obey, Abide," "To Win a Prince," "Big, Big Contest," "Twanger!," "A Potion," "Normal, Normal, Normal," "Garbage-Ella," "Tiny Light," "Forest of Silver," "But, I Love You," "Francis' Feast"

NOTES—*Twanger*, a musical for children, was produced for a limited engagement of three weeks. One of its songs, "Garbage-Ella," was later heard in the adult revue *Greenwich Village Follies* (see entry). Not to be confused with Lionel Bart's musical *Twang!!*, the legendary disaster about Robin Hood and his merry men which opened in London at the Shaftesbury Theatre on December 20, 1965, and closed after forty-three performances. But at least *Twang!!* was both recorded *and* released (by United Artists Records [LP # ULP-1116/SULP-1116; later reissued on LP by That's Entertainment Records [LP # TER-1055]). Which is more than you can say for poor *Pocahontas*, a West End flop which starred Anita Gillette in the title role. It opened at the Lyric Theatre on November 14, 1963, and closed after twelve performances. The musical was recorded by Decca Records (the respective numbers assigned to the stereo and monaural releases of the LP were # SKL-4569 and # LK-4569), and an advertisement in the musical's programme indicated the recording would be "available shortly" (some forty-five years later we're still waiting for it). To my knowledge, *Pocahontas* is the only British musical to be recorded and not released.

1680 The 25th Annual Putnam County Spelling Bee. THEATRE: 2econd (Second) Stage Theatre; OPENING DATE: February 7, 2005; PERFORMANCES: 48; BOOK: Rachel Sheinkin; LYRICS: William Finn; MUSIC: William Finn; DIRECTION: James Lapine; CHOREOGRAPHY: Dan Knechtges; SCENERY: Beowulf Boritt; COSTUMES: Jennifer Caprio; LIGHTING: Natasha Katz; MUSICAL DIRECTION: Vadim Feichtner; PRODUCER: The Second Stage Theatre (Carole Rothman, Artistic Director; Timothy J. McClimon, Executive Director)

CAST—Derrick Baskin (Mitch Mahoney), Deborah S. Craig (Marcy Park), Jesse Tyler Ferguson (Leaf Coneybear), Dan Fogler (William Barfee), Lisa Howard (Rona Lisa Peretti), Celia Keenan-Bolger (Olive Otrovsky), Jose Llana (Chip Tolentino), Jay Reiss (Douglas Panch), Sarah Saltzberg (Logainne Schwartzandgrubenierre)

The action occurs in a junior high school gym in the present time.

The musical was presented in one act.

MUSICAL NUMBERS—"The 25th Annual Putnam County Spelling Bee" (Company), "The Spelling Rules"/"My Favorite Moment of the Bee 1" (Jay Reiss, Lisa Howard, Spellers), "My Friend, the Dictionary" (Jay Reiss, Lisa Howard, Celia Keenan-Bolger, Company), "The First Goodbye" (Company), "Pandemonium" (Jose Llana, Company), "I'm Not That Smart" (Jesse Tyler Ferguson), "The Second Goodbye" (Company), "Magic Foot" (Dan Fogler, Company), "Pandemonium" (reprise)/"My Favorite Moment of the Bee 2" (Jose Llana, Derrick Baskin, Lisa Howard, Company), "Prayer of the Comfort Counselor" (Derrick Baskin, Company), "My Unfortunate Erection (Chip's Lament)" (Jose Llana), "Woe Is Me" (Sarah Saltzberg, Company), "I'm Not That Smart" (reprise) (Jesse Tyler Ferguson), "I Speak Six Languages" (Deborah S. Craig, Girls), "The 'I Love You' Song" (Celia Keenan-Bolger, Lisa Howard, Derrick Baskin), "Woe Is Me" (reprise) (Sarah Saltzberg, Company), "My Favorite Moment of the Bee 3"/"Second" (Lisa Howard, Celia Keenan-Bolger, Dan Fogler), Finale (Company), "The Last Goodbye" (Company)

NOTES—The revue-like musical, which dealt with a spelling bee contest among a group of nerdy kids, was the surprise hit of the season, and quickly moved to Broadway on May 2, 2005, where it opened at the Circle in the Square and played for 1,136 performances. The musical won Tony Awards for Best Book and Best Performance by a Featured Actor in a Musical (Dan Folger). For Broadway, one song ("We Like Spelling") was added, and the evening was divided into two acts. With Rachel Sheinkin's tongue-in-cheek book and William Finn's amiable score, the musical enjoyed a long life on Broadway and will probably have an even longer one in regional, community, and college theatre. As *C-R-E-P-U-S-C-U-L-E*, the work was first seen in 2002 as a non-musical by The Farm, an improvisational theatre company. The musical was first produced by the Barrington Stage Company in Sheffield, Massachusetts, on July 7, 2004. The Broadway cast recording was released by Ghostlight Records (CD # 7915584407-2).

1681 24 Inches. THEATRE: Theatre for the New City; OPENING DATE: October 7, 1982; PERFORMANCES: 15; BOOK: Robert Patrick; LYRICS: Robert Patrick; MUSIC: David Tice; SCENERY: John Jewell; LIGHTING: John Jewell; PRODUCER: Theater for the New City (George Bartenieff and Crystal Field, Artistic Directors)

CAST—Sandy Bigtree, Stephen Cross, Barry Greenberg, Kevin Hurley, Terry Talley, J.R. Wells, Stacia Gold, Nancy Crumpler, Jeff Lucchese

NOTES—The musical *24 Inches* was presented under an Off Off Broadway contract.

1682 22 Years. THEATRE: Stage 73; OPENING DATE: January 4, 1972; PERFORMANCES: 16; PLAY: Robert Sickinger; LYRICS AND MUSIC: Various writers; the score included songs by Charles Manson; DIRECTION: Robert Sickinger; SCENERY: Robert King; LIGHTING: Gary Marec; PRODUCERS: Jeff Britton in association with the Manhattan Theatre Club

CAST—King Morton (Prosecuting Attorney), Joan Grove (Linda Kasablan), Frank Girardeau (Charles Manson), Marc Handler (Digger, Guitarist), Diane Jayne (Flower Child), Barbara Marchant (Lynn), Julie Burgher (Katie), Gail Hayden (Gypsy), Kristin Marle (Sadie Mae Glutz), Louise Garone (Leslie Sankster), Robert Corwin (Holy Acid Head), Molly Larson (Hitchhiker), Curley Hurley (Dennis), Nikki Ana Dominguez (Missy), Dennis Kear (Bobbie, Defense Attorney), Ron Osborn (Terry), O.B. Lewis (Tex Watson), Chaz Palminteri (Randy), Loree Gold (Guitar Singer), Emanuel Kaufman (Defense Attorney), David Walker (Defense Attorney); Other Members of the Family (Jeanette Arnone, Tony Bruni, Tad Lathrop, Rita Ballard)

NOTES—A self-described "rockumentary," *22 Years* dealt with convicted multiple-murderer Charles Manson and his so-called "family." According to Mel Gussow in the *New York Times*, the musical portrayed Manson as an innocent victim of events; moreover, society created him and thus deserved him. The public didn't buy these questionable theses and the sympathetic portrait of Manson, and so the musical was gone in two weeks.

Gussow noted the production included six "inconsequential" songs, two of which were written by Manson (was he paid royalties?). The title referred to the twenty-two years Manson reportedly spent in prison between the ages of twelve and thirty-four, prior to the time of the notorious 1969 murders. In 1990, John Moran's opera *The Manson Family* was produced Off Off Broadway (see entry). For a musical which included Squeaky Fromme (a member of the Manson "family") in its cast of characters, see entry for *Assassins*.

1683 "2." "A New Musical Revue." THEATRE: Lincoln Center; OPENING DATE: January 23, 1978; PERFORMANCES: Unknown; LYRICS: Julie Mandel; MUSIC: Julie Mandel; DIRECTION: Clinton Atkinson; CHOREOGRAPHY: Bick Goss; MUSICAL DIRECTION: Donald Oliver; PRODUCER: Equity Library Theatre (George Wojtasik, Managing Director)

CAST—Ann Hodapp, Hal Waters

MUSICAL NUMBERS (number of acts unknown; all songs were performed by Ann Hodapp and Hal Waters; songs are listed in performance order)—"Two's a Nice Number," "Two Pieces of Bread," "Love Is a Two-Part Invention," "Dear Mr. Greene," "Baby Makes Two," "The Two-Note Rag," "Two Points of View," "We Are There," "Two to Tango," "In Two Words—Show Biz," "Two Things," "We Need Each Other," "A Tale of Two Cities," "I'm Two," "Twice on Matinee Days," "When We're Together," "One," "Two Is What It's All About," "Two's a Nice Number" (reprise)

NOTES—The liner notes for the cast album of the Off Off Broadway production *"2"* (released on Take Home Tunes Records [LP # THT 788]) noted the revue "sings about, and celebrates, the basic building block of society, one to one relationships—'2,'" (including how the number relates to psychology, sex, food, show business, office equipment, and the Bible). The revue seems to have disappeared after its initial performances at Lincoln Center, perhaps because its conception was all too one-note.

The song titles are taken from the cast recording.

Not to be confused with *Two* (see entry).

1684 Two. THEATRE: Van Dam Theatre; OPENING DATE: April 15, 1982; PERFORMANCES: 12; BOOK: Fredricka Weber; LYRICS: Misha Segal and Fredricka Weber; MUSIC: Misha Segal and Fredricka Weber; DIRECTION: Raymond Homer; CHOREOGRAPHY: Barbara Hanks; SCENERY: Seth Price; LIGHTING: Deborah Tulchin; MUSICAL DIRECTION: Michael Stockler; PRODUCER: T.L. Boston

CAST—Joe Godfrey (Dickie), Evelyn Page (Mother), Charles C. Welch (Father, Uncle Bud), Fredricka Weber (Frannie); Townspeople: Viki Boyle, Shaun Bushnell, Dennis Sullivan, Shaver Tillitt The action occurs during the 1940s in the small Illinois towns of Dwight and Beardstown.

MUSICAL NUMBERS (division of acts and song assignments unknown; Musical numbers listed in performance order)—"Illinois," "It Might Fall Off," "What Is Normal," "We Do Have," "I've Got a Secret," "Stop of Slushing," "I'll Be a Hairstylist to the Movie Stars," "The Answer to Life Is Death," "Ain't She Sweet," "Children Today," "I Did It!," "Frannie," "Do the Opposite," "I Feel Like I Lost Something," "One Door Opens," "My God Laughs," "Don't Lose That Spark"

NOTES—The musical may have been produced under an Off Off Broadway contract.

Not to be confused with *"2"* (see entry).

1685 2 by 5. "A Musical Cabaret." THEATRE: Village Gate Downstairs; OPENING DATE: October 19, 1976; PERFORMANCES: 57; LYRICS: Fred Ebb; MUSIC: John Kander; DIRECTION: Seth Glassman; SCENERY: Dan Leigh; COSTUMES: Dan Leigh; LIGHTING: Martin Tudor; MUSICAL DIRECTION: Joseph Clonick; PRODUCERS: Judy Gordon and Jack Temchin

CAST—D'Jamin Bartlett, Kay Cummings, Danny Fortus, Shirley Lemmon, Scott Stevensen

The revue was presented in two acts.

ACT ONE—Overture (Company), "Cabaret" (from *Cabaret*, 1966) (Company), "Wilkommen" (*Cabaret*, 1966) (Danny Fortus), "Yes" (*70, Girls, 70*, 1971) (Company), "Sing Happy" (*Flora, the Red Menace*, 1965) (Danny Fortus), "Mein Herr" (1972 film *Cabaret*) (Shirley Lemmon, D'Jamin Bartlett, Kay Cummings), "Seeing Things" (*The Happy Time*, 1968) (Scott Stevensen), "The World Goes 'Round" (1977 film *New York, New York*) (D'Jamin Bartlett), "Love Song" (a/k/a "Sara Lee"; independent song) (Danny Fortus), "The Money Song" (*Cabaret*, 1966) (Company), "Sign Here" (*Flora, the Red Menace*, 1965) (Kay Cummings), "My Own Best Friend" (*Chicago*, 1975) (Shirley Lemmon), "Losers" (independent song) (Danny Fortus, D'Jamin Bartlett), "Military Man" (see notes below) (Company), "Only Love" (*Zorba*, 1968) (Danny Fortus), "Why Can't I Speak?" (*Zorba*, 1968) (D'Jamin Bartlett, Scott Stevensen, Shirley Lemmon), "Me and My Baby" (*Chicago*, 1975) (Company), "Isn't This Better" (1975 film *Funny Lady*) (Kay Cummings)

ACT TWO—"Home" (*70, Girls, 70*, 1971) (Company), "Maybe This Time" (independent song; used in 1972 film *Cabaret*) (D'Jamin Bartlett), "Ring Them Bells" (independent song; used in the 1972 television special *Liza with a 'Z'*) (Kay Cummings), "Class" (*Chicago*, 1975) (Shirley Lemmon, Kay Cummings), "Broadway, My Street" (*70, Girls, 70*, 1971) (Shirley Lemmon, Kay Cummings, Scott Stevensen, Danny Fortus), "New York, New York" (1977 film *New York, New York*) (D'Jamin Bartlett), "On Stage" (independent song) (Company), "Ten Percent" (*Chicago*, 1975; dropped during production's pre-Broadway tryout) (Danny Fortus), "Razzle Dazzle" (*Chicago*, 1975) (Company), "A Quiet Thing" (*Flora, the Red Menace*, 1965) (Scott Stevensen), "Cabaret" (reprise) (*Cabaret*, 1966) (Company)

NOTES—This tribute to John Kander and Fred Ebb ran for just a few weeks, but a more successful revue of their songs (*And the World Goes 'Round*) opened in 1991 and ran for 408 performances (see entry). (Also, on February 4, 1976, the Manhattan Theatre Club presented another Kander and Ebb tribute, *A Kander & Ebb Cabaret*, which played for twelve performances; the cast included Kay Cummings and Tommy Breslin, the former of whom appeared in *2 by 5* later in the year.)

During the course of the *2 by 5*'s preview period as well as during its regular run, the following songs were also performed: "Marriage Sequence (He Wouldn't Sell Park Place)" (source unknown), "That's a Beginning, Isn't It?" (source unknown), "I Don't Care Much" (written for, but not used in, the original production of *Cabaret* [1966]; however, the number became a semi-standard, and was incorporated into later revivals of *Cabaret*), "Nowadays" (*Chicago*, 1975), "(Walking) Among My Yesterdays" (*The Happy Time*, 1968), and "I Don't Remember You" (*The Happy Time*, 1968).

Twenty-three years after "Military Man" was heard in *2 by 5*, the song was used in *Over & Over*, Kander and Ebb's disappointing musical version of Thornton Wilder's play *The Skin of Our Teeth* (1942) which played at the Signature Theatre in Arlington, Virginia, from January 6 through February 21, 1999; the song was performed by Dorothy Loudon and Mario Cantone, and was one of the musical highlights of the show. Sherie Rene Scott and David Garrison also appeared in the production, and Scott later recorded a song from the musical ("This Life") in her collection ... *Men I've Had* (Sh-K-Boom Records CD # 2000-2); in the musical, "This Life" was introduced by Beulah Watson and the chorus. *All About Us*, a revised version of *Over & Over*, opened at the Westport County Playhouse on April 14, 2007, with a cast which included Cady Huffman, Shuler Hensley, and Eartha Kitt. "Military Man" was also heard in this production, but "Someday, Pasadena," which had been performed by Scott in *Over & Over* and was one of the best songs in the score, was unaccountably omitted while "Nice People," possibly the worst song in the Kander and Ebb catalogue, was retained. Besides "This Life," one other song from *Over & Over*/*All About Us* has been recorded: "The Skin of Our Teeth" (introduced by David Garrison in *Over & Over*) can be heard on Brent Barrett's *The Kander & Ebb Album* (released by Varese Sarabande [CD # VSD-6044]), which, along with Neva Small's *My Place in the World* (released by Small Penny Enterprises, LLC [CD # NS-2211]), is one of the finest show music collections of recent years.

(For information about Betty Comden, Adolph Green, and Leonard Bernstein's unproduced musical version of *The Skin of Our Teeth*, see entries for *By Bernstein* and *The Madwoman of Central Park West*.)

1686 2 x 4. THEATRE: The Showplace; OPENING DATE: June 2, 1959; PERFORMANCES: Unknown; LYRICS: Mostly by Bob Bernstein; MUSIC: Alyson Skipp Hoyland, Warren B. Meyers, Harold Beebe, Nicholas Schachter, and Seth Rubenstein; DIRECTION: Bob Bernstein; CAST—Lynne Charnay, Doug Robinson, Saralou Cooper, Burit Bier

NOTES—Lewis Funke in the *New York Times* complained that the overstuffed revue *2 x 4* (which included twenty-three numbers) was presented as a "yammer-yammer cascade in a seemingly interminable torrent ... on a stage no larger than the title" of the show.

He mentioned it "probably" helped that audience members at the seventy-four-seat cabaret-theatre could drink and smoke during the performance.

1687 Two for Fun. "A Revue." THEATRE: Madison Avenue Playhouse; OPENING DATE: February 13, 1961; PERFORMANCES: 35; WRITTEN MATERIAL: Jack Woodford and Peter Goode; MUSIC: Lothar Perl and Silvio Masciarelli; DIRECTION: Mata and Hari; COSTUMES: Freddy Wittop; PRODUCERS: Madison Productions in association with Marshall Migatz; Bilee Steinberg, Associate Producer

CAST—Mata and Hari, with Lothar Perl; Simon Sadoff (Voices)

The revue was presented in two acts.

ACT ONE—"Kiss Me My Love," "Going Steady," "Woman on the Couch," "The Musical Clown," "The Lady Takes a Shower," "Keep Fit, Feel Better, Live Longer," "La Chanteuse," "Marionette Theatre"

ACT TWO—"Have Gun, Get Gold" (sung by Bob French), "The Lady Unobserved," "Carnegie Hall"

NOTES—*Two for Fun* was a mime revue, conceived, staged, and performed by Ruth Mata and Eugene Hari. The production included background music and at least one song.

Milton Esterow in the *New York Times* found Mata and Hari "excellent dancers and superb clowns," but noted that while some moments were "deliciously funny," others were "somewhat tiresome." He said one of the best sequences was "Have Gun, Get Gold," a comprehensive spoof of "almost every horse opera you ever saw." Other sketches dealt with rock 'n' roll fans, a young society matron and her analyst, and a bar-bell addict.

1688 Two for Tonight. THEATRE: Cherry Lane Theatre; OPENING DATE: December 28, 1939; PERFORMANCES: 30; SKETCHES: Ralph Berton and Mitchell Hodges; LYRICS: Ralph Berton, Eugene Berton, Charles Herbert, John LaTouche, Sylvia Marks, and Ben Raleigh; MUSIC: Ralph Berton, Eugene Berton, Charles Herbert, Berenice Kazounoff, and Bernie Wayne; DIRECTION: Max Scheck; SCENERY: Edwin Vanderbilt; COSTUMES: Doris Roberts; PRODUCER: The Promenaders

CAST—Charles Herbert, Grace Herbert, Billy Sands

MUSICAL NUMBERS (division of acts and song assignments unknown)—"Song of the Greasepaint" (lyric by John LaTouche, music by Berenice Kazounoff), "Personal Heaven" (lyric and music by Eugene and Ralph Berton), "Could You Use a New Friend?" (lyric and music by Eugene and Ralph Berton), "Call of the Wild" (lyric by Sylvia Marks, music by Berenice Kazounoff), "Masquerade" (lyric and music by Charles Herbert), "Windows" (lyric and music by Eugene and Ralph Berton), "Nursery" (lyric and music by Charles Herbert), "Five O'-Clock" (lyric by Ben Raleigh, music by Bernie Wayne), "Dancing Alone" (lyric and music by Eugene and Ralph Berton), "Blues" (lyric and music by John LaTouche), "Home Is Where You Hang Your Hat" (lyric by John LaTouche, music by Berenice Kazounoff), "Blasé" (lyric by John LaTouche, music by Berenice Kazounoff)

NOTES—*Two for Tonight*, one of the few Off Broadway musicals to open in the 1930s, is notable for being one of the earliest works by John La-Touche. The *New York Times* reported the "intimate revue" was cast with non-Equity performers.

1689 The Two Gentlemen of Verona. THEATRE: Delacorte Theatre/The Public Theatre; OPENING DATE: July 27, 1971; PERFORMANCES: 14; BOOK: John Guare and Mel Shapiro; LYRICS: John Guare; MUSIC: Galt MacDermot; DIRECTION: Mel Shapiro; CHOREOGRAPHY: Jean Erdman; MUSICAL DIRECTION: Margaret Harris; PRODUCER: The New York Shakespeare Festival (Joseph Papp, Producer; Bernard Gersten, Associate Producer) in cooperation with the City of New York (Hon. John V. Lindsay, Mayor; Hon. August Heckscher, Commissioner of Parks; and the New York State Council on the Arts) and the National Endowment for the Arts

CAST—Carla Pinza (Julia), Alix Elias (Lucetta), Raul Julia (Proteus), Clifton Davis (Valentine), Frederic Warriner (Antonio, Tavern Host), Jerry Stiller (Launce), Jose Perez (Speed), Norman Matlock (Duke of Milan), Frank O'Brien (Thurio), Jonelle Allen (Silvia), Alvin Lum (Eglamour); Street Urchins (Anthony Cuascut, Alex Velez); Citizens (Christopher Alden, Paul De John, Richard DeRusso, Richard Erickson, Brenda Feliciano, Sheila Gibbs, Jeff Goldblum, Albert Insinnia, Elizabeth Lage, Ken Lowrie, Gale McNeeley, Douglass Riddick, Madeleine Swift)

SOURCE—The play *The Two Gentlemen of Verona* (written during the 1590s [possibly 1598]) by William Shakespeare.

The action occurs in Verona, Milan, and in a forest.

The musical was presented in two acts.

NOTES—musical numbers from the summer production of *The Two Gentlemen of Verona* are not available, but are probably similar to the song list from the musical when it transferred to Broadway later in the year (see information below).

Soon after its run at the Delacorte Theatre in Central Park, the musical began a "mobile tour" which played throughout New York City for a total of twenty-three performances. As *Two Gentlemen of Verona*, the musical opened on Broadway at the St. James Theatre on December 1, 1971, for 614 performances; for Broadway, Diana Davila replaced Carla Pinza and John Bottoms replaced Jerry Stiller. The scenery was designed by Ming Cho Lee, and the costumes were by Theoni V. Alredge; the lighting was by Lawrence Metzler, and Dennis Nahat was credited with additional musical staging. The Broadway credits also included one dog (the character of Crab, performed by Phineas); the character of Milkmaid, performed by Sheila Gibbs; and Vissi D'Amore, enacted by Frank O'Brien and Georgyn Geetlein. Many of the chorus members who appeared in the summer production were also in the Broadway version (including Jeff Goldblum).

One chorus member who joined the Broadway production was Stockard Channing; she was later associated with the musical's lyricist and co-author John Guare when she appeared in three productions of his plays, creating the role of Ouisa Kittredge in the original production of Guare's finest work, *Six Degrees of Separation* (1990), *Four Baboons Adoring the Sun* (1992), and the 1986 revival of his brilliant black comedy *The House of Blue Leaves* (1971).

At best, *Two Gentlemen of Verona* was mildly entertaining. Its weak book offered a loose and loopy story-telling approach with hippy-dippy characterizations (the musical also labored, in vain, to make connections between fifteenth-century Italy and the United States' involvement in Vietnam). The scenery looked cheap, the choreography was bland, and the performances not particularly memorable. The show's strongest asset was Galt MacDermot's sunny score, which was somewhat hampered by Guare's weak and often puerile lyrics. Diana Davila made for a winningly ditzy Julia, and provided the show's best performance.

When the Tony Awards were presented, *Follies* (1971) won seven awards (Best Score, Best Actress, Best Direction, Best Choreography, Best Scenery, Best Costumes, and Best Lighting) but unaccountably the Tony voters gave *Two Gentlemen of Verona* the Best Book Award, and, most shockingly, the Best Musical Award. To this day, musical theater lovers still debate the controversial choice. But time has proven *Follies* the legendary musical and *Two Gentlemen of Verona* an also-ran (for the record, some thirty-four years after its premiere at the Delacorte, *Two Gentlemen of Verona* returned there on August 28, 2005, for a limited run of thirteen performances; this time around, there was no transfer to Broadway).

The Broadway cast album of *Two Gentlemen of Verona* was released on a 2-LP set by ABC-Dunhill Records (# BCSY-1001) and on CD by Decca Broadway Records (# 440-017-565-2). The musical opened in London at the Phoenix Theatre on April 26, 1973, for 237 performances, and the (one-LP) cast recording of the production was released by RSO Records (# RSO-SUPER-2394-110). Kilmarnock Records also released a recording of the score which was conducted by Galt MacDermot and included vocals by Sheila Gibbs and Ken Lowry (LP # KIL-72004). The script was published in a lavish edition by Holt, Rinehart & Winston in 1973, and was also included in the collection *Great Rock Musicals*, edited by Stanley Richards and published by Stein and Day in 1979.

The following musical numbers (and the performers listed below) are taken from the Broadway production.

ACT ONE—"Summer, Summer" (Ensemble), "I Love My Father" (Ensemble), "That's a Very Interesting Question" (Raul Julia, Clifton Davis), "I'd Like to Be a Rose" (Raul Julia, Clifton Davis), "Thou, Julia, Thou Hast Metamorphosed Me" (Raul Julia), "Symphony" (Raul Julia, Ensemble), "I Am Not Interested in Love" (Diana Davila), "Love, Is That You?" (Frank O'Brien, Georgyn Geetlein), "Thou, Proteus, Thou Has Metamorphosed Me" (reprise) (Diana Davila), "What Does a Lover Pack?" (Diana Davila, Raul Julia, Ensemble), "Pearls" (John Bottoms), "I Love My Father" (reprise) (Raul Julia), "Two Gentlemen of Verona" (Diana Davila, Alix Elias, Ensemble), "Follow the Rainbow" (Clifton Davis, Jose Perez, Raul Julia, John Bottoms, Diana Davila, Alix Elias), "Where's North?" (Clifton Davis, Jose Perez, Norman Matlock, Jonelle Allen, Frank O'Brien, Ensemble), "Bring All the Boys Back Home" (Norman Matlock, Frank O'Brien, Ensemble), "Love's Revenge" (Clifton Davis), "To Whom It May Concern Me" (Jonelle Allen, Clifton Davis), "Night Letter" (Jonelle Allen, Clifton Davis), "Love's Revenge" (reprise) (Clifton Davis, Raul Julia, Jose Perez, John Bottoms), "Calla Lily Lady" (Raul Julia)

ACT TWO—"Land of Betrayal" (Alix Elias), "Thurio's Samba" (Frank O'Brien, Norman Matlock, Ensemble), "Hot Lover" (John Bottoms, Jose Perez), "What a Nice Idea" (Diana Davila), "Who Is Sylvia" (Raul Julia, Frederic Warriner, Ensemble), "Love Me" (Jonelle Allen, Ensemble), "Eglamour" (Alvin Lum, Jonelle Allen), "Kidnapped" (Jonelle Allen, Norman Matlock, Raul Julio, Frank O'Brien, Ensemble), "Mansion" (Clifton Davis), "Eglamour" (reprise) (Jonelle Allen, Alvin Lum), "What's a Nice Girl Like Her" (Raul Julia), "Dragon Fight" ([unidentified performer], Alvin Lum, Raul Julia, Clifton Davis), "Don't Have the Baby" (Diana Davila, Alix Elias, Jose Perez, John Bottoms), "Love, Is That

You?" (reprise) (Frank O'Brien, Alix Elias), "Milkmaid" (John Bottoms, Sheila Gibbs), Finale: "I Love My Father" (reprise) (Company), "Love Has Driven Me Sane" (Company)

1690 Two Hearts Over Easy. THEATRE: Actors' Playhouse; OPENING DATE: August 24, 1994; PERFORMANCES: 39; BOOK: Robert W. Cabell; LYRICS: Robert W. Cabell; MUSIC: Robert W. Cabell; DIRECTION: Robert W. Cabell; CHOREOGRAPHY: Marvin Gardens; SCENERY: Tristan Wilson; COSTUMES: Maggie Anderson; LIGHTING: Bob Kneeland; MUSICAL DIRECTION: Seth Osburn; PRODUCERS: Michael and Barbara Ross in association with Evette Stark and Marvin Gardens

CAST—Melanie Dimitri (Maggie), Bill Ebbesmeyer (Jimmy), Randy Weiss (Rusty, Paul, Dad, Steven, Stripper), Maggie Wirth (Gina, Joanne, Mom)

The action occurs in The Whisper Café in New York City.

The musical was presented in two acts.

NOTES—The musical *Two Hearts Over Easy* told the story of two cousins, Jimmy, a gay man, and Maggie, a divorced woman, who meet every Sunday for brunch.

Stephen Holden in the *New York Times* noted that although the script meant to be "warm and cuddly," it was in fact "quite mean-spirited," and he found the two leading characters "selfish hysterics" who are "awash in self-pity." Holden reported that in her song "It Was My Favorite," Maggie described the happiest day of her life as the one in which she got her American Express Gold Card and went on a shopping spree. And Holden felt the evening's worst moment was the song "Erotic," in which Randy Weiss performed a striptease and invited audience members to put money (play money, which had been handed out to the audience during intermission) into his G-string. Another character, Gina, was a waitress in the restaurant who gets a role in an "'Off-Off-Off-Off Broadway' space-age adaptation of *Hamlet*." The musical had first been produced at the cabaret Don't Tell Mama.

1691 Two If by Sea. "A Revolutionary Musical." THEATRE: Circle in the Square (Downtown); OPENING DATE: February 6, 1972; PERFORMANCES: 1; BOOK: Priscilla B. Dewey and Charles Werner Moore; LYRICS: Priscilla B. Dewey; MUSIC: Tony Hutchins; additional music by Jeff Lass and John Nagy; DIRECTION: Charles Werner Moore; CHOREOGRAPHY: Edward Roll; SCENERY: John Doepp; COSTUMES: Julie Weiss; LIGHTING: Roger Morgan; MUSICAL DIRECTION: Jeff Lass; PRODUCER: The Tea Party Company

CAST—Kay Cole (Rachel/Rachel Revere), Jack Gardner (John/John Hancock), Judy Gibson (Lydia/Lydia Hancock), Rod Loomis (Hugh/Lord Percy), Joe Morton (Sam/Samuel Adams), Rick Podell (John/John Singleton Copley), Jan Ross (Dolly/Dolly Quincy), John Stratton (Thomas Richardson), John Witham (Paul/Paul Revere).

The action occurs in the present.

The musical was presented in two acts.

ACT ONE—"The American Revolution" (Company), "Paul Revere" (Joe Morton, Company), "Wouldn't It Be Fine" (Judy Gibson, Joe Morton), "Daddy's Footsteps" (John Stratton, Company), "There'll Be a Tomorrow" (Kay Cole, John Witham), "Stamp Out the Tea Tax" (Kay Cole, with Joe Morton, Jack Gardner, Judy Gibson, Rick Podell, John Witham), "You Can Do It" (Jan Ross, Rod Loomis), "Melt It Down" (John Witham, Rick Podell, Joe Morton, Jack Gardner), "Tea Dance" (Jack Gardner), Finale: "We're a Young Country" (Company)

ACT TWO—"Lawbreakers" (John Stratton, Company), "You Can't Turn Off the Stars" (Rod Loomis, John Witham, Company), "There'll Be a Tomorrow" (reprise) (John Witham, Kay Cole), "Be More Aggressive" (Judy Gibson, Jack Gardner), "Throw the Egg" (Rod Loomis, Rick Podell), "People Who Live on the Islands" (Jan Ross, Company), "Two If By Sea, I Think" (John Witham, Company), "Lanterns" (John Stratton), Finale (Company)

NOTES—*Two If by Sea* was an attempt to favorably compare dissidents of the 1970s with our Founding Fathers. This questionable conceit lasted for just one performance. Edith Oliver in the *New Yorker* found the musical's concept "foolish" and the score no more than "serviceable," but she praised the performers (who would surely be seen in "better shows" during the coming years). Clive Barnes in the *New York Times* noted that the musical (which told the story of a "hip Mr. Chips"-styled teacher who attempts to show the "relevance" of the American Revolution to his high school students) had lyrics which "limped," a book "better left unread," and music which at its best was as "effective as a barber shop trio." Barnes reported that the Boston Tea Party was depicted by having the cast throw tea bags at the audience; he said he picked up eleven tea bags (from boredom, not frugality), and only stopped when his wife reminded him that he drank only coffee.

1692 Two of Everything. THEATRE: Marymount Manhattan Theatre; OPENING DATE: October 14, 1976; PERFORMANCES: Unknown; BOOK: Andrew Rosenthal; LYRICS: Andrew Rosenthal; MUSIC: Andrew Rosenthal; DIRECTION: Andrew Rosenthal; CHOREOGRAPHY: Bilo Bryant; SCENERY: Michael Sharp; COSTUMES: Michael Sharp (?); LIGHTING: William F. Condee; MUSICAL DIRECTION: Elliot Finkel; PRODUCER: Leonard Patrick

CAST—Erik Rhodes (Joe), Lola Smith (Marianne Brooks), Elaine Swann (Mother Cramm), Michael Sedgwick (Lincoln Brooks), Thea Ramsey (Sallylee Polk), Sara Dillon (Octavia Brooks), Michael Oakes (Wally Packard), Joan Wetmore (Inez Packard), Fredda Kaufman (Mrs. Schwetzenbaum), Mary Jay (Mrs. Parsley), Bonnie Snyder (Isadora Hole), Sharron Miller (Marion Carter)

The action occurs in the Brooks' apartment in New York during spring of the present year.

The musical was presented in two acts.

ACT ONE—"Yes, Virginia" (Erik Rhodes), "I'd Rather Stay at Home with You" (Lola Smith, Elaine Swann, Sara Dillon, Thea Ramsey), "When I Asked You for a Match" (Sara Dillon, Michael Sedgwick), "I Want That" (Thea Ramsey), "Small Streak of Gray" (Sara Dillon, Joan Wetmore), "The First Time" (Lola Smith, Sara Dillon), "I'm Going Away for Awhile" (Michael Sedgwick), "In Vino Veritas" (Sara Dillon, Michael Sedgwick), "The Best of Friends" (Michael Sedgwick, Elaine Swann, Sara Dillon, Joan Wetmore, Erik Rhodes)

ACT TWO—"The Hard Core Gang's All Here" (Michael Sedgwick, Erik Rhodes), "Innocent as Hell" (Michael Sedgwick, Ladies), "I'd Go Home to My Mother" (Lola Smith), "How Nice for You" (Sara Dillon), "Two of Everything" (Michael Sedgwick, Michael Oakes), "Ne'er Do Well" (Elaine Swann), "The Best of Friends" (reprise) (Erik Rhodes), "Hamburger Heaven" (Thea Ramsey), "That's How the Whole Thing Began" (Michael Oakes, Lola Smith), "Time and Tide" (Michael Sedgwick), "Samedi Soir" (Sharron Miller), "As Long as You Live" (Sara Dillon, Joan Wetmore, Company), "Yes, Virginia" (reprise) (Erik Rhodes)

NOTES—*Two of Everything* was a revised version of Andrew Rosenthal's failed British musical *Innocent as Hell*, which opened at the Lyric Hammersmith on June 29, 1960, for just thirteen performances (the musical was directed by Vida Hope, and Anne Francine was among the cast members). Numbers from *Innocent as Hell* which weren't used in New York were "Breakfast Dance," "A Damned Good Man at the Bar," "My Place," and "You Never Had It So Good."

A few weeks before the musical opened at the Marymount, Rosenthal was interviewed in the *New York Times*. The article stated the Off Broadway run would be tantamount to a New Haven tryout, but no mention was made by either the interviewer or Rosenthal of the earlier London production. The interview also mentioned that Jeri Archer had been cast in the musical. But by the time the musical opened she was no longer with the company. Archer is perhaps best known for *Little Me* (not the 1962 musical, but the 1961 Patrick Dennis novel upon which the musical was based; Archer portrayed the fictitious Belle Poitrine in the classic photos which accompany the novel's text).

Three of Rosenthal's plays were seen on Broadway: *The Burning Deck* (1940, three performances); *Broken Journey* (1942, 23 performances); and *Horses in Midstream* (1953, four performances). Another play, *Third Person* (1955), never reached Broadway. As for *Two of Everything*, after its Off Broadway "tryout" it was never heard from again.

1693 (212). THEATRE: CSC Repertory Theatre; OPENING DATE: May 15, 1987; PERFORMANCES: 14 (estimated); BOOK: Victor Joseph; LYRICS: Victor Joseph; MUSIC: Donald Siegal; DIRECTION: Maggie L. Harrer; CHOREOGRAPHY: Maggie L. Harrer; Cheryl Spencer, Assistant Choreographer; SCENERY CONSULTANT: Evelyn Sakash; COSTUME CONSULTANT: Amanda J. Klein; LIGHTING CONSULTANT: Clarke W. Thornton; MUSICAL DIRECTION: Donald Siegal; PRODUCER: Musical Theatre Works (Anthony J. Stimac, Artistic Director; Mark Herko, Associate Artistic Director)

CAST—Elizabeth Austin (Jennifer), Vicki Lewis (Diane), Catherine Russell (Cindy), Cady Huffman (New Girl in Town), Peggy Atkinson (Frieda), Molly Stark (Gertie), Cynthia Darlow (Faye), Suzzanne Douglas (Winona Jackson), Mary Gordon Murray (Megan)

The action occurs in New York City at the present time.

The musical was presented in two acts (song assignments weren't credited in the program).

ACT ONE—"(212)," "It Isn't Over Yet," "I Want to Live on Jane Street," "Once Upon a Yesterday," "How to Be Hot," "It Isn't Over Yet" (reprise), "Lover, I'm Not Ready Yet for You," "(212)" (reprise), "Life Is the Café Carlyle," "I Never Saw Myself That Way," "Where Would I Be Today," "Pieces"

ACT TWO—"3 Girls, 6 Legs," "(212)" (reprise), "Almost a Woman," "Old Fashioned Love," "Sundays," "Hooker in the Snow," "Only the Dawn and I," "You're Weird but You're Wonderful"

1694 Two Pianos, Four Hands. THEATRE: Promenade Theatre; transferred to the Variety Arts Theatre on March 24, 1998; OPENING DATE: October 30, 1997; PERFORMANCES: 231; PLAY: Ted Dykstra and Richard Greenblatt; DIRECTION: Gloria Muzio; Andy McKim, Associate Director; SCENERY: Steve Lucas; COSTUMES: Steve Lucas; LIGHTING: Tharon Musser; PRODUCERS: David Mirvish, Ed Mirvish, Ben Specher, and William P. Miller; Brian Sewell, Executive Producer; Linda Intaschi, Associate Producer

CAST—Ted Dykstra, Richard Greenblatt

The play with music was presented in two acts.

ACT ONE—"D Minor Concerto, First Movement" (music by Johann Sebastian Bach), "Heart and Soul" (music by Hoagy Carmichael), "In My Little Birch Canoe" (music by Lelia Fletcher), "By the Stream" (music by Richard Greenblatt), "Our Band Goes to Town" (arranged by J.B. Duvernoy), "Sonatina No. 6 in F Major" (music by Ludwig van

Beethoven), "Sonatina Facile in C Major, First Movement" and "Sonata for One Piano"/"Four Hands in D Major, First Movement" (music by Wolfgang Amadeus Mozart), "In Der Halle des Bergkonigs"—*Peer Gynt* Suite I (music by Edvard Grieg), "D Minor Concerto, First Movement" (reprise) (music by Johann Sebastian Bach)

ACT TWO—"Prelude in D Flat Major" (music by Frederic Chopin), "Leyenda" (music by I. Albeniz), "Rondo for Two Pianos"/"Four Hands in C Major" (music by Frederic Chopin), "Fantasiestucke No. 2" (music by Robert Schumann), "Pathetique Sonata No. 8 in C Minor, First and Second Movements" (music by Ludwig van Beethoven), "Ballade No. 2 in F Major" (music by Frederic Chopin), "Mephisto Waltz No. 1" (music by Franz Liszt), Medley of Pop Tunes, "A Flat Impromptu" (music by Franz Schubert), "My Funny Valentine" (from *Babes in Arms*, 1937; music by Richard Rodgers), "Piano Man" (music by Billy Joel), "Mephisto Waltz" (Israel Horowitz' recording), "D Minor Concerto, First Movement" (reprise) (music by Johann Sebastian Bach), "Sheep May Safely Graze" (music by Johann Sebastian Bach)

NOTES—*Two Pianos, Four Hands* was originally produced at the Terragon Theatre in Toronto in 1994. The play with music told the often light-hearted but sometimes serious story of two musicians who strove to perfect their talents for careers in the concert hall but who never quite made the leap to the big time.

Peter Marks in the *New York Times* felt that despite the evening's "bloated" length of almost two-and-a-half hours, the piece never really developed its characters; further, the script's humor was "obvious" and "broadly comic." He regretted that he never really knew what music meant to the two pianists and what, if anything, they felt was lost when they "fell or were pushed off the concert track." One of the production's alternate performers was Andrew Lippa.

1695 2008½ (A Spaced Oddity). THEATRE: Truck and Warehouse Theatre; OPENING DATE: January 19, 1974; PERFORMANCES: 21; BOOK: Tom Eyen; LYRICS: Tom Eyen; MUSIC: Gary William Friedman; DIRECTION: Tom Eyen; CHOREOGRAPHY: Julie Arenel; SCENERY: T.E. Mason; COSTUMES: Bernard Roth; LIGHTING: Lawrance Steckman, Richard Monier, and Richard Jaklel; PRODUCERS: The New York Theatre Strategy, Inc.; a Theatre of the Eye Repertory Company production

CAST—Madeleine le Roux (Blonde Laura), Mary-Jenifer Mitchell (Annette Funkacello), Clark Gardner (Philip Head), William Duff-Griffin (The President of the U.S.A.), Debbie Wright (Ice Cream Lady [in white hat]), Ron Capozzoli (Vice President Cat Stevens), Marion Ramsey (Dora Ross), Denise Rogers (Super Chairwoman in Need), Erle Bjornstad (Maria Upstairs at the Downstairs), Peter Bartlett (General David Eisenhower), Anthony White (Steam Interviewer and Chief Mirror), Andre de Shields (The Old Movie), Frederica Washington (The Great Mirror Lady of the Planet Plastique)

The musical was presented in one act.

NOTES—*2008½ (A Spaced Oddity)* was presented for a limited engagement of twenty-one performances. It appears that immediately after its run at the Truck and Warehouse Theatre, the musical transferred to the New York Theatre Strategy on February 10. Tom Eyen's avant-garde-musical is all but forgotten today, but the names of the characters are amusing, and Clive Barnes' review in the *New York Times* indicates the evening was a light-hearted exercise in camp.

Barnes noted the plot was difficult to describe in a "family newspaper" (or even in a "family court"), but it dealt with the "not-too-far-distant future" (June 2008?) when the world is "ruled by female sexuality." While Barnes felt the evening wasn't consistent and that the self-described work-in-progress perhaps needed *more* progress, he liked Eyen's "lively eye for the ridiculous," and praised the Gary William Friedman's "attractive and tangy" score and Julie Arenal's "smoothly integrated" choreography.

1696 Uhuruh. THEATRE: City Center Downstairs; OPENING DATE: March 20, 1972; PERFORMANCES: 8; BOOK: Danny Duncan; LYRICS: Danny Duncan; MUSIC: Danny Duncan; DIRECTION: Danny Duncan; CHOREOGRAPHY: Danny Duncan; COSTUMES: Richmond Curry; LIGHTING: Kueleza Furaha; MUSICAL DIRECTION: Rick Appling; PRODUCERS: Franklin Fried and Bert Wainer in association with City Center of Music and Drama, Inc.

CAST—Danny Duncan, Blondell Breed, Gregory Burrell, Pasy Cain, Alice Alexander, Raymond Wade, Ebony Wright, David Gardner, Cyril Tyrone Hanna II, Walterine Ross, Pamela Swedon, Victor Willis, Earl Young, Samaki Zuri

NOTES—The short-lived topical revue *Uhuruh* had originally been produced in San Francisco. Clive Barnes in the *New York Times* noted that despite its stridency the revue was nonetheless monotonous. He singled out a second-act sequence set in a courtroom which debated the differences between "Mr. Black" and "Mr. Negro" as well as a sequence that defended Angela Davis. Barnes also mentioned the revue included a song about welfare mothers; a "cute" number about marijuana; and an "appealing" song about the "Bourgeois Black."

1697 The Umbrellas of Cherbourg. THEATRE: Martinson Hall/The Public Theatre; OPENING DATE: February 1, 1979; PERFORMANCES: 36; LIBRETTO: Jacques Demy; English translation by Sheldon Harnick in association with Charles Burr; lyric for "I Will Wait for You" by Norman Gimbel; MUSIC: Michel Legrand; introductions to Parts II and III by Steven Margoshes, based on themes by Michel Legrand; DIRECTION: Andrei Serban; Craig Zadan, Assistant Director; SCENERY: Michael Yeargan; COSTUMES: Jane Greenwood; LIGHTING: Ian Calderon; MUSICAL DIRECTION: Steven Margoshes; PRODUCER: The New York Shakespeare Festival (Joseph Papp, Director)

CAST—Stuart Baker-Bergen (Pierre, Minister, Customer), Stephen Bogardus (Jean, Waiter), Shirley Chester (Madame Germaine), Stefanianne Christopherson (Genevieve), Jennifer Governor (Francoise), Laurence Guittard (Cassard), Marc Jordan (Aubin), Joe Palmieri (Bernard, Postman), Dean Pitchford (Guy), Lizabeth Pritchett (Aunt Elise), Judith Roberts (Madame Emery), Maureen Silliman (Madeleine), Jeannine Taylor (Jenny), William Tost (Customer, Dubourg, Café Owner)

SOURCE—The 1964 film *L'Parapluis de Cherbourg* (*The Umbrellas of Cherbourg*), directed by Jacques Demy.

The action occurs in Cherbourg, France, from November 1957 to December 1963.

The musical was presented in three acts, with an intermission between acts two and three.

NOTES—Like the film upon which it was based, the musical *The Umbrellas of Cherbourg* was sung-through (the program didn't list individual musical numbers). The original film had three musical sequences which were fashioned into popular songs (translated into English by various lyricists), "I Will Wait for You," "Watch What Happens," and "I'm Falling in Love Again"; the first (with an English lyric by Norman Gimbel) was so popular that the stage adaptation wisely included it in the newly translated text for the Public Theatre production.

The familiar plot had touches of *Fanny* [1954], *The Most Happy Fella* [1956], and *The Baker's Wife* [1976; closed during pre-Broadway tryout; see entry for Off Off Broadway production]), not to mention the 1957 film *Wild Is the Wind* (which dealt with a farmer, his new wife, and a young ranch hand).

The Umbrellas of Cherbourg dealt with Genevieve and Guy, two young lovers who must separate when he's drafted into the army in 1957, the period of France's conflict in Algeria. When Genevieve discovers she's pregnant, she allows her mother to arrange a marriage to a wealthy middle-aged man who has always been infatuated with her. Upon Guy's return to civilian life, he discovers Genevieve has forsaken him, but he eventually finds love with another woman. A chance meeting in 1963 between Guy and Genevieve reveals Guy to be happy and content with his wife, his young child, and his job; but Genevieve seems doomed to unhappiness over the unwise choices she made as a younger woman.The bittersweet, romantic film was awash in pastel colors and unusual camera angles, and, of course, a sung-through film musical was unusual.

Joseph Papp's production of the stage adaptation was arguably the most romantic musical seen on a New York stage in the 1970s. The musical was thrillingly and beautifully sung, and the fluid staging by Andrei Serban (with an assist from Craig Zadan) deftly handled the love story which takes place over a six-year period. Further, the décor of the musical was breathtaking in its simple beauty. The stage was filled with movable plexiglass frosted panels which conveyed the sense of a world caught in a metaphorical rain shower. Further, umbrellas and balloons (the former in Magritte-like formations) festooned the stage.

For its thirty-six performances, *The Umbrellas of Cherbourg* was probably the hottest ticket in New York. Hours before a performance, would-be audience members found themselves in *A Cancellation Line*, hoping for a spare ticket or two. Some theatergoers didn't bother, for it seemed certain the musical would transfer to Broadway (according to rumor, the Booth Theatre). But, mysteriously, the transfer never happened, and so New York saw one of most romantic of all musicals for just those thirty-six performances.

While there was no recording of the Off Broadway production, the film's soundtrack was released by Philips Records (LP # PCC-616 [one LP] and LP # 6622031 [two LPs]; the CD was issued by Sony Classical Records [# SM2K-62678] with six bonus tracks). A September 1979 stage production in Paris was recorded by Accord Records (CD # 103262). A thirty-minute symphonic suite of music from the film (played by the London Symphony Orchestra and conducted by Michel Legrand) was released by Sony Music Japan International Inc. (CD # SICP-1562); the CD also included suites of music from two other films with background music by Legrand.

1698 The Uncommon Denominator. THEATRE: Mermaid Theatre; OPENING DATE: May 1, 1963; PERFORMANCES: 7; MATERIAL: Written by the performers; DIRECTION: Henry Jaglom; PRODUCER: Uncommon Company

CAST—Karen Black, Henry Jaglom, Peggy Pope, Leslie J. Stark

The revue was presented in two acts (sketch and song assignments unknown).

ACT ONE—"Letter from the Publisher," "Books," "Business," "Communication," "Dear Denominator," "Education," "Feature Story," "Fable," "Local," "New York Interview," "Lost and Found," "Dreams," "Medicine"

ACT TWO—"Modern Living," "Music," "People," "Press," "Request," "Letter to the Editor," "Science," "Show Business," "Sports," "Theology," "The World"

NOTES—The revue *The Uncommon Denominator* boasted it was a "new form of improvisational theatre," but new or not, it went nowhere. Milton Esterow in the *New York Times* felt the talented performers were in need of "uncommon material," and he lamented that overall the revue was uninteresting and gave the effect of an acting-school exercise. But Esterow had high praise for one sketch concerning a dentist accused of undermining the free enterprise system by endorsing *without compensation* a particular brand of toothpaste. His subversive act gets the American Medical Association, the Daughters of the American Revolution, and the House Committee on Un-American Activities into an uproar.

1699 Under Fire. THEATRE: The New York Shakespeare Festival's Touring Theatre; the production played in various New York City venues; OPENING DATE: August 6, 1980; PERFORMANCES: 19; BOOK AND LYRICS: Adapted from material by Elizabeth Swados, The *Under Fire* Company, Nikki Giovanni, Pedro Pietri, Michael Herr, Amiri Baraka, and Vanessa Howard; MUSIC: Elizabeth Swados; DIRECTION: Elizabeth Swados; CHOREOGRAPHY: Debbie Allen; SCENERY: David Jenkins; COSTUMES: Hilary Rosenfeld; LIGHTING: Arden Fingerhut; PRODUCER: The New York Shakespeare Festival (Joseph Papp, Director; Jason Steven Cohen, Production Supervisor)

CAST—Charlaine Woodard (Rastafarout), Gedde Watanabe (Agent Orange), Carol Lynn Maillard (Dawn 2Dusk), Mark Syers (C.C. Rider), Pi Douglass (Dark Star), David Schechter (Rover Dose), Paul Binotto (Ripple Vampyre), Karen Evans Kandel (Night Nurse), Jack Landron (Nito Pichiquino); The Funkin Doughnuts (David A. Dunaway, May-Pole Bar/Bass; Judith Fleisher, Glazed Over/Keyboards; Joel Diamond, Jelly Roll/Keyboards; David Sawyer, Boston Cream/Drums; Keith I. Loving, Kareem Puff/Guitar; Caroline Dutton, Éclair/Violin)

The action occurs "here," and the time is now.

The number of acts is unknown.

NOTES—Elizabeth Swados' *Under Fire* was presented free throughout New York City as part of the New York Shakespeare Festival's Summer Touring Theatre. But even free tickets might have been too high a price to pay for yet another preachy and earnest musical from Swados and Papp, works that were supported, in part, by taxpayers (via public funding from the New York State Council on the Arts as well as from the National Endowment for the Arts). In an interview with C. Gerald Fraser in the *New York Times*, Swados said the musical was based on interviews with young people who were concerning about drugs, the draft, unemployment, and "dishonesty." She also said the young people were "very worried" and "frightened" about their mental health, and they wondered if there was "any love left in the world."

Richard F. Shepard in the *New York Times* found the evening a "joyous doing," and said the antiwar and antidraft musical was more in the nature of a concert than a traditional book musical. He reported that some audience members "shouted wisecracks and comments" during the performance, and he felt this "happy irreverence" was somehow fitting for the occasion and gave the theatre-going experience the "quality" of "folk theatre." Shepard singled out the song "Crazy" (performed by Charlaine Woodard) as a "rouser" (the number wasn't listed in the program). A program note indicated "'King Heroin' is based on the traditional signified monkey poem," information perhaps obvious to some members of the audience but probably over the heads of most. The revue's humor appeared to be on the level of calling the band The Funkin Doughnuts.

Collaborators included trendy poet Nikki Giovanni as well as Amiri Baraka. Baraka, a/k/a LeRoi Jones, was later embroiled in a battle with the State of New Jersey when the state's governor announced his intention of stripping Baraka of his title of State Poet Laureate when Baraka allegedly made controversial statements regarding Jews and other non-Blacks. As LeRoi Jones, his controversial 1970 play *Slave Ship* was briefly seen Off Broadway; in *The Best Plays of 1969-1970*, Otis L. Guernsey, Jr., reported that Blacks in the audience were "told that their race mission is to destroy the white beast ... not necessarily [those Whites in the audience], but not necessarily *not.*"

Besides "King Heroin," the program listed the following sequences which were collaborations between Swados and specific performers (the program noted that much of the revue was based on improvisations by the actors): "Announcement by Rover Dose" (David Schechter), "Introduction of the Band"(Jack Landron), "Tele Type" (Gedde Watanabe, David Schechter, Jack Landron), "Who Are the Kids of the 80's" (David Schechter), "If I Had My Choice" (Gedde Watanabe), "Letters to the Lost" (Karen Evans Kandel, Charlaine Woodard, Carol Lynn Maillard), "When the Band Disbands" (David Schechter)

1700 Under the Bridge. THEATRE: Zipper Theatre; OPENING DATE: January 6, 2005; PERFORMANCES: 54; BOOK: Kathie Lee Gifford; LYRICS: Kathie Lee Gifford; MUSIC: David Pomeranz; additional music by David Pomeranz and Kathie Lee Gifford; DIRECTION: Eric Schaeffer; SCENERY: Jim Kronzer; COSTUMES: Anne Kennedy; LIGHTING: Chris Lee; MUSICAL DIRECTION: Paul Raiman; PRODUCERS: Lambchop Productions; Christine Gardner, Associate Producer

CAST—Dan Cooney (Jacques, Police Officer, Ensemble), Ed Dixon (Armand), Alexa Ehrlich (Evelyne), Thursday Farrar (Do-Gooder, Ensemble), Tamra Hayden (Do-Gooder, Ensemble), Florence Lacey (Mireli), Jacquelyn Piro (Madame Calcet), Greg Stone (Store Manager, Pierre, Monsieur Latour, Ensemble), Maggie Watts (Suzy), Andrew Blake Zutty (Paul), Eleasha Gamble (Ensemble), C. Mingo Long (Ensemble)

SOURCE—The 1958 novel *The Family Under the Bridge* by Natalie Savage Carlson.

The action occurs on the streets of Paris, December 15-December 24, 1952.

The musical was presented in two acts.

ACT ONE—"Paris" (Ed Dixon, Company), "You Will Meet with Adventure Today" (Florence Lacey), "You Will Meet with Adventure Today" (reprise) (Florence Lacey), "Half a Dream" (Ed Dixon, Children), "Under the Bridge" (Ed Dixon, Jacquelyn Piro), "Paris" (reprise) (Florence Lacey), "Paris" (reprise) (Ed Dixon), "The Marriage of Lady Tartine" (Children, Company), "It Was My Bridge!" (Ed Dixon), "This House Where We Live" (Maggie Watts), "You Will Meet with Adventure Today" (reprise) (Florence Lacey), "Do-Gooders' Lament" (Thursday Farrar, Tamra Hayden), "What Might Have Been" (Ed Dixon, Florence Lacey), "This Is the Gypsy Life!" (Florence Lacey, Gypsies), "What Kind of Mother Am I?" (Jacquelyn Piro, Thursday Farrar, Tamra Hayden, Ed Dixon)

ACT TWO—"This Is the Gypsy Life!" (reprise) (Company), "He Is with You" (Florence Lacey, Gypsies), "Christmas Is Everyone's Holiday" (Company), "You Will Meet with Adventure Today" (reprise) (Florence Lacey), "Do-Gooders' Lament" (reprise) (Thursday Farrar, Tamra Hayden, Dan Cooney), "What Might Have Been" (reprise) (Ed Dixon, Florence Lacey), "The Sum of a Man" (Florence Lacey, Andrew Blake Zutty), "As Long As We Have Us" (Jacquelyn Piro, Maggie Watts, Alexa Ehrlich), "I'm Going to Make a Clean Start" (Ed Dixon), "Something Called Love" (Ed Dixon), Finale (Ed Dixon, Company)

NOTES—The short-lived musical *Under the Bridge* dealt with a homeless Parisian family. Charles Isherwood in the *New York Times* noted the score was "competent if generic" and said the book needed some "finesse" because its story "lurches forward clumsily at times." Overall, he felt the production was "inert," partly because of the Zipper Theatre's "cramped" stage and Jim Kronzer's "oppressively drab set." The script was published by Samuel French, Inc., in 2006.

1701 Unfair to Goliath. THEATRE: Cherry Lane Theatre; OPENING DATE: January 25, 1970; PERFORMANCES: 76; SKETCHES: Ephraim Kishon (adapted by Herbert Appleman); LYRICS: Ephraim Kishon (adapted by Herbert Appleman); MUSIC: Menachem Zur; DIRECTION: Ephraim Kishon and Herbert Appleman; SCENERY: C. Murawski; COSTUMES: Pamela Scofield; LIGHTING: C. Murawski; MUSICAL DIRECTION: Menachem Zur; PRODUCERS: Edward Schreiber in association with Alexander Beck

CAST—Hugh Alexander, Jim Brochu, Jay Devlin, Corinne Kason, Laura May Lewis

The revue was presented in two acts.

ACT ONE—Overture (Menachem Zur), "The Danger of Peace Is Over" (Company), "In the Reign of Chaim" (Company), "A Bus Driver" (Company), "The Salesman (With a Suitcase)" (Jay Devlin, Jim Brochu, Hugh Alexander, Corinne Kason), "What Kind of Baby?" (Company), "The Patter of Little Feet" (Laura May Lewis, Jay Devlin, Corinne Kason), "The Oldtimer" (Hugh Alexander, Laura May Lewis), "A Parking Meter Like Me" (Hugh Alexander), "The Hardest Currency" (Company), "Unfair to Goliath" (Hugh Alexander, Corinne Kason, Laura May Lewis), "Hello" (Jay Devlin, Corinne Kason), "The Generation Gap" (Jim Brochu, Laura May Lewis), "The Sabra" (Jim Brochu), "Incognito" (Hugh Alexander, Jim Brochu, Corinne Kason, Laura May Lewis), "The Famous Rabbi" (Company), "A Brief Romance" (Hugh Alexander, Laura May Lewis), "Back to Back" (Jay Devlin, Jim Brochu), "2 × 2 = Schultz (A Famous Trial in Jerusalem)" (Jim Brochu, Jay Devlin, Hugh Alexander)

ACT TWO—Overture (Menachem Zur), "In the Desert" (Company), "When Moses Spake to Goldstein" (Company), "The Rooster and the Hen" (Corinne Kason), "Polygamy" (Hugh Alexander, Corinna Kason), "Waiting" (Hugh Alexander, Jay Devlin), "(A) Brief Romance" (Hugh Alexander, Laura May Lewis), "What Abraham Lincoln Once Said" (Company), "High Number Wins" (Hugh Alexander, Jay Devlin), "We're Together" (Jim Brochu, Jay Devlin, Corinne Kason), "Sallah and the Social Worker" (Jim Brochu, Hugh Alexander, Laura May Lewis, Corinne Kason), "The Song of Sallah Shabet" (Company), "It's a Country" (Company), "The Danger of Peace Is Over" (reprise) (Company)

NOTES—*Unfair to Goliath* was an evening of satiric sketches and songs based on material originally written by Ephraim Kishon (under the pseudonym of Khad-Gadya), a humorist who columns appeared in *Maariv*, a Hebrew newspaper published in Tel Aviv. Clive Barnes in the *New York Times* found the revue "sweet" and "engaging," but lacking "punch." He noted that the occasionally thin material was nonetheless bolstered by the show's "great virtue," its talented cast. As for the score, he found it "attractively vigorous, if painlessly forgettable." He also noted the evening was "very ethnic," and surmised that "Arabs" and those of "French extraction" might not find the revue to their liking.

During previews, the following songs and sketches were deleted: "The Israeli Wonder Plate," "An Easy Language," "The Brilliant Career of Professor Schapiro," "The Teacher's Lament," "A Short History of Tel Aviv," and "We Are the Pioneers."

1702 An Unfinished Song. THEATRE: Provincetown Playhouse; OPENING DATE: February 10, 1991; PERFORMANCES: 25; BOOK: James J. Mellon;

Lyrics: James J. Mellon; Music: James J. Mellon; Direction: Simon Levy; Scenery: Scott Bradley; Costumes: Jeffrey Ullman; Lighting: Robert M. Wierzel; Musical Direction: Mark Mitchell; Producers: Cheryl L. Fluehr and Starbuck Productions, Ltd.

Cast—Aloysius Gigl (Worth), Joanna Glushak (Debbie), Robert Lambert (Brad), Ken Land (Mort), Beth Leavel (Beth)

The musical was presented in two acts.

Act One—"Things We've Collected" (Aloysius Gigl, Beth Leavel, Robert Lambert, Joanna Glushak), "Balance the Plate" (Company), "Crossing Boundaries" (Ken Land), "The Frying Pan" (Beth Leavel), "Being Left Out" (Joanna Glushak, Robert Lambert, Ensemble), "As I Say Goodbye" (Beth Leavel), "Hobby Horses"/"How Could I Let You Leave Me" (Company)

Act Two—"New Hampshire Nights" (Beth Leavel), "Blonde Haired Babies" (Joanna Glushak), "Is That Love" (Robert Lambert, Aloysius Gigl, Ken Land), "Crossing Boundaries" (reprise) (Ken Land), "An Unfinished Song" (Ken Land), "We Were Here" (Aloysius Gigl, Beth Leavel, Robert Lambert, Joanna Glushak)

Notes—The musical *An Unfinished Song* dealt with four friends who gather together in order to close up the apartment of Michael, a young composer who has recently died. Two in the group, a man and a woman, are former lovers of Michael; the other two are a married couple he knew. As the four pack up Michael's belongings, they sing about him, and soon he appears among them as the past and present emerge and the five of them sing about their convoluted relationships with one other.

Stephen Holden in the *New York Times* found the evening a "talky soap opera in which everything important is expressed at least three times." He also noted the soft-rock score aspired to the "lyrical acuity" of Stephen Sondheim and William Finn but missed by a "mile." Holden indicated the musical's best moment was "The Frying Pan," a comic number that had almost nothing to do with the plot.

In 1995, the score was recorded by Tri-Angle Productions Records (unnumbered CD), and the singers included original cast member Beth Leavel. The album included three numbers not heard in New York ("Tightrope," "Keeping Score with Myself," and "Remember the Ocean") and omitted one number ("Being Left Out").

1703 Unlock'd

Notes—See entry for *The New York Musical Theatre Festival*.

1704 Unsung Cole.

"A Musical Entertainment." Theatre: Circle Theatre; Opening Date: June 23, 1977; Performances: 75; Lyrics: Cole Porter; Music: Cole Porter; Direction: Norman L. Berman; Choreography: Dennis Grimaldi; Scenery: Peter Harvey; Costumes: Carol Oditz; Lighting: Arden Fingerhut; Musical Direction: Leon Odenz; Producer: The Circle Repertory Company (Marshall W. Mason, Artistic Director; Jerry Arrow, Executive Director)

Cast—Gene Lindsey, Mary Louise, Maureen Moore, Anita Morris, John Sloman

The revue was presented in two acts.

Act One—"Pick Me Up and Lay Me Down" (written for the unproduced 1931 musical *Star Dust*) (Company), "Farming" (from *Let's Face It!*, 1941) (Company), "Thank You So Much, Mrs. Lowsborough-Goodby" (1934; possibly intended for *Anything Goes* [1934]) (Mary Louise, Gene Lindsey), "The Great Indoors" (*The New Yorkers*, 1930) (Anita Morris), "The Tale of an Oyster" (*Fifty Million Frenchmen*, 1929 [but dropped from that production soon after the Broadway opening]) (Maureen Moore), "Poor Young Millionaire" (1920s; source unknown) (John Sloman), "A Lady Needs a Rest" (*Let's Face It!*, 1941) (Mary Louise, Anita Morris, Maureen Moore), "Ours" (*Red Hot and Blue!*, 1936) (John Sloman, Maureen Moore), "Lost Liberty Blues" (French revue *La Revue des Ambassadeurs*, 1928) (Anita Morris), "Olga (Come Back to the Volga)" (British musical *Mayfair and Montmartre*, 1922) (Gene Lindsey, Company), "The Queen of Terre Haute" (dropped during tryout of *Fifty Million Frenchmen*, 1929) (Mary Louise), "Almiro" (French revue *La Revue des Ambassadeurs*, 1928; original lyric by Rene Pujol, English adaptation by Brian Ross) (Company), "Dancin' to a Jungle Drum" (*Seven Lively Arts*, 1944) (Maureen Moore), "Take Me Back to Manhattan"/"I Happen to Like New York" (both songs from *The New Yorkers*, 1930) (Gene Lindsey), "Why Don't We Try Staying Home" (written for, but not used in, *Fifty Million Frenchmen*, 1929) (John Sloman, Maureen Moore), "Give Me the Land" (written for, but not used in, *Silk Stockings*, 1955) (Company)

Act Two—"Abracadabra" (*Mexican Hayride*, 1944) (Mary Louise, Company), "When the Hen Stops Laying" (dropped during tryout of *Leave It to Me!*, 1938) (Mary Louise, Gene Lindsey), "That's Why I Love You" (written for, but not used in, *Fifty Million Frenchmen*, 1929) (Anita Morris, John Sloman), "Nobody's Chasing Me" (*Out of This World*, 1950) (Maureen Moore), "I'm Getting Myself Ready for You" (*The New Yorkers*, 1930) (Mary Louise, John Sloman, Company), "Just Another Page in Your Diary" (written for, but not used in, *Leave It to Me!*, 1938; later heard in regional production *Two Weeks with Pay* [1941]) (Anita Morris, Gene Lindsey, Mary Louise, John Sloman), "Goodbye Little Dream Goodbye" (written for, but not used in, 1936 film *Born to Dance*; was later dropped during tryout of *Red Hot and Blue!* [1936]; and was eventually heard in 1936 British musical *O Mistress Mine*) (Gene Lindsey), "After You, Who?" (*The Gay Divorce*, 1931) (Mary Louise), "Down in the Depths (on the Ninetieth Floor)" (*Red Hot and Blue!*, 1936) (Anita Morris), "Love for Sale" (*The New Yorkers*, 1930) (John Sloman), "I've Got Some Unfinished Business with You" (*Panama Hattie*, 1940) (Mary Louise), "Kate the Great" (written for, but not used in, *Anything Goes*, 1934) (Anita Morris), "If Ever Married I'm" (written for, but not used in, *Kiss Me, Kate*, 1948) (Maureen Moore), "Red Hot and Blue!" (*Red Hot and Blue!*, 1936) (Mary Louise, Anita Morris), "Swingin' the Jinx Away" (1936 film *Born to Dance*) (Company), "Friendship" (*DuBarry Was a Lady*, 1939) (Company)

Notes—*Unsung Cole* was a tribute to Cole Porter, and, like *By Bernstein* (1975; see entry), it emphasized relatively obscure songs and avoided the more familiar ones.

As *Unsung Cole (and classics too)*, the script was published by Samuel French, Inc., in 1981. There have been two film versions of Porter's life. In 1946, Hollywood gave his story the standard Hollywood treatment with *Night and Day*, in which Cary Grant played Porter. Although his performance has been criticized and many consider him miscast, Grant brought his customary crisp and debonair touch to the role. (Monty Woolley, whom Porter knew during his days at Yale, played himself in the film.) In 2004, a franker version of Porter's life and career was seen in *De-Lovely*, in which Kevin Kline played Porter (in one sequence, Kline watches Cary Grant in a scene from *Night and Day*!).

Incidentally, a few years before Cary Grant and Monty Woolley appeared together in *Night and Day*, their career paths crossed when Grant was signed by Warner Brothers to portray Sheridan Whiteside in the film version of George S. Kaufman and Moss Hart's 1939 play *The Man Who Came to Dinner*; Woolley, of course, had originated the role on Broadway (further, Rosalind Russell was announced for the role of Maggie Cutler, Whiteside's secretary, which had originally been portrayed on the stage by Edith Atwater). But Douglas W. Churchill in the *New York Times* reported that Grant withdrew from the film (in an apparently amicable parting with Warner Brothers), and that upon his completion of *Before the Fact* (later retitled *Suspicion*), he would appear in Columbia's *Bedtime Story*, which the company had purchased for Grant a year before and in which Grant would probably co-star with Irene Dunne (the film was eventually produced with Fredric March and Loretta Young in the leads).

In regard to the film version of *The Man Who Came to Dinner*, Churchill noted that an "intra-studio conflict" led to the "dissolution" of Grant's contract. One faction at the studio wanted the character of Sheridan Whiteside to be performed "in the Monty Woolley manner," and another wanted a plot utilizing the old "boy-meets-girl formula" in which the Whiteside character would be portrayed as a "young and romantic figure." Ultimately, Woolley was brought to Hollywood to recreate his stage role, and Bette Davis was signed to portray his secretary. In another crossing of career paths, both Grant and Woolley appeared together in the 1947 Christmas classic *The Bishop's Wife*.

1705 Untitled Play.

Theatre: Judson Poets' Theatre; Opening Date: 1967-1968 Theatre Season; Performances: Unknown; Play: Lanford Wilson; Lyrics: Al Carmines; Music: Al Carmines; Direction: Marshall W. Mason; Choreography: Remy Charlip and Aileen Passloff

Cast—Joy Bang, Claris Erickson, David Groh, Michael McClanathan, Michael Warren Powell, Rob Thirkield

Notes—Almost forty years before the 2006 Off Broadway musical *[title of play]*, there was *Untitled Play*, one of Lanford Wilson's earliest works to be seen in New York. The Off Off Broadway play included incidental songs by Al Carmines. Wilson's first Broadway play was the short-lived *The Gingham Dog*, which lasted for five performances in 1969. But he soon found success, including a Pulitzer Prize for *Talley's Folly* (1979). His Off Broadway play *The Hot L Baltimore* (1973) ran for 1,126 performances, and his other major plays include *Lemon Sky* (1970), *The Fifth of July* (1978), and *Burn This* (1987). In 1972, Wilson wrote the libretto of Lee Hoiby's operatic adaptation of Tennessee Williams' *Summer and Smoke* (see entry).

1706 Up Against It.

Theatre: LuEsther Hall/The Public Theatre; Opening Date: December 4, 1989; Performances: 16; Book: Tom Ross; Lyrics: Todd Rundgren; Music: Todd Rundgren; Direction: Kenneth Elliott; Choreography: Jennifer Muller; Scenery: B.T. Whitehill; Costumes: John Glaser; Lighting: Vivian Leone; Musical Direction: Tom Fay; Producer: The New York Shakespeare Festival (Joseph Papp, Director)

Cast—Stephen Temperley (Father Brodie, Old Man), Alison Fraser (Miss Drumgoole), Philip Casnoff (Ian McTurk), Joel McKinnon Miller (Mayor Terence O'Scullion), Roger Bart (Christopher Low), Tony Dibuono (Connie Boon), Mari Nelson (Rowena), Tom Aulino (Bernard Coates), Judith Cohen (Man in the Hole, Lilly Corbett), Marnie Carmichael (Georgina), Dan Tubb (Jack Ramsay), Scott Carollo (Guard), Ensemble (Brian Arsenault, Scott Carollo, Mindy Cooper, Dorothy R. Earle, Julia C. Hughes, Gary Mendelson, Jim Newman)

Source—*Up Against It*, an unproduced screenplay by Joe Orton.

The action occurs in the 1960s in a mythical place "not unlike England."

The musical was presented in two acts.

Act One—"When Worlds Collide" (Stephen Temperley, Joel McKinnon Miller, Tony Dibuono),

"Parallel Lines" (Alison Fraser), "Free, Male and Twenty-One" (Philip Casnoff, Roger Bart), "The Smell of Money" (Tom Aulino), "The Smell of Money" (waltz) (Mari Nelson), "If I Have to Be Alone" (Philip Casnoff), "Up Against It" (Dan Tubb, Company), "Life Is a Drag" (Dan Tubb, Philip Casnoff, Joel McKinnon Miller, Roger Bart, Stephen Temperley, Men), "Lilly's Address" (Judith Cohen, Company), "Love in Disguise" (Mari Nelson, Dan Tubb, Philip Casnoff, Roger Bart, Company)

ACT TWO—"You'll Thank Me in the End" (Tony Dibuono), "Maybe I'm Better Off" (Philip Casnoff, Dan Tubb), "From Hunger" (Roger Bart), "Entropy" (Alison Fraser, Dan Tubb, Philip Casnoff, Roger Bart, Company), "Parallel Lines" (reprise) (Philip Casnoff, Company), Finale (Company)

NOTES—Joe Orton had originally written the screenplay *Up Against It* as a vehicle for the Beatles, who rejected it. He later revised the work, but it remained unproduced until Tom Ross adapted the material for the book of the musical version.

The satire dealt with friends who, in order to avenge themselves on women who have victimized them, decide to assassinate the female prime minister.

Mel Gussow in the *New York Times* reported that the musical's creators "obliterated whatever charm existed in the [published] screenplay," and, to use the verb in one of the evening's "unnecessarily repeated" songs ("When Worlds Collide"), Gussow noted that "everything" collided in the musical ("book, score, direction, performances, even ... the scenery"). Gussow singled out "Parallel Lines" as the best song in the score (especially as sung in its reprise version by Philip Casnoff) and indicated the evening's least appealing song (apparently "Entropy") was a "coarse Spanish number" which Alison Fraser sang to a "Yorick-like skull."

1707 Up Eden. "A Farce Musical." THEATRE: Jan Hus Playhouse; OPENING DATE: November 27, 1968; PERFORMANCES: 7; BOOK: Robert Rosenblum and Howard Schuman; LYRICS: Robert Rosenblum and Howard Schuman; MUSIC: Robert Rosenblum; DIRECTION: John Bishop; CHOREOGRAPHY: Patricia (Pat) Birch; SCENERY: Gordon Micunis; COSTUMES: Gordon Micunis; LIGHTING: Louis Guthman; MUSICAL DIRECTION: Wally Harper; PRODUCERS: Jack Farren in association with Evan William Mandel; Vivian Farren, Associate Producer

CAST—BLYTHE DANNER (Violet Beam), DEBORAH DEEBLE (Iris Beam), PATTI KARR (Desiree Wildwood), GEORGE S. IRVING (Hannibal Beam), DENNY SHEARER (Buster Turnbull), BOB BALABAN (Oak Bainbridge), Laurie Hutchinson (Rose), Sally Soldo (Pee Wee), Richard Hall (Dexter), George Connolly (Jack), David Burrow (Mayor), Stacy McAdams (the Reverend), Barbara Porter (Hatti), Diana Goble (Prudence)

SOURCE—The musical was inspired by, and freely adapted from, Wolfgang Amadeus Mozart's opera *Cosi fan Tutte* (1790).

The action occurs in 1927 in various parts of Beam, a Utopian community founded in the nineteenth century as a refugee against Progress; Beam is situated in a hidden valley, somewhere in the innards of America.

The musical was presented in two acts.

ACT ONE—Prologue (Company), "Haven't You Wondered" (Deborah Deeble), "Wishy-Washy Woman" (Patti Karr), "Hannibal's Comin'" (Company), "Homesick" (George S. Irving, Company), "The Will" (Patti Karr, Deborah Deeble, Blythe Danner, George S. Irving, Bob Balaban, Denny Shearer, David Burrow), "Let Me Show You the World" (George S. Irving, Patti Karr), "Remember Me Smiling" (Deborah Deeble, Blythe Danner, George S. Irving, Company), "Passin' Through" (Bob Balaban, Denny Shearer), "A Playboy's Work Is Never Done" (Bob Balaban, Denny Shearer), "Nothing Ever Happens 'Til Two A.M." (Company)

ACT TWO—"The Mowla" (George S. Irving, Patti Karr, Company), "Was That Me Talking" (Blythe Danner), "The Virgin of Velez-Jermano" (George S. Irving, Patti Karr), "A Little More Like You" (Deborah Deeble, Denny Shearer), "No More Edens" (George S. Irving), Prologue (reprise) (Company), Finale (George S. Irving, Company)

NOTES—Very loosely based on the libretto of Mozart's opera *Cosi fan Tutte*, the musical *Up Eden* lasted less than a week. Clive Barnes in the *New York Times* reported the free-wheeling plot dealt with a religious Utopian town which is visited by a scoundrel who introduces modern-day 1920s life to the heretofore cloistered community. As the villain of the piece, George S. Irving provided "boisterous fun" and was "awful, but in the right way." Otherwise, the evening didn't seem to offer much in the way of entertainment. But with Irving and Patti Karr together performing such numbers as "The Mowla" and "The Virgin of Velez-Jermano," the musical must have had something going for it. As for Blythe Danner's performance, who knows? During the previous year she had appeared in the Alvin-Theatre-bound *Mata Hari* (see entry), which closed during its pre-Broadway tryout at the National Theatre in Washington, D.C., and almost thirty-five years passed before she finally made her debut in a Broadway musical. Perhaps the debut was too soon, because her performance as Phyllis Stone in the 2001 revival of *Follies* was a low point in an evening filled with low points (clueless direction, anemic choreography, weak leads, and dinner-theater décor). The most distinguished moments in the revival were all-too-brief turns by Polly Bergen, Betty Garrett, Joan Roberts, Jane White, Marge Champion, and Donald Saddler.

1708 Up from Paradise. "A New Musical." THEATRE: Jewish Repertory Theatre; OPENING DATE: October 25, 1983; PERFORMANCES: 12; BOOK: Arthur Miller; LYRICS: Arthur Miller; MUSIC: Stanley Silverman; DIRECTION: Ran Avni; "additional" musical staging by Stanley Silverman; SCENERY: Michael C. Smith; COSTUMES: Marie Anne Chiment; LIGHTING: Dan Kinsley; MUSICAL DIRECTION: Michael Ward; PRODUCER: The Jewish Repertory Theatre (Ran Avni, Artistic Director)

CAST—Len Cariou (God), Raymond Murcell (Azrael), Avery J. Tracht (Raphael), Richard Frisch (Uriel), Austin Pendleton (Adam), Alice Playten (Eve), Walter Bobbie (Lucifer), Paul Ukena, Jr. (Cain), Lonny Price (Abel)

SOURCE—The 1972 play *The Creation of the World and Other Business* by Arthur Miller.

The musical was presented in two acts.

ACT ONE—"The Lord Is a Hammer of Light" (Angels), "How Fine It Is (to Name Things)" (Austin Pendleton, Len Cariou, Angels), "When Night Starts to Fall" (Austin Pendleton), "Bone of Thy Bones" (Len Cariou), "Hallelujah" (Angels), "(In) The Center of Your Mind (Keep the Lord)" (Len Cariou, Austin Pendleton, Alice Playten, Angels), "It's Just Like I Was You" (Austin Pendleton, Alice Playten), "Recitative" (Len Cariou), "But If Something Leads to Good (Can It Be Bad?)" (Walter Bobbie), "I'm Me, We're Us" (Austin Pendleton, Alice Playten), "Curses" (Len Cariou), "Lonely Quartet" (Austin Pendleton, Alice Playten, Walter Bobbie, Len Cariou), "How Lovely Is Eve" (Walter Bobbie), "I Am the River" and "Waltz" (Alice Playten)

ACT TWO—Entr'acte (Orchestra), "All of That Made for Me" (Angels), "As Good as Paradise" (Austin Pendleton, Alice Playten, Paul Ukena, Jr., Lonny Price), "It Was So Peaceful Before There Was Man" (Len Cariou), "It Comes to Me" (Lonny Price), "I Don't Know What Is Happening to Me" (Paul Ukena, Jr., Lonny Price), "Why Can't I See God?" (Paul Ukena, Jr.), "All Love" (Alice Playten, Austin Pendleton, Lonny Price, Angels), "Passion" (Len Cariou), "Nothing's Left of God" (Walter Bobbie), "Never Seen the Garden Again" (Austin Pendleton, Alice Playten, Company)

NOTES—Arthur Miller's play *The Creation of the World and Other Business* (1972) was one of his weakest, less a play than an endlessly extended sketch. And with Adam, Eve, and Lucifer as its main characters, you kept waiting for the actors to break out in Sheldon Harnick and Jerry Bock's memorable songs from *The Diary of Adam and Eve*, the first act of *The Apple Tree* (1966). *Up from Paradise*, the Off Off Broadway musical version of *Creation*, was likewise dreary and drawn-out, and, yes, you kept waiting for the performers to break out in songs from the first act of *The Apple Tree*. Instead, you got forgettable songs by Miller and Stanley Silverman.

Besides its subject matter, there was another *Apple Tree* connection with *Creation* and *Paradise*, in the person of Barbara Harris, the golden delicious Eve of *The Apple Tree*. The first newspaper advertisements, flyers, and window cards for the pre-Broadway Kennedy Center engagement of *The Creation of the World and Other Business* at the Eisenhower Theatre listed Harris as the star. But at the first preview performance, Susan Batson, her understudy, played the role (and during the run of the tryout, Batson was replaced by Zoe Caldwell, the wife of the play's co-producer). But it was all for naught, and *Creation* lasted less than three weeks on Broadway. (Incidentally, the background music for *Creation* was composed by Stanley Silverman, who of course later wrote the score for *Up from Paradise*.)

Like *Creation*, *Up from Paradise* was first seen at the Kennedy Center (in a Musical Theatre Lab production). Austin Pendleton, Walter Bobbie, and Paul Ukena, Jr., created the roles of Adam, Lucifer, and Cain, roles they would later play in the New York production (in Washington, Patti Perkins was Eve, and Paul Ukena played God). During the Washington run, "The Mother of Mankind" (possibly an early version of "I Am the River" and "Waltz"), "A Terrible Feeling," and "Adorable" were heard. "Lamentation" may have been an early version of "Passion"; "The Loneliness Song" and "I'm Lonely" were probably rewritten as the "Lonely Quartet"; "I Am Me" may have been an early version of "I'm Me, We're Us"; "The Vengeance of God" may have been reworked as "Curses"; and "When Eve Is Alone" was reworked as "How Lovely Is Eve." The script was published by Samuel French, Inc., in 1984, and included a new finale ("I Know He Wants Us To Praise His Mornings").

1709 Upstairs at O'Neals'. THEATRE: O'Neals' 43rd Street Cabaret; OPENING DATE: October 29, 1982; PERFORMANCES: 308; SKETCHES: Douglas Bernstein, Denis Markell, and Archie T. Tridmorten; LYRICS: Michael Abbott, Douglas Bernstein, Martin Charnin, David L. Crane, John Forster, Seth Friedman, Murray Horwitz, Marta Kauffman, Michael Leeds, Denis Markell, Ronald Melrose, Michael Mooney, Jim Morgan, Charles Strouse, and Sarah Weeks; MUSIC: Michael Abbott, Douglas Bernstein, Martin Charnin, John Forster, Seth Friedman, Stephen Hoffman, Michael Leeds, Denis Markell, Ronald Melrose, Charles Strouse, Paul Trueblood, and Sarah Weeks; DIRECTION: Martin Charnin; CHOREOGRAPHY: Ed Love; SCENERY: Ray Recht; COSTUMES: Zoran; LIGHTING: Ray Recht; MUSICAL DIRECTION: David Krane; PRODUCERS: Martin Charnin, Michael O'Neal, Patrick O'Neal, and Ture Tufvesson

CAST—Douglas Bernstein, Randall Edwards, Bebe Neuwirth, Michon Peacock, Richard Ryder, Sarah Weeks; David Krane and Paul Ford (Pianos)

The revue was presented in one act.

MUSICAL NUMBERS—Overture (David Krane, Paul Ford), "Upstairs at O'Neals'" (lyric and music by Martin Charnin) (Company), "Stools" (lyric and music by Martin Charnin) (Bebe Neuwirth, Douglas Bernstein, Richard Ryder), "Cancun" (lyric and music by Michael Leeds and John Forster) (Richard Ryder), "Something" (lyric and music by Douglas Bernstein and Denis Markell) (Douglas Bernstein), "I Furnished My One Room Apartment" (lyric by Michael Mooney, music by Stephen Hoffman) (Sarah Weeks), "Little H and Little G" (lyric and music by Ronald Melrose) (Company), "The Ballad of Cy and Beatrice" (lyric by Jim Morgan, music by Paul Trueblood) (Randall Edwards), "Signed, Peeled, Delivered" (lyric and music by Ronald Melrose) (Richard Ryder, Company), "The Feet" (lyric by David L. Crane, Seth Friedman, and Marta Kauffman, music by Seth Friedman) (Company), "The Soldier and the Washerworker" (lyric and music by Ronald Melrose) (Bebe Neuwirth), "Table D'Hote" (sketch by Archie T. Tridmorten) (Douglas Bernstein, Richard Ryder, Randall Edwards), "Soap Operetta" (lyric by David L. Crane, Seth Friedman, and Marta Kauffman, music by Seth Friedman) (Company), "Talkin' Morosco Blues" (lyric by Murray Horowitz) (Richard Ryder, with guitar accompaniment by Willie Nininger [who also wrote the music]), "Mommas' Turn" (lyric and music by Douglas Bernstein and Denis Markell) (Bebe Neuwirth, Michon Peacock, Sarah Weeks), "We'll Be Right Back After This Message" (sketch by Douglas Bernstein and Denis Markell) (Bebe Neuwirth, Randall Edwards, Douglas Bernstein), "All I Can Do Is Cry" (lyric and music by Sarah Weeks and Michael Abbott) (Sarah Weeks), "Cover Girls" (lyric by David L. Crane, Seth Friedman, and Marta Kauffman, music by Seth Friedman) (Michon Peacock, Bebe Neuwirth, Randall Edwards, Douglas Bernstein), "Boy, Do We Need It Now" (lyric and music by Charles Strouse) (Michon Peacock, Company), Finale (Company)

NOTES—Like *R.S.V.P.* (see entry), the revue *Upstairs at O'Neals'* was reminiscent of Julius Monk's frolics of the 1950s and 1960s; its title, and even the size and format of its program, were evocative of Monk's legendary revues. Although *Upstairs at O'Neals'* ran over 300 performances, there were unfortunately no more editions in the series.

Upstairs at O'Neals' included songs by Charles Strouse and Martin Charnin, both of whom had contributed material to early Off Broadway revues. The cast included a new face, Bebe Neuwirth, a powerhouse performer who unfortunately never appears in enough musicals (but whenever she does, her presence is musical comedy nirvana).

Frank Rich in the *New York Times* liked the lively cast and praised Charnin's "energetic" and "bubbling" direction. He singled out a soap opera sequence which was presented as a Gilbert and Sullivan operetta ("Soap Operetta"), a feminist Irish folk song ("The Soldier and the Washerwoman" [Rich remarked that the song's "alternative gender references become increasingly complex"]), teenage models ("Cover Girls"), and a song in which an old-fashioned doll laments that she's not anatomically correct ("All I Can Do Is Cry").

One of the revue's numbers, "Talkin' Morosco Blues," dealt with the recent demolition of the legendary theatre (the Morosco, along with the Helen Hayes and the Bijou, had faced the wrecker's ball earlier in the year) and was sung by a Sixties' type protester. One of the most amusing songs was "Mammas' Turn," in which the critics' mothers (the mothers of "Frank," "Clive," "John," and "Mel" are among those mentioned) give their two-cents about the current state of New York theatre (and, by the way, they just loved *1600 Pennsylvania Avenue*, *Mata Hari*, *Oh, Brother!*, and *Via Galactica*). "Stools" was later heard in *The No-Frills Revue* (1987).

The sketch "The Gurus" was omitted during previews.

The cast album was released by Painted Smiles Records (LP # PS-1344), which was of course Ben Bagley's label, and he, too, was another name from the golden era of the Off Broadway revue.

1710 Urban Blight. THEATRE: City Center Stage I/Manhattan Theatre Club; OPENING DATE: June 19, 1988; PERFORMANCES: 12; SKETCHES: John Augustine, John Bishop, Christopher Durang, Jules Feiffer, Larry Fishburne, Charles Fuller, Nancy Giles, A.R. Gurney, Jr., E. Katherine Kerr, David Mamet, Terrence McNally, Arthur Miller, Shel Silverstein, Ted Tally, Wendy Wasserstein, Richard Wesley, and George C. Wolfe; LYRICS: Ed Kleban and Richard Maltby, Jr; MUSIC: Ed Kleban and David Shire; DIRECTION: John Tillinger and Richard Maltby, Jr; CHOREOGRAPHY: Charles Randolph-Wright; SCENERY: Heidi Landesman; COSTUMES: C.L. Hundley; LIGHTING: Natasha Katz; MUSICAL DIRECTION: Michael Skloff; PRODUCER: Manhattan Theatre Club (Lynne Meadow, Artistic Director; Barry Grove, Managing Director)

CAST—Larry Fishburne, Nancy Giles, E. Katherine Kerr, Oliver Platt, Faith Prince, Rex Robbins, John Rubinstein

The revue was presented in two acts.

ACT ONE—"Don't Fall for the Lights" (lyric by Richard Maltby, Jr., music by David Shire, dialogue by Terrence McNally, A.R. Gurney, Jr., and Richard Maltby, Jr.) (Company), "Feeding the Baby" (sketch by Shel Silverstein) (Faith Prince, John Rubinstein, Oliver Platt), "Cardinal O'Connor" (sketch by Christopher Durang) (Rex Robbins, John Rubinstein), "Fries and a Shake" (sketch by Larry Fishburne and Nancy Giles) (Faith Prince, Larry Fishburne, Nancy Giles, E. Katherine Kerr), Portrait #1: "Life Story" (lyric by Richard Maltby, Jr., music by David Shire) (Faith Prince), "White Walls" (sketch by A.R. Gurney, Jr.) (Rex Robbins, Oliver Platt), Portrait #2: "Miss Byrd" (lyric by Richard Maltby, Jr., music by David Shire) (Nancy Giles), "Transfiguration of Gerome" (Part I) (sketch by E. Katherine Kerr) (E. Katherine Kerr), "Subway Panhandlers" (sketch by John Augustine) (Oliver Platt, Larry Fishburne, John Rubinstein, E. Katherine Kerr), "Street Talk" (sketch by Terrence McNally) (Larry Fishburne, Nancy Giles), "Transfiguration of Gerome" (Part II) (sketch by E. Katherine Kerr) (E. Katherine Kerr, Oliver Platt), "Over There" (sketch by George C. Wolfe) (John Rubinstein, Nancy Giles), "Woman Stand-Up" (sketch by Christopher Durang) (Faith Prince), "Aerobicantata" (lyric by Richard Maltby, Jr., music by David Shire) (Oliver Platt, Rex Robbins, John Rubinstein, Nancy Giles, Faith Prince)

ACT TWO—"Bill of Fare" (lyric by Richard Maltby, Jr., music by David Shire) (John Rubinstein, Company), "Taxi from Hell" (sketch by Ted Tally) (Oliver Platt, Rex Robbins), "Transfiguration of Gerome" (Part III) (sketch by E. Katherine Kerr) (E. Katherine Kerr, Nancy Giles), "Speech to the Neighborhood Watch Committee" (sketch by Arthur Miller) (John Rubinstein), "Transfiguration of Gerome" (Part IV) (sketch by E. Katherine Kerr) (E. Katherine Kerr, Nancy Giles), "Smart Women/Brilliant Choices" (sketch by Wendy Wasserstein) (Faith Prince, Rex Robbins), "Rope-a-Dope" (sketch by Jules Feiffer) (Oliver Platt), Portrait #3: "There" (lyric by Richard Maltby, Jr., music by David Shire) (E. Katherine Kerr, Rex Robbins), "Where Were You When It Went Down?" (sketch by David Mamet) (John Rubinstein, Larry Fishburne), "Eliot's Coming" (sketch by Charles Fuller) (Nancy Giles), "Lonely Bohunks" (sketch by John Bishop) (Oliver Platt, E. Katherine Kerr), "Bernard's Lament" (sketch by Richard Wesley) (Larry Fishburne), "Andre's Mother" (sketch by Terrence McNally) (John Rubinstein, Faith Prince, Rex Robbins, E. Katherine Kerr), "Self-Portrait" (lyric and music by Ed Kleban) (John Rubinstein), "Don't Fall for the Lights" (reprise) (Company)

NOTES—*Urban Blight* was another revue about living in New York City, and, considering the impressive names among its writers and cast members, it's surprising the revue faded so quickly.

The revue, which emphasized the negative aspects of life in New York in 1988, was, according to Frank Rich in the *New York Times*, "uneven" and about thirty minutes too long. But he praised a number of sequences, including "Taxi from Hell," a sketch by Ted Tally about a non-English-speaking taxi driver (a "witty reworking" of Bud Abbott and Lou Costello's "Who's on First" routine), and George C. Wolfe's sketch "Over There," which dealt with the New Black Woman (an "aloof" television anchor) and the New White Man ("sensitive and aware but not guilty"). Rich also praised Richard Maltby, Jr., and David Shire's "several charming songs," including "Miss Byrd," an "old-time show stopper" performed by Nancy Giles in a "sizzling comic frenzy."

Three of the revue's songs ("Miss Byrd," "Life Story," and "There") surfaced in Maltby and Shire's 1989 revue *Closer Than Ever* (see entry), and can be heard on that show's cast recording. The liner notes for *Closer Than Ever*'s cast album indicated two songs heard in *Urban Blight* (but not listed in its program) were "You Want to Be My Friend?" and "There's Nothing Like It"); that another song ("Three Friends") was written for *Urban Blight* but not used; and that "One of the Good Guys" had been "completed" for *Urban Blight* (but apparently not used). All these songs can be heard on the cast recording of *Closer Than Ever*; Ed Kleban's "Self Portrait" was later heard in *A Class Act* (2000; see entry), and can be heard on that musical's cast recording.

1711 The Urban Crisis. THEATRE: Judson Poets' Theatre; OPENING DATE: Early 1970s (?); PERFORMANCES: Unknown; LYRICS: Al Carmines; MUSIC: Al Carmines

1712 Urinetown. "The Musical." THEATRE: American Theatre of Actors; OPENING DATE: May 6, 2001; PERFORMANCES: 58; BOOK: Greg Kotis; LYRICS: Greg Kotis and Mark Hollmann; MUSIC: Mark Hollmann; DIRECTION: John Rando; CHOREOGRAPHY: John Carrafa; SCENERY: Scott Pask; COSTUMES: Jonathan Bixby and Gregory Gale; LIGHTING: Brian MacDevitt; MUSICAL DIRECTION: Edward Strauss; PRODUCERS: Araca Group and Dodger Theatricals in association with TheatreDreams, Inc., and Lauren Mitchell

CAST—Jeff McCarthy (Officer Lockstock), Spencer Kayden (Little Sally), Nancy Opel (Penelope Pennywise), Hunter Foster (Bobby Strong), Jennifer Laura Thompson (Hope Cladwell), David Beach (Mr. McQueen), John Deyle (Senator Fipp), Ken Jennings (Old Man Strong, Hot Blades Harry), Rick Crom (Tiny Tom, Dr. Billeaux), Rachel Coloff (Soupy Sue, Cladwell's Secretary), Megan Lawrence (Little Becky Two Shoes, Mrs. Millennium), Victor W. Hawks (Robbie the Stockfish, Business Man # 1), Lawrence Street (Billy Boy Bill, Business Man # 2), Kay Walbye (Old Woman, Josephine Strong), Daniel Marcus (Officer Barrel), John Cullum (Caldwell B. Cladwell)

The action occurs in a Gotham-like city "sometime after the Stink years."

The musical was presented in two acts.

ACT ONE—Overture (Orchestra), "Urinetown" (Jeff McCarthy, Company), "It's a Privilege to Pee" (Nancy Opel, The Poor), "It's a Privilege to Pee" (reprise) (Jeff McCarthy, The Poor), "Mr. Cladwell" (John Cullum, The UGC Staff), "Cop Song" (Jeff McCarthy, Daniel Marcus, Cops), "Follow Your Heart" (Jennifer Laura Thompson, Hunter Foster), "Look at the Sky" (Hunter Foster, The Poor), "Don't

Be the Bunny" (John Cullum, John Deyle, David Beach, Jeff McCarthy, Daniel Marcus, Nancy Opel), Finale (Company)

ACT TWO—"What Is Urinetown?" (Company), "Snuff That Girl" (Ken Jennings, Megan Lawrence, The Poor), "Run, Freedom, Run!" (Hunter Foster), "Follow Your Heart" (reprise) (Jennifer Laura Thompson), "Why Did I Listen to That Man?" (Nancy Opel, Jennifer Laura Thompson, John Deyle, Jeff McCarthy, Daniel Marcus, Hunter Foster), "Tell Her I Love Her" (Spencer Kayden, Hunter Foster, The Poor), "We're Not Sorry" (The Poor), "We're Not Sorry" (reprise) (John Cullum, Nancy Opel), "I See a River" (Jennifer Laura Thompson, Megan Lawrence, Kay Walbye, Company)

NOTES—Even with its off-putting title (which the advertisements wisely kidded), *Urinetown* was a hit, and after its Off Broadway run it transferred to Broadway at Henry Miller's Theatre on September 20, 2001, for a run of 965 performances. The musical was nominated for ten Tony Awards (winning three, for Best Book, Best Score, and Best Direction), and the Broadway cast album was released by RCA Victor Records (CD # 09026-63821-2). The script was published by Faber and Faber, Inc., in 2003.

In its plot about big business exploiting the common man (all citizens are forced to use public restrooms, and pay for the privilege, no less), the musical spoofed agit-prop theatre of the 1930s (such as Marc Blitzstein's *The Cradle Will Rock* [see entry]), theatre music of the Kurt Weill variety, and even laughed at musical comedy conventions (the characters are aware they're in a musical; thus in the first act a character welcomes us to *Urinetown* ... that is, not "the place" but "the musical," and indicates he doesn't want to overload the audience with too much exposition; later, another one ponders the meaning of the musical ["Urinetown isn't so much a place as it is a metaphysical place"]).

The musical had first been produced Off Off Broadway at the Theatre of the Apes by the New York International Fringe Festival in August 1999.

With his performance in *Urinetown*, John Cullum continued one of the most remarkable careers in the history of post-World War II musicals. He made his Broadway debut as Sir Dinadan in the original 1960 production of *Camelot*; during the tryout of *On a Clear Day You Can See Forever* (1965), he replaced Louis Jourdan, and so it was Cullum who introduced the standard title song to Broadway audiences; he then appeared in *Shenandoah* (1975), winning his first Tony Award for Best Actor in a Musical; in 1978, he won his second Tony for *On the Twentieth Century*; and in 2007 was in the revival of *110 in the Shade*. He can he heard on the cast albums of all six of these musicals.

1713 Utopia! "A Musical." THEATRE: Folksbiene Playhouse; OPENING DATE: May 6, 1963; PERFORMANCES: 11; BOOK: William Klenosky; LYRICS: William Klenosky; MUSIC: William Klenosky; DIRECTION: Cecil Reddick; CHOREOGRAPHY: Melinda Taintor; SCENERY: Gary Meir Zeller; COSTUMES: Edith Arm; LIGHTING: Gary Meir Zeller; MUSICAL DIRECTION: Stephen Lawrence; PRODUCER: Billy K Productions

CAST—Lionel Galant (Walter Fahrenheit, Second Hawker, Gillette), Mike Templon (General Padgett), Ray Gilbert (Col. John Dooley), Leonard Josenhans (Dr. Knadel), Heinz Hohenwald (Dr. Otto Von Black), Elliot Cuker (Col. Ivan Grussky), Leon Benedict (Vyachheslav Selinky), Jim Savage (Paul Penbroke), Xander Chello (Harry Cooke), Lewis Pierce (Amos Hartstone), Vilma Vaccaro (Mary Hartstone), Susan Seifert (Elizabeth Pembroke), Dorothy Lancaster (Sarah Cooke), Marvin Davis (Gov. George Garfield), Guje Seastrom (Olga Terranova), Ed Zang (Tax Agent, Secretary General, NKVD Agent), Charles Listman (Radio Announcer, First Hawker, Hy Octane, Kilroy), Anthony Cointreau (French Delegate, Ensemble), Leonard Josenhanz (British Delegate), Scott Ray (Reporter, Ensemble), William J. Marshall (Indian Delegate), Gary Peterson (Bagelform Bra, Ensemble), Eppie Baker (Prudence), Annette Brandler (Ensemble), Judy Gallagher (Ensemble), Jeannette Hartunian (Ensemble), Meredith Pogue (Ensemble), Judy Suhocki (Ensemble)

The action occurs in April and October of 1962 (division of acts and song assignments unknown; musical numbers are listed in performance order).

MUSICAL NUMBERS—"Why Are We Here," "The Ballad of Utopia," "April in Siberia," "We've Got a Feeling in Our Bones," "You've Got the Devil in Your Eyes," "I Work for Pravda," "The Tax Collector's Soliloquy," "You Gotta Have a Destination," "The National Anthem of Utopia," "Utopia Ballet—Hooligan's Hop," "The Masses Are Asses," "What Am I Hangin' Around For?," "I Can't Pretend," "All You Need Is a Little Love"

NOTES—According to Louis Calta in the *New York Times*, *Utopia!*, a musical which satirized politics and other twentieth-century institutions, was singularly lacking in wit and freshness. Calta noted that William Klenosky, the musical's librettist, lyricist, and composer, had been a failed candidate for mayor in New York City's recent election. He had campaigned to "restore dignity" to the New York City school system, to clean up Times Square, and to end the harassment of motorists (whatever that meant).

Utopia! had a cast of twenty-seven performers! And this was Off Broadway in 1963. Quite a contrast to the downsized musicals of today's Broadway, when we're actually impressed if a musical offers more than fifteen or twenty performers. Today, the number of cast and orchestra members keeps going down (and, distressingly, a mini-trend has suddenly emerged in which the orchestra is dispensed with and the cast members themselves play musical instruments) and cheap-looking unit sets have become the norm. The only thing which goes up is the cost of the ticket (and let's not forget the "theatre restoration fee").

From twenty-seven cast members ... to one. William Klenosky returned to Off Broadway in 1967 with his one-man revue *Klenosky Against the Slings and Arrows of Outrageous Fortune* (see entry). One of the numbers in the new revue was called "Return to Utopia."

1714 Utterly Wilde!!! THEATRE: Next Stage Company; OPENING DATE: March 22, 1995; PERFORMANCES: 5; TEXT: Created from the words and writings of Oscar Wilde by Marc H. Glick; LYRICS: John Franceschina; MUSIC: John Franceschina; DIRECTION: Drew Scott Harris; LIGHTING: David Castaneda; MUSICAL DIRECTION: George Kramer; PRODUCER: Next Stage Company

CAST—Marc H. Glick (Oscar Wilde)

The action occurs in Paris at the Hotel D'Alsace in 1899.

The musical was probably presented in one act (all songs performed by Marc H. Glick)

MUSICAL NUMBERS—"Déjà Vu," "Two Loves," "I Want to Make Magic," "Wasted Days," "Dearest of All Boys," "Romantic Experience," "Joshua," "To My Wife," "I'll Never Give Up on Bosie," "Ballad of Reading Gaol"

NOTES—Like *Dear Oscar* and *It's Wilde!* (see entries), *Utterly Wilde!!!* was a musical biography of Oscar Wilde; while the other musicals had full casts, *Utterly Wilde!!!* was a one-man musical.

For musicals based on works by Oscar Wilde, see entries for *After the Ball* and *A Delightful Evening*, both based on *Lady Windermere's Fan*; *Dorian* (which also references *Dorian Gray*, another musical adaptation of the material [both musicals opened within a month of one another in 1990]); *Dorian Gray*, another musical adaptation (which opened in 1996); and *Ernest in Love* (which also references other musical adaptations of *The Importance of Being Earnest*).

1715 Vagabond Stars. "A New Musical." THEATRE: Jewish Repertory Theatre; OPENING DATE: May 29, 1982; PERFORMANCES: Unknown; BOOK: Nahma Sandrow; LYRICS: Alan Poul; MUSIC: Raphael Crystal; DIRECTION: Ran Avni; CHOREOGRAPHY: Bick Goss; SCENERY: Jeffrey Schneider; COSTUMES: Karen Hummel; LIGHTING: Phil Monat; MUSICAL DIRECTION: Raphael Crystal; PRODUCER: The Jewish Repertory Theatre (Ran Avni, Artistic Director)

CAST—Herbert Rubens (Mishke, Simkhe, Khatski, Willie, Shloyme), Dana Zeller-Alexis (Mashke, Bas-Sheve, Indian, Rivke), Susan Victor (Flossie, Bessie, Indian, Minna), Steve Yudson (Noyekh, Itsik, Jack, Indian), Steve Sterner (Zalmen, Khayim, Mr. Menachem Yosef, Yankl, Kalomfulo, Mr. Wolf)

The musical was presented in two acts.

ACT ONE—The Greenhorns: "Mishke and Mashke" (sketch by Joseph Lateuer; 1889) and American "Thievery" (sketch by Fishl Bimko; 1936) (Dana Zeller-Alexis, Herbert Rubens), Living in America: "Vi Derlebt Men Shoyn Amerike Tsu Zeyn" (lyric by H. Wohl, music by A. Lebedeff; 1921) and "Zay Gebentsht Du Fraye Land" (sketch by J.M. Rumshinsky and A. Shmulewitz; 1911) (Company), "Watch Your Step" (same title in Yiddish; sketch by J.M. Rumshinsky and Sam Lowenworth; 1922) (Steve Sterner), "Letter from Europe" (from *The Green Millionaire*; sketch by Abraham Schomer; 1915) (Steve Sterner, Steve Yudson), The Letter: "A Briveke Der Mamen" (sketch by S. Smulewitz; 1921) (Dana Zeller-Alexis), Messiah in America: "Messiah in America" (sketch by Moyshe Nadir; 1919) (Steve Yudson, Steve Sterner, Herbert Rubens, Susan Victor), "Steam, Steam, Steam" (same title in Yiddish; sketch by S. Lowenworth; 1930) (Steve Yudson, Steve Sterner, Herbert Rubens), Homeless: "Homeless" (sketch by Jacob Gordin; 1911) (Susan Victor, Dana Zeller-Alexis), Sabbath and the Holy Days: "Shabos, Yom Tov, Un Rosh Khodesh" (sketch by A. Goldfaden; date unknown) (Susan Victor), "Taking a Pitshke" (from *The Green Millionaire*; sketch by Abraham Schomer; 1915) (Steve Yudson, Steve Sterner), Romantic Medley: "Aza Yingele Vi Du" (lyric and music by J.M. Rumshinsky and I. Lilien; date unknown); "Oy Iz Dos a Meydel" (lyric and music by J.M. Rumshinsky and Molly Picon; date unknown); and "Ay, Gute Vaybele" (author[s] and date unknown) (Susan Victor, Steve Sterner, Steve Yudson, Herbert Rubens), Bronx Express: "Bronx Express" (sketch by Osip Dymov; 1925) (Steve Sterner, Hebert Rubens), "The Line Is Busy" (same title in Yiddish; sketch by J.M. Rumshinsky and L. Gilrod; 1918) (Company)

ACT TWO—Indians and Attorney Street: "Among the Indians" (sketch by H.I. Minikes; 1895) and "Attorney Street" (same title in Yiddish; author[s] and date unknown) (Herbert Rubens, Company), Bread: "Broyt" (sketch by H. Yablokoff; 1935) (Steve Yudson), My Greenhorn Cousin: "Di Grini Kuzine" (sketch by A. Schwartz and Hyman Prizant; 1922) (Dana Zeller-Alexis), "Goodbye" (from *The Green Millionaire*; sketch by Abraham Schomer; 1915) (Steve Yudson, Steve Sterner), She's Missing the Cherry on the Top: "Es Feylt Ir Di Rozhinke" (lyric and music by J.M. Rumshinsky and Molly Picon; date unknown) (Susan Victor, Dana Zeller-Alexis, Herbert Rubens), "Gerrara Here" (from *The Green Millionaire*; sketch by Abraham Schomer; 1915) (Steve Sterner, Steve Yudson), What Can I Do?: "Vos Zol Ikh Tun Az Ikh Hob Im Lib" (lyric and music by J.M. Rumshinsky and Molly Picon; 1925) (Susan Victor), Shop: "Shop" (sketch by H. Leivick; 1926) (Susan Victor, Steve Sterner),

The Plow: "Di Sokhe" (sketch by E. Zunser; date unknown) (Steve Sterner, Company), Riverside Drive: "Riverside Drive" (sketch by L. Kobrin; 1930) (Dana Zeller-Alexis, Herbert Rubens), Raisins and Almonds: "Rozhinkes Mit Mandlen" (sketch by A. Goldfaden; year unknown) (Dana Zeller-Alexis), Columbus, You Done Okay by Me: "Columbus, Ikh Hob Tsu Dir Gornit" (lyric and music by L. Friedsell and D. Meerovitz; date unknown) (Company)

NOTES—The Off Off Broadway revue *Vagabond Stars* offered sketches and songs which had been originally performed during the heyday of New York Yiddish theatre. All the material was performed in English, and was adapted by Nahma Sandrow, Alan Poul, and Raphael Crystal. Richard F. Shepard in the *New York Times* found the revue "great fun" and the performers "first-class." He noted that while the revue's style recalled *Tintypes* (see entry), the evening nonetheless went "its own entirely Jewish way."

1716 Valmouth. THEATRE: York Playhouse; OPENING DATE: October 6, 1960; PERFORMANCES: 14; BOOK: Sandy Wilson; LYRICS: Sandy Wilson; MUSIC: Sandy Wilson; DIRECTION: Vida Hope; CHOREOGRAPHY: Harry Naughton; SCENERY: Tony Walton; COSTUMES: Tony Walton; MUSICAL DIRECTION: Julian Stein; PRODUCERS: Gene Andrewski; produced with Barbara Griner and Morton Segal

CAST—Anne Francine (Mrs. Hurstpierpoint), Phillipa Bevans (Mrs. Thoroughfare), Eugene Roche (Father Colley-Mahoney), Alfred Toigo (Capt. Dick Thoroughfare), Gene Rupert (Lt. Jack Whorwood), Thom Koutsoukos (Ffines), Bill Mitchell (Nit), Mona Abboud (Fowler), Elly Stone (Sister Ecclesia), Beatrice Pons (Grannie Tooke), Nan Courtney (Thetis Tooke), Franklin Kiser (David Tooke), Beatrice Reading (Mrs. Yajnavalkya), Gail Jones (Niri-Esther), Rhoda Levine (Carry), Constance Carpenter (Lady Parvula de Panzoust), William Beck (Sir Victor Vatt), Janice O'Dell (Lady Saunter), Maureen Fritz (Madame Mimosa), Ralston Hill (Cardinal Pirelli), Vince Tampio (Doctor Dee)

SOURCE—The 1919 novel *Valmouth* by Ronald Firbank.

The musical was presented in two acts.

ACT ONE—"Valmouth" (Company), "Magic Fingers" (Beatrice Reading), "Mustapha" (Beatrice Reading), "I Loved a Man" (Nan Courtney), "All the Girls Were Pretty" (Anne Francine, Constance Carpenter, Phillipa Bevans), "What Do I Want with Love" (Franklin Kiser), "Just Once More" (Constance Carpenter, Beatrice Reading), "Lady of the Manor" (Gail Jones), "Big Best Shoes" (Beatrice Reading, Company), "Niri-Esther" (Alfred Toigo, Gene Rupert), "Cry of the Peacock" (Beatrice Reading, Gail Jones, Company)

ACT TWO—"Little Girl Baby" (Beatrice Reading, William Beck, Gail Jones), "The Cathedral of Clemenza" (Ralston Hill), "Only a Passing Phase" (Constance Carpenter), "Valmouth" (reprise) (Alfred Toigo), "Where the Trees Are Filled with Parrots" (Gail Jones), "My Talking Day" (Elly Stone), "I Will Miss You" (Beatrice Reading, Beatrice Pons), "Pinpipi's Sob of Love" (Anne Francine), "Where the Trees Are Filled with Parrots" (reprise) (Gail Jones), "Valmouth" (reprise) (William Beck)

NOTES—*Valmouth* opened in London on October 2, 1958, at the Lyric Opera House, Hammersmith, and on January 7, 1959, transferred to the Saville Theatre, for a total of 186 performances. It was a highly regarded piece, but, like another British musical, *The Crystal Heart* (1960; see entry), it was perhaps too brittle and special for mass popularity. Nonetheless, its reputation has lasted through the decades, and when the best of theatre music is discussed, *Valmouth* has an important place in that discussion.

Indeed, in 1960 Off Broadway offered *The Crystal Heart*, *Valmouth*, and *Kittiwake Island* (the latter opened a week after *Valmouth*; see entry) to adventurous Off Broadway theatergoers, affording them the opportunity of hearing some of the most exquisite theatre music ever written. But they had to be quick. In total, the three musicals ran for thirty performances.

The Burns Mantle Yearbook/The Best Plays of 1960-1961 noted that *Valmouth* was the most expensive Off Broadway musical yet. It cost $40,000 to mount (compared to $10,000 for *The Threepenny Opera*, $15,000 for *Little Mary Sunshine*, and $16,500 for *The Fantasticks*).

The plot of *Valmouth* (concerning the inhabitants of an English spa) was almost incidental to its musical charms, the most talked about song being "Big Best Shoes," introduced by Beatrice Reading (Cleo Laine succeeded her in the role when the production transferred to the Saville). The entire score was outstanding, with perhaps "Just Once More," "My Talking Day," "I Love a Man," "Where the Trees Are Green with Parrots," "Only a Passing Phase," and "All the Girls Were Pretty" deserving special mention.

The Off Broadway production offered Beatrice Reading reprising her original role of Mrs. Yajnavalkya, and Vida Hope (director), Harry Naughton (choreography), and Tony Walton (scenery and costumes) also repeated their London assignments.

Howard Taubman in the *New York Times* was disappointed with the book, but noted if you could "survive" the plot and dialogue, you would find much pleasure in the score, choreography, and décor. He noted that Wilson offered "graceful and insinuating" lyrics and "pleasant and lively" music; that Harry Naughton's choreography captured "a comic spirit in movement"; and that Tony Walton's costumes were "a delightful expression of an amused affection for the past."

There was one major change in the musical numbers between London and New York. Late in the second act, the London production included "Wedding Anthem" (for Mrs. Yajnavalkya and Grannie Tooke); this number wasn't used in New York, but a late second act number was added for Mrs. Hurstpierpoint ("Pinpipi's Sob of Love"). Also, in London, Lady Parvula's "Just Once More" was titled "Request Number."

It should be noted that Lady Parvula de Panzoust was performed by Constance Carpenter, who, with William Gaxton, introduced "My Heart Stood Still" and "Thou Swell" in the original Broadway production of Richard Rodgers and Lorenz Hart's *A Connecticut Yankee* (1927). Gail Jones, who played Niri-Esther, was the daughter of Lena Horne.

During *Valmouth*'s brief run, two of Sandy Wilson's musicals were playing Off Broadway (*The Boy Friend* was approaching the end of its two-year run; see entry). It appears there were a few cast changes before *Valmouth*'s opening; Eugene Roche replaced John Fostini, Thom Koutsoukos replaced Alfred White, and Franklin Kiser replaced Gregory White.

There are two *Valmouth* recordings (the Saville cast, with Cleo Laine as Mrs. Yajnavalkya, and a 1982 revival recording, with Beatrice Reading recreating her original role of Mrs. Yajnavalkya). The Saville cast recording was released by Pye Records (LP # NPL-18029 and # NSPL-18029; later issued on LP by PRT Records [# FBLP-8102]), and the revival was released by That's Entertainment Records (LP # TER-1019; later issued on CD by Jay Records [# CDJAY-1345]). It's interesting that the era saw another "spa" musical; Johnny Mercer and Harold Arlen's *Saratoga* opened on Broadway at the Winter Garden Theatre on December 7, 1959, for a disappointing run of eighty performances; thankfully, its memorable (if overlooked) score was preserved on the RCA Victor Records cast recording. The most successful "spa" musical of them all is Maury Yeston's *Nine* (1982).

1717 Vamps and Rideouts. THEATRE: Hudson Guild Theatre; OPENING DATE: February 2, 1982; PERFORMANCES: 12; BOOK MATERIAL: Betty Comden and Adolph Green, Arthur Laurents, Isobel Lennart, and Anita Loos; material adapted by Phyllis Newman and James Pentecost; LYRICS: See song list for credits; MUSIC: Jule Styne; DIRECTION: James Pentecost; CHOREOGRAPHY: Dennis Dennehy; SCENERY: Lawrence Miller; COSTUMES: "Co-ordinated by" Cynthia O'Neal; LIGHTING: David H. Murdock; MUSICAL DIRECTION: Eric Stern Producer: Hudson Guild Theatre (David Kerry Heefner, Producing Director)

CAST—Phyllis Newman, George Lee Andrews, Pauletta Pearson

The revue was presented in two acts (song assignments not listed in the program).

ACT ONE—Opening, *Bells Are Ringing* (book and lyrics by Betty Comden and Adolph Green, 1956): "It's a Perfect Relationship" "I Met a Girl," "People" (*Funny Girl*, 1964; lyric by Bob Merrill), Marriage Medley (songs not identified in program), "Long Before I Knew You" (*Bells Are Ringing*, 1956; lyric by Betty Comden and Adolph Green), "The Party's Over" (*Bells Are Ringing*, 1956; lyric by Betty Comden and Adolph Green), "Let's See What Happens" (*Darling of the Day*, 1968; lyric by E.Y. Harburg), "Ambition" (*Do Re Mi*, 1960; lyric by Betty Comden and Adolph Green), *Funny Girl* (book by Isobel Lennart, 1964), "I'm the Greatest Star" (lyric by Bob Merrill), *Peter Pan* (book by Betty Comden and Adolph Green, 1954), "Never Never Land" (lyric by Betty Comden and Adolph Green), "Make Someone Happy" (*Do Re Mi*, 1960; lyric by Betty Comden and Adolph Green)

ACT TWO—"Just in Time" (*Bells Are Ringing*, 1956; lyric by Betty Comden and Adolph Green), Beauty Contest Sequence: "I'm Just a Little Girl from Little Rock" (*Gentlemen Prefer Blondes*, 1949; lyric by Leo Robin), *Gentlemen Prefer Blondes* (script based upon the 1926 play of the same name by Anita Loos and John Emerson), "I Was a Shoo-In" (*Subways Are for Sleeping*, 1961; lyric by Betty Comden and Adolph Green), "My Fortune Is My Face" (*Fade Out-Fade In*, 1964; lyric by Betty Comden and Adolph Green), "Guess I'll Hang My Tears Out to Dry" (*Glad To See You*, which closed during its pre-Broadway tryout in 1944; lyric by Sammy Cahn), "Hey Look No Crying" (lyric by Susan Birkenhead; appears to be a song written independent of any production), *Mothers and Daughters*: *Hallelujah, Baby!* (book by Arthur Laurents, 1967), "My Own Morning" (lyric by Betty Comden and Adolph Green), *Gypsy* (book by Arthur Laurents, 1959), "Some People" (lyric by Stephen Sondheim), "Let Me Entertain You" (lyric by Stephen Sondheim), "All I Need Is the Girl" (*Gypsy*, 1959; lyric by Stephen Sondheim), The Women's Medley (songs not identified in the program; see notes below), "The Music That Makes Me Dance" (*Funny Girl*, 1964; lyric by Bob Merrill), "Together" (*Gypsy*, 1959; lyric by Stephen Sondheim)

NOTES—The Off Off Broadway revue *Vamps and Rideouts* was the second tribute to Jule Styne in the early 1980s; see entry for *Styne After Styne*.

The revue seems to have incorporated dialogue sequences from and anecdotes about some of Styne's musicals.

The cast of the revue included Phyllis Newman (Mrs. Adolph Green), who had appeared in the original 1961 Broadway production of Styne's *Subways Are for Sleeping*. One of the revue's sequences ("The Women's Medley") might have been a revised version of a similar sequence which appeared in Newman's 1978 revue *My Mother Was a Fortune-Teller* (see entry for more information).

1718 Vanessa. THEATRE: Metropolitan Opera House; OPENING DATE: January 15, 1958; PERFOR-

MANCES: Unknown; LIBRETTO: Gian-Carlo Menotti; MUSIC: Samuel Barber; DIRECTION: Gian-Carlo Menotti; CHOREOGRAPHY: Zachary Solov; SCENERY: Cecil Beaton; COSTUMES: Cecil Beaton; MUSICAL DIRECTION: Dimitri Mitropoulos; PRODUCER: The Metropolitan Opera; from a note in the program: "The production of *Vanessa* was made possible by a generous and deeply appreciated gift of the Francis Goelet Foundation."

CAST—Eleanor Steber (Vanessa), Rosalind Elias (Erika), Regina Resnik (The Old Baroness), Nicolai Gedda (Anatol), Giorgio Tozzi (The Old Doctor), George Cehanovsky (Nicholas), Robert Nagy (Footman)

The action occurs at Vanessa's country house in a Northern country, around 1905.

The opera was presented in four acts.

NOTES—For one of its rare world premieres, the Metropolitan ensured that the new opera *Vanessa* enjoyed a pedigree few such operas could hope for: Barber, Menotti, Mitropoulous, Beaton, Steber, Elias, Resnik, Tozzi, and Nagy provided contributions to ensure that the first performances of *Vanessa* would be memorable. And, indeed, *Vanessa* is a powerful work, one which has rightly found its place in the repertory of modern opera. The haunting Chekhovian-like story was set in a wintry "Northern" country. Vanessa, who has lived in her mansion as a recluse for twenty years, has kept all its mirrors shrouded as she awaits the return of her lover Anatol, who long ago deserted her. He returns, as a handsome young man, and while his name is Anatol, he reveals he's the son of her lover, who has since died. Anatol seduces Vanessa's niece, Erika, who miscarries his child and who rejects him because of his superficiality. Unaware of Anatol's relationship with Erika, Vanessa marries him, and they leave the mansion forever, to begin their new life together. As the opera ends, Erika prepares to live out her years as a recluse in the mansion, and she orders shrouds to be placed on all the mirrors.

The opera includes a few arias which have enjoyed a certain amount of popularity in concerts and on recordings ("He Has Come," "Must the Winter Come So Soon?," and "Under the Willow Tree"). Perhaps the most memorable sequence in the opera (indeed, one of the most powerful sequences in modern musical theatre) is the haunting "Quintet" ("To Leave, to Break"). The opera is also noteworthy for Gian-Carlo Menotti's participation, not only as director but as librettist. Normally, Menotti both wrote both the libretti and the music for his operas, and so *Vanessa* was an interesting departure for him. His libretto was remarkably tight and vivid, one of his strongest and most intense.

Howard Taubman in the *New York Times* said *Vanessa* was the "best" American opera ever seen on the Met's stage, and he praised the "impressive achievement" of Barber's score, including "a waltz, a country-dance, a hymn, a genial aria or two." As for the "grand" quintet, Taubman said it "packs an emotional charge ... that would be a credit to any composer anywhere today." Taubman also found Menotti's libretto "concise" in its evocation of a "lost, other-worldly mood." Taubman reported that Sena Jurinac was to have created the role of Vanessa for the world premiere, but because of an illness she was replaced by Eleanor Steber.

The production was recorded by RCA Victor on a 2-LP set (# ARL2-2094), and was later released on a 2-CD set by RCA Victor/BMG Classics Records (# 7899-2-RG). On February 1, 1958, the original production was broadcast live on radio. A 1978 production of the opera at the Spoleto Festival USA was shown on January 31, 1979, as part of the *Great Performances* series on public television.

Barber was commissioned by the Metropolitan to compose a new opera for the 1966 opening of their new theatre at Lincoln Center; unfortunately, *Antony and Cleopatra* (see entry) didn't match the success of his earlier Metropolitan premiere.

1719 Variety Obit. THEATRE: Cherry Lane Theatre; OPENING DATE: February 12, 1973; PERFORMANCES: 24; DIRECTION: Tom Moore Scenery: Peter Harvey; COSTUMES: Bruce Harrow; LIGHTING: Roger Morgan; PRODUCERS: Ruth Kalkstein, Patricia Gray, and Sidney Annis

NOTES—The evening consisted of two offerings by Ron Whyte; the first, *Welcome to Andromeda*, was a non-musical presented in two acts; the latter, *Variety Obit*, was a musical in one act. The above credits pertain to both productions. Clive Barnes in the *New York Times* reported that *Variety Obit* dealt with the death of the last surviving member of America's oldest show-business family. He found the music "tuneful" and "pleasant" if not "exactly memorable," and said the story had a "nostalgic lilt" to it which was "sweet but half-baked."

The cast was as follows: Andrea Marcovicci and Richard Cox (Singers), David Clennon (Narrator), Mel Marvin and Gary Mure (Musicians). The music was by Mel Marvin, and the lyrics by Ron Whyte.

MUSICAL NUMBERS—"This New World," "Central Park, 1917," "The Wolves of Kultur on a Bright and Silent Saturday," "Ellesburg, Ohio," "Song for Sunday," "Carnival," "This New World" (reprise)

The scripts of both *Welcome to Andromeda* and *Variety Obit* were published together in one volume by Samuel French, Inc., in 1973.

1720 The Vi-Ton-Ka Medicine Show. THEATRE: The American Place Theatre; OPENING DATE: October 4, 1983; PERFORMANCES: 14; PROJECT DIRECTOR: Glenn Hinson; C. Lee Jenner, Associate Project Director; Brooks McNamara, Staging Consultant; SCENERY: Marco A. Martinez-Galarce; C. Lee Jenner, Design Consultant; LIGHTING: Marco A. Martinez-Galarce; PRODUCER: The American Place Theatre (Wynn Handman, Director; Julia Miles, Associate Director)

CAST—Fred F. Bloodgood, James "Goober" Buchanan, Col. Buster Doss, Susan Gibney, Ernest W. Hayes, Dewitt "Snuffy" Jenkins, Tommy Kizziah, Harold Lucas, Randy Lucas, Dale Madden, Sr., Dale "Boots" Madden, Mary Smith McClain, Connie Mills, Homer "Pappy" Sherrill, Leroy Watts

The revue was presented in one act.

MUSICAL AND MEDICINE SHOW SEQUENCES—Overture (Dale Madden, Dale "Boots" Madden), Medicine Show Introduction (Col. Buster Doss), "The Hired Hands" (Dewitt "Snuffy" Jenkins, Harold Lucas, Randy Lucas, Homer "Pappy" Sherrill), "The Betting Bit" (Connie Mills, Leroy Watts), "Dixie Breakdown"/"Pig in a Pen"/"Alabama Jubilee" (The Hired Hands [Dewitt "Snuffy" Jenkins, Harold Lucas, Randy Lucas, Homer "Pappy" Sherrill]), "Ventriloquism"/"Ace in the Hole" (Col Buster Doss), "Alabama Jubilee" (reprise) (played on the fly spray) (James "Goober" Buchanan, Col. Buster Doss), "The Circus Organlog" (Dale Madden, Sr.), "The Vi-Ton-Ka Lecture" (Fred F. Bloodgood), "The King Bee" (James "Goober" Buchanan, Col. Buster Doss, Leroy Watts), "Old Blind Fiddler"/"Please Don't Talk About Me"/"I Love You Because" (Tommy Kizziah, Homer "Pappy" Sherrill), "Chair Dance" (Leroy Watts), "Candy Pitch" (Fred F, Bloodgood), "Dance Contest" (Dewitt "Snuffy" Jenkins, Harold Lucas, Randy Lucas, Homer "Pappy" Sherrill), "Don't the Moon Look Lonesome"/"St. Louis Blues" (Mary Smith McClain), "Wichita Kid Bullwhips" and "Sharpshooting" (Dale "Boots" Madden, Susan Gibney), "When the Saints Go Marching In" (Mary Smith McClain), "When the Saints Go Marching In" (reprise) (Company)

NOTES—According to *The Burns Mantle Yearbook/The Best Plays of 1983-1984*, the revue *The Vi-Ton-Ka Medicine Show* was an "authentic recreation of a medicine show ... including the simulated hawking of an all-purpose curative tonic." Although Mel Gussow in the *New York Times* noted the work was "apparently sincere" and "historical," he nonetheless found it "marginal entertainment" and concluded that the evening needed a dose of snake oil.

1721 Victoria. "A New Musical." THEATRE: The Theatre at Mama Gail's; OPENING DATE: September 20, 1975; PERFORMANCES: Unknown; BOOK: Christian Hamilton; LYRICS: Christian Hamilton; MUSIC: Marcia Hamilton; DIRECTION: Bruce Graham; CHOREOGRAPHY: B.J. Hanford; SCENERY: Terry Leong; COSTUMES: Terry Leong; LIGHTING: Winnie Sensiba; MUSICAL DIRECTION: Matthew Yasner; PRODUCER: Bruce Graham

CAST—Emma Cappello (Ballerina), David Clark (Canterbury), Bill Collins (Conygham), Dorie Donvito (Maid), W.P. Dremak (Running), Barry Hahn (York), Parks Hill (Bertie), Rachel Jeffreys (Victoria), Peter Johl (Melbourne), Linda Lauter (Miss Prim), Lynn Martin (Florence Nightengale), Michael A. Maurice (Albert), Barbara S. McCarthy (P.R. Lady), Lois Sanders (Duchess), Richard Stack (Ernest), Jim Swanson (Prinny), Karen Worronkoff (Miss Smiley)

The musical was presented in two acts.

ACT ONE—"Victoria's Christening" (David Clark, Company), "My Chick, My Chuck" (Lois Sanders), "Kings and Queens (Coronation Cakewalk)" (Rachel Jeffreys, Company), "A Hazardous Experiment" (Michael A. Maurice), "I Had to Laugh" (Peter Johl), "Pardon My Glow" (Rachel Jeffreys), "A Meeting of the Minds" (Michael A. Maurice), "The Grand Old Duke of York" (Lois Sanders, Company), "A Grand Diversion" (Company), "Ill-Natured Girls" (Richard Stack, Men), "A Near Thing" (Rachel Jeffreys), "The Wedding" (Company)

ACT TWO—"The Wedding Concluded" (Company), "After the Interval" (Richard Stack, Peter Johl, David Clark), "A Game of Whist" (Company), "Mine!" (Rachel Jeffreys), "Parabasis" (Company), "Yours, Use Me" (Michael A. Maurice), "Never Again" (Rachel Jeffreys, Lois Sanders, Company), "A Quiet Heart" (Michael A. Maurice), "Photographs" (Company), "Get Out of It" (Company), Finale: "Doin' the Windsor Walk" (Company)

NOTES—Despite such felicitous song titles as "Coronation Cakewalk" and "Doin' the Windsor Walk," *Victoria*, a musical about Queen Victoria and Prince Albert, went nowhere (even though its program indicated it was "Broadway-bound"), which is exactly where all musicals about the royal couple seem to go. Richard Maltby, Jr., and David Shire's *Love Match* floundered on the road in 1968, and *I and Albert* was a major flop in London in 1972 (and was, incidentally, the only musical Charles Strouse and Lee Adams wrote expressly for the London stage).

Mel Gussow in the *New York Times* found *Victoria* "diverting," and said the "compact entertainment" was more in the nature of a "chamber operetta" than a traditional Broadway musical. He noted that the score was "exuberant and unabashedly old-fashioned."

Victoria seems to have been presented in an elaborate workshop production at the Theatre and Restaurant at Mama Gail's. Gussow mentioned the restaurant-theatre (which was located at 22 Wooster Street [near Canal Street and in the southernmost part of SoHo]) was "attractive," "pleasant and comfortable," and "a most suitable environment."

1722 Vienna: Lusthaus. THEATRE: Newman Theatre/The Public Theatre; OPENING DATE: June 15, 1986; PERFORMANCES: 49; TEXT: Charles Mee, Jr; conceived by Martha Clarke and "created with" the Company; MUSIC: Richard Peaslee; "with the aid of" Johann Sebastian Bach, Eugene Friesen, and Johann Strauss; DIRECTION: Martha Clarke; CHOREOGRAPHY: Martha Clarke; SCENERY: Robert Israel; COSTUMES: Robert Israel; costume execution by Sandra Woodall; LIGHTING: Paul Gallo; PRODUCERS: The New York Shakespeare Festival (Joseph Papp, Producer; Jason Steven Cohen, Associate Producer) and the Music-Theatre Group/Lenox Arts Center (Lyn Austin, Producing Director, with Robert De Rothschild; Associate Producing Directors, Diane Wondisford and Mark Jones)

CAST—Rob Besserer, Brenda Currin, Timothy Doyle, Marie Fourcaut, Lotte Goslar, Robert Langdon-Lloyd, Rick Merrill, Gianfranco Paoluzi, Amy Spencer, Paola Styron, Lila York

The action occurs in Vienna around 1900 at the Lusthaus (Pleasure Pavilion). The music-dance-theatre piece was presented in one act.

NOTES—*Vienna: Lusthaus*, Martha Clarke's seemingly free-form music-dance-theatre piece, might appear to be unstructured and improvisational. But it (and all of Clarke's work) was tightly organized: it was first conceived by Clarke and then developed into a text written by Charles Mee, Jr., with music composed by Richard Peaslee (and others); moreover, the work was also a collaboration between the writers and the performers. Even the costumes affected the staging; in an interview with Jan Carr for a Kennedy Center *Stagebill* article, Clarke noted that costumes influenced how she created the movement and form of the choreography because how the performers wore their costumes provided insight into the characters they portrayed. The final result was a dream-like series of abstract vignettes depicting erotic interludes in Old Vienna, all of which appear to occur spontaneously and without outward logic. A program note indicated the Lusthaus was built prior to 1556, and that the octagonal building is located at the far end of the Prader.

Before transferring to the Public Theatre, the work had been seen Off Off Broadway on April 8, 1986, when it opened at Saint Clement's Theatre for a run of thirty-four performances. As *Vienna: Lusthaus (revisited)*, it was later revived at the New York Theatre Workshop on May 8, 2002, for 111 performances.

For a list of theatre works by Martha Clarke which are discussed in this book, see entry for *The Garden of Earthly Delights*.

1723 A View from the Bridge.

THEATRE: Metropolitan Opera House. OPENING DATE: December 5, 2002; PERFORMANCES: 7; LIBRETTO: Arnold Weinstein and Arthur Miller; MUSIC: William Bolcom; DIRECTION: Frank Galati; SCENERY: Santo Loquasto; COSTUMES: Santo Loquasto; LIGHTING: Duane Schuler; MUSICAL DIRECTION: Dennis Russell Davies; PRODUCER: The Metropolitan Opera Cast—Michael Devlin (Alfieri), Dale Travis (Louis), Tony Stevenson (Mike), Kim Josephson (Eddie), Isbabel Bayrakdarian (Catherine), Catherine Malfitano (Beatrice), Lynn Taylor (Woman), Glenn Bater (Man), Charlie Reid (Tony), Gregory Turay (Rodolpho), Richard Bernstein (Marco), Carole Wright (Old Woman), Patrick Carfizzi (First Officer), Anthony Laciura (Second Officer)

SOURCE—The 1955 play *A View from the Bridge* by Arthur Miller.

The action takes place in the Red Hook neighborhood of Brooklyn in the 1950s.

The opera was presented in two acts.

ACT ONE—Orchestral Introduction (Orchestra), "Red Hook" (Chorus, John Del Carlo, Glenn Bater), "Hey, Eddie!" (Dale Travis, Chorus, Tony Stevenson, Kim Josephson, Isabel Bayrakdarian), "Where You Goin' All Dressed Up?" (Kim Josephson, Isabel Bayrakdarian), "Beatrice! Hurry Up!" (Isabel Bayrakdarian, Kim Josephson, Catherine Malfitano), "Get Used to It, Eddie" (Catherine Malfitano, Kim Josephson, Isabel Bayrakdarian), "But When You're Gone" (Jim Josephson, Catherine Malfitano), "Now, Listen, Both a Yiz" (Kim Josephson), "Remember Vinnie Bolzano" (Chorus, Kim Josephson, Dale Travis, Tony Stevenson, Lynn Taylor, Charles Reid), "Eddie Was a Man" (John Del Carlo, Chorus), "You're on Your Own Now" (Charles Reid, Gregory Turay, Richard Bernstein), "Marco! Rodolpho!" (Catherine Malfitano, Richard Bernstein, Kim Josephson, Isabel Bayrakdarian, Gregory Turay), "Then When I Am Rich" (Gregory Turay, Richard Bernstein), "Rodolpho, Are You Married, Too?" (Isabel Bayrakdarian, Gregory Turay, Kim Josephson, Richard Bernstein), "I Sing Jazz, Too" (Gregory Turay, Isabel Bayrakdarian, Kim Josephson), "Eduardo, If You Let Us Sleep Here" (Richard Bernstein, Catherine Malfitano, Kim Josephson, Gregory Turay, Isabel Bayrakdarian), "Now There Was a Future He Must Face" (John Del Carlo), "It's After Eight O'Clock" (Kim Josephson, Catherine Malfitano), "Eddie, When Am I Gonna Be a Wife Again?" (Catherine Malfitano, Kim Josephson), "Eddie Never Knew He Had a Destiny" (Chorus), "Hey Eddie! Wanna Go Bowling Tonight?" (Tony Stevenson, Dale Travis, Kim Josephson), "Where'd You Go?" (Kim Josephson, Isabel Bayrakdarian, Gregory Turay), "I Love the Beauty of the View at Home" (a/k/a "New York Lights") Aria) (Gregory Turay), "Rodolpho, I Thought I Told You to Go In" (Kim Josephson, Gregory Turay, Isabel Bayrakdarian), "He's a Hit-and-Run Guy!" (Arietta) (Kim Josephson, Isabel Bayrakdarian, Catherine Malfitano), "Was There Ever Any Fella That He Liked for You?" (Aria) (Catherine Malfitano), "There's Nothing Illegal About It" (John Del Carlo, Kim Josephson, Chorus, Carole Wright), "You Know Where the Two of Them Went?" (Isabel Bayrakdarian, Kim Josephson, Catherine Malfitano, Richard Bernstein, Gregory Turay), "Whadddya Say, Marco?" (Kim Josephson, Gregory Turay, Richard Bernstein, Chorus, Catherine Malfitano, Isabel Bayrakdarian), "Eddie, You're Pretty Strong" (Richard Bernstein, Kim Josephson, Chorus)

ACT TWO—Orchestral Introduction (Orchestra), "Hey Guys! It's Whisky!" (Chorus, Charles Reid, Tony Stevenson, Kim Josephson, Dale Travis), "Rodolpho! Didn't They Hire You?" (Isabel Bayrakdarian, Gregory Turay), "It's True" (Gregory Turay, Isabel Bayrakdarian), "But You Do Not Know This Man" (Aria) (Isabel Bayrakdarian, Gregory Turay), "Somehow, Somehow" (Kim Josephson, Isabel Bayrakdarian, Gregory Turay, Chorus), "On December Twenty-Seventh I Saw Him Next" (Aria) (John Del Carlo), "He Won't Leave!" (Kim Josephson, John Del Carlo, Chorus, Dale Travis, Tony Stevenson), "Where Are They?" (Kim Josephson, Catherine Malfitano), "Eddie Has Something to Say, Katie" (Catherine Malfitano, Isabel Bayrakdarian, Kim Josephson), "Bea, Could I Take Two Pillows Up?" (Isabel Bayrakdarian, Kim Josephson, Catherine Malfitano, Patrick Carfizzi, Anthony Laciura), "That Man! I Accuse That Man!" (Richard Bernstein, Chorus, Kim Josephson, Patrick Carfizzi, Anthony Laciura), "To America I Sailed on a Ship Called Hunger" (Aria) (Gregory Turay), Orchestral Interlude (Orchestra), "For the Sake of My Sister" (Catherine Malfitano, Kim Josephson, Isabel Bayrakdarian), "Marco's Coming, Eddie" (Gregory Turay, Catherine Malfitano, Kim Josephson, Isabel Bayrakdarian, Chorus), "Come, Catherine" (Gregory Turay, Kim Josephson, Catherine Malfitano, Chorus), "Eddie, Listen to Me!" (Catherine Malfitano, Isabel Bayrakdarian, Kim Josephson, Richard Bernstein, Chorus, Gregory Turay), "Eddie Carbone!" (Richard Bernstein, Kim Josephson, Chorus, Gregory Turay, Catherine Malfitano, Dale Travis, Isabel Bayrakdarian), "Eyes Like Tunnels" (Chorus, John Del Carlo), "When the Tide Is Right" (Chorus, John Del Carlo)

NOTES—William Bolcom's opera *A View from the Bridge* was first performed in 1999 by the Lyric Opera of Chicago, and the Met's production represented the work's first New York performances.

The opera was well received; based on Arthur Miller's powerful play (which is arguably his masterwork), the taut libretto and rich score combined to make *A View from the Bridge* a memorable opera. Writing in the *New Yorker*, Alex Ross noted the score "works a Brittenesque psychological sprectrum" which reveals Eddie's obsession with his niece; at the same time, Bolcom offered a "rich anthology of dance tunes and ballads." *Variety*'s critic Chris Jones said the opera "crackles with power," and in *New York* Peter G. Davis noted the score was "apt and theatrically saavy, with a delicious feel for the underlying pop idioms" of the 1950s.

One aria in particular was singled out, Rodolpho's "I Love the Beauty of the View at Home" (a/k/a "New York Lights") in which he compared his hometown in Italy with New York City. Other powerful moments included Beatrice's "Eddie, When Am I Gonna Be a Wife Again?" and Rodolpho's "To America I Sailed on a Ship Called Hunger." Further, the introductory music for the second act was particularly striking. But one slightly disappointing aspect of the score was the interpolation of the pop ballad "Paper Doll" (by Johnny S. Black). Bolcom is a master of pastiche and popular music styles, and it would have been interesting had he composed his own version of a popular Fifties tune.

In 2007, the opera was presented by the Washington National Opera in a production which included three of the original cast members (Kim Josephson, Gregory Turay, and Catherine Malfitano). Reviewing the work for the *Washington Post*, Tim Page noted that Malfitano was "one of the great singing actresses of our time." As for the opera itself, Page called it a "remarkable accomplishment," and said Bolcom's score was one "of considerable invention and power" which "complements and enhances the action with rare acuity." The opera was recorded on a 2-CD set by New World Records (# 80588-2); the titles of the song sequences are taken from this recording. The libretto was published by Edward B. Marks Music Company and Bolcom Music in 1999.

For other lyric adaptations of Miller's plays, see entries for *The Crucible* and *Up from Paradise* (the entry for *The Crucible* includes information on an earlier operatic adaptation of *A View from the Bridge*).

1724 A View from Under the Bridge.

THEATRE: Square East; OPENING DATE: August 5, 1964; PERFORMANCES: 94; SCENES AND DIALOGUE: Created by the Company; LYRICS: Alan Arkin, David Arkin, Roger Bowen, Leigh Hunt, David Shepherd, and Paul Sills; MUSIC: William Mathieu and David Arkin; DIRECTION: Sheldon Patinkin; SCENERY: Ralph Alswang; stage photograph slides by Alan Arkin; LIGHTING: Dan Butt; MUSICAL DIRECTION: Probably by William Mathieu; PRODUCER: Norman Atkins

CAST—Alan Arkin, Barbara Dana, Severn Darden

The revue was presented in two acts.

NOTES—This was the seventh Second City revue to play Off Broadway, and Richard F. Shepard in the *New York Times* noted the company "still has the ludicrously offbeat touch" and "is still first rate in its class." Shepard singled out a number of sequences, including one on modern art, another on politics ("President Goldwater" announces that Canada isn't the threat it appears it be), and an "hilarious" spoof of Arthur Miller's *After the Fall* (which had opened earlier in the year).

For a complete list of the Second City revues which were presented in New York, see entry for *Seacoast of Bohemia*; also see Appendix T.

1725 Vinyl. THEATRE: Caffe Cino; OPENING DATE: October 31, 1967; PERFORMANCES: 16 (estimated); BOOK: Ronald Tavel; LYRICS: Ronald Tavel; MUSIC: John Harrill; DIRECTION: Harvey Tavel; CHOREOGRAPHY: Ronn Pratt; PRODUCER: Caffe Cino

CAST—Raymond Edwards, John Harrill, Sterling Houston, Norman Thomas Marshall, Mike St. Shaw, Mary Woronov

SOURCE—The 1965 film *Vinyl* (screenplay by Ronald Tavel; directed by Andy Warhol)

NOTES—For about ten years, the Caffe Cino was one of the centers of the Off Off Broadway theatre movement, and it flourished under the directorship of its founder, Joe Cino (1931-1967). But upon his death, the venue closed and Ron Tavel's *Vinyl* was one of the last productions to play there. Dan Sullivan in the *New York Times* reported that *Vinyl* was apparently an "indictment" of sado-masochism, and he noted the evening certainly gave enough "graphic" examples of the world of S & M, particularly one "hairy-chested" hood who likes to carve up his partners. Sullivan hilariously noted that throughout the evening "whips slash, chains lash, high-heeled boots stomp"; further, ribs were cracked, fingernails were yanked out, and eyeballs were squished. With his tongue planted firmly in his cheek, Sullivan surmised that the evening was really a "metaphor" about rebellious youth brought down by the system, but then added that perhaps "metaphor" was not exactly the "name" of *Vinyl*'s "game." Sullivan mentioned that the director (Harvey Tavel, the author's brother) and the choreographer (Ron Pratt) saw to it that the evening moved along with the "vividness of a highly specialized nightmare."

The best-known work to emerge from the Caffe Cino was *Dames at Sea* (see entry); prior to its Off Broadway production in December 1968, an abbreviated version of the musical had been seen there (as *Dames at Sea*, or *Golddiggers Afloat*).

1726 Violet. "A New Musical." THEATRE: Playwrights Horizons; OPENING DATE: March 11, 1997; PERFORMANCES: 32; BOOK: Brian Crawley; LYRICS: Brian Crawley; MUSIC: Jeanine Tesori; DIRECTION: Susan H. Schulman; CHOREOGRAPHY: Kathleen Marshall; SCENERY: Derek McLane; COSTUMES: Catherine Zuber; LIGHTING: Peter Kaczorowski; MUSICAL DIRECTION: Michael Rafter; PRODUCERS: Playwrights Horizons (Tim Sanford, Artistic Director; Leslie Marcus, Managing Director; Lynn Landis, General Manager) in association with AT&T OnStage; Ira Weitzman

CAST—Amanda Posner (Young Vi), Michael Medeiros (Leroy Evans, Waiter. Mechanic, Lead Radio Singer, Bus Driver 3, Earl), Lauren Ward (Violet), Stephen Lee Anderson (Father), Robert Westenberg (Bus Driver, Preacher, Rufus, Radio Singer, Bus Driver 4), Cass Morgan (Old Lady, Hotel Singer, Old Lady 2), Kirk McDonald (Creepy Guy, Bus Driver 2, Radio Singer, Billy Dean, Virgil), Paula Newsome (Woman with Fan, Music Hall Singer, Mabel), Roz Ryan (Woman Knitting, Landlady, Hotel Singer 2, Gospel Soloist), Michael McElroy (Flick), Michael Park (Monty) SOURCE—The short story "The Ugliest Pilgrim" by Doris Betts.

The action occurs in early September 1964 in North Carolina, Tennessee, Arkansas, and Oklahoma.

The musical was presented in two acts.

ACT ONE—Opening ("Water in the Well"/"Surprised") (Amanda Posner, Lauren Ward), "On My Way" (Lauren Ward, Company), "Luck of the Draw" (Stephen Lee Anderson, Amanda Posner, Lauren Ward, Michael Park, Michael McElroy), "Question and Answer" (Michael Park, Lauren Ward), "All to Pieces" (Lauren Ward, Michael Park, Michael McElroy), "Let It Sing" (Michael McElroy), "Who'll Be the One (If Not Me)" (Michael Medeiros, Kirk McDonald, Robert Westenberg), "You're Different" (Michael Park), "Lonely Stranger"/"Anyone Would Do" (Paula Newsome, Cass Morgan, Roz Ryan), "Lay Down Your Head" (Lauren Ward)

ACT TWO—"Lonely Stranger" (reprise) (Michael Medeiros), "Hard to Say Goodbye" (Lauren Ward, Michael McElroy), "Promise Me, Violet" (Lauren Ward, Michael Park, Michael McElroy), "Raise Me Up" (Roz Ryan, Robert Westenberg, Roz Ryan, Choir), "Down the Mountain" (Amanda Posner, Stephen Lee Anderson), "Raise Me Up" (reprise) (Lauren Ward), "Look at Me" (Lauren Ward, Amanda Posner), "That's What I Could Do" (Stephen Lee Anderson), "Promise Me, Violet" (reprise) (Michael McElroy, Lauren Ward), "Bring Me to Light" (Michael McElroy, Lauren Ward, Amanda Posner, Company

NOTES—*Violet*'s plot strained credibility. Set in 1964, the story dealt with Violet, a naïve young woman from a small town in North Carolina who was accidentally disfigured by her father when she was a little girl. She takes a bus to Oklahoma, where she hopes a televangelist will have God give her "a brand-new face." Along the journey, she takes up with two servicemen, Monty and Flick, the former White, the latter Black. At a stop-over in Memphis, Violet and Monty make love, and later in Oklahoma Violet doesn't receive any encouragement from the evangelist. In Arkansas, she meets Monty, who has signed up for a tour of duty in Vietnam. She rejects his offer to join him in San Francisco, and when she sees Flick at the bus station, it seems she has really loved him all the time, and so two go off together. Further, the story's subtext (one must look beyond scars and skin color in order to measure a person's value) was a trifle preachy and obvious for 1997. What saved the evening was Jeanine Tesori's intriguing score, which was recorded by Resmiranda Records (CD # RES-8037); the CD included two songs ("M &Ms" and "A Healing Touch") which weren't listed in the program. Audra McDonald's CD collection *How Glory Goes* included one of the musical's songs, "Lay Down Your Head." After its limited engagement at Playwrights Horizons, and despite having won the New York Drama Critics Award for Best Musical of the season, *Violet* faded. The musical didn't enjoy an extended Off Broadway run or a transfer to a Broadway theatre.

1727 Virgin. "A Rock Opera Concert." THEATRE: Village East Theatre; OPENING DATE: December 1, 1972; PERFORMANCES: Unknown; BOOK, LYRICS, AND MUSIC: The Mission; the Rev. John O'Reilly, Principal Author and Composer; SCENERY: Projections by Steve Loew; LIGHTING: Steve Loew; MUSICAL DIRECTION: Al Del Monte; PRODUCERS: Jay H. Fuchs and Elliott Taubenslag

CAST—Joe DeVito (Young Priest), Dorothy Lerner (Young Sister), Jim Rast (Conscience of Young Priest), Jay Pielecki (Bishop)

ACT ONE—"Ordination" (Jay Pielecki), "Ordination Theme" (lyric and music by John O'Reilly, Dorothy Lerner, and Joe DeVito) (Orchestra), "Young Man" (lyric and music by John O'Reilly and Rick Stott) (Jim Rast), "I'm Alone Today" (lyric and music by John O'Reilly and P. Coyne) (Dorothy Lerner), "See His Way" (lyric and music by John O'Reilly and Mike Merrell) (Company), "My Child" (lyric and music by John O'Reilly and Jerry Wisham) (Joe DeVito), "Don't Need Religion" (lyric and music by John O'Reilly and Mike Merrell) (performer unknown; sung on the recording by Mike Merrell), "Same Old Song" (lyric and music by John O'Reilly and Joe DeVito) (Joe DeVito), "Bless Me Father" (lyric and music by John O'Reilly) (Dorothy Lerner), "Kyrie Eleison" (lyric and music by John O'Reilly, Joe Venneri, and Al Del Monte) (Joe DeVito), "Merciful Jesus" (lyric and music by John O'Reilly) (Jim Rast), "No More Silence" (lyric and music by Joe Valentine) (Dorothy Lerner), "A Feeling" (lyric and music by John O'Reilly, Mike Merrell, Jim Rast, and Jerry Wisham) (Company)

ACT TWO—"Becoming One" (lyric and music by Joe Valentine) (Dorothy Lerner), "Sign in the Darkness" (lyric and music by John O'Reilly) (Joe DeVito), "No Choice" (lyric and music by John O'Reilly and Jim Rast) (Jim Rast), "Lost Love" (lyric and music by John O'Reilly and Joe Valentine) (Dorothy Lerner), "Got to Know" (lyric and music by John O'Reilly) (Joe DeVito and Dorothy Lerner), "Temple Turning Time" (lyric and music by John O'Reilly and Tom Troxell) (Joe DeVito, Jim Rast, Dorothy Lerner), "Everybody I Love You" (lyric and music by John O'Reilly and Jim Rast) (Joe DeVito, Jim Rast), "Listen to Me" (lyric and music by John O'Reilly and Jim Rast) (Jay Pielecki, Joe DeVito), "He Thinks I'm Weak" (lyric and music by John O'Reilly) (Jay Pielecki), "Why Not Leave" (lyric and music by John O'Reilly and Jim Rast) (performer unknown; sung on the recording by Rick Stott)), "What's It All About" (lyric and music by John O'Reilly) (Jim Rast), "We'll Never Let It Go" (lyric and music by John O'Reilly, Jerry Wisham, and Rick Stott) (Joe DeVito, Jim Rast, Dorothy Lerner)

NOTES—*Virgin* was written and composed by The Mission, a group of Roman Catholic priests who felt alienated by the Church and who disagreed with its tenets (especially the rule of celibacy). The plot of the rock opera dealt with priest and nun who fall in love.

Clive Barnes in the *New York Times* felt the musical's message was "admirable," but noted the story was told in a "murky" and "amateurish" style. He also found the music "not specially interesting" and the direction "not specially good."

The musical, which was recorded by Paramount Records on a 2-LP set (# PAS-8000), included original cast members and other singers (the song titles above are taken from the recording). The liner notes stated the musical was based on an original concept by Father John O'Reilly, and said the story specifically dealt with a newly ordained priest who faces the universal dilemma of following either his conscience or tradition (that is, the Church's rules).

Virgin was the first production to play the Village East, which had been formerly known as the Fillmore East.

1728 Voices from the Past

NOTES—See entry for *An Evening with Wolfgang Roth*.

1729 Volpone. THEATRE: Cherry Lane Theatre; OPENING DATE: July 6, 1953; PERFORMANCES: 45 (estimated); LIBRETTO: Alfred Perry; MUSIC: George Antheil; DIRECTION: Nelson Sykes; SCENERY: Robert Widder; COSTUMES: Joseph Braswell; MUSICAL DIRECTION: Rex Wilder; PRODUCER: Punch Opera (Nelson Sykes, General Director)

CAST—Willard Pierce or Kenneth Lane (Mosca), Gordon Myers or Robert Falk (Volpone), William Ross (Buono), Robert Falk or Ted Hart (Voltore), John Miller (Corbaccio), Anietje Mather (Pepita), Richard Roussin (Corvino), Martha Moore (Celia), Harriet Hill (Nina), Ted Hart, Dale Thompson, or Charles Radano (Magistrate)

SOURCE—The 1606 play *Volpone, or The Fox* by Ben Jonson.

The action occurs during a twenty-four-hour period in Venice during the sixteenth century.

The opera was presented in two acts.

NOTES—The opera *Volpone* had first been produced in January 1953 by the Opera Workshop at the University of Southern California.

Another lyric adaptation of *Volpone* is the 1964 Broadway musical *Foxy* (see entry for the 2000 revival presented by *Musicals Tonight!*), which starred Bert Lahr; set in the Klondike during the late-nineteenth-century gold rush, the Robert Emmett

Dolan and Johnny Mercer score is filled with delights, including "Bon Vivant," one of the best comedy songs in the history of the Broadway musical. Jonson's play was adapted for the opera stage a second time on March 10, 2004, when *Volpone* premiered at The Barnes at Wolf Trap in Vienna, Virginia, for three performances; the libretto was by Mark Campbell and the music by John Musto. The work was revived by Wolf Trap during the summer of 2007 for four performances.

Sly Fox, Larry Gelbart's non-musical adaptation of *Volpone*, was a Broadway hit in 1976, and was revived there in 2004.

1730 The Voyage. THEATRE: Metropolitan Opera House; OPENING DATE: October 12, 1992; PERFORMANCES: 6; LIBRETTO: David Henry Hwang; MUSIC: Philip Glass; DIRECTION: David Pountney; CHOREOGRAPHY: Quinny Sacks; SCENERY: Robert Israel; COSTUMES: Dunya Ramicova; LIGHTING: Gil Wechsler; MUSICAL DIRECTION: Bruce Ferden; PRODUCER: The Metropolitan Opera

CAST—Douglas Perry (Scientist, First Mate), Patricia Shuman (Commander), Kaaren Erickson (Ship's Doctor, Space Twin #1), Julien Robbins (Second Mate, Space Twin # 2), Tatiana Troyanos (Isabella), Timothy Noble (Columbus), Jane Shaulis (Earth Twin # 1), Jan Opalach (Earth Twin #2); Note: Early programs didn't list the performers (Jose Bercero, Ralph Di Rienzo, and Christopher Stocker) who portrayed the Crystal Bearers; according to the Metropolitan Opera's archives, these performers who portrayed the Crystal Bearers were listed beginning with the program for the October 16 performance (the Crystal Bearers were also included in the programs for the 1996 performances).

The action of the Prologue occurs in the present; act one: 15,000 years ago; act two: Granada and the Atlantic Ocean in 1492; act three: Earth and outer space, 2092; Epilogue, 1506.

The opera was presented in three acts.

NOTES—Philip Glass' epic concept opera *The Voyage* was commissioned by the Metropolitan in commemoration of the 500th anniversary of Christopher Columbus' voyage to the New World. It was somewhat indifferently received, but was revived at the Met in 1996 for six more performances. Curiously, the opera wasn't recorded, and for a number of years only a brief orchestral sequence ("Mechanical Ballet") was available on the Nonesuch Records CD *Philip Glass/Symphony No. 3* (# 79581-2); but in 2006 a complete 2-CD set of a German production (which was sung in English) was released by Orange Mountain Music Records (# OMM-0017). With the release of this important recording, one of the masterworks of modern musical theatre is now readily available so that musical theatre lovers may discover its haunting and chilling beauty.

For Glass and Hwang, the "voyage" is an eternal one: mankind is forever on a voyage, whether a metaphorical one of the mind or a literal one to faraway places on Earth or in the heavens. The prologue occurs in the present; the audience sees a scientist who though bound to his wheelchair is able to travel through space in his imagination (in the program notes, Glass wrote that the scientist was inspired by Stephen Hawking). The first act takes place fifteen thousand years ago during the Ice Age when four voyagers from another planet crash-land on Earth. Because their spaceship can no longer function, the travelers will never be able to return home. However, if sometime in the future the technology exists to build a new rocket ship, a combination of any two of the ship's four navigational crystals will direct the ship to the home planet. Each voyager takes a crystal and then embarks on his or her own journey of the newly discovered planet. Three of the voyagers envision the kind of world in which they would like to live: for one, a world of industrial power; for another, a world of spirituality; and for the third, a world of education.

The fourth voyager, the ship's commander, doesn't seek an abstract vision; she confronts her destiny in the here and now by encountering the natives of Earth (and they in turn await their encounter with her). In one of the most brilliant sequences of modern musical theatre, the commander sings of her fears and doubts in meeting the natives (the aria "What Will They Want from Me?"). Outside the spaceship, the natives too are fearful of their encounter with this alien being. Ironically, their song ("What Will She Want from Us?") is the same as the commander's, but with one amusing difference in the lyric. The commander wonders if the natives will want "color TV" and the natives wonder if the alien will want "photos in color"; the Ice Age is presumably far behind the commander's distant planet in terms of technology, and so while color photographs are available on Earth, there's no color television as of yet. When the commander and the natives finally meet, both she and the natives sing in gibberish (which the audience of course can't understand; in other words, the commander can't understand the natives, and they can't understand her; thus everyone on the stage hears gibberish [but with coloratura effects]). The entire sequence is told through Hwang's terse lyric and Glass' mesmerizing, pulsating, and rhythmic music.

The second act occurs in 1492; Columbus meets his fate on the thirty-second day of his voyage when "Paradise" is discovered in the New World. The third act takes place in 2092; two space crystals are found and man sets forth to travel to the home planet of the voyagers from fifteen thousand years ago. In the epilogue, the dying Columbus embarks on his final voyage, one which every living creature will eventually take.

For the music in the opening sequence of the second act, Glass created what is arguably the most ethereal and haunting music heard in lyric theatre since the premiere of Leonard Bernstein's *Candide* in 1956. An orchestral prelude is followed by the royal court of Spain singing "Admiral of the Ocean Sea," which in turn is followed by Queen Isabella's aria "Qui Navigant Mare Ennarent Pericula Eius (They That Sail on the Sea Tell of the Danger Thereof)"; the sequence concludes with the court and the queen singing in counterpoint. *The Voyage* was an ambitious opera with a concept perhaps not easily grasped on first viewing. (Glass and Hwang must have been appalled, but bemused, when a national political columnist lashed out at them for writing a blasphemous sequence in which the Virgin Mary gives herself to a group of natives; yes, this is how the columnist described the scene in which the commander and the natives meet for the first time.)

The fascinating story, combined with Glass' powerful and mesmerizing music, made *The Voyage* one of the most important musical works heard in New York since *Candide*. In 1996, *Floyd Collins* (see entry) joined *Candide*, *Follies*, and *The Voyage* as one of the four towering masterworks of modern American musical theatre.

The libretto of *The Voyage* was published by the Metropolitan Opera Guild in 1992. The opera's first performance, on Columbus Day, 1992, was broadcast live on radio.

For other lyric works about Christopher Columbus, see entry for *Columbus*.

1731 Wake Up, It's Time to Go to Bed! "Soundtheatre—A Concert of Contemporary Music." THEATRE: LuEsther Hall/The Public Theatre; OPENING DATE: May 16, 1979; PERFORMANCES: 31; BOOK: Carson Kievman; LYRICS: Carson Kievman; MUSIC: Carson Kievman; DIRECTION: Carson Kievman; SCENERY: Robert Yodice; COSTUMES: Robert Yodice; LIGHTING: Pat Collins; MUSICAL DIRECTION: David Arden; PRODUCER: The New York Shakespeare Festival (Joseph Papp, Director)

CAST—Keith Carradine (Orpheus), Joseph Kubera (Piano, Janitor, Orpheus Piano & Chorus), Dennis Masuzzo (Butler, Janitor, Orpheus Double Bass & Chorus), Lawrence Raiken (Butler, Janitor, Orpheus the Tenor), Michael Edwin Willson (Press Secretary, Janitor, Orpheus the Baritone), Sara Cutler (Maid, Janitor, Orpheus Harp & Chorus), Elizabeth C. Brown (Secretary, Janitor, Orpheus Flute and Chorus), Marty Ehrlich (Chauffer, Janitor, Orpheus Clarinet/Saxaphone & Chorus), David Arden (North American Conductor), Ellen Greene (United Nations Referee, Eurydice), Steven Paysen (European Percussionist, Orpheus Percussion & Chorus), Richard Sacks (Middle East Percussionist), William N. Moersch (Asian Percussionist, Orpheus Percussion & Chorus), David Van Tieghem (Sino/Soviet Percussionist), Susan Krongold (Heaven Violin #1, Orpheus Violin #2 & Chorus), Claudia Hafer (Heaven Violin #2, Orpheus Violin #1 & Chorus), Ruth Ann DeMarco (Heaven Viola), Erika Nelson Boras (Heaven Cello), Kurt Richards (Banker, Orpheus the Bass), Michael Pearlman (Boy Orpheus); Children (Renee Pearl and Sean Caposella); Additional Chorus (Erika Nelson Boras, Ruth Ann DeMarco, Richard Sacks, David Van Tieghen)

SOURCE—The Orpheus legend.

The musical was presented in two acts.

The program didn't list individual musical numbers; the following is a list of sequences taken from the program.

ACT ONE—Orpheus, The Temporary and Tentative Extended Piano (Curtain Raiser), Multinationals and the Heavens, Acquisition of wealth by the silvery moon; Cooperation in stormy weather, or breakfast on 5th Avenue; The breakdown of trade, or how I got to the New Hebrides Islands in the fog; Post script for string quartet

ACT TWO—[Wake Up, It's Time to Go to Bed!], Opus or not (preamble), Scenic Seen, Third stage scene, Scene 57, The scene, The late morning (postamble)

NOTES—*Wake Up, It's Time to Go to Bed!* was another evening at the Public which in part drew upon Greek legend for its source. The three-part presentation of "soundramas" from the "soundtheatre" was collectively titled *Wake Up, It's Time to Go to Bed!* and included two sequences for the first act ("The Temporary and Tentative Piano" and "Multinationals and the Heavens"); for the second act, the title sequence "Wake Up, It's Time to Go to Bed!" examined the Orpheus legend.

Ken Emerson in the *New York Times* reported that the "madcap" program's opening, the "Piano" sequence, dealt with a pianist and his piano, both "suspended in midair on a rickety scaffolding" while he plays arpeggios. His "poker-faced" household staff watches as he, his piano, and the scaffolding are swallowed up by an enormous mirror. The "Multinationals" sequence was even "wackier." It dealt in part with four dueling percussionists as well as the United Nations (represented by Ellen Greene in clown and referee drag), and its message seemed to say that money rules the world. Emerson noted that although the piece was impossible to take seriously, it was "entertaining" and it made one "laugh uproariously."

While the first two offerings were "tours de farce," Emerson felt the "Wake Up" sequence faltered; it was a "pretentious and banal" look at the Orpheus and Eurydice legend in Freudian terms (Keith Carradine and Ellen Greene played the leads). But Emerson mentioned that much of the music was "enthralling." Like the Public's *Blood* (1971, about Agamemnon; see entry) and *The Wedding of Iphigenia/Iphigenia in Concert* (1971; see entry) before it, the new musical and its irreverent look at the Orpheus legend was soon gone and quickly forgotten.

1732 Walk Down Mah Street! "A New Topical Musical Revue." THEATRE: Players Theatre; OPENING DATE: June 12, 1968; PERFORMANCES: 135; SKETCHES: Patricia Taylor Curtis; LYRICS: Patricia Taylor Curtis; MUSIC: Norman Curtis (Special material by James Taylor, Gabriel Levenson, and the members of the Next Stage Theatre Company); DIRECTION: Patricia Taylor Curtis; CHOREOGRAPHY: Patricia Taylor Curtis; SCENERY: Jack Logan; COSTUMES: Bob Rogers; LIGHTING: Bruce D. Bassman; MUSICAL DIRECTION: Apparently Norman Curtis; PRODUCER: Audience Associates, Inc.

CAST—The Next Stage Theatre Company (Denise Delapenha, Freddy Diaz, Lorraine Feather, Kenneth Frett, Vaughn Martinez, Gene Rounds)

The revue was presented in two acts.

ACT ONE—"We're Today" (Company), "Taxi!" (Gene Rounds), "Walk Down Mah Street" (Kenneth Frett), "Is She or Ain't She" (Denise Delapenha, Lorraine Feather), "Zap!" (Vaughn Martinez, Denise Delapenha), "If You Want to Get Ahead" (Freddy Diaz, Kenneth Frett, Gene Rounds, Denise Delapenha, Lorraine Feather), "Don't Be a Litterbug" (Vaughn Martinez), "Just One More Time" (Denise Delapenha, Freddy Diaz), "Walk Down Mah Street Courageous Award of the Year" (Gene Rounds), "Where and with What?" (Freddy Diaz, Vaughn Martinez, Denise Delapenha, Company), "I'm Just a Statistic" (Denise Delapenha, Freddy Diaz, Gene Rounds), "Minus One" (Kenneth Frett, Lorraine Feather), "Unknown Factor" (Lorraine Feather, Denise Delapenha), "Someday, If We Grow Up" (Vaughn Martinez), "Candid Camera" (Gene Rounds, Kenneth Frett), "Basic Black" (Company)

ACT TWO—"What Shadows We Are" (Freddy Diaz), "Want to Get Retarded?" (Denise Delapenha, Lorraine Feather), "What's for Dinner?" (Vaughn Martinez, Denise Delapenha), "Teeny Bopper" (Vaughn Martinez, Gene Rounds), "Plus One" (Lorraine Feather, Kenneth Frett), "Flower Child" (Kenneth Frett, Lorraine Feather), "For Four Hundred Years" (Gene Rounds), "Walk Down Mah Street Courageous Award of the Year" (reprise) (Kenneth Frett), "Don't Have to Take It Anymore" (Freddy Diaz, Gene Rounds, Denise Delapenha, Company), "Plus Two" (Lorraine Feather, Kenneth Frett), "Lonely Girl" (Vaughn Martinez), "The American Way" (Denise Delapenha), "Clean Up Your Own Backyard" (Freddy Diaz, Gene Rounds, Vaughn Martinez), "Walk Down Mah Street Courageous Award of the Year" (reprise) (Gene Rounds), "Walk, Lordy, Walk" (Kenneth Frett, Company), "Walk Down Mah Street" (Company)

NOTES—Despite its short run, *Walk Down Mah Street!*, a revue about racial issues, went through considerable revision by the authors. The six-member cast was eventually supplemented by a seventh performer (Anna Pagan), and during the run a number of songs and sketches were added ("The Buildings Slash the Sunlight," "Obie," "Mah House," "Better We Should Start All Over," and "Foster Child").

Richard F. Shepard in the *New York Times* liked the "bright, offbeat" evening which found its style somewhere between the "glib quick-laugh topical revue" and the "heavy we-hate-you Whitey" revue. Shepard felt the show was "intelligently assertive without threats or stridence." At one point, the revue wryly noted that a "Negro" can't get a taxi, but an "African" can. Further, one song ("Clean Up Your Own Backyard") had an anti-war message (this was 1968) and another ("Basic Black") looked towards racial equality and independence. Shepard mentioned the score included "lovely" ballads, and singled out "Just One More Time" (a "moving tune, beautifully sung").

1733 A Walk on the Wild Side. THEATRE: Musical Theatre Works; OPENING DATE: January 20, 1988; PERFORMANCES: 20; BOOK: Will Holt; LYRICS: Will Holt; MUSIC: Will Holt; DIRECTION: Pat Birch; CHOREOGRAPHY: Pat Birch; SCENERY: Michael Keith; COSTUMES: Amanda J. Klein; LIGHTING: Clarke W. Thornton; PRODUCER: Musical Theatre Works (Anthony J. Stimac, Artistic Director; Mark Herko, Associate Artistic Director

CAST—Mana Allen (Gladys), Brigid Brady (Kitty), David Brand (Schmidt), Jeb Brown (Dove), Rhonda Coullet (Hallie), Connie Fredericks (Lucille), Taylor Jenkins (Flora Lee), Irma Estel LaGuerre (Terasina), John Mineo (Finnerty), Kathi Moss (Reba), Catherine Newman (Frenchy), Gordon J. Weiss (Byron), K.C. Wilson (Fort)

SOURCE—The 1956 novel *A Walk on the Wild Side* by Nelson Algren.

The action occurs in East Texas and in New Orleans during the spring and summer of 1931.

The musical was presented in two acts (division of acts and song assignments unknown; songs listed in performance order).

MUSICAL NUMBERS—"Stay Away from Waycross," "Shut Out the Night," "That Old Piano Roll," "Don't Put Me Down for the Common Kind," "The Life We Lead," "The Rex Café," "Ingenuity," "When It Gets Right Down to Evening," "Cawfee Man," "Turtle Song," "A Walk on the Wild Side," "Loew's State and Orpheum," "Little Darling," "Night Time Women," "Strongman's Song," "Since the Night I Stood in the Dancehall Door," "The Way Home," "That Boy Can Read," "Heaviest Fight in New Orleans," "We Been in Love," "So Long"

NOTES—Set mostly in a New Orleans' bordello, Will Holt's Off Off Broadway musical *A Walk on the Wild Side* was based on Nelson Algren's novel, which is perhaps best remembered for its campy 1962 film version (which included a memorable background score by Elmer Bernstein).

1734 Walk Together Children (1968). THEATRE: Greenwich Mews Theatre; OPENING DATE: November 11, 1968; PERFORMANCES: 24; DIRECTION: Vinie Burrows (?); COSTUMES: Arthur McGee; LIGHTING: Fritz deBoer; PRODUCERS: Robert Hooks and Michael Tolan, in association with Ananse Productions

CAST—Vinie Burrows

The revue was presented in two acts.

ACT ONE—"John Brown's Body — Prelude, The Slaver" (by Stephen Vincent Benet), "Speech" (by Sojourner Truth), "Runagate Runagate" (Robert Hayden), "The Party" (by Paul Laurence Dunbar), "Life Cycle in the Delta" (by George Houston Bass), "Scarlet Woman" (by Fenton Johnson), "W.E.B. to Booker T." (by Dudley Randall), "Between the World and Me" (by Richard Wright)

ACT TWO—"Alberta K. Johnson" (by Langston Hughes), "Jazz Poem" (by Carl Wendell Hines), "I Know Jesus Heard Me" (by Charles Anderson), "Benediction" (by Bob Kaufman), "Revolutionary Cradle Song" (by Edward Reicher), "Conversation" (anonymous), "Jitterbugging in the Streets" (by Calvin Hernton), "Poem for Certain Cats" (by Roland Snellings), "Three Movements and a Coda" (by LeRoi Jones), "Status Symbol" (by Mari Evans), "Let America Begin Again" (by Langston Hughes)

NOTES—*Walk Together Children*, another revue depicting the Black experience in America, differed from others of its ilk because it was a one-woman show. Vinie Burrows presented an evening of prose, poetry, and occasional song, all of which centered around Black life from the times of slavery to the modern era.

Burrows also appeared in a revival of the revue in 1972 (see entry) which included a slightly different selection of material. That production was recorded by Spoken Arts Records.

Burrows was also in the Off Broadway revue, *Her Talking Drum* (1987; see entry), which provided dramatic and singing portraits of Black women from all over the world, and then she later appeared in a similar evening, *Sister! Sister!*, a one-woman show which opened at the American Place Theatre in an Off Off Broadway engagement beginning on October 29, 1992, for twenty performances (*Theatre World 1992-1993 Season* described it as "a collage of women's voices from around the world").

1735 Walk Together Children (1972). THEATRE: Mercer-Brecht Theatre; OPENING DATE: March 16, 1972; PERFORMANCES: 89; MATERIAL ADAPTED BY Vinie Burrows; GOWNS: Arthur McGee; MUSIC: Taped music by Brother Ahh (Robert Northen); PRODUCER: Ananse Productions

CAST—Vinie Burrows

The revue was presented in two acts.

ACT ONE—"Membrances" (by Jenny Proctor), "Speech" (by Sojourner Truth), "Runagate Runagate" (by Robert Hayden), "Slave Song" (anonymous), "The Party" (by Paul Laurence Dunbar), "Life Cycle in the Delta" (by George Houston Bass), "When My Uncle Willie Saw" (by Carol Freeman), "I Know Jesus Heard Me" (by Charles Anderson), "Scarlet Woman" (by Fenton Johnson), "W.E.B. to Booker T." (by Dudley Randall), "Between the World and Me" (by Richard Wright)

ACT TWO—"Alberta K. Johnson" (by Langston Hughes), "Two Jazz Poems" (by Carl Wendell Hines, Jr.), "U Name This One" (by Carolyn Rogers), "Benediction" (by Bob Kaufman), "Conversation" (anonymous), "Jitterbugging in the Streets" (by Calvin Hernton), "Brother Harlem Bedford Watts Tells Mr. Charlie Where It's At" (by Bobb Hamilton), "Three Movements and a Coda" (by Imamu Amiri Baraka [LeRoi Jones]), "When I Heard Dat White Man Say" (by Zack Gilbert), "Poem of Angela Yvonne Davis" (by Nikki Giovanni), "Poem to Complement Other Poems" (by Don L. Lee)

NOTES—*Walk Together Children* was a revival of an earlier production which had been produced Off Broadway in 1968 (see entry), and which had also featured Vinie Burrows; it dealt with the Black experience in America, and was a collection of poems and readings as well as some songs.

The new production was recorded by Spoken Arts Records.

Burrows returned in 1987 with an Off Broadway revue which offered dramatic and singing portraits of Black women from all over the world (see entry for *Her Talking Drum*). On October 29, 1992, she also performed in her Off Off Broadway one-woman show *Sister! Sister!* which opened at the American Place Theatre and played for twenty performances; similar in subject to *Her Talking Drum*, the work was described in *Theatre World 1992-1993 Season* as "a collage of women's voices from around the world."

1736 Walmartopia, The Musical! "A Musical on a Mission." THEATRE: Minetta Lane Theatre; OPENING DATE: September 3, 2007; PERFORMANCES: 136; BOOK: Catherine Capellaro; LYRICS: Andrew Rohn; MUSIC: Andrew Rohn; DIRECTION: Daniel Goldstein; CHOREOGRAPHY: Wendy Seyb; SCENERY: David Korins; COSTUMES: Miranda Hoffman; LIGHTING: Ben Stanton; MUSICAL DIRECTION: August Eriksmoen; PRODUCER: WMtopia, LLC

CAST—Sarah Bolt (Jamie, Guard, Others), Bradley Dean (Miguel, Zeb, Others), Stephen DeRosa (Dr. Normal, Otis, Others), Cheryl Freeman (Vicki Latrell), Nikki M. James (Maia Latrell), John Jellison (Scott "Scooter" Smiley, Others), (Justin) Brennen Leath (Darin, Alan, Others), Andrew Polk (Pearson, Lawrence, Others), Pearl Sun (Xu Fu, Counselor, Others), Scotty Watson (Sam Walton, Others), Helene Yorke (Hooters Girl, Daphne, Others)

The action in act one occurs in Madison, Wisconsin, during the present time; Act two occurs in Bentonville, Arkansas, thirty years later.

The musical was presented in two acts.

ACT ONE—"A New Age Has Begun" (Company), "American Dream" (Cheryl Freeman, Nikki M. James, Bradley Dean, Company), "March of the Executives" (John Jellison, Company), "Baby Girl" (Cheryl Freeman, Nikki M. James), "The Future Is Ours" (Stephen DeRosa, John Jellison), "A Woman's Place" (Cheryl Freeman, Nikki M. James, Company), "Flash Them Bootstraps" (Scotty Watson, Company), "Heave-Ho" (Stephen DeRosa, Company)

ACT TWO—"Walmartopia" (Company), "American Dream" (reprise) (Bradley Dean), "One-Stop Salvation" (Pearl Sun, Sarah Bolt, Cheryl Freeman, Nikki M. James, Bradley Dean), "The Future Is Ours" (reprise) (John Jellison, Andrew Polk), "These Bullets Are Freedom" (lyric and music by Steve Tyska) (Brennen Leath, Helene Yorke, Stephen DeRosa, Company), "Consume"/"American Dream" (reprise) (Scotty Watson, Bradley Dean, Company), "What Kind of Mother?" (Cheryl Freeman, Nikki M. James), "Outside the Big Box" (Company)

NOTES—*Walmartopia, The Musical!* was a satiric look at a Wal-Mart employee who is transported to the year 2037, where she finds that Wal-Mart has taken over every state in the union (except for Vermont, which is dominated by Ben and Jerry).

The program noted the musical "is not endorsed, sponsored or otherwise affiliated with, in any way, Wal-Mart Stores, Inc. or any affiliates of Wal-Mart Stores, Inc."

Caryn James in the *New York Times* found the evening a "genial grab bag of lost satirical opportunities," and noted the musical's concept was "tired on arrival." She also found the songs "uninspired." Frank Scheck in the *New York Post* mentioned that the musical's $65 tickets were a bargain compared to those of Broadway tickets, but also warned "you get what you pay for." He said the "mediocre" musical lurched between "seriousness and broad buffoonery, [failing] on both levels." He also mentioned that the book and lyrics lacked wit, the staging was "amateurish," and felt the performers should have taken part-time jobs at "you-know-where." A cast album was released on an unnamed and unnumbered label and included an "Uncle Sam's Commercial" sequence as well as playout music. The cast album was dedicated to the memory of Brennen Leath, who had died shortly after the musical's opening; his role was assumed by Demond Nasen, who is heard on the recording.

The musical had first been produced in 2005 by the Mercury Players at the Bartell Community Theatre in Madison, Wisconsin, and was later seen at the 2006 New York Fringe Festival.

1737 Waltz of the Stork (1982).

"A New Comedy with Music." THEATRE: Century Theatre; OPENING DATE: January 5, 1982; PERFORMANCES: 160; BOOK: Melvin Van Peebles; LYRICS: Melvin Van Peebles; MUSIC: Melvin Van Peebles (Additional lyrics and music by Ted Hayes and by Mark Barkan); DIRECTION: Melvin Van Peebles; SCENERY: Kurt Lundell; COSTUMES: Bernard Johnson; LIGHTING: Shirley Prendergast; MUSICAL DIRECTION: Bob Carten; PRODUCER: Melvin Van Peebles CAST—Melvin Van Peebles (Edward Aloyisus Younger), Bob Carten (Stillman), C.J. Critt (Phantoms, Memories, Back-Up Vocals), Mario Van Peebles (Phantoms, Memories, Back-Up Vocals)

The action occurs "now and before" in "wherever" and in Midtown Manhattan.

The musical was presented in two acts (song assignments weren't credited in the program).

ACT ONE—"There," "And I Love You," "The Apple Stretching," "Tender Understanding" (lyric and music by Ted Hayes), "The Apple Stretching" (reprise) (Orchestra), "Mother's Prayer," "My Love Belongs to You," "Weddings and Funerals" (lyric and music by Mark Barkan)

ACT TWO—"My Love Belongs to You" (reprise), "One Hundred and Fifteen," "Play It As It Lays," "The Apple Stretching" (reprise), "Shoulders to Lean On"

NOTES—Melvin Van Peebles had been twice represented on Broadway during the 1971-1972 season when his apostrophe-challenged musicals *Aint Supposed to Die a Natural Death* [1971] and *Dont Play Us Cheap* [1972]) opened.

Waltz of the Stork, which seems to have been produced under a Middle Broadway contract, had all the earmarks of a vanity production (Van Peebles was the show's book writer, lyricist, composer, producer, and star; the cast also included Van Peebles' son, Mario); and, indeed, the aimless, self-indulgent piece needed the firm hand of a director and producer who would demand a tighter and more coherent offering from the librettist, lyricist, composer, and star. But that didn't happen, and so the musical was in pretty much hopeless shape by the time it premiered (it nonetheless managed to hang on for the rest of the season).

The story, which dealt with the reminiscences (some real, some apparently fantasy) of Edward Aloysius Younger (Van Peebles), was less a book musical than a monologue with incidental songs and characters, and Christopher Sharp in *Women's Wear Daily* said the work might have been more entertaining as a coffee-house poetry reading. But the score included one catchy song (not by Van Peebles) called "(We All Get Together at) Weddings and Funerals," and this number was the show's highlight.

In 1984, Van Peebles revised the now self-styled "Comedy Musical." As *Waltz of the Stork Boogie*, the musical starred Harold Nichols in the role originally created by Van Peebles and included two new songs (see entry). *Waltz of the Stork* played at a small venue, the Century Theatre, which had formerly been the home of the famous nightclub Billy Rose's Diamond Horseshoe. Before it was named the Century, the venue was known as the Mayfair Theatre.

For another musical by Van Peebles, see entry for *Champeeen!* (which also references *Becky*, his proposed musical version of *Vanity Fair*).

1738 Waltz of the Stork Boogie (1984).

"Comedy Musical." THEATRE: Harry DeJur Henry Street Settlement Playhouse; OPENING DATE: July 12, 1984; PERFORMANCES: 20; BOOK: Melvin Van Peebles; LYRICS: Melvin Van Peebles; MUSIC: Melvin Van Peebles (Additional songs by Ted Hayes and Mark Barkan); DIRECTION: Melvin Van Peebles; CHOREOGRAPHY: Louis Johnson; SCENERY: Kurt Lundell; COSTUMES: Jeffrey N. Mazor; dancers' costumes by Quay Truitt; LIGHTING: William H. Grant III; PRODUCER: Henry Street Settlement's New Federal Theatre (Woodie King, Jr., Producer)

CAST—HAROLD NICHOLAS (Edward Aloysius Younger), Brewery Puppets (Brad Brewer, Puppet Master [Edward #4], Marvin Brown, Puppeteer [Edward #2], Glenngo King, Puppeteer [Edward #3], and David A.S. Marin, Puppeteer [Edward #1]), Dancers (Alfred L. Dove, Mercie Hinton, Rufus Jackson, Chiquita Ross, who also seem to have played the characters of Otis, Fast Eddie, John Jay, Junior, Lucille, Hazel, and Martha)

The action occurs "now and before" in "wherever" and in midtown Manhattan.

The musical was presented in two acts (song assignments weren't credited in the program).

ACT ONE—Overture, "So Many Bars," "And I Love You," "The Apple Stretching" (instrumental), "Tender Understanding" (lyric and music by Ted Hayes), "There," "Mother's Prayer," "My Love Belongs to You," "Jungle Party (No Escape)"

ACT TWO—"Weddings and Funerals" (lyric and music by Mark Barkan), "My Love Belongs to You" (reprise), "One Hundred and Fifteen," "The Apple Stretching" (reprise), "Play It as It Lays," "Shoulders to Lean On"

NOTES—The Off Off Broadway production of *Waltz of the Stork Boogie* was a revised version of *Waltz of the Stork*, which had played Off Broadway in 1982 (see entry).

For the revival, legendary dancer Harold Nicholas played the role originally created by Melvin Van Peebles, and the cast also included the Brewery Puppets. All numbers from the 1982 production were retained, and two were added, "So Many Bars" and "Jungle Party (No Escape)."

1739 Wanted.

"A New Musical." THEATRE: Cherry Lane Theatre; OPENING DATE: January 19, 1972; PERFORMANCES: 79; BOOK: David Epstein; LYRICS: Al Carmines; MUSIC: Al Carmines; DIRECTION: Lawrence Kornfeld; SCENERY: Paul Zalon; COSTUMES: Linda Giese; LIGHTING: Roger Morgan; MUSICAL DIRECTION: Susan Romann; PRODUCER: Arthur D. Zinberg

CAST—Andra Akers (Starr Faithful Brown), Reathel Bean (Billy the Kid), Jerry Clark (Babycakes), Cecelia Cooper (Opal), Frank Coppola (John Dillinger), June Gable (Shorty), MERWIN GOLDSMITH (Jacob Hooper), Lee Guilliatt (Ma Barker), John Kuhner (Deafy, Jelly Barker), Peter Lombard (Jesse James), Stuart Silver (Sheriff Sweet, Doc Barker), Gretchen Van Aken (Miss Susannah Figgit, Sister Powhatan Lace)

The musical was presented in two acts.

ACT ONE—"I Am the Man" (Peter Lombard), "Where Have You Been Up to Now?" (Reathel Bean, Andra Akers), "Outlaw Man" (Gretchen Van Aken), "Who's On Our Side?" (Merwin Goldsmith, Jerry Clark, June Gable), "Parasol Lady" (Merwin Goldsmith), "Jailhouse Blues" (Lee Guilliatt), "I Want to Ride with You" (Andra Akers, Reathel Bean), "You Do This" (Frank Coppola, June Gable, John Kuhner), "Guns Are Fun" (Frank Coppola)

ACT TWO—"I Do the Best I Can" (Lee Guilliatt, with Stuart Silver), "Wahoo!" (Stuart Silver, John Kuhner, Lee Guilliatt), "Whispering to You" (Jerry Clark, Merwin Goldsmith), "I Want To Blow Up the World" (June Gable), "The Indian Benefit Ball" (Gretchen Van Aken, with June Gable, Lee Guilliatt, Stuart Silver, John Kuhner, Frank Coppola), "The Lord Is My Light" (Peter Lombard, with Gretchen Van Aken, June Gable, Lee Guilliatt, Stuart Silver, John Kuhner, Frank Coppola), "It's Love" (Merwin Goldsmith), "As I'm Growing Older" (Lee Guilliatt, with Merwin Goldsmith)

NOTES—*Wanted* was another merry romp by Carmines & Company; it dealt with notorious outlaws of the American past who do battle with Jacob Hooper (read: J. Edgar Hoover). Of course, in Carmines' upside-down world, the bad guys were good, and the good guys bad. The subtext of the musical's politics may have been suspect, but the madcap book and Carmines' tinkling, ingratiating score won the day. Moreover, the high-camp musical was peopled with such knowing artists as Lee Guilliatt, Frank Coppola, Reathel Bean, and the always wonderful (and often underrated) June Gable, and was directed by Carmines' director of choice, Lawrence Kornfeld. Despite all the fun, the musical closed within a few weeks, and, unlike many of Carmines' musicals of the period, didn't leave behind a cast album.

Lyrics of four numbers ("Who's on Our Side?," "I Want to Ride with You," "I Do the Best I Can," and "The Lord Is My Light") were co-written by Carmines and David Epstein.

The musical had been previously produced at the Judson Poets' Theatre for two weeks, beginning on September 17, 1972. That production included most of the cast members who appeared in the Off Broadway version. Two numbers ("On the Run" and "Up in the Cut") used in the Judson version weren't included in the Off Broadway transfer. The program for the Judson production indicated that in addition to the four songs cited above, the lyrics for "Outlaw Man," "Guns Are Fun," and "The Indian Benefit Ball" were co-written by Carmines and Epstein.

1740 The Warrior. THEATRE: Metropolitan Opera House; OPENING DATE: January 11, 1947; PERFORMANCES: 2; LIBRETTO: Norman Corwin; MUSIC: Bernard Rogers; DIRECTION: Herbert Graf; SCENERY: Samuel Leve; COSTUMES: Mary Percy Schenck; MUSICAL DIRECTION: Max Rudolf; PRODUCER: The Metropolitan Opera

CAST—Mack Harrell (Samson), Regina Resnik (Delilah), Kenneth Schon (Officer), Irene Jordan (Boy), Philistine Lords (Anthony Marlowe, Felix Knight, John Baker, Osie Hawkins), Captains (John Garris, Thomas Hayward, William Hargrave)

The opera was presented in one act.

NOTE—The world premiere of *The Warrior* told the familiar story of Samson and Delilah (Mack Harrell and Regina Resnik). Reviewing the opera in the *New York Times*, Olin Downes found the work "singularly weak and ineffectual" without any "inspiration or dramatic intensity"; he also remarked that the music lacked "convincing" melodic ideas.

Downes also noted the libretto attempted to recreate Delilah in the mold of a modern woman by giving her a "suffragette speech" and having her sing in the vernacular (she remarks that the lords of the land are "all at sea"). The pillar to which Samson was chained looked puny and unrealistic, and Downes reported that he felt either "an impulse to laugh" or "to swear at the absurdity, the complete lack of illusion, and disproportion" of the pillar. It also seems that Samson was encased in a kind of box to restrain him, and Downes noted that Harrell's "length [protruded] from a little bit of department store tent" which wasn't big enough to contain him.

After its two initial performances, the work was never again seen at the Met. But another opera on the same subject, Camille Saint-Saens' *Samson et Dalila* (1877), has continued to enjoy frequent revivals there. In 1987, Regina Resnik appeared as Fraulein Schneider in the Broadway revival of *Cabaret*.

The Warrior was presented on a double bill with a revival of Engelbert Humperdinck's *Hansel and Gretel* (1893). The world premiere performance of *The Warrior* was broadcast live on radio.

1741 Washington Square. THEATRE: N.Y.U. University Theatre; OPENING DATE: October 13, 1977; PERFORMANCES: 6 (estimated); LIBRETTO: Kenward Elmslie; MUSIC: Thomas Pasatieri; DIRECTION: David Alden; SCENERY: Paul Steinberg; MUSICAL DIRECTION: Victor De Renzi; PRODUCER: The New York Lyric Opera Company

CAST—Sheri Greenawald (Catherine Sloper), Stephen Dickson (Morris Townsend), Judith Cristin (Aunt Lavinia), Marc Embree (Dr. Sloper)

SOURCE—The novel *Washington Square* (serialized in 1880 and published in book format in 1881) by Henry James.

The opera was presented in three acts.

NOTES—The world premiere of the opera *Washington Square* had taken place at the Michigan Opera Theatre in Detroit the previous year, and the New York Lyric Opera Company's production marked the opera's first showing in New York.

In his review for the *New York Times*, Allen Hughes noted that Thomas Pasatieri didn't opt for "facile tunes" or "obvious themes" and instead created a conservative score which was "coherent, tasteful and ... thoroughly operatic." Kenward Elmslie's libretto was commended for its "generally cogent dramatic line." *Newsweek* praised Pasatieri's "strong melodic gift," and found the score, "richly diverse" with a hymn, a comic patter number, a "beautiful" trio, and an "ingenious" transatlantic quartet (Catherine and Dr. Sloper in Venice, Morris and Aunt Lavinia in New York).

An earlier lyric adaptation of the novel was seen in Washington, D.C., in 1972; also titled *Washington Square*, the chamber musical offered an interesting number or two and boasted strong performances by its cast (Jeannie Carson [Catherine Sloper], Hurd Hatfield [Dr. Sloper], and Biff McGuire [Morris Townsend]); the musical's book was by Kenneth Jerome and Jerome Walman; the lyrics were by Jerome, and the music by Walman.

1742 Water Coolers. THEATRE: Dillon's; OPENING DATE: October 14, 2002; PERFORMANCES: 80; MATERIAL: Thomas Michael Allen, Joe Allen, Marya Grandy, David Nehls, and E. Andrew Sensenig; DIRECTION: William Wesbrooks; CHOREOGRAPHY: Timothy Albrecht; SCENERY: Michael Schweikardt; COSTUMES: Jeffrey Johnson Doherty; LIGHTING: John-Paul Szczepanski; MUSICAL DIRECTION: David Nehls; PRODUCERS: Steven Baruch, Marc Routh, Richard Frankel, Tom Viertel, Pete Herber, Ross Meyerson, Rodger Hess, and Ken Gentry

CAST—Marya Grandy (Judy), Adam Mastrelli (Steve), Kurt Robbins (Glen), Peter Brown (Frank), Elena Shaddow (Brooke)

The revue was presented in two acts.

ACT ONE—"Gather 'Round" (Company), "Panic Monday" (Elena Shaddow, with Adam Mastrelli, Kurt Robbins, Peter Brown), "In My Cube" (Marya Grandy, Company), "The Paranoia Chorus" (Company), "PC" (Kurt Robbins, Adam Mastrelli, Peter Brown), "The Great Pretender" (Kurt Robbins, Company), "A Song of Acceptance" (Adam Mastrelli), "And Hold Please" (Company), "The IT Cowboy" (Company), "In Windows2525" (Adam Mastrelli, Company)

ACT TWO—"Who Will Buy" (Company), "One Rung Higher" (Marya Grandy), "Chat Room" (Elena Shaddow, Company), "A Love Song" (Kurt Robbins, Adam Mastrelli, Peter Brown), "What You Want" (Elena Shaddow, Marya Grandy), "Just Another Friday" (Company), "Many Paths" (Company)

NOTES—The revue-like *Water Coolers* kidded modern-day office life (everything from cubicles to computers) with new lyrics set to well-known songs (the evening also included a few new songs as well).

Lawrence Van Gelder in the *New York Times* found the first act far too much in the style of a television sit-com; but in the second act, the heretofore glib characters became touchingly real, and suddenly the musical took on "attitude, wit and emotion." Van Gelder praised the "charming, talented" cast and the "brisk" direction by William Wesbrooks.

1743 The Way It Is!!! THEATRE: New Lincoln Theatre; OPENING DATE: December 2, 1969 (first day of preview performances); PERFORMANCES: Closed on January 20, 1970, after 60 preview performances; SKETCHES: Jerry Clark; LYRICS: Michael Greer and Kelly Montgomery; MUSIC: Buddy Bregman; DIRECTION: Buddy Bregman; CHOREOGRAPHY: Eddie Gasper; SCENERY: Mike Goldberg; COSTUMES: Gloria Gresham; LIGHTING: Joe Pacitti; MUSICAL DIRECTION: Jack Lee; PRODUCERS: Lee Hessel and Sam Fleishman

CAST—Jacqueline Britt, Deborah Bush, Jerry Clark, Gene Foote, Milton Earl Forrest, Ann Hodges, David Life, Renee Lippin, Veronica Redd

The revue was presented in two acts (sketch and song assignments unknown).

ACT ONE—"Adam and Eve," "Superman," "Does America Need a Third Party?," "Obscene Phone Call," "Goldberg's Gripe," "Smut Mail," "Generation Gap"/"I See in You," "Orgy," "Sexual Anonymous," "Shakespeare Today," "The Nude-Nik Hora," "Campus Life," "Pornography," "Tune of the Hickory Stick," "Could I Be Kidding Myself," "The Vice President and the Call Girl," "'Tis the Season," "Times Have Changed," "My Ghost Writer," "The Brand New Fourth Estate"

ACT TWO—"Local Hookers' Local," "Intermission Interviews," "I Feel So Lost," "Sexicare," "Operations Trade-In," "The Producers," "A Little Something on the Side," "Film Discussion Show," "Praise to the Blessed Builders," "Apollo 69," "Graffiti" "A Nude Encounter," "The Way It Is"

NOTES—The adult revue *The Way It Is!!!* never officially opened; it began previews on December 2, 1969, and closed on January 20, 1970, after playing sixty preview performances (an Off Broadway record which was bested just a few months later when *The Rise and Fall of the City of Mahagonny* played sixty-nine previews; see entry). The $65,000 production was an *Oh! Calcutta!* wannabe; with its closing, theatergoers were spared such numbers as "Obscene Phone Call," "Smut Mail," "Orgy," "Pornography," "Sexicare," "A Nude Encounter," and "The Nude-Nik Hora."

The New Lincoln Theatre was located in the Empire Hotel.

1744 We'd Rather Switch. THEATRE: Mermaid Theatre; OPENING DATE: May 2, 1969; PERFORMANCES: 256 (estimated); SKETCHES: Adapted by Walter M. Berger, from an idea by Mario Manzini; LYRICS: Larry Crane; MUSIC: Larry Crane; DIRECTION: Larry Crane; SCENERY: Frank Wakula; COSTUMES: Crane-Sterling Enterprises; MUSICAL DIRECTION: Lorenzo Fuller; PRODUCER: Mario Manzini

CAST—Wayne Clark (Mike), Maureen Sadusk (Gert), Karen Lynn (Ella), Diana Goble (Mae), Tony Carroll (Stud), Richard Schmeer (Al), Phillips Cross (Don), Ronnie Britton (Tom), Anastasia Jones (Betty)

The revue was presented in two acts (division of acts and sketch and song assignments unknown; sketches and songs are listed in performance order).

SKETCHES AND MUSICAL NUMBERS—"The Greatest Show on Earth," "The Premise," "The Strangest Show on Earth," "Flugel Street," "Stud Shows Us," "I'm Goin' Down to the River and Have Myself a Darn Good Cry," "On the Pier," "The Secrets of Claudimir," "A Man Isn't Old," "Mod Man of Manhattan," "Cuckoo's Nest," "We'd Rather Switch," "The Golden Gang," "The Candy Butcher," "The Rehash," "Ziffirelli Presents," "The Living Doll," "Villains Aren't Bad Anymore," "A Man Is Good for Something After All," "A Short History of Fashion," "Let's All Sing," "Let's Do It Over Again," Finale

NOTES—*We'd Rather Switch* had been previously produced in London. Mel Gussow in the *New York Times* reviewed the "depressingly tacky" production eight months after it opened, noting that the female performers did comic bits and the male performers stripped. He said he "very loosely" used the word "entertainment" to describe the revue, which wasn't a spoof but was instead "just an excuse for a male peep show." He found the performers "awkward and amateurish," and surmised that some of the casting came from muscle magazines. Gussow further noted that the producer (and professional escape artist) Mario Manzini must also be a "magician," because at the performance he attended there were fewer than twenty people in the audience ("only two of them, I think, female").

A recording of the revue on Varieties Records (LP # WRS-100) included nine numbers (one of which, "I'm Cute," wasn't heard in the New York); the album described the production as a "Groovy Newde Revue."

1745 A Wedding in Shtetel. "A Musical Comedy." THEATRE: Eden Theatre; OPENING DATE: February 9, 1975; PERFORMANCES: 12; BOOK AND LYRICS: William Siegel; adapted by Lillian Lux; DIRECTION: Pesach Burstein; MUSICAL DIRECTION: Renee Solomon

CAST—David Carey (Narrator, Mike), Janece Martel (Malka), Pesach Burstein (Eli Melach), Gerri-Ann Frank (Feigele), Karol Latowicz (Shimon), Robert Wayne (Ruben), Shmulik Goldstein (Levi), Elia Patron (Rabbi Issor'l), Mike Burstein (Yossele), Rochelle Relis (The Rebbitzin), Jaime Lewin (Guzik), Reizl Bozyk (Ruzha), Lillian Lux (Regina), William Gary (Dr. Boris Lazarow)

The action occurs in the village of Brinitze, Russia, before World War I, and in Kretshma, in the town of Zhmerkinka.

The musical was presented in two acts (division of acts and song assignments unknown; the songs are listed in performance order).

MUSICAL NUMBERS—"A Chasens in Shtetel," "Az Men Zicht, Gefint Men," "Feigalach Tzvei," "Oy Vay Tate," "Yossele and Feigele," "Wedding Ensemble," "An Actor's Life," "Without Him," "Yossele Entrance," "Sing a Happy Song," "Feigele, My Love," "Shabes Nuchn Kiegel," "Yossele's Dream," "Efsher Vet Geshen a Ness"

NOTES—Pesach Burstein and Lillian Lux headlined the Yiddish musical *A Wedding in Shtetel* (shtetl), which was booked for a special twelve-performance engagement. Their son Mike Burstein (later Burstyn) was one of Jim Dale's replacements in the original Broadway production of Cy Coleman's *Barnum* (1980), and in 1989 he starred as Mike Todd in Mitch Leigh's *Ain't Broadway Grand?*

The production of *A Wedding in Shtetel* was taped and released on videocassette by Jewish Video Library.

A cliché of Off Broadway Jewish-themed musicals was that they always seemed to center around a wedding, and there was always at least one song dealing with the subject. The pattern was evident even in Jewish-themed Broadway musicals, such as Jerry Herman's *Milk and Honey* (1961) which included a wedding number (appropriately titled "The Wedding"; in fact, the instrumental dance number "Independence Day Hora" had earlier been titled "Mazeltov," and its lyric dealt with a wedding). And of course *Fiddler on the Roof* (1964) offered a memorable wedding sequence.

1746 The Wedding of Iphigenia and Iphigenia in Concert. THEATRE: Martinson Hall/The Public Theatre; OPENING DATE: December 16, 1971; PERFORMANCES: 139; BOOK AND LYRICS: Doug Dyer, Peter Link, and Gretchen Cryer (lyrics adapted from Euripides); MUSIC: Peter Link; DIRECTION: Gerald Freedman; SCENERY: Douglas Schmidt; COSTUMES: Theoni V. Aldredge Lighting: Laura Rambaldi; MUSICAL DIRECTION: Peter Link (?); PRODUCER: The New York Shakespeare Festival Public Theatre (Joseph Papp, Producer; Bernard Gersten, Associate Producer)

CAST—Manu Tupou (Agamemnon), Madge Sinclair (Clytemnestra); the character of Iphigenia was portrayed by twelve actresses (presumably to emphasize the character's fragmented personality): Nell Carter, Margaret Dorn, Leata Galloway, Bonnie Guidry, Patricia Hawkins, Marta Heflin, Lynda Lee Lawley, Andrea Marcovicci, Julienne Marshall, Pamela Pentony, Marion Ramsey, Sharon Redd; Band: Goatleg (Henry "Bootsie" Normand, lead guitar; Chip McDonald, rhythm guitar; Leon Medica, bass guitar and steel guitar; Robert Patriquin, percussion; Fred Sherry, cello; Peter Link, acoustic guitar)

SOURCES—The 414-412 B.C. play *Iphigenia in Tauris* and the 410 B.C. play *Iphigenia in Aulis*, both by Euripides.

The musical was presented in two acts, *The Wedding of Iphigenia* and *Iphigenia in Concert*; the first act dealt with Agamemnon's sacrifice of Iphigenia; the second dealt with her life in Tauris.

The Wedding of Iphigenia: Opening (Madge Sinclair, Chorus), "What Has Your Tongue to Tell?" (Andrea Marcovicci, Julienne Marshall, Chorus), "On a Ship with Fifty Oars" (Julienne Marshall, Marion Ramsey, Chorus), "Ride on to the Highest Destiny" (Madge Sinclair, Chorus), "The Line Is Unbroken" (Chorus), "Who Will Lay Hands?" (Margaret Dorn, Chorus), "Oh What Bridal Song" (Chorus), "All Hail the King" (Chorus), "I Was the First to Call You Father" (Chorus), "This New Land" (Margaret Dorn, Chorus), "Lead Me On" (Nell Carter, Chorus), "I Was First to Call You Father" (reprise) (Marta Heflin, Chorus), "They Sing My Marriage Song at Home" (Nell Carter, Chorus), "Can't Stand in the Way of My Country" (Andrea Marcovicci, Marion Ramsey, Linda Lee Lawley, Leata Galloway), "All Greece" (Leata Galloway), "To Greece I Gave This Body of Mine" (Sharon Redd, Chorus), "Who Will Lay Hands?" (reprise) (Margaret Dorn), "Lead Me On" (reprise) (Pamela Pentony), "Come Let Us Dance" (Patrica Hawkins, Chorus), Finale (Marta Heflin, Chorus)

Iphigenia in Concert: "Lead Me On" (reprise) (Nell Carter, Chorus), "And Now, Part I" (Julienne Marshall, Lynda Lee Lawley, Andrea Marcovicci, Patricia Hawkins, Chorus), "And Now, Part II" (Nell Carter, Marta Heflin, Lynda Lee Lawley, Patricia Hawkins, Leata Galloway, Julienne Marshall, Chorus), "Last Night in a Dream" (Bonnie Guidry, Manu Tupou, Madge Sinclair, Chorus), "Your Turn Has Come" (Sharon Redd, Chorus), "I Wonder" (Pamela Pentony, with Nell Carter, Margaret Dorn, Sharon Redd, Julienne Marshall, Bonnie Guidry), "How Can I Tell My Joy" (Andrea Marcovicci, Chorus), "Gate Tender" (Marion Ramsey, Nell Carter, Marta Heflin, Leata Galloway), "Unhappiness Remembering Happiness" (Margaret Dorn, Bonnie Guidry, Chorus), "On a Ship with Fifty Oars" (reprise) (Henry "Bootsie" Normand, Chorus), "Crown Us with the Truth" (Lynda Lee Lawley, Chorus)

NOTES—Doug Dyer returned with another quickly forgotten rock-musical adaptation of a Greek tragedy (see entry for his earlier *Blood*, an adaptation of Aeschylus' trilogy *The Oresteia*). His double bill of two *Iphigenia* musicals soon disappeared (and so for that matter did Dyer).

Clive Barnes in the *New York Times* noted that *The Wedding of Iphigenia* was performed by twelve actresses, and he felt this fragmentation of the leading role was a gimmick which served no apparent dramatic purpose; further, he felt it was difficult to identify with the heroine's problems when she was portrayed by twelve different performers. As for *Iphigenia in Concert*, Barnes reported the characters chatted away as if they were on a television talk show or in a cozy coffee klatch; he criticized the "ingénue-level" of the performances, and said the evening was never more "childish" than when it tried to make Euripides "contemporary" and relevant. But Barnes was taken with Peter Link's score, and he called it "one of the best musical scores of the season — warm, vibrant and very appealing."

Incidentally, the musical's rock bank was called Goatleg.

In February 2008, James C. Nicola, the Artistic Director of the New York Theatre Workshop, announced that beginning with the 2008-2009 season the theatre would present *Encores!*-like concert revivals of three Off Broadway musicals each season. *Promenade* (see entry) is scheduled to inaugurate the series, and Nicola said the second production will be a "reworked" version of *The Wedding of Iphigenia* and *Iphigenia in Concert*; as of this writing, the third musical has yet to be announced.

1747 Weekend. "A New Musical." THEATRE: The Theatre at Saint Peter's Church; OPENING DATE: October 24, 1983; PERFORMANCES: 8; BOOK: Roger Lax; LYRICS: Roger Lax; MUSIC: Roger Lax; DIRECTION: David H. Bell; CHOREOGRAPHY: David H. Bell; SCENERY: Ursula Belden; COSTUMES: Sally Lesser; LIGHTING: Toni Goldin; MUSICAL DIRECTION: Clay Fullum; PRODUCER: The Midtown Arts Common at Saint Peter's Church (Edmund Anderson, Executive Director)

CAST—Justin Ross (Justin), Louise Edeiken (Louise), Gregg Edelman (Timothy), Carole-Ann Scott (Sally)

The action occurs in New York City at the present time.

The musical was presented in two acts.

ACT ONE—"Thank God It's Friday" (Company), "Lip Service" (Carole-Ann Scott), "This Song's for You" (Justin Ross, Louis Edekien), "Big Date Tonight" (Gregg Edelman, Carole-Ann Scott), "Lover, Sweet Lover" (Gregg Edelman), "The Man Next Door" (Carole-Ann Scott), "What's On?" (Justin Ross, Louise Edeiken), "Let's Have Dinner and Dance" (Justin Ross, Louise Edeiken), "Hangin' Out the Window" (Carole-Ann Scott), "Saturday Is Just Another Day" (Company), "Lucky Woman" (Gregg Edelman), "It's Sad to Say" (Justin Ross, Louise Edeiken), "Once You Take the Feeling Out" (Carole-Ann Scott), "See What Happens (When You Wait Too Long)" (Company), "Where Is She Now?" (Justin Ross, Louise Edeiken), "Cuddle In" (Gregg Edelman)

ACT TWO—"Baby, It Must Be Love" (Carole-Ann Scott), "Wake-Up Call" (Company), "A Man Wakes Up" (Gregg Edelman), "Seven Years Later" (Justin Ross, Louise Edeiken), "I Have Me" (Gregg Edelman), "I'll Never Want You Again" (Gregg Edelman), "Word Gets Around (The Silly Mementoes We Keep)" (Justin Ross, Louise Edeiken), "Dragon Lady" (Carole-Ann Scott, Justin Ross, Louise Edeiken), "What Time Is It?" (Company), "Sunday Makes a Difference" (Company)

NOTES—*Weekend* was yet another musical about young singles meeting and falling in love in Manhattan. Audiences had seen this story far too many times, and so *Weekend*'s first weekend was also its last.

Frank Rich in the *New York Times* said the evening was yet another *Company*-like musical which fell short of Stephen Sondheim's iconic work; further, it was also reminiscent of Sondheim's *Marry Me a Little* (see entry). But Rich noted that composer and lyricist Roger Lax was talented and that his score offered "signs of musicianship and wit." However, he indicated the music was too often "stubbornly monochromatic" and that "despair" was the score's "repetitive cri du coeur." Rich also reported that due to a vocal chord injury, Louise Edeiken was unable to sing on opening night; as a result, she "mutely" mimed her role while her understudy (Rosalyn Rahn) performed her songs.

1748 Weird Romance. "Two One-Act Musicals of Speculative Fiction." THEATRE: WPA Theatre; OPENING DATE: May 12, 1992; PERFORMANCES: 50; DIRECTION: Barry Harman; CHOREOGRAPHY: John Carrafa; SCENERY: Edward T. Gianfrancesco; COSTUMES: Michael Krass; LIGHTING: Craig Evans; MUSICAL DIRECTION: Kathy Sommer; PRODUCER: WPA Theatre (Kyle Renick, Artistic Director; Donna Lieberman, Managing Director)

NOTE—*Weird Romance* was comprised of two one-act musicals, *The Girl Who Was Plugged In* and *Her Pilgrim Soul.*

The Girl Who Was Plugged In; BOOK: Alan Brennert and David Spencer; LYRICS: David Spencer; MUSIC: Alan Menken

CAST—Valarie Pettiford (Shannana, Technician, Make-Up Specialist, GTX Lady, Script Supervisor),

Eric Riley (Zanth, Paramedic, Technician, Movement Coach), Ellen Greene (P. Burke), William Youmans (Vendor, Joe Hopkins), Sal Viviano (Paul), Marguerite MacIntyre (First Fan, Delphi), Jessica Molaskey (Second Fan, Mugger, Technician, Voice Coach, GTX Lady, Second Film Director), Danny Burstein (Third Fan, Paramedic, Technician, Reporter, First Film Director), Jonathan Hadary (Isham)

SOURCE—Based on a short story by James Tiptree, Jr.

The action occurs in a large metropolitan city in 2061.

MUSICAL NUMBERS—"Weird Romance" (Eric Riley, Valarie Pettiford) "Stop and See Me" (Ellen Greene), "That's Where We Come In" (Jonathan Hadary, Ellen Greene, Danny Burstein, Jessica Molaskey, Valarie Pettiford, Eric Riley), "Feeling No Pain" (Marguerite MacIntyre, William Youmans), "Pop! Flash!" (Eric Riley, Jessica Molaskey, Valarie Pettiford, Marguerite MacIntyre, Jonathan Hadary, William Youmans, Danny Burstein), "Amazing Penetration" (Jonathan Hadary, Jessica Molaskey, Valarie Pettiford), "Eyes That Never Lie" (Sal Viviano), "No One Can Do" (William Youmans, Ellen Greene), "Worth It" (Ellen Greene, Marguerite MacIntyre), "Eyes That Never Lie" (reprise) (Sal Viviano), "Worth It" (reprise) (Marguerite MacIntyre, Ellen Greene), Finale (Eric Riley, Valarie Pettiford), *Her Pilgrim Soul*; BOOK: Alan Brennert; LYRICS: David Spencer; MUSIC: Alan Menken

CAST—Danny Burstein (Daniel), Jonathan Hadary (Kevin), Holograms (Sal Viviano [Johnny Beaumont], William Youmans [Clown], Eric Riley [Boxer], Marguerite MacIntyre [Bride]), Jessica Molaskey (Carol), Valarie Pettiford (Rebecca), Ellen Greene (Nola), William Youmans (Chuck, Ruskin), Marguerite MacIntyre (Susan), Eric Riley (George Lester)

SOURCE—The short story "Her Pilgrim Soul" from Alan Brennert's 1990 short story collection *Her Pilgrim Soul and Other Stories*.

The action occurs on the day after tomorrow in Cambridge, Massachusetts.

MUSICAL NUMBERS—"My Ordinary World" (Danny Burstein, Jonathan Hadary), "Need to Know" (Danny Burstein), "You Remember" (Jonathan Hadary, Ellen Greene, Danny Burstein), "Another Woman" (Jessica Molaskey, Jonathan Hadary), "Pressing Onward" (Ellen Greene, Jonathan Hadary, William Youmans, Danny Burstein, Marguerite MacIntyre, Eric Riley), "I Can Show You a Thing or Two" (Sal Viviano), "A Man" (Jessica Molaskey, Valarie Pettiford), "Pressing Onward" (reprise) (William Youmans), "Someone Else Is Waiting" (Ellen Greene, Jonathan Hadary)

NOTES—Alan Menken's *Weird Romance* consisted of two one-act musicals which dealt with science fiction themes. *The Girl Who Was Plugged In* was about a homeless woman whose soul is transported into the body of a gorgeous android, and *Her Pilgrim Soul* told the story of a holograph which comes to life.

Despite their unusual subject matter, interesting casts, and surprisingly lavish productions, the two musicals were disappointingly tame and never overcame a certain amount of general blandness.

Mel Gussow in the *New York Times* praised *Her Pilgrim Soul*, "a melodious musical play" (which included "rapturous duets"). He also praised the "jaunty" lyrics, Ellen Greene's performance of "grace and disarming humor," and suggested that with more imaginative staging, expanded décor, and a few more songs, the work could stand alone as a full evening of musical theatre.

But Gussow was disappointed with *The Girl Who Was Plugged In*. He noted it contained a "cruel narrative" with little humanity, and its "overly complicated" story affected the book, lyrics, and music. But he felt Greene was very "affecting" in "Stop and See Me," which recalled the "poignancy" of Judy Holliday's rendition of "The Party's Over." During the run, the two acts were presented in *Plugged In*/*Pilgrim Soul* order, but later the running order was reversed. However, the script, which was published by Samuel French, Inc., in 1993, reverted to the original running order, which is presumably the "final" version of *Weird Romance*. During the run, the song "Great Unknown" was dropped from *The Girl Who Was Plugged In*. The published script included a more elaborate listing of reprises and overall song sequences, including the song "Happy in Your Work" for *Her Pilgrim Soul*.

The cast album was released by Columbia Records (CD # CK-53318).

1749 Well I Never! "A Musical Revue." THEATRE: Barbizon-Plaza Theatre; OPENING DATE: February 25, 1957; PERFORMANCES: 1; SKETCHES: Steven Vinaver; LYRICS: Steven Vinaver; MUSIC: Jonathan Tunick, Dan Silverstein, Harriet Josephs, Anthony Tuttle, and Steven Vinaver; DIRECTION: Steven Vinaver; SCENERY: John Kaufman; COSTUMES: John Kaufman; LIGHTING: John Kaufman; PRODUCER: Bard College

CAST—Students of Bard College (Aline Brown, Ronny Davis, Peter Feldman, Eliza Horsley, Michael Miller, Ruth Rosenheim, Peter Shaw)

The revue was presented in two acts.

ACT ONE—Opening (music by Harriet Josephs) (Company), "Pickle Week" (music by Dan Silverstein) (Michael Miller, Eliza Horsley), "He's a Hit!" (music by Harriet Josephs) (Peter Feldman, Ronny Davis, Michael Miller), "Passacaglia" (music by George Frederick Handel) (dance; choreographed by Steven Vinaver) (danced by Peter Shaw and Aline Brown), "New Neuroses for Old" (music by Steven Vinaver) (Michael Miller and Eliza Horsley, with Peter Feldman, Aline Brown, Ruth Rosenheim, and Ronny Davis), "Inspector Fink: A Melodrama, or You Take the High Road and I'll Take the Low Road and I'll be in Scotland Yard Before You" (sketch by Steven Vinaver) (Company), "Nothing" (music by Jonathan Tunick) (Aline Brown), "Motet for the Movies" (music by Jonathan Tunick) (Company)

ACT TWO—"Production Number" (music by Dan Silverstein and Anthony Tuttle) (Company), "Life in the Country" (music by Dan Silverstein) (Peter Feldman and Aline Brown), "Sixty-Four Thousand Bananas" (music by Dan Silverstein) (Ruth Rosenheim, Peter Feldman, Ronny Davis, and Peter Shaw), "The Pro Musica Antiqua" (music by Jonathan Tunick) (Eliza Horsley), "The Poet's Corner" (sketch by Steven Vinaver) (Peter Shaw, Eliza Horsley, Ruth Rosenheim, Aline Brown, Ronny Davis), "The Distaff Side" (music by Jonathan Tunick) (Peter Feldman, Announcer), "Adept and Scintillating" (Aline Brown, with Peter Feldman, Ronny Davis, Michael, Miller, Peter Shaw), "When You're in Love" (Eliza Horsley, with Peter Feldman and Peter Shaw), "The Troubles of the World" (Ruth Rosenheim, with Peter Feldman, Ronny Davis,, Michael Miller, Peter Shaw), "You Lied to Me" (music by Harriet Josephs) (Aline Brown; danced by Aline Brown, and Ronny Davis), Closing: "Snow" (music by Jonathan Tunick, words by Robert Frost) (Eliza Horsley, Ruth Rosenheim, Peter Feldman, Peter Shaw, and Ronny Davis)

NOTES—*Well I Never!* was a Bard College revue booked for one performance at the Barbizon-Plaza Theatre. It was the first New York hearings for both Steven Vinaver and Jonathan Tunick. Two numbers (the song "The Pro Musica Antiqua" and the sketch "The Poet's Corner" [a/k/a "The Poets' Corner"] were later used in the Off Broadway revue *Take Five* (1957; see entry), and were recorded on that show's cast album. A third, "Production Number," was later used in Vinaver's 1958 revue *Diversions* (see entry).

It was not all that unusual for college shows to sometimes play in legitimate theatres. As far back as 1907, the M.I.T. Tech Show *William, Willie and Bill* was performed at Boston's Colonial Theatre on April 25 and 26 of that year (with no less than Kurt Vonnegut [Sr.], Class of 1908, playing one of the three title roles, Bill).

1750 We'll Meet Again. THEATRE: 45th Street Theatre; OPENING DATE: July 27, 1995; PERFORMANCES: 79; WRITTEN BY Vicki Stuart; additional material by Ivan Menchell; LYRICS: See song list for credits; MUSIC: See song list for credits; DIRECTION: Johnny King; SCENERY: James Morgan; COSTUMES: Oleg Cassini; LIGHTING: Daniel Ettinger; MUSICAL DIRECTION: Paul Katz; PRODUCERS: Michael and Barbara Ross; Lois Teich

CAST—Paul Katz, Vicki Stuart

The revue was presented in one act.

MUSICAL NUMBERS—"Remember" (probably the song with lyric and music by Irving Berlin), "Look for the Silver Lining" (from *Sally*, 1920; lyric by B.G. [Buddy] DeSylva, music by Jerome Kern), "Beyond the Blue Horizon" (1930 film *Monte Carlo*; lyric by Leo Robin, music by Richard A. Whiting and W. Franke Harling), "The Army and the Navy and the Air Force," "There'll Always Be an England," "A Nightingale Sang in Berkeley Square" (lyric by Holt Marvell [Eric Maschwitz], music by Manning Sherwin), "Stick It on the Wall, Mrs. Riley," "Underneath the Arches" (lyric by Reginald Connelly, music by Bud Flanagan and Joseph McCarthy), "All Our Tomorrows" (lyric and music by Jimmy Kennedy), "The Thingummybob," "Dancing with My Shadow" (lyric and music by Harry Woods), "Wish Me Luck" (lyric by Phil Park, music by Harry Parr-Davis), "The Deepest Shelter in Town" (lyric and music by Leslie Julian Jones), "Love Letters," "P.S. I Love You" (lyric by Johnny Mercer, music by Gordon Jenkins), "Don't Sit Under the Apple Tree (With Anyone Else but Me)" (1942 film *Private Buckaroo*; lyric and music by Lew Brown, Charles Tobias, and Sam H. Stept), "Don't Get Around Much Anymore" (lyric by Bob Russell, music by Duke Ellington), "They're Either Too Young or Too Old" (1943 film *Thank Your Lucky Stars*; lyric by Frank Loesser, music by Arthur Schwartz), "You'll Never Know" (1943 film *Hello, Frisco, Hello*; lyric by Mack Gordon, music by Harry Warren), "Long Ago and Far Away" (1944 film *Cover Girl*; lyric by Ira Gershwin, music by Jerome Kern), "I'll Be Seeing You" (*Right This Way*, 1938; lyric by Irving Kahal, music by Sammy Fain), "These Foolish Things (Remind Me of You)" (British musical *Spread It Around*, 1936; lyric by Holt Marvell [Eric Maschwitz], music by James Strachey and Harry Link), "Luverly Bunch of Coconuts," "The White Cliffs of Dover" (lyric by Nat Burton, music by Walter Kent), "London by Night," "Yours" "You'd Be So Nice to Come Home To" (1943 film *Something To Shout About*; lyric and music by Cole Porter), "Lili Marlene" (lyric by Hans Liep, music by Norbert Schultze; English lyric by John Turner and Tommy Connoer [some sources give latter's name as Tommie Connor]), "Auf Wiedersehn" (*The Blue Paradise*, 1915; lyric by Herbert Reynolds, music by Sigmund Romberg), "We'll Meet Again" (lyric and music by Ross Parker and Hughie Charles)

NOTES—Vicki Stuart returned in *We'll Meet Again*, another revue which looked back on the British home front during World War II (see entry for *Smiling Through* [1994], which included much of the same material heard in *We'll Meet Again*).

For other revues with a similar theme, see entries for *Swingtime Canteen* (1995) and *When the Lights Go On Again* (2007).

We'll Meet Again was revived later in the season by the York Theatre Company, opening at the Theatre at St. Peter's on May 23, 1996.

The song "We'll Meet Again" no doubt received its most famous hearing during the explosive ending sequence of Stanley Kubrick's 1964 film *Dr. Strangelove*, or: *How I Learned to Stop Worrying and Love the Bomb*.

1751 We're Civilized? "A Musical Comedy." THEATRE: Jan Hus Playhouse; OPENING DATE: November 8, 1962; PERFORMANCES: 22; BOOK: Alfred Aiken; LYRICS: Alfred Aiken; MUSIC: Ray Haney; DIRECTION: Martin H. Cohen; CHOREOGRAPHY: Bhaskar; SCENERY: Jack H. Cornwell; COSTUMES: Sonia Lowenstein; LIGHTING: Roger Morgan; MUSICAL DIRECTION: Michael Leonard; PRODUCER: Randell Productions

CAST—Bert Niemark (Atahualpa), Sally De May (Juana), Roy Bhaskar (Garsilaso), Marty Ross (Manalac), Karen Black (Zinnina), Gus Sabin (Jack Smith), Peggy Pope (Barbara Jones), Diane Findlay (Toni Frazier), John McLeod (Bob Jason), Mark LaRoche (Larry Mack), Robert (Bob) E. Fitch (Ken Crocker), Diane Adler (Native), Eddie Barton (Native), Fred Benjamin (Native), Richard Goss (Native), Shari Green (Native), Toby Hinkes (Native), Danny Joel (Native), Eydi Renaud (Native), Christine Stewart (Native), Al Tipay (Native)

The musical was presented in two acts (song assignments unknown).

ACT ONE—"Brewing the Love Potion," "Too Old," "J.B. Pictures, Inc.," "Welcome Dance," "Everything Is Wonderful," "Knife Dance," "Me Atahualpa," "No Place to Go," "Lullaby Wind," "I Like," "Fertility Dance," "You Can Hang Your Hat Here," "I Like" (reprise), "You're Like," "Witch Song"

ACT TWO—"Mother Nature," "Procession," "Bad If He Does, Worse If He Doesn't," "Snake Dance," "Diversion," "Muted" (music by Michael Leonard), "Stretto," "Yankee Stay," "We're Civilized"

NOTES—With that title, *We're Civilized?* would at first appear to be a typical Off Broadway revue of the period. But it was in fact a book musical which dealt with a Hollywood crew and its misadventures while filming a movie on location in the ruins of a Peruvian Inca temple where a lost civilization of natives still thrives. Apparently the clash of cultures wasn't funny enough, and so the musical was gone in less than three weeks. The cast included Off Broadway perennial Robert Fitch, comic Peggy Pope, and Karen Black. Earlier in the year, Black had created the role of Philia during the out-of-town tryout of *A Funny Thing Happened on the Way to the Forum*, but was replaced by Preshy Marker (whatever happened to Preshy Marker?).

Bhaskar had duel functions in *We're Civilized?* As Bhaskar, he was the musical's choreographer, and as Roy Bhaskar he played the role of Garsilaso. *We're Civilized?* is important in the history of the American musical, because with it we at last discover Bhaskar's first name.

1752 We're Home. "Words and Music by Bob Merrill." THEATRE: Vineyard Theatre; OPENING DATE: October 19, 1984; PERFORMANCES: 24. ADAPTATION: Douglas Aibel and Stephen Milbank; LYRICS: Bob Merrill; MUSIC: Except where noted, all music by Bob Merrill; DIRECTION: Douglas Aibel; CHOREOGRAPHY: Pamela Sousa; SCENERY: James Wolk; COSTUMES: Amanda J. Klein; LIGHTING: Richard Lund; MUSICAL DIRECTION: Stephen Milbank; PRODUCER: The Vineyard Theatre (Barbara Zinn Krieger, Executive Director)

CAST—Ann Talman (Evelyn), Peter Frechette (Paul), Larry Keith (Ted), Rita Gardner (Anne)

The action occurs in a small city park during an evening in spring.

The revue was presented in two acts divided into three parts (with an intermission apparently between the first and second parts); the program didn't provide credits for song assignments.

ACT ONE—Part One—*I'm in a Tree:* "I'm in a Tree" (from *Prettybelle*, 1971 [closed during pre-Broadway tryout]; music by Jule Styne), "Nine O'-Clock" (*Take Me Along*, 1959), "Here I Am" (*Henry, Sweet Henry*, 1967), "Make Yourself Comfortable" (song written independent of a musical production), "Traveling" (*Breakfast at Tiffany's* [a/k/a *Holly Golightly*], 1966 [closed during Broadway previews]), "You Are Woman" (*Funny Girl*, 1964; music by Jule Styne), "I'm Naïve" (1965 television musical *The Dangerous Christmas of Red Riding Hood* [see entry for Off Off Broadway production]; music by Jule Styne)/"My Place in the World" (*The Prince of Grand Street*, 1978 [closed during pre-Broadway tryout]), "My Red Riding Hood" (*The Dangerous Christmas of Red Riding Hood*, 1965; music by Jule Styne), "Mira" (*Carnival!*, 1961)/"The Girl with Too Much Heart" (*The Prince of Grand Street*, 1978), "A Woman in Love" (*Henry, Sweet Henry*, 1967), "Stay with Me" (*Breakfast at Tiffany's*, 1966)

ACT TWO—Part Two—*People Watching People:* "The People Watchers" (*Henry, Sweet Henry*, 1967), "Nothing Is New in New York" (*Breakfast at Tiffany's*, 1966), "The Rich" (*Carnival!*, 1961), "The Party People" (*Breakfast at Tiffany's*, 1966), "I've Got a Penny" (*Breakfast at Tiffany's*, 1966), "To a Small Degree" (*Prettybelle*, 1971; music by Jule Styne), "How Could I Know?" (*Prettybelle*, 1971; music by Jule Styne), "Knights on White Horses" (*Take Me Along*, 1959; song written for 1985 Broadway revival), "Breakfast at Tiffany's" (*Breakfast at Tiffany's*, 1966), "The Home for Wayward Girls" (*Breakfast at Tiffany's*, 1966), "[In] The Company of Men" (*Take Me Along*, 1959; song written for 1984 Off Off Broadway revival; see entry), "She Wears Red Feathers" (independent song), "Pittsburgh, Pennsylvania" (independent song), "Sunshine Girl" (*New Girl in Town*, 1957; song identified as "Sunshine Girls" in program), "Flings" (*New Girl in Town*, 1957), "Grade 'A' Treatment" (*Breakfast at Tiffany's*, 1966), "Staying Young" (*Take Me Along*, 1959), "We're Home" (*Take Me Along*, 1959), "But Yours" (*Take Me Along*, 1959), "Waltz" (independent song?), Part Three—*When You're Alone*, "When Daddy Comes (Came) Home" (*Breakfast at Tiffany's*, 1966), "Do You Ever Go to Boston?" (*Henry, Sweet Henry*, 1967), "Alone in the World" (1962 television musical *Mr. Magoo's Christmas Carol*; music by Jule Styne), "People" (*Funny Girl*, 1964; music by Jule Styne)

NOTES—Even though character names were assigned to the four singers and there was a plot of sorts, the Off Off Broadway production of *We're Home* was not really a full-fledged book musical. The revue-like evening was for all purposes a tribute to lyricist and composer Bob Merrill (1920-1998) who enjoyed a few successes on Broadway (notably *New Girl in Town*, *Carnival!* and *Funny Girl* [for the latter he wrote the lyrics]) as well as a number of failures (some of which closed during their pre-Broadway tryouts, in New York previews, or shortly after their Broadway openings). However, even his flops left behind a number of pleasant songs, and *We're Home* was a welcome evening devoted to Merrill's theatre songs as well as a few numbers he wrote independent of musicals.

The evening included two songs from the 1965 television musical *The Dangerous Christmas of Red Riding Hood*, which was later adapted into an Off Off Broadway musical (see entry).

1753 We're Still Hot! THEATRE: The Theatre at Saint Luke's; OPENING DATE: February 15, 2005; PERFORMANCES: 96; BOOK: JJ McColl; LYRICS: JJ McColl; MUSIC: JJ McColl and Rueben Gurr; DIRECTION: Sue Wolf; SCENERY: Takeshi Kata; COSTUMES: Philip Heckman; LIGHTING: Gregory Cohen; MUSICAL DIRECTION: Alan J. Plado; PRODUCERS: Entertainment Events Inc. and Waxman Williams Entertainment with Robert Dragotta, in association with Scott Prisand, Marcia Roberts, and Danny Seraphine

CAST—Deborah Jean Templin (Kate), Marnee Hollis (Cynthia), Deirdre Kingsbury (Marnie), Jane Seaman (Zsu Zsu)

The revue was presented in two acts.

NOTES—Like the long-running *Menopause: The Musical* (see entry), *We're Still Hot!* was a revue-like musical about women in their middle years. But there was room for just one menopause musical on the New York stage, and so *We're Still Hot!* lasted only three months while *Menopause: The Musical* continued on, eventually running for over 1,700 performances. The evening dealt with a high school class reunion for members of the graduating class of 1970, and specifically focused on a musical revue being written for the reunion. Anita Gates in the *New York Times* wasn't always impressed with the soap-opera-like plot and the sometimes "painful" lyrics, but she found the characters occasionally "endearing" and a few of the songs and sketches amusing. The musical included a number of songs, including "Nothing Special," "Hormones," "Whirligig Glands," and "One Hell of a Woman" (Gates noted the latter was a "satisfying" anthem about one of the character's liberation).

We're Still Hot! was actually written and produced three years before *Menopause: The Musical* (the latter had premiered in Orlando, Florida, on March 28, 2001, while *We're Still Hot!* was first seen as *Menopositive! The Musical* at Vancouver's Firehall Arts Center in April 1998).

1754 Wet Paint. "A Musical Revue." THEATRE: Renata Theatre; OPENING DATE: April 14, 1965; PERFORMANCES: 16; SKETCHES: Pierre Berton, Tony Geiss, Stanley Handleman, Herbert Hartig, Dolly Jonah, Lois Balk Korey, Marc London, Paul Lynde, Pat McCormick, Judith Milan, David Panich, Bob Rosenblum, Paul Sand, and Howard Schuman; LYRICS: Martin Charnin, Anne Croswell, Tony Geiss, Ronny Graham, Sheldon Harnick, Herbert Hartig, Jennifer Konecky, Johnny Myers, and Giles O'Connor; MUSIC: Gerald Alters, Stan Davis, Tony Geiss, Ronny Graham, Sheldon Harnick, Bob Kessler, Jennifer Konecky, Johnny Myers, and Ed Scott; DIRECTION: Michael Ross; CHOREOGRAPHY: Rudy Tronto; SCENERY: David Moon; COSTUMES: (Joe) Mostoller; LIGHTING: David Moon; MUSICAL DIRECTION: Gerald Alters; PRODUCERS: Lee Reynolds and Isobel Robins, in association with Allan H. Mankoff

CAST—BILL MCCUTCHEON, PAUL SAND, Gene Allen, Isobel Robins, Hank Garrett, Linda Lavin

The revue was presented in two acts.

ACT ONE—Prologue: "How's Elsie" (writer uncredited) (Bill McCutcheon, Paul Sand, Gene Allen, Isobel Robins) Opening: "Walk Dog" (sketch by Pat McCormick and Marc London) (Company) "Red Moroccan Shoes" (sketch by Judith Milan, Howard Schuman, and Bob Rosenblum) (Linda Lavin, Isobel Robins), "Ventrioloquy" (sketch by Herbert Hartig) (Bill McCutcheon, Hank Garrett, Linda Lavin) "Concert Encore" (lyric and music by Sheldon Harnick) (Gene Allen) "Potato Salad" (sketch by Herbert Hartig and Lois Balk Korey) (Paul Sand, Hank Garrett, Isobel Robins) "Neville" (lyric and music by Tony Geiss) (Linda Lavin) "No Tickee" (sketch; freely adapted from the vaudeville sketch by Leslie H. Carter) (Bill McCutcheon, Hank Garrett, Isobel Robins) "On the Phone" (sketch by Stanley Handleman) (Gene Allen) "Cantata" (lyric by Herbert Hartig, music by Gerald Alters) (Paul Sand, Company) "Don't" (sketch by Herbert Hartig) (Gene Allen, Linda Lavin) "Little Woman" (sketch by Herbert Hartig) (Bill McCutcheon, Hank Garrett) "Cream in My Coffee" (lyric by Anne Croswell, music by Ed

Scott) (Gene Allen, Isobel Robins, Linda Lavin), "Shakespeare Revisited" (sketch by Pierre Berton) (Bill McCutcheon, Paul Sand, Gene Allen, Hank Garrett, Isobel Robins) "Love Affair" (lyric by Martin Charnin, music by Bob Kessler) (Linda Lavin), "Half-Way House" (sketch by Paul Sand) (Bill McCutcheon, Paul Sand, Linda Lavin) "Unrequited Love March" (lyric and music by Ronny Graham) (Company)

ACT TWO—"Puns" (lyric by Herbert Hartig, music by Gerald Alters) (Bill McCutcheon, Paul Sand, Linda Lavin) "The Computer" (sketch by David Panich) (Hank Garrett, Isobel Robins, Gene Allen) "I Know He'll Understand" (lyric and music by Johnny Myers) (Isobel Robins) "The Well Boiled Icicle" (sketch by Dolly Jonah) (Gene Allen, Linda Lavin) "Canary" (lyric by Giles O'Connor, music by Stan Davis) (Hank Garrett, Isobel Robins) "Street Scene" (sketch by Bob Hilliard) (Bill McCutcheon, Paul Sand) "Showstopper" (lyric and music by Johnny Myers) (Linda Lavin) "It Takes a Heap" (sketch by Tony Geiss and Paul Lynde) (Hank Garrett, Company) "These Things I Know Are True" (lyric and music by Jennifer Konecky) (Bill McCutcheon, Gene Allen, Hank Garrett, Linda Lavin, Isobel Robins) "On the Phone" (sketch by Stanley Handleman) (Gene Allen) "I Spy" (sketch by Judith Milan, Howard Schuman, and Bob Rosenblum) (Paul Sand, Linda Lavin) Finale (Company)

NOTES—Such clowns as Paul Sand and Linda Lavin couldn't keep the revue *Wet Paint* going for more than two weeks. But the following season they found themselves in a hit, the long-running *The Mad Show* (see entry).

One sketch ("Cryin' Shame" by Lawrence B. Eisenberg and Betty Freedman) may have been dropped before opening night. After the opening, the running order of the songs and sketches was considerably altered (for instance, "The Well Boiled Icicle" was moved from the second act to the opening of the first act, and "Red Moroccan Shoes" was moved from the first to the second act) and other numbers ("Potato Salad" and "Little Woman") were dropped altogether. Lewis Funke in the *New York Times* found the revue's title "incomprehensible," and noted that overall the evening added up "to something less than plus." But he singled out the sketch "Half-Way House," in which Linda Lavin played the role of a psychologist in a home for unwed fathers, one of whom is Paul Sand (who describes how he got into trouble when a group of girls took him into the park). Funke also singled out "Showstopper," "I Spy," "These Things I Know Are True," and Ronny Graham's "Unrequited Love March" (if memory serves, the latter was performed on a television show of the era [Jack Paar's late-night talk show?], and despite [or perhaps in spite of] its title, it was a merrily confident, aggressively optimistic, and assertively hopeful number).

"Showstopper" had originally been heard in *Talent '60*, a showcase production which was performed at the Majestic Theatre on March 22, 1960.

1755 What a Killing. "A Musical Comedy." THEATRE: Folksbiene Theatre; OPENING DATE: March 27, 1961; PERFORMANCES: 1; BOOK: Fred Hebert; LYRICS: George Harwell; additional lyrics by Joan Anania; MUSIC: George Harwell; DIRECTION: Gene Montefiore; CHOREOGRAPHY: Bob Hamilton; SCENERY: Robert Wightman; COSTUMES: Hugh Whitfield; LIGHTING: Robert Wightman; MUSICAL DIRECTION: Andrew Lesco; PRODUCER: Jack Collins

CAST—Paul Hartman (Chic), Al Mancini (Bookie, Florist, Chorus), Joel Abel (Customer, Bartender, Chorus), Ted Chapman (Golfbag Sam), Barney Martin (Big Mike), Lou Wills, Jr. (Lennie), Betty Secino (Rocky, Chorus), Margo DeBarr (Rocky, Chorus), Don Pottner (Rockette), John Anania (Tony Caro), Judy Lynn (Connie), John Carter (Dino), Chanin Hale (Norma), Barbara Ellers (Gladys, Chorus)

SOURCE—A story by Jack Waldron.

The action occurs in Chicago.

The division of acts is unknown, as are song assignments; however, the songs are listed in performance order.

MUSICAL NUMBERS—"The Chicago That I Know," "The Customer Is Always Right," "Troubled Lady," "Look at What It's Done," "I'm a Positive Guy," "Out of Luck with Luck," "Rockette's Dance," "Laughing Out Loud," "Here I Come," "Nobody Cheats Big Mike," "Fools Come and Fools Go," "The Race," "A Rag, a Bone, a Hank of Hair," "Face the Facts," "Oh, How I Love You," "Pride in My Work," "Lennie," "What a Killing"

NOTES—*What a Killing* has the dubious distinction of being the first Off Broadway musical to close on opening night. It appears to have been a *Guys and Dolls* wannabe, but there was room for only one musical about gamblers and horse-racing in the musical theatre canon, as *Let it Ride!* (1961) will unhappily attest.

The musical was told in the form of reminiscences by Chic of Chicago (played by Paul Hartman) about life in Chicago during the Prohibition era, and the main plot dealt with two nightclub owners who vie for the love of a singer. Howard Taubman in the *New York Times* felt the material offered "used goods, which were cheap when new" and noted the evening offered a "relentless march" of clichés, a book which was "simple-minded," and songs which didn't "rise above conventional standards and often [sank] below them." But Taubman found Hartman an "engaging personality" who could "deliver" a number, and he liked the idea of the musical's "hatchet trio" (a "dapper lad" named Rockette [Don Pottner] and "two statuesque babes," both named Rocky [Betty Secino and Margo DeBarr]), an "ominous" threesome who promised more in the way of diversion than the musical actually delivered.

1756 What About Luv? THEATRE: York Theatre; OPENING DATE: December 22, 1991; PERFORMANCES: 29; BOOK: Jeffrey Sweet; LYRICS: Susan Birkenhead; MUSIC: Howard Marren; DIRECTION: Patricia Birch; SCENERY: James Morgan; COSTUMES: Barbara Beccio; LIGHTING: Mary Jo Dondlinger; MUSICAL DIRECTION: Tom Helm; PRODUCER: The York Theatre Company (Janet Hayes Walker, Founder and Producing Director; Molly Pickering Grose, Managing Director)

CAST—Austin Pendleton (Harry Berlin), David Green (Milt Manville), Judy Kaye (Ellen Manville)

SOURCE—The 1964 play *Luv* by Murray Schisgal.

The action occurs in New York City during the recent past.

The musical was presented in two acts (song assignments and division of acts unknown; see entry for *Love* for song assignments and division of acts in that production).

MUSICAL NUMBERS—"Harry's Letter," "Polyarts U.," "Why Bother?," "Paradise," "It's Love!," "The Chart," "Ellen's Credo," "Somebody," "The Test," "How Beautiful the Night Is," "What a Life!," "Lady," "If Harry Weren't Here," "My Brown Paper Hat," "Do I Love Him?"

NOTES—The Off Off Broadway musical *What About Luv?* had previously been seen Off Broadway in 1984 as *Love* (which also starred Judy Kaye). For more information about the different versions of this musical (the first New York production, a regional theatre version, and a London mounting), see entry for *Love*.

1757 What Happened. THEATRE: Judson Poets' Theatre; OPENING DATE: 1963; PERFORMANCES: Unknown; WORDS: Gertrude Stein; text adapted by Al Carmines; MUSIC: Al Carmines; DIRECTION: Lawrence Kornfeld

NOTES—Based on a 1922 text by Gertrude Stein, the Off Off Broadway musical *What Happened* was a thirty-two-minute dance and performance piece. It was revived at the Judson Poets' Theatre five times during the next few years, and appears to be Al Carmines' first major theatre work. *What Happened* was the first of six adaptations by Carmines of Stein's works, all of them directed by Lawrence Kornfeld, who became the director most associated with the composer. For almost twenty years Kornfeld directed the premieres of many of Carmines' works, including his longest-running musical, *Promenade* (1969; see entry). See separate entries for Carmines' other five adaptations of works by Gertrude Stein: *In Circles* (1967), *The Making of Americans* (1972), *Listen to Me* (1974), *A Manoir* (1977), and *Dr. Faustus Lights the Lights* (1979).

1758 What's a Nice Country Like You Doing in a State Like This? (1973). "A Red, White & Blue Revue!" THEATRE: Upstage at Jimmy's; OPENING DATE: April 19, 1973; PERFORMANCES: 543; LYRICS: Ira Gasman; MUSIC: Cary Hoffman; DIRECTION: Miriam Fond; CHOREOGRAPHY: Miriam Fond; SCENERY: Billy Puzo; COSTUMES: Danny Morgan; LIGHTING: Richard Delehanty; MUSICAL DIRECTION: Arnold Goss; PRODUCER: Budd Friedman

CAST—Betty Lynn Buckley, Sam Freed, Bill La Vallee, Priscilla Lopez, Barry Michlin

The revue was presented in two acts.

ACT ONE—"It's a Political-Satirical Revue" (Company), "Liberal's Lament" (Barry Michlin), "I'm in Love With—" (Priscilla Lopez), "Massage a Trois" (Company), "Changing Partners" (Priscilla Lopez, Barry Michlin, Betty Lynn Buckley), "Crime in the Streets" (Sam Freed, Bill La Vallee, Barry Michlin), "I'm in Love With—" (reprise) (Priscilla Lopez), "Street Suite": "Street People" (Company), "It's Getting Better" (Bill La Vallee, Company), "I Like Me" (Betty Lynn Buckley, Company), "I'm in Love With—" (reprise) (Priscilla Lopez), "Male Chauvinist" (Sam Freed, Betty Lynn Buckley), "Primary Tango" (Priscilla Lopez, Company), "Johannesburg" (Barry Michlin), "New York Suite": "But I Love New York" (Priscilla Lopez, Sam Freed), "Why Do I Keep Going to the Theatre?" (Betty Lynn Buckley, Barry Michlin), "I Found the Girl of My Dreams on Broadway" (Sam Freed), "But I Love New York" (reprise) (Sam Freed, Betty Lynn Buckley, Priscilla Lopez), "A Mugger's Work Is Never Done" (Bill La Vallee), "But I Love New York" (reprise) (Company)

ACT TWO—"Kissinger und Kleindeinst und Klein" (Company), "Farewell First Amendment" (Company), "Why Johnny?" (Betty Lynn Buckley), "The Right Place at the Right Time" (Company), "Love Story" (Sam Freed, Priscilla Lopez), "I'm Not Myself Anymore" (Barry Michlin), "Porcupine Suite": "People Are Like Porcupines" (Barry Michlin, Bill La Valle, Betty Lynn Buckley), "On a Scale of One to Ten" (Barry Michlin, Betty Lynn Buckley), "Threesome" (Bill La Vallee, Betty Lynn Buckley, Barry Michlin), "Come on, Daisy" (Betty Lynn Buckley, Company), "Whatever Happened to the Communist Menace?" (Company), Finale (Company)

NOTES—Based on a concept by Ira Gasman, Cary Hoffman, and Bernie Travis, the long-running revue *What's a Nice Country Like You Doing in a State Like This?* was a self-described "Red, White & Blue Revue," but the emphasis was definitely on the blue, in this distinctly left-leaning piece. The revue had first been produced Off Off Broadway as *What's a Nice Country Like You Doing in a State Like This?* (or, *Who Got America in Trouble?*) for twenty performances at St. Peter's Gate Theatre on October 16, 1972; this production was directed by Miriam Fond and was produced by Theatre at Noon. The revue later transferred to the American Place Theatre on January 10, 1973, for twelve additional performances. For the Off Broadway run at Upstage at Jimmy's, Miriam Fond continued in her role as director, and Bill LaValle and Bill Michlin, two cast members from the October 1972 version, were also seen in this production. In order to remain topical, new numbers were added and others deleted during the run.

In *The Billy Barnes Revue* (see entry), a running gag was the "Whatever Happened To" songs, in which a cast member sang short numbers regarding past fads and celebrities. *What's a Nice Country* used a similar device with the "I'm in Love With—" songs; ultimately, there were five of these mini-numbers, depicting a hapless girl who's in love with a bisexual, a sado-masochist, a gay activist, a transvestite, and a priest (to show the dearth of wit in the revue, the priest turns out to be in love with a nun). A Canadian (?) 7" LP (RMSC Records # 747003) by the Young People's Theatre (with a cast which included Andrea Martin and Martin Short) was released with eight numbers, some from the 1973 production (with at least one updated number ["Haldeman und Ehrlichman und Klein"] and one new song ["Communist Menace"]).

There was also a 1976 British cast album released on Galaxy Records (LP # GAL-6004); titled *What's a Nice Country Like U.S. Doing in a State Like This?*, the recording was a combination of songs from the 1973 production as well as other ones updated or rewritten in the intervening years.

In 1986, Samuel French, Inc., published the script (which included much new material). The revue was revived three times, Off Off Broadway in 1984 as *What's a Nice Country Like You Still Doing in a State Like This?*; Off Broadway in 1985 as *What's a Nice Country Like You...Doing in a State Like This?*; and Off Off Broadway in 1996 as *What's a Nice Country Like You Doing in a State Like This?* (see entries).

1759 What's a Nice Country Like You...Doing in a State Like This? (1985).

THEATRE: Actors' Playhouse; OPENING DATE: July 31, 1985; PERFORMANCES: 252; LYRICS: Ira Gasman; MUSIC: Cary Hoffman; DIRECTION: Suzanne Astor Hoffman; based on the original staging by Miriam Fond; CHOREOGRAPHY: Suzanne Astor Hoffman; SCENERY: Charles Plummer; COSTUMES: Henrietta Louise Howard; MUSICAL DIRECTION: Dean Johnson; PRODUCERS: Alice Kopreski and Bick Goss

CAST—Missy Baldino, Jane Brucker, Steve Mulch, Hugh Panaro, Rob Resnick

The revue was presented in two acts.

ACT ONE—"Get Out of Here" (Company), "Church and State" (Steve Mulch, Rob Resnick), "What the Hell" (Jane Brucker), "I'm in Love With—" (Missy Baldino), "Terrorist Trio" (Hugh Panaro, Rob Resnick, Steve Mulch), "Hard to Be a Liberal" (Hugh Panero), "I'm in Love Withm—" (reprise) (Missy Baldino), "Male Chauvinist Pig of Myself" (Hugh Panaro), "Liberation Tango" (Jane Brucker), "Changing Partners" (Missy Baldino, Steve Mulch, Jane Brucker), "The Last One of the Boys" (Steve Mulch), "I'm in Love With—" (reprise) (Missy Baldino), "Runaway Suite," "Runaways" (Steve Mulch, Missy Baldino), "It's Getting Better" (Steve Mulch), "I Like Me" (Missy Baldino), "I'm in Love With—" (reprise) (Missy Baldino), "Update" (Company), "I Just Pressed a Button" (Rob Resnick), "Nuclear Winter" (Missy Baldino, Hugh Panaro), "New York Suite": "But I Love New York" (Company), "Girl of My Dreams" (Hugh Panaro), "A Mugger's Work Is Never Done" (Rob Resnick), "How'm I Doing?" (Steve Mulch)

ACT TWO—Entr'acte (Dean Johnson), "Why Do I Keep Going to the Theatre?" (Company), "Carlos, Juan, and Miguel" (Steve Mulch, Hugh Panaro, Rob Resnick), "Nicaragua" (Jane Brucker), "I'm Not Myself Anymore" (Rob Resnick), "I'm in Love With" (reprise) (Missy Baldino), "Keeping the Peace" (Company), "I'm in Love With—" (reprise) (Missy Baldino), "America, You're Looking Good" (Hugh Panaro), "They Aren't There" (Missy Baldino, Steve Mulch), "Farewell" (Company), "Fill-er Up" (Missy Baldino), "Porcupine Suite": "People Are Like Porcupines" (Company), "I'm Not Taking a Chance on Love" (Missy Baldino, Hugh Panaro), "Threesome" (Steve Mulch, Jane Brucker, Rob Resnick), "Scale of 1 to 10" (Hugh Panaro, Missy Baldino), "People Are Like Porcupines" (reprise) (Company), "Everybody Ought to Have a Gun" (Rob Resnick, Company), "Hallelujah" (Steve Mulch, Company), "Johannesburg" (Steve Mulch), "I'm in Love With—" (reprise) (Missy Baldino), "Take Us Back, King George" (Jane Brucker, Hugh Panaro, Rob Resnick, Steve Mulch), "Come On, Daisy" (Missy Baldino, Company), Finale (Company)

NOTES—This was New York's third visit from *What's a Nice Country* (see entries for *What's a Nice Country Like You Still Doing in a State Like This?* [Off Broadway, 1973] and *What's a Nice Country Like You Still Doing in a State Like This?* [Off Off Broadway, 1984]). The new production (*What's a Nice Country Like You...Doing in a State Like This?*) played Off Broadway for over six months, and included both old and new material. A fourth edition (as *What's a Nice Country Like You Doing in a State Like This?*) appeared in 1996 (see entry).

1760 What's a Nice Country Like You Doing in a State Like This? (1996).

THEATRE: Theatre Row Theatre; OPENING DATE: November 23, 1996; PERFORMANCES: 45; SKETCHES: Ira Gasman; LYRICS: Ira Gasman; MUSIC: Cary Hoffman; DIRECTION: Miriam Fond; SCENERY: Joseph Miklojcik, Jr; COSTUMES: Ann-Marie Wright; LIGHTING: Robert Bessoir; MUSICAL DIRECTION: Ken Lundie; PRODUCERS: Anne Strickland Squadron and Eric Krebs

CAST—David Edwards, Janine LaManna, Sean McCourt, Vontress Mitchell, Karyn Quackenbush

The revue was presented in one act (sketch and song assignments unknown).

MUSICAL NUMBERS—Opening, "Liberal's Lament," "Church & State," "One Night Stand," "Be Frank," "Farewell (First Amendment)," "Button A," "Militia Song," "I'm in Love," "M.C.P.," "The Last One of the Boys," "Coffee Bar Suite," "Honky," "Coalition," "Farrakhan," "Fill 'Er Up," "Reality Check," "Pee Wee," "I'm Not Myself," "Watch Your Language," "Homeless Suite," "Rights of Bill," "How Do I Say I Love You?," "New York Suite," "Daisy," Finale

NOTES—The Off Off Broadway edition of *What's a Nice Country Like You Doing in a State Like This?* was the revue's fourth major visit in a period of almost twenty five years. See entries for the original 1973 Off Broadway production; the 1984 Off Off Broadway production (as *What's a Nice Country Like You Still Doing in a State Like This?*); and the 1985 Off Broadway production (as *What's a Nice Country Like You...Doing in a State Like This?*).

1761 What's a Nice Country Like You Still Doing in a State Like This? (1984).

THEATRE: American Place Theatre; OPENING DATE: October 21, 1984; PERFORMANCES: 31; LYRICS: Ira Gasman; MUSIC: Cary Hoffman; DIRECTION: Miriam Fond; CHOREOGRAPHY: Miriam Fond; SCENERY: Neil Peter Jampolis; COSTUMES: David C. Woolard and Mary Grace Froehlich; LIGHTING: Anne Militello; MUSICAL DIRECTION: John Spalla; PRODUCER: The American Place Theatre (Wynn Handman, Director; Julia Miles, Associate Director)

CAST—Brent Barrett, Jack Landron, Krista Neumann, Patrick Richwood, Diana Szlosberg

The revue was presented in two acts.

ACT ONE—"Get Out of Here" (Company), "Hello, Mr. Church" (Jack Landron, Patrick Richwood), "I'm in Love With—" (Diana Szlosberg), "What the Hell" (Jack Landron), "Greatest Performance" (Company), "I'm in Love With—" (reprise) (Diana Szlosberg), "Johannesburg" (Patrick Richwood), "Who Put the Glitz in Fritz" (Krista Neumann), "It's Hard to Be a Liberal Today" (Brent Barrett), "Changing Partners" (Diana Szlosberg, Krista Neumann, Brent Barrett), "Male Chauvinist Pig" (Brent Barrett), "Street Suite," "Runaways" (Patrick Landron, Diana Szlosberg, Company), "It's Getting Better" (Patrick Richwood), "I Like Me" (Krista Neumann, Company), "I'm in Love With—" (reprise) (Diana Szlosberg), "Carlos, Juan & Miguel" (Brent Barrett, Jack Landron, Patrick Richwood), "Button A" (Patrick Richwood), "Nuclear Winter" (Brent Barrett, Diana Szlosberg), "There's No Such Thing" (Jack Landron), "New York Suite," "But I Love New York" (Diana Szlosberg, Brent Barrett), "I Found the Girl of My Dreams on Broadway" (Brent Barrett), "But I Love New York" (reprise) (Diana Szlosberg, Krista Neumann, Brent Barrett), "A Mugger's Work Is Never Done" (Patrick Richwood), "How'm I Doing?" (Jack Landron), "But I Love New York" (reprise) (Company)

ACT TWO—"Why Do I Keep Going to the Theatre?" (Company), "I'm in Love With—" (reprise) (Diana Szlosberg), "Keeping the Peace" (Company), "God Is Not Finished with Me Yet" (Jack Landron), "America, You're Looking Good" (Brent Barrett), "They Aren't There" (Diana Szlosberg), "Farewell" (Company), "I'm Not Myself Anymore" (Jack Landron), "Porcupine Suite": "People Are Like Porcupines" (Jack Landron, Diana Szlosberg, Patrick Richwood), "I'm Not Taking a Chance on Love" (Krista Neumann, Brent Barrett), "Threesome" (Diana Szlosberg, Jack Landron, Patrick Richwood), "Scale of 1 to 10" (Brent Barrett, Krista Neumann), "People Are Like Porcupines" (reprise) (Company), "I'm in Love With—" (reprise) (Diana Szlosberg), "The Four R's" (Krista Neumann), "Take Us Back" (Patrick Richwood, Brent Barrett, Jack Landron), "Come On, Daisy" (Krista Neumann, Company), Finale (Company)

NOTES—*What's a Nice Country Like You Doing in a State Like This?* was a left-leaning revue which had originally opened Off Broadway in 1973 and played for 543 performances (see entry). The revue returned in 1984 in an Off Off Broadway production under the slightly altered title *What's a Nice Country Like You Still Doing in a State Like This?*, and included a mixture of old and new material. There were also two more editions, the first in a 1985 Off Broadway production (as *What's a Nice Country Like You...Doing in a State Like This?*) and the second in a 1996 Off Off Broadway version (as *What's a Nice Country Like You Doing in a State Like This?*); see entries for these editions.

1762 When Hell Freezes Over, I'll Skate.

THEATRE: Urban Arts Corps Theatre; OPENING DATE: January 1979; PERFORMANCES: 12 (estimated); CONCEIVED BY: Vinnette Carroll; DIRECTION: Vinnette Carroll; SCENERY: Marty Kappell; LIGHTING: Rick Belzer; MUSICAL DIRECTION: Cleavant Derricks; PRODUCER: Urban Arts Corps (Vinnette Carroll, Artistic Director; Anita MacShane, Managing Director)

CAST—Lynne Clifton-Allen, Brenda Braxton, Clinton Derricks-Carroll, Cleavant Derricks, Jeffrey Anderson-Gunter, Alde Lewis, Jr., Marilynn Winbush

NOTES—Vinette Carroll's Off Off Broadway revue *When Hell Freezes Over, I'll Skate* was a collection of poetry by Paul Laurence Dunbar, Lindamichellebaron, Langston Hughes, and Nikki Giovanni as well as songs by H.B. Barnum and by Cleavant Derricks and Clinton Derricks-Carroll. Richard F. Shepard in the *New York Times* said that although Carroll referred to the production as "an evening of poetry," it was also "an evening of entertainment and theatre." He praised the "delectable feast" of performers, poetry, songs, and choreography, and noted that while the authors of the poems weren't specifically identified, one could nonetheless "sit back and relish" the material in "blissful ignorance" of (but "contented appreciation" for) the specific writers.

A few months after the Off Off Broadway opening, the revue was seen for two performances beginning on May 1, 1979, as part of the Black Theatre Festival U.S.A. at the Mitzi E. Newhouse Theatre at Lincoln Center. In 1979, the revue was shown on public television's *Great Performances/Theatre in America*, and was later produced at the Coconut Grove Playhouse beginning on July 14, 1983. In May 1984, the revue was seen at the Kennedy Center. In a *Stagebill* interview with Jeanne Brown, Vinnette Carroll said the revue was "about always looking on the bright side. It's a celebration; it's not a lecture on black history."

The following song list is taken from the Kennedy Center program (the song writers were identified, but the poets were not):

ACT ONE—(Mid–19th Century, The Rural South) "Lord, Hear Your Child A-Callin'" (lyric and music by Cleavant Derricks and Clinton Derricks-Carroll), "The Colored Band," "The Dance," "Jealous," "Protest," "The Party" (traditional), "A Frolic," "Itching Heels," "Discovered," "He Is My Horse," "Encouragement," "A Negro Love Song," "Little Liza Jane" (traditional), "When Malindy Sings," "Just Come from the Fountain" (traditional), "Ring Them Bells" (traditional), "Ride Up in the Chariot" (traditional), "Ain't Got Time to Die" (traditional), "No Hiding Place" (traditional), "Let the Church Roll On" (traditional), "Come On Down to the River" (lyric and music by H.B. Barnum), "No More Auction Block" (traditional), "We Raise the Wheat," "Lost in the Wilderness" (lyric and music by Cleavant Derricks and Clinton Derricks-Carroll), "An Ante-Bellum Sermon," "Honor to the Dying Lamb" (traditional), "Ride On, King Jesus" (traditional), "Movin' Up to Higher Ground" (lyric and music by H.B. Barnum)

ACT TWO—(Mid-to-Late 20th Century, The Urban North), "Philadelphia Blues" (lyric and music by H.B. Barnum), "These Are the Blues," "How Can You Fix Your Mouth," "Fat Man Blues" (lyric and music by Cleavant Derricks and Clinton Derricks-Carroll), "Why I Went Off My Diet," "I Got the Blues," "I Wish I Knew How It Would Feel," "Something's Going On" (lyric and music by H.B. Barnum), "Dance to That," "Club Heaven," "My Man," "Who Loves You, Baby?," "When Hell Freezes Over," "My Man Was Here Today," "I Like the Body," "Myth," "When I Do My Thing," "When I Went Downtown" (traditional), "You're the One," "Look at That Gal," "Because," "A Funny Thing," "Blue Rendezvous," "Ignorance," "Zerox," "I'm Just Looking," "There You Are" (lyric and music by H.B. Barnum), "Letter from a Wife," "No Good Night"/"Autumn"/"To Mareta," "Reaching Back," "Talking About Love," "Benign Neglect," "I Thought You Knew"/"Tried Me a River," "That Last Goodbye" (lyric and music by H.B. Barnum), "Alone," "A Trip," "Housecleaning," "Poem for Joyce," "Play the Games," "I Am Here," "No More Looking Back Rap" (lyric and music by H.B. Barnum), "Harlem Beat" (lyric and music by Cleavant Derricks and Clinton Derricks-Carroll), "The Gospel Truth," "No More Looking Back" (lyric and music by H.B. Barnum)

1763 When Pigs Fly (a/k/a Howard Crabtree's When Pigs Fly). "A Side-Splitting Musical Extravaganza!" THEATRE: Douglas Fairbanks Theatre; OPENING DATE: August 14, 1996; PERFORMANCES: 840; SKETCHES: Mark Waldrop; LYRICS: Dick Gallagher; DIRECTION: Mark Waldrop; Phillip George, Associate Director; SCENERY: Peter Hauser; COSTUMES: Howard Crabtree; LIGHTING: Peter Hauser; MUSICAL DIRECTION: Philip Fortenberry; PRODUCERS: Gail Homer Seay, Peter Hauser, and Jane M. Abernethy in association with Marc Howard Segan

CAST—Stanley Bojarski, John Traecy Egan, David Pevsner, Jay Rogers, Michael West (as "Howard")

The revue was presented in two acts.

ACT ONE—"When Pigs Fly" (Michael West, Company), "You've Got to Stay in the Game" (John Traecy Egan, Stanley Bojarski, Michael West, David Pevsner), "Torch #1" (Jay Rogers), "Light in the Loafers" (David Pevsner, John Traecy Egan), "Coming Attractions with Carol Ann": "Coming Attraction #1" (John Traecy Egan, Jay Rogers, David Pevsner, Michael West), "Coming Attraction #2" (Michael West, "Angel Voices"), "Coming Attraction #3" (Stanley Bojarski, John Traecy Egan, Jay Rogers), "Not All Man" (David Pevsner, Michael West), "Torch #2" (Jay Rogers), "A Patriotic Finale (You Can't Take the Color Out of Colorado)" (John Traecy Egan, Company)

ACT TWO—"Wear Your Vanity with Pride" (Company), "Hawaiian Wedding Day" (Michael West), "Shaft of Love" (Jay Rogers, John Traecy Egan, Stanley Bojarski, Michael West), "Sam and Me" (David Pevsner), "Bigger Is Better" (John Traecy Egan, Michael West), "Torch #3" (Jay Rogers), "Laughing Matters" (Jay Rogers), "Over the Top"/"When Pigs Fly" (reprise) (Michael West, Company)

NOTES—In 1993, Howard Crabtree was the driving force behind the popular gay-themed revue *Whoop-Dee-Doo!* (see entry). Two years later, he and Mark Waldrop conceived *When Pigs Fly*, another revue infused with a gay sensibility; it too was a success, and ran almost three times longer than its predecessor, for a total of 840 performances.

But Crabtree wasn't around to enjoy the new hit; he died on June 28, 1996, just a few days after completing the revue and five weeks before its Off Broadway opening. Ironically, five months earlier Jonathan Larson had died, never seeing the opening of his revised Off Broadway version of *Rent* (the work had been briefly staged in an Off Off Broadway production fifteen months earlier; see entry) and never knowing he had authored what was to become one of the biggest successes in Broadway history. Both Larsen and Crabtree came from very different traditions of musical theatre, the dramatic and the comic, and one can only regret they never lived to create more musicals in their respective genres.

As for *When Pigs Fly*, with the exception of Michael West, all the actors were referred to by their own names; the script, published by Samuel French, Inc., in 1999, indicates all future productions could use the names of the actors playing in the revue, with the exception of the role created by Michael West who plays "Howard, who is always Howard."

One of the revue's highlights was the "Coming Attractions" sequence in which Carol Ann, the desperate "artistic director" of the Melody Barn, is determined to bring her audiences "the best of Broadway — shows with zip, zing, and plenty of pizzazz!" But her production of *Rockabye Hamlet* didn't go over well. And a revue of obscure songs by Richard Rodgers (*You Don't Know Dick*) flopped, and another revue of Frank Loesser's World War II songs (*Brutally Frank*) bombed (it seems Carol Ann's audiences want *stories* with their musicals). So for her next season, Carol Ann will present three original musicals, and she offers the audience a peek at them: *Quasimodo!* (the hero sings "I've got a hunch...I'm in love!"); *Lord of the Fries* (an ordinary housewife buys a box of Ore-Ida crinkle-cuts which spell out a secret message from God); and *Annie 3* (the former tyke is now a *Hello, Dolly!*-styled diva who sings uptempo inspirational songs ["Life is a cabernet"]).

The cast album was released by RCA Victor Records (CD # 09026-68729-2).

1764 When the Lights Go On Again. "A New 1940's Musical." THEATRE: Triad Theatre; OPENING DATE: January 18, 2007; PERFORMANCES: Still running as of December 31, 2007; BOOK: Bill Daugherty; LYRICS: See song list for credits; MUSIC: See song list for credits; DIRECTION: Bill Daugherty; CHOREOGRAPHY: Lori Leshner; LIGHTING: Tonya Pierre; MUSICAL DIRECTION: Doyle Newmyer; PRODUCER: Max Weintraub

CAST—The Moonlighters — Bill Daugherty (Billy Allen), Paul Kropfl (Joe Parker), Christina Morrell (Nancy Sanders), Connie Pachl (Connie Sanders)

The action occurs in the Hotel Roosevelt in December 1941 and "over there."

The revue was presented in one act.

MUSICAL NUMBERS—"Show Your Linen, Miss Richardson" (lyric by Johnny Mercer, music by Hanighen), "Don't Wake Up My Heart" (lyric and music by Wendling, Meyer, and Lewis), "Humpty Dumpty Heart" (from 1941 film *Playmates*; lyric by Johnny Burke, music by Jimmy Van Heusen), "Moonlight Serenade" (lyric by Mitchell Parish, music by Glenn Miller), "It's Make Believe Ballroom Time" (lyric and music by Block, Green, and Stoner), "When the Lights Go On Again (All Over the World)" (lyric and music by Seller, Marcus, and Benjamin), "You're a Lucky Fellow, Mr. Smith" (1941 film *Buck Privates*; lyric and music by Don Raye, Sonny Burke, and Hughie Prince), "No Love, No Nothin'" (1943 film *The Gang's All Here*; lyric by Leo Robin, music by Harry Warren), "It's a Lovely Day Tomorrow" (*Louisiana Purchase*, 1940; lyric and music by Irving Berlin), "I Left My Heart at the Stage Door Canteen" (*This Is the Army*, 1942; lyric and music by Irving Berlin), "They're Either Too Young or Too Old" (1943 film *Thank Your Lucky Stars*; lyric by Frank Loesser, music by Arthur Schwartz), "The Flat Foot Floogie" (lyric and music by Gaillard, Stewart, and Green), "He's 1-A in the Army (and He's A-1 in My Heart)" (lyric and music by Evans), "The Starlit Hour" (lyric by Mitchell Parish, music by DeRose), "We Mustn't Say Goodbye" (1943 film *Stage Door Canteen*; lyric by Al Dubin, music by James V. Monaco), "Any Bonds Today?" (independent song, 1941; lyric and music by Irving Berlin), "Nancy (With the Laughing Face)" (lyric by Silvers, music by Jimmy Van Heusen), "My Sister and I" (lyric and music by Zaret, Whitney, and Kramer), "G.I. Jive" (lyric and music by Johnny Mercer), "Don't Sit Under the Apple Tree (With Anyone Else But Me)" (1942 film *Private Buckaroo*; lyric and music by Lew Brown, Charles Tobias, and Sam H. Stept), "(There'll Be a) Hot Time in the Town of Berlin" (lyric and music by Bushkin and DeVries), "The White Cliffs of Dover" (lyric by Nat Burton, music by Walter Kent)

NOTES—This Off Off Broadway revue-like musical *When the Lights Go On Again* was set in the Big Band era of the 1940s; the cast played the roles of a musical quartet called the Moonlighters, a group which has just hit the big time when Pearl Harbor is attacked. Frank Scheck in the *New York Post* said the musical was "one warm nostalgia trip," and he noted that the songs from the World War II era "perfectly recapture a wonderful and vanished musical era."

The program didn't identify specific songs; the above list is taken from the original cast recording (released by Thoroughbred Records CD # TBR-

104). The production included six other songs (not recorded for the cast album), including "Happiness Is Just a Thing Called Joe" (1943 film *Cabin in the Sky*; lyric by E.Y. Harburg, music by Harold Arlen). The musical was performed on an abbreviated schedule (often playing just two or three performances each weekend), extended its run until the end of the year, and after a brief hiatus re-opened at the Triad in 2008 for weekend performances.

For similar World War II-era musicals, see entries for *Smiling Through* (1994), *Swingtime Canteen* (1995), and *We'll Meet Again* (1995).

When the Lights Go On Again is not to be confused with *When the Lights Come On*, a play which opened in regional theatre during the same season as the musical's New York premiere. Written by Brian Letscher, the play about football opened on April 13, 2007, at the Purple Rose Theatre Company in Chelsea, Michigan.

1765 When the Owl Screams. THEATRE: Square East; OPENING DATE: September 12, 1963; PERFORMANCES: 141; SCENES AND DIALOGUE: Created by the Company; MUSIC: Tom O'Horgan; DIRECTION: Paul Sills; SCENERY: Ralph Alswang; LIGHTING: Dan Butt; PRODUCERS: Bernard Sahlins and Paul Sills

CAST—Bob Dishy, MacIntyre Dixon, Paul Dooley, Andrew Duncan, Barbara Harris, Anthony Holland

The revue was presented in two acts (sketch and song assignments unknown).

ACT ONE—"New Wine in Old Bottles," "Operation Kid's Toy," "How Not to Win a Boy Friend," "Pythagoras Tells How He Discovered That There Are 360 Degrees in a Circle," "Karate," "Shy Man in a Loud Drug Store," "TV Sidelights on the March on Washington," "Galileo Demonstrates His Discovery That a Feather and a Heavy Object Fall at the Same Rate of Speed," "The High Holidays," "Long Day's Voyage Home," "Two Cigarettes for One," "Sex and the Single Girl," "Homosexual Priests," "Teachers' Strike Meeting"

ACT TWO—"Christine Keeler's Testimonial," "DeGaulle and the Test Ban Treaty," "Roy Cohen," "The Unmarried Couple," "A Picture Is Worth a Thousand Words," "Open Mouth," "The Modern Poetry Quintet"

NOTES—*When the Owl Screams* was the fourth Second City revue to play Off Broadway; see entry for *Seacoast of Bohemia* for a complete list of the Second City revues which were presented in New York; also see Appendix T.

MacIntyre Dixon, one of the Stewed Prunes (see entry for *Stewed Prunes*), joined the troupe for this edition. According to Milton Esterow in the *New York Times*, Barbara Harris was a "radiant, wide-eyed pixie ... unfailingly delightful." He praised her "gushing" portrayal of a high school girl who tells a reporter she identifies with President Kennedy because she too is a president (of her high school sorority), and in a spoof of New York high school teachers on strike (an event which had taken place on the Sunday before the revue opened), her voice sounded like "steel nails being rubbed on sandpaper." (And she must have been terrific in the Christine Keeler sequence.) The revue continued to explore current political topics (DeGaulle, the civil rights march on Washington [which had taken place less than three weeks before the revue opened], the Ecumenical Council, and Roy Cohn) as well as modern mores ["Sex and the Single Girl"] and even traditional theatre (the plays of Eugene O'Neill in "Long Day's Voyage Home").

The group was ahead of the headlines in *Alarums and Excursions* (1962; see entry) when it dealt with Vietnam, and now it was about four decades ahead of the times in its sketch about "Homosexual Priests."

1766 Where's Mamie?
NOTES—See entry for *First Lady Suite*.

1767 Whispers on the Wind. "A New Musical." THEATRE: Theatre de Lys; OPENING DATE: June 14, 1970; PERFORMANCES: 15; BOOK: John B. Kuntz; LYRICS: John B. Kuntz; MUSIC: Lor Crane; DIRECTION: Burt Brinckerhoff; SCENERY: David F. Segal; COSTUMES: Joseph G. Aulisi; LIGHTING: David F. Segal; MUSICAL DIRECTION: Jack Holmes; PRODUCERS: Bruce W. Paltrow and Mitchell Fink, by special arrangement with Lucille Lortel Productions, Inc.

CAST—DAVID CRYER (Narrator), NANCY DUSSAULT (First Woman), Patrick Fox (First Man), R.G. Brown (Second Man), Mary Louise Wilson (Second Woman)

The action occurs in the present time, in the suburbs and later in the city.

The musical was presented in two acts.

ACT ONE—"Whispers on the Wind" (Company), "Welcome Little One" (Company), "Midwestern Summer" (Patrick Fox, Company), "Why and Because" (David Cryer), "Children's Games" (Company), "Miss Cadwallader" (Nancy Dussault), "Upstairs Downstairs" (David Cryer, Patrick Fox), "Strawberries" (Company)

ACT TWO—"Is There a City?" (Company), "Carmen Viscenzo" (R.G. Brown, Company), "Neighbors" (Mary Louise Wilson), "Apples and Raisins" (Company), "Things Are Going Nicely" (Patrick Fox, Company), "It Won't Be Long" (Company), "Prove I'm Really Here" (Nancy Dussault), Finale (Company)

NOTES—*Whispers on the Wind* dealt with a young man who leaves his suburban background in order to find his place in the big city. For a moment or two the musical seemed to be sliding into *Allegro* (1947) territory, with a bit of *Company* (1970) on the side. During the next season, another musical (*Love Me, Love My Children*; see entry) dealt with a similar theme, this time with a female protagonist.

Unfortunately, the bland, whimsical story never found its own voice, and the musical disappeared after two weeks. In order to push the wispy story along, the script utilized a narrator; further, all the characters were nameless; and the dialogue was written in pretentious blank verse. All this might have been tolerable had the score been strong, but at best the lyrics and music were mildly pleasant and not particularly memorable.

Sege in *Variety* said the musical had "nowhere to go and not much of interest to say"; on the other hand, Edith Oliver in the *New Yorker* found *Whispers on the Wind* "a charmer—fresh, modest, and with a rare light touch." (She also noted, rather curiously, that the musical "is what it is ... all-white and non-rock.")

The script, published by Samuel French, Inc., in 1971, didn't include the song "Why and Because," and at least one regional production of the show also omitted this song.

A cast recording of sorts exists. When the musical was presented in workshop at Lincoln Center, the staged reading was recorded as a souvenir (unnamed label # SS-492). The cast included David Cryer, Nancy Dussault, and Patrick Fox (with Karen Morrow and Joe Ponazecki in roles eventually played by Mary Louise Wilson and R.G. Brown). The album consisted of twelve songs and four reprises, including five songs not used in the Off Broadway production: "The Very First Girl (Boy)," "Down the Fields," "The Children's Sake," "In the Mind's Eye," and "Then in the Middle."

1768 The Whistling Wizard and the Sultan of Tuffet (1969)/Winnie the Pooh (revival). THEATRE: Bil Baird Theatre; OPENING DATE: December 20, 1969; PERFORMANCES: 167; BOOK: Alan Stern; LYRICS: Bil Baird; MUSIC: Alan Stern; DIRECTION: Gordon Hunt; MUSICAL DIRECTION: Alvy West; PRODUCER: The American Puppet Arts Council; Arthur Cantor, Executive Producer

CAST—Fania Sullivan (J.P.), Byron Whiting (Heathcliff), Bil Baird (Dooley [Wizard], Casbah), Frank Sullivan (Turtle, Ali Booby [Sultan]), Robert Gerstein (Pasha), Christopher Kemble (Sasha, Akimbo, Dragon), Olga Felgemacher (Princess Peekaboo)

The action occurs in the Country of Tuffet and Land of Beyond.

The musical was presented in two acts.

NOTES—For the 1969-1970 season, Bil Baird offered a new puppet musical, *The Whistling Wizard and the Sultan of Tuffet*, which played for 167 performances (see entries for 1970 and 1973 revivals). During the run, a revival of *Winnie the Pooh* (1967; see entry) was presented for a total of twenty-three performances. As with most of Bil Baird's puppet musicals, *A Pageant of Puppet Variety* was included on the program.

1769 The Whistling Wizard and the Sultan of Tuffet (1970). THEATRE: Bil Baird Theatre; OPENING DATE: October 17, 1970; PERFORMANCES: 33

NOTES—See entry for information about the original 1969 production of *The Whistling Wizard and the Sultan of Tuffet* (book by Alan Stern, and lyrics and music by Bil Baird and Alan Stern). For the record, the following cast members in the 1970 production were: Cary Antebi (Pasha), Bil Baird (Dooley, Casbah), Peter Baird (Birds, Animals), Pady Blackwood (Dragon), David Canaan (Sasha, Akimbo), Olga Felgemacher (Peekaboo, J.P.), Frank Sullivan (Ali Booby, Turtle), Byron Whiting (Heathcliff). As with virtually all Bil Baird puppet shows, the bill also included *A Pageant of Puppet Variety*, which demonstrated the techniques and the art of puppetry.

The Whistling Wizard was again revived in 1973 (see entry).

1770 The Whistling Wizard and the Sultan of Tuffet (1973). THEATRE: Bil Baird's Theatre; OPENING DATE: October 17, 1973; PERFORMANCES: 36; PRODUCERS: The American Puppet Arts Council (Arthur Cantor, Executive Producer); a Bil Baird Marionettes Production

NOTES—*The Whistling Wizard and the Sultan of Tuffet* had originally been produced on December 20, 1969, for 167 performances; its first revival was on October 17, 1970, for thirty-three performances (see entries for both productions.) The musical's book was by Alan Stern, and the lyrics and music were by Stern and Bil Baird.

The 1973 revival was directed by Frank Sullivan and Lee Theodore, and the musical direction was by Alvy West. The two-act musical was designed by Bil Baird, and the lighting was by Peggy Clark. The cast members were Peter Baird (Akimbo; Sasha; Flying Carpet), Olga Felgemacher (Princess Peekaboo, J.P.), Jonathan E. Freeman (Sultan, Turtle), John O'Malley (Dooley, Wizard, Dooley Bird, Camel Driver), Bill Tost (Casbah, Pasha, Dragon), and Byron Whiting (Heathcliff, Camel, Magic Lamp).

The revival was accompanied by *Bil Baird's Variety*.

1771 White Widow. THEATRE: INTAR Theatre; OPENING DATE: December 4, 1993; PERFORMANCES: 13; BOOK: Paul Dick; LYRICS: Paul Dick; MUSIC: Paul Dick; DIRECTION: John Margulis; SCENERY: Jack Mehler; COSTUMES: Crystal Thompson; LIGHTING: Jack Mehler; MUSICAL DIRECTION: Christopher McGovern; PRODUCER: PASSAJ Productions

CAST—William Broderick (Don Rosario), Diana

DiMarzio (Donna Raffaella), Jim Festante (Tonio), Tim Tucker (Carmelo), Anthony Razzano (Malacarne), Don Stansfield (Nesti), Mitch Poulos (Maresciallo), Carrie Wilshusen (Donna Cinzia), Kay Elise Kleinerman (Ornella), John Savarese (Peppuzzo), Jerry Rodgers (Babbio), Deborah Unger (Vendor), Andrea Bianchi (Vendor), Dewey Moss (Vendor)

SOURCE—The play *Mafia* by Mario Fratti.

The action occurs in Sicily.

The musical was presented in two acts (division of acts and song assignments unknown; the songs are listed in performance order).

MUSICAL NUMBERS—"The Stoning," "Fish, Lemons, Chickens," "Bel Paese," "The Game," "The Letter," "Law, Order, Justice," "Two Young People in Love," "Basic Sicilian," "Music for a Murder," "We Mourn," "Donna Cinzia's Love," "Four Proverbs," "So Little Time," "Don't You Understand," "Not I," "To Build Tomorrow," "Time to Prepare for Donna Cinzia," "Only Yesterday," "All for You," "Bel Paese" (reprise)

NOTES—The obscure Off Off Broadway musical *White Widow* is one of a number of short-running musicals set in Italy (see entry for *Fortuna*). As of this writing, the musical is scheduled to be produced at the Roy Arias Theatre for sixteen performances beginning on May 9, 2008. Subtitled "A Sicilian Musical Passion," the production's press release indicated the plot dealt with a man who is stoned to death in modern-day Sicily. A reporter investigating the stoning uncovers the shocking reason for the murder.

1772 **Whoop-Dee-Doo! (a/k/a Howard Crabtree's Whoop-Dee-Doo!).** "A Musical Extravaganza." THEATRE: Actors' Playhouse; OPENING DATE: June 29, 1993; PERFORMANCES: 258; LYRICS: Jack Feldman, Dick Gallagher, Peter Morris, David Rambo, Bruce Sussman, and Mark Waldrop; Dick Gallagher, Peter Morris, and Mark Waldrop also appear to have contributed dialogue/sketch material; MUSIC: Brad Ellis, Jack Feldman, Dick Gallagher, David Rambo, Eric Schorr, and Bruce Sussman; DIRECTION: Phillip George; ADDITIONAL STAGING AND TAP CHOREOGRAPHY: David Lowenstein; SCENERY: Bill Wood; COSTUMES: Howard Crabtree; LIGHTING: Tracy Dedrickson; MUSICAL DIRECTION: Fred Barton; PRODUCERS: The Glines and Postage Stamp Xtravaganzas; Charles Catanese, John Glines, and Michael Wantuck, Executive Producers

CAST—Howard Crabtree, Keith Cromwell, Tommy Femia, David Lowenstein, Peter Morris, Jay Rogers, Ron Skobel, Richard Stegman, Alan Tulin

The revue was presented in two acts.

ACT ONE—"Whoop-Dee-Doo!" (lyric by Peter Morris, music by Dick Gallagher) (Howard Crabtree, Jay Rogers, Company), "Stuck on You" (lyric by Mark Waldrop, music by Dick Gallagher) (Alan Tulin, David Lowenstein, Keith Cromwell), "Teach It How to Dance" (lyric and music by Dick Gallagher) (Peter Morris, Alan Tulin, David Lowenstein, Richard Stegman), "Elizabeth" (lyric and music by David Rambo) (Keith Cromwell), "Nancy: The Unauthorized Musical" (lyrics by Mark Waldrop, music by Dick Gallagher) (Tommy Femia, Richard Stegman, David Lowenstein, Howard Crabtree), "Tough to Be a Fairy" (lyric by Mark Waldrop, music by Dick Gallagher) (Jay Rogers, Alan Tulin, Peter Morris), "Blue Flame" (lyric and music by Dick Gallagher) (David Lowenstein), "A Soldier's Musical" (lyric by Peter Morris, music by Dick Gallagher) (Company)

ACT TWO—"It's a Perfect Day (for an Outing)" (lyric by Mark Waldrop, music by Dick Gallagher) (Company), "Last One Picked" (lyric by Mark Waldrop, music by Dick Gallagher) (Alan Tulin), "As Plain as the Nose on My Face" (lyric by Peter Morris, music by Eric Schorr), "I Was Born This Way" (lyric by Peter Morris, music by Dick Gallagher) (Richard Stegman), "You Are My Idol" (lyric by Peter Morris, music by Brad Ellis), "The Magic of Me" (lyric and music by Bruce Sussman and Jack Feldman), "My Turn to Shine" ("The Faux Finale") (lyric by Peter Morris, music by Dick Gallagher) (Ron Femia), "Less Is More" (lyric by Mark Waldrop, music by Dick Gallagher) (Howard Crabtree, Company)

NOTES—*Whoop-Dee-Doo!* was a gay-themed revue, now mostly remembered for its lavish, over-the-top costumes designed by Howard Crabtree, one of the musical's cast members who also "conceived, created and developed" the work along with Charles Catanese, Dick Gallagher, Phillip George, Peter Morris, and Mark Waldrop.

The revue spoofed Nancy Reagan ("Nancy: The Unauthorized Musical"); presented its own version of the play *A Soldier's Play* (here, *A Soldier's Musical*); and touched upon various gay icons such as Elizabeth Taylor (a song sang the praises of "Elizabeth Taylor Hilton Wilding Todd Fisher Burton Burton Warner Fortensky") and Judy Garland (who, in concert, acknowledges her audience ["I haven't seen so many beautiful boys all in one place since Liza's wedding to Peter Allen—if you know what I mean"] as well as various celebrities in the audience [such as June Allyson: "You can always depend on her"]).

One edgy number, "It's a Lovely Day (for an Outing)," managed to include in its lyric a number of A List celebrities whom the chorus hopes to invite for an "outing."

The "nearly original cast recording" was released by RCA Victor Records (CD # 09026-68231-2), and the script was published by Samuel French, Inc., in 1995.

Howard Crabtree's next (and posthumous) revue, *When Pigs Fly* (a/k/a *Howard Crabtree's When Pigs Fly*), was an even bigger hit, running over two years (see entry).

1773 **Whores, Wars & Tin Pan Alley.** "An Evening of Songs by Kurt Weill." THEATRE: The Bitter End; transferred to the Sheridan Square Playhouse on July 3, 1969; OPENING DATE: June 16, 1969; PERFORMANCES: 72; LYRICS: See song list for credits; MUSIC: Kurt Weill; PRODUCER: Allen Swift and Seymour Vall in association with I.P.C.

CAST—Martha Schlamme, Alvin Epstein, Ronald Clairmont (Piano)

The revue was presented in two acts (all songs performed by Martha Schlamme and Alvin Epstein).

ACT ONE—"Alabama Song" (from *The Rise and Fall of the City of Mahagonny*, 1930; English lyric by Bertolt Brecht), "Moritat" ("Ballad of Mack the Knife") (*The Threepenny Opera*, 1928; original German lyric by Bertolt Brecht, English lyric by Marc Blitzstein), "Barbara-Song" (*The Threepenny Opera*, 1928; original German lyric by Bertolt Brecht, English lyric by Marc Blitzstein), "Havana—Lied and Duet" (*The Rise and Fall of the City of Mahagonny*, 1930; original German lyric by Bertolt Brecht, English lyric by either Will Holt or Arnold Weinstein), "Instead-Of Song" (*The Threepenny Opera*, 1928; original German lyric by Bertolt Brecht, English lyric by Marc Blitzstein), "Ballad of Sexual Slavery" (*The Threepenny Opera*, 1928; original German lyric by Bertolt Brecht, English lyric by George Tabori), "Zuhhalterballade" ("Ballad of the Pimp and the Whore") (*The Threepenny Opera*, 1928; original German lyric by Bertolt Brecht, English lyric by Marc Blitzstein), "Seerrauber-Jenny" ("Pirate Jenny") (*The Threepenny Opera*, 1928; original German l, lyric by Bertolt Brecht, English lyric by Marc Blitzstein), "Kanonensong" ("Army Song" a/k/a "Recruitment Song") (*The Threepenny Opera*, 1928; original German lyric by Bertolt Brecht, English lyric by Marc Blitzstein), "Ballade vom Soldaten Weib" ("Ballad of the Soldier's Wife") (German lyric by Bertolt Brecht; English lyricist unknown; this 1946 song was the last collaboration between Brecht and Weill), "Essen" ("Eating") (*The Rise and Fall of the City of Mahagonny*, 1930; original German lyric by Bertolt Brecht, English lyric by Arnold Weinstein), "Wie Man Sich Bettet" ("As You Make Your Bed") (*The Rise and Fall of the City of Mahagonny*, 1930; original German lyric by Bertolt Brecht, English lyric by Will Holt)

ACT TWO—"Le Roi d'Aquitaine" (*Marie Galante*, 1934; lyric by Jacques Duval), Medley from *Johnny Johnson* (1936) (which specific songs were performed are unknown; lyrics by Paul Green), "That's Him" (*One Touch of Venus*, 1943; lyric by Ogden Nash), "Speak Low" (*One Touch of Venus*, 1943; lyric by Ogden Nash), "Susan's Dream" (*Love Life*, 1948; lyric by Alan Jay Lerner), "September Song" (*Knickerbocker Holiday*, 1938; lyric by Maxwell Anderson), "The Saga of Jenny" (*Lady in the Dark*, 1941; lyric by Ira Gershwin), "Lost in the Stars" (*Lost in the Stars*, 1949; lyric by Maxwell Anderson), Songs from *Happy End* (1929) (original German lyrics by Bertolt Brecht; English lyric for "The Sailor's Tango" by Will Holt): "The Mandalay Song," "The Sailor's Tango" "Surabaya Johnny," "Bilbao-Song," "The Survival Song" (*The Threepenny* Opera, 1928; original German lyric by Bertolt Brecht, English lyric by Marc Blitzstein), Finale

NOTES—*Whores, Wars & Tin Pan Alley* was another Kurt Weill tribute, and was in effect an unofficial revival of *The World of Kurt Weill in Song* (a/k/a *A Kurt Weill Cabaret*). See entry for 1963 production of *The World of Kurt Weill in Song* for more information about Off Broadway revues and musicals that featured music by Kurt Weill; also see Appendix O.

During the revue's run, the medley of songs from *Johnny Johnson* was deleted and "My Ship" (*Lady in the Dark*, 1941; lyric by Ira Gershwin) was added.

1774 **Who's Who, Baby?** THEATRE: Players Theatre; OPENING DATE: January 29, 1968; PERFORMANCES: 16; BOOK: Gerald Frank (not credited in program); LYRICS: Johnny Brandon; MUSIC: Johnny Brandon; DIRECTION: Marvin Gordon; CHOREOGRAPHY: Marvin Gordon; SCENERY: Alan Kimmel; COSTUMES: Alan Kimmel; LIGHTING: Marshall Williams; MUSICAL DIRECTION: Leslie Harnley; PRODUCERS: Edmund J. Ferdinard and Charlotte Schiff, by arrangement with George Wiener

CAST—Jacqueline Mayro (Carol Winslow), Marcia Lewis (Daisy), Danny Guerrero (Smitty), Frank Andre (Benny Hare), Glory Van Scott (Sabine), Gloria Kaye (Frankie), Tommy Breslin (Al), Tom Eatman (Louis), Ural Wilson (Jean), Humphrey Davis (Sir Peveril Ballantyne), Erik Howell (Toby a/k/a Lord MacLaren)

SOURCE—An early version of the book for the musical (apparently written by Guy Bolton) was based on the 1934 play *Who's Who* by Bolton and P.G. Wodehouse.

The action occurs in the present, here, there, and everywhere on the island of Manuella.

The musical was presented in two acts.

ACT ONE—"Island of Happiness" (Humphrey Davis, Ural Wilson, Tom Eatman, Jacqueline Mayro, Frank Andre, Glory Van Scott, Gloria Kaye, Marcia Lewis, Tommy Breslin, Danny Guerrero), "That'll Be the Day" (Erik Howell, Jacqueline Mayro), "Come-Along-a-Me, Babe" (Frank Andre, Tommy Breslin, Danny Guerrero, Gloria Kaye), "Nothin's Gonna Change" (Frank Andre, Gloria Kaye), "There Aren't Many Ladies in the Mile End Road" (Marcia Lewis), "Syncopatin'" (Jacqueline Mayro, Tom Eatman, Ural Wilson, Danny Guerrero, Frank Andre, Marcia Lewis, Tommy Breslin, Gloria Kaye, Erik Howell), "Syncopatin'" (reprise) (Tom Eatman, Ural Wilson, Danny Guerrero, Tommy Breslin, Gloria Kaye, Humphrey Davis),

"Voodoo" (Glory Van Scott, Tom Eatman, Ural Wilson), "How Do You Stop Loving Someone?" (Gloria Kaye, Erik Howell, Jacqueline Mayro, Frank Andre), "That'll Be the Day" (reprise) (Frank Andre)

ACT TWO—"Come-Along-a-Me, Babe" (reprise) (Erik Howell), Drums (Gloria Kaye, Tommy Breslin, Danny Guerrero, Erik Howell), "Feminine-inity" (Marcia Lewis, Jacqueline Mayro, Gloria Kaye, Glory Van Scott), "That's What's Happening, Baby" (Frank Andre, Glory Van Scott, Tom Eatman, Ural Wilson, Gloria Kaye, Erik Howell, Danny Guerrero, Tommy Breslin, Jacqueline Mayro, Marcia Lewis), "Me" (Frank Andre), "Syncopatin'" (reprise) (Frank Andre, Erik Howell, Humphrey Davis, Marcia Lewis, Ural Wilson, Tom Eatman, Tommy Breslin, Danny Guerrero), "Island of Happiness" (reprise) (Glory Van Scott, Ural Wilson, Tom Eatman), "Nobody to Cry To" (Jacqueline Mayro), "Feminine-inity" (reprise) (Marica Lewis, Humphrey Davis), Finale (Company)

NOTES—Despite its rather disappointing score, Johnny Brandon got by with *Cindy* (1964; see entry), which played for the better part of a year. But *Who's Who, Baby?* suffered from major book problems and was gone in two weeks.

Based on a 1934 play by P.G. Wodehouse and Guy Bolton, the musical's script went uncredited (through the preview period, apparently Gerald Frank was credited; in the meantime, Bolton refused program credits for the project although the musical's book seems to have been originally based on an early version which he had written).

The musical dealt with a young Scotsman and a leader of a rock group who discover they were mistakenly switched at birth and thus have been living each other's lives. So they exchange identities (and girlfriends), only to later switch back to their old lives. Dan Sullivan in the *New York Times* noted that the evening began as a "spoof of a drippy musical" and then almost immediately became what it was spoofing. He singled out "That's What's Happening, Baby" ("a good rhythm tune"), but found the other songs lacking. Incidentally, "Syncopatin'" was later heard in Brandon's 1979 musical *Suddenly the Music Starts* (see entry).

Jacqueline Mayro, who created the role of Baby June in the original Broadway production of *Gypsy* (1959), was here making her second appearance in an Off Broadway musical by Johnny Brandon (she had created the title role in *Cindy*). *Who's Who, Baby?* found Glory Van Scott in her second musical which included a number called "Voodoo" ("Voudou" in the original 1954 production of *House of Flowers*).

1775 Why Do I Deserve This? (Womit Haben wir das Verdient?). THEATRE: Barbizon-Plaza Theatre; OPENING DATE: January 18, 1966; PERFORMANCES: 12; SKETCHES: Kay and Lore Lorentz, Eckart Hachfeld, and Martin Morlock; LYRICS: Wolfgang Franke and Mischa Leinek; MUSIC: Werner Kruse (Krause), Emil Schuchardt, and Fritz Maldener; DIRECTION: Kay Lorentz; SCENERY: Fritz Butz; COSTUMES: Fritz Butz; LIGHTING: Peter Frass-Wolfsburg; PRODUCERS: Gert von Gontard and Felix G. Gerstman, in association with the Deutschen Theater, Inc.

CAST—Das Kom(m)odchen Company (Lore Lorentz, Karl-Heinz Gerdesmann, Ernst Hilbich, Kay Lorentz, Werner Vielhaber)

NOTES—The revue *Why Do I Deserve This?* (*Womit Haben wir das Verdient?*) was performed in German, and was the Kom(m)odchen Company's second revue to play the Barbizon-Plaza Theatre (see entry for *Between Whisky and Vodka* [1961]); during the next few years one or two more productions of (non-musical) German works and at least one Indian dance company were booked into the theatre.

The Kom(m)odchen Company was a satiric political troupe based in Dusseldorf, and Richard F. Shepard in the *New York Times* noted that their name was a play on words ("komodchen" meant "little comedy" and "kommodchen" meant "little drawer"). Shepard reported that the evening included a title song which asked why no one seems to like Germany; a number about how Germans can be easily assimilated into New York City because of the town's numerous German restaurants; and a sketch about two Berlin clowns, one from the East, the other from the West, and their different attitudes toward humor. There was also a strange sketch about a Jewish German actor who wants to play Shylock but is told that in Germany only "moral" plays (such as *The Diary of Anne Frank*) are produced. Shepard concluded that *Why Do I Deserve This?* was "gemutlicher evening."

1776 Why I Love New York. THEATRE: Judson Poets' Theatre; OPENING DATE: October 10, 1975; PERFORMANCES: Unknown; BOOK: Al Carmines; LYRICS: Al Carmines; MUSIC: Al Carmines; DIRECTION: Leonard Peters; CHOREOGRAPHY: Bob Herget; SCENERY: Jimmy Cuomo; COSTUMES: Carol Oditz; LIGHTING: Todd Lichienstein; MUSICAL DIRECTION: Al Carmines; PRODUCER: Judson Poets' Theatre

CAST—Cast included Philip Owens, Stephen Holt, Lou Bullock, David Summers, Lee Guilliatt, Emily Adams, Barbara Sandek, Jeffrey Knox, Judy Noble, Sandy Padilla, Alice Carey, Elly (Ellie) Schadt, Terence Burk, Jim Kaufman, Joseph Adorante, Essie Borden, Aldyn McKean, Margaret Wright, Beverly Wideman, Connie Campbell, Trisha Long, Billy Conway, Bob Helm, Paul Rounsaville, Mae Gautier, Darrell Husted, Joyce Beebe, Bill Altham, Alice Garraro, Patricia Triana, Van Moore The action occurs in New York City.

NOTES—Al Carmines' Off Off Broadway *Why I Love New York* was more in the nature of a revue than a book musical, and was, in the words of Mel Gussow in the *New York Times*, a "positively passionate" evening extolling Carmines' love for his adopted city. Gussow noted that while one sequence took place in the Museum of Modern Art, the show, with characters ranging from bums to prostitutes to hustlers, was "much more at home on seedy Eighth Avenue." He indicated the work was "suffused with radiant optimism and sentiment," and speculated that Carmines was in a sense a "counter-culture" Oscar Hammerstein II.

Gussow praised Carmines' score, including an "upbeat ... Judy Garlandish" "I'm Gonna Be a Star" (which was sung in the Port Authority Bus Terminal), a "rapturous" "How Do You Love a City?," and other "melodic" songs such as "Staten Island Barcarolle" and "New York Is So Hard." Gussow noted that whenever the musical was singing, it soared; but when it "stops to talk, it stands still." Including Carmines, the cast, and the chorus, the production boasted a total of forty-nine performers, among them members of Carmines' stock company, which included Lee Guilliatt, Essie Borden, and Margaret Wright, the latter portraying the Statue of Liberty "off her perch." One song from the musical ("A Woman Needs Approval Now and Then") surfaced in the 1982 revue *The Gospel According to Al* (see entry).

1777 Wild Men. "A Musical ... Sort Of." THEATRE: Westside Theatre; OPENING DATE: May 6, 1993; PERFORMANCES: 59; BOOK: Peter Burns, Mark Nutter, Rob Riley, and Tom Wolfe; LYRICS: Mark Nutter; MUSIC: Mark Nutter; DIRECTION: Rob Riley; CHOREOGRAPHY: Jim Corti; SCENERY: Griswold; COSTUMES: John Paoletti; LIGHTING: Geoffrey Bushor; MUSICAL DIRECTION: Lisa Yeargan; PRODUCERS: James D. Stern in association with Doug Meyer

CAST—Rob Riley (Stuart Penn), David Lewman (Donnie Lodge), George Wendt (Ken Finnerty), Peter Burns (Greg Neely), Joe Liss (Artie Bishop)

The action occurs at the present time in the North Woods.

The musical was presented in two acts (song assignments unknown).

ACT ONE—"Come Away," "What Stuart Has Planned," "True Value," "Wimmins," "Ooh, That's Hot," "We're Wild Men," "Lookit Those Stars"

ACT TWO—"The 'Un' Song," "It's You," "My Friend, My Father," "Get Pissed," "Now I Am a Man," "Come Away" (reprise)

NOTES—The short-lived musical *Wild Men* was about male bonding and took place during a weekend retreat in the wilderness. Jeffrey Sweet in *The Best Plays of 1992-1993* noted the musical often seemed like an extended sketch, but he nonetheless praised its "stupid comedy" (the kind that "only smart people can create") and he enjoyed Mark Nutter's score that parodied popular music.

Mel Gussow in the *New York Times* found the first act "fast and silly," and said the songs are "sung, stomped and shouted and often boast of their political correctness." But he felt the second act meandered ("like an improvisation or a vaudeville routine that knows no end"), and speculated the evening might have been more effective in one act.

1778 The Wild Party. THEATRE: City Center Stage I/Manhattan Theatre Club; OPENING DATE: February 24, 2000; PERFORMANCES: 54; BOOK: Andrew Lippa; LYRICS: Andrew Lippa; MUSIC: Andrew Lippa; DIRECTION: Gabriel Barre; CHOREOGRAPHY: Mark Dendy; SCENERY: David Gallo; COSTUMES: Martin Pakledinaz; LIGHTING: Kenneth Posner; MUSICAL DIRECTION: Stephen Oremus; PRODUCER: Manhattan Theatre Club (Lynne Meadow, Artistic Director; Barry Grove, Executive Producer)

CAST—JULIA MURNEY (Queenie), BRIAN D'ARCY JAMES (Burrs), Todd Anderson (Reno), Ron J. Todorowski (Kegs), Alix (Alexandra) Korey (Madelaine True), Raymond Jaramillo McLeod (Eddie), Megan Sikora (Peggy), James Delisco Beeks (Max), Felicia Finley (Rose Himmelsteen), Peter Kapetan (Sam Himmelsteen), Amanda Watkins (Ellie), Lawrence Keigwin (Jackie), Charles Dillon (Oscar d'Armano), Kevin Cahoon (Phil d'Armano), Kena Tangi Dorsey (Dolores), Jennifer Cody (Mae), Kristin McDonald (Nadine), IDINA MENZEL (Kate), TAYE DIGGS (Black), Charlie Marcus (The Neighbor), Steven Pasquale (The Cop)

SOURCE—The 1929 poem *The Wild Party* by Joseph Moncure March.

The action occurs in an apartment in 1929.

The musical was presented in two acts.

ACT ONE—"Queenie Was a Blonde" (Julia Murney, Brian d'Arcy James, Company), "The Apartment (Sunday Noon)" (Julia Murney, Brian d'Arcy James, Company), "Out of the Blue" (Julia Murney), "What a Party" (Company), "Raise the Roof" (Company), "Look at Me Now" (Idina Menzel), "Poor Child" (Idina Menzel, Taye Diggs, Julia Murney, Brian d'Arcy James), "An Old-Fashioned Love Story" (Alix Korey), "The Juggernaut" (Julia Murney, Taye Diggs, Idina Menzel, Brian d'Arcy James, Julia Murney), "A Wild, Wild Party" (Charles Dillon, Kevin Cahoon, Julia Murney, Brian d'Arcy James, Company), "Two of a Kind" (Raymond Jaramillo McLeod, Jennifer Cody), "Maybe I Like It This Way" (Julia Murney), "What Is It About Her?" (Brian d'Arcy James, Julia Murney)

ACT TWO—"The Life of the Party" (Idina Menzel), "Who Is This Man?" (Julia Murney), "I'll Be Here" (Taye Diggs), "Listen to Me" (Taye Diggs, Brian d'Arcy James, Idina Menzel, Julia Murney), "Let Me Drown" (Brian d'Arcy Jones, Idina Menzel, Company), "The Fight" (Company), "Mary Jane" (Peter Kapetan, James Delisco Beeks), "Come with

Me" (Julia Murney, Taye Diggs, Company), "Jackie's Last Dance" (Lawrence Keigwin), "Make Me Happy" (Brian d'Arcy James, Taye Diggs, Julia Murney), "How Did We Come to This?" (Julia Murney)

NOTES—As the theatrical fates would have it, *The Wild Party*, Joseph Moncure March's epic poem about a night-long Jazz Age party that goes terribly wrong, was the subject of two musicals during the 1999-2000 theatre season. Andrew Lippa's Off Broadway version opened first, on February 24, 2000, and then on April 13 Michael John LaChiusa's adaptation premiered on Broadway at the Virginia (now August Wilson) Theatre. With less than rave reviews, Lippa's version didn't transfer to Broadway. But even if it had received stellar reviews, LaChiusa's version was already booked at the Virginia, and perhaps possible investors for a Broadway transfer of Lippa's adaptation might have been scared off by the prospect of dueling wild parties during the same Broadway spring season. When LaChiusa's version opened, it was cooly received, possibly because the critics had just seen Lippa's adaptation two months earlier. So the two musicals in effect cancelled each other out, and LaChiusa's musical lasted only sixty-eight performances.

During the preview period of Lippa's version, the song "The Gal for Me" was dropped.

Happily, both scores were recorded, Lippa's on RCA Victor Records (CD # 09026-63695-2) and LaChiusa's on Decca Broadway Records (CD # 012-159-003-2), and so whether the listener saw one, both, or neither of the two versions, the scores themselves offer lyrically and melodically interesting scores and of course are also fascinating for comparison purposes (if only the Leroy Anderson-Arnold B. Horwitt *Wonderful Town* score were available for comparison to the Leonard Bernstein-Betty Comden-Adolph Green adaptation!).

There is actually a *third* score of *The Wild Party.* In 1975, the poem was filmed with screenplay, lyrics, and music by Walter Marks, who wrote the scores for the Broadway musicals *Bajour* (1964) and *Golden Rainbow* (1968) as well as the Off Off Broadway musical *Body Shop* (see entry for the latter). Marks' lively score was comprised of eight songs: "That Queenie of Mine," "Funny Man," "We're Goin' to a Wild Party," "I Am Serene Again" (an amusing Noel Coward spoof), "Singapore Sally," "The Herbert Hoover Drag," "Ain't Nothin' Bad About Feeling Good," and "Sunday Morning Blues." The film was co-produced by Merchant/Ivory Productions, and was directed by James Ivory. Patricia Birch was the choreographer, and Queenie was played by Raquel Welch.

1779 Wilder. THEATRE: Peter Jay Sharp Theatre; OPENING DATE: October 26, 2003; PERFORMANCES: 21; BOOK, LYRICS, AND MUSIC: Erin Cressida Wilson, Jack Herrick, and Mike Craver; DIRECTION: Lisa Portes; CHOREOGRAPHY: Jane Comfort; SCENERY: G.W. Mercier; COSTUMES: G.W. Mercier; LIGHTING: Jane Cox; MUSICAL DIRECTION: Jack Herrick; PRODUCERS: Playwrights Horizons (Tim Sanford, Artistic Director; Leslie Marcus, Managing Director; William Russo, General Manager); Ira Weitzman, Associate Producer

CAST—Mike Craver (Mike), John Cullum (Old Wilder), Jack Herrick (Jack), Lacey Kohl (Jessie, Melora), Jeremiah Miller (Wilder)

SOURCE—The play *Cross-Dressing in the Depression* by Erin Cressida Wilson.

The action occurs during the 1930s in a dilapidated brothel in Denver.

The musical was presented in one act.

NOTES—The musical *Wilder* dealt with an older man (John Cullum) who looks back on his younger self (Jeremiah Miller) when he once lived in the attic of a brothel.

Bruce Weber in the *New York Times* said the creators of the musical were trying for something different, but he felt the evening was a "lost cause," noting the work was "familiar," "pretentious," and, at eighty minutes, "tedious." He was also disappointed with the music, and said that beginning with the opening song ("Blow Out the Candle") the score was "lackluster."

John Cullum seems to be the only Broadway performer whose cast recording performances cover the longest time span. He was first heard on the original Broadway cast recording of *Camelot* (1960), when he created the role of Sir Dinadan. Forty-seven years later, his role of H.C. Curry was preserved on the 2007 revival cast recording of *110 in the Shade*, and in between he was represented on the cast albums of such musicals as *On a Clear Day You Can See Forever* (1965), *Shenandoah* (1975), *On the Twentieth Century* (1978), and *Urinetown* (2001).

1780 Will the Mail Train Run Tonight? THEATRE: New Bowery Theatre; OPENING DATE: January 9, 1964; PERFORMANCES: 8; BOOK: Malcolm L. LaPrade; LYRICS: Malcolm L. LaPrade; MUSIC: Alan Heim; DIRECTION: Jon Baisch; CHOREOGRAPHY: Lynne Fippinger; SCENERY: Gene Czernicki; COSTUMES: Joe Crosby; LIGHTING: Joseph Kreisel; MUSICAL DIRECTION: Possibly Helen Smith; PRODUCER: Jon Baisch

CAST—Fred Jackson (Truman Pendennis), Jerome Zeffren (Harold Stanfast), Peter Lombard (Simon Darkway), Ross Gifford (Dick Sneath), Naomi Riseman (Mrs. Hopewell), Barbara Cole (Prudence), Lela Lawrence (Carlotta Cortez)

SOURCE—A play by Hugh Nevill.

The action occurs in Upper New York State during the 1890s.

The musical was presented in two acts (song assignments unknown).

ACT ONE—"So Much to Be Thankful For," "Dearer to Me," "Nature's Serenade," "Honeymoon Choo-Choo," "Hickory, Dickory," "Comes the Dawn," "Paper Matches," "To Dream or Not to Dream," "Prudence, Have Faith," "Villainy"

ACT TWO—"Three Cowards Craven," "Vengeance," "This Decadent Age," "Heroism," "A Slip of a Girl," "Remember Him," "I'll Walk Alone," "Heroism (reprise)," "The Fall of Valor," "Age of Miracles," "Bitter Tears," "No Sacrifice," Finale

NOTES—Since the mid-1930s, Off Broadway had been spoofing old-time melodramas (see entries for *Murder in the Old Red Barn* [1936], *Naughty-Naught* [1937] and *The Fireman's Flame* [1937]). The latest such spoof played for just one week. (In 1970, another spoof appeared when *The Drunkard* opened.)

In his review of *Will the Mail Train Run Tonight?*, Lewis Funke in the *New York Times* answered the title's question: "Yes it did — interminably." He also mentioned it had been a "tough" month for trains, alluding to the "repaired" version of Tennessee Williams' *The Milk Train Doesn't Stop Here Anymore* which had "derailed" a week earlier (it ran for five performances; the earlier [1963] version of the play had lasted for sixty-nine performances). (For more information about "train" musicals, see entry for *Frimbo.*)

1781 Will They Ever Love Us on Broadway? THEATRE: AMAS Repertory Theatre; OPENING DATE: October 22, 1981; PERFORMANCES: 16; BOOK, LYRICS, AND MUSIC: Osayande Baruti (in consultation with Mabel Robinson and Coleridge-Taylor Perkinson); DIRECTION: Mabel Robinson; CHOREOGRAPHY: Mabel Robinson; SCENERY: Thomas Barnes; COSTUMES: Judy Dearing; LIGHTING: John Enea; MUSICAL DIRECTION: Fred Gripper; PRODUCER: AMAS Repertory Theatre (Rosetta LeNoire, Founder and Artistic Director)

CAST—J. Herbert Kerr, Jr. (Kwame Kombs), Marva Hicks (Jessie Day), L. Edmond Wesley (Sam Johnson), Roma Maffia (Rosita Consuela Rialto), William Lucas (I.A. Prince), Ed Battle (Rafael Fredericks), Fred Gripper (Rehearsal Pianist), Valencia Edner (Savanna Fredericks), Melodee Savage (Cast Member), James Judy (Ivan Dierch), Dwayne Grayman (George Jenkins)

The action occurs on the stage of a Broadway theatre in 1981.

The musical was presented in two acts.

NOTES—The show-business-themed *Will They Ever Love Us on Broadway?* was presented under an Off Off Broadway contract.

1782 Will You Marry Me? THEATRE: The Opera Ensemble of New York; OPENING DATE: March 8, 1989; PERFORMANCES: 3; LIBRETTO: Charles Kondek; MUSIC: Hugo Weisgall; DIRECTION: Charles Kondek; SCENERY: Russell Metheny; COSTUMES: Hope Hanafin; LIGHTING: Michael Giannitti; MUSICAL DIRECTION: Donald W. Johnson; PRODUCER: The Opera Ensemble of New York (John J.D. Sheehan, Executive Director; Jonathan Tunick, Music Director)

CAST—Andrea Broido, David Trombley

SOURCE—The 1904 play *A Marriage Has Been Arranged* by Alfred Sutro.

The action occurs in a hotel roof garden in New York City during the 1930s.

The opera was presented in one act.

NOTES—Hugo Weisgall's opera *Will You Marry Me?* was a world premiere, and it constituted one of three works in *An Evening of Music by Hugo Weisgall* which was presented by the Opera Ensemble of New York. The two other works were a revival of Weisgall's 1952 opera *The Stronger* (libretto by Richard Hart; the one-act opera was based on August Strindberg's play, which had its New York premiere in 1913) and the song cycle *The Golden Peacock* (based on Yiddish music and texts, the seven songs were performed in English translations by Albert Weisser).

Will You Marry Me? dealt with a self-made millionaire who sets his cap on a young socialite in search of a rich husband; but the young woman may not be amenable to the millionaire's proposal of marriage. Bernard Holland in the *New York Times* noted that David Trombley's performance was an "admirable achievement" because he was a last-minute replacement (for Michael Willson, whose name appeared on early flyers for the opera) and had to learn the role in one week.

1783 Williams & Walker. "A Musical Entertainment." THEATRE: American Place Theatre; OPENING DATE: March 9, 1986; PERFORMANCES: 77; PLAY: Vincent D. Smith; LYRICS: See song list for credits; MUSIC: See song list for credits; DIRECTION: Shauneille Perry; CHOREOGRAPHY: Lenwood Sloan; SCENERY: Marc D. Malamud; COSTUMES: Judy Dearing; LIGHTING: Marc D. Malamud; MUSICAL DIRECTION: Neal Tate; PRODUCERS: American Place Theatre (Wynn Handman, Director; Julia Miles, Associate Director) and Henry Street Settlement's New Federal Theatre

CAST—Ben Harney (Bert Williams), Vondie Curtis-Hall (George Walker), Neal Tate (Pianist)

The action occurs on June 10, 1910, in the backstage dressing quarters of Bert Williams at the Majestic Theatre in New York City.

The musical was presented in one act.

MUSICAL NUMBERS—"Magnetic Rag" (music by Scott Joplin), "Constantly" (lyric by Smith and Barris, music by Bert Williams), "Bon Bon Buddy" (lyric by Alex Rogers, music by Will Marion Cook), "Somebody Stole My Gal" (lyric and music by L. Wood), "Let It Alone" (lyric by Alex Rogers, music by Bert Williams), "Everybody Wants to See the Baby" (lyric by James Weldon Johnson, music by Bob Cole), "Save Your Money, John" (lyric and music by Alex Rogers and Les Copeland), "I'd Rather Have Nothin' All of the Time Than Somethin' for a

Little While" (lyric by John B. Lowitz, music by Bert Williams), "I'm a Jonah Man" (lyric and music by Alex Rogers), "Original Rag" (music by Scott Joplin), "Chocolate Drop (Original Cake Walk)" (music by Will Marion Cook)

NOTES—With his performance in the 1910 edition of the *Ziegfeld Follies*, Bert Williams (1874-1922) became the first Black Broadway star; he continued to appear on Broadway in seven more editions (1911, 1912, 1914, 1915, 1916, 1917, and 1919) of the *Follies*. His final Broadway appearance was in *Broadway Brevities*, two years before his death.

Prior to Williams' successes in the *Follies*, he and his partner George W. Walker had appeared in minstrel shows and then in various ragtime-styled vaudeville revues and musicals (their final joint stage appearance was in 1909). A program note for *Williams & Walker* stated theirs was "a sometimes painful, but heroic trail from minstrel show to the Broadway stage."

Although the program didn't include in its song list Williams' most famous number, the iconic "(I Ain't Never Done Nothing to) Nobody" (lyric by Alex Rogers, music by Williams), Mel Gussow in the *New York Times* referred to it and noted that Ben Harney's "soulful wail" brought forth the "full emotion" of the song.

Williams & Walker had been previously seen for twelve performances in an Off Off Broadway production at the New Federal Theatre beginning on February 5, 1986.

1784 The Wind in the Willows. THEATRE: New Victory Theatre; OPENING DATE: May 29, 1998; PERFORMANCES: 18; BOOK: Gerardine Clark; additional text by Dianne Adams and James McDowell; LYRICS: Dianne Adams and James McDowell; additional lyrics by Gerardine Clark and Katharine Clark; MUSIC: Dianne Adams and James McDowell; DIRECTION: Gerardine Clark and Anthony Salatino; CHOREOGRAPHY: Anthony Salatino; SCENERY: Beowulf Boritt; COSTUMES: Mirena Rada; LIGHTING: A. Nelson Ruger IV; MUSICAL DIRECTION: Dianne Adams; PRODUCERS: A Syracuse Stage Production (James A. Clark, Producing Director; Robert Moss, Artistic Director) in association with Syracuse University; also produced by The New 42nd Street Inc. (Cora Cahan, President; Lisa L. Post, Project Director)

CAST—Eric Collins (Mole), Timothy A. FitzGerald (Rat), Michael Poignand (Badger), Lee Zarrett (Toad), Steven X. Ward (Otter, Stoat), Lana Quintal (Squirrel, Stoat, Weasel, Portly), Stewart Gregory (Horse, Old Gaoler, Great Weasel, Stoat), Dee King (Policeman, Hedgehog, Stoat Sergeant), Price Waldman (Chief Magistrate, Bear, Weasel, Stoat), Stacey Sargeant (Gaoler's Daughter, Stoat, Weasel), Alan Souza (Rabbit, Stoat, Weasel), Beth Lapierre (Washerwoman, Stoat, Weasel), Martha Thomas (Stoat, Weasel, Fox)

SOURCE—The 1908 book *The Wind in the Willows* by Kenneth Grahame.

The action occurs in the pastoral countryside of Edwardian England.

The musical was presented in two acts (division of acts and song assignments unknown; the songs are listed in performance order).

MUSICAL NUMBERS—"The Wind in the Willows," "Song of the River," "Things with Wheels," "Song of the Wild Wood," "It's Time to Take the Toad in Hand," "Dulce Domum," "I, Glorious Toad," "Mercy-Justice," "The End of Toad," "Joy Shall Be Yours in the Morning," "Missing Him," "The Triumph of Toad," "Weapons Underscore," "Stoats Forever," "The Battle Song," Finale

NOTES—Lawrence Van Gelder in the *New York Times* praised the "ambitious" musical version of the classic children's story *The Wind in the Willows*. He found it "colorful, cheery, tuneful and spirited," and said the score was "consistently melodic" and the youthful cast "a definite plus."

On December 19, 1985, another musical adaptation of the material had been seen on Broadway at the Nederlander Theatre. Despite a pleasant score by Roger McCough and William Perry which included a superior ballad ("I'd Be Attracted," sung by Vicki Lewis [Mole] and David-James Carroll [Rat]), the musical closed after four performances; the cast also included Nathan Lane (Toad), P.J. Benjamin (Chief Weasel), and Scott Waara (Police Sergeant).

1785 The Winds of Change. THEATRE: AMAS Repertory Theatre; OPENING DATE: February 4, 1982; PERFORMANCES: 16; PERFORMANCES: 16; BOOK: Franklin C. Tramutola; LYRICS: Gary Romero; MUSIC: Joseph D'Agostino; DIRECTION: William Michael Maher; SCENERY: Tom Barnes; COSTUMES: Judy Dearing; LIGHTING: Ronald L. McIntyre; MUSICAL DIRECTION: Lea Richardson; PRODUCER: AMAS Repertory Theatre (Rosetta LeNoire, Founder and Artistic Director)

CAST—Richard T. Alpers (Mr. Holmes), Susan Berkson (Mrs. Holmes), Terry Kirwin (Ned Vann), Steve Correia (Master, Reporter), Nick DiVirgilio (Michaelko), Marjorie Gayle Edwards (Dancer, Reporter's Assistant), Jimmy Foster (Master, Managing Editor), Donald Grimme (Master, Reporter), Sonya Hensley (Nonnie, Sandy, Reporter's Assistant), Vicki Juditz (Lolo, Reporter's Assistant), Jon-David Kibbe (Eddy, Reporter, Master), Dinah Lenney (Mary Olcott), Robin Oxman (Hannah, Reporter's Assistant), Jack Sevier (Colonel Olcott), Molly Stark (H.P. Blavatsky)

The action occurs in New York City during the period 1872-1879.

The musical was presented in two acts.

NOTES—*The Winds of Change* was presented under an Off Off Broadway contract.

1786 Wine Lovers. "The Wine-Tasting Musical." THEATRE: Triad Theatre; OPENING DATE: December 1, 2007; PERFORMANCES: 6; BOOK: Travis Kramer Lyrics: Michael Green; MUSIC: Gary Negbaur; DIRECTION: Holly-Anne Ruggiero

CAST—Tuck Milligan, Eric Rubbe, Jessica Phillips

NOTES—The Off Off Broadway musical *Wine Lovers*, which played for a limited engagement of six performances, dealt with two members of a wine class who fall in love.

During each performance, audience members were offered six different wines to sample.

1787 Wings. (1975; Robert McLaughlin and Peter Ryan). THEATRE: Eastside Playhouse; OPENING DATE: March 16, 1975; PERFORMANCES: 9; BOOK: Robert McLaughlin and Peter Ryan; LYRICS: Robert McLaughlin and Peter Ryan; MUSIC: Robert McLaughlin and Peter Ryan; DIRECTION: Robert McLaughlin; CHOREOGRAPHY: Nora Christiansen; SCENERY: Karl Eigsti; COSTUMES: Shadow; LIGHTING: Karl Eigsti; MUSICAL DIRECTION: Larry Hochman; PRODUCER: Stephen Wells

CAST—Jerry Sroka (Pisthetairos), David Kolatch (Euelpides), David Pursley (Butler Bird, Insurance Salesman, Hercules), Jay E. Raphael (Epops [The King of the Birds]), Mary Sue Finnerty (Procne), Peter Jurasik (Cardinal, Barbarian God), James Howard Laurence (Male Tanager), Maureen Sadusk (Female Tanager, Birdwatcher), Barbara Rubenstein (Large-Breasted Bushtit, Poet), Nicholas Stannard (Dickcissel), Dan Held (Eagle, Construction Boss, Prometheus), Brenda Gardner (Macaw), Robin Wesley (Parrot, Iris), Sally Mitchell (Flamingo, Soothsayer), Stuart Pankin (Penguin, Land Developer, Zeus)

SOURCE—The 414 B.C. play *The Birds* by Aristophanes.

The action occurs on a mountain top.

The musical was presented in two acts.

ACT ONE—"Call of the Birds" (Mary Sue Finnerty, Jay E. Raphael, Birds), "O Sacrilege" (Birds), "The Human Species" (Brenda Gardner, Robin Wesley, Dan Held, Birds), "Time to Find Something to Do" (Jerry Sroka, Birds), "First I Propose" (Jerry Sroka), "First I Propose" (reprise) (Jay E. Raphael, Birds), "Comfort for the Taking" (Birds), "You'll Regret It" (Pests), "How Great It Is to Be a Bird" (Jay E. Raphael, Birds)

ACT TWO—"Rah Tah Tah Tio Beep Doo Doo" (Birds), "The Wall Song" (James Howard Laurence, Jay E. Raphael, Birds), "Take to the Air" (Birds), "Iris the Fleet" (Robin Wesley), "Iris the Fleet" (reprise) (Robin Wesley, Jerry Sroka, Birds), "The Great Immortals" (Brenda Gardner, David Pursley, Peter Jurasik, Birds), "Wings" (Company), "We're Gonna Make It" (Jerry Sroka, Dan Held, David Kolatch), Finale (Company)

NOTES—Clive Barnes in the *New York Times* felt that nothing much was wrong with this musical adaptation of Aristophanes' *Wings*, but he noted there wasn't much right with it, either. He indicated the musical followed the original story about two Athenians who travel to Cloud Cuckoo Land and there are persuaded by the king of the birds to build a wall separating mankind from the gods (the birds' rationale is that if smoke from man's religious offerings fails to penetrate into heaven, then the gods will lose their power and birds can become the rulers of the world). Barnes found the evening "extremely good-natured and perfectly harmless," with "eclectic" music, "serviceable if primitive" lyrics, and humor on the order of one goddess stating that "I'm immortal — besides, I can't die." Barnes was "especially taken" with Jerry Sroka's performance ("as if he were on leave from an Athenian road company of *Fiddler on the Roof*") and also praised the "flexible singing and dancing" of Jay E. Raphael (the King of the Birds) and Dan Held's roles as a "rather tattered" American eagle and an "extraordinarily nervy" Prometheus.

Besides *Wings*, Aristophanes' plays have been the source of a number of other musicals (*The Happiest Girl in the World* [1961]; Al Carmines' *Peace* [1967; see entry]; *Lysistrata* [1972]; Stephen Sondheim's *The Frogs* [1973]); and *Lyz!* [1999; see entry]). (*The Happiest Girl in the World* and *Lysistrata* were Broadway adaptations of *Lysistrata*, and are briefly discussed in the entry for *Lyz!*, an Off Off Broadway version of the material.)

Moreover, the play *Lysistrata* and even Aristophanes himself figure prominently in the plot of *The Athenian Touch* (1964; see entry).

Following in the great casting tradition of David Canary, who played a bird-watcher in *Kittiwake Island* (1960; see entry), the producers wisely cast Jay E. Raphael and Robin Wesley in *Wings*.

1788 Wings. (1993; Jeffrey Lunden). THEATRE: Newman Theatre/The Public Theatre; OPENING DATE: March 9, 1993; PERFORMANCES: 47; BOOK: Arthur Perlman; LYRICS: Arthur Perlman; MUSIC: Jeffrey Lunden; DIRECTION: Michael Maggio; SCENERY: Linda Buchanan; COSTUMES: Birgit Rattenborg Wise; LIGHTING: Robert Christen; MUSICAL DIRECTION: Bradley Vieth; PRODUCER: The New York Shakespeare Festival (Joseph Papp, Founder; JoAnne Akalaitis, Artistic Director)

CAST—Linda Stephens (Emily Stilson), William Brown (Doctor, Mr. Brambilla), Ora Jones (Nurse, Mr. Timmins), Hollis Resnik (Amy), Ross Lehman (Billy)

SOURCE—The 1978 play *Wings* by Arthur Kopit (which had originally been written as a radio play).

The action occurs over a period of two years.

The musical was presented in one act.

MUSICAL NUMBERS—"The New Daredevils of

the Air" (recording), "Catastrophe" (Linda Stephens), "The Hospital"/"Globbidge" (William Brown, Ora Jones, Linda Stephens), "Wait-Stop-Hold-Cut" (Linda Stephens), "My Name Then..." (Ora Jones, Linda Stephens, William Brown), "All in All" (Linda Stephens), "Let Me Call You Sweetheart" (instrumental), "Makey Your Naming Powers" (William Brown, Ora Jones, Linda Stephens), "I'll Come Back to That" (Linda Stephens, Hollis Resnik), "Let Me Call You Sweetheart #2" (Hollis Resnik, Linda Stephens), "I'll Come Back to That #2" (Linda Stephens), "Yum, Yummy, Yum" (Ora Jones, Linda Stephens), "I'll Come Back to That #3" (Linda Stephens), "Tither" (William Brown, Linda Stephens), "All in All #2" (Linda Stephens), "I Don't Trust Him" (Linda Stephens, William Brown), "Malacats" (William Brown, Linda Stephens, Ora Jones), "Needle" (Linda Stephens), Interlude—"Wings Theme" (Linda Stephens, Hollis Resnik), "Out on the Wing" (Linda Stephens, Hollis Resnik), "Out on the Wing #2" (Linda Stephens, Hollis Resnik), "I Wonder What's Inside" (Linda Stephens, Ross Lehman), "Let Me Call You Sweetheart"/"Therapy Scene" (Hollis Resnik, William Brown, Linda Stephens, Ross Lehman, Ora Jones), "A Recipe for Cheesecake" (Ross Lehman, Hollis Resnik, Patients), "Like the Clouds" (Linda Stephens), "Brownie Scene" (Ross Lehman, Linda Stephens), "Record Player Scene" (Hollis Resnik, Linda Stephens), "The New Daredevils of the Air" (reprise) (recording), "Preparing for the Flight" (Linda Stephens), "Winter Scene I" (Hollis Resnik, Linda Stephens), "Snow" (Linda Stephens, Hollis Resnik), "Winter Scene II" (Linda Stephens, Hollis Resnik), "Wings" (Linda Stephens)

NOTES—Arthur Kopit's 1978 play *Wings* and its musical adaptation told the story of Emily Stilson, a former aviatrix in her 70s who suffers a stroke. Presented from Emily's point of view, the story dealt with her rehabilitation and recovery. Although not written in a documentary or clinical style, the somewhat chilly but ultimately touching work studiously avoided sentimentality and instead presented Emily's story in a sometimes surreal and dream-like manner.

Both the original play (which later transferred to Broadway in 1979) and its musical adaptation opened at the Public's Newman Theatre. In the nonmusical version, Constance Cummings' memorable performance won her a Tony Award for Best Actress. For the musical, Linda Stephens received high praise (for certain performances, the role was played by Rita Gardner).

Frank Rich in the *New York Times* noted that at times the evening veered into television's "disease-of-the-week" territory; he also found the lyrics "linguistically conventional" and the dialogue "perfunctorily written." But he praised Jeffrey Lunden's "impressive" score, which "tickles the intellect" and offers "an alluring modernist musical shimmer." He reported that Lunden's score used splintered musical motifs to mirror the state of Emily's fragmented mind, with musical phrases constantly "regrouping and reconstituting themselves" in kaleidoscopic fashion.

The musical had first been produced in October 1992 at the Goodman Theatre in Chicago. Two years after the Off Broadway production closed, a cast recording was released by RCA Victor Records (CD # 09026-68323-2); for the recording, the role of Billy, which had been originated by Ross Lehman, was performed by Russ Thacker. The song list comes from the sequences on the cast recording.

1789 The Wings of the Dove. THEATRE: New York City Center; OPENING DATE: October 12, 1961; PERFORMANCES: 3; LIBRETTO: Ethan Ayer; MUSIC: Douglas Moore; DIRECTION: Christopher West; CHOREOGRAPHY: Robert Joffrey; SCENERY: Donald Oenslager; COSTUMES: Patton Campbell; MUSICAL DIRECTION: Julius Rudel; PRODUCER: The New York City Center of Music and Drama

CAST—Regina Sarfaty (Kate Croy), Paul Ukena (Homer Croy), Martha Lipton (Aunt Maud Lowder), John Reardon (Miles Dunster [in the novel, the character's name is Merton Densher]), Dorothy Coulter (Milly Theale), Mary Lesawyer (Susan Stringham), Norman Kelley (Lord Mark), Richard Fredricks (Steffans), Maurice Stern (Lecturer), Fredric Milstein (Guiliano); Players in "Janus" Ballet: Gerald Arpino and Paul Sutherland (Janus), Francoise Martinet (Goddess of Spring), Rita Bradley and Mary Ellen Jackson (Attendants of Goddess of Spring), Brunhilda Ruiz (Goddess of Winter), Suzanne Hammons and Marie Paquet (Attendants of Goddess of Winter), James DeBolt, James Howell, Nels Jorgensen, Lawrence Rhodes, and John Wilson (Warriors)

SOURCE—Henry James' 1902 novel *The Wings of the Dove*.

The action occurs in London and Venice in 1902.

The opera was presented in three acts.

ACT ONE—"There Was a Day" (Paul Ukena), "Kate, Would You Mind If We Were Poor?" (Regina Sarfaty, John Reardon), "I Can Bite Your Head Off Any Day" (Martha Lipton), "Dove Song" (Dorothy Coulter), "Susan and I Missed You" (Dorothy Coulter, Norman Kelley)

ACT TWO—"Everything Is Likely Looking" (Dorothy Coulter), "Although I Came from Boston" (Mary Lesawyer), "You Shall Have Money" (Regina Sarfaty, John Reardon), "I Have the One You See" (Dorothy Coulter, John Reardon)

ACT THREE—"Constanza Lepolelli Was the Daughter" (Dorothy Coulter), "Kate, Kate, What Have We Done" (John Reardon), "To Write This Letter" (Regina Sarfaty), "Can You Forgive Me?" (Regina Sarfaty, Martha Lipton)

NOTES—*The Wings of the Dove* was one of many new operas produced during the period by the New York City Opera Company, and, like most of the others, it fell into almost immediate obscurity. Harold C. Schonberg's review in the *New York Times* indicated Douglas Moore's music was "devoid of personality ... it suggests nobody"; he noted the score was "all skillful, all full of integrity, and all bland." The published edition of the score was a revised version of this production, and it included a second act sequence titled "Minstrel's Song" (for a new character, the Narrator).

Five years before the opera's premiere, a dramatic version of James' novel had been produced on Broadway. Titled *Child of Fortune*, the work was adapted by Guy Bolton and played for twenty-three performances at the Royale (now Bernard B. Jacobs) Theatre in 1956.

1790 Winnie the Pooh (1967). THEATRE: Bil Baird Theatre; OPENING DATE: November 23, 1967; PERFORMANCES: 185; BOOK: A.J. Russell; LYRICS: A.A. Milne and Hack Brooks; MUSIC: Jack Brooks; DIRECTION: Fania Sullivan; PRODUCERS: The American Puppet Arts Council; Executive Producer, Arthur Cantor

CAST—Franz Fazakas (Winnie the Pooh), Jerry Nelson (Piglet), Bil Baird (Eeyore), Fania Sullivan (Kanga), Byron Whiting (Roo, Tigger), Phyllis Nierendorf (Christopher Robin), Frank Sullivan (Rabbit, Owl), The Simon Sisters (Mice)

The action occurs in the 100 Aker Wood.

The musical was presented in two acts.

NOTES—This was another annual visit by Bil Baird and his puppeteers; act one consisted of *Winnie the Pooh*, which was based on A.A. Milne's books *Winnie-the-Pooh* (1926) and *The House at Pooh Corner* (1928), and act two was the perennial *A Pageant of Puppet Variety* (a/k/a *A Pageant of Puppetry*), in which puppeteers demonstrated their techniques and trade secrets. For some revivals, *Winnie the Pooh* was presented in two acts.

George Gent in the *New York Times* reported that the musical contained six songs to make children in the audience whistle; he also noted that the funniest sequence ("a comic episode of pure genius") dealt with Winnie's trying to "wiggle out of Rabbit's house with a tummy full of honey." As for the *Pageant* section of the evening, Gent said it included "a wild happening" to the tune of "Won't You Come Home, Bill Bailey" and a high-stepping chorus line of French ponies dancing the can-can.

During the run of *Winnie the Pooh*, revivals of two other puppet musicals joined the program (*People Is the Thing That the World Is Fullest Of*, six performances; and *Davy Jones' Locker*, five performances); see entries for other productions of these two musicals, and see entries for the revivals of *Winnie the Pooh* in 1969, 1971, 1972, and 1976 (the musical was also presented for twenty-three performances during the run of the 1969-1970 production of *The Whistling Wizard and the Sultan of Tuffet* [see entry]).

1791 Winnie the Pooh (1969). THEATRE: Bil Baird Theatre; OPENING DATE: March 7, 1969; PERFORMANCES: 58; BOOK: A.J. Russell; LYRICS: A.A. Milne and Jack Brooks; MUSIC: Jack Brooks; DIRECTION: Fania Sullivan; MUSICAL DIRECTION: Alvy West; PRODUCERS: The American Puppet Arts Council; Arthur Cantor, Executive Producer

CAST—Bil Baird (Eeyore), Franz Fazakas (Winnie-the-Pooh), Jerry Nelson (Piglet), Phyllis Nierendorf (Christopher Robin), The Simon Sisters (Mice), Fania Sullivan (Kanga), Frank Sullivan (Rabbit, Owl), Byron Whiting (Roo, Tigger)

NOTES—*Winnie the Pooh* had first been produced in 1967 for 185 performances (see entry). During the run of the 1969 revival (which included *A Pageant of Puppet Variety*), four performances of *The Wizard of Oz* (which had opened earlier in the season) were given on April 7 and 8 (see entries for 1968 and 1971 productions of *The Wizard of Oz*); the four *Oz* performances were accompanied by *A Pageant of Puppet Variety*. See entries for the 1971, 1972, and 1976 revivals of *Winnie the Pooh* (the musical was also presented for twenty-three performances during the run of the 1969-1970 production of *The Whistling Wizard and the Sultan of Tuffet* [see entry for the latter]).

1792 Winnie the Pooh (1971). THEATRE: Bil Baird's Theatre; OPENING DATE: March 27, 1971; PERFORMANCES: 48

NOTES—Bil Baird's spring season offered a revival of *Winnie the Pooh* as well as a new piece called *Bil Baird's Variety* (which probably was a new version of his popular *A Pageant of Puppet Variety* [a/k/a *A Pageant of Puppetry*], which had accompanied many of his previous offerings).

The original production of *Winnie the Pooh* had opened in 1967 and played for 185 performances (and was also revived in 1969, 1972, and 1976); see entries for all productions (the musical was also presented for twenty-three performances during the run of the 1969-1970 production of *The Whistling Wizard and the Sultan of Tuffet* [see entry]).

For the 1971 revival, the cast was as follows: Bil Baird (Eeyore, Owl), Peter Baird (Roo), Pady Backwood (Kanga, Rabbit), David Canaan (Tigger), Olga Felgemacher (Christopher Robin), The Simon Sisters (Mice), Frank Sullivan (Winnie the Pooh), Byron Whiting (Piglet).

1793 Winnie the Pooh (1972). THEATRE: Bil Baird's Theatre; OPENING DATE: October 29, 1972; PERFORMANCES: 44; PRODUCERS: The American Puppet Arts Council (Arthur Cantor, Executive Producer); a Bil Baird's Marionettes Production

NOTES—Based on the book by A.A. Milne, the

two-act revival of *Winnie the Pooh* was first presented by Bil Baird in 1967 for 185 performances (see entry). The book was by A.J. Russell, lyrics by A.A. Milne and Jack Brooks, and music by Jack Brooks. The cast was as follows: Bil Baird (Owl), Peter Baird (Roo), Pady Blackwood (Kanga, Rabbit), Olga Felgemacher (Christopher Robin), John O'Malley (Tigger), Simon Sisters (Mice), Frank Sullivan (Winnie-the-Pooh), William Tost (Eeyore), Byron Whiting (Piglet). The musical was directed by Lee Theodore, and musical direction was by Alvy West.

As usual, *Bil Baird's Variety* accompanied the main presentation.

During the previous summer (July 11 through July 21), the company presented a special puppet program titled *The Magic Onion*; it was written by Bil Baird, and played for eighteen performances.

See entries for the 1969, 1971, and 1976 revivals of *Winnie the Pooh* (the musical was also presented for twenty-three performances during the run of the 1969-1970 production of *The Whistling Wizard and the Sultan of Tuffet* [see entry]).

1794 Winnie the Pooh (1976). THEATRE: Bil Baird Theatre; OPENING DATE: January 24, 1976; PERFORMANCES: 111; PRODUCERS: The American Puppet Arts Council (Arthur Cantor, Executive Producer)

NOTES—Based on the stories by A.A. Milne, *Winnie the Pooh* had first been presented by Bil Baird in 1967 for 185 performances; it was also revived in 1969, 1971, and 1972 (see entries for all productions); the musical was also presented for twenty-three performances during the run of the 1969-1970 production of *The Whistling Wizard and the Sultan of Tuffet* [see entry]).

The two-act musical, set in and around the 100-acre wood, had a book by A. J. Russell, lyrics by A.A. Milne and Jack Brooks, and music by Jack Brooks. The musical was directed by Bil Baird; the scenery was by Howard Mandel; the lighting was by Peggy Clark; and the musical direction was by Alvy West. The puppets were designed and produced by Bil Baird and Susanna Baird.

The puppeteers were: William Tost (Winnie the Pooh); Peter Baird (Piglet); Brian Stashick (Eeyore); Rebecca Bondor (Kanga), Christopher Robin (Roo), Olga Felgemacher (Tigger, Owl); Steven Widerman (Tigger); Madeleine Gruen (Bee); and various puppeteers represented Moles, Spiders, Cows, Butterflies, Raccoons, and Bees.

The singing voices were: Bil Baird (Eeyore, Owl); Bill Marine (Winnie the Pooh); and Carly Simon and Lucy Simon (Mice).

Winnie the Pooh was accompanied by *Bil Baird's Variety*.

1795 With Glee

NOTES—See entry for *The New York Musical Theatre Festival*.

1796 The Wizard of Oz (1968). THEATRE: Bil Baird Theatre; OPENING DATE: November 27, 1968; PERFORMANCES: 118; BOOK: Bil Baird and Arthur Cantor; LYRICS: E.Y. Harburg; MUSIC: Harold Arlen; DIRECTION: Bil Baird and Arthur Cantor; MUSICAL DIRECTION: Alvy West; PRODUCERS: The American Puppet Arts Council; Arthur Cantor, Executive Producer

CAST—Bil Baird (Tanglefoot, Cowardly Lion), Franz Fazakas (Tin Woodman), Jerry Nelson (Toto, Wizard), Phyllis Nierendorf (Dorothy), Fania Sullivan (Aunt Em, Glinda), Frank Sullivan (Uncle Henry, Scarecrow), Byron Whiting (Kalidah, Guardian, Witch of the West)

SOURCE—The 1900 book *The Wonderful Wizard of Oz* by L. Frank Baum (who also wrote thirteen other *Oz* books) and the 1939 film adaptation by MGM.

The musical was presented in two acts.

NOTES—Dan Sullivan in the *New York Times* praised Bil Baird's adaptation of *The Wizard of Oz*, stating the production was a "grand way" to introduce children to the classic story. While the musical included songs from the 1939 film version (such as "Over the Rainbow" and "We're Off to See the Wizard"), Sullivan noted the script sometimes utilized sequences from the original novel which weren't seen in the film. He also praised the scenic effects, such as the "tiny" but "spectacular" sight of Dorothy's house spinning in the cyclone, and he singled out the puppet of Toto (he reported that before the "wary little black mutt" jumped into an action sequence, he would first tentatively back away in order to decide what to do). The musical was revived by Bil Baird during the 1971-1972 season, and played for a total of sixty-five performances in two slightly separated engagements (see entry). *The Wizard of Oz* was also briefly revived (for four performances) during the run of the 1969 revival of *Winnie the Pooh* (see entry for the latter).

The evening also included *A Pageant of Puppet Variety*.

1797 The Wizard of Oz (1971). THEATRE: Bil Baird's Theatre; OPENING DATE: October 30, 1971; PERFORMANCES: 65; PRODUCER: The American Puppet Arts Council (Arthur Cantor, Executive Producer); a Bil Baird's Marionettes Production

NOTES—*The Wizard of Oz* was originally produced by Bil Baird in 1968, when it played for 118 performances (see entry). The 1971 revival returned on April 28, 1972, for a total of sixty-five performances for the season. The musical was also presented for four performances during the run of the 1969 revival of *Winnie the Pooh* (see entry for the latter).

Based on the L. Frank Baum stories, the adaptation was by Arthur Cantor and Bil Baird; songs from the 1939 film were used (lyrics by E.Y. Harburg, music by Harold Arlen). The revival was directed by Gordon Hunt, and the cast was as follows: Peter Baird (Apparitions, Trees, Monkeys), Pady Blackwood (Aunt Em, Glinda, Tin Woodman), Olga Felgemacher (Dorothy), John O'Malley (Toto, Oz), Frank Sullivan (Uncle Henry, Scarecrow), Bill Tost (Tanglefoot, Cowardly Lion), Byron Whiting (Kalidah, Guardian, Witch of the West).

The bill also included the perennial *Bil Baird's Variety*, also directed by Gordon Hunt. For this production, a special finale was written by Pady Blackwood.

1798 A Woman Without a Man Is... "An Evening of Songs and Poetry." THEATRE: Theatre East; OPENING DATE: May 9, 1979; PERFORMANCES: 47; PRODUCER: Arthur Shafman International Ltd.

The revue was presented in two acts.

NOTES—The revue *A Woman Without a Man Is...* was a one-woman show of songs and poems performed by Martha Schlamme, who was accompanied by pianist Steve Blier. Curt Davis in the *New York Post* felt the title was wrong, that Schlamme was a woman "*with*," that is, a performer who "puts you at your ease" as you listen to her with a "grateful ear." He further noted that the show wasn't a "big Broadway bauble" but instead was a "precious little package filled with humanity."

The revue included songs by the following lyricists and composers: Bertolt Brecht and Kurt Weill (English lyric translations by Marc Blitzstein and Will Holt); Jacques Brel and Jerard Jouannest (English lyric translations by Eric Blau and Corinne Jacker); Kurt Tucholsky and Olaf Bienert (English lyric translations by Louis Golden); Stephen Sondheim; Melissa Manchester; Carole Bayer Sager; Carol Hall; Richard Maltby, Jr., and David Shire.

The revue also included poems by the following writers: Dorothy Parker, Edna St. Vincent Millay, e.e. cummings, Eve Merriam, Nikki Giovanni, Ntozake Shange, Bertolt Brecht (English translation by Eric Bentley), and Judith Viorst.

1799 Womit Haben wir das Verdient?

NOTES—See entry for *Why Do I Deserve This?*

1800 The Wonder Years. "The Musical." THEATRE: Top of the Gate/The Village Gate; OPENING DATE: May 25, 1988; PERFORMANCES: 23; BOOK: David Levy, Steve Liebman, David Holdgrive, and Terry LeBolt; LYRICS: David Levy; MUSIC: David Levy; DIRECTION: David Holdgrive; CHOREOGRAPHY: David Holdgrive; SCENERY: Nancy Thun; COSTUMES: Richard Schurkamp; LIGHTING: Ken Billington; MUSICAL DIRECTION: Keith Thompson; PRODUCERS: Russ Thacker and Dwight Frye

CAST—Alan Osburn (Ken), Louisa Flaningam (Carol), Adam Bryant (Scott), Meghan Duffy (Lynnie), Kathy Morath (Patti), Lenny Wolpe (Skippy)

The musical was presented in two acts.

ACT ONE—"Baby Boom Babies" (Company), "Thru You" (Adam Bryant, Louisa Flaningam), "Another Elementary School" (Company), "First Love" (Company), "Monarch Notes" (Meghan Duffy), "Teach Me How to Fast Dance" (Kathy Morath, Louisa Flaningam, Meghan Duffy), "Skippy A-Go-Go" (Lenny Wolpe, Company), "The Wonder Years" (Company), "Flowers from the Sixties" (Alan Osburn)

ACT TWO—"The Me Suite" (Company), "Pushing Thirty" (Kathy Morath), "Takin' Him Home to Meet Mom" (Adam Bryant), "The Girl Most Likely" (Louisa Flaningam), "The Wonder Years" (reprise) (Company)

NOTES—This short-lived revue-like musical *The Wonder Years* looked at a group of baby boomers from the time of their birth to the year 2019 (the fiftieth-anniversary of the Woodstock rock concert). Audiences weren't interested in the saga of these boomers' "wonder years," and so the musical was gone in less than three weeks.

Stephen Holden in the *New York Times* found the "innocuous" evening all too quick to rely on "pop-culture references and buzzwords" to instill in the audience a "shallow sense of shared recognition." Moreover, the writing lacked wit, and one number, "The Me Song," consisted entirely of one repeated word ("me"). Holden also noted that one song ("Flowers from the Sixties") oozed "glib sentimentality" while another one ("Pushing Thirty") exuded self-pity. Holden concluded that the sometimes "sour" evening (which left him with a "faintly rancid taste") revealed an "underlying meanness" toward women.

1801 Wonderful Lives. "A Musical Fantasy." THEATRE: The Glines; OPENING DATE: September 21, 1977; PERFORMANCES: 32; BOOK: James B. Ferguson; LYRICS: James B. Ferguson; MUSIC: James B. Ferguson; DIRECTION: James B. Ferguson; CHOREOGRAPHY: James B. Ferguson; SCENERY: James B. Ferguson; COSTUMES: James B. Ferguson; LIGHTING: Marcia Madeira; PRODUCER: The Glines (John Glines, Producer)

CAST—Deborah Stern, James B. Ferguson, Cynthia Cobey, Mark Lavender, Leslie Welles, Anne Connors, Jim David, Timothy Gray, Kathryn Cordes, Don Scotti, Christie Virtue, Loretta Edmonds, Jay Bennett, Rick Walsh

NOTES—The Off Off Broadway musical *Wonderful Lives* dealt with two roommates, a gay man (John B. Ferguson) and a straight woman (Cynthia Cobey), and their respective romances. Rob Baker in the *New York Daily News* felt that *Wonderful Lives* was the kind of musical "they don't make any more ... full of memorable songs, witty dialogue ... a lot of heart."

1802 The Wonderful World of Burlesque (First Edition). THEATRE: Mayfair Theatre; OPENING DATE: April 28, 1965; PERFORMANCES: 92; DIRECTION: LeRoy C. Griffith; CHOREOGRAPHY: Guy Martin; SCENERY: Ed McDonnell; COSTUMES: Monique Starr; LIGHTING: Peter Xantho; MUSICAL DIRECTION: Nick Alversano; PRODUCERS: LeRoy C. Griffith and William Berger

CAST—Yolanda Moreno, Julie Taylor, Al Anger, Earl Van, Bobbye Mack, Rick Perri, Barbara Curtis, Helena Jackman, Rosanna Faire, Danny Jacobs

The revue was presented in two acts.

MUSICAL NUMBERS—The Mayfairette, The M.C. and Mr. America, "Strip," "Love College," Mayfairette in Production Number with Rick Perri, "The Telephone Scene," "My Wedding Night," "The Drunk Sketch," Songs by Helena Jackman, "The School Room," "The Grande Duchess of Burlesque," Finale

NOTES—*The Wonderful World of Burlesque* was another attempt to match the success of Ann Corio's *This Was Burlesque* (see entry). It fared a little better than most such revues, and with the help of a second edition (see entry) managed to run well into the summer. The production gave twenty-nine performances a week, and LeRoy C. Griffith, one of the producers, said he hoped to introduce a new revue every month. But, as noted, the series lasted for just two editions.

Harry Gilroy in the *New York Times* noted the chorus of seven dancers had "leggy gracelessness" and "frozen-custard smiles," a combination which "has made burlesquegoers feel at home for decades." The Mayfair Theatre had first been the home of Billy Rose's Diamond Horseshoe nightclub, and then in its later years was known as the Century Theatre.

1803 The Wonderful World of Burlesque (Second Edition). THEATRE: Mayfair Theatre; OPENING DATE: May 24, 1965; PERFORMANCES: 117

NOTES—This was the second edition of *The Wonderful World of Burlesque* (see entry for first edition).

1804 Woody Guthrie. THEATRE: Cherry Lane Theatre; OPENING DATE: November 26, 1979; PERFORMANCES: 47; SCRIPT ADAPTED from the writings and songs of Woody (Woodrow Wilson) Guthrie (1912-1967) by George Boyd, Michael Diamond, and Tom Taylor; DIRECTION: George Boyd; SCENERY: Robert Blackman; COSTUMES: Robert Blackman; LIGHTING: Daniel Adams; PRODUCERS: Harold Leventhal and Michael Diamond in association with Alison H. Clarkson

CAST—Tom Taylor

The action occurs throughout the United States from the 1920s through the 1960s.

The revue was presented in two acts.

NOTES—If Woody Guthrie's music and social positions were your cup of tea, then you had just forty-seven chances to see Tom Taylor's one-man show about him; perhaps the biographical 1976 film *Bound for Glory* had been enough to satisfy Guthrie's fans. On the other hand, perhaps audiences didn't support the revue because they felt it might encourage some foolhardy producer to mount one about Guthrie's son, Arlo. Robert Palmer in the *New York Times* found Tom Taylor "riveting," but noted that the evening itself was "something of a mess" in its "windy invective," sketchiness, and lack of continuity. Palmer also reported the production gave short shrift to Guthrie's music. Another evening of Woody Guthrie (as *Woody Guthrie's American Song*) opened Off Off Broadway on December 6, 1998, by the Melting Pot Theatre at Theatre 3 for thirty-six performances (the cast included Ernestine Jackson); the production was conceived and adapted by Peter Glazer. The revue had been previously produced in regional theatre at the Northlight Theatre in Chicago on April 10, 1991, and also at Ford's Theatre in Washington, D.C. Another production of this revue was presented by the Pope Theatre Company in Manalapan, Florida; it was recorded by WG Records (CD # WG-1001) and released in 1994; the Florida cast included David M. Lutken and James J. Stein, Jr., both of whom later appeared in the Melting Pot Theatre production of the revue.

1805 Work and Win!, or Frank Manley's Fortune. "The New Horatio Alger Musical Comedy." THEATRE: West Park Theatre; OPENING DATE: 1978-1979 Season; PERFORMANCES: Unknown; BOOK: Ted Drachman and Mary Chaffee; LYRICS: Ted Drachman and Mary Chaffee; MUSIC: Ted Drachman and Mary Chaffee; DIRECTION: Pat Robertson; CHOREOGRAPHY: Denise Moses; SCENERY: Jeff Guzik; COSTUMES: Zoe Mathias; Shelby Brammer, Assistant; LIGHTING: Craig D. Tonelson; MUSICAL DIRECTION: Gregory J. Dlugos; PRODUCER: Experimental Theatre Project, Inc.

CAST—Peter Bubriski (Roland Blackwood, Robert Baron), Timothy Hall (Horatio Alger, St. Clair Sterling), Bary Phillips (Luck), Nancy Cook (Pluck), Ron Cosgrove (Frank Manley), Deborah Jean Templin (Albert), Mark Enis (Mickey Slade), Toni Wooster (Mother Magruder), Philip Jostrom (Randolph)

NOTES—The program didn't list musical numbers. The musical *Work and Win!*, or *Frank Manley's Fortune* was inspired by the stories of Horatio Alger, Jr. (1832-1899), the writer whose one-hundred-plus novels supported the theory that any American boy, even a poor one, could find monetary and worldly success through honesty and hard work. It appears the production was under an Off Off Broadway contract.

There have been at least four other Horatio Alger-inspired musicals. *Rags to Riches* was produced at the Kalita Humphreys Theatre at the Dallas Theatre Center on March 12, 1969, for eleven performances; the book was based on two of the Horatio Alger stories, and was written by Aurand Harris, who co-wrote the lyrics with Eva Franklin, who composed the score. Another regional musical version of the material was *Horatio*, which opened at Arena Stage in Washington, D.C., on June 14, 1974, with book and lyrics by Ron Whyte and music by Mel Marvin; the musical was produced by the American Conservatory Theatre at the Geary Theatre in San Francisco, where it opened on November 20, 1974, and played for twenty-eight performances. *Shine* ("The Horatio Alger Musical") opened in regional theatre in 1983; based on characters and incidents suggested by the Horatio Alger stories, the book was by Richard Seff and Richard Altman, lyrics by Lee Goldsmith, and music by Roger Anderson. In 1997, the Off Off Broadway musical *Bound to Rise* opened at the Medicine Show; the "Comic Musical Play" was inspired by the "rags-to-riches novels" of Horatio Alger; the book and lyrics were by Stephen Phillip Policoff and the music was by Robert Dennis.

1806 World of Illusion. THEATRE: Actors' Playhouse; OPENING DATE: June 24, 1964; PERFORMANCES: 71 (estimated); WRITTEN BY: Lionel Shepard; MUSIC: Alan De Mause; DIRECTION: Lionel Shepard; SCENERY: Slides by Rosalind Zaman; LIGHTING: Eric Gertner; MUSICAL DIRECTION: Alan De Mause (guitar), Lynn Cushman (flute); PRODUCER: Jay Stanwyck

CAST—Lionel Shepard, Hallie Goodman, Lily Tomlin, Daniel Landau, Richard Gilden (Narrator)

The revue was presented in two acts.

ACT ONE—Introduction, "Mime and Man in the Beginning," "The Pattern," "Rebirth and the Life Cycle," "The Pattern Continues," "The Cage," "William Overcast," "The Giant" "Rope"

ACT TWO—"The Jabberwock," "The Brass Ring," "The Golden Boat," "Improvisations," "Pastorale," "Rope"

NOTES—*World of Illusion* was an evening of mime told through narration, slides, films, and background music.

According to Louis Calta in the *New York Times*, the first act was an "ambitious chronology" of mankind (from the amoeba to the present day), but he felt the presentation was dull and monotonous when it should have been sardonic and imaginative. The second act was turned over to various improvisations. Calta felt they lacked "originality and bite," and noted that the Premise group (see entry) and Marcel Marceau had nothing to worry about.

World of Illusion appears to have been Lily Tomlin's first New York stage appearance.

1807 The World of Kurt Weill in Song (1963). THEATRE: The Howff; OPENING DATE: June 6, 1963; PERFORMANCES: 245; LYRICS: See song list for credits; MUSIC: Kurt Weill; CONTINUITY: Will Holt; DIRECTION: Will Holt; LIGHTING: John Morris; PRODUCERS: Tanya Chasman and E.A. Gilbert

CAST—Martha Schlamme, Will Holt

The revue was presented in two acts (all songs performed by Martha Schlamme and Will Holt).

ACT ONE—"Alabama Song" (from *The Rise and Fall of the City of Mahagonny*, 1930; English lyric by Bertolt Brecht), "Barbara's Song" (a/k/a "Barbara Song") and "Mack the Knife" (*The Threepenny Opera*, 1928; English lyrics by Marc Blitzstein, from the original German lyrics by Bertolt Brecht), "Duet" (*The Rise and Fall of the City of Mahagonny*, 1930; English lyric by Marc Blitzstein, from the original German lyric by Bertolt Brecht) "Housekeeping Duet"; and "Seer Auber Jenny" (a/k/a "The Black Freighter" and "Pirate Jenny") (*The Threepenny Opera*, 1928; English lyrics by Marc Blitzstein, from the original German lyrics by Bertolt Brecht), "Le Roi d'Aquitaine" (*Marie Galante*, 1934; English lyric by Marc Blitzstein, from the original French lyric by Jacques Deval), "Caesar's Death" (*The Silver Lake*, 1933; English lyric by Will Holt, from the original German lyric by George Kaiser)

ACT TWO—Piano Medley: "Along (On the Rio Grande)" (*Johnny Johnson*, 1936; lyric by Paul Green); "My Ship" (*Lady in the Dark*, 1941; lyric by Ira Gershwin); and "Speak Low" (*One Touch of Venus*, 1943; lyric by Ogden Nash), "Jenny" ("The Saga of Jenny") (*Lady in the Dark*, 1941; lyric by Ira Gershwin), "September Song" (*Knickerbocker Holiday*, 1938; lyric by Maxwell Anderson), "The Sailor's Tango" (*Happy End*, 1929; English lyric by Marc Blitzstein, from the original German lyric by Bertolt Brecht), "Surabaya Johnny" and "Bilbao Song" (*Happy End*, 1929; English lyrics by Marc Blitzstein, from the original German lyrics by Bertolt Brecht), "What Keeps a Man Alive?" (*The Threepenny Opera*, 1928; English lyric by Marc Blitzstein, from the original German lyric by Bertolt Brecht), "Lost in the Stars" and "Cry, the Beloved Country" (*Lost in the Stars*, 1949; lyrics by Maxwell Anderson)

NOTES—*The World of Kurt Weill in Song* (a/k/a *A Kurt Weill Cabaret*) appears to have been the first major composer "tribute" revue seen in New York. The revue opened the floodgates, and succeeding Off Broadway seasons seemed to offer one or more of such tributes. With the Broadway successes of *Side by Side by Sondheim* (1977) and *Ain't Misbehavin'* (1978; see entry), the composer and lyricist tribute revues became institutionalized, and at least one or more popped up during virtually every Broadway and Off Broadway season. And the worst was yet to come. Composer/lyricist tribute revues (and their offspring, the singer and singing-group tribute revues) were at least honest and presented their songs in a more or less straightforward revue-like manner.

But they soon morphed into the truly evil jukebox musical, which took songs originally written as independent pop tunes and shoehorned them into book musicals, forcing the songs to carry the weight of plot, character, and atmosphere. The most obvious example of the jukebox musical is the lamentable ABBAration *Mamma Mia!* (2001), which took ABBA songs and stitched them into a plot similar to the film *Buona Sera, Mrs. Campbell* (1969) and the Broadway musical *Carmelina* (1979).

The Kurt Weill tribute premiered on June 6, 1963, at The Howff, which included both a theatre (seating 115) and a coffeehouse. Located at 4 St. Marks Place in a venue previously known as The New Bowery Theatre, the revue was The Howff's inaugural production. Robert Shelton in the *New York Times* praised Martha Schlamme and Will Holt, saying they moved "in a casual, but growingly engrossing, fashion." Shelton also noted that Schlamme's "flexible" and "under-the-skin" interpretations of Weill should "dispel" the notion that Lotte Lenga had a "monopoly" on Weill's music. After playing out its scheduled three-week engagement at The Howff, the revue transferred to One Sheridan Square in late June. The *Times* noted "howff" was a Scottish word meaning "haunt, den, hang-out; a place where people gather to talk, drink, eat and sing," and mentioned that while the venue had previously been the home of a dance hall as well as two Off Broadway theatres, The Howff was off to an auspicious start with the Weill revue. But, unfortunately, The Howff seems to have had a short theatrical life.

After playing for most of the season for a total of 245 performances, the revue closed, but quickly returned for another engagement, playing an additional 164 performances in 1964 (see entry).

The revue's cast album was released by MGM Records (LP # ELSE-4180); it was titled *A Kurt Weill Cabaret*, and eventually later revivals of the revue adopted this title.

The World of Kurt Weill in Song was the first of many Off Broadway revues devoted to the music of Kurt Weill, who became something of a cottage industry there. Besides the long-running revival of *The Threepenny Opera*, there were two revivals of *Johnny Johnson* as well as the New York premiere of *The Rise and Fall of the City of Mahagonny* (see entries). After the original (and return engagement) of *The World of Kurt Weill in Song*, the revue was seen four more times (as *A Kurt Weill Cabaret*). It was first was produced in 1976 with Will Holt and Dolly Jonah (see entry), and then later with Martha Schlamme and Alvin Epstein in 1979, 1981, and 1984; see entries. In 1969, Schlamme and Epstein appeared in another Kurt Weill retrospective, *Whores, Wars and Tin Pan Alley* (see entry), which was for all purposes a revival of *A Kurt Weill Cabaret*. The two productions of *The World of Kurt Weill in Song*, the four productions of *A Kurt Weill Cabaret*, and *Whores, Wars and Tin Pan Alley* played for more than 600 performances.

In 1972, there was another Weill tribute, *Berlin to Broadway with Kurt Weill*, which was revived in 2000 (see entries). See Appendix O for a complete list of all Kurt Weill-related Off (and Off Off) Broadway revues and musicals.

1808 The World of Kurt Weill in Song (1964). THEATRE: Jan Hus Playhouse; OPENING DATE: May 12, 1964; PERFORMANCES: 164

NOTES—Martha Schlamme and Will Holt repeated their roles for the return engagement of the Kurt Weill tribute. See entry for original 1963 production as well as for information regarding productions of other Kurt Weill revues and musicals which played Off Broadway; also see Appendix O for Kurt Weill-related revues and musicals.

1809 The World of Kurt Weill. THEATRE: Theatre Arielle; OPENING DATE: July 7, 1992; PERFORMANCES: 28; DIALOGUE: Elliot Finkel and Milli Janz; LYRICS: See song list for credits; MUSIC: Kurt Weill; DIRECTION: Sharron Miller; LIGHTING: David Meade; MUSICAL DIRECTION: David Wolfson; PRODUCERS: Michael Ross and Eric Krebs

CAST—Juliette Koka

MUSICAL NUMBERS—"Sing Me Not a Ballad" (from *The Firebrand of Florence*, 1945; lyric by Ira Gershwin), American Love Medley (specific numbers performed in this sequence are unknown), "Pirate Jenny" (*The Threepenny Opera*, 1928; original German lyric by Bertolt Brecht), "Barbara-Song" (*The Threepenny Opera*, 1928; original German lyric by Bertolt Brecht), "Bilbao Song" (*Happy End*, 1929; original German lyric by Bertolt Brecht), "Je Ne T'aime Pas" (independent song; original French lyric by Maurice Magre, 1934), "That's Him" (*One Touch of Venus*, 1943; lyric by Ogden Nash), "Green-Up Time" (*Love Life*, 1948; lyric by Alan Jay Lerner), "Surabaya Johnny" (*Happy End*, 1929; original German lyric by Bertolt Brecht), "Nana's Lied" (a/k/a "Nannas Lied") (independent song; original German lyric by Bertolt Brecht, 1939), *The Rise and Fall of the City of Mahagonny* (1930; specific numbers performed in this sequence are unknown), War Medley (specific numbers performed in this sequence are unknown), "Buddy's on the Night Shift" (a/k/a "Buddy on the Nightshift"; lyric by Oscar Hammerstein II; apparently introduced in a 1942 U.S. Army Soldier Shows Production titled *Three Day's Pass*), "Soldier's Wife" (a/ka "Soldatenweib") (composed in 1946, this song was the final collaboration between Brecht and Weill), "Schickelgrubber" (a/k/a "Schickelgruber"; lyric by Howard Dietz; apparently introduced in a 1942 U.S. Army Soldier Shows Production titled *Three Day's Pass*), "How Can You Tell an American" (*Knickerbocker Holiday*, 1938; lyric by Maxwell Anderson), "Lost in the Stars" (*Lost in the Stars*, 1949; lyric by Maxwell Anderson), *Lady in the Dark* (1941; specific numbers performed in this sequence are unknown), "September Song" (*Knickerbocker Holiday*, 1938; lyric by Maxwell Anderson)

NOTES—It's unclear if the German and French songs were sung in translation.

Despite the similarity in titles of Juliette Koka's Off Off Broadway revue *The World of Kurt Weill* and the 1963 and 1964 productions of *The World of Kurt Weill in Song*, it appears Koka's evening wasn't based on the earlier tributes. *Theatre World 1992-1993 Season* indicates the new revue was "conceived" as well as performed by Koka.

For more information regarding Kurt Weill retrospectives, see entry for the 1963 production of *The World of Kurt Weill in Song*; also see Appendix O.

1810 The World of My America. THEATRE: Greenwich Mews Theatre; OPENING DATE: October 3, 1966; PERFORMANCES: 40; MATERIAL ADAPTED BY: Paulene Myers; MUSIC: Michael Hennagin; DIRECTION: Arthur A. Seidelman; CHOREOGRAPHY: Jimmie Fields; COSTUMES: Jesse Jacobs; LIGHTING: Willard Bond; PRODUCERS: Stella Holt-Apple Productions; Frances Drucker, Associate Producer

CAST—Paulene Myers

The revue was presented in three parts (possibly three acts).

NOTES—*The World of My America* (its full title may have been *Paulene Myers' One Woman Dramatization of The World of My America*) was in part an evening of readings from the poetry and writings of Langston Hughes, Sojourner Truth, and Paul Laurence Dunbar. The Off Off Broadway production was accompanied by dances and incidental music (which was taped).

Dan Sullivan in the *New York Times* reported that Myers had been performing her one-woman show on the West Coast for almost 10 years. He noted that for part of the evening Myers simply *recited* the poetry of Hughes and Dunbar and *told* the audience about Truth. But when she acted out vignettes of a tired wash-woman, a Harlem "chippie," and a young wife who sees her husband being lynched, Sullivan said "we are in on a performance." For here Myers wasn't describing, she was instead demonstrating and defining the soul of a people.

1811 The World's My Oyster. "A Musical." THEATRE: Actors' Playhouse; OPENING DATE: July 31, 1956; PERFORMANCES: 40; BOOK, LYRICS, AND MUSIC: Carley Mills and Lorenzo Fuller; DIRECTION: Jed Duane; CHOREOGRAPHY: Walter Nick and Louis Johnson (assisted by Lew Smith); SCENERY: Henry Buckmaster; COSTUMES: Lew Smith; LIGHTING: Tom Anderson; MUSICAL DIRECTION: Lorenzo Fuller; PRODUCER: Actors' Playhouse

CAST—Ned Wright (John D. Rockingchair), Lorenzo Fuller (Robert Fulton Brown), Jacqueline Barnes (Laura), Butterfly McQueen (Queen Elizabeth Victoria), Helen Furguson (Monday), Phil Hepburn (Windsor); Inhabitants of the Island: Helen Haynes, Plumath Brent, Jocelyn Martinez, Lew Smith, Linurte Wynn, Herman Howell

MUSICAL NUMBERS (division of acts and song assignments unknown; songs are listed in performance order)—"Shoeshine," "Rich Enough to Be Rude," "Footprints in the Sand," "Quiet Little Royal Household," "I Wouldn't Bother About You So Much," "Moola Makes the Hula Feel Much Cooler," "A Thing Like This," "The World's a Jug," "Merchandise," "The Finer Things of Life," "I Set My Heart on One to Love," "Just Before I Go To Sleep," "This Is the Life for Me," "Friendship Ain't No One Way Street," "It's the Human Thing to Do," "The Devil Is a Man You Know," Finale

NOTES—The forgotten *The World's My Oyster* has the distinction of being the very first Black Off Broadway musical. The plot dealt with a couple of New York con artists who travel to a small island with the intention of swindling pearls from the natives. The names of the characters (John D. Rockingchair, Queen Elizabeth Victoria), the titles of the songs ("Rich Enough to Be Rude," "Quiet Little Royal Household," "Moola Makes the Hula Feel Much Cooler"), and at least one cast member (Butterfly McQueen) suggest a quirky and irreverent piece, but Arthur Gelb in the *New York Times* found the musical's plot "dreary," and he noted the evening came "embarrassingly close to being an unwitting parody of *South Pacific*." Later in the season, Off Broadway's second Black musical met with greater success (see entry for *Simply Heavenly*).

"Rich Enough to Be Rude" was later heard in the 1962 revue *Look at Us* (see entry). "A Thing Like This" had first been heard in *Music, Music (see entry).*

1812 Worlds of Oscar Brown, Jr. THEATRE: Gramercy Arts Theatre; OPENING DATE: February 18, 1965; PERFORMANCES: 55; PRODUCER: Manon Productions

CAST—Oscar Brown, Jr.

NOTES—*Worlds of Oscar Brown, Jr.*, was a one-man revue of Brown performing his own songs, impressions, and improvisations. He returned to Off Broadway a few years later with his wife, Jean Pace, and Brazilian guitarist Sevuca, in the intimate revue *Joy* (1970; see entry), which ran for almost six months.

On July 29, 2003, an Off Off Broadway tribute-revue *Serenade the World: The Music and Words of Oscar Brown, Jr.* opened at the John Houseman Theatre with Genovis Albright and the Oscar Brown Trio; the two-act revue was conceived and produced by Eric Krebs.

In 2006, *The Story of Oscar Brown, Jr.*, a documentary about Brown, was released. It was later shown on public television in February 2007; as of this writing, it doesn't appear to have been released on DVD.

1813 The Wrecking Ball. THEATRE: Square East; OPENING DATE: April 15, 1964; PERFORMANCES: 126; SCENES AND DIALOGUE: Created by the Company; DIRECTION: Bob Dishy; Alan Arkin and Peter Kass, Co-Directors; SCENERY: Ralph Alswang; LIGHTING: Dan Butt; PRODUCERS: Charles Rubin, Murray Sweig, and Al Weinstein

CAST—Jack Burns, Bob Dishy, Severn Darden, Mina Kolb, Dick Schaal, Avery Schreiber

The revue was presented in two acts (sketch and song assignments unknown).

ACT ONE—"Umbrella Stand," "You Don't Look Jewish!," "From Mineola with Hate," "The Cabdriver of the Conventioneer," "Silent Spring," "Truckdrivers"

ACT TWO—"Blueboy," "Contact Lenses," "Open Mouth," "Orange Juice," "The Faith Healer"

NOTES—*The Wrecking Ball* was the sixth Second City revue to play Off Broadway. Brian O'Doherty in the *New York Times* felt it wasn't up to the edginess of its predecessors, but he nonetheless found the evening a "sound professional job" which offered a number of amusing sketches, including one in which a "pure Grant Wood" family visits their gay son who lives in Greenwich Village. The revue's material was created by the company, and no doubt included a few improvisations suggested by the audience.

For a complete list of Second City revues that were presented in New York, see entry for *Seacoast of Bohemia*; also see Appendix T.

1814 Wuthering Heights (1959; Carlisle Floyd). THEATRE: New York City Center; OPENING DATE: April 9, 1959; PERFORMANCES: 3; LIBRETTO: Carlisle Floyd; MUSIC: Carlisle Floyd; DIRECTION: Delbert Mann; CHOREOGRAPHY: Robert Joffrey; SCENERY: Lester Polakov; COSTUMES: Patton Campbell; MUSICAL DIRECTION: Julius Rudel; PRODUCER: The New York City Opera Company

CAST—Phyllis Curtin (Catherine Earnshaw), John Reardon (Heathcliff), Patricia Neway (Nelly), Frank Porretta (Edgar Linton), Jacquelynne Moody (Isabella Linton), Jon Crain (Hindley Earnshaw), Arnold Voketaitis (Mr. Earnshaw), Grant Williams (Joseph), Jack De Lon (Lockwood)

SOURCE—The 1847 novel *Wuthering Heights* by Emily Bronte.

The opera was presented in three acts.

NOTES—*Wuthering Heights*, Carlisle Floyd's second opera, has all but disappeared, but Howard Taubman in the *New York Times* indicated that while the work had its weak points, there were also many strong ones. He praised Floyd's adaptation of the lengthy novel, saying he brought "so much of it to life through his music." While Taubman felt that overall the music didn't match the intense drama of the story, he nonetheless praised many of the opera's musical sequences, such as the second act opening, a minuet, a waltz, and a passage at the end of the second act's first scene. The opera had first been produced by the Santa Fe Opera during Summer 1958.

Two of the opera's performers would soon introduce two classic songs in Broadway musicals. Later in the year, Patricia Neway created the role of the Mother Abbess in the original Broadway production of *The Sound of Music* and introduced "Climb Every Mountain." The following year, John Reardon, the opera's Heathcliff, sang "Make Someone Happy" in *Do Re Mi*.

Another operatic adaptation of the novel was by film composer Bernard Herrmann; the opera was recorded on a 3-CD set by Unicorn Records (Herrmann conducted).

In 1991, *Wuthering Heights: The Musical* by Bernard J. Taylor was recorded by Silva Screen Records (CD # SONGCD-904); this adaptation was apparently never staged.

In 1999, an Off Off Broadway musical version by Paul Dick was produced (see entry for *Wuthering Heights: A Romantic Musical*).

1815 Wuthering Heights: A Romantic Musical (1999; Paul Dick). THEATRE: Mint Theatre Space; OPENING DATE: October 23, 1999; PERFORMANCES: 16; BOOK: Paul Dick; LYRICS: Paul Dick; MUSIC: Paul Dick; DIRECTION: David Leidholdt; CHOREOGRAPHY: David Leidholdt; SCENERY: David Martin; COSTUMES: Robin L. Shane; LIGHTING: Frank DenDanto III; MUSICAL DIRECTION: Peter C. Mills; PRODUCER: PASSAJJ Productions

CAST—Darin S. Adams (Edgar), Ari Butler (Young Heathcliff), Lyssandra Cox (Mrs. Linton), Patti Davidson-Gorbea (Nellie), Timothy Ellis (Hindley), William Thomas Evans (Heathcliff), Jennifer Featherston (Cathy), Kelly Fleck (Isabella), Larry Rogowsky (Lockwood, Robert), Christian Stuck (Young Hindley), Laura Sweitzer (Young Cathy), John Taylor (Father, Linton), Danny Wiseman (Joseph)

SOURCE—The 1847 novel *Wuthering Heights* by Emily Bronte.

The action occurs on the Yorkshire Moors during the period of the early to mid 1800s.

The musical was presented in two acts (division of acts and song assignments unknown; the songs are listed in performance order).

MUSICAL NUMBERS—"Hymn to the House," "Catherine, Come Home," "Fly Across the Moor," "Flesh and Blood," "From Now On," "More Like a Lady," "Never Seen Anything Like It Before," "The Rules of Society," "Cath'rine," "I Can Hardly Believe It's You," "If I Were Edgar," "Dustin Now," "Go If You Want," "Caught," "Choose Love," "I Love Him," "Will I Wake Up Tomorrow?," "I Thought Only of You," "Fair Fight, Fight Fair," "Deal, Choose, Throw, Lose," "From the Very First Day," "Come with Me," "A Life Without Love," "Twenty Years from Now," "Never to Go," "Be There," Finale

NOTES—This Off Off Broadway musical adaptation of Emily Bronte's *Wuthering Heights* is at least the fourth lyric version of the classic novel. See entry for Carlisle Floyd's 1959 operatic adaptation, which also references two other musical versions.

1816 X (The Life and Times of Malcolm X). THEATRE: New York State Theatre; OPENING DATE: September 28, 1986; PERFORMANCES: Unknown; LIBRETTO: Thulani Davis; story by Christopher Davis; MUSIC: Anthony Davis; DIRECTION: Rhoda Levine; CHOREOGRAPHY: Rhoda Levine; Sylvia Bird-Leitner, Assistant Choreographer; SCENERY: John Conklin; image for backdrop designed by Romare Bearden; COSTUMES: Frances Nelson; LIGHTING: Curt Ostermann; MUSICAL DIRECTION: Christopher Keene; the orchestra also included the composer's own musical group, Episteme (Kamau Adilifu, Pheeroan Aklaff, Ray Anderson, Dwight Andrews, Marilyn Crispell, Martin Ehrlich, Mark Helias, Gerry Hemingway, J.D. Parran, Abdul Wadud); PRODUCER: The New York City Opera

CAST—Ben Holt (Malcolm Little, Malcolm X, El Hajj Malik El-Shabazz), Thomas Young (Street, Elijah Muhammad), Priscilla Baskerville (Louise Little, Queen Mother, Betty Shabazz), Marietta Simpson (Ella, Muslim), Mark S. Doss (Reginald), Armond Pressley (Young Malcolm Little), Raymond Bazemore (Garvey Preacher, Father, Player, Inmate, Garvey Orator, Muslim), Janice Dixon (Neighbor, Malcolm's Sweetheart, Teen, Muslim, Pilgrim), Sheryl Melvin (Neighbor, Beautician, Mother, Muslim, Pilgrim), Sonja Small (Teen, Dancer, Student, Muslim, Rioter), Robert Dixon (Young Man, Ballroom Dancer, Basketball Player, Muslim, Rioter), Sylvia Byrd-Leitner (Teen, Dancer, Student, Muslim, Pilgrim, Rioter), Reginald Pindell (Neighbor, Preacher, Player, Inmate, Muslim, Pilgrim, Fruit of Islam), Raven Wilkinson (Mother, Dancer, Muslim, Rioter), Kathleen Sanders (Dancer, Young Businesswoman, Rioter), Michael Gray (Neighbor, Bootblack, Player, Inmate, Youth, Paper Peddler, Muslim, Pilgrim), Kevin Deas (Neighbor, Laborer, Inmate, Muslim, Pilgrim), Irwin Reese (Neighbor, Player, Inmate, Professor, Muslim, Pilgrim, Fruit of Islam), Frank Walker (Delivery Boy, Fruit of Islam, Rioter), Ihsan Abdul-Rahiim (Used Clothes Salesman, Dancer, Drunk, Muslim, Rioter), Katherine White (Dancer, Young Woman, Rioter), Federico Edwards (Salesman, Fruit of Islam, Rioter), William Moize (Neighbor, Player, Inmate, Muslim, Pilgrim), Vanessa Ayers (Neighbor, Church Woman, Muslim, Pilgrim), Raeschelle Potter (Neighbor, Businesswoman, Muslim, Pilgrim), Cornelius White (Neighbor, Musician, Inmate, Youth, Muslim, Pilgrim), Kevin Short (Blind Man, Salesman, Player, Inmate, Numbers Runner, Muslim, Pilgrim, Fruit of Islam), Daryl Davis (Neighbor, Player, Inmate, Muslim, Pilgrim, Reporter), Ifetayo Abdul-Rahiim (Hilda Little, Muslim Girl, Rioter), Karla Simmons (Yvonne Little, Muslim Girl, Rioter), Melvin Coston (Young Reginald Little, Muslim Boy, Rioter), Rebecca Luker (Social Worker, The Blonde, Girl Friend, Reporter), Autris Page (Neighbor, Player, Inmate, Boy Friend, Muslim, Pilgrim, Fruit of Islam), Jonathan Green (Policeman, Guard, Pilgrim, Reporter), James Clark (Policeman, Guard, Pilgrim, Reporter), William Ledbetter (Policeman, Guard, Pilgrim, Reporter), Paul Parente (Policeman, Guard, Reporter, Rioter), Douglas Hamilton (Policeman, Guard, Rioter)

The action occurs in various places, including Lansing, Michigan, Boston, New York, and Phoenix, during the period 1931-1965.

The opera was presented in three acts.

NOTES—The opera *X (The Life and Times of Malcolm X)* received its world premiere in Philadelphia in 1984 at the American Music Theatre Festival. It was presented as a work-in-progress; a staged "sampler" of act one was offered as well as a concert presentation of portions of the second and third acts. Reviewing the New York premiere for the *New York Times*, Donald Henahan referred to the opera as a "romanticized" biography of Malcolm X, and noted the production recalled the "agitprop theatre" of the 1930s; he further noted that *X* was "message theatre" which wouldn't appeal to everyone. As for the music, he mentioned that except for "jazzy outbreaks" the score alternated between "monotonous chanting" and music of a "spiky, keyless line that no human voice outside contemporary opera has been known to sing."

In 1992, the opera was recorded on a 2-CD set by Gramavision Records (# R2-79470).

1817 Y2K, You're OK. THEATRE: Chicago City Limits Theatre; OPENING DATE: August 6, 1999; PERFORMANCES: 169; SKETCHES: Joe DeGise II, Denny Siegel, and Paul Zuckerman; IMPROVISATIONS: Chicago City Limits Company; DIRECTION: Paul Zuckerman; MUSICAL DIRECTION: Frank Spitznagel; PRODUCERS: Chicago City Limits (Paul Zuckerman, Executive Producer); Linda Gelman and Jay Stern

CAST—Jose DiGise II, Carol Kissin, Denny Siegel, Victor Varnado

NOTES—*Y2K, You're OK* was a combination of written and improvisational skits accompanied by incidental music.

1818 Yank! "A New Musical." THEATRE: The Gallery Players Theatre; OPENING DATE: October 20, 2007; PERFORMANCES: 12 (estimated); BOOK: David Zellnik; LYRICS: David Zellnik; MUSIC: Joseph Zellnik; DIRECTION: Igor Goldin; CHOREOGRAPHY: Jeffry Denman; SCENERY: Ray Klausen

("Scenic Consultant"); COSTUMES: Tricia Barsamian; LIGHTING: Ken Lapham; MUSICAL DIRECTION: Daniel Feyer; PRODUCER: The Gallery Players (Matt Schicker, Executive Director and President)

CAST—Bobby Steggert (Stu), Maxime de Toledo (Mitch), Tyson Kaup (Tennessee), James Stover (Czechowski), Daniel Shevlin (Professor), Chris Carfizzi (Rotelli), Todd Faulkner (Sarge, Scarlett), Matthew Marks (Melanie), Brian Mulay (India), Nancy Anderson (Louise, [and all other female roles]), Jeffry Denman (Artie), Jonathan Day (Dream Stu), Chad Harlow (Dream Mitch)

The action occurs during World War II.

The musical was presented in one act.

MUSICAL NUMBERS—"Remembering You" (Maxime de Toledo), "Yank" (Bobby Steggert, Ensemble), "Polishing Shoes" (James Stover, Tyson Kaup, Maxime de Toledo, Bobby Steggert), "Saddest Gal What Am" (Nancy Anderson, Boys), "Betty" (Tyson Kaup, Maxime de Toledo, James Stover, Bobby Steggert), "Click" (Jeffry Denman), "Click" (reprise) (Bobby Steggert), "Remembering You" (reprise)/"Letters" (Nancy Anderson, Bobby Steggert, Squad), "Blue Twilight" (Nancy Anderson), "A Couple of Regular Guys" (Maxime de Toledo, Bobby Steggert), "Movie Night: The Great Beyond!" (Nancy Anderson), "Your Squad Is Your Squad" (James Stover, Daniel Shevlin, Chris Carfizzi, Bobby Steggert, Maxime de Toledo), "Credit to the Uniform" (Nancy Anderson, Jeffry Denman, Bobby Steggert, Boys), "Just True" (Bobby Steggert, Maxime de Toledo), "Stuck in a Cell" (Todd Faulkner, Matthew Marks, Brian Mulay; ballet danced by Jonathan Day, Chad Harlow, and Company), "A Couple of Regular Guys" (reprise) (Bobby Steggert), "Remembering You" (reprise) (Maxime de Toledo)

NOTES—Produced in Brooklyn by the Gallery Players, the Off Off Broadway musical *Yanks!* dealt with the love affair between two men during World War II, one a reporter for *Yank* magazine and the other an Army private. A press release described the score as "suffused with songs in swing, big band and boogie-woogie styles."

The musical's demo recording includes many of the performers in the Brooklyn production. The musical had been produced as part of the 2005 New York Musical Theatre Festival.

1819 The Yellow Wood

NOTES—See entry for *The New York Musical Theatre Festival.*

1820 Yesterday Is Over.

THEATRE: Interart Theatre; OPENING DATE: June 18 (?), 1980; PERFORMANCES: 76 (estimated); PLAY: Mady Christian; LYRICS: Mady Christian; MUSIC: Bill Roscoe; DIRECTION: Margot Lewitin; CHOREOGRAPHY: Cheryl McFadden; SCENERY: Christina Weppner; COSTUMES: Jean Steinlein; LIGHTING: Frances Aronson; MUSICAL DIRECTION: David Tice; PRODUCER: Interart Theatre

CAST—Margot Lewitin (M.C.), Lucille Patton (Lucy), Elizabeth Franz (Neil), David Tice (Pianist)

The action occurs in an attic of a mansion on the Eastern Seaboard, sometime in the past.

The play with music was presented in two acts.

ACT ONE—"The Banco Number" (Lucille Patton, Elizabeth Franz), "Oh How I Loved Him" (Elizabeth Franz), "Sawing a Woman in Half" (Lucille Patton, Elizabeth Franz)

ACT TWO—"I'm in the Market for a Dream" (Margot Lewitin, Lucille Patton), "Yesterday Is Over" (Lucille Patton, Elizabeth Franz)

NOTES—*Yesterday Is Over*, which was produced under an Off Off Broadway contract, was a dour look at the once-famous twins the Dolly Sisters (Jennie [1892-1941] and Rosie [1892-1970]). With fame long behind them, they sit in an attic in their wheelchairs and hash over old feuds and rivalries as they reminisce about their glory days when they were the toasts of Broadway and Europe. The two had appeared in over a dozen Broadway revues and musicals between 1910-1924, including the 1911 edition of the *Ziegfeld Follies*. In 1945, Hollywood filmed their life story as *The Dolly Sisters* (which starred Betty Grable and June Haver).

John Corry in the *New York Times* reported that only the staff of the Interart theatre group (a company primarily devoted to producing plays by women) knew who wrote the play with music because the credited writers, "Mady Christian" and "Bill Roscoe," were pseudonyms. It's unclear why the name "Mady Christian" was chosen because it was so close to the name of Mady Christians (1900-1951), the actress who created the role of Mama in the long-running Broadway hit *I Remember Mama* (1944). Christians also originated the role of Sarah in the Broadway production of Lillian Hellman's *Watch on the Rhine* (1941; for the 1943 film version, the role was played by Bette Davis).

Frank Rich in the *New York Times* found the work a baffling evening which seemed to draw upon *Follies* (1971), *The Sunshine Boys* (1972), and even the 1962 film *What Ever Happened to Baby Jane?* for its inspiration. Further, he noted that the character of the M.C. seemed to be a "hybrid" of Joel Grey's M.C. in *Cabaret* (1966) and Beatrice Arthur's Vera in *Mame* (1966). Moreover, the work had a certain anti-male streak running through it; and, on top of that, Rich reported that out of nowhere the M.C. gave a "completely irrelevant" speech about the problems encountered by female blue-collar workers.

Rich said the dialogue sounded as if it had been "badly" translated from a "non-Latinate tongue," and he described the songs as "mock-Weill." Although the production's official opening was in the latter part of June, the play had begun performances on May 7, with a cast which included Lucille Patton, Elly Stone, and Virginia Stevens. By the June opening, the latter two performers were no longer in the play and Elizabeth Franz and Margot Lewitin had assumed their roles (Lewitin was also the production's director). The estimated number of performances include both preview and regular performances.

1821 Yiddle with a Fiddle.

THEATRE: Town Hall; OPENING DATE: October 28, 1990; PERFORMANCES: 55; BOOK: Isaiah Sheffer; LYRICS: Isaiah Sheffer; MUSIC: Abraham Ellstein; DIRECTION: Ran Avni; CHOREOGRAPHY: Helen Butleroff; SCENERY: Jeffrey Schneider; COSTUMES: Karen Hummel; LIGHTING: Robert Bessoir; MUSICAL DIRECTION: Lanny Meyers; PRODUCERS: Raymond Ariel and Lawrence Toppall

CAST—Emily Loesser (Yiddle), Mitchell Greenberg (Aryeh), Steve Sterner (Wagon Driver, Tavern Keeper, Rabbi, Mr. Becker), Michael Ingram (Kalamutke), Robert Michael Baker (Froym), Danny Rutigliano (Truck Driver, Zalmen Gold, Stationmaster, Professor Zinger), Andrea Green (Waitress, Cook, Stage Manager), Steven Fickinger (Chauffeur, Yossel), Rachel Black (Cook's Helper, Musician's Assistant), Patricia Ben Peterson (Teibele), Susan Flynn (Teibele's Mother, Channah); Townspeople, Tavern Patrons, City Folk (Steve Sterner, Danny Rutigliano, Andrea Green, Steven Fickinger, Rachel Black, Susan Flynn)

SOURCE—The 1936 film *Yidl Mitn Fidl* (screenplay and direction by Joseph Green).

The action occurs in Poland during Summer 1936.

The musical was presented in two acts.

ACT ONE—"Come Gather 'Round" (Emily Loesser), "If You Wanna Dance" (Emily Loesser, Villagers), "Music, It's a Necessity" (Mitchell Greenberg), "Yiddle with a Fiddle" (Emily Loesser, Mitchell Greenberg), "Come Gather 'Round" (reprise) (Emily Loesser), "New Rhythm" (Michael Ingram, Robert Michael Baker, Emily Loesser, Mitchell Greenberg, Townspeople), "Help Is on the Way!" (Michael Ingram, Robert Michael Baker, Emily Loesser, Mitchell Greenberg), "Yiddle with a Fiddle" (reprise) (Emily Loesser, Mitchell Greenberg, Michael Ingram, Robert Michael Baker), "I'll Sing" (Robert Michael Baker), "Hard as a Nail" (Emily Loesser, Tavern Patrons), "Man to Man" (Robert Michael Baker, Emily Loesser), "Oh Mama, Am I in Love" (Emily Loesser), "Travelling First Class Style" (Michael Ingram, Mitchell Greenberg, Emily Loesser, Robert Michael Baker, Steven Fickinger), "Badchen's Verses" (Steve Sterner), "Only for a Moment" (Patricia Ben Peterson), "Wedding Bulgar: Dance" (Wedding Guests), "Help Is on the Way!" (reprise) (Michael Ingram, Emily Loesser, Robert Michael Baker, Mitchell Greenberg, Patricia Ben Peterson)

ACT TWO—"Come Gather 'Round" (reprise) (Patricia Ben Peterson, Emily Loesser, Mitchell Greenberg, Robert Michael Baker, Michael Ingram), "Warsaw!" (Michael Ingram, Emily Loesser, Patricia Ben Peterson, Robert Michael Baker, Mitchell Greenberg), "How Can the Cat Cross the Water?" (Emily Loesser), "Yiddle with a Fiddle" (reprise) (Emily Loesser, Mitchell Greenberg, Patricia Ben Peterson, Robert Michael Baker, Michael Ingram, Passengers), "Stay Home Here with Me" (Susan Flynn, Michael Ingram), "Take It from the Top" (Susan Flynn, Patricia Ben Peterson, Emily Loesser), "Come Gather 'Round" (reprise) (Patricia Ben Peterson, Emily Loesser, Mitchell Greenberg, Robert Michael Baker, Michael Ingram), "Yiddle with a Fiddle" (reprise) (Emily Loesser, Mitchell Greenberg, Robert Mitchell Baker, Michael Ingram, Susan Flynn), "Only for a Moment" (reprise) (Patricia Ben Peterson, Steven Fickinger), "To Tell the Truth" (Emily Loesser), "We'll Sing" (reprise version of "I'll Sing" [?]; Emily Loesser, Robert Michael Baker, Ensemble), "Help Is on the Way!" (finale) (Ensemble)

NOTES—Based on the 1936 film *Yidl Mitn Fidl* which starred Molly Picon, the musical told the story of a young girl who disguises herself a boy in order to travel with her father throughout the Polish countryside where they earn their keep as musicians.

Richard F. Shepard in the *New York Times* said the evening "sparkles with fun and music," and he praised Emily Loesser in the leading role, noting that she shined with an "all-embracing bright-eyed impishness." Shepard reported that the music of Abraham Ellstein (1907-1963) had been set to new lyrics by Isaiah Sheffer, who also adapted the book. (The film's lyrics had been written by Itzik Manger.) He said the score was a "bumper crop" of Ellstein's music (tango, doo-wop, a touch of the Andrews Sisters, and a "special difficult-to-define music that is a recognizable Yiddish area code").

1822 Yoshe Kalb.

THEATRE: Eden Theatre; OPENING DATE: October 22, 1972; PERFORMANCES: 95; BOOK: David Licht; LYRICS: Isaac Dogim; MUSIC: Maurice Rauch; DIRECTION: David Licht; CHOREOGRAPHY: Lillian Shapero; SCENERY: Jorday Barry; and Donald DuVall ("Scenic Artist"); COSTUMES: Sylvia Friedlander; LIGHTING: Tom Meleck; MUSICAL DIRECTION: Renee Solomon; PRODUCERS: H. Rothpearl and S. Ehrenfield & Associates, and The Jewish Nostalgic Productions, Inc.

CAST—Warren Pincus (Narrator), Elia Patron (Psachye, Kune), Jaime Lewin (Moishe Chossed, Zanvil), Shmulik Goldstein (Mechala), Mordechai Yachson (Motye Godle, Schachne), Jacob Zanger (Isroel Avigdor), Isaac Dogim (Rabbi Reb Ezre, Rabbi Mayerel), Miriam Kressyn (Leah, Tsivye), David Opatoshu (Rabbi Reb Melech), David Ellis (Nachum [Yoshe Kalb]), Reizl Bozyk (Gittel), Helen Blay (Feige, Bashe-Dviore), Ruth Vool (Serele), Shifra Lerer (Aydele, Bayle-Dobe), Raquel Yossiffon (Malkele), Jack Rechtzeit (Abish, Rabbi from Le-jane), Jacob Ben-Ami (Rabbi from Krakow); Chassidim and Townspeople (Dale Carter, Jack Dyville, Susan Griss, Claire Hash, James Vaughan, Robert Yarri, Keith Driggs, Shanna Kanter)

SOURCE—The short story "Yoshe Kalb" by Israel Joshua Singer and its stage adaptation by Maurice Schwartz.

The action occurs in Russia in 1860 and 1875.

The musical was presented in two acts.

ACT ONE—"Ein Koloheinu" (Company), "Song of Joy" (Jacob Zanger, Elia Patron), "The Three Good Deeds" (Miriam Kressyn, Shifra Lerer, Reizl Bozyk), "Wedding Procession" (Company), "Chosen Doime le Meilech and Rikodle" (David Opatoshu, Company), "Malkele's Song" (Raquel Yossiffon), "Wedding Dance" (Comany), "Trio" (David Ellin, Elia Patron, Raquel Yossiffon)

ACT TWO—"Tsivye's Song" (Miriam Kressyn), "Badchen" (Jack Rechtzeit), "Beis (Bwis) Oilem (Iolem) Tantz" (Company), "Rosh Hashono" (Company)

NOTES—Based on Israel Joshua Singer's classic Jewish novel of the same name, *Yoshe Kalb* ran for three months, and was the second of three Jewish-themed musicals which opened during the 1972-73 Off Broadway season (see entries for *The Rebbitzen from Israel* and *The Grand Music Hall of Israel*).

The musical was performed in Yiddish, and told the story of a young Jewish scholar whose actions lead him to a loss of faith. He ultimately abandons his wife and his way of living, and creates a new life for himself under a different name; but he ultimately returns to his home after many years. The denouement was not unlike the popular 1982 film *The Return of Martin Guerre* in which family, friends, and fellow townsman question whether the returning wanderer is or is not an impostor. Clive Barnes in the *New York Times* found it fitting that *Yoshe Kalb* opened at the Eden Theatre since the Eden was the original home of Maurice Schwartz' fabled Yiddish theatre company; in fact, the original non-musical version of *Yoshe Kalb* had been first produced at the same theatre four decades earlier. As for the musical, Barnes reported that the production could be enjoyed even without a knowledge of Yiddish, and he praised both the cast and Maurice Rauch's "bright, tuneful and decently ethic" score.

(Following the original production of Schwartz' Yiddish adaptation, an English version by Fritz Blocki was produced at the National [now Nederlander] Theatre on December 28, 1933, for four performances.)

1823 You Never Know. THEATRE: Eastside Playhouse; OPENING DATE: March 12, 1973; PERFORMANCES: 8; BOOK: Rowland Leigh; LYRICS: Cole Porter; MUSIC: Cole Porter; DIRECTION: Robert Troie; SCENERY: Robert Troie; COSTUMES: Robert Troie; MUSICAL DIRECTION: Walter Geismar; PRODUCER: Stanley H. Handman

CAST—Dan Held (Baron Romer), Esteban Chalbaud (Gaston), Grace Theveny (Ida Courtney), Rod Loomis (Lord Baltin), Jamie Thomas (Lady Baltin)

SOURCE—The 1928 play *By Candlelight* (a/k/a *By Candle-Light*) by P.G. Wodehouse (adapted from the Austrian comedy by Siegfried [sometimes given as Sigfried] Geyer, Karl Farkas, and Robert Katscher).

The action occurs in Baron Romer's drawing room in 1938.

The musical was presented in two acts.

ACT ONE—"By Candlelight" (Dan Held), "Maria" (Esteban Chalbaud), "By Candlelight" (reprise) (Dan Held, Esteban Chalbaud), "Maria" (reprise) (Esteban Chalbaud), "I'm Going in for Love" (Lynn Fitzpatrick), "I'm Back in Circulation" (Grace Theveny), "From Alpha to Omega" (Lynn Fitzpatrick, Esteban Chalbaud)

ACT TWO—"You've Got That Thing" (Esteban Chalbaud), "What Shall I Do" (Lynn Fitzpatrick), "For No Rhyme or Reason" (Esteban Chalbaud, Lynn Fitzpatrick), "At Long Last Love" (Estaban Chalbaud), "Greek to You" (Jamie Thomas, Dan Held), "You Never Know" (Jamie Thomas), "Ridin' High" (Lynn Fitzpatrick, Esteban Chalbaud), "They All Fall in Love" (Lynn Fitzpatrick, Jamie Thomas, Esteban Chalbaud, Dan Held)

NOTES—*You Never Know* was a drawing room farce about a baron and his valet who exchange identities, only to find the two women whom they're seducing have done the same.

The original production of *You Never Know* opened on Broadway in 1938, and had the second shortest run (78 performances) of any Cole Porter musical (*Around the World* played for 74 performances in 1946). Porter had been seriously injured in a horseback-riding accident while writing the score, and by the time the musical opened it had undergone a prolonged and arduous tryout, which included song interpolations by other writers.

The 1973 revival, which had been produced in stock during the previous summer, lasted just one week. Clive Barnes in the *New York Times* gave his highest praise to the musical's décor, reporting that as the curtain rose the audience was treated to a silver and chromium art deco drawing room replete with a mauve Bauhaus sofa and white chairs. But after the initial delight of seeing the set, everything "was pretty much downhill." Barnes felt Porter would have been better served with a revue along the lines of *Oh Coward!* (see entry) and London's *Cowardy Custard*. The revival omitted the following songs from the original production: "I Am Gaston," "Au Revoir, Chez Baron," "Don't Let It Get You Down," "Good Evening, Princess," "What Is That Tune?," and "Yes, Yes, Yes," all with lyrics and music by Porter; "By Candlelight" and "Gendarme," lyrics by Rowland Leigh and music by Robert Katscher; "No (You Can't Have My Heart)," lyric and music by Dana Suesse; and "Let's Put It to Music," "Ladies' Room," and "Take Yourself a Trip," lyrics by Edwin Gilbert and music by Alex Fogerty.

The revival retained only six songs from the original New York production: "Maria," "From Alpha to Omega," "For No Rhyme or Reason," "At Long Last Love," "You Never Know," and "What Shall I Do?" (the latter with lyric by Rowland Leigh and music by Porter).

The revival used a song titled "By Candlelight," but it wasn't the same "By Candlelight" which had been heard in the Broadway production with a lyric by Rowland Leigh and music by Robert Katscher. The revival's song had been written by Porter but had never been used in the original production.

The revival interpolated the following songs: "I'm Going in for Love" and "I'm Back in Circulation" (both of which were deleted during the tryout of the original production), "You've Got That Thing" (from *Fifty Million Frenchmen*, 1929), "Greek to You" (from *Greek to You*, an unproduced musical written by Porter in 1937), "Ridin' High" (from *Red Hot and Blue!*, 1936), and "They All Fall in Love" (from the 1929 film *The Battle of Paris*).

During previews, Grace Theveny replaced Barbara Norris, and the number ""Looking at You" was dropped (the song had been introduced in *Wake Up and Dream*, which opened in London in early 1929, and premiered in New York later that year).

The revival was recorded as a private souvenir of the production, and was released by Blue Pear Records in the 1980s (LP # BP-1015). The album includes "What Is That Tune?," which, along with "Looking at You," was apparently performed only in previews (however, "Looking at You" wasn't recorded for the album).

A script of a 1991 production produced at the Pasadena Playhouse was published by Samuel French, Inc., in 2001; this version was based on the adaptation by Rowland Leigh, with a revised "additional adaptation" by Paul Lazarus; the cast included David Garrison, Harry Groener, Kurt Knudson, Donna McKechnie, Megan Mullally, and Angela Teek. It was recorded by Fynsworth Alley Records (CD # 302-062-108-2) in 2001 with some members from the 1991 production (Garrison, Groener, McKechnie, and Teek) as well as Kristin Chenoweth and Guy Haines.

1824 Young Abe Lincoln (1961). THEATRE: York Playhouse; OPENING DATE: April 3, 1961; PERFORMANCES: 18; BOOK: Richard N. Bernstein and John Allen; "special dialogue" by Arnold Sundgaard; LYRICS: Joan Javits; "special lyrics" by Arnold Sundgaard; MUSIC: Victor Ziskin; DIRECTION: Jay Harnick; CHOREOGRAPHY: Rhoda Levine; SCENERY: Fred Voelpel; COSTUMES: Fred Voelpel; LIGHTING: Fred Voelpel; MUSICAL DIRECTION: Victor Ziskin; PRODUCER: The Little Golden Theatre production (produced by Arthur Shimkin)

CAST—DARRELL SANDEEN (Abe Lincoln), Lou Cutell (William Berry), Joan Kibrig (Minnie), JUDY FOSTER (Ann Rutledge), Ray Hyson (John McNiel), Tom Noel (Bowling Green), Dan Resin (Ninian Edwards), Ken Kercheval (Josh), Robert Darnell (Jack Armstrong), Ralston Hill (Seth), Barbara Cornett (Hannah)

The action occurs in New Salem, Illinois, in 1833.

The musical was presented in two acts.

ACT ONE—"The Same Old Me" (Darrel Sandeen, Company), "Cheer Up, Cheer Up!" (Joan Kibrig, Lou Cutell), "You Can Dance" (Judy Foster, Darrell Sandeen), "Someone You Know" (Darrell Sandeen, Judy Foster), "I Want to Be a Little Frog in a Little Pond" (Darrell Sandeen, Tom Noel, Dan Resin, Lou Cutell, Ralston Hill, Barbara Cornett), "Don't P-P-Point Them Guns at Me" (Robert Darnell, Ray Hyson, Ken Kercheval), "The Captain Lincoln March" (Darrell Sandeen, Ken Kercheval, Tom Noel, Robert Darnell, Ray Hyson, Lou Cutell, Ralston Hill), "Run, Indian, Run" (Robert Darnell, Ken Kercheval, Ray Hyson, Lou Cutell, Ralston Hill, Darrell Sandeen)

ACT TWO—"Welcome Home Again" (Company), "Vote for Lincoln" (Dan Resin, Tom Noel, Robert Darnell, Ken Kercheval, Ray Hyson, Ralston Hill), "I Want to Be a Little Frog in a Little Pond" (reprise) (Darrell Sandeen, Townsmen), "Cheer Up, Cheer Up!" (reprise) (Joan Kibrig, Lou Cutell), "Frontier Politics" (Dan Resin, Robert Darnell, Tom Noel, Ken Kercheval, Ray Hyson, Ralston Hill), Finale (Darrell Sandeen, Company)

NOTES—*Young Abe Lincoln* had a serpentine run in New York. It first opened at the York Playhouse on April 3, for a run of eighteen performances, and then transferred to Broadway at the Eugene O'Neill Theatre on April 25, and played there for twenty-seven performances (the elusive playbill for the Broadway production seems to be the Holy Grail of Broadway Playbills). After its Broadway engagement, the musical returned to the York Theatre on May 10 and played there for forty-eight more performances. The musical also was performed thirty-four times at various New York City public schools.

In reviewing the musical's Broadway opening, Milton Esterow in the *New York Times* said the one-hour show (booked for an open run with prices ranging from seventy-five cents to $2.50) "should be a neighbor of the town's hit musicals for some time." He praised the "delightful" score, the "excellent" book, and the "fine" cast.

It appears that "The Clarey Grove Song" (a/k/a "We're from Clary's Grove" and "The Clary Grove Boys"), which was sung by the characters of Jack Armstrong, John McNeil, and Josh, was not in the first Off Broadway production and was added for Broadway. The song appears on the cast album, which was recorded by Golden Records (LP # 76), and reissued in 1975 by Wonderland Records (LP # WLP-76); the first recording identifies the number as "We're from Clary's Grove," and the reissue identifies the song as "The Clary Grove Boys."

Young Abe Lincoln was presented at Ford's Theatre in Washington, D.C., on February 16, 1971, for a run of three weeks; prior to that production, the musical had played a special performance at Town Hall (see entry).

1825 Young Abe Lincoln (1971). THEATRE: Town Hall; OPENING DATE: February 13, 1971; PERFORMANCES: 1; BOOK: Robert Larsen and John Allen; additional dialogue by Arnold Sundgaard; LYRICS: Joan Javits; additional lyrics by Arnold Sundgaard; MUSIC: Victor Ziskin; DIRECTION: Jay Harnick; SCENERY: Fred Voelpel; COSTUMES: Fred Voelpel; MUSICAL DIRECTION: Walter Mitchell Cree; PRODUCER: Performing Arts Repertory Theatre Foundation and New York University's Town Hall

CAST—Robert Larsen (Abe), Ann Hodapp (Ann Rutledge), Liz O'Neal (Minnie), Frank Groseclose (Judge Bowling Green), Herbert Duval (Jack Armstrong), Alan Easterby (John McNeil), James Rivers (Josh), John Remme (Bill Berry), Bailey Davis (Ninian Edwards)

NOTES—The revival of *Young Abe Lincoln* was presented for one performance only, in celebration of Lincoln's birthday. It included the following songs: "Same Old Me," "Cheer Up," "You Can Dance," "Someone You Know," "Frog," "Clarey Grove," "Don't Point Them Guns," "Drill," "Run Injuns," "Welcome Home," "Vote for Lincoln," and "Frontier Politics."

For further information, see entry for the original 1961 production.

1826 Young Goodman Brown. THEATRE: LaMama Experimental Theatre Club (ETC); OPENING DATE: February 16, 1995; PERFORMANCES: Unknown; LIBRETTO: Richard Foreman; MUSIC: Phillip Johnston; DIRECTION: David Herskovits; SCENERY: Erika Belsey; COSTUMES: David Zinn; LIGHTING: Lenore Doxsee; PRODUCERS: LaMama Experimental Theatre Club; co-produced by Target Margin Theatre

CAST—Jamie Callahan (Little Devil), David Eye (Young Goodman Brown), Michael Gans (Brown's Father), Nicole Halmos (Faith), Julie Fain Lawrence (Goody Cloyse), Randolph Curtis Rand (Minister), Suzanne Rose (Granddaughter), Henry Steele (Devil), Andrei Clark, Gretchen Krich, Jennifer Westfeldt, Amy Wilson

SOURCE—The 1835 short story "Young Goodman Brown" by Nathaniel Hawthorne.

NOTES—*Young Goodman Brown*, an Off Off Broadway adaptation of Nathaniel Hawthorne's short story about a New England Puritan's encounter with the devil, doesn't seem to have enjoyed any further productions. Ben Brantley in the *New York Times* found the chamber opera somewhat "static" and lacking in theatrical tension. But he praised Phillip Johnston's attractive music, which was "laced with jazz, Latin dance tunes, waltzes and modern dissonance," and noted the score suggested a "subversive, nightclub version" of Benjamin Britten's opera *Peter Grimes*.

For other lyric adaptations of Hawthorne's works, see entries for *Feathertop*, *The House of the Seven Gables*, and *Rappaccini's Daughter*.

1827 Your Own Thing. "A New Rock Musical." THEATRE: Orpheum Theatre; OPENING DATE: January 13, 1968; PERFORMANCES: 933; BOOK: Donald Driver; LYRICS: Hal Hester and Danny Apolinar; MUSIC: Hal Hester and Danny Apolinar; DIRECTION: Donald Driver; SCENERY: Robert Guerra; COSTUMES: Albert Wolsky; LIGHTING: Tom Skelton; MUSICAL DIRECTION: Charles Schneider; PRODUCERS: Zev Bufman and Dorothy Love, in association with Walter Gidaly

CAST—The Apocalypse (singing group): Danny Apolinar, John Kuhner, and Michael Valenti; Tom Ligon (Orson), Marian Mercer (Olivia), Leland Palmer (Viola), Rusty Thacker (Sebastian), Igors Gavon (Purser, Stage Manager), Imogene Bliss (Nurse)

SOURCE—The play *Twelfth Night* (written in either 1600 or 1601) by William Shakespeare.

The action occurs in New York City at the present time.

The musical was presented in one act.

MUSICAL NUMBERS—"No One's Perfect, Dear" (Rusty Thacker, Leland Palmer), "The Flowers" (Leland Palmer), "I'm Me! (I'm Not Afraid)" (Danny Apolinar, John Kuhner, Michael Valenti), "Baby! Baby!" (Danny Apolinar, John Kuhner, Michael Valenti, Leland Palmer), "Come Away, Death" (Rusty Thacker), "I'm On My Way to the Top" (Rusty Thacker), "She Never Told Her Love" (Leland Palmer), "Be Gentle" (Leland Palmer, Tim Ligon), "What Do I Know?" (Leland Palmer), "Baby! Baby!" (reprise) (Danny Apolinar, John Kuhner, Michael Valenti, Rusty Thacker, Leland Palmer), "The Now Generation" (Danny Apolinar, John Kuhner, Michael Valenti, Leland Palmer), "The Middle Years" (Rusty Thacker), "The Middle Years" (reprise) (Marian Mercer), "When You're Young and in Love" (Tim Ligon), "Hunca Munca" (Danny Apolinar, John Kuhner, Michael Valenti, Company), "Don't Leave Me" (Marian Mercer, Rusty Thacker, Tim Ligon), "Do Your Own Thing" (Company)

NOTES—*Your Own Thing* was the second Off Broadway musical adaptation of Shakespeare's *Twelfth Night* to open in January 1968. It was an immediate sensation, winning the New York Drama Critics' Award for Best Musical, only the second time an Off Broadway musical had been so honored (*The Golden Apple* [see entry] had been the first). The musical ran for over 900 performances; its script was published by Dell Publishing Co., Inc., in 1970 (in a volume which also included the text of *Twelfth Night*) and by Stein and Day in 1979 in the collection *Great Rock Musicals*, edited by Stanley Richards; RCA Victor Records (LP # LOC-1148 and # LSO-1148; CD # 09026-63582-2) recorded the cast album. The musical later played London; and the film rights reportedly sold for a half-million dollars (but a film version never materialized).

There was even a related RCA album, *Hal Hester Does His Own Thing/Music from Your Own Thing* (LP # LPM-3996 and # LSP-3996). This was the era when even an Off-Broadway musical could enjoy two or more separate recordings (see entries for *Hair* and *Salvation*). As for Broadway shows of the era, a hit musical could expect a number of recordings; for example, there are at least eight different versions of *Carnival!* (1961): the Broadway, London, and Mexico City cast albums as well as five instrumental and studio cast recordings. But when one now plays the cast recording of *Your Own Thing*, or reads the script, one wonders what all the excitement was about. Those New York critics who were always eager to ride A Streetcar Named Trendy rushed to embrace this so-called rock musical (but the always perceptive Martin Gottfried saw through it, and termed the enterprise "long-winded" and "half-baked"). The score wasn't much; there was a pleasant number or two (particularly "I'm On My Way to the Top"), but most of the songs were mild at best. "What Do I Know?" was so corny in its approximation of a wailing 1950s-styled ballad that it must have been written that way on purpose. And "The Now Generation," "Hunka Munca," and "Do Your Own Thing" were just words and musical notes strung together in search of ideas. Perhaps the show's superficially clever staging allowed it to get by with critics and audiences. Slide projections of celebrities, film clips, and comic-book balloons were used to make supposedly witty asides to the audience. The musical tried so hard to be "with it" that criticism of it was tantamount to confessing that one was hopelessly stuffy and not part of the show's celebration of the "now generation." But was a slide projection of Everett Dirksen allegedly saying he can never remember if Marlowe or Bacon wrote the line "If music be the food of love, play on" really expected to crack up the audience? Was a slide of John Wayne presumably complaining about the use of four-letter words in the theatre intended to make the audience double up with laughter? If so, then these supposedly clever asides which were interjected into the action were hopelessly passé, on the level of the era's weakest television variety-show writing.

And the purposely "youth"-driven dialogue was at once dated and tiresome (a character is described as "freaked out" and "on a bum trip"; other characters say "It's where I'm at" and "It's my bag").

And, of course, the musical had no problem mocking religious figures (specifically Christian ones, such as Jesus Christ and the Pope).

Marian Mercer (who appeared as Olivia) left the show soon after it opened (and before the cast album was recorded), and was replaced by Marcia Rodd (who is heard on the cast album); two weeks earlier Rodd had appeared as Viola in the month's first musical adaptation of *Twelfth Night*, the flop *Love and Let Love* (see entry).

Like so many trendy works, *Your Own Thing* has drifted into obscurity, an all-but-forgotten moment of late 1960s musicals. Unlike *Hair*, which had the benefit of Galt MacDermot's lively score and which institutionalized the concept musical, *Your Own Thing*'s liteweight score (too insubstantial to even be lightweight) and insubstantial story and characters have probably doomed the show to theatrical oblivion, making it an unlikely candidate for revival (except perhaps as a period piece).

For information on *Music Is* (1976) and *Play On!* (1997), two Broadway musicals adapted from *Twelfth Night*, as well as an Off Off Broadway version titled *What You Will*, see entry for *Love and Let Love*.

1828 You're a Good Man, Charlie Brown. "A New Musical Entertainment." THEATRE: Theatre 80 St. Marks; OPENING DATE: March 7, 1967; PERFORMANCES: 1,597; BOOK: "John Gordon" (see notes below); LYRICS: Clark Gesner; MUSIC: Clark Gesner; DIRECTION: Joseph Hardy; CHOREOGRAPHY: Pat Birch ("Assistant to the Director," and who may have contributed to the musical staging); SCENERY: Alan Kimmel; COSTUMES: Alan Kimmel; LIGHTING: Jules Fisher; MUSICAL DIRECTION: Joseph Raposo; PRODUCERS: Arthur Whitelaw and Gene Persson

CAST—Bob Balaban (Linus), Gary Burghoff (Charlie Brown), Karen Johnson (Patty), Skip Hinnant (Schroeder), Bill Hinnant (Snoopy), Reva Rose (Lucy)

SOURCE—The comic strip *Peanuts* by Charles M. Schulz

The musical was presented in two acts.

ACT ONE—"You're a Good Man, Charlie Brown" (Company), "Schroeder" (Reva Rose, Skip Hinnant), "Snoopy" (Bill Hinnant, Gary Burghoff), "My Blanket and Me" (Bob Balaban), "Kite" (Gary Burghoff), "Dr. Lucy (The Doctor Is In)" (Reva Rose, Gary Burghoff), "Book Report" (Gary Burghoff, Reva Rose, Bob Balaban, Skip Hinnant)

ACT TWO—"The Red Baron" (Bill Hinnant), "T.E.A.M. (The Baseball Game)" (Company), "Glee Club Rehearsal" (Company), "Little Known Facts" (Reva Rose, Bob Balaban, Gary Burghoff), "Suppertime" (Bill Hinnant), "Happiness" (Company)

NOTES—If you liked insufferable wistfulness, interminable coyness, and self-conscious out-of-the-mouths-of-babes (and-dog) bumper-sticker wisdom, then *You're a Good Man, Charlie Brown* was the show for you. Unaccountably, the musical played over four years and toured widely; the script was published by Random House in 1968; and two cast albums were released by MGM Records (LP # S1E-9-OC and LP # (LP # S1E-9-OC-X); the former was recorded live at an early performance at the theatre, 80 St. Marks, and the latter was recorded in a studio. A 1966 pre-production recording had been released by MGM Records via their Leo the Lion Records/King Leo Series (LP # LE-900), and its cast included Orson Bean as Charlie Brown, Composer-Lyricist Clark Gesner as Linus, Barbara Minkus as Lucy, and Bill Hinnant as Snoopy, a role he would record four times (on the pre-production, Off Broadway, and television albums). A television version was produced in 1972 on NBC's Hallmark Hall of Fame, with Wendell Burton in the title role and with one original cast member, Bill Hinnant (the soundtrack was released on Atlantic Records [LP # SD-7252]). In November 1985, a cartoon version of the musical was telecast on CBS. There was also a studio cast album released by Pickwick Records (LP # PC-3069 and # SPC-3069).

But the musical's hold on the public soon evaporated. Its two Broadway revivals were failures: the first opened on June 1, 1971, at the John Golden Theatre for just 31 performances; the second revival, which opened on February 4, 1999, at the Ambassador Theatre, lasted for 150 performances. Moreover, the London production, which opened at the Fortune Theatre on February 1, 1968, played for only 116 performances (some sources indicate 130); Don Potter performed as Snoopy, and other cast members included David Rhys Anderson and Gene Kidwell.

Incidentally, the 1999 Broadway revival included two new songs, "Beethoven Day" and "My New Philosophy," both with lyrics and music by Andrew Lippa; the latter was one of the revival's highlights, and it was performed by Kristin Chenoweth (as Sally), who won a Tony Award for Best Performance by a Featured Actress in a Musical. The cast also included B.D. Wong (Linus), Anthony Rapp (Charlie Brown), and Roger Bart (Snoopy); Bart also picked up a Tony Award, for Best Performance by a Featured Actor in a Musical. This revival was recorded by RCA Victor Records (CD # 09026-63384-2).

Clark Gesner's score was mild, and only one song was truly inspired, Snoopy's wing-ding vaudeville-styled number "Suppertime." Despite the promise of his Princeton Triangle Club shows, his Off Broadway revue contributions, and the major success of the original production of *You're a Good Man, Charlie Brown*, Gesner wrote just one new musical for Broadway, the 1979 one-performance flop *The Utter Glory of Morrissey Hall*. He was later heard from in the 1998 Off Broadway revue *The Jello Is Always Red* (see entry), which opened (and quickly closed) four years before his death in 2002. The writer of *Charlie Brown*'s book was "John Gordon," which was a collective pseudonym for Clark Gesner, the performers, and various members of the creative team.

It appears that two numbers ("Queen Lucy" for Reva Rose and Bob Balaban and "Peanuts' Potpourri" for Bill Hinnant, Bob Balaban, Skip Hinnant, Reva Rose, and Karen Johnson) were written for the third and fourth spots in the second act, and may have been performed during rehearsals or previews. By opening night they were replaced by one number ("Glee Club Rehearsal").

In 1982, *Snoopy* (see entry) opened Off Broadway; while not a sequel per se, the musical was no doubt inspired by the long-running success of *You're a Good Man, Charlie Brown*. The lyrics were by Hal Hackady, the music by Larry Grossman, and David Garrison played Snoopy. For an earlier (1976) version of the musical (as *Snoopy!!!*), Don Potter played the title role (he had also played Snoopy in the 1968 London production of *Charlie Brown*). In 1974, Gene Persson, one of the producers of *Charlie Brown*, presented another coy musical; titled *R.J.* during its tryout and *Rainbow Jones* on Broadway, it closed on opening night. The title character (played by Ruby Persson, the producer's wife, who had also appeared as Lucy in the television adaptation of *Charlie Brown*) spent most of her time in Central Park talking to imaginary animals.

1829 Yours, Anne. THEATRE: Playhouse 91; OPENING DATE: October 13, 1985; PERFORMANCES: 57; LIBRETTO: Enid Futterman; MUSIC: Michael Cohen; DIRECTION: Arthur Masella; MOVEMENT: Helena Andreyko; SCENERY: Franco Colavecchia; COSTUMES: Judith Dolan; LIGHTING: Beverly Emmons; MUSICAL DIRECTION: Dan Strickland; PRODUCERS: John Flaxman; Arlene Caruso, Associate Producer

CAST—Betty Aberlin (Mrs. Van Daan), Trini Alvarado (Anne Frank), David Cady (Peter Van Daan), Merwin Goldsmith (Mr. Van Daan), George Guidall (Mr. Frank), Hal Robinson (Mr. Dussel), Ann Talman (Margot Frank), Dana Zeller-Alexis (Mrs. Frank)

SOURCES—The book ANNE FRANK: *The Diary of a Young Girl* and the 1955 play *The Diary of Anne Frank* by Frances Goodrich and Albert Hackett.

The action occurs from June 12, 1942, to August 4, 1944, in Amsterdam, Holland.

The musical was presented in two acts.

ACT ONE—Prologue (Company), "Dear Kitty: I Am Thirteen Years Old" (Trini Alvarado), "Dear Kitty: It's a Dangerous Adventure" (Trini Alvarado), "An Ordinary Day" (Company), "Schlaf" (Dana Zeller-Alexis), "She Doesn't Understand Me" (Dana Zeller-Alexis, Trini Alvarado), "Dear Kitty: In the Night" (Trini Alvarado), "They Don't Have To" (Company), "Hollywood" (Trini Alvarado), "Dear Kitty: I Have a Nicer Side" (Trini Alvarado), "We Live with Fear" (Company), "A Writer" (George Guidall, Trini Alvarado), "I'm Not a Jew" (David Cady, Trini Alvarado), "The First Chanukah Night" (Company)

ACT TWO—"Dear Kitty: It's a New Year"/"We're Here" (Anne, Company), "Dear Kitty: My Sweet Secret" (Trini Alvarado), "My Wife" (Betty Aberlin, Merwin Goldsmith, George Guidall, Hal Robinson), "Dear Kitty: I Am Longing" (Trini Alvarado), "I Remember" (Company), "I Think Myself Out" (Trini Alvarado, David Cady), "Nightmare" (Trini Alvarado), "For the Children" (George Guidall, Dana Zeller-Alexis), "Something to Get Up For" (Ann Talman), "Dear Kitty: I Am a Woman" (Trini Alvarado), "When We Are Free" (Company), "Dear Kitty: I Still Believe" (Trini Alvarado)

NOTES—The critics were generally unimpressed by *Yours, Anne*, the lyric adaptation of Anne Frank's diary. Frank Rich in the *New York Times* noted the musical didn't deteriorate into a burlesque like Mel Brooks' *Springtime for Hitler* sequence in the 1967 film *The Producers*, but added that after sitting through a few minutes of the "soporific" production, one might well wish that it had. In his review for *Women's Wear Daily*, Howard Kissel said the adaptation was not "a necessary or useful effort," and *USA Today*'s Miriam Rubenstone suggested audiences would be better off buying the paperback of the diary rather than a ticket to the show.

However, Clive Barnes in the *New York Post* noted that while the score didn't offer any particularly memorable musical moments, he felt the work was "deepened by the semi-operatic approach," and said that overall the evening was "moving, poignant," and "tasteful."

That's Entertainment Records released the cast recording (LP # TER-1118), which included three sequences not listed in the theatre program ("Much Too Young," "I Am Only Fifteen," and "Something Is New").

In 1996, a "music-theatre piece" based on both *Yours, Anne* and ANNE FRANK: *The Diary of a Young Girl* premiered as *I Am Anne Frank* and included excerpts from the *Diary* as well as songs from *Yours, Anne*; the work was recorded by the Anne Frank Center USA (the CD was unlabelled and unnumbered) and was performed by Andrea Marcovicci and Stephen Bogardus. Songs retained from the original production were "Dear Kitty: I Am Thirteen Years Old," "Hollywood," "The First Chanukah Night," "Dear Kitty: In the Night, in the Dark," "Dear Kitty: I Am Longing," "I Remember," "I Think Myself Out," "Nightmare," and "I Am Not a Jew." Also included were a title song and another "Dear Kitty" sequence.

In 1995, another musical about the Anne Frank story also opened at Playhouse 91; see entry for *The Secret Annex*. And in February 2008, an operatic version of Anne Frank's *Diary* opened in Madrid.

1830 Zanna, Don't! "A Musical Fairy Tale." THEATRE: John Houseman Theatre; OPENING DATE: March 20, 2003; PERFORMANCES: 112; BOOK: Tim Acito; additional book material by Alexander Dinelaris; LYRICS: Tim Acito; additional lyrics by Alexander Dinelaris; MUSIC: Tim Acito; DIRECTION: Devanand Janki; CHOREOGRAPHY: Devanand Janki; SCENERY: Wade Laboissonniere and Tobin Ost; COSTUMES: Wade Laboissonniere and Tobin Ost; LIGHTING: Jeff Nellis; MUSICAL DIRECTION: Edward G. Robinson; PRODUCERS: Jack M. Dalgleish in association with Stephanie Joel; Susan R. Hoffman and Lisa Juliano, Associate Producers

CAST—Jai Rodriguez (Zanna), Anika Larsen (Roberta), Darius Nichols (Buck, Bronco), Amanda Ryan Paige (Candy, Loretta), Enrico Rodriguez (Mike), Robb Sapp (Tank, Tex), Shelley Thomas (Kate), Jared Zeus (Steve)

The musical was presented in one act.

MUSICAL NUMBERS—"Who's Got Extra Love?" (Jai Rodriguez, Ensemble), "I Think We Got Love" (Jared Zeus, Enrico Rodriguez), "I Ain't Got Time" (Anika Larsen, Ensemble), "Ride 'Em" (Shelley Thomas, Anika Larsen, Ensemble), "Zanna's Song" (Jai Rodriguez), "Be a Man" (Jai Rodriguez, Ensemble), "Don't Ask, Don't Tell" (Shelley Thomas, Jared Zeus), "Fast" (Darius Nichols, Robb Sapp, Amanda Ryan Paige), "I Could Write Books" (Enrico Rodriguez, Ensemble), "Don't You Wish We Could Be in Love?" (Anika Larsen, Enrico Rodriguez, Shelley Thomas, Jared Zeus, Jai Rodriguez), "Whatcha Got?" (Anika Larsen, Ensemble), "Do You Know What It's Like?" (Jared Zeus, Enrico Rodriguez, Shelley Thomas, Anika Larsen), "Zanna's Song" (reprise) (Jai Rodriguez), "'Tis a Far, Far Better Thing I Do"/"Blow Winds" (Jai Rodriguez, Ensemble), "Straight to Heaven" (Robb Sapp), "Someday You Might Love Me" (Jai Rodriguez), "Straight to Heaven" (reprise) (Ensemble)

NOTES—*Zanna, Don't!* took place in a high school where being gay is the norm and straight students are considered social outcasts; despite a somewhat edgy theme which probably seemed like the sure-fire ingredient for an Off Broadway hit, the musical ran for just a little over three months.

Perhaps the evening's highlight was the high school drama club's show *Don't Ask, Don't Tell*, a musical-within-the-musical which dealt with the issue of whether or not straights should be allowed in the military and if a gay-only military policy should be abandoned.

Bruce Weber in the *New York Times* found the evening full of "talent, warmth and polish," and he praised Tim Acito's "candy-flavored melodies" (which, he reported, had audience members lining up in the lobby after the show to order CDs of the cast album [which was released by PS Classics Records # PS-314]).

The musical had been previously produced by

Amas Musical Theatre at the Kirk Theatre on October 17, 2002.

1831 Zombie Prom. "A New Musical." THEATRE: Variety Arts Theatre; OPENING DATE: April 9, 1996; PERFORMANCES: 12 Book: John Dempsey; LYRICS: John Dempsey; MUSIC: Dana P. Rowe; DIRECTION: Philip Wm. McKinley; CHOREOGRAPHY: Tony Stevens; SCENERY: James Youmans; COSTUMES: Gregg Barnes; LIGHTING: Richard Nelson; MUSICAL DIRECTION: Darren R. Cohen; PRODUCERS: Nat Weiss in association with Randall L. Wreghitt

CAST—KAREN MURPHY (Delilah Strict), JESSICA-SNOW WILSON (Toffee), Cathy Trien (Coco), Natalie Toro (Ginger), Rebecca Rich (Candy), Marc Lovci (Joey), Stephen Bienskie (Jake), Jeff Skowron (Josh), RICHARD ROLAND (Jonny), RICHARD MUENZ (Eddie Flagrante)

SOURCE—A story by John Dempsey and Hugh M. Murphy.

The action occurs in the Nuclear Fifties.

The musical was presented in two acts.

ACT ONE—"Enrico Fermi High" (Jessica-Snow Wilson, Richard Roland, Cathy Trien, Rebecca Rich, Natalie Toro, Jeff Skowron, Marc Lovci, Stephen Bienskie, Karen Murphy), "Ain't No Goin' Back" (Jessica-Snow Wilson, Richard Roland, Kids), "Jonny Don't Cry" (Jessica-Snow Wilson, Girls), "Good as It Gets" (Jessica-Snow Wilson, Kids), "The C Word" (Jessica-Snow Wilson, Richard Roland, Kids), "Rules, Regulations, and Respect" (Karen Murphy, Kids), "Blast from the Past" (Richard Roland, Kids), "That's the Beat for Me" (Richard Muenz, Secretaries, Copy Boys), "The Voice in the Ocean" (Richard Roland, Jessica-Snow Wilson), "It's Alive" (Richard Roland, Karen Murphy, Kids), "Where Do We Go from Here" (Richard Roland, Jessica-Snow Wilson, Kids), "Trio (Case Closed)" (Richard Muenz, Karen Murphy, Richard Roland)

ACT TWO—"Then Came Jonny" (Karen Murphy, Richard Roland, Jessica-Snow Wilson, Kids), "Come Join Us" ('Ramona Meringue,' Motorwise Gasoline Guys, Richard Muenz, Richard Roland), "How Can I Say Goodbye?" (Richard Roland, Motorwise Gasoline Guys), "Easy To Say" (Jessica-Snow Wilson, Girls), "Expose" (Richard Muenz, Karen Murphy), "Isn't It?" (Kids), "Forbidden Love" (Jessica-Snow Wilson, Richard Roland, Kids), "The Lid's Been Blown" (Richard Muenz, Karen Murphy, Kids), "Zombie Prom" (Company)

NOTES—*Zombie Prom* was the season's second musical about zombies (see entry for *Zombies from the Beyond*). Both musicals had short engagements, but *Zombie Prom* seems to have been short-changed by both critics and audiences. It deserved a lengthy run.

With a witty book and a playful and often adventurous score which offered a new genre of theatre music (call it retro sci-fi operetta), *Zombie Prom* told the story of Toffee and Jonny, seniors who attend Enrico Fermi High School (Fermi is hailed as the "beloved father of the atomic bomb"). Because of Jonny's rebelliousness (this is the 1950s, after all, and so the rebel with a cause goes against the natural order of things by omitting the "h" from the spelling of his name), Toffee breaks up with Jonny, thus causing him to jump into the main nuclear waste treatment silo of the local neighborhood Francis Gary Powers Nuclear Plant (his death is "a tragic case of a hormonal imbalance resulting in a class three nuclear disaster"). But all is not lost, because Jonny returns from the dead as a zombie ("Gonna get me my diploma/And complete my senior year") and thus he and Toffee will be able to attend the all-important senior prom together (although "there are bound to be a lot of people out there who won't accept us as a couple").

The merry cast recording was released by First Night Records (CD # CAST-CD-66), and the very funny script was published by Samuel French, Inc., in 1996.

The published script included two songs not heard in the New York production or the recording ("At the Dance" and "How Do You Stand on Dreams?").

The musical had first been produced in February 1993 at the Red Barn Theatre in Key West, Florida, and then by the New River Repertory Theatre in Ft. Lauderdale. A subsequent New York workshop in February and March of 1995 included Kristin Chenoweth in the role of Toffee.

The musical played at the Landor Theatre in London from 20 October to 14 November 2009; further, a 36-minute film adaption in 2006 won the Best Short Film award at the Palm Beach International Film Festival.

1832 Zombies from the Beyond. THEATRE: Players Theatre; OPENING DATE: October 23, 1995; PERFORMANCES: 72; BOOK: James Valcq; LYRICS: James Valcq; MUSIC: James Valcq; DIRECTION: Pam Kriger; CHOREOGRAPHY: Pam Kriger; SCENERY: James Schuette; COSTUMES: James Schuette; LIGHTING: Ken Billington; MUSICAL DIRECTION: Andrew Wilder; PRODUCER: Colin Cabot

CAST—Michael Shelle (Major Malone), Robert Boles (Rick Jones), Suzanne Graff (Charlene [Charlie] Osmanski), Jeremy Czarniak (Billy Krutzik), Claire Morkin (Mary Malone), Matt McClanahan (Trenton Corbett), Susan Gottschalk (Zombina)

The action occurs at the Milwaukee Space Center and environs during May 1955.

The musical was presented in two acts.

ACT ONE—"The Sky's the Limit" (Michael Shelle, Robert Boles, Suzanne Graff, Jeremy Czarniak, Claire Morkin, Matt McClanahan), "The Rocket-Roll" (Robert Boles, Claire Morkin), "Second Planet on the Right" (Matt McClanahan, Claire Morkin), "Blast Off Baby" (Suzanne Graff, Robert Boles, Matt McClanahan), "Atomic Feet" (Jeremy Czarniak), "Big Wig" (Robert Boles), "In the Stars" (Claire Morkin, Ensemble), "Secret Weapon" (Susan Gottschalk), "Zombies from the Beyond" (Susan Gottschalk, Robert Boles, Zombettes)

ACT TWO—"Dateline: Milwaukee" (Michael Shelle, Matt McClanahan, Claire Morkin, Jeremy Czarniak), "Second Planet on the Right" (reprise) (Matt McClanahan, Claire Morkin), "The American Way" (Matt McClanahan, Claire Morkin, Michael Shelle) "I Am a Zombie" (Robert Boles, Company), "The Last Man on Earth" (Susan Gottschalk), "Breaking the Sound Barrier" (Susan Gottschalk, Company), "Keep Watching the Skies" (Michael Shelle, Company)

NOTES—With the huge success of *Little Shop of Horrors* (see entry), many producers believed any edgy and/or ironic science-fiction musical was a sure-fire box-office winner. But *Zombies from the Beyond* (like *Starmites* and *Return to the Forbidden Planet* before it and *Zombie Prom* [the *second* zombie musical of the 1995-1996 season!], *Space Trek*, and *Bat Boy: The Musical* after it) didn't make much of an impression, and so *Little Shop* remains the outstanding success of this limited genre (even the original 1975 Broadway production of *The Rocky Horror Show* was a flop, running only thirty-two performances). The script of *Zombies from the Beyond* (published by Dramatists Play Service, Inc., in 2007) reads well; the plot dealt with both Communists *and* alien beings threatening Milwaukee.

Appendices

Appendix A: Chronology

The following is a seasonal chronology of the 1,804 musicals discussed in this book. For a few entries, exact opening dates are unknown, and thus those musical's opening dates are estimated (these musicals are notated with an asterisk; for further information, the reader may refer to the specific entry for the musical). A double asterisk denotes the musicals closed prior to their official openings (*Bodo*, in fact, closed during rehearsals).

1909-1910
The Pipe of Desire

1911-1912
Mona

1912-1913
Cyrano

1913-1914
Madeleine

1916-1917
The Canterbury Pilgrims

1917-1918
The Dance in Place Congo
The Robin Woman: Shanewis

1918-1919
The Better 'Ole, or The Romance of Old Bill
The Legend
The Temple Dancer

1919-1920
The Greenwich Village Follies
Cleopatra's Night

1920-1921
Strut Miss Lizzie
The Greenwich Village Follies of 1920
A Fantastic Fricassee

1922-1923
The Grand Street Follies (First Edition)

1923-1924
The Grand Street Follies (Second Edition)

1924-1925
The Grand Street Follies (Third Edition)

1925-1926
Polly
Bad Habits of 1926

1926-1927
The Grand Street Follies (Fourth Edition)
The King's Henchman
The Grand Street Follies (Fifth Edition)

1929-1930
A Noble Rouge

1930-1931
Peter Ibbetson

1932-1933
The Emperor Jones

1933-1934
Merry Mount

1934-1935
In the Pasha's Garden

1935-1936
The Provincetown Follies
Entre-Nous
Murder in the Old Red Barn

1936-1937
Pepper Mill
Naughty-Naught '00
The Man Without a Country

1937-1938
The Fireman's Flame
Amelia Goes to the Ball

1938-1939
The Girl from Wyoming

1939-1940
Two for Tonight

1940-1941
No for an Answer
Paul Bunyan

1941-1942
The Island God

1946-1947
Naughty-Naught '00 (revival)
The Warrior
The Mother of Us All

1950-1951
*My Lucky Day**

1951-1952
A Night in Venice
Music, Music

1953-1954
Volpone
The Threepenny Opera
The Golden Apple
The Tender Land
Hello Out There
Malady of Love

1954-1955
Arabian Nights
I Feel Wonderful
Sandhog
Shoestring Revue
Once Over Lightly
Phoenix'55

1955-1956
The Threepenny Opera (return engagement)
Four Below
Pantaloon
The Littlest Revue
*Murder in 3 Keys** (*Black Roses, Dark Sonnet*, and *Simoon*)

1956-1957
By Hex
The World's My Oyster
The Son of Four Below
The Tempest
Susannah
Johnny Johnson
Shoestring '57
Well I Never!
Livin' the Life
Simply Heavenly

1957-1958
Kaleidoscope
The Best of Burlesque
The Italian Straw Hat
Take Five
In Your Hat
Simply Heavenly (return engagement)
Conversation Piece
The Sweet Bye and Bye
Vanessa
The Boy Friend
The Ballad of Baby Doe
Tale for a Deaf Ear
The Taming of the Shrew
The Pet Shop
The Robbers
The Good Soldier Schweik
Three by One (*A Game of Chance, The Rajah's Ruby*, and *Chanticleer*)
Nightcap
*Mr. Montage**

1958-1959
The Egg and I
Demi-Dozen
Diversions
A Party with Betty Comden and Adolph Green
Salad Days
Hamlet of Stepney Green
Of Mice and Men (Alfred Brooks)
On the Town
Fashion, or *Life in New York*
She Shall Have Music
Ole!
The Scarf
Wuthering Heights (Carlisle Floyd)
He Who Gets Slapped
The Triumph of St. Joan
Six Characters in Search of an Author
Once Upon a Mattress
Chic
Fallout
Leave It to Jane

1959-1960
2 x 4
The Billy Barnes Revue
Pieces-of-Eight
Four Below Strikes Back
Lend an Ear
Mis-Guided Tour
Billy Barnes Revue (return engagement)
The Kosher Widow
Little Mary Sunshine
Dinny and the Witches
The Follies of 1910
Parade (a/k/a *Jerry Herman's Parade*)
Russell Patterson's Sketchbook
Shakespeare in Harlem (*God's Trombones* and *Shakespeare in Harlem*)
The Crystal Heart
41 in a Sack
Miss Emily Adam
Gay Divorce
Oh, Kay!
The Fantasticks
Ernest in Love
*Taboo Revue** (a/k/a *Timothy Grey's Taboo Revue*)

1960-1961
Christopher's Wonders
A Delightful Season
Greenwich Village, U.S.A.
Dressed to the Nines
Valmouth
Kittiwake Island
The Shoemaker and the Peddler
Darwin's Theories
Kulka, Burr and Ollie
Stewed Prunes
The Premise
Beautiful Dreamer
Ballet Ballads
O, Oysters!!!
Bartleby
Two for Fun
Elsa Lancaster—Herself
The Tiger Rag
Double Entry (*The Bible Salesman* and *The Oldest Trick in the World*)
What a Killing
The Decameron
Hobo
Smiling the Boy Fell Dead
Young Abe Lincoln
The Tattooed Countess
A Curious Evening with Gypsy Rose Lee
Meet Peter Grant
*Ten-ish, Anyone?**

1961-1962
Paradise Island
I Want You
Fourth Avenue North
Hi, Paisano!
The Sap of Life
Between Whisky and Vodka
Seven Come Eleven
The Wings of the Dove
Another Evening with Harry Stoones
Bei Mir Bistu Schoen
The Crucible
O Marry Me!

Go Fight City Hall
Time, Gentlemen Please! (*Ridgeway's Late Joys*)
All in Love
Bella
'Toinette
Sing Muse!
Black Nativity
Signs Along the Cynic Route
All Kinds of Giants
Not While I'm Eating
Madame Aphrodite
Brecht on Brecht
Fortuna
Seacoast of Bohemia
Time, Gentlemen Please (Second Edition)
The Banker's Daughter
Fly Blackbird
The Golden Apple (revival)
This Was Burlesque
Pilgrim's Progress
Half-Past Wednesday
King of the Whole Damn World!
The Difficult Woman
Anything Goes
Alarums and Excursions
The Cats' Pajamas

1962-1963

Down in the Valley/*Look at Us*
The Kumquat in the Persimmon Tree
Sweet Miani
Digging for Apples
Ten Nights in a Barroom
O Say Can You See!
No Shoestrings
The Passion of Jonathan Wade
Dime a Dozen
Old Bucks and New Wings
We're Civilized?
Les Poupees des Paris
Riverwind
The Establishment
Graham Crackers
The Long Christmas Dinner
Best Foot Forward
New York Coloring Book
To the Water Tower
Man in the Moon
The Boys from Syracuse
The Uncommon Denominator
Utopia!
Put It in Writing
Four Faces East

1963-1964

The World of Kurt Weill in Song
The Living Premise
Tour de Four
Around the World in 80 Days
Money
Seven Come Eleven (Second Edition)
When the Owl Screams
A Political Party
Morning Sun
Gentlemen, Be Seated!
The Prince and the Pauper (George Fischoff)
Ballad for Bimshire
The Streets of New York
The Establishment
The Plot Against the Chase Manhattan Bank
Burlesque on Parade
The Stones of Jehoshaphat
Trumpets of the Lord
*What Happened**
Pimpernel!
Baker's Dozen
Will the Mail Train Run Tonight?
Jerico-Jim Crow
The Athenian Touch
Open Season at the Second City
The Last Savage
Cabin in the Sky
Jo
... And in This Corner
The Amorous Flea
Dynamite Tonight
Cindy
The Salad of the Mad Café
The Muffled Report
The Wrecking Ball
*Alice with Kisses***
Home Movies
The World of Kurt Weill in Song (Return Engagement)
International Playgirls '64
The Third Ear

1964-1965

All by Myself
World of Illusion
A View from Under the Bridge
That Hat!
The Game Is Up (First Edition)
Bits and Pieces XIV
Natalia Petrovna
Gogo Loves You
Good Luck
Hang Down Your Head and Die
That Five A.M. Jazz (production included musical *Five A.M. Jazz*)
Cambridge Circus
The Cradle Will Rock
Enchanting Melody
The Secret Life of Walter Mitty
Babes in the Wood
New Cambridge Circus
The Worlds of Oscar Brown, Jr.
The Game Is Up (Second Edition)
Lizzie Borden
The Decline and Fall of the Entire World as Seen Through the Eyes of Cole Porter Revisited (First Edition)
Wet Paint
The Wonderful World of Burlesque (First Edition)
That Thing at the Cherry Lane
The Prodigal Son
The Wonderful World of Burlesque (Second Edition)

1965-1966

The Game Is Up (Third Edition)
Mardi Gras!
Leonard Bernstein's Theatre Songs
Mackey of Appalachia
Pick a Number XV
Play That on Your Old Piano
Hotel Passionato
Hello, Charlie
Just for Openers
Miss Julie
Great Scot!
The Decline and Fall of the Entire World as Seen Through the Eyes of Cole Porter Revisited (a/k/a *New Cole Porter Revue*) (Second Edition)
The Mad Show
Jonah (Meyer Kupferman)
Why Do I Deserve This? (*Womit Haben wir das Verdient?*)
Pomegranada
Hooray! It's a Glorious Day ... and All That
The Return of the Second City in "20,000 Frozen Grenadiers"
Bohikee Creek

1966-1967

Below the Belt
Potluck!
Men and Dreams
Antony and Cleopatra
The World of My America
My Wife and I
Mixed Doubles
Autumn's Here!
Man with a Load of Mischief
Blitzstein!
The Penny Friend
By Jupiter
The Golden Screw
People Is the Thing That the World Is Fullest Of
Junebug Graduates Tonight!
The Harold Arlen Songbook
Shoemakers' Holiday
You're a Good Man, Charlie Brown
Dynamite Tonite!
Mourning Becomes Electra
Carricknabauna
Skits-Oh-Frantics!
Gorilla Queen
Davy Jones' Locker
Follies Burlesque '67
An Evening with the Times Square Two
Pins and Needles
Absolutely Freeee
*The Playoffs of Mixed Doubles**

1967-1968

In the Nick of Time
Klenosky Against the Slings and Arrows of Outrageous Fortune
Now Is the Time for All Good Men
Beyond Desire
Hair (Anspacher Theatre engagement)
Vinyl
In Circles
Curley McDimple
Take It from the Top
Winnie the Pooh
4 in Hand
Hair (Cheetah Theatre engagement)
Dark Horses
Love and Let Love
Have I Got One for You
Your Own Thing
Jacques Brel Is Alive and Well and Living in Paris
House of Flowers
Who's Who, Baby?
Oh, Say Can You See L.A.
Fun City
Photo Finish
Jerico-Jim Crow (revival)
Final Solutions
Bomarzo
Carry Nation
The Line of Least Existence
The Proposition (Jeremy Leven)
The Believers
*D.M.Z. Revue**
*Untitled Play**

1968-1969

Now
Frere Jacques
Walk Down Mah Street!
In Circles (revival) and *Songs by Carmines*
Instant Replay
The Fourth Wall
The Happy Hypocrite
Month of Sundays
Nine Rivers from Jordan
How to Steal an Election
Just for Love
Walk Together Children
Chad Mitchell's Counterpoint
Up Eden
The Wizard of Oz
Ballad for a Firing Squad
God Is a (Guess What?)
Dames at Sea
Get Thee to Canterbury
Horseman, Pass By
Peace
An Evening with Max Morath at the Turn of the Century
Of Thee I Sing
Winnie the Pooh
City Scene (a/k/a *Frank Gagliano's City Scene*) (production included musical *Paradise Gardens East*)
Salvation
Free Fall
We'd Rather Switch
Fiesta in Madrid

1969-1970

Promenade
Whores, Wars & Tin Pan Alley
Oh! Calcutta!
Pequod/*The Next Voyage*
Man Better Man
The Hoofers
Butterfly McQueen and Friends
The American Hamburger League
Salvation (revival)
From the Second City
*Mother Goose Go-Go**
Rondelay
Stomp (The Combine)
*The Way It Is!!!***
The Moon Dreamers
Sambo
Gertrude Stein's First Reader
The Whistling Wizard and the Sultan of Tuffet
*Christmas Rappings**
Love and Maple Syrup
Unfair to Goliath
The Last Sweet Days of Isaac (*The Elevator* and *I Want to Walk to San Francisco*)
Joy
Exchange
This Was Burlesque (revival)
I Dreamt I Dwelt in Bloomingdale's
Billy Noname
Show Me Where the Good Times Are
The House of Leather
Lyle
The Drunkard
Mod Donna
The Rise and Fall of the City of Mahagonny
Colette
The Me Nobody Knows
Akokawe

1970-1971

Whispers on the Wind
Golden Bat
Dames at Sea (revival)
Colette (revival)
The Whistling Wizard and the Sultan of Tuffet (revival)
Theatre of the Balustrade
To Be or Not to Be ... What Kind of a Question Is That?
Sensations
Touch
Moon Walk
Ali Baba and the 40 Thieves
*Elephant Steps**
*The Urban Crisis**
Stag Movie
Earthlight
Soon
The Shrinking Bride
It's Lynne Carter
Skye
Cooler Near the Lake
Do It Again!
Young Abe Lincoln (revival)
The Journey of Snow White
The Survival of St. Joan
Tarot
Look Where I'm At!
Blood
A Day in the Life of Just About Everyone
Nevertheless, They Laugh
The Proposition (Allan Albert)
Winnie the Pooh (revival)
The Red White and Black
Johnny Johnson (revival)
Six
Kiss Now
The Ballad of Johnny Pot
Godspell

1971-1972

Dance Wi' Me, or *The Fatal Twitch*
The Two Gentlemen of Verona
Leaves of Grass
Look Me Up
Drat!
F. Jasmine Addams
The Wizard of Oz
Love Me, Love My Children
Kumquats
Richard Farina: Long Time Coming and a Long Time Gone
Only Fools Are Sad
The Wedding of Iphigenia and *Iphigenia in Concert*
Peter and the Wolf
Anne of Green Gables (Norman Campbell)

*The Songs of Mao Tse-Tung**
*Song of Songs**
22 Years
Wanted
Two If by Sea
Grease
Walk Together Children (revival)
Summer and Smoke
Uhuruh
That's Entertainment
Dont Bother Me, I Cant Cope
God Bless Coney
Tommy
Cherry
Hard Job Being God
Hark!
One for the Money Etc.
Sweet Feet
The Beggar's Opera
The Big Show of 1928
*A Look at the Fifties**

1972-1973

Buy Bonds, Buster!
They Don't Make 'Em Like That Anymore
The Sunshine Train
Joan Curley McDimple (revival)
Mass
Safari 300
Ti-Jean and His Brothers
Speed Gets the Poppys
Aesop's Fables
Crazy Now
The Life of a Man
Berlin to Broadway with Kurt Weill
Lady Audley's Secret
Oh Coward!
The Rebbitzen from Israel
Lady Day: A Musical Tragedy
Yoshe Kalb
Religion
Winnie the Pooh
The Making of Americans
A Quarter for the Ladies Room
Twanger
Dear Oscar
Doctor Selavy's Magic Theatre
The Contrast
Virgin
The Bar That Never Closes
Say When
Step Lively, Boy!
The Blue Magi
Rainbow
The Trials of OZ
Davy Jones' Locker
Memphis Store-Bought Teeth
The Grand Music Hall of Israel
National Lampoon's Lemmings
Carmilla
Variety Obit
El Coca-Cola Grande (a/k/a *El Grande de Coca-Cola*)
You Never Know
Croesus and the Witch
Band-Wagon
The Karl Marx Play
Thoughts
Good Tomorrow
Smile, Smile, Smile
What's a Nice Country Like You Doing in a State Like This?
Hot and Cold Heros
Smith

1973-1974

Some People, Some Other People, and What They Finally Do
The Faggot
Antiques
Nicol Williamson's Late Show
Sisters of Mercy
My Mama the General
The Whistling Wizard and the Sultan of Tuffet (revival)
Lotta, or *The Best Thing Evolution's Ever Come Up With*
Markheim
Hard to Be a Jew (Sholom Secunda)
More Than You Deserve
Candide
The Life and Times of Joseph Stalin
Pinocchio
Let My People Come
2008½ (A Spaced Oddity)
Pigjazz
Fashion (Donald Pippin)
The Great McDaddy
Once I Saw a Boy Laughing...
Sextet
The Future
A Life in a Dream
Pop
Music! Music!
Ionescopade
Kaboom!
Ride the Winds
Judy: A Garland of Songs
Jacques Brel Is Alive and Well and Living in Paris (revival)
*Power**

1974-1975

Manhattan Follies
Listen to Me
The Big Winner
Gay Company
I'll Die If I Can't Live Forever
The Robber Bridegroom
Turquoise Pantomime
Just Libby
Street Jesus
How to Get Rid of It
Sgt. Pepper's Lonely Hearts Club Band on the Road
By Bernstein
The Prodigal Sister
Peter and the Wolf (revival)
Portfolio Revue
Pretzels
Broadway Dandies
The Charles Pierce Show
Hotel for Criminals
Bayou Legend
Diamond Studs
Dance with Me (revival)
Lovers
Man on the Moon
A Wedding in Shtetel
Bubbling Brown Sugar
Straws in the Wind
The Bone Room
*Sacred and Profane Love**
Alice in Wonderland
The National Lampoon Show
Ape Over Broadway
Wings (Robert McLaughlin and Peter Ryan)
Be Kind to People Week
Rhinegold
In Gay Company
Philemon
The Magic of Jolson!
God's Trombones
The Rainbow Rape Trick
A Chorus Line
A Matter of Time
Polly (revival)
The Red Blue-Grass Western Flyer Show
The $ Value of Man
The Glorious Age
Sweet Suite

1975-1976

A Musical Merchant of Venice
Boy Meets Boy
The Cast Aways
Victoria
Why I Love New York
The 5th Season
Christy
The Man with the Ragtime Blues
Men Women and why it won't work
Alice in Wonderland (revival)
Tania
A Mass Murder in the Balcony of the Old Ritz-Rialto
Boccaccio
Gift of the Magi
Tuscaloosa's Calling Me ...But I'm Not Going!
Columbus
Dear Piaf
Winnie the Pooh (revival)
Fire of Flowers
Apple Pie
The Bonus Army
The Polish Mime Theatre
Pouff
Fat Tuesday
Godsong
Dreamstuff
Le Bellybutton
I Paid My Dues
Tickles by Tucholsky
A Kurt Weill Cabaret
The Red Horse Animation
Das Lusitania Songspiel
Camp Meeting: 1840
*The Phantom Tollbooth**

1976-1977

Greenwich Village Follies
Beware the Jubjub Bird
Becoming
Montpelier Pizazz
Saints
Political Theatre Songs
Oh! Calcutta! (revival)
Those Darn Kids
Lovesong
The Club
Two of Everything
Davy Jones' Locker (revival)
2 by 5
Don't Step on My Olive Branch
The Beast: A Meditation on Beauty
Einstein on the Beach
Gauguin in Tahiti
The Second Shepherd's Play
Nightclub Cantata
Ichabod
The Cockeyed Tiger (or The Last, Final, Farewell Performance of Lilly Marlena Littleflea)
North Atlantic
Lulu
Grandpa
Memphis Is Gone
Castaways Mademoiselle Colombe
Piaf
Starting Here, Starting Now
Happy End
Movie Buff
For Love or Money
The Great McDaddy (revival)
The Confidence Man
Jacques Brel Is Alive and Well and Living in Paris (revival)
On-the Lock-In
Dance on a Country Grave
A Manoir
Der Ring Gott Farblonjet
New York City Street Show
*The Passion of Alice**

1977-1978

The 2nd Greatest Entertainer in the Whole Wide World
Love! Love! Love!
Unsung Cole
The Threepenny Opera (revival)
Camp Meeting
Children of Adam
For the Snark Was a Boojum, You See
Wonderful Lives
The Present Tense
Hot Grog
The Misanthrope
Survival
Washington Square
Nightsong
Bon Voyage
Fixed
Lyrical and Satirical: The Music of Harold Rome
Beowulf
Green Pond
An Evening with Wolfgang Roth (a/k/a *Voices from the Past*)
Joe Masiell Not at the Palace
Judy: A Garland of Songs (revival)
"2"
*Jacques Brel Is Alive and Well and Living in Paris** (revival)
By Strouse
Jacques Brel Is Alive and Well and Living in Paris (second revival of the season)
Ain't Misbehavin' Runaways
*Birdland**
A Bistro Car on the CNR
*Monsieur de Pourceaugnac**
Jigsaw
The Best Little Whorehouse in Texas
Boston Boston
The Last Vaudeville Show at Radio City Music Hall
The Class
*One and One**
Happy with the Blues
The Proposition (Allan Albert)
My Mother Was a Fortune-Teller
Rosa
Reunion
Funeral March for a One-Man Band
I'm Getting My Act Together and Taking It on the Road
Saint Joan of the Stockyards
Pins and Needles (revival)
Mahalia

1978-1979

Piano Bar
The American Dance Machine
The Coolest Cat in Town
*But Never Jam Today**
A Broadway Musical
Ain't Doin' Nothin' But Singin' My Song
Hot Dishes!
Music-Hall Sidelights
Laugh a Lifetime
Sparrow in Flight
In Praise of Death
Cartoons for a Lunch Hour
A Lady Needs a Change
Helen
In Trousers
Jimmy and Billy
Tune the Grand Up! Words and Music by Jerry Herman
Dancing in the Dark
My Old Friends
Take It from the Top
Streetsongs
*When Hell Freezes Over, I'll Skate**
*Shelley**
The Umbrellas of Cherbourg
Hillbilly Women
Says I, Says He
Telecast
It's So Nice to Be Civilized
*Success!**
Mary
Sterling Silver
The City Suite
Tip-Toes
Sancocho
Miss Havisham's Fire
Duel
Dispatches
Last Chance Revue
Saga
Encore
Suddenly the Music Starts
A Woman Without a Man Is ...
Festival
Wake Up, It's Time to Go to Bed!
Bea's Place
Strider: The Story of a Horse
Work and Win!, or *Frank Manley's Fortune**

1979-1980

Latinos
Miss Truth
Not Tonight, Benvenuto!
Scrambled Feet
The Madwoman of Central Park West
Sky High
The Beggar's Soap Opera
Someone's in the Kitchen with Dinah
Patch, Patch, Patch
Big Bad Burlesque!
The Jack the Ripper Review
The All Night Strut!
King of Schnorrers
Potholes
God Bless You, Mr. Rosewater
And Still I Rise

Postcard from Morocco
*How's the House?**
One Mo' Time!
Dr. Faustus Lights the Lights
Rebecca, the Rabbi's Daughter
A Kurt Weill Cabaret (revival)
Tongues
The Dream
Give My Regards to Leicester Square
Mama's Got a Job
Woody Guthrie
King of Schnorrers (return engagement)
Five After Eight
The Lullaby of Broadway, or *Harry Who?*
Before the Flood
Holeville
The Babes in Toyland
The Incredible Feeling Show
Say It with Music
*The Payoff**
Snapshot
Das Lusitania Songspiel
Hard Sell
Paris Lights
A Millionaire in Trouble
Fair Play for Eve
Jane White, Who?...
Elizabeth and Essex
The Derby (John Braden)
Shakespeare's Cabaret
The Canterbury Tales
Dunbar
The Housewives' Cantata
Changes
Star Treatment
An Evening with W.S. Gilbert
Censored Scenes from King Kong
Silverlake
Blues in the Night
The Haggadah
Sidewalkin'
Abi Gezunt
Song Night in the City
Tintypes
Fly with Me
Jam
Airtime
Fourtune
Black Broadway
Styne After Styne
Musical Chairs
It's Wilde!
*A One-Way Ticket to Broadway**
*Sinking Sinking**

1980-1981

The Lion and the Jewel
Turns
Chase a Rainbow
Fearless Frank
Billy Bishop Goes to War
Yesterday Is Over
Jazzbo Brown
The Pirates of Penzance, or *The Slave of Duty*
Under Fire
Gay Company Revisited
Betjemania
Girls, Girls, Girls
A Matter of Opinion
The Agony of Paul
Really Rosie
The Peanut Man, George Washington Carver
Scandal
Banjo Dancing, or *The 48th Annual Squitters Mountain Song Dance Folklore Convention and Banjo Contest ... And How I Lost*
Starmites
Frimbo
Ka-Boom!
Alice in Concert
Coming Attractions
Mama, I Want to Sing
Trixie True, Teen Detective
Dream Time
Hijinks!
Oh Me, Oh My, Oh Youmans
Shakespeare's Cabaret (revival)
Real Life Funnies
An Evening with Joan Crawford
Jacques Brel Is Alive and Well and Living in Paris (revival)
Summer Friends
In Trousers (revival)
Mo' Tea, Miss Ann?
A Reel American Hero
The Matinee Kids
Marry Me a Little
Bloolips in "Lust in Space"
T.S. Eliot: Midwinter Vigil(ante)
March of the Falsettos
It's Me, Sylvia!
Randy Newman's Maybe I'm Doing It Wrong
The Haggadah (revival)
Sister Aimee
The Crystal Tree
Ah, Men
I Can't Keep Running in Place
The Meehans
*Going Hollywood**

1981-1982

Harry Ruby's Songs My Mother Never Sang
Constance and the Musician
El Bravo!
The Heebie Jeebies
Close Enough for Jazz
The Laundry Hour
Jerry's Girls
Toulouse
The Derby (Robert MacDougall)
Louis
Everybody's Gettin' Into the Act
Pump Boys and Dinettes
Double Feature
Marlowe
Cotton Patch Gospel
The Roumanian Wedding
Will They Ever Love Us on Broadway?
Satyagraha
Pigjazz, II
Joseph and the Amazing Technicolor Dreamcoat
Child of the Sun
Tomfoolery
Head Over Heels
A Kurt Weill Cabaret (revival)
Snoopy
Francis
Waltz of the Stork
Oh, Johnny
Vamps and Rideouts
Alec Wilder/Clues to a Life
The Winds of Change
Lullabye and Goodnight
From Renoir—to Reagan
Livin' Dolls
I Take These Women
Nymph Errant
Maybe I'm Doing It Wrong
Poor Little Lambs
Lola
The Evangelist
*Sleeparound Town (Songs of Puberty)**
Letters to Ben
Bags
Five Points
Two
T.N.T.
Nightingale
Forbidden Broadway
Vagabond Stars

1982-1983

Blues in the Night (revival)
Social Intercourse: Pilgrim's Progress
A Drifter, the Grifter & Heather McBride
Cleavage
Life Is Not a Doris Day Movie
Herringbone
Broadway Scandals of 1928
All of the Above
Broken Toys!
Manhattan Rhythm
Little Shop of Horrors
The Death of Von Richthofen as Witnessed from Earth
Birdbath
Charlotte Sweet
R.S.V.P.
Pudding Lane
The Vi-Ton-Ka Medicine Show
Lennon
Corkscrews!
24 Inches
Bugles at Dawn
The 3 Travels of Aladin with the Magic Lamp
The Gospel According to Al
Rats
The Showgirl
Louisiana Summer
Upstairs at O'Neals'
Portrait of Jennie
*The Boogie-Woogie Rumble of a Dream Deferred**
Not-So-New Faces of '82
The Entertainer
The Little Prince (Ada Janik)
It's a Jungle Out There!
The Gilded Cage
Poppie Nongena
Adam
Miss Waters, to You
*America Kicks Up Its Heels***
The Rise of David Levinsky
A Bundle of Nerves
Champeeen!
On the Swing Shift
It's Better with a Band
From Brooks, with Love
Colette Collage
The Juniper Tree, A Tragic Household Tale (Wendy Kesselman)
Opening Night
The Cradle Will Rock (revival)
Jacques Brel Is Alive and Well and Living in Paris (revival)
The Mother of Us All (revival)
Egyptology: My Head Was a Sledgehammer
The Day, the Night
My Heart Is in the East

1983-1984

Taking My Turn
Sunday in the Park with George
American Passion
Banned in France
Non Pasquale
Dogs
The Brooklyn Bridge
Preppies
Basin Street
The Great American Backstage Musical
Dick Deterred
Serious Bizness
The Jewish Gypsy
Dementos
Of Mice and Men (Carlisle Floyd)
Blue Plate Special
It's Hard to Be a Jew (Alexander Yampolsky)
Weekend
Up from Paradise
The Buck Stops Here!
London Days and New York Nights
Tallulah
Crossroads Cafe
Sunset
Leftovers
Pahokee Beach
A Backers' Audition
One More Song/One More Dance
Lenny and the Heartbreakers
The Human Comedy
*Bodo***
Dinah! "Queen of the Blues"
Sarita
Bittersuite
Dr. Selavy's Magic Theatre (C'est La Vie)
Street Dreams (Helen Miller)
Sing Me Sunshine!
Babalooney
Selma
A ... My Name Is Alice
Judy: A Garland of Songs (revival)
Cummings and Goings
Hey, Ma ... Kaye Ballard
Orwell That Ends Well
The Road to Hollywood
Take Me Along
Pacific Overtures
The Nunsense Story
Not-So-New Faces of '84
The Me Nobody Knows (revival)
Mandrake
Love
Blackberries
Frozen Roses
Nite Club Confidential
Street Dreams (William Eaton)
Elizabeth and Essex (revival)
Broadway Babylon—The Musical That Never Was!
Brownstone
Abelard and Heloise
*Exhalations**

1984-1985

Golden Boy
Oh! Oh! Obesity
Waltz of the Stork Boogie
Shades of Harlem
The Chinese Magic Revue of Taiwan
Elvis Mania
Quilters
Rap Master Ronnie
The Games
Kuni-Leml, or *The Mismatch*
Feathertop
We're Home
What's a Nice Country Like You Still Doing in a State Like This? (revival)
Anonymous
Pacific Overtures (revival)
I Hear Music ... of Frank Loesser and Friends
Akhnaten
An Evening of Adult Fairy Tales (*Miss Chicken Little* and revival of *The Journey of Snow White*)
Jericho
Romance Language
Haarlem Nocturne
The Garden of Earthly Delights
Oy Mama! Am I in Love!
La Boheme
The Gifts of the Magi
Once on a Summer's Day
Diamonds
Horizons
A Kurt Weill Cabaret (revival)
Anne Reinking ... Music Moves Me
Jacques Brel Is Alive and Well and Living in Paris (revival)
Downriver
On the Lam
Tracers
Hang on to the Good Times
Streetheat
Sweet Will
3 Guys Naked from the Waist Down
Northern Boulevard
Carmines Sings Whitman Sings Carmines
An Evening with Ekkehard Schall
Taboo in Revue
The Making of Americans (revival)
Hollywood Opera
The Baker's Wife
In Trousers (revival)
Hannah Senesh
Manhattan Serenade
Penn & Teller
*Surf City***
Lies & Legends/The Musical Stories of Harry Chapin
Sit Down and Eat Before Our Love Gets Cold
Mayor
Tropicana

1985-1986

Ladies and Gentlemen, Jerome Kern
Dames at Sea (revival)
One Man Band
A Broadcast Baby
Options
What's a Nice Country Like

You ... Doing in a State Like This? (revival)
The Mystery of Edwin Drood
Tales of Tinseltown
Miss Gulch Returns!
Paradise
Angel Levine
The Lady of the Lake
Legs
Yours, Anne
The Special
Bingo!
Tatterdemalion
A Match Made in Heaven
Casanova
Hamelin
The Golden Land
Personals
Times and Appetites of Toulouse-Lautrec
Birth of a Poet
Just So
Nunsense
To Whom It May Concern
I Have a Dream
*Miami**
The Shop on Main Street
Sweet Will (revival)
Africanis Instructus
El Grande de Cola-Cola (revival)
Moby Dick
Halala!
La Belle Helene
To Feed Their Hopes
Williams & Walker
Living Color
Elisabeth Welch: Time to Start Living
Beehive
Sh-Boom!
Goblin Market
Just Once
Buskers
National Lampoon's Class of '86
Professionally Speaking

1986-1987

How I Survived High School
Vienna: Lusthaus
Sills & Company
Olympus on My Mind
Homecoming
Angry Housewives
X (The Life and Times of Malcolm X)
Back in the Big Time
Sex Tips for Modern Girls
Brownstone (revival)
Groucho: A Life in Revue
Hot Sake ... with a Pinch of Salt
Dori
Have I Got a Girl for You!
The Transposed Heads
Stardust
The Knee Plays
the CIVIL warS: a tree is best measured when it is down
Black Sea Follies
The Dangerous Christmas of Red Riding Hood
*A Romantic Detachment**
The Rise of David Levinsky (revival)
Dazy
Gay Divorce (revival)
The Hunger Artist
The Knife
Of Thee I Sing (revival)
Let 'Em Eat Cake
Staggerlee
Abyssinia
Standup Shakespeare
Prime Time
Funny Feet
Ready or Not
Shylock
The Little Show and Friends
Bittersuite (revival)
Cowboy
Three Postcards
(212)
No Way to Treat a Lady

1987-1988

Songs on a Shipwrecked Sofa
Bar Mitzvah Boy
Her Talking Drum
Strip!
Moms
Sayonara
Conrack
Julie Wilson from Weill to Sondheim
Sarafina!
Birds of Paradise
Tango Apasionado
Sophie
*Bittersuite** (revival)
Sing Hallelujah!
Oil City Symphony
One Two Three Four Five
Romance Romance (*The Little Comedy* and *Summer Share*)
The No-Frills Revue
Nixon in China
Mademoiselle Colombe (revival)
Davy Jones' Locker (revival)
*Millicent Montrose**
The Chosen
The River
A Walk on the Wild Side
Jacques Brel Is Alive and Well and Living in Paris (revival)
*Call Me Ethel!**
Struttin'
Liliane Montevecchi on the Boulevard
Alias Jimmy Valentine
Juan Darien
Ten Percent Revue
Robin's Band
Lucky Stiff
Bittersuite—One More Time (revival)
Kaye Ballard: Working 42nd Street at Last!
The Wonder Years

1988-1989

Godspell (revival)
Urban Blight
Miracolo d'Amore
Stranger Here Myself
The Blitzstein Project (*The Harpies* and *I've Got the Tune*)
Blues in the Night (revival)
Forbidden Broadway 1988
I Could Go On Lip-Synching!
Suds
The Taffetas
The Hired Man
The Middle of Nowhere
Sweethearts
1000 Airplanes on the Roof
Chu Chem
Desire Under the Elms
Songs of Paradise
Step Into My World
Together Again for the First Time
Will You Marry Me?
Prizes
Legends in Concert
Blame It on the Movies!
Laughing Matters
Showing Off

1989-1990

Sid Caesar & Company
The Red Sneaks
Buzzsaw Berkeley
The People Who Could Fly
Privates on Parade
Box Office of the Damned, Part 2
God's Trombones!
Paris '31
Closer Than Ever
Up Against It
Romance in Hard Times
Junon and Avos: The Hope
Forbidden Broadway 1990
A Spinning Tale
The Rothschilds
Dorian
Jonah (Elizabeth Swados)
Mama, I Want to Sing—Part II: The Story Continues
A Change in the Heir
Once on This Island
Further Mo'
Forever Plaid
Troubadour Hannah ... 1939

1990-1991

Jekyll and Hyde
Falsettoland
Broadway Jukebox
*The Manson Family/Helter Five-0**
Smoke on the Mountain
A Hard Time to Be Single
Pretty Faces
Yiddle with a Fiddle
Those Were the Days
Catch Me If I Fall
*Those Ringlings!**
Assassins
An Unfinished Song
Jeff Harnar Sings the 1959 Broadway Songbook
And the World Goes 'Round
Colette Collage (revival)
Love Lemmings
Pageant
Hydrogen Jukebox
Song of Singapore

1991-1992

Forbidden Broadway 19911/2
Prom Queens Unchained
Penn & Teller Rot in Hell
The Death of Klinghoffer
At Wit's End
Return to the Forbidden Planet
Tubes
Rags/Children of the Wind
I Won't Dance
Finkel's Follies
Big Noise of '92
Cinderella
The Ghosts of Versailles
What About Luv?
Chess
Just a Night Out!
Opal
Get Used to It!
Gunmetal Blues
Forbidden Broadway 1992
Groundhog
Ruthless!
Weird Romance (*The Girl Who Was Plugged In* and *Her Pilgrim Soul*)
Eating Raoul
The Marriage Contract

1992-1993

Casino Paradise
Balancing Act
Ethel Merman's Broadway
The World of Kurt Weill
The News in Review
A Rag on a Stick and a Star
Cut the Ribbons
The Voyage
Jacques Brel Is Alive and Well and Living in Paris (revival)
Juno
Bubbe Meises Bubbe Stories
A ... My Name Is Still Alice
The Shiek of Avenue B
Lightin' Out
Hello Muddah, Hello Fadduh!
Manhattan Moves
Madison Avenue
Theda Bara and the Frontier Rabbi
Forbidden Broadway 1993
Tapestry
One Foot Out the Door
Wings (Jeffrey Lunden)
Hey, Love
Back to Bacharach and David
Sondheim Putting It Together
Jack and Jill
Wild Men
Sharon

1993-1994

Prime Time Prophet
Piaf ... Remembered
Whoop-Dee-Doo! (a/k/a *Howard Crabtree's Whoop-Dee-Doo!*)
Songs from the Café Escargot
Annie Warbucks
The Little Prince (Rick Cummins)
Marilyn
Esther
Johnny Pye and the Foolkiller
Forbidden Broadway 1994
Black Rider
White Widow
First Lady Suite (*Eleanor Sleeps Here*, *Olio*, *Where's Mamie?*, and *Over Texas*)
The Petrified Prince
Ballet Russes
Hello Again
Ricky Jay & His 52 Assistants
Smiling Through
Avenue X
Stomp (Luke Cresswell and Steve McNicholas)
Amphigorey
American Enterprise
Fallen Angel
Bring in the Morning
Christina Alberta's Father
Hysterical Blindness and Other Southern Tragedies That Have Plagued My Life Thus Far
*A Song Floating**

1994-1995

Honky Tonk Highway
Faith Journey
That's Life!
Jelly Roll!
Two Hearts Over Easy
Ram in the Thicket
Rent
The Diva Is Dismissed
Nunsense 2: The Sequel
Inside Out
Das Barbecu
Body Shop
La Belle et la Bete
A Doll's Life
I Sent a Letter to My Love
Most Men Are
King Mackerel & The Blues Are Running
Young Goodman Brown
Jack's Holiday
Swingtime Canteen
Utterly Wilde!!!
Harvey Milk
Hundreds of Hats
Chez Garbo

1995-1996

john and jen
J.P. Morgan Saves the Nation
Identical Twins from Baltimore
Lust
Pets!
Time and the Wind
We'll Meet Again
The Secret Annex
Pomp Duck and Circumstance
Zombies from the Beyond
Pendragon
Songs for a New World
The Threepenny Opera (revival)
Splendora
Chinoserie
Bring in 'Da Noise, Bring in 'Da Funk
Jam in the Groove
Nunsense (revival)
A Haunted Deconstruction of Nathaniel Hawthorne's The House of the Seven Gables
Rendez-vous with Marlene
Too Jewish?
Sheba
Mata Hari
Bed and Sofa
Floyd Collins
The Green Bird
Forbidden Hollywood
Take It Easy
I Do! I Do!
Cowgirls
Zombie Prom
Tovah: Out of Her Mind!

1996-1997

I Love You, You're Perfect, Now Change
Born to Sing!
When Pigs Fly (a/k/a *Howard Crabtree's When Pigs Fly*)
The Cocoanuts
Disappearing Act
Dorian Gray
Magic on Broadway

Radio Gals
Forbidden Broadway Strikes Back!
The New Bozena
Nightmare Alley
A Brief History of White Music
What's a Nice Country Like You Doing in a State Like This? (revival) *Sharps, Flats & Accidentals*
Fyvush Finkel
No Way to Treat a Lady
Peter and Wendy
God's Trombones
The Portable Pioneer and Prairie Show
Capitol Steps
Space Trek
The Tokyo Shock Boys
Violet
Tap Dogs
Doctor! Doctor!
Saturn Returns: A Concert
The Green Heart
Nellie
*Rappaccini's Daughter**

1997-1998

Fairy Tales
Always ... Patsy Cline
On the Town (revival)
The Last Empress
The Irish ... And How They Got That Way
The Last Session
Momix
Secrets Every Smart Traveler Should Know
Two Pianos, Four Hands
Marco Polo
MindGames
Clue: The Musical
The Show Goes On
Hedwig and the Angry Inch
I Will Come Back
Tallulah's Party
Hot Klezmer
Emmeline
Savion Glover/Downtown
Dinah Was
Wind in the Willows

1998-1999

Symphonie Fantastique
The Jello Is Always Red
As Thousands Cheer
A New Brain
Nunsense-A-Men!
Jayson
Stupid Kids
*Billion Dollar Baby**
Queen of Hearts
Wuthering Heights: A Romantic Musical (Paul Dick)
Abby's Song
Forbidden Broadway Cleans Up Its Act!
Lyz!
Little by Little
Rollin' on the T.O.B.A.
James Naughton: Street of Dreams
Captains Courageous
Bright Lights, Big City
It Ain't Nothin' but the Blues
Queen of Hearts (revival)
Dream True/My Life with Vernon Dexter
Exactly Like You
Savion Glover: Downtown (revival)
Sorry, Wrong Number

1999-2000

Thwak
If Love Were All
Squonk
After the Fair
Summer 69
Naked Boys Singing!
A Good Swift Kick
Y2K, You're OK
The Donkey Show: A Midsummer Night's Disco
Shockheaded Peter
Stars in Your Eyes
James Joyce's The Dead
Sail Away
Central Park (*The Festival of Regrets, Strawberry Fields*, and *The Food of Love*)
Inappropriate
A Death in the Family
Jolson & Co.
The Bomb-itty of Errors
Our Sinatra
The Great Gatsby
Joyful Noise
Saturday Night
The Wild Party
The Big Bang
Look, Ma, I'm Dancin'!
Taking a Chance on Love
Postcards on Parade
Enter the Guardsman

2000-2001

The Bubbly Black Girl Sheds Her Chameleon Skin
Godspell (revival)
Berlin to Broadway with Kurt Weill (revival)
Imperfect Chemistry
4 Guys Named Jose ... and Una Mujer Named Maria!
The Gorey Details
Fame Takes a Holiday
A Class Act
American Rhapsody
Forbidden Broadway: A Spoof Odyssey
Book of the Dead (Second Avenue)
Foxy
Fermat's Last Tango
The House of the Seven Gables
Pete 'n' Keely
Time and Again
Suburb
Bat Boy
Newyorkers
Love, Janis
The IT Girl
Urinetown

2001-2002

tick, tick ... BOOM!
I Sing!
Once Around the City
Mr. President
The Spitfire Grill
Reefer Madness
Elaine Stritch at Liberty
Roadside
Roman Fever
Summer of '42
Forbidden Broadway: 20th Anniversary Celebration
The Last Five Years
Prodigal
Menopause: The Musical
That's the Ticket!

2002-2003

The Prince and the Pauper (Neil Berg)
Thunder Knocking on the Door
Harlem Song
Call the Children Home
Little Ham
A Man of No Importance
Water Coolers
Dudu Fisher: Something Old, Something New
Debbie Does Dallas
Bewilderness
Crowns
A View from the Bridge
The Seagull
Tommy Tune/White Tie and Tails
Little Fish
*Rain**
Radiant Baby
Heat Lighting
My Life with Albertine
Avenue Q
Zanna, Don't!
Little Women
Elegies
Hank Williams: Lost Highway
The Jackie Wilson Story
Dream a Little Dream
Boobs! The Musical (The World According to Ruth Wallis)

2003-2004

Mack the Knife
Thrill Me: The Leopold & Loeb Story
The Thing About Men
Sondheim: Opening Doors
Listen to My Heart
Wilder
Fame on 42nd Street
Golf: The Musical
Caroline, or Change
The Musical of Musicals
They Wrote That?
Ministry of Progress
Open Heart
Johnny Guitar
Chef's Theatre
Bare
The Joys of Sex
Here Lies Jenny

2004-2005

Children's Letters to God
Forbidden Broadway Summer Shock!
Junie B. Jones
From My Hometown
Let's Put on a Show!
Mandy Patinkin in Concert
People Be Heard
Absolutely Fascinating
Newsical
Gospel at Colonus Haroun and the Sea of Stories
The Immigrant
People Are Wrong!
Belle Epoque
Souvenir
After the Ball
Lone Star Love, or *The Merry Wives of Windsor, Texas*
Forbidden Broadway: Special Victims Unit
Under the Bridge
The 25th Annual Putnam County Spelling Bee
We're Still Hot!
Picon Pie
Lingoland
Altar Boyz
Lazer Vaudeville
Dessa Rose
Trolls
Songs from an Unmade Bed

2005-2006

Once Around the Sun
Dr. Sex
The Great American Trailer Park Musical
Bush Is Bad
Slut
Five Course Love
See What I Wanna See (*Kesa & Morito, Parts I & II, R Shomon*, and *Gloryday*)
Captain Louie
Infertility
Bingo
Almost Heaven: Songs of John Denver
The Little Prince (Rachel Portman)
The Ark
An American Tragedy
Mirette
The Seven
I Love You Because
Fanny Hill
[title of show]
Bernarda Alba
Grey Gardens
George M. Cohan Tonight!
Sidd
Jacques Brel Is Alive and Well and Living in Paris (revival)
A Fine and Private Place

2006-2007

Spring Awakening
Grendel
Shout!
The Fantasticks (revival)
Asylum: The Strange Case of Mary Lincoln
Evil Dead: The Musical
Mimi le Duck
Gauguin/Savage Light
How to Save the World and Find True Love in 90 Minutes
The Big Voice: God or Merman?
Kaos
Floyd and Clea Under the Western Sky
The First Emperor
Love in the Nick of Tyme
When the Lights Go On Again
Gutenberg! The Musical!
At Least It's Pink
misUnderstanding Mammy: The Hattie McDaniel Story
In the Heights
Adrift in Macao
Magpie
Be
The Juniper Tree (Philip Glass and Robert Moran)
Anne of Green Gables (Nancy Ford)
Passing Strange

June 1, 2007–December 31, 2007

Sessions
Forbidden Broadway: The Roast of Utopia
10 Million Miles
Gone Missing
The Last Year in the Life of Reverend Martin Luther King Jr. as Devised by Waterwell
Idol: The Musical
Neva Small: Not Quite an Ingenue
Walmartopia, The Musical!
Margaret Garner
The 2007 New York Musical Theatre Festival; musicals discussed under this entry are: *Austentatious, Bernice Bobs Her Mullet, The Brain from Planet X, Emma, Gemini The Musical, The Last Starfighter, Like Love, Little Egypt, Look What a Wonder Jesus Has Done, Love Kills, Love Sucks, Mud Donahue & Son, Platforms, The Rockae, Roller Derby, Such Good Friends, Tully (In No Particular Order), Unlock'd*, with *Glee*, and *The Yellow Wood*
Forbidden Broadway: Rude Awakening
Celia
Three Mo' Tenors
Greetings from Yorkville
Crossing Brooklyn
Yank!
Frankenstein
Make Me a Song/The Music of William Finn
The Glorious Ones
Black Nativity (2007)
Wine Lovers
Serenade
Queens Boulevard (the musical)
Cut to the Chase
A Kid's Life!

Appendix B: Discography

This is not a comprehensive discography for the productions discussed in this book but is instead intended to serve as a general guideline for the reader regarding which musicals in the book were recorded (including some private recordings). Generally, a recording's first release is listed, and, in some cases, its most recent release (e.g., for a musical which was first recorded on LP and then later reissued on CD, both recordings are listed). A few of the musicals on this list had no cast recording per se, but songs from the musicals were recorded on other albums. For example, Frederick Silver's 1978 revue *Sterling Silver* wasn't recorded, but six years later the cast album of a touring version of Silver's revue *In Gay Company* included five songs from *Sterling Silver*. As a result, *Sterling Silver* is listed in the discography, and the reader can reference the entry for *Sterling Silver* for specific information about which of its songs were later interpolated in, and recorded for, the cast album of *In Gay Company*. Similarly, the entry for *Gay Company* also references which songs had previously been used in *Sterling Silver* (note that each of Silver's various *Gay Company* revues had slightly different titles).

Another such example is the 1963 revue *New York Coloring Book*, which appears in this list even though a cast album of the production wasn't recorded; in the revue, Ronny White sang "Rocky on the Rocks," and later in the year the industrial revue *All About Life* included the song, which was again sung by Ronny White and thus constitutes an original cast performance of one of the songs from *New York Coloring Book*.

In a similar vein, there were no cast recordings for the 1970 production of *The Rise and Fall of the City of Mahagonny* and the 1979 production of *The Umbrellas of Cherbourg*; but for the reader who is unfamiliar with these scores and who wishes to hear them, the respective entries list various recordings of the scores.

Further, many of the entries in this book didn't receive Off Broadway cast recordings, but were recorded when their productions transferred to Broadway. For the discography, the Broadway cast albums are listed, and the reader can refer to specific entries for more information. In the case of the 1959 musical *She Shall Have Music*, there was no Off Broadway cast album, but a few years later a college production of the musical was recorded, and so the discography references that particular cast album.

Moreover, the 1968 Off Broadway production of *Ballad for a Firing Squad* (a revised version of *Mata Hari*, which closed during its 1967 pre–Broadway tryout) wasn't recorded; but the 1996 Off Off Broadway production of *Mata Hari* was, and since both productions shared the same basic score, both *Ballad for a Firing Squad* and *Mata Hari* are included in the discography, and the reader can refer to the specific entries for more information about which songs from the two productions were recorded.

The discography also includes cast albums which have been recorded (or are scheduled to be recorded).

A...My Name Is Alice
A...My Name Is Still Alice
Abyssinia
Adrift in Macao
After the Ball
Ain't Misbehavin'
Akhnaten
Alec Wilder/Clues to a Life
All in Love
The All Night Strut!
Altar Boyz
Always...Patsy Cline
And the World Goes 'Round
Anne of Green Gables (1971; Norman Campbell)
Anne of Green Gables (2007; Nancy Ford)
Annie Warbucks
Another Evening with Harry Stoones
Antony and Cleopatra
Anything Goes
Apple Pie
Arabian Nights
Around the World in 80 Days
As Thousands Cheer
Assassins
Asylum: The Strange Case of Mary Lincoln
Avenue Q
Avenue X
The Babes in Toyland
The Baker's Wife
Balancing Act
Ballad for a Firing Squad
The Ballad of Baby Doe
Ballet Ballads
Banjo Dancing
Bar Mitzvah Boy
Das Barbecu
Bare
Bat Boy
Be Kind to People Week
Bed and Sofa
Beehive
Bei Mir Bistu Schoen
The Believers
La Belle et la Bete
Below the Belt
Berlin to Broadway with Kurt Weill
Bernarda Alba
Best Foot Forward
The Best Little Whorehouse in Texas
The Best of Burlesque
Betjemania
The Big Bang
The Big Voice: God or Merman?
Billion Dollar Baby
The Billy Barnes Revue
Billy Bishop Goes to War
Billy Noname
Bingo
Birds of Paradise
A Bistro Car on the CNR
Blues in the Night
Bomarzo
Boobs! The Musical (The World According to Ruth Wallis)
The Boy Friend
Boy Meets Boy
Brecht on Brecht
Bright Lights, Big City
Bring in 'Da Noise, Bring in 'Da Funk
Brownstone
Bubbe Meises Bubbe Stories
Bubbling Brown Sugar
The Bubbly Black Girl Sheds Her Chameleon Skin
Bush Is Bad
Buy Bonds, Buster!
By Hex
By Jupiter
Cabin in the Sky
Cambridge Circus
Candide
The Canterbury Tales
Captain Louie
Carmilla
Caroline, or Change
Carry Nation
Casino Paradise
The Cast Aways/Castaways
Catch Me If I Fall
Charlotte Sweet
Chess
Chez Garbo
Children's Letters to God
A Chorus Line
Christmas Rappings
Christy
Cindy
A Class Act
Cleavage
Closer Than Ever
The Club
El Coca-Cola Grande (a/k/a *El Grande de Coca-Cola*)
The Cockeyed Tiger (or, The Last, Final, Farewell Performance of Lilly Marlena Littleflea)
Colette
Colette Collage
The Confidence Man
Contact
The Contrast
Conversation Piece
Corkscrews!
Cotton Patch Gospel
Cowgirls
The Cradle Will Rock
The Crucible
The Crystal Heart
Curley McDimple
Dames at Sea
Dance on a Country Grave
The Dangerous Christmas of Red Riding Hood
Darwin's Theories
A Death in the Family
The Death of Klinghoffer
Debbie Does Dallas
The Decline and Fall of the Entire World as Seen Through the Eyes of Cole Porter Revisited
Demi-Dozen
Desire Under the Elms
Dessa Rose
Diamond Studs
Diamonds
Doctor Selavy's Magic Theatre
A Doll's Life
Dont Bother Me, I Cant Cope
Down in the Valley
Downriver
Dream Time/My Life with Vernon Dexter
Dressed to the Nines
Duel
Dynamite Tonight (*Dynamite Tonite!*)
Eating Raoul
Einstein on the Beach
Elaine Stritch at Liberty
Elegies
Elephant Steps
Elsa Lanchester—Herself
Emmeline
Ernest in Love
Esther
Ethel Merman's Broadway
An Evening with Max Morath at the Turn of the Century
An Evening with W.S. Gilbert
Everybody's Gettin' Into the Act
Evil Dead: The Musical
Exchange
F. Jasmine Addams
The Faggot
Falsettoland
Fame on 42nd Street
The Fantasticks
Fashion (1974)
Fermat's Last Tango
Festival
A Fine and Private Place
Five After Eight
Five Course Love
Floyd Collins
Fly Blackbird
Fly with Me
Forbidden Broadway
Forbidden Broadway Cleans Up Its Act!
Forbidden Broadway: Rude Awakening
Forbidden Broadway: Special Victims Unit
Forbidden Broadway Strikes Back!
Forbidden Broadway 2001: A Spoof Odyssey
Forbidden Hollywood
Forever Plaid
Fortuna
Four Below Strikes Back
4 Guys Named Jose...and Una Mujer Named Maria!
Frankenstein
Gauguin/Savage Light
Gay Company
Gentlemen, Be Seated!
George M. Cohan Tonight!
Gertrude Stein's First Reader
Get Used to It!
The Gifts of the Magi
The Glorious Ones
Go Fight City Hall
Goblin Market
Godspell
The Golden Apple
Golden Boy
The Golden Land
The Golden Screw
Golf: The Musical
Gone Missing
The Good Soldier Schweik
Gospel at Colonus
The Grand Music Hall of Israel
Grease
The Great American Backstage Musical
The Great American Trailer Park Musical
The Green Bird
Greenwich Village, U.S.A.
Grey Gardens
Groucho: A Life in Revue
Gutenberg! The Musical!
Hair
Half-Past Wednesday

Hank Williams: Lost Highway
Hannah...1939
Happy End
Hard Job Being God
A Hard Time to Be Single
Hark!
Harlem Song
The Harpies
Have I Got One for You
Hedwig and the Angry Inch
Hello Again
Hello Out There
Hey, Love
Hey, Ma, Kaye Ballard
The Hired Man
Honky-Tonk Highway
Hotel Passionato
House of Flowers
The House of Leather
The House of the Seven Gables
The Housewives' Cantata
How to Save the World and Find True Love in 90 Minutes
How to Steal an Election
The Human Comedy
Hydrogen Jukebox
I Can't Keep Running in Place
I Do! I Do!
I Love You Because
I Love You, You're Perfect, Now Change
I Sing!
If Love Were All
I'm Getting My Act Together and Taking It on the Road
The Immigrant
In Circles
In Gay Company
In the Heights
In Trousers
Inappropriate
Infertility
Inside Out
The Irish...And How They Got That Way
It Ain't Nothin' but the Blues
The IT Girl
Jacques Brel Is Alive and Well and Living in Paris
James Joyce's The Dead
The Jello Is Always Red
Jerico-Jim Crow
Jerry's Girls
Joan
john and jen
Johnny Guitar
Johnny Johnson
Joseph and the Amazing Technicolor Dreamcoat
Joy
Juan Darien
Juno
Junon and Avos: The Hope
Just for Openers
Ka-Boom!
The Karl Marx Play
King Mackerel & the Blues Are Running
King of the Whole Damn World!
Kittiwake Island
Kuni-Leml
A Kurt Weill Cabaret
Lady of the Lake
The Last Five Years
The Last Session
The Last Sweet Days of Isaac
Leave It to Jane
Lend an Ear
Let 'Em Eat Cake
Let My People Come
Lies and Legends/The Musical Stories of Harry Chapin
Lightin' Out (as *Mark Twain's Blues*)
Lingoland
Listen to My Heart
Little by Little
Little Fish
Little Ham
Little Mary Sunshine
The Little Prince
Little Shop of Horrors
Little Women
The Littlest Revue
Lizzie Borden
Lola
Lone Star Love, or The Merry Wives of Windsor, Texas
Look, Ma, I'm Dancin'!
Love
Love and Let Love
Lovers
Lovesong
The Mad Show
Madison Avenue
The Madwoman of Central Park West
Make Me a Song
Mama, I Want to Sing
Mama, I Want to Sing—Part II: The Story Continues
Man in the Moon
A Man of No Importance
Man on the Moon
Man with a Load of Mischief
The Manson Family/Helter Five-O
March of the Falsettos
Marco Polo
Mardi Gras!
Marry Me a Little
Mass
Mata Hari
Mayor
The Me Nobody Knows
Menopause: The Musical
Merry Mount
Miss Gulch Returns!
Miss Julie
Mr. President
Mixed Doubles
Monsieur de Pourceaugnac
Most Men Are
The Mother of Us All
Mud Donahue & Son (as *My Vaudeville Man!*)
Musical Chairs
The Musical of Musicals
My Life with Albertine
The Mystery of Edwin Drood
Naked Boys Singing!
Natalia Petrovna
National Lampoon's Lemmings
Neva Small: Not Quite an Ingenue
A New Brain
New York Coloring Book
Newsical
A Night in Venice
Nightingale
Nite Club Confidential
Nixon in China
No for an Answer
The No-Frills Revue
No Way to Treat a Lady
Non Pasquale
North Atlantic
Now Is the Time for All Good Men
Nunsense
Nunsense-A-Men!
Nunsense 2: The Sequel
Nymph Errant
O Marry Me!
O Say Can You See!
Of Mice and Men (Carlisle Floyd, 1983)
Of Thee I Sing
Oh! Calcutta!
Oh Coward!
Oh, Johnny
Oh, Kay!
Oil City Symphony
Olympus on My Mind
On the Town
Once Around the Sun
Once on This Island
Once Upon a Mattress
One Foot Out the Door
One Man Band
One Mo' Time!
1000 Airplanes on the Roof
A One-Way Ticket to Broadway
Only Fools Are Sad
Opal
Options
Pacific Overtures
Pageant
Parade
A Party with Betty Comden and Adolph Green
Passing Strange
Paul Bunyan
Peace
People Is the Thing That the World Is Fullest Of
Personals
Pete 'n' Keely
Philemon
Piano Bar
Pieces-of-Eight
Pins and Needles
The Pirates of Penzance, or The Slave of Duty
Pomegranada
Poppie Nongena
Postcard from Morocco
Postcards on Parade
Les Poupees de Paris
The Premise
Preppies
The Prince and the Pauper (George Fischoff, 1963)
The Prince and the Pauper (Neil Berg, 2002)
Privates on Parade
Prodigal
Promenade
Pump Boys and Dinettes
Radio Gals
Rags/Children of the Wind
Rain
Rap Master Ronnie
Rappaccini's Daughter (*La Hija de Rappacini*)
Really Rosie
Reefer Madness
Rent
Return to the Forbidden Planet
Der Ring Gott Farblonjet
The Rise and Fall of the City of Mahagonny
Riverwind
Roadside
The Robber Bridegroom
Roman Fever
Romance Romance
The Rothschilds
Runaways
Ruthless!
Sail Away
Salad Days
Salvation
Sandhog
The Sap of Life
Sarafina!
Saturday Night
Saturn Returns: A Concert
Satyagraha
Scrambled Feet
Seacoast of Bohemia (*From the Second City* recordings are referenced in this entry)
The Seagull
The Second Shepherd's Play
The Secret Life of Walter Mitty
Secrets Every Smart Traveler Should Know
See What I Wanna See
Selma
Seven Come Eleven
She Shall Have Music
Sheba
Shockheaded Peter
Shoestring '57
Shoestring Revue
Shout!
The Show Goes On
Silence! The Musical
Silverlake
Simply Heavenly
Sing Muse!
Six Characters in Search of an Author
Smiling the Boy Fell Dead
Smoke on the Mountain
Sondheim: Opening Doors
Sondheim Putting It Together
A Song Floating
Song of Singapore
Songs for a New World
The Spitfire Grill
Spring Awakening
Standup Shakespeare
Starmites
Starting Here, Starting Now
Sterling Silver
Stranger Here Myself
Street Dreams
The Streets of New York
Streetsongs
Suburb
Summer of '42
Sunday in the Park with George
Sunset
The Survival of St. Joan
Susannah
The Sweet Bye and Bye
Swingtime Canteen
The Taffetas
Take Five
Take Me Along
Taking a Chance on Love
Taking My Turn
Tallulah
Tarot
Ten Percent Revue
The Tender Land
That's the Ticket!
The Thing About Men
This Was Burlesque Three Postcards
3 Guys Naked from the Waist Down
The Threepenny Opera
Thrill Me
Thunder Knocking on the Door
tick, tick...BOOM!
Time and Again
Tintypes
Tip-Toes
[title of show]
Tomfoolery
Tommy
Too Jewish?
Touch
Tovah: Out of Her Mind!
Trixie True, Teen Detective
Turns
Tuscaloosa's Calling Me...But I'm Not Going!
The 25th Annual Putnam County Spelling Bee
"2"
The Two Gentlemen of Verona
The Umbrellas of Cherbourgh
An Unfinished Song
Upstairs at O'Neals'
Urban Blight
Urinetown
Valmouth
Vanessa
A View from the Bridge
Violet
Virgin
The Voyage
Walk Together Children
Walmartopia, The Musical!
We'd Rather Switch
Weird Romance
What About Luv?
What's a Nice Country Like You Doing in a State Like This?
When Pigs Fly (a/k/a *Howard Crabtree's When Pigs Fly*)
When the Lights Go On Again
Whispers on the Wind
Whoop-Dee-Doo! (a/k/a *Howard Crabtree's Whoop-Dee-Doo!*)
Wings (Jeffrey Lunden, 1993)
The World of Kurt Weill in Song
X (The Life and Times of Malcolm X)
You Never Know
Young Abe Lincoln
Your Own Thing
You're a Good Man, Charlie Brown
Yours, Anne
Zanna, Don't!
Zombie Prom

Selected Recordings Which Feature Songs from Off Broadway Productions

Billy Barnes/*Billy Barnes Revued* (Various Artists) (Ducy Lee Recordings CD #DLR-900107)
William Bolcom/*William Bolcom Songs* (Carole Farley & William Bolcom) (Naxos Records CD#8-559249)
Liz Callaway/*The Story Goes On/Liz Callaway On & Off Broadway* (Varese Sarabande CD #VSD-5585)
Craig Carnelia/*Pictures in the Hall/Songs of Craig Carnelia* (Maureen Silliman and Craig Carnelia) (Original Cast Records CD #OC-914)
William Finn/*Infinite Joy/The Songs of William Finn* (Various Artists) (RCA Victor Records CD #09026-63766-2)
Rita Gardner/*Try to Remember/A Look Back at Off-Broadway* (Harbinger Records CD #HCD-2202)
Lauren Kennedy/*Songs of Jason Robert Brown* (PS Classics CD #PS-309)
Audra McDonald/*How Glory Goes* (Nonesuch Records CD #79580-2)
Sharon McNight/*In the Meantime* (Jezebel Music Records CD #OU-81-SS)
Jerome Moross/*Jerome Moross* (Various Artists) (Naxos Records CD #8-559086)
Jerome Moross/*Windflowers/The Songs of Jerome Moross* (Various Artists) (PS Classics CD #8-03607-01022-5)
Robert Morse and Charles Nelson Reilly/*A Jolly Theatrical Season* (DRG Records CD # 19101; originally released by Capitol Records LP #ST-1862)
Robert Nassif Lindsey/*Opal, Honky-Tonk Highway and Other Theatre Songs by Robert Nassif Lindsey* (Various Artists) (Original Cast Records CD #OC-9514)
Jerry Orbach/*Off Broadway* (Decca Broadway CD #012-159-254-2; originally released by MGM Records LP #E/ES-4056)
Emily Skinner/Alice Ripley/*Raw at Town Hall* (Kritzerland Records CD #KR-20011-0)
Neva Small/*My Place in the World* (Small Penny Enterprises, LLC Records CD #NS-2211)
Barbra Streisand/*A Happening in Central Park* (Columbia Records CD #9710)
Susan Watson/*Earthly Paradise* (Nassau Records CD #96598)
18 Interesting Songs from Unfortunate Shows (Various Artists) (Take Homes Tunes! LP #THT-777)

APPENDIX C: PUBLISHED SCRIPTS

The following is a list of published scripts for the revues and musicals discussed in this book. See entries for the names of publishers and the dates of publication, and also the specifics of certain titles (for example, *King of Schnorrers* and its revised version [which was titled *Tatterdemalion*] were published as *Petticoat Lane*). The list also includes titles which have been announced for publication (see entries for more information).

A...My Name Is Alice
A...My Name Is Still Alice
Adrift in Macao
After the Ball
Alice in Concert
The Amorous Flea
Angry Housewives
Anne of Green Gables
Anything Goes
Apple Pie
Assassins
Avenue Q
Avenue X
Babes in the Wood
Baker's Dozen
The Ballad of Baby Doe
Ballet Ballads
Das Barbecu
Bat Boy
Bed and Sofa
The Beggar's Opera
Best Foot Forward
The Big Bang
The Big Voice: God or Merman?
Billy Bishop Goes to War
Birds of Paradise
Bittersuite
Bomarzo
The Boy Friend
The Boys from Syracuse
Bubbling Brown Sugar
The Bubbly Black Girl Sheds Her Chamelon Skin
By Hex
Candide
Caroline, or Change
Charlotte Sweet
Chess
Children's Letters to God
A Chorus Line
A Class Act
The Club
Clue: The Musical
El Coca-Cola Grande (a/k/a *El Grande de Coca-Cola*)
The Contrast
Conversation Piece
Cowgirls
The Cradle Will Rock
Crowns
Curley McDimple
Cut the Ribbons
Dames at Sea
The Dangerous Christmas of Red Riding Hood
Debbie Does Dallas
The Derby (1981; Robert MacDougall)
Diamond Studs
Diamonds
Dinny and the Witches
A Doll's Life
Doctor! Doctor!
Dont Bother Me, I Cant Cope
Double Entry (*The Bible Salesman* and *The Oldest Trick in the World*)
Eating Raoul
Egyptology: My Head Was a Sledgehammer
The Entertainer
Evil Dead: The Musical
Falsettoland
Fashion (1974)
Festival
A Fine and Private Place
The Fireman's Flame
First Lady Suite
Five Course Love
Floyd Collins
Fly with Me
Gauguin/Savage Light
The Ghosts of Versailles
The Gifts of the Magi
The Girl from Wyoming
Goblin Market
God Bless You, Mr. Rosewater
The Golden Apple
Golden Boy
The Golden Screw
Golf: The Musical
Gone Missing
Gorilla Queen
Grease
The Great American Backstage Musical
The Great American Trailer Park Musical
The Great Gatsby
The Great McDaddy
The Green Heart
Grey Gardens
Groucho: A Life in Revue
Gunmetal Blues
Gutenberg! The Musical!
The Haggadah
Hair
Hamlet of Stepney Green
Hank Williams: Lost Highway
Head Over Heels
Hedwig and the Angry Inch
Hello Again
Hello Muddah, Hello Fadduh!
Hijinks!
The Hired Man
Home Movies
Honky-Tonk Highway
Hot Grog
House of Flowers
The Human Comedy
I Can't Keep Running in Place
I'll Die If I Can't Live Forever
I'm Getting My Act Together and Taking It on the Road
The Immigrant
In Trousers
Inside Out
It Ain't Nothin' but the Blues
The IT Girl
Jack's Holiday
Jacques Brel Is Alive and Well and Living in Paris
James Joyce's The Dead
Jerry's Girls
Johnny Guitar
Johnny Johnson
Johnny Pye and the Foolkiller
Jolson & Co.
Just So
The Karl Marx Play
King Mackerel & The Blues Are Running
King of Schnorrers Kittiwake Island
Kuni-Leml
The Last Savage
The Last Session
The Last Sweet Days of Isaac
Lend an Ear
Let 'Em Eat Cake
The Line of Least Existence
Little by Little
Little Ham
Little Mary Sunshine
Little Shop of Horrors
The Littlest Revue
Lust
The Mad Show
Madison Avenue
A Man of No Importance
March of the Falsettos
The Me Nobody Knows
Merry Mount
Mod Donna
Money
Musical Chairs
The Musical of Musicals
My Old Friends
The Mystery of Edwin Drood
Naughty Naught '00
A New Brain
Nightclub Cantata
No Way to Treat a Lady
Now Is the Time for All Good Men
Nunsense
Nymph Errant
O Marry Me!
Of Thee I Sing
Oh! Calcutta!
Oh Coward!
Olympus on My Mind
On the Town
Once Upon a Mattress
One for the Money Etc.
One Mo' Time!
1000 Airplanes on the Roof
Opal
Open Heart
Pacific Overtures
Pageant
Paradise Gardens East
Passing Strange
Peace
Personals
Pete 'n' Keely
Phoenix '55
Piano Bar
Postcard from Morocco
Postcards on Parade
Preppies
Pretzels
The Prince and the Pauper (2002; Neil Berg)
Privates on Parade
The Prodigal Sister
Prom Queens Unchained
Promenade
Pump Boys and Dinettes
Quilters
Radio Gals
Really Rosie
The Red Sneaks
Rent
Return to the Forbidden Planet
Der Ring Gott Farblonjet
The Rise and Fall of the City of Mahagonny
The Rise of David Levinsky
The Robber Bridegroom
Romance Romance
The Rothschilds
Runaways
Ruthless!
Salad Days
Sarita
Scrambled Feet
The Secret Life of Walter Mitty
See What I Wanna See
Serious Bizness
Show Me Where the Good Times Are
Simply Heavenly
Smith
Smoke on the Mountain
Song of Singapore
Souvenir
The Spitfire Grill
Splendora
Spring Awakening
Standup Shakespeare
Stardust
Starmites
Street Dreams
The Streets of New York
Strider: The Story of a Horse
Summer of '42
Sunday in the Park with George
The Sweet Bye and Bye
Swingtime Canteen
Taking My Turn
Tatterdemalion
Ten Percent Revue
The Threepenny Opera
Thrill Me

tick, tick ... BOOM!
Ti-Jean and His Brothers
Times and Appetites of Toulouse-Lautrec
To Whom It May Concern
Tongues
Tracers
Trixie True, Teen Detective
Turns (published as *Taking My Turn*)
The Two Gentlemen of Verona
Under the Bridge
Unsung Cole
Up from Paradise
Urinetown
Variety Obit
A View from the Bridge
The Voyage
Weird Romance (*The Girl Who Was Plugged In* and *Her Pilgrim Soul*)
What's a Nice Country Like You Doing in a State Like This?
When Pigs Fly (a/k/a *Howard Crabtree's When Pigs Fly*)
Whispers on the Wind
Whoop-Dee-Doo! (a/k/a *Howard Crabtree's Whoop-Dee-Doo!*)
You Never Know
Your Own Thing
You're a Good Man, Charlie Brown
Zombie Prom
Zombies from the Beyond

Appendix D: Filmography

This is a list of films, teleplays, and radio broadcasts of the musicals discussed in this book. In the interest of completeness and for the reader's reference, the list sometimes includes a source musical upon which an Off Broadway musical was based (such as the 1964 film musical *The Umbrellas of Cherbourg*, which was produced Off Broadway in 1979). For specific information, see entries for the musicals listed below.

Ain't Misbehavin'
Alice in Concert
Amelia Goes to the Ball
The American Dance Machine
...And in This Corner
Anne of Green Gables
Antiques
Antony and Cleopatra
The Ballad of Baby Doe
Best Foot Forward
The Better 'Ole
The Big Winner
Billy Barnes Revue
Billy Bishop Goes to War
Black Nativity
The Boy Friend
The Boys from Syracuse
Bubbe Meises Bubbe Stories
Cabin in the Sky
Candide
Central Park
A Chorus Line
Christmas Rappings
The Cocoanuts
Contact
The Cradle Will Rock
Dames at Sea
The Dangerous Christmas of Red Riding Hood
The Death of Klinghoffer
Down in the Valley
Elaine Stritch at Liberty
Emmeline
The Entertainer
Ernest in Love
Fame on 42nd Street
The Fantasticks
The First Emperor
Frankenstein
Forever Plaid
Gay Divorce
The Ghosts of Versailles
Godspell
The Golden Screw
Gospel at Colonus
Grease
The Great Gatsby
Hair
Hedwig and the Angry Inch
I Do! I Do!
I've Got the Tune
Jacques Brel Is Alive and Well and Living in Paris
Joseph and the Amazing Technicolor Dreamcoat
King Mackerel & The Blues Are Running
The Little Prince
Little Shop of Horrors
Little Women
Lizzie Borden
The Madwoman of Central Park West
Mama I Want to Sing
A Match Made in Heaven
The Me Nobody Knows
Merry Mount
Mother Goose Go-Go
Naked Boys Singing!
Nixon in China
Nunsense
Nunsense 2: The Sequel
Of Thee I Sing
Oh! Calcutta!
Oh Coward!
On the Town
Once Upon a Mattress
Pacific Overtures
Passing Strange
Paul Bunyan
Philemon
Pins and Needles
The Pirates of Penzance, or The Slave of Duty
Privates on Parade
Pump Boys and Dinettes
Rap Master Ronnie
Really Rosie
Reefer Madness
Rent
The Rise and Fall of the City of Mahagonny
Romance Romance
Sarafina!
Satyagraha
Scrambled Feet
Shockheaded Peter
Simply Heavenly
Sondheim Putting It Together
Stomp (1994)
The Streets of New York
Streetsongs
Summer and Smoke
Sunday in the Park with George
Taking My Turn
The Taming of the Shrew
This Was Burlesque
The Threepenny Opera
Tommy
The Triumph of St. Joan
Tubes
The Umbrellas of Cherbourg
Vanessa
The Voyage
The Warrior
A Wedding in Shtetel
When Hell Freezes Over, I'll Skate
You're a Good Man, Charlie Brown
Zombie Prom

Appendix E: Black Musicals and Revues

The following is a list of musicals and revues discussed in this book which have predominately Black stories, issues, themes, and characters:

Abyssnia
Adam
Ain't Misbehavin'
Akokawe
Ballad for Bimshire
Basin Street
Bayou Legend
The Believers
Billy Noname
Bingo!
Birdland
Black Broadway
Black Nativity (1961)
Black Nativity (2007)
Blackberries
Bohikee Creek
Born to Sing!
Bring in 'Da Noise, Bring in 'Da Funk
Bubbling Brown Sugar
The Bubbly Black Girl Sheds Her Chameleon Skin
But Never Jam Today
Butterfly McQueen and Friends
Cabin in the Sky
Caroline, or Change
Champeen!
Child of the Sun
Croesus and the Witch
Crowns
The Crystal Tree
The Day, the Night
Dessa Rose
Dinah! "Queen of the Blues"
Dinah Was
Dont Bother Me, I Cant Cope
Dunbar
The Egg and I
Elisabeth Welch: Time to Start Singing
Faith Journey
Fixed
Fly Blackbird
Further Mo'
God Is a (Guess What?)
God's Trombones
Godsong
Golden Boy
Gospel at Colonus
Haarlem Nocturne
Halala!
Harlem Song
Her Talking Drum
The Hoofers
Hot Dishes!
House of Flowers
I Have a Dream
It's So Nice to Be Civilized
The Jackie Wilson Story
Jam
Jam on the Groove
Jelly Roll!
Jericho
Jerico-Jim Crow
Joy
Junebug Graduates Tonight!
Just a Night Out!
Lady Day: A Musical Tragedy
The Last Years in the Life of Reverend Martin Luther King Jr. as Devised by Waterwell
The Lion and the Jewel
Little Ham
Louis
Louisiana Summer
Mahalia
Mama, I Want to Sing
Mama, I Want to Sing—Part II: The Story Continues
Man Better Man
Margaret Garner
Miss Truth
Miss Waters, to You
(mis)Understanding Mammy: The Hattie McDaniel Story
Moms
Once on This Island
One Mo' Time!
Paris '31
Passing Strange
The Peanut Man, George Washington Carver
Poppie Nongena
The Prodigal Sister
The Prodigal Son
Rollin' on the T.O.B.A.
Safari 300
Sambo
Sarafina!
Savion Glover/Downtown (1998)
Savion Glover: Downtown (1999)
Selma
Shades of Harlem
Shakespeare in Harlem
Simply Heavenly
Sing Hallelujah!
Sparrow in Flight
Staggerlee
Step Into My World
Street Dreams
Struttin'
The Sunshine Train
Survival
Take It from the Top (1979)
Take Me Along
Thoughts
Three Mo' Tenors
Thunder Knocking on the Door
Ti-Jean and His Brothers
Trumpets of the Lord
Uhuruh
Walk Down Mah Street!
Walk Together Children (1968)
Walk Together Children (1972)
Waltz of the Stork
Waltz of the Stork Boogie
When Hell Freezes Over, I'll Skate
Williams & Walker
The World of My America
The World's My Oyster
The Worlds of Oscar Brown, Jr.
X (The Life and Times of Malcolm X)

Appendix F: Children's Musicals and Revues

The following is a list of children's revues and musicals which are discussed in this book:

Abby's Song
Aladin
Ali Baba and the 40 Thieves
Alice in Wonderland (1975; Joe Raposo)
Anne of Green Gables (1971; Norman Campbell)
Anne of Green Gables (2007; Nancy Ford)
Band-Wagon
Bar Mitzvah Boy
Captain Louie
Captains Courageous
Children's Letters to God
Cut to the Chase
The Dangerous Christmas of Red Riding Hood
Davy Jones' Locker
Half-Past Wednesday
The Incredible Feeling Show
Jekyll and Hyde
Junie B. Jones
A Kid's Life!
Kukla, Burr and Ollie
The Little Prince (1982; Ada Janik)
The Little Prince (1993; Rick Cummins)
The Little Prince (2005; Rachel Portman)
Mirette
Mother Goose Go-Go
Pendragon
The People Who Could Fly
Peter and the Wolf
Peter and Wendy
The Phantom Tollbooth
Pinocchio
The Prince and the Pauper (1963; George Fischoff)
The Prince and the Pauper (2002; Neil Berg)
Really Rosie
Skye
Speed Gets the Poppys
A Spinning Tale
Those Darn Kids
Twanger
The Whistling Wizard and the Sultan of Tuffet
The Wind and the Willows
Winnie the Pooh
The Wizard of Oz

Appendix G: Gay Musicals and Revues

The following is an alphabetical list of musicals and revues discussed in this book which are essentially gay in nature (gay themes, issues, characters, and sensibility):

Ballet Russes
The Big Voice: God or Merman?
The Bloolips in "Lust in Space"
Boy Meets Boy
The Charles Pierce Show
Dear Oscar
Disappearing Act
Dream Time/My Life with Vernon Dexter
An Evening with Joan Crawford
The Faggot
Fairy Tales
Falsettoland
Fourtune
Fun City
Gay Company
Gay Company Revisited
Get Used to It!
Gorilla Queen
Harvey Milk
I Could Go On Lip-Synching!
I Will Come Back
In Gay Company
In Trousers
It's Lynne Carter
It's Wilde!
Jayson
The Knife
Lovers
A Man of No Importance
Manhattan Follies
March of the Falsettos
Most Men Are
Pageant
Privates on Parade
Prodigal
Radiant Baby
Songs from an Unmade Bed
Splendora
Ten Percent Revue
Trolls
Two Hearts Over Easy
An Unfinished Song
Utterly Wilde!!!
When Pigs Fly (a/k/a *Howard Crabtree's When Pigs Fly*)
Whoop-Dee-Doo! (a/k/a *Howard Crabtree's Whoop-Dee-Doo!*)
Wonderful Lives
Yanks!
Zanna, Don't!

Appendix H: Jewish Musicals and Revues

The following is an alphabetical list of musicals and revues discussed in this book which have predominately Jewish plots, themes, and characters:

Abi Gezunt
Angel Levine
Bar Mitzvah Boy
Bei Mir Bustu Schoen
The Big Winner
A Broadcast Baby
Bubbe Meises Bubbe Stories
The Chosen
Chu Chem
Dori
Dudu Fisher: Something Old, Something New
Enchanting Melody
Esther
The 5th Season
Final Solutions
Finkel's Follies
Fyvush Finkel
Go Fight City Hall
The Golden Land
Good Luck
The Grand Music Hall of Israel
The Haggadah (1980; 1981)
Hannah...1939
Hannah Senesh
Hard to Be a Jew (1973; Sholom Secunda)
Hello, Charlie
Hot Klezmer
Hot Sake...with a Pinch of Salt
The Immigrant
It's Hard to Be a Jew (1983; Alexander Yampolsky)
The Jewish Gypsy
Jonah (1966; Meyer Kupferman)
Jonah (1990; Elizabeth Swados)
King of Schnorrers
The Kosher Widow
Kuni-Leml, or The Mismatch
The Lady of the Lake
Laugh a Lifetime
The Marriage Contract
A Match Made in Heaven
Men and Dreams
Miami
A Millionaire in Trouble
My Heart Is in the East
My Lucky Day
My Mama the General
Only Fools Are Sad
Oy Mama! Am I in Love!
Picon Pie
Rag on a Stick and a Star
Rags/Children of the Wind
The Rebbitzen from Israel
Rebecca, the Rabbi's Daughter
The Rise of David Levinsky
The Rothschilds
The Roumanian Wedding
The Secret Annex
Sheba
The Shiek of Avenue B
The Shop on Main Street
The Showgirl
Songs of Paradise
The Stones of Jehoshaphat
That's Life!
Theda Bara and the Frontier Rabbi
Those Were the Days
To Be or Not to Be...What Kind of a Question Is That?
Too Jewish?
Unfair to Goliath
Vagabond Stars
A Wedding in Shtetel
Yiddle with a Fiddle
Yoshe Kalb
Yours, Anne

Appendix I: Women's Musicals and Revues

The following is an alphabetical list of musicals and revues discussed in this book which are either feminist in nature or which deal with women's issues:

A...My Name Is Alice
A...My Name Is Still Alice
Angry Housewives
Apple Pie
The Club
Crowns
Cut the Ribbons
A Doll's Life
Girls, Girls, Girls
The Housewives' Cantata

I Can't Keep Running in Place
I'm Getting My Act Together and Taking It on the Road
Inside Out
Lyz!
Menopause: The Musical
Mod Donna
The Mother of Us All
Nellie
A Quarter for the Ladies Room
Quilters
Scandal
Sex Tips for Modern Girls
Sit Down and Eat Before Our Love Gets Cold
To Feed Their Hopes
We're Still Hot!

Appendix J: Burlesque Musicals and Revues

The following is an alphabetical list of burlesque revues and musicals (as well as a one-woman, non-burlesque revue which starred a famous burlesque performer) which are discussed in this book:

The Best of Burlesque
Big Bad Burlesque!
Burlesque on Parade
A Curious Evening with Gypsy Rose Lee
Follies Burlesque '67
International Playgirls '64
Strip!
This Was Burlesque (1962)
This Was Burlesque (1970)
We'd Rather Switch
The Wonderful World of Burlesque (First Edition, April 1965)
The Wonderful World of Burlesque (Second Edition, May 1965)

Appendix K: Musicals Based on Writings of Lewis B. Carroll

The following is an alphabetical list of musicals discussed in this book which are based on Lewis B. Carroll's life or his writings (specifically, *Alice's Adventures in Wonderland* and *Through the Looking Glass*):

Alice
Alice in Concert
Alice in Wonderland (March 1975; November 1975; Joe Raposo)
Alice in Wonderland (circa 2007; TayWah)
Alice with Kisses
But Never Jam Today
For the Snark Was a Boojum, You See
Once on a Summer's Day
The Passion of Alice

Appendix L: Musicals and Revues Based on Writings of William Shakespeare

The following is an alphabetical list of musicals and revues discussed in this book which are based on the writings of William Shakespeare:

Antony and Cleopatra
Babes in the Wood (based on *A Midsummer Night's Dream*)
The Bomb-itty of Errors (*The Comedy of Errors*)
Boston Boston (*The Merry Wives of Windsor*)
The Boys from Syracuse (*The Comedy of Errors*)
Dick Deterred (*Richard III*)
The Donkey Show: A Midsummer Night's Disco
Dreamstuff (*The Tempest*)
Hamlet of Stepney Green
Live and Let Love (*Twelfth Night*)
Lone Star Love, or *The Merry Wives of Windsor, Texas*
Love Sucks (*Love's Labour's Lost*)
A Musical Merchant of Venice
Pop (*King Lear*)
Sensations (*Romeo and Juliet*)
Shakespeare in Harlem
Shakespeare's Cabaret (1980; 1981)
Shylock (*The Merchant of Venice*)
Standup Shakespeare
Sweet Will (1985; 1986)
The Taming of the Shrew
The Tempest
The Two Gentlemen of Verona
Your Own Thing (*Twelfth Night*)

Appendix M: Composer and Lyricist Tribute Revues

The following is an alphabetical list of revues discussed in this book which are composer/lyricist tributes; this list also includes works which used pre-existing songs of composers/lyricists for book musicals (for tributes to Al Carmines, see Appendix N; for Kurt Weill, Appendix O):

Ain't Misbehavin' (Thomas "Fats" Waller)
Alec Wilder/Clues to a Life
Almost Heaven: Songs of John Denver
American Rhapsody (George Gershwin)
And the World Goes 'Round (John Kander and Fred Ebb)
Back to Bacharach and David (Burt Bacharach and Hal David)
Beautiful Dreamer (Stephen Foster)
Beyond Desire (Felix Mendelssohn)
Blitzstein! (Marc Blitzstein)
The Blitzstein Project (Marc Blitzstein)
By Bernstein (Leonard Bernstein)
By Strouse (Charles Strouse)
A Class Act (Ed Kleban)
Closer Than Ever (Richard Maltby, Jr., and David Shire)
Dancing in the Dark (Arthur Schwartz)
The Decline and Fall of the Entire World as Seen Through the Eyes of Cole Porter Revisited (First Edition, March 1965)
The Decline and Fall of the Entire World as Seen Through the Eyes of Cole Porter Revisited (a/k/a *New Cole Porter Revue*) (Second Edition, December 1965)
Do It Again! (George Gershwin)
Dream a Little Dream (The Mamas and the Papas)
An Evening with W.S. Gilbert
George M. Cohan Tonight!
Hang on to the Good Times (Gretchen Cryer and Nancy Ford)
Happy with the Blues (Harold Arlen)
Harry Ruby's Songs My Mother Never Sang

Hey, Love (Mary Rodgers)
Hundreds of Hats (Howard Ashman)
I Hear Music…of Frank Loesser and Friends
If Love Were All (Noel Coward)
It's Better with a Band (David Zippel)
Jacques Brel Is Alive and Well and Living in Paris
The Jello Is Always Red (Clark Gesner)
Jerry's Girls (Jerry Herman)
Just Once (Cynthia Weil and Barry Mann)
Ladies and Gentlemen, Jerome Kern
A Lady Needs a Change (Dorothy Fields)
Leonard Bernstein's Theatre Songs
Lies and Legends/The Musical Stories of Harry Chapin
Lingoland (Kenward Elmslie)
Listen to My Heart (David Friedman)
The Little Show and Friends (Arthur Schwartz and Howard Dietz)
Love, Janis (Janis Joplin)
The Lullaby of Broadway, or Harry Who? (Harry Warren)
Lyrical and Satirical: The Music of Harold Rome
Make Me a Song (William Finn)
Manhattan Serenade (Louis Alter)
Maybe I'm Doing It Wrong (Randy Newman; 1982)
The Middle of Nowhere (Randy Newman)
Oh Coward! (Noel Coward)
Oh Me, Oh My, Oh Youmans! (Vincent Youmans)
A Party with Betty Comden and Adolph Green
Randy Newman's Maybe I'm Doing It Wrong (1981)
Richard Farina: Long Time Coming and a Long Time Gone
Say It with Music (Irving Berlin)
The Show Goes On (Tom Jones and Harvey Schmidt)
Sisters of Mercy (Leonard Cohen)
Sondheim: Opening Doors (Stephen Sondheim)
Sondheim Putting It Together (Stephen Sondheim)
A Song Floating (Philip Springer)
Star Dust (Mitchell Parish)
Starting Here, Starting Now (Richard Maltby, Jr., and David Shire)
Step Into My World (Micki Grant)
Styne After Styne (Jule Styne)
Taking a Chance on Love (John LaTouche)
Tapestry (Carole King)
That's Entertainment (Arthur Schwartz and Howard Dietz)
They Wrote That? (Cynthia Weil and Barry Mann)
Tomfoolery (Tom Lehrer)
Tune the Grand Up! Words and Music by Jerry Herman
2 by 5 (John Kander and Fred Ebb)
Unsung Cole (Cole Porter)
Vamps and Rideouts (Jule Styne)
We're Home (Bob Merrill)
Woody Guthrie

Appendix N: Al Carmines Musicals and Revues

The following is an alphabetical list of plays, revues (including tribute revues), and musicals discussed in this book which have lyrics and music by Al Carmines (in some cases, the lyrics were adapted by Carmines from other sources; see specific entries for information):

The Agony of Paul
The Beast: Meditation on Beauty
The Bonus Army
Camp Meeting
Camp Meeting: 1840
Carmines Sings Whitman Sings Carmines
Christmas Rappings
Dr. Faustus Lights the Lights
The Evangelist
An Evening of Adult Fairy Tales
Exhalations
The Faggot
The Future
Gorilla Queen
The Gospel According to Al
Home Movies
In Circles (1967, 1968)
In Praise of Death
Joan
The Journey of Snow White
The Life of a Man
The Line of Least Existence
Listen to Me
A Look at the Fifties
The Making of Americans (1972; 1985)
A Manoir
Peace
Pomegranada
Promenade
Religion
Romance Language (Carmines appeared as a performer in this production)
Sacred and Profane Love
Someone's in the Kitchen with Dinah
Song of Songs
Songs by Carmines (see entry for 1968 production of *In Circles*)
The Songs of Mao Tse-Tung
T.S. Eliot: Midwinter Vigil(ante)
Untitled Play
The Urban Crisis
Wanted
What Happened
Why I Love New York

Appendix O: Kurt Weill Musicals and Revues

The following is an alphabetical list of musicals and composer-tribute revues discussed in this book with music by Kurt Weill:

Berlin to Broadway with Kurt Weill (1972; 2000)
Brecht on Brecht
Down in the Valley
An Evening with Ekkehard Schall
An Evening with Wolfgang Roth
Happy End
Here Lies Jenny
Johnny Johnson (1956; 1971)
Julie Wilson: from Weill to Sondheim
A Kurt Weill Cabaret (1976; 1979; 1981; 1984)
The Rise and Fall of the City of Mahagonny
Silverlake
Stranger Here Myself
The Threepenny Opera (1954; 1955; 1977; 1995)
Whores, Wars and Tin Pan Alley
A Woman Without a Man Is…
The World of Kurt Weill
The World of Kurt Weill in Song (1963; 1964)

Appendix P: Ben Bagley Revues

The following is a chronological list of the Ben Bagley revues discussed in this book:

Shoestring Revue (1955)
The Littlest Revue (1956)
Shoestring '57 (1956)
No Shoestrings (1962)
The Decline and Fall of the Entire World as Seen Through the Eyes of Cole Porter Revisited (1965)
The Decline and Fall of the Entire World as Seen Through the Eyes of Cole Porter Revisited (Second Edition, 1965; a/k/a *New Cole Porter Revue*)

Appendix Q: Julius Monk Revues

The following is a chronological list of the Julius Monk revues discussed in this book:

Four Below (1956)
The Son of Four Below (1956)
Take Five (1957)
Demi-Dozen (1958)
Pieces-of-Eight (1959)
Four Below Strikes Back (1959)
Dressed to the Nines (1960)
Seven Come Eleven (First Edition, 1961)
Ten-ish, Anyone? (1961)
Dime a Dozen (1961)
Seven Come Eleven (Second Edition, 1963)
Baker's Dozen (1963)
Bits and Pieces XIV (1964)
Pick a Number XV (1965)
4 in Hand (1967)

Appendix R: Rod Warren Revues

The following is a chronological list of the Rod Warren revues discussed in this book:

...And in This Corner (1964)
The Game Is Up (First Edition, 1964)
The Game Is Up (Second Edition, 1965)
The Game Is Up (Third Edition, 1965)
Just for Openers (1965)
Below the Belt (1966)
Mixed Doubles (1966)
The Playoffs of Mixed Doubles (1967)
Dark Horses (1967)
Photo Finish (1968)
Instant Replay (1968)
Free Fall (1969)

Appendix S: Forbidden Broadway

The following is a chronological list of the *Forbidden Broadway* productions discussed in this book (see entries for specific information):

Forbidden Broadway (1982) (this production included new editions which were introduced in 1983, 1985, 1986, and 1987)
Forbidden Broadway 1988 (1988) (during run, title changed to *Forbidden Broadway 1989*)
Forbidden Broadway 1990 (1990)
Forbidden Broadway 1991½ (1991) (during run, *Forbidden Christmas*, a special edition of the revue, was presented)
Forbidden Broadway 1992 (1992) (during run, title changed to *The Best of Forbidden Broadway—10th Anniversary Edition*)
Forbidden Broadway 1993 (1993) (between the runs of the 1992 and 1993 editions, a special edition of *Forbidden Broadway Featuring Forbidden Christmas* was presented)
Forbidden Broadway 1994 (1993)
Forbidden Hollywood (1996)
Forbidden Broadway Strikes Back! (1996)
Forbidden Broadway Cleans Up Its Act! (1998)
Forbidden Broadway 2001: A Spoof Odyssey (2000)
Forbidden Broadway: 20th Anniversary Edition (2002)
Forbidden Broadway Summer Shock! (2004)
Forbidden Broadway: Special Victims Unit (2004)
Forbidden Broadway: The Roast of Utopia (2007)
Forbidden Broadway: Rude Awakening (2007)

Appendix T: Second City Revues

The following is a chronological list of the Second City revues discussed in this book (see entries for specific information):

Seacoast of Bohemia (1962)
Alarums and Excursions (1962)
To the Water Tower (1963)
When the Owl Screams (1963)
Open Season at the Second City (1964)
The Wrecking Ball (1964)
A View from Under the Bridge (1964)
The Return of the Second City in "20,000 Frozen Grenadiers" (1966)
From the Second City (1969)
Cooler Near the Lake (1971)
Orwell That Ends Well (1984)

Appendix U: Theatre "Curses"

For the "Italian Curse," see entry for *Fortuna*.
For the "New Orleans Curse," see entry for *Basin Street*.
For the "Adelphi Theatre Curse," see entry for *Nellie*.
For the "Hot Air Balloon Curse," see entry for *Nellie*.
For the "Silent Movie-Making Curse," see entry for *Theda Bara and the Frontier Rabbi*.
For the "Alexander Cohen Curse," see entry for *Lyle*.
For the "Joey Faye Curse," see entry for *Lyle*.
For the "Carmen Mathews Curse," see entry for *Sunday in the Park with George*.

Bibliography

For approximately 70 percent of the musicals discussed in this book, I used primary source material, such as playbills, programs, souvenir programs, flyers, window cards, posters, scripts (both published and unpublished), recordings, sheet music, and newspaper advertisements. But there were also many reference books and data bases which were invaluable to me in my research, and these are listed below.

I especially want to single out a few reference books, including the stalwart and indispensable *Best Plays* and *Theatre World* series; Ken Bloom's *American Song*; Richard C. Norton's *A Chronology of American Musical Theatre*; and Knopf's fascinating (and ongoing) series of collections devoted to the complete lyrics of Irving Berlin, Ira Gershwin, Lorenz Hart, Frank Loesser, Cole Porter, Oscar Hammerstein II, and Johnny Mercer. Bloom and Norton's books were particularly helpful for reality checks, and the Knopf series (as well as other collections of lyrics which are listed below) were helpful in ascertaining the precise titles of many songs. Moreover, the annuals in the *New York Theatre Critics' Reviews* series were extremely helpful.

I want to note that the *New York Times'* archives were invaluable for their treasure-trove of reviews (these reviews deserve to be collected in a volume of their own!), and I particularly want to mention the perceptive and entertaining reviews written by Clive Barnes, who not only reviewed, but *reported*; his comments often make one feel one actually saw the productions he wrote about.

I also want to mention that the Metropolitan Opera's database was extremely helpful. The list below in effect constitutes the basis for a solid library of books on musical theatre, and following the bibliography I've taken the liberty of listing a number of other books which are highly recommended for rounding out any musical-theatre library.

Baxter, Joan. *Television Musicals: Plots, Critiques, Casts and Credits for 222 Shows, Written for and Presented on Television, 1944–1996*. Jefferson, NC: McFarland, 1997.

Bloom, Ken. *American Song: The Complete Musical Theatre Companion, Second Edition, 1877–1995* (two volumes). New York: Schirmer Books, 1996. note: The first edition is worth tracking down because it includes many factual and witty asides by Bloom (two volumes; *American Song: The Complete Musical Theatre Companion, 1900–1984*; Facts on File Publications, 1985).

The Best Plays. As of this writing, the most recent edition of this venerable series is Jeffrey Eric Jenkins, editor, *The Best Plays Theatre Yearbook 2005-2006* (New York: Limelight Editions, 2007).

Day, Barry. *The Complete Lyrics of P.G. Wodehouse*. Lanham, Maryland: The Scarecrow Press, 2004.

_____. *Noel Coward: The Complete Lyrics*. New York: The Overlook Press, 1998.

Drew, David. *Kurt Weill: A Handbook*. Berkeley: University of California Press, 1987.

Farber, Douglas C., and Robert Viagas. *The Amazing Story of 'The Fantasticks': America's Longest-Running Play*. Pompton Plains, NJ: Limelight Editions, 2005. (This is the second edition of the book, which had originally been published in 1991.)

Fordin, Hugh. *The Movies' Greatest Musicals: Produced in Hollywood USA by the Freed Unit*. New York: Ungar, 1984.

Ganzl, Kurt. *The British Musical Theatre* (two volumes, 1865–1914, and 1915–1984). New York: Oxford University Press, 1986.

Gordon, Eric. *Mark the Music: The Life and Work of Marc Blitzstein*. New York: St. Martin's Press, 1989.

Gottfried, Martin. *Opening Nights: Theatre Criticism of the Sixties*. New York: G.P. Putnam's Sons, 1972.

Gottlieb, Robert, and Robert Kimball (editors). *Reading Lyrics*. New York: Pantheon Books, 2000.

Green, Stanley (editor). *Rodgers and Hammerstein Fact Book: A Record of Their Works Together and with Other Collaborators*. New York: The Lynn Farnol Group, 1980.

Hart, Dorothy, and Robert Kimball (editors). *The Complete Lyrics of Lorenz Hart*. New York: Alfred A. Knopf, 1986.

Hirschhorn, Clive. *The Hollywood Musical*. New York: Crown, 1981.

Kimball, Robert (editor). *The Complete Lyrics of Cole Porter*. New York: Alfred A. Knopf, 1983.

_____. *The Complete Lyrics of Ira Gershwin*. New York: Alfred A. Knopf, 1993.

Kimball, Robert, and Linda Emmet (editors). *The Complete Lyrics of Irving Berlin*. New York: Alfred A. Knopf, 2001.

Kimball, Robert, and Steve Nelson (editors). *The Complete Lyrics of Frank Loesser*. New York: Alfred A. Knopf, 2003.

Lewine, Richard, and Alfred Simon (editors). *Songs of the Theatre: A Definitive Index to the Songs of the Musical Stage*. New York: H.W. Wilson, 1984.

Norton, Richard C. *A Chronology of American Musical Theatre* (three volumes). New York: Oxford University Press, 2002.

Osato, Sono. *Distant Dances*. New York: Alfred A. Knopf, 1980.

Portantiere, Michael (editor). *The Theatremania Guide to Musical Theatre Recordings*. New York: Back Stage Books, 2004.

Sanders, Ronald. *The Days Grow Short: The Life and Music of Kurt Weill*. New York: Holt, Rinehart, and Winston, 1980.

Seeley, Robert, and Rex Bunnett. *London Musical Shows on Record 1889–1989: A Hundred Years of London's Musical Theatre*. Middlesex, Great Britain: General Gramophone Publications, 1989.

Stewart, John. *Broadway Musicals, 1943–2004*. Jefferson, NC: McFarland, 2006.

Stone, Wendell C. *Caffe Cino: The Birthplace of Off-Off-Broadway*. Carbondale: Southern Illinois University Press, 2005.

Suskin, Steven. *Show Tunes: The Songs, Shows, and Careers of Broadway's Major Composers*, revised and expanded third edition. New York: Oxford University Press, 2000.

Theatre World. As of this writing, the most recent edition of this invaluable series is John Willis and Ben Hodges, editors, *Theatre World Volume 61 2004-2005* (New York: Applause Theatre and Cinema Books, 2007).

Weales, Gerald. *American Drama Since World War II*. New York: Harcourt, Brace & World, 1962.

Wlaschin, Ken. *Gian Carlo Menotti on Screen: Opera, Dance and Choral Works on Film, Television and Video*. Jefferson, NC: McFarland, 1999.

- For books on the history of musical theatre, Ethan Mordden's wonderful series of books on twentieth-century American musical theatre is informative, witty, and enjoyable, and an absolute must for every serious theatre library:

Make Believe: The Broadway Musical in the 1920s. New York: Oxford University Press, 1997.

Sing for Your Supper: The Broadway Musical in the 1930s. New York: Palgrave MacMillan, 2005.

Beautiful Morning: The Broadway Musical in the 1940s. New York: Oxford University Press, 1999.

Coming Up Roses: The Broadway Musical in the 1950s. New York: Oxford University Press, 1998.

Open a New Window: The Broadway Musical in the 1960s. New York: Palgrave, 2001.

One More Kiss: The Broadway Musical in the 1970s. New York: Palgrave MacMillan, 2003.

The Happiest Corpse I've Ever Seen: The Last Twenty-Five Years of the Broadway Musical. Palgrave MacMillan, 2004.

- Probably the ultimate theatre book of its era is *The Season: A Candid Look at Broadway* by William Goldman (New York: Harcourt, Brace & World, 1969). This fascinating book follows the ups and downs of every Broadway show which opened during the 1967-1968 season.

- For books about flop shows, the following are essential:

Leonard, William Torbert. *Broadway Bound: A Guide to Shows That Died Aborning*. Metuchen, NJ: The Scarecrow Press, 1983.

Suskin, Steven. *Second Act Trouble: Behind the Scenes at Broadway's Big Musical Bombs*. New York: Applause Theatre & Cinema Books, 2006.

- For books about scenic design and/or show artwork, the following are especially recommended:

Davis, Paul. *Paul Davis: Posters & Paintings*. New York: E.P. Dutton, 1977.

Gilbert Lesser: Theatre Designs Etc. Introduction by Peter Shaffer. New York: INCR, 1987.

Harris, Andrew B. *The Performing Set: The Broadway Designs of William and Jean Eckart*. Denton: University of North Texas Press, 2006.

Hearn, Michael Patrick. *The Art of the Broadway Poster*. New York: Ballantine Books, 1980.

Henderson, Mary C. *Mielziner: Master of Modern Stage Design*. New York: Back Stage Books, 2001.

McMullan, John. *The Theatre Posters of James McMullan*. New York: Penguin Studio, 1998.

Mielziner, Jo. *Designing for the Theatre: A Memoir and a Portfolio*. New York: Bramhall House, 1965.

Nelson-Cave, Wendy. *Broadway Theatre Posters*. New York: SMITHMARK Publishers, 1993.

Rich, Frank with Lisa Aronson. *The Theatre Art of Boris Aronson*. New York: Alfred A. Knopf, 1987.

Suskin, Steven. *A Must See! Brilliant Broadway Artwork*. San Francisco: Chronicle Books, 2004.

Tumbusch, Tom. *Broadway Musicals: A History in Posters*. Dayton, OH: Tomart Publications, 2004.

- For books about Broadway (and other) theatres, the following are fascinating journeys into both past and present-day playhouses:

Henderson, Mary C. *The City and the Theatre: The History of New York Playhouses, a 250-Year Journey from Bowling Green to Times Square*. New York: Back Stage Books, 2004. (This is a revised and expanded edition of the original 1973 publication by James T. White.)

_____. *The New Amsterdam Theatre: The Biography of a Broadway Theatre*. New York: Hyperion, 1997.

Lee, Douglas Bennett, Roger L. Meersman, and Donn B. Murphy. *Stage for a Nation: The National Theatre/150 Years*. Lanham, Maryland: University Press of America, 1985.

Stein, Tobie S. *Boston's Colonial Theatre: Celebrating a Century of Theatrical Vision*. Boston: Colonial 2000, 2000.

Van Hoogstraten, Nicholas. *Lost Broadway Theatres*. New York: Princeton Architectural Press, 1991. (Revised, updated, and expanded edition published in 1997.)

- For books about specific musicals, a number of such exist, but probably the outstanding example in this field is *Show Boat: The Story of a Classic American Musical* by Miles Kreuger (New York: Oxford University Press, 1977).

- If the reader is unable to locate copies of the *New York Theatre Critics' Reviews* series, there are two books which offer samplings of the opening night reviews of musicals by New York critics:

Suskin, Steven. *Opening Nights on Broadway: A Critical Quotebook of the Golden Era of the Musical Theatre, Oklahoma! (1943) to Fiddler on the Roof (1964)*. New York: Schirmer Books, 1990.

_____. *More Opening Nights on Broadway: A Critical Quotebook of the Musical Theatre 1965 Through 1981*. New York: Schirmer Books, 1997.

Song Index

References are to entry numbers

"A Is For" 752
"A La Carte" 472
"A La Pimpernel" 1265
"A La What?" 616
"A L'Chayim, Men Shraybt T'noyim" 1032
"Aaron Harris" 813
"Aba Daba Honeymoon" 955
"Abandoned" 948
"Abbe's Appearance" 1250
"Abbie's Bird Song" 947
"Abby's Lament" 8
"Abby's Song" 3
"A B C" 1264
"ABC to XYZ" 1034
"The ABC's of Success" 1481
"Abduction" 643
"Abduction from the Ladder" 1415
"Abdullah" 1327
"Abi Gezint (Just a Little Bit of Health)" 1453
"Abi Gezunt (As Long As You're Healthy)" 604
"Abi Tsu Zein Mit Dir (As Long as I'm with You)" 492
"Abie and Me and the Baby" 1442
"Abio, Oalla, Bondoyika" 120
"Abortion" 114, 449
"About Israel" 1647
"About Puppets" 96
"About the Ompire" 250
"About Time" 473
"Above the Clouds" 1428
"Above the Law" 58
"Abracadabra" 1704
"Abraham, Martin and John" 736, 1096
"Absalom" 583
"Absent in the Spring" 1569
"Absent Minded" 1606
"Absinthe Frappe" 577
"Abyssinia" 8
"Academy Award" 115
"Academy Awards" (Logan) 1394
"Academy Awards" (Siegel and Hart) 986
"Accentuate the Positive" 662, 1571
"Accepting the Tolls" 1620
"According to Plan" 1638
"According to Plotnik" 1060
"L'Accordioniste" 1256, 1257
"Ace in the Hole" 1720
"Ace's Revelation" 730
"Ache in Acorn" 873
"Achoo-Cha-Cha (Gesundheit)" 1575
"Achtung!" 609
"The Acid Queen" 1655
"Ackabacka" 1487
"ACLU" 643
"Acre of Grass" 1153
"Acrobats" 1153
"Across the Lake" 741
"Act Like a Villager" 1331
"Acting and Hustling" 1337
"The Action Never Stops" 1345
"The Actor" (Brooks) 360
"The Actor" (Fieger) 1192
"The Actor's Fantasy" 444
"An Actor's Life" 1745
"An Actress" 874
"Actress on the Stage" 1327
"The Acutary Song" 738
"The Ad" 913
"Adagio" 635
"Adam & Eve" 450
"Adam and Eve" (Bregman) 1743
"Adam and Eve" (Kemp) 1662
"Adam and Eve" (Motta) 877
"Adam Clayton Powell" 556, 557
"Adaptations" 852
"Addio, Bambino" 1250
"Adela" 130
"Adelaide's Lament" 212
"Adept and Scintillating" 1749
"Adieu to Ballyshannon" 805
"Adios" 1480
"Adios Barrio" 203
"The Admonitory Hippopotamus" 49, 612
"Adolescents" 1133
"Adon Olam" 1212
"Adonais" 1443
"Adonis Leaving Venus" 1569
"Adoption Interrogation" 769
"Adrift in Macao" 10
"Ads Infinitum" 50
"Adultery" 743
"Adultery Waltz" 718
"Adunde" 1388
"Advance Man" 1618
"Advanced Civilizations" 1294
"The Advantages of Floating in the Middle of the Sea" 1213
"The Adventures of Businessman" 22
"Advertising for the Labor Party" 449
"Advice" 1594
"Advice for a Friend" 1441
"Advice to Producers" 1414
"The Aerialist, Leotard" 581
"Aerobicantata" 1710
"Aeronautics Revelation" 1338
"Afferdytie" 987
"Affirmation of Life" 602
"Afghanistan" 664
"Afraid of Rejection" 719
"Afraid of the Dark" 1522
"Afraid to Fall in Love" 822
"Africa" (Bicat) 873
"Africa" (Davis) 1239
"Africa" (Diop) 21
"Africa" (Leslee) 78
"Africa Burning in the Sun" 1401
"African Sequence" 120
"Afro Blue" 835
"Aft Ye" 1071
"After" 105
"After All" (Paul) 1361
"After All" (Schaefer) 788
"After Burton, Who?" 1431
"After Dark" 963
"After Dinner Drinks" 225
"After Forty" 861
"After I Go to Sleep" 1102
"L'After Lines" 542
"After Opening Night" 157
"After Rehearsal" 989, 990
"After School Special" 1243
"After That the Sweat Had Soaked My Uniform" 1139
"After the Fair" 14
"After the Gold Is Gone" 102
"After the Interval" 1721
"After Time" 1669
"After You, Who?" 567, 807, 1704
"After You've Gone" 746, 840, 1198, 1373
"Afternoon of a Faun" 95
"Afterward" 1379
"Afunani Amaphoyisa eSoweto (What Is the Army Doing in Soweto?)" 1401
"Again" 416
"Again We Meet to Celebrate" 941
"Against the Time" 949
"Age Is a State of Mind" 968
"Age Is Nothin'" 82
"Age of Bronze" 253
"Age of Elegance" 564, 807, 1527
"Age of Miracles" 1780
"An Aged, Aged Man" 27
"Agent" 1414
"Agent 008" 740
"The Agent Returns" 812
"Aggie" 1420
"The Aggie Song" 133
"Aggie's Song" 826, 827
"Agnes and Me" 332
"Agnus Dei" 873
"Agony Round" 321
"Ah, But Underneath" 1491, 1492
"Ah! Child" 362
"Ah, Febbre Perniciosa" 1374
"Ah, Heaven's Height Has Cracked!" 615
"Ah, Hum; Oh, Hum" 1445
"Ah, It's Love" 1638
"Ah, Maien Zeit!" 683
"Ah, May the Red Rose" 112
"Ah Me Poor Venus" 1569
"Ah, Men" (Holt) 16
"Ah, Men" (Menken) 1339
"Ah Mes Amis" 1623
"Ah, Our Germans" 658
"Ah! Sweet Mystery of Life" 1570
"Ah, Sweet Revenge" 1146
"Ah, Sweet Youth!" 1512
"Aha, Rheumatism!" 609
"Ahab" 1071
"Ahab and the Carpenter" 1071
"Ahab's Cabin" 1071
"Ahhhh" 755
"Aid to Vietnam" 1206
"Aiken Drum" 1085
"Aimee, Slay Me" 1470
"Aimez-Vous Bach?" 1662
"Ain't Gonna Let Nobody Turn Me 'Round" 470
"Ain't Got No" 649
"Ain't Got No Tears Left" 234
"Ain't Got Time to Die" 1762
"Ain't He Cute?" 463
"Ain't It a Pretty Night?" 1563
"Ain't It Awful, the Heat" 128
"Ain't It De Truth" 662
"Ain't It Funny" 745
"Ain't It Great to Have a Kid?" 769
"Ain't Losin' No Sleep" 1500
"Ain't Love Easy" 1650
"Ain't Marryin' Nobody" 1307
"Ain't Misbehavin'" 18, 35, 212
"Ain't No Goin' Back" 1831
"Ain't No Place Like Home" 456
"Ain't No Trouble" 922
"Ain't No Woman But You" 1366
"Ain't No Women There" 217
"Ain't Nobody" 1407
"Ain't Nobody Got a Bed of Roses" 1650
"Ain't She Cute?" 463
"Ain't She Sweet" 1684
"Ain't That Something?" (Alford) 1620
"Ain't That Something?" (Simpson and Wann) 864
"Ain't Worth a Dime" 216
"Ain't You Ashamed?" 255
"Air" 649
"Air Guitar" 45
"Air Jordans" 1407
"Airport '79" 897
"Airtime" 19
"AJ on the Subway" 328
"Akhnaten and Nefertiti" 20
"Akiwawa" 1388
"Alabama Bound" (aka "Alabamy Bound") 813
"Alabama Jubilee" 1720
"Alabama Song" (aka "Alabama-Song") 128, 879, 880, 882, 1773, 1807
"Alabamy Bound" (aka "Alabama Bound") 553, 993
"The Alabatross" 1662
"Alas for You" 595
"Alas, Good Friend" 1443
"Alas, the Stage" 1416
"Albert" 1315
"Alberta K. Johnson" 1734, 1735
"Alborada" 1033
"Alcatraz" 655
"Aldo Would Be Better Off Without You" 907
"Ale House Song" 1161
"Alexander's Discount Rag" 160
"Alexander's Ragtime Band" 457
"Alfie" 83
"Algae" 326
"Algonquin Anthem" 1586
"Alhambra Nights" 1287
"Alice" 785
"Alice Back Home" 1058
"Alice in Africa" 1058
"Alice in Italy" 1058
"Alice in Spain" 1058
"Alice on the Matterhorn" 1058
"Alien Love" 229
"Alison Dear" 572
"Alive and ... Well" 461
"Alive and Kicking" 132
"All a Matter of Strategy" 991
"All Aboard" 1060
"All Aboard for Broadway" 42, 570
"All About Evelyn" 121
"All About He" 48
"All About Him" 48
"All About Me" 48
"All Alone" 1154, 1467
"All American Male" 179
"All-American Sweetheart" 570
"The All-American Two-Step" 1603
"All Around the World" 1254
"All Blues" 1015
"All Blues Jam" 1407
"All Choked Up" 625
"All Dolled Up" 58
"All Fall Down" 41, 997, 1375
"All Flowers That Die" 1503
"All for a Dime" 858
"All for the Best" 595
"All for You" 1403, 1771
"All Girl Band" 1
"All Good Gifts" 595

"All Good Things" 667
"All Hail, King Dinny!" 384
"All Hail, to Dinny!" 384
"All I Can Do Is Cry" 1709
"All I Do Is Sing" 770
"All I Got Is You" 109
"All I Need" 400
"All I Need Is the Girl" 1717
"All I Really Want to Do Is Dance" 699
"All I Remember Is You" 434, 435
"All I See Is You" 1450
"All I Wanna Do Is Dance" 959
"All I Want for My Birthday" 485
"All I Wanted Was a Cup of Tea" 364
"All in a Day's Work" 1251
"All in All" 1788
"All in All #2" 1788
"All in Favor?" 673
"All in Fun" 428
"All in Love" 33
"All in the Name of Love" 1136
"All Is Need Is the Girl" 1546
"All Is Prepared" 1270
"All Is Well in the City" 1311
"All Kinds of Giants" 34
"All Long Island Gossips" 874
"All Love" 1708
"All Men Are Equal" 427
"All Men Is Crazy" 1366
"All My Anguish and My Sorrow" 1327
"All My Love" 993
"All My Tomorrows" 1210
"All My Yesterdays" 1354
"All of My Love" 229
"All of My Memories" 37
"All of That Made for Me" 1708
"All of Us Are Brothers" 41
"All of Us Are Niggers" 41
"All of You" 850
"All or Nothing at All" 1210
"All or Nothing Woman" 712
"All Our Tomorrows" 1482, 1750
"All Out of Tune" 639
"All Over My Mind" 464
"All Over the Place" 1584
"All Right" 471
"All Shook Up" 431
"All-Talking, All-Singing, All-Dancing" 1089
"All That Glisters Is Not Gold" (aka "All That Glisters") 1437, 1569
"All That I Know" 217
"All That It Takes" 105
"All That Jazz" 52, 1494
"All That's Known" 1515
"All the Children Sing" 742
"All the Days Are Dark. All the Days Are Long" 951
"All the Dearly Beloved" 733
"All the Flowers Turn to Snow" 786
"All the Girls Were Pretty" 1716
"All the Gods Have Gone Away" 1231
"All the Lovely Ladies" 297
"All the Magic Ladies" 692
"All the Men in My Life (Keep Getting Killed by Candarian Demons)" 462
"All the Pretty Little Horses" 1083
"All the Same to Me" 230
"All the Things You Are" 883
"All the Time in the World" (Hoffman) 1514
"All the Time in the World" (Jankowski) 539
"All the Way" 1210
"All the Way Down" 1072
"All the World Has Gone By" 1356
"All the World to Me" 1559
"All the World's" 908
"All the World's a Hold" 258
"All the Years" 272
"All Things Bright and Beautiful" 1027
"All Things New" 1052
"All Thinking's Done" 1601
"All This and Heaven Too" 1669
"All Those Who Want Their Hamburgers Rare, Raise Their Hand" 44
"All Through the Day" 883
"All Through the Night" 63
"All Tied Up on the Line" 385
"All to Pieces" 1726
"All We Have to Do" 808
"All Will Come to You" 1135
"All Ya' Gotta Do Is" 769
"All You Had to Do" 808
"All You Need Is a Little Love" 1713
"All You Need Is Confidence" 1194
"All You Want Is Always" 791
"All's Fair" 288
"All's Right on the Left Bank" 1385
"Allah" 844
"Allegheny Moon" 1575
"Alleluia" (Bernstein) 1029
"Alleluia" (Carmines) 286
"Alleluia" (Kennon) 484
"Alleluia, Alleluia" 1510
"The Allied High Command" 826
"Allied High Command" 827
"Alligator Dance" 107
"Alligator Meat" 634
"Alligator Romp" 960
"Alligators" 812
"Alligators All Around" 1340
"Allons" 1381
"Alma Mater" 625
"Alma Mater (Parody)" 625
"Alma's Poem" 224
"Almiro" 1704
"Almost a Woman" 1693
"Almost, But Not Quite" 1364
"Almost Everybody Suffers More Than Us" 720
"Almost Home" 1303
"Almost Like 1948" 511
"Almost Real" 1274
"Almost There" 219
"Almost Too Good to Be True" 661
"Almost Working" 1034
"Almosts, Maybes and Perhapses" 731
"Alone" (Brel) 792
"Alone" (Dorsey) 1117
"Alone" (Salzman) 738
"Alone" (Smyrl) 1183
"Alone" (Valenti) 989
"Alone at a Drive-In Movie" 625
"Alone at Last" 19
"Alone in the World" (Merrill) 1752
"Alone in the World" (Pen) 285
"Alone on the Road" 1002
"Alone Together" 348, 1606
"Alone Too Long" 886
"Alone with Me" 293
"Along the Seine (Rodeuse de Berges)" 1641
"Along the Way" 349
"Alouette" 963
"Alphabet" 27
"The Alphabet Song" 80
"Alphabet Soup" 1584
"Alphagenesis" 1659
"Also Spach Zarathrustra" 399
"Alternate Side" 1037
"Alternative Parking" 980
"Although I Came from Boston" 1789
"Alumnae Report" 381
"Always" 305, 1146
"Always a Bridesmaid" 739
"Always a Friend (Never a Lover)" 808
"Always, Always You" 692
"Always Autumn" 616
"Always Do as People Say You Should" 577
"Always for Science" 675
"Always Leave 'Em Wanting More" 980
"Always on the Way" 1458
"Always One Day More (Death of a Ballad)" 1447
"Always Remember" 1117
"Always Room for One More" 505
"Always Something There to Remind Me" 83, 1551
"Always Through the Changing" 92
"Always True to You in My Fashion" 367
"Am I Asking Too Much" 382
"Am I Blue" 180, 181, 182
"Am I Late?" 1058
"Am I Nuts" 1338
"Am I Ready for This?" 338
"Am I Supposed to Be Mad Today?" 665
"Am Yisroel Chai (Jewish People Will Live On)" 666
"Am Yisroel Khay!" 604
"Amazing Grace" 696, 736, 996
"Amazing Journey" 1655
"Ambition" (Bock) 511
"Ambition" (Styne) 1717
"Amedee, Amedee, It Isn't Too Late" 720
"Amelia" 130
"Amen" (Baron) 541
"Amen" (*God's Trombones!*) 592
"Amen" (Leake) 278
"Amen" (Mgcina) 1284
"Amen Response" 1672
"America" 911
"America, America" 602
"America First" 1255
"L'America Ha Fato per Te" 493, 1537
"America I Like You" 304
"America, Kick Up Your Heels" 41
"America, Kick Up Your Heels (A Choral Arrangement)" 41
"America Online" 1128
"America the Beautiful" 852
"America, You're Looking Good" 1759, 1761
"America — We're in New York" 65
"American Beauty" 469
"American Business" 920
"American Civil Liberties Union" 1273
"The American Clothes of Millicent Montrose" 1050
"An American Cripple Need Not Stand for the Star-Spangled Banner" 1263
"American Dream" (Copani) 1124, 1294
"American Dream" (Rohn) 1736
"The American Dream" 1622
"American Dream Girl" 877
"American Express — Italian Style" 557, 558
"American Family Plan" 1364
"American Flag" 602
"American Girls" 403
"American Impressions" 21
"(An) American in Paris" (Gershwin) 46, 73
"(An) American in Paris" (Roman) 529
"American Man on the Moon" 1007
"An American Odyssey" 871
"American Passion" 45
"The American Revolution" 1691
"American Rock" 602
"An American Tragedy" 1142
"The American Way" (Curtis) 1732
"The American Way" (Valc Q) 1832
"Amerike, Hurrah for Onkl Sem! (America, What a Name!)" 604
"An Amishman" 235
"Among the Indians" 1715
"Amoroso" 1179
"The Amorous Arrow" 661
"The Amorous Flea" 48
"Amos Gonna Give You Hell" 663
"L'Amour" 1410
"L'Amour Dangereux" 9
"Amour Time" 1508
"Amsterdam" (Brel) 792
"Amsterdam" (Stew and Rodewald) 1225
"The Amulet" 250
"Amyl, You're Back" 1149
"Ana, Goodbye" 1670
"Anchors Away" 892
"The Anchor's Aweigh" 775
"Ancient Land" 1670
"Ancient Oriental Custom" 1171
"And ..." 283
"... And a Drop of Lavendar Oil" 987
"And a Few More Questions" 1069
"And a Messenger Appeared" 1069
"And Freedom" 708
"And Furthermore" 203
"And God Said Unto Jacob" 1203
"And Her Golden Hair Was Hanging Down Her Back" 581
"And Hold Please" 1742
"And I Know" 1117
"And I Love You" 1737, 1738
"And I Thought You Beside Me" 1503
"And I Was Beautiful" 818
"And I Was Fired" 387
"And I'll Show You Something Else" 92
"And I'm There!" 461
"And If I Told You That I Want You" 990
"... And in This Corner" 50
"And It's Alright in the Summertime" 581
"And More" 1477
"And She Loved Me" 913
"And That Was He and She" 415
"And That Was Puerto Rico" 1434
"And That's Your Life" 1188
"And the Gods Heard Her Prayer" 1191
"... And the Pursuit of Happiness" 547
"And the Supremes" 1600
"And the Winner Is" 196
"And the World Goes 'Round" 52
"And Then I Wrote ..." 1261
"And Then There Were None" 1515
"And They All Call the Hatter Mad" 230
"And They're Off" 1121
"And We Were One" 1671
"And Will He Not Come Again?" 1568
"And Yet I Lived On" 391
"Andre's Mother" 1710
"Andrew Jackson James Tyrone" 1208
"Andrew's Aria" 947
"Anerca" 963
"Angel, Angel" 1203
"Angel Band" 1484
"Angel Eyes" 1210
"Angel Face" 1379
"An Angel Has a Message" 3
"Angel Mom" 1386
"Angel Mother, Angel Father" 1204
"Angel of Mercy" 683
"Angel Voices" 1763
"An Angel Will Go Before You" 673
"Angela's Flight Drama" 910
"Angela's Tango" 910
"Angelette March" 133
"Angelface" 395
"Angelica" 528
"Angeline" 1158, 1159
"Angelita" 1459
"Angels" 934
"Angel's Ballet" 831
"An Angel's Embrace" 541
"Angelus" 1255
"The Angles of Geometry" 1190
"Angry Guy" 1622
"Angry Inch" 680
"The Angry Young Men" 277
"The Animal Song" 1250
"Animal Trio" 1229
"Animals" 957
"Animule Ball" 813
"Ann Devine" 1394
"Anna Lee" 708
"Anna Louisa" 1635
"Anna Maria" 557
"Anna Nicole" 1128
"Anne of Green Gables" 56
"Anne's Song" 1419
"Annie Ain't Just Annie Anymore" 58
"Annie Green" 1158
"Annie Laurie" 1092
"Annie's Lament" 743
"Annie's Song" (Barkan) 224
"Annie's Song" (Denver) 37
"Annie's Thing" 1504
"Annie's Waltz" 789
"Anniversary Five" 469
"Anniversary Song" 993
"The Announcement" 1441
"Ann's Fantasy" 295
"Anon Comes Adonis" 1569

"Anonymous" 59
"Another April" 1102
"Another Bumper Crop" 1058
"Another Candle" 1218
"Another Chance" 749
"Another Country" 1356
"Another Cry" 208
"Another Day" (Courts) 828
"Another Day" (Friedman) 995
"Another Day" (Landron) 107
"Another Day" (Meyrelles) 1523
"Another Day" (Wood) 466
"Another Dead Cow" 106
"Another Drunken Cowboy" 1366
"Another Elementary School" 1800
"Another Girl Who's Just Like Me" 3
"Another Hundred People" 1491
"Another Letter" 14
"Another Life" 1512
"Another Love" 234
"Another Love Song" 1485
"Another Martini" 712
"Another Melody in F" 505
"Another Miracle of Judaism" 473
"Another Mr. Right" 55, 781
"Another Mister Right" 599
"Another National Anthem" 70
"Another Night" 83
"Another Op'nin', Another Show" 212, 367
"Another Place — Another World" 897
"Another Rabbi Outta the Hat" 1610
"Another Saturday Night in New York" 738
"Another Sleepless Night" 763, 765
"Another Soiree" 948
"Another Spring" 915
"Another Wedding Song" 300
"Another Winter in a Summer Town" 641
"The Answer" 828
"The Answer (The No Song)" 1379
"The Answer Is No" 983
"The Answer Song" 855
"Answer the Call" 703
"The Answer to Life Is Death" 1684
"Answering Machine" 1228
"Ant and Grasshopper (More Dialectic Inaction!)" 170
"An Ante-Bellum Sermon" 1762
"Anthem" (Anderson and Ulraeus) 275
"Anthem" (Brandt, Knight, and Lowery) 464
"Anthem" (Pen) 114
"The Anti-Establishment Rag" 542
"Anti-Romantic" 963
"Anticipation Blues" 1077
"Antioch Prison" 1253
"The Antique Man" 1218
"Antiques" 61, 235
"Ants" 280
"The Ants and the Cocoon" 11
"Anvil Chorus" 1176
"Any Bonds Today?" 1764
"Any Day Now" 76
"Any-Day-Now-Day" 88
"Any Old Time of Day" 83
"Any Other Way" 1008
"Any Spare Change?" 734
"Any Town" 372
"Anybody See Him Do It?" 995
"Anybody Wanna Buy a Little Love" 1030
"Anyone Can Make a Mistake" 80
"Anyone Can Play Bingo" 154
"Anyone Else" 299
"Anyone Who Had a Heart" 83, 1551
"Anyone Who's Anyone" 126, 852
"Anyone Would Do" 1726
"Anything Goes" 55, 63
"Anything You Want to Do, Dear" 1028
"Anytime" 39
"Anytime (I Am There)" 430, 997
"Anytime, Anywhere" 663
"Anyway You Bless" 1466
"Apache" 123, 1636
"Apartheid Love" 1113
"The Apartment" 171
"The Apartment (Sunday Noon)" 1778
"Apartment for Rent" 1394
"Apartment Lament" 718
"An Ape Can Save the World" 64
"Ape Over Broadway" 64
"Apollo 69" 1743
"The Apology" (Weiss) 161, 162, 163
"The Apology" (Young) 1604
"Apology to a Cow" 106
"Apostasy" 1349
"Appalachia and Mackey" 985
"Appearance" 461
"Appearance of the Life and Death Magicians" 1592
"Appearances" 402, 1327
"Appendectomy" 1384
"Appendectomy II" 1384
"Applause" 237
"The Apple Stretching" 1737, 1738
"Apples and Raisins" 1767
"The Applicant" (*Open Season at the Second City*) 1206
"The Applicant" (Swados) 1133
"Appreciation" 1475
"Apres Ski" 1427
"Apres Vous I" 1311
"April Child" 972
"The April Fools" 83
"April in Siberia" 1713
"April Showers" 829, 993
"April Song" 246
"April Twenty One" 364
"Aqua Vitae" 678
"Aquarius" 212, 649
"Aqui, Senor" 1336
"Arabella" 226
"Arbeter Froyen (Working Women)" 604
"The Arbiter's Song" 275
"Ardent Admirer" 1261
"Are There Any More Rosie O'Gradys?" 336
"Are We Downhearted?" 85
"Are We Ready?" 321
"Are You a Man" 1358
"Are You All Right?" 717
"Are You Alone?" 1416
"Are You Charles Waltz?" 44
"Are You Coming Bowling with Me Tonight, or Not?" 44
"Are You Lonesome Tonight" 1551
"Are You Saved from Sin" 1563
"Are You Still Holding My Hand?" 206
"Are You the Man Whose Name Is on the Paper" 720
"Are You the One" 1298
"Are You There with Another Girl" 83
"Are You Waiting for Vito?" 44
"Are You Washed in the Blood (of the Lamb)?" 1323, 1484
"Are You with Me?" 1133
"Aren't You Warm" 1539
"The Argument" 222
"Argument" (Andersson and Ulraeus) 275
"Argument" (Isen) 491
"Argument" (Sterner) 971
"Aria" 427
"Aria for a Cow" 727
"Aria of the Falling Body (Gymnopedie)" 363
"Ariel" 419
"Aries" 1397
"Arithmetic Times" 927
"Arizona" 465
"Arlington Hill" 1225
"Arm in Arm in Harmony" 855
"Armageddon" 1301
"Armanda's Sack" 583
"Armanda's Tarantella" 583
"Armies of the Right" 716
"Arms for the Love of Me" 1539
"The Army and the Navy and the Air Force" 1750
"Army Life" 1562
"The Army Song" (aka "[The] Army Song," "Canon Song," "Kanon Song," "Kanonensong," "Recruitment [Recruiting] Song" 689, 827, 879, 1626, 1773
"Arnold" 280
"Arnold and the Kennedys" 1128
"Around the Bend" 57
"Around the World" (Frankel) 641
"Around the World" (Young) 68, 1575
"Arpeggio" 1152
"The Arrangement" 1338
"The Arrest of Oscar Wilde at the Cadogan Hotel" 135
"The Arrival" (Grossman) 398
"The Arrival" (Justice and Ramirez) 1398
"Arrival at Pago-Pago" 1329
"Arrival in Christiania" 398
"The Arrival of the Postman" 1601
"Arrivederci" 352
"Arrivederci Roma" 1575
"Art" 1006
"Art for Art's Sake" 324
"Art Imitating Life" 444
"Art Is Forever" 403
"Art Is the Imitation of an Action (Beauty Is an Action)" 111
"Art Machine #1" 910
"The Art of Deceiving" 979
"The Art of Pleasing Me" 1057
"The Art of the Mime" 1447
"Art Song" 467
"Arthur in the Afternoon" 52
"An Artist Til the End" 276
"Artistic Confusion" 1385
"The Arts" 1447
"Arty" 1318
"As Adam" 903
"As Calm as the Ocean" 151
"As for the Future, I'll Dance" 1132
"As Good as Paradise" 1708
"As I Do" 276
"As I Say Goodbye" 1702
"As I'm Growing Older" 1739
"As If" 678
"As If I Weren't There" 1265
"As Long as I Can" 491
"As Long as I Can Sing" 929
"As Long as I Live" 165
"As Long as I'm with You" 555
"As Long as There Are Men" 404
"As Long as There's Music" 1210
"As Long As We Have Us" 1700
"As Long as You Live" 1692
"As Plain as the Nose on My Face" 1772
"As Time Goes By" 35
"As We Go Along" 1343
"As You Are" 434, 435
"As You Make Your Bed" 128, 1773
"Ashcan" 1291
"Asia" 1239
"Asia Avenue" 945
"Ask a Foolish Question" 616
"Ask and You Shall Receive" 1397
"Ask Me No Question" 41
"Ask the Doctor" 1149
"Ask Us Again" 324
"Assassination" 1294
"Assault Me" 1066
"The Asses Song" 449
"Assisi" 1671
"The Assistant Undersecretary of State for Human Rights" 1335
"The Assyrians" 726
"Astrociggy" 1072
"Astrology" 1397
"The Astronaut" 1318
"The Asylum Chorus" 826
"At a Georgia Camp Meeting" 1435
"At a Pantomime" 460
"At Kelly's (You're a Star)" 82
"At Last" 398
"At Last I Feel My Heart Awaking" 1316
"At Least I Know What's Killing Me" 892
"At Least There Are Parties" 873
"At Least We Can Say We've Been There" 1058
"At Liberty in Thebes" 1181
"At Long Last Love" 1210, 1823
"At My Age" 1
"At My Side" 463
"At Sea" 1584
"At the Agway" 1237
"At the Ball" 1060
"At the Ballet" 283
"At the Bottom Lookin' Up" 179
"At the Bottom of Your Heart" 1620
"At the Chat Noir" 547
"At the End of a Period of Time" 720
"At the End of the Day" 152
"At the Glen" 375
"At the Library" 877
"At the Middle of the Earth" 1020
"At the Movies" 1457
"At the Music Hall" 271
"At the Playland Jamboree" 336
"At the Prom" 683
"At the Seaside" 1639
"At the Sounding" 1404
"At the Theatre" 1637
"At the Zoo" 265
"At This Moment" 1407
"At Twenty-Two" 1447
"Atencion" 760
"A.T.F.D." 501
"Atlanta" 1219
"Atlanta Has Fallen" 1152
"Atlantic City" 1197
"Atomic Feet" 1832
"Attack and Fall" 20
"Attack of Banshees" 1522
"Attempt" 963
"Attention Must Be Paid" 196
"Attitude #1" 461
"Attitude #2" 461
"Attitude #3" 461
"Attitude #4" 461
"Attorney Street" 1715
"Au Revoir" 1476
"L'Audace, L'Audace et Plus L'Audace!" 871
"The Audition" 1218
"The Auditions" 1394
"Auditions" 492
"The Audley Family Honor" 884
"Auf Weidersehen (Weidersehn)" (Jessel) 1431
"Auf Weidersehen (Weidersehn)" (Jordan) 1379
"Auf Weidersehen (Weidersehn)" (Romberg) 1750
"Augusta! Augusta!" 92
"Augusta, What Are You Doing Here?" 92
"Augustus and the Soup" 1444
"Auld Lang Syne" 695
"Aunt Rose" 729
"Aunt? Now, I Haven't Done Any Shading Yet" 941
"Authentic" 808
"Auto Da Fe" 244
"The Auto Salon" 773
"Autumn" (Dowell) 1594
"Autumn" (Shire) 1524
"Autumn Leaves" 924
"Autumn Love" 308
"Autumn Night" 1016
"The Autumn of My Life" 976
"Autumn Salutation" 134
"Autumn's Here" 76
"Avalon" (Jolson, DeSylva and Rose) 993
"Avalon" (Tapper) 755
"Avant Garbage" 1276
"Avant the Guard" 820
"Ave Maria" 1431
"Ave Nelson" 857
"Avenue P" 1340
"Avenue Q Theme" 77
"The Average Man" 1034
"Aviatrix Love Song" 1326
"Avis" 87
"Avon Garde" 87
"Avreymele Melamed" 1203
"Avrum and Sore's Duet" 1502
"Awaiting You" 1404
"The Award" 1301
"Award of the Week" 1614
"Away" 1084
"Away, Away! (My Heart's On Fire)" 1270
"Away with Age" 1117
"The Awful Truth" 1340
"Awful Word and Awful Thoughts" 922
"Awkward Waltz" 396
"Ay, Gute Vaybele" 1715
"Ay Mi Dio" 1398
"Aye!" 673
"Ayers Rock/Uluru Song" 729
"The Ayes of Texas" 1318

"Der Ayznban (The Train)" 1619
"Az Der Rebbe Vill" 1032
"Az Men Zicht, Gefint Men" 1745
"Aza Yingele Vi Du" 1715
"Azoy Gich" 1212
"Azure Blue" 1469
"Azure Te" 1623

"B4" 154
"Ba-Ba-Ba" 602
"Ba-Boom" 626
"Ba-Boom-Ching" 1475
"The Babbitt and the Bromide" 1096
"Babes in the Wood" 80
"Babies on the Brain" 219
"Babkak Omar Aladdin Kassim" 727
"Baby" 2, 812
"Baby at 110" 1201
"Baby, Baby" (Hester and Apolinar) 1827
"Baby, Baby" (Sereda) 1432
"Baby Benjamin" 571
"Baby Bobby's Backyard" 552
"Baby Boom Babies" 1800
"Baby Doll" 180, 181, 182
"Baby Dolls" 1319
"Baby Face" 955
"Baby Girl" 1736
"Baby, I Love Your Biscuits" 703
"Baby, It Must Be Love" 1747
"Baby, It's a Matter of Life (All I Want to Do Is See It Through)" 699
"Baby, It's Cold Outside" 1176
"Baby It's You" 1551
"Baby Johann" 860
"Baby John" 1661
"Baby Makes Two" 1683
"The Baby Medley" 1478
"Baby Pictures" 1505
"Baby Rue" 175
"Baby Sitters Ball" 858
"The Baby Song" 739
"Baby, Sweet Baby" 1434
"Baby, Take Advantage of Me" 808
"Baby, That's Love" 466
"Baby, Won't You Please Come Home" 553
"Baby Workout" 790
"Baby You Bore Me" 638
"Baby, You Give Good Heart" 1149
"Baby, You Got What It Takes" 383
"Babysitter" 986
"Bacchis' Song" 124
"Bachelor's Dance (La Bouree du Celibataire)" 792
"Back and Forth" 114
"Back at the Seat of Power" 889
"Back Home" 1383
"Back Home Again" 37
"Back in Baby's Arms" 39
"Back in Business" 1491, 1492
"Back in Champagne-Urbana: Later That Night, Much Later, Much Much Later" 899
"Back in the Big Time" 82
"Back in the Gay Old Days" 1669
"Back in the World" 1562
"Back in the World Now" 386
"Back Legs" 1050
"Back Off" 1040
"Back on Base" 300
"Back on the Street" 1290
"Back So Soon?" 1181
"Back to Back" 1701
"Back to Genesis" 1395, 1396
"Back to My Babies" 1320
"Back to Nature" 1379
"Back to Nature with You" 1160
"Back to Our Story" 1366
"Back to the Play" 1181
"Back to Work" 1267, 1268
"Back with a Beat" 1558
"Backbone of Steel" 1320, 1321
"Background Music" 1045
"Background Song" 602
"Backstage" 626
"Backwards" 1678
"Bacteria" 1234
"Bad!" 1584
"Bad Bar Bebop" 1263
"Bad Blood" 825
"Bad Blow" 206
"Bad Boy" 646
"Bad But Good" 1124, 1537
"Bad Girl" 605
"Bad If He Does, Worse If He Doesn't" 1751
"Bad Luck" 383
"Bad News" 1014
"Bad Timing" 148, 1224
"Bad Whitey" 1620
"Badchen" 1822
"Badchen's Verses" 1821
"Baddest Mammyjammy" 1397
"The Bag with Which You Shop" 87
"Bagel-Shop Quartet" 1547
"Baggage" 1102
"Bailar!" 203
"Baker's Dozen" 87
"Baking with the BVM" 1155, 1157
"Bal Dans Ma Rue" 1256
"Le Bal de L'Amour" 240
"Balance the Plate" 1702
"Balancing" 338
"Balbec-by-the-Sea" 1103
"The Balboa" 840
"Balcony of the Faithful" 45
"The Bald Eagle and the Hairy Canaries" 871
"Balinasia" 1483
"The Ball" 1191
"Ball & Chain" 965
"Ball and Chain" 115
"Ball Routine" 1234
"Ballad" 299, 1037
"Ballad for a Firing Squad" 90
"Ballad for a Park" 160
"Ballad for Bimshire" 91
"Ballad for Christmas" 655
"Ballad in Bethelem" 1418
"Ballad in Which Macheath Begs All Men for Forgiveness" 1628
"Ballad of Adam and Eve" 856
"The Ballad of Baby Trygaeus" 1231
"The Ballad of Bedford Gaol" 1264
"The Ballad of Belle Boyd (Belle Boyd's Back in Town)" 569
"The Ballad of Booth" 70
"The Ballad of Caesar's Death" 1462
"Ballad of Castle Maiden" 708
"The Ballad of Cy and Beatrice" 1709
"The Ballad of Czolgosz" 70
"Ballad of Dependency" 1626
"Ballad of Dry Dock Country" 734
"The Ballad of Falstaff" 950
"The Ballad of Federal City" 1276
"The Ballad of Floyd Collins" 503
"The Ballad of Frimbo" 544
"Ballad of Gracious Living" 1628
"The Ballad of Guillermo" 499
"The Ballad of Guiteau" 70
"The Ballad of Happy Planet" 1508
"The Ballad of Harry Lewis" 685
"Ballad of Immoral Earnings" 1628
"The Ballad of Jack Eric Williams" 430
"The Ballad of Johnny Pot" 93
"The Ballad of Louis" 547
"Ballad of Mack (Mac) the Knife" 882, 1626, 1628, 1773
"The Ballad of Marcia LaRue" 1608
"Ballad of Mervyn Schwartz" 740
"Ballad of Oh" 486
"Ballad of Reading Gaol" 1714
"The Ballad of Robert Moses" 610
"Ballad of Sexual Obsession (Dependency) (Oppression) (Slavery)" 880, 882, 1628, 1773
"Ballad of Sheldon Roth" 1485
"Ballad of Sir Topaz" 572
"The Ballad of Sister Anne" 436
"The Ballad of Stonewall Jackson" 569
"Ballad of Tammy Brown" 469
"Ballad of Tancred" 366
"The Ballad of the Easy Life" 879, 1626
"Ballad of the Lily of Hell" 660
"Ballad of the Oak Tree" 501
"Ballad of the Pimp and the Whore" (aka "Zuhhalterballade") 880, 1773
"The Ballad of the Sad Café" 1133
"Ballad of the Soldier's Wife" (aka "Ballade vom Soldaten Weib"; "Soldatenweib"; "The Soldier's Wife" 880, 882, 1773, 1809
"Ballad of the Stag" 1179
"Ballad of the Tree" 60
"Ballad of the Triangle Fire" 604
"Ballad of the Victim" 461
"The Ballad of Utopia" 1713
"Ballad Singer" 32
"Ballad to the International" 60
"Ballade" 819
"Ballade No. 2 in F Major" 1694
"Ballade vom Soldaten Weib" (aka "Ballad of the Soldier's Wife"; "Soldatenweib"; "The Soldier's Wife") 880, 882, 1773, 1809
"Ballet" 60
"Ballet (Italian Interlude)" 1390
"Ballet Barre" 924
"Ballet Erotique" 636
"Ballet for San Damiano" 539
"Ballin'" 1396
"Ballin' the Jack" 55, 813
"Ballparks of the Gods" 377
"Ballroom Sequence" 291
"Baltimore" (Mahoney) 1108
"Baltimore" (Newman) 1049
"La Bamba" 1558
"Bamba Colora" 262
"Banana" 241
"Banana Oil" 263
"Bananas" 916
"The Banco Number" 1820
"Bang!" (Harris) 60
"Bang!" (Sondheim) 1027, 1492
"Bang, Bang" 365
"Bankrupt Blues" 393, 394
"The Banquet" 622
"Banquet in Honor" 1373
"Bantwana Besikolo" 1284
"The Baobabs" 938
"Baptist Fashion Show" 1225
"Barbara-Song" (aka "Barbara Song"; "The Barbara Song"; "Barbara's Song") 128, 689, 879, 880, 882, 1532, 1626, 1628, 1773, 1807, 1809
"Barbary Coast" 68
"Barbeque" 1547
"Barbecue for Two" 102
"B-A-R-B-E-R" 1194
"The Barbershop" 828
"Barbie and Ken" 1195
"Barcelona" 1491
"The Bard" 870
"The Bard in the Park" 352
"Bard to Verse" 472
"Bare Bones I" 926
"Bare Bones II" 926
"Bare Bones III" 926
"Bare Bones IV" 926
"Bare Facts" 81
"Barnabo" 366
"The Barnyard Song" 900
"The Baron" 1119
"Baron Samedi" 1388
"Baroness von Botzenheim" 609
"The Barquilleros (Los Barquilleros)" 488
"Barristers! It's Quarter Past!" 941
"Barry's Boys" 87, 160, 381
"The Baseball Game" 473, 997
"Basic" 1440
"Basic Black" 1732
"Basic Sicilian" 1771
"Basin Street Blues" 1096
"Basketball" 424
"Basketball Game" 278
"The Basketball Song" 1384
"Bastard for the Lord" 1392
"Bat Boy" 573
"Bath Parade" 66
"Bathos After the Funeral" 1614
"Bathroom" 1330
"Batting Order" 377
"Battle" 663
"The Battle" 827
"The Battle at Eagle Rock" 1107
"Battle Ballet" 194
"Battle Hymn of Groundhog" 643
"Battle Hymn of the Republic" 740, 815, 816, 1245
"Battle Hymn of the Rialto" 381
"Battle Montage" 224
"The Battle of Chicago" 968
"The Battle of Old Jim Crow" 815, 816
"The Battle of San Juan Hill" 826
"Battle of the Choruses" 983
"Battle of Trenton" 740
"The Battle Song" 1784
"Bayakhala" 651
"Bazaar-For the Lord" 333
"Bazoom" 598
"BBC-TV Presents" 22
"BBCBC" 241
"Be a Lover" 1161
"Be a Man" 1830
"Be a Mensch!" 1510
"Be Black" 1397
"Be Careful" 1598
"Be Flexible" 1362
"Be Frank" 1760
"Be Fruitful and Multiply" 878
"Be Gentle" 1827
"Be Good" 1584
"Be Good or Be Gone" 1317
"Be Happy" 210
"Be Honest, Dr. Dorn" 1416
"Be Kind to People Week" 109
"Be Kind to the Young" 1380
"Be Kind to Your Parents" 981
"Be Like a Basketball and Bounce Right Back" 214
"Be Like the Bluebird" 63
"Be More Aggressive" 1691
"Be My Baby" 1551
"Be My Bland Romantic Lead" 36
"Be My Lady" 308
"Be My Love" 1063
"Be Myself" 34
"Be Not Afraid" 1330
"Be Polite to Everybody" 1121
"Be Prepared" 1654
"Be There" 1815
"Be Very Careful" 571
"Be Witness to My Madness" 1057
"Be Yourself" 34
"Bea, Could I Take Two Pillows Up?" 1723
"The Beach House" 260
"Beach Scene" 1661
"Beams of Heaven" 1559
"Beans" 114
"Beans, Bacon and Gravy" 740
"The Bear, the Tiger, the Hamster and the Mole" 300
"Bea's Place" 110
"The Beast in Me" 1365
"The Beat Goes On" 115
"Beat, Little Pulse" 1652
"Beat Me, Daddy, Eight to the Bar" 35, 1571
"The Beat of the City" 292
"Beat the World" 987
"Beat This!" 1605
"Beata, Biax" 486
"Beaten by a Dead Man" 227
"Beatnik Love Affair" 1390
"Beatrice! Hurry Up!" 1723
"Beatriz" 1336
"Beauteous Is the Bride" 1531
"Beautiful" (Herman) 987
"Beautiful" (King) 1591
"Beautiful" (Sachs) 326
"Beautiful" (Shire) 1524
"Beautiful" (Sondheim) 1557
"Beautiful" (Springer) 1493
"Beautiful As Is" 431
"Beautiful Bright Blue Sky" 222
"The Beautiful Children" 575
"Beautiful Day" 864, 1076
"Beautiful Dreamer" 112, 695
"Beautiful for Once" 386
"Beautiful Heaven" 1004
"Beautiful Is Black" 1232
"Beautiful Man" 1072
"Beautiful Music" 726
"Beautiful People" (Brown and Tait) 1434
"Beautiful People" (Now) 1153
"Beautiful People" (Tomlin) 1255
"The Beautiful People" 605
"Beautiful Song" 812
"Beautiful Soup" 27
"Beautiful Storm" 1102

"Beautiful Sunday" 206
"The Beautiful Time" 606
"Beauty" 1046
"The Beauty in Her Bath and Her Admirer" 1293
"The Beauty of Numbers" 485
"Beauty Past All Dreaming" 404
"Beauty School Dropout" 625
"Beauty Secrets" 926, 948
"Beauty Treatment" 535
"Beauty Within" 1522
"Beaver Ball at the Bug Club" 1176
"Bebe Perdu" 1427
"Because" (Lennon and McCartney) 1426
"Because" (Mann) 1613
"Because, Because" (aka "Because") 1166, 1167
"Because I'm a Woman" 1025
"Because of Her" 338
"Because of Them All" 491
"Because of You" (Carmines) 920
"Because of You" (Salzman) 738
"Becky, Stay in Your Own Backyard" 1442
"Becoming Is a Lot Like Dying" 834
"Becoming One" 1727
"Bed" 338, 427
"Bed and Sofa #1" 114
"Bed and Sofa #2" 114
"Bed and Sofa #3" 114
"Bed and Sofa #4" 114
"Bed and Sofa #5" 114
"The Bed Was Not My Own" 683
"Bedtime Story" 350
"A Bedtime Story" (Ewing) 622
"A Bedtime Story" (Hartig) 616
"Beef Stew" 958
"The Beehive Dance" 115
"Beehive Polka" 1176
"Been There, Done That" 1117
"Been to Canaan" 1591
"Beep! Beep! Di Liebe Kimt" 1212
"Beer Barrel Polka" 1571
"Beer Is Best" 246
"Beetle Bailey, Won't You Please Come Home" 1263
"Before and After" 1431
"Before Breakfast" 1379
"Before I Fall" 1147
"Before I Kiss the World Goodbye" 348
"Before Invasion 1940" 135
"Before It's Too Late" 1380
"Before Stonewall" 1600
"Before the Curtain" 635
"Before the Music Motif Curtain" 637
"Before the Parade Passes By" 818
"Before the World Was Made" 707
"Before You Knew I Love You" 175
"Beggar and Poet" 529
"Beggars Can't Be Choosers" 654
"Begging the Question" 1441
"Begin the Beguine" 367, 1439
"Beginners Guide to Cruising (Pilgrim's Primer)" 564
"The Beginning" (Harper) 1424
"The Beginning" (Strouse) 1473
"The Beguine" 341
"Behave" 510
"Behind Dena's Back" 770
"Behind the Scenes" 287
"Behold the Coming of the Sun" 1476
"Bei Mir Bist Du Rap" 1607
"Bei Mir Bistu Schoen (To Me, You're Wonderful)" 119, 205, 1571, 1619
"Being Alive" 807, 1491, 1492, 1623
"Being Bouvier" 641
"Being for the Benefit of Mr. Kite" 1426
"Being for the Benefit of Mr. Kite II" 1426
"Being for the Benefit of Mr. Kite III" 1426
"Being Good (Isn't Good Enough)" 1546
"Being Left Out" 1702
"Being Made Love To" 626
"Bel Paese" 1771
"Believe" 1119
"Believe in Me, or I'll Be Leavin' You" 297
"Believe in You" 113
"Believe in Yourself" 489
"Believe Me" 1258
"Believe Us" 856
"Believers' Chants" 120
"Believers' Lament" 120
"Bella" 851
"Belladonna" 1336
"Belle" 727
"Belle Boyd, Where Have You Been?" 569
"Belle of New York" 922
"Belle of the Ball" (Anderson) 1521
"Belle of the Ball" (Childs) 222
"The Belle of the Ball and the Bull of the Brawl" 810, 1179
"Belle Plain" 91
"La Belle Province" 159
"Belle Raconte Son Histoire" 123
"Belle Retourne Chez Son Pere" 123
"La Belle va au Chateau" 123
"The Belles of Belle Harbor" 874
"Bellevue and the Judge" 643
"Bells" 1296
"The Bells" (Bristol, Gage and Stover) 1494
"The Bells" (*Time, Gentlemen Please!*) 1639
"Bells, Bells!" 1374
"Bells of St. Mark's" 1131
"Beloved" 14
"Below the Belt" 126
"Belt & Leather" 971
"Belz (Wonderful Girl of Mine)" 492
"Ben Hur" 507
"Benares Song" 879
"Benedicite" 1155, 1157
"Benedictine" 1192
"Benediction" (Carmines) 952
"Benediction" (Kaufman) 1734, 1735
"Benediction" (Telson) 615
"Benjamin Calypso" 833
"Benny's Dispatch" 760
"Berl, the Tailor (Opening a New Account)" 1203
"Berlin im Licht-Song" 689
"Berlin in Licht-Song (Berlin in Lights)" 1532
"Bernarda's Prayer" 130
"Bernardin" 1209
"Bernard's Lament" 1710
"Bernice, I Don't Believe You" 1245
"Bertha" 1460
"Bertha the Sewing Machine Girl" 1267
"Bertie's Annual Aria" 301
"Bertie's Waltz" 375
"Besame Mucho" 1245
"Besancon" 497
"Besides the Seaside" 135
"Bess, You Is My Woman Now" 1096
"Bessarabia" 819
"The Best for You" 413
"The Best Is None Too Good for Me" 9
"The Best Is Yet to Come" 1210
"Best Loved Girls" 1447
"The Best Man" 809
"The Best Man (I Never Had)" 1317
"Best Not to Get Involved" 1422
"The Best of All Possible Worlds" 244, 911
"The Best of Both Possible Worlds" 1045
"The Best of Both Worlds" 470
"Best of Friends" 949
"The Best of Friends" 1692
"The Best Part-Time Job in Town" 1309
"The Best Thing That Ever Has Happened" 1491
"The Best Things in Life Are Free" 955
"Best Way to Have the Blues" 949
"Best Wishes" 1069
"The Best Women in the World (Las Mejores Mujeres del Mundo)" 488
"Best Years of My Life" 1600
"The Best Years of Our Lives" 413
"Bestiario" 1133
"Bethena" 1643
"Betrayed" 834, 1161
"Betsy Moberly" 54
"Bette Davis" 783
"Better" (Kennon) 484
"Better" (Kleban) 296, 992, 1106
"Better Bein' Loved" 215
"A Better Day" 1537
"Better Days" 1449
"Better Fall Out of Love" 641
"Better Get a Grip" 359
"Better If I Died" 375
"Better Keep Your Promise" 653
"Better Leave Segregation Alone" 815, 816
"The Better Man Won" 1613
"Better Not to Know" 1084
"Better Place to Be" 916
"Better Safe Than Sorry" 1058
"Better Than Broadway" 1097
"A Better World" 41
"The Betting Bit" 1720
"Betty" 1818
"Betty Simpson" 60
"The Betty Song" 580
"Between an Ape and an Angel" 468
"Between Me and Myself" 529
"Between the Devil and the Deep Blue Sea" 165
"Between the Lines" 14
"Between the Sheets" 873
"Between the World and Me" 1734, 1735
"Beware as You Ride Through the Hollow" 76
"Beware the Thunder and the Light" 814
"Beyached" 1647
"Beyond" 3
"The Beyond Ballet" 1237
"Beyond Reproach" 942
"Beyond the Binge, I Want to Get Off" 1125
"Beyond the Blue Horizon" 1570, 1571, 1750
"Beyond the Clouds" 1221
"Beyond the Rule of the Khan" 1020
"A Beyzer Chulem" 1032
"Bicentennial March" 636
"A Bicycle Built for Two" 1092
"Bid Me Love" 972
"Bidding the World Farewell" 539
"Biddlebury Gap" 1289
"The Bide-a-Wee in Soho" 1626
"Bidin' My Time" 955
"Big" 476
"Big and Complicated" 114
"Big Apple" 834
"Big Baby" 81
"Big Bad Burlesque" 142
"The Big Ballet in the Sky" 552
"The Big Bang" 143
"Big Barry" 60
"Big Belinda Fatsquat" 820
"The Big-Bellied Bottle" 631
"Big Bertha" 606
"Big Best Shoes" 1716
"Big Betty's Song" 504
"Big, Big" 121
"Big, Big Contest" 1679
"Big Bill Murphy" 656
"Big Bird" 571
"The Big Bow-Wow" 1486
"Big Bright Green Pleasure Machine" 265
"Big Brother" 201
"Big Chief" 1518
"The Big City" 272
"Big City Dance" 1307
"Big Date Tonight" 1747
"Big Day Tomorrow" 667
"Big Dogs Run" 769
"Big Dreams" 949
"Big Hair" 755
"Big Ideas" 934
"Big Lucy" 78
"The Big Mac Tree" 610
"Big Man" 1551
"Big Money" (LaChiusa) 1422
"Big Money" (Mo' and Edwards) 1631
"Big Names, Big News" 1162
"Big Radio" 1459
"Big Red Plane" 248
"Big Sister Blues" 111
"Big Spender" 212
"The Big Walk" 1125
"Big Wig" 1832
"Big Wooden Shoes" 1618
"Bigger Is Better" 1763
"Bigger Than Both of Us" 241
"The Biggest Ain't the Best" 1155, 1157
"The Biggest Still Ain't the Best" 1159
"Bilbao Song" (aka "The Bilbao Song"; "Bilbao-Song") 128, 660, 689, 879, 880, 882, 1773, 1807, 1809
"The Bill" 1237
"Bill" 1096
"Bill and Willa" 643
"Bill Bailey" 96, 1239
"Bill Bailey (Won't You Please Come Home?)" 171, 1643
"Bill of Fare" 1710
"Bill Robinson Walk" 1373
"Billie's Bounce" 35
"Bill's Lament" 27
"Billy Noname" 152
"Billy's Blues" 415
"Billy's Law of Genetics" 997
"Bim-Bam-Bom" 1203
"Bing, Bang, Boom!" 391
"Bingo (Bingo Eli Yale)" 1282
"The Bingo Long Travelling All-Stars and Motor Kings" 153
"Biography" 1527
"Bird" 820
"Bird Chorus" 1133
"A Bird in a Cage" 812
"A Bird in a Gilded Cage" 577, 829, 1643
"Bird Lament" 1133
"Bird on a Wire" 1471
"The Bird Song" 27
"Bird Upon the Tree" 848
"Birdie Follies" 1476
"Birdies" 701
"Birdie's Lament" 1469
"Birdland" 156
"The Birds in the Sky" 726
"The Birds in the Trees" 726
"Birds of Paradise" 157
"Bird's Song (I Like Them)" 812
"The Birds That Left the Cage" 253
"Birmingham" 1036, 1334
"Birmingham Sunday" 1356
"Birth" 958
"Birth of a Beatnik" 638
"The Birth of Bingo" 154
"Birth of the Hermit (God of all the Magics)" 1592
"Birth to My Creation" 541
"A Birthday" 851, 972
"A Birthday Horoscope" 1527
"Birthday Party" 1551
"Birthday Serenade" 1131
"Birthday Song" 113
"Birthstone of the Death Squad" 1066
"BiSexual Blues" 123
"Bistro" 529
"Bit-Part Demon" 462
"The Bitch of Living" 1515
"The Bitch Scene" 947
"Bite Your Tongue" 682
"Bits & Pieces XIV" 160
"Bits and Pieces" 436
"Bits of Nonsense" 550
"The Bitter and the Sweet" 1048
"Bitter Green" 963
"Bitter Licci Nuts" 1448
"Bitter Tears" 1780
"The Bittersuite" 162, 163, 164
"Bittersweet" 1361, 1362
"Bizarbara's Wedding" 1522
"Black" 1038
"Black and Blue" 18, 165
"Black and Blue Plumps" 292
"Black and Tan Fantasy" 1373
"Black and White People" 788
"Black and White World" 778
"Black Annie" 960
"The Black-Black Song" 589
"Black Boy" 152
"Black Boys" 649
"Black Cockroach Pas de Deux" 552
"Black Coffee" (Dorsey) 1500

"Black Coffee" (Webster and Burke) 156, 1245, 1435
"The Black Freighter" 1807
"Black Is Beautiful" 109
"Black Magic Woman" 1556
"Black Man" 1397
"The Black One" 1225
"Black Pearls" 1566
"Black Rape" 1388
"Black Silence" 407
"Black Slacks" 1138
"Black Tie Waltz" 1320, 1321
"Black Up" 1505
"Black Velvet" 1304
"Black Woman" 777
"The Blackberry Vine (A Play)" 571
"Blackberry Wine" (Ford) 656
"Blackberry Wine" (Kociolek) 8
"Blackberry Winter" 23
"Blackest of Tresses" 1264
"Blackout" 207
"Blah, Blah, Blah" 46
"Blame It All on Me" 456
"Blame It on My Youth" 73
"Blame It on the Bossa Nova" 854
"Blame It on the Moon" 453
"Blame It on the Movies" 172
"Blame It on the Summer Night" 1328
"Blame It on These Times" 1375
"Blame the Reds" 844
"Blanket Over the Sorrows of Werther" 820
"Blasé" 1688
"Blast from the Past" 1831
"Blast Off Baby" 1832
"Bleecker Street" 698
"Bless Me Father" 1727
"Bless the Lord" 595
"Bless This House" 1218
"Bless This School" 381
"Bless You" 854
"Bless You, My Children" 1002
"Blessed Assurance" 196
"Blessed Be God" 1650
"A Blessing" 647
"Blimelech Tzvey (Two Flowers)" 1382
"The Blind Junkie" 493
"Blind Man's Buff" 1440
"Bliss" (Cain) 1110
"Bliss" (Carmines) 1311
"Blocks" 149
"A Blond in Bed" 1300
"Blonde Haired Babies" 1702
"The Blonde in the Bathing Suit" 1475
"The Blonde Song" 644
"The Blonde Under the Sheet" 1475
"Blondes and Brunettes, I Like Them All (Las Rubias y Las Morenas)" 488
"The Blonde's Song" 1460
"The Blood Done Sign My Name" 657
"Blood Done Signed My Name" 777
"Blood Lines" 1593
"Blood Red Roses" 972
"Blood Religion" 1333
"The Blood Saved Me" 166
"Bloodshed and Brotherhood" 350
"The Bloom Is Gone" 111
"The Bloom Is Off the Rose" 348
"Blooming in the Fall" 1323
"Les Blouses Blanches (The Ones in White)" 1256, 1257
"Blow, Blow Soft Winds" 382
"Blow, Bugles, Blow" 224
"Blow, Gabriel, Blow" 63
"Blow Hot, Blow Cold" 1016
"Blow Slow Kisses" 873
"Blow Top Blues #1" 382
"Blow Winds" 1830
"Blow Ye Winds" 740
"Blowin' in the Wind" 265
"Blowing Bubbles in the Bathtub" 215
"BLT" 638
"Blue Again" 886
"Blue and Troubled" 985
"The Blue Aspic" 49, 612
"Blue, Blue, Blue" 912
"Blue Blues" 180, 181, 182
"The Blue Book" 105
"Blue Book" 240
"Blue Eyes" 503
"The Blue Flame" 499
"Blue Flame" 1772
"Blue Gate Fields Hotel" 404
"Blue Grass (of Kentucky)" 1606
"Blue-Grass Dreamers" 1343
"The Blue Hen's Chick" 322
"Blue Jeans and Misery" 922
"Blue Monk" 156
"Blue Moon of Kentucky" 39
"Blue Pacific Blues" 1329
"Blue Plate Special" 179
"Blue Shadows" 1016
"Blue Suede Shoes" 205
"Blue Train" 156
"Blue Turning Grey Over You" 165
"Blue Twilight" 1818
"Blue Wind" 1515
"Bluebirds" 332
"Blueboy" 1813
"Blues" (Harris) 1605
"Blues" (Latouche) 1688
"Blues" (Silver; aka "The White Anglo-Saxon Protestant Blues") 1527
"Blues" (The Stewed Prunes) 261
"The Blues Ain't Nothing" 382
"The Blues Are Brewin'" 1016
"Blues for Minnis" 996
"Blues in the Night" 180, 181, 182, 662
"Blues Man" 777
"Blues Revelation" 1225
"Blues Was a Pastime" 1620
"The Blues: Quartet of the Defeated" 1229
"Board of Estimate" 1037
"The Boarder" 1361, 1362
"Boarding Houses" 285
"Boardwalkin' Blues" 257
"Boasting Song" 701
"Boatman" 257
"The Boatmen's Dance" 436
"Bob's Fantasy" 295
"Bobbie's Fantasy" 295
"Bobby Bear" 945
"Bobby the K" 1069
"Bobby Watson and the Family" 773
"Bobby's Song" 296
"Bobby's Songs" 86
"La Bodega" 607
"Bodoni County" 292
"Body and Soul" 1435
"Body Beautiful Beale" 641
"Body Count" 194
"Body, Mind and Soul" 38
"Bof Booof" 1407
"Bohemian Rhapsody" 1623
"Bojangles of Harlem" 886
"Bolero" (Davis) 388
"Bolero" (Offenbach) 124
"Bolt of Love" 1610
"Bon Bon Buddy" 1783
"Le Bon Mot" 1265
"Bon Soir" 924
"Bon Vivant" 538
"Bon Voyage" (Bernstein) 244
"Bon Voyage" (Offenbach) 190
"Bon Voyage" (Porter) 63
"Bon Voyeur" 1069
"Bond Sequence" 1184
"Bonds" 1381
"Bone of Thy Bones" 1708
"Bones" 1232
"Bonjour" 1138, 1652
"Bonne Entente" 963
"Bonny Boudreau" 1478
"Bonus #1" 1251
"Bonus #2" 1251
"Bonus #3" 1251
"Boogey Man" 225
"Boogie Bug" 1171
"Boogie Woogie" 553
"Boogie Woogie Ball" 1550
"Boogie Woogie Bugle Boy from Company 'B'" 1571
"Boogie-Woogie Rumble" 194
"The Book" 927
"Book Report" 1828
"Books" (Flaherty) 1006
"Books" (*The Uncommon Denominator*) 1698
"The Bookworm" 352
"Boola" 1282
"Boom!" (Friedman) 1255
"Boom!" (Leigh) 289
"Boom Boom" 430
"Boomer and Bunger" 1071
"Boompies" 1565
"Boost the Morale" 1171
"Boot Dance" 651
"Boot It Boy" 553
"Boots" 388
"Boots on the Floor" 1438
"Bop-A-Bye" 1192
"The Bop Will Never Die" 319
"Borders" 1458
"Bored" 407
"Boring Straight Song" 241
"Born Again" (Carmines) 111
"Born Again" (Eisenberg) 36
"Born for Better Things" 1196
"Born in America" 693
"Born in the USA" 1664
"Born Leader" 624
"Born Never Asked" 1664
"Born on a Bike" 1061
"Born to Be Together" 854
"Born to Be Wild" 1353
"Born to Entertain" 1386
"Born to Fly" 1410
"Born to Hand Jive" 625
"Born to Lose" 1183
"Born to Love" 229
"Born to Rock and Roll" 319
"Born to Schnorr" 1593
"Born to Sing" (Lemberg) 809
"Born to Sing" (Naylor) 196
"Born to Sing (Gospel)" 809
"Born Too Late" (Duke) 942
"Born Too Late" (Strouse) 237
"Borned" 1366
"Bosom Buddies" 818
"Boss Man" 963
"Boston in the Spring" 578
"Both Ends Against the Middle" 98
"Both Sides of the Coin" 1109
"The Bottle (Fantasy on Alcohol)" 1044
"Bottom's Up" 572
"Bottoms Up" 236
"Bougainvillea" 386
"Boughten Bride" 858
"The Bouillabaisse Song" 978
"Boule, Boulevard" 507
"The Boulevard of Broken Dreams" 924
"Bounce" 1491
"Bounce Back" 156
"Bound Away" (Braden) 408
"Bound Away" (Simpson and Wann) 710
"A Bowler Hat" 1213
"The Boy Actor" 1170
"Boy and Girl at the Movies" 1394
"Boy at His First Dance" 1457
"Boy Blue" 1397
"Boy, Do I Hate Horse Races" 76
"Boy, Do We Need It Now" 1709
"The Boy Friend" 199
"The Boy from ..." 986
"A Boy from Home" 1459
"The Boy I Left Behind Me" 236
"The Boy Is Perfect" 878
"A Boy Like You" 689
"Boy Meets Boy" 200
"Boy Meets Girl" 1483
"The Boy Next Door" 746
"Boy to Love" 1472
"Boychild" 152
"Boycott Trial Song" 1423
"The Boyfriend" 1149
"A Boy's Best Friend Is His Mother" 695
"Boys from the South" 1007
"The Boys in the Backroom" 1350
"The Boys of Summer" 377
"Boys Will Be Girls" 297
"Boys' Bunk" 1478
"B.P. II" 1439
"The Braggart's Song" 1161
"Brain Dead" 1121
"Brain Drain" 1508
"Brand New Eyes" 1306
"The Brand New Fourth Estate" 1743
"Brand New Wall-to-Wall Day" 1045
"Brand New World" 1328
"Branded a Tramp" 825
"Brandy in Your Champagne" 631
"The Brass Ring" 1806
"Brave New World" 222
"Brave You" 575
"The Bravest Little Boat" 1479
"Bravest of All" 1458
"Bravo for the Clown" ("Bravo Pour Le Clown") 361, 1256, 1257
"Bravo!" 947
"Bravo! Bravo!" (Donizetti) 1146
"Bravo! Bravo!" (Wallace) 673
"Brazil" 926
"Bread" 88
"Bread and Roses" 604
"Break-up Rag" 65
"Breakdown" 995
"Breakfast" 1485
"Breakfast at Tiffany's" 1752
"Breakfast in Harlem" 165
"A Breakfast Over Sugar" 763, 764
"Breakfast Over Sugar" 765
"Breakin' a Leg" 1543
"Breakin' the Spell" 1480
"The Breaking of So Great a Thing" 62
"Breaking the Penal Code with You" 573
"Breaking the Sound Barrier" 1832
"Breaking the Travel Ban" 1356
"Breathe" 1428
"Breathes There a Man with Soul So Dead?" 542
"Breathing In" 386
"Breathing the Air" 1358
"Breathless" 19
"Brendan's Dream" 545
"Brethren an' Sister'n" 1563
"Brewing the Love Potion" 1751
"Bridal Bouquet" 1477
"Bridal Fete" 66
"Briderlekh Tayere (Dear Brothers, Help)" 604
"Bridge of Coulaincourt" 924
"Bridge Over Troubled Daughters: A Kitchen in Champagne-Urbana, 9 P.M. on a Saturday Night" 899
"The Bridge Song" 220
"Bridge to the Future" 217
"Bridges" 61
"A Brief Dissertation on the Relevancy of a Liberal Education in a Contemporary Society" 357
"Brief Encounter" (Kaufman and Koreto) 1069
"Brief Encounter" (McAuliffe) 509, 949
"Brief Encounter" (*Russell Patterson's Sketchbook*) 1385
"(A) Brief Romance" 1701
"Bright College Days" 1654
"Bright College Years" 1282
"Bright Footed" 226
"Bright Lights" 785
"Bright Lights, Big City" 206
"Bright Morning Stars" 376
"Bright Side Somewhere" 1466
"Bright Spring Morn" 290
"Bright Young People" 1170
"Brighton Parade" 317
"A Brilliant Idea" 1155
"Brilliant!" 1050
"Bring All the Boys Back Home" 1689
"Bring Back Nelson Mandela" 1401
"Bring Back Swing" 159
"Bring Back the Roxy to Me" 415
"Bring Him Home" 1623
"Bring in 'da Noise Bring in 'da Funk" 207
"Bring in the Morning (Nicole Leach, Company), Let It Rain" 208
"Bring It On Home" 682
"Bring Me to Light" 1726
"Bring on the Loot" 1296
"Bring on Tomorrow" 474
"Bring Out Old Glory" 258
"Bring Out the Beast" 241
"Bring Out the Beast in Me" 1431
"Bringing in the Sheaves" 1484
"Bringing Up Badger" 297
"Briscoe, the Hero" 1004
"British Defense Minister Peter Thornycroft" 1091
"The British Free Enterprise Auction" 1381
"A British Subject" 1109
"Brittania Rules" 1069
"A Briveke Der Mamen" 1715
"A Brivele Der Mamen (A Letter to Mother)" 604
"Broadway" 64
"Broadway Baby" 341, 428
"Broadway Blossom" 148

"Broadway Blossoms" 1224
"Broadway Boogie Woogie" 296
"Broadway, Broadway" 809
"A Broadway Cinderella" 637
"Broadway in Dahomey" 165
"Broadway Melody" 1548
"A Broadway Musical" 210, 214, 237
"Broadway, My Street" 1685
"Broadway, New York" 1476
"Broadway Rhythm" 840
"Broadway Wedding" 215
"Broken & Bent" 216
"Broken Dialog" 1373
"Broken String Blues" 1464, 1465
"Brom and Katrina" 76
"B'rochos L'Havdoloh" 119
"Bronx Express" 1715
"Bronxville Darby and Joan" 1390
"Brooklyn" 217, 907
"Brooklyn Bridge" 328
"The Brooklyn Bridge" 1546
"Brother" 206
"Brother 2" 206
"The Brother Blues" 453
"Brother, Can You Spare a Dime?" 35, 604, 740, 1096
"Brother, Give Yourself a Shove" 660
"Brother Harlem Bedford Watts Tells Mr. Charlie Where It's At" 1735
"Brother Men" 655
"Brother Mountain" 1671
"Brother to Brother" 634
"Brother, Where Are You?" 835
"Brothers" 59
"The Brothers Came to Egypt" 833
"Brown Baby" 835
"Brown-Eyed Girl" 1434
"Brown Gal" 221
"Brown Paper Bag" 734
"Brown Penny" 707
"Brown-Shirted Cowboy" 1635
"The Brown-Skin Gal in the Calico Gown" 165
"Brownie Scene" 1788
"The Brownie Song" 1347
"Brownstone" 638
"Broyt" 1715
"Brtko, Tono Brtko" 1449
"The Brushing Song" 1594
"Bruxelles" 924
"Bubbe Meises Bubbe Stories" 220
"Bubble Gum" 624
"Bubbles in My Bonnet" 271
"Bubbles in the Bathtub" 1208
"Bubbling Brown Sugar" 221
"Bub's Song" 755
"The Buck Stops Here" (Lippman) 223
"The Buck Stops Here" (Nehls) 627
"The Buck Stops Here" (Schimmel) 378
"Buckhead-Dunwoody Diet Brigade" 1500
"Buckin' Barley" 1164
"Buckle Down, Winsocki" 132, 1611
"Bud" 411
"Buddha's Song" 1458
"Buddy Bolden's Blues" 813
"Buddy Bolden's Horn" 240
"Buddy Toupee — Live" 644
"Buddy's on the Night Shift" 1809
"The Buds of May" 453
"Bug" 142
"Bug Song" 983
"Bugle Call Rag" 1571
"Build a Bridge" 1404
"Build a Union" 1361
"Build on the Rock" 1484
"Building/Train" 427
"Bull Blood and Brandy" 379
"Bull Dog" 1282
"The Bullfight" 142
"The Bulls (Les Toros)" 792
"Bully Boys" 1444
"Bully Song" 197
"Bum Luck" 576
"Bumble Bee Freilach" 555
"Bump and Grind for God" 856
"Bump, Bump, Bump" 809
"Der Bumsen-Kratzentanz" 499
"A Bundle of Nerves" 225
"Bunnies" 1486
"The Bunny's Lament" 1125
"A Bunny's Mother" 550
"Bunyan's Farewell" 1229
"Bunyan's Good Morning" 1229
"Bunyan's Goodnight (I)" 1229
"Bunyan's Goodnight (II)" 1229
"Bunyan's Goodnight (III)" 1229
"Bunyan's Greeting" 1229
"Bunyan's Return" 1229
"Bunyan's Warning" 1229
"Bunyan's Welcome" 1229
"Buono Notte" 506
"The Burden of Life" 1006
"Bureau of Mutual Affairs" 396
"Burger Beguine" 861
"Burglar" 1647
"Buried Alive in the Mud" 151
"Burlesque" 1662
"Burlesque Is a Stamping Ground" 506
"Burn" 1423
"Burn, Baby, Burn" 152
"Burn On" 1036
"Burn This Town" 120
"Burnin' Hunk of Clay" 750
"Burnin' Luv" 1235
"Burnin' Up" 1363
"Burning a Witch" 1562
"The Burning Bush" 647
"Burning the Henrietta" 68
"burntangel@aol.com" 502
"Burundanga" 262
"The Bus (in Israel)" 1044
"A Bus Driver" 1701
"Bus from Amarillo" 133
"Bus Ride" 1176
"Bus Stop" 1661
"Das Busch Ist Schlecht" 227
"Bush Is Bad" 227
"Bush Is Bad Intro" 227
"Business" 1698
"Business as Usual" 1171
"Business Is an Art" 260
"Business Is Bad" 1468
"The Businessman" 938
"Buster, He's a Hot Dog Now" 1326
"Busy" 1294
"Busy, Busy, Busy" 1108
"Busy Busy Busy Correspondence Card" 1289
"Busy, Busy Day" 1108
"Busy Days" 960
"Busy Lady" 857
"But Alive" 237
"But Beautiful" 924
"But He's Mine" 627
"But I Do" 738
"... But I Don't Want to Talk About Her" 738
"But I Hear" 814
"But I Love New York" 1758, 1759, 1761
"But, I Love You" 1679
"But If Something Leads to Good (Can It Be Bad?)" 1708
"But in the Morning, No" 367
"But Never Jam Today" 230
"But Not for Me" 46, 428
"But, Oh, the Dreams" 331
"But Sir, You Stir Rebellion" 331
"But That's Why I Loved It! So Lurid and Preposterous" 941
"But the World Goes 'Round" 824
"But What I Say" 1103
"But When You're Gone" 1723
"But You Do Not Know This Man" 1723
"But You Go On" 58
"But Yours" 1752
"Butcher, Why Didn't You Kill Me?" 1063
"A Butler in the Abbey" 1546
"Buttercup" 1480
"The Buttercups" 552
"Butterfingers" 60
"The Butterfly" 1323
"Butterfly" 1670
"Butterfly Child" 1136
"Butterfly's Lament" 1319
"Button A" 1760, 1761
"Button Up Your Overcoat" 955
"Buy a Slave" 663
"Buy American" 1152
"Buy Bonds, Buster (Buy Bonds)" 232, 1163
"Buy My Pardons" 572
"Buying and Selling" 857
"Buzz Mirandy" 1543
"Bwis Iolem Tantz" 1822
"By Any Means Necessary" 470
"By Brecht and Weill" 547
"By Buddha This Duck Is Immortal!" 1235
"By Candlelight" 1823
"By Golly, That's It!" 362
"By Goona-Goona Lagoon" 600
"By Moonlight" 250
"By My Side" 595
"By Myself" (Schwartz) 348, 1606
"By Myself" (Slater) 719
"By Myself" (Sticco) 267
"By Strauss" 46
"By Ten Last Night" 1416
"By the Beautiful Black Sea" 170
"By the Glenside" 1399
"By the Mississinewah" 367
"By the Sea" 1491
"By the Stream" 1694
"By the Time I Forget Her" 1638
"By the Time I'm Forty" 1420
"By the Waters of Babylon" 647
"By the Way" 933
"By Way of Frank Ford" 950
"Bye and Bye" 409
"Bye Baby Bye" 1345
"Bye, Bye Baby" 965
"Bye Bye Birdie" 237
"Bye-Bye Brevoort" 942
"Bye, Bye, Conrack" 313
"Bye Bye Future" 610
"Bye Room" 830
"Bye the Time" 542
"B.Y.O.B." 646

"The C Word" 1831
"Cabaret" 52, 212, 1685
"The Cabaret Dies — The Cabaret Lives" 547
"The Cabdriver of the Conventioneer" 1813
"Cabin in the Rockies" 729
"Cabin in the Sky" 238
"Cabin in the Woods" 462
"Cacophony" (Rado) 1330
"Cacophony" (Satlin) 279
"Cadenza" 427
"Caesar's Death" 879, 1807
"Café Escargot" 1500
"Café Royale Rag Time" 1452
"Café Society" 1125
"The Cage" 1806
"Caius's Theme" 950
"Cajun Vitrine: The Ballad of Aout Anni" 926
"The Cake I Had" 641
"Cake Walkin' Babies from Home" 1198
"Cakewalk" (Carmines) 1231
"Cakewalk" (*Safari 300*) 1388
"Cakewalk Into Kansas City" 376
"Calcamania" 507
"Calendar Girls" 226
"California" 1539
"California Dreamin'" 411
"California, Here I Come" 829, 993
"California Love" 36
"California Style" 1153
"California Suite" 89
"La Calinda" 1385
"The Call" 503
"Call Back in the Morning" 939
"Call Back the Times" 258, 259
"Call from the Grave" 1626, 1628
"Call Him Papa" 528
"Call It Un-American" 1268
"Call Me Andre" 505
"Call Me Jasmine" 1042
"Call Me Lucky" 291
"Call Me Mister" 1096
"Call Me Pet Names" 481
"Call Me Ursula" 194
"Call of the Birds" 1787
"The Call of the Wild" 395
"Call of the Wild" (*Tour de Four*) 1661
"Call of the Wild" (*Two for Tonight*) 1688
"Call on a Veteran" 1077
"Call the Children Home" (Kayden) 240
"Call the Children Home" (Murphy) 105
"Call This a Guverment?" 922
"Call to Prayer" 1672
"Calla Lily Lady" 1689
"Called to the Simple Life" 1671
"The Calling" 38
"Calvary" 1672
"Calypso" (Denver) 37
"Calypso" (Ladd) 1475
"Calypso" (Moross) 600
"Cambrick Shirt" 1085
"The Camel Song" 781
"Camellias" 1102
"The Camel's Blues" (aka "The Camel's Song") 855
"The Cameo" 635
"Camera Wall" 206
"Camouflage" 219
"Camp" 126, 558, 1273
"Camp Let-Yourself-Go" 1649
"Campaign Song" (Holt) 1603
"Campaign Song" (Rome) 1608
"The Campfire" 1554
"Campfire Songs" 1154
"Campus Life" 1743
"Le Can Can" 1293
"Can-Can" 1641
"Can I Come Over, Please" 206
"Can I Do It All" 217
"Can I Stay Awhile?" 502
"Can I Touch You?" 605
"Can That Boy Fox Trot!" 1027
"Can the Big 'A' Beat" 897
"Can This Be a Toe-Print?" 870
"Can Ye Fancy That?" 345
"Can You Forgive Me?" 1789
"Can You Love" 1119
"Can You Read My Mind" 1651
"Can You See a Girl Like Me in the Role" 1447
"Can You Tell Me What's Happened to Kurtz?" 624
"Can You Type?" 1290
"Can You Use Any Money Today?" 428
"Canada at War" 151
"The Canarsie Diner" 1138
"The Canary" 1385
"Canary" 1754
"The Cancan Volunteers" 1092
"Canceling the Bar Mitzvah" 473
"Cancer Operation" 449
"Cancion del Enfermero" 262
"Cancun" 1709
"Candid Camera" 1415, 1732
"Candid Candidates" 1255
"Candle Blessing" 666
"Candlelight Graces a Woman's Face" 44
"Candlesticks" 754
"Candy Bar" 945
"Candy Butcher" 1615
"Candy Man" 777
"Candy Pitch" 1720
"Candy's Lament" 1164
"Cane Cutter's Ballet" 960
"Canis Minor Bolero Waltz" 1007
"The Cannon Song" 1628
"Cannonfire, It's Over" 1562
"Canon Song" 882
"Can't Breathe" 328
"Can't Can't" 1171
"Can't Help Lovin' That Man" 883, 955
"Can't Help Singing" 883
"Can't I?" 267
"Can't Keep It Down" 474
"Can't Leave Now" 1025
"Can't Make Love Without You" 1151
"Can't Nobody Do Me Like Jesus" 1466
"Can't Say for Sure" 1523
"Can't Stand to Sing" 1427
"Can't Stop Dreaming" 1618
"Can't Wait" 573
"Can't You Hear I'm Making Love to You" 398
"Can't You Just See Yourself?" 1651
"Cantabile" 170
"Cantata" 143, 1754
"Cantata for a First Date" 739
"Canteen Serenade" 232, 1163
"Canter Banter" 572
"Canterbury Day" 246
"Canticle of Pleasure" 539
"Canticle to the Wind" 1566
"Canto a la Habana" 262
"Canto Lucumi" 262

"Cao, Cao, Mani Picao" 262
"Cap-Pitulation" 773
"Cape Cod Girls" 740
"Capes" 820
"Capital of the World" 1264
"Capitalist Beguine" 1045
"Caprice" 135
"Capricious and Fickle" 1311
"Captain Gingah" 1639
"Captain Hook's Soliloquy" 234
"Captain Hook's Waltz" 1224
"Captain Jinks of the Horse Marines" 695
"The Captain Lincoln March" 1824
"Captain Louie" 248
"Captain of the Ship" 1508
"Captain Valentine's Song" 826
"The Captain's Jig" 979
"Captains of Courage" 1664
"Capture the Girl" 375
"Car Alarms" 1237
"Car Crash" 1373
"Car Wash" 399
"Le Carabine" 107
"Caramelos" 262
"Las Caras Lindas de Mi Gente Negra" 262
"Caravan" 1407
"The Card Game" 322, 476
"A Card Trick" 1235
"Cardboard Madonna" 453
"Cardinal O'Connor" 1710
"Cardology" 287
"Cardova the Bronx Casanova" 1658
"Careless Rhapsody" 236
"Carlos, Juan, and Miguel" 1759, 1761
"Carmen Viscenzo" 1767
"Carmilla stays" 250
"Carnegie Hall" 1687
"Carnegie Hall Pavane (Pavanne [sic])" 1185, 1186
"Carnival" (Holt) 1460
"Carnival" (Link) 1363
"Carnival" (Marvin) 1719
"Carnival (La Foule)" 361, 1256, 1257
"The Carnival" 503
"Carnival in Capri" 60
"Carnival Ride" 961
"A Carol" 93
"Carolina Rolling Stone" 1521
"Carolina's Lament" 878
"Caroline" (Brielle) 1135
"Caroline" (Newman) 1036, 1334
"Carousel" (Holton) 693
"Carousel" (Rodgers) 212
"Carousel (La Valse a Mille Temps)" (aka "Carousels and Cotton Candy") 792, 1162
"Carrara Marble" 1637
"A Carriage for Alida" 98
"A Carriage, You Hear It?" 1063
"Carrickfergus" 775
"Carricknabauna" 253
"Carried Away" (Bernstein) 1185, 1186
"Carried Away" (Venneri) 352
"Carrion Train" 464
"Carry Me Home" 950
"Carry On" 68
"Carry That Weight" 1426
"Carrying On" 136
"The Carter Song" 1297
"Caryl Ann" 407
"Casanova" 1160
"The Case of the Hum-Drum Killer" 1318
"Casey at the Bat" 1234, 1235
"Casey Jones" 740
"Cash for Your Trash" 18
"Cash Politics" 217
"Casino Paradise" 257
"The Cassions Are Rolling Along" 892
"Cast Call" 1576
"Cast of Thousands" 1624
"A Casting Call" 89
"Casting Director, Casting Director, Give Me a Part" 511
"A Castle in India" 1379
"Castle in the Air" 1493
"Castles in the Air" 822
"Castles in the Sand" 678
"A Casual Kind of Thing" 1646
"The Cat and the Rooster" 11
"Cat in the Box" 1251
"Catalogue Woman" 436
"Catastrophe" 1788
"Catch a Falling Star" 527
"Catch Me" 929
"Catch Me If I Fall" 260
"Catch on Fire" 777
"Catch Our Act at the Met" 1224
"Catering" 240
"Caterpillar's Advice" 27
"Catfish" 1317
"Cath'rine" 1815
"The Cathedral of Clemenza" 1716
"Catherine, Come Home" 1815
"The Catherine Maidman Show" 1048
"Cats' Creed" 1229
"Cat's in the Cradle" 916
"Cat's Meat" 436
"The Cats' Pajamas" 261
"The Cattle Are Asleep" 92
"Cattle Calls" 1548
"Cattlemen" 950
"Catullus Song" 915
"Caught" 1511, 1815
"Cause a Sensation" 1207
"Cause I'm Happy" 300
"A Cautionary Cantata" 1076
"Cautiously Optimistic" 1228, 1297
"Cavalcade of Curtain Calls" 919
"Cave Art" 1152
"Cavorting" 80
"Cawfee Man" 1733
"Cazanova" 1160
"C.C. Rider" 1198
"Cecilia" 96
"Celebrate!" 878
"Celebration" (Butler) 1423
"Celebration" (Cohen) 963
"Celebration" (Grant) 1307
"Celebration" (*Manhattan Rhythm*) 1015
"Celebration" (Msomi) 651
"Celebration" (Schmidt) 1451
"Celebration for a Gray Day" 1356
"Celia's Oye Como Va" 262
"Cell of the Well-to-Do" 1149
"Cemetery Plot" 1485
"Center Peace" 196
"Central Intelligence" 1649
"Central Park" (LaChiusa) 1422
"Central Park" (Mainieri, Martin and Brown) 1014
"Central Park, 1917" 1719
"Central Park on a Sunday Afternoon" 1678
"Ceremonial Chant" 1221
"Ceremonial March" 1221
"The Ceremony" 486
"C'Est Fini" 1385
"C'Est l'Amour Qui Fait Qu'on S'Aime" 361
"C'est Magnifique" 367
"C'Est Si Bon" 1575
"C'est Toujours la Meme Histoire" 1257
"Ceylon" 1109
"Chad" 666
"L'Chaim" 555
"Chain Gang" 527
"Chain of Love" 926
"The Chain Song" 1519
"Chain Store Daisy" 1267, 1268
"Chair Dance" 1720
"The Chair Dance" 1398
"Chalfalaya's Ballet" 996
"Chalhatchee" 703
"Chalk Dust Man" 1325
"Challenge to Love" 828
"Champagne" 1379
"Champagne and Kisses" 1007
"Champagne Charlie" 695
"Champagne Song" 1476
"Chan Ballet" 1348
"The Chance of a Lifetime" 1296
"Chance of You" 741
"Change" (Draesel) 1671
"Change" (Finn) 997, 1121
"Change, Change, Change" 1046
"Change in Direction" 710
"Change in the Air" 741
"Change of Scene" 957
"Change of Sky" 1493
"Change Your Immigrant Ways" 1442
"Changes" (Alper) 754
"Changes" (Brandon) 1467
"Changes" (Fieger) 268
"Changes" (Richmond) 1226
"Changes" (Strouse) 58
"Changes" (Taylor) 1289
"Changing" (Ashwander) 624
"Changing" (Ford) 656
"Changing" (Silver) 1458
"Changing Faces" 791
"Changing Partners" 1758, 1759, 1761
"Chanson" 88
"Chanson, Chanson, Chanson" 411
"Chanson Francais" 542
"Chant" 91
"La Chanteuse" 1687
"Chaos Ballet" 755
"Chapel of Love" 1551
"Chaperone" 260
"Chapter One" 676
"The Charade of the Marionettes" 1254
"Charisma" 722
"Charismatic" 653
"Charity" (Grand) 277
"Charity" (*Elsa Lanchester—Herself*) 436
"Charity Quartet" 1375
"Charles" (Riddle) 322
"Charles" (*Dark Horses*) 350
"Charles, This Isn't Easy for Me to Have to Say" 44
"Charleston" (Ellstein) 1342
"Charleston" (Gould) 148
"Charleston" (Johnson) 165
"Charleston Rag" 165
"Charleston Under the Moon" 215
"Charlie and Pepper" 742
"Charlie in a Field, Forever" 1018
"Charlie's Plaint" 1072
"Charlotte Sweet" 271
"The Charm" 253
"Charm Song" 296
"Charmed Life" 1400
"A Charmed Life" 1524
"Charming" 1134
"Charming! Charming! Charming!" 317
"Charmingly Insane" 1226
"The Chart" 961, 1756
"The Chase" (Baron) 541
"The Chase" (Dean) 76
"The Chase" (Kookoolis, Fagin) 1504
"The Chase" (Metcalf) 409
"The Chase" (Peterson) 710
"The Chase" (Pippin) 258, 259
"A Chasens in Shtetel" 1745
"Chasidik" 1647
"Chassene" 1342
"Chassene Hobn Iz Doch Zeyer Git (Marriage Is a Good Thing)" 1382
"Chat & Tea" 1321
"Chat Room" 1742
"Chattanooga Choo-Choo" 35
"Chatter" 403
"The Chatter of an Old Woman" 1449
"Chauncey's Tune" 105
"Cheap Chablis" 1558
"The Cheap Exit" 690
"Cheap Jack" 253
"Cheatin'" 1263
"Check It Out" 1117
"Checkers" 114
"Checking the Facts" 528
"Cheeky Kiki" 1289
"Cheer Up, Cheer Up!" 1824
"Cheerio, Old Boys" 1636
"Cheerleader" 992
"Cheers" (Adams) 1139
"Cheers" (Katsaros) 434, 435
"Cheese" 1335
"Cheese Nips" 588, 727
"Chekhov" 157
"Chelm" 1619
"Chelsea Song" 1471
"Cherry Street Café" 1328
"Cherry's Soliloquy" 274
"Cheshire Puss" 27
"The Chess Game" (Finn) 1019
"The Chess Game" (Gounod) 1373
"Chess Game #1" 275
"Chess Game #2" 275
"Chess Hymn" 275
"Chew Chewy Chow" 89
"Chez Adams (The Washingtons Come Too)" 1263
"Ch'hob Lib Teater (I Love the Theatre)" 1453
"Ch'hob Moyre Derfar" 1212
"Chi Town Strut" 996
"Chic" 277
"Chic Dogs" 396
"The Chic of Paris" 1293
"Chicago Bound" 207
"Chicago Drag" 105
"The Chicago Riot Rag" 207
"Das Chicago Song" 1069
"The Chicago That I Know" 1755
"The Chicken and the Frog" 690
"Chicken Is He" 1311
"The Chicken Song" 676
"Chicken Soup with Rice" 1340
"Chicken's a Popular Bird" 91
"Chico-Chico Chico-Layo Tico-Tico Pay-Pa-Payo Buena Vista de Banana by-the-Sea" (aka "Chico Chico") 232, 1163
"Chief Surgeon" 377
"Child Abuse" 719
"A Child Ill" 135
"A Child Is Born" 23
"The Child Is Born" 166
"Child of a Sweater" 36
"Child of Mine" 1441
"Child of Pure Unclouded Brow" 27
"Child of Sympathy" 1504
"Child of the Most High King" 777
"Child of the Shade" 582
"Child of the Sun" 278
"The Child Was a Girl" 439
"Childhood" 1354
"Childhood Days" 644
"Childhood Lullaby" 1445
"Children and Art" 1557
"Children Are a Blessing" 385
"Children Are for Loving" 1064
"Children, Children" 106
"Children, Go Where I Send Thee" 166
"Children Have It Easy" 1400
"Children of Adam" 279
"Children of Darkness" 1356
"Children of Love" 1423
"Children of the Heavenly King" 1404
"Children of the Wind" 1328
"The Children, They Grow Up" 510
"Children Today" 1684
"Children, Your Line Is Dragging" 777
"Children's Game" 689
"Children's Games" (*The Believers*) 120
"Children's Games" (Crane) 1767
"Children's Song" 716
"Children's Sour" 1315
"Chill Out!" 855
"Chilling Stream, Drink" 240
"Chin Up, Ladies" 818
"China" 979
"Chinatown" 1208
"Chinese Cha, Cha, Cha" 1066
"Chip & Dale Days" 750
"The Chipmunk" 812
"Chiquita Bonita" 203
"Chiribim" 1647
"Chloe" 171
"Chlorophyl Solly" 32
"Ch'ob Zich Areinge-Dreit (How Did I Get Into This?)" 1105
"Chocolate Covered Cherries" 220
"Chocolate Drop " 1783
"Chocolate Turkey" 701
"The Choice Is Yours" 90, 1031
"Choices" (Edwards, Harris) 113
"Choices" (Richmond) 1226
"Choir Practice" 913
"Choir Rehearsal" 1001
"Choo-Choo Honeymoon" 341
"Choo Choo Rap" 216
"Choose Love" 1815
"Choose to Be Happy" 641
"Chopin" 444
"Chorale" 1184
"Chorus" 1229
"Chorus Accusation" 1229
"Chorus Girl Blues" 85
"A Chorus Nun" 1158
"Chorus of Exiled Jews" 363
"Chorus of Exiled Palestinains" 363

"Chorus Questions Oedipus" 615
"The Chosen" 284
"Chosen Doime le Meilech and Rikodle" 1822
"Chosun Is Tangun's Land" 889
"Chrastine" 1337
"Christ Was Born" 166
"Christian Charity" 106
"Christian Cowboy" 1484
"Christina Alberta and I" 285
"Christine Keeler's Testimonial" 1765
"Christmas" (Gould) 135
"Christmas" (Lippa) 830
"Christmas" (Townshend) 1655
"A Christmas Buche" 271
"Christmas Carol" 1539
"Christmas Is Everyone's Holiday" 1700
"Christmas Is to Blame" 576
"Christmas Lullaby" 1498
"The Christmas Party" 1229
"Christmas Puppies" 1384
"Christmas Shopping" 1635
"Christmas Song" 1635
"Christmas Tree" 1149
"Christmas Trees" 535
"The Christmas Waltz" 1546
"Christopher" 1025
"Christopher Columbus" 165
"Christopher on the Air" 287
"Christopher, Pass the Warm Wine" 1063
"Christopher Street" 911
"Christy" 288
"Chromolume #7" 1557
"Chrysanthemum Tea" 1213
"La Chulapona" 1179
"Church and State" (aka "Church & State") 1759, 1760
"The Church in the Wildwood" 1484
"The Church of Birch" 1276
"Church of the World" 59
"Church Rulez" 38
"The Church Social" 600
"Chutzpah" 865, 866, 1593
"Ciao, Ciao, Bambino" 1521
"Cigarets" 529
"The Cigarette" 252
"Cigarette Dream" 933
"The Cigarette Song" 1311
"Les Cigarettes" 32
"Cindelia" 1283
"Cinderella" 1153
"Cinderella of Our Block" 85
"Cindy" 291, 698
"Cindy's Birthday" 1551
"Circa 1929" 616
"Circe, Circe" 600
"Circle" 916, 1363
"Circle of Life" 1623
"Circle Round" 1320, 1321
"The Circle Stomp" 207
"Circumstances" 1183
"Circus" (Fleischman) 226
"Circus" (*Tourquoise Pantomime*) 1662
"The Circus Is Coming" 1618
"Circus of Jade" 101
"The Circus of Voices" 271
"The Circus Organlog" 1720
"Ciribiribin" 1570
"Cirque-O-Pade" 773
"Cities of Light" 345
"Citizen Kong" 700
"The City" 20
"City Blues" 120
"City Hall" 1290
"City Lights" 313
"City of Dreams" 791
"City of the Angels" 150
"City Song" 1659
"City Walk" 1200
"The Civil War" 716
"Civilian Review Board" 1069
"Civilization" 428
"Civilization and the Nursery Rhyme" 1085
"Civilized" 884
"Clap Yo' Hands" 1172
"Clara Drum" 639
"Clarence's Turn" 200
"Clarinet Marmalade" 553
"Class" (Kander) 52, 1685
"Class" (Sondheim) 1403
"Class Act" 185
"The Class of 1984" 1335
"The Classic Queens" 1159
"Classical Music" 1299
"Classified Information" 542
"Clay and Frelinghuysen" 722
"The Clean Ones" 86
"Clean Up Your Own Backyard" 1732
"A Cleaner N.Y." 535
"Clear, Bright Morning" 13
"Cleavage" 297
"Cleopatra" 1393
"Cleopatterer" 902
"Clerk" 198
"Cliché" 161
"The Cliché Waltz" 162, 163, 164
"Click" 1818
"Client Service" 991
"Clifford, Where Are You?" 717
"The Climax" 649
"Climb" 387
"Climb That Mountain" 507
"Climb Up Here with Daddy on the Boom Boom" 1153
"Climb Up the Social Ladder (The New Blue D.A.R.)" 912
"Climbing Over Rocky Mountain" 1270
"Climbing Uphill" 890
"Clinging to the Rock" 453
"Clip Joint" 1475
"Cloak and Dagger" 241
"The Clock Keeps Ticking" 57
"The Clocks" 1274
"Clog Dance" 42
"A Close Call" 1143
"Close Enough for Jazz" 299
"Close Every Door" 833
"Close Harmony at Detroit (A Minstrel Show)" 622
"Close That Show" 1383
"Close to You" 83
"Close Your Eyes" (Chodosh) 1539
"Close Your Eyes" (Isen) 491
"Closed for Renovations" 939
"Closeness Begets Closeness" 48
"Closer" 1379
"The Closer I Get" 790
"Closer Than Ever" 300
"The Closest Star" 1548
"Closets Are a Necessary Fact of Life" 673
"Closeup of Jack Entering Room" 44
"Closing" 1258
"The Closing" 1274
"Closing Arguments" 643
"Closing Remarks" 1155, 1157
"Closing Song" 497
"Closing Time" 1317
"Clothes" 1384
"The Clothes Make the Man" 1311
"Clothes Make the Man" 1415
"Cloudburst" 1138
"Clouds" 1486
"The Clown" 1119
"The Clown Song" 1476
"The Club" 760
"Club Crawl" 206
"CNR" 159
"Co-Cobra Women" 907
"Co-operatin' Nature" 274
"Coalition" 1760
"Coaxing the Ivories" 1176
"Coaxing the Piano" 1176
"Coca Cola Girl" 614
"Cocaine" 1113
"A Cockeyed Vocalist" 511
"Cockling? Cackling" 941
"Cockney London" 436
"The Cockroach Song" 1299
"A Cocktail Party" 1394
"Cocktail Party Types" 1276
"Cocoanut Cream Pie" 726
"The Coconut Wireless" 1221
"The Cocotte" 1160
"The Code" 1135
"Code of the Licensed Pilot" 1566
"Code of the West" 949, 950
"Codependent with You" 610
"Coffee" (Kaplan) 1485
"Coffee" (LaChiusa) 1422
"Coffee" (Porter) 1160
"Coffee" (Salzman) 738
"Coffee (A Relativity)" 1447
"Coffee Bar Suite" 1760
"Coffee Cups and Gossip" 1513
"Coffee in a Cardboard Cup" 52
"Coffee Morning" 667
"Cohen Owes Me $97" 1442
"The Cohens Are Coming" 100
"Coin Routine" 1234
"Cold Box of Chicken" 261
"Cold Cash" (Beebe) 1678
"Cold Cash" (Herrick) 950
"Cold Cruel Dark" 54
"Cold Steel" 175
"Cold Turkey" 1661
"Cold's the Wind" 1446
"Coliseum" 143
"Collage" 1624
"Collecting of the Plaid" 381
"College of L'Amour" 598
"The College of Reality and Pragmatism" 780
"A College on Broadway" 505
"Collision Course" 995
"Colonel Clevis in West Berlin" 1415
"Color and Light" 1557
"Color Me White" 152
"Color My World" 1551
"The Color Red" 990
"Colorado Love Call" 766, 935
"Colorblind Blues" 573
"The Colored Band" 1762
"Colored Lights" 52
"Colorful" 237, 603
"Coloring Book" 1125
"The Colors of Paradise" 1513
"Columbus, Ikh Hob Tsu Dir Gornit" 1715
"Coma Baby" 206
"Come After Breakfast (Bring 'Long Your Lunch and Leave 'Fore Supper Time)" 457
"Come Again " 419
"Come Alive Again" 1513
"Come-Along-a-Me, Babe" 1774
"Come Along, Boys" 600
"Come Along Down" 1021
"Come Along with Me" 307
"Come Along with Us" 1153
"Come and Be Married" 1399
"Come and Go with Me" 815, 816
"Come and Help Yourself to America, or Frank in the Melting Pot" 483
"Come Avec!" 1635
"Come Away" 1777
"Come Away, Death" (Hester and Apolinar) 1827
"Come Away, Death" (Mulcahy) 1437
"Come Baby" 206
"Come Back, Baby" 785
"Come Back Home Baby" 123
"Come Back, Paddy Reilly" 775
"Come Back to Brooklyn" 814
"Come Be My Love" 499
"Come, Birdie, Come" 481
"Come Buy, Come Buy" 586
"Come by Here" 1559
"Come, Catherine" 1723
"Come Celebrate Our Reforms" 889
"Come Dance with Me" 1210
"Come Down" 1399
"Come Down Now" 1225
"Come, Elijah, Come" 1136
"Come Fly with Me" 1210
"Come Gather 'Round" 1821
"Come Here. Look" 363
"Come Home, Runaway" 408
"Come, I Will Be Your Mother" 834
"Come In and Browse" 415
"Come in from the Rain" 1106
"Come in My Mouth" 913
"Come In!" 609
"Come Into My Jungle" 208
"Come Join the Party" 616
"Come Join Us" 1831
"Come Little Children" 730
"Come Live with Me" (Leslee) 1519
"Come Live with Me" (Valenti) 851
"Come Live with Me and Be My Love" 1437
"Come Luv" 1117
"Come, O, Come (to Pittsburgh)" 1606
"Come of Age" 1574
"Come On" 206
"Come On Along" 1451
"Come On and Dance" 682
"Come On and Marry Me, Honey" 246
"Come on, Daisy" 1758, 1759, 1761
"Come On Down to the Ostrich Farm (Part I)" 1289
"Come On Down to the Ostrich Farm (Part II)" 1289
"Come On Down to the River" 1762
"Come on Down to the Sea" 710
"Come on Home" 1397
"Come On In" (Brandon) 968
"Come On In" (*Further Mo'*) 553
"Come On In" (Martin) 746
"Come On In" (Porter) 367
"Come On In (and Sit Right Down)" 39
"Come On in My Kitchen" 777
"Come on in the House" 1308
"Come On in This House" 255
"Come on Joan" 823
"Come On Outside and Get Some Air" 1652
"Come on Train" 464
"Come Out and Play" 703
"Come Rain or Come Shine" 383, 1210
"Come Raise Your Cup" 448
"Come Said My Soul" 903
"Come See About Me" 115
"Come, Sinner, Tonight's the Night" 1563
"Come Sweet Love" 366
"Come Take a Trip in My Airship" 1643
"Come to Bohemia" 637
"Come to Cuba" 1297
"Come to Jesus" 1404
"Come to Life" 308
"Come to Mama" 266
"Come to Me" 1390
"Come to Me, Bend to Me" 42
"Come to the Club Tonight" 301
"Come to the Road" 1659
"Come to Your Senses" 1634
"Come Together" 1426
"Come Tomorrow" 979
"Come Unto These Yellow Sands" 1437, 1569
"Come Up to My Place" 1185, 1186, 1224
"Come with Me" (Childs) 222
"Come with Me" (Dick) 1815
"Come with Me" (Eliran) 401, 1136
"Come with Me" (Friedman) 1441
"Come with Me" (Lippa) 1778
"Come with Me" (Rodgers) 201
"Come with Me ... We Know Love" 1082
"Come with Us" 59
"Come Ye Disconsolate" 736
"Comedy in Stripping" 506
"The Comedy of Love" 583
"Comes a Time" 884
"Comes the Dawn" 1780
"Comes the Revolution" (Gershwin) 912
"Comes the Revolution" (MacDermot) 860
"Comes the Right Man" 722
"Comfort and Joy" 106
"Comfort for the Taking" 1787
"The Comic" 1030
"Comin' Down the Quarters" 375
"Comin' Through the Rye" 170
"Coming and Going" 471
"Coming Attraction #1" 1763
"Coming Attraction #2" 1763
"Coming Attraction #3" 1763
"Coming Attractions" (Raniello) 1089
"Coming Attractions" (Strouse) 1473
"Coming Attractions with Carol Ann" 1763
"Coming Back Home" 1002
"The Coming of the Dawn" 541
"Coming Together, Going Together" 1168
"Coming True" 157
"Command Me" 78
"Comment Allez-Vous?" 1138
"Comments" 1356
"The Commercial" 22
"Commitment" 1076
"Common Little Catechism" 328
"Common Sense" 743
"Communicate" 1078

"Communication" (Brown, Tait) 1434
"Communication" (Harris) 60, 1605
"Communication" (*The Uncommon Denominator*) 1698
"Community Sing" 32
"Commute" 1547
"Companionship" 652
"The Company of Men" 1580
"Company of Men" 957
"Complications" 537
"Composer/Hung-Up Tango" 1414
"The Composers' Song" 1096
"The Composing of 'Tahiti Trot'" 170
"The Compromise Soft Shoe" 1635
"The Computer" 1754
"Comrades, Fill No Cup for Me" 112
"Con Edison" 415
"Concerning the Insecurity of the Human State" 1628
"Concert Encore" 1754
"Concert Reading at Town Hall" 550
"Concert Tonight" 45
"Concerto in B Flat for Bassoon, First Movement" 1439
"Concerto in F" 73
"Concerto in F, Allegro" 295
"Conchita Marquita Lolita Pepita Rosita Juanita Lopez" 1546
"Conclave" 59
"Conclusion" 435
"The Conclusion" 1109
"Conclusions" 1195
"Concrete and Steel" 1470
"Concrete Jungle" 804
"Coney-by-the-Sea" 1116
"The Coney Island" 587
"Coney Island" 778
"Coney Island Dream Ballet" 1185
"Conference" 124
"Conference Call (or Gray Flannel & How It Grew)" 160, 371
"The Confession" 1613
"Confession" (Flaherty) 1006
"Confession" (LaChiusa) 1422
"Confession" (Rubell) 403
"Confession" (Schwartz) 348, 1606
"Confession #2" 973
"Confession to a Park Avenue Mother (I'm in Love with a West Side Girl)" 1218
"Confessional" 509
"Confessions—1,2,3" 304
"La Confiance de la Bete en la Belle" 123
"Confide in Me" 1469
"Confidence" 1420
"Confiteor" 1029
"Conformity" 1239
"The Confrontation" (Andersson and Ulvaeus) 275
"The Confrontation" (Schmidt) 1253
"The Confrontation" (Springer) 714
"Confrontation Song" 1659
"Confusing Times" 1006
"Confusion" 1108
"Conga!" 911
"Congratulations!" 203
"Congratulations!" (McAnuff) 364
"Congratulations!" (Fremont) 1258
"Connected" 892
"Connected Forever" 665
"Connie" 225
"Consenting Adults" 968
"Consolation" 707
"Constance Insured" 963
"The Constant Nymphet" 531
"Constantinople" 1575
"Constantly" 1783
"Constanza Lepolelli Was the Daughter" 1789
"Construction of the Death-Life-Death Mandala Bridge" 1592
"Consuelo" 1119
"Consume" 1736
"The Consummate Picture" 391
"Contact Lenses" 1813
"Conte Dracula" 1293
"Contemporary Music" 32
"Contest Winner" 1315
"The Contraband Ball" 569
"Contracts in E Flat" 1548
"Contrasts" 287
"The Controversial Play's the Thing" 160
"Convent" 1007
"Convention Results" 638
"Conventional Wisdom" 1523
"Conversation" 1734, 1735
"Conversation Piece" (Bernstein) 911
"Conversation Piece" (Goggin and Solley) 667
"A Conversation Piece" (Dana) 1261
"A Conversation Piece" (Goggin) 1202
"Conversationalization" 1373
"Conversations" 61, 207
"Coo-Coo (Coo Coo)" 766, 935
"The Cook" 1158
"Cook American" 664
"Cooking (Cookin') Breakfast (for the One I Love)" 692, 1494
"Cooking for Henry" 143
"The Cooking Lesson" 773
"Cooks' Duet" 1229
"Cook's Tour" 415
"Cool" 812
"Cool Cape May" 507
"Cool Cats" 1251
"Cool, Cool Elbow" 926
"The Coolest Cat in Town" 319
"Coolie Gone" 1004
"The Coolie's Dilemma" 234
"Coonskin Cap" 464
"Cooper Square" 643
"Cooperation" 1661
"Cop Song" 1712
"Copacabana" 992, 1106
"Copenhagen" 180, 181
"Copenhagen, Denmark" 1058
"Copper's Creed" 716
"Cops and Mafia Out of the Bars!" 673
"Coquin de Printemps" 301
"Corey's Coming" 916
"Cornbean Pie" 1042
"Cornbread" 1562
"Corncake Inlet Inn" 864
"Cornelia" 1323
"Cornish Cliffs" 135
"The Coronation" 1303
"The Coronation of Akhnaten" 20
"Coronation Song" 1302
"Corporate Choreography" 299
"Correspondent's Correspondence" 194
"Corridors and Halls" 302
"Corruption" 1124, 1537
"Corsage" 1310
"Corti" 792
"Cosmetology" 1299
"Cosmic Incident" 1192
"Cossack" 32
"Cote Saint-Jacques" 1510
"Cottage by the Sea" 463
"Cotton Club Revue" 1388
"Cotton Club Stomp" 165
"Could Be" 121
"Could He Be You?" 678
"Could I Be Kidding Myself" 1743
"Could I Leave You?" 1492
"Could I?" 1117
"Could She Be the One" 1082
"Could Such a Face Be False" 259
"Could You Please Inform Us" 1304
"Could You Use a New Friend?" 1688
"Couldn't Be Happier" 1448
"Couldn't Hear Nobody Pray" 1466
"Couldn't I Un-Bake the Breads" 941
"Couldn't We" 504
"Count on My Love" 950
"Count Your Blessings" 1176
"Counter Melody" 1574
"Counterfeit Love" 404
"The Counterman" 65
"Counterpoint" (Friedman) 558
"Counterpoint" (McAuliffe) 509
"Country Boy/City Girl" 153
"Country Harmony" 960
"Country House" 1492
"Country Life" 1562
"The Country Nun" 1159
"A Country of the Mind" 823
"Country Song" 861
"Country Spell" 345
"Country Store Living" 1504
"Country That Is Missing" 647
"County" 135
"County Fair" 102
"County Mayo" 253
"The Couple" 449
"A Couple Fools" 1598
"Couple of Questions" 67
"A Couple of Regular Guys" 1818
"A Couple of Years from Now" 1033
"Couplet" 1342
"Couplet for Alfred" 1608
"Court Minuet" 1316
"Court of Conscience" 285
"Court-room Scene" 1615
"Court Room Scene" 226
"Courtroom Cantata" 463
"The Courtroom Scene" 1475
"Cousin Kevin" 1655
"Cover Girls" 1709
"Cover-Up #1" 2
"Cover-Up #2" 2
"Cover-Up #3" 2
"Covered in the Rear" 224
"Cowboy Song" 827
"The Cowboys" 740
"Cowboy's Burning Desire" 1171
"Cowboy's Dream" 950
"A Cowboy's Life" 740
"Cowgirls" 323
"Cozy Dreams Come True" 1052
"Crabbed Age and Youth" 1437
"Crack in the Record" 735
"The Cradle Song" 253
"The Cradle Will Rock" 324
"The Cranes Are Flying" 938
"Craniotomy" 1121
"The Crave" 813
"Crawlin' King Snake" 777
"Crazy" (Ballard) 93
"Crazy" (Nelson) 39
"Crazy" (Swados) 386
"Crazy 'Bout Ya' Baby" 527
"Crazy Ann Coulter" 227
"Crazy Crazy" 370
"Crazy Downtown" 685
"Crazy Girl, Loquita" 995
"Crazy House" 142, 506, 1615, 1616
"Crazy Jane on the Day of Judgment" 707
"Crazy, Man, Crazy" 1239
"Crazy Melody" 824
"Crazy New Words" 1138
"Crazy Now" 326
"Crazy People" 681
"Cream in My Coffee" 1754
"Cream of Mississippi" 1574
"Cream of Mush" 1267
"The Creation" 1436, 1672
"Creation" (Leake) 278
"Creation" (Rubell) 403
"Creation" (Kaplan) 1485
"The Creation of the Earth" 1592
"The Creature from the Last Offramp" 1478
"Creatures Go to Sleep in Peace" 834
"The Creature's Tale" 541
"Credit Card" 580
"Credit Face" 1361, 1362
"Credit Is Due" 942
"Credit to the Uniform" 1818
"Credo in Unum Deum ..." 1029
"Creeque Alley" 411
"Creole Belles" 1543
"Creole Love Call" 165
"Creon" 1072
"Creon Comes to Colonus: Come Home" 615
"Crick Crack" 413
"Cricket" 769
"Cricket Master" 135
"The Crickets Are Calling" 902
"(Cries in the) Common Marketplace" 87
"Crime in the Streets" 1758
"Criminal" 203
"Crisis in the Kitchen" 1500
"Criss-Cross-Wordless Puzzle" 622
"The Critic" 1473
"Critics" 969
"The Critic's Blues" 635
"Crocodile Lounge" 696
"Crocodiles Cry" 980
"Croft's Serenade" 476
"Le Croissant" 1265
"Croon-Spoon" 324
"Crooning" 1543
"Croquet" (Holt) 1460
"Croquet" (Taylor) 481
"The Cross Country Tour" 1245
"Cross Over—Off to John Henry's" 238
"Cross That River" 1135
"Cross Your Finger" 1477
"Crossbridge Dance" 697
"Crossing Boundaries" 1702
"Crossing Nation" 729
"Crossing the Red Sea" 647
"Crossroad Blues" 777
"Crossword Puzzle" 616, 1524
"The Crow and the Fox" 11
"Crown Me" 1311
"The Crows" 253
"Crucifixion" 1672
"The Cruelty Stomp" 1522
"Crush on You" 1331
"Cry" (Kociolek) 8
"Cry" (Kohlman) 527, 1575
"Cry, Baby" (aka "Cry, Baby, Cry") 981, 1608
"A Cry from the Coast" 36
"Cry of the Peacock" 1716
"Cry the Beloved Country" 128, 1807
"Crying My Heart Out" 221
"Crystal Glass" 240
"Crystal Palace" 1293
"Crystal Palaces" 949
"Crystal Wisdom" 71
"Cuando Volveras" 262
"Cuant Union" 1336
"Cuanta Calma" 1336
"Cuba" 262
"Cuba Si Yanqui No" 1276
"Cuban Love Song" 1570
"Cubes and Abstracts" 693
"Cucala" 262
"La Cucaracha" 746
"Cuchifrito Restaurant" 203
"Cuckold's Delight" 366
"Cuckold's Song" 963
"Cuckoo" 878
"Cuckoo Song" 1661
"Cuddle In" 1747
"The Cuddles Mary Gave" 1006
"Culture of Life" 227
"Culture Quiz" 1209
"The Culture Twist" 1276
"Cum Deum" 543
"The Cunnilingus Champion of Co. C" 913
"Cup" 820
"A Cup of Coffee" (Dahdah) 336
"A Cup of Coffee" (Manilow) 417
"Cup of Sugar" 837
"Cupid's Arrow" 1194
"Cups & Balls" 1234
"Cups and Balls Suite" 1234
"Curiosity" 1422
"Curiouser and Curiouser" (Larimer and Keyes) 230
"Curiouser and Curiouser" (Richmond) 1226
"Curley McDimple" 336
"Curley's Wife" 1164
"Current Events" 1384
"The Curse" 257
"The Curse of an Aching Heart" 417
"Curses" 1708
"Curtain Speech" 198
"The Customer Is Always Right" (Baron) 1618
"The Customer Is Always Right" (Harwell) 1755
"The Customer's Always Right" 1390
"The Customer's Nightmare (Eggs)" 545
"Cut Movie Songs" 1318
"Cut the Ribbons" 338
"Cuttin' Out" 934
"Cuttin' Out and Crossin' Over" 240
"Cutting a Girl in 3 Pieces" 287
"Cutting Hair (A Recitative)" 41
"Cutting in the Cane" 960

"Cyril Suitcase" 261
"Czardas" 1311
"Czardus" 1176

"D. and D. Rag" 1661
"D Minor Concerto, First Movement" 1694
"Daarlin' Man" 848
"Dad" 1283
"Dad Got Girls (Instead of Boys)" 1108
"Dada 1982" 547
"Daddy!" (Mayer) 362
"Daddy!" (Smit) 1338
"Daddy!" (Troup) 1245, 1571
"Daddy and Me" 41
"Daddy Blues" 16
"Daddy Doesn't Care" 1298
"Daddy Oh!" 304
"Daddy Will Not Come Walking Through the Door" 726
"Daddy Wouldn't Buy Me a Bow-Wow" 1639
"Daddy's Footsteps" 1691
"Daddy's Girl" (Bolin) 742
"Daddy's Girl" (Frankel) 641
"Daddy's Girl" (Lindsey) 703
"Daddy's Home" 1434
"Daddy's Playboy Magazines" 1084
"Dad's a Millionaire" 695
"Daedalus" 1395
"Daffodils and Mud I" 952
"Daffodils and Mud II" 952
"Dagger Dance" 134
"Daily Buzz" 120
"Daisies" 701
"Daisy" (Hoffman) 1760
"Daisy" (Wood) 1318, 1602
"Daisy Mae Blues" 959
"Dali Wam" 1623
"Dallas" (Finkel) 492
"Dallas" (Logan) 1394
"Dallas ... I'm Coming!" 365
"Damage" 1225
"Dames at Sea" 341
"Dami a Pani!" 609
"Damn!" 362
"Damned If You Do" 696
"Dan, You Idiot!" 673
"The Dance" (*Band-Wagon*) 96
"The Dance" (Kirshenbaum) 1554
"The Dance" (Swados) 1133
"The Dance" (*When Hell Freezes Over...*) 1762
"Dance (Beginning)" 20
"Dance (Conclusion)" 20
"Dance a Little Closer" 210
"Dance Around the World with Me" 1171
"Dance at the Ball Tonight" 290
"Dance at the Ritz" 396
"Dance at the Salon" 90, 1031
"Dance Band on the Titanic" 916
"Dance by Numbers" 1523
"Dance Contest" 1720
"Dance, Dance, Dance" (Barnes) 150
"Dance, Dance, Dance" (Brandon) 1550
"Dance Finale" 950
"The Dance Floor" 385
"Dance Guignole" 637
"Dance in the Studio" 285
"Dance, Little Lady" 1170
"Dance Me 'Cross the Stream" 995
"Dance, My Little One" 963
"Dance Night" 1048
"Dance of Distraction" 93
"Dance of Exhaustion" 1222
"Dance of Murder" 175
"Dance of Spiritual Arousal" 1522
"Dance of the Fans" 1410
"Dance of the Golden Apple" 682
"Dance of the Orient" 1615
"Dance of the Unemployed" 278
"Dance on a Country Grave" 345
"Dance 1" 427
"Dance Only with Me" 1224
"Dance L'Oriental" 1616
"Dance to the Music" 1556
"Dance 2" 427
"Dance with Me" (*Donkey Show*) 399
"Dance with Me" (Peters) 1348
"Dance with Me, Darling" 106
"Dance with Me, John" 1063
"Dance — Then and Now" 1616
"Dance: Ten, Looks: Three" 283
"Dancer" 1194
"The Dancer and the Dance" 1149
"Dancin' Free and Easy" 60
"Dancin' Shoes" (Eisenberg) 36
"Dancin' Shoes" (Lemberg) 809
"Dancin' to a Jungle Drum" 1704
"Dancin' with the One I Love" 410
"Dancing Alone" (Berton) 1688
"Dancing Alone" (Bolin) 742
"Dancing at the Grand Banquet" 889
"The Dancing Bandannas" 1066
"Dancing Dan" 1550
"Dancing Days and Stinkbombs" 436
"The Dancing Debutantes" 1315
"Dancing Dream" 1315
"Dancing in the Dark" 348, 1606
"Dancing in the Rain" 336
"Dancing in the Temple" 402
"The Dancing Master" 570
"Dancing Partners" 624
"The Dancing Rogue" 962
"Dancing Through Lifetimes" 464
"Dancing to the Rhythm of the Rain Drops" 1385
"Dancing to the Tick of Terror" 170
"Dancing with My Shadow" 1482, 1750
"Dancing with the Fools" 1328
"Dandelion" 1323
"Dandy Night Clerk, or How to Get On in the Hotel Trade" 483
"Danger Blues" 777
"Danger Men Working" 1538
"The Danger of Peace Is Over" 1701
"Dangerous Game" 1265
"The Dangling Conversation" 265
"Danilo's Rap" 643
"Danke Schon" 1304
"Danny Boy" 775
"Danny Boy (Cuchulain's Lament)" 1540
"Danny DeLuca" 664
"Danny's Plea" 284
"Dansa de la Arana" 948
"Danse Classique" 635
"Danza and Danzon" 1398
"Danza Espanola" 488
"D'Arcy's Aria" 805
"Dark Angel" 1670
"Dark as a Dungeon" 740
"Dark Horse" 1153
"Dark Horses" 350
"The Dark I Know Well" 1515
"The Dark Lady of the Senates" 1142
"Dark New England Night" 76
"Dark Night of My Soul" 926
"The Dark Side of My Love" 345
"Dark Tower" 207
"The Darkies Song" 589
"The Darkness" (Markoe) 271
"The Darkness" (Pen) 1503
"Darkness Song" 701
"Darktown Poker Club" 1543
"Darktown Strutters Ball" 681
"Darkwoods Lullaby" 1562
"Darling" 1585
"Darling, Let Me Teach You How to Kiss" 246
"Darn That Dream" 399, 1107
"Darwin's Calypso" 352
"Dasvadanya" 1162
"Dat Truck Da Is Trash" 922
"The Date" 1033
"Dateline: Milwaukee" 1832
"Daughter" 634
"A Daughter for Valentine's Day" 271
"Daughter of God" 727
"Daughter of Prospero" 727
"Daughters, Daughters" 111
"Daughter's Lullaby" 718
"David Garth" 664
"Davidson Approves the Deportation" 1329
"Davidson Fails in the Final Quartet" 1329
"Davidson Returns to Sadie's Room" 1329
"Davidson Speaks of Reforming Sadie" 1329
"Davidson's Aria Condemning Sin" 1329
"Davidson's Attempt to Break Up Sadie's Party" 1329
"Davidson's Body Is Discovered" 1329
"Davidson's Explanation and Aria" 1329
"Davidson's Reassurance" 1329
"Davy the Fat Boy" 1036, 1049, 1334
"Dawn in the Heart of Africa" 21
"Dawn's Unemployment History" 396
"Day After Day" (Britton) 575
"Day After Day" (Kupferman) 831
"Day After Day" (Schwartz) 1606
"Day and Night" 1419
"A Day Around Town Dance" 973
"The Day at the Sexmockena Mambo" 1468
"Day by Day" (Schwartz) 595
"Day by Day" (Stordahl and Weston) 1210
"Day Chorus" 363
"Day Dreams" 33
"The Day Goes By" 760
"The Day I Met My Friend" 741
"A Day in Jerusalem" 1441
"A Day in the Life" 1426
"A Day in the Life of a Fat Kid from Philly" 727
"A Day in the Life of a Tiger" 304
"A Day in the Park" 352
"Day In — Day Out" 1210
"Day of Judgement I" 572
"Day of Judgement II" 572
"The Day Off" 1557
"Day Oh Day" 1620
"The Day the Peace Action Broke Out" 558
"The Day We Greet the New Queen" 889
"Daybreak" (Copeland) 1601
"Daybreak" (Guettel) 503
"Daybreak" (Pen) 285
"Daydreams" (Baker) 1481
"Daydreams" (Evans) 280
"Dayenu Chant" 647
"Daylight Will Come in Such Short Time" 1601
"Days" 933
"Days Like This" 473
"The Days of My Youth" 1379
"Days of the Dancing" 1527
"The Days of the Dancing (Are Gone)" 758
"Days of the Dancing Are Gone" 564
"(Daytime) Sunday Television" 558
"Dayton, Ohio 1903" 1036, 1334
"De Bluebells" 1505
"La-De-Da-Da" 884
"De Medici Cha Cha" 910
"Dead" 865, 866, 1593
"Dead Bride-To-Be" 1263
"Dead End" 649
"Dead End Street" 1138
"Dead Men Tell No Tales" 884
"Dead Old Man" 1347
"Dead Pan" 145
"Dead Words" 1416
"Deadalus" 1396
"A Deal" 528
"The Deal" (Andersson and Ulvaeus) 275
"The Deal" (Bingham) 1072
"Deal, Choose, Throw, Lose" 1815
"Dealer" 1459
"Dean's Old-Fashioned All-American Down-Home Bar-B-Que Texas Eats" 499
"Dear Abbey" 50
"Dear Brother" 726
"Dear Children" 1503
"Dear Dad" (Barnes) 469
"Dear Dad" (Lippman) 223
"Dear Dad" (Sottile) 767
"Dear, Dear" 101
"Dear Death" 1485
"Dear Denominator" 1698
"Dear Diary" (Forrest) 1219
"Dear Diary" (Gordon) 705
"Dear Diary" (Oster) 385
"Dear Friend" 1380
"Dear God" 830
"Dear Heart" 1514
"Dear Icarus" 364
"Dear Jane" 1107
"Dear John — Help!" 550
"Dear Kitty: I Am a Woman" 1829
"Dear Kitty: I Am Longing" 1829
"Dear Kitty: I Am Thirteen Years Old" 1829
"Dear Kitty: I Have a Nicer Side" 1829
"Dear Kitty: I Still Believe" 1829
"Dear Kitty: In the Night" 1829
"Dear Kitty: It's a Dangerous Adventure" 1829
"Dear Kitty: It's a New Year" 1829
"Dear Kitty: My Sweet Secret" 1829
"Dear Lady" 1111
"Dear Lord Chesterfield" 316
"Dear Madame" 609
"Dear Max" 1251
"Dear Mr. Gershwin" 1326
"Dear Mr. Greene" 1683
"Dear Mr. Haring" 1325
"Dear Mr. Lincoln" 71
"Dear Mr. Merrick" 1548
"Dear Old Dad" 1481
"Dear Old Friend" 1060
"Dear Old Ireland" 775
"Dear Old Plants" 1237
"Dear Old Southland" 1543
"Dear Old Syracuse" 201
"Dear Ophelia" 588
"Dear Reader" 430
"Dear Sir" 979
"Dear Tom" 656
"Dearer to Me" 1780
"Dearest Mama (Letter Song)" 92
"Dearest Man" 393, 394
"Dearest Mother and Father (Letter Aria)" 439
"Dearest of All Boys" 1714
"Death and Reality" 716
"Death Beware" 572
"Death Come to My House" 591
"Death Comes Like a Thief" 1392
"Death Could Not Be Colder" 1020
"Death Dance" 869
"Death Duet" 1134
"Death Message" 1626
"Death of Cleopatra" 62
"The Death of Moses" 647
"Death of the Firstborn" 647
"Death, The Hanged Man and Eternity Take Their Places" 1592
"Debbie Benton" 365
"Debts" 69
"The Debutante's Ball" 1036, 1334
"Deca Dance" 969
"Deceive Me" 366
"December Nights" 151
"A Decent Job" 814
"Decide" 470
"Declaration" 1659
"Decorate the Human Face" 1451
"Dedicated to the One I Love" 411, 1551, 1575
"Dedication" 510
"Deductions" 780
"Deep in Alaska" 128
"Deep in Me" 661
"Deep in My Heart" 91
"Deep in My Mind" 1147
"Deep in the Bosom of the Family" 822
"Deep in the Dark" 1330
"Deep Purple" 1521
"Deeper" 1028
"Deeper in the Woods" 1367
"The Deepest Shelter in Town" 1482, 1750
"The Defection" 1273
"DeFiance Against Force" 21
"DeGaulle" 1394

"DeGaulle and the Test Ban Treaty" 1765
"Déjà Vu" 1714
"Delicate Secrets of Love" 1470
"Delicatessen" 1678
"Delicious Indignities" 1168
"Delighted, I'm Sure" 1403
"Delighted You Invited Me" 290
"Deliver My Soul" 208
"Delivery Boy" 19
"Della's Desire" 575
"Delle Rose's Turn" 700
"La Demande en Mariage d'Avenant" 123
"Demigod" 1
"Democracy Is Lunacy" 1331
"Democracy's Call" 826, 827
"The Demonstrators" 772
"Denial" 1128
"Denn Wie Man Sich Bettet" 879
"Dentist!" 939
"The Departure" 398
"The Departure for Rhododendron" 600
"The Depression Is Over" 41
"Deprogramming Song" 975
"Depths" 367
"The Deranged Cousins" 49, 612
"Le Dernier Pierrot" 924
"Dermott Donn MacMorna" 253
"Descending" 250
"Desert ... As Near as My Finger's End" 1020
"Desert Chorus" 363
"Desert Dessert" 855
"Desert Incident" 1058
"Desire" 185
"Desire Under the Elmsford Country Club Oaks" 1045
"Despair" 823
"Desperate" 332
"The Desperate Ones (Les Desesperes)" 792
"Desperation" 467
"Desperation Quintet" 409
"Dessau Dance Hall" 1451
"Dessert" 1379
"Destination Moon" 382
"Destiny" (Grusecki) 639
"Destiny" (Friedman) 1558
"Destroy Me" 858
"Destruction" 175
"Detective Story" 388
"Determination" 1034
"A Determined Woman" 1608
"Deuteronomy XVII Verse 2" 1395, 1396
"Developing" 1325
"The Devil in Your Eyes" 1035
"The Devil Is a Man You Know" 1811
"Devil Man" 1476
"Devil, Take Yourself Away" 1308
"The Devil to Pay" 1301
"Devil's Disguise" 1518
"The Devil's Song" 456
"Devoted to the Cause" 814
"Dewey and Sal" 159
"Di-a-wham" 1427
"Le Diable de la Bastille" 1257
"The Diagnostician" 1236
"Dialogue on Dalliance" 48
"Diamante" 1073
"Diamond Jubilee" 507
"Diamonds Are a Girl's Best Friend" 1546
"Diamonds Are Forever" (Barry) 1450
"Diamonds Are Forever" (Kander) 377
"Diamonds in the Mine" 1471
"Diana" (Engeran) 726
"Diana" (MacDermot) 1151
"Diary of a Church Mouse" 135
"Diaspora" 402
"Dibarti" 1133
"La Dicha Mia" 262
"Dick and Jane" 1168
"The Dictator Who Ran Away" 36
"Did I Ever Really Live?" 685
"Did I Make a Good Impression?" 466
"Did Not" 851, 972
"Did Ya Ever Have One of Those Days" 570
"Did You Ever Hear the Blues?" 1464, 1465
"Did You Notice?" 1263
"Di Demerung (The Twilight)" 1502
"Di Dinst (The Maid)" 1619
"Didn't He Ramble" 813, 996
"Didn't It Rain" 592, 996, 1363, 1466, 1672
"Didn't Know What I Wanted" 384
"Didn't Know What You Looked Like" 384
"Die Vampire, Die" 1645
"The Diehards" 858
"Diet" 942
"Le Dieu Bleu" 95
"Diff'rent" 1208
"The Difference Is Me" 710
"The Different Albertines" 1103
"A Different Drummer" 152
"A Difficult Transition" 1155, 1157, 1158
"Di Fon Fun Frayhayt (The Flag of Freedom)" 604
"Dig, Dig, Dig" 1311
"Dig That Mummy" 1385
"Dig We Must" 350
"Diga, Diga, Do" 165, 886, 1435
"Digging Stone" 1513
"Di Greene Kuzeene (My Little Cousin)" 492
"Di Grini Kuzine" 1715
"The Dildo Rag" 365
"Dim All the Lights" 1494
"Di Mame (The Mother)" 1619
"Dime" 1336
"Dime a Dozen" (Grossman) 1486
"Dime a Dozen" (Roy) 381
"Dimension 6 Rock" 1237
"The Dimple" 963
"The Dimple on My Knee" 1167
"Dimples" 1140
"Dinah" 681
"Dinah Washington" 382
"Le Diner" 123
"Ding-A-Ling, Ding-A-Ling" 349
"Ding Ding" 19
"Ding Dong Cocktail Party" 556, 557
"Ding Dong! The Witch Is Dead!" 662
"'Dink' Smith's Teen Age Band Party" 22
"Dink's Lament" 25
"Dinner" 67
"Dinner at the Murklines'" 1258
"Dinner Is Served" 952
"Dinner Minuet" 1008
"A Dinner Party" 1499
"Dino Repetti" 693
"Dino's in Love" 693
"Dior, Dior" 735
"Diplomacy" 682
"Directions" 1547
"The Director" (*Fourth Avenue North*) 535
"The Director" (*The Plot Against The Chase Manhattan Bank*) 1274
"Director Bob" 222
"Dirge for Two Veterans" 903
"Dirge of the Lone Woman" 253
"Dirty" 372
"Dirty Dish Rag" 718
"Dirty Is the Funniest Thing I Know" 1666
"Dirty Mind" 326
"Dirty No-Gooder (Gooder's) Blues" 182
"Dirty No-Gooder Blues" 181
"The Dirty Word Waltz" 877
"Dirty Words" 913
"Disappearing Act" 385
"Disappearing Water Ballet" 66
"Discarded Blues" 93
"Discipline" 750
"Disco" 1064
"Disco Circus" 399
"Disco Nights" 19
"Disco Rag" 319
"Disco Toyland" 81
"Discontented Blues" 1518
"Discotheque" 557, 558
"Discover the Man You Are" 404
"Discovered" 1762
"The Discovery" 767
"Discussion" 1460
"Dishes" 226
"Disney for Adults" 783
"Disneyland" 727
"Di Sokhe" 1715
"Dispensible" 844
"Disposable Woman" 614
"Disraeli" 1611
"The Disrespectful Summons" 612
"Dissatisfied Women" 952
"Dissection Section" 910
"A Dissertation on Transportation, or It All Started with the Wheel" 150
"Dissipation" 403
"The Distaff Side" 1749
"Distance" 750
"The Distant Shore" 460
"Diva" 157
"Diva Supreme" 1301
"Diversion" 1751
"Divertissement" 637
"Divorce" (Hardwick) 580
"Divorce" (Kaplan) 1485
"Divorce Has Brought Us Together" 1339
"Divorce Lament" 718
"Divorce, Of Course" 1331
"Dixie" 1543
"D*I*X*I*E" 507
"Dixie After Dark" 1521
"Dixie Breakdown" 1720
"Dixie Prelude" 716
"Djibuti!" 1058
"Do (Did) You Ever Cross Over to Sneden's?" 23
"Do a Little Exercise" 1604
"Do a Revue" 149, 150
"Do, Do, Do" 1172
"Do-Do-Re-Do" 1185
"Do-Gooders' Lament" 1700
"Do Horses Talk to Horses?" 878
"Do I Do It Through God?" 453
"Do I Improve My Lord" 927
"Do I Love Him?" 961, 1756
"Do I Need a Man?" 240
"Do I Shave?" 511
"Do I Still Have You" 391
"Do I Wonder" 120
"Do It" 101
"Do It Again!" 261
"Do It at Home" 770
"Do It for Willy" 308
"Do It Yourself" (Cohen) 1547
"Do It Yourself" (Harris) 1476
"Do It Yourself Playwriting" 22
"Do Me a Favor" 466
"Do My Eyes Deceive Me" 494
"Do Not Bruise the Fruit" 701
"Do Not Hurt the Queen" 889
"Do Right Woman" 115
"Do Something" 491
"Do Something Every Day for Jesus" 1412
"Do the Least You Can" 969
"Do the Necronomicon" 462
"Do the Opposite" 1684
"Do This, Do That" 1302
"Do Us a Favor" 682
"Do Wah Diddy Diddy" 1551
"Do What You Do" 948
"Do What You Must" 682
"Do What You Want to Do" 238
"Do Whatcha Gotta Do" 656
"Do You Care Too Much" 1397
"Do You Clean Birthday Suits?" 44
"Do You Ever Dream of Vienna?" 935
"Do You Ever Go to Boston?" 1752
"Do You Know?" 1434
"Do You Know the Land Where the Lemon Trees Bloom" 941
"Do You Know the Way to San Jose" 83
"Do You Know What It Means to Miss New Orleans?" 171
"Do You Know What It's Like?" 1830
"Do You Know What the Children Were Doing Today?" 402, 1327
"Do You Lie?" 1423
"Do You Mean to Stay Here?" 114
"Do You Not Remember Jeanie" 586
"Do You Recall the House of Leather?" 716
"Do You Remember?" 1582, 1677
"Do You Retreat?" 779
"Do You Suppose" 903
"Do You Think I'm Pretty?" 76
"Do You Think It's Alright?" 1655
"Do You Wanna Be Saved" 417
"Do You Want to Know a Secret" 1551
"Do Your Own Thing" 1827
"Do Your Thing, Miss Truth" 1064
"Doatsey Mae" 133
"The Doctor" 65
"Doctor" 71
"Doctor and Ella" 324
"The Doctor and His Creation" 1293
"Dr. Charlotte and Cordelia's House" 473
"Dr. Iatro" 1652
"Dr. Love" (Lindsey) 703
"Dr. Love" (Romanovsky and Phillips) 808
"Dr. Lucy (The Doctor Is In)" 1828
"Dr. Phil" 1128
"Dr. Rosalyn Green" 60
"Dr. Sex" 395
"Doctor's Canon" 643
"Doctors in The Chase Scene" 394
"Doctor's Office" 1091
"Doctor's Orals" 1206
"The Doctor's Out Today" 1309
"A Doctor's Prayer" 1309
"The Doctor's Wife" 395
"The Dodger Game" 377
"Does America Need a Third Party?" 1743
"Does Anybody Love You?" 200
"Does Broadway Need Some More Rats?" 1337
"Does He Think of Her" 1338
"Does Your Heart Beat for Me" 1521
"Doesn't Anybody Love Anymore" 913
"Doesn't It Bug You" 393, 394
"D-O-G" 332
"A Dog" 571
"A Dog Is a Man's Best Friend" 1252
"A Dog Outside a Store" 812
"The Dog, the Cat, the Squirrel" 1192
"The Dogface Jive" 1163
"Doggie in the Window" 1575
"Doggin' Me Around" 790
"Dogs Versus You" 973
"Dogtown" 916
"Doin' It by the Book" 1388
"Doin' the Finale First" 858
"Doin' the Neighborhood Rag" 1442
"Doin' the New Low Down (Low-Down)" 165, 886
"Doin' the Waltz" 494
"Doin' the Windsor Walk" 1721
"Doing My Job" 653
"Doing the High" 1504
"Doing the Psycho-Neurotique" 1576
"Doing the Reactionary" 1268
"Doing the Revolutionary" 1267
"Doing the Work" 1427
"Dolcey Jones" 112
"The Doll Song" 126, 556, 557
"The 'Dolly' Sisters" 852
"Dolores" 1016
"La Domaine de la Bete" 123
"Dombaye" 1388
"Domestication of Animals" 1234
"Domesticity" 1209
"Dominus Vobiscum" 1029
"Don Jose of Far Rockaway" 981
"Done Found My Lost Sheep" 1308
"Doney Gal" 740
"The Donkey and the Grasshopper" 11
"Donna Cinzia's Love" 1771
"La Donna e Mobile" 1623
"The Donor Dating Game" 769
"The Dons' Chorus" 1393

"Don't" (Hartig) 1754
"Don't" (Springer) 714
"Don't Advertise Your Man" 553
"Don't Ask" (Feinstein) 1052
"Don't Ask" (Silvestri) 1595
"Don't Ask, Don't Tell" 1830
"Don't Ask Her Another" 622
"Don't Ask Me" 33
"Don't Ask the Lady What the Lady Did Before" 861
"Don't Be a Litterbug" 1732
"Don't Be a Miracle" 969
"Don't Be Absurd" 381
"Don't Be Afraid" 660, 689
"Don't Be Anything Less Than Everything You Can Be" 1486
"Don't Be That Way" 1521
"Don't Be the Bunny" 1712
"Don't Betray His Love" 971
"Don't Blame Me" (Blum, Barker, and Martucci) 302
"Don't Blame Me" (McHugh) 886
"Don't Bother Me, I Can't Cope" 400
"Don't Bring Her Flowers"1181
"Don't Buy the Lie" 278
"Don't Call Me Trailer Trash" 323
"Don't Call Us" 175
"Don't Change the Way You Love Me" 1343
"Don't Come Easy" 1598
"Don't Cross Your Bridge" 820
"Don't Cry, Bo Peep" 81
"Don't Cry for Me" 919
"Don't Cry for Me, Argentina" 1540
"Don't Cry for Me, Barbra Streisand" 511
"Don't Dare Suggest It, Laurie" 941
"Don't Deny" 23
"Don't Depend on Watches, My Friend" 1190
"Don't Dilly Dally on the Way" 1482
"Don't Do It, Mr. Hermes" 1231
"Don't Do Sadness" 1515
"Don't Drop the Bomb" 1113
"Don't Dump on Eve" 468
"Don't Eat It" 1311
"Don't Ever Book a Trip on the IRT" 1585
"Don't Ever Leave Me" 883
"Don't Fall for the Lights" 1710
"Don't Fall Till (Until) You've Seen Them All" 1028
"Don't Feed the Animals" 1263
"Don't Feed the Plants" 939
"Don't Fence Me In" 1571
"Don't Forget" 1420
"Don't Forget 127th Street" 237, 603
"Don't Forget Your Mama" 1505
"Don't Get Around Much Anymore" 1750
"Don't Get Me Started" 1514
"Don't Give In" 1121
"Don't Give Up" 1450
"Don't Give Up the Hunt, Dr. Puffin" 870
"Don't Give Up Your Key" 665
"Don't Go Back to Baltimore" 1050
"Don't Go in the Lion's Cage Tonight" 457
"Don't Go to Bed Right Yet, Sam" 1563
"Don't Go to Strangers" 850
"Don't Grow Old" 729
"Don't Grow Old Gracefully" 61
"Don't Have to Take It Anymore" 1732
"Don't I Know You?" 461
"Don't It Feel Good" 1363
"Don't It Go to Show Ya Never Know" 939
"Don't Kiki Me" 1253
"Don't Know Much" 854
"Don't Know What I Expected" 644
"Don't Know What I'm Here For" 384
"Don't Know Why I Came Here" 384
"Don't Laugh" 992, 1106
"Don't Laugh at Me" 60
"Don't Leave Me" 1827
"Don't Leave Me This Way" 399
"Don't Let It Bother You" 1035
"Don't Let It Get You Down" 1651
"Don't Let Me Be Misunderstood" 1353
"Don't Let Me Go" 328
"Don't Let Them Take Checkers Away" 378
"Don't Let Them Take the Paramount" 160
"Don't Like Goodbyes" 715, 807
"Don't Live in Yesterday" 706
"Don't Look at Me That Way" 367
"Don't Look Down" 323
"Don't Lose That Spark" 1684
"Don't Love Me Like Othello" 505
"Don't Make Me Over" 83, 1551
"Don't Mess Around with Your Mother-in-Law" 463
"Don't Much Matter Any More" 105
"Don't Need Religion" 1727
"Don't Open the Door" 675
"Don't P-P-Point Them Guns at Me" 1824
"Don't Put Me Down for the Common Kind" 1733
"Don't Put Your Daughter on the Stage, Mrs. Worthington" 751
"Don't Quit While You're Ahead" 1109
"Don't Quote Me" 299
"Don't Rain on My Parade" 1546
"Don't Say Nothing Bad About My Body" 1046
"Don't Say Shoo-Be-Dobop" 319
"Don't Say Yes If You Want to Say No" 731
"Don't Say You Like Tchaikowsky" 1447
"Don't Sell It Cheap" 1203
"Don't Send That Boy" 1487
"Don't Set Me Free" 1623
"Don't Sit Under the Apple Tree" 1571, 1750, 1764
"Don't Sleep in the Subway" 115, 1450
"Don't Speak of Love to Me" 1131
"Don't Spill the Beans" 1365
"Don't Suck the Bones" 1203
"Don't Swat Your Mother, Boys" 417
"Don't Take Away All My Friends" 396
"Don't Take Off Your Mask in Bricksville" 922
"Don't Take Sides" 661
"Don't Take Your Love" 470
"Don't Tear Up the Horse Slips" 867
"Don't Tell Mary" 419
"Don't Tell Me" (MacDermot) 726
"Don't Tell Me" (Strouse) 214
"Don't Tell Me Everything" 219
"Don't Tell Me Too Many Lies" 708
"Don't the Moon Look Lonesome" 1720
"Don't Think About It" 791
"Don't Throw Me Out of the House, Father" 1092
"Don't Throw Your Love Away" 404
"Don't Touch Me" 1061
"Don't Turn Away from Love" 1390
"Don't Twist Her Mind" 969
"Don't Twist My Mind" 969
"Don't Wait Up" 1595
"Don't Wake Up My Heart" 1764
"Don't Wanna Be No Superstar" 1622
"Don't Wanna Be No Superstar I" 1622
"Don't Wanna Be No Superstar II" 1622
"Don't Wanna Be No Superstar III" 1622
"Don't Wish" 992, 1106
"Don't Worry 'Bout Me" 1251
"Don't You Believe" 431
"Don't You Come Inside My Head" 1345
"Don't You Ever Give It All Away" 975
"Don't You Leave Me Here" 813
"Don't You Love Everything About Show Biz" 766
"Don't You Love to Watch What People Do" 1135
"Don't You Understand" 1771
"Don't You Wish We Could Be in Love?" 1830
"Donuts for Defense" 232
"A Doodlin' Song" 616
"Doom Is Due at Dawn" 1219
"Doomed, Doomed, Doomed" 600
"Doop-De-Doop" 1447
"The Door Is Closed" 338
"The Door to Isle Goree" 207
"Doorman" 535
"Doors" 300
"Dope" 1030
"Dope Double Time" 1030
"Dope Rag" 1030
"Dorian Gray" 404
"Doris" 126, 557, 558
"Doris' Nightmare" 185
"Dormez-Vous" 1250
"Dorothy's 'Opener'" 1138
"Dorset" 135
"Dos Jueyes" 262
"Dos Yiddishe Shtetele" 1032
"Dost Thou" 1608
"Double" 1057
"Double Dummy Drill" 912
"Double Exposure" 1209
"Double Feature" 406
"Double-O Or Nothing" 87
"The Doubloom" 1071
"The Doubloon" 1071
"The Doubtful Guest" 49, 612
"Doughnuts for Defense" 1163
"The Douglass Decree" 814
"Dove Deceptions" 287
"Dove Song" 1789
"Down a Down, Down Derry" 1446
"Down Among the Grass Roots" 722
"Down at the Ol' Five-and-Dime" 1347
"Down by the Edge of the Sea" 864
"Down by the Riverside" 481
"Down by the Sea Shore" 507
"Down Down Down" 27
"Down in Honky Tonk Town" 1198
"Down in the Depths (on the 90th [Ninetieth] Floor)" 367, 692, 1704
"Down in the Sand" 943
"Down My Street" 1467
"Down on Me" (Copani) 493, 1537
"Down on Me" (Joplin) 965
"Down the Drain" 685
"Down the Field" 1282
"Down the Fire Valley" 820
"Down the Hall" 1310
"Down the Hatch" 288
"Down the Mountain" 1726
"Down There" 692
"Down to the Foodstore" 229
"Down to the Sea" 1254
"Down Under" 948
"Down Went McGinty" 1092
"Down with Love" 662
"Down with Whiskey" 1021
"Down Yonder" 1543
"Downriver" 408
"Downtown" 115, 1450
"Downtown Bohemian Slum" 1613
"D'Oyly Carte Blanche" 700
"Dozen Husbands" 693
"Draft Dodger Rag" 37
"Drag Tango" 1500
"Dragon Lady" 1747
"Drama" 444
"Drama Quartet" 1611
"A Dramatized Message" 472
"Drat!" 409
"Draw and Move" 1325
"Draw Me a Circle" 1604
"Draw Me a Door" 1325
"The Drawing Room" 22
"The Dreadful Story About Harriet and the Matches" 1444
"A dream" 250
"Dream" (Mercer) 35, 382
"Dream" (Barkan) 224
"The Dream" (Brandon) 152
"The Dream" (Guettel) 503
"The Dream" (Moskowitz) 819
"The Dream" (Sottile) 767
"The Dream" (Strouse) 1473
"Dream a Little Dream of Me" 411
"Dream Along with Me" 527
"Dream Babies" 1038
"Dream Ballet" 379
"Dream Come True" 755
"Dream House" 60
"Dream Like a Child" 161
"The Dream Lovers" 635
"Dream of Egypt" 308
"Dream of Hollywood" 1584
"Dream Smoke" 333
"The Dream Song of J. Alfred Kerouac" 1356
"Dream Toyland" 81
"Dream True" 413
"Dream with Me" 234
"Dreamboat from Dreamland" 232, 1163
"Dreamers" 276
"Dreaming" 1438
"Dreaming of Love" 393
"Dreaming of Reinhardt" 431
"Dreaming True" 505
"Dreams" (Carnives) 111
"Dreams" (Dorsey) 1500
"Dreams" (Hoffert) 572
"Dreams" (Satlin) 279
"Dreams" (Shaiman) 370
"Dreams" (*The Uncommon Denominator*) 1698
"Dreams Come True" 148
"Dreams Go By" 916
"Dreams of a Rarebit Fiend" 301
"Dreams of Heaven" 1622
"Dress Rehearsal Rag" 1471
"Dressed to Kill" 1138
"Dressed to the Nines" 415
"Dressing Room" 299
"The Dressing Room Shuffle" 742
"The Dressing Screen" 114
"Drift Away" 641
"Drill Team" 1153
"Drill Ye Tarriers, Drill" 740
"An Drinaun Donn" 253
"Drink Me" 27
"Drink with Me" 570
"Drinkin' Shoes" 1317
"Drinking Fool" 710
"Drinking Games" 742
"Drinking Song" 507
"A Drinking Song" 1203
"Drip, Drop, Tapoketa" 1420
"Drippin' and Droppin'" 1046
"The Drive-In" 1155, 1157
"Drive Me, Driver" 257
"Drizzling in New York" 941
"Le Droit d'Aimer" 1257
"Drug Free" 493
"The Drugstore" 1554
"Drugstore Scene" 324
"Drum Finale" 21
"Drume Negrita" 262
"Drummin'" 207
"Drums Communicate a Warm Welcome" 651
"Drums in My Heart" 955
"The Drunk Sketch" 1802
"Drunk!" 57
"The Drunkard" 938
"A Drunken Man's Praise of Sobriety" 707
"Drunkenness" 1051
"Dry Mouth with No Water" 1183
"The Dryer" 252
"Dual Pianists" 261
"Dubya We Love Ya" 1128
"The Duchess Song" 1146
"Duck Dispatch" 287
"Dudin' Up" 1164
"Duel" 34
"Dueling Keyboards" 1176
"Dueling Neurotics" 1149
"Duet" (Beeson) 947
"Duet" (Cohen) 1547
"Duet" (DeBenedictis) 1669
"Duet" (Katz) 963
"Duet" (Michael) 19
"Duet" (Secunda) 666
"Duet" (Sticco) 267
"Duet" (Strauss) 1131
"Duet" (Weill) 879, 1807
"Duet in the Hospital" 1462
"Duet for Mating Organisms" 552

"Duet of the Salesgirls" 1462
"Duet of the Woodcutters" 1462
"Dulce Domum" 1784
"Dummy Juggler" 614
"Dumplings" 259
"Duncan and Brady" 376
"Dungeons and Dragons" 162, 163, 164
"Duo Thoughts" 1147
"Dusky Shadows" 393, 394
"Dustbane: The Ballad of Minka" 1310
"Dusters, Goggles and Hats" 1594
"Dustin Now" 1815
"Dusty Roads" 1136
"Dutch Country Table" 76
"The Dutchman's Pants" 322
"Dutch's Song" 221
"Dvoyreh" 1382
"Dvoyreh Fun Rumeynie (Serba)" 1382
"Dwarfs' Song" 336
"Dying a Little a Lot Alone" 949
"A Dying Business" 667
"Dying Child" 860
"The Dying Cowboy" 578
"The Dying Schwann" 50
"The Dying Swan" 96

"E-Mail Love Notes" 755
"E MC2" 472
"The 'E' Medley" 1263
"Each Night Is a New Day" 407
"Each of Us" 865, 866, 1593
"Each Sin Brings" 1063
"Early Amphibians" 285
"Early Bird Eddie" 409
"Early Morning Rain" 718
"Early One Morning Blues" 120
"Early Sunday" 667
"Earth Dance" 1072
"Earth Fall" 1081
"The Earth Is the Lord's" 1671
"Earthly Paradise" 308
"Earthworms" 1072
"Easier Said Than Done" 1551
"Easier to Sing Than Say" 703
"The East Egdon Band" 345
"East Indian Love Call" 1263
"East Indian Needle Mystery" 1234
"East Is East" 942
"East of the Sun (and West of the Moon)" 1210
"East Side Moon" 1442
"The East Side Story" 277
"East Side, West Side" 87
"The Easter Bunny Polka" 507
"Easy" (Bernstein) 1029
"Easy" (Jordan) 1379
"Easy" (Menken) 1228
"Easy Breezy" 1117
"Easy Does It" 226
"Easy for Me" 653
"Easy for Them to Say" 1432
"Easy for You" (Bingham) 71
"Easy for You" (Strouse) 1328
"Easy Harvey — Don't Push" 673
"The Easy Life" (Magee) 633
"The Easy Life" (LaChiusa) 1250
"Easy Love" 110
"Easy to Be Hard" 649
"Easy to Love" 367
"Easy to Say" 1831
"Easy Winners" 457
"Eat" 1014
"Eat, Eat, Eat" 855
"Eat, Lord, and Enjoy" 1203
"Eat the Lunch" 1310
"Eat Your @*!#@*!@#! Cornflakes" 54
"Eating" 880, 882, 1773
"Eating Mushrooms" 27
"Eating Myself Up Alive" 1121
"Eating Raoul" 424
"Eave's Song" 1386
"E.C." 1073
"Eccch" 986
"Ecdysiasis" 1615
"Echo" 851, 972
"An Echo of Greco" 1385
"Echo Song" 661
"The Echo Waltz" 341
"Echoes" 19
"The Echoes of My Mind (Life)" 23
"Ecology" 109
"The Ecstasy and the Cure" 393
"Eddie Carbone!" 1723
"Eddie Has Something to Say, Katie" 1723
"Eddie, Listen to Me!" 1723
"Eddie Never Knew He Had a Destiny" 1723
"Eddie Was a Man" 1723
"Eddie, When Am I Gonna Be a Wife Again?" 1723
"Eddie, You're Pretty Strong" 1723
"Eddie's Always Here" 1195
"Edgar Allan Poe" 1486
"Edgar's Hoedown" 1162
"Edie" 1149
"Editorial" (Kaz) 1209
"Editorial" (Lewis) 664
"Edna Jones, The Elephant Girl" 1326
"Eduardo, If You Let Us Sleep Here" 1723
"Educated Feet" 1
"Education" 1698
"The Education of Peg" 1467
"Efsher Vet Geshen a Ness" 1745
"The Ego and the Id" 609
"Eight Bells" 1071
"Eight-Horse Parlay" 587
"8:00 Auto-Pilot" 198
"The Eighth Day" 1647
"The Eighth Floor" 1493
"Eighty Thousand Orgasms" 391
"Ein Koloheinu" 1822
"Eisenhower — Grandfather to the World" 952
"El-Al (A Nudnik)" 1647
"El Bravo" 203
"El Cuando Minuet" 379
"El Cumbachero" 262
"El Dorado" 563
"El Guaba" 262
"El Jibaro y el Politico" 897
"El Kazar" 1050
"El Mar" 1336
"El Tango de la Embasada" 712
"El Yerbero Moderno" 262
"Elbow Room" 1078
"Eldorado" 911
"Eleanor Roosevelt (A Discussion of Soup)" 41, 1375
"The Election Returns" 1091
"Election Spectacular" 1261
"Electric Blues" 649
"Elegy" 105
"Eleleu!" 74
"The Elements" 1654
"Elephant Drone" 431
"Elephant Heartbeats" 431
"Elephant Joke" 50
"Elephants" 431
"11th Hour Report" 352
"The Eleven Commandments" 663
"Elijah" 647
"Eliot ... Sylvia" 588
"Eliot's Coming" 1710
"Elip-Parcs" 1066
"Elizabeth" 1772
"Elizabeth I of Chosun" 889
"Elizabeth X. Oliphant" 1237
"Eliza's Breakdown" 67
"Ellen" 23
"Ellen's Credo" 1756
"Ellen's Lament" 961
"Ellesburg, Ohio" 1719
"Ellis Island (Ellis Island, So Awesome and Cold)" 604
"The Embassy Sidestep" 712
"Embraceable You" 46, 1095
"Emelia" 1025
"Emily, The M.B.A." 1
"Emmeline! Is It True? (Revelation)" 439
"Emmene-moi" 963
"Emmy Lou" 1318
"Emmy-Lou, Lafayette and the Football Team" 1309
"The Emperor Is a Man" 1134
"Emperor Man" 143
"The Emperor Me" 1358
"Empire City Music Hall" 1066
"The Empire Soiree" 151
"The Empire Strikes First" 1335
"Employment Office Dance" 1307
"Empty Bed" 424
"Empty or Full" 1052
"Empty Spaces" 968
"Empty World of Power" 1331
"En Rev'nant de la Revue" 1641
"Encantigo" 262
"The Encounter" 1200
"Encountering America" 602
"Encouragement" 1762
"The End" (Kessler) 472
"The End" (Lennon and McCartney) 1426
"The End of the Road" 828
"The End of the World" (Jankowski) 789
"The End of the World" (Kent) 1176, 1551
"The End of Toad" 1784
"An End to a Young Man" 1356
"Endangered Species" 1607
"Endgame" 275
"The Ending" (Gesner) 812
"The Ending" (Pen) 114
"Ending Up Alone" 949
"Endless Possibilities" 1523
"The Ends Justify the Means" 1025
"England Is Lovely" 1412
"England Swings" 1450
"England — The U.K" 364
"The English Class System" 449
"The English Country Life" 884
"The English Lesson" 317
"The English Rose" 200
"English version of Advise and Consent" 449
"The English Way to Die" 655
"Enough" 903
"The Enraged Telephone" 49
"Enrico Fermi High" 1831
"Ensemble" 159
"Ensigns' Lament" 1508
"Enter the Guardsman" 444
"Enter X. Oliphant" 1237
"Enter Xanthus" 1237
"Entering Gray Gardens" 641
"Entering Marion" 610
"Enterprise" 1384
"The Entertainer" 1110
"Entire History of the World in Two Minutes and Thirty-Two Seconds" 1448
"Entonces" 1336
"Entrance" 427
"Entrance of Chorus" 1229
"Entrance of Kings" 124
"Entrance of Martin and Top" 1601
"Entrance of the Sabaens" 1441
"Entrance Polonaise" 1008
"Entropy" 1706
"The Envelope, Please" 50, 126
"Epic (or, I'll Be Glad When You're Dead You Roskolnikov You)" 1448
"Epilogue" 963
"Epilogue in Suede" 716
"Epiphany" (Frank) 1306
"Epiphany" (Walker) 38
"Epistle of Love" 962
"Epitaph" (Clifton and Siegel) 1319
"Epitaph" (Valenti) 851
"Epitaph" (Weill) 1532
"An Epitaph" 972
"Epitaph for Marina" 1437
"The Equal of Kings" 425
"The Equation Cannot Be Solved" 1190
"Equilib" 279
"Equipment Song" 701
"The Equitable Distribution Waltz" 1309
"Equity Announcement Opening" 1427
"Erase Him" 1147
"Erie Canal" 740, 775
"Ernani! Ernani! Involami" 1639
"Ernest in Love" 448
"Es Feylt Ir Di Rozhinke" 1715
"The Escape" 486
"The Escargot Song" 1500
"Escorte-Moi" 377
"Eskimo Tableaux" 963
"Esmeralda" 185
"Espero No" 1336
"Espresso House" 638
"Ess, Ess, Mein Kindt" 1510
"Essen" 882, 1773
"The Establishment Route" 257
"The Establishment's Window on the World (I)" 449
"The Establishment's Window on the World (II)" 449
"E.T." 1149
"Etch a Sketch" 607
"Eternal Sleep" 615
"The Eternal Virgin" 1397
"Ethel" 350
"Ethiope's Ear" 864
"L'Etranger" 1256, 1257
"Etude" 229
"Etude in D Minor" 295
"Etude No. X" 963
"Eugenia" 1643
"Eulogy to Chlorophyl" 735
"Eunice" 135
"Euphoria" 957
"The European" 21
"Ev'ry Street's a Boulevard (in Old New York)" 1546
"Ev'ry Time" 1651
"Ev'ry Time We Say Goodbye" 367
"Ev'rybody Needs Somebody to Love" 1302
"Ev'rybody's Boppin'" 1138
"Ev'rybody's Gotta Eat" 1208
"Ev'rything I Love" 367
"Ev'rything I've Got" 236, 1651
"Eve" 976
"Eve Sweet Eve" 468
"Evelyn Woods" 664
"Even a Doctor Can Make a Mistake" 1652
"An Even Chance" 1040
"Even Though" 738
"Even When You Win, You Sometimes Lose" 1631
"Evenin'" 1521
"Evening" 1184
"The Evening News" 547
"Evening News (A Song of Success)" 483
"Evening Prayer" 1419
"Everlasting" 726
"Everlasting Vibe" 1237
"Every Afternoon at Four" 976
"Every Day" 1671
"Every Day a Little Death" 1492
"Every Day a New Day" 328
"Every Day for Four Years" 217
"Every Day Is Night" 157
"Every Day That Passes" 361
"Every Days" 1358
"Every Day's an Invention of Youth" 922
"Every Father" 175
"Every Fifteen Minutes, One More Will Be Shot" 363
"Every Goodbye Is Hello" 830
"Every Little Nothing" 766, 935
"Every Log in My House" 1323
"Every Man in London" 476
"Every Morning" 1071
"Every Now and Then" 1384
"Every Other Saturday Night" 408
"Every Poodle" 1404
"Every Saturday Night" 323
"Every Thursday Night" (Menken) 1339
"Every Thursday Night" (Martin-Silvestri) 1595
"Every Time I Look I See a Stranger" 834
"Every Time I Meet a Lady" 1028
"Every Time the Music Starts" 1097
"Every Time the Sun Goes Down" 362
"Every Woman Brings Something with Her" 834
"Everybody Dance" 1565
"Everybody Fits, Something About You" 38
"Everybody Gets It in the End" 572
"Everybody I Love You" 1727
"Everybody Loves a Single Girl" 357
"Everybody Loves a Tree" 985
"Everybody Loves Louis" 1557
"Everybody Loves My Baby" 681, 1198
"Everybody Needs Something" (Lawrence) 210
"Everybody Needs Something" (Silver) 1458
"Everybody Ought to Have a Gun" 1759
"Everybody Ought to Have a Maid" 1492
"Everybody Ought to Know" 1466
"Everybody Says" 328
"Everybody Says Don't" 1491

"Everybody Talking 'Bout Heaven" 780
"Everybody Wants to Be a Star" 1174
"Everybody Wants To Be in Love" 293
"Everybody Wants to Be Loved" 1261
"Everybody Wants to Be Remembered" 980
"Everybody Wants to See the Baby" 1783
"Everybody's Been Talkin'" 411
"Everybody's Doin' It" 457
"Everybody's Doing the Disco" 1550
"Everybody's Fantasy" 729
"Everybody's Gettin' Into the Act" 461
"Everybody's Gone to California" 1202
"Everybody's Got a Pitch" 785
"Everybody's Got the Right" 70
"Everybody's in the Know but Me" 22
"Everybody's Looking for Love" 1204
"Everybody's Running" 1504
"Everyday Devices" 302
"Everyone Has a Right to Love" 1342
"Everyone Has Something to Hide" 90, 1031
"Everyone Hates His Parents" 473
"Everyone Home but Me" 1484
"Everyone Looks Lonely" 1451
"Everyone Should Play a Musical Instrument" 582
"Everyone Tells Jason to See a Psychiatrist" 1019
"Everyone Tells Me" 820
"Everyone Worth Taking" 1061
"Everyone's Full of #%it" 1128
"Everyone's Here" 749
"Everything" 824, 1381, 1606
"Everything Changes" 1040, 1052
"Everything Comes to Those Who Wait" 504
"Everything Costs Money in New York" 850
"Everything Fine" 1119
"Everything for Roz" 1125
"Everything God Does Is Perfect" 453
"Everything Happens for the Best" (Gordon) 705
"Everything Happens for the Best" (Stone) 272
"Everything Happens to Me" 1210
"Everything Has a Time" 1323
"Everything I Know" 760
"Everything I Want Is Gone" 439
"Everything Is Changed" 726
"Everything Is Likely Looking" 1789
"Everything Is Only for a Little While" 834
"Everything Is Tinglin'" 1446
"Everything Is Wonderful" 1751
"Everything Leads Me to You" 550
"Everything Looks Beautiful" 92
"Everything Must Go" 1547
"Everything Old Is New Again" 1656
"Everything That You Are" 767
"Everything Under the Sun" 855
"Everything You Hate Is Right Here" 1678
"Everything's Coming Up Merman" 511
"Everything's Coming Up Roses" 1491, 1546
"Everything's Gonna Be All Right" 328
"Everything's Great" 237, 603
"Everything's Just Divine" 1265
"Everything's Lovely in the Morning" 603
"Everytime" 132
"Everywhere I Go" 1258
"Evil" 615
"The Evil Fairy and the Hippie" 877
"Evil Gal Blues" 382
"Evil Kindness" 615
"Evocation" 831
"Evolution" 1373
"Exactly Like You" (Coleman) 463
"Exactly Like You" (McHugh) 886
"Exactly the Same as It Was" 267
"The Examination" 27
"The Examination Song, or Get Me on That Boat" 483
"Exanaplanetooch" 649
"Excellent Idea for a Story" 1416
"Excelsior" 903
"Excerpt from 'Galaxy'" 1291
"The Exciting Life Blues" 1548
"Excuse Me" 92
"Excuse Me Baby" 1401
"Executive" 135
"The Exercise" 1158
"Exhibit A" 1403
"Exhortation" 1349
"L'Exile" 963
"Existential" 857
"Exit Atlantic City Scene" 1167
"Exit of Lumberjacks" 1229
"Exit Right" 1499
"Exits and Entrances" 259
"Das Exorcist" 700
"Exotic" 506
"Exotic Dance Team" 506
"Expect a Miracle" 1301
"Experience" (Kernochan) 1478
"Experience" (Schwartz) 1606
"Experiment" 1160
"Experiments in E.S.P." 287
"Experts" (Swados) 643
"Experts" (Weinberg) 573
"An Explanation" 287
"Expletive Deleted" 378
"The Exposé" 636
"Exposé" (Katz) 1584
"Exposé" (Rowe) 1831
"Exposition" (Goggin) 1158
"Exposition" (Young) 1604
"Exquisite Corpse" 680
"Exquisite Passions" 786
"Extra! Extra!" (Moore) 92
"Extra! Extra!" (Shimoda) 602
"Extramarital Relationships" 19
"Extraordinary Waiter" 1500
"Exuent Omnes" 1276
"Eye on New York" 126, 557, 558, 1142
"Eyes Like Tunnels" 1723
"The Eyes of Egypt" 634
"Eyesight to the Blind" 1655
"Ezekiel Saw the Wheel" 815, 816

"F. Jasmine Addams" 466
"Fa La" 434
"Fa-La-La" 1608
"Fable" 1698
"Fable of Chicken Little" 1162
"Fable of Emperor and Nightingale" 1162
"Fable of the Analyst and the Nightingale" 1162
"Fable of the Moth and the Flame" 1162
"Fable of the Nightingale and the Immigration Officer" 1162
"Fable of the Third Little Pig" 1162
"Fabulous Faker" 820
"The Fabulous Twenties" 547
"The Face of Love" 661
"A Face That Could Stop a Clock" 1493
"The Face That Launched a Thousand Ships" 124
"Face the Facts" 1755
"Face to Face" (Gari) 665
"Face to Face" (Naylor) 196
"Face to Face" (Swerdlow) 969
"Faces" 993
"Faces in a Crowd" 1550
"Faces, Names and Places" 1504
"Faces Without Names" 357
"Facing the Pirates" 393
"Fact and Fiction?" 206
"Facts and Figures" 616
"Facts!" (Bohmler and Adler) 644
"Facts!" (Swados) 1335
"Fade Away" 697
"Faded Levi Jacket" 385
"Faded Love" 39
"The Faerie Piper" 1477
"Faeries in My Mother's Flower Garden" 1326
"Fag Hag" 467
"Faggots!" 673
"Fahrenheit 451" 758
"Failure" 1379
"Faintly Macabre's Song" 1252
"The Fair Dissenter Lass" 972
"Fair Fight, Fight Fair" 1815
"The Fair Sex" 1608
"Fair Warning" 981
"The Fairy and the Hard Hat" 877
"Fairy Child" 1190
"Fairy Godmother's Beguine" 907
"A Fairy Tale" 267
"(A) Fairy Tale Come True" 1320, 1321
"Fairy-Tale Life" 1637
"Fairy Tales" (Clifton) 203
"Fairy Tales" (Portnoy and Angelo) 1296
"Fairytale" 293
"Faith" 693
"Faith Can Move a Mountain" 1001
"The Faith Healer" 1813
"Faith Is Such a Simple Thing" 823
"Fakir Tricks" 1235
"The Falcon" 1356
"Fall in Love with Me" 1545
"The Fall of Valor" 1780
"Fall Under the Spell" 1512
"Fallen Angel" 471
"Falling in Line" 471
"Falling in Love Again" 547, 1350
"Falling in Love Again Boogie" 1565
"Falling in Love with Love" 201
"Fallout Shelter" 1661
"Falsettoland" 473, 997
"Fame" (Bergersen) 1380
"Fame" (Bowie, Lennon, and Alomar) 1494
"Fame" (Gore) 474
"Fame" (*Manhattan Rhythm*) 1015
"Fame" (Matay) 1548
"Fame" (Raposo) 1468
"Family" 1201
"The Family" (Glass) 20
"A Family Affair" 1125
"The Family Affair" 1255
"The Family Danced" 1239
"Family Farewell" 529
"Family History" 1121
"Family Obligation" 563
"Family of Man" 1007
"Family of Misfits" 750
"The Family Plan" 1058
"Family Tree" 1108
"Family Trouble" 1447
"Famine" 663
"Famous Blue Raincoat" 1471
"Famous for Fifteen Minutes" 749
"Famous People Quotes" 377
"The Famous Rabbi" 1701
"Fan Dance" 1439
"Fan the Flame" 1420
"Fanatics #1" 377
"Fanatics #2" 377
"Fanatics #3" 377
"Fancy Forgetting" 199
"Fancy Meeting You Here" 973
"Fandango" 300
"Fanette (La Fanette)" 792
"Fanged Tango" 983
"Fanny" 981
"Fanny Dear" 1043
"Fantasiestucke No. 2" 1694
"Fantasy" 537
"Fantasy Come True" 837
"Fantasy for a Fool" 1077
"Far Away Island" 1566
"Far from Wonderful" 942
"Far-Off Lights" 703
"Far Rockaway" 867
"Faraway Land" 13
"Fare Thee Well" 357
"Fare-Thee-Well" 408
"Fare You Well" 569
"The Farewell" 492
"Farewell" (Hoffman) 1759, 1760, 1761
"Farewell" (Roy) 1261
"Farewell Dear Love" 1568, 1569
"Farewell, Family" 1400
"Farewell First Amendment" 1758
"Farewell, Goodbye" 827
"Farewell, Me Butty" 848
"Farewell, My Lovely" 1606
"Farewell Soft Life" 1327
"Farewell Song" 697
"The Farewell Song" 1502
"Farewell to Auld Lang Syne" 271
"Farewell to Dreams" 1570
"The Farewells" 745
"The Farmer and His Wife" 639
"Farmer Tan" 1317
"Farmers' Exit" 1229
"Farmers' Song" 1229
"Farming" 367, 1704
"Farrakhan" 1760
"Fascinating Rhythm" 35, 46, 171, 1096, 1656
"Fascinating Rhythme" 1293
"The Fashion Show" (Bobrowitz) 919
"The Fashion Show" (Solly) 1050
"Fashion Show" (Davis) 1069
"Fashion Show" (Gershwin) 912
"Fashions" 1161
"Fashions of the Day" 820
"Fast" 1830
"Fast Dance" 624
"Faster Than the Speed of Life" 1325
"Fat and Greasy" 18
"Fat City" 969
"The Fat Gram Song" 1046
"Fat Luigi" 416
"The Fatal Curse of Drink" 570
"Fatal Fascination" 1606
"The Fatality Hop" 225
"Fate of John Burgoyne" 740
"Fatha" 221
"Father Andrew's Lesson" 1303
"Father, Dear Father, Stop Testing" 1276
"Father Death Blues" 729
"Father, Father" 175
"Father, I Have Sinned" 1610
"A Father Now" 1622
"Father of Fathers" 300
"The Father of the Bride" 733
"A Father Speaks" 1652
"Father to Son" 1019
"Fathers and Mothers (And You and Me)" 726
"Fathers and Sons" (Carpenter) 1148
"Fathers and Sons" (Sloan) 1607
"Fathers and Sons" (Weiss) 161, 162, 163, 164
"Father's Daughter" 98
"Father's Day" (Deems) 858
"Father's Day" (Ruby) 672
"Father's Lament" 1231
"Fathers That Wear Rags" 1437
"Father's Waltz" 65
"Fats" 221
"The Faux Finale" 1772
"Faux Pas de la Dee Dah" 1014
"Faux Pas de Trois" 552
"Favorite Son" 1033
"Favorite Sons" 377
"Favorite Words" 915
"F.D.R. Jones" 1268
"Fear and Self-Loathing" 385
"Fearless Frank" 483
"Fear's Alive" 789
"Feast or Famine" 419
"Feathered Friends" 160
"Feather in My Shoe" 213
"Feature Story" 1698
"February Weather" 1500
"Feeble-Minded Idjet!" 1563
"Feed the Lions" 1422
"Feeding the Baby" 1710
"Feel at Home" 1319
"Feel the Beat" 653
"Feel the Heat" 82
"Feelin' Bleu" 1077
"A Feeling" 1727
"Feeling Good" 1315
"Feeling Rich" 1375
"Feelings" 465
"Feels Good" 767
"Feels Like Home" 1428
"Feet" (Roy) 1236
"Feet" (Yeston) 1201
"The Feet" 1709
"Feigalach Tzvei" 1745
"Feigele, My Love" 1745
"Fellatio 101" 913
"Felony" 1487
"Felt Up at the Airport" 1128
"Female Animal" 1197

"Female Encounters" 1143
"Feminine Companionship" 88
"Feminine-inity" 1774
"Femme Fatale" 1453
"Fennimore's Song" 1462, 1532
"Ferhuddled and Ferhexed" 235
"Fernando's Suicide" 1250
"Fern's Castle" 253
"Ferret Song" 1103
"Fertility Dance" 1751
"Festival" 663
"Festival Fever" 198
"Festival President" 32
"Fetus" 958
"Fever" 777, 1245
"A Few to Get Through" 856
"A Few Words About Matthew" 469
"Fiction Writer" 219
"Fiction Writer Duet" 219
"The Fiddle" 492
"Fiddle About" 1655
"The Fiddles Were Playing" 253
"Fidgety Feet" 1172
"Fidgety Phil" 1444
"Fido's Sympathy" 1229
"The Field Near the Cathedral at Chartres" 1356
"Fields of Athenry" 775
"Fiesta" 507
"Fiesta Brava" 1179
"Fiesta in Madrid" 488
"Fifteen Minutes" 750
"Fifteen Years" 1458
"The Fifth from the Right" 89, 1202
"Fifth Interlude" 299
"A Fifth of Beethoven" 399
"The Fifth Season" 489
"Fifty-Fifty" (Romshinsky) 220, 604
"Fifty-Fifty" (Smith) 1643
"Fifty Million Years Ago" 1451
"The 59th Street Bridge Song (Feelin' Groovy)" 265
"57 Street" 1015
"56 Cities" 1365
"Fifty Years of Making People Laugh" 614
"The Fight" (Britten) 1229
"The Fight" (Lippa) 1778
"The Fight (La Pelea)" 488
"Fight at the Market Place" 889
"Fight Fiercely, Harvard" 1654
"Fight on for Tannenbaum" 672
"Fight, Team, Fight" 1255
"Fight the Urge" 1110
"Fight to the Death" 1146
"Fighting for Pharoah" 400
"The Fights" 149, 150
"Figli" 59
"Filibuster" 1276
"Fill 'Er Up" (aka "Fill-er Up") 1759, 1760
"Fill It to the Top" 697
"Fill the Cup" 388
"Fill Up and Drink Up" 609
"Fill Up Your Cup with Sunshine" 1400
"Filling Out the Form" 1645
"The Filling Station" 1484
"Film Discussion Show" 1743
"Fin De Sickle" 1594
"The Final Chase" 1071
"Final Choral Blessing" 707
"The Final Clue" 302
"The Final Curtain" 783
"Final Dance" 95
"Final Declaration" 602
"Final Episode" 241
"The Final Hour" 1419
"Final Interlude" 299
"Final Judgment" 65
"The Finale" (Silvestri) 1595
"The Finale" (Stoner) 752
"Find a Way" (Marks) 185
"Find a Way" (Petsche) 416
"Find Her" 1228
"Find Me" 328
"Find Me a Body" 313
"Find Me a Hero" 1384
"Find Me a Primitive Man" 367
"Find My Way Alone" 93
"Find Out What They Like" 18
"Find Someone to Love (Song of the Soldier)" 968
"Find the Cost of Freedom" 1556
"Find the Queen, Kill the Fox" 889
"Find Yourself Something to Do" 1393
"Finding Home" 413
"A Fine and Private Place" 491
"The Fine Art of Schnorring" 865, 866
"Fine Clothes" 156
"Fine for the Shape I'm In" 1582, 1677
"The Fine Ladies" 92
"A Fine Romance" 35, 883, 886
"Fine Words and Fancy Phrases" 76
"The Finer Things of Life" 1811
"The Finger Song" 1311
"Fingerbreaker" 813
"Finif Sent (Five Cents)" 1453
"Finishing the Hat" 1557
"Finkel & Son" 555
"Finnegan's Wake" 775
"A Fiord Joke" 622
"Fire" 59, 773
"The Fire" 1637
"Fire Belles Gallop" 494
"Fire Escape" 760
"Fire, Fire" 591
"The Fire in My Heart" 539
"Fire in the Belly" 983
"Fire on the Mountains" 617
"Fireflies" 332
"The Fireman's Flame" 494
"Fireman's Song" 393, 394
"Firemen's Quartet" 884
"A Fireside, a Pipe and a Pet" 1326
"A Firestorm Consuming Indianapolis" 588, 727
"Fireworks" 760
"Fireworks Gallop" 1131
"First Act Crisis" 1072
"First Ballad Interlude" 1229
"First Born" 1307
"First Cat" 1251
"The First Chanukah Night" 1829
"First Child by 33" 1472
"First Dance" 1188
"First Day at the Academy" 57
"First Fig" 1222
"The First Goodbye" 1680
"First Grade" 328
"The First Hunt" 1071
"First I Propose" 1787
"First Impressions" 21
"First Interlude" 299
"The First Jam Session" 1398
"First Kid on the Block" 54
"The First Kiss" 1379
"First Lady and First Gent" 912
"The First Last Supper" 910
"First Laur and Von Luber Duet" 1462
"First, Let's Kill All the Lawyers" 1309
"First Love" 1800
"First Message" 1422
"The First Move" 1143, 1144
"First Night of Summer" 285
"First Ones There" 1058
"First Prize" 1254
"First Quarter" 1319
"First Rehearsal" 1006
"First Star" 1598
"First Step" 328
"First Things First" 1102
"The First Time" (Rosenthal) 1692
"The First Time" (Weinstein) 837
"First Time I Heard Ella" 788
"First Time I Heard Ellington" 788
"First Time I Saw You" 809
"The First to Know" 434, 435
"First to Walk Away" 1033
"The First Touch of Autumn" 406
"The First Volume of My Life" 820
"Fish, Lemons, Chickens" 1771
"Fish Song" 1445
"The Fish Soup Song" 1380
"Fisherman's Prayer" 1317
"The Fishermen of Kineret" 617
"The Five-Fifteen" 641
"Five Full Months" 927
"500 Miles" 411
"Five Hundred Garments" 1361, 1362
"Five Hundred Pages" 1361, 1362
"Five Minutes Ago" 1679
"Five More Minutes" 1143
"Five O'Clock" 1688
"Five O'Clock Tea" 305
"The Five of Us" 1618
"Five Plus One" 388
"Five to One" 720
"Fix It Scene" 1615
"Fixed" 501
"Fixin' to Die Rag" 1664
"Fixing a Hole" 1426
"The Flag of Death" 224
"The Flagmaker, 1775" 1498
"Flair" 1524
"Flame of Life" 1537
"Flamenco Dancer" 529
"Flamenco Song (Canto Flamenco)" 488
"Flaming Agnes" 733
"Flamingo Fuss" 64
"Flaminio Scala's Historical Journey to France" 583
"Flash Them Bootstraps" 1736
"The Flat Foot Floogie" 1764
"A Flat Impromptu" 1694
"Flattery" 277
"Flattery Will Get You Nowhere" 501
"Flaunting It" 1600
"Flavor of the Week" 1325
"Flavor of the Week (Part 2)" 1325
"The Fledgling" 352
"Flesh and Blood" 1815
"Flesh Rebels" 1139
"Fleshly Chain" 419
"Fleugel Street" 134
"Flibberty-Gibbet" 1451
"The Flickers" 1158
"Flight of the Phoenix" 162, 163
"The Flight of the Wasp" 542
"Flight to Health" 643
"Flim-Flam" 25
"Flim Flam Flooey (Flooie)" 232, 1163
"Flings" 1752
"Flip Religion" 386
"Flippin' Out!" 605
"Flirtation Dance" 1307
"Flirtation Scene" 226, 1615, 1616
"Flirtation Waltz" 1636
"The Floating Cabaret" 635
"The Flood" 1201
"Floozies" 926
"Florence" 1499
"Florence Quits" 275
"Florida by the Sea" 305
"Flotsam" 933
"The Flower" 1662
"A Flower" 1311
"Flower Child" 1732
"Flower Children" 1153
"Flower I Don't Need You Anymore" 1078
"Flower Scent Song" 507
"Flower Shop" 990
"The Flower Song" 464
"Flower Song" 1358
"The Flowers" 1827
"Flowers" 820
"The Flowers and the Rainbow" 279
"Flowers for Her Hair" 1638
"Flowers from the Sixties" 1800
"Flowery Waltz" 1636
"Flowing to the Sea" 835
"Floyd" 503
"Flushed Down the Pipes" 627
"Flushing Gaucho" 897
"Fly a Rainbow" 3
"Fly Across the Moor" 1815
"Fly Away" (Blatt) 676
"Fly Away" (Denver) 37
"Fly Away" (Flaherty) 375
"Fly Away" (Harris) 1476
"Fly Away" (Meyer) 1652
"Fly Away Rose" 1495
"Fly Blackbird" 504
"Fly By Night" 1606
"A Fly-By-Night Affair" 1091
"Fly Eagle Fly" 1348
"Fly Me to the Moon (In Other Words)" 1210
"Fly Now, Pay Later" 942
"Fly with Me" 416
"Flying" (Braden) 372
"Flying" (Kayden) 773
"Flying" (Lasser) 225
"Flying Dreams" 469
"Flying Home" 1498
"The Flying Linguinis (Pasta Medley)" 171
"Flying Milk and Runaway Plates" 1038
"Flying Robert" 1444
"Flying Somehow" 464
"The Fog" 1338
"Fog Song" 922
"Folgen A Tatten" 119
"Folies Bergeres" (Valenti) 990
"Folies Bergeres" (Yeston) 924
"Folk Song" 861
"The Folk Song Army" 1654
"The Folks Who Live on the Hill" 883
"Follow Him" 1083
"Follow Me" 78
"Follow Schmidt" 1635
"Follow the Drinkin' Gourd" 922
"Follow the Drinking Gourd" 815, 816
"Follow the Music Man" 653
"Follow the Rainbow" 1689
"Follow Where the Music Goes" 703
"Follow Your Heart" (Hollmann) 1712
"Follow Your Heart" (Jacobson) 1452
"Follow Your Heart" (Romanovsky and Phillips) 808
"Follow Your Star" 296
"Following in Father's Footsteps" 301
"Le Folly Bergere" 1058
"Fons Pietatis" 244
"Fonye Ganev (Ivan the Czar, The Rouge)" 604
"Food Chain" 864
"Food Chorus" 1229
"Food Is Love" 1072
"A Fool in Love" 115
"The Fool Is Born Into Pre-Life" 1592
"Fool Like Me" 1188
"Foolin' Ourselves" 149, 150
"Foolish Face" 1606
"Foolish Geese" 1495
"Foolish Heart" 1532
"Fools Come and Fools Go" 1755
"Fool's Song" 435
"Foot Note" 241
"Football in Depth" 986
"Footloose Youth and Fancy-Free (Fancy Free)" 1395, 1396
"Footprints" 1033
"Footprints in the Sand" 1811
"Footsteps" 1384
"For a Bride You Have Come" 253
"For a Little While" 1255
"For Alice" 36
"For Anne Gregory" 707
"For Bobbie" 37
"For Critics Only" 1447
"For Ever" 1395, 1396
"For Example" 705
"For Feet Only" 1291
"For Four Hundred Years" 1732
"For Love" 848
"For Love or Money" 121
"For Much in the World" 331
"For My Mary" 1328
"For No Rhyme or Reason" 1823
"For Now" 77
"For Old Time's Sake" 403
"For Once in My Life" 1083
"For Sarah Good Confessed" 331
"For the Children" 1829
"For the Good of Brotherhood" 539
"For the Good Times" 1537
"For the Harvest Safely Gathered" 76
"For the Love" 486
"For the Money" 1438
"For the People" 735
"For the Sake of My Sister" 1723
"For Those You Love" 1637
"For Two Minutes" 1107
"For What It's Worth" 1556
"For When You're Dead" 417
"For Whom?" 602
"For-Women-Only Poems" 1
"For You" 37
"Forbidden Broadway" 511
"Forbidden Love" 1831
"Forbidden Tropics" 1430
"'Fore Day Noon in the Mornin'" 91
"Foreign Affairs" 1192

"Forest for the Trees" 1513
"Forest, Forest" 1203
"Forest Hills 9 A.M." 206
"Forest of Silver" 1679
"The Forest Rangers" 766, 935
"Forever" 271
"Forever and Always" 1566
"Forever Friends" 1419
"Forever Mine" 240
"Forever Yours" 1191
"Forget" 1008
"Forget It" 781
"Forget Me Not" 1342
"Forget-Me-Not Lane" 1540
"Forget the Girl, Once and for All (Olivida esa Muchacha para Siempre)" 488
"Forget.me.knots" 1407
"Forgive Her, Forgive Her" 884
"Forgive Me" 1179
"Forgiveness" (Carmines) 614
"Forgiveness" (Micare) 1438
"Forgotten Dreams" 1521
"Forgotten Lullaby" 1513
"Forgotten Words" 556, 557
"Formidable" 924
"Fortune" (Berg) 1303
"Fortune" (Melrose) 537
"Forty Days" 831
"Forty-Five Minutes from Broadway" 570
"The Forty-Second Street Philharmonic" 1385
"The Forty-Seven Questions" 49, 612
"Forty-Three" 1485
"42-32-42" 1298
"42-32-42 (Soliloquies #1)" 1298
"42-32-42 (Soliloquies #2)" 1298
"42nd St. Blues" 1183
"42nd Street" 1030
"The Forum Looks Dark" 1374
"Foster Children" 1263
"Foul Weather Friend" 302
"Founders Come First, Then Profiteers" 1139
"The Fountain in the Garden" 296
"The Fountains Mingle" 1443
"Four" 1311
"Four & Twenty Years Ago" 1664
"Four Black Dragons" 1213
"Four Eyes" 708
"Four Fo' Me" 1543
"Four Green Fields" 1540
"Four Hands in C Major" 1694
"Four Hands in D Major, First Movement" 1694
"Four in Hand" 1168
"Four Japanese" 889
"Four Japanese Merchants" 889
"Four Jews in a Room Bitching" 997, 1019
"Four Little Angels of Peace (Are We)" 981, 1267
"Four Little Chests All in a Row" 941
"Four More Shopping Days" 1460
"Four Part Harmony" 537
"Four Part Invention" 159
"Four Proverbs" 1771
"The Four Questions" 647
"The Four R's" 1761
"Four Seasons" (Bargy) 638
"Four Seasons" (Roy) 415, 531
"The Four Seasons" 1037
"Four Square Blocks" 328
"4,000 Years" 175
"Four-Two-Two" 338
"Four Walls (and One Dirty Window) Blues" 181, 182
"Four Walls Blues" 180
"Four White Horses" 364
"14 Dwight Ave., Natick, Massachusetts" 430
"Fourteen Hours and Thirty-Seven Minutes" 87
"Fourth Avenue North" 535
"Fourth Interlude" 299
"Fourth of July" 197
"The Fourth Telegram" 726
"The Fox" 938
"The Fox and the Stork" 11
"Fox! Fox! Come Here Boy" 609
"Frances' Ballad" 580
"Francie" 1140
"Francis" 539
"Francis' Feast" 1679
"Frank Mills" 649
"Frankenstein" 419
"Frankie and Johnnies" 1611
"Frankie's Return" 1365
"Franklin" 1251
"Frannie" 1684
"Fraught" 1140
"A Freak-Out in Feathers" 783
"Freaks" 1119
"Freckled Fanny (Nini Peau d'Chien)" 1641
"Fred" 430
"Freddie and Flo" 1373
"Freddy Liked to Fugue (aka "Freddie's Fugue")" 564, 758
"Freddy, My Love" 625
"Free" 1331
"Free at Last" 736
"Free, Easy Guy" 1613
"Free Food and Frontal Nudity" 143
"Free for All" 1179
"Free, Male and Twenty-One" 1706
"Free Our Sons" 1670
"Free Speech, Free Thought, Free Love" 483
"Free the Tiger" 837
"Free Time" 1034
"Freedom" (Broderick) 470
"Freedom" (Feuer) 143
"Freedom" (Underwood) 556, 557, 558
"Freedom (Amen)" 736
"Freedom and All That" 436
"Freedom Anthem" 65
"The Freedom Choo Choo (Is Leaving [Leavin'] Today)" 232, 1163
"Freedom Diet" 1064
"Freedom Is Coming Tomorrow" 1401
"Freedom Land" 815, 816
"Freedom, Liberation" 1423
"The Freedom of the Press" 324
"Freedom Riders" 1274
"The Freedom Song" 86
"The Freedom Train" 569
"Freer Love" 113
"Freeze an' Melt" 886
"Freezing and Burning" 386
"Freight Train" 1225
"The French Fink" 871
"The French Lesson" (Edens) 1224
"The French Lesson" (Kim) 889
"The French Monologue" 1
"The French Song" 1
"French Thing Tango" 869
"French Tickler" 1149
"French with Tears" 1138
"Frere Jacques Rock" 543
"Fresh & Young" (sketch) 1448
"Fresh and Young" (song) 1448
"Fresh from Puerto Rico" 897
"Freud Is a Fraud" 109
"A Freudian Slip" 547
"Friar's Tune" 1424
"Fricassee of Chicken" 285
"Friday, Friday" 409
"Friday Night" 489
"Fridays" 712
"Fridays at Four" 296
"A Friend Like Me" 808
"A Friend Like You" 1008
"Friendly Fire" 892
"Friendly, Liberal Neighborhood" 1069
"A Friendly Little Game" 510
"Friendly Polka" 822
"A Friendly Vacation" 385
"Friends" (Cribari) 1283
"Friends" (Mettee) 1
"Friends" (Peretti, Creatore, and Weiss) 1480
"Friends" (Pottle) 34
"Friends" (Staudt and Copani) 1537
"Friends Ain't Supposed to Die" 151
"Friends for Life" 665
"Friends in High Places" 573
"Friends Like You" 1149
"Friendship" (Porter) 63, 367, 1704
"Friendship" (Slater) 719
"Friendship Ain't No One Way Street" 1811
"Friendship and Love" 930
"Friendship Duet" 1462
"Friendship for Dulles" 1276
"Fries and a Shake" 1710
"Frightened of the Dark" 409
"The Frimbo Special" 544
"Fritzie" 90, 1031
"The Frog and the Ox" 11
"The Frogs" 977
"Frogs Have So Much Spring" 1121
"The Frogs Perform" 1679
"A Frolic" 1762
"From Alpha to Omega" 1823
"From Atlanta to the Sea" 569
"From Chopin to Country" 323
"From Dust We Come" 673
"From El Barrio to Riverdale" 897
"From Here to Eternity" 1210
"From Here to Here" 1338
"From High" 1020
"From Hunger" 1706
"From Mineola with Hate" 1813
"From Now On" (Dick) 1815
"From Now On" (Edwards and Harris) 113
"From Now On" (Friedman) 995
"From Seventh Avenue to Seventh Heaven" 489
"From the Bottom of the Sea" 1380
"From the Convent" 1146
"From the Cradle to the Grave" 1192
"From the Moment" 698
"From the Top" 381
"From the Unisphere with Love" 160
"From the Very First Day" 1815
"From This Day" 990
"The Front Page" 1208
"Front Page News" 1143, 1144
"The Front Yard of the Moss Home" 1601
"Frontier Politics" 1824
"Frontier Rabbi" 1610
"Frozen Logger" 740
"The Frozen Man" 49, 612
"Fruits and Vegetables" 1330
"Fruits of Domestic Bliss" 385
"Frustration" 1504
"The Frying Pan" 1702
"Ft. Lauderdale" 415
"Fuel for the Fire" 1479
"Fugue" 238
"Fugue for Four Girls" 1038
"Fugue on a Hot Afternoon in a Small Flat" 1399
"Full" 1584
"Full Circle" 1538
"Full Fathom Five" 1568, 1569
"Fun" 1060
"Fun and Games" (McCreery) 1142
"Fun and Games" (Taylor) 1289
"Fun City" 550, 1475
"Fun Downtown-Uptown (From Downtown, We Move Uptown)" 604
"Fun, Food, and Fellowship" 1232
"Fun in the Morning" 852
"Fun with Your Doohinkus" 1427
"The Funeral" 130
"Funeral Dance" 42
"The Funeral Dirge" 1025
"Funeral March" 240
"Funeral March of the Marionettes" 1373
"Funeral of Amenhotep III" 20
"Funeral of Charleston" 85
"A funeral passed by" 250
"Funeral Procession" (Engeran) 1151
"Funeral Procession" (Picker) 439
"Funeral Tango (Tango Funebre)" 792
"Funky" 1558
"Funky Bessie" 809
"Funky-Butt Hall" 959
"Funky Dance" 1638
"Funky Eyes" 208
"Funky Love" 537
"Funky People" 1550
"Funky Piano Man" 110
"Funky World" 835
"The Funnies" 69
"Funny" 1577
"Funny Bunny" 226
"Funny Face" 1096
"Funny Feathers" 553
"Funny Feeling" 835
"Funny Gesture" 1499
"A Funny Heart" 1254
"A Funny Thing Happened (on My Way to Love)" 981
"Funny Wind-Up Toy" 216
"Furiant" 609
"Furs, Fortune, Fame, Glamor" 1298
"Further Comments" 834
"Further Particulars" 622
"Fusion" 610
"Future for Sale" 393, 394
"The Future Is Ours" 1736
"Future King of England" 1320, 1321
"The Future Looks Promising" 582

"G-Man" 1267
"Gabey's Comin' (Coming)" 234, 1186
"Gabrielle" 777
"Gad" 666
"A Gaggle of Celebrities" 1375
"A Gal in Calico" 348
"The Gal Who Took the Minutes" 1125
"Gala Galore" 198
"Gala Opening" 1261
"Gala Performance of the Opera" 620
"Galaxy Girl" 1048
"Galbraith" 450
"Galicianer Cabellero" 1105
"Galileo Demonstrates His Discovery That a Feather and a Heavy Object Fall at the Same Rate of Speed" 1765
"Gall Wasp Wedding" 395
"Gallop" 779
"Gallows Pole" 655
"A Gal's Got to Do What a Gal's Got to Do" 1326
"Galway Bay" 775
"The Gamble" 1439
"The Gamblin' Hand" 345
"Gambling" 257
"Game" 293
"The Game" (Blum, Barker, and Martucci) 302
"The Game" (Dick) 1771
"The Game" (Kayden) 240
"The Game Is Mate" 197
"The Game Is Over!" 160
"The Game Is Up" 556, 557, 558
"Game of Dance" 942
"The Game of Love" 989
"The Game of the Name" 780
"A Game of Whist" 1721
"The Game Show" 485
"Game Show Hosts" 36
"Games" (Eiler and Bargy) 1085
"Games" (Leake) 278
"The Games I Play" 1019
"The Gap: A Corner Booth Very Near the Orchestra at the Rainbow Room" 899
"Garbage" (Barnes) 469
"Garbage" (Harnick) 1448
"Garbage Can Blues" 417
"Garbage Court Round" 1302
"Garbage-Ella" 636, 1679
"Garbo" 1315
"The Garden" (Carmines) 1349
"The Garden" (Strouse) 1473
"A Garden for Two" 1330
"The Garden Is Green" 1052
"The Garden of Roses" 136
"The Garden Path to Hell" 1109
"Garden Song" 1659
"Garland Is My Man" 453
"Garland of Roses" 1480
"The Garment Trade" 1361, 1362
"Garter Song" 1348
"Gas Can" 175
"Gastrointestinal Rag" 1309
"The Gate in the Road" 1343
"Gather 'Round" 1742
"Gather Ye Rose Buds" 1446
"Gathering of Soldiers" 697
"The Gathering of the Clan" 160
"The Gatsby Bridge March" 1481
"Gaudeamus Igitur" 666
"Gauguin's Shoes" 296
"Gavotte" 431
"The Gay Agenda" 227
"A Gay Bar Cantata" 467
"Gay Bohemia" 1639
"Gay Caballeros" 1669

"Gay Guys" 469
"Gay Name Game" 1600
"The Gay Rap" 873
"Gazelles" 529
"G'bye" 1483
"Gebentsht Iz Amerike (Blessed Is America)" 604
"Gedaliah, the Tar Maker" 1203
"Gee, I'm Glad I'm No One Else but Me" 56
"Gee, Officer Krupke" 911
"Geendikt Iz Der Tog (Peasants Return from Work)" 1382
"Geisha Girl" 85
"The Geisha Song" 547
"Gelber Meets the Wolfgang" 616
"A Gem of a Pearl" 550
"Gemini" 1319
"Genealogy" 286
"The General" 858
"General DeGaulle's Agent" 1091
"The General Election" 1091
"General! General!" 1635
"General Sir Hugh M. Trenchard" 151
"General Store" 56
"The General's Gone to a Party" 912
"Generals' Pandemonium" 1181
"The Generation Gap" 1701
"Generation Gap" (Bregman) 1743
"Generation Gap" (Gari) 980
"Generation Gap" (Rusk) 542
"Generic Women" 54
"Genesis" 1363
"Genetic Engineering" 547
"Genie Ballet" 66
"Genius" 699
"Genius at Work" 547
"Genius Burns" 822
"Genteel" 98
"Gentle Afternoon" 658
"The Gentle Buffoon" 1358
"Gentle People" 814
"Gentle Rain" 1638
"Gentle Sighs" 1504
"Gentleman Caller" 153, 154
"Gentlemen, Be Seated" 569
"Gentlemen of Leisure" 975
"Gentlemen's Duel" 529
"Gentlemen's Resale Shop" 126
"Gentlemen's Understanding" 98
"Gentleness, Virtue" 1443
"Gently, Sirs, Gently" 331
"Gentrification" 385
"A Genuine Feminine Girl" 291
"Genuine Grade A Canadian Superstar" 159
"Genuine Limitation of Life" 265
"Geographically Undesirable" 919
"Geography" 509
"Geordie" 655
"George" (Goggin and Solley) 667
"George" (Kennon) 690
"Georgia on My Mind" 171, 1623
"Georgia Peach" 959
"Georgia Rose" 864
"Georgia Sand" 1160
"Georgie and I" 989, 990
"Georgy Girl" 1450
"Gerbils" 465
"German Evening" 1635
"Gerrara Here" 1715
"The Geshrunken Meshuggena Rag" 1607
"Get a Dog" 780
"Get a Job" 1434
"Get Alice" 1226
"Get an Education" 1397
"Get Away Jordan" 166
"Get Back" 934, 1426
"Get Happy" 662, 746, 955
"Get Her to Do It" 1135
"Get in Line" 1517
"Get It Together" 1388
"Get It While You Can" 965
"Get Me Out of Here" 1611
"Get Me to New York" 1325
"Get Naked" 326
"Get Off My Back" 1300
"Get Off My Lawn" 1218
"Get Off on Somebody Else" 1398
"Get Off the Pot" 672
"Get on the Raft with Taft" 722
"Get On with It" 916
"Get Out of Here" 1759, 1761
"Get Out of It" 1721
"Get Out of Town" 367
"Get Out the Vote" 722
"Get Outta Here, Peter" 1052
"Get Pissed" 1777
"Get Real" 227
"Get the Answer Now" 731
"Get the News" 1177
"Get Thee Behind Me" 1207
"Get Thee Behind Me, Satan!" 8
"Get Thee to Bed" 786
"Get Thee to Canterbury" 572
"Get Tough or Get Out" 907
"Get Up and Dance" 1148
"Get Up and Go, Lad" 697
"Get Used to It" (Magee) 633
"Get Used to It" (Weinberg) 573
"Get Used to It, Eddie" 1723
"Get While the Getting's Good" 153
"Get Your Rocks Off Rock" 1517
"Get Your Slice of Cake" 152
"Get Yourself a Geisha" 348
"Get Yourself Some Lovin'" 934
"Getaway" 416
"The Getaway Quintet" 676
"Gettin' Ready for Love" 1117
"Getting Better" 1426
"Getting from Day to Day" 975
"Getting Married Today" 1492
"Getting Older" 624
"Getting Ready for the Ball" 290
"Getting to Know You" 986
"Getzl, the Shoemaker (Aleph ... Beth)" 1203
"Gevalt! Vus Vet Zein Der Sof?" 1212
"Ghetto of My Mind" 208
"G.I. Jive" 1764
"G.I. Joe" 943
"Giannina Mia" 1570
"The Giant" 1806
"Giddyup" 1476
"The Gift" 575
"The Gift of Maggie (and Others)" 986
"The Gift of Trouble" 929
"Gifted Is" 1001
"Gifts of Love" 88
"The Gifts of the Magi" 576
"Gifts to You" 486
"Giglo, Shanklin and Mudd" 9
"Gigolo" 367
"Gimme a 'G'" 856
"Gimme-a-Break Heartbreak" 910
"Gimme a Good Digestion" 1253
"Gimme a Pigfoot (and a Bottle of Beer)" 35, 165, 171, 266, 996
"Gimme Shelter" 1664
"Gimme Some" 603
"Gin" 612
"Gin Rummy Rhapsody" 1608
"The Gin Song" 789
"Gina" (Blitzstein) 1140
"Gina" (Link and Courtney) 1396
"Ginger Brown" 165
"Ginger Wildcat" 773
"Gingerbread Girl" 969
"Gingham and Orchid" 599
"The Gipsy's Warning" 481
"Giraffe's Reprise" 855
"G-I-R-L" 1188
"The Girl and the Bat" 1293
"The Girl by the Gate in Old San Juan" 1475
"A Girl Can Go Wacky" 213
"The Girl Friend" 1096
"Girl He Adores" 693
"Girl in the Coffee" 1004
"Girl Machine" 926
"The Girl Most Likely" 1800
"The Girl Next Door" 1547
"Girl of My Dreams" 1759
"Girl of the Minute" 1524
"Girl of the Moment" 128
"Girl Power" 1215
"A Girl Really Needs a Woman" 834
"A Girl That You Meet in a Bar" 1479
"A Girl with a Ribbon" 332
"The Girl with Too Much Heart" 1752
"A Girl You Should Know" 1524
"Girl You're a Woman" 133
"Girlfriend" 1200
"Girlfriends for Life" 675
"Girls" (Porter) 367
"Girls" (Wittman and Shaiman) 943
"Girls" (Phillips) 1007
"Les Girls" 1304
"The Girls and the Dogs (Les Filles et les Chiens)" 792
"The Girls Are Back" 749
"The Girls in My Life" 1036
"The Girls in Short Supply" 626
"The Girls in Their Summer Dresses" 1415
"Girls Like Me" 1048
"Girls' Night Out" 154
"Girls of Madrid" 1179
"The Girls of Summer" 1027
"Girl's Song" 707
"The Girls Who Sell Orangeade" 1264
"The Girls Who Sit and Wait" 987
"Git Comfortable" 503
"Git It!" 939
"Give a Cheer" 1076
"Give a Damn (What You Do)" 959
"Give a Girl a Break!" 215
"Give a Little Helping Hand" 1011
"Give and Take" (Friedman) 1441
"Give and Take" (Jordan) 1379
"Give 'Em a Kiss" 1318
"Give 'Em a Lollipop and ..." 652
"Give 'Em Hell" 456
"Give 'Em What They Want" 599
"Give England Strength" 1381
"Give Her Back Her Music" 995
"Give Her to Me" 439
"Give Him a Great Big Kiss" 115
"Give Him the Oo-La-La" 367, 807
"Give It to Me" 913
"Give It Up" 222
"Give Me" 903
"Give Me a Pinch" 1604
"Give Me All the Money" 726
"Give Me an And" 297
"Give Me Excess of It" 1666
"Give Me Five Minutes More" 1546
"Give Me Love" (Barkan) 224
"Give Me Love" (Roullier) 1354
"Give Me More" 809
"Give Me My Robe" 62
"Give Me the Land" 1704
"Give Me the Love" 1398
"Give Me the Power" 9
"Give Me the Simple Life" 1082
"Give Me This Night" 499
"Give Me Time" 23
"Give Me Your Tired, Your Poor" 604
"Give My Best to the Blonde" 1061
"Give My Regards to Broadway" 570, 775, 993
"Give My Regards to Leicester Square" 581
"Give My Regards to Mott St." 942
"Give Our Regards to Broadway" 212
"Give the Bad Cat Some" 156
"Give the Child a Break" 196
"Give These Orders" 363
"Give Us Power" 1401
"Give Us This Day" 357
"Give Your Heart to Jesus" 1330
"Give Your Love" 1310
"Giving It Up for Love" 200
"Giving Life" 913
"Giza-on-the-Nile" 1264
"Glad Rag Doll" 955
"Glad to Be in the Service" 1002
"Glad to Know Ya" 1504
"Gladiators" 529
"Gladys Gutzman" 845
"The Glamorous Life" 1651
"Glamour Girls" 142
"Glee Club Rehearsal" 1828
"Glitter and Be Gay" 244, 911
"Global Glamor Girls" 1298
"Globbidge" 1788
"Globligated" 1330
"Gloria" 78, 1353
"Gloria in Excelsis" 1029
"Gloria in Excelsis Deo" 1155, 1157, 1159
"Gloria Tibi" 1029
"Gloriana" 434, 435
"Glorious" 1623
"Glorious Age" 582
"The Glorious Ones" 583
"The Glory of Each Morning" 208
"Glory Train" 1470
"Gloryday" 1422
"Go 'Way from My Window" 1350
"Go Ahead, Fire Me, George" 673
"Go Away" 1574
"Go Away, Mrs. Levittown" 198
"Go Back" 823
"Go Down Death" 1672
"Go Down Moses" 740, 815, 816
"Go for It" 1432
"Go! Go! Go!" 1058
"Go, Go, Go Guerillas" 1082
"Go, Go, Go, Joseph" 833
"Go If You Want" 1815
"Go It Alone Song" 1237
"Go Little Boat" 883
"Go Now" 1353
"Go Slow, Johnny" 1390
"Go Tell It on the Mountain" 166, 777
"Go There" 78
"Go to Sleep Early" 210
"Go to the Mirror!" 1655
"Go to the Wall" 449
"Go Up to the Mountain" 985
"Go Visit Your Grandmother" 210
"Go Where You Want to Go" 411
"Go Your Way with the Lord" 960
"The Goat" 1203
"Goat Play" 1274
"Goat Prologue" 184
"God" 958
"God Almighty Is Gonna Cut You Down" 1672
"God Be with You" 166, 1559, 1672
"God Bless" 1294
"God Bless All" 111
"God Bless All the Misfits" 587
"God Bless Coney" 587
"God Bless Everyone" 1438
"God Bless the Child" 221, 807, 1435
"God Bless the Fig Tree" 1480
"God Bless Us All" 614
"God Could Give Me Anything" 230
"God Does Not Need My Name" 331
"God Faithful" 647
"God Hates Fags" 469
"God Help Us" 785
"God, I Beg Your Forgiveness" 59
"God Is Black" 716
"God Is Good to Me" 304
"God Is in the People" 493, 1124
"God Is Not Finished with Me Yet" 1761
"God Is Smiling on You" 857
"God Is There" 413
"God Lead Us Along" 1672
"God Loves the Baptist" 730
"God Must Love a Fool" 365
"God Never Closes a Door" 741
"God of Mercy" 647
"God of Our Fathers" 1441
"God of Wrath" 468
"God Said" (Berstein) 1029
"God Said" (Kennon) 690
"God Save the City" 370
"God Save the King" 581
"God Save Us" 1666
"God Will Be" 1001
"God Will Take Care" 589
"Goddess of Liberty" 827
"The Goddess of Love" 989
"Godiva's Gambol" 635
"The Gods" 983
"God's Country" 993
"God's Favorite Choice" 1510
"God's Gift" 781
"God's Gonna Cut You Down" 815, 816

"God's in the People" 1537
"The Gods on Tap" 1181
"God's Song (That's Why I Love Mankind)" 1036, 1334
"Goeika" 602
"Gogo" 598
"A Goil Like Me" 993
"Goin' Back" 1450
"Goin' Back to That Feelin'" 113
"Goin' Down the Road" 740
"Goin' East — Chicago" 322
"Goin' East — New York" 322
"Goin' East — St. Louis" 322
"Goin' Home" 357, 681
"Goin' Home with My Children" 656
"Goin' to Broadway" 214
"Goin' to Chicago" 1388
"Goin' to Louisanne" 777
"Goin' Up the Country" 1556
"Going All the Way" 1310
"Going Back to Eden" 468
"Going Down" 649
"Going Down Slowly" 1518
"Going Home" 544
"Going It Alone" 892
"Going Native" 1566
"The Going Out" 1398
"Going-Staying" 1433
"Going Steady" 1687
"Going to Chicago" 729
"Going to Mrs. Brown's" 476
"Going to the Theatre" 1414
"Going Up" 1006
"Gold" 653
"The Gold Band" 375
"Gold! Gold!" 1512
"Gold Is a Fine Thing (Silver Aria)" 92
"Gold Rush in the Sky" 1152
"Goldberg's Gripe" 1743
"A Golden Age" 541
"The Golden Age of Smut" 1273
"The Golden Boat" 1806
"Golden Boy" 603
"The Golden Calf" 647
"The Golden Carnival" 637
"Golden Days" 1354
"Golden Eagle" 1152
"Golden Goblet" 366
"The Golden Rule Song" 589
"Golden Slave" 95
"Golden Slumbers" 1426
"The Golden Wedding" 492
"Goldenhair" 805
"Goldfinger" 1450
"Goldstein, Swank & Gordon" 220
"The Golfer's Psalm" 606
"Golfing Museum" 606
"Golf's Such a Naughty Game" 606
"Gondola Duet" 1131
"Gondola Song" 1131
"Gone" (Alford) 1620
"Gone" (Thomas) 1031
"Gone Are the Days" 505
"Gone Away Blues" 85
"Gone Everywhere But Home" 544
"Gone Missing" 607
"Gone on That Guy" 507
"Gone, the Mountains, the Shady Hills" 362
"Gone to the Movies" 1478
"The Gong Song" 504
"Gonna Be Somebody" 1505
"Gonna Get a Woman" 1603
"Gonna Get Right Some Day" 1151
"Gonna Run" 1296
"Gonna Teach Our Brothers" 1232
"Gonna Win" 378
"Gooch's Song" 818
"Good Advice" 685
"Good as Anybody" (Klein) 1083
"Good as Anybody" (Wood) 466
"Good as It Gets" 1831
"A Good Boy" 767
"Good-By Feet" 27
"Good Bye" 1215
"Good-Bye" 111, 453
"Good Bye Blues" 886
"Good-bye, Judy Garland" 673
"A Good Cigar (A Woman Is Only a Woman but a Good Cigar Is a Smoke)" 301, 577
"Good, Clean Brooklyn" 1412
"Good Connections" 1414
"Good Conservative Values I" 227
"Good Conservative Values II" 227
"Good Conservative Values III" 227
"Good Day" (Coleman) 463
"Good Day" (Eyerly) 717
"Good Enough" 742
"Good Evening, Ev'rybody, It's Been a Lovely Day" 609
"Good Evening, Gentlemen" 609
"Good Evening, Lady Windermere" 13
"Good Fer Nothin' Me" 766
"Good for Nothing" 698
"Good Friends" 237
"Good, Good, Good" 714
"Good, Good Times" 360
"Good Guys and Bad Guys" 1545
"Good Hearts, Rejoice" 1514
"Good Is Good" 417
"Good Little Boy" 1424
"Good Little Girls" 942
"Good Luck" (McAnuff) 364
"Good Luck" (Secunda) 874
"Good Luck to You" 1582, 1677
"A Good Man Is Hard to Find" 1373
"Good Morning" (Brown) 304
"Good Morning" (Shire) 1400
"Good Morning Color Photo" 897
"Good Morning, Dr. Puffin" 870
"Good Morning, Good Morning" 1426
"Good Morning, I'll Put You Through" 720
"'Good Morning!' ... It's The Beatles" 1018
"Good Morning, My Dove" 1179
"Good Morning Starshine" 649
"Good Morrow My Love" 766
"The Good News" 1537
"Good News" 1466
"Good Night, Irene" 777
"Good Night, Poor Harvard" 1282
"A Good Ol' Mammy Song" 215, 1208
"The Good Old American Way" 480
"Good Old Atwater" 902
"The Good Old Days" (Carmines) 614
"The Good Old Days" (Siegel) 1152
"Good Old Days" 1399
"A Good Old-Fashioned Revolutionary" 1480
"Good Old Girl" (Hall) 133
"Good Old Girl" (Martin) 1464
"Good Old Reliable Jake" 462
"The Good Old Ways" 33
"Good Ole Days" 1661
"Good Ole Days (of Sex)" 391
"Good or Bad" 682
"Good People of Leadville" 92
"The Good Ship Caledonia" 151
"Good Sports: Detroit Persons" 1
"Good Thing I Learned to Dance" 1
"Good Things Come" 271
"Good Times" 1037
"The Good Times Are Here" 1375
"Good Times Are Here to Stay" 341
"Good to Be Alive" 973
"Good Triumphs Over Evil" 1511
"Good Vibrations" (Grant) 400
"Good Vibrations" (Wilson) 1046, 1353
"A Good Week" 819
"Goodbye" (Dixon) 476
"Goodbye" (Finn) 430
"Goodbye" (Gould) 135
"Goodbye" (MacDermot) 1638
"Goodbye" (Manning) 489
"Goodbye" (Miranda) 760
"Goodbye" (Salzman) 738
"Goodbye" (Schomer) 1715
"Goodbye Again" 37
"Goodbye and Hello" 265
"Goodbye Flo" 570
"Goodbye for Now" 1491
"Goodbye, Girls, Hello, Yale" 1115, 1116
"Goodbye! Hello!" 1291
"Goodbye Hives" 587
"Goodbye. It's Time for Me to Die" 834
"Goodbye Johnny" 828
"Goodbye Little Dream Goodbye" 1704
"Goodbye, My City" 1445
"Goodbye, My Fancy" 903
"Goodbye, My Lady Love" 695
"Goodbye, My Sweet" 1008
"Goodbye Salome" 1367
"Goodbye Until Tomorrow" 890
"Goodbye, World" 1451
"Goodbyes" 1659
"Goodness Had Nothing to Do with It" 550
"Goodnight" (Brandon) 1550
"Goodnight" (Davis) 388
"Goodnight" (Finn) 764
"Goodnight" (Schmidt) 733
"Goodnight Hymn" 246
"Goodnight Mrs. Astor" 1196
"Goodnight, Sweet Molly" 249
"Goody, Goody" 1138
"Gordita Es Bonita" 920
"Gordo's Law of Genetics" 1121
"Gorgeous" 783
"Gorgeous Kay" 1607
"Gospel" 207
"The Gospel According to Rock" 45
"The Gospel According to the Leopard" 855
"Gospel Car" 1470
"Gospel: Great Day" 238
"Gossip" (Dowell) 1594
"Gossip" (Katsaros) 434, 435
"Gossip" (Smith) 510
"Gossip" (Sondheim) 1557
"Gossip I: Poor Sad Thing ..." 1514
"Gossip II: Up at Dawn ..." 1514
"Gossip III: Warms My Soul ..." 1514
"The Gossip Song" 80
"Gossiping Grapevine" 1576
"Got a Feelin'" 411
"Got a Notion" 710
"Got the World in the Palm of My Hand" 291
"Got to Be a Woman Now" 357
"Got To Find My Way" 1594
"Got to Get a Life" 1508
"Got to Know" 1727
"Got to Sing Me a Song" 1354
"Got un Zayn Mishpet Iz Gerekht (God and His Judgement Are Right)" 604
"Gotham Magazine" 206
"Gotta Be This or That" 527
"Gotta Dance" 954
"Gotta Get Back to You" 123
"Gotta Get Out" 203
"Gotta Get Outta Here" 1084
"Gotta Go West" 599
"Gotta Have a Passion" 272
"Gotta Have Me Go with You" 662
"Gotta Lot of Rhythm in My Soul" 39
"Gotta Pay" 985
"Gotta Pretend" 1034
"La Goulante du Pauvre Jean" 1256, 1257
"Grace" 469
"Grace's Nightmare" 770
"Gracias" 262
"Gracious Living Fantasy" 1403
"Grade 'A' Treatment" 1752
"Graduates of Mrs. Grimm's Learning" 716
"Graduation" 830
"The Graduation Eve Supper" 1601
"Graffiti" 1743
"Grain of Sand" 1136
"Grain of the Salt of the Earth" 288
"Gramophone on Full Blast Denouncing All Men" 1329
"Grand Banks Sequence" 249
"Grand Design" 468
"A Grand Diversion" 1721
"Grand Man" 1438
"Grand March" 569
"The Grand Old Duke of York" 1721
"Grand Opening" 371
"The Grand Parade" 1236
"Le Grand Rape" 636
"Grand Street" 1362
"Grand Tour of the Planets" 1081
"Grand Vizier's Lament" 66
"The Grande Duchess of Burlesque" 1802
"Grandfather Clock in the Hall" 1338
"Grandfathers (Ev'ry Baby's Best Friend)" 652
"Grandioso" 379
"Grandma Small" 387
"Grandma's Diary" 61
"Grandma's Feather Bed" 37
"Grandmere et Grandpere" 963
"Grandpa Meets the Boys" 1601
"Grandpa's Confrontation" 1601
"Granny's Advice" 222
"Granny's Song" 349
"Grant" 722
"Grass Between My Toes" 741
"The Grass Is Always Greener" (Botto) 858
"The Grass Is Always Greener" (Kander) 52
"Grasshop Song" 867
"Grateful" 1514
"Gratitude" 1385
"Gratuitous Nudity" 1110
"Gravel's Coming with Us" 1237
"The Graveyard" 1198
"Graveyard Chant" 107
"Graveyard Rap" 1427
"Gray" 1052
"Graze on My Lips" 1569
"Greased Lightin'" 625
"Greasy Lightnin'" 266
"Great" 450
"The Great-All-American-Power-Driven-Engine" 968
"The Great American TV Show" 627
"Great Balls of Fire" 1353
"A Great Big Kiss" 624
"Great Big Land" 902
"A Great Cathedral" 1671
"Great Connection" 326
"Great Day!" 955, 1096
"Great Explanations" 1427
"Great Gittin' Up Morning" 996
"The Great Highway" 1404
"The Great Immortals" 1787
"The Great Indoors" 1704
"Great Is Thy Faithfulness" 1002
"A Great Lady Golfer" 606
"Great Leap Forward" 664
"A Great Man's Child" 257
"Great Men, Great Days, or The King of the Café Royal" 483
"The Great One" 1293
"The Great Pretender" (Ram) 1046
"The Great Pretender" (*Water Coolers*) 1742
"The Great Purple Butterfly" 707
"Great Roles" 1548
"Great Scot" 631
"The Great Society Waltz" 126, 557, 558, 1273
"The Great Unknown" 1236
"The Great Waltz" 1291
"The Great White Way" 752
"The Great Wind" 1354
"Great Workers for the Cause" 56
"The Great Writer" 1486
"The Greatest Friend" 1613
"The Greatest Man of All" 483
"Greatest Performance" 1761
"The Greatest Practical Joke" 1422
"The Greatest Show" 1320
"Greatest Show on Earth" 1321
"Greathead Shield" 1399
"A Grecian Urn" 22
"Greed" 576
"Greed, Chasing the Thief, Barely Escapes Into Life and Horror" 1592
"Greedy" 502
"Greek Dance" 1160
"Greek to You" 1823
"The Green Automobile" 729
"Green, Chaney, Buster, Slyde" 207
"The Green Flash" 1052

"Green Gravel" 345
"Green Green Dress" 1634
"Green, Green, Green" 1323
"The Green Heart" 633
"The Green Line" 635
"A Green Place" 1287
"Green Pond" 634
"Green-Up Time" 1809
"Greenhorns" 1328
"Greenhouse Blues" 1493
"Greenspons" 1258
"The Greenwich Village Carnival" 637
"Greenwich Village Follies" 636
"Greenwich Village Quartette" 635
"The Greenwich Village Theatre" 635
"Greenwich Village, U.S.A." 638
"Greetings" 1291
"Greetings from the Paddlers on the Sheringham Front" 285
"Greetings from Yorkville" 639
"Greetings to All" 951
"Greetings to You, Sabbath Angels" 284
"Grenadiers" 361
"The Grenadiers (Los Granaderos)" 488
"Gretchen's Lament" 499
"Grey Cloud Over New York" 1200
"The Gripe of the Group" 87
"Gristedes" 1576
"Grocery Boy" 1517
"Groovy Green Man Groovy" 1330
"Gross Anatomy Lecture" 2
"The Ground Was Always in Play" 386
"Groundhog Has Won" 643
"Groundhog Is Becoming Important" 643
"Groundhog Is Going to Trial" 643
"The Group" (Holof, Metee, and Berkowitz) 2
"The Group" (Schalchlin) 892
"Group Analysis" 1448
"A Group Improvisation" 22
"Grovel, Grovel" 833
"Grow Big and Strong, Dear Prince" 889
"Grow for Me" 939
"Grow, Mrs. Goldfarb" 685
"Grow Up, Little Girl" 706
"Grow Where You're Planted" 1232
"Growing" 1148
"Growing Away from Me" 1591
"Growing Bo" 727
"Growing Older" 308
"Growing Up" (Ashwander) 624
"Growing Up" (Kaz) 1209
"Growing Up Catholic" 1155, 1157
"Grumpy Mood" 10
"Guadalajara" 1309
"Guaguanco" 897
"Guantanamera" 262, 533
"La Guarachera" 262
"Guardian Angels" 1383
"Guardians of This Land" 1285
"Guess I'll Hang My Tears Out to Dry" 1210, 1546, 1717
"The Guess-It Hour" 1196
"Guess What from Guess Who?" 1283
"Guess Who Was There" 371
"Guggenheim's Bald Eagle" 871
"Guide My Feet" 1623
"Guided by Love" 865, 866
"Guides" 1550
"Guilty" (Coleman) 463
"Guilty" (Fields) 1445
"Guilty" (*Manhattan Rhythm*) 1015
"The Guilty Ones" 1515
"Guinea Piggin" 1330
"Guiness, Woman" 1659
"Guinevere Among the Grapefruit Peels" 718
"Guitarist" 159
"The Gull in My Life" 277
"Gumby Gets a Nose" 1263
"Gun Scene" 65
"Gun Song" 70, 1492
"Gunfight" 277
"The Gunfighter" (Higgins and Silvestri) 825
"The Gunfighter" (Kent) 1348
"Gunga Dhin" 505
"Gunmetal Blues" 644
"Guns" 1493
"Guns Are Fun" 1739
"Gunze, Gunze, Gunze" 1066
"Guru" 1414
"Gus and Sadie Love Song" 324
"Gus' Triumph (One Verse)" 1375
"Gussy and the Beautiful People" 292
"Gusto" 1379
"Gutter of Love" 1427
"A Guy, A Guy, A Guy" 1164
"The Guy I Love" 1243
"The Guy Who Brought Me" 132
"Gvald Ich Vil Es (I Want It!)" 1382
"Gym Jam Boogie (Come Jam with Us)" 1174
"The Gypsy" 963
"Gypsy Dance" 1218
"A Gypsy Girl Named Carmen" 995
"Gypsy Tango" 431

"Ha-Cha" 263
"Haarlem Nocturne" 646
"Haberdashery Blues" 223
"The Habit" 381
"Hack 'Em" 710
"Had He Kissed Me Tonight" 1514
"Had to Get Up This Morning, Soon" 120
"Had to Give Up Gym" 553
"Hagar Chorus" 363
"Hagar Shipley" 963
"Haifi Melody" 1647
"Hail Britannia" 91
"Hail, Columbia" 852
"Hail, David" 663
"Hail, Hail" 1124, 1537
"Hail, Hallelujah" 1418
"Hail Hio" 1283
"Hail Mary" 1438
"Hail, the Mythic Smew" 870
"Hail the TV Commercial" 1218
"Hail to Peter" 255
"Hail to the Blood" 175
"Hail to the King" 866
"Hail to the Sultan" 66
"Hail to Thee!" 60
"Haim, the Goose-Herder" 1203
"Hair" 649
"Hair Pulling Ballet" 416
"The Haircut" 673
"The Hairdresser" 1158
"The Halala Song" 651
"Halevay Volt Ikh Singl Geven (I Wish I Were Single Again)" 1619
"Half a Couple" 293
"Half a Dream" 1700
"Half a World Away" 1148
"Half-Forgotten Teddy Bear" 981
"Half of Life" 237
"Half of the People" 1029
"Half-Remembered Melody" 949
"Half-Way House" 1754
"Halfway to Heaven" (Chapin) 916
"Halfway to Heaven" (Wheeler) 179
"Hall of Fame" 1615, 1616
"Hall of the Mountain King" 1439
"Hallelujah!" (Hoffman) 1759
"Hallelujah!" (Silverman) 1708
"Hallelujah!" (Youmans) 955
"Hallelujah, Baby!" 807, 1546
"Hallelujah Basketball" 952
"Hallelujah Day" 1423
"Hallelujah, He's on His Way" 408
"Halloween Hayride" 1154
"Hallucinations" 1388
"Halted at the Very Gates of Paradise (A Song of Frustration)" 483
"The Ham Kick" 105
"Ham-Some" 1174
"Hamakom" 100
"Hamburger Heaven" 1692
"Hamlet" 1328
"Hamlet, Prince of Skaters" 1448
"Hamletto" 32
"The Hamley Catalog" 1320
"Hammacher Schlemmer, I Love You" 1606
"Hammerstein's Music Hall" 1287
"Hana Wa" 602
"Hana, Yuki, Kaze" 602
"Hand in Hand" 121
"The Hand of Fate" 860
"A Handbag Is Not a Proper Mother" 448
"Handful of Keys" 18
"Handle Me with Care" 639
"Handle with Care" (Courts) 828
"Handle with Care" (Siegel and Hart) 986
"Hands Across the Table" 1521
"Hands Around" 1323
"The Hands of God" 791
"The Hands of Time" 541
"Handsome Husbands" 332
"Handsome Stranger" 564, 758
"Handy" 1547
"Handy Man Around the House" 1254
"Hang Down Your Head and Die" 655
"Hang Down Your Head, Jane Dooley" 87
"Hang on to the Good Times" 656
"Hangin' Out the Window" 1747
"Hanging Around" 1207
"Hanging Is My Only Sport" 117
"Hanging Johnny" 655
"Hanging Out" 1124
"Hanging Throttlebottom in the Morning" 912
"The Hangman's Plea" 379
"Hank Ladd" 1475
"Hannah Had a Son" 1513
"Hannah Will Take Care of You" 658
"Hannibal's Comin'" 1707
"A Happier Day" 541
"Happier Side" 1147
"Happiest Moment of My Life" 41
"The Happiest People" 272
"Happily Ever After" (Rodgers) 691, 1193
"Happily Ever After" (Sondheim) 1027
"Happily Ever After, After All" 267
"Happily the Days Are Running By" 484
"Happiness" 1828
"Happiness Is" 50, 126
"Happiness Is a Bird" 1261
"Happy" (Eyerly) 717
"Happy" (Gordon) 705
"Happy" (Grusecki) 639
"Happy Am I" 1117
"Happy Anniversary" 726
"Happy as the Day Is Long" 662
"Happy Birthday" (Ford) 656
"Happy Birthday" (MacDermot) 726
"Happy Birthday" (Mathieu) 1415
"Happy Birthday, Darling" 206
"Happy Birthday, Harry" 424
"Happy Birthday Sweet Sixteen" 1551
"Happy Day" 779
"Happy Days Are Here Again" 746, 1092
"The Happy Daze Saloon" 1603
"The Happy End" 660
"Happy Ending" (Weill) 128
"Happy Ending" (Levy) 290
"Happy Ending" (Schmidt) 478
"Happy Ending" (McHugh) 1294
"Happy Ending" (Jordan) 1379
"Happy Families" 1306
"Happy Feet" 955
"Happy House" 535
"A Happy Hukilau" 1221
"Happy Jest Bein' with Me" 215
"Happy Lament" 1066
"A Happy Life" 1051
"Happy Love Affair" 598
"Happy Me" 1294
"Happy New Year" 631
"Happy New Year, Darling" 1048
"Happy Rovin' Cowboy" 657
"Happy Shop" 1458
"Happy Stoned Song" 963
"The Happy Time" 52
"Happy Time" 1518
"Happy Tomorrow" 501
"Happy Wanderer" 1575
"The Happy Washerwoman" 1291
"The Happy Years" 277
"Harbor Lights" 382
"Harbour Lady" 1
"Harbour of Love" 1495
"Hard as a Nail" 1821
"Hard Candy Christmas" 133
"The Hard Core Gang's All Here" 1692
"Hard Hat Stetsons" 93
"Hard-Hat Woman" 2
"Hard Loving Loser" 1356
"Hard Sell" 664
"A Hard Time to Be Single" 665
"Hard Time War Time" 175
"Hard Times" (Herrick) 950
"Hard Times" (Paul) 1361, 1362
"Hard Times" (Sachs) 326
"Hard Times in the Mill" 814
"Hard to Be a Liberal" 1759
"Hard to Be a Pauper" 1051
"Hard to Be Diva" 1522
"Hard to Love" 634
"Hard to Say Goodbye" 1726
"Hard Word" 474
"Hardcore Porn" 1459
"The Hardest Currency" 1701
"Harem Dance" 1160
"Hari Krishna" 467
"Hark" 667
"Hark Hark, the Lark" 1568, 1569
"Hark! The Land Bids Me Tread No More Upon It" 62
"Harlem Blonde Bombshell" 21
"Harlem Follies" 809
"Harlem Hop" 1435
"Harlem River Quiver" 886
"Harlem Streets" 400
"Harlem Sweet Harlem" 221
"Harlem Tour" 221
"Harlem, You're My Girl" 934
"Harlots" 240
"A Harmless Peccadillo" 1412
"Harmonica" 145
"Harmonica Man" 643
"Harmony" (Kayden) 292
"Harmony" (Naylor) 196
"Harmony, Mass." 822
"Harmony, Sweet Harmoni" 74
"Harold Benched" 926
"Harold Wilson Honors Sir George Muffle" 1091
"The Harolds of This World" 100
"Harrigan" 570
"Harry the Hipster" 1576
"Harry, This Time We're Clapping for You" 223
"Harry's a Rat" 1228
"Harry's Letter" 1756
"Harry's Nightmare: Welcome Back, Mr. Witherspoon" 973
"Harry's Rag" 65
"Harry's Resolution" 961
"Harvest Hymn" 135
"Harvest Parlor Game" 926
"Harvey" (Finn) 1375
"Harvey" (Martin and Gray) 1611
"Harvey" (Wallace) 673
"Harvey and Sheila" 685
"Harvey. Come Home" 673
"Harvey Promised to Change the World" 1375
"Has Anybody Here Seen Kelly?" 775
"Has Anybody Seen Our Ship?" 751
"Has Anyone Here Seen My Daddy?" 409
"Has Anyone Here Seen Patti?" 511
"Haschich Fudge" 1222
"Hasseltown" 1659
"The Hat" 448
"Hat and Cane" 766
"A Hat and Cane Song" 1158, 1159
"Hat Crossover" 232
"Hate Song" (Barr) 415
"Hate Song" (Rodgers) 986

"Hats Off" 578
"Hattie's Time" 1343
"Haul on the Bow Line" 740
"Haunted Heart" 1221
"Hav-A-Havana" 1289
"Havana — Lied and Duet" 1773
"Have a Career" 1045
"Have a Drink" 194
"Have a Good Day" 272
"Have a Little Fun" 401, 1136
"Have a Little Sooth on Me" 74
"Have a Nice Day" 413
"Have Another Drink" 417
"Have Feet Will Dance" 886
"Have Gun, Get Gold" 1687
"Have I Got a Girl for You" (Blatt) 676
"Have I Got a Girl for You" (Gallagher) 675
"Have I Got a Girl for You" (Sondheim) 1492
"(Have I Stayed) Too Long at the Fair?" 149, 150
"Have Peace Jo" 941
"Have Piano and Hanky ... Will Travel" 550
"Have Some Pot" 93
"Have They Arrived? (Birth Scene)" 439
"Have They Ever Examined the State of Your Mind?" 609
"Have We Got a Number for You" 1252
"Have You Ever Been on the Stage?" 1414
"Have You Ever Seen a Prettier Little Congress?" 1381
"Have You Got a Lot to Learn" 1245
"Have You Got Charm?" 91
"Have You Heard I've Fallen in Love" 766
"Have You Seen ... ?" 1011
"Have You Seen Her?" 92
"Have You Seen Him, Did He Pass This Way?" 569
"Have You Seen the Princess?" 1679
"Haven't I Seen You Somewhere Before?" 1480
"Haven't We Met?" 1414
"Haven't You Had Enough?" 1416
"Haven't You Wondered" 1707
"Hawaiian Wedding Day" 1763
"Haynt iz Yomtev (Today Is a Holiday)" 1453
"The Hayride" 1237
"A Hazardous Experiment" 1721
"He" 933
"He Ain't Scared of Nothing" 263
"He and She" 201
"He Brought Me Out" 591
"He Called Me" 739
"He Can, I Can" 598
"He Comes Home Tired" 929
"He Could Show Me" 1154
"He Did It, She Did It!" 575
"He Didn't Leave It Here" 219
"He Didn't Oughter" 436
"He Eats" 860
"He Follows Me Around" 388
"He Gon' Stay" 313
"He Had the Callin'" 809
"He Is an Animal" 708
"He Is Coming" 1042
"He Is My Horse" 1762
"He Is My Son" 1458
"He Is with You" 1700
"He Knows Where to Find Me" 631
"He Lived By His Wits" 394
"He Looked at Me" 587
"He Loves Her" 1148
"He Loves to Make a Fuss" 1057
"He May Be Your Man but He Comes to See Me Sometimes" 165
"He Never Did That Before" 1499
"He Once Was Beautiful" 419
"He Plays the Cello" 1499
"He Reminds Her of His Father" 301
"He Says" 203
"He She We" 1274
"He Should Have Been Mine" 9
"He Thinks I'm Weak" 1727
"He Threw Out the Ball" 377
"He Tossed a Coin" 1381
"He Touched Me" 210
"He Was Thinking of You" 1402
"He Wasn't Talking to Me" 808
"He Who Loves Worst Loves Most" 1614
"He Won't Leave!" 1723
"He Wouldn't Care" 388
"Head Down the Road" 93
"Head in the Stars" 98
"The Head Song" 710
"Headlines" 1445
"The Headmaster Ritual" 1545
"Heads or Tails" (Andreopoulos) 646
"Heads or Tails" (Murfitt) 323
"The Healing Chant (I)" 948
"The Healing Chant (II)" 948
"Health Club Rap" 1300
"Hear Me, O Lord, I Beseech Thee" 1563
"Hear Me Out" 760
"Hear My Song" 1498
"Hear No Evil" 1329
"Hear the Birds" 1438
"Hear the Guns" 175
"Hear Your Voice" 697
"Hearing Voices" 643
"Heart an' Hand" 503
"Heart and Music" 997, 1121
"Heart and Soul" (Goodman) 206
"Heart and Soul" (Carmichael) 527, 1694
"The Heart's a Wonder" 288
"Heartbeat" 1635
"Heartbreak" 206
"Heartbreak Hall of Fame" 703
"Heartbreaker" 1298
"The Heat" 1554
"The Hear Is On" 1329
"Heat Wave" 69, 1315
"Heather's Fantasy Ballet" 295
"Heave-Ho" 1736
"Heaven" (Bone and Fenton) 501
"Heaven" (Carmines) 1349
"Heaven" (Montgomery) 958
"Heaven Come and Help Us Out" 255
"Heaven Help My Heart" 275
"Heaven Hop" 63
"Heaven in Your Eyes" 255
"Heaven Must Be Missing an Angel" 1623
"Heaven Must Have Been Smiling" 710
"Heaven on Earth" 1181
"Heaven to Me" 469
"Heavenly Body" 1142
"Heavenly Party" 1301
"Heavenly Sustenance" 1231
"Heaviest Fight in New Orleans" 1733
"Hebrew Benediction" 647
"Hector's Dream" 208
"Hector's Song" 600
"Hedwig's Lament" 680
"Heebie-Jeebie Furies" 175
"The Heebie Jeebies" 681
"The Heffley & Browne Secretarial School" 543
"Heidi, Are You There?" 742
"The Heirophant (Perfection) Passes Through Utopia" 1592
"The H'Elegant Homes of H'England" 1467
"Helen" 682
"Helen Is Always Willing" 600
"Helen Quit Your Yellin'" 1468
"Helena" 80
"Helena's Solution" 80
"Helicopter, Helicopter" 386
"Heliopolis" 1330
"Helium" 610
"Hell" (Carmines) 1349
"Hell" (Green and Stamper) 1315
"He'll Bring the Roses" 1511
"He'll Come to Me Crawling" 1539
"Hell Hath No Fury" 661
"He'll Never Know" 1224
"A Hell of a Hole" 912
"Hell of a Job" 143
"Hell to Pay" 755
"He'll Understand" 592, 1672
"Hellahahana" 149, 150
"Hello" (Davis) 388
"Hello" (Zur) 1701
"Hello Again" 683
"Hello, Boys" 1508
"Hello, Broadway!" 570
"Hello, Central, Give Me No Man's Land" 829
"Hello Central Park" 557
"Hello, Columbus" 556
"Hello Doc" 726
"Hello, Dolly" 818, 877
"Hello Egypt" 1245
"Hello, Everybody" 134, 1615, 1616
"The 'Hello Fellas' TV Special World Tour" 1622
"Hello, Ferryman" 1458
"Hello, Good Morning" 1166, 1167
"Hello, Hello" (MacDermot) 860
"Hello, Hello" (Moritz) 507
"Hello, Hello" (*Potluck!*) 1291
"Hello, Hello America!" 1212
"Hello Hubert" 1153
"Hello, I Love You, Goodbye" 1420
"Hello, I Must Be Going" 672
"Hello, It's Me Again" 278
"Hello, Jeremy" 873
"Hello, Little Chillin'!" 1085
"Hello, Little Girl" 1492
"Hello, Ma Baby" 1643
"Hello, Manhattan!" 1016
"Hello, Mr. Church" 1761
"Hello Muddah, Hello Fadduh" 685
"Hello, New York" 636
"Hello, Out There" 107
"Hello Peter We're Going Out" 873
"Hello Stranger!" 1512
"Hello Titanic" 1469
"Hello, Tom" 1033
"Hello, Tucky!" 993
"Hello Twelve, Hello Thirteen, Hello Love" 283
"Hello World" 152
"Hello Yank" 90, 1031
"A Helluva Day" 764
"Helluva Night" 372
"Help" 400
"Help Is on the Way" (Ellstein) 1821
"Help Is on the Way" (Friedman) 929
"Help Me Find a Way" 470
"Help Me Girl" 1551
"An Help Meet I" 468
"Help's on the Way" 502
"A Helping Hand and a Willing Heart" 407
"Henery the Eighth, I Am" 581
"Hennie Soup" 1375
"Henrietta's Elegy" 633
"Henry Is Where It's At" 1504
"Henry's Dream Theme" 1504
"Her Anxiety" 707
"Her Career" 338
"Her Husband" 114
"Her Majesty" 1426
"Her Royal Highness" 1320, 1321
"Her Song" 1283
"The Herb Song" 1380
"Here Am I" 1366
"Here and Now" 1554
"Here Are We" 34
"Here Beside Me" 1192
"Here Comes the Ballad" 388
"Here Comes the Hot Tamale Man" 553
"Here Comes the Night" 1402
"Here Comes the Peanut Man" 1232
"Here Comes the Rabbi" 587
"Here Comes the Sun" 234
"Here I Am" (Dolginoff) 1195
"Here I Am" (Kennon) 484
"Here I Am" (Menten) 716
"Here I Am" (Merrill) 1752
"Here I Am" (Sticco) 267
"Here I Am Again" 159
"(Here I Am on the) Bottom End of Bleecker Street" 605
"Here I Come" 1755
"Here I Go Bananas!" 1283
"Here I Stand" 257
"Here in a Bog" 395
"Here in Love" 285
"Here in My Bed" 1499
"Here in the Playbill" 214
"Here Is a Rural Fellow" 62
"Here It Happened" 717
"Here, Really Here" 1410
"Here They Come" 586
"Here They Come Now" 701
"Here Tonight Off-Broadway" 1077
"Here We Are" (Glines) 587
"Here We Are" (McAnuff) 364
"Here We Go" 465
"Here We Go Again" (Goldstein) 712
"Here We Go Again" (Turner) 850
"Here You Come Again" 854
"Heredity-Environment" 1481
"Here's a Love Song" 1348
"Here's My Secret" 938
"Here's That Rainy Day" 824, 1210
"Here's the Story" 71
"Here's the Thing" 1458
"Here's to the Crabgrass" 685
"Here's to the Health, and Here's to the Wealth of Bayard, Brandon and Bayard" 951
"Here's to You, Mrs. Rodreguez" 667
"Here's What a Mistress Ought to Be" 1440
"Hermes Finds a Friend" 1291
"Hero" 727
"Hero and Leander" 1404
"Hero of My Dreams" 66
"Hero Time" 1348
"Hero Worship" 1152
"Heroes" 952, 1283
"The Heroes Come Home" 600
"Heroism" 1780
"A Hero's Love" 1400
"Herr Jakob Schmidt" 880, 882
"Herringbone" 690
"He's a Comin'" 705
"He's a Hit!" 1749
"He's a Hit-and-Run Guy!" 1723
"He's a Peculiar Guy" 920
"He's a Tall Man" 820
"He's Back!" 673
"He's Beginning to Look a Lot Like Me" 357
"He's Coming" 1253
"He's Funny That Way" 1198, 1540
"He's Got the Whole World in His Hands" 120
"He's Gotta Go" 9
"He's Nice, He's Clean ..." 436
"He's Not an Aristocrat" 672
"He's Not for Me" 631
"He's Not There" 372
"He's 1-A in the Army" 1764
"He's So Near" 95
"He's So Shy" 854
"He's Sure the Boy I Love" 854
"He's the Child, the Child I Bore" 1418
"He's the Right Man (March)" 722
"He's Waltzing You Around" 788
"He's Wonderful" 1452
"Heterosexual" 450
"Hey!" 184
"Hey Boy" 1397
"Hey Chico" 203
"Hey, Eddie!" 1723
"Hey Eddie! Wanna Go Bowling Tonight?" 1723
"Hey General" 194
"Hey, Good Lookin'" 657, 1015
"Hey Groundhog" 643
"Hey Guys! It's Whisky!" 1723
"Hey Ho, the Wind and the Rain" 1568, 1569
"Hey, I'm Talkin' to You, Beethoven!" 313
"Hey Jack" 1459
"Hey Jacques" 924
"Hey, Joe" (Robinson) 1399
"Hey, Joe" (Strouse) 603
"Hey, Kid" (Preston) 1365
"Hey, Kid" (Riddle) 322
"Hey Kiddo, You're Through" 416
"Hey Lady" (Boesky and McCoy) 471
"Hey Lady" (Elliot) 1197
"Hey, Little Boy" 362
"Hey Look No Crying" 1717
"Hey, Ma" 692
"The 'Hey, Ma, You Were Right' Cantata" 61
"Hey, Mister!" 92
"Hey Now" 844

"Hey, Poppa" 824
"Hey, Sweet Momma" 986
"Hey, That's No Way to Say Good-bye (Goodbye)" 963, 1471
"Hey There Fans" 1524
"Hey There, Little Robin, I'm Back Agin" 1563
"Hey, There, Single Guy/Gal" 739
"Hey Twa Nah" 120
"Hey, What's This?" 831
"Hey, World" 915
"Heym ofn Range" 1658
"Hi" (Hurwit) 1433
"Hi" (Lasser) 1033
"Hi" (Young) 45
"Hi de hi de hi, Hi de hi de ho" 336
"Hi De Ho" 1591
"Hi-Fly" 156
"Hi Grandma" 719
"Hi, Mama!" 362
"Hi, Paisano" 693
"Hi There, Joan" 219
"Hi There!" 834
"Hi Ya Kid" 726
"Hickerie, Dickerie, Dock" 1085
"Hickory, Dickory" 1780
"Hide & Seek" 607
"High Adventure" 727
"High Air" 1399
"High and Low" 348, 1606
"High Class Bums" 370
"High Finance" 350
"The High Holidays" 1765
"High Hopes" 1210
"High in the Sky" 1374
"High Is Better Than Low" 1606
"High Lonesome" 175
"High Number Wins" 1701
"High Risk for Afraids" 1600
"The High Road" 1042
"High School" 580, 719
"High School Diplomas" 857
"High School Ladies at 5 (Five) O'Clock" 763, 764, 765
"High School Prom" 1206
"High Up" 1594
"Higher" (Butler) 1423
"Higher" (*The Sunshine Train*) 1559
"Higher" (Sly and the Family Stone) 1664
"Higher and Higher" (Brandon) 82
"Higher and Higher" (Jackson, Smith, and Miner) 55
"Higher and Higher" (Wilson) 790
"Higher Education" 134
"Higher Ground" 996
"Higher Than High" 1025
"Highway 57" 1317
"Highway Narrows" 326
"Highway of Your Heart" 1613
"Hija Mia" 1336
"Hillbilly Hambone" 696
"Hillbilly Women Go Home" 696
"The Hills of Tomorrow" 1491
"Him, Them, It, Her" 973
"Himalaya" 1020
"The Hinkey Dee" 570
"Hinky Dinky Parlez (Parlay) Vous (Voo)" 740, 1096
"Hinton Went Down" 229
"Hip Hooray" 556, 557
"Hip Hooray for America" 667
"Hip Hop Rant" 207
"Hip-Hop Ya Don't Stop" 804
"The Hired Hands" 1720
"His Eye Is on the Sparrow" 221, 736, 996, 1559
"His Family Tree" 1250
"His Highness" 290
"His Little World" 68
"His Own Peculiar Charm" 848
"His Rocking Horse Ran Away" 1571
"His Will Be Done" 166
"His Wonderful Eye" 1402
"The History of Stand-Up Comedy" 1622
"Hit 'Em Where It Hurts" 1135
"Hit Me with a Hot Note" 55
"Hit That Jive, Jack" 35
"Hit the Ladies" 725, 1097
"Hit the Road, Jack" 646, 1623
"Hitchhiking Across America" 997
"Hittin'" 207
"H.M.S. Brownstone" 160, 381, 535
"Ho, Hee" 120
"Ho-Hum" 1202
"Hob Mich Lieb" 119
"Hobby Horses" 1702
"The Hobo's Song" 1034
"Hockney-Blue Eyes" 910
"Hoedown" 1323
"Hoffa Love Is Better Than None" 1142
"Hog-Tie Your Man" 102
"Hoger and the Turks" 1502
"Hoger's Lament" 1502
"Hokunani" 1221
"Hokunani's Prayer" 1221
"Hold Down the Fort" 830
"Hold Me" (Lasser) 1033
"Hold Me" (Unknown) 535
"Hold Me, Bat Boy" 106
"Hold Me Gently" 183
"Hold Me Thusly" 304, 672
"Hold, Monsters!" 1270
"Hold My Baby Back" 1375
"Hold On" (Darway) 1538
"Hold On" (Gordon) 413
"Hold On" (McLean) 67
"Hold On" (Mo' and Edwards) 1631
"Hold On Tight" 682
"Hold That Crown" 267
"Hold the Fort" 740
"Hold Tight, Hold Tight" 1571
"Holden and Phoebe" 1069, 1273
"Holding the Bag" 416
"Holding to the Ground" 473
"Hole-in-the-Head Blues" 639
"Holiday in the Kibbutz" 617
"Holier Than Thou" 1155, 1157
"Hollow" 1072
"Hollow Days, Mellow Days" 844
"Hollow Faces" 1283
"Hollywood" (Cohen) 1829
"Hollywood" (Ellstein) 1342
"Hollywood" (Gallagher) 675
"Hollywood 'n' Vinyl" 89
"Hollywood Canteen" 1571
"Hollywood Folk Song" 1661
"Hollywood Has Got Her" 1149
"Hollywood Lullaby" 456
"Hollywood Opera" 700
"The Hollywood Piece" 1263
"Hollywood Rhythm" 599
"Hollywood Scene" 1466
"The Hollywood Sign" 1584
"Hollywood Surplus" 986
"Holy and Innocent" 1146
"Holy Ghost, Don't Leave Me" 166
"Holy Ghost Ride" 453
"Holy God" 1650
"Holy Ground" 775
"Holy Hanna" 110
"Holy Little World" 284
"The Holy Man and the New Yorker" 371, 1451
"Holy Mystery" 860
"Holy Spirit, Good Morning" 1402
"Home" (Berkowitz) 1060
"Home" (Carmines) 453
"Home" (Gershwin) 1172
"Home" (Hoffman) 1514
"Home" (Kander) 1685
"Home" (Kennon) 484
"Home" (Offenbach) 190
"Home" (Shimoda) 602
"Home" (Van Peebles) 266
"Home" (Weinberg) 1600
"Home Again" (King) 1591
"Home Again" (Schwartz) 248
"Home Away from Home" 698
"Home Ballet" 266
"Home Folks" 996
"Home for Christmas" 1577
"The Home for Wayward Girls" 1218, 1752
"A Home for You" 106
"Home from the Sea" 510
"The Home Front Farm Brigade" 1577
"Home in Mississippi" 149, 150
"Home Is a State of Mind" 922
"Home Is the Entire World" 333
"Home Is Where You Hang Your Hat" 1688
"A Home Movie" 1155, 1157
"Home Never Leaves You" 260
"Home on the Range" 261
"Home on the River" 864
"Home Study" 1209
"Home Sweet Home" (Goggin) 89
"Home Sweet Home" (Patterson) 1385
"Home Sweet Home" (Payne) 695
"Home Sweet Home" (Siegel) 1585, 1586
"Home Sweet Home" (Unknown) 553
"Home Town Girl" 1594
"Homeless" 1715
"The Homeless Lady's Revenge" 1121
"Homeless Suite" 1760
"Homely Woman" 1030
"Homesick" 1707
"Homesick for Hell" 1301
"Homesick in Our Hearts" 1566
"Hometown Blues of New Orleans" 240
"Homeward" 1060
"Homework" 930
"Hominy Grits" 641
"L'Homme a la Moto" 1257
"Homo Haven Fight Song" 1600
"Homosexual Priests" 1765
"Honest Confession Is Good for the Soul" 1396
"Honest Honore" 1652
"Honest John's Game" 203
"Honest Woman" 278
"Honest Women" (reprise version of "Honest Woman") 278
"Honesty" 416
"Honey and Lemon" 8
"Honey in the Honeycomb" 238
"Honey Love" 1434
"A Honey to Love" 1566
"Honeymoon Choo-Choo" 1780
"Honeymoon Dance" 395
"The Honeymoon Is Over" (Dolan) 538
"The Honeymoon Is Over" (Schmidt) 733, 1451
"The Honeymooners" 1069
"Honeypot" 1
"The Honeysuckle and the Bee" 1639
"Honeysuckle Rose" 18, 212, 221, 1350
"Honeysuckle Vine" 1636
"Hong Kong" 68
"Hong Kong Gong" 745
"Honky" 1760
"Honky Jewish Boy" 86
"Honky Tonk Blues" 657
"Honky Tonk Girl" 323
"Honky-Tonk Highway" 703
"Honky Tonk Merry Go Round" 39
"Honky Tonk Queens" 179
"Honolulu" 324
"Honor" 1379
"Honor Lost" 476
"Honor to the Dying Lamb" 1762
"An Honorary Colonel" 1412
"Honour" 33
"The Hook" 410
"Hooked!" 948
"Hooker in the Snow" 1693
"Hoola, from Coney Isle" 1543
"The Hooligan's Hop" 871
"Hooray for Hollywood" 428, 1096
"Hooray for Love" 662
"Hooray for the Judge" 1034
"Hooray for Us!" 622
"Hootenanny with Peter, Paul and Irving" 1276
"Hooters Air" 1128
"Hootsatsa" 1619
"Hope" 915
"Hopes an' Dreams" 313
"Hora" 119
"Horace!" 92
"Horace, What Is This?" 92
"Horehound Compound I" 1326
"Horehound Compound II" 1326
"Horehound Compound III" 1326
"Horn's Aria of Distress" 1329
"Horns of an Immoral Dilemma" 633
"The Horse" (Friedman) 1038
"The Horse" (Riddle) 322
"Horse Rise" 246
"Horsin' Around" 781
"Hose Boys" 494
"The Hospital" 1788
"Host of Hosts" 1595
"Hostess with the Mostess of Them All" 378
"Hot as Hades" 1476
"The Hot Canary" 1575
"Hot Chocolate and Marshmallow" 786
"Hot Feet" 886
"Hot Fun" 207
"Hot Grog" 710
"Hot Honey Rag" 1656
"Hot Ice" 1365
"Hot Lunch" 1
"Hot Monkey Love" 424
"Hot Pants Dance" 1307
"Hot Shot" 1301
"Hot Stuff" 1494
"Hot Tamale Tango" 766
"A Hot Time in the Old Town Tonight" 1643
"Hot Time in the Town of Berlin" 1764
"Hot Times in the Ole Town Tonight" 553
"Hot Tomato Soup" 1325
"Hot Water Bottles" 714
"Hotel Del Rio" 370
"Hotel Passionato" 714
"Hottentot Potentate" 1606
"Houdini Tricks" 1235
"The Hour for Thee and Me" 695
"The Hour Is Ripe" 1274
"A House Divided" 1152
"A House Full of People" 316
"House in Arlington" 1410
"A House Is Not a Home" (Bacharach) 83
"A House Is Not a Home" (Silver) 758
"The House of Don Pasquale" 1146
"House of Flowers" 669, 715
"A House of Gold" 657
"House of Joy" 476
"House of Leather Theme" 716
"House on Coney Island" 1195
"A House on the Ohio" 858
"House Rules" 323
"House Un-American Activities Blues Dream" 1356
"The House Watches" 947
"The House We Live In" 641
"A House with a Little Red Barn" 1196
"Housekeeping Duet" 1807
"Housewares Employee" 462
"The Housing Cha-Cha" 504
"How About Dinner at My Place?" 206
"How About Us Last Nite" 638
"How About You?" 511
"How About You and Me" 466
"How Am I Doin', Dad?" 667
"How Am I'm Gonna Make It?" 1308
"How America Got Its Name" 763, 764, 765
"How Are You Goin' to Wet Your Whistle" 457
"How Beautiful It Was" 1483
"How Beautiful the Night Is" 1756
"How Beautifully Blue the Sky" 1270
"How Black the Garden" 1416
"How Black Was My Valley" 241
"How Can 59 Million People Be So Dumb?" 227
"How Can Anyone So Sweet" 638
"How Can I Be Sure" 1551
"How Can I Keep from Singing" 777
"How Can I Leave Here?" 491
"How Can I Leave You Again" 37
"How Can I Lose You" 1404
"How Can I Say Goodbye?" 1831
"How Can I Tell?" 1076
"How Can I Tell Him She Loves Me?" 147
"How Can the Cat Cross the Water?" 1821
"How Can You Tell" 1450

"How Can You Tell an American?" 128, 1809
"How Can You Write a Song About Manhattan When They've All Been Written Before?" 497
"How Clear" 717
"How Come?" 280
"How Could I Know?" 1752
"How Could I Let You Leave Me" 1702
"How Could We Be Wrong?" 1160
"How Could You Do This to Someone Who Robbed for You? (Prison Music)" 1375
"How Dare He" 360
"How Did Freud Know?" 952
"How Did I Come Across" 1472
"How Did This Happen to Me" 489
"How Did We Come to This?" 1778
"How Do I Feel?" 1452
"How Do I Know You're Not Mad, Sir?" 962
"How Do I Say I Love You?" 1760
"How Do I Tell You?" 1237
"How Do They Ever Grow Up?" 867
"How Do You Die?" 958
"How Do You Do?" (Besoyan) 935
"How Do You Do?" (Engeran) 1151
"How Do You Do?" (Goldstein) 712
"How Do You Do?" (Lustig) 1051
"How Do You Do It Mabel" 457
"How Do You Find the Words?" 448
"How Do You Follow a Star" 3
"How Do You Get to the Desert?" 1050
"How Do You Keep the Music Playing?" 1210
"How Do You Like Your Men" 1298
"How Do You Love a Girl Like That?" 742
"How Do You Say?" 778
"How Do You Stop Loving Someone?" 1774
"How Does a King Decide" 1441
"How Does It Start?" 1433
"How Does She Do It?" 1301
"How Doth the Apple Butterfly" 1236
"How Dreamlike" 1330
"How Far Can You Follow" 1078
"How Fine It Is (to Name Things)" 1708
"How Glory Goes" 503
"How Good Is It" 1342
"How Great It Is to Be a Bird" 1787
"How Great Thou Art" 592
"How Heavy Do I Journey" 1569
"How High Can a [Little] Bird Fly" 1606
"How High the Moon" 1196, 1571
"How Hollywood Actresses Find Their Names (Part I)" 1218
"How Hollywood Actresses Find Their Names (Part II)" 1218
"How I Feel" 1038
"How I Got Over" 592
"How I Love Your Thingamajig" 726
"How I Saved Roosevelt" 70
"How It All Began" 492
"How Jolly Our Folly" 1152
"How Like Heaven" 1514
"How Little I Know" 1514
"How Little We Know (How Little It Matters)" 1210, 1493
"How Little We've Learned" 161, 162, 163
"How Long Has It Been" 66
"How Long Has This Been Going On?" 955
"How Long Have We Been in This House?" 951
"How Long's It Gonna Last, Sam?" 1563
"How Lovely, How Lovely" 652
"How Lovely Is Eve" 1708
"How Lovely to Be a Woman" 237
"How Low Can a Little Worm Go?" 1606
"How Lucky Can You Get" 52
"How Many" 1505
"How Many Rainbows" 1207
"How Many Women" 275
"How Marvin Eats His Breakfast" 763, 764, 765
"How Much Do You Want Me to Bear?" 815, 816
"How Much Love" 59
"How Much Money" 1063
"How Much to Buy My Dream?" 576
"How Nice for You" 1692
"How Not to Win a Boy Friend" 1765
"How Now Frau Brown?" 1091
"How Now Voyager" 700
"How Our Garden Grows — Fall" 1237
"How Our Garden Grows — Spring" 1237
"How Peaceful Is the Evening" 1608
"How Quick They Forget" 727
"How Shall I See You Through My Tears?" 615
"How She Glows" 1594
"How Should I Your True Love Know?" 1437
"How Solemn" 903
"How Soon Is Now?" 1545
"How Strange" 1671
"How Strange the Silence" 332
"How Strange You Are" 1063
"How Sweet Is Peach Ice Cream" 466, 1118
"How Sweet It Is to Be Loved by You" 1623
"How Sweetly Friendship Binds" 827
"How That Things Are Rough" 1635
"How the Body Falls Apart" 763, 765
"How They Do, Do" 571
"How Thou Art Changed" 1443
"How to Be Hot" 1693
"How to Become the Lightest Soldier in the History of the U.S. Army" 871
"How to Get Out of a Taxi" 1206
"How to Get Rich" 1635
"How to Get Rich Quick" 871
"How to Sell a Fall-Out Shelter" 1649
"How to Steal an Election" 722, 780
"How to Succeed in Business Without Really Trying" 1431
"How to Survive" 128, 1626
"How Was Your Day?" 712
"How We Get Down" 634
"How We Get the News" 573
"How We Met" 1234
"How We Would Like Our Man" 985
"How? What? Why?" 884
"How Will I Live Now" 889
"How Wonderful It Is" 93
"How Ya Gonna Keep 'Em Down on the Farm?" 1096
"How You've Changed" 276
"How Young You Were Tonight" 90, 1031
"How'd You Like to Spoon with Me?" 883
"How'm I Doin'" (Lewis) 664
"How'm I Doin'" (Strouse) 1037
"How'm I Doing?" 1759, 1761
"How's Chances?" 69
"How's Elsie" 1754
"How's It Gonna End?" 406
"How's Your Romance?" 367, 567
"How's Your Uncle" 886
"Howl Part II" 729
"H.R.H. and N.Y.C." 436
"Hudl Mitn Shtrudl (Hufl with the Shrtudl)" 1619
"Huggin' and Chalkin'" 1373
"Hula Hoop" 319
"Huliet Huliet Kinderlech (Children, Enjoy Yourselves)" 1382
"Hulla-Baloo-Balay" 1008
"Human, a Grace Note" 1020
"The Human Body" 391
"The Human Heart" 1191
"Human Nature" 1135
"Human Side of the News" 60
"The Human Species" 1787
"The Human Thing" 958
"Humanity" 1034
"A Hummingbird" 469
"Humor Without Tears" 241
"Humpin' Hips" 396
"Humpty Dumpty" 27
"Humpty Dumpty Heart" 1764
"Hunca Munca" 1827
"Hunchy" 1584
"A Hundred and Twenty-Fifth Street" 9
"A Hundred Easy Ways to Lose a Man" 1224
"A Hundred Thousand Ways" 316
"A Hundred Years Ago" 249
"Hundreds of Girls" 818
"Hundreds of Hats" 377, 727
"Hundreds of Stories" 760
"Hundsvieh" 65
"Hunker Down Cowboy" 322
"Hunky Dory" 237
"Huns/British" 1414
"The Hunters" 938
"Hunting Song" 1654
"Huntrer Trials" 135
"Hurdy-Gurdies" 361
"Hurricane" 634
"Hurry" 1029
"Hurry Home" 822
"Hurry, Hurry" 1291
"Hurry, Uncle Donal" 1438
"Hurt Somebody" 1631
"The Hurt They Write About" 1580
"Husband of Mine" 1264
"Husbands Beware" 979
"Hush" 592
"Hush, Here Come the Queen and Anthony" 62
"Hush-Hush" 1393
"Hush, Hush! Not a Word" 1270
"Hush My Sweet Children" 278
"Hush Now" 1434
"Hush Somebody's Calling My Name" 1623
"Hushabye" 740
"The Hustler: A Five-Minute Opera" 467
"Hustlers Hookers Whores" 370
"The Hustling Executive" 82
"Hymn" (aka "Hymn to Aten") 20
"Hymn" (Blitzsein) 848
"Hymn" (Britten) 1229
"Hymn" (Gould) 135
"Hymn" (Ekstrom) 391
"Hymn" (Weinberg) 573
"Hymn" (Sterner) 971
"The Hymn of Shame" 730
"A Hymn to Her" 1514
"Hymn to Intellectual Beauty" 1443
"Hymn to Peace" 128, 827
"A Hymn to Peace" 826
"Hymn to Spring" 643
"Hymn to the House" 1815
"Hymn to the Nobility" 460
"Hymne a L'Amour" 1256, 1257
"Hymns from the Darkness" 453

"I" 1060
"I Adore You" 550
"I Ain't Gonna Let Nobody Turn Me Around" 736
"I Ain't Got Time" 1830
"I Ain't Had My Fill" 194
"I Ain't Had Your Woman" 790
"I Ain't Looking Back" 179
"(I Ain't Never Done Nothing to) Nobody" 221, 1373
"I Ain't Surprised" 1563
"I Also Have a Heart (Tambien Yo, Tego Mi Corazoncito)" 488
"I Always Knew" 58
"I Always Thought the Army" 609
"I Am" 1058
"I Am a Child" 1397
"I Am a Cloud" 1330
"I Am a Handsome Prince" 834
"I Am a Little Worm" 831
"I Am a Pirate King" 460
"I Am a Preacher of the Lord" 453
"I Am a Prince" 290
"I Am a Splendid American Man" 32
"I Am a Tailor's Daughter" 147
"I Am a Travelling Poet" 1468
"I Am a Vietnam Veteran" 720
"I Am a Windsong" 278
"I Am a Zombie" 1832
"I Am All Ablaze" 246
"I Am Alone" 1416
"I Am an Absence" 834
"I Am an Animal" 1128
"I Am an Evangelist" 453
"I Am Beauty" 1514
"I Am Child" 1397
"I Am Easily Assimilated" 244
"I Am Famous" 927
"I Am Going to Dance" 1236
"I Am Here" 1034
"I Am Here at the Place Where Time Began" 720
"I Am Here to Stay" 1159
"I Am Home" 3
"I Am Hong Kye-Hun" 889
"I Am Hungry" 114
"I Am in Dance Class" 222
"I Am My Beloved" 614
"I Am No Longer Beautiful" 431
"I Am No One" 1139
"I Am Not Free" 1330
"I Am Not Gone" 1638
"I Am Not Interested in Love" 1689
"I Am Not Listening" 419
"I Am Not Old" 1582, 1677
"I Am Old and I Cannot Sleep" 1139
"I Am Playing Me" 1645
"I Am Reeling" 285
"I Am Royal" 1380
"I Am Saint Jacques' Pilgrim" 1437
"I Am Sick and Sullen" 62
"I Am Sick of Love" 975
"I Am the Boy" 654
"I Am the Landlord" 257
"I Am the Light" 1558
"I Am the Man" 790, 1739
"I Am the Next" 1035
"I Am the Nice Nurse" 1121
"I Am the President" 255
"I Am the Reverend Olin Blitch" 1563
"I Am the River" 1708
"I Am the Sign" 1392
"I Am the Very Model of a Modern Major-General" 1270
"I Am the Wife of Mao Tsetung" 1139
"I Am This Place" 293
"I Am Wearing a Hat" 763, 764, 765
"I Am You" 968
"I Am Yours" 89, 743
"I Been 'Buked and I Been Scorned" 815, 816
"I Been Up in Hell" 1307
"I Beg Your Pardon" 92
"I Believe" (Drake, et al.) 1487
"I Believe" (Eliran) 401, 1136
"I Believe" (Sheik) 1515
"I Believe" (Unknown) 1540
"I Believe" (Walker) 38
"I Believe in a New World" 1349
"I Believe in God" 1029
"I Believe in Music" 1096
"I Believe in Survival" 1392
"I Believe in the Man" 223
"I Believe in You" 1491
"I Believe in You and Me" 1623
"I Believe My Body" 913
"I Belong" 980
"I Belong Right Here" 107
"I Belong to Hollywood" 1584
"I Bless You" 59
"I Blow My Nose" 1222
"I Bought a Bicycle" 1107
"I Came to London" 476
"I Came to Town" 1638
"I Can Bend My Arms" 465
"I Can Bite Your Head Off Any Day" 1789
"I Can Carry a Tune" 726
"I Can Change!" 184
"I Can Cook, Too" 1185, 1186

"I Can Count on You" 731
"I Can Dance" 1451
"I Can Do Better Than That" 890
"I Can Do It Myself" 1620
"I Can Feel" 279
"I Can Feel Him" 1423
"I Can Give You Music" 1035
"I Can Hardly Believe It's You" 1815
"I Can Heal You" 1459
"I Can Hold You" 929
"I Can Keep Still" 1139
"I Can Learn" 235
"I Can Live with That" 739
"I Can Live with That!" 673
"I Can Make It" 279, 464
"I Can Never Get Anywhere on Time" 348
"I Can Never Go Home Again" 115
"I Can Paddle My Own Canoe" 1470
"I Can Pass" 1607
"I Can See Him Clearly" 1585
"I Can See It" 478
"I Can See You Here" 770
"I Can Sing" 1584
"I Can Stay" 57
"I Can Take It" 1594
"I Can't Be Bothered Now" 1656
"I Can't Believe It's Real" 980
"I Can't Believe That You're in Love with Me" 165
"I Can't Dance" 685
"I Can't Find My Wife" 1131
"I Can't Give You Anything but Love (Baby)" 18, 165, 886
"I Can't Go On" 444
"I Can't Help It" 790
"I Can't Help It (If I'm Still in Love with You)" 657
"I Can't Keep Running in Place" 731
"I Can't Make It Anymore" 605
"I Can't Pretend" 1713
"I Can't Recall" 633
"I Can't Remember" (Downs) 486
"I Can't Remember" (Frandsen, et al.) 1495
"I Can't Remember" (Moross) 569
"I Can't Remember" (Sankey) 605
"I Can't Remember Living Without Loving You" 781
"I Can't Sit Still" 1365
"I Can't Sleep" 764, 765
"I Can't Stop" 1345
"I Can't Stop Lovin' You" 777
"I Can't Take This Anymore!" 673
"I Can't Turn You Loose" 55
"I Can't Wait Till You Arrive" 1658
"I Can't Walk on Water" 1392
"I Cannot Give the Reasons" 1503
"I Cannot Tell Her So" 1364
"I Cannot Wait" 1424
"I Caught a Glimpse of the Man" 1595
"I Charmed the Wine" 1119
"I Choose You" 296
"I Come from Woodmere, Long Island!" 673
"I Could Always Go to You" 1243
"I Could Be Happy with You" 199
"I Could Dig You" 1397
"I Could Drive a Person Crazy" 1492
"I Could Fall in Love" 626
"I Could Go with the Wind" 1531
"I Could Never Be Your Lover Again" 19
"I Could Never Get Enough of You" 88
"I Could Never Rescue You" 890
"I Could Not Get Along Without a Song" 993
"I Could Write a Book" 382
"I Could Write Books" 1830
"I Could've Gone to Nashville" 1155, 1157
"I Couldn't Care Less" 1084
"I Couldn't Live Without Your Love" 1450
"I Couldn't Say" 215
"I Cried" 1575
"I Cried and I Cried" 736
"I Cut Their Throats" 107
"I Dare You Not to Dance" 338
"I Delight in the Sight of My Lydia" 870
"I Did It" (Chapin) 321
"I Did It" (Segal and Weber) 1684
"I Did It" (Willensky) 3
"I Did Not Sleep Last Night" 90
"I Didn't Raise My Boy to Be a Soldier" 1096
"I Didn't Raise My Girl to Be a Bunny" 783
"I Dig Action" 844
"I Dig Myself" 1678
"I Do! I Do!" 733, 1451
"I Do! I Do! (I Do Adore You)" 1451
"I Do! I Do! (Who Loves to Touch You?)" 1451
"I Do Like London" 1527
"I Do Like You" 1491
"I Do Love Thee" 1519
"I Do the Best I Can" 1739
"I Don't Agree" 819
"I Don't Ask About Tomorrow" 364
"I Don't Believe in Heroes Anymore" 1622
"I Don't Believe It" 1524
"I Don't Care" (Lenox & Sutton) 1643
"I Don't Care" (Long and Crozier) 1659
"I Don't Care" (Preston) 1365
"I Don't Eat a Thing" 1174
"I Don't Feel Anything" 1255
"I Don't Feel No Ways Tired" 736
"I Don't Find You Sexy Anymore" 1427
"I Don't Give a Damn for You" 1316
"I Don't Have a Name" 1207
"I Don't Hope for Great Things" 1330
"I Don't Hurt Anymore" 382, 383
"I Don't Know" 1029
"I Don't Know How to Be My Daddy's Father" 1343
"I Don't Know How to Have Sex" 225
"I Don't Know What Is Happening to Me" 1708
"I Don't Live Anywhere Anymore" 159
"I Don't Mind" 987
"I Don't Mind Being Funny" 1383
"I Don't Need a Man to Know I'm Good" 376
"I Don't Play with Humans" 216
"I Don't Remember Christmas" 1524
"I Don't Remember You" 52
"I Don't S-M-O-K-E Sermonette" 1289
"I Don't Say Anything" 770
"I Don't See Him Very Much Any More (Anymore)" 90, 1031
"I Don't See You" 1545
"I Don't Think I Like This Game" 216
"I Don't Think I'll Ever Love You" 101
"I Don't Trust Him" 1788
"I Don't Understand It" 1119
"I Don't Wanna Be a Loser" 1551
"I Don't Want Anymore Good Friends" 1472
"I Don't Want It" 754
"I Don't Want That You Don't Want" 1510
"I Don't Want to Be a Mirror Anymore" 834
"I Don't Want to Be Fired Again" 41
"I Don't Want to Bother Nobody" 1366
"I Don't Want to Feel What I Feel" 1375
"I Don't Want to Hear No But, But, But" 1398
"I Don't Want to Hold Back" 1472
"I Don't Want to Know" 818, 824, 924
"I Don't Want to Lose You" 1494
"I Don't Want to Set the World on Fire" 1494
"I Don't Want to Walk Without You, Baby" 1546
"I Don't Want to Watch TV" 971
"I Don't Worry About Tomorrow" 1001
"I Dread the Night" 502
"I Dream" 416
"I Dream About Frankie" 115
"I Dream of Jeannie" 112
"I Dreamed" 485
"I Dreamt About My Home" 175
"I Dreamt I Dwelt in Bloomingdale's" 734
"I Eat" 225
"I, Eliot Rosewater" 588
"I Fall in Love Too Easily" 1210, 1546
"I Fall to Pieces" 39
"I Feel Him Slipping Away" 765
"I Feel Like I Lost Something" 1684
"I Feel Like I'm Fixin' to Die Rag" 1556
"I Feel Like I'm Not Out of Bed Yet" 911, 1185, 1186
"I Feel Like I'm Sailing" 1121
"I Feel Love" 274
"I Feel So Lost" 1743
"I Feel So Much Spring" 1121
"I Feel So Terribly Alone" 13
"I Feel the Earth Move" (Glass) 427
"I Feel the Earth Move" (King) 1591
"I Feel Wonderful" 735
"I Find a Friend in You" 470
"I Float" 1503
"I Forget and I Remember" 614
"I Forgot My Bible" 439
"I Found a Friend" 712
"I Found a Song" 703
"I Found Him" 33, 1430
"I Found My Twin" 962
"I Found the Girl of My Dreams on Broadway" 1758, 1761
"I Fried All Night Long" 1174
"I Furnished My One Room Apartment" 1709
"I Gave It Away" 607
"I Get a Kick Out of You" 63, 1210
"I Get Embarrassed" 1580
"I Get Ideas" 35
"I Get Tired" 463
"(I Get) Carried Away" 1224
"I, Glorious Toad" 1784
"I Go by the Book" 1077
"I Go On" 1029
"I Got a Gal I Love" 1546
"I Got a Gal in Kalamazoo" 205
"I Got a Man Who Loves Me" 67
"I Got a Plan" 396
"I Got De Raff" 922
"I Got Faith in You" 1514
"I Got Four Kids" 252
"I Got It Bad (and That Ain't Good)" 221, 1435
"I Got It from Agnes" 1654
"I Got Life" 649
"I Got Lucky" 1192
"I Got Me" 58
"I Got Rhythm" 1435
"I Got Rhythm Too" 1030
"I Got That Other Lady's with My Baby Feeling" 216
"I Got the Beat" 207
"I Got the What?" 626
"I Got to Go" 470
"I Got You" 1551
"I Gotta Hear a Song" 215
"I Gotta Keep Movin'" 400
"I Gotta Little Time" 683
"I Gotta Make My Own Music" 861
"I Gotta Right to Sing the Blues" 180, 181, 182, 662
"I Guess He'd Rather Be in Colorado" 37
"I Guess I'll Have to Change My Plan" 348, 1606
"I Guess I'll Have to Change My Plans" 1091
"I Had a King" 963
"I Had a Son" 175
"I Had Myself a True Love" 669
"I Had to Go" 1384
"I Had to Laugh" (Hamilton) 1721
"I Had to Laugh" (Oster) 385
"I Had Twins" 201
"I Happen to Like New York" 1704
"I Hate Being Me" 834
"I Hate Colored People" 1423
"I Hate Dogs" 396
"I Hate Football" 752
"I Hate It" 1309
"I Hate Musicals" 1386
"I Hate Spring" 861
"I Hate the French" 206
"I Hate to Travel" 68
"I Hate Trains" 544
"I Hate You" 698
"I Have a Charge to Fulfill" 834
"I Have a Family" 765
"I Have a Friend at the Chase Manhattan Bank" 109
"I Have a Little Secret" 1512
"I Have a Noble Cock" 246
"I Have a Single Track Mind" 779
"I Have Always Collected" 276
"I Have Always Had a Plain Face" 44
"I Have Been Heavy" 1222
"I Have Changed" 855
"I Have Come to the Conclusion That I Am Unable to Compete in the Normal Labor Market" 44
"I Have Dreamed" 1210
"I Have Found" 997
"I Have Lived" 235
"I Have Me" 1747
"I Have My Brief" 1139
"I Have My Price" 1503
"I Have Never Been So Happy" 476
"I Have No Name" 1263
"I Have No Offspring" 1139
"I Have Not Lived in Vain" 865, 866, 1593
"I Have Not Told" 1020
"I Have Not Told One Half of What I Saw" 1020
"I Have Noticed a Change" 1144
"I Have Often Reflected That This Is No Ship" 363
"I Have Seen the Wind" 8
"I Have So Many Songs" 1121
"I Have the One You See" 1789
"I Have These Pains in My Back" 44
"I Have to Tell You" (Rome) 981
"I Have to Tell You" (Smit) 1338
"I Hear a Song" 401, 1136
"I Hear a Symphony" 115
"I Hear America Singing" 903
"I Hear an Army" 1623
"I Hear Bells" 1524
"I Hear Humming" 1143, 1144
"I Heard It" 1046
"I Heard My Mother Crying" 605
"I Held a Hope" 1147
"I Hold Your Hand in Mine" 1654
"I Hope He's Not Ashamed of Me" 705
"I Hope I Get It" 283
"I Hope I Never Get It" 391
"I Hope You're Happy" 1318
"I Hurry Home to You" 214
"I Imagine You're Upset" 106
"I Introduced" 367
"I Just Came to Say, 'I'm Gay'" 1128
"I Just Can't Move in Her Shadow" 338
"I Just Don't Know What to Do with Myself" 1450
"I Just Found Out" 861
"I Just Got in the City" 120
"I Just Have to Breathe" 83
"I Just Kissed My Nose Goodnight" 861
"I Just Pressed a Button" 1759

"I Just Slipped Away from My Wedding" 1447
"I Just Wanna Be Loved" 470
"I Just Want to Be a Star" 1155, 1157
"I Just Want to Be Happy" 1263
"I Just Want to Hold You for a While" 1428
"I Just Want to Know" 219
"I Just Want to Know That You're All Right" 272
"I Kept My Distance" 363
"I Knew a Girl in Barcelona" 779
"I Knew Her" 976
"I Knew I Could Fly" 1338
"I Knew It Was Wrong" 92
"I Knew It!" 1584
"I Knew That You Would Be My Love" 13
"I Knew the Music" 89
"I Know" 280
"I Know a Bank" 1519
"I Know a Fellow" 234
"I Know a Foul Ball" 912
"I Know a Place" 1450, 1551
"I Know He'll Understand" 1754
"I Know Him So Well" 275
"I Know How You Sell It" 701
"I Know How You Wonder" 352
"I Know, I Know" 366
"I Know I've Been Changed" 777
"I Know Jesus Heard Me" 1734, 1735
"I Know Loneliness" 858
"I Know Loneliness Quite Well" 1451
"I Know My Love" 235
"I Know My Wife" 1181
"I Know Not Love" 1569
"I Know Nothing" 439
"I Know Now" 1486
"I Know of a Place" 820
"I Know the Feeling" 260
"I Know Things Now" 1491
"I Know This House" 1637
"I Know What He's Up To" 693
"I Know What I Knows" 884
"I Know What I Saw" 1237
"I Know What Love Can Bring" 229
"I Know What You Saw" 1237
"I Know What You're Thinking" 44
"I Know You" 1460
"I Know You Too Well" 639
"I Know You're Here, Jeannine" 497
"I Landed on Him" 503
"I Lay Alone All Winter" 948
"I Left a Dream Somewhere" 631
"I Left My Heart at the Stage Door Canteen" 1764
"I Left You There" 89
"I Let the Moment Slip By" 1395
"I Lied" 907
"I Light a Light" 45
"I Like" (Dyer) 822
"I Like" (Haney) 1751
"I Like" (Shimoda) 602
"I Like America" 751
"I Like Girls" 602
"I Like Her" 743
"I Like How We All Dance Together" 1345
"I Like It" (Ballard) 93
"I Like It" (Friedman) 1582, 1677
"I Like It" (Gelber) 962
"I Like Me" 1758, 1759, 1761
"I Like the Job" 558
"I Like the Nose on Your Face" 494
"I Like to Lead When I Dance" 1210
"I Like to Win" 230
"I Like What I Do" 210
"I Like You, I Love You" 1345
"I Live a Little" 823
"I Live Alone" 634, 731
"I Live by My Wits" 393, 394
"I Live for Love" 979
"I Live in a Dive" 949
"I Live My Life in Color" 401
"I Live to Love" 1440
"I Look Down the Road" 1308
"I Lost the Rhythm" 942
"I Lost You" 1611
"I Love a Fool" 33
"I Love a Lad" 812
"I Love a Man" (Hasman) 1232
"I Love a Man" (Young) 1604
"'I Love a Man with a Uniform On' Polka" 1171
"I Love Ann" 858
"I Love Drugs" 206
"I Love Eggs" 1546
"I Love Everyone in the Wide, Wide World" 570
"I Love Everything That's Old" 1161
"I Love Harlem" 1435
"I Love Her So" 190
"I Love Him" (Dick) 1815
"I Love Him" (Rubell) 403
"I Love His Face" 1253
"I Love How You Love Me" 854
"I Love Me" 675
"I Love My Father" 1689
"I Love My Serfs" 184
"I Love My Wife" 733
"I Love Myself in Two" 834
"I Love Only You" 567
"I Love Order" 1253
"I Love Paris" 226, 924
"I Love Petite Belle" 1004
"I Love the Army" 194
"I Love the Beauty of the View at Home" 1723
"I Love the Dance" 1207
"I Love the Nightlife" 399
"I Love the Sun" 493
"I Love To Sing-A" 1651
"I Love to Travel" 68
"I Love What the Girls Have" 1038
"I Love What's Like You About Me and I Love in You What's Different from Me" 834
"I Love You" (Carmines) 453
"I Love You" (MacDermot) 1638
"I Love You" (Marren) 1287
"I Love You" (Porter) 1221
"I Love You All the Time" 1433
"I Love You Because" (Salzman) 738
"I Love You Because" (Unknown) 1720
"I Love You, Jimmy Valentine" 25
"I Love You More" 1057
"I Love You, You're Perfect, Now Change" 739
"The 'I Love You' Song" 1680
"I Love Your Brains" 1339
"I Love Your Laughing Face" 1364
"I Loved (J'Aimais)" 792
"I Loved a Man" 1716
"I Loved Him, but He Didn't Love Me" 367
"I Loved My Father" 391
"I Loved You When I Thought Your Name Was Ken" 499
"I Loves You, Porgy" 1096
"I-M-4-U" 1575
"I Made a Vow" 470
"I Made It to the Top" 749
"I Make Up This Song" 249
"I Married a Woman" 249
"I Married an Angel" 1282
"I May Be Fast" 436
"I May Be Gay" 227
"I May Blush from Anger" 1539
"I May Not Be Much" 808
"I Met a Girl" 1546, 1717
"I Met Harvey Like Most People Did" 673
"I Met My Love" 564
"I Miss My Home in Haarlem" 1495
"I Miss New York" 1499
"I Miss You" 470
"I Miss You, My Dear Queen" 889
"I Must Devise a Plan" 480
"I Must Go" 1416
"I Must Go Now" 279
"I Must Have Been Hysterical" 363
"I Must Have Been Stoned" 1128
"I Must Have That Man" 165, 886
"I Must Paint" 332
"I Must Smile" 661
"I Must Stay with Him" 419
"I Must Tell Jesus" 736
"I Need a Life" 1144
"I Need a Man to Love" 965
"I Need It Bad" 837
"I Need Me a Girl" 1103
"I Need One Man" 786
"I Need to Know" 493
"I Need to Speak to Matthew" 439
"I Need You" (Bussins and Olin) 109
"I Need You" (Secunda) 874
"I Never Do Anything Twice" 807, 924
"I Never Felt So Good Before" 609
"I Never Has Seen Snow" 212, 715
"I Never Knew" 741
"I Never Let Anyone Beat Me but You" 123
"I Never Let It Ruin My Day" 599
"I Never Made Money from Music" 1582, 1677
"I Never Said I Didn't Love You" 1375
"I Never Saw Myself That Way" 1693
"I Never Sing a Song" 1343
"I Never Spent Time with My Dad" 1428
"I Never Thought I'd See the Day" 9
"I Never Wanted to Love You" 1019
"I Now Pronounce" 717
"I Offer You My Heart" 13
"I Once Believed" 289
"I Only Know" 1196
"I Only Want the Best" 1263
"I Only Want to Be with You" 1450
"I Ought to Cry" 930
"I Paid My Dues" 740
"I Poured Me a Man" 1061
"I Professionisti" 1309
"I Put a Spell on You" 777
"I Put Watches Out of Time" 820
"I Question You" 1441
"I Ran" 933
"I Reach for a Star" 599, 781
"I Really Love You" 1108
"I Really Loved You" 1325
"I Really Think That Poverty Is Wrong" 1316
"I Remember" (Cohen) 1829
"I Remember" (Frandsen, et al.) 1495
"I Remember" (Singer) 543
"I Remember" (Sondheim) 807
"I Remember" (Taylor) 1289
"I Remember" (Valenti) 972
"I Remember" (Ward) 1374
"I Remember a Feeling Called Love" 834
"I Remember Him" 71
"I Remember Mama" 758
"I Remember Once" 1416
"I Remember Rosey" 197
"I Remember That" 1403
"I Remember the Cold" 439
"I Said Good Morning" 1224
"I Said No" 1546
"I Said, Oh No" 726
"I Saw a Man" 1311
"I Saw a Ship" 1085
"I Saw God" 370
"I Saw Her Again" 411
"I Saw the Light" 657
"I Saw the Rest of My Life" 1428
"I Saw Three Ships" 252
"I Say a Little Prayer" 1551
"I Say a Little Prayer for You" 83
"I See a River" 1712
"I See a Road" 386
"I See by the Papers" 871
"I See in You" 1743
"I See It Now" 23
"I See Myself" 276
"I See the Light" 706, 1504
"I See the People" 667
"I See the Streetlights" 706
"I See Your Face Before Me" 1606
"I Seek Him Here, I Seek Her There" 1349
"I Seen It with My Very Own Eyes" 1083
"I Set My Heart on One to Love" 1811
"I Shall Condemn" 59
"I Shall Hold This Tight" 951
"I Should Fall Through the Floor" 1412
"I Should Live So" 1341
"I Should Stay" 676
"I Shouldn't Love You" 1608
"I Sing" 742
"I Sing Jazz, Too" 1723
"I Sing the Rainbow" 1064
"I Sit in the Sun" 1393
"I Slept with a Zombie" 385
"I Sold My Heart to the Junkman" 115
"I Speak Six Languages" 1680
"I Spy" (Milan, et al.) 1754
"I Spy" (Moross) 569
"I Still Believe in You" 154
"I Still Haven't Found What I'm Looking For" 775
"I Still Hear It All" 1135
"I Still Love You" 993
"I Sure Like the Boys" 1
"I Swear I Won't Ever Again" 764, 765
"I Think About It All the Time" 328
"I Think I Like Her" 1554
"I Think I Like His Eyes" 45
"I Think I'm Falling for You" 1577
"I Think If You Could Talk Like This" 363
"I Think It's Going to Rain Today" 1036, 1049
"I Think Myself Out" 1829
"I Think the Kid Will Do" 726
"I Think Too Much of the Future" 665
"I Think We Got Love" 1830
"I Think You Should Know" 1243
"(I Think) I May Want to Remember Today" 1524
"I Thought About You" 1138
"I Thought I Was All Alone" 1255
"I Thought I Was Alone" 67
"I Thought Only of You" 1815
"I Thought, Why Me?" 255
"I to the World" 1519
"I Toe the Line" 1366
"I Took These Women" 743
"I Touch Myself Right Here" 465
"I Tried and I Tried and I Tried" 267
"I Try" 336
"I Try to Be Like the Rose" 717
"I Turn to Jesus" 120
"I Turned My Back" 384
"I Understand" 1185, 1186
"I Understand. You're Leaving Us" 941
"I Wait" 1020
"I Wait for a Ship" 128
"I Walk Alone" 229
"I Walk Ze Dogs" 1251
"I Wanna Be a Country Music Singer" 1343
"I Wanna Be Loved by You" 171, 382, 383
"I Wanna Be Ready" 470
"I Wanna Come Home" 387
"I Wanna Do Debbie" 365
"I Wanna Go Back to Dixie" 1654
"I Wanna Have Sex Tonight" 206
"I Wanna Hold Your Handel" 241
"I Wanna Make the World Laugh" 818
"I Want" 1152
"I Want a Daddy" 635
"I Want a Long Time Daddy" 428
"I Want a Real Man" 1538
"I Want a Surprise" 1364
"I Want Gas" 655
"I Want It All" 1623
"I Want More Out of Life Than This" 1517
"I Want Real" 510
"I Want That" 1692
"I Want the Best for Him" 463
"I Want the World to Know" 570
"I Want to Be a Bride" 1342
"I Want to Be a Jewish Girl" 819
"I Want to Be a Little Frog in a Little Pond" 1824

"I Want to Be Free of This Dream" 1345
"I Want to Be Happy" 740
"I Want to Be Somebody" 1348
"I Want to Be the Mayor" 1037
"I Want to Be with You" 603
"I Want to Be Your Congressman" 785
"I Want To Blow Up the World" 1739
"I Want to Get Off This Island" 1495
"I Want to Go Out Tonight" 1499
"I Want to Hear a Yankee Doodle Tune" 570
"I Want to Know You" 721
"I Want to Live" 152
"I Want to Live on Jane Street" 1693
"I Want to Make Magic" (Franceschina) 1714
"I Want to Make Magic" (Margoshes) 474
"I Want to Make You Cry" 1330
"I Want to Ride with You" 1739
"I Want to See It" 511
"I Want to See Peace Again" 1231
"I Want to Sing in Opera" 581
"I Want to Take 'Em Off for Norman Rockwell" 1385
"I Want to Walk in a Garden" 208
"I Want What I Want When I Want It" 1643
"I Want What You Want" 721
"I Want You" (Gordon) 1103
"I Want You" (Kanfer, et al.) 745
"I Want You" (Lennon and McCartney) 1426
"I Want You to Be ..." 260, 1472
"I Want Your Boyfriend" 665
"I Wanted to See the World" 332
"I Was a Black Sheep" 453
"I Was a Shoo-In" 1717
"I Was Beautiful" 86
"I Was Born in Virginia" 570
"I Was Born This Way" 1772
"(I Was Born to Do) The Two-a-Day" 1218
"I Was Here" 583
"I Was in the Closet" 316
"I Was Lost" 1134
"I Was Remembering This Morning the Days When I Was a Child" 951
"I Was Taught to Love" 1638
"I Wasn't Born to Die No Common Way" 107
"I Wasn't Home for Christmas" 219
"I Wasn't Prepared" 82
"I Went an' Found Myself a Cowboy" 1208
"I Went Back Home" 1384
"I Went Fishing with My Dad" 997
"I Went Out in the Evening" 253
"I Will Be Loved Tonight" 739
"I Will Come Back" 746
"I Will Dream of What I Saw" 130
"I Will Follow Him" 1551
"I Will Give Him Love" 109
"I Will Have Him" 962
"I Will Love You" 19
"I Will Miss You" 1716
"I Will Never Be the Same" 949
"I Will Never Find Another You" 1428
"I Will Remember You" 1670
"I Will See You" 945
"I Will Stay with You" 1071
"I Will Tarry" 1519
"I Will Trust in the Lord" 736
"I Wish I Could Forget You" 1491
"I Wish I Could Go Back to College" 77
"I Wish I Could Say" 1132
"I Wish I Could've Been There (Woodstock)" 37
"I Wish I Knew" (Gordon) 705
"I Wish I Knew" (Mo' and Edwards) 1631
"I Wish I Led This Kind of Life" 927
"I Wish I Was Dead" 1186
"I Wish I Were a Man" 726
"I Wish It So" 848, 1651
"I Wish It Was Over" 1341
"I Woke Up This Morning with My Mind Stayed on Freedom" 736
"I Woke Up Today" 175
"I Won't Be an Actor No More" 570
"I Won't Be Home for a Long, Long Time" 402
"I Won't Be There (When the Dawn Breaks)" 296
"I Won't Cross Over" 1201
"I Won't Cry Anymore" 383
"I Won't Dance" 883, 886, 1210
"I Won't Let It Happen to Me" 742
"I Won't Love a Soldier Boy (Soldier-Boy)" 258, 259
"I Won't Send Roses" 818
"I Won't Take No for an Answer" 379
"I Won't Worry" 1078
"I Wonder" (Hurwit) 1433
"I Wonder" (Sottile) 767
"I Wonder I Wonder" 1671
"I Wonder What Became of Me" 662
"I Wonder What's Inside" 1788
"I Wonder Why" 985
"I Wore It for My Love" 563
"I Work for Pravda" 1713
"I Work with Wood" 1107
"I Worship You" 367
"I Would Die" 1580
"I Would Give My Soul for That" 404
"I Would If I Could but I Can't" 1521
"I Would Like to Say" 1250
"I Wouldn't Be the First" 697
"I Wouldn't Bother About You So Much" 1811
"I Wouldn't Change a Thing" 1479
"I Wouldn't Go Back" 300
"I Wouldn't Have Believed It" 959
"I Wouldn't Say No" 1109
"I Wouldn't Take Nothing for My Journey Now" 1484
"The 'I' Word" 227
"I (You) Can't Have It All" 1613
"Icarus" (Goggin and Solley) 667
"Icarus" (Guettel) 1404
"Ice and Snow" 1513
"Ice Cream" (Goldberg) 229
"Ice Cream" (Weiss) 161, 162, 163, 164
"The Ice House Fire" 528
"The Ice Stage" 1293
"Ich Bin Gerecht (I'm Right)" 1382
"Ich Dank Eich Mein Liebe Fraynt" 1212
"Ich Habe Gelernt" 882
"Ich Hob Dich Tzufil Lieb (I Love You Too Much)" 492
"Ich Lib Dich (I Love You)" 1382
"Ich Traumt Du Kamst An Mich" 607
"Ich Trink in Sholof" 1032
"Ich Vel Eybik Dich Gedenken (I'll Always Remember You)" 1453
"Ich Vel Vartnoyf Dir (I Will Wait for You)" 1453
"Icicles" 1598
"I'd Be Attracted" 1784
"I'd Do Almost Anything to Get Out of Here and Go Home" 1253
"I'd Do It All Again" 23
"I'd Do It All Over" 1066
"I'd Forgotten How Beautiful She Could Be" 1364
"I'd Give It All for You" 1498
"I'd Give to Her the World in Diamonds" 716
"I'd Gladly Walk to Alaska" 870
"I'd Go Home to My Mother" 1692
"I'd Know How to Be Big" 1337
"I'd Know That Smile" 1021
"I'd Like to Be" 1600
"I'd Like to Be a Rose" 1689
"I'd Like to Propose a Bill" 9
"I'd Like to Spray the World" 370
"I'd Love to Be in Love with You" 1171
"I'd Rather Be a Fairy Than a Troll" 537
"I'd Rather Be Sailing" 997, 1121
"I'd Rather Dance Alone" 1243
"I'd Rather Have Nothin' All of the Time Than Somethin' for a Little While" 1783
"I'd Rather Stay at Home with You" 1692
"I'd Rather Wake Up by Myself" 886
"Id, Superego" 1646
"Ida Mae Cole Takes a Stance" 2
"Identity" 1225
"Idolize" 750
"If (If You Hadn't, But You Did)" 1224, 1546
"If Anybody Asked You Who I Am?" 166
"If De Boot Don't Fit You Can't Wear It" 1174
"If Ever Married I'm" 1704
"If Ever You Need Me" 1416
"If Harry Weren't Here" 961, 1756
"If He Be Dead" 1569
"If He Has a Girl" 468
"If He Knew" 1514
"If He Walked Into My Life" 818
"If He'd Only Been Gentle" 564, 758
"If He's Really Sly" 1418
"If I Ain't Got You" 1623
"If I Am Released" 643
"If I Am to Marry You" 1440
"If I Could" (Fieger) 360
"If I Could" (Goodall) 697
"If I Could Be Beautiful" 725, 1097
"If I Could Dance with You" 599
"If I Could Escape" 328
"If I Could Just Be Like Pete" 1428
"If I Could Live My Life Again" (DeBenedictis) 1669
"If I Could Live My Life Again" (Wilson) 357
"If I Could See the World (Through the Eyes of a Child)" 39
"If I Could Tell You" 1222
"If I Didn't Believe in You" 890
"If I Felt Any Younger Today" 1481
"If I Had A" 466
"If I Had a Million Dollars" 1038
"If I Had the Answers" 464
"If I Had Wings" 258
"If I Have the Will" 364
"If I Have to Be Alone" 1706
"If I Have to Live Alone" 88
"If I May" 1539
"If I Only Had" 835
"If I Profane" 1437
"If I Sing" 300
"If I Try" 1618
"If I Were" 1600
"If I Were a Rich Man" 555
"If I Were Edgar" 1815
"If I Were Only Someone" 34
"If I Were Pretty" 929
"If I Were You" 1303
"If I'm Honest with You" 328
"If-If-If-If" 652
"If It Can't Be Love" 1325
"If It Gives Us Nothing Else" 1548
"If It Hadn't Been for Me" 56
"If It Is True" 1103
"If It Were All True" 814
"If It's Love" (Brandon) 291
"If It's Love" (Lewis) 1196
"If Jesus Walked (the Earth Today)" 493, 1124, 1537
"If Life Is Only a Dream" 1020
"If Love Were All" 55, 428, 751
"If Love's Like a Lark" 870
"If Money Talks" 301
"If Music and Sweet Poetry Agree" 1437
"If Music Be the Food of Love" 1437
"If My Love You'll Be" 1316
"If Nicky Knew" 499
"If Not Fer You" 102
"If Only" (Donizetti) 1146
"If Only" (Steinman) 1082
"If Only a Little Bit Sticks" 100
"If Only, Ben" 915
"If Only He Were a Woman" 1585, 1586
"If Our Songs Still Make It" 665
"If She Came Back Again" 1610
"If She Could Only Feel the Same" 962
"If She Has Never Loved Before" 246
"If Stars Could Talk" 1326
"If That's What Everyone Wants" 82
"If the Crown Fits" 126, 852
"If the Rain's Gotta Fall" 42
"If the Sun Didn't Shine Each Day" 1034
"If There Is Someone Lovelier Than You" 348, 1606
"If There's Anything Left of Us" 497
"If There's Love Enough" 926
"If Things Go Awry" 1011
"If This Is Love" 1303
"If This Were My World" 1035
"If We Can't Lick 'Em, Join 'Em" 1207
"If We Catch the Next Train" 1063
"If We Don't Find a Well" 938
"If We Never Meet Again" 1328
"If We Only Have Love (Quand on N'a Que L'Amour)" 792
"If We Spent Our Lives in a Fishbowl" 497
"If What I Saw" 1638
"If You Are But a Dream" 1210
"If You Can Prove I'm in Love" 1194
"If You Can Stay" 1251
"If You Can't Join 'Em, Beat 'Em" 1666
"If You Did It Once" 652
"If You Find a True Love" 822
"If You Give Me Your Attention" 460
"If You Had Seen" 183
"If You Hadn't, But You Did" 1224
"If You Knew How I Love You" 813
"If You Knew Susie (Like I Know Susie)" 955, 993
"If You Knew Time" 27
"If You Know What's Good for You" 1307
"If You Let Me Make Love to You Then Why Can't I Touch You" 1396
"If You Like the Music" 824
"If You Listen to My Song" 464
"If You Love Me Please Don't Feed Me" 929
"If You Loved Me" 930
"If You Only Knew" 930
"If You Really Cared" 1011
"If You Really Loved Me" 770
"If You Run Into Bruno" 1485
"If You Try" 223
"If You Wanna Dance" 1821
"If You Wanna Keep Your Man" 1435
"If You Want to Get Ahead" 1732
"If You Want to Learn" 1111
"If You Were You" 505
"If You Will Dream of Me" 791
"If You're a Woman" 920
"If You're in Love" 1469
"If You're Proposing" 394
"If You've Got It, You've Got It" 291
"If You've Only Got a Moustache" 112, 695
"Iggie's Nightmare" 867
"Ikh Bin a Border Bay Mayn Vayb (I Am a Boarder at My Wife's House)" 604
"Ikh Breng Aykh a Grus Fun Di Trenches (I Bring You Greeting from the Trenches)" 604
"Iko Iko" 1518
"I'll Always Be There" 485
"I'll Always Love You" 726
"I'll Always Remember This Day" 190
"I'll Be a Hairstylist to the Movie Stars" 1684
"I'll Be Around" 23
"I'll Be Different" 434, 435

"I'll Be Gone to Freedom" 922
"I'll Be Here" 1778
"I'll Be Here Tomorrow" 818
"I'll Be Here with You" 929
"I'll Be Home" 1036, 1334
"I'll Be Seeing You" 1571, 1750
"I'll Be Someone Someday" 545
"I'll Be There" (Lindsey) 703
"I'll Be There" (Weiss) 161, 162, 163, 164
"I'll Be There When You Need Me" 850
"I'll Be Waitin'" 1348
"I'll Be with You in Apple Blossom Time" 1571
"I'll Be Your Secret" 502
"I'll Be Your Valentine" 637
"I'll Bet You're a Cat Girl" 292
"I'll Bring the Roses" 1511
"(I'll Build a) Stairway to Paradise" 1096
"I'll Call My Soul My Own" 404
"I'll Call You Lover" 573
"I'll Carry You an Inch" 831
"I'll Come Back to That" 1788
"I'll Come Back to That #2" 1788
"I'll Come Back to That #3" 1788
"I'll Come By" 1108
"I'll Dance You" 1192
"I'll Demonstrate" 255
"I'll Die If I Can't Live Forever" 752
"I'll Die Laughing" 1042
"I'll Do Anything" 983
"I'll Dream Your Dream" 322
"I'll Fly Away" 1484
"I'll Follow My Secret Heart" 317, 751
"I'll Get Out of Here" 1375
"I'll Get You Out of My Life" 1375
"I'll Give My Love a Ring" 246
"I'll Just Pretend" 1221
"I'll Learn a New Song Tomorrow" 511
"I'll Live a Million Years" 1484
"I'll Make a Place" 164
"(I'll Make Sure My Head Is Clearer) The Next Time I Love" 1218
"Ill-Natured Girls" 1721
"I'll Never Die (I'll Just Change My Address)" 1484
"I'll Never Fall in Love Again" 83
"I'll Never Give Up on Bosie" 1714
"I'll Never Leave You" 1037
"I'll Never Love This Way Again" 1494
"I'll Never Make It to the Top" 1252
"I'll Never Move a Mountain" 1477
"I'll Never Smile Again" 1210
"I'll Never Want You Again" 1747
"I'll Only Miss the Feeling" 1650
"I'll Pay the Check" 886
"I'll Play the Fool" 1494
"I'll Raise You" 92
"I'll Remember" 653
"I'll Remember Her" 751
"I'll Remember Spring" 1577
"I'll Scratch Your Back" 1550
"I'll See You Again" 751, 1096
"I'll See You in My Dreams" 171
"I'll Show Him" 56
"I'll Show You the World Tonight" 1379
"I'll Sing" 1821
"I'll Sing a Different Song Tomorrow" 949
"I'll Smile" 962
"I'll Stand by You" 1584
"I'll Stay, I'll Go" 1424
"I'll Still Love Jean" 631
"I'll Take a Quiet Road" 609
"I'll Take My Fantasy" 467
"I'll Take You Home Again, Kathleen" 775
"I'll Talk to Her" 289
"I'll Tell Stable" 1063
"I'll Tell You About My Family" 726
"I'll Think of You" 1575
"I'll Try It Your Way" 537
"I'll Try to Smile" 1108
"I'll Wait for Joe" 626
"I'll Walk Alone" 1546, 1780
"I'll Walk Every Step of the Way" 1484
"Ill Wind" 165
"The Illegitimate Daughter" 1166, 1167
"Illicit Love Affair" 907
"Illinois" 1684
"Illinois Fred" 469
"Illusion" 858
"Illusions" (Hollander) 1350
"Illusions" (Holt) 16
"I'm a Bitch" 1061
"I'm a Brokenhearted Blackbird" 886
"I'm a Dandy" 91
"I'm a Fool to Want You" 1210
"I'm a Gigolo" 367
"I'm a Girl that Likes to Go Along" 384
"I'm a Good Old Girl" 1464, 1465
"I'm a Jonah Man" 1783
"I'm a Litvak, She's a Galitz" 1658
"I'm a Lonely Man, Susannah" 1563
"I'm a Lonesome Woman" 501
"I'm a Member in Good Standing of a Reform Congregation" 44
"I'm a Pinkerton Man" 569
"I'm a Popular Man" 570
"I'm a Positive Guy" 1755
"I'm a Professional Now" 1315
"I'm a Rocket Tonight" 910
"I'm a Rotten Person" 930
"I'm a Run to the City of Refuge" 657
"I'm a Sleuth" 68
"I'm a Stranger Here Myself" 689, 1532
"I'm a Teacher" 313
"I'm a Very Patient Man" 1327
"I'm a Virgin" 844
"I'm a Well-Known, Respected Practitioner" 391
"I'm a Wow" 1538
"I'm Afire" 493
"I'm Afraid" (Lasser) 225
"I'm Afraid" (Schwerin) 1162
"I'm Afraid It's Love" 234
"I'm All It Takes to Make You Happy" 1354
"I'm All Smiles" 212
"I'm Alone Today" 1727
"I'm an Average Guy" 1428
"I'm an Upper East Side Neurotic" 920
"I'm Ashamed to Look the Moon in the Face" 635
"I'm at My Best in Love" 665
"I'm Available" 461
"I'm Awfully Strong for You" 570
"I'm Back" 1631
"I'm Back in Circulation" 1823
"I'm Bad" 107
"I'm Beautiful" 1584
"I'm Bettin' on You" 809
"I'm Betting on You" 1476
"I'm Blest" 1438
"I'm Blue" 1185
"I'm Bluer Than You" 1
"I'm Breaking Down" 764, 765
"I'm Calm" 1492
"I'm Coming 'Round to Your Point of View" 1025
"I'm Coming Home, Dear Lord" 592
"I'm Coming Out" 742
"I'm Countin' on You" 663
"I'm Different" 1049
"I'm Doin' It for Defense" 662
"I'm Entertainment" 511
"I'm Falling in Love with Someone" 1570
"I'm Fat" 1174
"I'm Feelin' Blue" 886
"I'm Feeling Better All the Time" 1264
"I'm Fixin' To Tell Y' 'Bout a Feller I Knowed" 1563
"I'm Flashing" 1046
"I'm Forever Blowing Bubbles" 134
"I'm Free" (Haber) 25
"I'm Free" (Townshend) 1655
"I'm Gay" 913
"I'm Gettin' Off Here" 25
"I'm Getting Myself Ready for You" 1704
"I'm Glad I Don't Act Anymore" 511
"I'm Glad I'm Here" 731
"I'm Glad I'm Not a Man" 942
"I'm Glad I'm Not Young Anymore" 555
"I'm Glad I'm Single" 1606
"I'm Glad to See You're Back" 436
"I'm Goin' Back" 1546
"I'm Going Away for Awhile" 1692
"I'm Going Golfing Tomorrow" 606
"I'm Going in for Love" 1823
"I'm Going to Find a Girl" 902
"I'm Going to Live Forever" 164
"I'm Going to Make a Clean Start" 1700
"I'm Going to Make You Beautiful" 1524
"I'm Going to Sit at the Welcome Table" 736
"I'm Going to Tell God All My Troubles" 221
"I'm Gonna Be John Henry" 1464, 1465
"I'm Gonna Be Rich" 1447
"I'm Gonna Be Strong" 854
"I'm Gonna Change the World" 1353
"I'm Gonna Cry" 681
"I'm Gonna Do My Thing" 120
"I'm Gonna Do What the Spirit Say Do" 777
"I'm Gonna Get Lit Up" 1482
"I'm Gonna Get Out Alive" 372
"I'm Gonna Have a Baby" 631
"I'm Gonna Hit Today" 934
"I'm Gonna Make It" (Roullier) 1354
"I'm Gonna Make It" (Schwerin) 857
"I'm Gonna Miss Those Tennessee Nights" 179
"I'm Gonna Sing, Sing, Sing" 657
"I'm Gonna Sit Right Down and Write Myself a Letter" 18
"I'm Gonna Teach You How to Cook" 273
"I'm Growing Up" 766
"I'm Grown Up" 100
"I'm Gwine Lie Down" 701
"I'm Happy" 121
"I'm Harvey Ellesworth Cheyne" 249
"I'm Having Lunch with Sarah" 1144
"I'm Here" (Romanovsky and Phillips) 808
"I'm Here" (Stevenson) 255
"I'm Here and You're Here" 834
"I'm His" 257
"I'm Home" (Freyer) 249
"I'm Home" (MacDermot) 726
"I'm in a Tree" 1752
"I'm in Like with You" (Bussins and Olin) 109
"I'm in Like with You" (Ross) 64
"I'm in Love" (Amber) 1341
"I'm in Love" (Hoffman) 1760
"I'm in Love" (Stoner) 752
"I'm in Love" (Viola) 678
"I'm in Love Again" 567
"I'm in Love! I'm in Love!" 1381
"I'm in Love With—" 1758, 1759, 1761
"I'm in Love with a Flyer" 1647
"I'm in Love with a Soldier Boy" 367
"I'm in Love with My Zoology Professor" 395
"I'm in Showbiz" 272
"I'm in the Market for a Dream" 1820
"I'm in the Mood for Love" 886
"I'm in the Show" 198
"I'm Innocence" 614
"I'm Jim Dale" 511
"I'm Just a Knave" 1226
"I'm Just a Little Girl from Little Rock" 1717
"I'm Just a Lucky So-and-So" 182
"I'm Just a Statistic" 1732
"I'm Just a Toy" 920
"I'm Just Holdin' On" 1466
"I'm Just Nuts About You" 1268
"I'm Just Simply Full of Jazz" 1435
"I'm Lazy" 1476
"I'm Leaving" (Schimmel) 378
"I'm Leaving" (Slater) 719
"I'm Leigh Hunt-Smith" 1523
"I'm Lise" 65
"I'm Living the Past" 352
"I'm Lonely" 1402
"I'm Losing You, Karl" 227
"(I'm) Mad About You" 751
"I'm Madame Margaret the Therapist" 823
"I'm Mathew P. Brady, the Camera Man" 569
"I'm Me!" 1827
"I'm Me, We're Us" 1708
"I'm Mother Nature of You All" 1476
"I'm My Own Grandpa" 1656
"I'm Naïve" 349, 1752
"I'm No Babe, Ma!" 1046
"I'm No Closer" 431
"I'm No Sure" 812
"I'm Not" 930
"I'm Not a Jew" 1829
"I'm Not a Killer" 462
"I'm Not Afraid of Anything" 1498
"I'm Not for You" 80
"I'm Not Getting Any Younger" 1452
"I'm Not Going Gently" 491
"I'm Not in Love with You" 1040
"I'm Not in Philadelphia" 237
"I'm Not My Mother" 929
"I'm Not Myself" 1760
"I'm Not Myself Anymore" 1758, 1759, 1761
"I'm Not Old" 1107
"I'm Not So Bright" 954
"I'm Not Taking a Chance on Love" 1759, 1761
"I'm Not That Smart" 1680
"I'm Nothing Without You" 1595
"I'm O.K., You're O.K." 1646
"I'm on My Own" 731
"I'm on My Way" (Friedman) 208
"I'm on My Way" (Traditional) 815, 816
"I'm On My Way to the Top" 1827
"I'm on the Look-Out" 908
"I'm on Your Side" 749
"I'm One of the Girls Who Sings Like a Boy" 511
"I'm Only a Woman" 865, 866, 1593
"I'm Only Human" 1428
"I'm Out" 1635
"I'm Peculiar That Way" 614, 952
"I'm Poor" 633
"I'm Probably Not Gonna Call" 1479
"I'm Pudding" 1402
"I'm Ready, I Have Money" 1063
"I'm Ready Now!" 539
"I'm Ready to Go" 417
"I'm Relieved to See You" 439
"I'm Saving Myself for a Soldier" 90, 1031
"I'm Saving Up to Buy a Home for Mother" 570
"I'm Seeing Things" 1265
"I'm Sick of the Whole Damn Problem" 504
"I'm Single" 170
"I'm Sitting on Top of the World" 829, 993
"I'm Snow White—A Human Woman" 834
"I'm So Bored" 752
"I'm So Fat" 919
"I'm So Glad" 120
"I'm So Happy for Her" 1472
"I'm So Happy, I Could Cry" 703
"I'm So Lonesome I Could Cry" 657
"I'm Someone Now" 1184
"I'm Sorry" (Denver) 37
"I'm Sorry" (Self) 115, 1575
"I'm Standing in This Room" 1624
"(I'm) Staying Young" 1580
"I'm Still Alive" 1670
"I'm Still Here" 428, 1373
"I'm Still in Love with My Zoology Professor" 395
"I'm Stumbling" 485

"I'm Sure of It" 391
"I'm Taking a Flight" 1484
"I'm Tellin' You" 657
"I'm the Boy Who Owns the Lights on Broadway" 507
"I'm the Breeze" 864
"I'm the Cockalorum" 1480
"I'm the First Girl (in the Second Row of the Third Scene of the Fourth Number)" 954
"I'm the Girl" 556
"I'm the Greatest Star" 1546, 1717
"I'm the Guy" 1226
"I'm the Hostess of a Bum Cabaret" 635
"I'm the Master of the City" 396
"I'm the One That Got Away" 644
"I'm the Trivium" 1252
"I'm the Victim Here" 633
"I'm the Woman You Wanted" 1586
"I'm Through with You" (Reiser) 95
"I'm Through with You" (Schmidt) 1366
"I'm Throwing a Ball Tonight" 367
"I'm Tired of Texas" 954
"I'm to Blame 1468
"I'm True to Them All" 570
"I'm Twirling" 730
"I'm Two" 1683
"I'm Ugly" 111
"I'm Using My Bible for a Roadmap" 1484
"I'm Way Ahead of the Game" 538
"I'm Your Bitch" 1061
"I'm Your Boogie Man" 399
"I'm Your Hoochie Coochie Man" 777
"I'm Yours Alone" 361
"The Image on Our Retina Has Gone. We Go On" 834
"Imaginary Coney Island" 1186
"Imagine Me" 676
"Imagine My Surprise" 1243
"Imagine That" 328
"Imagine the Audacity!" 1412
"Imagine You're Alive" 716
"Imagining You" 157
"The Immigration and Naturalization Rag" 237
"Immigration, Please" 616
"Immolation" 1522
"Imperfections" 197
"Imperial" 963
"An Important Announcement" 1276
"Important Papers" 995
"Impossibility" 1679
"Impossible" 1492
"Impressions" 976
"Improv/EDT" 1414
"Improvisation" 583
"The Improvisation" 752
"Improvisations" 1806
"Impulses Under Religion" 1349
"In a Bath Tea Shop" 135
"In a Brownstone Mansion" 98
"In a Foreign City" 10
"In-A-Gadda-Da-Vida" 1176
"In a Garden (A Mini-Opera)" 571
"In a Hundred Years" 667
"In a Little Town in California" 726
"In a Little While" 1193
"In a Perfect World" (Alasa' and Welch) 276
"In a Perfect World" (McLean) 67
"In a Pretty New Dress" 1063
"In a Schoolyard in Brooklyn" 1607
"In a Silly Mood" 237
"In a Story Book" 1302
"In America" 1361, 1362
"In an Orem Shtibele (In a Poor Little House)" 1619
"In and Out" 277
"In April" 1582, 1677
"In Atzind Vi Ahin" 1032
"In Bed with the Reader's Digest" 1448
"In Between" (Edens) 840
"In Between" (Link and Courtney) 1395, 1396
"In Between Gigs" 788
"In Bimini" 9
"In Boston" 197
"In Broken-Promise Land" 1584
"In Cahoots" 1668
"In Crowd" 411
"In Dat Great Gittin' Up Mornin'" 591
"In Der Halle des Bergkonigs" 1694
"In Dreams Begin Responsibilities" 1133
"In Front of the Screens" 637
"In Good Old Colony Times" 740, 814
"In Here" 385
"In His Own Words" 227
"In Italics" 1255
"In Izzenschnooken on the Lovely Essnezook Zee" 935
"In Java" 635
"In-Laws" 147
"In Love? In Love?" 1601
"In Love in Vain" 883
"In Love with the Expert Red" 814
"In Loving Memory" 538
"In Meinem Garten" 689
"In Memoriam Walter Ramsden" 135
"In My Cube" 1742
"In My Life" 824
"In My Little Birch Canoe" 1694
"In My Own Lifetime" 1381
"In My Silent Universe" 823
"(In My) Solitude" 156, 221
"In Nomine Dei" 1424
"In Nomine Patris" 1029
"In Old Chicago" 1069
"In Old Mexico" 1654
"In Old Santa Fe" 825
"In One" 1595
"In Our Childhood's Bright Endeavor" 660, 689
"In Our Community" 385
"In Our Fantasy" 837
"In Our Hands" 727
"In Our Hearts" 1514
"In Our Little Salon" 1468
"In Our Teeny Little Weeny Nest" 908
"In Praise of Women" 1492
"In Saint-Lazare (A St.-Lazare)" 1641
"In Secret Chambers" 1443
"In Shady Green Pastures" 592
"In Small and Simple Ways" 1514
"In Some Other Life" 683
"In That Great Gettin' Up Morning" 1672
"In the Baggage Car Ahead" 577
"In the Barrel House" 555
"In the Beginning" (Markoe) 468
"In the Beginning" (Yeston) 1201
"In the Beginning, God ..." 1239
"In the Beginning Was the Word" 286
"In the Bend of My Arm" 375
"In the Cards" 377
"(In) The Center of Your Mind (Keep the Lord)" 1708
"In the Closet" 610
"[In] The Company of Men" 1752
"In the Courtroom" 331
"In the Desert" 1701
"In the Hallway" 45
"In the Heights" 760
"In the Hills of Andalusia" 1179
"In the House" 1582
"In the Life" 975
"In the Middle of the Room" 1121
"In the Mirror's Reflection" 1650
"In the Mist of the Night" 1066
"In the Mood" 35, 1015, 1096, 1571
"In the Morning" (Gardner) 1470
"In the Morning" (Graham) 261
"In the Morning" (Traditional) 330
"In the Movies" 1403
"In the Name of Love" (Coleman) 463
"In the Name of Love" (Copani) 493, 1537
"In the Name of Love" (Motta) 877
"In the Park" 1037
"In the Parlor Be a Lady" 837
"In the Police Station" 1462
"In the Prison" 903
"In the Rainbow of My Mind" 359
"In the Reign of Chaim" 1701
"In the Sack" 1132
"In the Sky" 151
"In the Sleeping Line" 1384
"In the Stars" 1832
"In the Still of the Night (I'll Remember)" 1434
"In the Sunny Old South" 569
"In the Sweet By and By (Bye and Bye)" 1176, 1392
"In the Town" 1201
"In the Wee Small Hours of the Morning" 1210
"In the Wildest Dream" 402, 1327
"In There" 234
"In This House" 1677
"In Time" (Kaplan) 98
"In Time" (Kayden) 773
"In Times of War and Tumults" 827
"In Trousers " 763, 765
"In Two Words — Show Biz" 1683
"In Twos and Threes" 933
"In Vino Veritas" 1692
"In Westminster Abbey" 135
"In Windows2525" 1742
"In Yama" 1543
"In Yonder World (Luten's Song)" 460
"In Your Hands" 1504
"The Inanimate Tragedy" 49, 612
"The Inauguration Was Marvelous" 227
"Incantation" 1072
"Incantation to the T.M.I." 198
"The Incantations" 484
"Incest and Apples" 1319
"Inching Along" 1484
"The Incinerator Hour" 292
"Incog-Negroes" 1407
"Incognito" 1701
"Incomplete" 1319
"Incomprehensible" 743
"The Incorporation" 1072
"Increasingly Messy" 1321
"The Incredible Orlando" 1662
"Indecent Exposure" 1135
"Indecision" 1133
"Independence Day, July 4th, 1959" 871
"Independent" 1546
"The Independent Farmer" 481
"The Indian Benefit Ball" 1739
"Indian Love Call" 1570
"Indian Nuts" 60
"Indian Summer" 972
"Individuals" 472
"Indoor Games Near Newbury" 135
"Indus River" 602
"Industrialization" 207
"Inevitably Me (Young People's Soiree, 1870)" 1448
"Inexpensive Progress" 135
"Inexpensive Tango" 1495
"Infertile Love Song" 769
"Infinite Joy" 430
"Inflight Nudniks" 1647
"The Influence of Scotch" 161
"Influenza" 919
"The Ingenue" 781, 1254
"Ingenuity" 1733
"Ink" 375
"Inkslinger's Regret" 1229
"Inkslinger's Song" 1229
"Inner Thoughts: Just After the Final Playlet at St. Peter's, Now" 899
"Inner Thoughts: Just Before the Curtain at St. Peter's, Now" 899
"Innocence" 952
"Innocent as Hell" 1692
"An Innocent Man Is Never Hanged" 655
"Inoue Threatens King Kojong" 889
"The Ins and the Outs" 1276
"The Insect God" 612
"Inside" 1219
"Inside a Prison Cell" 651
"Inside Inside" 1448
"Inside Out" 770
"Inside the Inside of Another Person's Mind" 1300
"Inside the Wall" 431
"Inside Your Heart" 106
"Inspector Fink: A Melodrama, or You Take the High Road and I'll Take the Low Road and I'll Be in Scotland Yard Before You" 1749
"Inspiration" 1224
"Inspiration (The Futurist Love Song)" 505
"Inspirational Song" 705
"Instant Biographies" 1142
"Instant Gratification" 1325
"Instant Hate" 493
"Instant Magic" 1511
"Instead-Of Song" 1626, 1773
"Instinct" 338
"Institute for Psychodrama" 535
"Integration" 21
"Intercourse on the Internet" 837
"Interesting Use of Space" 910
"The Interlude" 224
"Interlude" 844
"Intermission Interviews" 1743
"Intermission Rag" 587
"The Intermission's Great" 234
"International Monopoly" 126, 558
"The International Rag" 171
"International Reporters' Song" 1117
"International Set" 1255
"Interpretations" 196
"Interrogation" 749
"The Interview" 350
"Interview" 986
"An Interview" 1192
"Interview on Soccer with Jomo Kenyatta" 449
"Interview with a Maid" 1647
"Interview with a Movie Star" 1385
"Intrigue" 402
"Introducin' Mr. Paris" 600
"Introduction" (Braden) 408
"Introduction" (Layton) 963
"Introductions" (Carmines) 834
"Introductions" (Meyer and Neuburge) 126
"Introductions" (Oil City Symphony) 1176
"Introductory Remarks" 1091
"Inutil (Useless)" 760
"The Invasion" 1221
"Invasion Exercise on the Poultry Farm" 135
"Investigation of Police Brutality" 1091
"The Invisible Man" 1473
"Invisible Man" 1611
"An invitation" 250
"Invitation" (Bingham) 1072
"Invitation" (Friedman) 1441
"Invitation to a Hanging" 1077
"The Invitation to Dance" 1601
"The Invitation to France" 583
"An Invitation to Sleep in My Arms" 1121
"Invitation to the Basketball" 60
"Invocation" 21
"Invocation and Instructions" 1492
"Io E' Te" 824
"Io Sono Cosi Stanco" 78
"Iowa" 664
"Iowa Summer" 639
"Ira, My Dope Fiend" 823
"Ireland" 434, 435
"Ireland: My Land of Dreams" 570
"Ireland's Eye" 848
"Iris" 1176
"Iris the Fleet" 1787
"Irish Ballad" 1654
"The Irish Washerwoman" 775
"Irish Washerwoman's Lament" 1636
"Irma la Douce" 924
"Irma's Candy Heaven" 877
"Iron Furnace" 1470
"Iron Horse" 729
"The Irving Irving Story" 986
"Is Everybody Happy?" 725

"Is He Nisardi?" 779
"Is His Care" 1672
"Is It Art?" 1339
"Is It Him or Is It Me?" 1532
"Is It Really So Strange?" 1545
"Is It Too Late" 857
"Is Massa Gwine to Sell Us Tomorrow?" 815, 816
"Is My Living in Vain" 196
"Is She or Ain't She" 1732
"Is That All There Is?" 861
"Is That Love" 1702
"Is That Remarkable?" 503
"Is Then His Fate Decreed, Sir?" 117
"Is There a City?" 1767
"Is There a Straight Man in the House" 1383
"Is There Anything I Can Do?" 1458
"Is There Room?" 1052
"Is There Someplace for Me" 1164
"Is There Something to What He Said?" 291
"Is This Fact?" 90, 1031
"Is This Love?" 1565
"Is This Really the End?" 1192
"Is This the Way?" 1445
"Isaac, the Baker (The Treasure)" 1203
"Isabel" (Hardwick) 338
"Isabel" (Torroba) 1179
"Isabella" 1133
"Isadora Duncan" 262
"Isangoma" 651
"Ish-Ga-Bibble (I Should Worry)" 1442
"Isizwe (The Nation Is Dying)" 1401
"Island of Happiness" 1774
"Island Ritual" 1483
"The Isle of Skye" 1477
"The Ism Song" 547
"Isn't It?" (Rowe) 1831
"Isn't It?" (Sondheim) 1403
"Isn't It a Pity" 46
"Isn't It Great to Be Rotten" 1469
"Isn't It Romantic" 55
"Isn't It Strange, Snowflakes Are Falling" 889
"Isn't It Strange That We Can Love Again?" 260
"Isn't It Time for the People" 1037
"Isn't It Wonderful" 1423
"Isn't She" 258, 259
"Isn't That a Wonderful Way to Die?" 1451
"Isn't That Clear" 1311
"Isn't That What Makes Life Worthwhile" 357
"Isn't This Better?" 52, 1685
"Israel Shall Live" 874
"Israeli Rhapsody" 617
"The Issue of the Floor Is" 673
"It" (Ewing) 622
"It" (McKibbins) 778
"It Ain't Easy" 279
"It Ain't Good" 1458
"It Ain't Nice Not to Play on Your Own Turf" 952
"It Ain't Over" 2
"It Ain't the Meat, It's the Motion" 1494
"It Ain't Us Who Makes The Wars" 605
"It Always Seems to Rain" 461
"It Can Only Happen in America" 411
"It Comes to Me" 1708
"It Could Be Calais" 1177
"It Could Only Happen in the Theatre" 271
"The IT Cowboy" 1742
"It Depends on How You Look at Things" 261
"It Depends on What You Pay" 478
"It Depends on What You're At" 246
"It Didn't Used to Be This Way" 1338
"It Doesn't Look Deserted to Me" 870
"It Doesn't Take a Genius" 627
"It Don't Mean a Thing (If It Ain't Got That Swing)" 35, 221, 1435
"It Feels Good" 933
"It Feels So Good to Be Alive Today" 113
"It Goes Without Saying" 1252
"It Had to Be You" 955
"It Had to Happen Sometime" 665
"It Happened One Night" 492
"It Happens Every Day" 693
"It Happens to the Best of Friends" 1521
"It Has Everything" 638
"It Is a Glorious Thing to Be Kevin Kline" 511
"It Is Almost Finished" 947
"It Is as if Our Earthly Life Were Spent Miserably" 363
"It Is Most Best" 1503
"It Is the Place" 938
"It Is Too Late" 1103
"It Is Well, Well with My Soul" 736
"It Isn't Easy" (Chapin) 321
"It Isn't Easy" (Pottle) 1040
"It Isn't Easy to Be a Jew" 1510
"It Isn't Over Yet" 1693
"It Isn't the End of the World" 219
"It Isn't the Same" 121
"It Isn't What You Did, It's What You Didn't" 912
"It Just Ain't a Party Without You" 36
"It Makes January Feel Like July" 197
"It Makes My Love Come Down" 180, 181, 182
"It May Be Life" 436
"It Might as Well Be Spring" 924
"It Might Fall Off" 1684
"It Moves" 503
"It Must Be Good for Me" 289
"It Must Be Love" 1483
"It Must Be Me" 911
"It Must Be So" 911
"It Never Entered My Mind" 1210
"It Never Was You" 879, 882
"It Only Takes a Moment" 818
"It Pays to Advertise" 638
"It Says Here" 1254
"It Seems So Strange" 1139
"It Seems to Me" 322
"It Seems We've Stood and Talked" 1255
"It Starts Over Here" 1228
"It Still Isn't Over" 1582, 1677
"It Takes a Heap" 1754
"It Takes a Man" 434, 435
"It Takes a Soldier" 194
"It Takes a Whole Lot of Human Feeling" 400
"It Takes a Woman" 818
"It Takes Time" 235, 359
"It Takes Two" 67
"It Took Them" 332
"It Was a Glad Adventure" 600
"It Was a Lover and His Lass" 1568, 1569
"It Was for Fashion's Sake" 480
"It Was Fun" 41
"It Was Good" 468
"It Was Good Enough for Grandpa" 1154
"It Was Just After One-Fifteen" 363
"It Was Kind of Lazy and Jolly" 922
"It Was Magnificent" 1671
"It Was Me" 1181
"It Was My Bridge!" 1700
"It Was Not Because of Gilbert Blythe" 57
"It Was So Peaceful Before There Was Man" 1708
"It Was Worth It" 401, 1136
"It Wasn't God Who Made Honky Tonk Angels" 39
"It Wasn't Meant to Happen" 1027
"It Will Be My Day" (Aznavour) 824
"It Will Be My Day" (Margo) 1035
"It Will Be Our Little Secret" 257
"It Won't Be Long" (Crane) 1767
"It Won't Be Long" (Kookoolis and Fagin) 1504
"It Won't Be Long Now" 71, 760
"It Won't Let Us Leave" 462
"It Would Have Been Wonderful" 58
"It Wouldn't Be So Bad" 372
"Italian Straw Hat" 1604
"Italian Street Song" 1570
"Itch, Itch, Itch" 855
"Itch to Be a Witch" 1331
"Itching Heels" 1762
"It'd Be Nice" 1433
"Itoh's Ambition" 889
"It's a Bang-Up Job" 92
"It's a Beautiful World" 1040
"It's a Boy" 1655
"It's a Boy's Life" 200
"It's a Bubbe Meise" 220
"It's a Country" 1701
"It's a Dolly" 200
"It's a Doris Day Morning" 919
"It's a Funny Thing" 219
"It's a Glorious Day" 705
"It's a Great Day for Hawaii" 1221
"It's a Great Day for the Irish" 840
"It's a Great Little World" (Cass) 1142
"It's a Great Little World" (Gershwin) 1644
"It's a Helluva Big Job" 934
"It's a Hit" 1585, 1586
"It's a Hot Night for Dancin'" 1563
"It's a Job" 370
"It's a Jungle Out There" (Brand) 780
"It's a Jungle Out There" (Brandon) 1300
"It's a Lie" 1083
"It's a Living" 865
"It's a Long, Long March to Kansas City" 304
"It's a Long Road Home" 76
"It's a Lovely Day Tomorrow" 1764
"It's a Lovely Night on the Hudson River" 494
"It's a Man's World" (Brown and Newsome) 1353
"It's a Man's World" (Carmines) 614
"It's a Mystery" 499
"It's a Nice Place to Visit" 638
"It's a Party" 338
"It's a Perfect Day (for an Outing)" 1772
"It's a Perfect Relationship" 1717
"It's a Political-Satirical Revue" 1758
"It's a Privilege to Pee" 1712
"It's a Rich Life" 927
"It's a Sign" 933
"It's a Simple Little System" 1546
"It's a Sin" 1438
"It's a Sin to Tell a Lie" (Davis) 1239
"It's a Sin to Tell a Lie" (Mayhew) 18
"It's a Sound Idea" 1063
"It's a Stretchy Day" 48
"It's a Sweet Life" 81
"It's a Well-Known Fact" 733
"It's After Eight O'Clock" 1723
"It's Alive" 1831
"It's All a Scheme" 889
"It's All About" 1052
"It's All Because of the Fire" 1316
"It's All for the Good of the People" 1480
"It's All in the Family" 1333
"It's All in the Mind" 1192
"It's All in the Point of View" 934
"It's All in the Timin'" 153
"It's All Music" 1188
"It's All Off" 1604
"It's All Right" 1577
"It's All Right God" 364
"It's All Right with Me" 367
"It's All Written in Your Genes" 755
"It's All Your Fault" 221
"It's an Art" 210
"It's Bad for Me" 1160
"It's Been a Hard Life" 1043
"It's Been a Long, Long Time" 1546
"It's Better to Give Than Receive" 865
"It's Better with a Band" 781
"It's Better with a Union Man" 981, 1268
"It's Beyond Me" 1607
"It's Called a Piano" 639
"It's Capital" 1077
"It's Christmas Today" 735
"(It's) Closing Time" 1527
"It's Comin' True" 676
"It's Coming Back to Me" 1258
"It's De-Lovely (Delovely)" 63, 367
"It's Delicious" 147
"It's Delightful to Be Married!" 1643
"It's Easy to Sing" 1393
"It's Easy When You Know How" 538
"It's Funny About Love" 667
"It's Getting Better" 1758, 1759, 1761
"It's Glorious" 1671
"It's Gonna Be Fun" 54
"(It's Gonna Be) Another Hot Day" 1451
"It's Gonna Rain!" 547
"It's Got to Be Bad to Be Good" 234
"It's Gotta Be Venus" 1215
"It's Great Fun" 609
"It's Great to Be Alive" 66
"It's Great to Be Back in the City" 206
"It's Great to Be Gay" 752
"It's Great to Be Single Again" 1045
"It's Great to Hate Yourself" 407
"It's Happening!" (Crom) 1383
"It's Happening!" (Unknown) 96
"It's Hard I Know" 1392
"It's Hard to Be a Liberal Today" 1761
"It's Hard to Be a Patriarch Today" 1607
"It's Heaven" 1562
"It's Hot Up Here" 1557
"It's Just a Little Awkward" 742
"It's Just Like I Was You" 1708
"It's Just Not Fair" 624
"It's Like a Movie" 1610
"It's Love" (Bernstein) 911, 1224
"It's Love" (Carmines) 1739
"It's Love" (Marren) 1756
"It's Love! So What?" 1045
"It's Lovely. My Father Swears by Him" 941
"It's Make Believe Ballroom Time" 1764
"It's Matrimonial Weather" 779
"It's Me They Talk About" 860
"It's Mine" 86, 1584
"It's Money That I Love" 1036, 1049, 1334
"It's My Fat!" 391
"It's My Party" 115, 1551
"It's My Time" 1320, 1321
"It's My Turn Now" 1550
"It's Never Easy" 627
"It's Never That Easy" 300
"It's Never Too Late to Fall in Love" 199
"It's Nice" 545
"It's Nice to Know" 57
"It's None of My Business" 491
"It's Not a Commercial, It's Art" 991
"It's Not a Real Wedding" 260
"It's Not as Good as Love (Tout ca Vaut pas l'Amour)" 1641
"It's Not Cruel to Forget Your Ma" 1540
"It's Not Easy Being Next" 1035
"It's Not Easy to Change Your Life" 113
"It's Not Irish" 848
"(It's) Not Cricket to Picket" 981, 1267, 1268
"It's Not Like We Have Forever" 276
"It's Not My Idea of a Gig" 1061
"It's Not Working Out" 497
"It's Only a Paper Moon (If You Believed in Me)" 662, 669
"It's Only a Play" 157
"It's Only the Best Yet" 484
"It's Our Time Now" 152
"It's Out of Our Hands" 1078
"It's Over" 865, 866, 1593
"It's Over, Miles" 721
"It's Positively You" 1060
"It's Possible" 289
"It's Pouring" 1108
"It's Quiet on the Potomac Tonight" 569
"It's Rainin'" 1388

"It's Raining on Prom Night" 625
"It's Really Easy Baking Bread" 1045
"It's Really You" 279
"It's Sad to Be Lonesome" 985
"It's Sad to Say" 1747
"It's Silk, I Feel It" 1192
"It's So Easy to Say" 870
"It's So Good" 1517
"It's So Heartwarming" 98
"It's So Nice to Be Civilized" 785
"It's (So) Nice to Cuddle in a Threesome" 614, 823
"It's So Peaceful in the Country" 23
"It's Still the Most Beautiful City" 1374
"It's Team Time" 952
"It's the End" 378
"It's the Going Home Together" 600
"It's the Hat That Makes the Lady" 407
"It's the Human Thing to Do" 1811
"It's the Loneliness, I Think" 1263
"It's the Strangest Thing" 57
"It's the Witching Hour by the Old Water Tower" 569
"It's Time" (Cipolla, et al.) 462
"It's Time" (Holt) 16
"It's Time to Come Home" 323
"It's Time to Take the Toad in Hand" 1784
"It's Today" 818
"It's Too Much" 316
"It's Tough to Be a Man" 1383
"It's True" 1723
"It's Us Again" 1245
"It's What You Do (That Makes Your Wishes Come True)" 290
"It's Wilde!" 786
"It's You" (Nutter) 1777
"It's You" (Willson) 1656
"It's You" (Wise) 341
"It's Your Turn" 1635
"Itsche" 119
"I've a Sweetheart in Each Star" 635
"I've Arrived" 1595
"I've Been a Bad Boy" 1143, 1144
"I've Been A-Begging" 1302
"I've Been Around the Horn" 272
"I've Been in Love" 636
"I've Been in Those Shoes" 214
"I've Been Living with the Blues" 777
"I've Been There" 23
"I've Been There Before" 300
"I've Been to a Marvelous Party" 428
"I've Been True to Myself" 1142
"I've Been Watching You" 1624
"I've Brushed My Teeth" 912
"I've Forgotten Abigail" 331
"I've Got a Crush on You" 1210
"I've Got a Date with a Dream" 181, 182
"I've Got a Feeling I'm Falling" 18
"I've Got a Feeling for Ophelia" 458
"I've Got a Girl" 364
"I've Got a Goose" 652
"I've Got a Light on You" 1523
"I've Got a Little Secret" 336
"I've Got a Man on the Moon" 1152
"I've Got a Penny" 1752
"I've Got a Plan" 962
"I've Got a Problem" 1108
"I've Got a Secret" 1684
"I've Got a Surprise for You" 1379
"I've Got a Wonderful Future" 1481
"I've Got It" 1113
"I've Got It Hidden" 858
"I've Got My Eye on You" 1365
"I've Got My Fingers Crossed" 18
"I've Got My Orders" 230
"I've Got Pizzazz" 1159
"I've Got Some Unfinished Business with You" 1704
"I've Got Something Better" 575
"I've Got Sperm in My Pocket" 769
"I've Got the 'You-Don't-Want-To-Play-With-Me' Blues" 199
"I've Got the Nerve to Be in Love" 1267, 1268
"I've Got the World on a String" 1210
"I've Got to Be Famous" 164
"I've Got to Be Me" 1623
"I've Got to Know" 855
"I've Got to Try Everything Once" 1585, 1586
"I've Got What It Takes" 1198
"I've Got You on My Mind" 367, 567
"I've Got You Under My Skin" 367, 850, 924, 1210
"(I've Got) Harlem on My Mind" 69
"I've Gotta Get Back to New York" 993
"I've Grown Accustomed to His Face" 1350
"I've Grown Accustomed to This Show" 511
"I've Had Everything but a Man" 64
"I've Just Been to a Wedding" 564
"I've Just Begun" 100
"I've Known a Lot of Guys" 726
"I've Made a Habit of You" 1606
"I've Made Up My Mind" 154
"I've Never Been a Violent Man" 363
"I've Never Been a Woman Before" 274
"I've Never Seen My Face Before" 439
"I've Never Seen the Back" 1063
"I've Noticed a Change" 1143
"I've Seen People Like Them Before" 1638
"I've Seen Shakespeare" 350
"I've Still Got My Bite" 785
"I've Still Got My Health" 367
"I've Told Every Little Star" 883
"I've Tried Before" 82
"Ivy Covered Cottage" 507
"Izigubhu" 651
"Izzie's Story" 1595

"J-Dogg's Lament" 1479
"J. Timothy Fielding III" 766
"The Jabberwock" 1806
"Jabberwocky" (Lunden) 1190
"Jabberwocky" (Swados) 27
"Jack and Jill" 1168
"Jack Ketch" 655
"The Jack the Ripper Waltz" 789
"Jackie (La Chanson de Jacky)" 792
"The Jackie Look" 1430
"Jackie's Last Dance" 1778
"Jack's Song" 1110
"Jackson" 697
"Jacob and Sons" 833
"Jacob and the Angel (Man's Fight Against Divine Power)" 1044
"Jacob in Egypt" 833
"Jacob's Ladder" 1672
"Jacques and Jeannine" 552
"Ja-Da" 171
"Jahweh and Allah Battle" 729
"Jail-House Blues" 786
"Jail-Life Walk" 1038
"Jail Song" 396
"Jailer, Jailer" 398
"Jailhouse Blues" (Carmines) 1739
"Jailhouse Blues" (Herman) 735
"Jake the Ball Player" 1442
"Jake's Blues" 278
"Jam" 1222
"Jam on the Groove" 804
"Jamaica Farewell" 527
"Jamais Encore" 1470
"Jambalaya (On the Bayou)" 657
"James Bond Theme" 1450
"Jamie's Song" 890
"Jane's Song (My Fish and I)" 1299
"Janet Get Up" 1582, 1677
"Janey's Song" 1479
"Janitor" 804
"The Janitor's Statement" 1422
"Japan's Choice" 889
"Japanese and Proud to Be" 1410
"Japanese Lesson" 602
"Japanese Production" 772
"Jason's Bar Mitzvah" 473
"Jason's Song" 947
"Jason's Therapy" 1019
"Jasper's Vision" 1109
"J'Attends un Navire (I Wait for a Ship)" 1532
"Java Jive" 35
"Jaywalkin'" 949
"Jazz" 1439
"J-a-z-z" 788
"Jazz Baby Learns Aesthetic Dancing" 622
"Jazz Ballet, Third Movement" 295
"Les Jazz Chics" 552
"Jazz Games" 226
"Jazz Poem" 1734
"Jazzbo Brown" 809
"Jazzman" 1591
"J.B. Pictures, Inc." 1751
"Je Cherche un Millionaire" 924
"Je M'en Fiche" 1594
"Je Ne Sais Pa Pa" 577
"Je ne t'Aime Pas (I Don't Love You)" 689, 1532, 1809
"Je Sais Que Vous Etes Gentil" 136
"Je Vous Aime" 1494
"Jealous" 1762
"Jealousy Duet" 128, 1626, 1628
"The Jean Harlow Story" 557
"Jeff's Plaints" 1072
"Jeff's Song" 1194
"Jehoshaphat Makes Up His Mind" 1531
"The Jello Is Always Red" 812
"Jelly Roll Blues" 813
"Jellybread Falls on Jellyside Down" 1174
"Jenny" (Bohmler and Adler) 644
"Jenny" (Ryan) 535
"Jenny" (Smit) 1338
"Jenny" (Sternberg) 571
"Jenny" (Weill) 1807
"Jenny Is Like an Angel" 860
"Jenny Kiss'd (Kissed) Me" 851, 972
"Jenny Made Her Mind Up" (aka "The Saga of Jenny" and "Jenny") 879
"Jenny Rebecca" 1650
"Jenny von Westphalen" 860
"Jericho Cotton Mill Blues" 814
"Jericho Massacre" 814
"The Jeroboam" 1071
"Jerry Likes My Corn" 641
"Jerry's Daughter" 1545
"Jerry's Dream ('Move Over, You Guys')" 545
"Jerry's Girls" 818
"Jersey" 60, 1605
"Jerusalem" (Draesel) 1671
"Jerusalem" (Eliran) 401
"Jesse James Robbed This Train" 376
"Jesse's Lullaby" 323
"The Jester's Tale" 1531
"Jesu Joy of Man's Desiring" 952
"Jesus Christ" 1423
"Jesus Christ, Xanthus Fucked Us" 1237
"Jesus Come Down" 605
"Jesus Is Mine" 1484
"Jesus Is My Captain" 736
"Jesus Is My Doctor" 391
"Jesus Is My Main Man" 1620
"Jesus, Light Up the World" 120
"Jesus Likes Me" 1427
"Jesus Loves Me" 1559
"The Jesus-Mary Game" 1349
"Jesus, My Consolation" 331
"Jesus the Mighty Conqueror" 1404
"Jet Ace" 1066
"The Jewel Stairs' Grievance" 1222
"Jews in Groups" 1607
"Jilted" 1166, 1167
"Jim" 19
"Jim Along Josie" 481
"Jim, Jam, Jumpin' Jive" 221
"Jimmy on the Lam" 1347
"Jimmy Takes a Hit" 1347
"Jimmy's Comin' Back" 25
"Jim's Song" 403
"The Jitterbug" 1435
"Jitterbugging in the Streets" 1734, 1735
"Joanne" 283
"Job Hunting in Sodom" 1263
"Job Interview" (Kaz) 1209
"Job Interview" (Rivers and Silverman) 556
"Joe and Paul's" 604
"Joe Papp" 430
"Joe Sanchez" 915
"Joe Worker" 324
"Joe's Fantasy" 295
"Joey's Song" 22
"The Jog" 348
"Johanna" 1491
"Johannesburg" 1758, 1759
"John B. Sails" 261
"John Bolton Has Feelings, Too" 227
"John Brown's Body" 740, 815, 816
"John Brown's Body — Prelude, The Slaver" 1734
"John D. Rockefeller" 395
"John Henry" (Martin) 1464
"John Henry" (Traditional) 740
"John Is Your Sweetheart" 1063
"John Loves Mary: A Television Studio in Los Angeles and Elsewhere" 899
"John Luke Puts the Bite on Henry" 1478
"John Paul" 933
"Johnny and Jimmy" 571
"Johnny Angel" 1551, 1575
"Johnny Blue Eyes" 1459
"Johnny Can't Decide" 1634
"Johnny Come Lately" 381
"Johnny Guitar" 825
"Johnny Has Gone for a Soldier" 740
"Johnny Head-in-Air" 1444
"Johnny, I Hardly Knew Ye" 775
"Johnny Is the Man for Me" 1171
"Johnny Johnson's Song" 827
"Johnny-O" 1399
"Johnny Over There" 820
"Johnny Space" 216
"Johnny Too Bad" 1388
"Johnny's Creed" 93
"Johnny's Cursing Song" 1399
"Johnny's Dream" 827
"Johnny's Melody (When Man Was First Created)" (aka "Johnny's Song" and "Listen to My Song") 827
"Johnny's Oath" 827
"Johnny's Song" 826
"Johnny's Song (Listen to My Song)" 128
"John's Song" 161, 162, 163
"Johny" 449
"Join Us" 462
"The Joint Is Jumpin'" 18
"The Joint Is Really Jumpin' Down at Carnegie Hall" 840
"Joke a Cola" 1330
"Jokes" 214
"Jolly Coppers on Parade" 1036, 1334
"Jolly Good Luck to the Girl Who Loves a Soldier" 1639
"(A) Jolly Theatrical Season" 1132, 1218
"Jonah" 249
"Johannesburg" 1761
"The Jonah Cliché" 1333
"Jonah Man" 1643
"Jonah's Melodrama" 831
"Jonah's Wail" 698
"Jonas et Latude" 1073
"Jonny" 1350
"Jonny Don't Cry" 1831
"Joseph All the Time" 833
"Josephine" (Cohan) 570
"Josephine" (Wolf) 1274
"Joseph's Coat" 833
"Joseph's Dreams" 833
"Josette" 773
"Josette's Theme" 960
"Joshua" 1714
"Joshua's Rap" 814
"The Journals" 1325
"The Journey" 572
"Journey Home" 969
"Journey — Shin Tsen" 1020

"A Journey That Never Ends" 930
"The Journey That Was Yours" 1020
"Journey to Ever" 820
"Journeys" 111
"Journey's End" 1548
"Journey's in the Mind" 1438
"Joy" (Ford) 656
"Joy" (Schmidt) 308
"Joy, Joy, Joy" (Gardner) 1470
"Joy, Joy, Joy" (Naylor) 1002
"The Joy of My Desiring" 780
"Joy 'Round My Brain" 1356
"Joy Shall Be Yours in the Morning" 1784
"Joy to the World" 166
"A Joyful Noise" 106
"Joyride" 864
"Joys of Manhattan Life" 752
"The Joys of Sex" 837
"J'pas Capable!" 1510
"Juan" 1228
"Juan Carlose Rosenbloom" 1356
"Juanita Craiga (for Juanita Craiga Weight Loss Centers)" 2
"Jub-Jub" 785
"Jubilatedo" 1159
"Jubilation" 321
"Jubilee" 696
"Jubilee: No Never" 615
"Judge Not" 241
"Judgement" (Brown, et al.) 1487
"Judgement" (Offenbach) 124
"The Judgement Day" 1672
"Judgement Day" (Ercole) 856
"Judgement Day" (Unknown) 1559
"The Judge's Decision" 643
"Judging Song" 985
"Judgment" 1042
"The Judgment" 1436
"Judy!" (Martin and Gray) 1611
"Judy!" (*The Salad of The Mad Cafe*) 1394
"The Judy Garland National Anthem" 50
"Judy's Turn to Cry" 115
"The Jug Song" 542
"The Juggernaut" 1778
"The Juggler" 1475
"Jui-Jitsu" 1315
"Juice of the Grape" 301
"Juke Box Saturday Night" 35
"Julia's Song" 417
"Julie" (Dooley) 698
"Julie" (Singer) 543
"Julie Is Mine" 277
"Julie's Prayer" 721
"Jump De Broom" 715
"Jump Down, Spin Around" 685
"Jump for Joy" 165
"Jumpin' Jehosephat" 652
"Jumpin' the Gun" 499
"Jumping from Rock to Rock" 230
"June Is Bustin' Out All Over" 42
"The June Taylor" 869
"Juney Graduates Tonight" 844
"Jungle Fever" 1584
"Jungle Hip Hop" 646
"Jungle Party (No Escape)" 1738
"Junk Food Boogie" 919
"Junk Man (The Old Fool) Passes Through Utopia" 1592
"Jupiter Ammon! The Poetry!" 941
"Jupiter Slept Here" 1181
"Just ... Like ... Me" 1361, 1362
"Just a Closer Walk with Thee" 39
"Just a Coupla Sisters" 1155, 1157
"Just a Feeling" 279
"Just a Gigolo" 924, 1350
"Just a Little Bit" 175
"Just a Little Italian Girl" 255
"Just a Little Joint with a Juke-Box" 132
"Just a Little Walk with Jesus" 592
"Just a Night Out" 850
"Just Another Friday" 1742
"Just Another Page in Your Diary" 1704
"Just Another Song" 297
"Just Another Year" 1188
"Just as I Am" 1333
"Just As It Should Be" 406
"Just Before Daylight" 156
"Just Before I Go To Sleep" 1811
"Just Between Us" 930
"Just Can't Help It" 1231
"Just Come from the Fountain" 1762
"Just Do It Without Me" 1251
"Just Don't Know What to Do with Myself" 83
"Just Flowers" 1226
"Just for Love" 851
"Just for Me" 866
"Just for Once" 886
"Just for Openers" 852
"Just Friends" 293
"Just Go" 1121
"Just Go Shopping" 385
"Just Go to the Movies" 818
"Just Got Me" 333
"Just Him" 1254
"Just in Case" 14
"Just in Time" 746, 850, 1224, 1546, 1717
"Just Laugh It Away" 1584
"Just Let Me Dream" 1618
"Just Let Me Get My Hands on Peace Again" 1231
"Just Let Me Love You" 276
"Just Like a Woman" (Dylan) 265
"Just Like a Woman" (Lewine) 1116
"Just Like a Young Man" 1146
"Just Like in the Movies: Production" 410
"Just Like in the Movies: Rehearsal" 410
"Just Like Love" 408
"Just Like the Ivy I'll Cling to You" 1639
"Just Like You" (Downs) 486
"Just Like You" (Lippa) 830
"Just Like You" (Shaiman) 370
"Just Look at Me" 609
"Just Look Where I Come From" 1559
"Just Lucky I Guess" 639
"Just My Luck" 200
"Just Not Now" 738
"Just Once" 55, 854
"Just Once More" 1716
"Just One More Time" (Curtis) 1732
"Just One More Time" (Fox) 1577
"Just One of Those Things" 367
"Just One Person" 1486
"Just One Step" 1498
"Just Our Way of Doing Business" 416
"Just Over the Line" 375
"Just Plain Folks" 1218
"Just Plain Will" 1574
"Just Rapping" 542
"Just Say NO" 198
"Just Sit Around" 1231
"Just Sit Back" 1290
"Just Sit Back and Relax" 1566
"Just So" 855
"Just Someone to Talk To" 1164
"Just Suppose" 972, 989
"Just Sweet Sixteen" 637
"Just the Facts" 1034
"Just the Way We're Bred" 730
"Just the Way You Are" 1163
"Just Then" 14
"Just to Look at Him" 1033
"Just True" 1818
"Just Trust Me" 643
"Just Whistle" 64
"Just You Watch My Step" 902
"(Just) Across the River" 1524
"The Justice Game" 1666
"Justice Is Knocking" 470
"Juvenile Fiction" 1668

"The K-Bomb" 871
"Ka Da Bing, Ka Da Bang" 413
"Kabuki Parody" 1206
"Kabuki Rock" 869
"Kaleidoscope" (Clamen) 1574
"Kaleidoscope" (Mandel) 101
"Kaleidoscope" (Sottile) 767
"Kaleidoscope 1" 926
"Kaleidoscope 2" 926
"Kaleidoscope 3" 926
"Kaleidoscope 4" 926
"Kalt Vi Ize (Cold as Ice)" 1105
"Kamikaze Kabaret" 1622
"Kangaroo Court" 216
"Kanon Song" (aka "[The] Army Song," "Canon Song," and "Kanonensong") 879
"Kanonensong" (aka " [The] Army Song," "Canon Song," and "Kanon Song") 880, 882, 1773
"Kansas City Blues" 1550
"Karate" 1765
"Ka-razy" 377
"Kasi Atta Bat" 377
"Kasrilevke Restoran (A Restaurant in Kasrilevke)" 1619
"Kate, Kate, What Have We Done" 1789
"Kate Kearney" 805
"Kate the Great" 1704
"Kate, Would You Mind If We Were Poor?" 1789
"Katerina's Aria" 170
"Katie O'Sullivan" 1399
"Katinka" 271
"Katydid" 656
"A Katzenjammer Kinda Song" 1668
"K.C. Line" 376
"Keep 'Em Busy, Keep 'Em Quiet" 1154
"Keep 'Em Flying" 556, 557, 558
"Keep Fit, Feel Better, Live Longer" 1687
"Keep Him Safe" 754
"Keep Holding On" 1207
"Keep Hope Alive" 493
"Keep in Touch" 598
"Keep It Cool" 396
"Keep It Low" 271
"Keep Me Out of the Cassion" 217
"Keep Movin'" 1505
"Keep Off the Grass" (Schwerin) 1162
"Keep Off the Grass" (Schwartz) 1606
"Keep on Dancing" 1433
"Keep Smilin' Through" 730
"Keep the Castle Warm" 290
"Keep the Cool" 543
"Keep the Home Fires Burning" 1571
"Keep Watching the Skies" 1832
"Keep Working" 975
"Keep Your Little Eye Upon the Main Chance, Mary" 316
"Keep Your Shirt On" 85
"(Keep) Your Hand in Mine" 1218
"Keepers of the Light" 469
"Keepin' It Together" 461
"Keepin' Out of Mischief Now" 18
"Keeping Posted" 664
"Keeping the Man" 1315
"Keeping the Peace" 1759, 1761
"Keishi Attu Za Battu, or The Three Challenges" 415
"Keith's, Pantages & Loews" 1177
"Kemo Kimo" 481
"Kennedy-Khrushchev Interview" 22
"Kennst du das Land, wo die Zitronen Bluhn?" 941
"Kentucky Babe" 1643
"Kesa" 1422
"Ketchum, Idaho" 1052
"Keys" 1225
"Keys to Your Heart" 886
"Khave and the Apple Tree" 1502
"A Khazndl Oyf Shabes (A Cantor for the Sabbath)" 1619
"Khrushchev, Castro and Klenosky" 871
"Khrushchev-Kennedy Interview" 1415
"Khrushchev-Kennedy Press Conference" 1649
"Kick It Around" 409
"Kick Me Again" 338
"Kickball Tournament" 845
"Kicker Brown" 280
"Kickin' the Corn Around" 578
"Kicks" 854
"Kid" 1135
"The Kid" 145
"Kid Go!" 207
"Kid, I Love You" 505
"Kid Stuff" 1245
"Kiddie T.V." 986
"Kiddush" 666
"Kids Are Out" 575
"Kids Are the Only Ones Who Get Work Today" 511
"Kid's World" 602
"Kilimanjaro" 1401
"The Kill" 1424
"Kill Me" 100
"Kill Time" 947
"Killarney's Lakes" 805
"Killer Cheer" 387
"Killer on the Line" 1143
"Killing Time" 1184
"Kimberly" 1545
"Kimen Vet der Sholom (Peace Will Come)" 1105
"The Kind of a Girl" 1021
"The Kind of a Woman" 1565
"The Kind of Guy" 1319
"The Kind of Man" 1161
"A Kind of Power" 814
"Kind Sir" 259
"Kinder Yohrn (Childhood Years)" 1382
"Kinderishe Seychi (Childishness)" 1453
"Kindness" 206
"Kindness and Love" 983
"Kindred Spirits" 56, 57
"The King" 938
"King" 464
"King and Courtesans" 889
"The King Becomes a Clown" 1538
"The King Bee" 1720
"King Cole" 376
"King David" 1333
"King Foo-Foo the First" 1302
"The King Goes Out to War" 170
"King Joe" 152
"King Mackerel & The Blues Are Running" 864
"King Neptune" 1476
"King of Animal Traps" 1235
"The King of Offal Court" 1303
"King of the Rock" 107
"King of the World" (Brown) 1498
"King of the World" (Larimer) 867
"The Kingdom of Addo" 413
"Kingdom of Country" 323
"Kingly Duties" 834
"Kings and Queens (Coronation Cakewalk)" 1721
"Kings Die Easy" 1356
"The King's Regiment" 1635
"Kingston Market" 527
"Kinks" 837
"Kinsey in the Eleventh Hour" 395
"Kish Im In Derfrish Im" 1212
"Kishinev" 402
"Kismet Quick" 1574
"Kiss a Lonely Wife" 577
"A Kiss for Cinderella" 1167
"Kiss Her Now" 818
"A Kiss Is a Poem" 543
"Kiss Me" 121
"Kiss Me My Love" 1687
"Kiss Me Sweet" 1198
"Kiss Now" 869
"Kiss of Myer" 685
"Kiss of the Spider Woman" 52
"Kiss Off" 226
"Kiss the Girl" 727
"Kissed on the Eyes" 658
"Kisses and Hugs" 1386
"Kissinger und Kleindeinst und Klein" 1758
"Kitchen Man" 180, 181, 182, 1198
"Kite" (Gesner) 1828
"Kite" (Griffin) 1598
"The Kite" 1582, 1677
"Kittens in the Snow" 1326
"Kittiwake Island" 870
"Kitty Hawk and Jockey's Ridge" 864
"Kitty Kat Song" 1476
"Kivkaq" 963
"Klansmen Song" 1423
"Klenosky vs. Thaler" 871
"The Kleptomaniac" 547
"A Kliene Soft Shoe" 492
"Klinghoffer's Death" 363
"The Klutzenhoffer Jingle" 1289
"Knee Play 1" 427

"Knee Play 2" 427
"Knee Play 3" 427
"Knee Play 4" 427
"The Knife" 873
"Knife Dance" 1751
"Knife Routine" 1234
"Knights and Kings" 1419
"Knights on White Horses" 1752
"Knock at the Door" 1228
"Knock Knock" 889
"Knock on Wood" 399
"Knocking Myself Out" 1518
"Knockout" 266
"Knocks" 773
"Knotty Problems" 287
"Know When to Leave the Party" 1001
"Know Your Man" 190
"Knowing When to Leave" 83
"Kojong's Imperial Conference" 889
"Kol, Rinah Vish'ah" 1203
"Kolya's Return" 114
"Komedy Kupboard" 1427
"Komedy Kupboard I" 1427
"Die Konzert" 22
"Koyft a Tsaytung! (Buy, Read a Paper!)" 604
"Koze Kubenini" 651
"Krazy Kat's Ball" 637
"The Kremlin Krawl" 507
"Kris, Look What You've Missed" 1110
"Kulturny" 1460
"Kum Leybke Tantsn (Come Dance, Leybke)" 604
"Kumquats" 877
"Kung Fu" 1124
"The Kuzari" 1102
"Kyrie Eleison" (Bernstein) 1029
"Kyrie Eleison" (O'Reilly, et al.) 1727

"L.A. Freeway" 991
"L.A. Incident" 464
"La La La" 582
"La, La, La, La" 92
"La-La-La-La-La-La" 834
"La La Land" 424
"Labor Relations: Mom-to-Be's Old Bedroom in Naperville, Just Outside of Chicago" 899
"Labyrinth" 1200
"Lac Des Scenes" 1142
"Ladder to the Lord" 284
"Ladies" 375
"The Ladies 'Sizing-Up' Trio and Dialog" 1329
"Ladies and Gentlemen" 1111
"Ladies and Gentlemen, Comrades and Friends" 1139
"Ladies and Renaissance" 1435
"The Ladies Come from Baltimore" 1392
"Ladies in Waiting" 652
"Ladies, Look at Yourselves" 975
"Ladies of Louisburg Square" 197
"Ladies of Quality" 979
"Ladies of the Ballet" 1021
"Ladies of the Evening" 201
"Ladies of the House" 638
"Ladies of the Night" 706
"Ladies Should Be Beautiful" 1341
"The Ladies Who Lunch" 428
"The Ladies Who Sing with a Band" 18
"Ladies' Choice Ballet" 201
"Lady" (Marren) 961, 1756
"Lady" (Unknown) 1015
"Lady Anne's Chastity Belt" 1469
"Lady B" 858
"Lady Bird" 126, 558, 1605
"Lady Bird Fly Away Home" 1276
"Lady by Choice" 544
"The Lady Can't Act" 403
"Lady Gets Me There" 105
"The Lady in the Harbor" 1637
"The Lady Is a Tramp" 824, 850, 1210
"The Lady Lies" 434, 435
"Lady Lingerie" 82
"Lady Love" 581
"Lady Luck" 1644
"A Lady Needs a Change" 886
"A Lady Needs a Rest" 1704
"A Lady of Leisure" 74
"Lady of Light" 1562
"A Lady of Sex" 622
"Lady of Spain" 527
"Lady of the Desert Sand" 1050
"Lady of the Manor" 1716
"The Lady on the Piano" 1202
"Lady One & One" 156
"Lady Play Your Mandolin" 73
"Lady Ride with Me" 216
"Lady St. Helier" 151
"Lady Seeks Gentleman" 741
"Lady Success" 1459
"The Lady Takes a Shower" 1687
"The Lady Unobserved" 1687
"Lady Vagabond" 1136
"Lady Wake Up" 86
"The Lady Was Made to Be Loved" 33
"The Lady Who Loved to Sing" 159
"Lak Jeem" 1570
"The Lake" 1338
"Lalasana, Jerusalem" 1284
"Lamb Stew Tonight" 1418
"Lambatomy" 1014
"The Lambeth Walk" 449
"Lament" (Bobrowitz) 919
"Lament" (Gonzalez) 858
"Lament (of a Decoy Cop)" 564
"Lament and Argument" 9
"Lament for a Man in Blue" 758
"Lament on Fifth Avenue" 1447
"Lament to an Elephant-Woman" 1011
"The Lamp Is Low" 1521
"The Lamplighter" 938
"Lamplighters" 1635
"Lamps" 1412
"Lancashire" 476
"The Land of Desolation" 111
"The Land Where There Is No Death" 828
"Land Where We'll Never Grow Old" 1323
"Landing of the Spirit of '76" 1139
"The Landlord" 492
"Language of Flowers" 444
"Languishing" 465
"The Lannan Shoe" 253
"Lanterns" 1691
"Larceny and Love" 538
"LaRue's Song" 1469
"Las Vegas" 149, 150
"Las Vegas Post-Blitz" 36
"Last" 1460
"The Last 'I Love New York' Song" 1037
"Last Call" 1149
"The Last Can of Hennie Soup" 1375
"Last Chance for Dinny" 384
"The Last Chance Revue" 919
"Last Chance Saloon" 926
"Last Chance Series" 919
"Last Confession" 707
"Last Day on the Job" 656
"The Last Elf Aria" 1512
"The Last Encounter" 435
"The Last Goodbye" 1680
"The Last Incantation" 484
"The Last Man on Earth" 1832
"The Last Minute Waltz" 16
"Last Night" 741
"Last Night When We Were Young" 662, 1210
"The Last of Hong Kye-Hun" 889
"The Last One of the Boys" 1759, 1760
"Last One Picked" 1772
"The Last Paradise" 1219
"Last Quarter" 1319
"The Last Rockette" 1218
"Last Rose of Summer" 695
"The Last Thing That I Want to Do Is Fall in Love" 919
"The Last Time I Saw Her Face" 963
"The Last Time I Saw Paris" 883
"The Last to Know" 240
"The Last Train" 1315
"Last Year" 1422
"LATE" 198
"Late Last Night" 1416
"The Late, Late Show" (Shuman) 720
"The Late, Late Show" (Unknown) 1614
"The Late News" 547
"The Late Show" 160
"Late Sleeping Day" 265
"Lately I've Been Feeling So Strange" 91
"Later" 277
"Later Amphibians" 285
"Later Than Spring" 1390
"The Latest" 32
"The Latin American Way" 1304
"Latin Feelings" 897
"Latin Girl" 255
"Laugh and the World Laughs" 900
"Laugh It Up" 291
"The Laughing Generals" 826, 827
"Laughing Matters" 1763
"Laughing Out Loud" 1755
"The Laughing Song" 1311
"The Laundry" 285
"Laundry Finish" 252
"The Laundry Hour" 900
"Laundry Quintet" 252
"Laurie ... You Know, Laurie" 1601
"Laurie, Laurie" 1601
"Laurie!—The Very Same, Madam" 941
"Laurie's Farewell" 1601
"Law and Order" (Brand) 722
"Law and Order" (Brandon) 968
"Law, Order, Justice" 1771
"Lawbreakers" 1691
"Lawn as White as Driven Snow" 1437
"Lawyers" 210, 214
"Lawyer's Lament" 643
"The Lawyer's Out Today" 1309
"Lawyerman" 1309
"Lay a Little Love on Me" 696
"Lay Down Your Head" 1726
"Layers of Underwear" 271
"Layin' in the Sand" 359
"Lazar's Heroes" 1384
"The Laziest Gal in Town" 367, 1350
"Lazy Afternoon" 600, 692
"Lead 'Em Around by the Nose" 297
"Lead Me to the Water" 1363
"Lead Us On" 196
"The Leader" 773
"The Leader of a Big-Time Band" 367
"Leader of the Pack" 205
"Leading My Own Parade" 1300
"Leaflets" 324
"The League of Nations" 912
"Leak in the Building" 166
"Leak Something to Me ..." 547
"Lean on Me" 409
"Lean Sideways on the Wind" 1503
"Leaning on the Everlasting Arms" 996
"Leap of Faith" 1301
"Learn Everything!" 56
"Learn to Be Lonely" 398
"Learn to Love" 120
"Learn Your Lessons Well" 595
"Learning" 1361
"Learning Is a Lot Like Forgetting" 834
"Learning Love" 48
"Least of All Love" 1162
"Leather Love" 1153
"Leave It to Jane" 902
"Leave It to Me" 25
"Leave It to the Girls" 58
"Leave the Stronger and the Lesser Things to Me" 1503
"Leave the Thinking to Men" 1593
"Leave the World Behind" 969
"Leave Your Fate to Fate" 755
"Leavin' Time" 662
"Leaving on a Jet Plane" 37
"Lebedeff Der Melich (The Songs of Aaron Lebedeff)" 1212
"Lebn Zol Kolombus! (Long Live Columbus)" 604
"The Lecture" 1192
"Left Alone to Be" 216
"Left Behind" 1515
"Left-Hand Arrangement" 778
"Left Hook" 502
"Left, Right, Left" 990
"Legacy" (Childs) 222
"Legacy" (Forster) 610
"Legalese" 1472
"Legend from Lake Malacen" 295
"The Legend of King Arthur" 539
"The Legend of Old Rufino" 539
"Legend of the Islands" 1566
"Legs" (Marvin) 907
"Legs" (Motta) 877
"Legs" (Spektor) 718
"Lekha Doydi, Ya Riboyn Olam, Sholem Aleykhem, Gut Vokh" 604
"Lemme Tell Ya" 1164
"Leningrad-What War Was It?" 170
"Lennie" 1755
"Lennie's Lemonade" 991
"Lenny and the Heartbreakers" 910
"Lenox Hill Laundramat" 535
"Lenten Thoughts of a High Angelican" 135
"Leonardo's Lemonade" 991
"Leonard's Lemonade" 991
"The Les Less Show" 1394
"Leslie's Dance" 295
"Leslie's Fantasy of Men's Combination" 295
"Leslie's Fantasy of Warm-Up Ballet" 295
"Leslie's Fantasy of Women's Combination" 295
"Less Is More" 1772
"Less Is More and More" 752
"The Lesson" 1303
"Lesson #8" 1557
"Lessons on Life" 48
"Let America Begin Again" 1734
"Let 'Em Eat Cake" 912
"Let Freedom Ring" 844
"Let Go" 1188
"Let Her Be" 1222
"Let Her Go" 338
"Let Him Love You" 486
"Let It All Hang Out" 542
"Let It Alone" 457, 1783
"Let It Be" 1494
"Let It Be Today" 113
"Let It Fall" 1392
"Let It Go" (Russ) 770
"Let It Go" (Silver) 1458
"Let It Sing" 1726
"Let It Snow! Let It Snow! Let It Snow!" 1546
"Let It Spin" 825
"Let Me Be a Kid" 1384
"Let Me Be Lonely" 83
"Let Me Be Myself" 85
"Let Me Be Something to You" 468
"Let Me Be the One" 767
"Let Me Believe in Me" 856
"Let Me Believe in You" 404
"Let Me Call You Sweetheart" 1788
"Let Me Call You Sweetheart #2" 1788
"Let Me Come In" 1038
"Let Me Down" 969
"Let Me Drown" (Holton) 693
"Let Me Drown" (Lippa) 1778
"Let Me Entertain You" 1717
"Let Me Explain" 491
"Let Me Go to Him" 83
"Let Me Go to the Sea" 130
"Let Me In" 385
"Let Me Look at You" 941
"Let Me Make Love to You" 123
"Let Me Not to the Marriage of True Minds" 1519
"Let Me Out" 370
"Let Me Show You a New Way to Love" 1207
"Let Me Show You the World" 1707
"Let Me Sing!" 636
"Let Me Sing My Song" 214
"Let Me Take You for a Ride" 1464, 1465
"Let Me Walk Among You" 106
"Let My People Come" 913
"Let My People Go" 591, 1436, 1672
"Let the Church Roll On" 1762
"Let the Day Perish When I Was Born" 975

"Let the Flowers Find Me" 712
"Let the Good Times Roll" (Goodman) 965
"Let the Good Times Roll" (Lee) 1494
"Let the Good Times Roll" (Moore and Theard) 777, 1623
"Let the Moment Slip By" 1396
"Let the Play Begin" 1274
"Let the Show Go On!" 856
"Let the Toast Pass" 972
"Let the World Begin" 1504
"Let Them Bleed" 1327
"Let There Be Books" 1671
"Let There Be Peace" 819
"Let Us Begin (What Are We Making Weapons For?)" 37
"Let Us Charm Each Other" 1380
"Let Us Examine What You Did" 1139
"Let Us Take (Quartet)" 717
"Let Us Take the Road" 117
"Let Yourself Go" 681
"Let's" 200
"Let's Abolish Holidays" 852
"Let's All Be Exactly and Precisely What We Are" 1161
"Let's All Go to the Lobby" 1030
"Let's Ball Awhile" 1464, 1465
"Let's Be Elegant or Die!" 822
"Let's Begin" 883
"Let's Bring Back Showbusiness" 1177
"Let's Bring Golf to the Gulf" 606
"Let's Burn Down the Cornfield" 1036
"Let's Call the Whole Thing Off" 924
"Let's Dance" 212
"Let's Do It for Adam" 9
"Let's Do It, Let's Fall in Love" 367
"Let's Do It Right" 161
"Let's Do Lunch" 808
"Let's Do Something" 324
"Let's Do Something New Tonight" 197
"Let's Do the Confessional" 1333
"Let's Evolve" 1481
"Let's Face the Music and Dance" 1014
"Let's Fall in Love Today" 735
"Let's Get It On" 1623
"Let's Get Lost in Now" 1395, 1396
"Let's Get One Thing Straight" 850
"Let's Get Started" 113
"Let's Get Together" 1556
"Let's Go" (Katz) 1584
"Let's Go" (Koch and Taylor) 545
"Let's Go Boating" 215
"Let's Go Down" 1397
"Let's Go Out" 1111
"Let's Go to the Dogs" 1476
"Let's Go to Tuscany" 1671
"Let's Have a Party" 535
"Let's Have a Rodgers and Hammerstein Affair" 752
"Let's Have a Simple Wedding" 341
"Let's Have Another Cup of Coffee" 69, 740
"Let's Have Dinner and Dance" 1747
"Let's Hear It for Daddy Moola (Moolah)" 393, 394
"Let's Hear It for Me" 272
"Let's Hear It for the Kid" 1050
"Let's Live It Over Again" 319
"Let's Live It Up" 1518
"Let's Misbehave" 63
"Let's Mop Up These Yankees and Go Back Home" 258
"Let's Not Get Married" 1385
"Let's Not Go Away This Summer" 535
"Let's Not Miss the Boat" 1148
"Let's Play a Love Scene" 474
"Let's Play Ball" 377
"Let's Play Let's Stay" 216
"Let's Play the Game" 402, 1327
"Let's Pretend" (Brandon) 291
"Let's Pretend" (Micare) 1438
"Let's Say Goodbye" 13, 1170
"Let's See What Happens" 1546, 1717
"Let's Spend an Hour" 1045
"Let's Step Out" 63
"Let's Take a Stroll Through London" 1393
"Let's Toast" 1303
"The Letter" (Ballard) 93
"The Letter" (Bingham) 71
"The Letter" (Dick) 1771
"The Letter" (Fields) 1445
"The Letter" (Goodman) 206
"The Letter" (Odenz) 1402
"The Letter" (Pen) 114
"The Letter" (Thompson) 1551
"The Letter (Me Charlotte Dear)" 271
"Letter Fantasy: Grand Street" 1361
"Letter from Europe" 1715
"Letter from Klemnacht" 398
"Letter from My Son" 1647
"Letter from the Publisher" 1698
"Letter #1" 791
"Letter #2" 791
"Letter #3" 791
"Letter #4" 791
"Letter of the Law" 1152
"The Letter of the Law" 538
"Letter Song" (Barnes) 469
"Letter Song" (Coward) 13
"Letter Suite" 616
"Letter to the Children" 398
"Letter to the Editor" 1698
"A Letter to the Rabbi" 1203
"Letters" (Aman, et al.) 1661
"Letters" (Zellnick) 1818
"The Letters" 1103
"Level with You" 1638
"Leviathan" 831
"Levine and His Flying Machine" 604
"Leyenda" 1694
"The L.I. Van Gogh Blue Period Gavotte" 1263
"A Li'l Ole Bitty Pissant Country Place" 133
"Liaisons Dangereuses (A Common Conjugal Problem)" 1077
"The Liar (Staggolee)" 1373
"Libby" 506
"The Liberal Campaign" 1091
"Liberal's Lament" 1758, 1760
"Liberate" 260
"Liberation Tango" 1759
"Liberia" 1072
"Liberty, Equality & Fraternity" 1265
"The Licorice Fields at Pontefract" 135
"The Lid's Been Blown" 1831
"Lie with Me" 293
"Liebeslied" 1628
"Das Lied Ist Aus" 1350
"Lieder Singer" 32
"Lies, Lies, Lies" 975
"Lieutenants of the Lord" 660
"Life" (Procter) 654
"Life" (Satlin) 279
"Life" (Slater) 719
"Life and All That" 930
"Life Can Pass You By" 1228
"Life Cry" 361
"Life Cycle in the Delta" 1734, 1735
"Life Don't Always Work Out" 1208
"Life in the Country" 1749
"Life Is a Balancing Act" 89
"Life Is a Bowl of Pits" 302
"Life Is a Drag" 1706
"Life Is But a Dream" 1404
"Life Is Funny" 945
"Life Is Good" 639
"Life Is Happiness Indeed" 244
"Life Is Just a Bowl of Cherries" 681
"Life Is Lovely" 598
"Life Is Perfect" 461
"Life Is So Beautiful" 819
"Life Is the Café Carlyle" 1693
"Life Is What You Make of It" 1188
"Life Isn't Easy, Agnes" 638
"Life of an Innocent Child" 1333
"The Life of Peter" 120
"The Life of the Party" 1778
"Life on Mars" 1494
"Life on the Inside" 393, 394
"Life on the Rocks" 272
"Life Story" 300, 1710
"The Life That I Planned for Him" 291
"The Life That Jack Built" 161, 162, 163, 164
"The Life That We Lead" 880, 882
"Life Upon the Wicked Stage" 883
"The Life We Lead" 1733
"A Life Without Her" 480
"A Life Without Love" 1815
"'Life' Is a Four-Letter Word" 1646
"The Lifeguard (on a Crowded Beach)" 1044
"The Lifeguards" 85
"Lifelines" 2
"Life's a Funny Proposition, After All" 570
"Life's Ambition" 781
"Life's Odyssey" 224
"Life's Railway to Heaven" 1484
"Life's Unanswerable Questions" 606
"Lifesaver" 943
"Lifeshine Ark I" 926
"Lifeshine Ark II" 926
"The Liffey Waltz" 848
"Lift Every Voice and Sing" (Scott) 1064
"Lift Every Voice and Sing" (Traditional) 736
"Lift Him Up" 615
"Lift Me Up" (McLean) 67
"Lift Me Up" (Telson) 615
"Lift Off!" 96
"Lift Up Your Voice!" 8
"Lifted" 1339
"Lifting Belly" 1222
"Lifting the Leather" 1618
"Liftoff to Love" 1235
"The Light" 453
"The Light Around the Corner" 856
"The Light Ballet" 1252
"Light Doesn't Last That Long" 322
"Light in the East" 1422
"Light in the Loafers" 1763
"Light Is Her Step on the Stair and the Floor" 951
"Light Is the Heart" 13
"Light My Fire" 265, 1664
"Light of the World" 595
"The Light of Your Love (La Luz de Tu Amor)" 208
"Light on My Feet" 296
"Light Our Way" 576
"Light Sings" 1038
"A Light Thing" 910
"Lighter Than a Light Thing" 910
"Lighting a Candle" 1518
"Lightnin' Bug" 8
"Like a Dream" 266
"Like a Lady" 785
"Like a Lily" 586
"Like a Park on Sunday" 279
"Like a Rolling Stone" 265
"Like a Wood in Ireland This Is" 439
"Like Carmen, Not Me!" 474
"Like Chocolate, Soldier?" 673
"Like Everybody Else" (Bernstein) 234
"Like Everybody Else" (Evans) 280
"Like Her or Not" 1294
"Like It Was" 1492
"Like Liza Does" 1337
"Like the Breeze Blows" 981
"Like the Clouds" 1788
"Like the Ming Tombs" 1139
"Like the Skyline" 1195
"Like They Do" 1500
"Like They Used To" 1554
"Like Yours" 685
"Lilac Tree" 504
"Lilacs Bring Back Memories" 1155, 1157
"Lili Is a Lady with a Suitcase Up Her Sleeve" 1348
"Lili Marlene" 1350, 1611, 1750
"Lilly's Address" 1706
"Lily of Laguna" 1540
"Lily Pad Tango" 690
"Limbo" 1349
"Limbrada's Daughters" 130
"Limehouse Blues" 171
"Limo to the Plaza" 45
"Lincoln and Soda" 722
"Lincoln Center" 415
"The Lincoln Waltz" 71
"Lincoln West" 1373
"Linda, Georgina, Marilyn and Me" 913
"Linda Quisqueya" 533
"Lindsay Was Prettier and Taller Than Klenosky and Who's Sorry Now?" 871
"The Line" 791
"The Line Is Busy" 1715
"Lines to a Reviewer" 1443
"Linger Awhile" 502
"Linger in Blissful Repose" 112
"Lingoland" 926
"The Lion and the Boar" 11
"The Lion and the Jewel" 927
"The Lion and the Mouse" 11
"Lion Dance" 1213
"Lip Service" 1747
"The Lippy Song" 1386
"Liquid Legerdemain" 287
"The Liquor Dealer's Dream" 660
"Lise Dear" 65
"List Song" 992, 1106
"Listen!" 222, 1020
"Listen, Davey" 654
"Listen, I Feel" 1311
"Listen Little Boy" 272
"Listen Lord — A Prayer" 1672
"Listen to Jesus, Jimmy" 1347
"Listen to Me" (Lippa) 1778
"Listen to Me" (O'Reilly and Rast) 1727
"Listen to Me Jesus" 1423
"Listen to My Heart" 929
"Listen to the Beat!" 149, 150
"Listen to the Children" 706
"Listen to the Music" 683
"Listen to the Voice" 1671
"Listen, World!" 272
"Listenin' to the Grand Ole Opry" 1343
"Listening" 388
"Listening for Sounds I've Never Heard (Looking for Things I've Never Seen)" 1475
"Litany" 1229
"Literary Cocktail Party" 1318
"Literary Jam/Jam/Band Jam, 'JAM'" 1222
"A Little Anisette (Mon Anisette)" 1641
"Little Babes That Sleep All Night" 1323
"Little Bat, What You Doin' Here?" 1563
"Little Bird" 927
"Little Birdies Learning How to Fly" 577
"Little Birds" 698
"A Little Bit" 788
"A Little Bit o' Glitter" 856
"A Little Bit of B.S." 1202
"A Little Bit of Soap" 1551
"A Little Bit of This" 406
"A Little Bit Off" 1524
"Little-Bitty Pretty One" 790
"Little Black Baby" 1388
"Little Black Tshombe" 1276
"Little Blue Star" 1331
"A Little Boo Boo" 1402
"Little Boy Blue" 1085
"The Little Boy Blues" 954
"Little Brother" 350
"A Little Bungalow" 305
"Little by Little I" 930
"Little by Little II" 930
"Little by Little III" 930
"Little by Little IV" 930
"Little by Little V" 930
"Little by Little VI" 930
"Little Children on the Grass" 453
"Little Darling" (Holt) 1733
"Little Darling" (Williams) 1575
"A Little Dental Music" 727
"Little Did I Dream" 1554
"Little Did I Know" 1362
"Little Did We Know" 1362
"Little Dog Blue" 867
"Little Fairies" 409
"Little Fish" (Freyer) 249
"Little Fish" (LaChiusa) 933
"Little Flower" 1232
"Little Fool" 1311
"A Little Game of Tennis" 908
"Little Girl" 1485
"Little Girl Baby" 1716
"Little Girl Blue" 965
"Little Girl Blues" 1142

"A Little Girl in the Night" 3
"Little Girl—Big Voice" 919
"Little Green Snake" 1580
"Little H and Little G" 1709
"A Little Happiness" 1243
"Little Hero" 1522
"A Little House for Me" 102
"A Little House in the Country" 476
"A Little Hustle" 930
"Little Jazz Bird" 46, 1172
"Little Known Facts" 1828
"Little Lamb" 1204
"Little League" 830
"A Little Learning" 878
"Little Little" 416
"Little Liza Jane" 1762
"A Little Love, A Little Money—I" 942
"A Little Love, A Little Money—II" 942
"Little Mary Sunshine" (Besoyan) 766, 935
"Little Mary Sunshine" (Studney) 1347
"Little Mister Tippy Toes" 690
"A Little Moosic to Soothe the Savage" 871
"A Little More Like You" 1707
"Little Nell" 976
"Little Old Lady in Black" 948
"The Little Ones' ABC" 1390
"Little Piece of Sugar Cane" 1367
"Little Rag Doll" 1008
"Little Reward" 252
"Little Rubik's Room" 36
"Little Shop of Horrors" 939
"A Little Something on the Side" 1743
"Little Sparrow" 957
"Little Sparrows" 93
"Little Star" 375
"A Little Starch Left" 1107
"Little Tear" 80
"The Little Things We Used to Do" 1304
"The Little Things You Do Together" 428, 1491
"A Little Valise" 301
"The Little Victrola" 829
"Little White Dog" 605
"Little Woman" 1754
"Little Women" 718
"Little Yellow Bird" 1639
"The Littleflea Hop" 304
"The Littlest Revue" 942
"Litvak/Galitsyaner" 1619
"Live Alone and Like It" 1492
"Live and Be Well" 915
"Live for the Moment" 1025
"Live It Up" 929
"Live Where You Can" 615
"Liverpool Sunset" 271
"Livin to the Beat" 410
"Livin'" 696
"Livin' Alone" 237
"A Livin' Doll" 943
"Livin' in a Hole" 676
"Livin' on Dreams" 1208
"Livin' Ragtime" 1373
"Living a Dream" 719
"The Living and the Dead" 805
"Living Color" 945
"Living in Luxury" 1148
"Living in New York" 1419
"Living in Sin" 297
"Living It Up" 238
"Living Love" 509
"Living Next Door to the Sun" 1511
"Living Out a Lie" 1428
"Living Pictures" 638
"Living the Good Life" 393
"Liza" 165
"Liza Lisi Dinga" 1284
"Lizzie" 947
"Lizzie Borden" 861
"Lizzie, Lizzie, Have You Tasted" 586
"Lizzie's Dressing Scene" 947
"Lizzie's Mad Scene" 947
"Lloyd's of London" 68
"Lloyds of London" 68
"Lo, Here the Gentle Lark" 1569
"Lo Que Me Gusta a Mi" 1402
"Lo Que Tiene" 1336
"Loadin' Time" 348
"The Lobster Quadrille" 27
"Local" 1698
"Local Hookers' Local" 1743
"Locked and Secluded" 1512
"Locker of Love" 1283
"The Locker Room" 952
"The Locket" 1204
"Loco-Motion" 1551
"Loehmann's" 1299
"Loew's Sheridan Square" 758
"Loew's State and Orpheum" 1733
"Logic!" 34
"Loki and Baldur" 398
"Lola" 436
"Lola in Bavaria" 948
"Lola-Lola" 1350
"Lolaland" 948
"Lollipop" 1574, 1575
"Lollipop Lane" 1142
"Lollipops and Roses" 1551
"Lollitapop" 226
"Lomir Freylach Zeyn" 1032
"Lomir Geyn a Polka Tantzn" 1032
"Lomir Loybn (Let Us Praise)" 1619
"London at Night" 13
"London Bridge" 1303
"London Bus" 241
"London by Night" 1750
"London Days and New York Nights" 949
"London Dierriere" 1255
"London Hilton" 450
"London Pride" 751
"London Town" 1316
"Lone Star Love" 950
"Lonely" 719
"Lonely Are They" 1153
"Lonely at the Top" 1036, 1049
"Lonely Bohunks" 1710
"Lonely Canary" 271
"Lonely Children" 1424
"Lonely Girl" 1732
"Lonely Heart" 69
"Lonely Heartache, Lonely Man" 535
"Lonely House" 128, 1532
"Lonely in Space" 910
"Lonely Is" 915
"Lonely Is the Life" 93
"Lonely Man" 535
"Lonely Man, Lonely Woman" 164
"Lonely Me" 234
"Lonely Neighbors" 1562
"Lonely Ones" 1420
"Lonely Pew" 1347
"Lonely Quartet" 1708
"Lonely Song and Dance Man" 1194
"The Lonely Sparrows of Wessex" 345
"Lonely Stranger" 1726
"Lonely Teardrops" 790
"Lonely Times" 113
"Lonely Town" 1185, 1186, 1224
"Lonely Town Dance" 1185
"Lonely Voice" 985
"Lonely Woman" 1045
"Lonesome in New York" 735
"Lonesome Longing Blues" 1543
"Lonesome of the Road" 1384
"Long Ago (and Far Away)" 883, 1750
"A Long Ago Love" 66
"Long Ago, or Yesterday?" 636
"The Long and Winding Road" 1426
"Long Before I Knew You" 1717
"Long Day's Voyage Home" 1765
"Long Distance" 19
"Long Distance Love" 1002
"Long Gone Lonesome Blues" 657
"The Long Goodbye" 1138
"The Long Grift" 680
"Long John Blues" 383, 1494
"Long Live Free Enterprise" 393, 394
"Long Live the Greedy" 1531
"Long Live the Queen" 230
"A Long, Long Time" 1467
"A Long, Long Way" 89
"Long Long Way to Heaven" 730
"Long May Our Comrades Prosper Well" 941
"Long Past Sunset" 726
"The Long Run" 444
"The Long Song" 1605
"A Long Story" 624
"Long Time No See" 535
"Long Time Travelling" 780
"A Long Way from Home" 655
"Longing" 1051
"Longing for Someone" 1646
"Longue Vie a la Famille!" 1510
"Look!" 472
"The Look" 991
"Look a Yonder" 120
"Look All Around You (See What's Happenin')" 968
"Look at Him" 971
"Look at Mama, the General!" 1105
"Look at Me" (Britton) 636
"Look at Me" (Dorsey) 1117
"Look at Me" (Gari) 980
"Look at Me" (Grant) 1307
"Look at Me" (Laird) 1386
"Look at Me" (Slade) 1393
"Look at Me" (Sticco) 267
"Look at Me" (Swados) 1345
"Look at Me" (Tesori) 1726
"Look At Me Go" 1670
"Look at Me, I'm Sandra Dee" 625
"Look at Me Joan" 823
"Look at Me Now" 1778
"Look at My Hands" 431
"Look at My Sister" 292
"Look at the Basin" 362
"Look at the Camera" 1320, 1321
"Look at the Children" 647
"Look at the Sky" 1712
"Look at the Stars" 938
"Look at Us" 785
"Look at What It's Done" 1755
"Look at What We're Saving from the Blaze" 1316
"Look Away" 74
"A Look Back" 492
"Look Closer, Love" 1250
"Look for a Sky of Blue" 766, 935
"Look for the Morning Star" 1465
"Look for the Silver Lining" 1096, 1750
"Look in the Mirror" 717
"Look Inside" 113
"Look, Look at Me" 820
"Look Ma, I Made It" 1159
"Look Me Over Closely" 1350
"The Look of Love" 83, 1551
"Look on Me" 889
"Look Out to the World" 959
"Look Through the Moongate" 1531
"Look Through the Window" 152
"Look to the Rainbow" 775
"Look Underneath" 61
"Look Up" 1452
"Look What Happened to Mabel" 818
"Look Where I'm At!" 957
"Look Who I Am, Surprise, Surprise!" 569
"Look Who's Coming to Harlem" 9
"Look Who's Evil Now" 462
"Look Who's Here" (Menken) 588
"Look Who's Here" (Solly) 1050
"Look Who's Throwing a Party" 1452
"The Looka Song" 1505
"Lookin' at the Moon" 1366
"Lookin' for Food" 1046
"Lookin' Good" 338
"Lookin' Good but Feelin' Bad" 18
"Lookin' Over from Your Side" 400
"Looking at the Sun" 1517
"Looking at Us" 1136
"Looking at You" 71
"Looking for a Boy" 1644
"Looking for a Candidate" 1608
"Looking for a Miracle" 323
"Looking for Love" 886
"Looking for Someone" (Rodgers) 986
"Looking for Someone" (Simons) 1290
"Looking for Space" 37
"Looking for the Action" 1649
"Looking for the Sunshine" 1577
"Looking Over My Life" 602
"Looking to the Sky" 1194
"Looking Up" 430
"Looking Up Quintet" 430
"Lookit Those Stars" 1777
"Looks Like It Might Rain" 385
"Looks Like Love" 461
"Looney Bin Administration" 1091
"Loose Change" 644
"Looza on the Block" 248
"Lopeziana" 1016
"The Lord Bless and Keep You" 1043
"The Lord Doesn't Rain Down Manna" 1323
"Lord, Don't Move This Mountain" 592
"The Lord Has Spared This Child" 439
"Lord Have Mercy" 959
"Lord, Hear Your Child A-Callin'" 1762
"Lord How Come Me Here" 1623
"Lord, How My Baby Has Grown" 362
"The Lord Is a Hammer of Light" 1708
"The Lord Is Blessing Me" 1002
"The Lord Is My Light" 1739
"The Lord Is My Shepherd (The Wake)" 439
"Lord Keep Us Day by Day" 196
"Lord We Thank Thee" 1338
"The Lord's Prayer" 1401
"The Lord's Work" 333
"Lordy" 113
"Lordy, the Flies" 1318
"Loretta" 980
"Lorna's Here" 237, 603
"Lorraine's Tape" 1040
"The Loser's Dream Team" 871
"Losers" 1685
"Losing Touch" 1472
"Lost" (Pockriss) 448
"Lost" (Sottile) 767
"Lost" (Wallowitch) 820
"Lost and Found" 1698
"Lost and Won" 197
"Lost at Sea" 1470
"The Lost Beat Swing" 207
"Lost Highway" 657
"Lost Horizon" 607
"Lost in Space" 943
"Lost in the Stars" 128, 1773, 1807, 1809
"Lost in the Wilderness" 1762
"Lost Liberty Blues" 1704
"Lost Love" 1727
"Lost My Cool" 319
"Lost New York" 1290
"A Lot of Heart" 1595
"A Lot of Livin' to Do" 237
"A Lot of Men" 726
"Lotta" 958
"Lottery Celebration" 147
"Loud and Tacky" 322
"Loud Enough" 45
"Loud Is Good" 781
"Louder! I Can't Hear You When the Philharmonic's Playing on Sheep Meadow" 550
"Louder Than Words" 1634
"Louie" (LaChiusa) 1422
"Louie" (Shaiman) 646
"Louise" 1198
"Louisiana 1927" 1049
"Louisiana Cajun Man" 960
"Louisiana Hayride" 348, 1606
"Louisiana Summer" 960
"Loumania" 1365
"Lounging at the Waldorf" 18
"Loup's Lament" 960
"A Lovable Fellow" 1131
"L-O-V-E" 1575
"Love" (Blane and Martin) 1245
"Love" (Marren) 961
"Love" (Smith) 1198
"Love" (Strouse) 58
"Love" (Wilson) 419
"Love a Stranger" 110
"Love Affair" 1754
"Love and Live On" 1188
"Love and Maple Syrup" 963
"Love at an Auction" 535
"Love at First Sight" 229
"Love at Robin Lake" 963
"Love Calls You by Your Name" 1471
"Love Came to Me" 175
"Love Child" 123
"Love College" 1802
"Love Come A-Callin'" 943
"Love Comes and Goes" 493
"Love Conquers All" 766
"Love Does" 1095

"Love Doesn't Grow on Trees" 121
"Love, Don't Be a Stranger" 469
"Love Duet" (Britten) 1229
"Love Duet" (Keating) 1522
"Love Duet" (Offenback) 124
"Love Duet" (Ost) 461
"Love Duet" (Rangstrom) 295
"Love Duet" (Weill) 128
"The Love Duet" 1398
"Love Duet (I Like the Way He Looks)" 959
"The Love Elixir" 504
"Love Essay" 915
"Love Everybody" 1085
"Love for Four" 945
"Love for Sale" 367, 382, 1015, 1282, 1704
"Love Gets in the Way" 749
"Love Got in the Way" 359
"Love Has Arrived" 1316
"Love Held Lightly" 669
"Love in Disguise" 1706
"Love in the Morning" 646
"Love in the Wings" 1414
"Love Is" (Berkowitz) 1060
"Love Is" (Charnin) 472
"Love Is" (Cribari) 1283
"Love Is" (Leigh) 289
"Love Is" (Weinstein) 721
"Love Is a Crazy Thing" 1263
"Love Is a Feeling" (Charlap) 1447
"Love Is a Feeling" (Koch and Taylor) 545
"Love Is a Four-Letter Word" 25
"Love Is a Fragile Thing" 1480
"Love Is a Game" 1179
"Love Is a Good Thing for You" 261
"Love Is a Many Splendored Thing" 527
"Love Is a Pain" 1480
"Love Is a Sickness" 915
"Love Is a Simple Thing" 861
"Love Is a Stranger" 352
"Love Is a Two-Part Invention" 1683
"Love Is a Two-Way Street" 1575
"Love Is Beautiful" 1124, 1537
"Love Is Blind" 997, 1019
"Love Is Coming Back" 1007
"Love Is Everything" 61
"Love Is for the Birds" 1475
"Love Is Here to Stay" 46
"Love Is International" 1341
"Love Is Like a Rose" 304, 672
"Love Is Like a Water Faucet" 194
"Love Is Lovely" 80
"Love Is Not a Sentiment Worthy of Respect" 308
"Love Is on Its Knees" 1585, 1586
"Love Is Paradise" 366
"Love Is Perjured Everywhere" 1519
"Love Is Simply Heavenly" 1464, 1465
"Love Is Still in Town" 942
"Love Is Still Love" 1608
"Love Is Sweeping the Country" 1166, 1167
"Love, Is That You?" 1689
"Love Is the Loveliest Love Song" 336
"(Love Is) A Game of Poker" 669
"(Love Is) The Tender Trap" 1210
"Love Isn't Born, It's Made" 348, 1138, 1571
"Love Isn't Everything" 733
"Love, It Hurts So Good" 981
"Love Knots" 434, 435
"Love Lesson" 962
"Love, Let Me Sing You" 130
"Love Letters" 1750
"Love Letters in the Sand" 1575
"Love Letters Written to My Mother" 160
"Love Life" 587
"Love Like That" 1225
"Love Looking Back at Me" 499
"Love! Love! Love!" (Brandon) 968
"Love! Love! Love!" (Offenbach) 190
"Love! Love! Love!" (Shimoda) 602
"Love, Love, Oh See Now" 507
"Love Loves the Difficult Things" 975
"Love Makes the World Go Round" 1115
"Love Match" 858
"Love Me" (Bargy) 638
"Love Me" (Ruffin) 1562
"Love Me a Little" 352
"Love Me As I Am" 1016
"Love Me, Baby!" 1331
"Love Me for What I Am" 763, 764, 765
"Love Me Just a Little Bit" 461
"Love Me Lightly" 113
"Love Me Love Me Dorothy Lamour La Sarong" 1330
"Love Me, Love My Children" 969
"Love Me or Leave Me" 1297
"Love Me Tomorrow (but Leave Me Alone Today)" 238
"Love Me Too" 985
"Love Means" 217
"Love Must Be Delicato" 1146
"The Love Nest" 1028
"Love Never Went to College" 1282
"Love-O-Meter" 54
"The Love of a Woman" 543
"Love of Long Ago" 1265
"Love of Money" 1407
"The Love of My Life" 1158
"The Love of Your Life" 1400
"Love on the Moon" 1192
"Love on the Street" 1574
"Love or Fear" 721
"Love Please Stay" 786
"Love Potion No. 9" 205
"Love Power" 400
"Love Runs Deeper Than Pride" 1363
"Love Scene" 65
"A Love Scene for Who?" 293
"Love Should Be Free" 348
"Love Song" (Beeson) 926
"Love Song" (Kander) 1685
"Love Song" (Kaplan) 147
"Love Song" (Neuner) 769
"Love Song" (Petsche) 416
"Love Song" (Silver) 1527
"Love Song" (Strouse) 1473
"Love Song" (Weill) 128, 1626
"A Love Song" (Allen, et al.) 1742
"A Love Song" (Shire) 616
"Love Song of W. Mark Felt" 227
"Love Song to a Monster" 1081
"Love Stays" 333
"Love Stolen" 1367
"Love Story" (Hoffman) 1758
"Love Story" (Kaz) 1209
"Love Story" (Newman) 1036, 1334
"Love Story" (Unknown) 1494
"Love Suffers Everything" 1253
"Love Takes Time" 1492
"The Love That Came Before" 260
"Love That Lives Forever" 404
"Love Them and Leave Them Alone" 1306
"Love Themes" 1255
"The Love They Write About" 1580
"Love Throws a Line" 1598
"Love Times One" 820
"Love Train" 1623
"Love Turned the Light Out" 238
"Love Unconquerable" 615
"Love Was a Stranger to Me" 705
"Love Was Just a Game" 183
"Love Who You Love" 1006
"Love Will Come Your Way" 985
"Love Will Conquer All" 246
"Love Will Find a Way" 221
"Love Wins Again" 1539
"Love-Wise" 926
"Love-Wise Anecdote" 926
"Love, You Are So Difficult" 74
"Lovely" 1492
"Lovely Bridesmaids" 332
"Lovely Day" 1622
"A Lovely Girl" 148
"Lovely Is the Breeze (Quartet)" 717
"Lovely Island" 332
"Lovely Ladies" 850
"Lovely Light" 616
"A Lovely Little Life" 2
"Lovely Rita" 1426
"Lovely to Look At" 883, 886
"A Lovely Way to Spend an Evening" 1210
"Lover" 1239, 1245
"Lover Come Back to Me" 382, 1245, 1570
"Lover, I'm Not Ready Yet for You" 1693
"Lover Like a Blind Man" 183
"Lover Lost" 1008
"Lover Man" 156, 181, 182
"Lover of Love" 1518
"Lover, Sweet Lover" 1747
"A Lover Waits" 80
"Lovers" (Hardwick) 580
"Lovers" (Menken) 1228
"Lovers" (Sterner) 971
"Lovers" (Tucholsky) 1635
"Lovers" (Wilson) 419
"The Lovers (Adolescence)" 1592
"Lovers and Losers" 23
"A Lover's Dream" 493
"Lovers in Love" 424
"Lovers Manage" 1057
"Lovers of Teruel" 361
"Lovers of the Lamplight" 1379
"Lover's Prayer" 1049
"Love's a Bond" 1403
"'Love's a Bond' Blues" 1403
"The Loves in My Life" 556
"Love's Labour Lost" 126
"Love's Melody" 638
"Love's Old Sweet Song" 695
"Love's Philosophy" 1443
"Love's Revenge" 1689
"Love's Sad Glance" 646
"Love's Sorrow" 323
"The Love's Still Growing" 1666
"Love's Too Mild a Word" 1237
"Lovesick Blues" (Mills and Friend) 39
"Lovesick Blues" (Williams) 657
"Lovesong" 1375
"Lovesongs and Lullabies" 878
"The Lovin" 410
"Lovin'" 968
"Lovin' Hands" 927
"Lovin' Tree" 110
"Loving Him" 143
"Loving Is a Lot Like Indifference" 834
"Loving You" (Driver) 1358
"Loving You" (Sondheim) 1491
"Low" 181
"Low Fidelity" 1125
"Lower Deck Diplomacy" 1058
"Lower the Bar" 1479
"Lower the Boom" 701
"Lowlife" 370
"Loxagane (Avalon)" 755
"Loyal American" 745
"Lozt Ayayn (Let Us In)" 604
"Luau Chant" 1221
"Lubov Nye Kartoshka" 1032
"Lucia" 1670
"Lucien" 361
"Lucille Camille Chenille" 845
"Luck, Be a Lady" 1210
"Luck of the Draw" 1726
"Lucky" (Bowman and Pole) 1316
"Lucky" (Flaherty) 973
"Lucky" (Guettel) 503
"Lucky Baby" 1033
"Lucky Day" (Morris and Shane) 1188
"Lucky Day" (Renzi) 959
"Lucky Heart" 1135
"Lucky Lindy" (Bauer and Wolfe) 1096
"Lucky Lindy" (Brand) 722
"Lucky Louie" 1538
"Lucky Love" 1033
"Lucky Me" 86
"Lucky Star" 190
"Lucky to Be Me" 1185, 1186, 1224
"Lucky Woman" 1747
"Lucy in the Sky with Diamonds" 1426
"Luis and Susana" 897
"Lullaby" (Ander, et al.) 175
"Lullaby" (Baton) 1419
"Lullaby" (Carmines) 952
"Lullaby" (Donizetti) 1146
"Lullaby" (Engeran) 1151
"Lullaby" (Finn) 41
"Lullaby" (Frank) 1306
"Lullaby" (Goggin and Solley) 667
"Lullaby" (Katsaros) 781, 855
"Lullaby" (LaChiusa) 130
"Lullaby" (Rodgers) 1193
"Lullaby" (Rue) 1333
"Lullaby" (Tucholsky) 1635
"Lullaby" (Weill) 128
"A Lullaby" 1652
"Lullaby for Luis" 1384
"Lullaby from Baby to Baby" 1384
"Lullaby of Broadway" 35, 212, 1096
"Lullaby of Night" 960
"Lullaby of the Plain" 578
"Lullaby Wind" 1751
"Lullabye" (Carmines) 111
"Lullabye" (Goggin) 1202
"Lullabye" (Gordon) 1103
"Lullabye" (Henderson) 333
"Lullabye" (Kennon) 690
"Lullabye" (Levenson) 293
"Lullabye" (Studney) 1347
"Lullabye to Myself" 678
"Lullabye — Baby Men" 465
"Lumberjacks' Chorus" 1229
"Lunacy (The Moon) Attempts To Abort the Fool-Fetus" 1592
"Lunch" 114
"Lunch Box" 845
"Lush Life" 180, 182
"Lust" (Heather Brothers) 979
"Lust" (Weill) 1532
"Lust for Life" 1545
"Luverly Bunch of Coconuts" 1750
"Lydia, The Tattooed Lady" 662
"Lying Here" 1424
"Lying Liars" 227
"Lyle" 980
"Lyle's Turn" 980
"Lyle's Wedding" 1661
"The Lynch-Him Song" 589
"The Lynchers' Prayer" 589
"The Lynching Blues" 207
"Lynn's Dream" 545

"M–" 1020
"Ma, Ma, Where's My Dad?" 1399
"Ma, She's Makin' Eyes at Me" 993
"MacDougal Street" 1315
"Mach Es Motkeh Noch Amol (Motkeh, Do It Again)" 1382
"Machest Mich Feelen Yinger" 119
"Macho!" 673
"Machst Mich Feelen Yinger" 119
"Mack Sennett, Where Are You Now?" 272
"Mack the Knife" 128, 879, 1651, 1807
"Mackey of Appalachia" 985
"MacMillan-Butler" 450
"Maco Light" 864
"Macumba" 873
"Mad About" 1290
"Mad About the Boy" 751, 1611
"Mad About You, Manhattan" 109
"Mad as the Mist and Snow" 707
"The Mad Ballet" 1604
"Mad Dogs and Englishmen" 751, 1170
"The Mad Hatters" 637
"Mad Mission" 1598
"The Mad Tea Party" 170
"Madam" 1057
"Madam & The Numbers Runner" 501
"Madam, I Beg You" 332
"Madame Albert K. Johnson" 1435
"Madame Arthur" 1641
"Madame Colette" 308
"Madame from Paree" 121
"Madame La Chanson" 159
"Madame Meets a Midget" 877
"Madame Tango's Particular Tango" 715
"Madame Z's" 1469
"Maddy's Piece" 1306
"Made for the Movies" 599
"Madeleine" (Brel) 792, 824

"Madeleine" (Kayden) 773
"Madeline" (Carmines) 1311
"Mademoiselle de Paris" 1641
"Mademoiselle in New Rochelle" 46
"'Mademoiselle Marie' Ballet" 954
"Madison Avenue" (Cherpakov and Moehl) 991
"Madison Avenue" (Simons) 1290
"Madly in Love" 942
"Madly in Love with You Am I" 1652
"Madness Murder" 175
"Madness. No. Mania. No." 941
"The Madness of Columbina" 583
"The Madness of Isabella" 583
"Madness to Act" 583
"Madonna" 907
"Madonna Isabella" 183
"Madriene" 295
"A Madrigal" (Besoyan) 766
"A Madrigal" (Brandt, et al.) 464
"Madrigal" 831
"The Madrigal Blues" 1025
"Madrigal Group" 32
"Madrigals" 431
"Magdalena" 130
"Maggie" 1394
"Maggie's Chant" 1042
"Maggie's Dream" 995
"Maggie's Opera: Oh Come to Me, My Love" 995
"The Magi Waltz" 575
"Magic Fingers" 1716
"Magic Foot" 1680
"Magic Licorice" 1679
"The Magic Number" 655
"The Magic of Me" 1772
"Magical Man" 333
"Magician" 772
"Magician Makes Good" 1385
"A Magician's Work" 727
"The Magillah" 871
"Magnetic" 1480
"Magnetic Rag" 1783
"La Magnifique Apparait" 123
"Mah Blushin' Rosie" 993
"Mahagonny" 879
"Maid of Honor" 1427
"Maid to Marry" 773
"Maiden's Voyage" 1058
"Mail Order Annie" 916
"The Main Floor" 545
"Main Street (in Tel Aviv — or Anywhere)" 1044
"Mais Qui" 1638
"Le Maitre de la Conte, or Maupassant Tells All" 483
"The Majority" 1335
"Make a Joyful Noise" 1650
"Make Believe World" 407
"Make Earth Glad" 1204
"Make Him Think I'm Still Pretty" 575
"Make It" 971
"Make It Another Old-Fashioned, Please" 367
"Make It in L.A." 945
"Make Me a Promise, Thomas" 1613
"Make Me a Song" 997
"Make Me a Star" 781
"Make Me a Willow Cabin" 1519
"Make Me Happy" 1778
"Make Our Garden Grow" 244, 911
"Make Someone Happy" 382, 1546, 1717
"Make the Heart Be Stone" 1140
"Make Them Hate" 493, 1124, 1537
"Make Them Hear You" 1623
"Make Trixie Make" 1459
"Make Way" 1201
"Make Way for My Lady" 1008
"Make Way for One More Dream" 1300
"Make You Mine" 1554
"Make Your Own Kind of Music" 115, 854
"Make Yourself Comfortable" 1752
"Makeout Moon" 1237
"Makeshift Into Elephants" 820
"Makey Your Naming Powers" 1788
"Makin' Believe" 734
"Makin' Guacamole" 102
"Makin' the Rounds" 1414
"Makin' Whoopee" 261, 955, 993, 1350, 1394
"Making" 963
"Making a Home" 1019
"Making a Star" 1565
"Making It" 537
"Making Love" 583
"Making Love with You" 837
"The Making of a Man" 381
"The Making of President Fink" 871
"Making Pies" 1598
"Making the Moonmoth Laugh" 1081
"Making Up for Lost Time" 57
"Making Up Ways" 296
"Makoti" 1284
"Malacats" 1788
"Malaguena" 871
"Male Chauvinist (Pig of My-self)" 1758, 1759, 1761
"Maletero" 897
"Malkele's Song" 1822
"Mall" 1547
"Malpractice" 1309
"Malpractice II" 1309
"Maluan Moon" 1566
"Malumbo" 379
"Mama" (Edwards and Harris) 113
"Mama" (Ngema and Masekele) 1401
"Mama Always Said" 1397
"Mama Don't Cry" 161, 162, 163, 164
"Mama Fantastic" 376
"Mama, Go Inside!" 92
"Mama, I Want to Sing" 1001
"Mama, I Want to Sit Down-stairs" 1607
"Mama Is Here" 321
"Mama Lazarus" 1392
"Mama Loves You" 1330
"Mama Mama" 1192
"Mama. There Are Things" 673
"Mama Told Me Not To Come" 1036
"Mama Who Bore Me" 1515
"Mama Will Be Waiting with the Dawn" 1219
"Mama Will Provide" 1191
"Mama You Better Watch Out for Your Daughter" 1082
"Maman" 605, 1031, 1096
"Mama's Advice" 712
"Mama's Arms" 778
"Mama's Boys" 1243
"Mama's Little Girl" 110
"Mamaw" 1317
"Mambo '52" 1107
"Mambo Ensembo" 1048
"Mambo Frimbo" 544
"Mambo Jambo" 555
"Mambo Malaysian" 10
"Mame" 818
"Mamenyu, or Elegy on the Triangle Fire Victims" 604
"Mamenyu Tayere (Dear Mama)" 1619
"Mamie Desdoume's Blues" 813
"Mamie Is Mimi" 42, 1052
"Mamma's Cooking" 509
"Mampondo Mse" 1284
"A Man" 1574
"The Man" 1330
"Man Alone Blues" 1066
"The Man and His Message" 1388
"The Man and the Man-nequin" 277
"The Man and the Telephone" 1192
"Man and Wife" 587
"Man and Wife Arguing to the First Movement of Beethoven's Symphony" 1457
"Man and Woman" 1239
"Man Around the House" 1554
"The Man at the Piano" 215, 1208
"The Man Below" 1438
"Man Better Man" 1004
"Man Bites Dog" 69
"A Man Could Go Quite Mad" 1109
"The Man-Eating Ape Waltz" 64
"A Man for the Age" 950
"Man from Glad" 708
"The Man I Could Have Been" 357
"The Man I Love" 46, 1096
"The Man I Want to Be" 1207
"Man I've Become" 1419
"The Man in the Gray Flannel Space Suit" 942
"Man in the Mirror" 1006
"The Man in the Moon" 818
"The Man in the Starched White Shirt" 1499
"The Man in the Window" 217
"A Man Is a Dog's Best Friend" 1252
"Man Is a Man's Best Friend" 48
"A Man Is Allowed to Change His Mind" 673
"Man Is for the Woman Made" 16
"Man Is For Woman Made" 851
"Man is Made for Woman" 962
"A Man Is Meant to Reason" 865, 1593
"Man Is Small" 190
"Man May Escape from Rope and Gun" 117
"A Man Named Dewey" 1514
"The Man Next Door" 1747
"A Man of No Importance" 1006
"Man on a Subway" 1297
"Man on the Street" 142
"The Man That Got Away" 662, 840
"Man That Is Born of a Woman" 975
"Man to Man" 1821
"Man to Man Talk" 1193
"A Man Up My Sleeve" 277
"The Man Upstairs" 238
"A Man Wakes Up" 1747
"Man Walking Down the Aisle" 1457
"A Man Who Isn't" 919
"The Man Who Made His Life Into a Work of Art" 483
"Man Who Makes Human Be-ings" 563
"The Man Who Owns Broad-way" 570
"A Man Who Speaks for Him-self" 1531
"The Man Who Wouldn't Sing Along with Mitch" 411
"Man with a Load of Mis-chief" 1008
"The Man with a Mirror in His Hat" 820
"Man with a Problem" 1069
"A Man with a Problem" 1076
"Man/Woman" 580
"Manchester" 649
"Manchild" 152
"Mancipation" 569
"(T)he Mandalay Song" 660, 879, 1773
"Mandrake" 1011
"Mandrake Hymn" 1011
"Mandy" 1543
"Manhattan" (*Akokawe*) 21
"Manhattan" (Rodgers) 382, 955, 1096
"Manhattan 4 A.M." 1129
"Manhattan Is My Favorite Rendezvous" 1066
"Manhattan Lullaby" 1550
"Manhattan Moves" 1014
"Manhattan Rhapsody" 1493
"Manhattan Serenade" 1016
"Manhattan Transfer" 85
"A Mania" 701
"The Manicurist" 1158
"Mannequine Lady" 110
"Manners" 550
"A Man's a Man for All That" 740
"Man's Inhumanity" 1448
"Mansion Hill" 644
"Mantra" 1646
"Manuelo" 578
"Manufacture and Sell" 1537
"Many a Fairer Face" 972
"Many Happy Returns" 948
"Many Moons Ago" 1193
"Many Paths" 1742
"Many Thousands Gone" 740
"Many Trades" 1051
"Many Ways to Skin a Cat" 538
"Mao Tse Tongue" 877
"The Maos Dance" 1139
"The Map Song" 1458
"Maple Leaf Rag" 457
"Marathon (Les Flamandes)" 792
"The Marathoners" 148
"Marble Arch to Leicester Square" 1639
"March" (*Fourth Avenue North*) 535
"March" (Kurka) 609
"March Ahead" 660
"March in the Right Direction" 547
"March, Little Soldiers" 317
"March of the Executives" 1736
"March of the Falsettos" 997, 1019
"March of the Vigilant Vassals" 48
"March of the Wooden Sol-diers" 81
"March of the Yuppies" 1037
"The March of Time" 300
"March vs. Waltz (Dialectic In-action!)" 170
"March You Off in Style" 867
"Marching for Peace" 381
"Marching Song" 1162
"Marching to Victory" 224
"Marco! Rodolpho!" 1723
"Marco's Coming, Eddie" 1723
"Marcus, My Friend" 726
"Marcy's Yours" 738
"Mardi Gras in Chicago" 996
"Mardi Gras Time" 1518
"The Mardi Gras Waltz" 1021
"The Marganiot" 617
"Margaret" 1228, 1297
"Margaret Thatcher" 1209
"Marginal People" 326
"Margret's Garden Aria" 947
"Marguerita" 1459
"Marguerite's Backyard" 635
"Maria" 1823
"Maria in Spats" 1218
"Marianne" 818
"Maria's Song" 727
"Marie" 1036, 1049, 1334
"Marieke" 792
"Marietta" 820
"Marilyn's Theme" 123
"A Marine, a Marine, a Ma-rine" 1329
"Marine's Hymn" 892
"Marionette Theatre" 1687
"Mariposa" 1222
"Marjorie Morningstar" 237
"Marjorie's Dream" 545
"Mark Me Tomorrow" 1449
"Market Day" (Blankman) 235
"Market Day" (Honigman) 1449
"Market Place" 889
"Market Song" 1131
"Marketing, Marketing" 1504
"Mark's All-Male Thanksgiv-ing" 430
"Mark's Fantasy" 295
"Marlene" 1183
"Marlon of the Plaza" 1394
"Marooned" 710
"The Marquis of Mince Pie" 460
"Marriage" 403, 404
"Marriage Counsel" 1460
"Marriage Is for Old Folks" 1420
"Marriage License Bureau" 772
"The Marriage of Lady Tar-tine" 1700
"A Marriage Proposal" 1019
"Marriage Song" 476
"Marriage Tango" 739
"Married Man" 1319
"A Married Man" 1362
"Married with Children" 828
"Married Yet!" 1510
"Marry an American" 200
"Marry Me" (Kander) 52
"Marry Me" (Springer) 714
"Marry Me a Little" 1027, 1491, 1492
"Marry Me. I Will" 834
"Marry the One You Love" 66
"Marry with Me" 926
"The Marrying Kind" 1637
"'Marrying' Duet" 1131
"Marshall's Blues" 65
"Marshall's Reply" 65
"Marsovia" 1570
"Marter!" 689
"Martha Graham" 664
"Martha Stewart: The Musical" 1128

"Martin Alone" 1601
"Martin and Top Enter the Farmyard" 1601
"Martin and Top Make Horseplay" 1601
"Martin, Martin" 1423
"Martina" 658
"Martin's Coming Up" 535
"Martirio" 130
"Marty's Room Is at the Top" 352
"Marvelous, Curious, and Strange" 484
"Marvin at the Psychiatrist" 1019
"Marvin Hits Trina" 1019
"Marvin Takes a Victory Shower" 763, 764
"Marvin's Giddy Seizures" 763, 764
"Marvin's Giddy Seizures I" 765
"Marvin's Giddy Seizures II" 765
"Mary" (Feuer) 424
"Mary" (Griffin) 1598
"Mary" (Hinsch) 1028
"Mary Alice, Don't Say Shit" 708
"Mary Ann" 851
"Mary, I'm a Fool" 44
"Mary Jane" 1778
"Mary Mack" 646
"Mary Margaret's House in the Country" 656
"Mary, Mother of God" 362
"Maryann" 972
"Mary's a Grand Old Name" 570
"Mary's Announcement" 1166
"Mary's Lament" 675
"Mary's Song" 789
"Ma's Entrance" 1601
"Mashoogie Boogie" 352
"Masks" 708
"Masochism Tango" 1654
"Masquerade" (Clifton) 1008
"Masquerade" (Herbert) 1688
"Masquerade" (Jordan) 1379
"Masquerade" (Stone) 272
"Masquerade Ball" 1666
"Massage a Trois" 1758
"Mass Market" 1646
"The Masses Are Asses" 1713
"Masses of Masses" 786
"The Master Class" 979
"Master, Master" 1148
"The Master Race Polka" 232
"Masters Song" 396
"Mata Hari" 766, 935
"The Matchmaker's Daughter" 878
"Material Universe" 1345
"Math Widow" 485
"Mathematical Quartet" 1309
"Mathilde" 792
"Matilda Jane" 510
"Matilda, Matilda" 527
"The Matinee" 852
"Matinee" 1033
"Matinee Girl" 1442
"The Mating Dance" 65
"Matsuri" 602
"Matter and Pills" 1011
"Matter of Opinion" 1034
"A Matter of Position" 1527
"A Matter of Time" (Margo) 1035
"A Matter of Time" (Marks) 185
"Matthew" 37
"Matthew Gurney?" 439
"Matthew! Everything I Want Is Gone" 439
"Matthew! If You Love Me (Love Duet)" 439
"Maud, the Bawd" 1440
"Mauricio and Nettie — Part I" 897
"Mawari Toro" 602
"Max" 899
"Maxie" 215
"Maxine!" 1659
"Maxwell's Silver Hammer" 1426
"May Day" 1225
"May I Dance with You?" 1089
"May I Have the Pleasure" 13
"May in Manhattan" 1385
"May the Force Be with You" 949
"Maybe" 1172
"Maybe for Instance" 856
"Maybe I Like It This Way" 1778
"Maybe I'm Better Off" 1706
"Maybe I'm Doing It Wrong" 1036, 1049, 1334
"Maybe I'm Lonely" 229
"Maybe It's Not Too Late" 185
"Maybe Some Weekend" 1084
"Maybe There's a Place" 582
"Maybe This Time" 52, 1685
"Maybe Tomorrow" 464
"Maybe We Just Made Love" 738
"Maybe You Can See Yourself" 279
"Mayn Alte Heym" 1619
"Mayn Rochele" 1382
"Mayor" 1037
"The Mayor Doesn't Care" 653
"The Mayor of Harlem" 165
"The Mayor of Memphis" 1042
"Mazel Bruche" 1212
"Mazel Tov" 1051
"Mazurka" 488
"Mazurka (El Pelele)" 1179
"M.C.P." (Hoffman) 1760
"M.C.P." (Spektor) 718
"The McPhails' Dialog" 1329
"Me" (Brandon) 1774
"Me" (Solly) 200
"Me, a Heap Big Injun" 935
"Me Alone" 1004
"Me and Bobby McGee" 115, 965
"Me and Dorothea" 1481
"Me and Jesus" 785
"Me and My Baby" 52, 1685
"Me and My Horse" 76
"Me and the Mountain" 190
"Me Atahualpa" 1751
"Me God, Please God" 1035
"The Me I Want to Be" 957
"Me, Me, Me" 980
"Me, Myself and I" 703
"Me So Far" 915
"The Me Suite" 1800
"Me, Too" 1613
"Meadowlark" 88
"A Meal to Remember" 273
"Mean as a Snake" 1367
"Mean Mr. Mustard" 1426
"Mean to Me" 18
"The Meanest Man in Town" 336
"Means to an End" 573
"The Means to an End" 1011
"Meanwhile, Back in Yonkers" 1258
"La Mecedora" 897
"The Mechanical Bird" 1134
"Medea in Disneyland" 1448
"Medeta, Medeta" 602
"Medic" 149, 150
"The Medicare Rock" 1276
"Medicine" 1698
"Medicine Man Blues" 391
"Mediocrity" 277
"Meditation" (Bailin) 253
"Meditation" (Michael) 19
"The Mediterranean Flavor" 617
"The Medium" (Allen, et al.) 535
"The Medium" (*Time, Gentlemen Please!*) 1639
"The Medium and the Husband's Statement" 1422
"Medley" 499
"The Meek Shall Inherit" 939
"Meet Me in St. Louis" 746
"Meet Me Round the Corner" 142
"Meet Me Tonight" 480
"Meet Mother in the Skies" 1484
"Meet the Blands" 424
"Meetin' Here Tonight" 166
"The Meeting" 1161
"(A) Meeting Here Tonight" 815, 816
"A Meeting of the Minds" (Crystal) 878
"A Meeting of the Minds" (Hamilton) 1721
"Meeting on Japan's Chosun Policy" 889
"The Meeting Song" 1237
"Meeting Tonight" 1401
"Meg and Joe" 161
"Megalopolis" 87
"Mein Hartz Flegt Zogen Mir" 119
"Mein Herr" 1685
"Melancholy Birdsong" 1500
"Melinda Schecker" 319
"Melisande" 1451
"Melody" 1483
"Melody from the Sky" 1016
"Melody I" 1459
"Melody II" 1459
"Melody of Manhattan" 636
"The Melon Ballet" 721
"Melt It Down" 1691
"Melvin" 1192
"Members Only" (Addison) 777
"Members Only" (Bates) 1110
"Membrances" 1735
"Memorabilia" 616
"Memories" (Panich) 858, 1318
"Memories" (Rorem) 926
"Memories" (*This Was Burlesque*) 1616
"Memories of Kong" 36
"Memories of LaFollette" 287
"Memories of You" 221
"Memphis Is Gone" 1042
"Men" (Baird) 274
"Men" (Meyrelles) 1523
"Men About Town" 751
"Men and Wives" 14
"Men Are Men" 453
"Men Are Never Lonely" 1045
"Men at Work" 1427
"Men Come with Guns" 65
"The Men in Bowler Hats" 1503
"The Men in My Life" 1464, 1465
"Men of Stone" 697
"Men on My Mind" 403
"Men Who Like Their Men" 385
"Mendel at Work" 473
"The Mendoza March" 1670
"Mene Mene Tekel" 1267, 1268
"The Menehune" 1221
"Men's Eyes" 873
"Menu Song" 1317
"Mephisto Waltz" 1694
"Mephisto Waltz No. 1" 1694
"Merano" 275
"Mercedes Benz" 965, 1556
"Merchandise" 1811
"The Merchandisers' Song" 275
"Merci Beaucoup, M. Godard" 1225
"Merciful Jesus" 1727
"Mercy-Justice" 1784
"Mercy Street" 1073
"The Merengue" 1434
"Merinda Love Song" 21
"Mermaid" 1014
"Mermaids" 1476
"The Mermaid's Evening Song" 695
"Merrill, Lynch, Pierce, Fenner and Clyde" 357
"Merrily We Roll Along" 1491
"Merrily We Roll Along #1" 1492
"Merrily We Roll Along #2" 1492
"Merrily We Roll Along #3" 1492
"Merrily We Roll Along #4" 1492
"Merrily We Roll Along #5" 1492
"Merry-Go-Round" (Britton) 636
"Merry-Go-Round" (Wood) 87
"A Merry Melody" 1203
"The Merry Widow Waltz" 1096
"Mescaline Hat Dance" 87
"Mesmerized" 250
"The Message" 1475
"A Message from the Backer" 1158
"The Message of the Cameo" 635
"Message to Michael" 83
"Message to My Mother" 657
"Messiah in America" 1715
"Messing Around" 553
"La Metamorphose" 123
"Metamorphosis Plus" 287
"Metaphor" 478
"Metaphorically Speaking" 448
"Meter Maid" 1290
"The Method" 1066
"Metropolitan Midge" 198
"Metropolitan Nocturne" 1016
"Metropolitan Opening" 69
"Metropolitan Opens in Old-Time Splendor" 69
"Met's Vets" 1415
"A Mexican Experience" 897
"Mexican Hat Dance" 685
"Mexico" (Dorsey) 1117
"Mexico" (Sottile) 767
"Mexico Lindo (y Querido)" 262, 533
"Mi-Komash Melon (What Is the Meaning?)" 492
"Miami" 1048
"Miani" 1566
"The Mice in Council" 11
"Mice of Means" 1251
"Michael" 1243
"Michael and Peter" 1128
"Michael Furey" 805
"Middle Aged" 718
"The Middle Class (Les Bourgeois)" 792
"Middle-Class-Liberal-Blues" 968
"Middle Class Revolution" 1424
"The Middle of Nowhere" 926, 1289
"Middle of the Sea" 1566
"The Middle Years" 1827
"Middlesex" 135
"Midnight at the Onyx" 1521
"Midnight Deadline Blastoff" 1007
"Midnight in the Museum" 1385
"Midnight Love Song" 110
"Midnight Lullabye" 1082
"Midnight Radio" 680
"The Midnight Show" 620
"Midnight Sun" 431
"Midnight Train to Georgia" 1494, 1623
"A Midrash" 647
"Midsummer Night" 80
"Midwestern Summer" 1767
"A Mighty Fortress" 589
"A Mighty Storm" 864
"Mignon" 976
"Migratory V" 1404
"The Mikado's Song" 460
"Mike" 1140
"Milady" 1522
"Milbeburg Joys" 813
"Mild, Mild Day" 1071
"The Mileage Millionaire" 544
"Milestones" (Davis) 156
"Milestones" (Unknown) 1407
"Miliaria Rubra" 471
"Military Life" 981
"Military Man" 1194, 1685
"Military Mutiny of 1882" 889
"Militia Song" 1760
"Milk and Honey" 818
"The Milk Train!" 673
"The Miller's Son" 1491, 1492
"Milles Fountain" 1045
"A Million Dollar Fiasco" 871
"Million Dollar Secret" 1373
"Million Dollar Smile (Billion Dollar Baby)" 148
"Million Goes to Million" 528
"Million Songs" 809
"A Million Windows and I" 1448
"Millions of Envelopes" 1081
"Milonga" 379
"Milord" 419, 1256, 1257
"The Milord's Waltz (Caballero de Gracia)" 488
"Milo's Discontent" 1252
"Mime and Man in the Beginning" 1806
"Mimosa and Me" 23
"Minaret" 1439
"Mind Over Matter" 1400
"Mind Your Business" 720
"Mind Your Own Business" 657, 777
"Mine" 912, 1721
"Mine Zien (My Son)" 1105
"Minimal" 1153
"Minimalament" 1439
"Mink, Mink, Mink" 1448
"Minnesota" 60, 1605
"Minnesota Strip" 1384
"Minnie from Trinidad" 840
"The Minnie Scene" 1616
"Minnie the Moocher" 35, 1623
"Minnie the Moocher's Wedding Day" 681
"Minnis in Eros" 996
"The Minnows and the Sharks" 381

"A Minor Catastrophe" 1155, 1157
"Minorities Is No Damn Good" 1276
"Minstrel Days" 1616
"Minstrel Parade" 112
"The Minstrel, the Jester and I" 1193
"Minuets from The Suites for Unaccompanied Cello" 1439
"Minus One" 1732
"A Minute, A Minute" 1152
"Minute by Minute" 175
"Mio Fratello (My Brother)" 1445
"Mir Forn Kayn Amerike (We're Going to America, Good-Bye, Mother Russia)" 604
"Mir Fur'n Kin Odess" 1032
"Mira" 1752
"Miracle Cure" 1655
"Miracle in Las Vegas" 287
"Miracle of Judaism" 473
"The Miracle Song" 38
"Miracle Town" 539
"A Miracle Would Happen" 890
"Miracles" (Hall) 1650
"Miracles" (Jones) 1487
"Mirage" 586
"Le Miroir" 123
"The Mirror" 717
"Mirror" 913
"The Mirror-Blue Night" 1515
"Mirrors and Shadows" 948
"Misconceptions" 769
"Le Miserere" 813
"Miserere" (Bicat) 873
"Miserere" (Kupferman) 831
"Misery Is" 986
"Mishke and Mashke" 1715
"A Mismatch Made in Hell" 610
"Miss America" (Harris) 1476
"Miss America" (Logan) 1394
"Miss Byrd" 300, 1710
"Miss Cadwallader" 1767
"Miss Crepe Myrtle" 1514
"Miss Dorothea Dix" 569
"Miss Emily Fleetwood" 1221
"Miss Euclid Avenue" 987
"Miss Glamouresse" 1215
"Miss Greenwich Village" 60
"Miss Gulch's 'Take Me, Please'" 1061
"Miss Heinschlinger" 60
"Miss Hi-Fie" 638
"Miss Hollywood" 772
"Miss Jenny's Ball" 1198
"Miss Julia" 1639
"Miss Julie's Taken Leave" 1063
"Miss Lulu White" 105
"Miss Marmelstein" 981
"Miss Mere" 661
"Miss Pearl Bailey" 783
"Miss Pinhead" 466
"Miss Subways" 550
"Miss Truth" 1064
"Miss Turnstiles (Dance)" 1185
"Miss Williams" 1261
"Missing" 206
"Missing Him" 1784
"Missing Person" 208
"Missing You, My Friend" 1188
"The Mission" 1171
"Mission Control" 1007
"Mississippi Mud" 553
"Mississippi U" 1276
"Missouri Mule" 1083
"Mr. (Mister) Off-Broadway" 371, 1451
"Mr. and Mrs. Dick Dickerson" 1668
"Mr. and Mrs. Fitch" 567
"Mr. and Mrs. Guardsman" 620
"Mr. and Mrs. Myth" 279
"Mr. Bojangles" 427
"Mister Boy" 504
"Mr. Brady Takes a Photograph" 569
"Mr. Bunbury" 448
"Mr. Cellophane" 52
"Mr. Chigger" 1083
"Mister Choi & Madame G" 430
"Mr. Cladwell" 1712
"Mr. Corbett" 535
"Mr. Fisby" 261
"Mr. Fixer" 718
"Mr. Flatfoot" 1365
"Mr. Gellman's Shirts" 252
"Mr. Graffiti" 1384
"Mr. Grogan, Wake Up" 726
"Mr. Harlem" 9
"Mr. Harris, It's All Over Now!" 483
"Mr. Hooper's Chanty" 13
"Mr. Horn Warns Sadie" 1329
"Mr. James Dillingham Young" 575
"Mr. Jelly Lord" 813
"Mr. John Brooke, Laurie's Tutor" 941
"Mr. Know It All" 319
"Mr. Know-It-All" 852
"Mr. Lee" 1575
"Mr. Maybe" 185
"Mister McGuffin" 10
"Mr. Might've Been" 722
"Mr. Money" 703
Mr. Phelps" 1311
"Mr. Playwright" 1207
"Mr. Potato Head" 945
"Mr. Premier, Distinguished Guests" 1139
"Mr. President" 1036, 1049
"Mister Producer" 1202
"Mr. Ravel" 1527
"Mr. Sandman" 1575
"Mr. Sloane" 1478
"Mr. Smith, Please Go Back to Washington" 350
"Mr. Sondheim" 1337
"Mister Spaceman" 1353
"Mr. Tambourine Man" 265
"Mr. Tanner" 916
"Mr. Tenniel" 510
"Mr. Tenniel, Reverend Dodgson" 510
"Mr. Tenniel, Reverend Dodgson, Lewis Carroll" 510
"Mr. Tornado I" 1427
"Mr. Tornado II" 1427
"Mr. Tornado III" 1427
"Mr. Wanamaker's Home" 50
"Mr. White, Mr. Black, Mr. Green" 654
"Mr. Witherspoon's Friday Night" 973
"mr. youse" 1222
"Mistress of the Senator" 683
"Misty" 850
"Misunderstanding" 963
"Mitch's Story" 10
"Miura's Audience with the King" 889
"The Mix" 386
"Mixed Doubles" 1069
"Mixed Emotions (If It's the Last Thing I Do)" 382
"Mixed Marriages" 1069, 1273
"Mixed-Up Media" 64
"Miya Sama Dinah Shore" 1263
"M'Lady Chatterley" 1261
"Mme. Nhu" 450
"Moanin' Low" 226
"Mobile, A Fascination" 1192
"Mobile-Texas Line" 376
"Mock Funeral March" 1229
"Mock Turtle Lament" 27
"Mockin' Bird Hill" 1575
"Mocking Bird" 569
"The Mocking of Hel Helson" 1229
"A Model of Decorum and Tranquility" 275
"Modern Artists" 858
"Modern Housing" 1460
"Modern Living" 1698
"The Modern Poetry Quintet" 1765
"The Modern Prometheus" 541
"Mofo, the Psychic Gorilla" 1234, 1235
"Moi" 1440
"Molecules" 1504
"Moll and Dick" 324
"Moll and Drugist" 324
"Moll and Gent" 324
"Mollie's Song" 1505
"Moll's Song" 324
"Molly" 667
"Molly Interlude" 1135
"Molly O'Reilly" 908
"Molotov Brothers" 552
"Mom, I Want to Be in Yiddish Vaudeville" 492
"Mom, I've Got Something to Tell You" 1149
"Mom Kills Child Comma Self" 36
"Mom Song" 1225
"Mom Will Be There" 338
"Mom! You Don't Understand!" 489
"The Moment Has Passed" 1311
"Moment in the Sun" 1441
"A Moment to Live" 1412
"Moment to Moment" 1320, 1321
"A Moment with You" 1027, 1403
"Moments" (Holt) 1558
"Moments" (Vales) 804
"Moments by the Sea" 1136
"Moments in Time" 1289
"Moments to Remember" 527
"Momma Said" 424
"Mommas' Turn" 1709
"Mommy Number Four" 338
"Mommy Says" 1207
"Mommy We Love You" 920
"Moms and Dads" 1258
"Mon Ami, My Friend" 826, 827
"Mon Dieu" 361, 1256, 1257
"Mon Homme" 1435
"Mon Marte" 59
"Mon Menage a Moi" 1256, 1257
"Mon Pays" 963
"Mona" 296
"Mona Lisa" 1494
"Monarch Notes" 1800
"Monday Monday" 411
"Monday Morning in the Mirror" 1637
"Monday Mornings" 229
"Money" 563
"Money (Money, Money, Money)" 1028
"Money in the Bank" 393, 394
"Money Is Honey" 164
"Money Isn't Everything" 538
"Money Isn't Everything, But" 957
"Money, Money, Money" 52, 824
"The Money Rolls In" 780
"The Money Song" (Kander) 1685
"The Money Song" (Lopez and Marks) 77
"The Money Song" (Rome) 981, 1608
"Money, Wealth, Gold" 147
"Monica & Mark" 430
"Monica's a Moonie" 1459
"Monkey in a Tree" 175
"A Monkey When He Loves" 332
"Monkeys and Playbills" 1645
"Monk's Merrie Minstrel Show!" 371
"Monody on the Death of a Platonist Bank Clerk" 135
"Monologue" 1299
"Monotheism" 59
"Monsier Toad" 261
"Monsieur Le Prefet" 190
"The Monster Mash" 1353
"Monster Medley" 1348
"The Monster's Song" 675
"Monstrous Events" 206
"Montage" (Adams and O'-Donnell) 1194
"Montage" (Baton) 1419
"Montage" (LaChiusa) 683
"Montage (I Was Blind)" 1303
"Montage (Now I See)" 1303
"Montana" (Baird) 274
"Montana" (Riddle) 322
"Montana Chem." 1403
"Monte Carlo" 973
"Monte Carlo Crossover" 42
"Monterey Fair" 1356
"Montgomery Moon" 614, 952
"Montgomery School Song" 952
"Moods" 822
"Moola Makes the Hula Feel Much Cooler" 1811
"Moon and Me" 1042
"Moon and Sand" 23
"Moon Dear" 989, 990
"Moon-Faced, Starry-Eyed" 128, 882
"Moon Madness" 80
"Moon of Alabama" 1532
"The Moon Song" 542
"Moon Walk" 1081
"Moon Watching" 712
"The Moon Woman" 583
"Moonblowfoofoo" 1081
"Moonfall" 1109
"Mooning" 625
"Moonlight" (Eliran) 401
"Moonlight" (Elliott) 1197
"Moonlight and You" 505
"Moonlight Cocktail" 221
"Moonlight Gambler" 1493
"Moonlight in Old Sicily" 78
"Moonlight Serenade" 1521, 1764
"Moonlight Sonata" 55
"Moonrock Candy Freak-Out" 1081
"Moonshiner" 775
"Moonshot" 1152
"Moosh, Moosh" 1330
"Moral Majority" 1383
"La Morale" 1146
"Morality" 1161
"More and More" 1432
"More Blood" 106
"More Coffee" 858
"More Drinking Games" 742
"The More I Hold You" 506
"The More I See People" 230
"More Is Less" 224
"More Like a Lady" 1815
"More Love" 1040
"More of Me to Love" 731
"More of the Same" 722
"More on the Same Subject" 547
"More Questions" 1069
"More Racquetball" 473
"More Songs" 1291
"More Than 5700 Years" 1607
"More Than Ever" 3
"More Than Ever Now" 1481
"More Than Friends" 822
"More Than I Asked For" 67
"More Than Love" (Copani/McHugh) 493
"More Than Love" (Driver and Haddow) 1414
"More Than Me" 1119
"More Than One Man in Her Life" 989, 990
"A More Than Ordinary Glorious Vocabulary" 33
"More Than You" 1119
"More Than You Deserve" 1082
"More Than You Know" 471
"More Unpleasantness" 947
"The More You Get" 393, 394
"The More You Ruv Someone" 77
"Morgan the Pirate" 1356
"Moritat" 880, 882, 1773
"The Moritat" 879
"Morito" 1422
"Morning" (Dansicker) 1184
"Morning" (Moss) 406
"The Morning After" (Arlen) 662
"The Morning After" (Bingham) 1072
"The Morning After" (Blank) 288
"Morning Anthem" 128, 1626
"Morning Glory Mountain" 179
"Morning in Madrid" 1048
"Morning Lecture and Its Results" 622
"Morning Light" (Coffin) 499
"Morning Light" (Unknown) 123
"Morning Sun" (Bernstein) 911
"Morning Sun" (Harper) 1424
"Morning Sun" (Klein) 1083
"Morning to Ye" 1071
"Mornings at Seven" 661
"Mornin's Lovely Rose" 110
"Morris" 1045
"Morris Life" 1144
"Mortality" 135
"Mos'ly Love" 1208
"Moscow Cheryomushki" 170
"Moses' Song" 663
"Most Confused Prince" 1331
"Most Done Traveling" 166
"The Most Heavenly Creature" 476
"Most Likely" 1310
"Most Men Are" 1084
"Most People" 407
"Most Popular and Most Likely to Succeed" 1668
"Most Unusual Pair" 636
"Motele" 1619
"Moteni" 927
"Motet" 963
"Motet for the Movies" 1749
"The Moth and the Flame" 975
"Mother" 80
"A Mother" 690
"Mother Africa's Day" 835

"Mother, Darling" (Frankel) 641
"Mother, Darling" (Schwerin) 857
"Mother Earth" 152
"Mother Goose Almanac" 1085
"Mother Hare's Prophecy" 600
"Mother Hare's Séance" 600
"Mother, I Am Not a Christian" 922
"Mother, I Need You" 71
"The Mother-in-Law" 772
"Mother Isn't Getting Any Younger" 494, 1116
"Mother Love" 582
"Mother Machree" 775
"Mother, May I Be Forgiven?" 730
"Mother Mustn't Know" 1416
"Mother Nature" 1751
"Mother of Man" 1282
"Mother of the Bride" 1117
"The Mother of the Bride" 1614
"Mother Peep" 773
"Mother Son" 1051
"A Mother with Sons" 1333
"The Motherland" 1255
"Motherload" 1432
"Motherly Love" 1161
"Mothers and Wives" 317
"Mother's Day" (Brandon) 968
"Mother's Day" (Grossman) 1486
"Mother's Gonna Make Things Fine" 1121
"A Mother's Heart" 3
"Mothers-in-Law" 467
"Mother's Love" 1419
"A Mother's Love" 1311
"A Mother's Love Song" 359
"Mother's March" 65
"Mothers of the Nation" 912
"Mother's Prayer" 1737, 1738
"A Mother's Smile" 695
"A Mother's Wish Is a Daughter's Duty" 884
"Motl Der Opereyter (Motl the Operator)" 604
"Motor Scooter" 1631
"Des Mots (Elio de Grandmont)" 963
"Mountain Top Duet" 275
"Mountain Speaks to Me" 425
"A mountebank" 250
"The Mounted Messenger" 1626
"The Mounties" 1570
"Mourning" 615
"The Mouse" 277
"Mouth So Charmful" 586
"Move" 1250
"Move Along" 279
"Move It On Over" 657
"Move On" 1557
"Move on Up a Little Higher (Jesus Is All)" 382, 996
"Move Over" 965
"Move Over, You Guys" 545
"Move to the Outskirts of Town" 790
"Movie" 529
"The Movie Cowboy" 1089
"Movie Fan" 638
"The Movie Game of Make Believe" 1348
"The Movie Guide to Love" 1263
"Movie House" 467
"Movie Moguls" 749
"Movie Montage" 147
"Movie Night: The Great Beyond!" 1818
"Movie Queen" 781
"Movie Stars" (Goldberg) 229
"Movie Stars" (Raniello) 1089
"The Movies" 1554
"Movies Were Movies" 818
"Movietown, U.S.A." 1089
"Movin'" 152
"Movin' Day" 699
"Movin' On" 1631
"Movin' Up to Higher Ground" 1762
"Moving" 1458
"Moving in with Linda" 1243
"Moving On" 1296
"Moving Too Fast" 890
"Mow" 1547
"The Mowla" 1707
"Mrs. Bodie" 1236
"Mrs. Davidson Awakes to Reality and Sadie Turns Her" 1329
"Mrs. Davidson's Aria of Distress" 1329
"Mrs. Davidson's Denunciation of Dancing" 1329
"Mrs. Finished Lament" 1034
"Mrs. Grimm" 716
"Mrs. Horn's Lament" 1329
"Mrs. Horn's Sad Vocalise and McPhails' Duet" 1329
"Mrs. Klinghoffer, Please Sit Down" 363
"Mrs. Lady Bird" 1091
"Mrs. Mary Middleton" 417
"Mrs. McGrath" 775
"Mrs. McPhail's Aria About the Fishermen" 1329
"Mrs. McPhail's Aria of Shame and Davidson's Vision" 1329
"Mrs. Mister and Reverend Salvation" 324
"Mrs. Muller!" 609
"Ms. Mae" 1
"Much as I Love You" 835
"Much More" 478
"Much More Alive" 491
"Much Too Soon" 1168
"Mucho Macho Trio" 424
"Muddy Waters" 1198
"The Muffin Song" 448
"A Mugger's Work Is Never Done" 1758, 1759, 1761
"Multi-Colored Bush" 1661
"Multitudes of Amys" 1491
"Mumble Nothing" 464
"Mumbo Jumbo" 1021
"Mummies at the Met" 206
"The Murder" 302
"Murder" (Beeson) 947
"Murder" (LaChiusa) 1422
"Murder" (Studney) 1347
"Murder" (Unknown) 1407
"Murder" (Woldin) 866, 1593
"Murderer's Home" 922
"Murmurings" 419
"The Murphy's Squabble" 1428
"Musak" 535
"Muse, Darling, Muse" 1231
"Muses" 469
"Museum Piece" 60
"Mushari's Waltz" 588
"Mushnik and Son" 939
"The Mushrooms Are Coming in Here" 720
"Music" (King) 1591
"Music" (*The Uncommon Denominator*) 1698
"Music Addiction" 1110
"The Music and the Mirror" 283
"The Music Box" 1190
"Music Business" 1459
"Music for a Murder" 1771
"The Music Goes 'Round and Around" 681
"The Music Hall" 308
"Music-Hall 1600" 241
"Music Hall Medley" 587
"Music Hall Shakespeare" 581
"Music in the Air" 1620
"Music in the City" 1136
"Music in the House" 848
"Music in This Mountain" 703
"Music, It's a Necessity" 1821
"Music Moves Me" 55
"Music, Music" (Fuller) 1095
"Music, Music" (Kookoolis and Fagin) 1504
"Music! Music! Music!" 1575
"Music of Love" 361
"The Music of Love" (Baron) 541
"The Music of Love" (Kennon) 1637
"Music of the Stricken Redeemer" 827
"The Music Still Plays On" 1121
"Music Teacher" 1616
"The Music That Makes Me Dance" 1546, 1717
"Music, When Soft Voices Die" 1443
"Musical Chairs" (Savage) 1097
"Musical Chairs" (Vitale) 1030
"The Musical Clown" 1687
"Musical Comedy Dream" 639
"The Musical Melange" 1584
"Musical Memories" 1176
"Musical Moments" 1176
"Musical Moon" 570
"Musicals in My Head" 926
"Musicians" 388
"Musketeers" 672
"Must Be a Witch in Town" 582
"Must Be Something" 1523
"Must've Been High" 1225
"Mustapha" 1716
"Muted" 1751
"Mutter Hast Du Mir Vergeben" 1350
"My Ambition" 469
"My Baby" 1427
"My Baby and Me" 271
"My Barbie Was the Tramp of the Neighborhood" 945
"My Best Friend" 223
"My Best Girl" 818
"My Bio Is (a) Blank" 89, 1202
"My Blanket and Me" 1828
"My Bod Is for God" 1113
"My Body" 1084
"My Body Wasn't Why" 583
"My Boy" (Frank) 1306
"My Boy" (Katzaros) 1071
"My Boyfriend's Back" 115
"My Brown Paper Hat" 961, 1756
"My Building Disappeared" 1200
"My Calling" 1607
"My Card" 121
"My Chance to Survive the Night" 763
"My Chick, My Chuck" 1721
"My Child" 1727
"My Children Searching" 1388
"My City" (Marren) 1287
"My City" (Strouse) 861, 1037
"My Coloring Book" 52
"My Country 'Tis of Thee" 470, 1398
"My Cozy Little Corner in the Ritz" 567
"My Cup Runneth Over" 733, 1451
"My Daddy Was Right" 745
"My Daddy's Dead" 362
"My Darling, Close Your Eyes" 1419
"My Daughter, My Angel" 1264
"My Daughter The Countess" 480
"My Day Has Come" 41
"My Dear" 194
"My, Dear, You're Down" 1374
"My Dearest Mary" 1443
"My Death (La Mort)" 792
"My Deepest Thoughts" 1195
"My Doggie" 60
"My Dogs" 430
"My Dream Is Through" 676
"My Dream of the South of France" 304, 672
"My Dreams" 1342
"My Ears" 431
"My Empty Bed" 915
"My Eternal Devotion" 448
"My Eyes Are Fully Open" 1270
"My Faith Looks Up to Thee" 1001
"My Father Is a Homo" 997
"My Father the Gangster" 257
"My Father Told Me" 570
"My Father Was a Peculiar Man" 1636
"My Father Was Right" 1303
"My Father's a Homo" 1019
"My Favorite Guy" 742
"My Favorite Mirage" 1050
"My Favorite Moment of the Bee 1" 1680
"My Favorite Moment of the Bee 2" 1680
"My Favorite Moment of the Bee 3" 1680
"My Final Fling" 1043
"My First" 16
"My First Girl" 1078
"My First Love" 1385
"My First Mistake" 855
"My First Solo Flight" 151
"My Forefathers" 673
"My Fortune Is My Face" 1717
"My Friend" (Russ) 64
"My Friend" (Stone) 960
"My Friend, My Father" 1777
"My Friend, the Dictionary" 1680
"My Friends, the Celebrities" 1125
"My Funny Valentine" 1694
"My Geranium" 409
"My Ghost Writer" 1743
"My G.I. Joey" 232, 1163
"My Girl" 1623
"My God Laughs" 1684
"My God Looked Down" 591
"My God Why Hast Thou Forsaken Me?" 831
"My Grandson Did, Who Was Two" 363
"My Handy Man Ain't Handy No More" 1373
"My Heart Belongs to Daddy" 367
"My Heart Is Crying" 790
"My Heart Is in the East" 1102
"My Heart Is Unemployed" 981
"My Heart Was So Free" 117
"My Heart Won't Learn" 332
"My Heart's a Marionette" 1152
"My Heart's Intact" 36
"My Hero's Grenades" 1319
"My High School Sweetheart" 763, 764, 765
"My Holiday" 1154
"My Holy Prayer" 183
"My Home Is in a Southern Town" 813
"My Home Town" (Brandon) 1550
"My Home Town" (Lehrer) 1654
"My Home's Across the Blue Ridge Mountains" 777
"My Husband" 1604
"My Husband Is Playing Around" 606
"My Husband Sleeps Tonight" 1046
"My Husband the Pig" 1492
"My, It's Been Grand" 1604
"My. Joy Beyond Measure, Mother!" 941
"My Junk" 1515
"My Key Don't Fit the Lock" 1638
"My Kind of Love" 333
"My Kind of Town (Chicago Is)" 1210
"My Kinda Love" 1016
"My Knees Are Weak" 860
"My Land" 401, 1136
"My Leviticus" 573
"My Life Is Love" 976
"My Life's a Musical Comedy" 752
"My Little Girl" 985
"My Little Grass Shack" 1575
"My Little Javanese" 635
"My Little Prairie Flower" 1366
"My Little Red Book" 83
"My Little Room" 230
"My Lola" 948
"My Lord, My Lord! Noblest of Men" 62
"My Love" (Bernstein) 244, 911
"My Love" (Pippin) 258, 259
"My Love Belongs to You" 1737, 1738
"My Love Is On the Way" 600
"My Love Is Waiting" 672
"My Love, My Love" 985
"My Love Song" 735
"My Love Will Come By" 91
"My Lovely Lad" 1446
"My Lover and His Wife" 1319
"My Lungs" 1330
"My Mammy" 829, 993
"My Man" (Barsha) 1505
"My Man" (Yvain) 553, 924, 1435
"My Man Blues" 1198
"My Man Don't Love Me" 844
"My Man Rocks Me" 777
"My Master Plan" 91
"My Meadow" 272
"My Mind on Freedom" 815, 816
"My Moppets, My Poppets and Me" 184
"My Mother Always Said" 1052
"My Mother Was a Fortune-Teller" 992, 1106
"My Mother Would Love You" 367
"My Mother's Clothes" 808
"My Mother's Mother and Your Mother's Mother Were Sisters" 951
"My Moustache Is Twitchin'" 1511
"My Movie of the Week" 643
"My Name" (Kernochan) 1478
"My Name" (Pen) 114
"My Name" (Rosenblum) 485

"A ... My Name Is Alice Poems" 1
"My Name Is Can" 1007
"My Name Is Man" 400
"My Name Is Timothy John" 1514
"My Name Then ..." 1788
"My Name's Abundance" 1231
"My New Friends" 992
"My New York" 293
"My Number Is Eleven" 701
"My Ol' Kentucky Rock and Roll Home" 1176
"My Old Friends" 1107
"My Old Kentucky Home" (Foster) 112
"My Old Kentucky Home" (Newman) 1036, 1334
"My Old Man" 614
"My One Consolation" 363
"My One Day" 223
"My One Great Love" 444
"My Only Love" (Brown) 1066
"My Only Love" (Dixon) 476
"My Only Son" 107
"My Ordeal" 1077
"My Own Best Friend" 807, 1685
"My Own Morning" 1717
"My Own, or True Love at Last" 483
"My Own Space" 807
"My Own United States" 1570
"My Parents' House" 229
"My Perfection" 403
"My Picture in the Papers" 600
"My Place in the World" 1752
"My Place or Yours?" 752
"My Play Is Full of Visions" 1416
"My Political Opinion" 1128
"My Poodle Puddles" 1386
"My Poor Wee Lassie (A Scottish Lament)" 483
"My Precious Mystery" 1478
"My Prince" 34
"My Red Riding Hood" 349, 1752
"My Religion" 1064
"My Sargeant Doesn't Look Like Big John Wayne" 1348
"My Secret Dream" 1253
"My Shining Hour" 1571
"My Ship" 128, 879, 1494, 1532, 1807
"My Simple Wish (Rich, Famous & Powerful)" 929
"My Sister and I" 1764
"My Sister Bess" 726
"My Sister-in-Law" 1083
"My Son" (Brown) 814
"My Son" (Buhrer) 861
"My Son" (Goodman) 206
"My Son" (Kaplan) 1485
"My Son-in-Law" 348
"My Son, The Doctor" 489
"My Son the Kibutsnik" 1647
"My Song" 19
"My Sort Of Ex-Boyfriend" 1650
"My Soul Weeps" 1103
"My Star" (Bone and Fenton) 501
"My Star" (Pottle) 34
"My Story" 1158
"My Sweetheart's the Mule in the Mine" 740
"My Talking Day" 1716
"My Terms" 1505
"My Thighs" 1046
"My Time" 725, 1097
"My Title Song" 480
"My Topic of Conversation Is You" 1521
"My True Heart" 848
"My Turn" 185
"My Turn to Shine" 1772
"My Type" 1132
"My Uncle's Mistress" 598
"My Unfortunate Erection" 1680
"My Very First Impression" 448
"My Way" 1210
"My Way Is Cloudy" 166
"My Wedding Night" 1802
"My White Knight" 929
"My Wife" 1829
"My Wife and I" 1108
"My World" 284, 285
"My World and Your World" 1221
"My Yiddisha Colleen" 1442
"My Yiddishe Mame" 1619
"Myrna P." 229
"Myrtle May's Birthday Party" 766
"Mysteries" 1441
"Mystery Date" 1551
"The Mystery of the Moon" 1668

"Nachas Fun Kinder" 119
"Nada" 1459
"Nagasaki Days" 729
"Naked Boys Singing!" 1110
"The Naked Dance" 105
"Naked Foot" 120
"The Naked Maid" 1110
"Name Dropping" 708
"The Name Game" 115
"The Name of God" (Carmines) 1349
"The Name of God" (Martell) 1443
"The Name of Love" 1109
"A Name of Our Own" 1261
"Name: Cockian" 1253
"Name: Emily Adam" 1060
"The Names" 1441
"Names" 415
"Names of the Trains" 544
"Namu Amida Butsu" 602
"Nana" 692
"Nana's Lied" 1809
"Nancy" (Cohen) 1471
"Nancy" (*Dark Horses*) 350
"Nancy (With the Laughing Face)" 1764
"Nancy: The Unauthorized Musical" 1772
"Nannas Lied" 1532
"Nanny" 415
"Naomi" 734
"Napoleon" 662
"Napoleon's Nightmare" 1250
"Narcissism Rag" 161, 162, 163, 164
"Narcissus" (Betjeman) 135
"Narcissus" (Nevin) 1643
"Narcissus" (Roman) 529
"The Narration" 647
"Narration" 196
"Narrative of Ismene" 615
"The Narrator" 612
"Nasality" 705
"Nashly, Calling Nashly" 362
"Natchitoches, Louisiana" 504
"Nathan, Nathan, What Are You Waitin' For?" 1442
"National Anthem" 952
"The National Anthem of Utopia" 1713
"National Brotherhood Week" 1654
"A National Disgrace" 71
"National Service Corps" 87
"The Natives Are Restless" 1066
"Natural Born Females" 1215
"Natural Woman" 1591
"A Natural Woman" 115
"Nature Hunt Ballet" 56
"Nature's Child" 1423
"Nature's Serenade" 1780
"Naughty Bird Tarantella" 1445
"Naughty Forty-Second Street" 1132, 1218
"Naughty Girls" 805
"Naughty-Naught" 1115, 1116
"Naughty, Naughty Nancy" 935
"The Naughty Nineties" 622
"Nausea Before the Game" 763, 764
"Navajo Woman" 453
"The Navel" 465
"Ne Me Quitte Pas" 924, 1162
"Ne'er Do Well" 1692
"Near the Cross" 1559
"A Near Thing" 1721
"Nearer My God to Thee" 736, 813
"'Neath the Southern Moon" 1570
"Neauville-Sur-Mer" 1160
"Necessarily Evil" 1301
"The Necessity of Being Cruel" 814
"Necrology" 1495
"Needle" 1788
"The Needle's Eye" 1323
"Negotiations at the Grand Banquet" 889
"La Negra Tiene Tumbao" 262
"A Negro Love Song" 1762
"Negro Prison Songs" 922
"Neighbors" (Crystal) 1102
"Neighbors" (Crane) 1767
"Neighbors Above, Neighbors Below" 219
"Nel Blue di Pinto di Blue" 1575
"Nellie Bly" 112
"Nellie, Don't Go" 1117
"Nellie Paves the Way" 1117
"Nelson" 818
"Nemt Eich a Man" 1212
"Nero, Caesar, Napoleon" 98
"Nervous" 1433
"Nessun Dorma" 1623
"N.E.T. and This Is Remote" 708
"Nettie and Mauricio — Part II" 897
"Network" 1290
"Never" (Alasa' and Welch) 276
"Never" (Micare) 1438
"Never Again" (Coward) 13
"Never Again" (Hamilton) 1721
"Never Any Time to Play" 1221
"Never Be a Servant" 1011
"Never Can Tell" 1250
"Never Disappointed Him" 1084
"Never Do a Bad Thing" 1164
"Never Ending Love" 1015
"Never Enough" 770
"Never Ever Land" 464
"Never Felt Better in My Life" 828
"Never Gonna Dance" 886
"Never Gonna Let You Go" 854
"Never Gonna Run Again" 240
"Never Had a Home" 370
"Never Have a Book" 1337
"Never Knew Love Like This Before" 399
"Never Left Home" 1337
"Never Look Back" 223
"Never Marry a Dancer" 348
"Never Met a Man I Didn't Like" 1512
"Never More" 1443
"Never, Never" 461
"Never Never Land" 1224, 1546, 1717
"Never, Never Leave Me" 957
"Never or Now" 260
"Never Pay Musicians What They're Worth" 1495
"Never Play Croquet" 27
"Never Say Die" 87
"Never Say Never" 179
"Never Say No" 478
"Never Seen Anything Like It Before" 1815
"Never Seen the Garden Again" 1708
"Never Speak Directly to an Emperor" 1134
"Never Stop Believing" 208
"Never Time to Dance" 791
"Never to Go" 1815
"Never Try Too Hard" 870
"Never Wait for Love" 1254
"Never Was There a Girl So Fair" 1167
"Nevermore" 317
"Nevertheless" (Larson and Rubins) 219
"Nevertheless" (Ruby) 672
"Nevertheless, They Laugh" 1119
"Neville" 1754
"A New Age Has Begun" 1736
"The New Aimee" 1470
"New Attitude" 1046
"New, Beautiful Man" 1613
"New Beginnings" 1207
"New Boy in Town" (Carmines) 614
"New Boy in Town" (Klein) 1083
"The New Daredevils of the Air" 1788
"A New Deal for Christmas" 58
"New Evaline" 605
"New Face in Town" 1149
"New-Fangled Tango" 924
"A New Generation" 835
"New Gun in Town" 708
"New Hampshire Nights" 1702
"New Hope for the Fabulously Wealthy" 227
"A New Italian Folk Song" 87
"New Kid in the Neighborhood" 248
"A New Kind of Husband" 545
"A New Life" 948
"A New Life Coming" 1524
"New Life on the Planet" 1002
"New Literature" 206
"New Love for Old Love" 1016
"New Loves for Old" 678
"The New Madness" 539
"New Math" 1654
"The New Me" 1320
"New Morning Is Dawning in Chosun" 889
"New Musketeers" 88
"The New Neuroses for Old" 1749
"The New Non-Union Usher Polka" 198
"New Orleans" 1543
"New Orleans Hot (Hop) Scop Blues" 180, 181, 182, 1198
"New Prisoner's Song" 376
"New Rhythm" 1821
"The New School, The Old School" 1040
"New Shoes" 301
"New Snow" 175
"The New Soft Shoe" 507
"New Song" 1620
"A New Song" (Bernstein) 1029
"A New Song" (Spektor) 718
"New Sun in the Sky" 348, 1606
"The New-Time Religion" 534
"New to Me" 1448
"New Wine in Old Bottles" 1765
"New Word" 571
"New Words" 1201
"New Words to an Old Love Song" 1315
"A New World" 143
"New World" 1466
"The New World" (Brown) 1498
"The New World" (Kennon) 484
"New World Coming" 854
"New Year's Eve" 398
"New Year's Eve at the Computer Center" 36
"New Years in Beirut, 1983" 1335
"New York" (*Akokawe*) 21
"New York" (Brown) 1066
"New York" (Stornaiuolo) 59
"New York City Cock Roach Blues" 1207
"New York Cliché" 1258
"The New York Coloring Book" 1605
"New York from the Air" 1678
"New York, Get Ready for Us" 749
"New York Has a New Hotel" 1430
"New York Interview" 1698
"New York Is a Festival of Fun" 1069, 1273
"New York Is a Party" 370, 646
"New York Lights" 1723
"New York Makes Me" 1325
"New York, New York" (Bernstein) 911, 1185, 1186, 1224
"New York, New York" (Kander) 1685
"New York, New York Dance" 1185
"New York on Five Dollars a Day" 160
"New York Skyscrapers" 21
"New York Suite" 1758, 1759, 1760, 1761
"New York Unknown" 907
"New York Without Bob" 852
"The New Yorker" 415
"Newest Girl in Town" 1548
"News" (Davis) 450
"News" (Pen) 114
"The News" (Bergman, et al.) 1149
"The News" (Ford) 656
"The News" (Lasser) 225
"News Flash" 1276
"News Has a Kind of Mystery" 1139
"News Item" 1460
"News of You" 626
"News Report" 1091
"Next" 1213
"Next (Au Suivant)" 792

"The Next Best Thing to Love" 296
"The Next Move" 1143
"Next! Next! Next!" 439
"Next on the Agenda" 673
"Next Season on Broadway" 899
"Next Stop: New York City" 89
"The Next Ten Minutes" 890
"Next Time" 300
"Next to Lovin', I Like Fightin'" 42
"Next Week: David and the Goliaths" 616
"N.G.N. Productions" 1584
"Ni-nana Waltz" 1131
"Nicaragua" 1759
"Nice" 973
"Nice 'n' Easy" 1210
"Nice as Any Man Can Be" 822
"Nice Baby" 1644
"Nice Day" 1228
"Nice Fella" 1164
"A Nice Girl Like You" 676
"Nice Girls Don't Do That" 1505
"Nice House We Got Here" 1164
"Nice Ladies" 1319
"A Nice Man Like That" 712
"Nice Running Into You" 1132
"Nice Shot" 44
"Nice Work If You Can Get It" 1656
"Nicer in Nice" 199
"Nicest Part of Me" 1043
"Nick" 1140
"Nickel Under the Foot" 324
"Nickel's Worth of Dreams" 626
"Nickolodean Holiday" 501
"Nicky Knows" 499
"Nigger Woman" 1423
"The Night" 114
"A Night Alone" 1243
"Night and Day" 212, 567, 1210
"A Night at the Bar" 742
"A Night at the Movies" 170
"Night at the Theatre" 403
"Night Chorus" 363
"Night Club" 1315
"Night Club Days" 436
"The Night Dolly Parton Was Almost Mine" 1317
"Night Fever" 1046
"The Night Gondolfo Got Married" 867
"Night! Healing Darkness!" 834
"Night Heat!" 1576
"Night Highway #1" 1018
"The Night I Bit John Simon" 1337
"Night Is a Weapon" 1392
"Night Lady" 123
"Night Letter" 1689
"Night Lites" 1478
"Night, Make My Day" 257
"A Night of Horror" 1293
"Night of Love" (Fischoff) 1410
"Night of Love" (Friedman) 1441
"Night of Shooting Stars" 1204
"Night of the Iguana" 1251
"Night of the Living Preppies" 1149
"Night on Bald Mountain" 295
"Night on Disco Mountain" 295
"A Night on the Gilboa Mountains" 617
"Night on the Town" 1184
"Night People" 1518
"Night Riders" 1232
"Night Song" 237
"Night Talk" 23
"The Night That I Met Phil" 1195
"The Night the Hurricane Struck" 1261
"Night Time" 570
"Night Time Women" 1733
"Night Train" 427
"Night Waltzes" 1492
"The Night Was Made for Love" 883
"The Night When We Were Young" 1577
"Night Wolf" 1459
"The Night You Decided to Stay" 1499
"Nightclub Interview" 1415
"Nightie-Night!" 1644
"Nightingale" (Earle) 366
"Nightingale" (Strouse) 1134
"Nightingale and Meadow Lark" 1111
"A Nightingale Sang in Berkeley Square" 35, 1482, 1750
"Nightmare" (Cohen) 1829
"Nightmare" (Ophir) 529
"The Nightmare" (Fields) 1445
"The Nightmare" (Ophir) 1253
"Nightmare Alley" 1135
"Nightmare on M Street: A Personnel Office in Washington, D.C., Now" 899
"The Nightmare Was Me" 975
"Nights of Sine" 21
"Nights When I'm Lonely" 681
"Nightshift" 790
"Nightsong" (Eliran) 1136
"Nightsong" (Strouse) 603
"Nightwalk" 1478
"Niihau Hula" 1221
"Nikki" 83
"The Nileside Cotillion" 1201
"9 to 5" 1015
"911 Emergency" 1121
"Nine Lives Blues" 1042
"Nine Long Months Ago" 391
"Nine O'Clock" 1752
"Nine People's Favorite Thing" 1645
"Nine to Twelve" 1335
"1918" 364
"1984" 206
"1950's Singing Group" 1388
"1945" 1558
"1943" 252
"1919" 377
"1960's Twist" 1388
"The 1934 Hot Chocolate Jazz Babies Revue" 214
"The 1920 Agricultural Exposition an' Fair" 313
"96,000" 760
"Niri-Esther" 1716
"Nirvana" 1538
"Nite Club" 1138
"Niwah Wechi" 777
"Niyayibona Lento Engiybonayo (Do You See What I See?)" 1401
"Nize Baby" 1442
"Nkosi Sikelela Lafrica" 1284
"Nkosi Sikeleli'Afrika" 1401
"No" (Davis) 450
"No" (Dun) 1020
"No" (Lunden) 1190
"No" (Woldin) 934
"No Better Way to Start a Case" 912
"No Big Deal" 1296
"No Bird That Sits" 253
"No Blacks, No Chicks, No Jews" 606
"No-Cal, Norma?" 44
"No Champagne" 1468
"No Choice" 1727
"No Choir of Angels" 697
"No Competition for Me" 1613
"No Comprenez, No Capish, No Versteh!" 912
"No Contest" 275
"No Crystal Stair" 501
"No Dessert" 708
"No Easy Way Down" 1591
"No Exit" 1274
"No Finale" 1066
"No for an Answer" 1140
"No Further Questions, Please" 463
"No Garlic Tonight" 74
"No, George, Don't" 1415
"No Give, No Take" 658
"No Good Can Come with Bad" 1109
"No Hard Feelings" 765
"No Hiding Place" 1762
"No Holdin' Back" 240
"No Holds Barred" 1317
"No-Holds Barred Press Conference" 871
"No, I Am Brave" 1270
"No Irish Need Apply" 775
"'No' Is a Word I Don't Fear" 499
"No Ketchup" 1164
"No Lies" 133
"No Life" 1557
"No Love in Lies" 959
"No Love, No Nothin'" 1764
"No, Love, You're Not Alone" 792
"No Man's as Wonderful" 1201
"No Man's Land" 827
"No, Mary Ann" 1491
"No Me Diga" 760
"No More" (LaChiusa) 1422
"No More" (Larson) 1634
"No More" (Sondheim) 1491
"No More Auction Block" 1762
"No More Edens" 1707
"No More Games" 279
"No More Magic" 958
"No More Mornings" 398
"No More Silence" 1727
"No More Than a Moment" 1031
"No, No, It Is a Natural Lie to Tell" 331
"No! No! No!" (Moore) 92
"No! No! No!" (Moskowitz) 819
"No. No. No Secrets" 439
"No Not Much" 527
"No One Believes ..." 1482
"No One Cared Like You" 1159
"No One Ever Knows" 491
"No One Ever Told Me Love Would Be So Hard" 537
"No One Had a Clue in Santiago" 995
"No One Inside" 770
"No One Is Alone" 1491
"No One, Jigsaw" 820
"No One Listens" 1283
"No One Will Know" 1119
"No One's Perfect" 685
"No One's Perfect, Dear" 1827
"No One's Toy" 992, 1106
"No Opening Number" 573
"No Place for Me" 1424
"No Place to Go" (Alper) 754
"No Place to Go" (Haney) 1751
"No Power on Earth Can E'er Divide" 117
"No Questions Asked" 943
"No Room at the Inn" 166
"No Room No Room" 27
"No Sacrifice" 1780
"No Sign of the Times" 1125
"No Small Roles" 1414
"No Tears in Heaven" 1484
"No Thank You from a Mocking Sun" 1034
"'No They Can't' Song" 1628
"No Tickee" 1754
"No Time to Cry" 959
"No Touch Mine" 869
"No True Love" 1440
"No Ways Tired" 1466
"No Women in the Bible" 1201
"Noah" 591
"Noah and the Ark" 1436
"Noah Built the Ark" 1672
"Noah Down the Stairs" 252
"Noah's Dove" 375
"Noah's Prayer" 67
"Nobody" 577
"Nobody But You" 692
"Nobody Cheats Big Mike" 1755
"Nobody Else" 299
"Nobody Ever Hears What I've Got to Say" 1300
"Nobody Home" 1135
"Nobody Knows That It's Me" 1149
"Nobody Knows You When You're Down and Out" 180, 181, 182
"Nobody Like the Lord" 166
"Nobody Loves a Fairy" 1482
"Nobody Makes a Pass at Me" 981, 1267, 1268
"Nobody Messes with Liza" 1128
"Nobody Needs a Man as Bad as That!" 215
"Nobody Needs to Know" 890
"Nobody Shoots No-One in Canada" 151
"Nobody Shtomps on My Shtudio" 1584
"Nobody Takes My Paradise from Me" 257
"Nobody to Cry To" 1774
"Nobody's Blues" 1207
"Nobody's Chasing Me" 1704
"Nobody's Doin' It Dance" 1448
"Nobody's Ever Gonna Step on Me" 41
"Nobody's Fault" 175
"Nobody's Gal" 1543
"Nobody's Heart" 236
"Nobody's Listening" 722
"Nobody's on Nobody's Side" 275
"Nobody's Perfect" 733, 1258
"Nobody's Valentine" 943
"Nocturne" (Rose) 159
"Nocturne" (Ross) 930
"Nokhumke, Mayn Zun (Nochum, My Son)" 1619
"Nomad" 1058
"Non-Bridaled Passion" 2
"Non Credo" 1029
"Non, Je Ne Regrette Rien" 361, 1256, 1257
"Non Merci!" 1510
"Nookie Time" 467
"Noon Sunday Promenade" 1449
"Nor Yiddish" 1032
"Nora, The Nursemaid's Door" 483
"Normal" 1485
"Normal Day" 1325
"A Normal Man Running" 1200
"Normal, Normal, Normal" 1679
"Normandy" 1193
"North American Shmear" 969
"North Atlantic" 1147
"North Coast Recollections" 135
"North-Northwest" 602
"Northchester" 1331
"Northern Boulevard" 1148
"Northfield, Minnesota" 376
"Nose Ahead" 1265
"Noses" 726
"Nosotros Venceremos" 740
"Nostalgia" 614
"Not a Care in the World" 238
"Not a Day Goes By" 1491
"Not All Man" 1763
"Not Allowed" 1600
"Not as I Was" 639
"Not at Home" 54
"Not Available in Stores!" 644
"Not Easy Being Green" 1106
"Not Every Day Can Be a Day of Shine" 1034
"Not for All the Rice in China" 69
"Not for Joe" 481
"Not Getting Any Younger" 714
"Not I" 1771
"Not in My Backyard!" 673
"Not Me" 1547
"Not Mine" 100
"Not Mister Right" 919
"Not My Day" 529
"Not Now" 434, 435
"Not Now, Not Here" 1031
"Not of Her World" 216
"Not on the Top" 492, 555, 1658
"Not on Your Tintype" 1092
"Not President, Please" 690
"Not So Bad" 249
"Not So Bad to Be Good" 238
"Not So Easy" (Allen, et al.) 535
"Not So Easy" (Bone and Fenton) 501
"The Not So Great White Way" 1548
"Not-So-New Faces" 1149
"Not So Young Love" 1379
"Not Tabu" 1566
"Not That Strong" 1084
"Not the Man I Married" 1128
"Not This Year" 249
"Not Today" 219
"Not Tonight" 1394
"Not Too Nice" 837
"Not While I'm Eating" 1152
"Not Your Cup of Tea" 208
"Not Your Heart" 333
"The Note" 719
"Nothin' But the Radio On" 1110
"Nothin' Funny" 333
"Nothin' Up" 1367
"Nothing" (Hamlisch) 283
"Nothing" (Marvin) 907
"Nothing" (Tunick) 1749
"Nothing But" 1558
"Nothing but a Fool" 835
"Nothing But the Blood of Jesus" 1484
"Nothing Can Possibly Change the Fact" 1316
"Nothing Can Replace a Man" 1138
"Nothing Can Stand in My Way" 497

"Nothing Counts But Love" 878
"Nothing Else to Do" 814
"Nothing Ever Happens 'Til Two A.M." 1707
"Nothing Ever Happens in Angel's Roost" 600
"Nothing Ever Happens in Greece" 682
"Nothing Ever Happens to Me" (Hartig and Balk) 858
"Nothing Ever Happens to Me" (Perry) 1320, 1321
"Nothing in Common" 929
"Nothing Is New in New York" 1752
"Nothing Is Sweeter Than You" 681
"Nothing Is Working Quite Right" 870
"Nothing Left but the Rope" 814
"Nothing Left But You" 922
"Nothing Like a Friend" 1467
"Nothing Poem" 1356
"Nothing Sacred" 542
"Nothing Seems the Same" 1043
"Nothing Stays" 14
"Nothing to Do with Love" 1243
"Nothing Ventured, Nothing Lost" 610
"Nothing Will Ever Be the Same" 14
"Nothingness and Being" 1209
"Nothing's Changed" 461
"Nothing's Left of God" 1708
"Nothin's Gonna Change" 1774
"Notre Pere" 1510
"November Elegy" 1356
"November in Kenya" 858
"Now" (Aman) 1153
"Now" (Bingham) 1072
"Now" (Jackson and Hatch) 504
"Now" (Lindsey) 1670
"Now" (Mulcahy) 1569
"Now" (Sondheim) 1492
"Now (It's Just the Gas)" 939
"Now and Then" (Conklin and Miller) 232
"Now and Then" (Yeston) 1201
"Now for the First Time" 697
"Now for the Pirates' Lair!" 1270
"The Now Generation" 1827
"Now I Am a Man" 1777
"Now I Am Ready" 1638
"Now I Know" 1670
"Now I Lay Me Down to Sleep" 1151
"Now I See" 845
"Now I'm Gonna Be Bad" 777
"Now Is All I Have" 1102
"Now Is Here" 1147
"Now Is the Time" 646
"Now Isn't That Lovely?" 1058
"Now It Is Night" 363
"Now It's Gone, Gone, Gone" 716
"Now Let the Weeping Cease" 615
"Now, Listen, Both a Yiz" 1723
"Now That I've Got My Strength" 236
"Now That We Are Alone" 1131
"Now That's Tap" 207
"Now the Day Is Done" 1131
"Now There Was a Future He Must Face" 1723
"Now We Go to the Right" 609
"Now We Pray" 856
"Now, Where Do You Suppose?" 92
"Now Who the Hell at This Hour?" 362
"Now You Are One of the Family" 975
"Now You're Married" 654
"Now You've Been to the Big Time" 920
"Nowadays" 1656
"Noways Tired" 1623
"Nowhere" 678
"Nowhere Man" 1426
"Nowhere Man II" 1426
"Nowhere to Run" 55
"N.S.A. (National Security Agency) Dope Calypso" 729
"Nuclear Winter" 1759, 1761
"A Nude Encounter" 1743
"Nude-Lewd" 64
"The Nude-Nik Hora" 1743
"Nude with Violin" 636
"Nuevo Laredo" 1603
"# 4 Humentash Lane" 1658
"Number 1 on Your Hit Parade" 1132
"Number 918" 38
"Number One" (Feuer) 143
"Number One" (Roberts) 263
"Number One Man" 1319
"Numberless Are the World's Wonders" 615
"Numbers" (Friedman) 1038
"Numbers" (Slater) 719
"Numbers in the Red Notebook" 729
"The Nun and the Restless" 1158
"Nunca" 1336
"Nunsense Is Habit-Forming" 1155, 1157, 1158
"Nunsense, the Magic Word" 1159
"Nursery" 1688
"The Nursery Frieze" 49, 612
"Nurse's Care" 391
"Nurse's Song" 257
"Nursie, Nursie" 581
"Nuthin for Nuthin" 698
"N.Y.C." 237
"Nymph Errant" 1160
"N.Y.U." 638

"O God Our Hearts Are Like the Trees" 1412
"O God with Grace" 717
"O, Grenada" 1335
"O Here It Is! And There It Is!" 1503
"O Love! O Death! O Ecstasy!" 1503
"O Marry Me!" 1161
"O Miserere" 244
"O, Miss Walkaround, Come Walking Out with Me" 569
"O Mistress Mine" (Leslee) 1519
"O Mistress Mine" (MacDermot) 860
"O Mistress Mine" (Mulcahy) 1568, 1569
"O My Soul" 1392
"O! Mysterious Hole" 1478
"O Negros Bahianos" 1388
"O' No" 837
"O-o-oh!" 609
"O, Oysters!" 1162
"O Pallas Athene" 1468
"O Sacrilege" 1787
"O Say Can You See" 232, 1163
"O Se Saoeste" 1639
"O Sov'reign Mistress" 62
"O Stomach of Mine, We Eat!" 528
"O, the Picnic at Manassas" 569
"O Vienna Waltz" 402
"O, What a Lovely Evening (Que, Hermosa Noche Me Espera)" 488
"O, What a Pain It Is to Part" 117
"O, What a War" 1082
"The Oath" 277
"Obedian March" 1060
"Obedience" 1330
"Obey, Abide" 1679
"Obituary" 1600
"The Object Lesson" 49, 612
"The Object of My Affection" 681
"Obscene Phone Call" 1743
"Observant in My Way" 1607
"Obsessed" 665
"Occupations" 828
"Ocean Chorus" 363
"Oceanography and Old Astronomy" 870
"O'Connell Bridge" 253
"October" 926
"Odalie" 407
"Odd Job Man" 916
"Odd or Even?" 1416
"Odds" 33
"Ode to a Hard Hat" 758
"Ode to a Junkie Player" 156
"Ode to a Scrapbook" 1661
"Ode to an Accidental Stabbing" 462
"Ode to an Eminent Daily" 381
"Ode to Colonus: Fair Colonus" 615
"Ode to Connie Carlson" 323
"Ode to Electricity" 752
"Ode to Jo" 323
"Ode to Love" 529
"Ode to Marcello" 676
"Ode to Steam" 544
"Ode to the One I Love" 979
"Ode to the West Wind" 1443
"An Ode to Those Anchor Men" 160
"Ode to Willie" 708
"Odem and the Khave Duet" 1502
"Odenemya" 492
"Odeon" 206
"Odun De" 777
"Oedipus and Antigone Enter Colonus" 615
"Oedipus Rex" 1654
"Oedipus's Curse" 615
"O'er Seas That Have No Beaches" 1503
"Of Thee I Sing" 1166, 1167
"Off Broadway Broads" 638
"Off Off Broadway" 1548
"Off the Map" 328
"Off-Time" 18
"Off to Fight the Hun" 151
"Off to the Races" 1109
"The Off Whites" 277
"An Office in the White House" 1276
"Office Romance" 991
"Office Under the Sky" 693
"An Official Welcome" 622
"Oh America!" 1209
"Oh Baby, Won't You Please Come Home" 55
"Oh, Beatriz" 1336
"Oh, Beautiful" 1231
"Oh, Better Far to Live and Die" 1270
"Oh, Boy! How I Love My Cigarettes!" 391
"Oh, Brother" (Jankowski) 539
"Oh, Brother" (Moritz) 507
"Oh! Calcutta!" 1168
"Oh, Canada" 963
"Oh Captain! My Captain!" 903
"Oh, Catch Me, Mr. Harris, 'Cause I'm Falling for You!" 483
"Oh Chicago!" 1209
"Oh, Come All You Faithful" 166
"Oh, Daddy, Daddy!" 1231
"Oh, Danny Boy" 790
"Oh Darling" 1426
"Oh-Dey-Nameya" 1658
"Oh, Diogenes!" 201
"Oh, Dry the Glistening Tear" 1270
"Oh, False One, You Have Deceived Me!" 1270
"Oh, Fine!" 1383
"Oh! Freedom" 740, 815, 816
"Oh Gee, I Love My G.I." 1554
"Oh God" (Henderson) 333
"Oh God" (Weinstein) 721
"Oh God, I'm Thirty" 159
"Oh, Gods of Love" 124
"Oh Happy Day" 1466
"Oh Happy We" 244, 911
"Oh, Heart of Love" 826, 827
"Oh, Heavenly Salvation" 128, 689
"Oh, How I Love You" 1755
"Oh How I Loved Him" 1820
"Oh, How Many Times, Mr. Parris" 331
"Oh, How We Love You, Mrs. Cornwall" 1380
"Oh I Am a Fork" 1330
"Oh, I Was Goin' A-Courtin'" 1601
"Oh, Is There Not One Maiden Breast" 1270
"Oh, It's You" 485
"Oh, Jerusalem in the Morning" 166
"Oh, Johnny" 1171
"Oh, Kay, You're Okay (Oh, Kay!)" 1172
"Oh! K-Y Chorale (or Beyond the Labia Majora)" 1432
"Oh, Lady Be Good" 1096
"Oh Lead Us Now" 1327
"Oh, Levittown!" 32
"Oh, Lord" 856
"(Oh Lord) Did I Get Too Far Away from You" 9
"Oh, Lorraine" 1040
"Oh Mama, Am I in Love" 1821
"Oh Mary Don't You Weep" 1466
"Oh, Men of Dark and Dismal Fate" 1270
"Oh Mio Snow White" 834
"Oh, Mr. Harris, You're a Naughty, Naughty Man!" 483
"Oh, Mr. Tabor" 92
"Oh, Mrs. Slade" 1374
"Oh, My Age" 1424
"Oh, My Mysterious Lady" 1224
"Oh, My Rose" 1107
"Oh, Oh, Cowboy" 322
"Oh! Oh! Obesity" 1174
"Oh, Oh, Oh" 1330
"Oh, Oh, Oh, O'Sullivan" 1399
"Oh, Pity the Man" 1302
"Oh, Please" 1580
"Oh, Pretty Woman" 1353
"Oh Say, Can You See?" 472
"Oh, Sell Me, Pretty Maiden" 1152
"'Oh Sponsor,' Said She, Jolly Old Sigmund Freud" 32
"Oh Succubus" 1610
"Oh Sunlight of No Light" 615
"Oh Take, Oh Take Those Lips Away" 62
"Oh, Terrible Lady" 1111
"Oh, the Gen'rals" 609
"Oh, the Scandal!" 1584
"Oh, the Shame" 1060
"Oh There Is Not One Maiden Fair Who Does Not Flutter at My Beauty" 511
"Oh, This Cannot Be Borne" 941
"Oh, Three Fun-Lovers Are We" 384
"Oh, to Be Stupid Again" 1499
"Oh Vienna" 1327
"Oh, What a Century It's Been" 13
"Oh What a Day I Thought I'd Die!" 1139
"Oh What a Difference" 738
"Oh, What a Filthy Night Court!" 324
"Oh What a Lovely View" 1383
"Oh, What a Man!" 1613
"Oh, What a Time We Had" 61
"Oh, What a Wedding!" 1146
"Oh, What a Wonderful Plan" 1035
"Oh What a Wonderful Vacation" 1469
"Oh, What Joy to Be Free" 1410
"Oh, William Morris" 919
"Oh, World" 1035
"Oh, Yeah" 67
"Oh! You Beautiful Girl" 570
"Oh, You Don't Need Wine to Have a Wonderful Time" 457
"Oh, You Wonderful Girl" 570
"Oh, Your Mother Is in Bed" 1222
"Ohio" 911, 1224
"Ohio Afternoon" 1176
"O.K., Goodbye" 1330
"Okage, Okage!" 602
"Okay" 930
"Okay, Let's Pray!" 609
"The Ol' Ark's A-Moverin'" 591
"Ol' Man River" 883, 1095, 1210
"Ol' Time Religion" 591
"Olayithi (It's All Right)" 1401
"Old Abe Lincoln Had a Farm" 1239
"The Old Apartment" 742
"Old Banjar" 375
"Old Blind Fiddler" 1720
"Old Cape Cod" 1575
"Old Clothes" 830
"Old College Avenue" 916
"The Old Days" 1030
"The Old Dope Peddler" 1654
"The Old Eight-Ten" 87
"Old Enough to Know Better" 225
"Old-Fashioned" 367
"An Old-Fashioned Ballad" 511
"An Old-Fashioned Chase Ballet" 1511

"Old Fashioned (Old-Fashioned) Girl" 80, 766
"Old-Fashioned Love" 165
"Old Fashioned Love" 1693
"An Old-Fashioned Love Story" 1778
"Old Flame" 385
"The Old Folks (Les Vieux)" 792
"The Old Folks at Home" 1343
"Old Friend" 656
"Old Friends" 1491, 1492
"Old Gals Are the Best Pals After All" 1326
"Old Glory" 259
"The Old Gray Mayor He Ain't What He Used to Be" 550
"The Old Habanera" 1179
"Old Hat Joke" 877
"The Old Hollywood Story" 132
"An Old Japanese Custom" 1385
"Old Kentucky Home" 1049
"The Old Lonesome Stranger" 1042
"Old MacDonald Had a Farm" 96
"An Old Maid" 884
"Old Man" 1036, 1049, 1334
"The Old Man" 1678
"The Old Man Says to the Old Woman" 720
"Old Man Won" 927
"Old Miss" 1125
"Old Mister Fate" 345
"Old Mom and Pop Lament" 788
"The Old Poet" 253
"The Old Rabbit Hole" 1392
"Old Sayin's" 848
"Old Scholar" 253
"An Old Shade of the Moulin Rouge" 1385
"The Old Soft Shoe" 861, 1196
"Old Things" 785
"An Old Time Girl" 1577
"Old Times, Good Times" 1558
"Old Tunes" 692
"The Old Vaudevillian" 1548
"Old White Tom" 504
"Old Wine in New Bottle" 927
"Old Woman of the Roads" 253
"The Oldtimer" 1701
"Ole!" 1179
"Ole Soft Core" 636
"Oleo" 112
"Olga (Come Back to the Volga)" 1704
"Olim! Olim!" 1462
"Olympics" (Driver and Haddow) 1414
"Olympics" (Unknown; possibly Harris) 1605
"Olympus Is a Lonely Town" 1181
"Omaha I'm Here" 453
"Ombra Mai Fu" 1623
"On a Boat to Somewhere" 1412
"On a Day Like This" 848
"On a Girl's Hard Life (Pobre Chica, La Que Tiene Que Servir)" 488
"On a Moonlit Night" 1619
"On a Scale of One to Ten" 1758
"On a Shoestring" 1447
"On a Train at Night" 544
"On and On" 419
"On and On and On" 912
"On Broadway" 212, 854, 1014
"On December Twenty-Seventh I Saw Him Next" 1723
"On Her Majesty's Service" 241
"On Her Own" 857
"On It Goes" 271
"On Living" 1133
"On Mahaneyheya" 1219
"On Moonrock Mountain" 1081
"On My Heart" 1510
"On My Knees Praying" 1559
"On My Own" (Ford) 1154
"On My Own" (Kole, et al.) 743
"On My Own" (Powell) 1125
"On My Planet" 938
"On My Side" 1419
"On My Way" 1726
"On Our Way" 227
"On Seeing an Old Poet in the Café Royal" 135
"On Stage" 1685
"On the Charts" 1504
"On the Checkerboard of Time We've All Played Our Parts. But the Heart Exists in Freedom" 834
"On the Clock on the Floor" 1500
"On the Day That I Marry" 130
"On the Day When the World Goes Boom" 698
"On the Death of Keats" 1443
"On the Deck of a Spanish Sailing Ship, 1492" 1498
"On the Ground at Last" 634
"On the Heavenly Side" 501
"On the Highway of Love" 739
"On the Inside" 372
"On the Line" 740
"On the odyllic influence of the moon" 250
"On the Other Hand" 348
"On the Phone" 1754
"On the Relative Merits of Education & Experience" 572
"On the Road" (Dixon) 476
"On the Road" (Gari) 980
"On the Road" (Melrose) 537
"On the Road Again" 1194
"On the Seashore by the Sea" 121
"On the Sunny Side of the Street" 886, 1435
"On the Swing Shift" 662
"On the Virtues of Being Canadian" 963
"On the Way Home to the Old Land" 402, 1327
"On the Willows" 595
"On with the Show" 1298
"On Your Own" 788
"Once a Week I Put My Television Set on the Windowsill" 44
"Once a Widow" 302
"Once and For All" 1119
"Once and Only Thing" 2
"Once Around the Sun" 1188
"Once Bit, Twice Shy" 1639
"Once I Had a Vision" 1671
"Once I Thought I'd Never Grow" 1601
"Once I Wondered" 68
"Once in a Blue Moon" 766, 935
"Once in Love with Amy" 1611
"Once Is Enough" 1066
"Once It Was Different" 1342
"Once More from the Top" 1143, 1144
"Once on a Summer's Day" 1190
"Once, Only Once" 661
"Once There Was a Melody" 1203
"Once Upon a Time" (Berkowitz) 1060
"Once Upon a Time" (Brandon) 291
"Once Upon a Time" (Lombardo and Loeb) 1221
"Once Upon a Time" (Strouse) 210, 237
"Once Upon a Time" (Swados) 1384
"Once Upon a Time and Long Ago" 1224
"Once Upon a Yesterday" 1693
"Once Upon the Natchez Trace" 1367
"Once You Take the Feeling Out" 1747
"Once You've Had a Little Taste" 1008
"Once You've Seen Everything" 701
"One" (Hamlisch) 283
"One" (Mandel) 1683
"1, 2, 3, 4, 5, 6" 395
"One Adam at a Time" 1479
"One and All" 371
"One and One" 1194
"One and Twenty" 851
"One and Two!" 431
"One Big Family" 388
"One Big Happy Family" 1452
"One Big Love" 1598
"One Big Union for Two" 1267, 1268
"One Billion Little Emperors" 610
"One Boy" 237
"One Came Before Her" 253
"One Cell" 1476
"One Day" 470
"One Day at a Time" 1550
"One Day, One Day, Congotay" 1004
"One Door Opens" 1684
"One Drop Alone" 1363
"One-Faced Woman" 1263
"One-Faced Woman Turns the Other Cheek" 1263
"One Fell Swoop" 288
"One Fine Day" 115
"One Foot in the Real World" 502
"One Foot Out the Door" 1195
"One for a Rainy Day" 1201
"One for My Baby (and One More for the Road)" 662, 1210
"One Happy Family" 1414
"One Helluva Bore" 858
"One Hippopotami" 685
"One Hour Mama" 553, 1373
"One Hundred and Fifteen" 1737, 1738
"One Hundred Virgins" 1379
"The One I Love" 683
"The One I Love (Belongs to Somebody Else)" 1210
"One in My Position" 379
"One Kind of Man" 920
"One Kind Word" 848
"One Kiss" (Leslie) 319
"One Kiss" (Romberg) 1570
"One Last Bop" 424
"One Last Embrace" 184
"One Last Kiss" 237
"One Less Bell to Answer" 83
"One Little Taste" 1250
"One Long Party" 410
"One Man Ain't Quite Enough" 662
"One Man Band" 1197
"One Monkey Don't Stop No Show" 1518
"One Moorish Girl" 130
"One More Angel in Heaven" 833
"One More Beautiful Song" 296
"One More Chance" 98
"One More Day" 643
"One More Kiss" 1651
"One More Study" 1335
"One More Time" (Kookoolis and Fagin) 1504
"One More Time" (Weiss) 164
"One Morning in May" 1521
"One Mother" 362
"One Night in Bangkok" 275
"One Night of Loneliness" 1066
"One Night Stand" (Hoffman) 1760
"One Night Stand" (McAuliffe) 949
"One Night Stand" (Richardson) 926
"One Night Stand" (Weinstein) 837
"One Night Stands" 1505
"One O'Clock Jump" 1015
"One of a Kind" 237
"One of the Beautiful People" 1143, 1144
"One of the Boys" 1620
"One of the Good Guys" 300
"One of Them" 219
"One of These Fine Days" 981
"One of Those Days" 149, 150
"One of Us" (Copani) 493, 1124, 1537
"One of Us" (Simpson and Bland) 710
"One of Us Cannot Be Wrong" 1471
"One of You" 979
"One on One" 1168
"One Rare Pair of Red Sneaks" 1345
"One Room" 1381
"One Rung Higher" 1742
"One-Sided Love" 749
"One Silk Shirt" 1197
"One Simple Song" 1119
"One Small Girl" 1191
"One Small Voice" 3
"One Step" 1524
"One Step at a Time" (Brown) 814
"One Step at a Time" (Moss) 406
"One Step Away" 1296
"One Step Closer" 627
"One Step Forward, Two Steps Back" 814
"One Step Further" 486
"One-Stop Salvation" 1736
"One Sweet Chile" 922
"One Sweet Moment" 1440
"One Thing After Another" 1011
"1000 Airplanes on the Roof" 1200
"1001" 1395, 1396
"One Ticket" 198
"One Track Mind" 148
"One, Two, Three" (Burisoff, et al.) 1450
"One, Two, Three" (Fremont) 1258
"One, Two, Three" (Kennon) 484
"One, Two, Three" (Perkinson) 1004
"One Was Johnny" 1340
"One Way Ticket" 1356
"A One-Way Ticket to Broadway" 1202
"One Week Later" 742
"The One Who Will Love Me" 1001
"One Woman Man" 407
"One-Woman Man" 1613
"One Wonderful Day" 1403
"One Word Is Too Often Profaned" 1443
"The One You Love" 1434
"The Ones in White" 361
"Onh-Honh-Honh!" 1483
"Only a Day Dream" 985
"Only a Heartbeat Away" 1144
"Only a Man" 235
"Only a Passing Phase" 1716
"An Only Child" 280
"Only Dreams" 563
"Only Fool" 1274
"Only Fools Are Sad" 1203
"Only for a Moment" 1821
"Only in America" 854
"Only Love" (Eliran) 401
"Only Love" (Herman) 987
"Only Love" (Kander) 52, 1685
"Only Love" (Sheffield) 297
"Only My Pillow Knows" 929
"Only One" 430, 997
"Only One Dance" 1414
"Only One Person's Opinion" 665
"Only One Shadow" 1477
"The Only Place for Me" 1107
"Only Right Here in New York City" 1678
"Only So Much I Can Give" 990
"Only the Dawn and I" 1693
"Only the Lonely" 1353
"Only the Paranoid Survive" 721
"The Only Thing Missing Is You" 607
"The Only Time We Have Is Now" 1052
"Only Two Allowed" 1274
"Only Yesterday" 1771
"Only You" 1046
"Oo-La-La" 308
"Ooh ... Forgive Me" 1111
"Ooh Child" 252
"Ooh, That's Hot" 1777
"Oom-Glick Blues" 1658
"Oom Pah Pah" 124
"Oooh Lah Lah" 506
"Oop Shoop" 1575
"OP" 156
"Opal" 1204
"Open a New Window" 818
"Open Air Market" 535
"Open All Night" 972
"Open Bright" 1431
"An Open Mind" 633
"Open Mouth" (*When the Owl Screams*) 1765
"Open Mouth" (*The Wrecking Ball*) 1813
"The Open Sea" 873
"Open the Door" (LaChiusa) 130
"Open the Door" (Swados) 643
"Open the Window!" 56
"Open Thou, My Lips, O Lord" 331
"Open Up Your Eyes to Love" 929
"Open Your Heart" 1480
"Opening Call of Drums" 21
"Opening Day" 1500
"Opening Doors" 1491
"An Opening for a Princess" 1193

"Opening Goulash" 685
"Opening Night" (Adams and O'Donnell) 1194
"Opening Night" (Preston) 1365
"Opening Night" (Taylor-Dunn, et al.) 1207
"The Opening Number" 752
"Opening Remarks" 1155, 1157
"Opening the Package" 1601
"The Opera" 675
"Opera Buffa" 758
"Opera in 3-D" 700
"Opera Star" 1379
"Operation Flea" 814
"Operation Kid's Toy" 1765
"Operation Tomorrow" 1121
"Operations Trade-In" 1743
"Operator" (Ahlert) 9
"Operator" (Rupert) 1622
"Operator" (Spivery) 35, 1494
"Opinions in Public" 1441
"Opium Song" 1476
"Opportunity" 266
"Opportunity Knocking" 1613
"Opposite You" 583
"Optimism" 746
"Optimistic" 1294
"Options" 1208
"Opus 9" 942
"Orange Juice" (Lawlor) 550
"Orange Juice" (*The Wrecking Ball*) 1813
"Oranges and Lemons" 1666
"Oranges from Seville" 948
"Oratorio" 1388
"Orbit" 1073
"The Order" 1671
"Ordering the Pizza" 1485
"Ordinary Boy" 1252
"An Ordinary Day" (Cohen) 1829
"An Ordinary Day" (Oster) 385
"An Ordinary Family" (Lewis) 1196
"An Ordinary Family" (Sticco) 267
"Ordinary Guy" 1595
"Ordinary Jo" 1523
"An Ordinary Man" 1593
"Ordinary People" (Grusecki) 639
"Ordinary People" (Legend) 1623
"Ordinary Things" 467, 614
"An Ordinary Town" 3
"Ordinary Women" 1432
"Ordination" 1727
"Ordination Theme" 1727
"Oregon" 71
"Organ Grinder's Swing" 1521
"The Organization Man" 1152
"Organize" 1671
"The Orgy" 1347
"Orgy" 1743
"Orient Yourself" 289
"Oriental" 1261
"The Origin of Love" 680
"An Original Musical" 1645
"Original Parkway" 926
"Original Rag" 1783
"Original Sin" 631
"Orlando at the Palais" 1662
"Ormiston's Blues" 1470
"Ornithology" 633
"An Orphan, I Am" 726
"Orphan in the Storm" 1451
"The Osbick Bird" 49
"Oscar" 1574, 1611
"Oscar Wilde Has Said It" 360
"The Osteopathy Rag" 1192
"Other Alternatives" 509
"The Other Day I Went to an Affair" 1057
"The Other One (Darling)" 1138
"The Other Other Woman" 1499
"Other People" 725, 1097
"Other People's Houses" 159
"Other Possibilities" 1226
"The Other Side of the Wall" (Montgomery) 48
"The Other Side of the Wall" (Roberts) 263
"The Other Side of Time" 359
"The Other Woman" 58
"Ounce of Prevention" 385
"Our Band Goes to Town" 1694
"Our Bright Summer Days Are Gone" 112
"Our Business Is News" 1177
"Our Cause Is Righteous" 194
"Our Crowd" 1255
"Our Day Will Come" 1494, 1551
"Our Decision" 59
"Our Ears" 1503
"Our Exchange Policy" 198
"Our Family Album" 1255
"Our Father" 1006, 1029
"Our Favorite Restaurant" 161, 162, 163
"Our Finest Customer" 633
"Our Home" 578
"Our household" 250
"Our Kids" 814
"Our Kind of War" 289
"Our Last Noble Attempt" 1231
"Our Little Captain" 1644
"Our Little Family" 1274
"Our New Best Friends" 50
"Our New Jerusalem" 284
"Our Night" 1296
"Our Night to Howl" 313
"Our Own Fanny Mendelssohn!" 941
"Our Padre" 135
"Our Polly Is a Sad Slut" 117
"Our Red Knight" 364
"Our Separate Ways" 1499
"Our Song" 486
"Our Special Love" 786
"Our Threepenny Hop" 436
"Our Time" 1491
"Our Time Together" 1107
"Our Wedding Day" 69
"Our World Within" 767
"Our Yesterday" 1577
"Ours" (Porter) 1704
"Ours" (Woldin) 1593
"Out-A-Town" 214
"Out at Sea" 778
"Out Here on My Own" 1015
"Out Last Dance Together" 406
"Out of Breath" 1393
"Out of Love" 272
"Out of Luck with Luck" 1755
"Out of My Sight" 830
"Out of Myself" 1306
"Out of Session" 50
"Out of Sight, Out of Mind" 886
"Out of the Blue" 1778
"Out of the Closets" 673
"Out of the Closets and Into the Streets!" 673
"Out of the Frying Pan" 1513
"Out of the Overlapping" 1503
"Out of Town" 357
"The Out-of-Towner" 1678
"Out on My Own" 1333
"Out on the Sea" 249
"Out On the Street" (Grant) 785
"Out On the Street" (Swados) 1384
"Out on the Streets" 86
"Out on the Wing" 1788
"Out on the Wing #2" 1788
"Out to Launch" 1468
"Outlaw Man" 1739
"Outracing Light" 1424
"Outside the Big Box" 1736
"The Outstanding Member" 667
"The Oval Office" 926
"Over and Over" (Herman) 735
"Over and Over" (Thiele) 1252
"Over Denver Again" 729
"Over Forty" 693
"Over Hill, Over Dale" 1568, 1569
"Over in Europe" 826, 827
"Over My Head" (Broderick) 470
"Over My Head" (Unknown) 736
"Over the Edge" (Giering) 328
"Over the Edge" (Link) 1363
"Over the Hill" 1309
"Over the Hill There Stands a Lady" 654
"Over the Hills and Far Away" 253
"Over the Moon" 114
"Over the Pacific" 963
"Over the Rainbow" 746, 1014
"Over the River and Into the Woods" 261
"Over the Top" 1763
"Over the Trenches" 1635
"Over There" (Cohan) 570, 604, 775, 1096
"Over There" (Wolfe) 1710
"Overture to the Dance" 789
"Ovinu Malkeynu" 604
"Own a Chulapona" 1179
"Owner of My Heart" 627
"Oy Der Pesach Pesach" 1341
"Oy, How I Hate That Fellow Nathan" 220
"Oy, I Like Him" 220
"Oy Iz Dos a Meydel" 1715
"Oy Mama" 492
"Oy Mama! Bin Ich Farleebt!" 1212
"Oy Vay Tate" 1745
"Oy, Yoy" 654
"Oyez! Oyez! Oyez!" 912
"Oyfin Veg Shteyt a Boym" 1658
"Oyfn Pripetshik (At the Fire-place)" 1619
"Oyfn Pripitchik" 1658
"Ozymandias" 1443

"P-P-P-Pain" 1289
"P.A. Announcement" 377
"The PAC Man" 610
"Paciencia y Fe (Patience and Faith)" 760
"Pacific Street" 507
"Pack Up Your Sins and Go to the Devil" 305, 1651
"Pack Up Your Sorrows" 1356
"Pack Up Your Troubles in Your Old Kit Bag" 1540, 1571
"Packin' Up" 166
"Packing the Trunk" 1616
"Packing Up" 765
"Padadooly" 754
"Padam" 1256, 1257
"The Padre Polka" 1159
"Paducah" 1448
"Pagan Love Song" 134, 171
"Pagan Love Song (Ballet)" 134
"Pagan Place" 1415
"Pageant in Exile" 419
"The Pageant of Plantagenet County" 1349
"Pageant of the Bleeding Heart" 419
"Pageant Song" 56
"Paging the Ether" 1326
"Pain" 52
"Pain in My Heart" 229
"Pain(e)" 1263
"Paint Me a Rainbow" 34
"Painted Ladies" 2
"Paintings of Clovis Trouille" 1168
"Pairs of One" 493
"The Palace of Pleasure" 948
"The Palace of the Czar" 1619
"Palermo" 78
"Palestine" 1418
"Palestine: Follow the Star" 1418
"Pamplona" 1274
"The Pan Handlers" 207
"Panassociative" 1072
"Pancho Villa" 376
"Pandarus' Song" 791
"Pandemonium" 1680
"Pandora" 636
"Pandora's Box" (Levinson) 976
"Pandora's Box" (Weinstein) 837
"Pandora's Waltz" 976
"Panic" 627
"Panic Ballet" 705
"Panic Monday" 1742
"Panic on a Planet" 1508
"A Panorama of Hassidic Life" 617
"Pantalone Alone" 583
"Panther" 1014
"Panties" 1478
"Pantomime" 1616
"Pantomine (A Melodrama with a Moral for Our Time)" 581
"Pantomime Dance" 609
"The Pantomime 'Super' to His Mask" 460
"Pantomime Wine" 226
"Pants" 1036
"Papa Bird" 61
"Papa De Da Da" 1198
"Papa Don't Love Mama Any-more" 1268
"Papa Is a Traveller" 402
"Papa, Let's Do It Again" 291
"Papa Says" 41
"Papa, You Won" 41
"Papa's Song" 1117
"Paper Matches" 1780
"Paper Tiger" 357
"Paperback Writer" 299
"Papi No" 1402
"Papirosn (Buy Cigarettes)" 604, 1619
"Parabasis" 1721
"Parade" (*The Cats' Pajamas*) 261
"Parade" (Barnes) 469
"Parade" (Fleischman) 226
"Parade" (Herman) 1218
"Parade" (Ibert) 779
"A Parade in Town" 1491
"Parade Rest" 1152
"Paradiddle" 1447
"Paradise" (Barsha) 1325
"Paradise" (Brown) 171
"Paradise" (Jarboe and Shield) 653
"Paradise" (Marren) 961, 1756
"Paradise" (Peretti, Creatore, and Weiss) 1480
"Paradise Island" 1221
"Paradise Lost" 1611
"Paradise Quartet" 468
"Paradise Quintet" 831
"Parakeet Counselor by Day — Nightingale by Night" 945
"Parallel Lines" 1706
"Paramount, Capitol and the Strand" 861
"Paramus, New Jersey, U.S.A." 1385
"The Paranoia Chorus" 1742
"Parasol Lady" 1739
"Pardon, Ma'am" 569
"Pardon, Mayn Her (Excuse Me, Sir)" 1453
"Pardon Me, Sir" 91
"Pardon Me While I Dance" 1364
"Pardon My Glow" 1721
"Paree" 507
"Parent/Kid Dance" 1384
"The Parents' Farewell" 1296
"Parfum d'Amour" 637
"Paris" (Glass) 427
"Paris" (Marren) 1287
"Paris" (Pine) 1057
"Paris" (Pomeranz) 1700
"Paris Artist" 772
"Paris Beauties" 1293
"Paris Canaille" 924
"Paris, I'm Prepared" 1218
"Paris in the Snow" 21
"Paris Is a City" 1052
"Paris Through the Window" 296
"Paris' Song" 124
"Parisian Pierrot" 751
"Parisian Street Scene" 506
"The Park" 1422
"Park Avenue Rapid Transit" 535
"A Parking Meter Like Me" 1701
"Parlor Songs" 1492
"Parnasse" 598
"Parnell's Plight" 805
"Part of It All" 1645
"Part of Me" 1574
"A Part of That" 890
"Part of the Crowd" 1078
"Part of the Plan" 279
"A Part of Us" 1191
"Part of Your World" 727
"Parting" 726
"Partners" (Pottle) 1040
"Partners" (Ramin) 957
"Party" (Levenson) 293
"Party" (Rubenstein) 1647
"The Party" (Dunbar) 1734, 1735
"The Party" (Traditional? Dunbar?) 1762
"A Party at Peter's Place" 255
"Party Doll" 1414
"Party Farewell" 1601
"Party Games" 461
"Party in Room 203" 200
"A Party in Southampton" 461
"The Party Is Where I Am" 1585, 1586
"Party Music Back in the House" 1601
"Party of the First Part" 60
"Party! Party!" 1487
"The Party People" 1752
"Party Scene" 957
"Party Time" 352

"Party's Gonna End" 393
"The Party's Over" 428, 1224, 1546, 1717
"The Party's Over Now" 1611
"Pas De Deux" (Carmines) 111
"Pas De Deux" (Friedman) 1441
"Pas De Deux" (Goehring) 884
"Pas de Six" 1439
"Pas de Trois pour la Psychologie Contemporaine" 552
"Pass a Little Love Around" 785
"Pass Her Along" 1367
"Pass the Bread and Butter, Brother Van" 322
"Pass the Flame" 222
"Pass the Wine" 3
"Passacaglia" 1749
"Passe-Pied" 635
"The Passenger's Always Right" 1390
"Passin' Through" 1707
"Passing" 610
"Passing Away" 586
"Passing By" 159
"Passing days" 250
"The Passing of a Friend" 770
"The Passing of Time" 1311
"Passing of Various Lives" 1356
"Passing Parade" 226
"Passing Phase" 1225
"Passion" 1708
"La Passion d'Avenant" 123
"Passion Street" 226
"Passionate Pourceaugnac" 1077
"Passover" (Finn) 430, 997
"Passover" (Martel) 663
"The Past Goes On" 1020
"Pastorale" 1806
"Pastrami Brothers" 1133
"Patch, Patch, Patch" 1228
"Patched-Up Day" 1493
"Pathetique Sonata No. 8 in C Minor, First and Second Movements" 1694
"Patience" 76
"Patience ... Charity ... Prudence ... Lucy" 439
"Patience and Gentleness" 379
"Patients, for the Use Of" 241
"Patient's Lament" 1309
"Patio Espanol" 488
"A Patriotic Fantasy" 1176
"Patriotic Finale" 142
"A Patriotic Finale (You Can't Take the Color Out of Colorado)" 1763
"The Patter of Little Feet" 1701
"The Pattern" 1806
"The Pattern Continues" 1806
"Patterns" 300
"Paul Revere" 1691
"Pause for Prayer" 919
"Le Pavillon" 123
"A Pawn for Wernher von Braun" 1142
"The Pawn Shop" 637
"Pay, Pay, Pay" 1108
"Pay Phone" 643
"Pay the Piper" 161
"Pay Them No Mind" 1
"Pay Your Royal Dues" 1320, 1321
"Pazzo" 1146
"PC" 1742
"PEACE" 542
"Peace" (Lewis) 996
"Peace" (Shimoda) 602
"Peace" (Unknown) 1559
"Peace Anthem" 1231
"Peace Ballet" 1231
"Peace Celebration Music" 1380
"The Peace Conference" 773
"Peace Love and Good Damn" 1397
"Peaceful Coexistence" 542
"Peaceful Little Town" 1366
"Peachum's Morning Hymn" 1628
"The Peanut Butter Affair" 160
"Peanut Song" 701
"Pear Tree Sextet" 246
"Pearl" 232
"The Pearl We Called Prague" 658
"Pearls" 1689
"Peas" 1419
"Peas in a Pod" 641
"The Peasants' Song" 675
"Pebble Waltz" 1083
"Peculiar" 257, 1251
"Dem Peddlers Brivele (The Peddler's Letter)" 604
"Pee Wee" 1760
"Peek in Pekin'" 505
"Peg" 1467
"Pegasus" 1404
"Peggy Hewitt & Misty del Giorno" 430
"Peking Watches the Stars" 1139
"The Pembroke Story" 149, 150
"The Pen" 1102
"Penalty" 1195
"Penguins Must Sing" 157
"Penis Envoy" 1432
"Penis Envy" 731
"Penniless Bums" 1546
"PEnnslyvania 1600" 1276
"Pennsylvania Polka" 1571
"Penny a Tune" 1328
"Penny Candy" 1140
"The Penny Candy Gum Machine" 1457
"A Penny for Your Thoughts" 505
"The Penny Friend" 1236
"A Penny Saved" 575
"Penny Whistle Sweet" 105
"Penthouse of Your Mind" 1007
"Pents-un-wreckum" 701
"Peonies" 1153
"People" (Styne) 1546, 1717, 1752
"People" (*The Uncommon Denominator*) 1698
"People Are Like Porcupines" 1758, 1759, 1761
"The People Are the Heroes Now" 1139
"People Are Up for Grabs" 1045
"People Are Wrong!" 1237
"People Collecting Things" 1339
"People Don't Do That" 1483
"The People in the Street" 357
"People Like Us" 1296
"People Like You" 582
"People, People" 1239
"People Stink" 1330
"The People Watchers" 1752
"People Who Live on the Islands" 1691
"The People You Know" 272
"The People's Choice" 1318
"Pep" 813
"Perdido" 165, 382, 1435
"Perennials" 1237
"Perfect" (Feldman) 1048
"Perfect" (LaChiusa) 933
"Perfect" (Valenti) 990
"Perfect Acts" 958
"Perfect Dialogue" 958
"The Perfect Family" 1310
"Perfect Feeling" 206
"Perfect Finite" 1499
"Perfect Harmony" 1134
"The Perfect Imbalance" 497
"The Perfect Life" 1197
"Perfect Man" 745
"A Perfect Pair" 742
"The Perfect Place on Christopher Street" 1084
"A Perfect Plan" 778
"The Perfect Romance" 738
"Perfect Stranger" (Howard) 1576
"Perfect Stranger" (Lindsey) 703
"Perfect Strangers" (Holmes) 1109
"Perfect Strangers" (Silverman) 1208
"Perfect Timing" 741
"A Perfect Tragedy" 403
"The Perfect Understanding" 360
"The Perfect Woman" 976
"Perfect Young Ladies" 199
"Perfection" (Bergersen) 1380
"Perfection" (Ost) 461
"Perfection" (Pockriss) 448
"Perfection" (Viola) 678
"A Perfectly Charming Visit" 714
"Perfidia" 527, 533
"A Period Piece" 338
"Perish the Baubles" 1161
"Perky Little Porn Star" 1110
"A Permanent Romance" 949
"Permission" 1146
"Peroration" 615
"Perpetual Anticipation" 1492
"Perpetual Care" 1251
"A Person Who Eats Meat" 963
"Personal Experiences" 651
"Personal Heaven" 1688
"Personality Plus" 1366
"Personals" (Choset) 915
"Personals" (Fremont) 1258
"Personals" (*Orwell That Ends Well*) 1209
"Personals" (Weinberg) 1600
"Pesach Has Come to the Ghetto" 647
"Pessimistic Voices, Part One" 730
"Pessimistic Voices, Part Two" 730
"Peter Pan" 1192
"Peter's Dream" 413
"Peter's Reprise" 1052
"Petite Belle Lily" 1004
"La Petite Oiseau" 290
"Petition" 638
"Petrouchka" 95
"Pets" (Oler) 1251
"Pets" (Porter) 567
"Petticoat Lane" 865, 1593
"Phantasmagoria at the Caravanserai" 1050
"Phantom Affair" 1263
"Phantom of the Opera" 564
"Pharoah's Chant" 647
"Pharoah's Dream Explained" 833
"Pharoah's Story" 833
"Pharoah's Tomb" 395
"Phil the Fluter" 1540
"The Philanthropist's Progress" 1076
"Philatelic" 381
"Philip & Elizabeth" 450
"The Philosopher Encounters the Tree of Life and Transcends His Intellect" 1592
"Philosophy" 543
"Phil's Medley" 685
"The Phobia Song" 1478
"Phoebe's Song" 476
"The Phoenix and the Turtle" 1437
"The Phone Call" 973
"Phone Calls" 719
"Phony Jo (Le Bluffeur)" 1641
"Photograph Song" 431
"Photographer" 410
"Photographs" (Hamilton) 1721
"Photographs" (Wilder) 23
"Phyllis Frog" 1679
"Physical" 1015
"Physical Fitness" 1069
"The Physician" 367, 1160
"Pianist's Fingers" 36
"Piano" 1527
"Piano Effects" 1624
"Piano Man" 1694
"Piano Phun" 1016
"Piano Players" 1493
"Piano Rollin' Rag" 457
"Picasso's Theme" 1538
"Pick a Bale of Cotton" 740
"Pick Dis Cotton, Lord" 120
"Pick Me" 499
"Pick Me a Flower" 547
"Pick Me Up and Lay Me Down" 1704
"Pick More Daisies" 1582, 1677
"Pick Up the Pieces" 886
"Pick Up Your Weapon" 1423
"Pick Yourself Up" 883
"Pickin' Up the Pieces" 8
"Picking Up the Pieces" 1243
"Pickle Week" 1749
"The Pickup" 461
"The Picture in the Hall" 1624
"A Picture Is Worth a Thousand Words" 1765
"Picture Me" (Blank) 288
"Picture Me" (Magee) 633
"Picture Me with You" 215
"The Picture of Dorian Gray" 403
"The Picture of Happiness" 1266
"Picture Perfect" 224
"Picture Postcard Place" 1306
"Picture Postcard Poifect" 1289
"Picture Yerself" 184
"Pictures and an Exhibition" 1030
"Pictures in the Sky" 960
"Pictures of You" 712
"Pie and Coffee" 626
"Piece of My Heart" 115, 965, 1556
"Pieces" 1693
"Pieces of Lives" 1323
"Pieces of My Life" 1419
"Pieces of Paper" 1294
"Pied Piper" 464
"Piel Canela" 533
"Pierre" 1340
"Pierre, The Great Lover" 1475
"Pig in a Pen" 1720
"The Pig Song" 1540
"Pigeon-Hole Time" 1258
"Pigeons of San Marco" 1131
"Piggyback Partners" 350
"A Pilgrim's Primer (Beginner's Guide to Cruising)" 758
"The Pill" 61
"The Pilot" 938
"The Pilot Meets the Prince" 938
"A Pimp Like That" 1518
"Pimp's Ballad" 689
"Pinball Wizard" 1655
"Pink Fish" 1228
"Pink Lady" 1030
"Pinky Panky Poo" 301
"Pinpipi's Sob of Love" 1716
"Pioneers" 903
"The Piper Must Be Paid" 197
"Pip's Song" 1071
"Piragua" 760
"Pirate Jenny" 128, 807, 879, 880, 882, 1540, 1626, 1628, 1773, 1807, 1809
"Pirates" 1209
"Pirates Song" 486
"A Pirate's Lament" 1021
"The Pirates' Life" 710
"Pirates' Polka" 1021
"The Pirate's Song" 366
"Pisa" 419
"The Piscean" 1397
"Piti's Song" 1449
"Pittsburgh, Pennsylvania" 1752
"Pity the Child" 275
"Place in Space" 1007
"A Place of My Own" 1380
"A Place Somewhere" 255
"Places I Fainted from Hunger" 1375
"The Plagues" 647
"Plaid" 606
"Plain, Clean, Average Americans" 588
"A Plain Song" 1527
"Plaisir D'Amour" 1494
"Le Plan" 123
"Plan B" 760
"Planet" 1476
"Planet of No Thigh Bulge" 580
"Planning the Bar Mitzvah" 473
"Plant a Radish" 478
"Play Away the Blues" 89, 1202
"Play Game" 1634
"Play Gypsies, Play" 1326
"Play It As It Lays" 1737, 1738
"Play Nice" 2
"Play to Win" 284
"Play with Me" 216
"A Playboy's Work Is Never Done" 1707
"The Played-Out Humorist" 460
"Playing Croquet" 935
"Playing Hostess" 461
"Playing Second Fiddle" 1155, 1157
"Playing the Part of the Maid" 1505
"Playoffs Opening" 1273
"A Playwright Remembered" 299
"The Plaza Waltz-Waltz" 381
"A Plea for Understanding" 1574
"Pleasant Company" 634
"Pleasantly Plump" 1339
"Please Come to My House" 1019
"Please, Dr. Fletcher?" 391
"Please Don't Make Me Be Good" 567
"Please Don't Make Me Hear That Song Again" 1134
"Please Don't Stop Him" 777
"Please Don't Talk About Me" 1720
"Please Don't Tell My Father" 719
"Please God" 1108
"Please Hello" 1213
"Please Hold" 198
"Please If You Don't Mind Baby" 1401
"Please Let Me Read" 1468
"Please Make Me Over" 1046

"Please Mr. Postman" 1551
"Please Understand" 1002
"(Please) Believe Me" 1631
"Pleased with Myself" 1524
"A Pleasure" 375
"Pleasure and Privilege" 1381
"Pleasures" 1358
"The Pledge" 948
"The Plot Against the Chase Manhattan Bank" 1274
"Plot and Counterplot" 969
"Plot Luck" 1318
"Plumbing" (Carmines) 1231
"Plumbing" (Porter) 1160
"The Plumed Knight" 722
"The Plunger" 952
"Plus One" (Carpenter) 1148
"Plus One" (Curtis) 1732
"Plus Two" 1732
"P.M. With Lufa" 1149
"Pockets" 576
"Poem" 196
"A Poem" 1394
"A Poem by William Blake" 588
"Poem for Certain Cats" 1734
"Poem of Angela Yvonne Davis" 1735
"Poem of Greetings" 21
"Poem to Complement Other Poems" 1735
"Poems" 1213
"Poems, Prayers and Promises" 37
"The Poet Is Cornered" 472
"The Poet's Corner" 1576, 1749
"Poindexter's Lament" 943
"Point Number" 1661
"Point of View" 1485
"Points" 1040
"Pointy's Lament" 1250
"Poison Hiding" 1423
"Poisoning Pigeons" 1654
"Les Poissons" 727
"The Poker Game" 1373
"Police Song" 1483
"Police!" 528
"Polishing Shoes" 1818
"Political Lady" 1608
"Political Science" 1036, 1049, 1334
"Polka" 609
"Polka a la Appalachia" 985
"Polka Furioso" 1131
"Pollution" 1239, 1654
"Polly's Lied (Song)" 1626, 1628
"Poltergeist Phemomena" 287
"Polyarts U" 961, 1756
"Polygamy" 1701
"Polythene Pam" 1426
"Poncia" 130
"The Pool" 933
"Poontang" 913
"Poor" 33
"Poor Bosie" 360
"Poor Boy" 393, 394
"Poor Charlotte" 933
"Poor Child" 1778
"Poor Dear Is Beside Himself" 673
"Poor Don Pasquale" 1146
"Poor Foolish Frightened Boy" 844
"Poor General" 194
"Poor Isabel" 379
"Poor Jenny" 654
"Poor Kitty Popcorn (or, The Soldier's Pet)" 695
"Poor Little Boy" 867
"The Poor Little Girls of Ontario" 963
"Poor Little Jesus" 166
"Poor Little Pierette" 199
"Poor Little Rhode Island" 1546
"Poor Little Rich Girl" 751, 1170
"A Poor Man" 1311
"A Poor Man at Parting" 1446
"Poor Mouse" 349
"The Poor People of Paris" 1540
"Poor Pitiful Rascals" 922
"Poor, Poor Joseph" 833
"Poor, Poor Pharoah" 833
"Poor Prune" 902
"Poor Sweet Baby" 1486
"Poor Teddy Bear" 786
"Poor Tied Up Darlin'" 1367
"Poor Unfortunate Souls" 727
"Poor, Unsuccessful and Fat" 1121
"Poor Wandering One" 1270
"Poor Warbling Star" 511
"Poor Young Millionaire" 1704
"Popcorn" 930
"Popcorn and Piss" 1030
"Popcorn II" 930
"The Pophams" 1172
"Poppin'" 1151
"Poppy Fields" 493
"Popular Love Song" 21
"Popularity" 42
"The Population Explosion" 1239
"Porcupine Suite" 1758, 1759, 1761
"Porky Done His Best" 1315
"Pornography" 1743
"Port Authority" 975
"Port of Debarkation" 1058
"Portfolio Girl" 665
"Portia's Plan" 1309
"Portman Kick" 1149
"Portofino" 371
"The Portrait" 1
"Portrait of a Freeze" 804
"Portrait of Jennie" 1287
"Posin'" 165
"Positively No (Construction Gang)" 553
"Possum Pie" 1297
"The Post" 299
"Post Card" 1485
"Post-Mortem" 1196
"Postcards on Parade" 1289
"Posterity" 1166
"Posterity Is Just Around the Corner" 1167
"Postlude" 730
"A Pot of Myrtle" 1604
"Pot Pourri from a Surrey Garden" 135
"Potato" 143
"Potato Salad" 1754
"Potatoes, Potatoes" 449
"Potential" 1084
"A Potion" 1679
"Potiphar" 833
"Potpourri" 1342
"Pour Le Sport" 1027
"Pour Me a Man" 1061
"Pour, O Pour the Pirate Sherry" 1270
"The POW-MIA Benefit Show" 1263
"Powder My Back" 1615, 1616
"Power!" (Bolcom) 257
"Power!" (Grossman) 398
"Power!" (Harper) 1424
"Power!" (Rich and Moritz) 1538
"Power!" (Swados) 1345
"Power Babies" 1607
"Power in the Air" 229
"The Power Lies Within" 1538
"Power of Dreams" 1419
"The Power of Negative Thinking" 942
"Power Play" 1294
"A Power Stronger Than Will" 701
"A Pox on Love and Wenching" 979
"Prairie Moon" 950
"Praise the Lord" 823
"Praise the Lord and Pass the Ammunition" 1571
"Praise to the Blessed Builders" 1743
"Praised Be My Lord" 1671
"Praised Be to the Lord Our Savior" 59
"Praises, Praises" 278
"Praises to the Sun! (Canticle of Our Brother Sun)" 539
"Praties They Grow Small" 740
"Pray" 1191
"Pray for the Lights to Go Out" 221
"Pray I Make P.A." 474
"Prayer" (Davis) 388
"Prayer" (LaChiusa) 1422
"Prayer" (Martel) 663
"Prayer" (Reiser) 95
"Prayer" (Traditional?) 591
"Prayer" (Unknown) 1388
"Prayer" (Yeston) 1201
"The Prayer" (Gordon) 1103
"The Prayer" (Levison) 404
"Prayer Chain" 1338
"A Prayer for Mama" 730
"Prayer of the Comfort Counselor" 1680
"Prayer Song" 216
"The Prayer That Got Away" 21
"Prayer to Masks" 21
"Prayers in the Delta" 386
"Preach the Good News" 1470
"The Preacher and the Nurse" 892
"Preacher Man" 968
"Preaching with Tuned Response" 615
"Precious Little Darkness" 101
"Precious Lord" 736, 1001
"Precious Memories" 1423
"Precious Mommy" 1562
"Precious Patterns" 809
"Precious to Me" 1512
"Precious Twins" 730
"Preference" 501
"Pregnancy" 449
"Prelude" (Glass) 427
"Prelude" (Swados) 647
"Prelude in D Flat Major" 1694
"Prelude to War" 486
"Prelude: Refrain, Verse 1, Verse 2" 20
"Preludes I, II, and III" 73
"Prematurely Air-Conditioned Supermarket" 427
"Premeditated Luck" 528
"The Premonition" 1569
"Prepare Ye the Way of the Lord" 595
"Preparing for the Flight" 1788
"The Preppy Song" 780
"The Presentation" 676
"Presentation" 261
"Presentation of Miss Turnstiles" 1186
"Presidents and Golf" 606
"The President's Dream" 1113
"Press" 1698
"Press a Dress" 1179
"Press Conference I" 485
"Press Conference II" 485
"Press Conference III" 485
"Pretend You're Him" 1063
"Prettiest Politician" 9
"Pretty" (Childs) 222
"Pretty" (Merrill) 658
"Pretty Boy" 1514
"Pretty Doll" 553
"Pretty Faces" 1298
"Pretty Flower" 1397
"Pretty Jack" 667
"A Pretty Kettle of Fish" 57
"Pretty Lady" (Britton) 575
"Pretty Lady" (Sondheim) 1213
"Pretty Lady" (Weiss) 161
"Pretty Like You Do" 1050
"Pretty Piggy" 27
"Pretty Woman" 465, 860
"Pretty Women" 1491, 1492
"The Pretzel Peddler" 22
"Pretzels" 1299
"Previous Lives" 1646
"Priceless Relics" 634
"The Pricklepear Bloom" 1367
"Pride" 413
"Pride and Freedom" 809
"Pride and Joy" 241
"Pride in My Work" 1755
"Priests" 1471
"Priggish, Mealy-Mouthed" 362
"The Prima Ballerina" 1159
"Prima Donna" (Leveillee) 598
"Prima Donna" (Russell) 32
"Prima Donna Fabulous" 750
"Primary Tango" 1758
"Prime Time" 1300
"Primers" 986
"The Prince and Me" 284
"Prince and Queen" 889
"Prince Charming" 403
"Prince Edward Skool" 50
"The Prince Is Coming" 1303
"The Prince Is Mad" 1302, 1303
"The Prince of Peace" 1304
"The Prince's Planet" 938
"Princes' Street" 631
"The Princess" 1319
"Princess" 1006
"The Princess and the Prince" 789
"Princess Di" 1149
"The Princess Lays a Golden Egg" 350
"The Princess of Herzogovinia" 948
"Princeton Pastorale" 1460
"The Principle of the Thing" 1108
"Principles" 1412
"Priorities" 1148
"Prison Camp Scene" 170
"Prison Life" 1562
"Prison Song" 1423
"Prisoner of War" 1647
"Prisoner's Lullaby" 1264
"La Prisonniere" 622
"Private Hunting Ground" 76
"Private Practice" 391
"Private Secretary" 1208
"Privates on Parade" 1304
"The Pro Musica Antiqua" 1576, 1749
"Problem" 472
"Problem After Problem" 1384
"The Problem with Us" 1508
"The Problems of a Shepherd" 1418
"Procession" (Haney) 1751
"Procession" (Perkinson) 1004
"Procession" (Shepp) 844
"Processional" (Jacobson) 1452
"Processional" (Springer) 284
"The Prodigal Has Returned" 1307
"The Prodigal Son" 1436
"The Producer Didn't Hire Me" 1132
"The Producers" 1743
"Production Number" (Silver) 1527
"Production Number" (Silverstein and Tuttle) 388, 1749
"The Professor" 1457
"Progress" 128
"Progressive Education" 1318
"Project Heal" 643
"Project Moon Shot" 1276
"Prologue" 1532
"Prom Date" 719
"Prom Dreams" 1325
"Promenade dans le Jardin" 123
"Promenade Theme" 1311
"The Promise" (Rue) 1333
"The Promise" (Weiss) 402
"Promise" 1063
"The Promise Broken" 1333
"Promise Me" 742
"Promise Me One Thing" 1514
"Promise Me, Violet" 1726
"Promise of Greatness" 1622
"The Promise of Living" 1601
"The Promise of Love" 808
"Promise of the Future" 1002
"Promise of the Morning" 1554
"The Promise That Was Kept" 1203
"Promises and Love" 1051
"Promises, Promises" 83
"Prop-Room Ballet" 1565
"Proper Due" 1161
"Prophesy" 175
"Prophet" 241
"A Proposal for Our Time" 812
"The Proposition" 541
"'The Prosecutor' at Death-Train Station Five" 1018
"The Prosperity Song" 1375
"Protect Me from Him" 1063
"Protest" 1762
"The Protest" 1253
"Proud Lady" 88
"Proud Mary" 115
"Proud of Your Boy" 727
"Prove I'm Really Here" 1767
"Proverb" 963
"Prozac, Ritalin, TrimSpa" 1128
"Prudence, Have Faith" 1780
"P.S. I Love You" 1750
"The Psalm of Jehoshaphat" 1531
"A Psalm of Peace" 663
"Psyched Out" 377
"(The) Psychiatry Song" 826, 827
"Psychological Warfare" 616
"P.T. Boat" 381
"P.T. Playwriting Kit" 1414
"PTA" 1066
"Puberty" 297
"Public Enemy Number .1" 102
"Public Enemy Number One" 63
"A Public Place" 977
"Public Service Announcement" 573
"Public Service Message" 919
"Puddin 'N' Tame" 467
"Puddin' Head" 1546
"Pudding Lane" 1316
"Puddles" 464
"Puff, My God, I'm Draggin'" 1046
"Puilly Fuisse" 1048

"Pull It Together (A Response)" 41
"Pull the Boat for Eli" 1115, 1116
"Pull Together" 1423
"Pullin' the Wool" 1077
"Pump Boys" 1317
"The Pump Song" 457
"Punch and Judy" 96
"Punk" 580
"Puns" 1754
"Puppet" 804
"Puppet Dream" 831
"Puppet on a String" 1450
"The Puppet Rebbe" 647
"Puppets & People" 261
"Puppy Love" 1575
"The Purest Kind of Guy" 1140
"Purgatory" 1349
"Purgatory U." 1035
"The Purification" 1398
"Purim" 1453
"Purim Song" 878
"Purple Hearted Soldiers" 1298
"Purple Sage in the Twilight" 1546
"Push and Pull (A Recitative)" 41
"Push Over for Love" 1315
"Pushcart Sellers" 1505
"Pushing Thirty" 1800
"The Pussy Cat Girl" 1616
"Put a Light in The Window" 1452
"Put 'Em in a Box" 1546
"Put Him In" 257
"Put in a Package and Sold" 656
"Put It All Down in the Diary" 1316
"Put It in Writing" 1318
"Put It on the (My) Tab" 644
"Put It Together" 41
"Put It Where the Moon Don't Shine" 376
"Put on a Happy Face" 237
"Put On Your Sunday Clothes" 818
"Put on Your Tatta, Little Girlie" 577
"Put That Down" 1063
"Put the Blame on Mamie" 1138
"Put the Fire Out" 1363
"Put Your Dreams Away (for Another Day)" 1210
"Puttin' on the Ritz" 1014, 1656
"Putting It Together" 1491, 1492, 1557
"Pygmies, Palms and Pirates" 1503
"Pyramid" 143
"Pyramus, Arise" 1437
"Pythagoras Tells How He Discovered That There Are 360 Degrees in a Circle" 1765

"Q.R.V." (Golub) 49
"Q.R.V." (Matz) 612
"Q.R.V. Also" 49
"Q.R.V. Too" 49
"Quadrille" 42
"Quail-Bagging" 950
"Quakin' and Shakin'" 386
"Quakin' for Aiken" 750
"Quand L-Amour Meurt" 1350
"Quand Vous Mourrez de Nos Amours" 963
"Quartet" (Barsha) 1325
"Quartet" (Fields) 1445
"Quartet" (Isen) 491
"Quartet" (Smit) 1338
"Quartet Agonistes" 271
"Quartet for Juggling Ensemble" 1439
"Quartet for Losers" 636
"Quartet of Swedes" 1229
"A Quartet with a Smile" 497
"Quartet: Sharp" 1362
"Que Aire" 1336
"Que Bueno Baila Usted" 262
"Que Es?" 1336
"Que Pasa, My Love?" 203
"Quebec Qui!" 1510
"The Queen" 449
"Queen Alice" 27
"The Queen and the New Order" 1091
"Queen Cobra" 1476
"Queen Gormlai" 253
"Queen Mab" 1424
"Queen Min Chased by the Beasts" 889
"Queen Min's Return" 889
"The Queen of Burlesque" 1616
"Queen of Hearts" 1320, 1321
"Queen of Hollywood" 1485
"Queen of Our Hearts" 805
"Queen of Spain" 1447
"The Queen of Terre Haute" 1704
"Queen Victoria" 963
"Queen Victoria's Benediction" 1289
"Queenie Take Me Home with You" 1326
"Queenie Was a Blonde" 1778
"Queenly Comments" 271
"Queequeg Dying" 1071
"Quelle Heure Est-Il?" 598
"Questa o Quella" 1623
"Questa Quela" 212
"Question and Answer" 1726
"The Question Is" 1466
"The Question Song" 1415
"Questions" (Brielle) 1135
"Questions" (Grant) 400
"Questions" (Kresley) 1069
"Questions for the Rain" 280
"Questions, Questions" (Evans) 280
"Questions, Questions" (Rado) 1330
"Quick Thoughts from AG!" 1407
"Quickly" 33
"Quiet" 1193
"Quiet by Myself" 410
"Quiet Country" 1659
"Quiet Evening" 1658
"A Quiet Girl" 911, 1224
"A Quiet Heart" 1721
"A Quiet Kind of Love" 1383
"Quiet Little Royal Household" 1811
"Quiet Morning" 575
"Quiet Place" 1043
"A Quiet Thing" 52, 210, 1685
"Quigley's Message" 197
"The Quilt" 1323
"Quiltin' and Dreamin'" 1323
"Quimbara" 262
"Quintet" 1131
"Quite Suddenly" 466
"Quittin' Time" (Ford) 1154
"Quittin' Time" (MacDermot) 1638
"The Quiz" 1155, 1157
"Quodlibet" 1637
"A Quoi Ca Sert l'Amour" 1257
"Quotation of the Day" 1235
"Quotations" 615
"Quote of the Day" 1234

"The Rabbi Who Promised to Wait" 1203
"A Rabbi's Daughter" 1442
"The Rabbit Habit" 506
"The Rabbit's Excuse" 27
"The Rabbit's House" 27
"The Race" 1755
"The Race of the Lexington Avenue Express" 371
"Racquetball Court" 473
"The Radio" 252
"Radio City Music Hall" 557, 1261
"Radio Dance" 658
"Radio Song" 1545
"Radio Waves" 431
"Raftery" 253
"Raftery's Repentence" 253
"A Rag, a Bone, a Hank of Hair" 1755
"Rag Doll Rag" 216
"Rag Mop" 1575
"A Rag on a Stick and a Star" 1327
"Raga" 1133
"The Rage" 60
"Rags" (Meyer) 1652
"Rags" (Strouse) 1328
"Rags to Riches" 527
"Ragtime" 60
"The Ragtime Dance" 1643
"Ragtime Man" 105
"Ragtime Max" 1605
"Ragtime Nightingale" 1643
"Rah, Rah" 582
"Rah, Rah, Rah, Rah" 395
"Rah Tah Tah Tio Beep Doo Doo" 1787
"Railroad Bill" 740
"The Railroad's Pushing North" 439
"Rain" (Carnelia) 1624
"Rain" (Flaherty) 1191, 1623
"Rain" (Leigh) 289
"Rain Over Manhattan" 1315
"Rain, Rain (Don't Go 'Way)" 23
"Rain Song #1" 67
"Rain Song #2" 67
"Rain Song #3" 67
"Rain Song #4" 67
"Rain Your Love on Me" 1154
"Rainbow" (Harris) 1476
"Rainbow" ("Over The Rainbow"; Arlen) 1014
"Rainbow" (Silverman) 1208
"Rainbow, Rainbow" 1527
"Rainbows" 930
"Raining in My Heart" 341
"Rainmaker" 1631
"Rainy Day Woman #12 and 35" 265
"A Rainy Night in Rio" 348
"Raise a Glass to Love!" 1510
"Raise Me Up" 1726
"Raise the Roof" 1778
"Raise Them Up Higher" 777
"Raise Up the Flagon" 1477
"Raising an Igloo" 1147
"Ram" 181, 182
"Ramona's Lament" 179
"Ranchera of the Lonesome Women" 897
"Randy Girls" 1153
"Rank and File" 164
"Rants and Raves" 385
"Rap" (aka "Roscoe's Rap"; Leslee) 78
"Rap" (Friedman) 1558
"Rap Master Ronnie" 1335
"Rape" 708
"Rape Ballet" 478
"Rape Me" 786
"Rape Music" 1018
"The Rape of Miss Goldberg" 763, 764, 765
"Rapid Reading Rachel" 1661
"The Rare Old Times" 775
"Rare Wines" 398
"The Rat-A-Tat-Tap" 1337
"Rat Trap" 653
"Ratched's Lament" 154
"Rats & People" 1294
"Rats and Mice and Fish" 398
"Ratta Tat Tat" 1348
"Raven Girl" 1356
"Raven the Magnet" 453
"Raving Beauty" 132
"Razz-Me-Tazz-Jazz" 1636
"Razzle Dazzle" 1685
"Razzy Dazzy" 105
"The RE-7" 151
"Re-Orient Yourself" 289
"Reach for the Sky!" 786
"Reach Out" 968
"Reach Out and Touch Her" 1274
"Reach Out for Me" 83
"Reach Out in the Darkness" 1551
"Reach Right Down" 1522
"Reaching, Touching" 1659
"Reaching Up" 770
"Read All About It" 1608
"Read My Mind" 721
"Read My Palm[s]" 431
"Ready Made" 1361
"Ready or Not" (Cohen) 1547
"Ready or Not" (Rose) 159
"Ready or Not" (Smit) 1338
"Ready to Go" 1081
"Real" 767
"The Real American Folk Song Is a Rag" 46
"The Real Coney Island" 1185, 1186
"Real Life" 1634
"Real Life Funnies" 1339
"A Real Life Lullabye" 230
"The Real McCoys" 672
"The Real Origin of the Black Bottom" 622
"The Real Thing" 986
"The 'Real' People's Party" 1263
"Reality Check" 1760
"Reality: The Turtle Awakens the Dealer" 1592
"Realize" 750
"A Really Lousy Day in the Universe" 1121
"Really Rosie" 1340
"The Realm of Passion (or The Soldier's Wife)" 989, 990
"Reap What You Sow" 1672
"Reason Died Last Night" 107
"A Reason for Living" 1300
"Reason to Marry" 693
"Dem Rebbn's Chassene" 1032
"The Rebel" 253
"Rebel Girl" 604
"Rebirth and the Life Cycle" 1806
"Recapitulation from Oedipus the King" 615
"Receive Us" 856
"Recess with Mrs. Grimm" 716
"Recipe" 8
"The Recipe" 161, 162, 163, 164
"A Recipe for Cheesecake" 1788
"The Recipe for Husbandry" 1446
"Recipe for Love" 101
"Recital" 1383
"Recitative" (Baton) 1419
"Recitative" (Meyer) 1652
"Recitative" (Silverman) 1708
"Recitativo" 1146
"Reckless Blues" 180, 181, 182
"The Reckoning" 271
"Reconciliation" 983
"Record Player Scene" 1788
"Recruitment (Recruiting) Song" (see "Army Song") 879, 882, 1773
"Red" 409
"Red as the Rose" 635
"The Red Baron" 1828
"Red, Blue, and White" 649
"Red Faces at the Kremlin" 41, 1375
"Red Hook" 1723
"Red Hot and Blue!" 367, 1704
"Red Hot Mamma" 32
"Red Iron Ore" 740
"The Red Kimono" 61
"Red Leather Wrist Watch" 860
"Red Letter Hope" 820
"Red Moroccan Shoes" 1754
"Red Queen" 27
"Red Roses for a Blue Lady" 1494
"Red Sails in the Sunset" 1315
"Red Sneaker Rap, Part I" 1345
"Red Sneaker Rap, Part II" 1345
"The Red Visitors" 1276
"The Redemption of Ebenezer Scrooge" 1152
"Redlining" 664
"Rednecks" 1049
"Reefer Madness!" 1347
"The Reefer Song" 18
"Reet Petite" 790
"Reflections" (Fischoff) 1410
"Reflections" (Jordan) 1379
"Reflections" (Swerdlow) 969
"Reflections in a Mirror" 1089
"Reflections on a Crystal Wind" 1356
"Refugees" 1478
"Regency Rakes" 317
"Regiment of Our Own" 136
"A Regular Family" 313
"Regular Fellas" 249
"Regulation Purple" 326
"Rehabilitation in America" 699
"The Rehearsal" 1048
"Rehearsal Break Skipping Dance" 170
"Reidhof's" 1379
"Reiffied Expression" 65
"Reindeer Moss" 1147
"The Rejected Lovers" 1192
"Rejoice" 1038
"The Relay Race" 485
"Release Yourself" 646
"Relic Seller Theme" 582
"Religions" 450
"The Religious Establishment" 823
"Remarkable" 745
"Remember?" (Berlin) 1750
"Remember?" (Friedman) 995
"Remember?" (Grant) 1307
"Remember?" (Sondheim) 807, 1492
"Remember (Walking in the Sand)" 115
"Remember Always to Give" 726
"Remember Caesar" 1307
"Remember Him" 1780
"Remember Joplin" 453
"Remember Love" 1392
"Remember Me" (Choset) 915
"Remember Me" (Coward) 13

"Remember Me" (LaChiusa) 933
"Remember Me" (Ogborn) 198
"Remember Me Smiling" 1707
"Remember November Third" 814
"Remember, Remember" 1445
"Remember Someone" 1550
"Remember That Day" 1358
"Remember That I Care" 1532
"Remember the Boy That Used to Call" 1601
"Remember the Dream" 416
"Remember the Horse" 780
"Remember the Moment" 673
"Remember the Time" 1512
"Remember There Was Me" 1309
"Remember to Call Me Master" 468
"Remember Today" 1287
"Remember Vinnie Bolzano" 1723
"Remember When I Hated You?" 701
"Remembering You" 1818
"Remembrance of Things Past" 758
"Remembrance Waltz" 552
"Remembrances" 564
"Remind Me" 861, 883, 886
"Rendezvous" 1209
"Renee's Lament" 850
"Renoir, Degas, Toulouse-Lautrec" 1447
"Rent-a-crowd" 1276
"Rent-a-Grandma" 61
"Report on Status" 919
"Repose" 884
"Reprise Me" 297
"The Republican Dilemma: Goldwater or Klenosky" 871
"Republicans" 997
"Request" 1698
"Requiem" (Carmines) 834
"Requiem" (Silverman) 393, 394
"Requiem" 393, 394, 834
"Requiem for Everyone" 381
"Requiem for Living" 897
"Requiem for the Queen" 350
"Required Reading" 299
"Reruns" 945
"Resale Shop" 558
"The Rescue" 1008
"Rescue Me" 55
"Residuals" 991
"Respect" 115, 1551
"Respectability" (Dolan) 538
"Respectability" (Rome) 981
"The Restaurant" 576
"Restless Heart" 981
"Resume" 637
"La Retour de Pere" 123
"Retreat" 1558
"The Return of Tennessee Williams' Heroine" 352
"Return to Africa" 1388
"Return to the Hive" 1200
"Return to Utopia" 871
"Reunion" (Crom) 1383
"Reunion" (Freedman and Kornfeld) 1354
"Reunion" (Kaz) 1209
"The Reunion" 1299
"Reunion: Outside the Metropolitan Tower on 57th Street, a Rainy November Afternoon" 899
"Le Reve" 1623
"The Revelation" 3
"A Revelation" 95
"Revelation" 1363
"Revelations" 106
"Revenge Song" 1384
"Revenge Tango" 1500
"Revisions" 1472
"Revival" 1447
"A Revival of Miss Ethel Barrymore in The School for Rivals" 622
"Revival on Broadway" 19
"Revolt of Islam" 1443
"Revolution Now" 1283
"The Revolutionary Costume for Today" 641
"Revolutionary Cradle Song" 1734
"Revue Hoedown" 1574
"A Revue on a Stool" 735
"Rewrite Your Own Story" 643
"Rex and Julie" 1394
"The Rex Café" 1733
"Rhapsody in Blue" 73
"Rhapsody in Blue Jeans" 1014
"Rhapsody on Broadway" 1014
"Rhinoplasty" 1607
"Rhode Island Is Famous for You" 348
"Rhode Island Tango" 588, 727
"Rhumba" 1636
"Rhumba Rita" 1202
"Rhumboogie" 1571
"Rhyme and Reason" 1252
"Rhymes and Reasons" 37
"Rhythm & Rhyme" 278
"Rhythm in Me" 38
"Rhythm in My Bones" 1315
"Rhythm Made a Success of Me" 1315
"The Rhythm of the Line" 1398
"Rhythms" 175
"The Ribbon Cutting: Hootspa" 1037
"Ribbons I Will Give Thee" 1446
"Ribbons of Gold" 995
"Riblah's Lament" 1531
"Rice Hulling Song" 107
"The Rich" 324, 1752
"Rich and Famous" 537
"Rich and Happy #1" 1492
"Rich and Happy #2" 1492
"Rich Enough to Be Rude" 407, 1811
"Rich Kids' Rag" 42
"Rich Man's Baby" 1500
"The Rich Man's Frug" 1291
"Riches" 1367
"Richie and Theresa" 1299
"Ricochet" (aka "Ricochet Romance") 1575
"The Riddle of You" 867
"The Riddle Song" 503
"Ride 'Em" 1830
"Ride Cowboy Ride" 578
"The Ride Home" 385
"Ride On, King Jesus" 1762
"Ride Out the Storm" 886
"Ride the Winds" 1358
"Ride Up in the Chariot" 1762
"Rider in the Rain" 1036, 1334
"Ridiculous" 563
"Ridin' High" 367, 1823
"Ridin' on the Moon" 662
"Riding for a Fall" 230
"Riding the Range (A Song of the Old West)" 483
"Right at the Start of It" 1606
"Right from the Start" 19
"The Right Hand Song" 391
"The Right Image" 919
"The Right Look" 1637
"Right Now" 1466
"The Right One Will Ask Me to Dance" 1586
"The Right Place at the Right Time" 1758
"Right Way" 504
"Rights of Bill" 1760
"Rigmarole? It's Another Game" 941
"A Rilly Great Shew" 1276
"Rim of a Rainbow" 1438
"A Ring Around the Moon" 1513
"Ring Iron" 1399
"Ring My Bell" 399
"A Ring of Gold in Texas" 102
"Ring, Ring the Bell" 1477
"Ring Them Bells" (Kander) 52, 1685
"Ring Them Bells" (Traditional) 1762
"Ringa Zinga" 492
"Ringaroundarosy" 234
"Ringmaster Song" 1476
"Rings on Her Fingers" 775
"The Rink" 52
"Rio" 463
"The Rio Grande" (aka "Oh, the Rio Grande" and "Along (On the Rio Grande)") 826, 827, 1807
"The Riobamba" 234
"Riot" 493, 1537
"Rip Around" 922
"Ripoff of Love" 1235
"The Rise & Fall of the City of Movieville" 1460
"Rise and Fall" 583
"Rise and Fly" 8
"Rise in Love" 279
"Rise, People of Chosun" 889
"Rise Up, Shepherd, and Follow" 166
"Rise Up!" 948
"Rising Expectations" 1635
"Rising, Up" 1422
"Risk Love" 499
"Rita Cheeta" 1504
"Rita from Argentina" 1668
"Rita's Confession" 973
"Rite of Spring" 95
"Ritual" 857
"Ritual for Murder" 889
"Ritual of Ruku" 1566
"The Ritual" 1035
"The River" (Leigh) 289
"The River" (Link) 1363
"River Deep, Mountain High" 115
"River of Fire" 102
"River Rats" 408
"River Song" 333
"The River Won't Flow" 1498
"Riverboat Shuffle" 1521
"Riverman" 1315
"Rivers Cannot Flow Upwards" 1134
"The River's in Me" 1363
"Rivers of Roses" 823
"Rivers to the South" 504
"Riverside Drive" 1715
"Riverside Nights" 436
"Riverwind" 1364
"The Riviera" 199
"Riviera Nights" 308
"Rivkele Dem Rebns" 1342
"The Road" 639
"The Road Ends Here" 830
"The Road I'm Taking" 220
"Road Kill" 627
"Road Song" 419
"The Road To" 1548
"The Road to Heaven" 606
"The Road to Lucy" 1613
"The Road to Paradise" 539
"The Road to You" 257
"Roadside" 1366
"Roadside Rest" 1206
"The Robbery" 1445
"Robert" 933
"Robert, Alvin, Wendell and Jo Jo" 1038
"Robert Mitchum" 1110
"Robert to the Rescue" 1155, 1157
"Roberta's Passion Play" 1250
"Robert's Song" 639
"Robinson Crusoe" 870
"Robot Man" 1353
"Rocco's Dream (Security)" 545
"The Rochelle Hudson Tango" 1447
"Rock" 820
"The Rock" 916
"Rock 'n' Roll" 681
"Rock 'n' Roll Party Queen" 625
"Rock 'n' Roll Star" 636
"Rock 1975" 1388
"Rock-a-Bye Your Baby with a Dixie Melody" 746, 829, 993
"A Rock and a Body" 285
"Rock and Roll Critic" 708
"Rock Back the Clock" 319
"Rock, Crane's Town" 602
"Rock Garden" 1168
"Rock Is My Way of Life" 1558
"Rock of Ages" 1484
"Rock Singer" 656
"Rock Sweet Baby" 766
"Rock with Jezebel" 1308
"Rock with Rock" 683
"Rockabye Child Jesus" 71
"Rockaway Beach" 359
"The Rocket-Roll" 1832
"Rockette's Dance" 1755
"Rockin' Around the Christmas Tree" 115
"A Rockin' Good Way" 383
"Rockin' My Soul" 278
"Rocking the Boat" 1025
"Rocky Mountain High" 37
"Rocky on the Rocks" 1125
"Rocky Road" 1323
"The Rocky Road to the White House" 1276
"Rococo Rag" 480
"Di Rod (The Circle)" 1619
"Rodents" 1337
"Rodeo" 869
"Rodeo Romeo" 102
"Rodgers and Hart" 1255
"Rodolpho, Are You Married, Too?" 1723
"Rodolpho, I Thought I Told You to Go In" 1723
"Rodolpho! Didn't They Hire You?" 1723
"The Roebling Plan" 217
"Roger Arrives" 1121
"Roger the Ox" 486
"Roger, the Rabbit" 1576
"The Rogue Song" 1570
"Le Roi D'Aquitaine" 882, 1773, 1807
"Role-Playing" 971
"Rolf Hochhuth Speaks" 1394
"Roll Call" 388
"The Roll of the Dice" 976
"Roll Out the Morning" 1504
"Roll the Union On" 740
"Roll Up the Ribbons" 733
"Roll Up Your Sleeves" 257
"Roll Your Yiddisha Eyes" 1442
"Roller Coaster Blues" 1192
"Roller Derby" 1448
"A Rollicking Band of Pirates We" 1270
"Rollin'" 1036, 1334
"Rollin' in Gold" 538
"Rollin' on the T.O.B.A." 1373
"Rolling Stone" 1594
"Romance" (Clifton) 1008
"Romance" (Secunda) 666
"Romance on the High Seas" 1058
"Romantic Experience" 1714
"Romeo and Juliet" 1347
"Ronald Reagan" 1069
"A Rondelay" 972
"Rondelay" 1379
"Rondo for Two Pianos" 1694
"Room for Improvement" 934
"Room for One" 1268
"Room in Bloomsbury" 199
"The Room Is Filled with You" 1451
"Room Service" 1153
"A Room with a View" 751, 1170
"The Roommate Beguine" 752
"Roommates" 907
"The Rooster and the Hen" 1701
"Rope" 1806
"Rope-a-Dope" 1710
"Rope Dancers" 96
"Ropin' Dogies" 1290
"Rosa" 1380
"Rosalie Murchison" 1228
"Rosalinde" 1437
"Rosamund's Dream" 1367
"Roscoe's Rap" (aka "Rap") 78
"The Rose" 938
"Rose" 1380
"The Rose Garden" 938
"Rose-Marie" 1570
"The Rose of Rangoon" 1495
"The Rose of Tralee" 775
"Rose Recovers" 252
"Roseland" 1433
"Roses" 276
"Rosetta" 221
"The Rosewater Foundation" 588
"Rosh Hashono" 1822
"Rosie" 1149
"Rosie Rosenblatt, Stop the Turkey Trot" 1442
"Rosita Rodriguez: Serenade" 1311
"Rothschilds and Sons" 1381
"Rough and Ready Man" 181, 182
"Roughly Speaking" 1158
"Roulez Tambours" 1257
"Roumeynishe Libe (Roumanian Love)" 1382
"Round About Midnight" 943
"Round and Round" 478, 699
"'Round Every Corner" 1450, 1551
"Round Midnite" 156
"The Round Up" 1335
"Routine Disruption" 926
"Row 10, Aisle 6, Bench 114" 1184
"Row, Row, Row" 1494
"Roy Cohen" 1765
"Royal Court Dance" 1388
"Royal Flush" 1226
"Royal Radio" 1326
"The Royal We" 789
"Rozinkes (Rozhinkes) Mit Mandlen (Raisins and Olives)" 492, 1715
"The Rubber Plant Song" 1219
"Ruby" 1521

"Rue de la Solitude" 820
"Ruin Them" 1584
"Ruined" 1467
"Ruins" 1160
"The Ruins" 20
"The Rule" 1671
"Ruler of My Heart" 1518
"The Rules of Society" 1815
"Rules of the Game" 789
"Rules, Regulations, and Respect" 1831
"Rules Shall Not Be Broken" 1190
"A Ruling Is a Ruling" 1510
"Rum and Coca-Cola" 1571
"Rumenye, Rumenye (Rumania)" 604, 1619
"Rumors" 288
"Rumpadee, Rumpadee" 1475
"The Run" 71
"Run" 224
"Run and Hide" 830
"Run, Freedom, Run!" 1712
"Run, Indian, Run" 1824
"Run, Musashi, Run" 1358
"Run River Run" 1363
"Run, Run" 1562
"Run, Run, Run Cinderella" 538
"Run Sinner Run" 1672
"Run with the Tide" 1306
"Runagate Runagate" 1734, 1735
"Runaway Suite" 1759
"Runaways" 1759, 1761
"Runnin' for Jesus" 1466
"Runnin' Wild" 955
"Running" 361
"Running About" 285
"Running Down the Sun" 969
"Running with the Night" 854
"Rupert Bear Song" 1666
"Rush of Speed" 1345
"Rushing the Season" 864
"A Russell Flint" 135
"Russell's Song" 1485
"The Russian Lesson" 1196
"Russian Waltz" 666
"The Russian Waltz" 819
"Ruth" 663
"Ruthie's Lullaby" 106
"Ruthless!" 1386

"The S & M Polka" 123
"S-E-X" 1125
"S — Sksk ... Every Face a Mask" 1020
"S — Sksk ... Spilled from a Fountain" 1020
"S'iz Kayle Gevorn (Everything Is Spoiled)" 604
"S'posin'" 221
"S'vet Zeyn a Chassene" 1032
"Sabbath Services" 100
"A Sabbath Song" 1203
"Saboteurs" 986
"The Sabra" 1701
"Sacrifice" 1072
"Sacrifice (Poor Mortals)" 1231
"Sacrifice Your Body" 1538
"Sad and Lonely Child" 1345
"Sad Eyed Lady in the Lowlands" 265
"The Sad Tale of the Beaux-hommes" 1191
"Saddest Gal What Am" 1818
"Saddle Tramp Blues" 323
"Sadie and Davidson Go for a Walk" 1329
"Sadie and Davidson's Confrontation" 1329
"Sadie and Davidson's First Confrontation" 1329
"Sadie and the Sailors" 1329
"Sadie Arrives" 1329
"Sadie/Davidson Duet" 1329
"Sadie's 'Always Running' Aria" 1329
"Sadie's Blues" 1329
"Sadie's Lament" 1329
"Sadie's Ordered Deported" 1329
"Sadie's Prayer Aria" 1329
"Sadie's Sympathy Fails with Mrs. Davidson" 1329
"S.A.D.U.S.E.A." 1304
"Safari a la Marilyn" 149
"Safe" (LaChiusa) 683
"Safe" (Wilson) 357
"Safe from Harm" 1073
"Safe Haven" 1236
"Safe in His Arms" 1466
"The Safe Scene" 1615
"Safe Sex Slut" 1600
"Safer in My Arms" 1143, 1144
"Safety in Numbers" (McWhinney) 1605
"Safety in Numbers" (Wilson) 199
"Safety Net" 502
"The Saga of Jenny" (aka "Jenny" and "Jenny Made Her Mind Up") 128, 689, 879, 880, 882, 1773, 1807
"Saga of Men and Marriage" 64
"The Saga of the Prima Ballerina" 773
"Sage" 1388
"Said I Wasn't Gonna Tell Nobody" 166
"Sail Away" (Coward) 1170, 1390
"Sail Away" (Newman) 1036, 1049, 1334
"Sailing" 1566
"Sailing On" 1228
"The Sailor of My Dreams" 341
"Sailor Tango" (aka "[The] Sailor's Tango," "[T]he Sailors' Tango") 128, 660, 879, 880, 882, 1773, 1807
"Sailor's Rebound" 831
"Sailor's Song" 476
"St. Andrews" 755
"Saint Genesius" 1379
"St. Louis Blues" 681, 777, 1720
"St. Patrick's Day Parade" 1290
"St. Paul's Steeple" 436
"St. Vincent's Isle" 1356
"The Saints Come In — Flying In" 910
"La Saisie des Meubles" 123
"Sake" 712
"The Salad of the Mad Café" 1394
"Sales Reproach" 987
"The Salesman (With a Suitcase)" 1701
"Salish Song of Longing" 963
"Sallah and the Social Worker" 1701
"Salley Gardens" 707
"Sally" (Metcalf) 409
"Sally" (Savage) 725, 1097
"The Sally Bright Self-Risin' Flour Song" 1343
"Sally Goodin'" 657
"Sally Simpson" 1655
"Saloon Piano" 376
"Saloon Talk" 1239
"Salsation" 399
"Salt Air" 567
"Salt and Pepper" 916
"Salty Dog" 553
"Salty Papa Blues" 382
"Salutations" 773
"Salvation" 1395, 1396
"Salve Madonna" 823
"Sam and Me" 1763
"Sam Hall" 655
"Sam, You Made the Pants Too Long" 1442
"The Samba" 1338
"Sambo Was a Bad Boy" 1397
"The Same Girl" 576
"The Same Old Me" 1824
"Same Old Song" 1727
"Same Old Song and Dance" 1656
"The Same Old Tune" 809
"Samedi Soir" 1692
"Samson's Epiphany" 1250
"Samson's Thoughts" 1250
"San Antonio Rose" 39
"San Fernando" 1076
"San Francisco" 1570
"San Francisco (Be Sure to Wear Some Flowers in Your Hair)" 411
"San Simeon Blues" 1648
"Sancocho" 1398
"Sanctify Me Holy" 1002
"Sand in My Eyes" 1393
"Sand Mountain Song" 864
"Sandhog Song" 1399
"The Sandman" 1034
"The Sandwich Girls" 637
"Sandy" 1650
"Sane and Normal Girls" 1046
"Santa Baby" 284, 1493
"Santa Barbara" 464
"Santa Claus" 32
"Santa Comin' Caroline" 252
"Santo Domingo" 908
"Santy Anno" 740
"Saposhkelekh (The Boots)" 1619
"Sara Jane" 716
"Sara Lee" 52, 1685
"Sarabande" 419
"Sarafina" 1401
"Sarah" 364
"Sarah Jackman" 685
"Sarah's Touch" 1143
"Sartor Sartoris" 1069
"Saskatchewan" 93
"Satan's Song" 922
"Satin Doll" 42, 55, 1435
"Satin-Skinned Doll" 333
"Satisfaction Guaranteed" 179
"Saturday Is Just Another Day" 1747
"Saturday Morning" 1400
"Saturday Night" (Pottle) 616
"Saturday Night" (Sondheim) 1027, 1403
"Saturday Night (Is the Loneliest Night of the Week)" 1210, 1546
"Saturday Night at the Rose and Crown" 1540
"Saturday Night in Kansas City" 153
"Saturday's Child" 1138
"Saturn Returns: The Flight" 1404
"Saturn Returns: The Return" 1404
"Saturn Rising" 1523
"The Saucer Song" 1393
"A saunter" 250
"Savage Light" 563
"Savannah" 238
"Save a Sinner Tonight" 1153
"Save Me a Seat" 892
"Save the Last Dance" 364
"Save the People" 595, 721
"Save the Village!" (Bargy) 638
"Save the Village!" (Herman) 1218
"Save Your Love for Me" 156
"Save Your Money, John" 1783
"Saved by Grace" 1518
"Saved!" 1301
"Savin' Souls" 1030
"Savoir Faire" 598
"Sawing a Couple in Half" 297
"Sawing a Woman in Half" (Roscoe) 1820
"Sawing a Woman in Half" (Silverman and Smith) 577
"Say 'Uncle'" 935
"Say Farewell" 1577
"Say Goodnight" 1514
"Say Hello to Your Feet" 934
"Say It Again" 646
"Say No More" 98
"Say Something Funny" 296
"Say When" 234
"Say Yes, Look No" 1161
"Say Your Goodbyes" 1427
"The Scabs Crawl In" 740
"Scale of 1 to 10" 1759, 1761
"Scandal" 1412
"Scandals!" 215
"Scandals' Finale" 215
"Scared" 93
"Scarlet Trimmings" 1440
"Scarlet Woman" 1734, 1735
"Scat" 78
"The Scat Song" 1521
"Scatty" 241
"Scene with the Grapes" 1610
"Scenes from Some Marriages (The People Gone)" 1258
"Schadenfreude" 77
"The Scheme" 375
"Schickelgrubber" 1809
"Schizophrenia 101A" 1149
"Schizophrenic" 32
"Schlaf" 1829
"Schleppin'" 1365
"Schmaltzy Waltz" 381
"The Schmooze" 930
"The Schmuel Song" 890
"School Board" 1152
"School Days" 1616
"School Daze" (*Big Bad Burlesque!*) 142
"School Daze" (Brown) 1430
"School Don't Mean a Damn Thing" 120
"School for Music" 1475
"School on Saturday Night" 36
"School Rap" 915
"The School Room" 1802
"Schoolboy Blues" 1666
"Schoolroom" 142
"Schottische" 1179
"Schroeder" 1828
"Schwartz" 1396
"Schweik, Schweik" 609
"Schweik!" 609
"Schwesters" 86
"Science" (Brielle) 1135
"Science" (Marvin) 958
"Science" (*The Uncommon Denominator*) 1698
"Science Fiction" 1239
"Scintillating Sophie" 296
"Scoobi-doo-Since You've Come" 834
"Scoobie Doo" 952
"Scorin' Makes a Girl Seem Old" 844
"Scotch on the Rocks" 1605
"Scotland the Brave" 527
"Scott? Are You Asleep?" 673
"Scott, He Can Still Hear You" 1084
"Scraps of Paper" 328
"Scratch Golfer" 606
"Scratch-My-Back" 506
"Scratched" 1385
"Screaming and Yelling" 1340
"Screaming Clocks" 1622
"Screaming Clocks (The Dummies Song)" 1622
"Screen Test" 450
"Screens of Memory" 1200
"Scrubby Dubby" 765
"Scrynatchkielooaw" 1384
"The Sculptors" 963
"The Scum of the Earth" 1040
"Scylla and Charybdis" 600
"The Sea" (Katsaros) 1071
"The Sea" (Link) 1363
"The Sea A Sound A Thing An Animal" 1020
"Sea Breeze" 710
"The Sea Gull" 977
"The Sea Is All Around Us" 1448
"Sea of Tranquility" 1081
"Sea Song" 1568, 1569
"Seagulls" 587
"The Seal" 1274
"Sean O'Dwyer" 253
"Séance Fantastique" 287
"Search for a Sign" 1204
"Search for Diana" 1151
"Search Party" 1478
"Searching for Love" 968
"Searching for Yesterdays" 968
"Sears and Roebuck Wedding Band" 1204
"Seaside Gold" 135
"Seaside Peace" 257
"The Seaside Spectacle" 507
"A Season You'll Never Forget" 198
"A Seasonal Sonata" 371
"Seasons' Greetings" 1261
"Sechaba" 1401
"Second Act Beginning" 1072
"Second Avenue and 12th Street Rag" 942
"Second Ballad Interlude" 1229
"Second Best" 1057
"The Second-Best Man" 852
"A Second Chance" 1670
"Second City Theme Song" 1649
"The Second Creation" 1201
"Second Date" 273
"Second Deck Diplomacy" 1058
"The Second Fight (La Pelea)" 488
"Second Glances" 1460
"The Second Goodbye" 1680
"Second Grade" 1243
"The Second Honeymoon" 1072
"Second Interlude" 299
"The Second Jam Session" 1398
"Second Laur and Von Luber Duet" 1462
"Second Message" 1422
"Second Murder Interlude" 947
"Second Planet on the Right" 1832
"Second Rhapsody" 73
"Second Thoughts" 1460
"The Second Time Around" 1210
"The Second Time Is Always Nicer" 654
"Secondary Characters" 1645
"Seconds" 1460
"A Secret" (Goggin) 385

"A Secret" (McHugh) 1294
"Secret Agent Man" 1551
"The Secret Life" 1420
"Secret Love" (Fain) 1245
"Secret Love" (Moore) 646
"The Secret of Life" 1646
"The Secret of the Tapping Shoes" 1668
"Secret Singing" 1140
"Secret Song" 639
"Secret Songs" 1029
"Secret Storms" 1459
"Secret Weapon" 1832
"Secretarial Pool" 222
"Secrets" 1287
"Secrets Men Should Know" 1219
"Security" 450
"Seduction" 152
"Seduction Deduction" 302
"Seduction, Literary Style" 1614
"Seduction Scene" 947
"Seduction Second Degree" 1072
"See" 969
"See Everything New" 1154
"See Her Smile" 1634
"See His Way" 1727
"See How the Sun Shines" 1624
"See I'm Smiling" 890
"See Me as a Man" 501
"See That Lady There" 219
"See the Light" 1283
"See the River Flow" 1392
"See the Sign of Judgment" 591
"See the U.S.A. in Your Chevrolet" 1575
"See Through Me" 1631
"See What Happens (When You Wait Too Long)" 1747
"See What I Wanna See" 1422
"See What Mr. Dodgson Gave Me" 1190
"See Ya in Tiajuana" 907
"Seeing London" 476
"Seeing Red" 1310
"Seeing Things" (Alter) 1016
"Seeing Things" (Kander) 1685
"Seer Auber Jenny" (aka "Seerrauber-Jenny," "The Black Freighter," and "Pirate Jenny") 1773, 1807
"Segue" 272
"Seizure of the Daughters" 615
"Seizure to Roam" 710
"Selena" 229
"Selene's Speech" 460
"Self Made Man" 1335
"Self-Made Woman" 1064
"Self Portrait" 296, 1710
"Self-Sacrificing Woman" 345
"Selma" 21, 1423
"Seminary Song" 701
"Semper, Semper" 1273
"The Senate" 1167
"The Senator from Minnesota" 1167
"Send in the Clowns" 212
"Send Me You" 1638
"Send the Marines" 1654
"Senor Doctor" 1336
"Senoras De La Noche" 1384
"Sensation" (Shire) 295
"Sensation" (Townshend) 1655
"Sensations" 1424
"Sensitive New-Age Guys" 2
"Sensitivity" 1193
"The Sensuous Woman" 877
"Sentimental Gentleman from Georgia" 681, 1521
"Sentimental Mood" 1407
"The Sentry Song" 460
"Separate but Equal" 1620
"Sephardic Lullaby" 865, 866
"September" 926
"September in the Rain" 382
"September Song" 128, 879, 880, 882, 1645, 1773, 1807, 1809
"Serena" 60
"Serenade" (Carmines) 453
"Serenade" (Donizetti) 1146
"Serenade" (Jankowski) 539
"Serenade" (Schwartz) 88
"Serenade Me, Sally, with a Ragtime Tune" 1442
"Serenade to a Wealthy Widow" 886
"The Sergeant's Chant" 827
"Serious Business" 755
"Sermon" (Barkan) 224
"Sermon" (Carmines) 1349
"Sermon" (Horowitz and DeShields) 646
"Sermon" (Johnston) 1610
"The Sermon" (Katsaros) 1071
"The Sermon" (Telson) 615
"Sermon Song" 1002
"Serve It Up" 1495
"Serve the Dog Right" 979
"Serves You Right" 78
"The Service" 545
"Service for Two" 50
"Serving the People" 653
"Session" 60
"'Set'" 637
"'Set' in Silver: The Naked Truth" 637
"Set Me Free" 1306
"Set Those Sails" 763, 764, 765, 997
"Sets" 511
"Settin' the Woods on Fire" 657
"Setting Sail" 1071
"Settling Up the Score" 1109
"Seumas-a-Ree" 253
"Seven Come Eleven" 1430
"Seven Dominicans" 1158
"Seven Foreign Envoys" 889
"Seven Lonely Days" 39
"The Seven Seas" 121
"Seven Years Later" 1747
"Seventeen Summers" 1083
"76 Foolish Things" 556, 557, 558
"Severin-Fennimore Duet" 1462
"Severin in Chains" 1462
"Severin's Revenge Aria" 1462
"Sew the Buttons On" 1364
"The Sewing Bee" 600
"Sex" 718
"Sex and the Single Girl" 1765
"Sex Can Be Funny" 1153
"Sex Is a Spectator Sport" 1035
"Sex Is Animal" 279
"Sex, Sex, Sex" 857
"Sexicare" 1743
"Sexperts" 424
"Sextet" (Clifton) 1008
"Sextet" (Kurka) 609
"Sextet" (Thomas) 90
"Sextette" 1439
"Sexual Anonymous" 1743
"Sexy Blues" 1373
"Sexy!" 1427
"Sgt. Pepper's Lonely Hearts Club Band" 1426
"Sh-Boom" 1434, 1575
"Sha Shtil (The Rabbi's Coming)" 1619
"Shabes Nuchn Kiegel" 1745
"Shabes, Shabes, Shabes (Welcoming the Sabbath)" 1619
"Shabos, Yom Tov, Un Rosh Khodesh" 1715
"Shade and Shadows" 1464
"Shades of Harlem" 1435
"The Shadow" 1512
"The Shadow Knows" 804
"Shadow Song" 1030
"Shadowplay" 644
"Shadows" (Hoffert) 572
"Shadows" (Penn and Teller) 1234, 1235
"Shadows" (Schwartz) 248
"Shadows Dance Behind You" 873
"Shadowy Forest of Garadufi Dance" 855
"The Shadrach and Meshach Show" 1333
"Shady Lady Bird" 132
"Shaft of Love" 1763
"Shaftway Danger" 326
"Shag Baby" 864
"Shainele" 1449
"Shakakh-Mones (Gifts for Purim)" 1619
"Shake Hands with a Millionaire" 1192
"Shake Hands with Your Uncle Max" 685
"Shake It and Break It" 553
"Shake, Rattle and Roll" 1353
"Shake, Shake, Shake" (Frandsen, et al.) 1495
"Shake, Shake, Shake" (Wilson) 790
"Shake the Foundation" 474
"Shakespeare Revisited" 1754
"Shakespeare Today" 1743
"Shakin' All Over" 1353
"Shakin' at the High School Hop" 625
"Shaking My Can in Front of Carnegie Hall" 783
"The Shaking of the Sheets" 1446
"Shaking the Blues Away" 305
"Shall I Be an Old Man's Darling" 417
"Shall I Compare Thee" 1519, 1569
"Shall I Compare Thee (to a Summer's Day?)" (Mulcahy) 1437, 1569
"Shall I Compare Thee (to a Summer's Day?)" (Leslee) 1519
"Shall We Dance" 1656
"Shalom" 818
"Shalom L'chaim!" 663
"Shalom Suez" 1105
"Sham Dancing" 1414
"The Shaman" 889
"Shame" 1064
"Shame on You" 289
"Shandu Mishoo-Ganah" 1058
"Shanghai Lil" 1656
"The Shanghai Rooster" 112
"Shanghai Sorcery" 287
"Shangri-La" 527
"Shaolin Temple of Hip-Hop" 804
"The Shape I'm In" 873
"The Shape of Things" 942
"A Share of Paradise" 1607
"Sharon's Waltz" 1438
"Sharp" 1361
"Sharpshooting" 1720
"Shattered Image" 135
"Shayles Tzim Rebb'n" 1032
"She" 123
"She Belonged to Me" 265
"She Called Me Fellow" 962
"She Came in Through the Bathroom Window" 1426
"She Can't Really Be" 316
"She Can't Resist Me" 259
"She Cries" 1498
"She Deserves Me" 1379
"She Didn't Say 'Yes'" 883
"She Dies" 1637
"She Doctor" 183
"She Doesn't Understand Me" 1829
"She Hasn't Got a Clue" 302
"She Is More to Be Pitied Than Censured" 458, 577
"She Just Walked In" 1076
"She Left Without a Word" 3
"She Looked at Me" 1422
"She Looks Upon His Lips" 1569
"She Loves Me Not" 300, 1400
"She Loves You" 338
"She Makes Me Laugh" 463
"She Makes You Think of Home" 1236
"She Never Knew What Hit Her" 1011
"She Never Told Her Love" 1827
"She Shall Have Music" 1440
"She Smiled at Me" 225
"She Sounds Very Happy. I Hope Laurie Feels the Same" 941
"She That Is Down Need Fear No Fall" 941
"She Told Me to Meet Her at the Gate" 581
"She Waits for Me" 249
"She Was K.C." 1624
"She Was One of the Early Birds" 577
"She Wears Red Feathers" 1752
"She Who Is Down Need Fear No Fall" 941
"She Would Be a Soldier" 258, 259
"Shears' Song" 1229
"Sheep May Safely Graze" 1694
"Sheep's Song" 244
"Sheik & E" 1407
"Sheik Song" 1476
"Shelby's Ad" 1513
"Sheldon Potts' Halftime Show" 845
"A 'Shell Game'" 935
"She'll Get the Business in the End" 1476
"She'll Get You Yet" 25
"She'll Thank Me" 1505
"Shema" 1510
"Shema Ysrael" 1441
"Shenandoah" 740, 1570
"Shepherd Song" 647
"Shepherd's Song" 1437
"Sheridan Square" 727
"Sherman's March to the Sea" 716
"Sherman's Mom" 326
"Sherry's Theme" 1310
"She's a Big White Mouse" 820
"She's a Fool" 115
"She's a Little Off" 444
"She's a Shame, Shame, Shame" 322
"She's a Star" 1365
"She's a Virgin" 1146
"She's a Woman" 434, 435
"She's an Actress" 990
"She's an Innocent" 995
"She's Asked for You" 941
"She's Comin' to Town" 1505
"She's Fifteen" 78
"She's Funny That Way (I Got a Woman, Crazy for Me)" 1198
"She's Getting' More Like the White Folks Every Day" 1643
"She's Going There Every Night" 581
"She's Got You" 39
"She's in Again" 1315
"She's Leaving Home" 1426, 1540
"She's My Girl" (Ford) 656
"She's My Girl" (Lehrer) 1654
"She's Not for Me" 631
"She's Not There" 1353
"She's Out There" 157
"She's Talking Out" 1420
"She's Tall, She's Tan, She's Terrific" 165
"Shetler-Lied" 499
"Shew! Fly, Don't Bother Me" 695
"A Shiduch Fin Himmel" 1032
"The Shiek of Avenue B" 1442
"Shifting Sounds" 207
"Shiloh" 569
"Shimmy" 959
"Shine" 1513
"Shine Down, Lord" 408
"Shine Moon" 1042
"Shine On, Harvest Moon" 1643
"Shine On, Harvey Bloom" 685
"A Shine on Your Shoes" 348, 1606
"Ship Without an Ocean" 67
"Shir Hamaylesn (Song of Blessings)" 1502
"Shirts" 45
"Shirts by the Millions (Orders! Orders!)" 912
"Shitla" 1620
"Shloymele-Malkele" 1619
"Shnel Loyfn Di Reder (The Wheels Turn Quickly)" 604
"Sho 'Nuff" 321
"Shockheaded Peter" 1444
"Shoes" 203
"Shoeshine" 1811
"The Shoop Shoop Song" 1353
"Shoot the Moon" 1513
"Shoot Them" 431
"The Shooting of Dan McGrew" 1639
"Shooting Star" 916
"Shooting Stars" 900
"Shooting Through a Girl" 287
"Shop" 1715
"The Shop on Main Street" 1449
"Shopkeepers Trio" 638
"Shopping" 545
"Shopping Around" 981
"Shopping Bag Lady" 1034
"Shopping Bag Man" 370
"The Shopping Waltz" 1361
"Shore Leave" 963
"Shores of Amerikay" 775
"Short People" 1036, 1049, 1334
"Short Story" 933
"Short Subjects" 1033
"A Shortage of Me" 1434
"The Shortest Day of the Year" 201
"Should I Tell Him" 1638
"Should I Wait" 470
"Should She Stay?" 834
"Should We?" 197
"Shoulda Been, Coulda Been Mine" 1508
"Shoulders to Lean On" 1737, 1738
"Shouldn't I Be Less in Love with You?" 739
"Shout, Sister, Shout" 681

"Shout!" 1450, 1551
"A Show" 1224
"A Show About Golf" 606
"Show and Tell" 845
"Show Business" 1698
"The Show Business Nobody Knows" 913
"Show Girl" 1611
"The Show Goes On" 1451
"Show Me" 701
"Show Me a Rose" 304, 672
"Show Me the Man" 372
"Show Me Where the Good Times Are" 1452
"The Show Must Go On" 1565
"Show Tune" (aka "Show Tune in 2/4," "Show Tune in 2/4 Time," "There Is No Tune Like a Show Tune") 1132, 1218, 1332
"Show You a Thing or Two" 106
"Show Your Linen, Miss Richardson" 1764
"Showbiz" 545
"Showcases" 639
"Shower of Sparks" 828
"Showmanship" 1477
"The Show's the Thing" 655
"Showstopper" 1754
"Showtime" 383
"Showtime Is Mine" 850
"Shpil Guitar" 1619
"Shrink" 1503
"Shteytl" 1453
"Shuffle the Cards" (Richardson) 948
"Shuffle the Cards" (Brielle) 1135
"Shuffle Your Feet and Just Roll Along" 886
"Shunned" 235
"Shut de Do'" 1466
"Shut Out the Light" 1664
"Shut Out the Night" 1733
"Shut Up and Dance" 267
"Shver Tzu Zine A Yid" 666
"Shy" 1193
"Shy Couple" 719
"Shy Man in a Loud Drug Store" 1765
"Si J'Etais Blanche" 171
"Si, Signora" 1146
"Si Vous Aimez Les Poitrines" 1160
"Siberia" 544
"Sibling Rivalry" 1309
"Siblings" 1485
"Sick Man" 450
"Sid Ol' Kid" 1580
"Sidd's Enlightenment" 1458
"Side by Side by Side" 1491
"Side of Fries" 179
"Side Street in Gotham" 1016
"The Sidestep" 133
"Sidewalks" 1459
"Sidewalks of Cuba" 1521
"The Sidi Bou Said Mystery" 287
"Sidney" (Aman) 1153
"Sidney" (Lacey) 616
"Siempre" 760
"Siesta" 379
"Las Siete Potencias and Despoho" 1398
"Sigh No More (Ladies)" 1568, 1569
"Sighing Softly to the River" 1270
"Sigma, Alpha, Iota" 323
"Sigmund Freud's Impersonation" 1049
"Sigmund Freud's Impersonation of Albert Einstein in America" 1036
"Sign Here" 1685
"Sign in the Darkness" 1727
"Sign of the Times" (Hatch) 1046
"Sign of the Times" (Kitsakos) 1418
"Sign Song" 1147
"Signed, Peeled, Delivered" 1709
"Signs" 1460
"Silence" 284, 1020
"Silence Is Golden" 1611
"Silent Cal" 722
"Silent E" 1654
"Silent Love" 1618
"Silent Movie" (LaChiusa) 683
"Silent Movie" (Pen) 114
"The Silent Spot" 1595
"Silent Spring" (Powell) 1125
"Silent Spring" (*The Wrecking Ball*) 1813
"Silent Summer Nights" 960
"Silk Suits" 1407
"Silky the Duke" 1459
"Silly Old Hat" 280
"Silly People" 1027
"Silo" 471
"Silver Earring" 91
"A Silver Pattern" 1527
"Silver Screen" 1089
"Silver Threads Among the Gold" 695
"Silvery Days" 1566
"A Silvery Song" 1148
"Simcha" 100
"Simon Says" 750
"Simon Smith" 1049
"Simon Smith and the Amazing Dancing Bear" 1036, 1334
"Simple As This" 1422
"Simple Boy" 1303
"Simple But Not an Ordinary Man" 223
"A Simple Country Wedding" 308
"Simple Creature" 933
"A Simple Holiday Song" 280
"Simple Humble Neighborhood" 1340
"A Simple Life" (Ford) 1154
"A Simple Life" (Kreisberg and Cale) 502
"Simple Little Things" 1451
"Simple Melody" (Renzi) 959
"Simple Melody" (*This Was Burlesque* [1962]) 1615
"Simple on Integration" 1373
"Simple Principles" 915
"A Simple Rotational System" 395
"A Simple Song" (Bernstein) 1029
"A Simple Song" (Silver) 1527
"Simple Things" 1472
"Simple Tune" 1431
"A Simple Wife" 572
"Simply Free" 754
"Sin Ballet" 1333
"Since Eve" 735
"Since Henry Ford Apologized to Me" 1442
"Since the Night I Stood in the Dancehall Door" 1733
"Since When?" 372
"Since You Came to This Town" 588, 727
"Since You Stayed Here" 219
"Sincere" 461
"Sincerely" 1575
"Sincerely, Harold Berlin" 961
"Sing a Happy Song" 1745
"Sing a Little Jingle" 681
"Sing a Song of Octopi" 1066
"Sing a Song of Sambo" 1397
"Sing, All Ye Women of the Lord" 730
"Sing Along" 1383
"Sing and Dance" 1299
"Sing, Damn You, Sing" 439
"Sing for Your Supper" 201
"Sing Hallelujah!" 1466
"Sing Happy" 807, 1685
"Sing, Jacques, Sing" 1265
"Sing Me a Song of Social Significance" 981, 1267, 1268
"Sing Me Not a Ballad" 1809
"Sing Me Sunshine" 1467
"Sing Muse!" 1468
"Sing Out in the Streets" 1264
"Sing Sing" 241
"Sing, Sing, Sing" 55, 1571
"Sing Something Simple" 1651
"Sing Sorrow" 1399
"Sing This All Together" 265
"Sing to Me, Mr. C." 527
"Sing We to Symmetry" 485
"Sing!" 283
"Singapore Sue" 341
"The Singer" 1398
"The Singer and the Song" 74, 892
"A Singer I Must Be" 654
"A Singer Must Be Free" 1134
"The Singer Must Die" 1471
"Singer Who Moves Well" 919
"Singin' a Song" 1197
"Singin' the Blues" 886
"Singin' to 'Em" 322
"Singing" 1476
"Singing Drums" 1388
"Singing Jesus" 1470
"Singing Wheels" 1385
"Single Man Drought" 739
"Singles on the Slopes" 350
"Sinking Sinking" 1469
"Sinner! Abomination! Whore!" 439
"Sir Galahad" 902
"Sir Greenbaum's Madrigal" 685
"Les Sirens" 95
"The Siren's Song" 902
"Si's Dilemma" 1637
"Si's Soliloquy" 1637
"Sister Aimee" 1470
"A Sister and Brother" 1679
"Sister Is My Daughter" 1470
"Sister Love" 1307
"Sister Paradise" 1183
"The Sisters" 586
"Sisters" (Berlin) 212
"Sisters" (Hardwick) 1
"Sisters" (Morgan) 1317
"Sisters of Healing" 8
"Sisters of Mercy" 1471
"Sisyphus" 1404
"Sit Down and Eat Before Our Love Gets Cold" 1472
"The Sit Down Song" 589
"Sit In — Wade In" 152
"Sitting Around" 449
"Sitting Around the Radio" 1139
"Sitting Becalmed in the Lee of Cuttyhunk" 1121
"Sitting in the Garden" 364
"Sitting in the Park" 1659
"The Situation Changes Overnight" 1011
"The Situation in Quebec" 1510
"Sivuk'ekuseni" 651
"Six" 1473
"Six Fucking Shades of Green" 386
"Six Hours as a Princess" 280
"Six Little Kids" 667
"Six O'Clock" 1661
"The Six O'Clock News" 1300
"16 Feet Beneath the Sea" 252
"1600 Pennsylvania Avenue" 1142, 1661
"Sixteen Soprony, Madame Kakonyi" 609
"Sixteen Tons" 527, 740
"Sixty-Four Thousand Bananas" 1749
"6' 2" and Ooh!" 850
"Size Places" 1388
"The Skate" 222
"Skate Away" 372
"Skateboard Acrobats" 1650
"Skating in the Bois" 1092
"Skeletons" 644
"The Skeletons' Dance" 1293
"Skibbereen" 775
"Skid Row Downtown" 727, 939
"Skidaddle" 416
"The Skies Have Gone Dry" 364
"Skippy A-Go-Go" 1800
"Skits-Oh-Frantics or How I Found Fun in Fun City" 1475
"Skiva" 1073
"Sklip, Dat, Doobee" 1297
"Sky and Sea" 835
"Sky, Sky" 654
"Skye Boat Song" 710
"The Sky's the Limit" (Naylor) 196
"The Sky's the Limit" (Valcq) 1832
"Slatey Fork" 985
"Slave Auction" 1388
"Slave Chant" 647
"The Slave Scene" 1398
"Slave Ships" 207
"Slave Song" 1735
"Slavery Chain Done Broke at Last" 815, 816
"Slaves' Dance" 62
"Slavite" 666
"Sleep" 1416
"Sleep, Laura, Sleep" 586
"Sleep Little Mouse" 831
"Sleep Little Red Object" 285
"Sleep My Child" 279
"Sleep, O Sleep" 98
"Sleep On" 460
"Sleep on Seven Flowers" 926, 1063
"Sleep Walkers Lament #1" 1298
"Sleep Walkers Lament #2" 1298
"Sleep Walkers Lament #3" 1298
"Sleeparound Town" 1478
"Sleepin' Around" 279
"A Sleepin' Bee" 662, 715
"Sleepy Hollow" 76
"Sleepy Man" 1367
"Sleepy Time Down South" 376
"Sleigh Ride" 1521
"The Sleigh with the Cream Colored Team" 1147
"Slewfoot Shuffle" 1636
"Slice of Life" 225
"Slick Chick (On the Mellow Side)" 383
"Slide a Little Closer" 102
"A Slight Detail (Promise Me a Rose)" 1580
"Slim's Song" 1229
"Slip Away" 1307
"A Slip of a Girl" 1780
"Slough" 135
"Slow Down Moses" 381
"Slow Rockin' Blues" 407
"A Slow Summer" 1095
"Slow Town Small Time Step" 110
"Slow't Dow" 285
"Slowly on Your Thighs" 1020
"Slugger Ryan" 1239
"Slumming" 1030
"The Slut of the World" 1479
"Slutterday Night" 1479
"Smackwater Jack" 1591
"Small Apartment" 1652
"Small Aria" 333
"A Small Restaurant" 424
"Small Streak of Gray" 1692
"Small Town" (Baker) 1481
"Small Town" (Haber) 25
"Small Town Blues" 750
"Small Town Girl" (Aman, et al.) 1661
"Small Town Girl" (Sherman) 365
"Small World" 1546
"The Smallest Stream" 130
"Smart" 734
"Smart People" 667
"Smart Women/Brilliant Choices" 1710
"Smash the Mirror" 1655
"The Smell of Money" 1706
"Smellamagoody Perfume" 1366
"Smellin' of Vanilla" 715
"Smelly Demon Swine" 1333
"The Smew Song" 870
"Smile" (Ercole) 856
"Smile" (Sondheim; music of "Send in the Clowns") 552
"Smile" (Turner, et al.) 746, 1575
"Smile and Be Gracious" 543
"A Smile Is Up" 109
"Smile Little Irish Girl" 255
"Smile of Your Dreams" 830
"Smile, Smile" 222
"Smile, Smile, Smile" 1480
"Smile Through the Pain" 742
"Smiles" 1643
"Smoke" 415
"A Smoke and a Good Cup o' Coffee" 825
"Smoke Detector" 664
"Smoke Gets in Your Eyes" 883, 1095
"Smoke on the Mountain" 1484
"Smoke Roly Poly" 735
"Smoke Signals" 50
"Smoke, Smoke" 59
"Smokey" 1373
"Smokin' Reefers" 348, 1606
"Smoking" 550
"Smoking on the Sabbath" 1203
"Smut Mail" 1743
"Snake" (Ander, et al.) 175
"Snake" (Margo) 1035
"The Snake" 938
"Snake Charmer" 1618
"Snake Dance" 1751
"The Snake Returns" 938
"Snap Back" 161, 162, 163, 164
"Snap Decision" 509
"Snap Your Fingers at Care" 637
"Snappy Answers" 986
"Snapshot" 1485
"Snapshots II" 1485

"Sneaker Prison" 1345
"Sneaky, Creepy Fellows" 1679
"Snip Snip" 1444
"Sniper" 916
"Snoopy" 1828
"Snoopy's Song" 1486
"Snow" (Lunden) 1788
"Snow" (Tunick) 1749
"Snow from Finland" 361
"Snow Song" 1228
"Snow White, My Daughter" 1348
"Snubbed" 349
"Snuff That Girl" 1712
"So Close" 461
"So Do I (Ode to Virginity)" 1025
"So Far" 316
"So Far Away" 1591
"So Far, So Good" 1143, 1144
"So Glad I'm Here" 592, 1672
"So Good to See You" 658
"So Help Me God" 1301
"So I Give You" 860
"So I Said to My Grandson" 363
"So Into You" 1494
"So It Goes" (Blatt) 676
"So It Goes" (Ross) 930
"So Little Time" (Dick) 1771
"So Little Time" (Grant) 400
"So Long" (Holt) 1733
"So Long" (Melnick) 10
"So Long as He Loves You" 535
"So Long, Baby" 1185, 1186
"So Long, Big Time" 662
"So Long, Dearie" 818
"So Long for Now" 232
"So, Long Marianne" 1471
"So Long Mom" 1654
"So Long Sammy" 400
"So Long, Yesterday" 745
"So Many Bars" 1738
"So Many Little Things" 206
"So Many Nights" 157
"So Many People" 1027, 1403, 1491
"So Much for Marriage" 86
"So Much in Common" 1144
"So Much Rain" 2
"So Much That I Know" 1504
"So Much to Be Thankful For" 1780
"(So Much) More Than I Asked For" 67
"So Raise the Banner High" 870
"So Says I" 922
"So Short the Day" 184
"So, So Sophie" 1177
"So Tell Your Children" 697
"So the Days Go By, and the Summers Fly" 941
"So They Call It New York" 316
"So They Killed Ferdinand!" 609
"So This Is the Movies" 1584
"So, We'll Go No More A-Roving" 851, 972
"So What" (Davis) 156
"So What" (Leslie) 319
"So What? Why Not!" 528
"So Ya Wanna Be a Toy" 216
"So You Found the Library" 439
"So You Let One of Our Trunks Get Stolen" 609
"So You Want to Be a Nun" 1155, 1157, 1158
"So You're Not from New York" 639
"Soap Is Good for You" 229
"Soap Opera" 161, 162, 163, 164
"Soap Operetta" 1709
"Sociable Amoeba" 415
"The Social Director's Song" 1460
"Social Intercourse" 461
"Social Security" 119
"Society Means Propriety" 786
"Society Wedding" 69
"Society's Child" 115
"Socks" 941
"Sodomangamor" 215
"Les Soeurs" 123
"Soft Shoe Freak" 263
"The Soft Spot" 856
"Softly, as in a Morning Sunrise" 1570
"Softly, Softly to the Garden" 1146
"Soho" (Lewis) 664
"Soho" (Wallowitch) 820
"Sojourner" 253
"Soldatenweib" (aka "Ballad of the Soldier's Wife," "Soldier's Wife," and "Ballade vom Soldaten Weib") 880, 882, 1773, 1809
"Soldier" 571
"The Soldier and the Washerworker" 1709
"Soldier Boy" 1171
"A Soldier Takes Pride in Saluting His Captain" 707
"A Soldier's Musical" 1772
"Soldier's Wife" (aka "Ballad of the Soldier's Wife," "Ballade vom Soldaten Weib," and "Soldatenweib") 880, 882, 1773, 1809
"Soldiers of Heaven Hold the Sky" 1139
"Soldiers of the Lord" 105
"Sole Brother" 1225
"Solidarity Forever" 740
"Soliloquy" (Kole, et al.) 743
"Soliloquy" (Lescsak) 1119
"Soliloquy" (Shimoda) 602
"Soliloquy in One Bar" 1475
"Solitary Star" 1333
"Solo for the Telephone" 1298
"Solo Thoughts" 1147
"Solomon" 1160
"Solomon Decide" 1441
"Solomon Song" 1532, 1626, 1628
"Solutions" 61
"Som'thin' from Nuthin'" 207
"Somber Wind" 1356
"Some Are Born Great" 962
"Some Bright Morning" 237
"Some Day They'll Come in That Door and Say: Good Morning, Good Morning, Mother!" 951
"Some Folks Do" 112
"Some Girls" 1191
"Some Girls Can Bake a Pie" 1167
"Some Glory in Their Birth" 1519, 1569
"Some Incredible Guy" 1362
"Some Killa Sh*" 1407
"Some Kind of Wonderful" 1591
"Some Minor Turbulence" 19
"Some of It's Good" 359
"Some of These Days" 171, 221
"Some Other Time" 911, 1185, 1186
"Some People" 1106, 1546, 1717
"Some Said They Were Crazy" 1399
"Some Say" 1191
"Some Sunday" 1603
"Some Sunny Day" 1543
"Some There Are Who Never Venture" 586
"Some Things Don't End" 1243
"Some Things Don't Have to End" 665
"Somebody" (Evans) 157
"Somebody" (Marren) 961, 1756
"Somebody (More or Less) Likes Me" 1523
"Somebody Else" (Friedman) 1582, 1677
"Somebody Else" (Steidl) 299
"Somebody Loves Me" 73, 1096
"Somebody, Somebody to Hold Me" 971
"Somebody Stole My Gal" 1783
"Somebody to Love" 1556
"Somebody Touched Me" 682
"Somebody Write Me a Love Song" 159
"Somebody's Friend" 892
"Somebody's Gotta Do Somethin'" 58
"Somebody's Knocking" 470
"Somebody's Stepping on My Olive Branch" 401
"Someday" (Cohen) 1547
"Someday" (Kaplan) 1485
"Someday" (Menken) 1339
"Someday" (Merrill) 658
"Someday I'll Find You" 751
"Someday I'll Walk" 1358
"Someday, If We Grow Up" 1732
"Someday, Maybe" 1440
"Someday Sometime" 1135
"Someday There'll Be Some One Up There with the Man in the Moon" 507
"Someday We'll All Be Free" 777
"Someday You Might Love Me" 1830
"Somehow I Must Find a Way Out" 396
"Somehow I'm Taller" 971
"Somehow, Somehow" 1723
"Someone" (Lindsey) 1204
"Someone" (Micare) 1438
"Someone a Lot Like You" 1163
"Someone Better Comes Along" 1469
"Someone Else Is Steppin' In" 777
"Someone Else Will Know" 1477
"Someone Else's Story" 275
"Someone I Could Love" 1021
"Someone in a Chair" 741
"Someone in a Tree" 1213
"Someone in My Life" 1527
"Someone Is Discovering Something" 643
"Someone Is Dying" 1562
"Someone Is Sending Me Flowers" 1448
"Someone Is Waiting" 1491
"Someone Like You" 381
"Someone Needs Me" 733
"Someone Special" 692
"Someone Such as Me" 528
"Someone to Come Home with Me Tonight" 1339
"Someone to Count On" 1652
"Someone to Dance with Me" 1554
"Someone to Do For" 1449
"Someone to Love" 1321
"Someone to Watch Over Me" 955, 1096, 1172
"Someone Who Touches Me" 873
"Someone You Know" 1824
"Someone's Moving In" 219
"Someone's Moving Out" 219
"Somethin' 'Bout Love" 1300
"Somethin' Cold to Drink" 715
"Something" (Bernstein and Markell) 1709
"Something" (Gallagher) 675
"Something Bad Is Happening" 473
"Something Beautiful" 1038
"Something Bound to Begin" 1084
"Something Called Love" 1700
"Something Different" 484
"Something Else" 1595
"Something Extra" 1215
"Something for Me" 991
"Something for Nothing" 1335
"Something for the Boys" 367
"Something for the Summer" 308
"Something Funny's Going On" 973
"Something Good" 428
"Something Good Will Happen Soon" 417
"Something Has Happened" 733
"Something I'm Supposed to Do" 959
"Something in a Birth" 1485
"Something in the Wind" 107
"Something Is Wrong with Everyone Today" 208
"Something More" (Matay) 1548
"Something More" (Silverman) 1208
"Something Must Be Done" 81
"Something New" (Blankman) 235
"Something New" (Evans) 157
"Something Nice Is Going to Happen" 336
"Something of My Own" 375
"Something on a Tray" 13
"Something Pretty" 1002
"Something Sentimental" 1188
"Something Special" (Fradrich) 1147
"Something Special" (Shaiman and Wittman) 943
"Something Tells Me" 1611
"Something to Believe In" (Baird) 274
"Something to Believe In" (Raniello) 1089
"Something to Do Tonight" 1184
"Something to Do with My Hands" 326
"Something to Do with Spring" 1170
"Something to Get Up For" 1829
"Something to Hold On To" 1043
"Something to Live For" 180
"Something to Remember Me By" 1002
"Something to Remember You By" 348, 1606
"Something Very Strange" 1390
"Something Wonderful" 95
"Something You Really Want" 1043
"Something's Always Happening by the River" 1224
"Something's Come Over Me" 1016
"Something's Coming" 911, 1491
"Something's Coming Up" 1494
"Something's Cooking at the Spitfire Grill" 1513
"Something's Going On" 1458
"Something's Gonna Happen Really Strange Tonight" 1219
"Something's Got a Hold on Me" 790
"Something's Gotta Give" 1138
"Something's Wrong with This Picture" 385
"Somethin's Brewin' in Gainesville" 321
"Somethin's Doin'" 682
"Sometime" 1095
"Sometimes" (Gordon) 1103
"Sometimes" (Schmidt) 1253
"Sometimes" (Swados) 1384
"Sometimes a Day Goes By" 52
"Sometimes a Mania" 1416
"Sometimes at Night" 260
"Sometimes I Dream" 1063
"Sometimes I Look at Him" 1237
"Sometimes I Wonder" 1445
"Sometimes I'm Happy" 383
"Sometimes the Sky Is Blue" 614
"Sometimes When We Touch" 854
"Somewhere" (Bernstein) 911
"Somewhere" (Schmidt) 308
"Somewhere Along the Road" 968
"Somewhere Down the Road" 854
"Somewhere in Your Eyes" 698
"Somewhere Out There" (Elliot) 1197
"Somewhere Out There" (Heather Brothers) 979
"Somewhere Out There" (Horner, et al.) 746
"Somewhere, Someone" 726
"Somewhere That's Green" 727, 939
"Somewhere Under the Rainbow" 1330
"Son of a Preacher Man" 1450
"Son of Africa" 1397
"A Son of the Beach" 1385
"Sonata for One Piano" 1694
"Sonata Pathetique, Opus 13" 323
"Sonatina Facile in C Major, First Movement" 1694
"Sonatina No. 6 in F Major" 1694
"Sondheim Song" 861
"Song" 972
"Song and Dance Man" 82
"A Song Floating" 1493
"Song for a Crowded Cabaret" 1297
"Song for a Hunter College Graduate" 377, 727
"Song for a Pinch Hitter" 377
"Song for Jesus" 1298
"A Song for Myself" 781
"Song for Sunday" 1719
"Song for the Dead" 1049
"The Song Is You" 1210
"Song of a Child Prostitute" 1384
"A Song of Acceptance" 1742
"Song of Economic Difficulty" 977

"The Song of Economic Difficulty" 978
"The Song of Economic Reality" 978
"Song of Escape" 814
"Song of Exposition" 1011
"Song of Identification" 814
"The Song of Indifference" 1635
"Song of Innocence and Experience" 997
"Song of Joy" 1822
"A Song of Lists" (aka "List Song") 992, 1106
"Song of Love" 1193
"Song of Mandalay" 1532
"Song of Me" 1524
"The Song of Milady Gutrun" 184
"Song of Mother Samuels" 8
"Song of My Fathers" 105
"Song of Myself" 903
"Song of Ojo" 21
"Song of Peace" 983
"Song of Praise" (McLean) 67
"Song of Praise" (Taylor-Dunn and Reaves-Phillips) 1207
"Song of Proverbs" 21
"The Song of Purple Summer" 1515
"Song of Ruth" 689
"The Song of Sallah Shabet" 1701
"Song of Sharon" 1438
"Song of Singapore" 1495
"Song of Sixpence" 1085
"Song of Solitude" 1103
"Song of Solomon" 1441
"Song of Songs" 647
"Song of Sorrow" 1388
"Song of the 13 Colonies" 76
"The Song of the Bat" 1140
"Song of the Bends" 1399
"Song of the Big Shot" 660, 689, 1532
"Song of the Bourgeois Beatnik" 718
"Song of the City of Hope" 1082
"Song of the Field" 8
"Song of the Frog" 1483
"Song of the Goddess" 827
"Song of the Golden Egg" 1082
"Song of the Greasepaint" 1688
"Song of the Guns" 128, 827
"Song of the Hired Man" 697
"Song of the Insufficiency of Human Endeavor" 1628
"Song of the King" 833
"Song of the LURP" 386
"Song of the Ma" 848
"The Song of the Mask" 661
"Song of the Nazi Dogs" 814
"Song of the Open Road" (Harte) 903
"Song of the Open Road" (Spektor) 718
"Song of the Orient" 1171
"The Song of the Queen Bee" 1447
"Song of the River" 1784
"Song of the Road" 1135
"The Song of the Samovar" 637
"Song of the Sea" 249
"Song of the Seasons" 1410
"Song of the Soldiers" 889
"Song of the United Racist Front" 814
"Song of the Wild Wood" 1784
"Song of the Witch" 1531
"Song of the Wounded Frenchmen" 827
"Song of Troubles" 1388
"Song of War" 21
"Song of Wisdom" 21
"Song of Yesterday" 1089
"Song of Youth" 719
"Song Song" 279
"Song to Endangered Species" 86
"Song to Sing" 1330
"A Song Whose Time Has Come" 949
"Song Writer's Awards" 1066
"Songs" 1291
"Songs My Mama Sang" 323
"The Songs My Mother Used to Sing to Me" 672
"Songs Of" 37
"Songs of Peace and War" 128
"Sonnet" 1057
"Sonny Boy" 829, 993
"The Sonny-Boy Slave Song" 589
"Sono Come Tu Mi Vuoi" 807
"Sonqoba" 651
"Sons" 1381
"Sons Of ... (Fils De ...)" 792
"Sons of Greentree" 1481
"Soon" (Draesel) 1671
"Soon" (Kaplan) 1485
"Soon" (Kookoolis and Fagin) 1504
"Soon-ah Will Be Done" 591
"Soon I'll Be Done" 1388
"Soon It's Gonna Rain" 478
"Soon One Morning" 1672
"Sooner or Later" 1492
"Sophia" 972
"Sophie-Louise" 107
"Sophie's Love Song" 1505
"Sophie's Waltz" 1505
"Sophisticated Lady" 134, 180, 1521
"Sophisticated Swing" 1521
"The Sorcerer" 963
"Sorcerer's Dance" 647
"Sore's Lullaby" 1502
"The Sorghum Sisters" 2
"Sorrow" 333
"The Sorrow Born of Dreams" 541
"Sorry-Grateful" 1492
"Sorry Her Lot" 1270
"Sorry Wrong Valley" 1611
"A Sort of Courting Song" 316
"Soul Food" 1373
"Soulless a Faery Dies" 707
"Sound and Light" 1290
"The Sound of a Ragtime Band" 8
"The Sound of Laughter" 407
"Sound of Love" 1328
"The Sound of Money" 981
"The Sound of Muzak" 300, 616
"Sound Off" 194
"Sound Side" 864
"The Soundkeeper's Song" 1252
"Sounds" (Friedman) 1038
"Sounds" (Harper) 1424
"Sounds of Silence" 693
"Sounds of the Day" 1604
"Sounds of the Night" 1604
"Sounds Pretty Risky" 1374
"Soup" 1505
"Soup Song" 740
"Soup's On (The Dying Nun Ballet)" 1155, 1157
"Sous le Ciel de Paris (Under Paris Skies)" 1256, 1257
"South American, Polite and Rude" 32
"South American Way" 1476
"Southbound Train" 471
"Southern Charm" 313
"Southern Comfort" 463
"Souvenirs" 1125
"Soy Antillana" 262
"Space" 413
"Space Age" 852
"Space Idiocy" 1153
"Spaceship" 427
"Spaghetti Song" 1131
"Spain" 1623
"Spanish Cape" 1015
"Spanish Lady" 253
"Spanish Mazurka" 948
"Spanish Panic" 1193
"A Spanish Shawl" 1315
"Spare Some Change" 644
"The Spare to the Heir" 1320, 1321
"Sparks" 10, 1655
"Spawning" 1073
"Speak in Silence" 528
"Speak Low" 128, 879, 1773, 1807
"Speak No Love" 531
"Speaking French" 973
"Speaking of Pals" 148
"A Special!" 1510
"A Special Boy" 564, 758
"Special Bulletin" 1072
"Special Day" 486
"Special Guest Spot" 1149
"(A) Special Man" 493, 1124, 1537
"The Specials Today" 1121
"Le Spectre de la Rose" 95
"Speech" (Thorne) 528
"Speech" (Truth) 1734, 1735
"Speech to the Neighborhood Watch Committee" 1710
"Speed" 364
"Speed Kills" 1153
"Speed of Light" 1007
"Speed Typists" 556
"Speed Won't Get Me" 1511
"Speeding Time" 1591
"The Spelling Rules" 1680
"Spend an Evening in Caroline" 681
"Spics" 897
"Spider and the Fly" 1085
"Spies" 1014
"Spiffin' Up Ziggy's" 248
"Spike's Turn" 1508
"Spin! Spin! Spin!" 1512
"Spinning Song" (Brown) 814
"Spinning Song" (Colby) 652
"A Spinning Tale" 1512
"Spirit of Beauty" 419
"Spirit of the Forest" 1073
"Spirit of the Line" 1325
"The Spirit of Your Father" 1002
"Spirit Song" 497
"Spirits of Banality and Hate!" 834
"The Spiritual" 506
"Spirograph" 945
"Spitball (Me Lord)" 321
"Splendor in the Grass" 1517
"Splendor in the Grass Ballet" 1517
"Spoken Aria" 823
"Spoleto" 1069, 1125
"Spooky Stuff" 1234
"Spores" 610
"The Sporting House Professor Blues" 105
"Sports" 1698
"Le Spot Hot" 381
"A Spot of Tea" 14
"Spring" 1499
"Spring Beauties" 1311
"Spring Cleaning" 219
"Spring Day" 484
"Spring Doth Let Her Colours Fly" 942
"Spring Frolic: Rose Garden" 301
"Spring Is on My Side" 425
"The Spring of Next Year" 818
"Spring, Sun and Flowers" 96
"Spring Will Come Again" 234
"Springhill Mine Disaster" 963
"Springtime at Vassar" 22
"Spunk" 1433
"Sputnik (Fellow Traveler)" 1073
"Square Dance" 1083
"Squeek" 1162
"Squeeze Me" 18
"Squeeze Me in the Rain" 1310
"Squeeze, Squeeze, Squeeze" 991
"S.S. Commodore Ebenezer McAfee III" 538
"The Stabbing Campaign" 1091
"Stag Movie" 1517
"Stage Blood" 791
"Stage Coach" 241
"Stage Door" 226
"Stage Manager's Song" 1066
"Staggerlee" 1518
"Stairway to the Stars" 382, 1521
"Stalling for Time" 54
"The Stallion" 130
"Stamp Out the Tea Tax" 1691
"La Stampa de Feeta" 552
"Stand Back" 1399
"Stand by Me" (Katsaros) 1071
"Stand by Me" (Penn) 1392
"Stand by Me" (Telson) 615
"The Stand-In" 506
"Stand Straight and Tall" 778
"Stand Up" (Davis) 450
"Stand Up" (Swados) 1345
"Stand Up and Cheer" 1177
"Stand Up and Flex" 160
"Stand Up for Jesus" 1559
"Stand Up the Fatherland" 364
"Standing and Waiting" 1458
"Standing in Line" 1375
"Standing in Need" 1558
"Standing in the Middle of the Road" 1637
"Standing in the Need of Prayer" 736
"Standing on the Corner" 212
"Standing with Henry!" 1412
"Stanislaw" 1414
"Star Crazy" 1016
"Star Dust" 1521
"A Star Is Born" 1181
"Star Letters" 280
"The Star Number" 64
"The Star of the Show" 626
"A Star on the Monument" 1154
"Star Song" 1330
"The Star-Spangled Banner" 695, 1014, 1556
"Star-Spangled Breakdown" 1014
"The Star Spot" 783
"Star Stepping Stranger" 1007
"Star Tar" 341
"Star Wars Cantina" 1015
"Starburst" 1007
"Staring" 926, 948
"Staring at the Moon" 387
"Starlight" 930
"The Starlit Hour" 1764
"Starmites" 1522
"Starring Me" 1050
"Starry Cold Night" 1330
"Stars" (Friedman) 607
"Stars" (Steady) 410
"The Stars" (Alper) 754
"The Stars" (*Band-Wagon*) 96
"The Stars" (Portman) 938
"Stars and Bars" 1330
"Stars and Lovers" 336
"Stars and Stripes Forever" 1643
"Stars and the Moon" 1498
"Stars Fell on Alabama" 1521
"Stars in My Eyes" 1584
"Stars in Your Eyes" 1523
"Stars of the Morning" 1102
"The Stars Seem So Low Tonight" 352
"Stars with Stripes" 622
"The Stars — Leah" 754
"Starsong" 1202
"Starting from Scratch" 1385
"Starting Here, Starting Now" 1524
"Starting Out Again" 27
"Starting Over" 742
"Starved" 1290
"Starvin' to Death on the Government Claim" 1285
"State Fair" 1338
"The State Film Industry at Work" 170
"State of the Kingdom" 34
"Statehood Hula" 371
"Station Break" 149, 150
"Station L-O-V-E" 85
"Station Syren" 135
"Stations of the Cross" 253
"The Statue (La Statue)" 792
"Status Quo" 1267, 1268
"Status Symbol" 1734
"Stay" (Barsha) 1325
"Stay" (LaChiusa) 1250
"Stay" (Levinson) 404
"Stay Ahead of the People" 255
"Stay Away from Waycross" 1733
"Stay Awhile" 1585, 1586
"Stay Close to the Music" 1002
"Stay East, Young Man" 578
"Stay, Frederic, Stay!" 1270
"Stay Home Here with Me" 1821
"Stay in My Life" 206
"Stay in the Field" 815, 816
"Stay in Your Own Back Yard" 377
"Stay on the Path" 582
"Stay on the Side of the Angels" 13
"Stay, We Must Not Lose Our Senses" 1270
"Stay with Me" (Lipson) 1331
"Stay with Me" (McKibbins) 778
"Stay with Me" (Merrill) 1752
"Stay with Me Baby" 78
"Stay with Me, Nora" 398
"Stayin' Awake" 1046
"Staying Alive" 1452
"Staying In" 948
"Staying Young" 1752
"Steady Job" 716
"Steal Away" 591
"Steal My Thunder" 1084
"Steal with Style" 1367
"Steam, Steam, Steam" 604, 1715
"The Steam Train" 1498
"Steel Guitars and Barking Seals" 1261
"Step Back" 461
"Step Into My World" 785
"Step Into the Light" 1301
"Step Into Their Shoes" 778
"Step Lively Boy" 194
"Step Out in Front" 81

"Stephanie" 60
"Stephen Dowling Botts" 922
"Stepping to the Stars" 1007
"Stick Around" 237, 603
"Stick It on the Wall, Mrs. Riley" 1750
"Stick with Me, Kid" 934
"Sticks and Stones" 222
"Stiff Upper Lip" 1172
"Still" (Brady) 1245
"Still" (Cohen) 1143, 1144
"Still Be Me?" 1117
"Still Here with Me" 497
"Still Hurting" 890
"Still More Questions" 1069
"A Still Small Voice" 1363
"Still Waters" 1493
"Stimela Sasezola" 1401
"Stirring Soup" 431
"Stitch in Time" 1447
"Stoats Forever" 1784
"Stock Exchange Day" 976
"Stock Report" 1318
"The Stockboy Blues" 65
"Stockhausen Potpourri" 1395, 1396
"Stocks-Sports-Weather" 664
"The Stolen Melody" 635
"Stolen Sneakers" 624
"Stomp Your Foot Upon the Floor" 1601
"Stompin' at the Savoy" 55, 180, 182, 221
"Stone Song" 1020
"Stone the Crows" 833
"Stoned" 1225
"Stoned in Saigon" 386
"Stonefire" 1562
"The Stones of Jehoshaphat" 1531
"Stonewall Serenade" 469
"The Stoning" 1771
"Stools" 1709
"Stop, Do Not Go On" 615
"Stop Kidding Yourself" 491
"Stop, Ladies, Pray!" 1270
"Stop Look Listen" 1623
"Stop of Slushing" 1684
"Stop Seeing Reinhardt" 431
"Stop the Presses Finale" 725
"Store-Bought Suit" 600
"Stories" 255
"The Stork" 436
"Storm" 476
"Storm Ballet" 1060
"The Storm Is Passing Over" 736
"Storm's A-Brewin'" 627
"Stormy Monday Blues" 221
"Stormy Weather" 662, 1096
"Story of a Life" 916
"The Story of Alice" 1431
"The Story of Black Broadway" 165
"The Story of Cruel Frederick" 1444
"The Story of My Life" (Bernstein) 234
"The Story of My Life" (Schmidt) 1451
"Story of My Life" 683
"The Story of Nelly O." 547
"The Story of Ooooh!" 877
"The Story of the Man That Went Out Shooting" 1444
"The Story of the Opera" 1196
"The Story That History Won't Tell" 1477
"The Storyteller" 21
"Stouthearted Men" 1096, 1570
"Stowaway" 1435
"Straight" 1504
"Straight, No Chaser" 156
"Straight to Heaven" 1830
"A strange Agony" 250
"Strange Bedfellows" 461
"Strange. From Inside the House" 439
"Strange Fruit" 171, 777, 1620
"Strange Little Man" 1427
"A Strange May Seem Strange That's True" 1601
"Strange Men You Cannot Satisfy" 1139
"A Strange Thing" 431
"Strange Weather" 352
"Strangely" 1164
"Stranger" 198
"Stranger Blues" 1631
"A Stranger Here" 754
"Stranger in His World" 1618
"Strangers in the Night" 1210
"Strangers on a Train" 60
"Strangler Martin" 449
"Straw Into Gold" 1512
"Strawberries" 1767
"Strawberries, Pickles and Ice Cream" 493, 1124, 1537
"Strawberry-Blueberry" 393, 394
"Strawberry Day" 869
"Strawberry Fields Forever" 1426
"Stray Cat" 1042
"The Stream" 1363
"The Street" (Gordon) 1103
"The Street" (Kanfer, et al.) 745
"The Street Act" 1263
"Street Corner Song" 86
"Street Cries" 91, 1569
"A Street in Greenwich Village" 635
"Street Jesus" 493, 1537
"Street Lady" 580
"Street Music" 159
"Street People" (Hoffman) 1758
"Street People" (Lindsey) 1670
"Street People" (Swados) 643
"Street People's Anthem" 86
"Street Rap" 82
"Street Scene" (Axelrod and Hart) 616
"Street Scene" (Hilliard) 1754
"Street Scene" (Warren) 542
"The Street Singer" 145
"Street Singer" 993
"Street Song" 661
"Street Suite" 1758, 1761
"Street Talk" (McNally) 1710
"Street Talk" (Steady) 410
"A Streetcar Is a Horsecar" 672
"Streetheat" 1538
"Streets" 359
"The Streets of Antioch" 1253
"The Streets of Bed-Stuy" 968
"The Streets of Dublin" 1006
"The Streets of Madrid (Las Calles de Madrid)" 488
"Stretto" 1751
"The Strike" 9
"Strike Up the Band" 955
"Strike!" 814
"Strike! America" 602
"String of Pearls" 301
"Strip" 1802
"Strip Tease" 134
"Strolling" 221
"Strolling Down Broadway" 1550
"Strolling Through the Park" 417
"Strongman's Song" 1733
"Struggle in Vain" 124
"Struttin' with Some Barbeque" 959
"The Struwwelpeter Overture" 1444
"Stubb's Song" 1071
"Stuck in a Cell" 1818
"Stuck on the Windshield of Life" 1558
"Stuck on You" 1772
"Stuck-Up" 1154
"A Stud and a Babe" 739
"The Student Robin Hood of Pilsen" 85
"Studs" 225
"Study of the Human Figure" 910
"Stuff" 1550
"The Stuff" 1347
"Stupid Kids" 1545
"Stupid Things I Won't Do" 997
"Stupidly in Love" 1309
"Stuttering Song" 701
"Sub-Babylon" 975
"Subito (Nearer to the Lire)" 1146
"Subscribe!" 198
"Substitute" 1057
"Suburb" 1547
"Suburban Lullaby" 1142
"Suburban Retreat" 1254
"Suburban Rose" 718
"Suburbia Square Dance" 126, 558, 667
"Subway" (Altman) 858
"Subway" (Baldwin, et al.) 708
"Subway" (Cummings) 1066
"Subway" (Kander, et al.) 1014
"Subway Panhandlers" 1710
"Subway Rag" 388
"Subway Ride" 1186
"Subway Rider" 785
"Subway to Coney Island" 587
"Subways Are for Skiing" 50
"Success" (Jordan) 1379
"Success" (Matay) 1548
"Success" (Romanovsky and Phillips) 808
"The Success Song" 1500
"Success Stories" 461
"Such a Beautiful World" 98
"Such a Little King" 815, 816
"Such a Merry Party" 935
"Such a Moment" 1020
"Such Beautiful Snow" 951
"A Sucker's Soliloquy" 123
"Sudden Beauty" 550
"Sudden Death Overtime" 159
"Suddenly" (Levinson) 976
"Suddenly" (Valenti) 989
"Suddenly, Last Tuesday" 1430
"Suddenly Love" 1097
"Suddenly Seymour" 727, 939
"Suddenly She Was There" 1290
"Suddenly Somehow" 1428
"Suddenly Stop and Think" 34
"Suddenly the Day Looks Sunny" 1367
"Suddenly the Music Starts" 1550
"Suddenly You're a Stranger" 980
"Suffer" 185
"Suffragettes March" 1412
"Sugar" 1634
"Sugar Daddy" 680
"Sugar Daddy Blues" 1348
"The Suicide" 1394
"Suicide Rap" 1289
"Suite" 293
"Suite for a Growing Corpse" 720
"Suite for Five Letters" 1168
"Suite in Three Movements for Diverse Juggling Instruments" 1439
"Suite Limousine" 1077
"Sullivan Street Flat" 575
"The Sum of a Man" 1700
"Sumer Is Icumen In" 942
"Summer Afternoons" 1419
"Summer Fancy" 14
"Summer in New York" 616
"A Summer in Ohio" 890
"Summer in the City" 1556
"Summer Love" (Laws) 1078
"Summer Love" (Pasatieri) 1416
"Summer Nights" 625
"A Summer Romance" 277
"Summer Stock" 1460
"Summer, Summer" 1689
"Summer Wind" 1210
"Summer's Breeze" 1149
"Summer's Nice" 1231
"Summertime" 212, 965, 1296
"Summoned by Bells" 135
"Sun and Fun" 135
"The Sun Comes Up" 754
"Sun Down" 667
"The Sun Is Coming Up" 1601
"The Sun Rises" 98
"The Sun Shines Brighter" 902
"The Sun Shines In" 1428
"The Sun Won't Set" 1492
"Sunday" (Larson) 1634
"Sunday" (Sondheim) 1491, 1557
"Sunday" (Styne) 1546
"Sunday Brunch" 638
"Sunday in the Park" 1267, 1268
"Sunday in the Park with George" 1557
"Sunday Makes a Difference" 1747
"Sunday Morning Social Call" 345
"Sunday School Boys" 1618
"Sunday Sweetheart" 813
"Sunday Television" 556, 557
"Sundays" 1693
"Sunflower" 323
"Sung-Fu" 1030
"The Sunlight" 1503
"Sunny" 883
"Sunny, Sunny Moon" 1007
"Sunnyside Lane" 1304
"Sunrise" (Frandsen, et al.) 1495
"Sunrise" (Miranda) 760
"Sunrise" (Valcq) 1513
"Sunrise Melody" 1326
"Sunrise Semester" 535
"The Suns That Daily Rise" 831
"Sunset Boulevard" 1611
"Sunset City" 1558
"Sunset Dreams" 1558
"Sunsets" 938
"Sunshine" (Alford) 1620
"Sunshine" (Moritz) 507
"Sunshine" (Sternberg) 571
"Sunshine and Shadows" 1618
"Sunshine Girl" 1752
"Sunshine on My Shoulders" 37
"Sunshine Tomorrow" 466
"The Sunshine Train" 1559
"Super Bad" 1550
"Super Wasp" 919
"Superhero Girl" 1522
"Superman" 1743
"Supermarket" (Schwerin) 857
"Supermarket" (Warren) 556, 557
"Supersonic" 858
"Superstar" (Leslie) 319
"Superstar" (Russell and Bramlett) 1623
"Superwoman" 1307
"Supper Club" 692
"The Supper Ends" 1601
"Supper, Half an Hour!" 941
"Supper Time" 69
"Suppertime" 939, 1828
"Supported Adagio" 295
"The Supreme Court Saved from Fire" 1375
"Sur la Table" 766
"Sur le Plage" 199
"Sur le Quais" 213
"Surabaya Johnny" 128, 660, 689, 879, 880, 882, 1532, 1773, 1807, 1809
"Surabaya-Santa" 1498
"Sure of His Love" 1595
"Sure Thing" 883
"Sure, You Betcha, Georgie" 227
"Surface" 1225
"Surgery" 780
"Surprise Me" 297
"Surprise!" 1181
"Surprise! Surprise!" 271
"Surprised" 1726
"Surprising People" 773
"Surrounded by Women" 111
"Survival" 1562
"Survival of the Fittest" 1361, 1362
"Survival Song" (Meyers) 65
"Survival Song" (Weill) 882
"The Survival Song" 1773
"Survive" 1451
"Survivor: Beltway Scumbag Edition" 227
"Survivors" 789
"Susan and I Missed You" 1789
"Susan Atkins on Night Highway" 1018
"Susan's Dream" 689, 1773
"Susan's Song" 1659
"The Suspects Polka" 789
"Suspended Animation" 319
"Suspension" 1234
"Suzanne" 1471
"Swamps of Home" 1193
"Swan and Edgar's" 360
"Swanee" 73, 829, 993, 1540
"Swanee River" 716
"Swanee River Overture" 716
"Swanislavsky" 1611
"Sweat Song" 1399
"Sweeping Through the City" 196
"Sweet and Hot" 662
"Sweet and Low-Down" 46, 1644
"Sweet Angeline" 1543
"Sweet Beginning" 924
"Sweet Bitter Candy" 643
"Sweet Charity" 1385
"Sweet Chitty Chatty" 222
"Sweet Day" 13
"Sweet Dreams" (Gibson) 39
"Sweet Dreams" (Stewart) 646
"Sweet Eternity" 364
"Sweet Fantasy" 1136
"Sweet Feet" 1565
"Sweet Freedom" 854
"Sweet Georgia Brown" 221, 1435
"Sweet Henry Loves You" 1504
"Sweet Home Chicago" 777
"Sweet Hour of Prayer" 591, 592, 736

"Sweet Jesus, Blessed Savior" 1392
"Sweet Jesus What a Mess" 1063
"Sweet Little Jesus Boy" 166
"Sweet Longings" 1582, 1677
"Sweet Lorraine" 1521
"Sweet Man" 553
"Sweet Mary" 333
"Sweet Memories" 1177
"Sweet Polly Plunkett" 1492
"Sweet Popularity" 570
"Sweet Refrain" 278
"Sweet Seasons" 1591
"Sweet Song of India" 1575
"Sweet Substitute" 813
"Sweet Sue's" 1258
"Sweet Talkin' Guy" 115
"Sweet Time" 1603
"Sweet Words" 975
"Sweet Words Don't Scare My Lady" 665
"The Sweetest Songs Remain To Be Sung" 279
"Sweethearts" 1570
"Sweetie Dear" 553
"Sweetness" 698
"Swell" 154
"Swell Shampoo Song" 1245
"Swing-a-Ding-a-Ling" 336
"Swing a Li'l Funk Into Gang" 1407
"Swing Low" 1559
"Swing Low Sweet Chariot" 221, 592
"Swing, Swing, Swing" 424
"Swing Your Heart to le Bon Dieu" 1510
"Swingin' for Science" 395
"Swingin' the Jinx Away" 1704
"Swinging" 935
"Swinging Shepherd's Blues" 1452
"Swingle Songsters" 1427
"Swiss Family Trapp" 977
"Swoop of the Moopem" 701
"The Swordfight" 710
"Les Sylphides" 95
"Sylvan Ballet" 349
"The Symbolic Death and Rebirth" 393
"Sympathy" 698
"Sympathy for the Devil" 1664
"Symphonie" 1057
"Symphony" 1689
"Symphony No. 3, Final Movement" 295
"Symphony No. 4 in G" 295
"Symphony Number 9 (Fourth Movement excerpt)" 1439
"Symphony Rap" 646
"The Syncopated Clock" 1521
"Syncopatin'" 1550, 1774

"'T Ain't Nobody's Biz-ness If I Do" 18, 266
"'T' for Texas" 777
"T-Party" 535
"T'ai Chi" 338
"T'Ain't Kosher" 119
"Ta-Ra-Ra Boom-De-Ay!" 1643
"Table D'Hote" 1709
"Table Talk" 1073
"Table Tango" 693
"Tableau" 60
"Tables" 96
"Taboo or Not Taboo" 509
"Tabor Owns the Big Hotel" 92
"Tabulation" 1255
"Tackle That Temptation with a Time Step" 1157
"Tacky Closing" 1383
"Tacky Opening" 1383
"Taewongun's Regency" 889
"Tag" 930
"Taggin'" 1325
"Tahiti Duet" 911
"Taiko" 1439
"Taiko Drums" 1410
"Takarazuka Girl" 1410
"Take a Bow" 809
"Take a Break" 644
"Take a Chance" (Douglass) 121
"Take a Chance" (Taylor-Dunn and Reaves-Phillips) 1207
"Take a Chance on Me" 1058
"Take a Good Look Around" 987
"Take a Knife" 1072
"Take a Little Time" 1102
"Take a Look" (Goggin and Solley) 667
"Take a Look" (Levenson) 293
"Take a Look at Life" 274
"Take a Look at That" 267
"Take a Pick" 572
"Take a Ride" 1058
"Take a Stand" 196
"Take a Trippie with a Hippie" 534
"Take a Vacation" 456
"Take Away the Darkening Sky" 889
"Take Back the Heart" 481
"Take Back Your Gold" 577
"Take by Giving" 224
"Take Care" 1040
"Take Care of Your Heart" 404
"Take Courage, Daughter" 823
"Take Courage Heart" 920
"Take Every Opportunity" 745
"Take Five" 1015
"Take Hold the Crutch" 1038
"Take It Easy" (Fox) 1577
"Take It Easy" (McHugh) 886
"Take It from a Pal" 1511
"Take It from the Top" 1821
"Take It Off, Tammy!" 391
"Take It Right Back" 180, 181, 182
"Take It Slow, Joe" 662
"Take Me" (Pippin) 480
"Take Me" (Stoner) 752
"Take Me Along" 1580
"Take Me As I Am" 1373
"Take Me Away" (Bargy) 638
"Take Me Away" (Forrest) 1219
"Take Me Away, Roy Rogers" 926
"Take Me Back" 1299
"Take Me Back to Manhattan" 63, 1704
"Take Me Back to Texas" 1163
"Take Me-Find Me" 1045
"Take Me for a Buggy Ride" 180, 181, 182
"Take Me Home, Country Roads" 37
"Take Me Home with You" (Tierney) 1251
"Take Me Home with You" (Wilson) 913
"Take Me in Your Arms" 1521
"Take Me Into You" 1613
"Take Me Out to the Ball-game" 377
"Take Me, Please" 1061
"Take Me to Central Park" 1066
"Take Me to Heart" 1523
"Take Me to the World" 1491
"Take Me Up" 1363
"Take More Out of Life" 220
"Take My Hand in Friendship" 1264
"Take My Hand, Precious Lord" 996
"Take My Mother Home" 591
"Take My World Away" 930
"Take Off the Coat" 1608
"Take, Oh Take" 1519
"Take, Oh Take (Those Lips Away)" (Leslee) 1519
"Take, Oh Take (Those Lips Away)" (Mulcahy) 1568, 1569
"Take on the Road" 1631
"Take That Smile Off Your Face" 1335
"Take the 'A' Train" 221, 1435
"Take the Boat" 1338
"Take the Book" 1140
"Take the Bus" 160
"Take the Comforting Hand of Jesus" 754
"Take the Glamor Out of War" 386
"Take the High Way" 196
"Take the Lord God" 1308
"Take the Picture" 749
"Take the Picture First" 1152
"Take the Skinheads Bowling" 1545
"Take Them Away, They'll Drive Me Crazy" 695
"Take This Hammer" 740
"Take to the Air" 1787
"Take Two" 1584
"Take Us Back" 1761
"Take Us to the Forest" 1134
"Take What You Can" 364
"Taken at Her Word" 1142
"Takin' Him Home to Meet Mom" 1800
"Takin' My Time" 1317
"Taking a Chance on Love" 182, 238
"Taking a Pitshke" 1715
"Taking Chances" 1298
"Taking Inventory" 379
"The Taking of Rhododendron" 600
"Taking Off the Robe" 1168
"Taking Our Turn" 1582, 1677
"Taking Responsibility" 1155, 1157
"Taking the Cure" 822
"The Tale of a Shirt" 305
"The Tale of Pudding Lane" 1316
"The Tale of the Caliph Stork" 96
"The Tale of the (an) Oyster" 367, 861, 1704
"The Tale of the Soldier's Wife" 689
"A Tale of Two Cities" 1683
"Talent" 1365, 1386
"The Talent Contest" 203
"Talk" 366
"Talk About the Men" 1319
"Talk About the Weather" 1103
"Talk, Talk, Talk" (Grant) 1307
"Talk, Talk, Talk" (Sheffer) 599
"Talk to Me" (Berkowitz) 1060
"Talk to Me" (Clifton and Siegel) 1319
"Talk to Me" (Giering) 328
"Talk to Me" (Stein) 277
"Talk to Me, Baby" 538
"Talk to My Machine" 36
"A Talk with One's Conscience" 1531
"Talk Your Feelings" 1550
"Talkin' Blues" 1183
"Talkin' Morosco Blues" 1709
"Talking About Love" 1401
"Talking Man" 226
"Talking to People" 785
"Talking Union" 740
"Tallahassie Lassie" 277
"Tallulah" 1585, 1586
"Tallulahbaloo" 1585, 1586
"Tam" 637
"Tamara, Queen of the Nile" 1309
"The Taming" 938
"Tan 'n' Hot" 232
"Tan Manhattan" 165
"Tanabata" 1410
"Tangled Tangents" 1330
"Tangled Up Puppet" 916
"The Tango" 147, 199
"Tango" (Fremont) 1258
"Tango" (Gaburo) 1636
"Tango" (Silverman) 215
"Tango" (Weill) 1462
"Tango(-)Ballad (Ballade)" 128, 879, 1626
"Tango Melody" 305
"Tango Rehearsal" 147
"Tankhum" 492
"Tantalize" 1077
"Tante Helene" 807
"Tanya" 348
"The Tap Combination" 283
"Tap Dance" 705
"Tap Dance Drill" 569
"Tap My Potential" 1607
"Tap Your Troubles Away" 818, 1656
"Tapestry" 1591
"Tappin' In" 506
"Tarantella" 1131
"The Tarantula" 488
"Tarot" 1592
"Tarts" 510
"Taru Bawo" 1284
"Tate House" 1018
"Tatenyu" 1212
"Tattooed Woman" 1594
"The Tax Collector's Soliloquy" 1713
"Tax Time, USA" 1066
"Taxi" (Chapin) 916
"Taxi" (Curtis) 1732
"Taxi" (Duquesnay, et al.) 207
"Taxi" (Lennon and McCartney) 1014
"Taxi from Hell" 1710
"Taxis at Midnight" 100
"Tchaikovsky" 170
"Tchaikovsky Romance" 666
"Tchort Vasmi (To Hell with It!)" 666
"Tea" 277
"The Tea and I" 735
"Tea Chanty" 1447
"Tea Dance" 1691
"Tea for Three" 1226
"Tea for Two" 55
"Tea in the Rain" 1154
"Tea Party" (Bargy) 638
"Tea Party" (Bergersen) 332
"The Tea Party" (Herman) 818
"The Tea Party" (Lunden) 1190
"Tea Service" 476
"The Tea Song" 826
"Tea Song" 827
"Tea-Tea-Tea" 714
"Teach It How to Dance" 1772
"Teach Me" 1670
"Teach Me How" 1321
"Teach Me How to Fast Dance" 1800
"Teach Me How to Move" 1458
"Teach Me Tonight" 382
"Teach the Children" 582
"Teach Your Children Well" 1556
"The Teachers' Argument" 474
"The Teacher's Out Today" 1309
"Teachers' Strike Meeting" 1765
"(Teaching) Third Grade" 1386
"The Teachings" 615
"Teaka's Dance" 107
"T.E.A.M. (The Baseball Game)" 1828
"Team, Team, Team" 912
"Tear Down the Wall" 284
"Tear Jerk" 739
"Tear Me Down" 680
"Tears" (Harte) 903
"Tears" (Sachs) 326
"Tears" (Wallach) 1605
"Tears and Tears Ago" 1298
"Tears of Ice" 101
"Technical Assistants in Vietnam" 22
"Teddy Da Roose" 1643
"Teenager in Love" 205
"Teeny Bopper" 1732
"Teeny Tiny" 692
"Teeny-Weeny Genie" 66
"Teeter Totter Tessie" 1196
"Tel-Aviv" 1341
"Tel-Aviv, I Love You" 1647
"The Telegram" 641
"The Telepathetique" 491
"A Telephone Call" 926
"Telephone Conversation" 21
"The Telephone Dance" 42
"The Telephone Hang-Up" 126, 852
"The Telephone Scene" 1802
"Telephone Song" 820
"Telephones" 359
"Tell 'Em the Truth" 1347
"Tell a Handsome Stranger" 935
"Tell a Little Lie or Two" 1089
"Tell Her" 1353
"Tell Her I Love Her" 1712
"Tell Her You Care" 1638
"Tell Him, These Boots Are Made for Walking" 1551
"Tell Me" (Richman) 506
"Tell Me" (Ross) 930
"Tell Me" (Woldin) 865, 866, 1593
"Tell Me a Lie" 825
"Tell Me Goodbye" 1083
"Tell Me I'm Good" 1485
"Tell Me the Story of Your Life" 598
"Tell Me What the Rain Is Saying" 1203
"Tell Me What to Do" 19
"Tell Me, Where Is Fancy Bred?" 1437
"Tell Me Who I Am" 976
"Tell Me Why" (Edwards and Spaeth) 1521
"Tell Me Why" (Flaherty) 1006
"Tell Me Why I Love Him" 293
"Tell Me You Know Me" 717
"Tell Me You Love Me" 1146
"Tell Me Your Secret" 485
"Tell the Boys" 1450
"Temperance Polka" 1481
"The Temperance Song" 216
"Temperance Trio" 112
"The Temple" 20
"Temple Turning Time" 1727
"Temporary Thing" 1485
"Temporary Woman Blues" 1045
"Le Temps" 924
"The Temptation" 1436
"Temptation" (Leake) 278
"Temptation" (Markoe) 468
"Temptation" (Rubell) 403
"Tempting Salome" 860

"Tempura's Song" 10
"Tempus Fugit" 1348
"10 in 1" 1234
"10 Million Miles" 1598
"Ten Cent Piece of the Pie" 257
"Ten Cents a Dance" 212
"Ten Commandments" 647
"Ten Days Ago" 1330
"Ten Dollars Closer" 365
"Ten in One" 1135
"Ten Per Cent Orlon" 381
"Ten Percent" 210, 1685
"The Ten-Percent Solution: An 18th Floor Office at the Most Powerful Talent Agency on Earth" 899
"Ten Petticoats" 375
"The Ten Plagues" 663
"The Ten Ruble Note" 1203
"Ten Thousand Feet in the Air" 1171
"Ten Year Blues" 643
"Ten Years" 690
"The Tender Land" 1601
"Tender Understanding" 1737, 1738
"The Tenement Lullaby" 58
"Tenement Scene" 1218
"Tengu" 1358
"Tennessee Waltz" 790, 1575
"Tennessee Williams' Heroine" 352
"The Tenor" 261
"Tenting Tonight" 740
"Teresa" 693
"Terre Haute" 1460
"Terrible" 375
"The Terrible Robber Men" 253
"Terrible Tuesday" 785
"Terrorist Trio" 1759
"Tess's Torch Song" 662
"The Test" (Aman, et al.) 1661
"The Test" (Jacobson) 1452
"The Test" (Marren) 1756
"Test Tube Baby" 1337
"Testimony" (Swados) 643
"Testimony" (Tucholsky) 1635
"A Tete a Tete" 1604
"Texas Chainsaw Manicurist" 945
"Texas Has a Whorehouse in It" 133
"Texas Wind" 950
"Thad's Journey" 1083
"Thank God" 657
"'Thank God' Chorus Reprise" 1263
"Thank God for the Civil War" 535
"Thank God for the Volunteer Fire Brigade" 588, 727
"Thank God I'm a Country Boy" 37
"Thank God It's Friday" 1747
"Thank Heaven for You" 400
"Thank You" (Bernstein) 1029
"Thank You" (Carmines) 1311
"Thank You" (Choset) 915
"Thank You" (Ngema and Masekela) 1401
"Thank You Doctor" 1046
"Thank You Lord" (Traditional) 736, 1559
"Thank You Lord" (Grant) 1307
"Thank You, San Francisco!" 673
"Thank You So Much, Mrs. Lowsborough-Goodby" 1704
"Thank You, Thank You" 758
"Thank You, Thank You All" 1601
"Thank Your Lucky Stars and Stripes" 1571
"Thanks" 903
"Thanks a Lot" 219
"Thanks to Mom" 463
"Thanks to You" 415
"Thanksgiving" 469
"That-a-Way" 436
"That Ain't Right" (Cole) 18
"That Ain't Right" (Woldin) 934
"That Ain't Right (Cuttin' Contest)" 1631
"That Boy Can Read" 1733
"That Boy's Not Good Enough for You" 223
"That Certain Feeling" 1644
"That Certain Look" 1661
"That Crick Oughta Be Right About Here" 1563
"That Day Will Come" 1177
"That Dirty Book" 395
"That Face" 807
"That Farm Out in Kansas (Down on the Old Kansas Farm)" 1028
"That First Hello" 461
"That Gal Is a High Born Lady" 695
"That Girl" (Haber) 25
"That Girl" (Warrender) 945
"That Girl with the Curls" 636
"That Happy Melody" 509
"That Is What I Give to You" 1467
"That Isn't Done" 1142
"That Kid's Gonna Make It" 89
"That Kind of Neighborhood" 1403
"That Lady from Eng-a-land" 884
"That Latin Lure" 203
"That Little Monosyllable" 316
"That Man" 32
"That Man! I Accuse That Man!" 1723
"That Might (May) Have Satisfied Grandma" 1028
"That Mister Man of Mine" 341
"That Moment Is Now" 1354
"That Old Black Magic" 1138
"That Old Feeling" 73
"That Old Piano Roll" 1491, 1733
"That Quartet" 1092
"That Revue" 1132
"That Smile" 1111
"That Something Special" 492
"That Sound" 225
"That Special Day" 631
"That Special Night" 1310
"That Switched-On Feeling" 542
"That Time of Year" 1519
"That Tired Feeling" 1016
"That Touch" 1358
"That Trip Across the Rhine" 136
"That Was My Way" 830
"That Was Your Life" 1177
"That Woman in the Mirror" 338
"That Woman Is Me" 850
"That'll Be the Day" (Brandon) 1774
"That'll Be the Day" (Holly) 205
"That's A Plenty" 171
"That's a Very Interesting Question" 1689
"That's a Woman" 463
"That's All" 1245
"That's an Egg Cream!" 1442
"That's Business" 1458
"That's Crazy" 1601
"That's Enough" 996
"That's Enough for Me" 997, 1375
"That's Enough for Me Duet" 1375
"That's Entertainment" 73, 212, 348, 1606
"That's Grown Up" 100
"That's Her Life" 1594
"That's Him" 128, 807, 880, 882, 1773, 1809
"That's How I Love the Blues" 132
"That's How It Goes" 1438
"That's How It Is" 1102
"That's How It Starts" 1580
"That's How Rhythm Was Born" 681
"That's How the Whole Thing Began" 1692
"That's How You Get Your Kicks" 638
"That's How You Play Golf" 606
"That's My Girl" 23
"That's Right, Mr. Syph" 292
"That's Right!" 1083
"That's the Beat for Me" 1831
"That's the Kind of Woman" 58
"That's the Problem with Solitaire; You Always Need a King" 941
"That's the Way of the World" 399
"That's the Way They Like It" 372
"That's the Way to Make It Move" 544
"That's What a Friend's For" 1043
"That's What He Did" 912
"That's What I Could Do" 1726
"That's What Living's All About" 1467
"That's What Love Does to Me" 497
"That's What the Bible Say" 194
"That's What the Public Wants" 745
"That's What They Said" 1523
"That's What'll Happen to Me" 225
"That's What's Gonna Happen" 738
"That's What's Happening, Baby" 1774
"That's Where I'm Bound" 249
"That's Why" 1661
"That's Why I Love My Man" 627
"That's Why I Love You" 1704
"That's Why I Love You So" 790
"That's Why I'm Here Tonight" 1385
"That's Your Thing, Baby (It's Not Mine)" 605
"Theater Party" 1548
"Theatre in the Round" 638
"Theatre-Party Ladies" 1414
"Theatre Quadrille" 1440
"Theatre Relationships" 1548
"Theatres" 1661
"The Theatre's in the Dining Room" 415
"Them as Has Gets" 926
"Them Conkheads" 207
"Theme from Peyton Place" 411
"Themselves" 149, 150
"Then Came Jonny" 1831
"Then Frederic" 1270
"Then I'd Be Satisfied with Life" 1643
"Then Let Me the Canakin Clink" 1437
"Then When I Am Rich" 1723
"Then You'll Remember Me" 695
"Theologian Theme" 582
"Theology" 1698
"Therapy" (Dolginoff) 1195
"Therapy" (Larson) 1634
"Therapy — Part 2" 1195
"Therapy — Part 3" 1195
"There" (Peebles) 1737, 1738
"There" (Shire) 300, 1710
"There Ain't No Busy Signals (on the Hot Line to God)" 321
"There Ain't No Flies on Jesus" 1396
"There Ain't No Virgins in Queens" 45
"There Are Girls" 1638
"There Are Happy Endings" 1250
"There Are Moments" 419
"There Are So Many Things That a Vampire Can Do" 1610
"There Are So Many Things That a Vampire Can't Do" 1610
"There Are Such Things" 1096
"There Are Times" 1638
"There Are Times in Life" 1052
"There Are Ways of Gettin' Things Done" 682
"There Are Worse Shows I Could Do" 511
"There Are Worse Things I Could Do" 625
"There Aren't Many Ladies in the Mile End Road" 1774
"There Can Be One and There Can Be Two" 834
"There Comes a Time" (Herman) 987
"There Comes a Time" (Traditional?) 591
"There Goes a Mad Old Man" 48
"There Goes My Gal" 985
"There Goes the Ball Game" 52
"There Goes Time" 74
"There Has to Be a Reason" 8
"There I'd Be" 148
"There Is a Bird" 1327
"There Is a Fountain Filled with Blood" 1484
"There Is a Mystery" 1671
"There Is a Time" (Aznarour) 807
"There Is a Time" (Draesel) 1671
"There Is Always You" 971
"There Is an Old Tradition" 1510
"There Is Life Outside Your Apartment" 77
"There Is No Avenue" 1050
"There Is No Difference" 598
"There Is No Other Way" 1213
"There Is No Tune Like a Show Tune" (aka "Show Tune") 1132, 1218, 1332
"There Is Only One Thing to Be Sure Of" 90
"There Is Power in the Blood" 1484
"There Is Room" 1052
"There Is That in Me" 903
"There It Is Again" 902
"There Must Be Something More" 1671
"There Never Was a Baby Like My Baby" 428
"There Now. That's Better" 439
"There Once Was a King (The Song of the Rose)" 717
"There She Goes" (Larson and Rubens) 219
"There She Goes" (Margoshes) 474
"There She Is" 398
"There Was a Day" 1789
"There Was a Girl" 222
"There Was a Hen" 860
"There Was a Knight, Once" 941
"There Was a Place" 1201
"There Was a Time" 882
"There Was a Woman" 1443
"There Was Once a Little Village" 317
"There Where the Young Men Go" 360
"There Will Be a Miracle" 1422
"There Will Never Be Another You" 1091
"There Won't Be Trumpets" 1027
"There You Are" 725, 1097
"There You Go Again" (Ander, et al.) 175
"There You Go Again" (Britton) 575
"There'll Always Be an England" 1750
"There'll Be a Hot Time in the Old Town Tonight" 1198
"There'll Be a Tomorrow" 1691
"There'll Be England Again" 1109
"There'll Be Some Changes Made" 382
"There's a Bagel on the Piano" 1251
"There's a Big Job Waiting for You" 1483
"There's a Broken Heart for Every Light on Broadway" 577
"There's a Doctor" 1655
"There's a Girl" (Besdyan) 80
"There's a Girl" (Wittman and Shaiman) 943
"There's a Girl in the Heart of Wheeling, West Virginia" 672
"There's a Grand Flag Flyin'" 507
"There's a Land" 1404
"There's a Look to Him" 333
"There's a Man" 1672
"There's a New Place" 255
"There's a Place Called Omaha, Nebraska" 672
"There's a Price" 3
"There's a Rainbow at the End" 1147
"There's a Shout" 1404
"There's a War Going On" 1184
"There's a War in Mississippi" 470
"There's a Woman" 14
"There's Always a Woman" 1491
"There's Always Someone Who'll Tell You 'No'" 752
"There's Always Something Fishy About the French" 317
"There's Another World" 308

"There's Art in My Revenge" 910
"There's Goin' to Be a Wedding" 1154
"There's Gonna Be a Commission" 655
"There's Good News Tonight" 1232
"There's Got to Be Love" 985
"There's Gotta Be a Villain" 867
"There's Gotta Be Something Better Than This" 886
"There's Love in the Country" 716
"There's No Business Like Show Business" 428
"There's No Room for People Anymore" 277
"There's No Such Thing" 1761
"There's Nothing Illegal About It" 1723
"There's Nothing Left to Give Away" 1274
"There's Nothing Like a Clean Room to Sweep You Off Your Feet" 699
"There's Nothing Like a Spree" 1131
"There's Nothing Like It" 300
"There's Nothing New Under the Sun" 831
"There's Only One Way to End Your Prayers" 1159
"There's Only So Much I Can Give" 989
"There's Something Special" 959
"There's Something Worse Than Living Alone" 949
"There's the Moon" 246
"There's Trouble in His Brain" 1121
"These Acres" 1594
"These Are the Corridors of Power" 673
"These Are the Jokes" 492
"These Are Worth Fighting For" 232, 1163
"These Boots Are Made for Walkin'" 1450
"These Bullets Are Freedom" 1736
"These Charming People" 1644
"These Children Are in Love" 1111
"These Foolish Things (Remind Me of You)" 181, 681, 1210, 1750
"These Four Walls" 1419
"These Girls Never Saw a Spirit" 331
"These Hands" 541
"These Southern States That I Love" 376
"These Things I Know Are True" 1754
"These Were the Faces" 386
"They" (Larimer and Keyes) 230
"They" (Richardson) 926
"They 4-F'd My Billy" 844
"They All Fall in Love" 1823
"They Aren't There" 1759, 1761
"They Call Me the Virgin Mary" 823
"They Can't Take That Away from Me" 1210, 1656
"They Didn't Ask" 1638
"They Didn't Believe Me" 382, 883
"They Die" 444
"They Don't Have To" 1829
"They Don't Make 'Em Like That Anymore" 1611
"They Don't Write 'Em Like That Anymore" 746
"They Don't Write Songs Like That Anymore" 61
"They Had to Change" 484
"They Just Got Married" 1036, 1049
"They Keep Coming" 400
"They Left Me" 752
"They Lost the Revolution" 1113
"They Say" (Bock) 1381
"They Say" (Oster) 385
"They That Buildeth a Wall Against Man" 871
"They Were My Pals" 304
"They Were You" 478
"They'll Say I've Been Dreaming" 962
"They'll Tell You Everything" 395
"They're All Cowgirls to Me" 323
"They're Always Entertaining" 1160
"They're Either Too Young or Too Old" 348, 1750, 1764
"They're Going Sailing" 1338
"They're Here" (Mayer) 362
"They're Here" (Siegel) 44
"They're Here" (Ward) 1374
"They're Killing the Pope" 59
"They've Got to Complain" 1108
"They've Gotcha on the Hutska" 874
"They've Put Up a New Lampost" 44
"They've Taken My Man Away" 1316
"The Thief" 277
"Thief in the Night" 1493
"The Thief of Cups Looks to Death as Refuge" 1592
"The Thief's Statement" 1422
"Thievery!" (Bimko) 1715
"Thievery!" (Unknown) 1407
"A Thimbleful of Believin'" 1412
"Thin" 770
"A Thing Like This" 1095, 1811
"The Thing That Johnny Did" 1142
"Things Ain't as Nice" 985
"Things Are Going Nicely" 1767
"Things Are Going Well Today" 1448
"Things Are Most Mysterious" 1057
"Things Change, Jo" 941
"Things Get Broken" 1029
"Things Have Never Been Better" 215
"Things I Can't Forget" 157
"Things I Didn't Know I Loved" 1133
"Things Look Different" 770
"Things Starting to Grow Again" 1231
"The Things That Are Done by a Don" 1393
"Things We've Collected" 1702
"Things Were Much Better in the Past" 980
"Things Were Out" 1678
"Things Will Be Different" 658
"Things Will Never Be the Same" 1321
"Things with Wheels" 1784
"The Thingummybob" 1750
"Think About Tomorrow" 424
"Think Big" 830
"Think Mink" 291
"Think of Me" 919
"Think Positive" 54
"Thinkers and Drinkers" 206
"Thinking About You" 1375
"Thinking of You" (Carmines) 920
"Thinking of You" (Donaldson) 955
"Thinking of You" (Ruby) 672, 692
"Thinking the Impossible" 1523
"Thinking the Unthinkable" 1335
"Third Avenue" 507
"Third Avenue El" 371, 942
"Third Ballad Interlude" 1229
"The Third Degree of Love" 505
"Third Interlude" 299
"The Third Lady" 1153
"Thirteen" 280
"1348" 366
"13 Meschanskaia Lane" 114
"The Thirties" 149, 150
"Thirties" 1451
"30 Miles from the Banks of the Ohio" 727
"Thirty Little Aspirins" 1228
"Thirty Miles from the Banks of the Ohio" 588
"Thirty Odd Years" 130
"Thirty Seconds" 991
"The Thirty-Third President" 223
"This Amazing London Town" 1381
"This Angel's Arrivin'" 255
"This Bitter Earth" 382, 383
"This Bright Morning" 990
"This Can't Be Love" 201, 382
"This City Is a Kisser" 869
"This Could Be the End" 1219
"This Could Be the Start of Something Big" 1245
"This Darkness" 1392
"This Darling Industry" 599
"This Dawn" 258, 259
"This Decadent Age" 1780
"This Empty Place" 83
"This Funny World" 824
"This Guy's in Love with You" 83
"This Had Better Come to a Stop" 1019
"This Heat" 1083
"This House" 733
"This House Is Built" 1631
"This House Where We Live" 1700
"This Is a Changing World" 1170
"This Is a Dollar Bill" 745
"This Is a Great Country" 210
"This Is a Real, Slow Drag" 1077
"This Is a Very Special Day" 1064
"This Is About Food" 1505
"This Is All I Ask" 1363
"This Is All Very New to Me" 428
"This Is England" 1265
"This Is How It Goes" 413
"This Is How It Is" 1562
"This Is How the World Was Made" 384
"This Is How the World Will End" 384
"This Is Indeed My Lucky Day" 1668
"This Is It" 299, 348
"This Is Like the Dress I Never Had" 1601
"This Is Love" 858
"This Is My House" 743
"This Is My Night To Howl" 538
"This Is My Promise" 1327
"This Is My Song" 1582, 1677
"This Is New York" 1430, 1431
"This Is Nice" 1031
"This Is Norina?" 1146
"This Is Not the End" (Forrest) 1219
"This Is Not the End" (Ward) 14
"This Is Not the Promised Land" 257
"This Is Not What I Had Planned" 1135
"This Is One River I Can't Cross" 1428
"This Is Only the Beginning" 662
"This Is Our World" 1151
"This Is Paradise" 877
"This Is the Day" (Freitas) 379
"This Is the Day" (Friedman) 1441
"This Is the End" 1201
"This Is the Girl for Me" 76
"This Is the Gypsy Life!" 1700
"This Is the Life" (Besoyan) 766
"This Is the Life" (Strouse) 237, 603
"This Is the Life for Me" 1811
"This Is the Man" 1671
"This Is the Moment" 1623
"This Is the Premier" 1276
"This Is the Solution" 71
"This Is the Song That We Sing" 273
"This Is the Way I Do" 657
"This Is the World" 1325
"This Is What I Do When I'm Angry" 1384
"This Is What I Got for Not Listening to My Mother" 1385
"This Is Where I Belong" 372
"This Is Where We Met" 86
"This Is Your Day!" 1046
"This Is Your Year 1976" 1035
"This Isn't a Gentlemen's War Anymore" 569
"This Isn't How I Imagined a Trial to Be" 643
"This Isn't Tomorrow" 626
"This Job Is for the Birds" 198
"This Life's the Right One for Me" 216
"This Little Light" 1388
"This Lullabye Is for You" 110
"This Moment" 1035
"This Moment Is Mine" 1298
"This Must Be the End" 1219
"This New Identity" 278
"This New World" 1719
"This Night" 749
"This Old Guitar" 37
"This Old Ship" 120
"This One Thing I'll Do" 1412
"This One's for Me" 1558
"This Plum Is Too Ripe" 478
"This Side of the Tracks" 627
"This Song's for You" 1747
"This State of Affairs" 80
"This Time Next Year" 1661
"This Time Tomorrow" 100
"This Train" 740
"This Tuxedo Is Mine!" 1254
"This Used to Be a Nice, Normal Neighborhood" 673
"This Used to Be an Old Irish Neighborhood" 673
"This War Gets Old" 386
"This Was the War, What Did It Do for Me and You? ... Didn't It, Did It?" 569
"This Was the Week That Wasn't" 1394
"This Way Out" 1574
"This Wide Woods" 1513
"This Will Be Our Life" 277
"This World" (Bernstein) 244
"This World" (Friedman) 1038
"This Year of Disgrace" 1142
"Tho' I Had Never Meant to Tell You" 779
"Thor" 381
"Those ABC's" 856
"Those Birds Flying Above Us" 363
"Those Canaan Days" 833
"Those Endearing Young Charms" 775
"Those Magic Changes" 625
"Those Tassels on Her Boots" 695
"Those Were the Days" (Hold) 1603
"Those Were the Days" (Oddie) 241
"Those Were the Days" (Raskin) 1450, 1619
"Those Were the Days" (Strouse) 237
"Those Who Speak" 1358
"Those Who Want the Best" 665
"Those You've Known" 1515
"Thou, Julia, Thou Hast Metamorphosed Me" 1689
"Thou, Proteus, Thou Has Metamorphosed Me" 1689
"Thou Shalt Not Be Afraid" 386
"Thou Venerable Head" 1071
"Though I'm a Little Angel" 1007
"A Thought Occurs" 424
"Thoughteasy" 858
"Thoughts" (Alford) 1620
"Thoughts" (Dowell) 1594
"Thoughts by a River" 1274
"A Thousand and One Nights" 66
"A Thousand Hands" 1052
"A Thousand Kisses" 1569
"A Thousand Miles Away" 1434
"A Thousand Summer Nights" 78
"Thousand, Thousand" 1004
"Thread the Needle" 1323
"The Threads Remain" 1503
"Three-Bedroom House" 106
"Three B's" 132
"The Three Bells" 1575
"Three Cans of Film" 388
"Three Cheers for Yankee Doodle!" 604
"Three Cigarettes in an Ashtray" 39
"Three Coins in the Fountain" 527, 1546
"Three Cowards Craven" 1780
"Three Dance Classes" 222
"Three Doctors' Wives" 1309
"The Three Eiffels" 277
"The Three Faces of Sam" 472
"Three Fierce Men" 1331
"¾ for Three" 690
"Three Friends" 300
"3 Girls, 6 Legs" 1693

"The Three Good Deeds" 1822
"Three Graces" 805
"'Three Guys Naked from the Waist Down' Theme" 1622
"Three Handsome Young Princes Have Been Here" 834
"The Three Horsemen of the Metropolis" 1274
"Three Impressions" 1192
"Three in a Hospital Room" 1228
"Three Jolly Pigeons" 805
"Three Latin Tales" 897
"Three Lazzi" 583
"Three-Letter Word" 573
"The Three Little Fishes" 672
"Three Little Fishes" 1571
"Three Little Maids" 323
"Three Little Maids from Broadway Town" 622
"Three Little Queens of the Silver Screen" 908
"Three Little Sailors (Los Marineritos)" 488
"Three Little Words" 672
"Three Loves" 1448
"Three Men on a Date" 132
"Three Menu Songs" 393, 394
"Three Midrash" 647
"The Three Mo' Way" 1623
"Three Movements and a Coda" 1734, 1735
"Three Phases of Eve" 700
"Three Poems" 1222
"Three Postcards" 1624
"¾ Drag" 676
"Three Seconds" 765
"Three Serving Wenches" 1316
"The Three Sisters Who Are Not Sisters (A Murder Mystery)" 571
"Three Songs to the One Burden" 707
"Three Steps Forward" 1201
"Three Sunny Rooms" 1328
"30/90" 1634
"Three to the Bar" 1142
"Three Truths" 1200
"The Three-Way" 837
"Threesome" (Hoffman) 1758, 1759, 1761
"Threesome" (Weinberg) 1600
"Thrice Fairer" 1569
"The Thrill Is Gone" 777
"Thrill of Adventure" 1303
"The Thrill of First Love" 1019
"The Thrill of the Chase" 297
"Throttle Throttlebottom" 912
"Through a Keyhole" 69
"Through All the Employments of Life" 117
"Through the Mountain" 503
"Through the Years" 221
"Throw It Out" 1121
"Throw It Out the Window" 1016
"Throw Out the Lifeline" 587
"Throw Out the Yellow Journalists ..." 729
"Throw the Egg" 1691
"Throw the House Out the Window" 379
"Throwdown in Windsor" 950
"Thru You" 1800
"Thursday" 1222
"Thus Weary of the World" 1569
"Thy Neighbor and Thy Shelter" 1276
"Ti Moune" 1191
"Tick Behind Tock" 1252
"Tick-Tock" 261
"The Ticker" 1113
"Ticker Tape" 301
"Tickle Me" 1036, 1049, 1334
"Tickles" 1635
"Tico-Tico" 924, 1571
"Ties" 261
"Tiger" 529
"Tiger Lady" 386
"Tiger Rag" 457, 813
"Tiger Rag Blues" 1636
"Tiger, Tiger" 1048
"Tiger Woods" 606
"A Tight-Knit Family" 997, 1019
"Til Death Do They Part" 633
"'Til Our Good Luck Comes Along" 408
"'Til the End of Time" 78
"Tilibim" 1647
"Till I Met You" 403
"Till I'm Gone" 471
"Till the Bird Sings" 1460
"Till the Clouds Roll By" 883
"Till Tomorrow" 575
"Tiller Routine" 1160
"Tim Vander Beek" 1299
"Timbuctoo" 672
"Time" (Brown) 835
"Time" (Douglass) 121
"Time" (Finn) 1121
"Time After Time" 1210, 1546
"Time and Music" 1121
"Time and the Wind" 1638
"Time and Tide" (Kessler) 1161
"Time and Tide" (Rosenthal) 1692
"Time and Time Again" (Kennon) 1637
"Time and Time Again" (Powell) 1125
"Time and Time Again" (Shire) 1400
"Time Brings About a Change" 400
"Time Flies" 858
"Time for Another Affair" 1431
"Time Goes By" 1451
"Time Goes Faster" 1380
"The Time Has Come" 938
"Time Heals Everything" 818
"Time Is a Travellin' Show" 1035
"The Time Is Come" 486
"The Time Is Now" 1423
"Time Marches On" 716
"The Time of My Life" 1393
"The Time of the Cuckold" 616
"Time on Our Side" 781
"Time Out! Did I Just Hear What I Heard?" 673
"Time Passes" (Courts) 828
"Time Passes" (Finn) 1375
"Time Passes So Quickly" 1349
"Time Passing" 697
"Time Stands Still in Truro" 1287
"Time to Call It Quits" 638
"Time to Find Something to Do" 1787
"Time to Go" 183
"Time to Go Home" (Roberts) 1613
"Time to Go Home" (Vitale) 1030
"Time to Let Go" 1320, 1321
"Time to Live" 1361
"Time to Make a Drawing" 845
"Time to Prepare for Donna Cinzia" 1771
"Time to Say Goodnight" 1142
"Time to Think of Myself" 996
"Time to Wake Up" 765
"Time Was" 857
"Time We Talked" 693
"Time Will Be" 822
"Time, You Old Gypsy Man" 861, 1493
"Timeless" 864
"Timeline" 830
"Times Divine" 786
"Times Have Changed" 1743
"Times Have Changed (Los Tiempos Han Cambiado)" 488
"Times Like This" 973
"Times Square Ballet" 1185, 1186
"The Times They Are A-Changing (A'Changin')" 265, 1556
"Timid Frieda (Les Timides)" 792
"Timing and Lighting" 260
"Tin Can Incantation" 1460
"Tin Cap" 655
"Tina, My Daughter" 1386
"Tina Seeks Solace" 1301
"Tina's Finest Hour" 1301
"Tina's Mother" 1386
"Tinsel" 556, 557, 558
"Tinseltown Tattletale" 1584
"Tiny International Empire" 416
"Tiny Light" 1679
"Tiny Little Pieces" 1479
"Tiny Room" 954
"Tiny, the Champion" 1004
"Tiny Town" 415
"Tiny's Entrance" 1229
"Tiny's Song" 1229
"Tip-Toes" 1644
"Tippecanoe and Tyler, Too" 722
"Tippity Top" 416
"Tippy's Immolation" 700
"Tips" 1317
"Tips from Tina" 1301
"Tired Heroes" 401
"'Tis a Far, Far Better Thing I Do" 1830
"'Tis of Thee" 1331
"'Tis the Season" 1743
"'Tis Time" 419
"'Tis Woman That Seduces All Mankind" 117
"Titania's Philosophy" 80
"Titanic Panic" 1469
"Tite Street" 360
"Tither" 1788
"The Title" 506
"T,morra, T,morra" 669
"T.N.D.P.W.A.M." 1317
"To a Skylark" 1443
"To a Small Degree" 1752
"To America I Sailed on a Ship Called Hunger" 1723
"To an Isle in the Water" 707
"To Anacreon in Heaven" 695
"To Augusta" 419
"To Bath Derry-O" 33
"To Be a Captain" 1508
"To Be at Sea" 873
"To Be King" 34
"To Be Loved" 790
"To Be Loved for Who I Am" 470
"To Be or Not to Be" 272
"To Belgrade!" 609
"To Belong" 60, 1605
"To Build Tomorrow" 1771
"To Bury Caesar" 241
"To Catch a King" 864
"To Cheerfulness Inclining (Work Song)" 439
"To Conquer the Land" 1204
"To Dance Is to Fly" 1538
"To Dream or Not to Dream" 1780
"To Err Is Human" 547
"To Feel So Needed" 1082
"To Find True Love" 1480
"To Get It Off My Chest" 1011
"To Harriet" 1443
"To Have a Child" 114
"To Health" 874
"To Hell with It, I'm Going to Have Fun" 1192
"To Jane" 1443
"To Love Again" 61
"To Love and Be Loved" 1210
"To Love Is to Live" 109
"To Love Is to Serve" 1002
"To Love Somebody" 965
"To Model" 206
"To My Dear and Loving Husband" 972
"To My Wife" 1714
"To Ochun" 1402
"To Play This Part" 1386
"To Please the Woman in Me" 288
"To P.O." 729
"To Poe: Over the Planet, Air Albany-Baltimore" 729
"To Russia with Love" 1255
"To Sing" 1499
"To Sir, with Love" 115, 1450
"To Soothe the Savage Beast" 277
"To Tell the Truth" (Caruso and Levine) 616
"To Tell the Truth" (Ellstein) 1821
"To the Dead of Family Wars" 1384
"To the Dentist" 535
"To the Ends of the Earth" 1483
"To the Harbormaster" 1133
"To the Ladies" 301
"To the People of England" 1443
"To Thirst and Find No Fill" 1443
"To Touch the Sky" 1504
"To Whit—To Whoo" 652
"To Whom It May Concern" 1650
"To Whom It May Concern Me" 1689
"To Win a Prince" 1679
"To Wit" 461
"To Write This Letter" 1789
"To You I Gave My All" 1635
"To Your Health" 819
"The Toad's Lament" 676
"Toast of the Town" 1476
"Toast to Harlem" 1373
"Today" (Fremont) 1258
"Today" (Roullier) 1354
"Today I Found Me" 1538
"Today I Met the Boy I'm Gonna Marry" 1551
"Today I Sing the Blues" 1623
"Today I'm Smiling Rainbows" 599
"Today Is Love" 1316
"Today Is on Me" 25
"Today Is the First Day of the Rest of My Life" 1524
"Today Will Be" 493, 1537
"Today's Just Yesterday's Tomorrow" 143
"Today's the Day" 74
"Together" (Engeran) 1151
"Together" (Moritz) 507
"Together" (Moskowitz) 819
"Together" (Styne) 1717
"Together as One" 1512
"Together Forever" 733, 926
"Together So Long" 1333
"Togetherness" 492
"'Toinette" 1652
"Token Gesture" 350, 1273
"Tokyo, Mon Amour" 50, 556
"Toll Basket" 326
"Tolling Early in the Morning" 947
"Tom" 683
"Tom and Huck's Argument" 408
"Tom Tom Toddle (Tom, Tom, Toddle)" 1028
"Tommy" 136
"Tommy Can You Hear Me?" 1655
"Tommy's Holiday Camp" 1655
"Tomorrow" (Ekstrom) 391
"Tomorrow" (Moritz) 507
"Tomorrow" (Raniello) 1089
"Tomorrow" (Strouse) 237
"Tomorrow Is Here" 1254
"Tomorrow Is Saint Valentine's Day" 1437
"Tomorrow Is the First Day of the Rest of My Life" 1396
"Tomorrow Night" 1258
"The Tomorrow Waltz" 1264
"Tomorrow When the World Comes Crashing Down Around Our Ears" 714
"Tomorrow's Woman" 641
"Tone Deaf" 610
"Tonight" 911
"Tonight I Am Happy" 206
"Tonight Is the Night" 1618
"Tonight Was Like the First Night" 444
"Tonight Will Be Fine" 1471
"Tonight You Belong to Me" 1575
"Tonight You Dance with Me" 1379
"Tonight You See My Face" 253
"Tonight's the Flight" 1468
"Tonight's the Night" (Brandon) 291
"Tonight's the Night" (Savage) 1097
"Tonite Will Be Fine" 963
"Tony 'n' Cleo" 1245
"The Tony Award Song" 1645
"Tony Sarg" 635
"Too Darn Hot" 212
"Too Fat to Fit" 1245
"Too Good" 461
"Too Hot to Handel" 1263
"Too Many Questions" 472
"Too Many Sondheims" 511
"Too Many Women in My Life" 656
"Too Much Botox" 1128
"Too Much Money Blues" 456
"The Too Much Motet" 65
"Too Old" 1751
"Too Old for Love" 1594
"Too Plump for Prom Night" 1298
"Too-Ra-Loo-Ra-Loo-Ra" 775
"Too Tired to Love" 869
"Too Young" 1594
"Tool for You" 424
"Toot Toot Tootsie! (Goodbye)" 829, 993
"Toothloose in Rome" 1447
"Top o' Silo" 926
"Top of the List" 1318
"Top Secret Personal Beeswax" 845
"Torch #1" 1763

"Torch #2" 1763
"Torch #3" 1763
"The Torch Song" 783
"Torching My Way Through Life" 82
"Tormented" 379
"Toro Mata" 262
"Torture" (Clifton) 203
"Torture" (Csontos) 1469
"Torture Chamber" 1293
"Totally Fucked" 1515
"Touch and Go" 388
"Touch But My Lips" 1568
"Touch Kiss" 869
"Touch Me" 1398, 1515
"Touch My Hand" 1303
"Touch of Paris" 1265
"Touch the Earth" 780
"Touch'd by Romance" 507
"Touche's Salon" 926
"Tough Cookies" 1135
"Tough Dogs" 396
"Tough to Be a Fairy" 1772
"A Tough Town" 89, 1202
"Tour de Four" 1661
"A Tour of the World" 1276
"A Tour of Washington" 1276
"Tourist Madrigal" 1539
"Les Tourments de la Bete" 123
"Tout le Monde" 345
"Tower of Babble" 595
"The Town Clerk's Views" 135
"Town Without Pity" 1551
"Toy Bird" 96
"Toyland" 1643
"Toymaker" 253
"Tra Gog Vo In Dein Whole (I Will Not Tell a Soul)" 1384
"Tra-La-La" 285
"The Track" 1407
"Traditional Seder" 1341
"Trafalgar Square" 1091
"Traffic Island" 241
"The Tragedy of Miss Potato Sack" 1584
"A Tragic Queen" 550
"The Tragicale Historie of Queen Isaboo II" 735
"The Tragique Kingdom" 610
"The Train" (Harris) 544
"The Train" (Pen) 114
"Train" 464
"Train 1" 427
"Le Train du Ciel (The Heaven Train)" 1532
"Train Song" 960
"Train to Johannesburg" 128
"Train Walking" 544
"Trains and Boats and Planes" 83
"Trains or Me" 544
"Tramp! Tramp! Tramp!" 1570
"Tran-Quil" 1066
"The Tranquil Boxwood" 1326
"Transfiguration of Gerome" 1710
"Transformation" 1361
"The Transformation" 1362
"The Transformer" 506
"Transformer Scene" 1616
"Transition" 1635
"Transplant" (Botwin) 1058
"Transplant" (Wells) 171
"Transportation" 1042
"The Trap" 1254
"Trapped" 1072
"Trash" 1
"Trashin' and Tourin'" 45
"The Trashy Effeminate Hoodlum" 730
"Travel" 1524
"Travel Light" 754
"Travelin' Blues" 1373
"Travelin' Light" 1493
"Travelin' Man" 869
"Traveling" 1752
"Travellin' On" 466
"Travelling First Class Style" 1821
"Travelling Song" 1636
"Treasure to Bury" 710
"Trebetherick" 135
"Treble" 616
"The Tree" (Friedman) 1038
"The Tree" (Silverman) 50, 126
"The Tree and the Sun" 1302
"Tree-House Scene" 926
"The Tree Song" 333
"The Trees and the Ax" 11
"The Trees in the Mountains Are Cold and Bare" 1563
"Trench Coat" 858
"Trendell Terry" 1228
"The Trial" (Lunden) 1190
"The Trial" (Meyers) 65
"Trial 1" 427
"Trial 2/Prison" 427
"The Trial of Throttlebottom" 912
"The Trial of Wintergreen" 912
"The Trials of Tom" 1303
"Triangle Song" 64
"Tribes" 663
"Tribute" 919
"A Tribute" 1176
"The Tribute" 350, 542
"Tricephalous You" 1646
"Trick of Fate" 929
"Trick or Treat" 248
"Tricks" 396
"Tricks of the Trade" 791
"Trilogy" 1318
"Trina and Mendel's House" 473
"Trina's Song" 997, 1019
"Trinity" (Bingham) 59
"Trinity" (Stornaiuolo) 1072
"Trinity's Theme" 278
"Trink's Narration" 1522
"Trio" (Beeson) 947
"Trio" (Kaplan) 1485
"Trio" (Pottle) 1040
"Trio" (Rauch) 1822
"Trio" (Strouse) 1131
"Trio (Case Closed)" 1831
"Trio Con Brio" 556, 1661
"Trio for Four" 1547
"Trio for Three Buddies" 385
"Trio II" 1485
"Trip" (Friedman) 208
"Trip" (Strouse) 1473
"Trip Tick Talking Blues" 605
"Tripartite Intervention and the Atami House Conspiracy" 889
"Tripe Seller's Lament" 655
"Triple Tango" 1574
"Triplets" 348, 1606
"Tripping" 1659
"Tristan and Isolated" 50
"The Triumph of Toad" 1784
"Trixie True, Teen Detective" 1668
"Trixie's on the Case!" 1668
"Les Trois Cloches" 1256, 1257
"The Trolley Song" 746
"Trolls" 1669
"Trombones Ensemble" 592
"Tropical Island Breezes" 633
"Tropical Storm" 1139
"Troubador" 535
"The Troubadour" 1671
"Troubadour of the Lord" 1671
"Trouble" 450
"Trouble in Mind" 553, 1373
"Trouble in Tahiti" 911
"Trouble Is a Man" 23
"Trouble Man" 128
"The Trouble with Geraniums" 1503
"The Trouble with Me" 235
"Trouble with Me" 54
"The Trouble with Miss Manderson" 1447
"Troubled Lady" 1755
"Troubled Waters" 1559
"The Troubles of the World" 1749
"Il Trovatore" 1543
"Trowl the Bowl" 1446
"Troyerik Zayn Darf Men Nit (Why Be Sad?)" 604
"Truck Stop" 16
"The Truckdriver" 1206
"Truckdrivers" 1813
"Truckin'" 165
"The Trucks" 971
"True Blue Lou" 73
"True Confessions" (Goggin) 1158
"True Confessions" (Silver) 564
"True Love" 39, 1479
"True Love at the Star-Lite Tonight" 499
"True Love's Hand" 1638
"The True Tale of Pocahontas" 143
"True to Me" 444
"True Value" 1777
"Truly My Soul" 1650
"Trumpeter, Blow Your Golden Horn" 1166, 1167
"Trust Me Tango" 1512
"Trust No One" 712
"Trust the Wind" 929
"Trust Your Heart" 995
"The Truth About a Big Fish Story" 1649
"The Truth About Camille" 277
"Truth and Consequences" 1218
"Truth and Lies (Dialectic Inaction!)" 170
"Truth Cannot Be Treason" 1007
"Try (Just a Little Bit Harder)" 115, 965
"Try a Little Harder" 164
"Try a Trio" 1517
"Try Makin' Peace" 1601
"Try Me" 865
"Try Not to Need Her" 338
"Try the Sky" 869
"Try to Make the Best of It" 980
"Try to Remember" 478, 1451
"Try Try Again" (Botwin, et al.) 1058
"Try Try Again" (Fuller) 1511
"Try, Try, Try" 550
"Trying Hard" 1620
"Trying to Get Back on My Feet Again" 1333
"Tschaikowsky" 882
"Tsin" 637
"Tsivye's Song" 1822
"Tsong Gou" 1020
"Tsuris" 915
"Tu Voz" 262
"Tulip Print Waltz" 690
"A Tulip Told a Tale" 672
"Tulip Told a Tale" 304
"Tumbling" 1028
"Tunbridge Wells" 285
"Tune in My Heart" 284
"Tune in Tomorrow" 313
"Tune of the Hickory Stick" 1743
"Tune to Take Away" 1431
"Tuned-Out" 19
"Tupapau" 563
"Turkey Baster Baby" 1600
"Turn Around" 1319
"Turn Back, O Man" 595
"Turn Her Out" 975
"Turn It Around" 321
"The Turn My Life Is Taking" 582
"The Turn-On Song" 350
"Turn Tail and Run!" 92
"Turn the Tide" 102
"Turn to Him" 1232
"Turn to Me" 328
"Turn, Turn, Turn (To Everything There Is a Season)" 1556
"Turn Up the Spotlight" 1155, 1157
"Turned Off to Turning On" 706
"Turoola" 1566
"Turtle Blues" 965
"Turtle Song" 1733
"The Turtle Thus with Plaintive Crying" 117
"Tutti" 935
"TUU" 1073
"Tuxedo Junction" 35
"T.V. Nik" 986
"TV Sidelights on the March on Washington" 1765
"Twanger!" 1679
"Tweedle Dee" (Scott) 1575
"Tweedle Dee" (Wilson) 790
"Tweedledee for President" 912
"Tweedledum and Tweedledee" 27
"'Tween a Rock an' a Hard Place" 503
"Twelve Children" 375
"The Twelve Days After Christmas" 1527
"Twelve Days of Christmas" 1162
"Twelve Gates" 592
"Twelve O'Clock Song" 1440
"12:30" 411
"The Twenties Are Here to Stay" 1172
"The Twentieth Century" 143
"Twentieth Century Blues" 751
"Twentieth Reunion" 161, 162, 163, 164
"20 Fans" 133
"28 Men" 1399
"Twenty-Eight Men" 903
"The 25th Annual Putnam County Spelling Bee" 1680
"25 Points" 1635
"25 Years" 497
"Twenty-five Miles" 159
"Twenty-Four Hours from This Moment" 752
"24 Hours from Tulsa" 83
"Twenty-Four Hours of Lovin'" 133
"$29.50" 1162
"22 Rue Danou" 1052
"Twenty Years" (Carmines) 971
"Twenty Years" (Harte) 903
"Twenty Years from Now" 1815
"Twice as Nice" 179
"Twice on Matinee Days" 1683
"Twilight" (Berg) 1303
"Twilight" (Johnston) 250
"Twilight Zone" 504
"Twinkle Little Star" 1085
"Twinkle, Twinkle Little Star" 230
"Twinkling Eyes" 505
"Twins" 837
"T-w-i-n-s" 1399
"Twist and Shout" 411
"A Twist of Fate" 89
"Twist, Shimmy and Shake" 1615
"Two-a-Day" 818
"Two Against the World" 990
"Two Asian Ladies" 143
"Two Bags" 1058
"2 × 2" 1237
"Two by Two" 1481
"2 × 2 = Schultz (A Famous Trial in Jerusalem)" 1701
"Two Cents Worth of Plain" 942
"Two Cigarettes for One" 1765
"Two Days Later" 742
"Two Different Worlds" 929
"Two Doves" 586
"Two Eyes" 1438
"Two-Faced Woman" 1606
"Two Fairy Tales" 1027
"Two Falls to a Finish" 701
"Two for a Quarter, Three for a Dime" 359
"Two for the Road" 824
"Two for the Telephone" 1152
"Two-Four-Four" 338
"Two French Grenadiers" 1416
"Two Gentlemen of Verona" 1689
"The Two Graces" 1574
"Two Grown-Up People at Play" 357
"Two Heads" 1367
"Two Hearts" 1111
"Two If By Sea, I Think" 1691
"Two Is Company" 746
"Two Is What It's All About" 1683
"Two Jazz Poems" 1735
"Two Keys" 539
"Two Kinsman" 1109
"Two Ladies in De Shade of the Banana Tree" 715
"Two Little Angels" 1311
"Two Little Bits of Metal" 1601
"Two Little Pussycats" 1420
"Two Lonely Guys" 465
"Two Lovers" 1025
"Two Loves" 1714
"Two Men" 419
"The Two Miss Browns" 1142
"Two Nobodies in New York" 1645
"The Two-Note Rag" 1683
"Two of a Kind" (Lippa) 1778
"Two of a Kind" (Paul) 1361, 1362
"Two of Everything" 1692
"Two of Me" 1582
"Two of Us" 1677
"The Two of Us" 81
"Two Part Invention in D Minor" 1439
"Two People" 510
"Two Pieces of Bread" 1683
"Two Points of View" 1683
"Two Quintets" 947
"The Two Robertas" 773
"Two Should Be Harmonious" 786
"Two Sleepy People" 18
"Two Steps Forward" 2
"Two Strangers" 564, 758
"Two Strings to a Bow" 851
"Two Things" 1683
"2000 Miles" 605
"Two to Tango" 1683
"(212)" 1693
"Two Villagers" 1458
"Two Way Play" 1447
"Two Weeks" 57

"Two Young People in Love" 1771
"Two's a Nice Number" 1683
"Tyburn Jig" 979
"Tyger, Tyger" 304
"Tyler My Boy" 149, 150
"Typical American Consumer" 991
"Typical New Yorkers" 1290
"Tyrone's Rap" 474
"Tzi Tsu Zein Ich Zein Du? (Why Do I Have To Be Here?)" 492

"U Jehova: Poppie Uzubale" 1284
"U Name This One" 1735
"Ugly Boy" 106
"Ugly Chile" 1373
"Uh-Huh" 1048
"Uh-Oh" 60
"The Uh Oh Could It Be That I'm an Oh No Tango" 919
"Ulterior Motive" 379
"Ulysses' Soliloquy" 600
"Umbrella Stand" 1813
"Un Bon Mouvement" 436
"Un Canadian Errant" 963
"Un, Dieux, Trois" 1652
"The 'Un' Song" 1777
"Unaccustomed As I Am" 622
"Unanswered Questions" 497
"Unbelievable" 23
"The Unbeliever" 165
"Unchained Melody" 55
"The Uncle Bergie Evans Show" 1261
"Uncle Billy" 690
"Uncle Billy's Travellin' Family Show" 1366
"The Uncle Dan Song" 1219
"The Uncle Huck-a-Buck Song" 207
"Uncle Sam Rag" 886
"Uncle Sam Wants Who?" 556
"Uncrowned Queen of California" 948
"Undecided" 527
"Under a Bridge at Night (Sous le Ponts de Paris)" 1641
"Under a Tree" 870
"Under My Wing" 154
"Under Paris Skies (Sous le Ciel de Paris)" 1256, 1257
"Under Secretary" 1276
"Under Separate Cover" 296
"Under the Bamboo Tree" 165, 171
"Under the Bridge" 1700
"Under the Greenwood Tree" 1568, 1569
"Under the Spotlight" 1337
"Under the Sun" 835
"Under the Tree" 1451
"Under the Wonder" 820
"Underneath a Dragon Moon" 1477
"Underneath the Arches" 1482, 1540, 1750
"Underneath the Harlem Moon" 1494
"Understand It" 464
"Undertaker" 1282
"Underture" 1655
"Underwater Study #5" 1073
"Undesirable" 19
"The Undiscovered Son" 1384
"Uneasy Armchairs" 285
"Unemployment" 545, 1299
"An Unexpected Discovery" 1155, 1157
"Unexpected Love" 345
"Unexpectedly" 98
"Unexpurgated Version" 415
"Unfair to Goliath" 1701
"Unfinished Business" 1554
"Unfinished Song" 486
"An Unfinished Song" 1702
"Unforgettable" 382
"Ungrateful" 379
"Unhappy Bella" 972
"The Union Is Behind Us" 814
"The Union League (Cloistered from the Noisy City)" 912
"Union Maid" 740
"Union Square" 912
"United Kingdom" 789
"United Nations on the March" 170
"Universe Song" 820
"Unknown Factor" 1732
"The Unknown Quantity (A Mystery Play)" 622
"The Unknown Soldier" 1664
"The Unknown Vegetable" 612
"Unlikely Lovers" 473, 997
"Unmanly" 1040
"The Unmarried Couple" 1765
"Unpleasantries and Introductions" 947
"Unpredictable You" 1135
"The Unreconstructed Rebel" 376
"Unrequited Love" 1311
"Unrequited Love March" 1754
"Unseen Buds" 903
"Until" 1066
"Until [Till] the Real Thing Comes Along" 681
"Until My Luck Comes Rolling Along" 570
"Until the Likes of You" 288
"Until the World Needs Me Again" 889
"Untitled Opening Number" 1645
"Untogether Cinderella" 1397
"The Untrue Pigeon" 1384
"An Unusual Normal" 1671
"Unveil My Eyes" 471
"Unworthy of Your Love" 70
"Up Against It" 1706
"Up and At 'Em" 912
"Up and Down" 1424
"Up Chickamauga Hill" 827
"Up Front Behind" 785
"Up in Heaven" 1231
"Up in the Air" 635
"Up on the Roof" 1591
"Up There" 692
"Up to My Tits in Water" 1432
"Up to Your Ears in Souvenirs" 1016
"Up, Up, Up" 992
"Up Where the People Are" 42
"Update" 1759
"Upper Birth" 1254
"Upper East Side Blues" 991
"Uprising of the Old Line Units" 889
"Ups and Downs" 907
"Upside Down" 820
"Upstairs at O'Neals" 1709
"Upstairs at the Downstairs" 60
"Upstairs at the Downstairs Waltz" 1576
"Upstairs Downstairs" 1767
"Uptown" (Mann and Weil) 854
"Uptown" (Strouse) 1328
"Uptown, Downtown" 1027, 1491
"Uptown Dreamer's Express" 1538
"'A' Uptown Express" 1459
"Urban Allegro" 1383
"Urban Legend" 1084
"The Urge to Merge" 1066
"Urinetown" 1712
"U.S. Patent Office" 1153
"Us Two" 232, 1163
"US vs. USSR" 275
"The Use of the Colon" 57
"Useful Phrases" 1390
"Useless Desires" 1598
"Useless Song" 128, 1626
"The Uses of Television" 1209
"U.S.S.R." 114
"Usted Abuso" 262
"Utopia" 1592
"Utopia Ballet — Hooligan's Hop" 1713
"Utter Ecstasy" 1254
"Uyamemeza Ungoma" 1401

"Vacation" 1317
"The Vagabond Student" 1142
"The Vain Man" 938
"Valentine Pas de Deux" 637
"Valentine Song" 113
"Valentine's Tango" 827
"Valerie's Decision" 1458
"Valley of Jewels" 66
"Valmouth" 1716
"Val's Ballad" 580
"Valse Empire" 637
"Valse Triste" 461
"Value" 60
"The Vamp and Friends" 150
"The Vamp and the Friends" 149
"Van Buren" 722
"Vanilla Soda" 820
"Vanya" 1647
"The Varsity Students Rag" 135
"Vatch Your Step!" 604
"Vatican" 59
"The Vatican Rag" 1654
"Vaudeville" 1177
"Vaudeville Chase" 431
"Vaudeville for Jean Harlow" 926
"Vaudeville, Kosher Style" 492
"The Vault" 837
"V.D." 719
"Vedi La Vita (Look at Life)" 1445
"Vee Zenen Meine Zibn Gute Yur (Where Are My Seven Good Years?)" 492
"Vegetable Reggie" 271
"Veit! Veit!" 1212
"Velcome to Shul" 1610
"Velvet Vest" 857
"Vend-A-Buddy" 1415
"Vending Machine" 21
"Vendors" 377
"Vendor's Song" 91
"Venetcia" 766
"Venezia Vento" 1020
"Vengeance" (Heather Brothers) 979
"Vengeance" (Heim) 1780
"Venice" 430
"Ventriloquism" 1720
"Ventriloquist & Dummy" 1133
"Ventriloquy" 1754
"The Venulia" 1310
"The Venus and Adonis Suite" 1437
"Venus and Young Adonis" 1569
"Venus de Milo" (Darewski and Knight) 136
"Venus de Milo" (Springer) 1493
"Ver Der Ershter Vet Lakhn (Who Will Laugh First?)" 1619
"Verdun" 1635
"Verily, Verily" 493
"Vernon" 1030
"Veronica Takes Over" 1163
"Very Far Away" 1340
"A Very Full and Productive Day" 1236
"A Very Funny Thing" 1143
"A Very Good Night" 1300
"Very Influential Politicos" 1276
"A Very Lonely King" 663
"Very New York" 1527
"A Very Single Man" 499
"Very Soft Shoes" 1193
"Very Truly Yours, Rosy Red Pants Angela" 741
"A Very Young Man" 1343
"Vest Pocket Bert Williams" 1543
"Veterinarian" 260
"Vi Derlebt Men Shoyn Amerike Tsu Zeyn" 1715
"Vi Erlich Rein" 1212
"Vi Shver S'iz Tsu Sheyden (How Hard to Leave Old Homes)" 604
"The Vi-Ton-Ka Lecture" 1720
"The Vice President and the Call Girl" 1743
"Vickie Lawrence" 580
"The Victim Dream" 65
"Victim of Normality" 1432
"Victim Update #1" 424
"Victim Update #2" 424
"Victim Update #3" 424
"Victim Update #4" 424
"Victims of the Darkness" 1518
"Victims of the Past" 61
"Victoria" 1611
"Victoria's Christening" 1721
"Victory March" 1577
"Vict'ry (Victory) Polka" 1546
"La Vida es un Carnaval" 262
"La Vida Eternal" 38
"Video Bleeptones" 910
"Video Boys" 808
"Video Dreamboy" 910
"Video Enigma" 910
"La Vie en Rose" 924, 1256, 1257
"The View from My Window" 357
"View from the Hill" 719
"A View from the Top" 1362
"Vigil" 1486
"Vignette" 942
"The Village Inn" 135
"Village Lad" 638
"Village Vignette" 638
"Villains of History" 1338
"Villainy" 1780
"The Vineyard" 1158
"Violet Eyes" 740
"Violet's Confession" 721
"The Viper's Drag" 18
"Virgin" 719
"The Virgin of Velez-Jermano" 1707
"The Virgin Polka" 698
"Virgins Are Like the Fair Flower" 117
"Virtual Sexuality" 185
"Virtual Vivian" 610
"The Virtuoso" 644
"Vis-à-vis" 465
"Vision of Cleopatra's Barge" 62
"Visiting Hours" (Silver) 1527
"Visiting Hours" (Wilson) 357
"Visiting Rights" 1433
"Viva La Diva" 143
"Viva La Matinee" 198
"Vivaldi" 1582, 1677
"Vivi's" 926
"Vodka" 46
"A Voice" 410
"A Voice Foretold" 615
"The Voice in the Ocean" 1831
"The Voice of God" 1264
"A Voice: Refrain" 410
"Voices" (Kaplan) 1485
"Voices" (Silver) 1458
"The Voices in My Head" 721
"Voices of the Children" 297
"Voila" 88
"Volare" 1521, 1575
"The Volcano" 1478
"Voodoo" (Brandon) 1774
"Voodoo" (Unknown) 1388
"Voodoo Dance" 960
"Vos Zol Ikh Tun Az Ikh Hob Im Lib" 1715
"Vote for Crane" 748
"Vote for Lincoln" 1824
"The Voting Machine" 1206
"Le Voyage du Pere" 123
"Voyeur and His Conscience" 529
"Vu Nemt Men Parnose? (How Do I Make a Living?)" 604

"Wabash 4-7473" 1448
"Wacky Dust" 73
"Wade in the Water" (Duke) 238
"Wade in the Water" (Traditional) 740, 1308
"The Wages of Sin" 1109
"Wahoo!" 1739
"Wait" 1504
"Wait and See" (Copani) 493, 1124, 1537
"Wait and See" (Heather Brothers) 979
"Wait for Me" 1048
"Wait for the Ragged Soldiers" 609
"Wait-Stop-Hold-Cut" 1788
"Wait 'Til It Dawns" 1181
"Wait 'Til the Sun Shines, Nellie" 695
"Wait Till Tomorrow" 902
"Wait Till You See Her" 236, 1106
"Wait Till You See My Baby Do the Charleston" 1198
"Waitin'" (Arlen) 662, 715
"Waitin'" (Leslee) 78
"Waitin' for the Evening Mail" 577
"Waitin' on the Women" 290
"Waiting" (Bowles) 1011
"Waiting" (Hirsch) 1028
"Waiting" (Lasser) 225
"Waiting" (McHugh) 1294
"Waiting" (Pen) 285
"Waiting" (Swados) 1133
"Waiting" (Tucholsky) 1635
"Waiting" (Zur) 1701
"Waiting Around for the Sondheim Show" 511
"Waiting for Life" 1191
"Waiting for Our Wave" 943
"Waiting for the Bus of Life" 919
"Waiting for the Curtain" 1298
"Waiting for the Kiss to Come" 1610
"Waiting for the Men" 1399
"Waiting for the Messiah" 1203
"Waiting for the Train" 1644
"Waiting Game" 945
"Waiting in the Wings" (Bohmler) 444

"Waiting in the Wings" (Sheffer) 599
"Waiting in the Wings" (Silver) 1527
"Waiting Song" 1388
"Waiting Trio" 739
"The Waitress" (Flagg) 852
"The Waitress" (Forster) 1299
"Wake the Dead" 805
"Wake Up" 504
"Wake Up and Dream" 367
"Wake Up, Caesar" 143
"Wake-Up Call" 1747
"Wake Up, Sun" 785
"Wake Us with Your Song" 284
"The Waking Nightmare" 541
"Waking This Morning" 1133
"Waking Up Alone" 510
"Waldemar" 1635
"A Walk" 114
"Walk" 206
"The Walk" 1554
"Walk Dog" 1754
"Walk Down Mah Street" 1732
"Walk Down Mah Street Courageous Award of the Year" 1732
"Walk in Love" 1650
"Walk Just a Few Feet" 9
"Walk Like a Man" 205
"Walk, Lordy, Walk" 1732
"Walk On" 410
"Walk On By" 83, 1551
"Walk on Home" 175
"Walk on the Water" 222
"A Walk on the Wild Side" 1733
"Walk Through That (the) Golden Gate" 1476
"Walk to De Grave" 715
"The Walk to the Well" 938
"Walk Together" 470
"Walkin'" (Hasman) 1232
"Walkin'" (Satlin) 279
"Walkin' After Midnight" 39
"Walkin' Blues" 777
"Walkin' in the Rain" 409
"Walkin' Sally" 1015
"Walkin' the Dog" 785
"Walkin' to School" 1547
"Walking After Midnight" 777
"Walking All the Way to Rome" 539
"Walking Down Broadway" 481, 695
"Walking Down the Road" 1318
"Walking in Space" 649
"Walking in the Rain" 854
"Walking in the World" 969
"Walking on a Thin Line" 1664
"Walking the Dog" 194
"Walking with Jesus" 278
"Walking with Peninnah" 1420
"Walking with You, Two by Two" 101
"The Wall Song" 1787
"Wall Street" (Simons) 1290
"Wall Street" (Walsh and Goldenberg) 1014
"Wall Street" (Wise) 341
"Wallowing in the Mire" 1363
"Wallpaper" 406
"The Walls Are Closing In" 1320, 1321
"Walmartopia" 1736
"The Walrus and the Carpenter" 27
"Walter Kerr" 1069
"The Walter Mitty March" 1420
"Walt's Truth" 1258
"Waltz" (Dowell) 1594
"Waltz" (Merrill) 1752
"Waltz" (Pine) 1057
"Waltz" (Reiser) 95
"Waltz" (Silverman) 1708
"A Waltz for Two Balloons" 357
"Waltz of Lise's Childhood" 65
"Waltz of the Cameleopard" 408
"Waltz with Me, Lady" 667
"Waltzing in the Shadow" 569
"The Wanderer" 1034
"Wanderin' in the Wilderness" 1363
"Wanderin' Man" 102
"Wandering Stranger" 927
"Wandering Walking Everyday" 834
"Wang Dang Doodle" 777
"Wanna Get Married" 1679
"Wanna Go to Heaven" 255
"Want to Get Retarded?" 1732
"Wanta, Hope to Feel at Home" 1164
"Wantage Bells" 135
"Wanted to Dine" 1638
"Wanting" 1328
"Wanting You" 1570
"The War" 114
"War" (Baton) 1419
"War" (Downs) 486
"War" (Martell) 1443
"War Against War" 1635
"War and Peace (Dialectic Inaction!)" 170
"War and Poverty" 1614
"War and Rebellion" 1004
"War Babies" 1038
"War Is Good Business" 1424
"War Is Made for Generals" 194
"War Is Not Good" 222
"War Song" 1471
"Ward Off Puberty Chant" 1478
"Warm as the Autumn Light" 92
"Warm Breezes at Twilight" 1566
"Warm Mist" 71
"Warm-Up Ballet" 295
"Warm Winter" 1192
"Warner Wolf #1" 377
"Warner Wolf #2" 377
"Warner Wolf #3" 377
"Warner Wolf #4" 377
"The Warning" 1441
"The Warrior's Song" 124
"Warsaw!" 1821
"Was It Good for You Too?" 1168
"Was It Something That I Said" 293
"Was That Me Talking" 1707
"Was There Ever Any Fella That He Liked for You?" 1723
"Was This in the Book?" 1020
"Was Y'ever at Such a Nice Square Dance, Little Bat?" 1563
"Wash Your Sins Away" 1423
"Washed Away" 1154
"Washington Is Your Home" 1276
"Washington Square" (Britton) 575
"Washington Square" (Herman) 1132
"Wasn't Easy" 1050
"Wasn't It Fine" 1245
"Wasn't That a Mighty Day!" 166
"Wasted Days" 1714
"Wasted Life Blues" 180, 181, 182
"Wastin' Time" 934
"Watch Dog Theme" 133
"Watch Me Move" 431
"Watch Me Put My Right Foot" 431
"Watch Out for the Bump" 1290
"Watch Through the Night" 1418
"Watch Your Language" 1760
"Watch Your Step" 1715
"Watcha Wanna Do?" 106
"Watching" 1659
"Watching All the Pretty Young Men" 1
"Watching the Big Parade Go By" 1400, 1524
"Watching the News" 1485
"The Water and the Flame" 449
"Water in the Well" 1726
"The Water Is Wide" 313
"Water on the Brain" 60
"Water Pollution" 87
"The Water Through the Trees" 219
"Water Wears the Stone" 1441
"The Waterfall" 1363
"Waterfaucet Blues" 646
"Waterloo" 1315
"The Waters of the Spa" 1011
"The Waterworks Madrigal" 1594
"Watery Blue" 1338
"Wave of Manhattan" 1545
"The Way" 1468
"Way Back Home" 1513
"A Way Back to Then" 1645
"Way Down Deep" 610
"Way Down in Lil' Old Texas" 121
"Way Down on the Inside" 1631
"Way Downtown" 657
"The Way Home" 1733
"The Way It Is" 1743
"The Way It Should Be" 1366
"The Way of My Father" 1339
"A Way of Showing I Love You" 1338
"Way of the World" 1320, 1321
"Way Out West" 68
"Way Over Yonder" 1591
"The Way West" 413
"The Way You Look Tonight" 883, 886, 1210
"Wayside Inn" 1008
"Wayward the Air This Morning" 1020
"The Wayward Wimple" 1158
"We All Could Be Jewish If We Tried a Little Harder" 1607
"We All Gotta Stand" 983
"We Always Get Our Man" 1131
"We Are" 1294
"We Are All Dead Men" 647
"We Are But Patters of Paint" 404
"We Are China" 1134
"We Are Dancing in the Temple" 1327
"We Are Descended" 375
"We Are Family" 399
"We Are Friends" 985
"We Are God's Forgotten People" 1419
"We Are Guerrillas" 1401
"We Are No Longer Strangers" 814
"We Are Not Strangers" 1384
"We Are One" 1037
"We Are Soldiers" 1672
"We Are Sorry for You" 363
"We Are Such Stuff as Dreams Are Made On" 1020
"We Are the Altar Boys" 38
"We Are the Champions" 1623
"We Are the Clouds" 1330
"We Are the Police" 699
"We Are the Shakers" 790
"We Are the Stonewall Girls!" 673
"We Are the Whores (Liberation Song)" 1072
"We Are There" 1683
"We Are Water" 1598
"We Ate the Money" 1337
"We Been in Love" 1733
"We Believe" 1650
"We Belong" 980
"We Belong Together" 1002
"We Beseech Thee" 595
"We Broke Up!" 365
"We Came Along Too Late" 219
"We Came Together" 1517
"We Can Be Kind" 929
"We Can Be Proud" 848
"We Can Make It" 52
"We Can Save the World and Find True Love" 721
"We Can Talk to Each Other" 1524
"We Can Work It Out" 1551
"We Can't Finish" 983
"We Can't Go On Like This!" 1016
"We Can't Go On This Way" 1466
"We compare notes" 250
"We Could Rent a Movie" 1084
"We Couldn't Handle It, Jamie" 206
"We Dance" (Flaherty) 1191
"We Dance" (Merrill) 658
"We Did It" 82
"We Didn't Ask to Be Born" 734
"We Do Have" 1684
"We Do Not Belong Together" 1557
"We Don't Talk Anymore" 599
"We Don't Understand Our Children" 1393
"We Don't Waste Food" 1117
"We Doubt You, Papa" 860
"We Dwell in Our Hearts" 289
"We Found Love Our Own Way" 769
"We Go On" 468
"We Go Together" 625
"We Gon' Jump Up" 91
"We Got a Future" 1164
"We Got a Job to Do" 1184
"We Got a Movement" 470
"We Got Grounds, Good Ole Boys" 9
"We Got Love" 638
"We Got Married" 61
"We Got to Get Organized" 321
"We Got Troubles" 985
"We Got What We Wanted" 907
"We Gotta Get Out of This Place" 854
"We Gotta Put the Sun Back in the Sky" 681
"We Have Come So Far" 1327
"We Have Loved Forever" 1208
"We Have Never Met" 1604
"We Have the Pope" 59
"We Have to Die?" 1384
"We Have to Go Away" 1063
"We Have to Lead the Fight" 814
"We Is Wonderful" 1058
"We Just Had Sex" 1225
"We Kept the Faith" 9
"We Kiss" 683
"We Knew How to Live" 403
"We Know a Secret Secret" 652
"We Know What You Want and We Got It" 1385
"We Know Where We've Been" 1078
"We Light Our Lamps" 938
"We Like Things the Way They Are" 360
"We Live on Borrowed Time" 929
"We Live with Fear" 1829
"We Love a Conference" 401
"We Love You Conrad" 237
"We Make a Promise" 152
"We Met" 481
"We Might Play All Night" 1225
"We Miss Ike" 1431
"We Mourn" 1771
"We Must Not Look" 586
"We Must Talk" 1146
"We Mustn't Say Goodbye" 1764
"We Need a Few More Servants" 1146
"We Need a Little Christmas" 818
"We Need Each Other" 1683
"We Need Money" 95
"We Need More Love" 1559
"We No Longer Need Confucius" 1139
"The We of Me" 466
"We Paint Life" 1538
"We Place Our Faith in Good King Charles' Hands" 1316
"We Praise the Lord" 1441
"We Put the Music" 1218
"We Raise the Wheat" 1762
"We Said We Wouldn't Look Back" 1393
"We Saw a Movie Together" 406
"We Saw Everybody There" 714
"We Say OUI!" 1510
"We See It All" 198
"We Shall Be Changed" 166
"We Shall Discuss, Jaffrey ... Jaffrey ..." 717
"We Shall Meet in the Great Hereafter" 1154
"We Shall Not Be Moved" 736, 740, 1643, 1672
"We Shall Overcome" 470, 736, 815, 816, 1423, 1672
"We Shall Release You" 1283
"We Shall Return" 889
"We Shall Rise Again" 889
"We Should Care" 305
"We Should Talk" 219
"We Sing America" 1268
"We Sit in the Window" 431
"We Stand Together on This Old—" 941
"We Stand Together on This Old/New Day" 941
"We Still Love Her" 1505
"We Stood at the Harbour" 1020
"We Thank You" 979
"We Thought You'd Make Us Proud" 995
"We Wanna Star" 636
"We Want the Pope" 59
"We Want You to Be the First Ones to Know" 1431

"We, We, We" 1066
"We Were Born by Chance" 1636
"We Were Dancing" 1170
"We Were Friends" 1650
"We Were Here" 1702
"We Were Together" 170
"We Were Young" 824
"We Will All Go Together" 1654
"We Will Always Walk Together" 413
"We Will Fight for Our Land" 1401
"We Will Never Die" 462
"We Will Rock You" 1623
"We Wish the World a Happy Yule" 349
"We Wish We Was in Blighty" 136
"We Women" 1057
"We Won't Take It Back" 1606
"We Worked the Whole Thing Out" 1016
"Wealthy, Shmelthy, as Long as You're Healthy" 1521
"Weapons Underscore" 1784
"Wear a Little Grin" 658
"Wear Your Vanity with Pride" 1763
"Weather Report # 1" 643
"Weather Report # 2" 643
"Weather Report # 3" 643
"Weather Report # 4" 643
"Weather Song" 1326
"A-Weaving" 271
"W.E.B. to Booker T." 1734, 1735
"We'd Like to Go Back" 545
"The Wedding" (Finn) 1477
"The Wedding" (Greenberg and Goldwasser) 1237
"The Wedding" (Hamilton) 1721
"The Wedding" (Laws) 1078
"The Wedding" (Meyers) 65
"The Wedding" (Satlin) 279
"The Wedding" (Traditional) 604
"Wedding Ball" 1151
"Wedding Bands" 278
"Wedding Bulgar: Dance" 1821
"The Wedding Celebration" 1531
"Wedding Ceremony" 1367
"The Wedding Ceremony" 1146
"The Wedding Concluded" 1721
"Wedding Dance" (Gebirtig) 1382
"Wedding Dance" (Kaplan) 147
"Wedding Dance" (Rauch) 1822
"Wedding Ensemble" 1745
"A Wedding in Cherokee County" 1036
"The Wedding of the Flowers" 1326
"Wedding Pantomime" 661
"Wedding Procession" 1822
"Wedding Song" (Cribari) 1283
"Wedding Song" (Finn) 765
"Wedding Song" (Shire) 300
"Wedding Song" (Weill) 1626
"Wedding Song" (Weinberg) 1600
"Wedding Song for the Less Well-Off" 1628
"Wedding Vows" 739
"Wedding, Wedding" 58
"The Wedding: Khosn-Kale Mazl Tov (Congratulations to the Bride and Groom)" 1619
"A Wedding! A Wedding!" 822
"Weddings and Funerals" 1737, 1738
"Weddings Bands" 278
"Wednesday" 206
"Wednesday Matinee" 350
"The Wee Scotsman" 877
"Weed, Weed, Weed" 328
"Week-End Shopping" 638
"The Weekend" 267
"Weekend" 1460
"A Weekend Affair" 567
"A Weekend at the Club" 1045
"A Weekend in the Country" 1491
"Weep" 907
"Weep Not" 591
"The Weeping Chandelier" (Golub) 49
"The Weeping Chandelier" (Matz) 612
"The Weeping Song" 476
"Wei Yi Shu Xian Sheng" 1325
"The Weight" 265, 1556
"Weird Fun" 216
"Weird Interlude: A Good Table at a Bad Restaurant " 899
"Welcome" (Bernstein) 234
"Welcome" (Goggin) 1155
"Welcome" (Holt) 1460
"Welcome" (Leigh) 289
"Welcome" (Patterson) 1385
"Welcome" (Silver) 564
"Welcome" (Simons) 1290
"Welcome" (Townshend) 1655
"The Welcome" 615
"Welcome Banana" 1330
"Welcome, Bienvenue" 89
"Welcome Dance" 1751
"A Welcome for Louie" 248
"Welcome Home" 825
"Welcome Home Again" 1824
"Welcome, Ladies" 889
"Welcome Little One" 1767
"Welcome, Mr. Anderson" 785
"Welcome Song" 91, 246
"Welcome to Broadway" 920
"Welcome to Goodies" 396
"Welcome to Greece" 1181
"Welcome to Holiday Inn" 886
"Welcome to Kanagawa" 1213
"Welcome to Kindergarten, Mrs. Johnson" 1
"Welcome to London" 476
"Welcome to My L.A." 222
"Welcome to My World" 240
"Welcome to Paradise" 1219
"Welcome to Paradise Part II" 1219
"Welcome to the AfterMath" 485
"Welcome to the Calmer House" 1365
"Welcome to the Merry-Go-Round" 1361
"Welcome to the Moon" 1007
"Welcome to the Mud" 1618
"Welcome to the Theatre" 237
"Welcome to the World" (Flaherty) 1006
"Welcome to the World" (Lippa) 830
"Welcome to This Window" 644
"Welcome Washington" 378
"Welcome, Welcome" 758
"The Well" (Bailin) 253
"The Well" (Portman) 938
"Well, All Right, Okay, You Win" 1350
"We'll Always Stay in Love" 352
"We'll Be Right Back After This Message" 1709
"The Well Boiled Icicle" 1754
"Well, Did You Evah!" 367, 1210
"Well Done, Da Costa" 1593
"We'll Find a Dream Somewhere" 631
"We'll Find a Way" 1468
"We'll Have a Party" 360
"We'll Have (Give) a Wonderful Party" 1028
"We'll Have Tomorrow" 727
"(Well) I Wonder" 321
"Well, It Ain't" 986
"We'll Live All Over Again" 238
"We'll Meet Again" 1482, 1750
"We'll Never Let It Go" 1727
"Well, Schweik" 609
"Well, Schweik, How'd Things Go Today?" 609
"We'll Sing" 1821
"We'll Sleep with the Radio On" 45
"We'll Still Be Friends" 190
"We'll Suffer Together" 714
"Well, Tell Us More" 1374
"The Well-to-Do Waltz" 644
"Well, Well" 717
"Well, Yes, He's a Friend" 720
"Wendy" 1428
"Wenn Nur Ein Traum das Leben Ist" 1020
"Wenzeni Na" 1284
"Wer Wird Denn Weinen" 1350
"We're a Little Family" 726
"We're a Little Nervous Tonight" 989
"We're a Team" 153
"We're a Travelin' Trio" 323
"We're a Young Country" 1691
"We're Alive" 848
"We're All in a Hell of a Mess" 609
"We're Almost There" 1207
"We're Back" 786
"We're Betting on You" 472
"We're Civilized" 1751
"We're Everywhere" 1600
"We're Four of the Three Musketeers" 304
"(We're) Goin' to Atlanta" 321
"We're Going to De Moines" 453
"We're Gonna Do It Good" 1518
"We're Gonna Fly" 143
"We're Gonna Have a Wedding" 631
"We're Gonna Howl Tonight" 349
"We're Gonna Look Back" 468
"We're Gonna Love It (While It Lasts)" 321
"We're Gonna Make It" 1787
"We're Gonna See the Voodoo Queen" 1021
"We're Gonna Turn On Freedom" 152
"We're Gonna Win" 722
"We're Having a Party" 985
"We're Having a Very Fine Summer" 609
"We're Here" 1829
"We're Home" 1580, 1752
"Were I Laid on Greenland Coast" 117
"We're in a Race" 1221
"(We're in It for) The Long Haul" 502
"We're in the Army" 1577
"We're Just Friends" 738
"We're Looking for a Piano" 1393
"We're Needed Here" 1219
"We're Not Gonna Take It" 1655
"We're Not Sorry" 1712
"We're Not Who We Think We Are" 497
"We're # 1" 272
"We're Off" (Lewine) 494
"We're Off" (Solly) 1050
"We're on a Shelf in Your Attic" 216
"We're on the Highway to Heaven" 681
"We're Only Lovers" 360
"We're Rats" 653
"We're Rich" 1495
"We're Saving Ourselves for Yale" 1282
"We're Strangers Who Sleep Side by Side" 752
"We're the Ads" 1268
"We're the Nuns to Come To" 1158, 1159
"We're the People" 147
"Were This to Prove a Feather in My Hat" 870
"We're Today" 1732
"We're Together" 1701
"We're Wanted" 1021
"We're Wild Men" 1777
"Were You Saying Something" 316
"Were You There" 591, 592, 1672
"Wernher von Braun" 1654
"West End Saga" 241
"West Indies Blues" 553
"Westchester Cathedral" 1255
"Western Approaches Ballet" 1304
"Western Movies" 602
"Western Union Boy" 1229
"Western Union Boy's Song" 1229
"The Westfall Murder" 142
"Westport!" 1576
"We've Been Chums for Fifty Years" 581
"We've Been North" 1601
"We've Come This Far by Faith" 736
"We've Done All Right" 100
"We've Got a Feeling in Our Bones" 1713
"We've Got Each Other" 1296
"We've Got Quite a Future" 82
"We've Got to Clean Out the Freezer" 1155, 1157, 1158
"We've Had Our Moments" 825
"We've Just Begun" 600
"Whaddaya Say Kid" 93
"Whadddya Say, Marco?" 1723
"Whaddya Read?" 96
"A Whale of a Story" 66
"What a Bore" 676
"What a Catastrophe" 1159
"What a Country" 237
"What a Curious Girl" 714
"What a Day" (Henderson) 333
"What a Day" (Jarboe and Shield) 653
"What a Day for a Wonderful Day" 957
"What a Day for Me" 1265
"What a Difference (Diff'rence) a Day Made (Makes)" 156, 382, 383
"What a Fine Day for an Auction Sell" 408
"What a Fine Young Man!" 190
"What a Fool I've Been" 697
"What a Friend We Have in Jesus" 730
"What a Gift" 573
"What a Handsome Little Fellow" 979
"What a Killing" 1755
"What a Life" (Frietas) 379
"What a Life" (Marren) 961, 1756
"What a Life" (Marvin) 1446
"What a Long Cold Winter!" 822
"What a Lovely Dream" 528
"What a Lovely Evening" 92
"What a Lovely Night" 362
"What a Lovely Thing" 639
"What a Night!" 714
"What a Pair" 819
"What a Party" 1778
"What a Pity" 66
"What a Place That Was" 1020
"What a Ride I" 1622
"What a Ride II" 1622
"What a Shame" 631
"What a Sight" 67
"What a Story" 71
"What a Waste" 911
"What a Wedding" 291
"What About Me" (Ballard) 93
"What About Me" (Crom) 1128
"What About Today" 1524
"What About Us?" 1251
"What Abraham Lincoln Once Said" 1701
"What Alan Likes" 742
"What Am I Doing?" 300
"What Am I Forbidden Now?" 947
"What Am I Hangin' Around For?" 1713
"What Am I Supposed to Do?" 726
"What an Evening" 720
"What an Honor!" 184
"What Are They Doing to Us Now?" 981
"What Are You Looking For, Horace?" 92
"What Are You Proposing" 393, 394
"What Are You Running From, Mister?" 957
"What Became of Love" 1493
"What Became of the People We Were?" 1082
"What Becomes of the Broken Hearted" 646
"What Broadway Needs Is More Rats" 1337
"What Can I Do?" 830
"What Can I Do for You" 1330
"What Can I Say" 1638
"What Can It Be" (Stornaiuolo) 59
"What Can It Be" (Urbont) 33
"What Can You Do with a Man?" 201
"What Choices Are Left for Me?" 1117
"What Could Be More Romantic" 1221
"What Could I Have Done?" 643
"What Dark November Thoughts" 404

"What Did I Do Right?" 2
"What Did I Do Wrong?" 968
"What Did You Expect?" 491
"What Did You Put in That Look?" 1152
"What Do (What Would) We Do?" 1045
"What Do I Believe In" 786
"What Do I Care?" 200
"What Do I Do Now" (Melrose) 537
"What Do I Do Now" (Wilson) 357
"What Do I Have to Do?" 663
"What Do I Know?" 1827
"What Do I Want with Love" 1716
"What Do People Do?" 219
"What Do They Care?" 1264
"What Do They Know About Love Uptown" 638
"What Do We Care If It Rains" 1446
"What Do We Do?" 1045
"What Do We Do It For?" 738
"What Do Women Most Desire" 246
"What Do Women Want?" 1505
"What Do Ya Know" 385
"What Do You Do" (Lasser) 225
"What Do You Do" (Woldin) 865, 866
"What Do You Intend to Do?" 92
"What Do You Think I Am?" 132
"What Do You Win When You Win?" 1001
"What Does a Lover Pack?" 1689
"What Does Atlanta Mean to Me" 321
"What D'ya Wanna Be?" 667
"What Ever Happened" 293
"What Good Are You?" 1152
"What Good Can Drinking Do?" 965
"What Good Does Loneliness Do?" 712
"What Good Is Love?" 981, 1267, 1268
"What Good's A Mambo?" 1434
"What Happened?" 609
"What Happened Here?" 1327
"What Happened, What?" 289
"What Happens to Life" 1038
"What Has Become of Beauty?" 569
"What Has Happened?" 935
"What Have We Done" 1388
"What He'd Say" 1195
"What I Almost Said" 791
"What I Am" 741
"What I Could Have Done Tonight" 725, 1097
"What I Did for Love" 283
"What I Had in Mind" 102
"What I Hope For and What I Get" 501
"What I Like Is You" 781
"What I Want Is a Proper Cup of Coffee" 581
"What I Want to Be" 1661
"What I Was Dreamin' Of" 929
"What I Wonder" 823
"What I'd Had in Mind" 929
"What If?" (Dolginoff) 1084
"What If?" (Giering) 328
"What If?" (Kaplan) 1485
"What If?" (Shaiman) 370
"What If I Asked Her for a Dance?" 406
"What If We ..." 731
"What I'm Longing to Say" 902
"What I'm Looking For" (Bitterman) 497
"What I'm Looking For" (Steidl) 299
"What Is a Friend For?" 715
"What Is a Friend?" 835
"What Is a Letter" 27
"What Is a Melodrama?" 1511
"What Is a Queen" 467
"What Is a Woman" 74, 733
"What Is a Woman Like?" 972
"What Is, Ain't" 1514
"What Is Funny" 497
"What Is Good for Depression" 1636
"What Is It?" (Carmines) 834
"What Is It?" (Ladd) 1475
"What Is It About Her?" 1778
"What Is Liberty?" 1316
"What Is Love?" (Blankman) 235
"What Is Love?" (Valenti) 851, 972, 989
"What Is Missing in My Life" 1298
"What Is Normal" 1684
"What Is Real" 14
"What Is She Doing Here" 850
"What Is There to Say?" (Brandon) 968
"What Is There to Say?" (Duke) 1651
"What Is There to Sing About" 1473
"What Is This Malady?" 1077
"What Is This Sensation?" 714
"What Is This Thing Called Love?" 367
"What Is Urinetown?" 1712
"What Is Wrong with Alma" 224
"What Is Your Name?" 693, 989
"What It's Like to Be a Legend" 456
"What Keeps a Man Alive?" 1807
"What Keeps Mankind Alive?" 1628
"What Kind of Baby?" 1701
"What Kind of Girl Is She?" 1645
"What Kind of Life Is That?" 1318
"What Kind of Life Is This?" 542
"What Kind of Man Is He?" 480
"What Kind of Mother?" 1736
"What Kind of Mother Am I?" 1700
"What Kind of Parents" 1424
"What Land Is This?" 791
"What Makes Me Love Him" 992, 1106
"What Makes the Special Special" 1510
"What Makes Ye Go a Whaling?" 1071
"What Marriage Is" 1485
"What Might Have Been" (Pomeranz) 1700
"What Might Have Been" (Thomas) 90, 1031
"What Month Was Jesus Borned In?" 166
"What More Can I Say?" 473
"What More Do I Need?" 1403, 1491
"What Now?" 398
"What Now My Love" 824
"What of Love?" 1637
"The What on Earth Is Going On Tango" 1146
"What Ought We to Do?" 1270
"What People Really Do When the Lights Are Low" 395
"What Price Have I Paid?" 1309
"What Real True Friends Are For" 1511
"What Shadows We Are" 1732
"What Shall I Believe in Now?" 120
"What Shall I Do" 1823
"What Shall I Sing?" 1144
"What Should I Do?" 491
"What Stuart Has Planned" 1777
"What Style!" 1008
"What the ... ?" 462
"What the Hell" 1759, 1761
"What the Hell Am I Doing Here?" 1433
"What the Prince Is Saying" 1250
"What the Song Should Say" 1624
"What the World Needs Now" 83
"What Then?" (Duffy) 707
"What Then?" (Thomas) 90
"What There Is" 27
"What Thou See'st When Thou Dost Awake" 1437
"What Time Is Grey" 1200
"What Time Is It?" 1747
"What to Do?" 867
"What to Wear?" 778
"What We Go Through" 214
"What We Have Here Is Not What It Seems" 673
"What We Need Around Here" 1107
"What Will Daddy Say?" 1392
"What Will Happen to Me" 1548
"What Will Happen to Me Now?" 404
"What Will People Think?" 1510
"What Word of the Children?" 331
"What World Do You Live In?" 1237
"What Would Elvis Do?" 1159
"What Would I Do?" 473
"What Would You Do in My Place?" 873
"What Would You Say to Your Son?" 697
"What You Are" (Griffin) 1598
"What You Are" (Jordan) 1379
"What You Gonna Name Your Baby?" 166
"What You Looked Like" 1638
"What You Mean to Me" 873
"What You See Is What You Get" 1037
"What You Want" 1742
"What You'd Call a Dream" 377
"Whatcha Got?" 1830
"Whatever Happened" (Aman, et al.) 1661
"Whatever Happened" (DeBenedictis) 1669
"Whatever Happened To" (Barnes) 150
"Whatever Happened To" (Bissel, et al.) 350
"Whatever Happened to Spring" 407
"Whatever Happened to the Communist Menace?" 1758
"Whatever Happened to the Good Old Days" 109
"Whatever Happened to Tomorrow?" 1511
"Whatever It Happens to Be" 1183
"Whatever It Takes" 1135
"Whatever Turns You On" 913
"What're You Doin'?" 1042
"What's a Body to Do?" 690
"What's a Gang Without a Guy Named Muggsy?" 705
"What's a Guy Like You Doin' in a Place Like This?" 1154
"What's a Mama For?" 867
"What's a Show" 1447
"What's Cooking?" 1318
"What's Destined to Be" 874
"What's for Dinner?" 1732
"What's Goin' On" 725
"What's Gone Wrong" 1348
"What's Gonna Happen to Me" 1504
"What's Good About Good Morning?" 1116
"What's His Name" 1611
"What's in a Name?" (Kemeny) 1512
"What's in a Name?" (Roberts) 556
"What's in a Name?" (Venneri) 352
"What's in It for Me?" 825
"What's in the Air?" 1154
"What's It All About" 1727
"What's It Gonna Take (To Make It Clear Across the Lake)?" 633
"What's Love Got to Do with It" 1046
"What's Missing in My Life" 1298
"What's My Name?" 878
"What's New at the Zoo?" 210
"What's On?" 1747
"What's So Special About a Special?" 1510
"What's the Fun of Being King (If the King Is Poor?)" 652
"What's the Mail?" 990
"What's the Name of the Hotel" 1385
"What's the Name of What's-His-Name?" 652
"(What's the Use of Being) Miserable with You" 1606
"What's the Use?" 911
"What's Wrong with Me?" 366
"What's Wrong with That?" 1328
"What's Your Hurry, Mister?" 25
"What's Your Name?" 279
"What's Your Sign, Mr. Simpson?" 667
"Whatshisname" 1319
"Wheels" 2
"The Wheels Keep Turnin'" 153
"When" (Sherwin) 85
"When" (Sticco) 267
"When" (Kleinbort) 861
"When a Felon's Not Engaged in His Employment" 1270
"When a Gentleman's Well Dressed He's Well Prepared" 1467
"When a Jew Sings" 1342
"When a Lady Has a Piazza" 436
"When a Maid Wears Purple Stockings" 1446
"When a Pimp Meets a Whore" 975
"When a Robin Leaves Chicago" 870
"When a Woman Loves a Man" 180, 181, 182
"When After You Pass My Door" 16
"When Any Woman Makes a Running Issue Out of Her Flesh" 975
"When Daddy Comes (Came) Home" 1752
"When Daises Pied" 1568
"When Daisies Pied" 1569
"When Did the End Begin?" 949
"When Did You Leave Me?" 360
"When Do We Dance?" 1644
"When Every Man Is Everyman" 194
"When Everything Human Has Failed You" 834
"When First She Met Mark Antony" 62
"When Frederic Was a Little Lad" 1270
"When He Calls Half-Hour" 1476
"When Hope Goes" 1513
"When I Am in Charge" 280
"When I Am Lost" 726
"When I Asked You for a Match" 1692
"When I Come Home at Night" 1084
"When I Consider the Heavens" 1650
"When I Die" 809
"When I Do a (Tap) Dance for You" 1585, 1586
"When I Drink with My Love" 332
"When I Feel Like Moving" 400
"When I Get the Call" 376
"When I Grow Up (I Wanna Be a G-Man)" (aka "The G-Man Song") 1268
"When I Have You" 769
"When I Heard Dat White Man Say" 1735
"When I Heard, I Was in a State of Shock" 673
"When I Leave" 1043
"When I Look Up" 321
"When I Love Again" 735
"When I Make Up My Mind" 858
"When I Met Her" 406
"When I Rise" 785
"When I Take My Lady" 1021
"When I Take My Sugar to Tea" 681
"When I Touch His Garment" 1308
"When I Was a Child" (MacDermot) 1638
"When I Was a Child" (Wilson) 357
"When I Was a Cowboy" 376
"When I Was a Kid" 1306
"When I Was a Lad" 460
"When I Was a Little Cuckoo" 367
"When I Was a Man" 873
"When I Was Learning to Read" 50, 126
"When I Was One-and-Twenty" 972

"When I Woke Up" 1139
"When I'll Miss Him" 1195
"When I'm Gone" 740
"When I'm in a Quiet Mood" 1465
"When I'm Playin' the Palace" 818, 824
"When I'm Sixty-Four" 1426, 1656
"When I'm with Her" 1410
"When I'm Your Woman" 9
"When I've Done the Best I Can" 996
"When Icicles Hang by the Wall" 1568, 1569
"When Ilujinle Joins the World" 927
"When in Disgrace" 1519
"When Irish Eyes Are Smiling" 1092
"When It All Comes True" 52
"When It Gets Right Down to Evening" 1733
"When It Grows Dark My Lord" 1327
"When It's All Goin' Out and Nothin' Comin' In" 1643
"When It's Sweetpea Time in Georgia" 1326
"When Life Gives You Lemons" 845
"When Love Calls" 819
"When Lovely Lady" 805
"When Lovers Fall in Love" 1379
"When Mabel Comes in the Room" 818
"When Maggie Died" 1042
"When Malindy Sings" 1762
"When Moses Spake to Goldstein" 1701
"When My Dreams Come True" 305
"When My Love Swears" 1569
"When My Man Sails Home" 1021
"When My Sugar Walks Down the Street" 1282
"When My Uncle Willie Saw" 1735
"When Nations Come Together" 912
"When Night Starts to Fall" 1708
"When One Deems a Lady Sweet" 870
"When Pigs Fly" 1763
"When Rosie Lived on Essex Street" 604
"When the Bluebirds Fly All Over the World" 232, 1163
"When the Earth Stopped Turning" 430, 997
"When the Foeman Bares His Steel" 1270
"When the Hen Stops Laying" 1704
"When the Kids Get Married" 733
"When the Lady Passes" 486
"When the Lamp" 419
"When the Lamp Is Shattered" 1443
"When the Lights Go On Again" 1764
"When The Midnight Choo-Choo Leaves for Alabam'" 1656
"When the Money Comes In" 626
"When the Music Played" 721
"When the Nylons Bloom Again" 18
"When the Record Player's On" 1343
"When the Red, Red Robin Comes Bob, Bob, Bobbin' Along" 740, 829
"When the Right One Comes Along" 1365
"When the Roll Is Called Up Yonder" 1484
"When the Saints Come Home" 1349
"When the Saints Go Marching In" 1096, 1720
"When the Season's Over" 1618
"When the Summer Comes Again" 436
"When the Summer Moon Comes 'Long" 1282
"When the Sun Refused to Shine" 790
"When the Tide Is Right" 1723
"When the Time Comes" 1319
"When the Vampire (When a Woman) Exits Laughing" 1028
"When the Village Goes to Sleep" 638
"When the Whistle Blows" 278
"When the Wine Gets Cold" 889
"When the Wings of the Wind Take Me Home" 1385
"When the World Was Young" 1350
"When Time Takes Your Hand" 48
"When Tomorrow Comes" (Dansicker) 1184
"When Tomorrow Comes" (Jacobson) 1452
"When We All Get to Heaven" 1002
"When We Are Free" 1829
"When We Are Together" 493
"When We Are Wed" 927
"When We See a Pretty Girl We Whistle" 109
"When We Were Young" 600
"When We're in Love" 1116
"When We're Married" 972
"When We're Together" 1683
"When Will It End?" (Butler) 1423
"When Will It End?" (Yeston) 1201
"When Will the Music Be Gone" 1319
"When Will They Finish New York?" 1125
"When Will You Learn" 223
"When Worlds Collide" 1706
"When You Are Old and Grey" 1654
"When You Are on the Coast" 1527
"When You Are Together" 1124
"When You Care" 892
"When You Come Home to Me" 890
"When You Come to the End of Your Rainbow" 215
"When You Find Somebody" 1472
"When You Find You're a Broken-Down Critter" 460
"When You Had Left Our Pirate Fold" 1270
"When You Live in New York" 260
"When You Look in the Eyes of a Mule" 1543
"When You Looked at Me for the First Time" 834
"When You Love New York" 899
"When You Love Really" 1638
"When You Meet an Angel" 469
"When You Smile" 58
"When You Talk to a Lady Like Me" 1066
"When You Want Me" 1390
"When You Were a Lad" 253
"When You Write Greek Comedy" 74
"When You're Far Away from New York Town" 348
"When You're Home" 760
"When You're in Love" (Reiser) 95
"When You're in Love" (Tunick, et al.) 1749
"When You're Intimate with the Czar" 95
"When You're Not the Same" 1263
"When You're Older" 624
"When You're Shot at the Movies" 1030
"When You're Smiling" 1540
"When You're the Only One" 217
"When You're Young and in Love" 1827
"When You've Loved Your Man" 809
"When Your Hair Has Turned to Silver" 654
"When Your Lover Has Gone" 182
"Whenever He Needs a Miracle" 67
"Whenever I Dream" 1121
"Whenever You Want Me" 272
"Where" (Blitzstein) 848, 1140
"Where" (Slater) 719
"Where Am I Going" 886
"Where and with What?" 1732
"Where Are the Blossoms?" 572
"Where Are the Girls of Yesterday" 246
"Where Are the Snows?" 733
"Where Are They?" 1723
"Where Are Those People Who Did Hair" 1384
"Where Are You Going Wearing That Shawl from Manila? (Donde vas con Manton de Manila)" 488
"Where Are You Tonight?" 78
"Where Are Your Children?" 149, 150
"Where Can the Rich and the Poor Be Friends" 1539
"Where Did It Go?" (Schmidt) 1451
"Where Did It Go?" (Steinman) 1082
"Where Did Our Love Go?" 115
"Where Did Robinson Crusoe Go with Friday on Saturday Night?" 829, 993
"Where Did That Little Dog Go?" 1486
"Where Did the Dream Go?" 968
"Where Did the Summer Go To?" 56
"Where Did the World Go?" 359
"Where Did We Go Wrong?" 852
"Where Did You Come From?" 44
"Where Do All the Old Soldiers Go?" 197
"Where Do I Go" 293, 649
"Where Do I Go from Here?" (Carter, et al.) 120
"Where Do I Go from Here?" (Sterner) 971
"Where Do I Stand?" 1467
"Where Do People Go" 1384
"Where Do We Go from Here" 1831
"Where Do You Go" 780
"Where Does a Man Begin?" 631
"Where Does It Get You?" 1306
"Where Does Love Go" 1591
"Where Does One Turn To" 276
"Where Have I Been" (Fisher) 1043
"Where Have I Been" (Morrock) 1646
"Where Have I Been All My Life?" 509, 949
"Where Have You Been Asked the Doctor" 1200
"Where Have You Been Up to Now?" 1739
"Where I Belong" 330
"Where I Come From" 1287
"Where I Want to Be" 275
"Where in the World?" 1057
"Where Is Away?" 1467
"Where Is Love?" 78
"Where Is Matthew Going?" 56
"Where Is My Mommy, Please?" 1002
"Where Is She Now?" 1747
"Where Is That Man?" 1194
"Where Is That Rainbow" 631
"Where Is the Knight for Me" 1446
"Where Is the Lost and Found of London?" 285
"Where Is the Man" 1089
"Where Is the Man for Me?" 409
"Where Is the News?" 1276
"Where Is the One" 23
"Where Is the Place, Kid?" 149
"Where Is the Rainbow" 89, 1202
"Where Is the Warmth?" 88
"Where Oh Where Is My Baby Darlin'?" 1367
"Where or When" 1210
"Where Shall I Find Him (Her)?" 1390
"Where Shall I Go?" 120
"Where the Bee Sucks" 1568, 1569
"Where the Blue Horses" 963
"Where the Boys Are" 115, 205, 1551, 1575
"Where the Bulls Are" 50
"Where the Elite Meet — Carnegie Hall" 550
"Where the Hell Is Annie?" 1147
"Where the Mona Lisa Was Hung" 1276
"Where the Trees Are Filled with Parrots" 1716
"Where There's Smoke" (Roberts) 557
"Where There's Smoke" (Silver) 564
"Where Tina Gets It From" 1386
"Where Was I When They Passed Out the Luck?" 210
"Where Was It That We Met" 889
"Where Were You" (Amber) 1341
"Where Were You" (Brown) 1066
"Where Were You When It Went Down?" 1710
"Where Will I Be Next Wednesday Night?" 731
"Where Will I Lie Down?" 815, 816
"Where Would I Be Today" 1693
"Where Would We Be Without Perverts?" 752
"Where Would You Be?" 754
"Where You Been Hiding Til (Till) Now" 393, 394
"Where You Go" 1410
"Where You Goin' All Dressed Up?" 1723
"Where You Lead" 1591
"Where'd You Go?" 1723
"Wherefore Are Thou, Romeo" 87
"Where's Antony?" 62
"Where's Boris" 1218
"Where's My Love A-Wonderin'?" 1380
"Where's My Picture?" 338
"Where's North?" 1689
"Where's Seth?" 44
"Where's That Martin Boy" 1423
"Wherever He Ain't" 818
"Wherever You Go" 663
"Which Can See Further, An Ant or an Eagle" 871
"Which Side Are You On" 696, 740
"The Whiffenpoof Song" 1096, 1282
"While My Lady Sleeps" 1570
"While the City Sleeps" 603
"While the Iron Is Hot" 1255
"While They Were Sleeping" 857
"While We're Young" 23
"While Yet a Boy" 1443
"Whip Dance" 42
"The Whip Dance" 948
"Whip Her to Death!" 1139
"Whipperwill" 258, 259
"The Whirligig Stomp" 207
"Whirling in Circles" 278
"A Whirlwind of Wizardry" 287
"Whiskey in the Jar" 740
"Whispering" 1515
"Whispering Hope" (Hawthorne) 1484
"Whispering Hope" (Winner) 417, 695
"Whispering Pines" 1326
"Whispering to You" 1739
"Whispers" 790
"Whispers on the Wind" 1767
"Whistles" 175
"The White Anglo-Saxon Protestant Blues" (aka "Blues") 1527
"White Boys" 649
"White Cargo" 1615, 1616
"The White Cliffs of Dover" 1096, 1482, 1540, 1750, 1764
"White Cowboy Hat" 502
"White Faced Throng" 253
"White Heat" 1606
"White House Comics" 87
"White House Resident" 718
"White Is the Dove" 388
"The White Knight" 27
"White Liberal to the Rescue" 313

"White Milk and Red Blood" 375
"The White Queen" 27
"White Rabbit" 265, 1556
"White Roses Red" 27
"White Russian New Year" 535
"White Sheeting" 860
"The White Ship" 265
"White Trash Motel" 656
"White Walls" 1710
"The White Whale" 1071
"White Widow" 1073
"White Wings" 1092
"Whitechapel Life" 789
"The Whiteness" 1071
"The Whites" 277
"Whizzer Brown" 764
"Whizzer Going Down" 763, 765
"Who?" (Aznavour) 824
"Who?" (Kern) 165, 883
"Who Am I" (Brandon) 291
"Who Am I" (Eliran) 1136
"Who Am I" (Hatch) 1450
"Who Am I" (Mark) 359
"Who Am I" (Strouse) 214
"Who Am I, Who Are You, Who Are We?" 1236
"Who Are These Men?" 673
"Who Are These People?" 1134
"Who Are They to Me?" 1449
"Who Are We" 1330
"Who Are You?" (Carmines) 834
"Who Are You?" (Meyer) 1440
"Who Are You?" (White) 1058
"Who Are You Anyway?" 1637
"Who Broke the Lock?" 777
"Who But You?" 1077
"Who Can Benefit You Most?" 1671
"Who Can Control the Human Heart" 1151
"Who Can I Turn To (When Nobody Needs Me)?" 1623
"Who Can Say?" 493, 1124, 1537
"Who Cares?" 1166, 1167, 1577
"Who Cares for Love? (Que Te Importa Que No Venga)" 488
"Who Did Langston Love?" 573
"Who Do They Think They Are?" 825
"Who Do We Thank!" 752
"Who Does She Think She Is?" 957
"Who Gives a Damn" 1209
"Who Gives a Hey" 1446
"Who He? Don't Know!" 32
"Who Hit Me?" 908
"Who Is Hannah?" 658
"Who Is It?" 362
"Who Is It? The Grocery Boy" 44
"Who Is Like Unto Thee" 647
"Who Is She?" 453
"Who Is Sylvia?" 1568, 1569
"Who Is the Lucky Girl to Be?" 1167
"Who Is the Man" 717
"Who Is This Child" 3
"Who Is This Man?" (Friedman) 1441
"Who Is This Man?" (Lippa) 1778
"Who Is This Man?" (Paul) 1361, 1362
"Who Is This Man?" (Rue) 1333
"Who Is This Man?" (Telson) 615
"Who Is This Paragon?" 1111
"Who Is This Woman" 1219
"Who Knows Better Than I" 1078
"who knows if the moon's a balloon" 1222
"Who Makes Much of a Miracle?" 903
"Who Needs It" 1440
"Who Needs Presents" 576
"Who Needs Who?" 196
"Who Put Out the Light That Lit the Candle That Started the Fire That Started the Flame Deep Down in My Heart" 698
"Who Put the Bomp" 205, 854
"Who Put the Glitz in Fritz" 1761
"Who Says You Always Have to Be Happy?" 214
"Who Shall Tell the Sorrow?" 362
"Who the Hell Do These Wise Guys Think They Are?" 1309
"Who Threw the Overalls in Mrs. Murphy's Chowder?" 775
"Who Walks Like a Scarecrow" 76
"Who Wants to Live in New York?" 1491
"Who Wants to Work?" 1076
"Who Were You with Last Night?" 1639
"Who? Where? What?" 652
"Who: Whom" 1168
"Who Will Be There" 1432
"Who Will Believe in My Verse" 1569
"Who Will Bring Her Home" 1345
"Who Will Buy" 1742
"Who Will Count the Stitches?" 1323
"Who Will Dance with the Blind Dancing Bear" 1650
"Who Will Go to the War When It Comes?" 609
"Who Will I Be?" 734
"Who Will It Be?" 643
"Who Will the Next Fool Be" 1317
"Who Will You Marry Then?" 697
"Who Would Have Thought?" 345
"Who Would Have Thought It?" 1637
"Who Would Write Something Like That?" 44
"Who You Are" 1320, 1321
"Who You Gonna Blame?" 196
"Whoa, Baby" 1148
"Whoa Boy" 919
"Who'd Believe?" 1452
"Who'd Ever Guessed It?" 275
"Who'd Have Guessed It?" 1147
"Whoever You Are, I Love You" 83
"Whole" 610
"Whole Lotta Real Good Feeling" 1550
"Whole World" 1439
"The Whole World Revolves Around You" 855
"The Whole World Will Be Watching" 1595
"Who'll Be the One (If Not Me)" 1726
"Who'll Prop Me Up in the Rain" 926
"Who's Afraid of I. J. Fox" 87
"Whoop De Doo" 582
"Whoop-Dee-Doo!" 1772
"Whoopee!" (aka "Whoopie") 304, 672
"The Whores Behind the Doors" 948
"Who's Gonna Be the Winner?" 148
"Who's Gonna Teach the Children?" 785
"Who's Got Extra Love?" 1830
"Who's New" 949
"Who's Next" 1654
"Who's on First" 377
"Who's on Our Side?" 1739
"Who's Perfect?" 867
"Who's Perfect for You?" 867
"Who's Sorry Now?" 1353
"Who's That Bubbly Black Girl?" 222
"Who's That Man?" 573
"Who's That Woman?" 807
"Who's the Fool?" 504
"Who's the Girl" 369
"Who's the Greatest?" 912
"Who's the Mac" 804
"Who's the Thief?" 833
"Who's This Chick?" 834
"Who's This Geezer Hitler?" 1540
"Who's Who" 725, 1097
"Who's Who in the Cast" 1254
"Whose Baby Are You?" 1011
"Whose Hands Are These" 1143
"Whose Idea Was This?" 864
"Whose Is the Love" 1443
"Whose Izzy Is He?" 1442
"Why" (Baron) 541
"Why" (Finn) 41
"Why" (Klein) 1083
"Why" (Kole) 743
"Why" (Larson) 1634
"Why" (Leslee) 78
"Why" (Morrock) 1646
"Why" (Styne) 100
"Why Ain't We Got a Dome?" 569
"Why Am I Afraid To Love" 1171
"Why Am I So Happy?" 1134
"Why and Because" 1767
"Why Are We Here" 1713
"Why Bless My Soul" 609
"Why Bother?" 1756
"Why Can't He Be Like Me" 100
"Why Can't I See God?" 1708
"Why Can't I Speak?" 1685
"Why Can't I Walk Through That Door?" 308
"Why Can't It Be?" 706
"Why Can't Me and You?" 785
"Why Can't We?" 67
"Why Can't We Turn Back the Clock?" 633
"Why? Cause I'm a Guy" 739
"Why Did I Do It" 100
"Why Did I Forget?" 643
"Why Did I Listen to That Man?" 1712
"Why Did It Have to Be You" 990
"Why Did Ya Go?" 1117
"Why Did You Have to Be a Lawyer?" 463
"Why Did You Have to Come Into My Life?" 979
"Why Did You Make Me Love You?" 1326
"Why Do I Keep Going to the Theatre?" 1758, 1759, 1761
"Why Do I Love Bennie?" 1151
"Why Do I Love You?" 1644
"Why Do I Only" 1472
"Why Do I See God?" 1204
"Why Do the Wrong People Travel?" 428, 1390
"Why Do We Dance?" 1523
"Why Doesn't He Come?" 362
"Why Doesn't She Call on Me?" 2
"Why Don't I Leave Him" 1319
"Why Don't They Believe Me" 1132
"Why Don't We Run Away" 781
"Why Don't We Switch?" 1302
"Why Don't We Try Staying Home" 1704
"Why Don't You Believe Me?" 464
"Why Girls Leave Home" 622
"Why Go Anywhere at All?" 348
"Why Grow Up" 1108
"Why, Hail! It's Dinny!" 384
"Why Hast Thou Done Evil to These People?" 647
"Why, Hepzibah" 717
"Why How Now Madam Flirt" 117
"Why Is It I Just Don't Belong" 501
"Why Is It the Woman Who Pays?" 13
"Why Is My Verse So Barren" 1569
"Why Johnny?" 1758
"Why, Love?" 1102
"Why, Mrs. Doe!" 92
"Why Must I Be a Teenager in Love?" 1353
"Why Not?" (Camilo, et al.) 55
"Why Not?" (Feinstein) 1052
"Why Not?" (McKibbins) 778
"Why Not Leave" 1727
"Why Robert, Why" 71
"Why Should He" 717
"Why Should I Wait for a Prophet?" 1418
"Why Should They Know About Paris?" 480
"Why Should This a Desert Be?" 1437
"Why Should We Talk" 1472
"Why Shouldn't I?" (Meyer) 1652
"Why Shouldn't I?" (Porter) 567
"Why Speak of Money?" 912
"Why Try Hard to Be Good" 1164
"Why Was I Born" 883
"Why We Do It" 975
"Why We Tell the Story" 1191
"Why Wives" 33
"Wichita Kid Bullwhips" 1720
"Wichita Vortex Sutra" 729
"Wicked Little Town" 680
"A Wicked Man" 448
"The Wicked Man" 1457
"Wide-Awake Morning" 1445
"Widow's Lament" 194
"Widow's Testimony" 1011
"Wie Man Sich Bettet" 1773
"Wife Beating Song" 975
"The Wife's Statement" 1422
"Wig in a Box" 680
"Wigs" 22
"Wild" 1475
"Wild and Reckless" 1366
"Wild Bird" 1513
"The Wild Blue" 1447
"Wild Blue Yonder" 892
"Wild Cherry River" 1493
"Wild Kingdom" 1045
"Wild Montana Skies" 37
"Wild Strawberries" 1299
"A Wild, Wild Party" 1778
"Wild Women" (Cox) 55
"Wild Women" (Elliott and Rose) 411
"Wild Women" (Unknown) 553
"Wild Women Don't Have the Blues" 181, 182
"Wildcat Moan" 950
"Wildflowers" 571
"Wilkommen" 212, 1685
"The Will" (Katsaros) 1071
"The Will" (Rosenblum) 1707
"Will Answer All Sincere Replies" 1168
"Will He Ever Know?" 962
"Will I Wake Up Tomorrow?" 1815
"Will My Real Love Please Stand Up" 1125
"Will She Not Come Again" 1519
"Will Someone Remember Me?" 1669
"Will That Ever Happen to Me?" 1554
"Will They Remember" 545
"Will You?" 641
"Will You Be My Yvette?" 1510
"Will You Buy Any Tape?" 1437
"Will You Love Me in December as You Do in May?" 695
"Will You Love Me Tomorrow" 1591
"Will You Remember" 1570
"Will You Still Love Me Tomorrow" 115
"Willa" 1420
"Willard Scott" 643
"William Overcast" 1806
"Willie" 391
"Willie the Weeper" 94
"Willing to Go" 1631
"Willmouse" 419
"Willow in the Wind" 669
"The Willow Song" 1437
"Willow Weep for Me" 180, 181, 182
"Willow, Where We Met Together (Willow Song)" 92
"Willow, Willow, Willow" 1583
"Willy's Prize" 36
"Wilt Thou Be Gone, Love?" 695
"Wimmen's Ways" 835
"Wimmins" 1777
"Win and Lose" 161, 162, 163, 164
"Win for Us, Guys" 952
"Win the War for Lili" 1171
"Wind Around Me" 1063
"The Wind in the Willows" 1784
"The Wind-Up" 1073
"Wind-Up in New York City" 216
"Windchild" 1659
"Winded" 19
"The Window of Appearances" 20
"Window to the Soul" 1110
"Window to Window" 1110
"Windows" 1688
"Windy" 1450

"Wine, Women and Song" 1131
"Wings" 1787, 1788
"Wings Theme" 1788
"Wings to Fly" 278
"Winin' Boy" 813
"Winner" 1035
"Winner Take All" 25
"Winners" 603
"Winners, Losers" 147
"Winning Is Half the Fun" 952
"Winning Is Just the Beginning" 1159
"Winter Comes in Summer" 948
"Winter in New York" 377
"Winter Is Here" 933
"Winter Lady" 1471
"Winter of the Mind" 1287
"The Winter Rose" 884
"Winter Scene I" 1788
"Winter Scene II" 1788
"Wintergreen for President" 1166, 1167
"Winthrop Mackworth Redivivus" 135
"Wipe Out Games" 773
"Wipeout" 1353
"Wipeout at Panic Point" 943
"Wisconsin, or Kenosha Canoe" 1196
"The Wise" 289
"Wiser Than You Realize" 468
"Wish" 1287
"A Wish for a Prince" 889
"Wish I May" 132
"Wish I Was Anywhere Else" 265
"Wish Me Luck" (Moskowitz) 819
"Wish Me Luck" (Parr-Davis [Davies]) 1482, 1750
"Wish You Were Here" 981
"Wishful Thinking" 646
"Wishin' and Hopin'" 115, 1450
"Wishing and Hoping" 1551
"Wishing for a Victory" 1327
"Wishing Song" 1221, 1364
"Wishy-Washy Woman" 1707
"Witch Song" 1751
"Witchcraft" 1210, 1576
"With a Guitar" 1443
"With a Little Help from My Friends" 1426, 1556
"With a Sword in My Buckle" 1302
"With a World to Conquer" 856
"With a Yo Ho Heave Ho" 1221
"With Borrowed Money" 287
"With Cat-Like Tread, Upon Our Prey We Steal" 1270
"With Festive Pride" 1131
"With Lincoln and Liberty" 722
"With Love" 563
"With So Little to Be Sure Of" 1491
"With the Dawn" 1219
"With You in Mind" 1518
"Within This Empty Space" 1253
"Without a Song" 692, 1210
"Without Him" 1745
"Without Me" (Baron) 1618
"Without Me" (LaChiusa) 1618
"Without My Wife" 114
"Without My Work" 114
"Without Rules" 952
"Without You" 765
"The Wizard's Birthday" 287
"Woe Is Me" (Finn) 1680
"Woe Is Me" (Procter) 654
"The Woeful Waking" 612
"Woke Up This Morning" 470, 1672
"W*O*L*D*" 916
"The Wolf and the Lamb" 1647
"Wolf Song" 3
"Wololo!" 1401
"Wolverines" 813
"The Wolves and the Jackal" 11
"The Wolves of Kultur on a Bright and Silent Saturday" 1719
"A Woman" 1265
"Woman (La Femme)" 1641
"A Woman, a Lover, a Friend" 790
"A Woman Alone" 398
"Woman and Waif" 778
"A Woman at Home" 991
"Woman Child" 1307
"The Woman I Love" 823
"A Woman in Love" 1752
"The Woman in Me" (Marks) 185
"The Woman in Me" (Smith) 510
"A Woman in My Bathroom" 973
"A Woman in Search of Happiness" 1250
"Woman in the Moon" 1106
"A Woman Is Just a Female" 357
"A Woman Left Lonely" 965
"A Woman Like You" 1402
"Woman Makes the Man" 598
"A Woman Must Never Grow Old" 1364
"A Woman Must Think of These Things" 1364
"A Woman Needs Approval Now and Then" 614
"Woman Never Understan'" 715
"The Woman of the Century" 89
"Woman of the World" 78, 308
"Woman of the Year" 511
"Woman on the Couch" 1687
"Woman on the Run" 656
"Woman Power" 1319
"A Woman Rarely Ever" 316
"Woman Stand-Up" 1710
"Woman That I Am" 1298
"Woman to Me" 1441
"Woman to Woman" 634
"A Woman Waits for Me" 903
"Woman Who Acts Like a Man" 1117
"A Woman's Much Better Off Alone" 1594
"A Woman's Place" 1736
"The Woman's Touch" 1172
"Woman's Work" 3
"The Women" 194
"Women!" 366
"Women and Men" 1433
"Women Are Here to Stay" 1131
"Women Behind Desks" 2
"Women in Love" 537
"Women Is Losers" 965
"Women on the Move" 991
"Women Simple" 33
"Women with Women — Men with Men" 467
"Women's Chants" 983
"Women's Medley" 992
"A Wonder" 1008
"The Wonder of a Kingdom" 1446
"Wonder Where My Heart Is" 1440
"The Wonder Years" 1800
"Wonderful" 1181
"Wonderful Bad" 235
"Wonderful Burlesque Days" 142
"Wonderful Country" 780
"Wonderful Dog" 1478
"Wonderful Good" 235
"The Wonderful Machine" 1481
"Wonderful Time Up There" 1484
"Wonderful Way of Life" 1385
"Wonderful, Wonderful" 1551
"Wonderful, Wonderful, Wonderful" 160
"The Wonderful World of Wearables" 1048
"The Wonderful World-Wide Fair" 87
"Wondering" (Brandt, et al.) 464
"Wondering" (Slater) 719
"Wonderland" (Childs) 222
"Wonderland" (Lunden) 1190
"Wonderland" (Smith) 510
"Wonderland March" 510
"The Wonderland of Love" 705
"Wonderland Theme" 510
"Wonders from the Himalayas" 287
"Wonderworld" 1016
"Wondrin'" 56
"Won't Someone Give John Lindsay?" 350
"Won't You Buy My Sweet Blooming Lavender?" 436
"Won't You Charleston with Me?" 42, 199
"Won't You Come Home, Disraeli?" 685
"Won't You Come Home, Judge Crater" 160
"Won't You Come to the Party" 1236
"The Wooden People" 279
"Wooden Sign" 1237
"Woodstock" 1556
"Woodstock's Theme" 1486
"The Woogie Boogie" 232
"Wooing in the Woods" 1527
"Woolworth's" 370
"A Word from Our Sponsor" 415
"A Word from Reverend Mother" 1158
"A Word from the Reverend Mother" 1155, 1157
"Word Game" 1102
"Word Gets Around (The Silly Mementoes We Keep)" 1747
"The Word Is Love" 1524
"The Word of the Lord" 1029
"The Word of Your Body" 1515
"The Word to the Action" 616
"Wordfall" 206
"Wordless Dentistry" 1649
"The Words" 56
"Words" (Davis) 1239
"Words" (Springer) 284
"The Words We Whisper Cha-Cha" 1048
"Words Will Pay My Way" 1078
"Words Without Song" 908
"Words, Words, Words" 361
"Wordsworth" 1252
"Work" 1505
"Work It!" 1669
"Work Me, Lord" 965
"Work On, Pray On" 591
"Work Song" 1399
"Work Song: It's All Right for You" 697
"Work the Wound" 1225
"The Worker and the Shirker" 1072
"Workin' Thru School" 1232
"Working for the Government" 505
"Working in the Name of King" 1423
"Working Man's Shuffle" 1458
"Working Woman" 665
"The Workings of the Heart" 541
"Workout" 603
"Works of Charity" 1471
"The World" 1698
"The World According to Snoopy" 1486
"World at Large" 149, 150
"World at Large #1 (no. 1)" 149, 150
"World at Large #2 (no. 2)" 149, 150
"World at Large Preview" 149, 150
"The World at My Window" 14
"World Beyond the Pane" 1419
"World Creation" 860
"The World Goes 'Round" 1685
"A World I'll Make for Me" 1354
"The World Is Full of Loneliness" 726
"The World Is Getting Better" 878
"The World Is Mean" 1626
"The World Is Round" 1330
"The World Is Yours" 614
"The World Keeps Going Round" 785
"World Keeps Turnin'" 1388
"The World of Confusion" 1604
"World of Men" 950
"A World of My Own" 391
"The World She Writes" 583
"The World Spins" 1073
"World Through the Eyes of a Baby" 1457
"A World to Win" 1481
"The World Today" 1236
"The World Was Dancing" 1498
"World Without End" (Brandon) 1029
"World Without End" (Weiss) 162
"World Without Pain" 958
"A World Without Us" 402, 1327
"The World's a Jug" 1811
"The World's a Stage" 266
"The World's Greatest Loser?" 871
"The World's Greatest Magical Act" 401
"Worlds Apart" 1296
"The Worm Has Turned" 23
"Worry About the Blues Tomorrow" 1577
"Worrying" 624
"Wot's 'Is Name" 360
"Would-ja?" 85
"Would That I" 1446
"Would You Believe Me" 550
"Would You Give a Damn?" 502
"Woulda Coulda Shoulda" 788
"Wouldn't I" 316
"Wouldn't It Be a Dream" 165
"Wouldn't It Be Fine" 1691
"Wow Wow Wow" 27
"WPA Blues" 657
"Wrap Up" 926
"Wrapped, Tied, and Tangled" 1559
"The Wrath of Achilles" 1468
"Write a Letter" 1600
"Write About Me" 1337
"Write Him a Challenge" 962
"A Writer" 1829
"The Writer" 1152
"Writing Down the Story of My Life" 845
"Writing Lesson" 571
"The Wrong Blues" 23
"The Wrong Guy" 328
"Wrong Kind of Man" 1132
"Wrong Note Rag" 911, 1224
"The Wrong Plan" 60
"A Wrong Song" 214
"Wu Chang-Ching and Taewongun" 889
"The Wuggly Ump" 612
"The Wykehamist" 135
"Wyoming" 413
"Wyoming Intro" 413
"Wyoming Lullaby" 1543

"Xanthus, I'm Getting Nervous" 1237
"Xanthus Saves" 1237

"Ya Duele" 1336
"Ya Got Me" 1186
"Ya Gotta Be Female" 1194
"Ya Won't Complain" 1147
"Ya, Ya" 120
"Yacht Club Swing" 18
"Yamacraw" 313
"Yank" 1818
"Yankee Boy" 1328
"The Yankee Doodle Boy" (aka "Yankee Doodle Dandy" and "[I'm a] Yankee Doodle Dandy") 570, 740, 775, 1085, 1096, 1643
"Yankee Doodle Dandy-O" 740
"Yankee Doodle Londoner" 949
"Yankee Man" 1228, 1297
"Yankee Stay" 1751
"Yankev and Rokhl Duet" 1502
"Yankle Deedan Doodah Rag" 1263
"Yardbird Suite" 156
"Ye Shall Know the Truth" 871
"Yeah" 1623
"A Year Is a Day" 332
"The Year of Jubilo" 376
"Year of the Child" 473
"The Year of the Child" 997
"Yearning" 819
"The Years Are Burning" 1392
"Years from Now" 989, 990
"Yehi Rutzoin" 1341
"Yellow Drum" 926
"Yellow Flower" 861
"Yellow Man" 1036, 1049, 1334, 1494
"Yellowstone" 37
"Yenki Doodl Fort Uptown (Yankee Doodle Rides Uptown)" 604
"Yenta Power" 210, 214
"Yes" (Finn) 1121
"Yes" (Kander) 52, 1685
"Yes" (Ross) 930
"Yes Alexandra, No Alexandra" 990
"Yes, and Your Barbara" 1374
"Yes, Aunt" 332
"Yes, I Horrify You" 1374
"Yes, I See a Woman" 461

"Yes, I Thank You, Thank You, Thank You" 736
"Yes, Mamma" 369
"Yes, Sir, That's My Baby" 955, 1096
"Yes, Siree" 371
"Yes, Virginia" 1692
"Yes, We Can" 1159
"Yes, Yes, I Love You" 961
"Yes, Yes, Yes" 1263
"Yes! Mistress It's a Pity" 1401
"Yes/No" 643
"Yesterday I Left the Earth" 1007
"Yesterday I Loved You" 1193
"Yesterday I Was You" 274
"Yesterday Is Over" (Meyers) 65
"Yesterday Is Over" (Roscoe) 1820
"Yesterday Was Such a Lovely Day" 91
"Yesterdays" 883
"Yesterday's Champagne" 743
"Yesterday's Lover" 159
"Yeverechecha" 1341
"Yiddish International Radio Hour" 1619
"A Yiddish Lied (A Jewish Song)" 1453
"Yiddish Rag" 1442
"Yiddish Vaudeville Tonight" 492
"Yiddisha Charleston" 1442
"Yiddisha Luck and Irisha Love" 1442
"Yiddisha Nightingale" 1442
"Yiddishe Tzores" 666
"Yiddisher Father" 654
"Yiddishkeit" 1032
"Yiddle with a Fiddle" 1821
"The Yidisha Charleston" 604
"Yidl Mitn Fidl (Yiddle with His Fiddle)" 604
"Yitgadel" 673
"Yo" 666
"Yo, Chlo" 770
"Yo Es Hora" 1336
"Yo Vivire" 262
"Yo, Vu Nemt Men Di Eydes (Where Shall We Find the Witnesses?)" 604
"Yo-Yo" 1615
"Yodelin' Dixieland" 1138
"Yoga Class" 721
"Yolanda's" 424
"Yoo-Hoo, Raymond, Breakfast Is Ready" 44
"Yoofry" 926
"Yosef's Tango" 1502
"Yoshke Fort Avek (Yoshke's Going Away)" 1619
"Yosl Ber" 1619
"Yosl, Yosl" 1619
"Yossel, Yossel (Joseph, Joseph)" 492
"Yossele and Feigele" 1745
"Yossele Entrance" 1745
"Yossele's Dream" 1745
"You" 1550
"You (Tu)" 208
"You Ain't Heard Nothin' Yet" 993
"You, Alone; A Mansion of Stone" 941
"You Always Wear Black" 1416
"You and I" (Andersson and Ulvaeus) 275
"You and I" (Bricusse) 824
"You and I" (Metcalf) 409
"You & I & Love" 1228
"You and Me" 55
"You and the Night and the Music" 348, 1606
"You Are" 812
"You Are Always Complaining of Your Suffering" 363
"You Are Bugging Me" 378
"You Are Everything" 1494
"You Are for Loving" 132
"You Are Here" 1458
"You Are My Child" 1001
"You Are My Destiny" 889
"You Are My Gold" 786
"You Are My Idol" 1772
"You Are My Solace" 1342
"You Are One of a Kind" 456
"You Are Right" 717
"You Are Something Very Special" 1089
"You Are Still My Boy" 321
"You Are Tahiti" 1402
"You Are the King of Chosun" 889
"You Are the Magic" 403
"You Are the One" 1441
"You Are the Only One for Me (Tu Eres Ese)" 488
"You Are the Only Song" 916
"You Are There" 1117
"You Are Woman" 1752
"You Are You" 856
"You Be You and I'll Be Me" 834
"You Been a Good Ol' Wagon" 959
"You Belong to Me" 1575
"You Better Take Time To Pray" 1308
"You Better Watch Out for Me" 497
"You Blew That B**** Away" 462
"You Blow Hot and Cold" 1300
"You Boys Are Gonna Get Me in Such Trouble" 1121
"You Break My Heart" 615
"You Call This a Promise?" 1333
"You Came from Outer Space" 1661
"You Came to Me as a Young Man" 971
"You Can Be a New Yorker Too" 861, 1037
"You Can Be My Friend" 845
"You Can Beat the System" 1398
"You Can Dance" (Unknown) 1015
"You Can Dance" (Ziskin) 1824
"You Can Dance with Any Girl at All" 42
"You Can Do It" (Brandon) 1467
"You Can Do It" (Hutchins) 1691
"You Can Hang Your Hat Here" 1751
"You Can Kill Love" 656
"You Can Leave Your Hat On" 1036, 1049, 1334
"You Can Never Know My Mind" 656
"You Can Own the Whole World" 359
"You Can Tell a Book" 1232
"You Can't Have Anything" 1345
"You Can't Have Everything" 1061
"You Can't Have Me" 1671
"You Can't Hurry Love" 1551
"You Can't Judge the World" 543
"You Can't Keep a Good Man Down" 790
"You Can't Let Romance Die" 1375
"You Can't Make Love" 448
"You Can't Turn Off the Stars" 1691
"You Cannot Be a Beauty Queen Forever" 67
"You Could Do Worse" 1048
"You Could Hurt Me" 308
"You Could've Been a Big-Time Pimp" 844
"You Could've Told Me" 110
"You Couldn't Be Cuter" 883
"You Dance Real Well!" 1601
"You Devil You" 745
"You Didn't Hear It" 1655
"You Do Something to Me" 567
"You Do This" 1739
"You Don't Have To" 1345
"You Don't Have to Say You Love Me" 115, 1450, 1551
"You Don't Have to Stand There" 673
"You Don't Know Paree" 924
"You Don't Know Why" 1562
"You Don't Look Jewish!" 1813
"You Don't Need It" 692
"You Don't Own Me" 115, 1551
"You Don't Show Me Your Stories Anymore" 206
"You Don't Understand" 1384
"You Embraced Them!" 363
"You Fascinate Me So" 371
"You Fill My Arms" 1441
"You Gave Me Love" 975
"You Gave Your Word of Honor" 1063
"You Gay Dog You!" 714
"You Get Me High" 1153
"You Get What You Give" 1512
"You Go to My Head" 1350
"You Got Me" 1185
"You Got Me Crazy" 1375
"You Got to Be Clever" 1330
"You Gotta Believe" 1226
"You Gotta Die Sometime" 473
"You Gotta Do What You Gotta Do" 1495
"You Gotta Give 'Em a Show" 153
"You Gotta Go Tap Dancing Tonight" 704
"You Gotta Have a Destination" 1713
"You Gotta Keep Making Ends Meet" 1316
"You Gotta Takes Pains" 424
"You Had Me Anyhow" 266
"You Have ..." 1661
"You Have Cast Your Shadow on the Sea" 201
"You Have Everything" 1606
"You Have No Idea" 1031
"You Have the Ring" 444
"You Have To" 1294
"You Heard It Here First" 89
"You I Like" 210, 987
"You Interest Me" 398
"You Just Gotta Be You" 3
"You Knew I Was No Good" 1518
"You Know My Music" 656
"You Know We'll Meet with Your Confrere the Democratic Candidate If He Should Win" 1139
"You Know What I Mean" 491
"You Know Where the Two of Them Went?" 1723
"You Know Who" 599
"You Know Who I Am" 1471
"You Know Your Love Is True" 190
"You Lied to Me" 1749
"You Like Me" 185
"You Little So-and-So" 1350
"You Live in Flowers" 1330
"You Look Like Me" 701
"You Look Like My Valley" 322
"You Made It Possible, Dear" 1177
"You Made Me Love You (I Didn't Want to Do It)" 692, 829, 840, 955, 993
"You Make Me Feel So Young" 1210
"You May Be the Someone" 76
"You Must Believe in Miracles #1" 67
"You Must Believe in Miracles #2" 67
"You Must Believe in Miracles #3" 67
"You Must Believe in Miracles #4" 67
"You Must Forget" 1119
"You Must Remember" 403
"You Must See Evita" 511
"You Mustn't Be Discouraged" 210
"You Mustn't Eat People" 1348
"You Naughty, Naughty Men" 577
"You Need a Lift (Darling)" 1585, 1586
"You Need a Song" 1483
"You Never Can Tell" 986
"You Never Give Me Your Money" 1426
"You Never Know" 1823
"You Never Know the Mind of a Woman" 682
"You Never Know What Hit You — When It's Love" 1608
"You Never Know Who's Behind You" 791
"You Never Miss the Water" 76
"You Never Really Know" 120
"You Never Saw" 249
"You Never See the Sun" 697
"You Never Take Me Anywhere" 461
"You Only Fool Me 'Cause I Want You To" 107
"You Only Get One Chance" 214
"You Oughta Be in Pictures" 681
"You Poor Thing" 848
"You Puzzle Me" 398
"You Really Should See Amadeus" 511
"You Said So Yourself" 1066
"You Said You Loved Me" 742
"You See Before You What Fashion Can Do" 480
"You See in Me a Bobby" 271
"You Sent for Me?" 1111
"You Sexy Thing" 399
"you shall above all things" 1222
"You Shall Drink Miura's Wine" 889
"You Shall Have Money" 1789
"You Should Dance" 1428
"You Should See Him Now" 1618
"You Show Me Yours" 636
"You Still Don't Know" 219
"You Take Paris" 1594
"You Think I Got Rhythm?" 400
"You Think It's Easy to Love Her" 1505
"You Turn Me On" 743
"You Turned the Tables on Me" 1016
"You Wanna Be My Friend" 300
"You Want to Mourn" 1399
"You Were a Hell of a Crowd Tonight" 304
"You Were Dead, You Know" 244
"You Were Meant for Me" 492
"You Were There" 751
"You Who Have Taught Me to Love" 712
"You Will Do Great Things" 1458
"You Will Go to That Court" 331
"You Will Meet with Adventure Today" 1700
"You Will Never Get Into This Restaurant" 1613
"You Will See Hogg" 1443
"You Won at Poker" 1139
"You Won't Believe Me" 60, 1605
"You Won't Die Alone" 1084
"You Won't Do Any Business If You Haven't Got a Band" 570
"You Won't Say No" 605
"You Wouldn't Be You" 100
"You Wrong Me" 23
"You, You, You" 1575
"You'd Be Amazed" 1008
"You'd Be So Nice to Come Home To" 1750
"You'd Better Tell Her!" 575
"You'd Take Him Away" 615
"Youkali: Tango Habanera" 689, 1532
"You'll Always Be My Baby" 929
"You'll Be King" 1441
"You'll Be Sorry" 919
"You'll Do" 662
"You'll Fit Right In" 82
"You'll Go Away with Me" 1422
"You'll Have to Change" 289
"You'll Have to Put a Nightie on Aphrodite" 1282
"You'll Never Get Away from Me" 1546
"You'll Never Get to Heaven" 83
"You'll Never Know" 1571, 1750
"You'll Never See Me Run" 781
"You'll Never Walk Alone" 1002
"You'll Regret a Killing Spree" 1237
"You'll Regret It" 1787
"You'll Still Be There" 1172
"You'll Thank Me in the End" 1706
"Young Americans" 945
"Young and Agile" 1290
"Young and Foolish" 1265
"Young at Heart" 1210
"Young Day" 401
"Young Days" 1136
"The Young Dreamer" 1254
"Young Dreams" 1354
"Young Enough to Dream" 1397
"Young Girl" 1353
"Young I Was" 972
"Young Ladies in Town" 740

"Young Man" (Henderson) 333
"Young Man" (O'Reilly and Stott) 1727
"Young Man, Young Man" 591
"Young Nhudanycke" 858
"The Young Sailor's Lesson" 977, 978
"Younger Generation" 751
"A Younger Man" 58
"Younger Men Grow Older" 1388
"Youngest President" 1318
"Your Cheatin' Heart" 39, 657
"Your Day Begins Tonight" 727
"Your Eyes Are Blue" 1027
"Your Eyes Danced" 1565
"Your Father's Eyes" 541
"Your Feet's Too Big" 18
"Your Flight Was Smooth, I Hope?" 1139
"Your Good Morning" 1132, 1218
"Your High Note!" 271
"Your Highness Is Beautiful" 889
"Your Home Away from Home" 564
"Your Home Within My Life" 240
"Your Lips and Me" 763
"Your Love Is My Love" 1550
"Your Move" 293
"Your Name May Be Paris" 1468
"Your Prince" 741
"Your Proof Contains a Hole" 485
"Your Show" 36
"Your Squad Is Your Squad" 1818
"Your Sticks, Your Hat, Your Hand" 290
"Your Time Has Come" 706
"Your Time Will Come" 196
"Your Valentine" 1060
"Your Way of Loving" 467
"Your Words Were Music" 14
"You're a Big Boy Now" 852
"You're a Good Boy" 995
"You're a Good Man, Charlie Brown" 1828
"You're a Grand Old Flag" 570, 775, 1643
"You're a Hero Now" 485
"You're a Little Young for the Job" 726
"You're a Long, Long Way from America" 1390
"You're a Lucky Fellow, Mr. Smith" 1764
"You're a Natural" 185
"You're Already There" 929
"You're Beautiful" (Contet) 361
"You're Beautiful" (Solly) 200
"You're Dancing Inside Me" 220
"You're Different" 1726
"You're Divine" 109
"You're Dreaming" 969
"You're Even Better Than You Think You Are" 997
"You're Far from Wonderful" 942
"You're Getting Warmer" 1143, 1144
"You're Gonna Miss Me" 1554
"You're Gonna Need Somebody" 1174
"You're Gorgeous, You're Fantastic" 705
"You're in Love" (Porter) 567
"You're in Love" (Raposo) 1468
"You're in New York Now" 1483
"You're in the Army Now" 827
"You're Just in Love" 1575
"You're Like" 1751
"You're Loving Me" 1358
"You're Lucky" 132
"You're Mine" 157
"You're My Everything" 96
"You're My Favorite Lullabye" 975
"You're My Friend" 1207
"You're My Happiness" 1452
"You're My Last Chance" 319
"You're My Love" 1423
"You're My Lullaby" 1188
"You're My Man" 472
"You're My World" (Bindi) 1450
"You're My World" (Perry) 1320, 1321
"You're My Yaller Flower" 861
"You're Never Fully Dressed without a Smile" 237
"You're Not" 1420
"You're Not Getting Older" 161, 162, 163
"You're Not Ready" 1335
"You're Not the Mayor" 1037
"You're Not the Type" 1606
"You're Not Unique" 873
"You're Nothing" 388
"You're Off to See the World" 1571
"You're on the Radio" 431
"You're On Your Own" 663
"You're on Your Own Now" 1723
"You're Sensational" 1210
"You're So Good, John" 25
"You're So Indifferent" 1521
"You're Something More Than I Bargained For" 160
"You're the Best Thing That Ever Happened to Me" 778
"You're the Bottom" 469
"You're the Cream in My Coffee" 171, 1350, 1494
"You're the Fairest Flower" 766, 935
"You're the Most Impossible Person" 1652
"You're the Only One" 631
"(You're the) Sweet Beginning" 652
"You're the Top" 63, 367
"You're the Woman I Want to Be" 1061
"You're There" 929
"You're There Too" 1201
"You're Tired of Dancing" 1063
"You're Too Far Away" 1160
"You're Too Smart" 985
"You're Weird but You're Wonderful" 1693
"You're Wonderful" 388
"You're You" 1585, 1586
"Yours" 1750
"Yours, Use Me" 1721
"Youth Speaks Out" 1276
"You've Brightened Up My Day" 408
"You've Got a Friend" 1591
"You've Got It" 682
"You've Got Parts" 769
"You've Got That Thing" 1823
"You've Got the Devil in Your Eyes" 1713
"You've Got the Right Key but the Wrong Keyhole" 1198, 1435
"You've Got to Be a Tiger, Tiger" 304
"You've Got to Die to Be Born Again" 279
"You've Got to Get Rid of It" 720
"You've Got to Go Down" 740
"You've Got to Keep Building" 1107
"You've Got to Let Go" 1219
"You've Got to Stay in the Game" 1763
"You've Got to Stay Real Cool" 1174
"You've Got Yourself a Bunch of Woman" 1231
"You've Gotta Have a Passion" 272
"You've Lost That Lovin' Feeling" 854
"You've Never Seen" 1111
"You've Outstayed Your Welcome" 653
"You've Said That There's a Certain Well-Known Tree" 1139
"You've Taken My Blues and Gone" 1373
"Yum, Yummy, Yum" 1788
"Yuppie Love" 1113

"Zalinka" 963
"Zanna's Song" 1830
"Zap!" 1732
"Zasho " 651
"Zay Gebentsht Du Fraye Land" 1715
"Zebra Club" 926
"Zei Gezent" 683
"Zi Vet Kumen Fun Di Berg (She'll Be Coming from the Mountains)" 604
"Zibuyile Emasisweni (It's Finally Happening)" 1401
"Ziegeuner" 1170
"Zim Zam Zee" 1115, 1116
"Zing! Went the Strings of My Heart" 746, 840
"Zip" 428
"Zip Community" 1331
"Zisana Abantwane" 1284
"Zollst Mich Gedenk'n" 1212
"Zombie Prom" 1831
"Zombies from the Beyond" 1832
"Zoom" 986
"Zuhhalterballade" (aka "Ballad of the Pimp and the Whore") 880, 1773
"The Zulu Stomp" 1394
"Zum Gali, Gali" 740
"Zut Alors" 1066

Name Index

References are to entry numbers

A.D. Philip 1330
Aaida, Mariann 1579
Aaron, Adina 1329
Aaron, Paul 969, 1396, 1606
Aaronson, Jack 1289
Abaldo, Joseph 773
Abar, James 1143
Abbasi, Sophia 1320
Abbey, Lucinda 1481
Abbott, Annie 347, 1081
Abbott, Bud 377
Abbott, Charles 1511
Abbott, Chuck 949
Abbott, George 201, 1193, 1670
Abbott, Loretta 1064, 1300
Abbott, Michael 1141, 1709
Abbott, Richard 1278
Abbott, Ron 623
Abboud, Mona 616, 1716
Abbriano, Anthony 706
Abdul, Paula 1347
Abdulov, Alexander 849
Abdul-Rahiim, Ifetayo 1816
Abdul-Rahiim, Ihsan 1816
Abel, Chele 504, 822
Abel, Joel 1755
Abel, Jonathan 481
Abel, Marc 403
Abel, Marietta 481
Abel, Ron 172
Abell, David 1029
Abelson, Robert 1619
Abena, Gary 30
Aber, Christopher 914
Aberlin, Betty 27, 558, 753, 852, 1829
Abernethy, Jane M. 1763
Abernethy, Thomas G. 1475
Abeson, Anthony 1370
Able, Will B. 121, 572, 677
Abraham, Christine 1020
Abraham, F. Murray 1562
Abrahams, Jody 1338, 1575
Abrahamsen, Geraldine 626
Abrahamson, Neil 1233
Abramovitz, Jill 845
Abrams, Judith Ann 463
Abrams, Larry 1107
Abrams, Steve 1524
Abramski, Joe 1267
Abramson, Deborah 130
Abravanel, Wayne 811
Abravaya, Victor 713
Abromov, Anatoly 849
Abruzzo, Charles 194
Abuba, Ernest 1213, 1214
The Abyssinian Baptist and Institutional Radio Choirs 615
Acaro, Bob 1124
Accardo, Michael 1434
Acevedo, Herbert 786
Achilles, Peter 1341
Achziger, Lowell B. 595
Acito, Tim 1073, 1830
Acker, Kathy 158
Acker, Mitch 1025
Ackerman, Dorine 121
Ackerman, Emily 607
Ackerman, Loni 218, 377, 1250, 1524
Ackerman, Meyer 751, 806
Ackerman, Robert Allan 773, 1042
Ackerman, Sally 1163
Ackerman, Shelle 800
Acomb, Jen 746
Acosta, Mercedes 1588
Acree, Donald 313, 1039
Adair, Alan 1229
Adair, Erin 226
Adami, Valerie 1660
Adamo, Mark 941
Adams, April 337
Adams, Becky 1310
Adams, Betsy 1381
Adams, Chris 210
Adams, Christopher 210
Adams, Daniel 1804
Adams, Darin S. 1815
Adams, David 475, 1015, 1388
Adams, Dianne 1194, 1784
Adams, Don 1576
Adams, Emily 759, 823, 1349, 1776
Adams, J. Edward 501
Adams, J.B. 58, 89
Adams, Jean 1021
Adams, Jeffrey 82
Adams, John 363, 1139
Adams, Jon-Alan 789
Adams, Kenny 60, 1164, 1221
Adams, Kevin 296, 399, 680, 1225, 1515, 1545
Adams, Lee 214, 237, 603, 858, 942, 1100, 1447, 1448
Adams, Nelle 603
Adams, Pamela 316, 1196, 1346
Adams, Robert K. 1594
Adams, Ruth 82
Adams, Samuel 1691
Adams, Spence 221
Adams, Trude 911
Adamson, David 1470
Adamson, Harold 68
Adan, Richard 118
Adano, Erni 107
Adano, Ernie 1531
Adderly, Nat 996
Addinsell, Richard 1142
Addison, Bernard 569
Addison, John 445
Adelaar, Jesse 1128
Aden, Cecil 1369
Adilifu, Kamau 1816
Adkins, Angelo 1544
Adkins, Gilbert 1021
Adkins, Paul Spencer 294
Adkins, Walter 1570
Adler, Arlene 254, 488
Adler, Bruce (Brucie) 147, 585, 604, 608, 666, 874, 1362, 1619
Adler, Diane 1751
Adler, Gary 38, 77
Adler, Gil 303
Adler, Jerry 1113
Adler, Julius 585, 874
Adler, Marion 2, 444, 644
Adler, Morris 782, 1026
Adler, Peter Hermann 1587
Adler, Stella 826
Adler, Steven 179, 511
Admire, Jere 1185
Adolfi, Jack 706
Adoniadis, Sofia 1346
Adorante, Joseph 1030, 1776
Adri 361
Adrian, Max 1576
Adshead, Patricia 398, 567, 697, 773, 794, 865, 866, 1593
Adu, Frank 885
Aduba, Uzo 1429
Adzima, Nancy 869, 958
Aft 1648
Ageloff, Betty 1399
Agin, Debbie 1615
Agin, Susan 808
Agmon, Yaacov 1203
Agress, David 210
Agress, Ted 955
Aguero, Juan Manuel 118
Aguila, Kevin Del 38
Aguilar, David 1083
Aguirre, Paul 983
Ahearn, Michael 254
Ahern, Steve 967
Ahitov, Arik 742
Ahlert, Richard 9
Ahmad, Irfan 1233
Ahola, Helen 600
Ahrens, Lynn 375, 583, 973, 1006, 1100, 1101, 1191
Ahronheim, Albert 143, 391, 424, 769, 1251
Ahumada, Jose 68
Aibel, Douglas 77, 114, 285, 413, 658, 848, 1237, 1503, 1645, 1752
Aidman, Charles 1488
Aiken, Alfred 1751
Aikman, Julia 1543
Ailes, Roger 773, 1297
Ailey, Alvin 62, 815, 816, 1029
Ainslee, Winifred 66
Ainslie, Scott 321
Ajayi, Afolabi 20, 21, 1004
Akalaitis, JoAnne 1344, 1788
Akana, Marian 1320
Akerlind, Christopher 122, 471, 859, 1422
Akers, Andra 1739
Akers, Karen 800
Aki, Haru 1169, 1398
Akinlana, Babfemi 20
Aklaff, Pheeroan 1816
Ako 1410
Alagia, Mary 1615
Alailima, Marie 562
Alan 1393
Alan, Charles 1115
Alasa, Michelangelo 276
Alatter, Hanan 938
Albano, John 1182
Albee, Edward 104
Albergo, Mina 1016
Albert, Allan 1313, 1314
Albert, Ernest 136
Albert, Eugene 36
Albert, Louis 266, 1015
Albert, Lynne E. 601
Albert, Margot 1311
Albert, Wil 384
Alberti, Janet 1257
Alberts, Eunice 331
Albery, Shana 328
Albrecht, Gretchen 599, 948
Albrecht, Johanna 1473, 1522
Albrecht, Timothy 1742
The Albrights 772
Alcock, Merle 868
Alda, Alan 352
Alda, Frances 298, 340, 988
Alden, Christopher 673, 1532, 1689
Alden, David 1741
Alden, Michael 892
Alden, Tod 1618
Aldene, Greta 274, 693
Alderfer, Eric 1028
Aldin, Sandra 1660
Aldous, Brian 1674
Aldredge, Theoni (Vachlioti) 27, 58, 90, 175, 277, 283, 306, 307, 649, 992, 1096, 1481, 1492, 1513, 1628, 1633, 1746
Aldredge, Thomas (Tom) 1052, 1295
Aldrich, Janet 979, 1301
Aldridge, Amanda 391
Aldridge, Erbert 891
Aleandri, Emelise 1294
Alers, Yassmin 208
Alessandrini, Gerard 377, 511, 512, 513, 514, 515, 516, 517, 518, 519, 520, 521, 522, 523, 524, 525, 526, 1067
Alessi, Paul 1151
Aletter, Frank 566
Alevy, Maurice 379
Alexander, Adinah 1141, 1547
Alexander, Alice 1696
Alexander, Brooks 120
Alexander, Calvin 1
Alexander, Cheryl 222, 934
Alexander, David 944
Alexander, Hugh 1701
Alexander, Jace 70, 1188
Alexander, James 205
Alexander, Jason 1243
Alexander, John 1587
Alexander, Larry 852, 1661
Alexander, Layne R. 1202
Alexander, Mimi 693
Alexander, Patricia 284
Alexander, Ross 976
Alexander, Sharon 1321, 1435
Alexander, Taro 1188
Alexander, Tory 1011
Alexis, Connie L. 179
Alfano, Peter 15
Alfiorova, Irena 849
Alfonso, Gerald 1177
Alford, Lamar 595, 1080, 1620
Alford, Larry 818
Alfreds, Michael 1011
Alger, Tim 1548
Alice, Mary 1580, 1620
Alinder, Dallas 1620, 1666
Alisi, Art 826
Alk, Howard 22, 1415, 1649
All, Harriet 601
Allair, John 423
Allan, Lewis 609, 1000
Allan, Maude 1278
Allan, Richard 1267
Allan, Ted 289
Allburn, Peter P. 1128
Alldredge, E. Don 1043
Allegro, Joe 273
Allen, Deborah (Debbie) 1633
Allen, Charles 115
Allen, Barbara 475
Allen, Billie 116, 187, 333, 1065
Allen, D.R. 722
Allen, Debbie 107, 959, 1699
Allen, Elizabeth 908
Allen, Gene 1754
Allen, George 535
Allen, Glenn Seven 491, 1110
Allen, Jeffrey 719
Allen, Jennifer 37, 954, 1289, 1366, 1427
Allen, Joe 1742
Allen, John 360, 1488, 1824, 1825
Allen, Jonelle 649, 716, 1689
Allen, Judy 346
Allen, Lee 65
Allen, Lewis 151
Allen, Mana 1733
Allen, Marc, III 834, 1311
Allen, Marianna 15, 184, 1668
Allen, Dr. Niathan 278

Allen, Norman 572
Allen, Peter 1504
Allen, Ralph G. 377
Allen, Raymond 705, 1621
Allen, Richard 648
Allen, Richie 821
Allen, Sasha 103
Allen, Scott 283
Allen, Seth 426, 664, 1057, 1082
Allen, Thomas Michael 1742
Allen, Vera 620, 621
Allen, Whitney 404, 1067
Allen, William B. 761
Allen, Woody 616
Allen-Dutton, Jordan 189
Aller, John 1048
Alley, Fred 1513
Allgood, Anne 712, 1390
Allison, Bernie 1384
Allison, Fred 962
Allison, Karl 406, 692
Allison, Patti 476, 886
Allmon, Clint 133
Alloway, Jackie 236
Allport, Catherine 397
Allwood, Peter 1233
Almagor, Dan 542, 1203
Almistad, Jimmy 1070
Almon, John Paul 3
Almond, Todd 1237
Almonte, Vilma 897
Almquist, Dean Lyman 384
Almquist, Phillip 591
Almy, Brooks 58, 267, 1456
Alogna, Michael 877
Aloni, Yona 1341
Alonso, Odon 488
Alper, I. 1032
Alper, Steve (Steve M.) (a/k/a Stephen M.) 576, 596, 754, 828, 1141
Alper, Yakov 1212
Alperin, Yankele 819, 1032, 1051, 1212, 1342, 1382, 1453
Alpers, Richard 1040
Alpers, Richard T. 1785
Alperstein, Max 1131
Alpert, Herb 668
Alport, Katherine 713
Alsop, Peter 681
Alston, Barbara 91
Alston, Johnetta 1638
Alston, Kenneth D., Jr. 1623
Alston, Peggy 313
Alstrom, Ed 411
Alswang, Ralph 1256, 1649, 1724, 1765, 1813
Altamura, John 1542
Altay, Derin 444, 1321
Alter, Louis 1016
Alterman, Charlie 37
Alterman, Michael 969
Alters, Gerald 858, 1604, 1754
Altglass, Max 1047
Altham, Bill 15, 1776
Althaus, Harry 1187
Althouse, Paul 245, 905, 988, 1369
Altman, A. Arthur 319
Altman, Jane 743, 1392
Altman, Jay 1145
Altman, Jean 319
Altman, Richard 277
Altman, Shelly 780
Altman, Sig 858
Alton, Bill 422
Alton, Walter George 1589
Alvarado, Rachel 983, 1186
Alvarado, Trini 596, 1384, 1829
Alvarez, Carmen 367, 1604
Alvarez, Gabriel Enrique 1325
Alvarez, Lynne 897
Alvarez, Marie 1315
Alvarez, Wally 1040
Alvary, Lorenzo 62
Alversano, Nick 1802
Alvey, Maurice 379
Alvin, Farah 738
Alvin, Robert 1599
Alvy, Dan 749
Alymer, Jennifer 47
Alzado, Peter 346
Aman, John 661, 1153, 1166, 1661
Amaral, Bob 626
Amato, Pasquale 340
Amber, Lili 1341
Amberly, Liz 1370
Ambos, Frank 1092
Ameen, Kim 1094, 1349
Ament, Shaelyn 1327
Ames, Dorothy 977
Ames, Elliot 1331
Ames, Jerry 704
Ames, Lottie 1543
Ames, Paul V. 567
Amic-Angelo, Andrew 1477
Amigo, Lichiana 768
Ammon, Richard 147
Amora, Carmelo 1145
Amoros, Larry 1663
Amos, Keith 1039, 1569
Amouris, Yanni 362
Amparan, Belen 62
Amundeen, Oscar 1278
An, So Youn 889
Anania, Joan 1755
Anania, John 1755
Anania, Michael 246, 267, 374, 854, 929, 1410, 1513
Ananian, Paolo 340, 868
Anchel, David 1034, 1405
Anco, Nancy 1221
Andalman, Jean 101, 662, 1169, 1620
Ander, Alex 175
Ander, Calvin 946
Anders, Karen 766
Anders, Katie 1166, 1202
Andersen, Christine 913
Andersen, D.R. 159
Andersen, Dennis 259
Andersen, Kyle 101
Anderson, Adele 6
Anderson, Arden 1440, 1621
Anderson, Arthur 762, 1438, 1636
Anderson, Blake 1426
Anderson, Chris 1237
Anderson, Christian 1577
Anderson, Christine 372, 1155
Anderson, Clint 535
Anderson, Craig 345, 653
Anderson, Dale 1197
Anderson, Dave 601
Anderson, David 550, 1016
Anderson, Delroy 1629
Anderson, Dorothea 591
Anderson, Edmund 1747
Anderson, Elman R. 307, 357, 1446, 1527
Anderson, Emmett 1145
Anderson, Ethel 1570
Anderson, Evelyn Norton 822
Anderson, Frank 1412
Anderson, Greg 1287
Anderson, Heidi 510
Anderson, Hjordis 834
Anderson, Jim 701
Anderson, Joan 1636
Anderson, John Murray 635
Anderson, Jonathan 655
Anderson, Keith 469
Anderson, Kyle 101
Anderson, Larry 66
Anderson, Lawrence 721
Anderson, Leroy 1101
Anderson, Maggie 1690
Anderson, Many Ann 950
Anderson, Marilyn 212
Anderson, Maxwell 843
Anderson, Melissa Rain 1637
Anderson, Nancy 296, 476, 829, 1818
Anderson, Peter 1679
Anderson, Philip 124
Anderson, Ray 1816
Anderson, Robert 127, 468, 1085
Anderson, Sean 1022
Anderson, Sidney 214
Anderson, Stephen Lee 503, 643, 848, 1726
Anderson, Steve 920
Anderson, Sue 768
Anderson, Sydney 214
Anderson, T. Weldon 1516
Anderson, Todd 1778
Anderson, Tom 1811
Anderson, Valerie 402
Anderson, William 821
Anderson, William D. 1079
Anderson, Wilton 552
Anderson-Gunter, Jeffrey 1762
Andersson, Benny 275
Andewski, Gene 63
Andoniadis, George 427
Andrade, Debra Ann 1221
Andrade, Patricia 1221
Andrade, Paulette 1221
Andre 1566
Andre, Frank 1153, 1774
Andre, Margot 1278
Andre, Yvette 1315
Andrea, Jennie 92, 1131, 1474
Andreas, Christine 23
Andreas, Sara 1425
Andres, Barbara 662, 1629
Andresakis, Andrea 1117
Andrews, Bart 64
Andrews, Christine 1134
Andrews, David 1589
Andrews, Dwight 1816
Andrews, Earnest 1388
Andrews, George Lee 1524, 1717
Andrews, Jennifer Lee 979
Andrews, Julie 1492
Andrews, Linda 1030
Andrews, Marnie 780
Andrews, Martin 1140
Andrews, Nancy 324, 987, 989, 1636
Andrews, Sam 965
Andrews, Tige 1627
Andrewski, Gene 1716
Andreyev, Leonid 677
Andreyko, Helena 15, 42, 1829
Andrini, Kathy 1668
Andrisano, Gui 59, 171, 312, 1678
Andros, Douglas 1256, 1595
Ane, Renee 562
Angel, Anthony 702
Angela, June 1410
Angelescu, Jackie 3, 58
Angelo, Judy Hart 1296
Angelos, Bill 1574
Angelos, William 1318
Angelou, Maya 51
Anger, Al 1802
Anglin, Florence 88
Anglund, Dale 1112
Anglund, Robert 1483
Aniston, John 935
Ankeny, Mark 275, 658
Anker, Charlotte 1100
Anne, Alleen 1615
Anne, Jean 1276
Annis, Sidney 1488, 1719
Ano, Bonnie 341, 342
Anselmo, Andy Thomas 918, 1540
Anselmo, Santa 600
Anson, Barbara 722
Antaramian, Jacqueline 754
Antebi, Cary 24
Antheil, George 1729
Anthony, Eugene J. 1670
Anthony, Grace 868
Anthony, John D. 1029
Anthony, Judith 1552
Anthony, Michael 571
Anthony, Philip 533
Anthony, Ralph 545
Anthony, Rick 349
Anthony, Robert 1662
Anthony, Stephen G. 657
Anthorne, Allison 1477
Antoine, Tex 1078
Antonacci, Greg 346, 347, 1666
Antonio, James 389
Antony, John 1031
Antoon, A.J. 1495
Anyanzwa, Kennedy Malumbe 167
Anzell, Hy 939, 1517
Apfelbaum, William M. 103
Aplon, Boris 867
Apolinar, Danny 268, 1827
Appel, Charles 761
Appel, Eric 397
Appleby, Ryan 248, 1366
Appleman, Herbert 1701
Appleyard, Amy 439, 941
Appling, Rick 1696
Apter, Jeffrey 823, 834, 1231
Apuzzo, Richard 1360
Aquilina, Corinne 1046
Aquilino, Dominic 717
Arakawa, Jun 602
Arbacj, Richard 666
Arbogast, Lili 1160
Arcelo, John 1145
Arcenas, Loy 78, 370, 375, 1006, 1191, 1624
Archer, Harry 446
Archer, Julie 1248
Archer, Nicholas 444
Archibald, William 332, 1380
Arcilla, Marie-France 67, 1450, 1458
Ard, Kenneth D. 1025
Ardao, David 833, 1309
Arden, David 1731
Arden, Michael 103
Ardolino, Emile 1168
Arenal, Julie 8
Arendt, Julian 459
Arenel, Julie 1695
Arensault, Brian 1487
Arent, Arthur 1268
Argento, Dominick 256, 1062, 1288
Ari, Robert 829
Arian, Michael D. 1330
Ariel 373
Ariel, Raymond 819, 1032, 1212, 1342, 1382, 1821
Ariela 617
Arima, Stafford 38, 273, 280
Arison, Amir 1322
Aristedes, John 1131
Arizmendi, Peter "Bam Bam" 804
Arkelian, Marina 1134
Arkin, Alan 22, 1415, 1724, 1813
Arkin, David 1724
Arkin, Michael 1049
Arlen, Bob 1420
Arlen, Harold 662, 669, 715, 1796
Arlen, Howard 1141
Arlen, Suellen 1035
Arluck, Elliot 1041
Arluck, Neal 581
Arm, Edith 1713
Armani, Giorgio 899
Arment, Gwen 214, 545
Armerson, Fred 1145
Armijo, Lilian 379
Armitage, Karole 1225
Armstrong, Adrienne 1014
Armstrong, August 549
Armstrong, Bess 1079
Armstrong, Betty Coe 826
Armstrong, David Glenn 1068
Armstrong, Marilyn 488
Armstrong, Reed 1204
Armstrong, Will Steven 254, 1063, 1137, 1227
Armstrong, William 12, 1087, 1284
Armstrong, William Steven 1239
Armus, Sidney 826
Arneson, Christopher 1139
Arno, Dwight 15
Arnold, Barry 225, 336, 372, 390, 445, 582, 602, 833, 963, 1309, 1480, 1659
Arnold, Bob 454, 1584
Arnold, Jacqueline 206
Arnold, Jean 371, 1576
Arnold, Jeanne 117
Arnold, Jennifer 1031
Arnold, Michael 1381, 1498
Arnold, Monroe 456, 902
Arnon, Valerie 1203
Arnone, Jeanette 1682
Arnone, John 1034, 1052, 1094, 1519, 1520, 1641
Aroeste, Joel 43
Aron, Adele 566
Aronson, Arthur 119, 608
Aronson, Billy 1351
Aronson, Boris 1088
Aronson, Frances 41, 77, 102, 689, 690, 786, 1019, 1094, 1219, 1339, 1520, 1820
Aronson, Henry 1188, 1622
Aronstein, Martin 166, 291, 341, 649, 1035, 1072, 1082, 1083, 1096, 1189, 1291, 1397, 1483, 1633
Arpino, Gerald 609, 1789
Arredondo, Rosa Evangelina 668
Arriaga, Luis 897
Arriaga, Xiomara 897
Arrick, Larry 253
Arrocho, Ray 897
Arrow, Jerry 1704
Arsenault, Brian 1706
Artemieva, Ludmilla 849
Arthur, Beatrice 277, 566, 1448, 1626, 1627
Arthur, Carol 368
Arthur, Donald 92
Arthur, George K. 1315
Arthur, Helen 618, 619, 620, 621
Arthur, Ken 57, 537, 845
Arthur, Perry 700, 1522
Artpark Opera Chorus 1405
Aruj, Silvia 1135
Arundhati 1625
Arvia, Ann 1637
Asbury, Anthony B. 648
Asbury, Cleve 1048
Asch, Andrew 295

Ascher, Carollyne 323
Aschinger, Brian 697
Aschmann, Charles 66
Ash, Chayele 1051
Ash, Jeffrey 1053
Ash, Luba 918
Ash, Randl 1215
Ash, Walter 1679
Ashe, Jennifer 1469
Ashe, Rosemary 1316
Asher, David 833
Asher, Frances 975
Asher, Lawrence 284
Asher, Steve 1245
Ashford, Rob 1613, 1637
Ashley, Christopher 69, 102, 233, 1129
Ashley, Frank 156
Ashley, George 397
Ashley, Mary Ellen 416, 492, 1279, 1550
Ashlyn, Joan 1166
Ashman, Howard 377, 414, 588, 727, 939, 1100, 1339
Ashmanskas, Brooks 755, 1498
Ashton, Linda 415, 558, 1273
Ashton, Michael 1160
Ashwander, Donald 624, 1003
Ashwell, Ariel 839
Askey, Darrell J. 68
Askin, Peter 680
Assaf, Michele 208, 1031, 1538
Assante, Armand 183
Assoluta, Fanny Cerito 1358
Astin, John 1626, 1627
Astin, Skylar 1515
Astley, Edward 1432
Astley, Susan 1432
Atandian, Daria 118
Athas, Nick 1420
Atherton, Robert 92, 609
Atkins, Arthur 1140
Atkins, Charles 569
Atkins, Jayson 1349
Atkins, Norman 1221, 1619, 1724
Atkins, Win 246
Atkinson, Clinton (Clinton J.) (Clint) 505, 1028, 1147, 1160, 1683
Atkinson, David 33, 609, 677, 1021
Atkinson, Delroy 1629
Atkinson, Don 969
Atkinson, Peggy 86, 224, 467, 1693
Atlglass, Max 868
Attie, Paulette 442, 1066, 1424
Attile, Larry 1376
Attles, Joseph (C.) 221, 238, 815, 816, 1308
Attractions, Lily Turner 797
Attridge, Rachel 679
Atwater, Carle E. 712
Atwell, Rick 884, 1538
Atwood, Bob 336
Atwood, Robert 15
Auberjonois, Anne 227
Aubrey, Michael 684, 1440
Aubrey, Monte 261
Aubrey-Jones, Jay 1389
Auburn, David 1634
Auden, W.H. 1229, 1241
Audisio, Pietro 245, 1369
Audre 317, 1318
Audrei-Kairen 1148
Audy, Robert 1069
August, Joan 254, 1083
August, Ted 1604
Augustine, Jim 607
Augustine, John 1710
Augustus, Nicholas 1670
Aulicino, Armand 1445
Aulino, Tom 1706
Aulisi, Joseph G. 44, 466, 1013, 1455, 1666, 1767
Aull, Dorothy 1193
Aurnou, Ely 441
Aurthur, Gretchen Alan 1263
Austell, Jan 1419
Austen, Phyllis 1315
Austin, Bethe B. 57, 741
Austin, David A. 738
Austin, Douglas 1618
Austin, Elizabeth 416, 678, 1181, 1584, 1693
Austin, Lyn 12, 358, 393, 561, 691, 713, 728, 839, 847, 1087, 1133, 1535, 1722
Avant 964
Avedisian, Paul 697
Avery, Henry 949
Avian, Bob 283, 1492
Aviks, Valda 1391
Avila, Homer 1139, 1487
Avilas, Carlos 863
Aviles, Miguel 1139
Avnet, Brian 1426
Avni, Ran 289, 878, 1102, 1441, 1449, 1505, 1510, 1607, 1610, 1663, 1708, 1715, 1821
Axe, Ronald 160, 616
Axelrod, Cathleen 614
Axelrod, Dave 1261
Axelrod, David 160, 616, 1076, 1114
Axtell, Barry 89, 1155, 1156, 1157, 1159
Ayars, Bo 247
Aycock, Janet 343
Ayer, Ethan 1789
Ayer, Ethel 1509
Ayers, Charleen 1333
Ayers, Heather 499
Ayers, Mitchell 1021
Ayers, Raymond 1416
Ayers, Vanessa 1816
Ayler, Ethel 1464
Aylward, Tony 320, 566
Ayres, Mitchell 68
Aza, Estelle 1131
Azar, Michelle 1251
Azarow, Martin 1066
Azenberg, Emanuel 1619
Azenberg, Karen 1310
Azito, Antonio (Tony) 229, 660, 1270, 1346, 1628
Aziza, De'adre 1225
Azpilicueta, Jaime 262

B, Hank 1015
Ba Ba Ba Babalooney Band 79
Baba 50
Babafemi 1015
Babatunde, Obba 603
Babb, Roger 647
Babbish, Lenny 1158
Babcock, David 1427
Babe, Thomas 240, 257
Babidge, Darrell 362
Babin, Michael 979
Bach, Johann Sebastian 1069, 1722
Bacharach, Burt 83
Bacher, John 1080
Backar, Sol 529
Bacmeister, Nelia 1151
Bacon, Kevin 1282
Bada, Angelo 1249, 1369
Bade, Tom 907
Badger, Mary M. 1230
Badolato, Bill 819, 1048
Badolato, Dean 574, 1032, 1270
Badyna, Glen 1419
Bae, Geon Ryeong 889
Baer, Cynthia 935, 987, 1163
Baer, Joe 549
Baevsky, Sonya 505
Baez, Osvaldo 1179
Baffa, Diana 1221
Bagden, Ron 1425
Bagley, Ben 367, 368, 861, 1142, 1431, 1447, 1448
Bagneris, Vernel 553, 813, 1198, 1518
Baila, Wendy 712, 1362
Bailey, Adrian 214
Bailey, Alan 1484
Bailey, Bill 139
Bailey, Dennis 416, 678, 1296, 1309, 1392
Bailey, G.W. 1366
Bailey, Hillary (C.) 1252, 1348, 1494
Bailey, Jim 504
Bailey, Karen 510
Bailey, Russell 1481
Bailey, Sonia 960, 1039
Bailey, Victoria 633
Bailin, Harriet 253
Bain, Paul 1161
Baird, Bil 24, 1768, 1790, 1791, 1796
Baird, Bobbi 1475
Baird, Campbell 922
Baird, Mary E. 789
Baird, Peter 24
Baird, Peter S. 356
Baird, Tom 274
Bairnsfather, Captain Bruce 136
Baisch, Jon 1780
Baisley, Helen 92, 609
Bakanic, Bob 1254
Baker, Allen 654
Baker, Bertilla 71, 419, 1428
Baker, Blanche 1282
Baker, Carol 712
Baker, Darrin 930
Baker, David 124, 858, 1254, 1267, 1447, 1448, 1481, 1574
Baker, Dylan 1650
Baker, Earl 1029, 1672
Baker, Eppie 1713
Baker, Gaylynn 566
Baker, Gregg 1022
Baker, Henry 1183, 1397
Baker, Henry Judd 927
Baker, James 369
Baker, Jean-Claude 924
Baker, Joe 633
Baker, Keith 31, 453
Baker, Lawrence, Jr. 132
Baker, Lenny 292, 1562
Baker, Marilyn Cantor 980
Baker, Mark 49, 244, 628, 969, 1378, 1669
Baker, Matthew 552
Baker, Raymond 1314
Baker, Rita 297
Baker, Robert Michael 213, 1607, 1821
Baker, Ron 673, 1023
Baker, Scott 1033
Baker, Word 478, 753, 894, 1154, 1365, 1383, 1481
Baker-Bergen, Stuart 27, 1697
Baker-Jones, Shaun 82
Baker-Lee, Marie 1487
Bakula, Scott 210, 781, 1622
Balaban, Bob 580, 1707, 1828
Balaban, Cherry 858
Balach, Nancy Maria 1336
Balan, Courtney 738
Balcourt, Jon 750
Baldassare, Helen 581, 1158
Baldassari, Michael (Mike) 103, 1406, 1407
Baldauff, Patrick 187
Baldet, Damian 607
Balding, Ivor David 986, 1666
Baldino, Missy 1759
Baldoni, Gail 290, 829, 1328
Baldonieri, Louis 82, 153, 1660
Baldwin, Bill 785
Baldwin, Bryant 1538
Baldwin, Clive 906
Baldwin, Duncan 578
Baldwin, Islish 708
Baldwin, Kate 227, 1491
Baldwin, Katisha 349
Baldwin, Phillip 1651
Baldwin, Roberta Plutzik 1547
Balek, Agatha 1449
Balestrieri, Anthony 92, 1474
Balfour, William 1145
Balin, Ed 235
Balin, Richard 543
Balk, H. Wesley 716, 1062
Balk, Lois 858
Ball, Diane 1119
Ball, George 322
Ball, Jenny 118
Ball, Jonathan 794
Ball, Samuel C. 1358
Ball, William 1111, 1474
Ballard, Beverly 722
Ballard, Clint, Jr. (Clinton) 93, 696, 1343
Ballard, Kaye 367, 600, 692, 861
Ballard, Richard 1217
Ballard, Rita 1682
Ballard, Shane 767
Ballentine, Margaret 494
Ballou, David R. 987, 1319, 1445
Bamber, Sherry 1177
Bamberger, Carl 1244, 1368
Bamesberger, Karin Reed 1419
Bamford, George 708
Band, Hugo 716
Banfield, Scott 223
Bang, Joy 1705
Bank, West 864
Bankey, Christopher 824
Banks, Ernie 1423
Banks, Finesse 768
Banks, Renee 839
Bannister, Harry 1092
Bannon, Jeff 385
Banta, John 1050
Bantay, John 1213, 1214
Bantry, Bryan 692
Barab, Seymour 1621
Baraka, Amiri 1699
Baral, Vicki 916
Barall, Michi 1322
Baranski, Christine 311, 1411, 1557
Barat, Elayne 1080
Baray, John 1214
Barbaree, Bruce 1305
Barbaro, Lucy 1145
Barbeau, Adrienne 625, 1517
Barbeau, Francois 1655
Barber, Ellen 551, 1072
Barber, Elmer 1229
Barber, Ira 1040
Barber, Samuel 62, 1718
Barbera, Noelle 1336
Barbieri, Peter, Jr. 1428
Barbosa, James 1081
Barbour, Elly 1300
Barbour, Virginia 1116
Barcan, Nan 403
Barcelo, Randy 214, 885, 1037, 1080, 1426
Barclay, Humphrey 241
Barclay, Jered 1433
Barclay, William 46, 129, 285, 314, 586, 848, 1363, 1503
Barcliff, Norman 578
Barcus, Steve 1366
Bard, Aza 1116
Barden, Doug 1560
Barend, Robert 1460
Barenfeld, Lori 1252, 1494
Barer, Marshall 986, 1192, 1193, 1430
Barge, David Winston 153
Bargy, Jeanne 638, 1085
Bari, Charles 484, 789
Barie, B.J. 1340
Barilla, John 1505
Barisich, Kyle 362, 717
Barkan, Mark 224, 652, 1737, 1738
Barkdull, Les 564, 758
Barker, Amy 538
Barker, Howard 80, 766, 935, 987
Barker, Jean 1287
Barker, Sean 958
Barker, Sheila 1435
Barker, Sheila D. 313
Barker, Shirley 635
Barker, Wayne 302, 573
Barkley, Lynnette 1365
Barklie, Lance 121
Barksdale, Rebecca 735
Barlow, Anna Marie 652
Barlow, David 632
Barlow, Howard 621, 622
Barlow, Jean 743
Barlow, Richard 638
Barlow, Roxane 1347
Barnao, Anthony 146
Barnard, Francis 944
Barnes, Alli 954
Barnes, Bill 1252, 1494
Barnes, Billy 149, 150, 172, 1183
Barnes, Camille 1543
Barnes, Cary L. 156
Barnes, Cheryl 1029
Barnes, Eric 474
Barnes, Eric Lane 469
Barnes, Gregg 144, 374, 385, 1215, 1551, 1831
Barnes, Irving 944, 1221
Barnes, Irving D. 68
Barnes, Jacqueline 1811
Barnes, Katherine 68, 1021
Barnes, Margie 1633
Barnes, Marjorie 629, 857
Barnes, Paul 714
Barnes, Richard C. 1333
Barnes, Rob 682, 1397
Barnes, Rolf 1578
Barnes, Scott 929
Barnes, Terry 856
Barnes, Theo 392, 756, 757, 920, 928, 998, 1017
Barnes, Thomas 1781
Barnes, Tom 153, 500, 545, 960, 1065, 1148, 1785
Barnes, Virginia 1131
Barnes, Willie C. 839
Barnett, Ellen 1134
Barnett, J. Cameron 995
Barnett, Ken 755
Barnett, Micki 768
Barnett, Nate 214, 1358
Barnett, Randy 237
Barnett, Vince 145
Barney, Ann 1131
Barney, Jay 140, 1028
Barnhart, Jennifer 77
Barnicle, Andrew 1011
Baron, Alan 1026
Baron, Art 1495
Baron, David 1617, 1618

Baron, Evalyn 483, 491, 695, 731, 818, 1323, 1414, 1514
Baron, Jamie 79
Baron, Mark 541
Baron, Natasha 1310
Baron, Sheldon 478
Barone, Anthony 1434
Barone, John 100
Barone, Richard 206
Barr, Kathy 507
Barr, Michael 415
Barr, Richard 104, 409
Barracuda, John (Johnny) 255, 591, 1633
Barrajanos, Daniel 715
Barratt, Watson 1587
Barre, Gabriel 88, 184, 491, 703, 801, 830, 1250, 1353, 1523, 1554, 1646, 1778
Barreca, Christopher 130
Barrett, Bea 1627
Barrett, Brent 300, 364, 1287, 1761
Barrett, Daniel 805
Barrett, Gene 489, 1341
Barrett, Glenn 713
Barrett, James 1543
Barrett, Joe 200, 626
Barrett, John 759
Barrett, Leslie 1107
Barrett, Lorraine 833
Barrett, Mace 1582
Barrett, Mark 1618
Barrett, Michael 325
Barrett, Raina 1168
Barrett, Ric 461
Barrie, Barbara 84, 707
Barrie, Richard 1272
Barrile, Anthony 768
Barron, David 484, 820, 979
Barron, Malita 442
Barrosse, Paul 79
Barrosse, Paul "Skippy" 79
Barrow, Bernard 1517
Barrow, Will 546
Barroy, Michael 620
Barroy, Michel 618
Barrozo, Jean 66
Barry, Alberta 1291
Barry, J.J. 548
Barry, Jorday 1822
Barry, Raymond 426
Barry, Raymond J. 660
Barry, Zoe 1278
Barsamian, Tricia 1818
Barsha, Debra 1197, 1325, 1499, 1505, 1571
Barsky, Barbara 56, 320
Barstow, Richard 1616
Bart, Roger 1706
Barta, Becky 541
Barteaux, Judson 1485
Bartel, Paul 424
Bartenieff, George 701, 702, 925, 1182, 1681
Barth, Dorian 920, 998, 1077, 1349
Barth, Gene 1060
Barth, Mary Christine 554
Barth, Misty 834, 920, 1349
Barth, Nicole 1644
Barthelme, Donald 1534
Bartholomae, Philip 635
Bartholomew, Frank 32
Bartholomew, John 1595
Bartik, Ottokar 344
Bartis, John 735, 1447
Bartkowski, Jules 1321
Bartlett, D'jamin 23, 183, 582, 976, 1685
Bartlett, Jeff 572
Bartlett, Jud 112
Bartlett, Neil 1444
Bartlett, Paul 922
Bartlett, Peter 233, 794, 1695
Bartlett, Richard 135
Bartlett, Scott 1561
Bartley, Robert 302, 463
Barton, Alexander 124
Barton, Eddie 1320, 1751
Barton, Edith O'Hara Lee 200
Barton, Edward 1592
Barton, Fred 511, 526, 626, 1061, 1470, 1772
Barton, George E. 1269
Barton, Mark 499
Barton, Reggie 1419
Bartow, Arthur 957, 1424
Bartow, Nevett 31
Bartu, Janet 976
Baruch, Moishe 1341
Baruch, Steven 102, 108, 479, 1235, 1461, 1495, 1742
Baruti, Osayande 1781
Bash, Phyllis 1268
Bashkow, Jack 1519
Basile, Frank 1049
Basile, Mark 1670
Basile, Sal 695
Baskerville, Priscilla 496, 1816
Baskin, Derrick 1680
Basquin, Peter 173
Bass, Bill 1169
Bass, Emory 104, 236, 277, 566
Bass, Jules 1078
Bass, Tania 533
Bassett, Ralph 256, 1062
Bassman, Bruce D. 1732
Batch, James 985
Batchelder, William H. 401
Batchelor, Ruth 1319
Bateman, Tony 1639, 1640
Bates, James 1655
Bates, Jeff 9, 105, 1065, 1216, 1544
Bates, Kathy 1094
Bates, Lawson 1464
Bates, Leslie 359
Bates, Linda 902
Bates, Rawley 63
Bates, Stephen 3, 1110
Baton, William Charles 1419
Batson, Susan 649
Batt, Bryan 518, 522
Battaglia, Richard 15, 1673
Batteau, Robin 1150
Batterberry, Michael 535
Battista, Lloyd 539, 865, 866, 1456
Battle, Ed 59, 194, 1781
Battle, Hinton 462
Battle, Lois 1488
Battles, Daniel 1349
Battley, David 1091
Batwin, Arlene 834
Baudez, Yveline 957
Bauer, George 875, 908
Bauer, Irvin S. 1373
Bauer, Richard 183
Baughan, Terry 308
Baughman, Renee 283, 1096, 1483
Baum, Joanne 1386
Baum, Roberta 175
Baum, Susan J. 197, 299, 308, 310
Bauman, Henry 1229
Bauman, Mordecai 1229, 1399
Bautier, Michele 1521
Bavan, Yolande 130, 715, 831, 903, 1396
Bawtree, Michael 234
Baxt, George 942
Baxter, Cash 631
Baxter, Connie 654
Baxter, Ernest 21
Baxtresser, Suzanne 647
Bay, Howard 134, 1111, 1399
Bayer, Julius 245
Bayes, Sammy 1083
Bayes, Sammy Dallas 664
Baylis, Barbara 1618
Baylis, John 74, 332
Bayliss, Gene 652
Bayne, Trudy 1268
Bayona, Jose 897
Bays, Robert 197
Bazemore, Raymond 1816
Beaber, Jack 33
The Beach Boys 1560
Beach, Albert 1661
Beach, David 1607, 1712
Beach, Gary 225, 237, 773, 1098, 1480
Beal, Jerry 773
Beall, Alex 1080
Beals, Frederic 9
Bean, David 940, 1604
Bean, Reathel 192, 252, 554, 834, 920, 925, 971, 1231, 1335, 1378, 1484, 1501, 1739
Bean, Shoshana 597
Beane, Douglas Carter 69
Bear, Emily 811
Beard, Betsy 1028, 1279
Beard, Henry 1114
Beard, Mark 727
Bearden, Romare 1816
Beaton, Cecil 1718
Beattie, Paul 1052
Beatts, Anne 1114
Beatty, Ethel 221, 1307
Beatty, Ethel S. 153
Beatty, Herbert 947
Beatty, John Lee 806, 943, 1234, 1235, 1488, 1495
Beatty, Talley 91, 152, 194, 230, 504, 715
Beaty, Richard 1655
Beaubian, Susan 803, 1232
Beaumont, John H. 1153
Beaumont, Ralph 80
Beauvais, Jeanne 199
Beazer, Tracee 1325
Beccio, Barbara 1756
Becham, Larl 1388
Becher, John C. 1605
Bechtolf, Sven-Eric 26
Beck, Alexander 1701
Beck, Emily 240
Beck, Frances 985
Beck, John 1241
Beck, Lisa 216
Beck, William 1716
Beckelman, Laurie 207
Becker, Barbara 1474
Becker, Bruce 542
Becker, Kaitlin 863
Becker, Lee 616, 944, 1192
Becker, Peter 1055
Becker, Randy 1014
Beckerman, Mara 271, 1389
Becket, Roger 844
Beckett, Daniel 1233
Beckett, Samuel 1168
Beckham, William 243
Beckley, Connie 427
Beckman, Claire 889
Becknell, Howard 405, 1539
Beddow, Margery 360
Bedford, Lou 1256
Bedford, Suzanne 308, 408
Bedrosian, Alexander 1483
Beebe, Lucius 1092
Beebe, Hank 1678
Beebe, Harold 745, 1162, 1686
Beebe, Joyce 1349, 1776
Beech, Jackie 15, 392
Beechman, Laurie 833
Beeks, James Delisco 1778
Beer, Alice 618
Beers, Francine 867
Beers, Sarah 607
Beery, Lee 1259, 1473
Beery, Leigh 658, 948
Beeson, Jack 686, 947, 1086, 1506, 1564
Begley, Kim 47
Behan, Keri 1416
Behar, Howard 124, 153, 712, 1434
Behar, Samuel 140
Behn, Noel 436, 448, 566
Beigelman, Mark 586
Beil, Jeff 742
Beinhorn, Joseph 1302
Beker, Israel 782, 1026
Belasco, Jacques 490
Belcher, Daniel 941
Belcher, Wendy Jo 1522
Belcon, Natalie Venetia 77, 222, 583
Belden, Ursula 731, 1323, 1747
Belew, Bill 87, 160
Belgrave, Cynthia 803, 844, 876
Belin, Alexandre 1655
Belink, Susan 60
Belkin, Jeanna 1604
Belknap, Allen R. 310, 976, 1283
Bell, Barbara A. 322
Bell, David H. 267, 1747
Bell, Edith 1172
Bell, Francesca 1172
Bell, Gene 145
Bell, Hunter 1645
Bell, Jennifer 1525
Bell, Kelvyn 167
Bell, Ken 713
Bell, Kristen 1347
Bell, Madeline 166
Bell, Marty 273, 890
Bell, Mary 140
Bell, Melvin, III 167
Bell, Richard 1472
Bell, Vanessa 203, 1001, 1580
Bell-Ranske, Jutta 1597
Bellaver, Lee 256, 1062
Belle, Bonita 33
Belles, Nelle's 134
Bellesen, Pearl 1432
Belli, Mary Lou 468
Belline, Dennis 1504
Bellis, Dorothy 1543
Bellwood, Peter 450
Belmonte, Vicki 1155
Belogorsky, Jacob 441
Belong, Nik 369
Belousov, Vladimir 849
Belsey, Erika 1826
Belson, Edmund 1420
Belton, Nicholas 1103
Beltzer, John 1054
Belushi, John 1112, 1113, 1114
Belzer, Rick 653, 974, 1025, 1762
Ben, Jacqueline 1221
Ben-Ami, Jacob 1822
Benanti, Laura 1637
Ben-Ari, Neal 1201
Benczak, Margaret 186, 224, 250
Bender, Carol 1445
Bender, Howard 574
Bender, Patty 1046
Bendixen, Deborah 539
Bendorff, Robert 452
Beneby, Lehman 8
Benedetto Snyder, Patricia Di 43
Benedict, Gail 401
Benedict, Leon 1713
Benenate, Mia 767
Benesch, Vivienne 122
Beneville, J. Richard 1480
Beniades, Ted 528, 1481
Benish, Jeff 470
Ben-Israel, Ron 1500
Benjamin, Carla 326
Benjamin, Fred 221, 785, 1021, 1504, 1751
Benjamin, James 835
Benjamin, Joseph 1364
Benjamin, Romelda T. 103
Benjamin, Shawn 1345
Ben-Miriam, J. 782
Bennet, Matthew 1326
Bennett 319
Bennett, Albert S. 333
Bennett, Doris 1435
Bennett, Fran 91
Bennett, Fred 1194
Bennett, James Stewart 396
Bennett, Jay 1801
Bennett, Joan Sterndale 1639, 1640
Bennett, Keith 1181
Bennett, Mark 1499
Bennett, Matthew 503, 703, 730
Bennett, Michael 283
Bennett, Peter 696
Bennett, Richard 581
Bennett, Richard P. 1408
Bennett, Terry 217
Bennett, Timothy 229
Bennett-Gordon, Eve 12
Benoit, David 523
Benskin, Sammy 91, 152, 291
Benson, C.J. 116
Benson, Cindy 424
Benson, Deborah 410
Benson, Ellen 397
Benson, Jeffrey 505
Benson, Maggie 1
Benson, Robby 1205
Benson, Robin 390
Bensussen, Melia 967
Bentley, Carlton H. 1140
Bentley, Eric 389, 1346
Bentley, Lorrie 1164
Bentley, Mary Denise 514
Bentley, Ron 488
Bentley, Ronald 254
Benton, Nicholas 1472
Benton, Robert 1168
Bentz, Douglas 1035
Benville, Richard 274
Benzinger, Suzy 129, 733, 926, 1366, 1451, 1581
Benzoni, Peter 779
Berberian, Ara 574
Bercero, Jose 1730
Berdahl, Roger 1527
Berdeen, Robert 93
Berdini, Kevin 1146
Berenson, Stephen 299
Beretta, Joanne 301, 308, 309, 370
Berezkin, Sergey 849
Berezowsky, Sol 898
Berg, Barry 725, 1097
Berg, Christopher 1532
Berg, Lisa 684
Berg, Neil 1303
Berg, Oliver 1445
Berg, Patricia 940
Berg, Richard 703
Berg, Spence 998
Berg, Tracy 475
Berg, Winifred 147
Bergasse, Joshua 248
Bergelson, Ilene 1310

Bergen, Jerry 1385
Berger, Ellis 711
Berger, James N., Jr. 1623
Berger, Jesse Ira 190, 1151
Berger, Keith 216
Berger, Lauree 1153
Berger, Stephen 685, 1138
Berger, Susan 345, 1367
Berger, Ted 1446
Berger, Walter M. 1744
Berger, William 1802
Bergeron, George 1298
Bergersen, Baldwin 318, 332, 534, 1380
Bergeson, Scott 256
Bergman, Brenda 1007, 1149
Bergman, Lee 1041
Bergman, Michael 719
Bergman, Norman 1542
Bergquist, Eleanor 1539
Bergstrom, Lorraine 33, 652
Bergwall, James Curt 736, 1423
Bergy, Jean 1661
Beris, David M. 697
Berk, David 1040, 1493, 1501
Berk, Lara 1340
Berk, Phyllis 604
Berk, Tony 36
Berke, Stanley 1445
Berkeley, Edward 710, 1392
Berkman, Lee 1115
Berkow, Jay 829
Berkowitz, Dan 2
Berkowitz, Judith 701
Berkowitz, Sol 1060
Berkowsky, Paul B. 1074
Berkson, Michael 655, 1452
Berkson, Susan 329, 1160, 1785
Berl, Christine 1244
Berlin, Alexandra 450
Berlin, Irving 69, 305, 1067, 1101, 1408
Berlin, Thom 1500
Berlind, Roger 172, 486, 765, 1545
Berlioz, Hector 1572
Berman, Boaz 108
Berman, David 1268
Berman, Gail 833
Berman, Karen 95
Berman, Marjorie 1323
Berman, Matt 205, 747, 929, 1577, 1663
Berman, Norman L. 794, 1228, 1541, 1704
Berman, Rob 1006, 1491
Berman, Susan 364
Bermel, Albert 389, 632
Bern, Mina 898, 1510, 1619
Bernacchio, Dorian 842
Bernard, Bob 68, 569
Bernard, Charles 809
Bernard, David 574
Bernard, Francis 1264
Bernard, Jackie 505
Bernard, Kevin 950
Bernard, Mitchell 284, 1485
Bernardi, Cynthia 173
The Bernays 1315
Bernette, Sheila 1639, 1640
Bernfield, Lynne 1149
Bernhard, George 105
Bernheim, Shirl 1517
Bernsohn, Sophie 619
Bernstein, Aline 619, 620, 621, 622
Bernstein, Bob 1686
Bernstein, Douglas 2, 84, 299, 685, 1037, 1141, 1421, 1454, 1709
Bernstein, Leonard 234, 244, 911, 1029, 1185, 1186
Bernstein, Leslie 995
Bernstein, Linda 1349
Bernstein, Lisa 1600
Bernstein, Richard 1554
Bernstein, Richard N. 1824
Bernstein, Robert A. 1574
Bernstein, Sid 909
Bernstein, Stanley 909
Bernstein, Sue Renee 1679
Berresse, Michael 305, 1645
Berrian, Bill 1409
Berrien, Jenelle 1478
Berrings, Hank 258
Berry, Ada 1151
Berry, Alison 1629
Berry, Carolyne 730
Berry, Charles 785
Berry, Gabriel 500, 673, 1182, 1402
Berry, Judy 1139
Berry, Ken 149, 150
Berry, Loni 1434
Berry, Marilyn 1464
Berry, Stephanie R. 358
Bertelson, Harold 1131
Berthiaume, Kevin 1419
Berti, Mark A. 505
Bertolotto, Caterina 1665
Berton, Eugene 1688
Berton, Pierre 1754
Berton, Ralph 1688
Bertoncini, Gene 535
Beruh, Joseph 595, 870, 902, 1311, 1626
Beruk, Igor 1395
Bes-Arlene 1475
Besoyan, Rick 80, 766, 935
Besserer, Rob 728, 1055, 1722
Besserer, Robert 122
Bessette, Mimi 224, 1204
Bessoir, Robert (Bob) 247, 492, 555, 1316, 1442, 1760, 1821
Besson, Cassia 1592
Best, Michael 574
Besuner, Pearl 440
Beteta, Michelle 156, 1509
Bethel, Pepsi 813, 1518
Bethencourt, Francis 450
Bethke, Lars 474
Betley, Marge 499
Bettis, John 892
Bettis, Sara 600, 1131
Bettis, Valerie 490
Betts, Doris 1726
Betts, Jack 16, 638
Betz, Donna Lee 1476
Beudert, Mark 1270
Bevan, Alison 1668
Bevans, Phillipa 1716
Bevel, Charles 777
Beverley, Trazana 592, 593
Beverly, Dale A. 1320
Bevins, Michael 1458
Bey, Andy 1034
Bey, Salome 969
Beyer, John 985
Beyer, William 620, 621
Bhabha, Satya 1322
Bhartonn, Edward Q. 1426
Bhaskar, (Roy) 772, 1751
Bhise, Swati Gupte 1665
Biagi, Michael 1656
Biagini, Sal 1467
Bianca, Robert 778
Bianchi, Andrea 1771
Bianchini, Karen 1512
Bianco, Carla 206
Bianco, Joe 456
Bianco, Tony Lo 490
Bianconi, Nancy 146, 1260
Biano, Rich 1240
Bibb, Leon 798, 1399
Bible, Frances 92, 331
Bicat, Nick 873
Bichel, Ken 183
Bick, Debra 1077
Bickell, Ross 1304
Biddle, Christine Mortimer 1538
Bidgood, James 693, 1166
Bieber, Ethel 705
Bieff, Neil 1585
Bieff-Herrera 480
Bielawska, Grayzyna 1275
Bielecki, Bob 1200
Bielski, Czeslaw 1275
Bien, Annie 1487
Bienskie, Stephen 721, 892, 1831
Bier, Burit 1686
Bierbower, Neil 539
Biermann, Wolf 389
Bigelow, Susan 377, 1147
Biggam, Glenn 1131
Biggins, Christopher 1316
Biggs, Casey 325
Bigham, Abra 1150
Bigtree, Norma 336
Bigtree, Sandy 1681
Bilbrey, Scott 680
Bill 535
Billett, Don 603, 625
Billig, Robert 133, 288, 692, 866, 939, 1129
Billings, James 827
Billingsly, Rustin 1028
Billington, Ken 55, 58, 181, 208, 359, 377, 400, 474, 629, 992, 1129, 1205, 1299, 1462, 1486, 1521, 1546, 1575, 1585, 1613, 1620, 1622, 1637, 1645, 1800, 1832
Bilowit, Ira J. 1164
Bimonte, David 1318
Bimson, Wanda 1094
Binder, Christine 890
Binder, Jay 678, 1009
Binder, S. 506
Bindiger, Emily 1471
Bines, David 379
Bingham, June 71
Bingham, Susan Hulsman 1072
Bingham, Vincent 207
Binion, Sandy 997
Binkley, Howell 1073, 1250, 1325, 1513
Binkley, Lane 101
Binotto, Paul 865, 866, 1699
Biondi, Michael 1016
Biondo, Santa 1249
Birch, Patricia (Pat) 43, 45, 203, 244, 376, 463, 466, 528, 625, 660, 710, 741, 1038, 1340, 1459, 1482, 1733, 1756, 1828
Birch, Patricia (Pat) 1707
Bird, Jacqueline 1174
Bird, John 449, 1091
Bird, Rudolph 1138
Bird, Thomas 1664
Bird-Leitner, Sylvia 1816
Birdwell, Thom (Thomas) 18, 105, 603, 1064, 1467
Birkenhead, Susan 1, 865, 866, 961, 1593, 1756
Birn, David 471
Birnbaum, Steven L. 370, 1011
Birnkrant, Arthur 353, 356
Bisaccia, Bob 159
Bischoff, John 362, 717
Bishoff, Joel 739
Bishop, Adelaide 1474
Bishop, Andre 41, 70, 122, 130, 251, 315, 375, 430, 473, 583, 683, 690, 763, 973, 1006, 1019, 1048, 1121, 1191, 1219, 1478, 1553, 1557, 1624
Bishop, Carole (Kelly) 268, 283, 886, 1258
Bishop, D. 258
Bishop, David 948, 1048
Bishop, Fred 545
Bishop, John 232, 822, 1707, 1710
Bishop, Kenyon 136
Bishop, Ronald 1562
Bishop, Steven 154
Bishop, Stuart 1440, 1566, 1652
Bishop, Teddy 768
Biskup, Bill 466
Bissell, Gene 350, 1069, 1273
Bissinger, Robert (Rob) 395, 802
Bitsko, Richard 1316
Bittan, Roy 663
Bitterman, Michael 497
Bittern, Arwin 904
Bittner, Jack 234, 254, 360, 1400
Bivens, Diane 1633
Bixby, Jonathan 69, 305, 1441, 1712
Bixler, Valerie Leigh 1595
Bizar, Francine 997
Bizet, Georges 1100
Bjornson, Maria 938
Bjornstad, Erle 1695
Black, Aaron 167
Black, Arnold 389
Black, Brent 1410, 1441
Black, Colette 374
Black, Collette 1577
Black, David 241, 483, 1396
Black, Don 100
Black, Jimmy Clark 7
Black, Karen 1698, 1751
Black, Lewis 900
Black, Malcolm 1265
Black, Mel 190
Black, Phil 1177, 1388
Black, Rachel 1328, 1821
Black, Royana 1048
Black-Brown, Shirley 214
Blackburn, Charles 191, 1253, 1286
Blackhurst, Klea 154, 1326
Blackman, Jack 851, 980
Blackman, Robert 657, 965, 1804
Blackton, Jack 667, 793, 857, 1318
Blackwell, Donald 940
Blackwell, Susan 1645
Blackwell-Cook, Deborah (Debbie) 592, 593
Blackwood, Linda 15
Blackwood, Pady 24, 356
Blaine, Curtis 461, 915
Blaine, Terry 396
Blair, Diane 274
Blair, Nanette 66
Blair, Pamela 133, 283, 406, 1339
Blair, Richard 87, 126, 350, 556, 557, 558, 821, 852
Blaisdell, Geoffrey 1250
Blake, Arthur 1611
Blake, Curtis 1466
Blake, David 116
Blake, Ebony 167
Blake, George 1385
Blake, Josh 726
Blake, Kathleen 1412
Blake, Marsha Stephanie 1322
Blake, Michael 910
Blake, Paul 822, 1661
Blake, Russell 1398
Blake, Sydney 258, 480
Blakely, Wendy 423
Blakeslee, Carolyn 1086
Blakeslee, Susanne 163, 513, 514, 516, 517
Blakey, Evelyn 814
Blakley, Ronee 1558
Blanchard, Steven (Steve) 541, 825, 1071
Blanco, Michael 418
Bland, Hubert 1131
Bland, Steve 1001
Bland, Steven 171
Blanda, John 1331
Blane, Ralph 132, 1101, 1574
Blane, Steven 1541
Blank, Lawrence J. 288
Blankenbuehler, Andy 760, 1186, 1289
Blankenship, Hal 960
Blankenship, Joseph L. 31
Blankenship, Paul 309, 398, 435
Blankfort, Jase 413
Blankman, Howard 235
Blasdale, Justin 190
Blaska, Felix 561, 859, 1055
Blass, Yago 379
Blatt, Beth 922
Blatt, Jerry 676
Blau, Eric 226, 304, 402, 720, 740, 792, 793, 797, 798, 1162, 1327
Blau, Louis C. 642
Blau, Renee 220
Blausen, Whitney 314, 713, 1446
Blaxill, Peter 545
Blay, Helen 1822
Blaymore, Enid 725, 1097
Blazer, Judith (Judy) 130, 267, 683, 791
Bleach, Julian 1444
Blecher, Hilary 1284
Bleckmann, Theo 195
Bledsoe, Gilbert 1272
Bleezarde, Gloria 1125, 1605
Blevins, Michael 86
Bleyer, Mick 563
Blickenstaff, Heidi 1645
Blier, Steven 880, 881
The Blind Boys of Alabama 615
Bliss, Imogene 1827
Bliss, Janet 1034
Bliss, Tamara 441
Blitenthal, Dan 819
Blitz, R.D. 1531
Blitzstein, Marc 173, 174, 324, 325, 843, 848, 1100, 1140, 1268, 1626, 1627
Bloch, Ivan 855
Bloch, Max 245, 868, 1369
Blocher, Walter, Jr. 1264, 1636
Block, Dean 1494
Block, Dick 313
Block, Frederic 1309
Block, Larry 311
Blodgett, Carol 1302
Bloecher, Ted 1445
Blommaert, Susan 577
Bloodgood, Fred F. 1720
The Bloolips 176
Bloom, Leo 745, 1058
Bloomgarden, Kermit 602, 773
Blossom, Henry 1101
Blossom, Robert 104
Blount, Helon 336, 408, 504, 1108, 1319, 1364, 1485
Blount, Roy, Jr. 377
Blount, Tanya 196
Blue, Arlana 1426

Blue, Dan 1272
Blue, Diana 105
Blue, Pete 133
Blue, Samual, Jr. 1004
Blue Man Group Band 1674
Bluestone, Debbie 1134
Bluestone, Dena 1134
Blum, Baruch 1105
Blum, David 318
Blum, Galen 302
Blum, Joel 599, 606
Blum, Moshe 1212
Blumberg, Carla 708
Blumberg, David A. 685
Blume, Robert R. 1025
Blume, Bobby 312
Blume, Jurgen 1281
Blumenfeld, Mara 583
Blumenfeld, Norman 1464, 1465
Blumenfeld, Robert 599, 1250, 1593
Blumenthal, Francesca 2, 1421
Blumenthal, Leslie 1438
Blumenthal, Vicky 768
Bluth, Fred 409
Blyden, Larry 779
Blythe, Brian 71
Blythe, Susan 1060
Blyweiss, Jessica 863
Boak, Mike 919
Boas, Peg 1370
Bobbie, Walter 409, 625, 1708
Bobbitt, Wendy 1144
Bobb-Semple, Ron 153
Bobby, Anne (Marie) 596, 643, 726
Bobrowitz, Dave 918
Bochette, Alyce 363
Bock, Jerry 1005, 1100, 1381, 1431
Bocksch, Wolfgang 1386
Bodanzky, Artur 245
Boddie-Henderson, Deirdre 1351
Boder, Lada 1134
Bodie, Scott 1194
Bodin, Duane 203
Bodle, Jane 926, 1187
Bodnar, Amy 1428
Bodo, Yakov 1051
Bodry, Penelope (Anne) 386, 464, 1628
Boerum, Laura 1453
Boesky, Billy 471
Boevers, Jessica 778
Bogan, Karen 833
Bogard, Mitchell 1519
Bogardus, Janet 496
Bogardus, Stephen 473, 484, 1019, 1143, 1389, 1697
Bogart, Anne 999
Bogart, Joanne 1099
Bogdanov, Michael 950
Boggs, Gail 244, 975, 1633
Boggs, Lisa 313
Bogin, Abba 60
Bogin, Bernard 1626
Bogok, Gusti 909
Bohachevsky, George 488
Bohanek, James 503
Bohanna, Bob 423
Bohmer, Ron 521, 706, 837, 1613
Bohmler, Craig 444, 644
Bohn, George 1149, 1467
Boisseau, Juanita 1435
Bojar, Alvin 1096
Bojarski, Stanley 1763
Boland, Bill 750
Bolansi 1626
Bolcom, William 257, 421, 422, 1455, 1723
Boles, Glen 381
Boles, Robert 1648, 1832
Bolin, Eli 742
Bolin, Shannon 1311
Boller, Barbara 1029
Bollin, Mariann 66
Bolt, Sarah 1736
Bolton, Guy 63, 902, 1172, 1644
Bolton, John 499
Bolton, John Keene 290
Bolton, Joyce 510
Bommer, Lawrence 1230
Bonafons, Ken 81, 789
Bonazzi, Elaine 1062, 1063, 1462
Bond, Christopher 462
Bond, Clint, Jr. 365
Bond, Francine 1221
Bond, Linda Thorsen 1571
Bond, Sudie 701, 1431
Bond, Willard 1810
Bondi, Don 219, 1622
Bonds, D.B. 67, 997
Bonds, R.J. 1664
Bonds, Rufus, Jr. 1375
Bone, Gene 501, 535
Boneck, Naomi 66
Boneli, Olivia 1563
Bonelle, Dick 372, 980
Bonetti, Mary 868
Bonfiglio, Giuseppe 298, 344
Bonham, Eugene 1229
Boni, John 1069, 1114
Bonine, Marsha 1589
Bonnard, Philippe 1101
Bonnell, Don 274, 1535
Bonnell, Donn 1021
Bonnell, Stephen 799
Bonney, Jo 1429
Bonus, Ben 898
Bonwit, Elsie 85
Boockvor, Steven 1021
Booke, Sorrell 831
Bookman, Kirk 69, 280, 374, 463, 633, 741, 856, 1466
Boone, Frank 187
Boone, Gerri 349
Booth, Charles 1131
Booth, Debra 1020
Booth, Jon Randall 1189
Booth, Randy 1560
Boothe, Power 1087
Boras, Erika Nelson 1731
Borczon, Becky 967
Borde, Percival 21, 255, 1004
Borden, Eugene 136
Borden, Flora 85
Borden, William H. (Bill) 535
Borg, Julianne 941
Borgatta, Mia 1487
Borges, Yamil 203, 1665
Borget, Arnold 708
Bori, Lucrezia 1249
Borice, Andre 1145
Borio, Gene 200
Boris, Ruthanna 1179
Boritt, Beowulf 67, 273, 657, 721, 738, 890, 1479, 1680, 1784
Borle, Christian 430, 1306
Bormann, James 985
Bormet, Garry 1033
Bornstein, Stephen L. 25
Boros, Frank J. 461, 712, 1398
Boroson, Andy 607
Borow, Rena Berkowicz 1502
Borowitz, Katherine 909
Borowka, Mel 1571
Borrelli, Jim 625
Borrie, Alexandra 175, 660
Borrit, Beowulf 57
Borritt, Beowulf 1188
Borrus, Janet 1376
Borsch, Ben 1029
Borsuk, Alice 987
Bortniker, Larry 395
Bortolussi, Sophie 859
Borts, Joanne 604
Borum, Mark 863
Bos, John H. 1066
Bosco, Bob 1331
Bosco, Philip 1628
Bosotina, James 1445
Boss, Bill 9, 1646
Bossy, Michelle 10
Boston, Gretha 777
Boston, T.L. 1158, 1684
Bostwick, Barry 306, 625, 716, 1504
Bosveld, Alice 15, 759, 1349
Boswell, John 83
Boswell, Vet 681
Boswell, William 752
Bottari, Michael 14, 476, 749, 1204
Bottcher, Ron 62, 1088, 1227
Botti, Susan 1020
Botting, Ronald 293
Botto, Louis 87, 415, 531, 858, 1142, 1431
Bottomley, Rita 1394
Bottoms, John 346, 347, 699, 1057
Bottoms, Ronald 293
Botwin, Shirley 1058
Bouchard, Richard 1655
Boucher, Francine 1655
Boucher, Gene 62
Boucher, Gloria 697
Boudreau, Robin 41, 929, 1270
Boudreaux, Darleen 401
Bouie, John 1464, 1465
Bouley, Frank 66
Bounds, Catherine 1029
Bourcier, Gerard P. 900
Bourne, Alex 1629
Bourneuf, Phillip 494
Bourskaya, Ina 1249
Bousard, Joe 1274, 1302
Boutsikaris, Dennis 551
Boutte, Duane 222
Bouwer, Marc 746
Bova, Anthony 171, 1032
Bova, Joseph (Joe) 324, 1185, 1193
Bovasso, Bernard X. 1080
Bovasso, Julie 235, 384, 1080
Bovshow, Buzz 838
Bowab, John 1424
Bowden, Beth 310
Bowden, Jonny 54, 1049, 1149
Bowden, Joyce Leigh 88, 703, 1146
Bowen, Alex 413
Bowen, Bobby 200
Bowen, Jeff 1645
Bowen, Jessica 1117
Bowen, John 1508
Bowen, Roger 1415, 1724
Bowen, Shawtane Monroe 1429
Bowen, Thomas 539
Bowen-Roberts, Mimi 1066
Bower, Beverly 1583
Bowers, Alexander S. 1340
Bowers, Clent 171
Bowers, J. Bradley 328
Bowers, Jamie 1192
Bowers, Robert 380
Bowers, Teresa (Terry) 53, 1405
Bowers, The Reverend Thomas Dix 1316
Bowie, Joe 363
Bowles, Anthony 1011
Bowling, Lynn 485, 1289
Bowman, Jason W. 43
Bowman, Joan 944, 1448
Bowman, John 1187
Bowman, Margaret 657
Bowman, Regis 1646
Bowman, Rob 267, 428
Bowman, Robert 1316
Bowne, Richard 322, 1071, 1378
Bowyer, Bob 552
Boxall, Patti 226
Boxhorn, Jerry 507
Boyar, Sully 1455
Boyce, James 1640
Boyd, Christopher 697
Boyd, D'ambrose 934
Boyd, David 1226
Boyd, Elisse 858, 1261
Boyd, George 1804
Boyd, Guy 1238
Boyd, James 1655
Boyd, Jason 615
Boyd, Julianne 2, 662, 855, 981
Boyd, Thomas 631
Boyden, Peter 258
Boyer, Averie 767
Boyer, Henry 1021
Boyett, Robert 1187
Boylan, Malcolm Stuart 379
Boylan, Mary 175, 336, 337, 1617
Boyle, Juanita 226
Boyle, Peter 1614
Boyle, Robert Ott 907, 1361
Boyle, Viki 1684
Boynton, Peter 1194
Boynton, Wesley 621
Boys, Kenneth 1646
Bozarth, Danny 1500
Bozeman, Beverley 942
Bozinoff, Lillian 1221
Bozyk, Reizl 147, 819, 1032, 1212, 1342, 1382, 1453, 1745, 1822
Bracken, Fred 1061, 1530
Brackman, Jacob 1101
Braddock, Shane 950
Braden, Bill 1562
Braden, John 372, 408, 500, 834, 1041, 1523
Bradford, Alberta 400
Bradford, Alex 166, 400
Bradford, Don 752
Bradford, Doug 1226
Bradley, Alfred Bruce 1518
Bradley, Brad 305
Bradley, Brown 1379
Bradley, Bruce Vernon 581
Bradley, Henry 1183
Bradley, Jerry 1470
Bradley, Joanne 1646
Bradley, Rita 1789
Bradley, Scott 376, 1702
Bradley, Stephan 362
Bradshaw, Dean 892
Bradshaw, Jared 395, 519, 520
Brady, Brigid 1733
Brady, James Edmund 748
Brady, Patrick Scott (S.) 300, 691, 1245
Bragg, Melvyn 697
Bragin, Bill 1225
Braidech, Sheila 1244
Braine, John 450
Bramble, Mark 434, 435
Bramlette, Sally 745, 935
Brammer, Shelby 1805
Branch, Erin 349
Branch, Susan 685
Brand, David 1301, 1733
Brand, Gibby 258, 259, 1339
Brand, Oscar 722, 780
Brand, Robert 1203
Brandeaux, Pal 1615
Brandeis, Odna 622
Branden, Joey 1600
Brandin, Walter 1131
Brandler, Annette 74, 1713
Brandman, Michael 1614
Brandon, Charles (A.) 199, 1152, 1164, 1464, 1465
Brandon, Johnny 17, 82, 152, 291, 682, 968, 1300, 1467, 1550, 1774
Brandt, David 510
Brandt, George 150
Brandt, Mike 464
Brandy, Tamara 142
Brandzel, Robert 1358
Brannigan, Robert P. 1096
Bransdorf, John 309
Brasington, Alan 271, 1437, 1527
Braslau, Sophie 1369
Brass, Stacey Lynn 1375
Brassard, Gail 38, 280, 285, 770, 848, 1381, 1498
Brasser, Victoria 990
Braswell, John 101, 250, 1494, 1536
Braswell, Joseph 1093, 1729
Bratt, George 619, 620, 622
Bratt, J. 898
Braun, Ralph 1034
Braun, Roger 1194
Braunstein, Alan 1250
Bravo, Amy Elizabeth 1068
Brawer, Jacques 782
Brawn, Geoffrey 853
Braxton, Brenda 934, 1762
Bray, Kelly 1429
Bray, Kim 68
Brayley, Sally 62
Brazo, Ed 1202
Brazwell, Damon W. 1004
Brazzle, Dorothy 815
Breaker, Daniel 1225
Breaux, Marc 1486
Brechner, Stanley 100, 305, 711, 1328, 1361, 1381
Brecht, Bertolt 455, 459, 660, 843, 1360, 1391, 1626, 1627, 1628, 1629
Brecht, Mary 801, 1657
Bredehorst, Inge 66
Bredt, James 661
Breed, Blondell 1696
Breedlove, Joe 1001
Breedlove, Joella 116, 630, 682
Breen, Jeni 983
Breen, Joseph 224
Breger, Peter 1607
Bregman, Buddy 1743
Brehm, Heide 1240
Breitbart, Howard 247
Brel, Jacques 792, 1162
Bremers, Beverly Ann 1038
Bremseth, Lloyd 869
Brenn, Jani 1072
Brennan, Eileen 935
Brennan, James 476
Brennan, Kathleen 26
Brennan, Maureen 244, 1437, 1521
Brennan, Nora 1113
Brennan, Tom 33
Brenner, Janet 300
Brenner, Janis 910
Brenner, William 1367
Brent, Frank 425
Brent, Jerry 867
Brent, John 22
Brent, Plumath 1811

Brent, Romney 1160
Brentano, Felix 686, 1000, 1217
Brentano, Robyn 397
Brenton, Jack 408
Brents, Frank 425
Breslin, Tom (Tommy) 360, 1081, 1097, 1774
Bress, Rachel 1547
Breton, J. Robert 1606
Breton, Tomas 488
Brett, Jason 97, 916
Brett, Kelly 1629
Breuer, Lee 615, 1248, 1344
Brevis, Skip 115
Brevoort, Deborah 929
Brewer, Brad 1738
Brewer, James 1062
Brewer, Robert 345, 1343
Brewer, Sherri 107
Brewer-Moore, Cathy 1028
Brian, Michael 364, 576, 910
Briansky, Oleg 95
Briar, Suzanne 1593
Brice, Carol 569
Brice, Eugene 1227
Bricking, Joe 1343
Bricklin, Jonathan 110
Brickman, Marshall 1069, 1534
Bricusse, Leslie 1101
Bridge, Betsy 1131
Bridges, Deborah Lynn 809
Bridges, Kenneth 1510
Bridges, Mark 653
Bridges, Robert 322
Briel, Joel 403
Brielle, Jonathan 1135
Brier, Kathy 106, 1303
Brigel, Stockton 852
Briggle, Stockton 642
Briggs, Cynthia 1592
Briggs, Johari 1487
Briggs, Pat 1351
Bright, Michael 1098
Bright, Richard 1562
Brightman, Julian 954
Brill, Justin 67
Brimm, Thomas M., II 1183
Brinckerhoff, Burt 1767
Briner, Allison 929, 1353
Brink, Robert 398, 567
Brinker, Lynn 360
Brinsmade, Sallie 1163
Briones, Anton 1425
Brisbane, Ruth 177, 420
Briskin, Arthur V. 1647
Bristol, Gary 950
Britt, Jacqueline 969, 1029, 1743
Brittan, Robert 567
Britten, Benjamin 1229
Britten, Bill 319
Britton, Christina 171
Britton, Jeff 159, 208, 259, 705, 1035, 1038, 1682
Britton, John 268
Britton, Patricia 1112
Britton, Ronnie 575, 636, 708, 1660, 1679, 1744
Britton, Sherry 134
Bro, Erika 1349
Bro, Judith 856
Broaddus, John-Eric 732
Broadhurst, Kent 536
Broadman, Matilda 1131
Broadous, Rosita 255
Broadway, Bob 715, 815
Broady, Marie-Elizabeth 1252
Brochin, Kathleen 802
Brochu, Jim (James) 146, 892, 1477, 1647, 1701
Brock, Sue 611
Brockett, Don 142, 535, 1565
Brocklin, Jeffrey 1410
Brockmeier, William 575
Brockmeyer, John D. 1359
Brocksmith, Roy 117, 394, 1279, 1628
Brockus, Sarah 825
Broderick, George 470
Broderick, James 826
Broderick, William 403, 1278, 1771
Broderson, Margaret 1021
Brodhead, Pat 1003
Brody, Jonathan 424, 1110, 1610
Broecker, Tom 496
Brofsky, Kevin 1148
Brogan, Michael 948
Brogdon, Ben 133
Brogger, Ivar 848
Brogran, Michael 948
Brohn, Bill 197, 1147
Broich, Madame 136
Broido, Andrea 1782
Brokaw, Mark 78
Bromelmeier, Martha 612, 1046
Bromer, Steve 294
Bromfield, Valri 580
Bron, Eleanor 449, 1091
Bronfman, Edgar M. 208
Brongo, Laurie 1548
Brook, Fiona 1577
Brook, Sara 400, 851, 1078
Brooke, William 752
Brooke-Taylor, Tim 241, 1122
The Brooklyn Philharmonia 1405
Brooks, Alfred 1164
Brooks, David 98, 1399, 1421
Brooks, Donald 48, 381
Brooks, Donald L. 124, 1617
Brooks, Evelyn 1043
Brooks, Hack 1790
Brooks, Jack 1790, 1791
Brooks, Jeff 310, 314
Brooks, Juanita 1518
Brooks, Lawrence 1364
Brooks, Melvin (Mel) 1192
Brooks, Norman 993
Brooks, Patricia 331, 902, 1111, 1227
Brooks, Sharon K. 803, 1232
Brooks, Sydney 197
Brophy, Edmund 1566
Brossman, Lynn 337
Brosten, Harve 1181, 1377, 1595
Brotherton, Pamela 1023
Broughton, Barbara 1251
Broughton, Phillip 446
Brous, Nancy 470
Brovsky, Linda 717, 1336
Brower, Alfred 578
Brower, Jay 369
Brower, Kay 369, 566
Brown, Aline 388, 1749
Brown, Allan 64
Brown, Andrew 1015
Brown, Ann 1456
Brown, Arthur B. 512, 1251
Brown, Barry M. 992
Brown, Beverly 1359
Brown, Bill 50
Brown, Blaine 1673
Brown, Blair 805
Brown, Buck 814
Brown, Carter 901
Brown, Charles 630, 876, 1509
Brown, Charlie 1395
Brown, Chuck 1214, 1449
Brown, Clark 12
Brown, Daniel 109
Brown, Dave 483
Brown, David 74
Brown, Debra 574
Brown, Debria 331
Brown, Donna 1065
Brown, Dorothy 1278
Brown, Elizabeth 1672
Brown, Elizabeth C. 1731
Brown, Ericka 1359
Brown, Esther 1307
Brown, Eudora 717, 1374
Brown, Flo 1487
Brown, Garrett M. 1045
Brown, Graham 589, 629, 630, 1004
Brown, Gwendolyn 1567
Brown, Ian 1539
Brown, J. Terry 33
Brown, Jack 152
Brown, Jason C. 983
Brown, Jason Robert 273, 890, 1250, 1498
Brown, Jeb 1733
Brown, Joyce 90, 1300
Brown, Juanita 1029
Brown, Ka-Ron 1398
Brown, Kate Hunter 814
Brown, Katherine Mary 1541
Brown, Kelly 277
Brown, Kermit 976
Brown, Kim 768, 1134
Brown, Larry W. 1373
Brown, Leonard (Duke) 1384
Brown, Lew 1101
Brown, Lewis 256
Brown, Lisa 133
Brown, Mark Alton 387
Brown, Marvin 1738
Brown, Mary 816
Brown, Michael 87, 160, 371, 415, 418, 531, 771, 942, 971, 1205, 1421, 1430, 1576
Brown, Moses 815
Brown, Norman 1661
Brown, Oscar, Jr. 835, 1812
Brown, Patricia 272
Brown, Patrika 571, 663
Brown, Patti 1633
Brown, Paul 226
Brown, Pendleton 1504, 1567, 1628
Brown, Peter 1426, 1742
Brown, R.G. 556, 557, 558, 852, 1767
Brown, Renee Monique 668
Brown, Roger 465
Brown, Ron 1066
Brown, Ronald K. 330
Brown, Roo 1, 2
Brown, Rudy 1330
Brown, Russell 1638
Brown, Ruth 266, 1518
Brown, Scott 645
Brown, Sharon 334, 920, 1349
Brown, Slade 714, 1473
Brown, Stan 1205
Brown, Steve 258, 259, 316, 480, 695, 1541
Brown, Terry 1343
Brown, Timothy 1029
Brown, Trevor 645
Brown, Walter P. 1221
Brown, Warwick 908, 1192
Brown, Willex 1434
Brown, William 1137, 1788
Brown, William F. 87, 160, 214, 722, 1259, 1430
Brown, Zoe 1433
Browne, Paul 539
Brownell, Barbara 93
Browning, Dolph 1449
Browning, Kirk 1413
Browning, Lucielle 40, 1010
Browning, Robert 1511
Browning, Rod 1488
Browning, Susan 12, 381, 822
Brownlee, John 40, 1541
Brubaker, Robert 256, 1062
Bruce, Allan 631
Bruce, Merlin 867
Bruce, Sharon 212
Bruce, Shelley 215
Bruce, Thomas 478, 479
Brucker, Jane 1759
Bruder, Karolyn 66
Bruder, Patricia 1400
Bruder, Patsy 944
Brumage, Bruce H. 1033
Brummel, Barbara 1297
Brummel, David 1310
Bruneau, Ralph 218, 865, 866, 1392
Brunetti, David 180, 182, 445
Brunetti, Ted 78
Bruni, Tony 1682
Brunke, Heinrich 168, 872
Bruno, Carmelo 15
Bruno, Mandy 541
Bruns, Philip (Phil) 677, 1430
Brunyate, Roger 1374
Brushingham, Marcia 124, 1287
Bruskin, Perry 659
Brussell, Judy 814
Bruzzese, Elizabeth 194
Bryam, Amick 1326
Bryan, Brantz M., Jr. 287
Bryan, C.B. (a/k/a C.B. and C.D.B.) 535, 1276
Bryan, James 1017
Bryan, Jeffrey 105
Bryan, Kenneth 726, 833
Bryan, Wayne 486
Bryant, Adam 82, 800, 1800
Bryant, Ben 93, 324, 655
Bryant, Bilo 1692
Bryant, David 435
Bryant, Dean 1306
Bryant, Hazel S. 927
Bryant, Stephen 673, 1020
Bryce-Laporte, Camila 1252
Brydon, Angela 474
Bryggman, Larry 1072
Brys, Carol 154, 1508
Bua, Gene 279
Bubbles, John W. 165
Bubriski, Peter 1805
Bucci, Mark 1583
Buccio, Sam 468
Buchanan, Daisy 628
Buchanan, James "Goober" 1720
Buchanan, Linda 1788
Buchholz, Frederick (Fred) 544, 725, 864, 1036, 1317
Buchs, Sherry 200
Buchsbaum, Jeffrey 1419, 1586
Buck, Dennis 758
Buck, Heather 670
Buck, Randy 1301, 1359
Buck, Susan Hum 347
Buckingham, Matthew 872
Buckingham, Oliver 1117
Buckler, Curt Mitchell 1050
Buckley, Betty 93, 430, 1109
Buckley, Betty Lynn 1758
Buckley, Candy 130, 1052, 1250
Buckley, Emerson 92, 331, 569, 677
Buckley, Erick 249
Buckley, Faye 1293
Buckley, Hal 324, 448, 1152, 1431
Buckley, Ralph 1297
Buckley, Robert A. 14, 829, 1289, 1581
Buckmaster, Henry 1811
Bucknell, Nathaniel 15, 392
Buckner, Clay 950
Buckreus, Stefen 988
Bucks, Sherri 1151
Bucksey, Colin 263
Budd, Norman 140
Buddeke, Kat 11
Budin, Rachel 1472
Buele, Carol H. 545
Buell, Bill 25, 643, 1322
Buell, William 326
Bufalino, Brenda 1208
Bufano, Rocco 707
Buff, Jim 12, 170, 999
Buffaloe, Katharine 25, 833, 1146
Buffington, Joe 719
Buffington, Suzanne 1070
Bufman, Zev 833, 1827
Bugg, Randy 1562
Buglisi, Jocqulyn 666
Buhrer, Suzanne 350
Bukowiecki, Alan 395
Bullard, Brian 1270
Bullard, Gene 902
Bullock, Donna 453, 1287
Bullock, Lou 243, 392, 467, 920, 928, 1277, 1387, 1776
Bulmash, Jay S. 1377
Buloff, Joseph 489, 666
Bulos, Yusef 658, 1392
Bumgardner, Jim 940
Bumpass, Rodger 623, 1113
Bumpus, Jason 750
Bunce, David 43
Bundonis, Al 1428
Bundt, Ronald M. 1033
Bundy, Laura 1386
Bunin, Keith 1598
Bunn, David Alan 934, 1373
Bunnell, Jane 256
Bunt, George 416, 884, 1348
Bunting, Richard 1608
Bunton, Anissia 196
Buntzman, David 452
Burba, Blake 206, 1351, 1404
Burbridge, Edward 589, 1004, 1633
Burch, Fred 45
Burch, Shelly 25
Burchett, Beverly 124
Burchfield, Betty Ann 427
Burchfield, Ritty 397
Burchinal, Frederick 628
Burckhardt, Jacob 397
Burden, Laverne 705
Burden, William 47
Burdick, David 260
Burdick, Scott 1542
Burg, Brad 1346
Burgess, Elizabeth 33
Burgess, Granville 197, 313
Burgess, Grover 621
Burgess, Mary 569
Burgess, Walter 1393
Burghardt, Arthur 1057
Burgher, Julie 1682
Burghoff, Gary 1828
Burgie, Irving (Lord Burgess) 91
Burgstaller, Ludwig 1010
Burk, Terence 15, 1387, 1776
Burk, Terry 1349
Burke, Billy 1590
Burke, Cameron 133
Burke, Deirdre 1442
Burke, Georgia 187
Burke, Gerard A. 369
Burke, Karen 221
Burke, Karen G. 785
Burke, Lee 494
Burke, Louis F. 321

Burke, Michele 199
Burke, Peggy 1315
Burke, Richard 411
Burke, Terry 1349
Burke, Tim 1110
Burke, Veronica 1117
Burke, William 1278
Burkett, Shannon 1545
Burkette, Judith 1161
Burkhardt, Eric 1329
Burkhardt, Gerry 133
Burkholder, Scott 1665
Burks, Charles 379, 631, 705
Burks, Donny 152
Burlingame, Lloyd 93, 652, 902, 1265, 1420, 1603
Burman, Matt 162
Burmester, Leo 479
Burnell, Buster 1177
Burnett, Brevard 1543
Burnett, Carol 1193
Burnett, Connie 1221
Burnett, Howard J. 225
Burney, Harry L., III 194
Burney, Steve 483
Burns, Andrea 760, 1390, 1403, 1498
Burns, Arthur 1005
Burns, George E. 698
Burns, Helen 1393
Burns, Jack 1813
Burns, Joe 231
Burns, Peter 1777
Burns, Reese 112
Burns, Scott 1565
Burns, Theresa 750
Burnside, Molly 85
Burnside, Richard 550
Burr, Charles 1697
Burr, Lonnie 957
Burrell, Gregory 1696
Burrell, Pamela 226, 1541
Burrell, Terry (Teresa) 37, 855, 1581
Burris, Dean Burris 581
Burrough, Roslyn 1569
Burroughs, William S. 168
Burrow, David 1707
Burrows, Vinie 688, 1734, 1735
Bursky, Jay 133
Burstein, Danny 1390
Burstein, Lonnie 676
Burstein, Mike 1745
Burstein, Pesach 1105, 1341, 1745
Burstin, Joseph 226
Burstyn, Mike 1381
Burt, Elaine 750
Burton, Brenda 991
Burton, Donald 1304
Burton, Irving 289, 624, 1003
Burton, Jenny 1363
Burton, Keith 1623
Burton, Margaret 1639, 1640
Burton, Miriam 91, 501, 1227, 1465
Burton, Sarah 317
Burton, Warren 542, 649, 771, 1255
Burwell, Basil 253
Busackino, Barbara 1572
Busch, Charles 633, 1571
Bush, Deborah 1743
Bush, Jonathan 826
Bush, Linda 836
Bush, Michael 633
Bush, Norman 21, 589, 1004
Bush, Phillip 1200
Bush, Ronald 1621
Bush, Thommie 125, 152, 221, 400, 649
Bushnell, Shaun 1684
Bushor, Geoffrey 1777
Bushor, Janet 227
Buskin, David 1150
Buss, Tesha 679
Bussert, Meg 1309
Bussey, Raymond 1080
Bussins, Jack 109
Busto, Julia 397
Butcher, George 1633
Buterbaugh, Keith 990
Butler, Alistair 278
Butler, Ari 1815
Butler, Bill 369
Butler, Bruce 850
Butler, Buddy 1004
Butler, Christopher 1599
Butler, Don 255
Butler, Gregory 689
Butler, Henry 1088
Butler, James 729
Butler, James E. 380
Butler, John 944
Butler, Joseph Campbell 1504
Butler, Kerry 106, 1306
Butler, Mark Anthony 1384
Butler, Paul Lindsay 497, 1570
Butler, Rhoda 480
Butler, Ron 1547
Butler, Sam 615
Butler, Thomas Isaiah 1423
Butler, Todd 601
Butleroff, Helen 567, 811, 1251, 1607, 1821
Butt, Dan 1724, 1765, 1813
Butt, Joseph 681
Butterell, Jonathan 1006, 1422
Button, Jeanne 572, 1154, 1424, 1454
Buttram, Jan 480, 794
Butts, Barry 1029
Butts, T. Baomi 420
Butz, Fritz 1775
Butz, Norbert Leo 890
Buzzi, Ruth 80, 87, 558, 1058
Byatt, Irene 236
Byers, Jim 1592
Byers, Ralph 1250, 1557
Bykov, Vladislav 849
Byrd, Carolyn 107
Byrd, Debra 646
Byrd, John 1267
Byrde, Edye 803
Byrd-Leitner, Sylvia 1816
Byrne, David 872
Byrne, Gaylea 33
Byrne, Jack 905
Byrne, Jennifer 462
Byrne, Joseph Carl 905
Byrne, Michael 1119
Byrne, Richard 938
Byrne, Terrence B. 1389
Byrne, Terry 680
Byrnes, Kevin 397
Byrns, Renee 366

Cabalero, Roxann 1670
Caballero, Shirley 631
Caballos, Rene 1588
Cabell, Robert W. 1298, 1690
Cable, Christopher 417, 740
Cabot, Ceil 371, 381, 415, 1261, 1430, 1490, 1576
Cabot, Colin 1832
Cabot, Joe 772
Cabral, Mel 1291
Cacciatore, Jayne 408
Cacoyannis, Michael 1088
Cade, James 1552
Cade, Jim 698
Cadenhead, Ian 366
Cadiff, Andrew 218, 219, 1622
Cadman, Charles Wakefield 1369
Cady, David 1829
Cady, Scott 1663
Caesar, Adolph 629
Caesar, Robert 235
Caesar, Sid 1457
Caffey, Marion 171, 1037
Caffey, Marion J. 1623
Caffin, John 1242
Cahan, Cora 175, 777, 1439, 1444, 1784
Cahill, Edwin 71
Cahill, Paul 336
Cahill, Tom 908
Cahn, Cathy 1486
Cahn, David 785
Cahn, Larry 1285
Cahn, Sammy 942
Cahoon, Kevin 1778
Cain, Marie 146, 892
Cain, Pasy 1696
Cain, Tim 597
Cairns, Angus 1504
Cairns, Anthony 1444
Calabro, Tony 15, 1077, 1389, 1673
Calarco, Joe 502
Calderon, Ian 720, 793, 1697
Calderone, Michael 1240
Caldwell, Ben 1074
Caldwell, David 519, 520, 521
Caldwell, George 1525, 1631
Caldwell, Jay 615
Caldwell, Keith 1668
Caldwell, Roberta 816
Caldwell, Stephen 1338
Caldwell, Walter 1270, 1579
Caldwell, Zoe 306
Cale, David 502
Caleb, John 1214, 1287
Calhoun, Jeff 641, 1199
Calkins, Michael 81, 361, 968, 1471
Callahan, Jamie 1826
Callan, Christopher 319
Callan, Michael 100
Callas, May 1174
Callaway, Joe A. 91
Callaway, Liz 219, 1033, 1143, 1201, 1513
Callaway, Thomas 414
Callicutt, Jonathan 365
Callman, Nancy 1449
Calloway, Northern J. 466, 959, 1038
Calpito, Isaac 103
Calvert, Carter 777, 1608
Calvert, James 1349
Calvert, Robert 64, 1349
Calzado, Martha 488
Camacho, Blanca 897, 1402
Camacho, Lew 91
Cambridge, Ed 91, 425
Cambridge, Godfrey 946
Cambus, George 1117
Cameron, David 278
Cameron, Faye 1660
Cameron, George 1500
Cameron, John 1122
Cameron, Linda 395
Cameron, Lisa 1070
Cameron, Lorna 1655
Cameron, Nancy 1287
Cameron, Richard 138
Camien, Laura 1645
Camille 1330, 1522
Camp, Barbara Ann 613
Camp, Duane 1578
Camp, Ray 1360
Camp, Richard 377
Camp, Samantha 889
Campanella, Philip 1268, 1304, 1540
Campbell, Alan 10, 194
Campbell, Alison 596
Campbell, Alison H. 190
Campbell, Bill 1293
Campbell, Carolee 481
Campbell, Carolyn 1135
Campbell, Charles 400
Campbell, Chris 304
Campbell, Christian 1347
Campbell, Christine 420, 1646
Campbell, Colin 136
Campbell, Connie 1349, 1776
Campbell, David 1403
Campbell, Ed 1349
Campbell, Elaine 56
Campbell, Jason Scott 1054
Campbell, Jermaine 1340
Campbell, Jerry 814
Campbell, Larry 124, 493, 500, 814, 1537
Campbell, Margot 66
Campbell, Mark 1499, 1514
Campbell, Nancy 1629
Campbell, Norman 56
Campbell, Patton 254, 631, 947, 1063, 1111, 1789, 1814
Campbell, Robby 504
Campbell, Sande 338, 667, 1008
Campbell, Tisha 1039, 1340
Campbell, Toni 1453
Campbell, Torri 1382
Campisi, Tony 1094
Campone, Merv 159
Canaan, David 24
Canary, David 693, 870
Canary, John 288
Canavan, Linda 866
Canemaker, John 920, 998, 1265, 1604
Canestro, Paul 1389
Canning, James 625
Cannistraro, Mark 469
Cannon 1252
Cannon, Alice 827, 1008, 1043, 1148, 1228
Cannon, Mike 103
Cano, Jose Andres Ocampo 1660
Canonico, Gerard 280, 1303
Cantanese/Lauze 573
Cantania, Eric 362
Cantin, Jim 919
Cantor, Arthur 28, 29, 79, 96, 353, 354, 355, 356, 433, 602, 733, 1005, 1239, 1246, 1247, 1266, 1318, 1653, 1768, 1770, 1790, 1791, 1793, 1794, 1796, 1797
Cantor, David 1381
Cantor, Rachel 248
Cantor, Robin 1537
Cantrell, Nick 725
Cantril, Ken 235
Capalbo, Carmen 609, 1360, 1626, 1627
Capecce, Victor (Vittorio) 501, 565
Capellaro, Catherine 1736
Capewell, James 1629
Capillupo, Rinaldo 698
Caplin, Catherine 819, 1212
Caplin, Martha 170
Capo, Pedro 262
Capobianco, Tito 188, 488
Capodilupo, Tony 1455
Capone, Clifford 784, 1299
Capone, Tony 1390
Caposella, Sean 1731
Capote, Truman 715
Capozzoli, Ron 1426, 1695
Cappello, Emma 1721
Cappy, Ted 384
Caprin, Sandra 869
Caprio, Jennifer 1680
Cara, Irene 18, 958, 1038
Caraballo, Sunilda 262
Caradimas, Lana 1446
Card, June 569
Card, Mary 382
Cardenas, Henry 262
Carder, Tom 833
Cardin, Pierre 849
Cardwell, Jay 892, 1156, 1157
Cardy, Kathleen 15
Carelle, Linda 1382
Carelli, Gabor 62, 891
Carey, Alice 1387, 1776
Carey, Bob 535, 870, 902
Carey, David 147, 489, 666, 1341, 1342, 1382, 1453, 1745
Carey, Frank 1307
Carey, Norman 361
Carfagno, Randy 356
Carfizzi, Chris 1818
Cariddi, Vanessa 717
Cariou, Len 443, 1708
Caristi, Vincent 1664
Carl, Fred 222
The Carl Murray Singers 1559
Carlin, Paul 13
Carlin, Phyllis 505
Carlin, Tony 658
Carlisle, Kevin 944
Carlo, Don 254, 488
Carlos 863
Carlos, Laurie 1579
Carlos, Rosemary 1601
Carlow, Richard 1026
Carlsen, Allan 1520
Carlson, Ann 729
Carlson, Bill 1131
Carlson, Deborah 1089
Carlson, Sally Anne 63
Carlson, Sara 1054
Carlton, Bob 979, 1353
Carlton, Graeme 1264
Carlton, Joel 755, 1084
Carlton, Maurice 1579
Carlyle, Jane 66, 68
Carlyle, Warren 1479
Carmel, Kate 301, 1133
Carmello, Carolee 102, 296, 430, 683, 830
Carmichael, Bill 186, 511
Carmichael, Marnie 1706
Carmichael, Pat 1380
Carmichael, Patricia 1299
Carmine, Michael 1402
Carmines, Al (Alvin) 15, 111, 192, 242, 243, 251, 286, 392, 453, 465, 467, 554, 613, 614, 701, 756, 757, 759, 823, 834, 920, 925, 928, 952, 998, 999, 1017, 1231, 1277, 1280, 1311, 1349, 1376, 1387, 1489, 1496, 1501, 1673, 1705, 1739, 1757, 1776
Carnahan, Michael 1623
Carnelia, Craig 2, 377, 1141, 1624
Carney, Grace 1107, 1349
Carol, Cecil 1145
Carol, Jacqueline 636
Carollo, Scott 1706
Caron, Charles 1119
Caron, Sandra 963, 1352
Carpens, Ben 1229
Carpenter, Carleton 1148
Carpenter, Catherine 597
Carpenter, Constance 1670, 1716
Carpenter, Larry 419, 1094, 1304
Carpenter, Pamela 591
Carpenter, Thelma 1223, 1677
Carpenter, Wia 709

Carpinello, James 1545
Carr, Allan 1013
Carr, Eddie 1021
Carr, Jimmie 1145
Carr, Kenneth 1397
Carr, Leon 1420
Carr, Osmond 460
Carr, Robert K. 1419
Carr, Sharon 738
Carra, Alexis 474
Carra, Lawrence 870, 902
Carradine, Keith 1731
Carrafa, John 1547, 1712, 1748
Carrick, Christopher 1501
Carrie, John 1134
Carrillo, Jaime Robert 167
Carrington, Barry 470
Carroad, Andrea L. 1494
Carroll, Albert 618, 619, 620, 621, 622
Carroll, Chris 1297
Carroll, Danny 80, 201, 1142
Carroll, David (-James) 186, 1035
Carroll, Eddie 906
Carroll, Edward P. 1197
Carroll, Eleanor 618
Carroll, Jean 226
Carroll, Jonathan 1423
Carroll, Joyce 944
Carroll, June 693, 1431, 1448, 1661
Carroll, Lewis B. 510
Carroll, Mollie 136
Carroll, Nancy E. 89, 1156, 1159
Carroll, Pat 1185
Carroll, Ronn 873, 1006
Carroll, Tony 1744
Carroll, Vinnette 166, 194, 230, 327, 400, 592, 593, 1308, 1526, 1672, 1762
Carroll, Yvonne 652, 693
Carron, Arthur 1010
Carrothers, Richard 642
Carrubba, Philip 359, 833
Carruthers, James 976
Carruthers, Mike 247
Carsey, Keith 121
Carson, Heather 576, 1612
Carson, Trudy 68
Cartell, Nick 541
Carten, Bob 266, 1737
Carter, Alice E. 1064
Carter, Ann 1066
Carter, Benjamin 120
Carter, Charlene 201
Carter, Dale 1822
Carter, David W. 745, 1295
Carter, Desmond 1101
Carter, Dixie 1433
Carter, Genna 126
Carter, John 776, 1399, 1755
Carter, Larry 542, 771, 1255
Carter, Lynne 550
Carter, Myra 1666
Carter, Nell (N.) 18, 109, 165, 1504, 1746
Carter, Ralph 860
Carter, Sara 1131
Carter, Vicki H. 981
Carter, Vicki Helms 662
Carter-Hicks, Stephen 954
Cartier, Deidre 661
Cartwright, Carroll L. 1376
Carty, Cheryl 218
Carucci, Frank 319, 1646
Caruso, Arlene 1829
Caruso, Daniel 1368
Caruso, Dee 87, 126, 160, 556, 557, 558, 616, 1142, 1576
Caruso, Fran 708
Caruso, Fred M. 738, 1128
Caruso, Joseph George 171
Caruso, Tarry 599
Caruso, Thomas 154, 1052
Carusone, Leo P. 1157
Carvajal, Celia 1325
Carvajal, Celina 1325
Carver, Brent 1103
Carvi-Bozza, Mina 547
Cary, Claiborne 34, 875, 1481
Cary, Robert 749, 1586
Casanave, Carolyn 54, 225
Casanova, Jimmy 1131
Casapini, Ann 1670
Cascio, Gigi 261
Cascone, Michael 971
Case, Allen 1193
Case, Ron 1204
Case, Ronald 14, 476, 749
Case, Russ 1264
Casel, Ayodele 1406, 1407
Casella, Matt 765
Casey, Lawrence 847, 1087
Casey, Michael 1443
Casey, Peter 889
Casey, Warren 625
Cash, Rosalind 589, 844, 1004
Cashin, Tom 133, 1411
Cashman, John 226, 1483
Cashone, Regina 1537
Caskey, Bill 74
Caskey, Marilyn 314
Casler, Richard 332, 715
Casman, Nellie 1453
Casnoff, Philip 314, 699, 849, 865, 1706
Casolari, Bruno David 747
Cason, Barbara 87, 160, 1170
Casoria, Christopher 1320
Casper, Richard 1268
Cass, Carol 786
Cass, Lee 33, 714
Cass, Ronald 1142, 1431
Cassan, Claudine 785
Cassan-Jellison, Claudine 162
Cassel, Walter 92, 1587
Cassen, Jackie 490
Cassidy, Jack 1399
Cassidy, Joe 929
Cassidy, Martin J. 63, 1364
Cassidy, Patrick 70
Cassier, Brian 747
Cassilly, Richard 1583, 1596
Cassini, Oleg 1750
Cassmore, Judy 226
Casson, Claudine 161
Castaldo, Ralph 1671
Castaneda, David 387, 1714
Castang, Veronica 773
Castay, Leslie 979
Castel, Nico 188, 488, 1063, 1137
Castellino, Bill 749, 832
Castello, Glenn M. 1679
Castle, Diana 1049
Castle, Gene 132
Castle, Joyce 122, 256, 451
Castle, Marc 1030, 1376
Castle, Matt 926, 1056, 1322
Castleman, Ronald A. 897
Castonguay, Veronica 552
Castrigno, Tony 53, 275, 887
Castro, Hector "Tito" 122
Catalano, Frank 1618
Catalano, Jason 189
Catan, Daniel 1336
Catanese, Charles 1772
Cates, Gene 1538
Cates, Kristy 193
Cates, Steven 59
Cathey, Dalton 1349
Cation, Kathryn 397
Catlett, Mary Jo 480
Cato, Bob 571
Catt, Christopher 576
Cattermole, Paul 1233
Cava, Anthony 1660
Cavanagh, Maura 326
Cavander, Kenneth 183
Cave, Lisa Dawn 603
Cave, Victoria Lecta 1135
Cavenaugh, Kathryn H. 673
Cavenaugh, Matthew (Matt) 641, 673
Cavey, George 1446
Cea, Kim 1128
Cecil, Joe 834
Cecuona, E. 1619
Cehanovsky, George 868, 1010, 1047, 1249, 1718
Cele, Baby 1401
Celian, Charles 1424
Celik, Hassan 1281
Cella, Susan 794, 1056
Ceniceros, Lorna 331
Centracco, Cookie 1516
Cerabone, Raymond 1511
Cerdan, Esteban 1145
Ceres, Vela 1615
Cerf, Kurt 32
Cernovich, Nicola 701, 1672
Cernovitch, Nicholas 1655
Cerullo, Jonathan (Stewart) 463, 1482
Cesa, Jamie 892, 965, 1110
Cesario, Greg 1418
Cesario, Michael J. 725, 1097
Chabeau, Ray 1177
Chad, Harrison 252
Chadman, Christopher 348, 1143
Chaffee, Mary 1267, 1805
Chafkin, Martin 1226
Chaikin, Peter 654
Chaikin, Robin 654
Chaikin, Shami 647, 648
Chalbaud, Esteban 392, 1349, 1823
Chaleff, Jim 1355
Challee, William 622
Challenger, Rudy 1360
Chalmers, Cary 1025
Chalmers, Thomas 1369
Chalmers, Toni-Maria 1434
Chamberlain, Andrea 1347
Chamberlin, Kevin 69, 1484
Chamberlin, Lee 1544
Chambers, Carol 133
Chambers, Craig 133
Chambers, David 634, 958, 1285
Chambers, Ernest 415, 693
Chambers, Ernest A. 160
Chambers, Marilyn 125
Chambers, Renee 906
Chambers, Robert 935, 987
Chambers, Tara 476
Chambers, Terrence 397
Chambers, Tom 1233
Chamlee, Mario 40
Champagne, Michael 161, 162, 163, 164
Champlin, Donna Lynne 1103
Chan, Donald 1028, 1394
Chandler, Brian Evaret 153, 603
Chandler, David 170
Chandler, Jack 1270
Chandler, Jennie 1616
Chandler, Mildred 63
Chandler, Nat 1584
Chandler, Stan 527
Chandler, Stephen 1611
Chandler, Terry 255
Chaney, David 1606
Chaney, Jan 1163
Chaney, Lon 704
Chang, Craig 647, 648
Channing, Carol 1140
Chansky, Dorothy 217, 1169
Chanze, La 1191
Chaoge, Wang 495
Chapin, Eleanor 1531
Chapin, Harry 321, 916
Chapin, Miles 1282
Chapin, Schuyler G. 1029
Chapin, Tom 321
Chapman, David 125, 316, 501, 646, 903, 1096, 1189, 1504, 1517
Chapman, Dianne Finn 461
Chapman, Graham 241, 1122
Chapman, Linda S. 206
Chapman, Stuart 458
Chapman, Ted 598, 1755
Chapman, Topsy 553, 1198
Chapman, Tracy Nicole 252
Chapman, William 66, 1583
Chappell, Vickie D. 1034
Charalambides, Costas 1625
Charbonneau, Dianne 1589
Charisse, Zan 42, 955
Charlap, Moose 1100, 1447
Charles, Bob 985
Charles, Edward 1661
Charles, Lee 944
Charles, Paul 132
Charles, Robert 985
Charles, Todd 1182
Charles, Walter 754
Charleston, Natalie 766
Charlie, Uncle 79
Charlip, Remy 831, 1501, 1705
Charlsen, Nadine 843, 924, 1117
Charlson, Natalie 80, 199, 1605, 1661
Charnas, Fran 35
Charnas, Jonathan 1079
Charnay, Lynne 276, 1686
Charney, Eva 1124, 1361
Charney, Jordan 655
Charney, Lynne 1160
Charney, Miriam 1391
Charney, Sherry 1453
Charney, Tzili 749
Charnin, Martin 58, 84, 90, 237, 472, 535, 858, 899, 1031, 1096, 1100, 1112, 1141, 1184, 1261, 1318, 1630, 1709, 1754
Charnin, Sasha 229, 1141
Chartoff, Melanie 972
Chase, Bill 121
Chase, Chevy 1113, 1114
Chase, Debra 1359
Chase, Elyot 695
Chase, Jean 1252
Chase, Jo Flores 140
Chase, Norman 827
Chase, Paula Leggett 1321
Chase, Stanley 1626, 1627
Chasin, Susan 15, 759
Chasman, Tanya 1807
Chastain, Don 503
Chastonay, Jeanette 1007
Chatfield, Emily Knapp 1323
Chatzky, Jeremy 1237
Chaves, Esther Jane 562
Chaves, Richard 1664
Chebance, Sylvianne 563
Checco, Al 902, 908
Cheek, Jean 785, 803, 1232, 1525, 1550
Cheevers, Nancy 1083
Chello, Xander 1713
Chelsi, Lawrence (Larry) 600, 1440
Chen, Shi-Zheng 282
Chenoweth, Kristin 443, 1121
Chepulis, Kyle 838
Cheremeteff, Angel 704
Cheretun, Debbie 273
Cherin, Robert 236
Cherney, Christopher 702
Chernuck, Dorothy 361
Cherpakov, Gary 991, 1171
Cherry, Eleanor 420
Cherry, Nora 1538
Cherry, Vivian 854, 1404
Chesney, Leon "Mister Twister" 804
Chesnut, Jerry Plummer 1189
Chester, Gregory, II 790
Chester, Ken 574
Chester, Shirley 1697
Chesterman, Mary 920, 1201, 1349
Chestnut, Jim 1124
Chestnut, Morris 964
Chestnutt, Jim 1171
Chesworth, Jonathan 1629
Chesworth, Kate 1629
Chetter, Shirley 1349
Chew, Lee 322
Chianese, Dominic 90, 292
Chiasson, Gilles 485, 643, 1351
Chiba, Kiyoko 602
Chicas, Roy 208
Chierseka, Peggy 423
Chiffy, Richard 9
Child, Marilyn 467, 1119
Childers, Michael 1168
Childs, Casey 10, 240, 741
Childs, Kirsten 222
Childs, Lucinda 427
Chilton, Nola 1192
Chiment, Marie Anne 717, 1160, 1708
Chin, Connie 1487
Chinn, Lori (Tan) 107, 1147
Chinn, Sandra 552
Chiodo, Louis 1099
Chiodo, Tom 302
Chiriaeff, Ludmilla 1655
Chisholm, Anthony 1664
Chisholm, Erik 1093
Chismar, Nancy 42
Chizik, Tedrian 1349
Cho, Eun Jung 889
Cho, Irene 552
Chobanian, Haig 1445
Choder, Jill 132, 183
Chodosh, Richard (B.) 1142, 1539
Choi, Hyung O 889
Choi, Im Su 889
Choi, Mu Yeol 889
Choi, Se Hwan 889
Chong, Ping 282, 560
Chonishvilli, Sergey 849
Chookasian, Lili 891
Choset, Charles 915, 1040
Chotto, Ryan Christopher 474
Chouinard, Wayne 1024
Chris, Marilyn 844
Chriss, Soney 985
Christen, Robert 1788
Christian, Chris 1080
Christian, Mady 1820
Christian, Troy 906
Christians, William 61
Christiansen, Nora 1787
Christiansen, Tracy 1507
Christianson, Bob 81
Christie, Olga 1131
Christin, Judith 574
Christmas, David 341, 588
Christmas, Eric 1393
Christofferson, Nancy 1231
Christopher, Don 962
Christopher, Kevin 955, 1611

Christopher, Russell 62
Christopher, Sybil 1514
Christopherson, Indira 672
Christopherson, Stefanianne 1697
Christy, Anna 47
Chrysan, Demosthenes 1322
Chryst, Gary 55, 1199, 1462
Chu, Nancy S. 1547
Chuma, Natalia 1418
Chun, Anne 889
Chunayev, Boris 849
Chung, Yu Jung 1416
Churba, Laurie 1612
Church, Jordan 991
Church, Joseph 260, 456
Church, Stanley 90
Churchman, Calvin 1355
Churchman, Shawn 385
Churgin, Joanna 1392
Churney, Russell 6
Cibula, Nan 1146
Ciesla, Diane 290
Cilento, Wayne 54, 283, 854, 1290, 1595
Cimino, Leonard 490
Cimino, Leonardo 1588
Cina, John 884
Cincione, Theresa 574
Cinko, Paula 1319
Cioffi, Janice 66
Cipolla, Frank 462
Cissel, Chuck 283
Citarella, Joseph A. 451
Citygirl, Geeta 1322
Ciulla, A.C. 222
Claar, E. Alyssa 1556
Claflin, Rick 1030
Clairmont, Ronald 1773
Clamen, Dolores 1574
Clancy, Elizabeth Hope 1225
Claney, Howard 1594
Clanton, Rony 1579
Claps, Louise 1030, 1660
Clapsaddle, Robert 844
Clarence Williams 3rd 425
Clark, Alexander 1115
Clark, Andrei 1826
Clark, Bobby 1586
Clark, Casey Erin 541
Clark, Christine 294
Clark, Dane 204
Clark, David 1721
Clark, Eliza 1204
Clark, Gerardine 1784
Clark, Graham 574
Clark, Irene 1041
Clark, J.H. 1028, 1147
Clark, James 1462, 1816
Clark, James A. 1784
Clark, James Nisbet 304, 792, 795, 824
Clark, Jerry 1255, 1739, 1743
Clark, Jim 505
Clark, John (Peter) 68
Clark, Katharine 1784
Clark, Keith 1671
Clark, Lillian 1047
Clark, Michael 541
Clark, Nevin 136
Clark, Peggy 68, 149, 578, 1097, 1221, 1239, 1626, 1627
Clark, Peter 1021
Clark, Randy 906
Clark, Sarah 1434
Clark, Sarah C. 59
Clark, Thais 1198
Clark, Tony 243, 467, 823, 920, 928, 998
Clark, Victoria 1491
Clark, Wayne 575, 1660, 1744
Clark, Winston 812
Clarke, Bill 3, 385
Clarke, Evelyn 1315
Clarke, Gordon B. 324
Clarke, Hope 2, 62, 400, 715, 1291
Clarke, Martha 122, 561, 728, 859, 1020, 1055, 1722
Clarke, Marty 74
Clarke, Richard 1666
Clarke, Sarah 170
Clarkson, Alison H. 1804
Clarkson, Grady 316
Clary, Robert 68
Clary, Roy 962
Clausen, Richard 329
Clay, Louise 1379
Clay, Omar 629
Clay, Paul 206
Claycomb, Laura 640
Clayton, Charles 1416
Clayton, Don Allan 369
Clayton, Lawrence 330, 1375, 1404, 1591
Cleale, Lewis 1637
Cleary, Karen 324
Cleese, John 241, 1122
Clegg, Julia 1316
Clement, Maris 214, 626
Clement, Wilhelmina 1436
Clemente, Aixa 1537
Clemente, Steve "Mr. Wiggles" 804
Clements, Ann 1539
Clements, David 1137
Clements, Jehan 708
Clements, Joy 331
Clements, Mark 1613
Clements, Otis 534
Clemons, Vivian 745
Clenn, Gregory 850
Clerk, Clive 283
Clevenger, Joann 1198, 1518
Cleverie, Ann 578
Cliff, Lora Lee 290
Clifford, Mary 1412
Clifford, Pamela 88
Clifton, John 159, 203, 1008, 1319, 1378, 1531
Clifton-Allen, Lynne 194, 1762
Cline, Fred 1539
Cline, Hal 184
Cline, Jesse 1040
Clinger, Bijou 217
Clinton, Larry 1477
Clonick, Joseph 1685
Cloran, Matthew 198
Close, Del 1261
Cloud, Roderick 8
Clow, James 848
Clugston, Glen 74
Clyburn, Rose 1466
Clydesdale, Debi 1320
Coats, William Alan 1585
Cobb, Cynthia 1226
Cobey, Cynthia 1801
Cobler, Jann 395
Coburn, Charles 136
Coburn, Joan 735, 1627
Coburn, Mrs. Charles 136
Cochran, Cathy 1666
Cochran, Kevin 922
Cochran, Mabel 317
Cochren, Felix E. 205, 603, 1001
Cockett, Kalani 1221
Coco, James 352, 824
Coddington, Christopher 789
Codori, Joe 1066, 1185
Cody, Jennifer 365, 1554, 1778
Coe, George 471
Coe, John 844
Coe, John A. 660, 831
Coe, Peter 1473
Coffin, Frederick 588
Coffin, Gregg 499
Cogan, Suzanne 1615
Coggin, Barbara 64, 840, 841, 985, 1343, 1676
Coghill, Nevill 246
Cohan, George M. 570
Cohen, Al 572
Cohen, Allen 1297
Cohen, Anne 1314
Cohen, Coleman 1661
Cohen, Darren R. 997, 1831
Cohen, David 175, 1256
Cohen, Douglas J. 280, 1143, 1144
Cohen, Edward M. 289, 1505, 1510, 1607, 1610
Cohen, Eric 1395
Cohen, Esther 1351
Cohen, Frederic 1564
Cohen, Gary P. 541
Cohen, Greg 168
Cohen, Gregory 914, 994, 1753
Cohen, Hanoch 898
Cohen, Herb 7
Cohen, Jason Steven 387, 426, 496, 664, 873, 910, 975, 1109, 1146, 1250, 1375, 1664, 1699, 1722
Cohen, Joel C. 1245
Cohen, Joseph 1001
Cohen, Joseph J. 51, 420
Cohen, Joyce 376
Cohen, Judith 1505, 1706
Cohen, Jules 838
Cohen, Leonard 1471
Cohen, Leonard M. 1449
Cohen, Margery 128, 234, 1149, 1222, 1524
Cohen, Mark 814
Cohen, Martin B. 772
Cohen, Martin H. 1751
Cohen, Michael 126, 556, 557, 558, 852, 1069, 1273, 1829
Cohen, Myron 617
Cohen, Robert 1226
Cohen, Robert S. 1547
Cohen, Samuel D. 1285
Cohen, Sharleen Cooper 1441
Cohen, Sheila Rachel 423
Cohen, Shura 1284
Cohen, Sy 543
Cohen, Ze'eva 490
Cohenour, Patti 1109
Cohn, Sam 528
Coid, Marshall 1055, 1519
Cointreau, Anthony 1713
Coker, Bebe 1070
Coker, Jenna 462, 474
Cokorinos, Philip 574, 1023
Colacino, Richard 201
Colaneri, Joseph 451
Colavecchia, Franco 256, 1595, 1829
Colbert, Rachel 1120
Colbin, Kaila 349
Colbin, Rod 987
Colby, Michael 271, 1147, 1149, 1584
Colby, Robert 652
Colby, Ronald 22
Cole, Barbara 1780
Cole, Chris 1029
Cole, Christopher 706, 1138
Cole, Doug 681
Cole, J.J. 51
Cole, Jack 188
Cole, Kay 132, 283, 656, 1184, 1197, 1330, 1365, 1426, 1486, 1691
Cole, Michael 413, 1329
Cole, Nora 194, 643, 1089, 1186
Cole, Nora M. 127, 255
Cole, Roz 1383
Cole, Stephen 14
Colella, Jenn 1479
Coleman, Amy 892
Coleman, Charles 181
Coleman, Cy 371, 377, 463, 616, 1534
Coleman, Don 185
Coleman, Grisha 768
Coleman, James 1660
Coleman, Jane 1029
Coleman, Kia 716
Coleman, Larry 1559
Coleman, Ross 1281
Coleman, Sammy 1029
Coleman, Walter 815
Coles, Honi 165
Coles, Zaida 107, 1267
Coley, Aisha 927
Coley, Dottie 1559
Colker, Jerry 1622
Coll, Jean Michel 1281
Collamore, Jerome 1604
College, Bard 1749
Colley-Lee, Myrna 927, 1580
Colli, Mark C. 1281
Collier, Constance 1249
Collier, Marie 1088
Collier, Naomi 609
Collin, Kathy 1131
Collings, Nancy 706, 1310
Collins, A.M. 54
Collins, Bethanne 198
Collins, Bill 1721
Collins, Cathy 506
Collins, Courtenay 424, 1327
Collins, Cynthia 1608
Collins, David 1632
Collins, Douglas 1399
Collins, Eric 1784
Collins, Jack 1755
Collins, Jaycee 121
Collins, Julia 1207
Collins, Kathy Ellen 821
Collins, Ken 191, 1253
Collins, Lester 1253
Collins, Margaret 1145
Collins, Neatha 1291
Collins, Pat 65, 158, 372, 394, 943, 1485, 1628, 1731
Collins, Patricia 1604
Collins, Paul 294
Collins, Ray 7, 697
Collins, Rise 180
Collins, Stephen 263, 1113, 1492
Collins, Steve 1082
Collins, Zebedee 1174
Collins-Langhorne, Georgia 1001
Collis, Arthur 99
Coloff, Rachel 1712
Colon, Brunilda 118
Colpman, Nora 435
Colreavy, Sinead 1438
Colson, Jacque Lynn 920
Colston, Robert 87, 381, 531, 534, 1259, 1380
Colt, Alvin 93, 517, 518, 519, 520, 521, 522, 523, 524, 525, 526, 600, 942, 944, 1067, 1254
Colt, Ethel 1578
Colton, Chevi 154, 1048, 1161
Colton, Jacque Lynn 756, 757, 920
Colum, Padraic 253
Columbus, Tobie 913
Colyer, Austin 352, 1452
Colyer, Carlton 1636
Combs, Hadley 1416
Combs, Steven 574
Comden, Betty 234, 377, 398, 1100, 1185, 1186, 1224, 1534, 1717
Comer, Edmund 1233
Comfort, Jane 1779
Comor, Henry 851, 972
Compton, Dean 1330
Compton, Gardner 1168
Compton, Linda 649
Comstock, Eric 1210
Conant, Michael 915
Concepcion, Nickemil 1186
Concerts, B.F. 326
Condee, William F. 1692
Conderman, Susan 708
Condon, Dennis 906
Cone, Carole 654
Cone, Peggy 654
Cone, Rhett 654
Cone, Tom 690
Conforti, Gino 1179, 1481
Conforti, Tony 1025, 1435
Congden, David 292
Congress, Judy 109
Conkerite, Zenobia 860
Conklin, Bill 232, 1163
Conklin, John 366, 574, 676, 1062, 1400, 1816
Conlee, John Ellison 633, 727
Conley, Brian 1469
Conley, Harry 1616
Conley, Matt 720
Conley, Robert 76, 1446
Conley, Shannon 471
Conlon, James 47
Conlow, Peter 34, 199, 1448, 1636
Conn, Didi 632
Connaughton, Kevin 1512
Connell, David 266
Connell, Gordon 117, 371, 415, 726, 1261, 1318, 1390
Connell, Jane 371, 409, 528, 599, 601, 1142, 1261, 1318, 1390, 1602, 1627
Connell, Tim 1438
Connelly, Peter 950
Conner, Bar Dell 278
Conner, Bardell 996
Conner, Bruce 695
Connerton, Martha 552
Connes, Keith 1021
Connolley, Denise 913
Connolly, George 1707
Connolly, Michael 695
Connor, Catherine 112
Connor, Mark F. 1438
Connor, Maureen 1019
Connors, Anne 1801
Connors, Kevin 1301
Connors, Sharon Ferry 1469
Conradt, Mark 631
Conroy, Frances 580, 1376
Conroy, Jarlath 1006
Conroy, Maryellen 1316
Consoer, Dianne 609
Constant, George 1300
Constanten, Tom 1592
Constantine, Deborah 1428, 1638
Conte, Andrea Del 488
Conte, Edward R. 1419
Conte, John 772
Conte, Josie 1544
Contreras, Gloria 1276
Contreras, Ray 386, 1214, 1384, 1535
Contrucci, Lance 1113
Conversano, Frank 427, 872
Converse, Frederick S. 1269
Converse, Tony 1613
Converse-Roberts, William 1376

Convy, Bert 149, 390, 1083
Conway, Bert 1140
Conway, Bill 1017
Conway, Billy 1776
Conway, Curt 1140, 1652
Coogan, Jackie 145
Cook, Candy 599
Cook, Carole 1326
Cook, Charles "Cookie" 165
Cook, G. Richardson 410
Cook, Gregory 636
Cook, Jill 1290
Cook, MacRae 1412
Cook, Mildred 317
Cook, Nancy 1805
Cook, Patrick 249
Cook, Peter 449, 450, 1091
Cook, Pierre 196, 1002
Cook, Roderick 1170
Cook, Victor 647, 648, 1071
Cook, Victor Trent 1375
Cook, Wendy 1629
Cooke, Barbara Lee 1618
Cooke, Sally 795, 797
Cooke, Wanda 33
Cookson, Peter 316
Cool, Walter 985
Coon, David 1029
Coonen, Paula 1041
Cooner, Robert 743, 990
Cooner, Sharon 887
Cooney, Dan 1700
Cooper, Adrienne 1502
Cooper, Bob, Jr. 1412
Cooper, Brian 538, 808
Cooper, Cecelia 1739
Cooper, Charlotte 119
Cooper, Chuck 78, 252, 1631
Cooper, Denise 323
Cooper, Edwin 132
Cooper, Judith 716
Cooper, Keith D. 697
Cooper, Lawrence 4, 1165
Cooper, Lee 996
Cooper, Lilli 1515
Cooper, Marilyn 274, 1250
Cooper, Mindy 499, 1706
Cooper, Neil 575
Cooper, Pamela 108
Cooper, Randi 991
Cooper, Rene 1615
Cooper, Reni 1060
Cooper, Robert M. 221
Cooper, Saralou 638, 1686
Cooper, Sheila Tronn 1290
Cooper, Tiffany 185
Cooper, Tod 809
Cooper-Hecht, Gail 100, 359, 452, 1251, 1386, 1467, 1607, 1619, 1623
Coopersmith, Jerome 90, 1031
Copani, Peter 493, 1124, 1294, 1537
Cope, Pat 705
Copelan, Sheila 60
Copeland, Aaron 1241, 1601
Copeland, Bill 1360
Copeland, Carolyn Rossi 280, 576, 596, 828, 830, 1204, 1303, 1484
Copeland, Jane 66
Copeland, Joan 317, 369
Copeland, Maurice 1343
Copeland, Stephanie 1042, 1367
Copenhaver, Charles 876
Copley, John Singleton 1691
Copley, Johnathan 125
Copp, Aaron 1110
Coppicus, F.C. 1241
Coppin, Grace 494
Coppola, Anton 944, 947
Coppola, Frank 467, 920, 1739
Coppola, Nicholas 877
Coppola, William J. 1279
Corato, Lou 841, 1354, 1676
Coray, Catherine 999
Corbett, Dee 1652
Corbett, Gretchen 1562
Corbett, Michael 1033
Corbin, Al 481
Corbin, Clayton 1308
Corby, Joseph 90
Corcoran, Daniel 325
Corcoran, Mary 1648
Corday, Ken 601
Cordes, Kathryn 1392, 1801
Cordon, Norman 40, 776, 1010
Cordova, Richard 839, 1087
Cordtz, Wendell 111, 392, 1017
Corey, Herb 638
Corey, Jill 1595
Corigliano, John 574
Corio, Ann 1615, 1616
Corker, John 940
Corley, Nick 697, 1305, 1381
Corman, Avery 1477
Corn, Rosalind 1221
Cornett, Barbara 1824
Cornett, Ewel 1041
Corney, Emily 474
Cornwell, Eric 161, 163, 1173
Cornwell, Jack (H.) 867, 1163, 1751
Correa, Deardra 488
Correia, Steve 1785
Corren, Donald 1403, 1654
Correy, Jim 15
Corrick, Jeffery 1050
Corrin, George 735, 870, 902
Corry, James 786
Corsaro, Frank 254, 1165, 1350, 1552
Cort, Bud 542
Corteggiano, Joseph 451
Cortez, Natalie 1458
Cortez, Ricky 983
Corti, Jesse 203, 975
Corti, Jim 234, 244, 1777
Cortland, Kenneth 915
Corts, Christopher 395
Corum, Pete 321
Corvino, Alfredo 1131
Corwen, Carol 174
Corwin, Norman 1740
Corwin, Robert 1682
Cory, Ken 1226
Cory, Kenneth 109
Coryell, Essie Jane 1185
Cosden, Robert 74
Cosgrove, Caprice 1240
Cosgrove, Ron 1805
Cosier, E. David, Jr. 1381
Cosson, Steven 607
Costa, Natalie 1670
Costa, Richard 1544
Costa, Rico 295
Costabile, David 252, 1120
Costa-Greenspon, Muriel 720
Costain, Dan 56
Costanza, Marie 1052
Costello, Lee 349
Costello, Lou 377
Costello, Robert 436
Coster, Nicolas 791, 1163
Costigan, Ken 1446
Coston, Melvin 1816
Costumes, Grace 861
Cota, Keith 661
Cotsirilos, Stephanie 65, 634, 1553, 1568, 1569
Cotton, Robert 380
The Cotton Pickers 321
Cottrel, Karen 1016
Coucill, Christopher 184, 1610
Coulianos, Peter 1029
Coullet, Rhonda 323, 1367, 1733
Coulson, Christian 1233
Coulter, Dorothy 1789
Courson, Robert 37
Courtney, C.C. 1395, 1396
Courtney, Frederick 834
Courtney, James 574
Courtney, Nan 507, 1716
Courtney-James, Geene 1475
Courts, Randy 2, 576, 791, 828
Coury, Clay 162, 1158
Cousin, Tome 122
Coutlangus, Corrine 110
Couture, Simone 505
Cover, A.D. 260
Cowan, Edie 939
Cowan, Edwardyne 485
Cowan, Janet 1131
Cowan, Marianne 1092
Coward, Noel 13, 317, 751, 1100, 1170, 1390
Cowdery, Jim 983
Cowell, Stanley 885
Cowen, Marion 1278
Cowles, Frances 621, 622
Cowley, Christopher 1535
Cox, Caroline 396
Cox, Catherine 765, 781, 1335
Cox, Christie 95
Cox, Christopher 175
Cox, Jane 1374, 1479, 1779
Cox, Louise 340
Cox, Lyssandra 1815
Cox, Natania 1305
Cox, Richard 27
Cox, Susan 1389
Cox, Tyrone 1015
Cox, Veanne 252, 1113, 1454
Cox, William 390, 879, 1644
Cox, William R. 1119
Coyle, Bruce (W.) 612, 1032, 1309, 1389, 1438, 1485, 1585
Coyle, J.J. 743, 1119
Coyle, Jerry 1171
Crabbe, Gary 350, 1273
Crabtree, D. Matt 808
Crabtree, Don 133, 1360
Crabtree, Howard 1763, 1772
Craft, Barry 1139
Craft, Tom 952
Craig, Bradford 714, 1604
Craig, Casey 1480
Craig, Dagmar 1465
Craig, David 1254
Craig, Deborah S. 1680
Craig, Joel 1585
Craig, Kyle 808
Crain, Jon 1563, 1601, 1814
Crandall, Victoria 822
Crane, David 1, 811, 1243
Crane, David L. 1709
Crane, Debra 1359
Crane, Larry 1744
Crane, Lor 1767
Crane, Warren 352
Craney, Trudy Ellen 1139
Cratsley, David Bruce 295
Craven, Richard 160, 535
Craver, Mike 376, 1176, 1326, 1484, 1779
Craver, P.M. (Mike) 1326
Crawford, Ann 697
Crawford, Cheryl 204, 306, 307, 718, 875
Crawford, Jared 207
Crawford, Jen "J5" 79
Crawford, Joe 591
Crawford, Kathy 867
Crawford, Mary 676
Crawford, Mona 1475
Crawford, Rockin' Ronny 79
Crawford, Steven 397
Crawley, Brian 1726
Cray, Richard 284
Crayhon, Joseph 745
Creamer, Henry 1543
Crean, Jam 200
Creatore, Luigi 1480
Cree, Walter Mitchell 1825
Creed, Barbara 908
Creed, Kay 488
Creek, Luther 1006
Creekmore, Hubert 1179
Cregor, Lauren 896
Creighton, Georgia 15, 614, 990, 1085, 1236, 1673
Creighton, Orda 1278
Creley, Jack 1393
Crespi, Lee 757, 1231
Crespo, Emillio 188
Cresson, James 693
Cresswell, Luke 1530
Creyton, Barry 1421
Criado, Vincente 614
Cribari, Donna 1283
Crichton, Don 1574
Crider, Amanda 362, 717
Crinkley, Raymond 1282
Criscuolo, Lou 372
Criscuolo, Louis 705, 1483
Crisp, Mike 1469
Crispell, Marilyn 1816
Criss, Michael 1333
Cristin, Judith 1741
Cristler, Samuel 574
Criswell, Kim 1521
Critt, C.J. 1737
Crittenden, Jordan 1488
Critz, Darren 1237
Crivello, Anthony 847
Crivello, Mary Lou 319, 1646
Crochet, Laurie 1382
Crofoot, Alan 1360
Croft, Dwayne 628
Croft, Paddy 805
Croft, Richard 640
Croiter, Jeff 10, 444, 491, 711, 721, 738, 802, 845, 950
Crom, Rick 1128, 1383, 1508, 1712
Cromelin, Carey 99
Cromer, A. Harrison 695
Cromer, Harold 42, 313, 803, 1183
Cromwell, David 476
Cromwell, J.T. 1215
Cromwell, John 1116
Cromwell, Keith 1245, 1772
Crook, Beth 940
Crook, Mervin 121
Crook, Richard 773
Croom, Gabriel A. 668
Crosby, B.J. 668
Crosby, Don 1310
Crosby, Erin 519, 1450
Crosby, Joe 112, 199, 1780
Cross, Julie 362
Cross, Murphy 146, 610, 955
Cross, Phillips 1744
Cross, Richard 1062, 1111, 1413
Cross, Stephen 1681
Crossland, Ann 37
Crossley, Karen 1343
Croswell, Anne 313, 448, 1101, 1754
Crothers, Sam 1037
Crotty, Edward 224
Crouch, Julian 1444
Crouch, Michael 1171
Crouch, W. Michael 224
Crouse, Lindsay Ann 1081
Crouse, Russel 63
Crow, Carl 1661
Crowder, Bill 1155, 1156, 1157
Crowder, Jack 504
Crowe, Gillian 187
Crowe, Gordon 1168, 1606
Crowie, Margaret 1029
Crowley, Alison 612
Crowley, Ann 442
Crowley, Ed 649, 722
Crowley, Edward 745
Crozier, Jim 1659
Cruise, Julee 1325, 1353
Crumb, Ann 770, 825, 1328
Crumpler, Nancy 1681
Crutcher, T. Renee 333
Crutchfield, Buddy 391, 444
Cruz, Angelo 897
Cruz, Cintia 1398
Cruz, Frank 268
Cruze, Josh 1664
Cryer, Dan 399
Cryer, David 274, 990, 998, 1029, 1154, 1286, 1539, 1767
Cryer, Gretchen 57, 179, 656, 753, 894, 1154, 1650, 1746
Crystal, Raphael 878, 1102, 1715
Csontos, David 1469
Cuascut, Anthony 1689
The Cubiculo 918
Cuccioli, Bob (Robert) 52, 444, 802, 1056, 1381
Cuddy, Mark 499
Cuervo, Alma 263, 285, 1323, 1503
Cuevas, Ruben 1340
Cuff, Reneta 768
Cuka, Frances 445
Cuker, Elliot 1713
Culbertson, Caroline 876
Culkin, Joan 537
Cullen, Jack 965
Cullman, Joan 424
Cullum, John 1712, 1779
Culton, Dawn 734
Cumbo, Rashamella 82
Cumming, Richard 1445
Cummings, Claudia 294, 1405
cummings, e.e. 334
Cummings, Gretel 426, 701, 1628
Cummings, Jack, III 328
Cummings, Joanne 1582
Cummings, Kay 1685
Cummings, Lawrence 538
Cummings, Suzanne 1542
Cummings, Tony 765
Cummins, Jeremy 873
Cummins, Rick 1607
Cunliffe, Jerry 379
Cunningham, Bill 1666
Cunningham, Glenn 1029
Cunningham, Jo Ann 1173
Cunningham, Joan 1349
Cunningham, JoAnn 1451
Cunningham, John 157, 191, 348, 678, 962, 1048, 1265, 1485
Cunningham, Johnny 1248
Cunningham, Lisa Ann 434
Cunningham, Mary 591
Cunningham, Olma 405
Cunningham, Robin 196
Cunningham, Roger 434, 1288, 1391
Cunningham, Ronnie 236
Cunningham, Ryan 738
Cunningham, Thomas E. 983
Cuomo, Jimmy 1089, 1387, 1776
Cupo, Steven 1548
Curelop, Shepard 1116

Curlee, Karen 1575
Curless, John 445, 1143
The Curley Company 336
Curley, Dennis 920
Curley, George 415, 478, 1076
Curley, Wilma 1131
Curnock, Richard 884
Curran, Gerard 43
Curran, Keith 855, 1037, 1089
Curran, Sean 670, 805, 1103
Currie, Donald 1566
Currie, Richard 1359
Currin, Brenda 728, 1722
Curry, John 1304
Curry, Richmond 1696
Curry, Rosa 72, 668
Curry, Ruthann 1434
Curry, Virgil 50, 60, 556, 557, 1566
Curtan, James 1477
Curtin, Catherine 965
Curtin, Jane 1299, 1313
Curtin, Jim 374
Curtin, Phyllis 1227, 1563, 1587, 1814
Curtis, Norman 1732
Curtis, Barbara 1802
Curtis, Donna 884, 1154
Curtis, Frank 1139
Curtis, Jack 1535
Curtis, Keene 306
Curtis, Norman 1732
Curtis, Pat 821
Curtis, Patricia Taylor 1732
Curtis, Robin 293
Curtis, Roger 397
Curtis, Vera 340
Curtis, William C. 876
Curtis-Hall, Vondie 1049, 1783
Cushman, Lynn 1806
Cushman, Nancy 360
Cutell, Lou 987, 1824
Cuthbertson, Clarence 470
Cuties, Burley 1616
Cutler, Ben 494
Cutler, Sara 1731
Cypkin, Diane 147, 819, 1026, 1051
Cyr, Myriam 632
Cyrus, Jim 64, 420, 1297
Czarniak, Jeremy 749, 1832
Czekalska, Ewa 1275
Czernicki, Gene 1780
Czolczynski, Paul 1051

D, Eva 790
Dabdoub, Jack 66, 912, 948, 1167
Dabney, Ronald 1040
Dabney, Sheila 27, 648, 1402, 1625
D'Abruzzo, Stephanie 77, 738
Dacal, Janet 760
Da Costa, Morton 1452
Dadd, Kyle 1195
Dadds, Marcia 1300
Dade, Herb 1487
Dadral, Sonell 1233
Daffi 1080
Daggett, John 967
D'Agostino, Joseph 1785
Dahdah, Robert 336, 337, 1617
Dahill, Frank 158
Dahl, Carolyn 543
Dahl, Gail 110, 664
Dahl, Tracy 574
Dahlen, Michael 1120
The Daidalos Brothers 1281
Daigle, Vickie 1616
Dailey, Stephen 731
Dailey, Will 731
Daily, Patricia 586
Dain, Frank 248
Daines, John 1316
Dakin, Christine 666
D'Alby, Pierre 401
Dale, Grover 42, 472, 865, 866, 1199
Dale, Jim 1304
Dale, Karen Lynn 1287
Dale, Toby 66
Daleman, Rob 462
D'alesandro, Annette 1599
D'alessio, Arthur 1226
Daley, Cass 145
Daley, Stephen 481
Dalgleish, Jack M. 1830
Dallaire, Michel 1281
Dallas, Walter 1074
Dallos, Chris 1053, 1458
Dalrymple, Jean 140
Daltirus, Lisa 1022
Dalton, Kathie 1021
Dalton, Lezlie 1641
Dalton, Nancy 93
Dalton, Sasha 382
Dalton, William 232
Daly, Kevin 1452
Dalzell, Shirley 1566
Damari, Shoshana 617
Damaschke, Bill 596
Damashek, Barbara 1323
D'Amato, Anthony 625
d'Amboise, Charlotte 1146, 1660
d'Amboise, Christopher 1146
d'Amboise, Jacques 1379
D'ambrosio, Frank 454
D'ambrosio, Genie 834
Damiano, Tony 329
D'Amico, Kirk 1518
Damon, Bruno 1030, 1660
Damon, Cathryn 201, 1131, 1420, 1452
Damon, Stuart 201
Damrosch, Walter 340, 1010
Dana, Barbara 1724
Dana, Bill 160, 371, 1261
Dana, Dick 226
Dana, F. Mitchell 422, 672, 835, 979, 1245
Dancy, Virginia 1030
D'Andrea, Carole 86
Dane, Clarissa 929
Danek, Michael 142
Danen, Myrna 693
Danese, Connie 316, 773
Danford, Andrea 35
D'angelo, Louis 298, 868, 905, 1010, 1047, 1249
Dangerfield, Deborah 1542
Danias, Starr 203
Daniel, Diana 842
Daniele, Graciela 27, 130, 375, 430, 580, 583, 683, 873, 886, 933, 1109, 1121, 1191, 1270, 1588
Danieley, Jason 503
Danielle, Marlene 939, 1025
Danielle, Susan 1644
Danielpour, Richard 1022
Daniels, Christopher Leo 983
Daniels, Danny 132, 1447
Daniels, David 98, 1172, 1265
Daniels, Dennis 203
Daniels, Edgar 1440
Daniels, Elinor 1131
Daniels, Lisa 768
Daniels, Marc 1254
Daniels, Melanie 1435
Daniels, Paul (S.) 41, 70, 251, 473, 690, 973, 1048, 1191, 1219, 1478, 1557, 1624
Daniels, Sharon 1139
Daniels, Stan 1100, 1101, 1431
Daniels, Walker 572, 649
Daniels, Zelie (Zelle) 284, 1223
Danielsen, Carl 1669
Danko, Harold 1034
Dann, Sam 1678
Danna 1653
Danner, Blythe 1707
Danner, Dorothy Frank 1062
Danner, Harry 190
Dansicker, Michael 35, 372, 1184
Dansky, Peter 1439
Dante, Dena 379
Dante, Nicholas 283, 1483
Dantuono, Mike 345, 720, 820
Danz, Cassandra 475
Danzig, Sylvia 1361
D'aquila, Kenny 215
Dar, Ruth 1203
Dara, Joyce 153
D'Arcangelo-Mayer 427
d'arcy, David 1278
D'arcy, Mary 84
Darcy, Pattie 115
Darden, Michael 1580
Darden, Severn 1206, 1415, 1461, 1649, 1724, 1813
Darewski, Herman 136
Darian, Anita 616, 1409, 1445, 1474
Darion, Joe 1101
Darius, Tony 488
Darke, Alison 1233
Darling, Candy 599
Darling, Joan 946, 1295
Darling, Robert E. 32, 60
Darling, Sandra 1111
Darlow, Cynthia 1693
Darnell, Bob 1185
Darnell, Caroline Worth 1420
Darnell, Robert 1824
Darnutzer, Don 37, 657, 754, 777
Darom, Ari 562
Darrah, James 1421
Darrenkamp, John 574
Darrow, Harry 675
Darrow, Harry Silverglat 1348
Darrow, Richard 734
Darwin, Cress 1169
Darwin, Leslie 1050
Darzin, Daina 913
Da Sylva, Howard 134, 324, 1399
Datcher, Irene 361
Daugherty, Bill 1764
Dauphinais, Marcel 1013
Dauria, Debra 1300
Davenport, David 1261
Davenport, Joan 507
Davenport, John 11
Davenport, Ken 38
Davenport, Pembroke 66, 1221
Davey, Chris 1629
Davey, Shaun 805
David, Bob 235
David, Clifford 201, 324
David, Daniel 297
David, Hal 83
David, Jean 1080
David, Jeff 1242
David, Jim 83, 1801
David, Keith 12, 23, 186, 647, 1065, 1270
David, Linda 636, 1660
David, Lou 705
David, Michael 117, 234, 244, 376, 634, 660, 699, 885, 1279
David, Nina 142
David-Little, Alan 588
Davidsohn, George 441
Davidson, Carlos 706, 768
Davidson, Gordon 1029
Davidson, Ilana 846
Davidson, Jan 376
Davidson, Jez 1355
Davidson, John 1302
Davidson, Lorraine 913
Davidson, Michael 572
Davidson, Richard M. 445
Davidson, Ruth 363
Davidson, Suzanne Schwartz 2, 1357
Davidson-Gorbea, Patti 1815
Davie, Erin 583, 769
Davies, Andrew 483
Davies, Brian 805
Davies, Dennis Russell 1723
Davies, Joseph 822
Davies, Victor 127
Davila, Andrea 349
Davis, Andrew 1411
Davis, Ann 144
Davis, Anthony 1816
Davis, Bailey 1825
Davis, Barbara 1559
Davis, Billy 107
Davis, Buster 100, 132, 1239, 1254
Davis, Carl 388, 450
Davis, Carlos 1296
Davis, Chee 63
Davis, Cherry 987, 1060, 1440
Davis, Christopher 1816
Davis, Clayton 1171
Davis, Clifton 390, 707, 722, 1689
Davis, Clinton Turner 107
Davis, Daryl 1816
Davis, Dawn 9
Davis, Deborah 1434
Davis, Edith 376
Davis, Edward H. 631, 1560
Davis, Eisa 1225
Davis, Gail 125
Davis, Gordon 1278
Davis, Guy 1579
Davis, Hal 565, 1309
Davis, Harris 488
Davis, Humphrey 445, 1774
Davis, J.B. 1552
Davis, Janice 59, 1434
Davis, Jeff 17, 267, 272, 451, 673, 678, 740, 912, 968, 1023, 1039, 1167, 1287, 1358
Davis, Joe 152
Davis, John H.P. 1340
Davis, John Henry 1190
Davis, Joseph Warren 194
Davis, Kery 196
Davis, Kevin 615
Davis, Lawrence E. 1189
Davis, Lindsay (W.) 52, 127, 394, 552, 682, 910, 990, 1109, 1304
Davis, Lorrie 720
Davis, Marcy 1548
Davis, Marguerite 1394
Davis, Marvin 1713
Davis, Mary Bond 730
Davis, Michael 33, 1264, 1311, 1487
Davis, Michael Rees 1023
Davis, Murphy 1514
Davis, Ossie 91, 153, 1579
Davis, Paul E. 1060
Davis, Penny 696
Davis, Peter 12
Davis, Randy A. 668
Davis, Ron 268
Davis, Ronny 1749
Davis, Ryan J. 1479
Davis, S.J. 203
Davis, Sam 122
Davis, Samantha 196
Davis, Scott 1320, 1321
Davis, Sheila Kay 939, 1351
Davis, Sid 1069, 1273
Davis, Sidney 350
Davis, Stan 1754
Davis, Sylvia 1107, 1216
Davis, Thulani 1816
Davis, Todd 593
Davis, Vicki 1300
Davis, Virginia 815
Davis, William 1198
Davison, Lesley 87, 126, 160, 415, 558, 1259, 1421, 1430, 1605
Davison, Robert 1331
Davisson, Charles 566
Dawn, Roxy 713
Dawson, Audrey 1349
Dawson, Craig 808
Dawson, Curt 16
Dawson, Gregory 631
Dawson, Kate 444
Dawson, Suzanne 272, 626
Dawud, David 51
Day, Barry 13
Day, Connie 267, 955
Day, Cora Lee 1423
Day, Craig 1618
Day, David 463
Day, Denise 1359
Day, Janet 605
Day, Janine 1359
Day, Jennie 1543
Day, Jonathan 1818
Day, Leslie 116
Day, Leslie V. 51
Day, Linda 591
Day, Marie 56
Day, Nola 600
Dayag, George 1221
Days, Maya 1188
Dayton, R. Michael 960
Deacon, Simon 808
Deal, Dennis 1138
Dean, Bradley 1736
Dean, David J. 554
Dean, Gerri 1038, 1397
Dean, Jo 834
Dean, Kathi 566
Dean, Laura 2, 45, 260, 484, 596, 1243
Dean, Leamond 317
Dean, Mary Kay 378
Dean, Norman 76
Dean, Steve 649
Dean, Virginia L. 1014
DeAnda, Peter 716
De Andres, Vicente 108
Deane, Michael Howell 883
De Antonio, Adrienne 613
Dearing, Judy 9, 105, 162, 278, 382, 592, 688, 718, 736, 832, 959, 1064, 1074, 1148, 1191, 1207, 1307, 1423, 1579, 1781, 1783, 1785
Deas, Gerald W. 1174
Deas, Kevin 846, 1816
DeBaer, Jean 1042
de Barge, Flotilla 1500
DeBarr, Margo 1755
DeBartol, Dick 1066
DeBauer, Judy 1348
de Benedet, Rachel 10
Debenedetto, Joey 410
DeBenedictis, Dick 1669
de Berry, David 1412
DeBiase, Gemma 403
Deblinger, Ann 1287
deBlois, Kat 1548
DeBoer, Franklin 756, 1231

deBoer, Fritz 1734
DeBolt, James 1789
De Bono, Jerry 1574
DeBord, Jason 418
DeBoy, David 391
de Brugada, Philippe 636
De Camp, June 180
Decareau, Dick 25, 249, 990
Dechazza, Pepe 238
DeChristopher, Dave 1102
Deckard, Diane 350
Decker, Edwin 842
Decker, Lindsey 604
DeClue, Denise 1230
De Cormier, Robert 1399
DeCristo, Al 1650
DeDea, Robert 1134
De Dio, Harry 488
Dedrickson, Tracy 573, 1772
Dee, Debbi 1550
Dee, Ruby 1579
Deeble, Deborah 1707
Deegan, John Michael 123, 485, 1301, 1547, 1569
Deeks, Jeane (Jean) 201, 1604
Deem, George 1673
Deems, Mickey 63, 858
Deering, Nancy 1216
Deering, Olive 1140
Deeter, J.M. 136
Deeting, Sally 395
DeFelice, Harold 377
De Fesi, Ron 4
Deffaa, Chip 570
DeFilipps, Rick 1028, 1160
Defiris, Samantha 768
Deflorian, Daria 859
DeForest, Charles 1305
Defrere, Desire 1010
DeGaetani, Thomas 951
DeGange, Anny 284
deGhelder, Stephen 1343, 1398
DeGise, Joe, II 1817
DeGregorie, Frank 397
De Groat, Andrew 397, 427, 917
De Groff, Dale 190, 397
de Groot, Myra 1431
Deguchi, Makoto 1674
de Guzman, Dr. Daniel 1179
De Guzman, Jossie 210, 648, 975, 1384
de Haas, Darius 222
Dehass, Debra 1134
DeHaven, Gloria 676
Deign, Peter 1131
Deihim, Sussan 1625
DeJesus, Enrique Cruz 167
de Jesus, Robin 760
De John, Paul 1689
De Jong, Constance 1405
De Koven, Reginald 245
DeKoven, Roger 1541
Delahanty, Richard 177
Delaney, Sandra 397
Delano, Lee 1457
DeLany, Carolyn 322
Delapenha, Denise 393, 1732
de Lappe, Gemze 304, 1254
DeLaria, Lea 933, 1186
Delate, Brian 1664
De Laurentis, Semina 675, 920, 1017, 1155, 1159, 1349
Delehanty, Richard 1758
De Leporte, Rita 1047
Delgado, Margarita 799
D'elia, Maria 1080
D'elia, Vincent 906
DeLise, Doreen 1134
Dell, Gabriel 528
Dell, Marlene 301, 1185
Dell, Patricia 1506
Della-Penna, Philip 1152
Delmer, Lee 1163
Deloatch, Gary 1633
De Lon, Jack 92, 609, 944, 1360, 1587, 1814
DeLong, Lorraine 226
DeLorenzo, Michael 1538
DeLorenzo, Stephen 95
DelPazzo, Bob 310
Delson, Mary 393
Delu, Dahl 969
De Luca, John 194
de Luce, Virginia 277
De Luise, Dom 33, 60, 68, 652
de Luise, Jerry 528
de Mailly, Diane 1027, 1558
DeMaio, Peter 1420
DeMaio, Tommy 1298
De Marco, Ronnie 1035
DeMarco, Ruth Ann 1731
DeMarie, David 684
De Martin, Imelda 48
Demas, Carole 625, 722, 1083, 1379
De Matteis, Giancarlo 59
De Mattis, Ray 203, 567
De Mause, Alan 1806
De May, Sally 1751
De Mayo, Peter 600
Dembaugh, William 891
DeMendez, Doris 152
de Menil, Christophe 294
Demenkoff, Tom 740
Dementchoukov, Vassili 1281
De Mers, Jean 1412
DeMetz, Kay 190
DeMichael, Carmen 95
De Michele, Joseph V. 148, 398, 463, 812, 930, 1031, 1144, 1451
DeMirjian, Denise 255, 1648
Demone, Richard 342, 993
DeMora, Robert 945
De Moravia, Yvonne 1144
Demos, Nick 997
Dempsey, Jackie 1516
Dempsey, Jerome 1109, 1628
Dempsey, John 1831
Dempsey, Mark 1168
Dempsey, William 481
Dempster, Curt 1190
Demy, Jacques 1697
den Ende, Joop van 474
Denby, Edwin 1241
Denda, Elena 488
DenDanto, Frank, III 1815
Dendy, Mark 802, 1778
Dengel, Jake 528, 1455
Denham, Stacey 294
Deni, Katherine 1469
Denis, Andre 56
Denise, Carol 1638
Denison, Ken 37
Denison, Robert G. 316
Denisov, Viktor 849
Denman, Jeffry 751, 1110, 1818
Dennehy, Brian 1411
Dennehy, Dennis 271, 322, 505, 1028, 1147, 1148, 1160, 1569, 1584, 1717
Dennen, Barre 535
Denney, Dodo 121, 1481
Dennigan, Gib 957
Denning, Nancy 869
Dennis, Al 1594
Dennis, Alfred 1272, 1604
Dennis, Carol 186, 1074, 1146, 1363, 1568
Dennis, Charles 397, 427
Dennis, Robert 535, 1168
Dennis, Ronald 283, 1081, 1085, 1166
Dennison, John 33, 92, 609
Dennison, Mac 1615
Denny, Christopher 16
Denton, Jim 1011
Denvir, Jason 1629
de Oni, Christofer 116, 1670
De Paola, Paul 62
de Paree, Les Belles 506
De Paris, Wilbur 1021
Depasquale, Richard 1476
de Pass, Paul 81, 297, 564, 758, 781, 1297, 1560, 1668
DePietro, Peter 302
de Ramos, Jeannet Rollins 238
Derbas, Frank 448
Derbeneva, Tatiana 849
Derefinko, Rod 990
De Renzi, Victor 1741
Der Meulen, Howard Van 842
DeRosa, Pat 1350
DeRosa, Rob 551, 1124
DeRosa, Stephen 778, 838, 1129, 1736
De Rosario, Carmen Torrido 897
de Rothschild, Robert 284, 561, 675, 1722
DeRoy, Jamie 997
Derr, Hume 85
Derricks, Cleavant 230, 1375, 1762
Derricks, Marguerite 296
Derricks-Carroll, Clinton 230, 255, 1762
deRuiter, Albert 1029
DeRusso, Richard 1689
Derx, Hallam B. 1283
Desai, Angel 222
DeSal, Frank 957
DeSalvo, Allison 49, 612
DeSalvo, Anne 580, 588
DeSantis, John 214
De Segurola, Andres 988
Deshane, Terri 68
De Shields, Andre 18, 167, 171, 257, 646, 809, 855, 1521, 1695
DeSisto, A. Michael 767
Desko, Tanya 1390
Desmond, Brian 369
Desmond, Mona 136
Desmond, Paula 1307
DeSoto, Edward 490
DeSousa, Melissa 1370
Destin, Mark 935
DeSylva, B.G. [Buddy] 1101
De Sylva, William 171
de Toledo, Maxime (Alvarez) 717, 1374, 1416, 1818
Detrick, Don 214
Detweiler, Lowell 1082
Deutchman, Lois 586, 1176, 1197
Deutsch, Joshua 1233
Deutsch, Patti 542
Deveraux, Kam 772
DeVerne, Ellen 1525
De Ves, Silvia Garcias 108
Devin, Richard 869
Devine, Barry 1145
Devine, Elizabeth 695
Devine, Erick 57
Devine, Jeanne 1265
Devine, Jerry 48
Devine, Kelly 541
Devine, Loretta 214, 927, 996, 1064
DeVito, Danny 1455
DeVito, Joe 1727
De Vito, Karen 1258
DeVito, Karla 1205
Devivo, Liz 1134
Devlin, Jay 224, 1701
Devlin, Jon 1015
Devlin, Joyce 76
Devlin, Michael 188, 1137
Devlin, Sandra 126, 557, 558, 705, 852, 1265, 1603
DeVoe, Kevin 105, 785
DeVore, Jesse 120
DeVore, Jesse L., Jr. 470
De Vos, Will 122
DeVries, Michael 249, 1338
Dew, Lori 1131
De Waart, Edo 1139
DeWeerdt, Lee 768
Dewey, Judy 184
Dewey, Priscilla B. 1691
Dewhirst, Donald 1131
De Witt, David 889
DeWitt, Fay 1138, 1447
DeWolfe, Thomas 1176
Dexter, Terry 964
Deyle, John 1380, 1712
De Young, Cliff 1666
DeYoung, Michelle 495
Dezina, Kate 12, 764
Dhimos, Christine 1040
D'honau, Dorothy 1193
Diamond, Barry 536
Diamond, Eric 210
Diamond, Joel 1699
Diamond, Matthew 969
Diamond, Michael 1804
Diamond, Nancy E. 552
Diamond, Pat 66
Diamond, Tom 1516
Diaz, Freddy 1732
Diaz, Horace 337, 955
Diaz, Justino 62
Diaz, Natascia (A.) 206, 802, 1403
Diaz, Rodolfo 1402
Diazmunoz, Eduardo 1336
di Bella, Vito 859
DiBianco, Karen 401
DiBuono, Tom 526
DiBuono, Toni 512
Dibuono, Tony 1706
Dicello, Robert 1655
Dick, Paul 1589, 1771, 1815
Dick, Sylvia 944
Dickens, Hamp 236
Dickerson, Christi 964
Dickey, John 1618
Dickinson, Debra 310, 567, 824
Dickinson, Dorothy 779
Dickinson, Emily 1376
Dickinson, Janet 519, 520
Dickinson, Remmel Tyndall 997
Dickinson, Shelley 1351
Dickinson, Sherrylee 1512
Dickinson-Cargasacchi, Alexis 1226
Dicks, Gene A. 844
Dickson, Donald 1010
Dickson, Dorothy 124
Dickson, Miles 1626
Dickson, Muriel 40
Dickson, Stephen 1741
DiConstanzo, Justine 185
DiCrescenzo, Louis "El Rukn" 79
diDario, Linda 1098
Di Dia, Maria 689, 1674
Dieffenbach, Jimmy 280
Diehl, Crandall 600
Diekmann, Nancy Kassak 1351
Dietrich, Dena 291
Dietrich, Gary 1462
Dietrich, Max 1281
Dietz, Howard 348, 940, 1101, 1606
Dietz, Susan 10
di Franco, Loretta 574
DiFusco, John 1664
DiGennaro, Joseph 1419
Di Gesu, Traci 1327
Diggs, Elizabeth 1056
Diggs, Ramone 1623
Diggs, Taye 1778
DiGiacoma, Jerry 1081
DiGise, Jose, II 1817
Dignan, Pat 838
DiLallo, Susan 1607
Di Leone, Leon 697
Dileva, Anthony 1331
Dillard, William 803
Dille, David 115, 1363
Dillehay, Kaylyn 246
Dillingham, Leslie 562
Dillon, Barney 1629
Dillon, Charles 1778
Dillon, Denny 302
Dillon, Sara 1692
Dillon, Tom 1616
Dillon, Tony 4
Dilworth, Gordon 1399
Dimaggio, John 1240
DiMaggio, Vincenza 1080
DiMarzio, Diana 1771
Di Mauro, Gary 1040
Diminno, Nick 1535
Dimino, Richard 1015
Dimitri, Melanie 1690
di Nascemi, Maita 294
D'Incecco, Joan 132
Dinelaris, Alexander 1830
Dingenary, Gene 1539
Dinotto, Paul 682
Dinroe, Dorothy 120
Dionisio, Gabriel "Kwikstep" 804
DiPasquale, Frank 1610
DiPietro, Joe 739, 967, 1613
DiPinto, John 610
Diquinzio, Mark 333, 799, 1070, 1232
Director, Roger 664
Di Rienzo, Ralph 1730
Dishy, Bob 236, 277, 1206, 1765, 1813
Diskin, Ellyn 423
Disney, Darren 1590
Disque, Diane 329
Disraeli, Joe 543
Ditsky, Stuart A. 1556
Dittman, Dean 324
Divine, Grace 1249
DiVirgilio, Nick 1785
Divito, Lynda 1441
Dixon, Don 864
Dixon, Ed 234, 476, 689, 865, 866, 1029, 1056, 1071, 1456, 1700
Dixon, Edwin 293
Dixon, Eleanora 494, 1115
Dixon, Harland 1177
Dixon, Janice 1816
Dixon, Jerry 206, 222, 1129, 1191, 1581, 1634
Dixon, MacIntyre 261, 958, 986, 1461, 1528, 1641, 1654, 1765
Dixon, Mildred 1543
Dixon, Robert 1816
Dlamini, Dumisani 1401
Dlamini, Khumbuzile 1401
Dlamini, Lindiwe 1401
Dlamini, Ntomb'khona 1401
D'Lugoff, Art 205, 877, 963, 1162, 1198, 1209, 1457, 1466, 1654
D'Lugoff, Burt 877, 963, 1198
Dlugos, Gregory 1644
Dlugos, Gregory J. 1805
D'monroe 610

Dobbs, Jeffrey 1525
Dobie, Paul 284
Dobriansky, Andrij 574
Dobrish, Jeremy 679, 837
Dobson, Jamyl 1429
Dobson, Rebecca 1472
Dobson, West 883
Doby, Kathryn 68, 1177
Dockery, Leslie 115, 278, 546, 850, 934, 1207, 1373
Dodd, John (P.) 613, 1080, 1356
Dodd, Johnny 1476
Dodge, Jerry 1400, 1424, 1446
Dodge, Marcia Milgrom 300, 577, 919, 949, 1326, 1375
Dodson, Colleen 1033
Dodson, Leigh 1029
Dodson, Owen 107
Doemland, Ann 759
Doepp, John 1691
Doerr, James 720
Doerr, Mark 1438
Doerr, Mary Jane 566, 902
Doff, Gerard S. 1659
Doggett, Norma 236
Dogim, Isaac 489, 1822
Doh, Jeong Ju 889
Dohanos, Peter 448
Doherty, "Papa" Denny 411
Doherty, Dennis 1007
Doherty, Denny 411
Doherty, Jeffrey Johnson 1742
Dokuchitz, Jonathan 222, 778
Dolan, Clinton 112
Dolan, Judith 325, 377, 833, 1250, 1582, 1829
Dolan, Leo 1316
Dolan, Robert Emmett 538, 1101
Dolgenas, Hillel 229
Dolginoff, Stephen 1084, 1195, 1630
Doliner, Roy 1337
Doll, Lauren 1516
Dollarhide, Don 436
Dolven, Nils Olaf 1425
Domanski, Deborah 362
Domingo, Colman 1225
Domingo, Placido 495
Dominguez, Nikki Ana 1682
Dominico, Michael 601, 1385
Donahoe, Emily 1322
Donahoe, Jim 712
Donahue, James 857
Donahue, John 1288
Donahue, Theodore P., Jr. 483
Donaldson, Norma 1319
Dondlinger, Mary Jo 88, 308, 309, 398, 435, 479, 570, 656, 733, 926, 930, 1031, 1071, 1099, 1144, 1213, 1214, 1289, 1366, 1451, 1756
Donegan, James 519
Donelson, Ginger 99
Donhowe, Gwyda 214, 678
Doniec, Kazimierz 1275
Doninelli, Aida 1249
Donizetti, Gaetano 1146
Donnelly, Candice 264, 670, 739
Donnelly, Ken 1097
Donnelly, Terry 775
Donner, Mary 731
Donnerfield, Gail 872
Donohoe, Joe 1425
Donohue, Jack 1131
Donohue, Janet 1171
Donovan, Bryan T. 413
Donovan, Gerry 1661
Donovan, Joe 1330
Donovan, Nancy 1098
Donvito, Dorie 1721
Doo, Euwilde 1221
Doohan, James 1353
Dooley, Jerry 920
Dooley, John 698
Dooley, Paul 472, 677, 1461, 1626, 1649, 1765
Doran, Johnny 466
Dore, Louise 1655
Dorfman, Herbert 173
Dorfman, Robert 41
Doria, Elena 1221
Doria, Lotte 535
Dorish, John 1565
Dorman, Tracy 362, 1419
Dorn, Augusta 1229
Dorn, Carol 703
Dorn, Harding 66
Dorn, Margaret 175, 1746
Dornya, Maria 1111
Doro, Marianna 1089
Dorsen, Annie 1225
Dorsey, Brian J. 1054
Dorsey, Jaz 1117, 1500
Dorsey, Kena Tangi 1778
Dorsey, Kent 1551
Dorsey, Robert 1029
D'Orso, Wisa 858, 1152, 1185
Dorward, Mary Anne 1048, 1646
Doshi, Marcus 1322
Dosing, David 170
Doskocil, Melanie 994
Doss, Col. Buster 1720
Doss, Mark S. 1816
Dossett, John 539, 683, 725, 866
Dostis, Isaac 993
Doubleday, Kay 384
Doucette, Adrienne 915
Dougherty, Dennis 457, 707
Dougherty, J.P. 313, 675
Dougherty, Mindy 1425
Douglas, Jerry 1379
Douglas, Mike 1163
Douglas, Mitch 1009
Douglas, M.K. 292
Douglas, Pi 274
Douglas, Rogelio, Jr. 262
Douglas, Suzzanne 1693
Douglass, Charles 927
Douglass, Jane 121
Douglass, Philip 1131
Douglass, Pi 17, 370, 1699
Douglass, Stephen 600
Doumanian, Jean 627
Doumnian, Jean 383
Dova, Nina 543, 735, 1541
Dove, Alfred L. 1738
Dove, Ulysses 294
Dow, Dorothy 1086
Dow, Garrison 1015
Dow, Richard 1001
Dow, Susan 1296
Dowd, Harrison 779
Dowd, Janet 307
Dowd, M'el 314
Dowdy, Anthony 1434
Dowel, Clif 581
Dowell, Clif 581
Dowell, Coleman 1594
Downey, Robert, Jr. 45
Downey, Stephen 46
Downing, David 589, 629, 1004
Downs, Frederic 1627
Downs, Leslie-May 1655
Downs, Michael E. 685, 832
Downs, Sarah 403
Downs, Stephen 486
Doxsee, Lenore 1237, 1826
Doyle, Marcy 834
Doyle, Timothy 1722
Doyle, William 1551
Doyle-Murray, Brian 318, 1112
Dozer, David 1274
Drabinsky, Garth H. 214
Drachman, Ted 1805
Draesel, Bert 1671
Dragonette, Jessica 621
Dragotta, Robert 1753
Drake, Allan 772
Drake, David 1215
Drake, Donna 185, 193, 283, 1128
Drake, Dorothy 815, 816, 1308
Drakeford, Charliese 630
Draper, Anne 253
Draper, Paul 569
Draves, J. Kevin 193
Drayton, Cisco 1002
Drayton, Malissa 196
Drell, Jo 1617
Dremak, W.P. 1721
Dresher, Paul 1592
Dreskin, William 1243
Dressinger, Philip 1054
Drew, Bill 506, 1236
Drew, George 1107
Drews, Pam 377
Drews, Richard 574
Drew-Wilkinson, Katie 1168
Drexler, Rosalyn 701, 925
Drielsma, Diane 1160
Driggs, Keith 1822
Drischell, Ralph 1628
Driscoll, Ryan 1554
Driver, David 1237
Driver, Donald 1827
Driver, John 279, 1358, 1414
Droscoski, Carolyn 1159
Drost, Andrew 938
Druary, John 1413, 1563, 1596
Drucker, Frances 815, 1810
Drum, Leonard 567, 858, 1161, 1185, 1467
Drummond, David 1655
Drummond, David (K.) 1568, 1569
Drummond, Jack 284, 987
Drummond, Nolan 113
Druzhkin, Andrey 849
Dry, Marion 1139
Dryden, Dan 1200
Drzewinska, Danuta Kisiel 1275
Duane, Jed 1811
Duarte, Emanuel 1221
Duarte, Josephine 1221
Duberman, Martin 1504
Dubey, Matt 1483
DuBois, Amanda 103
DuBois, Peter 252, 1225, 1422
du Bois, Raoul Pene 1131, 1379
DuBose, Albert L. 611
Du Brock, Neal 1562
Duca, Lennie Del, Jr. 319, 1025
Duchamp, Alain 713
Duda, Andrea 1409
Dudley, Jennifer 439, 941
Duell, William 1376, 1626, 1627, 1628
Duer, Fred 172
Duff-Griffin, William 426, 1695
Duffield, Davis 1056
Duffy, Colin 1552
Duffy, John 707
Duffy, Marty 913
Duffy, Meghan 1800
Duggan, Annmarie 302, 829
Duguay, Brian 404
DuHoffman, Karl 1186
Duke, I. Milton 1267
Duke, Irving Milton 752
Duke, Karen 98
Duke, Mary 613
Duke, Milton 1511, 1603
Duke, Stuart 213, 830
Duke, Vernon 238, 942, 1101
Dukes, Lena 1543
Dukore, Lawrence 876
Dula, Jason 926
Dulaney, Renee 1025
Dulchin, Edwin 972, 989, 990
Dulin, Michael 575
Dumakude, Thuli 358, 651, 839, 1284
Dumaresq, William 726
Dumas, Deborah 1285
Dumas, Jennifer 965, 1110
du Maurier, Basil 143
Dumont, Harold 501
Dumrose, Boyd 1468
Dun, Tan 495, 1020
Dunaway, David A. 1699
Dunbar, Ann 1231
Dunbar, Kimberly Reid 995
Dunbar, Paul Laurence 420
Duncan, Andrew 22, 1415, 1649, 1765
Duncan, Cleone 56
Duncan, Danny 1696
Duncan, Harry 1413
Duncan, Laura Marie 679
Duncan, Mary 299
Duncan, Ryan 38, 954
Duncan, Stuart 390, 595, 1480
Dundas, Shane 1632
Dunedin, Myrtle 1116
Dunfee, Katharine 1072
Dunford, Judith 1185
Dunham, Clarke 359, 722, 1038, 1582, 1622, 1677
Dunham, David 734
Dunham, Joan 272, 821
Dunkel, Eugene (B.) 494, 578, 1115
Dunkel, George 1640
Dunkle, Jonathan 1645
Dunleavy, Timothy 943
Dunley, Jennifer 628
Dunlop, Charles L. 963
Dunlop, Peter 1566
Dunmore, Helen 1543
Dunn, Edward 225
Dunn, Griffin 311
Dunn, Jeffrey 785
Dunn, Joanna 1629
Dunn, Mark 1674
Dunn, Mary 223
Dunn, Mignon 1563
Dunn, Monte 265
Dunn, Robin 960, 1065
Dunn, Sally Mae 954
Dunn, Stephanie 768
Dunn, Thomas 607
Dunne, Murphy 548
Dunne, Stephan 1283
Dunno, Glenn 121
Dunnock, Mildred 306, 332
Dunsmore, Dee 1615
Duntiere, Victor 66
DuPois, Starletta 156
du Pont, Paul 1086
Dupuis, Catherine 1327
Duquesnay, Ann 116, 207, 803, 1001
Duquette, Joe 1040
Duran, Michael 59
Durang, Christopher 10, 978, 1492, 1710
Durant, Bernie, Jr. 166
Dure, Gerard 768, 1134
Durfee, Duke 1472
Durham, Christopher 1383
Durham, Colleen 749
Durham, Earl 761
Durham, Richard 337
Durkin, Betsy 74
Durkin, Peter 1316
Dusenbury, Karen 216
Dushon, Jean 682
Du Shon, Jean 181, 333
DuSold, Robert 1052
Dussault, Nancy 388, 531, 1767
Duteil, Jeff 510
Dutton, Caroline 1699
Dutton, Charles S. 615
Dutton, Nick 1629
Duva, Robert 1656
Duval, Funda 1238
Duval, Herbert 1825
Duval, Jose 1445, 1604
DuVall, Donald 1822
Duvaughn, Dolores 1615
Duwico 1446
Duwon, Tony 790
Dux, Francis 481, 745, 1060, 1265
Duykers, John 1139
Dvorett, Barbara 1618
Dvorsky, George 343, 435, 912, 1167, 1245
Dweir, Irv 1078
Dwyer, Bonnie 1021
Dwyer, Nick 1530
Dwyer, Tom 1157
Dwyer, Walter 535
Dyer, Bill 1669
Dyer, Doug 175, 1746
Dyer, Margaret 1298
Dyer, William 87, 822, 852, 858, 1255
Dykstra, Ted 1694
Dynan, Kelly 563
Dyson, Erika 512, 513, 514, 515, 516
Dyville, Jack 1089, 1822
Dzigan, Shimon 898

Eaddy, Paul 1487
Eagan, Daisy 805
Eagan, Jason 72
Eager, Edward 569, 661
Earle, Carla 165
Earle, Dorothy R. 1706
Earle, Edward 366, 1097, 1452, 1566
Earley, Candice 564, 758, 989
Early, Dan 1136
Easley, Douglas 194
Easley, Homles 271
East, Virginia Clark 1015
Easterbrook, Randall 695, 1097
Easterby, Alan 1825
Easterling, Gary 266, 709
Eastman, Donald 372, 1022, 1402, 1625
Eastman, Joan 705
Easton, Florence 868, 1597
Easton, Jack 147
Easton, Richard 1393
Eastwood, Gini 663
Eatman, Tom 1774
Eaton, Bekka 79
Eaton, Billy 1308
Eaton, Bob 909
Eaton, Lothair 1157
Eaton, Sally 649
Eaton, William 1535
Eaves, Dashiell 805, 1238
Ebb, Fred 52, 236, 377, 783, 1083, 1100, 1101, 1318, 1685
Ebbesmeyer, Bill 1690
Ebbin, Michael 591
Ebel, Elizabeth M. 1671
Eberhart, Nelle Richmond 1369

Eberly, Kevin 1591
Ebersole, Christine 443, 599, 634, 641
Ebert, Joyce 331
Echoles, Rueben D. 790
Echols, Angeles 1518
Echols, Frank 1161
Eck, Marsha Louis 466
Eckard, Helen 842
Eckart, Jean 600, 944, 1193, 1424
Eckart, William 600, 944, 1193, 1424
Eckert, Bob 997
Eckert, Ella 1249
Eckert, Robert 1554
Eckles, Robert 1242
Ecklund, Peter 544
Eckstein, George 149
Eddleman, Jack 631, 908
Eddy, Bill 101
Eddy, David 74
Eddy, Sarah 1530
Eddy, William 369
Edeards, Nazig 1171
Edegran, Lars 1198
Edeiken, Louise 799, 883, 912, 1167, 1650, 1747
Edelman, Gregg 1347, 1449, 1491, 1747
Edelstein, Stephen P. 794
Eden, Paul 1221
Eden, Susan 1661
Edenfield, Dennis 322, 1119
Edery, Gerard 402
Edgar, David 378
Edgar, Kate 1353
Edgerton, Annie 1321
Edgerton, Jeff 633, 1637
Edgerton, Sandy 172
Edloe 1395
Edlun, Thom 501
Edmead, Wendy 205, 1250
Edmonds, Audrey 578
Edmonds, Bob 266
Edmonds, Christopher 726
Edmonds, Loretta 1801
Edmonds, Louis 366, 448
Edmonds, Robert 105, 709, 842, 959
Edmondson, Mel 420, 591, 959
Edmunds, Dallas 1604
Edmunds, Kate 1365, 1558
Edner, Valencia 1781
Edwards, Anderson 1631
Edwards, Annie Joe 329
Edwards, Ben 284
Edwards, Brandt 283
Edwards, Carrie 1543
Edwards, Christopher 1193
Edwards, David 163, 164, 395, 1760
Edwards, Eugene 68, 91, 152, 785, 1029, 1221
Edwards, Federico 1816
Edwards, Gail 113
Edwards, Jason 825
Edwards, Jim 1618
Edwards, Kathleen 85
Edwards, Marjorie Gayle 500, 1785
Edwards, Maurice 600, 654, 826, 1060, 1161, 1578
Edwards, Mel 550
Edwards, Michele 759, 1387, 1489
Edwards, Omar 1406, 1407
Edwards, Randall 1709
Edwards, Raymond 1725
Edwards, Robert 1539
Edwards, Robin 510
Edwards, Ron 1288
Edwards, Ryan 117
Edwards, Sally 1599
Edwards, Thomas 66, 1221
Edwards, Tom 179
Edward-Stevens, Michael 648, 1625
Efe, Amber 1429
Effron, Edward 490
Effron, Howard (P.) 1025, 1435
Egan, John Traecy 1763
Egener, Minnie 245, 868, 1249
Eggingon, Paul 836
Ehlert, Maddie 933
Ehlert, Matthew 700
Ehlinger, Mary 1353
Ehman, Don 1204
Ehnes, Fred 572
Ehrenreich, Jake 832
Ehrhardt, Frank 92
Ehrhardt, Peter M. 1644
Ehrler, Anita 824
Ehrlich, Alexa 1700
Ehrlich, Jon 1201
Ehrlich, Martin 1816
Ehrlich, Marty 1731
Ehrlinger, Mary 323
Ehrman, Don 1484
Eichel, Paul 1504
Eichelberger, Ethyl 233, 1359
Eichenberger, Rebecca 375
Eichler, Alan 1540
Eichner, Billy 742
Eidman, Earl 111, 823, 834, 952
Eigsti, Karl 408, 544, 625, 833, 860, 1183, 1787
Eikenberry, Jill 117, 958, 1392
Eilber, Janet 42
Eiler, Jim 1085
Eilers, Jim Paul 766, 1132
Einenkel, Robert 1599
Einhorn, Frederick 811
Einhorn, Hy 617
Einhorn, Marvin 538
Einhorn, Susan 260, 731
Einwick, Joan Ann 66
Eis, Elizabeth 1562
Eiseman, Paul 706
Eisenberg, Emanuel 1268
Eisenberg, Lawrence B. 1274
Eisenberg, Lee 377
Eisenberg, Michael 36
Eisenberg, Ned 632
Eisenberg, Ron 265
Eisenhauer, Peggy 252, 375, 424, 428, 668, 683, 933, 965, 1121, 1588, 1598
Eisenhower, Jennie 1547
Eisler, Chuck 265, 1096, 1531
Eisler, Hanns 459
Eisner, Gloria 1131
Eisner, Jamie Lee 309, 706
Ekson, Larrio 831, 1055
Ekstrom, Peter 391
Elaine, Judith 15, 1673
Elbert, Wayne 156
Elborne, Daniel 3
Elder, Eldon 16, 1083, 1254
Elder, Jennifer 1007
Elder, Judith 1092
Eley, Val 333
Eley, Valerie K. 1363
Elftman, Kurt 403
Elgar, Ann 947
Elias, Alix 1689
Elias, Doren 836
Elias, Michael 1280
Elias, Rosalind 62, 1718
Elias, Tom 297
Eliasberg, Jan P. 1391
Elic, Joseph (Josip) 902, 1517, 1627
Elice, Eric 364, 900, 1036
Eliot, Captain Arthur 136
Eliran, Ron 401, 617, 1136
Elisa, Alexander 167
Eliscu, Edward 98
Elisha, Rina 718
Elkins, Doug 838, 1439
Elkins, Flora 1302
Elkins, Hillard 1168, 1169
Ellenburg, Eric 111, 1387
Eller, Celia 35
Ellers, Barbara 1755
Ellin, David 585, 819, 1032, 1212, 1342, 1382, 1453
Ellington, Duke 1100
Ellington, Justin 1429
Ellington, Mercedes 165, 809, 1021
Ellington, William 175
Elliot, Clint 1360
Elliot, J. Arthur 109
Elliot, Marc 1197
Elliott, Denise 266
Elliott, Donald 636
Elliott, Erin 1073
Elliott, Kenneth 633, 1571, 1706
Elliott, Patricia 234, 1279
Elliott, Robert 87, 1259, 1430
Elliott, Shawn 792, 797, 1379
Elliott, Stephen 944
Elliott, William 186, 609, 1146, 1270
Elliottt, Scott 77
Ellis, Barbara 1659
Ellis, Bob 569, 1021
Ellis, Brad 514, 515, 516, 517, 524, 525, 1772
Ellis, David 1822
Ellis, Gina 1544
Ellis, James H. 1571
Ellis, Jim 1350
Ellis, Joan 133
Ellis, Kellie 750
Ellis, Leslie 1381
Ellis, May 403
Ellis, Mitch 1320
Ellis, Perry 1141
Ellis, Rina 1341
Ellis, Robert 68
Ellis, Sam 854
Ellis, Scott 52, 695, 725, 1097
Ellis, Sheila 1001
Ellis, Terrance T. 358
Ellis, Thom 1029
Ellis, Timothy 1815
Ellis, Todd 750
Ellisen, Eric 1512
Ellison, Todd 296
Ellner, Ed 36
Ellstein, Abraham 1342, 1821
Ellsworth, Elinor 1343
Elmer, George 338
Elmer, George Allison 740
Elmer, Jimi 288
Elmore, Leo 1001
Elmore, Ruth 1288
Elmore, Stephen (Steve) 341, 601, 987, 1258
Elmslie, Kenward 926, 947, 948, 1063, 1100, 1289, 1416, 1447, 1564, 1741
Elson, Donald 1626
Elston, Robert 669
Emamjomeh, Shawn 689
Embree, Marc 439, 1329, 1741
Embs, Lisa 943
Emens, Homer F. 245
Emerson, Eric E. 1664
Emerson, Susan 1159, 1285
Emery, Rick 725, 1097, 1147
Emery, Ted 632
Emmanuel, Donna 660
Emmery, Kenneth 68
Emmet, Robert 349
Emmons, Beverly 294, 427, 832, 973, 1114, 1119, 1143, 1282, 1424, 1611, 1657, 1829
Emmons, David 97
Emmons, Don 337, 705
Emmons, Shirlee 1564
Emo, Ann R. 349
Emonts, Ann 219, 311, 1290, 1654
Enea, John 1781
Engel, David 527
Engel, Ellen Bogan 384
Engel, Georgia 338, 1196, 1644
Engel, Lehman 1000
Engel, Mary 779
Engelbach, Jerry 1011
Engelman, Arnold 185, 410, 1632
Engelman, Wilfred 1010
Engels, Charles 136
Engeran, Virgil 1151
Englander, Carrie 1134
Engle, Dale 1354
Englebach, Jerry 174
Engles, Judy 542
English, Anna 1465
English, Donna 522, 524, 1386, 1581
English, Ellia 171, 194, 313, 646, 964
English, Stephen 392
English, Todd 273
Englund, Patricia 22
Engquist, Richard 434, 435, 878, 934, 1102
Engstrom, Jon 1644
Engstrom, Robert 468, 1346
Engvick, William 112, 1192
Enis, Mark 396, 1660, 1805
Ennis, Luce 1193
Enoch, Verdon 91
The Enrico Kuklafraninalli Puppets 732
Enrique, Dionis 118
Enstad, Luther 713
Enten, Boni 1168, 1396
Enterprises, Crane-Sterling 1744
Enters, Warren 1152
Entertainment, Ignite! 808
Entwistle, John 1655
Ephram, Bobby 1177
Eppens, Phil 1115
Epperson, C. Jane 1338
Epperson, John 732
Epps, Sheldon 180, 181, 182
Epstein, Alvin 422, 880, 881, 882, 1773
Epstein, Dasha 102, 533
Epstein, David 192, 1739
Epstein, Donny 418
Epstein, Julius J. 1403
Epstein, Laura 397
Epstein, Mark 422
Epstein, Philip G. 1608
Epstein, Pierre 588, 1311
Epstein, Steven 742
Erat, Will 597
Ercole, Joe 856
Erdman, Jean 562, 1689
Erdman, Wendy 562
Erdmann, Eugenia V. 1505
Erdmann, Louis O. 1505
Ergener, Sibel 1671
Eric, David 93, 312
Ericksen, Edward 1244
Erickson, Arthur 1077
Erickson, Claris 1705
Erickson, Kaaren 1730
Erickson, Phil 232
Erickson, Richard 1689
Ericson, June 481, 530, 1192, 1490
Ericson, Richard 395
Eriksmoen, August 755, 1736
Eriksson, Bo 965
Erkkila, Dan 1625
Erlenborn, Struan 541
Erler, Noel 902
Ermides, Peter 1305
Ernotte, Andre 114, 285, 311, 586, 1503, 1558
Erskine, Anna 494, 1115
Ertischek, Dana 1310
Erwin, Michael 284
Esch, Dieter 1281
Eshelman, Drew 13
Eskow, Jerome 504, 1164, 1370
Esparza, Raul 1634
Espinosa, Louis 21
Espinoza, Brandon 249
Esposito, Chaz 984
Esposito, Laurence J. (Larry) 539, 789, 1033
Esposito, Mark 148, 395
Esposito, Vickie 1240
Essary, Lisa 243, 293
Esser, Carl 532
Essex, Francis 1142
Estes, Jack 288
Estes, Michael 1028
Estevez, Aramis 392
Estevez, Oscar 399
Estey, Carol 15, 1035
Estey, Suellen 164, 232, 974, 1480
Esther, Queen 668
Estin, Timothy 1117
Estrada, Roy 7
Estrin, Melvyn J. 833
Estrow, Herbert 66
Estwanik, Michael 1571
Esty, Robert 980, 1511
Etheridge, Dorothy 600
Etjen, Jeff 1011
Ettinger, Daniel 1215, 1456, 1750
Ettinghausen, Thomas 1029
Eubanks, Barbara 1288
Eubler, Vaughn 1227
Eula, Joe 166
Euster, Roger 458
Eustis, Oskar 1225, 1422, 1631
Evan, Rob 1303
Evan, Robert 825
Evanko, Ed 969
Evans, Al 494
Evans, Alan 913
Evans, Albert 1138, 1215
Evans, Allan 951
Evans, Barbara 1058
Evans, Ben 524
Evans, Beverly 331, 569
Evans, Clarke 1361
Evans, Claudette 470
Evans, Craig 233, 484, 588, 939, 1498, 1748
Evans, David 1, 69, 157, 280, 683, 685, 1427, 1461
Evans, Dickie 357
Evans, Dillon 1379
Evans, Don 9, 959, 996, 1460
Evans, Douglas C. 541
Evans, Freida 745, 1531
Evans, Harvey 58, 599, 1433
Evans, Joan 379
Evans, Joan V. 1535
Evans, Julie Dingman 1450
Evans, June 66
Evans, Karen 386, 1133, 1384
Evans, Kellie D. 196
Evans, Lloyd 1552
Evans, Maruti 1458
Evans, Meredith 1177

Evans, Ray 1101
Evans, Robert L. 470
Evans, Shakiem 474
Evans, Suzannah 649
Evans, Venida 934
Evans, William Thomas 1815
Evans-Kandel, Karen 999
Everett, Bridget 72
Everett, Horace 1601
Everett, Paul 456, 695
Everett, Sonny 1653
Everett, Timmy 944
Evering, Jim 1318
Evering, Valerie Monique 1345
Everly, Jack 59
Evers, Brian 725
Eversole, Charles 1320
Everson, Patricia Ann 1466
Evins, Donny Ray 906
Ewing, Madelyn Bell 965
Ewing, Max 622
Ewing, Tim 308, 1214
Eye, David 1826
Eyen, Tom 1661, 1695
Eyerly, Scott 717
Eyes, Ted 1054

Faber, Christy 395
Faber, Mary 502, 845, 1479
Faber, Ron 393, 973, 1391, 1641
Fabian, Douglas 248
Fabian, Robert 483
Fabiani, Joel 753
Fabricatore, Gene 221
Fabrici, Dan 1383
Fabrique, Tina 8, 375
Factora, Marshall 43
Fadoul, Paul B. 743
Fafa'n, Inaya 208
Fagan, Valerie 520, 523, 524
Fagerbakke, Bill 84
Fagin, Scott 1504
Fahey, MaryAnn 920
Fain, Sammy 68
Fair, Tony 922
Fairbanks, Douglas, Jr. 402
Fairbanks, Nola 1131
Fairchild, Charlotte 1236
Fairchild, George 1140
Faircloth, Alison 57
Faire, Rosanna 1802
Fairservis, Elf 378
Faison, Donald "Shun" 1345
Faison, Frankie R. 630
Faison, George 214, 383, 400, 501, 1633
Faison, Sandy 610
Faistl, Karen 1438
Faita, Josef 1609
Falabella, John 86, 159, 181, 321, 678, 786, 1039, 1343, 1378, 1585, 1664
Falchi, Carlos 196
Falco, Bruce 1146
Falco, Philine 1249
Falcon, Cosmo Richard 877
Falk, Mike 1343
Falk, Robert 1729
Falk, Willy 435, 1135
Falkenstein, Eric 997
Fallon, Larry 268
Fallon, Siobhan 940
Fallon, Thomas Mark 451
Fallon, Tom 1565
Falls, Charles B. 635
Fanelli, F. 319
Fanene, Fisaga Taoni 1221
The Fantasy Factory 1030
Farber, Norman 1394
Farber, Sandy 80
Farer, Ronnie 260
Fargo, Jerry 834, 998
Fargue, Anne 1013
Farhangfar, Fahimeh 397
Farhangfar, Nasar 397
Faria, Arthur 18, 225, 372, 1668
Faria, Luiz-Ottavio 1186
Farin, Paul 434, 453, 614
Farina, Marilyn 1155, 1158
Farina, Michael J. 476
Farina, Richard 1356
Farjeon, Bert 622
Farkas, Rob 1346
Farley, Bill 1066
Farley, Dan 1470
Farley, Edward J. 1469
Farmer, Arsenia 768
Farnsworth, Carla 401
Farnsworth, Ralph 686
Farr, Christopher 695
Farr, Kimberly 218, 219, 1082
Farr, Lowell 1161
Farr, Rex 1538
Farrant, Robert 1316
Farrar, Thursday 69, 1700
Farrell, Isabelle 1566
Farrell, John 1556
Farrell, John B. 647
Farrell, Kevin 1205
Farrell, Shellie 1254
Farrell, Tim 1416
Farrell, Walter 1587
Farrelly, Patrick 1438
Farren, Jack 1707
Farren, Vivian 1707
Farrington, Annette 1134
Farrington, Hubert 66
Farrugio, Matthew 1131
Fascinato, Jack 875
Faso, Laurie 582
Fass, Stephen 273
Fata, Wesley 314
Fatone, Charles 367, 368
Faulkner, Todd 1818
Faull, Ellen 254, 947
Faussett, Hudson 1385
Faust, Robert 561
Fay, Meagan (a/k/a Meagen) 741, 1209
Fay, Patricia 352
Fay, Sally 1141
Fay, Terry 578
Fay, Tom 739, 751, 1201, 1482, 1706
Fayad, Dameon 1349
Faye, Denise 1588
Faye, Joey 319, 980
Faye, Vini 134
Fayer, Art 1592
Fazakas, Franz 1790, 1791, 1796
Feagan, Leslie 1186
Fearing, Gordon 1119
Fearl, Clifford 599
Fearnley, John 124, 1223
Fearon, Ed 852, 1661
Feather, Lorraine 1732
Featherston, Jennifer 1815
Febvre, Curtis Le 1148
Fedder, Norman J. 223
Feder 140
Fedor, March Adrian 1208
Fedorin, Rose 1267
Fee, Dorothy 1587
Feeney, George 661
Fegan, Paul 373
Fehlandt, Tina 363
Feichtner, Vadim 430, 742, 1680
Feiffer, Jules 389, 1168, 1710
Feig, Jonathan 1384
Feigenbaum, Michael 108
Feigin, Michael 1134
Fein, Bernie 1627
Feiner, Harry 290
Feingold, Michael 122, 660, 843, 1149, 1150, 1641
Feinsinger, Mary 711
Feinstein, Brian 1052
Feinstein, Martin 1029
Feist, Gena 345
Feist, Gene 219, 445, 881, 1098, 1267, 1268, 1304, 1540
Feivelowitz, Ben 441
Feld, Eliot 1186, 1399
Felder, Mark 349
Feldman, Jack 311, 1048, 1772
Feldman, Joan 1066
Feldman, Karol 1453
Feldman, Peter 388, 1749
Feldon, Barbara 338
Feldshuh, Tovah 685, 1534, 1586, 1663
Feldstein, Robert D. 1468, 1594
Felgemacher, Olga 24, 1768
Feliciano, Brenda 118, 1689
Felix, Stanford 362, 717
Feliz, Georgina 897
Fellman, Ray 248
Fellner, Jenny 328
Felstein, Robert 538
Felty, Janice 363
Femia, Tommy 746, 1772
Fenhagen, James 907
Feniger, Susan 273
Fennelly, Bill 541
Fennelly, Liam 1029
Fenning, Stephen 184, 1039, 1486
Fenster, Nancy 601
Fenton, Howard 501, 535
Fenton, James 670
Fenwick, Chris 1052, 1422
Fenwick, Gillie 1393
Fenwick, John 56
Ferden, Bruce 294, 1730
Ferden, Dennis 1283
Ferdinard, Edmund J. 1774
Ferencz, George 1222
Ferguson, Bobby C. 1330
Ferguson, Helen 238
Ferguson, James B. 1801
Ferguson, Jesse Tyler 933, 1129, 1186, 1680
Ferguson-Acosta, Dennis 1402, 1588
Fergusson, Honora 122
Ferland, Danielle 1219, 1557
Fernandez, Jose 203, 474, 1038
Fernandez, Lai-Si 262
Fernandez, Manuel J. 507
Fernandez, Peter Jay 1187, 1631
Fernandez, Stacia 950
Fernhoff, Rosina 481
Ferra, Max 897, 1402, 1588
Ferracane, Rusty 444, 1618
Ferrall, Gina 476, 1390
Ferrand, Louise 1131
Ferrante, Elena 906
Ferrante, Evan 1381
Ferrante, Frank 642
Ferrara, Peter 925
Ferrari, Gisele 295
Ferrari, Marianne 1338
Ferraris, Claire 490
Ferraro, Elizabeth 985
Ferraro, John 1641
Ferrell, Andy 246
Ferrell, Ron 214
Ferrell, Tim 1029
Ferrell, Tyra 372, 886
Ferrer, Norma 1297
Ferreri, Bob 706
Ferrerra, Everaldo 835
Ferri, Virginia 549
Ferrone, Fran 434
Ferrone, Rod 1467
Fertig, Steve 1232
Fesco, Michael 507, 1058
Fesco, Michael E. 783
Festante, Jim 1771
Fetter, Ted 446, 494, 578, 1115, 1116
Fetzko, Donald C. 379
Feuchtwang, Rachel 1444
Feuer, Jed 143, 424
Feury, Joseph 86
Fevola, Lana 1660
Feyer, Daniel 462, 1818
Fialka, Ladislav 1609
Fibich, Felix 441, 1051, 1342, 1382
Fickinger, Steve (Steven) 842, 960, 1821
Fickman, Andy 1347
Fiedelman, Rosie Lani 760
Fieger, Addy (O.) 268, 360, 1421
Field, Alice 54
Field, Crystal 702, 925, 1182, 1681
Field, Daniel Thomas 895, 1380
Field, Robin 955, 1511
Field, Ronald (Ron) 63
Fielder, Michael 1425
Fielding, Fenella 307
Fields, Clare 1141
Fields, Dorothy 886, 1101
Fields, Eddie 1543
Fields, Florence 1145
Fields, Frank (Gaskin) 1445
Fields, Jessica 995
Fields, Jimmie 1810
Fields, Ken 1440
Fields, Leonard 1543
Fields, Lillian (a/k/a Lilian) 112, 1400
Fields, Linda 361
Fields, Richard 1592
Fields, Ronnie 1364
Fields, Sammy 31
Figa, Stewart 819, 1032, 1212
Figueroa, Anaysha 1002
Filiato, Phillip 490
Filler, Deborah 1505
Finch, David 474
Finch, R. Thomas 708
Finck, David 1469
Finck, Werner 459
Findlay, Diane (J.) 567, 907, 1480, 1751
Fine, Laura 290
Fineman, Lori 328
Finger, Leonard 225
Fingerhut, Arden 27, 179, 552, 580, 634, 647, 1042, 1057, 1184, 1699, 1704
Fingleton, Anthony 1296
Finguerra, James 349, 397
Fink, Dann 1458
Fink, John 1455
Fink, Mitchell 1767
Fink, Richard Paul 628
Finkel, Alicia 884
Finkel, Barry 322, 979
Finkel, Elliot 492, 1105, 1341, 1692, 1809
Finkel, Fyvush 492, 555, 585, 608
Finkel, Ian 555
Finkelstein, Richard 43
Finkelstien, Norman 1566
Finkle, David 126, 350, 542, 771, 852, 1069, 1141, 1255, 1259, 1273
Finley, Felicia 222, 525, 1778
Finley, Gracie 56
Finley, Pat 638
Finlow, Fiona 1629
Finn, Ben 1477
Finn, Frank 1131
Finn, William 41, 430, 473, 763, 764, 765, 997, 1019, 1121, 1375, 1588, 1680
Finnan, Tommy, III 507
Finnegan, Jack 507
Finnell, Jay 1547
Finner, Leigh 1034
Finnerty, Mary Sue 1787
Finston, Betsy 1607
Finston, Mona 81
Fiordellisi, Angelina 675
Fiorella, Albert (Al) 66, 1221
Fiorillo, Elisa 334
Fippinger, Lynne 1780
Firestone, I.W. 782
Firment, Marilyn 577
Firmin, Tyne 1054
Firth, David 135
Fischer, Allison 1303
Fischer, Bob 287
Fischer, Howard 1115
Fischer, Lisa 196
Fischer, Lori 323
Fischer, William S. 869
Fischoff, George 153, 563, 1302, 1410
Fisdbein, Zenon 779
Fish, Donald 991
Fish, Michael (Mike) 196, 813, 1579
Fish, William 136
Fishback, John 1297
Fishburne, Larry 1710
Fisheman, Carol 330
Fisher, Anne 1050
Fisher, Barry 1128
Fisher, Betsy 910
Fisher, Carrie 263
Fisher, Douglas 543
Fisher, Dudu 418
Fisher, Gail 1465
Fisher, Harrison 93, 217
Fisher, Jim 318
Fisher, Judy 1395
Fisher, Jules 33, 98, 132, 207, 252, 367, 368, 375, 428, 449, 504, 598, 601, 638, 652, 661, 668, 683, 705, 911, 965, 1007, 1163, 1218, 1311, 1357, 1364, 1426, 1504, 1598, 1636, 1666, 1828
Fisher, Linda 84, 183, 860
Fisher, Lola 1131
Fisher, Mary L. 179
Fisher, Nelle 134, 600, 601, 1385
Fisher, Rick 938
Fisher, Rob 1403
Fisher, Robert (Writer) 642
Fisher, Robert (Rob) (Conductor) 907, 1403, 1668
Fisher, Sanford H. 899
Fisher, William 1043
Fishko, Robert S. 263, 324, 1169
Fishman, Carol 933, 1187, 1357, 1403
Fistos, John 659
Fitch, Bob (Robert) (Robert E.) 63, 68, 212, 274, 332, 652, 696, 908, 1060, 1751
Fitch, Pauline 696
Fite, Mark 297
Fitter, Joey 68
Fitzgerald, Ara 586, 975, 1334, 1503
Fitzgerald, Christopher 645, 1403
Fitzgerald, Ed 1395
Fitzgerald, Geraldine 1438, 1540, 1580, 1650

Fitzgerald, Judy 1608
Fitzgerald, Kathy 1421
Fitzgerald, Neil 253
Fitzgerald, Paul 365
Fitzgerald, Peter J. 1235
Fitz-Gerald, Timothy A. 1784
FitzGibbon, John 562
Fitzgibbons, Mark 325
Fitzhugh, Ellen 55, 377, 690, 848, 1150
Fitzpatrick, Allen 791, 1031, 1052, 1381
Fitzpatrick, Burton 374
Fitzpatrick, Colleen 58, 1338, 1410
Fitzpatrick, Jim 290
Fitzpatrick, Joe 374
Flack, Nanette 1145
Flagello, Ezio 62, 891
Flagg, Fannie 852
Flagg, Tom 359, 948, 1366
Flaherty, Stephen (Steve) 162, 375, 583, 973, 1006, 1100, 1101, 1191, 1454
Flair, Nicholas 901
Flam, Shira 1026
Flanagan, Charles 1679
Flanagan, William 104
Flanigan, Lauren 451, 574
Flaningam, Louisa 873, 1204, 1455, 1800
Flannigan, Bob 229
Flansburgh, John 1237
Flasher, Pete 263
Flateman, Charles 668
Flauto, Elizabeth 248
Flavelle, Robert 600
Flavin, Tim 1270
Flaxman, John 1829
Fleck, Kelly 1815
Fleet, Ian 403
Fleischman, David 226
Fleisher, Judith 1133, 1384, 1699
Fleishman, Sam 1743
Fleming, Adam 103
Fleming, Conn 1343
Fleming, Daisy 1543
Fleming, Eugene 240
Fleming, Joyce 322
Fleming, Juanita 86
Fleming, Leopoldo F. 1384
Fleming, Michael 807
Fleming, Renee 574
Fleming, Ruth 1000
Fleming, Sam 1303
Fleming, Sarah 1563
Flender, Nicole 1032
Flershem, Merry 466
Flesh, Ed 235
Fless, Scott 653, 1365
Fletcher, Allen 331, 1227
Fletcher, Jack 44, 48, 371, 381, 408, 530, 822, 980, 1031, 1360, 1490, 1602
Fletcher, Jay 831
Fletcher, Robert 132, 652, 827, 1179, 1574
Flexer, Dorothy (or Dorothea) 868
Flick, Pat 290
Flicker, Theodore J. 745, 946, 1295
Flink, Michael 1128
Flinn, Denny Martin 957
Flood, Amy 552
Flood, John 779
Flood, Randy 9
Florek, Dann 1392
Florence, Tyler 273
Flores, Elizabeth 146
Flores, Victoria 1179
Flower, Nathan 983
Flower, Tyrone 196
Flowers, Kim 1487
Flowers, Martha 1221, 1620
Flowers, Nathylin 1085
Flowers, Wayland 877
Floyd, Carlisle 1024, 1165, 1227, 1563, 1814
Floyd, Carmen Ruby 330
Floyd, Charles 1058
Floyd, Patricia R. 195
Fludd, Quitman, III 203, 420
Fluehr, Cheryl L. 1702
Fluger, Marty 1252
Fluhr, Helene Anne 505
Flyer, Herbert 698
The Flying Karamazov Brothers 1439
Flynn, David 1493
Flynn, Denny Martin 1452
Flynn, J. Lee 105, 249, 1423
Flynn, James 538
Flynn, James V. 198
Flynn, Jim 198
Flynn, John 954
Flynn, Peter 845
Flynn, Susan 185, 213, 1821
Flynn, Terrance 1084
Flynn, Thomas 1229
Foa, Barrett 597
Fobair, David 1050
Fodor, Joleen 80, 631
Fogarty, Melissa 256
Fogler, Dan 1680
Foil, Homer 710, 1077
Fojo, Gerry 262
Fokin, Igor 849
Foley, Ellen 907
Foley, John 376, 1077, 1317, 1484
Foley, Peter 1499
Foley, Robert 1599
Followell, James 302, 313, 527
Fond, Miriam 177, 565, 788, 1045, 1758, 1759, 1760, 1761
Fondo, Fredericka 1131
Fontaine, Joel 878
Fontaine, Luther 1305
Fontana, Santino 479
Fonte, Henry 770
Foos, Kimberly 549
Foote, Don 74
Foote, Gene 121, 1298, 1743
Foote, Jay 50, 601
Forbes, Alex 1054
Forbes, Amy D. 404
Forbes, Barbara 213
Forbes, Donna Liggitt 1480
Forbes, Kenneth 1116
Forbes, Richard 1283
Ford, Barry 1160
Ford, Carl 166
Ford, Clebert 91, 105, 116, 927, 1633
Ford, David Patrick 1428
Ford, Joan 1101
Ford, Nancy 57, 338, 656, 753, 894, 1154
Ford, Paul 1012, 1709
Ford, Phyllis 1385
Ford, Rodney 979, 1353
Ford, Sara Jean 479
Ford, Suzanne 1011
Forde, Edmund 1278
Forde, Larry 1176
Forella, Ronn 268
Foreman, Jo Ann 613
Foreman, Jofka 1134
Foreman, Richard 12, 158, 393, 394, 426, 431, 713, 1628, 1826
Forer, Daniel 238
Forero, Luis 62
Forges, Johne 266
Forlow, Ted 408, 1216, 1381
Forman, Jacques 423
Forman, Norman 867
Forman, Richard 393
Forman, Sam 742
Forman, Terry 1236
Formand, William 869
Formosa, Roger 808
Fornara, Timothy 1233
Fornes, Maria Irene 1311, 1402
Fornia, Rita 1075
Forrest, Milton Earl 1743
Forrest, Robert 1219
Forrester, Joel 144
Forsmo, Ronald 4
Forster, John 610, 1299, 1312, 1709
Forster, Victoria 1378
Forsyth, Betty 288
Forsythe, Charles 1196
Forsythe, Henderson 133, 209
Fort, Syvilla 421, 1308
Forte, Mozelle 91
Fortenberry, Philip 512, 513, 1763
Fortier, Daniel 1151
Fortune, John 449
Fortus, Daniel (Danny) 357, 1268, 1685
Foss, Harlan (S.) 294, 1007, 1462
Fosse, Bob 1291
Foster, Alberta 1543
Foster, Christopher 15
Foster, Dan 769
Foster, Frances 21, 589, 996, 1004
Foster, Herb 791, 1390
Foster, Hunter 541, 1554, 1712
Foster, Jimmy 1785
Foster, John 948
Foster, Judy 1824
Foster, Margaret 1058
Foster, Marvin 15, 333
Foster, Nell 1131
Foster, Norah 1589
Foster, Peg 987
Foster, Scott Richard 1428
Foster, Stephen 112
Fote, Dee Dee 113
Fotopoulos, Mark 626
Fountain, Clarence 615
Fountain, Eli 1406, 1407
Fourcaut, Marie 561, 1055, 1722
Fowkes, Conard 1605
Fowler, Beth 1202, 1296
Fowley, Doug 423
Fox, Carol 1661
Fox, Derek 1024
Fox, Elliot 10
Fox, Herschel 898
Fox, Ivy 59, 1186
Fox, James 66, 245, 1369
Fox, Janet 1594
Fox, Kevin 703
Fox, Maxine 625
Fox, Patrick 175, 1767
Fox, Ray Errol 312
Fox, Raymond 1577
Fox, Robert 1545
Fox, Sonny 1582
Fox, Susan 147
Foy, Cathy 1495
Foy, Harriett D. 330, 770, 950, 1479, 1544
Foy, Kenneth (Ken) 208, 610, 1290, 1361, 1362, 1527, 1546
Fracht, J. Albert 74
Fracker, Richard 729
Fradkin, Philip (Phil) 601, 1594
Fradrich, James (Jim) 545, 575, 1147
Fram, Joel 830
Frame, Don 1419
France, Hal 1023
Frances, Norma 918
Franceschina, John 272, 564, 758, 1714
Francine, Anne 214, 1716
Francis, Allan 678
Francis, Donna 1542
Francis, Gerald G. 400
Francis, Nick 1615, 1616
Francis, Stacy 196
Francis, William 416, 587
Francisco, William 450, 1162, 1379, 1400
Franck, Eric 166
Francks, Don 911
Franco, Ramon 1398
Franco, Samuel 742
Frandsen, Erik 1495
Frank, Andrew 1458
Frank, Barry 1177
Frank, Benno D. 1236
Frank, Chris 950
Frank, Daniel 505
Frank, David 740, 1433
Frank, Dick 1343
Frank, Dorothy 1193
Frank, Gerald 1774
Frank, Gerri-Ann 489, 1105, 1745
Frank, Jim 345
Frank, Judy 1154
Frank, Mathew 1306
Frank, Ruella 279
Frankau, Edla 619, 620, 621, 622
Franke, Paul 62, 891
Franke, Wolfgang 1775
Frankel, Daniel 1652
Frankel, Frances 204
Frankel, Gene 204, 565, 1470
Frankel, Jessica 538
Frankel, Richard 102, 220, 479, 770, 1234, 1235, 1461, 1495, 1590, 1742
Frankel, Scott 641, 1492
Frankel, Shelley 68
Frankenstein, Karen 1336
Franklin, Abigail 577, 1365
Franklin, Barbara 1393
Franklin, Bonnie 409
Franklin, Danny 1166
Franklin, Helen 1116
Franklin, J.E. 1307
Franklin, Jim 63
Franklin, Joan Rice 1472
Franklin, Marcus Carl 252
Franklin, Marion 1308
Franklin, Pat 1423
Franklin, Tony 386
Franks, Dobbs 867
Franks, Laurie 68, 725, 726, 821
Franqui, Hermes 1291
Franz, Al 110
Franz, Elizabeth 1820
Franz, Joy 70, 162, 705, 731, 1097, 1166, 1654
Franz, Joyce 1056
Franzblau, William 462
Frasch, Charles 369
Frascoli, Michele 1292
Fraser, Alexander 1187, 1403
Fraser, Alison 115, 633, 763, 1019, 1306, 1390, 1571, 1584, 1706
Fraser, Ann 616
Fraser, Bert 88, 1670
Frass-Wolfsburg, Peter 1775
Fratantoni, Diane 89
Fratti, Mario 1589
Frawley, Kathryn 689, 769
Frawley, Mark 385, 1610
Frazer, Susanna 1641
Frazier, Carrie 1252
Frazier, Cliff 592, 593
Frazier, Douglas (a/k/a Douglass V.) 960, 1065
Frazier, Grenoldo 109, 156, 333, 592, 709, 1074
Frazier, Lynn 133
Frazier, Michael 311
Frazier, Steve 1333
Frazza, Lisa 897
Freas, Dianna 1538
Frechette, Peter 672, 1752
Frecon, Laura 30, 1260
Fredericks, Charles 1543
Fredericks, Connie 8, 1733
Fredericks, Norman 68
Frediani, Romano 994
Fredric, Arthur 1345
Fredrick, Vicki 1135
Fredricks, Richard 569, 947, 1227, 1789
Fredricks, Rita 183
Fredrickson, Joel 1456
Fredrik, Burry 246, 366, 1299
Fredriks, Martin 66
Free, Kevin R. 546
Free, Stan 209, 224, 442
Freed, Les 76
Freed, Sam 244, 345, 1758
Freedman, Betty 1274
Freedman, Danny 636
Freedman, Gerald 306, 307, 649, 1005, 1185, 1367, 1397, 1504, 1746
Freedman, Melvin H. 1354
Freedson, John 518, 520, 521, 522, 523, 524, 525, 526, 1067
Freeman, Al, Jr. 629, 946, 1672
Freeman, Cheryl 8, 474, 1736
Freeman, Elliot 1399
Freeman, Gladys 1559
Freeman, Janeece Aisha 67
Freeman, Jonathan 296, 1186, 1390
Freeman, Stan 73, 1350, 1421
Freeman, Steven A. (Steve) 412, 1151
Freeman, Stu 663
Freeman, Tom 697
Freeman, Yvette 383, 1337
Freeman-McDaniels, John 53
Freidman, Alan 852
Freifeld, Harry 441
Freiman, Louis 119, 608, 874, 1104
Freitag, Dorothea 277, 316, 1072, 1142, 1447
Freitas, Richard 379
Fremont, Rob 1258
French, Arthur 589, 1004
French, James 1565
French, Michael 1423
Freni, Rosemarie 1062
Frenock, Larry 984
Freschi, Bob 1166, 1287
Fresco, Zohar 711
Freshman, Florie 1124
Frett, Kenneth 630, 1358, 1360, 1398, 1732
Freudenberger, Daniel 710, 1411
Frey, Michael 105, 1174, 1423
Freydberg, James B. 1612, 1622
Freyer, Frederick 249
Fri, Sean 679
Friarson, Andrew 1001
Friberg, Carl 611
Fried, Barbara 761

Fried, Franklin 1696
Fried, Howard 92, 609
Fried, J.M. 1420
Fried, Michael 881, 1098, 1268, 1540
Fried, Scott 719
Friedberg, Billy 942
Friedberg, Martin Harvey 548
Friedel, Molly 1455
Frieden, Norman 173
Friedlander, Jane 63
Friedlander, Sylvia 1822
Friedman, Alan (Foster) 350, 542, 556, 558, 771, 852, 1255, 1261
Friedman, Barbara M. 1138
Friedman, Budd 1758
Friedman, Charles 1268
Friedman, David 200, 588, 833, 855, 929
Friedman, Gary William 208, 995, 1038, 1039, 1441, 1558, 1582, 1677, 1695
Friedman, Joel Phillip 1243
Friedman, Kim 1082
Friedman, Leo 238
Friedman, Lewis 916, 1049
Friedman, Martin 972
Friedman, Michael 607
Friedman, Samuel J. 150
Friedman, Sanford 134
Friedman, Seth 1243, 1709
Friedman, Sol 618, 619
Friedman, Stephanie 363, 1139
Friedman, Susan 878
Friedman, Tracy 916, 1049
Friend, Irma 1145
Friend, Robert 1203
Frierson, Andrea 1191, 1467
Frierson, Andrew 996, 1227
Fries, Jerry 1254
Friesen, Eugene 561, 1722
Friesen, Rick 1391
Frigerio, Claudio 1249
Frimet, Adrienne 125
Frink, Robert 831
Frisa, Lucille A. 1349
Frisch, Bob 275
Frisch, Richard 53, 831, 1029, 1087, 1708
Frisque, Chad 1333
Fritchie, Wayne 1395
Fritz, Maureen 1716
Fritzius, Harry 384
Froehlich, Marcy 1505
Froehlich, Mary Grace 1761
Frosher, Jon 1636
Frost, Jenni 769
Frumkin, Peter 346, 347
Frye, Dwight 1800
Frye, Elinor 1330
Fu, Haijing 495
Fuchs, Harry 490
Fuchs, Jay H. 390, 536, 1176, 1727
Fuchs, Leo 119
Fuchs, Peter 705
Fucillo, John 1383
Fuentes, Maria 768
Fugett, Joseph 500
Fuhrman, Debbi 374
Fujii, Timm 289, 1214
Fulford, David 481
Fulham, Mary 475
Fuller, Charles 1509, 1710
Fuller, Dean 1192, 1193, 1483
Fuller, Janice 1094
Fuller, Jeff 268
Fuller, Larry 1462, 1606
Fuller, Lorenzo 1095, 1511, 1744, 1811
Fuller, Penny 443, 1121, 1172
Fullerton, Joyce 456
Fullum, Ronald Clay 225, 234, 894, 1190, 1279, 1747
Fulton, Andrea 1379
Fulton, Larry 1207
Funes, Mimi 68, 1021
Funk, Sally 497
Fuqua, V.C. 986
Furaha, Kueleza 1696
Furber, Douglas 1101
Furguson, Helen 1811
Furman, Jay 668
Furman, Jill 760
Furman, Roger 482
Furman, Roy 1656
Furst, Jeff 380
Furst, Tim 1439
Furth, George 531
Futterman, Enid 1287, 1829
Fyfe, Jim 1304

Gabbert, Kenny "Ken Swift" 804
Gaberman, Alexander 1250
Gable, June 244, 311, 357, 884, 1072, 1143, 1260, 1520, 1641, 1739
Gabor, Arnold 868, 1047
Gabriel, Joseph 994
Gabriel, Gloria 1221
Gabriel, Lucy 994
Gabrieli, Lena 686
Gabriner, William 194
Gaburo, Kenneth 1636
Gaff, Billy 1025
Gage, Gary 409
Gagliano, Frank 292
Gagnon, Richard 713
Gagnon, Roland 117, 660
Gaige, Russell 779
Gailli, Rosina 1047
Gainer, Joan 1272
Gaines, Andrew 1601
Gaines, David 1141
Gaines, Davis 364, 945, 1201
Gaines, Frederick 716
Gaines, Leslie "Bubba" 165
Gaines, Reg E. 207, 1407
Gaines, Thomas 1163
Gainza, Henry 533
Gaither, Mareda 1399
Gaithers, Lita 777
Gal, Martin 858
Gal, Riki 401
Galan, Esperanza 1023
Galant, Lionel 1713
Galanti, Nino 68, 1021
Galantich, Tom 398, 990
Galasso, Michael 397
Galati, Frank 1723
Galberaith, Kim 1156
Galbraith, P.J. 1160
Galbraith, Philip 1160
Gale, Catherine Anne 398
Gale, Ellyn 1389
Gale, Gregory (A.) 69, 1613, 1712
Galeano, Gia 709
Gales, Martron 194, 1305, 1525
Galgour, Warren 1000
Galiano, Joseph 488
Galiber, Doris 68, 1021, 1221
Galina, Gita 608, 684
Gallager, Helen 1585
Gallagher, Billy 1145
Gallagher, Dick 475, 675, 1607, 1763, 1772
Gallagher, Helen 214, 731, 1057, 1635
Gallagher, Jennifer 659
Gallagher, Jerry 934
Gallagher, John, Jr. 1515
Gallagher, Judy 1713
Gallagher, Larry 115
Gallagher, Michael 214
Gallardo, Edward 995, 1250
Gallavan, Rick 1664
Galle, Myrna 1446
Gallegly, David 200
Gallet, Coralee 362
Galletti, Christopher 1634
Galli, Rosina 298, 344, 1597
Galligan, David 172
Gallin, Susan 323
Gallion, Roni 210
Gallione, Gale 329
Gallo, Barry R. 174
Gallo, David 103, 222, 462, 1121, 1450, 1545, 1778
Gallo, Joie 359, 1560
Gallo, Paul 70, 157, 186, 311, 551, 561, 728, 1055, 1109, 1186, 1643, 1722
Gallo, Rosemary 985
Gallogly, John 915, 1040
Galloway, Chris 809
Galloway, Jane 370, 1094, 1624
Galloway, Leata 603, 726, 1082, 1504, 1666, 1746
Galonsky, Denise 1469
Galvin, Gene (D.) 336, 337, 1171, 1617
Galvin, James 1131
Galway, Gregory W. 945
Gamache, Laurie 305
Gamba, Dolores 497
Gambatese, Jennifer 1347
Gamberoni, Kathryn 1023
Gambino, Kimberly 1134
Gamble, Eleasha 1700
Gamble, Julian 240
Gamboni, Ciro A. 1414
Gampel, Abigail 475
Gamson, Arnold 1583
Ganay, Lydia Punkus 617
Gandolfi, Alfredo 1047, 1249
Gandy, Sue 1285
Gang, Meredith 397
Gannaway, Lynne 159, 244, 414, 856, 1541
Gannon, Teresa 1131, 1601
Gans, Michael 1826
Gantry, Don 86
Garber, Victor 70
Garbiel, Inia 1636
Garcia, Alba Bonal 108
Garcia, Chamaco 203
Garcia, David 474
Garcia, Dolores 333, 1148
Garcia, Dolores Elena 1283
Garcia, Helena D. 1001
Garcia, Louis 490
Garcia, Nino 488
Garden, George 920
Gardens, Marvin 1690
Gardiner, Rick 758
Gardiner, Rodney 896
Gardner, Arron 693
Gardner, Brenda 1107, 1787
Gardner, Bunk 7
Gardner, Christine 1700
Gardner, Clark 1695
Gardner, David 1696
Gardner, Gary 1033
Gardner, Jack 1691
Gardner, Jake 941
Gardner, Janise 66
Gardner, Jeff 284, 1327
Gardner, Joe 803
Gardner, Patricia Ann 1419
Gardner, Rick 564
Gardner, Rita 324, 478, 1677, 1752
Gardner, Thomas 1071
Gardner, Worth 1466, 1470
Garfein, Jack 455, 882
Garffield, Matthew 58
Garfield, David 655
Garfield, Matt 739
Gargiulo, Terese 297
Gari, Brian 665
Gari, Janet 980
Garin, Michael 1495
Garland, Grace 892
Garland, Jamil (K.) 156, 194, 682
Garland, Nicholas 449
Garland, Patricia 283, 1483
Garland, Trish 1096
Garlid, Karl 759
Garner, Andre 546, 934
Garner, Jay 133
Garner, Jerri 224
Garner, Josie 1570
Garner, Larry 1509
Garner, Patrick 1187
Garnett, Chip 244, 886
Garnett, Gale 1471
Garon, Jay 16
Garone, Louise 1682
Garrambone, Joe 1537
Garrard, Alice 920, 1349
Garraro, Alice 1776
Garrett, Frederick 629
Garrett, Hank 1754
Garrett, Joy 417, 571, 1196
Garrett, Russell 1215
Garrett, Steven 1438
Garrett, Tom 907
Garrey, Colin 93, 1349
Garrick, Kathy 172, 765
Garrigan, Gerald 317, 826
Garringer, Nelson 550, 1259
Garrison, David 733, 912, 1486
Garrison, Mary Catherine 365
Garrison, Sean 652
Garside, Brad 945
Garson, Toby 980
Gartlan, Anne 217
Garver, Kristen 439
Garvey-Blackwell, Jennifer 77, 1237
Gary, Harold 1221
Gary, William 147, 1105, 1745
Garza, Troy 537
Garzia, Bernie 1303
Garzo, Jane 1288
Gasarch, Mark 588
Gasco, Ernesto 1146
Gascon, Gabriel 963
Gash, Kent (B.) 194, 240
Gaskill, William 445
Gaskin, Karl 1134
Gaskins, Deloris 1072
Gasman, Ira 1534, 1758, 1759, 1760, 1761
Gaspard, Raymond L. (Ray) 382, 731, 1432
Gaspard, Tamara 804
Gasper, Eddie 1291, 1743
Gaston, John 1416
Gaston, Ken 1085
Gaston, Lyd-Lyd 1410
Gaston, Penny 1446
Gatchell, R. Tyler, Jr. 52
Gately, David 374
Gates, Jim 1081
Gathers, Anissa 262
Gathright, Margaret 1385
Gatling, Arphelius Paul 1029
Gattelli, Christopher 10, 38, 721, 738
Gaud, Nameck 1281
Gaudet, Christie 1518
Gaudin, Kevin 1014
Gaughan, Jack 434
Gaul, Patricia 347, 1330
Gaumes, Reuben 873
Gaunt, Emily 983
Gauthier, Juliette 621
Gautier, Mae 1776
Gavon, Igors 464, 1279, 1541, 1827
Gawronski, Mieczyslaw 1275
Gaxton, William 1221
Gay, Bob 600
Gay, John 117, 1278, 1279
Gay, Noel 1101
Gaye, Albie 352, 735
Gayer, Josepha 439
Gayle, Marianne 902
Gayle-Swimmer-Anthony 507
Gaylor, Angela 411
Gaylor, Hal 265
Gaynes, Edmund 30, 104, 125, 132, 146, 466, 826, 1118, 1260, 1311, 1669
Gaynes, George 421, 422
Gaynor, Avril 1316
Gaynor, Charles 908
GeBauer, Judy 1348
Gebirtig, Mordechay 1382
Gedda, Nicolai 891, 1718
Geddes, Jill 391, 398
Geddes, Norman Bel 298, 905, 1369
Geddis, Ralph 622
Gedge, James 1296
Gee, Kevin John 682, 1223, 1300, 1509, 1550
Gee, Simone 289
Geer, Shippen 535
Geer, Will 481, 707
Geffen, David 939
Geffert, Eleanor R. 68
Gehling, Andrew 57
Gehman, Martha 1252
Gehman, Murrel 250
Gehman, Richard 235
Gehrecke, Frank 638, 1661
Geidt, Jeremy 449, 1091
Geier, Erik 105, 1644
Geiger, Mary Louise (M.L.) 739, 1345
Geiser, Maxine 1140
Geismar, Walter 1823
Geiss, Tony 1069, 1259, 1754
Gelbart, Larry 1201
Gelber, Stanley Jay 962
Gelfer, Steven 42
Gelfman, Sam W. 745
Gelke, Becky 133, 233, 1650
Gellar, Steve 918
Geller, Bruce 33, 944, 1430
Gelling, Hayley 1233
Gelman, Linda 36, 1817
Gemignani, Alexander 77
Gemignani, Paul 70, 377, 1557
Gemme, Chuck 1316
Gemmell, Don 1639, 1640
Gendron, Lyn 1015
Genelle, Joanne 1467
Genke, John 562
Gennaro, Liza 42
Gennaro, Peter 58, 1535
Geno, Alton 297
Genovese, June 1221
Gensler, Merlyn 66
Gentles, Avril 1160
Gentry, Celia 812
Gentry, Joseph M. 68
Gentry, Ken 1742
Gentry, Michael J. 68
Gentry, Minnie 844
Geoffreys, Stephen 726, 1503
Geoffroy, Zita-Ann 373
George, Andre 1014
George, Betty 1095
George, Hal 1468
George, Joseph 1652

George, Lovette 424, 633
George, Patricia 1029
George, Phillip 514, 515, 516, 518, 519, 520, 521, 522, 523, 524, 525, 526, 1450, 1763, 1772
George, Rhett G. 1325
Gerard, Barbara 456
Gerard, Ben 236
Gerard, Danny 473
Gerard, Gregory Taft 1613
Gerard, Linda 955, 993
Gerard, Phil 1131
Gerard, Theseus 1530
Gerb, Lynn (Lyn) 581, 713, 903
Gerber, Ella 1636
Gerber, Jay 652
Gerdes, George 1650
Gerdesmann, Karl-Heinz 1775
Gere, Richard 1356, 1504
Gerety, Peter 828
Gerhart, Michael 275
Gericke, Carol 1029
Gerlach, Ginger 631
Germain, Sarah 702
German, Edward 460
Germann, Greg 70
Gerro, Henry 5
Gershenson, Sue Anne 1381
Gershwin, George 46, 390, 912, 1101, 1166, 1167, 1172, 1644
Gershwin, Ira 46, 390, 843, 912, 1101, 1166, 1167, 1172, 1644
Gerson, Karen 217, 656
Gerstad, John 803, 1272
Gerstein, Robert 1768
Gersten, Bernard 65, 122, 130, 175, 283, 315, 346, 375, 430, 583, 683, 753, 1006, 1057, 1121, 1183, 1291, 1384, 1401, 1665, 1689, 1746
Gerstman, Felix (G.) 137, 1775
Gertler, Bonnie 768
Gertner, Eric 756, 1806
Gerut, Rosalie 1502
Gesek, Tad 187
Gesner, Clark 87, 160, 812, 1259, 1828
Gets, Malcolm 683, 848, 1121
Gettelfinger, Sara 641
Getter, Philip M. 321
Getz, John 1367
Gewandter, Holly 220
Geyer, George 66
Geyer, Josh 767
Geyra, Ellida 779
Ghaffari, Mohammad 1625
Ghazal, Edward 609
Ghebremichael, Asmeret 760, 950
Ghostley, Alice 569, 944, 1399
Giacosa, Giuseppe 186
Giagni, D.J. 70, 1243
Giaimo, Anthony 820
Giambattista, Ann Marie 1015
Giambri, Phillip 292
Giampa, Wade 1028
Gianfrancesco, Edward T. 143, 233, 484, 588, 934, 939, 1748
Gianiotis, Anna 1283
Giannelli, Christina 1650
Giannetta, Lucia 597
Gianniel, Christina 427
Giannini, (A.) Christina 153, 434, 445, 1016, 1635
Giannini, Vittorio 1587
Giannitti, Michael 1782
Giardino, Frank 768
Giardino, Pamela 1139
Gibb, Melinda 83
Gibba, Steve 734
Gibbs, Nancy Nagel 143, 892
Gibbs, Phyllis 1659
Gibbs, Raymond 188, 1137
Gibbs, Sheila 1191, 1384, 1689
Gibney, Susan 471, 1720
Gibson, B.G. 1426
Gibson, Darren 1186
Gibson, Darryl 195
Gibson, Edwin Lee 1429
Gibson, Joanne 480
Gibson, Jon 1200
Gibson, Judy 1197, 1424, 1691
Gibson, Marie 1131
Gibson, Nathan 940
Gibson, Sandra 704
Gibson, Teri 1025
Gibson, William 384
Gibson-Clark, Tanya 240
Gidaly, Walter 1827
Giddens, Duke 1131
Gideon, Steve 1138
Giehse, Therese 1241
Giering, Jenny 328, 1499
Giese, Linda 1739
Giffin, Norman 62, 1131
Gifford, Kathie Lee 929, 1700
Gifford, Ross 1780
Gigl, Aloysius 1303, 1702
Giguere, Edi 1641
Giladi, Moti 1647
Gilb, Melinda 210, 1551
Gilbert, Alan 1586
Gilbert, Barbara 1125, 1318
Gilbert, David 362, 717, 1374, 1416
Gilbert, E.A. 1807
Gilbert, Gerry 1655
Gilbert, Gloria 1131
Gilbert, Henry F. 344
Gilbert, Hy 153, 1410
Gilbert, Lou 421, 422
Gilbert, Mira 173
Gilbert, Raphael 68
Gilbert, Ray 91, 1221, 1713
Gilbert, Robert 459
Gilbert, Ronnie 1625
Gilbert, Tony 1410, 1441
Gilbert, W.S. 1270
Gilchrist, Rebecca 710
Gilden, Richard 1806
Gildersleeve, Allen 104
Gildon, Rob 362
Gile, Bill 886, 1057, 1668
Giles, Anthony 1146
Giles, Nancy 15, 1037, 1710
Giletto, John B. 345
Gilfillan, Sue Ann 317
Gilford, Jack 912, 1167, 1192, 1193
Gilford, Ross 177
Gill, Geula 490
Gill, Jackie 1240
Gill, Michael 300
Gill, Ray 225, 1375
Gillam, Lucie 235
Gilland, Anne 376
Gillaspy, John 1587
Gilleland, Lou Anne 36
Gillers, Ina 1349
Gillespie, Christie 494
Gillespie, Christina 33, 199, 448, 1438
Gillespie, Conor 828
Gillespie, Judy 190
Gillespie, Judy Kay 68
Gillespie, Lee 708, 1679
Gillespie, Robert 483
Gillespie, Sean 33
Gillespie, Tinker 360
Gillett, Eric Michael 541, 1637
Gillette, Anita 848, 1385
Gillette, Cynthia 426
Gillette, Priscilla 600, 1596
Gilliam, Gwen 668
Gilliam, Michael 172, 1046
Gilliam, Philip 1480, 1559
Gilliard, Jacquelyn 278
Gilliard, John 1543
Gillies, Don 963
Gilliland, Jane 1539
Gillis, Margie 561
Gillis, Mary Jo 631
Gilman, Judith 870
Gilmore, Craig 1561
Gilmore, Gerald 12
Gilmore, Paul 1145
Gilmore, Victoria 19
Gilmour, Graeme 1444
Gimbel, Norman 1447, 1448, 1697
Ginastera, Alberto 188
Gindi, Roger Alan 781
Gines, Christopher 1210
Gingold, Marvin 441
Ginnetti, Marie 288
Ginsberg, Allen 729
Ginsburg, Ned (Paul) 1305, 1458
Ginza, Joey 127, 785, 1171
Giombetti, Karen 1109
Giordano, Frank 542, 571
Giordano, Jonathan 1441
Giordano, Vincent 994
Giovannetti, Tony 412
Giovanni, Caesar 875
Giovanni, Kearran 103
Giovanni, Michael San 1441
Giovanni, Nikki 1699
Girardeau, Frank 1682
Girdler, Deb G. 1470
Girven, Howard 661
Girvin, T. Galen 1283
Girvin, Terri 730
Gisondi, John 16, 419
Gitlin, Murray 600
Gitonga, Brian Kamau 167
Gittens, Hugh 1388
Gitter, Chaim 1331
Gittler, Barbara 809
Gitto, George 1160
Gitzy, Andrew 538, 1608
Giudici, Joanne 1618
Giuffre, Joseph 948
Gizienski, George 486
Gjakonovski, Martin 1281
Glaab, Caryl 1674
Gladd, William 1646
Glade, Carol 80
Gladke, Peter 68, 1021, 1221
Gladstein, Renee 1382
Gladstone, Lydia 1419
Glant-Linden, Andrew 100
Glanville, Maxwell 885
Glaser, Cathy 1634
Glaser, John 1706
Glaser, Milton 1460
Glasgow, Jenny 1349
Glass, Adrian 920
Glass, Philip 20, 123, 294, 427, 729, 846, 1200, 1344, 1405, 1730
Glassman, Allan 451
Glassman, Seth 1685
Glaudini, John 1303
Glavin, Stephen 1109
Glaze, Sugar 134
Glazener, Janet 883, 1184
Glazer, Jay 362
Gleason, Helen 1047
Gleason, James 320, 1573
Gleason, John 1340, 1459
Gleason, Laurence 1376
Gleason, William 319
Gleaton, David 1081
Gleen, Laura 490
Glenn, Alice 236
Glenn, Kevin 814
Glenn, Robert 1436
Glennon, Kimberly 167
Glenn-Smith, Michael 1189, 1228, 1253
Glick, Gideon 1515
Glick, Marc H. 1714
Glick, Mari 890
Glick, Norman R. 613
Glickman, Stanley A. 35
Glickman, Will 1100
The Glines 573
Glines, John 587, 1531, 1772, 1801
Glist, Alan 1442
Glist, Kathi 1442
Glover, Abron 1406, 1407
Glover, Beth 185, 1301
Glover, Bill 1672
Glover, Corey 471
Glover, John 844
Glover, Keith 1631
Glover, Savion 207, 1406, 1407
Glovsky, Jeff 1671
Glushak, Joanna 910, 916, 1048, 1702
Glushanok, Masai 1134
Glynn, Carlin 133
Gmoser, Andrew 769
Gnys, Chuck 1562
Goble, Diana 1707, 1744
Gochman, Len 360, 1678
Gockel, Fred 76
Godby, Jack 1098
Godfrey, Joe 1684
Godreau, Miguel 1398
Godwin, Heather 15
Goeddertz, Charles 1124
Goehring, George 884
Goehring, Gerald 541
Goetz, Edward 171
Goetz, Marty 1565
Goetz, Sariva 1514
Goetzinger, Mark 1204
Goff, Charles 88, 1109, 1481, 1670
Goffin, Gerry 854, 1591
Goggin, Dan 89, 667, 1155, 1156, 1157, 1158, 1159, 1202
Gohl, James F. 572
Going, John 948
Goland, Arnold 1409
Gold, Beverly 1660
Gold, Felice 441
Gold, Harry 1666
Gold, Jonathan 284
Gold, Loree 1682
Gold, Marilyn 441
Gold, Michael E. 58
Gold, Robert Alan 478
Gold, Robin J. 1553
Gold, Rochelle 441
Gold, Stacia 1681
Goldberg, Andy 189
Goldberg, Hal 1381
Goldberg, Howard 229
Goldberg, Jerry 542, 1468
Goldberg, Leonard 1085
Goldberg, Mark 1554
Goldberg, Mike 1743
Goldberg, Missy 58
Goldberg, Phil 918
Goldberg, Roz 46
Goldberg, Rube 1385
Goldberg, Stan 1038
Goldberg, Whoopi 668
Goldblatt, Aaron 1163
Goldblatt, Hanan 401
Goldblum, Jeff 1689
Goldemberg, Rose Leiman 1260, 1505
Golden, Annie 67, 70, 370, 394, 1052, 1113, 1186, 1238, 1404
Golden, Jenny 1134
Golden, Ken 1161
Golden, Lee 979
Golden, Louis 1635
Golden, Norman 359, 1361
Golden, Peter 36
Golden, Ruth 256
Golden, Toni 1106
Golden, William 92, 1131
Goldenberg, Stuart D. 1174
Goldenberg, William 852
Goldenthal, Elliot 632, 640, 839, 1665
Goldfarb, Sidney 1665
Goldgran, Henry 1647
Goldie, Jack 578
Goldin, Igor 1818
Goldin, Toni 1171, 1747
Golding, Jeff 949
Golding, Ron 1522
Golding, Stephen 1092
Goldman, Donald (H.) 1008, 1346
Goldman, Herrick 305, 597, 1425
Goldman, Jenny Rebecca 293
Goldman, Jerry 472
Goldman, Lee 138
Goldman, Matt 1674
Goldman, Nina 122
Goldman, Shalom 20
Goldman, Sharon 696
Goldman, Sherwin M. 604
Goldmark, Sandra 328
Goldray, Martin 729, 1200
Goldrich, Zina 845
Goldschneider, Ed 1128
Goldsmith, Abe 472
Goldsmith, Lee 1433
Goldsmith, Merwin 186, 912, 1167, 1339, 1739, 1829
Goldstein, Bruce 1073
Goldstein, Daniel 1736
Goldstein, David 1599
Goldstein, Gail 668
Goldstein, Jerome I. 712
Goldstein, Jess 300, 1184, 1643
Goldstein, Jonathan 471
Goldstein, Owen H. 1679
Goldstein, Shmulik 147, 666, 1647, 1745, 1822
Goldstein, Steven 257
Goldstein, Ted 920
Goldstick, Oliver 383
Goldstone, Bob 71, 220, 319, 978, 1392
Goldwasser, Robin 1237
Goler, Lauren 833
Golkin, Dewey 1236
Golkin, Jeffrey 1236
Golladlay, Nancy 708
Golomb, Sheldon 867
Golub, Mark S. 751
Golub, Peter 49, 1499
Gomez, Armour 1015
Gondek, Juliana 673
Gonzales, Keith 834
Gonzalez, Ernesto 1358
Gonzalez, Guillermo 1398, 1655
Gonzalez, Lissette 533
Gonzalez, Lydia 1452
Gonzalez, Mandy 760
Gonzalez, Raoul 858
Goo, Kwang-Mo 1416
Goodall, Howard 697
Goodbrod, Gregg 1637
Goode, Edna 116, 996

Goode, Jennifer 362
Goode, Joseph 147
Goode, Peter 1687
Goodeve, Piper 57
Goodis, Marvin 68
Goodloe, Robert 62
Goodman, Alice 363, 1139
Goodman, Arthur 74
Goodman, Bill 991
Goodman, David 668
Goodman, Dody 368, 530, 1218, 1447, 1448
Goodman, Douglas F. 1
Goodman, Grace 834, 1349
Goodman, Hallie 1806
Goodman, Harry 543
Goodman, Lorraine 1505
Goodman, Margaret 960
Goodman, Paul 831
Goodman, Paul Scott 206
Goodman, Pegi 18, 664
Goodman, Robyn 38, 764, 1634
Goodman, Ruth 505
Goodman, Susan 1146
Goodmanson, Tim 185
Goodrich, Bruce 711, 907, 1350, 1442, 1670
Goodridge, Chad 1225
Goodridge, Ted 1021
Goodrow, Garry 1114, 1461
Goodsight, Larry 1310
Goodson, Germaine 82
Goodspeed, Don 633
Goodun, Elfeigo N., III 790
Goodwin, John 110
Goodwin, Karen Walter 58, 67
Goodwin, Kia Joy 1039
Goodwin, Mary 1543
Goodwin, Michael 307
Goodwin, Theodore 621
Goofy, Baby 1365
Goor, Carolyn 819, 1032, 1212
Gorbea, Carlos 244
Gordon, Arthur 705
Gordon, Barry H. 1097
Gordon, Bruce 494, 578
Gordon, Carl 630
Gordon, David 1329
Gordon, Don 1611
Gordon, Elmer 410
Gordon, Everett 368, 598
Gordon, Garry 600
Gordon, George 1176
Gordon, Haskell 912, 1365, 1644
Gordon, Janet Davidson 247
Gordon, Jeanne 298
Gordon, John 1828
Gordon, Jon 1495
Gordon, Judy 1685
Gordon, Kyle 607
Gordon, Marie 858
Gordon, Mark 1614
Gordon, Marvin 291, 598, 944, 980, 1043, 1153, 1166, 1300, 1455, 1647, 1774
Gordon, Michael David 702
Gordon, Peggy 595, 1573
Gordon, Peter 158, 243
Gordon, Ricky Ian 413, 1103
Gordon, Rita 200
Gordon, Robert H. 66
Gordy, Wayne 1370
Gore, Altovise 226
Gore, James 1308
Gore, Jim 935
Gore, Kathy 1221
Gore, Leigh Gibbs 4, 374
Gore, Tiffany 1629
Gorey, Edward 49, 612
Gorham, George H. 267
Gorka, John 2
Gorman, Andrew 223
Gorman, Angela 1369
Gorman, Michael 105
Gorman, Pat 1283
Gormley, Clare 47
Gorney, Walt 1057
Gorra, Olivia 1336
Gorrill, Liz 1072
Gorrill, Maggie 214
Gorrill, Maggy 86
Gorrin, John 1358
Gorrin, Michael 654
Gorsey, Renee 1274
Gorst, Helen 66
Gorzelnik (Gorzelnick), Christopher (Chris) (Cris) 983, 1240
Goslar, Lotte 1241, 1291, 1722
Gosney, Clare 819, 1032
Goss, Arnold 1758
Goss, Bick 232, 272, 734, 1274, 1302, 1361, 1527, 1683, 1715, 1759
Goss, Richard 1751
Goss, Robert 1179
Goss, Wade T. Pretlow 603
Gostinsky, Jacob 782
Gotlieb, Ben 1032
Gottermeyer, Eileen 1659
Gottfried, Howard 1436
Gottfried, Martin 100
Gottlieb, Michael 892
Gottschalk, Susan 1832
Gotwald, David 948
Gough, Amy 1416
Gough, Lloyd 98, 1140
Gough, Matthew 1629
Gough, Shawn 273
Gould, Charles W. 1258
Gould, Dennis I. 113
Gould, Ellen 220
Gould, Gordon 1541
Gould, John 135
Gould, Lecretia 1566
Gould, Morton 1100
Gould, Peter David 909
Goulston, Andre 241
Governor, Jennifer 1697
Gowers, Patrick 449
Goz, Harry 68, 1221
Goz, Maggie 1221
Goz, Michael 1441
Gozzi, Carlo 632
Graae, Jason 484, 527, 685, 855, 945, 1181, 1521, 1584
Grabowski, Christopher 1351
Grace, Ginger 1476
Grace, Michael L. 1486
Graden, David 588, 1486, 1575
Grader, Robert 1050
Grades, Fred 1085
Gradl, Christine 567
Grady, Eileen 66
Graebler, Mary 197
Grael, Barry Alan 735, 1142, 1539
Graf, Herbert 1740
Graf, Walter 1229
Graff, Lillian 25
Graff, Randy 1, 296, 1268
Graff, Steve 1387
Graff, Suzanne 1832
Graff, Todd 45, 157, 293
Graham, Arthur 891, 1227
Graham, Boyd 143, 424, 888, 919
Graham, Bruce 1621, 1721
Graham, Colin 574
Graham, Dan 1565
Graham, Deborah 1486
Graham, Elaine R. 1633
Graham, Gary 1659
Graham, Gerrit 1461
Graham, Holter 1450
Graham, June Lee 1615
Graham, Marla 1660
Graham, Ronny 531, 542, 616, 1076, 1141, 1448, 1576, 1754
Graham, Samaria 1134
Graham, Stephen 151, 1443
Graham, Susan 47, 628
Graham, William 766, 935
Graham-Geraci, Phillip 971
Graham-Knighton, Rita 1423
Graig, Candice 1064
Gram, Jonathan 1029
Gramm, Donald 1063, 1596
Grammer, Kelsey 1557
Grammis, Adam 406, 886
Granata, Dona 639, 1411
Grand, Murray 277, 535, 858, 1192, 1421, 1490
Grandi, Lois 366, 867
Grandison, J. Hamilton 591
Grandy, Fred 1299, 1312
Grandy, Marya 627, 1742
Graneto, Madeline Ann 486, 765
Graneto, Phillip 255
Graney, John Link 206
Granger, Dick 1142
Granger, Milton 485, 491
Granite, Judith 1562
Grannum, Karen 107
Granrud, Jenny 1068
Grant, Craig Anthony 470
Grant, Douglas 1038
Grant, Eva 1160
Grant, Kate Jennings 1325, 1554
Grant, Matthew 284
Grant, Maxwell 1448
Grant, Micki 194, 324, 327, 400, 504, 785, 911, 1307, 1525, 1526
Grant, Nanci 465
Grant, Sean 208
Grant, Suzanne 1029
Grant, William H., III 59, 240, 420, 592, 1423, 1738
Graphenreed, Timothy 45
Grasso, Arthur 352
Graubart, Judy 1069, 1273, 1352
Gravatt, Lynda 330
Gravell, Hazel 1086
Graves, Denyce 640
Graves, Eileen 1315
Graves, Linda 1618
Graves, Ruthanna 194
Graves, Yolanda 1065, 1307
Gravis, Frank 463
Gray, Charles 655
Gray, Dolores 599
Gray, Douglas 790
Gray, Jack [Timothy] 1101
Gray, Jennifer Uphoff 1547
Gray, John 151
Gray, Kevin 88, 873, 948, 1213, 1214
Gray, Malcolm 378
Gray, Margery 63
Gray, Michael 1816
Gray, Patricia 1719
Gray, Rudy 116
Gray, Stuart 1333
Gray, Teresa 1131
Gray, Timothy 746, 827, 1574, 1611, 1801
Grayman, Dwayne 785, 1781
Grayson, Bobby 1287
Grayson, John 1405
Grayson, Lee 909
Grayson, Mel 501
Grayson, Milton B., Jr. 883
Grayson, Richard 916
Grayson, Rick 684
Graziano, Maria 68
Graziano, Richard 958
Graziano, Stephen 888, 919
Grean, Robin 789
Greb, Doris 944
Grec, George 675
Greca, Barbara 101
Greco, Lois 1283
Grecyzlo, George 709
Green, Adolph 234, 377, 398, 1100, 1185, 1186, 1224, 1534, 1717
Green, Amanda 811, 1442
Green, Andrea 801, 1821
Green, Bob 775
Green, Chuck 704
Green, Cora 1543
Green, David 1048, 1190, 1756
Green, Dawn 196
Green, Del 161
Green, Dennis 414, 588
Green, Ghanniyya 358
Green, Helena 1134
Green, James 1543
Green, Jenna Leigh 103
Green, Joanna 763
Green, John Martin 1509
Green, Jonathan 673, 1023, 1062, 1816
Green, Lanny 396
Green, Laura 1600
Green, Martyn 253
Green, Mary-Pat 244
Green, Michael 1786
Green, Norma 1140
Green, Paul 826, 827, 1100
Green, Penny 1131
Green, Peter 293
Green, Robert 1108
Green, Rodney 809
Green, Rueben 9
Green, Scott 1600
Green, Shari 1751
Green, Simon 6
Green, Susan 1252
Green, Sylvan 1315
Green, Terry 1221
Green, Vivian 964
Greenawald, Sheri 1741
Greenbaum, John 404
Greenberg, Barry 1681
Greenberg, Edward M. 928
Greenberg, Edwin 1264
Greenberg, Gordon 802, 1479
Greenberg, Helen 967
Greenberg, Judith 834
Greenberg, Julia 1237
Greenberg, Mitchell 1821
Greenberg, Richard 728
Greenberg, Rob 471
Greenberg, Rocky 1133
Greenberg, Steven A. 784
Greenblatt, Karin 397
Greenblatt, Kenneth D. 837
Greenblatt, Richard 1694
Greenburg, Dan 1168
Greenburg, Jack 1145
Greene, Alan 61
Greene, Benton 1429
Greene, Billy (M.) 578, 1315
Greene, Ellen 939, 1628, 1731
Greene, Ethel 1131
Greene, Harriet 1229
Greene, Javotte S. 1464
Greene, Joyce E. 439
Greene, Juanita 591
Greene, Lyn 70
Greene, Milton 1152
Greene, Stanley 1464, 1465
Greener, Dorothy 598, 902, 1447, 1448
Greenfield, Debra 216, 1025
Greenfield, Ellen 930
Greenfield, Josh 736
Greenfield, Rose 119, 608
Greenhill, Donald 927
Greenhouse, Joel 675
Greenhut, Andrew 357
Greenspon, Muriel (Costa) 488, 1111, 1161
Greenstein, Jennifer 768
Greenstein, Michael 819, 1051, 1212, 1342, 1382, 1453
Greenwald, Nancy 1356
Greenwald, Patricia 1571
Greenwald, Robert 505, 1356
Greenwald, Tom 830
Greenwell, Charles 1029
Greenwell, Peter 1639
Greenwood, Deanna 1045
Greenwood, Jane 122, 186, 561, 628, 805, 873, 950, 1006, 1020, 1137, 1491, 1606, 1697
Greenwood, Joshua 863
Greenwood, Michael 284, 755
Greer, Jean 1331
Greer, Michael 1743
Gregg, Jacqueline 1240
Gregg, Jess 322
Gregori, Robert 188
Gregorian, Oshin 362, 717
Gregory, Chester, II 790
Gregory, Count 506, 1616
Gregory, David 858, 1268
Gregory, Helen 727
Gregory, Jay 232
Gregory, Joe 1131
Gregory, Stewart 1784
Gregory, Virginia 1253
Greif, Michael 206, 641, 1351
Grenham, Sheila 562
Grenier, Bernard 597, 606, 934
Grenier, Zach 158
Grenoldo 1207
Gresham, Gloria 1452, 1743
Grey, Christian 1420
Grey, DeMarest 357
Grey, Joel 443, 942, 1462
Grey, Larry 1160
Grey, Timothy 1574
Gribben, Eve 1308
Gribble, Bebe 1560
Grice, Jan 834
Grice, Wayne 187
Grifasi, Joe 660, 1109, 1146, 1187, 1411
Griffen, Joyce 1030, 1085, 1307, 1388, 1423
Griffin, Brent 43
Griffin, Emma 499
Griffin, Gerri 682
Griffin, Hayden 873
Griffin, Jerry 1398
Griffin, Marian Tomas 775
Griffin, Patty 1598
Griffin, Rodney 697
Griffin, Suzanne 1638
Griffin, Tamzin 1444
Griffin, Terri 165
Griffin, Victor 1582
Griffith, Diane 235
Griffith, Donald M. 1035
Griffith, LeRoy C. 1802
Griffith, Mary Beth 1438
Griffith-Haynie, Madelyn 322
Griffiths, Bob 1586
Griffiths, Horald 175
Griffiths, Paul 1020
Griggs, George 679
Griggs, Steve 679
Grignon, Monica 200, 708

Grigsby, Kimberly 754, 845, 1325, 1499, 1515
Grillo, Joanne 490
Grimaldi, Dennis 58, 345, 731, 1343, 1704
Grimaldi, John 1373
Grimaldi, Kathleen 994
Grimes, Charles 197
Grimes, Erroll 1487
Grimes, Nichols 324
Grimes, Tammy 942, 990, 1558
Grimes, Taryn 45
Grimes, Tiny 704
Grimley, Dorothy 717, 1374
Grimme, Donald 1785
Grinage, Dakeeta 803
Grindstaff, Robert 1359
Griner, Barbara 166, 1716
Gripper, Fred 996, 1781
Gripper, Frederic 1001, 1580
Grisetti, Josh 13
Griss, Susan 1822
Griswald, Mary 1230
Griswold 1777
Griswold, Putnam 340, 1075
Grite, Ester 397
Grodin, Charles 705
Groenendaal, Cris 539, 981
Groener, Harry 751
Groff, Jonathan 1515
Groff, Nancy 1223, 1305
Groh, David 1705
Gromelski, Brad 1283
Gromis, Karen B. 461
Gromov, Leonid 849
Groom, Malcolm 1567
Grooters, Robert 1086
Gropman, David 151
Grose, Molly Pickering 88, 1071, 1456, 1756
Grose, Robert Paine 352
Groseclose, Frank 98, 1825
Gross, Arnold 25, 360, 857, 1035
Gross, Daniel 362
Gross, Kerrie 1134
Gross, Yeeshas 418
Grossbart, Jack 103
Grosser, Maurice 1086
Grossman, Allen 406
Grossman, Bill 345
Grossman, Herbert 1667
Grossman, Ken 802
Grossman, Larry (Lawrence) 55, 377, 398, 1142, 1150, 1486
Grossman, Lisa 1194
Grossman, Robert 1109
Grossman, Shirley 1276
Grossman, Walt 38
Grove, Barry 18, 84, 179, 249, 296, 348, 633, 643, 656, 662, 672, 886, 943, 1129, 1184, 1201, 1339, 1459, 1492, 1546, 1637, 1710, 1778
Grove, James 605
Grove, Jessica 57
Grove, Joan 1682
Grover, Stanley 980
Groves, Napiera Daniele 206
Groves, Paul 495
Groves, Robin 1392
Gruda, Blythe 328
Grudeff, Marian 415
Gruden, Kevin 1232
Gruenberg, Louis 440
Gruenewald, Thomas 1485
Gruenewald, Tom 1008
Gruenwald, Tom 1274
Grund, Francoise 1625
Grunen, Gerta 1660
Grunfeld, Ginny 505
Grunheim, Joel 1488
Grupper, Adam 1144
Grusecki, Robert 639, 1378
Gruson, Harris 1252
Gualtieri, Tom 1110
Guare, John 1689
Guarino, Robin 1374
Guarino, Vicki 1226
Guastaferro, Dom 214
Guber, Zev 899
Guc, David 1098
Gudde, Lynda 649
Guerra, Robert 957, 1827
Guerrasio, John 1094
Guerrero, Danny 667, 1774
Guess, Alvaleta 78
Guest, Christopher 1113, 1114
Guettel, Adam 503, 1404
Guevara, Dedre 1345
Guggenheimer, Elinor 1290
Gugleotti, George 1294
Guida, Maria 1270
Guidall, George 1829
Guidera, Joseph Martin 563
Guidry, Bonnie 1746
Guilbert, Ann 149
Guile, Helen 331
Guilford, Carol 779
Guillaume, Robert 65, 504, 1096
Guilliatt, Lee 111, 243, 467, 554, 756, 757, 759, 823, 834, 920, 928, 998, 1017, 1277, 1387, 1739, 1776
Guilmartin, Ken 361, 958
Guimond, Steven 713
Guinevere, Camelot 631
Guiteras, Carmela 614
Guiterman, Arthur 1010
Guittard, Laurence 1697
Gulla, Amanda 1252
Gunderman, David 267
Gundersen, Arne 565, 1045
Gunderson, Anne 623
Gunderson, Don 112, 1264
Gunderson, Steve 83, 1551
Gunn, Moses 187, 844
Gunn, Nathan 47
Gunn, Nicholas 839, 1109, 1588
Gunnip, David 958
Gunther, Peter 359
Gunther, William 898
Gunton, Bob 364, 660, 1644
Gupta, Dipu 717
Gurian, Andy 397
Gurin, Robin 1450
Gurlitz, Eugene 100
Gurner, Jeff 499
Gurney, A.R., Jr. 1710
Gurney, John 1010
Gurr, Rueben 1753
Gurwin, Danny 525
Guske, Bill 213, 316
Guskin, Harold 138
Gustafson, Denise 872
Gustafson, Gloria 609
Gustafson, Karen 903, 1007, 1319, 1379, 1452
Gustafson, Robert 249
Gustafson, William 868
Gustavson, Tylar 423
Gustern, Joe 284
Guthman, Louis 1707
Guthman, Pamela 703
Guthrie, Clay 940
Guthrie, David 1035
Guthrie, Woody "Woodrow Wilson" 1804
Gutierrez, Gerald 325, 1048, 1201, 1390
Gutierrez, Phyllis 1390
Gutierrez-Soto, Ben 125
Gutknecht, Carol 256, 1165
Gutterman, Barbara 793
Gutterman, Cindy 965
Gutterman, Jay 657, 965
Gutwillig, Mike 1510
Gutzi, Mary 100, 873, 1591
Guy, Bette 352
Guy, Jasmine 115
Guy Lombardo and His Royal Canadians 68, 1221
Guyll, Judy 472, 638, 1594
Guzik, Jeff 1805
Gwynne, Fred 1082
Gyimes, William 425
Gyuzo 1653

Haack, Bruce 876
Haack, Charles 1382, 1453
Haagensen, Erik 491
Haas, Cathy 684
Haas, Holly 1154
Haas, Karen 1418
Haber, Bill 751
Haber, Bob 25
Haber, Carl 216
Haber, John L. 376, 544, 864, 950
Haberman, Linda 157, 1143
Habunek, Vlado 1137
Hachfeld, Eckart (a/k/a Eckard) 137, 1775
Hack, Sam 1248
Hack, Steven 319
Hackady, Hal 25, 930, 1486
Hacker, Linda 692
Hacker, Seymour 823
Hackett, Lester 235
Hackett, Mandy 1225, 1422
Hadary, Jonathan 70, 311, 588, 1201, 1654
Hadary, Nettie 1140
Hadas, Edward 397
Haddad, Robert 1142, 1574
Haddon, James 984
Haddow, Jeffrey 1414
Hadebe, Congo 1401
Hadjidakis, Mijos 1619
Hadley, Bob 76, 1475
Hadley, Henry 298
Hadley, Jerry 628
Hadley, Jonathan 1301, 1441, 1610
Haefner, Susan M. 778
Haen, Mark 808
Haenschen, Walter 621
Hafer, Claudia 1731
Hafner, Julie J. 301, 789
Hafner, Tom 1296, 1470, 1585
Hafney, Julie J. 633
Hagalili, Sonia 604
Hagan, Aaron 43, 741
Hagan, Howard 110, 1354
Hagegard, Hakan 574
Hagen, Reigh 1080
Hager, Linda Rae 734
Hager, Louis Busch 544, 1317
Hager, Max 372, 1349
Hagerty, Mike 1209
Haggart, John 622
Hagins, Marshall 948
Hague, Albert 685, 1100
Hahn, Barry 1721
Hahn, Julianna 1577
Haid, Charles 595
Haig, Peter 1072
Hailey, Keara 845
Haimes, Todd 219, 1304
Haimsohn, George 341, 342, 343, 1153
Haine, David 745
Haines, Jim 289
Haines, Judith Finn 904
Haines, Karron 1500
Hairston, William 815, 816
Haizlip, Melissa 153
Haker, Neta 108
Halcott, Gary 500
Hale, Birdie M. 313
Hale, Chanin 1755
Hale, Fiona 1028
Hale, Marian 610
Haley, Daniel 1068
Halford, Quinn 613
Hall, Adelaide 165
Hall, Adrian 1364
Hall, Berniece 709, 1672
Hall, Bill 417
Hall, Brad "Skippy" 79
Hall, Brad "Thing" 79
Hall, Carl 1638
Hall, Carol 1, 2, 133, 1650
Hall, Celeste 142
Hall, Davis 644
Hall, Debbie 1671
Hall, Delores 133, 726, 883
Hall, Dennis Michael 1303
Hall, Diana 417
Hall, George 308, 371, 448
Hall, Glenn 1269
Hall, Grayson 660
Hall, Iris 1543
Hall, John 856
Hall, Juanita 1021
Hall, Kimberly 229
Hall, Margaret 199, 472
Hall, Pamela 146, 543, 669, 1078, 1118, 1260, 1669
Hall, Richard 1707
Hall, Rick 790
Hall, Ronnie 1125
Hall, Steven (F.) (Steve) 308, 313, 1025, 1646
Hall, Suzanne 9
Hall, Timothy 1314, 1805
Halley, Sharon 434, 818
Hallick, Ned 159
Hallick, Nick 1391
Halliday, Bud 1543
Halliday, Buzz 1152, 1318
Halliday, Lynne 248
Halligan, T.J. 1163
Hally, Martha 54
Halmos, Nicole 1826
Halpern, Jeff 102
Halpern, Julie 1419
Halpern, Megan K. 519, 520, 521, 523
Halpner, Michael 349
Halverson, Lynn 1298
Hambleton, T. Edward 600, 710, 944, 1083, 1193, 1254, 1399, 1411
Hamburger, Anne 838
Hamel, Juliana 15
Hamil, Harriet 85
Hamil, Kathryn 85
Hamilton, Bob 1755
Hamilton, Christian 1721
Hamilton, David 256
Hamilton, Douglas 1816
Hamilton, Evelyn 1145
Hamilton, George 1550
Hamilton, Holly 1360, 1388
Hamilton, Jillian C. 1544
Hamilton, John F. 1164
Hamilton, Kelly 345, 1389, 1668
Hamilton, Lance 317
Hamilton, Lawrence 182, 1363
Hamilton, Marcia 1721
Hamilton, Nancy 1196
Hamilton, Patrick 653
Hamilton, Peter 870
Hamilton, Rita 1469
Hamilton, Roger 714
Hamilton, Stephen 1514
Hamilton, Victoria 1002
Hamingson, Andrew D. 1515, 1598
Hamlin, Peter 1349
Hamlisch, Marvin 126, 160, 283, 557, 558, 1141
Hamm, Margie 510
Hammarstrom, David Lewis 1618
Hammel, Lori 518
Hammer, James P., Jr. 49
Hammer, Jerry 1350
Hammer, Richard 1356
Hammer, Roberta 1080
Hammer, Valerie 562
Hammerlee, Patricia 1447
Hammerstein, James 739, 1678
Hammerstein, Oscar, II 505, 1100
Hammett, Gordon 192
Hammil, John 1169
Hammond, Blake 1186
Hammond, Earl 944
Hammond, Jane 1115
Hammond, Thomas 160, 381, 1236, 1259
Hammond, Will 1429
Hammons, Suzanne 1789
Hammons, Thomas 363, 1139
Hamparian, Peter 598
Hample, Stuart 280
Hampton, Dawn 638
Hampton, Donald 1256
Hampton, Jay 478
Hampton, Mark 681, 1149
Hamza, Jerry 657
Hanafin, Hope 194, 576, 1782
Hanan, Stephen 1270
Hanan, Stephen Mo 829
Hanayagi, Suzushi 872
Hancock, Fred Jason 116
Hancock, John 1691
Hancock, Louis 1559
Hancock, Lydia 1691
Hancock, Robert 81
Hand, Margot 481, 1539
Handakas, James Paul 497
Handleman, Stanley 1754
Handler, Evan 1541
Handler, Marc 1682
Handley, Alan 494, 1115
Handman, Stanley H. 1823
Handman, Wynn 314, 688, 860, 1222, 1534, 1641, 1720, 1761, 1783
Handwerger, Roshi 873
Handzlik, Anna 1140
Handzlik, Jean 1601
Hanerfield, Andrew 834
Haney, Ray 1751
Hanford, B.J. 1616, 1721
Hanford, Charles 388
Hanggi, Kristin 103
Hanion, Brendan 1356
Hanke, Christopher J. 474
Hankiewicz, Wojciech 1275
Hankin, Larry 1264
Hanks, Barbara 1684
Hanley, Dell 1611
Hanley, Ellen 201, 1576
Hanley, Katie 625
Hanlon, Colin 738
Hanlon, Julia 397
Hanlon, Mary-Ellen 200
Hanna, Cyril Tyrone, II 1696
Hanna, Ruth 66
Hannan, Joe 1487
Hannan, Thomas 972
Hanning, Geraldine 545, 1354
Hannington, Annette 796
Hannum, Kristie 567
Hansen, Irwin 1385

Hansen, Randy 434
Hansen, Ronn 74
Hansen-Young, Diana 1052
Hanson, Dave 1113
Hanson, Howard 1047
Hanson, Kelly 13
Hanson, Margot 1154
Hanson, Suzan 729
Hao, William 562
Harada, Ann 77, 1201
Harada, Deborah 1410
Haran, Mary-Cleere 700
Harausz, Stephen 1171
Harbach, Otto 1028
Harbachick, Stephen 1217
Harbaugh, John 1349
Harbison, John 628
Harbur, Chris 1425
Harburg, E.Y. 1100, 1796
Harby, Melanie Sue 1323
Hardeman, Daria 106
Harder, Caren 1334
Harder, James 74
Hardin, Faser 1556
Hardin, Jerry 1231
Harding, Jan Leslie 158
Hardwick, Cheryl 1, 338, 580, 656, 818
Hardwick, Mark 702, 1176, 1317, 1326
Hardy, Cherry 317
Hardy, Jim 734
Hardy, Joseph 715, 1539, 1828
Hardy, Michele 569
Hardy, Stephani 1141
Hardy, Wade L., III 434
Hardy, William, Jr. 996
Hare, David 873
Harelik, Mark 657, 754
Hargate, Bill 48, 63, 166, 601, 1594, 1604
Hargitay, Mickey 506
Hariday, Barbara 1391
Hariton, Gerry 916
Harkins, John 421
Harkins, Kay 1145
Harless, Dee 600
Harley, Lucille 1065
Harley, Margot 325, 332, 448
Harley, Pamela 1039
Harlow, Chad 1818
Harman, Barry 1181, 1377, 1595, 1748
Harman, Paul 785, 1361, 1442
Harmon, Heather Rochelle 994
Harmon, Irving 1475
Harmon, Jeffrey 1370
Harmon, Johnny 291
Harmon, Peggy 364, 586
Harmon, Steve 980
Harms, Marianne 353, 1239
Harnar, Jeff 810
Harner, Peggy 1079
Harney, Ben 219, 372, 400, 1783
Harnich, Aaron 365
Harnick, Jay 811, 1254, 1824, 1825
Harnick, Sheldon 858, 942, 1005, 1100, 1381, 1447, 1448, 1481, 1574, 1697, 1754
Harnley, Leslie 535, 1166, 1774
Harpel, Curt 1216
Harper, Jack 605
Harper, James 325
Harper, Jessica 393, 394, 1356
Harper, Kate 1309
Harper, Kay 780
Harper, Natasha 538
Harper, Olivia Virgil 873
Harper, Richard 493, 1124, 1294
Harper, Robert Alan 1309
Harper, Rosie 58
Harper, Ves 815
Harper, Wally 1424, 1473, 1707
Harper, William Jackson 1322
Harpre, Ves 815
Harradine, Archie 1639, 1640
Harrah, Verna 1347
Harrell, Gordon Lowry 1426
Harrell, Gregory 1022
Harrell, Hugh, III 9
Harrell, Mack 1667, 1740
Harrer, Maggie L. 1693
Harriell, Marcy 933
Harrigan, Charles 1464, 1465
Harrill, John 613, 1725
Harriman, P. Chelsea 1309
Harrington, Delphi 87
Harrington, Don 408
Harrington, Donald 250
Harrington, Hamtree 1543
Harrington, Laura 328
Harrington, Wendall K. 69, 1656
The Harris Sisters 1476
Harris, Albert 989, 990, 1521
Harris, Andrew B. 505
Harris, Ann 1476
Harris, Barbara 421, 904, 1206, 1360, 1415, 1765
Harris, Barley 1343
Harris, Carol 915
Harris, Charlene 255
Harris, Charlise 1035
Harris, Cynthia 1376
Harris, Daniel 469, 1010
Harris, Dede 1634
Harris, Dina 441
Harris, Drew Scott 474, 1056, 1366, 1451, 1714
Harris, Ellyn 980
Harris, Eloise 1476
Harris, Frederic 1476
Harris, Garland 1349
Harris, Gary 548, 1064, 1412, 1415
Harris, George, II 613
Harris, George, III 613
Harris, Herbert 134
Harris, Hilda 91, 574, 815, 816
Harris, Howard 544, 1077
Harris, J.L. 152
Harris, Jason 1618
Harris, Jay
Harris, Jay (H.) 46, 444, 462
Harris, Jayne Ann 1476
Harris, Jeff (Steve) 60, 1605
Harris, Jeremy 416, 974, 1678
Harris, John 918, 951
Harris, Johnny 1308
Harris, Jon 816
Harris, Joseph 1005
Harris, Julius 187
Harris, Julius W. 589, 1004
Harris, Kevin 278
Harris, Kymberly 983
Harris, Liana 1050
Harris, Linda 1318
Harris, Lloyd 68, 460, 1043, 1179
Harris, Lowell 822, 1029
Harris, Lulu Belle 1476
Harris, Margaret 589, 1689
Harris, Natalia 58
Harris, Peter Lind 359
Harris, Rosalind 1153, 1361
Harris, Sam 113
Harris, Scott 309, 828, 1204
Harris, Stacey 950
Harris, Steven 1575
Harris, T.J. 1670
Harris, Ted 1041
Harris, Timmy 857, 1415
Harris, Tom 625
Harris-Jekins, Lillette 1509
Harrison, Alan 1432
Harrison, Anthony 389
Harrison, Geneva 1278
Harrison, Gregory 172, 765
Harrison, Janice 809
Harrison, Jim 1066
Harrison, Lanny 1080
Harrison, Llewellyn 9, 382, 592, 1432
Harrison, Mark 1416
Harrison, Michael 572
Harrison, Paul Carter 629, 630, 885
Harrison, Peter 362, 453, 614, 828, 941, 1204, 1484
Harrison, Ray 766, 935, 1116, 1163
Harrison, Seth 1620
Harrison, Simone 349
Harrison, Stanley Earl (E.) 8, 194
Harrison, Tony 389
Harriss, Tom 556, 557, 558, 852
Harriton, Maria 1131
Harrity, Rory 160, 535
Harrod, Christopher 1251
Harrold, Jack 1111, 1462
Harrold, Orville 298
Harron, Donald 56
Harrow, Bruce 1719
Harrow, Joseph 1229
Harrow, Nancy 820
Harry, Jackee' 9, 214, 278, 377
Harsh, Roy D. 68
Hart, Adam 1207
Hart, Bruce 616, 1261
Hart, David 435
Hart, Enid 684
Hart, James 1637
Hart, Jean 1122
Hart, Jerry 1383
Hart, Joe 1160, 1240
Hart, Kathy 1054
Hart, Linda 627, 943
Hart, Lloyd David 372
Hart, Lorenz 201, 236, 505, 1100, 1101
Hart, Mary Ann 729
Hart, Max 66
Hart, Moss 69, 940
Hart, Nat 1293
Hart, Richard T. 73
Hart, Sara 458
Hart, Stan 986
Hart, Ted 1729
Hart, Teddy 1116
Hart, Virginia 779
Harte, Stan, Jr. 903
Harten, Lenn 1445
Harth, Laura 1062
Harth, Robert J. 1491
Hartig, Herbert (Herb) 531, 616, 858, 1142, 1152, 1447, 1754
Hartley, Cheryl 147
Hartley, Jan 37, 262, 282, 411
Hartley, Lanny 383
Hartley, Richard 196, 1002
Hartley, Stewart 1002
Hartman, David 1041
Hartman, J.P. 1320
Hartman, Jan 4, 490
Hartman, Mark 13, 1608
Hartman, Paul 1755
Hartmere, John, Jr. 103
Hartnett, Mickey 1361
Hartney, Brick 576
Hartney, Joseph 781
Hartunian, Jeannette 1713
Hartwell, Julie 494, 1115
Harve, Georgette 1543
Harvey, Alan 1080
Harvey, Dyane 278, 420, 1633
Harvey, Elwyn 317
Harvey, Gregory 1370, 1434
Harvey, James 535
Harvey, Katherine 1131
Harvey, Michael 660
Harvey, Nick 1212
Harvey, Peter 341, 342, 343, 464, 705, 827, 857, 986, 1076, 1318, 1433, 1534, 1562, 1704, 1719
Harvey, Rita 1303, 1608
Harvuot, Clifford 62, 891
Harwell, George 1755
Harwood, James 638, 1161
Harwood, Jill 1380
Harwood, Robert 188
Hase, Thomas 282
Hash, Burl 234, 244, 376, 660, 1279, 1592
Hash, Claire 1822
Hasiej, Julian 1275
Haskell, David 595
Haskell, Judith 974
Haskins, Nancy 287
Haskins, Susan 101
Hasman, Melvin 1232
Hasson, Tom 944
Hasting, Tony 463
Hastings, Hal 1193
Hastings, John 275, 781
Hastings, Mark 190
Hastings, Tom 752
Hatch, David 241, 1122
Hatch, James 504
Hatch, Joel 58
Hatchett, Frank 255
Hatchett, John 1158
Hathaway, Lois 1331
Hauer, Mary Elizabeth 1034
Haug, Peggy Marie 1021
Haugen, Eric T. 67, 1303
Haugen, Kristine 1595
Haughton, David 1662
Haupt, Paulette 285, 586
Hauptmann, Elisabeth 660
Hausam, Wiley 207, 1186, 1404
Hausen, Ray 598
Hausen, Roy 33
Hauser, Peter 1763
Havens, Richard 187
Havens, Richie 1388
Haverty, Doug 770
Haviland, Susan 101
Havlovic, Ed 510
Hawkes, Albert 621
Hawkins, Beth 66
Hawkins, Bruce 603
Hawkins, Eileen 284
Hawkins, Holly 1648
Hawkins, Ira 333
Hawkins, John 246, 295
Hawkins, Michael 962
Hawkins, Patricia 1746
Hawkins, Phyre 167
Hawkins, Robert 1227
Hawkins, Tom 708
Hawkins, Wood 1315
Hawks, Colleen 395
Hawks, Victor W. 1712
Hawley, Colette 78
Hawthorne-Bey, James 944
Hay, Curtis 755
Hayden, Gail 1682
Hayden, Ken 11
Hayden, Larry 100, 695
Hayden, Lee 15
Hayden, Michael 375
Hayden, Naura 109
Hayden, Tamra 398, 1700
Haydn, Maury 1566
Hayeem, Benjamin (Ben) 422, 528
Hayes, Aleta 282
Hayes, Diane 278
Hayes, Ernest W. 1720
Hayes, Every 803
Hayes, Hugh 689, 1110
Hayes, James 494
Hayes, Janet 190, 223, 600
Hayes, Jason 1508
Hayes, Lois 803
Hayes, Mark D. 790
Hayes, Pamela 772
Hayes, Steve 1158
Hayes, Ted 1737, 1738
Haygood, Bob 1291
Hayling, Patricia 501
Hayman, Lillian 1465
Haynes, Bruce 1029
Haynes, Cynthia 1589
Haynes, Helen 1811
Haynes, Teshina 333
Haynes, Tiger 86, 959, 1582, 1677
Haynes, Virginia Ellyn 985
Haynsworth, Brian 812
Hays, David 1393, 1481, 1564, 1667
Hays, John 448
Hayward, Harriet 888
Hayward, Michael 442
Hayward, Thomas 1131
Hayward-Jones, Michael 319, 599
Haywood, Lorna 951
Haywood, Mary 66
Haywood, Nancy 1083
Haze, Ralf Paul 194
Hazell, Assata 959
Head, Eric 1042
Headley, Shari 196
Hearn, Dennis 1147
Hearn, George 284, 707
Hearn, Roma 56
Heath, David 803
Heath, David Cochran 836
Heath, Eileen 1655
Heath, Gordon 278
Heath, Louise 1004
Heath, Sigrid 972
The Heather Brothers 979
Heather, Alfred 1145
Heatherly, James 1084, 1310
Heawood, John 317, 371, 1490, 1576
Hebert, Fred 1755
Hebert, Gail 537
Hecht, Joshua 92, 609, 1137, 1563, 1596
Hecht, Paul 1546
Heckman, Philip 1450, 1753
Heckscher, Hon. August 1689
Hecktman, Jeffrey B. 754
Hector, Hortense 1145
Hedge, Bill 288, 989
Hedges, David 761
Hedges, Marta 1467
Hedwig, Ula 643, 854, 975
Heed, Helen 1145
Heefner, David Kerry 218, 613, 1485, 1717
Heeley, Desmond 1569
Heffernan, Colleen 1389
Heffernan, John 490
Heffernan, Tracy O'Neil 960
Heflin, Marta 1395, 1396, 1504, 1746
Hefner, Raina 101
Hegel-Cantarella, Luke 845, 997
Heggie, Jake 1499

Heggins, Amy N. 1250
Heglerski, Kathleen 1062
Heider, Fred 1385
Heidinger, Bram 1669
Heifner, Jack 978, 1094, 1520
Heighley, Bruce 360
Heikin, Nancy 186, 1146, 1270
Heim, Alan 1780
Heim, Cynthia Leigh 1441
Heimann, Robert Paul 374
Heinberg, Allan 658
Heineman, Lori 1312
Heinemann, Gelia 1265
Heinemann, Larry 1674
Heinmiller, Glenn 35
Heinsohn, Elisa 1212
Heisler, Laura 1238
Heisler, Marcy 845
Heist, Karl 243, 364
Heit, Molly 834
Heitzman, Michael 154
Held, Dan 209, 1787, 1823
Helias, Mark 1816
Helle, Estelle 622
Hellems, Greg 1338
Heller, Adam 754, 878, 997, 1102, 1505, 1510
Heller, Alfred 460, 1016
Heller, Buck 786, 968
Heller, Eugene 925, 1066
Heller, George 619, 620, 621, 622
Heller, Laura 129
Heller, Liz 1632
Heller, Marc 82
Heller, Robert 789
Helliker, Steve 798, 800
Hellman, Bonnie 372, 1079
Hellstrom, Emily 399
Helm, Bob 1776
Helm, Tom 1756
Helmers, June 827
Helmond, Katherine 860
Helmore, Tom 715
Helms, Joe 68
Helpern, Lauren 72
Helton, Percy 1115
Heltzel, Sarah 1416
Hemingway, Alan 1226
Hemingway, Gerry 1816
Hemphill, Barry 120
Hemsley, Gilbert V., Jr. 1029, 1062
Hemsley, Winston DeWitt 232
Hendel, Ruth 38
Hendel, Stephen (Steve) 1634
Hendersen, Robert 244
Hendershott, Carmen 834
Henderson, Anthony 195
Henderson, Don 488, 569
Henderson, Helen 642
Henderson, Joe 1543
Henderson, Luther 333, 996, 1065, 1606
Henderson, Maggie 1316
Henderson, Melanie 1038, 1459
Henderson, Peter 1042
Henderson, Ray 436, 1101
Henderson, William J. 340
Hendra, Tony 962, 1114, 1483
Hendrick, Carol L. 720
Hendricks, Alonzo 425
Hendricks, Paul Vincent 593
Hendrickson, Benjamin 1541
Hendrickson, Ned 121, 380
Hendrickson, Stephen 1592
Hendry, Tom 393, 394
Henig, Andi 408
Heninburg, Gustav 120
Henley, Kenneth 1483
Hennagin, Michael 1810
Hennelly, Rachel 95
Hennes, Tom 322
Hennessey, Nina 299, 334
Hennessy, Amy E. 255
Hennessy, Dennis D. 642
Henning, Magnus 1241
Henning, Ted 1080
Henriksen, Daryl 729
Henriksen, Eve 76, 1475
Henritze, Bette 958
Henritze, Patricia 1252
Henry, Chad 54
Henry, Debra 1328
Henry, Joshua 760, 1425
Henry, Markas 627, 892, 929
Henry, Mary Pat 378
Henry, Peggie 1559
Henry, Suzanne (M.) 180, 1027
Henry, Tom 1321
Hensel, Christopher 1151
Henske, Judy 598
Hensley, Dale 1390
Hensley, Shuler 627
Hensley, Sonya 278, 1785
Henstock, Leslie 541
Hepburn, Betsy 201, 1063
Hepburn, Phil 1811
Herald, Sebastian 573
Herb, Gary 1365
Herber, Pete 249, 1742
Herbert, A.P. 124
Herbert, Carol 1244
Herbert, Charles 1688
Herbert, Dawn Le Ann 1644
Herbert, Grace 1688
Herbert, Lila 254
Herbert, Ralph 66
Herbert, Victor 81, 988, 1101
Herbst, Jeffrey (Jeff) 267, 398
Herd, Kermit 98
Herd, Richard 761
Herendeen, Frederick 1315
Herget, Bob 15, 201, 242, 1452, 1489, 1776
Herko, Fred 701
Herko, Mark (S.) 8, 25, 1693, 1733
Herlick, Jety 1041
Herman, Cynthia 1367
Herman, Danny 142, 1135
Herman, Gary H. 675
Herman, Harold 1272
Herman, Ian 2
Herman, Jerry 735, 818, 987, 1132, 1218, 1676
Herman, Maxine 1592
Herman, Renee 488
Hermany, Richard 1083, 1221
Hermione 1414
Hernan, Harold 654
Hernandez, Alan 1013
Hernandez, Ali 1535
Hernandez, Benjamin 1535
Hernandez, Jene 995
Hernandez, Luis 379
Hernandez, Oscar 533
Hernandez, Riccardo 207, 252, 330, 428, 668, 670, 933, 1325
Herndon, Ruby 1131
Hero, Maria 1452
Herr, Michael 1699
Herrera, John 186, 760, 916, 1109
Herrera, Lorenzo 686
Herrera, Manuel 1429
Herrick, Jack 950, 1779
Herrig, Robert 15, 1673
Herrington, Keith 68
Herrington, Shelly 1151
Herrmann, Keith 1100, 1310, 1377
Herrod, Bro 417
Herron, Joe 1636
Herschenfeld, Ethan 670
Hersi, Kyme S. 603
Herskovits, David 1237, 1826
Herter, Miles 453, 465
Herter, William 649
Hertz, Alfred 340, 1075, 1269
Hertzog, Irit 1453
Herz, Renee Semes 64
Herzig, Sig 68, 1021
Herzog, Arthur, Jr. 85
Hess, Bob 1264
Hess, David 375, 1306
Hess, Linda 284
Hess, Nancy 474
Hess, Rodger (a/k/a Roger H. and Roger) 323, 471, 1290, 1742
Hess, William 481, 1229
Hessel, Lee 1743
Hester, Hal 1827
Hester, Richard 1665
Hester, Tom 870
Heth, Peter David 288
Hettinger, Charles 1338
Hettlich, Sabine 1281
Heughens, Todd 408
Heusinger, George 1679
Hevner, Suzanne 89, 1158, 1338
Hewes, Maybin 1447
Hewes, Robert 1531
Hewett, Christopher 201, 236, 766, 1448, 1452
Hewett, Peggy 41, 1181, 1375, 1452
Hewitt, Johanna 1629
Hewitt, Lonnie 420
Hewitt, Paul 223
Hewitt, Sandi 221
Heyblum, I. 898
Heyer, Bill 384, 1162, 1254, 1678
Heyer, Rome 1678
Heyer, Rosemarie (Rosemary) 236, 661, 955, 957
Heyer, Thom 39
Heyman, Burt 548
Heymann, Henry 569
Heymann, Jerry 1077
Hiatt, Ron 1469
Hiatt, Teri 1015
Hibbard, David 296, 522
Hibbert, Edward 1304
Hickey, John 115
Hickey, Louise 42
Hickey, William 367, 1185
Hicklen, Cliff 124, 1016
Hicklin, Walker 919
Hicklin, Walter 1624
Hickman, Brent 1291
Hickok, John 233, 741, 1188
Hicks, Bill 376
Hicks, D'atra 1002
Hicks, Gene 1494
Hicks, Laura 325
Hicks, Leonard 1080, 1116
Hicks, Leslie 576
Hicks, Marva 252, 1518, 1631, 1781
Hicks, Munson 81, 183, 1313
Hicks, Reese 1429
Hicks, Rodney 546, 802
Hicks, Shauna 233
Hidalgo, Allen 424, 533, 915
Hiferty, Eileen 66
Higashi, Yutaka 602
Higdon, Gloria 91
Higginbotham, Diane 1029
Higginbotham, Robin 1577
Higgins, Joel 243, 825
Higgins, John Michael 1113
Higgins, Katie 510
Higgins, Patience 1384, 1406
Higginsen, Vy 196, 1001, 1002
Higginsen-Wydro, Knoelle 1002
High, John 1028
Highland, Jerry 599
Highstein, Jene 1344
Hightower, Loren 944
Hightower, Tex 1131
Higlen, David 217
Hiibel, Millie B. 738
Hiken, Gerald 284, 1541
Hiken, Nat 942
Hilbich, Ernst 1775
Hilbrandt, James 613
Hilferty, Susan 1103, 1439, 1515
Hilfiger, Ally 3
Hill, Andrew 1572
Hill, Bobby 400
Hill, Dan 854
Hill, Dorothy 1116
Hill, Dule 207
Hill, Erin 703, 1237, 1351, 1353
Hill, Erol 1004
Hill, Eunice 1062
Hill, Gregory 1441
Hill, Harriet 1729
Hill, Jeannie 872
Hill, Jessie 125
Hill, John 103
Hill, John-Edward 1243
Hill, Jozie 124
Hill, Katherine 125
Hill, Kathy Burke 1469
Hill, Lawrence W. 1670
Hill, Parks 1721
Hill, Ralston 117, 309, 828, 1539, 1716, 1824
Hill, Richard 246
Hill, Ron 1349
Hill, Valerie 469, 1600
Hillebrand, Elizabeth 846
Hiller, Bernardo 666, 1051
Hillman, George 336, 337
Hillman, Gerald Paul 1348
Hillman, Nancy Tribush (N.T.) 1348
Hillner, John 1289
Hillock, Jeff 1567
Hills, Beverly 1542
Hills, Bruce 462
Hills, Randy 1223
Hillyer, Kazuko 768, 1275
Hillyer, Reiko 768
Hilton, Ralph 397
Hilton, Richard 799
Himberg, Philip 1079
Himell, Jon 1320
Hindemith, Paul 951
Hindman, James 1245, 1366
Hinds, Ruby 294
Hines, Dennis 1633
Hines, Gregory 165, 180
Hines, Joyce 987
Hines, Patrick 710
Hinkes, Toby 1751
Hinkley, Del 722, 1504
Hinman, Kelly 1370
Hinnant, Bill 34, 44, 415, 587, 1259, 1318, 1828
Hinnant, Skip 1828
Hinshaw, William 340, 1075
Hinson, Bonnie 1483
Hinson, Glenn 1720
Hinton, James, Jr. 104
Hinton, Mercie 927, 1738
Hinton, Michael 1672
Hipkens, Robert 1495
Hipkins, Billy 25
Hippen, Lynn 81
Hiratzka, Marilyn 1147
Hirsch, Greg 395
Hirsch, Gregory Allen 1013
Hirsch, John 336
Hirsch, Louis A. 1028
Hirsch, Michael 1644, 1650
Hirsch, Nurit 1105
Hirsch, Penelope 780
Hirschhorn, Larry 997
Hirschhorn, Robert 731, 1314
Hirsh, Gary 1592
Hiskey, Iris 1405
Hitchcock, Joyce 940
Hitt, Tom 365
Hjalmarson, Jenni 95
Hlengwa, Lindiwe 1401
Hlengwa, Zandile 1401
Hlibok, Bruce 1384
Ho, Alvin 281
Hoag, George 620, 621, 622
Hoag, Judith 1641
Hoare, Charlotte 1233
Hoare, James 1233
Hobard, Rick 1379
Hobart, Sebastian 1223
Hobbs, Reginald 1434
Hobbs, Robert 1145
Hobbs, Wayne 1022
Hobson, I.M. 41, 672
Hobson, James 1360
Hobson, Richard (Dick) 1042
Hochhauser, Jeff 1610
Hochman, Larry 1107, 1197, 1339, 1787
Hocking, Leah 359, 515, 658, 1613
Hodapp, Ann 461, 483, 587, 716, 1045, 1081, 1202, 1683, 1825
Hodas, Martin 1379
Hodes, Gloria 301
Hodes, Stuart 158, 1083
Hodge, Jeannette 1308
Hodges, Ann 121, 1743
Hodges, Barney 816
Hodges, Joy 822
Hodges, Mitchell 1688
Hodgkiss, Lynn 1066
Hodshire, Allen 638
Hoefler, Charles E. (Chuck) 993, 1678
Hoel, Edson 92
Hoel, Jill 510
Hoenig, Karin 834
Hoesl, Joseph 1155, 1156, 1157
Hoff, Louise 1254
Hoff, Marie 876
Hoff, Robin 1268
Hoffenstein, Samuel 567
Hoffert, Paul 572
Hoffler, William 231
Hoffman, Avi (Ber) 492, 604, 1361, 1362, 1502, 1658
Hoffman, Bill 52
Hoffman, Billy 410
Hoffman, Cary 1758, 1759, 1760, 1761
Hoffman, Clarence 654
Hoffman, Constance 632, 640
Hoffman, G. Wayne 653
Hoffman, Gary 518, 521, 525
Hoffman, Heinrich 1444
Hoffman, Helen 1343
Hoffman, Jack 360
Hoffman, Jane 44, 360
Hoffman, Jay K. 1356
Hoffman, Kent 1586
Hoffman, Marlene 1182
Hoffman, Miranda 1736
Hoffman, Miriam 1502
Hoffman, Pamela 548
Hoffman, Philip 1328
Hoffman, Ralph 366, 1021
Hoffman, Stephen 1499, 1514, 1709

Hoffman, Susan (R.) 248, 1830
Hoffman, Suzanne Astor 1759
Hoffman, William M. 574
Hoffmeisterova, Lucie 1609
Hofmann, Isabella 1209
Hofsiss, Jack 1143, 1197, 1282, 1514
Hogan, Maggie 1412
Hogya, Giles 420, 1348
Hoh, Richard Charles 80, 743
Hohenwald, Heinz 1713
Hohn, Amy 413
Hoiby, Lee 1111, 1413, 1552
Holamon, Ken 856
Holbrook, Curtis 1325
Holby, Grethe 427
Holcenberg, David 154, 375, 583
Holcombe, Ernest 1229
Holcombe, Gary 821
Holden, Danette 778
Holden, Hal 1166
Holden, Steve 1153
Holder, Christian 153
Holder, Donald 78, 174, 313, 430, 627, 632, 837, 990, 1006, 1187, 1403
Holder, Laurence 500
Holdgreiwe, David 948, 1470
Holdgrive, David 1585, 1800
Holding, Dodger Stage 1012
Holdridge, Lee 852, 1661
Holgate, Danny 400, 682
Holgate, Ron (Ronald) 179, 698, 705, 1097
Holger 1251
Holiday, Hope 66
Holiday, Leila 1045
Hollaender, Friedrich (a/k/a Frederick Hollander) 459
Holland, Anthony 22, 421, 728, 1765
Holland, Barry 979
Holland, Dennis 995
Holland, Patrick 124
Holland, Stevie 995
Hollar, Lloyd 1242
Holleran, Mark 81
Holleran, Tom 81
Hollerith, Charles, Jr. 48, 713, 1133
Hollerman, Ed 735
Holley, Juanda LaJoyce 814
Holley, Patty 973
Holley, Robert Bruce 112
Holliday, David 1119
Holliday, Mark 74
Hollis, Esther 867
Hollis, Marnee 1753
Hollis, Tommy 12, 1219
Hollister, David 858, 1079
Hollmann, Erica 856
Hollmann, Mark 1712
Holloway, Stanley 1315
Hollrah, Patrice 105
Holly, Dennis 1050
Holly, Joy 1021
Holly, Robert Bruce 1302
Holm, Celeste 443
Holm, Hanya 600
Holm, John Cecil 132
Holm, Jorg 26, 168
Holm, Klaus 600, 942, 944, 1254
Holman, Bryce 48
Holman, Libby 853
Holman, Lola 996
Holmes, Jack 232, 415, 805, 935, 1163, 1430, 1431, 1539, 1767
Holmes, Jake 1459
Holmes, Jered 1606
Holmes, Jerry 669
Holmes, John, Jr. 601
Holmes, Lois 705
Holmes, Michael 110
Holmes, Peter 471
Holmes, Prudence Wright 660, 1279
Holmes, Richard 285
Holmes, Rupert 1109
Holmes, Scott 377
Holmes, Steven 548
Holof, Georgia (Bogardus) 1, 2
Holofcener, Larry 1100, 1142, 1431
Holsclaw, Doug 1418
Holse, Glenn 149, 150
Holt, Ben 1816
Holt, Fritz 992, 1546
Holt, Janice (L.) 171, 223
Holt, Sandy 548
Holt, Stella 33, 1308, 1464, 1465
Holt, Stephen 1349, 1359, 1776
Holt, Will 16, 879, 911, 1038, 1039, 1352, 1460, 1558, 1582, 1603, 1677, 1733, 1807
Holter, Bill 1276
Holton, Robert 693
Holtzman, Willy 718
Holzman, Winnie 1, 157, 1427
Homan, Melissa 397
Homberg, Terri 599
Homer, Louise 1075, 1269
Homer, Raymond 1684
Homewood, Charles 748
Honan, Mark 290
Honigman, Saul 1449
Honkamp, Helen 876
Honzack, Carl 1131
Hood, Janet 537
Hood, Regina Reynolds 1148, 1174
Hook, Walter 912, 1167
Hooker, Brian 1075
Hookey, Paul 834
Hooks, BeBe Drake 629
Hooks, Bill 908
Hooks, Bobby Dean (Robert) 91
Hooks, David 600, 1399
Hooks, Robert 629, 1734
Hooper, Colin 182
Hooper, Grace D. 619
Hooper, Lee 1029
Hoover, Paul 1305
Hoover, Richard 1429, 1613
Hope, Stephen 469, 833
Hope, Vida 1716
Hope, Wanetta 231
Hopkins, Bruce 467, 675, 920, 952
Hopkins, Janet 574
Hopkins, Kaitlin 103, 106, 627, 828
Hopkins, William 453, 465, 614
Hoppenstein, Reuben 402, 800
Hopson, Jimmy B. 1349
Horan, Bonnie 1040
Horen, Michael 661
Horenstein, Jonathan 1441
Horn, Barbara Lee 1452
Horn, Lew 1604
Horne, Charles G. 396
Horne, Lance 1068, 1499
Horne, Marilyn 574
Horne, Nat 68, 1221
Horne, William 1086
Horner, Chuck 980
Hornish, Rudy 1098
Hornor, Charlene 66
Hornung, Richard 1361
Horowitz, Cheryl Suzanne 505
Horowitz, Herschel 1276
Horowitz, Jeffrey 1345
Horowitz, Jimmy 1025, 1216
Horowitz, Nancy 642
Horowitz, Rochelle 441
Horowitz, Ronnie 642
Horrocks, Esther 1185
Horsey, Christopher 1590
Horsley, Eliza 1749
Horstman, Martha 1522
Horton, Arnold 397
Horton, Damon 196
Horton, Joanna 1233
Horton, Malcolm 1617
Horton, Ron 1559
Horvath, Jan 275, 799, 1467
Horwitt, Arnold B. 1100
Horwitz, David 244, 1483
Horwitz, Dominque 168
Horwitz, Murray 628, 646, 664, 1709
Hosbein, James 320, 360
Hoshko, John 1669
Hoshour, Robert 1025, 1410
Hosie, Bill 56
Hosiej, Urszula 1275
Hoskins, Jim 783
Hostettler, Andy 153
Hotchner, A.E. 463
Hotopp, John J. 758
Hotopp, Michael (J.) 81, 297, 338, 564, 642, 781, 1135, 1527, 1668
Hotrich, Garrett 844
Hott, Jordan 341, 342, 343, 1483
Hoty, Dee 1243
Houck, Ted, Jr. 246
Houdina, Mary Jane 408, 1593
Hough, Paul 1230
Houghton, James 1322
Houghton, Norris 600, 944, 1193, 1254, 1399
Hould-Ward, Ann 855, 1048, 1052, 1205, 1243, 1557
Hourie, Troy 167, 1210
House, Carl 872
House, Richard 1233
House, Ron 303, 623
Houseman, John 325
Houston, Cissy 1582
Houston, Douglas 1196
Houston, Mary 533
Houston, Sterling 1725
Houston, Wanda 610
Houta, Rony 1453
Hoven, Louise 869
Hover, Chuck 1599
Hovis, Jim 598
Howard, Alan 867
Howard, Arthur 184, 1362
Howard, Bart 415, 535, 1261, 1576
Howard, Bette 1174
Howard, Brian 750
Howard, Dennis 258
Howard, Elizabeth 175
Howard, G.A. 174
Howard, Greg 510
Howard, Henrietta Louise 1759
Howard, Kathleen 905, 1369
Howard, Laurie Williams 1391
Howard, Lee 736
Howard, Lisa 1680
Howard, Michael 1161
Howard, Myron 1221
Howard, Peter 433, 1196, 1224
Howard, Robin 696
Howard, Stephannie Hampton 1633
Howard, Vanessa 1699
Howe, Eleanor 834
Howe, Gwyda Don 1379
Howe, Juliet Grinnel 1320
Howell, Eleanor 815, 816
Howell, Erik 1774
Howell, Herman 1811
Howell, James 1789
Howell, John 1192
Howell, Michael W. 657
Howell, Rita 698, 935
Howell, Roger 710
Howes, Sally Ann 805
Howie, Betsy 323
Howse, Lola 913
Howson, Betty 1145
Howson, Frank 1145
Hoy, Bruce 66
Hoyland, Alyson Skipp 1686
Hoylen, Tony 1049, 1351
Hoyt, John 1601
Hoyt, Ken 612
Hoyt, Robert 1329
Hruska, Millie 121
Hsing-Kuo, Wu 495
Huang, Dou Dou 495
Hubbard, Alma 1464
Hubbard, Bruce 334, 975
Hubbard, Jane 1252
Hubbard, Lloyd 1166
Hubbell, Jeffrey 1525
Hubert, Janet 330
Hudacs, Chris 30
Huddleston, Paul 1137
Hudes, Quiara Alegria 760
Hudson, Charles 61, 631, 857
Hudson, Helen 870
Hudson, John Paul 949
Hudson, Laurie 1114
Hudson, Rodney 27, 41, 386
Hudson, Travis 572, 1043, 1594
Hudson, Walter 675
Huff, Harry 882
Huffington, Anita 235
Huffman, Cady 1693
Huffman, Mike 492
Huffman, Ted 362, 717
Huffmaster, Ellen 1229
Huge, Adrian 1444
The Hugh Porter Gospel Singers 815
Hughes, Alexandra 4
Hughes, Allen Lee 54, 1191, 1323, 1518
Hughes, Austin 340
Hughes, Barbarell 897
Hughes, Dickson 783
Hughes, John 1252
Hughes, Julia C. 1706
Hughes, Ken 1349
Hughes, Kim 1054
Hughes, Kristin 1577
Hughes, Langston 166, 167, 501, 815, 816, 843, 1308, 1464, 1465
Hughes, Michael 371
Hughes, Paula D. 1486
Hughes, Rhetta 592, 1222, 1580
Hughes, Richard B. 121
Hugill, J. Randall (Randy) 124, 246
Hugo, John Adam 1597
Hugot, Marceline 285
Hulce, Thomas 1478
Hulce, Tom 1515, 1598
Hulett, Michael 105
Hulicius, Otto 620, 621, 622
Hull, Charles 811
Hull, Don 121
Hull, Mylinda 273
Hull, Tom 734
Hulovo, Emilika 1131
Hulswit, Mark 209
Hume, Michael 1029
Hume, Michael J. 456
Humes, Bibi 1340
Hummel, Karen 878, 1102, 1510, 1715, 1821
Hummel, Martin 934
Hummel, Sayrah 1360
Hummel, Tamara 1336
Humphrey, Richard 1596
Humphreys, Kathryn 98
Hundley, C.L. 1710
Hunnery, Bill 1367
Hunnikin, Douglas 488
Hunsaker, Michael 929
Hunt, Amanda 1425
Hunt, Arthur 935
Hunt, Daryl 1389
Hunt, Eugenie 535
Hunt, Gordon 1768
Hunt, Joe 265
Hunt, Leigh 1724
Hunt, Lorraine 628
Hunt, Pamela 232, 1099
Hunt, Peter 421, 676, 1400
Hunt, Robert 193
Hunt, Scott 1389
Hunt, W.M. 582, 1028, 1362
Hunt, William E. 883, 1559
Hunter, Anne 578
Hunter, Barbara 1115
Hunter, Ian McLellan 538
Hunter, JoAnn 229
Hunter, Kathryn 396
Hunter, Marion 1066, 1287
Hunter, Penelope 1276
Hunter, Phyllis 4
Hunter, Susan 373
Hunter, Suzy 488
Hunter, Timothy (Tim) 385, 1215, 1523, 1554
Hunter, Walt 1558
Hunter, William "Gregg" 785, 1232, 1509, 1550
Huntington, Rex 1616
Huntley, Jobe 1308
Hunziker, Peter 863
Huot, Denise 253
Hurd, Hugh 1605
Hurley, Brian 642
Hurley, Curley 1682
Hurley, Jamie 1556
Hurley, Kevin 1681
Hurley, Laurel 1131
Hurney, Kate 112, 1087
Hursey, Sherry 765
Hurst, David 421
Hurst, James 90
Hurt, Mary 852
Hurt, Maybeth 1082
Hurwit, Lawrence 1433
Hurwitz, Deborah 185
Hurwitz, Nathan 743
Hurwitz, Sophie 619
Husmann, Ron 957
Hussung, Will 588
Husted, Darrell 1776
Huston, Jon 1360
Huston, Michael 195
Huston, Philip 578
Hutcheson, Jon 505
Hutchins, Jeannie 427
Hutchins, Tony 1691
Hutchinson, David 439
Hutchinson, Laurie 1707
Hutchinson, Ron 1411
Hutchison, Brian 1238
Hutton, Bill 172, 486, 833
Hutton, C.A. 81, 1595
Huxhold, Kristin 13
Hwang, David Henry 1200, 1730

Hwarng, Wern-Ying 730
Hyacinth, Rommel 1300
Hyams, Barry 529
Hyatt, Maggie 175
Hyer, June 987
Hyland, Lily (M.) 618, 619, 620, 621
Hyland, Sarah 641
Hyman, Earle 831
Hyman, Fracaswell 456
Hyman, Larry 172, 1048
Hyman, Pamela 768
Hyman, Robert 833
Hymen, Julia 397
Hymes, Deeda 226
Hynd, Ghretta 615
Hynes, Eliabeth 1462
Hynes, Holly 88
Hyslop, Jeff 56
Hyson, Ray 1824
Hyun, Cho Kyoo 872
Hyun, Soon Chul 889

I, Robert 370
Iacangelo, Peter 1628
Iacona, Lorenzo 859
Iacono, Paul 1390
Iacovelli, Josh 30
Ian, Janis 1520
Ianni, Richard 74
Iannucci, Michael P. 1615, 1616
Iasella, Paula 453
Iauco, Dianne 256
Ibert, Jacques 779
Ibrahim, El Tahra 1014
Ide, Richard 944
Igarashi, Gerri 1214
Iglesias, Antonio 1398
Iglesias, Enrique 533
Iglesias, Franco 488
Iglesias, Lisa 333
Ihde, Martha 155
Ikeda, Thomas 1213, 1214
Illes, Mary 13, 275
Illica, Luigi 186
Immer, Andrea 273
Imperato, Anthony 1384
Infante, Isidro 262
Ing, Alvin 1473
Ing, Michael 1139
Ingalls, James F. 47, 363, 1103, 1139
Inge, Matthew 709
Ingham, Tom 1652
Inghram, Elizabeth 13
Ingle, Doug 1494
Ingle, John 971
Ingram, Donna P. 959
Ingram, Kate 453, 614
Ingram, Michael 284, 828, 1071, 1296, 1677, 1821
Ingram, Tad 364, 614, 1541
Ingram-Young, Donna 153
The Ink Spots 145
The Inner Sanctum 605
Innerarity, Memrie 301, 681
Innvar, Christopher 503, 1121, 1637
Insinnia, Albert 414, 1669, 1689
Insull, Sigrid 246, 308, 1677
Intaschi, Linda 1694
Intrabartolo, Damon 103
Introcaso, John C. 329
Iobst, Anne 158
Iorio, Jim 859
Ioucelli, Vincenze 136
Irby, Dean 813, 1198, 1509, 1561
Ireland, James 198
Ireland, Joe 1559
Irish, Steve 1327
Irizarry, Frank 897
Irizarry, Vincent 909
Irons, Leslie 437
Irungu, Francis Kimani 167
Irvin, Syrena 1064
Irving, George S. 609, 1101, 1311, 1608, 1707
Irving, Jack 550
Irving, John 448
Irving, Jonathan 800
Irwin, Bill 1641
Irwin, Diane 915
Irwin, Elizabeth 767
Irwin, Jack 132
Irwin, Robin 1610
Irwin, Ted 1459
Isaacs, Pamela 313, 1129
Isen, Richard 491
Isenman, Don 507
Ishay, Galia 1203
Ishee, Suzanne 979
Isola, Kevin 1120
Israel, Neil 292
Israel, Robert 20, 122, 439, 728, 1055, 1405, 1722, 1730
Ito, Genji 1625
Ito, Teiji 562
Ivancic, Mark 1119
Ivanina, Elena 170
Ivanoff, Alexandra 301, 459, 1055, 1629
Ivanov, Kalina 223
Ivers, Mitchell 1535
Ives, Agnes 1140
Ivey, Judith 580
Ivie, Kelly 505
Izrahi, Isaac 899

Jabara, Paul 649
Jablons, Karen 764, 1527
Jack, Angel 1476
Jack, Tracy 167
Jackins, David L. 1512
Jackman, Helena 1221, 1802
Jackman, Kent C. 1174
Jackness, Andrew 2, 311, 804
Jackowski, Ronald 734
Jackson, Anne 204
Jackson, C. 504
Jackson, C. Tod 824
Jackson, Chequita 736, 1579
Jackson, Chris 1638
Jackson, Christopher 760, 1022
Jackson, Clay Harper 1186
Jackson, Clifford 1229
Jackson, Delilah 231
Jackson, Ernestine 219, 709, 959, 1335, 1441, 1505
Jackson, Fred 1274, 1780
Jackson, Jeffrey 541
Jackson, Jill 231
Jackson, Josephine 120
Jackson, Karen 8
Jackson, Kyle-Scott 1216
Jackson, Lat 1542
Jackson, Leon 214
Jackson, Leonard 860, 1307
Jackson, Mark 4
Jackson, Mary Ellen 1789
Jackson, Melinda 1014
Jackson, Nagle 87, 160
Jackson, Oliver, Jr. 1495
Jackson, Patty Ann 277
Jackson, Paul 1653
Jackson, Peter 1292
Jackson, Richard 336
Jackson, Robert 655, 715
Jackson, Robert Jason 222
Jackson, Rufus 194, 1738
Jackson, Saadiya 349
Jackson, Tod 944, 1035, 1119
Jackson, Troi C. 1509
Jacob, Norman 630, 1659
Jacob, Steven 184, 653
Jacobowitz, Anna 684
Jacobs, Barbara 1655
Jacobs, Danny 1802
Jacobs, Debra 299
Jacobs, Edward T. 81
Jacobs, Eric 834
Jacobs, Hal 1132
Jacobs, Hank 1508
Jacobs, Harvey 401
Jacobs, Jacob 119, 608, 684, 1104
Jacobs, Jesse 1810
Jacobs, Jessie 384
Jacobs, Jim 625
Jacobs, Marian Lerman 1303
Jacobs, Max 158
Jacobs, Paul 1112, 1114
Jacobson, Danny 1560
Jacobson, Helen 504
Jacobson, Henrietta 585, 874
Jacobson, Irving 585, 874, 1104
Jacobson, Jim 1031
Jacobson, John 1034
Jacobson, Kenneth 1452
Jacobson, Libbie 280
Jacobson, Ruth 1087
Jacobson, Steven M. 995
Jacobsson, Peter 95
Jacoby, Mark 427, 444
Jacques, Martyn 1444
Jaffe, Arnold 1229
Jaffe, Jill 122, 728, 859
Jaffe, Morris 809
Jaffe, Orly 1453
Jagel, Frederick 762
Jagger, Mick 1666
Jaglom, Henry 1698
Jahan, Marine 185
Jaklel, Richard 1695
Jakubovuc, Jaroslav (Yaron) 1136
Jakubowitz, Joe 708
Jalenak, Jan 653
Jamal, Sati 629
James, Brian 1279
James, Brian d'arcy 503, 1778
James, David 1094
James, Elmore 800
James, Hilary 309
James, Jessica 215
James, Kimo 404
James, Lester (Les) 1218, 1603
James, Marcia 266, 603
James, Nikki M. 130, 1736
James, Ray 698, 935
James, Robert 1443
James, Stephanie Renee 1363
James, Stephen 259, 634, 662
James, Ted 1259
James, Tommy 1406
James, Toni-Leslie 130, 375, 430, 683, 933, 1121, 1631
James, Vanessa 11
James, William 1483
Jameson, Joyce 149
Jamison, Betsy 786
Jamison, Judith 1029
Jamison, Marshall 1116
Jampolis, Neil Peter 203, 400, 408, 527, 739, 1335, 1379, 1452, 1595, 1761
Jane, Suzanne 1315
Janelli, Carl 638
Janezic, Barbara 332
Janick and Arnaut 66
Janik, Ada 334, 725
Janik, Nina 334
Janivier, Janie 735
Janki, Devanand 845, 1830
Jankowski, Stephen (Steve) 539, 789
Janowitz, Marc 518, 519, 520, 521, 523, 1067
Janus, Lester 1221
Janus, Stanley 1221
Janusz, Tom 464
Janz, Milli 1257, 1809
Jaquillard, Denis H. 1281
Jarboe, Richard 653
Jarchow, Bruce 1461
Jarecki, Divonne 471
Jared, Robert 1558, 1654
Jarnac, Dorothy 942
Jaroslow, Ruth 121, 831
Jarosz, Judith-Mari 1062
Jarrett, Bella 1242
Jarrett, Jennifer 630
Jarrett, Jerry 809, 1635
Jarrett, Jim 63
Jarvis, Graham 693, 1082, 1666
Jarvis, Lucy 849
Jarvis, Scott 903
Jason, Karen 1613
Jason, Mitchell 1185, 1452
Jason, Peter 93, 976
Jason, Robert 358
Jasper, Jinny 1616
Jasper, Zina 1080
Javerbaum, David 1547
Javits, Joan 714, 1824, 1825
Javits, Marion 655
Javore, James 887, 979, 1087
Jay, Bobby 854
Jay, Claude 470
Jay, Don 885, 959, 1183
Jay, Leticia 704
Jay, Mary 1595, 1692
Jay, Ricky 1357
Jay, Stanley 481
Jay, Stephen 55, 203, 1199
Jay, William 589, 1004
Jay-Alexander, Richard 418
Jaybe, Dwight 1659
Jayme, William North 254
Jayne, Brian 918
Jayne, Diane 1682
Jayne, Dwight 918
Jaynes, Carl H. 1370
Jbara, Gregory 675, 1304
Jean, Stephanie 1508
Jeanpierre, Francoise 834, 920, 1349
Jecko, Timothy 408
Jefferson, Rosetta 9
Jeffrey, Clare 1393
Jeffrey, Jim 1676
Jeffreys, Rachel 1721
Jeffries, Jay 509, 542, 550, 771, 949, 1150
Jeffries, Will 1033
Jeffrin, Hal 711
Jellison, John 70, 71, 162, 755, 909, 1121, 1736
Jemmott, Angel 596
Jenison, Tim 1235
Jenkins, Athalie 136
Jenkins, Capathia 252, 597, 1068
Jenkins, Daniel 413, 828
Jenkins, David 54, 179, 220, 805, 975, 1143, 1282, 1296, 1411, 1521, 1591, 1655, 1699
Jenkins, Dewitt "Snuffy" 1720
Jenkins, Esther 1017
Jenkins, George 68, 1021, 1221
Jenkins, Mark 253
Jenkins, Michael A. 1554
Jenkins, Raymond 768
Jenkins, Taylor 1733
Jenn, Myvanwy 999
Jenner, C. Lee 1720
Jenness, Sean 72
Jennings, James 1379
Jennings, John 1364
Jennings, Ken 49, 1037, 1052, 1438, 1712
Jennings, Sandra 138
Jensby, Wesley 1536
Jensen, Carol-Leigh 1108
Jensen, Don (Donald) 17, 63, 82, 268, 304, 720, 740, 793, 798, 800, 801, 968, 1301, 1327, 1635
Jensen, Elida 1566
Jeong, Young Ju 889
Jeoung, Woo Jeong 889
Jepson, Helen 762
Jepson, J.J. 1043
Jerome, Adele 1140
Jerome, Kenny 350
Jerome, Timothy 117, 308, 599, 1250, 1299
Jerro, Steve 215
Jervey, EllenMarie 1040
Jessel, Ray 415, 1431
Jestin, Jennifer 1094
Jeter, Michael 27, 203
Jewell, John 1681
Jewett, Marilyn 1445
Jewett, Tom 874
Jianli, Gao 495
Jiler, John 78
Jillette, Penn 1234, 1235
Jillson, Ken 1571
Jim, Marion 1221, 1358
Jima, Iwo "Buddy" 79
Jin, Ha 495
Jo, Sara 1117
Jo-Ann, Ebony 330, 603
Joaquin, Amador 562
Jobin, Raoul 776
Jobson, Jade 899
Jochim, Keith 203
Joe, Lutz 1281
Joel, Danny 274, 1751
Joel, Stephanie 1830
Joerder, Norb 64, 840, 1676
Joffe, Ed 737
Joffrey, Robert 609, 826, 1789, 1814
Joglar, Frank 287
Johann, Dallas 274
Johann, John 76, 1617
Johann, Zita 620
Johannson, Rhoda 1116
Johanos, Jennifer 901
Johanson, Don 42, 1027
Johanson, Robert 246, 1410
Johl, Peter 1721
John, Mary W. 306, 307, 360
John, Tom 1452
John, Tom H. 958
Johnnene, Robert 212
Johns, Clay 417, 827, 1611
Johns, Kurt T. 1438
Johnson, Alan 55, 90, 114, 496
Johnson, Allayne 1119
Johnson, Allynne 171
Johnson, Anderson 156
Johnson, Andrea J. 983
Johnson, Anita 846
Johnson, Ann 247
Johnson, Arny 566
Johnson, Arte 1448
Johnson, Bayn 336
Johnson, Bernard 82, 238, 255, 333, 542, 589, 682, 818, 1004, 1509, 1544, 1638, 1737
Johnson, Bert (K.) 362, 717
Johnson, Betsey 1153
Johnson, Bill 215, 1333
Johnson, Bjorn 1378
Johnson, Bob 649
Johnson, Bosha 700, 1355, 1522

Johnson, Brian Charles 1515
Johnson, Bryan 1067
Johnson, Charles A., III 194
Johnson, Crystal 1001
Johnson, Daniel Timothy 1671
Johnson, David Lawrence 726
Johnson, Dean 1519, 1759
Johnson, Deborah 1392
Johnson, Donald W. 1782
Johnson, Dorothy 1140
Johnson, Doug 1317
Johnson, Edward 868, 1041, 1047, 1249
Johnson, Eric 599, 1470, 1585
Johnson, Frank 985
Johnson, Heather 1336
Johnson, Helen 578
Johnson, Howard 1115
Johnson, Ian 221
Johnson, Ida 944
Johnson, Jack 295, 1431, 1661
Johnson, Jacqueline 1483
Johnson, James A. (Arthur) 603, 1538
Johnson, James Weldon 591
Johnson, Jeannie 1166
Johnson, Jeremy 42, 105
Johnson, John 979
Johnson, Jordan 1022
Johnson, Jose 615
Johnson, Joseph 768
Johnson, Judy 566
Johnson, Julie 102, 1366
Johnson, Justine 1481
Johnson, Karen 752, 1828
Johnson, Key 1542
Johnson, Leilani 177
Johnson, Leona 400
Johnson, Lianne 1383
Johnson, Louis 166, 266, 352, 589, 603, 809, 816, 844, 1064, 1604, 1638, 1738, 1811
Johnson, Marilyn 152
Johnson, Marilyn J. 788
Johnson, Mary 1559
Johnson, Mary Lea 1037
Johnson, Maurice 768
Johnson, Mel 867, 968, 1232, 1335, 1437
Johnson, Mel, Jr. 968, 1232, 1335, 1437
Johnson, Nancy 949
Johnson, Natalie Joy 103, 721
Johnson, Onni 648
Johnson, Paul L. 1338
Johnson, Reginald Vel 156, 230
Johnson, Richard 1500
Johnson, Roger 1272
Johnson, Ronny 693
Johnson, Samuel M. 427
Johnson, Sandra 250
Johnson, Scott 259, 347, 1268
Johnson, Scott L. 999
Johnson, Seri 769
Johnson, Shane 803
Johnson, Sy 181
Johnson, Taborah 1519
Johnson, Terry A. 260
Johnson, Tina 179, 285, 486, 855
Johnson, Todd Alan 1128
Johnson, Tommi 194
Johnson, Virginia 1550
Johnson, Yvette 107, 221
Johnson-White, Carolyn 615
Johnston, Audre 86, 652
Johnston, Ben 250
Johnston, Bob 1610
Johnston, Brian 1316
Johnston, Denis 1137, 1474
Johnston, Gail 752, 1021, 1446, 1539
Johnston, Jane A. 638
Johnston, Keith 78
Johnston, Nancy 391, 945, 1514
Johnston, Phillip 1826
Johnston, Romain 735, 870
Johnstone, Vicki 1029
Johnstone, Will B. 446
Jolles, Annette 930
Jolley, Nick 217, 1135
Jolliff, Kristin 660, 989
Jolo, Norman Dello 1667
Jon, David 728, 1055
Jonah, Dolly 879, 1460, 1603, 1754
Jonas, Joanne 595
Jonas, Nita 652
Jones, Adelaide 1543
Jones, Alberta 1543
Jones, Allan 145
Jones, Anastasia 1744
Jones, Anne 1193
Jones, Bambi 8
Jones, Bill 949
Jones, Bill T. 1429, 1487, 1515
Jones, Bradley 319
Jones, Bruce C. 844
Jones, Cadden 769
Jones, Charles 719
Jones, Charlotte (A.) 631, 827, 1594
Jones, Christine 365, 632, 1238, 1515
Jones, Clyde 8
Jones, David C. 48, 867
Jones, Debra Lynn 295
Jones, Dennis 1589
Jones, Dexter 1305, 1544
Jones, Donald G. (Don) 219, 289, 1089, 1437
Jones, Duane 1580
Jones, Duane L. 1001
Jones, Elinor 306, 307
Jones, Fred 944
Jones, Gail 1716
Jones, George 1092
Jones, Gloria 68, 105
Jones, Gregory 1406
Jones, Gwendolyn 941
Jones, Herman LeVern 736
Jones, James Earl 187
Jones, Jason King 444
Jones, Jay Aubrey 124, 1070
Jones, Jeffrey (Duncan) 364, 958
Jones, Jeffrey M. 838
Jones, Joe 913
Jones, John 42, 286
Jones, John Randolph 1242
Jones, Johnnie 756
Jones, Judd 1152
Jones, Kevin 216, 453
Jones, Lauren (Gloria) 91
Jones, Leilani 182
Jones, Libby 506
Jones, Ludie 1435
Jones, Lyman 1283
Jones, Mamie 876
Jones, Mark 12, 728, 839, 1722
Jones, Marlowe 1229
Jones, Marzetta 1398
Jones, Meachie 266
Jones, Michael 1378
Jones, Neil 1013
Jones, Ora 1788
Jones, Pamela 831
Jones, Pattie Darcy 1591
Jones, Paul 1312
Jones, Ray Anthony 501
Jones, Rebecca Naomi 1225
Jones, Reed 55
Jones, Reuben 1233
Jones, Rhodessa 1487
Jones, Robert Anthony 1303
Jones, Seth 398, 965
Jones, Shaun 105
Jones, Simon 1304
Jones, Steven 1181, 1377
Jones, Steven R. 688
Jones, Tom 191, 306, 307, 308, 309, 371, 478, 479, 531, 733, 858, 1056, 1100, 1253, 1259, 1286, 1366, 1447, 1451
Jones, Vanessa A. 1591
Jones, Vicki 1174
Jones, Walton 961
Jones, William 1029
Jons, Joelle 98, 1652
Jonsson, Judyann 589
Joplin, Laura 965
Joplin, Michael 965
Jordan, Bob 1648
Jordan, Clifford, Jr. 885
Jordan, Eddie 1207
Jordan, G. Adam 60
Jordan, Hal 1379
Jordan, Irene 1740
Jordan, Leslie 730
Jordan, Lynda 92
Jordan, Marc 572, 1628, 1697
Jorgensen, Nels 609, 1789
Jorgenson, Rhodie 62
Jose, Santana 897
Josef, William 1655
Josefsberg, David 38, 837, 1479
Josenhans(hanz), Leonard 1713
Joseph, Bob 1297
Joseph, Jackie 149
Joseph, Jeffrey 1461
Joseph, Peter 98, 226, 1119
Joseph, Rowan 1591
Joseph, Stephen M. 1038
Joseph, Victor 1693
Josephs, Harriet 1749
Josephs, Therese 136
Joslyn, Betsy 309
Jostrom, Philip 1805
Joubert, Elsa 1284
Joughin, James 606
Jovanovich, Brandon 1336
Jowsey, Nancy 44
Joy, Bernie 1179, 1440
Joy, Carol 425
Joy, James Leonard 1449, 1485
Joy, Lynda 171
Joy, Robert 364, 910
Joy, Signa 885
Joyce 1356
Joyce, Dan 363
Joyce, Evelyn 1179
Joyce, Joe 299, 1215
Joyce, Kimee 1579
Joyce, Robert 748
Joyner, Jerry 613
Juday, Jeff 742
Judd, Michael 1438
Jude, Patrick 275, 370, 647, 1025
Juden, Dorothy 1131
Judge, Jane 1058
Judge, Kevin 541
Judin, Sue 1434
Juditz, Vicki 1785
Judkins, Antoine "Doc" 804
Judson, Lester 277
Judy, James 184, 186, 260, 838, 1201, 1781
Jue, Francis 413, 1214
Jules, Anny 1325
Julia, Raul 292, 1367, 1689
Julian, Doris 333
Julian, Kimm 439
Juliano, Frank 1283
Juliano, Lisa 1830
Julien, Jay 241
Jumper, Alexandra 1390
Jun, Rosanne 66
Jung, Philipp 157, 300, 990, 992, 1106, 1190
Junion, Nancy 745, 1041
Junquera, Victor Gabriel 1639, 1640
Jurasik, Peter 1787
Juriga, George 56
Jurist, Irma 389, 1273
Jurkiewicz, Harold 709
Jurman, Karl 916
Justice, Clare 698
Justice, Jimmy 370, 1360, 1398
Justice, Milton 978
Jutard, Pascale 1586
Jutras, Simon 1510

Kaalund, Raymond 704
Kabatchnik, Amnon 654
Kabatznick, Brian 790
Kaczorowski, Peter (A.) 220, 315, 641, 804, 1375, 1495, 1591, 1726
Kadison, Luba 489
Kadri, Ron Cadry 1240
Kaehler, Deadra 294
Kael, Dan 1607
Kaftan, Jiri 1609
Kagan, Ido 108
Kahan, Judy 1299, 1313
Kahan, Marvin 453, 614
Kahane, Gabriel 1630
Kahl, Howard 112
Kahlil, Alisha 647
Kahn, Joseph 826
Kahn, Judy 403
Kahn, Kelli 1550
Kahn, Madeline 126, 852, 1069, 1273, 1311
Kahn, Michael 1603
Kahn, Ricardo 777
Kahn, Sarilee 662
Kaikkonen, Gus 290
Kail, Thomas 760
Kairson, Ursuline 1001
Kaiser, Amy 53, 887
Kaiser, George 1462
Kajiwara, Mari 1029
Kakatsakis, Charles 1652
Kalan, Charles 972
Kaldenberg, Keith 66, 92, 609, 1360, 1587
Kaleem, Barry Amyer 156
Kalegi, Sylvia 1274
Kaley, David 1128
Kalfin, Robert 100, 117, 234, 244, 376, 634, 660, 695, 844, 885, 1279, 1541, 1592
Kaliban, Bob 616
Kalich, Jacob 874
Kalkstein, Ruth 963, 1488, 1719
Kallaghan, Kathie 509
Kallan, Randi 1511
Kaller, Sheryl 10
Kalliel, Sean 1226
Kalmanowich(witch), Harry 585, 684
Kalmar, Bert 672
Kaluski, Drew 1590
Kaluski, Yankele 1453
Kamau, Mary Wambui 167
Kaminski, Tom 870
Kamlot, Robert 448
Kamm, Tom 294
Kampman, Ellen 66
Kanbar, Maury 1080
Kandel, Karen 1248
Kandel, Karen Evans 1699
Kandel, Paul 973, 1133
Kander, John 52, 317, 377, 783, 1100, 1101, 1685
Kane, Allegro 425, 1464, 1465
Kane, Andrea 839
Kane, Anthony 1582
Kane, Arleen 1582
Kane, Bradley 1557
Kane, Donna 343
Kane, Francis 1495
Kane, Irene 1627
Kane, Jean 714
Kane, John 705
Kane, Kris 983
Kane, Lucille 714
Kane, Mary 1399
Kane, Maureen 714
Kane, Ray 1130
Kane, Ronnie 1095
Kane, Trish 1600
Kane, Whitford 618, 620
Kane, Wyman 317
Kanfer, Stefan 745
Kanter, Shanna 1822
Kantor, Karen 35
Kantor, Kenneth 309, 1449
Kantor, Mitchell 485
Kantorski, Suzanne 362
Kantrowitz, Jason 271, 610, 1054, 1281, 1584, 1645
Kaokept, Adam 1425
Kapelos, John 1209
Kapetan, Peter 833, 1181, 1778
Kapitan, Mark 372
Kaplan, Caryn 284
Kaplan, Claire 1073
Kaplan, Herbert 203, 678, 869, 992, 1106, 1485
Kaplan, Jonathan 1328
Kaplan, Jordan 1666
Kaplan, Lisa 505
Kaplan, Mary Jo 101
Kaplan, Michael 1143
Kaplan, Shirley 367, 368
Kaplan, Sol 98, 147
Kaplin, Stephen 632, 702, 839, 1248, 1665
Kapner, Sara 248, 280
Kappell, Marty 230, 1762
Kapton 636
Karachentzov, Nikolai 849
Karamazoff, Sergej 1281
Karant, Glenn 1376
Karasiov, Denis 849
Karaty, Tommy 291
Karavan, Dani 1203
Karchmer, Charles 1522
Karel, Chuck 272, 416
Karel, Jane 1021
Karen, Fia 1218
Karger, Barbara 1439
Kariuki, Muchiri 167
Karl, Andy 38, 1479
Karliss, Gregory V. 1330
Karmazin, Sharon 38
Karmon, Jonathan 401, 617
Karnaushkin, Alexander 849
Karnecki, Zbigniew 1275
Karner, Chris 1193
Karnilova, Maria 858
Karp, Barbara 73
Karp, Charles Mayer 1567
Karp, Jonathan 721
Karr, Patti 718, 1078, 1097, 1475, 1485, 1707
Karras, Athan 366
Karrell, Maria 397
Karrol, Toni 506
Kary, Michael 474
Kasak, John 1542
Kasdan, Michael 409
Kase, William 1660
Kasha, Lawrence (N.) 63, 73, 1218
Kasher, Charles 332
Kashka 1207

Kashkin, Allan 1321
Kaslow, Susan 86
Kason, Corinne 857, 1701
Kason, James 1661
Kasprow, Dawn 717
Kass, Alan 109
Kass, Peter 1813
Kassir, John 583, 1347, 1622
Kassoff, Marla 1660
Kastl, Paul 132
Kastner, Ron 645, 1187
Kaszynski, Suzanne 842, 1408
Kata, Takeshi 607, 1753
Kate, Sally 648
Kates, Robert Alexander 1659
Katis, Merry Lynn 773, 1606
Kato, Andrew 189
Kato, Sukae 602
Katsaros, Doug (Douglas) 1, 2, 377, 434, 435, 463, 855, 1071
Katz, Allan 1495
Katz, Cheryl 1195
Katz, Christina 918
Katz, Leon (Leo) 998, 999
Katz, Michael 924
Katz, Michele Arlette 1349
Katz, Natasha 38, 300, 639, 643, 1176, 1197, 1631, 1656, 1680, 1710
Katz, Paul 1067, 1584, 1750
Katz, Steven 505
Katz, Tracy 284
Katzman, Drew 191, 1253, 1286
Katzmann, Laurie 712
Kauahi, Norman Wendall 1410
Kauffman, Jean 1362
Kauffman, Jeannie 116, 118
Kauffman, Marta 1, 811, 1243, 1709
Kauflin, Jack 472
Kaufman, Bill 126, 556, 557, 558, 852, 1069
Kaufman, Emanuel 1682
Kaufman, Fredda 1692
Kaufman, George S. 305, 912, 940, 1166, 1167
Kaufman, Hank 128
Kaufman, Ibi 782
Kaufman, Jim 1776
Kaufman, John 1749
Kaufman, Kel 949
Kaufman, Martin R. 567, 843, 861, 924, 1651
Kaufman, Philip S. 456
Kaufmann, Eduard 1281
Kaufmann, Kathy 1370
Kaup, Tyson 1818
Kaur, Vidya 1348
Kava, Caroline 314, 1628
Kawalek, Nancy 1541
Kay, Beatrice 145, 1315
Kay, Bradley 523
Kay, Megan 464
Kay, Tina 142
Kayden, Mildred 240, 338, 773
Kayden, Spencer 1712
Kaye, Anne 676, 1154, 1360
Kaye, Bradley 518, 522, 524, 525, 526, 863, 1067
Kaye, Gloria 317, 1774
Kaye, Howard 934
Kaye, John 1231
Kaye, Judy 374, 961, 1507, 1756
Kaye, Marla R. 378
Kaye, Robert R. 236
Kaye, William 1265
Kaz, Fred 22, 318, 548, 1209
Kazan, Lainie 870
Kazanoff, Paul 1391
Kazaras, Peter 574
Kazounoff, Berenice 1688
Keagy, Grace 1097
Keal, Anita 1511
Keale, Nalani 1221
Kean, Norman 183, 214, 237, 401, 457, 1169
Kean, Peter 1620
Keane, Dillie 6
Keane, Michael Edo 282
Kear, Dennis 1682
Kearne, Audrey 1131
Kearney, Lynn 288
Kearns, Martha T. 288
Keating, Barry 700, 1355, 1522
Keating, Charles 1006
Keats, Erza Jack 248
Keatts, John 1259
Keehbauch, Ann 1285
Keeling, Deborah 205, 850
Keels, Jim 9
Keen, Alan 205
Keen, Elizabeth 117, 183, 1106, 1190, 1279
Keen, Stan 371, 1576
Keenan, Joseph 299
Keenan-Bolger, Celia 933, 1554, 1680
Keene, Christopher 20, 673, 1165, 1405, 1816
Keene, Theodora 136
Kehr, Don 45, 726, 1109
Kehrig, Diana 488
Keigwin, Lawrence 1778
Keith, D. 67
Keith, David 1391
Keith, Gertrude 1092
Keith, Isham 494, 1115
Keith, Larry 252, 1048, 1361, 1752
Keith, Lynda 574
Keith, Michael 25, 1733
Keith, Warren 158
Kekana, Fana (David) 1284, 1561
Kekanoho, Joe 1221
Kekuewa, Sonny 1221
Kelakos, Eleni 1648
Kelepovska, Natasha 66, 1131
Kellard, Bill 1106, 1343
Kelleher, Ann 1189
Keller, Ben 60, 1206
Keller, Jeff 244, 1243
Keller, John 1446
Keller, Ramona 252
Kellery, Kate 1343
Kellett, Robert 1171
Kelley, Hilary 91
Kelley, Norman 331, 609, 677, 1227, 1789
Kellin, Orange 1198
Kellogg, Christine 172
Kellogg, John 1042
Kellogg, Marjorie 133, 634, 1397
Kellogg, Mary Ann 1200
Kellogg, Peter 929
Kellogg, Riley 1552
Kellstrom, Gail 345
Kelly, Brian 42
Kelly, Catherine 1329
Kelly, Charisse 803
Kelly, David Patrick 394, 414, 583, 909, 1426
Kelly, Dennis 1547
Kelly, Donna 463
Kelly, Drew 1671
Kelly, Eric 693
Kelly, Frank 497, 1215
Kelly, Glen 1383, 1421
Kelly, Hubert 1124
Kelly, Jack 396
Kelly, Janey 110
Kelly, Jean Louisa 778
Kelly, John 66, 805, 1055, 1131
Kelly, Joy 1070
Kelly, Jude 1444
Kelly, Kate 345, 509
Kelly, Katherine 591
Kelly, Kathleen 1303
Kelly, Kathleen Rosamond 1298
Kelly, Kevin 67
Kelly, Martha 539
Kelly, Mary Pat 3
Kelly, Michael 3, 392
Kelly, Mickey 3
Kelly, Patricia 1640
Kelly, Randy 770
Kelly, Ritamarie 675
Kelly, Ruth 1131
Kelly, Sean 377, 1112, 1114
Kelly, Sondra 574
Kelly, Thomas 173
Kelm, Joan 331
Kelman, Debra 842
Kelso, Betsy 627
Kelton, Gene 258, 316, 480
Kelton, Patti 68
Kemble, Christopher 1768
Kemeny, A. 1512
Kemeny, C.E. 1512
Kemmerling, Michael 456, 1030
Kemp, Lindsay 1662
Kempson, Voight 127, 326, 342
Kenan, Dodi 834
Kendall, Elaine 1648
Kendall, Jo 241
Kendall, Trent Armand 106
Kendrick, D. Polly 830
Kener, David 1362, 1502
Kenley, Joan 1265
Kenn, Dana 1303
Kenneally, Jerri 369
Kennedy, Anne 502, 1479, 1700
Kennedy, Beau 1305
Kennedy, Clive 611
Kennedy, Craig 453, 612, 614
Kennedy, Mimi 664, 710
Kennedy, R. Lee 328
Kennedy, William 652
Kennedy, Zona 76
Kennel, Laurice Simmons 1022
Kennel, Louis 379
Kennett, Karl 377
Kenney, Janet 1029
Kennon, Skip 484, 690, 1297
Kennon, Walter Edgar 1637
Kennon-Wilson, James 1021
Kenny, Doug 1114
Kenny, Jack 1362
Kent, Edgar 619, 620
Kent, Edmond 619
Kent, Gordon 1348
Kent, Guy 201
Kent, Jeffrey 738, 825
Kent, Linda 1029
Kent, Mildred 578
Kent, Peter 902
Kent, Stapleton 1092
Kentner, Joe 864
Kenway, Albert 136
Kenyon, Jennifer 469
Kenyon, Larry 1293
Kenyon, Laura 1514
Kenyon, Neal 153, 199, 341, 342, 343, 1483, 1539
Keogh, Tom 421
Keohavong, P.I. 1073
Kepros, Nicholas 1641
Kercheval, Ken 128, 1824
Kermoyan, Michael 504, 1399
Kern, Jerome 883, 902, 1101
Kern, Jill 768
Kern, Mina 441
Kern, Teddy 1030
Kernan, David 1491
Kerner, Ethel 1131
Kerner, Norberto 1107
Kernochan, Sarah 1478
Kerns, Jane 1589
Kerns, Linda 1194, 1201, 1484
Kerns, Rhoda 1448
Kerr, E. Katherine 1710
Kerr, Elaine 316
Kerr, Herbert 266
Kerr, J. Herbert, Jr. 500, 1781
Kerr, Janet 191, 1286
Kerr, Jean 1101
Kerr, Nancy 56
Kerr, Walter 1101
Kerry, Joyce 1163
Kershaw, Whitney 539
Kert, Larry 268, 912, 1096, 1167, 1362
Kerz, Leo 1563, 1596
Kesselman, Wendy 847
Kessler, Kurt 1131
Kessler, Marc 1656
Kessler, Merle 1392
Kessler, Michael 1014
Kessler, Robert (Bob) 858, 1161, 1261, 1318, 1754
Kessler, Zale 1162
Kett, Carissa 362
Kevin-Robert 1600
Key, Eugene 814
Key, Tom 321
Keyes, Daniel 192, 705
Keyser, Stephanie 1536
Keyte, Shula 1233
Kezer, Glenn 1175, 1311
Khalsa, Hari Dam Kaur 927
Khoury, Cynthia 1285
Khoutieff, Jeannine 1541
Khumalo, Leleti 1401
Khumalo, Sibiniso 1401
Khuzwayo, Mhlathi 1401
Kia, Carolee 1221
Kiara, Dorothy 516
Kibbe, Jon-David 1785
Kibler, Belva 1086
Kibrig, Joan 317, 1824
Kieller, Deborah 1552
Kiesler, Frederick (J.) 762, 1217
Kiesman, Jeremy 1590
Kievman, Carson 1731
Kilborn, Michael 1278
Kilborne, William S., Jr. 678
Kilgarriff, Patricia 1637
Kilgour, Adam 876
Kilian, Leslie Ann 378
Kilik, Howard 1671
Killam, Tracy 1391
Killiam, Paul 1116
Killian, Scott 910
Kilmer, Theodore 334
Kilpatrick, Joan 823, 834, 952
Kilpatrick, Mary 322
Kim, Do Hyeong 889
Kim, Do Kyung 889
Kim, Hae Shik 1655
Kim, Hak Jun 889
Kim, Hak Muk 889
Kim, Hakjun 889
Kim, He Jung 889
Kim, Hee Gab 889
Kim, Ho Jin 889
Kim, Hyun Dong 889
Kim, Hyun Sook 889
Kim, Kwang Lim 889
Kim, Min Soo 889
Kim, Peter 72
Kim, Randy 860
Kim, Shane 673
Kim, Soo Jin 889
Kim, Sung Ki 889
Kim, Taewon 889
Kim, Willa 10, 421, 435, 528, 754, 1311
Kim, Wonjung 889
Kim, Young Hwan 889
Kim, Young Ju 889
Kim, Young Ok 889
Kimball, Chad 597, 1103
Kimball, Christina Kumi 214
Kimball, Robert 1029
Kimball, Steve 1392
Kimball, Wendy 960
Kimbrough, Charles 33
Kimbrough, Fred 201, 236
Kimes, Bruce 490
Kimmel, Alan 73, 238, 442, 1774, 1828
Kimmel, Bruce 1126
Kimmel, Jess 384
Kimmel, Joel 73
Kimmell, Marcia 904
Kimmons, Ken 509
Kincaid, Leslie 706
Kinch, Myra 1564
Kind, Richard 1209
Kindberg, Wendell 322, 840, 841, 842, 1354, 1408, 1477, 1676
Kinder, Suzanne 920
Kindle, Tom 1349
Kindred, Graham 1260, 1669
King, Anthony 645
King, Bradley Clayton 133
King, Carole 1340, 1591
King, Cleo 2
King, Curtis, Jr. 854
King, David L. 153
King, Dee 1784
King, Denis 1304
King, Donna 133
King, Elizabeth 184
King, Glenngo 1738
King, Jim 15
King, John Michael 676
King, Johnny 1750
King, Larry 376
King, Larry L. 133
King, Lawrence 234
King, Michael Patrick 72
King, Molly 821
King, Patsi 1185, 1193
King, Paul L. 1023
King, Raymond 207
King, Richard 200
King, Robert 1682
King, Rosalie 815, 816
King, Shirley 1095
King, Teresa 823, 834, 920, 925
King, Wilson 326
King, Woodie, Jr. 9, 105, 156, 266, 278, 382, 592, 593, 709, 736, 959, 1174, 1287, 1307, 1423, 1579, 1738
Kingery, Larry 125
Kingman, Dan 254, 488
Kingsbury, Deirdre 1753
Kingsley, Evelyn 98, 489, 1647
Kingsley, Gershon 324, 504, 714, 867
Kingston, Morgan 1597
Kinkman, Tamara 697
Kinney, Debbie 125
Kinney, Sharon 764, 915
Kinsey, Bennett 357
Kinsey, Tony 449
Kinsley, Dab 878
Kinsley, Dan 1510, 1708
Kipnis, Claude 1044
Kipnis, Dinah 1044

Kirby, Bruce 1448
Kirby, J. David 121
Kirby, Jan 379
Kirby, Joel 294
Kirby, Ric 1310
Kirchner, Lisa 713, 726, 1629
Kirk, Al 885
Kirk, Keith Byron 430, 1121
Kirk, Tom 1402
Kirker, Janet 665
Kirkham, Mark 1349
Kirkham, Willi 1470
Kirkpatrick, Kathi 834
Kirksey, Kirk 1307
Kirkwood, James 283
Kirkwood, Kevin Smith 721
Kirle, Bruce 389
Kirns, Roberta 1487
Kirsch, Carolyn 283, 1595
Kirsch, Jay 1477
Kirsh, Bob 727
Kirshenbaum, David 398, 1554
Kirtland, Louise 725
Kirwin, Terry 1486, 1785
Kiser, Franklin 1716
Kiser, Terry 292, 707, 1082
Kishon, Ephraim (E.) 898, 1026, 1701
Kissane, Joseph 505
Kissin, Carol 1817
Kit McClure and Her All-Girl Orchestra 144
Kitsakos, Steve 1418
Kitt, Eartha 1052
Kizziah, Tommy 1720
Klaif, Sharon 1242
Klain, Margery 102
Klapmeyer, Renee 462
Klappas-Pariseau, Pam 143
Klashman, Michael 398
Klausen, Ray 1245, 1818
Klausner, Brachah 529
Klausner, Terri 114, 586, 656, 916
Klausner, Willette Murphy 1623
Klavan, Laurence 114
Kleban, Edward (Ed) 283, 296, 1710
Kleiman, Harlan P. 676
Klein, Adam 1020
Klein, Allen Edward 985
Klein, Amanda (J.) 8, 299, 577, 1232, 1693, 1733, 1752
Klein, Bob (Robert) 1352
Klein, Christopher 827
Klein, I.W. 989
Klein, Joseph 827
Klein, Joy 961
Klein, Larry 22, 1415
Klein, Maxine 869
Klein, N.A. 1146
Klein, Neal 186
Klein, Paul 1083
Klein, Randy 699, 786
Klein, Reid 870
Klein, Will 198
Kleinbort, Barry 1421, 1651
Kleinerman, Kay Elise 1771
Kleinhesselink, Pauline 1229
Kleinsinger, George 1101
Klementowicz, Paul 658
Klenosky, William (J.) 871, 1713
Kletter, Debra J. 23, 180, 370, 577, 919, 1027, 1334, 1365, 1624
Klewan, Suzanne 709
Kline, Kevin 138, 207, 345, 387, 496, 1250, 1270
Kline, Linda 296, 1102
Kline, Norman 44, 1514
Kling, Irene Frances 117
Klingman, Ari Zohar 404
Klitz, Jeffrey 1573
Klucevsek, Guy 282
Kluger, Bruce 856
Klugman, Kate 1034
Kmeck, George 249, 1560
Knaiz, Judy (Judith) 556, 557, 1446, 1606
Knapp, Jacqueline 696
Knapp, Sarah 754, 1141, 1204
Knauer, Ian 302
Knechtges, Dan 1680
Knee, Allan 359
Kneebone, Tom 1393
Kneeland, Bob 1690
Kneeland, Richard 360
Knight, Adam 1233
Knight, Darwin 461, 572, 667, 1108, 1173, 1319
Knight, Eric W. 238
Knight, June 226
Knight, Michael 464
Knight, Percival 136
Knight, Ronald 902
Knight, Shirley 660
Knight, William 192, 1169
Knisely, George 621
Knittel, Wolfgang 720, 1635
Knoblauh, M.T. 575
Knoll, Lesley Ann 66
Knowles, Christopher 397
Knowles, Liz 632
Knowles, Mark 730
Knowles, Michael 644
Knowles, Michael D. 1537
Knowlton, Sarah 1351
Knox, Dorothy 578
Knox, Jeffrey 1776
Knox, Marion 156
Knudson, Kurt 599, 1557
Knull, Chuck 1283
Kobart, Ruth 609, 1021, 1179, 1474, 1564
Kobatake, Risa 804
Kobayashi, Yukiko 602
Kobin, Joan 1676
Koch, David 275
Koch, George 545
Kociolek, Ted 8, 1410
Kocis, Stephen 38
Koebel, Kristina 42
Koenig, Tommy 1113
Koerber, Betty 870
Kogel, George 1481
Koger, Jeffrey S. 1556
Kohan, Alan 1318
Kohl, Lacey 1779
Kohner, Joy 1136
Kohoe, Sheila 1071
Koka, Juliette 1256, 1257, 1809
Kolas, Mary Lynn 955
Kolatch, David 1787
Kolb, Bliss 1439
Kolb, Mina 705, 1461, 1813
Kolb, Norbert U. 474, 1362
Kolber, Larry 854
Kolber, Lynne 1134
Kole, Debby 906
Kole, Hilary 1210
Kole, Robert 743
Koletzke, Peter 910
Kolinski, Joseph 491, 695, 726, 949, 1637
Kolitz, Ziv 490
Koll, Frances 68
Kolmes, Matthew 1340
Kolo, Fred 1607
Koloc, Bonnie 726
Kolodney, Nancy 834
Komar, Arthur 1621
Komara, Lisa 362
Komolova, Valentina 849
Kon, Henoch 441
Kondek, Charles 451, 1782
Konecky, Jennifer 1754
Kong, Gayln 1214
Konicus, Naomi 455
Konopka, Albin 778, 999
Konrardy, Nancy 1113
Kook, Edward F. 969
Kookoolis, Joseph M. 1504
Koots, Calvin 951
Kootsher, Alan Lee 125
Kopelan, Iris 1483
Kopfstein-Penk, Alicia 1029
Kopreski, Alice 1759
Kops, Bernard 654
Kopyc, Frank (W.) 203, 660, 912, 1167, 1283
Korbich, Eddie 70, 424, 596, 1581
Kordel, John 74, 1379
Koreto, Paul 126, 556, 557, 558, 852, 1069
Korey, Alix (Alexandra) 41, 484, 515, 791, 818, 929, 1144, 1270, 1375, 1547, 1778
Korey, Lois (Balk) 531, 1754
Korf, Gene R. 52
Korf, Mia 596, 1410
Korie, Michael 641, 673
Korins, David 502, 1225, 1736
Korman, Cliff 475
Korman, Jess J. 745
Kornfeld, Lawrence 392, 613, 701, 756, 831, 925, 928, 998, 1017, 1231, 1311, 1739, 1757
Kornfeld, Robert 1354
Kornfeld, Sarah 392
Kornick, Kevin 1516
Korthaze, Dick 1119, 1254
Korzen, Anne 192
Korzen, Annie 1510
Kosarin, Michael 1037
Kosik, Frank 1670
Kosis, Tom 144, 408
Kostalik-Boussom, Linda 1624
Kostroff, Michael 302, 1434
Kotis, Greg 1712
Kotite, Toni 424
Kotler, Jill 1434
Kotlowitz, Dan 883
Kottke, David 42, 401
Kotze, Sandra 1284
Koutoukas, H.M. 1280
Koutsoukos, Thom 722, 1716
Kovarova, Ludmilla 1609
Kowal, Marsha 916
Kowal, Ted 434
Kozak, Michael 1140
Kozinn, Marshall H. 949
Kozlov, Gennady 849
Koztowski, Jerzy 1275
Kraber, Tony 98, 578, 1164
Krachmalnick, Samuel 254
Kragen, Ken 916
Krahnert, Matthias 1281
Krajicek, Julie Signitzer 711
Krakowski, Jane 1048
Kraman, Lawrence 1228, 1339
Kramarich, Irene 1563
Kramer, Bruce 294
Kramer, Carla 36
Kramer, George 1714
Kramer, Glenn 1263, 1467
Kramer, Joel 184, 259
Kramer, Les 1385
Kramer, Milton 97
Kramer, Nathaniel 1347
Kramer, Stanley 819, 1212
Kramer, Terry Allen 645, 1347
Kramer, Travis 1786
Krane, David 42, 972, 1709
Krantz, Mark 668
Kranz, Carl 362
Krasnansky, Jennifer 1240
Krasner, Vivian 1337
Krass, Michael 727, 973, 1326, 1545, 1598, 1748
Kratochvilova, Zdenka 1609
Kraus, Andrew 653
Kraus, Lewis 235
Kraus, Sarah 1416
Krause, Karl (Patrick) 488, 1552
Krause, Marc 604
Krause, Richard 569, 947, 1063, 1111, 1621
Krause, Werner (Kruse) 137, 1775
Krausz, Diane F. 685
Krausz, Rob 685
Kravat, Jerry 518, 521, 525, 603, 1037
Kravets, Richard 11
Krawetz, Andrew 1660
Krawford, Gary 360, 402
Krebs, Beatrice 92
Krebs, Eric 143, 213, 247, 452, 492, 555, 606, 651, 866, 934, 979, 1240, 1362, 1593, 1638, 1658, 1760, 1809
Kreidler, Louis 340
Kreiger, Barbara Zinn 1503
Kreiner, Marty 1661
Kreisberg, Jonathan 502
Kreisel, Joseph 1780
Kreitzberg, Danny 920, 998, 1349
Krell, Jeff 808
Krenz, Frank 1482, 1495
Kreppel, Paul 146, 582, 610, 685, 1313
Kresley, Ed 350, 852, 1069, 1255
Kresley, Edmond 1149, 1150, 1522
Kress, Mark H. 825
Kressin, Lianne 1297
Kressyn, Miriam 119, 147, 489, 608, 666, 684, 1822
Kreste, Mary 1601
Kreuder, Peter 1241
Krich, Gretchen 1826
Krieger, Barbara Zinn 114, 285, 413, 658, 848, 1752
Krieger, Henry 1662
Kriger, Pam 1832
Kriger, Sam 914
Krikorian, Shari 1544
Krimsky, Jerrold 494, 578, 1115
Krimsky, John 449, 450, 494, 578, 1091, 1092, 1639, 1640
Kripi, Jack 1200
Krisher, Richard 1636
Kristen, Ilene 322, 625, 1037
Kristin, Karen 1274
Kristofer, Lou 1236
Kritzer, Leslie 597, 627
Krivoshei, David 401
Kroenke, Whitney 742
Kroeze, Jan 397
Krofft, Marty 1293
Krofft, Sid 1293
Krohn, David 1291
Kroll, Abe 82
Krone, George 601
Krone, Gerald 1265
Kroner, John 246, 892, 1595
Krones, Fred H. 181, 1554
Krones, Kip Richard 486
Krongold, Susan 1731
Kronold, Richard 1242
Kronzer, Jim 1700
Kroopf, Milton 505
Kropfl, Paul 1764
Kroschell, Joan 661, 705, 1539
Krown, Hans 960
Krueger, Ellen 453
Krug, Ruth 1086
Kruge, Phoebe 66
Kruger, Dan 81, 1343
Kruger, Joan 1131
Kruger, Karen 1194
Kruger, Ottilie 1116
Krugman, Ken 1514
Krummins, Eddie 1577
Krupa, Anatol 1275
Krupska, Dania 1172, 1448, 1604
Kruse, Werner 1241
Kuahulu, Dukie 1221
Kubala, Michael 55, 214, 406
Kubera, Joseph 1731
Kuczewski, Ed 1030
Kudakiewicz, Feliks 1275
Kudisch, Marc 443, 583, 1422, 1613
Kudriavtsev, Dimitri 849
Kuehl, Craig 392, 998, 1231
Kuehl, Matt 612
Kuemmerle, Clyde 1561
Kuestner, Charles 1131
Kuhlman, Kim 1015
Kuhlman, Ron 283
Kuhn, Hans Peter 294
Kuhn, Judy 69, 413, 1109
Kuhner, John 716, 928, 1592, 1739, 1827
Kukoff, Ben 1605
Kukoff, Bernie 739, 1613
Kulerman, Ruth 1438
Kuller, Doris 292
Kulukundis, Eddie 263
Kunath, Gerd 168
Kunkle, Connie 1016
Kuntz, John (B.) 884, 1153, 1767
Kupferman, Meyer 831
Kupfrian, Russ 1522
Kupperstein, Gordon 712
Kupris, Maija 1370
Kurilla, Dorothy 779
Kurisu-Chan 1674
Kurka, Robert 609
Kurlan, David 1131
Kurland, Rachel 981
Kurnitz, Julie 467, 757, 823, 834, 920, 928, 998, 1147, 1231, 1280, 1501
Kurnitz, Lyz 834, 920
Kurowski, Ron 1310
Kurowski, Susan 198
Kurshals, Raymond 349
Kurt, Stefan 26, 168
Kurtz, John Henry 1025
Kurtz, Linda 955
Kurtz, Marcia 831
Kurtz, Norman 385
Kurtzuba, Stephanie 837, 1128, 1577
Kushnarenko, Irena 849
Kushner, James 1019
Kushner, Tony 252
Kusner, Jon 1373
Kuss, Richard 140
Kutner, Daniel 738
Kutner, Michael 155
Kux, Bill 1554
Kuznetsov, Villor 849
Kuznetsov, Vladimir 849
Kwak, Min Kyeng 889
Kwartin, Paul 1140
Kya-Hill, Robert 466, 1580
Kybart, Peter 1666
Kyd, Joanna 920
Kyle, Dana 1367
Kyle, Don 1409
Kyrieleison, Jack 1470
Kyte, Mary 41, 237, 588, 1643, 1654

La Barbera, John T. 859
LaBenz, Joe, IV 1340
Laboissonniere, Wade 1830
Labour, Elaine 935
LaBourdette, Katie 906
Lacamoire, Alex 760
Lacen, Modesto 262
Lacey, Bill 616
Lacey, Florence 434, 1546, 1565, 1700
Lacey, Matthew 1421
Lach, Mary Ann 1525
La Chance, Julie 1608
LaChance, Manette 266
La Chane, Julie 1145
LaChanze 222, 375
Lachinsky, Amy 1207
LaChiusa, Michael John 2, 130, 233, 496, 683, 933, 1250, 1422
Lachman, Ronald A. 73
Lackey, Herndon 514, 1109
LaCorte, Lisa 59
LaCroix, Denise 510
la Cuesta, Jose de 1148
Lacy, Deborah 475
Lacy, Tom 962, 1446
Ladd, Hank 1475
Ladenhelm, Paul 1391
Laderman, Ezra 1023
Ladson, Rick 259
LaDuca, David 1353
LaDuca, Phil 229, 1321
Laev, James 614
LaFarga, Nina 760
LaFerla, Sandro 1098
Laffer, Hong-Van 1629
Lafferty, Thom 65
Laffey, Bruce 725
La Forge, Eleanor 698
La Fosse, Robert 628, 1514
la Fuente, Benjamin de 1416
Lage, Elizabeth 1689
LaGravanese, Richard 1
La Guardia, Midge 827
LaGuerre, Irma Estel 1733
Lahm, David 940
Lahr, John 377, 428
Laibson, Michael David 752, 1343
Laine, Cleo 1109
Lainez, Manuel Mujica 188
Laird, Chris 133
Laird, Marvin 1386
Laisne, Stephane 1281
Lake, Randy 1508
The Lake Sisters 1543
Lakeman, Alfred 1204
Lally, Dale 752
Lally, James 1003
Lam, Diane 1214
Lam, Zoie 289, 1410
Lamal, Christopher 101
Lamanna (LaManna), Janine (Jeanine) 273, 1610, 1760
Lamb, Don 87, 160, 381
Lamb, Mary Ann 105
Lamb, Myrna 65, 1072
Lamb, Rael 1039, 1307
Lamb, Stephen 834
Lamb, Sybil 66
Lambert, Jane 369
Lambert, Robert 1702
Lambert, Sally 1062
Lambert, Sherry 1021, 1060
Lambrinos, Theodore (Ted) 68, 1177
Lambrinos, Vassili 693
The Lamb's Club 1119
Lammers, Paul 942, 1447
Lamont, Robin 595, 1573, 1620
Lamos, Mark 264, 628, 670
LaMott, Nancy 781
La Motta, Johnny 587
Lampert, Emma 1451
Lampert, Rachel 1057
Lampl, Suzanne 1073
Lancaster, Dorothy 1713
Lanchester, Elsa 436
Land, David 833
Land, Ken 364, 1702
Landais, Aline 1625
Landau, Daniel 1806
Landau, Elie (Ely) 284, 418
Landau, Leonard M. 974
Landau, Lucy 448
Landau, Natasha 604
Landau, Tina 413, 503, 1404
Landek, Violetta 201, 236
Lander, David 1052
Lander, Judith 88
Lander, Judy 128, 963
Landers, Gayle Kelly 1079
Landers, Matt 1595
Landes, Frances 1109
Landes, Francine 1055, 1109
Landesman, Fran 949
Landesman, Heidi 699, 1036, 1048, 1334, 1710
Landi, Jami 121
Landi, Michael 550
Landi, Phil 1364
Landis, Bebe (Sacks) 288, 915
Landis, Erol K.C. 43
Landis, Jeanette 771, 848, 1255
Landis, Lynn 503, 791, 805, 1726
Landis, Sam 866
Landon, Hal, Sr. 1618
Landon, Maryellen 1028
Landron, Jack 107, 359, 1579, 1699, 1761
Landrum, Kinny 1025
Landry, Carole 1655
Landry, Glenda 56
Landwehr, Hugh 696
Landy, Christopher 1419
Lane, Allen W. 197
Lane, Allen Walker 1305
Lane, Burton 1100
Lane, Diane 1384
Lane, Donya 463
Lane, Frances 826
Lane, Kenneth 1729
Lane, Nancy 283
Lane, Nathan 443, 961
Lane, Stewart F. 267, 424
Laney, Lanier 99
Lang, Alyson 1435
Lang, Barbara 63, 1379
Lang, Eric 1007
Lang, Harold 367, 1185
Lang, Pearl 666
Lang, Stephen 16
Lang, Steven 420
Lang, Tony 1585
Lang, Victoria 36, 825, 929, 1450
Langan, Kevin 439
Langdon, Gwynn 1315
Langdon-Lloyd, Robert 1722
Lange, Anne 158
Lange, Bobbi 867
Langel, Jodie 742
Langer, Christine 1478
Langerstrom, Karen 1174
Langley, Gary (R.) 976, 1537
Langworth, Joe 1441
Langworthy, David 1551
Langworthy, Norma 1551
Lanier, Jane 825
Lanin, George 876
Lankston, John 256, 673, 1023, 1062, 1137, 1552
Lanman, Victoria 1584
Lanning, Jerry 128, 1043, 1390, 1433
Lansbury, Edgar 595, 1311
Lanteri, Joe 233
Lanyer, Charles 27
Lanzaroni, Bhen 722
Lanzillotti, Leonore 68
la Pena, George de 859
Lapham, Ken 712, 1818
Lapidus, Jerry 500
Lapierre, Beth 1784
Lapine, James 473, 1019, 1121, 1557, 1680
Lapira, Liza 206
LaPlount, Craig 19
LaPrade, Malcolm L. 1780
Larabee, Louise 1481
Laraia, Frank 675
Larbi, Babafumi Ohene Kwado 171
Larch, Louise Lerch 868
Lardner, Ring, Jr. 538
Large, Norman 1462
Larimer, Robert (Bob) 788, 867
Larin, Alexey 849
Larin, Manon 1655
Larke, Paula 958
Larkey, Joan 1008, 1078, 1396
Larkin, Christopher 200
Larkin, Jay 410
Larmon, Leila 1409
Larmore, Jennifer 47
Larned, Mel 1448
LaRocco, Rob 781
LaRoche, Mark 772, 1751
La Roche, Mary 578
La Rosa, Gary 906
La Rosa, Julius 214
Larry, Sheldon 406, 1376
Lars, Byron 282
Larsen, Anika 721, 1425, 1830
Larsen, Carl 1274
Larsen, Jonathan 1351
Larsen, Linda 1166
Larsen, Liz 154, 653, 930, 1121, 1129
Larsen, Morten Gunnar 813
Larsen, Robert 1825
Larsen, William 478, 1265
Larson, Bev 731, 1472
Larson, Francis 505
Larson, Jill 1427
Larson, Jonathan 838, 1634
Larson, Ken 1303
Larson, Linda Marie 396
Larson, Molly 1682
Larson, Peter 218, 219, 829
Larson, Tom "Yogi Bubba" 79
Lasher, Albert C. 405
Lasiter, John 997
Lasker, Harvey 1177
Laskey, Byron 882
Lasko, Gene 490
Lass, Jeff 1691
Lassen, Fred 10
Lasser, Brian 225, 1033, 1141
Lasser, Louise 1614
Latessa, Dick (Richard) 41, 377, 414, 601, 848, 1060, 1253, 1265
Lathan, John 285, 1351
Lathram, Elizabeth 279
Lathrop, Alton 221, 629
Lathrop, Marion 908
Lathrop, Tad 1682
Latimer, Jeffrey 462
Latimer, John 1092
LaTouche, John 92, 238, 244, 600, 601, 942, 1092, 1100, 1101, 1241, 1581, 1688
La Tourneaux, Robert 1397
Latowicz, Karol 1342, 1453, 1745
Latta, Richard 934, 1138, 1157
Lauber, Liza 45
Lauderdale, Jim 321
Lauer, Marion 1221
Laufer, Armin 988
Laufer, Murray 56, 1393
Laughlin, Jane 68
Laughlin, Sharon 1072
Laughton, Charles 436
Lauinger, Joe 983
Lau-Kee, Valerie 1300, 1410
Laun, Elna 226
Laur, Robert W. 1287
Lauren, Cynde 1151
Laurence, James Howard 1787
Laurence, Larry 1131
Laurenson, Diana 1015
Laurenti, Mario 245, 1369
Laurents, Arthur 157, 992, 1106, 1717
Laurents, Clyde 582, 1221
Lauricella, Ruth 1512
Laurita, Annie 505
Lauter, Linda 1721
Lautner, Joe 870, 1192
LaVallee, Bill 177
Laveau, Albert 1633
Lavel, Dick 1095
Lavelle, Pat 414
Lavender, Mark 1801
Lavergneau, Rene 709
La Verni, Marie 1145
Lavin, Christine 2
Lavin, Linda 535, 558, 714, 986, 1172, 1754
Lavine, Audrey 322, 681
Lavine, Michael 148
Lavon, Garrick 960
LaVon, Lora 845
Law, Jenny Lou 531, 908
Lawhead, Mark 1007
Lawhon, Carol 1314
Lawing, Skip 1541
Lawless, Sean 1512
Lawless, Sue 185, 272, 338, 564, 758, 761, 1153, 1290, 1361, 1362, 1446, 1527, 1644
Lawley, Lynda Lee 1746
Lawlor, James Reed 550, 1108
Lawn, Sand 484, 1173
Lawrence, Eddie 1100, 1627
Lawrence, Elliott 1035
Lawrence, Helena 1131
Lawrence, Henry 1131
Lawrence, Jerome 954
Lawrence, Josie 1160
Lawrence, Julie Fain 838, 1826
Lawrence, Lela 1780
Lawrence, Mal Z. 1250
Lawrence, Megan 1712
Lawrence, Melinda 1655
Lawrence, Miriam 1221
Lawrence, Stephen (a/k/a Steven) 1, 852, 1069, 1142, 1154, 1488, 1713
Lawrence, Tony 1001
Lawrence, Vera Brodsky 190
Lawrence, Yvette 208
Lawrie, Ted 112
Laws, Eloise 777
Laws, Maury 1078
Laws, Sam 238
Lawson, Daniel 1188, 1306
Lawson, Denis 979
Lawson, Douglas M. 157
Lawson, Kevin 95
Lawson, Leigh 751
Lawson, Leslie 853
Lawson, Roger 81, 152, 370, 386, 1267
Lax, Roger 1747
Layton, Joe 1185, 1193
Layton, Joseph 1131
Layton, Turner 1543
Lazansky, Ed 392, 928, 998
Lazansky, Edward 1017
Lazarus, Paul 672, 1243
Lazarus, Sara Louise 810, 1663
Lazer, Peter 1562
Lazowski, Yurek 66
Lea, Barbara 1045
Leabo, Loi 1412
Leach, Dan 76, 1666
Leach, Kitty 586
Leach, Nicole 208, 474
Leach, Wilford 186, 250, 726, 1109, 1146, 1270
Leacock, Victoria 1634
Leadbetter, Betsy Ann 1483
Leader, Charles 976
League, Michelle 1134
Leake, Damien 278, 708
Leake, Roy, Jr. 765
Leake, Sundy (Leigh) 785, 1070
Leaming, Susan 505
Lean, Roberta 585
Lear, Evelyn 435, 1088
Lear, Robert N. 1437
Learned, James 349
Leary, Leer Paul 1556
Leasor, James 957
Leath, Justin Brennen 1736
Leath, Ron 1108
Leather, Captain 944
Leavel, Beth 213, 950, 1702
Leavitt, Gerald 1131
Leavitt, Max 1179
Leavitt, Phillip 505
Lebeaux, Annie 801, 1505
LebHar, Dione H. 777
LeBlanc, Christopher 1660
LeBolt, Terry 1800
Lebowsky, Babs Warden 1493
Lebowsky, Stanley (Stan) 87, 160, 1259
LeBrun, Barbara 1094
Lecesne, James 1197
LeCompte, Jo Ann 946
Ledbetter, Victor 439
Ledbetter, William 256, 673, 1023, 1062, 1137, 1816
LeDonne, Denise 359
Ledoux, Paul 411
Lee, Andrea 1160
Lee, Baayork 283, 731, 1343
Lee, Bernice 1117
Lee, Bobby 109, 1480
Lee, Carl 420
Lee, Cheena 212
Lee, Chris 6, 1700
Lee, Darren 1250
Lee, Deborah 613
Lee, Eugene 784, 1631
Lee, Franne 185, 244, 424, 473, 1538
Lee, Gihieh 1499
Lee, Gypsy Rose 335
Lee, He Jeong 889
Lee, Hee Jung 889
Lee, Irving (A.) (Allen) 268, 709, 869, 1358
Lee, Jack 528, 957, 1424, 1743
Lee, Jack F. 1507
Lee, Jae Gu 889
Lee, Jae Hwan 889
Lee, Janda 1080
Lee, Jennifer Paulson 1523
Lee, Ji Eun 889
Lee, Ji Youn 889
Lee, Jo Ann 494
Lee, Keri 1186
Lee, Kyoung Woo 889
Lee, Leslie 603

Lee, Mable (M.) (Mabel) 82, 704, 1550
Lee, Minerva 1543
Lee, Ming Cho 58, 188, 649, 1397
Lee, Onike 885, 1388
Lee, Ralph 1231
Lee, Robert E. 954
Lee, Saja 772
Lee, Sang Ryul 889
Lee, Sondra 435, 464
Lee, Stephen 1304
Lee, Sun Mun 889
Lee, Sung Ho 889
Lee, Woo Jong 889
Lee, Yasmine 1073
Lee, Yolanda 278
Leeds, Doug 1538
Leeds, Jordan 738, 739
Leeds, Michael 685, 711, 1141, 1454, 1573, 1709
Leeds, Nancy 631
Leeds, Phil 98, 714, 1021, 1481
Leeka, Carter 510
Leeka, Lori 510
Leeman, Joanne 507
Leeper, Ray 767
Lees, Bob 698, 783
Leete, Richard 759
Leff, Keri 45
Legendary Soul Stirrers 615
LeGrady, Tom 535
Legrand, Michel 1697
LeGros, John 591
Lehew, Stephen 1379, 1568, 1569
Lehl, Philip 727
Lehman, Alfred (Al) 598, 870, 902, 1420
Lehman, Jeanne 926
Lehman, John 856
Lehman, Orin 44
Lehman, Paul 405
Lehman, Ross 1788
Lehman, Susan 328, 509, 1420
Lehmann, Jo Anna (a/k/a JoAnn) 215, 598
Lehr, LeRoy 628
Lehr, Wilson 1164
Lehrer, Ernest 453, 465, 1040
Lehrer, Tom 1654
Leib, Russell 1035
Leiber, Jerry 854
Leibman, Ron 1146
Leidholdt, David 1815
Leigh, Carolyn 371, 616, 1447, 1576
Leigh, Courtney 3
Leigh, Dan 64, 113, 414, 1045, 1685
Leigh, Mitch 289
Leigh, Rowland 1823
Leight, Warren 475, 1037
Leighton, Jan 1385
Leighton, Paul 1347
Leinek, Mischa 1775
Leinsdorf, Erich 1563, 1596
Leisek, Liz 1298
Leisten, Annette 81
Leith, Alan 1316
Leland, Corey 863
Leland, Robert 384
Lema, Julia 203, 214, 788, 934
LeMassena, William 466
Lemay, Maurice 1655
Lemback, Michael 54
Lembeck, Harvey 1254
Lemberg, Stephen M. 809
Lemenager, Nancy 1135
Lemmo, Josephine 389
Lemmon, Shirley 1483, 1685
Lenat, Jesse (Sinclair) 503, 1188, 1351
Lench, Katherine 1171
Leneham, John 1459
Lenehan, Gene 1135
Lenehan, John 197
l'Enjoleur, Julot 713
Lenn, Robert 1221, 1566
Lennart, Isobel 1717
Lenney, Dinah 1785
Lennon, John 1168, 1426, 1666
Lenny, Jim 1386
Lenny, Kim Lang 1386
LeNoire, Rosetta 51, 59, 107, 116, 124, 127, 153, 171, 197, 221, 223, 238, 313, 333, 359, 420, 500, 591, 644, 682, 712, 785, 803, 885, 960, 995, 1001, 1009, 1016, 1065, 1070, 1148, 1207, 1223, 1232, 1300, 1305, 1370, 1434, 1467, 1509, 1525, 1544, 1550, 1781, 1785
Lenox, Adriane 115, 252, 383, 749
Lenya, Lotte 204, 1626, 1627
Leo, Tom 1082
Leon, Dorothy 625
Leon, Geoff 225, 1196, 1480
Leon, James 104
Leon, Rick 703
Leon, Ruth 46
Leon, Tania 726
Leonard, Donna Lee 68
Leonard, Francine 1281
Leonard, Joan 68
Leonard, Lu 1119
Leonard, Michael 877, 1751
Leonard, Richard J. 341, 661
Leonard, Roger 360, 807
Leonardo, Joseph 539, 781
Leonardos, Urylee 152, 501
Leone, John 78
Leone, Vivian 659, 732, 1491, 1706
Leong, Terry 821, 1321, 1721
Leongrande, Ernest 1274
Leonhardt, Robert 245
Leonhart, Jay 1421
Leonora, Lily 136
Leonov, Andrey 849
Leporska, Zoya 1164, 1409, 1552
Lerer, Shifra 147, 1212, 1342, 1453, 1822
Leritz, Lawrence 193
Lerman, April 1340
Lerman, Liz 170
Lerner, Alan Jay 843, 1096, 1100
Lerner, Bob 350
Lerner, Diki 1447
Lerner, Dorothy 1727
Lerner, Gene 128, 129
Lerner, Sharon 356
LeRoy, Gloria 121, 1452
LeRoy, Hal 76
LeRoy, Peggy 1594
Lesawyer, Mary 92, 331, 609, 1474, 1789
Lesco, Andrew 1755
Lescsak, Richard 1119
Leshner, Lori 1764
Lesko, Andrew Orestes 761
Lesko, John 821, 1096
Leslee, Ray 78, 1519
Leslie, Bud 383
Leslie, Carol 918
Leslie, Charles 1045
Leslie, Diane 319
Lesniak, Shanna 717
Lessac, Michael 1437
Lessane, Leroy 93
Lesser, Gene 117, 183, 1471
Lesser, Sally (J.) 939, 1222, 1353, 1365, 1391, 1747
Lessner, Joanne Sydney 485
Lester, Amy 42
Lester, Ketty 238
Letang, Ellie (Eleanor) 153, 1467, 1550
LeTang, Henry 82, 153, 212, 1467, 1550
Lett, Gordon 1560
Letta, Linda 562
Lettich, Sheldon 1664
Levandoski, Frank 1349
Levans, Daniel 49, 612
Levant, Dee Dee 591
Levant, Lila 1511
Levda, Yakov 849
Leve, Harriet Newman 1530
Leve, Samuel 1740
Leveillee, Claude 598
Leven, Jeremy 1312
Levenson, Gabriel 1732
Levenson, Jeanine T. 349
Levenson, Keith 58, 293
Levenson, Seth 293
Leventhal, Harold 1804
Lever, Johnetta 224
Leveridge, Lynn Ann 117
Levering, Kate 463
Levern 1423
Levi, Baruk 1620
Levi, Gabriel 362
Levi, Richard 284
Levin, Chaim 1051
Levin, Ira 1101
Levin, Jane 649
Levin, Natalie 1336
Levin, Sylvan 1474
Levin, Yoav 863
Levine, Bill 87, 126, 160, 556, 557, 558, 1142, 1576
Levine, Daniel C. 612, 1110
Levine, David I. 821
Levine, Elliot 1264
Levine, Florence 619
Levine, Gary 1054
Levine, James 574, 628
Levine, Lainie 902
Levine, Maurice 912, 1167, 1582
Levine, Rhoda 324, 362, 481, 507, 707, 745, 941, 962, 1440, 1716, 1816, 1824
Levine, Sam 734
Levine, Susan 1310
Levine, Wally 735
Levine, William 616
Levinson, Gary (David) 310, 404, 976
Levinson, Jason 538
Levis, Melissa 837
Levit, Ben 41, 690
Levit, Helen 1616
Levithan, Robert 397, 1197
Levitt, Barry 82, 1212, 1582
Levitt, Betty 1084
Levitt, Bruce 288
Levitt, Harold 1084
Levitt, Sandy 819, 1026, 1212, 1382
Levitt, Sanford 213
Levy, Arnold H. 884
Levy, Charles 566
Levy, Dan 290
Levy, David 1800
Levy, Dorothy 844
Levy, Eric 464
Levy, Esther 647, 648, 1625
Levy, Franklin R. 172, 486, 765
Levy, H. Ross 414
Levy, Jacques 192, 474, 604, 1168, 1169
Levy, Jonathan 1455
Levy, Lorie Cowen 1634
Levy, Madeline 1145
Levy, Marvin David 1088
Levy, Mayra 397
Levy, Simon 1702
Levy, Steven M. 385, 610, 1610
Levy, Ted L. 1406
Lew, Richard 736
Lewandowski, John S. 647
Lewenstein, Oscar 483
Lewin, Jack 1210
Lewin, Jaime 147, 1105, 1745, 1822
Lewin, John 972
Lewine, Richard 446, 494, 578, 1092, 1115, 1116
Lewis, Abigail 376
Lewis, Alde, Jr. 959, 1762
Lewis, Bertha 1521
Lewis, Bobo 858, 1677
Lewis, Boncellia 1070, 1160
Lewis, Brenda 947
Lewis, Carol Jean 682, 1534
Lewis, Charles 1659
Lewis, David 1520
Lewis, Gwen 136
Lewis, Ilene 501
Lewis, J.J. 1595
Lewis, Jenifer 203, 387, 781, 1470
Lewis, Jim 1588
Lewis, John (Richard) 664, 996, 1314, 1335
Lewis, Kecia 375
Lewis, Ken "Krasher" 1235
Lewis, Kenneth 987
Lewis, Laura May 1358, 1701
Lewis, Lee 632
Lewis, Lucille 66
Lewis, Marcia 587, 1048, 1376, 1774
Lewis, Michael 1356
Lewis, Morgan 494, 1115, 1196
Lewis, Nadine 827
Lewis, Nicole 1425, 1458
Lewis, Norm 249, 375
Lewis, Norman 1589
Lewis, O.B. 1682
Lewis, Peter 450
Lewis, Rick 949, 1575
Lewis, Shannon 273
Lewis, Shawn 775
Lewis, Vicki 54, 225, 233, 1201, 1486, 1538, 1693
Lewis-Evans, Kecia 1191, 1370, 1650
Lewisohn, Irene 618, 620, 621
Lewitin, Margot 1231, 1820
Lewk, Bill 1117
Lewman, David 1777
Lewsen, Charles 450
Leynse, Andrew 10, 240
Libbon, Robert P. 1235
Libby, Dennis 716
Liberatore, Joseph 867
Libertini, Dick (Richard) 261, 986, 1528
Liberto, Don 112, 870, 955
Libin, Paul 98, 301, 422, 466, 613, 823
Lichienstein, Todd 1776
Licht, David 441, 666, 1822
Lichtefeld, Michael 484, 791
Lichtenberg, Lonnie 216
Lichtenstein, Harvey 912, 1139, 1167
Liderbach, John C. 505
Lieberman, Donna 233, 1748
Lieberman, Iris 1610
Liebermann, Rolf 137
Lieberson, Kenneth 155
Lieberson, Will 161, 1648
Liebgold, Leon 119, 684, 782, 1032, 1382
Liebling, Howard 126, 160, 557, 1259
Liebman, Joseph 507
Liebman, Steve 142, 1800
Liebowitz, Robert 397
Lieder, Rose 494
Liederman, Susan 623
Lief, Arthur 98
Lien, Mimi 1322
Lifchitz, Max 636
Life, David 1743
Life, Larry 1267
Life, Regge 223, 1232
Lifton, Betsy 182
Lifton, Betty Jean 1081
Lifton, Deborah 362
Ligeti, Peter 747
Lightdale, Hallie 1453
Lightstone, James F. 412
Lightstone, Nina 412
Ligon, Kevin 284
Ligon, Tom 1827
Lihamba, Amandina 20
Liker, George 944
Lile, David 197
Lilig, Jane 1265
Lillis, Joseph (H., Jr.) 288, 319
Lilly, Crystal 156, 501
Lin, Jodi 1322
Lincoln, Michael 14, 222, 285, 751, 1238, 1571
Lind, Kirsten 1338
Lind, Oona 216
Lind, Robert 54
Lind, Trinity 54
Lindemann, Gary 995
Lindemann, Sarah 888
Linden, Hal 63
Linderman, Ed 213, 773, 1026, 1212
Linders, Jeanie 1046
Lindfors, Viveca 204
Lindsay, Elizabeth 372
Lindsay, Gene 1668
Lindsay, Hon. John V. 1689
Lindsay, Howard 63
Lindsay, Kevin 1038
Lindsey, Gene 310, 598, 1704
Lindsey, Kathleen 1046
Lindsey, Robert Nassif 703, 1204, 1670
Lineberger, James 1562
Lines, Harry 809, 1026
Linhart, Buzzy 1666
Link, Peter 1101, 1363, 1395, 1396, 1746
Linn-Baker, Mark 27, 364, 900, 1036, 1187, 1334
Linsenmann, George W. 160
Linstrum, Jon 1444
Linville, Joanne 826
Lion, Margo 668
Lionarons, John S. 1323
Liotta, Jerome 745
Lipitz, Mark 1508
Lipkin, Dick 613
Lipman, David 414
Lipner, Nancy 1380
Lippa, Andrew 273, 830, 1778
Lippin, Renee 1743
Lippman, Richard A. 223
Lipps, Gary 1029
Lippy, Ira 1321
Lipson, Ann K. 1331
Lipson, Laurie 796
Lipton, Dan 933
Lipton, Holly (T.) 419, 1136
Lipton, James 1060
Lipton, Martha 1789
Lipton, Matthew 15, 920, 1349
Lipton, Michael C. 834
Lipton, Richard 467
Lisa, Luba 1611

Lisanby, Charles 33
Lishner, Leon 1626
Lisitza, Lorinda 129
Liss, Joe 1777
Lissauer, Robert 667
Lister, Dorothy 1166
Listman, Charles 1713
Litanny, Danny 1203
Litchfield, Sandt 1476
Litomy, Leslie 1092, 1115
Litt, Jim 326
Litt, Richard 378
Little, Eugene 959, 1633
Little, Gwenlynn 1062
Little, Valisia Lekae 37
Little, Wes 1188
The Little Hippodrome 564
Litvin, Mark 195, 1404
Litvinoff, Seymour 911
Litwin, Alicia 808
Litwin, Wallace 367, 368
Litz, Katherine 332, 925, 928, 1017, 1387
Litzsinger, Sarah E. 1135
Liu, Betty 505
Lively, William Fleet 990
Livengood, Jerry B. 295
Livingston, Jason 1508
Livingston, Jay 1101
Livingston, Robert H. 492, 722, 1038, 1039, 1582, 1677
Livingston, Ruth 369
Livingston, William 374
Livingstone, Annie 1560
Livsey, Christopher 1325
Ljungberg, Gota 1047
Llana, Jose 1186, 1404, 1680
Lloyd, Bert 1565
Lloyd, Christopher 660
Lloyd, Jason Robert 384
Lloyd, John Robert 384
Lloyd, John W. 624
Lloyd, John-Bedford 1287
Lloyd, Ken 876
Lloyd, Lewis 1400
Lloyd, Linda 1029
Lloyd, Norman 600
Lloyd, Pamela 1310
Lloyd, Stephen 112
Lo, Randon 833
Loaf, Meat 1082, 1330
Loar, Rosemary 15, 1326
Lobban, Lynn 1323
Lobel, Adrianne 1, 47, 865, 1139, 1186, 1187
LoBianco, Robert 872, 1200
Lobos, Olga Villa 1179
Lochner, Don 1242
Locilento, Nick 1338
Lock, Kevin 597
Lock, Rebecca 1233
Locke, Robert 59
Lockhart, Laurel 223
Lockhart, Warren 1486
Lockheart, Paula 1495
Lockin, Danny 1083
Locnikar, Jill 749
Loden, Barbara 529
Lodin, Jeff 1296
Loeb, John Jacob 66, 1021, 1221
Loeb, Philip 1192
Loebell, Marc 620, 621, 622
Loesser, Emily 1571, 1651, 1821
Loesser, Frank 1100, 1619
Loew, Steve 636, 1727
Loewe, Frederick 1100
Loffredo, Peter 1119
Logan, Danny 1394
Logan, George 136
Logan, Jack 972, 1732
Logue, Christopher 449
Logue, Spain 65
Lohmann, Otto 121, 698
Lohr, Aaron 103, 1325, 1422
Lokos, Allan 76
Lollos, John 962
Lombard, Dick 59
Lombard, Kirk 658
Lombard, Peter 192, 1739, 1780
Lombardi, Linda 1435
Lombardo, Carmen 66, 1021, 1221
Lombardo, George 1512
Lombardo, Guy 66, 68, 1221
Lombardo, Rick 1584
Lombardozzi, Terri 1398
Lomonaco, Michael 273
Londner, Rosita 5
London, Chet 1445
London, Frank 872
London, George 891
London, Marc 1420, 1754
London, Margot Ross 770
The London Four 1315
Long, Avon 221, 504, 569
Long, C. Mingo 1700
Long, David 844
Long, Garrett 1513
Long, John 117, 958, 1279
Long, Kenn 1659
Long, Loretta 1267
Long, Mark T. 752
Long, Quincy Long 1238
Long, Sue 1477
Long, Susan 390
Long, Tamara 341
Long, Trisha 11, 111, 243, 928, 1017, 1222, 1349, 1776
Long, William Ivey 45, 70, 315, 597, 641, 692, 1197, 1282, 1514, 1651, 1663
Long, Zola 1062
Longbottom, Robert (Bobby) 1215, 1223, 1644
Longwell, Karen 1389
Longworth, David 950
Lonner, Mara 216
Loomer, Lisa 2, 1077
Loomis, Deborah 860
Loomis, Mike 247
Loomis, Rod 1691, 1823
Loos, Anita 598, 1717
Loose, John 1636
Looze, Karen 922
Lopardo, James 198
Loper, Paul 59
Lopez, Belkys 768
Lopez, Cynthia 118
Lopez, J. Victor 920, 1349
Lopez, Priscilla 760, 1129, 1146, 1641, 1758
Lopez, Robert 77
Loquasto, Santo 41, 765, 1588, 1723
Lor, Denise 25, 1386, 1647
Lorca, Robert (Roberto) 379, 488
Lord, Rhonda Liss 1405
Lord, Sylvia 261
Lorentz, Kay 137, 1775
Lorentz, Lore 137, 1775
Loreto, Richard 1015, 1358
Lorey, Rob 538, 954
Lorge, Dana 109
Lorick, Robert 667, 1202
Loring, Marcia 1349
Lorino, Lynn Gay 1172
Lorraine, Janice 59, 1016
Lortel, Lucille 433, 455, 1318, 1627
Lorwin, Liza 1248
los Reyes, Imelda de 208
Losey, Jana 1516
Lotito, Mark 791, 828, 1289
Lou, Cindy 58
Loud, David 52, 1219, 1472
Louden, Tony 276
Loudon, Dorothy 443
Louis, Barbb 197
Louis, Michael 965
Louis, Murray 910
Louise, Mary 221, 504, 1065, 1221, 1509, 1550, 1704
Louise, Merle 271, 1604
Louise, Sara 1452
Louizos, Anna 38, 77, 280, 760, 1634
Loux, Constance 140
Lovci, Marc 1831
Love, Dorothy 268, 1827
Love, Douglas A. 1363
Love, Edward (Ed) 1, 107, 263, 1633, 1709
Love, Kermit 494, 1115, 1116
Lovejoy, Deirdre 658, 755
Loveless, David 83
Lovelle, Herb 313, 1370
Lovett, Marcus 691
Loving, Keith I. 1699
Lovitt, Shifee 819, 1032
Low, Beth-Lynne 1604
Low, Betty 1060
Low, Stephani 86
Lowe, Gwen Hillier 215, 1644
Lowe, Jane 1117
Lowe, Larry 1207, 1283, 1307
Lowe, Ralph 66, 1385
Lowell, Alan 1131
Lowell, Robert 389
Lowenstein, David 1450, 1544, 1772
Lowenstein, Sonia 698, 1265, 1751
Lowenthal, Jason 1608
Lowery, Robert J. 464
Lowman, Jay 1668
Lowman, Sarah 695
Lowrie, Ken 1689
Lowry, Marcella 959
Lowstetter, Ken 1377
Lowther, George Vaughn 1043
Ltd, Free Space 1089
Ltd, Saffron 807
Luard, Nicholas 449
Lubar, Cynthia 397
Lubell, Lily 618, 619, 620, 621, 622
Lucas, Craig 23, 1027, 1624
Lucas, David 605
Lucas, H. Scott 480
Lucas, Harold 1720
Lucas, J. Frank 133
Lucas, Jeanne 1286
Lucas, Jonathan 50, 556, 557, 600, 1431
Lucas, Randy 1720
Lucas, Roxie 512, 526
Lucas, Steve 1694
Lucas, William 1781
Lucchese, Jeff 1681
Luce, William 1410
Lucille 216
Luck, Tracie 1022
Luckinbill, Laurence 707
Ludd, Patricia 434
Ludgin, Chester 92, 331, 609, 677, 1667
Ludlam, Charles 1359
Ludlum, John Plumer 1315
Ludwig, James 14, 830, 1547
Lueders, Mary Cross 1552
Luening, Otto 1086
Luetters, Ray 697
Luft, Uriel G. 1655
Luftig, Hal 83, 189
Luftig, Stacey 1607
Luhrman, Henry 737
Luigs, Jim 102
Luiken, Carol 221, 417
Luker, Rebecca 1816
Lukes, Ivan 1609
Luks, Jonathan 1151
Luksch, Paul M. 1423
Lum, Alvin (K.U.) 289, 712, 1147, 1689
Luman, Carl 1131
Lumbard, Dirk 343
Lumley, Lauren 897
Lumpkin, Bruce 1556
Luna, Frank 1429
Lund, Alan 56
Lund, Art 1164
Lund, Blanche 1393
Lund, Kenny 1345
Lund, Richard 1752
Lundell, Kert (Kurt) 598, 715, 1504, 1737, 1738
Lunden, Clara 408
Lunden, Jeffrey 1190, 1788
Lundie, Ken 213, 322, 606, 1561, 1585, 1760
Lundy, Pat 17, 116, 968, 1064
Lupino, Richard 567, 697
LuPone, Patti 41, 325, 443
LuPone, Robert 283, 412, 909
Lupton, Heather 1392
Lurenz, Betty 906
Lusby, Vernon 367
Luscombe, George 44
Luskin, Jean 833
Lussier, R. Robert 120, 1446
Lustberg, Arch 400, 1276, 1678
Lustgarten, Diana 505
Lustig, Alexander 1032, 1051, 1342, 1453
Lustig, Andrew 1548
Lustig, I. 898
Lustig, Joseph 1618
Lustik, Marlena 1177
Lutgenhorst, Manuel 1462
Luthy, Elaine 397
Lutken, David M. 703, 1285, 1523
Luvinsky, Leonid 849
Lux, Lillian 1105, 1341, 1745
Luxembourg, Ella 1080
Luz, Franc 939
Luzier, Aimee M. 697
Lydiard, Robert (Bob) 64, 500, 827
Lyle, Kevin 248
Lyman, Debra 236
Lyman, Dorothy 44, 1242
Lynbeck, Edmund 1256
Lynch, Brid 253
Lynch, Dennis 1021
Lynch, Jayne Ackley 59
Lynch, John 374
Lynch, Luke 224, 1016, 1148
Lynch, Kenneth, Jr. 698
Lynch, Michael 15
Lynch, Sharon 854
Lynch, Tertia 657
Lynch, Thomas (Tom) 10, 55, 203, 315, 1103, 1422, 1643, 1654
Lynde, Janice 1219
Lynde, Paul 1754
Lyndeck, Edmund 68, 1670
Lyng, Nora Mae 511, 1584
Lynn, Betty 1379, 1477
Lynn, David 548
Lynn, Deidre 1331
Lynn, Jari 68
Lynn, Joan 226
Lynn, Joe 408
Lynn, Jonathan 241
Lynn, Joyce 76, 822
Lynn, Judy 1755
Lynn, Karen 1744
Lynn, Kathy 408
Lynn, Lee 1388
Lynn, Mara 1615
Lynn, Regina 76, 1154
Lynn, Rosamond 1035
Lynn, Tobie 63
Lynne, Michael 189
Lyon, Marissa 636
Lyon, Milton 1268
Lyon, Rick 77
Lyons, Deb 1612
Lyons, Deedee 68
Lyons, Jason 248, 462, 760, 1188, 1450
Lyons, Jeff 513, 514
Lyons, Lynn 1095
Lyons, Neil 396
Lysinger, Pat 1196

Mabley, Edward 53, 190, 887
Mabray, Stuart 501
Mabry, LaDonna 8, 1670
MacAaron, Francesca 124
Macadam, Adam 1359
Macan, Joanne 213
Macaulay, Joseph 867
Macbeth, Robert 1183
MacBryde, Phyllis 823, 952, 1349
Maccahan, Doc 601
MacCallum, Robert 198, 789
MacCardell-Fossel, Hart 1327
Maccaulay, Joseph 1481
MacDermot, Galt 649, 726, 784, 860, 1510, 1534, 1638, 1689
MacDevitt, Brian 100, 249, 496, 1410, 1712
MacDonald, Cathy 101
Macdonald, David Andrew 633
MacDonald, Donald 578
MacDonald, Joyce 822
Macdonald, Roberta 601, 1058
MacDougall, Robert 373
Mace, Paul 1038
MacGregor, Scottie 1652
MacHale, Deborah 1389
Machat, Martin J. 1471
Machitto, Martin 984
Machiz, Herbert 571
Macho, Carole Joan 1480
Macintosh, Joan 386, 1391
MacIntyre, Marguerite 58, 1031, 1144
Mack, Bobbye 1802
Mack, Helen 620
Mack, Robert 938
Mack, Stan 1339
Mack, Steve 1343
Mackabee, Tim 1645
MacKay, Bruce 104
MacKay, Morgan 1148
Mackay, Phoebe 199
MacKaye, Percy 245
MacKenzie, Arthur 1243
Mackenzie, Doan 1157
MacKenzie, Flora 56
MacKenzie, Jamie 385
MacKenzie, Philip 316
MacKenzie, Will 733, 1083, 1096, 1318
Mackes, Steve 193
Mackey, Bill 630
Mackey, William Wellington 152
Mackie, Bob 1245
Mackintosh, Cameron 939, 1654
MacKintosh, Robert 208, 633, 714, 737, 1305, 1571
Mackintosh, Woods 1384
Macklin, Albert 1282
Macklin, Valerie 1544

MacLane, Gretchen 831
MacLaren, Lord 1774
Maclarty, Scott 217
MacMahon, Aline 618, 619
MacMillan, Louis 1440, 1566
MacMurdo, Judy 1319
Macpherson, Joseph 868
MacRae, Arthur 1447, 1448
MacRae, Heath 57
MacRae, Heather 473, 1523
Macrie, Christine 1316
MacShane, Anita 194, 230, 1762
MacSweeney, Maurice 1233
Macurdy, John 62, 1088, 1474
Macy, Bill 1168
Maddalena, James 363, 1139
Madden, Dale "Boots" 1720
Madden, Dale Sr. 1720
Madden, Danny 1363
Madden, Jim 1428
Madden, John 1029
Madden, Sharon 509
Madden, Stephanie 255
Madeira, Marcia 975, 1304, 1456, 1665, 1801
Madero, Ralph 993
Madiou, Robert 1015
Madison, Tracey E. 43
Madrick, Jeffrey 784
Madsen, Ethel 66
Madzirov, Zoran 1281
Maeda, Jun 1625
Maestro, Lorna Del 1131
Maffei, Gary 1128
Maffia, Roma 1781
Maganini 481
Magee, Michael 1187
Magee, Rusty 633, 642, 775
Mages, Libby Adler 890
Maggart, Brandon 542, 1097, 1290, 1318, 1468, 1534
Maggio, Michael 1788
Maggiore, Charles 1045
Magid, Karen 1283
Magid, Larry 474, 1495
Magid, Paul 1439
Magnanti, Dick 1347
Magnini, Margaretta 587
Magnus, Robin 1013
Magnusen, Michael 486
Magnuson, Merilee 348, 599
Magradey, Jack 599
Maguire, Erin 499
Maguire, George (F.) 246, 310, 1279
Maguire, Kelli 1428
Maguire, Roberta 318
Mahaffey, Valerie 483
Mahan, Chris 1179
Maharaj, Rajendra Ramoon 995
Maher, James (Jim) 68, 1193
Maher, William Michael 197, 500, 545, 644, 1207, 1785
Mahin, John 85
Mahlaba, Cosmas 1401
Mahlangu, Lorraine 651
Mahler, Yael 108
Mahon, John 1242
Mahone, Juanita 156
Mahoney, Bill 1108
Mahoney, Billie 226
Mahoney, John 1677
Mahoney-Bennett, Kathleen 49, 658, 770, 1160
Mahowald, Joseph 950
Maillard, Brian 1556
Maillard, Carol (Lynn) 630, 785, 1699
Mailman, Bruce 101, 467
Maimone, Kasia 838
Mainelli, Jono 1067
Maiocco, David K. 746
Maiorano, Robert 95
Mais, Michele 203
Maisano, Joel 991
Maitner, Rob 469
Majeski, Marilyn 1320
Makeba, Miriam 1619
Makgoba, Paul 20
Makman, Michael 543
Malamet, Marsha 414
Malamud, Marc D. 1783
Malas, Spiro 331, 828
Malatesta, Peter 1383
Malatesta, Pompilio 245, 1047
Malbin, Elaine 68, 1221
Maldener, Fritz 1775
Maldonado, David 262
Maldonado-Lopez, Rafi 262
Malec, Paul 437
Maleczech, Ruth 122, 1344
Malenfant, Lloyd 56
Malina, Joel 1381
Malina, Stuart 1310
Mallin, Erika 1322
Mallin, Glen 535
Malloy, Judy 3, 1204
Malloy, Ullaine 1116
Malone, Beth 154
Malone, Deborah 358, 1124
Malone, Gabrielle 122, 859
Malone, Justin 848
Malone, Mark 1394
Malone, Mike 1580
Malone, Penny 858
Maloney, Bill 920, 1349
Maloney, Jennifer 738
Maloney, Maureen 259, 752, 1379
Maloney, Peter 714
Malouf, Juman 365
Maltby, Evan Charney 717
Maltby, Richard, Jr. 18, 300, 616, 656, 691, 943, 1210, 1400, 1524, 1540, 1612, 1622, 1710
Maltifano, Richard 734
Mamales, George 366
Mambo, Kevin 1188
Mamet, David 1357, 1710
Manachino, Francis 1131
Manahan, George 439, 670, 941, 1022
Manalli, Carlo 902
Manassee, Jackie 358
Manasseri, Michael 54, 1560
Manchester, Joe 1420
Manchester, Melissa 741
Mancini, Al 745, 1755
Mandel, Adrian 1453
Mandel, Evan William 1707
Mandel, Frank 1028
Mandel, Julie 1683
Mandel, Mel 1107
Mandel, Mordechai 819
Mandel, Tom 101
Mandell, Michael 1121, 1187, 1375
Mandis, Renos 1592
Mandracchia, Charles 1298
MaNeil, Cornell 1596
Manetto, Corinna 317
Mangan, Frank 1060
Manger, Itzik 441, 1502
Mango, Angelo 902
Manheim, Kate 426
Manheim, Ralph 1628
Manilow, Barry 417, 1153
Manilow, Edna 1676
Manim, Mannie 1401
Manings, Alan 942
Manis, James 536
Manisoff, Manuel (M.) 1092, 1140
Mankoff, Allan H. 1295, 1754
Manley, Mark 408, 1028, 1147
Mann, Allan 423
Mann, Barry 854, 1612
Mann, Buddy (Budd) 601, 1265, 1302
Mann, Delbert 1814
Mann, Erika 1241
Mann, Fred C., III 1398
Mann, Gubi 388, 1185
Mann, Irene 578
Mann, J. Patrick 456
Mann, Joan 566
Mann, Johnny 708
Mann, Judi 743
Mann, Klaus 1241
Mann, Lores 1177
Mann, Michael 322
Mann, Patrick 51, 116, 785, 1550
Mann, Paul 397, 427
Mann, Philip 618, 619, 620
Mann, Raina 1029
Mann, Ronald 1065
Mann, Ruth 578
Mann, Sylvia 291
Mann, Ted 664
Mann, Terrence 70
Mann, Theodore 301, 466, 823, 1481, 1672
Mann, Thomas 1665
Manna, Charlie 1447
Manners, Marlene 1385
Mannhardt, Renata 1517
Manning, Allan 1443
Manning, Dan 1484
Manning, David 1347
Manning, Dick 489
Manning, Ellen 1343
Manning, Irene 1594
Manning, Jane 368, 582
Manning, Laura 61
Manning, Lina 197
Manning, Steve 1131
Mannings, Muriel 1399
Mannion, Elizabeth 1474
Manno, Jesse 901
Manno, Karen 1494
Manocherian, Barbara 10, 997
Manocherian, Jennifer (R.) 10, 685, 1454
Manosalvas, Alfonso 488
Manousos, Kathleen 1134
Mansell, Lilene 310
Mansfield, Gail 1189
Mansfield, Scott 125, 920, 1189, 1524
Manson, Alan 1175
Manson, Charles 1682
Mansson, Michel 1599
Mansur, Susan 133, 463, 1386
Mantell, Marc 749
Mantello, Joe 1006
Manuel, Caren Lyn 1188
Manulis, John Bard 1632
Manus, Mara 252, 1225, 1325, 1422
Manzano, Sonia 595
Manzari, Robert 989, 1279
Manzi, Tony 132
Manzini, Mario 1744
Mapes, H. Pierson 1385
Maraden, Frank 426
Maraffi, Matthew 1260, 1669
Maran, Elaine 293
Maras, Nancy 505
Maravell, Peter 1399
Marc, Peter 172
Marcante, Mark 702, 1182
Marcee, Susanne 1062
Marcel, Jerry 1356
Marcel, Joyce 1356
Marcella, Lou 891
Marcelle, Melba 1145
Marcelo, Alicia 466
March, Bill 575
March, Calvin 891
March, Ellen 1267
March, Liska 784
March, Stephen 1674
Marchant, Barbara 1682
Marcheret, Charlotte 1085
Marchese, Joe 148
Marchetti, Gianni 1146
Marciona, Anthony 229, 1562
Marco, Fredric 223
Marco, Mitchell 231
Marcone, Lance 636
Marcosson, Lory 1660
Marcovicci, Andrea 1746
Marcum, Kevin 599, 1557
Marcus, Charlie 1778
Marcus, Dain 924
Marcus, Daniel 100, 186, 284, 644, 1712
Marcus, David 684
Marcus, Jason 1554
Marcus, Leslie 78, 222, 502, 503, 641, 791, 805, 1103, 1238, 1513, 1726, 1779
Marcus, Mesaline 1615
Marcy, George 90, 655, 942, 1447
Mardirosian, Tom 660
Marec, Gary 1682
Maredi, Selaelo Dan 1561
Marek, Dan 62, 92
Marek, Rochelle 1531
Maret, Erza Jack 1183
Maret, Joyce 236, 884, 1604
Marez Oyens, Conrad de 349
The Marganiot 617
Margaret, Mary 121
Margo, Philip F. 1035
Margolies, Abe 909, 1360
Margolis, David 293
Margolis, Rebecca 121
Margolis, Zora 1072
Margoshes, Steven (Steve) 334, 474, 1082, 1330, 1697
Margulies, Ellen 1610
Margulis, John 155, 1671, 1771
Mari, Floria 867, 935
Maria, J.D. 1586
Mariani, Michael 1443
Mariano, Patti 42
Maricheck, Gary 1054
Maricle, Marijane 649, 944
Maridjan-Koop, Oliva 363
Marie, Julienne 201
Marie-Antoinette 652
Marie-Lee, Jean 957
Mariglio, Franck 1660
Marik, Carol 1033
Marin, David A.S. 1738
Marineau, Barbara 163, 1006
Mariner, Gregg 626
Marino, John 1256, 1257
Marino, Tony 1213, 1214
Marinos, Peter 840, 841
Marion, George, Jr. 66
Maris, Ellen 1349
Mark, Lowell E. 359
Mark, Michael 321
Mark, Zane 207, 668
Marke, Jeffrey 1182
Markee, Dwayne 377
Markell, Denis 2, 84, 1141, 1421, 1454, 1709
Markey, Enid 481
Markham, Marcella 1626
Markham, Marion 940, 1151
Markham, Shelly 81, 232
Markina the Amazon Woman 1542
Markinson, Keith 863
Markinson, Martin 1486
Markoe, Gerald (Jay) (Jerry) 271, 468, 1149
Markowitz, Ella 619
Markowitz, Jeffrey M. 273
Marks, Arthur W. 1458
Marks, Dennis 1261
Marks, Ken 206, 933
Marks, Linda 1029
Marks, Matthew 1818
Marks, Robert 1171
Marks, Sylvia 1688
Marks, Walter 185, 531, 1100, 1259
Marlay, Andrew 1173
Marle, Kristin 1682
Marley, Andrew 1541
Marlowe, Alan 676
Marlowe, Marion 74
Marlowe, Paul 379
Maroulis, Jeanette 66
Marr, Richard 61, 360, 989, 1264, 1265
Marraccini, Carol 1021
Marran, Howard 961
Marre, Albert 289
Marrell, Lani 960
Marren, Howard 1287, 1756
Marriner, Gregg 223, 246, 500, 1016, 1065, 1207
Marriott, John 1164
Marrow, Esther 996
Mars, Kenneth 63
Marsciano, Mary 1212
Marsden, Les 642
Marsee, Susanne 256, 1023
Marsh, Bernard J. 1518, 1544
Marsh, Christopher 1161
Marsh, Don 1162
Marsh, Emily 1140
Marsh, Joe 474
Marsh, Lynn 56
Marshak, Alma 676
Marshall, Clarice 363
Marshall, David Alan 1336
Marshall, Dodie 1636
Marshall, Donna 237
Marshall, Donna Lee 726, 1459
Marshall, Gay 802
Marshall, James 425
Marshall, Jennifer Kathryn 1390
Marshall, Julienne 221, 1746
Marshall, Kathleen 69, 1403, 1726
Marshall, Ken 907
Marshall, Larry 214, 648, 975, 1029, 1082, 1625
Marshall, Lee 474
Marshall, Mort 1483
Marshall, Norman Thomas 613, 1725
Marshall, Richard 236, 920, 1506
Marshall, Rob 55, 194, 907, 1250
Marshall, Roberta 1066
Marshall, Sid 1397
Marshall, William 1166
Marshall, William J. 1713
Marsico, Frank 562
Marsolais, Ken 586, 920
Marston, Merlin 1664
Marta, Cecila 1538
Martel, Janece 1341, 1745
Martel, Tom 663
Martel, William 74, 1166
Martell, Fred 976
Martell, Ralph 1443
Martenez, Frank G. 442
Martin, Andrea 664
Martin, Angel 1537

Martin, Ann-Ngaire 1184
Martin, Barney 1475, 1755
Martin, Brian 688
Martin, Campbell 990
Martin, Charles 425
Martin, Colette 254
Martin, David 1464, 1465
Martin, David (Stone) 609, 1815
Martin, Deonne 82
Martin, Donald 1131
Martin, Dorothy 479
Martin, D'urville 238
Martin, Elliot 1326
Martin, Erin 858, 1649
Martin, Ethel 1524
Martin, Eva Boucherite 108
Martin, Frank 539, 1596
Martin, Gary 95
Martin, Gay 834
Martin, Gerry 1337
Martin, Glenn 4
Martin, Guy 1802
Martin, Herb 865, 866, 1593
Martin, Hugh 132, 954, 1101, 1574, 1611
Martin, Janis 891
Martin, Jeffrey (Jeff) 511, 1591
Martin, Jim 1487
Martin, John 1671
Martin, Judith 624, 1003
Martin, Kathryn 985
Martin, Ken 226
Martin, Ken "Slim" 379
Martin, Leila 448, 818, 1253, 1265
Martin, Luc 1281
Martin, Lynn 1446, 1721
Martin, Manuel (Jr.) 118, 897
Martin, Marjorie 1326
Martin, Michael X. 114, 249, 791
Martin, Nina 1055
Martin, Norman 550, 1318
Martin, Peter 46, 518, 522, 525, 526, 1156, 1421
Martin, Randal 486
Martin, Randy 109
Martin, Riccardo 340, 1075, 1269
Martin, Richard J. 31
Martin, Ron 1424
Martin, Ruth 1131
Martin, Sheryl 197
Martin, Stephen G. 377
Martin, Susie 132
Martin, Thomas 1131
Martin, Virginia 232
Martin, William 712, 1148
Martina, Tiger 994
Martindale, Margo 39
Martinet, Francoise 609, 1789
Martinez, Augusto 955
Martinez, Christopher 1325
Martinez, Jocelyn 1811
Martinez, Jose 1039
Martinez, Louise 1077
Martinez, Manual 897
Martinèz, Mario 1425
Martinez, Paula Denise 118
Martinez, Richard 632
Martinez, Vaughn 1732
Martinez-Galarce, Marco A. 1720
Martini, Richard 474, 916
Martinson, Martin 382
Martirano, Christian 1054
Martone, Marco 61
Martucci, Vinnie 302
Martyn, Greg 909
Martyn, Nevil 1679
Maruhashi, Setsuko 1410
Marvell, Cindy 901
Marvin, Blanche 654
Marvin, Charles S. 535
Marvin, Gaar 66
Marvin, Mel 314, 485, 551, 634, 907, 958, 1279, 1285, 1446, 1643
Marx, Amanda 15
Marx, Arthur 642
Marx, Jeff 77
Marx, Robert 999
Mary 749
Marzullo, Stephen (Steve) 1191, 1499
Mascari, Karen 994
Masciarelli, Silvio 1687
Masekela, Hugh 1401
Masella, Arthur 256, 377, 1829
Masella, Joni 319, 833
Maseng, Don 1203
Masenheimer, David 424, 1250
Masiell, Joe 291, 720, 795, 797, 824, 903, 1035, 1146, 1424, 1635
Maslow, Sophie 147, 489, 1399, 1445
Mason, Cameron 283
Mason, Doris 411
Mason, Edith 245
Mason, Gabrielle 779
Mason, Gaylord C. 1272
Mason, Karen 52, 225, 691, 1033
Mason, Marilyne 68
Mason, Marshall W. 1704, 1705
Mason, Michael 925
Mason, Richard G. 779
Mason, T.E. 467, 1349, 1455, 1695
Mason, Virginia 655
Massas, Elaine 976
Massee, Michael 1258
Massey, Cal 885
Massey, Michael 665
Massi, Bernice 857
Massimi, Robert 1571
Massimo, Gene 528
Massue, Nicholas 1010
Masswohl, George 1637
Masten, Boyd 981
Master, Yin-Yang 495
Masteroff, Joe 374, 807
Masters, Vicki 39
Masterson, Peter 133
Mastrantonio, Mary Elizabeth 726, 873, 1557
Mastrelli, Adam 1742
Mastrocola, Frank 907
Mastrone, Frank 1591
Masuoka, Gary Kenji 712
Masuzzo, Dennis 1731
Mata and Hari 1687
Matalon, Vivian 1507
Mataresse, Tony 1276
Matay, Steven J. 1548
Matheo, Len 697
Mather, Anietje 1729
Mather, Ted 1651
Matheson, Murray 1172
Mathews, Carmen 1557
Mathews, Steve 81
Mathias, Zoe 1805
Mathieu, William 22, 1352, 1415, 1724
Mathis, Claude 506, 1616
Mathis, Clover 1029
Matlack, Deborah 124
Matlock, Norman 153, 333, 860, 1638, 1689
Matlovsky (Matlowsky), Samuel 826, 1164, 1192, 1360, 1626
Matson, R.J. 247
Matsui, Yoshiko 1410
Matsunaga, Merle 1487
Matsuno, Yoshie 602
Matsusaka, Tom 1213, 1214, 1304, 1358
Mattaliano, Christopher 451
Mattaliano, Peter 789
Matter, Jack 573
Mattfeld, Marie 340
Matthew, Dana 730
Matthews, Art 902
Matthews, Edward RF 396
Matthews, Erin 1347
Matthews, Evan 1525, 1671
Matthews, Gerry 87, 160, 371, 381, 415, 530, 1261, 1490, 1576
Matthews, J. Gordon 319
Matthews, Jeffrey 1427
Matthews, Jon 1376, 1384
Matthews, Joy Lynn 71, 1046
Matthews, Junius 618, 619, 620, 622
Matthews, Karen 358, 690
Matthews, Michael 282
Matthews, Moose 1517
Matthews, Robert 304
Matthews, Tom 1476
Mattison, Jerry 1163
Mattox, Brenda 834
Mattox, Matt 1193
Matusewitch, Peter 1294
Matyas, Maria 1010
Matz, Jerry 1361
Matz, Peter 201, 612, 1192
Mau, Lester J.N. 1213
Mauceri, John 244
Maude-Roxby, Roddy 450
Maul, Betty 414
Maull, Kyla 349
Maultsby, Carl 17
Maurer, Michael 408, 705, 1083
Maurice, Marcus 1301
Maurice, Michael A. 1721
Maurin, Osvaldo 379
Maury, Richard F. 1448
Mauser, Rudi 1281
Mauthe, Denise 1096
Mavimbela, Thandani 1401
Maws'on, Elizabeth 56
Maxine and Bobby 1116
Maxmen, Mimi 1, 492, 1362
Maxon, Norman 1672
Maxwell, Adriana 1327
Maxwell, Jan 770, 1491
Maxwell, Linn 1087
Maxwell, Mitchell 54, 102, 181, 196, 284, 804, 1554, 1653
Maxwell, Victoria 182, 196, 804, 1554
May, Deborah 544
May, Deven 106
May, Earl 1495
May, Elaine 1614
May, Jim 490
May, Lorry 490
May, Mark 967
May, Marnee 1117
May, Pegge 423
Mayans, Nancy 1102
Maye, Anita 631
Maye, Carolyn 112, 1594
Mayer, Bradley J. 1632
Mayer, Jerry 865, 866, 1048
Mayer, Jo 1089, 1136
Mayer, Lottie 66
Mayer, Michael 727, 1515, 1545, 1598
Mayer, Neal 227
Mayer, William 362
Mayes, Sally 102, 300, 1245
Mayhew, Ina 736
Maylond, Sara 1098
Mayman, Lee 981
Maynard, Tyler 38
Mayo, Don 285
Mayo, James E. 580, 1505
Mayo, Joan 972
Mayo, Pamela 702
Mayro, Jacqueline 291, 851, 1774
Maysoner, Gene 274
Mazey, Duane 1542
Mazin, Stan 486
Mazor, Jeff 1065
Mazor, Jeffrey N. 420, 803, 1738
Mazurki, Mike 1172
Mazursky, Paul 1447
Mazza, Richard 1636
Mazzeo, Roger 78
Mazzini, Herbert 66
Mazzotta, Lesley 196
Mbambo, Nonhlanhla 1401
Mbugua, Gladys Wanjiku 167
McAdams, Stacy 1707
McAfee, Diane 63, 121
McAfee, Don 631
McAfee, Wes 565, 788
McAliece, F. J. 277
McAllen, Kathleen Rowe 275, 726, 833, 1296
McAnally, Dave 423
McAndrew, Bob 1207
McAneny, Susan 869
McAnuff, Des 364, 699
Mcart, Jan 601
McArthur, Michael 789
McAssey, Michael 565, 1223
McAteer, Kathryn 1037
McAuliffe, Jason 509, 949, 1150
McBain, Robert 1316
McBride, Billie 880
McBride, Michele 256, 1023
McBroom, Amanda 1, 2
McCabe, Eileen 725, 1097
McCabe, Jennifer 1054
McCall, Janet 304, 601, 720, 1594
McCall, Lynne 329
McCall, Nancy 518, 522, 525, 526, 681, 1421
McCall, Richie 359, 1016
McCallum, David 1637
McCallum, Davis 1322
McCallum, John 1174
McCann, Christopher 1391
McCann, Gene 737, 1611
McCann, Mary 1515
McCarroll, Earl 246
McCarroll, Ernest 1559
McCarry, Charles (E.) 703, 730, 789, 830
McCarthy, Barbara S. 1721
McCarthy, Bob 489
McCarthy, Ed 825
McCarthy, Elaine J. 778
McCarthy, Gerry 1160
McCarthy, Jeff 413, 576, 1712
McCarthy, Joseph 1101
McCarthy, Laura 1595
McCarthy, Theresa 503, 1404
McCarthy, Wayne 1550
McCarti, Eddie 613
McCartney, Ellen 78
McCartney, Liz 154
McCartney, Mary 64
McCartney, Paul 1426
McCarty, Conan 1520
McCarty, Ernest 382, 734
McCarty, Michael 973
McCauley, Bill 461
McCauley, Bobbie 844
McCauley, Judith 822
McCauley, Lois 600
McChesney, Ernest 1474
McClain, Marcia 372, 1330
McClain, Mary Smith 1720
McClain, Saundra 124, 1307
McClaine, Stephanie 469
McClain-Moore, Susan 960
McClam, DeLandis 668
McClanahan, Matthew (Matt) 1410, 1832
McClanahan, Rue 1420
McClanathan, Michael 1705
Mcclaren, Ian 620
McClary, Ron 1556
McClatchy, J.D. 439, 640
McCleister, Tom (Thom) 86, 1579
McClellan, Casey 1544
McClellan, Clark 968
McClendon, Afi 1191
McClennahan, Charles 1002
McClimon, Timothy J. 1680
McClung, Joffre 1469
McClure, Michael 373
McColl, Ian 410
McColl, JJ 1753
McCollum, John 1111
McCollum, Kevin 760, 1645
McComb, Bill 377
McComiskey, Bill 1411
McConahay, Liz 1421
McConnell, Mary Jo 1046
McConnell, Ty 316, 480, 972, 989, 1311
McConnie, Marilyn 1004
McCord, Joe 1592
McCorkle, David 823, 1182
McCormack, Mic 1508
McCormick, Cara-Duff 1098
McCormick, Gilmer 595
McCormick, Jane 1443
McCormick, Mary Ann 574
McCormick, Michael 271, 1006, 1303
McCormick, Parker 1272
McCormick, Pat 1754
McCormick, Robert 25, 979, 1353
McCorry, Marion 773
McCourt, Frank 775
McCourt, Sean 703, 1006, 1285, 1760
McCoy, Eleanor 854
McCoy, Kerry 906
McCoy, Michael 227, 845
McCoy, W. David 71
McCracken, David 15
McCrane, Paul 386
McCrary, Marc 121
McCreary, Kelly 1425
McCreery, Bud 87, 367, 368, 371, 531, 942, 1142, 1261, 1318, 1447, 1448
McCullers, Carson 466
McCulloh, Barbara 878
McCurry, Carolyn 1367
McCurry, John (R.) 116, 153, 591, 710, 1370
McCurry, Michael 803, 1522
McCutcheon, Bill 616, 722, 1142, 1754
McCutcheon, Ray 816
McCutcheon, Sherry 735, 908
McDaniel, William Foster 177, 240
McDermott, Kevin 49, 612
McDermott, Phelim 1444
McDermott, Sean 240
McDevitt, Bob 93
McDonach (McDonagh), Paul 782, 1212
McDonald, Cherie 1659

McDonald, Chip 1746
McDonald, Daniel Leroy 302
McDonald, David B. 512
McDonald, Hugh 241
McDonald, James 826
McDonald, Jeffrey D. 174
McDonald, Kirk 1031, 1403, 1726
McDonald, Kristin 1778
McDonald, Susan 1066
McDonald, Tanny 117, 253, 539, 828, 848
McDonald, William 569
McDonnell, Ed 1802
McDonnell, Graeme (F.) 801, 1327
McDonnell, Susan 124
McDonough, Glenn 81
McDonough, John 1438
McDonough, Ray 1066
McDorman, Jackson 469
McDowell, James 1784
McDowell, Paul 458
McEachran, Michael 721
McEathron, Laurie 1560
McElhiney, Rick 865, 866
McElroy, Michael 385, 1631, 1726
McElwaine, Jack 1359
McElwaine, James 910, 1522
McEntee, Donna 295
McEwen, Odette 379
McFadden, Cheryl 1820
McFarland, Robert 1165, 1462
McFate, Joseph 1067
McGarity, Jerry 102
McGee, Arthur 630, 1734, 1735
McGee, Kirk 1556
McGee, Robin L. 148, 778
McGehee, Eivie 1082
McGhee, Brownie 1465
McGill, Everett 1380
McGill, Georgia 1216
McGill, Moeisha 1612
McGillin, Howard 69, 186, 1109
McGinty, Joe 1237
McGlinn, John 912, 1167
McGourty, Patricia 259, 364, 426, 544, 1270, 1296, 1480
McGovern, Christopher 749, 1441, 1607, 1771
McGovern, Don 1440
McGovern, Maureen 218, 912, 1167
McGown, Ellen 199
McGrane, Paul Anthony 1103
McGrath, Bob 1018
McGrath, George 393, 394, 426, 756, 757, 999, 1231, 1628
McGrath, Katherine 1006
McGrath, Michael 305, 463, 512, 515, 526, 1421
McGrath, William 1564
McGraw, Nancy 1156
McGraw, Steve 518, 522, 525, 526, 1156, 1421, 1573
McGreevey, Annie 1593
McGregor, Dion 415
McGregor, Francisco 1503
McGroder, Carol 582
McGroder, Jack 110, 1028, 1081, 1147
McGuigan, Marcy 1571
McGuire, John T., III 43
McGuire, Margaret 1077
McGuire, Margot 1320
McGuire, Rose 749, 1441
McGuirk, Sean 948
McGunnigle, Kathi 1040
McHaffey, Robert 1302
McHale, Deborah 345
McHale, Gannon 474
McHale, Martin 985
McHugh, Burke 638
McHugh, David 493, 1124, 1294
McHugh, Joanne 1186
Mchunu, Linda 1401
McIlroy, Geraldine 951
McInnis, Bill 834, 920
McIntosh, Dale 221
McIntyre, Dianne 9, 592, 629, 630, 1580
McIntyre, Gerry 213, 1191, 1458
McIntyre, Karen 1522
McIntyre, Roger 1349
McIntyre, Ronald L. 960, 1785
McIver, Ray 589
McKay, Anthony 1472
McKay, Ian 807
McKay, Maureen 1022
McKay, Tony 1004
McKayle, Donald 777, 1291, 1672
McKean, Aldyn 1776
McKearney, Kathleen 190
Mckechnie, Donna 58, 283, 338, 443, 1096
McKee, Joseph 256
McKeehan, Mayla 88, 308
McKellar, John 1661
McKenna, Barney 1565
Mckenzie, Branice 1435
McKenzie, Rita 239, 452, 1492
McKeown, Douglas 460
McKergow, Helen 1655
McKernon, John 813
McKerrs, Terrance (Terrence) 1379, 1409
McKibbins, Paul 778
McKim, Andy 1694
McKinley, Ann 705
McKinley, David 680
McKinley, Mary 360
McKinley, Philip William (Wm.) 915, 1632, 1831
McKinley, Tom 218, 1622
McKinney, Gayle 996
McKinney, John 551, 695, 1094
McKinney, Marie 702, 1016
McKinney, Tom 577
McKneely, Joey 633, 848
McKoy, Winsome 1200
McLain, John 43, 604, 1538
McLain, Marcia 159
McLane, Derek 249, 496, 627, 683, 950, 1129, 1403, 1598, 1637, 1726
McLane, Jason 1617
McLane, Judith 990
McLane, Judy 825
McLaren, Conrad 1343
Mclaren, Ian 621
McLaughlin, Dennis 1066
McLaughlin, Kathy 66
McLaughlin, Robert 1787
McLaughlin, Vickie 1070
McLean, Michael 67
McLean, Sharlene 56
McLee, Svetlana 201, 1147
McLeod, Debbie 81, 1028
McLeod, John 1751
McLeod, Raymond Jaramillo 1778
McLeod, Ronnie 196
McLerie, Allyn Ann 348, 422
McLernon, Pamela 1338
McLucas, Rod 505
McLucas, W. Scott 398
McLuckey, William 891
McLure, James 1094
McMahon, Caroline 1103
McMahon, Jim 1258
McMahon, John 171
McMahon, Virginia 826
McMartin, John 641, 935, 1057
McMichael, Lewis 620, 621
McMillan, Adjora Faith 1207
McMillan, Colleen 1556
McMillan, Geraldine 673
McMillan, Kenneth 80, 766, 867
McMillan, Larry 1644
McMillan, Lisa 749
McMillan, Sarah 1233
McMullen, Kenneth (Ken) 124, 359
McNabb, Barry 1571, 1669
McNalley, Maureen 1058
McNally, John D. 266
McNally, Sean 1110
McNally, Terrence 1006, 1710
McNamara, Betty 366
McNamara, Brooks 1720
McNamara, Dyanne M. 746
McNamara, Eileen 398
McNamara, Maureen 486
McNamara, Robert 15
McNamara, Rosemary 253, 705, 1323
McNaughton, Charles 136
McNaughton, Stephen (Steve) 272, 833
McNeeley, Gale 1689
McNeely, Reginald 1500
McNeil, Angela 1060
McNeil, Claudia 1464
McNeil, Lonnie 767
McNeill, Lloyd 1064
McNeill, Robert 596
McNicholas, Jim 808
McNicholas, Steve 1530
McNicholl, BT 148, 778
McNickle, Jim 223
McNickle, Sean 1408
McNitt, David 940
McNutt, Eileen 759
McPhatter, Willie James 166
McPherson, Cynthia 500
McPherson, Megan 1389
McPherson, Ryan 670
McPhillips, Edward (J.) 360, 661
McQueen, Armelia 18
Mcqueen, Butterfly 74, 231, 1811
McQuiggan, John A. 157, 707
McRae, Arthur 1142
McRae, Calvin 56, 214
McRae, Charles A. 1464
McRoberts, Jeffrey 1149, 1150
McRoberts, Sally 1131
McSpadden, Becky Thatcher 1679
McVety, Drew 950
McVey, J. Mark 275, 1451
McWhinney, Michael 50, 126, 350, 415, 556, 558, 771, 852, 1069, 1125, 1142, 1255, 1273, 1605
McWhorter, Mitzie 902
McWilliams, Caroline 183
McWilliams, Patric 1648
McWilliams, Ralph 1254
McWilliams, Robert 910
Mead, Lewis 1098
Meade, David 1809
Meader, George 868
Meadow, Leslie 1021
Meadow, Lynne 18, 84, 179, 249, 296, 312, 348, 633, 643, 656, 662, 672, 886, 943, 1024, 1129, 1184, 1201, 1339, 1459, 1492, 1546, 1637, 1710, 1778
Meadows, Kristen 483
Meadows, Michael 127, 197, 682, 1426, 1509
Meadows, Nancy 1028, 1160
Meadows, Pauline 578
Means, Jesse, II 1186
Meara, Anne 1
Mears, DeAnn 366
Medak, Susan 1225
Medeiros, John 373
Medeiros, Michael 1726
Medica, Leon 1746
Medici, John 993
Medico, Michael Del 734
Medina, Wilfredo 222
Medley, Cassandra 1
Medow, Jill 1079
Mee, Charles (L., Jr.) 122, 1322, 1722
Meehan, Danny 368, 1162, 1481
Meehan, Harry 494, 1092, 1115
Meehan, Kelly 1560
Meehan, Thomas 58, 1141
Meek, Deanne 439
Meersman, Peter 324
Meffe, Robert 922
Meglio, Eleanor 1520
Megna, Ave Maria 1083
Mehler, Jack 469, 727, 1771
Mehr, Rachel 867
Mehring, Walter 459
Mehta, Zubin 1088
Meibach, Ina (Lea) 10, 101
Meier, Gustav 1137
Meier, Ron 1298
Meiere, Hildreth 245
Meinert, Silva 1221
Meister, Norman 113
Meit, Marvin R. 54, 284
Meitz, Millie 1445
Melamed, Johanna 505
Melano, Fabrizio 71
Melanson, Patricia 1450
Melcek, Tom 666
Melcher, Tamara 904
Melchior, Lauritz 66
Meldrum, Verity Anne 1316
Meleck, Tom 147, 666, 1822
Melemele, Honey Sanders 1221
Melendez, Joseph 995
Melendez, Maria 1179
Melfi, Leonard 1168, 1567
Meljie, Myron 1021
Mell, Randle 325
Mellen, Patrick 541
Mellman, Kenny 72
Mellon, Christopher 1671
Mellon, James J. 309, 492, 1702
Mellor, Stephen 1222
Mellow, Stephen 722
Melman, David 813
Melman, Susan 813
Melnick, Marjorie 217
Melnick, Peter 10
Melnik, Bertha 797
Melo, Jerry 935
Melone, Milena 468
Melrose, Ronald 55, 537, 1486, 1709
Melvin, Elsie 1145
Melvin, Robert 1001
Melvin, Sheryl 1816
Memel, Steven 648
Mence, Len 1172
Menchell, Ivan 1482, 1750
Mendelson, Gary 1310, 1706
Mendelson, James 717
Menden, Susan 1066
Mendick, Charles 1140
Mendieta, Wilson 262
Mendiola, Michael 57, 538, 1608
Mendoza, Dorothy 1661
Mendoza, Orville 10
Menendez, Brad 95
Menken, Alan 377, 588, 939, 1100, 1149, 1150, 1228, 1243, 1297, 1339
Menken, Steve 393
Menotti, Gian-Carlo 40, 776, 891, 1718
Mensoff, Richard 1069
Menten, Dale F. 716
Mentzer, Susanne 495
Menzel, Idina 1422, 1778
Mercado, Hector Jaime 1029, 1398
Mercado, Rafael Dantes 897
Mercedes, Ronny 248, 995
Mercer, Franklin 1465
Mercer, Johnny 538, 1100, 1101
Mercer, Marian 50, 556, 557, 714, 1827
Merchant, Jan 133
Merchant, Karen 454
Merchant, Tyler 57
Mercier, G.W. 114, 260, 413, 499, 643, 658, 839, 1237, 1345, 1779
Mercurio, Gregory John 475
Meredith, Lee 725, 1097
Meredith, Morley 891
Meredíz, Olga 203, 623, 726, 760, 975, 1510
Merkerson, S. Epatha 9
Merle, Sandi 743
Merner, George 56
Merriam, Eve 301
Merrick, Jimmy 1095
Merrigal, Alice 985
Merrill, Bob 349, 658, 1100, 1580, 1752
Merrill, Ellen 1140
Merrill, Jimmy 259
Merrill, Paul 217
Merrill, Rick 1722
Merrill, Scott 1626, 1627
Merriman, Eve 1536
Merring, Michelle 1508
Merritt, George 1250, 1337, 1525
Merritt, Rhonda 1419
Merritt, Theresa 466, 592, 593, 1672
Mers, Rockland 510
Merson, Susan 1094
Meryl, Cynthia 1527
Meryon, Charles 1506
Merzon, Jill 373
Messios, Kyriacos 1233
Meszel, Maz 1647
Metcalf, Ronald P. 1363
Metcalf, Steven 409
Metheny, Russell 1782
The Metropolitan Opera 40, 47, 298, 340, 440, 574, 762, 776, 868, 891, 905, 988, 1010, 1088, 1249, 1269, 1369, 1597, 1730, 1740
Mettee, David 1, 2
Metternich, Mary Lynne 841
Metz, Janet 154, 473
Metz, Robert Roy 1486
Metzgar, Bonnie 1186, 1404
Metzger, Rita 92, 1474
Metzler, Lawrence 884
Mews, Peter 56
Meyer, Deed (a/k/a Dede) 1440, 1531, 1652
Meyer, Donna 345, 1268
Meyer, Doug 1777

Meyer, Jeffrey 1227
Meyer, John 531, 556, 557, 558, 616, 852, 1069, 1261, 1431
Meyer, Joseph 834
Meyer, Leo 433, 507, 746
Meyer, Mary 920
Meyer, Zoya 1131
Meyerhoff, Tom O. 1049
Meyers, Donald (Don) 1021, 1445
Meyers, Lanny 1361, 1362, 1442, 1534, 1821
Meyers, Larry 708
Meyers, Leo B. 772
Meyers, Nicholas 65, 304
Meyers, Peter 1142
Meyers, Sarah 938
Meyers, Stanley 1142
Meyers, Timothy 625, 710, 789, 1459
Meyers, Warren B. 1574, 1686
Meyerson, Ross 1742
Meyn, Karen 1312
Meyrelles, Chip 1523
Mezvinsky, Kenneth Waissman 203
Mgcina, Sophie 1284
Mhlongo, Ndaba 1401
Micare, Franklin 1438
Michael, Gerry 605
Michael, Keith 1338
Michael, Kevin 605
Michael, Paul 655, 827, 1221, 1468, 1566
Michael, Richard 1029
Michael, Timi 144
Michael, Tom 19
Michaels, Adam 1110
Michaels, Barbara 1131
Michaels, Bert 161, 576, 903
Michaels, Devon 873
Michaels, Jay 808
Michaels, Jerryn 575
Michaels, Laura 1038
Michaelson, Dennis 1035
Michalovic, Michael 819, 1212, 1453
Michalski, Raymond 62, 1088
Michele, Lea 1515
Michelle, Laiona 167
Michelle, Melanie 708
Michelmore, Ellen 1556
Michels, Jeanne 624
Michener, Dean 600, 944
Micheni, Dennis Mutwiri 167
Michlin, Barry 1599, 1758
Mickelsen, David 1370
Mickens, Jan 62, 1620
Mickens, Valois 500, 1625
Mickey, Leilani 461
Micoleau, Tyler 72, 645
Micunis, Gordon 822, 1707
Middleton, Robert 1119
Middleton, Tony 238, 1504
Mieholes, Nicky 263
Miele, Jonathan 884
Mielziner, Jo 440, 969, 1047
Mieszkuc, Ruth 1518
Migatz, Marshall 1687
Mignini, Carolyn 664, 886, 907, 1190, 1643
Miho 1410
Miji, Eric 1213
Mikesell, Emily 950, 1326
Mikeulewicz, Mil 1346
Miklojcik, Joseph, Jr. 1760
Miko, Joyce 569
Miksits, Frances 1520
Mikulewicz, Bil 319
Milan, Joe 60
Milan, Judith 1754
Milanese, Bob 693
Milazzo, Ann Marie (Ann-marie) 206, 643, 832
Milbank, Stephen 658, 1503, 1752
Milburn, Brendan 1499
Miles, David 1561
Miles, Julia 314, 528, 688, 1222, 1534, 1641, 1720, 1761, 1783
Miles, Robin 838
Miles, Roland 1131
Miles, Sara 55
Miles, Sylvia 784, 1272
Miles, William 940
Milford, Kim 943, 1082, 1558
Milford, Penelope 1356
Milgrim, Lynn 292
Milikin, Paul 1287
Militello, Anne (E.) 1335, 1402, 1502, 1532, 1625, 1761
Millar, Gregory 1563, 1596
Millard, Vincent 1331
Mille, Antoinette 1570
Miller, Albert 1221
Miller, Alice 1221
Miller, Amy 58
Miller, Anne 1029
Miller, Arthur 1356, 1708, 1710, 1723
Miller, Barbara 962
Miller, Bill 281, 1125
Miller, Bob 232, 735, 1163
Miller, Bruce 412, 1432
Miller, Buzz 188, 304, 1558
Miller, Caitlin 365
Miller, Chris 1499
Miller, Court 434
Miller, Craig 855, 1377, 1482, 1668
Miller, Deborah 56
Miller, Donald 1405
Miller, Dutch 714
Miller, Earl F. 615
Miller, Edward 80, 1284
Miller, Elinor 1445
Miller, Eve-Lynn 58
Miller, Fred 1677
Miller, Georgia 1221
Miller, Helen 1536
Miller, Ira 548
Miller, James M. 297
Miller, Jan 66
Miller, Jason 1242
Miller, Jeff 156
Miller, Jeffrey 1370, 1544
Miller, Jennifer 954
Miller, Jeremiah 1779
Miller, Joel McKinnon 1706
Miller, John 1729
Miller, Karen D. 764
Miller, Kathleen 716
Miller, Kellis 254, 569, 1137
Miller, Kenn 1525
Miller, Kevin 1560
Miller, Lance 1536
Miller, Lani 1360
Miller, Lawrence 1197, 1199, 1717
Miller, Lorna 578
Miller, Lucille 1221
Miller, Luke 399
Miller, Lyle 790
Miller, Lynne 15, 920, 1349
Miller, M. Paige 706
Miller, Maralyn S. 112
Miller, Margaret 1182
Miller, Margot 1136
Miller, Marilyn S. 710
Miller, Marilyn Suzanne 580
Miller, Marla 1194
Miller, Marquette 815, 816
Miller, Marsha Trigg 297
Miller, Martha 660
Miller, Mary 836
Miller, Maura 59
Miller, Mel 538, 1608
Miller, Michael 1029, 1409, 1749
Miller, Miriam 1148
Miller, Page 466
Miller, Paul 89, 1156, 1159
Miller, R. Michael 1507
Miller, Richard 192, 1360
Miller, Richard A. 400
Miller, Robert (Bob) 381
Miller, Robert Strong 703, 1310
Miller, Robin 341, 342, 343
Miller, Ron 274
Miller, Ronnita 1329
Miller, Sharon 1432
Miller, Sharron 93, 667, 969, 1409, 1692, 1809
Miller, Skedge 566, 1440
Miller, Steve 505
Miller, Timothy 65
Miller, Tod 1517
Miller, Trudy 682
Miller, Walter "Dutch" 598
Miller, William P. 58, 837, 1694
Miller, Wynne 235
Miller-Moffatt 822
Millett, Tim 223
Milligan, Tuck 461, 1786
Milliken, Mary Sue 273
Mills, C. Richard 107, 1307
Mills, Carley 1811
Mills, Connie 1720
Mills, George 1192
Mills, Greg 13
Mills, Harlan 920
Mills, Jason 521
Mills, Jerry Leath 864
Mills, Peter C. 1815
Mills, Steve 1615, 1616
Mills, Thomas 538, 954, 1608
Millstein, Jack 341, 342, 343, 1483
Milne, A.A. 1790, 1791
Milne, John 819
Milnes, Sherrill 1088
Milo, Roy 108
Milrad, Robert 1273
Milson, Deborah 170
Milstein, Fredric 1789
Milton, Edna 133
Milton, James 577, 1503
Mimd, Gerald L.C. 420
Mimms, Lee 1326
Minahan, Greg 42
Minard, Gordon 827, 1360
Minarik, Fran 1428
Mindich, Stacey 997
Mine, Nonoru 602
Mineo, John 113, 1588, 1733
Miner, Jan 366
Miner, Sandy 834
Minford, Robert 826
Minichiello, Michael 1516, 1571
Minion, Devron 1065
Minjer, Harold 620, 621
Minkov, Taly 108
Minkus, Barbara 160, 1379
Minnelli, Liza 132
Minnick, Wendell 582, 700, 1380
Minning, Steven 567
Minor, Irene 1131
Minskoff, Lee 1305
Minskoff, Maggie 961
Mintun, John 572
Mintz, Brent 1279
Mintz, Melanie 854
Mintz, Thelma 119, 608, 684
Mintzer, Heide 675
Mintzer, William (Bill) 117, 183, 464, 587, 809, 885, 1279
Minyard, Melissa 983
Miranda, Evan 1384
Miranda, Lin-Manuel 760
Miranda, Sylvia 493
Miriam, Phyllis 385
Mironchik, James (Jim) (Steven) 404, 825, 1117, 1148, 1298, 1502
Mirvish, David 1694
Mirvish, Ed 1694
Mishenko, Matalia 849
Mishkin, Chase 610, 806, 1656
Misita, Michael 1409
Misiuro, Wojciech 1275
Miskell, Brad 1109, 1171
Mistarka, Essie 121
Miss Hollywood 772
Mitchel, Arthur 66
Mitchel, Jodi 653
Mitchell, Adrian 389
Mitchell, Ann 48
Mitchell, Bernardine 615
Mitchell, Bill 1716
Mitchell, Blu 964
Mitchell, Bob 289
Mitchell, Brenda 255, 785
Mitchell, Byron 332
Mitchell, Chad 265
Mitchell, David 65, 306, 307, 488
Mitchell, Deborah 82
Mitchell, Esther 618, 619, 620
Mitchell, Gregory 1199, 1588
Mitchell, James 944
Mitchell, Jerry 249, 599, 680, 1201
Mitchell, John Cameron 680, 683
Mitchell, Ken 1358
Mitchell, Lauren 1712
Mitchell, Loften 91, 221, 255, 1065
Mitchell, Mark 1702
Mitchell, Mary-Jenifer 1114, 1695
Mitchell, Melanie 1575
Mitchell, Peter J. 1659
Mitchell, Robert 86
Mitchell, Ruth 244
Mitchell, Sally 1787
Mitchell, Sinclair 668
Mitchell, Vontress 1760
Mitorotondo, Michael 82, 1151
Mitri, Michael F. 541
Mitropoulos, Dimitri 1718
Mitrovich, Andra 965
Mittenzwei, Veronica 129
Mitty, Nomi 226, 598
Mitzenmacher, Charlotte 1291
Mix, Timothy 1022
Mixon, Tom 235, 735, 858, 1185, 1193
Mizelle, Vance 246
Mjaanes, Otto 701
Mlaba, Pat 1401
Mlotek, Zalmen 604, 782, 1619
Mo, Keb' 1631
Moayed, Arian 1322
Moccia, Jodi 641
Modereger, J. Robin (J.R.) (Jeff) 305, 799, 1328, 1470
Moe, Elaine 1648
Moehl, Robert 991
Moench, Dennis 474
Moerer, Kim 1011
Moersch, William N. 1731
Moffat, Lynn 859, 1429, 1499
Moffitt, Jules 235
Mofokeng, Mubi 1401
Mohr, Marcia 669
Mohr, Matthew 859
Moise, Solo 1051, 1342
Moitaza, Rob 423
Moize, William 1816
Mokone, Tsepo 1284
Mola, Mary 1194
Molaskey, Jessica 413, 1006, 1498
Molinaro, Thom 199, 388
Moline, Patricia 840
Molinelli, Elise 954
Moliter, Elizabeth 1441
Moll, Dick 1594
Moll, Jonathan D. 703
Mollenhauer, Heidi 374, 1305
Mollin, Fred 1612
Molloy, Irene 1598
Molnar, Karen 1508
Molnar, Robert 1179
Molock, Bob 1620
Moloney, Mick 1411
Molthen, Jack 1560
Monaco, Robert 1068
Monat, Phil 46, 52, 114, 129, 476, 586, 596, 658, 730, 848, 1049, 1102, 1251, 1361, 1363, 1449, 1494, 1503, 1715
Moncrieff, Mary Jane 68, 1221
Monet, Gaby 1385
Monferdini, Carole 301, 789
Monier, Richard 1695
Monk, Debra 70, 1176, 1317
Monk, Julius 87, 160, 371, 381, 415, 531, 534, 1259, 1261, 1430, 1431, 1490, 1602
Monk, Meredith 560, 1280
Monk, Robby 624, 1290, 1541
Monk, Terence 1379
Monley, Adam 476
Monroe, Bruce (B.) 109, 1194, 1443
Monroe, Dale 277
Monroe, Donna 1452
Monroe, Josh 139, 1632
Monroe, Marianne 1512
Monson, Lex 592, 1672
Mont, Jeff 1182
Montalvo, Doreen 760
Montano, Alexandra 123
Montano, Robert 1186
Monte, Adrienne Del 319
Monte, Al Del 1727
Monte, George Del 92, 609, 1474, 1587
Monte, Marrielle 906
Montefiore, David 819, 1032
Montefiore, Gene 1755
Montel, Michael 748, 847
Montell, Jermaine 1325
Monteux, Pierre 344
Montevecchi, Liliane 924
Montgomery, Andre 1141
Montgomery, Barbara 501, 630, 1620
Montgomery, Bruce 48
Montgomery, Janice Lynne 1397
Montgomery, Joan 1149, 1349
Montgomery, John 972
Montgomery, Kelly 1743
Montgomery, Paul 1235
Montgomery, Robert 85, 634, 958
Montgomery, Ronald 56
Montgomery, Susanne 127
Montgomery, Zoelle 392, 454
Monti, Anthony 1226
Montresor, Beni 891
Monzione, David 1644
Moody, Carolyn 834, 920
Moody, Debbie 834
Moody, Duane A. 1623

Moody, Jacquelynne 1814
Moody, James 682, 709, 1509
Moody, Janette 501
Moody, Michael R. 1201
Moon, David (Dave) 745, 946, 1295, 1599, 1754
Moon, Hyo Jung 889
Moon, Joseph F. 112
Moon, Keith 1655
Moon, Marjorie 603
Moon, Sylvia 91
Moonen, Rick 273
Mooney, Ellie 863
Mooney, Maureen 1072
Mooney, Michael 1709
Mooney, Robert 290
Mooney, William 803
Moonves, Leslie 486
Moore, Al 1543
Moore, Anne 1556
Moore, Barbara 1015
Moore, Brennan 1636
Moore, Charles 68, 91, 152, 188, 715
Moore, Charles Werner 1691
Moore, Charlotte 13, 570, 775, 914
Moore, Crista 157, 1328, 1523
Moore, Cy 1169
Moore, Dana 1250
Moore, Donald C. 1380
Moore, Douglas 92, 254, 1789
Moore, Elizabeth 588
Moore, G. Eugene 1270
Moore, H. Thomas 551
Moore, James 913, 1543
Moore, Jason 77
Moore, Jessica Care 196
Moore, Jim 1185
Moore, John J. 1007
Moore, Judith 453, 979, 1250, 1557
Moore, Lloyd 615
Moore, Lorraine 196, 1002
Moore, Maggie 1237
Moore, Martha 1729
Moore, Marvin 1475
Moore, Maureen 109, 237, 496, 1704
Moore, Mavor 56
Moore, Melba 790
Moore, Michael 1514
Moore, Nita 275
Moore, Perry 278
Moore, R.G. 454
Moore, Rhonda 1487
Moore, Robert 1116
Moore, Roy 1146
Moore, Ruth 789
Moore, Sally 1131
Moore, Tim 975
Moore, Tom 625, 1719
Moore, Tracy 823, 1360
Moore, Van 1776
Moore, Vivian 815
Moorehead, Verma 816
Mopsy 722, 1038
Morales, Haydee 262
Morales, Lilana 488
Morales, Mark 319
Morales, Millie 897
Moran, Alan 66
Moran, Don 962
Moran, James 826
Moran, John 195, 1018
Moran, Martin 503, 999, 1006, 1190
Moran, Michael P. 657
Moran, Paul 1066
Moran, Peter 1470
Moran, Robert 846
Moranzoni, Roberto 905, 1369, 1597
Morath, Kathryn 27
Morath, Kathy 1309, 1485, 1800
Morath, Max 457, 901
Morcum, James Steward 955
Mordden, Ethan 1024
Mordecai, Benjamin 1631
Mordente, Lisa 54, 854, 1025
Mordoh, Abraham 819, 1453
Morea, Gabor 601, 1666
Morea, Robert 779, 1531
Moreau, Peter 1080
Morehead, Ronald K. 404
Moreland, Donald 187
Moreno, Deborah 1147
Moreno, Donato 763
Moreno, Soni 1625
Moreno, Yolanda 1802
Morenzie, Leon 304, 1633
Morera, James 717
Morfee, Scott 607
Morgan, Agnes 618, 619, 620, 621, 622
Morgan, Alfred 1131
Morgan, Andre 333
Morgan, Cass 186, 503, 544, 656, 754, 770, 864, 873, 1317, 1726
Morgan, Charles F. 190
Morgan, Christopher L. 934
Morgan, Clark 425
Morgan, Danny 177, 667, 1045, 1380, 1758
Morgan, Denise 1065, 1648
Morgan, Dennis A. 809
Morgan, Dotty 337
Morgan, Eric 889
Morgan, Ethel A. 1030
Morgan, James 14, 71, 88, 148, 190, 213, 308, 398, 435, 463, 476, 485, 491, 567, 570, 656, 778, 812, 829, 914, 926, 930, 948, 1031, 1056, 1071, 1099, 1144, 1151, 1213, 1214, 1289, 1306, 1366, 1451, 1482, 1507, 1547, 1581, 1750, 1756
Morgan, Jim 1149, 1709
Morgan, Judy 318
Morgan, Juliette 538
Morgan, Lee 37
Morgan, Robbi 337
Morgan, Roger 306, 307, 321, 343, 390, 466, 784, 827, 831, 860, 958, 998, 1231, 1534, 1691, 1719, 1739, 1751
Morgan, Tom 621
Morgenstern, Sam 1161
Morginsky, Martin 1445
Moriber, Brooke Sunny 805, 1103
Morick, Jeanine 260
Moritz, Albert 507
Moritz, Dwayne 1098
Morkin, Claire 1832
Morley, Carol 50, 342, 556, 557, 1290, 1483, 1488
Morley, Karen 98
Morley, Ruth 284, 331, 609, 1227, 1360, 1534, 1667
Morley, Sheridan 751
Morlino, Jim 1591
Morlock, Martin 1775
Morningstar, Carter 1448
Morocco 772
Morokoff, Paul 506
Moross, Jerome 569, 600, 601
Morozova, Zinaida 849
Morrell, Christina 1764
Morris, Anita 42, 1704
Morris, Christine 426
Morris, Edward 350, 1255
Morris, Edwin H. 1447
Morris, James 112, 1131
Morris, Janet Moody 68
Morris, Jay Hunter 640
Morris, Jennifer R. 607
Morris, Joan 257
Morris, Joanne 1349
Morris, John 649, 1221, 1254, 1807
Morris, Jonathan 317
Morris, Kenny 539, 800, 808
Morris, Kimi 1190
Morris, Leander 1070
Morris, Lee 1475
Morris, Libby 853
Morris, Lisa 1441
Morris, Margaret 910
Morris, Mark 363, 1139
Morris, Marti 244
Morris, Matthew S. 1630
Morris, Melissa 462
Morris, Michael 1444
Morris, Nat 278
Morris, Peter 607, 1772
Morris, Peter Charles 1450
Morris, Robert 1188
Morris, Steven 1188
Morris, Tyjuana 247
Morris, William 745
Morris, Zoie 668
Morrisey, Bob 442, 773
Morrison, Adrienne 618, 619
Morrison, Ann 36, 412, 586
Morrison, Eleanor 578
Morrison, Fraser 1530
Morrison, Lee 1315
Morrison, Matthew 1598
Morrison, Paul 66, 80, 686, 1000
Morrison, Peggy 150
Morrison, Richard 397, 427
Morrison, Toni 1022
Morrison, William 45, 1478
Morrissey, Paul 1007
Morrissey, Ray 1440
Morrock, Richard 1646
Morrow, Karen 201, 1096, 1468
Morrow, Milo 1072, 1397
Morrow, Rob 284
Morrow, Scott D. 666
Morse, Barry 1393
Morse, Muriel 1603
Morse, Richard 34
Morse, Tilda 535
Morsell, Fred 1107
Morss, Chester 1259
Mortifee, Ann 963
Mortimer, Jennie 101
Mortimer, Sally 66
Morton, Brooks 1364
Morton, George E., III 1423
Morton, Joe 740, 1078, 1395, 1396, 1691
Morton, Joy Venus 1030
Morton, King 1682
Morton, Linda 255
Morton, Richard 497
Morton, Tommy 942
Morton, Vince 1370
Morton, Winn (Winniford) 68, 236, 980, 1021, 1221, 1483
Moscartolo, Jonas 1135
Mosel, Tad 987
Moseley, Felicia 1487
Moseley, Page 1282
Moser, Nina 1522
Moser, Phillip 1380
Moser, William F. 1508
Moses, Burke 479
Moses, Denise 1805
Moses, Gilbert 959
Moses, Ken 877
Mosher, Gregory 805, 1401, 1665
Mosher, Evan 619
Mosher, Susan (Sue) 83, 1551
Mosiman, Marnie 1380
Moskowitz, Martin 819
Mosley, Milledge 310, 927
Moss, Dewey 1771
Moss, Helen 1315
Moss, Jane 763
Moss, Jeffrey 406
Moss, Jeffrey B. 147, 489, 603, 666, 1037
Moss, Kathi 394, 625, 710, 789, 1733
Moss, Kurt 1276
Moss, Larry 350, 771, 1069, 1273
Moss, Maia A. 1054
Moss, Robert 763, 794, 1079, 1355, 1553, 1784
Mosse, Spencer 426, 480, 1411, 1471, 1635
Mostel, Joshua (Josh) 1057, 1313, 1534
Mostel, Zero 1192
Mostoller, (Joe) 1754
Mott, Michael 1153
Mott, Reverie 362
Motta, Gustavo 877
Motyka, Bill 299
Motyka, Tad 989
Moulson, Robert 1165
Mourning, Inez 906
Mowatt, Anna Cora 481
Mowell, Shelley 1447, 1448
Mowry, Greg 1584
Moy, Nanci 983
Moyer, Allen 69, 641
Moyer, Mimi 1408
Moyes, Dennis W. 1338
Mrozek, Christian 1281
Msomi, Mandla 651
Msomi, Welcome 358, 651
Mucci, Anthony 161
Mucci, Kimberly 223, 960
Muckle, Charles 1070
Muehsam, Erich 1241
Muelle, Maison 340
Mueller, Frederic 369
Mueller, Zizi 250, 1471
Muenz, Richard 300, 1831
Mufson, Lauren 643
Mugleston, Linda 1186
Mulay, Brian 1818
Mulcahy, John 1366
Mulcahy, Lance 350, 542, 708, 1255, 1273, 1437, 1568, 1569, 1661
Mulch, Steve 1759
Mulett, Toni 897
Mulford, Florence 340
Mulheren, Michael 249, 503, 791
Mulholland, Kathryn 1278
Muligan, Joe 1216
Mullen, David 1560
Mullen, William 1278
Muller, Chris 1120
Muller, Ernst 1309
Muller, Jane 79
Muller, Jennifer 364, 1187, 1706
Muller, Romeo 1078
Mulligan, Grady 726
Mullikin, Bill 199
Mullin, Stephen 241
Mullins, The Reverend Andrew J.W. 1316
Mullins, Carol 397, 999
Mullins, Michael 1349
Mullins, Patrick 155
Mulrean, Linda 860
Mulvaney, Lon 412
Mulvey, Mike 1040
Mulvihill, Brendan 1411
Mumaw, Barton 600
Munda, Valerie 654
Mundi, Billy 7
Munford, Gordon 76
Munger, Kendra 1320
Munier, Leon 1107
Munjee, Tara 505
Munoz, Isai Jess 1416
Munoz, Javier 760
Munoz, Rodney 95, 741
Munso, Felix 1264
Murakoshi, Suzen 1410
Murawski, C. 316, 605, 611, 1701
Murcell, Raymond (Ray) 53, 713, 887, 1510, 1708
Murdock, David H. 1717
Murdy, Rachel Benbow 399
Mure, Glenn 326, 1378
Murfitt, Mary 323, 1176
Murger, Henri 186
Murin, David 86, 157, 179, 181, 267, 484, 721, 1546
Murin, Patti 1056
Murney, Christopher 699
Murney, Julia (K.) 296, 1031, 1637, 1778
Murnoch, Michael 995
Murphy, Charles 1196
Murphy, Donna 157, 539, 683, 1109, 1304, 1454, 1495
Murphy, Drew 113, 417
Murphy, Edward, Jr. 649
Murphy, Emmet 1577
Murphy, Judy 759
Murphy, Karen 1831
Murphy, Kevin 1347
Murphy, Lambert 340, 1075
Murphy, Matt 38
Murphy, Morna 1443
Murphy, Olive 253
Murphy, Patricia 1674
Murphy, Sally 130, 1006
Murphy, Shamus 1342
Murphy, Stephanie 194
Murphy, Susan 475, 1394
Murphy, Turk 105
Murphy, William, III 1283
Murphy-Palmer, Kathleen 1002
Murray, Art 1
Murray, Bill 1112
Murray, Billy 85
Murray, Braham 655
Murray, Carl 1559
Murray, Charles "C.B." 116, 682, 1509
Murray, Christopher 1222
Murray, David 1590
Murray, Don 1483
Murray, John Horton 574
Murray, Kathleen 870, 902
Murray, Lee 1131
Murray, Mary Gordon 1, 179, 873, 1201, 1513, 1693
Murray, Michael 985
Murray, Rachel 363
Murray, S. Barkley 81
Murray, Sharon 1151
Murray-Walsh, Merrily 1022
Murril, Herbert 1241
Musaeus, Louise 1597
Musayelian, Irena 849
Musco, Tony 144
Muselli, Fred 1080
Musiat, Andrzej 1275
Musselman, David 162, 1176
Musser, Tharon 283, 715, 806, 873, 1193, 1492, 1694
Muzio, Gloria 220, 1694

Myers, Bernard 95
Myers, Brooke 158
Myers, Edward 1264
Myers, Gordon 1729
Myers, JD 240
Myers, Joanna 1511
Myers, John Bernard 571
Myers, Johnny 1754
Myers, Laurie Alyssa 1195
Myers, Lou 1579
Myers, Mary 123
Myers, Nancy 160, 979
Myers, Nancy Jo 1548
Myers, Paulene 1810
Myers, Peter 1431
Myers, Sellwyn 494
Myers, Shelley 510
Myers, Stanley 449
Myers, Tom 1540
Myers, Troy 1250, 1538
Myerson, Alan 22
Myhers, John 277
Myler, Randal 37, 411, 657, 754, 777, 965
Mylett, Jeffrey 595, 1620
Myrvik, Norman 1217
Mysell, Bella 585
Mysels, George 379

Nabel, Bill 848
Nadeau, Nicky 1293
Nadler, Mark 46, 1442
Nadler, Shelia 363
Naegele, Matthias 170
Nagai, Reiko 602
Nagakura, Kyoichi 602
Nagano, Kent 363
Nagara, Jun 1300
Nagatsu, Hiroko 1410
Nager, Jesse 474
Nagy, John 1691
Nagy, Robert 62, 1718
Nahan, Laurent 1608
Nahat, Dennis 958
Naify, Marshall 716
Naim, Sharon Ben 108
Naimo, Jennifer 49, 435, 1650
Najimy, Kathy 83
Nakachi, Mari 1631
Nakagawa, Jon 114, 285, 658, 848
Nakagawa, Setsuko 602
Nakajima, Kumiko 1410
Nakao, Kenji 289
Nalepka, Brian 1656
Nally, Danielle 273
Namanworth, Phillip 492
Nambu 1653
Nancy-Suzanne 255
Napoli, Tony 1418
Napolitano, Peter 1040, 1670
Narayan, Manu 1458
Nardone, Jeff 563
Narizzano, Dino 654
Nash, Brian J. 328
Nash, Joe 944
Nash, Matthew 1673
Nash, Ogden 843, 942
Nash, Raphael 960
Nash, Ron 653, 1589
Nason, Brian 13, 411
Nassau, Paul 472
Nastasi, Frank 291, 1455
Nathan, Jamie Beth 915
Nathan, Stephen 595
Nation, Billy 1145
Nation, Tony 525
Natkowski, Richard 236
Naufts, Geoffrey 1187
Naughton, Amanda 727, 1067, 1375
Naughton, David 610, 1282
Naughton, Greg 791
Naughton, Harry 1716
Naughton, James 806
Nault, Fernand 1655
Naumkin, Yury 849
Navaja, Flaco 1429
Navarre, Ron 1591
Navon, Ruthi 401
Nayden, Mark 778
Naylor, Charles 1475
Naylor, Ian 913
Naylor, Wesley (W.) 196, 1002
Ndlovu, Nandi 1401
Neal, Brynn 1669
Neal, Joseph 65, 162, 304, 402, 720, 795, 798, 801, 1270, 1480, 1635
Nealon, Mary T. 162, 1176
Neals, Lawrence A., Jr. 839
Nealy, Milton Craig 1191
Nease, Bud 948
Nease, Byron 163
Neate, Ken 331
Nebreda, Vicente 609
Neck, Throgs 402
Nederlander, James L. 1347
Nederlander, James M. 1656
Nee, Michael 1263
Nee, Michael (James) 1263
Needham, Ann 600
Neeley, Ted 1426
Neff, John 609
Neff, Morty 379
Negbaur, Gary 1786
Negin, Louis 963
Negron, Rick 1536, 1538
Negus, Chris 1029
Nehls, David 627, 1742
Nehring, Karl-Heinz 455
Neiden, Daniel 643, 659, 1327, 1505
Neiditch, Max 441
Neighbors, George 698
Neil, Julian 456
Neil, Roger 164, 1348, 1414
Neill, Hailie 123
Neill, Jeffrey K. 61, 64, 840, 841, 842, 1354, 1408, 1676
Neill, William 1462
Neilson, Astrid 66
Neilson, Richard 1163
Neiman, Rod 1020
Neishloss, Curt 699
Nelis, Tom 1429
Nellis, Jeff 778, 1210, 1421, 1830
Nelson, Alva 205
Nelson, Ann 1179
Nelson, Beau 1385
Nelson, Brian 49
Nelson, Bruce 1678
Nelson, Doug 1439
Nelson, Eva 547
Nelson, Frances 1816
Nelson, Gail 237, 1096, 1473
Nelson, Gene 1096
Nelson, Herbert 547
Nelson, Jen 1385
Nelson, Jerry 1790, 1791, 1796
Nelson, Keith 175
Nelson, Kenneth 478, 858, 1400
Nelson, Lispet 1221
Nelson, Madeleine Yayodele 688
Nelson, Mari 1706
Nelson, Mennie F. 1174
Nelson, Mervyn 1420
Nelson, Nan-Lynn 1384
Nelson, Novella 707, 715
Nelson, Portia 371, 600, 929
Nelson, Randy 1439
Nelson, Richard 219, 260, 263, 268, 364, 409, 654, 698, 699, 805, 839, 865, 866, 1048, 1103, 1152, 1199, 1243, 1353, 1473, 1514, 1557, 1831
Nelson, Ruth 307
Nelson, Steve 542, 771, 1255
Nemec, Mike 510
Nemetz, Lee 1192, 1445
Nemetz, Lenora 41, 1565
Nemhauser, Frank 910
Nemser, Alec 719
Nemser, Bob 719
Neptune, Peter 854
Nesby, Ann 1466
Nesha 852
Ness Philip, John Van 1585
Ness, Pedar (Peter) 241, 1122
Nessell, Alfie 920
Neu, James 397
Neu, Thea 951, 1639, 1640
Neuberger, Jan 267, 272, 285, 1328
Neufeld, Peter 52
Neuland, Jennifer F. (L.) 58, 703
Neuman, David 1193
Neuman, Joan 1030
Neumann, Heinz 1481
Neumann, Krista 246, 1761
Neuner, Chris 769
Neusom, Daniel 1434
Neuwirth, Bebe 443, 689, 1365, 1709
Neville, Marcus 224, 814, 1052
Neville-Andrews, John 303, 623
Nevins, Zebra 201, 1131
New, Babette 779
New, Nancy 1079
Neway, Patricia 1083, 1413, 1474, 1583, 1814
Newberry, Doyle 1274
Newborn, Barbary 369
Newborn, Scott 725
Newburge, David 1517
Newby, Jerry 1193
Newcomb, Don 233
Newcome, Chuck 197
Newell, Erika 43
Newhall, William 1544
Newland, Eric 161
Newley, Anthony 1101
Newman, Andrew Hill 157
Newman, Arthur 92, 609, 1131, 1563, 1583, 1587, 1596
Newman, Catherine 1733
Newman, David 1168
Newman, Harold J. 1350
Newman, Jim 37, 610, 1706
Newman, Linda 1227
Newman, Molly 1323
Newman, Neal 1389
Newman, Paula 403
Newman, Peter 1348
Newman, Phyllis 735, 992, 1048, 1106, 1132, 1427, 1534, 1717
Newman, Randy 1036, 1049, 1334
Newman, Ronnie 1541
Newman, Rosalind 289
Newman, Stephen D. 1279
Newman, William 117
Newmyer, Doyle 1764
Newport, Elaina 247
Newsome, Paula 69, 1726
Newton, Adele 1601
Newton, John 190, 1433
Newton-Brown, Michael 442, 537
Ngan, Dimacula 1617
Ngema, Mbongeni 1401
Ngema, Nhlanhla 1401
Nhlanhla, Thandekile 1401
Nicelli, Angelo 66
Nicholas, Bryan 1398
Nicholas, Harold 82, 1738
Nicholas, Robert 719
Nicholaw, Casey 273, 1250
Nicholls, Allan 1426
Nichols, Billy 1534
Nichols, Bobb 1636
Nichols, Bud 1132
Nichols, Darius 845, 1830
Nichols, Linda 1405
Nichols, Mike 151, 806, 1519
Nichols, Noreen 980
Nichols, Peter 1304
Nicholson, Alan 1194
Nicholson, Robert 1010
Nicholson, Terry 705, 1119
Nichtern, Claire 98
Nick, Walter 1811
Nickell, April 1425
Nickerson, Dawn 1364
Nickerson, E. Lynn 1007
Nicol, Lesslie 1008
Nicola, James C. 206, 414, 859, 1351, 1429, 1499
Nicolaisen, Kari 1305
Nicolas, Claire 1244
Nicole, Diane 212
Nicoletti, L.A. 1116
Nicoll, Charles 1058
Nicoll, Fay 1342
Nicoll, Jonathan 231
Niehenke, Walter 312, 1270
Nielsen, Diana Lee 68
Nielsen, Kristine 632
Niemark, Bert 1751
Niemtzow, Annette 108
Nierendorf, Phyllis 1790, 1791, 1796
Nieske, David 1494
Nieuwenhuis, Hans 1405
Nieves, Richard 201, 1021
Nieves, Sandra 118
Nigh, Tom 1577
Nighbert, David 224
Nighbert, Stephanie 19
Nightingale, Bill 1283
Nikolais, Alwin 910, 1291
Niland, Peter 834
Niles, Barbara 320, 414, 419, 1212
Nimkoff, Mark 363
Nimnicht, Darren 910
Nisbet, Lindy 486
Nisenson, Amanda 362
Nishikata, Satoshi 1653
Niven, Kip 58
Niven, Sally 1154
Nixon, April 950
Nixon, Marni 805, 1204, 1582
The N.N.N. Company 89
Noa, Alii 1221
Nobbs, Keith 1545
Nobel, Iona 66
Nobel, Michael 1297
Noble, James 421
Noble, Judy 1349, 1776
Noble, Mae 620, 621, 622
Noble, Timothy 1730
Nocciolino, Albert 916, 1049
Noel, Andrea 1679
Noel, Daniel 726
Noel, Tom 98, 1008, 1164, 1221, 1824
Noh, David 1030
Noire, Rosetta Le 238, 885
Nolasco, Elvis 262
Nolen, Joyce 312, 1035
Nolen, Timothy 256
Nolfi, Ed 961, 1021
Nolin, Denise 1138
Noling, David 1011
Noll, Christiane 240, 491, 541, 930
Nollman, Barbara 704
Nolte, Bill 1390
Nomikos, Andreas 609, 677
Noodt, Brian 1148
Noonan, Brian 395
Noonan, John 1376
Noonan, Roger 1151
Noone, James 170, 296, 323, 633, 741, 1219, 1386, 1670
Norbert, James 1217
Norbo, Zahra 779
Nordon, Denise 1108
Nordstrom, Ben 612
Nordstrom, Cynthia 462
Norfleet, Cecelia 885
Normal, Nerida 216
Norman, Carl 381, 415, 1261, 1430
Norman, Dara 394
Norman, Grant 825
Norman, Hal 253
Norman, Jay 93, 1358
Norman, Kay 63
Norman, Marek 364
Norman, Rende Rae 1362
Normand, Henry “Bootsie” 1746
Normoyle, Tracie 198
Norris, Christopher 1420
Norris, Dallett 1231
Norris, Rufus 1412
Norris, Ruth Ann 322
Norris, Shirley 1445
Northen, Robert 1735
Northmore, Jack 56
Norton, Coe 1594
Norton, Richard 424
Norvind, Nailea 1617
Norwick, Douglas 179, 215, 672, 1339, 1546, 1582
Norwood 1002
Norworth, Jack 377
Noto, Lore 478, 779
Nottage, Lynn 2
Notzan, Shlomo 1203
Nova, Ars 72
Novak, Joseph 988, 1597
Novoa, Salvador 188
Nowak, Christopher 690
Noy, Michael 1203
Ntinga, Themba 1561
Nudelman, M. 898
Nugent, Nancy Elliott 1185
Nugent, Rodney 1370
Nuki, Christine 1336
Numark, Michael 505
Nunes, John 1671
Nunes, Paul 1146, 1363
Nunn, Alice 535
Nuphar, Eylon 108
Nurock, Kirk 1395, 1396
Nute, Don 920
Nutter, Mark 1777
Nye, Gene 419, 1094, 1520
Nygh, Anna 303
Nygren, James 1131
Nype, Russell 884, 1585

Oakes, Betty 61, 1399, 1440
Oakes, Gary 201, 1446
Oakes, Michael 1692
Oakley, G. William 105
Oakley, Scott 1149, 1150
Oaks, Lois Ann 601
Ober, Margaret 245
O’Boyle, William 1653
Obrecht, Martha 1494
O’Brien, Erin 848
O’Brien, Frank 848, 1616, 1689
O’Brien, Geoffrey 654

O'Brien, Hazel 136
O'Brien, Joe 654
O'Brien, John 573
O'Brien, Sylvia 360, 1161
O'Brien, Vince 902
O'Brien, Virginia 145
O'Brien, Andy 1411
O'Byrne, Bryan 1058
Ocasio, Rosemarie 598
Ochoa, Steven 1139
O'Connell, Charlie 394
O'Connell, Connie 376
O'Connell, Maggie 1287
O'Connell, Marilyn 1287
O'Connell, Patricia 1562
O'Connell, Patrick 1200
O'Connor, Brian Brucker 1113
O'Connor, Daniel 110
O'Connor, Giles 1754
O'Connor, J.T. 746
O'Connor, Kevin 562, 1042
O'Connor, Leland 1221
O'Connor, Shamus 1259
Oddie, Bill 241, 1122
Oddo, John 806
Odegaard, Myron 822
O'Dell, Janice 1716
Odenz, Leon 1030, 1402, 1704
Odette, Marchant 1580
Oditz, Carol 551, 681, 699, 1665, 1704, 1776
Odom, Ben 615
O'Donnell, Josie 974
O'Donnell, Mark 974
O'Donnell, Mary 1438
O'Donnell, Mary Eileen 1011
O'Donnell, Richard 1194
O'Donnell, Sally 1644
Odorisio, Rob 755, 770
Odums, Rick 255
Oei, David 12
Oenslager, Donald 40, 92, 1789
Oesterman, Phil 270, 913, 1542
Ofer, Roy 108
Offenbach, Jacques 124, 190, 1619
Offner, Deborah 847
Offt, Tom 1096, 1268
O'Flaherty, Douglas 144, 770
O'Flaherty, Joseph 318
O'Flaherty, Michael 695, 1650
O'Flynn, Eddie 902
Ofrane, Etan 1381
Ofrane, Josh 1381
Ogando, Edie 1134
Ogawa, Toshiro 1580
Ogborn, Michael James 198
Ogden, Connie 1310
Oglesby, Thomas 1367
O'Grady, Christine 328
O'Grady, Dan 172
O'Hara, Brian 1476
O'Hara, Edith 1548, 1659
O'Hara, Jenny 655, 1397
O'Hara, Jill 649, 655
O'Hara, John 198
O'Hara, Kelli 1103
O'Hara, Lyle 1661
O'Hara, Paige 575, 626, 912, 1167
O'Hare, Brad 1624
O'Hearn, Robert 1043, 1165
O'Hearn, Steve 1516
O'Horgan, Tom 1206, 1426, 1649, 1765
Ohrenstein, Dora 1200
Oirich, Steven (Steve) 500, 1124, 1290
Oka, Marc C. 289
Okazaki, Alan 1551
O'Keefe, Paul 88
Oken, Stuart 97, 916
Okerson, Doris 944
Okerson, Doug 1305
Okun, Alexander 1584, 1665
O'Kun, Lan 1574
Olaf, Pierre 1604
Olana 1520
Olcott, Emery 541
Oldfather, Craig 322
O'Leary, Chris 991
O'Leary, Kevin 661
Oleksa (a/k/a Jeanette Oleska) 23, 180, 1027, 1334
Olesky, Marek 1275
Olheim, Helen 40
Olim, Dorothy 478, 601, 1265
Olin, Ellsworth 109
Olivares, Luis 488
Olive, Marcy 1589
Oliver, Barrie 1315
Oliver, Bill 601
Oliver, Don 120, 960
Oliver, Donald 1683
Oliver, Helen 1131
Oliver, Jesse 1066
Oliver, Leon 470
Oliver, Lynn 1349
Oliver, Robert R. 479
Oliver, Thelma 291, 504, 715
Oliver-Norman, Peter 15
Oliviero, Lodovico 1010
Olivo, Karen 760
Olmon, Wynn 935
Olmos, Milton 1221
Olmstead, Remington 494
Olmsted, Jeffrey 419
Olon, John 1568, 1569
Olon-Scrymgeour, John 1062
Olrod, David 1530
Olsen, Bob 1388
Olsen, Gayle Swymer 4
Olsen, Ingrid 1419
Olsen, Robert 1484
Olsen, Steve 273
Olson, Bob 877, 1166
Olson, Marcus 70
Olson, Murray 1154
Olson, Stephen 1498
Olsson, Bjorn 129
Olstad, Dena 293, 497
O'Malley, Kerry 206
O'Malley, Mary W. 985
O'Malley, Sean 356
O'Malley, Tom 121
O'Mara, Terry 534
Omero, Costas 955
Omeron, Guen 1131
Omura, June 363
O'Neal, Cynthia 1427, 1519, 1717
O'neal, Frederick 91
O'Neal, Liz 1825
O'Neal, Michael 1709
O'Neal, Patrick 1709
O'Neil, F.J. 121
O'Neil, J.R. 1145
O'Neil, Paddie 1316
O'Neill, Dick 676
O'Neill, Eugene 440
O'Neill, James 697
O'Neill, Lisa 1469
Oney, Judy 1349
Ono, Yoko 1666
Onyango, Akki 1589
Opalach, Dorothy 259
Opalach, Jan 1730
Opatoshu, David 147, 1822
Opatz, Mari 1139
Opel, Nancy 727, 1243, 1557, 1712
Ophir, Shai K. 529
O'Quinn, Terry 710
Oquita, Ric 282
Oram, Harold L. 120
Orange, Fredi 1388
Orbach, Jerry 324, 478
Orbach, Ron 916
Ordassy, Carlotta 891
Ordynski, Richard 245, 298, 905, 1369, 1597
O'Reilly, Ciaran 13, 570, 775, 914
O'Reilly, The Reverend John 1727
O'Reilly, Rosemary 826
Orem, Susan 142
Oremus, Stephen 1634, 1778
Oren, Christine 42
Orfaly, Alexander (Alex) 827, 1279, 1358, 1360
Orfeh 627
Orgal, Yehiel 1203
Orin, Renee 1452, 1677
Orkin, Therese 1568
Orlando, Joyce 379, 1166
Orloff, Penny 1462
Orlow, Elzbieta 1275
Orman, Roscoe 996
Ormond, Michael 563
O'Rourke, P.J. 1114
Orselli, Raimonda 1596
Ortega, Juana 488
Orth, Robert 673
Ortman, George 235
Orton, Erik 67
Orum, Cathy 1509
Osakalumi, Adesola "D'incred-ible" 804
Osaki, Shay'anne 1221
Osato, Sono 1192
Osberg, Susan 800
Osborn, Ron 1682
Osborne, Eunice 1278
Osborne, John 445
Osborne, Robert 170
Osbun, Eric 680
Osburn, Alan 1800
Osburn, Seth 1690
Oscar, Brad 516, 517
Oscar, Gail 1045
Osco, Bill 30
Oser, Julie 944
O'Shaughnessy, Bronwyn 1337
O'Shea, Sally 1512
O'Shea, Tom 1337
Oshrin, Sidney S. 735
Osin, Fred 676
Osorio, Richard 1330
Ossa, Mossa 1080
Ossig, Drik 26
Ost, Bob 461, 1149, 1150
Ost, Tobin 37, 1425, 1830
Osteman, Georg 1359
Oster, Mike 385
Osterman, Curt 345
Osterman, Georg 1182
Ostermann, Curt 345, 1380, 1816
Osterwald, Bibi 600
Ostler, Bruce "Skippy" 79
Ostling, Dan 583
Ostrin, Art 1148, 1311, 1628
Ostrow, Carol 129, 711
Ostrow, Stuart 45
Ostrowski, Gordon 717
O'Sullivan, Anne 848
O'Sullivan, Michael 962
O'Sullivan, Patrick 1331
Osuna, Tracy 1660
Otero, Geisha 255
Otis, Jeannine 156
Otis, Phoebe 1611
O'Toole, Austin 902
Ott, E. Suzan 770
Otte, Charles 123
Ottenheimer, Albert M. 779
Otto, Liz 734, 1196, 1274
Ouelette, Gratian 1661
Ourisman, Jamie 767
Ousley, John Mack 1560
Ouzounian, Richard 159
Ovchinnikov, Rady 849
Overbey, Kelly 1188
Overett, Adam 845
Ovington, Erma 1543
Owen, Carmen 71
Owen, Donna 254, 488
Owen, Hanna 488
Owen, Jeanne 1278
Owen, Louise 805
Owen, Lynn 1329
Owen, Richard 1329
Owen, Richard, Jr. 1329
Owens, Anne-Marie 439
Owens, Dan 934
Owens, Elizabeth 345, 445
Owens, Eric 640
Owens, Frank 1435
Owens, Jill 1644
Owens, Philip (a/k/a Phillip Owen) 467, 834, 920, 1387, 1776
Owens, Rochelle 860
Oxberry, Cindy C. 4
Oxley, J. Leonard 333
Oxman, Robin 1785
Oyebola, Ifatumbo 20
Oyelowo, David 1629

Paaz, Nira 62, 529
Pabon, Jorge "Fabel" 804
Pace, Atkin 855
Pace, Jean 835
Pace, Michael 1365
Pachl, Connie 1764
Pacho, Andrew 1139
Pacitti, Joe 1743
Paddison, Gordon 179
Padgett, Billy 125
Padgett, Donald 1477
Padilla, Evelyn 349
Padilla, Louis 377, 726, 873
Padilla, Sandy 823, 834, 920, 1280, 1349, 1776
Padron, Aurelio 203, 1483
Padula, Edward 400
Pagan, Antoine 897
Pagan, Evelyn 897
Page, Autris 1816
Page, Betty 1543
Page, Carolann 71, 496, 1046, 1139
Page, Don 1445
Page, Evelyn 1684
Page, Frank 550
Page, Jacqueline 985
Page, Ken 18, 959
Page, Patricia L. 644
Page, Stan 601
Pagent, Robert 821
Paget, Daniel 962
Paget, Dennis 909
Pahl, Ellen 173
Pai, Ian 1674
Paige, Amanda Ryan 1830
Paige, Frances 1131
Paige, Joan 1021
Paige, Kelley 1148
Paisner, Dina 1400, 1412
Pake, Greg 1376
Pakledinaz, Martin 1560, 1778
Palazola, Tori Lynn 39
Palermo, Alex 74, 1060, 1594
Paley, Joel 1386
Palin, Pat 1445
Palmer, Artie 1385
Palmer, D. 1591
Palmer, David 241
Palmer, Elizabeth (P.) 695, 1323
Palmer, Jeree 1435
Palmer, Joni 152, 214
Palmer, Leland 342, 1827
Palmer, Skip 1153
Palmer, Steve 1627
Palmer, Winthrop 1060
Palmieri, Joseph (Joe) 117, 244, 1697
Palminteri, Chaz 1682
Palomo, Martinez 488
Paltrinieri, Giordano 1047, 1249
Paltrow, Bruce W. 1767
Palumbo, Patti 1021
Paluzzi, Pamela 1471
Pamplin, Kevin 1629
Panaro, Hugh 933, 1759
Pandel, Ted 876
Pandor, Miriam 1445
Panetta, George 867
Pang, Joanna 1410
Panian, Maggie 3
Panian, Susan Kelly 3
Panich, David 472, 858, 1318, 1754
Panis, Reuben 861
Panizza, Ettore 762, 776
Pankin, Stuart 582, 1787
Panko, Tom 274, 357, 1152, 1196
Pann, Tony Michael 796
Panthaky, Kay 897
Pantojas, Antonio 1013
Panzer, Linda 940
Panzer, Marty 1153
Paoletti, John 1230, 1777
Paoli, Diana 287
Paoluccio, Tricia 365
Paoluzi, Gianfranco 1722
Papa, Victor 1124
Papandreas, Johniene 1160
Papas, Theodore 1219
Papay, Raymond 488, 1137
Papezik, Rudolf 1609
Papi, Gennaro 298
Papis, Zbigniew 1275
Papotto, Giovanni 859
Papp, Ilona 223
Papp, Joseph 27, 65, 175, 283, 346, 364, 386, 426, 561, 580, 647, 649, 664, 726, 753, 832, 873, 900, 910, 958, 975, 1055, 1057, 1072, 1109, 1146, 1183, 1270, 1291, 1375, 1384, 1398, 1502, 1532, 1628, 1633, 1657, 1664, 1689, 1697, 1699, 1706, 1722, 1731, 1746, 1788
Pappas, John 984
Pappas, Shelly 1342, 1382
Pappas, Theodore 311, 370, 377, 690
Pappas, Victor 660
Paquereau, Paul 1075
Paquet, Marie 609, 1789
Paradiso, Roger 1412
Paraiso, Nicky 500
Pararozzi, Robert 1042
Pardee, E. Bette 985
Pardes, Erika 505
Parell, Nancy 1259
Parent, Gayle 126, 350, 557, 558, 771, 852
Parent, Richard 49
Parente, Paul 1816
Parente, Teresa 1389
Parfenyuk, Nikolai 849
Parham, Kitty 166
Parichy, Dennis 97, 133, 325, 362, 717, 909, 1234, 1235
Paris, Jackie 393

Parise, Tony 89, 1215
Pariseau, Kevin 1479
Parish, Mitchell 779, 1521
Park, Dick 488
Park, Dong Woo 889
Park, Joshua 1306
Park, Kolleen 889
Park, Michael 683, 1726
Park, Sang Hoe 889
Park, Scott 399
Park, Youn Cho 1625
Parker, Alecia 646
Parker, Carse David 1419
Parker, Daniel 1536
Parker, Dorothy 972
Parker, E. Huntington 1611
Parker, H.W. 1075
Parker, Howard 1193
Parker, Janet Lee 598
Parker, Lew 48
Parker, Pam 1470
Parker, Patrick 948, 1585
Parker, Rochelle 500
Parker, Roxann 486
Parker, Salli 572
Parker, Sara 101
Parker, Toby 1384, 1522
Parks, Beverly 996
Parks, Don 87, 822, 852, 858, 1255
Parks, Freeman 1475
Parks, John 1029
Parks, Monica 153
Parks, Trina 268, 715
Parlato, Dennis 435, 675, 683, 791, 873, 1071, 1378, 1456
Parlow, Shane T. 1591
Parmeggiani, Frida 168
Parmelee, Eva 142
Parnell, Peter 1376, 1478
Parnes, Joey 207
Parr, Stephen 1505
Parran, J.D. 1816
Parrinello, Catherine 1050
Parrinello, Richard 1483
Parriott, John (Proctor) 716, 1592
Parris, Hamilton 1633
Parris, Steven J. 1160
Parrish, Elizabeth 826, 935, 1364
Parry, Sally E. 1354, 1676
Parry, William 70, 319, 372, 375, 386, 873, 1057, 1187, 1426, 1557
Parsi, Bruce Hall 1405
Parsinsen, Jennifer 474
Parson, Mary Jean 1400
Parsons, Charlotte 1117
Parsons, Estelle 434, 1261, 1360
Parsons, Jennifer 1323
Partier, Justin A. 995
Partington, Arthur 1448
Partington, Jeanne 1447
Partner, Mycroft 458
Parva, Cynthia 1290
Parva, Michael 1584
Parver, Michael 63
Pasatieri, Thomas 1416, 1741
Pascal, Stephen 348, 662, 886, 1459, 1546
Pasekoff, Marilyn 513, 1309
Pashalinski, Lola 426, 1182, 1359
Pask, Scott 189, 859, 1712
Paskin, Murray 605
Pasle, Tom 350, 1273
Pasqual, Julie 1288
Pasquale, Liz 397
Pasquale, Steven 1006, 1513, 1778
Pasquineli, Joanne 535
Pass, Lenny 1226
Passerell, Mark 1213, 1214
Passloff, Aileen 831, 1705
Passolt, Barbara 153
Passos, John Dos 864
Pasternack, Barbara 57, 845
Patek, Patrick J. 52
Patel, Neil 689, 837, 1499, 1612, 1645
Patelis, George 985, 1445
Patik, Vickie 243
Patinkin, Mandy 873, 1012, 1557
Patinkin, Sheldon 1230, 1352, 1724
Paton, Angela 373
Paton, Lucille 65
Patricia, Jim 156
Patrick, Fred 98
Patrick, Julian 254, 600, 1137, 1193
Patrick, Leonard 1692
Patrick, Neal 63
Patrick, Robert 1681
Patricola, Tom, Jr. 1177
Patriquin, Robert 1746
Patron, Elia (Elias) 147, 489, 666, 1745, 1822
Pattavina, Joanne 1391
Patten, Caymichael 1335
Pattenden, Mark 1629
Patterson, Charles H. 105
Patterson, Chuck 470, 682, 996
Patterson, Howard Jay 1439
Patterson, Jackie 153
Patterson, James 709, 1390
Patterson, Kelly 1016
Patterson, Kraig 363
Patterson, Lorna 54
Patterson, Phil 1346
Patterson, Raymond 278
Patterson, Robert 891
Patterson, Russell 1385
Patterson, Ruth Cleary 1385
Patterson, Vaughn 811
Patton, Lucille 1279, 1820
Patton, Monica L. 3, 934
Patton, Will 1391
Patuto, Matthew 1138
Paul, Alan 625
Paul, Bobby 1361, 1362
Paul, Don 1509
Paul, Jeff 940
Paul, Linda 1015
Paul, Madeline 275
Paul, Moira 66
Paul, Rene 317
Paul, Shelly 873
Paul, Stephanie 374
Paul, Steven 980
Paul, Thomas 1227
Paul, Tina 406, 658, 907, 1575, 1588
Paul, Vicki 803, 1147
Paulee, Mona 987
Paulette, Larry 913
Pauley, Wilbur 574, 670
Paulino, Peter M. 1676
Paull, Jarna 1010
Paull, Morgan 1605
Paulmann, Annette 26, 168
Paulo, Kathy 562
Paulsen, Beverly Ann 1177
Paulson, Erica L. 653
Paulus, Diane 399, 768
Pausel, George 510
Paveglio, Marjorie 66
Pavelka, Michael 182
Pavell, Barbara 1440
Pavlides, Frances 488
Pavlik, Nicholas 369
Pawk, Michele 14, 683, 1347
Paxton, Jill 983
Payne, Carl 1134
Payne, Gregory 397
Payne, Jim 856, 1089, 1151, 1194, 1443, 1548
Payne, Virginia 1594
Paynter, Lynn 1141
Paysen, Steven 1731
Paz, Rafi 617
Pazzo, Bob Del 976
Peabody, Christopher (Chris) 1354, 1676
Peachena 913
Peacock, Chiara 1536
Peacock, Michon 969, 1096, 1606, 1709
Pearce, Damon 116
Pearl, Barry 582
Pearl, Kenneth 1029
Pearl, Renee 1731
Pearle, Gary 1643, 1654
Pearlman, Jerry 985
Pearlman, Michael 1731
Pearlman, Nan 406
Pearlman, Stan 1608
Pearlman, Stephen 1048, 1265
Pearson, Cynthia (I.) 171, 960, 1423
Pearson, David P. 883
Pearson, Pat 1066
Pearson, Pauletta 278, 544, 682, 818, 1509, 1546, 1717
Pearson, Rush 79
Pearson, Tania L. 30
Pearsons, Lyle 869
Pearthree, Michael 497
Pease, Robert 193
Peaslee, Richard 183, 389, 728, 1055, 1722
Peate, Patricia Flynn 17
Pechet, Howard 642
Pechner, Gerhard 891
Peck, Richard 1200
Pedersen, Michael 140
Pederson, Hal James 212
Pedi, Christine 517, 521, 522, 525, 526
Pedi, Tom 867
Peek, Brent 612, 1046, 1450
Peerce, Harry 1382
Pegasus III 138
Pegg, Scott 1117
Pehlivanian, Raffi 1305
Peierls, Tim 227
Peil, Mary Beth 69, 157, 1552
Peipers, David H. 1014, 1141
Peirce, Morrie 1264
Pelc, Donna 1040
Peled, JoAnna 1133
Pelish, Thelma 226
Pelkey, Sanita 66
Pell, Peter 277
Pell, Reef 1488
Pell, Stephen 1263
Pell, William 1288
Pellegrino, George 538
Pelletier, Carol Ann 282
Peloquin, Noell 1131
Pelton, Carmen 1087
Peluso, Claudia 255
Pelzig, Daniel 1129, 1304
Pemberton, Michael 1403
Pen, Polly 114, 246, 271, 285, 577, 586, 1190, 1503
Penagos, Isabel 188, 488
Pendell, Marilyn 66
Pendergast, Shirley 1544
Pendleton, Austin 1708, 1756
Pendleton, Lucy 1536
Pendleton, Moses 1073
Pengas, Avram 711
Penn, Bill 104, 235, 405, 1125, 1318, 1468, 1605
Penn, Edward (Ed) 360, 1108, 1166, 1196, 1511, 1676
Penn, Gina 1029
Penn, Jacqueline 1360
Penn, Leo 1164
Penn, Robert 332, 1221
Penn, William 1392
Pennington, Diane 1025
Pennington, Gail 88
Pennington, Mark 59, 1016
Penta, Michael C. 1166
Pentecost, Del 365
Pentecost, George 1534
Pentecost, James 1717
Pentony, Pamela 1504, 1746
Penzner, Seymour 274, 1034
Pepe, Neil 1515, 1598
Peppell, Stacy 1389
Pepper, Allan 854
Pepper, Emily 541
Pepusch, Johann Christoph 117
Percassi, Don 283
Percy, Lord 1691
Perea, Carol 1177
Perera, Cristina 294, 1139
Peress, Lorca 1117
Peress, Maurice 1029
Peretti, Hugo 1480
Peretz, Susan 696
Perez, Jose 1689
Perez, Luis 1205, 1513, 1588, 1631
Perez, Margie 45
Perez, Paul Andrew 679
Perez-Carrion, Edwin 1600
Perfect, Rose 1131
Pergament, Lola 1161
Perillo, Mary 910
Perkins, Carol 1235
Perkins, Drew 657
Perkins, Patti 258, 316, 611, 658, 1006, 1036, 1228, 1334, 1437, 1678
Perkins, Paula Smith 1469
Perkins, Susan 1636
Perkinson, Coleridge-Taylor 589, 629, 630, 1004, 1781
Perkuhn, Jackie 867
Perl, Arnold 134, 1399
Perl, Lothar 1687
Perley, William 718, 789
Perlman, Adam 328
Perlman, Arthur 1190, 1788
Perlman, Max 193, 608, 684, 1212
Perlov, Yitzchok 666
Perlowin, Ginny 1193
Perman, Don 1427
Perowksy, Frank 268
Perr, Harvey 1433
Perren, Dennis 1268
Perri, Irene 1152, 1440
Perri, Rick 1802
Perri, Valerie 1184
Perrie, Ernestine 112
Perrier, Michael 972
Perrin, Adrian S. 1145
Perrin, Margaret 87
Perrin, Scott 1210, 1421
Perrineau, Harold (Jr.) 78, 596
Perrotta, Sal 404
Perry, Alan D. 83
Perry, Alfred 1729
Perry, Alvin 156
Perry, Carol 68, 1021
Perry, Charles 196
Perry, Claudia 1320, 1321
Perry, Dein 1590
Perry, Douglas 4, 1024, 1405, 1730
Perry, E. Martin 1027
Perry, Elaine 1140
Perry, Elizabeth 86
Perry, Eugene 363, 451
Perry, Herbert 439
Perry, Jamila 313
Perry, Jean 1308
Perry, Jennifer 1156
Perry, John Bennett 93, 1029, 1078, 1154, 1452
Perry, Karen 156, 207
Perry, Keith 989
Perry, Louis 256, 1023
Perry, Lynnette 284
Perry, Marsha 1232
Perry, Peter 417
Perry, Phillip 59
Perry, Robert 330, 1347
Perry, Ross 673
Perry, Shauneille 107, 1307, 1783
Perry, Steve 851
Perry, Steven 1502
Perryman, Al 996
Persichetti, Lauren 1077
Persson, Gene 1486, 1828
Pertel, Thomas 1416
Peskow, Karen 214
Pesola, Robert 224
Pessano, Jan 435
Peter, Frances 369
Peters, Bernadette 336, 341, 1119, 1236, 1557
Peters, Florence 1182
Peters, George 33
Peters, Joan 91
Peters, Judy 1095
Peters, Lauri 324
Peters, Leonard 551, 1776
Peters, Maitland 1676
Peters, Mark 1084
Peters, Roberta 891
Peters, Shannon Reyshard 208
Peters, Stephanie 1348
Peters, Steve 1599
Peters, Suzanne 1359
Peters, William 900
Petersen, Erika 466, 734
Peterson, Alan 908
Peterson, Brian 1292
Peterson, Carmen 345, 1343
Peterson, Christy 1131
Peterson, Conrad 1655
Peterson, Curt 439
Peterson, Eric 151
Peterson, Gary 1713
Peterson, Jess 1679
Peterson, Jon 570
Peterson, Kurt 25, 234, 248, 342
Peterson, Lenka 203, 1323
Peterson, Mary 89
Peterson, Mary Nemecek 404
Peterson, Maurice 709
Peterson, Nora 1258, 1392
Peterson, Patricia Ben 284, 1510, 1821
Peterson, Patrick 1195
Peterson, Robbyn 1469
Peterson, Thom (J.) 422, 922
Petina, Irra 1047
Petit, Chris 1240
Petit, Lenard 839
Petito, Robert 403
Petrak, Rudolf 1596
Petrakis, Mark 364
Petrarca, David 383
Petricoff, Elaine 667, 695, 1202, 1268, 1358
Petrides, Avra 175
Petrie, Daniel 1083
Petrie, George 578
Petrilli, Stephen 290
Petrillo, Steven 1428
Petrino, Debbie 1040, 1223

Petro, Michael 1017
Petroski, Adam 714, 1021
Petrow, Mischa 303
Petrucelli, Rick 1628
Petruk, Connie 1237
Petsche, Bruce 416
Pettet, Ashley 58
Pettiford, Valarie 883, 1588
Pettrey, Brugh 15
Petty, Jason 657
Petty, Ross 461, 786
Pevsner, David 1327, 1328, 1763
Pew, Brian 223
Peyser, Penny 376
Peyton, Bruce 484
Peyton, Caroline 186, 726, 1146
Pezza, Francis 1331
Pezza, Mariner James 1512
Pfluger, Jean-Paul 1629
Phares, Keith 938
Phelps, Don 1539
Phelps, Dwayne 194, 603
Phelps, Eleanor 1115
Phelps, Lyon 834
Philibert, John 601
The Philip Glass Ensemble 123, 1200
Philipp, Karen 279
Philips, Bob 1173
Philips, Mardi 171, 1449, 1521
Philipson, Glen 768
Phillips, Amy Jo 1298
Phillips, Arlene 1662
Phillips, Arte 711
Phillips, Bary 1805
Phillips, Bob 510, 814, 1232, 1310
Phillips, Clayton 1289
Phillips, David 1310
Phillips, Don 66
Phillips, Eddie 1172
Phillips, Garrison 1117
Phillips, Graham 47, 938
Phillips, Jessica 1786
Phillips, John 1007
Phillips, Lorraine 1621
Phillips, Marishka (Shanice) 1207, 1535
Phillips, Mary Bracken 2, 710, 957, 1029
Phillips, Michelle R. 1238
Phillips, Miriam 654
Phillips, Pam Drews 323
Phillips, Paul 808
Phillips, Rosalind 66
Phillips, Sandra 709, 1509
Phillips, Stanley 352
Phillips, Teri 655
Phillips, Tim 603
Phipps, Brian 1287
Phoenix, Reggie 927
Physioc, Joseph Allen 1145
Piacentini, Anne 1119
Piazzolla, Astor 1588
Picard, Daphne 578
Picard, Larry 769
Picardo, Bob 1392
Picco, Millo 298, 868, 1047, 1249
Piccoli, Pier Paolo (P.P.) 825, 929, 1450
Pichette, Joe 186, 1146, 1182, 1270
Pickart, Christopher 39
Picker, Tobias 47, 439
Pickrell, Piper 576, 799
Picon, Molly 5, 874
Pictures, Universal 133
Piday, Louie 860
Piech, Jennifer 14, 979
Pieczuro, Janusz 1275
Piekarski, Peter 223
Pielecki, Jay 1727
Pierantozzi, Victor 1566
Pierce, Charles 270
Pierce, Edward 1306
Pierce, Joan 134
Pierce, John 578
Pierce, Lewis 1229, 1713
Pierce, Morrie 528
Pierce, Verna Jeanne 848
Pierce, Victoria 343
Pierce, Willard 1729
Pierce, William 1080
Pieris, Catherine 1599
Pierre, Christopher 1064
Pierre, Olivier 483
Pierre, Tonya 227, 1764
Pierson, Edward 254
Pierson, Harold 68, 238
Pierson, William 1468, 1480
Pieters, Barbara 423
Pieters, Rick 423
Pietkiewcz, Ewa 397
Pietri, Pedro 1699
Pietrs, Roman 399
Piette, W. Fredric 1229
Pigliavento, Michele 883, 1016
Pignuola, Dawn Noel 474
Pilkenton, Pamela 1169, 1398
Pilla, Candida 569
Pillich, Gualberto 1313
Pinchot, Bronson 1282
Pincus, Warren 1644, 1822
Pincus-Gani, Lydia 1453
Pincusoff, Reva 1655
Pindell, Reginald 1816
Pinhasik, Howard 308, 398, 1040
Pinhiero, Alfred Godot 397
Pini-Corsi, Antonio 340, 988
Pinkins, Tonya 252, 500
Pinkney, Eboyn Jo-Ann 1001
Pinkney, Scott 1160
Pinkston, Robert 1308
Pinnock, Jaja 1617
Pinto, Cola 564, 758
Pinto, Fabrizia 872
Pinza, Carla 715, 1689
Piper, Frank 366
Pippin, Don 258, 259, 283, 316, 480
Pippy, Katelyn 248
Piro, Jacquelyn 67, 1547, 1700
Piro, Sal 1226
Pistone, Charles 1456
Pitcher, Joanne 920
Pitchford, Dean 1392, 1697
Piteo, Paul 116
Pitilli, Lawrence 493
Pitkin, William 232, 360, 569, 1043, 1626, 1627
Pitluck, Sherman 1609
Pitot, Genevieve 944
Pitre, Andre 964
Pitt, Joel 822
Pitt, John 242
Pittelman, Ira 1515, 1598
Pitts, John 1489
Pitzer, Bruce 1469
Pivar, Amy 682, 1487, 1509
Piven, Byrne 1164
Pizer, Brian 288
Placzek, Ron 215, 1208
Plado, Alan J. 1753
Plakias, Nick 1392
Plamondon, Andre 140
Plano, Gerald 1636
Plant, Richard 947
Platt, Jon B. 518, 520, 521, 522, 523, 524, 525, 526
Platt, Livingston 344
Platt, Martin 689
Platt, Oliver 1710
Platt, Victoria 313, 1134
Platts, Ronald 1308
Playten, Alice 252, 496, 1114, 1201, 1311, 1708
Pleasants, Philip 1376
Pleshette, John 1455
Plimpton, Martha 647
Plimpton, Shelley 649, 1133
Pliska, Greg 1285, 1499
Pliskin, Marci 505
Ploner, George 87
Plotch, Adam Paul 1381
Plotnick, Jack 1442
Plowman, Robert 1147
Plummer, Amanda 27
Plummer, Charles 1759
Plunkett, Michael 979
Plunkett, Stephen 607
Plymale, Trip 345, 1367
Poacquadio, Peter 544
Pockriss, Hal 425
Pockriss, Lee 313, 448, 1101
Pocock, Jo 1444
Pocorobba, Tom 235
Podell, Rick 232, 1691
Pogue, Meredith 1713
Poignand, Michael 1784
Poitier, Pamelia 1579
Polacco, Giorgio 988
Polacheck, Charles 1140
Polakov, Lester 1814
Poland, Albert 101, 708, 1154, 1231, 1349, 1659
Polcovar, Carol 1577
Polcsa, Juliet 1049
Pole, Rupert 1140
Pole, Tony 1316
Polenz, Robert 65, 279, 1343, 1485
Polenzani, Matthew 628
Poleo, Dom 693
Poleshuck, Jesse 612, 639, 1046
Polite, Raquel 208
Polk, Andrew 1736
Polk, Ivson 603
Pollack, Carrie 1577
Pollack, Deborah 142
Pollard, John 995
Pollard, Jonathan 739, 1613
Pollard, Kevin 1444
Pollard, Sherrand 578
Pollitt, Barbara 839, 1665
Pollock, Alice Leal 298
Pollock, Bernard 82
Pollock, Michael 677, 1583, 1596, 1601
Pomeranz, David 1700
Pompeii, James 638
Pompeii, Jim 201
Ponce, Ramona 475
Pond, Helen 128, 201, 236, 566, 631, 654, 1161, 1170, 1203, 1440, 1481
Pons, Beatrice 1716
Ponselle, Rosa 905
Pontillo, Larry J. 575
Pontone, Alexandra J. 148
Pontrelli, Paul 248
Pool, Betsy M. 229
Poole, Wakefield 957
Poor, Harold 1635
Poor, Harris 1087
Pooras, Patriccio 188
Poore, Dennis 1648
Pope, Murray 1653
Pope, Peggy 1698, 1751
Pope, Sabrynaah 592, 593
Pope, Stephanie M. 105, 223
Popkin, Gary 1661
Poplaski, William 1462
Popova, Nina 66
Popp, Carolyn 697
Popwell, Albert 238
Porcher, Nananne 1398
Pordum, Herbert (J.) 68, 1021
Porgina, Ludmilla 849
Porrello, Joseph 1288
Porretta, Frank 677, 1227, 1360, 1667, 1814
Porter, Barbara 1389, 1707
Porter, Billy 1325, 1498
Porter, Brent J. 64
Porter, Cathy 832
Porter, Cole 63, 367, 368, 566, 567, 1101, 1160, 1223, 1704, 1823
Porter, Gregory 777
Porter, Howard 221, 629, 1620
Porter, Jeff 863
Porter, Joan 550
Porter, Mike 263
Porter, Professor Hugh 815, 816
Porter, Richard L. 1462
Porter, Scott 38
Porter, Stan 147, 489, 666, 793
Portes, Lisa 1779
Portman, Rachel 938
Portnoy, Gary 1296
Porto, Gary 1258, 1367
Posin, Kathryn 1396
Posner, Amanda 1726
Posner, Kenneth 323, 828, 1386, 1634, 1778
Posnick, Michael 660
Post, Charles 600
Post, Leah 1382
Post, Lisa L. 1784
Post, Lu Ann 884
Postel, Steve 1568, 1569
Postel, Suzan 643
Postell, Steve 471
Poston, Tom 134
Potamkin, Lexie 37
Potamkin, Victor H. 1619
Pothier, Nancy 719
Potok, Chaim 284
Potter, Jane 1484
Potter, Karen 468
Potter, Louise 1233
Potter, Michael 105
Potter, Raeschelle 1816
Pottle, Sam 34, 160, 448, 616, 1040, 1076
Pottner, Don 1755
Potts, George 626
Potts, Michael 641, 1187, 1351
Potts, Nancy 707, 1330
Poul, Alan 1715
Poulos, George 771
Poulos, Jim 1103
Poulos, Mitch 1771
Pountney, David 1730
Poutous, Constantine 1080
Povia, Charlotte 569
Povinelli, Mark 122
Powell, Ed 528
Powell, Janet 1330
Powell, Jennifer 362
Powell, Jerry 50, 126, 556, 601, 771, 1069, 1125, 1255, 1605
Powell, John 56
Powell, Kobie 313
Powell, Lee 1400
Powell, Lovelady 1364
Powell, Michael Warren 1705
Powell, Pepper 1616
Powell, Ricky 959
Powell, Thomas (Tom) 1131, 1601
Powell-Parker, Marianne 414
Power, Helen 1233
Power, Will 1429
Powers, Amy 290
Powers, Michelle 276
Powers, Neva Rae 968
Powers, Orlando 719
Powers, William 628
Powich, Christopher 239, 452
Pracht, Mary Ellen 62
Prager, Stanley 1192
Prather, Tom Ross 1108
Pratt, Alvin Ronn 629
Pratt, John 535
Pratt, Ronn 1174, 1725
Preece, K.K. 246
Preisser, Alfred 167
Preljocaj, Angelin 640
Premice, Josephine 715
Premus, Judy 1442
Prendergast, Shirley 9, 266, 278, 959, 1579, 1737
Prentice, Amelia 213
Prescott, Betty 619
Prescott, Dick 1021
Prescott, Jane 1315
Prescott, John A. 324
Prescott, Ken 17
Prescott, Richard 68
Presnell, Harve 58
Press, Jack 1145
Press, Peter 755
Press, Susane 1679
Pressel, Marc 1409
Pressgrove, Larry 280, 1645
Pressley, Armond 1816
Pressley, Brenda (D.) 51, 52, 182, 420
Pressman, Kenneth 972
Pressner, Stan 1439, 1674
Preston, Barry 42
Preston, Corliss 697
Preston, Don 7
Preston, Kay 985
Preston, Michael 1439
Preston, Rob 1365
Preston, Robert W. 582, 708, 1524
Preston, Tony 1388
Preston-Smith, Roger 1380
Presutti, Joyce A. 1046
Previn, Andre 1100
Prevost, Mary Anne 1467
Prianti, Gary 1032, 1212
Price, Alison 1340
Price, Cynthia 1254
Price, Don 404, 507, 857, 1025
Price, Gerald 779, 1626
Price, Gilbert 504, 815, 1311, 1473
Price, Jim 103, 106
Price, Leontyne 62
Price, Lonny 296, 848, 1328, 1381, 1641, 1708
Price, Lorin (E.) (Ellington) 1452, 1636
Price, Mark deSolla 1585
Price, Paige 273
Price, Paul B. 1163
Price, Robert 66
Price, Seth 1684
Price, Sherill 1043, 1236
Price, Tim Rose 873
Price-McKenney, Sterling 570
Prida, Dolores 118, 533
Pridgen, Rodney 1292, 1644
Priebe, James F. 1048
Priest, Steve 15
Prieto, Astrid 349
Prieur, Don 1483
Primont, Marian 695
Primrose, Alek 902, 1666
Prince, Boo-Boo 25
Prince, Charles 805, 1103
Prince, Clayton 706, 1535
Prince, Daisy 890, 1250, 1498

Prince, Faith 25, 473, 642, 945, 1006, 1710
Prince, Ginger 1677
Prince, Harold 244, 377, 1250, 1462
Pringle, Postell 1429
Pringle, Val 1360
Printz, Edward 826
Prinzo, Joseph 734
Prior, Candice 42
Prisand, Scott 1753
Pritchard, John 1142
Pritchard, Lauren 1515
Pritchard, Ted 1096
Pritchett, Jennifer 190
Pritchett, Lizabeth 291, 860, 1697
Pritchett, Willie 1464, 1465
Privette, Pamela 76
Procopio, Rennie 235
Procter, Robert 654
Proctor, Gerald E. 380
Proctor, James D. 1140
Proctor, Philip 48
Proett, Daniel 1113
Profeta, Katherine 632
Prokhorov, Vladimir 849
Prokhorova, Valentina 849
The Promenaders 1688
Prosser, Julie 770
Prostack, Edward 1608
Prostak, Edward 954
Prouty, Debbi Bier 42
Provenza, Rosario 1074
Provost, Sarah 1248
Pruitt, Debra 362
Pruitt, Richard 106
Prymus, Ken 1135
Przygrodska, Olga 1609
Psacharopoulos, Nikos 947, 1063, 1650
Ptaszynski, Andre 1353
Ptaszynski, Rebecca 1353
Pucci, Peter 1238, 1322
Puccini, Giacomo 186
Pucklis, Lee 696
Pudenz, Steve 378, 1392
Puente, Ricardo 533
Puerto, Arturo Rafael 1398
Pugh, Ted 272, 676, 761, 1153
Pugliese, Frank 859
Pugliese, Joseph 42
Puleo, Robert 1512
Pulliam, James 1074
Pulliam, Zelda 8
Pulman, Liza 6
Pulos, Virginia 884, 1480
Pulver, Lara 1233
Purdham, David 1190, 1641
Purdum, Ralph 34, 1021, 1221
Purdy, Mary 475
Purdy, Stephen 541
Pure Love and Pleasure 423
Puri, Rajika 1665
Purnhagen, Gregory 123
Purpuro, Sandra 1310
Pursley, David 467, 554, 660, 834, 1231, 1787
Pusilo, Robert 120, 316, 611
Putch, William 1448
Puzo, Billy 177, 1758
Pye, Viola 1145

Qaiyum, Gregory J. 189
Qaiyum, Jeffrey 189
Quackenbush, Karyn 633, 1015, 1296, 1560, 1760
Quaigh Theatre 820
Quandt, Stephen 39
Quaney, Barbara 745, 1076, 1440
Quebec, Herb 1070
Queenan, Charles 944
Quesenbery, Whitney 651, 1593
Quick, Louise 23, 125
Quick-Bowen, Louise 133
Quigley, Chip 512, 513, 514, 515, 516, 517, 1215
Quigley, Myra 1418
Quilico, Gino 574
Quilty, John 1117
Quincy, Dolly 1691
Quincy, George 1391
Quinlan, Bill 1321
Quinn 399
Quinn, Brian 1223
Quinn, Cynthia 1073
Quinn, Patrick 515, 1421
Quinn, Terry 1392
Quint, Robert 33
Quintal, Lana 1784
Quintavalla, Tony 669
Quintero, Jose 827, 1667
Quinton, Everett 1359
Quitman, Cleo 166, 238

Raab, Marni 538
Rabb, Jonathan 485
Rabbino, D. Bruce 63, 121, 745
Raben, Larry 527
Rabke, Kelli 954
Rabu, Renald 1655
Raby, Roger Allan 121
Racette, Patricia 47, 439
Racey, Noah 954
Racheff, James 8, 755
Rachel, Annie (Ann) 1395, 1396, 1604
Rachins, Alan 1168
Rachman, Lee 1256
Racioppi, James 877
Rackmil, Gladys 992
Rada, Mirena 77, 1784
Radano, Charles 1729
Radawan-Dana, Mireille 363
Radcliffe, Rosemary 1471
Radcliffe, Shirley J. 1580
Radelat, Paul 118
Radigan, Michael 212, 1096
Radner, David 1013
Radner, Gilda 1112
Rado, James 649, 655, 1330
Rado, Ted 1330
Radunz, Dale 1669
Rae, Charlotte 942, 1626
Rae, Margaret 92
Raedler, Dorothy 1621
Rael, Elsa 972
Raflo, Paula 897
Rafner, B.E. 1618
Rafter, Michael 1011, 1610, 1726
Ragni, Gerome 649, 655
Rago, Jerry 1117
Ragotzy, Jack 867
Ragusa, Michele 10
Rahman, Aishah 885
Rahn, Patsy 969
Raiff, Stan 271
Raiford, Steven 1023
Raiken, Lawrence (Larry) 1361, 1362, 1442, 1731
Raiman, Paul 1700
Raimondo, Robert 295
Rainbow, Harry 732
Rainbow, James 197, 1288
Raine, Michael 742
Raines, Walter 333, 715
Rainey, DanaShavonne 668
Rainey, William 1278
Rains, Jack 1221
Raitt, James 1215, 1521
Raitt, Jayson 997
Rakka-Thamm 983
Rakov, Theresa 161
Rakov, Victor 849
Raleigh, Ben 1688
Raley, Wade 377, 873, 1340
Ralstin, Monte 1223, 1660
Ralston, Curt 64
Ramage, Edmond 573, 1050
Ramback, Gary 1021
Rambaldi, Laura 346, 1222, 1746
Ramblin, Lute 1248
Rambo, David 1772
Ramer, Jack 734
Ramicova, Dunya 47, 363, 439, 1139, 1730
Ramin, Jordan 957
Ramirez, Bardo S. 77
Ramirez, Ramiro (Ray) 669, 1398
Ramis, Harold 1112
Ramos, Louis 1080
Ramos, Luis 1370
Ramos, Richard 958
Ramsel, Gena 824
Ramsey, Gordon 76, 564, 758
Ramsey, John 869
Ramsey, Kevin 9, 59, 546, 960, 1518, 1535
Ramsey, Logan 826, 1636, 1652
Ramsey, Marion 390, 1504, 1695, 1746
Ramsey, Remak 655
Ramsey, Stanley 1065
Ramsey, Thea 1692
Ramsey, Van 565, 1470
Rand, Randolph Curtis 1826
Rand, Sally 145
Randall, Benjie 395
Randall, Bob 1652
Randall, Dick 1594
Randall, Jenelle Lynn 837, 1612
Randall, Lisa 1542
Randall, Tony 443
Randell, Bob 535
Randich, Jean 838
Rando, John 1712
Randolph, James 153, 603, 1521
Randolph, Jerry "Flow Master" 804
Randolph, Jimmy 91
Randolph, Mimi 33, 822
Randolph-Wright, Charles 387, 1710
Ranes, Quinton 109
Raney, Joel 1138
Raney, Susie Vaughan 1660
Raniello, John 1089
Rankin, Arthur, Jr. 1078
Rankin, Zane 552
Ransom, Lucinda 1021
Raphael, Bette-Jane 536
Raphael, Gerrianne 66, 199, 404, 448, 535, 1409, 1457, 1626
Raphael, Jay E. 1787
Raphael, Marilyn 1095
Rapier, Trisha 606, 1428
Rapoport, Julie 768
Raposo, Joseph (Joe) 631, 715, 986, 1468, 1828
Rapp, Anthony 1351
Rappaport, Katherine 717
Raseen, Robin 1331
Rasely, George 1010
Rasey, Adelle 90
Rashad, Phylicia 130
Raskind, Philis 801
Rasmuson, Judy 314, 623, 1196
Rasmussen, Zora 943
Rast, Jim 1727
Rath, Debora 196
Rathburn, Roger 279
Ratkevich, Paul 200
Ratshin, Bernard 1131
Ratzer, Beth 1226
Rauber, Richard 1092
Rauch, Maurice 684, 1822
Rausch, Caroline 1161
Ravelo, Henry 118, 1213
Raven, Elsa 1221
Raven, Yolanda R. 1096
Raver, Kim 768
Ravinett, Ted 347
Ravinsky, Linda 1595
Ravitz, Mark 1666
Rawlings, Alice 31
Rawlings, Herbert Lee, Jr. 546, 1064
Rawlings, Paul 468
Rawlings, Theodore 213
Rawls, Henry C. 470
Rawn, Jean 1062
Ray, Anje 120
Ray, Bob 1013
Ray, Connie 1484
Ray, Ellen 236
Ray, James 1424
Ray, Joe 915, 1040
Ray, Katherine 1029
Ray, Kathryn 397
Ray, Leslie 1573
Ray, Leslie Ann 192
Ray, Ozzie 955
Ray, Robert 1509
Ray, Robin 1654
Ray, Ruth 1621
Ray, Scott 601, 1713
Raymond, Art 1341
Raymond, Janet 1539
Rayner, Jean 1639, 1640
Rayon, Pierre 1464
Rayow, Steven 379
Rayson, Benjamin 660
Rayson, Jonathan 10
Raywin, Hal 652
Raz, Rivka 401
Razzano, Anthony 1771
Razzle 1449
Re, Tommy 329
Rea, Kitty 414
Rea, Oliver 1116
Read, Ben 1590
Read, Mary 1315
Reade, Jeff 960
Reading, Beatrice 1716
Reagan, Deborah 1314
Reagan, Ronald 1149
Reale, Robert 1187
Reale, Willie 1187
Reams, Lee Roy 1290, 1527
Reardon, Greg 1331
Reardon, John 1088, 1111, 1552, 1789, 1814
Reardon, Peter 474
Reaux, Angelina 865, 866, 1102, 1389, 1532
Reaux, Roumel 1544
Reaves-Phillips, Sandra 105, 266, 553, 1174, 1207, 1373
Reavey, Jean 820
Rebega, Larri 491
Rebholz, Emily 645
Rebic, Don 1118
Rebolledo, Julian 995, 1336
Recht, Raymond C. (Ray) 84, 419, 718, 899, 1053, 1709
Rechtzeit, Jack 147, 489, 666, 782, 1032, 1822
Rechtzeit, Seymour 608
Red, Rhythm 704
Redd, Randy 1289
Redd, Sharon 1633, 1746
Redd, Veronica 1360, 1743
Reddick, Cecil 1713
Reddin, Keith 233, 445
Redding, Edward C. 531, 1576
Reddon, Nancy 752
Reddy, Brian 325
Reddy, Robert 1359
Redel, Jessica 256
Redfield, Liza 65, 466, 1060, 1072
Redgrave, Lynn 443
Redlich, Don 600, 1367
Redlin, Richard 1551
Redman, Scott Robert 347
Redmon, Robynne 451, 673
Redmond, Marge 1254
Redmond, Phoebe 1064
Redwine, Skip 367
Reece, Angharad 1233
Reece, Stoney 1426
Reed, Alaina 1, 764, 1426
Reed, Arvillie Ann 1221
Reed, Bernard 384, 745
Reed, Billy 226
Reed, Bobby 200
Reed, Darryl Alan 383
Reed, Ernie 133
Reed, Fay 1660
Reed, Gary 1226
Reed, Jacqueline 779
Reed, Jonathan Beck 1366
Reed, Mary Ann 1041
Reed, Sandy 1604
Reed, Tom 66
Reed, Vivian 221, 1606
Reedy, M. Kilburg 934
Rees, Adrian 1353
Rees, Roger 689, 846, 1006
Reese, Bob 149
Reese, Irwin 1816
Reese, Roxanne 1437
Reeves, Gregory 904
Refaeli, Nizan 108
Reffert, Danielle Ingrid 158
Refregier, Anton 1241
Regalson, Roz 1453
Regan, J.P. 120
Regan, Joe 1652
Regan, Patti 149, 1142
Regan, Woody 1327
Regev, Evi 462
Regst, Bruce 1487
Rehn, Rita 954, 1610
Rehnolds, Lette 1420
Reiber, Julie 1054
Reich, Adina 819, 1342, 1382
Reich, Bob 248
Reich, Herbert 858
Reichard, Daniel 1325, 1613
Reid, Alonzo G. 1070
Reid, Ilene 154
Reid, James (Allen) 1058
Reid, John 1349, 1589
Reid, Kay 507
Reid, Kevin 974
Reid, M.W. 424, 1398
Reid, Stephen O. 919
Reidy, Kilty 950
Reiersen, Kristin 717
Reiff, Linda 768, 1134
Reiley, Orrin 662
Reilley, Kevin 373
Reilley, Victor 1192
Reilly, Charles Nelson 472, 908, 1218
Reilly, Jacqueline 64, 740, 798, 841
Reilly, William Spencer 1363
Reily, George Wolf 378
Reinblatt, George 462
Reiner, Marcel 340, 988
Reinert, Christian 1416
Reinert, Ted 378
Reinhart, Taylor 1120

Reinheimer, David 215
Reinheimer, John 215
Reinking, Ann 55, 689, 1199
Reis, Eda 1140
Reis, Helena 708
Reisch, Michele 271, 1343, 1373, 1584
Reisel, Zvi 1647
Reiser, David 95
Reiser, Joseph 11
Reisman, Jane 48, 1595
Reisman, Michael 123
Reiss, Albert 245, 340, 1075
Reiss, Jay 1680
Reissa, Eleanor 100, 323, 1032, 1212, 1342, 1354, 1362, 1382, 1502, 1619
Reiter, Dean (H.) 111, 258
Reiter, Fran 428
Reiter, Tom 1610
Reiter, Val 493
Reith, Jeanne 836
Reither, Toni 68, 1021
Reitman, David 1212
Reitman, Ivan 1112
Reitz, Dana 427
Reizner, June 87, 160, 1069, 1259
Relis, Rochelle 441, 1745
Remeny, Ronny 1252
Remme, John 599, 1825
Rempel, Gene 918
Remus, Jorie 693
Renan, Emile 609, 677
Renaud, Eydi 1751
Renault, Norma 1393
Renault, Paul 572
Renay, Diane 1116
Rendin, Burt 920, 1349
Rene, Nikke 1191
Rene, Norman 23, 180, 370, 577, 919, 1027, 1334, 1365, 1624
Renee, Debbe 1079
Rengier, John 235
Renha, Rita 1305
Reni and Suzi 1615
Renick, Kyle 233, 383, 469, 484, 727, 1498, 1748
Rennagel, Marilyn 406, 765, 847, 1535
Rennalls, Natasha 1441
Reno, Phil 275, 1135
Renschler, Eric 154
Renschler, Eric L. (Lowell) 742, 892
Renzi, Marta 763, 764, 1478
Renzi, Michael 959
Reola, Candy 1221
Repicci, William 1516, 1571
Replansky, Naomi 1391
Repole, Charles 25
Resbury, Ronald 427
Reschiglian, Vincenzo 298
Rescigno, Richard 1660
Reseen, Robin 200, 545, 1151
Resiman, Jane 527
Resin, Dan 1078, 1193, 1824
Resnick, Rob 1759
Resnik, Hollis 1788
Resnik, Regina 1718, 1740
Resseguie, Lew 743
Resstab, Barbara 399
Resto, Guillermo 363
Restrepo, Jose 474
Reterski, Jerry 1275
Revere, Paul 1691
Revere, Rachel 1691
Rexroad, David 410
Rexsite, Seymour 119, 684
Rey, Antonia 488
Reyes, Gabriel 1469
Reyes, Joselin 262
Reyno 156, 630
Reynolds, Bill 467, 920
Reynolds, Brad J. 1016
Reynolds, Dorothy 1393
Reynolds, Jonathan 1546
Reynolds, Kwami 349
Reynolds, Lee 1754
Reynolds, Lette 1420
Reynolds, Molly 444
Reynolds, Paul B. 587
Reynolds, Tim 1231
Reynolds, Tobi 1041
Rhian, Geff 1014
Rhind, D. Kevin 552
Rhodes, Betty 797, 798
Rhodes, Elise 1254
Rhodes, Erik 307, 1692
Rhodes, Joseph 857
Rhodes, Lawrence 1789
Rhodes, Nancy 434, 1288, 1391
Rhodes, Robert 1145
Rhodes, Tran William 940
Rhodes, Willard 686
Rhodes, William 1000
Rhomberg, Vince 1028
Riashentsev, Uri 1541
Ribbink, Tom 112, 1577
Ribble, Michele 549
Riberto, Vel 809
Ribnikov, Alexis 849
Ricardo 506
Ricci, Rosalin 884
Rice, Jim 1585
Rice, Keith (R.) 1437, 1668
Rice, M. (Michael) 1326
Rice, Marie 427
Rice, Michael 89, 675, 717, 1155, 1156, 1159
Rice, Susan 1
Rice, Tim 275, 833
Rich, Beverly 343
Rich, Geoffrey 77
Rich, James 133, 833, 943, 1146
Rich, Jospeh 1382
Rich, Lucille 1115
Rich, Nancy 1089
Rich, Rebecca 1285, 1831
Rich, Sylvester 378
Rich, Tony 35
Richard 850
Richard, Mae 338, 1586
Richard, Raquel 1345
Richards, Carol 350
Richards, Cynthia 1029
Richards, Dick 506
Richards, Don 858
Richards, Geriane 1481
Richards, Gordon 1145
Richards, Jeff 955
Richards, Jeffrey 627
Richards, Jess 35, 972, 974, 1097, 1196, 1348
Richards, Jessie (Janet) 768, 1039
Richards, Jim 1089
Richards, Jon 902
Richards, Kurt 1731
Richards, Mae 1585
Richards, Martin 1037
Richards, Paul David 435
Richards, Penelope 1483
Richards, Reve 971, 998, 1030
Richardson, Alex 717
Richardson, Barbara 537
Richardson, Cathy 965
Richardson, Charles 12
Richardson, Claibe 948, 1100, 1259, 1261, 1447
Richardson, Cornella 1543
Richardson, Daryl 1538
Richardson, Desmond 640
Richardson, Jamaal 333
Richardson, Jane 423
Richardson, Jocko 1226
Richardson, Lea 223, 278, 960, 1785
Richardson, Morgan 42
Richardson, Robert E. 82, 152, 968, 1467
Richardson, Roy S. 1242
Richardson, Walter 1029
Richenthal, Richard 1053
Richert, Ted 820
Richetelle, Charles 834
Richie, Chuck 1522
Richie, Lionel 854
Richkin, Jerry 1194
Richman, Rebecca 119
Richman, Sol 506
Richman, Stanley 506
Richman-Maurer-Richards 506
Richmond, Caryn 1025
Richmond, David 142
Richmond, Elizabeth 1195
Richmond, Gary 1226
Richter, Carolyn 93
Richter, Will 74
Richwood, Patrick 1761
Ricker, Lucille 1131
Rickett, Edmond 619, 622
Ricketts, Jim 1149, 1150
Rickman, Allen Lewis 1610
Riddell, Richard 20, 1405
Riddick, Martin 156
Riddick, Douglass 1689
Riddle, Cynthia 863
Riddle, George 582
Riddle, Richard 322
Riddle, Steven 322
Riddley, Johnny 815
Riddock, Lita 954
Rideout, Leenya 1285
Ridge, John 1628
Ridge, John David 42, 292
Ridgely, Tom 896
Riebling, Tia 45, 284
Riedel, Steve 124
Rieder, Thomas 66
Riegert, Peter 263
Riehl, Bob 76
Rieser, Allan 404
Rieser, Terry 410, 678, 696, 1149
Riesman, Michael 846
Rieti, Vittorio 1244
Rigali, Alfred L. 1092
Rigdon, Kevin 882, 1357
Riggins, Norman 827
Rigol, Joey 284
Rigott, T. Robert 749
Riley, Betsy 43
Riley, Bob 1160
Riley, Ed 935
Riley, Eric 709, 934, 1191, 1300
Riley, Eugene 885
Riley, Frances 951
Riley, Jack 578
Riley, Larry 214, 377, 544, 1036, 1459, 1546
Riley, Marin 397
Riley, Michael 1024
Riley, Rob 1777
Riley, Robert Maurice 501
Rind, Maurice 851
Rinehimer, David 699
Ringbom, Jon 1284
Ringham, Nancy 224, 910, 1149, 1150, 1378
Rink, Scott 328
Rintala, Troy 1305
Rio, Michael Del 1660
Rio, Noemi Del 248
Rios, Linda 740
Rios, Rosemary 118
Rioseco, Eduardo 474
Ripka, Keith 1660
Ripley, Alice 273, 805
Ripley, Mary Jane 1564
Ripplinger, Jody 1237
Rippner, William W. 1592
Rise, Jim 913
Riseman, Naomi 989, 1780
Riser, Terry 681
Rish, Oliver 1030
Riss, Sheldon 1340
Rita, Rui 1421
Ritarossi, Louis 1538
Ritchie, Estelle 369
Ritman, William 104, 528, 630, 875, 1291, 1385
Ritt, Martin 1140
Ritter, Evan 1080
Ritter, Kathryn 244
Ritterman, H. 1647
Rittman, William 867, 1272
Riva, William 1447
Rivas, Armando 118
Rivera, Carmen 262
Rivera, Chita 1448
Rivera, Eileen 1425
Rivera, Frank 897
Rivera, Frederick 1592
Rivera, Jennifer 941
Rivera, Julio Enrique 1487
Rivera, Manolo 488
Rivera, Mario 1398
Rivera, Martin 971, 1030
Rivera, Michael 603
Rivera, Peter A. 1354
Rivera, Walter 1426
Rivers, James 1825
Rivers, Jimmy 1236
Rivers, Joan 556
Rivlin, Esther 1391
Rivlin, Michael 397
Rizhov, Sergey 849
Rizzio, R.H. 61
Rizzo, Bob 1016
Rizzo, John 1674
Rizzo, Michael 272, 1538
Roach, Kevin Joseph 1674
Roane, Mildred 1116
Roark, Patricia 1287
Roark, Peter 676
Robbins, Carrie (F.) 117, 203, 296, 483, 625, 660, 1057, 1279, 1340, 1459, 1471
Robbins, Chuck 796
Robbins, Gil 1078
Robbins, Jana 35, 213, 308, 1635, 1644
Robbins, Jane Marla 140
Robbins, Jerome 1601
Robbins, Julien 1730
Robbins, Kurt 769, 1742
Robbins, Mary Ann 1098
Robbins, Norman 290
Robbins, Rex 381, 534, 1259, 1430, 1710
Robbins, Robert CuilloJana 738
Robbins, Steve 1419
Robbins, Tom 325, 855
Robbins-Zust, Maia 901
Roberson, Ken 77, 78, 205, 668, 1545
Roberson, Rudy 503, 975, 1373
Roberson, Virgil 624
Roberson, Will 1551
Robert 54, 960
Roberts, Andy 263
Roberts, Chapman 78, 181, 969, 1395, 1396
Roberts, Chauncey 1207
Roberts, Christopher G. 983
Roberts, Dennis 884
Roberts, Doris 1688
Roberts, Emilie 1443
Roberts, Howard (A.) 681, 1672
Roberts, Irene 66
Roberts, Jason 1426
Roberts, Jerrell 964
Roberts, Jimmy 2, 739, 1613
Roberts, Joli 600
Roberts, Judith 1697
Roberts, Ken 1539
Roberts, Lance 526, 1232
Roberts, Les 556, 557, 558
Roberts, Marcia 1753
Roberts, Michael 606, 906, 1131, 1221
Roberts, Michael Anthony 1207
Roberts, Michelle 1679
Roberts, Mike 66
Roberts, Neal 1591
Roberts, Nick 19
Roberts, Ralph 1431
Roberts, Rhoda 1452
Roberts, Richard 1349
Roberts, Robin Sanford 777
Roberts, Ruth 483, 692, 961, 1028
Roberts, Sarah 1401
Roberts, The Reverend William D. 1316
Robertson, Alene 58
Robertson, Frances 456
Robertson, Geoff 1666
Robertson, Jane 232, 1035
Robertson, Joel 401
Robertson, Margaret 963
Robertson, Pat 1805
Robertson, Rudy 538
Robertson, Scott 84, 886, 949, 974, 1149
Robertson, Stewart 264
Robertson, Victor 1623
Robertson, Warren 379
Robey, Wilson 705
Robichaux, John 1198
Robin, Jean-Claude 646
Robin, Sy 1408
Robins, Isobel 1754
Robins, Kenneth 910
Robinson, Alma 649
Robinson, Andre 1388
Robinson, Angela 240, 1325
Robinson, Anne 198
Robinson, Bartlett 1115
Robinson, Ben 675
Robinson, Beverly 465
Robinson, Carol 548
Robinson, Charlie 226, 1615
Robinson, Chris 71
Robinson, David 1301
Robinson, Dee 482, 550
Robinson, Donna 454
Robinson, Douglas (Doug) 1152, 1686
Robinson, Earl 1399
Robinson, Edward G. 1593, 1830
Robinson, Experience 1370
Robinson, Fatima 1325
Robinson, Hal 88, 1043, 1829
Robinson, Jack 1153
Robinson, James 740
Robinson, Kathy 1146, 1514
Robinson, Lois 779
Robinson, Lorie 1384
Robinson, Mabel 17, 116, 996, 1207, 1781
Robinson, Martin (P.) 647, 648, 939
Robinson, Muriel 929, 1297
Robinson, Nell 322, 1316

Robinson, Richard 1069
Robinson, Roger 885, 1049
Robinson, Ronn 1644
Robinson, Shari Sue 145
Robinson, Venustra K. 1384
Robinson, Vicki Sue 1356, 1504
Robison, Barry 664
Robman, Steven 1411
Robson, Christopher 20
Rocco, Mary 712, 1011
Rocco, Tom 404
Roccosalva, John 1449
Roche, Eugene 1420, 1716
Roche, John Francis (F.) 618, 619, 621, 622
Roche, Sebastian 632
Roche, Tami 1616
Roche, Tudi 1296
Rochelle, Florence 1179
Rochelle, Lisa 1607
Rock, Jeff 831
Rockman, Wendy 1134
Rockoff, Isaac 1577
Rockwell, Eric 1099
Rockwell, Jeffrey 1618
Rockwell, Penny 675
Rodale, J. I. 1531, 1652
Rodas, Mary 994
Rodd, Marcia 731, 962, 1163
Roderick, Ray 67, 1303
Rodewald, Heidi 1225
Rodgers, Bob 149, 150
Rodgers, Chev 289
Rodgers, Eileen 63, 277
Rodgers, Enid 1160
Rodgers, Jerry 918, 1331, 1771
Rodgers, Les 1474
Rodgers, Lou 92, 361, 1360
Rodgers, Mary 353, 356, 691, 986, 1193, 1574
Rodgers, Richard 201, 236, 505, 1100, 1101
Rodgers, Rod 1291, 1307, 1383
Rodgers, Shev 572
Rodin, Roberta 1081
Rodman, David J. 1659
Rodriguez, Al 1370
Rodriguez, Charlie J. 682
Rodriguez, Domingo A. 369, 1264
Rodriguez, Edward 720, 740
Rodriguez, Enrico 474, 1830
Rodriguez, Jai 1830
Rodriguez, Nicholas 37
Rodriguez, Ralph 1015
Rodriguez, Wong, Goff 1350
Roe, Patricia 1636
Roeburt, John 772
Roeder, Charles (Chas) (W.) 840, 841, 842, 1354, 1408, 1676
Roediger, Rolf 1293
Roemer, Richard 161
Roerick, William 1666
Roffman, Frederick S. 64
Roffman, Rose 661, 1467
Rogers, Adam 1055
Rogers, Bernard 1740
Rogers, Bob 1732
Rogers, Brent 224
Rogers, Brie 983
Rogers, Cynthia 494
Rogers, David 237, 550, 858
Rogers, Denise 1695
Rogers, Doug 507, 1517
Rogers, Irma 90
Rogers, James E. 1452
Rogers, Jay 297, 1763, 1772
Rogers, Jeanne 566
Rogers, Kevin 203
Rogers, Mickie 1177
Rogers, Natalie 1105
Rogers, Poli 897, 1670
Rogers, Robert 587, 1265
Rogers, Ronald 442, 944
Rogers, Roy 255
Rogers, Shoshanna 572
Rogers, Vinnie 1603
Rogers, Willie 615
Rogerson, Bob 513
Rogness, Peter 83, 1298
Rogow, David 1026
Rogowsky, Larry 1815
Rohan, Richard 814
Rohn, Andrew 1736
Rohn, Jennifer 294
Rohrbacker, Jacquiline 3
Roi, Tony 906
Roland, Mark 1338
Roland, Richard 1831
Roland, Steve 66, 1430
Rolandi, Gianna 1062
Rolant, Arlena 255
Rolfe, Wendy A. 471
Rolfing, Tom 539
Roll, Edward 1691
Rolland, Grace 578
Rolle, Esther 21, 589, 1004
Roller, Cleve 1599
Roller, Justin 1608
Roller, Theo 1342
Rollins, Pierce 1276
Rollins, Rowena 232, 319
Rolph, Marti 1392
Romagnoli, Joe 1290
Romaguera, Joaquin 188, 567, 990, 1137
Roman, Andrew 757
Roman, Bob 366
Roman, Dini 488
Roman, Eliseo 597, 760
Roman, Martin 529
Roman, Murray 1614
Roman, Paul Reid 504
Romanello, Paul 1671
Romann, Fidel 33
Romann, Susan 480, 1311, 1739
Romano, Christy Carlson 1523
Romano, Michael 273
Romano, Tom 1385
Romanovsky, Ron 808
Rome, Harold 981, 1100, 1101, 1267, 1268, 1608
Romeo, John 43
Romero, Federico 1179
Romero, Gary 1785
Romero, Jill 1370
Romero, Miguel 1082
Romero, Rafael 1462
Romero, Roger "Orko" 804
Romoff, Colin 737, 1651
Romoff, Douglas 737
Ron, Beverly 918
Ron, Shoshana 898
Ronan, John 1294
Ronan, Robert 1446
Ronci, Donald 401
Rondo, George 398
Roney, Edmund 766
Ronstadt, Linda 186, 1270
Rook, Willie 1562
Rooks, Lois 74
Rooney, Deborah 275
Rooney, Jan Chamberlin 914
Rooney, Mickey 914
Rooney, Wallace 1241
Roony, Jeanette 654
Roos, Casper 912, 1167, 1221
Roos, Delmar 1264
Roos, Joanna 619, 622
Root, Frank 232
Root, Lynn 238
Root, Melina 503
Roquemore, Cliff 1423
Rorem, Ned 1063, 1368
Rosa, Dennis 1287, 1560
Rosalie 326
Rosario, Carmen 1402
Rosario, Francisco 897
Rosato, Mary Lou 325
Roscoe, Bill 1820
Rose, Anika Noni 252
Rose, Edmund 1179
Rose, Emmett 134
Rose, George 1109, 1270
Rose, Jeffrey 1050
Rose, L. Arthur 1101
Rose, Louisa 101
Rose, Margot 753
Rose, Michael 483
Rose, Patrick 159
Rose, Philip 359, 1107
Rose, R.A. 1145
Rose, Renee 959, 1021, 1633
Rose, Renee Louise 68
Rose, Reva 1828
Rose, Rhonda 378
Rose, Richard 391
Rose, Shelby 1608
Rose, Stephen 1556
Rose, Susan R. 833
Rose, Suzanne 1826
Rosen, Abigail 895
Rosen, E. David 1476
Rosen, Edward 1029
Rosen, Herschel 147
Rosen, Jeff 965
Rosen, Jonathan 1494
Rosen, Robert 1025
Rosenak, David S. 1034, 1190
Rosenberg, Irene 1100
Rosenberg, Jan 271
Rosenberg, Michael S. 69
Rosenberg, Stuart 1032
Rosenberg, Susan 706
Rosenblat, Barbara 973
Rosenblum, Ava 1659
Rosenblum, Bob 1754
Rosenblum, Glenn 1361
Rosenblum, Joshua 227, 413, 485, 1204, 1665
Rosenblum, Pauly 441
Rosenblum, Robert 1707
Rosenblum, Susan 1659
Rosenfeld, Hilary 386, 710, 975, 1036, 1384, 1699
Rosenfeld, Moishe 604, 1051, 1619
Rosenfield, Betsy 171
Rosenfield, Stephen 1297
Rosenheim, Ruth 1749
Rosenshein, Neil 574, 1024
Rosenstock, Kimberly 72
Rosenstock, Susan 325
Rosental, Chayele 684
Rosenthal, Andrew 1661, 1692
Rosenthal, Jack 100
Rosenthal, Steve 1548
Rosenzweig, Rose 585
Rosica, Tom 1080
Rosing, Vladimir 92
Rosko 45
Rosner, Frank M. 329
Rosner, Paul 1431, 1447
Ross, Anita 1568
Ross, Barbara 813, 1257, 1690, 1750
Ross, Ben 1140
Ross, Bertram 820, 827
Ross, Blair 463, 730
Ross, Brad 930
Ross, Chiquita 927, 1738
Ross, David 779, 858
Ross, Eliza 616
Ross, Hank 865
Ross, Howard 1253
Ross, Hugh 600, 1229
Ross, Jack 1512
Ross, Jamie 87, 160, 1170, 1236
Ross, Jan 1691
Ross, Jane 1636
Ross, Joe 332, 472, 1604
Ross, Julia 601
Ross, Justin 537, 732, 1082, 1141, 1747
Ross, Madeline 620
Ross, Martin 957
Ross, Marty 1751
Ross, Michael 714, 1256, 1690, 1754, 1809
Ross, Robert 578, 780
Ross, Sandra (L.) 630, 850, 1001
Ross, Soara-Joye 375
Ross, Stephen 64
Ross, Steve 747
Ross, Stuart (H.) 260, 313, 527, 681, 700, 794, 1149, 1150, 1325
Ross, Suzanne, Jr. 67
Ross, Ted 266
Ross, Tom 1706
Ross, Walterine 1696
Ross, William 659, 1729
Rossen, Howard 1026
Rossetti, Christina 586
Rossi, Angelo del 1410
Rossi, Giulio 245
Rossi, Tony 991
Rossomme, Richard 989
Rosson, Paul 345
Rost, Leo 1025, 1216
Rosten, Norman 1023
Roston, Karen 408, 580, 809
Roswell, Maggie 1461
Roswick, Janis 1228
Rotardier, Amanda 1040
Rotardier, Kelvin 1029
Rotblatt, Steve 989
Rotem, Reut 108
Roth, Ana 1252
Roth, Ann 133, 448, 566
Roth, Bernard 1695
Roth, Daryl 83, 102, 189, 300, 668, 1591
Roth, Debbi 768
Roth, Jordan 399
Roth, Laurence 373
Roth, Michael (S.) 364, 459, 672, 1036, 1238
Roth, Richard 397
Roth, Robert 1435
Roth, Robert Jess 1143
Roth, Susan 1216
Roth, Wolfgang 204, 459, 826, 1541
Rothier, Leon 1249
Rothkopf, David (J.) 299
Rothlein, Arlene 756, 757, 1231
Rothman, Carole 2, 330, 764, 933, 1187, 1357, 1403, 1680
Rothman, Diana 1029
Rothpearl, Harry (H.) 147, 489, 666, 1822
Rothstein, Arlene 1231
Rothstein, Barbara 929
Rotondaro, Stephen 1138
Rotondi, Michael 1353
Rough, Robert 1029
Roulet, Bill 1349
Roullier, Ron 1354
Roulston, Allison 50
Rounds, Danny (Dan) 105, 200, 319
Rounds, David 690, 1076
Rounds, Gene 1732
Roundtree, Jean 1543
Roundtree, Richard 1004
Rounsaville, Paul 15, 834, 1349, 1776
Rouse, Barbara 1660
Roussel, Daniel 1013
Roussin, Richard 1729
Routh, Marc (Mark) 108, 479, 770, 1235, 1495, 1590, 1742
Routledge, Patricia 1270
Routman, Steve 926
Roux, Madeleine le 1695
Roven, Glen 1
Rovescalli, Antonio 340
Rovin, Robert 126, 714, 716, 1069
Rowe, Bertram 1086
Rowe, Dana P. 1831
Rowe, Hansford 873
Rowe, Mannie 1655
Rowe, Shawneen 1500
Rowett, William 1349
Rowland, Douglas 1115
Rowland, Jeff 1632
Rowser, Bertin 208, 500
Roxbury, Ronald 1029
Roy, Jeffrey 359
Roy, Nancy 331
Roy, Peggy Le 601
Roy, Rene 1226
Roy, Ron 385
Roy, Will 1137
Roy, William 84, 87, 160, 381, 415, 531, 843, 886, 1223, 1236, 1261, 1430
Royce, Rosita 1131
Royer, Joseph 1010
Rozie, Keith 500, 960, 1065
Rozier, Fletcher 816
Rozier, Sheva 772
Rozlach, Zygmunt 1275
Roznowski, Robert (Rob) 739, 749, 922
Rozon, Gilbert 462
Rozovsky, Mark 1541
Rozsa, Shawn 597
Rubbe, Eric 1786
Rubbico, Kathleen 1456
Rubell, Irene 403
Rubell, Michael 403
Ruben, Paul 1149
Rubens, Herbert 1715
Rubenstein, Barbara 1787
Rubenstein, Eli 1647
Rubenstein, Madelyn 653
Rubenstein, Seth 1686
Rubenstein, Steve 347
Rubin, Aaron 1192
Rubin, Charles 1813
Rubin, Ira 361
Rubin, Lisa Gould 401
Rubin, Menachem 585, 654
Rubin, Steven 653, 1377
Rubine, Sarah 1647
Rubinek, Saul 699
Rubino, Michael 1462
Rubins, Josh 218, 219
Rubinson, David 324
Rubinstein, Carol 1154
Rubinstein, John 1710
Rubinstein, Mary 750
Rubin-Vega, Daphne 130, 1351
Rubman, Marc 302
Ruby, Harry 672
Ruckdeschel, Karl A. 1669
Ruddy, Robert 609
Rudel, Anthony 1111
Rudel, Julius 188, 609, 947, 1062, 1111, 1227, 1462, 1552, 1789, 1814
Ruderman, Jordin 399
Rudesill, Joni 1051, 1342
Rudin, Scott 1545
Rudina, Tatiana 849
Rudley, Marion 1140
Rudner, Sara 1291
Rudnick, Paul 1282

Rudnitskaya, Yelena 849
Rudnitsky, Sergey 849
Rudolf, Max 1740
Rudolph, Buddy 1071
Rudolph, Florence 298
Rudolph, Jerome 652
Ruduk, Oleg 849
Rudy, Lisa 1015
Rudy, Martin 1272
Rue, John 983
Rue, Steve 1333
Ruen, Kathleen 1084
Ruff, Ruff 1279
Ruffin, Clovis 861
Ruffin, Eric 811
Ruffin, Gary 1562
Ruffin, Hank 1562
Ruffin, Stan 1562
Ruger, A. Nelson, IV 1784
Ruggiero, Dom 1419
Ruggiero, Holly-Anne 1786
Ruggiero, Rob 997
Ruhala, Mark 294
Ruhl, Pat 415
Ruisinger, Thomas 25
Ruiz, Anthony 897
Ruiz, Brunhilda 609, 1789
Ruiz, Carlos Giovanni 897
Ruiz, Randy 1384
Rule, Charles 66
Rule, Jim 1394
Rummler, Tom 34
Rumshinsky, Joseph 1104
Rumshinsky, Murray 585
Runanin, Boris 1254
Rundgren, Todd 1706
Runner, Joseph L. 545
Runolfsson, Anne 791, 929
Ruocco, John 727, 755
Ruoff, Lane 410
Rupert, Gene 1716
Rupert, Michael 430, 473, 486, 1019, 1492, 1622
Ruperto, Eddie 897
Rupnik, Kevin 961
Rupp, Craig 1628
Ruppe, David 1349
Rush, Deborah 27, 347, 699, 1036, 1057, 1334
Rush, Jo Anna 1208
Rush, Susan 417, 1514
Rushton, Christianne 362, 717
Rusk, James 126, 542, 556, 557, 616, 1069, 1273
Ruska, Dani 216
Ruskin, Coby 1140
Ruskin, Jeanne 1411
Ruslander, Daniel 1276
Russ, Adryan 770
Russak, Gerard 379
Russel, Rec 68, 569
Russell, A.J. 1790, 1791
Russell, Anna 32
Russell, Bill 537, 1215
Russell, Catherine 1693
Russell, Charles 317
Russell, Craig 1013
Russell, Donn 844
Russell, Evelyn 277, 1185, 1605
Russell, Forbesy 718, 1343
Russell, Ginny 1666
Russell, Jack 379, 1131
Russell, Jay 633
Russell, Jim 277, 507, 638
Russell, John 682
Russell, John C. 1545
Russell, Robert 1100
Russell, Walter S. 226
Russo, James 578
Russo, Ronald G. 1525
Russo, William 11, 222, 502, 641, 1103, 1222, 1230, 1238, 1513, 1779
Russom, Leon 1168
Rustin, Dan 535, 1477
Rutigliano, Danny 1821
Rutledge, Meredith 1536
Rutz, Richard 954
Ruyle, Bill 561, 632, 728
Ruysdael, Basil 245, 340, 1075
Ryack, Rita 726, 1478
Ryall, William 434, 1366
Ryan, Charles 1079, 1595
Ryan, Chilton 535
Ryan, Conny 1615
Ryan, Harry 1616
Ryan, J. Keith 1290
Ryan, Kevin 42
Ryan, Owen 1177
Ryan, Peter 1787
Ryan, Roz 1726
Ryan, Shannon 1469
Ryan, Steve 1376
Ryanharrt, Shyrl 110
Rybeck, Alex 810
Rybin, Susan 897
Rychtarik, Richard 66, 776, 1244
Rydell, Charles 236, 1420
Ryder, Alfred 1140
Ryder, Amy 1298, 1660
Ryder, Donald 91
Ryder, Mark 1445
Ryder, Ric 275
Ryder, Richard 634, 1258, 1279, 1335, 1709
Rydzeski, Mary Ann 68, 1021, 1221
Ryer, Alexana 105, 223
Ryness, Bryce 328
Ryskind, Morrie 912, 1166, 1167

Sabado, Keith 363
Sabath, Bruce 983
Sabel, Shelly 365
Sabella, David 538
Sabella, Ernie 1367
Sabellico, Richard 305, 343, 545, 1328
Sabin, David 12, 1154, 1296, 1628
Sabin, Gus 1751
Sablow, Jane 1223, 1305
Sacco, John 1117
Sachar, Moshe 819, 1105
Sachinis, Richard 840
Sachs, C. Colby 95
Sachs, Norman 326, 1107
Sachse, Leopold 40
Sackeroff, David 200, 773
Sacks, Merrylen 1242
Sacks, Quinny 1730
Sacks, Richard 1731
Saddler, Donald 46, 128, 604, 737, 1083, 1651, 1670
Sadler, Bill 909
Sado, Alexander 849
Sadoff, Simon 1687
Sadoski, Felix 1104
Sadusk, Maureen 246, 920, 998, 1146, 1744, 1787
Saez, Ramon 1281
Saffran, Christina 55
Sager, Sarah 1024
Sahlins, Bernard 22, 318, 548, 1206, 1209, 1352, 1415, 1649, 1765
Saich, Nick 1233
Sainer, Lioner 1145
St. Benedict's Youth Choir 402
St. Clair, Robert 226
St. Cyr, Tommy 346
St. Darr, Deborah 244
St. Germain, Mark 2, 576, 791, 828, 855, 1071
St. James, Maximilian 1389
St. John, Eve 820
St. Laurent, Michael 1013
St. Louis, David 668
St. Louis, Louis 208, 625, 1360, 1504
St. Luke's, Orchestra of 846
St. Shaw, Mike 1725
Saint, Carroll 1627
Saint, David 1513
Saint-Jean, Andre R. 68
Saito, Shoichi 602
Saito, Yasunori 602
Saitta, Paul 1060
Sakamoto, Nancy 294
Sakash, Evelyn 8, 1141, 1575, 1693
Sakren, Jared 138
Saks, Gene 826
Saks, Gidon 673
Sala, Ed 825
Sala, Janet "Planet" 1476
Salamando, Peter 616
Salamandyk, Tim 633
Salamida, Danita 474
Salamone, Louis S. 30, 146, 1118
Salas, Nicolette 658
Salata, Gregory 1256
Salatino, Anthony 1022, 1784
Saldamando, Peter 1661
Saldana, Theresa 820, 1098, 1124
Salee, Marion 1626
Salem, Marc 1053
Salerno, Lauren 1015
Salerno, Ray 1394
Sales, Wilferd 425
Salfas, Richard 990
Salgado, Luis 760, 1425
Salguero, Sophia 240, 632, 1186
Salinaro, Dom 201
Salis, Nancy 824
Salisbury, Frances (Fran) 591, 682, 927, 1307, 1509
Salka, Benjamin 742
Salle, David 158
Salley, Herbert 844
Sallid, Otis (A.) 278, 662, 996, 1534
Salls, Carla 1252, 1494
Salmere, Toni 920
Salmon, Scott 1082, 1606
Salo, Nancy 82
Saloman, Nancy 1636
Salt, Waldo 353, 356, 1399
Saltz, Amy 1659
Saltzberg, Sarah 1680
Saltzman, Esta 874
Saltzman, Joel 1150
Saltzman, Mark 1, 2
Saltzman, Michael 1104
Saltzman, Simon L. 292
Salvatore, John 1215
Salzman, Eric 1665
Salzman, Joshua 738
Samayoa, Caesar 240
Sambogna, Adolph 1221
Sameth, Marten 600
Sammler, B.J. 400
Samoff, Marjorie 1665
Samplin, Ian 362
Sampson, June 1393
Sampson, Linda 460, 613
Samson, Susan Madden 311
Samuel, D. Peter 435, 1365
Samuels, David 268
Samuels, Gayle 809
Samuels, Jason 1406, 1407
Samuels, Tracey 1179
Sanborn, John 910
Sanchez, Jennifer 563
Sanchez, Jennifer M. 1547
Sanchez, Justo 1405
Sanchez, Marcelino 1459
Sanchez, Xiomara Laugart 262
Sand, Paul 714, 986, 1649, 1754
Sandall, Andrea 1016
Sandburg, Tricia 1616
Sandeen, Darrell 1824
Sandefur, James D. 1201
Sandek, Barbara 243, 392, 920, 1349, 1776
Sanderbeck, Kelly 1148
Sanders, Dan 11
Sanders, David 1146
Sanders, Donna 417, 1430
Sanders, Honey 528, 1440
Sanders, Howard 166
Sanders, Ira 287
Sanders, Jackie 323, 1571
Sanders, Jay O. 580, 764, 950
Sanders, Kathleen 1816
Sanders, Lois 1721
Sanders, Marta 133
Sanders, Paulette 125
Sanderson, Austin K. 240
Sanderson, Kirsten 496
Sandifur, Virginia 272, 1442, 1483
Sandish, Dale 49
Sandler, Peretz 1382
Sandler, Suki 323
Sandler, Will B. 1672
Sandrow, Nahma 878, 1715
Sands, Billy 1688
Sands, Diana 60, 425, 946
Sands, Donna 409
Sands, Dorothy 620, 621, 622
Sands, Peter 1318
Sandy, Gary 1242
Sanek, Barbara 920
Sanford, Isabel 425
Sanford, Jane 1080
Sanford, Lathan 478
Sanford, Rani 68
Sanford, Tim 222, 502, 503, 641, 791, 805, 1103, 1238, 1513, 1726, 1779
Sango 1653
Sanine, Alexander 440
Sankey, Tom 605
Sankowich, Lee D. 1358
Sansegundo, Carlos 925
Sansegundo, Ruth 925
Sansone, Peter 1452
Sansone, Rik 1556
Santana, Martiza 768
Santana, Orlando 399
Santana, Shirley 768
Santell, Marie 258, 417, 693, 1330, 1424
Santelmo, Anthony (Jr.) 1056, 1321
Santen, Kathy 1238
Santiago, Manuel 1183
Santiago, Saundra 130
Santinelli, Ralph 1081
Santoangelo, Michael R. 166
Santoni, Reni 1614
Santora, Bud 118
Santore, Lorraine 951
Santoriello, Alex 124, 1378
Santucci, Bob 1030
Santuccio, Valerie 396
Santvoord, Van 825
Sanyal, Debargo 1322
Saperstein, Jerry 1435
Saperstein, Paula 1244
Sapio, Maurice 340
Sapoff, Robert 305
Sapolsky, Robert 1062
Sapp, Robb 825, 1425, 1830
Sappington, Margo 1146, 1168, 1169, 1305, 1665
Sappio, Alfred 988
Saputo, Peter J. 190, 588, 1434
Sarakatsannis, Melanie 439
Sarallen 1620
Sarandon, Chris 263
Sarell, Charles 121
Sarfaty, Regina 677, 1217, 1474, 1789
Sarge, Brendan Fay 867
Sargeant, Stacey 1054, 1784
Sargent, Herb 664
Sargent, Joe 1192
Sargent, Stacey 668
Sarner, Joyce M. 1508, 1571
Sarno, Janet 1562
Sarnoff, Rosita 1, 1133, 1335
Sarofeen, Anne 663
Saroyan, Lucy 734
Saroyan, William 686
Sartor, Michael 1150
Sasser, James 1547
Sasso, Dick 416
Sassone, Vincent 1508
Sataraka, Peter 1221
Sater, Steven 1515
Saternow, Tim 1516
Satie, Stephanie 773, 1081
Satlin, Stan 279
Sato, Kenkichi 602
Satterfield, Laine 195
Satuloff, Robert 551, 907
Saucier, Marie 66
Sauer, Bernard 1032, 1341
Sauer, Clayton 1660
Saunders, Andrea 152
Saunders, Janet 212
Saunders, Karen 801
Saunders, Lois Ann 631
Saunders, Marilyn 1480
Saunders, Mary 575
Saunders, Velma 768
Sauter, Joe 291
Savage, Aileen 599, 800
Savage, Elliott 90
Savage, J. Brandon 193
Savage, Jack 878
Savage, Jim 1713
Savage, John 1424
Savage, Keith 25, 599
Savage, Lesley 725, 1097
Savage, Melodee 1065, 1375, 1781
Savage, Tom 725, 1097
Savarese, John 1771
Saver, Jeffrey 973
Saverance, Deborah 256
Savidge, Mary 1393
Savin, Ron Lee 539, 1365, 1538
Saviola, Camille 54, 700, 1365, 1588
Savitsky, Carol Cogan 929
Savoca, John 1599
Sawyer, David 1384, 1625, 1699
Sawyer, Mark 1454
Sawyer, Mary Le 1131
Sawyer, Michael (Mike) 291, 357
Sawyer, Tom 1562
Sawyer, W. Brent 57
Saxon, Wanda 1221
Saxon, William 92, 1474
Saxton, Lydia 1453
Sayer, Stanley 725, 1264
Sayers, Denni 938
Sayger, Jim 1342
Sbano, Jim 125
Scaccia, Tony 1013
Scalici, Jack 304
Scalzo, Joseph 213
Scammon, Cheryl 138
Scanga, Richard 1666

Scanlan, Dick 1215
Scanlan, John 140
Scanlon, Barbara 164, 435
Scardino, Don 78, 406, 582, 596, 656, 699, 753, 791
Scarfe, Alan 12, 170
Scarlato, Richard 1435
Scarpelli, Glenn 1538
Scatamacchia, Charlie 1089
Scatuorchio, Tee 1600
Scenery, More Than Just 49
Schaal, Dick 1206, 1813
Schacher, Richard (A.) 718, 796, 1226
Schachner, Dan 597
Schachter, Nicholas 1686
Schadt, Elly (Ellie) 1387, 1776
Schaechter, Ben 1607, 1658
Schaefer, David 567
Schaefer, Hal 788
Schaefer, Paul S. 1103
Schaeffer, Carl 696
Schaeffer, Eric 1700
Schaeffer, Joseph 1481
Schaeffer, Mary 1315
Schaeffer, Sandra Jean 488
Schafer, Milton 1101
Schafer, Reuben 100, 1349
Schafer, Susan 256
Schaffel, Marla 285, 444
Schaffner, James 362, 717
Schak, John 191, 1286
Schalchlin, Steve 146, 892
Schall, David 1354
Schall, Ekkehard 455
Schallenberg, Chuck 510
Schallenberg, Sherri 510
Schanker, Larry 79
Schapira, Joel 708
Schapiro, Herb 208, 1038, 1039
Scharer, Jonathan 513, 514, 515, 516, 517, 537
Scharer, Robert 1215
Scharf, Stephen 1330
Schary, Dore 61
Schauler, Eileen 1137
Schechter, Ben 782, 1026
Schechter, David 386, 643, 647, 648, 659, 700, 1133, 1384, 1699
Schechtman, Saul 472
Scheck, Max 1688
Scheckel, Joan 999
Scheeder, Louis W. 377
Scheeler, Bob 803
Scheer, Gene 47
Scheer, Jennifer 538
Scheffler, John 278
Scheifer, Neil 749
Scheitinger, Tony 643
Schelhammer, Robert 1182
Schellenbach, Kate 1384
Schenck, Elliott 136
Schenck, Mary Percy 1740
Schenker, Joel (W.) 875, 969
Scher, John 1632
Scherer, John 408, 883, 1296
Scherker, Cara Samantha 1425
Schertler, Nancy 3, 473
Scheu, Peter A. 1151
Schevers, Susan 1379
Schickele, Peter 1168
Schicker, Matt 1818
Schickling, John 66
Schielke, Joanna 460, 1034, 1198
Schiera, Thom 203
Schierhorn, Paul 900
Schiff, Charlotte 1774
Schiff, Dan 979
Schiff, Larry 1283
Schifrin, Lalo 51
Schimkat, Arnd D. 1281
Schimmel, John 1317, 1384
Schimmel, William 378, 459, 847
Schindeldecker, Cody 328
Schipa, Tito, Jr. 1146
Schippers, Thomas 62, 891, 1601
Schirmer, Gus, Jr. 199, 566
Schissler, Jeffrey 153, 230, 567, 675, 748, 854, 861, 1176
Schlamme, Martha 880, 881, 882, 1078, 1773, 1807
Schlee, Robert 393, 713, 1391, 1628
Schlefer, Mack 957
Schlegel, Carl 245, 1597
Schlegel, Jeanne 112
Schlein, Hap 556, 557, 1035
Schlesinger, Sarah 1184
Schlittne, Tianna 1389
Schloss, Edwin W. 129, 433
Schloss, Sybele 1241
Schlossberg, Jerry 1678
Schlossberg, Julian 751, 806, 1656
Schlossberg, Lili 768
Schlosser, Peter 648
Schmeer, Richard 1744
Schmid, Tom 889, 1321
Schmidt, Ann 85, 618, 619, 620
Schmidt, Douglas (W.) 364, 625, 1340, 1384, 1459, 1628, 1746
Schmidt, Erica 365, 1238
Schmidt, Harvey 191, 306, 307, 308, 309, 371, 478, 479, 733, 858, 1056, 1100, 1253, 1259, 1286, 1366, 1447, 1451
Schmidt, Maggie 373
Schmidt, Marie 1249
Schmidt, Paul 26, 170
Schmidt, S. Ryan 767, 1581
Schmidt, Sara 474, 755
Schmidt, Stephen 468
Schmitt, Kate 647
Schmitz, Ted 362
Schmorr, Robert 62, 1368
Schneider, Charles 1827
Schneider, Denise 768
Schneider, Evelyn 834
Schneider, Jana 1109, 1595
Schneider, Jeffrey 1102, 1510, 1715, 1821
Schneider, Jon Norman 1322
Schneider, Robert T. 1556
Schneider, Schorling 1660
Schneider, Stan 1626
Schnoll, Jo Ann 768
Schnuck, Terry E. 1054
Schob, Hank 403, 454
Schochen, Seyril 1636
Schoeffler, Paul 398, 1144
Schoenfeld, Mae 585
Schoep, Arthur 600
Schofield, Barbara 1469
Scholes, Michael 1316
Scholtz, Christa 672
Scholz, Walter Rosen 1409
Schomaker, Mike 1077
Schon, Bonnie 1606
Schon, Kenneth 1131, 1740
Schonfeld, Jeremy 1054
Schonfeld, Joel 1458
Schoonmaker, Charles 603, 1287
Schopp, Cathi 1177
Schorr, Eric 1772
Schorr, Moshe 1382
Schottenfeld, Barabra 1472
Schottenfeld, Barbara 260, 731, 1472
Schowalter, Mark 47
Schrager, Sara 1147
Schramm, David 325
Schrank, Joseph 1267
Schreiber, Avery 1206, 1813
Schreiber, Edward 1701
Schreiber, John 668
Schreiber, Robert 965
Schrock, Robert 1110
Schroder, William 948
Schroeder, Aaron 80
Schroeder, Erica 1450
Schroeder, Michael 676
Schroeder, Wayne 1303
Schuberg, Carol 275
Schuchardt, Emil (Emile) 137, 1775
Schuck, (Conrad) John 1134, 1238
Schuck, Karen 1108
Schuette, James 195, 503, 1404, 1832
Schuler, Duane 256, 495, 628, 1723
Schull, Richard B. 1208
Schulman, Susan H. 484, 692, 791, 1637, 1726
Schulman, Tony 1077
Schultz, Armand 1513
Schultz, Charley 226
Schultz, Dwight 551
Schultz, Frederick 260
Schultz, Michael (A.) 589, 1620
Schumacher, Ruth 66
Schuman, Howard 263, 1707, 1754
Schumer, Yvette 1125
Schurkamp, Richard 463, 1800
Schuster, Alan (J.) 54, 102, 142, 181, 284, 804, 1653
Schuster, Diana 310
Schustik, Bill 963
Schuyler, Thom 1042
Schwab, Buddy 199, 368, 472, 1261
Schwab, Sophie 865, 866, 981
Schwantes, Leland 1029, 1035
Schwantes, Neal 190
Schwartz, Arthur 348, 621, 940, 1101, 1606
Schwartz, Ben 768, 1134
Schwartz, Bob 587
Schwartz, Bonnie Nelson "Skippy" 79
Schwartz, Bruce 246
Schwartz, Deah 904
Schwartz, Diane 767
Schwartz, Gary 249, 284
Schwartz, Gwen Gibson 1276
Schwartz, Jerome J. 714
Schwartz, Marc 103
Schwartz, Mark 1046, 1450
Schwartz, Morton 1524
Schwartz, Nancy 101
Schwartz, Noel 1008
Schwartz, Sally 1470
Schwartz, Scott 1144, 1634
Schwartz, Sidney 1276
Schwartz, Stephen 2, 88, 248, 595, 596, 597, 1029, 1100, 1243, 1328, 1534
Schwartz, Susan L. 365
Schwartz, Suzanne J. 1454
Schwarz, Aviva 1203
Schwarz, Robert 403
Schweid, Carole 279, 1149
Schweikardt, Michael 1742
Schweizer, David 1499
Schwerin, Doris 857, 1162
Schwering, Elizabeth 331
Schwinn, Ron 274
Schwisow, James 374
Scioli, Tony 1469
Sclafani, Sal 796
Scofield, Pamela 491, 1484, 1523, 1554, 1701
Scooler, Zvee 647, 648, 666
Scooter, Earl 854
Scopeletis, James 565
Scordino, Bruno C. 61
Scotford, Sybil 1172
Scott, Alan 125
Scott, Alice 366
Scott, Allan 834
Scott, Besseye Ruth 709
Scott, Bobby 384
Scott, Brad 124
Scott, Brian H. 1499
Scott, Bruce 62, 90, 1424
Scott, Bryant 1551
Scott, Carole-Ann 1747
Scott, Christopher 143, 185, 284, 606, 811, 1251
Scott, Dennis 1272
Scott, Ed 1754
Scott, Ernie 803, 1070
Scott, Harold 278, 425
Scott, Helena 66, 98
Scott, Henry E., III 792
Scott, J. Blake 620, 621, 622
Scott, James 586, 658
Scott, Joel 125
Scott, John 619
Scott, Kenyon 1145
Scott, Lauren 1412
Scott, Lindsay 103
Scott, Mal 1227
Scott, Michael 133, 788
Scott, Molly 58
Scott, Norman 62, 891
Scott, Oz 996
Scott, Robyn 247
Scott, Sharon E. 153
Scott, Sherie Rene 365, 890
Scott, Susan Elizabeth 343, 565
Scott, Ted 324
Scott, Vernon Landix 294
Scott, Zenzele 850
Scotti, Don 1801
Scotti, Tricia 1237
Scoullar, John 326, 1343
Scourby, Stephanie 1399
Scruggs, Sharon 297
Scudder, Rose 215
Seabolt, Frank 600
Seabury, Jack 43
Seader, Richard 1582
Seale, Douglas 884
Seale, ouglas 884
Sealey, Carol B. 434
Seaman, George 235
Seaman, Jane 1753
Searcy, Nicholas 396
Searcy, Paul 231
Searles, Grace 1278
Sears, Sally 1582
Sears, Shawn 1508
Seary, Kim 1432
Seasongood, Eda 1410, 1560
Seastrom, Guje 1713
Seaton, Joanna 1160
Seaton, Johnny 437
Seawell, Brockman 1323
Seay, Gail Homer 1763
Secino, Betty 1385, 1755
Seckinger, Regina Anna 282
Seckinger, Sarah 767
Seckler, Beatrice 1445
Secter, David 572
Sector, Arnold 1021
Secunda, Sholom 119, 608, 666, 874
Sedgwick, Michael 1692
Seegar, Sara 448
Seelbach, Michael 1347
Seeley, Stephanie 1031
Seetoo, Keelee 289
Seff, Sherie 856
Segal, David (F.) 2, 86, 152, 292, 360, 716, 894, 1168, 1300, 1582, 1606, 1677, 1767
Segal, Erich 1468
Segal, George 902, 1295
Segal, Jonathan L. 780
Segal, Kathrin King 465, 789, 1253, 1286
Segal, Lynda 22, 1415, 1528
Segal, Misha 1684
Segal, Morton 1716
Segan, Eleanor 1377
Segan, Marc Howard 1763
Segovia, Yolanda 218
Seibel, Paula 1087
Seidel, Virginia 599
Seidelman, Arthur A. 1810
Seiden, Darren M. 145
Seiden, Jackie 679
Seiden, Stan 145
Seidman, Amy 865, 866
Seidman, Stanley 895
Seifert, Susan 1713
Seiffert, Alan F. 81
Seignious, Geri 68, 91
Seignious, Juliet 591
Seiler, Chris 1216
Seiter, Ken 545, 1408
Seitz, W. Thomas 1539
Selby, Margaret 804
Selby, Susan 804
Seldes, Marian 490, 1390
Selee, Marion 1627
Seletsky, Harold 711
Sell, Janie 84, 234, 342, 350, 588, 1069, 1184, 1273, 1339, 1459
Sellars, Lawrence 1080
Sellars, Peter 363, 1139
Seller, Jeffrey 760
Sellers, Jim 1230
Sellwood, Tom 1233
Seltzer, David J. 466
Selwyn, Florence 85
Selzer, Diana 1140
Semans, William H. 716
Semashko, Lilia 849
Sembach, Johannes 245
Semes, Renee 244
Semien, Steiv 116, 194
Semlitz, Stephen 1634
Semmler, Pamela 1139
Semos, Murray 957
Sendak, Maurice 1340
Sendzimir, Stanley 920
Sener, Alan 1146
Seng, Kathy 1560
Senger, John 1236
Senn, Herbert 128, 201, 236, 566, 631, 654, 1161, 1170, 1203, 1440, 1481
Sensenig, E. Andrew 1742
Sensiba, Winnie 1721
Senske, Rebecca 1466
Seo, Byrung Goo 889
Seo, Seung Jun 889
Seo, Shuhei 538
Seppe, Christopher 271, 1560
Septee, Moe 1619
Serabian, Lorraine 403, 1420
Serafin, Tullio 440, 868, 1047, 1249
Seraphine, Danny 1753
Serbagi, Midhat 574
Serban, Andrei 1697
Serebrov, Muni 874
Sereda, John 1432

Serotsky, Aaron 541
Serra, Hal 268
Serra, Raymond 1025
Serralles, Jeanine 1117
Serrano, Adriana 1054
Serrano, Charlie (Charles) 197, 203, 833, 1001, 1146
Serrano, Nestor 377
Serrecchia, Michael 283, 884
Sesma, Thom 69, 289
Sessa, Jay 1559
Setlock, Mark 1351
Setrakian, Mary 309, 404, 658
Setterfeld(field), Valda 158, 397
Setzer, Milton 34, 236, 1636
Sevec, Christine 1551
Sevier, Jack 217, 1593, 1785
Sevra, Robert 971
Sewall, Sally 366
Sewell, Brian 1694
Sewell, Danny 884, 1098
Sexton, Anne 972
Sexton, Coleen 679
Seyb, Wendy 1736
Seymour, Dan 116
Seymour, James 789, 1242
Seymour, John Laurence 762
Sgarro, Louis 62
Shaber, David 317
Shacket, Mark 38
Shacochis, Mike 11
Shactman, Murray I. 708
Shaddock, Pamela 1223
Shaddow, Elena 1742
Shade, Clarencia 470
Shade, Ellen 676
Shaer, Carol Sue 1185
Shaffer, Peter 450
Shaffer, Robert B. 1591
Shagi, Eli 1105
Shaheen, Dan 308, 733
Shaiman, Marc 370, 475, 646, 943
Shakespeare, William 62, 201, 414, 972, 1098, 1149, 1437, 1519, 1568, 1569
Shalet, Diane 1385
Shalit, Willa 1197
Shaller, Liza 612
Shamir, Amiram (Ami) 1044, 1647
Shamos, Jeremy 645
Shand, Kevin 399
Shane, Bob 532
Shane, Hal 1656
Shane, Joe 1188
Shane, Rita 1062
Shane, Robert 867, 1060
Shane, Robin L. 1815
Shanet, Howard 505
Shaney, Frank 11
Shangilia Youth Choir of Kenya 167
Shanina, Yelena 849
Shank, Corey 1281
Shank, Richard C. 121
Shankel, (C.) Lynne 38, 305, 1554, 1613
Shanks, Priscilla 632
Shanline, Susan 1522
Shannon, Eileen 957
Shanson, Esther 1629
Shanstrom, David 1302
Shapero, Lillian 1822
Shapiro, Anne 1240
Shapiro, Danial 910
Shapiro, Debbie 181
Shapiro, Harry 1145
Shapiro, Ira 1556
Shapiro, Mel 860, 1689
Shapiro, Richard K. 716
Shapiro, Ron 1326
Sharak, Marlaine 66
Sharkey, Dan 249, 950
Sharma, Barbara 172, 766, 1604
Sharma, Fran Kirmser 1458
Sharman, Jim 1666
Sharnock, Emma 1629
Sharp, Cathy 1655
Sharp, Michael 416, 445, 681, 1692
Sharpe, Billy 499, 1508
Sharpe, John 1448
Sharr, Yoel 1647
Sharron, Kristina 1416
Shatskin, Charles 750
Shaulis, Jane 574, 1462, 1730
Shaw, Bob 186, 973, 1109, 1146, 1270
Shaw, Brian 238
Shaw, Deborah 909, 1461
Shaw, Guillermo Fernandez 1179
Shaw, Howard 66, 1131
Shaw, Jane Catherine 1248
Shaw, Kendall 571
Shaw, Leon 199
Shaw, Louis 1131
Shaw, Marcia 601
Shaw, Marcie 186, 1146, 1270
Shaw, Paula 380, 613
Shaw, Peter 1749
Shaw, Philip 197
Shaw, Vanessa 124, 358
Shaw-Robinson, Charles 325
Shawhan, April 822, 1072
Shawn, Allen 1057
Shawn, Dick 569, 1417
Shawn, Dorothy 891, 1131
Shawn, Michael 1363, 1483
Shawn, Peter 90
Shay, Rita 235
Shay, Sylvia 384, 535
Shayne, Alan 448
Shea, Jean 332
Shea, Roger 1595
Sheahan, Tim 840
Shealy, Lauren 926
Shearer, Dennis J. (Denny) 42, 442, 803, 1070, 1707
Shearman, Alan 303, 623
Shearon, James K. 716
Shecter, Ben 1236
Sheehan, Alexia Hess 775
Sheehan, Ciaran 775
Sheehan, John J.D. 1782
Sheehan, Mike 376
Sheek, Charles C. 295
Sheens, Nathan 1590
Sheer, Rosemarri 1172
Sheets, J.C. 799
Sheffer, Isaiah 209, 389, 1361, 1362, 1442, 1821
Sheffer, Jonathan 377
Sheffield, Buddy 297
Sheffield, David 297
Sheffield, Dick 297
Sheffield, Don 915
Sheffield-Dewees, James 1345
Sheik, Duncan 1499, 1515
Shein, Kate 2
Sheinkin, Rachel 1425, 1680
Sheintsiss, Oleg 849
Shel, Claudia 803
Shelembe, Pumi 1401
Shell, Dick 329
Shell, Martha 1062
Shelle, Michael 1832
Shellenberger, James 1575
Shelley, Carole 406, 1450
Shelley, Gladys 598, 1385
Shelley, Joshua 93, 745, 1254, 1464, 1465
Shelley, Percy Bysshe 1443
Shelley, Robert 357
Shelton, Chad 941
Shelton, Ray 1030
Shelton, Reid 258, 1008
Shendell, Len 1469
Shenoy, Nandita J. 1441
Shepard, Drey 350, 1069
Shepard, Harold 100, 789
Shepard, Joan 1274, 1302
Shepard, Karen 1021
Shepard, Lionel 1806
Shepard, Matthew 1428
Shepard, Maura 83
Shepard, Richmond 1586
Shepard, Sam 1168
Shepherd, David 1415, 1724
Shepherd, Gwen 180
Shepherd, Lee 1664
Shepley, Michael 259
Shepp, Archie 844, 885
Sheppard, Hugo 1233
Sheppard, Julie 906, 1383
Shepperd, Drey 852, 1255
Sher, Gloria 42
Sherer, Jonathan 512
Sheridan, John 821, 1546
Sheridan, Liz 44, 90, 534, 587, 660, 1259
Sheridan, Matthew 1645
Sheridan, Maura 83
Sheridan, Wayne 545
Sheriff, Noam 1044
Sherman, Allan 685
Sherman, Andrew 365
Sherman, Arthur 784, 1152
Sherman, Bruce 796
Sherman, Carlos 66, 1131
Sherman, Charles 940
Sherman, Garry 1415
Sherman, Geoffrey 1143
Sherman, Kim D. 910, 1499
Sherman, Lee 98
Sherman, Loren 70, 219, 424, 1049, 1243, 1304, 1427
Sherman, Lori 469, 727, 1498
Sherman, Lowell 1112
Sherman, Martin 1599
Sherrill, Homer "Pappy" 1720
Sherry, Fred 1746
Sherwin, Manning 85
Sherwin, Mimi 246
Sherwood, Holly 652
Sherwood, Toba 883
Sherwood, Wayne 259, 827
Shevelove, Burt 353, 1239
Shevlin, Daniel 1818
Shew, Tim 873
Sheward, Debby 1522
Shibaoka, Masakazu 518, 521, 522, 525
Shibata, Shuji 1653
Shield, Harvey 653
Shiffman, Adam 767
Shimazaki, Saturo 872
Shimberg, Hinks 1654
Shimerman, Armin 1628
Shimkin, Arthur 1824
Shimoda, Itsuro 602
Shimono, Sab 1358
Shin, Hyo In 889
Shinsui, Sansho 602
Shiomi, R.A. 1300
Shipley, Sandra 1187
Shipp, John Wesley 1472
Shire, David 300, 616, 1400, 1524, 1652, 1710
Shirky, Clay 349
Shirvis, Barbara 673
Shiryayev, Vladimir 849
Shives, Sara 1645
Shi-Zheng, Chen 1020
Shlenker, Sidney (L.) 203, 833, 1138
Shnaider, Dan 920
Shobey, Norman 835
Shoenfeld, Mae 874
Shonert, Jeff 940
Shookhoff, David 1024
Shoop, Laura 130
Shoop, Linda 226
Shor, Miriam 680
Shore, Allen M. 527
Shore, Elaine 844
Shore, Harris 223, 1079
Shore, Lois 620, 621, 622
Shoremount, Amy 1374, 1416
Shorenstein, Carole J. 1560
Shorr, William 831
Short, Bobby 165, 368
Short, Kevin 574, 1816
Short, Sylvia 601, 1411
Shorter, Beth 1398
Shorter, James 1
Short-Goldsen, Martha 629
Shortt, Paul 422
Shoshanna 711
Shostakovich, Dmitri 170
Showell, Jill 851
Shriver, Chris J. 229
Shriver, Lisa 13, 206, 837
The Shubert Organization 1519
Shucraft, Wilhemena 1543
Shue, Larry 1109
Shukat, Scott 1228
Shull, Richard B. 44, 544
Shulman, A. 898
Shulman, Michael 70
Shultz, Philip 224
Shuman, Alice 857
Shuman, Earl 1420
Shuman, Mort 720, 792, 793
Shuman, Patricia 1730
Shurin, Sande 1567
Shurr, Buff 1265
Shusharin, Nikolai 849
Shuster, Alan J. 196
Shuttleworth, Barbara 1552
Shyre, Paul 16
Siatkowski, Jim 789
Sibanda, Seth 651, 1284, 1561
Sica, Joy Lynne 472
Sicangco, Eduardo 102, 644, 912, 1167, 1514
Sicari, Joseph R. 341, 962
Sickinger, Robert 1682
Sicuso, Tony 1320
Sidman, Sarah 262
Sieben, Pearl 993
Siebert, Charles 306
Siegal, Don 1297
Siegal, Donald 1693
Siegal, June 1
Siegel, Arthur 44, 261, 861, 1142, 1152, 1319, 1431, 1448, 1585, 1586, 1661
Siegel, Denny 1817
Siegel, June 2, 718, 1045, 1607
Siegel, Larry 701, 986
Siegel, Maxwell 1430
Siegel, William 1342, 1745
Siegfried, Dorothy 1131
Siegfried, Irene 1481
Siegfried, Mandy 1545
Siegler, Ben 1376
Siegler, Steve 1240
Siegmeister, Elie 53, 887
Siegmund, Ronald 1281
Sielski, Carolyn 256
Siena, Jerold 256, 1368
Sierra, Miguel 118
Siff, Ira 467, 554, 647, 648, 823, 834, 920, 952, 1349
Siford, Daniel 249
Sigel, David 1531
Siggins, Jeff 63
Sigler, Scott 454, 465
Sigmond, Ainsley 1227
Signore, Don 493, 1294
Signoretti, Toni 834
Sigrist, Susan 1026
Sigyn 566
Sikes, Pat 66
Sikora, Megan 1778
Silas, Eddie 869
Silberberg, Joseph 441
Silberg, David 1527
Silberman, David, Jr. 1152
Silberman, Joel 924, 1199, 1258, 1340
Siletti, Mario 935
Silliman, Maureen 1624, 1697
Sillman, Leonard 44
Sills, Beverly 92, 1474
Sills, Carol 1461
Sills, Paul 22, 421, 422, 1206, 1415, 1461, 1649, 1724, 1765
Sills, Rachel 1461
Sills, Stephanie 464
Silva, Chris 731
Silva, Nino 352
Silvano, Frank 506
Silver, Ben 702
Silver, Bob 802
Silver, Doug 1458
Silver, Fred (Frederick) 550, 564, 565, 758, 1259, 1527, 1640
Silver, Joan Micklin 2, 314, 1036, 1334
Silver, Joe 442, 1161, 1455
Silver, Joshua 181, 182
Silver, Kaz 854
Silver, Raphael D. 1036
Silver, Rhonda 802
Silver, Ronald (Ron) 958, 1082
Silver, Stuart (Stu) 243, 347, 920, 998, 1739
Silver, Susan 849
Silvera, Jack I. 754
Silver-Friedl, David G. 391
Silverglat, Harry 537, 1136, 1169
Silverman, Adam 1120
Silverman, Jefrey 215, 1039, 1208
Silverman, Jon D. 1243
Silverman, Mary (D.) 713, 1133
Silverman, Maura 319
Silverman, Maxwell 1272
Silverman, Stanley 12, 170, 393, 394, 431, 713, 1087, 1599, 1628, 1708
Silverman, Treva 50, 87, 126, 556, 771, 1142, 1255, 1273
Silverstein, Dan 1749
Silverstein, Shel 1710
Silverstein, Steven 561
Silvestri, Martin 825, 1595
Silvestri, Robi 1429
Sim, Keong 1325
Siman, Barbara 1037
Simard, Jennifer 395, 521, 523, 739, 1251, 1613
Simerson, Brian 1073
Simione, Donn 348
Simkin, Diane 1455
Simmonds, Catherine 1629
Simmons, Andrew 1113
Simmons, Bonnie 1028, 1270
Simmons, Chandra 850
Simmons, Collette 13
Simmons, Daniel 1084
Simmons, Doree 1399
Simmons, J.K. 102, 157, 267
Simmons, Jamie 1021
Simmons, Karla 1816
Simmons, Matty 1113

Simmons, Michael 1113
Simmons, Pat 34
Simmons, Stanley 464, 1152, 1524, 1620
Simmons, Ted, Jr. 124
Simms, Ellen 1525
Simms, Laura 1080
Simms, Lise 105
Simon, Avi 505
Simon, Carly 1354
Simon, E. Francis 384
Simon, Eddie 1300
Simon, Herb 595
Simon, Ilona 274
Simon, James L. 804, 1554
Simon, Joanna 188
Simon, John 87
Simon, Lawrence 357
Simon, Letty 1118
Simon, Lisa 915, 1469
Simon, Lucy 1, 1354
Simon, Marilyn 1616
Simon, Norman 359
Simon, Robert 621, 1140
Simon, Ted 556
The Simon Sisters 1790, 1791
Simone, Diedre 1080
Simonian, Norberto Carlos 1588
Simons, Hal 129
Simons, Ted 63, 350, 1290
Simonson, Lynn 705, 1119
Simpson, Bland 376, 710, 864, 950
Simpson, Carole 156, 449, 450, 1091
Simpson, Corey 901
Simpson, Dennis 1189
Simpson, Frank 448
Simpson, Julia 1434
Simpson, Marietta 1816
Simpson, Rick 376
Simpson, Robert 366, 1480
Simpson, Scott 1569
Simpson, Steve 156
Sims, Sandman 704
Sincere, Jean 1058
Sinclair, Madge 175, 885, 1072, 1633, 1746
Sinclair, Sandra 1487
Sinclair, Stephen 1513
Sinclair, Thomas Lee (Tom) 572, 788, 865, 866
Sinclaire, Honey 494
Sindler, Merrill 34
Singer, Ada 441
Singer, Benjamin C. 837
Singer, David 675
Singer, Gerald 543
Singer, James R. 213
Singer, Norman 56, 488, 1081, 1096
Singer, Perry 1405
Singer, Steve (Steven) 215, 699
The Singing Comedians 721
Singleton, Harry 528
Singleton, Karen 1522
Sinisi, Rosaria 358
Sink, Jim 270
Sinkler, David 1150
Sinkus, David 825
Siravo, Joseph 1441
Siretta, Dan 1442, 1644
Sirlin, Jerome 451, 729, 791, 1023, 1200
Sirotin, Alexander 782
Sirugo, Bella 344
Sirugo, Carol 344
Sislan, Stephan 1479
Sislian, Nicole 991
Sissons, Narelle 262, 1326, 1374
Sisti, Michelan 36
Sisto, Rocco 859, 1641
Sitomer, Gary 248
Sivuca 835
Skala, Lilia 1449
Skelton, Joni 510
Skelton, Thomas R. (Tom) 128, 284, 1360, 1562, 1827
Skiles, Steve 1154
Skinner, Emily 476, 805, 1103
Skinner, Peter G. 138
Skinner, Randy 3, 950
Skipper, Michael 804
Skipper, William 1152
Sklar, Marrin 458
Sklar, Paul 1263
Sklar, Roberta 676
Skloff, Michael 1, 387, 811, 1243, 1710
Skobel, Ron 1772
Skowron, Jeff 1128, 1831
Skweyiya, Kipizane 1401
Sky, Don 121
Skybell, Steven 413
Slade, Julian 1393
Slade, Renee 226
Slade, Stuart 1566
Slagel, Donald 1621
Slane, Stephan 908
Slappy, Sheila 196
Slater, Glenn (Glen) 719, 1129, 1607
Slater, Herbert 816
Slater, Mary Jo 1524
Slaton, Don 132
Slattery, Mary 1252
Slaughter, Randy 349
Slavenska, Mia 66
Slavin, Gary 227, 770
Slawson, Brian 737
Sliker, Peter 62, 92, 609, 1474
Sloan, Carolyn 2, 1607
Sloan, David 1389
Sloan, Lee 1160
Sloan, Lenwood (O.) 688, 1783
Sloane, A. Baldwin 635
Sloane, Barbara 591
Sloane, Joyce 1209
Sloane, Steven 640
Sloman, John 1375, 1704
Sloman, Larry 1113
Slone, Joyce 1095
Slough, Kelly 1139
Slover, Tim 836
Slovick, Sam 45
Slutsker, Peter 305, 1143
Slyde, Jimmy 704
Small, Bob 834
Small, Mary 1433
Small, Marya 625
Small, Michael 778
Small, Neva 90, 466, 604, 919, 1029, 1118, 1452, 1546
Small, Sally 1647
Small, Sonja 1816
Smartt, Suzanne 1034
Smedes, Tom 965, 1110
Smeian, Pavel 849
Smiley, Polly 578
Smit, Michael 1338
Smith, Alan Michael 1050
Smith, Alie 1338
Smith, Baker 642
Smith, Benny 705
Smith, Beth 1634
Smith, Bill 376
Smith, Cameron 717
Smith, Carl 1530
Smith, Christopher 985
Smith, Chuck 1626
Smith, Clayton Dean 328
Smith, Cynthia 1443
Smith, Cyril 1315
Smith, D.P. 448, 1594
Smith, David 569, 1227
Smith, David Rae 1462, 1552
Smith, Deborah 9, 706, 1039
Smith, Delos 1636
Smith, Derek 632
Smith, Donna 598
Smith, Doras 66
Smith, E.A. 412
Smith, Eleanor 957
Smith, Elwood 504
Smith, Ennis 785, 788, 1470
Smith, Erica Arlis 1174
Smith, Erin 362
Smith, Erin Elizabeth 1374
Smith, Ernest Allen (A.) 279, 725, 743, 1097, 1216, 1414, 1646
Smith, Ethel 140
Smith, Eugene 61
Smith, Felton 675, 1155, 1156, 1157, 1158, 1159
Smith, Garnett 360, 1446
Smith, Gary 1218, 1474
Smith, Gerald 1153
Smith, Greg 273
Smith, Gregory 877
Smith, Hazel 1002
Smith, Helen 1780
Smith, Jabbo 1198
Smith, Jeffrey R. 1547, 1581
Smith, Jennifer 267
Smith, Jessica 1248
Smith, Jim 1098, 1131
Smith, Joanie 910
Smith, John J. 1221, 1621
Smith, Joseph 591, 645
Smith, Juliet 657
Smith, Karen 132
Smith, Kathleen 1222, 1391
Smith, Keith 717
Smith, Kelly 362, 717
Smith, Kenneth 1596
Smith, Larry 1015
Smith, Len, Jr. 1116
Smith, Lenore 843
Smith, Lew 1811
Smith, Lois 696
Smith, Lola 1692
Smith, Louise 648
Smith, Marisa 1427
Smith, Mavis 768
Smith, Mich R. 1438
Smith, Michael C. 434, 576, 1708
Smith, Michael R. 1610
Smith, Miles 1029
Smith, Milton 1229
Smith, Miranda 1486
Smith, Norwood 1131
Smith, Oliver 393, 1029, 1134, 1601
Smith, Paul E. 420
Smith, Peter 100
Smith, Peter L. 452
Smith, Peyton 396
Smith, Polly P. 279
Smith, Q. 474
Smith, Ralph 101
Smith, Rex 219, 726, 1270
Smith, Richard K. 842
Smith, Ricky 248
Smith, Robert 700
Smith, Robert Lewis 1467
Smith, Robin 697
Smith, Rodney 768
Smith, Rome 1627
Smith, Ronaeld 636
Smith, Ronn 15
Smith, Salicia 822
Smith, Sandra 66
Smith, Sanford L. 1280
Smith, Scott 510
Smith, Sheila 788, 1566, 1574, 1582
Smith, Sheridan 1233
Smith, Sid 1349
Smith, Stan 510
Smith, Stephen J. 255
Smith, Sydney 456
Smith, Terry Alan 19, 373
Smith, Truman 132
Smith, Vernon Jeffrey 1015
Smith, Vincent D. 1783
Smith, Walter Reed 578
Smith, Ward 61
Smith, Wynonna 809
Smithies, Richard 326, 460
Smoak, Madelyn 376
Smoke Rise 1562
Smolko, John 858, 1185
Smulyan, Jane 808
Smyrl, David Langston 1183
Smyth, Deborah Gilmour 836
Smyth, Robert 836
Smythe, Kit 1318
Snadowsky, Stanley 854
Snape, Edward 6
Sneed, Allysia C. 809
Sneed, Gary 971, 1069
Snelling, Dietrich 299
Snelling, Lillia 1269
Snelson, Nicole Ruth 721
Snikowski, William 1042
Snitow, Charles 1229
Snow, Clarence 1466
Snow, Harry 1193
Snow, Norman 312
Snow, Tom 854
Snowdon, Ted 934, 1507
Snyder, Adam 1040
Snyder, Bonnie 1692
Snyder, Carleton 1475
Snyder, Dee 994
Snyder, Janet 1655
Snyder, Scotty 397
Soares, Leonard 1221
Soboil, Maggie 1284
Soboloff, Arnold 235, 598, 1096, 1452
Sockwell, Sally 1079
Soeder, Fran 308, 1213, 1214, 1449
Soelistyo, Julyana 583
Soffer, Shirley 397
Soglow, Otto 1385
Soifer, Norman 613
Soiffer, Freda 1096
Sojola, Phumzile 1623
Sokal, Dennis 1080
Sokel, Gloria 1626
Sokol, Lawrence E. 1433
Sokol, Marilyn 117, 209, 1346, 1361, 1457, 1668
Sokoll, Zelig Sokoll 1589
Sokoloff, Alexander 288
Sokolow, Anna 1563, 1596
Soldo, Sally 1707
Solia, Janice 1595
Solis, Jeffrey 17, 413, 1223
Solley, Marvin 667, 1202
Solly, Bill 200, 626, 853, 1050
Solms, Kenny 126, 350, 557, 558, 771, 852
Solomon, Alison 1425
Solomon, Mark 458
Solomon, Nicholas 4, 374
Solomon, Renee 489, 666, 819, 1051, 1342, 1382, 1453, 1745, 1822
Solomons, Gus, Jr. 823, 834
Solov, Zachary 867, 1718
Soloway, Leonard 610, 678, 1585, 1656
Soltes, Dafna 1342
Somack, Jack 1455
Somers, Asa 1188
Somerville, Phyllis 834, 1513
Sommer, Kathy 1377, 1591, 1748
Sommers, Avery 1207, 1398
Sommers, Chet 1041
Sommers, Michael 747
Somner, Pearl 152, 753
Sondergaard, Hester 1140
Sonderskov, Bob 442
Sondheim, Stephen 70, 244, 843, 986, 1027, 1213, 1214, 1403, 1491, 1492, 1557
Sondheimer, Hans 488, 1552
Sonner, Marilyn 121
Sontag, Donna 142, 1470
Sooy, Janet 1029
Soper, Gay 135
Sophiea, Cynthia 1250
Soreanu, Mary 819, 1212, 1342, 1382, 1453
Sorel, Diane 1136
Sorensen, Joel 670
Sorenson, Arthur Alan 497
Sorenson, Joel 1022
Sorge, Joey 1403
Soriero, Patrice 1521
Sorkin, Joan Ross 1068
Soroca, Karen 1648
Soroka, Heather Lee 828
Sorrell, Rozlyn 1550
Sorteberg, Rachel 1618
Sorvino, Paul 3
Sosa, Emilio 330, 1325, 1429
Sosin, Donald 174, 1160, 1314
Sothern, Georgia 772
Soto, Judy 453, 789, 1232
Sottile, Michael (S.) 643, 767, 832
Soule, Robert 277, 436, 504, 638, 1364, 1594, 1636
Soules, Dale 958, 1082, 1339
Sousa, Pamela 1181, 1377, 1438, 1752
Souza, Alan 1784
Soyinka, Wole 927
Sozen, Joyce 49
Sozzi, Sebastian 3
Spackman, Lisa 1050
Spaisman, Zypora (Ziporah) 441, 782, 1026
Spalla, John 700, 1150, 1761
Spangler, Amy 1634
Spangler, Andy 1181
Spangler, David 1029
Spangler, Walt 411, 1347
Spano, Nealla 1427
Spano, Nelsena Burt 470
Sparkes, Lenora 988, 1269
Sparks, Lee 456
Sparrow, Carol 256
Spaull, Guy 1483
Speace, Amy 983
Spear, David 486
Spearritt, Hannah 1233
Specher, Ben 1694
Speck, Jules 340, 988
Spector, Arnold 68, 1221
Spector, Donald 994
Spector, Phil 854
Spektor, Eryk 718
Spektor, Mira J. 718
Speller, Betsy 121
Speller, Rob 1066
Speller, Robert 1660
Spellman, Larry 1457
Spelvin, George 494, 1092, 1116, 1181
Spelvin, Hadra 619
Spence, Chenault 342, 501, 667
Spencer, Amy 1722
Spencer, Bob 611, 1468

Spencer, Cheryl 1693
Spencer, Christine 91, 333
Spencer, David 186, 1100
Spencer, Jonathan 195
Spencer, Lillian 136
Spencer, Robert 1433
Spencer, Ron 1283
Spencer, Vernon 726, 1537
Sperling, Howard 743
Sperling, Ted 503, 1121, 1375, 1404, 1422
Spero, Arete 661
Speros, Tia 1575, 1593
Spiegel, Terry 225
Spiering, Frank, Jr. 1274
Spillane, Sherri 957
Spiller, Marshall (S.) 718, 1044
Spina, Cristina 859
Spindler, Tracy 1204
Spinella, Stephen 805
Spinelli, Larry 1504
Spiner, Brent 1557
Spingler, Doug 1021
Spinner, Geri 1021
Spinney, Mel 318
Spinola, Marina 216
Spiotta, Daniel 71
Spirito, Joseph 1322
Spiro, Bernie (Bernard) 288, 1449
Spiro, Joan 288
Spiroff, Tom 1138
Spitz, Alan 414
Spitznagel, Frank 1817
Spivak, Adam 474
Spivak, Allen 474, 1495
Spivey, Aaron 533, 606
Spohn, Leslie 217, 696
Spolan, Jeffrey 1079
Spoletini, Giuseppe 362, 717
Sponseller, Howard L., Jr. 773
Spradbury, John 1662
Sprecher, Ben 58, 281, 837
Springer, Ashton 35, 382, 1373
Springer, Philip 284, 714, 1447, 1493, 1576
Sprouse, Angela 1065
Sprung, Sandy 1166
Spurlock, Estelle E. 1029
Squadron, Anne Strickland 979, 1760
Squibb, June 199, 259, 551, 908, 1142
Squire, Katherine 696
Sririn, Alexander 849
Sroka, Jerry 319, 1787
Stabile, Bill 780, 1057, 1222
Stabin, Sarah 441
Stacey, Richard 1233
Stack, Richard 1166, 1721
Stacy, Faun 1138
Stadlen, Lewis J. 244, 1181, 1201
Stadler, Ido 108
Stafford, Ken-Michael 329
Stafford, Tina 1493
Stahl, Cordell 730
Stahl, Stephen 1320, 1321
Stahl, William 619
Staiges, Tony 1557
Staller, David 13, 14, 1608
Stambler, Bernard 331, 677, 1217
Stamm, Kurt 1210, 1612
Stamper, Dave 1315
Stamps, Philip A. 1308
Stan, Peter 711
Stanczyk, Laura 404
Stander, Scott 452
Stanek, Jim 249, 541, 1479
Stange, Stanislaus 1101
Stanger, Russell 1413
Stanhope, Theodore 1315
Stanley, Chuck 224
Stanley, Dorothy 343
Stanley, Gordon 434, 435, 833, 922, 981, 1071
Stanley, Pat 616
Stannard, Nicholas 1787
Stansfield, Don 1771
Stantley, Ralph 1468
Stanton, Anthony 290
Stanton, Ben 273, 742, 1736
Stanton, Frank H. 957
Stanton, Harry 987
Stanton, Jane 1173
Stanton, Joyce 175
Stanton, Mary 1193
Stanton, Phil 1674
Stanwyck, Jay 1603, 1806
Stanzel, John 1655
Stapleton, Chris 1181
Stapleton, Julieanne 1333
Star, Lee 343
Starbuck, Joshua (Josh) 1326, 1454, 1600
Starbuck, Larry 85
Stark, Bruce W. 1504
Stark, Evette 1690
Stark, Leslie J. 1698
Stark, Molly 15, 53, 61, 434, 814, 1660, 1693, 1785
Stark, Robert 960
Stark, Sally 341
Stark, Walter 1248
Starkey, Jack 175
Starkie, Martin 246
Starling, Lynn 92
Starobin, Michael 41, 473, 763, 764, 873, 1019, 1109
Starr, Bill 1119
Starr, Blaze 226
Starr, Monique 1802
Starr, Rima 1408
Starr, Wayne 972
Starrett, Ken 698
Start, Carole 329
Stauber, Lauren 768
Stauch, Bonnie 172
Staudenmayer, Edward 463, 518
Staudt, Christian (Chris) 493, 1124, 1294, 1537
Stauffer, Blaire 528
Stauffer, Richard 478
Staunton, Kim 688
Staw, Ryszard 1275
Steadman, Frances 166
Steady, Walker 410
Stearns, Elizabeth 696
Steber, Eleanor 1718
Steber, John 788
Steck, Hazel 121
Steckman, Lawrance 1695
Stecko, Joseph 693, 870, 902, 1364, 1420
Stecko, Robert 113
Steeden, Tim 1629
Steefel, Jeffrey 596
Steele, Henry 1826
Steele, J.D. 615
Steele, Jevetta 615
Steele, Robert L. 236, 1236, 1517
Steele, Wes 1592
Steen, Jan 572
Steere, Clifton 725, 951
Steere, James 821
Steese, Michael 43
Stefanini, Prima 1531
Stefanowicz, Janus 789
Stefko, Karen 1408
Steggert, Bobby 1818
Stegman, Richard 990, 1772
Steichen, Gerald 938
Steidl, Scott 299
Steifelman, Leslie 689
Steigauf, Patricia 453
Stein, Anthony 248
Stein, Cassie 785
Stein, Debra 205, 313, 527, 1591
Stein, Douglas 473, 1019, 1478
Stein, Erik 249
Stein, Gertrude 392, 571, 756, 928, 1086, 1087, 1757
Stein, Harry 377
Stein, Jane 1449
Stein, Jared 1425
Stein, Joseph 88, 848, 1100, 1328, 1580
Stein, Joseph, Jr. 1138
Stein, Julian 63, 277, 478, 652, 1400, 1440, 1481, 1716
Stein, Lana 712
Stein, Meridee 248, 768, 1134
Steinberg, Ben 1399
Steinberg, Bilee 1687
Steinberg, David 1352
Steinberg, Lori 1285
Steinberg, Paul 673, 1532, 1741
Steinberg, Richard 1487
Steinberg, Samuel 1453
Steiner, Irwin 1136
Steiner, Loreal 470
Steiner, Rick 627
Steiner, Steve 58, 703, 712, 1353
Steinhart, Jon 72
Steinlein, Jean 1820
Steinman, Jim 312, 1082, 1355
Steinman, Lisa M. 1676
Steinmann, Herbert 33
Stell, John 1198
Stell, Joseph 535
Stella, Tim 733
Stellman, Maxine 1010
Stenborg, James 1213, 1584
Stenta, Henry 362
Stepanchenko, Sergey 849
Stephanya 32
Stephen, Joe 666
Stephen, Prima (K.) 770, 1030
Stephens, Charles Robert 941
Stephens, Claudia 828
Stephens, Dick 582
Stephens, Harry 1664
Stephens, Linda 1788
Stephens, Mark Edgar 1310
Stephens, Norman 1635
Stephens, Perry 915
Stephens, Ray 1363
Stephens, Ty 546, 1435
Stephenson, Nikki 167
Stephenson, Tom 836
Stepniak, Jerzy 1275
Stepowany, Michael 95
Stepp, Walt 922
Stepter, Trellis 632
Sterling, Clark 1585
Sterling, Lynn 959
Stern, Alan 24, 1768
Stern, Alfred 384
Stern, Allan 369
Stern, Cheryl 1607
Stern, Deborah 1801
Stern, Eric 129, 284, 308, 1214, 1546, 1654, 1717
Stern, James D. 1530, 1777
Stern, Jamie 403
Stern, Jay 1594, 1817
Stern, Jenny Lee 1321
Stern, Kimberly 100
Stern, Kurt 1269
Stern, Lenny 761
Stern, Maurice 331, 1789
Stern, Pat 794
Stern, Rachel 1556
Stern, Rudi 490
Stern, T. 1591
Sternberg, Ann 571
Sterne, Richard 140
Sterner, Steve 971, 1011, 1102, 1505, 1510, 1607, 1715, 1821
Sterner, Steven 1260
Sterrett, T.O. 645
Steuer, Gary P. 1503
Stevens, Allan 786
Stevens, Carl 145
Stevens, Chris 397
Stevens, Fisher 1048, 1522
Stevens, Fran 292, 1279
Stevens, Garn 625
Stevens, Gloria 1193
Stevens, Jane Kip 1163
Stevens, Jere 600
Stevens, Jeremy 536
Stevens, Jodi 185
Stevens, Joel 1391, 1418
Stevens, Judy 17
Stevens, Larry 336
Stevens, Lisa 154
Stevens, Marti 1172
Stevens, Roger L. 695, 1029
Stevens, Ronald "Smokey" 1373
Stevens, Shadoe 38
Stevens, Susan 1267
Stevens, Tony 81, 93, 185, 1096, 1441, 1831
Stevensen, Scott 110, 1685
Stevenson, Jim 1193
Stevenson, McLean 616
Stevenson, Robert 1029
Stevenson, Rudy 255
Stew 1225
Steward, Ron 120, 1397
Stewart, Charles 196, 1002
Stewart, Christine 1751
Stewart, Christopher 1232
Stewart, Daniel 401, 1144
Stewart, Don 80, 822
Stewart, Ellen 1536
Stewart, Gene 615
Stewart, Grant 255, 988
Stewart, Jack 1316
Stewart, Jaye 1373
Stewart, Jim 1149
Stewart, John 254, 1137
Stewart, John (Johnny) 332, 1594
Stewart, Kim C. 333
Stewart, Larry J. 420, 803
Stewart, Leon 486
Stewart, Maggie 630
Stewart, Mark 549
Stewart, Melvin 1464, 1465
Stewart, Mike (Michael) 434, 435, 858, 942, 1447, 1448
Stewart, Patricia 132
Stewart, Princess 166
Stewart, Ray 191
Stewart, Ronni 1335
Stewart, Seth 760
Stewart, Susan 1616
Stewart, William 1672
Sticco, Dan 267
Stich, Teresa 1086
Stickney, Thom 1660
Stigwood, Robert 1013, 1426
Stiller, Jerry 600, 1689
Stillman, Bob 641, 892, 1141, 1404
Stillman, Richard 246
Stillman, Robert 577, 948
Stilwell, Gene 1151
Stimac, Anthony (J.) 8, 25, 258, 259, 309, 316, 480, 611, 907, 1141, 1378, 1386, 1670, 1693, 1733
Stinchfeld, George 494
Stinnett, Edward 66
Stinnette, Dorothy 902
Stites, Kevin 1186, 1637
Stith, James 1165
Stitt, Georgia 14, 1523
Stitt, Milan 869
Stock, Jeffrey 1499
Stockdale, Muriel 229, 586, 1263, 1503
Stocker, Christopher 1730
Stocker, Leonard 1140, 1229
Stockhammer, Elizabeth 1079
Stockler, Michael (Lee) 406, 1684
Stockley, Travis L. 14
Stockman, Todd 1182
Stockton, Cheryl Lee 216
Stockwell, Jeremy 1331
Stockwell, Jock 253
Stoddard, Haila 884, 894, 961, 1562
Stoeckle, Robert 246
Stokes, Heather Ann 1298
Stokes, Jesse L. 1040
Stokes, Richard L. 1047
Stole, Mink 144
Stolin, Sonia 1587
Stollak, Clare 49, 612
Stoller, Michael 1516
Stoller, Mike 854
Stone, Anna 1187
Stone, Betty 1131
Stone, David (S.) 541, 806
Stone, Douglas 1080
Stone, Edward 271
Stone, Elly 304, 792, 795, 800, 801, 1161, 1162, 1716
Stone, Federick 1079
Stone, Fred 1639, 1640
Stone, Greg 423, 1108, 1554, 1700
Stone, Harold 448
Stone, Harry 272
Stone, Jerald B. 572
Stone, Jon 1076
Stone, Kris 1547
Stone, Mark 291
Stone, Marshall 92
Stone, Mimi 1265
Stone, Peter 1534
Stone, Robin 1028
Stone, Rocky 960
Stone, Rosetta 397
Stone, Wilson 1393
Stoneback, Ric 1160
Stoneburner, Sam 448, 1510
Stonefelt, Kay 807
Stoner, Joyce 752
Stoner, Patrick 752
Stonn, Caleb 1013
Storch, Larry 942
Storey, David 642, 855, 1472
Storm, Doug 106
Storm, Wayne 535
Stornaiuolo, Vincenzo 59
Storr, Sue 1444
Stotts, Sally 910
Stotz, Larry 697
Stoudnour, David J. 1659
Stough, Raymond 9, 1579
Stout, Adrian 1444
Stout, Mary 100, 267, 749, 1305
Stout, Stephen 973
Stovall, Count 278
Stovall, James 375, 1375, 1523
Stover, James 1818
Stover, Nancy 834, 1349
Stovola, Charlie 725
Straiges, Tony 377, 1184
Straight, Willard 74
Strain, Ralph 1192, 1430

Stram, Henry 170, 285, 325, 791, 999, 1422
Strand, Gwendolyn 501
Strang, Hilary 1432
Strang, Lloyd 62
Strange, Sherrie 1423
Strasberg, Lee 696
Stratas, Teresa 574, 891
Strater, Christopher 253
Stratford, Bert 725, 1097
Strathairn, David 179
Stratton, Albert 307
Stratton, John 1691
Strauss, Bill 247
Strauss, Edward 1038, 1712
Strauss, Haila 878, 1102, 1268, 1297, 1510
Strauss, Harold L. 801
Strauss, Jane 1441
Strauss, Johann 1131, 1722
Strauss, John 422, 942, 1083
Strauss, Marilyn 1317
Strauss, Natalie 1646
Strauss, Oscar 1101
Strauss, Wally 86
Strawbridge, Stephen 130, 383, 583, 726, 1020, 1641
Strayhorn, Dan 214, 1207, 1398
Strayhorn, Melinda Moore 1469
Straz, Jim 404, 1419
Streep, Meryl 27
Street, Lawrence 1712
Streisand, Barbra 60
Streitz, Paul 991, 1171
Strickland, Bruce 736
Strickland, Daniel (Dan) 50, 556, 557, 558, 1273, 1829
Strickler, Dan 311
Stricklin, Debra 496
Stringer, Marcie 1594
Stringfellow, Jean 1636
Stritch, Elaine 428, 1390
Strohmeier, Robert (F.) 279, 904, 1113, 1414, 1435, 1540
Strole, Phoebe 1515
Strom, A. William 388
Strom, Myrna 969
Strom, William 232
Stroman, Guy 527, 1650
Stroman, Messeret 850
Stroman, Susan 52, 210, 315, 725, 945, 1097, 1410
Stroming, Gil 1590
Strong, Edward 699
Strong, Tao 600, 1440
Strouse, Charles 58, 214, 237, 603, 942, 1037, 1100, 1134, 1328, 1447, 1448, 1473, 1709
Strouse, Irving 85
Strummer, Peter 670
Stryon, Polly 561
Stuart, Charles 1679
Stuart, Eddie 1177
Stuart, Fabian 1604
Stuart, Harvey 472
Stuart, Jana 935
Stuart, Jane 337
Stuart, John 906
Stuart, Lynne 1676
Stuart, Mark 1177, 1647
Stuart, Mary 1177
Stuart, Michel 283, 748
Stuart, Pat 140
Stuart, Patricia Quinn 291, 969, 1038
Stuart, Ronald 1599
Stuart, Sebastian 370
Stuart, Vicki 1482, 1750
Stuarti, Enzo 1131
Stubbs, George 1183
Stubbs, Kerry 647, 648
Stubbs, Louise 1307
Stubbs, Michelle 127
Stuck, Christian 1321, 1815
Studley, Kate 1317
Studney, Dan 1347
Stuhlbarg, Michael 122
Sturchio, Malcolm (Mal) 215, 1208, 1427, 1461
Sturge, Tom 1328, 1441, 1610, 1619
Sturges, Leayha 821
Sturiale, Grant 848, 1181, 1381, 1535
Sturm, Jason 289
Sturm, Justin 1604
Sturm, Katherine 1604
Sturner, Lynda 847
Sturrock, Don 51
Styles, Joy 934
Styles, Stephanie 938
Styne, Jule 100, 349, 1100, 1546, 1717
Styne, Karyn 1221
Styron, Paola 122, 728, 1055, 1722
Suanda, Endo 1625
Suarez, Ilka 792
Suave, Gloria 1522
Suber, Kate 1186
Subik, Jeff 248
Subjack, Jenny 1248
Sublett, Robbie Collier 607
Suckling, Jenny-Lynn 193
Sudduth, Skip 1598
Suehsdorf, David 632
Suffrin, Herb 261, 761
Sugarman, Lianna 1134
Sugarman, Richard 1655
Sugihara, William 504
Suhocki, Judy 1713
Sukis, Lilian 1088
Sullivan, Arthur 460, 1270
Sullivan, Brad 844, 1517
Sullivan, Deidre 140
Sullivan, Dennis 1684
Sullivan, Fania 353, 1239, 1768, 1790, 1791, 1796
Sullivan, Frank 24, 1768, 1790, 1791, 1796
Sullivan, Gary 171
Sullivan, Howard 1115
Sullivan, James 1172
Sullivan, Jo 737, 1164, 1626, 1627, 1651
Sullivan, John 940
Sullivan, John Carver 395, 812, 930, 1099
Sullivan, Kelly 1056
Sullivan, Kitty 1083
Sullivan, KT 2, 46, 1514
Sullivan, Marc 1474
Sullivan, Matthew 1660
Sullivan, Maxine 1107
Sullivan, Nick 950
Sullivan, Nicole 768
Sullivan, Patrick 605, 1356
Sullivan, Patrick Ryan 154
Sullivan, Paul 44, 51, 107, 127, 197, 545, 682, 783, 785, 971, 1467, 1509, 1550
Sullivan, Peggy 505, 632
Sullivan, Roger 1041
Sullivan, Sheila 236
Sullo, Teresina 1345
Sumac, Yma 1234, 1235
Sumler, Kathleen 593
Summerfield, Robin 1538
Summerford, Denise 1450
Summerhays, Jane 1222
Summers, Caley 894
Summers, David 15, 243, 467, 1367, 1776
Summers, Elaine 756
Summers, Joan 1063
Summers, Lee 546, 934
Summers, Leon, Jr. 1065, 1232
Summerson, Kim 196
Sumter, Gwen 493
Sun, Pearl 1429, 1736
Sunday, Carlton 1086
Sundelius, Marie 245, 1369
Sunder 124
Sundgaard, Arnold 870, 1824, 1825
Sundine, John Patrick 1007
Sunguroff, Tamara Bering 1541
Supree, Burt 831, 1280
Surace, Sal 1435
Surita, Wilfred 212
Surmont, Elisa 610
Surovy, Nicolas 1471
Surver, Marc 288
Susanne, Jackie 578
Susin 876
Suskin, Steven 527
Susskind, David 1585
Sussman, Bruce 311, 1048, 1772
Sussman, Don 1652
Sussman, Sadie 620, 621
Sussman, Sally 622
Susswein, Joan 1676
Suter, Andrea 709
Suter, Stanley 598
Suter, William P. 1363
Sutherin, Joseph M. 678
Sutherland, Brian 86, 267, 599, 1199
Sutherland, Paul 1789
Sutphen, Melissa 920, 1349
Suttell, V. Jane 1023, 1079
Sutter, William P. 929
Sutton, Carol 1518
Sutton, Christopher 606
Sutton, Henry 867
Sutton, Jimmy 1349
Sutton, Rob 67
Sutton, Sheryl L. 427
Suvall, Doug 854
Suzeau, Patrick 666
Svar, John 1259
Svejcar, Eric 802, 1479
Svitzer, Daud 216
Swados, Elizabeth 27, 386, 643, 647, 648, 768, 832, 975, 1133, 1335, 1345, 1384, 1625, 1699
Swados, Kim 98
Swaebe, Philip 35
Swaine, Jim 1349
Swan, Allen 920
Swan, Jon 11
Swan, Kathleen 1380
Swan, Marion (Waits) 920, 1349
Swan, Richard 1029
Swann, Crist 1434
Swann, Elaine 1692
Swann, Francis 507, 1221
Swansen, Larry 1343
Swanson, Bea 288
Swanson, Britt 920
Swanson, Don 42, 212, 1337
Swanson, Jim 1721
Swanson, Sue 902
Swanson, Suzi 212
Swarbrick, Carol 409, 582
Sward, Anne 113
Swarm, Sally Ann 442, 1016
Swarthout, Gladys 1047
Swartz, Marlene 174, 1011, 1674
Swasey, Robert W. 1456
Swayne, Viola 1272
Swayne, William 136
Swedlund, Kristina 1240
Swedon, Pamela 1696
Swee, Daniel 218
Sweeney, Bill 1346
Sweeney, Deborah 834
Sweeney, Kelley 43
Sweeney, Kevin 1410
Sweeney, Paula 577
Sweeney, Terry 99
Sweet, Jeffrey (Jeff) 43, 741, 961, 1297, 1756
Sweig, Murray 1813
Sweitzer, Laura 1815
Swenson, Linda 175, 860
Swenson, Swen 42, 601
Swenson, Will 10
Swerdlow, Elizabeth 969
Swerdlow, Robert 969
Swerdlow, Stan 720
Swetland, William 481
Swift, Allen 1078, 1107, 1773
Swift, Barbara 453
Swift, Chris 1629
Swift, Judith 764
Swift, Madeleine 1689
Swiggard, Bill 1042
Swimmer, Saul 507
Swindley, Ted 39
Swinsky, Morton 668
Swymer, Gayle 1166
Sydow, Jack 48
Syers, Mark 1699
Syke, Robin 398, 1031
Sykes, Curtis 1040
Sykes, Nelson 1093, 1729
Sylbert, Paul 331, 1162, 1583
Sylvan, Carole 1065
Sylvan, Sanford 363, 1139
Symington, Donald 369, 1455
Symonette, Lys (Bert) 204, 1462
Symons, Charlotte 40
Synder, Carleton 1475
Synder, William 317
Szczepanski, John-Paul 755, 1742
Szlosberg, Diana 1761
Szwaja, Krzysztof 1275
Szwejbka, Michael 1329
Szymkowicz, Gloria 295

Tabachnik, Kenneth 82
Tabacknick, Ken 170
Tabakin, Steven 252, 1422
Tabisel, Brett 1554
Tabor, David 543
Tabori, George 204
Taccone, Tony 1225
Tackaberry, Celia 305
Tadlock, Bob 425
Taffner, Don 1353
Taggart, Vince 605
Tagliarino, Salvatore 551
Tahse, Martin 1083
Taines, Andrew 15, 73, 1673
Taintor, Melinda 1713
Tait, Eric V., Jr. 1434
Takazauckas, Albert 1258
Taketa, Edward Akio 910
The Tal U'matar 617
Talayco, Lucille 1589
Talbert, Christopher 1608
Talbert, David E. 964
Talbert, Lyn 964
Talbot, Sharon 718, 1389
Taliaferro, Hugh 1661
Taliarino, Salvatore 210
Talley, Terry 1681
Tally, Ted 311, 1710
Talmadge, Bob 626
Talman, Ann 960, 1503, 1752, 1829
Talmud, Blanche 618, 620, 621, 622
Talus, Pamela 464
Talyn, Olga 1449, 1584
Tamagna, Nick 1416
Tamaroff, Marsha 1021
Tamasik, Laszlo 1655
Tamber, Selma 366
Tambornino, Jeff 408
Tamburro, Frances 376
Tamen, Jack 343
Tamir, Moshe 1051
Tampio, Vince 1716
Tamres, Abram 1131
Tan, Victor En Yu 36, 53, 731, 759, 764, 887, 996, 1134, 1183, 1489
Tanaka, Yoshihico 1625
Tananis, Robert 564, 758, 1595
Tandet, A. Joseph 1176
Tandy, Spencer 681
Tanji, Lydia 1674
Tanker, Andre 1633
Tanner, Melinda 1338
Tanner, Tony 259, 661, 833, 1098, 1296, 1309
Tannis, Ron 423
Tanno, Guy 743
Tanno, Rita 735
Tansey, June 9
Tantleff, Jack Z. 1252
Tanzy, Jan 1083
Taormina, Latifah 1586
Taphorn, Peggy 567
Tapla, Jose 1620
Tapp, Steve 171
Tapper, Albert (M.) 755, 1428
Tara, Elaine 1636
Tara, Judy 1636
Taradash, Marcia 1599
Tarallo, Barry 833, 1270
Taras, John 1086
Tardi, Paul 223
Tarlet, Nathalie 1281
Tarleton, Diane 197
Tarlow, Florence 392, 1311, 1501
Taros, George 669, 851
Tarr, William 366
Tarr, Yvonne 366
Tarraglia, Bob 1480
Tarshis 1238
Tartaglia, John 77
Tartel, Michael 361, 990, 1483
Tarver, Ben 1008
Tarver, Bernard J. 43
Task, Maggie 1365
Tassone, George 1435
Tatad, Robert 845
Tate, Barbara 105, 1423
Tate, Charles 631
Tate, Dennis 187
Tate, Jimmy (W.) 82, 207
Tate, Katrina 790
Tate, Kevin Ricardo 252
Tate, Marzetta 124, 712
Tate, Nancy 918
Tate, Neal 9, 107, 712, 959, 1307, 1397, 1423, 1544, 1550, 1783
Tate, Robert 922, 1328, 1600
Tatum, Marianne 577
Taubenslag, Elliott (E.) 719, 1727
Taubenslag, Michael 719
Tauber, Chaim 608
Taubin, Amy 393
Taussig, Lynn 92
Tavel, Harry 613
Tavel, Harvey 1725
Tavel, Ronald 613, 1725
Taverner, Sonia 1655
Tavori, Eyal 108
Tawney, Ria 655

Tay, David A. 3
Taylor, Andy 285, 703, 848
Taylor, Beth 854
Taylor, Billy 927
Taylor, Bonnie Sue 1015
Taylor, Chance 1406
Taylor, Clarence 1349
Taylor, Clarice 21, 425, 589, 1004, 1074
Taylor, Clifton 57, 146, 1298
Taylor, David 275, 1296
Taylor, Deems 481, 868, 1249
Taylor, Dwight 566, 567
Taylor, Ed 1065
Taylor, Edwin 136
Taylor, Ethel 1543
Taylor, George 1411
Taylor, Gina 115
Taylor, Hiram 1089
Taylor, Holland 306, 480
Taylor, Howard 136
Taylor, Jackie 790
Taylor, James (A.) 261, 655, 1732
Taylor, Jason 1633
Taylor, Jeannine 695, 1697
Taylor, Jennifer 965
Taylor, Jeremy James 1233, 1629
Taylor, John 1815
Taylor, Jonathan 369
Taylor, Julie 506, 1802
Taylor, June 68, 1021, 1221
Taylor, Kendal J. 1618
Taylor, King 1116
Taylor, Kirk 1580
Taylor, Lark 136
Taylor, Laura 985
Taylor, Laurence 955, 1629
Taylor, Loomis 1075
Taylor, Marian 17
Taylor, Mark Anthony 1250
Taylor, Mary Ann 1147
Taylor, Morris 297
Taylor, Noel 1272
Taylor, Regina 330
Taylor, Renee 384, 1614
Taylor, Robert U. 117, 183, 480, 660, 885, 1279, 1471, 1659
Taylor, Robin 486, 1156
Taylor, Ron 777, 939
Taylor, Rose Mary 969
Taylor, Russ 545
Taylor, Steven 1289
Taylor, Susan 1655
Taylor, Theda 631, 908
Taylor, Tiffany 302
Taylor, Todd 1173
Taylor, Tom 1804
Taylor-Corbett, Lynne 88, 285, 424, 1610
Taylor-Dunn, Corliss 197, 1207
Taymor, Julie 632, 640, 647, 648, 839, 1665
Taynton, David 472
TayWah 30
Tazewell, Paul 252, 383, 428, 474, 668, 760, 941, 1186, 1187
Tchakirides, Bill 1358
Tebelak, John-Michael 582, 595, 596, 597, 856
Tebesli, Ilsebet Anna 65
Tebo, Mitchell Steven 142
Teddy Wilson Trio 449, 450
Tedick, Feodore 66, 1221
Tee, Richard 1001
Teer, Barbara Ann 120, 701
Tees, John, III 46
Teeter, Lara 1670
Teeters, Clarence 359
Tegani, Riccardo 245
Teich, Lois 1482, 1750
Teijelo, Gerald 822
Teitelbaum, Maurice 705
Teitelbaum, Paula 782
Tekosky, Valarie 790
Teller 1234, 1235
Telson, Bob 615
Telva, Marion 1249
Temchin, Jack 303, 1685
Temperley, Davy 1050
Temperley, Stephen 1507, 1706
Temple, Renny 1678
Temple, Shirley 1375
Temple Emanu-El Choir 402
Templeton, Jan 87
Templin, Deborah Jean 1753, 1805
Templon, Mike 1713
Tempo, Chuck 1353
Tempo, Joe 506
Tennen, Steven 278, 959
Tenney, Del 1141
Tennyson, Alfred Lord 972
Tennyson, Paula 66, 1021
Teplitzky, Lee 453, 454
Tepper, Arielle 668, 805, 890
Tepper, Eileen 719
Tepper, Ruth 397
Ter-Arutunian, Rouben 1311, 1413
Teresa 488
Terheyden, Jerry 1639, 1640
Terjeson, Arthur 76
Terrel, Elwin Charles, II 554, 623, 1198, 1349
Terrell, Betty 1021
Terrell, Stephen 102
Terriss, Elaine 403
Terry, Cliff 1232
Terry, Edith 1131
Terry, Jacob 374
Terry, Jonathan 403
Terry, Mary Ellen 1447
Terry, Megan 1620
Terry, Robert 1412
Terry, Sylvia 815, 1308
Tesich, Steve 1, 2
Tesler, Monica 1032
Tesori, Jeanine 252, 1726
Tesreau, Krista 229
Tessier, Claude 599
Tessler, Fred 499
Testa, Mary 685, 763, 873, 919, 973, 1011, 1121, 1149, 1150, 1186, 1422
Tetirick, Robert 246
Tetley, Glen 528
Tetro, Renee 822
Thacker, Cheryl 301, 564, 1133
Thacker, Russ (Rusty) 360, 1096, 1189, 1644, 1800, 1827
Thalken, Joseph 1499
Thau, Harold 37
Thayer, David 836
Thee, Christian 409
Theis, Howard 1182
Thek, Paul 397
Theodore, Donna 345
Theodore, Laura 115
Theodore, Lee 42, 663
Theveny, Grace 1823
Theyard, Harry 331, 1227
Thiele, Bob 1252
Thiemele, Aka Jean Claude 108
Thiergaard, Judith 1031, 1648
Thies, Melissa 1617
Thigpen, Lynne 1643
Thigpen, Martha 1062
Thirkield, Rob 1705
Thole, Cynthia 1160
Thoma, Carl 1038
Thomann, Eric 1434
Thomas, Allen 768
Thomas, Anita L. 501
Thomas, Carlo 453
Thomas, Carryl 1629
Thomas, Chris 266
Thomas, David 1083
Thomas, Debbie 1108
Thomas, Eb 1563
Thomas, Edward 90, 374, 1031, 1100
Thomas, Evelyn 1633
Thomas, Frank 380
Thomas, Freyda-Ann (Freyda) 64, 599
Thomas, Frozine 553
Thomas, Hank 1435
Thomas, Hugh 478
Thomas, Ivan 124
Thomas, J.T. 706
Thomas, Jamie 1823
Thomas, Jess 62
Thomas, Joseph 1620
Thomas, Keith Lamelle 668
Thomas, Ken 1066
Thomas, Leon 1183
Thomas, Linda 1084
Thomas, Marie 400
Thomas, Martha 1784
Thomas, Megan Lynn 453, 454
Thomas, Michael 1655
Thomas, Michael Tilson 912, 1167
Thomas, Michelle 1233
Thomas, Mike 732
Thomas, Powys 1393
Thomas, Rick 1209
Thomas, Robert L. 790
Thomas, Rudolph 1217
Thomas, Sally 1248
Thomas, Shelley 1830
Thomas, Tammy 719
Thomas, Todd 1139
Thomas, Vickie 844
Thomas, Walter 99
Thomas, William, Jr. 1149, 1150, 1282
Thome, David K. 1438
Thome, Maria 379
Thompson, Blanche 1543
Thompson, Bob 581, 1660
Thompson, Chris 485
Thompson, Cle 420
Thompson, Clive 166, 1029
Thompson, Crystal 1771
Thompson, Dale 1729
Thompson, Darcy 1305
Thompson, Donald V. 1363
Thompson, Ella 91
Thompson, Evan 1135, 1360
Thompson, Evelyn 844
Thompson, Frank 128, 366, 1029
Thompson, Fred 1644
Thompson, Jay 371, 405, 1193, 1255, 1318, 1574
Thompson, Jeffrey V. 959, 1373, 1580
Thompson, Jennifer Laura 398, 933, 1712
Thompson, Keith 297, 1800
Thompson, Kent 777
Thompson, Kevin E. 19
Thompson, Laura 564
Thompson, Linda 574
Thompson, R. Randy 1469
Thompson, Randall 621
Thompson, Ray 1464
Thompson, Ron Stacker 420
Thompson, Rosemary 996
Thompson, Tazewell 8, 1022
Thompson, Tommy 376, 950
Thompson, Trance 1110
Thomsen, Mark 256
Thomsen, Richard 658
Thomson, R.H. 958
Thomson, Scott 983
Thomson, Virgil 1086, 1087
Thorell, Clarke 950, 1403
Thorn, Alphie 940
Thornberry, Lee 902
Thorne, Clif 1067
Thorne, Dyanne 1615
Thorne, Francis 528
Thorne, Nellie 578
Thorne, Raymond 58, 342, 611, 788, 912, 1008, 1167
Thornton, Clarke W. 8, 25, 258, 1141, 1378, 1409, 1670, 1693, 1733
Thornton, Daryl 1615
Thornton, Sandra 93, 480, 571
Thornton, Vanessa 333
Thoroman, Eric 967
Thorsell, Karen 369
The Three Kayes 1644
Throne, Malachi 1677
Thumhart, Frank 605
Thun, Nancy 1800
Thuna, Lee 1452
Thurman, Uma 195
Thurn, Jane 23, 672, 1027
Thurston, Ted 1483, 1582, 1677
Tiala, Crystal 391
Tibaldeo, Camille 101, 250, 1494
Tibbett, Lawrence 440, 762, 868, 1047, 1249
Tibbs, Deloyd 1131
Tice, David (Dave) 834, 1017, 1231, 1387, 1617, 1681, 1820
Tichler, Rosemarie 195, 207, 387, 496, 1186, 1250, 1404
Tick, Donald 1486
Ticotin, Nancy 2, 130
Tierce, Pattie 297
Tierney, Bill 1636
Tierney, Harry 1101
Tierney, Thomas 748
Tiffany, Marie 245, 298, 1369
Tiffany, Patty 172
Tiffany, Robert 1338
Tigar, Ken 1312
Tighe, Kelly 37
Tilden, Helen 136
Tilford, Joseph P. 1466
Tilford, Mike 247
Tiller, Jennifer 938
Tiller, Ted 48
Tilley, Martin 483
Tillinger, John 1242, 1710
Tillitt, Shaver 948, 1684
Tillman, Jimmy 790
Tillman, Judith 322
Tillotson, John 184
Tilton, Deborah 1418
Tilton, James 90, 401, 710, 1168, 1169, 1330
Tilton, Thomas 620
Timberlake, Craig 1474
Timbers, Alex 645
Timerman, Alec 305, 1212, 1328
Timmers, Jack 1467
Timmons, John 1071
Timmons, Rodester 1399
Timms, Rebecca 275
Tina, Devi 379
Tine, Hal 818
Tinling, Ted 550
Tinnerello, Sal 550
Tipay, Al 1751
Tiplady, Neil 1530
Tipton, Jennifer 151, 386, 660, 805, 1146, 1270, 1384
Tiraco, Joseph 575
Tirado, Candido 262
Tirrell, Donald (Don) Bailey 481, 587
Tischler, Audrey 712, 1434
Tisdale, Christianne 476, 485
Tishler, Elaine 1267
Titunik, Gail 110, 1338
Titus, Alan 1029, 1062, 1552
Titus, David 730, 1157
Tobias, Barbara 1160
Tobias, Fred 87, 160, 237, 1259
Tobias, Willard 85
Tobie, Ellen 445
Tobin, DeNessa 266
Tobin, Kathleen 632
Tobin, Margaret 326, 1346
Tobin, Matthew 201, 980, 1562
Tobin, Timothy 1025
Tobin, Tom Matthew 857
Toblini, Fabio 680, 1054
Todaro, Mary Jo 889
Todd, Albert 849
Todd, Ivan 708
Todd, Judson S. 1448
Todd, Michael 1131
Todd, Mrs. Judson 63
Todd, Nick 369
Todd, Paris 1611
Todorowski, Ron J. 1778
Tofel, Tom 1392
Toguri, David 263
Toibin, Niall 483
Toigo, Alfred 1716
Tokayer, Sheindi 701
Tolan, Michael 1734
Tolan, Peter 899
Tolan, RJ 597
Toland, John 1604
Tolivar, Julie 950
Tolka, Mary Ann 1331
Tolken, James 1445
Toller, Ernst 1241
Tolson, Pat 1440
Tolson, Ron 1349
Tom, Lauren 1146
Toma, Heather 1139
Tomaino, Anita 1537
Tomal, George 66
Tomasovic, Tom 1671
Tomasson, Verna 1302
Tomaszewski, Henryk 1275
Tomine, Lorne 1655
Tomlin, Lily 126, 771, 1255, 1806
Tomlinson, Cabell 195
Tomlinson, Charles D. 1636
Tompkins, Claudia 1030
Toms, Patti 56
Tone, Franchot 140
Tone, Richard 735, 1218
Tonelson, Craig D. 1805
Toner, Thomas 551
Toomim, Yosef 782
Toon, Terpsie 803, 1595
Topliff, Stanley 1585
Toppall, Lawrence 1442, 1821
Toppe, Andris 1655
Topping, Susan 1494
Toran, Peter 786
Torchia, Lee 1589
Torenzo, Carmen 1226
Torgersen, Elizabeth 1380, 1412
Torigi, Richard 188
Tormey, John 569
Toro, Natalie 995, 1831
Torren, Frank 883, 1040
Torres, Andy 152, 959, 1232, 1550
Torres, Maria 399, 533

Torres, Omar 897
Torres, Robert 1016
Torrey, Marguerite 136
Torrill 1350
Torroba, Federico Moreno 1179
Torsiglieri, Anne 1187
Torti, Robert 1347
Toser, David 225, 570, 775, 886, 1015, 1410, 1517, 1527, 1644, 1668
Tost, William 356, 1697
Toth, Melissa 1120
Toti, Jerome 1021
Totten, Christopher 1630
Touchstone 1592
Toumine, Lorne 1655
Tourag, Vincent Normen 1264
Toussaint, Allen 1518
Toussaint, Mari 589, 1004
Tovar, Candace 599
Tovar, Juan 1336
Towey, John (M.) 588, 1102
Towne, B. 1619
Townsend, Bross 382
Townsend, Dwight 745
Townsend, K.C. 745
Townsend, Robert 1579
Townshend, Pete 1655
Toy, Christine 89, 1171, 1214, 1410
Toy, Mary Mon 1177
Toyser, Ronald 74
Tozzi, Giorgio 1718
Tozzi, Kipp 1146
Tracht, Avery J. 1087, 1708
Tracy, Arthur 145
Tracy, H.C. 762
Tracy, Jim 1664
Traines, Andrew 246
Tramel, Jay 1032
Tramon, Carl 1478
Tramutola, Franklin C. 1785
Trano, Gina 567
Trask, Stephen 680
Traub, Franziska 1281
Traubel, Helen 1010
Travers, Sy 177, 1272
Traxler, Mark 1310
Tray, Elias 1361
Traylor, Gene 748
Treacher, Arthur 1221
Treadwell, Tom 1031
Trebor, Robert 1077
Trees, Amanda 1078
Trefousse, Roger 257
Trehey, Robert 1474
Trehy, Bob 1131
Trehy, John 62, 1131
Treiber, Eleanor 974
Treigle, Norman 331, 1227, 1563, 1601
Trenyce 964
Trepanier, Danielle 1281
Trevens, Janine Nina 349
Trevisani, Wayne 1321
Treyz, Russell 321, 1378
Triana, Patricia 1776
Tribush, Nancy 655, 1168
Trice, Phillip 194
Tridmorten, Archie T. 1709
Trien, Cathy 1134, 1831
Triffitt, Nigel 1590
Trimble, Susan 789
Trinder, Marisa 1007
Trinidad, Kay 103
Trinkoff, Donna 789, 915, 950, 995
Tripolino, Joseph 1331
Tripp, Rickey 760
Trisler, Joyce 631, 1318
Triwush, Ken 328, 703
Trofimov, Gennady 849
Troie, Robert 1256, 1823
Trombley, David 1782
Tronto, Rudy 201, 1097, 1420, 1440, 1480, 1754
Tronzo, Michael 1029
Troob, Daniel (Danny) 1214, 1313
Troobnick, Eugene (Gene) 22, 422, 1415, 1649
Trooper 599
Trotman, Jim 91, 425
Trott, Karen 633, 1150, 1541, 1624
Trott, Pat 1221
Trouille, Clovis 1168
Trout, Charles 1278
Troutman, Ron 200, 537
Trova, Ernest 421
Trovato, Vincent 930, 1328
Troy, Doris 1002
Troy, Louise 317, 1162
Troyanos, Tatiana 1730
Trudeau, Gary 1335
Trudeau, Jacqueline 223
True, Kathleen 706
Trueblood, Paul 87, 348, 531, 1149, 1709
Trueman, Paula 618, 619, 620, 621, 622
Truesdale, Tad 591, 1388
Truitt, Quay 266, 1738
Trujillo, Sergio 103, 627
Trullinger, George 906
Trunz, Barbara 110
Trydel, John 1131
Tse-Tung, Mao 1501
Tshabalala, Linda 651
Tsuai, Yung Yung 1410
Tsypin, George 363
Tubb, Dan 1706
Tubert, Susana 533
Tucci, Lin 1156
Tucci, Louis 1353
Tucci, Maria 707
Tucholsky, Kurt 459, 1635
Tucker, Al 1177
Tucker, Bob 955, 1107
Tucker, Christian 1505
Tucker, Don 1, 350, 771
Tucker, Gregory 922
Tucker, Jeffrey 1022
Tucker, John 922
Tucker, Laura 1020
Tucker, Louis 1071
Tucker, Michael 623
Tucker, Tim 1771
Tucker, Wayne 324
Tudor, Martin 113, 410, 414, 753, 1685
Tudor, Ray 902, 987
Tufvesson, Ture 1709
Tuite, Bertha 619
Tulchin, Deborah 171, 1148, 1684
Tulcin, Ted 1631
Tulin, Alan 1772
Tumas, Sally Ann 1250
Tune, Tommy (T.) 133, 301, 748, 1656
Tunezi, Gene 1318, 1460, 1661
Tung, Allan 1213, 1214
Tunick, Jonathan 1576, 1749, 1782
Tunie, Tamara 105, 240, 1441, 1650
Tunkeler, J. 898
Tupou, Manu 1746
Tupper, Rettadel 944
Turash, Stephanie 686, 831, 1000
Turco, Tony 1595
Turcotte, Helene 1281
Turk, Bruce 632
Turley, Myra 412
Turley, Richard 1007
Turman, Glynn 844
Turnage, Dawn 349
Turnbull, Laura 492
Turner, Anya 639
Turner, Charles 421, 1429
Turner, Claramae 188, 488
Turner, Eva 704
Turner, Gayle (L.) 927, 1493
Turner, George 1397
Turner, Glenn 1186
Turner, Jim 175
Turner, Lily 378, 793, 795, 824, 1161
Turner, Richard 850
Turner, Roland 756
Turner, Susan 850
Turner, Wyetta 165
Turoff, Robert 569, 601, 987
Turque, Mimi 284, 1628
Tursi, Daniel 750
Tursky, Vladimir 849
Turturice, Robert 215, 1208
Tuthill, Bob 493
Tuthill, Patricia 1186
Tuttle, Anthony 1749
Tuttle, Day 85
Twain, Norman 1130, 1365
Twiggy 751
Twine, Linda 252, 330
Twist, Basil 1248
Twitchell, Audrey 641
Twohill, William 604
Twomey, John 663
Tyce, Claudia 1145
Tyler, Chase 1645
Tyler, Ed 1566
Tyler, Steve 791
Tyler, Timothy 1281
Tyler, Veronica 951
Tyler, Willie 1543
Tynan, Kenneth 1168
Tyne, George 1626
Tyner, Charles 826
Tynes, Antoinette 593
Tyree, Neilan 144
Tyrone, Keith 153
Tyrrell, Tara 819, 1032, 1212
Tyson, Cicely 1672
Tyson, Pamala 1423
Tyspin, George 640
Tzu, Susan 595

Ubarry, Hechter 289, 1376
Udall, Lynn 377
Uecker, Korliss 574
Uggams, Leslie 181, 1631
Uhry, Alfred 412, 1367
Ukena, Paul, Jr. 133, 713, 1628, 1708
Ulanet, Rachel 1403
Ulisse, Arthur 66
Ulissey, Catherine 922
Ullett, Nic 962
Ullman, Douglas, Jr. 479
Ullman, Jeffrey 1702
Ullman, Robert 1080
Ullrich, Mattie 802, 1237
Ulvaeus, Bjorn 275
Underwood, Franklin (Franklyn) (Frank) 550, 556, 557, 558, 783, 1069
Underwood, Jason 1478
Unger, David W. 1245
Unger, Deborah 1771
Unger, Robert 187
Upbin, Shari 1034, 1198
Uppman, Theodor 1227
Urban, Joseph 868, 1249
Urban, Ruth 136
Urbano, Tony 1293
Urbont, Jacques (Jack) 33, 415, 944, 1430, 1517
Urdang, Terry 1216
Urich, Tom 1446, 1539
Urmston, Ken 638
Utley, Byron 1568, 1665
Utzig, Greg 737, 1540
Uziel, Phyllis 1177

Vaccaro, Danny 1157
Vaccaro, John 372
Vaccaro, John Adams (A.) 303, 904, 1414
Vaccaro, Vilma 720, 1713
Vachon-Coco, LizaGrace 1030
Vail, Seymour 722
Vajda, Frederick 868
Valbor, Kirsten 1131
Valcq, James 1513, 1832
Valdez, Zulma 1230
Valencia, Ereine "Honey Roc Well" 804
Valenne, Valerie 1315
Valente, Jean 747
Valenti, Michael 851, 972, 989, 990, 1827
Valenti, Tom 273
Valentine, Albert 1627
Valentine, James 317
Valentine, Tony 848
Vales, Ernie 804
Valfer, Shelley 397
Valin, Israel 1105
Vall, Seymour 851, 1773
Valle, Peter del 971
Vallejo, Alvaro 1416
Vallejo, Diego 118
Vallier, Jo Anne 86
Vallo, George 1453
Vallone, Eddie 1256
Valmonte, Dea 1281
Valor, Henrietta 159, 480, 488, 652, 793
Van, Earl 1802
Van, Gus 1177
Van, Vinnie 380
Van Aken, Gretchen 111, 243, 380, 920, 928, 998, 1739
Van Allen, Leo T. 679
Van Antwerp, John 494, 578, 1115, 1116
Van Antwerp, Ted 215
Vanarelli, Mario 693
Vanase, Paul 1030
Vance, Dana 84
Vanderbilt, Edwin 1688
Vanderpool, Charles 142
Vanderpool, Freda T. 630
Vandertholen, Jon 1670
Vando, David 224
Van Dorpe, Gloria 66
Van Duyne, Elisa 10
Van Dyke, Steven 1015
Van Fleet, David 1579
Van Grack, Brad 247
Van Griethuysen, Ted 332, 1161
Van Hoogstraten, Nicholas 825
Van Horn, Bill 1556
Van Ingen, Elisabeth 1055
Van Norden, Peter 1437
Vannuys, Ed 588
Van Peebles, Mario 266, 1580, 1737
Van Peebles, Melvin 266, 1737, 1738
Van Pelt, Lois 66
Van Scott, Glory 152, 504, 968, 1035, 1064, 1308, 1774
Van Scoyk, Bob 942
Vanterpool, Audrey 944
Vanterpool, Freda T. 629, 927
Van Tieghem, David 1731
van Treuren, James 1287, 1669
van Treuren, Martin 1287
Van Valkenburgh, Deborah 943
Van Vliet, Julia N. 808
Van Vooren, Monique 1007
Van Voorhis, Gail 64
Van Wey, Adelaide 1229
van Witsen, Leo 1564, 1596
Varela, Andrew 1441
Varga, Andrea 1425
Varga, Joseph (A.) 403, 1011, 1454
Vargas, Ovi 597
Varnado, Victor 1817
Varnay, Astrid 776
Varney, Amelia 291
Varney, Carleton 1383
Varnik, Reet Roos 276
Varona, Jose 188, 488
Varone, Doug 47
Varrone, Gene 66, 599, 878
Vaselle, Renata 90, 236
Vassi, Marco 101
Vassiliev, Vladimir 849
Vaszuez, Jorge 1538
Vaucresson, Robert, Jr. 500
Vaughan, David 286, 467, 756, 952, 1231, 1280
Vaughan, Jack 134
Vaughan, James 1822
Vaughan, Katharine 870
Vaughan, Melanie 1557
Vaughn, D. Jonathan 396
Vaughn, David 199, 445, 823
Vaughn, Kimberly 360
Vaux, Lyn 229
Vayne, Kyra 1639
Vazules, James 826
Veazey, Jeff 981
Vecchio, Charles Del 1040
Vechetova, Bozena 1609
Vega, Daphne Rubin 273
Vega, Juan 1402
Vehr, Bill 1359
Veille, Fayn Le 236
Velasco, Javier 83, 1551
Velasco, Vi 90
Velasquez, David Navarro 1664
Velez, Alex 1689
Velez, Martha 1599
Velie, Jay 140
Velis, Andrea 62, 574, 891
Veljohnson, Reginald 194, 1174, 1518
Venable, Sarah 346
Venneri, Darwin 352
Venora, Lee 677, 1583, 1667
Ventriss, Jennie 731
Ventura, Frank 1141
Venuta, Benay 1319
Venza, Jac 1185
Verakus, Steven 1080
Verberkmoes, Robert E. 1058
Verdesca, Albert 1098
Verdolino, Annette 1134
Verheyen, Mariann 442
Vermeulen, James 143, 189
Vermont, Ted 1264
Vernacchio, Dorian 1263
Verney, Richard 1627
Vernon, Michael 483
Very, Raymond 673
Vessels, R.T. 885
Vestoff, Floria 1385
Vestoff, Virginia 183, 332, 368, 472, 962, 1008, 1057
Vetere, John 1389
Vetkin, S. 1541
Vetrano, Stephen 290
Viana, Marta 379
Vichey, Luben 1044
Vickery, John 364

Victor, Dee 481
Victor, Larry 665
Victor, Lucia 17, 152, 361, 682
Victor, Marc 1179
Victor, Susan 1102, 1715
Vida, Richard 934
Vidal, Gore 1101
Vidal, Marta 333
Vidnovic, Martin 479, 916, 1181
Vielhaber, Werner 1775
Viertel, Jack 102, 1637
Viertel, Thomas (Tom) 102, 108, 479, 1235, 1461, 1495, 1742
Viesta, John 154
Vieth, Bradley 1450, 1788
Vietti, Alejo 997
Vig, Joel 1386
Vigil, Marcos 362
Vigoda, Bob 1276
Vigon, Barry 1560
Vilanch, Bruce 486
Villaire, Holly 588
Villamil, Jaclynn 705
Villani, Paul 43
Villanueva, Erico 632
Villechaize, Herve 1080
Villella, Edward 944
Vinaver, Steven 388, 450, 986, 1318, 1576, 1749
Vincent Millay, Edna St. 616, 868, 972
Vincent, A.J. 979
Vincent, Allen 620
Vincent, Christian 1325
Vincent, Chuck 21
Vincent, Holly 834
Vincent, Lawrence 105, 266
Vining, John 394, 1087
Vinocur, Burt 1348
Vinovich, Stephen (Steve) 406, 664, 961, 1219, 1367, 1380
Viola, Albert T. 678
Viracola, Fiddle 15, 86, 345, 532, 908
Virolas, Jassen 1186
Virtue, Christie 1801
Visconti, Tony 1054
Viscuso, Annie 768
Visitor, Alexandra 42
Vita, Michael 1160, 1606
Vitacco, Lou 417
Vitale, Adriano 66
Vitale, Bill 64, 1030
Vitali, Michael 43
Vitella, Sel 359, 1098
Viti, Geraldine 600
Vivano, Sal 213, 260
Viverito, Sam 25, 338
Viverito, Vince 383
Vivian, Ann 980
Vivian, Robert 1092
Vivian, Ruth 136
Viviano, Sal 606
Vivino, Jimmy 854
Vivona, Jerome 1586
Vlastnik, Frank 1403
Vode, Tim 1338
Voelpel, Fred 472, 655, 1168, 1196, 1483, 1605, 1824, 1825
Voet, Doug 833
Vogel, David 720, 1412
Vogel, Ed 493, 1124, 1537
Vogel, Frederic B. 979
Vogel, James 1382, 1453
Vogel, Marvin 85
Vogel, Sona 1226
Vohs, Frank 408, 1041, 1264
Voice, Kaye 825
Voight, Jon 1162
Voketaitis, Arnold 254, 1474, 1814
Volavkova 1008
Volkoff, Andrew 1328
von Gontard, Gert 137, 1462, 1775
Von Brandenstein, Rizia 406
Von Furstenberg, Betsy 140
Von Mayrhauser, Jennifer 263, 582
Vonnegut, Edith 588
Von Scherler, Sasha 317
Von Tilzer, Albert 377
Von Wymetal, Wilhelm 868, 1249
Vool, Ruth 1822
Voorhees, David 1029
Vosburgh, David 1362, 1483
Voskovec, George 204, 1175
Vossbrink, Heinz 168
Votipka, Thelma 1010
Votolato, Nina 1660
Voyce, Kaye 689, 1374
Voznesensky, Andrey 849
Vriezelaar, Clint 1470
Vroman, Lisa 435, 873, 990, 1456
Vucci, Ralph 68, 1221
Vukotich, Helen 66

Waas, Cinthia 781
Wachholtz, Becky 510
Wachholtz, Ron 510
Wachtel, Jeffrey 97
Wada, Emi 495
Wadden, Terese 71
Waddy, Henrietta 166
Wade, Mark 1580
Wade, Nancy 293
Wade, Raymond 1696
Wade, Stephen 97
Wade, Tryphena 167
Wade, Uel 961, 1143, 1287
Wade, Warren 63, 1481
Wadley, Steve 1030
Wadsworth, Adrian 1131
Wadud, Abdul 1816
Wager, Michael 204, 1236
Wagg, Jim 229
Waggett, Ellen 1419
Waggoner, Jamie 1333
Wagner, Daryl 906
Wagner, Frank 87, 160, 381, 415, 534, 722, 1259, 1430
Wagner, Gerard 1343
Wagner, Janet 951
Wagner, Kathryn 1223
Wagner, Nancy 510
Wagner, Robin 283, 369, 1360, 1426, 1492
Wagner, Ruth 60
Wagner, Sanghi 872
Wagner, Thomas 1431
Wagner, William 363
Wagoner, Dan 111, 286, 554, 759, 920
Wagreich, Ian 1134
Wahl, Kirby 712
Wainer, Bert 265, 1696
Wainwright, Lennal 1004
Waissman, Kenneth 625
Wait, Robert R. 1108
Waite, Genevieve 1007
Waite, John Thomas 1098
Waithe, William R. 333
Waits, Richard E. 1054
Waits, Tom 26, 168
Wakefield, Henriette 868, 1047
Wakefield, Scott 1660
Wakula, Frank 1744
Walbye, Kay 1028, 1712
Walcott, Derek 1633
Walcott, Jacqueline 944
Wald, Adam 1508
Wald, Shelley 1505
Walden, Grant 132, 360
Walden, Russell 1641
Walden, Stanley 707, 1168, 1169
Waldman, Frederic 1564
Waldman, Jennifer 679
Waldman, Price 1784
Waldman, Robert 412, 1367
Waldman, Susan 981
Waldon, Louis 925
Waldron, Michael 305, 1028, 1542
Waldrop, Mark 691, 929, 1089, 1245, 1763, 1772
Walenta, Edmund 68, 1021, 1221
Wales, Judee 1538
Walke, Gillian 545
Walken, Christopher (Ronald) 132, 805
Walken, Glenn 132
Walker, Barbara 497
Walker, Berta 1358
Walker, Bill 1540
Walker, Bonnie 63, 1483
Walker, Charles 4, 1541
Walker, Clara 1559
Walker, Dan 618, 619, 620
Walker, Daniel L. 775
Walker, David 1682
Walker, Don 619
Walker, Douglas 1097
Walker, Frank 1816
Walker, Fredi 290
Walker, Jaison 8, 1039
Walker, Janet Hayes 88, 308, 398, 435, 948, 1031, 1071, 1144, 1213, 1456, 1756
Walker, Joe 750
Walker, Jon Patrick 365
Walker, Joseph A. 120, 593
Walker, June 578
Walker, June L. 507
Walker, Lynne Del 1029
Walker, Megan Valerie 1554
Walker, Michael Patrick 38
Walker, Nancy 1254
Walker, Natalie 1025
Walker, Paul 325
Walker, Peter 1107
Walker, Ray 275
Walker, Suzanne 125, 969
Walker, Tom 462
Walker, Ula 844
Walker, William 891
Walker, Zoe 1070
Wall, Joan 1244
Wallace, Art 714, 1154, 1594
Wallace, Ashley 863
Wallace, Barbara 66
Wallace, Charles E. 668
Wallace, Emett "Babe" 107
Wallace, Jerry 235
Wallace, John 693
Wallace, Marcia 536
Wallace, Nicole-Capri 1333
Wallace, Roy 820
Wallace, Royce 1192
Wallace, Stewart 673
Wallace, Timothy 345
Wallach, Barbara 1221
Wallach, D. Brian 1043
Wallach, Ira 857, 1192, 1254, 1481, 1605
Wallach, Jeffrey 437
Wallach, Kathy 1252
Wallach, Lorna 1062
Wallem, Linda 899
Wallen, Linda 162
Waller, Peggy Jean 1169
Wallerstein, Lothar 776
Walling, Stratton 1147, 1287
Wallis, Ruth 193
Wallman, Jan 1125
Wallowitch, John 820
Walsh, Amy 1637
Walsh, Barbara 157, 1523
Walsh, Elizabeth 990
Walsh, James A. 1320, 1321
Walsh, Juanita 1070
Walsh, Martin 246
Walsh, Rick 1801
Walsh, Thomas (Thommie) J. 133, 283, 639, 973, 1096
Walt, William James 1409
Walter, Cy 535, 1661
Walters, Kelly 246
Walters, Susan 608, 684
Walters, William 1670
Walther, Denise 11
Walton, Bob 1296
Walton, Debra M. 222
Walton, Emma 1514
Walton, Hugh 469
Walton, Jim 52, 142, 273, 1521
Walton, Matthew 1629
Walton, Tony 13, 317, 751, 1663, 1716
Waltzer, Bernard 91, 226
Waltzer, Jack 826
Wangare, Phresia 167
Wanhel, Jeff 1641
Wann, Jim 376, 377, 544, 710, 864, 1317
Wanshel, Jeff 699
Wantuck, Michael 1772
Wanzandae, Psyche 885
Warchoff, Milton 1229
Ward, Dale 681
Ward, Donald 200, 626
Ward, Douglas Turner 629, 630, 850, 1004
Ward, Elizabeth 633
Ward, Elizabeth Caitlin 1422
Ward, Elsa 220
Ward, Henry 136
Ward, Janet 696
Ward, Joe Patrick 730
Ward, Ken 856, 1337
Ward, Lauren 463, 791, 1403, 1637, 1726
Ward, Lisa 1252
Ward, Matthew 14, 518, 522
Ward, Michael 394, 408, 1222, 1568, 1569, 1708
Ward, Nancee 134
Ward, Nancy 1419
Ward, Olivia 1580
Ward, Patricia 1300
Ward, Paula 1151
Ward, Peggy 161
Ward, Phylis 64, 1098
Ward, Robert 4, 331, 677, 1217, 1374
Ward, Ryan 462
Ward, Steven 768, 1134
Ward, Steven X. 208, 1784
Ward, Tim 1281
Ward, Toni 1399
Wardell, Brandon 462
Ware, Jeff 976
Warfield, Chris 324
Warfield, Donald 1079
Warfield, Joe 935
Warfield, Joel 1163
Warhol, Andy 421, 1007
Waring, Paula 944
Waring, Richard 1142
Warmflash, Stuart 1434
Warncke, Margaret 1025
Warner, Candace 1434
Warner, Elise 68, 1021
Warner, Joseph 1288
Warner, Milt 226, 1615
Warner, Nicole 1416
Warner, Rick 192, 1189
Warner, Sherman 699
Warners, Robert 1199
Warning, Dennis 821
Warnock, Elinore 1315
Warrack, David 1045
Warren, Angela 665
Warren, Annette 944
Warren, David 1375
Warren, Elton 1254
Warren, Harry 974
Warren, Jeff 908
Warren, Jennifer Leigh 8, 939
Warren, Leonard 776
Warren, Mary Mease 629
Warren, Renee 833
Warren, Rod 50, 87, 126, 350, 415, 542, 556, 557, 558, 771, 852, 1069, 1142, 1255, 1261, 1273, 1430, 1661
Warren, Tom 345
Warren, Vincent 332, 1655
Warren-Cooke, Barbara 1232, 1434
Warrender, Scott 102, 945
Warrilow, David 1344
Warriner, Frederic 481, 1689
Warshofsky, David 1376
Warszawski, Marek 1382
Warwick, Henry 136
Warwick, Norman 1131
Warwick, Veni 1369
Washburn, Jack 1221
Washington, Don Corey 592, 593
Washington, Frederica 1695
Washington, Kenneth 166
Washington, Lamont 815
Washington, Michael Benjamin 1403
Washington, Vernon 238
Wass, Ted 310
Wassell, Marilyn 320
Wasser, Scott 1240
Wasserman, Allan 311
Wasserman, Bryna 147
Wasserman, Dale 944
Wasserman, Molly 1160
Wassermann, Molly 1048
Wasserstein, Wendy 664, 1048, 1079, 1710
Wasson, David 496
Wassong, Linda 46
Watanabe, Gedde 386, 1282, 1699
Waterkotte, Joseph A. 1323
Watermeier, Ethan 362
Waters, Bernard 256
Waters, Daryl 8, 207, 668, 1429
Waters, Hal 698, 1683
Waters, Kyle 403
Waters, Skip 959
Waters, Sylvia 1029
Watford, Myk 657
Watkins, Amanda 755, 1479, 1778
Watkins, Brea 1022
Watkins, Gordon 844
Watkins, Harry 1543
Watkins, John Piilani 1221
Watkins, Steven Ray 837
Watroba, Sharon 1011
Watson, Becky 305
Watson, Brian 1274, 1354
Watson, Chester 609, 1587, 1667
Watson, Edna 400
Watson, Henry Kip 68
Watson, Janet 308, 309, 479, 485, 733, 789, 828, 926, 1204, 1213, 1214, 1449, 1451, 1581

Watson, Jessica 1629
Watson, Jim 376
Watson, John 65
Watson, Kip 1021
Watson, Lee 609, 987, 1319, 1445
Watson, Lisa 850
Watson, Michael Orris 1190
Watson, Patti (Ann) 68, 1021
Watson, Peggy Ann 1440
Watson, Rita 272
Watson, Ron 1021
Watson, Scotty 1736
Watson, Shari 81
Watson, Susan 191, 507, 908
Watt, Kathryn 56
Watt, Nina 1055
Watt, Patricia 965
Watters, Hal 128, 1473
Watts, Dion 816
Watts, Elizabeth 779
Watts, LaRue 1119
Watts, Leroy 1720
Watts, Maggie 1056, 1700
Watts, William E. 1140
Waxman, Anita 1053
Waxman, Herschel 1080
Waxman, Jeff 710, 1343
Way, Catherine 1323
Way, Lillo 229
Wayland, Newton 128
Wayne, Bernie 1475, 1688
Wayne, Cliff 98
Wayne, Hayden 1567
Wayne, Paula 132, 274, 693
Wayne, Robert 1745
Weatherly, Christal 1322
Weathersbee, Gary 270, 467, 708, 1017, 1349
Weatherstone, James 391
Weaver, Diane 736
Weaver, Fritz 68
Weaver, Jane 1229
Weaver, Jimmy 996
Weaver, Sigourney 978
Weaver, Thom 541, 679, 1630
Webb, Alyce 91
Webb, Barbara Ann 1021
Webb, Brian 754
Webb, Carolyn 266
Webb, Chloe 511
Webb, Cris 834
Webb, Elmon 1030
Webb, Geoffrey 955, 1639, 1640
Webb, Kenneth 567
Webb, Peter 1514
Webber, Andrew Lloyd 833, 1233, 1629
Weber, Erika 474
Weber, Fredricka 1684
Weber, Lawrence 1440, 1449
Weber, Lynne 65
Weber, Rex 1177
Weber, Richard 1609
Webley, Erin 1554
Webster, Margaret 1587
Webster, Virginia 1406, 1407
Wechsler, Gil 574, 1730
Wechter, Meredith 349
Wedekind, Frank 459
Weeden, Bill 126, 350, 542, 771, 852, 1069, 1141, 1255, 1259, 1273
Weeden, Janet 470
Weekes, Pauline 591
Weeks, Alan 152, 214, 1171, 1183, 1606
Weeks, Sarah 1141, 1709
Weems, Andrew 632
Weems, Deborah 414
Weideman, Japhy 995
Weidman, Charles 942
Weidman, John 70, 315, 377, 1213, 1214
Weidmann, Jennie 329
Weigert, Rene 1043
Weikel, Chris 404
Weil, Cynthia 854, 1612
Weil, Melissa 739
Weil, Robert 660, 1107, 1193
Weil, Tim 88, 1351, 1598
Weilding, Chris 680
Weiler, Norman 989
Weill, Kurt 128, 129, 459, 660, 689, 826, 827, 843, 879, 880, 882, 1100, 1360, 1462, 1532, 1626, 1627, 1628, 1629, 1773, 1807, 1809
Weill, Robert 1475
Weill, Sanford I. 1491
Weille, Blair 771, 1058, 1661
Weiman, Kate 328
Weinberg, Edwin 1661
Weinberg, Myron 134
Weinberg, Richard G. 754
Weinberg, Tom Wilson 573, 1600
Weiner, David 1429
Weiner, Ellis 81
Weiner, Erik 189
Weiner, Mark 708
Weiner, Meri 1537
Weiner, Randy 399
Weiner, Stephen 1129
Weiner, Stuart 291
Weiner, Vi 708
Weingartner, Mark 505
Weinrib, Len 149
Weinstein, Al 1813
Weinstein, Arnold 257, 421, 422, 528, 1206, 1723
Weinstein, David 837
Weinstein, Robert S. 1659
Weinstein, Seth 721
Weinstein, Sol 160
Weinstock, Adam 385
Weinstock, Richard 1478
Weintraub, Cindy 1252, 1494
Weintraub, Fred 598
Weintraub, Max 1764
Weintraub, Scooter 965
Weis, Jean-Guilliaum 363
Weisgall, Hugo 451, 1137, 1474, 1782
Weishar, Joseph 1060
Weisman, Sam 916
Weiss, David N. 224, 251, 1553
Weiss, Elliot 23, 156, 161, 162, 163, 164, 402, 1327
Weiss, George (David) 1100, 1480
Weiss, Gordon J. 1733
Weiss, Jeff 392
Weiss, Jonathan 1113
Weiss, Julie 1691
Weiss, Larry 1228
Weiss, Marc B. 84, 234, 646, 1433, 1560
Weiss, Nat 1831
Weiss, Noel 34
Weiss, Norman 309, 1449
Weiss, Peter Eliot 1432
Weiss, Randall 1560
Weiss, Randy 1690
Weiss, Rebecca 402
Weiss, Sarah 402
Weiss, Stanley G. 1060
Weissler, Barry 81
Weissler, Fran 81, 646
Weissmann, Polaire 618, 619, 620, 622
Weist, Stan 1517
Weitzenhoffer, Max 424, 1317, 1622, 1635
Weitzman, Ira 222, 430, 1103, 1513, 1726, 1779
Welbeck-Browne, Vassie 593
Welbes, George 1168, 1175
Welch, Charles C. 588, 652, 1684
Welch, David 276
Welch, Elisabeth 165, 433
Welch, Kenneth (Ken) 858, 1448, 1475
Welch, LaTonya 359
Welch, Miriam 1035
Weldon, Charles 629, 630, 1356
Weldon, Kevin B. 1410
Weldy, Frederick 157, 1427
Weller, David 1505
Weller, Michael 1082
Welles, Karen 1313
Welles, Leslie 1679, 1801
Wellington, Richard 1316
Wells, Anita 196
Wells, B.J. 468
Wells, Billy K. 171
Wells, Carveth 417
Wells, Craig 19, 89, 309, 516, 517
Wells, Deanna 1438
Wells, J.R. 1681
Wells, Kathy 1294
Wells, Matthew 653
Wells, Phradie 1249
Wells, Stephen 1622, 1787
Wells, Tico 855, 1535, 1538
Welsh, Kenneth 1519
Welty, Eudora 942
Welzer, Irving 1309
Wendel, Elmarie 80, 367, 698, 935, 1163, 1604
Wendell, Lynn 1221
Wender, Rebecca 122, 859
Wendorf, Vernon 1021
Wendt, Angela 72, 206, 1351
Wendt, George 1777
Wendt, William 705
Wengerd, Tim 561
Wentworth, Richard 1596
Wentworth, Scott 444, 644, 878
Wenz, Carol 210, 1089, 1150, 1348
Weppner, Christina 731, 1472, 1820
Werkheiser, John 976, 1537
Wermuth, Paul 1548
Werner, Fred, Jr. 566
Werner, Howard 685
Werner, Ken 125
Wernick, Richard 1142
Wernli, Carol 213
Wersinger, Robert 122, 859
Werth, Amanda 505
Werthmann, Colleen 607
Wertimer, Ned 698, 714
Wesbrooks, William 1742
Wesley, L. Edmond 420, 803, 1781
Wesley, Richard 1710
Wesley, Robin 582, 1787
Wesson, Josh 273
West, Alvy 353, 1239, 1768, 1791, 1796
West, Bernie 1172
West, Christopher 951, 1789
West, David 195
West, Edwin 1440
West, Gene 713
West, Julie 1487
West, Maria 254, 488
West, Matt 1052
West, Michael 520, 523, 524, 1067, 1763
Westberg, Bonnie 1202
Westberg, Britt 1252
Westbrook, Frank 1475
Westenberg, Robert 364, 741, 1726
Westergaard, Louise 46
Westergard, Lance 62
Westerhoff, Peter 510
Westerman, Dale 631
Westerman, Tom 419
Westfall, John David 1222
Westfeldt, Jennifer 1826
Westlein, Richard 101
Weston, Jack 88
Weston, Jim 93
Weston, Larry 1194
Wetmore, Joan 1692
Wetzel, Arleen 1242
Wever, Russ 657
Wexler, Bradley 960
Wexler, J. 1591
Wexler, Jerry 1198
Wexler, Peter 214, 237, 947
Wexler, Robert 960
Wexler, Yale 1192
Whaley, Charlotte 867
Whaley, Michael 193
Wharton, Leigh 68
Whately, Frank 1233
Whedon, Tom 34, 160, 1076
Wheeler, Barbara 611
Wheeler, Chris 1410
Wheeler, Gary James 629
Wheeler, Harris 179
Wheeler, Hugh 244, 1213, 1214, 1462
Wheeler, Jedediah 729, 872, 1200
Wheeler, John 1587
Wheeler, Monte 778
Wheeler, Sandra 271
Wheetman, Dan 657, 777
Whelan, Christian 1054, 1669
Wheless, Bill 1066
Whisted, Don 212
Whitaker, Grenna 1388
Whitaker, Mical 927, 1435
Whitchurch, Missy 217
White, Anemone 1333
White, Anthony 1695
White, Boysie 1002
White, Calvin 166
White, Carl D. 892, 965, 1110
White, Cornelius 1816
White, David A. 683, 1403
White, Diz 303, 623
White, Dorothy 92
White, Greg 1157
White, Helen 1278
White, Jane 16, 807, 948, 1058, 1193, 1250, 1390
White, Jane Douglass 822
White, Jerri L. 1333
White, Julie 973
White, Katherine 1816
White, Kenna 904
White, L. Keith 1333
White, Lillias 83, 330, 1375
White, Lilly 134
White, Michael 263, 1168
White, Miles 268, 357, 1319
White, Onna 435
White, Phyllis 1369
White, Richard 434, 1410
White, Robert 951
White, Roxanne 1348
White, Stephen Len 4
White, Stuart 740
White, Susan A. 182, 1155
White, Terri 301, 748, 1159
White, Tom 107
White, Tony 704
Whitefield, Bill 749
Whitehead, Fannie 856
Whitehead, Mary 663
Whitehead, Paxton 1379
Whitehead, Ron 1136
Whitehead, Torri 719
Whitehill, B.T. 1571, 1706
Whitehill, Clarence 1269
Whitehill, Jane Margaret 346
Whitehouse, Anthony 221, 255
Whitehurst, Victor 769
Whitelaw, Arthur 132, 238, 1486, 1575, 1620, 1828
Whiteley, Benjamin (Ben) 799, 1390
Whiteley, Larry 1166, 1477
Whitfield, Alice 792
Whitfield, Arthur 631
Whitfield, Hugh 1755
Whitfield, Lynn 630
Whiting, Byron 24, 1768, 1790, 1791, 1796
Whiting, Jack 600
Whiting, Margaret 390, 1582
Whitley, Todd 573
Whitman, Allister C. 985
Whitman, Mary Lynn 1179
Whitman, Walt 903
Whitmore, Maud 56
Whitney, Adrienne 1360
Whitney, Robert 1029
Whitten, Dan 802
Whitten, Laurie 1050
Whitten, Victoria 994
Whittlesey, Derek 350
Whitty, Jeff 77
Whyte, Ron 259, 551
Whyte, Ronny 1125
Wicke, Hal 1081
Wickenheiser, Michael D. 190
Wickstrom, Robert 362
Widder, Robert 1729
Widdoes, Kathleen 13, 117, 259
Wideman, Beverly 716, 1354, 1387, 1776
Wideman, Susan 1349
Widholm, Jerry Dale 510
Widney, Stone 1078
Wiegert, Rene 1170
Wiemer, Whitney 295
Wiener, George 1774
Wiener, Jenny 72
Wiener, Sally Dixon 177
Wierzel, Robert (M.) 264, 729, 791, 1022, 1074, 1200, 1702
Wiesel, Elie 647, 648
Wieselman, Douglas 1439
Wietrzychowski, Stanley 1540
Wiggin, Tom 943
Wiggins, Carmiletta 1070
Wiggins, James H., Jr. 1353
Wightman, Robert 1755
Wigura, Wladyslaw 1275
Wikoff, Jack 1077
Wilbur, Richard 244
Wilcher, James "Red" 409, 553
Wilcox, Patricia (Patty) 182, 280, 284
Wilcox, Wayne 627
Wilcynski, Gregg 144
Wilde, Oscar 1714
Wilder, Alec 870, 1192, 1448
Wilder, Andrew 402, 1513, 1832
Wilder, Anne 1
Wilder, Baakari 207
Wilder, Carrie 1016
Wilder, Clinton 104
Wilder, Duane 894
Wilder, Gene 421
Wilder, Rex 1093, 1729
Wilder, Thornton 951

Wildhorn, Frank 668
Wile, Joan 371
Wiles, Quinton 1469
Wiley, Flo 501
Wiley, Irene 839
Wiley, Major 669
Wiley, Tomianne 409
Wilfert, Sally 997, 1303
Wilford, Anne 904
Wilke, Ray 663
Wilkens, Bob 697
Wilkerson, Arnold 400, 649
Wilkerson, John 3
Wilkes, Benjamin 1131
Wilkes, Fiona 1530
Wilkes, Patricia 1192
Wilkie, Alice 1435
Wilkie, Andrew 1590
Wilkins, Julia 859
Wilkins, Lee 808
Wilkinson, Kate 1343
Wilkinson, Leslie 76
Wilkinson, Raven 1816
Wilkof, Lee (S.) 54, 70, 939, 1297
Willard, Fred 1352
Willard, Frederick 49
Willauer, Marguerite 1063
Willens, Doris 1258
Willensky, Elliot 3
Willes, Christine 1432
Willett, John 1628
Willetts, Sandra 1029
Williams, Arthur 756, 757
Williams, Barbara 1539
Williams, Beth 454
Williams, Bill 11
Williams, Bradley 673
Williams, Brandon 950
Williams, Brock 815, 816
Williams, Carl 378
Williams, Carlton 591
Williams, Casey 1434
Williams, Charles 1543
Williams, Charles LaVont 266, 1064, 1423
Williams, Clyde 127
Williams, Danrell 495
Williams, Darius Keith 1525
Williams, Darnell 682
Williams, Dennis 630
Williams, Dick 1314
Williams, Dorian 107, 1388
Williams, Dudley 1029, 1291
Williams, Duke 1465
Williams, Ellis (E.) 1191, 1398
Williams, Fiona 1134
Williams, Freida 646
Williams, Grace 1183
Williams, Grant 92, 1474, 1587, 1814
Williams, Hank 657
Williams, Harold 1535
Williams, Jack Eric 1376, 1628
Williams, Jason F. 328
Williams, Jennifer 957
Williams, John H. 1518
Williams, John R. 467, 1045
Williams, Julie 1131
Williams, Keith 105
Williams, Ken 507
Williams, Lenny 247
Williams, Liz 507
Williams, Lowell 1284
Williams, Lucky 1535
Williams, Lynne Ann 1670
Williams, M. Drue 195
Williams, Margo 501
Williams, Marion 166
Williams, Marshall 196, 589, 1002, 1774
Williams, Mathew J. 749, 811
Williams, Matt 1205
Williams, Mattie 166
Williams, Megan 363
Williams, Mr. 1076
Williams, Ralph 827
Williams, Richard 423, 996
Williams, Robert T. 74, 291, 1078, 1274
Williams, Ron 497
Williams, Ryan 462
Williams, Sally 910
Williams, Sam 1439
Williams, Samm-Art 156
Williams, Sammy 283
Williams, Sandra Courtney 1207
Williams, Sandy 1580
Williams, Selena 613
Williams, Sundra (Jean) 107, 706
Williams, Sylvia "Kuumba" 1198
Williams, Ted 1147
Williams, Teddy 212, 1308
Williams, Timothy 1600
Williams, Treat 249, 1334
Williams, Tyrone 1001
Williams, Valerie 1470
Williams, Vanessa 1197
Williams, Wes 1080
Williams, Zinda 769
Williamson, Bruce 531, 632, 771, 826, 1261, 1661
Williamson, Christine M. 1556
Williamson, Jama 365
Williamson, Marcus 147, 666
Williamson, Nicol 445, 1130
Williamson, Ruth 184, 633
Williamson, Sonny Boy 1655
Williford, Lou 791
Willinger, Kathy 200
Willis, Nikki 1131
Willis, Sally 303
Willis, Scott 1467
Willis, Susan 582, 962
Willis, Tom 175
Willis, Victor 629, 1307, 1696
Willison, Walter 215, 1208
Willoughby, Ronald 192, 834, 920, 1349
Willoughby, Tanya 854
Willows, Linda 1035
Wills, Lou, Jr. 1755
Wills, Ray 296, 1381
Willson, Michael (Edwin) 186, 726, 873, 1146, 1270, 1731
Willson, Parker 125
Wilmshurst, Carolyn 1163
Wilner, John 642
Wilner, Lori 658, 659, 1619
Wilshusen, Carrie 485, 1441, 1771
Wilson, Amy 1826
Wilson, Andrea 565
Wilson, Anita 1004
Wilson, Anna 399
Wilson, Anne 1081
Wilson, Archie 730
Wilson, Billy 959
Wilson, Bob 510
Wilson, Carl 831, 1080
Wilson, Carrie 1311
Wilson, Chandra 252, 1186
Wilson, Derby 704
Wilson, Diane 682, 785, 1001
Wilson, Earl, Jr. 357, 913
Wilson, Edith 165
Wilson, Elizabeth 1259
Wilson, Erin Cressida 1665, 1779
Wilson, Flip 1177
Wilson, Jackie 790
Wilson, James 910
Wilson, Jeffrey 1308
Wilson, Jessica-Snow 1831
Wilson, Joe, Jr. 934
Wilson, Joe Lee 885
Wilson, John 693, 1789
Wilson, John W. 1412
Wilson, Julie 658, 843
Wilson, K.C. 539, 1593, 1628, 1733
Wilson, Katie 1233
Wilson, Lanford 1552, 1705
Wilson, Lohr 857
Wilson, Mary Jane 33
Wilson, Mary Louise 381, 415, 534, 641, 1430, 1767
Wilson, Mitzi 1399
Wilson, Pamela Ann 319
Wilson, Patrick 206
Wilson, Rainn 1120
Wilson, Randal 419
Wilson, Robert 26, 168, 294, 397, 427, 872, 917
Wilson, Robin 9
Wilson, Sandy 199, 1716
Wilson, Scat 1388
Wilson, Stan 314
Wilson, Theodore 589
Wilson, Tom 395
Wilson, Trey 1243, 1643
Wilson, Tristan 1690
Wilson, Tug Wilson 59, 171, 960
Wilson, Ural 91, 1774
Wilzak, Crissy 283
Wimmer, Rebecca J. 983
Winberry, T. 361
Winbush, Marilynn 194, 230, 1762
Wincelberg, Shimon 1203
Winchu, Laeleen 1655
Winde, Beatrice 844, 1201
Windheim, Marek 440, 762, 1047, 1249
Windsor, John 401, 486
Winer, Margarite 1469
Winfield, Hemsley 440
Wingate, Martha 364
Wingate, Peter 1308
Wingert, Melanie 290
Wing-Porter, Mary 322
Winiarski, Jo 738
Wink, Chris 1674
Winkler, Peter 1309
Winkler, Richard 45, 125, 194, 259, 395, 416, 642, 681, 907, 976, 1037, 1296, 1623
Winkworth, Mark 1098
Winner, Andrew 1599
Winnerman, Lawrence J. 37
Winnick, Jay Brian 290, 538
Winningham, Mare 1598
Winograde, Joshua 938
Winsett, Betty 1131, 1223
Winslow, Darryl 462
Winslow, Pippa 1204
Winslow, Rain 1254
Winson, Suzi 1155
Winston, Alice 826
Winston, Hattie 152, 589, 629, 688, 1004, 1038, 1308, 1397
Winston, Lee 1065
Winston, Morton 238
Winston, Tarik 313
Winter, Elinor 1131
Winter, Keith 1409
Winter, Michael 1120
Winters, Anne 585, 874
Winters, Ben H. 1479
Winters, David 652, 1399
Winters, Nancy 12, 394, 426, 764, 910, 999, 1033, 1079, 1535
Winters, Newton 682
Winters, Renee 132
Wintersteller, Lynne 300, 576, 741, 1362
Winther, Michael 129, 1298, 1325, 1499
Winthrop, Brian 1435
Wipf, Alex 192, 483, 534, 1284
Wirth, Maggie 1690
Wirtshafter, Tom 607, 1523
Wise, Birgit Rattenborg 1788
Wise, Deborah Anne 647
Wise, James Scott 1491
Wise, Jim 341, 342, 343, 1318
Wise, Maggie 15, 392, 834, 920
Wise, Mike 486
Wise, Scott 296
Wiseman, Danny 1815
Wiseman, Philip 317
Wisner, James J. (Jimmy) 279, 304, 1216, 1414
Wisniak, Kasimierz 1275
Wisniski, Ron 1593
Wiswell, Andy 663
Witcover, Walt 1460
Witham, John 1691
Witham, Tricia 246
Witherspood, Herbert 1269
Witherspoon, Dwight 736
Witherspoon, Ernest 593
Witherspoon, Herbert 1075
Withey, Barbara 1655
Witkin, Stephen 1310
Witsger, Brad 1644
Wittenborn, Paul 1081
Wittman, Scott 943
Wittop, Freddy 1687
Wittstein, Ed 309, 381, 478, 479, 733, 734, 866, 894, 1593, 1672
Wizoreck, Barry 1014
Wodarz, Hans-Peter 1281
Wodehouse, P.G. 63, 902, 1101, 1172
Wohl, David 1287
Wohl, Jack 289
Wojak, Regina 779
Wojewodski, Bob (Bobby) 763, 1042
Wojtasik, George 799, 1683
Woldin, Judd 865, 866, 934, 1593
Wolf, Bill 1182
Wolf, Catherine 1048
Wolf, Richard R. 1274
Wolf, Sue 1753
Wolf, Teresa 359
Wolfe, Brian 434
Wolfe, Burton 786
Wolfe, Elissa 1485
Wolfe, George C. 195, 207, 252, 387, 428, 496, 668, 1186, 1219, 1250, 1325, 1404, 1710
Wolfe, James 868, 1047
Wolfe, John Leslie 217
Wolfe, Karin 76, 132, 822
Wolfe, Leslie Anne 725, 1097
Wolfe, Tom 1777
Wolfe, Wendy 304, 740, 1270, 1595
Wolff, Art 179, 552, 1234
Wolff, Beverly 254
Wolff, Greta 92
Wolff, Mark 1389
Wolfson, David 1301, 1370, 1570, 1809
Wolfson, John 460
Wolfson, Martin 85, 619, 1140
Wolin, Rob 1321
Wolin, Robert F. 1320
Wolk, James 883, 1580, 1752
Wolkowitz, Morton 1530
Wolpe, Lenny 218, 1037, 1800
Wolshonak, Derek 42, 819, 1032, 1212
Wolsk, Gene 205, 527
Wolsky, Albert 55, 1199, 1827
Wolvin, Roy 1116
Womack, Norman 1302
Womble, Andre 21
Wondisford, Diane 12, 691, 728, 839, 1722
Wong, Anthony 732
Wong, B.D. 69
Wong, Goff, Rodriguez 1350
Wong, Janet 1171
Wong, Randall 673
Wonsek, Paul 218
Wood, Bill 1772
Wood, Binky 107
Wood, Christal 45
Wood, Ellie 1652
Wood, Frank 1515
Wood, G. 87, 415, 466, 531, 858, 870, 1318, 1430, 1447, 1448
Wood, Joy 1029
Wood, Kelly 1242
Wood, Marcia 1446
Wood, Norma Jean 716
Wood, Raymond 200
Wood, Susan 424
Wood, Virginia 940
Woodall, James 815
Woodall, Oliver 567
Woodall, Sandra 1722
Woodard, Charlaine 1, 370, 656, 1219, 1699
Woodard, Patricia 15
Woodberry, David P. 427
Woodbridge, Patricia 386, 1133
Woodeson, Nicholas 84
Woodford, Jack 1687
Woodhouse, Debbie 1343
Woodhouse, Sam 777
Wooding, Rodney 197
Woodley, Becky 1207
Woodman, Branch 385
Woodman, Britt 544
Woodman, Jeff 1482
Woodruff, Kelly 229
Woodruff, Robert 1439, 1657
Woods, Allie 21, 589, 1004
Woods, Carol 182, 496
Woods, Josephine 1464, 1465
Woods, Michele-Denise 325
Woods, Rejinald 167
Woods, Richard 1124, 1418
Woods, Tim 1653
Woods, Willie 844
Woodson, Deborah 1525
Woodson, Roger 177
Woodson, Sally 1173
Woodson, William 317
Woodward, Bliss 1229
Woodward, Charles 409
Woodward, Greer 1607
Woolard, David 659, 1335
Woolard, David C. 2, 3, 57, 103, 189, 222, 224, 399, 411, 596, 691, 837, 1129, 1219, 1375, 1761
Woolever, Harry 1652
Wooley, Michael-Leon 3
Woolf, Steven 1367
Woolley, Reginald 1639, 1640
Woolsey, Michael-Leon 72
Woolsey, Wysandria 302
Wooster, Ann 397
Wooster, Toni 1805
Wootten, Christopher 151
Wopat, Tom 159

Worby, Joshua 505
Worden, Marvin 686
Workman, Jason 114
World, Robert 1044
World, Sascha 1044
Worley, Jo Anne 714, 986, 1605
Wormer, Sally 397
Wormley, Iony L. 918
Woronov, Mary 1725
Worra, Caroline 941
Worronkoff, Karen 1721
Worth, Caroline 870
Worth, Maggie 1021
Worth, Matthew 1416
Worth, Wendy 359
Worthing, Gerrie 1115
Woyasz, Laura 1103
Wragge, Betty 1380
Wrangler, Jack 25
Wray, Deborah 888
Wray, Phoebe 532
Wreghitt, Randall L. 1831
Wren, Rene 136
Wrenn, Bob 1287
Wright, Andrea 171, 856
Wright, Ann (Anne)-Marie 811, 1760
Wright, Ben 1219
Wright, Charles Michael 678
Wright, Charles Randolph 1034
Wright, David C. 991, 1171
Wright, Debbie 1695
Wright, Doug 233, 641
Wright, E.H. 1620
Wright, Ebony 1696
Wright, Elaine 284
Wright, Garland 419, 978, 1094, 1520
Wright, Helena-Joyce 1300
Wright, James 120
Wright, Jonathan B. 1515
Wright, Katherine 1412
Wright, Kevin R. 208
Wright, Margaret 111, 243, 823, 834, 928, 998, 1017, 1231, 1277, 1280, 1349, 1501, 1776
Wright, Mark 894
Wright, Martin 1040
Wright, Mary Catherine 907, 1643
Wright, Ned 809, 1811
Wright, Nicholas 938
Wright, Peter 895
Wright, Russel 620
Wright, Samuel E. 1290
Wright, Susan J. 1646
Wrightson, Ann (G.) (Annie) 1, 763, 1478, 1507
Wu, Shih-hui 1608
Wullen, Elizabeth 1083
Wulp, John 528
Wuorinen, Charles 670
Wurger, Bernard F. 822
Wurschmidt, Sigrid 364
Wurtzel, Fred 1299
Wurtzel, Stuart 406, 582, 1620
Wuthrich, Terry 1664
Wyatt, Eda 66
Wyatt, John 1383
Wyatt, Kelly 1627
Wyatt, Mona Yvette 1016
Wyche, Mimi 814, 1190
Wyche, Ron 1151
Wyche, Ronald 153, 1423
Wydro, Ken 196, 1001, 1002
Wyeth, Howard 1360
Wyler, Sharon Jane 1349
Wylie, Betty Jane 127
Wylie, Teressa 408
Wyman, George 256
Wyman, Nicholas 54, 271, 1190, 1222
Wymetal, Wilhelm Von, Jr. 762, 1047
Wyndham, Victoria 1255, 1380
Wynkoop, Christopher 255, 1410, 1595
Wynn, Kevin 9
Wynn, Linurte 1811
Wynroth, Alan 346, 1080

Xantho, Peter 772, 1802
Xenia-Ortiz, Roxana 505
Xifo, Ray 1628
Ximenez, Chavo 488
Xulu, Michael 651

Yablokoff, Bella (Bela) Mysell (Maisel) 819, 1382
Yachsen (Yachson), Mordecal (Mordechai) 119, 1822
Yadon, Dennis 1333
Yaffe, Hila 108
Yaffee, Ben 140, 1140
Yakim, Moni 265, 792, 793, 795, 797, 1635
Yamada, Sylvia 1410
Yamaguchi, Eiko 223, 960, 1214, 1410
Yamamoto, Ronald 1213, 1214
Yampolsky, Alexander 782
Yan, Victor En Tu 392
Yancy, Madeline 1543
Yaney, Denise 841
Yang, In Ja 889
Yang, Young il 889
Yankee, Daddy 262
Yankee, Pat 105
Yao, Qi 495
Yarborough, Bertram 1172
Yarborough, Sara 1029
Yarbrough, Camille 1397
Yaroshko, Michelle 769
Yarri, Robert 1166, 1822
Yasner, Matthew 1721
Yates, Craig 1119
Yates, Ken 916
Yates, Lynnen 729
Yates, Vern 1216
Yauger, Maria 1131
Yavne, Maria 92, 1131
Yazbeck, Tony 476
Yazbek, George 840
Yde, Bob 663
Yeager, Fabian 1181
Yeargan, Lisa 1777
Yeargan, Michael (H.) 27, 234, 264, 383, 628, 1007, 1287, 1697
Yeats, W.B. 707
Yeh, Ching 1080
Yehle, William 1487
Yehudith 441
Yellen, Harriet 521
Yellen, Sherman 1168, 1381
Yellin, Harriet 518, 520, 522, 523, 524, 525, 526, 1067
Yen, Ann 712
Yenque, Teresa 1398
Yerxa, Alison 615
Yesckas, Emmanual 897
Yeston, Maury 1201
Yi, Mun Yol 889
Yian, Hao Jiang 495
Yimou, Zhang 495
Ynes 962
Yoder, Jerry 653
Yodice, Robert 1731
Yorinks, Arthur 846
York, Donald 1558
York, James 1222
York, Lila 561, 1722
York, Peter 1379
York, Rachel 375, 1492
York, Richard 201
York, Y. 976
The York Players 190
Yorke, Helene 1736
Yorke, Sally 435, 1016, 1171
Yorkin, Beulah 1145
Yorks, Julia 1321
Yoshida, Peter 1300
Yoshii, Kumiko 1554
Yoshimura, Akira 580, 1518
Yossiffon, Raquel 489, 666, 1051, 1822
Youmans, James 680, 1250, 1375, 1523, 1554, 1831
Youmans, Vincent 1173
Youmans, William 1201, 1327
Youn, Chan 889
Younes, Lisa 1617
Young, Amy Felices 247
Young, Aston 1004
Young, Caryl Gabrielle 360
Young, Cy 388, 531, 582, 1431, 1604
Young, David 58
Young, Donald 42
Young, Earl 1696
Young, Ed Reynolds 1428
Young, Eric Jordan 375, 933, 1067, 1491
Young, Eugenie 136
Young, Greg 395
Young, James 105
Young, Janice Kay 373
Young, Linda E. 255
Young, Marie 488
Young, Neal 812
Young, Priscilla 1221
Young, Rebecca 193
Young, Ronald 416, 1173
Young, Thomas 363, 419, 1519, 1816
Young, William B. 1027
Young, Willie Fong 45
Youngsman, Christopher 612
Younin, Wolf 147
Yount, Kenneth M. (Ken) 289, 419, 675, 1169, 1414, 1485
Yousef, Tish 985
Youtt, Jene 761, 1130
Yu, Hee Sung 889
Yucis, Raymond 1349
Yudson, Steve 1715
Yue, Fan 495
Yuen, Chan Kwok 282
Yueyang, Mother of 495
Yule, Don 254, 569, 673, 1063
Yun, Ho Jin 889
Yurman, Lawrence 586, 641, 1571
Yzraely, Yossi 1203
Zablocki, Jenna 983
Zacharias, Emily 289, 1181
Zachary, Alaina Warren 203
Zachos, Ellen 940, 1223
Zadan, Craig 1697
Zadikian, Margaux 1186
Zadorzny, John 1131
Zagaeski, Mark 1133
Zagnit, Stuart 878, 973, 1067, 1260, 1593
Zagottis, Frank 973
Zahn, Mary 1221
Zajick, Dolora 47
Zakariasen, William 609
Zaken, Remy 248, 1325, 1515
Zakes, Carin Marie 293
Zakharov, Mark 849
Zakharova, Alexandra 849
Zakkai, Jamil 831
Zakowska, Donna 859, 1190
Zakrzewaki, Paul 1424
Zaks, Jerry 70, 1643
Zala, Nancy 756
Zalkind, Debra 133
Zalon, Paul 1739
Zaman, Rosalind 1806
Zambalis, Stella 574, 846
Zambello, Francesca 47, 439, 938
Zande, Michael 834
Zane, Arnie 1487
Zang, Edward (Ed) 1057, 1082, 1279, 1628, 1713
Zanger, Jacob 1822
Zappa, Frank 7
Zarai, Yohanan 1203
Zaremba, Elisabeth 58
Zaremba, Kathryn 58
Zarle, Brandy 1187
Zarley, Matt 1328
Zarrett, Lee 1784
Zarro, Ron 708
Zaslow, Michael 86, 183
Zayenda, Edmund 1104
Zbornik, Kristine 456, 518, 746
Zeavin, Carol 170
Zee, Allan 66
Zeeman, Sandra 820
Zeffirelli, Franco 62
Zeffiro, William 1577
Zeffren, Jerome 1780
Zeiberg, Madeline 940
Zeidman, Jeffrey 1084
Zeitlin, Meredith 742
Zeitz, Jhonny 216
Zelaya, Gloria 897
Zeldis, Joshua 441
Zeldis, Lou 1291
Zelenin, Yury 849
Zeller, Gary Meir 1713
Zeller, Mark 289, 878
Zeller, Marvin 66
Zeller, Robert 1063, 1229
Zeller-Alexis, Dana 1715, 1829
Zellnik, David 1818
Zellnik, Joseph 1818
Zelon, Helen 1011
Zemarel, Jamie 247
Zemel, Alan 822
Zender, Marguerite 1145
Zeno, Norman 446
Zenobia 384, 740
Zetter, Lois 714
Zettler, Michael 780, 1222
Zeus, Jared 1830
Zhang, Ruth 1322
Zhivova, Valeria 849
Zhou, Zheng 123
Zieff, Rick 1505
Zielinski, Scott 413, 503, 644
Zielonka, Jana 738, 995
Ziemba, Karen 52, 567, 599, 733, 907, 1305
Zien, Chip 377, 473, 763, 1019, 1121, 1228, 1339, 1358, 1480
Ziferstein, Gail 504
Zihlman, Dana 950
Ziman, Jerrold 958
Ziman, Richard 305, 1327
Zimberg, Stuart 463, 801
Zimmerman, Anne F. 1186
Zimmerman, Edward 369, 1462
Zimmerman, Mark 912, 1167, 1410
Zinberg, Arthur D. 467, 1739
Zinger, Pablo 1588
Zinn, Barbara 23
Zinn, David 1499, 1634, 1826
Zinn, Randolyn 1094
Zinnato, Stephen 1303
Zinni, Lisa L. 67
Zipf, Raymond Skip 960
Zipf, Skip 347
Zippel, David 1, 377, 781, 855, 1149, 1150
Zippel, Joanne (L.) 855, 1149
Zippin, Louis 1030
Zipprodt, Patricia 987, 1083, 1557, 1558
Ziske, Carol Anne 466
Ziskie, Daniel (Dan) 259, 318
Ziskin, Victor 1824, 1825
Zitko, Peggy Ann 1028
Zmed, Adrian 67, 424
Znidarsic, John 1067
Zola, Greg 1403
Zollinger, Betty 66
Zollo, Dolly 1315
Zollo, Marge 1315
Zoran 1709
Zorich, Louis 710
Zozhen, Jania 822
Zschau, Marilyn 951
Zuber, Catherine 249, 323, 791, 1135, 1403, 1637, 1726
Zucker, Milton 779
Zuckerman, John 717
Zuckerman, Michael 459
Zuckerman, Paul 1817
Zuckerman, Stephen 907
Zuckmayer, Carl 459
Zukowski, Zbigniew 1275
Zulema 809
Zulu, Thandi 1401
Zungolo, Al 698
Zur, Menachem 1701
Zuri, Samaki 1696
Zuspan, Peter 1329
Zutty, Andrew
Zutty, Andrew (Blake) 280, 1700
Zutz, Carl 1641
Zwane, Paula 1179
Zweibel, Alan 377
Zwick, Joel 346, 347
Zwiegbaum, Steve 1616
Zyla, David R. 302

Theatre Index

References are to entry numbers

Abbey Theatre 1559
Abingdon Theatre/Arts Complex 563, 1630
Academy Theatre 906
Acorn Theatre 6
Actor's (Actors) Outlet Theatre (Center) 349, 1298, 1377
Actor's (Actors) Temple Theatre 146, 1118
The Actors Studio 696
Actors' Playhouse 200, 216, 407, 461, 537, 645, 1027, 1089, 1110, 1124, 1175, 1263, 1314, 1364, 1432, 1460, 1570, 1600, 1618, 1669, 1690, 1759, 1772, 1806, 1811
Alice Tully Hall/Lincoln Center 846, 872, 1003, 1329
All Soul's Church Theatre 940
All Souls Fellowship Hall 842
AMAS Musical/Repertory Theatre 51, 59, 116, 124, 127, 153, 171, 197, 223, 313, 333, 359, 420, 500, 682, 712, 785, 803, 950, 960, 1001, 1009, 1016, 1065, 1070, 1148, 1207, 1223, 1232, 1300, 1305, 1370, 1434, 1467, 1509, 1525, 1544, 1550, 1781, 1785
AMDA Theatre 904
American Jewish Theatre 100, 209, 1328, 1361, 1381
American Music Hall 494, 578, 1092, 1115
American Place Theatre 1, 305, 314, 325, 688, 831, 860, 1014, 1222, 1340, 1514, 1534, 1641, 1720, 1761, 1783
American Theatre of Actors 95, 1712
Anderson Theatre 874, 1360, 1562, 1666
Anderson Yiddish Theatre 608
Anspacher Theatre/The Public Theatre 27, 65, 186, 346, 649, 726, 753, 958, 1057, 1225, 1422
Apollo Theatre 615, 668, 790, 1064
Ark Theatre 1522
Ars Nova Theatre 72
Astor Place Playhouse 1603, 1672
Astor Place Theatre 101, 304, 571, 720, 740, 793, 824, 904, 968, 1036, 1049, 1074, 1231, 1561, 1674
Atlantic Theatre Company 1515
Attic Theatre/Brooklyn Academy of Music 699
Audrey Wood Theatre 878, 961
Baird's Theatre 96
The Ballroom 237, 257, 700
Ballroom Theatre 737, 1138
Barbarann Theatre Restaurant 1524
Barbizon-Plaza Theatre 137, 317, 379, 1192, 1393, 1447, 1594, 1647, 1749, 1775
Barrow Street Theatre 607, 896
Beacon Theatre 768, 964, 1200, 1426
Belmont Theatre 109
Bert Wheeler Theatre 64, 76, 231, 288, 336, 1194, 1331, 1475
Bijou Theatre 357, 880, 1358, 1433
Bil Baird (Baird's) Theatre 24, 28, 29, 353, 354, 355, 1239, 1246, 1247, 1266, 1768, 1769, 1770, 1790, 1791, 1792, 1793, 1794, 1796, 1797
Billie Holiday Theatre 603
Biltmore Theatre 1005
The Bitter End 265, 1312, 1773
Blackfriars' Guild 985
Blue Angel Theatre 533, 1210, 1215, 1571
Boltax Theatre 974
Booth Theatre 136
Bottom Line Theatre 854, 857
Bouwerie Lane Theatre 341, 661
Bowery Theatre 876
Brander Matthews Theatre/Hall/Columbia University 686, 1000, 1086, 1229
The Brook 1418
Brooklyn Academy of Music 26, 123, 168, 244, 294, 363, 560, 660, 729, 885, 1279, 1405
Bruno Walter Auditorium/Library and Museum of the Performing Arts, The New York Public Library at Lincoln Center 274, 841, 1006, 1018, 1408, 1477, 1683
BTA Theatre 1033
Burstein Theatre 1105

Cabaret/Manhattan Theatre Club 18, 312, 348, 662, 886
Café Society 1125
Caffe Cino 1725
Carnegie Hall 783
Carnegie Hall Playhouse 150, 507, 826, 1185
Carnegie Playhouse 134
Carter Theatre 856, 1151, 1443, 1548
Casino East Theatre 1615
The Cathedral Church of St. John the Divine 402
Central Arts Cabaret 611
Century Center for the Performing Arts 612, 825
Century Theatre 97, 1545, 1737
Chanin Auditorium 1241
Cheetah Theatre 650
Chelsea Playhouse 775, 1508
Chelsea Theatre Center 459, 844
Chelsea Theatre Center/Upstairs 1340
Chelsea Westside Cabaret Theatre 279
Chelsea('s) Westside Theatre 1541, 1678
Chernuchin Theatre/American Theatre of Actors 103, 224, 1479, 1677
Cherry Lane Theatre 144, 220, 300, 384, 446, 448, 460, 566, 595, 659, 756, 770, 935, 1093, 1120, 1141, 1153, 1155, 1205, 1224, 1278, 1290, 1481, 1523, 1575, 1605, 1636, 1688, 1701, 1719, 1729, 1739, 1804
Cheryl Crawford Theatre/Chelsea Theatre Center/Westside Arts Center/Theatre 271, 382, 695, 731, 1019, 1585
Chicago City Limits Theatre 1817
Christian C. Yegen Theatre 1304
The Christian C. Yegen Theatre/Roundabout Theatre Company 219
Church of St. Paul and St. Andrew 107, 221, 591
Church of the Holy Trinity 562
Circle in the Square (Downtown) 113, 301, 377, 466, 471, 586, 653, 685, 753, 823, 1176, 1528, 1592, 1691
Circle Repertory Company Theatre 509, 1208
Circle Theatre 1704
City Center 55th Street Theatre 1096, 1655
City Center Downstairs 486, 1696
City Center Little Theatre 319
City Center Stage I/Manhattan Theatre Club 249, 1492, 1710, 1778
City Center Stage II/Manhattan Theatre Club 296, 1129, 1201, 1637
City Center Theatre 4, 374, 488
City Lights Theatre 809
Club 53 83
Club El Flamingo 399
The Club Room at Sardi's 781
Colonnades Theatre/Lab 1317, 1437
Columbia College Theatre 1230
The Common/The Theatre at St. Peter's Church 406, 539, 1282, 1643
Connelly Theatre 328
Cort Theatre 136
Cricket Playhouse 1473
Cricket Theatre 34, 291, 636, 654
Criterion Center 1551
Criterion Center Stage Left 172
CSC Repertory Theatre 8, 1693
Cubiculo Theatre 497, 918, 1354

Delacorte Theatre/The Public Theatre 1109, 1146, 1186, 1270, 1291, 1628, 1633, 1689
Dillon's Theatre 769, 1742
Diplomat Cabaret Theatre 125
Direct Theatre 310, 976
Dodger Stages 38, 627, 754, 1012, 1099, 1458
Don't Tell Mama 239, 665, 703, 945, 1568
Donnell Theatre 1202
Dorothy B. Williams Theatre/Here Arts Center 1572
Douglas Fairbanks Theatre 143, 325, 521, 523, 524, 525, 651, 1067, 1155, 1159, 1284, 1556, 1593, 1763
DownStage/Manhattan Theatre Club 1184
Downstairs at the Upstairs 126, 531, 558, 1273, 1602
The Downstairs Room 530, 1490, 1576
Downstairs/New York City Center 295
Downtown Theatre 199, 388, 1058
Drifting Traffic Theatre 1567
The Duke on 42nd Street Theatre 167, 1513
Duo Theatre 276
The Duplex 162, 1061, 1158

Earl Carroll Theatre 1543
East 74th Street Theatre/Playhouse 48, 94, 332, 366, 714, 1172, 1445
Eastside Playhouse 316, 548, 884, 894, 1130, 1196, 1480, 1787, 1823
Eden Theatre 147, 326, 489, 625, 666, 1168, 1483, 1745, 1822
Edison Theatre 183, 267, 400, 663, 827, 879, 1169, 1203, 1452, 1606, 1619
18th Street Playhouse 329, 814
Eighty Eights 691
85th Street Playhouse 1464
Ellen Stewart Theatre 306, 307, 716, 1080
Elysian Playhouse 1030
En Garde Arts 838
Encompass, The Music Theatre 434, 1288, 1391
Ensemble Studio Theatre 1190
Entermedia Theatre 133, 203, 588, 833, 909, 1560, 1582
The Entermedia's Second Story Theatre 549
Equity (Library) Theatre 799, 1028, 1160
Exchange (Westbeth) Theatre 713

The Felt Forum/Madison Square Garden Center 81, 145, 490, 617
54th Street Theatre Cabaret at Studio 54 1538
The First All Children's Theatre 1134
First City Theatre 798
Folksbiene Playhouse/Theatre 441, 782, 1026, 1041, 1713, 1755
Forlini's Restaurant 389
Fortune Theatre 292, 707, 1356
45 Bleecker 189
45th Street Theatre 750, 808, 1257, 1750
41st Street Theatre 31, 32, 166, 436, 529, 1276, 1436, 1440
47th Street Theatre 139, 385, 416, 519, 520, 521, 697, 813, 892, 1110, 1157, 1350, 1373
14th Street Y 538, 954, 1608
Fourth Street Theatre 779

The Gallery Players Theatre 1818
Gansevoort Theatre 1145
Garrick Theatre 7, 120, 423
Gate Theatre 291, 636, 698, 1161, 1264, 1517
The Gene Frankel Theatre (and Media Center) 565, 1147, 1470
The Glines 573, 1801

Good Shepherd-Faith Church 1392
Gramercy Arts Theatre 60, 121, 369, 448, 458, 757, 1265, 1313, 1578, 1812
Gramercy Theatre 383, 546
Grand Central Station on Terminal Tracks 39 to 42 544
Greenwich House Theatre 69
Greenwich Mews Theatre 238, 242, 253, 816, 1179, 1226, 1308, 1599, 1734, 1810
Greenwich Street Theatre 1117
Greenwich Village Theatre 85, 136, 477, 635, 637
Grove Street Playhouse 1320

Harold Clurman Theatre 412, 455, 545, 678, 865, 882, 883, 1321
Harry DeJur Henry Street Settlement Playhouse/New Federal Theatre 9, 266, 709, 1738
Hartley Theatre 1077
Heckscher Theatre 1002
Helen Carey Playhouse/Brooklyn Academy of Music 1644
Helen Hayes Theatre 1085
Henry Street Settlement's New Federal Theatre/Playhouse 278, 996
The Howff 1807
Hudson Guild Theatre 218, 345, 1106, 1143, 1485, 1717
Hudson West Theatre/Playhouse 1379, 1616
Hunter College Playhouse 1609

IBIS Theatre 1421
The Improvisation 752
INTAR Theatre 118, 897, 1338, 1402, 1588, 1771
Interart Theatre 1820
International Cabaret Theatre 212
Irish Repertory Theatre 13, 570, 775, 914

Jack Lawrence Theatre 855, 1323
Jan Hus Auditorium/House/Playhouse/Theatre 74, 98, 425, 457, 550, 719, 867, 1008, 1396, 1707, 1751, 1808
Jane Street Theatre 365, 680, 1054, 1634
Jason's Park Royal Theatre 949
Jerry Kravat's Club 320
Jewish Repertory Theatre 289, 1102, 1449, 1505, 1510, 1610, 1708, 1715
Joan and Sanford I. Weill Recital Hall/Carnegie Hall 1390
Joann's Silver Lining Cabaret Theatre 1569
John C. Borden Auditorium/Manhattan School of Music/Opera Theatre 717, 1336
John Houseman Theatre 213, 247, 452, 492, 555, 606, 901, 934, 979, 1110, 1235, 1245, 1326, 1362, 1638, 1658, 1830
Jones Beach Theatre (formerly Marine Stadium and then Jones Beach Marine Theatre) 66, 68, 1021, 1131, 1221
Joyce Theatre 45, 55, 1199
Judith Anderson Theatre 404, 922, 1333, 1577
Judson Hall Playhouse 1302
Judson Poets' Theatre 15, 111, 192, 243, 286, 392, 554, 759, 834, 920, 925, 928, 952, 998, 1017, 1277, 1280, 1349, 1387, 1489, 1496, 1501, 1673, 1705, 1711, 1757, 1776
Juilliard Concert Hall 951
Juilliard Opera Theatre 1564
Juilliard School Theatre 1217
Julia Miles Theatre 1110, 1450

Kaufman Theatre 567, 813, 843, 861, 924, 1651
Kaufmann Auditorium/92nd Street YM-YWHA 624
The Kirk Theatre at Theatre Row 30, 679
Krofft Theatre (The York Playhouse) 1293
Kuklapolitan Room/Hotel Astor 875

LaMama Experimental Theatre Club (ETC) 1536, 1826
Lamb's Theatre 280, 321, 343, 470, 552, 576, 596, 733, 828, 830, 836, 994, 1119, 1181, 1204, 1260, 1303, 1461, 1484, 1486
Latin Quarter 646
Lenox Arts Center/Saint Clement's Episcopal Church 358, 1087
Lepercq Space/Brooklyn Academy of Music 397, 482, 1344
The Lexington Avenue Young Men's and Young Women's Hebrew Association 1244, 1368
Linda Gross Theatre 1598
Lion Theatre 419, 1094, 1520
The Little Church Around the Corner 981
The Little Hippodrome 564
Little Shubert Theatre 248, 474, 657, 1623, 1656
Little Theatre 1007
Lone Star Theatre 991
Louis Abron Arts for Living Center/Henry Street Settlement's New Federal Theatre 736, 1174, 1423
Lucille Lortel Theatre 57, 433, 473, 642, 751, 845
LuEsther Hall/The (Joseph Papp) Public Theatre 647, 648, 1183, 1398, 1404, 1706, 1731

Madison Avenue Playhouse 112, 352, 535, 1152, 1687
Maidman Playhouse 287, 528, 745, 1385, 1539
Main Theatre/New York Stage Works 19
Majestic Theatre/Brooklyn Academy of Music 282
La Mama Experimental Theatre Club (ETC) 250, 475, 1625
Manhattan Punchline 789
Manhattan School of Music/Opera Theatre 362, 1374, 1416
Manhattan Theatre Club 1024
Manhattan Theatre Club at City Center Theatre (The Space at City Center Theatre) 656
Manhattan Theatre Club/Stage II 643
The (Martin R.) Kaufman Theatre 567, 813, 843, 861, 924, 1586, 1651
Martinique Theatre 33, 422, 613, 869, 870, 1659
Martinson Hall/The (Joseph Papp) Public Theatre 175, 195, 386, 832, 1250, 1384, 1697, 1746
Marymount Manhattan College/Theatre 258, 1411, 1692
Masque Theatre 1394
Master Theatre 275
Maverick Theatre 742
Mayfair Theatre 91, 335, 347, 504, 585, 655, 1177, 1341, 1388, 1802, 1803
Mazer Theatre 418
McAlpin Rooftop Theatre 117, 409, 480, 980
McGinn/Cazale Theatre 1612
McMillin Theatre/Columbia University 505
Mecca Auditorium 1140
Mercer Arts Center 11, 303
Mercer-Brecht Theatre 1511, 1735
Mercer-Hansbury Theatre 963
Mercer-O'Casey Theatre 61, 464, 667, 969
Mercer-Shaw Arena 1313
Mercury Theatre 704, 1242, 1455
Mermaid Theatre 1698, 1744
Merrymount Manhattan Theatre 710
Metropolitan Opera House 40, 47, 62, 245, 298, 340, 344, 427, 440, 495, 574, 628, 762, 776, 868, 891, 905, 988, 1010, 1047, 1075, 1088, 1249, 1269, 1369, 1597, 1718, 1723, 1730, 1740
Michael's Pub 73
Minetta Lane Theatre 54, 102, 182, 323, 499, 755, 804, 890, 1243, 1622, 1631, 1632, 1653, 1736
Mint Theatre Space 1815
The Mitzi E. Newhouse Theatre/Lincoln Center Theatre 122, 130, 315, 375, 430, 583, 683, 927, 1121, 1401, 1665
Musical Theatre Works 25, 408, 907, 1378, 1584, 1670, 1733

Nat Horne (Musical) Theatre 510, 743
National Winter Garden Theatre on Hudson Street 1543
Neighborhood Playhouse 618, 619, 620, 621, 622
New Anderson Theatre 1166
New Bowery Theatre 1780
New Federal Theatre 105, 156, 959, 1287, 1579
New Follies Theatre 636
New Lincoln Theatre 1743
New Palladium 1112
New Theatre 44, 835, 986, 1170, 1565
New Victory Theatre 632, 777, 1248, 1439, 1444, 1784
New World Stages 262, 721, 997, 1052
New World Stages/Stage 4 1110
(New York) City Center 3, 56, 92, 569, 609, 677, 849, 947, 1063, 1073, 1081, 1111, 1227, 1233, 1413, 1474, 1563, 1583, 1587, 1596, 1601, 1629, 1667, 1789, 1814
The New York Shakespeare Festival's Touring Theatre 1699
New York Stageworks 373
New York State Theater 20, 188, 254, 256, 264, 439, 451, 640, 670, 673, 889, 938, 941, 1020, 1022, 1023, 1062, 1137, 1165, 1462, 1552, 1816
New York Theatre Ensemble 1589
New York Theatre Workshop 206, 859, 1351, 1429, 1499
Newman Theatre/The (Joseph Papp) Public Theatre 207, 252, 283, 364, 428, 873, 910, 975, 1055, 1082, 1325, 1375, 1722, 1788
Next Stage Company 1714
92nd Street Y 53, 887
Norman Thomas Theatre 898
N.Y.U. University Theatre 1741

Oak Room/Algonquin Hotel 810
Off Center Theatre 895
Off On Broadway Theatre 437
Old Knickerbocker Music Hall 1116
One Sheridan Square 638, 807, 1400, 1672
O'Neals' Times Square/Club Broadway (O'Neals' 43rd Street Cabaret) 99, 215, 1427, 1709
The Opera Ensemble of New York 1782
Opera House/Brooklyn Academy of Music 158, 912, 917, 1139, 1167
Orpheum Theatre 63, 80, 142, 176, 277, 291, 356, 456, 587, 652, 822, 935, 939, 987, 1038, 1043, 1107, 1330, 1446, 1494, 1530, 1827
The Other Stage/The Public Theatre 426, 580, 664, 900, 1657

Palsson's/Supper Club 163, 164, 320, 511, 1573
Paper Mill Playhouse 1410
Paper Moon Cabaret 210
Park Royal Cabaret Theatre 796
Park Royal Theatre 293, 725, 1297
Performance Space 122 1516
Perry Street Theatre 36, 49, 255, 396, 1345
Persian Room/Plaza Hotel 1013
Peter Jay Sharp Theatre 1428, 1779
The Peter Norton Space/Signature Theatre Company 395, 1322
Phoenix Theatre 600, 942, 944, 1083, 1193, 1254, 1399
Playbox Studio 1294
Players Theatre 302, 391, 506, 575, 746, 935, 971, 995, 1034, 1171, 1218, 1283, 1301, 1346, 1386, 1420, 1476, 1566, 1646, 1732, 1774, 1832
The Playhouse 1256
Playhouse 46 180, 1216
Playhouse 46/St. Clement's Church 43
Playhouse 91 290, 749, 1046, 1419, 1438, 1441, 1512, 1607, 1829
Playhouse 91/Jewish Repertory Theatre 1663
Playhouse II 784
Playhouse on Vandam 730
Playhouse Theatre 159, 297, 360, 400, 401, 866, 1035
Playwrights Horizons 41, 70, 78, 170, 222, 251, 311, 473, 502, 503, 641, 690, 763, 791, 805, 973, 989, 1019, 1048, 1079, 1103, 1191, 1219, 1238, 1355, 1376, 1478, 1553, 1557, 1624, 1726
PLaza 9- Music Hall 318, 342, 955, 1611
PLaza 9- Room 87, 160, 534, 1259
PLaza 9- Theatre 381, 1409
Plaza 9 Music Theatre 337
Pocket Theatre 722
Portfolio Studio/Theatre 191, 1253, 1286
The Premise 946, 1295, 1614
The President Theatre 1448
Primary Stages 240, 741
Princess Theatre 263, 483
The Production Company Theatre 577, 1334
Promenade Theatre 37, 157, 184, 259, 260, 281, 390, 595, 692, 765, 806, 811, 1214, 1296, 1311, 1363, 1417, 1613, 1694
Provincetown Playhouse 79, 173, 493, 605, 701, 732, 734, 851, 858, 993, 1008, 1095, 1163, 1164, 1315, 1537, 1702
The Public Theatre 1072, 1397, 1529

Quaigh Theatre 155, 161, 217, 1648
Queens Theatre in the Park/Playwrights Horizons 794

The Raymond J. Greenwald Theatre 711
Renata Theatre 472, 908, 1272, 1465, 1754
Reprise Room at Dillon's 1210
Rialto Theatre 181, 246, 1025, 1097, 1348
Richard Allen Center for Culture and Art/Manhattan Community College 1580
Ritz Theatre 1504
Riverside Theatre 1671
Riverwest Theatre 320, 706
Rodale Theatre 1531
Roundabout Theatre 1267
Roundabout Theatre/Stage One 1268, 1540
Roundabout Theatre/Stage Two 1098
The Roundtable/King Arthur's Room 532
Royal Playhouse 481

St. Bart's Playhouse 135, 1316, 1595
St. Bart's Playhouse/Soho Rep 174
St. Clement's 1042, 1284
St. Clement's Church 1367
St. Clement's Theatre 12, 394, 561, 728, 839, 847, 999, 1380, 1535
St. Luke's Theatre 154
St. Malachy's Theatre 442
St. Marks (Mark's) Playhouse 21, 589, 629, 1004
St. Peter's Gate Theatre 177
St. Peter's Theatre 71

St. Stephen's Church 1650
Salon Zazou 1281
Samuel Beckett Theatre 983
The Sanctuary 815
Saval Theatre 403
Savoy Theatre 1015
Second Avenue Theatre 284, 604, 675, 1104, 1518
The Second Stage 764
Second Stage Theatre 2, 1187, 1357
The 78th Street Theatre Lab 780
Sheridan Square Playhouse 261, 572, 602, 902, 962, 1155, 1773
The Showplace 766, 1132, 1528, 1574, 1686
Shubert Theatre 637
Silver Lining 626
Snapple Theatre Center 479
Soho Playhouse 639
Soho Rep Theatre 1011
Song of Singapore Theatre 1495
South Street Theatre 16, 82, 1039, 1197, 1240
The Space/New York City Center 1487
Square East 22, 241, 367, 368, 1122, 1206, 1352, 1415, 1649, 1724, 1765, 1813
Stage 73 132, 187, 669, 761, 1236, 1488, 1682
Stage Arts Center/Actors Outlet Theatre Center 229
Stage Arts Theatre 322
Stage I/New World Stages 462
Stage One 1412
Stage One/Roundabout Theatre Company 445, 881
Stardust Theatre 518, 525
Steve McGraw's 527, 1454
Strollers Theatre-Club 449, 450, 1091, 1639, 1640
Studio Theatre/Playwrights Horizons 1019
Sullivan Street Playhouse 478, 1621
Susan Bloch Theatre 1432, 1600
Susan Stein Shiva Theatre/The (Joseph Papp) Public Theatre 387, 496, 1502, 1532, 1664
Sylvia and Danny Kaye Playhouse/Hunter College 1506

Teatro La Tea 1425
Ted Hook's Onstage Theatre 818, 888
Tempo Playhouse 235
Theater at St. Clement's/The Musical Theatre Lab of St. Clement's 1343
Theatre 3 1135
Theatre 4 1110, 1482
Theatre 5 1068
Theatre 80 St. Marks 1828
Theatre 802 543
Theatre 890 1519
Theatre Arielle 788, 1257, 1809
The Theatre at Mama Gail's 361, 1045, 1721
The Theatre at Saint Luke's 1753
Theatre de Lys 90, 128, 151, 204, 232, 268, 341, 598, 630, 715, 735, 911, 1044, 1078, 1154, 1307, 1318, 1471, 1620, 1626, 1627, 1668, 1767
Theatre East 512, 513, 514, 515, 516, 517, 536, 786, 871, 1251, 1274, 1383, 1798
Theatre for the New City 372, 702, 915, 1040, 1182, 1617, 1681
Theatre Four 35, 93, 138, 140, 201, 236, 272, 324, 582, 631, 676, 705, 718, 773, 903, 957, 1046, 1108, 1299, 1424, 1604, 1635
Theatre Guinevere 370, 1365
Theatre Marquee 1060, 1440, 1652
Theatre of the Riverside Church 214, 501, 592, 1285
Theatre Off Park 17, 581, 644, 732, 990, 1084, 1521
Theatre Row Theatre 767, 1327, 1760
Theatre Space/Madison Avenue Baptist Church 465
59E59 Theatres 10, 339
The 13th Street Theatre 417
13th Street Theatre 708
37 Arts Theatre 67, 541, 760
The 3 Muses Opening Date: January 17, 1980 468
The 3 Muses Theatre 547
Three Muses Theatre 86
Times Square Theatre 1543
T.O.M.I. 320, 1469
Town Hall 5, 165, 748, 795, 797, 800, 819, 1032, 1051, 1212, 1342, 1382, 1442, 1453, 1821, 1825
Triad Theatre 46, 129, 193, 227, 522, 526, 1156, 1421, 1764, 1786
Tribeca Arts Center 593
The Trocadero 1500
Trocadero Cabaret at Don't Tell Mama 1195
Truck and Warehouse Theatre 152, 467, 1359, 1662, 1695
Tudor Room/The Commodore Hotel 820
22 Steps Theatre 992
2econd (Second) Stage Theatre 330, 933, 1403, 1680

Ukranian Hall 1660
Union Square Theatre 106, 108, 196, 424, 1590, 1591
Upstage at Jimmy's 853, 1758
UpStage/Cabaret/Manhattan Theatre Club 84, 179, 672, 943, 1339, 1459, 1546
Upstairs at Channel VII 840
Upstairs at Greene Street 1150
Upstairs at Jimmy's 758
Upstairs at Studio 54 929, 1128
Upstairs at the Downstairs 50, 350, 371, 415, 542, 556, 557, 616, 771, 852, 1069, 1076, 1142, 1255, 1261, 1430, 1431
Upstairs/The Village Gate 1
Urban Arts Corps Theatre 230, 1762
Urban Arts Theatre 194, 327, 1526

Van Buren Theatre 1337
Van Dam Theatre 977, 1468, 1679, 1684
Vanities Theatre/Chelsea Theatre Center 978
Variety Arts Theatre 39, 58, 208, 610, 837, 1347, 1353, 1406, 1407, 1554, 1694, 1831
Variety Arts Theatre/Manhattan Theatre Club 633
La Vie En Rose 1292
Village Arena Theatre 1659
Village East Theatre 1727
Village Gate (All Venues) 115, 205, 225, 270, 334, 553, 623, 792, 801, 850, 877, 913, 916, 919, 967, 972, 1037, 1113, 1114, 1133, 1136, 1162, 1198, 1209, 1310, 1319, 1335, 1395, 1414, 1435, 1457, 1466, 1527, 1558, 1575, 1654, 1678, 1685, 1800
Village Theatre 226, 411, 738, 772, 965
Vineyard Theatre 23, 77, 114, 285, 413, 658, 848, 1237, 1503, 1645, 1752
Vineyard/Dimson Theatre 444

Washington Square Theatre 380
West Bank Café 198, 378, 1228
West Bank Downstairs Theatre 864
West Park Theatre 1805
West Side Theatre 1066
West Side Y Arts Center 1472
Westbeth Theatre/Center 110, 185, 410, 551, 1493
Westside Arts Theatre/Downstairs 681, 1234
Westside Chelsea Theatre 1258
Westside Mainstage 1149
Westside Theatre 52, 89, 234, 376, 634, 1189, 1777
Westside Theatre/Downstairs 338, 492, 1053
Westside Theatre/Upstairs 739, 821
Wings Theatre Company 1050
Wonderhorse Theatre 299, 453, 454, 1173, 1389
Workshop Theatre/Sarah Lawrence College 1252
WPA Theatre 233, 414, 469, 484, 727, 1498, 1748
Writers' Stage Theatre 1661

Yiddish Anderson Playhouse (Phyllis Anderson Theatre) 119, 684
York Playhouse/Theatre 48, 104, 148, 149, 166, 421, 601, 693, 1716, 1824
York Theatre Company 14, 88, 190, 308, 309, 398, 435, 463, 476, 485, 491, 597, 747, 778, 812, 829, 863, 899, 926, 930, 948, 984, 1031, 1056, 1071, 1099, 1144, 1213, 1289, 1306, 1309, 1366, 1451, 1456, 1507, 1547, 1581, 1747, 1765

Zankel Hall/Carnegie Hall 1491
Zipper Theatre 689, 802, 1188, 1700